Standard Catalog of

WORLD COINS

Seventeenth Century

1601-1700

4th OFFICIAL Edition

Colin R. Bruce II
Senior Editor

Thomas Michael
Market Analyst

Harry Miller
U.S. Market Analyst

George Cuhaj
Editor

Merna Dudley
Coordinating Editor

Deborah McCue
Database Specialist

Randy Thern
Numismatic Cataloging Supervisor

Special Contributors

Al Boulanger **Craig Keplinger**
Robert Mish **Paul Montz**
N. Douglas Nicol **Erik J. van Loon**

Bullion Value (BV) Market Valuations

Valuations for all platinum, gold, palladium and silver coins of the more common, basically bullion types, or those possessing only modest numismatic premiums are presented in this edition based on the market levels of:

$950 per ounce for **gold**

$18.50 per ounce for **silver**

Published by

700 East State Street • Iola, WI 54990-0001
715-445-2214 • 888-457-2873
www.krausebooks.com

Our toll-free number to place an order or obtain
a free catalog is (800) 258-0929.

Library of Congress Control Number: 2008928408

ISBN-13: 978-0-89689-708-3
ISBN-10: 0-89689-708-7

Designed by Stacy Bloch
Edited by Randy Thern

Printed in United States of America

ACKNOWLEDGMENTS

Many individuals have provided valuable contributions complementing this fourth edition. While all can not be acknowledged here, special appreciation is extended to the following individuals and organizations who have exhibited a special dedication - verifying historical information, technical data, coin listings, reviewing market valuations and loaning coins to photograph - for this edition.

Dr. Lawrence A. Adams
Stephen Album
Esko Ahlroth
Don Bailey
Mitchell A. Battino
Allen G. Berman
Joseph Boling
Al Boulanger
Klaus Bronny
Xavier Calicó
Ralph A. Cannito
Adolfo Cayón
Clemente Cayón
Raul Chirilá
Scott E. Cordry
Jerry Crain
Jean-Paul Divo
Frederic Droulers
Mike Dunigan
Graham P. Dyer
Wilhelm R. Eglseer
Jack Erb
George Falcke
John Ferm
Thomas Fitzgerald
Arthur Friedberg
Kent Froseth
Tom Galway
Dr. Roberto Ganganelli
Bruce Griffith
Ron Guth
Marcel Häberling
Flemming Lyngbeck Hansen
Wade Hinderling
Serge Huard
Clyde Hubbard
Louis Hudson
Robert E. Johnston
Robert W. Julian
Børge R. Juul
John K. Kallman
Craig Keplinger
Lawrence C. Korchnak
Ronachai Krisadaolarn
Samson Kin Chiu Lai
Joseph E. Lang
Jürgen Mikeska
Juozas Minikevicius
Robert Mish
Paul Montz
Horst-Dieter Müller
N. Douglas Nicol
Dr. Alex Oguy
Frank Passic
Marc Pelletier
Jens Pilegaard
Kent Ponterio
Rick Ponterio
Mircea Raicopal
Remy Said
Dhr. J. Scheper
Dr. Wolfgang Schuster
Daniel Frank Sedwick
Olav Sejeroe
Saran Singh
Clark Smith
Jørgen Sømod
Dr. Sebastian Steinbach
Alim A. Sumana
M. Louis Teller
Gunnar Thesen
Frank Timmerman
Archie Tonkin
Anthony Tumonis
Erik J. Van Loon
David F. Walker
Justin C. Wang
Paul Welz
Stewart Westdal
Ertekin Yenisey

AUCTION HOUSES AND DISTRIBUTORS

Baldwin's Auctions LTD
Classical Numismatic Group
Dix Noonan Webb Ltd.
Dmitry Markov Coins & Medals
Jean Elsen S.A.
Frankfurter Münzhandlung
Gorny & Mosch - Giessener Münzhandlung
Ira & Larry Goldberg Coins & Collectibles, Inc.
Heidelberger Münzhandlung Herbert Grün e.K.
Helios Numismatik
Heritage World Coin Auctions
Hess-Divo, AG
Gerhard D. Hirsch Nachfolger
Thomas Høiland Auktioner A/S
Fritz Rudolf Künker Münzhandlung
Maison Palombo
Auktionshaus Meister & Sonntag
Moneti i Medali
Münzhandlung Harald Möller GmbH
Münz Zentrum - Köln
Noble Numismatics, Pty. Ltd.
Numismatica Ars Classica
Numismatik Lanz München
Ponterio & Associates
Dr. Busso Peus Nachfolger
Bruun Rasmussen
Auktionshaus H.D. Rauch GmbH
Riibe Mynthandel AS
Laurens Schulman BV
Sotheby's
Spink
Stack's - Coin Galleries
UBS AG
Jean Vinchon Numismatique
Westfälische Auktionsgesellschaft
World Wide Coins of California

SOCIETIES and INSTITUTIONS

American Numismatic Association
American Numismatic Society
British Museum
Numismatics International
Smithsonian Institution

TABLE OF CONTENTS

Title 1
Copyright 2
Acknowledgments 3
Introduction 5
Country Index 6
How To Use This Catalog 10
Standard International Numeral Systems 16
Foreign Exchange 17
Instant Identifier 19
Hejira Date Conversion Chart 18
Gold Bullion Chart 24
Guide to International Numerics 23

INTRODUCTION

Welcome to our new 4th edition of the 17th Century Standard Catalog of World Coins. This most recent version of our ever changing and evolving series of comprehensive reference catalogs is designed to meet the needs of those with serious interest in the coins of our numismatic heritage. More than half of the pages within this reference are devoted to early European coinage, with a significant portion of this book displaying the vast array of Germanic coins stuck during this time period.

Still, the Standard Catalog of World Coins 1601-1700 provides an abundance of coin listing for nations around the globe. You will find coins from worldwide territories of the European powers, including issues meant for circulation in Portuguese India, Spanish Netherlands and Colonial North America, countermarked coins from Brazil and cob coins from Colombia and Bolivia. Listings for the remnants of the Hapsburg Empire can be found throughout this volume with coins struck for use in Austria, Bohemia, Hungary and Salzburg. Coins of Spain, France and the French States are here as well, alongside crowns from Transylvania, plus coins from the Middle Eastern areas of Turkey and Syria.

But some of the greatest areas of interest probably reside with this catalogs listings for pre-unified territories. The massive section for German States coinage has experienced a complete revision for all values on minor coins, crowns and thalers, and gold ducats and their multiples. The same is true of the Swiss Cantonal issues, coinage of the Provinces of the Netherlands and those coins struck for use in the various Italian States and cities. All of these collecting areas have witnessed a great rebirth of activity and very significant boosts to individual coin values.

It just goes to show that the classics never go out of style. There will always be a healthy market for coins of this era, hammered or milled, specialists will always be interested in 17th Century types.

So this easy to use catalog, arranged in a basic alphabetic fashion by country, with groupings for political structure, coinage type and denomination to help better organize the data, will always be an important volume in any numismatic library. You will find photographs of many 17th Century coins, information on metal content, obverse and reverse descriptions, legends, types and variety details, date listings and of course values presented in multiple grades of preservation. In short, just about all the information you could want on the classic coins of the old world and its early extensions into the East and West of the globe.

All this data has not come easily into the book you hold before you. A generation of numismatists has worked diligently to lay the foundations on which current experts can build and to them we own a debt of gratitude.

Continuing this work are some eighty contributing coin dealers, collectors and researchers who have lent their knowledge to the compiling of this new edition, providing our staff with updated values, new images, newly discovered dates and expanded listings. The accuracy of the data offered in this volume is assured through their kind assistance. To them we offer a heartfelt "Thank you!" for their generosity and dedication to the advancement of our shared field of coin collecting.

Finally to you, the reader, we extend our wishes that you may enjoy using this catalog as much as we enjoyed it's production. Look it over, put it to good use and please let us know if you have any comments or questions.

Best Wishes,

The Editorial Staff of the
Standard Catalog of World Coins

COUNTRY INDEX

Aachen 278
Ahlen 279
Ahmadnagar 1004
Ahnholt 292
Aire 267
Albera 1046
Algeria 29
Algeries 29
Alsace 279
Amsterdam 1186
Angolia 30
Anhalt 284
Anhalt-Bernburg 287
Anhalt-Dessau 287
Anhalt-Harzgerode 288
Anhalt-Kothen 289
Anhalt-Plotzkau 290
Anhalt-Zerbst 290
Anklam 292
Aragon 1311
Arakan 1000
Arenberg 292
Armenia 30
Arquata 1046
Artois 1321
Assam 1000
Auersperg 81
Augsburg 293
Austria 30
Austrian Netherlands 112
Austrian States 81
Avignon 1107
Azerbaijan 115
Bacaim 1020
Bacaim & Chaul 1020
Baden 299
Baglana 1003
Bamberg 303
Barby 306
Barcelona 1311
Basel 1355
Batenburg 1187
Bavaria 307
Beckum 319
Beeskow 319
Benculen 1241
Bentheim-Bentheim 319
Bentheim-Tecklenburg-Rheda 320
Berlin 322
Berlin & Kolln 323
Bermuda 115
Bern 1358
Besancon 323
Bhatgaon 1181
Biberach 324
Bidar 1005
Bijapur 1005
Bocholt 324
Bohemia 115
Bohemian Estates 135
Boisbelle & Henrichemont 267
Bolivia 143
Bologna 1109
Bombay Presidency 1012
Bouillon & Sedan 267
Bozzolo 1046
Brabant 1187
Brabant 1322
Brandenburg 324
Brandenburg-Ansbach 352
Brandenburg-Bayreuth 357
Brandenburg-Franconia 361
Brazil 152
Breda 1187
Breisach 361
Bremen 362
Bremen & Verden 368
Breslau 371
British India 1012
Brixen 81
Bromberg 1262
Brunswick 373
Brunswick-Bevern 376
Brunswick-Dannenberg 377
Brunswick-Harburg 378
Brunswick-Hitzacker 380
Brunswick-Luneburg-Calenberg 381
Brunswick-Luneburg-Calenberg-Hannove 401
Brunswick-Luneburg-Celle 403
Brunswick-Wolfenbuttel 422
Bucheim 450
Burgmilchling 450
Burgundy 269
Camenz 450
Cammin 451
Campi 1047
Casale 1048
Castiglione Dei Gatti 1050
Castiglione Delle Stiviere 1050
Catalonia 1313
Central Asia 156
Ceylon 158
Chateau-Renaud 269
China, Empire 161
Chur 1361
Cisterna 1052
Cleves 454
Cochin 1020
Coesfeld 455
Colmar 455
Cologne 456
Colombia 184
Compiano 1052
Constance 461
Cooch Behar 1003
Corvey 64
Cottbus 466
Courland 188
Cremona 1053
Crimea 189
Cuneo 1053
Dai Viet 1437
Damao 1020
Danish India 1014
Danzig 1262
Deccan Sultanates 1004
Denmark 190
Desana 1053
Deventer 1188
Dietrichstein 82
Diu 1020
Dombes 271
Dominican Republic 214
Dortmund 467
Drossen 468
Dulmen 468
Dutch Guiana 214
Dutch India 1018

East Friesland 468
Eger 136
Eggenberg 83
Egypt 215
Eichstatt 471
Einbeck 472
Elbing 1268
Elburg 1191
Electorial Pfalz 681
Ellwangen 473
Emden 474
England 891
Erbach 475
Erbach-Breuberg 476
Erbach-Furstenau 476
Erfurt 476
Essen 479
Estonia 217
Ferrara 1112
Finstingen 480
Flanders 1330
France 219
Franconia 480
Franconian Circle 480
Frankenthal 482
Frankfurt am Main 482
Frankfurt am Oder 489
Fraustadt 1272
Freiburg 1365
Freiburg im Breisgau 489
Freising 490
French India 1020
French States 267
Friedberg 490
Friedland 136
Friesland 1191
Fugger 492
Fugger-Pfirt 493
Fugger-Babemhausen 492
Fugger-Babenhausen-Wellenburg 493
Fugger-Glott 493
Fugger-Nordendorf 493
Fulda 493
Furstenberg 494
Furstenberg-Heiligenberg 494
Furstenwalde 495
Furth 495
Garsten 85
Gazzoldo 1056
Gelderland 1196
Geneva 1366
Genoa 1056
German States 277
Gerona 1318
Glarus 1368
Glatz 85
Glogau 495
Gluckstadt 212
Goa 1021
Goldberg 495
Golkonda 1006
Gorlitz 496
Gorze 496
Goslar 496
Gottingen 498
Great Britain 891
Greifswald 499
Groningen and Ommeland 1200
Gronsfeld 499
Gubbio 1114
Guben 500
Gustalla 1061
Guttenburg 500
Hagenau 500
Halberstadt 501
Haldenstein 1368
Hall 504
Haltern 504
Hamburg 504
Hameln 513
Hamm 516
Hanau 517
Hanau-Lichtenberg 517
Hanau-Munzenberg 520
Hannover 522
Hatzfeld 524
Hatzfeld-Gleichen 524
Hatzfeld-Wildenburg-Krottorf 524
Heid & Bleid 525
Helfenstein 525
Helfenstein-Gundelfingen 525
Helfenstein-Wiesensteig 525
Henneberg 525
Henneberg-Ilmenau 526
Herford 527
Hermannstadt 1424
Hersfeld 528
Hesse-Cassel 528
Hesse-Darmstadt 542
Hesse-Homburg 545
Hesse-Marburg 545
Hildesheim 545
Hohengeroldseck 551
Hohenlohe 551
Hohenlohe-Langenburg 553
Hohenlohe-Neuenstein-Neuenstein 553
Hohenlohe-Neuenstein-Oehringen 554
Hohenlohe-Neuenstein-Weikersheim 555
Hohenlohe-Pfedelbach 555
Hohenlohe-Waldenburg-Schillingfurst 555
Hohenlohe-Waldenburg-Waldenburg 556
Hohenzollern-Hechingen 556
Hohenzollern-Sigmaringen 557
Hohnstein 557
Holland 1204
Huizen 1211
Hungary 925
India, British 1012
India, Danish 1014
India, Dutch 1018
India, French 1020
India, Independent Kingdoms 1000
India, Moghal Empire 940
India, Portuguese 1020
Ingolstadt 558
Iran 1023
Iraq 1035
Ireland 1036
Isenburg 558
Isny 559
Italian States 1045
Jagerndorf 559
Jahore 1164
Jaintiapur 1007
Janid 156
Japan 1144
Java 1242
Jever 561
Julich 564
Julich-Berg 566
Julich-Cleve-Berg 569
Kachar 1008
Kampen 1211
Kathmandu 1182

Kaufbeuren ... 570
Kedah ... 1165
Kempten ... 570
Kingdom of Bhatgaon ... 1181
Kingdom of Kathmandu ... 1182
Kngdom of Patan ... 1184
Kolln ... 572
Korea ... 1146
Koshu ... 1146
Krim ... 189
Kristianstad ... 1354
Kronstadt ... 1425
Krossen ... 572
Kustrin ... 572
Kutch ... 1008
Kyritz ... 572
Laufenburg ... 1370
Lauingen ... 572
Leeuwarden ... 1214
Leiningen ... 572
Leiningen-Dagsburg-Falkenburg ... 572
Leiningen-Leiningen ... 573
Leiningen-Schaumburg-Kleeberg ... 574
Libya ... 1150
Liege ... 1151
Lindau ... 575
Lippe ... 575
Lippe-Detmold ... 575
Lithuania ... 1158
Livonia ... 1161
Livorno ... 1062
Loano ... 1063
Lobkowitz-Sternstein ... 140
Lobsenz ... 1272
Lorraine ... 579
Lowenberg ... 582
Lowenstein-Wertheim ... 582
Lowenstein-Wertheim-Rochefort ... 582
Lowenstein-Wertheim-Virneburg ... 585
Lubeck ... 585
Lucca ... 1064
Luckau ... 591
Luneburg ... 592
Luxembourg ... 1333
Luzern ... 1370
Maccagno ... 1065
Madras Presidency ... 1013
Madurai ... 1009
Magdeburg ... 594
Mainz ... 604
Majorca ... 1318
Malay Peninsula ... 1164
Maldive Islands ... 1165
Malta, Order of ... 1166
Mansfeld ... 612
Mansfeld-Artern ... 613
Mansfeld-Bornstedt ... 617
Mansfeld-Eigentliche-Hinterort ... 621
Mansfeld-Eisleben ... 627
Mansfeld-Friedeburg ... 629
Mansfeld-Schraplau ... 629
Mantua ... 1066
Maratha Confederacy ... 1010
Mark ... 630
Marsberg ... 630
Maryland ... 1435
Masegra ... 1075
Massa Di Lunigiano ... 1075
Massachusetts ... 1435
Mecklenburg-Gustrow ... 631
Mecklenburg-Schwerin ... 634
Mecklenburg-Strelitz ... 638
Memmingen ... 638
Messerano ... 1076
Metz ... 638
Mexico ... 1171
Milan ... 1080
Minden ... 640
Mirandola ... 1081
Mittweida ... 641
Modena ... 1082
Moghal Empire ... 940
Mompelgart ... 641
Monaco ... 1174
Montfort ... 642
Morocco ... 1177
Muhlhausen Alsace ... 646
Muhlhausen Thuringen ... 646
Munster ... 647
Munsterberg ... 653
Munsterberg-Oles ... 653
Murbach & Luders ... 657
Namur ... 1334
Naples & Sicily ... 1084
Narva ... 217
Nassau ... 657
Navarre ... 1319
Nepal ... 1180
Netherlands ... 1185
Netherlands East Indies ... 1240
Neuchatel ... 1372
Neuruppin ... 657
Nevers & Rethel ... 272
New England ... 1435
New Jersey ... 1436
New Yorke ... 1437
Nijmegen ... 1215
Nordhausen ... 657
Northeim ... 658
Norway ... 1242
Nurnberg ... 659
Oldenburg ... 669
Olmutz ... 85
Oran ... 29
Orange ... 274
Order of Malta ... 1166
Ortenburg ... 89
Osnabruck ... 672
Ottingen ... 675
Ottingen-Ottingen ... 675
Ottingen-Wallerstein-Wallerstein ... 678
Overyssel ... 1216
Paderborn ... 678
Papal City States ... 1107
Papal States ... 1085
Papal States Papacy ... 1086
Parma ... 1115
Passau ... 680
Patan ... 1184
Peru ... 1252
Pfalz ... 681
Pfalz-Neuburg ... 685
Pfalz-Simmern ... 688
Pfalz-Sulzbach ... 689
Pfalz-Veldenz ... 689
Pfalz-Zweibrucken ... 691
Piacenza ... 1117
Piombino ... 1118
Pisa ... 1118
Poland ... 1254
Pomerania ... 693
Pomerania-Settin ... 693
Pomerania-Wolgast ... 700
Portugal ... 1276

Portuguese India 1020
Posen 1272
Prenzlau 707
Quedlinburg 707
Ragusa 1285
Rantzau 710
Ratzeburg 710
Ravensberg 712
Ravensburg 714
Reckheim 112
Regensburg 714
Regenstei 722
Retegno 1119
Reuss 722
Revel 217
Ronco 1121
Rosenberg 140
Roussillon 1320
Rovegno 1121
Russia 1286
Sabbioneta 1121
Saint Gall 1373
Salzburg 89
San Martino 1121
Santo Domingo 214
Sardinia 1121
Savoy 1122
Sayn-Altenkirchen 794
Sayn-Berleburg 795
Sayn-Hackenberg-Altenkirchen 796
Sayn-Wittgenstein-Hohnstein 796
Schaffhausen 1374
Schaumburg-Lippe 800
Schaumburg-Pinneberg 800
Schleswig-Holstein 807
Schleswig-Holstein-Glucksburg 808
Schleswig-Holstein-Gottorp 808
Schleswig-Holstein-Norburg 811
Schleswig-Holstein-Ploen 812
Schleswig-Holstein-Sonderburg 812
Schlick 140
Schwarzburg 813
Schwarzburg-Arnstadt 815
Schwarzburg-Rudolstadt 815
Schwarzburg-Sondershausen 816
Schwarzenberg 817
Schweinfurt 817
Schwyz 1376
Scotland 1289
Seborga 1126
Shaybanid 157
S-Heerenberg 1203
Sicily 1127
Silesia 818
Silesia-Liegnitz-Brieg 829
Sinkang Province 184
Sinzendorf 108
Sitten 1377
Soest 839
Solferino 1127
Solms 839
Solms-Braunfels 839
Solms-Heruletz 840
Solms-Hohensolms 840
Solms-Laubach 842
Solms-Lich 842
Solms-Roedelheim 843
Solothurn 1377
Sorau 844
Spain 1295
Spain-Local 1311
Spanish Netherlands 1320
Speyer 844
Stade 845
Stolberg 845
Stolberg-Stolberg 846
Stolberg-Wernigerode 848
Stralsund 848
Strassburg 853
Sulz 856
Swabian Circle 856
Sweden 1337
Swiss Cantons 1355
Syria 1386
Tassarolla 1127
Telgte 856
Teutonic Order 856
Thann 859
Thorn 1273
Torriglia 1129
Tournai 1334
Tranquebar 1014
Transylvania 1388
Trautson 108
Tresana 1129
Tricerro 1129
Trier 860
Tripoli 1150
Tripura 1010
Troppau-Jaegendorf 110
Tunis 1427
Tunisia 1427
Turkey 1428
Tuscany 1129
Ulm 864
United States 1435
Urbino 1132
Uri 1378
Valencia 1320
Venice 1132
Vercelli 1143
Verdun 275
Vergagni 1143
Vietnam 1437
Vijayanagar 1011
Waldeck 865
Weissenburg 865
Werden & Helmstaedt 866
Werne 867
West Friesland 1225
Westphalia 867
Wismar 867
Wolfenbuttel 870
Wolgast 871
Wollwarth 871
Worms 871
Wurttemberg 874
Wurttemberg-Oels 883
Wurzburg 885
Yemen 1438
Zeeland 1231
Zug 1379
Zurich 1380
Zutphen 1235
Zwolle 1236

HOW TO USE THIS CATALOG

This catalog series is designed to serve the needs of both the novice and advanced collectors. It pro-vides a comprehensive guide to over 400 years of world coinage. It is generally arranged so that persons with no more than a basic knowledge of world history and a casual acquaintance with coin collecting can consult it with confidence and ease. The following explanations summarize the general practices used in preparing this catalog's listings. However, because of specialized requirements, which may vary by country and era, these must not be considered ironclad. Where these standards have been set aside, appropriate notations of the variations are incorporated in that particular listing.

ARRANGEMENT

Countries are arranged alphabetically. Political changes within a country are arranged chronologically. In countries where Rulers are the single most significant political entity a chronological arrangement by Ruler has been employed. Distinctive sub-geographic regions are listed alphabetically following the countries main listings. A few exceptions to these rules may exist. Refer to the Country Index for assistance in locating any given entity.

Diverse coinage types relating to fabrication methods, revaluations, denomination systems, non-circulating categories and such have been identified, separated and arranged in logical fashion. Chronological arrangement is employed for most circulating coinage, i.e., Hammered coinage will normally precede Milled coinage, monetary reforms will flow in order of their institution. Non-circulating types such as Essais, Piefors, Patterns, Trial Strikes, Mint and Proof sets will follow the main listings, as will Medallic coinage and Token coinage.

Within a coinage type coins will be listed by denomination, from smallest to largest. Numbered types within a denomination will be ordered by their first date of issue.

IDENTIFICATION

The most important step in the identification of a coin is the determination of the nation of origin. This is generally easily accomplished where Western alphabets are used. In this time period the use of Latin leg-ends on larger denominations and just shields and initials of the ruler for smaller value coins abound. Only through the familiarity of the monarchial portraits, shields, legend abbreviations or an indication of currency systems are they identifiable. Use of the Country Index is sometimes required.

Collectors have the greatest difficulty with coins that do not bear legends or dates in the Western systems. These include coins bearing Cyrillic lettering, attributable to Bulgaria, Russia, the Slavic states and Mongolia, the Greek script peculiar to Greece, Crete and the Ionian Islands; The Amharic characters of Ethiopia, or Hebrew in the case of Israel. Dragons and sunbursts along with the distinctive word characters attribute a coin to the Asian countries of China, Japan, Korea, Tibet, Viet Nam and their component parts.

There are instances in which a little schooling in the rudiments of foreign languages can be most helpful. In general, colonial possessions of countries using the Western alphabet are similarly identifiable as they often carry portraits of their current rulers, the familiar lettering, sometimes in combination with a compan-ion designation in the local language.

The most difficult coins to identify are those bearing only Persian or Arabic script and its derivatives, found on the issues of nations stretching in a wide swath across North Africa and East Asia, from Morocco to Indonesia, and the Indian subcontinent coinages which surely are more confusing in their vast array of Nagari, Sanskrit, Ahom, Assamese and other local dialects found on the local issues of the Indian Princely States. Although the task of identification on the more modern issues of these lands is often eased by the added presence of Western alphabet legends, a feature sometimes adopted as early as the late 19th Cen-tury, for the earlier pieces it is often necessary for the uninitiated to laboriously seek and find.

Except for the cruder issues, however, it will be found that certain characteristics and symbols fea-tured in addition to the predominant legends are typical on coins from a given country or group of coun-tries. The toughra monogram, for instance, occurs on some of the coins of Afghanistan, Egypt, the Sudan, Pakistan, Turkey and other areas of the late Ottoman Empire. A predominant design feature on the coins of Nepal is the trident; while neighboring Tibet features a lotus blossom or lion on many of their issues.

To assist in identification of the more difficult coins, we have assembled the **Instant Identifier** section presented on the following pages. This is designed to provide a point of beginning for col-lectors by allowing them to compare unidentified coins with photographic details from typical issues.

We also suggest reference to the **Index of Coin Denominations** presented here and also the comprehensive **Country Index**, where the inscription will be found listed just as it appears on the coin for nations using the Western alphabet.

DATING

Coin dating is the final basic attribution consideration. Here, the problem can be more difficult because the reading of a coin date is subject not only to the vagaries of numeric styling, but to calendar variations caused by the observance of various religious eras or regal periods from country to country, or even within a country. Here again with the exception of the sphere from North Africa through the Orient, it will be found that most countries rely on Western date numerals and Christian (AD) era reckoning, although in a few instances, coin dating has been tied to the year of a reign or government. The Vatican, for example dates its coinage according to the year of reign of the current pope, in addition to the Christian-era date.

Countries in the Arabic sphere generally date their coins to the Muslim era (AH), which commenced on July 16, 622 AD (Julian calendar), when the prophet Mohammed fled from Mecca to Medina. As their calendar is reckoned by the lunar year of 354 days, which is about three percent (precisely 2.98%) shorter than the Christian year, a formula is required to convert AH dating to its Western equivalent. To convert an AH date to the approximate AD date, subtract three percent of the AH date (round to the closest whole number) from the AH date, and then add 622. A chart for converting all AH years from 1010 (July 2, 1601) to 1450 (May 25, 2028) is included in this edition.

The Muslim calendar is not always based on the lunar year (AH), however, causing some confusion, particularly in Afghanistan and Iran, where a calendar based on the solar year (SH) was introduced around 1920. These dates can be converted to AD by simply adding 621. In 1976 the government of Iran implemented a new solar calendar based on the foundation of the Iranian monarchy in 559 BC. The first year observed on the new calendar was 2535 (MS), which commenced March 20, 1976. A reversion to the traditional SH dating standard occurred a few years later.

Several different eras of reckoning, including Christian and Muslim (AH), have been used to date coins of the Indian subcontinent. The two basic systems are the Vikrama Samvat (VS), which dates from Oct. 18, 58 BC, and the Saka era, the origin of which is reckoned from March 3, 78 AD. Dating according to both eras appears on various coins of the area.

Coins of Thailand (Siam) are found dated by three different eras. The most predominant is the Buddhist era (BE), which originated in 543 BC. Next is the Bangkok or Ratanakosindsok (RS) era, dating from 1781 AD; followed by the Chula-Sakarat (CS) era, dating from 638 AD. The latter era originated in Burma and is used on that country's coins.

Other calendars include that of the Ethiopian era (EE), which commenced seven years, eight months after AD dating; and that of the Jewish people, which commenced on Oct. 7, 3761 BC. Korea claims a legendary dating from 2333 BC, which is acknowledged in some of its coin dating. Some coin issues of the Indonesian area carry dates determined by the Javanese Aji Saka era (AS), a calendar of 354 days (100 Javanese years equal 97 Christian or Gregorian calendar years), which can be matched to AD dating by comparing it to AH dating.

The following table indicates the year dating for the various eras, which correspond to 1997 in Christian calendar reckoning, but it must be remembered that there are overlaps between the eras in some instances.

Christian era (AD)	-1997
Muslim era (AH)	-AH1418
Solar year (SH)	-SH1376
Monarchic Solar era (MS)	-MS2556
Vikrama Samvat (VS)	-VS2054
Saka era (SE)	-SE1919
Buddhist era (BE)	-BE2540
Bangkok era (RS)	-RS216
Chula-Sakarat era (CS)	-CS1359
Ethiopian era (EE)	-EE1989
Jewish era	-5757
Korean era	-4330
Javanese Aji Saka era (AS)	-AS1930
Fasli era (FE)	-FE1407

Coins of Oriental origin - principally Japan, Korea, China, Turkestan and Tibet and some modern gold issues of Turkey - are generally dated to the year of the government, dynasty, reign or cyclic eras, with the dates indicated in Oriental characters which usually read from right to left. In recent years, however, some dating has been according to the Christian calendar and in Western numerals. In Japan, Oriental character dating was reversed to read from left to right in Showa year 23 (1948 AD).

More detailed guides to less prevalent coin dating systems, which are strictly local in nature, are presented with the appropriate listings.

Some coins carry dates according to both locally observed and Christian eras. This is particularly true in the Arabic world, where the Hejira date may be indicated in Arabic numerals and the Christian date in Western numerals, or both dates in either form.

The date actually carried on a given coin is generally cataloged here in the first column under the term, Date. If an AD date appears, the AD is not necessarily indicated, while other dating types are generally identified by the two initial Era abbreviations used in the dating table in this section.

A date listed in the column, which does not actually appear on a given coin is generally enclosed by parentheses. Undated coins are indicated by the letters ND in the date column and the estimated year of issue in parentheses.

Timing differentials between some era of reckoning particularly the 354-day Muslim and 365-day Chris-tian years, cause situations whereby coins which carry dates for both eras exist bearing two year dates from one calendar combined with a single date from another.

ARRANGEMENT

Some catalog numbers assigned in this volume are based on established references. This practice has been observed for two reasons: First, when world coins are listed chronologically they are basically self- cataloging; second, there was no need to confuse collectors with totally new numeric designations where appropriate systems already existed. As time progressed we found many of these established systems incomplete and inadequate. Many of these have been replaced with new KM numbers with appropriate cross-referencing.

Some of the coins listed in this catalog are identified or cross-referenced by numbers assigned by R.S. Yeoman (Y#), or slight adaptations thereof, in his *Modern World Coins*, and *Current Coins of the World*. For the pre-Yeoman dated issues, the numbers assigned by William D. Craig (C#) in his *Coins of the World* (1750-1850 period), 3rd edition, have generally been applied.

In some countries, listings are cross-referenced to Robert Friedberg's (FR#) *Gold Coins of the World* or *Coins of the British World*. Major Fred Pridmore's (P#) studies of British colonial coinage are also refer-enced, as are W.H. Valentine's (V#) references on the *Modern Copper Coins of the Muhammadan States*. Coins issued under the Chinese sphere of influence are assigned numbers from E. Kann's (K#) *Illustrated Catalog of Chinese Coins* and T.K. Hsu's (Su) work of similar title.

DENOMINATIONS

The second basic consideration to be met in the attribution of a coin is the determination of denomination. Since denominations are usually expressed in numeric, rather than word form on a coin, this is usually quite easily accomplished on coins from nations, which use Western numerals, except in those instances where issues are devoid of any mention of face value, and denomination must be attributed by size, metal-lic composition or weight. Coins listed in this volume are generally illustrated in actual size. Where size is critical to proper attribution, the coin's millimeter size is indicated.

The sphere of countries stretching from North Africa through the Orient, on which numeric symbols gen-erally unfamiliar to Westerners are employed, often provide the collector with a much greater challenge. This is particularly true on nearly all pre-20th Century issues. On some of the more modern issues, West-ern style numerals, usually presented in combination with the local numeric system, are becoming more commonplace.

Determination of a coin's currency system can also be valuable in attributing the issue to its country of origin. A comprehensive alphabetical index of denominations or currency names, applicable to the countries as cataloged in this volume, with all individual nations of use for each, is presented in this section.

The included table of ***Standard International Numeral Systems*** presents charts of the basic numeric designations found on coins of non-Western origin. Although denomination numerals are generally prominently displayed on coins, it must be remembered that these are general representations of characters, which individual coin engravers may have rendered in widely varying styles. Where a numeric or script denominations designation form is peculiar to a given coin or country, such as the script used on some Persian (Iranian) issues, they are so indicated or illustrated in conjunction with the appropriate listings.

MINTAGES

Quantities minted of each date are indicated where that information is available, generally stated in millions, often rounded off to the nearest 10,000 pieces. On quantities of a few thousand or less, actual mintages are generally indicated.

The abbreviation "Inc. Above" means Included Above, while "Inc. Below" means Included Below. The designation "Est." beside a mintage figure indicates the number given is an estimate or mintage limit.

MINT AND PRIVY MARKS

The presence of distinctive, but frequently inconspicuously placed, mintmarks indicates the mint of issue for many of the coins listed in this catalog. An appropriate designation in the date listings or general type information notes the presence, if any, of a mint mark on a particular coin type. On individual dates these letters will follow the date, or a mints name or mark might be mentioned in a note field for the type.

The presence of mint and/or mintmaster's privy marks on a coin in non-letter form is indicated by incor-porating the mint letter in lower case within parentheses adjoining the date; i.e. 1727(a). The corresponding mark is illustrated or identified in the introduction of the country.

A listing format by mints of issue has been adopted for some countries - including France, Spain and Mexico - to allow for a more logical arrangement. In these instances, the name of the mint or its mint mark letter or letters is presented in the general note field of each issue.

Where listings incorporate mintmaster initials, they are always presented in capital letters separated from the date; i.e., 1765 MF. The different mintmark and mintmaster letters found on the coins of any country, state or city of issue are always shown at the beginning of listings.

METALS

At the beginning of each date listing, the metallic composition of each coin denomination is listed, and thereafter, whenever a change in metal occurs. The traditional coinage metals and their symbolic chemical abbreviations used in this catalog are:

Platinum - (PT)	Copper - (Cu)
Gold - (Au)	Brass -
Silver - (Ag)	Copper-nickel - (CN)
Billion -	Lead - (Pb)
Nickel - (Ni)	Steel -
Zinc - (Zn)	Tin - (Sn)
Bronze - (Ae)	Aluminum - (Al)

During the 17th and 18th centuries, most of the world's coins were struck of copper or bronze, silver and gold.

OFF-METAL STRIKES

Off-metal strikes previously designated by "(OMS)" which also included the wide range of error coinage struck in other than their officially authorized compositions have been incorporated into Pattern listings along with special issues, which were struck for presentation or other reasons.

Collectors of Germanic coinage may be familiar with the term "Abschlag" which quickly identifies similar types of coinage struck in off metals from the circulating types.

PRECIOUS METAL WEIGHTS

Listings of weight, fineness and actual silver (ASW), gold (AGW), platinum or palladium (APW) content of most machine-struck silver, gold, platinum and palladium coins are provided in this edition. These designations will be found incorporated in the listings immediately beneath illustrations or in conjunction with type changes wherever these factors could be determined.

The ASW, AGW and APW figures were determined by multiplying the gross weight of a given coin by its known or tested fineness and converting the resulting gram or grain weight to troy ounces, rounded to the nearest ten-thousandth of an ounce. A silver coin with a 24.25 gram weight and .875 fineness, for example, would have a fine weight of approximately 21.2188 grams, or a .6822 ASW, a factor that can be used to accurately determine the intrinsic value for multiple examples.

The ASW, AGW or APW figure can be multiplied by the spot price of each precious metal to determine the current intrinsic value of any coin accompanied by these designations.

WEIGHTS AND FINENESSES

Coin weights are indicated in grams (abbreviated "g") along with fineness where the information is of value in differentiating between types. These weights are based on 31.103 grams per troy (scientific) ounce, as opposed to the avoirdupois (commercial) standard of 28.35 grams. Actual coin weights are gen-erally shown in hundredths or thousands of a gram; i.e., .500 SILVER 2.9200g.

As the silver and gold bullion markets have advanced and declined sharply in recent years, the fineness and total precious metal content of coins has become especially significant where bullion coins - issues which trade on the basis of their intrinsic metallic content rather than numismatic value - are concerned. In many instances, such issues have become worth more in bullion form than their nominal collector values or denominations indicate.

Establishing the weight of a coin can also be valuable for determining its denomination. Actual weight is also necessary to ascertain the specific gravity of the coin's metallic content, an important factor in determining authenticity.

TROY WEIGHT STANDARDS

24 Grains = 1 Pennyweight
480 Grains = 1 Ounce
31.103 Grams = 1 Ounce

UNIFORM WEIGHTS

15.432 Grains = 1 Gram
0.0648 Gram = 1 Grain

AVOIRDUPOIS STANDARDS

27-11/32 Grains = 11 Dram
437-1/2 Grains = 1 Ounce
28.350 Grams = 1 Ounce

COUNTERMARKS/COUNTERSTAMPS

There is some confusion among collectors over the terms "countermark" and "counterstamp" when applied to a coin bearing an additional mark or change of design and/or denomination.

To clarify, a countermark might be considered similar to the "hall mark" applied to a piece of silverware, by which a silversmith assured the quality of the piece. In the same way, a countermark assures the quality of the coin on which it is placed, as, for example, when the royal crown of England was countermarked (punched into) on segmented Spanish reales, allowing them to circulate in commerce in the British West Indies. An additional countermark indicating the new denomination may also be encountered on these coins.

Countermarks are generally applied singularly and in most cases indiscriminately on either side of the "host" coin.

Counterstamped coins are more extensively altered. The counterstamping is done with a set of dies, rather than a hand punch. The coin being counterstamped is placed between the new dies and struck as if it were a blank planchet as found with the Manila 8 reales issue of the Philippines.

PHOTOGRAPHS

To assist the reader in coin identification, every effort has been made to present actual size photographs of every coinage type listed. Obverse and reverse are illustrated, except when a change in design is restricted to one side, and the coin has a diameter of 39mm or larger, in which case only the side required for identification of the type is generally illustrated. All coins up to 60mm are illustrated actual size, to the nearest 1/2mm up to 25mm, and to the nearest 1mm thereafter. Coins larger than 60mm diameter are illustrated in reduced size, with the actual size noted in the descriptive text for the type. Where slight change in size is important to coin type identification, actual millimeter measurements are stated.

TRADE COINS

A number of nations, particularly European colonial powers and commercial traders, minted silver trade coins to facilitate commerce with the local populace of Africa, the Arab countries, the Indian sub-continental, Southeast Asia and the Far East. Within the European continent some gold coinage weights and denomination designations were widely adopted to facilitate trade. Such coins generally circulated at a value based on the weight and fineness of their silver or gold content, rather than their stated denomination. Examples include the sovereigns of Great Britain and the gold ducat issues of Austria, Hungary and the Netherlands. Trade coinage will be found listed at the end of the domestic issues.

VALUATIONS

Values quoted in this catalog represent the current retail market and are compiled from recommendations provided and verified through various source documents and specialized consultants. **It should be stressed, however, that this book is intended to serve only as a guide for evaluating coins, actual market conditions are constantly changing and additional influences, such as particularly strong local demand for certain coin series, fluctuation of international exchange rates and worldwide collection patterns must also be considered.** ****Publication of this catalog is not intended as a solicitation by the pub-lisher, editors or contributors to buy or sell the listed coins at the prices indicated.****

All valuations are stated in U.S. dollars, based on careful assessment of the varied international col-lector market. Valuations for coins priced below $100.00 are generally stated in full amounts - i.e. 37.50 or 75.00 - while valuations at or above that figure are rounded off in even dollars with a comma added to indicate thousands of dollars in value - i.e. $110.00 is expressed 110 and $1250.00 is expressed 1,250.

It should be noted that when particularly select uncirculated or proof-like examples of uncirculated coins become available they could be expected to command proportionately high premiums. Such examples in reference to choice Germanic Thalers are referred to as "erst schlage" or first strikes.

TOKEN COINAGE

At times local economic conditions have forced regular coinage from circulation or found mints unable to cope with the demand for coinage, giving rise to privately issued token coinage substitutes. British tokens of the late 1700s and early 1880s, and the German and French and French Colonial emergency emissions of the World War I era are examples of such tokens being freely accepted in monetary trans-actions over wide areas. Tokens were likewise introduced to satisfy specific restricted needs, such as the leper colony issues of Brazil, Colombia and the Philippines.

This catalog includes introductory or detailed listings with "Tn" prefixes of many token coinage issues, particularly those which enjoyed wide circulation and where the series was limited in diversity. More complex series, and those more restricted in scope of circulation are generally not listed, although a rep-resentative sample may be illustrated and reference provided to more specialized catalogs.

SIEGE COINAGE

During the 17th and 18th centuries the realities of warfare sometimes left a city or region with shortages of various necessity items, including coinage. When blockades, attacks or sieges restricted the flow of coinage to an area, officials often took steps to provide emergency issues. These types of coins will be found cataloged under the designations of Siege, Emergency or Necessity coinage, after the standard circulating coinage types.

MEDALLIC ISSUES

Medallic issues are segregated following the regular issue listings. Grouped there are coin-type issues, which can generally be identified as commemoratives produced to the country's established coinage standards but without the usual indicator of denomination. These pieces may or may not feature designs adapted from the country's regular issue or commemorative coinage, and may or may not have been issued in conjunction with related coinage issues.

RESTRIKES, COUNTERFEITS

Deceptive restrike and counterfeit (both contemporary and modern) examples exist of some coin issues. Where possible, the existence of restrikes is noted. Warnings are also incorporated in instances where particularly deceptive counterfeits are known to exist. Collectors who are uncertain about the authenticity of a coin held in their collection, or being offered for sale, should take the precaution of having it authenticated by the American Numismatic Association Authentication Bureau, 818 N. Cascade, Colorado Springs, CO 80903. Their reasonably-priced certification tests are widely accepted by collec-tors and dealers alike.

EDGE VARIETIES

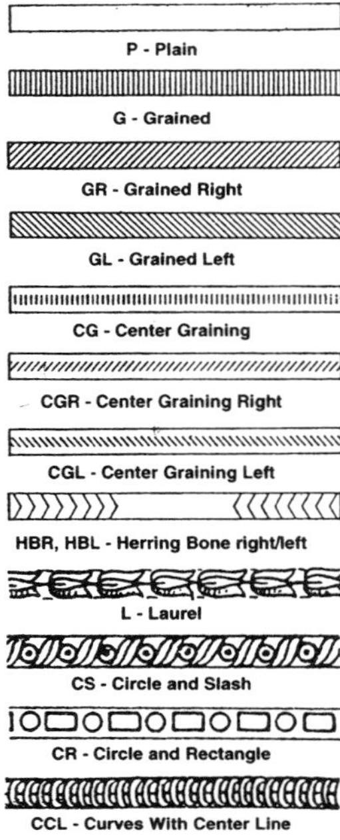

CONDITIONS

Wherever possible, coin valuations are given in four or five grades of preservation. On most early "cob" issues and some crude hammered and dump coinage, coin valuations have been limited to three grades of preservation to conform to the standards of these fields. Proof issues are indicated by the word "Proof" next to the date, with valuation proceeded by the word "value" following the mintage.

There are almost no grading guides for world coins. What follows is an attempt to help bridge that gap until a detailed, illustrated guide becomes available.

In grading world coins, there are two elements to look for: 1) Overall wear, and 2) loss of design details, such as strands of hair, feathers on eagles, designs on coats of arms, etc.

The age, rarity or type of a coin should not be a consideration in grading.

Grade each coin by the weaker of the two sides. This method appears to give results most nearly con-sistent with conservative American Numismatic Association standards for U.S. coins. Split grades, i.e., F/VF for obverse and reverse, respectively, are normally no more than one grade apart. If the two sides are more than one grade apart, the series of coins probably wears differently on each side and should then be graded by the weaker side alone.

Grading is determined by the amount of overall wear and loss of design detail evident on each side of the coin. On coins with a moderately small design element, which is prone to early wear, grade by that design alone. For example, the 5-ore (KM#554) of Sweden has a crown above the monogram on which the beads on the arches show wear most clearly. So, grade by the crown alone.

For **Brilliant Uncirculated** (BU) grades there will be no visible signs of wear or handling, even under a 30-power microscope. Full mint luster will be present. Ideally no bags marks will be evident.

For **Uncirculated** (Unc.) grades there will be no visible signs of wear or handling, even under a 30- power microscope. Bag marks may be present.

For **Almost Uncirculated** (AU), all detail will be visible. There will be wear only on the highest point of the coin. There will often be half or more of the original mint luster present.

On the **Extremely Fine** (XF or EF) coin, there will be about 95% of the original detail visible. Or, on a coin with a design with no inner detail to wear down, there will be a light wear over nearly all the coin. If a small design is used as the grading area, about 90% of the original detail will be visible. This latter rule stems from the logic that a smaller amount of detail needs to be present because a small area is being used to grade the whole coin.

The **Very Fine** (VF) coin will have about 75% of the original detail visible. Or, on a coin with no inner detail, there will be moderate wear over the entire coin. Corners of letters and numbers may be weak. A small grading area will have about 66% of the original detail.

For **Fine** (F), there will be about 50% of the original detail visible. Or, on a coin with no inner detail, there will be fairly heavy wear over all of the coin. Sides of letters will be weak. A typically coin found in it's natural state will often appear as dirty or dull. A small grading area will have fewer than 50% of the original detail.

On the **Very Good** (VG) coin, there will be about 25% of the original detail visible. There will be heavy wear on all of the coin.

The **Good** (G) coin's design will be clearly outlined but with substantial wear. Some of the larger detail may be visible. The rim may have a few weak spots of wear.

On the **About Good** (AG) coin, there will typically be only a silhouette of a large design. The rim will be worn down into the letters if any.

Strong or weak strikes, partially weak strikes, damage, corrosion, attractive or unattractive toning, dip-ping or cleaning should be described along with the above grades. These factors affect the quality of the coin just as do wear and loss of detail, but are easier to describe.

In the case of countermarked/counterstamped coins, the condition of the host coin will have a bearing on the end valuation. The important factor in determining the grade is the condition, clarity and completeness of the countermark itself. This is in reference to countermarks/counterstamps having raised design while being struck in a depression.

Incuse countermarks cannot be graded for wear. They are graded by the clarity and completeness including the condition of the host coin, which will also have more bearing on the final grade/valuation determined.

STANDARD INTERNATIONAL GRADING TERMINOLOGY AND ABBREVIATIONS

	PROOF	UNCIRCULATED	EXTREMELY FINE	VERY FINE	FINE	VERY GOOD	GOOD	POOR
U.S. and ENGLISH SPEAKING LANDS	PRF	UNC	EF or XF	VF	F	VG	G	PR
BRAZIL	—	(1)FDC or FC	(3) S	(5) MBC	(7) BC	(8) BC/R	(9) R	UT GeG
DENMARK	M	0	01	1+	1	1÷	2	3
FINLAND	00	0	01	1+	1	1?	2	3
FRANCE	FB Flan Bruni	FDC Fleur de Coin	SUP Superbe	TTB Très très beau	TB Très beau	B Beau	TBC Très Bien Conservée	BC Bien Conservée
GERMANY	PP Polierte Platte	STG Stempelglanz	VZ Vorzüglich	SS Sehr schön	S Schön	S.G.E. Sehr gut erhalten	G.E. Gut erhalten	Gering erhalten
ITALY	FS Fondo Specchio	FDC Fior di Conio	SPL Splendido	BB Bellissimo	MB Molto Bello	B Bello	M	—
JAPAN	—	未使用	極美品	美品	並品	—	—	—
NETHERLANDS	— Proef	FDC Fleur de Coin	Pr. Prachtig	Z.f. Zeer fraai	Fr. Fraai	Z.g. Zeer goed	G	—
NORWAY	M	0	01	1+	1	1÷	2	3
PORTUGAL	—	Soberba	Bela	MBC	BC	MREG	REG	MC
SPAIN	Prueba	SC	EBC	MBC	BC+	BC	RC	MC
SWEDEN	Polerad	0	01	1+	1	1?	2	—

STANDARD INTERNATIONAL NUMERAL SYSTEMS

PREPARED ESPECIALLY FOR THE **STANDARD CATALOG OF WORLD COINS**

WESTERN	0	½	1	2	3	4	5	6	7	8	9	10	50	100	500	1000
ROMAN			I	II	III	IV	V	VI	VII	VIII	IX	X	L	C	D	M
ARABIC-TURKISH	٠	١/٢	١	٢	٣	٤	٥	٦	٧	٨	٩	١٠	٥٠	١٠٠	٥٠٠	١٠٠٠
MALAY-PERSIAN	٠	١/٢	١	٢	٣	۴	۵	٦ or ۶	٧	٨	٩	١٠	۵٠	١٠٠	۵٠٠	١٠٠٠
EASTERN ARABIC	۰	۱/۲	۱	۲	۳	۴	۵	۶	۷	۸	۹	۱۰	۵۰	۱۰۰	۵۰۰	۱۰۰۰
HYDERABAD ARABIC	۰	۱/۲	۱	۲	۳	۴	۵	۶	۷	۸	۹	۱۰	۵۰	۱۰۰	۵۰۰	۱۰۰۰
INDIAN (Sanskrit)	०	१/२	१	२	३	४	५	६	७	८	९	१०	५०	१००	५००	१०००
ASSAMESE	০	১/২	১	২	৩	৪	৫	৬	৭	৮	৯	১০	৫০	১০০	৫০০	১০০০
BENGALI	০	১/২	১	২	৩	৪	৫	৬	৭	৮	৯	১০	৫০	১০০	৫০০	১০০০
GUJARATI	૦	૧/૨	૧	૨	૩	૪	૫	૬	૭	૮	૯	૧૦	૫૦	૧૦૦	૫૦૦	૧૦૦૦
KUTCH	०	१/२	१	२	३	४	५	६	७	८	९	१०	५०	१००	५००	१०००
DEVAVNAGRI	०	१/२	१	२	३	४	५	६	७	८	९	१०	५०	१००	५००	१०००
NEPALESE	०	१/२	१	२	३	४	५	६	७	८	९	१०	५०	१००	५००	१०००
TIBETAN	༠	༡/༢	༡	༢	༣	༤	༥	༦	༧	༨	༩	༡༠	༥༠	༡༠༠	༥༠༠	༡༠༠༠
MONGOLIAN	᠐	᠑/᠒	᠑	᠒	᠓	᠔	᠕	᠖	᠗	᠘	᠙	᠑᠐	᠕᠐	᠑᠐᠐	᠕᠐᠐	᠑᠐᠐᠐
BURMESE	၀	၁/၂	၁	၂	၃	၄	၅	၆	၇	၈	၉	၁၀	၅၀	၁၀၀	၅၀၀	၁၀၀၀
THAI-LAO	๐	๑/๒	๑	๒	๓	๔	๕	๖	๗	๘	๙	๑๐	๕๐	๑๐๐	๕๐๐	๑๐๐๐
JAVANESE	꧐		꧑	꧒	꧓	꧔	꧕	꧖	꧗	꧘	꧙	꧑꧐	꧕꧐	꧑꧐꧐	꧕꧐꧐	꧑꧐꧐꧐
ORDINARY CHINESE JAPANESE-KOREAN	零	半	一	二	三	四	五	六	七	八	九	十	十五	百	百五	千
OFFICIAL CHINESE			壹	貳	叁	肆	伍	陸	柒	捌	玖	拾	拾伍	佰	佰伍	仟
COMMERCIAL CHINESE			〡	〢	〣	〤	〥	〦	〧	〨	〩	十	〥十	〡百	〥百	〡千
KOREAN		반	일	이	삼	사	오	육	칠	팔	구	십	오십	백	오백	천
GEORGIAN			ა	ბ	გ	დ	ე	ვ	ზ	ჱ	თ	ი	ნ	რ	ფ	ჵ
			11 [illegible]	20 კ	30 ლ	40 მ	50 ნ	60 ჲ	70 ო	80 პ	90 ჟ	100 რ	200 ს 300 ტ	400 უ	600 ქ 700 ღ	800 ყ
ETHIOPIAN	◆		፩	፪	፫	፬	፭	፮	፯	፰	፱	፲	፶	፻	፭፻	፲፻
				20 ፳	30 ፴	40 ፵		60 ፷	70 ፸	80 ፹	90 ፺					
HEBREW			א	ב	ג	ד	ה	ו	ז	ח	ט	י	נ	ק	תק	
				20 כ	30 ל	40 מ		60 ס	70 ע	80 פ	90 צ		200 ר 300 ש	400 ת	600 תר 700 תש	800 תת
GREEK			Α	Β	Γ	Δ	Ε	ΣΤ	Ζ	Η	Θ	Ι	Ν	Ρ	Φ	Α
				20 Κ	30 Λ	40 Μ	60 Ξ	70 Ο	80 Π		200 Σ	300 Τ	400 Υ	600 Χ	700 Ψ	800 Ω

Foreign Exchange Table

The latest foreign exchange rates below apply to trade with banks in the country of origin. The left column shows the number of units per U.S. dollar at the official rate. The right column shows the number of units per dollar at the free market rate.

Country	Official #/$	Market #/$
Afghanistan (New Afghani)	50	–
Albania (Lek)	89	–
Algeria (Dinar)	61	–
Andorra uses Euro	.724	–
Angola (Readjust Kwanza)	75	–
Anguilla uses E.C. Dollar	2.65	–
Antigua uses E.C. Dollar	2.65	–
Argentina (Peso)	3.14	–
Armenia (Dram)	301	–
Aruba (Florin)	1.79	–
Australia (Dollar)	1.29	–
Austria (Euro)	.724	–
Azerbaijan (New Manat)	.81	–
Bahamas (Dollar)	1.0	–
Bahrain Is. (Dinar)	.377	–
Bangladesh (Taka)	68.5	–
Barbados (Dollar)	2.0	–
Belarus (Ruble)	2,113	–
Belgium (Euro)	.724	–
Belize (Dollar)	1.96	–
Benin uses CFA Franc West	475	–
Bermuda (Dollar)	1.0	–
Bhutan (Ngultrum)	46	–
Bolivia (Boliviano)	7.0	–
Bosnia-Herzegovina (Conv. marka)	1.35	–
Botswana (Pula)	7.06	–
British Virgin Islands uses U.S. Dollar	1.00	–
Brazil (Real)	2.01	–
Brunei (Dollar)	1.44	–
Bulgaria (Lev)	1.41	–
Burkina Faso uses CFA Fr.West	475	–
Burma (Kyat)	6.43	1,250
Burundi (Franc)	1,191	–
Cambodia (Riel)	4,124	–
Cameroon uses CFA Franc Central	475	–
Canada (Dollar)	1.07	–
Cape Verde (Escudo)	79	–
Cayman Islands (Dollar)	0.82	–
Central African Rep.	475	–
CFA Franc Central	475	–
CFA Franc West	475	–
CFP Franc	86	–
Chad uses CFA Franc Central	475	–
Chile (Peso)	571	–
China, P.R. (Renminbi Yuan)	6.82	–
Colombia (Peso)	2,195	–
Comoros (Franc)	356	–
Congo uses CFA Franc Central	475	–
Congo-Dem.Rep. (Congolese Franc)	551	–
Cook Islands (Dollar)	1.73	–
Costa Rica (Colon)	554	–
Croatia (Kuna)	5.15	–
Cuba (Peso)	1.00	27.00
Cyprus (Euro)	.724	–
Czech Republic (Koruna)	17.94	–
Denmark (Danish Krone)	5.40	–
Djibouti (Franc)	176	–
Dominica uses E.C. Dollar	2.64	–
Dominican Republic (Peso)	35	–
East Caribbean (Dollar)	2.65	–
Ecuador (U.S. Dollar)	1.00	–
Egypt (Pound)	5.45	–
El Salvador (U.S. Dollar)	1.00	–
Equatorial Guinea uses CFA Franc Central	475	–
Eritrea (Nafka)	15	–
Estonia (Kroon)	11.33	–
Ethiopia (Birr)	9.7	–
Euro		.724–
Falkland Is. (Pound)	.568	–
Faroe Islands (Krona)	5.40	–
Fiji Islands (Dollar)	1.65	–
Finland (Euro)	.724	–
France (Euro)	.724	–
French Polynesia uses CFP Franc	86	–
Gabon (CFA Franc)	475	–
Gambia (Dalasi)	23.6	–
Georgia (Lari)	1.41	–
Germany (Euro)	.724	–
Ghana (New Cedi)	1.16	–
Gibraltar (Pound)	.568	–
Greece (Euro)	.724	–
Greenland uses Danish Krone	5.40	–
Grenada uses E.C. Dollar	2.65	–
Guatemala (Quetzal)	7.50	–
Guernsey uses Sterling Pound	.568	–
Guinea Bissau (CFA Franc)	475	–
Guinea Conakry (Franc)	4,833	–
Guyana (Dollar)	204	–
Haiti (Gourde)	39	–
Honduras (Lempira)	18.9	–
Hong Kong (Dollar)	7.77	–
Hungary (Forint)	177	–
Iceland (Krona)	113	–
India (Rupee)	46.63	–
Indonesia (Rupiah)	9,480	–
Iran (Rial)	9,717	–
Iraq (Dinar)	1,178	–
Ireland (Euro)	.724	–
Isle of Man uses Sterling Pound	.568	–
Israel (New Sheqalim)	3.46	–
Italy (Euro)	.724	–
Ivory Coast uses CFA Franc West	475	–
Jamaica (Dollar)	72	–
Japan (Yen)	105	–
Jersey uses Sterling Pound	.568	–
Jordan (Dinar)	.71	–
Kazakhstan (Tenge)	120	–
Kenya (Shilling)	73	–
Kiribati uses Australian Dollar	1.29	–
Korea-PDR (Won)	2.2	425
Korea-Rep. (Won)	1,231	–
Kuwait (Dinar)	.267	–
Kyrgyzstan (Som)	36.8	–
Laos (Kip)	8,553	–
Latvia (Lats)	.513	–
Lebanon (Pound)	1,501	–
Lesotho (Maloti)	8.48	–
Liberia (Dollar)	63.5	–
Libya (Dinar)	1.23	–
Liechtenstein uses Swiss Franc	1.13	–
Lithuania (Litas)	2.5	–
Luxembourg (Euro)	.724	–
Macao (Pataca)	8.0	–
Macedonia (New Denar)	43	–
Madagascar (Franc)	1,700	–
Malawi (Kwacha)	140	–
Malaysia (Ringgit)	3.46	–
Maldives (Rufiya)	12.8	–
Mali uses CFA Franc West	475	–
Malta (Euro)	.724	–
Marshall Islands uses U.S.Dollar	1.00	–
Mauritania (Ouguiya)	232	–
Mauritius (Rupee)	29	–
Mexico (Peso)	11.13	–
Moldova (Leu)	10.25	–
Monaco uses Euro	.724	–
Mongolia (Tugrik)	1,145	–
Montenegro uses Euro	.724	–
Montserrat uses E.C. Dollar	2.65	–
Morocco (Dirham)	8.14	–
Mozambique (New Metical)	24	–
Myanmar (Burma) (Kyat)	6.42	–
Namibia (Rand)	8.48	–
Nauru uses Australian Dollar	1.29	–
Nepal (Rupee)	74.6	–
Netherlands (Euro)	.724	–
Netherlands Antilles (Gulden)	1.79	–
New Caledonia uses CFP Franc	86	–
New Zealand (Dollar)	1.51	–
Nicaragua (Cordoba Oro)	19.6	–
Niger uses CFA Franc West	475	–
Nigeria (Naira)	118	–
Northern Ireland uses Sterling Pound	.568	–
Norway (Krone)	6.0	–
Oman (Rial)	.385	–
Pakistan (Rupee)	78	–
Palau uses U.S.Dollar	1.00	–
Panama (Balboa) uses U.S.Dollar	1.00	–
Papua New Guinea (Kina)	2.53	–
Paraguay (Guarani)	4,002	–
Peru (Nuevo Sol)	2.99	–
Philippines (Peso)	47.13	–
Poland (Zloty)	2.48	–
Portugal (Euro)	.724	–
Qatar (Riyal)	3.64	–
Romania (New Leu)	2.77	–
Russia (Ruble)	25.9	–
Rwanda (Franc)	550	–
St. Helena (Pound)	.568	–
St. Kitts uses E.C. Dollar	2.65	–
St. Lucia uses E.C. Dollar	2.65	–
St. Vincent uses E.C. Dollar	2.65	–
San Marino uses Euro	.724	–
Sao Tome e Principe (Dobra)	14,682	–
Saudi Arabia (Riyal)	3.75	–
Scotland uses Sterling Pound	.568	–
Senegal uses CFA Franc West	475	–
Serbia (Dinar)	55.66	–
Seychelles (Rupee)	8.25	–
Sierra Leone (Leone)	2,981	–
Singapore (Dollar)	1.45	–
Slovakia (Sk. Koruna)	21.97	–
Slovenia (Euro)	.724	–
Solomon Islands (Dollar)	7.7	–
Somalia (Shilling)	1,407	–
Somaliland (Somali Shilling)	1,800	4,000
South Africa (Rand)	8.47	–
Spain (Euro)	.724	–
Sri Lanka (Rupee)	108	–
Sudan (Pound)	2.14	–
Surinam (Dollar)	2.75	–
Swaziland (Lilangeni)	8.47	–
Sweden (Krona)	7.04	–
Switzerland (Franc)	1.14	–
Syria (Pound)	51	–
Taiwan (NT Dollar)	32.28	–
Tajikistan (Somoni)	3.4	–
Tanzania (Shilling)	1,162	–
Thailand (Baht)	34.1	–
Togo uses CFA Franc West	475	–
Tonga (Pa'anga)	1.96	–
Transdniestra (Ruble)	–	–
Trinidad & Tobago (Dollar)	6.25	–
Tunisia (Dinar)	1.28	–
Turkey (New Lira)	1.31	–
Turkmenistan (Manat)	14,250	–
Turks & Caicos uses U.S. Dollar	1.00	–
Tuvalu uses Australian Dollar	1.29	–
Uganda (Shilling)	1,683	–
Ukraine (Hryvnia)	5.17	–
United Arab Emirates (Dirham)	3.673	–
United Kingdom (Sterling Pound)	.568	–
Uruguay (Peso Uruguayo)	21.72	–
Uzbekistan (Sum)	1,330	–
Vanuatu (Vatu)	106.5	–
Vatican City uses Euro	.724	–
Venezuela (New Bolivar)	2.15	5.7
Vietnam (Dong)	16,585	–
Western Samoa (Tala)	2.7	–
Yemen (Rial)	199	–
Zambia (Kwacha)	3,500	–
Zimbabwe (Dollar)	149.495	–

HEJIRA DATE CONVERSION CHART

HEJIRA (Hijira, Hegira), the name of the Muslim era (A.H. = Anno Hegirae) dates back to the Christian year 622 when Mohammed "fled" from Mecca, escaping to Medina to avoid persecution from the Koreish tribemen. Based on a lunar year the Muslim year is 11 days shorter.

*=Leap Year (Christian Calendar)

AH Hejira	AD Christian Date
1010	1601, July 2
1011	1602, June 21
1012	1603, June 11
1013	1604, May 30
1014	1605, May 19
1015	1606, May 19
1016	1607, May 9
1017	1608, April 28
1018	1609, April 6
1017	1608, April 28
1018	1609, April 6
1019	1610, March 26
1020	1611, March 16
1021	1612, March 4
1022	1613, February 21
1023	1614, February 11
1024	1615, January 31
1025	1616, January 20
1026	1617, January 9
1027	1617, December 29
1028	1618, December 19
1029	1619, December 8
1030	1620, November 26
1031	1621, November 16
1032	1622, November 5
1033	1623, October 25
1034	1624, October 14
1035	1625, October 3
1036	1626, September 22
1037	1627, Septembe 12
1038	1628, August 31
1039	1629, August 21
1040	1630, July 10
1041	1631, July 30
1042	1632, July 19
1043	1633, July 8
1044	1634, June 27
1045	1635, June 17
1046	1636, June 5
1047	1637, May 26
1048	1638, May 15
1049	1639, May 4
1050	1640, April 23
1051	1641, April 12
1052	1642, April 1
1053	1643, March 22
1054	1644, March 10
1055	1645, February 27
1056	1646, February 17
1057	1647, February 6
1058	1648, January 27
1059	1649, January 15
1060	1650, January 4
1061	1650, December 25
1062	1651, December 14
1063	1652, December 2
1064	1653, November 22
1065	1654, November 11
1066	1655, October 31
1067	1656, October 20
1068	1657, October 9
1069	1658, September 29
1070	1659, September 18
1071	1660, September 6
1072	1661, August 27
1073	1662, August 16
1074	1663, August 5
1075	1664, July 25
1076	1665, July 14
1077	1666, July 4
1078	1667, June 23
1079	1668, June 11
1080	1669, June 1
1081	1670, May 21
1082	1671, may 10
1083	1672, April 29
1084	1673, April 18
1085	1674, April 7

AH Hejira	AD Christian Date
1086	1675, March 28
1087	1676, March 16*
1088	1677, March 6
1089	1678, February 23
1090	1679, February 12
1091	1680, February 2*
1092	1681, January 21
1093	1682, January 10
1094	1682, December 31
1095	1683, December 20
1096	1684, December 8*
1097	1685, November 28
1098	1686, November 17
1099	1687, November 7
1100	1688, October 26*
1101	1689, October 15
1102	1690, October 5
1103	1691, September 24
1104	1692, September 12*
1105	1693, September 2
1106	1694, August 22
1107	1695, August 12
1108	1696, July 31*
1109	1697, July 20
1110	1698, July 10
1111	1699, June 29
1112	1700, June 18
1113	1701, June 8
1114	1702, May 28
1115	1703, May 17
1116	1704, May 6*
1117	1705, April 25
1118	1706, April 15
1119	1707, April 4
1120	1708, March 23*
1121	1709, March 13
1122	1710, March 2
1123	1711, February 19
1124	1712, Feburary 9*
1125	1713, January 28
1126	1714, January 17
1127	1715, January 7
1128	1715, December 27
1129	1716, December 16*
1130	1717, December 5
1131	1718, November 24
1132	1719, November 14
1133	1720, November 2*
1134	1721, October 22
1135	1722, October 12
1136	1723, October 1
1137	1724, September 19
1138	1725, September 9
1139	1726, August 29
1140	1727, August 19
1141	1728, August 7*
1142	1729, July 27
1143	1730, July 17
1144	1731, July 6
1145	1732, June 24*
1146	1733, June 14
1147	1734, June 3
1148	1735, May 24
1149	1736, May 12*
1150	1737, May 1
1151	1738, April 21
1152	1739, April 10
1153	1740, March 29*
1154	1741, March 19
1155	1742, March 8
1156	1743, Febuary 25
1157	1744, February 15*
1158	1745, February 3
1159	1746, January 24
1160	1747, January 13
1161	1748, January 2
1162	1748, December 22*
1163	1749, December 11
1164	1750, November 30
1165	1751, November 20
1166	1752, November 8*
1167	1753, October 29
1168	1754, October 18
1169	1755, October 7
1170	1756, September 26*
1171	1757, September 15
1172	1758, September 4
1173	1759, August 25
1174	1760, August 13*
1175	1761, August 2
1176	1762, July 23

AH Hejira	AD Christian Date
1177	1763, July 12
1178	1764, July 1*
1179	1765, June 20
1180	1766, June 9
1181	1767, May 30
1182	1768, May 18*
1183	1769, May 7
1184	1770, April 27
1185	1771, April 16
1186	1772, April 4*
1187	1773, March 25
1188	1774, March 14
1189	1775, March 4
1190	1776, February 21*
1191	1777, February 91
1192	1778, January 30
1193	1779, January 19
1194	1780, January 8*
1195	1780, December 28*
1196	1781, December 17
1197	1782, December 7
1198	1783, November 26
1199	1784, November 14*
1200	1785, November 4
1201	1786, October 24
1202	1787, October 13
1203	1788, October 2*
1204	1789, September 21
1205	1790, September 10
1206	1791, August 31
1207	1792, August 19*
1208	1793, August 9
1209	1794, July 29
1210	1795, July 18
1211	1796, July 7*
1212	1797, June 26
1213	1798, June 15
1214	1799, June 5
1215	1800, May 25
1216	1801, May 14
1217	1802, May 4
1218	1803, April 23
1219	1804, April 12*
1220	1805, April 1
1221	1806, March 21
1222	1807, March 11
1223	1808, February 28*
1224	1809, February 16
1225	1810, Febauary 6
1226	1811, January 26
1227	1812, January 16*
1228	1813, Janaury 26
1229	1813, December 24
1230	1814, December 14
1231	1815, December 3
1232	1816, November 21*
1233	1817, November 11
1234	1818, October 31
1235	1819, October 20
1236	1820, October 9*
1237	1821, September 28
1238	1822, September 18
1239	1823, September 18
1240	1824, August 26*
1241	1825, August 16
1242	1826, August 5
1243	1827, July 25
1244	1828, July 14*
1245	1829, July 3
1246	1830, June 22
1247	1831, June 12
1248	1832, May 31*
1249	1833, May 21
1250	1834, May 10
1251	1835, April 29
1252	1836, April 18*
1253	1837, April 7
1254	1838, March 27
1255	1839, March 17
1256	1840, March 5*
1257	1841, February 23
1258	1842, February 12
1259	1843, February 1
1260	1844, January 22*
1261	1845, January 10
1262	1845, December 30
1263	1846, December 20
1264	1847, December 9
1265	1848, November 27*
1266	1849, November 17
1267	1850, November 6

AH Hejira	AD Christian Date
1268	1851, October 27
1269	1852, October 15*
1270	1853, October 4
1271	1854, September 24
1272	1855, September 13
1273	1856, September 1*
1274	1857, August 22
1275	1858, August 11
1276	1859, July 31
1277	1860, July 20*
1278	1861, July 9
1279	1862, June 29
1280	1863, June 18
1281	1864, June 6*
1282	1865, May 27
1283	1866, May 16
1284	1867, May 5
1285	1868, April 24*
1286	1869, April 13
1287	1870, April 3
1288	1871, March 23
1289	1872, March 11*
1290	1873, March 1
1291	1874, February 18
1292	1875, Febuary 7
1293	1876, January 28*
1294	1877, January 16
1295	1878, January 5
1296	1878, December 26
1297	1879, December 15
1298	1880, December 4*
1299	1881, November 23
1300	1882, November 12
1301	1883, November 2
1302	1884, October 21*
1303	1885, October 10
1304	1886, September 30
1305	1887, September 19
1306	1888, September 7*
1307	1889, August 28
1308	1890, August 17
1309	1891, August 7
1310	1892, July 26*
1311	1893, July 15
1312	1894, July 5
1313	1895, June 24
1314	1896, June 12*
1315	1897, June 2
1316	1898, May 22
1317	1899, May 12
1318	1900, May 1
1319	1901, April 20
1320	1902, april 10
1321	1903, March 30
1322	1904, March 18*
1323	1905, March 8
1324	1906, February 25
1325	1907, February 14
1326	1908, February 4*
1327	1909, January 23
1328	1910, January 13
1329	1911, January 2
1330	1911, December 22
1332	1913, November 30
1333	1914, November 19
1334	1915, November 9
1335	1916, October 28*
1336	1917, October 17
1337	1918, October 7
1338	1919, September 26
1339	1920, September 15*
1340	1921, September 4
1341	1922, August 24
1342	1923, August 14
1343	1924, August 2*
1344	1925, July 22
1345	1926, July 12
1346	1927, July 1
1347	1928, June 20*
1348	1929, June 9
1349	1930, May 29
1350	1931, May 19
1351	1932, May 7*
1352	1933, April 26
1353	1934, April 16
1354	1935, April 5
1355	1936, March 24*
1356	1937, March 14
1357	1938, March 3
1358	1939, February 21
1359	1940, February 10*

AH Hejira	AD Christian Date
1360	1941, January 29
1361	1942, January 19
1362	1943, January 8
1363	1943, December 28
1364	1944, December 17*
1365	1945, December 6
1366	1946, November 25
1367	1947, November 15
1368	1948, November 3*
1369	1949, October 24
1370	1950, October 13
1371	1951, October 2
1372	1952, September 21*
1373	1953, September 10
1374	1954, August 30
1375	1955, August 20
1376	1956, August 8*
1377	1957, July 29
1378	1958, July 18
1379	1959, July 7
1380	1960, June 25*
1381	1961, June 14
1382	1962, June 4
1383	1963, May 25
1384	1964, May 13*
1385	1965, May 2
1386	1966, April 22
1387	1967, April 11
1388	1968, March 31*
1389	1969, march 20
1390	1970, March 9
1391	1971, February 27
1392	1972, February 16*
1393	1973, February 4
1394	1974, January 25
1395	1975, January 14
1396	1976, January 3*
1397	1976, December 23*
1398	1977, December 12
1399	1978, December 2
1400	1979, November 21
1401	1980, November 9*
1402	1981, October 30
1403	1982, October 19
1404	1984, October 8
1405	1984, September 27*
1406	1985, September 16
1407	1986, September 6
1409	1987, August 26
1409	1988, August 14*
1410	1989, August 3
1411	1990, July 24
1412	1991, July 13
1413	1992, July 2*
1414	1993, June 21
1415	1994, June 10
1416	1995, May 31
1417	1996, May 19*
1418	1997, May 9
1419	1998, April 28
1420	1999, April 17
1421	2000, April 6*
1422	2001, March 26
1423	2002, March 15
1424	2003, March 5
1425	2004, February 22*
1426	2005, February 10
1427	2006, January 31
1428	2007, January 20
1429	2008, January 10*
1430	2008, December 29
1431	2009, December 18
1432	2010, December 8
1433	2011, November 27*
1434	2012, November 15
1435	2013, November 5
1436	2014, October 25
1437	2015, October 15*
1438	2016, October 3
1439	2017, September 22
1440	2018, September 12
1441	2019, September 11*
1442	2020, August 20
1443	2021, August 10
1444	2022, July 30
1445	2023, July 19*
1446	2024, July 8
1447	2025, June 27
1448	2026, June 17
1449	2027, June 6*
1450	2028, May25

GERMAN STATES INSTANT IDENTIFIER

Aachen

Anhalt (Joint Coinage)

Anhalt-Bernberg

Arenberg

Augsburg

Augsburg

Baden

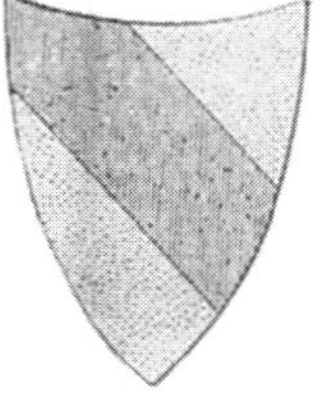
Baden

Bamberg

Bamberg

Bavaria

Bentheim

Berlin

Biberach

Brandenburg Old City

Brandenburg New City

Brandenburg Ansbach

Bremen

Bretzenheim

Brunswick

Brunswick-Luneburg

Brunswick-Wolfenbuttel

Chur Pfalz

Cologne

Constance

Dessau

Dortmund

Eichstadt

Emden

Erfurt Mainz

Erfurt

Essen

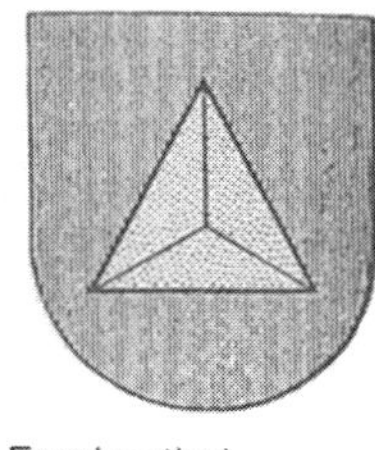
Frankenthal

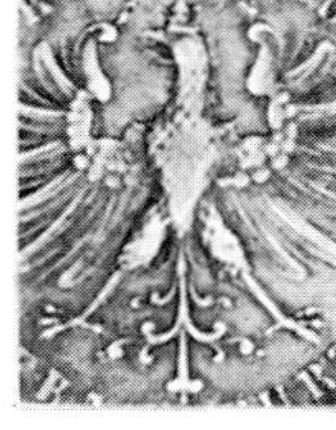
Frankfurt am Main

Frankfurt am Main

Frankfurt am Oder

Friedberg

Fugger

Fulda

Fulda

Furstenberg

Furth

GERMAN STATES INSTANT IDENTIFIER

German Empire

German New Guinea

Glogau

Gorlitz

Goslar

Gottingen

Greifswald

Hagenau

Hall in Swabia

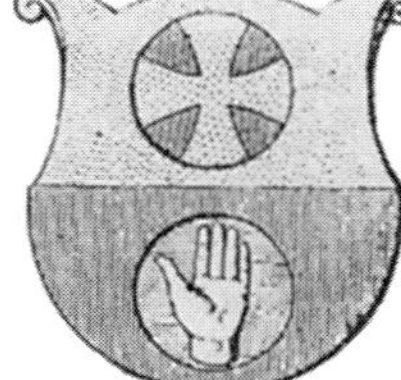
Hall in Swabia

Hamburg

Hamburg

Hamm

Hanau

Hanau-Munzenberg

Hannover

Hannover

Hannover

Heilbronn

Herford

Hersfeld

Hesse-Cassel

Hesse-Cassel

Hesse-Darmstadt

Hesse-Homburg

Hildesheim

Hildesheim

Hohenlohe-Neuenstein-Oehringen

Hohenzollern

Hohenzollern-Hechingen

Jever

Julich-Berg

Kaufbeuren

Kempten

Landau

Liegnitz

Lindau

Lippe-Detmold

Lowenstein-Wertheim

Lubeck

Lubeck

Luneburg

GERMAN STATES INSTANT IDENTIFIER

Magdeburg

Mainz

Mainz

Mecklenburg-Strelitz

Memmingen

Muhlhausen

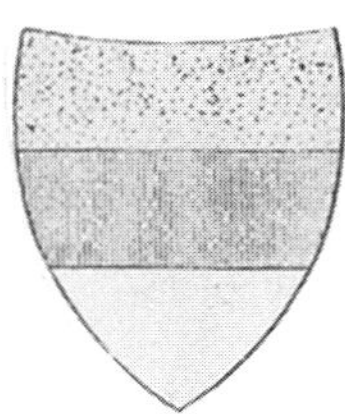
Munster

Munsterberg

Nassau

Nordhausen

Nurnberg

Oldenburg

Oldenburg

Oldenburg

Osnabruck

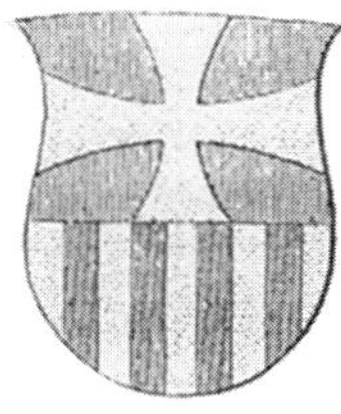
Paderborn

Paderborn

Passau

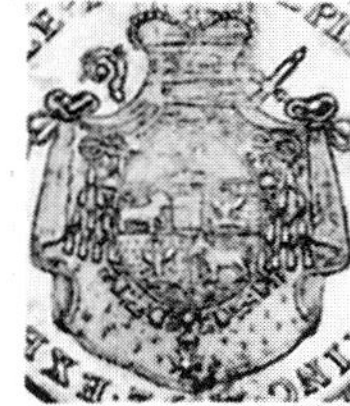
Passau

Prussia

Quedlinburg

Regensburg

Reuss-Greiz

Rhenish Confederation

Rostock

Rostock

Rothenburg

Rottweil

Saint Alban

Saxe-Altenburg

Saxe-Coburg-Gotha

Saxe-Meiningen

Saxe-Saalfield

Saxe-Weimar

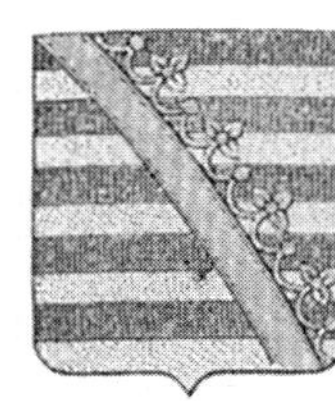
Saxony

Saxony

Schaumburg-Lippe

Schmalkalden

Schwarzburg

Schwarzburg-Rudolstadt

Schwarzburg-Sondershausen

Schwarzenberg

GERMAN STATES INSTANT IDENTIFIER

Solms-Laubach Speyer Stade Stolberg-Stolberg Stralsund Teutonic Order Trier

Waldeck-Pyrmont Wismar Wismar Worms Wurttemberg Wurzburg Wurzburg

A GUIDE TO INTERNATIONAL NUMERICS

	ENGLISH	CZECH	DANISH	DUTCH	ESPERANTO	FRENCH
1/4	one-quarter	jeden-ctvrt	én kvart	een-kwart	unu-kvar'ono	un-quart
1/2	one-half	jeden-polovieni or pul	én halv	een-half	unu-du'one	un-demi
1	one	jeden	én	een	unu	un
2	two	dve	to	twee	du	deux
3	three	tri	tre	drie	tri	trois
4	four	ctyri	fire	vier	kvar	quatre
5	five	pet	fem	vijf	kvin	cinq
6	six	sest	seks	zes	ses	six
7	seven	sedm	syv	zeven	sep	sept
8	eight	osm	otte	acht	ok	huit
9	nine	devet	ni	negen	nau	neuf
10	ten	deset	ti	tien	dek	dix
12	twelve	dvanáct	tolv	twaalf	dek du	douze
15	fifteen	patnáct	femten	vijftien	dek kvin	quinze
20	twenty	dvacet	tyve	twintig	du'dek	vingt
24	twenty-four	dvacet-ctyri	fire og tyve	twintig-vier	du'dek kvar	vingt-quatre
25	twenty-five	dvacet-pet	fem og tyve	twintig-vijf	du'dek kvin	vingt-cinq
30	thirty	tricet	tredive	dertig	tri'dek	trente
40	forty	ctyricet	fyrre	veertig	kvar'dek	quarante
50	fifty	padesát	halvtreds	vijftig	kvin'dek	cinquante
60	sixty	sedesát	tres	zestig	ses'dek	soixante
70	seventy	sedmdesát	halvfjerds	zeventig	sep'dek	soixante dix
80	eighty	osemdesát	firs	tachtig	ok'dek	quatre-vingt
90	ninety	devadesát	halvfems	negentig	nau'dek	quatre-vingt-dix
100	one hundred	jedno sto	et hundrede	een-honderd	unu-cento	un-cent
1000	thousand	tisíc	tusind	duizend	mil	mille

	GERMAN	HUNGARIAN	INDONESIAN	ITALIAN	NORWEGIAN	POLISH
1/4	ein viertel	egy-negyed	satu-suku	uno-guarto	en-fjeerdedel	jeden-c weirc
1/2	einhalb	egy-fél	satu-setengah	un-mezzo	en-halv	jeden-polowa
1	ein	egy	satu	uno	en	jeden
2	zwei	kettö	dud	due	to	dwa
3	drei	három	tiga	tre	tre	trzy
4	vier	négy	empot	quattro	fire	cztery
5	fünf	öt	lima	cinque	fem	piec'
6	sechs	hat	enam	sei	seks	szes'c'
7	sieben	hét	tudjuh	sette	sju	siedem
8	acht	nyolc	delapan	otto	atte	osiem
9	neun	kilenc	sembilan	nove	ni	dziewiec'
10	zehn	tí z	sepuluh	dieci	ti	dziesiec'
12	zwölf	tizenketto	duabelas	dodici	tolv	dwanas' cie
15	fünfzehn	tizenöt	lima belas	quindici	femten	pietnas'cie
20	zwanzig	húsz	dua pulah	venti	tjue or tyve	dwadzies'cia
24	vierundzwanzig	húsz-négy	dua pulah-empot	venti-quattro	tjue-fire or tyve-fire	dwadzies'cia-cztery
25	fünfundzwanzig	húsz-öt	dua-pulah-lima	venti-cinque	tjue-fem or tyve-fem	dwadzies'cia-piec
30	dreissig	harminc	tigapulah	trenta	tredve	trydzies'ci
40	vierzig	negyven	empat pulah	quaranta	forti	czterdries'ci
50	fünfzig	otven	lima pulah	cinquanta	femti	piec'dziesiat
60	sechzig	hatvan	enam pulah	sessanta	seksti	szes'c'dziesiat
70	siebzig	hetven	tudjuh pulu	settanta	sytti	siedemdziesiat
80	achtzig	nyolvan	delapan puluh	ottonta	atti	osiemdziesiat
90	neunzig	kilencven	sembilan puluh	novanta	nitty	dziewiec'dziesiat
100	ein hundert	egy-száz	satu-seratus	uno-cento	en-hundre	jeden-sto
1000	tausend	ezer	seribu	mille	tusen	tysiac

	PORTUGUESE	ROMANIAN	SERBO-CROATIAN	SPANISH	SWEDISH	TURKISH
1/4	um-quarto	un-sfert	jedan-ceturtina	un-cuarto	en-fjärdedel	bir-ceyrek
1/2	un-meio	o-jumatate	jedan-polovina	un-medio	en-hälft	bir-yarim
1	um	un	jedan	uno	en	bir
2	dois	doi	dva	dos	tva	iki
3	trés	trei	tri	tres	tre	üc
4	quatro	patru	cetiri	cuatro	fyra	dört
5	cinco	cinci	pet	cinco	fem	bes
6	seis	sase	sest	seis	sex	alti
7	sete	sapte	sedam	siete	sju	yedi
8	oito	opt	osam	ocho	atta	sekiz
9	nove	noua	devet	nueve	io	dokuz
10	dez	zece	deset	diez	tio	on
12	doze	doisprezece	dvanaest	doce	tolv	on iki
15	quinze	cincisprezece	petnaest	quince	femton	on bes
20	vinte	douazeci	dvadset	veinte	tjugu	yirmi
24	vinte-quatro	douazeci-patru	dvadesel-citiri	veinticuatro	tjugu-fyra	yirmi-dört
25	vinte-cinco	douazeci-cinci	dvadeset-pet	veinticinco	tjugu-fem	yirmi-bes
30	trinta	treizeci	trideset	treinta	trettio	otuz
40	quarenta	patruzeci	cetrdeset	cuarenta	fyrtio	kirk
50	cinqüenta	cincizeci	padeset	cincuenta	femtio	elli
60	sessenta	saizeci	sezdeset	sesenta	sextio	altmis
70	setenta	saptezeci	sedamdeset	setenta	sjuttio	yetmis
80	oitenta	optzeci	osamdeset	ochenta	attio	seksen
90	noventa	novazeci	devedeset	noventa	nittio	doksan
100	un-cem	o-suta	jedan-sto	cien	en-hundra	bir-yüz

GOLD BULLION VALUE CHART

Oz.	700.00	710.00	720.00	730.00	740.00	750.00	760.00	770.00	780.00	790.00	800.00	810.00	820.00	830.00	840.00	850.00	860.00	870.00	880.00	890.00	900.00
0.001	0.70	0.71	0.72	0.73	0.74	0.75	0.76	0.77	0.78	0.79	0.80	0.81	0.82	0.83	0.84	0.85	0.86	0.87	0.88	0.89	0.90
0.002	1.40	1.42	1.44	1.46	1.48	1.50	1.52	1.54	1.56	1.58	1.60	1.62	1.64	1.66	1.68	1.70	1.72	1.74	1.76	1.78	1.80
0.003	2.10	2.13	2.16	2.19	2.22	2.25	2.28	2.31	2.34	2.37	2.40	2.43	2.46	2.49	2.52	2.55	2.58	2.61	2.64	2.67	2.70
0.004	2.80	2.84	2.88	2.92	2.96	3.00	3.04	3.08	3.12	3.16	3.20	3.24	3.28	3.32	3.36	3.40	3.44	3.48	3.52	3.56	3.60
0.005	3.50	3.55	3.60	3.65	3.70	3.75	3.80	3.85	3.90	3.95	4.00	4.05	4.10	4.15	4.20	4.25	4.30	4.35	4.40	4.45	4.50
0.006	4.20	4.26	4.32	4.38	4.44	4.50	4.56	4.62	4.68	4.74	4.80	4.86	4.92	4.98	5.04	5.10	5.16	5.22	5.28	5.34	5.40
0.007	4.90	4.97	5.04	5.11	5.18	5.25	5.32	5.39	5.46	5.53	5.60	5.67	5.74	5.81	5.88	5.95	6.02	6.09	6.16	6.23	6.30
0.008	5.60	5.68	5.76	5.84	5.92	6.00	6.08	6.16	6.24	6.32	6.40	6.48	6.56	6.64	6.72	6.80	6.88	6.96	7.04	7.12	7.20
0.009	6.30	6.39	6.48	6.57	6.66	6.75	6.84	6.93	7.02	7.11	7.20	7.29	7.38	7.47	7.56	7.65	7.74	7.83	7.92	8.01	8.10
0.010	7.00	7.10	7.20	7.30	7.40	7.50	7.60	7.70	7.80	7.90	8.00	8.10	8.20	8.30	8.40	8.50	8.60	8.70	8.80	8.90	9.00
0.020	14.00	14.20	14.40	14.60	14.80	15.00	15.20	15.40	15.60	15.80	16.00	16.20	16.40	16.60	16.80	17.00	17.20	17.40	17.60	17.80	18.00
0.030	21.00	21.30	21.60	21.90	22.20	22.50	22.80	23.10	23.40	23.70	24.00	24.30	24.60	24.90	25.20	25.50	25.80	26.10	26.40	26.70	27.00
0.040	28.00	28.40	28.80	29.20	29.60	30.00	30.40	30.80	31.20	31.60	32.00	32.40	32.80	33.20	33.60	34.00	34.40	34.80	35.20	35.60	36.00
0.050	35.00	35.50	36.00	36.50	37.00	37.50	38.00	38.50	39.00	39.50	40.00	40.50	41.00	41.50	42.00	42.50	43.00	43.50	44.00	44.50	45.00
0.060	42.00	42.60	43.20	43.80	44.40	45.00	45.60	46.20	46.80	47.40	48.00	48.60	49.20	49.80	50.40	51.00	51.60	52.20	52.80	53.40	54.00
0.070	49.00	49.70	50.40	51.10	51.80	52.50	53.20	53.90	54.60	55.30	56.00	56.70	57.40	58.10	58.80	59.50	60.20	60.90	61.60	62.30	63.00
0.080	56.00	56.80	57.60	58.40	59.20	60.00	60.80	61.60	62.40	63.20	64.00	64.80	65.60	66.40	67.20	68.00	68.80	69.60	70.40	71.20	72.00
0.090	63.00	63.90	64.80	65.70	66.60	67.50	68.40	69.30	70.20	71.10	72.00	72.90	73.80	74.70	75.60	76.50	77.40	78.30	79.20	80.10	81.00
0.100	70.00	71.00	72.00	73.00	74.00	75.00	76.00	77.00	78.00	79.00	80.00	81.00	82.00	83.00	84.00	85.00	86.00	87.00	88.00	89.00	90.00
0.110	77.00	78.10	79.20	80.30	81.40	82.50	83.60	84.70	85.80	86.90	88.00	89.10	90.20	91.30	92.40	93.50	94.60	95.70	96.80	97.90	99.00
0.120	84.00	85.20	86.40	87.60	88.80	90.00	91.20	92.40	93.60	94.80	96.00	97.20	98.40	99.60	100.80	102.00	103.20	104.40	105.60	106.80	108.00
0.130	91.00	92.30	93.60	94.90	96.20	97.50	98.80	100.10	101.40	102.70	104.00	105.30	106.60	107.90	109.20	110.50	111.80	113.10	114.40	115.70	117.00
0.140	98.00	99.40	100.80	102.20	103.60	105.00	106.40	107.80	109.20	110.60	112.00	113.40	114.80	116.20	117.60	119.00	120.40	121.80	123.20	124.60	126.00
0.150	105.00	106.50	108.00	109.50	111.00	112.50	114.00	115.50	117.00	118.50	120.00	121.50	123.00	124.50	126.00	127.50	129.00	130.50	132.00	133.50	135.00
0.160	112.00	113.60	115.20	116.80	118.40	120.00	121.60	123.20	124.80	126.40	128.00	129.60	131.20	132.80	134.40	136.00	137.60	139.20	140.80	142.40	144.00
0.170	119.00	120.70	122.40	124.10	125.80	127.50	129.20	130.90	132.60	134.30	136.00	137.70	139.40	141.10	142.80	144.50	146.20	147.90	149.60	151.30	153.00
0.180	126.00	127.80	129.60	131.40	133.20	135.00	136.80	138.60	140.40	142.20	144.00	145.80	147.60	149.40	151.20	153.00	154.80	156.60	158.40	160.20	162.00
0.190	133.00	134.90	136.80	138.70	140.60	142.50	144.40	146.30	148.20	150.10	152.00	153.90	155.80	157.70	159.60	161.50	163.40	165.30	167.20	169.10	171.00
0.200	140.00	142.00	144.00	146.00	148.00	150.00	152.00	154.00	156.00	158.00	160.00	162.00	164.00	166.00	168.00	170.00	172.00	174.00	176.00	178.00	180.00
0.210	147.00	149.10	151.20	153.30	155.40	157.50	159.60	161.70	163.80	165.90	168.00	170.10	172.20	174.30	176.40	178.50	180.60	182.70	184.80	186.90	189.00
0.220	154.00	156.20	158.40	160.60	162.80	165.00	167.20	169.40	171.60	173.80	176.00	178.20	180.40	182.60	184.80	187.00	189.20	191.40	193.60	195.80	198.00
0.230	161.00	163.30	165.60	167.90	170.20	172.50	174.80	177.10	179.40	181.70	184.00	186.30	188.60	190.90	193.20	195.50	197.80	200.10	202.40	204.70	207.00
0.240	168.00	170.40	172.80	175.20	177.60	180.00	182.40	184.80	187.20	189.60	192.00	194.40	196.80	199.20	201.60	204.00	206.40	208.80	211.20	213.60	216.00
0.250	175.00	177.50	180.00	182.50	185.00	187.50	190.00	192.50	195.00	197.50	200.00	202.50	205.00	207.50	210.00	212.50	215.00	217.50	220.00	222.50	225.00
0.260	182.00	184.60	187.20	189.80	192.40	195.00	197.60	200.20	202.80	205.40	208.00	210.60	213.20	215.80	218.40	221.00	223.60	226.20	228.80	231.40	234.00
0.270	189.00	191.70	194.40	197.10	199.80	202.50	205.20	207.90	210.60	213.30	216.00	218.70	221.40	224.10	226.80	229.50	232.20	234.90	237.60	240.30	243.00
0.280	196.00	198.80	201.60	204.40	207.20	210.00	212.80	215.60	218.40	221.20	224.00	226.80	229.60	232.40	235.20	238.00	240.80	243.60	246.40	249.20	252.00
0.290	203.00	205.90	208.80	211.70	214.60	217.50	220.40	223.30	226.20	229.10	232.00	234.90	237.80	240.70	243.60	246.50	249.40	252.30	255.20	258.10	261.00
0.300	210.00	213.00	216.00	219.00	222.00	225.00	228.00	231.00	234.00	237.00	240.00	243.00	246.00	249.00	252.00	255.00	258.00	261.00	264.00	267.00	270.00
0.310	217.00	220.10	223.20	226.30	229.40	232.50	235.60	238.70	241.80	244.90	248.00	251.10	254.20	257.30	260.40	263.50	266.60	269.70	272.80	275.90	279.00
0.320	224.00	227.20	230.40	233.60	236.80	240.00	243.20	246.40	249.60	252.80	256.00	259.20	262.40	265.60	268.80	272.00	275.20	278.40	281.60	284.80	288.00
0.330	231.00	234.30	237.60	240.90	244.20	247.50	250.80	254.10	257.40	260.70	264.00	267.30	270.60	273.90	277.20	280.50	283.80	287.10	290.40	293.70	297.00
0.340	238.00	241.40	244.80	248.20	251.60	255.00	258.40	261.80	265.20	268.60	272.00	275.40	278.80	282.20	285.60	289.00	292.40	295.80	299.20	302.60	306.00
0.350	245.00	248.50	252.00	255.50	259.00	262.50	266.00	269.50	273.00	276.50	280.00	283.50	287.00	290.50	294.00	297.50	301.00	304.50	308.00	311.50	315.00
0.360	252.00	255.60	259.20	262.80	266.40	270.00	273.60	277.20	280.80	284.40	288.00	291.60	295.20	298.80	302.40	306.00	309.60	313.20	316.80	320.40	324.00
0.370	259.00	262.70	266.40	270.10	273.80	277.50	281.20	284.90	288.60	292.30	296.00	299.70	303.40	307.10	310.80	314.50	318.20	321.90	325.60	329.30	333.00
0.380	266.00	269.80	273.60	277.40	281.20	285.00	288.80	292.60	296.40	300.20	304.00	307.80	311.60	315.40	319.20	323.00	326.80	330.60	334.40	338.20	342.00
0.390	273.00	276.90	280.80	284.70	288.60	292.50	296.40	300.30	304.20	308.10	312.00	315.90	319.80	323.70	327.60	331.50	335.40	339.30	343.20	347.10	351.00
0.400	280.00	284.00	288.00	292.00	296.00	300.00	304.00	308.00	312.00	316.00	320.00	324.00	328.00	332.00	336.00	340.00	344.00	348.00	352.00	356.00	360.00
0.410	287.00	291.10	295.20	299.30	303.40	307.50	311.60	315.70	319.80	323.90	328.00	332.10	336.20	340.30	344.40	348.50	352.60	356.70	360.80	364.90	369.00
0.420	294.00	298.20	302.40	306.60	310.80	315.00	319.20	323.40	327.60	331.80	336.00	340.20	344.40	348.60	352.80	357.00	361.20	365.40	369.60	373.80	378.00
0.430	301.00	305.30	309.60	313.90	318.20	322.50	326.80	331.10	335.40	339.70	344.00	348.30	352.60	356.90	361.20	365.50	369.80	374.10	378.40	382.70	387.00
0.440	308.00	312.40	316.80	321.20	325.60	330.00	334.40	338.80	343.20	347.60	352.00	356.40	360.80	365.20	369.60	374.00	378.40	382.80	387.20	391.60	396.00
0.450	315.00	319.50	324.00	328.50	333.00	337.50	342.00	346.50	351.00	355.50	360.00	364.50	369.00	373.50	378.00	382.50	387.00	391.50	396.00	400.50	405.00
0.460	322.00	326.60	331.20	335.80	340.40	345.00	349.60	354.20	358.80	363.40	368.00	372.60	377.20	381.80	386.40	391.00	395.60	400.20	404.80	409.40	414.00

GOLD BULLION VALUE CHART

Oz.	700.00	710.00	720.00	730.00	740.00	750.00	760.00	770.00	780.00	790.00	800.00	810.00	820.00	830.00	840.00	850.00	860.00	870.00	880.00	890.00	900.00
0.470	329.00	333.70	338.40	343.10	347.80	352.50	357.20	361.90	366.60	371.30	376.00	380.70	385.40	390.10	394.80	399.50	404.20	408.90	413.60	418.30	423.00
0.480	336.00	340.80	345.60	350.40	355.20	360.00	364.80	369.60	374.40	379.20	384.00	388.80	393.60	398.40	403.20	408.00	412.80	417.60	422.40	427.20	432.00
0.490	343.00	347.90	352.80	357.70	362.60	367.50	372.40	377.30	382.20	387.10	392.00	396.90	401.80	406.70	411.60	416.50	421.40	426.30	431.20	436.10	441.00
0.500	350.00	355.00	360.00	365.00	370.00	375.00	380.00	385.00	390.00	395.00	400.00	405.00	410.00	415.00	420.00	425.00	430.00	435.00	440.00	445.00	450.00
0.510	357.00	362.10	367.20	372.30	377.40	382.50	387.60	392.70	397.80	402.90	408.00	413.10	418.20	423.30	428.40	433.50	438.60	443.70	448.80	453.90	459.00
0.520	364.00	369.20	374.40	379.60	384.80	390.00	395.20	400.40	405.60	410.80	416.00	421.20	426.40	431.60	436.80	442.00	447.20	452.40	457.60	462.80	468.00
0.530	371.00	376.30	381.60	386.90	392.20	397.50	402.80	408.10	413.40	418.70	424.00	429.30	434.60	439.90	445.20	450.50	455.80	461.10	466.40	471.70	477.00
0.540	378.00	383.40	388.80	394.20	399.60	405.00	410.40	415.80	421.20	426.60	432.00	437.40	442.80	448.20	453.60	459.00	464.40	469.80	475.20	480.60	486.00
0.550	385.00	390.50	396.00	401.50	407.00	412.50	418.00	423.50	429.00	434.50	440.00	445.50	451.00	456.50	462.00	467.50	473.00	478.50	484.00	489.50	495.00
0.560	392.00	397.60	403.20	408.80	414.40	420.00	425.60	431.20	436.80	442.40	448.00	453.60	459.20	464.80	470.40	476.00	481.60	487.20	492.80	498.40	504.00
0.570	399.00	404.70	410.40	416.10	421.80	427.50	433.20	438.90	444.60	450.30	456.00	461.70	467.40	473.10	478.80	484.50	490.20	495.90	501.60	507.30	513.00
0.580	406.00	411.80	417.60	423.40	429.20	435.00	440.80	446.60	452.40	458.20	464.00	469.80	475.60	481.40	487.20	493.00	498.80	504.60	510.40	516.20	522.00
0.590	413.00	418.90	424.80	430.70	436.60	442.50	448.40	454.30	460.20	466.10	472.00	477.90	483.80	489.70	495.60	501.50	507.40	513.30	519.20	525.10	531.00
0.600	420.00	426.00	432.00	438.00	444.00	450.00	456.00	462.00	468.00	474.00	480.00	486.00	492.00	498.00	504.00	510.00	516.00	522.00	528.00	534.00	540.00
0.610	427.00	433.10	439.20	445.30	451.40	457.50	463.60	469.70	475.80	481.90	488.00	494.10	500.20	506.30	512.40	518.50	524.60	530.70	536.80	542.90	549.00
0.620	434.00	440.20	446.40	452.60	458.80	465.00	471.20	477.40	483.60	489.80	496.00	502.20	508.40	514.60	520.80	527.00	533.20	539.40	545.60	551.80	558.00
0.630	441.00	447.30	453.60	459.90	466.20	472.50	478.80	485.10	491.40	497.70	504.00	510.30	516.60	522.90	529.20	535.50	541.80	548.10	554.40	560.70	567.00
0.640	448.00	454.40	460.80	467.20	473.60	480.00	486.40	492.80	499.20	505.60	512.00	518.40	524.80	531.20	537.60	544.00	550.40	556.80	563.20	569.60	576.00
0.650	455.00	461.50	468.00	474.50	481.00	487.50	494.00	500.50	507.00	513.50	520.00	526.50	533.00	539.50	546.00	552.50	559.00	565.50	572.00	578.50	585.00
0.660	462.00	468.60	475.20	481.80	488.40	495.00	501.60	508.20	514.80	521.40	528.00	534.60	541.20	547.80	554.40	561.00	567.60	574.20	580.80	587.40	594.00
0.670	469.00	475.70	482.40	489.10	495.80	502.50	509.20	515.90	522.60	529.30	536.00	542.70	549.40	556.10	562.80	569.50	576.20	582.90	589.60	596.30	603.00
0.680	476.00	482.80	489.60	496.40	503.20	510.00	516.80	523.60	530.40	537.20	544.00	550.80	557.60	564.40	571.20	578.00	584.80	591.60	598.40	605.20	612.00
0.690	483.00	489.90	496.80	503.70	510.60	517.50	524.40	531.30	538.20	545.10	552.00	558.90	565.80	572.70	579.60	586.50	593.40	600.30	607.20	614.10	621.00
0.700	490.00	497.00	504.00	511.00	518.00	525.00	532.00	539.00	546.00	553.00	560.00	567.00	574.00	581.00	588.00	595.00	602.00	609.00	616.00	623.00	630.00
0.710	497.00	504.10	511.20	518.30	525.40	532.50	539.60	546.70	553.80	560.90	568.00	575.10	582.20	589.30	596.40	603.50	610.60	617.70	624.80	631.90	639.00
0.720	504.00	511.20	518.40	525.60	532.80	540.00	547.20	554.40	561.60	568.80	576.00	583.20	590.40	597.60	604.80	612.00	619.20	626.40	633.60	640.80	648.00
0.730	511.00	518.30	525.60	532.90	540.20	547.50	554.80	562.10	569.40	576.70	584.00	591.30	598.60	605.90	613.20	620.50	627.80	635.10	642.40	649.70	657.00
0.740	518.00	525.40	532.80	540.20	547.60	555.00	562.40	569.80	577.20	584.60	592.00	599.40	606.80	614.20	621.60	629.00	636.40	643.80	651.20	658.60	666.00
0.750	525.00	532.50	540.00	547.50	555.00	562.50	570.00	577.50	585.00	592.50	600.00	607.50	615.00	622.50	630.00	637.50	645.00	652.50	660.00	667.50	675.00
0.760	532.00	539.60	547.20	554.80	562.40	570.00	577.60	585.20	592.80	600.40	608.00	615.60	623.20	630.80	638.40	646.00	653.60	661.20	668.80	676.40	684.00
0.770	539.00	546.70	554.40	562.10	569.80	577.50	585.20	592.90	600.60	608.30	616.00	623.70	631.40	639.10	646.80	654.50	662.20	669.90	677.60	685.30	693.00
0.780	546.00	553.80	561.60	569.40	577.20	585.00	592.80	600.60	608.40	616.20	624.00	631.80	639.60	647.40	655.20	663.00	670.80	678.60	686.40	694.20	702.00
0.790	553.00	560.90	568.80	576.70	584.60	592.50	600.40	608.30	616.20	624.10	632.00	639.90	647.80	655.70	663.60	671.50	679.40	687.30	695.20	703.10	711.00
0.800	560.00	568.00	576.00	584.00	592.00	600.00	608.00	616.00	624.00	632.00	640.00	648.00	656.00	664.00	672.00	680.00	688.00	696.00	704.00	712.00	720.00
0.810	567.00	575.10	583.20	591.30	599.40	607.50	615.60	623.70	631.80	639.90	648.00	656.10	664.20	672.30	680.40	688.50	696.60	704.70	712.80	720.90	729.00
0.820	574.00	582.20	590.40	598.60	606.80	615.00	623.20	631.40	639.60	647.80	656.00	664.20	672.40	680.60	688.80	697.00	705.20	713.40	721.60	729.80	738.00
0.830	581.00	589.30	597.60	605.90	614.20	622.50	630.80	639.10	647.40	655.70	664.00	672.30	680.60	688.90	697.20	705.50	713.80	722.10	730.40	738.70	747.00
0.840	588.00	596.40	604.80	613.20	621.60	630.00	638.40	646.80	655.20	663.60	672.00	680.40	688.80	697.20	705.60	714.00	722.40	730.80	739.20	747.60	756.00
0.850	595.00	603.50	612.00	620.50	629.00	637.50	646.00	654.50	663.00	671.50	680.00	688.50	697.00	705.50	714.00	722.50	731.00	739.50	748.00	756.50	765.00
0.860	602.00	610.60	619.20	627.80	636.40	645.00	653.60	662.20	670.80	679.40	688.00	696.60	705.20	713.80	722.40	731.00	739.60	748.20	756.80	765.40	774.00
0.870	609.00	617.70	626.40	635.10	643.80	652.50	661.20	669.90	678.60	687.30	696.00	704.70	713.40	722.10	730.80	739.50	748.20	756.90	765.60	774.30	783.00
0.880	616.00	624.80	633.60	642.40	651.20	660.00	668.80	677.60	686.40	695.20	704.00	712.80	721.60	730.40	739.20	748.00	756.80	765.60	774.40	783.20	792.00
0.890	623.00	631.90	640.80	649.70	658.60	667.50	676.40	685.30	694.20	703.10	712.00	720.90	729.80	738.70	747.60	756.50	765.40	774.30	783.20	792.10	801.00
0.900	630.00	639.00	648.00	657.00	666.00	675.00	684.00	693.00	702.00	711.00	720.00	729.00	738.00	747.00	756.00	765.00	774.00	783.00	792.00	801.00	810.00
0.910	637.00	646.10	655.20	664.30	673.40	682.50	691.60	700.70	709.80	718.90	728.00	737.10	746.20	755.30	764.40	773.50	782.60	791.70	800.80	809.90	819.00
0.920	644.00	653.20	662.40	671.60	680.80	690.00	699.20	708.40	717.60	726.80	736.00	745.20	754.40	763.60	772.80	782.00	791.20	800.40	809.60	818.80	828.00
0.930	651.00	660.30	669.60	678.90	688.20	697.50	706.80	716.10	725.40	734.70	744.00	753.30	762.60	771.90	781.20	790.50	799.80	809.10	818.40	827.70	837.00
0.940	658.00	667.40	676.80	686.20	695.60	705.00	714.40	723.80	733.20	742.60	752.00	761.40	770.80	780.20	789.60	799.00	808.40	817.80	827.20	836.60	846.00
0.950	665.00	674.50	684.00	693.50	703.00	712.50	722.00	731.50	741.00	750.50	760.00	769.50	779.00	788.50	798.00	807.50	817.00	826.50	836.00	845.50	855.00
0.960	672.00	681.60	691.20	700.80	710.40	720.00	729.60	739.20	748.80	758.40	768.00	777.60	787.20	796.80	806.40	816.00	825.60	835.20	844.80	854.40	864.00
0.970	679.00	688.70	698.40	708.10	717.80	727.50	737.20	746.90	756.60	766.30	776.00	785.70	795.40	805.10	814.80	824.50	834.20	843.90	853.60	863.30	873.00
0.980	686.00	695.80	705.60	715.40	725.20	735.00	744.80	754.60	764.40	774.20	784.00	793.80	803.60	813.40	823.20	833.00	842.80	852.60	862.40	872.20	882.00
0.990	693.00	702.90	712.80	722.70	732.60	742.50	752.40	762.30	772.20	782.10	792.00	801.90	811.80	821.70	831.60	841.50	851.40	861.30	871.20	881.10	891.00
1.000	700.00	710.00	720.00	730.00	740.00	750.00	760.00	770.00	780.00	790.00	800.00	810.00	820.00	830.00	840.00	850.00	860.00	870.00	880.00	890.00	900.00

HOW TO USE THE DVD

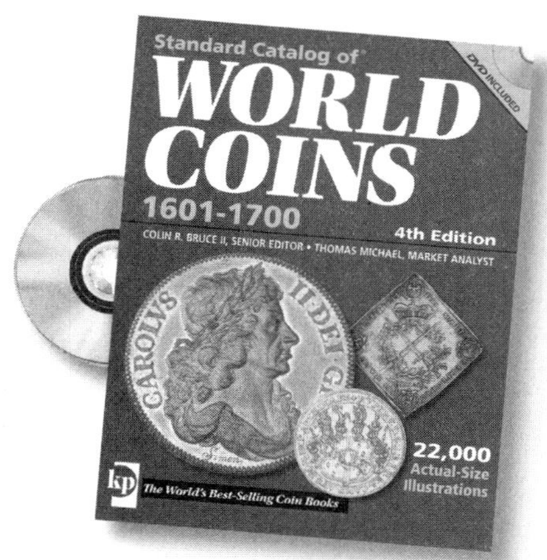

This DVD is PC and Macintosh® compatible when used with Adobe Acrobat Reader® version 6.0 or later. A step-by-step free download of Adobe Acrobat Reader® 8 is available at www.adobe.com. Adobe Reader® 8 was used in creating the instructions that follow.

To help you successfully navigate through the PDF document, several types of searches are available.

USING BOOKMARKS

Click on the Bookmarks icon to open the Bookmarks window. Use these links to go to specific points of interest. To scroll through pages in each section, use the arrows at the top of the screen (see next page for instructions to find page navigators).

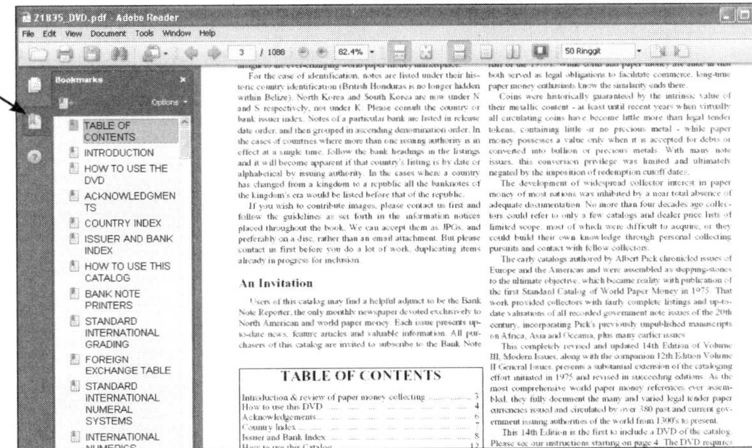

USING THE FIND BOX

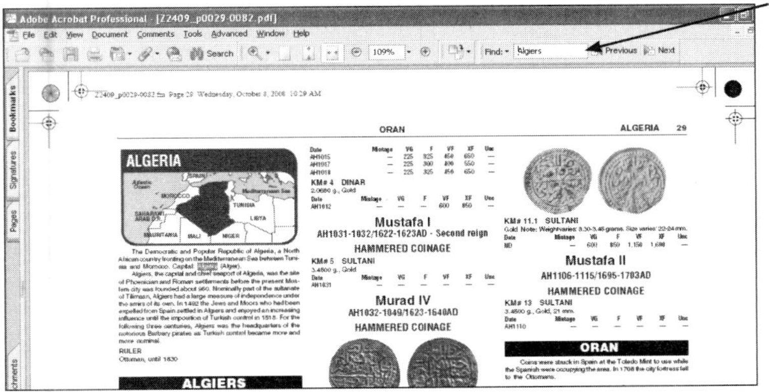

Locate the find box in the tool bar and enter the word(s) you are searching for.

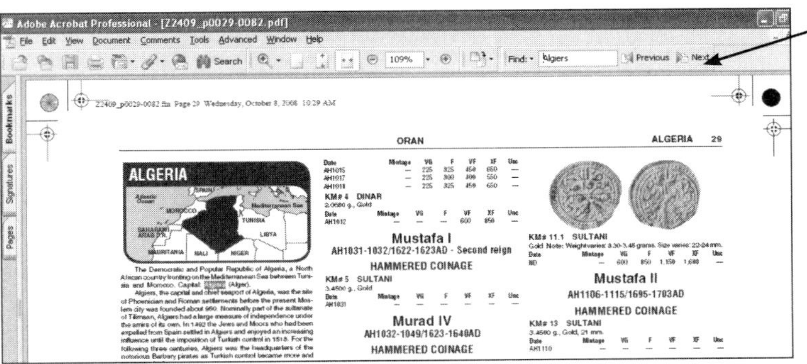

To navigate through the results of your search, use the Find Next icon.

USING THE SEARCH OPTION

Locate the Search button by choosing Customize Toolbars in the Tools pull-down menu. Check Search (binocular icon) to have the Search option available in the toolbar.

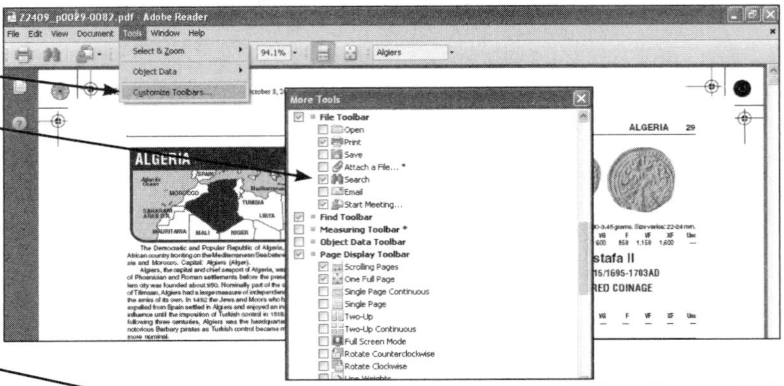

Click on the Search icon to open the Search dialog box.

In the Search dialog box, enter the word(s) you are searching for and click on the Search button.

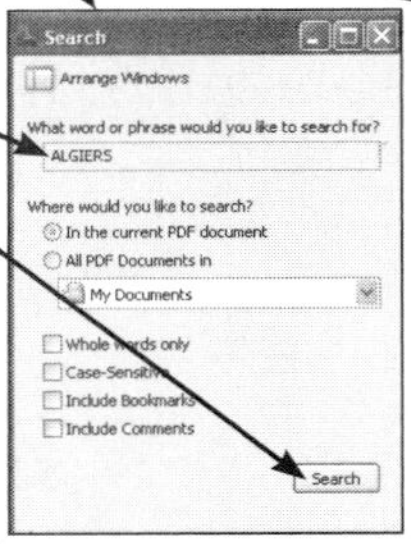

The list of results will appear in the dialog box. Click on the listings to view each page that contains your searched word(s).

To begin a new word search, click on the New Search button.

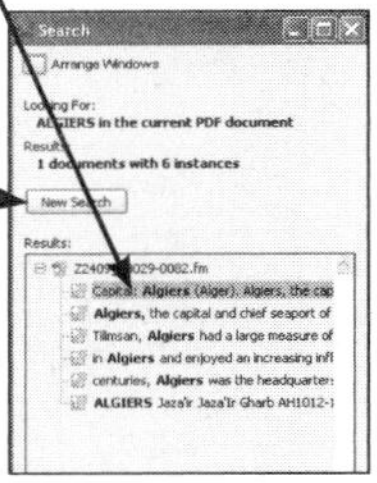

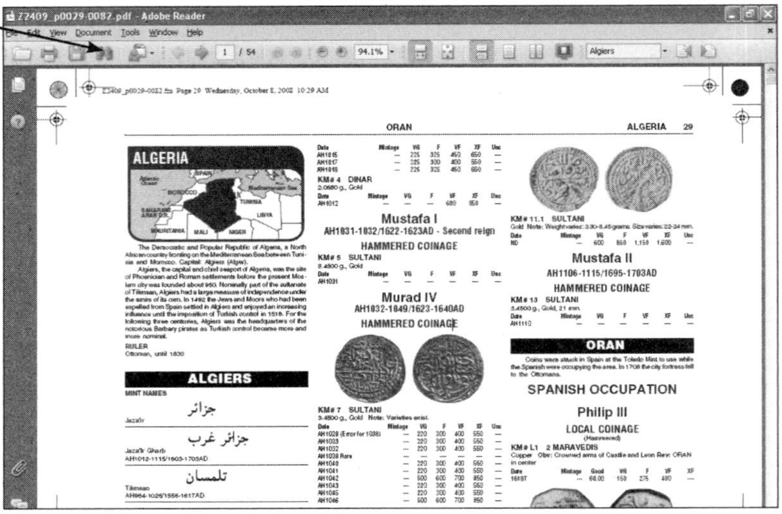

USING PAGE NAVIGATORS

Activate the Page Navigator Toolbar by choosing Customize Toolbars in the Tools pull-down menu. Check each tool as shown at right. You are now able to page through the PDF document by using the arrows at the top of the screen or by entering a page number you wish to view.

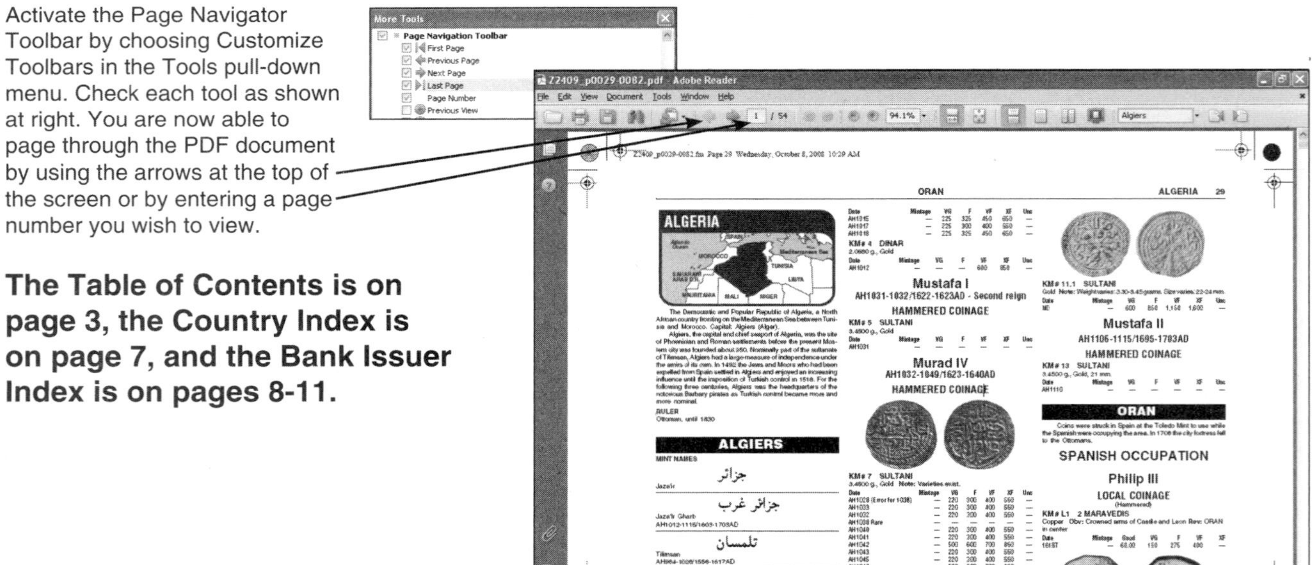

The Table of Contents is on page 3, the Country Index is on page 7, and the Bank Issuer Index is on pages 8-11.

You may also enlarge the images of the paper money up to 400% for easy viewing

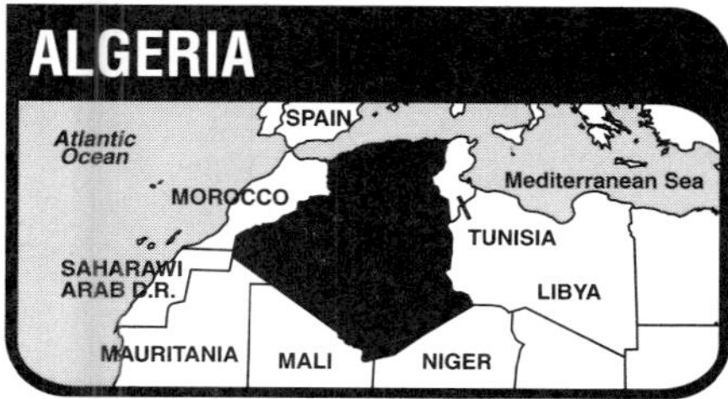

The Democratic and Popular Republic of Algeria, a North African country fronting on the Mediterranean Sea between Tunisia and Morocco. Capital: Algiers (Alger).

Algiers, the capital and chief seaport of Algeria, was the site of Phoenician and Roman settlements before the present Moslem city was founded about 950. Nominally part of the sultanate of Tilimsan, Algiers had a large measure of independence under the amirs of its own. In 1492 the Jews and Moors who had been expelled from Spain settled in Algiers and enjoyed an increasing influence until the imposition of Turkish control in 1518. For the following three centuries, Algiers was the headquarters of the notorious Barbary pirates as Turkish control became more and more nominal.

RULER

Ottoman, until 1830

ALGIERS

MINT NAMES

جزائر

Jaza'ir

جزائر غرب

Jaza'Ir Gharb

AH1012-1115/1603-1703AD

تلمسان

Tilimsan

AH964-1026/1556-1617AD

NOTE: The dots above and below the letters are integral parts of the letters, but for stylistic reasons, are occasionally omitted.

MONETARY SYSTEM

(Until 1847)

14-1/2 Asper (Akche, Dirham Saghir) = 1 Kharub
2 Kharuba = 1 Muzuna
24 Muzuna = 3 Batlaka (Pataka) = 1 Budju

NOTE: Coin denominations are not expressed on the coins, and are best determined by size and weight. The silver Budju weighed about 13.5 g until AH1236/1821AD, when it was reduced to about 10.0 g. The fractional pieces varied in proportion to the Budju. They had secondary names, which are given in the text. In 1829 three new silver coins were introduced and Budju became Tugrali-rial, Tugrali-batlaka = 1/3 Rial = 8 Muzuna and Tugralinessflik = 1/2 Batlaka = 4 Muzuna. The gold Sultani was officially valued at 108 Muzuna, but varied in accordance with the market price of gold expressed in silver. It weighed 3.20-3.40 g. The Zer-i Mahbub was valued at 80 Muzuna & weighed 2.38-3.10 g.

OTTOMAN

Ahmed I

AH1012-1026/1603-1617AD

HAMMERED COINAGE

KM# A3 MANGIR

2.5200 g., Copper

Date	Mintage	Good	VG	F	VF	XF
AH1012 Rare	—	—	—	—	—	—

KM# B3 SULTANI

3.4000 g., Gold

Date	Mintage	VG	F	VF	XF	Unc
ND Rare	—	—	—	—	—	—

KM# 3 SULTANI

Gold **Note:** Weight varies: 3.08-3.45 grams. Varieties exist.

Date	Mintage	VG	F	VF	XF	Unc
AH1011 (Error)	—	300	400	600	800	—
AH1012	—	225	300	400	550	—
AH1102 (Error); Rare	—	—	—	—	—	—

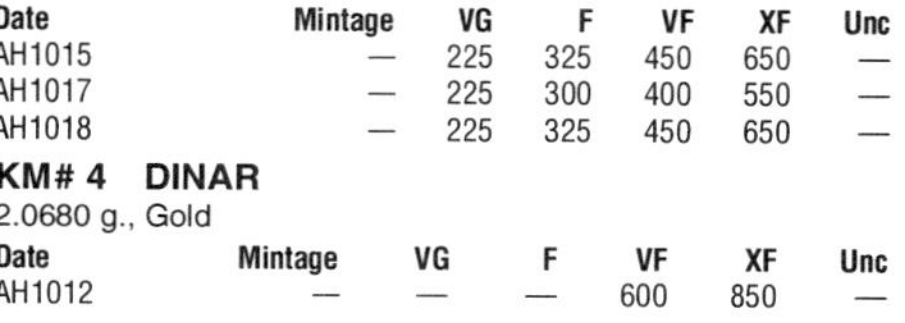

Date	Mintage	VG	F	VF	XF	Unc
AH1015	—	225	325	450	650	—
AH1017	—	225	300	400	550	—
AH1018	—	225	325	450	650	—

KM# 4 DINAR

2.0680 g., Gold

Date	Mintage	VG	F	VF	XF	Unc
AH1012	—	—	—	600	850	—

Mustafa I

AH1031-1032/1622-1623AD - Second reign

HAMMERED COINAGE

KM# 5 SULTANI

3.4500 g., Gold

Date	Mintage	VG	F	VF	XF	Unc
AH1031	—	—	—	—	—	—

Murad IV

AH1032-1049/1623-1640AD

HAMMERED COINAGE

KM# 7 SULTANI

3.4500 g., Gold **Note:** Varieties exist.

Date	Mintage	VG	F	VF	XF	Unc
AH1028 (Error for 1038)	—	220	300	400	550	—
AH1033	—	220	300	400	550	—
AH1032	—	220	300	400	550	—
AH1038 Rare	—	—	—	—	—	—
AH1040	—	220	300	400	550	—
AH1041	—	220	300	400	550	—
AH1042	—	500	600	700	850	—
AH1043	—	220	300	400	550	—
AH1045	—	220	300	400	550	—
AH1046	—	500	600	700	850	—

Ibrahim

AH1049-1058/1640-1648AD

HAMMERED COINAGE

KM# 9 SULTANI

Gold, 21-22 mm. **Note:** Weight varies: 3.00-3.46 grams. Size varies.

Date	Mintage	VG	F	VF	XF	Unc
AH1049	—	225	400	500	650	—
AH1050//1049	—	225	400	550	700	—
Note: 1050 on obverse, 1049 on reverse						
AH10xx	—	225	400	500	650	—
AH1051	—	225	400	500	650	—
AH1052	—	225	400	500	650	—

Mehmed IV

AH1058-1099/1648-1687AD

HAMMERED COINAGE

KM# 11.2 SULTANI

Gold **Note:** Varieties exist.

Date	Mintage	VG	F	VF	XF	Unc
AH1058	—	—	—	—	—	—
AH1061	—	220	285	375	500	—
AH1076	—	220	285	375	500	—
AH1078	—	220	285	375	500	—
AH1086	—	220	285	375	500	—
AH1090	—	220	285	375	500	—
AH1092	—	220	285	375	500	—

KM# 11.1 SULTANI

Gold **Note:** Weight varies: 3.30-3.45 grams. Size varies: 22-24 mm.

Date	Mintage	VG	F	VF	XF	Unc
ND	—	600	850	1,150	1,600	—

Mustafa II

AH1106-1115/1695-1703AD

HAMMERED COINAGE

KM# 13 SULTANI

3.4500 g., Gold, 21 mm.

Date	Mintage	VG	F	VF	XF	Unc
AH1110	—	—	—	—	—	—

ORAN

Coins were struck in Spain at the Toledo Mint to use while the Spanish were occupying the area. In 1708 the city fortress fell to the Ottomans.

SPANISH OCCUPATION

Philip III

LOCAL COINAGE

(Hammered)

KM# L1 2 MARAVEDIS

Copper **Obv:** Crowned arms of Castile and Leon **Rev:** ORAN in center

Date	Mintage	Good	VG	F	VF	XF
1618T	—	60.00	150	275	400	—

KM# L2 4 MARAVEDIS

Copper **Obv:** Crowned arms of Castile and Leon **Rev:** ORAN

Date	Mintage	Good	VG	F	VF	XF
1618	—	60.00	150	275	400	—

KM# L4 4 MARAVEDIS

Copper **Obv:** Crowned arms of Castile and Leon **Rev:** Crowned 'IHS' below 'ORAN'

Date	Mintage	Good	VG	F	VF	XF
1691	—	—	—	—	—	—

KM# L3 8 MARAVEDIS

Copper **Obv:** Crowned arms of Castile and Leon **Rev:** ORAN in center of legend

Date	Mintage	Good	VG	F	VF	XF
1618	—	50.00	125	250	375	—

KM# L5 8 MARAVEDIS

Copper **Obv:** Crowned arms of Castile and Leon **Rev:** Crowned 'IHS' below 'ORAN'.

Date	Mintage	Good	VG	F	VF	XF
1691	—	—	—	—	—	—

ANGOLA

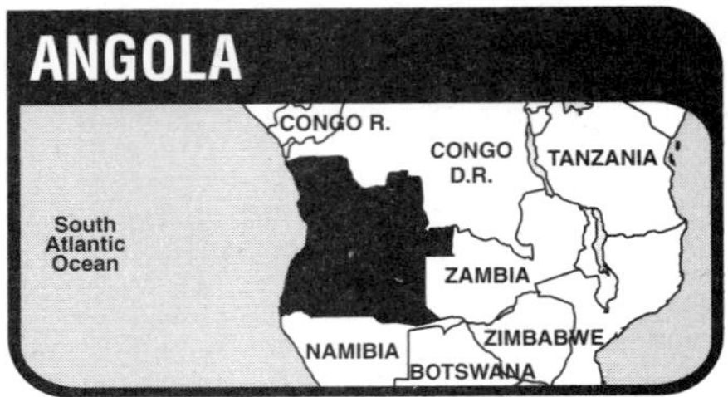

Angola is a country on the west coast of southern Africa. The population is predominantly Bantu in origin.

Angola was discovered by Portuguese navigator Diogo Cao in 1482. Portuguese settlers arrived in 1491, and established Angola as a major slaving center which sent about 3 million slaves to the New World.

RULER

Portuguese until 1975

MONETARY SYSTEM

(Until 1860)

50 Reis = 1 Macuta

PORTUGUESE COLONY

COLONIAL COINAGE

KM# 3 5 REIS (V)

Copper **Note:** The 1749 V Reis formerly listed here as KM#6 can be found under Brazil KM#159. This coin was struck for Brazil but also circulated in Angola.

Date	Mintage	VG	F	VF	XF	Unc
1695	—	275	475	800	1,750	—
1696	—	250	450	775	1,750	—

KM# 2 10 REIS (X)

Copper **Note:** The 1715-1749 X Reis formerly listed here as KM#4 can be found under Brazil KM#108 and KM#142. These coins were struck for Brazil but also circulated in Angola.

Date	Mintage	VG	F	VF	XF	Unc
1693 Unique	—	—	—	—	—	—
1694	—	100	200	350	750	—
1696	—	70.00	145	250	450	—
1697	—	20.00	40.00	80.00	175	—
1699	—	20.00	40.00	80.00	175	—

KM# 1 20 REIS (XX)

Copper **Note:** Similar to 5 Reis, KM#3. The 1715-1749 XX Reis formerly listed here as KM#5 can be found under Brazil KM#109 and KM#143. These coins were struck for Brazil but also circulated in Angola.

Date	Mintage	VG	F	VF	XF	Unc
1693	—	90.00	250	475	750	—
1694	—	60.00	110	225	400	—
1695	—	65.00	120	250	425	—
1697	—	8.00	16.00	35.00	75.00	—
1698	—	8.00	16.00	35.00	75.00	—
1699	—	7.50	14.00	28.00	65.00	—

ARMENIA

Presently the Republic of Armenia (formerly Armenian S.S.R.) is bounded in the north by Georgia, to the east by Azerbaijan and to the south and west by Turkey and Iran (Persia). It has an area of 11,506 sq. mi. (29,800 sq. km).

The earliest history of Armenia records continuous struggles with expanding Babylonia and later Assyria. In the sixth century B.C. it was called Armina. Later under the Persian empire it enjoyed the position of a vassal state. Conquered by Macedonia, it later defeated the Seleucids and Greater Armenia was founded under the Artaxis dynasty. Christianity was established in 303 A.D. which led to religious wars with the Persians and Romans who divided it into two zones of influence. The Arabs succeeded the Persian Empire of the Sassanids which later allowed the Armenian princes to conclude a treaty in 653 A.D. In 862 A.D. Ashot V was recognized as the "prince of princes" and established a throne recognized by Baghdad and Constantinople in 886 A.D. The Seljuks overran the whole country and united with Kurdistan which eventually ran the new government. In 1240 A.D. onward the Mongols occupied almost all of western Asia until their downfall in 1375 A.D. when various Kurdish, Armenian and Turkoman independent principalities arose. After the defeat of the Persians in 1516 A.D. the Ottoman Turks gradually took control over a period of some 40 years, with Kurdish tribes settling within Armenian lands. In 1605 A.D. the Persians moved thousands of Armenians as far as India developing prosperous colonies. Persia and the Ottoman Turks were again at war, with the Ottomans once again prevailing. The Ottomans later gave absolute civil authority to a Christian bishop allowing them free enjoyment of their religion and traditions.

RULER

Persian, until 1724

MINT NAMES

Revan, (Erevan, now Yerevan)

OTTOMAN EMPIRE

STANDARD COINAGE

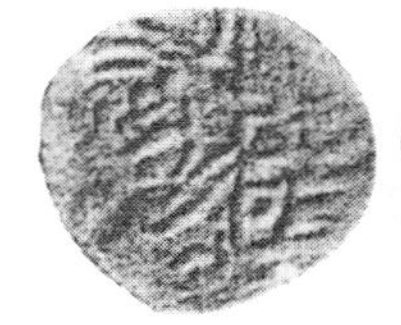

KM# 6 DIRHEM

1.9000 g., Silver **Obv:** Toughra **Rev:** Duribe Revan

Date	Mintage	VG	F	VF	XF	Unc
AHxxxx Rare	—	—	—	—	—	—

Mustafa I

STANDARD COINAGE

KM# 10 DIRHEM

1.8400 g., Silver **Obv:** Toughra with 4 lines **Rev:** Ruler and mint name

Date	Mintage	VG	F	VF	XF	Unc
AH1031 Rare	—	—	—	—	—	—

AUSTRIA

Presently the Republic of Austria, a parliamentary democracy located in mountainous central Europe, has an area of 32,374 sq. mi. (83,850 sq. km.) and a population of 8.08 million. Capital: Wien (Vienna). Austria is primarily an industrial country. Machinery, iron, steel, textiles, yarns and timber are exported.

The territories later to be known as Austria were overrun in pre-Roman times by various tribes, including the Celts. Upon the fall of the Roman Empire, the country became a margravate of Charlemagne's Empire. Premysl II of Otaker, King of Bohemia, gained possession in 1252, only to lose the territory to Rudolf of Habsburg in 1276. Thereafter, until World War I, the story of Austria was conducted by the ruling Habsburgs.

During the 17th century, Austrian coinage reflected the geopolitical strife of three wars. From 1618-1648, the Thirty Years' War between northern Protestants and southern Catholics produced low quality, "kipperwhipper" strikes of 12, 24, 30, 60, 75 and 150 Kreuzer. Later, during the Austrian-Turkish War, 1660-1664, coinages used to maintain soldier's salaries also reported the steady division of Hungarian territories. Finally, between 1683 and 1699, during the second Austrian-Turkish conflict, new issues of 3, 6 and 15 Kreuzers were struck, being necessary to help defray mounting expenses of the war effort.

RULERS

Rudolf II, 1576-1612
Matthias II, 1612-1619
Ferdinand II, 1619-1637
Ferdinand III, 1637-1657
Leopold I, 1657-1705

MINT MARKS

A, W, WI - Vienna (Wien)
(a) - Vienna (Wien)
AI,AL-IV,C-A,E,GA - Karlsburg (Alba Iulia, Transylvania)
B,K,KB - Kremnica (Kremnitz, Hungary)
BE,BE/V,BEZ,B.T. - Bistrice (Romania)
CB,CI,CI-BI(NI),CW,H,HS - Hermannstadt (Sibiu) (Transylvania)
CV (1693-94),FT,KV (1694-1700) - Klausenburg (Cluy, Transylvania)
D - Salzburg
D,G,GR - Graz (Styria)
F, HA - Hall
G,H,P-R - Gunzburg
GM - Mantua (Mantova)
(h) Shield - Vienna (Wien)
M - Milan (Milano, Lombardy)
MB 1693-1697, 1702 - Breh (Brzeg)
NB - Nagybanya (Baia Mare, Hungary)
O - Olmutz (Olomouc)
O - Oravicza (Oravita, Hungary)
S - Schmollnitz (Smolnik, Hungary)
V - Venice (Venice, Venetia)
(v) Eagle - Hall
W - Breslau (Wroclaw, Vratislav, Poland)

MINT IDENTIFICATION

To aid in determining an Austrian (Habsburg) coin's mint it is necessary to first check the coat of arms. In some cases the coat of arms will dominate the reverse. The Hungarian Madonna and child is a prime example. On more traditional Austrian design types the provincial coat of arms will be the only one on the imperial eagle's breast. When a more complicated coat of arms is used the provincial arms will usually be found in the center or at the top center usually overlapping neighboring arms.

Legend endings frequently reflect the various provincial coats of arms. Sometimes mint marks appear on coins such as the letter W for Breslau. Mintmaster's and mint officials' initials or symbols also appear and can be used to confirm the mint identity.

The following pages will present the mint name, illustrate or describe the provincial coats of arms, legend endings, mint marks, and mint officials' initials or symbols with which the mint identity can be determined.

AUGSBURG MINT

BRUNN MINT

(Brno)
(in Moravia)

MINT MARKS

Privy Mark	Description	Date	Names
	Circled B	1624, 1625, 1627	

MINT OFFICIALS' INITIALS

Initials	Dates	Names
GR	1621-23	Georg Ritter

HG	1624	Hans Gebhart
BZ	1624	B. Zwirner

MINT OFFICIALS' PRIVY MARKS

Privy Mark	Description	Date	Names
CW(c) - cw	CW monogram	1623-27	Christoph Wonsiedler
(cs) -	Crenalated square	1621-23	Cons. De Witte
(ct) -	Circle in triangle or triangle in circle	1646-48	Johann Jan Conrad Richthausen
(d)	Dot in center of diamond		
(h) -	Conjoined HP, metal hook	1619-20	Peter Hema
		1619-22	Hans Peca
(o)	Dot in triangle		
(s)	Snowflake		

FÜRTH MINT

(in Bavaria)

Coat of arms, like Vienna, fills the lower left quarter of the shield on the imperial eagle's breast.

MINT OFFICIALS' INITIALS

Initials	Date	Name
CS	1630	Conrad Stutz, in Nurnberg

GRAZ MINT

(in Province of Styria)

Coat of arms, rampant panther similar to Bohemian lion, usually found on imperial eagle's breast. Legend usually ends: STY, STYR or STYRIAE.

MINT MARKS

D, G, GR - Graz (Styria)

MINT OFFICIALS' INITIALS

Initials	Dates	Names
CH, SH	1665-66	Sebastian Haydt
HCK	1657-65	Hans Caspar Khendimayer
IA	1694-1705	Johann Jacob Aigmann
IAN	1670-1694	Johann Anton Nowak
IGH	1671-73	-
IGW, IW	1671	Johann Georg Weiss
L	1660-82	-
MAX K		Maximillian Konig, engraver
M-IS	1649	Hans Ulrich Mark
MM	1690	Michael Miller, engraver

MINT OFFICIALS' PRIVY MARKS

Privy Mark	Description	Dates	Names
(m) - M	Stylized M	1648-49	Hans Ulrich Mark

HALL MINT

(in Tyrol)

Coat of arms are on eagle's breast. Legends usually end: TYR or TYROL.

MINT OFFICIALS' INITIALS

Initials	Dates	Names
CO, co	1613-18	Christoph Orber
IAK	1693-1701, 1704, 1706	Johann anton Konig, die-cutter

KLAGENFURT MINT

(in Province of Carinthia)

Coat of arms usually found in legend or as the middle arms on the imperial eagle's breast. Legend usually ends CAR or CARINTHIAE. This mint closed in 1622 and moved to Saint Veit.

MINT OFFICIALS' INITIALS

PS - P. Sigharter

KRAIN MINT

MAINZ MINT

(Germany)

MINT OFFICIALS' PRIVY MARK

Privy Mark	Description	Dates	Names
(s) -		1685	Ulrich Burkhart Wildering

NEUBURG am INN MINT

(in upper Austria)

Coat of arms, like Vienna, or quartered arms on imperial eagle's breast.

MINT OFFICIALS' PRIVY MARK

Privy mark	Description	Date	Name
(t) -	Triangle	1664-65	Bartholomaus Triangel

NIKOLSBURG MINT

(Mikulov)

(in Moravia)

For coat of arms, see Vienna. This mint opened in 1627 and closed in 1628.

MINT OFFICIALS' PRIVY MARKS

Privy marks	Description	Dates	Names
CW	C above W	1625	Christoph Wansidler

OLMÜTZ MINT

(Olomouc)

(in Moravia)

Coat of arms, see Vienna. This mint was captured and occupied by Sweden from June, 1642 until July, 1650 when it moved to Brunn. In 1664 it was closed.

MINT MARKS

1620, 1624, 1628

MINT OFFICIALS' INITIALS

Initials	Dates	Names
BZ	1620-24	Balthasar Zwirner, mintmaster
CC	1619-20	Cristoph Cantor
GR	1621-23	Georg Ritter, die cutter
HH	1636	Jan Krystof Huber, warden

MINT OFFICIALS' PRIVY MARKS

Privy Mark	Description	Dates	Names
ICH	C above IH	1635-36	Tobias Sonnenschein, mintmaster
		1636-38	Mrs. Dorota Sonnenschein
MF	Ligate MF, MF and anchor between crescents	1625-27, 29-35	Martin Fritsch
(a) -	Anchor	1628-40	-
(d) -	Crenalated diamond	1622-23	-
(h) -	HP & hook	1621	Peter Hema
(i)	Lamb in oval	1638-42	Adam Schafer, mintmaster
(l)	Leaf		
(o)	O in circle		

SAINT POLTEN MINT

Coat of arms, see Vienna.

MINT OFFICIALS' PRIVY MARKS

Privy mark	Description	Dates	Names
(c) -	Inverted chevron in circle	1624-25	Matthias Fellner v. Feldegg
(d)	Double trefoil in circle	1624-25	Johann Joachim Edling
			Donat Starkh, die-cutter
(f) - II E	Fleur de lis in circle between II & E	1625	Johann Joachim Edling
(r) -	Rosette	1625-26	Martin Turba

SAINT VEIT MINT

(in Carinthia)

Coat of arms, see Klagenfurt, are usually found on top center of the massive coat of arms on the imperial eagle's breast. Legend usually ends CAR or CARINTHIAE. This mint moved from Klagenfurt and opened in October, 1622. It closed in 1720.

MINT OFFICIALS' INITIALS

Initials	Dates	Names
CCS	1696	Carl Georg Christoph Strauss v. Straussenegg
CS	1690, 1692-1700	
DS	1622	Donat Stockh, die-cutter
GCVS	1689, 1693	Carl Georg Christoph
GSVS	1689, 91, 94	Strauss V. Straussenegg
G, GS,	1668-72	Georg Christoph Strauss v.
GCS		Straussenegg
HGP	1630, 38, 42	Hans Georg Perro
HL, LS	1693	-
IGR, IR	1679-89	John Georg Rabensteiner
IIP, IP	1699-1705	Johann Josef Preiss
IW	1700	-
P	1627	H. G. Perro
p-HS	1649	H. J. Stadler

MINT OFFICIALS' MONOGRAMS

Monogram	Description	Dates	Names
(g) - HG	HG monogram	1627-28	Hans Georg, die-cutter
(h) - M	HM monogram	1623-25	Hans Matz
(is) - IS	IS monogram	1645, 50, 54, 57	H. J. Stadler
(m) - MH	MH monogram		
(p) -	PS monogram	1624-28	Paul Sigharter

VIENNA MINT

(Wien)

Coat of arms, usually found in the legend or as the middle arms on a multiple arms shield or alone on the imperial eagle's breast. Legend usually ends TY, TYR or TYROL.

MINT OFFICIALS' INITIALS

Initials	Dates	Names
AP	1628, 30	Andreas Peter, die-cutter
BZ	1624	Balthasar Zwirner
CH	1610-11	Caspar Haidler, die-cutter
CM	1609-12	Christian Maler, die-cutter
DS	1624-37	Donat Starkh, die-cutter
HH	1659	?
HS	1655, 57-58	Hans Stadler
IMH, MH	1680-1736	Johann Michael Hofmann

MINT OFFICIALS' PRIVY MARKS

Privy mark	Description	Dates	Names
(b)	Bird		
(bs) -	Bird standing in circle	1637-48	Hans Jacob Stadler

Privy mark	Description	Date	Name
(bw) -	Rooster walking right	1605-12, 22	Andreas Handl
(c) -	Chevrons within circles	1648-59	Johann Conrad Richthausen
(ca) -	CA monogram	1660-65	Andrea Cetto
(cv) -	Crowned CV monogram in circle	1636-37	Virgilius Constanz v. Vestenburg
(lf) -	Floweret	1659-60	Franz Faber
(ic)	Inverted chevron & inverted Y	1612-17, 19-36	Matthias Feliner v.Feldegg
(if)	Large flower	1622-23	Martin Turba, warden
(mm) -	MM monogram	1679-95, 1703-05, 07-08	Matthias Mittermayer
(r) -	Rosette	1659-60, 66-79	Franz Faber v. Rosenstock
(ri) -	Ring	1588-1604	Lorenz Huebmer
(t) -	Tree on shield	1617-19	Isaias Jessensky
(v)	VC monogram in circle		

WÜRZBURG MINT

(in Germany)

Coat of arms, like Vienna.

MINT OFFICIALS' PRIVY MARKS

Privy mark	Description	Date	Name
(a) -	Stylized A	1685	

EMPIRE

STANDARD COINAGE

KM# 10 4 HELLER (Vierer)

Silver **Ruler:** Rudolf II **Obv:** Coat of arms within legend **Rev:** Eagle in inner circle **Mint:** Hall **Note:** Prev. KM#580.

Date	Mintage	VG	F	VF	XF	Unc
1601	—	55.00	110	195	300	—
1603	—	55.00	110	195	300	—
1604	—	55.00	110	195	300	—
1605	—	55.00	110	195	300	—
1606	—	55.00	110	195	300	—

KM# 11 PFENNIG

Silver **Ruler:** Ferdinand II **Obv:** Griffin in shield with date above in diamond **Mint:** Graz **Note:** Uniface. Varieties exist. Prev. KM#555.

Date	Mintage	VG	F	VF	XF	Unc
1601	—	8.00	17.00	27.50	48.00	—
1602	—	8.00	17.00	27.50	48.00	—
1603	—	8.00	17.00	27.50	48.00	—
1604	—	8.00	17.00	27.50	48.00	—
1605	—	8.00	17.00	27.50	48.00	—
1608	—	8.00	17.00	27.50	48.00	—
(1)609	—	8.00	17.00	27.50	48.00	—
1610	—	8.00	17.00	27.50	48.00	—
1611	—	8.00	17.00	27.50	48.00	—
1612	—	8.00	17.00	27.50	48.00	—
1613	—	—	—	—	—	—
Note: Reported, not confirmed						
1614	—	8.00	17.00	27.50	48.00	—
1615	—	8.00	17.00	27.50	48.00	—
1616	—	8.00	17.00	27.50	48.00	—
1617	—	8.00	17.00	27.50	48.00	—

KM# 12 PFENNIG

Silver **Ruler:** Ferdinand II **Obv:** Divided arms with date above in diamond **Mint:** Klagenfurt **Note:** Uniface. Varieties exist. Local issue for Archduke Ferdinand. Prev. KM#985.

Date	Mintage	VG	F	VF	XF	Unc
1601	—	12.00	25.00	42.00	70.00	—
1602	—	12.00	25.00	42.00	70.00	—
1603	—	12.00	25.00	42.00	70.00	—
1604	—	12.00	25.00	42.00	70.00	—
1605	—	12.00	25.00	42.00	70.00	—
1606	—	12.00	25.00	42.00	70.00	—
1607	—	12.00	25.00	42.00	70.00	—
1608	—	12.00	25.00	42.00	70.00	—
1609	—	12.00	25.00	42.00	70.00	—
1610	—	12.00	25.00	42.00	70.00	—
1612	—	12.00	25.00	42.00	70.00	—
1613	—	12.00	25.00	42.00	70.00	—
1614	—	12.00	25.00	42.00	70.00	—
1616	—	12.00	25.00	42.00	70.00	—
1617	—	12.00	25.00	42.00	70.00	—
1618	—	12.00	25.00	42.00	70.00	—

KM# 133 PFENNIG

Billon **Ruler:** Matthias II **Obv:** Shield of arms divides date in diamond **Mint:** Vienna **Note:** Uniface. Prev. KM#1725.

Date	Mintage	VG	F	VF	XF	Unc
1612	—	—	—	—	—	—

KM# 466 PFENNIG

Billon **Ruler:** Ferdinand II **Obv:** Shield of arms at center of diamond, date at sides and top **Mint:** Graz **Note:** Uniface. Varieties exist. Prev. KM#335.

Date	Mintage	VG	F	VF	XF	Unc
1624	—	9.00	22.00	45.00	75.00	—
1625	—	9.00	22.00	45.00	75.00	—
1626	—	9.00	22.00	45.00	75.00	—
1627	—	9.00	22.00	45.00	75.00	—
1628	—	9.00	22.00	45.00	75.00	—
1629	—	9.00	22.00	45.00	75.00	—
1630	—	9.00	22.00	45.00	75.00	—
1631	—	9.00	22.00	45.00	75.00	—
1632	—	9.00	22.00	45.00	75.00	—
1633	—	9.00	22.00	45.00	75.00	—
1634	—	9.00	22.00	45.00	75.00	—
1635	—	9.00	22.00	45.00	75.00	—
1636	—	9.00	22.00	45.00	75.00	—
1637	—	9.00	22.00	45.00	75.00	—

KM# 467 PFENNIG

Billon **Ruler:** Ferdinand II **Obv:** Carinthian arms in diamond, one digit of date on each side **Mint:** Saint Veit **Note:** Uniface. Prev. KM#1585.

Date	Mintage	VG	F	VF	XF	Unc
1624 (g)	—	30.00	50.00	90.00	150	—
1625 (h)	—	30.00	50.00	90.00	150	—
1627 (g)	—	30.00	50.00	90.00	150	—
1629 (g)	—	30.00	50.00	90.00	150	—

KM# 765 PFENNIG

Billon **Ruler:** Ferdinand III **Obv:** Date numerals left and right **Mint:** Saint Veit **Note:** Varieties exist. Uniface. Prev. KM#1620.

Date	Mintage	VG	F	VF	XF	Unc
1631	—	5.00	12.00	22.00	50.00	—
1636	—	5.00	12.00	22.00	50.00	—
1637	—	5.00	12.00	22.00	50.00	—
1639	—	5.00	12.00	22.00	50.00	—
1652	—	5.00	12.00	22.00	50.00	—
1653	—	5.00	12.00	22.00	50.00	—
1654	—	5.00	12.00	22.00	50.00	—

KM# 826 PFENNIG

Billon **Ruler:** Ferdinand III **Obv:** Oval shield of arms **Mint:** Graz **Note:** Uniface. Prev. KM#415.

Date	Mintage	VG	F	VF	XF	Unc
1637	—	4.00	9.00	18.00	30.00	—
1638	—	4.00	9.00	18.00	30.00	—
1639	—	4.00	9.00	18.00	30.00	—
1640	—	4.00	9.00	18.00	30.00	—

KM# 848 PFENNIG

Billon **Ruler:** Ferdinand III **Obv:** Flat-topped shield of arms **Mint:** Graz **Note:** Prev. KM#416.

Date	Mintage	VG	F	VF	XF	Unc
1638	—	4.00	9.00	18.00	30.00	—

KM# 847 PFENNIG

Billon **Ruler:** Ferdinand III **Obv:** Crowned arms divide date **Mint:** Glatz **Note:** Uniface. Prev. KM#290.

Date	Mintage	VG	F	VF	XF	Unc
1638	—	—	—	—	—	—

KM# 906 PFENNIG

Billon **Ruler:** Ferdinand III **Obv:** Oval arms **Mint:** Saint Veit **Note:** Prev. KM#1621.

Date	Mintage	VG	F	VF	XF	Unc
1642	—	5.00	12.00	22.00	50.00	—
1645	—	5.00	12.00	22.00	50.00	—
1649	—	5.00	12.00	22.00	50.00	—

KM# 905 PFENNIG

Billon **Ruler:** Ferdinand III **Obv:** Arms in cartouche at center of diamond, date at sides and bottom **Mint:** Graz **Note:** Prev. KM#417.

Date	Mintage	VG	F	VF	XF	Unc
1642	—	4.00	9.00	18.00	30.00	—
1643	—	4.00	9.00	18.00	30.00	—
1645	—	4.00	9.00	18.00	30.00	—
1647	—	4.00	9.00	18.00	30.00	—

KM# 923 PFENNIG

Billon **Ruler:** Ferdinand III **Obv:** Date at sides and top **Mint:** Graz **Note:** Varieties exist. Prev. KM#418.

Date	Mintage	VG	F	VF	XF	Unc
1645	—	4.00	9.00	18.00	30.00	—
1648	—	4.00	9.00	18.00	30.00	—
1649	—	4.00	9.00	18.00	30.00	—
1650	—	4.00	9.00	18.00	30.00	—
1653	—	4.00	9.00	18.00	30.00	—

KM# 945 PFENNIG

Billon **Ruler:** Ferdinand III **Obv:** Small shield of arms divides date in diamond, F above shield, W below **Mint:** Vienna **Note:** Uniface. Prev. KM#1815.

Date	Mintage	VG	F	VF	XF	Unc
1647	—	10.00	20.00	40.00	70.00	—
1648	—	10.00	20.00	40.00	70.00	—

KM# 994 PFENNIG

Billon **Ruler:** Ferdinand III **Obv:** Flat-topped shield of arms at center of quatrefoil, date at sides and bottom **Mint:** Graz **Note:** Prev. KM#419.

Date	Mintage	VG	F	VF	XF	Unc
1656	—	4.00	9.00	18.00	30.00	—
1657	—	4.00	9.00	18.00	30.00	—

KM# 1111 PFENNIG

Billon **Ruler:** Leopold I **Obv:** Carinthian arms in diamond, one digit of date on each side **Mint:** Saint Veit **Note:** Uniface. Prev. KM#1635.

Date	Mintage	VG	F	VF	XF	Unc
1658	—	5.00	10.00	20.00	45.00	—
1659	—	5.00	10.00	20.00	45.00	—
1660	—	5.00	10.00	20.00	45.00	—
1664	—	5.00	10.00	20.00	45.00	—
1669	—	5.00	10.00	20.00	45.00	—
1681	—	5.00	10.00	20.00	45.00	—
1682	—	5.00	10.00	20.00	45.00	—
1684	—	5.00	10.00	20.00	45.00	—
1690	—	5.00	10.00	20.00	45.00	—
1693	—	5.00	10.00	20.00	45.00	—
1695	—	5.00	10.00	20.00	45.00	—
1696	—	5.00	10.00	20.00	45.00	—

KM# 1168 PFENNIG

Billon **Ruler:** Leopold I **Obv:** Oval arms divide date **Mint:** Graz **Note:** Uniface. Prev. KM#445.

Date	Mintage	VG	F	VF	XF	Unc
1660	—	5.00	10.00	20.00	40.00	—
1661	—	5.00	10.00	20.00	40.00	—
1662	—	5.00	10.00	20.00	40.00	—
1666	—	5.00	10.00	20.00	40.00	—
1671	—	5.00	10.00	20.00	40.00	—
1673	—	5.00	10.00	20.00	40.00	—
1674	—	5.00	10.00	20.00	40.00	—
1675	—	5.00	10.00	20.00	40.00	—

KM# 1286 PFENNIG

Billon **Ruler:** Leopold I **Obv:** Oval arms in diamond **Mint:** Graz **Note:** Varieties exist. Prev. KM#446.

Date	Mintage	VG	F	VF	XF	Unc
1676	—	5.00	10.00	20.00	40.00	—
1677	—	5.00	10.00	20.00	40.00	—
1678	—	5.00	10.00	20.00	40.00	—
1679	—	5.00	10.00	20.00	40.00	—
1680	—	5.00	10.00	20.00	40.00	—
1682	—	5.00	10.00	20.00	40.00	—
1684	—	5.00	10.00	20.00	40.00	—
1685	—	5.00	10.00	20.00	40.00	—
1686	—	5.00	10.00	20.00	40.00	—
1687	—	5.00	10.00	20.00	40.00	—
1688	—	5.00	10.00	20.00	40.00	—
1689	—	5.00	10.00	20.00	40.00	—
1691	—	5.00	10.00	20.00	40.00	—
1692	—	5.00	10.00	20.00	40.00	—
1693	—	5.00	10.00	20.00	40.00	—

KM# 13 2 PFENNIG

Silver **Ruler:** Ferdinand II **Obv:** Two crowned shields with date below in trilobe **Mint:** Klagenfurt **Note:** Uniface. Varieties exist. Local issue for Archduke Ferdinand. Prev. KM#986.

Date	Mintage	VG	F	VF	XF	Unc
1601	—	10.00	20.00	35.00	65.00	—
1602	—	10.00	20.00	35.00	65.00	—
1603	—	10.00	20.00	35.00	65.00	—
1604	—	10.00	20.00	35.00	65.00	—
1605	—	10.00	20.00	35.00	65.00	—
1606	—	10.00	20.00	35.00	65.00	—
1607	—	10.00	20.00	35.00	65.00	—
1608	—	10.00	20.00	35.00	65.00	—
1609	—	10.00	20.00	35.00	65.00	—
1610	—	10.00	20.00	35.00	65.00	—
1611	—	10.00	20.00	35.00	65.00	—
1612	—	10.00	20.00	35.00	65.00	—
1613	—	10.00	20.00	35.00	65.00	—
1614	—	10.00	20.00	35.00	65.00	—
1615	—	10.00	20.00	35.00	65.00	—
1616	—	10.00	20.00	35.00	65.00	—
1617	—	10.00	20.00	35.00	65.00	—
1618	—	10.00	20.00	35.00	65.00	—

KM# 14 2 PFENNIG

Silver **Ruler:** Ferdinand II **Obv:** Two crowned shields with date below, in trilobe **Mint:** Graz **Note:** Uniface. Varieties exist. Prev. KM#556.

Date	Mintage	VG	F	VF	XF	Unc
(1)601	—	8.00	17.00	27.50	48.00	—
(1)602	—	8.00	17.00	27.50	48.00	—
(1)603	—	8.00	17.00	27.50	48.00	—
(1)604	—	8.00	17.00	27.50	48.00	—
(1)605	—	8.00	17.00	27.50	48.00	—
1606	—	8.00	17.00	27.50	48.00	—
(1)608	—	8.00	17.00	27.50	48.00	—
(1)610	—	8.00	17.00	27.50	48.00	—
(1)611	—	8.00	17.00	27.50	48.00	—
(1)612	—	8.00	17.00	27.50	48.00	—
(1)613	—	8.00	17.00	27.50	48.00	—
(1)614	—	8.00	17.00	27.50	48.00	—
(1)615	—	8.00	17.00	27.50	48.00	—
(1)616	—	8.00	17.00	27.50	48.00	—
(1)617	—	8.00	17.00	27.50	48.00	—

KM# 251 2 PFENNIG

Billon **Ruler:** Ferdinand II **Mint:** Klagenfurt **Note:** Uniface. Three shields of arms, one above two. Prev. KM#950.

Date	Mintage	VG	F	VF	XF	Unc
ND	—	20.00	40.00	70.00	120	—

KM# 252 2 PFENNIG

Billon **Ruler:** Ferdinand II **Obv:** Three shields of arms, top shiled divides date **Mint:** Saint Veit **Note:** Varieties exist. Uniface. Prev. KM#1586.

Date	Mintage	VG	F	VF	XF	Unc
ND	—	25.00	45.00	85.00	145	—
1620	—	25.00	45.00	85.00	145	—
1623	—	25.00	45.00	85.00	145	—
1623 (m)	—	25.00	45.00	85.00	145	—
1624	—	25.00	45.00	85.00	145	—
1624 (m)	—	15.00	25.00	50.00	100	—
1625 (m)	—	15.00	25.00	50.00	100	—
1625 (h)	—	15.00	25.00	50.00	100	—
1625 (p)	—	18.00	35.00	60.00	120	—
1626 (p)	—	18.00	35.00	60.00	120	—
1627 (p)	—	18.00	35.00	60.00	120	—

KM# 377 2 PFENNIG

Billon **Ruler:** Ferdinand II **Obv:** Three shields of arms, one above two, date divided by top shield **Mint:** Graz **Note:** Uniface. Varieties exist. Prev. KM#336.

Date	Mintage	VG	F	VF	XF	Unc
1622	—	9.00	22.00	45.00	75.00	—
1623	—	9.00	22.00	45.00	75.00	—
1624	—	9.00	22.00	45.00	75.00	—
1625	—	9.00	22.00	45.00	75.00	—
1626	—	9.00	22.00	45.00	75.00	—
1627	—	9.00	22.00	45.00	75.00	—
1628	—	9.00	22.00	45.00	75.00	—
1629	—	9.00	22.00	45.00	75.00	—
1630	—	9.00	22.00	45.00	75.00	—
1631	—	9.00	22.00	45.00	75.00	—
1632	—	9.00	22.00	45.00	75.00	—

KM# 435 2 PFENNIG

Silver **Ruler:** Ferdinand II **Obv:** Three coat of arms **Mint:** Krain **Note:** Uniface. Prev. KM#1010.

Date	Mintage	VG	F	VF	XF	Unc
1623 K Rare	—	—	—	—	—	—

KM# 564 2 PFENNIG

Billon **Ruler:** Ferdinand II **Obv:** Large shields **Mint:** Saint Veit **Note:** Varieties exist. Uniface. Prev. KM#1587.

Date	Mintage	VG	F	VF	XF	Unc
1625	—	18.00	35.00	60.00	120	—
1626	—	18.00	35.00	60.00	120	—
1627	—	18.00	35.00	60.00	120	—

KM# 565 2 PFENNIG

Silver **Ruler:** Ferdinand II **Obv:** Crown above two shields of arms divides flat date **Mint:** Vienna **Note:** Uniface. Prev. KM#1765.

Date	Mintage	VG	F	VF	XF	Unc
1625	—	—	—	—	—	—

KM# 566 2 PFENNIG

Silver **Ruler:** Ferdinand II **Obv:** Shields reversed, crown divides arched date **Mint:** Vienna **Note:** Prev. KM#1766.

Date	Mintage	VG	F	VF	XF	Unc
1625	—	10.00	30.00	50.00	85.00	—
1626	—	10.00	30.00	50.00	85.00	—
1627	—	10.00	30.00	50.00	85.00	—
1628	—	10.00	30.00	50.00	85.00	—
1629	—	10.00	30.00	50.00	85.00	—
1630	—	10.00	30.00	50.00	85.00	—
1631	—	10.00	30.00	50.00	85.00	—
1632	—	10.00	30.00	50.00	85.00	—
1633	—	10.00	30.00	50.00	85.00	—
1634	—	10.00	30.00	50.00	85.00	—
1635	—	10.00	30.00	50.00	85.00	—
1636	—	10.00	30.00	50.00	85.00	—

KM# 688 2 PFENNIG

Billon **Ruler:** Ferdinand II **Obv:** Two-digit date between bottom two shields **Mint:** Saint Veit **Note:** Prev. KM#1588.

Date	Mintage	VG	F	VF	XF	Unc
(16)28	—	20.00	40.00	75.00	135	—
(16)29	—	20.00	40.00	75.00	135	—
(16)30	—	20.00	40.00	75.00	135	—

KM# 741 2 PFENNIG

Billon **Ruler:** Ferdinand III **Obv:** Crowned "F III" above two shield of arms, crown divides date **Mint:** Glatz **Note:** Uniface. Prev. KM#291.

Date	Mintage	VG	F	VF	XF	Unc
1630 (p)	—	8.00	15.00	27.50	48.00	—
1631 (p)	—	8.00	15.00	27.50	48.00	—
1637 (h)	—	8.00	15.00	27.50	48.00	—
1638 (h)	—	8.00	15.00	27.50	48.00	—

KM# 801 2 PFENNIG

Billon **Ruler:** Ferdinand II **Obv:** Heart-shaped shields **Mint:** Graz **Note:** Prev. KM#337.

Date	Mintage	VG	F	VF	XF	Unc
1633	—	9.00	22.00	45.00	75.00	—
1634	—	9.00	22.00	45.00	75.00	—
1635	—	9.00	22.00	45.00	75.00	—
1637	—	9.00	22.00	45.00	75.00	—

KM# 804 2 PFENNIG

Billon **Ruler:** Ferdinand III **Obv:** Oval arms **Mint:** Saint Veit **Note:** Varieties exist. Uniface. Prev. KM#1622.

Date	Mintage	VG	F	VF	XF	Unc
1634	—	6.00	13.00	25.00	60.00	—
1637	—	6.00	13.00	25.00	60.00	—
1638	—	6.00	13.00	25.00	60.00	—
1640	—	6.00	13.00	25.00	60.00	—
1641	—	6.00	13.00	25.00	60.00	—
1642	—	6.00	13.00	25.00	60.00	—
1645	—	6.00	13.00	25.00	60.00	—
1646	—	6.00	13.00	25.00	60.00	—
1648	—	6.00	13.00	25.00	60.00	—
1649	—	6.00	13.00	25.00	60.00	—
1651	—	6.00	13.00	25.00	60.00	—
1653	—	6.00	13.00	25.00	60.00	—
1655	—	6.00	13.00	25.00	60.00	—

KM# 827 2 PFENNIG

Billon **Ruler:** Ferdinand III **Obv:** Larger, longer shields, arched date above crown **Mint:** Vienna **Note:** Prev. KM#1816.

Date	Mintage	VG	F	VF	XF	Unc
1637	—	8.00	16.00	30.00	50.00	—
1638	—	8.00	16.00	30.00	50.00	—
1639	—	8.00	16.00	30.00	50.00	—
1640	—	8.00	16.00	30.00	50.00	—
1641	—	8.00	16.00	30.00	50.00	—
1642	—	8.00	16.00	30.00	50.00	—
1643	—	8.00	16.00	30.00	50.00	—
1647	—	8.00	16.00	30.00	50.00	—
1653	—	8.00	16.00	30.00	50.00	—

KM# 849 2 PFENNIG

Billon **Ruler:** Ferdinand III **Obv:** Three shields of arms **Mint:** Graz **Note:** Varieties exist. Uniface. Prev. KM#420.

Date	Mintage	VG	F	VF	XF	Unc
1638	—	4.00	9.00	18.00	33.00	—
1639	—	4.00	9.00	18.00	33.00	—
1640	—	4.00	9.00	18.00	33.00	—
1641	—	4.00	9.00	18.00	33.00	—
1642	—	4.00	9.00	18.00	33.00	—
1643	—	4.00	9.00	18.00	33.00	—
1644	—	4.00	9.00	18.00	33.00	—
1645	—	4.00	9.00	18.00	33.00	—
1646	—	4.00	9.00	18.00	33.00	—
1647	—	4.00	9.00	18.00	33.00	—
1648	—	4.00	9.00	18.00	33.00	—
1651	—	4.00	9.00	18.00	33.00	—
1653	—	4.00	9.00	18.00	33.00	—
1655	—	4.00	9.00	18.00	33.00	—
1656	—	4.00	9.00	18.00	33.00	—
1657	—	4.00	9.00	18.00	33.00	—

KM# 872 2 PFENNIG

Billon **Ruler:** Ferdinand III **Obv:** Flat-topped shields **Mint:** Graz **Note:** Prev. KM#872.

Date	Mintage	VG	F	VF	XF	Unc
1639	—	5.00	10.00	20.00	40.00	—

KM# 891 2 PFENNIG

Billon **Ruler:** Ferdinand III **Obv:** Three shields ov arms - one above two, top shield divides date **Mint:** Glatz **Note:** Prev. KM#292.

Date	Mintage	VG	F	VF	XF	Unc
1641 GW	—	7.00	14.00	25.00	45.00	—
1644 GW	—	7.00	14.00	25.00	45.00	—

KM# 1112 2 PFENNIG

Silver **Ruler:** Leopold I **Obv:** Bottom shields flat at center **Mint:** Saint Veit **Note:** Uniface. Prev. KM#1636.

Date	Mintage	VG	F	VF	XF	Unc
1658	—	8.00	16.00	35.00	65.00	—
1664	—	8.00	16.00	35.00	65.00	—

KM# 1131 2 PFENNIG

Billon **Ruler:** Leopold I **Obv:** Three shields of arms **Mint:** Graz **Note:** Varieties exist. Uniface. Prev. KM#447.

Date	Mintage	VG	F	VF	XF	Unc
1659	—	4.00	8.00	16.00	35.00	—
1660 L	—	4.00	8.00	16.00	35.00	—
1661 L	—	4.00	8.00	16.00	35.00	—
1662 L	—	4.00	8.00	16.00	35.00	—
1666 L	—	4.00	8.00	16.00	35.00	—
1669 L	—	4.00	8.00	16.00	35.00	—
1671 L	—	4.00	8.00	16.00	35.00	—
1672 L	—	4.00	8.00	16.00	35.00	—
1673 L	—	4.00	8.00	16.00	35.00	—
1674 L	—	4.00	8.00	16.00	35.00	—
1675 L	—	4.00	8.00	16.00	35.00	—
1676 L	—	4.00	8.00	16.00	35.00	—
1677 L	—	4.00	8.00	16.00	35.00	—
1678 L	—	4.00	8.00	16.00	35.00	—
1679 L	—	4.00	8.00	16.00	35.00	—
1680 L	—	4.00	8.00	16.00	35.00	—
1682 L	—	4.00	8.00	16.00	35.00	—
1682	—	4.00	8.00	16.00	35.00	—
1685	—	4.00	8.00	16.00	35.00	—
1686	—	4.00	8.00	16.00	35.00	—
1688	—	4.00	8.00	16.00	35.00	—
1692	—	4.00	8.00	16.00	35.00	—
1698	—	4.00	8.00	16.00	35.00	—
1700	—	4.00	8.00	16.00	35.00	—

KM# 1195 2 PFENNIG

Silver **Ruler:** Leopold I **Obv:** Three shields of arms - one above two, top shield divides date in straight line **Mint:** Vienna **Note:** Varieties exist. Uniface. Prev. KM#1850.

Date	Mintage	VG	F	VF	XF	Unc
1662	—	6.00	12.00	25.00	48.00	—
1664	—	6.00	12.00	25.00	48.00	—
1665	—	6.00	12.00	25.00	48.00	—
1667	—	6.00	12.00	25.00	48.00	—
1668	—	6.00	12.00	25.00	48.00	—
1669	—	6.00	12.00	25.00	48.00	—
1670	—	6.00	12.00	25.00	48.00	—
1671	—	6.00	12.00	25.00	48.00	—
1672	—	6.00	12.00	25.00	48.00	—
1675	—	6.00	12.00	25.00	48.00	—
1676	—	6.00	12.00	25.00	48.00	—
1680	—	6.00	12.00	25.00	48.00	—
1681	—	6.00	12.00	25.00	48.00	—
1683	—	6.00	12.00	25.00	48.00	—
1684	—	6.00	12.00	25.00	48.00	—
1685	—	6.00	12.00	25.00	48.00	—

KM# 1228 2 PFENNIG

Silver **Ruler:** Leopold I **Obv:** Bottom shields round **Mint:** Saint Veit **Note:** Uniface. Prev. KM#1637.

Date	Mintage	VG	F	VF	XF	Unc
1665	—	7.00	13.00	27.50	60.00	—
1668	—	7.00	13.00	27.50	60.00	—
1679	—	7.00	13.00	27.50	60.00	—
1683	—	7.00	13.00	27.50	60.00	—
1691	—	7.00	13.00	27.50	60.00	—
1693	—	7.00	13.00	27.50	60.00	—
1695	—	7.00	13.00	27.50	60.00	—

KM# 1337 2 PFENNIG

Silver **Ruler:** Leopold I **Obv:** Three shields of arms - one above two, divided date in arc **Mint:** Vienna **Note:** Varieties exist. Uniface. Prev. KM#1851.

Date	Mintage	VG	F	VF	XF	Unc
1686	—	6.00	12.00	25.00	48.00	—
1687	—	6.00	12.00	25.00	48.00	—
1688	—	6.00	12.00	25.00	48.00	—
1689	—	7.00	14.00	27.50	55.00	—
1690	—	6.00	12.00	25.00	48.00	—
1691	—	6.00	12.00	25.00	48.00	—
1692	—	6.00	12.00	25.00	48.00	—
1693	—	6.00	12.00	25.00	48.00	—
1694	—	6.00	12.00	25.00	48.00	—
1698	—	6.00	12.00	25.00	48.00	—
1699	—	6.00	12.00	25.00	48.00	—
1700	—	6.00	12.00	25.00	48.00	—

KM# 132 VIERER (4 Heller)

Silver **Ruler:** Maximilian **Mint:** Hall **Note:** Prev. KM#760.

Date	Mintage	VG	F	VF	XF	Unc
ND(1612-19)	2,311,000	100	200	350	650	—

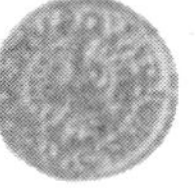

KM# 235 VIERER (4 Heller)

Silver **Ruler:** Leopold **Mint:** Hall **Note:** Prev. KM#785.

Date	Mintage	VG	F	VF	XF	Unc
ND(1619)	—	12.50	25.00	37.50	70.00	—

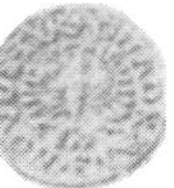

KM# 955 VIERER (4 Heller)

Silver **Ruler:** Ferdinand Charles **Obv:** Austrian shield **Rev:** Eagle **Mint:** Hall **Note:** Prev. KM#825.

Date	Mintage	VG	F	VF	XF	Unc
ND(1648-62)	289,000	10.00	20.00	35.00	60.00	—

KM# 956 VIERER (4 Heller)

Silver **Ruler:** Ferdinand Charles **Rev:** Eagle with wreath **Mint:** Hall **Note:** Prev. KM#826.

Date	Mintage	VG	F	VF	XF	Unc
ND(1648-62)	2,483,000	10.00	20.00	35.00	60.00	—

KM# 31 KREUZER

Silver **Ruler:** Rudolf II **Obv:** Bust, date below **Rev:** Two crosses at 45 degree angle with shield in circle at center **Mint:** Hall **Note:** Prev. KM#581.

Date	Mintage	VG	F	VF	XF	Unc
1602	—	25.00	50.00	100	185	—
1603	—	25.00	50.00	100	185	—

KM# 51 KREUZER

Silver **Ruler:** Rudolf II **Obv:** Inner circle and two-digit date **Mint:** Hall **Note:** Prev. KM#582.

Date	Mintage	VG	F	VF	XF	Unc
(16)04	—	25.00	50.00	100	185	—

KM# 52 KREUZER

Silver **Ruler:** Rudolf II **Obv:** Inner circle **Rev:** Inner circle **Mint:** Hall **Note:** Prev. KM#583.1.

Date	Mintage	VG	F	VF	XF	Unc
1604	—	20.00	40.00	80.00	165	—
1605	—	20.00	40.00	80.00	165	—
1606	—	20.00	40.00	80.00	165	—
1607	—	20.00	40.00	80.00	165	—
1608	—	20.00	40.00	80.00	165	—
1609	—	20.00	40.00	80.00	165	—
1610	—	20.00	40.00	80.00	165	—
1611	—	20.00	40.00	80.00	165	—

KM# 61 KREUZER

Silver **Ruler:** Rudolf II **Obv:** Two-digit date **Mint:** Hall **Note:** Prev. KM#584.

Date	Mintage	VG	F	VF	XF	Unc
(16)05	—	25.00	50.00	100	185	—
(16)08	—	25.00	50.00	100	185	—
(16)09	—	25.00	50.00	100	185	—

KM# 62 KREUZER

Silver **Ruler:** Rudolf II **Obv:** 1605 **Rev:** 1602 **Mint:** Hall **Note:** Mule. Prev. KM#585.

Date	Mintage	VG	F	VF	XF	Unc
1605-02	—	150	300	500	800	—

KM# 116 KREUZER

Silver **Ruler:** Rudolf II **Mint:** Vienna **Note:** Prev. KM#1710.

Date	Mintage	VG	F	VF	XF	Unc
1610	—	—	—	—	—	—

KM# 53.1 KREUZER

Silver **Ruler:** Rudolf II **Mint:** Hall **Note:** Thick planchet. Prev. KM#583.2.

Date	Mintage	VG	F	VF	XF	Unc
1610	—	22.00	45.00	90.00	175	—

KM# 134 KREUZER

Silver **Ruler:** Maximilian **Mint:** Hall **Note:** Prev. KM#761.

Date	Mintage	VG	F	VF	XF	Unc
ND(1612) CO	58,000	200	375	700	1,150	—
1613	142,000	200	375	700	1,150	—
1615	62,000	200	375	700	1,150	—
1616 CO	78,000	200	375	700	1,150	—
1617	62,000	200	375	700	1,150	—
1618 CO	214,000	200	375	700	1,150	—

KM# 185 KREUZER

Silver **Ruler:** Ferdinand II **Obv:** Bust right in inner circle **Rev:** Crowned arms in inner circle, date in legend **Mint:** Klagenfurt **Note:** Local issue for Archduke Ferdinand. Prev. KM#987.

Date	Mintage	VG	F	VF	XF	Unc
1614	—	100	175	300	500	—

KM# 236 KREUZER

Silver **Ruler:** Leopold **Obv:** Austrian arms **Rev:** Eagle arms on double cross **Mint:** Hall **Note:** Prev. KM#786.

Date	Mintage	VG	F	VF	XF	Unc
ND(1619-22)	—	7.00	15.00	30.00	55.00	—

KM# 253 KREUZER

Silver **Ruler:** Leopold **Obv:** Robed bust **Rev:** Eagle shield on double cross **Mint:** Hall **Note:** Prev. KM#787.

Date	Mintage	VG	F	VF	XF	Unc
ND	—	7.00	15.00	30.00	55.00	—

KM# 254 KREUZER

Silver **Ruler:** Ferdinand II **Obv:** Laureate bust right in inner circle, value at bottom **Rev:** Long cross with arms at center in inner circle **Mint:** Klagenfurt **Note:** Varieties exist. Prev. KM#951.

Date	Mintage	VG	F	VF	XF	Unc
ND	—	20.00	40.00	70.00	120	—

KM# 255 KREUZER

Silver **Ruler:** Ferdinand II **Obv:** Bust right **Rev:** Arms in double cross **Mint:** Klagenfurt **Note:** Prev. KM#952.

Date	Mintage	VG	F	VF	XF	Unc
ND	—	20.00	40.00	70.00	120	—

KM# 285 KREUZER

Silver **Ruler:** Ferdinand II **Obv:** Bust right **Rev:** Panther shield on double eagle **Mint:** Graz **Note:** Prev. KM#338.

Date	Mintage	VG	F	VF	XF	Unc
ND	—	10.00	20.00	35.00	60.00	—
1621	—	10.00	20.00	35.00	60.00	—

KM# 286 KREUZER

Silver **Ruler:** Ferdinand II **Obv:** Laureate bust right in inner circle **Rev:** Crowned imperial eagle with value on breast in inner circle **Mint:** Vienna **Note:** Prev. KM#1767.

Date	Mintage	VG	F	VF	XF	Unc
1621	—	12.50	25.00	45.00	70.00	—
1622 (c)	—	12.50	25.00	45.00	70.00	—
1624 (c)	—	12.50	25.00	45.00	70.00	—
1630	—	12.50	25.00	45.00	70.00	—

KM# 378 KREUZER

Silver **Ruler:** Ferdinand II **Obv:** Bust with plain collar **Mint:** Graz **Note:** Prev. KM#339.

Date	Mintage	VG	F	VF	XF	Unc
1622	—	10.00	20.00	35.00	60.00	—

KM# 379 KREUZER

Silver **Ruler:** Ferdinand II **Obv:** Bust with ruffled collar **Mint:** Graz **Note:** Prev. KM#340.

Date	Mintage	VG	F	VF	XF	Unc
1622	—	10.00	20.00	35.00	60.00	—
1623	—	10.00	20.00	35.00	60.00	—

KM# 381 KREUZER

Silver **Ruler:** Ferdinand II **Mint:** Vienna **Note:** Kipper Kreuzer. Prev. KM#1769.

Date	Mintage	VG	F	VF	XF	Unc
1622 (c)	—	—	—	—	—	—

KM# 380 KREUZER

Silver **Ruler:** Ferdinand II **Obv:** Bust with ruffled collar **Mint:** Graz **Note:** Kipper Kreuzer. Prev. KM#341.

Date	Mintage	VG	F	VF	XF	Unc
1622	—	10.00	20.00	35.00	60.00	—

KM# 437 KREUZER

Silver **Ruler:** Ferdinand II **Obv:** Laureate bust right in inner circle, value below, date below bust **Rev:** Long cross with arms at center in inner circle **Mint:** Saint Veit **Note:** Varieties exist. Prev. KM#1589.

Date	Mintage	VG	F	VF	XF	Unc
1623	—	18.00	30.00	50.00	100	—
1624	—	18.00	30.00	50.00	100	—
1624 (h)	—	15.00	25.00	45.00	90.00	—
1625 (p)	—	15.00	25.00	45.00	90.00	—
1626 (p)	—	15.00	25.00	45.00	90.00	—
1627 (p)	—	15.00	25.00	45.00	90.00	—
1627 (p)	—	16.00	28.00	50.00	100	—
1627 (p)	—	16.00	28.00	50.00	100	—
1628 (g)	—	16.00	28.00	50.00	100	—

KM# 479 KREUZER

Silver **Ruler:** Ferdinand II **Obv:** Bust right **Rev:** Small shield between eagle, value on eagle **Mint:** Brunn **Note:** Prev. KM#200.

Date	Mintage	VG	F	VF	XF	Unc
1624 B-CW	—	—	—	—	—	—

KM# 480 KREUZER

Silver **Ruler:** Ferdinand II **Rev:** Without shield below eagle **Mint:** Brunn **Note:** Prev. KM#201.

Date	Mintage	VG	F	VF	XF	Unc
1624 B-CW	—	8.00	17.00	33.00	60.00	—
1624 CW	—	8.00	17.00	33.00	60.00	—
1624 B	—	8.00	17.00	33.00	60.00	—
1625 B-CW	—	8.00	17.00	33.00	60.00	—
1625 CW	—	8.00	17.00	33.00	60.00	—
1626 CW	—	8.00	17.00	33.00	60.00	—

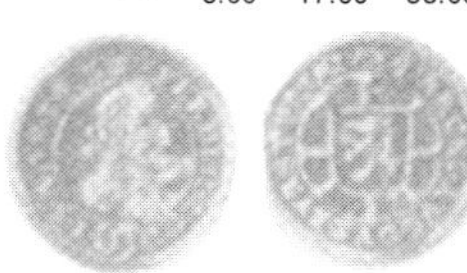

KM# 481 KREUZER

Silver **Ruler:** Ferdinand II **Obv:** Panther shield on double cross **Mint:** Graz **Note:** Prev. KM#342.

Date	Mintage	VG	F	VF	XF	Unc
1624	—	10.00	20.00	35.00	60.00	—
1626	—	10.00	20.00	35.00	60.00	—
1630	—	10.00	20.00	35.00	60.00	—
1631	—	10.00	20.00	35.00	60.00	—

KM# 484 KREUZER

Silver **Ruler:** Ferdinand II **Obv:** Bust right with ruffled collar **Rev:** Value on double eagle **Mint:** Nikolsburg **Note:** Prev. KM#1220.

Date	Mintage	VG	F	VF	XF	Unc
1624 N-CW	—	40.00	70.00	120	200	—
1624 N	—	40.00	70.00	120	200	—
1627 N	—	40.00	70.00	120	200	—
1628 N	—	40.00	70.00	120	200	—

KM# 486 KREUZER

Silver **Ruler:** Ferdinand II **Obv:** Laureate bust right, date below **Rev:** Long cross with shield of arms at center **Mint:** Saint Polten **Note:** Prev. KM#1570.

Date	Mintage	VG	F	VF	XF	Unc
1624	—	30.00	50.00	80.00	150	—

KM# 487 KREUZER

Silver **Ruler:** Ferdinand II **Obv:** Laureate bust right in inner circle **Rev:** Crowned imperial eagle with shield on breast in inner circle, date in legend **Mint:** Saint Polten **Note:** Varieties exist. Prev. KM#1571.

Date	Mintage	VG	F	VF	XF	Unc
1624 (c)-IIE	—	25.00	45.00	75.00	140	—
1624 (c)-(d)	—	25.00	45.00	75.00	140	—
1624 (d)	—	25.00	45.00	75.00	140	—
1625 (c)-IIE	—	25.00	45.00	75.00	140	—

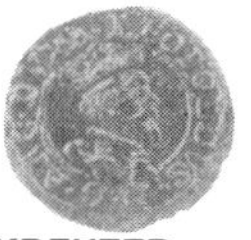

KM# 575 KREUZER

Silver **Ruler:** Leopold **Obv:** Crowned bust **Rev:** Eagle shield on double cross **Mint:** Hall **Note:** Prev. KM#788.

Date	Mintage	VG	F	VF	XF	Unc
ND(1625-32)	—	7.00	15.00	30.00	55.00	—

KM# 577 KREUZER

Silver **Ruler:** Ferdinand II **Obv:** Bust right **Rev:** Value on double eagle **Mint:** Olmutz **Note:** Varieties exist. Prev. KM#1230.

Date	Mintage	VG	F	VF	XF	Unc
1625 MF	—	8.00	17.00	33.00	60.00	—
1626 MF	—	8.00	17.00	33.00	60.00	—
1627 MF	—	8.00	17.00	33.00	60.00	—
1628 O	—	8.00	17.00	33.00	60.00	—
1629 O	—	8.00	17.00	33.00	60.00	—
1630 O	—	8.00	17.00	33.00	60.00	—
1630 MF-O	—	8.00	17.00	33.00	60.00	—
1631 MF-O	—	8.00	17.00	33.00	60.00	—
1632 MF	—	8.00	17.00	33.00	60.00	—
1632	—	8.00	17.00	33.00	60.00	—
1633 MF	—	8.00	17.00	33.00	60.00	—
1633	—	8.00	17.00	33.00	60.00	—
1634	—	8.00	17.00	33.00	60.00	—
1634 MF	—	8.00	17.00	33.00	60.00	—
1635 O-ICH	—	8.00	17.00	33.00	60.00	—
1635 ICH	—	8.00	17.00	33.00	60.00	—
1636 O-ICH	—	8.00	17.00	33.00	60.00	—
1636 O-HH	—	8.00	17.00	33.00	60.00	—

KM# 625 KREUZER

Silver **Ruler:** Ferdinand II **Rev:** Date divided below arms **Mint:** Saint Veit **Note:** Varieties exist. Prev. KM#1590.

Date	Mintage	VG	F	VF	XF	Unc
1626 (p)	—	16.00	28.00	50.00	100	—
1627 (g)	—	16.00	28.00	50.00	100	—
1628 (g)	—	16.00	28.00	50.00	100	—
1629	—	16.00	28.00	50.00	100	—
1630	—	16.00	28.00	50.00	100	—
1631	—	16.00	28.00	50.00	100	—
1636	—	16.00	28.00	50.00	100	—
1637	—	16.00	28.00	50.00	100	—

KM# 668 KREUZER

Silver **Ruler:** Ferdinand II **Obv:** Bust right with plain collar **Mint:** Nikolsburg **Note:** Prev. KM#1221.

Date	Mintage	VG	F	VF	XF	Unc
1627 N	—	40.00	70.00	120	200	—
1628 N	—	40.00	70.00	120	200	—

KM# 689 KREUZER

Silver **Ruler:** Ferdinand III **Obv:** Bust right **Rev:** Rampant lion **Mint:** Glatz **Note:** Prev. KM#293.

Date	Mintage	VG	F	VF	XF	Unc
1628	—	—	—	—	—	—
1628 (c)	—	—	—	—	—	—

KM# 690 KREUZER

Silver **Ruler:** Ferdinand III **Rev:** Shield on double cross **Mint:** Glatz **Note:** Prev. KM#294.

Date	Mintage	VG	F	VF	XF	Unc
1628	—	8.00	17.00	33.00	60.00	—
1628 (c)	—	8.00	17.00	33.00	60.00	—
1628 (p)	—	8.00	17.00	33.00	60.00	—
1629 (p)	—	8.00	17.00	33.00	60.00	—
1630 (p)	—	8.00	17.00	33.00	60.00	—
1631 (p)	—	8.00	17.00	33.00	60.00	—
1632 (h)	—	8.00	17.00	33.00	60.00	—
1633 (h)	—	8.00	17.00	33.00	60.00	—
1635 (h)	—	8.00	17.00	33.00	60.00	—
1636 (h)	—	8.00	17.00	33.00	60.00	—

KM# 766 KREUZER

Silver **Ruler:** Ferdinand II **Obv:** Bust with plain collar **Mint:** Vienna **Note:** Varieties exist. Prev. KM#1768.

Date	Mintage	VG	F	VF	XF	Unc
1631 (c)	—	12.50	25.00	45.00	70.00	—
1631 (v)	—	12.50	25.00	45.00	70.00	—
1633	—	12.50	25.00	45.00	70.00	—
1634	—	12.50	25.00	45.00	70.00	—
1635	—	12.50	25.00	45.00	70.00	—
1636 (v)	—	12.50	25.00	45.00	70.00	—

KM# 779 KREUZER

Silver **Ruler:** Ferdinand II **Obv:** Flat-topped shield **Mint:** Graz **Note:** Prev. KM#344.

Date	Mintage	VG	F	VF	XF	Unc
1632	—	10.00	20.00	35.00	60.00	—
1633	—	10.00	20.00	35.00	60.00	—

KM# 778 KREUZER

Silver **Ruler:** Ferdinand II **Obv:** Heart-shaped shield **Mint:** Graz **Note:** Prev. KM#343.

Date	Mintage	VG	F	VF	XF	Unc
1632	—	10.00	20.00	35.00	60.00	—

KM# 802 KREUZER

Silver **Ruler:** Ferdinand II **Obv:** Without denomination below bust **Mint:** Graz **Note:** Prev. KM#345.

Date	Mintage	VG	F	VF	XF	Unc
1633	—	10.00	20.00	35.00	60.00	—

KM# 805 KREUZER

Silver **Ruler:** Ferdinand II **Obv:** Denomination below bust **Mint:** Graz **Note:** Prev. KM#346.

Date	Mintage	VG	F	VF	XF	Unc
1634	—	10.00	20.00	35.00	60.00	—
1635	—	10.00	20.00	35.00	60.00	—
1636	—	10.00	20.00	35.00	60.00	—

KM# 829 KREUZER

Silver **Ruler:** Ferdinand III **Obv:** Bust right **Rev:** Value on imperial eagle **Mint:** Olmutz **Note:** Prev. KM#1252.

Date	Mintage	VG	F	VF	XF	Unc
1637 O	—	8.00	18.00	35.00	65.00	—
1638 O	—	8.00	18.00	35.00	65.00	—
1639 O	—	8.00	18.00	35.00	65.00	—
1640 O	—	8.00	18.00	35.00	65.00	—
1641 O	—	8.00	18.00	35.00	65.00	—

KM# 830 KREUZER

Silver **Ruler:** Ferdinand III **Obv:** Laureate bust right in inner circle **Rev:** Crowned imperial eagle with value on breast in inner circle **Mint:** Vienna **Note:** Varieties exist. Prev. KM#1817.

Date	Mintage	VG	F	VF	XF	Unc
1637	—	10.00	20.00	35.00	65.00	—
1639	—	10.00	20.00	35.00	65.00	—
1641	—	10.00	20.00	35.00	65.00	—
1643	—	10.00	20.00	35.00	65.00	—
1644	—	10.00	20.00	35.00	65.00	—
1647	—	10.00	20.00	35.00	65.00	—

KM# 850 KREUZER

Silver **Ruler:** Ferdinand III **Obv:** Portrait and titles of Ferdinand III **Mint:** Graz **Note:** Varieties exist. Prev. KM#850.

Date	Mintage	VG	F	VF	XF	Unc
1638	—	10.00	20.00	35.00	65.00	—
1639	—	10.00	20.00	35.00	65.00	—
1640	—	10.00	20.00	35.00	65.00	—
1641	—	10.00	20.00	35.00	65.00	—
1644	—	10.00	20.00	35.00	65.00	—
1645	—	10.00	20.00	35.00	65.00	—
1646	—	10.00	20.00	35.00	65.00	—
1648	—	10.00	20.00	35.00	65.00	—
1650	—	10.00	20.00	35.00	65.00	—
1652	—	10.00	20.00	35.00	65.00	—
1654	—	10.00	20.00	35.00	65.00	—

KM# 873 KREUZER

Silver **Ruler:** Ferdinand III **Mint:** Saint Veit **Note:** Prev. KM#1623.

Date	Mintage	VG	F	VF	XF	Unc
1639	—	12.00	25.00	48.00	80.00	—
1640	—	12.00	25.00	48.00	80.00	—
1641	—	12.00	25.00	48.00	80.00	—
1642	—	12.00	25.00	48.00	80.00	—
1645	—	12.00	25.00	48.00	80.00	—
1647	—	12.00	25.00	48.00	80.00	—
1649	—	12.00	25.00	48.00	80.00	—
1650	—	12.00	25.00	48.00	80.00	—
1651	—	12.00	25.00	48.00	80.00	—
1652	—	12.00	25.00	48.00	80.00	—
1655	—	12.00	25.00	48.00	80.00	—
1657	—	12.00	25.00	48.00	80.00	—

KM# 892 KREUZER

Silver **Ruler:** Ferdinand III **Mint:** Graz **Note:** Klippe. Prev. KM#423.

Date	Mintage	VG	F	VF	XF	Unc
1641	—	—	—	—	—	—

KM# 946 KREUZER

Silver **Ruler:** Ferdinand Charles **Obv:** Crowned bust **Rev:** Arms **Mint:** Hall **Note:** Prev. KM#827.

Date	Mintage	VG	F	VF	XF	Unc
ND(1647-62)	2,344,000	10.00	20.00	35.00	60.00	—

KM# 1133 KREUZER

Silver **Ruler:** Leopold I **Obv:** Young bust right, value below **Rev:** Crowned imperial eagle, date in legend **Mint:** Glatz **Note:** Prev. KM#323.

Date	Mintage	VG	F	VF	XF	Unc
1659 GW	—	8.00	17.00	33.00	60.00	—

KM# 1134 KREUZER

Silver **Ruler:** Leopold I **Obv:** Portrait and titles of Leopold I **Mint:** Graz **Note:** Varieties exist. Prev. KM#448.

Date	Mintage	VG	F	VF	XF	Unc
1659	—	8.00	17.00	33.00	65.00	—
1660	—	8.00	17.00	33.00	65.00	—
1662	—	8.00	17.00	33.00	65.00	—
1664	—	8.00	17.00	33.00	65.00	—
1665	—	8.00	17.00	33.00	65.00	—

KM# 1135 KREUZER

Silver **Ruler:** Leopold I **Obv:** Laureate bust right in laurel inner circle **Rev:** Arms on St. George and St. Andrew crosses in laurel inner circle **Mint:** Hall **Note:** Prev. KM#620.

Date	Mintage	VG	F	VF	XF	Unc
ND	—	12.00	25.00	40.00	65.00	—

KM# 1136 KREUZER

Silver **Ruler:** Leopold I **Obv:** Solid inner circle **Rev:** Solid inner circle **Mint:** Hall **Note:** Prev. KM#621.

Date	Mintage	VG	F	VF	XF	Unc
ND	—	12.00	25.00	40.00	65.00	—

KM# 1137 KREUZER

Silver **Ruler:** Leopold I **Mint:** Saint Veit **Note:** Varieties exist. Prev. KM#1638.

Date	Mintage	VG	F	VF	XF	Unc
1659	—	14.00	30.00	60.00	100	—
1662	—	14.00	30.00	60.00	100	—
1665	—	14.00	30.00	60.00	100	—
1668	—	14.00	30.00	60.00	100	—
1679 IR	—	14.00	30.00	60.00	100	—
1681 IR	—	14.00	30.00	60.00	100	—
1682 IR	—	14.00	30.00	60.00	100	—
1683 IR	—	14.00	30.00	60.00	100	—
1685 IR	—	14.00	30.00	60.00	100	—
1689 IR	—	14.00	30.00	60.00	100	—
1693 GCS	—	14.00	30.00	60.00	100	—
1695 CS	—	14.00	30.00	60.00	100	—
1696 CCS	—	14.00	30.00	60.00	100	—
1700 IP	—	14.00	30.00	60.00	100	—

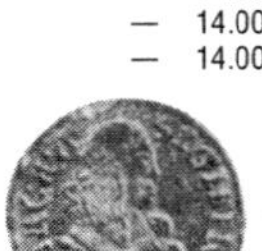

KM# 1208 KREUZER

Silver **Ruler:** Sigismund Franz **Mint:** Hall **Note:** Prev. KM#850.

Date	Mintage	VG	F	VF	XF	Unc
ND(1663-65)	1,052,000	10.00	20.00	35.00	60.00	—

KM# 1229 KREUZER

Silver **Ruler:** Leopold I **Mint:** Vienna **Note:** Varieties exist. Prev. KM#1852.

Date	Mintage	VG	F	VF	XF	Unc
1665	—	8.00	17.00	33.00	60.00	—
1666	—	8.00	17.00	33.00	60.00	—
1667	—	8.00	17.00	33.00	60.00	—
1668	—	8.00	17.00	35.25	65.00	—
1669	—	8.00	17.00	33.00	60.00	—
1670	—	8.00	17.00	33.00	60.00	—
1672	—	8.00	17.00	33.00	60.00	—
1673	—	8.00	17.00	33.00	60.00	—
1674	—	8.00	17.00	35.25	65.00	—
1675	—	8.00	17.00	33.00	60.00	—
1676	—	8.00	17.00	33.00	60.00	—
1677	—	8.00	17.00	33.00	60.00	—
1681	—	8.00	17.00	33.00	60.00	—
1695	—	8.00	17.00	33.00	60.00	—
1696	—	8.00	17.00	33.00	60.00	—
1697	—	8.00	17.00	33.00	60.00	—
1698	—	8.00	17.00	33.00	60.00	—
1699	—	8.00	17.00	33.00	60.00	—
1700	—	8.00	17.00	33.00	60.00	—

KM# 1240 KREUZER

Silver **Ruler:** Leopold I **Obv:** Portrait and titles of Leopold I **Rev:** Date divided below arms **Mint:** Graz **Note:** Varieties exist. Prev. KM#449.

Date	Mintage	VG	F	VF	XF	Unc
1666	—	8.00	17.00	33.00	60.00	—
1667	—	8.00	17.00	33.00	60.00	—
1669	—	8.00	17.00	33.00	60.00	—
1670	—	8.00	17.00	33.00	60.00	—
1672	—	8.00	17.00	33.00	60.00	—
1673	—	8.00	17.00	33.00	60.00	—
1674	—	8.00	17.00	33.00	60.00	—
1675	—	8.00	17.00	33.00	60.00	—
1676	—	8.00	17.00	33.00	60.00	—
1677	—	8.00	17.00	33.00	60.00	—
1678	—	8.00	17.00	33.00	60.00	—
1679	—	8.00	17.00	33.00	60.00	—
1680	—	8.00	17.00	33.00	60.00	—
1682	—	8.00	17.00	33.00	60.00	—
1684	—	8.00	17.00	33.00	60.00	—
1685	—	8.00	17.00	33.00	60.00	—
1686	—	8.00	17.00	33.00	60.00	—
1688	—	8.00	17.00	33.00	60.00	—
1690	—	8.00	17.00	33.00	60.00	—
1691	—	8.00	17.00	33.00	60.00	—
1692	—	8.00	17.00	33.00	60.00	—
1693	—	8.00	17.00	33.00	60.00	—
1694	—	8.00	17.00	33.00	60.00	—
1695	—	8.00	17.00	33.00	60.00	—
1696	—	8.00	17.00	33.00	60.00	—
1697	—	8.00	17.00	33.00	60.00	—
1698	—	8.00	17.00	33.00	60.00	—
1699	—	8.00	17.00	33.00	60.00	—
1700	—	8.00	17.00	33.00	60.00	—

KM# 1355 KREUZER

Silver **Ruler:** Leopold I **Mint:** Hall **Note:** Prev. KM#622.

Date	Mintage	VG	F	VF	XF	Unc
1691	—	15.00	30.00	45.00	70.00	—
1692	—	15.00	30.00	45.00	70.00	—
1693	—	15.00	30.00	45.00	70.00	—
1694	—	15.00	30.00	45.00	70.00	—
1695	—	15.00	30.00	45.00	70.00	—

KM# 1381 KREUZER

Silver **Ruler:** Leopold I **Obv:** Laureate bust of Leopold I right in inner circle **Rev:** Crowned double-headed eagle with value on breast in inner circle, crown divides date **Mint:** Augsburg **Note:** Prev. KM#5.

Date	Mintage	VG	F	VF	XF	Unc
1695A	2,892,000	—	—	—	—	—

KM# 1383 KREUZER

Silver **Ruler:** Leopold I **Rev:** Value on breast of eagle **Mint:** Vienna **Note:** Prev. KM#1853.

Date	Mintage	VG	F	VF	XF	Unc
1695	—	12.00	25.00	40.00	70.00	—

KM# 1397 KREUZER

Silver **Ruler:** Leopold I **Mint:** Hall **Note:** Varieties exist. Prev. KM#623.

Date	Mintage	VG	F	VF	XF	Unc
1699	1,339,000	15.00	30.00	45.00	70.00	—

KM# 124 2 KREUZER

Silver **Ruler:** Ferdinand II **Obv:** Half-figure right in inner circle **Rev:** Crowned arms in inner circle, date in legend **Mint:** Klagenfurt **Note:** Varieties exist. Local issue for Archduke Ferdinand. Prev. KM#988.

Date	Mintage	VG	F	VF	XF	Unc
1611	—	65.00	125	200	350	—
1614	—	65.00	125	200	350	—
1616	—	65.00	125	200	350	—
1617	—	65.00	125	200	350	—

KM# 382 2 KREUZER

Silver **Ruler:** Leopold **Obv:** Tyrolean eagle **Rev:** Four-line inscription, value below in roman numerals **Mint:** Hall **Note:** Prev. KM#789.

Date	Mintage	VG	F	VF	XF	Unc
1622	—	12.00	25.00	48.00	80.00	—
1623	—	12.00	25.00	48.00	80.00	—

KM# 383 2 KREUZER

Silver **Ruler:** Ferdinand II **Obv:** Double eagle **Rev:** Crowned oval arms **Mint:** Saint Veit **Note:** Prev. KM#1000.

Date	Mintage	VG	F	VF	XF	Unc
1622	—	—	—	—	—	—

KM# 384 2 KREUZER

Silver **Ruler:** Ferdinand II **Obv:** Crowned bust right **Rev:** Heraldic imperial eagle **Mint:** Saint Veit **Note:** Prev. KM#1001.

Date	Mintage	VG	F	VF	XF	Unc
1622	—	—	—	—	—	—

KM# 490 2 KREUZER

Silver **Ruler:** Ferdinand II **Obv:** Laureate bust right **Rev:** Crowned arms in inner circle **Mint:** Saint Veit **Note:** Varieties exist. Prev. KM#1591.

Date	Mintage	VG	F	VF	XF	Unc
1624 (m)	—	30.00	50.00	90.00	150	—
1625 (m)	—	30.00	50.00	90.00	150	—

KM# 488 2 KREUZER

Silver **Ruler:** Ferdinand II **Obv:** Laureate bust right **Rev:** Crowned shield with lion **Mint:** Graz **Note:** Varieties exist. Prev. KM#347.

Date	Mintage	VG	F	VF	XF	Unc
1624	—	15.00	30.00	55.00	85.00	—
1625	—	15.00	30.00	55.00	85.00	—
1626	—	15.00	30.00	55.00	85.00	—
1627	—	15.00	30.00	55.00	85.00	—

KM# 489 2 KREUZER

Silver **Ruler:** Ferdinand II **Obv:** Laureate bust right **Rev:** Denomination below shield **Mint:** Graz **Note:** Prev. KM#348.

Date	Mintage	VG	F	VF	XF	Unc
1624	—	15.00	30.00	50.00	85.00	—

KM# 15 3 KREUZER

Silver **Ruler:** Ferdinand II **Obv:** Crowned bust right, value below **Rev:** Three shields, points together, date in legend **Mint:** Graz **Note:** Prev. KM#557.

Date	Mintage	VG	F	VF	XF	Unc
1601	—	—	—	—	—	—
(1)601	—	—	—	—	—	—

KM# 16 3 KREUZER

Silver **Ruler:** Ferdinand II **Obv:** Crowned half-figure right in inner circle **Rev:** Crowned arms in inner circle, date in legend **Mint:** Klagenfurt **Note:** Varieties exist. Local issue for Archduke Ferdinand. Prev. KM#989.

Date	Mintage	VG	F	VF	XF	Unc
1601	—	40.00	100	175	300	—
1602	—	40.00	100	175	300	—
1603	—	40.00	100	175	300	—
1604	—	40.00	100	175	300	—
1605	—	40.00	100	175	300	—
1606	—	40.00	100	175	300	—
1607	—	40.00	100	175	300	—
1608	—	40.00	100	175	300	—
1609	—	40.00	100	175	300	—
1610	—	40.00	100	175	300	—
1611	—	40.00	100	175	300	—
1612	—	40.00	100	175	300	—
1613	—	40.00	100	175	300	—
1614	—	40.00	100	175	300	—
1617	—	40.00	100	175	300	—
1618	—	40.00	100	175	300	—
1619	—	40.00	100	175	300	—

KM# 17 3 KREUZER

Silver **Ruler:** Rudolf II **Obv:** Portrait right **Rev:** Heraldic imperial eagle **Mint:** Vienna **Note:** Prev. KM#1711.

Date	Mintage	VG	F	VF	XF	Unc
1601	—	35.00	75.00	145	225	—
1603	—	35.00	75.00	145	225	—
1604	—	35.00	75.00	145	225	—
1610	—	35.00	75.00	145	225	—

KM# 32 3 KREUZER

Silver **Ruler:** Ferdinand II **Obv:** Inner circles added **Rev:** Inner circles added **Mint:** Graz **Note:** Varieties exist. Prev. KM#558.

Date	Mintage	VG	F	VF	XF	Unc
1602	—	30.00	65.00	120	200	—
1603	—	30.00	65.00	120	200	—
1605	—	30.00	65.00	120	200	—
1606	—	30.00	65.00	120	200	—
1607	—	30.00	65.00	120	200	—
1608	—	30.00	65.00	120	200	—
1609	—	30.00	65.00	120	200	—
1613	—	30.00	65.00	120	200	—
1617	—	30.00	65.00	120	200	—

KM# 41 3 KREUZER

Silver **Ruler:** Rudolf II **Obv:** Armored bust in ruffled collar right in inner circle, date below bust **Rev:** Three shields with value below in inner circle **Mint:** Hall **Note:** Prev. KM#586.

Date	Mintage	VG	F	VF	XF	Unc
1603	—	75.00	150	285	475	—

KM# 42 3 KREUZER

Silver **Ruler:** Rudolf II **Obv:** Laureate armored bust right within inner circle **Rev:** Value above three shields within inner circle **Mint:** Hall **Note:** Prev. KM#587.

Date	Mintage	VG	F	VF	XF	Unc
1603	—	45.00	90.00	180	350	—
1604	—	45.00	90.00	180	350	—

KM# 43.1 3 KREUZER

Silver **Ruler:** Rudolf II **Obv:** Bust right, high ruffled collar **Rev:** Value encircled above three shields without inner circle **Mint:** Hall **Note:** Prev. KM#588.1.

Date	Mintage	VG	F	VF	XF	Unc
1603	—	45.00	90.00	180	350	—
1605	—	45.00	90.00	180	350	—

KM# 43.2 3 KREUZER

Silver **Ruler:** Rudolf II **Mint:** Hall **Note:** Thick planchet. Prev. KM#588.2.

Date	Mintage	VG	F	VF	XF	Unc
1605	—	45.00	90.00	180	350	—

KM# 91 3 KREUZER

Silver **Ruler:** Matthias II **Mint:** Vienna **Note:** Coronation commemorative. Prev. KM#1727.

Date	Mintage	VG	F	VF	XF	Unc
1608 CH	—	15.00	30.00	55.00	85.00	—

KM# 117 3 KREUZER

Silver **Ruler:** Rudolf II **Obv:** Laureate bust right with ruffled collar divides date **Rev:** Value above three shields within inner circle **Mint:** Hall **Note:** Prev. KM#589.

Date	Mintage	VG	F	VF	XF	Unc
1610	—	35.00	75.00	150	300	—
1611	—	35.00	75.00	150	300	—

KM# 125 3 KREUZER

Silver **Ruler:** Rudolf II **Obv:** Laureate bust right, ruffled collar **Rev:** Value below three shields without inner circle **Mint:** Hall **Note:** Prev. KM#590.

Date	Mintage	VG	F	VF	XF	Unc
1611	—	35.00	75.00	150	300	—

KM# 135 3 KREUZER

Silver **Ruler:** Maximilian **Obv:** Armored bust right, ruffled collar **Rev:** Three shields with date encircled above within inner circle **Mint:** Hall **Note:** Prev. KM#762.

Date	Mintage	VG	F	VF	XF	Unc
ND(1612) CO	40,000	350	600	1,000	1,500	—
1613	56,000	350	600	1,000	1,500	—
1616	16,000	350	600	1,000	1,500	—
1617 CO	7,999	350	600	1,000	1,500	—
1618	18,000	350	600	1,000	1,500	—

KM# 161 3 KREUZER

Silver **Ruler:** Matthias II **Obv:** Armored bust in ruffled collar right in inner circle **Rev:** Crowned imperial eagle with sword and sceptre in inner circle, date in legend **Mint:** Vienna **Note:** Prev. KM#1728.

Date	Mintage	VG	F	VF	XF	Unc
1613 (c)	—	12.00	25.00	50.00	80.00	—
1616	—	12.00	25.00	50.00	80.00	—

KM# 186 3 KREUZER

Silver **Ruler:** Matthias II **Obv:** Head in ruffled collar right in inner circle **Rev:** Crowned imperial eagle in inner circle, value below, date in legend **Mint:** Vienna **Note:** Prev. KM#1726.

Date	Mintage	VG	F	VF	XF	Unc
1614 (c)	—	10.00	20.00	35.00	60.00	—
1615	—	10.00	20.00	35.00	60.00	—
1617 (t)	—	10.00	20.00	35.00	60.00	—
1618	—	10.00	20.00	35.00	60.00	—
1619	—	10.00	20.00	35.00	60.00	—

KM# 215 3 KREUZER

Silver **Ruler:** Ferdinand II **Obv:** Bust divides date **Mint:** Graz **Note:** Varieties exist. Prev. KM#559.

Date	Mintage	VG	F	VF	XF	Unc
1617	—	40.00	80.00	150	235	—

KM# 225 3 KREUZER

Silver **Ruler:** Matthias II **Obv:** Bust right **Rev:** Heraldic imperial eagle **Mint:** Vienna **Note:** Prev. KM#1729.

Date	Mintage	VG	F	VF	XF	Unc
1618 (t)	—	12.00	25.00	50.00	80.00	—
1619	—	12.00	25.00	50.00	80.00	—

KM# 226 3 KREUZER

Silver **Ruler:** Matthias II **Mint:** Vienna **Note:** Klippe. Prev. KM#1730.

Date	Mintage	VG	F	VF	XF	Unc
1618	—	—	—	—	—	—
1619	—	—	—	—	—	—

KM# 238 3 KREUZER

Silver **Ruler:** Leopold **Obv:** Robed bust **Rev:** Three shields within circle **Mint:** Hall **Note:** Prev. KM#790.

Date	Mintage	VG	F	VF	XF	Unc
ND(1619-25)	—	10.00	20.00	35.00	65.00	—

KM# 256 3 KREUZER

Silver **Ruler:** Ferdinand II **Mint:** Vienna **Note:** Varieties exist. Prev. KM#1770.

Date	Mintage	VG	F	VF	XF	Unc
1620 (c)	—	12.00	22.00	40.00	65.00	—
1621 (c)	—	12.00	22.00	40.00	65.00	—
1622 (c)	—	12.00	22.00	40.00	65.00	—
1622 (c)	—	12.00	22.00	40.00	65.00	—
1622 (r)	—	12.00	22.00	40.00	65.00	—
1623 (c)	—	12.00	22.00	40.00	65.00	—
1624 (c)	—	12.00	22.00	40.00	65.00	—
1624 (c)-BZ	—	12.00	22.00	40.00	65.00	—
1625 (c)	—	12.00	22.00	40.00	65.00	—
1626 (c)	—	12.00	22.00	40.00	65.00	—
1627 (c)	—	12.00	22.00	40.00	65.00	—
1628 (c)	—	12.00	22.00	40.00	65.00	—
1629 (c)	—	12.00	22.00	40.00	65.00	—
1630 (c)	—	12.00	22.00	40.00	65.00	—
1631 (c)	—	12.00	22.00	40.00	65.00	—
1632 (c)	—	12.00	22.00	40.00	65.00	—
1633 (c)	—	12.00	22.00	40.00	65.00	—
1634 (c)	—	12.00	22.00	40.00	65.00	—
1635 (c)	—	12.00	22.00	40.00	65.00	—
1636 (c)	—	12.00	22.00	40.00	65.00	—
1636 (v)	—	12.00	22.00	40.00	65.00	—
1637 (v)	—	12.00	22.00	40.00	65.00	—

KM# 288 3 KREUZER

Silver **Ruler:** Ferdinand II **Obv:** Crowned imperial eagle with value on breast in inner circle **Rev:** Crowned arms in order collar and inner circle, crown divides date **Mint:** Graz **Note:** Prev. KM#353.

Date	Mintage	VG	F	VF	XF	Unc
1621	—	20.00	40.00	75.00	125	—
1622	—	20.00	40.00	75.00	125	—

KM# 290 3 KREUZER

Silver **Ruler:** Ferdinand II **Obv:** Large crowned bust right in inner circle **Rev:** Crowned imperial eagle with arms on breast, date in legend, value below **Mint:** Klagenfurt **Note:** Varieties exist. Prev. KM#954.

Date	Mintage	VG	F	VF	XF	Unc
1621	—	35.00	65.00	125	200	—

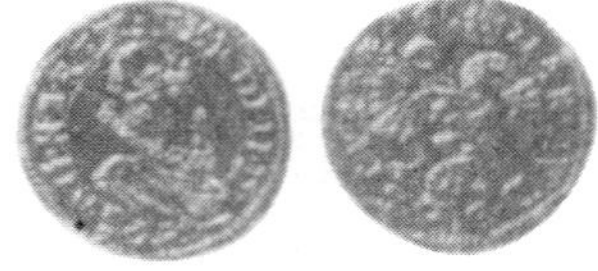

KM# 287 3 KREUZER

Silver **Ruler:** Ferdinand II **Obv:** Crowned bust right in inner circle **Rev:** Crowned imperial eagle with shield on breast, crown divides date **Mint:** Graz **Note:** Kipper 3 Kreuzer. Varieties exist. Prev. KM#349.

Date	Mintage	VG	F	VF	XF	Unc
1621	—	15.00	25.00	45.00	75.00	—
1622	—	15.00	25.00	45.00	75.00	—
1623	—	15.00	25.00	45.00	75.00	—

KM# 289 3 KREUZER

Silver **Ruler:** Ferdinand II **Obv:** Crowned imperial eagle in inner circle, value below **Mint:** Klagenfurt **Note:** Kipper 3 Kreuzer. Prev. KM#953.

Date	Mintage	VG	F	VF	XF	Unc
1621	—	35.00	65.00	125	200	—

KM# 387 3 KREUZER

Silver **Ruler:** Ferdinand II **Obv:** Bust right **Rev:** Heraldic double eagle **Mint:** Brunn **Note:** Prev. KM#202.

Date	Mintage	VG	F	VF	XF	Unc
1622 (h)	—	9.00	18.00	35.00	65.00	—
1624 B-BZ	—	9.00	18.00	35.00	65.00	—
1624 B-CW	—	9.00	18.00	35.00	65.00	—
1624 CW	—	9.00	18.00	35.00	65.00	—
1625 CW	—	9.00	18.00	35.00	65.00	—
1626 CW	—	9.00	18.00	35.00	65.00	—
1627 CW	—	9.00	18.00	35.00	65.00	—

KM# 388 3 KREUZER

Silver **Ruler:** Ferdinand II **Obv:** Crowned bust right in ornamented inner circle, date below bust **Rev:** Crowned imperial eagle in inner circle, value below **Mint:** Graz **Note:** Prev. KM#354.

Date	Mintage	VG	F	VF	XF	Unc
1622	—	20.00	40.00	75.00	125	—
1623	—	20.00	40.00	75.00	125	—

KM# 389 3 KREUZER

Silver **Ruler:** Ferdinand II **Obv:** Bust in plain circle **Mint:** Graz **Note:** Prev. KM#355.

Date	Mintage	VG	F	VF	XF	Unc
1622	—	20.00	40.00	75.00	125	—

KM# 390 3 KREUZER

Silver **Ruler:** Ferdinand II **Obv:** Small crowned bust **Mint:** Klagenfurt **Note:** Prev. KM#955.

Date	Mintage	VG	F	VF	XF	Unc
1622	—	35.00	65.00	125	200	—

KM# 391 3 KREUZER

Silver **Ruler:** Ferdinand II **Obv:** Crowned imperial eagle in inner circle, value below **Rev:** Arms in cartouche, date in legend **Mint:** Klagenfurt **Note:** Varieties exist. Prev. KM#956.

Date	Mintage	VG	F	VF	XF	Unc
1622	—	35.00	65.00	125	200	—

KM# 393 3 KREUZER

Silver **Ruler:** Ferdinand II **Obv:** Crowned bust right in inner circle **Rev:** Crowned imperial eagle in inner circle, value below, date in legend **Mint:** Saint Veit **Note:** Prev. KM#1592.

Date	Mintage	VG	F	VF	XF	Unc
1622	—	12.00	25.00	45.00	85.00	—
1623	—	12.00	25.00	45.00	85.00	—

KM# 493 3 KREUZER

Silver **Ruler:** Ferdinand II **Obv:** Laureate bust right in inner circle, value below **Rev:** Three shields of arms, points together, in inner circle, date at top **Mint:** Graz **Note:** Varieties exist. Prev. KM#350.

Date	Mintage	VG	F	VF	XF	Unc
1624	—	15.00	25.00	45.00	75.00	—
1625	—	15.00	25.00	45.00	75.00	—
1626	—	15.00	25.00	45.00	75.00	—

KM# 498 3 KREUZER

Silver **Ruler:** Ferdinand II **Obv:** Bust right with ruffled collar **Mint:** Saint Polten **Note:** Varieties exist. Prev. KM#1572.

Date	Mintage	VG	F	VF	XF	Unc
1624 (c)	—	18.00	35.00	65.00	125	—
1624 (d)	—	18.00	35.00	65.00	125	—
1625 (c)	—	—	—	—	—	—
1625 (d)	—	18.00	35.00	65.00	125	—
1625 (r)	—	18.00	35.00	65.00	125	—
1626 (r)	—	18.00	35.00	65.00	125	—

KM# 499 3 KREUZER

Silver **Ruler:** Ferdinand II **Mint:** Saint Veit **Note:** Varieties exist. Prev. KM#1593.

Date	Mintage	VG	F	VF	XF	Unc
1624 (h)	—	10.00	20.00	40.00	75.00	—
1624 (h)	—	10.00	20.00	40.00	75.00	—
1625 (h)	—	10.00	20.00	40.00	75.00	—
1625 (h)	—	10.00	20.00	40.00	75.00	—
1625 (p)	—	10.00	20.00	40.00	75.00	—
1626 (p)	—	10.00	20.00	40.00	75.00	—
1627 (g)	—	10.00	20.00	40.00	75.00	—
1627 (p)	—	10.00	20.00	40.00	75.00	—
1628 (g)	—	10.00	20.00	40.00	75.00	—
1628 (p)	—	10.00	20.00	40.00	75.00	—
1628	—	10.00	20.00	40.00	75.00	—
1629	—	10.00	20.00	40.00	75.00	—
1630 (g)	—	10.00	20.00	40.00	75.00	—
1630	—	10.00	20.00	40.00	75.00	—
1631	—	10.00	20.00	40.00	75.00	—
1632	—	10.00	20.00	40.00	75.00	—
1633	—	10.00	20.00	40.00	75.00	—
1634	—	12.00	25.00	50.00	90.00	—
1635	—	10.00	20.00	40.00	75.00	—
1636	—	10.00	20.00	40.00	75.00	—
1637	—	10.00	20.00	40.00	75.00	—

KM# 494 3 KREUZER

Silver **Ruler:** Ferdinand II **Obv:** Bust right **Rev:** Value above three coat of arms and ornamentation **Mint:** Krain **Note:** Prev. KM#1011.

Date	Mintage	VG	F	VF	XF	Unc
1624 Rare	—	—	—	—	—	—

KM# 496 3 KREUZER

Silver **Ruler:** Ferdinand II **Obv:** Bust right with ruffled collar **Rev:** Heraldic double eagle **Mint:** Nikolsburg **Note:** Prev. KM#1222.

Date	Mintage	VG	F	VF	XF	Unc
1624 Z	—	35.00	65.00	120	200	—
1627 N	—	35.00	65.00	120	200	—

KM# 497 3 KREUZER

Silver **Ruler:** Ferdinand II **Obv:** Bust right with ruffled collar **Rev:** Heraldic imperial eagle **Mint:** Olmutz **Note:** Prev. KM#1231.

Date	Mintage	VG	F	VF	XF	Unc
1624 BZ/(l)	—	8.00	17.00	33.00	60.00	—
1626 MF	—	8.00	17.00	33.00	60.00	—
1627 MF	—	8.00	17.00	33.00	60.00	—
1627 O	—	8.00	17.00	33.00	60.00	—
1628 O	—	8.00	17.00	33.00	60.00	—
1628 OL	—	8.00	17.00	33.00	60.00	—
1637 O	—	8.00	17.00	33.00	60.00	—

KM# 500 3 KREUZER

Silver **Ruler:** Ferdinand II **Mint:** Saint Veit **Note:** Prev. KM#1594.

Date	Mintage	VG	F	VF	XF	Unc
1624	—	12.00	25.00	50.00	90.00	—

KM# 501 3 KREUZER

Silver **Ruler:** Ferdinand II **Obv:** Date below bust **Mint:** Saint Veit **Note:** Varieties exist. Prev. KM#1595.

Date	Mintage	VG	F	VF	XF	Unc
1624	—	12.00	25.00	50.00	90.00	—
1628	—	12.00	25.00	50.00	90.00	—
1629	—	12.00	25.00	50.00	90.00	—

KM# 582 3 KREUZER

Silver **Ruler:** Ferdinand II **Mint:** Brunn **Note:** Klippe. Prev. KM#203.

Date	Mintage	VG	F	VF	XF	Unc
1625 CW	—	—	—	—	—	—

KM# 583 3 KREUZER

Silver **Ruler:** Leopold **Obv:** Crowned bust **Mint:** Hall **Note:** Prev. KM#791.

Date	Mintage	VG	F	VF	XF	Unc
ND(1625-32)	—	10.00	20.00	40.00	70.00	—

KM# 584 3 KREUZER

Silver **Ruler:** Ferdinand II **Obv:** Bust right with plain collar **Mint:** Nikolsburg **Note:** Prev. KM#1233.

Date	Mintage	VG	F	VF	XF	Unc
1625 N-(c)	—	35.00	65.00	120	200	—
1627 N	—	35.00	65.00	120	200	—
1627 N-(c)	—	35.00	65.00	120	200	—
1628 N	—	35.00	65.00	120	200	—

KM# 626 3 KREUZER

Silver **Ruler:** Ferdinand II **Mint:** Graz **Note:** Varieties exist. Prev. KM#351.

Date	Mintage	VG	F	VF	XF	Unc
1626	—	15.00	25.00	45.00	75.00	—
1627	—	15.00	25.00	45.00	75.00	—
1628	—	15.00	25.00	45.00	75.00	—

KM# 669 3 KREUZER

Silver **Ruler:** Ferdinand III **Obv:** Bust right **Rev:** Three shields in circle **Mint:** Glatz **Note:** Varieties exist. Prev. KM#295.

Date	Mintage	VG	F	VF	XF	Unc
1627	—	8.00	17.00	35.00	65.00	—
1627 (c)	—	8.00	17.00	35.00	65.00	—
1628 (c)	—	8.00	17.00	35.00	65.00	—
1628 G-(p)	—	8.00	17.00	35.00	65.00	—
1628 AP	—	8.00	17.00	35.00	65.00	—
1628 (p)	—	8.00	17.00	35.00	65.00	—

KM# 692 3 KREUZER

Silver **Ruler:** Ferdinand III **Rev:** Crowned arms **Mint:** Glatz **Note:** Prev. KM#296.

Date	Mintage	VG	F	VF	XF	Unc
1628 (p)	—	8.00	17.00	35.00	65.00	—
1629 (p)	—	8.00	17.00	35.00	65.00	—
1630 (p)	—	8.00	17.00	35.00	65.00	—
1630 H	—	8.00	17.00	35.00	65.00	—
1631 (p)	—	8.00	17.00	35.00	65.00	—
1631 (h)	—	8.00	17.00	35.00	65.00	—
1632 (p)	—	8.00	17.00	35.00	65.00	—
1632 (h)	—	8.00	17.00	35.00	65.00	—
1633 (h)	—	8.00	17.00	35.00	65.00	—
1634 (h)	—	8.00	17.00	35.00	65.00	—
1635 (h)	—	8.00	17.00	35.00	65.00	—
1636 (h)	—	8.00	17.00	35.00	65.00	—
1637 (h)	—	8.00	17.00	35.00	65.00	—

KM# 693 3 KREUZER

Silver **Ruler:** Ferdinand II **Obv:** Bust right with plain collar **Mint:** Olmutz **Note:** Varieties exist. Prev. KM#1232.

Date	Mintage	VG	F	VF	XF	Unc
1628 O	—	8.00	17.00	33.00	60.00	—
1629 O	—	8.00	17.00	33.00	60.00	—
1630 O	—	8.00	17.00	33.00	60.00	—
1630 (a)	—	8.00	17.00	33.00	60.00	—
1631 O	—	8.00	17.00	33.00	60.00	—
1632 (a)	—	8.00	17.00	33.00	60.00	—
1632 O	—	8.00	17.00	33.00	60.00	—
1633 (a)	—	8.00	17.00	33.00	60.00	—
1634 (a)	—	8.00	17.00	33.00	60.00	—
1635 MF	—	8.00	17.00	33.00	60.00	—

KM# 694 3 KREUZER

Silver **Ruler:** Ferdinand II **Obv:** Date **Rev:** Date **Mint:** Saint Veit **Note:** Prev. KM#1596.

Date	Mintage	VG	F	VF	XF	Unc
1628	—	12.00	25.00	50.00	90.00	—

KM# 709 3 KREUZER

Silver **Ruler:** Ferdinand II **Mint:** Graz **Note:** Varieties exist. Prev. KM#352.

Date	Mintage	VG	F	VF	XF	Unc
1629	—	15.00	25.00	45.00	75.00	—
1630	—	15.00	25.00	45.00	75.00	—
1631	—	15.00	25.00	45.00	75.00	—
1632	—	15.00	25.00	45.00	75.00	—
1633	—	15.00	25.00	45.00	75.00	—
1634	—	15.00	25.00	45.00	75.00	—
1635	—	15.00	25.00	45.00	75.00	—
1636	—	15.00	25.00	45.00	75.00	—
1637	—	15.00	25.00	45.00	75.00	—

KM# 743 3 KREUZER

Silver **Ruler:** Ferdinand II **Mint:** Furth **Note:** Similar to 1 Thaler, KM#746. Prev. KM#285.

Date	Mintage	VG	F	VF	XF	Unc
1630 F Rare	—	—	—	—	—	—

KM# 832 3 KREUZER

Silver **Ruler:** Ferdinand III **Rev:** Crowned imperial eagle **Mint:** Glatz **Note:** Varieties exist. Prev. KM#297.

Date	Mintage	VG	F	VF	XF	Unc
1637 (r)	—	10.00	20.00	38.00	75.00	—
1637 G	—	10.00	20.00	38.00	75.00	—
1638 G	—	10.00	20.00	38.00	75.00	—
1639 G	—	10.00	20.00	38.00	75.00	—
1640 G	—	10.00	20.00	38.00	75.00	—
1640 GW	—	10.00	20.00	38.00	75.00	—

KM# 833 3 KREUZER

Silver **Ruler:** Ferdinand III **Obv:** Portrait and titles of Ferdinand III **Mint:** Graz **Note:** Prev. KM#424.

Date	Mintage	VG	F	VF	XF	Unc
1637	—	15.00	25.00	45.00	80.00	—
1673	—	15.00	25.00	45.00	80.00	—
1638	—	15.00	25.00	45.00	80.00	—
1639	—	15.00	25.00	45.00	80.00	—
1640	—	15.00	25.00	45.00	80.00	—
1641	—	15.00	25.00	45.00	80.00	—
1642	—	15.00	25.00	45.00	80.00	—
1643	—	15.00	25.00	45.00	80.00	—
1644	—	15.00	25.00	45.00	80.00	—
1645	—	15.00	25.00	45.00	80.00	—
1646	—	15.00	25.00	45.00	80.00	—
1647	—	15.00	25.00	45.00	80.00	—
1648	—	15.00	25.00	45.00	80.00	—
1649	—	15.00	25.00	45.00	80.00	—
1650	—	15.00	25.00	45.00	80.00	—
1651	—	15.00	25.00	45.00	80.00	—
1652	—	15.00	25.00	45.00	80.00	—
1653	—	15.00	25.00	45.00	80.00	—
1654	—	15.00	25.00	45.00	80.00	—
1655	—	15.00	25.00	45.00	80.00	—
1656	—	15.00	25.00	45.00	80.00	—
1657	—	15.00	25.00	45.00	80.00	—

KM# 834 3 KREUZER

Silver **Ruler:** Ferdinand III **Obv:** Bust right **Rev:** Heraldic double eagle **Mint:** Olmutz **Note:** Prev. KM#1253.

Date	Mintage	VG	F	VF	XF	Unc
1637 O	—	10.00	20.00	35.00	65.00	—
1638 O	—	10.00	20.00	35.00	65.00	—
1639 O	—	10.00	20.00	35.00	65.00	—
1640 O	—	10.00	20.00	35.00	65.00	—
1640 (s)	—	10.00	20.00	35.00	65.00	—
1641 O	—	10.00	20.00	35.00	65.00	—
1641 (s)	—	10.00	20.00	35.00	65.00	—

KM# 835 3 KREUZER

Silver **Ruler:** Ferdinand III **Mint:** Saint Veit **Note:** Varieties exist. Prev. KM#1624.

Date	Mintage	VG	F	VF	XF	Unc
1637	—	12.00	25.00	50.00	85.00	—
1638	—	12.00	25.00	50.00	85.00	—
1639	—	12.00	25.00	50.00	85.00	—
1640	—	12.00	25.00	50.00	85.00	—
1641	—	12.00	25.00	50.00	85.00	—
1642	—	12.00	25.00	50.00	85.00	—
1643	—	12.00	25.00	50.00	85.00	—
1644	—	12.00	25.00	50.00	85.00	—
1645	—	12.00	25.00	50.00	85.00	—
1646	—	12.00	25.00	50.00	85.00	—
1647	—	12.00	25.00	50.00	85.00	—
1648	—	12.00	25.00	50.00	85.00	—
1649	—	12.00	25.00	50.00	85.00	—
1650	—	12.00	25.00	50.00	85.00	—
1652	—	12.00	25.00	50.00	85.00	—
1653	—	12.00	25.00	50.00	85.00	—
1655	—	12.00	25.00	50.00	85.00	—
1657	—	12.00	25.00	50.00	85.00	—

KM# 836 3 KREUZER

Silver **Ruler:** Ferdinand III **Mint:** Saint Veit **Note:** Klippe. Prev. KM#1625.

Date	Mintage	VG	F	VF	XF	Unc
1637	—	—	—	—	—	—

KM# 837 3 KREUZER

Silver **Ruler:** Ferdinand III **Mint:** Vienna **Note:** Varieties exist. Prev. KM#1818.

Date	Mintage	VG	F	VF	XF	Unc
1637 (b)	—	12.00	25.00	45.00	75.00	—
1638 (b)	—	12.00	25.00	45.00	75.00	—
1639 (b)	—	12.00	25.00	45.00	75.00	—
1640 (b)	—	12.00	25.00	45.00	75.00	—
1641 (b)	—	12.00	25.00	45.00	75.00	—
1642 (b)	—	12.00	25.00	45.00	75.00	—
1643 (b)	—	12.00	25.00	45.00	75.00	—
1644 (b)	—	12.00	25.00	45.00	75.00	—
1645 (b)	—	12.00	25.00	45.00	75.00	—
1646 (b)	—	12.00	25.00	45.00	75.00	—
1647 (b)	—	12.00	25.00	45.00	75.00	—
1651 (b)	—	12.00	25.00	45.00	75.00	—
1657 (c)	—	12.00	25.00	45.00	75.00	—

KM# 851 3 KREUZER

Silver **Ruler:** Ferdinand Charles **Rev:** Three shields **Mint:** Hall **Note:** Prev. KM#828.

Date	Mintage	VG	F	VF	XF	Unc
1638	688,000	8.00	17.00	35.00	65.00	—

KM# 852 3 KREUZER
Silver **Ruler:** Ferdinand Charles **Obv:** Crowned bust right divides date **Rev:** Two shields, value below **Mint:** Hall **Note:** Prev. KM#829.

Date	Mintage	VG	F	VF	XF	Unc
1638	1,100,000	8.00	17.00	33.00	60.00	—
1639	2,133,000	8.00	17.00	33.00	60.00	—
1640	1,308,000	8.00	17.00	33.00	60.00	—
1641	1,563,000	8.00	17.00	33.00	60.00	—
1642	2,353,000	8.00	17.00	33.00	60.00	—
1643	1,877,000	8.00	17.00	33.00	60.00	—
1644	1,907,000	8.00	17.00	33.00	60.00	—
1645	1,927,000	8.00	17.00	33.00	60.00	—
1646	2,344,000	8.00	17.00	33.00	60.00	—
1647	898,000	8.00	17.00	33.00	60.00	—
1648	1,727,000	8.00	17.00	33.00	60.00	—
1649	—	8.00	17.00	33.00	60.00	—
1650	1,787,000	8.00	17.00	33.00	60.00	—
1651	1,494,000	8.00	17.00	33.00	60.00	—
1652	1,594,000	8.00	17.00	33.00	60.00	—
1653	—	8.00	17.00	33.00	60.00	—
1654	1,910,000	8.00	17.00	33.00	60.00	—
1655	1,891,000	8.00	17.00	33.00	60.00	—
1656	1,971,000	8.00	17.00	33.00	60.00	—
1657	2,185,000	8.00	17.00	33.00	60.00	—
1658	3,377,000	8.00	17.00	33.00	60.00	—
1659	—	8.00	17.00	33.00	60.00	—
1660	3,909,000	8.00	17.00	33.00	60.00	—
1661	6,431,000	8.00	17.00	33.00	60.00	—
1662	5,113,000	8.00	17.00	33.00	60.00	—

KM# 893 3 KREUZER
Silver **Ruler:** Ferdinand III **Obv:** Robed bust right **Mint:** Glatz **Note:** Varieties exist. Prev. KM#298.

Date	Mintage	VG	F	VF	XF	Unc
1641 GW	—	10.00	20.00	38.00	75.00	—
1642 GW	—	10.00	20.00	38.00	75.00	—
1643 GW	—	10.00	20.00	38.00	75.00	—
1644 GW	—	10.00	20.00	38.00	75.00	—
1645 GW	—	10.00	20.00	38.00	75.00	—
1646 GW	—	10.00	20.00	38.00	75.00	—
1647 GW	—	10.00	20.00	38.00	75.00	—
1648 GW	—	10.00	20.00	38.00	75.00	—
1649 GW	—	10.00	20.00	38.00	75.00	—
1650 GW	—	10.00	20.00	38.00	75.00	—
1651 GW	—	10.00	20.00	38.00	75.00	—
1652 GW	—	10.00	20.00	38.00	75.00	—
1653 GW	—	10.00	20.00	38.00	75.00	—
1654 GW	—	10.00	20.00	38.00	75.00	—
1658 GW	—	10.00	20.00	38.00	75.00	—
1659 GW	—	10.00	20.00	38.00	75.00	—

KM# 947 3 KREUZER
Silver **Ruler:** Ferdinand III **Mint:** Graz **Note:** Klippe. Prev. KM#425.

Date	Mintage	VG	F	VF	XF	Unc
1647	—	—	—	—	—	—

KM# 1114 3 KREUZER
Silver **Ruler:** Ferdinand III **Mint:** Glatz **Note:** Posthumous issue. Prev. KM#299.

Date	Mintage	VG	F	VF	XF	Unc
1658 G	—	—	—	—	—	—

KM# 1115 3 KREUZER
Silver **Ruler:** Leopold I **Obv:** Portrait right and titles of Leopold I **Rev:** Three shields in inner circle, date at top **Mint:** Graz **Note:** Varieties exist. Prev. KM#450.

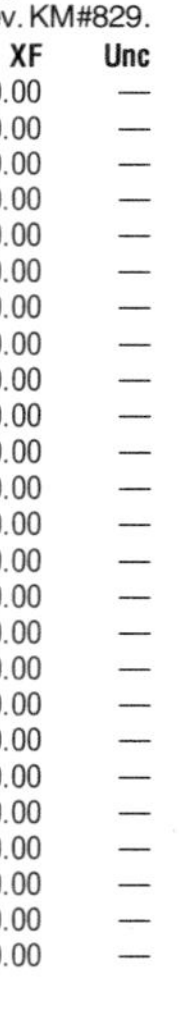

Date	Mintage	VG	F	VF	XF	Unc
1658 HCK	—	8.00	17.00	33.00	60.00	—
1659 HCK	—	8.00	17.00	33.00	60.00	—
1659 L	—	8.00	17.00	33.00	60.00	—
1660 HCK	—	8.00	17.00	33.00	60.00	—
1660 L	—	8.00	17.00	33.00	60.00	—
1661 L	—	8.00	17.00	33.00	60.00	—
1662 L	—	8.00	17.00	33.00	60.00	—
1662	—	8.00	17.00	33.00	60.00	—
1663 L	—	8.00	17.00	33.00	60.00	—
1664 L	—	8.00	17.00	33.00	60.00	—
1665 SH	—	8.00	17.00	33.00	60.00	—
1666 SH	—	8.00	17.00	33.00	60.00	—
1666	—	8.00	17.00	33.00	60.00	—
1667	—	8.00	17.00	33.00	60.00	—
1668	—	8.00	17.00	33.00	60.00	—
1669 IGN	—	8.00	17.00	33.00	60.00	—
1669 IAN	—	8.00	17.00	33.00	60.00	—
1670 IGW	—	8.00	17.00	33.00	60.00	—
1671 IAN	—	8.00	17.00	33.00	60.00	—
1673 IAN	—	8.00	17.00	33.00	60.00	—
1674 IAN	—	8.00	17.00	33.00	60.00	—
1675 IAN	—	8.00	17.00	33.00	60.00	—
1676 IAN	—	8.00	17.00	33.00	60.00	—
1677 IAN	—	8.00	17.00	33.00	60.00	—
1678 IAN	—	8.00	17.00	33.00	60.00	—
1679 IAN	—	8.00	17.00	33.00	60.00	—
1681 IAN	—	8.00	17.00	33.00	60.00	—
1682 IAN	—	8.00	17.00	33.00	60.00	—
1684 IAN	—	8.00	17.00	33.00	60.00	—
1686 IAN	—	8.00	17.00	33.00	60.00	—
1688 IAN	—	8.00	17.00	33.00	60.00	—
1693	—	8.00	17.00	33.00	60.00	—
1694	—	8.00	17.00	33.00	60.00	—
1695 IA	—	8.00	17.00	33.00	60.00	—
1696 IA	—	8.00	17.00	33.00	60.00	—
1697 IA	—	8.00	17.00	33.00	60.00	—
1698 IA	—	8.00	17.00	33.00	60.00	—
1699 IA	—	8.00	17.00	33.00	60.00	—
1700 IA	—	8.00	17.00	33.00	60.00	—

KM# 1116 3 KREUZER
Silver **Ruler:** Leopold I **Obv:** Bust right in inner circle **Obv. Legend:** LEOPOLDVS • D • G • R • I • .... **Rev:** Three shields in inner circle **Mint:** Saint Veit **Note:** Varieties exist. Prev. KM#1639.

Date	Mintage	VG	F	VF	XF	Unc
1658	—	10.00	22.50	45.00	90.00	—
1659	—	10.00	22.50	45.00	90.00	—
1661	—	10.00	22.50	45.00	90.00	—
1662	—	10.00	22.50	45.00	90.00	—
1663	—	10.00	22.50	45.00	90.00	—
1664	—	10.00	22.50	45.00	90.00	—
1665	—	10.00	22.50	45.00	90.00	—
1666	—	10.00	22.50	45.00	90.00	—
1667	—	10.00	22.50	45.00	90.00	—
1668 GCS	—	10.00	22.50	45.00	90.00	—
1668 GS	—	10.00	22.50	45.00	90.00	—
1669	—	10.00	22.50	45.00	90.00	—
1669 GCS	—	10.00	22.50	45.00	90.00	—
1680 IR	—	10.00	22.50	45.00	90.00	—
1681 IR	—	10.00	22.50	45.00	90.00	—
1682 IR	—	10.00	22.50	45.00	90.00	—
1683 IR	—	10.00	22.50	45.00	90.00	—
1686 IR	—	10.00	22.50	45.00	90.00	—
1692 CS	—	10.00	22.50	45.00	90.00	—
1693 C-S	—	10.00	22.50	45.00	90.00	—
1695 CS	—	10.00	22.50	45.00	90.00	—
1695 I-R	—	10.00	22.50	45.00	90.00	—
1695 IA	—	10.00	22.50	45.00	90.00	—
1695	—	10.00	22.50	45.00	90.00	—
1696 CS	—	10.00	22.50	45.00	90.00	—
1696 C-S	—	10.00	22.50	45.00	90.00	—
1696	—	10.00	22.50	45.00	90.00	—
1697 CS	—	10.00	22.50	45.00	90.00	—
1697	—	10.00	22.50	45.00	90.00	—
1698 CS	—	10.00	22.50	45.00	90.00	—
1699 CS	—	10.00	22.50	45.00	90.00	—
1699 IP	—	10.00	22.50	45.00	90.00	—
1700 IP	—	10.00	22.50	45.00	90.00	—
1700 CS	—	10.00	22.50	45.00	90.00	—
1700 IW	—	10.00	22.50	45.00	90.00	—

KM# 1117 3 KREUZER
Silver **Ruler:** Ferdinand III **Mint:** Vienna **Note:** Posthumous issue. Prev. KM#1819.

Date	Mintage	VG	F	VF	XF	Unc
1658 (c)	—	—	—	—	—	—

KM# 1140 3 KREUZER
Silver **Ruler:** Leopold I **Obv:** Young bust right, value below **Rev:** Crowned imperial eagle, date in legend **Mint:** Glatz **Note:** Prev. KM#324.

Date	Mintage	VG	F	VF	XF	Unc
1659 GW	—	8.00	17.00	33.00	60.00	—
1660 GW	—	8.00	17.00	33.00	60.00	—

KM# 1141 3 KREUZER
Silver **Ruler:** Leopold I **Rev:** Vienna arms below eagle **Mint:** Vienna **Note:** Varieties exist. Prev. KM#1854.

Date	Mintage	VG	F	VF	XF	Unc
1659	—	8.00	17.00	35.00	65.00	—
1659 HH	—	8.00	17.00	35.00	65.00	—
1660	—	8.00	17.00	35.00	65.00	—

KM# 1169 3 KREUZER
Silver **Ruler:** Leopold I **Rev:** Vienna arms on breast of eagle **Mint:** Vienna **Note:** Varieties exist. Prev. KM#1855.

Date	Mintage	VG	F	VF	XF	Unc
1660 (ca)	—	8.00	17.00	33.00	60.00	—
1661 (ca)	—	8.00	17.00	33.00	60.00	—
1662 (ca)	—	8.00	17.00	33.00	60.00	—
1663 (ca)	—	8.00	17.00	33.00	60.00	—
1664 (ca)	—	8.00	17.00	33.00	60.00	—
1665 (ca)	—	8.00	17.00	33.00	60.00	—
1666 (r)	—	8.00	17.00	33.00	60.00	—
1667 (r)	—	8.00	17.00	33.00	60.00	—
1668 (r)	—	8.00	17.00	33.00	60.00	—
1669 (r)	—	8.00	17.00	33.00	60.00	—
1670 (r)	—	8.00	17.00	33.00	60.00	—
1672 (r)	—	8.00	17.00	33.00	60.00	—
1673 (r)	—	8.00	17.00	33.00	60.00	—
1674 (r)	—	8.00	17.00	33.00	60.00	—
1693	—	—	—	—	—	—
1694	—	—	—	—	—	—
1695	—	—	—	—	—	—

KM# 1209 3 KREUZER
Silver **Ruler:** Sigismund Franz **Mint:** Hall **Note:** Prev. KM#851.

Date	Mintage	VG	F	VF	XF	Unc
1663	9,705,000	8.00	17.00	33.00	60.00	—
1664	5,624,000	8.00	17.00	33.00	60.00	—
1665	2,728,000	8.00	17.00	33.00	60.00	—

KM# 1231 3 KREUZER
Silver **Ruler:** Leopold I **Obv:** Value below bust right **Rev:** Shield on double eagle's breast, crown above **Mint:** Neuburg am Inn **Note:** Varieties exist. Prev. KM#1215.

Date	Mintage	VG	F	VF	XF	Unc
1665	—	5.00	8.00	15.00	30.00	—

KM# 1245 3 KREUZER
Silver **Ruler:** Leopold I **Mint:** Hall **Note:** Varieties exist. Prev. KM#624.

Date	Mintage	VG	F	VF	XF	Unc
1667	—	8.00	17.00	33.00	60.00	—
1668	—	8.00	17.00	33.00	60.00	—
1669	—	8.00	17.00	33.00	60.00	—
1670	—	8.00	17.00	33.00	60.00	—
1671	—	8.00	17.00	33.00	60.00	—
1672	—	8.00	17.00	33.00	60.00	—
1673	—	8.00	17.00	33.00	60.00	—
1674	—	8.00	17.00	33.00	60.00	—
1675	—	8.00	17.00	33.00	60.00	—
1676	—	8.00	17.00	33.00	60.00	—

Date	Mintage	VG	F	VF	XF	Unc
1677	—	8.00	17.00	33.00	60.00	—
1678	—	8.00	17.00	33.00	60.00	—
1679	—	8.00	17.00	33.00	60.00	—
1680	—	8.00	17.00	33.00	60.00	—
1681	—	8.00	17.00	33.00	60.00	—
1682	—	8.00	17.00	33.00	60.00	—
1683	—	8.00	17.00	33.00	60.00	—
1684	—	8.00	17.00	33.00	60.00	—
1685	—	8.00	17.00	33.00	60.00	—
1686	—	8.00	17.00	33.00	60.00	—
1687	—	8.00	17.00	33.00	60.00	—
1688	—	8.00	17.00	33.00	60.00	—
1689	—	8.00	17.00	33.00	60.00	—
1690	—	8.00	17.00	33.00	60.00	—

KM# 1346 3 KREUZER

Silver **Ruler:** Leopold I **Rev:** Ornamental shields, value below **Mint:** Hall **Note:** Prev. KM#625.

Date	Mintage	VG	F	VF	XF	Unc
1690	—	8.00	17.00	33.00	60.00	—
1691	—	8.00	17.00	33.00	60.00	—

KM# 1356 3 KREUZER

Silver **Ruler:** Leopold I **Obv:** Value below bust **Mint:** Hall **Note:** Varieties exist. Prev. KM#626.

Date	Mintage	VG	F	VF	XF	Unc
1692	—	8.00	17.00	33.00	60.00	—
1693	—	8.00	17.00	33.00	60.00	—
1694	—	8.00	17.00	33.00	60.00	—

KM# 291 4 KREUZER

Silver **Ruler:** Leopold **Obv:** Tirolean eagle **Rev:** Five-line inscription **Mint:** Hall **Note:** Prev. KM#792.

Date	Mintage	VG	F	VF	XF	Unc
1621	—	20.00	35.00	65.00	120	—

KM# 33.1 6 KREUZER

Silver **Ruler:** Rudolf II **Obv:** Armed bust in ruffled collar right in inner circle **Rev:** Four shields in angles of cross in inner circle, date in legend **Mint:** Hall **Note:** Prev. KM#591.1.

Date	Mintage	VG	F	VF	XF	Unc
1602	—	35.00	75.00	145	300	—
ND(1603)	—	—	—	—	—	—

KM# 33.2 6 KREUZER

Silver **Ruler:** Rudolf II **Mint:** Hall **Note:** Thick planchet. Prev. KM#591.2.

Date	Mintage	VG	F	VF	XF	Unc
1602	—	35.00	75.00	145	300	—

KM# 53 6 KREUZER

Silver **Ruler:** Rudolf II **Obv:** Date below bust **Mint:** Hall **Note:** Prev. KM#592.

Date	Mintage	VG	F	VF	XF	Unc
1604	—	35.00	75.00	145	300	—

KM# 75 6 KREUZER

Silver **Ruler:** Rudolf II **Rev:** Oval shields in angles of cross **Mint:** Hall **Note:** Prev. KM#593.

Date	Mintage	VG	F	VF	XF	Unc
1606	—	35.00	75.00	145	300	—

KM# 76 6 KREUZER

Silver **Ruler:** Rudolf II **Obv:** Bust left, date below **Rev:** Four oval shields in angles of cross **Mint:** Hall **Note:** Prev. KM#594.

Date	Mintage	VG	F	VF	XF	Unc
1606	—	35.00	75.00	145	300	—

KM# 136 6 KREUZER

Silver **Ruler:** Maximilian **Obv:** Bust right within inner circle **Rev:** Plain Austrian shield on bottom **Mint:** Hall **Note:** Prev. KM#763.

Date	Mintage	VG	F	VF	XF	Unc
ND(1612)	—	350	650	1,100	1,650	—

KM# 137 6 KREUZER

Silver **Ruler:** Maximilian **Obv:** Bust right with high ruffled collar **Rev:** Ornamented shields **Mint:** Hall **Note:** Prev. KM#764.

Date	Mintage	VG	F	VF	XF	Unc
ND(612)	—	350	650	1,100	1,650	—

KM# 139 6 KREUZER

Silver **Ruler:** Maximilian **Obv:** Bust right, high ruffled collar **Rev:** Plain Hapsburg shield at bottom **Mint:** Hall **Note:** Prev. KM#766.

Date	Mintage	VG	F	VF	XF	Unc
ND(1612)	—	350	650	1,100	1,650	—

KM# 292 6 KREUZER

Silver **Ruler:** Leopold **Obv:** Tirolean eagle **Rev:** Four-line inscription, value below in romzan numerals **Mint:** Hall **Note:** Prev. KM#793.

Date	Mintage	VG	F	VF	XF	Unc
1621	—	18.00	35.00	75.00	150	—
1622	—	18.00	35.00	75.00	150	—
1623	—	18.00	35.00	75.00	150	—

KM# 744 6 KREUZER

Silver **Ruler:** Ferdinand II **Mint:** Furth **Note:** Similar to 1 Thaler, KM#746. Prev. KM#286.

Date	Mintage	VG	F	VF	XF	Unc
1630 Rare	—	—	—	—	—	—

KM# 1185 6 KREUZER

Silver **Ruler:** Leopold I **Mint:** Vienna **Note:** Varieties exist. Prev. KM#1856.

Date	Mintage	VG	F	VF	XF	Unc
1661	—	8.00	18.00	35.00	60.00	—
1662	—	8.00	18.00	35.00	60.00	—
1664	—	8.00	18.00	35.00	60.00	—
1665	—	8.00	18.00	35.00	60.00	—
1674	—	8.00	18.00	35.00	60.00	—
1676	—	8.00	18.00	35.00	60.00	—
1677	—	8.00	18.00	35.00	60.00	—
1678	—	8.00	18.00	35.00	60.00	—
1679	—	8.00	18.00	35.00	60.00	—
1680	—	8.00	18.00	35.00	60.00	—
1681	—	8.00	18.00	35.00	60.00	—
1682	—	8.00	18.00	35.00	60.00	—
1683	—	8.00	18.00	35.00	60.00	—
1684	—	8.00	18.00	35.00	60.00	—
1685	—	8.00	18.00	35.00	60.00	—
1686	—	8.00	18.00	35.00	60.00	—
1687	—	8.00	18.00	35.00	60.00	—
1688	—	8.00	18.00	35.00	60.00	—
1689	—	8.00	18.00	35.00	60.00	—
1690	—	8.00	18.00	35.00	60.00	—
1691	—	8.00	18.00	35.00	60.00	—
1692	—	8.00	18.00	35.00	60.00	—

KM# 1196 6 KREUZER

Silver **Ruler:** Leopold I **Rev:** Date in legend **Mint:** Vienna **Note:** Prev. KM#1857.

Date	Mintage	VG	F	VF	XF	Unc
1662	—	—	—	—	—	—

KM# 1233 6 KREUZER

Silver **Ruler:** Leopold I **Obv:** Leopold I **Mint:** Graz **Note:** Varieties exist. Prev. KM#452.

Date	Mintage	VG	F	VF	XF	Unc
1665 SH	—	10.00	20.00	35.00	70.00	—
1669 IGW	—	10.00	20.00	35.00	70.00	—
1670 IGW	—	10.00	20.00	35.00	70.00	—
1670 IAN	—	10.00	20.00	35.00	70.00	—
1671 IGW	—	10.00	20.00	35.00	70.00	—
1672 IAN	—	10.00	20.00	35.00	70.00	—
1673 IAN	—	10.00	20.00	35.00	70.00	—
1674 IAN	—	10.00	20.00	35.00	70.00	—
1675 IAN	—	10.00	20.00	35.00	70.00	—

KM# 1234.1 6 KREUZER

Silver **Ruler:** Leopold I **Obv:** Hair style in curls **Mint:** Neuburg am Inn **Note:** Prev. KM#1216.1.

Date	Mintage	VG	F	VF	XF	Unc
1665	—	5.00	7.00	14.00	30.00	—

KM# 1234.2 6 KREUZER

Silver **Ruler:** Leopold I **Obv:** Hair style wavy **Mint:** Neuburg am Inn **Note:** Prev. KM#1216.2.

Date	Mintage	VG	F	VF	XF	Unc
1665	—	5.00	7.00	14.00	30.00	—

KM# 1257 6 KREUZER

Silver **Ruler:** Leopold I **Obv:** Laureate bust right, value below **Mint:** Saint Veit **Note:** Varieties exist. Prev. KM#1640.

Date	Mintage	VG	F	VF	XF	Unc
1669 G-S	—	25.00	55.00	125	225	—
1670 G-S	—	25.00	55.00	125	225	—
1671 G-S	—	25.00	55.00	125	225	—

Date	Mintage	VG	F	VF	XF	Unc
1671	—	25.00	55.00	125	225	—
1672 G	—	25.00	55.00	125	225	—
1672	—	25.00	55.00	125	225	—
1673	—	25.00	55.00	125	225	—
1674	—	25.00	55.00	125	225	—
1675	—	25.00	55.00	125	225	—

KM# 1288 6 KREUZER

Silver **Ruler:** Leopold I **Obv:** Crowned arms in order collar and inner circle, crown divides date **Mint:** Graz **Note:** Varieties exist. Prev. KM#453.

Date	Mintage	VG	F	VF	XF	Unc
1676 IAN	—	10.00	20.00	35.00	70.00	—
1679 IAN	—	10.00	20.00	35.00	70.00	—
1680 IAN	—	10.00	20.00	35.00	70.00	—
1681 IAN	—	10.00	20.00	35.00	70.00	—
1682 IAN	—	10.00	20.00	35.00	70.00	—
1683 IAN	—	10.00	20.00	35.00	70.00	—
1684 IAN	—	10.00	20.00	35.00	70.00	—
1685 IAN	—	10.00	20.00	35.00	70.00	—
1686 IAN	—	10.00	20.00	35.00	70.00	—
1687 IAN	—	10.00	20.00	35.00	70.00	—
1688 IAN	—	10.00	20.00	35.00	70.00	—
1689 IAN	—	10.00	20.00	35.00	70.00	—
1690 IAN	—	10.00	20.00	35.00	70.00	—
1691 IAN	—	10.00	20.00	35.00	70.00	—
1692 IAN	—	10.00	20.00	35.00	70.00	—

KM# 1307 6 KREUZER

Silver **Ruler:** Leopold I **Obv:** Value in Roman numerals, without inner circle **Rev:** Without inner circle, arms in oval shield **Mint:** Saint Veit **Note:** Prev. KM#1641.

Date	Mintage	VG	F	VF	XF	Unc
1680	—	40.00	80.00	150	275	—
1680 IR	—	40.00	80.00	150	275	—
1681 IR	—	40.00	80.00	150	275	—
1682 IR	—	40.00	80.00	150	275	—

KM# 1317 6 KREUZER

Silver **Ruler:** Leopold I **Obv:** Without inner circle **Rev:** Without inner circle **Mint:** Graz **Note:** Prev. KM#454.

Date	Mintage	VG	F	VF	XF	Unc
1682	—	12.00	25.00	45.00	80.00	—

KM# 1322 6 KREUZER

Silver **Ruler:** Leopold I **Obv:** Inner circle added **Mint:** Saint Veit **Note:** Prev. KM#1642.

Date	Mintage	VG	F	VF	XF	Unc
1683 IR	—	40.00	80.00	150	275	—
1684 IR	—	40.00	80.00	150	275	—
1686 H-L	—	40.00	80.00	150	275	—
1690 CS	—	40.00	80.00	150	275	—

KM# 1334 6 KREUZER

Silver **Ruler:** Leopold I **Obv:** With inner circle **Rev:** With inner circle **Mint:** Saint Veit **Note:** Prev. KM#1643.

Date	Mintage	VG	F	VF	XF	Unc
1685	—	40.00	80.00	150	275	—
1686	—	40.00	80.00	150	275	—

KM# 1340 6 KREUZER

Silver **Ruler:** Leopold I **Obv:** Laureate bust right in inner circle **Rev:** Crown above two ornamental shields, value below, crown divides date **Mint:** Hall **Note:** Prev. KM#628.

Date	Mintage	VG	F	VF	XF	Unc
1687	—	8.00	18.00	35.00	70.00	—

KM# 1366 6 KREUZER

Silver **Ruler:** Leopold I **Obv:** Value in Arabic numeral below bust **Mint:** Hall **Note:** Prev. KM#1366.

Date	Mintage	VG	F	VF	XF	Unc
1693	—	8.00	18.00	35.00	70.00	—
1694	123,000	8.00	18.00	35.00	70.00	—

KM# 1644x 6 KREUZER

Silver **Ruler:** Leopold I **Obv:** Without inner circle **Rev:** Flat-topped shield, without inner circle **Mint:** Saint Veit

Date	Mintage	VG	F	VF	XF	Unc
1693 C-S	—	30.00	60.00	135	250	—

KM# 1374 6 KREUZER

Silver **Ruler:** Leopold I **Obv:** Value in Roman numeral below bust **Mint:** Hall **Note:** Prev. KM#630.

Date	Mintage	VG	F	VF	XF	Unc
1694	Inc. above	8.00	18.00	35.00	70.00	—

KM# 438.1 10 KREUZER

Silver **Ruler:** Leopold **Obv:** Rounded features on small bust **Mint:** Hall **Note:** Prev. KM#794.1.

Date	Mintage	VG	F	VF	XF	Unc
1623	—	30.00	60.00	120	200	—
1624	—	30.00	60.00	120	200	—

KM# 438.2 10 KREUZER

Silver **Ruler:** Leopold **Obv:** Angular features on large bust **Rev:** Rosettes flank arms **Mint:** Hall **Note:** Prev. KM#794.2.

Date	Mintage	VG	F	VF	XF	Unc
1625	—	30.00	60.00	120	200	—

KM# 589.1 10 KREUZER

Silver **Ruler:** Leopold **Mint:** Hall **Note:** Prev. KM#795.1.

Date	Mintage	VG	F	VF	XF	Unc
1625	—	20.00	40.00	75.00	135	—
1626	—	20.00	40.00	75.00	135	—
1627	—	20.00	40.00	75.00	135	—
1628	—	20.00	40.00	80.00	145	—
1629	—	20.00	40.00	80.00	145	—
1630	—	15.00	35.00	65.00	125	—

KM# 589.2 10 KREUZER

Silver **Ruler:** Leopold **Obv:** Bust with striped sash **Mint:** Hall **Note:** Prev. KM#795.2.

Date	Mintage	VG	F	VF	XF	Unc
1632	—	15.00	35.00	65.00	125	—

KM# 695 10 KREUZER

Silver **Ruler:** Ferdinand II **Mint:** Saint Veit **Note:** Prev. KM#1597.

Date	Mintage	VG	F	VF	XF	Unc
1628	—	20.00	40.00	75.00	135	—
1637	—	20.00	40.00	75.00	135	—

KM# 696 10 KREUZER

Silver **Ruler:** Ferdinand II **Obv:** Value divides date below bust **Mint:** Saint Veit **Note:** Prev. KM#1598.

Date	Mintage	VG	F	VF	XF	Unc
1628	—	25.00	50.00	90.00	150	—

KM# 1142 10 KREUZER

Silver **Ruler:** Leopold I **Rev:** Value in arabic numerals **Mint:** Vienna **Note:** Prev. KM#1858.

Date	Mintage	VG	F	VF	XF	Unc
1659	—	—	—	—	—	—

KM# 1210 10 KREUZER

Silver **Ruler:** Sigismund Franz **Obv:** Armored bust right **Rev:** Crown above arms divides date **Mint:** Hall **Note:** Prev. KM#852.

Date	Mintage	VG	F	VF	XF	Unc
1663	252,000	15.00	25.00	45.00	80.00	—

KM# 1318 10 KREUZER

Silver **Ruler:** Leopold I **Obv:** Leopold I right, value below shoulder **Rev:** Three oval shields below date **Mint:** Graz **Note:** Varieties exist. Prev. KM#455.

Date	Mintage	VG	F	VF	XF	Unc
1682	—	25.00	50.00	100	185	—

KM# 1320 10 KREUZER
Silver **Ruler:** Leopold I **Obv:** Older bust right, value in Roman numerals **Rev:** Vienna arms on breast of eagle **Mint:** Vienna **Note:** Prev. KM#1859.

Date	Mintage	VG	F	VF	XF	Unc
1682	—	25.00	50.00	90.00	150	—

KM# 1319 10 KREUZER
Silver **Ruler:** Leopold I **Mint:** Saint Veit **Note:** Prev. KM#1645.

Date	Mintage	VG	F	VF	XF	Unc
1682 IR	—	30.00	60.00	135	250	—

KM# 295 12 KREUZER
Billon **Ruler:** Ferdinand II **Obv:** Bust with ruffled collar right in inner circle **Rev:** Crowned double-headed eagle in inner circle, value below, date in legend **Mint:** Vienna **Note:** 12 Kipper Kreuzer. Varieties exist. Prev. KM#1771.

Date	Mintage	VG	F	VF	XF	Unc
1621	—	15.00	25.00	45.00	75.00	—

KM# 195 15 KREUZER
Silver **Ruler:** Ferdinand II **Obv:** Crowned bust right in inner circle, value below **Rev:** Crowned cruciform arms in inner circle, crown divides date **Mint:** Graz **Note:** Prev. KM#560.

Date	Mintage	VG	F	VF	XF	Unc
1615	—	—	—	—	—	—

KM# 394 15 KREUZER
Silver **Ruler:** Ferdinand II **Obv:** Bust right **Rev:** Heraldic imperial eagle **Mint:** Brunn **Note:** Prev. KM#204.

Date	Mintage	VG	F	VF	XF	Unc
1622	—	—	—	—	—	—
1623	—	—	—	—	—	—

KM# 395 15 KREUZER
Silver **Ruler:** Ferdinand II **Mint:** Brunn **Note:** Klippe. Prev. KM#205.

Date	Mintage	VG	F	VF	XF	Unc
1622	—	—	—	—	—	—
1623	—	—	—	—	—	—

KM# 1144 15 KREUZER
Silver **Ruler:** Leopold I **Mint:** Vienna **Note:** Varieties exist. Prev. KM#1860.

Date	Mintage	VG	F	VF	XF	Unc
1659	—	15.00	28.00	60.00	125	—

KM# 1145 15 KREUZER
Silver **Ruler:** Leopold I **Obv:** Inner circles added **Rev:** Inner circles added **Mint:** Vienna **Note:** Varieties exist. Prev. KM#1861.

Date	Mintage	VG	F	VF	XF	Unc
1659	—	10.00	22.00	40.00	85.00	—
1660	—	10.00	22.00	40.00	85.00	—
1661	—	10.00	22.00	40.00	85.00	—
1662	—	10.00	22.00	40.00	85.00	—

KM# 1170 15 KREUZER
Silver **Ruler:** Leopold I **Rev:** Crown divides date **Mint:** Vienna **Note:** Varieties exist. Prev. KM#1862.

Date	Mintage	VG	F	VF	XF	Unc
1660	—	10.00	20.00	40.00	80.00	—
1663	—	10.00	20.00	40.00	80.00	—
1664	—	10.00	20.00	40.00	80.00	—
1674	—	10.00	20.00	40.00	80.00	—
1675	—	10.00	20.00	40.00	80.00	—
1676	—	10.00	20.00	40.00	80.00	—
1683	—	10.00	20.00	40.00	80.00	—
1684	—	10.00	20.00	40.00	80.00	—
1685	—	10.00	20.00	40.00	80.00	—
1693	—	10.00	20.00	40.00	80.00	—
1694	—	10.00	20.00	40.00	80.00	—
1695	—	10.00	20.00	40.00	80.00	—
1696	—	10.00	20.00	40.00	80.00	—

KM# 1186 15 KREUZER
Silver **Ruler:** Leopold I **Obv:** Value in Roman numeral below **Mint:** Graz **Note:** Varieties exist. Prev. KM#456.

Date	Mintage	VG	F	VF	XF	Unc
1661/0	—	10.00	20.00	40.00	80.00	—
1663	—	10.00	20.00	40.00	80.00	—
1664 L	—	10.00	20.00	40.00	80.00	—
1664 SH	—	10.00	20.00	40.00	80.00	—
1664	—	10.00	20.00	40.00	80.00	—
1665 SH	—	10.00	20.00	40.00	80.00	—

KM# 1187 15 KREUZER
Silver **Ruler:** Leopold I **Obv:** Ornamented inner circle **Mint:** Graz **Note:** Prev. KM#457.

Date	Mintage	VG	F	VF	XF	Unc
1661	—	10.00	20.00	40.00	80.00	—

KM# 1197 15 KREUZER
Silver **Ruler:** Leopold I **Obv:** Tall, awkward laureate bust to top of coin **Mint:** Vienna **Note:** Prev. KM#1863.

Date	Mintage	VG	F	VF	XF	Unc
1662	—	12.00	25.00	45.00	90.00	—

KM# 1198 15 KREUZER
Silver **Ruler:** Leopold I **Obv:** Ornamented inner circle **Mint:** Vienna **Note:** Varieties of ornamentation exist. Prev. KM#1864.

Date	Mintage	VG	F	VF	XF	Unc
1662	—	12.00	25.00	45.00	90.00	—
1663	—	12.00	25.00	45.00	90.00	—

KM# 1211 15 KREUZER
Silver **Ruler:** Leopold I **Obv:** Laureate bust right, value below **Rev:** Round shield within order chain on eagle's breast **Mint:** Saint Veit **Note:** Prev. KM#1646.

Date	Mintage	VG	F	VF	XF	Unc
1663	—	20.00	40.00	85.00	175	—
1663 H-S	—	20.00	40.00	85.00	175	—
1664	—	20.00	40.00	85.00	175	—
1675	—	20.00	40.00	85.00	175	—

KM# 1219 15 KREUZER
Silver **Ruler:** Sigismund Franz **Obv:** Armored bust right, value below **Rev:** Crown above two shields **Mint:** Hall **Note:** Prev. KM#853.

Date	Mintage	VG	F	VF	XF	Unc
1664	2,249,000	10.00	20.00	40.00	80.00	—

KM# 1220.1 15 KREUZER
Silver **Ruler:** Leopold I **Obv:** Legend breaks between R and I **Obv. Legend:** DG • R • • - I • S • **Mint:** Neuburg am Inn **Note:** Prev. KM#1217.1.

Date	Mintage	VG	F	VF	XF	Unc
1664	—	12.00	25.00	50.00	100	—

KM# 1220.2 15 KREUZER
Silver **Ruler:** Leopold I **Obv:** Legend breaks between G and R **Obv. Legend:** DG • - R • I • S • **Mint:** Neuburg am Inn **Note:** Prev. KM#1217.2.

Date	Mintage	VG	F	VF	XF	Unc
1664	—	12.00	25.00	50.00	100	—

KM# 1235 15 KREUZER
Silver **Ruler:** Leopold I **Obv:** Value in Arabic numerals, plain inner circle **Mint:** Graz **Note:** Prev. KM#458.

Date	Mintage	VG	F	VF	XF	Unc
1665 SH	—	10.00	20.00	40.00	80.00	—

KM# 1279 15 KREUZER
Silver **Ruler:** Leopold I **Mint:** Graz **Note:** Varieties exist. Prev. KM#459.

Date	Mintage	VG	F	VF	XF	Unc
1675 IAN	—	10.00	20.00	40.00	80.00	—
1676 IAN	—	10.00	20.00	40.00	80.00	—
1677 IAN	—	10.00	20.00	40.00	80.00	—
1678 IAN	—	10.00	20.00	40.00	80.00	—
1679 IAN	—	10.00	20.00	40.00	80.00	—
1680 IAN	—	10.00	20.00	40.00	80.00	—
1682 IAN	—	10.00	20.00	40.00	80.00	—
1689 IAN	—	10.00	20.00	40.00	80.00	—
1694 IAN	—	10.00	20.00	40.00	80.00	—

KM# 1280 15 KREUZER
Silver **Ruler:** Leopold I **Mint:** Saint Veit **Note:** Prev. KM#1647.

Date	Mintage	VG	F	VF	XF	Unc
1675 G-S	—	20.00	40.00	85.00	175	—
1675 GC-S	—	20.00	40.00	85.00	175	—

KM# 1281 15 KREUZER
Silver **Ruler:** Leopold I **Obv:** Plain inner circle **Rev:** Plain inner circle **Mint:** Saint Veit **Note:** Prev. KM#1648.

Date	Mintage	VG	F	VF	XF	Unc
1675 GC-SS	—	20.00	40.00	85.00	175	—
1689 GC-VS	—	20.00	40.00	85.00	175	—
1693	—	20.00	40.00	85.00	175	—
1693 GC-VS	—	20.00	40.00	85.00	175	—

KM# 1289 15 KREUZER
Silver **Ruler:** Leopold I **Mint:** Hall **Note:** Varieties exist. Prev. KM#631.

Date	Mintage	VG	F	VF	XF	Unc
1676	—	10.00	20.00	40.00	80.00	—
1687	—	10.00	20.00	40.00	80.00	—
1691	—	10.00	20.00	40.00	80.00	—
1694	—	10.00	20.00	40.00	80.00	—
1697	—	10.00	20.00	40.00	80.00	—

KM# 1302 15 KREUZER
Silver **Ruler:** Leopold I **Obv:** Bust right, value in Roman numerals **Rev:** Crowned imperial eagle **Mint:** Saint Veit **Note:** Varieties exist. Prev. KM#1649.

Date	Mintage	VG	F	VF	XF	Unc
1679 I-G-R	—	16.50	35.00	65.00	125	—
1680 I-R	—	16.50	35.00	65.00	125	—
1681 I-R	—	16.50	35.00	65.00	125	—
1689 GS-VS	—	16.50	35.00	65.00	125	—
1690 CS	—	16.50	35.00	65.00	125	—
1693	—	16.50	35.00	65.00	125	—
1693 C-S	—	16.50	35.00	65.00	125	—
1693 L-S	—	16.50	35.00	65.00	125	—
1693 GCS	—	16.50	35.00	65.00	125	—
1693 GC-VS	—	16.50	35.00	65.00	125	—
1694	—	16.50	35.00	65.00	125	—
1694 C-S	—	16.50	35.00	65.00	125	—
1694 G-S	—	16.50	35.00	65.00	125	—
1694 GS-VS	—	16.50	35.00	65.00	125	—
1695	—	16.50	35.00	65.00	125	—
1696	—	16.50	35.00	65.00	125	—
1697 C-S	—	16.50	35.00	65.00	125	—
1697	—	16.50	35.00	65.00	125	—
1700	—	16.50	35.00	65.00	125	—

KM# 1335 15 KREUZER
Silver **Ruler:** Leopold I **Mint:** Mainz **Note:** The House of Hohenlohe. Varieties exist. Prev. KM#1175.

Date	Mintage	VG	F	VF	XF	Unc
1685 (s)	—	15.00	30.00	60.00	120	—
1685 B-W	—	15.00	30.00	60.00	120	—
1685 VB Monogram /W-(S)	—	15.00	30.00	60.00	120	—

KM# 1336 15 KREUZER
Silver **Ruler:** Leopold I **Mint:** Wurzburg **Note:** Struck by the House of Hohenlohe. Prev. KM#1989.

Date	Mintage	VG	F	VF	XF	Unc
1685 (a)	—	—	—	—	—	—

KM# 1341 15 KREUZER
Silver **Ruler:** Leopold I **Rev:** Value below shields **Mint:** Hall **Note:** Prev. KM#632.

Date	Mintage	VG	F	VF	XF	Unc
1687	—	10.00	20.00	40.00	80.00	—

KM# 1344 15 KREUZER
Silver **Ruler:** Leopold I **Obv:** Laurreate armored bust right, wavy hair **Rev:** Crown above two shields, value below **Mint:** Hall **Note:** Prev. KM#633.

Date	Mintage	VG	F	VF	XF	Unc
1688	—	10.00	20.00	40.00	80.00	—
1690	—	10.00	20.00	40.00	80.00	—

KM# 1375 15 KREUZER
Silver **Ruler:** Leopold I **Obv:** Laureate bust right, roman numeral value below shoulder **Rev:** Crown divides date above complex arms within order chain **Mint:** Graz **Note:** Prev. KM#460.

Date	Mintage	VG	F	VF	XF	Unc
1694	—	10.00	20.00	40.00	80.00	—
1694 IA	—	10.00	20.00	40.00	80.00	—
1695 IA	—	10.00	20.00	40.00	80.00	—
1696 IA	—	10.00	20.00	40.00	80.00	—

KM# 301 24 KREUZER
Silver **Ruler:** Ferdinand II **Obv:** Bust right **Rev:** Heraldic imperial eagle **Mint:** Brunn **Note:** Prev. KM#206.

Date	Mintage	VG	F	VF	XF	Unc
1621 (h)	—	13.00	32.50	50.00	100	—
1622	—	13.00	32.50	50.00	100	—
1623	—	13.00	32.50	50.00	100	—

KM# 302 24 KREUZER
Silver **Ruler:** Ferdinand II **Mint:** Brunn **Note:** Klippe. Prev. KM#207.

Date	Mintage	VG	F	VF	XF	Unc
1621	—	—	—	—	—	—
1622	—	—	—	—	—	—
162x	—	—	—	—	—	—

KM# 303 24 KREUZER
Silver **Ruler:** Ferdinand II **Obv:** Laureate bust right in inner circle **Rev:** Crowned imperial eagle in inner circle, value below **Mint:** Graz **Note:** 24 Kipper Kreuzer. Prev. KM#356.

Date	Mintage	VG	F	VF	XF	Unc
1621	—	25.00	50.00	90.00	150	—
1622	—	25.00	50.00	90.00	150	—

KM# 305 24 KREUZER
Billon **Ruler:** Ferdinand II **Obv:** Laureate bust right in inner circle **Rev:** Crowned imperial eagle in inner circle, value below, date in legend **Mint:** Vienna **Note:** 24 Kipper Kreuzer. Varieties exist. Prev. KM#1772.

Date	Mintage	VG	F	VF	XF	Unc
1621	—	12.00	22.00	45.00	85.00	—
1622	—	12.00	22.00	45.00	85.00	—
1623	—	12.00	22.00	45.00	85.00	—

KM# 399 24 KREUZER
Silver **Ruler:** Ferdinand II **Obv:** Crowned bust right in ornamented inner circle **Rev:** Crowned imperial eagle in inner circle, value below, crown divides date **Mint:** Saint Veit **Note:** Varieties exist. Prev. KM#1599.

Date	Mintage	VG	F	VF	XF	Unc
1622	—	—	—	—	—	—
1623	—	—	—	—	—	—

KM# 397 24 KREUZER
Silver **Ruler:** Ferdinand II **Obv:** Crowned bust right **Rev:** Crowned imperial eagle with arms on breast, value below, crown divides date **Mint:** Saint Veit **Note:** 24 kipper Kreuzer. KM#384 is a product of either the Saint Veit or Klagenfurt Mints. Prev. KM#1002.

Date	Mintage	VG	F	VF	XF	Unc
1622	—	—	—	—	—	—

KM# 442 24 KREUZER
Silver **Ruler:** Ferdinand II **Obv:** Plain inner circle **Mint:** Saint Veit **Note:** Varieties exist. Prev. KM#1600.

Date	Mintage	VG	F	VF	XF	Unc
1623	—	—	—	—	—	—

KM# 309 30 KREUZER
Silver **Ruler:** Ferdinand II **Obv:** Bust right **Rev:** Heraldic imperial eagle **Mint:** Brunn **Note:** Prev. KM#208.

Date	Mintage	VG	F	VF	XF	Unc
1621 (h)	—	—	—	—	—	—

KM# 310 30 KREUZER
Silver **Ruler:** Leopold **Mint:** Hall **Note:** Prev. KM#796.

Date	Mintage	VG	F	VF	XF	Unc
1621	—	250	450	750	1,200	—
1623	—	250	450	750	1,200	—

KM# 316 48 KREUZER
Silver **Ruler:** Ferdinand II **Obv:** Bust right **Rev:** Heraldic imperial eagle **Mint:** Olmutz **Note:** Prev. KM#1233.

Date	Mintage	VG	F	VF	XF	Unc
1621 BZ	—	—	—	—	—	—
1622 BZ	—	—	—	—	—	—

KM# 317 48 KREUZER
Billon **Ruler:** Ferdinand II **Mint:** Vienna **Note:** 48 kipper Kreuzer. Varieties exist. Prev. KM#1773.

Date	Mintage	VG	F	VF	XF	Unc
1621 (c)	—	10.00	20.00	40.00	70.00	—
1622 (c)	—	10.00	20.00	40.00	70.00	—
1623 (b)	—	10.00	20.00	40.00	70.00	—
1623 (c)	—	10.00	20.00	40.00	70.00	—

KM# 311 48 KREUZER
Silver **Ruler:** Ferdinand II **Obv:** Bust right **Rev:** Heraldic imperial eagle **Mint:** Brunn **Note:** Prev. KM#209.

Date	Mintage	VG	F	VF	XF	Unc
1621 (h)	—	14.00	30.00	50.00	100	—
1622 (h)	—	14.00	30.00	50.00	100	—

KM# 312 48 KREUZER
Silver **Ruler:** Ferdinand II **Mint:** Brunn **Note:** Klippe. Prev. KM#210.

Date	Mintage	VG	F	VF	XF	Unc
1621 (h)	—	—	—	—	—	—

KM# 313 48 KREUZER
Silver **Ruler:** Ferdinand II **Obv:** Crowned imperial eagle with value on breast in inner circle **Rev:** Crowned arms in order collar and inner circle, crown divides date **Mint:** Graz **Note:** 48 Kipper Kreuzer. Prev. KM#357.

Date	Mintage	VG	F	VF	XF	Unc
1621	—	15.00	30.00	55.00	100	—

KM# 314 48 KREUZER
Silver **Ruler:** Ferdinand II **Obv:** Crowned imperial eagle with

value on breast in inner circle **Rev:** Crowned oval arms in order collar and inner circle, date in legend **Mint:** Klagenfurt **Note:** Varieties exist. Prev. KM#957.

Date	Mintage	VG	F	VF	XF	Unc
1621	—	40.00	80.00	150	250	—
1622	—	40.00	80.00	150	250	—

KM# 405 48 KREUZER

Silver **Ruler:** Ferdinand II **Obv:** Crowned bust right in inner circle **Rev:** Crowned imperial eagle with panther shield on breast in inner circle, crown divides date **Mint:** Graz **Note:** Prev. KM#358.

Date	Mintage	VG	F	VF	XF	Unc
1622	—	15.00	30.00	55.00	100	—

KM# 406 48 KREUZER

Silver **Ruler:** Ferdinand II **Obv:** Ornamented inner circle **Mint:** Graz **Note:** Prev. KM#359.

Date	Mintage	VG	F	VF	XF	Unc
1622	—	15.00	30.00	55.00	100	—

KM# 407 48 KREUZER

Silver **Ruler:** Ferdinand II **Obv:** Date below bust **Mint:** Graz **Note:** Prev. KM#360.

Date	Mintage	VG	F	VF	XF	Unc
1622	—	15.00	30.00	55.00	100	—
1623	—	15.00	30.00	55.00	100	—

KM# 408 48 KREUZER

Silver **Ruler:** Ferdinand II **Obv:** Plain inner circle **Mint:** Graz **Note:** Prev. KM#361.

Date	Mintage	VG	F	VF	XF	Unc
1622	—	15.00	30.00	55.00	100	—
1623	—	15.00	30.00	55.00	100	—

KM# 409 48 KREUZER

Silver **Ruler:** Ferdinand II **Obv:** Crowned bust right in inner circle **Rev:** Crowned imperial eagle in inner circle, value at bottom, crown divides date **Mint:** Klagenfurt **Note:** Varieties exist. KM#409 is a product of either the Klagenfurt or Saint Veit mints. Prev. KM#958.

Date	Mintage	VG	F	VF	XF	Unc
1622	—	40.00	80.00	150	250	—
1623	—	40.00	80.00	150	250	—

KM# 410 48 KREUZER

Silver **Ruler:** Ferdinand II **Mint:** Saint Veit **Note:** 48 Kipper Kreuzer. Prev. KM#A1601.

Date	Mintage	VG	F	VF	XF	Unc
1622	—	—	—	—	—	—

KM# 443 48 KREUZER

Silver **Ruler:** Ferdinand II **Obv:** Date **Mint:** Klagenfurt **Note:** Prev. KM#959.

Date	Mintage	VG	F	VF	XF	Unc
1623	—	40.00	80.00	150	250	—

KM# 243 60 KREUZER

Silver **Ruler:** Leopold **Obv:** Bust right divides date **Rev:** Crowned arms **Mint:** Hall **Note:** Similar to 1 Thaler, KM#264.1. Prev. KM#798.

Date	Mintage	VG	F	VF	XF	Unc
ND(1619)	—	60.00	120	225	375	—
1623	—	60.00	120	225	375	—
16Z4	—	60.00	120	225	375	—

KM# 321 60 KREUZER

Silver **Ruler:** Ferdinand II **Obv:** Bust right **Rev:** Heraldic imperial eagle **Mint:** Brunn **Note:** Prev. KM#211.

Date	Mintage	VG	F	VF	XF	Unc
1621 (d)	—	16.50	32.50	60.00	125	—
1621 (d)-(h)	—	16.50	32.50	60.00	125	—
1621 (h)	—	16.50	32.50	60.00	125	—

KM# 322 60 KREUZER

Silver **Ruler:** Leopold **Obv:** Crown above two shields **Rev:** Legend **Mint:** Hall **Note:** Prev. KM#797.

Date	Mintage	VG	F	VF	XF	Unc
1621	—	300	550	900	1,500	—
1622	—	300	550	900	1,500	—
1623	—	300	550	900	1,500	—

KM# 323 60 KREUZER

Silver **Ruler:** Ferdinand II **Obv:** Bust right **Rev:** Heraldic imperial eagle **Mint:** Olmutz **Note:** Prev. KM#1234.

Date	Mintage	VG	F	VF	XF	Unc
1621 BZ/(I)	—	25.00	45.00	80.00	135	—
1621 BZ	—	25.00	45.00	80.00	135	—

KM# 411 75 KREUZER

Silver **Ruler:** Ferdinand II **Obv:** Bust right **Rev:** Heraldic imperial eagle **Mint:** Brunn **Note:** Prev. KM#212.

Date	Mintage	VG	F	VF	XF	Unc
1622	—	16.50	35.00	65.00	120	—
1622 (d)	—	16.50	35.00	65.00	120	—

KM# 412 75 KREUZER

Silver **Ruler:** Ferdinand II **Mint:** Brunn **Note:** Klippe. Prev. KM#213.

Date	Mintage	VG	F	VF	XF	Unc
1622	—	—	—	—	—	—

KM# 413 75 KREUZER

Silver **Ruler:** Ferdinand II **Obv:** Crowned bust right in inner circle **Rev:** Crowned imperial eagle with panther shield on breast in inner circle, crown divides date **Mint:** Graz **Note:** 75 Kipper Kreuzer. Prev. KM#362.

Date	Mintage	VG	F	VF	XF	Unc
1622	—	30.00	60.00	100	175	—

KM# 415 75 KREUZER

Silver **Ruler:** Ferdinand II **Obv:** Crowned bust right in inner circle, value at bottom **Rev:** Crowned imperial eagle in inner circle, crown divides date **Note:** 75 Kipper Kreuzer. Varieties exist. This coin is a product of either the Saint Veit or Klagenfurt Mints. Prev. KM#1003.

Date	Mintage	VG	F	VF	XF	Unc
1622	—	100	200	350	600	—

KM# 416 75 KREUZER

Silver **Ruler:** Ferdinand II **Obv:** Oval arms on eagle **Note:** This coin is a product of either the Saint Veit or Klagenfurt Mints. Prev. KM#1004.

Date	Mintage	VG	F	VF	XF	Unc
1622	—	—	—	—	—	—

KM# 417 75 KREUZER

Billon **Ruler:** Ferdinand II **Obv:** Laureate bust right in inner circle **Rev:** Crowned imperial eagle in inner circle, date in legend **Mint:** Vienna **Note:** 75 Kipper Kreuzer. Varieties exist. Prev. KM#1774.

Date	Mintage	VG	F	VF	XF	Unc
1622 (b)	—	15.00	25.00	50.00	90.00	—

KM# 414 150 KREUZER

Silver **Ruler:** Ferdinand II **Obv:** Ornamented inner circle **Rev:** Panther shield on breast in inner circle **Mint:** Graz **Note:** 150 Kipper Kreuzer. Varieties exist. Prev. KM#363.

Date	Mintage	VG	F	VF	XF	Unc
1622	—	50.00	100	175	300	—

KM# 423 150 KREUZER

Billon **Ruler:** Ferdinand II **Obv:** Bust right with high ruffled collar, value below **Rev:** Crowned double imperial eagle, shield on breast **Mint:** Vienna **Note:** 150 Kipper Thaler Kreuzer. Varieties exist. Prev. KM#1775.

Date	Mintage	VG	F	VF	XF	Unc
1622 (b)	—	14.00	27.50	48.00	90.00	—
1622 (c)	—	14.00	27.50	48.00	90.00	—
1622 (r)	—	14.00	27.50	48.00	90.00	—
1623 BZ	—	14.00	27.50	48.00	90.00	—

KM# 422 150 KREUZER

Silver **Ruler:** Ferdinand II **Obv:** Bust right **Rev:** Heraldic imperial eagle **Mint:** Graz **Note:** Prev. KM#1235.

Date	Mintage	VG	F	VF	XF	Unc
1622 (I) Rare	—	—	—	—	—	—
1623 (I) Rare	—	—	—	—	—	—

KM# 418 150 KREUZER

Silver **Ruler:** Ferdinand II **Obv:** Bust right **Rev:** Heraldic imperial eagle **Mint:** Brunn **Note:** Prev. KM#214.

Date	Mintage	VG	F	VF	XF	Unc
1622 (s)	—	20.00	40.00	90.00	175	—
1622	—	20.00	40.00	90.00	175	—
1623	—	20.00	40.00	90.00	175	—

KM# 419 150 KREUZER

Silver **Ruler:** Ferdinand II **Obv:** Plain inner circle **Mint:** Graz **Note:** Varieties exist. Prev. KM#364.

Date	Mintage	VG	F	VF	XF	Unc
1622	—	50.00	100	175	300	—

KM# 420 150 KREUZER

Silver **Ruler:** Ferdinand II **Note:** 150 Kipper Kreuzer. Varieties exist. This coin is a product of either the Saint Veit or Klagenfurt Mints. Prev. KM#1005.

Date	Mintage	VG	F	VF	XF	Unc
1622	—	125	250	400	700	—

KM# 424 150 KREUZER

Billon **Ruler:** Ferdinand II **Mint:** Vienna **Note:** Klippe. Prev. KM#1776.

Date	Mintage	VG	F	VF	XF	Unc
1622 (b)	—	14.00	27.50	48.00	80.00	—
1622 (r)	—	14.00	27.50	48.00	80.00	—

KM# 444 150 KREUZER

Silver **Ruler:** Ferdinand II **Mint:** Olmutz **Note:** Klippe. Prev. KM#1236.

Date	Mintage	VG	F	VF	XF	Unc
1623 (l) Rare	—	—	—	—	—	—

KM# 1246 1/10 THALER

Silver **Ruler:** Leopold I **Obv:** Crowned half-figure right with sword and sceptre, value below **Rev:** Crowned eagle in order collar and inner circle **Mint:** Hall **Note:** Prev. KM#634.

Date	Mintage	VG	F	VF	XF	Unc
ND	—	80.00	175	350	600	—

KM# 1247 1/10 THALER

Silver **Ruler:** Leopold I **Mint:** Hall **Note:** Prev. KM#635.

Date	Mintage	VG	F	VF	XF	Unc
1667	—	100	200	400	650	—

KM# 1248 1/10 THALER

Silver **Ruler:** Leopold I **Obv:** Date in front of figure **Mint:** Hall **Note:** Prev. KM#636.

Date	Mintage	VG	F	VF	XF	Unc
1667	—	100	200	400	650	—

KM# 20 1/4 THALER

Silver **Ruler:** Rudolf II **Obv:** Armored bust in ruffled collar right in inner circle **Rev:** Crowned imperial eagle with sword and scepter in inner circle, date in legend **Mint:** Vienna **Note:** Prev. KM#1712.

Date	Mintage	VG	F	VF	XF	Unc
1601	—	—	—	—	—	—

KM# 44 1/4 THALER

Silver **Ruler:** Rudolf II **Obv:** Armored bust in ruffled collar right in inner circle, date below bust **Rev:** Crowned flat-topped shield in order collar in inner circle **Mint:** Hall **Note:** Prev. KM#595.

Date	Mintage	VG	F	VF	XF	Unc
1603	—	50.00	100	175	300	—
1604	—	50.00	100	175	300	—

KM# 54 1/4 THALER

Silver **Ruler:** Rudolf II **Obv:** Laureate bust right, high ruffled collar **Rev:** Crowned oval arms in garlands in inner circle **Mint:** Hall **Note:** Prev. KM#596.

Date	Mintage	VG	F	VF	XF	Unc
1604	—	50.00	100	175	300	—
1605	—	50.00	100	175	300	—

KM# 55 1/4 THALER

Silver **Ruler:** Rudolf II **Obv:** Laureate armored bust left, date below **Rev:** Crowned complex arms **Mint:** Hall **Note:** Prev. KM#597.

Date	Mintage	VG	F	VF	XF	Unc
1604	—	60.00	120	200	350	—

KM# 140 1/4 THALER

Silver **Ruler:** Rudolf II **Obv:** Bust left in laurel inner circle **Mint:** Hall **Note:** Prev. KM#598.

Date	Mintage	VG	F	VF	XF	Unc
1612	—	60.00	120	200	350	—

KM# 141 1/4 THALER

Silver **Ruler:** Maximilian **Mint:** Hall **Note:** Similar to 1 Thaler, KM#205.1. Prev. KM#755.

Date	Mintage	VG	F	VF	XF	Unc
1612	—	400	750	1,250	2,000	—
ND	—	400	750	1,250	2,000	—

KM# 162 1/4 THALER

Silver **Ruler:** Maximilian **Obv:** Bust right **Rev:** Crowned arms with Teutonic Order cross **Mint:** Hall **Note:** Prev. KM#756.

Date	Mintage	VG	F	VF	XF	Unc
1613	—	400	750	1,250	2,000	—

KM# 163 1/4 THALER

Silver **Ruler:** Maximilian **Mint:** Hall **Note:** Klippe. Prev. KM#757.

Date	Mintage	VG	F	VF	XF	Unc
1613	—	—	—	—	—	—

KM# 324 1/4 THALER

Silver **Ruler:** Ferdinand II **Obv:** Half figure right, holding scepter, in inner circle **Rev:** Three shields, points together **Mint:** Graz **Note:** Struck with dies of 3 Kreuzer, weight of 1/4 Thaler. Klippe. Prev. KM#561.

Date	Mintage	VG	F	VF	XF	Unc
ND Rare	—	—	—	—	—	—

KM# 325 1/4 THALER

Silver **Ruler:** Ferdinand II **Obv:** Crowned bust right in inner circle **Rev:** Crowned imperial eagle with oval arms on breast in inner circle **Mint:** Klagenfurt **Note:** Varieties exist. Prev. KM#960.

Date	Mintage	VG	F	VF	XF	Unc
ND	—	200	400	650	1,250	—

KM# 326 1/4 THALER

Silver **Ruler:** Ferdinand II **Obv:** Date below bust **Mint:** Klagenfurt **Note:** Prev. KM#961.

Date	Mintage	VG	F	VF	XF	Unc
1621	—	200	400	650	1,250	—

KM# 327 1/4 THALER

Silver **Ruler:** Ferdinand II **Obv:** Crown divides date **Mint:** Klagenfurt **Note:** Prev. KM#962.

Date	Mintage	VG	F	VF	XF	Unc
1621	—	200	400	650	1,250	—

KM# 328 1/4 THALER

Silver **Ruler:** Ferdinand II **Rev:** Crown divides date **Mint:** Klagenfurt **Note:** Prev. KM#963.

Date	Mintage	VG	F	VF	XF	Unc
1621	—	200	400	650	1,250	—

KM# 329 1/4 THALER

Silver **Ruler:** Ferdinand II **Obv:** Laureate bust right in inner circle **Rev:** Crowned imperial eagle in inner circle, date in legend **Mint:** Vienna **Note:** Prev. KM#1777.

Date	Mintage	VG	F	VF	XF	Unc
1621	—	50.00	100	200	350	—
1623	—	50.00	100	200	350	—

KM# 445 1/4 THALER

Silver **Ruler:** Ferdinand II **Obv:** Laureate bust, date below bust **Rev:** Crowned arms in Order collar and inner circle **Mint:** Graz **Note:** Prev. KM#365.

Date	Mintage	VG	F	VF	XF	Unc
1623	—	30.00	60.00	120	200	—
1630	—	30.00	60.00	120	200	—
1634	—	30.00	60.00	120	200	—
1638/4	—	30.00	60.00	120	200	—

KM# 590 1/4 THALER

Silver **Ruler:** Leopold **Mint:** Hall **Note:** Prev. KM#799.

Date	Mintage	VG	F	VF	XF	Unc
ND(1625)	—	60.00	120	225	375	—
1626	—	60.00	120	225	375	—
1629	—	60.00	120	225	375	—
1632	—	50.00	100	200	350	—

KM# 591 1/4 THALER

13.5700 g., Silver **Ruler:** Ferdinand II **Mint:** Graz **Note:** Klippe. Weight of 1/2 Thaler. Prev. KM#367.

Date	Mintage	VG	F	VF	XF	Unc
1625	—	—	—	—	—	—

KM# 506 1/4 THALER

Silver **Ruler:** Ferdinand II **Obv:** Small bust right in inner circle **Mint:** Vienna **Note:** Prev. KM#1778.

Date	Mintage	VG	F	VF	XF	Unc
1625	—	50.00	100	200	350	—

KM# 672 1/4 THALER

Silver **Ruler:** Ferdinand II **Obv:** Laureate bust right in inner circle **Mint:** Vienna **Note:** Prev. KM#1779.

Date	Mintage	VG	F	VF	XF	Unc
1627 (c)	—	40.00	90.00	180	300	—
1628 (c)	—	40.00	90.00	180	300	—
1629 (c)	—	40.00	90.00	180	300	—
1630 (c)	—	40.00	90.00	180	300	—
1631 (c)	—	40.00	90.00	180	300	—
1632 (c)	—	40.00	90.00	180	300	—
1633 (c)	—	40.00	90.00	180	300	—
1634 (c)	—	40.00	90.00	180	300	—
1635 (c)	—	40.00	90.00	180	300	—
1636 (v)	—	40.00	90.00	180	300	—

KM# 670 1/4 THALER

Silver **Ruler:** Ferdinand II **Mint:** Graz **Note:** Klippe. Prev. KM#366.

Date	Mintage	VG	F	VF	XF	Unc
1627	—	—	—	—	—	—

KM# 671 1/4 THALER

14.0000 g., Silver **Ruler:** Ferdinand II **Mint:** Graz **Note:** Prev. KM#368.

Date	Mintage	VG	F	VF	XF	Unc
1627	—	—	—	—	—	—

KM# 815 1/4 THALER

Silver **Ruler:** Ferdinand II **Mint:** Vienna **Note:** Klippe. Prev. KM#1780.

Date	Mintage	VG	F	VF	XF	Unc
1636 Rare	—	—	—	—	—	—

KM# 838 1/4 THALER

Silver **Ruler:** Ferdinand III **Obv:** Laureate bust right in inner circle **Mint:** Vienna **Note:** Varieties exist. Prev. KM#1820.

Date	Mintage	VG	F	VF	XF	Unc
1637	—	150	250	400	650	—
1639	—	150	250	400	650	—
1640	—	150	250	400	650	—
1641	—	150	250	400	650	—
1642	—	150	250	400	650	—
1643	—	150	250	400	650	—
1644	—	150	250	400	650	—
1645	—	150	250	400	650	—
1646	—	150	250	400	650	—
1647	—	150	250	400	650	—
1648	—	150	250	400	650	—

KM# 874 1/4 THALER

Silver **Ruler:** Ferdinand III **Mint:** Vienna **Note:** Klippe. Prev. KM#1821.

Date	Mintage	VG	F	VF	XF	Unc
1639	—	—	—	—	—	—

KM# 927 1/4 THALER

Silver **Ruler:** Ferdinand Charles **Mint:** Hall **Note:** Similar to 5 Ducat, KM#793. Prev. KM#831.

Date	Mintage	VG	F	VF	XF	Unc
ND(1646)	—	80.00	160	275	450	—

KM# 982 1/4 THALER

Silver **Ruler:** Ferdinand Charles **Obv:** Armored bust right, value below **Rev:** Crowned arms within order chain **Mint:** Hall **Note:** Prev. KM#830.

Date	Mintage	VG	F	VF	XF	Unc
1654	—	75.00	150	250	400	—

KM# 1173.1 1/4 THALER

Silver **Ruler:** Leopold I **Obv:** Laureate bust right, value below, lion face on shoulder **Rev:** Crowned arms within order chain **Mint:** Hall **Note:** Prev. KM#637.1.

Date	Mintage	VG	F	VF	XF	Unc
ND	—	90.00	185	350	600	—

KM# 1173.2 1/4 THALER

Silver **Ruler:** Leopold I **Obv:** Denomination below lion's head on shoulder **Rev:** Crowned complex arms within order chain **Mint:** Hall **Note:** Prev. KM#637.2.

Date	Mintage	VG	F	VF	XF	Unc
ND	—	90.00	185	350	600	—

KM# 1271 1/4 THALER

Silver **Ruler:** Leopold I **Mint:** Vienna **Note:** Prev. KM#1865.

Date	Mintage	VG	F	VF	XF	Unc
1671 Rare	—	—	—	—	—	—

KM# 1376 1/4 THALER

Silver **Ruler:** Leopold I **Mint:** Graz **Note:** Prev. KM#461.

Date	Mintage	VG	F	VF	XF	Unc
1694 IA	—	50.00	100	185	300	—

KM# 21 1/2 THALER

Silver **Ruler:** Ferdinand II **Obv:** Crowned half figure right, holding scepter, in inner circle **Rev:** Crowned arms in Order collar, date in legend **Mint:** Klagenfurt **Note:** Varieties exist. Local issue for Archduke Ferdinand. Prev. KM#990.

Date	Mintage	VG	F	VF	XF	Unc
1601	—	65.00	125	200	350	—
1602	—	65.00	125	200	350	—
1610	—	65.00	125	200	350	—
1611	—	65.00	125	200	350	—

KM# 22 1/2 THALER

Silver **Ruler:** Rudolf II **Mint:** Vienna **Note:** Prev. KM#1713.

Date	Mintage	VG	F	VF	XF	Unc
1601	—	100	200	350	600	—
1602	—	100	200	350	600	—
1605	—	100	200	350	600	—
1606	—	100	200	350	600	—
1607	—	100	200	350	600	—
1608	—	100	200	350	600	—
1609	—	100	200	350	600	—

KM# 35 1/2 THALER

Silver **Ruler:** Ferdinand II **Obv:** Crowned half figure right holding scepter, in inner circle **Rev:** Crowned arms in Order collar, date in legend **Mint:** Graz **Note:** Prev. KM#562.

Date	Mintage	VG	F	VF	XF	Unc
1602 Rare	—	—	—	—	—	—

KM# 45 1/2 THALER

Silver **Ruler:** Rudolf II **Mint:** Hall **Note:** Prev. KM#599.

Date	Mintage	VG	F	VF	XF	Unc
1603	—	125	250	400	700	—

KM# 64 1/2 THALER

Silver **Ruler:** Rudolf II **Mint:** Vienna **Note:** Klippe. Prev. KM#1714.

Date	Mintage	VG	F	VF	XF	Unc
1605	—	—	—	—	—	—

KM# 92 1/2 THALER

Silver **Ruler:** Matthias II **Mint:** Vienna **Note:** Coronation commemorative. Prev. KM#1731.

Date	Mintage	VG	F	VF	XF	Unc
1608 CH	—	200	350	675	1,150	—

KM# 93 1/2 THALER

Silver **Ruler:** Matthias II **Mint:** Vienna **Note:** Klippe. Prev. KM#1732.

Date	Mintage	VG	F	VF	XF	Unc
1608 CH	—	—	—	—	—	—

KM# 101 1/2 THALER

Silver **Ruler:** Matthias II **Obv:** Portrait right **Rev:** Heraldic imperial eagle **Mint:** Vienna **Note:** Prev. KM#1733.

Date	Mintage	VG	F	VF	XF	Unc
1609	—	—	—	—	—	—

KM# 142 1/2 THALER

Silver **Ruler:** Rudolf II **Obv:** Bust right in rope inner circle, date in front of bust **Mint:** Hall **Note:** Prev. KM#600.

Date	Mintage	VG	F	VF	XF	Unc
1612	—	120	225	375	650	—

KM# 164 1/2 THALER

Silver **Ruler:** Matthias II **Obv:** Armored bust in ruffled collar right **Mint:** Vienna **Note:** Prev. KM#1734.

Date	Mintage	VG	F	VF	XF	Unc
1613 (c)	—	125	250	425	750	—
1615	—	125	250	425	750	—
1616	—	125	250	425	750	—
1617	—	125	250	425	750	—
1617 (t)	—	125	250	425	750	—
1618	—	125	250	425	750	—
1619	—	125	250	425	750	—

KM# 260 1/2 THALER

Silver **Ruler:** Ferdinand II **Mint:** Klagenfurt **Note:** Varieties exist. Prev. KM#964.

Date	Mintage	VG	F	VF	XF	Unc
ND	—	65.00	125	235	400	—

KM# 261 1/2 THALER

Silver **Ruler:** Ferdinand II **Mint:** Vienna **Note:** Prev. KM#1781.

Date	Mintage	VG	F	VF	XF	Unc
1620 (c)	—	35.00	75.00	135	225	—
1621 (c)	—	35.00	75.00	135	225	—
1622 (c)	—	35.00	75.00	135	225	—
1623 (c)	—	35.00	75.00	135	225	—
1624 (c)	—	35.00	75.00	135	225	—

KM# 330 1/2 THALER

Silver **Ruler:** Ferdinand II **Obv:** Date below bust **Mint:** Klagenfurt **Note:** Varieties exist. Prev. KM#965.

Date	Mintage	VG	F	VF	XF	Unc
1621	—	65.00	125	235	400	—

KM# 331 1/2 THALER

Silver **Ruler:** Ferdinand II **Rev:** Crown divides date **Mint:** Klagenfurt **Note:** Prev. KM#966.

Date	Mintage	VG	F	VF	XF	Unc
1621	—	65.00	125	235	400	—

KM# 446 1/2 THALER

Silver **Ruler:** Ferdinand II **Mint:** Graz **Note:** Prev. KM#369.

Date	Mintage	VG	F	VF	XF	Unc
1623	—	35.00	75.00	135	225	—
1624	—	35.00	75.00	135	225	—
1625	—	35.00	75.00	135	225	—
1627	—	35.00	75.00	135	225	—

KM# 447 1/2 THALER

Silver **Ruler:** Leopold **Mint:** Hall **Note:** Prev. KM#800.

Date	Mintage	VG	F	VF	XF	Unc
1623	—	60.00	120	225	375	—
1624	—	60.00	120	225	375	—

KM# 511 1/2 THALER

Silver **Ruler:** Ferdinand II **Obv:** Bust right **Rev:** Heraldic imperial eagle **Mint:** Brunn **Note:** Prev. KM#215.

Date	Mintage	VG	F	VF	XF	Unc
1624 B-CW	—	—	—	—	—	—

KM# 513 1/2 THALER

Silver **Ruler:** Ferdinand II **Obv:** Laureate bust right in inner circle **Rev:** Crowned arms in Order collar in inner circle, date in legend **Mint:** Saint Polten **Note:** Prev. KM#1573.

Date	Mintage	VG	F	VF	XF	Unc
1624 IIE Rare	—	—	—	—	—	—
1625 IIE Rare	—	—	—	—	—	—

KM# 514 1/2 THALER

Silver **Ruler:** Ferdinand II **Obv:** Plain collar **Mint:** Vienna **Note:** Varieties exist. Prev. KM#1782.

Date	Mintage	VG	F	VF	XF	Unc
1624 (c)	—	35.00	75.00	135	225	—
1625 (c)	—	35.00	75.00	135	225	—
1626 (c)	—	35.00	75.00	135	225	—
1627 (c)	—	35.00	75.00	135	225	—
1628 (c)	—	35.00	75.00	135	225	—
1629 (c)	—	35.00	75.00	135	225	—
1630 (c)	—	35.00	75.00	135	225	—
1631 (c)	—	35.00	75.00	135	225	—
1632 (c)	—	35.00	75.00	135	225	—
1633 (c)	—	35.00	75.00	135	225	—
1634 (c)	—	35.00	75.00	135	225	—
1635 (c)	—	35.00	75.00	135	225	—
1636 (c)	—	35.00	75.00	135	225	—
1636 (v)	—	35.00	75.00	135	225	—

KM# 515 1/2 THALER

Silver **Ruler:** Ferdinand II **Mint:** Vienna **Note:** Prev. KM#1784.

Date	Mintage	VG	F	VF	XF	Unc
1624 (c)	—	40.00	80.00	145	250	—

KM# 592.1 1/2 THALER

Silver **Ruler:** Leopold **Obv:** Horizontal stripes below breast plate **Rev:** Crown above arms **Mint:** Hall **Note:** Prev. KM#801.1.

Date	Mintage	VG	F	VF	XF	Unc
1625	—	60.00	120	225	375	—
1626	—	60.00	120	225	375	—
1629	—	60.00	120	225	375	—
1632	—	40.00	90.00	175	300	—

KM# 592.2 1/2 THALER

Silver **Ruler:** Leopold **Obv:** Dot in square pattern below breast plate **Mint:** Hall **Note:** Prev. KM#801.2.

Date	Mintage	VG	F	VF	XF	Unc
1629	—	60.00	120	225	375	—

KM# 673 1/2 THALER

Silver **Ruler:** Ferdinand II **Mint:** Graz **Note:** Klippe. Prev. KM#370.

Date	Mintage	VG	F	VF	XF	Unc
1627	—	—	—	—	—	—
1629	—	—	—	—	—	—

KM# 698 1/2 THALER

Silver **Ruler:** Ferdinand II **Mint:** Graz **Note:** Klippe. Weight of 1 Thaler. Prev. KM#371.

Date	Mintage	VG	F	VF	XF	Unc
1627	—	—	—	—	—	—

KM# 710 1/2 THALER

Tin **Ruler:** Ferdinand II **Mint:** Graz **Note:** Prev. KM#370a.

Date	Mintage	VG	F	VF	XF	Unc
1629/7	—	—	—	—	—	—

KM# 807 1/2 THALER

Silver **Ruler:** Ferdinand II **Mint:** Vienna **Note:** Klippe. Prev. KM#1783.

Date	Mintage	VG	F	VF	XF	Unc
1635 (c) Rare	—	—	—	—	—	—

KM# 839 1/2 THALER
Silver **Ruler:** Ferdinand III **Mint:** Vienna **Note:** Prev. KM#1822.

Date	Mintage	VG	F	VF	XF	Unc
1637 (b)	—	75.00	150	275	450	—
1638 (b)	—	75.00	150	275	450	—
1639 (b)	—	75.00	150	275	450	—
1640 (b)	—	75.00	150	275	450	—
1641 (b)	—	75.00	150	275	450	—
1642 (b)	—	75.00	150	275	450	—
1643 (b)	—	75.00	150	275	450	—
1644 (b)	—	75.00	150	275	450	—
1645 (b)	—	75.00	150	275	450	—
1646 (b)	—	75.00	150	275	450	—
1647 (b)	—	75.00	150	275	450	—
1648 (b)	—	75.00	150	275	450	—
1649 (c)	—	75.00	150	275	450	—

KM# 854 1/2 THALER
Silver **Ruler:** Ferdinand III **Obv:** Portrait and titles of Ferdinand III **Rev:** Crowned arms in Order collar and inner circle **Mint:** Graz **Note:** Prev. KM#426.

Date	Mintage	VG	F	VF	XF	Unc
1638	—	30.00	65.00	125	200	—

KM# 855 1/2 THALER
Silver **Ruler:** Ferdinand III **Mint:** Graz **Note:** Klippe. Prev. KM#427.

Date	Mintage	VG	F	VF	XF	Unc
1638	—	100	175	300	500	—

KM# 856 1/2 THALER
Silver **Ruler:** Ferdinand III **Mint:** Vienna **Note:** Klippe. Prev. KM#1823.

Date	Mintage	VG	F	VF	XF	Unc
1638	—	—	—	—	—	—

KM# 974 1/2 THALER
0.8330 Silver **Ruler:** Ferdinand III **Mint:** Vienna **Note:** Prev. KM#1824.

Date	Mintage	VG	F	VF	XF	Unc
1651 (c)	—	90.00	175	300	525	—
1652 (c)	—	90.00	175	300	525	—
1653 (c)	—	90.00	175	300	525	—
1655 (c)	—	90.00	175	300	525	—
1656 (c)	—	90.00	175	300	525	—

KM# 983 1/2 THALER
Silver **Ruler:** Ferdinand Charles **Mint:** Hall **Note:** Prev. KM#832.

Date	Mintage	VG	F	VF	XF	Unc
1654	—	90.00	175	300	500	—

KM# 1002 1/2 THALER
0.8330 Silver **Ruler:** Ferdinand III **Obv:** Large head reaches top of coin, date below bust **Mint:** Vienna **Note:** Prev. KM#1825.

Date	Mintage	VG	F	VF	XF	Unc
1657	—	90.00	175	300	525	—

KM# 1147 1/2 THALER
Silver **Ruler:** Leopold I **Obv:** Young laureate bust right in inner circle **Mint:** Hall **Note:** Prev. KM#638.

Date	Mintage	VG	F	VF	XF	Unc
ND	—	70.00	150	325	600	—

KM# 1148 1/2 THALER
Silver **Ruler:** Leopold I **Obv:** KM#638 **Rev:** Archduke Ferdinand Karl **Mint:** Hall **Note:** Mule. Prev. KM#639.

Date	Mintage	VG	F	VF	XF	Unc
ND	—	70.00	150	325	600	—

KM# 1149 1/2 THALER
Silver **Ruler:** Leopold I **Mint:** Hall **Note:** Prev. KM#640.

Date	Mintage	VG	F	VF	XF	Unc
ND	—	70.00	150	325	600	—

KM# 1150 1/2 THALER
Silver **Ruler:** Leopold I **Obv:** Similar to KM#640 with value below bust **Mint:** Hall **Note:** Prev. KM#641.

Date	Mintage	VG	F	VF	XF	Unc
ND	—	70.00	150	325	600	—

KM# 1151 1/2 THALER
0.8330 Silver **Ruler:** Leopold I **Obv:** Laureate bust right in inner circle **Rev:** Crowned imperial eagle in inner circle, crown divides date **Mint:** Vienna **Note:** Varieties exist. Prev. KM#1866.

Date	Mintage	VG	F	VF	XF	Unc
1659 Rare	—	—	—	—	—	—
1664	—	—	—	—	—	—
1671	—	100	165	275	450	—

KM# 1258 1/2 THALER
Silver **Ruler:** Leopold I **Mint:** Graz **Note:** Varieties exist. Prev. KM#462.

Date	Mintage	VG	F	VF	XF	Unc
1669 IGW	—	40.00	80.00	145	235	—
1674 IAN	—	40.00	80.00	145	235	—
1676 IAN	—	40.00	80.00	145	235	—
1678 IAN	—	40.00	80.00	145	235	—
1684 IAN	—	40.00	80.00	145	235	—
1694	—	40.00	80.00	145	235	—
1696	—	40.00	80.00	145	235	—

KM# 1368 1/2 THALER
0.8330 Silver **Ruler:** Leopold I **Obv:** Thin bust right in inner circle **Rev:** Crowned imperial eagle in inner circle, crown divides date **Mint:** Vienna **Note:** Varieties exist. Prev. KM#1867.

Date	Mintage	VG	F	VF	XF	Unc
1693	—	40.00	100	175	300	—

KM# 25 THALER
Silver **Ruler:** Rudolf II **Obv:** Armored bust in ruffled collar right **Mint:** Vienna **Note:** Dav. #3002. Prev. KM#1715.

Date	Mintage	VG	F	VF	XF	Unc
1601	—	65.00	125	200	350	—
1602	—	65.00	125	200	350	—
1603	—	65.00	125	200	350	—
1604	—	65.00	125	200	350	—
1605	—	65.00	125	200	350	—
1606	—	65.00	125	200	350	—
1607	—	65.00	125	200	350	—
1608	—	65.00	125	200	350	—
1609	—	65.00	125	200	350	—

KM# 23 THALER
Silver **Ruler:** Ferdinand II **Obv:** Crowned and armored half figure with scepter on shoulder right in inner circle **Rev:** Crowned flat-topped arms in Order collar of The Golden Fleece, date in legend at upper left **Mint:** Graz **Note:** Dav. #3307. Prev. KM#563.

Date	Mintage	VG	F	VF	XF	Unc
1601	—	125	225	425	750	—
1602	—	125	225	425	750	—

KM# 24 THALER
Silver **Ruler:** Ferdinand II **Mint:** Klagenfurt **Note:** Dav. #3314. Local issue for Archduke Ferdinand. Prev. KM#991.

Date	Mintage	VG	F	VF	XF	Unc
1601/0	—	100	200	375	625	—
1601	—	100	200	375	625	—
1602	—	100	200	375	625	—
1609	—	100	200	375	625	—
1610	—	100	200	375	625	—
1611	—	100	200	375	625	—
1612	—	100	200	375	625	—
1613	—	100	200	375	625	—
1614	—	100	200	375	625	—
1615	—	100	200	375	625	—
1616	—	100	200	375	625	—
1617	—	100	200	375	625	—
1618	—	100	200	375	625	—
1619	—	100	200	375	625	—
1620	—	100	200	375	625	—

KM# 36 THALER

Silver **Ruler:** Ferdinand II **Obv:** KM#566 **Rev:** KM#563 **Mint:** Graz **Note:** Dav. #3310A. Mule. Klippe. Prev. KM#567.

Date	Mintage	VG	F	VF	XF	Unc
1602 Rare	—	—	—	—	—	—

KM# 37.1 THALER

28.2800 g., Silver **Ruler:** Rudolf II **Obv:** Date below draped armored bust, clasp on shoulder **Mint:** Hall **Note:** Dav. #3005. Prev. KM#601.1.

Date	Mintage	VG	F	VF	XF	Unc
1602	—	50.00	100	175	350	—
1603	—	50.00	100	175	350	—
1605	—	50.00	100	175	350	—

KM# 37.2 THALER

Silver **Ruler:** Rudolf II **Obv:** Bust with tassel behind neck, without drapery or clasp **Mint:** Hall **Note:** Dav. #3005B. Varieties exist. Prev. KM#601.2.

Date	Mintage	VG	F	VF	XF	Unc
1605	—	50.00	100	175	350	—
1606	—	50.00	100	175	350	—
1607	—	50.00	100	175	350	—
1612	—	50.00	100	175	350	—

KM# 37.3 THALER

Silver **Ruler:** Rudolf II **Obv:** Longer ribbon tails, without tassel **Mint:** Hall **Note:** Dav. #3005C. Prev. KM#601.3.

Date	Mintage	VG	F	VF	XF	Unc
1605	—	50.00	100	175	350	—

KM# 56.1 THALER

Silver **Ruler:** Rudolf II **Obv:** Legend broken at lower right between R-OM: **Mint:** Hall **Note:** Dav. #3005A. Prev. KM#602.1.

Date	Mintage	VG	F	VF	XF	Unc
1604	—	50.00	100	175	350	—

KM# 56.2 THALER

Silver **Ruler:** Rudolf II **Obv:** Legend broken at lower right between RO-M: **Mint:** Hall **Note:** Varieties exist. Prev. KM#602.2.

Date	Mintage	VG	F	VF	XF	Unc
1605	—	50.00	100	175	350	—

KM# 65 THALER

Silver **Ruler:** Ferdinand II **Rev:** Inner circle added **Rev. Legend:** DVX • BVRGVND... **Mint:** Graz **Note:** Dav. #3307A. Prev. KM#564.

Date	Mintage	VG	F	VF	XF	Unc
(1)605	—	100	200	400	700	—

KM# 81 THALER

Silver **Ruler:** Rudolf II **Obv:** Front of armored bust through inner circle, date in legend above **Mint:** Hall **Note:** Dav. #3006. Prev. KM#603.

Date	Mintage	VG	F	VF	XF	Unc
1607	—	50.00	100	175	350	—
1609	—	50.00	100	175	350	—
1610	—	50.00	100	175	350	—

KM# 82 THALER

Silver **Ruler:** Rudolf II **Obv:** Bust with Alchemistry symbols on shoulder **Rev:** Cronwed complex arms within order chain **Mint:** Hall **Note:** Dav. #3006A. Prev. KM#604.

Date	Mintage	VG	F	VF	XF	Unc
1607	—	50.00	100	175	350	—

KM# 94 THALER

Silver **Ruler:** Ferdinand II **Rev:** Round Order collar without inner circle **Mint:** Graz **Note:** Dav. #3308. Prev. KM#565.

Date	Mintage	VG	F	VF	XF	Unc
1608	—	100	200	400	700	—

KM# 95 THALER

Silver **Ruler:** Rudolf II **Obv:** Different armored bust right in inner circle **Mint:** Hall **Note:** Dav. #3006B. Prev. KM#605.

Date	Mintage	VG	F	VF	XF	Unc
1608	—	50.00	100	175	350	—

KM# 96 THALER

Silver **Ruler:** Matthias II **Mint:** Vienna **Note:** Coronation commemorative. Prev. KM#1735.

Date	Mintage	VG	F	VF	XF	Unc
1608 CH Rare	—	—	—	—	—	—

KM# 102 THALER

Silver **Ruler:** Ferdinand II **Rev:** Inner circle within order collar **Mint:** Graz **Note:** Dav. #3310. Prev. KM#566.

Date	Mintage	VG	F	VF	XF	Unc
1609	—	75.00	150	300	650	—
1610	—	75.00	150	300	650	—

KM# 103 THALER

Silver **Ruler:** Matthias II **Obv:** Crowned bust in ruffled collar right in inner circle **Rev:** Crowned arms in Order collar in inner circle, date in legend **Mint:** Vienna **Note:** Titles as King of Bohemia. Dav. #3037. Prev. KM#1736.

Date	Mintage	VG	F	VF	XF	Unc
1609	—	125	250	425	750	—
1610	—	125	250	425	750	—

KM# 104 THALER

Silver **Ruler:** Matthias II **Obv:** Larger crowned bust with crown touching inner circle **Mint:** Vienna **Note:** Titles as King of Bohemia. Dav. #3038. Prev. KM#1737.

Date	Mintage	VG	F	VF	XF	Unc
1609	—	300	550	950	1,600	—

KM# 122 THALER

Silver **Ruler:** Matthias II **Obv:** Smaller bust in inner circle **Mint:** Vienna **Note:** Titles as King of Bohemia. Dav. #3039. Prev. KM#1738.

Date	Mintage	VG	F	VF	XF	Unc
1610	—	125	250	425	750	—
1611	—	125	250	425	750	—

KM# 118.1 THALER

Silver **Ruler:** Rudolf II **Obv:** Date in front of bust with additional shoulder ornamentation, legend divided **Obv. Legend:** RO-IM: **Rev:** Crowned complex arms within order chain **Mint:** Hall **Note:** Dav. #3007. Prev. KM#606.1.

Date	Mintage	VG	F	VF	XF	Unc
1610	—	50.00	100	175	350	—

KM# 118.2 THALER

Silver **Ruler:** Rudolf II **Obv:** Laureate armored bust right, ornaments on armor, date at right **Rev:** Crowned complex arms within order chain **Rev. Legend:** ...TIROL **Mint:** Hall **Note:** Dav. #3007C. Prev. KM#606.2.

Date	Mintage	VG	F	VF	XF	Unc
1610	—	50.00	100	175	350	—

KM# 118.3 THALER

Silver **Ruler:** Rudolf II **Obv:** Laureate armored bust right, date at right **Rev:** Crowned complex arms **Rev. Legend:** ...TIRO **Mint:** Hall **Note:** Dav. #3007D. Prev. KM#606.3.

Date	Mintage	VG	F	VF	XF	Unc
1610	—	50.00	100	175	350	—

KM# 118.4 THALER

Silver **Ruler:** Rudolf II **Obv:** Armored bust right, legend divided. **Obv. Legend:** DG: - RO. **Rev:** Crowned complex arms within order chain **Rev. Legend:** ...TIRO **Mint:** Hall **Note:** Dav. #3007A. Prev. KM#606.4.

Date	Mintage	VG	F	VF	XF	Unc
1610	—	50.00	100	175	350	—

KM# 120 THALER

Silver **Ruler:** Rudolf II **Obv:** Laureate armored bust right, legend divided **Obv. Legend:** ROM-: IM: **Rev:** Crowned complex arms **Mint:** Hall **Note:** Dav. #3007B. Prev. KM#607.

Date	Mintage	VG	F	VF	XF	Unc
1610	—	50.00	100	175	350	—

KM# 121 THALER

Silver **Ruler:** Rudolf II **Obv:** Cloaked bust without horn on shoulder **Rev:** Ornamented shield **Mint:** Hall **Note:** Dav. #3008. Prev. KM#608.

Date	Mintage	VG	F	VF	XF	Unc
1610	—	50.00	100	175	350	—

KM# 126.1 THALER

Silver **Ruler:** Rudolf II **Obv:** Draped bust with lion's head on shoulder in laurel wreath, unbroken legend **Mint:** Hall **Note:** Dav. #3009A. Prev. KM#609.1

Date	Mintage	VG	F	VF	XF	Unc
1611	—	55.00	110	200	400	—

KM# 126.2 THALER

Silver **Ruler:** Rudolf II **Obv:** Legend broken at lower right **Mint:** Hall **Note:** Dav. #3009. Prev. KM#609.2.

Date	Mintage	VG	F	VF	XF	Unc
1611	—	55.00	110	200	400	—
161Z	—	55.00	110	200	400	—

KM# 130 THALER

Silver **Ruler:** Matthias II **Obv:** Crowned bust in ruffled collar right in inner circle **Rev:** Crowned arms in Order collar in inner circle, date in legend **Mint:** Vienna **Note:** Titles as King of Bohemia. Dav. #3040. Prev. KM#1739.

Date	Mintage	VG	F	VF	XF	Unc
1611	—	350	650	1,150	1,850	—
1612	—	350	650	1,150	1,850	—

KM# 144 THALER

Silver **Ruler:** Matthias II **Obv:** Smaller bust and crown **Mint:** Vienna **Note:** Titles as King of Bohemia. Dav. #3041. Prev. KM#1740.

Date	Mintage	VG	F	VF	XF	Unc
1612	—	350	650	1,150	1,850	—
1613	—	350	650	1,150	1,850	—

KM# 143 THALER

Silver **Ruler:** Rudolf II **Obv:** Bust divides date **Mint:** Hall **Note:** Dav. #3010. Prev. KM#610.

Date	Mintage	VG	F	VF	XF	Unc
1612	—	55.00	110	200	400	—

KM# 165 THALER

Silver **Ruler:** Maximilian **Obv:** Bust right in decorated inner circle **Mint:** Hall **Note:** Dav. #3315. Prev. KM#767.

Date	Mintage	VG	F	VF	XF	Unc
ND	—	250	450	775	1,600	—

KM# 37.4 THALER

28.1800 g., Silver **Ruler:** Rudolf II **Obv:** Laureate bust right, longer ribbon tails, without tassel **Obv. Legend:** RUDOLPHVS II • DG • RO.IM • SEM • AV • GE • HVNG • BOH • REX **Rev:** Crowned arms in order chain **Rev. Legend:** NEC NON ARCHIDVCES AV:DVC:BVR:COM:TIRO **Mint:** Hall **Note:** Dav.#3005C.

Date	Mintage	VG	F	VF	XF	Unc
1612	—	50.00	100	175	350	—

KM# 166 THALER

Silver **Ruler:** Maximilian **Obv:** Laurels form inner circle **Rev:** Laurels form inner circle; continuous legend with date below bust **Mint:** Hall **Note:** Dav. #3316. Prev. KM#768.

Date	Mintage	VG	F	VF	XF	Unc
1613	—	75.00	150	265	525	—

KM# 167 THALER

Silver **Ruler:** Maximilian **Obv:** Larger bust dividing legend at lower right with date **Mint:** Hall **Note:** Dav. #3317. Prev. KM#769.1.

Date	Mintage	VG	F	VF	XF	Unc
1613	—	75.00	150	265	525	—

KM# 168 THALER

Silver **Ruler:** Maximilian **Obv:** Bust divides date **Mint:** Hall **Note:** Dav. #3318. Prev. KM#769.2.

Date	Mintage	VG	F	VF	XF	Unc
1613	—	75.00	150	265	525	—

KM# 169 THALER

Silver **Ruler:** Matthias II **Obv:** Laureate, armored bust right in inner circle **Rev:** Crowned imperial eagle with shield on breast with sword and scepter in inner circle, date in legend **Mint:** Vienna **Note:** Titles as Emperor. Dav. #3043. Prev. KM#1741.

Date	Mintage	VG	F	VF	XF	Unc
1613	—	125	250	425	750	—
1614	—	125	250	425	750	—

KM# 187 THALER

Silver **Ruler:** Ferdinand II **Rev:** Crowned arms in Order collar in inner circle, crown divides date **Mint:** Graz **Note:** Dav. #3311. Prev. KM#568.

Date	Mintage	VG	F	VF	XF	Unc
1614	—	65.00	145	350	900	—
1617	—	65.00	145	350	900	—
1618	—	65.00	145	350	900	—

KM# 188.1 THALER

Silver **Ruler:** Maximilian **Obv:** Date in front of bust with Co below **Mint:** Hall **Note:** Dav. #3319. Prev. KM#770.1.

Date	Mintage	VG	F	VF	XF	Unc
1614 CO	—	200	350	575	1,150	—

KM# 188.2 THALER

Silver **Ruler:** Maximilian **Obv:** Bust divides date with Co below **Mint:** Hall **Note:** Dav. #3320. Prev. KM#770.2.

Date	Mintage	VG	F	VF	XF	Unc
1614 Co	—	200	350	575	1,150	—

KM# 188.3 THALER

Silver **Ruler:** Maximilian **Obv:** Bust divides punctuated date with large CO below **Mint:** Hall **Note:** Dav. #3321. Prev. KM#770.3.

Date	Mintage	VG	F	VF	XF	Unc
1615 CO	—	50.00	100	200	400	—

KM# 188.4 THALER

Silver **Ruler:** Maximilian **Obv:** Bust divides date with small co below **Mint:** Hall **Note:** Dav. #3321A. Prev. KM#770.4.

Date	Mintage	VG	F	VF	XF	Unc
1615 co	—	50.00	100	200	400	—

KM# 188.5 THALER

Silver **Ruler:** Maximilian **Obv:** Smaller bust divides date with small co below **Mint:** Hall **Note:** Dav. #3321B. Prev. KM#770.5.

Date	Mintage	VG	F	VF	XF	Unc
1615 co	—	50.00	100	200	400	—

KM# 196 THALER

Silver **Ruler:** Matthias II **Rev:** Larger crown above eagle **Mint:** Vienna **Note:** Titles as Emperor. Dav. #3044. Prev. KM#1742.

Date	Mintage	VG	F	VF	XF	Unc
1615	—	125	250	425	750	—
1616	—	125	250	425	750	—

KM# 205.1 THALER

Silver **Ruler:** Maximilian **Obv:** Bust with large drapery divides date with small co below **Mint:** Hall **Note:** Dav. #3322. Prev. KM#771.1.

Date	Mintage	VG	F	VF	XF	Unc
1616 co	—	50.00	100	200	400	—

KM# 205.2 THALER

Silver **Ruler:** Maximilian **Obv:** With CO in legend below bust **Mint:** Hall **Note:** Dav. #3322A. Prev. KM#771.2.

Date	Mintage	VG	F	VF	XF	Unc
1616 CO	—	50.00	100	200	400	—

KM# 206 THALER

Silver **Ruler:** Matthias II **Rev:** Smaller crown above eagle **Mint:** Vienna **Note:** Titles as Emperor. Dav. #3046. Prev. KM#1743.

Date	Mintage	VG	F	VF	XF	Unc
1616	—	125	250	425	750	—
1617	—	125	250	425	750	—

KM# 216 THALER

Silver **Ruler:** Ferdinand II **Rev:** Date in legend **Mint:** Graz **Note:** Dav. #3312. Prev. KM#569.

Date	Mintage	VG	F	VF	XF	Unc
1617	—	50.00	100	220	575	—

KM# 217 THALER

Silver **Ruler:** Ferdinand II **Obv:** Crowned bust without scepter **Rev:** Crown divides date **Mint:** Graz **Note:** Dav. #A3312. Prev. KM#570.

Date	Mintage	VG	F	VF	XF	Unc
1617	—	50.00	100	220	575	—
1618	—	50.00	100	220	575	—

KM# 221 THALER

Silver **Ruler:** Matthias II **Obv:** Laureate bust with wide ruffle **Mint:** Vienna **Note:** Titles as Emperor. Dav. #3048. Varieties exist. Prev. KM#1744.

Date	Mintage	VG	F	VF	XF	Unc
1617	—	125	250	425	750	—
1618	—	125	250	425	750	—
1619	—	125	250	425	750	—

KM# 218.1 THALER

Silver **Ruler:** Maximilian **Obv:** Small bust divides date with small outlined CO below **Mint:** Hall **Note:** Dav. #3323. Prev. KM#772.1.

Date	Mintage	VG	F	VF	XF	Unc
1617 co	—	40.00	90.00	175	350	—

KM# 218.2 THALER

Silver **Ruler:** Maximilian **Obv:** Bust barely dividing legend, with CARENTA **Mint:** Hall **Note:** Dav. #3323A. Prev. KM#772.2.

Date	Mintage	VG	F	VF	XF	Unc
1617	—	40.00	90.00	175	350	—

KM# 218.3 THALER

Silver **Ruler:** Maximilian **Obv:** Bust with lance rest on chest **Obv. Legend:** ...CAREN **Mint:** Hall **Note:** Dav. #3323B. Prev. KM#772.3.

Date	Mintage	VG	F	VF	XF	Unc
1617	—	40.00	90.00	175	350	—

KM# 218.4 THALER

Silver **Ruler:** Maximilian **Obv:** With CO in legend below bust **Obv. Legend:** MAXIMIL: DG: ARG: - :oo: AV: DVX: BVR: STIR: **Mint:** Hall **Note:** Dav. #3323C. Prev. KM#772.4.

Date	Mintage	VG	F	VF	XF	Unc
1617	—	35.00	80.00	165	275	—

KM# 218.5 THALER

Silver **Ruler:** Maximilian **Obv. Legend:** MAXIMIL: DG: AR-C: oo: AV: DVX: BVR: STIR: **Mint:** Hall **Note:** Dav. #3323D. Prev. KM#772.5.

Date	Mintage	VG	F	VF	XF	Unc
1617	—	35.00	80.00	160	250	—

KM# 218.6 THALER

28.4700 g., Silver **Ruler:** Maximilian **Obv:** Bust right divides date **Obv. Legend:** *MAXIMIL: DG: ARC: - :OO: AV: DVX: BUR: STIR **Rev:** Crowned arms **Rev. Legend:** ET: CARN: MAG: PRVSS: AD: COM: H: ET: TIROL **Mint:** Hall **Note:** Dav.#3323V.

Date	Mintage	VG	F	VF	XF	Unc
1617	—	50.00	100	175	350	—

KM# 219 THALER

Silver **Ruler:** Maximilian **Obv:** Bust with lance rest on shoulder **Mint:** Hall **Note:** Dav. #A3324. Prev. KM#773.

Date	Mintage	VG	F	VF	XF	Unc
1617	—	30.00	70.00	150	225	—

KM# 220 THALER

Silver **Ruler:** Maximilian **Obv:** Bust with shoulder ornamentation **Mint:** Hall **Note:** Dav. #A3324. Prev. KM#782.

Date	Mintage	VG	F	VF	XF	Unc
1617	—	30.00	70.00	150	225	—

KM# 227.1 THALER

Silver **Ruler:** Maximilian **Obv:** Bust right divides date, high ruffled collar, cross on chain around neck **Obv. Legend:** MAXIMIL: DG...CARN **Rev:** Crowned complex arms **Mint:** Hall **Note:** Dav. #3324. Prev. KM#774.1.

Date	Mintage	VG	F	VF	XF	Unc
1618	—	40.00	80.00	165	275	—

KM# 227.2 THALER

Silver **Ruler:** Maximilian **Obv:** Ruffled collar bust right divides date **Obv. Legend:** MAXIMILI: DG...CARN: **Rev:** Crowned arms **Mint:** Hall **Note:** Dav. #3324A. Prev. KM#774.2.

Date	Mintage	VG	F	VF	XF	Unc
1618	—	35.00	80.00	160	250	—

KM# 228 THALER

Silver **Ruler:** Matthias II **Mint:** Vienna **Note:** Titles as Emperor. Dav. #3048A. Klippe. Prev. KM#1745.

Date	Mintage	VG	F	VF	XF	Unc
1618 Rare	—	—	—	—	—	—

KM# 244 THALER

Silver **Ruler:** Ferdinand II **Obv:** Crowned bust right in inner circle **Rev:** Crowned imperial eagle with oval arms on breast in inner circle **Mint:** Klagenfurt **Note:** Varieties exist. Prev. KM#967.

Date	Mintage	VG	F	VF	XF	Unc
ND Rare	—	—	—	—	—	—

KM# 245 THALER

Silver **Ruler:** Matthias II **Rev:** Ornament after "TYR..." **Mint:** Vienna **Note:** Titles as Emperor. Dav. #3049. Prev. KM#1746.

Date	Mintage	VG	F	VF	XF	Unc
1619	—	125	250	425	750	—

KM# 262.1 THALER

Silver **Ruler:** Ferdinand II **Obv:** Date below bust, legend **Obv. Legend:** FERDINANDVS • II • DG • RO • IM • S • A • GER • H • B • REX • **Rev:** Crowned imperial eagle with round arms, legend **Rev. Legend:** ARCHI • AVSTRIA • DVX • BVRGVN • STYRIAE • ETC • **Mint:** Graz **Note:** Prev. KM#372.1.

Date	Mintage	VG	F	VF	XF	Unc
1620	—	65.00	125	250	400	—

KM# 262.2 THALER

Silver **Ruler:** Ferdinand II **Obv. Legend:** ...D • G • - RO • IMP • S • A • G • HVN • ET • BO • REX • **Rev. Legend:** ...B-VRGVNDIAE... **Mint:** Graz **Note:** Varieties exist. Dav. #3098. Prev. KM#372.2.

Date	Mintage	VG	F	VF	XF	Unc
1620	—	65.00	125	250	400	—

KM# 264.1 THALER

28.3800 g., Silver **Ruler:** Leopold **Obv. Legend:** LEOPOLDVS: NECNON: CAETERI: D: G: ARCHID: AUSTRI **Rev. Legend:** DVC: BVRG: STYR: CAR: ET: CARN: COM: TYROL: **Mint:** Hall **Note:** Dav. #3328. Prev. KM#802.1.

Date	Mintage	VG	F	VF	XF	Unc
1620	—	60.00	125	300	500	—
1621	—	60.00	125	300	500	—

KM# 264.2 THALER

Silver **Ruler:** Leopold **Obv:** Bust right divides date **Obv. Legend:** *LEOPOLDVS: D: G: A: ANEC: NON CAETERI: ARCH: AUST **Rev:** Crowned arms with furls at upper left and right **Rev. Legend:** DVX BVRG: STIR: CAR-ET: CARN: COM: TIRO **Mint:** Hall **Note:** Dav.#3329.

Date	Mintage	VG	F	VF	XF	Unc
16Z0	—	60.00	125	300	500	—

KM# 264.3 THALER

Silver **Ruler:** Leopold **Obv:** Bust right divides date **Obv. Legend:** * LEOPOLDVS: D: G: A: NEC: NON CAETERI: ARCH: AUST **Rev:** Crowned plain arms **Rev. Legend:** DVX BVRG: STIR: CAR-ET: CARN: COM: TIRO **Mint:** Hall **Note:** Dav. #3329V.

Date	Mintage	VG	F	VF	XF	Unc
16Z0	—	60.00	125	300	500	—

KM# 264.4 THALER

Silver **Ruler:** Leopold **Obv:** Bust right divides date **Obv. Legend:** * LEOPOLDVS: D: G: A: NEC: NON CAETERI: ARCH: AUST **Rev:** Crowned slightly ornate arms **Rev. Legend:** DVX BVRG: STIR: CA-RET: CARN: COM: TI • **Mint:** Hall **Note:** Dav. #3329.

Date	Mintage	VG	F	VF	XF	Unc
16Z0	—	60.00	125	300	500	—

KM# 264.5 THALER

28.7900 g., Silver **Ruler:** Leopold **Obv. Legend:** LEOPOLDVS D G ARCHID AUSTRIAE DVX BVRG S CAES M...ET RELIQ **Rev. Legend:** ARCHIDVC GVBERNATOR PLENARIVS COM TIROL **Mint:** Hall **Note:** Portrait varieties exist. Prev. KM#802.2.

Date	Mintage	VG	F	VF	XF	Unc
16Z1	—	60.00	125	300	500	—
16ZZ	—	60.00	125	300	500	—
16Z3	—	60.00	125	300	500	—
16Z4	—	60.00	125	300	500	—
16Z5	—	60.00	125	300	500	—

KM# 264.6 THALER

28.6600 g., Silver **Ruler:** Leopold **Obv:** Bust right divides date **Obv. Legend:** *LEOPOLDVS: D: G: ARCHID: AVSTRIAE DVX BVRG S CAES: M ET R LI **Rev:** Crowned arms with small ornaments left and right **Mint:** Hall **Note:** Dav. #3330V.

Date	Mintage	VG	F	VF	XF	Unc
16ZZ	—	30.00	125	300	500	—
16Z4	—	60.00	125	300	500	—

KM# 265 THALER

Silver **Ruler:** Ferdinand II **Rev:** Crown divides date **Mint:** Klagenfurt **Note:** Varieties exist. Dav. #3112. Prev. KM#968.

Date	Mintage	VG	F	VF	XF	Unc
1620	—	125	250	400	650	—

KM# 266 THALER

Silver **Ruler:** Ferdinand II **Rev:** Flat-topped shield of arms **Mint:** Klagenfurt **Note:** Dav. #3114. Prev. KM#969.

Date	Mintage	VG	F	VF	XF	Unc
1620	—	125	275	450	800	—

KM# 268.1 THALER

Silver **Ruler:** Ferdinand II **Mint:** Vienna **Note:** Dav. #3074. Prev. KM#1785.1.

Date	Mintage	VG	F	VF	XF	Unc
16Z0	—	65.00	125	200	350	—

KM# 268.2 THALER

Silver **Ruler:** Ferdinand II **Obv:** Laureate wreath without bow **Rev:** Crowned double eagle, shield on breast surrounded by order chain **Mint:** Vienna **Note:** Dav. #3076. Prev. KM#1785.2.

Date	Mintage	VG	F	VF	XF	Unc
16Z0 (c)	—	50.00	100	175	300	—
16Z1 (c)	—	50.00	100	175	300	—

KM# 263 THALER

Silver **Ruler:** Ferdinand II **Obv. Legend:** ...ROM. IMP. S. A. GER... **Rev:** Arms in flat-topped shield, date divided at top **Mint:** Graz **Note:** Dav. #3099. Prev. KM#374.

Date	Mintage	VG	F	VF	XF	Unc
1620	—	65.00	125	250	400	—

KM# 335 THALER

Silver **Ruler:** Ferdinand II **Obv:** Standing figure right between two shields **Rev:** Heraldic imperial eagle **Mint:** Brunn **Note:** Prev. KM#216.

Date	Mintage	VG	F	VF	XF	Unc
1621 GR-(h) Rare	—	—	—	—	—	—
1621 GR Rare	—	—	—	—	—	—
1622 GR Rare	—	—	—	—	—	—

KM# 347 THALER

Silver **Ruler:** Ferdinand II **Obv:** Standing Kaiser holding sceptre and orb **Rev:** Crowned imperial eagle, arms on breast, date in legend left of crown **Mint:** Olmutz **Note:** Klippe. Dav. A3147. Prev. KM#A1237.

Date	Mintage	VG	F	VF	XF	Unc
1621 BZ	—	750	1,250	2,000	3,000	—
1622	—	750	1,250	2,000	3,000	—

KM# 336 THALER

Silver **Ruler:** Ferdinand II **Obv:** Date below bust **Obv. Legend:** ...D-G. RO. IM...HV. BO. REX **Rev:** Round arms on eagle's breast **Rev. Legend:** DVX-BVRGVN. STYRIAE. ETC. **Mint:** Graz **Note:** Varieties exist. Dav. #3100. Prev. KM#373.

Date	Mintage	VG	F	VF	XF	Unc
1621	—	65.00	125	250	400	—

KM# 337 THALER

Silver **Ruler:** Ferdinand II **Obv. Legend:** ...HV. B. REX. **Rev:** Date divided above by crown **Rev. Legend:** ...ET. **Mint:** Graz **Note:** Dav. #3102. Prev. KM#375.

Date	Mintage	VG	F	VF	XF	Unc
1621	—	65.00	125	250	400	—

KM# 338 THALER

Silver **Ruler:** Ferdinand II **Obv:** Laureate bust with ruffled collar right divides date **Rev:** Crowned complex arms within order chain **Mint:** Hall **Note:** Dav. #A3125. Prev. KM#615.

Date	Mintage	VG	F	VF	XF	Unc
1621	—	125	250	450	1,100	—
1622	—	125	250	450	1,100	—
1623	—	125	250	450	1,100	—

KM# 339 THALER

Silver **Ruler:** Ferdinand II **Obv:** Tall, thin crowned bust **Rev:** Crown divides date **Mint:** Klagenfurt **Note:** Dav. #3118. Prev. KM#970.

Date	Mintage	VG	F	VF	XF	Unc
1621	—	650	1,200	2,000	3,500	—

KM# 340 THALER

Silver **Ruler:** Ferdinand II **Obv:** Crowned bust with high ruffled collar right, date below **Rev:** Crowned double eagle with shield on breast **Mint:** Klagenfurt **Note:** Varieties exist. Dav. #3115. Prev. KM#971.

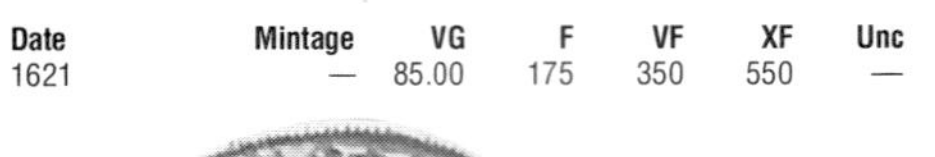

Date	Mintage	VG	F	VF	XF	Unc
1621	—	85.00	175	350	550	—

KM# 341 THALER

Silver **Ruler:** Ferdinand II **Obv:** Crown divides date **Rev:** Order chain surrounds shield on crowned double eagle's breast **Mint:** Klagenfurt **Note:** Varieties exist. Dav. #3116. Prev. KM#972.

Date	Mintage	VG	F	VF	XF	Unc
1621	—	85.00	175	350	550	—

KM# 342 THALER

Silver **Ruler:** Ferdinand II **Rev:** Oval arms **Mint:** Klagenfurt **Note:** Dav. #3116. Prev. KM#A973.

Date	Mintage	VG	F	VF	XF	Unc
1621 Rare	—	—	—	—	—	—

KM# 343 THALER

Silver **Ruler:** Ferdinand II **Obv:** Date below bust **Obv. Legend:** S. A. G. HV. BO. REX **Mint:** Klagenfurt **Note:** Dav. #3120. Prev. KM#B973.

Date	Mintage	VG	F	VF	XF	Unc
1621	—	85.00	175	350	550	—

KM# 344 THALER

Silver **Ruler:** Ferdinand II **Obv:** Crowned bust divides date at collar height **Mint:** Klagenfurt **Note:** Dav. #3121. Varieties exist. Prev. KM#973.

Date	Mintage	VG	F	VF	XF	Unc
1621	—	85.00	175	350	550	—

KM# 345 THALER

Silver **Ruler:** Ferdinand II **Obv:** Bust divides date at shoulder height **Mint:** Klagenfurt **Note:** Dav. #3121A. Prev. KM#A974.

Date	Mintage	VG	F	VF	XF	Unc
1621	—	85.00	175	350	550	—

KM# 348 THALER

Silver **Ruler:** Ferdinand II **Mint:** Vienna **Note:** Klippe. Dav. #3076A. Prev. KM#1786.

Date	Mintage	VG	F	VF	XF	Unc
16Z1 (c) Rare	—	—	—	—	—	—

KM# 346 THALER

Silver **Ruler:** Ferdinand II **Obv:** Ornamented inner circle **Rev:** Round arms **Mint:** Klagenfurt **Note:** Dav. #3121A. Varieties exist. Prev. KM#974.

Date	Mintage	VG	F	VF	XF	Unc
1622	—	85.00	175	350	550	—

KM# 451 THALER

19.8700 g., Silver **Ruler:** Ferdinand II **Mint:** Brunn **Note:** Klippe. Prev. KM#216a.

Date	Mintage	VG	F	VF	XF	Unc
1623 GR Rare	—	—	—	—	—	—

KM# 452 THALER

Silver **Ruler:** Ferdinand II **Obv:** Laureate bust with high ruffled collar right, date below **Obv. Legend:** ...I: S: A: G: H: B: REX. **Rev:** Crowned arms in order chain **Rev. Legend:** ...AVST: DVX:-BVR: STYRIAE: ETC. **Mint:** Graz **Note:** Dav. #3103. Prev. KM#376.

Date	Mintage	VG	F	VF	XF	Unc
1623	—	40.00	110	200	300	—

KM# 453 THALER

Silver **Ruler:** Ferdinand II **Obv:** Plain collar on Ferdinand **Mint:** Graz **Note:** Dav. #3104. Prev. KM#377.

Date	Mintage	VG	F	VF	XF	Unc
16Z3	—	35.00	100	175	250	—
16Z4/3	—	35.00	100	175	250	—
16Z4	—	35.00	100	175	250	—

KM# 454 THALER

Silver **Ruler:** Ferdinand II **Obv:** Shield added on each side of Kaiser **Mint:** Olmutz **Note:** Klippe. Dav. #3147. Prev. KM#B1237.

Date	Mintage	VG	F	VF	XF	Unc
1623	—	750	1,250	2,000	3,000	—

KM# 455 THALER

Silver **Ruler:** Ferdinand II **Obv:** Bust right in inner circle, date below bust **Rev:** Crowned arms in Order collar and inner circle **Mint:** Saint Veit **Note:** Dav. #A3123. Prev. KM#1601.

Date	Mintage	VG	F	VF	XF	Unc
1623	—	125	250	400	800	—

KM# 456 THALER

Silver **Ruler:** Ferdinand II **Obv:** Older bust **Mint:** Vienna **Note:** Dav. #3078. Prev. KM#A1787.

Date	Mintage	VG	F	VF	XF	Unc
1623 (c)	—	50.00	100	175	300	—
1624 (c)	—	50.00	100	175	300	—

KM# 521 THALER

Silver **Ruler:** Ferdinand II **Obv:** Laureate bust right in laurel wreath border **Rev:** Crowned complex arms within order chain **Mint:** Graz **Note:** Dav. #3106. Prev. KM#379.

Date	Mintage	VG	F	VF	XF	Unc
1624	—	35.00	100	175	250	—
1625	—	35.00	100	175	250	—
1626	—	35.00	100	175	250	—

KM# 531 THALER

Silver **Ruler:** Ferdinand II **Mint:** Vienna **Note:** Dav. #3087. Varieties exist. Prev. KM#1790.

Date	Mintage	VG	F	VF	XF	Unc
1624 (c)	—	100	175	300	500	—
1625 (c)	—	100	175	300	500	—

KM# 526 THALER

Silver **Ruler:** Ferdinand II **Obv:** Laureate armored bust right, date below **Rev:** Crowned complex arms within order chain **Mint:** Saint Veit **Note:** Dav. #3123. Varieties exist. Prev. KM#1602.

Date	Mintage	VG	F	VF	XF	Unc
1624 (m)	—	75.00	150	300	650	—
1625 (m)	—	75.00	150	300	650	—
1625 (p)	—	75.00	150	300	650	—

KM# 517.1 THALER

19.8700 g., Silver **Ruler:** Ferdinand II **Obv:** Laureate bust with high ruffled collar right **Rev:** Order chain surrounds shield on double eagle breast **Mint:** Brunn **Note:** Dav. #3144. Prev. KM#217.1.

Date	Mintage	VG	F	VF	XF	Unc
1624 B/HG-(c)	—	200	400	650	1,000	—
1624 B-(c)	—	200	400	650	1,000	—

KM# 517.2 THALER

19.8700 g., Silver **Ruler:** Ferdinand II **Obv:** Legend in circle followed by D. G... **Obv. Legend:** FERDINANDVS. II. B **Mint:** Brunn **Note:** Dav. #3146. Prev. KM#217.2.

Date	Mintage	VG	F	VF	XF	Unc
1624 B/HG	—	200	400	650	1,000	—
1624 B-(c)	—	200	400	650	1,000	—
1624 (c)	—	200	400	650	1,000	—

KM# 518 THALER

19.8700 g., Silver **Ruler:** Ferdinand II **Mint:** Brunn **Note:** Klippe. Dav. #3146A. Prev. KM#218.

Date	Mintage	VG	F	VF	XF	Unc
1624 (c) Rare	—	—	—	—	—	—

KM# 519 THALER

16.5500 g., Silver **Ruler:** Ferdinand II **Mint:** Brunn **Note:** Klippe. Prev. KM#218a.

Date	Mintage	VG	F	VF	XF	Unc
1624 B-(c) Rare	—	—	—	—	—	—

KM# 520 THALER

Silver **Ruler:** Ferdinand II **Obv:** Without Roman numeral II in legend **Mint:** Graz **Note:** Dav. #3104A. Prev. KM#378.

Date	Mintage	VG	F	VF	XF	Unc
1624	—	35.00	100	175	250	—

KM# 522 THALER

Silver **Ruler:** Ferdinand II **Mint:** Hall **Note:** Dav. #3330A. Klippe. Prev. KM#803.

Date	Mintage	VG	F	VF	XF	Unc
1624	—	—	—	—	—	—

KM# 525.1 THALER

Silver **Ruler:** Ferdinand II **Obv:** Laureate bust right **Obv. Legend:** FERDINANDVS. II. D., mint mark, G. R. I. S. A. G. HV. BO. REX **Rev:** Crowned arms in Order chain, date **Rev. Legend:** ARCHID. AVS. DVX. -BVR. CO. TYR **Mint:** Saint Polten **Note:** Dav. #3092. Prev. KM#1574.1.

Date	Mintage	VG	F	VF	XF	Unc
1624 (c)-IIE	—	350	600	1,000	1,750	—
1624 (d)	—	350	600	1,000	1,750	—

KM# 525.2 THALER

Silver **Ruler:** Ferdinand II **Obv:** Bust in laurel wreath **Obv. Legend:** FERDINANDVS: II: D:, mint mark, : G. R: I: S: A: G: HV: BO: REX: **Mint:** Saint Polten **Note:** Dav. #3093. Prev. KM#1574.2.

Date	Mintage	VG	F	VF	XF	Unc
1625 (d)	—	350	600	1,000	1,750	—

KM# 525.3 THALER

Silver **Ruler:** Ferdinand II **Obv:** Bust in laurel wreath within circle **Mint:** Saint Polten **Note:** Dav. #3094. Prev. KM#1574.3.

Date	Mintage	VG	F	VF	XF	Unc
1625 (c)	—	350	600	1,000	1,750	—

KM# 525.4 THALER

Silver **Ruler:** Ferdinand II **Obv:** Bust in inner circle, mint mark divides IL-E below **Obv. Legend:** ...G. H. B. REX. **Rev:** Smaller Order chain **Mint:** Saint Polten **Note:** Dav. #3095. Prev. KM#1574.4.

Date	Mintage	VG	F	VF	XF	Unc
1625 (d)-IIE	—	350	600	1,000	1,750	—

KM# 525.5 THALER

Silver **Ruler:** Ferdinand II **Obv:** Bust in three circles **Obv. Legend:** ...G. R. IM. S. A. G. H. B. REX. **Mint:** Saint Polten **Note:** Dav. #3096. Prev. KM#1574.5.

Date	Mintage	VG	F	VF	XF	Unc
1625 (r)	—	350	600	1,000	1,750	—

KM# 527 THALER

Silver **Ruler:** Ferdinand II **Obv:** Half-length figure right **Rev:** Five shields below crown **Mint:** Vienna **Note:** Dav. #3080. Prev. KM#B1787.

Date	Mintage	VG	F	VF	XF	Unc
1624 (c)	—	150	300	500	800	—

KM# 528 THALER
Silver **Ruler:** Ferdinand II **Obv:** Bust with ruffled collar right, legend without II **Mint:** Vienna **Note:** Dav. #3081. Prev. KM#C1787.

Date	Mintage	VG	F	VF	XF	Unc
1624 (c)	—	100	175	300	500	—

KM# 529 THALER
Silver **Ruler:** Ferdinand II **Obv:** Laureate armored bust right **Rev:** Crown above five shields **Mint:** Vienna **Note:** Dav. #3085. Prev. KM#1789.

Date	Mintage	VG	F	VF	XF	Unc
1624 (c)	—	100	175	300	500	—

KM# 530 THALER
Silver **Ruler:** Ferdinand II **Obv:** Larger head and different drapery **Rev:** Different crown, differently shaped shields **Mint:** Vienna **Note:** Dav. #3086. Prev. KM#A1789.

Date	Mintage	VG	F	VF	XF	Unc
1624 (c)	—	150	300	500	800	—

KM# 532 THALER
Silver **Ruler:** Ferdinand II **Obv:** Bust with thick striated collar right **Rev:** Crown above five shields with decorations between **Mint:** Vienna **Note:** Dav. #3083. Prev. KM#A1790.

Date	Mintage	VG	F	VF	XF	Unc
1624 (c)	—	100	175	300	500	—

KM# 533 THALER
Silver **Ruler:** Ferdinand II **Obv:** Bust with thin striated collar right **Rev:** Rearranged shields **Mint:** Vienna **Note:** Dav. #3084. Prev. KM#B1790.

Date	Mintage	VG	F	VF	XF	Unc
1624 (c)	—	100	175	300	500	—

KM# 534 THALER
Silver **Ruler:** Ferdinand II **Mint:** Vienna **Note:** Dav. #3087A. Klippe. Prev. KM#1791.

Date	Mintage	VG	F	VF	XF	Unc
1624 (c) Rare	—	—	—	—	—	—

KM# 599 THALER
Silver **Ruler:** Ferdinand II **Mint:** Vienna **Note:** Dav. #3091. Varieties exist. Prev. KM#1787.

Date	Mintage	VG	F	VF	XF	Unc
1625 (c)	—	35.00	100	175	300	—
1626/5 (c)	—	35.00	100	175	300	—
1626 (c)	—	35.00	100	175	300	—
1627 (c)	—	35.00	100	175	300	—
1628 (c)	—	35.00	100	175	300	—
1629 (c)	—	35.00	100	175	300	—
1630 (c)	—	35.00	100	175	300	—
1631 (c)	—	35.00	100	175	300	—
1632 (c)	—	35.00	100	175	300	—
1633 (c)	—	35.00	100	175	300	—
1634 (c)	—	35.00	100	175	300	—
1635 (c)	—	35.00	100	175	300	—
1636 (c)	—	35.00	100	175	300	—
1636 (v)	—	35.00	100	175	300	—
1637 (v)	—	35.00	100	175	300	—
1638 (v)	—	35.00	100	175	300	—

KM# 600 THALER
Silver **Ruler:** Ferdinand II **Mint:** Vienna **Note:** Klippe. Dav. #3091A. Varieties exist. Prev. KM#1788.

Date	Mintage	VG	F	VF	XF	Unc
1625 (c) Rare	—	—	—	—	—	—
1628 (c) Rare	—	—	—	—	—	—
1630 (c) Rare	—	—	—	—	—	—
1633 (c) Rare	—	—	—	—	—	—
1634 (c) Rare	—	—	—	—	—	—
1635 (c) Rare	—	—	—	—	—	—
1637 (v) Rare	—	—	—	—	—	—

KM# 598 THALER
Silver **Ruler:** Ferdinand II **Obv:** Armored laureate bust right **Obv. Legend:** ... COM. TYR. **Mint:** Vienna **Note:** Similar to KM#599. Dav. #3088. Prev. KM#D1787.

Date	Mintage	VG	F	VF	XF	Unc
1625 (c)	—	50.00	100	175	300	—

KM# 628 THALER
Silver **Ruler:** Ferdinand II **Rev:** Ornamented shield of arms, different crown **Mint:** Graz **Note:** Dav. #3108. Varieties exist. Prev. KM#380.

Date	Mintage	VG	F	VF	XF	Unc
1626	—	35.00	100	175	250	—
1627	—	35.00	100	175	250	—
1628	—	35.00	100	175	250	—
1629	—	35.00	100	175	250	—
1630	—	35.00	100	175	250	—
1631/0	—	35.00	100	175	250	—
1631	—	35.00	100	175	250	—

KM# 629.1 THALER
Silver **Ruler:** Leopold **Obv:** Crossed half figure in armor with sword and scepter, date in front **Rev:** Crowned arms with decorations on sides **Mint:** Hall **Note:** Dav. #3337. Prev. KM#804.1.

Date	Mintage	VG	F	VF	XF	Unc
1626	—	45.00	100	175	275	—
1627	—	45.00	100	175	275	—

KM# 629.2 THALER
Silver **Ruler:** Leopold **Obv:** Different armor **Rev:** Order chain around arms **Rev. Legend:** ...TIROLIS **Mint:** Hall **Note:** Dav. #3338. Prev. KM#804.2.

Date	Mintage	VG	F	VF	XF	Unc
1628	—	45.00	100	175	275	—
1630	—	45.00	100	175	275	—
1632	—	45.00	100	175	275	—

KM# 629.3 THALER

Silver **Ruler:** Leopold **Rev. Legend:** ...AVSTIÆ (error) **Mint:** Hall **Note:** Dav. #3338A. Prev. KM#804.3.

Date	Mintage	VG	F	VF	XF	Unc
1632	—	35.00	85.00	145	250	—

KM# 629.4 THALER

Silver **Ruler:** Leopold **Obv:** Crowned 1/2-length figure right with sceptre and sword **Obv. Legend:** LEOPOLDVS • D: G: ARCHIDVX • AVSTRIÆ **Rev:** Crowned arms within order chain **Rev. Legend:** DVX • BVRGVND: — COMES • TIROLIS **Mint:** Hall **Note:** Dav. #3338B. Prev. KM#804.4.

Date	Mintage	VG	F	VF	XF	Unc
1632	—	35.00	85.00	145	250	—

KM# 630 THALER

Silver **Ruler:** Leopold **Mint:** Hall **Note:** Dav. #3337A. Klippe. Prev. KM#A805.

Date	Mintage	VG	F	VF	XF	Unc
1626	—	500	900	1,800	3,500	—

KM# 631 THALER

Silver **Ruler:** Ferdinand II **Obv:** Bust in laurel wreath **Rev:** Fuller Order chain **Mint:** Saint Polten **Note:** Dav. #3097. Varieties exist. Prev. KM#1574.6.

Date	Mintage	VG	F	VF	XF	Unc
1626 (r)	—	350	600	1,000	1,750	—

KM# 677 THALER

28.4000 g., Silver **Ruler:** Leopold **Subject:** Wedding of Leopold and Claudia **Obv:** Crowned busts of royal couple right within inner circle **Rev:** Imperial eagle within inner circle **Mint:** Hall **Note:** Mule. Struck on 1/2 Thaler dies. Dav. #3334. Prev. KM#806.

Date	Mintage	VG	F	VF	XF	Unc
ND Rare	—	—	—	—	—	—

KM# 678 THALER

Silver **Ruler:** Ferdinand II **Mint:** Saint Veit **Note:** Dav. #3124. Varieties exist. Prev. KM#1603.

Date	Mintage	VG	F	VF	XF	Unc
1627 (g)	—	75.00	150	300	650	—
1628 (g)	—	75.00	150	300	650	—
1632	—	75.00	150	300	650	—

KM# 675 THALER

Silver **Ruler:** Ferdinand III **Obv:** Armored bust of Ferdinand III wearing ruffled collar right **Rev:** Crowned ornate oval arms in Order chain **Mint:** Glatz **Note:** Dav. #3356. Prev. KM#300.

Date	Mintage	VG	F	VF	XF	Unc
1627 (c)	—	350	600	1,000	1,750	—
1627 AP	—	350	600	1,000	1,750	—

KM# 676 THALER

Silver **Ruler:** Ferdinand II **Obv:** Date below bust **Rev:** Crowned ornamented shield of arms **Mint:** Graz **Note:** Klippe. Prev. KM#382.

Date	Mintage	VG	F	VF	XF	Unc
1627 Rare	—	—	—	—	—	—

KM# 699.1 THALER

Silver **Ruler:** Ferdinand III **Obv:** Armored bust of Ferdinand III wearing wide ruffled collar right **Rev:** Crowned ornate flat-topped arms in Order chain **Mint:** Glatz **Note:** Varieties exist. Dav. #3357. Prev. KM#301.1.

Date	Mintage	VG	F	VF	XF	Unc
1628 (p)	—	250	500	900	1,500	—
1629 (p)	—	250	500	900	1,500	—

KM# 699.2 THALER

Silver **Ruler:** Ferdinand III **Obv:** Without HP monogram **Mint:** Glatz **Note:** Dav. #3357A. Prev. KM#301.2.

Date	Mintage	VG	F	VF	XF	Unc
1629	—	250	500	900	1,500	—

KM# 699.3 THALER

Silver **Ruler:** Ferdinand III **Obv:** Armored bust of Ferdinand III wearing narrow ruffled collar right **Mint:** Glatz **Note:** Dav. #3361. Prev. KM#301.3.

Date	Mintage	VG	F	VF	XF	Unc
1629 HG	—	250	500	900	1,500	—

KM# 700 THALER
Silver **Ruler:** Ferdinand II **Obv:** Laureate bust right with ruffled collar **Mint:** Olmutz **Note:** Dav. #3148. Prev. KM#1237.

Date	Mintage	VG	F	VF	XF	Unc
1628 H-N(I) Rare	—	—	—	—	—	—
1630 (o)/M-F Rare	—	—	—	—	—	—

KM# 711 THALER
Silver **Ruler:** Ferdinand III **Rev:** Crowned plain arms in Order chain **Mint:** Glatz **Note:** Dav. #3360. Prev. KM#302.

Date	Mintage	VG	F	VF	XF	Unc
1629 (p)	—	250	500	900	1,500	—
1630 (p)	—	250	500	900	1,500	—
1630	—	250	500	900	1,500	—
1631 (h)	—	250	500	900	1,500	—

KM# 713 THALER
Silver **Ruler:** Ferdinand III **Obv:** Armored bust of Ferdinand III wearing wide ruffled collar right, HP monogram below **Rev:** Hungarian shield at left, and Bohemian shields at right, Vienna shield at bottom in legend **Mint:** Glatz **Note:** Dav. #3359. Prev. KM#304.

Date	Mintage	VG	F	VF	XF	Unc
1629 (p)	—	350	650	1,500	2,500	—
1630 (p)	—	350	650	1,500	2,500	—

KM# 712 THALER
Silver **Ruler:** Ferdinand III **Rev:** Radiant Madonna and child with HP monogram below **Rev. Legend:** FECIT MAGNA POTENS **Mint:** Glatz **Note:** Varieties exist. Dav. #3358. Prev. KM#303.

Date	Mintage	VG	F	VF	XF	Unc
1629 (h)	—	350	650	1,500	2,500	—

KM# 714 THALER
Silver **Ruler:** Ferdinand III **Rev:** Radiant Madonna and child with HP monogram below **Rev. Legend:** FECIT MAGNA POTENS **Mint:** Glatz **Note:** Dav. #3359A. Prev. KM#A304.

Date	Mintage	VG	F	VF	XF	Unc
1629 (h)//(h)	—	350	600	1,000	1,750	—

KM# 746 THALER
Silver **Ruler:** Ferdinand II **Mint:** Furth **Note:** Dav. #3167. Prev. KM#287.

Date	Mintage	VG	F	VF	XF	Unc
1630 CS Rare	—	—	—	—	—	—

KM# 747 THALER
Silver **Ruler:** Ferdinand III **Obv:** Armored bust of Ferdinand III wearing wide ruffled collar 3/4 right **Rev:** Crowned ornate arms in Order chain **Mint:** Glatz **Note:** Dav. #3362. Prev. KM#305.

Date	Mintage	VG	F	VF	XF	Unc
1630 (p) Rare	—	—	—	—	—	—

KM# 748 THALER
Silver **Ruler:** Ferdinand II **Obv:** Ornamented inner circle **Mint:** Graz **Note:** Dav. #3110A. Prev. KM#383.

Date	Mintage	VG	F	VF	XF	Unc
1630 Rare	—	—	—	—	—	—

KM# 749.1 THALER
Silver **Ruler:** Ferdinand II **Obv. Legend:** ...D. G. ROM. IMP. S. A. G. H. BO. REX. **Rev:** Large crown and arms **Rev. Legend:** ...BVRG... **Mint:** Graz **Note:** Dav. #3110. Prev. KM#384.

Date	Mintage	VG	F	VF	XF	Unc
1630	—	35.00	100	175	250	—
1631	—	35.00	100	175	250	—
1632	—	35.00	100	175	250	—
1632/1	—	35.00	100	175	250	—
1633	—	35.00	100	175	250	—
1633/2	—	35.00	100	175	250	—
1636	—	35.00	100	175	250	—

KM# 749.3 THALER
Silver **Ruler:** Ferdinand II **Rev:** Crowned plain shield without ornamentation **Mint:** Graz **Note:** Dav. #3110B. Prev. KM#384.3.

Date	Mintage	VG	F	VF	XF	Unc
1631	—	35.00	100	175	250	—
1632	—	35.00	100	175	250	—

KM# 750 THALER
Silver **Ruler:** Ferdinand II **Mint:** Graz **Note:** Dav. #3110C. Klippe. Prev. KM#385.

Date	Mintage	VG	F	VF	XF	Unc
1632 Rare	—	—	—	—	—	—
1633/2 Rare	—	—	—	—	—	—
1636 Rare	—	—	—	—	—	—

KM# 783 THALER
Silver **Ruler:** Leopold **Rev. Legend:** ...TIROLI. **Mint:** Hall **Note:** Prev. KM#A804.3.

Date	Mintage	VG	F	VF	XF	Unc
1632	—	22.50	45.00	90.00	165	—

KM# 784 THALER
Silver **Ruler:** Leopold **Obv:** Fancier embroidery on jacket **Mint:** Hall **Note:** Prev. KM#A804.4.

Date	Mintage	VG	F	VF	XF	Unc
1632	—	22.50	45.00	90.00	165	—

KM# 785 THALER

Silver **Ruler:** Leopold **Mint:** Hall **Note:** Dav. #3338C. Klippe. Prev. KM#805.

Date	Mintage	VG	F	VF	XF	Unc
1632	—	450	750	1,650	3,000	—

KM# 816 THALER

Silver **Ruler:** Ferdinand III **Obv:** Robed bust of Ferdinand III right **Rev:** Crowned ornate arms in Order chain **Mint:** Glatz **Note:** Dav. #A3363. Prev. KM#306.

Date	Mintage	VG	F	VF	XF	Unc
1636 O Rare	—	—	—	—	—	—

KM# 817 THALER

Silver **Ruler:** Ferdinand II **Obv. Legend:** FERDINAN: II: D • - G • **Mint:** Graz **Note:** Dav. #3111. Prev. KM#381.

Date	Mintage	VG	F	VF	XF	Unc
1636	—	35.00	100	175	250	—

KM# 840 THALER

0.8330 Silver **Ruler:** Ferdinand III **Obv:** Laureate bust with lace collar right **Rev:** With flat-topped shield on breast **Mint:** Vienna **Note:** Dav. #3174. Varieties exist. Prev. KM#1826.

Date	Mintage	VG	F	VF	XF	Unc
1637 (b)	—	65.00	125	200	350	—
1638 (b)	—	65.00	125	200	350	—
1639 (b)	—	65.00	125	200	350	—
1640 (b)	—	65.00	125	200	350	—
1641 (b)	—	65.00	125	200	350	—
1642 (b)	—	65.00	125	200	350	—
1643 (b)	—	65.00	125	200	350	—
1644 (b)	—	65.00	125	200	350	—
1645 (b)	—	65.00	125	200	350	—
1646 (b)	—	65.00	125	200	350	—
1647 (b)	—	65.00	125	200	350	—
1648 (b)	—	65.00	125	200	350	—
1648 (c)	—	65.00	125	200	350	—
1649 (c)	—	65.00	125	200	350	—

KM# 841 THALER

0.8330 Silver **Ruler:** Ferdinand III **Mint:** Vienna **Note:** Klippe. Dav. #3174A. Prev. KM#1827.

Date	Mintage	VG	F	VF	XF	Unc
1637 Rare	—	—	—	—	—	—

KM# 857 THALER

Silver **Ruler:** Ferdinand III **Obv:** Laureate bust, date below **Rev:** Crowned ornamental arms with flat-topped shield **Mint:** Graz **Note:** Dav. #3185. Prev. KM#428.

Date	Mintage	VG	F	VF	XF	Unc
1638	—	45.00	100	250	500	—

KM# 858 THALER

Silver **Ruler:** Ferdinand III **Mint:** Saint Veit **Note:** Dav. #3192. Prev. KM#1626.

Date	Mintage	VG	F	VF	XF	Unc
1638	—	75.00	150	300	650	—
1642	—	75.00	150	300	650	—

KM# 881 THALER

Silver **Ruler:** Ferdinand III **Obv:** Punctuated date below bust - 1.6.4.0. **Mint:** Graz **Note:** Dav. #3186. Prev. KM#429.

Date	Mintage	VG	F	VF	XF	Unc
1640	—	45.00	100	250	500	—

KM# 882 THALER

0.8330 Silver **Ruler:** Ferdinand III **Obv:** Oval shield on eagle **Mint:** Vienna **Note:** Dav. #3175. Varieties exist. Prev. KM#1828.

Date	Mintage	VG	F	VF	XF	Unc
1640 (b)	—	75.00	150	250	400	—
1641 (b)	—	75.00	150	250	400	—
1643 (b)	—	75.00	150	250	400	—
1645 (b)	—	75.00	150	250	400	—

KM# 883 THALER

0.8330 Silver **Ruler:** Ferdinand III **Mint:** Vienna **Note:** Dav. #3175A. Prev. KM#1829.

Date	Mintage	VG	F	VF	XF	Unc
1640 Rare	—	—	—	—	—	—
1641 Rare	—	—	—	—	—	—

KM# 895 THALER

Silver **Ruler:** Ferdinand III **Obv:** Ornamental inner circle **Rev:** Date divided above crown **Mint:** Graz **Note:** Dav. #3187. Prev. KM#430.

Date	Mintage	VG	F	VF	XF	Unc
1641	—	45.00	100	250	500	—

KM# 896 THALER

Silver **Ruler:** Ferdinand III **Mint:** Graz **Note:** Dav. #3187A. Klippe. Prev. KM#431.

Date	Mintage	VG	F	VF	XF	Unc
1641	—	300	600	1,200	2,000	—

KM# 920 THALER

Silver **Ruler:** Ferdinand III **Obv:** Plain inner circles **Rev:** Date above crown **Mint:** Graz **Note:** Dav. #3189. Prev. KM#432.

Date	Mintage	VG	F	VF	XF	Unc
1644	—	35.00	100	200	450	—
1646	—	35.00	100	200	450	—
1650	—	35.00	100	200	450	—

KM# 924 THALER

Silver **Ruler:** Ferdinand III **Mint:** Saint Veit **Note:** Dav. #3194. Varieties exist. Prev. KM#1627.

Date	Mintage	VG	F	VF	XF	Unc
1645	—	75.00	150	300	650	—
1649	—	75.00	150	300	650	—
1650	—	75.00	150	300	650	—
1654	—	75.00	150	300	650	—
1657	—	75.00	150	300	650	—

KM# 929.1 THALER

Silver **Ruler:** Ferdinand III **Obv. Legend:** FERDINANDVS. III. D: G: MM. R: I: S: A: G: HVN: BO: REX. **Rev. Legend:** ARCHID: AVS: D: VX:, arms, BVR: C: TYR: C:, date **Mint:** Brunn **Note:** Dav. #3216. Prev. KM#223.1.

Date	Mintage	VG	F	VF	XF	Unc
1646 (o)	—	550	1,000	1,650	2,500	—
1648 (o)	—	550	1,000	1,650	2,500	—

KM# 929.2 THALER

Silver **Ruler:** Ferdinand III **Obv. Legend:** ...ROM: IM: SE: AV: GE: HV: BO: REX. **Rev:** Eagle arms below eagle **Mint:** Brunn **Note:** Dav. #3217. Prev. KM#223.2.

Date	Mintage	VG	F	VF	XF	Unc
1647 (t)	—	550	1,000	1,650	2,500	—

KM# 932.1 THALER

Silver **Ruler:** Ferdinand Charles **Obv:** Bust right with date in front **Rev:** Crowned arms in Order chain **Mint:** Hall **Note:** Dav. #3365. Prev. KM#833.1.

Date	Mintage	VG	F	VF	XF	Unc
1646	—	75.00	150	275	550	—

KM# 932.2 THALER

Silver **Ruler:** Ferdinand Charles **Obv:** Older, larger bust **Rev:** Smaller arms **Mint:** Hall **Note:** Dav. #3366. Prev. KM#833.2.

Date	Mintage	VG	F	VF	XF	Unc
1652	—	75.00	150	275	550	—

KM# 932.4 THALER

Silver **Ruler:** Ferdinand Charles **Obv:** Larger bust dividing legend at top **Rev:** Date above crown **Mint:** Hall **Note:** Dav. #3368. Prev. KM#833.4.

Date	Mintage	VG	F	VF	XF	Unc
1662	—	175	350	550	900	—

KM# 930 THALER

Silver **Ruler:** Ferdinand III **Obv:** Date below bust **Rev:** Date divided by crown **Mint:** Graz **Note:** Dav. #3189A. Prev. KM#433.

Date	Mintage	VG	F	VF	XF	Unc
1646//1646	—	35.00	100	200	450	—

KM# 931 THALER

Silver **Ruler:** Ferdinand III **Mint:** Graz **Note:** Dav. #3189B. Klippe. Prev. KM#434.

Date	Mintage	VG	F	VF	XF	Unc
1646//1646	—	225	400	600	1,000	—

KM# 957 THALER

Silver **Ruler:** Ferdinand III **Obv:** Larger laureate bust **Obv. Legend:** FERDINAND. III. D. G. ROM. IMP. S. A. G. H. B. REX. **Mint:** Graz **Note:** Dav. #3190. Prev. KM#435.

Date	Mintage	VG	F	VF	XF	Unc
1648	—	35.00	100	250	500	—
1649	—	35.00	100	250	500	—
1650	—	35.00	100	250	500	—
1651	—	35.00	100	250	500	—
1653	—	35.00	100	250	500	—
1654	—	35.00	100	250	500	—

KM# 958 THALER

0.8330 Silver **Ruler:** Ferdinand III **Obv:** Bust with plain collar **Rev:** Flat-topped shield of arms **Mint:** Vienna **Note:** Dav. #3177. Prev. KM#1830.1.

Date	Mintage	VG	F	VF	XF	Unc
1648	—	85.00	165	300	550	—
1649	—	85.00	165	300	550	—

KM# 959 THALER

0.8330 Silver **Ruler:** Ferdinand III **Obv:** Bust with plain collar and lapels **Mint:** Vienna **Note:** Dav. #3179. Prev. KM#1830.2.

Date	Mintage	VG	F	VF	XF	Unc
1648	—	85.00	165	300	550	—
1649	—	85.00	165	300	550	—

KM# 972 THALER

0.8330 Silver **Ruler:** Ferdinand III **Mint:** Vienna **Note:** Dav. #3180. Prev. KM#1831.

Date	Mintage	VG	F	VF	XF	Unc
1650 (c)	—	85.00	165	300	550	—

KM# 975 THALER

0.8330 Silver **Ruler:** Ferdinand III **Obv:** Bust with heavy drapery **Mint:** Vienna **Note:** Dav. #3181. Prev. KM#1832.

Date	Mintage	VG	F	VF	XF	Unc
1651 (c)	—	85.00	165	300	550	—

KM# 977 THALER

0.8330 Silver **Ruler:** Ferdinand III **Obv:** Bust with light drapery **Mint:** Vienna **Note:** Dav. #3183. Varieties exist. Prev. KM#1833.

Date	Mintage	VG	F	VF	XF	Unc
1652 (c)	—	100	200	375	750	—
1653 (c)	—	100	200	375	750	—
1654 (c)	—	100	200	375	750	—
1655 (c)	—	100	200	375	750	—

KM# 933.3 THALER

Silver **Ruler:** Ferdinand Charles **Obv:** Older, thinner bust **Mint:** Hall **Note:** Dav. #3367. Prev. KM#833.3.

Date	Mintage	VG	F	VF	XF	Unc
1654	—	50.00	120	250	500	—

KM# 1003 THALER

Silver **Ruler:** Ferdinand III **Obv:** Older laureate bust with short beard, date above **Mint:** Graz **Note:** Dav. #3191. Prev. KM#436.

Date	Mintage	VG	F	VF	XF	Unc
1657 HCK	—	200	350	600	1,150	—

KM# 1004 THALER

0.8330 Silver **Ruler:** Ferdinand III **Obv:** Large bust **Rev:** Crowned oval arms **Mint:** Vienna **Note:** Dav. #A3184. Prev. KM#1834.

Date	Mintage	VG	F	VF	XF	Unc
1657 (c)	—	100	200	350	750	—

KM# 1005 THALER

0.8330 Silver **Ruler:** Ferdinand III **Obv:** Small laureate bust right in plain inner circle, punctuated date below bust **Rev:** Crowned arms in flat-topped shield in Order collar and inner circle **Mint:** Vienna **Note:** Dav. #3184. Prev. KM#1835.

Date	Mintage	VG	F	VF	XF	Unc
1657	—	100	200	350	750	—

KM# 1118 THALER

Silver **Ruler:** Leopold I **Mint:** Vienna **Note:** Dav. #3223. Prev. KM#1868.

Date	Mintage	VG	F	VF	XF	Unc
1658 (c)	—	350	700	1,250	2,500	—

KM# 1156 THALER

Silver **Ruler:** Leopold I **Obv:** Laureate bust right, wavy hair **Rev:** Hapsburg arms on breast of eagle **Mint:** Vienna **Note:** Dav. #3224. Prev. KM#1869.

Date	Mintage	VG	F	VF	XF	Unc
1659 (c)	—	300	550	1,100	2,000	—

KM# 1175 THALER

Silver **Ruler:** Leopold I **Obv:** Laureate bust right, date above **Obv. Legend:** LEOPOLDVS. -D. G. R.I. S. A. G. H. ET. B. REX. **Rev. Legend:** ... BVR. STYRIAE. ET. C. **Mint:** Graz **Note:** Dav. #3231. Prev. KM#463.

Date	Mintage	VG	F	VF	XF	Unc
1660	—	250	400	650	1,000	—
1662	—	250	400	650	1,000	—
1669 IGW	—	250	400	650	1,000	—

KM# 1176 THALER

Silver **Ruler:** Leopold I **Mint:** Saint Veit **Note:** Varieties exist. Dav. #3236. Prev. KM#1652.

Date	Mintage	VG	F	VF	XF	Unc
1660	—	400	750	1,250	2,250	—
1670	—	400	750	1,250	2,250	—

KM# 1200 THALER

Silver **Ruler:** Sigismund Franz **Rev:** Date above crown **Mint:** Hall **Note:** Dav. #3369. Prev. KM#854.

Date	Mintage	VG	F	VF	XF	Unc
1662 Rare	5,415	—	—	—	—	—

KM# 1237 THALER

Silver **Ruler:** Leopold I **Obv:** KM#643 **Rev. Legend:** DVV. BVRGVNDI: -COM: TYROLIS. **Mint:** Hall **Note:** Dav. #3239. Mule. Prev. KM#1237.

Date	Mintage	VG	F	VF	XF	Unc
1665	—	40.00	100	175	350	—

KM# 1238 THALER

Silver **Ruler:** Leopold I **Obv:** With lion's head in shoulder drapery **Rev. Legend:** ARCHID: AVST: -DVX. BV: CO: TYR **Mint:** Hall **Note:** Dav. #3240. Prev. KM#643.

Date	Mintage	VG	F	VF	XF	Unc
1665	—	40.00	100	175	350	—
1668	—	40.00	100	175	350	—

KM# 1239.1 THALER

Silver **Ruler:** Sigismund Franz **Obv. Legend:** ...AVS: **Rev:** Crown divides dates **Mint:** Hall **Note:** Dav. #3370. Prev. KM#855.1.

Date	Mintage	VG	F	VF	XF	Unc
1665	39,000	125	250	400	750	—

KM# 1239.2 THALER

Silver **Ruler:** Sigismund Franz **Obv. Legend:** ...AVST: **Rev:** Crown divides dates **Mint:** Hall **Note:** Dav. #3370A. Prev. KM#855.2.

Date	Mintage	VG	F	VF	XF	Unc
1665	Inc. above	125	250	400	750	—

KM# 1268.1 THALER

Silver **Ruler:** Leopold I **Rev:** Vienna arms on breast of eagle **Mint:** Vienna **Note:** Dav. #3225. Prev. KM#1870.1.

Date	Mintage	VG	F	VF	XF	Unc
1670 (r)	—	75.00	135	275	475	—

KM# 1268.2 THALER

Silver **Ruler:** Leopold I **Obv:** Large bust divides legend at bottom **Rev:** Larger Vienna arms **Mint:** Vienna **Note:** Dav. #3226. Prev. KM#1870.2.

Date	Mintage	VG	F	VF	XF	Unc
1671 (r)	—	65.00	125	250	450	—

KM# 1272 THALER

Silver **Ruler:** Leopold I **Obv. Legend:** ROM: IM: SE: AV: GE: HVN: BOH: **Rev:** Date divided by crown above arms **Mint:** Graz **Note:** Dav. #3232. Prev. KM#464.

Date	Mintage	VG	F	VF	XF	Unc
1671 IGW	—	60.00	125	250	400	—
1672 IAN	—	60.00	125	250	400	—
1674 IAN	—	60.00	125	250	400	—
1676 IAN	—	60.00	125	250	400	—
1678 IAN	—	60.00	125	250	400	—
1682 IAN	—	60.00	125	250	400	—
1684 IAN	—	60.00	125	250	400	—
1687 IAN	—	60.00	125	250	400	—
1688 IAN	—	60.00	125	250	400	—

KM# 1275.1 THALER

Silver **Ruler:** Leopold I **Obv:** Older bust **Rev:** Complex heart-shaped arms on eagle's breast **Mint:** Vienna **Note:** Dav. #3227. Prev. KM#1871.1.

Date	Mintage	VG	F	VF	XF	Unc
1672 Rare	—	—	—	—	—	—

KM# 1275.2 THALER

Silver **Ruler:** Leopold I **Obv. Legend:** ...G. H. ET. B. REX. **Rev. Legend:** ARCHID. AVST. (mint mark)DVX. B. COM. TYR. **Mint:** Vienna **Note:** Dav. #3228. Prev. KM#1871.2.

Date	Mintage	VG	F	VF	XF	Unc
1681 Rare	—	—	—	—	—	—
1683 With mint mark	—	—	—	—	—	—
1683	—	—	—	—	—	—

KM# 1275.3 THALER

Silver **Ruler:** Leopold I **Obv:** Older portrait **Rev. Legend:** ...TYRO: 16 (crown) **Mint:** Vienna **Note:** Dav. #3229. Prev. KM#1871.3.

Date	Mintage	VG	F	VF	XF	Unc
1692	—	35.00	100	175	300	—
1693	—	35.00	100	175	300	—
1695	—	35.00	100	175	300	—

KM# 1275.4 THALER
Silver **Ruler:** Leopold I **Obv:** Older portrait **Rev. Legend:** ...TYRO: 16: (crown) **Mint:** Vienna **Note:** Dav. #3229A. Prev. KM#1871.4.

Date	Mintage	VG	F	VF	XF	Unc
1695	—	35.00	100	175	300	—

KM# 1275.5 THALER
Silver **Ruler:** Leopold I **Obv:** Fatter bust **Rev. Legend:** ...TYRO **Mint:** Vienna **Note:** Dav. #3230. Prev. KM#1871.5.

Date	Mintage	VG	F	VF	XF	Unc
1696	—	35.00	100	175	300	—
1698	—	35.00	100	175	300	—
1699	—	35.00	100	175	300	—
1700	—	35.00	100	175	300	—

KM# 1303.1 THALER
Silver **Ruler:** Leopold I **Obv:** Armored bust without lion's head in shoulder drapery **Rev:** Crowned arms within Order chain **Mint:** Hall **Note:** Dav. #3241. Prev. KM#644.1.

Date	Mintage	VG	F	VF	XF	Unc
1679	—	30.00	90.00	150	300	—
1680	—	30.00	90.00	150	300	—
1682	—	30.00	90.00	150	300	—
1683	—	30.00	90.00	150	300	—
1686	—	30.00	90.00	150	300	—

KM# 1303.2 THALER
Silver **Ruler:** Leopold I **Obv:** Bust with lion's head in ornate shoulder drapery **Rev:** Crowned arms within Order chain **Mint:** Hall **Note:** Dav. #3243. Prev. KM#644.2.

Date	Mintage	VG	F	VF	XF	Unc
1691	—	30.00	90.00	150	300	—
1693	—	30.00	90.00	150	300	—
1694	—	30.00	90.00	150	300	—

KM# 1303.3 THALER
Silver **Ruler:** Leopold I **Obv:** Legend continuous below bust **Rev:** Crowned arms within Order chain **Mint:** Hall **Note:** Dav. #3244. Prev. KM#644.3.

Date	Mintage	VG	F	VF	XF	Unc
1694	—	30.00	90.00	150	300	—

KM# 1303.4 THALER
Silver **Ruler:** Leopold I **Obv:** Old laureate bust right in inner circle **Obv. Legend:** LEOPOLDVS • D: G: ROM: IMP: SE: A: G: H: B: REX • **Rev:** Crowned arms within Order chain **Rev. Legend:** ARCHID: AVST: DVX: BV: COM: TYR: **Mint:** Hall **Note:** Dav. #3245. Varieties exist. Prev. KM#644.4.

Date	Mintage	VG	F	VF	XF	Unc
1694 IAK	—	30.00	90.00	150	300	—
1695	—	30.00	90.00	150	300	—
1695 IAK	—	30.00	90.00	150	300	—
1696 IAK	—	30.00	90.00	150	300	—
1698	—	30.00	90.00	150	300	—
1700	—	30.00	90.00	150	300	—

KM# 1303.5 THALER
Silver **Ruler:** Leopold I **Obv:** Narrow bust **Rev:** Crowned arms within Order chain **Mint:** Hall **Note:** Dav. #3245A. Prev. KM#644.5.

Date	Mintage	VG	F	VF	XF	Unc
1696	—	30.00	90.00	150	300	—
1699	—	30.00	90.00	150	300	—

KM# 1308 THALER
Silver **Ruler:** Leopold I **Mint:** Hall **Note:** Dav. #3241A. Klippe. Prev. KM#645.

Date	Mintage	VG	F	VF	XF	Unc
1680 Rare	—	—	—	—	—	—

KM# 1321 THALER
Silver **Ruler:** Leopold I **Obv:** Older laureate bust right **Rev:** Crowned arms in Order collar, crown divides date **Mint:** Saint Veit **Note:** Varieties exist. Dav. #3237. Prev. KM#1653.

Date	Mintage	VG	F	VF	XF	Unc
1682 I-R Rare	—	—	—	—	—	—
1693 H-L	—	700	1,150	1,850	3,200	—

KM# 1348.1 THALER
Silver **Ruler:** Leopold I **Obv. Legend:** ...D. G. (decoration) ROM: IMP: SE: AV: G: H: B: REX: **Mint:** Graz **Note:** Dav. #3233. Prev. KM#465.1.

Date	Mintage	VG	F	VF	XF	Unc
1690	—	40.00	100	175	325	—

KM# 1348.2 THALER

Silver **Ruler:** Leopold I **Obv. Legend:** ...D. G. -R. I. S. A... **Mint:** Graz **Note:** Dav. #3234. Prev. KM#465.2.

Date	Mintage	VG	F	VF	XF	Unc
1693	—	40.00	100	175	325	—

KM# 1348.3 THALER

Silver **Ruler:** Leopold I **Obv. Legend:** ...D. G. spray ROM: OIMP:... **Mint:** Graz **Note:** Varieties exist. Dav. #3235. Prev. KM#465.3.

Date	Mintage	VG	F	VF	XF	Unc
1698	—	40.00	100	175	325	—

KM# 1349 THALER

Silver **Ruler:** Leopold I **Obv:** Laureate bust within inner circle, lion face on shoulder **Rev:** Crowned arms in order chain, crown divides date **Mint:** Hall **Note:** Dav. #3242. Prev. KM#646.

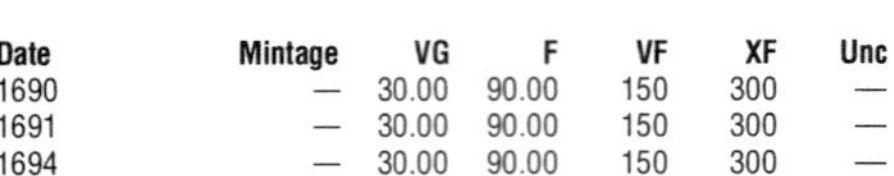

Date	Mintage	VG	F	VF	XF	Unc
1690	—	30.00	90.00	150	300	—
1691	—	30.00	90.00	150	300	—
1694	—	30.00	90.00	150	300	—

KM# 1408 THALER

Silver **Ruler:** Leopold I **Mint:** Vienna **Note:** Dav. #3230A. Klippe. Prev. KM#1873.

Date	Mintage	VG	F	VF	XF	Unc
1700 Rare	—	—	—	—	—	—

KM# 786 1-1/4 THALER

Silver **Ruler:** Ferdinand II **Obv:** Laureate bust right in inner circle, date below bust **Rev:** Crowned arms in Order collar and inner circle **Mint:** Graz **Note:** Klippe. Prev. KM#386.

Date	Mintage	VG	F	VF	XF	Unc
1632 Rare	—	—	—	—	—	—

KM# 537 1-1/2 THALER

Silver **Ruler:** Ferdinand II **Obv:** Laureate bust right in inner circle **Rev:** Crown above five shields of arms in inner circle, date in legend **Mint:** Vienna **Note:** Klippe. Dav. #A3083. Prev. KM#1792.

Date	Mintage	VG	F	VF	XF	Unc
1624 (c) Rare	—	—	—	—	—	—

KM# 26 2 THALER

Silver **Ruler:** Ferdinand II **Obv:** Crowned and armored half figure with scepter on shoulder in inner circle **Rev:** Crowned flat-topped arms in Order collar of The Golden Fleece in inner circle, date in legend at upper left **Mint:** Graz **Note:** Dav. #3306. Prev. KM#571.

Date	Mintage	VG	F	VF	XF	Unc
1601 Rare	—	—	—	—	—	—
1602 Rare	—	—	—	—	—	—

KM# 27 2 THALER

Silver **Ruler:** Ferdinand II **Mint:** Graz **Note:** Dav. #3306A. Klippe. Prev. KM#572. Illustration reduced.

Date	Mintage	VG	F	VF	XF	Unc
1601	—	2,000	3,500	6,000	10,000	—

KM# 57.1 2 THALER

57.1900 g., Silver **Ruler:** Rudolf II **Obv. Legend:** RVDOLPHVS II: DG... **Mint:** Hall **Note:** Dav. #3004. Prev. KM#611.1.

Date	Mintage	VG	F	VF	XF	Unc
1604	—	220	425	825	1,500	—

KM# 57.2 2 THALER

Silver **Ruler:** Rudolf II **Obv:** Bust of Rudolph II right in inner circle **Obv. Legend:** RVDOLPHVS II: DG: ROM: IM: SEM: AV: GER: HV: BO: REX • **Mint:** Hall **Note:** Dav. #3004. Legend error. Prev. KM#611.2.

Date	Mintage	VG	F	VF	XF	Unc
1604	—	325	600	1,200	2,000	—

KM# 69 2 THALER

Silver **Ruler:** Ferdinand II **Rev. Legend:** DVX • BVRGUNDI... **Mint:** Graz **Note:** Dav. #A3307. Prev. KM#575.

Date	Mintage	VG	F	VF	XF	Unc
1605 Rare	—	—	—	—	—	—

KM# 70 2 THALER

Silver **Ruler:** Ferdinand II **Mint:** Graz **Note:** Dav. #A3307A. Klippe. Prev. KM#576.

Date	Mintage	VG	F	VF	XF	Unc
1605 Rare	—	—	—	—	—	—

KM# 83 2 THALER

Silver **Ruler:** Rudolf II **Obv:** Armored bust in ruffled collar right **Mint:** Vienna **Note:** Dav. #3001. Prev. KM#1716.

Date	Mintage	VG	F	VF	XF	Unc
1607	—	450	750	1,250	2,000	—

KM# 105 2 THALER

Silver **Ruler:** Ferdinand II **Rev. Legend:** DVX • BVRGUNDI... **Mint:** Graz **Note:** Dav. #3309. Prev. KM#577.

Date	Mintage	VG	F	VF	XF	Unc
1609 Rare	—	—	—	—	—	—

KM# 106 2 THALER

Silver **Ruler:** Ferdinand II **Mint:** Graz **Note:** Dav. #A3309. Klippe. Prev. KM#578.

Date	Mintage	VG	F	VF	XF	Unc
1609 Rare	—	—	—	—	—	—

KM# 107 2 THALER

Silver **Ruler:** Matthias II **Obv:** Crowned bust in ruffled collar right in inner circle **Rev:** Crowned arms in Order collar in inner circle, date in legend **Mint:** Vienna **Note:** Titles as designated King of Bohemia. Dav. #A3037. Prev. KM#1747.

Date	Mintage	VG	F	VF	XF	Unc
1609 Rare	—	—	—	—	—	—

KM# 123 2 THALER
Silver **Ruler:** Ferdinand II **Mint:** Klagenfurt **Note:** Dav. #3313. Similar to 1 Thaler, KM#24. Local issue for Archduke Ferdinand. Prev. KM#992.

Date	Mintage	VG	F	VF	XF	Unc
1610 Rare	—	—	—	—	—	—
1611 Rare	—	—	—	—	—	—
1613 Rare	—	—	—	—	—	—
1620 Rare	—	—	—	—	—	—

KM# 131 2 THALER
Silver **Ruler:** Matthias II **Mint:** Vienna **Note:** Titles as King of Bohemia. Dav. #A3040. Prev. KM#1748.

Date	Mintage	VG	F	VF	XF	Unc
1611 Rare	—	—	—	—	—	—

KM# 145 2 THALER
Silver **Ruler:** Matthias II **Obv:** Smaller bust and crown **Mint:** Vienna **Note:** Titles as King of Bohemia. Dav. #A3041. Prev. KM#1749.

Date	Mintage	VG	F	VF	XF	Unc
1612	—	2,000	4,000	6,000	9,500	—

KM# 170 2 THALER
Silver **Ruler:** Maximilian **Mint:** Hall **Note:** Dav. #A3316. Similar to 1 Thaler, KM#166. Prev. KM#775.

Date	Mintage	VG	F	VF	XF	Unc
1613 Rare	—	—	—	—	—	—

KM# 189 2 THALER
Silver **Ruler:** Matthias II **Obv:** Laureate, armored bust right in inner circle **Rev:** Crowned imperial eagle with shield on breast with sword and scepter in inner circle, date in legend **Mint:** Vienna **Note:** Titles as Emperor. Dav. #A3042. Prev. KM#1750.

Date	Mintage	VG	F	VF	XF	Unc
1614	—	1,000	1,850	3,250	5,500	—

KM# 197 2 THALER
Silver **Ruler:** Matthias II **Rev:** Larger crown above eagle **Mint:** Vienna **Note:** Titles as Emperor. Dav. #A3044. Prev. KM#1751.

Date	Mintage	VG	F	VF	XF	Unc
1615	—	950	1,750	3,000	5,000	—

KM# 207 2 THALER
Silver **Ruler:** Matthias II **Rev:** Smaller crown above eagle **Mint:** Vienna **Note:** Titles as Emperor. Dav. #3045. Prev. KM#1752.

Date	Mintage	VG	F	VF	XF	Unc
1616	—	1,000	1,850	3,250	5,500	—
1617	—	1,000	1,850	3,250	5,500	—

KM# 229.1 2 THALER
Silver **Ruler:** Matthias II **Obv:** Laureate bust with wide ruffle **Mint:** Vienna **Note:** Titles as Emperor. Dav. #A3047. Thick planchet. Prev. KM#1753.1.

Date	Mintage	VG	F	VF	XF	Unc
1618	—	1,000	1,850	3,250	5,500	—

KM# 229.2 2 THALER
Silver **Ruler:** Matthias II **Mint:** Vienna **Note:** Titles as Emperor. Thin planchet. Prev. KM#1753.2.

Date	Mintage	VG	F	VF	XF	Unc
1619	—	1,000	1,850	3,250	5,500	—

KM# 271 2 THALER
Silver **Ruler:** Ferdinand II **Obv:** Crowned half-length figure right **Rev:** Crowned arms **Mint:** Klagenfurt **Note:** Prev. KM#975.

Date	Mintage	VG	F	VF	XF	Unc
1620 Rare	—	—	—	—	—	—

KM# 272 2 THALER
Silver **Ruler:** Ferdinand II **Obv:** Crowned bust right in inner circle **Rev:** Crowned imperial eagle with flat-topped shield of arms on breast in inner circle, crown divides date **Mint:** Klagenfurt **Note:** Dav. #3113. Varieties exist. Prev. KM#976.

Date	Mintage	VG	F	VF	XF	Unc
1620	—	550	1,050	1,950	3,100	—

KM# 356 2 THALER
Silver **Ruler:** Ferdinand II **Obv:** Tall, thin crowned bust **Mint:** Klagenfurt **Note:** Dav. #3117. Prev. KM#977.

Date	Mintage	VG	F	VF	XF	Unc
1621 Rare	—	—	—	—	—	—

KM# 273.1 2 THALER
Silver **Ruler:** Ferdinand II **Mint:** Vienna **Note:** Dav. #A3074. Similar to 1 Thaler, KM#268.1. Prev. KM#1793.1.

Date	Mintage	VG	F	VF	XF	Unc
16Z0	—	325	550	1,000	1,650	—

KM# 273.2 2 THALER
Silver **Ruler:** Ferdinand II **Obv:** Without bow knot on laureate wreath **Mint:** Vienna **Note:** Dav. #3075. Similar to 1 Thaler, KM#268.1. Prev. KM#1793.2.

Date	Mintage	VG	F	VF	XF	Unc
16Z1	—	325	550	1,000	1,650	—
16Z2	—	325	550	1,000	1,650	—

KM# 273.3 2 THALER
Silver **Ruler:** Ferdinand II **Obv:** Older bust **Mint:** Vienna **Note:** Dav. #3077. Varieties exist. Prev. KM#1793.3.

Date	Mintage	VG	F	VF	XF	Unc
1623	—	325	550	1,000	1,650	—
1624	—	325	550	1,000	1,650	—

KM# 273.4 2 THALER
Silver **Ruler:** Ferdinand II **Obv:** Older ruffld collar laureate bust right **Obv. Legend:** + FERDINANDVS • II • D: G • RISAVG • G • HVN • BOH • REX **Rev:** Jeweled crown above imperial eagle **Rev. Legend:** ARCHID • AVS • DVX • (shield) BUR • GO • TYR • **Mint:** Vienna **Note:** Dav.#3079.

Date	Mintage	VG	F	VF	XF	Unc
1624	—	325	550	1,000	1,650	—

KM# 355 2 THALER
Silver **Ruler:** Ferdinand II **Obv:** Crowned bust with high ruffled collar right, lion's face on shoulder **Obv. Legend:** FERDINANDVS • II • D • G • ROM • IMP • S • A • GER • HVNG • ET • BO • REX • **Rev:** Crowned imperial eagle, complex arms within order chain on breast **Rev. Legend:** ARCHI • AVSTRIAE • DVX •. B - VRGVNDIAE • STYRIAE • ETC • **Mint:** Graz **Note:** Dav. #3301A. Varieties exist. Prev. KM#387.

Date	Mintage	VG	F	VF	XF	Unc
1621	—	275	550	1,000	1,650	—

KM# 357 2 THALER
Silver **Ruler:** Ferdinand II **Obv:** Crowned bust right **Rev:** Heraldic imperial eagle **Mint:** Klagenfurt **Note:** Prev. KM#978.

Date	Mintage	VG	F	VF	XF	Unc
1621 Rare	—	—	—	—	—	—

KM# 457 2 THALER
Silver **Ruler:** Ferdinand II **Obv:** Standing figure right **Rev:** Heraldic imperial eagle **Mint:** Brunn **Note:** Klippe. Prev. KM#219.

Date	Mintage	VG	F	VF	XF	Unc
1623 GR Rare	—	—	—	—	—	—

KM# 545 2 THALER
Silver **Ruler:** Ferdinand II **Obv:** Laureate bust with plain collar right in inner circle **Rev:** Crown above five shields of arms in inner circle, date in legend **Mint:** Vienna **Note:** Dav. #3082. Prev. KM#1795.

Date	Mintage	VG	F	VF	XF	Unc
1624	—	325	550	1,000	1,650	—
1625	—	325	550	1,000	1,650	—

KM# 546 2 THALER
Silver **Ruler:** Ferdinand II **Mint:** Vienna **Note:** Dav. #3082A. Klippe. Prev. KM#1796.

Date	Mintage	VG	F	VF	XF	Unc
1624 Rare	—	—	—	—	—	—

KM# 541 2 THALER
Silver **Ruler:** Ferdinand II **Obv:** Bust right **Rev:** Heraldic imperial eagle **Mint:** Brunn **Note:** Dav. #3145. Prev. KM#220.

Date	Mintage	VG	F	VF	XF	Unc
1624 B-(c) Rare	—	—	—	—	—	—

KM# 542 2 THALER
Silver **Ruler:** Ferdinand II **Mint:** Brunn **Note:** Hexagonal klippe. Dav. #3145A. Prev. KM#221.

Date	Mintage	VG	F	VF	XF	Unc
1624 B-(c) Rare	—	—	—	—	—	—

KM# 544 2 THALER
Silver **Ruler:** Ferdinand II **Obv:** Laureate half-figure right in inner circle **Mint:** Vienna **Note:** Dav. #A3080. Prev. KM#1794.

Date	Mintage	VG	F	VF	XF	Unc
1624	—	3,250	5,000	7,250	10,500	—

KM# 610 2 THALER
Silver **Ruler:** Ferdinand II **Rev:** Different decorations between shields **Mint:** Vienna **Note:** Dav. #A3087. Prev. KM#A1795.

Date	Mintage	VG	F	VF	XF	Unc
1625 (c) Rare	—	—	—	—	—	—

KM# 609.1 2 THALER
Silver **Ruler:** Leopold **Obv:** Crowned half-length armored figure with sword and scepter **Rev:** Wreath above crowned eagle **Mint:** Hall **Note:** Dav. #3335. Prev. KM#807.1.

Date	Mintage	VG	F	VF	XF	Unc
ND(1625)	—	195	350	825	1,400	—

KM# 609.2 2 THALER
Silver **Ruler:** Leopold **Obv:** Date in front of figure **Rev:** Large wreath above eagle **Mint:** Hall **Note:** Dav. #3336. Prev. KM#807.2.

Date	Mintage	VG	F	VF	XF	Unc
ND(1625)	—	195	325	775	1,350	—

KM# 611 2 THALER
Silver **Ruler:** Ferdinand II **Rev:** Crowned imperial eagle in inner circle, date in legend **Mint:** Vienna **Note:** Dav. #3090. Varieties exist. Prev. KM#1797.

Date	Mintage	VG	F	VF	XF	Unc
1625 (c)	—	325	550	1,000	1,650	—
1626 (c)	—	325	550	1,000	1,650	—
1629 (c)	—	325	550	1,000	1,650	—
1631 (c)	—	325	550	1,000	1,650	—
1633 (c)	—	325	550	1,000	1,650	—
1634 (c)	—	325	550	1,000	1,650	—
1636 (v)	—	325	550	1,000	1,650	—

KM# 605 2 THALER
Silver **Ruler:** Ferdinand II **Obv:** Laureate bust right in inner circle of laurel, date below bust **Rev:** Crowned flat-topped arms in Order collar and inner circle **Mint:** Graz **Note:** Dav. #3105. Prev. KM#388.

Date	Mintage	VG	F	VF	XF	Unc
1625	—	275	550	1,000	1,650	—

KM# 606 2 THALER
Silver **Ruler:** Ferdinand II **Mint:** Graz **Note:** Dav. #3105A. Klippe. Prev. KM#389.

Date	Mintage	VG	F	VF	XF	Unc
1625 Rare	—	—	—	—	—	—

KM# 607 2 THALER
Silver **Ruler:** Ferdinand II **Obv:** Date above bust **Rev:** Crowned oval arms **Mint:** Graz **Note:** Dav. #3107. Prev. KM#390.

Date	Mintage	VG	F	VF	XF	Unc
1625	—	275	550	1,050	1,750	—
16Z6/5	—	275	550	1,050	1,750	—
1632/30/26	—	275	550	1,050	1,750	—

KM# 608 2 THALER
Silver **Ruler:** Ferdinand II **Mint:** Graz **Note:** Dav. #3107A. Klippe. Prev. KM#391.

Date	Mintage	VG	F	VF	XF	Unc
1625	—	550	1,050	1,950	3,300	—
1626	—	550	1,050	1,950	3,300	—

KM# 639 2 THALER
Silver **Ruler:** Leopold **Subject:** Wedding of Leopold and Claudia **Obv:** Conjoined busts of Leopold and Claudia right **Rev:** Crowned eagle within inner circle, legend around **Mint:** Hall **Note:** Dav. #3331. Prev. KM#808.

Date	Mintage	VG	F	VF	XF	Unc
ND(1626)	—	120	250	550	875	—

KM# 640 2 THALER
Silver **Ruler:** Leopold **Mint:** Hall **Note:** Dav. #3331A. Klippe. Prev. KM#809.

Date	Mintage	VG	F	VF	XF	Unc
ND(1626) Rare	—	—	—	—	—	—

KM# 641 2 THALER
Silver **Ruler:** Leopold **Obv:** More ornate crowns and robes **Rev:** Larger wreath above eagle **Mint:** Hall **Note:** Dav. #3332. Prev. KM#810.

Date	Mintage	VG	F	VF	XF	Unc
ND(1626)	—	140	275	725	1,300	—

KM# 643 2 THALER
Silver **Ruler:** Leopold **Obv:** Similar to KM#808. **Rev:** Wreath surrounds crowned eagle's head, without inner circle **Mint:** Hall **Note:** Dav. #3333. Prev. KM#822.

Date	Mintage	VG	F	VF	XF	Unc
ND(1626)	—	—	—	—	—	—

KM# A644 2 THALER
Silver **Ruler:** Leopold **Obv:** Jugate busts right **Obv. Legend:** LEOPOLDVS • ARCHID • AVS • ET • CLAVDIA • ARCHIDVCISA • AVS • MEDIC **Rev:** Wreath around crowned head of eagle with wings outspread **Rev. Legend:** ARCHIDVX: AVST: DVX: BVR: COM: TYROLIS **Shape:** Klippe **Mint:** Hall

Date	Mintage	VG	F	VF	XF	Unc
ND(1626)	—	—	—	—	—	—

KM# 642 2 THALER
Silver **Ruler:** Leopold **Obv:** Similar to KM#808. **Rev:** Similar to KM#810 **Mint:** Hall **Note:** Dav. #A3334. Mule. Prev. KM#821.

Date	Mintage	VG	F	VF	XF	Unc
ND(1626)	—	—	—	—	—	—

KM# 644 2 THALER
Silver **Ruler:** Leopold **Obv:** KM#808 **Rev:** Obverse KM#810 **Mint:** Hall **Note:** Dav. #A3334. Mule. Prev. KM#823.

Date	Mintage	VG	F	VF	XF	Unc
ND(1626)	—	—	—	—	—	—

KM# 680 2 THALER
Silver **Ruler:** Ferdinand III **Obv:** Armored bust of Ferdinand III wearing ruffled collar right **Rev:** Crowned ornate oval arms in Order chain **Mint:** Glatz **Note:** Dav. #A3356. Prev. KM#307.

Date	Mintage	VG	F	VF	XF	Unc
1627 (c) Rare	—	—	—	—	—	—

KM# 609.3 2 THALER
Silver **Ruler:** Leopold **Mint:** Hall **Note:** Dav. #A3338. Similar to 1 Thaler, KM#629.3. Prev. KM#807.3.

Date	Mintage	VG	F	VF	XF	Unc
1628	—	195	325	775	1,350	—

KM# 716 2 THALER
Silver **Ruler:** Ferdinand III **Rev:** Crowned plain arms in Order chain **Mint:** Glatz **Note:** Dav. #A3360. Prev. KM#A308.

Date	Mintage	VG	F	VF	XF	Unc
1629 (p) Rare	—	—	—	—	—	—

KM# 715 2 THALER
Silver **Ruler:** Ferdinand III **Rev:** Crowned ornate arms **Mint:** Glatz **Note:** Dav. #A3361. Prev. KM#308.

Date	Mintage	VG	F	VF	XF	Unc
1629 HG Rare	—	—	—	—	—	—

KM# 717 2 THALER
Silver **Ruler:** Ferdinand III **Mint:** Glatz **Note:** Similar to 1 Thaler, KM#712. Dav. #A3358. Prev. KM#309.

Date	Mintage	VG	F	VF	XF	Unc
1629 (p) Rare	—	—	—	—	—	—

KM# 718 2 THALER
Silver **Ruler:** Ferdinand II **Rev:** Similar to 1 Thaler, KM#1237 **Mint:** Olmutz **Note:** Dav. #3149. Prev. KM#1238.

Date	Mintage	VG	F	VF	XF	Unc
1629 (o) Rare	—	—	—	—	—	—

KM# 751 2 THALER

Silver **Ruler:** Ferdinand III **Mint:** Glatz **Note:** Similar to 1 Thaler, KM#747. Dav. #A3362. Prev. KM#310.

Date	Mintage	VG	F	VF	XF	Unc
1630 (p) Rare	—	—	—	—	—	—

KM# 769 2 THALER

Silver **Ruler:** Ferdinand II **Mint:** Graz **Note:** Klippe. Dav. #3109B. Prev. KM#394.

Date	Mintage	VG	F	VF	XF	Unc
1631 Rare	—	—	—	—	—	—

KM# 768 2 THALER

56.8300 g., Silver **Ruler:** Ferdinand II **Obv:** Plain inner circle, date below bust **Rev:** Ornamental shield of arms **Mint:** Graz **Note:** Dav. #A3109. Prev. KM#392.

Date	Mintage	VG	F	VF	XF	Unc
1631	—	275	550	1,000	1,650	—

KM# 876.1 2 THALER

Silver **Ruler:** Ferdinand III **Obv:** Laureate bust right, date below **Rev:** Crowned oval arms **Mint:** Graz **Note:** Dav. #A3186. Broad planchet. Prev. KM#437.1.

Date	Mintage	VG	F	VF	XF	Unc
1639	—	275	500	1,100	2,400	—
1641/39	—	275	500	1,100	2,400	—

KM# 876.2 2 THALER

Silver **Ruler:** Ferdinand III **Rev:** Crowned flat-topped arms **Mint:** Graz **Note:** Dav. #B3186. Thick planchet. Prev. KM#437.2.

Date	Mintage	VG	F	VF	XF	Unc
1640	—	275	500	1,100	2,200	—
1641/0	—	275	500	1,100	2,200	—

KM# 897 2 THALER

Silver **Ruler:** Ferdinand II **Mint:** Graz **Note:** Dav. #A3109A. Posthumous date. Prev. KM#393.

Date	Mintage	VG	F	VF	XF	Unc
1640/31	—	275	550	1,000	1,650	—

KM# 884 2 THALER

Silver **Ruler:** Ferdinand III **Obv:** Laureate bust right in inner circle **Rev:** Crowned imperial eagle with flat-topped shield on breast in inner circle, date in legend **Mint:** Vienna **Note:** Dav. #3173. Varieties exist. Prev. KM#1836.

Date	Mintage	VG	F	VF	XF	Unc
1640 Rare	—	—	—	—	—	—
1641 Rare	—	—	—	—	—	—

KM# 925 2 THALER

Silver **Ruler:** Ferdinand III **Rev:** Oval arms **Mint:** Vienna **Note:** Dav. #3176. Prev. KM#1837.

Date	Mintage	VG	F	VF	XF	Unc
1645 Rare	—	—	—	—	—	—

KM# 933 2 THALER

Silver **Ruler:** Ferdinand III **Obv:** Without scalloped inner circle **Rev:** Crowned oval arms, date divided above **Mint:** Graz **Note:** Dav. #3188. Prev. KM#438.

Date	Mintage	VG	F	VF	XF	Unc
1646	—	275	500	825	1,400	—

KM# 934 2 THALER

Silver **Ruler:** Ferdinand Charles **Obv:** Uncrowned bust with lion face on shoulder **Mint:** Hall **Note:** Dav. #3363. Prev. KM#834.

Date	Mintage	VG	F	VF	XF	Unc
ND(1646)	—	165	325	750	1,250	—

KM# 937 2 THALER

Silver **Ruler:** Ferdinand Charles **Mint:** Hall **Note:** Klippe. Prev. KM#835.

Date	Mintage	VG	F	VF	XF	Unc
ND(1646) Rare	—	—	—	—	—	—

KM# 960 2 THALER
Silver **Ruler:** Ferdinand III **Mint:** Brunn **Note:** Dav. #3215. Similar to 1 Thaler, KM#929.1. Prev. KM#224.

Date	Mintage	VG	F	VF	XF	Unc
1648 (o) Rare	—	—	—	—	—	—

KM# 967 2 THALER
Silver **Ruler:** Ferdinand III **Mint:** Saint Veit **Note:** Dav. #3193. Varieties exist. Prev. KM#1628.

Date	Mintage	VG	F	VF	XF	Unc
1649	—	275	550	1,100	2,050	—
1650	—	275	550	1,100	2,050	—
1654	—	275	550	1,100	2,050	—
1657	—	275	550	1,100	2,050	—

KM# 968 2 THALER
Silver **Ruler:** Ferdinand III **Obv:** Armored bust right **Rev:** Flat-topped shield on eagle's breast **Mint:** Vienna **Note:** Dav. #3178. Prev. KM#A1838.

Date	Mintage	VG	F	VF	XF	Unc
1649 Rare	—	—	—	—	—	—

KM# 976 2 THALER
Silver **Ruler:** Ferdinand III **Mint:** Graz **Note:** Dav. #A3190. Similar to 3 Thaler, KM#877. Prev. KM#442.

Date	Mintage	VG	F	VF	XF	Unc
1651	—	275	500	825	1,400	—

KM# 984 2 THALER
56.5100 g., Silver **Ruler:** Ferdinand Charles **Obv:** Uncrowned bust with armored shoulder **Mint:** Hall **Note:** Dav. #3363A. Prev. KM#836.

Date	Mintage	VG	F	VF	XF	Unc
ND(1654)	—	140	300	750	1,250	—

KM# 985 2 THALER
57.2600 g., Silver **Ruler:** Ferdinand Charles **Obv:** Crowned bust with armored shoulder **Mint:** Hall **Note:** Dav. #3364. Prev. KM#837.

Date	Mintage	VG	F	VF	XF	Unc
ND(1654)	—	275	550	1,100	2,400	—

KM# 986 2 THALER
Silver **Ruler:** Ferdinand Charles **Obv:** Crowned bust with lion face on shoulder **Mint:** Hall **Note:** Dav. #3364A. Prev. KM#845.

Date	Mintage	VG	F	VF	XF	Unc
ND(1654)	—	375	725	1,400	2,750	—

KM# 992 2 THALER
Silver **Ruler:** Ferdinand III **Obv:** Laureate bust right with light drapery, date below bust in inner circle **Rev:** Crowned arms in flat-topped shield in Order collar and inner circle **Mint:** Vienna **Note:** Dav. #3182. Prev. KM#1838.

Date	Mintage	VG	F	VF	XF	Unc
1655 Rare	—	—	—	—	—	—

KM# 1269x 2 THALER
Silver **Ruler:** Leopold I **Mint:** Graz **Note:** Varieties exist. Dav. #A3232. Prev. KM#466. Illustration reduced.

Date	Mintage	VG	F	VF	XF	Unc
1670 IAN	—	275	600	1,300	2,200	—
1670 IGW	—	275	600	1,300	2,200	—
1675 IAN	—	275	600	1,300	2,200	—
1678 IAN	—	275	600	1,300	2,200	—
1682 IAN	—	275	600	1,300	2,200	—
1684 IAN	—	275	600	1,300	2,200	—

KM# 1119.1 2 THALER
56.5300 g., Silver **Ruler:** Leopold I **Obv:** Lion's head in shoulder drapery **Mint:** Hall **Note:** Dav. #3247. Prev. KM#648.1.

Date	Mintage	VG	F	VF	XF	Unc
ND(1670)	—	165	325	825	1,550	—

KM# 1119.2 2 THALER
Silver **Ruler:** Leopold I **Obv:** Lion's head in ornate shoulder drapery **Mint:** Hall **Note:** Dav. #3249. Prev. KM#648.2.

Date	Mintage	VG	F	VF	XF	Unc
ND	—	165	325	825	1,550	—

KM# 1121 2 THALER
Silver **Ruler:** Leopold I **Obv:** Similar to 2 Thaler, KM#648 **Rev. Legend:** DVX • BVRGVNDIAE • COMES • TYROLIS **Mint:** Hall **Note:** Dav. #3253. Prev. KM#658.

Date	Mintage	VG	F	VF	XF	Unc
ND	—	110	220	550	1,400	—

KM# 1323 2 THALER
Silver **Ruler:** Leopold I **Obv:** Bust right in inner circle **Rev:** Crowned arms in Order collar, crown divides date **Mint:** Saint Veit **Note:** Dav. #3238. Prev. KM#1654.

Date	Mintage	VG	F	VF	XF	Unc
1683/2	—	1,250	2,200	3,500	5,000	—

KM# 1120.1 2 THALER
Silver **Ruler:** Leopold I **Obv:** Armored bust without lion's head **Mint:** Hall **Note:** Dav. #3250. Prev. KM#656.1.

Date	Mintage	VG	F	VF	XF	Unc
ND	—	120	275	650	1,450	—

KM# 1120.2 2 THALER
Silver **Ruler:** Leopold I **Obv:** Lion's head in ornate shoulder drapery **Mint:** Hall **Note:** Dav. #3251. Prev. KM#656.2.

Date	Mintage	VG	F	VF	XF	Unc
ND	—	12.00	275	650	1,450	—

KM# 1338 2 THALER
Silver **Ruler:** Leopold I **Obv:** Finer style armored bust, hair curls in rows **Mint:** Hall **Note:** Dav. #3252. Prev. KM#657.

Date	Mintage	VG	F	VF	XF	Unc
ND1686-96	—	110	250	600	1,400	—

KM# 645 2-1/2 THALER
Silver **Ruler:** Ferdinand II **Obv:** Laureate bust right in inner circle of laurel, date at top **Rev:** Crowned oval arms in Order collar and inner circle **Mint:** Graz **Note:** Klippe. Prev. KM#395.

Date	Mintage	VG	F	VF	XF	Unc
1626/5 Rare	—	—	—	—	—	—

KM# 59 3 THALER
Silver **Ruler:** Rudolf II **Mint:** Hall **Note:** Dav. #3003. Prev. KM#612.

Date	Mintage	VG	F	VF	XF	Unc
1604	—	825	1,400	2,400	4,500	—

KM# 190 3 THALER
Silver **Ruler:** Matthias II **Obv:** Laureate, armored bust right in inner circle **Rev:** Crowned imperial eagle with shield on breast with sword and scepter in inner circle, date in legend **Mint:** Vienna **Note:** Titles as Emperor. Dav. #B3042. Prev. KM#1754.

Date	Mintage	VG	F	VF	XF	Unc
1614 Rare	—	—	—	—	—	—

KM# 208 3 THALER
Silver **Ruler:** Matthias II **Obv:** Smaller crown above eagle **Mint:** Vienna **Note:** Titles as Emperor. Dav. #A3045. Prev. KM#1755.

Date	Mintage	VG	F	VF	XF	Unc
1616 Rare	—	—	—	—	—	—
1617 Rare	—	—	—	—	—	—

KM# 230 3 THALER
Silver **Ruler:** Matthias II **Obv:** Laureate bust with wide ruffle **Mint:** Vienna **Note:** Titles as Emperor. Dav. #3047. Thick planchet. Prev. KM#1756.

Date	Mintage	VG	F	VF	XF	Unc
1618 Rare	—	—	—	—	—	—

KM# 359 3 THALER
Silver **Ruler:** Ferdinand II **Obv:** Crowned bust right in inner circle **Rev:** Crowned imperial eagle in inner circle, arms in flat-topped circle, crown divides date **Mint:** Graz **Note:** Dav.#3101. Prev.#KM396.

Date	Mintage	VG	F	VF	XF	Unc
1621 Rare	—	—	—	—	—	—

KM# 547 3 THALER
Silver **Ruler:** Ferdinand II **Obv:** Laureate bust right **Obv. Legend:** FERDINANDVS. II. B in circle; D. G. R. I. S. A. G. H. B. REX. **Rev:** Crowned imperial eagle **Rev. Legend:** ARCHID. AVS. DVX, arms, BVR. MA. MO., date, CW **Mint:** Brunn **Note:** Dav. #A3145. Prev. KM#222.

Date	Mintage	VG	F	VF	XF	Unc
1624 B-(c) Rare	—	—	—	—	—	—

KM# 615 3 THALER
Silver **Ruler:** Ferdinand II **Mint:** Graz **Note:** Dav. #A3107. Prev. KM#397.

Date	Mintage	VG	F	VF	XF	Unc
1625	—	850	1,500	2,500	4,650	—

KM# 616 3 THALER
Silver **Ruler:** Ferdinand II **Obv:** Laureate bust right with lion face on shoulder, laureate chain surrounds **Rev:** Crowned round

complex arms within order chain **Mint:** Graz **Note:** Dav. #A3107A. Klippe. Prev. KM#399.

Date	Mintage	VG	F	VF	XF	Unc
1625	—	—	—	7,000	9,000	—
1626/5	—	—	—	7,000	9,000	—

KM# 617.1 3 THALER

Silver **Ruler:** Leopold **Mint:** Hall **Note:** Dav. #A3335. Similar to 2 Thaler, KM#609.1 Prev. KM#811.1.

Date	Mintage	VG	F	VF	XF	Unc
ND(1625)	—	1,400	2,500	3,850	5,500	—

KM# 617.2 3 THALER

Silver **Ruler:** Leopold **Mint:** Hall **Note:** Dav. #A3336. Similar to 2 Thaler, KM#807.2. Prev. KM#811.2.

Date	Mintage	VG	F	VF	XF	Unc
1626	—	1,400	2,500	3,850	5,500	—

KM# 647 3 THALER

Silver **Ruler:** Ferdinand II **Obv:** Undivided date at top **Rev:** Oval arms **Mint:** Graz **Note:** Dav. #B3107. Prev. KM#398.

Date	Mintage	VG	F	VF	XF	Unc
1626/5	—	825	1,500	2,500	4,000	—
1632/30/26	—	825	1,500	2,500	4,000	—

KM# 648 3 THALER

Silver **Ruler:** Leopold **Subject:** Wedding of Leopold and Claudia **Mint:** Hall **Note:** Dav. #A3331. Prev. KM#812.

Date	Mintage	VG	F	VF	XF	Unc
ND(1626)	—	—	—	—	—	—
ND(1626) Rare	—	—	—	—	—	—

KM# 649 3 THALER

Silver **Ruler:** Leopold **Mint:** Hall **Note:** Dav. #A3331A. Klippe. Prev. KM#813.

Date	Mintage	VG	F	VF	XF	Unc
ND(1626) Rare	—	—	—	—	—	—

KM# 721 3 THALER

Silver **Ruler:** Ferdinand III **Mint:** Glatz **Note:** Similar to 1 Thaler, KM#699.1. Dav. #A3361. Prev. KM#311.

Date	Mintage	VG	F	VF	XF	Unc
1629 (p) Rare	—	—	—	—	—	—

KM# 770 3 THALER

Silver **Ruler:** Ferdinand II **Obv:** Plain inner circle, date below bust **Rev:** Ornamental shield of arms **Mint:** Graz **Note:** Dav. #3109. Prev. KM#400.

Date	Mintage	VG	F	VF	XF	Unc
1631	—	950	1,650	3,250	5,500	—

KM# 787 3 THALER

Silver **Ruler:** Ferdinand II **Obv:** Laureate bust right in inner circle **Rev:** Crowned imperial eagle in inner circle, date in legend **Mint:** Vienna **Note:** Varieties exist. Prev. KM#1798.

Date	Mintage	VG	F	VF	XF	Unc
1632 Rare	—	—	—	—	—	—
1636 Rare	—	—	—	—	—	—

KM# 877 3 THALER

Silver **Ruler:** Ferdinand III **Obv:** Laureate bust, date below **Rev:** Crowned arms **Mint:** Graz **Note:** Dav. #LS290. Broad planchet. Prev. KM#439. Illustration reduced.

Date	Mintage	VG	F	VF	XF	Unc
1639 Rare	—	—	—	—	—	—
1641 Rare	—	—	—	—	—	—

KM# 885 3 THALER

Silver **Ruler:** Ferdinand III **Obv:** Laureate bust right in inner circle **Rev:** Crowned imperial eagle with flat-topped shield on breast in inner circle, date in legend **Mint:** Vienna **Note:** Dav. #A3173. Prev. KM#1839.

Date	Mintage	VG	F	VF	XF	Unc
1640 Rare	—	—	—	—	—	—

KM# 886 3 THALER

Silver **Ruler:** Ferdinand III **Rev:** Oval arms **Mint:** Vienna **Note:** Dav. #A3175. Prev. KM#1840.

Date	Mintage	VG	F	VF	XF	Unc
1640 Rare	—	—	—	—	—	—

KM# 961 3 THALER

Silver **Ruler:** Ferdinand III **Mint:** Brunn **Note:** Dav. #3214. Similar to 1 Thaler, KM#929.1. Prev. KM#225.

Date	Mintage	VG	F	VF	XF	Unc
1648 (o) Rare	—	—	—	—	—	—

KM# 1122.1 3 THALER

Silver **Ruler:** Leopold I **Mint:** Hall **Note:** Similar to 2 Thaler, KM#1119.1. Dav. #3246. Prev. KM#655.1.

Date	Mintage	VG	F	VF	XF	Unc
ND Rare	—	—	—	—	—	—

KM# 1122.2 3 THALER

Silver **Ruler:** Leopold I **Mint:** Hall **Note:** Similar to 2 Thaler, KM#1119.2. Dav. #3248. Prev. KM#655.2.

Date	Mintage	VG	F	VF	XF	Unc
ND Rare	—	—	—	—	—	—

KM# 1388 3 THALER

Silver **Ruler:** Leopold I **Mint:** Vienna **Note:** Dav. #A3229. Similar to 1 Thaler, KM#1275.3. Prev. KM#1910.

Date	Mintage	VG	F	VF	XF	Unc
1695 Rare	—	—	—	—	—	—

KM# 650 3-1/4 THALER

94.0000 g., Silver **Ruler:** Ferdinand II **Obv:** Laureate bust right in inner circle of laurel, date in legend above head **Rev:** Crowned oval arms in Order collar and inner circle **Mint:** Graz **Note:** Prev. KM#401.

Date	Mintage	VG	F	VF	XF	Unc
1626 Rare	—	—	—	—	—	—

KM# 191 4 THALER

Silver **Ruler:** Matthias II **Obv:** Laureate, armored bust right in inner circle **Rev:** Crowned imperial eagle with shield on breast with sword and scepter in inner circle, date in legend **Mint:** Vienna **Note:** Titles as Emperor. Dav. #3042. Prev. KM#1757.

Date	Mintage	VG	F	VF	XF	Unc
1614 Rare	—	—	—	—	—	—

KM# 618 4 THALER

Silver **Ruler:** Ferdinand II **Obv:** Laureate bust right in inner circle **Rev:** Crown above five shields of arms in inner circle, date in legend **Mint:** Vienna **Note:** Dav. #A3087A. Prev. KM#1799.

Date	Mintage	VG	F	VF	XF	Unc
1625 Rare	—	—	—	—	—	—

KM# 788 4 THALER

Silver **Ruler:** Ferdinand II **Rev:** Crowned imperial eagle in inner circle, date in legend **Mint:** Vienna **Note:** Dav. #3089. Varieties exist. Struck with Thaler and double thaler dies. Prev. KM#1800.

Date	Mintage	VG	F	VF	XF	Unc
1632 Rare	—	—	—	—	—	—

KM# 908 4 THALER

Silver **Ruler:** Ferdinand III **Obv:** Laureate bust right in inner circle **Rev:** Crowned imperial eagle in inner circle, date in legend **Mint:** Vienna **Note:** Dav. #A3173. Prev. KM#1841.

Date	Mintage	VG	F	VF	XF	Unc
1642 Rare	—	—	—	—	—	—

KM# 962 4 THALER

113.7500 g., Silver **Ruler:** Ferdinand III **Mint:** Brunn **Note:** Dav. #A3214. Similar to 1 Thaler, KM#929.1. Prev. KM#226.

Date	Mintage	VG	F	VF	XF	Unc
1648 (o) Rare	—	—	—	—	—	—

KM# 551 5 THALER

Silver **Ruler:** Ferdinand II **Obv:** Old ruffled bust right **Rev:** Crowned imperial eagle, shield on breast **Mint:** Vienna **Note:** Dav. #A3077. Prev. KM#A1801.

Date	Mintage	VG	F	VF	XF	Unc
1624 (c) Rare	—	—	—	—	—	—

KM# 550 5 THALER

Silver **Ruler:** Ferdinand II **Obv:** Laureate bust right with ruffled collar **Rev:** Crown above five shields of arms, crowned imperial eagle **Mint:** Vienna **Note:** Prev. KM#1801.

Date	Mintage	VG	F	VF	XF	Unc
1624 Rare	—	—	—	—	—	—

KM# 552 5 THALER

Silver **Ruler:** Ferdinand II **Obv:** Bust with plain collar **Mint:** Vienna **Note:** Prev. KM#1802.

Date	Mintage	VG	F	VF	XF	Unc
1624 Rare	—	—	—	—	—	—

KM# 619 5 THALER

Silver **Ruler:** Ferdinand II **Obv:** Laureate bust right in inner circle of laurel, date below bust **Rev:** Crowned arms in flat-topped shield in Order collar and inner circle **Mint:** Graz **Note:** Dav. #3105. Prev. KM#402.

Date	Mintage	VG	F	VF	XF	Unc
1625 Rare	—	—	—	—	—	—

KM# 361 12-1/2 THALER

Silver **Ruler:** Ferdinand II **Obv:** Silesian eagle within legend; M and HR in corners **Mint:** Glogau **Note:** Uniface. Klippe. Prev. KM#332.

Date	Mintage	VG	F	VF	XF	Unc
1621 Rare	—	—	—	—	—	—

REVOLUTIONARY COINAGE

1620-1621

KM# 237 3 KREUZER
Silver **Ruler:** Ferdinand II **Obv:** Checkered eagle **Rev:** Monument **Mint:** Brunn **Note:** Prev. KM#230.

Date	Mintage	VG	F	VF	XF	Unc
1619	—	25.00	36.00	70.00	120	—
1619 (h)	—	25.00	36.00	70.00	120	—
1620 (h)	—	25.00	36.00	70.00	120	—

KM# 239 3 KREUZER
Silver **Ruler:** Ferdinand II **Obv:** Eagle **Rev:** Monument **Mint:** Olmutz **Note:** Prev. KM#1255.

Date	Mintage	VG	F	VF	XF	Unc
1619 CC	—	10.00	18.00	36.00	60.00	—
16Z0 CC	—	10.00	18.00	36.00	60.00	—

KM# 241 12 KREUZER
Silver **Ruler:** Ferdinand II **Obv:** Eagle **Rev:** Monument **Mint:** Olmutz **Note:** Prev. KM#1256.

Date	Mintage	VG	F	VF	XF	Unc
1619 CC	—	12.00	27.50	48.00	70.00	—
1620 CC	—	12.00	27.50	48.00	70.00	—
16Z0 BZ	—	12.00	27.50	48.00	70.00	—

KM# 240 12 KREUZER
Silver **Ruler:** Ferdinand II **Obv:** Checkered eagle **Rev:** Monument **Mint:** Brunn **Note:** Prev. KM#231.

Date	Mintage	VG	F	VF	XF	Unc
1619 HP	—	35.00	60.00	120	240	—
1620 (h)	—	35.00	60.00	120	240	—

KM# 257 12 KREUZER
Silver **Ruler:** Ferdinand II **Mint:** Brunn **Note:** Klippe. Prev. KM#232.

Date	Mintage	VG	F	VF	XF	Unc
1620 (h)	—	—	—	—	—	—

KM# 242 24 KREUZER
Silver **Ruler:** Ferdinand II **Mint:** Olmutz **Note:** Similar to 48 Kreuzer, KM#259. Prev. KM#1257.

Date	Mintage	VG	F	VF	XF	Unc
1619 CC	—	12.00	27.50	55.00	90.00	—
1619	—	12.00	27.50	55.00	90.00	—
1620 CC	—	12.00	27.50	55.00	90.00	—

KM# 259 48 KREUZER
Silver **Ruler:** Ferdinand II **Mint:** Olmutz **Note:** Prev. KM#1258.

Date	Mintage	VG	F	VF	XF	Unc
1620 BZ	—	15.00	37.50	80.00	135	—
1621 BZ	—	15.00	37.50	80.00	135	—

KM# 267 THALER
Silver **Ruler:** Ferdinand II **Mint:** Olmutz **Note:** Prev. KM#1259.

Date	Mintage	VG	F	VF	XF	Unc
1620 CC Rare	—	—	—	—	—	—
1620 BZ Rare	—	—	—	—	—	—

KM# 276 5 DUCAT
17.5000 g., 0.9860 Gold 0.5547 oz. AGW **Ruler:** Ferdinand II **Mint:** Olmutz **Note:** Struck with 1 Thaler dies, KM#267. Prev. KM#1262.

Date	Mintage	VG	F	VF	XF	Unc
1620 BZ Rare	—	—	—	—	—	—

KM# 278 10 DUCAT
35.0000 g., 0.9860 Gold 1.1095 oz. AGW **Ruler:** Ferdinand II **Mint:** Olmutz **Note:** Struck with 1 Thaler dies, KM#267. Prev. KM#1263.

Date	Mintage	VG	F	VF	XF	Unc
1620 BZ Rare	—	—	—	—	—	—

KM# 279 25 DUCAT
87.5000 g., 0.9860 Gold 2.7737 oz. AGW **Ruler:** Ferdinand II **Mint:** Olmutz **Note:** Struck with 1 Thaler dies, KM#267. Prev. KM#1264.

Date	Mintage	VG	F	VF	XF	Unc
1620 BZ Rare	—	—	—	—	—	—

TRADE COINAGE

KM# 1282 1/12 DUCAT
0.2917 g., 0.9860 Gold 0.0092 oz. AGW **Ruler:** Leopold I **Obv:** Laureate bust right in inner circle, value at shoulder **Rev:** Crowned imperial eagle **Mint:** Vienna **Note:** Prev. KM#1874.

Date	Mintage	VG	F	VF	XF	Unc
1675	—	100	165	325	725	—

KM# 1283 1/6 DUCAT
0.5834 g., 0.9860 Gold 0.0185 oz. AGW **Ruler:** Leopold I **Obv:** Laureate bust right, value at shoulder **Rev:** Crowned imperial eagle in inner circle **Mint:** Vienna **Note:** Prev. KM#1875.

Date	Mintage	VG	F	VF	XF	Unc
1675	—	165	275	425	825	—

KM# 1261 1/4 DUCAT
0.8750 g., 0.9860 Gold 0.0277 oz. AGW **Ruler:** Leopold I **Obv:** Laureate bust right in inner circle, value at shoulder **Rev:** Crowned imperial eagle **Mint:** Graz **Note:** Prev. KM#467.

Date	Mintage	VG	F	VF	XF	Unc
ND	—	100	220	350	775	—
1669	—	100	220	350	775	—

KM# 1377 1/4 DUCAT
0.8750 g., 0.9860 Gold 0.0277 oz. AGW **Ruler:** Leopold I **Obv:** Laureate bust right in inner circle, value at shoulder **Rev:** Crowned imperial eagle **Mint:** Vienna **Note:** Prev. KM#1876.

Date	Mintage	VG	F	VF	XF	Unc
1694	—	140	220	425	825	—

KM# 1284 1/3 DUCAT
1.1667 g., 0.9860 Gold 0.0370 oz. AGW **Ruler:** Leopold I **Obv:** Laureate bust right in inner circle, value at shoulder **Rev:** Crowned imperial eagle in inner circle **Mint:** Vienna **Note:** Prev. KM#1877.

Date	Mintage	VG	F	VF	XF	Unc
1675	—	140	250	450	875	—

KM# 969 1/2 DUCAT
1.7500 g., 0.9860 Gold 0.0555 oz. AGW **Ruler:** Ferdinand Charles **Obv:** Armored bust right **Rev:** Tyrolean eagle with shield of arms on breast **Mint:** Hall **Note:** Prev. KM#838.

Date	Mintage	VG	F	VF	XF	Unc
ND(1649)	—	185	375	1,100	1,950	—

KM# 1389 1/2 DUCAT
1.7500 g., 0.9860 Gold 0.0555 oz. AGW **Ruler:** Leopold I **Obv:** Laureate bust right in inner circle **Rev:** Crowned imperial eagle in inner circle **Mint:** Vienna **Note:** Prev. KM#1878.

Date	Mintage	VG	F	VF	XF	Unc
1695	—	165	275	525	1,000	—

KM# 6 DUCAT
3.5000 g., 0.9860 Gold 0.1109 oz. AGW **Ruler:** Ferdinand II **Obv:** Ferdinand standing facing divides date in inner circle **Rev:** Crowned arms in Order collar **Mint:** Klagenfurt **Note:** Prev. KM#993.

Date	Mintage	VG	F	VF	XF	Unc
ND	—	220	450	1,250	2,350	—
1598	—	220	450	1,250	2,350	—
1599	—	220	450	1,250	2,350	—
1601	—	220	450	1,250	2,350	—
160Z	—	220	450	1,250	2,350	—
1602	—	220	450	1,250	2,350	—
1604	—	220	450	1,250	2,350	—
1606	—	220	450	1,250	2,350	—
1607	—	220	450	1,250	2,350	—

KM# 28 DUCAT
3.5000 g., 0.9860 Gold 0.1109 oz. AGW **Ruler:** Rudolf II **Mint:** Vienna **Note:** Prev. KM#1717.

Date	Mintage	VG	F	VF	XF	Unc
1601	—	220	450	1,250	2,500	—
1602	—	220	450	1,250	2,500	—
1603	—	220	450	1,250	2,500	—
1604	—	220	450	1,250	2,500	—
1605	—	220	450	1,250	2,500	—
1606	—	220	450	1,250	2,500	—
1607	—	220	450	1,250	2,500	—
1608	—	220	450	1,250	2,500	—

KM# 5.1 DUCAT
3.5000 g., 0.9860 Gold 0.1109 oz. AGW **Ruler:** Ferdinand II **Obv:** Crowned and armored standing figure of Ferdinand facing holding sceptre over right shoulder, date between feet **Obv. Legend:** FERDINANDVS - D.G. ARCHIDVX. **Rev:** Crowned 12-fold arms with central shield of Styria in Spanish shield, Order of Golden Fleece around, date divided at left under crown and at right **Rev. Legend:** AVSTRIÆ. DVX. - BVRGVNDI. STYRI. **Mint:** Graz **Note:** Prev. KM#573. Fr.#(119).

Date	Mintage	VG	F	VF	XF	Unc
(1)608//(1)608	—	275	550	1,300	2,500	—

KM# 5.2 DUCAT
3.5000 g., 0.9860 Gold 0.1109 oz. AGW **Ruler:** Ferdinand II **Obv:** Crowned and armored standing Ferdinand facing with hands on hips **Obv. Legend:** FERDINANDV - S - D.G. ARCHIDVX. **Rev:** Crowned 12-fold arms with central shield of Styria in Spanish shield divide date, Order of Golden Fleece around **Rev. Legend:** AVSTRIÆ. DVX. - BVRGVNDI. STYRI. **Mint:** Graz **Note:** Fr.#119.

Date	Mintage	VG	F	VF	XF	Unc
1609	—	300	600	1,200	2,000	—

KM# 5.3 DUCAT
3.5000 g., 0.9860 Gold 0.1109 oz. AGW **Ruler:** Ferdinand II **Obv:** Crowned and armored Ferdinand facing holding sceptre over right shoulder, date between feet **Obv. Legend:** FERDINANDV - S - D.G. ARCHIDVX **Rev:** Crowned 12-fold arms with central shield of Styria in Spanish shield, Order of Golden Fleece around, date divided by crown at top **Rev. Legend:** AVSTRIÆ. DVX. - BVRG. STYRIÆ. **Mint:** Graz **Note:** Fr.#119.

Date	Mintage	VG	F	VF	XF	Unc
1610	—	300	600	1,200	2,000	—

KM# 5.4 DUCAT
3.5000 g., 0.9860 Gold 0.1109 oz. AGW **Ruler:** Ferdinand II **Obv:** Standing crowned and armored Ferdinand holding sceptre over right shoulder, date between feet **Obv. Legend:** FERDINANDV - D. - G. ARCHIDVX. **Rev:** Crowned oval 8-fold arms in baroque frame, Order of Golden Fleece around, date divided by crown at top **Rev. Legend:** AVSTRIÆ. DVX. - BVRG. STYRIÆ. **Mint:** Graz **Note:** Fr.#119.

Date	Mintage	VG	F	VF	XF	Unc
1613	—	300	600	1,200	2,000	—

KM# 97 DUCAT
3.5000 g., 0.9860 Gold 0.1109 oz. AGW **Ruler:** Ferdinand II
Obv: Standing figure right divides date in inner circle
Mint: Klagenfurt **Note:** Prev. KM#994.

Date	Mintage	VG	F	VF	XF	Unc
1608	—	220	450	1,250	2,350	—
1609	—	220	450	1,250	2,350	—
1610	—	220	450	1,250	2,350	—
1611	—	220	450	1,250	2,350	—
1612	—	220	450	1,250	2,350	—
1613	—	220	450	1,250	2,350	—
1614	—	220	450	1,250	2,350	—
1615	—	220	450	1,250	2,350	—
1616	—	220	450	1,250	2,350	—
1617	—	220	450	1,250	2,350	—
1618	—	220	450	1,250	2,350	—
1619	—	—	—	—	—	—
1620	—	—	—	—	—	—

KM# 108 DUCAT
3.5000 g., 0.9860 Gold 0.1109 oz. AGW **Ruler:** Maximilian
Mint: Hall **Note:** Prev. KM#777.

Date	Mintage	VG	F	VF	XF	Unc
ND(1609-12)	5,539	425	1,250	3,500	6,000	—

KM# 109 DUCAT
3.5000 g., 0.9860 Gold 0.1109 oz. AGW **Ruler:** Matthias II **Obv:** Bust right **Rev:** Crowned arms **Mint:** Vienna **Note:** Prev. KM#1758.

Date	Mintage	VG	F	VF	XF	Unc
1609	—	175	375	1,100	2,000	—
1610	—	175	375	1,100	2,000	—
1611 (b)	—	175	375	1,100	2,000	—
1612 (c)	—	175	375	1,100	2,000	—

KM# 147 DUCAT
3.5000 g., 0.9860 Gold 0.1109 oz. AGW **Ruler:** Matthias II **Obv:** Matthias standing right with scepter and orb **Rev:** Crowned imperial eagle with large shield **Mint:** Vienna **Note:** Prev. KM#1759.

Date	Mintage	VG	F	VF	XF	Unc
1612	—	220	450	1,400	2,200	—
1613	—	220	450	1,400	2,200	—
1614	—	220	450	1,400	2,200	—
1617 (c)	—	220	450	1,400	2,200	—
1617 (t)	—	220	450	1,400	2,200	—
1618	—	220	450	1,400	2,200	—

KM# 146 DUCAT
3.5000 g., 0.9860 Gold 0.1109 oz. AGW **Ruler:** Maximilian
Obv: Armored figure standing 3/4 right **Rev:** Crowned arms
Mint: Hall **Note:** Prev. KM#778.

Date	Mintage	VG	F	VF	XF	Unc
ND(1612)	—	425	1,250	3,500	6,000	—

KM# 171 DUCAT
3.5000 g., 0.9860 Gold 0.1109 oz. AGW **Ruler:** Ferdinand II
Rev: Crowned ornamented oval arms **Mint:** Graz **Note:** Prev. KM#574.

Date	Mintage	VG	F	VF	XF	Unc
1613	—	375	850	2,200	5,500	—
1616	—	375	850	2,200	5,500	—
1617	—	375	850	2,200	5,500	—

KM# 231 DUCAT
3.5000 g., 0.9860 Gold 0.1109 oz. AGW **Ruler:** Maximilian **Obv:** Arms of Tyrol in inner circle **Rev:** Crowned arms of Austria in inner circle **Mint:** Hall **Note:** Interregnum in Tyrol. Prev. KM#781.

Date	Mintage	VG	F	VF	XF	Unc
1618	1,971	550	1,650	3,650	6,500	—
1619	—	550	1,650	3,650	6,500	—

KM# 246 DUCAT
3.5000 g., 0.9860 Gold 0.1109 oz. AGW **Ruler:** Leopold
Mint: Hall **Note:** Prev. KM#814.

Date	Mintage	VG	F	VF	XF	Unc
ND(1619) Rare; CO monogram	—	—	—	—	—	—

KM# 247 DUCAT
3.5000 g., 0.9860 Gold 0.1109 oz. AGW **Ruler:** Friedrich von der Pfalz **Obv:** Ferdinand II standing facing in inner circle **Rev:** Crowned arms in inner circle, crown divides date **Mint:** Klagenfurt **Note:** Prev. KM#979.

Date	Mintage	VG	F	VF	XF	Unc
ND	—	220	450	1,100	1,950	—
1619	—	220	450	1,100	1,950	—
1620	—	220	450	1,100	1,950	—
1621	—	220	450	1,100	1,950	—
1622	—	220	450	1,100	1,950	—

KM# 248 DUCAT
3.5000 g., 0.9860 Gold 0.1109 oz. AGW **Ruler:** Matthias II **Obv:** Matthias standing facing **Mint:** Vienna **Note:** Prev. KM#1760.

Date	Mintage	VG	F	VF	XF	Unc
1619	—	220	450	1,400	2,200	—

KM# 274 DUCAT
3.5000 g., 0.9860 Gold 0.1109 oz. AGW **Ruler:** Ferdinand II
Mint: Vienna **Note:** Prev. KM#1803.

Date	Mintage	VG	F	VF	XF	Unc
1620 (c)	—	140	250	550	1,650	—
1622 (c)	—	140	250	550	1,650	—
1628 (c)	—	140	250	550	1,650	—
1629 (c)	—	140	250	550	1,650	—
1630 (c)	—	140	250	550	1,650	—
1631 (c)	—	140	250	550	1,650	—
1632 (c)	—	140	250	550	1,650	—
1633 (c)	—	140	250	550	1,650	—
1634 (c)	—	140	250	550	1,650	—

KM# 363 DUCAT
3.5000 g., 0.9860 Gold 0.1109 oz. AGW **Ruler:** Ferdinand II
Obv: Seated figure **Rev:** Heraldic imperial eagle **Mint:** Klagenfurt
Note: Prev. KM#980.

Date	Mintage	VG	F	VF	XF	Unc
1621	—	750	1,650	3,850	6,750	—

KM# 364 DUCAT
3.5000 g., 0.9860 Gold 0.1109 oz. AGW **Ruler:** Ferdinand II
Obv: Seated figure **Rev:** Heraldic imperial eagle **Mint:** Klagenfurt
Note: Prev. KM#995.

Date	Mintage	VG	F	VF	XF	Unc
1621	—	750	1,650	3,850	6,750	—

KM# 425 DUCAT
3.5000 g., 0.9860 Gold 0.1109 oz. AGW **Ruler:** Ferdinand II
Obv: Facing ruler seated on throne in inner circle **Rev:** Crowned imperial eagle in inner circle, crown divides date **Mint:** Graz
Note: Prev. KM#403.

Date	Mintage	VG	F	VF	XF	Unc
1622	—	275	550	1,150	2,200	—
1623	—	275	550	1,150	2,200	—
1625	—	275	550	1,150	2,200	—
1627	—	275	550	1,150	2,200	—

KM# 426 DUCAT
3.5000 g., 0.9860 Gold 0.1109 oz. AGW **Ruler:** Ferdinand II
Obv: Seated figure **Rev:** Heraldic imperial eagle **Mint:** Saint Veit
Note: Prev. KM#1604.

Date	Mintage	VG	F	VF	XF	Unc
1622	—	220	450	1,100	2,000	—
1625	—	220	450	1,100	2,000	—

KM# 460 DUCAT
3.5000 g., 0.9860 Gold 0.1109 oz. AGW **Ruler:** Ferdinand II
Mint: Graz **Note:** Prev. KM#404.

Date	Mintage	VG	F	VF	XF	Unc
1623	—	175	300	625	1,800	—
1625	—	175	300	625	1,800	—
1627	—	175	300	625	1,800	—
1629	—	175	300	625	1,800	—
1631	—	175	300	625	1,800	—
1633	—	175	300	625	1,800	—

KM# 620 DUCAT
3.5000 g., 0.9860 Gold 0.1109 oz. AGW **Ruler:** Leopold
Obv: Crowned bust **Mint:** Hall **Note:** Prev. KM#817.

Date	Mintage	VG	F	VF	XF	Unc
ND(1625-30)	—	—	—	—	—	—
1631	—	—	—	—	—	—

KM# 657 DUCAT
3.5000 g., 0.9860 Gold 0.1109 oz. AGW **Ruler:** Ferdinand II
Mint: Hall **Note:** Prev. KM#616.

Date	Mintage	VG	F	VF	XF	Unc
ND(ca.1626)	—	325	650	1,400	3,250	—

KM# 681 DUCAT
3.5000 g., 0.9860 Gold 0.1109 oz. AGW **Ruler:** Ferdinand II
Obv: Standing figure right **Rev:** Heraldic imperial eagle
Mint: Saint Veit **Note:** Prev. KM#1605.

Date	Mintage	VG	F	VF	XF	Unc
1627	—	220	450	1,100	2,000	—

KM# 722 DUCAT
3.5000 g., 0.9860 Gold 0.1109 oz. AGW **Ruler:** Ferdinand III
Obv: Ferdinand III standing facing 3/4 right **Rev:** Crowned arms in Order chain, crown divides date **Mint:** Glatz **Note:** Prev. KM#312.

Date	Mintage	VG	F	VF	XF	Unc
1629 (p)	—	175	425	875	2,200	—
1631 (p)	—	175	425	875	2,200	—
1631 (h)	—	175	425	875	2,200	—
1636 (h)	—	175	425	875	2,200	—

KM# 723 DUCAT
3.5000 g., 0.9860 Gold 0.1109 oz. AGW **Ruler:** Ferdinand II
Obv: Ferdinand II standing right **Rev:** Heraldic imperial eagle
Mint: Olmutz **Note:** Prev. KM#1239.

Date	Mintage	VG	F	VF	XF	Unc
1629 (o)	—	220	450	1,100	2,000	—

KM# 757 DUCAT

3.5000 g., 0.9860 Gold 0.1109 oz. AGW **Ruler:** Leopold **Obv:** Standing figure with scepter facing front **Rev:** Standing saint **Mint:** Hall **Note:** Prev. KM#816.

Date	Mintage	VG	F	VF	XF	Unc
ND(1630-32)	—	350	1,000	2,750	4,250	—

KM# 758 DUCAT

3.5000 g., 0.9860 Gold 0.1109 oz. AGW **Ruler:** Ferdinand II **Obv:** Bust right **Mint:** Olmutz **Note:** Prev. KM#1240.

Date	Mintage	VG	F	VF	XF	Unc
1630 MF	—	275	550	1,400	2,750	—

KM# 771 DUCAT

3.5000 g., 0.9860 Gold 0.1109 oz. AGW **Ruler:** Leopold **Obv:** Arms in Order chain, legend **Obv. Legend:** LEOPOLDVS. D-G:... **Rev:** St. Leopold standing facing with banner, holding church model in left hand **Note:** Posthumous issue. Fr.#119a. Prev. KM#283.

Date	Mintage	VG	F	VF	XF	Unc
ND(1631-34)	—	1,150	2,300	4,600	7,800	—

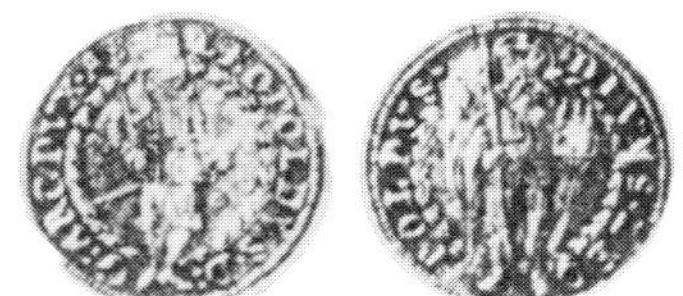

KM# 772 DUCAT

3.5000 g., 0.9860 Gold 0.1109 oz. AGW **Ruler:** Leopold **Obv:** Standing figure of Leopold right in inner circle **Rev:** Standing figure of St. Leopold right with banner in inner circle **Mint:** Hall **Note:** Prev. KM#815.

Date	Mintage	VG	F	VF	XF	Unc
ND	—	300	1,000	2,750	3,850	—
1631	—	300	1,000	2,750	3,850	—

KM# 808 DUCAT

3.5000 g., 0.9860 Gold 0.1109 oz. AGW **Ruler:** Ferdinand Charles **Obv:** Armored bust right **Rev:** Crowned oval arms in Order collar **Mint:** Hall **Note:** Prev. KM#839.

Date	Mintage	VG	F	VF	XF	Unc
ND Rare	—	—	—	—	—	—

KM# 809 DUCAT

3.5000 g., 0.9860 Gold 0.1109 oz. AGW **Ruler:** Ferdinand Charles **Obv:** Standing figure of Ferdinand Karl right in laurel circle **Rev:** Standing figure of St. Leopold facing with banner in laurel circle **Mint:** Hall **Note:** Prev. KM#840.

Date	Mintage	VG	F	VF	XF	Unc
ND	—	220	450	1,400	2,000	—

KM# 861 DUCAT

3.5000 g., 0.9860 Gold 0.1109 oz. AGW **Ruler:** Ferdinand III **Mint:** Saint Veit **Note:** Klippe. Prev. KM#1630.

Date	Mintage	VG	F	VF	XF	Unc
1638	—	325	550	1,250	2,750	—

KM# 859 DUCAT

3.5000 g., 0.9860 Gold 0.1109 oz. AGW **Ruler:** Ferdinand III **Rev:** Crowned imperial eagle in Order chain **Mint:** Glatz **Note:** Prev. KM#313.

Date	Mintage	VG	F	VF	XF	Unc
1638 G	—	175	425	875	2,200	—
1640 GW	—	175	425	875	2,200	—
1641 GW	—	175	425	875	2,200	—
1645 GW	—	175	425	875	2,200	—
1647 GW	—	175	425	875	2,200	—

KM# 860 DUCAT

3.5000 g., 0.9860 Gold 0.1109 oz. AGW **Ruler:** Ferdinand III **Obv:** Ferdinand III standing facing in inner circle **Rev:** Crowned imperial eagle, crown divides date **Mint:** Graz **Note:** Prev. KM#440.

Date	Mintage	VG	F	VF	XF	Unc
1638	—	175	425	800	1,950	—
1640	—	175	425	800	1,950	—
1643	—	175	425	800	1,950	—
1644	—	175	425	800	1,950	—
1645	—	175	425	800	1,950	—
1647	—	175	425	800	1,950	—
1648	—	175	425	800	1,950	—
1652	—	175	425	800	1,950	—
1657	—	175	425	800	1,950	—

KM# 878 DUCAT

3.5000 g., 0.9860 Gold 0.1109 oz. AGW **Ruler:** Ferdinand III **Obv:** Ferdinand III standing right in inner circle **Rev:** Crowned imperial eagle in inner circle **Mint:** Vienna **Note:** Prev. KM#1842.

Date	Mintage	VG	F	VF	XF	Unc
1639	—	160	325	575	1,650	—
1641	—	160	325	575	1,650	—
1642	—	160	325	575	1,650	—
1645	—	160	325	575	1,650	—
1646	—	160	325	575	1,650	—
1647	—	160	325	575	1,650	—

KM# 948 DUCAT

3.5000 g., 0.9860 Gold 0.1109 oz. AGW **Ruler:** Ferdinand III **Obv:** Laureate bust right **Rev:** Crowned imperial eagle, crown divides date **Mint:** Brunn **Note:** Prev. KM#227.

Date	Mintage	VG	F	VF	XF	Unc
1647	—	300	550	1,100	2,000	—

KM# 949 DUCAT

3.5000 g., 0.9860 Gold 0.1109 oz. AGW **Ruler:** Ferdinand III **Obv:** Ferdinand III standing right in inner circle **Rev:** Crowned imperial eagle, date in legend **Mint:** Saint Veit **Note:** Prev. KM#1629.

Date	Mintage	VG	F	VF	XF	Unc
1647	—	275	500	1,000	1,800	—

KM# 950 DUCAT

3.5000 g., 0.9860 Gold 0.1109 oz. AGW **Ruler:** Ferdinand III **Obv:** Crowned shield of arms added at each side of standing figure **Mint:** Vienna **Note:** Prev. KM#1843.

Date	Mintage	VG	F	VF	XF	Unc
1647	—	160	325	575	1,650	—
1648	—	160	325	575	1,650	—
1651	—	160	325	575	1,650	—
1652	—	160	325	575	1,650	—
1653	—	160	325	575	1,650	—
1654	—	160	325	575	1,650	—
1655	—	160	325	575	1,650	—
1656	—	160	325	575	1,650	—
1657	—	160	325	575	1,650	—

KM# 1158 DUCAT

3.5000 g., 0.9860 Gold 0.1109 oz. AGW **Ruler:** Leopold I **Obv:** Laureate head right in inner circle **Rev:** Crowned imperial eagle in inner circle, crown divides date **Mint:** Graz **Note:** Prev. KM#468.

Date	Mintage	VG	F	VF	XF	Unc
1659	—	200	425	825	1,750	—
1661	—	200	425	825	1,750	—
1667	—	200	425	825	1,750	—

KM# 1159 DUCAT

3.5000 g., 0.9860 Gold 0.1109 oz. AGW **Ruler:** Leopold I **Obv:** Leopold I on horseback right **Mint:** Graz **Note:** Prev. KM#469.

Date	Mintage	VG	F	VF	XF	Unc
1659	—	875	2,500	4,750	7,900	—
1660	—	875	2,500	4,750	7,900	—
1661	—	875	2,500	4,750	7,900	—

KM# 1181 DUCAT

3.5000 g., 0.9860 Gold 0.1109 oz. AGW **Ruler:** Leopold I **Mint:** Graz **Note:** Prev. KM#471.

Date	Mintage	VG	F	VF	XF	Unc
1660	—	130	350	725	1,550	—
1661	—	130	350	725	1,550	—
1667	—	130	350	725	1,550	—
1676 IAN	—	130	350	725	1,550	—
1679 IAN	—	130	350	725	1,550	—
1680 IAN	—	130	350	725	1,550	—
1682 IAN	—	130	350	725	1,550	—

KM# 1182 DUCAT

3.5000 g., 0.9860 Gold 0.1109 oz. AGW **Ruler:** Leopold I **Obv:** Leopold standing right flanked by crowned shields in inner circle **Rev:** Crowned imperial eagle in inner circle, date in legend **Mint:** Vienna **Note:** Prev. KM#1879.

Date	Mintage	VG	F	VF	XF	Unc
1660	—	275	550	1,100	2,200	—

KM# 1212 DUCAT

3.5000 g., 0.9860 Gold 0.1109 oz. AGW **Ruler:** Sigismund Franz **Obv:** Bust right **Rev:** Crowned arms in Order collar **Mint:** Hall **Note:** Prev. KM#856.

Date	Mintage	F	VF	XF	Unc	BU
ND(1663-65) Rare	4,233	—	—	—	—	—

KM# 1250 DUCAT

3.5000 g., 0.9860 Gold 0.1109 oz. AGW **Ruler:** Leopold I **Obv:** Laureate bust right **Rev:** Crowned arms in Order collar **Mint:** Hall **Note:** Prev. KM#649.

Date	Mintage	VG	F	VF	XF	Unc
ND(1667)	—	550	1,250	2,650	5,300	—

KM# 1251 DUCAT

3.5000 g., 0.9860 Gold 0.1109 oz. AGW **Ruler:** Leopold I **Obv:** Laureate bust right in inner circle **Rev:** Crowned imperial eagle in inner circle, crown divides date **Mint:** Vienna **Note:** Prev. KM#1880.

Date	Mintage	VG	F	VF	XF	Unc
1667	—	130	350	725	1,300	—
1668	—	130	350	725	1,300	—
1671	—	130	350	725	1,300	—
1673	—	130	350	725	1,300	—
1676	—	130	350	725	1,300	—
1680	—	130	350	725	1,300	—

KM# 1255 DUCAT

3.5000 g., 0.9860 Gold 0.1109 oz. AGW **Ruler:** Leopold I **Obv:** Laureate bust right in inner circle **Rev:** Crowned imperial eagle, date at upper left **Mint:** Saint Veit **Note:** Prev. KM#1655.

Date	Mintage	VG	F	VF	XF	Unc
1668 GS	—	220	450	875	1,950	—
1670	—	220	450	875	1,950	—

KM# 1290 DUCAT

3.5000 g., 0.9860 Gold 0.1109 oz. AGW **Ruler:** Leopold I **Obv:** Leopold standing facing in ornamental inner circle **Rev:** Crowned arms in Order collar, crown divides date **Mint:** Graz **Note:** Prev. KM#470.

Date	Mintage	VG	F	VF	XF	Unc
1676 IAN	—	275	550	1,100	2,200	—

KM# 1123 DUCAT

3.5000 g., 0.9860 Gold 0.1109 oz. AGW **Ruler:** Leopold I **Rev:** Crowned round arms in Order collar **Mint:** Hall **Note:** Prev. KM#650.

Date	Mintage	VG	F	VF	XF	Unc
ND	—	550	1,250	2,650	5,300	—

KM# 1124 DUCAT

3.5000 g., 0.9860 Gold 0.1109 oz. AGW **Ruler:** Leopold I **Obv:** Laureate bust right in inner circle **Rev:** Crowned arms with concave sides in Order collar **Mint:** Hall **Note:** Prev. KM#651.

Date	Mintage	VG	F	VF	XF	Unc
ND	—	550	1,250	2,650	5,300	—

KM# 1125 DUCAT

3.5000 g., 0.9860 Gold 0.1109 oz. AGW **Ruler:** Leopold I **Obv:** Laureate armored bust right in inner circle **Rev:** Crowned arms in Order collar in inner circle **Mint:** Hall **Note:** Prev. KM#652.

Date	Mintage	VG	F	VF	XF	Unc
ND	—	550	1,250	2,650	5,300	—

KM# 1309 DUCAT
3.5000 g., 0.9860 Gold 0.1109 oz. AGW **Ruler:** Leopold I **Obv:** Laureate bust right in inner circle **Rev:** Crowned imperial eagle, crown divides date **Mint:** Saint Veit **Note:** Prev. KM#1656.

Date	Mintage	VG	F	VF	XF	Unc
1680 IR	—	175	425	800	1,750	—
1682 IR	—	175	425	800	1,750	—
1687	—	175	425	800	1,750	—
1690 CS	—	175	425	800	1,750	—

KM# 1324 DUCAT
3.5000 g., 0.9860 Gold 0.1109 oz. AGW **Ruler:** Leopold I **Obv:** Older portrait **Rev:** Crowned oval arms **Mint:** Graz **Note:** Prev. KM#472.

Date	Mintage	VG	F	VF	XF	Unc
1683 IAN	—	130	350	725	1,550	—
1684 IAN	—	130	350	725	1,550	—
1686 IAN	—	130	350	725	1,550	—
1687 IAN	—	130	350	725	1,550	—
1689 IAN	—	130	350	725	1,550	—

KM# 1325 DUCAT
3.5000 g., 0.9860 Gold 0.1109 oz. AGW **Ruler:** Leopold I **Obv:** Large laureate bust right divides legend **Rev:** Crowned imperial eagle, crown divides date **Mint:** Vienna **Note:** Prev. KM#1890.

Date	Mintage	VG	F	VF	XF	Unc
1683	—	130	350	725	1,300	—
1684	—	130	350	725	1,300	—
1685	—	130	350	725	1,300	—
1686	—	130	350	725	1,300	—
1687	—	130	350	725	1,300	—
1689	—	130	350	725	1,300	—
1693	—	130	350	725	1,300	—
1694	—	130	350	725	1,300	—
1695	—	130	350	725	1,300	—
1697	—	130	350	725	1,300	—
1700	—	130	350	725	1,300	—

KM# 1372 DUCAT
3.5000 g., 0.9860 Gold 0.1109 oz. AGW **Ruler:** Leopold I **Obv:** Large laureate bust right to edge of coin **Rev:** Crowned arms in Order collar, crown divides date **Mint:** Graz **Note:** Prev. KM#473.

Date	Mintage	VG	F	VF	XF	Unc
1693	—	450	875	1,750	3,250	—

KM# 1410 DUCAT
3.5000 g., 0.9860 Gold 0.1109 oz. AGW **Ruler:** Leopold I **Obv:** Laureate bust right **Rev:** Crowned imperial eagle, crown divides date **Mint:** Saint Veit **Note:** Prev. KM#1657.

Date	Mintage	VG	F	VF	XF	Unc
1700	—	220	450	875	1,950	—

KM# 110 2 DUCAT
7.0000 g., 0.9860 Gold 0.2219 oz. AGW **Ruler:** Maximilian **Mint:** Hall **Note:** Similar to 1 Ducat, KM#146. Prev. KM#779.

Date	Mintage	VG	F	VF	XF	Unc
ND(1609)	—	725	1,500	4,250	7,500	—

KM# 172 2 DUCAT
7.0000 g., 0.9860 Gold 0.2219 oz. AGW **Ruler:** Matthias II **Mint:** Vienna **Note:** Varieties exist. Prev. KM#1761.

Date	Mintage	VG	F	VF	XF	Unc
1613	—	375	925	2,750	6,350	—
1615	—	375	925	2,750	6,350	—
1616	—	375	925	2,750	6,350	—
1619	—	375	925	2,750	6,350	—

KM# 275 2 DUCAT
7.0000 g., 0.9860 Gold 0.2219 oz. AGW **Ruler:** Ferdinand II **Obv:** Ferdinand II standing right **Mint:** Vienna **Note:** Prev. KM#1804.

Date	Mintage	VG	F	VF	XF	Unc
1620 (c)	—	325	800	2,000	5,200	—
1621 (c)	—	325	800	2,000	5,200	—
1622 (c)	—	325	800	2,000	5,200	—
1623 (c)	—	325	800	2,000	5,200	—
1624 (c)	—	325	800	2,000	5,200	—
1626 (c)	—	325	800	2,000	5,200	—
1627 (c)	—	325	800	2,000	5,200	—
1628 (c)	—	325	800	2,000	5,200	—
1629 (c)	—	325	800	2,000	5,200	—
1630 (c)	—	325	800	2,000	5,200	—
1631 (c)	—	325	800	2,000	5,200	—
1632 (c)	—	325	800	2,000	5,200	—
1633 (c)	—	325	800	2,000	5,200	—
1634 (c)	—	325	800	2,000	5,200	—
1635 (c)	—	325	800	2,000	5,200	—

KM# 365 2 DUCAT
7.0000 g., 0.9860 Gold 0.2219 oz. AGW **Ruler:** Ferdinand II **Obv:** Ruler seated facing throne in inner circle **Rev:** Crowned imperial eagle in inner circle, crown divides date **Mint:** Graz **Note:** Prev. KM#405.

Date	Mintage	VG	F	VF	XF	Unc
1621	—	450	925	2,200	5,300	—
1627	—	450	925	2,200	5,300	—

KM# 682 2 DUCAT
7.0000 g., 0.9860 Gold 0.2219 oz. AGW **Ruler:** Ferdinand II **Obv:** Standing figure right **Rev:** Heraldic imperial eagle with oval arms **Mint:** Saint Veit **Note:** Struck with 1 Ducat dies. Prev. KM#1606.

Date	Mintage	VG	F	VF	XF	Unc
1627 (g)	—	800	1,600	3,200	6,000	—

KM# 724 2 DUCAT
7.0000 g., 0.9860 Gold 0.2219 oz. AGW **Ruler:** Ferdinand III **Obv:** Ferdinand III standing right **Rev:** Madonna and child **Mint:** Glatz **Note:** Prev. KM#314.

Date	Mintage	VG	F	VF	XF	Unc
1629 (p)	—	475	1,050	3,050	6,300	—
1630 (p)	—	475	1,050	3,050	6,300	—
1631 (p)	—	475	1,050	3,050	6,300	—
1631 (h)	—	475	1,050	3,050	6,300	—

KM# 725 2 DUCAT
7.0000 g., 0.9860 Gold 0.2219 oz. AGW **Ruler:** Ferdinand II **Obv:** Uncrowned figure standing right **Rev:** Heraldic imperial eagle **Mint:** Olmutz **Note:** Prev. KM#1241.

Date	Mintage	VG	F	VF	XF	Unc
1629 (o) MF	—	350	725	1,950	4,600	—

KM# 760 2 DUCAT
7.0000 g., 0.9860 Gold 0.2219 oz. AGW **Ruler:** Ferdinand II **Obv:** Crowned figure **Mint:** Olmutz **Note:** Prev. KM#1242.

Date	Mintage	VG	F	VF	XF	Unc
1630	—	450	875	2,200	5,300	—

KM# 789 2 DUCAT
7.0000 g., 0.9860 Gold 0.2219 oz. AGW **Ruler:** Ferdinand Charles **Obv:** Armored bust right **Rev:** Tyrolean eagle with shield of arms on breast **Mint:** Hall **Note:** Prev. KM#841.

Date	Mintage	VG	F	VF	XF	Unc
ND(1632-62)	—	950	2,150	4,650	8,500	—

KM# 790 2 DUCAT
7.0000 g., 0.9860 Gold 0.2219 oz. AGW **Ruler:** Ferdinand II **Mint:** Klagenfurt **Note:** Prev. KM#981.

Date	Mintage	VG	F	VF	XF	Unc
1632	—	475	925	2,500	6,000	—

KM# 791 2 DUCAT
7.0000 g., 0.9860 Gold 0.2219 oz. AGW **Ruler:** Ferdinand II **Obv:** Standing figure **Rev:** Shield-shaped arms **Mint:** Saint Veit **Note:** Prev. KM#1607.

Date	Mintage	VG	F	VF	XF	Unc
1632	—	800	1,600	3,300	6,200	—

KM# 899 2 DUCAT
7.0000 g., 0.9860 Gold 0.2219 oz. AGW **Ruler:** Ferdinand III **Obv:** Ferdinand III standing right in inner circle **Rev:** Crowned imperial eagle in inner circle **Mint:** Vienna **Note:** Prev. KM#1844.

Date	Mintage	VG	F	VF	XF	Unc
1641	—	325	800	2,200	5,000	—
1642	—	325	800	2,200	5,000	—
1643	—	325	800	2,200	5,000	—
1644	—	325	800	2,200	5,000	—
1645	—	325	800	2,200	5,000	—
1646	—	325	800	2,200	5,000	—
1647	—	325	800	2,200	5,000	—
1648	—	325	800	2,200	5,000	—
1649	—	325	800	2,200	5,000	—
1650	—	325	800	2,200	5,000	—
1652	—	325	800	2,200	5,000	—
1653	—	325	800	2,200	5,000	—
1654	—	325	800	2,200	5,000	—
1656	—	325	800	2,200	5,000	—
1657	—	325	800	2,200	5,000	—

KM# 909 2 DUCAT
7.0000 g., 0.9860 Gold 0.2219 oz. AGW **Ruler:** Ferdinand Charles **Obv:** Ferdinand Karl on horseback right above city view **Mint:** Hall **Note:** Prev. KM#842.

Date	Mintage	VG	F	VF	XF	Unc
1642	—	700	1,500	3,500	6,000	—

KM# 936 2 DUCAT
7.0000 g., 0.9860 Gold 0.2219 oz. AGW **Ruler:** Ferdinand III **Mint:** Saint Veit **Note:** Prev. KM#1631.

Date	Mintage	VG	F	VF	XF	Unc
1646	—	350	850	2,250	5,200	—
1648	—	350	850	2,250	5,200	—

Date	Mintage	VG	F	VF	XF	Unc
1652	—	350	850	2,250	5,200	—
1653	—	350	850	2,250	5,200	—
1655	—	350	850	2,250	5,200	—

KM# 973 2 DUCAT

7.0000 g., 0.9860 Gold 0.2219 oz. AGW **Ruler:** Ferdinand III **Obv:** Ferdinand III standing facing in inner circle **Rev:** Crowned arms in inner circle, crown divides date **Mint:** Graz **Note:** Prev. KM#441.

Date	Mintage	VG	F	VF	XF	Unc
1650	—	375	950	2,350	5,300	—

KM# 1160 2 DUCAT

7.0000 g., 0.9860 Gold 0.2219 oz. AGW **Ruler:** Leopold I **Mint:** Saint Veit **Note:** Prev. KM#1659.

Date	Mintage	VG	F	VF	XF	Unc
1659	—	850	1,650	3,750	8,000	—

KM# 1161 2 DUCAT

7.0000 g., 0.9860 Gold 0.2219 oz. AGW **Ruler:** Leopold I **Obv:** Leopold standing left flanked by shields of arms **Rev:** Crowned imperial eagle, date in legend **Mint:** Vienna **Note:** Prev. KM#1891.

Date	Mintage	VG	F	VF	XF	Unc
1659	—	475	1,000	2,750	7,700	—

KM# 1183 2 DUCAT

7.0000 g., 0.9860 Gold 0.2219 oz. AGW **Ruler:** Leopold I **Obv:** Laureate bust right **Rev:** Crowned imperial eagle in inner circle, date in legend **Mint:** Vienna **Note:** Prev. KM#1892.

Date	Mintage	VG	F	VF	XF	Unc
1660	—	525	1,100	3,150	9,000	—
1661	—	525	1,100	3,150	9,000	—
1662	—	525	1,100	3,150	9,000	—

KM# 1223 2 DUCAT

7.0000 g., 0.9860 Gold 0.2219 oz. AGW **Ruler:** Leopold I **Obv:** Older laureate bust right in inner circle **Rev:** Crowned imperial eagle in inner circle, crown divides date **Mint:** Vienna **Note:** Prev. KM#1893.

Date	Mintage	VG	F	VF	XF	Unc
1664	—	525	1,100	3,150	9,000	—
1669	—	525	1,100	3,150	9,000	—
1682	—	525	1,100	3,150	9,000	—

KM# 1276 2 DUCAT

7.0000 g., 0.9860 Gold 0.2219 oz. AGW **Ruler:** Leopold I **Obv:** Older laureate bust right in inner circle **Rev:** Crowned arms in Order collar, crown divides date **Mint:** Graz **Note:** Prev. KM#474.

Date	Mintage	VG	F	VF	XF	Unc
1672 IAN	—	475	1,000	2,750	7,700	—
1674 IAN	—	475	1,000	2,750	7,700	—
1676 IAN	—	475	1,000	2,750	7,700	—
1678 IAN	—	475	1,000	2,750	7,700	—
1680 IAN	—	475	1,000	2,750	7,700	—
1682 IAN	—	475	1,000	2,750	7,700	—
1684 IAN	—	475	1,000	2,750	7,700	—
1685 IAN	—	475	1,000	2,750	7,700	—
1687/6 IAN	—	475	1,000	2,750	7,700	—

KM# 1126 2 DUCAT

7.0000 g., 0.9860 Gold 0.2219 oz. AGW **Ruler:** Leopold I **Obv:** Laureate bust right in inner circle **Rev:** Crowned eagle with wreath around head in inner circle **Mint:** Hall **Note:** Prev. KM#653.

Date	Mintage	VG	F	VF	XF	Unc
ND(1680)F	—	550	1,150	3,250	9,250	—

KM# 1312 2 DUCAT

7.0000 g., 0.9860 Gold 0.2219 oz. AGW **Ruler:** Leopold I **Obv:** Laureate bust right **Rev:** Crowned imperial eagle, crown divides date **Mint:** Saint Veit **Note:** Prev. KM#1660.

Date	Mintage	VG	F	VF	XF	Unc
1681 IR	—	825	1,650	3,850	8,750	—
1685 IR	—	825	1,650	3,850	8,750	—
1686 HL/VP	—	825	1,650	3,850	8,750	—

KM# 77 3 DUCAT

10.5000 g., 0.9860 Gold 0.3328 oz. AGW **Ruler:** Rudolf II **Mint:** Vienna **Note:** Prev. KM#1718.

Date	Mintage	VG	F	VF	XF	Unc
1606	—	2,750	4,700	7,250	12,500	—

KM# 806 3 DUCAT

10.5000 g., 0.9860 Gold 0.3328 oz. AGW **Ruler:** Ferdinand II **Mint:** Graz **Note:** Klippe. Prev. KM#411.

Date	Mintage	VG	F	VF	XF	Unc
1634 Rare	—	—	—	—	—	—

KM# 910 3 DUCAT

10.5000 g., 0.9860 Gold 0.3328 oz. AGW **Ruler:** Ferdinand Charles **Obv:** Ferdinand Karl on horseback right in circle of arms **Mint:** Hall **Note:** Prev. KM#843.

Date	Mintage	VG	F	VF	XF	Unc
1642	—	1,150	3,150	7,250	10,500	—

KM# 995 3 DUCAT

10.5000 g., 0.9860 Gold 0.3328 oz. AGW **Ruler:** Ferdinand III **Obv:** Laureate bust right in inner circle **Rev:** Crowned imperial eagle in inner circle **Mint:** Vienna **Note:** Struck with 1 Ducat dies, KM#950. Prev. KM#1845.

Date	Mintage	VG	F	VF	XF	Unc
1656	—	825	1,550	4,400	8,000	—

KM# 1127 3 DUCAT

10.5000 g., 0.9860 Gold 0.3328 oz. AGW **Ruler:** Leopold I **Obv:** Laureate bust right in inner circle **Rev:** Crowned imperial eagle in inner circle **Mint:** Hall **Note:** Prev. KM#654.

Date	Mintage	VG	F	VF	XF	Unc
ND	—	750	1,700	4,500	9,250	—

KM# 148 4 DUCAT

14.0000 g., 0.9860 Gold 0.4438 oz. AGW **Ruler:** Matthias II **Mint:** Joachimstal **Note:** Prev. KM#A890.

Date	Mintage	VG	F	VF	XF	Unc
1612 Rare	—	—	—	—	—	—

KM# 366 4 DUCAT

14.0000 g., 0.9860 Gold 0.4438 oz. AGW **Ruler:** Ferdinand II **Obv:** Laureate bust right in inner circle **Rev:** Crowned imperial eagle in inner circle **Mint:** Vienna **Note:** Prev. KM#1805.

Date	Mintage	VG	F	VF	XF	Unc
1621 (c)	—	—	—	—	—	—
1622 (c)	—	1,100	2,750	6,500	10,000	—
1628 (c)	—	1,100	2,750	6,500	10,000	—
1634 (c)	—	1,100	2,750	6,500	10,000	—

KM# 683 4 DUCAT

14.0000 g., 0.9860 Gold 0.4438 oz. AGW **Ruler:** Ferdinand II **Obv:** Standing figure right **Rev:** Heraldic imperial eagle **Mint:** Saint Veit **Note:** Klippe. Struck with 1 Ducat dies. Prev. KM#1608.

Date	Mintage	VG	F	VF	XF	Unc
1627	—	2,750	4,700	8,750	12,500	—

KM# 1128 4 DUCAT

14.0000 g., 0.9860 Gold 0.4438 oz. AGW **Ruler:** Leopold I **Obv:** Young laureate bust right in inner circle **Rev:** Crowned imperial eagle in inner circle **Mint:** Saint Veit **Note:** Prev. KM#1661.

Date	Mintage	VG	F	VF	XF	Unc
1658	—	1,300	2,750	6,500	10,500	—

KM# 1162 4 DUCAT

14.0000 g., 0.9860 Gold 0.4438 oz. AGW **Ruler:** Leopold I **Mint:** Vienna **Note:** Prev. KM#1894.

Date	Mintage	VG	F	VF	XF	Unc
1659	—	1,300	2,750	6,500	10,500	—

KM# 1203 4 DUCAT

14.0000 g., 0.9860 Gold 0.4438 oz. AGW **Ruler:** Leopold I **Mint:** Vienna **Note:** Prev. KM#1896.

Date	Mintage	VG	F	VF	XF	Unc
1662	—	1,300	2,750	6,500	10,500	—

KM# 84 5 DUCAT

17.5000 g., 0.9860 Gold 0.5547 oz. AGW **Ruler:** Rudolf II **Mint:** Vienna **Note:** Prev. KM#1719.

Date	Mintage	VG	F	VF	XF	Unc
1607	—	4,600	7,200	10,500	17,000	—

KM# 179 5 DUCAT

17.5000 g., 0.9860 Gold 0.5547 oz. AGW **Ruler:** Matthias II **Mint:** Vienna **Note:** Thick planchet. Struck with 1/2 Thaler dies, KM#164. Prev. KM#1762.

Date	Mintage	VG	F	VF	XF	Unc
1613	—	1,200	2,400	4,950	9,900	—
1617	—	1,200	2,400	4,950	9,900	—
1618	—	1,200	2,400	4,950	9,900	—

KM# 277 5 DUCAT

17.5000 g., 0.9860 Gold 0.5547 oz. AGW **Ruler:** Ferdinand II **Mint:** Vienna **Note:** Prev. KM#1806.

Date	Mintage	VG	F	VF	XF	Unc
1620 (c)	—	725	1,600	3,450	6,900	—
1621 (c)	—	725	1,600	3,450	6,900	—
1622 (c)	—	725	1,600	3,450	6,900	—
1623 (c)	—	725	1,600	3,450	6,900	—

KM# 367 5 DUCAT

17.5000 g., 0.9860 Gold 0.5547 oz. AGW **Ruler:** Ferdinand II **Obv:** Crowned bust right **Rev:** Heraldic imperial eagle **Mint:** Saint Veit **Note:** Prev. KM#1609.

Date	Mintage	VG	F	VF	XF	Unc
1621 Rare	—	—	—	—	—	—

KM# 553 5 DUCAT

17.5000 g., 0.9860 Gold 0.5547 oz. AGW **Ruler:** Ferdinand II **Obv:** Bust with plain collar **Rev:** Five coats of arms **Mint:** Vienna **Note:** Prev. KM#1807.

Date	Mintage	VG	F	VF	XF	Unc
1624 (c)	—	725	1,600	3,450	6,900	—

KM# 660 5 DUCAT

17.5000 g., 0.9860 Gold 0.5547 oz. AGW **Ruler:** Ferdinand II **Rev:** Crowned imperial eagle in inner circle **Mint:** Vienna **Note:** Prev. KM#1808.

Date	Mintage	VG	F	VF	XF	Unc
1626 (c)	—	725	1,600	3,450	6,900	—
1627 (c)	—	725	1,600	3,450	6,900	—
1628 (c)	—	725	1,600	3,450	6,900	—
1632 (c)	—	725	1,600	3,450	6,900	—
1634 (c)	—	725	1,600	3,450	6,900	—
1636 (c)	—	725	1,600	3,450	6,900	—
1637 (v)	—	725	1,600	3,450	6,900	—
1637 (v)	—	725	1,600	3,450	6,900	—

KM# 659 5 DUCAT

17.5000 g., 0.9860 Gold 0.5547 oz. AGW **Ruler:** Leopold **Subject:** Wedding of Leopold and Claudia **Mint:** Hall **Note:** Prev. KM#818.

Date	Mintage	VG	F	VF	XF	Unc
ND(1626) Rare	—	—	—	—	—	—

KM# 684 5 DUCAT

17.5000 g., 0.9860 Gold 0.5547 oz. AGW **Ruler:** Ferdinand II **Obv:** Uncrowned bust right **Rev:** Crowned arms **Mint:** Saint Veit **Note:** Prev. KM#1610.

Date	Mintage	VG	F	VF	XF	Unc
1627 (g) Rare	—	—	—	—	—	—

KM# 726 5 DUCAT

17.5000 g., 0.9860 Gold 0.5547 oz. AGW **Ruler:** Ferdinand II **Obv:** Bust right **Rev:** Heraldic imperial eagle **Mint:** Olmutz **Note:** Struck wtih 1 Thaler dies, KM#718. Prev. KM#1243.

Date	Mintage	VG	F	VF	XF	Unc
1629 (o)	—	775	1,650	3,500	7,400	—

KM# 761 5 DUCAT

17.5000 g., 0.9860 Gold 0.5547 oz. AGW **Ruler:** Ferdinand II **Mint:** Olmutz **Note:** Struck wtih 1 Thaler dies, KM#700. Prev. KM#A1244.

Date	Mintage	VG	F	VF	XF	Unc
1630 (o) MF	—	775	1,650	3,500	7,400	—

KM# 793 5 DUCAT
17.5000 g., 0.9860 Gold 0.5547 oz. AGW **Ruler:** Ferdinand Charles **Mint:** Hall **Note:** Prev. KM#844.

Date	Mintage	VG	F	VF	XF	Unc
ND(1632-46) Rare	—	—	—	—	—	—

KM# 792 5 DUCAT
17.5000 g., 0.9860 Gold 0.5547 oz. AGW **Ruler:** Ferdinand II **Obv:** Bust right **Rev:** Crowned arms **Mint:** Graz **Note:** Prev. KM#406.

Date	Mintage	VG	F	VF	XF	Unc
1632	—	900	1,750	4,600	8,000	—
1633	—	900	1,750	4,600	8,000	—

KM# 819 5 DUCAT
17.5000 g., 0.9860 Gold 0.5547 oz. AGW **Ruler:** Ferdinand III **Mint:** Glatz **Note:** Fr.#192. Prev. KM#315.

Date	Mintage	VG	F	VF	XF	Unc
1636 (h)	—	1,300	2,750	6,600	10,500	—

KM# 863 5 DUCAT
17.5000 g., 0.9860 Gold 0.5547 oz. AGW **Ruler:** Ferdinand III **Mint:** Saint Veit **Note:** Struck wtih 1 Thaler dies, KM#858. Prev. KM#1632.

Date	Mintage	VG	F	VF	XF	Unc
1638 Rare	—	—	—	—	—	—

KM# 912 5 DUCAT
17.5000 g., 0.9860 Gold 0.5547 oz. AGW **Ruler:** Ferdinand III **Obv:** Laureate bust right **Rev:** Crowned imperial eagle, arms on breast, holding upright sword and scepter **Mint:** Vienna **Note:** Struck with 1/2 Thaler dies, KM#839. Prev. KM#1846.

Date	Mintage	VG	F	VF	XF	Unc
1642	—	650	1,200	2,750	6,300	—
1643	—	650	1,200	2,750	6,300	—
1644	—	650	1,200	2,750	6,300	—
1646	—	650	1,200	2,750	6,300	—
1655	—	650	1,200	2,750	6,300	—

KM# 1163 5 DUCAT
17.5000 g., 0.9860 Gold 0.5547 oz. AGW **Ruler:** Leopold I **Obv:** Leopold laureate bust right **Rev:** Crowned imperial eagle **Mint:** Vienna **Note:** Prev. KM#1895.

Date	Mintage	VG	F	VF	XF	Unc
1659 Rare	—	—	—	—	—	—

KM# A1203 5 DUCAT
17.5000 g., 0.9860 Gold 0.5547 oz. AGW **Ruler:** Leopold I **Obv:** Laureate bust right **Obv. Legend:** LEOPOLDVS DG R.... **Rev:** Crowned imperial eagle **Rev. Legend:** ARCHD • AVS • D • BVR • COM • TIRO **Mint:** Vienna **Note:** Prev. KM#PnC22, PnD22, PnF22. Fr#262.

Date	Mintage	VG	F	VF	XF	Unc
1661 ca	—	—	—	8,500	13,500	—
1662 ca	—	—	—	8,500	13,500	—
1663 ca	—	—	—	8,500	13,500	—

KM# 1263 5 DUCAT
17.5000 g., 0.9860 Gold 0.5547 oz. AGW **Ruler:** Leopold I **Obv:** Leopold bust right **Rev:** Crowned imperial eagle **Mint:** Vienna **Note:** Prev. KM#1897.

Date	Mintage	VG	F	VF	XF	Unc
1669 Rare	—	—	—	—	—	—

KM# 1270 5 DUCAT
17.5000 g., 0.9860 Gold 0.5547 oz. AGW **Ruler:** Leopold I **Obv:** Laureate bust right in inner circle **Rev:** Crowned imperial eagle in inner circle **Mint:** Graz **Note:** Prev. KM#475.

Date	Mintage	VG	F	VF	XF	Unc
1670 IGW	—	775	1,750	4,800	9,400	—
1671 IW	—	775	1,750	4,800	9,400	—
1672	—	775	1,750	4,800	9,400	—
1690 IAN	—	775	1,750	4,800	9,400	—

KM# 98 6 DUCAT
21.0000 g., 0.9860 Gold 0.6657 oz. AGW **Ruler:** Rudolf II **Mint:** Vienna **Note:** Struck with 1 Thaler dies, KM#25. Prev. KM#1722.

Date	Mintage	VG	F	VF	XF	Unc
1608 Rare	—	—	—	—	—	—

KM# 111 6 DUCAT
21.0000 g., 0.9860 Gold 0.6657 oz. AGW **Ruler:** Rudolf II **Mint:** Vienna **Note:** Struck with 1/2 Thaler dies, KM#22. Prev. KM#1723.

Date	Mintage	VG	F	VF	XF	Unc
1609 Rare	—	—	—	—	—	—

KM# 661 6 DUCAT
21.0000 g., 0.9860 Gold 0.6657 oz. AGW **Ruler:** Leopold **Subject:** Wedding of Leopold and Claudia **Mint:** Hall **Note:** Similar to 5 Ducat, KM#818 but klippe. Prev. KM#819.

Date	Mintage	VG	F	VF	XF	Unc
ND(1626) Rare	—	—	—	—	—	—

KM# 702 6 DUCAT
21.0000 g., 0.9860 Gold 0.6657 oz. AGW **Ruler:** Ferdinand II **Obv:** Bust right **Rev:** Crowned imperial eagle **Mint:** Vienna **Note:** Struck with 1/2 Thaler dies, KM#514. Prev. KM#1809.

Date	Mintage	VG	F	VF	XF	Unc
1628 Rare	—	—	—	—	—	—

KM# 701 6 DUCAT
21.0000 g., 0.9860 Gold 0.6657 oz. AGW **Ruler:** Ferdinand II **Obv:** Bust right **Rev:** Crowned arms **Mint:** Saint Veit **Note:** Struck with 1 Thaler dies, KM#678. Prev. KM#1611.

Date	Mintage	VG	F	VF	XF	Unc
1628 (g) Rare	—	—	—	—	—	—

KM# 794 6 DUCAT
20.9000 g., 0.9860 Gold 0.6625 oz. AGW **Ruler:** Ferdinand II **Obv:** Bust right **Rev:** Crowned arms **Mint:** Graz **Note:** Prev. KM#407.

Date	Mintage	VG	F	VF	XF	Unc
1632	—	1,450	3,000	7,200	11,000	—

KM# 864 6 DUCAT
21.0000 g., 0.9860 Gold 0.6657 oz. AGW **Ruler:** Ferdinand III **Mint:** Saint Veit **Note:** Struck wtih 1 Thaler dies, KM#858. Prev. KM#A1633.

Date	Mintage	VG	F	VF	XF	Unc
1638 Rare	—	—	—	—	—	—

KM# 938 6 DUCAT
21.0000 g., 0.9860 Gold 0.6657 oz. AGW **Ruler:** Ferdinand III **Mint:** Brunn **Note:** Similar to 10 Ducats, KM#939.1. Prev. KM#228.

Date	Mintage	VG	F	VF	XF	Unc
1646 (o)	—	1,450	3,000	6,600	10,500	—

KM# 150 6-1/2 DUCAT
22.7500 g., 0.9860 Gold 0.7212 oz. AGW **Ruler:** Rudolf II **Obv:** Laureate bust of Rudolph II right **Rev:** Crowned arms **Mint:** Ensisheim **Note:** Prev. KM#A276.

Date	Mintage	VG	F	VF	XF	Unc
1611 Rare	—	—	—	—	—	—

KM# 773 7 DUCAT
24.5000 g., 0.9860 Gold 0.7766 oz. AGW **Ruler:** Ferdinand II **Obv:** Bust right **Rev:** Crowned arms **Mint:** Graz **Note:** Prev. KM#408.

Date	Mintage	VG	F	VF	XF	Unc
1631 Rare	—	—	—	—	—	—

KM# 865 7 DUCAT
24.5000 g., 0.9860 Gold 0.7766 oz. AGW **Ruler:** Ferdinand III **Mint:** Saint Veit **Note:** Struck wtih 1 Thaler dies, KM#858. Prev. KM#1633.

Date	Mintage	VG	F	VF	XF	Unc
1638 Rare	—	—	—	—	—	—

KM# 151 8 DUCAT
28.0000 g., 0.9860 Gold 0.8876 oz. AGW **Ruler:** Matthias II **Mint:** Vienna **Note:** Struck with 1 Thaler dies, KM#130. Prev. KM#A1763.

Date	Mintage	VG	F	VF	XF	Unc
1612 Rare	—	—	—	—	—	—

KM# 232 8 DUCAT
28.0000 g., 0.9860 Gold 0.8876 oz. AGW **Ruler:** Ferdinand II **Mint:** Klagenfurt **Note:** Struck with 1 Thaler dies, KM#24. Prev. KM#999.

Date	Mintage	VG	F	VF	XF	Unc
1618 Rare	—	—	—	—	—	—

KM# 662 8 DUCAT
28.0000 g., 0.9860 Gold 0.8876 oz. AGW **Ruler:** Leopold **Subject:** Wedding of Leopold **Obv:** Crowned busts of the royal couple right **Rev:** Crowned imperial eagle right **Mint:** Hall **Note:** Prev. KM#820.

Date	Mintage	VG	F	VF	XF	Unc
ND(1626) Rare	—	—	—	—	—	—

KM# 727 8 DUCAT
28.0000 g., 0.9860 Gold 0.8876 oz. AGW **Ruler:** Ferdinand III **Mint:** Glatz **Note:** Struck with 1 Thaler dies, KM#699.3. Fr.#191. Prev. KM#316.

Date	Mintage	VG	F	VF	XF	Unc
1629 HG Rare	—	—	—	—	—	—

KM# 795 8 DUCAT
28.0000 g., 0.9860 Gold 0.8876 oz. AGW **Ruler:** Ferdinand II **Obv:** Bust right **Rev:** Crowned arms **Mint:** Saint Veit **Note:** Struck with 1 Thaler dies, KM#678. Prev. KM#1612.

Date	Mintage	VG	F	VF	XF	Unc
1632	—	—	—	14,000	20,000	—

KM# 866 8 DUCAT
28.0000 g., 0.9860 Gold 0.8876 oz. AGW **Ruler:** Ferdinand III **Mint:** Saint Veit **Note:** Struck wtih 1 Thaler dies, KM#858. Prev. KM#A1634.

Date	Mintage	VG	F	VF	XF	Unc
1638 Rare	—	—	—	—	—	—

KM# 728 9 DUCAT
31.5000 g., 0.9860 Gold 0.9985 oz. AGW **Ruler:** Ferdinand III **Mint:** Glatz **Note:** Struck with 1 Thaler dies, KM#699.3. Fr.#190. Prev. KM#317.

Date	Mintage	VG	F	VF	XF	Unc
1629 HG Rare	—	—	—	—	—	—

KM# 796 9 DUCAT
31.5000 g., 0.9860 Gold 0.9985 oz. AGW **Ruler:** Ferdinand II **Obv:** Bust right **Rev:** Crowned arms **Mint:** Saint Veit **Note:** Struck with 1 Thaler dies, KM#678. Prev. KM#1613.

Date	Mintage	VG	F	VF	XF	Unc
1632 Rare	—	—	—	—	—	—

KM# 1256 9 DUCAT
31.5000 g., 0.9860 Gold 0.9985 oz. AGW **Ruler:** Leopold I **Mint:** Hall **Note:** Struck with 1 Thaler dies, KM#1238. Prev. KM#647.

Date	Mintage	VG	F	VF	XF	Unc
1668 Rare	—	—	—	—	—	—

KM# 85 10 DUCAT
35.0000 g., 0.9860 Gold 1.1095 oz. AGW **Ruler:** Rudolf II **Mint:** Vienna **Note:** Struck with 1 Thaler dies, KM#25. Prev. KM#1721.

Date	Mintage	VG	F	VF	XF	Unc
1607 Rare	—	—	—	—	—	—

KM# 155 10 DUCAT
35.0000 g., 0.9860 Gold 1.1095 oz. AGW **Ruler:** Matthias II **Mint:** Vienna **Note:** Struck with 1 Thaler dies, KM#144. Prev. KM#B1763.

Date	Mintage	VG	F	VF	XF	Unc
1612	—	1,200	2,250	4,500	8,500	—

KM# 181 10 DUCAT
35.0000 g., 0.9860 Gold 1.1095 oz. AGW **Ruler:** Matthias II **Mint:** Vienna **Note:** Struck with 1/2 Thaler dies, KM#164. Prev. KM#1763.

Date	Mintage	VG	F	VF	XF	Unc
1613 (c) Rare	—	—	—	—	—	—

KM# 192 10 DUCAT
35.0000 g., 0.9860 Gold 1.1095 oz. AGW **Ruler:** Matthias II **Mint:** Vienna **Note:** Struck with 1 Thaler dies, KM#169. Prev. KM#A1764.

Date	Mintage	VG	F	VF	XF	Unc
1614 Rare	—	—	—	—	—	—

KM# 198 10 DUCAT
35.0000 g., 0.9860 Gold 1.1095 oz. AGW **Ruler:** Matthias II **Mint:** Vienna **Note:** Struck with 1 Thaler dies, KM#196. Prev. KM#B1764.

Date	Mintage	VG	F	VF	XF	Unc
1615 Rare	—	—	—	—	—	—

KM# 211 10 DUCAT
35.0000 g., 0.9860 Gold 1.1095 oz. AGW **Ruler:** Matthias II **Mint:** Vienna **Note:** Struck with 1 Thaler dies, KM#206. Prev. KM#1764.

Date	Mintage	VG	F	VF	XF	Unc
1616 Rare	—	—	—	—	—	—

KM# 368 10 DUCAT
3.5000 g., 0.9860 Gold 0.1109 oz. AGW **Ruler:** Ferdinand II **Obv:** Bust right **Rev:** Crowned arms **Mint:** Hall **Note:** Prev. KM#617.

Date	Mintage	VG	F	VF	XF	Unc
1621 Rare	—	—	—	—	—	—

KM# 369 10 DUCAT
35.0000 g., 0.9860 Gold 1.1095 oz. AGW **Ruler:** Ferdinand II **Obv:** Crowned bust right **Rev:** Heraldic imperial eagle **Mint:** Klagenfurt **Note:** Prev. KM#982.

Date	Mintage	VG	F	VF	XF	Unc
1621 Rare	—	—	—	—	—	—

KM# 370 10 DUCAT
35.0000 g., 0.9860 Gold 1.1095 oz. AGW **Ruler:** Ferdinand II **Obv:** Ruffled collar **Mint:** Olmutz **Note:** Prev. KM#1244.

Date	Mintage	VG	F	VF	XF	Unc
1621 BZ Rare	—	—	—	—	—	—
1628 (o) Rare	—	—	—	—	—	—

KM# 371 10 DUCAT
35.0000 g., 0.9860 Gold 1.1095 oz. AGW **Ruler:** Ferdinand II **Obv:** Bust right **Rev:** Crowned imperial eagle **Mint:** Vienna **Note:** Struck with 1 Thaler dies, KM#268.2. Prev. KM#1810.

Date	Mintage	VG	F	VF	XF	Unc
16Z1 (c)	—	2,500	4,150	7,700	12,000	—
16ZZ/1 (c)	—	2,500	4,150	7,700	12,000	—

KM# 622 10 DUCAT
35.0000 g., 0.9860 Gold 1.1095 oz. AGW **Ruler:** Ferdinand II **Mint:** Vienna **Note:** Struck with 1 Thaler dies, KM#599. Prev. KM#1811.

Date	Mintage	VG	F	VF	XF	Unc
1625 (c)	—	2,500	4,150	7,700	12,000	—
1626 (c)	—	2,500	4,150	7,700	12,000	—
1628 (c)	—	2,500	4,150	7,700	12,000	—
1630 (c)	—	2,500	4,150	7,700	12,000	—
1631 (c)	—	2,500	4,150	7,700	12,000	—
1636 (v)	—	2,500	4,150	7,700	12,000	—
1637 (v)	—	2,500	4,150	7,700	12,000	—

KM# 703 10 DUCAT
35.0000 g., 0.9860 Gold 1.1095 oz. AGW **Ruler:** Ferdinand III **Mint:** Glatz **Note:** Struck with 1 Thaler dies, KM#699.1. Fr.#189. Prev. KM#318.

Date	Mintage	VG	F	VF	XF	Unc
1628 (p) Rare	—	—	—	—	—	—

KM# 729 10 DUCAT
35.0000 g., 0.9860 Gold 1.1095 oz. AGW **Ruler:** Ferdinand III **Mint:** Glatz **Note:** Struck with 1 Thaler dies, KM#699.3. Fr.#189. Prev. KM#319.

Date	Mintage	VG	F	VF	XF	Unc
1629 HG Rare	—	—	—	—	—	—

Note: Hess-Divo Auction 267, 5-96, Unc. realized $22,500

KM# 730 10 DUCAT
35.0000 g., 0.9860 Gold 1.1095 oz. AGW **Ruler:** Ferdinand II **Obv:** Plain collar **Mint:** Olmutz **Note:** Prev. KM#1245.

Date	Mintage	VG	F	VF	XF	Unc
1629 (o) Rare	—	—	—	—	—	—
1630 (o) MF Rare	—	—	—	—	—	—
1633 (o) Rare	—	—	—	—	—	—
1636/3 (o) Rare	—	—	—	—	—	—

KM# 803 10 DUCAT
35.0000 g., 0.9860 Gold 1.1095 oz. AGW **Ruler:** Ferdinand II **Obv:** Bust right **Rev:** Crowned arms **Mint:** Graz **Note:** Prev. KM#409.

Date	Mintage	VG	F	VF	XF	Unc
1633 Rare	—	—	—	—	—	—

KM# 867 10 DUCAT
35.0000 g., 0.9860 Gold 1.1095 oz. AGW **Ruler:** Ferdinand III **Mint:** Saint Veit **Note:** Struck wtih 1 Thaler dies, KM#858. Prev. KM#1634.

Date	Mintage	VG	F	VF	XF	Unc
1638 Rare	—	—	—	—	—	—

KM# 900 10 DUCAT
35.0000 g., 0.9860 Gold 1.1095 oz. AGW **Ruler:** Ferdinand III **Mint:** Vienna **Note:** Struck with 1 Thaler dies, KM#840. Prev. KM#A1848.

Date	Mintage	VG	F	VF	XF	Unc
1641 (b) Rare	—	—	—	—	—	—
1642 (b) Rare	—	—	—	—	—	—

KM# 913 10 DUCAT
35.0000 g., 0.9860 Gold 1.1095 oz. AGW **Ruler:** Ferdinand III **Obv:** Large laureate bust right **Rev:** Crowned imperial eagle, arms on breast, holding upright sword and scepter **Mint:** Vienna **Note:** Struck with 1 Thaler dies, KM#839. Prev. KM#1847.

Date	Mintage	VG	F	VF	XF	Unc
164Z (b)	—	2,750	4,400	8,500	12,500	—
1643 (b)	—	2,750	4,400	8,500	12,500	—

KM# 926 10 DUCAT
35.0000 g., 0.9860 Gold 1.1095 oz. AGW **Ruler:** Ferdinand III **Mint:** Vienna **Note:** Struck with 1 Thaler dies, KM#882. Prev. KM#B1848.

Date	Mintage	VG	F	VF	XF	Unc
1645 (b) Rare	—	—	—	—	—	—

KM# 939.1 10 DUCAT
35.0000 g., 0.9860 Gold 1.1095 oz. AGW **Ruler:** Ferdinand III **Obv:** With inner beaded circle **Rev:** With inner beaded circle **Mint:** Brunn **Note:** Prev. KM#229.2.

Date	Mintage	VG	F	VF	XF	Unc
1648 (o) Rare	—	—	—	—	—	—

KM# 939.2 10 DUCAT
35.0000 g., 0.9860 Gold 1.1095 oz. AGW **Ruler:** Ferdinand III **Obv:** Without inner beaded circle **Rev:** Without inner beaded circle **Mint:** Brunn **Note:** Struck with 1 Thaler dies, KM#929.1. Prev. KM#229.1.

Date	Mintage	VG	F	VF	XF	Unc
1646 (o) Rare	—	—	—	—	—	—

KM# 993 10 DUCAT
35.0000 g., 0.9860 Gold 1.1095 oz. AGW **Ruler:** Ferdinand III **Obv:** Large, more ornate laureate bust right **Mint:** Vienna **Note:** Prev. KM#1848.

Date	Mintage	VG	F	VF	XF	Unc
1655	—	3,000	5,000	9,000	14,000	—

KM# 996 10 DUCAT
35.0000 g., 0.9860 Gold 1.1095 oz. AGW **Ruler:** Ferdinand III **Obv:** Small laureate bust right **Mint:** Vienna **Note:** Prev. KM#1849.

Date	Mintage	VG	F	VF	XF	Unc
1656	—	2,750	4,500	8,500	12,500	—
1657	—	2,750	4,500	8,500	12,500	—

KM# 1326 10 DUCAT
35.0000 g., 0.9860 Gold 1.1095 oz. AGW **Ruler:** Leopold I **Mint:** Hall **Note:** Struck with 1 Thaler dies, KM#1303.1. Prev. KM#A659.

Date	Mintage	VG	F	VF	XF	Unc
1683 Rare	—	—	—	—	—	—

KM# 1327 10 DUCAT
Gold **Ruler:** Leopold I **Obv:** Leopold I laureate bust right in inner circle **Rev:** Crowned arms in Order chain, crown divides date **Mint:** Saint Veit **Note:** Struck with 2 Thaler dies, KM#1323. Prev. KM#1662.

Date	Mintage	VG	F	VF	XF	Unc
1683/2	—	—	—	14,000	20,000	—

KM# 1350 10 DUCAT
35.0000 g., 0.9860 Gold 1.1095 oz. AGW **Ruler:** Leopold I **Obv:** Armored laureate bust right **Obv. Legend:** LEOPOLDVS: D: ROM: IMP: S: A: G: H: B: REX: **Rev:** Crowned arms within Order chain **Rev. Legend:** ARCHID: AVST: DVX: BV: CO: TYR • 16 **Mint:** Hall **Note:** Struck with 1 Thaler dies, KM#1349. Prev. KM#659.

Date	Mintage	VG	F	VF	XF	Unc
1690 Rare	—	—	—	—	—	—

KM# 731 12 DUCAT
42.0000 g., 0.9860 Gold 1.3314 oz. AGW **Ruler:** Ferdinand III **Mint:** Glatz **Note:** Struck with 1 Thaler dies, KM#699.3. Fr.#188. Prev. KM#322.

Date	Mintage	VG	F	VF	XF	Unc
1629 HG Rare	—	—	—	—	—	—

KM# 797 12 DUCAT
42.0000 g., 0.9860 Gold 1.3314 oz. AGW **Ruler:** Ferdinand II **Obv:** Bust right **Rev:** Crowned arms **Mint:** Saint Veit **Note:** Struck with 1 Thaler dies, KM#678. Prev. KM#1614.

Date	Mintage	VG	F	VF	XF	Unc
1632 Rare	—	—	—	—	—	—

KM# 820 12 DUCAT
42.0000 g., 0.9860 Gold 1.3314 oz. AGW **Ruler:** Ferdinand II **Obv:** Bust right **Rev:** Heraldic imperial eagle **Mint:** Olmutz **Note:** Prev. KM#1246.

Date	Mintage	VG	F	VF	XF	Unc
1636/3 (o) Rare	—	—	—	—	—	—

KM# 1264 12 DUCAT
42.0000 g., 0.9860 Gold 1.3314 oz. AGW **Ruler:** Leopold I **Obv:** Laureate bust right **Rev:** Crowned imperial eagle **Mint:** Vienna **Note:** Prev. KM#A1899.

Date	Mintage	VG	F	VF	XF	Unc
1669 Rare	—	—	—	—	—	—

KM# 1313 12 DUCAT
42.0000 g., 0.9860 Gold 1.3314 oz. AGW **Ruler:** Leopold I **Mint:** Vienna **Note:** Struck with 1 Thaler dies, KM#1275.2. Prev. KM#1899.

Date	Mintage	VG	F	VF	XF	Unc
1681 Rare	—	—	—	—	—	—

KM# 821 15 DUCAT
52.5000 g., 0.9860 Gold 1.6642 oz. AGW **Ruler:** Ferdinand II **Obv:** Bust right **Rev:** Heraldic imperial eagle **Mint:** Olmutz **Note:** Prev. KM#1247.

Date	Mintage	VG	F	VF	XF	Unc
1636/3 (o) Rare	—	—	—	—	—	—

KM# 372 20 DUCAT
70.0000 g., 0.9860 Gold 2.2190 oz. AGW **Ruler:** Ferdinand II **Obv:** Crowned bust right **Rev:** Heraldic imperial eagle **Mint:** Olmutz **Note:** Prev. KM#1248.

Date	Mintage	VG	F	VF	XF	Unc
1621 BZ Rare	—	—	—	—	—	—

KM# 427 20 DUCAT
70.0000 g., 0.9860 Gold 2.2190 oz. AGW **Ruler:** Ferdinand II **Obv:** Crowned bust right **Rev:** Heraldic imperial eagle **Mint:** Klagenfurt **Note:** Prev. KM#983.

Date	Mintage	VG	F	VF	XF	Unc
1622 Rare	—	—	—	—	—	—

KM# 664 20 DUCAT
70.0000 g., 0.9860 Gold 2.2190 oz. AGW **Ruler:** Leopold **Subject:** Wedding of Leopold and Claudia **Mint:** Hall **Note:** Struck with 3 Thaler dies, KM#648. Prev. KM#824.

Date	Mintage	VG	F	VF	XF	Unc
ND(1626) Rare	—	—	—	—	—	—

KM# 822 20 DUCAT
70.0000 g., 0.9860 Gold 2.2190 oz. AGW **Ruler:** Ferdinand II **Obv:** Bust right with value XX stamped in field **Rev:** Crowned arms **Mint:** Graz **Note:** Prev. KM#410.

Date	Mintage	VG	F	VF	XF	Unc
1636 Rare	—	—	—	—	—	—

KM# 823 20 DUCAT
70.0000 g., 0.9860 Gold 2.2190 oz. AGW **Ruler:** Ferdinand II **Obv:** Bust right **Mint:** Olmutz **Note:** Prev. KM#1249.

Date	Mintage	VG	F	VF	XF	Unc
1636/3 (o) Rare	—	—	—	—	—	—

KM# 940 20 DUCAT
70.0000 g., 0.9860 Gold 2.2190 oz. AGW **Ruler:** Ferdinand Charles **Mint:** Hall **Note:** Struck with 2 Thaler dies, KM#934. Prev. KM#849.

Date	Mintage	VG	F	VF	XF	Unc
ND(1646) Rare	—	—	—	—	—	—

PATTERNS

Including off metal strikes

KM#	Date	Mintage	Identification	Mkt Val
PnPR1	1602	—	Ducat. Silver. Klippe.	—
PnPR2	1604	—	Maley Groschen. Gold. KM#1295.	—
PnPR3	1604	—	3 Kreuzer. Gold. KM#1297. Weight of 1 Ducat.	—
PnKN2	1604	—	Klein Pfennig. Gold. KM#1015	—
PnJO1	1607	—	1/4 Thaler. Gold. KM#867, weight of 3 Ducat.	—
PnHA1	1612	—	Kreuzer. Gold. KM#583	—
PnHA2	ND(1612-19)	—	Vierer. Gold. Weight of 1/4 Ducat, KM#760.	—
PnVI6	1613	—	3 Kreuzer. Gold. KM#1728, weight of 3 Ducat.	—
PnVI9	1616	—	3 Kreuzer. Gold. KM#1728, weight of 5 Ducat.	—
PnSV1	ND	—	Kreuzer. Gold. Weight of 1/2 Ducat.	—
PnSV2	1621	—	48 Kreuzer. Gold. Weight of 4 Ducat.	—
PnKL1	ND	—	Kreuzer. Gold. KM#951, weight of 1/2 Ducat.	—
PnKL2	ND	—	Kreuzer. Gold. KM#952, weight of 1/2 Ducat.	—
PnKL3	1621	—	48 Kreuzer. Gold. KM#957, weight of 4 Ducat.	—
PnKL4	1622	—	48 Kreuzer. Gold. KM#958, weight of 4 Ducat.	—
PnSV3	1622	—	48 Kreuzer. Gold. Weight of 4 Ducat.	—
PnPR24	1623 (e)	—	10 Ducat. Silver. KM#1400. Weight of 1 Thaler.	—
PnPR25	1623 (e)	—	10 Ducat. Silver. KM#1400. Weight of 2 Thaler.	—
PnPR26	1623 (e)	—	10 Ducat. Silver. KM#1400. Weight of 3 Thaler.	—
PnPR28	1624 (c)	—	10 Ducat. Silver. KM#1400. Weight of 1 Thaler.	—
PnHA3	ND(1625-32)	—	Kreuzer. Gold. Weight of 1/2 Ducat, KM#788.	—
PnHA4	1626	—	10 Kreuzer. Bronze. KM#795.	—
PnSV4	1627	—	Thaler. Gold. Weight of 5 Ducat; KM#1603.	—
PnSV5	1628	—	10 Kreuzer. Gold. Weight of 2 Ducat; KM#1597.	—
PnSV6	1628	—	10 Kreuzer. Gold. Weight of 3 Ducat; KM#1597.	—
PnSV7	1628	—	10 Kreuzer. Gold. Weight of 3 Ducat; KM#1598.	—
PnKL5	1628	—	10 Kreuzer. Gold. Weight of 3 Ducat.	—
PnKL6	1628	—	10 Kreuzer. Gold. Weight of 2 Ducat.	—
PnHA8	ND(1632)	—	2 Thaler. Pewter. KM#807.	—
PnSV11	1637	—	3 Kreuzer. Gold. Weight of 1 Ducat; KM#1624.	—
PnSV12	1637	—	3 Kreuzer. Gold. Weight of 1 Ducat; KM#1625. Klippe.	—
PnSV13	1638	—	2 Pfennig. Gold. KM#1622.	—
	1638	—	2 Pfennig. Gold. KM#1622.	—
PnSV14	1638	—	3 Kreuzer. Gold. Weight of 1 Ducat. KM#1622.	—
PnSV15	1638	—	3 Kreuzer. Gold. Weight of 1 Ducat. KM#1625. Klippe.	—
PnGR9	1638/4	—	2 Ducat. Gold.	—
PnPR29	1639	—	Ducat. Silver. KM#1417. Klippe.	—
PnSV21	1639	—	Pfennig. Gold. KM#1620.	—
PnSV22	1639	—	Kreuzer. Gold. KM#1623; weight of 1/2 Ducat.	—
PnSV23	1640	—	Kreuzer. Gold. KM#1623; weight of 1/2 Ducat.	—
PnSV24	1641	—	2 Pfennig. Gold. KM#1622.	—
PnSV25	1642	—	2 Pfennig. Gold. KM#1622.	—
PnHA9	1642	—	2 Ducat. Silver. KM#842.	—
PnVI18	1642	—	2 Pfennig. Gold. KM#1816.	—
PnVI19	1644	—	2 Pfennig. Gold. KM#1850.	—
PnGR10	1644	—	2 Pfennig. Gold. KM#420	—
PnGR11	1645	—	Pfennig. Gold. KM#418	—
PnGR12	1645	—	Kreuzer. Gold. KM#422; weight of 1/2 Ducat.	—
PnGR13	1646	—	Kreuzer. Gold. KM#422	—
PnHA11	ND(1647-62)	—	Kreuzer. Gold. KM#827.	—
PnVI20	1647	—	2 Pfennig. Gold. KM#1816.	—
PnGR14	1648	—	2 Pfennig. Gold. KM#420	—
PnSV26	1653	—	Pfennig. Gold. KM#1620.	—
PnSV27	1653	—	2 Pfennig. Gold. KM#1622; weight of 1/4 Ducat.	—
PnKN4	1654	—	Pfennig. Lead. KM#1100	—
PnJO3	1659	—	Thaler. Lead. KM#935	—
PnJO5	1663	—	15 Kreuzer. Gold. KM#932	—
PnJO6	1663	—	1/4 Thaler. Lead. KM#933	—
PnJO7	1663	—	1/2 Thaler. Lead. KM#934	—
PnJO4	1664	—	15 Kreuzer. Lead. KM#932	—
PnVI22	1696	—	15 Kreuzer. Brass.	—

AUSTRIAN STATES

BURGAU
MUNICH • (GERMANY)
VIENNA • (AUSTRIA)
SALZBURG
STYRIA
TYROL
GURK
• BRIXEN
• AUERSPERG

TRIAL STRIKES

KM#	Date	Mintage	Identification	Mkt Val
TSHA1	ND(1626)	—	2 Thaler. Lead. KM#822.	—

AUERSPERG

Auersberg

The Auersperg princes were princes of estates in Austrian Carniola, a former duchy with estates in Laibach and Silesia, a former province in southwestern Poland and Swabia, one of the stem-duchies of medieval Germany. They were elevated to princely rank in 1653, and the following year were made dukes of Muensterberg, which they ultimately sold to Prussia.

RULER
Johann Weikard, 1615-1677

MONETARY SYSTEM
120 Kreuzer = 1 Convention Thaler

PRINCIPALITY

STANDARD COINAGE

KM# 3 THALER
Silver **Ruler:** Johann Weikard **Obv:** Facing bust with date below **Rev:** Crowned arms in Order chain **Note:** Dav. #3371.

Date	Mintage	VG	F	VF	XF	Unc
1654	—	900	1,400	2,250	3,500	—

TRADE COINAGE

KM# 10 DUCAT
3.5000 g., 0.9860 Gold 0.1109 oz. AGW **Ruler:** Johann Weikard **Obv:** Bust of Johann Weikhard in inner circle **Rev:** Shield of arms in inner circle

Date	Mintage	VG	F	VF	XF	Unc
ND	—	350	800	1,500	2,900	—

BRIXEN

A city near the Brenner Pass that was the seat of a bishopric from 992. The bishops were given the coinage right in 1179. Brixen was given to Austria in 1802.

RULER
Karl of Austria, 1613-1624

NOTE: Ruler listing includes only coin issuers and not all bishops.

BISHOPRIC

STANDARD COINAGE

KM# 5 3 KREUZER
Silver **Ruler:** Karl of Austria

Date	Mintage	VG	F	VF	XF	Unc
1614	—	22.50	45.00	80.00	175	—
1620	—	22.50	45.00	80.00	175	—

KM# 6 THALER
Silver **Ruler:** Karl of Austria **Obv:** Bust right **Rev:** Several coast of arms **Note:** Dav. #3457.

Date	Mintage	VG	F	VF	XF	Unc
1614	—	600	1,000	2,000	3,250	—

KM# 7 THALER
Silver **Ruler:** Karl of Austria **Note:** Dav. #3459.

Date	Mintage	VG	F	VF	XF	Unc
1615	—	600	1,000	2,000	3,250	—
1618	—	600	1,000	2,000	3,250	—

KM# 8 2 THALER
Silver **Ruler:** Karl of Austria **Obv:** Bust right **Rev:** Several coat of arms **Note:** Dav. #3456.

Date	Mintage	VG	F	VF	XF	Unc
1614 Rare	—	—	—	—	—	—

KM# 17 2 THALER
Silver **Ruler:** Karl of Austria **Note:** Similar to 1 Thaler, KM#7. Dav. #3458.

Date	Mintage	VG	F	VF	XF	Unc
1618	—	2,250	3,500	—	—	—

KM# 10 3 THALER
Silver **Ruler:** Karl of Austria **Obv:** Bust right **Rev:** Several coat of arms **Note:** Dav. #3456A.

Date	Mintage	VG	F	VF	XF	Unc
1614 Rare	—	—	—	—	—	—

KM# 11 4 THALER
Silver **Ruler:** Karl of Austria **Obv:** Bust right **Rev:** Several coat of arms **Note:** Dav. #3456B.

Date	Mintage	VG	F	VF	XF	Unc
1614 Rare	—	—	—	—	—	—

TRADE COINAGE

KM# 18 1/2 DUCAT
1.7500 g., 0.9860 Gold 0.0555 oz. AGW **Ruler:** Karl of Austria **Obv:** Bust of Karl right **Rev:** Crowned arms flanked by mitred arms

Date	Mintage	VG	F	VF	XF	Unc
1618	—	575	1,200	2,750	4,000	—

KM# 12 DUCAT
3.5000 g., 0.9860 Gold 0.1109 oz. AGW **Ruler:** Karl of Austria **Obv:** Bust of Karl right **Rev:** Crowned arms flanked by mitred arms

Date	Mintage	VG	F	VF	XF	Unc
1614	—	800	1,700	3,350	6,000	—
1618	—	800	1,700	3,350	6,000	—

KM# 13 3 DUCAT
10.5000 g., 0.9860 Gold 0.3328 oz. AGW **Ruler:** Karl of Austria **Obv:** Bust of Karl right in inner circle **Rev:** Crowned arms in inner circle

Date	Mintage	VG	F	VF	XF	Unc
1614 Rare	—	—	—	—	—	—

KM# 15 5 DUCAT
17.5000 g., 0.9860 Gold 0.5547 oz. AGW **Ruler:** Karl of Austria **Obv:** Bust of Karl right in inner circle **Rev:** Crowned arms in inner circle

Date	Mintage	VG	F	VF	XF	Unc
1614 Rare	—	—	—	—	—	—

KM# 16 7 DUCAT
24.5000 g., 0.9860 Gold 0.7766 oz. AGW **Ruler:** Karl of Austria **Note:** Struck with 1 Thaler dies, KM#6.

Date	Mintage	VG	F	VF	XF	Unc
1614 Rare	—	—	—	—	—	—

KM# 20 10 DUCAT
35.0000 g., 0.9860 Gold 1.1095 oz. AGW **Ruler:** Karl of Austria **Note:** Struck with 1 Thaler dies, KM#7.

Date	Mintage	VG	F	VF	XF	Unc
1618 Rare	—	—	—	—	—	—

DIETRICHSTEIN

A noble Carinthian family traceable from 1000, it was not until after 1500 that the first coins were made. The coinage was sporadic and Karl Ludwig was the last to issue coins in 1726.

RULERS

Pulsgau Line
Sigismund Ludwig, 1631-1664
Sigismund Helfried, 1664-1698
Karl Ludwig, 1698-1732
Nicolsburg Line
Ferdinand Josef, 1655-1698

NOTE: Ruler listing includes only coin issuers and not all rulers of the various line of this family.

COUNTY

STANDARD COINAGE

KM# 5 1/2 KREUZER (2 Pfennig)
Copper Or Billon **Ruler:** Sigismund Ludwig **Obv:** Crowned arms **Note:** Uniface.

Date	Mintage	VG	F	VF	XF	Unc
1650	—	45.00	85.00	170	300	—

KM# 1 THALER
Silver **Ruler:** Sigismund Ludwig **Rev:** Double eagle above large crowned arms **Note:** Dav. #3372. Varieties exist.

Date	Mintage	VG	F	VF	XF	Unc
1638	—	165	325	550	875	—
1644	—	165	325	550	875	—
1647	—	165	325	550	875	—

KM# 7 THALER
Silver **Ruler:** Sigismund Ludwig **Rev:** Large double eagle above small crowned arms **Note:** Dav. #3373.

Date	Mintage	VG	F	VF	XF	Unc
1640	—	175	350	575	925	—
1641	—	175	350	575	925	—

KM# 9 THALER
Silver **Ruler:** Sigismund Ludwig **Rev:** Larger arms with Order chain around **Note:** Dav. #3374. Varieties exist.

Date	Mintage	VG	F	VF	XF	Unc
1646	—	165	325	550	875	—
1651	—	165	325	550	875	—
1653	—	165	325	550	875	—

KM# 12 THALER
Silver **Ruler:** Sigismund Helfried **Obv:** Bust right **Rev:** Crowned arms **Note:** Dav. #3375.

Date	Mintage	VG	F	VF	XF	Unc
1664	—	375	650	1,150	2,000	—

KM# 10 2 THALER
Silver **Ruler:** Sigismund Ludwig **Note:** Similar to 1 Thaler, KM#7. Dav. A3373.

Date	Mintage	VG	F	VF	XF	Unc
1641	—	1,200	2,000	3,500	6,000	—

TRADE COINAGE

KM# 8 DUCAT
3.5000 g., 0.9860 Gold 0.1109 oz. AGW **Ruler:** Sigismund Ludwig **Obv:** Bust right in inner circle **Rev:** Crowned imperial eagle with F III on breast over small arms in inner circle

Date	Mintage	VG	F	VF	XF	Unc
1640	—	725	1,400	3,300	5,500	—
1651	—	725	1,400	3,300	5,500	—

KM# 2 5 DUCAT
17.5000 g., 0.9860 Gold 0.5547 oz. AGW **Ruler:** Sigismund Ludwig **Note:** Struck with 1 Thaler dies, KM#6.

Date	Mintage	VG	F	VF	XF	Unc
1638 Rare	—	—	—	—	—	—

KM# 3 6 DUCAT
21.0000 g., 0.9860 Gold 0.6657 oz. AGW **Ruler:** Sigismund Ludwig **Note:** Struck with 1 Thaler dies, KM#9.

Date	Mintage	VG	F	VF	XF	Unc
1638 Rare	—	—	—	—	—	—

KM# A12 6 DUCAT
21.0000 g., 0.9860 Gold 0.6657 oz. AGW **Ruler:** Sigismund Ludwig **Note:** Struck with 1 Thaler dies, KM#9.

Date	Mintage	VG	F	VF	XF	Unc
1653 Rare	—	—	—	—	—	—

KM# 11 10 DUCAT
35.0000 g., 0.9870 Gold 1.1106 oz. AGW **Ruler:** Sigismund Ludwig **Note:** Struck with 1 Thaler dies, KM#7.

Date	Mintage	VG	F	VF	XF	Unc
1641 Rare	—	—	—	—	—	—

KM# B12 10 DUCAT
35.0000 g., 0.9870 Gold 1.1106 oz. AGW **Ruler:** Sigismund Ludwig **Note:** Struck with 1 Thaler dies, KM#9.

Date	Mintage	VG	F	VF	XF	Unc
1653 Rare	—	—	—	—	—	—

COUNTY

Nikolsburg Line

STANDARD COINAGE

KM# 20 THALER
Silver **Ruler:** Ferdinand Josef **Obv:** Bust right **Rev:** Crowned arms **Note:** Dav. #3376.

Date	Mintage	VG	F	VF	XF	Unc
1695	—	175	350	600	950	—

TRADE COINAGE

KM# 21 DUCAT
3.5000 g., 0.9860 Gold 0.1109 oz. AGW **Ruler:** Ferdinand Josef **Obv:** Bust of Ferdinand Josef right **Rev:** Crowned arms in order collar; date divided at top

Date	Mintage	VG	F	VF	XF	Unc
1695	—	825	1,500	3,850	6,250	—
1696	—	825	1,500	3,850	6,250	—

EGGENBERG

An old Styrian family first mentioned in 1448. Two members made free barons in 1598 after service in the Dutch wars. Made a prince in 1623. Bought Italian properties of Aquileia and Gradiska in 1641. Passed to Herberstein in 1774 after death of the line.

RULERS
Johann Ulrich, 1623-1634
Johann Anton, 1634-1649
Johann Christoph, 1649-1710
Johann Seyfried, 1649-1713

PRINCIPALITY

STANDARD COINAGE

KM# 19 3 KREUZER
Silver **Ruler:** Johann Anton

Date	Mintage	VG	F	VF	XF	Unc
1647	—	45.00	90.00	165	275	—
1649	—	45.00	90.00	165	275	—

KM# 52 3 KREUZER
Silver **Ruler:** Johann Christoph

Date	Mintage	VG	F	VF	XF	Unc
1677	—	32.00	65.00	125	245	—

KM# 39 1/4 THALER
Silver **Ruler:** Johann Christoph

Date	Mintage	VG	F	VF	XF	Unc
1655	—	175	350	625	1,000	—
1658	—	175	350	625	1,000	—

KM# 40 1/2 THALER
Silver **Ruler:** Johann Christoph

Date	Mintage	VG	F	VF	XF	Unc
1654	—	275	550	1,000	1,650	—
1658	—	275	550	1,000	1,650	—

KM# 5 THALER
Silver **Ruler:** Johann Ulrich **Obv:** Crowned arms **Rev:** Heraldic double eagle **Note:** Dav. #3377.

Date	Mintage	VG	F	VF	XF	Unc
1625	—	600	1,000	1,650	2,750	—

KM# 6 THALER
Silver **Ruler:** Johann Ulrich **Note:** Similar to 2 Thaler, KM#7. Dav. #3379.

Date	Mintage	VG	F	VF	XF	Unc
1625	—	600	1,000	1,650	2,750	—

KM# 8 THALER
Silver **Ruler:** Johann Ulrich **Obv:** Crowned arms in order chain, 1-6-2-5 **Note:** Dav. #3380. Varieties exist.

Date	Mintage	VG	F	VF	XF	Unc
1629 Rare	—	—	—	—	—	—

KM# 9 THALER
Silver **Ruler:** Johann Ulrich **Obv:** EG and scroll below ruffled bust **Rev:** Crowned oval arms in order chain, date in legend **Note:** Dav. #3382.

Date	Mintage	VG	F	VF	XF	Unc
1629	—	285	525	875	1,450	—

KM# 15 THALER
Silver **Ruler:** Johann Ulrich **Rev:** Crowned shield shaped arms **Note:** Dav. #3383.

Date	Mintage	VG	F	VF	XF	Unc
1630	—	275	500	1,000	1,650	—
1631	—	275	500	1,000	1,650	—
1633	—	275	500	1,000	1,650	—

KM# 16 THALER
Silver **Ruler:** Johann Ulrich **Obv:** Date below ruffled bust **Note:** Dav. #3384. Varieties exist.

Date	Mintage	VG	F	VF	XF	Unc
1633 Rare	—	—	—	—	—	—

KM# 20 THALER
Silver **Ruler:** Johann Anton **Obv:** Bust right **Rev:** Crowned arms, date divided **Note:** Dav. #3385.

Date	Mintage	VG	F	VF	XF	Unc
1638	—	550	900	1,450	2,500	—

KM# 25 THALER
Silver **Ruler:** Johann Anton **Rev:** Date left of crown **Note:** Dav. #3387.

Date	Mintage	VG	F	VF	XF	Unc
1642	—	145	285	525	1,150	—
1643	—	145	285	525	1,150	—
1644	—	145	285	525	1,150	—

KM# 27 THALER
Silver **Ruler:** Johann Anton **Obv:** Older bust, different drapery **Rev:** Ornate arms in order chain **Note:** Dav. #3389.

Date	Mintage	VG	F	VF	XF	Unc
1644	—	220	375	650	1,300	—
1649	—	220	375	650	1,300	—

KM# 28 THALER

Silver **Ruler:** Johann Anton **Note:** Klippe. Dav. #3389A. Illustration reduced.

Date	Mintage	VG	F	VF	XF	Unc
1644 Rare	—	—	—	—	—	—

KM# 32 THALER

Silver **Ruler:** Johann Anton **Obv:** Bust divides legend at top **Rev:** Crowned ornate, oval arms **Note:** Dav. #3390.

Date	Mintage	VG	F	VF	XF	Unc
1645	—	300	550	1,100	1,800	—

KM# 33 THALER

Silver **Ruler:** Johann Christoph **Obv:** 2 facing busts above date **Rev:** Crowned oval with 6 smaller arms **Note:** Klippe. Dav. #3391.

Date	Mintage	VG	F	VF	XF	Unc
1652 Rare	—	—	—	—	—	—

KM# 37 THALER

Silver **Ruler:** Johann Christoph **Obv:** 2 facing busts below date **Rev:** Crowned oval arms **Note:** Dav. #3392. Previous KM#36.

Date	Mintage	VG	F	VF	XF	Unc
1653	—	220	375	600	1,000	—

KM# 41 THALER

Silver **Ruler:** Johann Christoph **Obv:** 2 facing busts above date, scroll border in inner circle **Note:** Dav. #3393. Previously KM#38.

Date	Mintage	VG	F	VF	XF	Unc
1654	—	140	220	375	650	—

KM# 45 THALER

Silver **Ruler:** Johann Christoph **Obv:** Longer busts **Rev:** Different frame around arms **Note:** Dav. #3395.

Date	Mintage	VG	F	VF	XF	Unc
1658	—	140	220	375	650	—

KM# 46 1-1/4 THALER

Silver **Ruler:** Johann Christoph **Note:** Similar to 1 Thaler, KM#39. Dav. #A3395.

Date	Mintage	VG	F	VF	XF	Unc
1658 Rare	—	—	—	—	—	—

KM# 7 2 THALER

Silver **Ruler:** Johann Ulrich **Obv:** Crowned arms **Rev:** Heraldic double eagle **Note:** Dav. #3378.

Date	Mintage	VG	F	VF	XF	Unc
1625	—	2,000	3,500	6,000	9,500	—

KM# 10 2 THALER

Silver **Ruler:** Johann Ulrich **Note:** Similar to 1 Thaler, KM#9. Dav. #3381.

Date	Mintage	VG	F	VF	XF	Unc
1629	—	700	1,150	2,000	3,500	—

KM# 26 2 THALER

Silver **Ruler:** Johann Anton **Note:** Similar to 1 Thaler, KM#25. Dav. #3386.

Date	Mintage	VG	F	VF	XF	Unc
1642	—	825	1,400	2,200	3,850	—
1643	—	825	1,400	2,200	3,850	—
1644	—	825	1,400	2,200	3,850	—

KM# 29 2 THALER

Silver **Ruler:** Johann Anton **Obv:** Bust extends to edge of coin on bottom **Rev:** Crowned arms **Note:** Dav. #3388.

Date	Mintage	VG	F	VF	XF	Unc
1644	—	825	1,400	2,200	3,850	—
1649	—	825	1,400	2,200	3,850	—

KM# 38 2 THALER

Silver **Ruler:** Johann Christoph **Note:** Similar to 1 Thaler, KM#36. Dav. #A3392. Previously KM#37.

Date	Mintage	VG	F	VF	XF	Unc
1653	—	825	1,400	2,200	3,850	—

KM# 47 2 THALER

Silver **Ruler:** Johann Christoph **Note:** Similar to 1 Thaler, KM#39. Dav. #3394. Previously KM#41.

Date	Mintage	VG	F	VF	XF	Unc
1658	—	825	1,400	2,200	3,850	—

KM# 30 3 THALER

Silver **Ruler:** Johann Anton **Note:** Similar to 2Thaler, KM#29. Dav. A3388.

Date	Mintage	VG	F	VF	XF	Unc
1644 Rare	—	—	—	—	—	—

KM# 31 4 THALER
Silver **Ruler:** Johann Anton **Note:** Similar to 1 Thaler, KM#25. Dav. #A3386.

Date	Mintage	VG	F	VF	XF	Unc
1644 Rare	—	—	—	—	—	—

TRADE COINAGE

KM# 22 DUCAT
3.5000 g., 0.9860 Gold 0.1109 oz. AGW **Ruler:** Johann Anton **Obv:** Bust of Johann Anton right **Rev:** Crowned arms

Date	Mintage	VG	F	VF	XF	Unc
1638	—	3,500	5,500	8,000	13,500	—

KM# 43 DUCAT
3.5000 g., 0.9860 Gold 0.1109 oz. AGW **Ruler:** Johann Christoph **Obv:** Busts of Johann Christoph and Johann Seyfried facing in inner circle **Rev:** Crowned arms in inner circle

Date	Mintage	VG	F	VF	XF	Unc
1654	—	3,850	6,000	8,750	15,000	—

KM# 34 5 DUCAT
17.5000 g., 0.9860 Gold 0.5547 oz. AGW **Ruler:** Johann Christoph **Note:** Struck with 1 Thaler dies, KM#35.

Date	Mintage	VG	F	VF	XF	Unc
1652 Rare	—	—	—	—	—	—

KM# 49 5 DUCAT
17.5000 g., 0.9860 Gold 0.5547 oz. AGW **Ruler:** Johann Christoph **Note:** Struck with 1 Thaler dies, KM#39.

Date	Mintage	VG	F	VF	XF	Unc
1658 Rare	—	—	—	—	—	—

KM# 18 8 DUCAT
28.0000 g., 0.9860 Gold 0.8876 oz. AGW **Ruler:** Johann Ulrich **Note:** Struck with 1 Thaler dies, KM#9.

Date	Mintage	VG	F	VF	XF	Unc
1629	—	—	—	13,500	18,500	—

KM# 35 10 DUCAT
35.0000 g., 0.9860 Gold 1.1095 oz. AGW **Ruler:** Johann Christoph **Note:** Struck with 1 Thaler dies, KM#35.

Date	Mintage	VG	F	VF	XF	Unc
1652 Rare	—	—	—	—	—	—

KM# A36 10 DUCAT
35.0000 g., 0.9860 Gold 1.1095 oz. AGW **Ruler:** Johann Christoph **Note:** Struck with 1 Thaler dies, KM#38.

Date	Mintage	VG	F	VF	XF	Unc
1654 Rare	—	—	—	—	—	—

KM# 36 15 DUCAT
52.5000 g., 0.9860 Gold 1.6642 oz. AGW **Ruler:** Johann Christoph **Note:** Struck with 1 Thaler dies, KM#35.

Date	Mintage	VG	F	VF	XF	Unc
1652 Rare	—	—	—	—	—	—

GARSTEN

A Benedictine Abbey located in Upper Austria endowed by the Margrave Ottokar in the Steiermark. The Abbot issued a thaler for the official jubilee of the city of Steyer and the Ironmakers Guild in 1679.

ABBEY

STANDARD COINAGE

KM# 5 THALER
Silver **Ruler:** Roman Rauscher von Steyr **Obv:** 11-line inscription within sprays **Rev:** 3 shields in frame, bishop miter above **Note:** Dav. #3460.

Date	Mintage	VG	F	VF	XF	Unc
1679	—	575	975	1,650	3,000	—

GLATZ

COUNTY

STANDARD COINAGE

KM# 5 THALER
Silver **Ruler:** Georg Friedrich von Hardegg **Obv:** Helmeted arms **Rev:** St. George slaying the dragon separating the date **Note:** Dav. #3396.

Date	Mintage	VG	F	VF	XF	Unc
1613 Rare	—	—	—	—	—	—

OLMUTZ

In Moravia

Olmutz (Olomouc), a town in the eastern part of the Czech Republic which was, until 1640, the recognized capital of Moravia, obtained the right to mint coinage in 1144, but exercised it sparingly until the 17th century, when it became an archbishopric.

RULERS
Franz von Dietrichstein
Prince-Bishop, 1599-1636
Johann XIX Ernst von Plattenstein, 1636-1637
Leopold Wilhelm of Austria, 1637-1662
Karl Josef of Austria, 1663-1664
Karl II von Liechtenstein-Castelcorn, 1664-1695
Karl III Josef Herzog von Lothringen, 1695-1711

BISHOPRIC

STANDARD COINAGE

KM# 60.1 HELLER
Silver **Ruler:** Franz **Obv:** 3 shields on trilobe below hat, bottom of shields point towards center of coin **Note:** Uniface. Prev. KM#5.1.

Date	Mintage	Good	VG	F	VF	XF
(1)614	—	15.00	25.00	35.00	65.00	90.00

KM# 60.2 HELLER
Silver **Ruler:** Franz **Obv:** 3 shields on trilobe below hat, bottom of shields pont towards bottom of coin **Note:** Uniface. Prev. KM#5.2.

Date	Mintage	Good	VG	F	VF	XF
ND	—	15.00	25.00	35.00	50.00	80.00
(1)615	—	8.00	12.00	25.00	40.00	70.00
(1)616	—	8.00	12.00	25.00	40.00	70.00
(1)617	—	8.00	12.00	25.00	40.00	70.00

KM# 316 1/2 KREUZER
Silver **Ruler:** Leopold Wilhelm **Obv:** 3 shields on trilobe **Note:** Prev. KM#A50.

Date	Mintage	Good	VG	F	VF	XF
ND	—	15.00	25.00	35.00	65.00	90.00

KM# 318 1/2 KREUZER
Silver **Ruler:** Karl II **Obv:** 3 shields, 1/2 in parenthesis **Note:** Uniface. Varieties exist. Prev. KM#86.

Date	Mintage	VG	F	VF	XF	Unc
1681	—	20.00	35.00	60.00	100	—
1682	—	15.00	30.00	50.00	80.00	—
1683	—	10.00	20.00	35.00	60.00	—
1684	—	15.00	30.00	50.00	80.00	—

KM# 325 1/2 KREUZER
Silver **Ruler:** Karl II **Obv:** 3 shields, denomination - S 1/2 S **Note:** Uniface. Prev. KM#95.

Date	Mintage	VG	F	VF	XF	Unc
1694	—	15.00	30.00	50.00	80.00	—
1695	—	15.00	30.00	50.00	80.00	—

KM# 15 KREUZER
Silver **Ruler:** Franz **Obv:** Arms on cross **Rev:** Mitre with sword and staff **Note:** Varieties exist. Prev. KM#6.

Date	Mintage	VG	F	VF	XF	Unc
ND	—	18.00	30.00	50.00	90.00	—

KM# 185 KREUZER
Silver **Ruler:** Leopold Wilhelm **Obv:** Bust right **Rev:** 3 shields in trilobe **Rev. Legend:** ...PRO., PRIN. or PRINC **Note:** Varieties exist. Prev. KM#50.

Date	Mintage	VG	F	VF	XF	Unc
1650	—	7.00	15.00	30.00	60.00	—
1651	—	6.00	12.00	25.00	55.00	—
(16)52	—	7.00	15.00	30.00	60.00	—
1652	—	7.00	15.00	30.00	60.00	—
1653	—	7.00	15.00	30.00	60.00	—
(16)53	—	7.00	15.00	30.00	60.00	—
(16)54	—	—	—	—	—	—
1654	—	5.00	10.00	20.00	50.00	—
1655	—	6.00	12.00	25.00	55.00	—

KM# 190.1 KREUZER
Silver **Ruler:** Leopold Wilhelm **Rev. Legend:** C. or COMES **Note:** Prev. KM#52.1.

Date	Mintage	VG	F	VF	XF	Unc
1656	—	8.00	16.00	38.00	70.00	—
1658	—	8.00	16.00	38.00	70.00	—

KM# 190.2 KREUZER
Silver **Ruler:** Leopold Wilhelm **Obv:** Bust right **Rev:** 2 shields in circle **Note:** Prev. KM#52.2.

Date	Mintage	VG	F	VF	XF	Unc
1658	—	7.00	15.00	30.00	60.00	—
1659	—	8.00	16.00	32.00	65.00	—

KM# 62 2 KREUZER
Silver **Ruler:** Franz **Obv:** Arms below hat **Rev:** 2 shields with staff and sword **Note:** Prev. KM#7.

Date	Mintage	VG	F	VF	XF	Unc
ND	—	25.00	40.00	75.00	120	—

KM# 63 3 KREUZER
Silver **Ruler:** Franz **Obv:** Bust 3/4 profile **Rev:** 3 shields in trilobe **Note:** Prev. KM#11.

Date	Mintage	VG	F	VF	XF	Unc
(1)614	—	10.00	20.00	35.00	65.00	—
(1)616	—	10.00	20.00	35.00	65.00	—
(1)617	—	10.00	20.00	35.00	65.00	—

KM# 50 3 KREUZER
Silver **Ruler:** Franz **Obv:** Arms below hat **Rev:** Madonna and child **Note:** Prev. KM#8.

Date	Mintage	VG	F	VF	XF	Unc
ND	—	—	—	—	—	—

KM# 51 3 KREUZER
Silver **Ruler:** Franz **Obv:** Bust right **Rev:** 3 shields in trilobe **Note:** Prev. KM#9.

Date	Mintage	VG	F	VF	XF	Unc
ND	—	10.00	20.00	35.00	65.00	—

KM# 52 3 KREUZER
Silver **Ruler:** Franz **Obv:** Bust right **Rev:** Ornamentation between shields **Note:** Varieties exist. Prev. KM#10.

Date	Mintage	VG	F	VF	XF	Unc
ND	—	10.00	20.00	35.00	65.00	—

KM# 90 3 KREUZER
Silver **Ruler:** Franz **Obv:** Bust right **Rev:** 3 shields in circle **Note:** Varieties exist. Prev. KM#12.

Date	Mintage	VG	F	VF	XF	Unc
(1)618	—	10.00	20.00	35.00	65.00	—
(1)619	—	10.00	20.00	35.00	65.00	—
(16)19	—	20.00	30.00	45.00	75.00	—

KM# 186 3 KREUZER
Silver **Ruler:** Leopold Wilhelm **Obv:** Bust right **Rev:** 3 shields with ornamentation, date **Rev. Legend:** ...PRIN **Note:** Varieties exist. Prev. KM#51.

Date	Mintage	VG	F	VF	XF	Unc
1650	—	10.00	20.00	35.00	70.00	—
1651	—	10.00	20.00	35.00	70.00	—
1652	—	20.00	25.00	40.00	80.00	—
1654	—	7.00	15.00	30.00	60.00	—
1655	—	7.00	15.00	30.00	60.00	—

KM# 192.1 3 KREUZER
Silver **Ruler:** Leopold Wilhelm **Obv:** Bust right **Rev:** 3 shields with ornamentation, date **Rev. Legend:** ...CO. or COM **Note:** Prev. KM#53.1.

Date	Mintage	VG	F	VF	XF	Unc
1656	—	7.00	15.00	30.00	60.00	—
1657	—	7.00	15.00	30.00	60.00	—
(16)5.7.	—	7.00	15.00	30.00	60.00	—

KM# 192.2 3 KREUZER
Silver **Ruler:** Leopold Wilhelm **Rev:** 2 shields in circle **Note:** Prev. KM#53.2.

Date	Mintage	VG	F	VF	XF	Unc
1658	—	7.00	15.00	30.00	60.00	—
1659	—	7.00	15.00	30.00	60.00	—

KM# 192.3 3 KREUZER
Silver **Ruler:** Leopold Wilhelm **Rev:** Arms below mitre and crown **Note:** Prev. KM#53.3.

Date	Mintage	VG	F	VF	XF	Unc
1660	—	8.00	16.00	38.00	70.00	—
1662	—	12.00	30.00	50.00	85.00	—

KM# 227.1 3 KREUZER
Silver **Ruler:** Karl II **Obv:** Small bust right within inner circle **Rev:** Arms **Note:** Many varieties exist. Prev. KM#65.1.

Date	Mintage	VG	F	VF	XF	Unc
1664	—	6.00	15.00	30.00	50.00	—
1667	—	6.00	15.00	30.00	50.00	—
1668	—	5.00	12.00	25.00	40.00	—
1669	—	4.00	10.00	22.50	38.00	—

KM# 227.2 3 KREUZER
Silver **Ruler:** Karl II **Obv:** Large bust right breaks inner circle ote: Many varieties exist. Prev. KM#65.2.

Date	Mintage	VG	F	VF	XF	Unc
1665	—	5.00	12.00	25.00	40.00	—
1666	—	5.00	12.00	25.00	40.00	—
1667	—	5.00	12.00	25.00	40.00	—
1668	—	2.00	10.00	25.00	40.00	—
1669	—	2.00	10.00	22.50	38.00	—
1670	—	2.00	10.00	22.50	38.00	—
Note: More than 150 varieties exist for this date.						
1673	—	6.00	15.00	30.00	50.00	—

KM# 227.3 3 KREUZER
Silver **Ruler:** Karl II **Rev:** Arms, SAS below, date at top **Note:** Prev. KM#65.3.

Date	Mintage	VG	F	VF	XF	Unc
1676	—	—	—	—	—	—

Note: Existance is questionable. SAS is an abbreviation for die cutter Simon Andreas Sinopi, who worked at the mint from 1677 to 1684 and 1689 to 1699.

KM# 227.4 3 KREUZER
Silver **Ruler:** Karl II **Rev:** Round or oval arms, without SAS **Note:** Prev. KM#65.4.

Date	Mintage	VG	F	VF	XF	Unc
1693	—	5.00	12.00	25.00	40.00	—

KM# 227.5 3 KREUZER
Silver **Ruler:** Karl II **Rev:** Round or oval arms, SAS below, date at top **Note:** Varieties exist. Prev. KM#65.5

Date	Mintage	VG	F	VF	XF	Unc
1695	—	5.00	12.00	25.00	40.00	—

KM# 335 3 KREUZER
Silver **Ruler:** Karl III Josef **Obv:** Bust right **Rev:** Crowned arms on cross **Note:** KM#335 has more than 5 minor varieties. Prev. KM#102.

Date	Mintage	VG	F	VF	XF	Unc
1699	—	15.00	42.00	75.00	100	—

KM# 236.1 6 KREUZER
Silver **Ruler:** Karl II **Obv:** Small bust right **Rev:** Arms, legends ends with date **Note:** Prev. KM#71.1.

Date	Mintage	VG	F	VF	XF	Unc
1665	—	10.00	20.00	40.00	80.00	—
1669	—	10.00	20.00	40.00	80.00	—

KM# 236.2 6 KREUZER
Silver **Ruler:** Karl II **Obv:** Large bust right **Rev:** Round arms, date divided by mitre and crown **Note:** Prev. KM#71.2.

Date	Mintage	VG	F	VF	XF	Unc
1673	—	10.00	20.00	40.00	80.00	—
1674	—	9.00	18.00	37.50	75.00	—
1675	—	9.00	18.00	37.50	75.00	—
1676	—	10.00	20.00	40.00	80.00	—
1677	—	12.00	22.50	45.00	85.00	—
1678	—	10.00	20.00	40.00	80.00	—
1679	—	12.00	22.50	45.00	85.00	—
1685	—	12.00	22.50	45.00	85.00	—
1693	—	9.00	18.00	37.50	75.00	—

KM# 236.3 6 KREUZER
Silver **Ruler:** Karl II **Rev:** SAS below arms **Note:** Prev. KM#71.3

Date	Mintage	VG	F	VF	XF	Unc
1678	—	12.00	22.50	45.00	85.00	—
1680	—	9.00	18.00	37.50	75.00	—
1681	—	12.00	22.50	45.00	85.00	—
1682	—	9.00	18.00	37.50	75.00	—
1683	—	10.00	20.00	40.00	80.00	—
1684	—	10.00	20.00	40.00	80.00	—

KM# 210 15 KREUZER
Silver **Ruler:** Leopold Wilhelm **Obv:** Bust right **Rev:** Arms below mitre and crown **Note:** Varieties exist. Prev. KM#58.

Date	Mintage	VG	F	VF	XF	Unc
1659	—	20.00	45.00	70.00	120	—
1661	—	20.00	45.00	70.00	120	—
1662	—	25.00	50.00	90.00	150	—

KM# 225 15 KREUZER
Silver **Ruler:** Karl Josef **Obv:** Bust facing **Rev:** Arms topped by mitre and crown **Note:** Prev. KM#60.

Date	Mintage	VG	F	VF	XF	Unc
1663	—	40.00	75.00	150	250	—
1664	—	35.00	75.00	150	250	—

KM# 230 15 KREUZER
Silver **Ruler:** Karl II **Obv:** Bust facing **Rev:** Arms **Note:** Prev. KM#66.

Date	Mintage	VG	F	VF	XF	Unc
1664	—	35.00	70.00	120	200	—

KM# 231.1 15 KREUZER
Silver **Ruler:** Karl II **Obv:** Bust right **Rev:** Arms, legend ends with date **Note:** Prev. KM#80.1.

Date	Mintage	VG	F	VF	XF	Unc
1664	—	20.00	35.00	60.00	100	—

KM# 231.2 15 KREUZER
Silver **Ruler:** Karl II **Rev:** Round arms, date at top between mitre and crown **Note:** Prev. KM#80.2.

Date	Mintage	VG	F	VF	XF	Unc
1675	—	20.00	35.00	60.00	100	—
1676	—	15.00	25.00	45.00	70.00	—
1677	—	35.00	50.00	100	180	—

KM# 231.3 15 KREUZER
Silver **Ruler:** Karl II **Rev:** Oval arms, SAS below **Note:** Prev. KM#80.3.

Date	Mintage	VG	F	VF	XF	Unc
1679	—	20.00	40.00	70.00	130	—

KM# 231.4 15 KREUZER
Silver **Ruler:** Karl II **Rev:** Heart-shaped arms **Note:** Prev. KM#80.4.

Date	Mintage	VG	F	VF	XF	Unc
1686	—	20.00	40.00	70.00	130	—

KM# 231.5 15 KREUZER
Silver **Ruler:** Karl II **Rev:** Arms straight on top, round on the bottom **Note:** Prev. KM#80.5.

Date	Mintage	VG	F	VF	XF	Unc
1687	—	20.00	35.00	60.00	120	—
1688	—	25.00	45.00	75.00	135	—
1689	—	25.00	45.00	75.00	135	—
1690	—	25.00	45.00	75.00	135	—
1691	—	25.00	45.00	75.00	135	—
1693	—	20.00	35.00	60.00	120	—
1694	—	20.00	35.00	60.00	120	—

KM# 231.6 15 KREUZER
Silver **Ruler:** Karl II **Rev:** Arms with two-tablet bottom **Note:** Prev. KM#80.7.

Date	Mintage	VG	F	VF	XF	Unc
1692	—	25.00	45.00	70.00	125	—
1693	—	20.00	35.00	60.00	100	—
1694	—	12.00	20.00	40.00	90.00	—

KM# 231.7 15 KREUZER
Silver **Ruler:** Karl II **Rev:** SAS below arms **Note:** Prev. KM#80.6

Date	Mintage	VG	F	VF	XF	Unc
1694	—	12.00	20.00	40.00	90.00	—

KM# 65 GULDEN (1/2 Thaler)
Silver **Ruler:** Franz **Obv:** Bust right **Rev:** Madonna and child, 2 shields **Note:** Prev. KM#13.

Date	Mintage	VG	F	VF	XF	Unc
ND Rare	—	—	—	—	—	—

KM# 75 GULDEN (1/2 Thaler)
Silver **Ruler:** Franz **Obv:** Bust 3/4 profile **Rev:** Madonna and child, 2 shields **Note:** Prev. KM#14.

Date	Mintage	VG	F	VF	XF	Unc
ND Rare	—	—	—	—	—	—

KM# 195 GULDEN (1/2 Thaler)
Silver **Ruler:** Leopold Wilhelm **Obv:** Bust right **Rev:** Arms with crown and miter **Note:** Prev. KM#A52.

Date	Mintage	VG	F	VF	XF	Unc
1656 Rare	—	—	—	—	—	—

KM# 196 1/2 THALER
Silver **Ruler:** Leopold Wilhelm **Obv:** Bust right **Rev:** Arms below mitre and crown **Note:** Prev. KM#A56.

Date	Mintage	VG	F	VF	XF	Unc
1656 Rare	—	—	—	—	—	—

KM# 20 THALER
Silver **Ruler:** Franz **Obv:** 3 shields in cloverleaf, 8 in center **Rev:** Saint Wenceslaus standing with arms at right, holding flag **Note:** Dav. #3461. Prev. KM#16.

Date	Mintage	VG	F	VF	XF	Unc
ND(1608-14) Rare	—	—	—	—	—	—

KM# 21 THALER
Silver **Ruler:** Franz **Obv:** Bust 3/4 profile **Rev:** Madonna and child behind 2 shields **Rev. Legend:** A-LA-RVM... **Note:** Dav. #3465. Varieties exist. Prev. KM#17.

Date	Mintage	VG	F	VF	XF	Unc
ND	—	800	1,500	2,500	4,000	—

KM# 22 THALER
Silver **Ruler:** Franz **Obv:** Bust right **Obv. Legend:** FRAN • CARD • A... **Rev:** Madonna and child **Note:** Dav. #3463. Varieties exist. Prev. KM#18.

Date	Mintage	VG	F	VF	XF	Unc
ND	—	1,000	2,000	3,500	5,500	—

KM# 35 THALER
Silver **Ruler:** Franz **Note:** Klippe. Dav. #3468A. Prev. KM#22.

Date	Mintage	VG	F	VF	XF	Unc
ND Rare	—	—	—	—	—	—

KM# 36 THALER
Gold Plated Silver **Ruler:** Franz **Note:** Klippe. Prev. KM#22a.

Date	Mintage	VG	F	VF	XF	Unc
ND Rare	—	—	—	—	—	—

KM# 45 THALER
Silver **Ruler:** Franz **Obv:** Narrower bust **Rev. Legend:** AL-A-RVM **Note:** Dav. #3466. Prev. KM#19.

Date	Mintage	VG	F	VF	XF	Unc
ND	—	800	1,500	2,500	4,000	—

KM# 55 THALER
Silver **Ruler:** Franz **Rev. Legend:** AL-LA-RVM **Note:** Dav. #3467. Prev. KM#20.

Date	Mintage	VG	F	VF	XF	Unc
ND	—	800	1,500	2,500	4,000	—

KM# 67 THALER
Silver **Ruler:** Franz **Rev. Legend:** A-LA-RVM **Note:** Dav. #3468. Prev. KM#21.

Date	Mintage	VG	F	VF	XF	Unc
ND Rare	—	—	—	—	—	—

KM# 76 THALER
Gold Plated Silver **Ruler:** Franz **Rev:** Madonna and child, 2 shields **Note:** Dav. #3469. Prev. KM#23.

Date	Mintage	VG	F	VF	XF	Unc
ND Rare	—	—	—	—	—	—

KM# 100 THALER
Silver **Ruler:** Franz **Obv:** Capped bust right **Rev:** Madonna and child behind 2 shields **Note:** Dav. #3470. Prev. KM#35.

Date	Mintage	VG	F	VF	XF	Unc
1624	—	900	1,800	3,000	5,000	—

KM# 101 THALER
Silver **Ruler:** Franz **Obv:** Bare bust right **Rev:** Madonna and child divide date above 2 shields **Note:** Dav. #3471. Prev. KM#36.

Date	Mintage	VG	F	VF	XF	Unc
1624	—	600	1,200	2,000	3,500	—

KM# 102 THALER
Silver **Ruler:** Franz **Note:** Klippe. Dav. #3471A. Prev. KM#37.

Date	Mintage	VG	F	VF	XF	Unc
1624 Rare	—	—	—	—	—	—

KM# 110 THALER
Silver **Ruler:** Franz **Obv:** Hatted arms **Rev:** Madonna and child on a half moon, date in legend **Note:** Dav. #3473. Prev. KM#38.

Date	Mintage	VG	F	VF	XF	Unc
1626 Rare	—	—	—	—	—	—

KM# 130 THALER
Silver **Ruler:** Franz **Obv:** Bust right **Rev:** Larger Madonna and child behind smaller shields, P-A and 1-6-2-8 below **Note:** Dav. #3474. Prev. KM#41.

Date	Mintage	VG	F	VF	XF	Unc
1628 P-A	—	600	1,200	2,000	3,500	—

KM# 131 THALER
Silver **Ruler:** Franz **Rev:** Oval shields, 16-28 below **Rev. Legend:** A-LL-ARVM... **Note:** Dav. #3475. Prev. KM#42.

Date	Mintage	VG	F	VF	XF	Unc
1628 Rare	—	—	—	—	—	—

KM# 140 THALER
Silver **Ruler:** Franz **Obv:** Date below bust **Rev:** Madonna and child above 2 small oval shields **Note:** Dav. #3477. Prev. KM#43.

Date	Mintage	VG	F	VF	XF	Unc
1629 Rare	—	—	—	—	—	—
1630 Rare	—	—	—	—	—	—

KM# 165 THALER
Silver **Ruler:** Franz **Obv:** Scroll work within inner circle **Rev:** Madonna and child above 2 shields, divided date below, scroll work in inner circle **Note:** Dav. #3478. Prev. KM#46.

Date	Mintage	VG	F	VF	XF	Unc
1634 Rare	—	—	—	—	—	—
1636 Rare	—	—	—	—	—	—

KM# 205 THALER
Silver **Ruler:** Leopold Wilhelm **Obv:** Armored bust right **Rev:** Arms topped by mitre and crown with mitre dividing date **Note:** Dav. #3479. Prev. KM#56.

Date	Mintage	VG	F	VF	XF	Unc
1658 Rare	—	—	—	—	—	—

KM# 245 THALER
Silver **Ruler:** Karl II **Obv:** Bust right **Obv. Legend:** CAROLVS • EX • COMM **Rev:** Capped arms divide date **Rev. Legend:** REGIAE - CAPELLAE • BOHEMAE **Note:** Dav. #3480. Prev. KM#72.

Date	Mintage	VG	F	VF	XF	Unc
1666 Rare	—	—	—	—	—	—

KM# 260 THALER
Silver **Ruler:** Karl II **Obv. Legend:** CAROL' D: G' EPVS... **Rev. Legend:** REG: - CAP: BOHE: ... **Note:** Dav. #3481. Prev. KM#76.

Date	Mintage	VG	F	VF	XF	Unc
1671	—	275	550	900	1,500	—

KM# 278 THALER
Silver **Ruler:** Karl II **Obv. Legend:** DVX • S • R • I • PCEPS **Note:** Dav. #3482. Prev. KM#81.

Date	Mintage	VG	F	VF	XF	Unc
1676	—	275	550	900	1,500	—

KM# 294 THALER
Silver **Ruler:** Karl II **Obv:** Larger bust breaks legend at top **Rev:** Arms with crown and mitre above, date in ornamentation at sides **Note:** Dav. #3484. Prev. KM#82.

Date	Mintage	VG	F	VF	XF	Unc
1678	—	275	550	900	1,500	—

KM# 320 THALER
Silver **Ruler:** Karl II **Obv:** Smaller bust in inner circle **Rev:** Date between crown and mitre above arms **Note:** Dav. #3485. Prev. KM#87.

Date	Mintage	VG	F	VF	XF	Unc
1683	—	300	600	1,000	1,750	—

KM# 327 THALER
Silver **Ruler:** Karl II **Obv:** Large bust breaks legend at top **Rev:** Mitre, date above crown divide legend at top **Note:** Dav. #3486. Prev. KM#96.

Date	Mintage	VG	F	VF	XF	Unc
1695	—	175	350	600	900	—

KM# 25 1-1/2 THALER
Silver **Ruler:** Franz **Obv:** Bust 3/4 profile **Rev:** Madonna and child, 2 shields **Note:** Dav. #3462. Prev. KM#24.

Date	Mintage	VG	F	VF	XF	Unc
ND Rare	—	—	—	—	—	—

KM# 37 2 THALER
Silver **Ruler:** Franz **Obv:** Bust right **Rev:** Madonna and child, 2 shields **Note:** Dav. #3464. Prev. KM#25.

Date	Mintage	VG	F	VF	XF	Unc
ND Rare	—	—	—	—	—	—

KM# 111 2 THALER
Silver **Ruler:** Franz **Obv:** Arms below crown, mitre and staff **Rev:** Madonna and child on a half moon **Note:** Dav. #3472. Prev. KM#39.

Date	Mintage	VG	F	VF	XF	Unc
1626 Rare	—	—	—	—	—	—

KM# 150 2 THALER
Silver **Ruler:** Franz **Obv:** Bust right, date below **Rev:** Madonna and child above 2 shields **Note:** Dav. #3476. Prev. KM#45.

Date	Mintage	VG	F	VF	XF	Unc
1630 Rare	—	—	—	—	—	—

KM# 296 2 THALER
Silver **Ruler:** Karl II **Note:** Similar to 1 Thaler, KM#82. Dav. #3483. Prev. KM#83.

Date	Mintage	VG	F	VF	XF	Unc
1678 Rare	—	—	—	—	—	—

KM# 26 3 THALER
Silver **Ruler:** Franz **Obv:** Bust right **Rev:** Madonna and child, 2 shields **Note:** Dav. #A3464.

Date	Mintage	VG	F	VF	XF	Unc
ND Rare	—	—	—	—	—	—

TRADE COINAGE

KM# 240 1/12 DUCAT

0.2917 g., 0.9860 Gold 0.0092 oz. AGW **Ruler:** Karl II **Obv:** Bust right **Rev:** Eagle **Note:** Prev. KM#A67.

Date	Mintage	VG	F	VF	XF	Unc
ND Rare	—	—	—	—	—	—

KM# 256 1/6 DUCAT

0.5833 g., 0.9860 Gold 0.0185 oz. AGW **Ruler:** Karl II **Obv:** Bust right **Rev:** Crowned and mitred arms **Note:** Prev. KM#68.

Date	Mintage	VG	F	VF	XF	Unc
ND	—	75.00	130	300	500	—

KM# 262 1/6 DUCAT

0.5833 g., 0.9860 Gold 0.0185 oz. AGW **Ruler:** Karl II **Obv:** Bust right **Rev:** Eagle with star on breast **Note:** Prev. KM#77.

Date	Mintage	VG	F	VF	XF	Unc
1671	—	100	170	350	600	—

KM# 80 1/4 DUCAT

0.8750 g., 0.9860 Gold 0.0277 oz. AGW **Ruler:** Franz **Obv:** Crowned F **Rev:** Cardinal's hat above arms **Note:** Prev. KM#27.

Date	Mintage	VG	F	VF	XF	Unc
ND	—	65.00	125	275	475	—
1616	—	65.00	125	275	475	—

KM# 252 1/4 DUCAT

0.8750 g., 0.9860 Gold 0.0277 oz. AGW **Ruler:** Karl II **Obv:** Bust right **Rev:** Arms **Note:** Prev. KM#69.

Date	Mintage	VG	F	VF	XF	Unc
ND	—	—	—	—	—	—

Note: Reported, not confirmed

KM# 170 1/2 DUCAT

1.7500 g., 0.9860 Gold 0.0555 oz. AGW **Ruler:** Franz **Obv:** Arms of Dietrichstein **Rev:** Arms of Olmutz **Note:** Prev. KM#47.

Date	Mintage	VG	F	VF	XF	Unc
1636	—	200	350	800	1,600	—

KM# 175 1/2 DUCAT

1.6600 g., 0.9860 Gold 0.0526 oz. AGW **Ruler:** Karl II **Obv:** Bust right **Rev:** Coat of arms **Note:** Prev. KM#67.

Date	Mintage	VG	F	VF	XF	Unc
ND	—	200	350	700	1,500	—

KM# 263 1/2 DUCAT

1.6600 g., 0.9860 Gold 0.0526 oz. AGW **Ruler:** Karl II **Obv:** Bust right **Rev:** Arms **Note:** Prev. KM#A70.

Date	Mintage	VG	F	VF	XF	Unc
ND Rare	—	—	—	—	—	—

KM# 115 DUCAT

3.5000 g., 0.9860 Gold 0.1109 oz. AGW **Ruler:** Franz **Obv:** Arms below hat **Rev:** Madonna and child facing seated in inner circle **Note:** Varieties exist. Prev. KM#40.

Date	Mintage	VG	F	VF	XF	Unc
1626	—	350	550	1,500	2,850	—
1628	—	350	550	1,500	2,850	—
1629	—	350	550	1,500	2,850	—
ND	—	350	550	1,500	2,850	—

KM# 207 DUCAT

3.5000 g., 0.9860 Gold 0.1109 oz. AGW **Ruler:** Leopold Wilhelm **Obv:** Bust right **Rev:** 2 shields of arms topped by mitre and crown **Note:** Prev. KM#57.

Date	Mintage	VG	F	VF	XF	Unc
1658	—	500	1,000	2,000	3,500	—

KM# 280 DUCAT

3.5000 g., 0.9860 Gold 0.1109 oz. AGW **Ruler:** Karl II **Obv:** Bust right **Rev:** Crowned and mitred arms **Note:** Prev. KM#89.

Date	Mintage	VG	F	VF	XF	Unc
1676	—	300	500	900	1,750	—
1684	—	300	500	900	1,750	—
ND	—	300	500	900	1,750	—

KM# 267 2 DUCAT

7.0000 g., 0.9860 Gold 0.2219 oz. AGW **Ruler:** Karl II **Obv:** Bust right in inner circle **Rev:** Crowned and mitred arms **Note:** Prev. KM#85.

Date	Mintage	VG	F	VF	XF	Unc
1672	—	400	1,000	2,150	3,750	—
1678	—	400	1,000	2,150	3,750	—
1680	—	400	1,000	2,150	3,750	—
1684	—	400	1,000	2,150	3,750	—
1691	—	400	1,000	2,150	3,750	—
1693	—	400	1,000	2,150	3,750	—
ND	—	400	1,000	2,150	3,750	—

KM# 220 3 DUCAT

10.5000 g., 0.9860 Gold 0.3328 oz. AGW **Ruler:** Leopold Wilhelm **Obv:** Bust right **Rev:** Crowned and mitred arms

Date	Mintage	VG	F	VF	XF	Unc
1660	—	600	1,250	2,750	5,000	—

KM# 298 3 DUCAT

10.5000 g., 0.9860 Gold 0.3328 oz. AGW **Ruler:** Karl II **Obv:** Bust right **Rev:** Crowned and mitred arms **Note:** Prev. KM#88.

Date	Mintage	VG	F	VF	XF	Unc
1678	—	600	1,250	2,750	5,000	—

KM# 30 4 DUCAT

13.6600 g., 0.9860 Gold 0.4330 oz. AGW **Ruler:** Franz **Obv:** Bust right **Rev:** Madonna with child behind small CoA **Note:** Struck with 1/2 Thaler dies of KM#15.

Date	Mintage	VG	F	VF	XF	Unc
ND Rare	—	—	—	—	—	—

KM# 197 4 DUCAT

14.0000 g., 0.9860 Gold 0.4438 oz. AGW **Ruler:** Leopold Wilhelm **Obv:** Bust right in inner circle **Rev:** Arms topped by mitre and crown in inner circle **Note:** Prev. KM#54.

Date	Mintage	VG	F	VF	XF	Unc
1656	—	—	—	—	—	—

Note: Reported, not confirmed

KM# 250 4 DUCAT

13.6600 g., 0.9860 Gold 0.4330 oz. AGW, 36 mm. **Ruler:** Karl II **Obv:** Bust of Karl II, right, in circle **Rev:** CoA with straight vertical lines

Date	Mintage	VG	F	VF	XF	Unc
1666 Rare	—	—	—	—	—	—

KM# 301 4 DUCAT

12.7200 g., 0.9860 Gold 0.4032 oz. AGW **Ruler:** Karl II **Obv:** Bust right **Rev:** Arms, topped by mitre and crown **Note:** Prev. KM#A78.

Date	Mintage	VG	F	VF	XF	Unc
1678 Rare	—	—	—	—	—	—

KM# 300 4 DUCAT

12.7200 g., 0.9860 Gold 0.4032 oz. AGW, 45 mm. **Ruler:** Karl II **Obv:** Bust of Karl II right, breaks inner circle at top **Rev:** CoA nearly round **Note:** Struck with Thaler dies of KM#294.

Date	Mintage	VG	F	VF	XF	Unc
1678 Rare	—	—	—	—	—	—

KM# 160 5 DUCAT

17.5000 g., 0.9860 Gold 0.5547 oz. AGW **Ruler:** Franz **Obv:** Bust right, within circle **Rev:** Madonna with child **Note:** Struck with 1/2 Thaler dies of KM#65.

Date	Mintage	VG	F	VF	XF	Unc
ND Rare	—	—	—	—	—	—

KM# 161 5 DUCAT

17.5000 g., 0.9860 Gold 0.5547 oz. AGW **Ruler:** Franz **Obv:** Bust 3/4 profile **Rev:** Madonna with child **Note:** Struck with 1/2 Thaler dies of KM#75.

Date	Mintage	VG	F	VF	XF	Unc
ND Rare	—	—	—	—	—	—

KM# 167 5 DUCAT

17.5000 g., 0.9860 Gold 0.5547 oz. AGW, 38.5 mm. **Ruler:** Franz **Obv:** Bust right, cuts inner circle at top **Obv. Legend:** FRAN•CARD •A•DIETRICHSTAIN•EPS•OLOMVC•8 **Rev:** Madonna wearing 4 point crown; child above 2 straight shield; Dietrichstein on left and Olmutz on right **Rev. Legend:** SVB VMBRAA LA RVM TVARVM **Edge:** Plain **Note:** Struck with Thaler dies, KM#140. Prev. KM#15.

Date	Mintage	F	VF	XF	Unc	BU
1634 Rare	—	—	—	—	—	—

KM# 269 5 DUCAT

17.5000 g., 0.9860 Gold 0.5547 oz. AGW, 37.5 mm. **Ruler:** Karl II **Obv:** Bust of Karl II right **Rev:** CoA **Note:** Struck with 1/2 Thaler dies of an unknown type. Prev. KM#78.

Date	Mintage	VG	F	VF	XF	Unc
1672	—	1,500	3,000	5,000	8,000	—
1672 PRNICEPS error	—	2,500	4,000	6,000	9,000	—
1676	—	1,500	3,000	5,000	8,000	—
1678	—	1,500	3,000	5,000	8,000	—
ND	—	1,500	3,000	5,000	8,000	—

KM# 303 5 DUCAT

17.5000 g., 0.9860 Gold 0.5547 oz. AGW, 44 mm. **Ruler:** Karl II **Obv:** Bust of Karl II right **Rev:** CoA **Note:** Struck with Thaler dies of KM#294.

Date	Mintage	VG	F	VF	XF	Unc
1678	—	1,500	3,000	5,000	8,000	—

KM# 330 5 DUCAT

17.5000 g., 0.9860 Gold 0.5547 oz. AGW, 44 mm. **Ruler:** Karl II **Obv:** Bust of Karl II right **Rev:** CoA **Note:** Struck with Thaler dies of KM#327.

Date	Mintage	VG	F	VF	XF	Unc
1695	—	1,500	3,000	5,000	8,000	—

KM# 168 6 DUCAT

20.2000 g., 0.9860 Gold 0.6403 oz. AGW **Ruler:** Franz **Obv:** Bust right **Rev:** Madonna with child and shield **Note:** Struck with Thaler dies of KM#165.

Date	Mintage	VG	F	VF	XF	Unc
1634 Rare	—	—	—	—	—	—

KM# 305 6 DUCAT

20.6200 g., 0.9860 Gold 0.6536 oz. AGW, 36 mm. **Ruler:** Karl II **Obv:** Bust right in inner circle **Rev:** Arms topped by mitre and crown in inner circle **Note:** Struck with 1/2 Thaler dies of an unknown type. Prev. KM#70.

Date	Mintage	VG	F	VF	XF	Unc
1678	—	2,000	3,500	6,000	10,000	—

KM# 306 6 DUCAT

20.6200 g., 0.9860 Gold 0.6536 oz. AGW, 45 mm. **Ruler:** Karl II **Obv:** Bust right, touches top **Rev:** Arms below mitre and crown which touch outer boarder **Note:** Struck with Thaler dies of KM#294.

Date	Mintage	VG	F	VF	XF	Unc
1678	—	2,000	3,500	6,000	10,000	—

KM# 155 8 DUCAT

26.2500 g., 0.9860 Gold 0.8321 oz. AGW, 45 mm. **Ruler:** Franz **Obv:** Bust right in inner circle **Rev:** Madonna with child in Gloriole **Note:** Struck with Thaler dies of KM#140.

Date	Mintage	VG	F	VF	XF	Unc
1630	—	2,000	3,500	6,000	10,000	—

KM# 308 8 DUCAT

28.0000 g., 0.9860 Gold 0.8876 oz. AGW **Ruler:** Karl II **Note:** Struck with 1 Thaler dies, KM#294. Prev. KM#92.

Date	Mintage	VG	F	VF	XF	Unc
1678 Rare	—	—	—	—	—	—

KM# 332 9 DUCAT

30.9800 g., 0.9860 Gold 0.9820 oz. AGW, 44.5 mm. **Ruler:** Karl II **Obv:** Bust right **Rev:** Arms topped by mitre and crown in inner circle **Note:** Struck with Thaler dies of an unknown type.

Date	Mintage	VG	F	VF	XF	Unc
1695	—	—	—	—	—	—

Note: Reported, not confirmed

KM# 135 10 DUCAT

35.0000 g., 0.9860 Gold 1.1095 oz. AGW **Ruler:** Franz **Rev:** Madonna **Note:** Struck with 1 Thaler dies, KM#130. Prev. KM#49.

Date	Mintage	VG	F	VF	XF	Unc
1628 P-A Rare	—	—	—	—	—	—

KM# 172 10 DUCAT

35.0000 g., 0.9860 Gold 1.1095 oz. AGW **Ruler:** Franz **Note:** Struck with Thaler dies of KM#165.

Date	Mintage	VG	F	VF	XF	Unc
1636 Rare	—	—	—	—	—	—

KM# 120 10 DUCAT

35.0000 g., 0.9860 Gold 1.1095 oz. AGW **Ruler:** Franz **Note:** Struck with Thaler dies of KM#20.

Date	Mintage	VG	F	VF	XF	Unc
ND Rare	—	—	—	—	—	—

KM# 121 10 DUCAT
35.0000 g., 0.9860 Gold 1.1095 oz. AGW **Ruler:** Franz
Obv: Three shields in cloverleaf **Rev:** Saint Wenzeslaus standing
Note: Struck with Thaler dies of KM#20.

Date	Mintage	VG	F	VF	XF	Unc
ND Rare	—	—	—	—	—	—

KM# 198 10 DUCAT
35.0000 g., 0.9860 Gold 1.1095 oz. AGW **Ruler:** Leopold Wilhelm **Obv:** Bust right in inner circle **Rev:** Arms topped by mitre and crown in inner circle **Note:** Prev. KM#55.

Date	Mintage	VG	F	VF	XF	Unc
1656 Rare	—	—	—	—	—	—
1658 Rare	—	—	—	—	—	—

KM# 265 10 DUCAT
35.0000 g., 0.9860 Gold 1.1095 oz. AGW **Ruler:** Karl II
Obv: Bust right, within inner circle **Note:** Struck with 1 Thaler dies, KM#260. Prev. KM#93.

Date	Mintage	VG	F	VF	XF	Unc
1671	—	3,000	5,500	9,500	15,000	—

KM# 282 10 DUCAT
35.0000 g., 0.9860 Gold 1.1095 oz. AGW **Ruler:** Karl II **Obv:** Bust right, within inner circle **Note:** Struck with Thaler dies of KM#278.

Date	Mintage	VG	F	VF	XF	Unc
1676	—	3,000	5,500	9,500	15,000	—

KM# 310 10 DUCAT
35.0000 g., 0.9860 Gold 1.1095 oz. AGW **Ruler:** Karl II **Obv:** Bust right, dividing legend at top **Note:** Struck with Thaler dies of KM#294.

Date	Mintage	VG	F	VF	XF	Unc
1678	—	3,000	5,500	9,500	15,000	—

KM# 312 11 DUCAT
38.0300 g., 0.9860 Gold 1.2055 oz. AGW, 47.5 mm.
Ruler: Karl II **Obv:** Bust right **Rev:** Coat of arms **Note:** Struck with Thaler dies of KM#294.

Date	Mintage	VG	F	VF	XF	Unc
1678 Rare	—	—	—	—	—	—

KM# 284 20 DUCAT
69.2000 g., 0.9860 Gold 2.1936 oz. AGW, 48.5 mm.
Ruler: Karl II **Obv:** Bust right **Rev:** Coat of arms **Note:** Struck with Thaler dies of KM#278.

Date	Mintage	VG	F	VF	XF	Unc
1676 Rare	—	—	—	—	—	—

KM# 286 30 DUCAT
104.0000 g., 0.9860 Gold 3.2967 oz. AGW, 48 mm.
Ruler: Karl II **Obv:** Bust right **Rev:** Coat of arms **Note:** Struck with Thaler dies of KM#278.

Date	Mintage	VG	F	VF	XF	Unc
1676 Rare	—	—	—	—	—	—

PATTERNS

Including off metal strikes

KM#	Date	Mintage	Identification	Mkt Val
Pn1	ND	—	Thaler. Pewter.	—
Pn2	1624	—	Thaler. Pewter.	—

ORTENBURG

A district of Carinthia with its own counts from c.1100 to 1421. Eventually it became property of the emperor who assigned it to a Spanish noble in 1524. This line died out in 1640. The Widmanns, an Italian family, ruled from 1640 to 1662 and produced the only coins. In 1662 Ortenburg passed to Porcia and was finally mediatized to Austria in 1805.

RULER
Christopher Widmann, 1640-1660

COUNTY

STANDARD COINAGE

KM# A3 1/2 THALER (Show - Schau)
Silver **Ruler:** Christopher Widmann **Obv:** Bust of Hans Widman right **Obv. Legend:** HANS WIDMAN AIGENTVMBSHERR DER (1631) **Rev:** Helmeted shield **Rev. Legend:** HER SCHAFTEN SOMMERÖGG VND PATERNIAN

Date	Mintage	VG	F	VF	XF	Unc
1631	—	—	—	—	—	—

KM# 3 THALER
Silver **Ruler:** Christopher Widmann **Note:** Dav. #3397.

Date	Mintage	VG	F	VF	XF	Unc
1656	—	230	400	700	1,150	—

TRADE COINAGE

KM# 6 DUCAT
3.5000 g., 0.9860 Gold 0.1109 oz. AGW **Ruler:** Christopher Widmann **Obv:** Bust in cardinal's garb **Rev:** Circular arms below cardinal's hat, date in legend

Date	Mintage	VG	F	VF	XF	Unc
1658	—	1,500	3,300	5,400	7,800	—

KM# 7 2 DUCAT
7.0000 g., 0.9860 Gold 0.2219 oz. AGW **Ruler:** Christopher Widmann **Note:** Similar to 1 Ducat, KM#6.

Date	Mintage	VG	F	VF	XF	Unc
1657 Rare	—	—	—	—	—	—

KM# 4 5 DUCAT
17.5000 g., 0.9860 Gold 0.5547 oz. AGW **Ruler:** Christopher Widmann **Note:** Struck with 1 Thaler dies, KM#3.

Date	Mintage	VG	F	VF	XF	Unc
1656	—	2,400	4,200	7,200	11,500	—

KM# 5 10 DUCAT
35.0000 g., 0.9860 Gold 1.1095 oz. AGW **Ruler:** Christopher Widmann **Note:** Struck with 1 Thaler dies, KM#3.

Date	Mintage	VG	F	VF	XF	Unc
1656 Rare	—	—	—	—	—	—

SALZBURG

A town on the Austro-Bavarian frontier which grew up around a monastery and bishopric that was founded circa 700. It was raised to the rank of archbishopric in 798. In 1803 Salzburg was secularized and given to an archduke of Austria. In 1803 it was annexed to Austria but years later passed to Bavaria, returning to Austria in 1813. It became a crownland in 1849, remaining so until becoming part of the Austrian Republic in 1918.

RULERS
Wolfgang Dietrich von Raitenau, 1587-1612
Marcus Sitticus, Graf van Hohenems, 1612-1619
Paris, Graf von Lodron, 1619-1653
Guidobald, Graf von Thun und Hohenstein 1654-1668
Maximilian Gandolph, Graf von Küenburg, 1668-1687
Johann Ernst, Graf von Thun und Hohenstein, 1687-1709

MONETARY SYSTEM
4 Pfenning = 1 Kreutzer
120 Kreutzer = 1 Convention Thaler

ARCHBISHOPRIC

STANDARD COINAGE

KM# 6 HELLER
Silver **Ruler:** Wolfgang Dietrich **Obv:** Shield of arms with date above in diamond **Rev:** Shield of arms in diamond

Date	Mintage	VG	F	VF	XF	Unc
1607	—	10.00	20.00	40.00	70.00	—
1608	—	10.00	20.00	40.00	70.00	—

KM# 33 HELLER
Silver **Ruler:** Markus Sittich **Obv:** Shield of arms with date above and/or at sides in diamond **Rev:** Shield of arms in diamond with annulets in corners

Date	Mintage	VG	F	VF	XF	Unc
1614	—	5.50	12.00	20.00	45.00	—
1615	—	5.50	12.00	20.00	45.00	—
1616	—	5.50	12.00	20.00	45.00	—
1618	—	5.50	12.00	20.00	45.00	—

KM# 72 HELLER
Silver **Ruler:** Paris **Obv:** Shield of arms divides date, "P" above **Note:** Kipper Heller. Uniface.

Date	Mintage	VG	F	VF	XF	Unc
1621	—	6.00	12.00	20.00	45.00	—
1622	—	6.00	12.00	20.00	45.00	—

KM# 10 PFENNING
Silver **Ruler:** Wolfgang Dietrich **Obv:** Shield of arms divides W-T, date below in diamond **Note:** Uniface.

Date	Mintage	VG	F	VF	XF	Unc
1610	—	5.50	12.00	20.00	45.00	—
1611	—	5.50	12.00	20.00	45.00	—

KM# 11 PFENNING
Silver **Ruler:** Markus Sittich **Obv:** Shield of arms, date above in diamond **Note:** Uniface.

Date	Mintage	VG	F	VF	XF	Unc
(1)612	—	5.50	12.00	20.00	45.00	—
1612	—	5.50	12.00	20.00	45.00	—
(1)613	—	5.50	12.00	20.00	45.00	—
(1)614	—	5.50	12.00	20.00	45.00	—
(1)615	—	5.50	12.00	20.00	45.00	—
(1)616	—	5.50	12.00	20.00	45.00	—
(1)617	—	5.50	12.00	20.00	45.00	—
(1)618	—	5.50	12.00	20.00	45.00	—
(1)619	—	5.50	12.00	20.00	45.00	—

KM# 55 PFENNING
Silver **Ruler:** Paris **Obv:** Cap above two shields of arms in trilobe, date below **Note:** Uniface.

Date	Mintage	VG	F	VF	XF	Unc
(1)620	—	6.00	12.00	25.00	50.00	—

KM# 73 PFENNING
Silver **Ruler:** Paris **Obv:** Cap above two shields of arms in trilobe, date below **Note:** Kipper Pfenning.

Date	Mintage	VG	F	VF	XF	Unc
(1)621	—	6.00	12.00	25.00	50.00	—
(1)622	—	6.00	12.00	25.00	50.00	—

KM# 82 PFENNING
Silver **Ruler:** Paris **Obv:** Shield of arms, "P" above **Rev:** Shield of arms, with date above

Date	Mintage	VG	F	VF	XF	Unc
1623	—	5.00	10.00	20.00	45.00	—
1624	—	5.00	10.00	20.00	45.00	—
1625	—	5.00	10.00	20.00	45.00	—
1626	—	5.00	10.00	20.00	45.00	—
1627	—	5.00	10.00	20.00	45.00	—
1628	—	5.00	10.00	20.00	45.00	—
1629	—	5.00	10.00	20.00	45.00	—
1630	—	5.00	10.00	20.00	45.00	—
1631	—	5.00	10.00	20.00	45.00	—
1632	—	5.00	10.00	20.00	45.00	—
1633	—	5.00	10.00	20.00	45.00	—

Date	Mintage	VG	F	VF	XF	Unc
1634	—	5.00	10.00	20.00	45.00	—
1635	—	5.00	10.00	20.00	45.00	—
1636	—	5.00	10.00	20.00	45.00	—
1638	—	5.00	10.00	20.00	45.00	—
1639	—	5.00	10.00	20.00	45.00	—
1640	—	5.00	10.00	20.00	45.00	—
1641	—	5.00	10.00	20.00	45.00	—
1642	—	5.00	10.00	20.00	45.00	—
1643	—	5.00	10.00	20.00	45.00	—
1644	—	5.00	10.00	20.00	45.00	—
1645	—	5.00	10.00	20.00	45.00	—
1646	—	5.00	10.00	20.00	45.00	—
1647	—	5.00	10.00	20.00	45.00	—
1648	—	5.00	10.00	20.00	45.00	—
1649	—	5.00	10.00	20.00	45.00	—
1650	—	5.00	10.00	20.00	45.00	—
1652	—	5.00	10.00	20.00	45.00	—
1653	—	5.00	10.00	20.00	45.00	—

KM# 157 PFENNING

Silver **Ruler:** Guidobald **Obv:** Date above two shields of arms, G below **Note:** Uniface.

Date	Mintage	VG	F	VF	XF	Unc
1654	—	—	—	—	—	—

KM# 174 PFENNING

Silver **Ruler:** Guidobald **Obv:** Date above two shields, different right shield, G below

Date	Mintage	VG	F	VF	XF	Unc
1655	—	4.00	8.00	18.00	35.00	—
1656	—	4.00	8.00	18.00	35.00	—
1657	—	4.00	8.00	18.00	35.00	—
1658	—	4.00	8.00	18.00	35.00	—
1659	—	4.00	8.00	18.00	35.00	—
1660	—	4.00	8.00	18.00	35.00	—
1661	—	4.00	8.00	18.00	35.00	—
1662	—	4.00	8.00	18.00	35.00	—
1663	—	4.00	8.00	18.00	35.00	—
1664	—	4.00	8.00	18.00	35.00	—
1665	—	4.00	8.00	18.00	35.00	—
1666	—	4.00	8.00	18.00	35.00	—
1667	—	4.00	8.00	18.00	35.00	—
1668	—	4.00	8.00	18.00	35.00	—

KM# 186 PFENNING

Silver **Ruler:** Maximilian Gandolph **Obv:** Date above two shields, different right shield, MG below **Note:** Uniface.

Date	Mintage	VG	F	VF	XF	Unc
1668	—	4.00	8.00	18.00	35.00	—
1669	—	4.00	8.00	18.00	35.00	—
1670	—	4.00	8.00	18.00	35.00	—
1671	—	4.00	8.00	18.00	35.00	—
1672	—	4.00	8.00	18.00	35.00	—
1673	—	4.00	8.00	18.00	35.00	—
1674	—	4.00	8.00	18.00	35.00	—
1675	—	4.00	8.00	18.00	35.00	—
1676	—	4.00	8.00	18.00	35.00	—
1677	—	4.00	8.00	18.00	35.00	—
1678	—	4.00	8.00	18.00	35.00	—
1679	—	4.00	8.00	18.00	35.00	—
1680	—	4.00	8.00	18.00	35.00	—
1681	—	4.00	8.00	18.00	35.00	—
1682	—	4.00	8.00	18.00	35.00	—
1683	—	4.00	8.00	18.00	35.00	—
1684	—	4.00	8.00	18.00	35.00	—
1685	—	4.00	8.00	18.00	35.00	—
1686	—	4.00	8.00	18.00	35.00	—
1687	—	4.00	8.00	18.00	35.00	—

KM# 5 2 PFENNING

Silver **Ruler:** Wolfgang Dietrich **Obv:** Three shields in trilobe, date below **Note:** Uniface.

Date	Mintage	VG	F	VF	XF	Unc
1601	—	5.50	12.00	20.00	45.00	—
(1)601	—	5.50	12.00	20.00	45.00	—
1603	—	5.50	12.00	20.00	45.00	—
(1)603	—	5.50	12.00	20.00	45.00	—
1604	—	5.50	12.00	20.00	45.00	—
1605	—	5.50	12.00	20.00	45.00	—
(1)606	—	5.50	12.00	20.00	45.00	—
(1)607	—	5.50	12.00	20.00	45.00	—
(1)608	—	5.50	12.00	20.00	45.00	—
(1)610	—	5.50	12.00	20.00	45.00	—
(1)611	—	5.50	12.00	20.00	45.00	—

KM# 12 2 PFENNING

Silver **Ruler:** Markus Sittich **Obv:** Shield of arms, hat above in trilobe, date below **Note:** Uniface.

Date	Mintage	VG	F	VF	XF	Unc
1612	—	5.50	12.00	20.00	45.00	—
(1)612	—	5.50	12.00	20.00	45.00	—
(1)613	—	5.50	12.00	20.00	45.00	—
1614	—	5.50	12.00	20.00	45.00	—
1615	—	5.50	12.00	20.00	45.00	—
1616	—	5.50	12.00	20.00	45.00	—
1617	—	5.50	12.00	20.00	45.00	—
1618	—	5.50	12.00	20.00	45.00	—
1619	—	5.50	12.00	20.00	45.00	—
1661 Error date	—	5.50	12.00	20.00	45.00	—

KM# 268 2 PFENNING

Silver **Ruler:** Johann Ernst **Obv:** Date above 2 shields, "IE" below **Note:** Uniface.

Date	Mintage	VG	F	VF	XF	Unc
1688	—	4.00	8.00	16.00	30.00	—
1689	—	4.00	8.00	16.00	30.00	—
1690	—	4.00	8.00	16.00	30.00	—
1691	—	4.00	8.00	16.00	30.00	—
1692	—	4.00	8.00	16.00	30.00	—
1693	—	4.00	8.00	16.00	30.00	—
1694	—	4.00	8.00	16.00	30.00	—
1695	—	4.00	8.00	16.00	30.00	—
1696	—	4.00	8.00	16.00	30.00	—
1697	—	4.00	8.00	16.00	30.00	—
1698	—	4.00	8.00	16.00	30.00	—
1699	—	4.00	8.00	16.00	30.00	—
1700	—	4.00	8.00	16.00	30.00	—

KM# 83 1/2 KREUZER

Silver **Ruler:** Paris **Obv:** Hat above shield of arms **Rev:** Shield of arms, value divides date at top

Date	Mintage	VG	F	VF	XF	Unc
1623	—	4.00	8.00	16.00	30.00	—
1624	—	4.00	8.00	16.00	30.00	—
1625	—	4.00	8.00	16.00	30.00	—
1627	—	4.00	8.00	16.00	30.00	—
1629	—	4.00	8.00	16.00	30.00	—
1630	—	4.00	8.00	16.00	30.00	—
1631	—	4.00	8.00	16.00	30.00	—
1633	—	4.00	8.00	16.00	30.00	—
1635	—	4.00	8.00	16.00	30.00	—
1636	—	4.00	8.00	16.00	30.00	—
1637	—	4.00	8.00	16.00	30.00	—
1638	—	4.00	8.00	16.00	30.00	—
1640	—	4.00	8.00	16.00	30.00	—
1642	—	4.00	8.00	16.00	30.00	—
1643	—	4.00	8.00	16.00	30.00	—
1645	—	4.00	8.00	16.00	30.00	—
1646	—	4.00	8.00	16.00	30.00	—
1647	—	4.00	8.00	16.00	30.00	—
1648	—	4.00	8.00	16.00	30.00	—
1649	—	4.00	8.00	16.00	30.00	—
1651	—	4.00	8.00	16.00	30.00	—
1652	—	4.00	8.00	16.00	30.00	—
1653	—	4.00	8.00	16.00	30.00	—

KM# 158 1/2 KREUZER

Silver **Ruler:** Guidobald **Obv:** Value divides date above two shields of arms, G above

Date	Mintage	VG	F	VF	XF	Unc
1654	—	3.50	7.00	16.00	30.00	—
1655	—	3.50	7.00	16.00	30.00	—
1656	—	3.50	7.00	16.00	30.00	—
1657	—	3.50	7.00	16.00	30.00	—
1658	—	3.50	7.00	16.00	30.00	—
1659	—	3.50	7.00	16.00	30.00	—
1660	—	3.50	7.00	16.00	30.00	—
1661	—	3.50	7.00	16.00	30.00	—
1662	—	3.50	7.00	16.00	30.00	—
1663	—	3.50	7.00	16.00	30.00	—
1665	—	3.50	7.00	16.00	30.00	—
1667	—	3.50	7.00	16.00	30.00	—

KM# 221 1/2 KREUZER

Silver **Ruler:** Maximilian Gandolph **Obv:** Value divides date above two shields of arms, different right shield, MG below **Note:** Uniface.

Date	Mintage	VG	F	VF	XF	Unc
1671	—	4.00	8.00	16.00	30.00	—
1677	—	4.00	8.00	16.00	30.00	—
1680	—	4.00	8.00	16.00	30.00	—
1681	—	4.00	8.00	16.00	30.00	—
1682	—	4.00	8.00	16.00	30.00	—
1683	—	4.00	8.00	16.00	30.00	—
1684	—	4.00	8.00	16.00	30.00	—
1685	—	4.00	8.00	16.00	30.00	—
1686	—	4.00	8.00	16.00	30.00	—
1687	—	4.00	8.00	16.00	30.00	—

KM# 247 1/2 KREUZER

Silver **Ruler:** Johann Ernst **Obv:** Value divides date above 2 shields , "IE" below **Note:** Uniface.

Date	Mintage	VG	F	VF	XF	Unc
1687	—	4.00	8.00	16.00	30.00	—
1688	—	4.00	8.00	16.00	30.00	—
1689	—	4.00	8.00	16.00	30.00	—
1690	—	4.00	8.00	16.00	30.00	—
1691	—	4.00	8.00	16.00	30.00	—
1693	—	4.00	8.00	16.00	30.00	—
1694	—	4.00	8.00	16.00	30.00	—
1695	—	4.00	8.00	16.00	30.00	—
1696	—	4.00	8.00	16.00	30.00	—
1697	—	4.00	8.00	16.00	30.00	—
1698	—	4.00	8.00	16.00	30.00	—
1699	—	4.00	8.00	16.00	30.00	—
1700	—	4.00	8.00	16.00	30.00	—

KM# 84 KREUZER

Silver **Ruler:** Paris **Obv:** Hat above shield of arms **Obv. Legend:** PARIS D G ARCHIEPS **Rev:** Round arms in eight-armed cross, date in legend

Date	Mintage	VG	F	VF	XF	Unc
1623	—	4.00	8.00	18.00	35.00	—
1624	—	4.00	8.00	18.00	35.00	—
1627	—	4.00	8.00	18.00	35.00	—
1628	—	4.00	8.00	18.00	35.00	—
1629	—	4.00	8.00	18.00	35.00	—
1630	—	4.00	8.00	18.00	35.00	—
1631	—	4.00	8.00	18.00	35.00	—
1632	—	4.00	8.00	18.00	35.00	—
1633	—	4.00	8.00	18.00	35.00	—
1634	—	4.00	8.00	18.00	35.00	—
1636	—	4.00	8.00	18.00	35.00	—
1637	—	4.00	8.00	18.00	35.00	—
1638	—	4.00	8.00	18.00	35.00	—
1639	—	4.00	8.00	18.00	35.00	—
1640	—	4.00	8.00	18.00	35.00	—
1641	—	4.00	8.00	18.00	35.00	—
1642	—	4.00	8.00	18.00	35.00	—
1643	—	4.00	8.00	18.00	35.00	—
1644	—	4.00	8.00	18.00	35.00	—
1645	—	4.00	8.00	18.00	35.00	—
1646	—	4.00	8.00	18.00	35.00	—
1647	—	4.00	8.00	18.00	35.00	—
1648	—	4.00	8.00	18.00	35.00	—
1649	—	4.00	8.00	18.00	35.00	—
1650	—	4.00	8.00	18.00	35.00	—
1651	—	4.00	8.00	18.00	35.00	—
1652	—	4.00	8.00	18.00	35.00	—
1653	—	4.00	8.00	18.00	35.00	—

KM# 159 KREUZER

Silver **Ruler:** Guidobald **Obv. Legend:** GVIDOBALD D G AR EPS **Rev:** Round arms in eight-armed cross in inner circle, date in legend

Date	Mintage	VG	F	VF	XF	Unc
1654	—	4.00	8.00	18.00	35.00	—
1655	—	4.00	8.00	18.00	35.00	—
1656	—	4.00	8.00	18.00	35.00	—
1657	—	4.00	8.00	18.00	35.00	—
1658	—	4.00	8.00	18.00	35.00	—
1659	—	4.00	8.00	18.00	35.00	—
1660	—	4.00	8.00	18.00	35.00	—
1661	—	4.00	8.00	18.00	35.00	—
1662	—	4.00	8.00	18.00	35.00	—
1663	—	4.00	8.00	18.00	35.00	—
1664	—	4.00	8.00	18.00	35.00	—
1665	—	4.00	8.00	18.00	35.00	—
1666	—	4.00	8.00	18.00	35.00	—
1667	—	4.00	8.00	18.00	35.00	—
1668/7	—	4.00	8.00	18.00	35.00	—
1668	—	4.00	8.00	18.00	35.00	—

KM# 185 KREUZER

Silver **Ruler:** Guidobald **Obv. Legend:** GVIDOBALD D G ARCHI EPS **Rev:** Date divided at top

Date	Mintage	VG	F	VF	XF	Unc
1660	—	6.00	12.00	25.00	40.00	—
1661	—	6.00	12.00	25.00	40.00	—
1662	—	6.00	12.00	25.00	40.00	—
1663	—	6.00	12.00	25.00	40.00	—

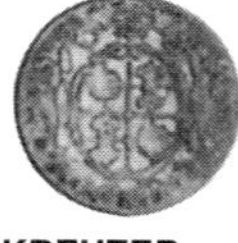

KM# 187 KREUZER

Silver **Ruler:** Maximilian Gandolph **Obv. Legend:** MAX GAND DG AR EPS **Rev:** Round arms in eight-armed cross, date in legend

Date	Mintage	VG	F	VF	XF	Unc
1668	—	4.00	8.00	18.00	35.00	—
1669	—	4.00	8.00	18.00	35.00	—
1670	—	4.00	8.00	18.00	35.00	—
1671	—	4.00	8.00	18.00	35.00	—
1672	—	4.00	8.00	18.00	35.00	—
1673	—	4.00	8.00	18.00	35.00	—
1674	—	4.00	8.00	18.00	35.00	—
1675	—	4.00	8.00	18.00	35.00	—
1676	—	4.00	8.00	18.00	35.00	—
1677	—	4.00	8.00	18.00	35.00	—
1678	—	4.00	8.00	18.00	35.00	—
1679	—	4.00	8.00	18.00	35.00	—

Date	Mintage	VG	F	VF	XF	Unc
1680	—	4.00	8.00	18.00	35.00	—
1681	—	4.00	8.00	18.00	35.00	—
1682	—	4.00	8.00	18.00	35.00	—
1683	—	4.00	8.00	18.00	35.00	—
1684	—	4.00	8.00	18.00	35.00	—
1685	—	4.00	8.00	18.00	35.00	—
1686	—	4.00	8.00	18.00	35.00	—

KM# 226 KREUZER

Silver **Ruler:** Maximilian Gandolph **Obv. Legend:** MAX GAND DG ARCHIEPS **Rev:** Date at top in legend

Date	Mintage	VG	F	VF	XF	Unc
1674	—	6.00	12.00	25.00	40.00	—
1675	—	6.00	12.00	25.00	40.00	—
1676	—	6.00	12.00	25.00	40.00	—

KM# 248 KREUZER

Silver **Ruler:** Johann Ernst9 **Obv:** Oval arms with cardinals' hat above **Obv. Legend:** IO : ERNEST : D : G : ARCHIEP **Rev:** Round shield within double cross and circle

Date	Mintage	VG	F	VF	XF	Unc
1687	—	4.00	8.00	16.00	30.00	—
1688	—	4.00	8.00	16.00	30.00	—
1689	—	4.00	8.00	16.00	30.00	—
1690	—	4.00	8.00	16.00	30.00	—
1691	—	4.00	8.00	16.00	30.00	—
1692	—	4.00	8.00	16.00	30.00	—
1693	—	4.00	8.00	16.00	30.00	—
1694	—	4.00	8.00	16.00	30.00	—
1695	—	4.00	8.00	16.00	30.00	—
1696	—	4.00	8.00	16.00	30.00	—
1697	—	4.00	8.00	16.00	30.00	—
1698	—	4.00	8.00	16.00	30.00	—
1699	—	4.00	8.00	16.00	30.00	—
1700	—	4.00	8.00	16.00	30.00	—

KM# 276 2 KREUZER

Silver **Ruler:** Johann Ernst **Obv:** Hat above two shields of arms, value below **Rev. Legend:** SALZB/LAND/MINZ/1692

Date	Mintage	VG	F	VF	XF	Unc
1692	—	5.00	10.00	15.00	35.00	—

KM# 85 2 KREUZER (1/2 Landbatzen)

Silver **Ruler:** Paris **Obv:** Hat above two shields of arms in inner circle **Obv. Legend:** PARIS D G ARCHIEPS SALIS **Rev:** St. Rupert in inner circle, value below, date in legend

Date	Mintage	VG	F	VF	XF	Unc
1623	—	7.00	18.00	36.00	60.00	—

KM# 86 2 KREUZER (1/2 Landbatzen)

Silver **Ruler:** Paris **Obv. Legend:** PARIS D G ARCHIEPS **Rev:** Shield of arms in inner circle, value below, date above shield

Date	Mintage	VG	F	VF	XF	Unc
1623	—	6.00	12.00	25.00	40.00	—
1624	—	6.00	12.00	25.00	40.00	—
1625	—	6.00	12.00	25.00	40.00	—
1626	—	6.00	12.00	25.00	40.00	—
1629	—	6.00	12.00	25.00	40.00	—
1630	—	6.00	12.00	25.00	40.00	—
1631	—	6.00	12.00	25.00	40.00	—
1632	—	6.00	12.00	25.00	40.00	—
1633	—	6.00	12.00	25.00	40.00	—
1635	—	6.00	12.00	25.00	40.00	—
1636	—	6.00	12.00	25.00	40.00	—
1637	—	6.00	12.00	25.00	40.00	—

KM# 280 2 KREUZER (1/2 Reichsbatzen)

Silver **Ruler:** Johann Erns **Obv:** Cardinals' hat above oval shield **Rev:** Oval shield within frame and circle with divided date above, value below

Date	Mintage	VG	F	VF	XF	Unc
1694	—	6.00	12.00	25.00	40.00	—
1695	—	6.00	12.00	25.00	40.00	—
1696	—	6.00	12.00	25.00	40.00	—
1697	—	6.00	12.00	25.00	40.00	—
1698	—	6.00	12.00	25.00	40.00	—
1699	—	6.00	12.00	25.00	40.00	—
1700	—	6.00	12.00	25.00	40.00	—

KM# 74 3 KREUZER

Silver **Ruler:** Paris **Obv:** Hat above two shields of arms in inner circle **Rev:** St. Rupert in inner circle, value below, date in legend

Date	Mintage	VG	F	VF	XF	Unc
1621	—	40.00	80.00	175	300	—
1622	—	40.00	80.00	175	300	—

KM# 156 3 KREUZER

Silver **Ruler:** Paris **Obv:** Hat above shield of arms, value below **Obv. Legend:** PARIS D G ARCHIEPS **Rev:** Shield of arms, date in legend **Note:** Kipper 3 Kreuzer.

Date	Mintage	VG	F	VF	XF	Unc
1653	—	25.00	48.00	95.00	210	—

KM# 228 3 KREUZER

Silver **Ruler:** Maximilian Gandolph **Obv:** Two shields of arms, date above, value below in inner circle **Obv. Legend:** MAX GAND... **Rev:** St. Rupert with salt box and crozier in inner circle

Date	Mintage	VG	F	VF	XF	Unc
1678	—	6.00	15.00	35.00	50.00	—
1679	—	6.00	15.00	35.00	50.00	—
1680	—	6.00	15.00	35.00	50.00	—
1681	—	6.00	15.00	35.00	50.00	—
1682	—	6.00	15.00	35.00	50.00	—
1683	—	6.00	15.00	35.00	50.00	—
1684	—	6.00	15.00	35.00	50.00	—
1685	—	6.00	15.00	35.00	50.00	—

KM# 249 3 KREUZER

Silver **Ruler:** Johann Ernst **Obv. Legend:** IO ERNEST...

Date	Mintage	VG	F	VF	XF	Unc
1687	—	6.00	15.00	35.00	50.00	—
1688	—	6.00	15.00	35.00	50.00	—
1689	—	6.00	15.00	35.00	50.00	—
1690	—	6.00	15.00	35.00	50.00	—
1691	—	6.00	15.00	35.00	50.00	—
1692	—	6.00	15.00	35.00	50.00	—

KM# 277 4 KREUZER (Batzen)

Silver **Ruler:** Johann Ernst **Obv:** Hat above two shields of arms, value below **Rev. Legend:** SALZB / LAND / MINZ / 1692

Date	Mintage	VG	F	VF	XF	Unc
1692	—	6.00	15.00	30.00	45.00	—

KM# 77 6 KREUZER

Silver **Ruler:** Paris **Obv:** Hat above shield of arms in inner circle **Rev:** St. Rupert in inner circle, value below, date in legend **Note:** Kipper 6 Kreuzer.

Date	Mintage	VG	F	VF	XF	Unc
(i)622	—	60.00	120	240	425	—
1622	—	60.00	120	240	425	—

KM# 78 12 KREUZER

Silver **Ruler:** Paris **Obv:** Hat above shield of arms in inner circle **Rev:** St. Rupert in inner circle, value below, date in legend **Note:** Kipper 12 Kreuzer.

Date	Mintage	VG	F	VF	XF	Unc
1622	—	90.00	180	300	475	—

KM# 230 15 KREUZER

Silver **Ruler:** Maximilian Gandolph **Obv:** Hat above shield of arms **Obv. Legend:** MAX GAND... **Rev:** St. Rupert in inner circle, value below, date in legend

Date	Mintage	VG	F	VF	XF	Unc
1681	—	12.50	25.00	45.00	90.00	—
1683	—	12.50	25.00	45.00	90.00	—
1684	—	12.50	25.00	45.00	90.00	—
1685	—	12.50	25.00	45.00	90.00	—
1686	—	12.50	25.00	45.00	90.00	—

KM# 250 15 KREUZER

Silver **Ruler:** Johann Ernst **Obv. Legend:** IO ERNEST...

Date	Mintage	VG	F	VF	XF	Unc
1687	—	12.50	25.00	45.00	90.00	—
1688	—	12.50	25.00	45.00	90.00	—
1689	—	12.50	25.00	45.00	90.00	—
1690	—	12.50	25.00	45.00	90.00	—
1692	—	12.50	25.00	45.00	90.00	—

KM# 278 15 KREUZER

Silver **Ruler:** Johann Ernst **Rev:** Saints Rupert and Virgil in diamond with value below in Arabic numerals

Date	Mintage	VG	F	VF	XF	Unc
1694	—	22.50	42.00	95.00	145	—

KM# 279 15 KREUZER

Silver **Ruler:** Johann Ernst **Rev:** Value in Roman numerals

Date	Mintage	VG	F	VF	XF	Unc
1694	—	22.50	42.00	95.00	145	—

KM# 56 24 KREUZER

Silver **Ruler:** Paris **Obv:** Hat above shield of arms in inner circle **Rev:** St. Rupert in inner circle, value below, date in legend **Note:** Kipper 24 Kreuzer.

Date	Mintage	VG	F	VF	XF	Unc
1620	—	120	210	350	600	—
1621	—	120	210	350	600	—

KM# 75 48 KREUZER

Silver **Ruler:** Paris **Obv:** Hat above value and two shields of arms in inner circle **Rev:** St. Rupert in inner circle, date in legend **Note:** Kipper 48 Kreuzer.

Date	Mintage	VG	F	VF	XF	Unc
1621	—	70.00	150	270	475	—

KM# 60 120 KREUZER

Silver **Ruler:** Paris **Obv:** Hat above value above two shields of arms within inner circle **Note:** Kipper 120 Kreuzer.

Date	Mintage	VG	F	VF	XF	Unc
1620 Rare	—	—	—	—	—	—
1621 Rare	—	—	—	—	—	—
1622 Rare	—	—	—	—	—	—

KM# 79 1/9 THALER

Silver **Ruler:** ParisObv: Hat above shield of arms **Obv. Legend:** PARIS D G... **Rev:** St. Rupert in inner circle, value below, date in legend

Date	Mintage	VG	F	VF	XF	Unc
1622	—	40.00	80.00	150	250	—
1624	—	40.00	80.00	150	250	—
1626	—	40.00	80.00	150	250	—
1627	—	40.00	80.00	150	250	—
1628	—	40.00	80.00	150	250	—
1630	—	40.00	80.00	150	250	—
1633	—	40.00	80.00	150	250	—
1634	—	40.00	80.00	150	250	—
1635	—	40.00	80.00	150	250	—
1636	—	40.00	80.00	150	250	—
1638	—	40.00	80.00	150	250	—
1640	—	40.00	80.00	150	250	—
1642	—	40.00	80.00	150	250	—
1643	—	40.00	80.00	150	250	—
1644	—	40.00	80.00	150	250	—

KM# 150 1/9 THALER

Silver **Ruler:** Paris **Note:** Klippe.

Date	Mintage	VG	F	VF	XF	Unc
1643	—	50.00	100	185	300	—
1644	—	50.00	100	185	300	—

KM# 180 1/9 THALER

Silver **Ruler:** Guidobald

Date	Mintage	VG	F	VF	XF	Unc
1656	—	45.00	90.00	150	250	—
1660	—	45.00	90.00	150	250	—
1666	—	45.00	90.00	150	250	—

KM# 179 1/9 THALER

Silver **Ruler:** Guidobald **Note:** Similar in design to KM#180.

Date	Mintage	VG	F	VF	XF	Unc
1656	—	70.00	145	240	350	—

KM# 214 1/9 THALER

Silver **Ruler:** Maximilian Gandolph **Note:** Klippe.

Date	Mintage	VG	F	VF	XF	Unc
1669	—	45.00	90.00	160	270	—
1672	—	45.00	90.00	160	270	—
1673	—	45.00	90.00	160	270	—

KM# 222 1/9 THALER

Silver **Ruler:** Maximilian Gandolph **Obv. Legend:** MAX GAND D G... **Note:** Similar in design to KM#180.

Date	Mintage	VG	F	VF	XF	Unc
1673	—	45.00	90.00	165	285	—

KM# 269 1/9 THALER

Silver **Ruler:** Johann Erns **Obv. Legend:** IO ERNEST D G... **Note:** Similar in design to KM#180.

Date	Mintage	VG	F	VF	XF	Unc
1688	—	45.00	90.00	150	250	—

KM# 270 1/9 THALER

Silver **Ruler:** Johann Ernst **Note:** Klippe.

Date	Mintage	VG	F	VF	XF	Unc
1688	—	45.00	90.00	150	250	—

KM# 7.1 1/8 THALER

Silver **Ruler:** Wolfgang Dietrich **Obv:** Oval arms with value above in inner circle **Obv. Legend:** WOLF TEO D G... **Rev:** St. Rupert in inner circle, date in legend

Date	Mintage	VG	F	VF	XF	Unc
ND	—	250	500	900	1,500	—

KM# 7.2 1/8 THALER

Silver **Ruler:** Wolfgang Dietrich

Date	Mintage	VG	F	VF	XF	Unc
1607	—	165	300	550	900	—
1609	—	165	300	550	900	—
1610	—	165	300	550	900	—
1612	—	165	300	550	900	—

KM# 8 1/8 THALER

Silver **Ruler:** Wolfgang Dietrich **Note:** Klippe.

Date	Mintage	VG	F	VF	XF	Unc
1609	—	150	275	500	850	—
1610	—	150	275	500	850	—
1612	—	150	275	500	850	—

KM# 14 1/8 THALER

Silver **Ruler:** Markus Sittich, **Note:** Klippe.

Date	Mintage	VG	F	VF	XF	Unc
1612	—	250	450	750	1,200	—
1613	—	250	450	750	1,200	—
1615	—	250	450	750	1,200	—
1616	—	250	450	750	1,200	—

KM# 13 1/8 THALER

Silver **Ruler:** Markus Sittich, **Obv. Legend:** MARCVS SITTICVS D G...

Date	Mintage	VG	F	VF	XF	Unc
1612	—	200	400	650	1,000	—
1613	—	200	400	650	1,000	—
1614	—	200	400	650	1,000	—
1615	—	200	400	650	1,000	—
1616	—	200	400	650	1,000	—

KM# 57 1/8 THALER

Silver **Ruler:** Paris**Obv:** Shield of arms with value above, in inner circle **Obv. Legend:** PARIS D G...

Date	Mintage	VG	F	VF	XF	Unc
1620	—	45.00	90.00	165	275	—
1622	—	45.00	90.00	165	275	—
1623	—	45.00	90.00	165	275	—
1624	—	45.00	90.00	165	275	—

KM# 106 1/8 THALER

Silver **Ruler:** Paris **Note:** Klippe.

Date	Mintage	VG	F	VF	XF	Unc
1627	—	60.00	120	200	350	—

KM# 107.1 1/6 THALER

Silver **Ruler:** Paris**Obv:** Madonna and child above shield of arms in inner circle **Obv. Legend:** PARIS D G... **Rev:** St. Rupert with value above arms in inner circle, date in legend

Date	Mintage	VG	F	VF	XF	Unc
1627	—	50.00	100	185	300	—
1628	—	50.00	100	185	300	—
1630	—	50.00	100	185	300	—
1634	—	50.00	100	185	300	—

KM# 108 1/6 THALER

Silver **Ruler:** Paris**Note:** Klippe.

Date	Mintage	VG	F	VF	XF	Unc
1627	—	65.00	120	225	375	—
1642	—	65.00	120	225	375	—
1646	—	65.00	120	225	375	—
1647	—	65.00	120	225	375	—
1648	—	65.00	120	225	375	—
1651	—	65.00	120	225	375	—
1652	—	65.00	120	225	375	—

KM# 107.2 1/6 THALER

Silver **Ruler:** Paris**Rev:** Round shield below St. Rupert

Date	Mintage	VG	F	VF	XF	Unc
1638	—	75.00	135	250	400	—
1642	—	75.00	135	250	400	—
1645	—	75.00	135	250	400	—
1646	—	75.00	135	250	400	—
1648	—	75.00	135	250	400	—

KM# 160 1/6 THALER

Silver **Ruler:** Guidobald **Note:** Klippe.

Date	Mintage	VG	F	VF	XF	Unc
1654	—	35.00	70.00	135	225	—
1656	—	35.00	70.00	135	225	—
1658	—	35.00	70.00	135	225	—
1661	—	35.00	70.00	135	225	—
1663	—	35.00	70.00	135	225	—
1666	—	35.00	70.00	135	225	—

KM# 181 1/6 THALER

Silver **Ruler:** Guidobald **Obv:** Hat above shield of arms **Obv. Legend:** GUIDOBALD D G... **Rev:** St. Rupert in inner circle, value below, date in legend

Date	Mintage	VG	F	VF	XF	Unc
1656	—	40.00	80.00	145	240	—
1658	—	40.00	80.00	145	240	—
1661	—	40.00	80.00	145	240	—
1666	—	40.00	80.00	145	240	—

KM# 215 1/6 THALER

Silver **Ruler:** Maximilian Gandolph **Note:** Klippe.

Date	Mintage	VG	F	VF	XF	Unc
1669	—	60.00	100	175	300	—
1674	—	60.00	100	175	300	—
1677	—	60.00	100	175	300	—
1679	—	60.00	100	175	300	—

KM# 227 1/6 THALER

Silver **Ruler:** Maximilian Gandolph **Obv. Legend:** MAX GAND D G...

Date	Mintage	VG	F	VF	XF	Unc
1677	—	100	175	275	450	—

KM# 251 1/6 THALER

Silver **Ruler:** Johann Ernst **Obv. Legend:** IO ERNEST D G... **Note:** Klippe.

Date	Mintage	VG	F	VF	XF	Unc
1687	—	—	—	—	—	—
1688	—	100	200	300	500	—

KM# 15 1/4 THALER

Silver **Ruler:** Markus Sittich **Obv:** Hat above shield of arms dividing date **Obv. Legend:** MARCVS SITTICVS D. G. **Rev:** St. Rupert in inner circle, value below

Date	Mintage	VG	F	VF	XF	Unc
1612	—	200	350	600	1,000	—
1613	—	200	350	600	1,000	—

KM# 16 1/4 THALER

Silver **Ruler:** Markus Sittich **Note:** Klippe.

Date	Mintage	VG	F	VF	XF	Unc
1612	—	175	300	500	850	—
1613	—	175	300	500	850	—

KM# 35 1/4 THALER

Silver **Ruler:** Markus Sittich **Note:** Klippe.

Date	Mintage	VG	F	VF	XF	Unc
1614	—	100	200	350	600	—
1615	—	100	200	350	600	—
1616	—	100	200	350	600	—

KM# 34 1/4 THALER

Silver **Ruler:** Markus Sittich **Rev:** Date at end of outer legend

Date	Mintage	VG	F	VF	XF	Unc
1614	—	150	250	450	700	—
1615	—	150	250	450	700	—
1616	—	150	250	450	700	—

KM# 58 1/4 THALER

Silver **Ruler:** Paris **Note:** Klippe.

Date	Mintage	VG	F	VF	XF	Unc
1620	—	100	200	300	550	—
1622	—	100	200	300	550	—

KM# 80 1/4 THALER

Silver **Ruler:** Paris **Obv:** Hat above shield of arms **Obv. Legend:** PARIS D G... **Rev:** St. Rupert in inner circle, date in legend

Date	Mintage	VG	F	VF	XF	Unc
1622	—	120	220	400	650	—

KM# 88 1/4 THALER

Silver **Ruler:** Paris **Note:** Klippe.

Date	Mintage	VG	F	VF	XF	Unc
1624	—	80.00	150	250	450	—
1625	—	80.00	150	250	450	—

Date	Mintage	VG	F	VF	XF	Unc
1626	—	80.00	150	250	450	—
1631	—	80.00	150	250	450	—
1638	—	80.00	150	250	450	—
1639	—	80.00	150	250	450	—
1651	—	80.00	150	250	450	—
1652	—	80.00	150	250	450	—

KM# 97 1/4 THALER

Silver **Ruler:** Paris **Rev:** St. Rupert in inner circle, value below, date in legend

Date	Mintage	VG	F	VF	XF	Unc
1625	—	100	200	350	600	—
1626	—	100	200	350	600	—
1639	—	100	200	350	600	—
1652	—	100	200	350	600	—

KM# 98 1/4 THALER

Silver **Ruler:** Paris**Obv:** Madonna and child above shield of arms **Obv. Legend:** PARIS D G... **Rev:** St. Rupert above value and arms in inner circle, date in legend

Date	Mintage	VG	F	VF	XF	Unc
ND	—	100	200	350	600	—
1626	—	100	200	350	600	—
1633	—	100	200	350	600	—
1634	—	100	200	350	600	—
1636	—	100	200	350	600	—
1637	—	100	200	350	600	—
1640	—	100	200	350	600	—
1642	—	100	200	350	600	—

KM# 103 1/4 THALER

Silver **Ruler:** Paris **Note:** Klippe.

Date	Mintage	VG	F	VF	XF	Unc
1626	—	70.00	135	245	450	—
1633	—	70.00	135	245	450	—
1636	—	70.00	135	245	450	—
1640	—	70.00	135	245	450	—
1642	—	70.00	135	245	450	—

KM# 140 1/4 THALER

Silver **Ruler:** Paris**Subject:** Cathedral Dedication **Note:** Similar to 1/2 Thaler, KM#141.

Date	Mintage	VG	F	VF	XF	Unc
1628	—	—	—	—	—	—

KM# 161 1/4 THALER

Silver **Ruler:** Guidobald **Note:** Klippe.

Date	Mintage	VG	F	VF	XF	Unc
1654	—	50.00	100	175	375	—
1658	—	50.00	100	175	375	—
1668	—	50.00	100	175	375	—

KM# 182 1/4 THALER

Silver **Ruler:** Guidobald **Obv:** Hat above shield of arms **Obv. Legend:** GVIDOBALDVS D G... **Rev:** St. Rupert in inner circle, value below, date in legend

Date	Mintage	VG	F	VF	XF	Unc
1656	—	65.00	125	200	400	—
1658	—	65.00	125	200	400	—
1660	—	65.00	125	200	400	—
1661	—	65.00	125	200	400	—
1663	—	65.00	125	200	400	—

KM# 216 1/4 THALER

Silver **Ruler:** Maximilian Gandolph **Obv:** Hat above shield of arms **Obv. Legend:** MAXIM GANDOL D G...

Date	Mintage	VG	F	VF	XF	Unc
1669	—	50.00	100	200	325	—
1672	—	50.00	100	200	325	—
1675	—	50.00	100	200	325	—

KM# 231 1/4 THALER

Silver **Ruler:** Maximilian Gandolph **Obv:** Inscription **Obv. Inscription:** MAX / GAND EX CO / MIT DE KOEN / BURG ARCHIEP ET / PR SALISBS SED / AP LEG SAZCVLO / VNDECIMO FVN / DATI ARCHI / EPTVS **Rev:** Hat above shield of arms divides date, triangle above

Date	Mintage	VG	F	VF	XF	Unc
1682	—	60.00	120	230	400	—

KM# 245 1/4 THALER

Silver **Ruler:** Maximilian Gandolph **Obv:** Hat above two shields of arms **Obv. Legend:** MAXIM GANDOL D G... **Rev:** St. Rupert in inner circle, value below, date in legend

Date	Mintage	VG	F	VF	XF	Unc
1684	—	120	240	350	600	—

KM# 246 1/4 THALER

Silver **Ruler:** Maximilian Gandolph, **Note:** Klippe.

Date	Mintage	VG	F	VF	XF	Unc
1684	—	65.00	125	225	375	—

KM# 252 1/4 THALER

Silver **Ruler:** Johann Ernst **Obv:** Hat above two shields of arms in inner circle **Obv. Legend:** IO ERNEST D G... **Note:** Klippe.

Date	Mintage	VG	F	VF	XF	Unc
1687	—	45.00	90.00	165	275	—

KM# 281 1/4 THALER

Silver **Ruler:** Johann Ernst **Obv:** Hat above shield of arms

Date	Mintage	VG	F	VF	XF	Unc
1694	—	65.00	120	200	350	—

KM# 282 1/4 THALER

Silver **Ruler:** Johann Ernst**Obv:** Madonna and Child above shield of arms in inner circle **Rev:** St. Rupert above value and arms in inner circle, date in legend

Date	Mintage	VG	F	VF	XF	Unc
1694	—	30.00	60.00	125	250	—
1695	—	30.00	60.00	125	250	—
1696	—	30.00	60.00	125	250	—

Date	Mintage	VG	F	VF	XF	Unc
1699	—	30.00	60.00	125	250	—
1700	—	30.00	60.00	125	250	—

KM# 294 1/4 THALER

Silver, 30 mm. **Ruler:** Franz Anton **Subject:** Enthronement of the archbishop **Obv:** Bust of Franz Anton right, star below bust **Rev:** Legend, date below **Rev. Legend:** IN MANV DOMINI SORTS MEA

Date	Mintage	VG	F	VF	XF	Unc
1699	—	95.00	195	325	550	—

KM# 17 1/2 THALER

Silver **Ruler:** Markus Sittich **Obv:** Hat above shield of arms, hat divides date **Obv. Legend:** MARCVS SITTICVS D G... **Rev:** St. Rupert in inner circle

Date	Mintage	VG	F	VF	XF	Unc
1612	—	325	600	1,000	1,650	—

KM# 18 1/2 THALER

Silver **Ruler:** Markus Sittich **Note:** Klippe.

Date	Mintage	VG	F	VF	XF	Unc
1612	—	275	500	825	1,400	—

KM# 37 1/2 THALER

Silver **Ruler:** Markus Sittich **Note:** Klippe.

Date	Mintage	VG	F	VF	XF	Unc
1614	—	150	300	550	900	—
1615	—	150	300	550	900	—
1617	—	150	300	550	900	—
1619	—	150	300	550	900	—

KM# 36 1/2 THALER

Silver **Ruler:** Markus Sittich **Rev:** Date at end of legend

Date	Mintage	VG	F	VF	XF	Unc
1614	—	225	400	700	1,150	—
1615	—	225	400	700	1,150	—
1617	—	225	400	700	1,150	—

KM# 59 1/2 THALER

Silver **Ruler:** Paris **Obv:** Hat above shield of arms in inner circle **Obv. Legend:** PARIS D G... **Rev:** St. Rupert in inner circle, date in legend **Note:** Klippe.

Date	Mintage	VG	F	VF	XF	Unc
1620	—	350	600	1,000	1,650	—
1622	—	350	600	1,000	1,650	—

KM# 76 1/2 THALER

Silver **Ruler:** Paris **Obv:** Hat above shield of arms in inner circle **Rev:** St. Rupert in inner circle, value below, date in legend **Note:** Kipper 1/2 Thaler.

Date	Mintage	VG	F	VF	XF	Unc
1621	—	85.00	175	300	500	—
1622	—	100	200	350	600	—

KM# 90 1/2 THALER

Silver **Ruler:** Paris **Note:** Klippe. Varieties exist.

Date	Mintage	VG	F	VF	XF	Unc
1624	—	250	400	750	1,350	—
1625	—	250	400	750	1,350	—
1626	—	250	400	750	1,350	—
1627	—	250	400	750	1,350	—
1629	—	250	400	750	1,350	—
1631	—	250	400	750	1,350	—
1636	—	250	400	750	1,350	—
1638	—	250	400	750	1,350	—
1639	—	250	400	750	1,350	—

KM# 89 1/2 THALER

Silver **Ruler:** Paris **Obv:** Madonna and child above shield of arms in inner circle **Rev:** St. Rupert above arms in inner circle

Date	Mintage	VG	F	VF	XF	Unc
1624	—	350	600	1,000	1,650	—
1625	—	350	600	1,000	1,650	—
1626	—	350	600	1,000	1,650	—
1627	—	350	600	1,000	1,650	—

KM# 141 1/2 THALER

14.5500 g., Silver **Ruler:** ParisSubject: Cathedral Dedication

Date	Mintage	VG	F	VF	XF	Unc
1628	—	60.00	120	210	350	—

KM# 188 1/2 THALER

Silver **Ruler:** Maximilian Gandolph **Obv:** Hat above shield of arms, date divided below in inner circle **Obv. Legend:** MAXIMM. GANDOLPH... **Rev:** St. Rupert in inner circle

Date	Mintage	VG	F	VF	XF	Unc
1668	—	175	300	500	850	—

KM# 189 1/2 THALER

Silver **Ruler:** Maximilian Gandolph

Date	Mintage	VG	F	VF	XF	Unc
1668	—	65.00	140	250	500	—

KM# 232 1/2 THALER

Silver **Ruler:** Maximilian Gandolph **Subject:** 1100th Year of the Bishopric

Date	Mintage	VG	F	VF	XF	Unc
1682	—	60.00	120	240	475	—

KM# 253 1/2 THALER

Silver **Ruler:** Johann Ernst **Obv:** Hat above shield of arms, date divided near bottom in inner circle **Rev:** SS. Rupert and Virgil

Date	Mintage	VG	F	VF	XF	Unc
1687	—	45.00	85.00	165	290	—
1694	—	45.00	85.00	165	290	—
1695	—	45.00	85.00	165	290	—
1698	—	45.00	85.00	165	290	—
1699	—	45.00	85.00	165	290	—
1700	—	45.00	85.00	165	290	—

KM# 19 THALER

Silver **Ruler:** Markus Sittich **Obv:** Similar to KM#38 but date divided near bottom of arms **Note:** Dav. #3488.

Date	Mintage	VG	F	VF	XF	Unc
1612	—	120	300	475	775	—
1613	—	120	300	475	775	—

KM# 20 THALER

Silver **Ruler:** Markus Sittich **Note:** Dav. #A3488. Klippe.

Date	Mintage	VG	F	VF	XF	Unc
1612	—	265	650	1,100	1,800	—
1613	—	265	650	1,100	1,800	—

KM# 39 THALER

Silver **Ruler:** Markus Sittich **Note:** Klippe. Dav. #A3492.

Date	Mintage	VG	F	VF	XF	Unc
1614	—	265	650	1,100	1,800	—
1615	—	265	650	1,100	1,800	—
1616	—	265	650	1,100	1,800	—
1617	—	265	650	1,100	1,800	—
1618	—	265	650	1,100	1,800	—
1619	—	265	650	1,100	1,800	—

KM# 38 THALER

Silver **Ruler:** Markus Sittich **Rev:** Date in legend **Note:** Dav. #3492.

Date	Mintage	VG	F	VF	XF	Unc
1614	—	120	300	475	775	—
1615	—	120	300	475	775	—
1616	—	120	300	475	775	—
1617	—	120	300	475	775	—
1618	—	120	300	475	775	—
1619	—	120	300	475	775	—

KM# 28 THALER

Silver **Ruler:** Markus Sittich **Obv:** Tower **Rev:** Saint on throne **Note:** Klippe. Mule. Dav. #3493.

Date	Mintage	VG	F	VF	XF	Unc
ND/1615 Rare	—	—	—	—	—	—
1593/1615 Rare	—	—	—	—	—	—
1593/1617 Rare	—	—	—	—	—	—

KM# 61 THALER

Silver **Ruler:** Paris **Obv. Legend:** PARIS D G... **Note:** Dav. #3497.

Date	Mintage	VG	F	VF	XF	Unc
1620	—	50.00	115	190	325	—
1621	—	50.00	115	190	325	—
1622	—	50.00	115	190	325	—
1623	—	50.00	115	190	325	—
1624	—	50.00	115	190	325	—

KM# 62 THALER

Silver **Ruler:** Paris **Note:** Dav. #3497A. Klippe.

Date	Mintage	VG	F	VF	XF	Unc
1620	—	170	425	725	1,100	—
1622	—	170	425	725	1,100	—

KM# 87 THALER

Silver **Ruler:** Paris **Obv:** Madonna above shield of arms **Rev:** St. Rupert standing facing **Note:** Dav. #3504. Varieties exist.

Date	Mintage	VG	F	VF	XF	Unc
1623	—	36.00	90.00	160	325	—
1624	—	36.00	90.00	160	325	—
1625	—	36.00	90.00	160	325	—
1626	—	36.00	90.00	160	325	—
1627	—	36.00	90.00	160	325	—
1628	—	36.00	90.00	160	325	—
1629	—	36.00	90.00	160	325	—
1630	—	36.00	90.00	160	325	—
1631	—	36.00	90.00	160	325	—
1632	—	36.00	90.00	160	325	—
1633	—	36.00	90.00	160	325	—
1634	—	36.00	90.00	160	325	—
1635	—	36.00	90.00	160	325	—
1636	—	36.00	90.00	160	325	—
1637	—	36.00	90.00	160	325	—
1638	—	36.00	90.00	160	325	—
1639	—	36.00	90.00	160	325	—
1640	—	36.00	90.00	160	325	—
1641	—	36.00	90.00	160	325	—
1642	—	36.00	90.00	160	325	—
1643/2	—	36.00	90.00	160	325	—
1644	—	36.00	90.00	160	325	—
1645	—	36.00	90.00	160	325	—
1646	—	36.00	90.00	160	325	—
1647	—	36.00	90.00	160	325	—
1648	—	36.00	90.00	160	325	—
1649	—	36.00	90.00	160	325	—
1650	—	36.00	90.00	160	325	—
1651	—	36.00	90.00	160	325	—
1652	—	36.00	90.00	160	325	—
1653	—	36.00	90.00	160	325	—

KM# 91 THALER

Silver **Ruler:** Paris **Note:** Dav. #3504A. Klippe.

Date	Mintage	VG	F	VF	XF	Unc
1624	—	170	425	725	1,100	—
1625	—	170	425	725	1,100	—

Date	Mintage	VG	F	VF	XF	Unc
1628	—	170	425	725	1,100	—
1629	—	170	425	725	1,100	—
1631	—	170	425	725	1,100	—
1632	—	170	425	725	1,100	—
1636	—	170	425	725	1,100	—
1638	—	170	425	725	1,100	—

KM# 110 THALER

Silver **Ruler:** Paris **Subject:** Consecration of the Cathedral **Note:** Dav. #3499.

Date	Mintage	VG	F	VF	XF	Unc
1628	—	75.00	190	325	450	—

KM# 162 THALER

Silver **Ruler:** Guidobald, **Obv. Legend:** GVIDOBALD D G... **Note:** Dav. #3505.

Date	Mintage	VG	F	VF	XF	Unc
1654	—	36.00	90.00	160	325	—
1655	—	36.00	90.00	160	325	—
1656	—	36.00	90.00	160	325	—
1657	—	36.00	90.00	160	325	—
1658	—	36.00	90.00	160	325	—
1659	—	36.00	90.00	160	325	—
1660	—	36.00	90.00	160	325	—
1661	—	36.00	90.00	160	325	—
1662	—	36.00	90.00	160	325	—
1663	—	36.00	90.00	160	325	—
1664	—	36.00	90.00	160	325	—
1665	—	36.00	90.00	160	325	—
1666	—	36.00	90.00	160	325	—
1667	—	36.00	90.00	160	325	—
1668	—	36.00	90.00	160	325	—

KM# 190 THALER

Silver **Ruler:** Maximilian Gandolph **Obv. Legend:** MAX: GAND: D: G:... **Note:** Dav. #3508. Illustration reduced.

Date	Mintage	VG	F	VF	XF	Unc
1668	—	36.00	90.00	160	325	—
1669	—	36.00	90.00	160	325	—
1670	—	36.00	90.00	160	325	—
1671	—	36.00	90.00	160	325	—
1672	—	36.00	90.00	160	325	—
1673	—	36.00	90.00	160	325	—
1674	—	36.00	90.00	160	325	—
1675	—	36.00	90.00	160	325	—
1677	—	36.00	90.00	160	325	—
1680	—	36.00	90.00	160	325	—
1685	—	36.00	90.00	160	325	—
1686	—	36.00	90.00	160	325	—

KM# 233 THALER

Silver **Ruler:** Maximilian Gandolph **Subject:** 1100th Year of the Bishopric **Note:** Dav. #3509.

Date	Mintage	VG	F	VF	XF	Unc
MDCLXXXII (1682)	—	75.00	190	325	575	—
1682 PS	—	—	—	—	—	—

KM# 254 THALER

Silver **Ruler:** Johann Ernst **Obv:** Madonna and child above Cardinals' hat and shield **Obv. Legend:** IO: ERNEST: D:G: ... **Rev:** St. Rupert above shield in frame, date in legend **Rev. Legend:** S: RUDBERTUS: EPS .... **Note:** Dav.#1234.

Date	Mintage	F	VF	XF	Unc	BU
1687	—	90.00	160	325	600	—
1688	—	90.00	160	325	600	—
1690	—	90.00	160	325	600	—
1691	—	90.00	160	325	600	—
1692	—	90.00	160	325	600	—
1693	—	90.00	160	325	600	—
1694	—	90.00	160	325	600	—
1695	—	90.00	160	325	600	—
1696	—	90.00	160	325	600	—
1697	—	90.00	160	325	600	—
1698	—	90.00	160	325	600	—
1699	—	90.00	160	325	600	—
1700	—	90.00	160	325	600	—

KM# 43 1-1/2 THALER

Silver **Ruler:** Markus Sittich **Obv:** Hat above oval shield of arms in inner circle **Obv. Legend:** MARCVS. SITTICVS. D. G... **Rev:** St. Rupert in inner circle, date in legend **Note:** Klippe. Dav. #3491.

Date	Mintage	VG	F	VF	XF	Unc
1617 Rare	—	—	—	—	—	—

KM# 21 2 THALER

Silver **Ruler:** Markus Sittich **Obv:** Hat above oval shield of arms in inner circle, date divided near bottom of arms **Obv. Legend:** MARCVS. SITTICVS. D. G... **Rev:** St. Rupert in inner circle **Note:** Klippe. Dav. #3487.

Date	Mintage	VG	F	VF	XF	Unc
1612 Rare	—	—	—	—	—	—
1613 Rare	—	—	—	—	—	—

KM# 40 2 THALER

Silver **Ruler:** Markus Sittich **Note:** Dav. #3490. Similar to 1 Thaler, KM#39.

Date	Mintage	VG	F	VF	XF	Unc
1614	—	950	1,450	2,250	3,500	—
1615	—	950	1,450	2,250	3,500	—
1616	—	950	1,450	2,250	3,500	—
1617	—	950	1,450	2,250	3,500	—
1618	—	950	1,450	2,250	3,500	—
1619	—	950	1,450	2,250	3,500	—

KM# 44 2 THALER

Silver **Ruler:** Markus Sittich **Note:** Dav. #3490A. Similar to 1 Thaler, KM#38.

Date	Mintage	VG	F	VF	XF	Unc
1617 Rare	—	—	—	—	—	—

KM# 63 2 THALER

Silver **Ruler:** Paris **Obv. Legend:** PARIS D G... **Note:** Dav. #3496. Similar to 1 Thaler, KM#62. Klippe.

Date	Mintage	VG	F	VF	XF	Unc
1620	—	750	1,250	2,000	3,000	—

KM# 92 2 THALER

Silver **Ruler:** Paris **Note:** Dav. #3503. Similar to 1 Thaler, KM#87. Klippe.

Date	Mintage	VG	F	VF	XF	Unc
1624	—	450	750	1,250	2,000	—
1625	—	450	750	1,250	2,000	—
1629	—	450	750	1,250	2,000	—
1631	—	450	750	1,250	2,000	—
1632	—	450	750	1,250	2,000	—
1636	—	450	750	1,250	2,000	—

KM# A111 2 THALER

Silver **Ruler:** Paris **Subject:** Consecration of the Cathedral **Note:** Dav. #3498.

Date	Mintage	VG	F	VF	XF	Unc
1628	—	900	1,500	2,500	3,500	—

KM# 111 2 THALER

Silver **Ruler:** Paris **Note:** Dav. #3498A. Klippe.

Date	Mintage	VG	F	VF	XF	Unc
1628	—	1,450	2,250	3,500	5,000	—

KM# 138 2 THALER

Silver **Ruler:** Paris**Note:** Dav. #3503A. Similar to 1 Thaler, KM#87.

Date	Mintage	VG	F	VF	XF	Unc
1629	—	500	900	1,500	2,500	—

KM# 113 2 THALER

Silver **Ruler:** Maximilian Gandolph **Obv:** City view of Salzburg **Obv. Legend:** MAX: GAND: D: G... **Note:** Dav. #3507. Illustration reduced.

Date	Mintage	VG	F	VF	XF	Unc
ND Rare	—	—	—	—	—	—

KM# 48 3 THALER

Silver **Ruler:** Markus Sittich **Obv:** Hat above oval shield of arms in inner circle **Obv. Legend:** MARCVS. SITTICVS. D. G... **Rev:** St. Rupert in inner circle, date in legend **Note:** Dav. #3489. Klippe.

Date	Mintage	VG	F	VF	XF	Unc
1618 Rare	—	—	—	—	—	—

KM# 81 3 THALER

Silver **Ruler:** Paris **Obv. Legend:** PARIS D G... **Note:** Dav. #3495. Klippe. Similar to 1 Thaler, KM#62.

Date	Mintage	VG	F	VF	XF	Unc
1622 Rare	—	—	—	—	—	—

KM# 99 3 THALER

Silver **Ruler:** Paris **Obv:** Madonna and child above shield of arms in inner circle **Rev:** St. Rupert above shield of arms in inner circle, date in legend **Note:** Dav. #3502. Klippe.

Date	Mintage	VG	F	VF	XF	Unc
1625	—	1,250	2,000	3,000	4,500	—
1629	—	1,250	2,000	3,000	4,500	—
1631	—	1,250	2,000	3,000	4,500	—

KM# 114 3 THALER

Silver **Ruler:** Paris **Subject:** Consecration of the Cathedral **Note:** Dav. #3498B. Similar to 1 Thaler, KM#110.

Date	Mintage	VG	F	VF	XF	Unc
1628 Rare	—	—	—	—	—	—

KM# 115 3 THALER

Silver **Ruler:** Paris **Note:** Dav. #3498C. Klippe.

Date	Mintage	VG	F	VF	XF	Unc
1628 Rare	—	—	—	—	—	—

KM# 64 4 THALER

Silver **Ruler:** Paris **Obv:** Hat above shield of arms in inner circle **Obv. Legend:** PARIS. D. G... **Rev:** St. Rupert in inner circle, date in legend **Note:** Dav. #3494. Klippe.

Date	Mintage	VG	F	VF	XF	Unc
1620 Rare	—	—	—	—	—	—

KM# 100 4 THALER

Silver **Ruler:** Paris **Note:** Dav. #3501. Klippe. Illustration reduced.

Date	Mintage	VG	F	VF	XF	Unc
1625 Rare	—	—	—	—	—	—
1629 Rare	—	—	—	—	—	—
1632 Rare	—	—	—	—	—	—

KM# 101 4 THALER

Silver **Ruler:** Paris **Note:** Dav. #3501A. Design similar to KM#100.

Date	Mintage	VG	F	VF	XF	Unc
1625 Rare	—	—	—	—	—	—

KM# 116 4 THALER

Silver **Ruler:** Paris **Subject:** Consecration of the Cathedral **Note:** Dav. #3498D.

Date	Mintage	VG	F	VF	XF	Unc
1628 Rare	—	—	—	—	—	—

KM# 117.1 4 THALER

Silver **Ruler:** Paris **Note:** Dav. #3498E. Klippe. Illustration reduced.

Date	Mintage	VG	F	VF	XF	Unc
1628 Rare	—	—	—	—	—	—

KM# 117.2 4 THALER

Silver **Ruler:** Paris **Note:** Three-sided klippe.

Date	Mintage	VG	F	VF	XF	Unc
1628 Rare	—	—	—	—	—	—

KM# 118 4 THALER

Silver **Ruler:** Maximilian Gandolph **Obv:** City view of Salzburg in inner circle **Obv. Legend:** MAX: GAND: D: G:... **Rev:** Hat above oval arms, a saint seated at each side in inner circle **Note:** Dav. #3506.

Date	Mintage	VG	F	VF	XF	Unc
ND Rare	—	—	—	—	—	—

KM# 119 5 THALER

Silver **Ruler:** Paris **Subject:** Consecration of the Cathedral **Note:** Dav. #3498F. Klippe. Similar to 4 Thaler, KM#117.1.

Date	Mintage	VG	F	VF	XF	Unc
1628 Rare	—	—	—	—	—	—

KM# 120 6 THALER

Silver **Ruler:** Paris **Subject:** Consecration of the Cathedral **Note:** Dav. #3498G. Klippe.

Date	Mintage	VG	F	VF	XF	Unc
1628 Rare	—	—	—	—	—	—

KM# 139 6 THALER

Silver **Ruler:** Paris **Note:** Dav. #3500. Similar to KM#145.

Date	Mintage	VG	F	VF	XF	Unc
1629 Rare	—	—	—	—	—	—

KM# 145 6 THALER

Silver **Ruler:** Paris **Note:** Dav. #3500A.

Date	Mintage	VG	F	VF	XF	Unc
1631 Rare	—	—	—	—	—	—

COUNTERMARKED COINAGE

1681

Prior to 1681 the confusion of the various types of Germanic coinage continued, particularly in regards to the many debased coins in circulation. In order to save his country from greater difficulties, Max Gandolph Kuenburg in 1681, ordered that all thalers and half thalers in circulation be countermarked with the Arms of the See including the date 1681. As the charge for this was one kreuzer for each thaler and two pfennige for each half thaler, the desired result was not attained. Partly through fear of innovation, partly through meanness, very few coins were handed in and all these countermarked pieces are comparitively rare.

KM# 217 GROSCHEN

Silver **Ruler:** Maximilian Gandolph **Countermark:** Arms of the See, date **Note:** Countermark on Bohemia-Prague Mint 1 Groschen of Wenceslaus III.

CM Date	Host Date	Good	VG	F	VF	XF
ND(1681)	1601-19 Rare	—	—	—	—	—

KM# 218 1/2 GULDEN

Silver **Ruler:** Maximilian Gandolph **Countermark:** Arms of the See, date **Note:** Countermark on Germany-Brandenburg 1/2 Gulden.

CM Date	Host Date	Good	VG	F	VF	XF
ND1681	1671 Rare	—	—	—	—	—
ND(1681)	1671 Rare	—	—	—	—	—

KM# 219 GULDEN

Silver **Ruler:** Maximilian Gandolph **Countermark:** Arms of the See, date **Note:** Countermark on Germany-Reuss-Schleiz Gulden.

CM Date	Host Date	Good	VG	F	VF	XF
1681	1678 Rare	—	—	—	—	—
ND(1681)	1678 Rare	—	—	—	—	—

KM# A229 2/3 THALER

Silver **Ruler:** Maximilian Gandolph **Countermark:** Arms of the See **Note:** Countermark on Goslar 24 Mariengroschen, KM#69.

CM Date	Host Date	Good	VG	F	VF	XF
ND(1681)	1674 CH	—	275	450	650	—

KM# 229.9 THALER

Silver, 40 mm. **Ruler:** Maximilian Gandolph **Countermark:** Arms of the See, date **Note:** Countermarked on Austria, Hall mint 1 Thaler, Dav.#3005.

CM Date	Host Date	Good	VG	F	VF	XF
ND(1681)	1607	—	—	—	—	—

KM# 229.2 THALER

Silver **Ruler:** Maximilian Gandolph **Countermark:** Arms of the See, date **Note:** Countermark on Austria - Hall Mint 1 Thaler, Dav. #3125.

CM Date	Host Date	Good	VG	F	VF	XF
ND(1681)	1622	—	450	750	1,250	1,800

KM# 229.3 THALER

Silver **Ruler:** Maximilian Gandolph **Countermark:** Arms of the See, date **Note:** Countermark on Austria - Hall Mint 1 Thaler, Dav. #3330.

CM Date	Host Date	Good	VG	F	VF	XF
ND(1681)	1632	—	450	750	1,250	1,800

KM# 229.4 THALER

Silver **Ruler:** Maximilian Gandolph **Countermark:** Arms of the See, date **Note:** Countermark on Austria - Hall Mint 1 Thaler, Dav. #3370.

CM Date	Host Date	Good	VG	F	VF	XF
ND(1681)	1665	—	450	750	1,250	1,800

KM# 229.6 THALER

Silver **Ruler:** Maximilian Gandolph **Countermark:** Arms of the See, date **Note:** Countermark on Austria - Salzburg 1 Thaler of Maximiliam Gandolf von Kuenberg.

CM Date	Host Date	Good	VG	F	VF	XF
ND(1681)	1624	—	500	900	1,500	2,000

KM# 229.5 THALER

Silver **Ruler:** Maximilian Gandolph **Countermark:** Arms of the See, date **Note:** Countermark on Austria - Salzburg 1 Thaler of Wolf Dietrich von Raitenau.

CM Date	Host Date	Good	VG	F	VF	XF
ND(1681)	ND(1612)	—	500	900	1,500	2,000

KM# 229.1 THALER

Silver **Ruler:** Maximilian Gandolph **Countermark:** Arms of the See, date **Note:** Countermark on Austria 1 Thaler of Leopold I.

CM Date	Host Date	Good	VG	F	VF	XF
ND(1681)	1621	—	450	750	1,250	1,800

KM# 229.8 THALER

Silver **Ruler:** Maximilian Gandolph **Countermark:** Arms of the See, date **Note:** Countermark on Germany - Teutonic Order 1 Thaler, Dav. #5848.

CM Date	Host Date	Good	VG	F	VF	XF
ND(1681)	1603	—	400	700	1,200	1,750

KM# 229.7 THALER

Silver **Ruler:** Maximilian Gandolph **Countermark:** Arms of the See, date **Note:** Countermark on Austria - Salzburg 1 Thaler, Dav. #3505.

CM Date	Host Date	Good	VG	F	VF	XF
ND(1681)	1654	—	400	700	1,200	1,750
ND(1681)	1665	—	400	700	1,200	1,750

TRADE COINAGE

KM# 51 GOLDGULDEN

0.6850 g., 0.9040 Gold 0.0199 oz. AGW **Ruler:** Markus Sittich, Graf von Hohenems 1612-1619 **Obv:** Two shields below hat in inner circle **Rev:** St. Rupert standing divides date in inner circle

Date	Mintage	VG	F	VF	XF	Unc
1619	—	900	1,750	3,750	6,000	—

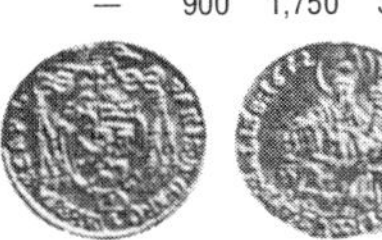

KM# 155 1/4 DUCAT

0.8750 g., 0.9860 Gold 0.0277 oz. AGW **Ruler:** Paris **Obv:** Arms below hat, value below **Obv. Legend:** PARIS... **Rev:** St. Rupert seated facing half right

Date	Mintage	VG	F	VF	XF	Unc
1652	—	100	200	400	750	—

KM# 163 1/4 DUCAT

0.8750 g., 0.9860 Gold 0.0277 oz. AGW **Ruler:** Guidobald **Obv. Legend:** GVIDOB...

Date	Mintage	VG	F	VF	XF	Unc
1654	—	60.00	100	180	265	—
1655	—	60.00	100	180	265	—
1658	—	60.00	100	180	265	—
1659	—	60.00	100	180	265	—
1660	—	60.00	100	180	265	—
1662	—	60.00	100	180	265	—
1668	—	100	175	400	550	—

KM# 191 1/4 DUCAT

0.8750 g., 0.9860 Gold 0.0277 oz. AGW **Ruler:** Maximilian Gandolph **Obv. Legend:** MAX GAND...

Date	Mintage	VG	F	VF	XF	Unc
1668	—	60.00	100	200	300	—
1669	—	60.00	100	200	300	—
1670	—	60.00	100	200	300	—
1671	—	60.00	100	200	300	—
1672	—	60.00	100	200	300	—
1675	—	60.00	100	200	300	—
1676	—	60.00	100	200	300	—
1678	—	60.00	100	200	300	—
1682	—	60.00	100	200	300	—
1686	—	60.00	100	200	300	—

KM# 255 1/4 DUCAT

0.8750 g., 0.9860 Gold 0.0277 oz. AGW **Ruler:** Johann Ernst **Obv:** Cardinals' hat above oval shield **Obv. Legend:** IO ERNEST... **Rev:** St. Rupert, value within oval circle below

Date	Mintage	VG	F	VF	XF	Unc
1687	—	50.00	90.00	185	285	—
1688	—	50.00	90.00	185	285	—
1699	—	50.00	90.00	185	285	—
1700	—	50.00	90.00	185	285	—

KM# 151 1/2 DUCAT

1.7500 g., 0.9860 Gold 0.0555 oz. AGW **Ruler:** Paris **Obv:** Arms below hat **Obv. Legend:** PARIS... **Rev:** St. Rupert seated facing

Date	Mintage	VG	F	VF	XF	Unc
1643	—	85.00	150	350	600	—
1644	—	85.00	150	350	600	—
1648	—	85.00	150	350	600	—
1649	—	85.00	150	350	600	—
1650	—	85.00	150	350	600	—
1651	—	85.00	150	350	600	—
1652	—	85.00	150	350	600	—

KM# 152 1/2 DUCAT

1.7500 g., 0.9860 Gold 0.0555 oz. AGW **Ruler:** Paris **Note:** Klippe.

Date	Mintage	VG	F	VF	XF	Unc
1643	—	125	200	500	800	—
1644	—	125	200	500	800	—
1649	—	125	200	500	800	—
1650	—	125	200	500	800	—

KM# 164 1/2 DUCAT

1.7500 g., 0.9860 Gold 0.0555 oz. AGW **Ruler:** Guidobald **Obv. Legend:** GVIDO...

Date	Mintage	VG	F	VF	XF	Unc
1654	—	75.00	125	225	350	—
1658	—	75.00	125	225	350	—
1659	—	75.00	125	225	350	—
1662	—	75.00	125	225	350	—
1663	—	75.00	125	225	350	—
1664	—	75.00	125	225	350	—
1665	—	75.00	125	225	350	—
1666	—	75.00	125	225	350	—

KM# 192 1/2 DUCAT

1.7500 g., 0.9860 Gold 0.0555 oz. AGW **Ruler:** Maximilian Gandolph **Obv. Legend:** MAX GAND...

Date	Mintage	VG	F	VF	XF	Unc
1668	—	65.00	110	250	400	—
1669	—	65.00	110	250	400	—
1670	—	65.00	110	250	400	—
1684	—	65.00	110	250	400	—
1686	—	65.00	110	250	400	—

KM# 193 1/2 DUCAT

1.7500 g., 0.9860 Gold 0.0555 oz. AGW **Ruler:** Maximilian Gandolph **Note:** Klippe.

Date	Mintage	VG	F	VF	XF	Unc
1668	—	110	165	350	600	—

KM# 256 1/2 DUCAT

1.7500 g., 0.9860 Gold 0.0555 oz. AGW **Ruler:** Johann Ernst **Obv:** Cardinals' hat above oval shield **Obv. Legend:** IO : ERNEST : D : G : ...
Rev: St. Rupert **Rev. Legend:** SALISBVRG • 1705 • S: RVD....

Date	Mintage	VG	F	VF	XF	Unc
1687	—	75.00	125	275	450	—
1690	—	75.00	125	275	450	—
1699	—	75.00	125	275	450	—
1700	—	75.00	125	275	450	—

KM# 2 DUCAT

3.5000 g., 0.9860 Gold 0.1109 oz. AGW **Ruler:** Wolfgang Dietrich **Obv:** Oval 6-fold arms with central shield of Raitenau, legate's hat above **Obv. Legend:** WOLF. TEOD. D.G. AREPS. SAL. A.S.L. **Rev:** St. Rupert seated on throne holding salt cellar and crozier, date at end of legend **Rev. Legend:** SANCTVS. RVDBERTVS. EPS. SALZ. **Note:** Fr.#662.

Date	Mintage	VG	F	VF	XF	Unc
160Z	—	300	700	1,500	2,000	—

KM# 3 DUCAT

3.5000 g., 0.9860 Gold 0.1109 oz. AGW **Ruler:** Wolfgang Dietrich **Obv:** Oval 6-fold arms with central shield of Raitenau, legate's hat above **Obv. Legend:** WOLF. TEOD. D.G. AREPS. SAL. A.S.L. **Rev:** Saint seated on throne holding salt cellar and crozier, date at end of legend **Rev. Legend:** SANCTVS. RVDBERTVS. EPS. SALZ. **Shape:** Klippe **Note:** Fr.#663.

Date	Mintage	VG	F	VF	XF	Unc
160Z	—	500	1,000	2,000	3,000	—

KM# 22 DUCAT

3.5000 g., 0.9860 Gold 0.1109 oz. AGW **Ruler:** Markus Sittich **Obv:** Arms below hat **Obv. Legend:** MARC SIT... **Rev:** St. Rupert seated facing

Date	Mintage	VG	F	VF	XF	Unc
161Z	—	250	500	1,000	1,850	—
1613	—	250	500	1,000	1,850	—
1614	—	250	500	1,000	1,850	—
1615	—	250	500	1,000	1,850	—
1616	—	250	500	1,000	1,850	—
1617	—	250	500	1,000	1,850	—
1618	—	250	500	1,000	1,850	—

KM# 29 DUCAT

3.5000 g., 0.9860 Gold 0.1109 oz. AGW **Ruler:** Markus Sittich **Note:** Klippe.

Date	Mintage	VG	F	VF	XF	Unc
1613	—	350	800	1,600	2,200	—
1614	—	350	800	1,600	2,200	—

KM# 65 DUCAT

3.5000 g., 0.9860 Gold 0.1109 oz. AGW **Ruler:** Paris **Obv. Legend:** PARIS...

Date	Mintage	VG	F	VF	XF	Unc
1620	—	145	285	550	900	—
1622	—	145	285	550	900	—
1623	—	145	285	550	900	—
1625	—	145	285	550	900	—
1627	—	145	285	550	900	—
1629	—	145	285	550	900	—
1630	—	145	285	550	900	—
1631	—	145	285	550	900	—
1632	—	145	285	550	900	—
1633	—	145	285	550	900	—
1634	—	145	285	550	900	—
1635	—	145	285	550	900	—
1636	—	145	285	550	900	—
1637	—	145	285	550	900	—
1638	—	145	285	550	900	—
1639	—	145	285	550	900	—
1640	—	145	285	550	900	—
1641	—	145	285	550	900	—
1642	—	145	285	550	900	—
1643	—	145	285	550	900	—
1644	—	145	285	550	900	—
1645	—	145	285	550	900	—
1646	—	145	285	550	900	—
1647	—	145	285	550	900	—
1648	—	145	285	550	900	—
1649	—	145	285	550	900	—
1650	—	145	285	550	900	—
1652	—	145	285	550	900	—
1653	—	145	285	550	900	—

KM# 109 DUCAT

3.5000 g., 0.9860 Gold 0.1109 oz. AGW **Ruler:** Paris **Shape:** Klippe

Date	Mintage	VG	F	VF	XF	Unc
1627	—	300	750	1,500	2,250	—
1628	—	300	750	1,500	2,250	—
1631	—	300	750	1,500	2,250	—
1632	—	300	750	1,500	2,250	—
1634	—	300	750	1,500	2,250	—
1636	—	300	750	1,500	2,250	—
1637	—	300	750	1,500	2,250	—
1638	—	300	750	1,500	2,250	—
1640	—	300	750	1,500	2,250	—
1641	—	300	750	1,500	2,250	—
1642	—	300	750	1,500	2,250	—
1644	—	300	750	1,500	2,250	—
1645	—	300	750	1,500	2,250	—
1646	—	300	750	1,500	2,250	—
1647	—	300	750	1,500	2,250	—
1648	—	300	750	1,500	2,250	—
1649	—	300	750	1,500	2,250	—
1650	—	300	750	1,500	2,250	—
1651	—	300	750	1,500	2,250	—

KM# 165 DUCAT

3.5000 g., 0.9860 Gold 0.1109 oz. AGW **Ruler:** Guidobald **Obv. Legend:** GVIDOBALD...

Date	Mintage	VG	F	VF	XF	Unc
1654	—	120	225	550	900	—
1655	—	120	225	550	900	—
1656	—	120	225	550	900	—
1657	—	120	225	550	900	—
1658	—	120	225	550	900	—
1659	—	120	225	550	900	—
1660	—	120	225	550	900	—
1661	—	120	225	550	900	—
1662	—	120	225	550	900	—
1663	—	120	225	550	900	—
1664	—	120	225	550	900	—
1665	—	120	225	550	900	—
1666	—	120	225	550	900	—
1667	—	120	225	550	900	—
1668	—	120	225	550	900	—

KM# 175 DUCAT

3.5000 g., 0.9860 Gold 0.1109 oz. AGW **Ruler:** Guidobald **Note:** Klippe.

Date	Mintage	VG	F	VF	XF	Unc
1655	—	140	275	650	1,200	—
1657	—	140	275	650	1,200	—
1666	—	140	275	650	1,200	—

KM# 195 DUCAT

3.5000 g., 0.9860 Gold 0.1109 oz. AGW **Ruler:** Maximilian Gandolph **Note:** Klippe.

Date	Mintage	VG	F	VF	XF	Unc
1668	—	250	550	1,150	2,250	—
1669	—	250	550	1,150	2,250	—
1672	—	140	275	650	1,250	—
1674	—	140	275	650	1,250	—

KM# 194 DUCAT

3.5000 g., 0.9860 Gold 0.1109 oz. AGW **Ruler:** Maximilian Gandolph **Obv. Legend:** MAX GAND...

Date	Mintage	VG	F	VF	XF	Unc
1668	—	200	450	950	1,850	—
1669	—	200	450	950	1,850	—
1670	—	120	220	500	900	—
1671	—	120	220	500	900	—
1672	—	120	220	500	900	—
1673	—	120	220	500	900	—
1674	—	120	220	500	900	—
1675	—	120	220	500	900	—
1676	—	120	220	500	900	—
1677	—	120	220	500	900	—
1678	—	120	220	500	900	—
1679	—	120	220	500	900	—
1680	—	120	220	500	900	—
1681	—	120	220	500	900	—
1682	—	120	220	500	900	—
1683	—	120	220	500	900	—
1684	—	120	220	500	900	—
1685	—	120	220	500	900	—
1686	—	120	220	500	900	—
1687	—	120	220	500	900	—

KM# 257 DUCAT

3.5000 g., 0.9860 Gold 0.1109 oz. AGW **Ruler:** Johann Ernst **Obv:** Cardinals' hat above oval shield **Obv. Legend:** IO : ERNEST : .... **Rev:** St. Rupert **Rev. Legend:** S: RVDBERTVS • EPS • SALISBVRG •

Date	Mintage	VG	F	VF	XF	Unc
1687	—	130	275	650	1,250	—
1688	—	130	275	650	1,250	—
1689	—	130	275	650	1,250	—
1690	—	130	275	650	1,250	—
1691	—	130	275	650	1,250	—
1692	—	130	275	650	1,250	—
1693	—	130	275	650	1,250	—
1694	—	130	275	650	1,250	—
1695	—	130	275	650	1,250	—
1696	—	130	275	650	1,250	—
1697	—	130	275	650	1,250	—
1698	—	130	275	650	1,250	—
1699	—	130	275	650	1,250	—
1700	—	130	275	650	1,250	—

MB# 461 2 DUCAT

7.0000 g., 0.9860 Gold 0.2219 oz. AGW, 28 mm. **Ruler:** Wolfgang Dietrich **Obv:** Oval 6-fold arms with central shield of Raitenau, legate's hat above **Obv. Legend:** WOLF. TEOD. D.G. - AREPS. SAL. A.S.L. **Rev:** 2 saints seated facing each other

Rev. Legend: + S. RVDBERTVS. ET. S. VIRGILIVS. EPI. SALZ. **Note:** Fr.#658. Klippe.

Date	Mintage	VG	F	VF	XF	Unc
ND(1587-1612)	—	275	500	900	1,500	—

MB# 460 2 DUCAT

7.0000 g., 0.9860 Gold 0.2219 oz. AGW **Ruler:** Wolfgang Dietrich **Obv:** Oval 6-fold arms with central shield of Raitenau, legate's hat above **Obv. Legend:** WOLF. TEOD. D.G. - AREPS. SAL. A.S.L. **Rev:** 2 saints seated facing each other **Rev. Legend:** + S. RVDBERTVS. ET. S. VIRGILIVS. EPI. SALZ. **Note:** Fr.#659.

Date	Mintage	VG	F	VF	XF	Unc
ND(1587-1612)	—	275	500	900	1,500	—

MB# 462 2 DUCAT

7.0000 g., 0.9860 Gold 0.2219 oz. AGW **Ruler:** Wolfgang Dietrich **Note:** Fr.#659. Klippe.

Date	Mintage	VG	F	VF	XF	Unc
ND(1587-1612)	—	900	1,650	3,000	5,000	—

KM# 4.1 2 DUCAT

7.0000 g., 0.9860 Gold 0.2219 oz. AGW **Ruler:** Wolfgang Dietrich **Obv:** Oval 6-fold arms with central shield of Raitenau, legate's hat above **Obv. Legend:** WOLF • TEOD • D.G • AREPS • SAL • A:S •L: **Rev:** St. Rupert seated on throne holding salt cellar and crozier, date at end of legend **Rev. Legend:** SANCTVS. RVDBERTVS. EPS. SALZ. **Note:** Fr.#660.

Date	Mintage	VG	F	VF	XF	Unc
1601	—	275	525	1,150	2,150	—
1602	—	275	525	1,150	2,150	—
160Z	—	275	525	1,150	2,150	—
1603	—	275	525	1,150	2,150	—
1604	—	275	525	1,150	2,150	—
1605	—	275	525	1,150	2,150	—
1606	—	275	525	1,150	2,150	—
1607	—	275	525	1,150	2,150	—
1608	—	275	525	1,150	2,150	—
1609	—	275	525	1,150	2,150	—
1610	—	275	525	1,150	2,150	—
1611	—	275	525	1,150	2,150	—

KM# 23 2 DUCAT

7.0000 g., 0.9860 Gold 0.2219 oz. AGW **Ruler:** Markus Sittich **Obv. Legend:** MARCVS SITTICVS

Date	Mintage	VG	F	VF	XF	Unc
1612	—	400	950	1,850	3,000	—
1613	—	400	950	1,850	3,000	—
1614	—	400	950	1,850	3,000	—
1616	—	400	950	1,850	3,000	—

KM# 9 2 DUCAT

7.0000 g., 0.9860 Gold 0.2219 oz. AGW **Ruler:** Wolfgang Dietrich **Rev:** St. Rupert and St. Virgil **Note:** Klippe.

Date	Mintage	VG	F	VF	XF	Unc
ND	—	500	1,100	3,250	5,500	—

KM# 30 2 DUCAT

7.0000 g., 0.9860 Gold 0.2219 oz. AGW **Ruler:** Markus Sittich **Note:** Klippe.

Date	Mintage	VG	F	VF	XF	Unc
1613	—	500	1,100	2,250	4,500	—
1615	—	500	1,100	2,250	4,500	—

KM# 93 2 DUCAT

7.0000 g., 0.9860 Gold 0.2219 oz. AGW **Ruler:** Paris **Note:** Klippe.

Date	Mintage	VG	F	VF	XF	Unc
1624	—	500	1,100	3,500	5,500	—
1634	—	500	1,100	3,500	5,500	—
1638	—	500	1,100	3,500	5,500	—
1639	—	500	1,100	3,500	5,500	—
1640	—	500	1,100	3,500	5,500	—
1641	—	500	1,100	3,500	5,500	—
1642	—	500	1,100	3,500	5,500	—
1643	—	500	1,100	3,500	5,500	—
1644	—	500	1,100	3,500	5,500	—
1645	—	500	1,100	3,500	5,500	—
1646	—	500	1,100	3,500	5,500	—
1648	—	500	1,100	3,500	5,500	—
1651	—	500	1,100	3,500	5,500	—

KM# 105 2 DUCAT

7.0000 g., 0.9860 Gold 0.2219 oz. AGW **Ruler:** Paris **Note:** Klippe.

Date	Mintage	VG	F	VF	XF	Unc
1626	—	500	1,100	3,500	5,750	—

KM# 104 2 DUCAT

7.0000 g., 0.9860 Gold 0.2219 oz. AGW **Ruler:** Paris **Obv:** Madonna above arms in inner circle **Obv. Legend:** PARIS... **Rev:** St. Rupert standing with arms below in ornate inner circle

Date	Mintage	VG	F	VF	XF	Unc
1626	—	400	1,000	3,000	5,250	—

KM# 121 2 DUCAT

7.0000 g., 0.9860 Gold 0.2219 oz. AGW **Ruler:** Paris **Obv:** Cathedral divides date with saints at sides in inner circle, arms below **Rev:** Reliquary carried by eight bishops, two angels below religuary in inner circle

Date	Mintage	VG	F	VF	XF	Unc
1628	—	—	—	—	—	—

KM# 122 2 DUCAT

7.0000 g., 0.9860 Gold 0.2219 oz. AGW **Ruler:** Paris **Obv:** Arms below hat **Obv. Legend:** PARIS... **Rev:** St. Rupert seated facing half right

Date	Mintage	VG	F	VF	XF	Unc
1628	—	400	900	2,850	5,000	—
1629	—	400	900	2,850	5,000	—
1631	—	400	900	2,850	5,000	—
1633	—	400	900	2,850	5,000	—
1634	—	400	900	2,850	5,000	—
1647	—	400	900	2,850	5,000	—
1648	—	400	900	2,850	5,000	—

KM# 166 2 DUCAT

7.0000 g., 0.9860 Gold 0.2219 oz. AGW **Ruler:** Guidobald **Obv. Legend:** GVIDO-BALDVS... **Rev:** St. Rupert seated facing

Date	Mintage	VG	F	VF	XF	Unc
1654	—	300	700	1,850	3,250	—
1659	—	300	700	1,850	3,250	—
1662	—	300	700	1,850	3,250	—

KM# 196 2 DUCAT

7.0000 g., 0.9860 Gold 0.2219 oz. AGW **Ruler:** Maximilian Gandolph **Obv:** Cardinal's hat above shield **Obv. Legend:** MAX GAND... **Rev:** Figure seated 1/4 left

Date	Mintage	VG	F	VF	XF	Unc
1668	—	250	500	1,000	2,000	—
1673	—	250	500	1,000	2,000	—

KM# 223 2 DUCAT

7.0000 g., 0.9860 Gold 0.2219 oz. AGW **Ruler:** Maximilian Gandolph **Note:** Klippe.

Date	Mintage	VG	F	VF	XF	Unc
1673	—	550	1,150	3,000	5,000	—

KM# 234 2 DUCAT

7.0000 g., 0.9860 Gold 0.2219 oz. AGW **Ruler:** Maximilian Gandolph **Subject:** 1100th Anniversary of Salzburg **Obv:** Radiant symbol above Cardinal's hat over shield **Rev:** Inscription

Date	Mintage	VG	F	VF	XF	Unc
1682	—	375	750	1,950	3,500	—

KM# 272 2 DUCAT

7.0000 g., 0.9860 Gold 0.2219 oz. AGW **Ruler:** Johann Ernst **Note:** Klippe.

Date	Mintage	VG	F	VF	XF	Unc
1688	—	350	700	1,850	3,250	—

KM# 271 2 DUCAT

7.0000 g., 0.9860 Gold 0.2219 oz. AGW **Ruler:** Johann Ernst **Obv:** Arms **Obv. Legend:** IO ERNEST... **Rev:** Saint Rupert on throne

Date	Mintage	VG	F	VF	XF	Unc
1688	—	275	550	1,350	2,500	—

MB# 467 3 DUCAT

10.5000 g., 0.9860 Gold 0.3328 oz. AGW **Ruler:** Wolfgang Dietrich **Obv:** Oval 6-fold arms with central shield of Raitenau, legate's hat above **Obv. Legend:** WOLF. TEOD. D.G. AREPS. SAL. A.S.L. **Rev:** 2 saints seated facing each other **Rev. Legend:** S. RVDBERTVS. ET. S. VIRGILIVS. EP. **Note:** Fr.#656.

Date	Mintage	VG	F	VF	XF	Unc
ND(1587-1612)	—	1,350	2,500	4,500	7,500	—

MB# 471 3 DUCAT
10.5000 g., 0.9860 Gold 0.3328 oz. AGW **Ruler:** Wolfgang Dietrich **Obv:** Oval 6-fold arms with central shield of Raitenau, legate's hat above **Obv. Legend:** WOLF. TEOD. D.G. AREPS. SAL. A.S.L. **Rev:** 2 saints seated facing each other **Rev. Legend:** S. RVDBERTVS. ET. S. VIRGILIVS. EP. **Note:** Fr.#656.

Date	Mintage	VG	F	VF	XF	Unc
ND(1587-1612)	—	1,350	2,500	4,500	7,500	—

MB# 468 3 DUCAT
10.5000 g., 0.9860 Gold 0.3328 oz. AGW **Ruler:** Wolfgang Dietrich **Obv:** Oval 6-fold arms with central shield of Raitenau, legate's hat above **Obv. Legend:** WOLF. TEOD. D.G. AREPS. SAL. A.S.L. **Rev:** 2 saints seated facing each other **Rev. Legend:** S. RVDBERTVS. ET. S. VIRGILIVS. EP. **Note:** Fr.#657. Klippe.

Date	Mintage	VG	F	VF	XF	Unc
ND(1587-1612)	—	1,500	2,650	4,750	7,750	—

MB# 465 3 DUCAT
10.5000 g., 0.9860 Gold 0.3328 oz. AGW, 35.5 mm. **Ruler:** Wolfgang Dietrich **Obv:** Saint seated on throne holding salt cellar and crozier, oval 6-fold arms with central shield of Raitenau below **Obv. Legend:** SANCTVS. RVDBE - RTVS. EPS. SALISBV. **Rev:** Tower in storm-tossed sea, winds from clouds to either side blowing on it, date at end of legend **Rev. Legend:** + IN. DOMINO. SPERANS. NON. INFIRMABOR. **Note:** FR.#687/695.

Date	Mintage	VG	F	VF	XF	Unc
ND(1587-1612)	—	1,250	2,250	4,250	7,000	—

MB# 466 3 DUCAT
10.5000 g., 0.9860 Gold 0.3328 oz. AGW **Ruler:** Wolfgang Dietrich **Obv:** Saint seated on throne holding salt cellar and crozier, oval 6-fold arms with central shield of Raitenau below **Obv. Legend:** SANCTVS. RVDBE - RTVS. EPS. SALISBV. **Rev:** Tower in storm-tossed sea, winds from clouds to either side blowing on it, date at end of legend **Rev. Legend:** + IN. DOMINO. SPERANS. NON. INFIRMABOR. **Note:** Fr.#688. Klippe.

Date	Mintage	VG	F	VF	XF	Unc
ND(1587-1612)	—	1,350	2,500	4,500	8,000	—

MB# 470 3 DUCAT
10.5000 g., 0.9860 Gold 0.3328 oz. AGW **Ruler:** Wolfgang Dietrich **Obv:** Oval 6-fold arms with central shield of Raitenau, legate's hat above **Obv. Legend:** WOLF. TEOD. D.G. - AREPS. SAL. AP. SE. L. **Rev:** Saint seated on throne holding salt cellar and crozier **Rev. Legend:** SANCTVS. RVDBERTVS. EPS. SALZBV. **Note:** Fr#657. Klippe.

Date	Mintage	VG	F	VF	XF	Unc
ND(1587-1612)	—	1,650	3,000	5,000	8,500	—

MB# 469 3 DUCAT
10.5000 g., 0.9860 Gold 0.3328 oz. AGW **Ruler:** Wolfgang Dietrich **Obv:** Oval 6-fold arms with central shield of Raitenau, legate's hat above **Obv. Legend:** WOLF. TEOD. D.G. - AREPS. SAL. A.S.L. **Rev:** 2 saints seated facing each other **Rev. Legend:** + S. RVDBERTVS. ET. S. VIRGILIVS. EPI. SALZ. **Note:** Fr.#(657). Klippe.

Date	Mintage	VG	F	VF	XF	Unc
ND(1587-1612)	—	1,750	3,150	5,000	8,500	—

MB# 472 3 DUCAT
10.5000 g., 0.9860 Gold 0.3328 oz. AGW **Ruler:** Wolfgang Dietrich **Obv:** 2 adjacent shields of Salzburg and Keutschach joined by hanger loop above, date below **Obv. Legend:** 2 saints seated facing each other **Rev:** + S. RVDBERTVS. ET. S. VIRGILIVS. EPI. SALZ. **Note:** Klippe.

Date	Mintage	VG	F	VF	XF	Unc
ND(1513)//(1587-1612)	—	—	—	—	—	—

Note: Mule. Obv. die of MB#48 used with rev. die of MB#469.

KM# 24 3 DUCAT
10.5000 g., 0.9860 Gold 0.3328 oz. AGW **Ruler:** Markus Sittich **Note:** Klippe.

Date	Mintage	VG	F	VF	XF	Unc
1612	—	650	1,450	3,500	6,000	—

KM# A46 3 DUCAT
10.5000 g., 0.9860 Gold 0.3328 oz. AGW **Ruler:** Markus Sittich **Note:** Klippe.

Date	Mintage	VG	F	VF	XF	Unc
1617	—	—	1,700	4,000	7,000	—

KM# 45 3 DUCAT
10.5000 g., 0.9860 Gold 0.3328 oz. AGW **Ruler:** Markus Sittich **Obv:** Arms below hat **Obv. Legend:** MARCVS SITTICVS... **Rev:** St. Rupert seated facing

Date	Mintage	VG	F	VF	XF	Unc
1617	—	550	1,300	3,000	5,500	—

KM# 66 3 DUCAT
10.5000 g., 0.9860 Gold 0.3328 oz. AGW **Ruler:** Paris **Obv. Legend:** PARIS...

Date	Mintage	VG	F	VF	XF	Unc
1620	—	700	1,500	3,850	6,500	—

KM# 94 3 DUCAT
10.5000 g., 0.9860 Gold 0.3328 oz. AGW **Ruler:** Paris **Note:** Klippe.

Date	Mintage	VG	F	VF	XF	Unc
1624	—	650	1,400	3,650	6,000	—
1629	—	650	1,400	3,650	6,000	—
1638	—	650	1,400	3,650	6,000	—
1642	—	650	1,400	3,650	6,000	—

KM# 123 3 DUCAT
10.5000 g., 0.9860 Gold 0.3328 oz. AGW **Ruler:** Paris **Obv:** Cathedral divides date with saints at sides in inner circle, arms below **Rev:** Reliquary carried by eight bishops, two angels below reliquary in inner circle

Date	Mintage	VG	F	VF	XF	Unc
1628	—	500	1,150	2,750	4,750	—

KM# 146 3 DUCAT
10.5000 g., 0.9860 Gold 0.3328 oz. AGW **Ruler:** Paris **Obv:** Madonna above arms in inner circle **Obv. Legend:** PARIS... **Rev:** St. Rupert standing with arms below in ornate inner circle

Date	Mintage	VG	F	VF	XF	Unc
1631	—	700	1,500	3,850	6,500	—
1638	—	700	1,500	3,850	6,500	—
1642	—	700	1,500	3,850	6,500	—

KM# 183 3 DUCAT
10.5000 g., 0.9860 Gold 0.3328 oz. AGW **Ruler:** Guidobald **Obv:** Arms below hat in inner circle **Obv. Legend:** GVIDOBALDVS... **Rev:** Cathedral with saints at sides in inner circle

Date	Mintage	VG	F	VF	XF	Unc
1656	—	750	1,800	4,000	6,500	—

KM# 220 3 DUCAT
10.5000 g., 0.9860 Gold 0.3328 oz. AGW **Ruler:** Maximilian Gandolph **Obv:** Arms below hat **Obv. Legend:** MAXIM GANDOL... **Rev:** St. Rupert seated facing

Date	Mintage	VG	F	VF	XF	Unc
1670	—	725	1,800	4,000	6,750	—
1673	—	725	1,800	4,000	6,750	—

KM# 224 3 DUCAT
10.5000 g., 0.9860 Gold 0.3328 oz. AGW **Ruler:** Maximilian Gandolph **Note:** Klippe.

Date	Mintage	VG	F	VF	XF	Unc
1673	—	1,000	2,150	4,750	7,500	—

KM# 235 3 DUCAT
10.5000 g., 0.9860 Gold 0.3328 oz. AGW **Ruler:** Maximilian Gandolph **Subject:** 1100th Anniversary of Salzburg **Obv:** Arms below radiant triangle in inner circle **Obv. Legend:** A. MAX GAND. **Rev:** Five standing saints; five-line inscription in exergue

Date	Mintage	VG	F	VF	XF	Unc
1682	—	575	1,300	3,000	5,000	—

KM# 236 3 DUCAT
10.5000 g., 0.9860 Gold 0.3328 oz. AGW **Ruler:** Maximilian Gandolph **Subject:** 1100th Anniversary of Salzburg **Obv:** Nine-line inscription **Rev:** Arms below radiant triangle

Date	Mintage	VG	F	VF	XF	Unc
1682	—	650	1,450	3,750	6,000	—

KM# 275 3 DUCAT
10.5000 g., 0.9860 Gold 0.3328 oz. AGW **Ruler:** Johann Ernst **Obv. Legend:** IOAN ERNEST...

Date	Mintage	VG	F	VF	XF	Unc
1690	—	600	1,250	3,000	5,000	—

MB# 477 4 DUCAT
14.0000 g., 0.9860 Gold 0.4438 oz. AGW, 33.5 mm. **Ruler:** Wolfgang Dietrich **Obv:** 4-fold arms of Salzburg and Raitenau (globe), legate's hat above **Obv. Legend:** WOLF. TEOD. D.G. ARE - PS. SALZ. AP. SE. LEG. **Rev:** 2 saints seated facing eaach other **Rev. Legend:** S. RVDBERTVS. ET S. VIRGILIVS. EP. **Note:** Fr.#654.

Date	Mintage	VG	F	VF	XF	Unc
ND(1587-1612)	—	3,250	6,000	9,500	16,500	—

MB# 478 4 DUCAT
14.0000 g., 0.9860 Gold 0.4438 oz. AGW, 34 mm. **Ruler:** Wolfgang Dietrich **Obv:** Oval 6-fold arms with central shield of Raitenau, legate's hat above **Obv. Legend:** WOLF. TEOD. D.G. AREPS. SAL. A.S.L. **Rev:** 2 saints seated facing each other **Rev. Legend:** S. RVDBERTVS. ET. S. VIRGILIVS. EP. **Note:** Fr.#654.

Date	Mintage	VG	F	VF	XF	Unc
ND(1587-1612)	—	3,250	6,000	9,500	16,500	—

MB# 476 4 DUCAT
14.0000 g., 0.9860 Gold 0.4438 oz. AGW **Ruler:** Wolfgang Dietrich **Obv:** Oval 6-fold arms with central shield of Raitenau, legate's hat above **Obv. Legend:** WOLF. TEOD. D.G. AREPS. SAL. A.S.L. **Rev:** 2 saints seated facing each other **Rev. Legend:** S. RVDBERTVS. ET. S. VIRGILIVS. EP. **Note:** Fr.#655. Klippe. 36.5 x 36.5 mm.

Date	Mintage	VG	F	VF	XF	Unc
ND(1587-1612) Rare	—	—	—	—	—	—

MB# 474 4 DUCAT
14.0000 g., 0.9860 Gold 0.4438 oz. AGW **Ruler:** Wolfgang Dietrich **Obv:** Saint seated on throne holding salt cellar and crozier, oval 6-fold arms with central shield of Raitenau below **Obv. Legend:** SANCTVS. RVDBE - RTVS. EPS. SALISBV. **Rev:** Tower in storm-tossed sea, winds from clouds to either side blowing on it, date at end of legend **Rev. Legend:** + IN. DOMINO. SPERANS. NON. IMFIRMABOR. **Note:** Fr.#693.

Date	Mintage	VG	F	VF	XF	Unc
ND(1587-1612)	—	2,250	4,750	8,500	13,500	—

MB# 475 4 DUCAT
14.0000 g., 0.9860 Gold 0.4438 oz. AGW **Ruler:** Wolfgang Dietrich **Obv:** Saint seated on throne holding salt cellar and crozier, oval 6-fold arms with central shield of Raitenau below **Obv. Legend:** SANCTVS. RVDBE - RTVS. EPS. SALISBV. **Rev:** Tower in storm-tossed sea, winds from clouds to either side blowing on it, date at end of legend **Rev. Legend:** + IN. DOMINO. SPERANS. NON. INFIRMABOR. **Note:** Fr.#694. Klippe.

Date	Mintage	VG	F	VF	XF	Unc
ND(1587-1612)	—	3,250	6,000	9,500	16,500	—

KM# 25 4 DUCAT
14.0000 g., 0.9860 Gold 0.4438 oz. AGW **Ruler:** Markus Sittich **Obv:** Arms below hat **Obv. Legend:** MARCVS SITTICVS... **Rev:** St. Rupert seated facing

Date	Mintage	VG	F	VF	XF	Unc
161Z	—	1,000	2,600	5,500	9,000	—
1614	—	1,000	2,600	5,500	9,000	—
1615	—	1,000	2,600	5,500	9,000	—
1617	—	1,000	2,600	5,500	9,000	—

KM# 41 4 DUCAT
14.0000 g., 0.9860 Gold 0.4438 oz. AGW **Ruler:** Markus Sittich

Date	Mintage	VG	F	VF	XF	Unc
1615	—	1,000	2,600	5,500	9,000	—
1616	—	1,000	2,600	5,500	9,000	—
1618	—	1,000	2,600	5,500	9,000	—

KM# 67 4 DUCAT
14.0000 g., 0.9860 Gold 0.4438 oz. AGW **Ruler:** Paris **Obv:** Arms below hat **Obv. Legend:** PARIS... **Rev:** St. Rupert seated facing

Date	Mintage	VG	F	VF	XF	Unc
1620	—	800	1,800	4,000	6,500	—

KM# 68 4 DUCAT
14.0000 g., 0.9860 Gold 0.4438 oz. AGW **Ruler:** Paris **Note:** Klippe.

Date	Mintage	VG	F	VF	XF	Unc
1620	—	1,000	2,250	5,000	7,500	—

KM# 95 4 DUCAT
14.0000 g., 0.9860 Gold 0.4438 oz. AGW **Ruler:** Paris

Date	Mintage	VG	F	VF	XF	Unc
1624	—	1,000	2,250	5,250	8,000	—
1625	—	1,000	2,250	5,250	8,000	—
1629	—	1,000	2,250	5,250	8,000	—
1638	—	1,000	2,250	5,250	8,000	—

KM# 96 4 DUCAT
14.0000 g., 0.9860 Gold 0.4438 oz. AGW **Ruler:** Paris **Note:** Klippe.

Date	Mintage	VG	F	VF	XF	Unc
1624	—	1,500	3,600	8,000	12,000	—

KM# 124 4 DUCAT
14.0000 g., 0.9860 Gold 0.4438 oz. AGW **Ruler:** Paris

Date	Mintage	VG	F	VF	XF	Unc
1628	—	550	1,200	2,500	4,000	—

KM# 125 4 DUCAT
14.0000 g., 0.9860 Gold 0.4438 oz. AGW **Ruler:** Paris **Note:** Klippe.

Date	Mintage	VG	F	VF	XF	Unc
1628	—	750	1,600	3,750	6,000	—

KM# 176 4 DUCAT
14.0000 g., 0.9860 Gold 0.4438 oz. AGW **Ruler:** Guidobald **Obv. Legend:** GVIDOBALDVS...

Date	Mintage	VG	F	VF	XF	Unc
1655	—	750	1,600	3,750	6,000	—

KM# 197 4 DUCAT
14.0000 g., 0.9860 Gold 0.4438 oz. AGW **Ruler:** Maximilian Gandolph **Obv. Legend:** MAXIMIL GANDOLPH...

Date	Mintage	VG	F	VF	XF	Unc
1668	—	900	2,000	4,500	7,000	—

KM# 225 4 DUCAT
14.0000 g., 0.9860 Gold 0.4438 oz. AGW **Ruler:** Maximilian Gandolph **Obv:** Arms below hat **Obv. Legend:** MAXIM GANDOL... **Rev:** St. Rupert seated facing

Date	Mintage	VG	F	VF	XF	Unc
1673	—	1,000	2,500	5,500	9,000	—

KM# 237 4 DUCAT
14.0000 g., 0.9860 Gold 0.4438 oz. AGW **Ruler:** Maximilian Gandolph **Subject:** 1100th Anniversary of Salzburg **Obv:** Arms below radiant triangle in inner circle **Obv. Legend:** A MAX GAND... **Rev:** Five standing saints; five-line inscription in exergue

Date	Mintage	VG	F	VF	XF	Unc
1682	—	575	1,200	2,750	4,500	—

KM# 258 4 DUCAT
14.0000 g., 0.9860 Gold 0.4438 oz. AGW **Ruler:** Johann Ernst **Obv. Legend:** IOAN ERNESTUS...

Date	Mintage	VG	F	VF	XF	Unc
1687	—	575	1,200	2,750	4,750	—

MB# 482 5 DUCAT
17.5000 g., 0.9860 Gold 0.5547 oz. AGW **Ruler:** Wolfgang Dietrich **Obv:** 4-fold arms of Salzburg and Raitenau (globe), legate's hat above **Obv. Legend:** WOLF. TEOD. D.G. ARE - PS. SALZ. AP. SE. LEG. **Rev:** 2 saints seated facing each other **Rev. Legend:** S. RVDBERTVS. ET S. VIRGILIVS. ET S. VIRGILIVS. EP. **Note:** Fr.#653.

Date	Mintage	VG	F	VF	XF	Unc
ND(1587-1612)	—	3,250	6,000	9,500	16,500	—

MB# 481 5 DUCAT
17.5000 g., 0.9860 Gold 0.5547 oz. AGW **Ruler:** Wolfgang Dietrich **Obv:** Saint seated on throne holding salt cellar and crozier, oal 6-fold arms with central shield of Raitenau below **Obv. Legend:** SANCTVS. RVDBE - RTVS. EPS. SALISBV **Rev:** Tower in storm-tossed sea, winds from clouds to either side blowing on it, date at end of legend **Rev. Legend:** + IN. DOMINO. SPERANS. NON. INFIRMABOR. **Note:** Fr.#684. Klippe.

Date	Mintage	VG	F	VF	XF	Unc
ND(1587-1612)	—	3,250	6,000	9,500	16,500	—

MB# 480 5 DUCAT

17.5000 g., 0.9860 Gold 0.5547 oz. AGW **Ruler:** Wolfgang Dietrich **Obv:** Saint seated on throne holding salt cellar and crozier, oval 6-fold arms with central shield of Raitenau below **Obv. Legend:** SANCTVS. RVDBE - RTVS. EPS. SALISBV. **Rev:** Tower in storm-tossed sea, winds from clouds to either side blowing on it, date at end of legend **Rev. Legend:** + IN. DOMINO. SPERANS. NON. INFIRMABOR. **Note:** Fr.#692.

Date	Mintage	VG	F	VF	XF	Unc
ND(1587-1612)	—	2,250	4,750	8,500	13,500	—

KM# 27 5 DUCAT

17.5000 g., 0.9860 Gold 0.5547 oz. AGW **Ruler:** Markus Sittich **Note:** Klippe.

Date	Mintage	VG	F	VF	XF	Unc
1612	—	2,000	4,000	7,000	12,000	—
1617	—	2,000	4,000	7,000	12,000	—

KM# 26 5 DUCAT

17.5000 g., 0.9860 Gold 0.5547 oz. AGW **Ruler:** Markus Sittich **Obv:** Arms below hat **Obv. Legend:** MARCVS SITTICVS... **Rev:** Tower in stormy sea

Date	Mintage	VG	F	VF	XF	Unc
1612	—	1,000	2,500	5,500	9,000	—

KM# 69 5 DUCAT

17.5000 g., 0.9860 Gold 0.5547 oz. AGW **Ruler:** Paris **Obv. Legend:** PARIS... **Rev:** St. Rupert seated facing

Date	Mintage	VG	F	VF	XF	Unc
1620	—	1,500	2,850	6,500	10,000	—

KM# 126 5 DUCAT

17.5000 g., 0.9860 Gold 0.5547 oz. AGW **Ruler:** Paris **Obv:** Cathedral divides date with saints at sides in inner circle, arms below **Rev:** Reliquary carried by eight bishops, two angels below reliquary, in inner circle

Date	Mintage	VG	F	VF	XF	Unc
1628	—	850	1,650	4,000	7,000	—

KM# 127 5 DUCAT

17.5000 g., 0.9860 Gold 0.5547 oz. AGW **Ruler:** Paris **Note:** Klippe.

Date	Mintage	VG	F	VF	XF	Unc
1628	—	1,500	2,850	6,500	10,000	—

KM# 177 5 DUCAT

17.5000 g., 0.9860 Gold 0.5547 oz. AGW **Ruler:** Guidobald **Obv. Legend:** GVIDOBALDVS...

Date	Mintage	VG	F	VF	XF	Unc
1655	—	850	1,750	4,000	6,500	—

KM# 198 5 DUCAT

17.5000 g., 0.9860 Gold 0.5547 oz. AGW **Ruler:** Maximilian Gandolph **Obv. Legend:** MAXIMIL GANDOLPH...

Date	Mintage	VG	F	VF	XF	Unc
1668	—	1,000	2,250	5,000	7,500	—

KM# 199 5 DUCAT

17.5000 g., 0.9860 Gold 0.5547 oz. AGW **Ruler:** Maximilian Gandolph **Obv:** Arms below hat **Obv. Legend:** MAXIMIL GANDOLPH... **Rev:** St. Rupert seated facing

Date	Mintage	VG	F	VF	XF	Unc
1668	—	1,000	2,500	5,500	9,000	—

KM# 238 5 DUCAT

17.5000 g., 0.9860 Gold 0.5547 oz. AGW **Ruler:** Maximilian Gandolph **Subject:** 1100th Anniversary of Salzburg **Obv:** Arms below radiant triangle in inner circle **Obv. Legend:** A MAX GAND... **Rev:** Five standing saints; five-line inscription in exergue

Date	Mintage	VG	F	VF	XF	Unc
1682	—	1,000	2,250	5,000	8,000	—

KM# 259 5 DUCAT

17.5000 g., 0.9860 Gold 0.5547 oz. AGW **Ruler:** Johann Ernst **Obv:** Arms below hat in inner circle **Obv. Legend:** IOAN ERNESTUS... **Rev:** Two saints seated, facing each other with croziers, church in foreground

Date	Mintage	VG	F	VF	XF	Unc
1687	—	750	1,450	3,250	5,000	—

MB# 485 6 DUCAT

21.0000 g., 0.9860 Gold 0.6657 oz. AGW **Ruler:** Wolfgang Dietrich **Obv:** 2 adjacent shields of arms, Salzburg on left, Raitenau (globe) on right, legate's hat above **Obv. Legend:** WOLF. TEOD. D.G. AREPS. SAL. AP. SE. LE. **Rev:** 2 saints seated facing each other **Rev. Legend:** + S. RVDBERTVS. ET S. VIRGILIVS. EPI. SALZBVRGN. **Note:** Fr.#652.

Date	Mintage	VG	F	VF	XF	Unc
ND(1587-1612) Rare	—	—	—	—	—	—

KM# 42 6 DUCAT

21.0000 g., 0.9860 Gold 0.6657 oz. AGW **Ruler:** Markus Sittich **Obv. Legend:** SANCTVS RUDBERTVS... **Note:** Klippe.

Date	Mintage	VG	F	VF	XF	Unc
1616	—	2,000	4,500	8,000	12,000	—
1617	—	2,000	4,500	8,000	12,000	—

KM# 46 6 DUCAT

21.0000 g., 0.9860 Gold 0.6657 oz. AGW **Ruler:** MarkusSittich

Date	Mintage	VG	F	VF	XF	Unc
1617	—	1,750	4,000	7,000	10,000	—

KM# 49 6 DUCAT

21.0000 g., 0.9860 Gold 0.6657 oz. AGW **Ruler:** Markus Sittich **Obv. Legend:** MARCVS SITTICVS...

Date	Mintage	VG	F	VF	XF	Unc
1618	—	1,750	4,000	7,000	10,000	—

KM# 128 6 DUCAT

21.0000 g., 0.9860 Gold 0.6657 oz. AGW **Ruler:** Paris **Obv:** Madonna above arms in inner circle **Obv. Legend:** PARIS • D:G: ARCHI EPS • SALIS • 1625
Rev: St. Rupert standing with arms below in ornate inner circle

Date	Mintage	VG	F	VF	XF	Unc
1625	—	2,500	4,500	8,000	12,000	—
1628	—	2,500	4,500	8,000	12,000	—

KM# 129 6 DUCAT

21.0000 g., 0.9860 Gold 0.6657 oz. AGW **Ruler:** Paris **Obv:** Cathedral divides date with saints at sides in inner circle, arms below **Rev:** Reliquary carried by eight bishops, two angels below reliquary, in inner circle

Date	Mintage	VG	F	VF	XF	Unc
1628	—	950	1,850	4,250	7,500	—

KM# 178 6 DUCAT

21.0000 g., 0.9860 Gold 0.6657 oz. AGW **Ruler:** Guidobald **Obv:** Arms below hat in inner circle **Obv. Legend:** GVIDOBALDVS... **Rev:** Cathedral with saints at sides in inner circle

Date	Mintage	VG	F	VF	XF	Unc
1655	—	1,250	3,000	5,000	7,750	—

KM# 200 6 DUCAT

21.0000 g., 0.9860 Gold 0.6657 oz. AGW **Ruler:** Maximilian Gandolph **Obv:** Arms below hat **Obv. Legend:** MAXIMIL GANDOLPH... **Rev:** St. Rupert seated facing

Date	Mintage	VG	F	VF	XF	Unc
1668	—	1,750	4,000	7,000	10,000	—

KM# 201 6 DUCAT

21.0000 g., 0.9860 Gold 0.6657 oz. AGW **Ruler:** Maximilian Gandolph **Obv:** Arms below hat in inner circle **Obv. Legend:** MAXIMIL GANDOLPH... **Rev:** Two saints seated, facing each other with croziers, church in foreground

Date	Mintage	VG	F	VF	XF	Unc
1668	—	1,250	3,000	5,000	7,000	—

KM# 239 6 DUCAT

21.0000 g., 0.9860 Gold 0.6657 oz. AGW **Ruler:** Maximilian Gandolph **Obv:** Arms below radiant triangle in inner circle **Obv. Legend:** A MAX GAND... **Rev:** Five standing saints; five-line inscription in exergue

Date	Mintage	VG	F	VF	XF	Unc
1682	—	1,750	4,000	7,000	10,000	—

KM# 260 6 DUCAT

21.0000 g., 0.9860 Gold 0.6657 oz. AGW **Ruler:** Johann Ernst **Obv. Legend:** IOAN ERNESTUS...

Date	Mintage	VG	F	VF	XF	Unc
1687	—	1,100	2,750	5,000	8,000	—

MB# 487 7 DUCAT

24.5000 g., 0.9860 Gold 0.7766 oz. AGW **Ruler:** Wolfgang Dietrich **Obv:** 2 adjacent shields of arms, Salzburg on left, Raitenau (globe) on right, legate's hat above **Obv. Legend:** WOLF. TEOD. D.G. AREPS. SAL. AP. SE. LE. **Rev:** 2 saints seated facing each other **Rev. Legend:** + S. RVDBERTVS. ET S. VIRGILIVS. EPI. SALZBVRGN. **Note:** Fr.#651.

Date	Mintage	VG	F	VF	XF	Unc
ND(1587-1612) Rare	—	—	—	—	—	—

KM# 50 7 DUCAT

24.5000 g., 0.9860 Gold 0.7766 oz. AGW **Ruler:** Markus Sittich, Graf **Obv:** Arms below hat **Obv. Legend:** MARCVS SITTICVS... **Rev:** Tower in stormy sea **Note:** Klippe.

Date	Mintage	VG	F	VF	XF	Unc
1618	—	2,500	6,000	10,000	14,000	—

KM# 240 7 DUCAT

24.5000 g., 0.9860 Gold 0.7766 oz. AGW **Ruler:** Maximilian Gandolph **Subject:** 1100th Anniversary of Salzburg **Obv. Legend:** A MAX GAND...

Date	Mintage	VG	F	VF	XF	Unc
1682 Rare	—	—	—	—	—	—

KM# 261 7 DUCAT
24.5000 g., 0.9860 Gold 0.7766 oz. AGW **Ruler:** Johann Ernst **Obv:** Arms below hat in inner circle **Obv. Legend:** IOAN ERNESTUS... **Rev:** Two saints seated, facing each other with croziers, church in foreground

Date	Mintage	VG	F	VF	XF	Unc
1687	—	2,000	4,250	7,500	11,500	—

MB# 491 8 DUCAT
28.0000 g., 0.9860 Gold 0.8876 oz. AGW **Ruler:** Wolfgang Dietrich **Obv:** 2 adjacent shields of arms, Salzburg on left, Raitenau (globe) on right, legate's hat above **Obv. Legend:** WOLF. TEOD. D.G. AREPS. SAL. AP. SE. LE. **Rev:** 2 saints seated facing each other **Rev. Legend:** + S. RVDBERTVS. ET S. VIRGILIVS. EPI. SALZBVRGN. **Note:** Fr.#650.

Date	Mintage	VG	F	VF	XF	Unc
ND(1587-1612) Rare	—	—	—	—	—	—

MB# 490 8 DUCAT
28.0000 g., 0.9860 Gold 0.8876 oz. AGW **Ruler:** Wolfgang Dietrich **Obv:** Saint seated on throne holding salt cellar and crozier, oval 6-fold arms with central shield of Raitenau below **Obv. Legend:** SANCTVS. RVDBE—RTVS. EPS. SALISBV. **Rev:** Tower in storm-tossed sea, winds from clouds to either side blowing on it, date at end of legend **Rev. Legend:** IN. DOMINO. SPERANS. NON. INFIRMABOR. **Note:** Fr.#691.

Date	Mintage	VG	F	VF	XF	Unc
ND(1587-1612)	—	3,500	6,000	10,000	17,500	—

KM# 31 8 DUCAT
28.0000 g., 0.9860 Gold 0.8876 oz. AGW **Ruler:** Markus Sittich **Obv:** Arms below hat **Obv. Legend:** MARCVS SITTICVS... **Rev:** Tower in stormy sea

Date	Mintage	VG	F	VF	XF	Unc
1613	—	2,500	6,000	10,000	14,000	—

KM# 70 8 DUCAT
28.0000 g., 0.9860 Gold 0.8876 oz. AGW **Ruler:** Paris **Obv. Legend:** PARIS... **Rev:** St. Rupert seated facing

Date	Mintage	VG	F	VF	XF	Unc
1620	—	2,250	5,000	8,500	12,500	—

KM# 71 8 DUCAT
28.0000 g., 0.9860 Gold 0.8876 oz. AGW **Ruler:** Paris **Note:** Klippe.

Date	Mintage	VG	F	VF	XF	Unc
1620	—	—	—	10,000	15,000	—

KM# 102 8 DUCAT
28.0000 g., 0.9860 Gold 0.8876 oz. AGW **Ruler:** Paris, **Obv:** Maddona above arms in inner circle **Obv. Legend:** PARIS... **Rev:** St. Rupert standing with arms below in ornate inner circle

Date	Mintage	VG	F	VF	XF	Unc
1625	—	3,250	7,500	12,000	17,500	—
1628	—	3,250	7,500	12,000	17,500	—

KM# 130 8 DUCAT
28.0000 g., 0.9860 Gold 0.8876 oz. AGW **Ruler:** Paris **Obv:** Cathedral divides date with saints at sides in inner circle, arms below **Rev:** Reliquary carried by eight bishops, two angels below reliquary in inner circle

Date	Mintage	VG	F	VF	XF	Unc
1628	—	2,250	5,000	8,500	12,000	—

KM# 131 8 DUCAT
28.0000 g., 0.9860 Gold 0.8876 oz. AGW **Ruler:** Paris **Note:** Klippe.

Date	Mintage	VG	F	VF	XF	Unc
1628 Rare	—	—	—	—	—	—

KM# 167 8 DUCAT
28.0000 g., 0.9860 Gold 0.8876 oz. AGW **Ruler:** Guidobald **Obv:** Arms below hat **Obv. Legend:** GVIDOBALDVS... **Rev:** Cathedral with saints at sides in inner circle

Date	Mintage	VG	F	VF	XF	Unc
1654	—	2,250	5,000	8,500	12,000	—

KM# 202 8 DUCAT
28.0000 g., 0.9860 Gold 0.8876 oz. AGW **Ruler:** Maximilian Gandolph **Obv:** Arms below hat in inner circle **Obv. Legend:** MAXIMIL GANDOLPH... **Rev:** Two saints seated facing each other with croziers, church in foreground

Date	Mintage	VG	F	VF	XF	Unc
1668	—	2,250	5,000	8,500	12,000	—

KM# 241 8 DUCAT
28.0000 g., 0.9860 Gold 0.8876 oz. AGW **Ruler:** Maximilian Gandolph **Subject:** 1100th Anniversary of Salzburg **Obv:** Arms below radiant triangle in inner circle **Obv. Legend:** A MAX GAND... **Rev:** Five standing saints; five-line inscription in exergue

Date	Mintage	VG	F	VF	XF	Unc
1682	—	2,500	6,000	10,000	14,000	—

KM# 262 8 DUCAT
28.0000 g., 0.9860 Gold 0.8876 oz. AGW **Ruler:** Johann Ernst **Obv. Legend:** IOAN ERNESTUS...

Date	Mintage	VG	F	VF	XF	Unc
1687	—	2,250	5,000	8,500	12,000	—

KM# 203 9 DUCAT
31.5000 g., 0.9860 Gold 0.9985 oz. AGW **Ruler:** Maximilian Gandolph **Obv:** Arms below hat in inner circle **Obv. Legend:** MAXIMIL GANDOLPH... **Rev:** Two saints seated facing each other with croziers, church in foreground

Date	Mintage	VG	F	VF	XF	Unc
1668	—	2,250	5,000	8,500	12,500	—

KM# 32 10 DUCAT
35.0000 g., 0.9860 Gold 1.1095 oz. AGW **Ruler:** Markus Sittich **Note:** Klippe.

Date	Mintage	VG	F	VF	XF	Unc
1613 Rare	—	—	—	—	—	—

KM# 47 10 DUCAT
35.0000 g., 0.9860 Gold 1.1095 oz. AGW **Ruler:** Markus Sittich **Obv:** Arms below hat **Obv. Legend:** MARCVS SITTICVS... **Rev:** Tower in stormy sea

Date	Mintage	VG	F	VF	XF	Unc
1617	—	3,000	7,000	12,000	17,500	—

KM# 132 10 DUCAT
35.0000 g., 0.9860 Gold 1.1095 oz. AGW **Ruler:** Paris

Date	Mintage	VG	F	VF	XF	Unc
1628	—	2,000	3,750	6,750	9,500	—

KM# 134 10 DUCAT
35.0000 g., 0.9860 Gold 1.1095 oz. AGW **Ruler:** Paris **Obv:** Madonna above arms in inner circle **Obv. Legend:** PARIS... **Rev:** St. Rupert standing, arms below

Date	Mintage	VG	F	VF	XF	Unc
1628	—	3,250	7,500	12,000	17,500	—
1631	—	3,250	7,500	12,000	17,500	—

KM# 133 10 DUCAT
35.0000 g., 0.9860 Gold 1.1095 oz. AGW **Ruler:** Paris **Note:** Klippe. Illustration reduced.

Date	Mintage	VG	F	VF	XF	Unc
1628	—	2,500	6,000	10,000	14,000	—

KM# 168 10 DUCAT
35.0000 g., 0.9860 Gold 1.1095 oz. AGW **Ruler:** Guidobald **Obv:** Arms below hat **Obv. Legend:** GVIDOBALDVS... **Rev:** Cathedral with saints at sides in inner circle

Date	Mintage	VG	F	VF	XF	Unc
1654	—	3,000	6,500	10,000	14,000	—

KM# 204 10 DUCAT
35.0000 g., 0.9860 Gold 1.1095 oz. AGW **Ruler:** Maximilian Gandolph **Obv:** Arms below hat in inner circle **Obv. Legend:** MAX GAND... **Rev:** Two saints seated facing each other with croziers, church in foreground

Date	Mintage	VG	F	VF	XF	Unc
1668	—	3,000	6,750	11,500	16,500	—

KM# 205 10 DUCAT
35.0000 g., 0.9860 Gold 1.1095 oz. AGW **Ruler:** Maximilian Gandolph **Note:** Klippe.

Date	Mintage	VG	F	VF	XF	Unc
1668 Rare	—	—	—	—	—	—

KM# 242 10 DUCAT
35.0000 g., 0.9860 Gold 1.1095 oz. AGW **Ruler:** Maximilian Gandolph **Subject:** 1100th Anniversary of Salzburg

Date	Mintage	VG	F	VF	XF	Unc
1682	—	2,250	5,000	8,500	12,000	—

KM# 243 10 DUCAT
35.0000 g., 0.9860 Gold 1.1095 oz. AGW **Ruler:** Maximilian Gandolph **Note:** Klippe.

Date	Mintage	VG	F	VF	XF	Unc
1682	—	2,500	6,000	10,000	14,000	—

KM# 263 10 DUCAT
35.0000 g., 0.9860 Gold 1.1095 oz. AGW **Ruler:** Johann Ernst **Obv. Legend:** IOAN ERNESTUS... **Rev:** Two saints seated facing

Date	Mintage	VG	F	VF	XF	Unc
1687	—	2,000	3,750	6,750	9,500	—

MB# 495 12 DUCAT
42.0000 g., 0.9860 Gold 1.3314 oz. AGW **Ruler:** Wolfgang Dietrich **Obv:** 2 adjacent shields of arms, Salzburg on left, Raitenau (globe) on right, legate's hat above **Obv. Legend:** WOLF. TEOD. D.G. AREPS. SAL. AP. SE. LE. **Rev:** 2 saints seated facing each other **Rev. Legend:** + S. RVDBERTVS. ET S. VIRGILIVS. EPI. SALZBVRGN. **Note:** Fr.#648.

Date	Mintage	VG	F	VF	XF	Unc
ND(1587-1612) Rare	—	—	—	—	—	—

KM# 53 12 DUCAT
42.0000 g., 0.9860 Gold 1.3314 oz. AGW **Ruler:** Markus Sittich **Note:** Struck with 1 Thaler dies, KM#19.

Date	Mintage	VG	F	VF	XF	Unc
1612 Rare	—	—	—	—	—	—

KM# 135 12 DUCAT
42.0000 g., 0.9860 Gold 1.3314 oz. AGW **Ruler:** Paris **Obv:** Cathedral divides date with saints at sides in inner circle, arms below **Rev:** Reliquary carried by eight bishops, two angels below reliquary in inner circle

Date	Mintage	VG	F	VF	XF	Unc
1628 Rare	—	—	—	—	—	—

KM# 169 12 DUCAT
42.0000 g., 0.9860 Gold 1.3314 oz. AGW **Ruler:** Guidobald **Obv. Legend:** GVIDOBALDVS...

Date	Mintage	VG	F	VF	XF	Unc
1654	—	—	—	13,500	18,500	—

KM# A207 12 DUCAT
42.0000 g., 0.9860 Gold 1.3314 oz. AGW **Ruler:** Maximilian Gandolph **Obv:** Arms below hat in inner circle **Obv. Legend:** MAXIMIL GRANDOLPH... **Rev:** Two saints seated facing each other with croziers, church in foreground

Date	Mintage	VG	F	VF	XF	Unc
1668	—	—	—	12,000	16,000	—

KM# A208 12 DUCAT
42.0000 g., 0.9860 Gold 1.3314 oz. AGW **Ruler:** Maximilian Gandolph **Obv. Legend:** MAXIMIL GANDOLPH... **Note:** Prev. KM#206.

Date	Mintage	VG	F	VF	XF	Unc
1668 Rare	—	—	—	—	—	—

KM# 207 12 DUCAT
42.0000 g., 0.9860 Gold 1.3314 oz. AGW **Ruler:** Maximilian Gandolph **Note:** Klippe.

Date	Mintage	VG	F	VF	XF	Unc
1668 Rare	—	—	—	—	—	—

KM# 244 12 DUCAT
42.0000 g., 0.9860 Gold 1.3314 oz. AGW **Ruler:** Maximilian Gandolph **Subject:** 1100th Anniversary of Salzburg **Obv:** Arms below radiant triangle in inner circle **Obv. Legend:** A MAX GAND... **Rev:** Five standing saints; five-line inscription in exergue **Note:** Klippe.

Date	Mintage	VG	F	VF	XF	Unc
1682 Rare	—	—	—	—	—	—

KM# 264 12 DUCAT
42.0000 g., 0.9860 Gold 1.3314 oz. AGW **Ruler:** Johann Ernst **Obv:** Arms below hat in inner circle **Obv. Legend:** IOAN ERNESTUS... **Rev:** Two saints seated facing each other with croziers, church in foreground

Date	Mintage	VG	F	VF	XF	Unc
1687 Rare	—	—	—	—	—	—

KM# 54 14 DUCAT
49.0000 g., 0.9860 Gold 1.5533 oz. AGW **Ruler:** Markus Sittich **Note:** Struck with 1 Thaler dies, KM#19.

Date	Mintage	VG	F	VF	XF	Unc
1612 Rare	—	—	—	—	—	—

KM# 208 15 DUCAT
52.5000 g., 0.9860 Gold 1.6642 oz. AGW **Ruler:** Maximilian Gandolph **Obv:** Arms below hat in inner circle **Obv. Legend:** MAXIMIL GRANDOLPH... **Rev:** Two saints seated facing each other with croziers, church in foreground

Date	Mintage	VG	F	VF	XF	Unc
1668 Rare	—	—	—	—	—	—

KM# 265 15 DUCAT
52.5000 g., 0.9860 Gold 1.6642 oz. AGW **Ruler:** Johann Ernst, Graf **Obv. Legend:** IOAN ERNESTUS...

Date	Mintage	VG	F	VF	XF	Unc
1687 Rare	—	—	—	—	—	—

MB# 560 16 DUCAT
56.0000 g., 0.9860 Gold 1.7752 oz. AGW **Ruler:** Wolfgang Dietrich **Obv:** Saint seated on throne holding salt cellar and crozier, oval 6-fold arms with central shield of Raitenau below **Obv. Legend:** SANCTVS. RVDBE — RTVS. EPS. SALISBV. **Rev:** Tower in storm-tossed sea, winds from clouds to either side blowing on it, R.N. date in legend **Rev. Legend:** RESISTIT + MDXCIII + IMMOTA. **Note:** Fr.#675.

Date	Mintage	VG	F	VF	XF	Unc
MDXCIII (1593) Rare	—	—	—	—	—	—

KM# 136 16 DUCAT
56.0000 g., 0.9860 Gold 1.7752 oz. AGW **Ruler:** Paris **Obv:** Cathedral divides date with saints at sides in inner circle, arms below **Rev:** Reliquary carried by eight bishops, two angels below reliquary in inner circle

Date	Mintage	VG	F	VF	XF	Unc
1628 Rare	—	—	—	—	—	—

KM# 170 16 DUCAT
56.0000 g., 0.9860 Gold 1.7752 oz. AGW **Ruler:** Guidobald **Obv. Legend:** GVIDOBALDVS...

Date	Mintage	VG	F	VF	XF	Unc
1654 Rare	—	—	—	—	—	—

MB# 497 20 DUCAT
70.0000 g., 0.9860 Gold 2.2190 oz. AGW, 40 mm. **Ruler:** Wolfgang Dietrich **Obv:** 2 adjacent shields of arms, Salzburg on left, Raitenau (globe) on right, legate's hat above **Obv. Legend:** WOLF. TEOD. D.G. AREPS. SAL. AP. SE. LE. **Rev:** 2 saints seated facing each other **Rev. Legend:** + S. RVDBERTVS. ET S. VIRGILIVS. EPI. SALZBVRGN. **Note:** Fr.#647.

Date	Mintage	VG	F	VF	XF	Unc
ND(1587-1612) Rare	—	—	—	—	—	—

KM# 137 20 DUCAT
70.0000 g., 0.9860 Gold 2.2190 oz. AGW **Ruler:** Paris **Obv:** Cathedral divides date with saints at sides in inner circle, arms below **Obv. Legend:** ECCLES: METROP: SALISB: DEDICATVR 25 SEPT: APARIDE... **Rev:** Reliquary carried by eight bishops, two angels below reliquary in inner circle

Date	Mintage	VG	F	VF	XF	Unc
1628	—	—	—	16,500	26,500	—

KM# 171 20 DUCAT
70.0000 g., 0.9860 Gold 2.2190 oz. AGW **Ruler:** Guidobald **Obv:** Arms below hat **Obv. Legend:** GVIDOBALDVS... **Rev:** Cathedral with saints at sides in inner circle

Date	Mintage	VG	F	VF	XF	Unc
1654	—	—	—	12,500	17,000	—

KM# 209 20 DUCAT
70.0000 g., 0.9860 Gold 2.2190 oz. AGW **Ruler:** Maximilian Gandolph **Obv. Legend:** MAXIMIL GANDOLPH...

Date	Mintage	VG	F	VF	XF	Unc
1668 Rare	—	—	—	—	—	—

KM# 210 20 DUCAT
70.0000 g., 0.9860 Gold 2.2190 oz. AGW **Ruler:** Maximilian Gandolph **Note:** Klippe. Illustration reduced.

Date	Mintage	VG	F	VF	XF	Unc
1668 Rare	—	—	—	—	—	—

KM# 266 20 DUCAT
70.0000 g., 0.9860 Gold 2.2190 oz. AGW **Ruler:** Johann Ernst **Obv. Legend:** IOAN ERNESTUS...

Date	Mintage	VG	F	VF	XF	Unc
1687	—	—	—	16,500	22,500	—

KM# 172 24 DUCAT
84.0000 g., 0.9860 Gold 2.6627 oz. AGW **Ruler:** Guidobald, **Obv:** Arms below Bishops hat **Obv. Legend:** GVIDOBALDVS • D:G: ARCHI: EPS: SALISBVRG: SED: AP: LEG: **Rev:** Bishops holding up Cathedral within inner circle **Rev. Legend:** SS: RVDBERTVS • ET • VIRGILIVS • PATRONI • SALISBVRGENSES •

Date	Mintage	VG	F	VF	XF	Unc
1654 Rare	—	—	—	—	—	—

KM# 212 25 DUCAT
87.5000 g., 0.9860 Gold 2.7737 oz. AGW **Ruler:** Maximilian Gandolph **Note:** Klippe.

Date	Mintage	VG	F	VF	XF	Unc
1668 Rare	—	—	—	—	—	—

KM# 211 25 DUCAT
87.5000 g., 0.9860 Gold 2.7737 oz. AGW **Ruler:** Maximilian Gandolph **Obv:** Arms below hat in inner circle **Obv. Legend:** MAXIMIL GANDOLPH... **Rev:** Two saints seated facing each other with croziers, church in foreground

Date	Mintage	VG	F	VF	XF	Unc
1668 Rare	—	—	—	—	—	—

KM# 213 44 DUCAT
140.0000 g., 0.9860 Gold 4.4379 oz. AGW **Ruler:** Maximilian Gandolph **Obv:** Arms below hat in inner circle **Obv. Legend:** MAXIMIL GANDOLPH... **Rev:** Two saints seated facing each other with croziers, church in foreground

Date	Mintage	VG	F	VF	XF	Unc
1668 Rare	—	—	—	—	—	—

KM# 173 50 DUCAT
175.0000 g., 0.9860 Gold 5.5474 oz. AGW **Ruler:** Guidobald **Obv:** Arms below hat **Obv. Legend:** GVIDOBALDVS... **Rev:** Cathedral with saints at sides in inner circle **Note:** Klippe.

Date	Mintage	VG	F	VF	XF	Unc
1654 Rare	—	—	—	—	—	—

KM# 267 50 DUCAT
175.0000 g., 0.9860 Gold 5.5474 oz. AGW **Ruler:** Johann Ernst **Obv:** Arms below hat in inner circle **Obv. Legend:** IOAN ERNESTUS... **Rev:** Two saints seated facing each other with croziers, church in foreground

Date	Mintage	VG	F	VF	XF	Unc
1687 Rare	—	—	—	—	—	—

PATTERNS

Including off metal strikes

KM#	Date	Mintage	Identification	Mkt Val
Pn1	(1)610	—	2 Pfenning. Gold. KM#5.	—
Pn2	(1)613	—	2 Pfenning. Gold. KM#12.	—
Pn3	1615	—	2 Pfenning. Gold. KM#12.	—
Pn4	(1)617	—	Pfenning. Gold. KM#11.	—
Pn5	(1)618	—	Pfenning. Gold. KM#11.	—
Pn6	1628	—	4 Ducat. Silver. KM#124.	—

KM#	Date	Mintage	Identification	Mkt Val
Pn7	1628	—	10 Ducat. Lead. KM#132.	—
Pn8	1636	—	Kreuzer. Gold. KM#84.	—
Pn9	1638	—	1/4 Thaler. Gold. KM#88.	—

SINZENDORF

An old Austrian house which was divided into two branches. The elder line was advanced to the rank of count in 1613. His successors seemingly acquired the mint right a few years later. They became extinct in 1766.

Members of the younger line, who became counts in 1653 and princes in 1803, struck no coins.

RULERS
Pilgrim III, 1579-1620
Georg Ludwig, 1616-1680
Christian Ludwig, 1681-1687
Philipp Ludwig, 1687-1742

COUNTY

STANDARD COINAGE

KM# 4 1/2 THALER
Silver **Ruler:** Georg Ludwig **Obv:** Capped bust of Georg Ludwig right **Rev:** Crowned arms in order collar

Date	Mintage	VG	F	VF	XF	Unc
1676	—	275	500	875	1,500	—

KM# 5 THALER
Silver **Ruler:** Georg Ludwig **Obv:** Capped bust of Georg Ludwig right **Rev:** Crowned arms in order collar **Note:** Dav. #3414.

Date	Mintage	VG	F	VF	XF	Unc
1676	—	475	800	1,400	2,200	—

TRADE COINAGE

KM# 6 DUCAT
3.5000 g., 0.9860 Gold 0.1109 oz. AGW **Ruler:** Georg Ludwig **Obv:** Bust of Georg Ludwig right **Rev:** Crowned arms in Order collar **Note:** Fr. #3289.

Date	Mintage	VG	F	VF	XF	Unc
1676	—	775	1,650	3,750	6,500	—

TRAUTSON

An old Tyrolean family that traced its lineage back to 1134. During the reign of Paul Sixtus I (1589-1621), who was Imperial Governor of the Tyrol, the mint right was given to this house. Members of this house held high imperial offices until 1775 when the house passed to Auersperg.

RULERS
Paul Sixtus I, 1589-1621
Johann Franz, 1621-1663
Franz Eusebius, 1663-1728
Johann Leopold, 1663-1724

PRINCIPALITY

STANDARD COINAGE

KM# 5 3 KREUZER
Silver **Ruler:** Paul Sixtus I **Obv:** Bust right **Rev:** Coat of arms

Date	Mintage	VG	F	VF	XF	Unc
ND	—	15.00	25.00	40.00	75.00	—
1617	—	15.00	25.00	40.00	75.00	—
1618	—	15.00	25.00	40.00	75.00	—
1619	—	15.00	25.00	40.00	75.00	—

KM# 21 3 KREUZER
Silver **Ruler:** Paul Sixtus I **Obv:** Eagle **Rev:** Arms

Date	Mintage	VG	F	VF	XF	Unc
1621	—	12.00	20.00	38.00	70.00	—

KM# 25 1/4 THALER
Silver **Ruler:** Johann Franz

Date	Mintage	VG	F	VF	XF	Unc
1634	—	180	325	550	950	—

KM# 26 1/4 THALER
Silver **Ruler:** Johann Franz **Rev:** Crowned oval arms

Date	Mintage	VG	F	VF	XF	Unc
1634	—	250	425	650	1,150	—

KM# 27 1/4 THALER
Silver **Ruler:** Johann Franz **Rev:** Crowned shield-shaped arms

Date	Mintage	VG	F	VF	XF	Unc
1639	—	285	475	775	1,350	—

KM# A7 1/2 THALER
Silver **Ruler:** Paul Sixtus I **Note:** Similar to 1 Thaler, KM#20.

Date	Mintage	VG	F	VF	XF	Unc
ND(1615-21)	—	750	1,450	2,700	4,750	—

KM# 6 1/2 THALER
Silver **Ruler:** Paul Sixtus I **Obv:** Eagle **Rev:** Arms **Note:** Varieties exist.

Date	Mintage	VG	F	VF	XF	Unc
1620	—	245	475	850	1,450	—

KM# 8.1 THALER
Silver **Ruler:** Paul Sixtus I **Obv:** Bust right, bare headed, cape with order collar **Note:** Dav. #3418.

Date	Mintage	VG	F	VF	XF	Unc
1617	—	220	375	650	1,100	—

KM# 7 THALER
Silver **Ruler:** Paul Sixtus I **Obv:** Bust right with hat **Note:** Dav. 3416

Date	Mintage	VG	F	VF	XF	Unc
1617	—	500	825	1,400	2,000	—

KM# 8.2 THALER
Silver **Ruler:** Paul Sixtus I **Obv:** Larger bust **Note:** Similar to KM#8.3. Dav. #3422.

Date	Mintage	VG	F	VF	XF	Unc
1618	—	125	200	325	550	—

KM# 8.3 THALER
Silver **Ruler:** Paul Sixtus I **Note:** Dav. #3423.

Date	Mintage	VG	F	VF	XF	Unc
1619	—	125	200	325	550	—
16Z0	—	125	200	325	550	—

KM# 9 THALER
Silver **Ruler:** Paul Sixtus I **Obv:** Bow knot on shoulder **Note:** Dav. #3425.

Date	Mintage	VG	F	VF	XF	Unc
16Z0	—	125	200	325	550	—

KM# 20 THALER
Silver **Ruler:** Paul Sixtus I **Obv:** Arms in order chain **Rev:** Crowned double headed eagle above crown **Note:** Dav. #3426.

Date	Mintage	VG	F	VF	XF	Unc
ND	—	375	725	1,250	2,200	—

KM# 28.1 THALER
Silver **Ruler:** Johann Franz **Rev:** Double eagle above helmeted arms **Note:** Dav. #3427.

Date	Mintage	VG	F	VF	XF	Unc
1634	—	220	375	650	1,100	—
1635	—	220	375	650	1,100	—

KM# 28.2 THALER
Silver **Ruler:** Johann Franz **Obv:** Large bust **Rev:** Similar to KM#28.3 **Note:** Dav. #3428.

Date	Mintage	VG	F	VF	XF	Unc
1634	—	220	375	650	1,100	—

KM# 28.3 THALER
Silver **Ruler:** Johann Franz **Note:** Dav. #3429.

Date	Mintage	VG	F	VF	XF	Unc
1636	—	200	350	600	1,000	—
1637	—	200	350	600	1,000	—

Date	Mintage	VG	F	VF	XF	Unc
1638	—	200	350	600	1,000	—
1639	—	200	350	600	1,000	—

KM# 10 2 THALER

Silver **Ruler:** Paul Sixtus I **Note:** Similar to 1 Thaler, KM#7. Dav. #3415.

Date	Mintage	VG	F	VF	XF	Unc
1617 Rare	—	—	—	—	—	—

KM# 11.1 2 THALER

Silver **Ruler:** Paul Sixtus I **Note:** Similar to 1 Thaler, KM#8.1. Dav. #3417.

Date	Mintage	VG	F	VF	XF	Unc
1617	—	850	1,400	2,200	3,250	—

KM# 11.2 2 THALER

Silver **Ruler:** Paul Sixtus I **Obv:** Bare head right, cape with chain hung all across **Note:** Dav. #3421.

Date	Mintage	VG	F	VF	XF	Unc
1618	—	850	1,400	2,200	3,250	—

KM# 11.3 2 THALER

Silver **Ruler:** Paul Sixtus I **Obv:** Larger bust with bow knot on shoulder **Note:** Dav. #3424.

Date	Mintage	VG	F	VF	XF	Unc
1620	—	850	1,400	2,200	3,250	—

KM# 12 2 THALER

Silver **Ruler:** Paul Sixtus I **Note:** Klippe. Dav. #3424A.

Date	Mintage	VG	F	VF	XF	Unc
16Z0 Rare	—	—	—	—	—	—

KM# 13.1 3 THALER

Silver **Ruler:** Paul Sixtus I **Note:** Similar to 1 thaler, KM#8.1. Dav. #3424A.

Date	Mintage	VG	F	VF	XF	Unc
1617 Rare	—	—	—	—	—	—

KM# 13.2 3 THALER

Silver **Ruler:** Paul Sixtus I **Note:** Dav. #3420.

Date	Mintage	VG	F	VF	XF	Unc
1618	—	2,000	3,250	4,750	6,500	—

KM# 14 4 THALER

Silver **Ruler:** Paul Sixtus I **Note:** Similar to 1 Thaler, KM#7. Dav. #A3415.

Date	Mintage	VG	F	VF	XF	Unc
1617 Rare	—	—	—	—	—	—

KM# 15 4 THALER

Silver **Ruler:** Paul Sixtus I **Note:** Similar to 1 Thaler, KM#11.2. Dav. #3419.

Date	Mintage	VG	F	VF	XF	Unc
1618 Rare	—	—	—	—	—	—

KM# 16 6 THALER

Silver **Ruler:** Paul Sixtus I **Note:** Similar to 2 Thaler, KM#11.2. Dav. #A3419.

Date	Mintage	VG	F	VF	XF	Unc
1618 Rare	—	—	—	—	—	—

TRADE COINAGE

KM# 29 1/4 DUCAT

0.8750 g., 0.9860 Gold 0.0277 oz. AGW **Ruler:** Johann Franz **Obv:** Bust right

Date	Mintage	VG	F	VF	XF	Unc
1635	—	300	650	1,350	2,000	—

KM# 17 DUCAT

3.5000 g., 0.9860 Gold 0.1109 oz. AGW **Ruler:** Paul Sixtus I

Date	Mintage	VG	F	VF	XF	Unc
ND	—	1,000	2,000	3,750	6,500	—

KM# 30 DUCAT

3.5000 g., 0.9860 Gold 0.1109 oz. AGW **Ruler:** Johann Franz **Obv:** Bust right **Rev:** Crowned imperial eagle above crowned arms

Date	Mintage	VG	F	VF	XF	Unc
1634	—	450	875	2,000	3,250	—
1638	—	450	875	2,000	3,250	—

KM# 18 4 DUCAT

14.0000 g., 0.9860 Gold 0.4438 oz. AGW **Ruler:** Paul Sixtus I

Date	Mintage	VG	F	VF	XF	Unc
1618	—	1,650	3,250	5,500	9,750	—

KM# 19 5 DUCAT

1.7500 g., 0.9860 Gold 0.0555 oz. AGW **Ruler:** Paul Sixtus I

Date	Mintage	VG	F	VF	XF	Unc
1620	—	1,350	2,750	4,500	7,750	—

KM# 22 10 DUCAT

35.0000 g., 0.9860 Gold 1.1095 oz. AGW **Ruler:** Paul Sixtus I **Note:** Struck with 1 Thaler dies.

Date	Mintage	VG	F	VF	XF	Unc
1617 Rare	—	—	—	—	—	—

KM# 23 10 DUCAT

35.0000 g., 0.9860 Gold 1.1095 oz. AGW **Ruler:** Paul Sixtus I **Note:** Struck with 1 Thaler dies, KM#8.2.

Date	Mintage	VG	F	VF	XF	Unc
1618 Rare	—	—	—	—	—	—

KM# A31 10 DUCAT

35.0000 g., 0.9860 Gold 1.1095 oz. AGW **Ruler:** Johann Franz **Note:** Struck with 1 Thaler dies, KM#28.3.

Date	Mintage	VG	F	VF	XF	Unc
1638 Rare	—	—	—	—	—	—

TROPPAU-JAEGENDORF

Troppau was an old upper Silesian duchy with its capital in the town of the same name located 90 miles southeast of Breslau. The capital of an Upper Silesian duchy Troppau fell to Austria 1528-1614 except for a short period in the 1550's. In 1614 Count Carl of Liechtenstein was created duke of Troppau for his military services. This coinage was intended for circulation in Troppau and in Jaegendorf.

RULERS

Carl, 1614-1627
Karl Eusebius, 1627-1684

MINT OFFICIALS' INITIALS & MONOGRAMS

Initials	Description	Dates	Names
BH	Ligate H	1614-16	Burghard Haase
CC	Crossed flags divide CC	1617-29	Krystof Cantor
	M above W		Michal Wilke
(j)	JZ monogram	1616-17	Jan Ziesler
(t)	TS monogram	1629-30	Tobias Sommerschein

DUCHY

JOINT COINAGE

KM# 1 3 KRAJCAR

Silver **Ruler:** Carl **Obv:** Bust of Carl right **Rev:** Capped ornate shield

Date	Mintage	VG	F	VF	XF	Unc
1614 BH	—	35.00	65.00	120	200	—

KM# 2 3 KRAJCAR

Silver **Ruler:** Carl **Rev:** Capped eagle

Date	Mintage	VG	F	VF	XF	Unc
1614 BH	—	40.00	70.00	135	225	—

KM# 3 3 KRAJCAR

Silver **Ruler:** Carl **Rev:** 2 ornate shields capped

Date	Mintage	VG	F	VF	XF	Unc
1614 BH	—	40.00	70.00	135	225	—

KM# 13 3 KRAJCAR

Silver **Ruler:** Carl **Rev:** 2 plain shields capped

Date	Mintage	VG	F	VF	XF	Unc
1615 BH	—	25.00	50.00	100	200	—
1615 (t)	—	25.00	50.00	100	200	—
1616 BH	—	25.00	50.00	100	200	—
1616 (t)	—	25.00	50.00	100	200	—
1617 (t)	—	25.00	50.00	100	200	—
1618 (f) c	—	25.00	50.00	100	200	—
1619 (f) c	—	25.00	50.00	100	200	—

KM# 32 KREUZER

Silver **Ruler:** Karl Eusebius **Obv:** Bust of Karl right **Rev:** Capped shield of arms

Date	Mintage	VG	F	VF	XF	Unc
1629 MW	—	35.00	60.00	120	225	—

KM# 33 3 KREUZER

Silver **Ruler:** Karl Eusebius **Obv:** Bust of Karl right **Rev:** Capped shield of arms

Date	Mintage	VG	F	VF	XF	Unc
1629 (t)	—	30.00	50.00	100	185	—

KM# 5 THALER

Silver **Ruler:** Carl **Obv:** Bust right **Rev:** Capped and helmeted arms **Note:** Dav. #3430.

Date	Mintage	VG	F	VF	XF	Unc
(1)614 BH	—	1,600	2,700	4,200	6,000	—

KM# 6 THALER

Silver **Ruler:** Carl **Rev:** Capped and helmeted arms divide B-H at lower edge **Note:** Dav. #3431.

Date	Mintage	VG	F	VF	XF	Unc
1614 BH	—	1,600	2,700	4,200	6,000	—

KM# 7 THALER

Silver **Ruler:** Carl **Rev:** Plain field arms divide B-H **Note:** Dav. #3432.

Date	Mintage	VG	F	VF	XF	Unc
1614 BH	—	1,600	2,700	4,200	6,000	—

KM# 14 THALER

Silver **Ruler:** Carl **Obv:** Different portrait **Rev:** 2 shields capped and helmeted **Note:** Dav. #3434.

Date	Mintage	VG	F	VF	XF	Unc
1615 BH	—	725	1,300	2,200	3,850	—
1616 BH	—	725	1,300	2,200	3,850	—

KM# 28 THALER

Silver **Ruler:** Carl **Obv:** Smaller bust **Rev:** Troppau arms at right **Note:** Dav. #3435.

Date	Mintage	VG	F	VF	XF	Unc
1619 CC	—	750	1,400	2,300	4,000	—

KM# 29 THALER

Silver **Ruler:** Carl **Rev:** Troppau arms at left **Note:** Klippe. Dav. #3435A. Illustration reduced.

Date	Mintage	VG	F	VF	XF	Unc
1619 CC Rare	—	—	—	—	—	—

KM# 30 THALER

Silver **Ruler:** Carl **Rev:** Troppau arms at right **Note:** Klippe. Dav. #3435B.

Date	Mintage	VG	F	VF	XF	Unc
1619 CC Rare	—	—	—	—	—	—

KM# 35 THALER

Silver **Ruler:** Karl Eusebius **Obv:** Bust right **Rev:** Crowned arms, date in legend **Note:** Dav. #3437.

Date	Mintage	VG	F	VF	XF	Unc
1629 MW	—	1,600	2,700	4,200	6,000	—

KM# 15 2 THALER

Silver **Ruler:** Carl **Obv:** Bust right **Rev:** Capped shield of arms **Note:** Dav. #A3432.

Date	Mintage	VG	F	VF	XF	Unc
1615 BH	—	4,200	6,500	9,000	12,000	—

KM# 17 2 THALER

Silver **Ruler:** Carl **Note:** Similar to 1 Thaler, KM#14. Dav. #3433.

Date	Mintage	VG	F	VF	XF	Unc
1616 BH	—	2,750	4,500	6,500	10,000	—

KM# 19 2 THALER

Silver **Ruler:** Carl **Obv:** Bust right in sprays **Rev:** Capped shield of arms in sprays **Note:** Dav. #3436.

Date	Mintage	VG	F	VF	XF	Unc
ND Rare	—	—	—	—	—	—

KM# 20 3 THALER
Silver **Ruler:** Carl **Note:** Similar to 2 Thaler, KM#19. Dav. #3436A.

Date	Mintage	VG	F	VF	XF	Unc
ND Rare	—	—	—	—	—	—

KM# 21 4 THALER
Silver **Ruler:** Carl **Note:** Similar to 2 Thaler, KM#19. Dav. #3436B.

Date	Mintage	VG	F	VF	XF	Unc
ND Rare	—	—	—	—	—	—

KM# 22 5 THALER
Silver **Ruler:** Carl **Obv:** Bust right **Obv. Legend:** CAROLVS D • G • PRINCEPS DE LICHTENSTEIN **Rev:** Crowned arms **Rev. Legend:** DVX OPPAVIÆ - ET CARNOVIA ... **Note:** Dav. #3436C. Illustration reduced.

Date	Mintage	VG	F	VF	XF	Unc
ND Rare	—	—	—	—	—	—

JOINT TRADE COINAGE

KM# 8 DUCAT
3.4900 g., 0.9860 Gold 0.1106 oz. AGW **Ruler:** Carl **Obv:** Bust of Carl right in inner circle **Rev:** Capped shield of arms in inner circle **Note:** Restrikes exist.

Date	Mintage	VG	F	VF	XF	Unc
1614 BH	—	600	1,200	2,150	4,200	—
1617	—	600	1,200	2,150	4,200	—
1618	—	600	1,200	2,150	4,200	—

KM# 9 2 DUCAT
7.0000 g., 0.9860 Gold 0.2219 oz. AGW **Ruler:** Carl **Obv:** Bust of Carl right in inner circle **Rev:** Capped ornate shield of arms in inner circle

Date	Mintage	VG	F	VF	XF	Unc
1614 BH	—	2,500	4,800	7,800	12,000	—
1616	—	2,500	4,800	7,800	12,000	—

KM# 10 3 DUCAT
10.5000 g., 0.9860 Gold 0.3328 oz. AGW **Ruler:** Carl **Obv:** Bust of Carl right in inner circle **Rev:** Crowned shield of arms in inner circle, date in legend

Date	Mintage	VG	F	VF	XF	Unc
1614 Unique	—	—	—	—	—	—

KM# 16 3 DUCAT
10.5000 g., 0.9860 Gold 0.3328 oz. AGW **Ruler:** Carl **Rev:** 2 shields capped in inner circle

Date	Mintage	VG	F	VF	XF	Unc
(1)618 CC	—	—	—	—	7,500	—

KM# 27 3 DUCAT
10.5000 g., 0.9860 Gold 0.3328 oz. AGW **Ruler:** Carl **Note:** Klippe.

Date	Mintage	VG	F	VF	XF	Unc
1619 Restrike	—	—	—	—	500	—

KM# 25 4 DUCAT
14.0000 g., 0.9860 Gold 0.4438 oz. AGW **Ruler:** Carl **Obv:** Bust of Carl right in inner circle

Date	Mintage	VG	F	VF	XF	Unc
1618	—	—	7,500	12,500	18,000	—

KM# A16 5 DUCAT
17.5000 g., 0.9860 Gold 0.5547 oz. AGW **Ruler:** Carl **Obv:** Bust of Carl right in inner circle **Rev:** Capped shield of arms in inner circle

Date	Mintage	VG	F	VF	XF	Unc
1615 BH	—	—	7,500	12,500	18,000	—

KM# 24 6 DUCAT
21.0000 g., 0.9860 Gold 0.6657 oz. AGW **Ruler:** Carl **Obv:** Bust of Carl right in inner circle

Date	Mintage	VG	F	VF	XF	Unc
1617	—	—	—	—	20,000	—

KM# 23 10 DUCAT
35.0000 g., 0.9860 Gold 1.1095 oz. AGW **Ruler:** Carl **Note:** Struck with 1 Thaler dies, KM#14.

Date	Mintage	VG	F	VF	XF	Unc
1616	—	—	—	—	25,000	—

AUSTRIAN NETHERLANDS

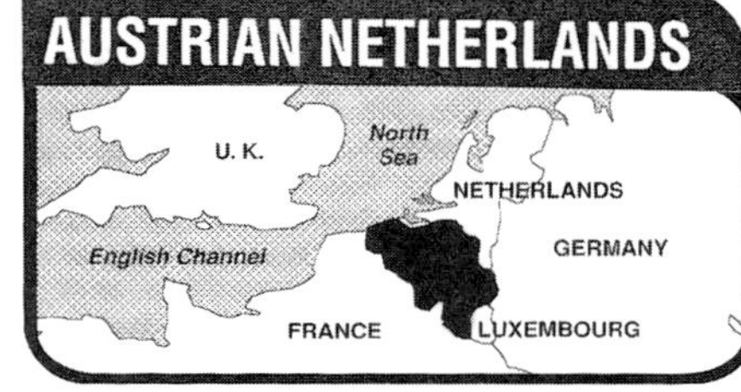

The Austrian Netherlands, which corresponds roughly to present-day Belgium, came into being on April 11, 1713, when the Treaty of Utrecht awarded the lands to Austria as part settlement following the war with Spain. It passed to France in 1795, was part of the Kingdom of Netherlands from 1815 to 1830, and became the present Belgium as the result of the revolution of 1830 against William I, Prince of Orange and King of the Netherlands.

RECKHEIM

A barony in Limburg which was raised to a county in 1624. Was in the hands of the van Lynden family and mediatized in 1803.

RULERS
Herman of Aspremont- Lynden, 1590-1603
Ernst, 1603-1636
Ferdinand, 1636-1665
Francois-Gobert and Ferdinand-Gobert of Aspremont-Lynden, 1665-1703

IMPERIAL BARONY

MILLED COINAGE

KM# 1 1/4 THALER (1/4 Daalder)
7.3100 g., Silver **Ruler:** Herman **Obv:** Helmeted arms **Obv. Legend:** HERM. DE LYNDEN. LIB. BAR. IMP. IN RECHEM **Rev:** Crowned imperial eagle **Rev. Legend:** RVDOLP. II. ROM. IMP. SEMPER (.) AVG (.) **Edge:** Plain

Date	Mintage	Good	VG	F	VF	XF
ND(1590-1603) Rare	—	—	—	—	—	—

KM# 2 THALER (Daalder)
29.2500 g., Silver **Ruler:** Herman **Obv:** Helmeted arms **Obv. Legend:** .HERM. DE. LYNDEN. LIB. BAR. IMP. IN. RECHEM **Rev:** Crowned imperial eagle **Rev. Legend:** *RVDOLP. II. ROM. IMP. SEMP(ER). AVG.* **Edge:** Plain **Note:** Cross-reference number Dav. #8689.

Date	Mintage	Good	VG	F	VF	XF
ND(1590-1603) Rare	—	—	—	—	—	—

COUNTY

STANDARD COINAGE

KM# 21 DUIT
Copper **Ruler:** Ernst **Obv:** Shield of arms in inner circle **Rev:** TRA/REC/HEM in inner circle, date in legend at top

Date	Mintage	Good	VG	F	VF	XF
1616	—	12.00	25.00	50.00	80.00	135

KM# 22 DUIT
Copper **Ruler:** Ernst **Obv:** Crowned arms **Rev:** FRI / CIR / date in wreath of leaves **Note:** Varieties exist.

Date	Mintage	Good	VG	F	VF	XF
1617	—	7.00	15.00	30.00	55.00	100
1619	—	7.00	15.00	30.00	55.00	100
1620	—	7.00	15.00	30.00	55.00	100
1621	—	7.00	15.00	30.00	55.00	100
1631	—	7.00	15.00	30.00	55.00	100
1632	—	7.00	15.00	30.00	55.00	100
1633	—	7.00	15.00	30.00	55.00	100
1634	—	7.00	15.00	30.00	55.00	100

KM# 23 DUIT
Copper **Ruler:** Ernst **Obv:** Crowned arms **Obv. Legend:** NISI. DEVS-NOBISCVM **Rev:** FRI / DER / 1619 in laurel wreath

Date	Mintage	Good	VG	F	VF	XF
1619	—	10.00	20.00	40.00	70.00	125

KM# 30 DUIT
Copper **Ruler:** Ernst **Obv:** Crowned arms **Rev:** FRI / DER / date in laurel wreath

Date	Mintage	Good	VG	F	VF	XF
1620	—	10.00	20.00	40.00	70.00	125
1621	—	10.00	20.00	40.00	70.00	125

KM# 45 DUIT
Copper **Ruler:** Ernst **Rev:** FRI/SA/1633 in wreath and leaves

Date	Mintage	Good	VG	F	VF	XF
1633	—	10.00	20.00	40.00	70.00	125

KM# 47 DUIT
Copper **Ruler:** Ernst **Obv:** Shield of arms in laurel branches **Rev:** IMP / R with eagle above

Date	Mintage	Good	VG	F	VF	XF
ND	—	10.00	20.00	40.00	70.00	125

KM# 48 DUIT
Copper **Ruler:** Ernst **Obv:** Crowned arms in laurel branches **Rev:** BVL / LONEN / SIS in wreath, shield at bottom

Date	Mintage	Good	VG	F	VF	XF
ND	—	10.00	20.00	40.00	70.00	125

KM# 49 DUIT
Copper **Ruler:** Ernst **Rev:** FRI/CUA

Date	Mintage	Good	VG	F	VF	XF
ND	—	10.00	20.00	40.00	70.00	125

KM# 51 DUIT
Copper **Ruler:** Ferdinand **Obv:** Crowned arms **Rev:** FRI / CIR / date

Date	Mintage	Good	VG	F	VF	XF
ND	—	6.00	12.00	20.00	35.00	65.00
1638	—	6.00	12.00	20.00	35.00	65.00
1639	—	6.00	12.00	20.00	35.00	65.00
1641	—	6.00	12.00	20.00	35.00	65.00
1642	—	6.00	12.00	20.00	35.00	65.00
1643	—	6.00	12.00	20.00	35.00	65.00
1644	—	6.00	12.00	20.00	35.00	65.00
1646	—	6.00	12.00	20.00	35.00	65.00
1651	—	6.00	12.00	20.00	35.00	65.00
1653	—	6.00	12.00	20.00	35.00	65.00
1655	—	6.00	12.00	20.00	35.00	65.00
1661	—	6.00	12.00	20.00	35.00	65.00

KM # 52 DUIT

Copper **Ruler:** Ferdinand **Obv:** Crowned arms **Rev:** FER / DIN / 1640 in wreath

Date	Mintage	Good	VG	F	VF	XF
ND	—	10.00	20.00	40.00	70.00	125
1640	—	10.00	20.00	40.00	70.00	125

KM # 87 DUIT

Copper **Ruler:** Francois-Gobert and Ferdinand-Gobert **Obv:** Crowned arms in palm branches

Date	Mintage	Good	VG	F	VF	XF
ND	—	10.00	20.00	40.00	70.00	125

KM # 88 DUIT

Copper **Ruler:** Francois-Gobert and Ferdinand-Gobert **Obv:** Shield of arms in garland

Date	Mintage	Good	VG	F	VF	XF
ND	—	10.00	20.00	40.00	70.00	125

KM # 89 DUIT

Copper **Ruler:** Francois-Gobert and Ferdinand-Gobert **Rev:** TRA / REC in quatrelobe

Date	Mintage	Good	VG	F	VF	XF
ND	—	10.00	20.00	40.00	70.00	125

KM # 90 DUIT

Copper **Ruler:** Francois-Gobert and Ferdinand-Gobert **Rev:** TRA / REC / HEM in wreath

Date	Mintage	Good	VG	F	VF	XF
ND	—	10.00	20.00	40.00	70.00	125

KM # 92 DUIT

Copper **Ruler:** Francois-Gobert and Ferdinand-Gobert **Obv:** Crowned eagle shield in palm branches **Rev:** TRA / REC / HEM in wreath

Date	Mintage	Good	VG	F	VF	XF
ND	—	10.00	20.00	40.00	70.00	125

KM # 96 DUIT

Copper **Ruler:** Francois-Gobert and Ferdinand-Gobert **Obv:** Bend sinister in shield

Date	Mintage	Good	VG	F	VF	XF
ND	—	10.00	20.00	40.00	70.00	125

KM # 97 DUIT

Copper **Ruler:** Francois-Gobert and Ferdinand-Gobert **Obv:** Crowned arms with lion supporters **Rev:** TRA/REC/NEM in wreath

Date	Mintage	Good	VG	F	VF	XF
ND	—	12.00	25.00	50.00	80.00	135

KM # 93 DUIT

Copper **Ruler:** Francois-Gobert and Ferdinand-Gobert **Rev:** DA/E TR/TRIA in inner circle and wreath **Note:** Legend: D(ENARIUS) AE (REUS) T(ERRITORII) R(ECKHEIMANSIS) I(MPERIALIS) A(SPREMONTIS), other legend varieties exist.

Date	Mintage	Good	VG	F	VF	XF
ND	—	10.00	20.00	40.00	70.00	125

KM # 46 DUIT

Copper **Ruler:** Ernst **Obv:** Crowned arms in wreath **Rev:** TRAN / MOESA / A.R. in wreath **Note:** Varieties exist.

Date	Mintage	Good	VG	F	VF	XF
ND	—	10.00	20.00	40.00	70.00	125

KM # 91 DUIT

Copper **Ruler:** Francois-Gobert and Ferdinand-Gobert **Obv:** Crowned oval arms **Rev:** O: D / FER / DIN in wreath **Note:** Varieties exist.

Date	Mintage	Good	VG	F	VF	XF
ND	—	10.00	20.00	40.00	70.00	125

KM # 94 DUIT

Copper **Ruler:** Francois-Gobert and Ferdinand-Gobert **Obv:** Ornamental shield of arms with cross of Lynden at bottom **Rev:** IN / REC / KVM in wreath **Note:** Varieties exist.

Date	Mintage	Good	VG	F	VF	XF
ND	—	10.00	20.00	40.00	70.00	125

KM # 95 DUIT

Copper **Ruler:** Francois-Gobert and Ferdinand-Gobert **Obv:** Ornamentation in bottom of shield of arms **Rev:** TRA / REC / KUM **Note:** Varieties exist.

Date	Mintage	Good	VG	F	VF	XF
ND	—	10.00	20.00	40.00	70.00	125

KM # 98 DUIT

Copper **Ruler:** Francois-Gobert and Ferdinand-Gobert **Rev:** TRAREC in quatrelobe **Note:** Varieties exist.

Date	Mintage	Good	VG	F	VF	XF
ND	—	12.00	25.00	50.00	80.00	135

KM # 85 DUIT

Copper **Ruler:** Ferdinand **Obv:** Small shield of arms, 2 digit date at top right **Rev:** FRI / CIA / R in wreath

Date	Mintage	Good	VG	F	VF	XF
(16)64	—	10.00	20.00	40.00	70.00	125

KM# 86 DUIT

Copper **Ruler:** Ferdinand **Obv:** Laurel branches around arms

Date	Mintage	Good	VG	F	VF	XF
(16)64	—	10.00	20.00	40.00	70.00	125

KM# 99 DUIT

Copper **Ruler:** Francois-Gobert and Ferdinand-Gobert **Obv:** Ornamental shield with ornamentation below bend **Rev:** FRAN / EG. LV / R.M in wreath **Note:** Varieties exist.

Date	Mintage	Good	VG	F	VF	XF
ND	—	12.00	25.00	50.00	80.00	135

KM# 100 DUIT

Copper **Ruler:** Francois-Gobert and Ferdinand-Gobert **Obv:** Crowned arms with lion supporters, VVTREH below **Rev:** / TRAREC / 1681 in quatrelobe **Note:** Varieties exist.

Date	Mintage	Good	VG	F	VF	XF
1681	—	12.00	25.00	50.00	80.00	135

KM# 68 1/2 LIARD (Gigot)

Copper **Ruler:** Ferdinand **Obv:** Crowned arms in inner circle **Obv. Legend:** FER...DE. REC **Rev:** Crowned arms on cross fleury, R-M at sides

Date	Mintage	Good	VG	F	VF	XF
ND	—	30.00	50.00	90.00	160	—

KM# 69 1/2 LIARD (Gigot)

Copper **Ruler:** Ferdinand **Obv:** Crowned arms **Rev:** Crowned double cross between 3 shields of arms, 2 above

Date	Mintage	Good	VG	F	VF	XF
ND	—	25.00	40.00	75.00	135	—

KM# 70 1/2 LIARD (Gigot)

Copper **Ruler:** Ferdinand **Rev:** Value divided at bottom

Date	Mintage	Good	VG	F	VF	XF
ND	—	25.00	40.00	75.00	135	—

KM# 71 1/2 LIARD (Gigot)

Copper **Ruler:** Ferdinand **Obv:** Crowned different arms in inner circle **Obv. Legend:** COM. REC

Date	Mintage	Good	VG	F	VF	XF
ND	—	25.00	40.00	75.00	135	—

KM# 72 1/2 LIARD (Gigot)

Copper **Ruler:** Ferdinand **Obv:** Crowned different arms (bend sinister) in inner circle **Obv. Legend:** MON. NO. DE. REC

Date	Mintage	Good	VG	F	VF	XF
ND	—	25.00	40.00	75.00	135	—

KM# 73 1/2 LIARD (Gigot)

Copper **Ruler:** Ferdinand **Rev:** Value divided at bottom

Date	Mintage	Good	VG	F	VF	XF
ND	—	25.00	40.00	75.00	135	—

KM# 74 1/2 LIARD (Gigot)

Copper **Ruler:** Ferdinand **Obv:** Crowned arms with bend **Obv. Legend:** FERDI. C. D. LIN. REC

Date	Mintage	Good	VG	F	VF	XF
ND	—	25.00	40.00	75.00	135	—

KM# 67 1/2 LIARD (Gigot)

Copper **Ruler:** Ferdinand **Obv:** Crowned arms **Obv. Legend:** REC. BAR. IN. BORS **Rev:** Crown above cross fleury **Rev. Legend:** FER-COM-LIN

Date	Mintage	Good	VG	F	VF	XF
1646	—	25.00	50.00	90.00	160	—

KM# 18 LIARD

Copper **Ruler:** Ernst **Obv:** Crown above 3 shields of arms, 2 above 1 **Obv. Legend:** ERNESTVS. DE. LYNDEN. LIBER **Rev:** Crowned arms **Rev. Legend:** BARO. IMPER. IN. RECHEM

Date	Mintage	Good	VG	F	VF	XF
ND	—	15.00	30.00	60.00	90.00	175

KM# 19 LIARD

Copper **Ruler:** Ernst **Obv:** Crowned arms divide A-I in inner circle **Rev:** Crowned arms divide P-P in inner circle

Date	Mintage	Good	VG	F	VF	XF
ND	—	15.00	30.00	60.00	90.00	175

KM# 15 LIARD

Copper **Ruler:** Ernst **Obv:** Bust of Emest left **Obv. Legend:** ERNESTVS. DE. LYNDEN. LIBER **Rev:** Crowned arms **Rev. Legend:** BARD. IMPERIALIS. IN. RECHEIM **Note:** Varieties exist.

Date	Mintage	Good	VG	F	VF	XF
ND	—	18.00	35.00	65.00	100	185
1614	—	18.00	35.00	65.00	100	185

KM# 16 LIARD

Copper **Ruler:** Ernst **Obv:** Crown above 3 shields of arms, 2 above 1 **Obv. Legend:** ERNESTVS. DE. LYNDEN. LIBER **Rev:** Crowned arms **Rev. Legend:** BARO. IMPERI. RECHEIM **Note:** Varieties exist.

Date	Mintage	Good	VG	F	VF	XF
ND	—	15.00	30.00	60.00	90.00	175

KM# 17 LIARD

Copper **Ruler:** Ernst **Obv:** Crowned arms **Obv. Legend:** ERNESTVS. DE. LYNDEN. LIBER **Rev:** Crown above 3 shields of arms, 2 above 1 **Rev. Legend:** BARO. IMPERIALIS. IN. REKEIM **Note:** Varieties exist.

Date	Mintage	Good	VG	F	VF	XF
ND	—	15.00	30.00	60.00	90.00	175

KM# 20 LIARD

Copper **Ruler:** Ferdinand **Obv:** Crown above 3 shields of arms, 2 above 1 **Obv. Legend:** FERD. COM. DE. LIN. RECHEM **Rev:** Crowned arms divide date in inner circle **Rev. Legend:** FERDIN. ET. ELISABETH **Note:** Varieties exist.

Date	Mintage	Good	VG	F	VF	XF
1611(sic) Error	—	10.00	20.00	40.00	70.00	150
1640	—	10.00	20.00	40.00	70.00	150
1641	—	10.00	20.00	40.00	70.00	150
1645	—	10.00	20.00	40.00	70.00	150
1646	—	10.00	20.00	40.00	70.00	150

KM# 61 LIARD

Copper **Ruler:** Ferdinand **Obv:** Soldier with sword above shoulder divides R-O in inner circle **Obv. Legend:** DOMINVS. MIHI. ADIVTOR **Rev:** Crowned arms on cross in inner circle **Rev. Legend:** MON. NOVA. COM. D. REC

Date	Mintage	Good	VG	F	VF	XF
ND	—	15.00	30.00	60.00	90.00	165

KM# 62 LIARD

Copper **Ruler:** Ferdinand **Obv:** Soldier with sword above shoulder divides F-R in inner circle

Date	Mintage	Good	VG	F	VF	XF
ND	—	15.00	30.00	60.00	90.00	165

KM# 64 LIARD

Copper **Ruler:** Ferdinand **Obv:** Soldier with sword above shoulder divides F-O in inner circle **Obv. Legend:** COM. DE. LIND. REC **Rev. Legend:** FERD. II. DG. ROM. IMP

Date	Mintage	Good	VG	F	VF	XF
ND	—	15.00	30.00	60.00	90.00	165

KM# 58 LIARD

Copper **Ruler:** Ferdinand **Rev:** Crowned differnet arms in inner circle

Date	Mintage	Good	VG	F	VF	XF
ND	—	18.00	35.00	65.00	100	185

KM# 56 LIARD

Copper **Ruler:** Ferdinand **Obv:** Bust of Ferdinand left **Obv. Legend:** FERDINAN. COME **Rev:** Crowned arms **Rev. Legend:** DOMINVS. CO. BORS

Date	Mintage	Good	VG	F	VF	XF
ND	—	18.00	35.00	65.00	100	185

KM# 59 LIARD

Copper **Ruler:** Ferdinand **Obv:** Crowned arms in inner circle **Obv. Legend:** FERDINANDVS...REC **Rev:** Crown above F-R and double cross in inner circle **Rev. Legend:** FERDINANDVS. III. D. G. RO. IM **Note:** Varieties exist.

Date	Mintage	Good	VG	F	VF	XF
ND	—	15.00	30.00	60.00	90.00	165

KM# 60 LIARD

Copper **Ruler:** Ferdinand **Obv:** Crowned different arms in inner circle **Note:** Varieties exist.

Date	Mintage	Good	VG	F	VF	XF
ND	—	15.00	30.00	60.00	90.00	165

KM# 57 LIARD

Copper **Ruler:** Ferdinand **Obv:** Crowned bust of Emperor Ferdinand III left **Obv. Legend:** FERDINANDUS. DG. RO. IMP **Rev:** Crowned arms divide date in inner circle **Rev. Legend:** BARO. BORS. THIEN

Date	Mintage	Good	VG	F	VF	XF
1640	—	18.00	35.00	65.00	100	185
1641	—	18.00	35.00	65.00	100	185

KM# 55 LIARD

Copper **Ruler:** Ferdinand **Obv:** Crown above 3 shields of arms, 2 above 1 **Obv. Legend:** FERD. COM. DE. LIN. RECHEM **Rev:** Crowned arms divide date **Rev. Legend:** BARO. DE. BORS. THIEN

Date	Mintage	Good	VG	F	VF	XF
1640	—	15.00	30.00	60.00	90.00	165

KM# 63 LIARD

Copper **Ruler:** Ferdinand **Rev:** Date above crown

Date	Mintage	Good	VG	F	VF	XF
1640	—	15.00	30.00	60.00	90.00	165

KM# 66 LIARD

Copper **Ruler:** Ferdinand **Obv:** Crowned different arms divide date in inner circle **Obv. Legend:** F. C. ASPREM. ET. REC. Z **Rev. Legend:** DEVS. PROTECTOR. NOSTER **Note:** Varieties exist.

Date	Mintage	Good	VG	F	VF	XF
1644	—	15.00	30.00	60.00	90.00	165

KM# 80 LIARD

Copper **Ruler:** Ferdinand **Obv:** Bust of Ferdinand right **Obv. Legend:** MONETANOVA. COMITIS. AS. Z **Rev:** Crowned arms of Zeeland, date in legend at upper left **Rev. Legend:** DEVS. PROTECTOR. NOR 1657 **Note:** Varieties exist.

Date	Mintage	Good	VG	F	VF	XF
1657	—	12.00	25.00	50.00	85.00	160

KM# 81 LIARD

Copper **Ruler:** Ferdinand **Rev:** Crown divides date **Note:** Varieties exist.

Date	Mintage	Good	VG	F	VF	XF
1657	—	12.00	25.00	50.00	85.00	160

KM# 105 3 KREUZER
Billon **Ruler:** Ernst **Obv:** Crowned arms **Obv. Legend:** MONETA. NO. ARG. R. 3. D **Rev:** Crowned imperial eagle with value on breast **Rev. Legend:** FER. II. D. G. RO. IMP. S. AV

Date	Mintage	Good	VG	F	VF	XF
ND	—	90.00	175	325	550	—

KM# 4 SOL (1/2 Gros Stuiver)
Billon **Ruler:** Ernst **Obv:** St. Peter kneeling between 2 shields of arms in inner circle **Obv. Legend:** SS - PETRV-PATR **Rev:** Long cross with stars in angles in inner circle **Rev. Legend:** SIT NOMEN DOMINI BENEDICTVM E. C. D. R...SSI. S. W

Date	Mintage	Good	VG	F	VF	XF
ND	—	125	250	400	700	—

KM# 5 SOL (1/2 Gros Stuiver)
Billon **Ruler:** Ernst **Obv:** Crowned arms divide value (1-S) in inner circle **Obv. Legend:** E. C. ASPREMONT. REP **Rev:** Ornamental cross with rosette at center **Rev. Legend:** DEVS. PROT. ECTO. NOST **Note:** Varieties exist.

Date	Mintage	Good	VG	F	VF	XF
ND	—	65.00	125	200	375	—

KM# 6 SOL (1/2 Gros Stuiver)
Billon **Ruler:** Ferdinand **Obv:** Crowned arms **Obv. Legend:** F. C. ASPREMON...OS **Rev:** Ornate cross **Rev. Legend:** DEVS PROT-ECTO NOST

Date	Mintage	Good	VG	F	VF	XF
ND	—	65.00	125	200	375	—

KM# 7 SOL (1/2 Gros Stuiver)
Silver **Ruler:** Ferdinand **Obv:** Different arms

Date	Mintage	Good	VG	F	VF	XF
ND	—	65.00	125	200	375	—

KM# 8 2 SOLS (2 Stuiver Gros)
Billon **Ruler:** Ernst **Obv:** St. Peter kneeling between 2 shields of arms in inner circle **Obv. Legend:** S. S. PETRV-M PATRO **Rev:** Long cross with stars in angles in inner circle **Rev. Legend:** SIT. NOMEN. DNI. BENEDICTVM/ E. C. D. R. 1 ST. S. W **Note:** Varieties exist.

Date	Mintage	Good	VG	F	VF	XF
ND	—	150	300	500	850	—

KM# 9 3 SOLS (3 Stuiver)
Silver **Ruler:** Ernst **Obv:** Crowned arms in sprays **Obv. Legend:** ERNESTVS. COMES. IMP. RO...RE **Rev:** Floriated cross with lion at center in inner circle **Rev. Legend:** SIDERVS. PRONOBIS. QVIS. COR...

Date	Mintage	Good	VG	F	VF	XF
ND	—	60.00	120	200	375	—

KM# 10 4 SOLS (4 Stuivers)
Silver **Ruler:** Ernst **Obv:** Crowned arms in inner circle **Obv. Legend:** ERNESTVS. DE. LVNDEN. LI **Rev:** Crowned double-headed eagle in inner circle **Rev. Legend:** BARON. IMPEV. IN. RECH. IIII-ST **Note:** Varieties exist.

Date	Mintage	Good	VG	F	VF	XF
ND	—	75.00	150	300	550	950

KM# 12 4 SOLS (4 Stuivers)
Silver **Ruler:** Ernst **Rev:** Different arms **Note:** Varieties exist.

Date	Mintage	Good	VG	F	VF	XF
ND	—	50.00	100	200	350	700

KM# 11 4 SOLS (4 Stuivers)
Silver **Ruler:** Ernst **Obv:** Crowned double-headed eagle in inner circle **Obv. Legend:** MATH. II. D. G. ROM. IMP. SEMP. AVGV **Rev:** Different crowned arms in inner circle **Rev. Legend:** MO: NO: ARG. RECHEIM. IIII. ST

Date	Mintage	Good	VG	F	VF	XF
ND	—	40.00	85.00	165	285	550

KM# 33 4 SOLS (4 Stuivers)
Silver **Ruler:** Ernst **Obv:** Crowned double-headed eagle in inner circle **Obv. Legend:** FERDINAN. II. D. E. ROM. IMP. SE. AUG **Rev:** Crowned different arms divide date in inner circle **Rev. Legend:** ERNESTVS. COMES. DE. RECHEIM **Note:** Varieties exist.

Date	Mintage	Good	VG	F	VF	XF
1626	—	60.00	120	250	400	750

KM# 35 1/3 ESCALIN (Peerdeken)
Billon **Ruler:** Ernst **Obv:** RECM in exergue **Rev:** Different arms on cross

Date	Mintage	Good	VG	F	VF	XF
ND	—	50.00	100	165	285	—

KM# 34 1/3 ESCALIN (Peerdeken)
Billon **Ruler:** Ernst **Obv:** Knight on horseback brandishing sword to right in inner circle, REHM in exergue **Rev:** Arms on cross in inner circle **Rev. Legend:** MONET. A. NOVA-RECH-MENSIS **Note:** Varieties exist.

Date	Mintage	Good	VG	F	VF	XF
ND	—	50.00	100	165	285	—

KM# 36 ESCALIN
Silver **Ruler:** Ernst **Obv:** Rampant lion to left holding sword and shield in inner circle **Obv. Legend:** ERNESTVS. DE. IS. ER. COMES **Rev:** Crowned arms divide date in inner circle **Rev. Legend:** IMPERI-ALIS. IN. RECHEM

Date	Mintage	Good	VG	F	VF	XF
1626	—	90.00	180	300	525	—

KM# 43 ESCALIN
Silver **Ruler:** Ernst **Obv:** Crowned arms in branchs in inner circle, date above crown **Rev:** Floreated cross in inner circle **Rev. Legend:** DEVS. FORTI. ET. SPES-NOSTR

Date	Mintage	Good	VG	F	VF	XF
1629	—	60.00	120	200	375	—

KM# 50 ESCALIN
Silver **Ruler:** Ernst **Obv:** Rampant lion left holding sword and shield in inner circle **Obv. Legend:** MONETA. NOVA. COM. R. DEVS. MEVS. ADIVTOR **Rev:** Crowned different arms divide date in inner circle **Rev. Legend:** ER-NESTVS-COM-ES. IM. DR-C **Note:** Varieites exist.

Date	Mintage	Good	VG	F	VF	XF
1636	—	75.00	150	250	425	—

KM# 65 ESCALIN
Silver **Ruler:** Ferdinand **Obv. Legend:** FERDINANDVS. ET. ELISABETH. CO **Rev:** Arms similar to those of Spain divides date **Rev. Legend:** VISA. IN. NIMOD

Date	Mintage	Good	VG	F	VF	XF
1640	—	60.00	120	200	375	—

KM# 38 PATARD
Silver **Ruler:** Ferdinand **Obv:** Crowned arms without inner circle **Rev:** Ornate cross **Rev. Legend:** MONE NOVA ARGE RECH

Date	Mintage	Good	VG	F	VF	XF
ND	—	50.00	100	185	325	—

KM# 37 PATARD
Silver **Ruler:** Ferdinand **Obv:** Crowned arms in inner circle **Obv. Legend:** FERDINANDVS. CO. IN. RE(C)HEI **Rev:** Ornate cruciform **Rev. Legend:** DEVS. PROT. ECTO. NOST **Note:** Varieties exist.

Date	Mintage	Good	VG	F	VF	XF
ND	—	50.00	100	185	325	—

KM# 39 FLORIN (Gulden - 24 Mariengroschen)
Silver **Ruler:** Ferdinand **Obv:** Shield of arms with 3 helmets above **Obv. Legend:** FRANC. ET. FERD. FRAT. COM. IN. ASPERM. ET. RECKE **Rev:** XXIII / MARIEN / GROSCHEN at center **Rev. Legend:** GRAFL. RECKHEIM. MVNT

Date	Mintage	Good	VG	F	VF	XF
ND	—	—	—	—	—	—

KM# 40 1/16 THALER (1/16 Daalder-Peerdeken)
Billon **Ruler:** Ernst **Obv:** Crowned arms divide date in inner circle **Obv. Legend:** ERNESTVS. COMES. DE. RECHE M **Rev:** Crowned imperial eagle with value on breast in inner circle **Rev. Legend:** FERDINAN. II. DG. RO. IM. SEM. AV

Date	Mintage	Good	VG	F	VF	XF
16Z6	—	85.00	165	275	475	—

KM# 24 1/4 THALER (1/4 Daalder)
Silver **Ruler:** Ernst **Obv:** Crowned arms divide in inner circle **Obv. Legend:** ERNESTVS. DE. LYNDEN. LI. BA. IN. IM. R **Rev:** Crowned imperial eagle **Rev. Legend:** FERDINAND. II. D. G. RO. IM. S. AU

Date	Mintage	Good	VG	F	VF	XF
1619	—	120	225	345	550	950

KM# A13 1/4 THALER (1/4 Daalder)
Silver **Ruler:** Ernst **Obv:** Helmeted arms **Obv. Legend:** (Heart) ERNESTVS. DE LYNDEN. LI. BA. IN. R. **Rev:** Crowned imperial eagle **Rev. Legend:** FERDINAND. II. DG. RO. IM. S. AV.

Date	Mintage	Good	VG	F	VF	XF
ND(1619-36)	—	—	—	—	—	—

KM# 101 2/3 THALER (2/3 Daalder)
Silver **Ruler:** Francois-Gobert and Ferdinand-Gobert **Obv:** Bust of Francois-Gobert to right **Obv. Legend:** OMNIA. FORTITVDINE: ST. PRVDSENTIA **Rev:** Crowned arms in palm branches, date above crown **Rev. Legend:** FR. G. ET. FERG. COM. DE. A. ET. R. FR

Date	Mintage	Good	VG	F	VF	XF
1687 Rare	—	—	—	—	—	—

KM# 31 THALER (Daalder)
Silver **Ruler:** Ernst **Obv:** Helmeted arms **Obv. Legend:** ERNESTVS. DE. LYNDEN. LI: BA: IMP. IN. REC **Rev:** Crowned double-headed eagle in inner circle **Rev. Legend:** MATHIAS. D. G. ELEC. ROM. IMP. SEMP-AVE **Note:** Dav. #4505.

Date	Mintage	Good	VG	F	VF	XF
ND Rare	—	—	—	—	—	—

KM# 32 THALER (Daalder)
Silver **Ruler:** Ernst **Obv:** Helmeted arms **Obv. Legend:** ERNESTVS. DE. LYNDEN. L. B. A. IMP. RECHEM **Rev:** Crowned imperial eagle, crown divides date **Rev. Legend:** FERDINANDVS. II. D. G. ROM. IM. SEM. AV **Note:** Dav. #4507.

Date	Mintage	Good	VG	F	VF	XF
16Z0 Rare	—	—	—	—	—	—

KM# 28 2 THALER (2 Daalder)
Silver **Ruler:** Ernst **Obv:** Helmeted arms **Obv. Legend:** ERNESTVS. DE. LYNDEN. LI: BA: IMP. IN. REC **Rev:** Crowned imperial eagle **Rev. Legend:** MATHIAS. D. G. ELEC. ROM. IMP. SEMP-AVE **Note:** Dav. #4504.

Date	Mintage	Good	VG	F	VF	XF
ND Rare	—	—	—	—	—	—

KM# 29 2 THALER (2 Daalder)
Silver **Ruler:** Ernst **Obv:** Helmeted arms **Obv. Legend:** ERNESTVS. DE. LYNDEN. L. B. A. IMP. RECHEM **Rev:** Crowned imperial eagle, crown divides date **Rev. Legend:** FERDINANDVS. II. D. G. ROM. IM. SEM. AV **Note:** Klippe. Dav. #4506.

Date	Mintage	Good	VG	F	VF	XF
16Z0 Rare	—	—	—	—	—	—

TRADE COINAGE

KM# 3 GOLDGULDEN (Florin D'or)
3.5000 g., 0.9860 Gold 0.1109 oz. AGW **Ruler:** Herman **Obv:** Helmeted arms **Obv. Legend:** HERM. DE LYNDEN LIB. BAR-IMP-IN-RECKEM **Rev:** Crowned imperial eagle **Rev. Legend:** RVDOLP • ROM • IMP • SEMPER • AVG • **Note:** Previous KM#41. Fr.#232a.

Date	Mintage	Good	VG	F	VF	XF
ND	—	300	550	1,100	2,000	3,250

KM# 42 GOLDGULDEN (Florin D'or)
3.5000 g., 0.9860 Gold 0.1109 oz. AGW **Ruler:** Ferdinand **Obv:** Soldier standing left with banner **Obv. Legend:** FERD: ASPREMON: LIND: RECHEIM. COM. **Rev:** Helmeted arms **Rev. Legend:** BEAT. GOB. COM.-ASPEREMON **Note:** Fr.#232b.

Date	Mintage	Good	VG	F	VF	XF
ND	—	350	650	1,250	2,000	3,250

Ancient home of Scythian tribes and known under the Romans as Albania and to the Arabs as Arran, the country of Azerbaijan was formed at the time of its invasion by Seliuk Turks and grew into a prosperous state under Persian suzerainty. From the 16th century the country was a theatre of fighting and political rivalry between Turkey, Persia and later Russia. Baku was first annexed to Russia by Czar Peter I in 1723 and remained under Russian rule for 12 years. After the Russian retreat the whole of Azerbaijan north of the Aras River became a khanate under Persian control. Czar Alexander I, after an eight-year war with Persia, annexed it in 1813 to the Russian empire.

RULERS

Mehmed III, AH1003-1012/1595-1603AD
Ahmed I, AH1012-1026/1603-1617AD

MINT NAMES

گنجه

Ganja (Elisabethpol, Kirovabad)

نخجوان

Nakhjavan

شماخي شماخه

Shemakhi

شيروان شروان

Shirvan

MONETARY SYSTEM

100 Qapik = 1 Manat

OTTOMAN

Ahmed I

HAMMERED COINAGE

MB# 56 BESLIK

1.8000 g., Silver **Obv:** Toughra **Rev:** Perso-Turkish-*duribe Shirvan* **Mint:** Shirvan **Note:** Varieties exist.

Date	Mintage	Good	VG	F	VF	XF
AHxxx	—	80.00	150	400	—	—

MB# 22 BESLIK

Silver **Obv:** Toughra **Rev:** Perso-Turkish-*duriba Shirvan* **Mint:** Shirvan **Note:** Weight varies 1.40-1.80 grams. Size varies 24-25 millimeters. Varieties of obverse exist.

Date	Mintage	Good	VG	F	VF	XF
AH1012	—	80.00	150	400	—	—
AHxxxx	—	80.00	150	400	—	—
AH1013	—	80.00	150	400	—	—
AH1014	—	80.00	150	400	—	—

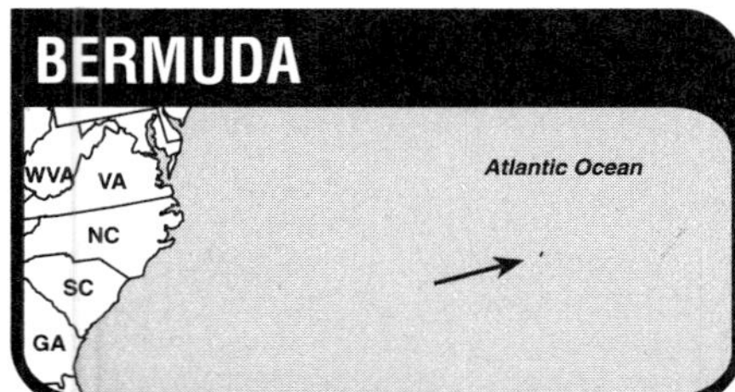

Situated in the western Atlantic Ocean 660 miles (1,062 km.) east of North Carolina, has an area of 20.6 sq. mi. (53 sq. km).

Bermuda was discovered by Juan de Bermudez, a Spanish navigator, in about 1503. British influence dates from 1609 when a group of Virginia-bound British colonists under the command of Sir George Somers was shipwrecked on the islands for 10 months. The islands were settled in 1612 by 60 British colonists from the Virginia Colony and became a crown colony in 1684. The earliest coins issued for the island were the "Hogge Money" series of 2, 3, 6 and 12 pence, the name derived from the pig in the obverse design, a recognition of the quantity of such animals then found there. The next issue for Bermuda was the Birmingham coppers of 1793; all locally circulating coinage was demonetized in 1842, when the currency of the United Kingdom became standard. Internal autonomy was obtained by the constitution of June 8, 1968.

BRITISH COLONY

HOGGE MONEY COINAGE

Coins of great rarity, sometimes known as "Hogge" money. Undated and struck in brass (or a brass alloy), originally silver washed, the Bermuda atmospheric conditions soon removed any trace of silver. Coins with a silver trace are of very great rarity. It has been alleged that denominations of one penny and four pence exist, but these are unknown.

KM# 1 2 PENCE (II Pence)

1.7000 g., Brass **Issuer:** Sommer Islands Company **Obv:** Hog standing facing left, II above **Rev:** Two-masted sailing ship between S and I

Date	Mintage	Good	VG	F	VF	XF
ND(c.1616) *16-18 known	—	—	—	—	—	—

Note: Stack's John J. Ford, Jr. Part XVIII, 5-07, VF-25 realized $86,250

KM# 2 3 PENCE (III Pence)

1.9600 g., Brass **Issuer:** Sommer Islands Company **Obv:** Hog standing facing left, III above **Rev:** Two-masted sailing ship between S and I

Date	Mintage	Good	VG	F	VF	XF
ND(c.1616) Rare	—	—	—	—	—	—

KM# 3 6 PENCE (VI Pence)

3.8000 g., Brass **Issuer:** Sommer Islands Company **Obv:** Hog facing left, VI above within circle **Obv. Legend:** SOMMER * ILANDS * **Rev:** Three-masted sailing ship, large portholes

Date	Mintage	Good	VG	F	VF	XF
ND(c.1616) *37 known	—	—	—	—	—	—

Note: Heritage Long Beach sale, 5-08, AU-50 realized $43,125; Spink sale 5010, 6-05, VF-XF realized $15,235

KM# 4 6 PENCE (VI Pence)

3.8000 g., Brass **Issuer:** Sommer Islands Company **Rev:** Small portholes

Date	Mintage	Good	VG	F	VF	XF
ND(c.1616)	—	—	—	—	—	—

Note: A combined total of *37 examples of all VI Pence are known

KM# A5 12 PENCE (XII Pence)

5.8600 g., Brass **Issuer:** Sommer Islands Company **Obv:** Hog facing left, XII above within circle **Obv. Legend:** SOMMER * ILANDS * **Rev:** Three-masted sailing ship with three small sails

Date	Mintage	Good	VG	F	VF	XF
ND(c.1616) *18 Known	—	—	—	—	—	—

KM# A6 12 PENCE (XII Pence)

5.8600 g., Brass **Issuer:** Sommer Islands Company **Rev:** Large sails

Date	Mintage	Good	VG	F	VF	XF
ND(c.1616) *6 known	—	—	—	—	—	—

Note: Stack's John J. Ford, Jr. Part XVIII, 5-07, EF-40 realized $109,250

Böhmen

The large and important Kingdom of Bohemia is located in Central Europe between Bavaria and Austria on the south, Saxony and Silesia on the north, Franconia and the Upper Palatinate to the west, and the Margraviate of Moravia to the east. The region was early settled by the Celtic Boii and controlled by the Czechs, a Slavic people, from the fifth century. Bohemia was at first a duchy and produced a series of rulers dating from the late 9th century. The first hereditary king was Wladislaw II, who ruled 1140-1173. During the later Middle Ages, the kingdom was acquired through marriage to various dynasties of the region, notably the Margraves of Moravia, the Electors of Brandenburg and emperors as well. By the late 15th century, the ruler was another Wladislaw II, a son of the King of Poland, and he was also the King of Hungary. His son, Ludwig, was killed in 1526 at the Battle of Mohacz, fighting against the Turks. His sister was the wife of Emperor Ferdinand I and thus, Bohemia passed to the Hapsburgs.

Bohemia, however, was an electoral monarchy and the king was chosen by the leading nobles at the capital, Prague. In most instances, the succession of one emperor to the next made electing the new emperor as king of Bohemia a mere formality. Very often, the heir apparent to the emperor was elected King of Bohemia prior to his father's passing. By the early 17th century, Protestantism had made great inroads among the Czech nobility and anti-Catholic/anti-Hapsburg sentiments were at a peak. Before Emperor Matthias died in 1619, the nobles had been forced to elect Archduke Ferdinand (II) in 1617. When two governors, appointed by Matthias, were thrown from a window of the palace in Prague in May 1618, in what became known as the Defenestration of Prague, the event precipitated a revolt by the Bohemian Estates (Die böhmischen Stände). The Estates were constituted of the noble lords, the knights and the cities, who deposed Emperor Ferdinand II as king and elected the Protestant Friedrich V, Count Palatine and Elector of the Rhine, in his place. Hostilities had already begun between some of the Protestant German princes and the Emperor, but the elevation of Friedrich to the Bohemian throne galvanized imperial resolve and made the new king's reign very short. Coinage was struck under the authority of firstly, the Estates, and then King Friedrich. The Hapsburgs regained Bohemia in 1620 and except for the later short reign of Karl Albrecht of Bavaria in 1741-42, continued until 1918, although it ceased to be viewed as a separate entity after the dissolution of the Holy Roman Empire by Napoleon in 1806.

RULERS

Ludwig, 1516-1626
Rudolf II, 1572-1612
Matthias, 1612-19
Friedrich von der Pfalz, 1619-20
Ferdinand II, 1620-37
Ferdinand III, 1637-57
Leopold I, 1657-1705

MINT MARKS

A – Vienna Mint
(c) – crossed hammers, 1695, 1711-12
S – Schmöllnitz Mint

BUDWEIS MINT

MINT OFFICIALS' INITIALS & PRIVY MARKS

Letters or Initials	Privy mark	Date	Name
(bf)=	Dog's head left in shield	1584-1611	Christoph Mattighofer, mintmaster
(bg)=	Dog's head left, but not in shield	1584-1611	Christoph Mattifghofer, mintmaster

ARMS

Crowned lion rampant, usually to left.

GLATZ MINT

(in Bohemia)

Coat of arms, like Vienna, on imperial eagle's breast, legends end like Breslau. This mint closed in 1660.

MINT MARKS

G, g, Glatz, 1628

MINT OFFICIALS' INITIALS and PRIVY MARKS

Initials	Dates	Names
AP	1627-28	Andreas Peter, die-cutter
G	1637-38	-
GW	1658-60	Georg Werner
HG	1629	Huser Glacensis, die-cutter
IR	1632	-
O	1636	Vacant

Privy Mark	Description	Dates	Names
(b)=	Circles in circle with wavy line	1627-28	Johann Jacob Huser
(r)=	Ligate HR	1631-36	Hans Rossner
(h)=	HP monogram	1628-31	Peter Hema

JOACHIMSTHAL MINT

Letters or Initials	Privy marks	Date	Name
(ah)=	Double fleur de lis in circle	1600-04	Christoph Taubenreutter, mintmaster
(ai)=		1604-06	Hans Gipfel, mintmaster
(aj)=	Lion's head left	1606-20	Centurio Lengefelder, mintmaster
(ak)=	Bird's wing	1621-37	Gregor Steinmüller, mintmaster
(al)=		1637-49	David Knobloch, mintmaster
(am)=	Bird flying left	1649-50	Johann Freistein, mintmaster
(an)=	Crown	1650-68	Johann Jakob Kittner, mintmaster
(ao)=		1668-70	Paul Wenzel Seling, mintmaster

KUTTENBERG MINT

Letters or Initials	Privy mark	Date	Name
(y)=	Goat's head left	1599-1603	Hans Spiess, mintmaster
(z)=	Eagle's head left in circle or shield	1603-1608	David Enderle, mintmaster
(aa)=		1608-12	Paul Skréta Sotnovsky von Závorice, mintmaster
(bb)=		1612-13	Johann Sultys, mintmaster
(cc)=	Bird left holding pole over wing	1614-15	August Schmilauer, mintmaster
(dd)=		1616-17, 1632-33	Vacant mintmaster's position
(ee)=		1617-32	Sebastian Hölzl, mintmaster
(ff)=		1633-35	Hans Prunz, mintmaster
(gg)=		1635	Lorenz Neumann, mint contractor
(hh)=	Arm left holding 3 arrows	1636-43	Daniel Kavka, mintmaster
(ii)=	Arm left holding hammer	1651-77	Gregor Hackl, mintmaster
(jj)=	CK or CK	1677-1702	Christoph Kroh, mintmaster

PRAGUE MINT

(Praha)
(in Bohemia)

Coat of arms on imperial eagle's breast. Legend usually ends BO, BOH, BOHEMIAE REX

Letters or Initials	Privy marks	Date	Name
(j)=		1600-09	Hans Lasanz, mintmaster
(k)=	Bird's wing	1609-10	Samuel Salvart, mintmaster
(l)=		1610-30	Benedikt Huebiner, mintmaster
(m)=		1619-20	Skréta Sotnovsky, mintmaster
(n)=	Upper half of griffin left	1623-25	Hans Suttner, mintmaster
(o)=	Boar's head right, I behind	1630-31	Eliseus du Bois, mintmaster
(p)=		1631-37	Tobias Schuster, mintmaster
(q)=		1637-66	Jakob W. Wolker, mintmaster
(qx)=		Used in 1651 only	Jakob W. Wolker
(r)=		1655-62	Christoph Margolik, mintmaster
(s)=		1668-88	Anton von Janinalli, mintmaster
(t)=	Crown and/or MV	1688-94	Matthias Vaist, mintmaster
PM		1694, 1710-11	Prague mint, during vacancies
GE		1694-1710	Gregor Egerer, mintmaster

KINGDOM

STANDARD COINAGE

MB# 238 HELLER

Silver **Ruler:** Rudolf II **Mint:** Kuttenberg **Note:** Uniface. Crowned R divides date. Varieties exist.

Date	Mintage	VG	F	VF	XF	Unc
1606	—	—	—	—	—	—

MB# 331 HELLER

Silver **Ruler:** Rudolf II **Obv:** Crowned R divides R - B, date below **Mint:** Kuttenberg **Note:** Uniface.

Date	Mintage	VG	F	VF	XF	Unc
1601	—	30.00	60.00	125	200	—
160Z	—	30.00	60.00	125	200	—
1603	—	30.00	60.00	125	200	—
1604	—	30.00	60.00	125	200	—
1605	—	30.00	60.00	125	200	—
1606	—	30.00	60.00	125	200	—
1607	—	30.00	60.00	125	200	—
1608	—	30.00	60.00	125	200	—
1609	—	30.00	60.00	125	200	—
1610	—	30.00	60.00	125	200	—
1611	—	30.00	60.00	125	200	—
161Z	—	30.00	60.00	125	200	—

KM# 150 HELLER

Silver **Ruler:** Matthias II **Obv:** Crowned M divides R - B, date below **Mint:** Kuttenberg **Note:** Uniface. Prev. KM#1045.

Date	Mintage	VG	F	VF	XF	Unc
1613	—	30.00	60.00	125	200	—
1614	—	30.00	60.00	125	200	—
1615	—	30.00	60.00	125	200	—
1616	—	30.00	60.00	125	200	—
1617	—	30.00	60.00	125	200	—
1618	—	30.00	60.00	125	200	—
1619	—	30.00	60.00	125	200	—

KM# 12 PFENNIG

Silver **Ruler:** Rudolf II **Obv:** Crowned Bohemian lion left in inner circle **Rev:** Date in center of empty field **Mint:** Joachimstal **Note:** Prev. KM#860.

Date	Mintage	VG	F	VF	XF	Unc
1602 (ah)	—	—	—	—	—	—

MB# 246 PFENNIG

Silver **Ruler:** Rudolf II **Obv:** Crowned Bohemian lion left in circle, date **Obv. Legend:** RVDOL. SECVN **Mint:** Kuttenberg **Note:** Uniface. Prev. KM#1016.

Date	Mintage	VG	F	VF	XF	Unc
1601	—	10.00	20.00	35.00	65.00	—
1602	—	10.00	20.00	35.00	65.00	—
1603	—	10.00	20.00	35.00	65.00	—
1604	—	10.00	20.00	35.00	65.00	—
1607	—	10.00	20.00	35.00	65.00	—
1608	—	10.00	20.00	35.00	65.00	—
1609	—	10.00	20.00	35.00	65.00	—
1610	—	10.00	20.00	35.00	65.00	—
1611	—	10.00	20.00	35.00	65.00	—

KM# 13 PFENNIG

Silver **Ruler:** Rudolf II **Obv:** Crowned Bohemian lion left in inner circle, date **Obv. Legend:** RVDOL. II. D.G... **Mint:** Kuttenberg **Note:** Klippe. Prev. KM#1017.

Date	Mintage	VG	F	VF	XF	Unc
1601	—	—	—	—	—	—

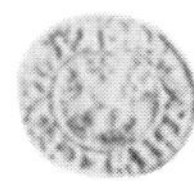

KM# 108 PFENNIG

Silver **Ruler:** Matthias II **Obv:** Crowned Bohemian lion left in circle, date **Obv. Legend:** MATHI. SECVN. **Mint:** Kuttenberg **Note:** Uniface. Prev. KM#1046.

Date	Mintage	VG	F	VF	XF	Unc
1612	—	25.00	45.00	100	180	—

KM# 175 PFENNIG

Silver **Ruler:** Matthias II **Obv:** Lion right, date **Obv. Legend:** MATTHIAS. R.B. **Mint:** Kuttenberg **Note:** Prev. KM#1047.

Date	Mintage	VG	F	VF	XF	Unc
1615	—	25.00	45.00	100	180	—
1616	—	25.00	45.00	100	180	—

KM# 202 PFENNIG

Silver **Ruler:** Matthias II **Obv:** Lion left **Mint:** Kuttenberg **Note:** Prev. KM#1048.

Date	Mintage	VG	F	VF	XF	Unc
1617	—	25.00	45.00	100	180	—
1618	—	25.00	45.00	100	180	—
1619	—	25.00	45.00	100	180	—

KM# 207 PFENNIG

Silver **Ruler:** Matthias II **Obv:** Legend, date **Obv. Legend:** MATTHIAS. R.H.B. **Mint:** Kuttenberg **Note:** Prev. KM#1049.

Date	Mintage	VG	F	VF	XF	Unc
1618	—	25.00	45.00	100	180	—

KM# 178 GROSCHEN

Silver **Ruler:** Matthias II **Obv:** Crowned Bohemian lion left **Rev:** Crowned imperial eagle **Mint:** Joachimstal **Note:** Prev. KM#880.

Date	Mintage	VG	F	VF	XF	Unc
1615 (aj)	—	35.00	75.00	145	275	—
1617 (aj)	—	35.00	75.00	145	275	—
1618 (aj)	—	35.00	75.00	145	275	—

MB# 233 GROSCHEN

Silver **Ruler:** Rudolf II **Obv:** Bohemian lion left, titles of Rudolf II **Rev:** Crowned imperial eagle **Mint:** Kuttenberg **Note:** Varieties exist. Prev. KM#1020.

Date	Mintage	VG	F	VF	XF	Unc
1601 (y)	—	16.00	32.00	60.00	100	—
1602 (y)	—	16.00	32.00	60.00	100	—
1603 (z)	—	16.00	32.00	60.00	100	—
1604 (z)	—	16.00	32.00	60.00	100	—
1605 (z)	—	16.00	32.00	60.00	100	—
1608 (z)	—	16.00	32.00	60.00	100	—
1609 (z)	—	16.00	32.00	60.00	100	—
1609 (aa)	—	16.00	32.00	60.00	100	—
1610 (aa)	—	16.00	32.00	60.00	100	—

MB# 260 GROSCHEN

Silver **Ruler:** Rudolf II **Obv:** Bohemian lion left **Obv. Legend:** * RVDOL • II • D G - R • I • S • A • G • H • B O • R **Rev:** Crowned imperial eagle **Rev. Legend:** ARCHID • AVST • DVX • B • M • M • **Shape:** Square **Mint:** Kuttenberg **Note:** Klippe. Prev. KM#1021.

Date	Mintage	VG	F	VF	XF	Unc
1604 (z)	—	—	—	—	—	—

KM# 192 GROSCHEN

Silver **Ruler:** Matthias II **Obv:** Crowned Bohemian lion left **Rev:** Crowned imperial eagle **Mint:** Kuttenberg **Note:** Prev. KM#1052.

Date	Mintage	VG	F	VF	XF	Unc
1616 (dd)	—	12.00	25.00	40.00	75.00	—
1617 (ee)	—	12.00	25.00	40.00	75.00	—
1618 (ee)	—	12.00	25.00	40.00	75.00	—
1619 (ee)	—	12.00	25.00	40.00	75.00	—

MB# 251 GROSCHEN

Silver **Ruler:** Rudolf II **Obv:** Bohemian lion left, titles of Rudolf II **Rev:** Crowned imperial eagle **Mint:** Prague **Note:** Varieties exist. Prev. KM#1296.

Date	Mintage	VG	F	VF	XF	Unc
1601 (j)	—	20.00	35.00	55.00	90.00	—
1604 (j)	—	20.00	35.00	55.00	90.00	—
1605 (j)	—	20.00	35.00	55.00	90.00	—

KM# 155 GROSCHEN

Silver **Ruler:** Matthias II **Obv:** Crowned Bohemian lion left in circle, titles of Matthias **Rev:** Crowned imperial eagle, Austria-Burgundy arms on breast, date in legend **Mint:** Prague **Note:** Prev. KM#1383.

Date	Mintage	VG	F	VF	XF	Unc
1613 (l)	—	12.00	25.00	40.00	75.00	—
1615 (l)	—	12.00	25.00	40.00	75.00	—
1616 (l)	—	12.00	25.00	40.00	75.00	—
1617 (l)	—	12.00	25.00	40.00	75.00	—
1618 (l)	—	12.00	25.00	40.00	75.00	—
1619 (l)	—	12.00	25.00	40.00	75.00	—
ND (l)	—	12.00	25.00	40.00	75.00	—

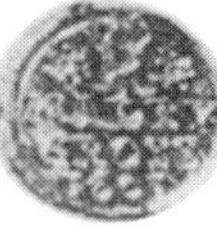

MB# 241 MALEY GROSCHEN

Silver **Ruler:** Rudolf II **Obv:** Crowned Bohemian lion left in circle, titles of Rudolf II **Rev:** Crowned R, value, and date **Mint:** Joachimstal **Note:** Prev. KM#861.

Date	Mintage	VG	F	VF	XF	Unc
1601 (ag)	—	5.00	10.00	22.00	45.00	—
1601 (ah)	—	5.00	10.00	22.00	45.00	—
1602 (ah)	—	5.00	10.00	22.00	45.00	—
ND (ag)	—	5.00	10.00	22.00	45.00	—
1603 (ah)	—	5.00	10.00	22.00	45.00	—
1604 (ah)	—	5.00	10.00	22.00	45.00	—
1606 (aj)	—	10.00	20.00	35.00	65.00	—
1607 (aj)	—	10.00	20.00	35.00	65.00	—
1608 (aj)	—	10.00	20.00	35.00	65.00	—
1609 (aj)	—	10.00	20.00	35.00	65.00	—
1610 (aj)	—	10.00	20.00	35.00	65.00	—
1611 (aj)	—	10.00	20.00	35.00	65.00	—
161Z (aj)	—	10.00	20.00	35.00	65.00	—

MB# 298 MALEY GROSCHEN

Silver **Ruler:** Rudolf II **Mint:** Joachimstal **Note:** Klippe. Prev. KM#864.

Date	Mintage	VG	F	VF	XF	Unc
1607 (aj)	—	—	—	—	—	—
1609 (aj)	—	—	—	—	—	—
1611 (aj)	—	—	—	—	—	—

KM# 47 MALEY GROSCHEN

Silver **Ruler:** Rudolf II **Rev:** Crowned R divides date, value below **Mint:** Joachimstal **Note:** Prev. KM#862.

Date	Mintage	VG	F	VF	XF	Unc
1604 (ai)	—	16.00	32.00	55.00	100	—
1605 (ai)	—	16.00	32.00	55.00	100	—
1606 (ai)	—	16.00	32.00	55.00	100	—

KM# 48 MALEY GROSCHEN

Silver **Ruler:** Rudolf II **Mint:** Joachimstal **Note:** Klippe. Prev. KM#863.

Date	Mintage	VG	F	VF	XF	Unc
1604 (ai)	—	—	—	—	—	—

KM# 111 MALEY GROSCHEN

Silver **Ruler:** Matthias II **Obv:** Crowned M divides date, value below **Mint:** Joachimstal **Note:** Prev. KM#879.

Date	Mintage	VG	F	VF	XF	Unc
1612 (aj)	—	30.00	60.00	125	245	—

KM# 203 MALEY GROSCHEN

Silver **Ruler:** Matthias II **Obv:** Crowned Bohemian lion left **Rev:** Crowned M divides date above value **Mint:** Joachimstal **Note:** Prev. KM#879.

Date	Mintage	VG	F	VF	XF	Unc
1617 (aj)	—	30.00	60.00	125	245	—
1618 (aj)	—	30.00	60.00	125	245	—
1619 (aj)	—	30.00	60.00	125	245	—

MB# 269 MALEY GROSCHEN

Silver **Ruler:** Rudolf II **Obv:** Bohemian lion rampant left in circle **Obv. Legend:** RVDOL.II.D.G.-R.I.S.A.G.H.B.R. **Rev:** Crowned 'R' between two floral ornaments, three-line inscription with date below. **Rev. Inscription:** MALEY/GROSS/(date) **Mint:** Kuttenberg **Note:** Klippe. Prev. KM#1019.

Date	Mintage	VG	F	VF	XF	Unc
1606 (z)	—	—	—	—	—	—
1607 (z)	—	—	—	—	—	—

MB# 250 MALEY GROSCHEN

Silver **Ruler:** Rudolf II **Obv:** Crowned Bohemian lion left in circle, titles of Rudolf II **Rev:** Crowned R, value, and date **Mint:** Kuttenberg **Note:** Varieties exist. Prev. KM#1018.

Date	Mintage	VG	F	VF	XF	Unc
1601 (y)	—	5.00	12.00	30.00	55.00	—
160Z (y)	—	5.00	12.00	30.00	55.00	—
1603 (y)	—	5.00	12.00	30.00	55.00	—
1603 (z)	—	4.00	8.00	20.00	38.00	—
1604 (z)	—	4.00	8.00	20.00	38.00	—
1605 (z)	—	4.00	8.00	20.00	38.00	—
1606 (z)	—	4.00	8.00	20.00	38.00	—
1607 (z)	—	4.00	8.00	20.00	38.00	—
1608 (aa)	—	4.00	8.00	20.00	38.00	—
1608 (z)	—	4.00	8.00	20.00	38.00	—
1609 (aa)	—	4.00	8.00	20.00	38.00	—
1610 (aa)	—	4.00	8.00	20.00	38.00	—
1611 (aa)	—	4.00	8.00	20.00	38.00	—
161Z	—	4.00	8.00	20.00	38.00	—

KM# 76 MALEY GROSCHEN

Silver **Ruler:** Rudolf II **Mint:** Kuttenberg **Note:** Klippe. Prev. KM#1019.

Date	Mintage	VG	F	VF	XF	Unc
1606	—	—	—	—	—	—
1607	—	—	—	—	—	—

KM# 110 MALEY GROSCHEN

Silver **Ruler:** Matthias II **Obv:** Crowned Bohemian lion left in circle, titles of Matthias **Rev:** Crowned M above value, date **Mint:** Kuttenberg **Note:** Prev. KM#1051.

Date	Mintage	VG	F	VF	XF	Unc
1612 (bb)	—	12.00	22.00	40.00	85.00	—
1613 (bb)	—	12.00	22.00	40.00	85.00	—
1614 (bb)	—	12.00	22.00	40.00	85.00	—

KM# 153 MALEY GROSCHEN

Silver **Ruler:** Matthias II **Obv:** Crowned Bohemian lion left **Rev:** Crowned M divides date above value **Mint:** Kuttenberg **Note:** Prev. KM#1051.

Date	Mintage	VG	F	VF	XF	Unc
1613 (ee)	—	10.00	20.00	35.00	65.00	—
1615 (ee)	—	10.00	20.00	35.00	65.00	—
1617 (ee)	—	10.00	20.00	35.00	65.00	—
1618 (ee)	—	10.00	20.00	35.00	65.00	—
1619 (ee)	—	10.00	20.00	35.00	65.00	—

MB# 240 MALEY GROSCHEN

Silver **Ruler:** Rudolf II **Obv:** Crowned Bohemian lion left in circle, titles of Rudolf II **Rev:** Crowned R, value, and date **Mint:** Prague **Note:** Prev. KM#1295.

Date	Mintage	VG	F	VF	XF	Unc
1601 (j)	—	14.00	22.50	42.00	85.00	—
160Z (j)	—	14.00	22.50	42.00	85.00	—
1604 (j)	—	14.00	22.50	42.00	85.00	—
1605 (j)	—	14.00	22.50	42.00	85.00	—
1606 (j)	—	14.00	22.50	42.00	85.00	—
1609 (j)	—	14.00	22.50	42.00	85.00	—
1609 (k)	—	14.00	22.50	42.00	85.00	—

KM# 75 MALEY GROSCHEN

Silver **Ruler:** Rudolf II **Obv:** Crowned Bohemian lion left in circle, titles of Rudolf II **Rev. Legend:** ZVM / NEVEN / IAHR / date **Mint:** Prague **Note:** New Year Commemorative

Date	Mintage	VG	F	VF	XF	Unc
1606 (j)	—	—	—	—	—	—

KM# 177 MALEY GROSCHEN

Silver **Ruler:** Matthias II **Obv:** Crowned Bohemian lion left **Rev:** Crowned M **Mint:** Prague **Note:** Prev. KM#1325.

Date	Mintage	VG	F	VF	XF	Unc
1615 (l)	—	38.00	75.00	150	250	—
1616 (l)	—	38.00	75.00	150	250	—
1617 (l)	—	38.00	75.00	150	250	—

KM# 191 MALEY GROSCHEN

Silver **Ruler:** Matthias II **Obv:** Crowned Bohemian lion left **Rev:** Crowned M divides date above value **Mint:** Prague **Note:** Prev. KM#1326.

Date	Mintage	VG	F	VF	XF	Unc
1616	—	35.00	60.00	120	200	—
1617	—	35.00	60.00	120	200	—
1617 (l)	—	35.00	60.00	120	200	—
1618 (l)	—	35.00	60.00	120	200	—
1619	—	35.00	60.00	120	200	—

KM# 233 1/4 KREUZER

Silver **Ruler:** Ferdinand II **Obv:** Bohemian lion arms divide date in rhombus **Mint:** Kuttenberg **Note:** Uniface. Prev. KM#1066.

Date	Mintage	VG	F	VF	XF	Unc
1620	—	30.00	40.00	75.00	135	—
1623	—	30.00	40.00	75.00	135	—
1624	—	30.00	40.00	75.00	135	—
1625	—	30.00	40.00	75.00	135	—
1626	—	30.00	40.00	75.00	135	—
1628	—	30.00	40.00	75.00	135	—
1629	—	30.00	40.00	75.00	135	—
1630	—	30.00	40.00	75.00	135	—
1633	—	30.00	40.00	75.00	135	—

KM# 280 1/4 KREUZER

Silver **Ruler:** Matthias II **Obv:** Crowned Bohemian lion left, 4 below, all in circle **Rev. Legend:** FER. II. D.G. R.B., date **Mint:** Kuttenberg **Note:** Uniface. Prev. KM#1065.

Date	Mintage	VG	F	VF	XF	Unc
16Z1	—	35.00	80.00	150	225	—
16Z1 (ee)	—	35.00	80.00	150	225	—
16ZZ	—	35.00	80.00	150	225	—

KM# 442 1/4 KREUZER

Silver **Ruler:** Ferdinand III **Obv:** Bohemian lion arms divide date in rhombus **Mint:** Kuttenberg **Note:** Prev. KM#1100.

Date	Mintage	VG	F	VF	XF	Unc
1640	—	25.00	50.00	90.00	150	—
1654	—	25.00	50.00	90.00	150	—

KM# 387 1/2 KREUZER

Silver **Ruler:** Ferdinand II **Obv:** Date above crown over two adjacent arms of imperial eagle and Bohemian lion **Mint:** Joachimstal **Note:** Uniface. Prev. KM#890.

Date	Mintage	VG	F	VF	XF	Unc
1626 (ak)	—	65.00	120	185	300	—
1629 (ak)	—	65.00	120	185	300	—

KM# 443 1/2 KREUZER

Silver **Ruler:** Ferdinand III **Obv:** Date above crown over two adjacent arms of imperial eagle and Bohemian lion **Mint:** Joachimstal **Note:** Prev. KM#910.

Date	Mintage	VG	F	VF	XF	Unc
1640 (al)	—	—	—	—	—	—

KM# 477 1/2 KREUZER

Silver **Ruler:** Ferdinand III **Obv:** Crowned Bohemian lion left, F-III divided above, date to right **Mint:** Joachimstal **Note:** Prev. KM#911.

Date	Mintage	VG	F	VF	XF	Unc
1651	—	100	175	275	—	—
1652 (an)	—	100	175	275	—	—

KM# 281 1/2 KREUZER

Silver **Ruler:** Ferdinand II **Obv:** Rampant lion left **Mint:** Kuttenberg **Note:** Prev. KM#1067.

Date	Mintage	VG	F	VF	XF	Unc
1621	—	25.00	50.00	90.00	150	—

KM# 321 1/2 KREUZER

Silver **Ruler:** Ferdinand II **Obv:** Crowned Bohemian lion left in trelobe divides F-II, date below **Mint:** Kuttenberg **Note:** Uniface. Prev. KM#1068.

Date	Mintage	VG	F	VF	XF	Unc
1622	—	25.00	50.00	90.00	150	—
1623	—	25.00	50.00	90.00	150	—

KM# 340 1/2 KREUZER

Silver **Ruler:** Ferdinand II **Obv:** Date above crown over two adjacent arms of imperial eagle and Bohemian lion **Mint:** Kuttenberg **Note:** Prev. KM#1069.

Date	Mintage	VG	F	VF	XF	Unc
1623	—	20.00	50.00	90.00	135	—
1624	—	20.00	50.00	90.00	135	—
1626	—	20.00	50.00	90.00	135	—
1627	—	20.00	50.00	90.00	135	—
1628	—	20.00	50.00	90.00	135	—
1629	—	20.00	50.00	90.00	135	—
1630	—	20.00	50.00	90.00	135	—
1631	—	20.00	50.00	90.00	135	—
1632	—	20.00	50.00	90.00	135	—
1633	—	20.00	50.00	90.00	135	—
1634	—	20.00	50.00	90.00	135	—

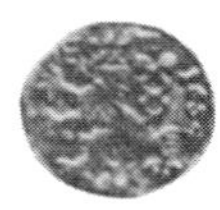

KM# 479 1/2 KREUZER

Silver **Ruler:** Ferdinand III **Obv:** Crowned Bohemian lion left, F-III divided above, date to right **Mint:** Kuttenberg **Note:** Prev. KM#1101.

Date	Mintage	VG	F	VF	XF	Unc
1654 (ii)	—	20.00	40.00	70.00	180	—
1656 (ii)	—	20.00	40.00	70.00	180	—

KM# 490 1/2 KREUZER

Silver **Ruler:** Leopold I **Obv:** Crowned Bohemian lion left **Mint:** Kuttenberg **Note:** Uniface. Varieties exist. Prev. KM#1115.

Date	Mintage	VG	F	VF	XF	Unc
1661 (ii)	—	4.00	9.00	18.00	30.00	—
1663 (ii)	—	4.00	9.00	18.00	30.00	—
1667 (ii)	—	4.00	9.00	18.00	30.00	—
1668 (ii)	—	4.00	9.00	18.00	30.00	—
1669 (ii)	—	4.00	9.00	18.00	30.00	—
1670 (ii)	—	4.00	9.00	18.00	30.00	—
1674 (ii)	—	4.00	9.00	18.00	30.00	—
1675 (ii)	—	4.00	9.00	18.00	30.00	—
1678 (jj)	—	4.00	9.00	18.00	30.00	—
1680 (jj)	—	4.00	9.00	18.00	30.00	—
1681 (jj)	—	4.00	9.00	18.00	30.00	—
1683 (jj)	—	4.00	9.00	18.00	30.00	—
1686 (jj)	—	4.00	9.00	18.00	30.00	—
1688 (jj)	—	4.00	9.00	18.00	30.00	—
1689 (jj)	—	4.00	9.00	18.00	30.00	—
1690 (jj)	—	4.00	9.00	18.00	30.00	—
1691 (jj)	—	4.00	9.00	18.00	30.00	—
1692 (jj)	—	4.00	9.00	18.00	30.00	—
1693 (jj)	—	4.00	9.00	18.00	30.00	—
1694 (jj)	—	4.00	9.00	18.00	30.00	—
1696 (jj)	—	4.00	9.00	18.00	30.00	—
1697 (jj)	—	4.00	9.00	18.00	30.00	—
1698 (jj)	—	4.00	9.00	18.00	30.00	—
1699 (jj)	—	4.00	9.00	18.00	30.00	—
1700 (jj)	—	4.00	9.00	18.00	30.00	—

KM# 385 1/2 KREUZER

Silver **Ruler:** Ferdinand II **Obv:** Date above crown over two adjacent arms of imperial eagle and Bohemian lion, all in trefoil **Mint:** Prague **Note:** Uniface. Prev. KM#1365.

Date	Mintage	VG	F	VF	XF	Unc
1626 (l)	—	10.00	20.00	40.00	70.00	—

KM# 388 1/2 KREUZER

Silver **Ruler:** Ferdinand I **Obv:** Crown above two shields of arms, date above crown **Mint:** Prague **Note:** Uniface.

Date	Mintage	VG	F	VF	XF	Unc
1626 (e)	—	—	—	—	—	—
1629 (e)	—	—	—	—	—	—

KM# 386 1/2 KREUZER

Silver **Ruler:** Ferdinand II **Obv:** Three-digit date at bottom **Mint:** Prague **Note:** Prev. KM#1366.

Date	Mintage	VG	F	VF	XF	Unc
1628	—	5.00	10.00	22.00	45.00	—

KM# 483 1/2 KREUZER

Silver **Ruler:** Ferdinand III **Obv:** Crowned Bohemian lion left, F-III divided above, date to right **Mint:** Prague **Note:** Prev. KM#1405.

Date	Mintage	VG	F	VF	XF	Unc
1655 (r)	—	20.00	40.00	70.00	180	—

KM# 484 1/2 KREUZER

Silver **Ruler:** Leopold I **Obv:** Crowned L divides date, mintmaster's symbol and "1/2" all in laurel wreath **Mint:** Prague **Note:** Prev. KM#1425.

Date	Mintage	VG	F	VF	XF	Unc
1658 (r)	—	5.00	10.00	20.00	40.00	—
1661 (r)	—	5.00	10.00	20.00	40.00	—
1662 (r)	—	5.00	10.00	20.00	40.00	—
1663 (r)	—	5.00	10.00	20.00	40.00	—

KM# 560 1/2 KREUZER

Silver **Ruler:** Leopold I **Obv:** Two adjacent shields, L and first half of date in left, Bohemian lion and last half of date in right, crown above, "1/2" in center, mintmaster's symbol below **Mint:** Prague **Note:** Prev. KM#1425.

Date	Mintage	VG	F	VF	XF	Unc
1665 (r)	—	6.00	12.00	25.00	50.00	—

KM# 602 1/2 KREUZER

Silver **Ruler:** Leopold I **Obv:** Crowned rampant lion left, "L-I" divided by lion's head, date down right side **Mint:** Prague **Note:** Uniface. Varieties exist. Prev. KM#1425.

Date	Mintage	VG	F	VF	XF	Unc
1695 GE	—	5.00	10.00	20.00	40.00	—
1698 GE	—	5.00	10.00	20.00	40.00	—
1699 GE	—	5.00	10.00	20.00	40.00	—
1700 GE	—	5.00	10.00	20.00	40.00	—

KM# 368 KREUZER

Silver **Ruler:** Ferdinand II **Obv:** Crowned imperial eagle, value on breast in inner circle **Rev:** Rampant lion left in inner circle, date in legend **Mint:** Joachimstal **Note:** Prev. KM#891.

Date	Mintage	VG	F	VF	XF	Unc
1624 (ak)	—	10.00	20.00	35.00	65.00	—
1627 (ak)	—	10.00	20.00	35.00	65.00	—
1634 (ak)	—	10.00	20.00	35.00	65.00	—

KM# 444 KREUZER

Silver **Ruler:** Ferdinand III **Obv:** Head of Ferdinand III right in inner circle **Rev:** Crowned imperial eagle in inner circle, date in legend **Mint:** Joachimstal **Note:** Prev. KM#912.

Date	Mintage	VG	F	VF	XF	Unc
1640 (al)	—	35.00	65.00	125	200	—
1641 (al)	—	35.00	65.00	125	200	—
1643 (al)	—	35.00	65.00	125	200	—
1646	—	35.00	65.00	125	200	—

KM# 446 KREUZER

Silver **Ruler:** Ferdinand III **Obv:** Laureate bust of Ferdinand III **Rev:** Crowned imperial eagle **Mint:** Joachimstal **Note:** Prev. KM#913.

Date	Mintage	VG	F	VF	XF	Unc
1640 (al)	—	40.00	75.00	145	225	—
1651 (an)	—	40.00	75.00	145	225	—
1652 (an)	—	40.00	75.00	145	225	—
1653 (an)	—	40.00	75.00	145	225	—

KM# 550 KREUZER

Silver **Ruler:** Leopold I **Obv:** Laureate bust of Leopold I, value below **Rev:** Crowned imperial eagle **Mint:** Joachimstal **Note:** Prev. KM#930.

Date	Mintage	VG	F	VF	XF	Unc
1660 (an)	—	75.00	135	225	—	—

KM# 322 KREUZER

Silver **Ruler:** Ferdinand II **Obv:** Crowned Bohemian lion left in circle, titles of Ferdinand II and date **Rev:** Imperial eagle in circle, orb on breast with "1" **Mint:** Kuttenberg **Note:** Known struck on thick flan. Prev. KM#1070.

Date	Mintage	VG	F	VF	XF	Unc
1622	—	25.00	45.00	80.00	150	—

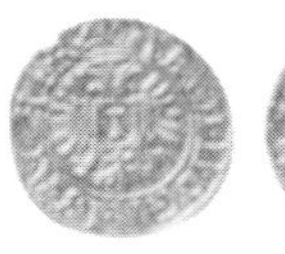 

KM# 367 KREUZER

Silver **Ruler:** Ferdinand II **Obv:** Crowned imperial eagle, "I" in shield on breast, titles of Ferdinand II **Rev:** Crowned Bohemian lion left in circle, date in legend **Mint:** Kuttenberg **Note:** Prev. KM#1071.

Date	Mintage	VG	F	VF	XF	Unc
1624 (ee)	—	10.00	20.00	35.00	65.00	—
1625 (ee)	—	10.00	20.00	35.00	65.00	—
1627 (ee)	—	10.00	20.00	35.00	65.00	—

KM# 393 KREUZER

Silver **Ruler:** Ferdinand II **Obv:** Laureate bust right, titles of Ferdinand II **Rev:** Crowned imperial eagle, "I" in shield on breast, date in legend **Mint:** Kuttenberg **Note:** Prev. KM#1072.

Date	Mintage	VG	F	VF	XF	Unc
1627 (ee)	—	35.00	60.00	125	250	—

KM# 480 KREUZER

Silver **Ruler:** Ferdinand III **Obv:** Laureate bust of Ferdinand III **Rev:** Crowned imperial eagle **Mint:** Kuttenberg **Note:** Prev. KM#1102.

Date	Mintage	VG	F	VF	XF	Unc
1654 (ii)	—	50.00	90.00	175	250	—

KM# 485 KREUZER

Silver **Ruler:** Leopold I **Obv:** Young laureate bust right, "1" below **Rev:** Crowned imperial eagle **Mint:** Kuttenberg **Note:** Prev. KM#1116.

Date	Mintage	VG	F	VF	XF	Unc
1659 (ii)	—	7.00	15.00	30.00	65.00	—
1660 (ii)	—	7.00	15.00	30.00	65.00	—
1661 (ii)	—	7.00	15.00	30.00	65.00	—
1663 (ii)	—	7.00	15.00	30.00	65.00	—
1664 (ii)	—	7.00	15.00	30.00	65.00	—
1665 (ii)	—	7.00	15.00	30.00	65.00	—
1666 (ii)	—	7.00	15.00	30.00	65.00	—
1667 (ii)	—	7.00	15.00	30.00	65.00	—
1668 (ii)	—	7.00	15.00	30.00	65.00	—
1671 (ii)	—	7.00	15.00	30.00	65.00	—
1672 (ii)	—	7.00	15.00	30.00	65.00	—
1675	—	7.00	15.00	30.00	65.00	—

KM# 582 KREUZER

Silver **Ruler:** Leopold I **Obv:** Older laureate bust right, "1" below **Rev:** Crowned imperial eagle, crown divides date **Mint:** Kuttenberg **Note:** Varieties exist. Prev. KM#1117.

Date	Mintage	VG	F	VF	XF	Unc
1680 (jj)	—	7.00	15.00	30.00	65.00	—
1681 (jj)	—	7.00	15.00	30.00	65.00	—
1683 (jj)	—	7.00	15.00	30.00	65.00	—

Date	Mintage	VG	F	VF	XF	Unc
1684 (jj)	—	7.00	15.00	30.00	65.00	—
1686 (jj)	—	7.00	15.00	30.00	65.00	—
1687 (jj)	—	7.00	15.00	30.00	65.00	—
1688 (jj)	—	7.00	15.00	30.00	65.00	—
1689 (jj)	—	7.00	15.00	30.00	65.00	—
1690 (jj)	—	7.00	15.00	30.00	65.00	—
1691 (jj)	—	7.00	15.00	30.00	65.00	—
1692 (jj)	—	7.00	15.00	30.00	65.00	—
1693 (jj)	—	7.00	15.00	30.00	65.00	—
1694 (jj)	—	7.00	15.00	30.00	65.00	—
1696 (jj)	—	7.00	15.00	30.00	65.00	—
1697 (jj)	—	7.00	15.00	30.00	65.00	—
1698 (jj)	—	7.00	15.00	30.00	65.00	—
1699 (jj)	—	7.00	15.00	30.00	65.00	—
1700 (jj)	—	7.00	15.00	30.00	65.00	—

KM# 604 KREUZER

Silver **Ruler:** Leopold I **Rev:** Date divided by crown and legend **Rev. Legend:** BOEMISCHE - LAND. MVN(T)Z **Mint:** Kuttenberg

Date	Mintage	VG	F	VF	XF	Unc
1695 (ll)	—	—	—	—	—	—

KM# 392 KREUZER

Silver **Ruler:** Ferdinand II **Obv:** Laureate bust right, titles of Ferdinand II **Rev:** Crowned imperial eagle, "I" in shield on breast, date in legend **Mint:** Prague **Note:** Prev. KM#1367.

Date	Mintage	VG	F	VF	XF	Unc
1624 (e)	—	10.00	20.00	35.00	65.00	—
1627 (l)	—	10.00	20.00	35.00	65.00	—
1637 (q)	—	10.00	20.00	35.00	65.00	—

KM# 411 KREUZER

Silver **Ruler:** Ferdinand III **Obv:** Bust right, value (I) below, titles of Ferdinand III **Rev:** Crowned imperial eagle, Bohemian arms on breast, date in legend **Mint:** Prague **Note:** Prev. KM#1406.

Date	Mintage	VG	F	VF	XF	Unc
1637	—	25.00	45.00	75.00	135	—
1638 (q)	—	25.00	45.00	75.00	135	—
1639 (q)	—	25.00	45.00	75.00	135	—
1640 (q)	—	25.00	45.00	75.00	135	—
1642 (q)	—	25.00	45.00	75.00	135	—

KM# 408 KREUZER

Silver **Ruler:** Ferdinand III **Obv:** KM#411 **Rev:** KM#392 **Mint:** Prague **Note:** Mule.

Date	Mintage	VG	F	VF	XF	Unc
1637	—	—	—	—	—	—

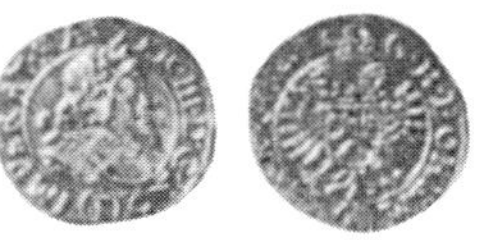

KM# 445 KREUZER

Silver **Ruler:** Ferdinand III **Obv:** Laureate bust of Ferdinand III **Rev:** Crowned imperial eagle **Mint:** Prague **Note:** Prev. KM#1407.

Date	Mintage	VG	F	VF	XF	Unc
1639 (q)	—	15.00	30.00	60.00	100	—
1641 (q)	—	15.00	30.00	60.00	100	—
1642 (q)	—	15.00	30.00	60.00	100	—
1645 (q)	—	15.00	30.00	60.00	100	—
1646 (q)	—	15.00	30.00	60.00	100	—
1653 (q)	—	15.00	30.00	60.00	100	—

KM# 491 KREUZER

Silver **Ruler:** Leopold I **Obv:** Young laureate bust right, value "1" in oval below, titles of Leopold I **Rev:** Crowned imperial eagle, oval Bohemian arms on breast, date in legend **Mint:** Prague **Note:** Prev. KM#1427.

Date	Mintage	VG	F	VF	XF	Unc
1659 (r)	—	7.00	15.00	30.00	65.00	—
1660 (r)	—	7.00	15.00	30.00	65.00	—
1663 (r)	—	7.00	15.00	30.00	65.00	—
1670 (s)	—	7.00	15.00	30.00	65.00	—
1673 (s)	—	7.00	15.00	30.00	65.00	—

KM# 605 KREUZER

Silver **Ruler:** Leopold I **Rev. Legend:** BOEMISCHE - LANDMVNTZ **Mint:** Prague

Date	Mintage	VG	F	VF	XF	Unc
1695 GE	—	—	—	—	—	—

KM# 603 KREUZER

Silver **Ruler:** Leopold I **Obv:** Young laureate bust right with long wig, value in oval below, titles of Leopold I **Rev:** Crowned imperial eagle holding sword and scepter in talons, oval Bohemian arms on breast, date divided by crown **Mint:** Prague **Note:** Varieties exist. Prev. KM#1427.

Date	Mintage	VG	F	VF	XF	Unc
1695 GE	—	6.00	12.00	25.00	50.00	—
1696 GE	—	6.00	12.00	25.00	50.00	—
1697 GE	—	6.00	12.00	25.00	50.00	—
1698 GE	—	6.00	12.00	25.00	50.00	—
1699 GE	—	6.00	12.00	25.00	50.00	—
1700 GE	—	6.00	12.00	25.00	50.00	—

KM# 204 3 KREUZER

Silver **Ruler:** Matthias II **Mint:** Joachimstal **Note:** Titles of Matthias. Prev. KM#881.

Date	Mintage	VG	F	VF	XF	Unc
1617	—	30.00	65.00	135	265	—
1618	—	30.00	65.00	135	265	—

KM# 283 3 KREUZER

Silver **Ruler:** Ferdinand II **Obv:** Imperial eagle **Rev:** Rampant lion left **Mint:** Joachimstal **Note:** Prev. KM#892.

Date	Mintage	VG	F	VF	XF	Unc
1621	—	12.00	25.00	50.00	90.00	—

KM# 327 3 KREUZER

Silver **Ruler:** Ferdinand II **Obv:** Laureate bust in inner circle, value below **Rev:** Crowned imperial eagle in inner circle, date in legend **Mint:** Joachimstal **Note:** Prev. KM#893.

Date	Mintage	VG	F	VF	XF	Unc
1622 (e)	—	10.00	20.00	40.00	75.00	—
1623 (E)	—	10.00	20.00	40.00	75.00	—

KM# 193 3 KREUZER

Silver **Ruler:** Matthias II **Obv:** Crowned rampant lion **Rev:** Crowned imperial eagle **Mint:** Kuttenberg **Note:** Varieties exist. Prev. KM#1050.

Date	Mintage	VG	F	VF	XF	Unc
1616	—	20.00	35.00	65.00	110	—
1617	—	20.00	35.00	65.00	110	—
1618	—	20.00	35.00	65.00	110	—
1619	—	20.00	35.00	65.00	110	—

KM# 394 3 KREUZER

Silver **Ruler:** Ferdinand II **Mint:** Kuttenberg **Note:** Klippe. Prev. KM#1077.

Date	Mintage	VG	F	VF	XF	Unc
1637	—	—	—	—	—	—

KM# 415 3 KREUZER

Silver **Ruler:** Ferdinand II **Obv:** Bare head **Mint:** Kuttenberg **Note:** Prev. KM#1103.

Date	Mintage	VG	F	VF	XF	Unc
1638	—	15.00	27.00	45.00	85.00	—
1639	—	15.00	27.00	45.00	85.00	—
1640	—	15.00	27.00	45.00	85.00	—
1641	—	15.00	27.00	45.00	85.00	—

KM# 606 3 KREUZER

Silver **Ruler:** Leopold I **Obv:** Laureate bust right in inner circle **Mint:** Kuttenberg **Note:** Varieties exist. Prev. KM#1120.

Date	Mintage	VG	F	VF	XF	Unc
1695 (jj)	—	7.00	12.00	25.00	55.00	—
1696 (jj)	—	7.00	12.00	25.00	55.00	—
1697 (jj)	—	7.00	12.00	25.00	55.00	—
1698 (jj)	—	7.00	12.00	25.00	55.00	—
1699 (jj)	—	7.00	12.00	25.00	55.00	—
1700 (jj)	—	7.00	12.00	25.00	55.00	—

KM# 590 3 KREUZER

Silver **Ruler:** Leopold I **Obv:** Bust left in long wig **Rev:** Crowned imperial arms with sword and scepter **Mint:** Prague **Note:** Varieties exist. Prev. KM#1430.

Date	Mintage	VG	F	VF	XF	Unc
1688 MV	—	10.00	22.00	40.00	75.00	—
1691 MV	—	10.00	22.00	40.00	75.00	—
1693 MV	—	10.00	22.00	40.00	75.00	—
1694 MV	—	10.00	22.00	40.00	75.00	—
1694 PM	—	10.00	22.00	40.00	75.00	—
1694 GE	—	7.00	15.00	30.00	60.00	—
1695 GE	—	7.00	15.00	30.00	60.00	—
1696 GE	—	7.00	15.00	30.00	60.00	—
1697 GE	—	7.00	15.00	30.00	60.00	—
1698 GE	—	7.00	15.00	30.00	60.00	—
1699 GE	—	7.00	15.00	30.00	60.00	—
1700 GE	—	7.00	15.00	30.00	60.00	—

KM# 326 3 KREUZER (Groschen)

Silver **Ruler:** Ferdinand II **Obv:** Laureate bust in inner circle, value below **Rev:** Crowned imperial eagle in inner circle, date in legend **Mint:** Joachimstal **Note:** Prev. KM#893.

Date	Mintage	VG	F	VF	XF	Unc
1622 (ak)	—	—	—	—	—	—
1623 (ak)	—	—	—	—	—	—

KM# 371 3 KREUZER (Groschen)

Silver **Ruler:** Ferdinand II **Rev:** Crowned imperial eagle, value below **Mint:** Joachimstal **Note:** Prev. KM#894. Varieties exist.

Date	Mintage	VG	F	VF	XF	Unc
1624 (ak)	—	7.00	15.00	28.00	55.00	—
1625 (ak)	—	7.00	15.00	28.00	55.00	—
1626 (ak)	—	7.00	15.00	28.00	55.00	—
1627 (ak)	—	7.00	15.00	28.00	55.00	—
1628 (ak)	—	7.00	15.00	28.00	55.00	—
1629 (ak)	—	7.00	15.00	28.00	55.00	—
1630 (ak)	—	7.00	15.00	28.00	55.00	—
1631 (ak)	—	7.00	15.00	28.00	55.00	—
1632 (ak)	—	7.00	15.00	28.00	55.00	—
1633 (ak)	—	7.00	15.00	28.00	55.00	—
1634 (ak)	—	7.00	15.00	28.00	55.00	—
1635 (ak)	—	7.00	15.00	28.00	55.00	—
1636 (ak)	—	7.00	15.00	28.00	55.00	—
1637 (ak)	—	7.00	15.00	28.00	55.00	—

KM# 414 3 KREUZER (Groschen)

Silver **Ruler:** Ferdinand III **Obv:** Head right in inner circle, value (3) below **Rev:** Crowned imperial eagle, date in legend **Mint:** Joachimstal **Note:** Prev. KM#914.

Date	Mintage	VG	F	VF	XF	Unc
1638 (al)	—	35.00	70.00	125	225	—
1639 (al)	—	35.00	70.00	125	225	—
1640 (al)	—	35.00	70.00	125	225	—
1641 (al)	—	35.00	70.00	125	225	—
1642 (al)	—	35.00	70.00	125	225	—
1643 (al)	—	35.00	70.00	125	225	—

KM# 464 3 KREUZER (Groschen)

Silver **Ruler:** Ferdinand III **Obv:** Laureate head right in inner circle, value below **Rev:** Crowned imperial eagle, date in legend **Mint:** Joachimstal **Note:** Prev. KM#915. Varieties exist.

Date	Mintage	VG	F	VF	XF	Unc
1643 (al)	—	30.00	55.00	110	200	—
1644 (al)	—	30.00	55.00	110	200	—
1645 (al)	—	30.00	55.00	110	200	—
1646 (al)	—	30.00	55.00	110	200	—
1647 (al)	—	30.00	55.00	110	200	—
1648 (al)	—	30.00	55.00	110	200	—
1649 (am)	—	30.00	55.00	110	200	—
1650 (am)	—	30.00	55.00	110	200	—
1651 (an)	—	30.00	55.00	110	200	—
1654 (an)	—	30.00	55.00	110	200	—
1657 (an)	—	30.00	55.00	110	200	—

KM# 492 3 KREUZER (Groschen)

Silver **Ruler:** Leopold I **Obv:** Laureate bust of Leopold I right, value below **Rev:** Crowned imperial eagle **Mint:** Joachimstal **Note:** Prev. KM#931.

Date	Mintage	VG	F	VF	XF	Unc
1659 (an)	—	35.00	65.00	115	185	—
1660 (an)	—	35.00	65.00	115	185	—
1663 (an)	—	35.00	65.00	115	185	—

KM# 234 3 KREUZER (Groschen)

Silver **Ruler:** Ferdinand II **Obv:** Crowned imperial eagle, value (3) below, Austria-Burgundy arms on breast, titles of Ferdinand II **Rev:** Crowned Bohemian lion left in circle, date in legend **Mint:** Kuttenberg **Note:** Prev. KM#1073.

Date	Mintage	VG	F	VF	XF	Unc
1620 (ee)	—	15.00	30.00	50.00	90.00	—
1621 (ee)	—	15.00	30.00	50.00	90.00	—

KM# 325 3 KREUZER (Groschen)

Silver **Ruler:** Ferdinand II **Obv:** Laureate bust right, value (3) below, titles of Ferdinand II **Rev:** Crowned imperial eagle, Austria-Burgundy arms on breast, date in legend **Mint:** Kuttenberg **Note:** Prev. KM#1074.

Date	Mintage	VG	F	VF	XF	Unc
1622	—	15.00	30.00	50.00	90.00	—
1622 (ee)	—	15.00	30.00	50.00	90.00	—

KM# 370 3 KREUZER (Groschen)

Silver **Ruler:** Ferdinand II **Obv:** Bust right in ruffled collar **Rev:** Crowned imperial eagle **Mint:** Kuttenberg **Note:** Prev. KM#1075.

Date	Mintage	VG	F	VF	XF	Unc
1624 (ee)	—	7.00	12.00	25.00	55.00	—
1625 (ee)	—	7.00	12.00	25.00	55.00	—
1626 (ee)	—	7.00	12.00	25.00	55.00	—
1627 (ee)	—	7.00	12.00	25.00	55.00	—
1628 (ee)	—	7.00	12.00	25.00	55.00	—
1629 (ee)	—	7.00	12.00	25.00	55.00	—
1630 (ee)	—	7.00	12.00	25.00	55.00	—
1631 (ee)	—	7.00	12.00	25.00	55.00	—
1631	—	7.00	12.00	25.00	55.00	—
1632 (ee)	—	7.00	12.00	25.00	55.00	—
1633	—	7.00	12.00	25.00	55.00	—
1633 (dd)	—	7.00	12.00	25.00	55.00	—
1633 (ee)	—	7.00	12.00	25.00	55.00	—
1633 (ff)	—	7.00	12.00	25.00	55.00	—
1634 (dd)	—	7.00	12.00	25.00	55.00	—
1634 (ff)	—	7.00	12.00	25.00	55.00	—

KM# 405 3 KREUZER (Groschen)

Silver **Ruler:** Ferdinand II **Mint:** Kuttenberg **Note:** Prev. KM#1076. Varieties exist.

Date	Mintage	VG	F	VF	XF	Unc
1635 (dd)	—	7.00	12.00	25.00	55.00	—
1636 (hh)	—	7.00	12.00	25.00	55.00	—
1637 (hh)	—	7.00	12.00	25.00	55.00	—

KM# 413 3 KREUZER (Groschen)

Silver **Ruler:** Ferdinand III **Obv:** Bust of Ferdinand III right **Rev:** Crowned imperial eagle **Mint:** Kuttenberg **Note:** Prev. KM#1076.

Date	Mintage	VG	F	VF	XF	Unc
1638 (hh)	—	7.00	12.00	25.00	55.00	—
1639 (hh)	—	7.00	12.00	25.00	55.00	—
1640 (hh)	—	7.00	12.00	25.00	55.00	—
1641 (hh)	—	7.00	12.00	25.00	55.00	—

KM# 449 3 KREUZER (Groschen)

Silver **Ruler:** Ferdinand III **Obv:** Laureate bust of Ferdinand III right **Rev:** Crowned imperial eagle **Mint:** Kuttenberg **Note:** Prev. KM#1104 and #1105. Varieties exist.

Date	Mintage	VG	F	VF	XF	Unc
1641 (hh)	—	12.00	22.00	40.00	65.00	—
1642 (hh)	—	12.00	22.00	40.00	65.00	—
1654 (ii)	—	12.00	22.00	40.00	65.00	—
1655 (ii)	—	12.00	22.00	40.00	65.00	—
1656 (ii)	—	12.00	22.00	40.00	65.00	—
1657 (ii)	—	12.00	22.00	40.00	65.00	—

KM# 487 3 KREUZER (Groschen)

Silver **Ruler:** Leopold I **Obv:** Laureate bust right **Rev:** Crowned imperial eagle **Mint:** Kuttenberg **Note:** Prev. KM#1118.

Date	Mintage	VG	F	VF	XF	Unc
1658 (ii)	—	8.00	16.00	32.00	60.00	—
1659 (ii)	—	8.00	16.00	32.00	60.00	—
1660 (ii)	—	8.00	16.00	32.00	60.00	—
1661 (ii)	—	8.00	16.00	32.00	60.00	—
1662 (ii)	—	8.00	16.00	32.00	60.00	—
1663 (ii)	—	8.00	16.00	32.00	60.00	—
1664 (ii)	—	8.00	16.00	32.00	60.00	—
1665 (ii)	—	8.00	16.00	32.00	60.00	—
1666 (ii)	—	8.00	16.00	32.00	60.00	—
1667 (ii)	—	8.00	16.00	32.00	60.00	—
1668 (ii)	—	8.00	16.00	32.00	60.00	—
1669 (ii)	—	8.00	16.00	32.00	60.00	—

KM# 568 3 KREUZER (Groschen)

Silver **Ruler:** Leopold I **Obv:** Large laureate bust right **Mint:** Kuttenberg **Note:** Prev. KM#1119.

Date	Mintage	VG	F	VF	XF	Unc
1670 (ii)	—	8.00	16.00	32.00	60.00	—
1671 (ii)	—	8.00	16.00	32.00	60.00	—
1673 (ii)	—	8.00	16.00	32.00	60.00	—
1675 (ii)	—	8.00	16.00	32.00	60.00	—
1676 (ii)	—	8.00	16.00	32.00	60.00	—
1677 (ii)	—	8.00	16.00	32.00	60.00	—
1678 (jj)	—	8.00	16.00	32.00	60.00	—
1679 (jj)	—	8.00	16.00	32.00	60.00	—

KM# 580 3 KREUZER (Groschen)

Silver **Ruler:** Leopold I **Obv:** Large laureate bust right **Rev:** Crowned imperial arms **Mint:** Kuttenberg **Note:** Prev. KM#1120.

Date	Mintage	VG	F	VF	XF	Unc
1679 (jj)	—	10.00	22.00	40.00	70.00	—
1680 (jj)	—	10.00	22.00	40.00	70.00	—
1681 (jj)	—	10.00	22.00	40.00	70.00	—
1682 (jj)	—	10.00	22.00	40.00	70.00	—
1683 (jj)	—	10.00	22.00	40.00	70.00	—
1684 (jj)	—	10.00	22.00	40.00	70.00	—
1685 (jj)	—	10.00	22.00	40.00	70.00	—
1686 (jj)	—	10.00	22.00	40.00	70.00	—
1687 (jj)	—	10.00	22.00	40.00	70.00	—
1688 (jj)	—	10.00	22.00	40.00	70.00	—
1689 (jj)	—	10.00	22.00	40.00	70.00	—
1690 (jj)	—	10.00	22.00	40.00	70.00	—
1691 (jj)	—	10.00	22.00	40.00	70.00	—
1692 (jj)	—	10.00	22.00	40.00	70.00	—
1693 (jj)	—	10.00	22.00	40.00	70.00	—
1694 (jj)	—	10.00	22.00	40.00	70.00	—

KM# 282 3 KREUZER (Groschen)

Silver **Ruler:** Ferdinand II **Obv:** Crowned imperial eagle, value (3) below, Austria-Burgundy arms on breast, titles of Ferdinand II **Rev:** Crowned Bohemian lion left in circle, date in legend **Mint:** Prague **Note:** Prev. KM#1368.

Date	Mintage	VG	F	VF	XF	Unc
16Z1 (l)	—	8.00	16.00	32.00	65.00	—

KM# 324 3 KREUZER (Groschen)

Silver **Ruler:** Ferdinand II **Obv:** Laureate bust right, value (3) below, titles of Ferdinand II **Rev:** Crowned imperial eagle, Austria-Burgundy arms on breast, date in legend **Mint:** Prague **Note:** Prev. KM#1369.

Date	Mintage	VG	F	VF	XF	Unc
1622 (l)	—	12.00	25.00	45.00	85.00	—
1623 (l)	—	10.00	22.00	40.00	75.00	—

KM# 369 3 KREUZER (Groschen)

Silver **Ruler:** Ferdinand II **Obv:** Bust right in ruffled collar **Rev:** Crowned imperial eagle **Mint:** Prague **Note:** Prev. KM#1370. Varieties exist.

Date	Mintage	VG	F	VF	XF	Unc
1624 (n)	—	8.00	15.00	30.00	60.00	—
1625 (l)	—	8.00	15.00	30.00	60.00	—
1625 (n)	—	8.00	15.00	30.00	60.00	—
1626 (l)	—	8.00	15.00	30.00	60.00	—
1626 (n)	—	8.00	15.00	30.00	60.00	—
1627 (l)	—	8.00	15.00	30.00	60.00	—
1628 (l)	—	8.00	15.00	30.00	60.00	—
1629 (l)	—	8.00	15.00	30.00	60.00	—
1630 (l)	—	8.00	15.00	30.00	60.00	—
1630 (o)	—	8.00	15.00	30.00	60.00	—
1631 (o)	—	8.00	15.00	30.00	60.00	—
1631 (p)	—	8.00	15.00	30.00	60.00	—
1632 (p)	—	8.00	15.00	30.00	60.00	—
1633 (p)	—	8.00	15.00	30.00	60.00	—
1634 (p)	—	8.00	15.00	30.00	60.00	—
1635 (p)	—	8.00	15.00	30.00	60.00	—
1636 (p)	—	8.00	15.00	30.00	60.00	—
1637 (p)	—	8.00	15.00	30.00	60.00	—
1637 (q)	—	8.00	15.00	30.00	60.00	—
1638 (q)	—	8.00	15.00	30.00	60.00	—

KM# 409 3 KREUZER (Groschen)

Silver **Ruler:** Ferdinand II **Mint:** Prague **Note:** Prev. KM#1371. Klippe.

Date	Mintage	VG	F	VF	XF	Unc
1637 (q) Rare	—	—	—	—	—	—

KM# 412 3 KREUZER (Groschen)

Silver **Ruler:** Ferdinand III **Obv:** Bare-headed bust right, value below **Rev:** Crowned imperial eagle **Mint:** Prague **Note:** Prev. KM#1408.

Date	Mintage	VG	F	VF	XF	Unc
1638 (q)	—	10.00	20.00	38.00	75.00	—
1639 (q)	—	10.00	20.00	38.00	75.00	—
1640 (q)	—	10.00	20.00	38.00	75.00	—
1641 (q)	—	10.00	20.00	38.00	75.00	—

KM# 448 3 KREUZER (Groschen)

Silver **Ruler:** Ferdinand III **Obv:** Laureate bust right **Rev:** Crowned imperial eagle **Mint:** Prague **Note:** Prev. KM#1409.

Date	Mintage	VG	F	VF	XF	Unc
1640 (q)	—	9.00	18.00	36.00	70.00	—
1641 (q)	—	9.00	18.00	36.00	70.00	—
1642 (q)	—	9.00	18.00	36.00	70.00	—
1643 (q)	—	9.00	18.00	36.00	70.00	—
1644 (q)	—	9.00	18.00	36.00	70.00	—
1645 (q)	—	9.00	18.00	36.00	70.00	—
1646 (q)	—	9.00	18.00	36.00	70.00	—
1647 (q)	—	9.00	18.00	36.00	70.00	—
1648 (q)	—	9.00	18.00	36.00	70.00	—
1649 (q)	—	9.00	18.00	36.00	70.00	—
1650 (q)	—	9.00	18.00	36.00	70.00	—
1651 (q)	—	9.00	18.00	36.00	70.00	—
1652 (q)	—	9.00	18.00	36.00	70.00	—
1653 (q)	—	9.00	18.00	36.00	70.00	—
1654 (q)	—	9.00	18.00	36.00	70.00	—
1655 (q)	—	9.00	18.00	36.00	70.00	—
1655 (r)	—	9.00	18.00	36.00	70.00	—
1656 (r)	—	9.00	18.00	36.00	70.00	—
1657 (r)	—	9.00	18.00	36.00	70.00	—

KM# 486 3 KREUZER (Groschen)

Silver **Ruler:** Leopold I **Obv:** Young bust right **Rev:** Crowned imperial arms **Mint:** Prague **Note:** Prev. KM#1428. Varieties exist.

Date	Mintage	VG	F	VF	XF	Unc
1658 (r)	—	15.00	30.00	55.00	90.00	—
1659 (r)	—	15.00	30.00	55.00	90.00	—
1660 (r)	—	15.00	30.00	55.00	90.00	—
1661 (r)	—	15.00	30.00	55.00	90.00	—
1662 (r)	—	15.00	30.00	55.00	90.00	—
1663 (r)	—	15.00	30.00	55.00	90.00	—

KM# 554 3 KREUZER (Groschen)

Silver **Ruler:** Leopold I **Obv:** Older laureate bust right **Rev:** Crowned imperial arms **Mint:** Prague **Note:** Prev. KM#1429.

Date	Mintage	VG	F	VF	XF	Unc
1664 (r)	—	10.00	22.00	40.00	70.00	—
1668 (r)	—	10.00	22.00	40.00	70.00	—
1670 (s)	—	10.00	22.00	40.00	70.00	—
1675 (s)	—	10.00	22.00	40.00	70.00	—
1676 (s)	—	10.00	22.00	40.00	70.00	—
1677 (s)	—	10.00	22.00	40.00	70.00	—
1678 (s)	—	10.00	22.00	40.00	70.00	—
1679	—	10.00	22.00	40.00	70.00	—

KM# 555 6 KREUZER

Silver **Ruler:** Leopold I **Obv:** Laureate bust right **Rev:** Crowned imperial eagle with sword and scepter **Mint:** Prague **Note:** Prev. #1431.

Date	Mintage	VG	F	VF	XF	Unc
1664 (r)	—	12.00	25.00	45.00	85.00	—
1665 (r)	—	12.00	25.00	45.00	85.00	—
1674 (s)	—	12.00	25.00	45.00	85.00	—
1678 (s)	—	12.00	25.00	45.00	85.00	—
1681 (s)	—	12.00	25.00	45.00	85.00	—
1682 (s)	—	12.00	25.00	45.00	85.00	—
1683 (s)	—	12.00	25.00	45.00	85.00	—

KM# 573 6 KREUZER

Silver **Ruler:** Leopold I **Obv:** Laureate bust right, value "VI" in oval below, titles of Leopold I **Rev:** Crowned imperial eagle, Bohemian arms on breast, holding sword and scepter in talons, date in legend **Mint:** Prague

Date	Mintage	VG	F	VF	XF	Unc
1674 (s)	—	—	—	—	—	—

KM# 584 6 KREUZER

Silver **Ruler:** Leopold I **Obv:** Laureate bust right **Mint:** Prague **Note:** Varieties exist. Prev. #1431 and #1432.

Date	Mintage	VG	F	VF	XF	Unc
1684 (s)	—	12.00	25.00	45.00	85.00	—
1685 (s)	—	12.00	25.00	45.00	85.00	—
1686 (s)	—	12.00	25.00	45.00	85.00	—
1687 (s)	—	12.00	25.00	45.00	85.00	—
1688 MV	—	20.00	40.00	75.00	120	—
1689 MV	—	20.00	40.00	75.00	120	—
1691 MV	—	20.00	40.00	75.00	120	—

KM# 591 6 KREUZER

Silver **Ruler:** Leopold I **Rev:** Date divided by crown at top **Mint:** Prague **Note:** Prev. KM#1430.

Date	Mintage	VG	F	VF	XF	Unc
1688 MV	—	6.00	12.00	25.00	65.00	—
1691 MV	—	6.00	12.00	25.00	65.00	—
1692	—	6.00	12.00	25.00	65.00	—
1693	—	6.00	12.00	25.00	65.00	—

KM# 286 12 KREUZER

Silver **Ruler:** Ferdinand II **Obv:** Laureate bust right **Rev:** Crowned imperial eagle **Mint:** Kuttenberg **Note:** Prev. KM#1078.

Date	Mintage	VG	F	VF	XF	Unc
1621 (ee)	—	—	—	—	—	—

KM# 285 12 KREUZER

Silver **Ruler:** Ferdinand II **Obv:** Bust right in ruffled collar **Rev:** Crowned imperial eagle **Mint:** Prague **Note:** Prev. KM#1372.

Date	Mintage	VG	F	VF	XF	Unc
1621 (l)	—	15.00	30.00	50.00	90.00	—

KM# 329 15 KREUZER

Silver **Ruler:** Ferdinand II **Obv:** Laureate bust in ruffled collar right in inner circle, value below **Rev:** Crowned imperial eagle **Mint:** Joachimstal **Note:** Prev. KM#895.

Date	Mintage	VG	F	VF	XF	Unc
1622 (ak)	—	65.00	120	200	325	—
1623 (ak)	—	65.00	120	200	325	—

KM# 552 15 KREUZER

Silver **Ruler:** Leopold I **Obv:** Laureate bust of Leopold I right, value below **Rev:** Crowned imperial eagle **Mint:** Joachimstal **Note:** Prev. KM#932.

Date	Mintage	VG	F	VF	XF	Unc
1663 (an) Rare	—	—	—	—	—	—

KM# 287 15 KREUZER

Silver **Ruler:** Ferdinand II **Obv:** Laureate bust right **Rev:** Crowned imperial eagle **Mint:** Kuttenberg **Note:** Prev. KM#1079.

Date	Mintage	VG	F	VF	XF	Unc
1621 (ee)	—	65.00	120	200	325	—
1622 (ee)	—	65.00	120	200	325	—

KM# 596 15 KREUZER

Silver **Ruler:** Leopold I **Obv:** Laureate bust right **Rev:** Crowned imperial eagle **Mint:** Kuttenberg **Note:** Prev. KM#1121.

Date	Mintage	VG	F	VF	XF	Unc
1694 CK	—	15.00	25.00	45.00	90.00	—
1695 CK	—	15.00	25.00	45.00	90.00	—
1696 CK	—	15.00	25.00	45.00	90.00	—

KM# 328 15 KREUZER

Silver **Ruler:** Ferdinand II **Obv:** Bust right in ruffled collar **Rev:** Crowned imperial eagle **Mint:** Prague **Note:** Prev. KM#1373.

Date	Mintage	VG	F	VF	XF	Unc
1622 (l)	—	15.00	25.00	40.00	75.00	—
1623 (l)	—	15.00	25.00	40.00	75.00	—

KM# 494 15 KREUZER

Silver **Ruler:** Leopold I **Obv:** Laureate bust right **Rev:** Crowned imperial eagle **Mint:** Prague **Note:** Prev. KM#1433.

Date	Mintage	VG	F	VF	XF	Unc
1659 (r)	—	15.00	25.00	45.00	85.00	—
1663 (r)	—	15.00	25.00	45.00	85.00	—
1664 (r)	—	15.00	25.00	45.00	85.00	—

KM# 574 15 KREUZER

Silver **Ruler:** Leopold I **Obv:** Laureate bust with long wig right **Rev:** Crowned imperial eagle **Mint:** Prague **Note:** Varieties exist. Prev. KM#1433.

Date	Mintage	VG	F	VF	XF	Unc
1674 (s)	—	15.00	25.00	45.00	90.00	—
1693 MV	—	15.00	25.00	45.00	90.00	—
1693 (t) MV	—	15.00	25.00	45.00	90.00	—
1694 MV	—	17.50	30.00	65.00	125	—
1694 PM	—	22.00	50.00	95.00	160	—
1694 GE	—	22.00	50.00	95.00	160	—
1695 GE	—	22.00	50.00	95.00	160	—
1696 GE	—	22.00	50.00	95.00	160	—

KM# 330 24 KREUZER

Silver **Ruler:** Ferdinand II **Obv:** Laureate bust right, value below **Rev:** Crowned imperial eagle **Mint:** Kuttenberg **Note:** Prev. KM#1080.

Date	Mintage	VG	F	VF	XF	Unc
1622 (ee)	—	—	—	—	—	—

KM# 342 24 KREUZER

Silver **Ruler:** Ferdinand II **Obv:** Bust right in ruffled collar **Rev:** Crowned imperial eagle **Mint:** Prague **Note:** Prev. KM#1374.

Date	Mintage	VG	F	VF	XF	Unc
1623 (l)	—	15.00	25.00	45.00	85.00	—

KM# 288 30 KREUZER

Silver **Ruler:** Ferdinand II **Obv:** Laureate bust right **Rev:** Crowned imperial eagle **Mint:** Kuttenberg **Note:** Prev. KM#1081.

Date	Mintage	VG	F	VF	XF	Unc
1621 (ee)	—	—	—	—	—	—

KM# 245 30 KREUZER

Silver **Ruler:** Ferdinand II **Obv:** Laureate bust right in ruffled collar **Rev:** Crowned imperial eagle **Mint:** Prague **Note:** Prev. KM#1375.

Date	Mintage	VG	F	VF	XF	Unc
1620 (m)	—	45.00	90.00	165	275	—
1621 (l)	—	45.00	90.00	165	275	—
1621 (m)	—	45.00	90.00	165	275	—
1622	—	45.00	90.00	165	275	—

KM# 289 37 KREUZER

Silver **Ruler:** Ferdinand II **Obv:** Laureate bust right **Rev:** Crowned imperial eagle **Mint:** Kuttenberg **Note:** Prev. KM#1082.

Date	Mintage	VG	F	VF	XF	Unc
1621 (ee)	—	125	325	575	1,000	—
1622 (ee)	—	125	325	575	1,000	—

KM# 290 37-1/2 KREUZER

Silver **Ruler:** Ferdinand II **Obv:** Laureate bust right **Rev:** Crowned imperial eagle **Mint:** Kuttenberg **Note:** Prev. KM#1083.

Date	Mintage	VG	F	VF	XF	Unc
1621 (ee)	—	—	—	—	—	—

KM# 295 48 KREUZER

Silver **Ruler:** Ferdinand II **Obv:** Laureate bust right in inner circle **Mint:** Joachimstal **Note:** Prev. KM#896.

Date	Mintage	VG	F	VF	XF	Unc
1621 (ak)	—	—	—	—	—	—

KM# 294 48 KREUZER

Silver **Ruler:** Ferdinand II **Obv:** Laureate bust right **Rev:** Crowned imperial eagle **Mint:** Kuttenberg **Note:** Prev. KM#1084.

Date	Mintage	VG	F	VF	XF	Unc
1621 (ee)	—	115	250	500	850	—

KM# 293 48 KREUZER

Silver **Ruler:** Ferdinand II **Obv:** Laureate bust right in ruffled collar **Rev:** Crowned imperial eagle **Mint:** Prague **Note:** Prev. KM#1376.

Date	Mintage	VG	F	VF	XF	Unc
1621 (l)	—	115	250	500	850	—
1622 (l)	—	115	250	500	850	—

KM# 297 60 KREUZER

Silver **Ruler:** Ferdinand II **Obv:** Laureate bust right in ruffled collar, value below **Rev:** Crowned imperial eagle **Mint:** Joachimstal **Note:** Prev. KM#897.

Date	Mintage	VG	F	VF	XF	Unc
1621 (aj)	—	115	250	500	850	—
1621 (ak)	—	115	250	500	850	—

KM# 260 60 KREUZER

Silver **Ruler:** Ferdinand II **Obv:** Laureate bust right **Rev:** Crowned imperial eagle **Mint:** Kuttenberg **Note:** Prev. KM#1085.

Date	Mintage	VG	F	VF	XF	Unc
1620 (ee)	—	30.00	60.00	120	225	—
1621 (ee)	—	30.00	60.00	120	225	—

KM# 259 60 KREUZER

Silver **Ruler:** Ferdinand II **Obv:** Laureate bust right in ruffled collar **Rev:** Crowned imperial eagle **Mint:** Prague **Note:** Prev. KM#1377.

Date	Mintage	VG	F	VF	XF	Unc
1620 (m)	—	120	275	525	900	—
1620 (n)	—	120	275	525	900	—
1621 (l)	—	120	275	525	900	—

KM# 262 70 KREUZER
Silver **Ruler:** Friedrich von der Pfalz **Obv:** Value below bust **Mint:** Prague **Note:** Prev. KM#1331.

Date	Mintage	VG	F	VF	XF	Unc
1620 (m)	—	—	—	—	—	—

KM# 264 70 KREUZER (1/2 Taler)
Silver **Ruler:** Ferdinand II **Obv:** Laureate bust right **Rev:** Crowned imperial eagle **Mint:** Kuttenberg **Note:** Prev. KM#1086.

Date	Mintage	VG	F	VF	XF	Unc
1620 (ee)	—	110	240	450	750	—
1621 (ee)	—	110	240	450	750	—

KM# 331 75 KREUZER (1/2 Taler)
Silver **Ruler:** Ferdinand II **Obv:** Laureate bust right in ruffled collar **Rev:** Crowned imperial eagle in inner circle, date in legend **Mint:** Joachimstal

Date	Mintage	VG	F	VF	XF	Unc
1622 (ak)	—	—	—	—	—	—
1623 (ak)	—	—	—	—	—	—

KM# 299 75 KREUZER (1/2 Taler)
Silver **Ruler:** Ferdinand II **Obv:** Laureate bust right **Rev:** Crowned imperial eagle **Mint:** Kuttenberg **Note:** Prev. KM#1087.

Date	Mintage	VG	F	VF	XF	Unc
1621 (ee)	—	85.00	160	275	600	—
1622 (ee)	—	85.00	160	275	600	—

KM# 298 75 KREUZER (1/2 Taler)
Silver **Ruler:** Ferdinand II **Obv:** Laureate bust right in ruffled collar **Rev:** Crowned imperial eagle in inner circle, date in legend **Mint:** Kuttenberg **Note:** Prev. KM#1378.

Date	Mintage	VG	F	VF	XF	Unc
1621 (l)	—	75.00	140	225	575	—
1622 (l)	—	75.00	140	225	575	—
1623 (l)	—	75.00	140	225	575	—
1623 (n)	—	75.00	140	225	575	—

KM# 307 120 KREUZER (Taler)
Silver **Ruler:** Ferdinand II **Obv:** Laureate bust right in ruffled collar **Rev:** Crowned imperial eagle **Mint:** Joachimstal **Note:** Prev. KM#899.

Date	Mintage	VG	F	VF	XF	Unc
1621 (ak)	—	50.00	100	185	300	—
1622 (ak)	—	50.00	100	185	300	—

KM# 305.1 120 KREUZER (Taler)
Silver **Ruler:** Ferdinand II **Obv:** Laureate bust right in ruffled collar **Rev:** Crowned imperial eagle **Mint:** Kuttenberg **Note:** Prev. KM#1088.

Date	Mintage	VG	F	VF	XF	Unc
1621 (ee)	—	65.00	130	240	375	—
1622 (ee)	—	65.00	130	240	375	—

KM# 305.2 120 KREUZER (Taler)
Silver **Ruler:** Ferdinand II **Obv:** Value as (1110) **Mint:** Kuttenberg **Note:** Prev. KM#1089.

Date	Mintage	VG	F	VF	XF	Unc
1621 (ee) Error	—	75.00	150	270	350	—

KM# 266 120 KREUZER (Taler)
Silver **Ruler:** Ferdinand II **Obv:** Laureate bust right in ruffled collar **Rev:** Crowned imperial eagle **Mint:** Prague **Note:** Prev. KM#1379.

Date	Mintage	VG	F	VF	XF	Unc
1620 (m)	—	45.00	90.00	165	275	—
1621 (l)	—	45.00	90.00	165	275	—

KM# 304 120 KREUZER (Taler)
Silver **Ruler:** Ferdinand II **Mint:** Prague **Note:** Klippe. Prev. KM#1380.

Date	Mintage	VG	F	VF	XF	Unc
1621 (l) Rare	—	—	—	—	—	—

KM# 268 140 KREUZER (Taler)
Silver **Ruler:** Ferdinand II **Obv:** Laureate bust right in ruffled collar **Rev:** Crowned imperial eagle **Mint:** Kuttenberg **Note:** Prev. KM#1090.

Date	Mintage	VG	F	VF	XF	Unc
1620 (ee)	—	85.00	160	300	500	—
1621 (ee)	—	85.00	160	300	500	—

KM# 267 140 KREUZER (Taler)
Silver **Ruler:** Ferdinand II **Obv:** Laureate bust right in ruffled collar **Rev:** Crowned imperial eagle **Mint:** Prague **Note:** Prev. KM#1381.

Date	Mintage	VG	F	VF	XF	Unc
1620 (m)	—	50.00	100	185	300	—
1621 (l)	—	50.00	100	185	300	—

KM# 310 150 KREUZER (Taler)
Silver **Ruler:** Ferdinand II **Obv:** Laureate bust right in ruffled collar **Rev:** Crowned imperial eagle **Mint:** Joachimstal **Note:** Prev. KM#900.

Date	Mintage	VG	F	VF	XF	Unc
1621 (ak)	—	40.00	90.00	165	250	—
1622 (ak)	—	40.00	90.00	165	250	—
1623 (ak)	—	40.00	90.00	165	250	—

KM# 309 150 KREUZER (Taler)
Silver **Ruler:** Ferdinand II **Obv:** Laureate bust right in ruffled collar **Rev:** Crowned imperial eagle **Mint:** Kuttenberg **Note:** Prev. KM#1091.

Date	Mintage	VG	F	VF	XF	Unc
1621 (ee)	—	45.00	90.00	150	250	—
1622 (ee)	—	45.00	90.00	150	250	—
1623 (ee)	—	45.00	90.00	150	250	—

KM# 308 150 KREUZER (Taler)
Silver **Ruler:** Ferdinand II **Obv:** Value below bust **Mint:** Prague **Note:** Prev. KM#1382.

Date	Mintage	VG	F	VF	XF	Unc
1621 (l)	—	35.00	65.00	110	200	—
1622 (l)	—	35.00	65.00	110	200	—
1623 (n)	—	35.00	65.00	110	200	—

KM# 333 300 KREUZER (2 Taler)

Silver **Ruler:** Ferdinand II **Obv:** Laureate bust right in ruffled collar, value below bust **Rev:** Crowned imperial eagle **Mint:** Kuttenberg **Note:** Prev. KM#1092.

Date	Mintage	VG	F	VF	XF	Unc
1622 (ee)	—	70.00	145	270	450	—

KM# 432 1/8 THALER (1/2 Reichsort)

Silver **Ruler:** Ferdinand III **Obv:** Bust right in circle, titles of Ferdinand III **Rev:** EIN / HALB / REICHS / ORTH / date in oval baroque frame, titles continuous **Mint:** Prague **Note:** Prev. KM#1410.

Date	Mintage	VG	F	VF	XF	Unc
1639 (q)	—	800	1,400	2,250	3,500	—
1648 (q)	—	—	—	—	—	—

Note: Reported, not confirmed

MB# 277 1/4 THALER

Silver **Ruler:** Rudolf II **Obv:** Young armored bust in ruffed collar right in inner circle **Rev:** Crowned double-headed eagle with sword and scepter in inner circle, date in legend **Mint:** Joachimstal **Note:** Varieties exist. Prev. KM#865.

Date	Mintage	VG	F	VF	XF	Unc
160Z (ah)	—	65.00	135	250	450	—
1604 (ai)	—	65.00	135	250	450	—

KM# 20 1/4 THALER

Silver **Ruler:** Rudolf II **Mint:** Joachimstal **Note:** Klippe. Prev. KM#866.

Date	Mintage	VG	F	VF	XF	Unc
1602 (ah) Rare	—	—	—	—	—	—

KM# 62 1/4 THALER

Silver **Ruler:** Rudolf II **Mint:** Joachimstal **Note:** Klippe. Prev. KM#868.

Date	Mintage	VG	F	VF	XF	Unc
1605 Rare	—	—	—	—	—	—

KM# 61 1/4 THALER

Silver **Ruler:** Rudolf II **Obv:** Older bust **Rev:** Crowned imperial eagle with square-topped shield n breast, without sword and scepter **Mint:** Joachimstal **Note:** Prev. KM#867.

Date	Mintage	VG	F	VF	XF	Unc
1605 (aj)	—	65.00	135	250	450	—
1607 (aj)	—	65.00	135	250	450	—
1610 (aj)	—	65.00	135	250	450	—

KM# 116 1/4 THALER

Silver **Ruler:** Matthias II **Obv:** Crowned bust right in inner circle **Rev:** Crowned arms divide date in order collar **Mint:** Joachimstal **Note:** Prev. KM#882.

Date	Mintage	VG	F	VF	XF	Unc
1612 (aj)	—	50.00	90.00	185	350	—

KM# 194 1/4 THALER

Silver **Ruler:** Matthias II **Obv:** Bust in ruffled collar right in inner circle **Rev:** Crowned imperial eagle in inner circle, date in legend **Mint:** Joachimstal **Note:** Prev. KM#883.

Date	Mintage	VG	F	VF	XF	Unc
1616 (aj)	—	40.00	80.00	160	275	—
1617 (aj)	—	40.00	80.00	160	275	—
1618 (aj)	—	40.00	80.00	160	275	—

KM# 209 1/4 THALER

Silver **Ruler:** Ferdinand II **Obv:** Crowned full-length armored figure turned slightly to right holding scepter and orb, titles of Ferdinand II **Rev:** Crowned imperial eagle in inner circle, date in legend **Mint:** Joachimstal **Note:** Mule. Prev. KM#884.

Date	Mintage	VG	F	VF	XF	Unc
1618 (aj) Rare	—	—	—	—	—	—

KM# 312 1/4 THALER

Silver **Ruler:** Ferdinand II **Obv:** Laureate bust right, titles of Ferdinand II **Rev:** Crowned imperial eagle, Austria-Burgundy arms on breast, date in legend **Mint:** Joachimstal

Date	Mintage	VG	F	VF	XF	Unc
1621 (ak)	—	—	—	—	—	—

KM# 345 1/4 THALER

Silver **Ruler:** Ferdinand II **Obv:** Standing figure holding orb and scepter in inner circle **Rev:** Crowned imperial eagle in inner circle **Mint:** Joachimstal **Note:** Prev. KM#901.

Date	Mintage	VG	F	VF	XF	Unc
1623 (ak)	—	125	275	550	950	—
1624 (ak)	—	125	275	550	950	—
1625 (ak)	—	125	275	550	950	—
1627 (ak)	—	125	275	550	950	—
1628 (ak)	—	125	275	550	950	—

KM# 434 1/4 THALER

Silver **Ruler:** Ferdinand III **Obv:** Bare bust of Ferdinand III right in inner circle **Rev:** Crowned imperial eagle in inner circle, date in legend **Mint:** Joachimstal **Note:** Prev. KM#916.

Date	Mintage	VG	F	VF	XF	Unc
1639 (al)	—	125	275	550	950	—
1643 (al)	—	125	275	550	950	—
1656 (al)	—	125	275	550	950	—

KM# 495 1/4 THALER

Silver **Ruler:** Leopold I **Obv:** Laureate bust of Leopold I right **Rev:** Crowned imperial eagle **Mint:** Joachimstal **Note:** Prev. KM#933.

Date	Mintage	VG	F	VF	XF	Unc
1659 (an) Rare	—	—	—	—	—	—
1663 (an) Rare	—	—	—	—	—	—

KM# 34 1/4 THALER

Silver **Ruler:** Rudolf II **Obv:** Armored bust right, titles of Rudolf II **Rev:** Crowned imperial eagle **Mint:** Kuttenberg **Note:** Prev. KM#1025.

Date	Mintage	VG	F	VF	XF	Unc
1603 (z)	—	45.00	75.00	145	250	—
1604 (z)	—	45.00	75.00	145	250	—
1605 (z)	—	45.00	75.00	145	250	—
1606	—	45.00	75.00	145	250	—
1609 (aa)	—	45.00	75.00	145	250	—
1610 (aa)	—	45.00	75.00	145	250	—
1611 (aa)	—	45.00	75.00	145	250	—

KM# 60 1/4 THALER

Silver **Ruler:** Rudolf II **Mint:** Kuttenberg **Note:** Klippe. Prev. KM#1026.

Date	Mintage	VG	F	VF	XF	Unc
1605 (z)	—	—	—	—	—	—
1607 (z)	—	—	—	—	—	—

KM# 158 1/4 THALER

Silver **Ruler:** Matthias II **Obv:** Bust in ruffled collar right **Rev:** Crowned imperial eagle **Mint:** Kuttenberg **Note:** Varieties exist. Prev. KM#1053.

Date	Mintage	VG	F	VF	XF	Unc
1613 (bb)	—	185	350	700	1,200	—
1614 (cc)	—	185	350	700	1,200	—
1615 (cc)	—	185	350	700	1,200	—
1616 (dd)	—	185	350	700	1,200	—
1617 (ee)	—	185	350	700	1,200	—
1618 (ee)	—	185	350	700	1,200	—
1619 (ee)	—	185	350	700	1,200	—

KM# 344 1/4 THALER

Silver **Ruler:** Ferdinand II **Obv:** Laureate bust right in ruffled collar **Rev:** Crowned imperial eagle **Mint:** Kuttenberg **Note:** Varieties exist. Prev. KM#1093.

Date	Mintage	VG	F	VF	XF	Unc
1623 (ee)	—	110	240	450	750	—
1624 (ee)	—	110	240	450	750	—
1625 (ee)	—	110	240	450	750	—
1626 (ee)	—	110	240	450	750	—
1627 (ee)	—	110	240	450	750	—
1628 (ee)	—	110	240	450	750	—
1629 (ee)	—	110	240	450	750	—
1630 (ee)	—	110	240	450	750	—
1631 (ee)	—	110	240	450	750	—
163Z (ee)	—	110	240	450	750	—
1633 (dd)	—	110	240	450	750	—
1633 (ff)	—	120	275	550	925	—
1634 (ff)	—	120	275	550	925	—
1637 (hh)	—	120	275	550	925	—
1638 (hh)	—	120	275	550	925	—

KM# 416 1/4 THALER

Silver **Ruler:** Ferdinand III **Obv:** Bust of Ferdinand III right **Rev:** Crowned imperial eagle **Mint:** Kuttenberg **Note:** Prev. KM#1106.

Date	Mintage	VG	F	VF	XF	Unc
1638 (hh)	—	150	300	550	950	—
1641 (hh)	—	150	300	550	950	—

MB# 252 1/4 THALER

Silver **Ruler:** Rudolf II **Obv:** Young armored bust of Rudolf II right **Rev:** Crowned imperial eagle **Mint:** Prague **Note:** Varieties exist.

Date	Mintage	VG	F	VF	XF	Unc
1601 (y)	—	85.00	175	300	525	—
160Z (y)	—	85.00	175	300	525	—

KM# 15 1/4 THALER

Silver **Ruler:** Rudolf II **Obv:** Full-length crowned and armored figure, turned slightly right, holding scepter and orb, small crowned shields of Bohemia left and Hungary right, titles of Rudolf II **Rev:** Crowned imperial eagle, arms of Austria-Burgundy on breast, date in legend **Mint:** Prague **Note:** Prev. KM#1298.

Date	Mintage	VG	F	VF	XF	Unc
1601 (j)	—	300	550	900	1,500	—
1602 (j)	—	300	550	900	1,500	—

KM# 21 1/4 THALER

Silver **Ruler:** Rudolf II **Mint:** Prague **Note:** Klippe. Prev. KM#1299.

Date	Mintage	VG	F	VF	XF	Unc
1602 (j)	—	—	—	—	—	—

KM# 33 1/4 THALER

Silver **Ruler:** Rudolf II **Mint:** Prague **Note:** Klippe. Prev. KM#1301.

Date	Mintage	VG	F	VF	XF	Unc
1603 (j)	—	—	—	—	—	—
1605 (j)	—	—	—	—	—	—
1605	—	—	—	—	—	—

KM# 49 1/4 THALER

Silver **Ruler:** Rudolf II **Obv:** Armored bust right, titles of Rudolf II **Rev:** Crowned imperial eagle **Mint:** Prague **Note:** Prev. KM#1300.

Date	Mintage	VG	F	VF	XF	Unc
1604 (j)	—	300	550	950	1,600	—
1605	—	300	550	950	1,600	—
1607 (j)	—	300	550	950	1,600	—
1608 (j)	—	300	550	950	1,600	—
1609	—	300	550	950	1,600	—
1610 (k)	—	300	550	950	1,600	—
1611 (l)	—	300	550	950	1,600	—

KM# 115 1/4 THALER

Silver **Ruler:** Matthias II **Obv:** Crowned bust right, titles of Matthias **Rev:** Crowned four-fold arms with central shield of Austria-Burgundy divide date, surrounded by Order of the Golden Fleece, date in legend **Mint:** Prague **Note:** Prev. KM#1328.

Date	Mintage	VG	F	VF	XF	Unc
1612 (l)	—	—	—	—	—	—

KM# 157 1/4 THALER

Silver **Ruler:** Matthias II **Obv:** Bust right, titles of Matthias **Rev:** Crowned imperial eagle, arms of Austria-Burgundy on breast with chain of order around, date in legend **Mint:** Prague **Note:** Prev. KM#1329.1.

Date	Mintage	VG	F	VF	XF	Unc
1613 (l)	—	200	400	700	1,500	—
1614 (l)	—	200	400	700	1,500	—
1616 (l)	—	200	400	700	1,500	—
1617 (l)	—	200	400	700	1,500	—
1618 (l)	—	200	400	700	1,500	—

KM# 179 1/4 THALER

Silver **Ruler:** Matthias II **Mint:** Prague **Note:** Thick planchet. Prev. KM#1329.2.

Date	Mintage	VG	F	VF	XF	Unc
1615	—	—	—	—	—	—

KM# 372 1/4 THALER

Silver **Ruler:** Ferdinand II **Mint:** Prague **Note:** Klippe. Prev. KM#1385.

Date	Mintage	VG	F	VF	XF	Unc
1623 (n) Rare	—	—	—	—	—	—
1624 (n) Rare	—	—	—	—	—	—

KM# 343 1/4 THALER

Silver **Ruler:** Ferdinand II **Obv:** Standing figure of Ferdinand II **Rev:** Crowned imperial eagle, crowned Bohemian arms surrounded by Order of the Golden Fleece on breast, date in legend **Mint:** Prague **Note:** Varieties exist. Prev. KM#1384.

Date	Mintage	VG	F	VF	XF	Unc
1623 (n)	—	75.00	140	250	575	—
1624 (n)	—	75.00	140	250	575	—
1625 (n)	—	75.00	140	250	575	—
1625 (l)	—	75.00	140	250	575	—
1630 (l)	—	75.00	140	250	575	—
1630 (o)	—	75.00	140	250	575	—
1631 (p)	—	75.00	140	250	575	—
1632 (p)	—	75.00	140	250	575	—
1633 (p)	—	75.00	140	250	575	—
1635 (p)	—	75.00	140	250	575	—
1637 (q)	—	75.00	140	250	575	—

KM# 346 1/4 THALER

Silver **Ruler:** Ferdinand II **Mint:** Prague **Note:** Weight of 1/2 Thaler. Prev. KM#1386.

Date	Mintage	VG	F	VF	XF	Unc
1623 Rare	—	—	—	—	—	—

KM# 433 1/4 THALER

Silver **Ruler:** Ferdinand III **Obv:** Bare-headed bust right **Rev:** Crowned imperial eagle **Mint:** Prague **Note:** Prev. KM#1411.

Date	Mintage	VG	F	VF	XF	Unc
1639 (q)	—	100	200	350	550	—
1640 (q)	—	100	200	350	550	—
1641 (q	—	100	200	350	550	—

KM# 462 1/4 THALER

Silver **Ruler:** Ferdinand III **Obv:** Laureate bust right **Rev:** Crowned imperial eagle **Mint:** Prague **Note:** Varieties exist. Prev. KM#1412.

Date	Mintage	VG	F	VF	XF	Unc
1642 (q)	—	100	200	350	550	—
1646 (q)	—	100	200	350	550	—
1647 (q)	—	100	200	350	550	—
1648 (q)	—	100	200	350	550	—
1653 (q)	—	100	200	350	550	—
1655 (q)	—	100	200	350	550	—
1656 (q)	—	100	200	350	550	—
1656 (r)	—	100	200	350	550	—
1657 (r)	—	100	200	350	550	—

KM# 592 1/4 THALER

Silver **Ruler:** Leopold I **Obv:** Laureate bust right **Rev:** Crowned imperial eagle with sword and scepter **Mint:** Prague **Note:** Varieties exist. Prev. KM#1435.

Date	Mintage	VG	F	VF	XF	Unc
1693 (t) MV	—	125	275	550	950	—
1693 (t)	—	125	275	550	950	—
1695 GE	—	125	275	550	950	—

KM# 593 1/4 THALER

Silver **Ruler:** Leopold I **Obv:** Bust right in inner circle **Rev:** Crowned imperial eagle in inner circle, value below, crown divides dates **Mint:** Prague **Note:** Prev. KM#1434.

Date	Mintage	VG	F	VF	XF	Unc
1693 MV	—	375	650	1,150	—	—

Note: Value on reverse is 1/2-an error coin

KM# 67 1/2 THALER

Silver **Ruler:** Rudolf II **Obv:** Armored bust right in inner circle **Rev:** Crowned imperial eagle in inner circle, date in legend **Mint:** Budweis **Note:** Prev. KM#235.

Date	Mintage	VG	F	VF	XF	Unc
1605 (bf)	—	35.00	70.00	145	250	—
1606 (bf)	—	35.00	70.00	145	250	—
1608 (bf)	—	35.00	70.00	145	250	—
1609 (bf)	—	35.00	70.00	145	250	—
1610 (bf)	—	35.00	70.00	145	250	—

MB# 262 1/2 THALER

Silver **Ruler:** Rudolf II **Obv:** Young armored bust in ruffled collar right in inner circle **Rev:** Crowned imperial eagle with sword and scepter in inner circle, date in legend **Mint:** Joachimstal **Note:** Prev. KM#869.

Date	Mintage	VG	F	VF	XF	Unc
1601 (ah)	—	115	250	500	850	—

KM# 23 1/2 THALER

Silver **Ruler:** Rudolf II **Obv:** Young armored bust in ruffled collar in inner circle **Mint:** Joachimstal **Note:** Klippe. Prev. KM#875.

Date	Mintage	VG	F	VF	XF	Unc
1602 (ah) Rare	—	—	—	—	—	—
1603 (ah) Rare	—	—	—	—	—	—

KM# 52 1/2 THALER

Silver **Ruler:** Rudolf II **Mint:** Joachimstal **Note:** Klippe. Prev. KM#873.1.

Date	Mintage	VG	F	VF	XF	Unc
1604 (ai) Rare	—	—	—	—	—	—
1608 Rare	—	—	—	—	—	—

KM# 51 1/2 THALER

Silver **Ruler:** Rudolf II **Obv:** Older bust **Rev:** Crowned imperial eagle with square-topped shield on breast, without sword and scepter **Mint:** Joachimstal **Note:** Prev. KM#872.

Date	Mintage	VG	F	VF	XF	Unc
1604 (ai)	—	100	200	350	600	—
1606 (ai)	—	100	200	350	600	—
1606 (aj)	—	100	200	350	600	—
1607 (aj)	—	100	200	350	600	—
1609 (aj)	—	100	200	350	600	—
1610 (aj)	—	100	200	350	600	—

KM# 50 1/2 THALER

Silver **Ruler:** Rudolf II **Mint:** Joachimstal **Note:** Struck from dies of 1/4 Taler, MB#277. Prev. KM#871.

Date	Mintage	VG	F	VF	XF	Unc
1604 (ai) Rare	—	—	—	—	—	—

KM# 66 1/2 THALER

Silver **Ruler:** Rudolf II **Mint:** Joachimstal **Note:** Prev. KM#873.2. Struck from 1/4 Taler dies, KM#867.

Date	Mintage	VG	F	VF	XF	Unc
1605 (aj) Rare	—	—	—	—	—	—
1608 (aj) Rare	—	—	—	—	—	—

KM# 118 1/2 THALER

Silver **Ruler:** Rudolf II **Obv:** Crowned and ruffled bust right in inner circle **Rev:** Crowned arms divide date in order collar **Mint:** Joachimstal **Note:** Prev. KM#885.

Date	Mintage	VG	F	VF	XF	Unc
1612 (aj) Rare	—	—	—	—	—	—

KM# 195 1/2 THALER

Silver **Ruler:** Matthias II **Obv:** Bust right in inner circle **Rev:** Crowned imperial eagle in inner circle, date in legend **Mint:** Joachimstal **Note:** Prev. KM#886.

Date	Mintage	VG	F	VF	XF	Unc
1616 (aj)	—	—	—	—	—	—

KM# 350 1/2 THALER

Silver **Ruler:** Ferdinand II **Obv:** Standing figure **Rev:** Crowned imperial eagle **Mint:** Joachimstal **Note:** Prev. KM#902.

Date	Mintage	VG	F	VF	XF	Unc
1623 (ak)	—	85.00	160	275	600	—
1624 (ak)	—	85.00	160	275	600	—
1625 (ak)	—	85.00	160	275	600	—
1626 (ak)	—	85.00	160	275	600	—
1627 (ak)	—	85.00	160	275	600	—
1628 (ak)	—	85.00	160	275	600	—

KM# 436 1/2 THALER

Silver **Ruler:** Ferdinand III **Obv:** Bare-headed bust of Ferdinand III right **Rev:** Crowned imperial eagle **Mint:** Joachimstal **Note:** Prev. KM#917.

Date	Mintage	VG	F	VF	XF	Unc
1639 (al) Rare	—	—	—	—	—	—

KM# 437 1/2 THALER

Silver **Ruler:** Ferdinand III **Obv:** Laureate bust right **Rev:** Crowned imperial eagle **Mint:** Joachimstal **Note:** Prev. KM#918.

Date	Mintage	VG	F	VF	XF	Unc
1639 (al) Rare	—	—	—	—	—	—
1643 (al) Rare	—	—	—	—	—	—
1656 Rare	—	—	—	—	—	—

KM# 496 1/2 THALER

Silver **Ruler:** Leopold I **Obv:** Laureate bust of Leopold I right **Rev:** Crowned imperial eagle **Mint:** Joachimstal **Note:** Prev. KM#934.

Date	Mintage	VG	F	VF	XF	Unc
1659 (an) Rare	—	—	—	—	—	—

Note: Restrike reported

MB# 253 1/2 THALER

Silver **Ruler:** Rudolf II **Obv:** Armored bust of Rudolf II right **Rev:** Crowned imperial eagle **Mint:** Kuttenberg **Note:** Varieties exist. Prev. KM#1027.

Date	Mintage	VG	F	VF	XF	Unc
1601 (y)	—	115	250	500	850	—
160Z (y)	—	115	250	500	850	—

KM# 22 1/2 THALER

Silver **Ruler:** Rudolf II **Mint:** Kuttenberg **Note:** Klippe.

Date	Mintage	VG	F	VF	XF	Unc
1602 Rare	—	—	—	—	—	—

KM# 35 1/2 THALER

Silver **Ruler:** Rudolf II **Obv:** Bust right of Rudolf II **Rev:** Crowned imperial eagle **Mint:** Kuttenberg **Note:** Prev. KM#1029.

Date	Mintage	VG	F	VF	XF	Unc
1603 (z)	—	85.00	165	300	500	—
1604 (z)	—	85.00	165	300	500	—
1605 (z)	—	85.00	165	300	500	—
1606 (z)	—	85.00	165	300	500	—
1608 (z)	—	85.00	165	300	500	—
1610 (aa)	—	85.00	165	300	500	—
1611 (aa)	—	85.00	165	300	500	—

KM# 65 1/2 THALER

Silver **Ruler:** Rudolf II **Mint:** Kuttenberg **Note:** Klippe. Struck from 1/4 Taler dies, KM#34. Prev. KM#1030.

Date	Mintage	VG	F	VF	XF	Unc
1605 (z) Rare	—	—	—	—	—	—

Note: Stack's International sale 3-88 VF realized $15,400. Leu Numismatik Auction 75, 10-99, XF realized $38,665.

KM# 160 1/2 THALER

Silver **Ruler:** Matthias II **Obv:** Bust in ruffled collar right **Rev:** Crowned imperial eagle **Mint:** Kuttenberg **Note:** Prev. KM#1054.

Date	Mintage	VG	F	VF	XF	Unc
1613 (bb)	—	350	725	1,125	1,800	—
1614 (cc)	—	350	725	1,125	1,800	—
1615 (cc)	—	350	725	1,125	1,800	—
1616 (ee)	—	350	725	1,125	1,800	—
1617 (ee)	—	350	725	1,125	1,800	—
1618 (ee)	—	350	725	1,125	1,800	—
1619 (ee)	—	350	725	1,125	1,800	—

KM# 230 1/2 THALER

Silver **Ruler:** Matthias II **Mint:** Kuttenberg **Note:** Prev. KM#1055. Struck on thick flan from dies of 1/4 Taler, KM#158.

Date	Mintage	VG	F	VF	XF	Unc
1619 (ee) Rare	—	—	—	—	—	—

KM# 349 1/2 THALER

Silver **Ruler:** Ferdinand II **Obv:** Standing figure of Ferdinand **Rev:** Crowned imperial eagle **Mint:** Kuttenberg **Note:** Prev. KM#1094. Varieties exist.

Date	Mintage	VG	F	VF	XF	Unc
1623 (ee)	—	35.00	75.00	145	285	—
1624 (ee)	—	35.00	75.00	145	285	—
1625 (ee)	—	35.00	75.00	145	285	—
1626 (ee)	—	35.00	75.00	145	285	—
1627 (ee)	—	35.00	75.00	145	285	—
1628 (ee)	—	35.00	75.00	145	285	—
1629 (ee)	—	35.00	75.00	145	285	—
1630 (ee)	—	35.00	75.00	145	285	—
1631 (ee)	—	35.00	75.00	145	285	—
163Z (ee)	—	35.00	75.00	145	285	—
1633 (dd)	—	35.00	75.00	145	285	—
1633 (ff)	—	35.00	75.00	145	285	—
1634 (ff)	—	35.00	75.00	145	285	—

KM# 418 1/2 THALER

Silver **Ruler:** Ferdinand III **Obv:** Bare-headed bust right **Rev:** Crowned imperial eagle **Mint:** Kuttenberg **Note:** Prev. KM#1107.

Date	Mintage	VG	F	VF	XF	Unc
1638 (hh)	—	120	250	450	750	—
1641 (hh)	—	120	250	450	750	—

KM# 466 1/2 THALER

Silver **Ruler:** Ferdinand III **Obv:** Laureate bust of Ferdinand III **Rev:** Crowned imperial eagle **Mint:** Kuttenberg **Note:** Prev. KM#1111.

Date	Mintage	VG	F	VF	XF	Unc
1643 (hh) Rare	—	—	—	—	—	—

KM# 570 1/2 THALER

Silver **Ruler:** Leopold I **Obv:** Laureate bust right **Rev:** Crowned imperial eagle **Mint:** Kuttenberg **Note:** Prev. KM#1122.

Date	Mintage	VG	F	VF	XF	Unc
1671 (ii) Rare	—	—	—	—	—	—

KM# 610 1/2 THALER

Silver **Ruler:** Leopold I **Obv:** Older bust right **Rev:** Crowned imperial eagle **Mint:** Kuttenberg **Note:** Prev. KM#1123.

Date	Mintage	VG	F	VF	XF	Unc
1695 (jj) Rare	—	—	—	—	—	—

MB# 323 1/2 THALER

Silver **Ruler:** Rudolf II **Obv:** Standing figure **Rev:** Crowned imperial eagle **Mint:** Prague **Note:** Varieties exist. Prev. KM#1302.

Date	Mintage	VG	F	VF	XF	Unc
1601 (j)	—	200	450	750	1,250	—
160Z (j)	—	200	450	750	1,250	—
1603 (j)	—	200	450	750	1,250	—
1604 (j)	—	200	450	750	1,250	—
1606 (J)	—	200	450	750	1,250	—

KM# 16 1/2 THALER

Silver **Ruler:** Rudolf II **Obv:** Standing figure, half right, holding scepter and orb, shield of arms on each side **Mint:** Prague **Note:** Prev. KM#1302.

Date	Mintage	VG	F	VF	XF	Unc
1601	—	200	400	750	1,250	—
1602	—	200	400	750	1,250	—
1603	—	200	400	750	1,250	—
1606	—	200	400	750	1,250	—
1608	—	200	400	750	1,250	—
1609 (b)	—	200	400	750	1,250	—
1610 (b)	—	200	400	750	1,250	—
1610 (c)	—	200	400	750	1,250	—
1611	—	200	400	750	1,250	—

KM# 24 1/2 THALER

Silver **Ruler:** Rudolf II **Mint:** Prague **Note:** Klippe. Prev. KM#1032.

Date	Mintage	VG	F	VF	XF	Unc
160Z (j) Rare	—	—	—	—	—	—
1604 (j) Rare	—	—	—	—	—	—

KM# 77 1/2 THALER

Silver **Ruler:** Rudolf II **Obv:** Armored bust right in ruffled collar **Rev:** Crowned imperial eagle **Mint:** Prague **Note:** Prev. KM#1304.

Date	Mintage	VG	F	VF	XF	Unc
1606 (j)	—	250	450	800	1,350	—
1608 (j)	—	250	450	800	1,350	—
1609 (k)	—	250	450	800	1,350	—
1610 (k)	—	250	450	800	1,350	—
1610 (l)	—	250	450	800	1,350	—
1611 (l)	—	250	450	800	1,350	—

KM# 97 1/2 THALER

Silver **Ruler:** Matthias II **Rev:** 15-fold arms **Mint:** Prague **Note:** Prev. KM#1330.

Date	Mintage	VG	F	VF	XF	Unc
1611 (l) Rare	—	—	—	—	—	—

KM# 98 1/2 THALER

Silver **Ruler:** Matthias II **Obv:** Crowned and ruffled bust right in inner circle **Mint:** Prague **Note:** Prev. KM#1331.

Date	Mintage	VG	F	VF	XF	Unc
1611 (l) Rare	—	—	—	—	—	—
1612 (l) Rare	—	—	—	—	—	—

KM# 119 1/2 THALER

Silver **Ruler:** Matthias II **Obv:** Three crowned busts to right, names and titles of Masimilian I, Karl V, and Ferdinand I **Rev:** Imperial eagle, Castile-Austria arms on breast, titles continuous **Mint:** Prague **Note:** Prev. KM#1333.

Date	Mintage	VG	F	VF	XF	Unc
ND(1612-19) Rare	—	—	—	—	—	—

KM# 159 1/2 THALER

Silver **Ruler:** Rudolf II **Obv:** Bust right **Rev:** Crowned imperial eagle **Mint:** Prague **Note:** Prev. KM#1332.

Date	Mintage	VG	F	VF	XF	Unc
1613 (l)	—	200	475	825	1,500	—
1614 (l)	—	200	475	825	1,500	—
1615 (l)	—	200	475	825	1,500	—
1616 (l)	—	200	475	825	1,500	—
1617 (l)	—	200	475	825	1,500	—
1618 (l)	—	200	475	825	1,500	—
1619 (l)	—	200	475	825	1,500	—

KM# 335 1/2 THALER

Silver **Ruler:** Ferdinand II **Mint:** Prague **Note:** Klippe. Prev. KM#1389.

Date	Mintage	VG	F	VF	XF	Unc
1622 (n)	—	200	300	500	950	—
1625 (l)	—	250	350	650	1,150	—

KM# 348 1/2 THALER

Silver **Ruler:** Ferdinand II **Mint:** Prague **Note:** Klippe. Prev. KM#1389. Struck from 1/4 Taler dies, KM#343 on square flan.

Date	Mintage	VG	F	VF	XF	Unc
16Z3 (n) Rare	—	—	—	—	—	—

KM# 347 1/2 THALER

Silver **Ruler:** Ferdinand II **Obv:** Standing figure of Ferdinand II **Rev:** Crowned imperial eagle **Mint:** Prague **Note:** Varieties exist. Prev. KM#1387.

Date	Mintage	VG	F	VF	XF	Unc
1623 (n)	—	100	220	425	800	—
1624 (n)	—	100	220	425	800	—
1625 (n)	—	100	220	425	800	—
1625 (l)	—	100	220	425	800	—
1626 (l)	—	100	220	425	800	—
1630 (l)	—	100	220	425	800	—
1630 (o)	—	100	220	425	800	—
1631 (p)	—	100	220	425	800	—
1632 (p)	—	100	220	425	800	—
1633 (p)	—	100	220	425	800	—
1635 (p)	—	100	220	425	800	—
1637 (q)	—	100	220	425	800	—

KM# 397 1/2 THALER

Silver **Ruler:** Ferdinand II **Mint:** Prague **Note:** Muled with 1/4 Thaler die. Prev. KM#1388.

Date	Mintage	VG	F	VF	XF	Unc
1631 (g) Rare	—	—	—	—	—	—

KM# 417 1/2 THALER

Silver **Ruler:** Ferdinand III **Obv:** Bare-headed bust right in lace collar **Rev:** Crowned imperial eagle **Mint:** Prague **Note:** Prev. KM#1413.

Date	Mintage	VG	F	VF	XF	Unc
1638 (q)	—	65.00	125	200	350	—
1639 (q)	—	65.00	125	200	350	—
1640 (q)	—	65.00	125	200	350	—
1641 (q)	—	65.00	125	200	350	—

KM# 452 1/2 THALER

Silver **Ruler:** Ferdinand III **Obv:** Laureate bust right in lace collar **Rev:** Crowned imperial eagle **Mint:** Prague **Note:** Prev. KM#1414.

Date	Mintage	VG	F	VF	XF	Unc
1641 (q)	—	65.00	125	200	350	—
1644 (q)	—	65.00	125	200	350	—
1646 (q)	—	65.00	125	200	350	—
1647 (q)	—	65.00	125	200	350	—
1648 (q)	—	65.00	125	200	350	—
1649 (q)	—	65.00	125	200	350	—
1653 (q)	—	65.00	125	200	350	—
1655 (rr)	—	65.00	125	200	350	—
1656 (rr)	—	65.00	125	200	350	—

KM# 577 1/2 THALER

Silver **Ruler:** Leopold I **Obv:** Small laureate bust right **Rev:** Crowned imperial eagle **Mint:** Prague **Note:** Prev. KM#1436.

Date	Mintage	VG	F	VF	XF	Unc
1676 (s)	—	100	200	350	600	—

KM# 594 1/2 THALER

Silver **Ruler:** Leopold I **Obv:** Large laureate bust right **Rev:** Crowned imperial eagle holding sword and scepter **Mint:** Prague **Note:** Prev. KM#1438.1.

Date	Mintage	VG	F	VF	XF	Unc
1693 MV	—	110	240	450	750	—
1693 (t)	—	110	240	450	750	—

KM# 609 1/2 THALER

Silver **Ruler:** Leopold I **Mint:** Prague **Note:** Prev. KM#1438.2.

Date	Mintage	VG	F	VF	XF	Unc
1695 GE	—	80.00	150	275	450	—

MB# 257 THALER

Silver **Ruler:** Rudolf II **Obv:** Bust right **Rev:** Stylized crowned imperial eagle **Mint:** Budweis **Note:** Varieties exist. Dav. #3029. Prev. KM#236.

Date	Mintage	VG	F	VF	XF	Unc
1601 (bg)	—	375	550	1,000	1,650	—
160Z (bg)	—	375	550	1,000	1,650	—
1603 (bg) Rare	—	—	—	—	—	—

KM# 36 THALER

Silver **Ruler:** Rudolf II **Obv:** Bust right, lion below **Rev:** Crowned imperial eagle **Mint:** Budweis **Note:** Dav. #3030. Prev. KM#237.

Date	Mintage	VG	F	VF	XF	Unc
1603 (bf)	—	70.00	140	220	375	—
1604 (bf)	—	70.00	140	220	375	—
1605 (bf)	—	70.00	140	220	375	—
1606 (bf)	—	70.00	140	220	375	—
1607 (bf)	—	70.00	140	220	375	—
1608 (bf)	—	70.00	140	220	375	—
1609 (bf)	—	70.00	140	220	375	—
1610 (bf)	—	70.00	140	220	375	—
1611 (bf)	—	70.00	140	220	375	—

MB# 256 THALER

Silver **Ruler:** Rudolf II **Obv:** Young armored bust in ruffled collar right **Rev:** Crowned imperial eagle with sword and scepter **Mint:** Joachimstal **Note:** Dav. #3020. Varieties exist.

Date	Mintage	VG	F	VF	XF	Unc
1601 (ah)	—	60.00	110	195	375	—
160Z (ah)	—	60.00	110	195	375	—
1603 (ah)	—	60.00	110	195	375	—
1604 (ah)	—	60.00	110	195	375	—

KM# 27 THALER

Silver **Ruler:** Rudolf II **Obv:** Wide bust right **Rev:** Eagle with square-topped shield on breast without sword and scepter **Mint:** Joachimstal **Note:** Varieties exist. Dav. #3021. Prev. KM#875.

Date	Mintage	VG	F	VF	XF	Unc
1602 (ah) Rare	—	—	—	—	—	—
1604 (ah) Rare	—	—	—	—	—	—
1604 (ai) Rare	—	—	—	—	—	—
1605 (ai) Rare	—	—	—	—	—	—
1606 (ai) Rare	—	—	—	—	—	—
1606 (aj) Rare	—	—	—	—	—	—
1607 (aj) Rare	—	—	—	—	—	—
1608 (aj) Rare	—	—	—	—	—	—
1609 (aj) Rare	—	—	—	—	—	—

KM# 122 THALER

Silver **Ruler:** Rudolf II **Obv:** Crowned bust right in inner circle **Rev:** Crowned arms divide date in order collar **Mint:** Joachimstal **Note:** Prev. KM#876.

Date	Mintage	VG	F	VF	XF	Unc
1610 Rare	—	—	—	—	—	—
1611 Rare	—	—	—	—	—	—
1612 (aj) Rare	—	—	—	—	—	—

KM# 94 THALER

Silver **Ruler:** Rudolf II **Obv:** Older bust **Mint:** Joachimstal **Note:** Prev. KM#876.

Date	Mintage	VG	F	VF	XF	Unc
1610 (c) Rare	—	—	—	—	—	—
1611 (c) Rare	—	—	—	—	—	—
1612 (c) Rare	—	—	—	—	—	—

KM# 93 THALER

Silver **Ruler:** Rudolf II **Obv:** Crowned bust right in ruffled collar **Rev:** Crowned shield in collar of the Golden Fleece **Mint:** Joachimstal **Note:** Dav. #3022. Prev. KM#876.

Date	Mintage	VG	F	VF	XF	Unc
1610 aj Rare	—	—	—	—	—	—
1611 aj Rare	—	—	—	—	—	—
1612 aj Rare	—	—	—	—	—	—

KM# 121.1 THALER

Silver **Ruler:** Rudolf II **Obv:** Crowned and armored bust **Mint:** Joachimstal **Note:** Dav. #3067. Prev. KM#887.1. Thick planchet variety exists.

Date	Mintage	VG	F	VF	XF	Unc
1612 (aj)	—	165	325	600	1,000	—

KM# 121.2 THALER

Silver **Ruler:** Rudolf II **Mint:** Joachimstal **Note:** Thick planchet.

Date	Mintage	VG	F	VF	XF	Unc
1612 aj	—	200	375	725	1,150	—

KM# 125 THALER

Silver **Ruler:** Matthias II **Mint:** Joachimstal **Note:** Thick planchet. Prev. KM#887.2.

Date	Mintage	VG	F	VF	XF	Unc
1612	—	165	325	550	875	—

KM# 163 THALER

Silver **Ruler:** Matthias II **Obv:** Bust in ruffled collar right in inner circle **Rev:** Crowned imperial eagle in inner circle, date in legend **Mint:** Joachimstal **Note:** Prev. KM#888. Dav. #3068. Varieties exist.

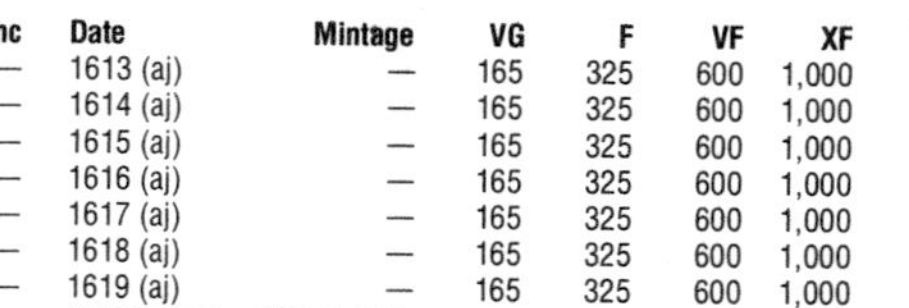

Date	Mintage	VG	F	VF	XF	Unc
1613 (aj)	—	165	325	600	1,000	—
1614 (aj)	—	165	325	600	1,000	—
1615 (aj)	—	165	325	600	1,000	—
1616 (aj)	—	165	325	600	1,000	—
1617 (aj)	—	165	325	600	1,000	—
1618 (aj)	—	165	325	600	1,000	—
1619 (aj)	—	165	325	600	1,000	—

KM# 314 THALER

Silver **Ruler:** Ferdinand II **Obv:** Laureate bust right in inner circle **Mint:** Joachimstal **Note:** Prev. KM#903.

Date	Mintage	VG	F	VF	XF	Unc
1621 (e)	—	325	600	1,000	1,650	—
1622 (e)	—	325	600	1,000	1,650	—

KM# 313 THALER

Silver **Ruler:** Ferdinand II **Obv:** Laureate bust right in inner circle **Rev:** Crowned imperial eagle, date in legend **Mint:** Joachimstal **Note:** Prev. KM#314. Dav. #3140.

Date	Mintage	VG	F	VF	XF	Unc
1621 (ak)	—	325	600	1,000	1,650	—
1622 (ak)	—	325	600	1,000	1,650	—

KM# 356 THALER

Silver **Ruler:** Ferdinand II **Mint:** Joachimstal **Note:** Dav. #3141. Prev. KM#904. Varieties exist.

Date	Mintage	VG	F	VF	XF	Unc
1623 (ak)	—	37.50	100	175	275	—
1624 (ak)	—	37.50	100	175	275	—
1625 (ak)	—	37.50	100	175	275	—
1626 (ak)	—	37.50	100	175	275	—
1627 (ak)	—	37.50	100	175	275	—
1630 (ak)	—	37.50	100	175	275	—
1631 (ak)	—	37.50	100	175	275	—
1632 (ak)	—	37.50	100	175	275	—

KM# 439 THALER

Silver **Ruler:** Ferdinand III **Obv:** Bust right in inner circle **Rev:** Crowned imperial eagle in inner circle, date in legend **Mint:** Joachimstal **Note:** Dav. #3208. Prev. KM#919.

Date	Mintage	VG	F	VF	XF	Unc
1639 (al)	—	110	195	325	550	—
1641 (al)	—	110	195	325	550	—
1642 (al)	—	110	195	325	550	—
1643 (al)	—	110	195	325	550	—

KM# 467 THALER

Silver **Ruler:** Ferdinand III **Obv:** Laureate bust right in inner circle **Rev:** Crowned imperial eagle in inner circle, date in legend **Mint:** Joachimstal **Note:** Dav. #3210. Prev. KM#920.

Date	Mintage	VG	F	VF	XF	Unc
1643 (al)	—	110	195	325	550	—
1644 (al)	—	110	195	325	550	—
1656 (an)	—	110	195	325	550	—

KM# 498 THALER

Silver **Ruler:** Leopold I **Obv:** Laureate bust of Leopold I right **Rev:** Crowned imperial eagle **Mint:** Joachimstal **Note:** Prev. KM#935. Dav. #3281. Restrikes reported.

Date	Mintage	VG	F	VF	XF	Unc
1659 (an) Rare	—	—	—	—	—	—

MB# 255 THALER

Silver **Ruler:** Maximilian II **Obv:** Young armored bust in ruffled collar right, lion and three dots below **Rev:** Crowned imperial eagle **Mint:** Kuttenberg **Note:** Dav. #8079. Varieties exist. Prev. KM#1031.

Date	Mintage	VG	F	VF	XF	Unc
1601 (y)	—	85.00	140	220	425	—
160Z (y)	—	85.00	140	220	425	—

KM# 26 THALER

Silver **Ruler:** Rudolf II **Obv:** Older, wider bust in ruffled collar **Mint:** Kuttenberg **Note:** Varieties exist. Dav. #3028. Prev. KM#1034.

Date	Mintage	VG	F	VF	XF	Unc
1602 (y)	—	70.00	140	220	375	—
1603 (y)	—	70.00	140	220	375	—
1603 (z)	—	70.00	140	220	375	—
1604 (z)	—	70.00	140	220	375	—
1605 (z)	—	70.00	140	220	375	—
1606 (z)	—	70.00	140	220	375	—
1607 (z)	—	70.00	140	220	375	—
1608 (z)	—	70.00	140	220	375	—
1608 (aa)	—	70.00	140	220	375	—
1609 (z)	—	70.00	140	220	375	—
1609 (aa)	—	70.00	140	220	375	—
1610 (aa)	—	70.00	140	220	375	—
1611 (aa)	—	70.00	140	220	375	—
1612 (aa)	—	70.00	140	220	375	—

KM# 28 THALER

Silver **Ruler:** Rudolf II **Obv:** Lion below older bust, without dots **Mint:** Kuttenberg **Note:** Prev. KM#1032.

Date	Mintage	VG	F	VF	XF	Unc
1602	—	70.00	140	220	375	—

KM# 37 THALER

Silver **Ruler:** Rudolf II **Obv:** Older, larger bust, lion and arabesques below **Mint:** Kuttenberg **Note:** Prev. KM#1033.

Date	Mintage	VG	F	VF	XF	Unc
1603 (c)	—	70.00	140	220	375	—

KM# 120 THALER

Silver **Ruler:** Rudolf II **Obv:** Crowned and armored bust right **Mint:** Kuttenberg **Note:** Dav. #3069. Prev. KM#1056.

Date	Mintage	VG	F	VF	XF	Unc
1612 (aa)	—	165	275	450	725	—
1612 (bb)	—	165	275	450	725	—
1613 (aa)	—	165	275	450	725	—
1613 (bb)	—	165	275	450	725	—

KM# 162 THALER

Silver **Ruler:** Matthias II **Obv:** Bust in ruffled collar **Rev:** Crowned imperial eagle **Mint:** Kuttenberg **Note:** Prev. KM#1057. Dav. #3071. Varieties exist.

Date	Mintage	VG	F	VF	XF	Unc
1613 (bb)	—	115	200	350	575	—
1614 (bb)	—	115	200	350	575	—
1614 (cc)	—	115	200	350	575	—
1615 (cc)	—	115	200	350	575	—
1615 (dd)	—	115	200	350	575	—
1616 (aa)	—	115	200	350	575	—
1616 (cc)	—	115	200	350	575	—
1616 (dd)	—	115	200	350	575	—
1616 (ee)	—	115	200	350	575	—
1617 (ee)	—	115	200	350	575	—
1618 (ee)	—	115	200	350	575	—
1619 (ee)	—	115	200	350	575	—

KM# 210 THALER

Silver **Ruler:** Matthias II **Obv:** Smaller bust right in inner circle **Mint:** Kuttenberg **Note:** Prev. KM#1058.

Date	Mintage	VG	F	VF	XF	Unc
1618	—	140	220	375	600	—
1619	—	140	220	375	600	—

KM# 355 THALER
Silver **Ruler:** Ferdinand II **Obv:** Standing figure of Ferdinand **Rev:** Crowned imperial eagle **Mint:** Kuttenberg **Note:** Dav. #3143. Prev. KM#1095. Varieties exist.

Date	Mintage	VG	F	VF	XF	Unc
1623 (ee)	—	45.00	115	200	400	—
1624 (ee)	—	45.00	115	200	400	—
1625 (ee)	—	45.00	115	200	400	—
1626 (ee)	—	45.00	115	200	400	—
1627 (ee)	—	45.00	115	200	400	—
1628 (ee)	—	45.00	115	200	400	—
1629 (ee)	—	45.00	115	200	400	—
1630 (ee)	—	45.00	115	200	400	—
1631 (ee)	—	45.00	115	200	400	—
163Z (ee)	—	45.00	115	200	400	—
1633 (ee)	—	45.00	115	200	400	—
1633 (dd)	—	45.00	115	200	400	—
1633 (ff)	—	45.00	115	200	400	—
1634 (ff)	—	45.00	115	200	400	—
1636 (ff)	—	45.00	115	200	400	—
1636 (hh)	—	45.00	115	200	400	—
1637 (hh)	—	45.00	115	200	400	—

KM# 421 THALER
Silver **Ruler:** Ferdinand III **Obv:** Bare-headed bust right **Rev:** Crowned imperial eagle **Mint:** Kuttenberg **Note:** Dav. #3212. Prev. KM#1108.

Date	Mintage	VG	F	VF	XF	Unc
1638 (hh)	—	110	195	325	550	—
1639 (hh)	—	110	195	325	550	—
1641 (hh)	—	110	195	325	550	—

KM# 440 THALER
Silver **Ruler:** Ferdinand III **Obv:** Laureate bust right **Rev:** Crowned imperial eagle **Mint:** Kuttenberg **Note:** Dav. #3213. Prev. KM#1109.

Date	Mintage	VG	F	VF	XF	Unc
1639 (hh)	—	110	195	325	550	—
1641 (hh)	—	110	195	325	550	—
1643 (hh)	—	110	195	325	550	—

KM# 497 THALER
Silver **Ruler:** Ferdinand III **Obv:** Large laureate bust right **Rev:** Crowned imperial eagle **Mint:** Kuttenberg **Note:** Dav. #3282. Prev. KM#1124.

Date	Mintage	VG	F	VF	XF	Unc
1659 (ii) Rare	—	—	—	—	—	—
1666 (ii)	—	450	775	1,300	1,950	—
1669 (ii)	—	450	775	1,300	1,950	—
1671 (ii)	—	450	775	1,300	1,950	—

KM# 612 THALER
Silver **Ruler:** Leopold I **Obv:** Older large laureate bust right **Rev:** Crowned imperial eagle **Mint:** Kuttenberg **Note:** Prev. KM#1126. Dav. #3284.

Date	Mintage	VG	F	VF	XF	Unc
1695 (jj)	—	325	600	1,000	1,650	—

MB# 300 THALER
Silver **Ruler:** Rudolf II **Obv:** Standing figure **Mint:** Prague **Note:** Dav. #8075. Prev. KM#1305. Varieties exist.

Date	Mintage	VG	F	VF	XF	Unc
1601 (j)	—	165	325	550	875	—
1602 (j)	—	165	325	550	875	—
1602	—	165	325	550	875	—

MB# 305 THALER
Silver **Ruler:** Rudolf II **Mint:** Prague **Note:** Klippe. Prev. KM#1306.

Date	Mintage	VG	F	VF	XF	Unc
1602 Rare	—	—	—	—	—	—

KM# 17 THALER
Silver **Ruler:** Rudolf II **Obv:** Standing figure, half right, holding scepter and orb, shield of arms on each side **Rev:** Crowned imperial eagle with shield on breast in inner circle, date in legend **Mint:** Prague **Note:** Prev. KM#1305.

Date	Mintage	VG	F	VF	XF	Unc
1601	—	165	325	550	875	—
1602	—	165	325	550	875	—

KM# 29 THALER
Silver **Ruler:** Rudolf II **Obv:** Armored bust in ruffled collar right in inner circle, ornamentatin in lower border **Mint:** Prague **Note:** Prev. KM#1306.

Date	Mintage	VG	F	VF	XF	Unc
1602 Rare	—	—	—	—	—	—

KM# 25 THALER
Silver **Ruler:** Rudolf II **Obv:** Armored bust in ruffled collar **Rev:** Crowned imperial eagle **Mint:** Prague **Note:** Varieties exist. Dav. #3019. Prev. KM#1307.

Date	Mintage	VG	F	VF	XF	Unc
1603 (j)	—	165	325	550	950	—
1604 (j)	—	165	325	550	950	—
1605 (j)	—	165	325	550	950	—
1606 (j)	—	165	325	550	950	—
1607 (j)	—	165	325	550	950	—
1608 (j)	—	165	325	550	950	—
1609 (k)	—	165	325	550	950	—
1610 (k)	—	165	325	550	950	—
1610 (l)	—	165	325	550	950	—
1611 (l)	—	165	325	550	950	—

KM# 53 THALER
Silver **Ruler:** Rudolf II **Mint:** Prague **Note:** Klippe. Dav. #3019A. Prev. KM#1308.

Date	Mintage	VG	F	VF	XF	Unc
1604 (j) Rare	—	—	—	—	—	—
1606 (j) Rare	—	—	—	—	—	—
1607 (j) Rare	—	—	—	—	—	—

KM# 100 THALER
Silver **Ruler:** Rudolf II **Obv:** Crowned bust right **Rev:** Crowned shield in collar of the Golden Fleece **Mint:** Prague **Note:** Dav. #3057. Prev. KM#1334.

Date	Mintage	VG	F	VF	XF	Unc
1611 (l)	—	275	525	1,000	1,600	—
ND	—	275	500	925	1,500	—

KM# 101 THALER
Silver **Ruler:** Rudolf II **Obv:** Crowned bust right in ruffled collar **Rev:** Crowned shield in collar of the Golden Fleece **Mint:** Prague **Note:** Dav. #3058. Prev. KM#1335.

Date	Mintage	VG	F	VF	XF	Unc
1611 (l)	—	165	325	550	875	—
1612 (l)	—	165	325	550	875	—

KM# 124 THALER

Silver **Ruler:** Matthias II **Obv:** Bust right in ruffled collar **Rev:** Maximilian I, Charles V and Ferdinand I **Mint:** Prague **Note:** Dav. #3064.

Date	Mintage	VG	F	VF	XF	Unc
ND (l)	—	725	1,350	2,750	5,000	—

KM# 123 THALER

Silver **Ruler:** Matthias II **Obv:** Crowned conjoined busts of Maximilian I, Charles V and Ferdinand I **Rev:** Crowned imperial eagle **Mint:** Prague **Note:** Dav. #3066. Prev. KM#1339.

Date	Mintage	VG	F	VF	XF	Unc
ND(1612-19)	—	725	1,350	2,750	5,000	—

KM# 126 THALER

Silver **Ruler:** Matthias II **Obv:** Bust of Matthias right in inner circle **Rev:** Crowned busts of Maximilian I, Charles V, and Ferdinand I right in inner circle **Mint:** Prague **Note:** Prev. KM#1338.

Date	Mintage	VG	F	VF	XF	Unc
ND	—	650	1,150	2,000	3,500	—

KM# 161 THALER

Silver **Ruler:** Matthias II **Obv:** Bust right in ruffled collar **Rev:** Crowned imperial eagle **Mint:** Prague **Note:** Prev. KM#1336. Dav. #3061.

Date	Mintage	VG	F	VF	XF	Unc
1613 (l)	—	85.00	175	350	575	—
1614 (l)	—	85.00	175	350	575	—
1615 (l)	—	85.00	175	350	575	—
1616 (l)	—	85.00	175	350	575	—
1617 (l)	—	85.00	175	350	575	—
1618 (l)	—	85.00	175	350	575	—
1619 (l)	—	85.00	175	350	575	—

KM# 180 THALER

Silver **Ruler:** Matthias II **Obv:** Bust right in ruffled collar **Rev:** Crowned imperial eagle in inner circle, date in legend **Mint:** Prague **Note:** Klippe. Dav. #3061A. Prev. KM#1337.

Date	Mintage	VG	F	VF	XF	Unc
1615 (l) Rare	—	—	—	—	—	—

KM# 270 THALER

Silver **Ruler:** Ferdinand II **Obv:** Crowned full-length armored figure holding scepter and orb, turned slightly right, crowned arms of Bohemia and Electoral Pfalz to left and right, titles of Friedrich **Rev:** Round five-fold arms, date in legend **Mint:** Prague **Note:** Prev. KM#99(1558).

Date	Mintage	VG	F	VF	XF	Unc
1620 (m)	—	—	—	—	—	—

KM# 354 THALER

28.8500 g., Silver **Ruler:** Ferdinand II **Rev:** Arms of Bohemia on eagle's breast **Mint:** Prague **Note:** Prev. KM#1390.1. Dav. #3136.

Date	Mintage	VG	F	VF	XF	Unc
1623 (n)	—	42.00	110	185	350	—
1624 (n)	—	42.00	110	185	350	—
1625 (n)	—	42.00	110	185	350	—
1625 (l)	—	42.00	110	185	350	—
1626 (l)	—	42.00	110	185	350	—
1627 (l)	—	42.00	110	185	350	—
1628 (l)	—	42.00	110	185	350	—
1629 (l)	—	42.00	110	185	350	—
1630 (l)	—	42.00	110	185	350	—
1630 (o)	—	42.00	110	185	350	—
1631 (o)	—	42.00	110	185	350	—
1631 (p)	—	42.00	110	185	350	—
1632 (p)	—	42.00	110	185	350	—
1633 (p)	—	42.00	110	185	350	—
1634 (p)	—	42.00	110	185	350	—
1635 (p)	—	42.00	110	185	350	—
1637 (p)	—	42.00	110	185	350	—
1637 (q)	—	42.00	110	185	350	—
1638 (q)	—	42.00	110	185	350	—

Note: 1638 coins are posthumous

KM# 353 THALER

Silver **Ruler:** Ferdinand II **Obv:** Full-length crowned and armored figure slightly right, with scepter and orb, crowned arms of Bohemia and Hungary to left and right, titles of Ferdinand II **Rev:** Crowned imperial eagle, Austria-Burgundy arms on breast, date in legend **Mint:** Prague

Date	Mintage	VG	F	VF	XF	Unc
1623 (n)	—	—	—	—	—	—

KM# 376 THALER

Silver **Ruler:** Ferdinand II **Obv:** No arms to left or right of figure **Mint:** Prague

Date	Mintage	VG	F	VF	XF	Unc
1624 (n)	—	—	—	—	—	—

KM# 377 THALER

Silver **Ruler:** Ferdinand II **Mint:** Prague **Note:** Klippe. Dav. #3136A. Prev. KM#1391.1.

Date	Mintage	VG	F	VF	XF	Unc
1624 (n) Rare	—	—	—	—	—	—

KM# 389 THALER

Silver **Ruler:** Ferdinand II **Obv:** Standing figure, "g" between feet **Mint:** Prague **Note:** Dav. #3136C. Prev. KM#1403. Varieties exist.

Date	Mintage	VG	F	VF	XF	Unc
1626 (l)	—	42.00	110	185	350	—

KM# 395 THALER

Silver **Ruler:** Ferdinand II **Obv:** Standing figure, slightly right, holding orb and scepter, titles of Ferdinand II **Rev:** Crowned imperial eagle **Mint:** Prague **Note:** Dav. #3137. Prev. KM#1392.

Date	Mintage	VG	F	VF	XF	Unc
1629 (l)	—	45.00	120	200	375	—
1630 (l)	—	45.00	120	200	375	—
1631 (p)	—	45.00	120	200	375	—

KM# 420 THALER

Silver **Ruler:** Ferdinand III **Obv:** Bare-headed bust right in lace collar **Rev:** Crowned imperial eagle **Mint:** Prague **Note:** Dav. #3204. Prev. KM#1415.

Date	Mintage	VG	F	VF	XF	Unc
1638 (q)	—	85.00	165	275	475	—
1639 (q)	—	85.00	165	275	475	—
1640 (q)	—	85.00	165	275	475	—
1641 (q)	—	85.00	165	275	475	—

KM# 453 THALER

Silver **Ruler:** Ferdinand III **Obv:** Laureate bust right **Rev:** Crowned imperial eagle **Mint:** Prague **Note:** Dav. #3205. Prev. KM#1416.

Date	Mintage	VG	F	VF	XF	Unc
1641 (q)	—	85.00	165	275	475	—
1642 (q)	—	85.00	165	275	475	—
1643 (q)	—	85.00	165	275	475	—
1644 (q)	—	85.00	165	275	475	—
1645 (q)	—	85.00	165	275	475	—
1646 (q)	—	85.00	165	275	475	—
1647 (q)	—	85.00	165	275	475	—
1648 (q)	—	85.00	165	275	475	—
1649 (q)	—	85.00	165	275	475	—
1653 (q)	—	85.00	165	275	475	—
1656 (r)	—	85.00	165	275	475	—

KM# 575 THALER
Silver **Ruler:** Leopold I **Obv:** Laureate bust right **Rev:** Crowned imperial eagle holding sword and scepter **Mint:** Prague **Note:** Prev. KM#1439. Dav. #3278.

Date	Mintage	VG	F	VF	XF	Unc
1674 (s) Rare	—	—	—	—	—	—

KM# 611 THALER
Silver **Ruler:** Leopold I **Obv:** Large laureate bust right in long wig, lion's head at shoulder **Rev:** Crowned imperial eagle holding sword and scepter **Mint:** Prague **Note:** Prev. KM#1440.1. Dav. #3279.

Date	Mintage	VG	F	VF	XF	Unc
1695 GE	—	130	250	450	925	—

KM# 616 THALER
Silver **Ruler:** Leopold I **Obv:** Large laureate bust right in long wig, without lion head at shoulder **Mint:** Prague **Note:** Prev. KM#1440.2. Dav. #1006.

Date	Mintage	VG	F	VF	XF	Unc
1696 GE	—	120	200	350	850	—

MB# 319 1-1/2 THALER
Silver **Ruler:** Franz II **Obv:** Laureate bust right, titles of Franz II **Mint:** Prague **Note:** Dav. #A8075.

Date	Mintage	VG	F	VF	XF	Unc
1594 (i)	—	—	—	—	—	—

KM# 128 1-1/2 THALER
Silver **Ruler:** Matthias II **Obv:** Bust right in ruffled collar **Rev:** Crowned busts of Maximilian, Charles V, and Ferdinand I **Mint:** Prague **Note:** Prev. KM#1340. Dav. #A3063.

Date	Mintage	VG	F	VF	XF	Unc
ND (I) Rare	—	—	—	—	—	—

KM# 127 1-1/2 THALER
Silver **Ruler:** Matthias II **Obv:** Crowned busts of Maximilian, Charles V, and Ferdinand I **Rev:** Crowned imperial eagle **Mint:** Prague **Note:** Prev. KM#1341.

Date	Mintage	VG	F	VF	XF	Unc
ND(1612-19) Rare	—	—	—	—	—	—

KM# 91 2 THALER
Silver **Ruler:** Rudolf II **Mint:** Budweis

Date	Mintage	VG	F	VF	XF	Unc
1609 (bf) Rare	—	—	—	—	—	—

MB# 312 2 THALER
Silver **Ruler:** Rudolf II **Obv:** Young armored bust in ruffled collar right in inner circle **Rev:** Crowned imperial eagle with sword and secpter in inner circle, date in legend **Mint:** Joachimstal **Note:** Dav. #8077, A3020. Prev. KM#877.

Date	Mintage	VG	F	VF	XF	Unc
1602 (ah)	—	—	—	—	—	—
1603 (ah)	—	—	—	—	—	—

KM# 71 2 THALER
Silver **Ruler:** Rudolf II **Obv:** Older armored bust right, lion and two arabesques below **Mint:** Joachimstal **Note:** Dav. #A3021. Prev. KM#878.1.

Date	Mintage	VG	F	VF	XF	Unc
1605 (ai) Rare	—	—	—	—	—	—
1606 (ai) Rare	—	—	—	—	—	—

KM# 90 2 THALER
Silver **Ruler:** Rudolf II **Obv:** Without arabesques below bust **Mint:** Joachimstal **Note:** Prev. KM#878.2.

Date	Mintage	VG	F	VF	XF	Unc
1609 (aj) Rare	—	—	—	—	—	—

KM# 211 2 THALER
Silver **Ruler:** Matthias II **Obv:** Bust in ruffled collar right in inner circle **Rev:** Crowned imperial eagle, date in legend **Mint:** Joachimstal **Note:** Dav. #A3068. Prev. KM#889.

Date	Mintage	VG	F	VF	XF	Unc
1618 (aj) Rare	—	—	—	—	—	—

KM# 315 2 THALER
Silver **Ruler:** Ferdinand II **Obv:** Laureate bust right in inner circle **Rev:** Crowned imperial eagle in inner circle, date in legend **Mint:** Joachimstal **Note:** Prev. KM#905.

Date	Mintage	VG	F	VF	XF	Unc
1621 (ak) Rare	—	—	—	—	—	—

KM# 362 2 THALER
Silver **Ruler:** Ferdinand II **Obv:** Ferdinand II standing holding orb and scepter in inner circle **Mint:** Joachimstal **Note:** Prev. KM#906. Dav. #A3141.

Date	Mintage	VG	F	VF	XF	Unc
1623 (ak)	—	600	1,100	1,800	2,700	—
1624 (ak)	—	600	1,100	1,800	2,700	—
1625 (ak)	—	600	1,100	1,800	2,700	—
1626 (ak)	—	600	1,100	1,800	2,700	—
1627 (ak)	—	600	1,100	1,800	2,700	—
1630 (ak)	—	600	1,100	1,800	2,700	—
1631 (ak)	—	600	1,100	1,800	2,700	—
1632 (ak)	—	600	1,100	1,800	2,700	—

KM# 454 2 THALER
Silver **Ruler:** Ferdinand III **Obv:** Bare head of Ferdinand III right in inner circle **Rev:** Crowned imperial eagle in inner circle, date in legend **Mint:** Joachimstal **Note:** Prev. KM#921. Dav. #3207.

Date	Mintage	VG	F	VF	XF	Unc
1641 (al) Rare	—	—	—	—	—	—
1643 (al) Rare	—	—	—	—	—	—

KM# 38 2 THALER
Silver **Ruler:** Rudolf II **Rev:** Oval four-fold arms of Bohemia and Hungary with central shield of Austria-Burgundy on eagle's breast **Mint:** Kuttenberg **Note:** Dav. #3027. Prev. KM#1035.

Date	Mintage	VG	F	VF	XF	Unc
1603 (Y)	—	—	—	—	—	—

KM# 39 2 THALER
Silver **Ruler:** Rudolf II **Obv:** Bust right, lion below **Rev:** Crowned imperial eagle **Mint:** Kuttenberg **Note:** Dav. #3027A. Prev. KM#1036.

Date	Mintage	VG	F	VF	XF	Unc
1603 (z)	—	80.00	150	240	425	—
1604 (z)	—	80.00	150	240	425	—
1605 (z)	—	80.00	150	240	425	—
1606 (z)	—	80.00	150	240	425	—
1607 (z)	—	80.00	150	240	425	—
1608 (z)	—	80.00	150	240	425	—
1608 (aa)	—	80.00	150	240	425	—
1609 (aa)	—	80.00	150	240	425	—
1610 (aa)	—	80.00	150	240	425	—
1611 (aa)	—	80.00	150	240	425	—

KM# 70 2 THALER
Silver **Ruler:** Rudolf II **Mint:** Kuttenberg **Note:** Klippe. Dav. #3027B. Prev. KM#1037.

Date	Mintage	VG	F	VF	XF	Unc
1605 (z) Rare	—	—	—	—	—	—

KM# 130 2 THALER
Silver **Ruler:** Matthias II **Obv:** Large crowned bust right **Rev:** Crowned shield divides date in order collar **Mint:** Kuttenberg **Note:** Dav. #A3069. Prev. KM#1059.

Date	Mintage	VG	F	VF	XF	Unc
1612 (aa) Rare	—	—	—	—	—	—
1612 (bb) Rare	—	—	—	—	—	—

KM# 166 2 THALER
Silver **Ruler:** Matthias II **Obv:** Large bust right **Rev:** Crowned imperial eagle **Mint:** Kuttenberg **Note:** Dav. #3070. Prev. KM#1060 and #1061. Varieties exist.

Date	Mintage	VG	F	VF	XF	Unc
1613 (bb)	—	725	1,200	2,000	3,300	—
1614 (bb)	—	725	1,200	2,000	3,300	—
1615 (cc)	—	725	1,200	2,000	3,300	—
1616 (aa)	—	725	1,200	2,000	3,300	—
1616 (dd)	—	725	1,200	2,000	3,300	—
1617 (ee)	—	725	1,200	2,000	3,300	—
1618 (ee)	—	725	1,200	2,000	3,300	—
1619 (ee)	—	725	1,200	2,000	3,300	—

KM# 361 2 THALER
Silver **Ruler:** Ferdinand II **Obv:** Standing figure of Ferdinand II holding orb and scepter **Rev:** Crowned imperial eagle **Mint:** Kuttenberg **Note:** Prev. KM#1096. Dav. #3142. Varieties exist.

Date	Mintage	VG	F	VF	XF	Unc
1623 (ee)	—	600	1,100	1,800	3,000	—
1624 (ee)	—	600	1,100	1,800	3,000	—
1625 (ee)	—	600	1,100	1,800	3,000	—
1626 (ee)	—	600	1,100	1,800	3,000	—
1627 (ee)	—	600	1,100	1,800	3,000	—
1628 (ee)	—	600	1,100	1,800	3,000	—
1630 (ee)	—	600	1,100	1,800	3,000	—
1631 (ee)	—	600	1,100	1,800	3,000	—
1632 (ee)	—	600	1,100	1,800	3,000	—
1634 (ff)	—	600	1,100	1,800	3,000	—

KM# 422 2 THALER
Silver **Ruler:** Ferdinand III **Obv:** Bare-headed bust right **Rev:** Crowned imperial eagle **Mint:** Kuttenberg **Note:** Prev. KM#1110. Dav. #3211.

Date	Mintage	VG	F	VF	XF	Unc
1638 (hh) Rare	—	—	—	—	—	—

KM# 564 2 THALER
Silver **Ruler:** Leopold I **Obv:** Bust right **Rev:** Crowned imperial eagle **Mint:** Kuttenberg

Date	Mintage	VG	F	VF	XF	Unc
1666 Rare	—	—	—	—	—	—

MB# 320 2 THALER

Silver **Ruler:** Matthias II **Obv:** Armored bust in ruffled collar right **Rev:** Crowned imperial eagle **Mint:** Prague **Note:** Dav. #3018. Prev. KM#1309.

Date	Mintage	VG	F	VF	XF	Unc
1602 (j)	—	600	1,000	2,000	3,500	—
1603 (j)	—	600	1,000	2,000	3,500	—
1604 (j)	—	600	1,000	2,000	3,500	—
1605 (j)	—	600	1,000	2,000	3,500	—
1606 (j)	—	600	1,000	2,000	3,500	—
1608 (j)	—	600	1,000	2,000	3,500	—
1609 (j)	—	600	1,000	2,000	3,500	—
1609 (k)	—	600	1,000	2,000	3,500	—
1610 (k)	—	600	1,000	2,000	3,500	—
1610 (l)	—	600	1,000	2,000	3,500	—
1611 (l)	—	600	1,000	2,000	3,500	—

KM# 54 2 THALER

Silver **Ruler:** Rudolf II **Mint:** Prague **Note:** Klippe. Dav. #3018A.

Date	Mintage	VG	F	VF	XF	Unc
1604 (j) Rare	—	—	—	—	—	—
1606 (j) Rare	—	—	—	—	—	—

KM# 103 2 THALER

Silver **Ruler:** Rudolf II **Obv:** Crowned bust right **Rev:** Crowned shield in collar of the Order of the Golden Fleece **Mint:** Prague **Note:** Prev. KM#1342. Dav. #A3057.

Date	Mintage	VG	F	VF	XF	Unc
1611 (l) Rare	—	—	—	—	—	—

KM# 104 2 THALER

Silver **Ruler:** Rudolf II **Obv:** Crowned bust right in ruffled collar **Rev:** Crowned shield in collar of the Order of the Golden Fleece **Mint:** Prague

Date	Mintage	VG	F	VF	XF	Unc
1611 (l)	—	1,000	1,650	2,750	4,500	—
1612 (l)	—	1,000	1,650	2,750	4,500	—

KM# 131 2 THALER

Silver **Ruler:** Matthias II **Obv:** Crowned conjoined busts of Maximilian I, Charles V and Ferdinand I **Rev:** Crowned imperial eagle **Mint:** Prague **Note:** Dav. #3065. Prev. KM#1349.

Date	Mintage	VG	F	VF	XF	Unc
ND(1612-19) (l) Rare	—	—	—	—	—	—

KM# 132 2 THALER

Silver **Ruler:** Matthias II **Obv:** Bust of Matthias right **Rev:** Crowned bust of Maximilian I, Charles V and Ferdinand I **Mint:** Prague **Note:** Dav. #B3063. Prev. KM#1348.

Date	Mintage	VG	F	VF	XF	Unc
ND(1612-19) Rare	—	—	—	—	—	—

KM# 165 2 THALER

Silver **Ruler:** Matthias II **Obv:** Bust right in ruffled collar **Rev:** Crowned imperial eagle **Mint:** Prague **Note:** Dav. #3060. Prev. KM#1344.

Date	Mintage	VG	F	VF	XF	Unc
1613 (l)	—	275	600	1,400	2,750	—
1614 (l)	—	275	600	1,400	2,750	—
1615 (l)	—	275	600	1,400	2,750	—
1616 (l)	—	275	600	1,400	2,750	—
1618 (l)	—	275	600	1,400	2,750	—
1619 (l)	—	275	600	1,400	2,750	—

KM# 184 2 THALER

Silver **Ruler:** Matthias II **Obv:** Matthias standing flanked by shield **Rev:** Crowned imperial eagle **Mint:** Prague **Note:** Dav. #3062. Prev. KM#1346.1.

Date	Mintage	VG	F	VF	XF	Unc
1615 (l)	—	725	1,300	2,200	3,850	—
1616 (l)	—	725	1,300	2,200	3,850	—
1617 (l)	—	725	1,300	2,200	3,850	—
1619 (l)	—	725	1,300	2,200	3,850	—

KM# 181 2 THALER

Silver **Ruler:** Matthias II **Obv:** Full-length figure of emperor turned slightly to right, holding orb and scepter, small crowned shield of Bohemian arms at left, Hungarian to right, titles of Matthias **Rev:** Crowned imperial eagle, arms of Austria-Burgundy on breast, chain of order around, date in legend **Mint:** Prague **Note:** Thick planchet. Dav. #3062A. Prev. KM#1347.

Date	Mintage	VG	F	VF	XF	Unc
1615 (l)	—	725	1,200	2,100	3,600	—
1618	—	725	1,200	2,100	3,600	—

KM# 183 2 THALER

Silver **Ruler:** Matthias II **Obv:** Bust right in ruffled collar **Rev:** Crowned imperial eagle **Mint:** Prague **Note:** Klippe. Dav. #3060A. Prev. KM#1345.

Date	Mintage	VG	F	VF	XF	Unc
1615 (l) Rare	—	—	—	—	—	—

KM# 359 2 THALER

Silver **Ruler:** Ferdinand II **Obv:** Laureate bust right **Rev:** Crowned imperial eagle **Mint:** Prague **Note:** Prev. KM#1393.

Date	Mintage	VG	F	VF	XF	Unc
1623 (n) Rare	—	—	—	—	—	—

KM# 360 2 THALER

Silver **Ruler:** Ferdinand II **Obv:** Standing figure of Ferdinand II **Rev:** Crowned imperial eagle **Mint:** Prague **Note:** Prev. KM#1394. Dav. #3135. Varieties exist.

Date	Mintage	VG	F	VF	XF	Unc
1623 (n) Rare	—	—	—	—	—	—
1629 (l) Rare	—	—	—	—	—	—
1630 (l) Rare	—	—	—	—	—	—
1632 (p) Rare	—	—	—	—	—	—

KM# 358 2 THALER

Silver **Ruler:** Ferdinand II **Mint:** Prague **Note:** Dav. #3134.

Date	Mintage	VG	F	VF	XF	Unc
1623 (n) Rare	—	—	—	—	—	—

KM# 396 2 THALER
Silver **Ruler:** Ferdinand II **Obv:** Laureate bust facing in ruffled collar **Rev:** Crowned imperial eagle **Mint:** Prague **Note:** Prev. KM#1395. Dav. #3138.

Date	Mintage	VG	F	VF	XF	Unc
1630 (l) Rare	—	—	—	—	—	—

KM# 198 2-1/2 THALER
Silver **Ruler:** Matthias II **Obv:** Matthias standing holding scepter and orb in inner circle **Rev:** Crowned imperial eagle in inner circle; date in legend **Mint:** Prague **Note:** Klippe.

Date	Mintage	VG	F	VF	XF	Unc
1616 (c) Rare	—	—	—	—	—	—

KM# 455 3 THALER
Silver **Ruler:** Ferdinand III **Obv:** Bare head of Ferdinand III **Mint:** Joachimstal **Note:** Prev. KM#923. Dav. #3206.

Date	Mintage	VG	F	VF	XF	Unc
1641 (al) Rare	—	—	—	—	—	—

KM# 472 3 THALER
Silver **Ruler:** Ferdinand III **Obv:** Laureate head of Ferdinand III **Mint:** Joachimstal **Note:** Prev. KM#924. Dav. #B3209.

Date	Mintage	VG	F	VF	XF	Unc
1644 (al) Rare	—	—	—	—	—	—

KM# 40 3 THALER
Silver **Ruler:** Rudolf II **Obv:** Armored bust in ruffled collar right **Rev:** Crowned imperial eagle, oval shield on breast **Mint:** Kuttenberg **Note:** Dav. #3026. Prev. KM#1038.

Date	Mintage	VG	F	VF	XF	Unc
1603 Rare	—	—	—	—	—	—

KM# 41 3 THALER
Silver **Ruler:** Rudolf II **Obv:** Bust right in ruffled collar **Rev:** Crowned imperial eagle, flat-topped shield on breast **Mint:** Kuttenberg **Note:** Dav. #3026A. Prev. KM#1039.

Date	Mintage	VG	F	VF	XF	Unc
1603 (z) Rare	—	—	—	—	—	—
1607 (z) Rare	—	—	—	—	—	—
1608 (z) Rare	—	—	—	—	—	—

MB# 324 3 THALER
Silver **Ruler:** Rudolf II **Mint:** Prague **Note:** Dav. #A8074.

Date	Mintage	VG	F	VF	XF	Unc
1603 (y) Rare	—	—	—	—	—	—

KM# 135 3 THALER
Silver **Ruler:** Matthias II **Obv:** Bust of Matthias right in ruffled collar **Rev:** Crowned conjoined busts of Maximilian I, Charles V, and Ferdinand I **Mint:** Prague **Note:** Prev. KM#1352. Dav. #C3063.

Date	Mintage	VG	F	VF	XF	Unc
ND (l) Rare	—	—	—	—	—	—

KM# 134 3 THALER
Silver **Ruler:** Matthias II **Obv:** Crowned bust of Maximilian I, Charles V, and Ferdinand I **Rev:** Crowned imperial eagle **Mint:** Prague **Note:** Prev. KM#1353.

Date	Mintage	VG	F	VF	XF	Unc
ND(612-19) Rare	—	—	—	—	—	—

KM# 199 3 THALER
Silver **Ruler:** Matthias II **Obv:** Matthias standing holding scepter and orb **Rev:** Crowned imperial eagle **Mint:** Prague **Note:** Dav. #B3059. Prev. KM#1351.

Date	Mintage	VG	F	VF	XF	Unc
1616 (l) Rare	—	—	—	—	—	—

KM# 364 3 THALER
Silver **Ruler:** Matthias II **Mint:** Prague **Note:** Prev. KM#365.

Date	Mintage	VG	F	VF	XF	Unc
1623 (n) Rare	—	—	—	—	—	—

KM# 473 4 THALER
Silver **Ruler:** Matthias II **Obv:** Laureate bust right in inner circle **Rev:** Crowned imperial eagle in inner circle, date in legend **Mint:** Joachimstal **Note:** Prev. KM#925. Dav. #3209.

Date	Mintage	VG	F	VF	XF	Unc
1644 (al) Rare	—	—	—	—	—	—

KM# 42 4 THALER
Silver **Ruler:** Rudolf II **Obv:** Armored bust in ruffled collar right **Rev:** Crowned imperial eagle **Mint:** Kuttenberg **Note:** Prev. KM#35. Dav. #A3026.

Date	Mintage	VG	F	VF	XF	Unc
1603 (z) Rare	—	—	—	—	—	—
1604 (z) Rare	—	—	—	—	—	—

KM# 137 4 THALER
Silver **Ruler:** Matthias II **Obv:** Bust of Matthias right **Rev:** Crowned busts of Maximilian I, Charles V, and Ferdinand I **Mint:** Prague **Note:** Prev. KM#1354. Dav. #3063.

Date	Mintage	VG	F	VF	XF	Unc
ND (l) Rare	—	—	—	—	—	—

KM# 187 5 THALER
Silver **Ruler:** Matthias II **Obv:** Matthias standing holding scepter and orb **Rev:** Crowned imperial eagle **Mint:** Prague **Note:** Prev. KM#1355. Dav. #3059.

Date	Mintage	VG	F	VF	XF	Unc
1615 (l) Rare	—	—	—	—	—	—
1619 (l) Rare	—	—	—	—	—	—

KM# 400 6 THALER
Silver **Ruler:** Ferdinand II **Obv:** Standing figure of Ferdinand holding orb and scepter **Rev:** Crowned imperial eagle **Mint:** Kuttenberg **Note:** Prev. KM#1097. Dav. #A3142.

Date	Mintage	VG	F	VF	XF	Unc
1631 (ee) Rare	—	—	—	—	—	—

TRADE COINAGE

KM# 587 1/4 DUCAT
0.8750 g., 0.9860 Gold 0.0277 oz. AGW **Ruler:** Leopold I **Obv:** Laureate bust right, titles of Leopold I **Rev:** Crowned imperial eagle holding sword and scepter in talons, Bohemian arms on breast, date divided by crown at top, titles continuous **Mint:** Kuttenberg **Note:** Prev. KM#1128.

Date	Mintage	VG	F	VF	XF	Unc
1690 (jj) Rare	—	—	—	—	—	—

KM# 598 1/4 DUCAT
0.8750 g., 0.9860 Gold 0.0277 oz. AGW **Ruler:** Leopold I **Obv:** Older laureate bust right in long wig **Rev:** Crowned imperial eagle with sword and scepter **Mint:** Kuttenberg **Note:** Prev. KM#1441.

Date	Mintage	VG	F	VF	XF	Unc
1694 PM	—	150	300	500	875	—
1694 GE	—	150	300	500	875	—
1695 GE	—	150	300	500	875	—

KM# 588 1/2 DUCAT
1.7500 g., 0.9860 Gold 0.0555 oz. AGW **Ruler:** Rudolf II **Mint:** Kuttenberg **Note:** Prev. KM#1129.

Date	Mintage	VG	F	VF	XF	Unc
1690 (jj) Rare	—	—	—	—	—	—

KM# 79 1/2 DUCAT
1.7500 g., 0.9860 Gold 0.0555 oz. AGW **Ruler:** Rudolf II **Subject:** New Years **Mint:** Prague **Note:** Prev. KM#1311.

Date	Mintage	VG	F	VF	XF	Unc
1606	—	—	—	—	—	—

KM# 562 1/2 DUCAT
1.7500 g., 0.9860 Gold 0.0555 oz. AGW **Ruler:** Rudolf II **Obv:** Laureate bust right **Rev:** Crowned imperial eagle **Mint:** Prague **Note:** Prev. KM#1442.

Date	Mintage	VG	F	VF	XF	Unc
1665 (r)	—	165	325	550	900	—

KM# 614 1/2 DUCAT
1.7500 g., 0.9860 Gold 0.0555 oz. AGW **Ruler:** Rudolf II **Obv:** Laureate bust right **Rev:** Crowned imperial eagle with sword and scepter **Mint:** Prague **Note:** Prev. KM#1442.

Date	Mintage	VG	F	VF	XF	Unc
1695 GE	—	165	325	550	900	—

MB# 316 DUCAT
Silver **Ruler:** Rudolf II **Rev:** Arms of Austria-Burgundy on breast of eagle with Order of the Golden Fleece **Mint:** Prague **Note:** Varieties exist. Prev. KM#1312.

Date	Mintage	VG	F	VF	XF	Unc
1601 (j)	—	120	220	550	900	—
1602 (j)	—	120	220	550	900	—
1603 (j)	—	120	220	550	900	—
1604 (j)	—	120	220	550	900	—
1605 (j)	—	120	220	550	900	—

KM# 81 DUCAT
Silver **Ruler:** Rudolf II **Rev:** Crowned imperial eagle **Mint:** Prague **Note:** Varieties exist. Prev. KM#1313.

Date	Mintage	VG	F	VF	XF	Unc
1606 (j)	—	120	220	550	900	—
1608 (j)	—	120	220	550	900	—
1609 (k)	—	120	220	550	900	—
1610 (k)	—	120	220	550	900	—
1610 (l)	—	120	220	550	900	—
1611 (l)	—	120	220	550	900	—

KM# 106 DUCAT
Silver **Ruler:** Matthias II **Obv:** Matthias standing dividing date **Rev:** St. Wenceslas **Mint:** Prague **Note:** Prev. KM#1356.

Date	Mintage	VG	F	VF	XF	Unc
1611 (l)	—	200	350	750	1,500	—
1612 (l)	—	200	350	750	1,500	—
ND (l)	—	200	350	750	1,500	—

KM# 168 DUCAT
Silver **Ruler:** Matthias II **Obv:** Matthias standing flanked by two shields **Rev:** Crowned imperial eagle **Mint:** Prague **Note:** Prev. KM#1357.

Date	Mintage	VG	F	VF	XF	Unc
1613 (l)	—	165	325	600	1,000	—
1614 (l)	—	165	325	600	1,000	—
1615 (l)	—	165	325	600	1,000	—
1616 (l)	—	165	325	600	1,000	—
1617 (l)	—	165	325	600	1,000	—
1618 (l)	—	165	325	600	1,000	—
1619 (l)	—	165	325	600	1,000	—

KM# 275 DUCAT
Silver **Ruler:** Ferdinand II **Obv:** Standing figure of Ferdinand II between two shield, with Golden Fleece **Rev:** Crowned imperial eagle **Mint:** Prague **Note:** Varieties exist. Prev. KM#1396.

Date	Mintage	VG	F	VF	XF	Unc
1620 (m)	—	150	250	600	1,000	—
1623 (n)	—	150	250	600	1,000	—
1626 (l)	—	150	250	600	1,000	—
1627 (l)	—	150	250	600	1,000	—
1628 (l)	—	150	250	600	1,000	—
1629 (l)	—	150	250	600	1,000	—
1630 (l)	—	150	250	600	1,000	—
1630 (o)	—	150	250	600	1,000	—
1631 (o)	—	150	250	600	1,000	—
1632 (p)	—	150	250	600	1,000	—
1633 (p)	—	150	250	600	1,000	—
1634 (p)	—	150	250	600	1,000	—
1635 (p)	—	150	250	600	1,000	—
1636 (p)	—	150	250	600	1,000	—
1637 (p)	—	150	250	600	1,000	—
1637 (q)	—	200	300	750	1,250	—

KM# 390 DUCAT
Silver **Ruler:** Ferdinand II **Obv:** Shield without Golden Fleece **Mint:** Prague **Note:** Prev. KM#1397.

Date	Mintage	VG	F	VF	XF	Unc
1626 (l)	—	150	250	600	1,000	—
1627 (l)	—	150	250	600	1,000	—
1628 (l)	—	150	250	600	1,000	—

KM# 424 DUCAT
Silver **Ruler:** Ferdinand III **Obv:** Bare head right in lace collar **Rev:** Crowned imperial eagle **Mint:** Prague **Note:** Prev. KM#1417.

Date	Mintage	VG	F	VF	XF	Unc
1638 (q)	—	165	275	650	1,100	—
1639 (q)	—	165	275	650	1,100	—
1640 (q)	—	165	275	650	1,100	—

KM# 457 DUCAT

Silver **Ruler:** Ferdinand III **Obv:** Laureate bust right in lace collar **Rev:** Crowned imperial eagle **Mint:** Prague **Note:** Prev. KM#1418.

Date	Mintage	VG	F	VF	XF	Unc
1641 (q)	—	150	250	600	1,000	—
1645 (q)	—	150	250	600	1,000	—
1646 (q)	—	150	250	600	1,000	—
1648 (q)	—	150	250	600	1,000	—
1649 (q)	—	150	250	600	1,000	—
1651 (q)	—	150	250	600	1,000	—
1652 (q)	—	150	250	600	1,000	—
1655 (r)	—	150	250	600	1,000	—
1656 (r)	—	175	275	700	1,200	—

KM# 500 DUCAT

Silver **Ruler:** Ferdinand III **Obv:** Youthful bust right **Rev:** Crowned imperial eagle **Mint:** Prague **Note:** Prev. KM#1443.

Date	Mintage	VG	F	VF	XF	Unc
1659 (r) Rare	—	—	—	—	—	—

KM# 578 DUCAT

Silver **Ruler:** Ferdinand III **Obv:** Older laureate bust right in inner circle **Rev:** Crowned imperial eagle with sword and scepter in inner circle **Mint:** Prague **Note:** Varieties exist. Prev. KM#1444.

Date	Mintage	VG	F	VF	XF	Unc
1676 (s)	—	150	250	600	1,000	—
1680 (s)	—	150	250	600	1,000	—
1684 (s)	—	150	250	600	1,000	—
1685 (s)	—	150	250	600	1,000	—
1692 MV	—	150	250	600	1,000	—
1693 (t) MV	—	150	250	600	1,000	—
1693 MV	—	150	250	600	1,000	—
1694 MV	—	150	250	600	1,000	—

KM# 599 DUCAT

3.5000 g., 0.9860 Gold 0.1109 oz. AGW **Ruler:** Leopold I **Obv:** Older laureate bust right without inner circle **Rev:** Crowned imperial eagle with sword and scepter without inner circle **Mint:** Prague **Note:** Prev. KM#1445. Varieties exist.

Date	Mintage	VG	F	VF	XF	Unc
1694 PM	—	165	275	650	1,100	—
1694 GE	—	165	275	650	1,100	—
1695 GE	—	165	275	650	1,100	—
1696 GE	—	165	275	650	1,100	—
1698 GE	—	165	275	650	1,100	—
1699 GE	—	165	275	650	1,100	—
1700 GE	—	165	275	650	1,100	—

KM# 138 2 DUCAT

7.5000 g., 0.9860 Gold 0.2377 oz. AGW **Ruler:** Rudolf II **Mint:** Joachimstal

Date	Mintage	VG	F	VF	XF	Unc
1612 (aj) Rare	—	—	—	—	—	—

KM# 382 2 DUCAT

7.0000 g., 0.9860 Gold 0.2219 oz. AGW **Ruler:** Ferdinand II **Obv:** Ferdinand II standing right between two shields **Rev:** Crowned imperial eagle **Mint:** Joachimstal **Note:** Prev. KM#907.

Date	Mintage	VG	F	VF	XF	Unc
1625 (ak)	—	325	1,000	1,950	3,250	—

KM# 569 2 DUCAT

7.0000 g., 0.9860 Gold 0.2219 oz. AGW **Ruler:** Ferdinand II **Obv:** Laureate bust right **Rev:** Crowned imperial eagle **Mint:** Kuttenberg **Note:** Prev. KM#1130.

Date	Mintage	VG	F	VF	XF	Unc
1670 (ii) Rare	—	—	—	—	—	—

KM# 55 2 DUCAT

7.5000 g., 0.9860 Gold 0.2377 oz. AGW **Ruler:** Rudolf II **Obv:** Armored bust right, titles of Rudolf II **Rev:** Crowned imperial eagle, arms of Austria-Burgundy on breast, titles continuous, date **Mint:** Prague **Note:** Struck from 1/4 Thaler dies, KM#45.

Date	Mintage	VG	F	VF	XF	Unc
1604 (j)	—	325	775	1,650	2,750	—
1609 (k)	—	325	775	1,650	2,750	—
1610 (l)	—	325	775	1,650	2,750	—
1611 (l)	—	325	775	1,650	2,750	—

KM# 82 2 DUCAT

7.5000 g., 0.9860 Gold 0.2377 oz. AGW **Ruler:** Rudolf II **Obv:** Armored bust right, titles of Rudolf II **Rev:** Crowned imperial eagle, arms of Austria-Burgundy on breast, titles continuous, date **Mint:** Prague **Note:** Prev. KM#1314.

Date	Mintage	VG	F	VF	XF	Unc
1606	—	325	775	1,650	2,750	—
1610	—	325	775	1,650	2,750	—

KM# 173 2 DUCAT

7.5000 g., 0.9860 Gold 0.2377 oz. AGW **Ruler:** Matthias II **Obv:** Bust right in wreath and feather cap **Rev:** Crowned inscription in laureate wreath **Mint:** Prague **Note:** Fr.#13. Prev. KM#1358.

Date	Mintage	VG	F	VF	XF	Unc
1614 (l)	—	300	550	1,000	1,800	—
1618 (l)	—	300	550	1,000	1,800	—

KM# 365 2 DUCAT

7.5000 g., 0.9860 Gold 0.2377 oz. AGW **Ruler:** Ferdinand II **Obv:** Standing figure of Ferdinand II, two shields flanking **Rev:** Crowned imperial eagle **Mint:** Prague **Note:** Fr. #40. Varieties exist. Prev. KM#1398.

Date	Mintage	VG	F	VF	XF	Unc
1623 (l)	—	245	475	950	1,700	—
1623 (p)	—	245	475	950	1,700	—
1624 (l)	—	245	475	950	1,700	—
1624 (n)	—	245	475	950	1,700	—
1627 (l)	—	245	475	950	1,700	—
1628 (l)	—	245	475	950	1,700	—
1629 (l)	—	245	475	950	1,700	—
1630 (o)	—	245	475	950	1,700	—
1631 (p)	—	245	475	950	1,700	—
1632 (p)	—	245	475	950	1,700	—
1633 (p)	—	245	475	950	1,700	—
1634 (p)	—	245	475	950	1,700	—
1635 (p)	—	245	475	950	1,700	—
1636 (p)	—	245	475	950	1,700	—
1637 (p)	—	245	475	950	1,700	—
1637 (q)	—	245	475	950	1,700	—

KM# 366 2 DUCAT

7.0000 g., 0.9860 Gold 0.2219 oz. AGW **Ruler:** Ferdinand II **Obv:** Ferdinand II standing facing half right flanked by two shields **Rev:** Crowned imperial eagle in inner circle, date in legend **Mint:** Prague **Note:** Prev. KM#1398.1.

Date	Mintage	VG	F	VF	XF	Unc
1623 (c)	—	240	475	950	1,700	—

KM# 425 2 DUCAT

7.0000 g., 0.9860 Gold 0.2219 oz. AGW **Ruler:** Ferdinand II **Obv:** Bare-headed bust right in lace collar **Rev:** Crowned imperial eagle **Mint:** Prague **Note:** Prev. KM#1419.

Date	Mintage	VG	F	VF	XF	Unc
1638 (q)	—	270	550	1,100	2,000	—
1639 (q)	—	270	550	1,100	2,000	—
1640 (q)	—	270	550	1,100	2,000	—

KM# 458 2 DUCAT

7.0000 g., 0.9860 Gold 0.2219 oz. AGW **Ruler:** Ferdinand III **Obv:** Laureate bust right **Rev:** Crowned imperial eagle **Mint:** Prague **Note:** Varieties exist. Prev. KM#1420.

Date	Mintage	VG	F	VF	XF	Unc
1641 (q)	—	240	475	950	1,700	—
1642 (q)	—	240	475	950	1,700	—
1643 (q)	—	240	475	950	1,700	—
1644 (q)	—	240	475	950	1,700	—
1645 (q)	—	240	475	950	1,700	—
1646 (q)	—	240	475	950	1,700	—
1647 (q)	—	240	475	950	1,700	—
1648 (q)	—	240	475	950	1,700	—
1650 (q)	—	240	475	950	1,700	—
1651 (q)	—	240	475	950	1,700	—
1651 (qx)	—	240	475	950	1,700	—
1652 (q)	—	240	475	950	1,700	—
1653 (q)	—	240	475	950	1,700	—
1654 (q)	—	240	475	950	1,700	—
1655 (q)	—	240	475	950	1,700	—
1655 (r)	—	240	475	950	1,700	—
1656 (r)	—	240	475	950	1,700	—
1657 (r)	—	240	475	950	1,700	—

KM# 501 2 DUCAT

7.0000 g., 0.9860 Gold 0.2219 oz. AGW **Ruler:** Leopold I **Obv:** Young laureate bust right **Rev:** Crowned imperial eagle **Mint:** Prague **Note:** Prev. KM#1446.

Date	Mintage	VG	F	VF	XF	Unc
1659 (r)	—	375	775	1,650	2,750	—
1660 (r)	—	375	775	1,650	2,750	—
1662 (r)	—	375	775	1,650	2,750	—

KM# 585 2 DUCAT

7.0000 g., 0.9860 Gold 0.2219 oz. AGW **Ruler:** Leopold I **Obv:** Older laureate bust right **Rev:** Crowned imperial eagle with sword and scepter **Mint:** Prague **Note:** Prev. KM#1447.

Date	Mintage	VG	F	VF	XF	Unc
1684 (s)	—	375	825	1,750	3,000	—

KM# 85 3 DUCAT

10.5000 g., 0.9860 Gold 0.3328 oz. AGW **Ruler:** Rudolf II **Mint:** Joachimstal **Note:** Struck from 1/4 Thaler dies, KM#232.

Date	Mintage	VG	F	VF	XF	Unc
1607 (aj) Rare	—	—	—	—	—	—

KM# 43 3 DUCAT

10.5000 g., 0.9860 Gold 0.3328 oz. AGW **Ruler:** Rudolf II **Rev:** Crowned shield **Mint:** Prague **Note:** Prev. KM#1315.

Date	Mintage	VG	F	VF	XF	Unc
1603 (j)	—	1,000	1,750	3,500	6,500	—
1604 (j)	—	1,000	1,750	3,500	6,500	—
1605 (j)	—	1,000	1,750	3,500	6,500	—

KM# 56 3 DUCAT

10.5000 g., 0.9860 Gold 0.3328 oz. AGW **Ruler:** Rudolf II **Mint:** Prague **Note:** Struck with 1/4 Thaler dies, KM#228.

Date	Mintage	VG	F	VF	XF	Unc
1604 (j)	—	1,000	1,750	3,500	6,500	—

KM# 83 3 DUCAT

10.5000 g., 0.9860 Gold 0.3328 oz. AGW **Ruler:** Rudolf II **Mint:** Prague **Note:** Prev. KM#1316.

Date	Mintage	VG	F	VF	XF	Unc
1606	—	1,000	1,750	3,500	6,500	—

KM# 80 3 DUCAT

10.5000 g., 0.9860 Gold 0.3328 oz. AGW **Ruler:** Matthias II **Rev:** Crowned imperial eagle **Mint:** Prague **Note:** Prev. KM#1359.

Date	Mintage	VG	F	VF	XF	Unc
1606 (j)	—	1,500	2,500	4,000	8,000	—

KM# 139 3 DUCAT
10.5000 g., 0.9860 Gold 0.3328 oz. AGW **Ruler:** Rudolf II **Mint:** Prague **Note:** Similar to 1/2 Thaler, KM#265.

Date	Mintage	VG	F	VF	XF	Unc
1612 (l) Rare	—	—	—	—	—	—

KM# 205 3 DUCAT
10.5000 g., 0.9860 Gold 0.3328 oz. AGW **Ruler:** Rudolf II **Mint:** Prague **Note:** Prev. KM#1359.

Date	Mintage	VG	F	VF	XF	Unc
1617 (l)	—	1,500	2,500	4,000	8,000	—

KM# 140 4 DUCAT
14.0000 g., 0.9860 Gold 0.4438 oz. AGW **Ruler:** Matthias II **Mint:** Joachimstal

Date	Mintage	VG	F	VF	XF	Unc
1612 (aj) Rare	—	—	—	—	—	—

KM# 57 4 DUCAT
14.0000 g., 0.9860 Gold 0.4438 oz. AGW **Ruler:** Rudolf II **Rev:** Crowned imperial eagle **Mint:** Prague **Note:** Prev. KM#1317. Struck with 1/2 Thaler dies, MB#323.

Date	Mintage	VG	F	VF	XF	Unc
1604 (j)	—	1,500	2,500	4,750	8,500	—

KM# 426 4 DUCAT
14.0000 g., 0.9860 Gold 0.4438 oz. AGW **Ruler:** Ferdinand III **Mint:** Prague **Note:** Struck with 1/2 Thaler dies, KM#417.

Date	Mintage	VG	F	VF	XF	Unc
1638 (q) Rare	—	—	—	—	—	—

KM# 475 4 DUCAT
14.0000 g., 0.9860 Gold 0.4438 oz. AGW **Ruler:** Ferdinand III **Mint:** Prague **Note:** Struck with 1/2 Thaler dies, KM#452.

Date	Mintage	VG	F	VF	XF	Unc
1644 (q) Rare	—	—	—	—	—	—

KM# 470 5 DUCAT
17.5000 g., 0.9860 Gold 0.5547 oz. AGW **Ruler:** Ferdinand III **Mint:** Joachimstal **Note:** Struck with 1/2 Thaler dies, KM#437.

Date	Mintage	VG	F	VF	XF	Unc
1643 (al)	—	2,000	3,500	6,500	10,000	—
1644 (al)	—	2,000	3,500	6,500	10,000	—

KM# 565 5 DUCAT
17.5000 g., 0.9860 Gold 0.5547 oz. AGW **Ruler:** Leopold I **Obv:** Laureate bust right **Rev:** Crowned imperial eagle **Mint:** Kuttenberg **Note:** Prev. KM#1131.

Date	Mintage	VG	F	VF	XF	Unc
1669 (ii) Rare	—	—	—	—	—	—

MB# 327 5 DUCAT
17.5000 g., 0.9860 Gold 0.5547 oz. AGW **Ruler:** Rudolf II **Obv:** Rudolf II standing **Mint:** Prague **Note:** Prev. KM#1318. Struck from dies or intended dies for 1/2 Thaler, MB#323.

Date	Mintage	VG	F	VF	XF	Unc
1603 (j)	—	1,650	3,250	6,500	10,000	—
1604 (j)	—	1,650	3,250	6,500	10,000	—
1605 (j)	—	1,650	3,250	6,500	10,000	—
1606 (j)	—	1,650	3,250	6,500	10,000	—
1610 (k)	—	1,650	3,250	6,500	10,000	—
1610 (l)	—	1,650	3,250	6,500	10,000	—
1611 (l)	—	1,650	3,250	6,500	10,000	—

KM# 73 5 DUCAT
17.5000 g., 0.9860 Gold 0.5547 oz. AGW **Ruler:** Rudolf II **Obv:** Rudolf II standing **Mint:** Prague **Note:** Struck from 1/2 Thaler dies, KM#77.

Date	Mintage	VG	F	VF	XF	Unc
1605 (j) Rare	—	—	—	—	—	—

KM# 141 5 DUCAT
17.5000 g., 0.9860 Gold 0.5547 oz. AGW **Ruler:** Matthias II **Obv:** Rudolf II standing **Mint:** Prague **Note:** Struck from Thaler dies, KM#123.

Date	Mintage	VG	F	VF	XF	Unc
ND(1612-19) Rare	—	—	—	—	—	—

KM# 170 5 DUCAT
17.5000 g., 0.9860 Gold 0.5547 oz. AGW **Ruler:** Matthias II **Obv:** Matthias standing **Mint:** Prague **Note:** Prev. KM#1360.

Date	Mintage	VG	F	VF	XF	Unc
1612 (l) Rare	—	—	—	—	—	—
1613 (l) Rare	—	—	—	—	—	—
1615 (l) Rare	—	—	—	—	—	—
1616 (l) Rare	—	—	—	—	—	—
1618 (l) Rare	—	—	—	—	—	—
1619 (l) Rare	—	—	—	—	—	—

KM# 142 5 DUCAT
17.5000 g., 0.9860 Gold 0.5547 oz. AGW **Ruler:** Matthias II **Obv:** Bust right in ruffled collar **Rev:** Crowned imperial eagle **Mint:** Prague

Date	Mintage	VG	F	VF	XF	Unc
1612 (l) Rare	—	—	—	—	—	—

KM# 277 5 DUCAT
17.5000 g., 0.9860 Gold 0.5547 oz. AGW **Ruler:** Ferdinand II **Mint:** Prague **Note:** Struck from Thaler dies, KM#270.

Date	Mintage	VG	F	VF	XF	Unc
1620 (m) Rare	—	—	—	—	—	—

KM# 317 5 DUCAT
17.5000 g., 0.9860 Gold 0.5547 oz. AGW **Ruler:** Ferdinand II **Obv:** Standing figure of Ferdinand II between two shields **Rev:** Crowned imperial eagle **Mint:** Prague **Note:** Varieties exist. Prev. KM#1399.

Date	Mintage	VG	F	VF	XF	Unc
1621 (l)	—	1,450	2,000	3,300	5,400	—
1622 (l)	—	1,450	2,000	3,300	5,400	—
1623 (n)	—	1,450	2,000	3,300	5,400	—
1624 (n)	—	1,450	2,000	3,300	5,400	—
1628 (l)	—	1,450	2,000	3,300	5,400	—
1629 (l)	—	1,450	2,000	3,300	5,400	—
1631 (p)	—	1,450	2,000	3,300	5,400	—
1633 (p)	—	1,450	2,000	3,300	5,400	—
1634 (p)	—	1,450	2,000	3,300	5,400	—
1635 (p)	—	1,450	2,000	3,300	5,400	—
1636 (p)	—	1,450	2,000	3,300	5,400	—
1637 (p)	—	1,450	2,000	3,300	5,400	—
1637 (q)	—	1,450	2,000	3,300	5,400	—

KM# 428 5 DUCAT
17.5000 g., 0.9860 Gold 0.5547 oz. AGW **Ruler:** Ferdinand III **Obv:** Bare-headed bust right in lace collar **Rev:** Crowned imperial eagle **Mint:** Prague **Note:** Prev. KM#1421. Struck with 1/2 Thaler dies, KM#417.

Date	Mintage	VG	F	VF	XF	Unc
1638 (q)	—	1,200	1,800	3,250	5,400	—
1640 (q)	—	1,200	1,800	3,250	5,400	—

KM# 459 5 DUCAT
17.5000 g., 0.9860 Gold 0.5547 oz. AGW **Ruler:** Ferdinand III **Obv:** Laureate bust right **Rev:** Crowned imperial eagle **Mint:** Prague **Note:** Prev. KM#1421. Struck with 1/2 Thaler dies, KM#452.

Date	Mintage	VG	F	VF	XF	Unc
1641 (q)	—	1,450	2,000	3,300	5,400	—
1642 (q)	—	1,450	2,000	3,300	5,400	—
1643 (q)	—	1,450	2,000	3,300	5,400	—
1644 (q)	—	1,450	2,000	3,300	5,400	—
1645 (q)	—	1,450	2,000	3,300	5,400	—
1647 (q)	—	1,450	2,000	3,300	5,400	—
1648 (q)	—	1,450	2,000	3,300	5,400	—
1654 (q)	—	1,450	2,000	3,300	5,400	—
1655 (r)	—	1,450	2,000	3,300	5,400	—

KM# 502 5 DUCAT
17.5000 g., 0.9860 Gold 0.5547 oz. AGW **Ruler:** Leopold I **Obv:** Young laureate bust right **Rev:** Crowned imperial eagle **Mint:** Prague **Note:** Prev. KM#1448.

Date	Mintage	VG	F	VF	XF	Unc
1659 (r)	—	1,200	1,800	2,650	5,500	—
1661 (r)	—	1,200	1,800	2,650	5,500	—

KM# 557 5 DUCAT
17.5000 g., 0.9860 Gold 0.5547 oz. AGW **Ruler:** Leopold I **Obv:** Older laureate bust right **Rev:** Crowned imperial eagle **Mint:** Prague **Note:** Prev. KM#1449.

Date	Mintage	VG	F	VF	XF	Unc
1664 (r)	—	1,100	1,700	2,400	5,250	—
1675 (s)	—	1,100	1,700	2,400	5,250	—
1676 (s)	—	1,100	1,700	2,400	5,250	—
1689 MV	—	1,100	1,700	2,400	5,250	—
1691 MV	—	1,100	1,700	2,400	5,250	—

KM# 95 6 DUCAT
0.9860 Gold **Ruler:** Leopold I **Mint:** Prague

Date	Mintage	VG	F	VF	XF	Unc
1610 (l) Rare	—	—	—	—	—	—

KM# 143 6 DUCAT
0.9860 Gold **Ruler:** Leopold I **Mint:** Prague **Note:** Struck with Thaler dies, KM#124.

Date	Mintage	VG	F	VF	XF	Unc
ND(1612-19) (l) Rare	—	—	—	—	—	—

KM# 318 10 DUCAT
35.0000 g., 0.9860 Gold 1.1095 oz. AGW **Ruler:** Ferdinand II **Obv:** Bust right **Rev:** Crowned imperial eagle **Mint:** Joachimstal **Note:** Struck with Thaler dies, KM#314. Prev. KM#908.

Date	Mintage	VG	F	VF	XF	Unc
1621 (ak) Rare	—	—	—	—	—	—

KM# 44 10 DUCAT
35.0000 g., 0.9860 Gold 1.1095 oz. AGW **Ruler:** Rudolf II **Mint:** Kuttenberg **Note:** Prev. KM#1041.

Date	Mintage	VG	F	VF	XF	Unc
1603 (y) Rare	—	—	—	—	—	—

KM# 402 10 DUCAT
35.0000 g., 0.9860 Gold 1.1095 oz. AGW **Ruler:** Ferdinand II **Obv:** Standing figure of Ferdinand II holding globe and scepter **Rev:** Crowned imperial eagle **Mint:** Kuttenberg **Note:** Prev. KM#1098.

Date	Mintage	VG	F	VF	XF	Unc
1633 (dd) Rare	—	—	—	—	—	—

KM# 566 10 DUCAT
35.0000 g., 0.9860 Gold 1.1095 oz. AGW **Ruler:** Leopold I **Obv:** Laureate bust right **Rev:** Crowned imperial eagle **Mint:** Kuttenberg **Note:** Prev. KM#1132.

Date	Mintage	VG	F	VF	XF	Unc
1669 (ii) Rare	—	—	—	—	—	—

MB# 308 10 DUCAT
35.0000 g., 0.9860 Gold 1.1095 oz. AGW **Ruler:** Rudolf II **Obv:** Rudolf II standing **Rev:** Crowned imperial eagle **Mint:** Prague **Note:** Prev. KM#1319. Varieties exist.

Date	Mintage	VG	F	VF	XF	Unc
1589 (i)	—	4,500	7,500	11,000	16,500	—
1597 (i)	—	4,500	7,500	11,000	16,500	—
1599 (i)	—	4,500	7,500	11,000	16,500	—
1601 (j)	—	4,500	7,500	11,000	16,500	—
1603 (j)	—	4,500	7,500	11,000	16,500	—
1604 (j)	—	4,500	7,500	11,000	16,500	—
1605 (j)	—	4,500	7,500	11,000	16,500	—
1606 (j)	—	4,500	7,500	11,000	16,500	—
1608 (j)	—	4,500	7,500	11,000	16,500	—
1610 (k)	—	4,500	7,500	11,000	16,500	—
1610 (l)	—	4,500	7,500	11,000	16,500	—
1611 (l)	—	4,500	7,500	11,000	16,500	—

KM# 30 10 DUCAT
35.0000 g., 0.9860 Gold 1.1095 oz. AGW **Ruler:** Rudolf II **Obv:** Armored bust in ruffled collar **Rev:** Crowned imperial eagle **Mint:** Prague

Date	Mintage	VG	F	VF	XF	Unc
1602 Rare	—	—	—	—	—	—
1602 (j) Rare	—	—	—	—	—	—
1604 (j) Rare	—	—	—	—	—	—

KM# 146 10 DUCAT
35.0000 g., 0.9860 Gold 1.1095 oz. AGW **Ruler:** Matthias II **Mint:** Prague **Note:** Struck with Thaler dies, KM#101.

Date	Mintage	VG	F	VF	XF	Unc
1612 (l) Rare	—	—	—	—	—	—

KM# 144 10 DUCAT
35.0000 g., 0.9860 Gold 1.1095 oz. AGW **Ruler:** Matthias II **Mint:** Prague **Note:** Struck with Thaler dies, KM#123.

Date	Mintage	VG	F	VF	XF	Unc
ND(1612-19) Rare	—	—	—	—	—	—

KM# 145 10 DUCAT
35.0000 g., 0.9860 Gold 1.1095 oz. AGW **Ruler:** Matthias II **Mint:** Prague **Note:** Struck with Thaler dies, KM#124.

Date	Mintage	VG	F	VF	XF	Unc
ND(1612-19) (l) Rare	—	—	—	—	—	—

KM# 171 10 DUCAT
35.0000 g., 0.9860 Gold 1.1095 oz. AGW **Ruler:** Matthias II **Obv:** Matthias standing right, holding sceptre and orb withing inner circle **Rev:** Crowned imperial eagle, shield on breast **Mint:** Prague **Note:** Prev. KM#1361, 1362, 1364.

Date	Mintage	VG	F	VF	XF	Unc
1613 (l) Rare	—	—	—	—	—	—
1616 (l) Rare	—	—	—	—	—	—
1617 (l) Rare	—	—	—	—	—	—
1618 (l) Rare	—	—	—	—	—	—
1619 (l) Rare	—	—	—	—	—	—

KM# 278 10 DUCAT
35.0000 g., 0.9860 Gold 1.1095 oz. AGW **Ruler:** Ferdinand II **Mint:** Prague **Note:** Struck with Thaler dies, KM#270. Prev. KM#1400.

Date	Mintage	VG	F	VF	XF	Unc
1620 (m)	—	2,500	3,750	5,500	9,000	—

KM# 319 10 DUCAT
35.0000 g., 0.9860 Gold 1.1095 oz. AGW **Ruler:** Ferdinand II **Obv:** Standing figure of Ferdinand II between two shields **Rev:** Crowned imperial eagle **Mint:** Prague **Note:** Prev. KM#1400. Varieties exist.

Date	Mintage	VG	F	VF	XF	Unc
1621 (l)	—	2,500	3,750	5,500	9,000	—
1622 (l)	—	2,500	3,750	5,500	9,000	—
1623 (n)	—	2,500	3,750	5,500	9,000	—
1624 (n)	—	2,500	3,750	5,500	9,000	—
1625 (l)	—	2,500	3,750	5,500	9,000	—
1627 (l)	—	2,500	3,750	5,500	9,000	—
1628 (l)	—	2,500	3,750	5,500	9,000	—
1629 (l)	—	2,500	3,750	5,500	9,000	—
1630 (o)	—	2,500	3,750	5,500	9,000	—
1631 (p)	—	2,500	3,750	5,500	9,000	—
1633 (p)	—	2,500	3,750	5,500	9,000	—
1634 (p)	—	2,500	3,750	5,500	9,000	—
1635 (p)	—	2,500	3,750	5,500	9,000	—
1636 (p)	—	2,500	3,750	5,500	9,000	—
1637 (p)	—	2,500	3,750	5,500	9,000	—
1637 (q)	—	2,500	3,750	5,500	9,000	—

KM# 380 10 DUCAT
35.0000 g., 0.9860 Gold 1.1095 oz. AGW **Ruler:** Ferdinand II **Obv:** Standing figure of Ferdinand II without shields **Rev:** Crowned imperial eagle **Mint:** Prague **Note:** Prev. KM#1401.

Date	Mintage	VG	F	VF	XF	Unc
1624 (n)	—	2,500	4,000	6,000	9,500	—

KM# 401 10 DUCAT
35.0000 g., 0.9860 Gold 1.1095 oz. AGW **Ruler:** Ferdinand II **Obv:** Facing bust in ruffled collar **Rev:** Crowned imperial eagle **Mint:** Prague **Note:** Prev. KM#1402. Struck with Thaler dies, KM#395.

Date	Mintage	VG	F	VF	XF	Unc
1631 (p) Rare	—	—	—	—	—	—

KM# 429 10 DUCAT
35.0000 g., 0.9860 Gold 1.1095 oz. AGW **Ruler:** Ferdinand III **Obv:** Bare-headed bust right in lace collar **Rev:** Crowned imperial eagle **Mint:** Prague **Note:** Prev. KM#1422. Struck with Thaler dies, KM#420.

Date	Mintage	VG	F	VF	XF	Unc
1638 (q)	—	2,500	3,750	6,000	10,000	—
1639 (q)	—	2,500	3,750	6,000	10,000	—
1640 (q)	—	2,500	3,750	6,000	10,000	—

KM# 460 10 DUCAT
35.0000 g., 0.9860 Gold 1.1095 oz. AGW **Ruler:** Ferdinand III **Obv:** Laureate bust right in lace collar **Rev:** Crowned imperial eagle **Mint:** Prague **Note:** Prev. KM#1423. Struck with Thaler dies, KM#453.

Date	Mintage	VG	F	VF	XF	Unc
1641 (q)	—	2,500	3,750	6,000	10,000	—
1642 (q)	—	2,500	3,750	6,000	10,000	—
1643 (q)	—	2,500	3,750	6,000	10,000	—
1644 (q)	—	2,500	3,750	6,000	10,000	—
1645 (q)	—	2,500	3,750	6,000	10,000	—
1646 (q)	—	2,500	3,750	6,000	10,000	—
1647 (q)	—	2,500	3,750	6,000	10,000	—
1648 (q)	—	2,500	3,750	6,000	10,000	—
1651 (q)	—	2,500	3,750	6,000	10,000	—
1652 (q)	—	2,500	3,750	6,000	10,000	—
1654 (q)	—	2,500	3,750	6,000	10,000	—
1655 (r)	—	2,500	3,750	6,000	10,000	—

KM# 503 10 DUCAT
35.0000 g., 0.9860 Gold 1.1095 oz. AGW **Ruler:** Leopold I **Obv:** Laureate bust right **Rev:** Crowned imperial eagle **Mint:** Prague **Note:** Prev. KM#1450.

Date	Mintage	VG	F	VF	XF	Unc
1659 (r)	—	2,500	3,750	6,000	10,000	—
1661 (r)	—	2,500	3,750	6,000	10,000	—
1663 (r)	—	2,500	3,750	6,000	10,000	—

KM# 558 10 DUCAT
35.0000 g., 0.9860 Gold 1.1095 oz. AGW **Ruler:** Leopold I **Obv:** Laureate bust right **Rev:** Crowned imperial eagle with sword and scepter **Mint:** Prague **Note:** Prev. KM#1451.

Date	Mintage	VG	F	VF	XF	Unc
1664 (r)	—	2,500	3,750	6,000	10,000	—
1675 (s)	—	2,500	3,750	6,000	10,000	—

KM# 147 15 DUCAT

Gold **Ruler:** Matthias II **Mint:** Prague **Note:** Struck with Thaler dies, KM#123.

Date	Mintage	VG	F	VF	XF	Unc
ND(1612-19) Rare	—	—	—	—	—	—

KM# 148 20 DUCAT

Gold **Ruler:** Matthias II **Mint:** Prague **Note:** Struck with Thaler dies, KM#101.

Date	Mintage	VG	F	VF	XF	Unc
1612 (l) Rare	—	—	—	—	—	—

KM# 189 25 DUCAT

Gold **Ruler:** Matthias II **Mint:** Prague **Note:** Klippe. Struck with Thaler dies, KM#181.

Date	Mintage	VG	F	VF	XF	Unc
1615 (l) Rare	—	—	—	—	—	—

BOHEMIAN ESTATES

STANDARD COINAGE

KM# 214 HELLER

Silver **Ruler:** Friedrich von der Pfalz **Obv:** Crowned F divides R - B, date below **Mint:** Kuttenberg **Note:** Uniface. Prev. KM#1064.

Date	Mintage	VG	F	VF	XF	Unc
1619	—	—	—	—	—	—
Note: Reported, not confirmed						
1620	—	80.00	160	250	400	—

KM# 213 HELLER

Silver **Ruler:** Friedrich von der Pfalz **Obv:** Crowned FRI divides R - B, date below **Mint:** Kuttenberg **Note:** Uniface. Prev. KM#1160.

Date	Mintage	VG	F	VF	XF	Unc
1619	—	100	180	275	450	—

KM# 215 HELLER

Silver **Ruler:** Friedrich von der Pfalz **Obv:** Crowned FII divides R - B, date below **Mint:** Kuttenberg **Note:** Uniface. Prev. KM#1160.

Date	Mintage	VG	F	VF	XF	Unc
1619	—	120	200	300	500	—
1620	—	120	200	300	500	—

KM# 216 PFENNIG

Silver **Ruler:** Friedrich von der Pfalz **Obv:** Crowned Bohemian lion left in circle, legend, date **Obv. Legend:** IN. DEO. F.(OR)T.(I)T. (U)D.O. **Mint:** Kuttenberg **Note:** Uniface. Prev. KM#1155.

Date	Mintage	VG	F	VF	XF	Unc
1619	—	125	225	350	550	—

KM# 217 PFENNIG

Silver **Ruler:** Friedrich von der Pfalz **Obv:** Crowned Bohemian lion right in circle, legend, date **Obv. Legend:** FRIDER. REX. BO **Mint:** Kuttenberg **Note:** Uniface. Prev. KM#1161.

Date	Mintage	VG	F	VF	XF	Unc
1619	—	85.00	165	275	450	—
1620	—	85.00	165	275	450	—

KM# 232 PFENNIG

Silver **Ruler:** Friedrich von der Pfalz **Obv:** Crowned Bohemian lion left, legend, date **Obv. Legend:** FRIDER. REX. B. **Mint:** Kuttenberg **Note:** Uniface. Prev. KM#1162.

Date	Mintage	VG	F	VF	XF	Unc
1620	—	85.00	165	275	450	—

KM# 218 KREUZER

Silver **Ruler:** Friedrich von der Pfalz **Obv:** Large crown over date in circle **Obv. Legend:** MONE. REG. BOHEMI. **Rev:** Crowned Bohemian lion to right in circle, value "I" at bottom **Rev. Legend:** IN. DEO. FOR - TITVDO. **Mint:** Kuttenberg **Note:** Prev. KM#1156.

Date	Mintage	VG	F	VF	XF	Unc
1619 (ee)	—	90.00	175	275	450	—

KM# 220 3 KREUZER (Groschen)

Silver **Ruler:** Friedrich von der Pfalz **Obv:** Large crown after date **Rev:** Crowned Bohemian lion left, value below **Mint:** Joachimstal **Note:** Prev. KM#940.

Date	Mintage	VG	F	VF	XF	Unc
1619 (aj)	—	40.00	80.00	150	300	—

KM# 219 3 KREUZER (Groschen)

Silver **Ruler:** Friedrich von der Pfalz **Obv:** Large crown over date, MONET REGNI BOHEMIAE **Rev:** Crowned Bohemian lion left in circle, value (3) at bottom, IN DEO FOR - TITVDO **Mint:** Kuttenberg **Note:** Kipper 3 Kreuzer. Prev. KM#1157.

Date	Mintage	VG	F	VF	XF	Unc
1619 (ee)	—	60.00	100	180	300	—

KM# 224 12 KREUZER

Silver **Ruler:** Friedrich von der Pfalz **Obv:** Crown over date **Rev:** Crowned Bohemian lion left **Mint:** Joachimstal **Note:** Prev. KM#941.

Date	Mintage	VG	F	VF	XF	Unc
1619 (aj)	—	40.00	80.00	150	300	—
1620 (aj)	—	40.00	80.00	150	300	—

KM# 223 12 KREUZER

Silver **Ruler:** Friedrich von der Pfalz **Obv:** Crown above date **Rev:** Bohemian lion, value at bottom **Mint:** Kuttenberg **Note:** Prev. KM#1158.

Date	Mintage	VG	F	VF	XF	Unc
1619 (ee)	—	50.00	100	200	450	—

KM# 236 12 KREUZER

Silver **Ruler:** Friedrich von der Pfalz **Obv:** Crowned bust right **Rev:** Crossed arms **Mint:** Kuttenberg **Note:** Prev. KM#1163.

Date	Mintage	VG	F	VF	XF	Unc
1620 (ee)	—	70.00	120	200	325	—

KM# 222 12 KREUZER

Silver **Ruler:** Friedrich von der Pfalz **Obv:** Crown above date **Rev:** Bohemian lion, value at bottom **Mint:** Prague **Note:** Kipper. Prev. KM#91 (1550).

Date	Mintage	VG	F	VF	XF	Unc
1619 (l)	—	25.00	50.00	100	185	—

KM# 235 12 KREUZER

Silver **Ruler:** Friedrich von der Pfalz **Obv:** Crowned bust right, value (12) below, titles of Friedrich **Rev:** Crowned two-fold arms of Bohemia and Electoral Pfalz, date in legend **Mint:** Prague **Note:** Kipper. Prev. KM#92 (1551).

Date	Mintage	VG	F	VF	XF	Unc
1620 (m)	—	25.00	50.00	100	185	—

KM# 228 24 KREUZER

Silver **Ruler:** Friedrich von der Pfalz **Obv:** Crown over date **Rev:** Crowned Bohemian lion left **Mint:** Joachimstal **Note:** Prev. KM#942.

Date	Mintage	VG	F	VF	XF	Unc
1619 (aj)	—	35.00	85.00	160	275	—
1620 (aj)	—	35.00	85.00	160	275	—

KM# 239 24 KREUZER

Silver **Ruler:** Friedrich von der Pfalz **Obv:** Crowned bust right, value (24) below, titles of Friedrich **Rev:** Ornate squarish two-fold arms of Bohemia and Electoral Pfalz divide date, titles continuous **Mint:** Joachimstal **Note:** Prev. KM#945.

Date	Mintage	VG	F	VF	XF	Unc
(16)20 (aj)	—	85.00	160	265	425	—

KM# 242 24 KREUZER

Silver **Ruler:** Friedrich von der Pfalz **Rev:** Round arms **Mint:** Joachimstal **Note:** Prev. KM#946.

Date	Mintage	VG	F	VF	XF	Unc
1620 (aj)	—	40.00	90.00	175	275	—

KM# 227 24 KREUZER

Silver **Ruler:** Friedrich von der Pfalz **Obv:** Crown over date **Rev:** Bohemian lion left **Mint:** Kuttenberg **Note:** Prev. KM#1159.

Date	Mintage	VG	F	VF	XF	Unc
1619 (ee)	—	25.00	50.00	90.00	175	—
1620 (ee)	—	25.00	50.00	90.00	175	—

KM# 238 24 KREUZER

Silver **Ruler:** Friedrich von der Pfalz **Obv:** Crowned bust right, value (24) below, titles of Friedrich **Rev:** Ornate squarish two-fold arms of Bohemia and Electoral Pfalz divide date, titles continuous **Mint:** Kuttenberg **Note:** Prev. KM#1164. Known struck on thick flan of unknown weight.

Date	Mintage	VG	F	VF	XF	Unc
(16)20 (ee)	—	80.00	150	250	400	—

KM# 241 24 KREUZER

Silver **Ruler:** Friedrich von der Pfalz **Obv:** Crowned bust right, value (24) below, titles of Friedrich **Rev:** Round six-fold arms **Mint:** Kuttenberg **Note:** Prev. KM#1165.

Date	Mintage	VG	F	VF	XF	Unc
1620 (ee)	—	40.00	90.00	175	275	—

KM# 243 24 KREUZER

Silver **Ruler:** Friedrich von der Pfalz **Obv:** Smaller bust **Rev:** Round six-fold arms **Mint:** Kuttenberg **Note:** Prev. KM#1166.

Date	Mintage	VG	F	VF	XF	Unc
1620 (ee)	—	45.00	95.00	185	300	—

KM# 226 24 KREUZER

Silver **Ruler:** Friedrich von der Pfalz **Obv:** Crown over date **Rev:** Bohemian lion left **Mint:** Prague **Note:** Kipper. Prev. KM#93 (1552)

Date	Mintage	VG	F	VF	XF	Unc
1619 (l)	—	30.00	75.00	145	250	—
1620 (m)	—	30.00	75.00	145	250	—

KM# 237 24 KREUZER

Silver **Ruler:** Friedrich von der Pfalz **Obv:** Crowned bust right, value (24) below, titles of Friedrich **Rev:** Ornate squarish two-fold arms of Bohemia and Electoral Pfalz divide date, titles continuous **Mint:** Prague **Note:** Kipper. Prev. KM#94

Date	Mintage	VG	F	VF	XF	Unc
(16)20 (m)	—	80.00	150	250	400	—

KM# 240 24 KREUZER

Silver **Ruler:** Friedrich von der Pfalz **Obv:** Crowned bust right, value (24) below, titles of Friedrich **Rev:** Round six-fold arms with central shield of Electoral Pfalz, date in legend **Mint:** Prague **Note:** Known struck on thick flan of unlisted weight. Prev. KM#95.1 (1554)

Date	Mintage	VG	F	VF	XF	Unc
1620 (m)	—	45.00	100	200	350	—

KM# 250 48 KREUZER

Silver **Ruler:** Friedrich von der Pfalz **Obv:** Value below bust **Mint:** Joachimstal

Date	Mintage	VG	F	VF	XF	Unc
1620 (aj)	—	125	245	475	900	—

KM# 249 48 KREUZER

Silver **Ruler:** Friedrich von der Pfalz **Obv:** Crowned bust right **Rev:** Shield-shaped arms **Mint:** Joachimstal **Note:** Prev. KM#947.

Date	Mintage	VG	F	VF	XF	Unc
1620 (aj)	—	125	245	475	900	—

KM# 253 48 KREUZER

Silver **Ruler:** Friedrich von der Pfalz **Obv:** Large bust **Rev:** Crown above large arms **Mint:** Joachimstal **Note:** Prev. KM#948.

Date	Mintage	VG	F	VF	XF	Unc
1620 (aj)	—	120	225	450	850	—

KM# 248 48 KREUZER

Silver **Ruler:** Friedrich von der Pfalz **Obv:** Value at bottom **Rev:** Date in margin **Mint:** Kuttenberg **Note:** Prev. KM#1167.

Date	Mintage	VG	F	VF	XF	Unc
1620 (ee)	—	100	200	350	—	—

KM# 252 48 KREUZER
Silver **Ruler:** Friedrich von der Pfalz **Obv:** Large bust **Rev:** Crown above large arms **Mint:** Kuttenberg **Note:** Prev. KM#1168.

Date	Mintage	VG	F	VF	XF	Unc
1620 (ee)	—	85.00	175	300	—	—

KM# 256 48 KREUZER
Silver **Ruler:** Friedrich von der Pfalz **Obv:** Ruffled collar bust right **Rev:** Crowned round seven-fold arms **Mint:** Kuttenberg **Note:** Prev. KM#1169.

Date	Mintage	VG	F	VF	XF	Unc
1620 (ee)	—	75.00	145	250	575	—

KM# 255 48 KREUZER
Silver **Ruler:** Friedrich von der Pfalz **Mint:** Prague **Note:** Klippe.

Date	Mintage	VG	F	VF	XF	Unc
1620 (m)	—	—	—	—	—	—

KM# 254.1 48 KREUZER
Silver **Ruler:** Friedrich von der Pfalz **Obv:** Large bust **Rev:** Crowned round seven-fold arms **Mint:** Prague **Note:** Prev. KM#96.1 (1555).

Date	Mintage	VG	F	VF	XF	Unc
1620 (m)	—	110	220	450	800	—

KM# 254.2 48 KREUZER
Silver **Ruler:** Friedrich von der Pfalz **Obv:** Crowned small bust right **Rev:** Crowned round seven-fold arms **Mint:** Prague **Note:** Prev. KM#96.2 (1705).

Date	Mintage	VG	F	VF	XF	Unc
1620 (m)	—	110	220	450	800	—
1621 (m)	—	110	220	450	800	—

KM# 251 48 KREUZER
Silver **Ruler:** Friedrich von der Pfalz **Obv:** Large bust **Rev:** Crown above large arms **Mint:** Prague **Note:** Prev. KM#97(1556).

Date	Mintage	VG	F	VF	XF	Unc
1620 (m)	—	175	350	675	1,150	—

KM# 258 60 KREUZER
Silver **Ruler:** Ferdinand II **Obv:** Laureate bust right, value below **Rev:** Round coat of arms **Mint:** Kuttenberg **Note:** Prev. KM#1170.

Date	Mintage	VG	F	VF	XF	Unc
1620 (ee)	—	40.00	75.00	150	275	—

KM# 263 70 KREUZER
Silver **Ruler:** Ferdinand II **Obv:** Value below bust **Mint:** Kuttenberg **Note:** Prev. KM#1171.

Date	Mintage	VG	F	VF	XF	Unc
1620 (ee)	—	—	—	—	—	—

TRADE COINAGE

KM# 274 DUCAT
Silver **Ruler:** Friedrich von der Pfalz **Obv:** Crowned bust right, titles of Friedrich **Rev:** Arms of Electoral Pfalz superimposed on crowned Bohemian lion to left, date below, titles continuous **Mint:** Prague

Date	Mintage	VG	F	VF	XF	Unc
1620	—	1,650	2,200	3,500	5,000	—
1620 (m)	—	1,650	2,200	3,500	5,000	—

KM# 272 DUCAT
Silver **Ruler:** Friedrich von der Pfalz **Obv:** Crowned full-length armored figure right, holding scepter, titles of Friedrich **Rev:** Crowned four-fold arms in circle, titles continuous **Mint:** Prague **Note:** Prev. KM#100(1559).

Date	Mintage	VG	F	VF	XF	Unc
ND(1620) Rare	—	—	—	—	—	—

KM# 273 DUCAT
Silver **Ruler:** Friedrich von der Pfalz **Obv:** Crowned full-length armored figure right, holding orb and scepter **Rev:** Ornately-shaped arms, date in legend **Mint:** Prague **Note:** Prev. KM#101(1560).

Date	Mintage	VG	F	VF	XF	Unc
1620 (m) Rare	—	—	—	—	—	—

EGER

The town of Eger (Czech – Cheb) is located on the Ohre River, 86 miles (144 kilometers) west of Prague, and gave its name to the region surrounding it. The district was first mentioned in 870 as part of the margraviate of East Franconia. Ludwig the Bavarian, in order to procure the imperial throne, pledged Eger to the Bohemian crown for 20,000 silver marks in 1314 (reigned as Ludwig III, 1314-47). Emperor Karl IV of Bohemia (1347-78) allowed the town to begin issuing coins in 1349. Eger also struck a number of coins in the early 16th century and again just before and during the Thirty Years' War. The town was the site of the murder of the imperial general Wallenstein on 25 February 1634 (see Friedland). A few siege coins were struck in Eger in 1743 during the War of the Austrian Succession.

ARMS:

2-fold divided horizontally, upper field has upper half of an eagle with spread wings, the lower field is filled with a cross-hatch pattern.

References:

S = Hugo Frhr. Von Saurma-Jeltsch, ***Die Saurmasche Münzsammlung deutscher, schweizerischer und polnischer Gepräge von etwa dem Beginn der Groschenzeit bis zur Kipperperiode***, Berlin, 1892.

Sch = Wolfgang Schulten, ***Deutsche Münzen aus der Zeit Karls V.***, Frankfurt am Main, 1974.

Sn = Gerhard Schön, ***Deutscher Münzkatalog 18. Jahrhundert***, Munich, 1984.

Sn (AE) = Günter Schön, ***Katalog der Kupfermünzen des Römisch-Deutschen Reiches im 16., 17. und 18. Jahrhundert,*** Graz, 1978.

FREE CITY

STANDARD COINAGE

KM# 1 PFENNIG (Weisspfennig)
Copper **Obv:** Oval city arms, date at end of legend **Obv. Legend:** VIER HERRN ... **Note:** Ref. Sn(AE)#1. Uniface.

Date	Mintage	VG	F	VF	XF	Unc
1616	—	12.00	30.00	55.00	85.00	—

KM# 2 PFENNIG (Weisspfennig)
Copper **Obv:** Oval city arms, date at end of legend, final 'N' reversed **Obv. Legend:** VIER HERRN ... **Note:** Ref. Sn(AE)#2. Uniface.

Date	Mintage	VG	F	VF	XF	Unc
1618	—	12.00	30.00	55.00	85.00	—

KM# 3 PFENNIG (Weisspfennig)
Copper **Obv:** Round city arms, date at end of legend, final 'N' reversed **Obv. Legend:** VIER HERRN ... **Note:** Ref. Sn(AE)#3. Uniface.

Date	Mintage	VG	F	VF	XF	Unc
1622	—	12.00	30.00	55.00	85.00	—

KM# 4 PFENNIG (Weisspfennig)
Copper **Obv:** Oval city arms, date at end of legend **Obv. Legend:** ★ HERRN. O E V N G V R **Note:** Ref. Sn(AE)#4. Uniface.

Date	Mintage	VG	F	VF	XF	Unc
1628	—	10.00	25.00	45.00	75.00	—

FRIEDLAND

Albrecht Wenzel Eusebius von Wallenstein, prominent leader of the empire until his assassination in 1634, was made count of the empire in 1622, duke of Friedland in 1623, duke of Sagan in 1627 and was duke of Mecklenburg from 1628 to 1632. During this time Wallenstein became powerful and had additional ambitions even to the reorganization of the empire. This was seen as a threat by higher powers in the empire and Wallenstein was assassinated February 25, 1634.

RULER
Albrecht von Wallenstein, 1583-1634

COUNTY

STANDARD COINAGE

KM# 66 1/2 KREUZER
Billon **Ruler:** Albrecht as Duke of Friedland, Sagan, and Mecklenburg **Obv:** 3 shields 1 above 2, top shield divides date **Note:** Uniface.

Date	Mintage	VG	F	VF	XF	Unc
1632	—	16.00	30.00	50.00	90.00	—

KM# 5 3 KREUZER
Silver **Ruler:** Albrecht as Duke of Friedland **Obv:** Bust of Albrecht 1/2 right in inner circle **Rev:** Crowned eagle shield in inner circle, date divide by crown **Rev. Legend:** SAO. ROM. IMPERI. PRINCES **Note:** Varieties exist.

Date	Mintage	VG	F	VF	XF	Unc
1626	—	15.00	25.00	45.00	90.00	—

KM# 11 3 KREUZER
Silver **Ruler:** Albrecht as Duke of Friedland **Obv:** Bust of Albrecht right in inner circle **Note:** Varieites exist.

Date	Mintage	VG	F	VF	XF	Unc
1627	—	15.00	25.00	40.00	75.00	—
1697 Error	—	15.00	25.00	40.00	75.00	—

KM# 12 3 KREUZER
Silver **Ruler:** Albrecht as Duke of Friedland **Rev:** Date in legend at upper left **Note:** Varieites exist.

Date	Mintage	VG	F	VF	XF	Unc
1627	—	18.00	30.00	48.00	90.00	—
1628	—	18.00	30.00	48.00	90.00	—

KM# 24 3 KREUZER
Silver **Ruler:** Albrecht as Duke of Friedland and Sagan **Note:** Varieties exist.

Date	Mintage	VG	F	VF	XF	Unc
1628	—	15.00	25.00	40.00	75.00	—
1629	—	15.00	25.00	40.00	75.00	—
1630	—	15.00	25.00	40.00	75.00	—

KM# 32 3 KREUZER
Silver **Ruler:** Albrecht as Duke of Friedland and Sagan **Obv:** Bust of Albrecht 1/2 right in inner circle **Note:** Varieties exist.

Date	Mintage	VG	F	VF	XF	Unc
1629	—	17.00	27.50	44.00	85.00	—
1630	—	17.00	27.50	44.00	85.00	—

KM# 51 3 KREUZER

Silver **Ruler:** Albrecht as Duke of Friedland, Sagan, and Mecklenburg **Obv:** Bust of Albrecht right in inner circle **Note:** Varieties exist.

Date	Mintage	VG	F	VF	XF	Unc
1630	—	15.00	30.00	50.00	90.00	—
1631	—	15.00	30.00	50.00	90.00	—
1632	—	15.00	30.00	50.00	90.00	—
1633	—	15.00	30.00	50.00	90.00	—
1634	—	15.00	30.00	50.00	90.00	—

KM# 50 3 KREUZER

Silver **Ruler:** Albrecht as Duke of Friedland, Sagan, and Mecklenburg **Rev:** 3 shields with points together in inner circle **Note:** Titles of Duke of Friedland, Sagan and Mecklenburg. Varieties exist.

Date	Mintage	VG	F	VF	XF	Unc
1630	—	15.00	30.00	50.00	90.00	—
1631	—	15.00	30.00	50.00	90.00	—

KM# 6 1/2 GULDEN

Silver **Ruler:** Albrecht as Duke of Friedland **Obv:** Bust of Albrecht 1/2 right in inner circle **Rev:** Crowned eagle shield with rosettes at sides, date divided by crown **Note:** Titles of Duke of Friedland. Varieties exist.

Date	Mintage	VG	F	VF	XF	Unc
1626	—	750	1,500	3,000	—	—
1627	—	750	1,500	3,000	—	—

KM# 25 1/2 GULDEN

Silver **Ruler:** Albrecht as Duke of Friedland and Sagan **Obv:** Bust of Albrecht right in inner circle **Rev:** Date left of crown in legend, plain field at sides of shield **Note:** Titles of Duke of Friedland and Sagan.

Date	Mintage	VG	F	VF	XF	Unc
1628	—	1,150	2,500	5,500	—	—

KM# 58 1/2 GULDEN

Silver **Ruler:** Albrecht as Duke of Friedland, Sagan, and Mecklenburg **Obv:** Bust of Albrecht 1/2 right in inner circle **Rev:** Crowned arms in order collar in inner circle, date in legend **Note:** Titles of Duke of Friedland, Sagan and Mecklenburg.

Date	Mintage	VG	F	VF	XF	Unc
1631	—	650	1,250	2,750	4,750	—
1632	—	650	1,250	2,750	4,750	—
1633	—	650	1,250	2,750	4,750	—

KM# 68 1/2 GULDEN

Silver **Ruler:** Albrecht as Duke of Friedland, Sagan, and Mecklenburg **Note:** Klippe.

Date	Mintage	VG	F	VF	XF	Unc
1633	—	950	1,800	3,600	6,000	—

KM# 7 GULDEN

Silver **Ruler:** Albrecht as Duke of Friedland **Obv:** Bust of Albrecht 1/2 right in inner circle **Rev:** Crowned eagle shield in inner circle, date divided by crown **Rev. Legend:** DOMINUS. PROTECTOR. MEVS **Note:** Titles of Duke of Friedland.

Date	Mintage	VG	F	VF	XF	Unc
1626	—	1,200	2,500	5,500	—	—

KM# 8 GULDEN

Silver **Ruler:** Albrecht as Duke of Friedland **Rev. Legend:** SAC. ROM. IMPERI. PRINCEPS **Note:** Varieties exist.

Date	Mintage	VG	F	VF	XF	Unc
1626	—	1,000	2,000	4,200	8,000	—

KM# 26 GULDEN

Silver **Ruler:** Albrecht as Duke of Friedland and Sagan **Obv:** Bust of Albrecht right in inner circle **Note:** Titles of Duke of Friedland and Sagan. Varieties exist.

Date	Mintage	VG	F	VF	XF	Unc
1628	—	1,250	2,750	6,000	—	—

KM# 33 GULDEN

14.3600 g., Silver **Ruler:** Albrecht as Duke of Friedland and Sagan **Obv:** Large bust of Albrecht 1/2 right in inner circle

Date	Mintage	VG	F	VF	XF	Unc
1629	—	1,500	3,000	6,500	—	—

KM# 38 GULDEN

Silver **Ruler:** Albrecht as Duke of Friedland, Sagan, and Mecklenburg **Rev:** Crown breaks outer legend, date in legend at upper left **Note:** Dav. #3448.

Date	Mintage	VG	F	VF	XF	Unc
1629	—	950	1,650	2,750	5,000	—

KM# 40 GULDEN

Silver **Ruler:** Albrecht as Duke of Friedland, Sagan, and Mecklenburg **Obv. Legend:** ALBERTVS D: G: DVX MEGAP:.. **Rev:** Crowned arms divides "G-E" in order collar, date in legend **Note:** Dav. #3450.

Date	Mintage	VG	F	VF	XF	Unc
1629 GE	—	1,000	1,750	2,950	5,500	—

KM# 52 GULDEN

Silver **Ruler:** Albrecht as Duke of Friedland, Sagan, and Mecklenburg **Note:** Klippe. Titles of Duke of Friedland, Sagan and Mecklenburg.

Date	Mintage	VG	F	VF	XF	Unc
1630	—	1,750	3,500	6,000	9,000	—

KM# 59 GULDEN

Silver **Ruler:** Albrecht as Duke of Friedland, Sagan, and Mecklenburg **Rev:** Crowned arms in order collar in inner circle, date in legend **Note:** Varieties exist.

Date	Mintage	VG	F	VF	XF	Unc
1631	—	950	1,750	3,250	6,000	—
1632	—	1,000	2,200	4,000	6,500	—
1633	—	1,000	2,200	4,000	6,500	—

KM# A9 1/4 THALER

Silver **Ruler:** Albrecht as Duke of Friedland **Obv:** Bust of Albrecht **Rev:** Crowned arms **Rev. Legend:** DEVS PROTECTOR MEVS **Note:** Klippe.

Date	Mintage	VG	F	VF	XF	Unc
1626	—	325	650	1,100	1,950	—

KM# 9 THALER

Silver **Ruler:** Albrecht as Duke of Friedland **Rev:** Small crown **Rev. Legend:** DOMINUS. PROTECTOR. MEVS **Note:** Dav. #3438. Varieties exist.

Date	Mintage	VG	F	VF	XF	Unc
1626	—	775	1,650	3,300	5,500	—

KM# 10 THALER

Silver **Ruler:** Albrecht as Duke of Friedland **Rev:** Large crown **Rev. Legend:** SAC. ROM. IMPERIL. PRINCEPS **Note:** Dav. #3439. Varieties exist.

Date	Mintage	VG	F	VF	XF	Unc
1626	—	725	1,400	2,750	5,000	—
1627	—	750	1,450	2,850	5,150	—

KM# 13 THALER

Silver **Ruler:** Albrecht as Duke of Friedland **Rev:** Plain field at sides of arms, date in legend **Note:** Dav. #3440. Varieties exist.

Date	Mintage	VG	F	VF	XF	Unc
1627	—	725	1,400	2,750	4,950	—
1628	—	725	1,400	2,750	4,950	—

KM# 14 THALER

Silver **Ruler:** Albrecht as Duke of Friedland **Rev:** Scrolls at sides of shield **Note:** Dav. #3441. Varieties exist.

Date	Mintage	VG	F	VF	XF	Unc
1627	—	725	1,400	2,850	5,100	—
1628	—	725	1,400	2,850	5,100	—

KM# 27 THALER

Silver **Ruler:** Albrecht as Duke of Friedland and Sagan **Note:** Dav. #3442. Varieties exist.

Date	Mintage	VG	F	VF	XF	Unc
1628	—	825	1,500	2,500	4,700	—

KM# 28 THALER

Silver **Ruler:** Albrecht as Duke of Friedland and Sagan **Note:** Dav. #3443. Varieties exist.

Date	Mintage	VG	F	VF	XF	Unc
1628	—	825	1,500	2,500	4,700	—

KM# 34 THALER

Silver **Ruler:** Albrecht as Duke of Friedland and Sagan **Obv:** Similar to KM#35 **Rev:** Crowned arms with decorations at sides in inner circle, date in legend **Note:** Dav. #3444. Varieties exist.

Date	Mintage	VG	F	VF	XF	Unc
1629	—	925	1,650	2,750	4,950	—

KM# 37 THALER

Silver **Ruler:** Albrecht as Duke of Friedland, Sagan, and Mecklenburg **Obv:** Date below bust **Rev:** Crowned arms in order collar **Note:** Dav. #3447.

Date	Mintage	VG	F	VF	XF	Unc
1629	—	975	1,750	3,000	5,200	—

KM# 39 THALER

Silver **Ruler:** Albrecht as Duke of Friedland, Sagan, and Mecklenburg **Obv. Legend:** ALBERTVS. D. G. DVX. ME-GA. FRI. ET. SA. P. VA **Note:** Dav. #3449.

Date	Mintage	VG	F	VF	XF	Unc
1629	—	975	1,750	3,000	5,200	—

KM# 53 THALER

Silver **Ruler:** Albrecht as Duke of Friedland, Sagan, and Mecklenburg **Obv. Legend:** ALBERT. D. G. DVX. ME-GA. FRID. ET. SA. PR. VA **Note:** Dav. #3451.

Date	Mintage	VG	F	VF	XF	Unc
1630	—	975	1,750	3,000	5,200	—

KM# 54 THALER

Silver **Ruler:** Albrecht as Duke of Friedland, Sagan, and Mecklenburg **Obv. Legend:** ALBERT. D.G. DVS. MEGA.. **Rev:** Crowned arms in order collar in inner circle, date in legend, ornamentation above crown **Note:** Dav. #3452.

Date	Mintage	VG	F	VF	XF	Unc
1630	—	1,000	1,850	3,200	5,800	—

KM# 60 THALER

Silver **Ruler:** Albrecht as Duke of Friedland, Sagan, and Mecklenburg **Obv. Legend:** ALBERT. D. G. DVX. MEGA. FRID. ET. SAG. PR. VAN **Note:** Dav. #3455. Varieties exist.

Date	Mintage	VG	F	VF	XF	Unc
1631	—	975	1,800	3,200	5,500	—
1632	—	975	1,750	3,000	5,200	—
1633	—	1,150	2,000	3,500	6,250	—

KM# 36 THALER

Silver **Ruler:** Albrecht as Duke of Friedland and Sagan **Rev:** Mint mark at bottom in outer legend **Mint:** Sagan **Note:** Dav. #3446. Struck at Sagan Mint.

Date	Mintage	VG	F	VF	XF	Unc
1629 S-HZ Rare	—	—	—	—	—	—

KM# 35 THALER

Silver **Ruler:** Albrecht as Duke of Friedland and Sagan **Obv. Legend:** ...DUX. FRIDLA. ET. SAGANAE **Mint:** Wismar **Note:** Dav. #3445. Struck at Wismar Mint.

Date	Mintage	VG	F	VF	XF	Unc
1629 Rare	—	—	—	—	—	—

Note: Leu Numismatik Auction 75, 10-99, VF realized $12,000

KM# 0068 1-1/2 THALER

Silver **Ruler:** Albrecht as Duke of Friedland, Sagan, and Mecklenburg **Note:** Klippe. Similar to 1 Thaler, KM#60. Dav. #3454.

Date	Mintage	VG	F	VF	XF	Unc
1633 Rare	—	—	—	—	—	—

KM# 15 2 THALER

Silver **Ruler:** Albrecht as Duke of Friedland **Rev. Legend:** SACRI. ROMANI. IMPE. PRINCEPS **Note:** Dav. #A3439.

Date	Mintage	VG	F	VF	XF	Unc
1627 Rare	—	—	—	—	—	—

KM# 16 2 THALER

Silver **Ruler:** Albrecht as Duke of Friedland **Rev:** Plain field at sides of arms, date in legend **Note:** Dav. #A3440.

Date	Mintage	VG	F	VF	XF	Unc
1627 Rare	—	—	—	—	—	—

Note: Leu Numismatik Auction 75, 10-99 VF realized $19,665

KM# 17 2 THALER

Silver **Ruler:** Albrecht as Duke of Friedland **Rev:** Scrolls at sides of shield **Note:** Dav. #A3441.

Date	Mintage	VG	F	VF	XF	Unc
1627 Rare	—	—	—	—	—	—

KM# 67 2 THALER

Silver **Ruler:** Albrecht as Duke of Friedland, Sagan, and Mecklenburg **Note:** Similar to 1 Thaler, KM#60.

Date	Mintage	VG	F	VF	XF	Unc
1632 Rare	—	—	—	—	—	—

TRADE COINAGE

KM# 19 DUCAT

3.4500 g., 0.9860 Gold 0.1094 oz. AGW **Ruler:** Albrecht as Duke of Friedland **Rev:** Crowned oval arms in inner circle, date in legend

Date	Mintage	VG	F	VF	XF	Unc
1627	—	500	1,250	2,500	4,500	—

KM# 20 DUCAT

3.2000 g., 0.9860 Gold 0.1014 oz. AGW **Ruler:** Albrecht as Duke of Friedland **Rev:** Crowned straight sided shield in inner circle; date in legend

Date	Mintage	VG	F	VF	XF	Unc
1627	—	500	1,250	2,500	4,500	—
1628	—	500	1,250	2,500	4,500	—

KM# 29 DUCAT

3.4000 g., 0.9860 Gold 0.1078 oz. AGW **Ruler:** Albrecht as Duke of Friedland and Sagan **Obv:** Bust of Albrecht right in inner circle **Rev:** Crowned round arms in cartouche in inner circle, date in legend **Note:** Varieties exist.

Date	Mintage	VG	F	VF	XF	Unc
1628	—	500	1,250	2,500	4,500	—
1629	—	500	1,250	2,500	4,500	—

KM# 41 DUCAT

3.4000 g., 0.9860 Gold 0.1078 oz. AGW **Ruler:** Albrecht as Duke of Friedland and Sagan **Obv:** Bust of Albrecht with broad face **Rev:** Crowned arms in order chain, date in legend

Date	Mintage	VG	F	VF	XF	Unc
1629	—	500	1,250	2,500	4,500	—

KM# 55 DUCAT

3.4000 g., 0.9860 Gold 0.1078 oz. AGW **Ruler:** Albrecht as Duke of Friedland, Sagan, and Mecklenburg **Obv:** Bust of Albrecht with pointed face

Date	Mintage	VG	F	VF	XF	Unc
1630	—	750	1,450	2,750	4,500	—

KM# 61 DUCAT

3.4900 g., 0.9860 Gold 0.1106 oz. AGW **Ruler:** Albrecht as Duke of Friedland, Sagan, and Mecklenburg **Obv:** Bust of Albrecht with large head **Rev:** Crowned arms in order collar, date in legend

Date	Mintage	VG	F	VF	XF	Unc
1631	—	750	1,450	2,750	4,500	—

KM# 62 DUCAT

3.4200 g., 0.9860 Gold 0.1084 oz. AGW **Ruler:** Albrecht as Duke of Friedland, Sagan, and Mecklenburg **Obv:** Small head **Note:** Varieties exist.

Date	Mintage	VG	F	VF	XF	Unc
1631	—	725	1,400	2,700	4,250	—
1633	—	725	1,400	2,700	4,250	—
1634	—	725	1,400	2,700	4,250	—

KM# 18 DUCAT

3.4800 g., 0.9860 Gold 0.1103 oz. AGW **Ruler:** Albrecht as Duke of Friedland **Obv:** Bust of Albrecht 1/2 right in inner circle **Rev:** Crowned arms in cartouche in inner circle, date in legend **Mint:** Gitschin

Date	Mintage	VG	F	VF	XF	Unc
1627	—	500	1,250	2,500	4,500	—

KM# 63 2 DUCAT

6.8000 g., 0.9860 Gold 0.2156 oz. AGW **Ruler:** Albrecht as Duke of Friedland, Sagan, and Mecklenburg **Rev:** Crowned arms in order collar, date in legend **Note:** Varieties exist.

Date	Mintage	VG	F	VF	XF	Unc
1631	—	—	—	—	—	—

Note: Leu Numismatik Auction 75, 10-99, XF realized $16,665

Date	Mintage	VG	F	VF	XF	Unc
1633	—	1,300	2,200	3,750	6,000	—
1634	—	1,100	2,000	3,250	5,500	—

KM# 21 2 DUCAT

6.9000 g., 0.9860 Gold 0.2187 oz. AGW **Ruler:** Albrecht as Duke of Friedland **Obv:** Bust of Albrecht 1/2 right in inner circle **Rev:** Crowned arms in inner inner circle, date in legend **Mint:** Gitschin

Date	Mintage	VG	F	VF	XF	Unc
1627	—	3,500	6,500	10,000	—	—

KM# 30 5 DUCAT

17.4000 g., 0.9860 Gold 0.5516 oz. AGW **Ruler:** Albrecht as Duke of Friedland **Obv:** Bust of Albrecht right in inner circle

Date	Mintage	VG	F	VF	XF	Unc
1628 Rare	—	—	—	—	—	—

KM# 42 5 DUCAT

17.2000 g., 0.9860 Gold 0.5452 oz. AGW **Ruler:** Albrecht as Duke of Friedland and Sagan **Obv:** Bust of Albrecht 1/2 right in inner circle **Rev:** Crowned arms in order collar, date in legend

Date	Mintage	VG	F	VF	XF	Unc
1629 Rare	—	—	—	—	—	—

KM# 22 5 DUCAT

17.1300 g., 0.9860 Gold 0.5430 oz. AGW **Ruler:** Albrecht as Duke of Friedland **Obv:** Bust of Albrecht 1/2 right in inner circle **Rev:** Crowned arms in inner circle, date in legend **Mint:** Gitschin

Date	Mintage	VG	F	VF	XF	Unc
1627 Rare	—	—	—	—	—	—

Note: Leu Numismatik Auction 75, 10-99, VF realized $32,000

KM# 56 5 DUCAT

17.2000 g., 0.9860 Gold 0.5452 oz. AGW **Ruler:** Albrecht as Duke of Friedland, Sagan, and Mecklenburg **Obv:** Head of Albrecht completely within inner circle **Mint:** Sagan

Date	Mintage	VG	F	VF	XF	Unc
1630	—	—	—	—	—	—

Note: Leu Numismatik Auction 75, 10-99, better than VF realized, $11,335

KM# 64 5 DUCAT

17.3500 g., 0.9860 Gold 0.5500 oz. AGW **Ruler:** Albrecht as Duke of Friedland, Sagan, and Mecklenburg **Obv:** Bust of Albrecht with pointed face 1/2 right in inner circle **Mint:** Sagan

Date	Mintage	VG	F	VF	XF	Unc
1631 Rare	—	—	—	—	—	—
1633 Rare	—	—	—	—	—	—
1634 Rare	—	—	—	—	—	—

KM# 31 10 DUCAT

34.6000 g., 0.9860 Gold 1.0968 oz. AGW **Ruler:** Albrecht as Duke of Friedland **Obv:** Bust of Albrecht right in inner circle

Date	Mintage	VG	F	VF	XF	Unc
1628 Rare	—	—	—	—	—	—

KM# 43 10 DUCAT

34.9000 g., 0.9860 Gold 1.1063 oz. AGW **Ruler:** Albrecht as Duke of Friedland and Sagan **Obv:** Bust of Albrecht 1/2 right in inner circle

Date	Mintage	VG	F	VF	XF	Unc
1629 Rare	—	—	—	—	—	—

KM# 44 10 DUCAT

34.6000 g., 0.9860 Gold 1.0968 oz. AGW **Ruler:** Albrecht as Duke of Friedland, Sagan, and Mecklenburg

Date	Mintage	VG	F	VF	XF	Unc
1629 Rare	—	—	—	—	—	—
1630 Rare	—	—	—	—	—	—

KM# 23 10 DUCAT

34.5000 g., 0.9860 Gold 1.0936 oz. AGW **Ruler:** Albrecht as Duke of Friedland **Obv:** Bust of Albrecht 1/2 right in inner circle **Rev:** Crowned oval arms in cartouche in inner circle **Mint:** Gitschin

Date	Mintage	VG	F	VF	XF	Unc
1627 Rare	—	—	—	—	—	—

KM# 65 10 DUCAT

34.6000 g., 0.9860 Gold 1.0968 oz. AGW **Ruler:** Albrecht as Duke of Friedland, Sagan, and Mecklenburg **Obv:** Bust of Albrecht with pointed face 1/2 right in inner circle **Rev:** Crowned arms in order collar in inner circle, date in legend **Mint:** Gitschin

Date	Mintage	VG	F	VF	XF	Unc
1631 Rare	—	—	—	—	—	—

Note: Leu Numismatik Auction 75, 10-99, XF realized, $38,665. Stack's International sale 3-88 VF realized $15,400.

KM# 57 10 DUCAT

34.6000 g., 0.9860 Gold 1.0968 oz. AGW **Ruler:** Albrecht as Duke of Friedland, Sagan, and Mecklenburg **Mint:** Sagan

Date	Mintage	VG	F	VF	XF	Unc
1630 GE Rare	—	—	—	—	—	—

LOBKOWITZ-STERNSTEIN

The Bohemian lords of Lobkowitz had long distinguished themselves in the service of the Holy Roman Empire. For his role on the side of the emperor in the opening phase of the Thirty Years' War, Dzenko Adalbert was given the countship of Sternstein in Upper Bavaria in 1623 and raised to the rank of Prince of the Empire. The lands in Bavaria were mediatized in 1805.

RULERS

Zdenko Adalbert, 1623-1628
Wenseslaus Franz Eusebius, 1628-1677
Ferdinand August Leopold, 1677-1715

MINT MARKS

VI = Vienna Mint

PRINCIPALITY

STANDARD COINAGE

KM# 7 1/2 THALER

Silver **Ruler:** Franz Joseph Maximilian **Obv:** Bust of Franz Joseph Maximillan right **Rev:** Crowned and mantled arms

Date	Mintage	VG	F	VF	XF	Unc
1615	—	—	—	—	—	—

Note: Reported, not confirmed

KM# 5 THALER

Silver **Ruler:** Zdenko Adalbert **Obv:** Bust of Zdenko Adalbert right **Rev:** Crowned 4-fold arms of Lobkowitz and Zerotin, surrounded by chain of the Order of the Golden Fleece **Note:** Show Thaler.

Date	Mintage	VG	F	VF	XF	Unc
ND	—	—	—	—	—	—

TRADE COINAGE

KM# 6 DUCAT

3.5000 g., 0.9860 Gold 0.1109 oz. AGW **Ruler:** Ferdinand August Leopold **Obv:** Armored bust right **Rev:** Crowned arms

Date	Mintage	VG	F	VF	XF	Unc
ND	—	1,650	2,750	5,000	7,500	—

ROSENBERG

The counts of Rosenberg in Bohemia trace their origins back to the lords of Krumlau in the second half of the 12th century. Two lines were established early, but only the elder branch in Krumlau issued coins. In 1592, Count Wilhelm was raised to the rank of prince and awarded the right to strike coins. The line came to an end in 1611 and title passed to the Habsburgs until 1622, then to Eggenberg until 1719 and finally to Schwarzenberg from that year. The younger branch was raised to

Count of the Empire in 1648 and then prince in 1790. The various territories of Rosenberg were mediatized during the Napoleonic Empire. All coinage of Rosenberg was produced at the Reichenstein mint in Silesia.

RULERS

Elder Line

Peter Wok von Ursini, 1592-1611

ARMS:

Upper and lower fields divided by horizontal bar in which an eel, upper field a 5-petaled rose, lower field 5 alternately shaded bars diagonally from upper left to lower right.

REFERENCES:

COUNTSHIP

STANDARD COINAGE

MB# 37 PFENNIG

Silver **Ruler:** Peter Wok von Ursini **Obv:** Rosenberg arms, 'W' above **Note:** Uniface.

Date	Mintage	VG	F	VF	XF	Unc
ND(1592-1611)	—	6.00	12.00	25.00	50.00	—

SCHLICK

Heinrich Schlick was the Bürgermeister (mayor) of Lazan in western Bohemia, but owned land in Passaun (Bassano in Italy, north of Vicenza and Padua) and Weisskirchen (at that time, Ujvár in Hungary, now in Romania) 45 miles (75 kilometers) east of Belgrade. Heinrich was given a patent for bearing a coat of arms by Emperor Sigismund (1410-37) in 1416. His son, Caspar (1436-49), was given the title of Count of Bassano in 1437. Therefore, Schlick was always included as the family name, but the title was Count of Passaun and Weisskirchen. The count obtained the mint right in 1489 and began coining silver from the mines of Joachimsthal and Michaelsburg about 1517. The large Guldengroschen struck from the mined silver came to be called a Joachimsthaler, later shorted to "Thaler", the origin of the "dollar" in English. The mint right was confiscated by the Bohemian crown in 1528 and Joachimsthal was also made a royal mint in 1545. The mint right was restored to the family in 1626. The last coins of Schlick were struck in the 1760's and by the dissolution of the Holy Roman Empire by Napoleon in 1806 the mint right was forfeited. The line of counts continued well into the 19th century, however.

RULERS

Georg Ernst, 1547-1612
Heinrich IV, 1612-1650
Franz Ernst, 1650-1675
Franz Josef, 1675-1740
Leopold Josef, 1675-1723

ARMS:

Schlick – 3 annulets divided by inverted 'V', 2 annulets to left and right of point, third lower inside the inverted figure.

Passaun (Bassano) – 2 rampant panthers facing each other and holding crenelated tower between them. This is usually the central shield of the family's manifold arms.

Weisskirchen – lion rampant left holding church model in left front paw.

REFERENCE:

S = Hugo Frhr. Von Saurma-Jeltsch, ***Die Saurmasche Münzsammlung deutscher, schweizerischer und polnischer Gepräge von etwa dem Beginn der Groschenzeit bis zur Kipperperiode,*** Berlin, 1892

Sch = Wolfgang Schulten, ***Deutsche Münzen aus der Zeit Karls V.*** Frankfurt am Main, 1974.

COUNTY

STANDARD COINAGE

KM# 5 KREUZER

Silver **Ruler:** Heinrich IV **Obv:** Arms **Rev:** Crowned imperial eagle with value on breast

Date	Mintage	VG	F	VF	XF	Unc
1630	—	18.00	28.00	50.00	90.00	—

KM# 6 3 KREUZER

Silver **Ruler:** Heinrich IV **Obv:** Arms **Rev:** Heraldic imperial eagle

Date	Mintage	VG	F	VF	XF	Unc
1628	—	12.00	22.00	42.00	75.00	—
1631	—	12.00	22.00	42.00	75.00	—
1632	—	12.00	22.00	42.00	75.00	—
1635	—	12.00	22.00	42.00	75.00	—
1637	—	12.00	22.00	42.00	75.00	—
1638	—	12.00	22.00	42.00	75.00	—

KM# 7 1/2 THALER

Silver **Ruler:** Heinrich IV

Date	Mintage	VG	F	VF	XF	Unc
1627	—	120	200	350	600	—

KM# 20.1 1/2 THALER

Silver **Ruler:** Franz Ernst **Obv:** Madonna with child and St. Anne, above crowned arms **Rev:** Double-headed imperial eagle with large heads

Date	Mintage	VG	F	VF	XF	Unc
1661	—	85.00	165	300	500	—

KM# 20.2 1/2 THALER

Silver **Ruler:** Franz Ernst **Obv:** Madonna with child and St. Anne, above crowned arms **Rev:** Double-headed imperial eagle with small heads **Rev. Legend:** LEOPOLD: ROM: IMP: - SEMPER • AVGVSTVS

Date	Mintage	VG	F	VF	XF	Unc
1661	—	300	525	875	1,450	—

KM# 25 1/2 THALER

Silver **Ruler:** Franz Josef **Obv:** Madonna with child with St. Anne separating S-A behind arms, small shield in legend separating I-G **Rev:** Crowned double-headed imperial eagle with arms on breast

Date	Mintage	VG	F	VF	XF	Unc
1677	—	240	425	775	1,200	—

KM# 8.1 THALER

Silver **Ruler:** Heinrich IV **Obv:** Crowned imperial eagle with arms on breast **Rev:** Madonna and child with St. Anne separating S-A behind arms, small shield in legend separating I-G **Note:** Dav. #3398.

Date	Mintage	VG	F	VF	XF	Unc
1627	—	145	240	425	725	—

KM# 8.2 THALER

Silver **Ruler:** Heinrich IV **Obv:** Madonna and child with St. Anne closer together behind oval arms separating date **Rev. Legend:** FERDINANDVS • I • ROM • IMP • SEMPER • AVGVSTVS **Note:** Dav. #3399.

Date	Mintage	VG	F	VF	XF	Unc
1629	—	145	240	425	725	—
1630	—	145	240	425	725	—

KM# 8.3 THALER

Silver **Ruler:** Heinrich IV **Obv:** Madonna and child with St. Anne dividing SAN-NA **Note:** Dav. #3400.

Date	Mintage	VG	F	VF	XF	Unc
1630	—	145	240	425	725	—

KM# 8.4 THALER

Silver **Ruler:** Heinrich IV **Obv:** Madonna and child with St. Anne dividing S. A-NNA **Note:** Dav. #3401.

Date	Mintage	VG	F	VF	XF	Unc
1632	—	145	240	425	725	—

KM# 8.5 THALER

Silver **Ruler:** Heinrich IV **Obv:** Shield dividing S. AN-NA **Note:** Dav. #3402.

Date	Mintage	VG	F	VF	XF	Unc
1634	—	145	240	425	725	—

KM# 8.6 THALER

Silver **Ruler:** Heinrich IV **Note:** Klippe. Dav. #3402A.

Date	Mintage	VG	F	VF	XF	Unc
1634 Rare	—	—	—	—	—	—

KM# 8.7 THALER

Silver **Ruler:** Heinrich IV **Rev. Legend:** FERDINAND: III • ROM - IMP • SEMPER • AVGVST **Note:** Klippe. Dav. #3404. Varieties exist.

Date	Mintage	VG	F	VF	XF	Unc
1641	—	145	240	425	725	—
1642	—	145	240	425	725	—

KM# 8.8 THALER

Silver **Ruler:** Heinrich IV **Note:** Klippe. Dav. #3404A.

Date	Mintage	VG	F	VF	XF	Unc
1641 Rare	—	—	—	—	—	—
1642 Rare	—	—	—	—	—	—

KM# 8.9 THALER

Silver **Ruler:** Heinrich IV **Obv:** Order chain around arms **Note:** Dav. #3406.

Date	Mintage	VG	F	VF	XF	Unc
1644	—	150	250	450	750	—

KM# 9 THALER

Silver **Ruler:** Heinrich IV **Obv:** Larger figures above shield **Note:** Almost every date is a different variety. Dav. #3408.

Date	Mintage	VG	F	VF	XF	Unc
1645	—	145	240	425	725	—
1646	—	145	240	425	725	—
1647	—	145	240	425	725	—
1648	—	145	240	425	725	—
1649	—	145	240	425	725	—

KM# 21.1 THALER

Silver **Ruler:** Franz Ernst **Obv:** Madonna and child with St. Anna above shield divides SAN NA **Rev:** Crowned double-headed imperial eagle with shield on breast **Rev. Legend:** FERDINAND: III... **Note:** Dav. #3409.

Date	Mintage	VG	F	VF	XF	Unc
1651	—	145	240	425	725	—
1652	—	145	240	425	725	—
1654	—	145	240	425	725	—

KM# 21.2 THALER

Silver **Ruler:** Franz Ernst **Obv:** Madonna and child with St. Anna above shield divides SAN NA **Rev:** Crowned double-headed imperial eagle with shield on breast **Rev. Legend:** LEOPOLDVS. I. ROM... **Note:** Dav. #3410.

Date	Mintage	VG	F	VF	XF	Unc
1658	—	150	250	450	750	—

KM# 21.3 THALER

Silver **Ruler:** Franz Ernst **Obv:** Madonna and child with St. Anne in cloud above crowned arms **Rev:** Crowned double-headed imperial eagle with shield on breast **Note:** Every date is a different variety. Dav. #3412.

Date	Mintage	VG	F	VF	XF	Unc
1660	—	145	240	425	725	—
1661	—	145	240	425	725	—
1663	—	145	240	425	725	—

KM# 26 THALER

Silver **Ruler:** Franz Josef **Obv:** Madonna and child with St. Anne in cloud above crowned arms dividing date and breaking legend at top and bottom **Obv. Legend:** Titles of Franz Josef **Rev:** Crowned double-headed imperial eagle with shield on breast, within circle of beads **Rev. Legend:** Titles of Leopold **Note:** Dav. #3413.

Date	Mintage	VG	F	VF	XF	Unc
1677	—	250	450	750	1,250	—

KM# 10 1-1/2 THALER

Silver **Ruler:** Heinrich IV **Note:** Klippe. Similar to 1 Thaler, KM#8.7. Dav. #A3404.

Date	Mintage	VG	F	VF	XF	Unc
1642 Rare	—	—	—	—	—	—

KM# 11.1 2 THALER

Silver **Ruler:** Heinrich IV **Note:** Similar to 1 Thaler, KM#8.4. Dav. #A3401.

Date	Mintage	VG	F	VF	XF	Unc
1632	—	875	1,450	2,250	3,500	—

KM# 11.2 2 THALER

Silver **Ruler:** Heinrich IV **Note:** Similar to 1 Thaler, KM#8.5. Dav. #A3402.

Date	Mintage	VG	F	VF	XF	Unc
1634	—	875	1,450	2,250	3,500	—

KM# 11.3 2 THALER

Silver **Ruler:** Heinrich IV **Note:** Klippe. Similar to 1 Thaler, KM#8.5. Dav. #A3402A.

Date	Mintage	VG	F	VF	XF	Unc
1634 Rare	—	—	—	—	—	—

KM# 12 2 THALER

Silver **Ruler:** Heinrich IV **Note:** Klippe. Dav. #3403.

Date	Mintage	VG	F	VF	XF	Unc
1641	—	900	1,500	3,000	6,000	—
1642	—	900	1,500	3,000	6,000	—

KM# 11.4 2 THALER

Silver **Ruler:** Heinrich IV **Note:** Similar to 1 Thaler, KM#8.7. Dav. #A3403.

Date	Mintage	VG	F	VF	XF	Unc
1642 Rare	—	—	—	—	—	—

KM# 11.5 2 THALER

Silver **Ruler:** Heinrich IV **Note:** Similar to 1 Thaler, KM#8.9. Dav. #3405.

Date	Mintage	VG	F	VF	XF	Unc
1644	—	875	1,450	2,250	3,500	—

KM# 16 2 THALER

Silver **Ruler:** Heinrich IV **Note:** Similar to 1 Thaler, KM#9. Dav. #3407.

Date	Mintage	VG	F	VF	XF	Unc
1645	—	875	1,450	2,250	3,500	—

KM# 22.1 2 THALER

Silver **Ruler:** Franz Ernst **Note:** Similar to 1 Thaler, KM#21.1. Dav. #A3409.

Date	Mintage	VG	F	VF	XF	Unc
1651 Rare	—	—	—	—	—	—

KM# 22.2 2 THALER

Silver **Ruler:** Franz Ernst **Note:** Similar to 1 Thaler, KM#21.3. Dav. #3411.

Date	Mintage	VG	F	VF	XF	Unc
1660 Rare	—	—	—	—	—	—

KM# 13 3 THALER
Silver **Ruler:** Heinrich IV **Note:** Similar to 1 Thaler, KM#8.9. Dav. #A3405.

Date	Mintage	VG	F	VF	XF	Unc
1644 Rare	—	—	—	—	—	—

TRADE COINAGE

KM# 14 DUCAT
3.5000 g., 0.9860 Gold 0.1109 oz. AGW **Ruler:** Heinrich IV
Obv: Madonna and child with St. Anne above arms in inner circle **Rev:** Crowned imperial eagle in inner circle **Rev. Legend:** FERDINAND:II • DG: ROM: IMP: SEMP: AV:

Date	Mintage	VG	F	VF	XF	Unc
1628	—	375	650	1,500	3,500	—
1629	—	375	650	1,500	3,500	—
1630	—	—	—	—	—	—
1631	—	375	650	1,500	3,500	—
1634	—	375	650	1,500	3,500	—
1636	—	375	650	1,500	3,500	—
1637	—	375	650	1,500	3,500	—
1638	—	375	650	1,500	3,500	—

KM# A19 5 DUCAT
17.5000 g., 0.9860 Gold 0.5547 oz. AGW **Ruler:** Heinrich IV
Obv: Madonna and child with St. Anne above arms in inner circle **Rev:** Crowned imperial eagle in inner circle **Note:** Struck with 1 Thaler dies, KM#9.

Date	Mintage	VG	F	VF	XF	Unc
1634	—	2,000	3,250	5,500	8,500	—
1646	—	2,000	3,250	5,500	8,500	—
1649	—	2,000	3,250	5,500	8,500	—

KM# B19 5 DUCAT
17.5000 g., 0.9860 Gold 0.5547 oz. AGW **Ruler:** Franz Ernst
Note: Struck with 1 Thaler dies, KM#21.1. Previous KM#19.

Date	Mintage	VG	F	VF	XF	Unc
1652 Rare	—	—	—	—	—	—

KM# 23 5 DUCAT
17.5000 g., 0.9860 Gold 0.5547 oz. AGW **Ruler:** Franz Ernst
Obv: Crowned imperial eagle **Rev:** Madonna, child and St. Anne

Date	Mintage	VG	F	VF	XF	Unc
1661	—	2,250	3,750	6,500	9,500	—
1662	—	2,250	3,750	6,500	9,500	—

KM# 17 10 DUCAT
35.0000 g., 0.9860 Gold 1.1095 oz. AGW **Ruler:** Heinrich IV
Note: Struck with 1 Thaler dies, KM#8.1.

Date	Mintage	VG	F	VF	XF	Unc
1627 Rare	—	—	—	—	—	—

KM# 18 10 DUCAT
35.0000 g., 0.9860 Gold 1.1095 oz. AGW **Ruler:** Heinrich IV
Note: Struck with 1 Thaler dies, KM#8.

Date	Mintage	VG	F	VF	XF	Unc
1634 Rare	—	—	—	—	—	—

KM# 19 10 DUCAT
35.0000 g., 0.9860 Gold 1.1095 oz. AGW **Ruler:** Heinrich IV
Note: Struck with 1 Thaler dies, KM#9.

Date	Mintage	VG	F	VF	XF	Unc
1646 Rare	—	—	—	—	—	—

BOLIVIA

Bolivia, a landlocked country in west central South America, has an area of 424,165 sq. mi. (1,098,580 sq. km.).

Much of present day Bolivia was first dominated by the Tiahuanaco Culture ca.400 BC. It had in turn been incorporated into the Inca Empire by 1440AD prior to the arrival of the Spanish, in 1535, who reduced the Indian population to virtual slavery. When Joseph Napoleon was placed upon the throne of occupied Spain in 1809, a fervor of revolutionary activity quickened throughout Alto Peru - culminating in the 1809 Proclamation of Liberty. Sixteen bloody years of struggle ensued before the republic, named for the famed liberator Simon Bolivar, was established on August 6, 1825. Since then Bolivia has survived more than 16 constitutions, 78 Presidents, 3 military juntas and over 160 revolutions.

The Imperial City of Potosi, founded by Villarroel in 1546, was established in the midst of what is estimated to have been the world's richest silver mines (having produced in excess of 2 billion dollars worth of silver).

The first mint, early in 1574, used equipment brought over from Lima. Before that it had been used at La Plata where the operation failed. The oldest type was a cob with the Hapsburg arms on the obverse and cross with quartered castles and lions on the reverse. To the heraldic right of the shield (at the left as one faces it) is a "p" and, under it, the assayer's initial, although in some early examples the "P" and assayer can appear to the right of the shield. While production at the "Casa de Moneda" was enormous, the quality of the coinage was at times so poor that some 50 were condemned to death by their superiors.

Therefore, by royal decree of February 17, 1651, the design was changed to the quartered castles and lions for the obverse and two crowned pillars of Hercules floating above the waves of the sea for the reverse. A new transitional series was introduced in 1651-1652 followed by a new standard design in 1652 and as the last cob type continued on for several years along with the milled pillars and bust pieces from 1767 through 1773. In the final years under Charles III the planchet is compact and dumpy, very irregular and of poor style, contrasting sharply with their counterpart denominations of the pillar and bust types.

Rarely, and at very high prices, we may be offered almost perfectly round cobs, with the dies well-centered, showing the legend and date completely. These have gained importance in the last decades and are known as "royal" or "presentation" pieces. Every year a few of these specimens were coined, using dies in excellent condition and a specially prepared round planchet, to prove the quality of the minting to the Viceroy or even to the King.

Most pre-decimal coinage of independent Bolivia carries the assayers' initials on the reverse near the rim to the left of the date, in 4 to 5 o'clock position. The mint mark or name appears in the 7 to 8 o'clock area.

RULER
Spanish until 1825

MINT MARKS
PTA monogram - La Plata (Sucre)
P or PTS monogram - Potosi

ASSAYERS' INITIALS

There is little information available to establish the chronology of the assayers during the reign of Phillip II, 1555-1598, so the assayers initials are listed in alphabetical order. Calbeto in *Compendio de las Piezas de Ocho Reales* describes a piece with A overstruck over B, indicating A was later.

Initial	Date	Name
B	1596-1605	Hernando Ballesteros
C	1613	Augustin de la Quadra (Cuadra)
C	1678-79	Manuel de Cejas
E	1651-78	Antonio de Ergueta
F	1697-1701	?
M	1616-17	Juan Munoz
O	1649-51	Juan Rodriguez de Rodas
P	1620-31	Pedro Perez de Carrion
P	1622-26, 28-29, 46-47	Luis de Peralta
P, PO	1624-26	Pedro Martin de Palencia
Q	1613-17	Augustin de la Quadra
R	191-1618	Gaspar Ruiz
R	1605-13	?
R	1645-48	Felipe Ramirez Arellano
R, RL	1591-98, 1610-13, 18-23, 27-36, 44-48	Balthasar Ramos Leceta
T	1618-23, 27-36, 44-48	Juan Ximenez de Tapia
TR	1636-48	Pedro Trevino
V	1646	Geronimo Velasquez
V, VR	1679-84	Pedro de Villar
Z	1647-49	Pedro Zambrano

SYMBOLS

Letter and Symbol	Dates	Name
(c)=	1697	Sebastian de Chavarria
(o)=	1649-51	Juan Rodrigues de Roas
(t)R=	1636-40	Pedro Trevino
(tr)R=	1640-43	Pedro trevino
(tre)R=	1643-97	?

NOTE: These names are based on data put forth by Dr. E.A. Sellschopp in Las *Acunaciones de las Cecas de Lima, La Plata Y Potosi*, J. Pelliceri Bru in *Glosario de Maestros de Ceca y Ensayadores* and archival research in the *Casa Moneda Nacional de Bolivia.*

MONETARY SYSTEM
16 Reales = 1 Escudo

COLONIAL

COLONIAL COB COINAGE

KM# A6 1/4 REAL
Silver **Ruler:** Philip III

Date	Mintage	Good	VG	F	VF	XF
ND(1598-1605)P B Rare	—	—	—	—	—	—

KM# 11.1 1/2 REAL
1.6921 g., 0.9310 Silver 0.0506 oz. ASW **Ruler:** Philip III
Obv: Monogram without assayer's initial or mint mark

Date	Mintage	Good	VG	F	VF	XF
ND	—	50.00	90.00	125	175	—

KM# 6.1 1/2 REAL
1.6921 g., 0.9310 Silver 0.0506 oz. ASW **Ruler:** Philip III
Obv: Mint mark and assayer's initials flanking PHILIPPVS monogram **Obv. Legend:** PHILIPPVS III D G

Date	Mintage	Good	VG	F	VF	XF
ND(1598-1605)P B-P Rare	—	—	—	—	—	—
ND(1605-13)P P-R	—	50.00	100	135	175	—
ND(1605-13)P R-P	—	50.00	100	135	175	—
ND(1613-17)P P-Q	—	50.00	100	135	175	—
ND(1613-17)P Q-P	—	50.00	100	135	175	—
1617P M Rare	—	—	—	—	—	—
1618P PAL Rare	—	—	—	—	—	—
1618P T/PAL Rare	—	—	—	—	—	—
1618P T Rare	—	—	—	—	—	—

KM# 6.2 1/2 REAL
1.6921 g., 0.9310 Silver 0.0506 oz. ASW **Ruler:** Philip III
Obv: Without mint mark

Date	Mintage	Good	VG	F	VF	XF
ND(1613-17)P Q	—	50.00	100	135	175	—
ND(1616-17)P M	—	50.00	100	135	175	—

KM# 6.3 1/2 REAL
1.6921 g., 0.9310 Silver 0.0506 oz. ASW **Ruler:** Philip III
Obv: Assayer's initials and mint mark to left of monogram
Obv. Legend: PHILIPPVS III DG

Date	Mintage	Good	VG	F	VF	XF
ND(1605-13)P R	—	50.00	100	135	175	—
ND(1618-21)P T	—	50.00	100	135	175	—

KM# A12 1/2 REAL
1.6917 g., 0.9310 Silver 0.0506 oz. ASW **Ruler:** Philip IV
Rev: Pillars and waves **Rev. Legend:** POTOSI ANO 1652 EL PERU **Rev. Inscription:** ...PL-V-SV above L-T-RA

Date	Mintage	Good	VG	F	VF	XF
1652P	—	100	150	250	375	—

KM# A12.2 1/2 REAL
1.6921 g., 0.9310 Silver 0.0506 oz. ASW **Ruler:** Philip III
Rev. Legend: POTOSI ANO 1652 EL PERU **Rev. Inscription:** ...PL-V-SV above L-T-RA

Date	Mintage	Good	VG	F	VF	XF
1652P	—	100	150	250	375	—

KM# A12.3 1/2 REAL
1.6921 g., 0.9310 Silver 0.0506 oz. ASW **Ruler:** Philip III
Rev. Inscription: ...P-LV-SV above LT-R-A

Date	Mintage	Good	VG	F	VF	XF
1652P	—	100	150	250	375	—

KM# A12.4 1/2 REAL
1.6921 g., 0.9310 Silver 0.0506 oz. ASW **Ruler:** Philip III
Rev. Inscription: ...PL-VS-VL above T-R-A

Date	Mintage	Good	VG	F	VF	XF
1652P	—	100	150	250	375	—

KM# A12.5 1/2 REAL
1.6921 g., 0.9310 Silver 0.0506 oz. ASW **Ruler:** Philip III
Rev. Inscription: ...P-LV-SV above L-TR-A

Date	Mintage	Good	VG	F	VF	XF
1652P	—	100	150	250	375	—

KM# A12.6 1/2 REAL
1.6921 g., 0.9310 Silver 0.0506 oz. ASW **Ruler:** Philip III
Rev. Inscription: ...P-LV-SV above L-T-RA

Date	Mintage	Good	VG	F	VF	XF
ND(1652)P	—	100	150	250	375	—

KM# A12.7 1/2 REAL
1.6921 g., 0.9310 Silver 0.0506 oz. ASW **Ruler:** Philip IV
Obv: PHILIPPVS monogram superimposed on Cross of Jerusalem

Date	Mintage	Good	VG	F	VF	XF
1656P	—	100	150	250	375	—

KM# B12 1/2 REAL

1.6921 g., 0.9310 Silver 0.0506 oz. ASW **Ruler:** Philip IV **Obv:** Monogram of PHILIPVS IIII superimposed on Cross of Jerusalem **Rev:** Crowned arms **Note:** Previous KM#A12.1.

Date	Mintage	Good	VG	F	VF	XF
ND(1653-66)P Date off flan	—	8.00	15.00	30.00	60.00	—
1654/3P PE Rare	—	—	—	—	—	—
1654P PER Rare	—	—	—	—	—	—
1654P E PE	—	37.50	82.50	150	235	—
1654P E	—	32.50	60.00	115	185	—
1655P	—	32.50	60.00	115	185	—
1655P PH	—	37.50	82.50	150	235	—
1657P	—	32.50	60.00	115	185	—
1658P E	—	32.50	60.00	115	185	—
1659P E	—	37.50	82.50	150	235	—
1660P E	—	37.50	82.50	150	235	—
1661P E	—	37.50	82.50	150	235	—
1662P E	—	32.50	60.00	115	185	—
1663P E	—	37.50	82.50	150	235	—
1664P E	—	37.50	82.50	150	235	—
1665P E	—	32.50	60.00	115	185	—
1666P E	—	37.50	82.50	150	235	—

KM# C12 1/2 REAL

1.6917 g., 0.9310 Silver 0.0506 oz. ASW **Ruler:** Philip IV **Obv:** Cross of Jerusalem with lions and castles in quarters **Obv. Legend:** PHILIPPVS IIII DG **Rev:** PHILIPPVS monogram superimposed on Cross of Jerusalem with P-H-5-2 in quadrants

Date	Mintage	Good	VG	F	VF	XF
1652P Rare	—	—	—	—	—	—

KM# 22 1/2 REAL

1.6921 g., 0.9310 Silver 0.0506 oz. ASW **Ruler:** Philip IV **Obv:** Cross of Jerusalem, lions and castles in quarters, partial date below **Rev:** CAROLVS monogram, date below

Date	Mintage	Good	VG	F	VF	XF
ND(1667-1700)P Date off flan	—	6.00	9.00	20.00	35.00	—
1667P	—	32.50	50.00	90.00	165	—
1668P	—	32.50	50.00	90.00	165	—
1669P	—	32.50	50.00	90.00	165	—
1670P	—	32.50	50.00	90.00	165	—
1671P	—	18.50	27.50	50.00	110	—
1672P	—	18.50	27.50	50.00	110	—
1673P	—	18.50	27.50	50.00	110	—
1674P	—	18.50	27.50	50.00	110	—
1675P	—	18.50	27.50	50.00	110	—
1676P	—	18.50	27.50	50.00	110	—
1677P	—	32.00	50.00	90.00	165	—
1678P	—	32.00	50.00	90.00	165	—
1679/8P	—	32.50	50.00	90.00	165	—
1679P	—	28.00	37.50	70.00	135	—
1680P	—	25.00	35.00	60.00	120	—
1681P	—	25.00	35.00	60.00	120	—
1682P	—	25.00	35.00	60.00	120	—
1683/82P	—	25.00	35.00	60.00	120	—
1683P	—	22.50	30.00	55.00	115	—
1684P	—	22.50	30.00	55.00	115	—
1685P	—	22.50	30.00	55.00	115	—
1686P	—	22.50	30.00	55.00	115	—
1687P	—	22.50	30.00	55.00	115	—
1688P	—	22.50	30.00	55.00	115	—
1689P	—	22.50	30.00	55.00	115	—
1690P	—	22.50	30.00	55.00	115	—
1691P	—	22.50	30.00	55.00	115	—
1692P	—	22.50	30.00	55.00	115	—
1693P	—	22.50	30.00	55.00	115	—
1694P	—	22.50	30.00	55.00	115	—
1695P	—	22.50	30.00	55.00	115	—
1696P	—	32.50	50.00	90.00	165	—
1697P	—	22.50	30.00	55.00	115	—
1698P	—	22.50	30.00	55.00	115	—
1699P	—	22.50	30.00	55.00	115	—
1700P	—	22.50	30.00	55.00	115	—

KM# 7 REAL

3.3834 g., 0.9310 Silver 0.1013 oz. ASW **Ruler:** Philip III **Obv. Legend:** PHILIPPVS III D G HISPANIARVM **Note:** Previous KM#7.1.

Date	Mintage	Good	VG	F	VF	XF
ND(1596-1605)P B Rare	—	—	—	—	—	—
ND(1598-1621)P Date off flan	—	30.00	50.00	75.00	100	—
ND(1605-13)P small R	—	40.00	65.00	100	150	—
ND(1613-17)P Q	—	37.50	60.00	90.00	135	—
ND(1616-17)P M	—	37.50	60.00	90.00	135	—
1617P M Rare	—	—	—	—	—	—
1618P PAL/M Rare	—	—	—	—	—	—
1618P T Rare	—	—	—	—	—	—
1620P T Rare	—	—	—	—	—	—

KM# 12 REAL

3.3834 g., 0.9310 Silver 0.1013 oz. ASW **Ruler:** Philip IV **Obv. Legend:** PHILIPPVS IIII D G HISPANIARVM **Note:** Prev. KM#12.4.

Date	Mintage	Good	VG	F	VF	XF
ND(1622)P Date off flan	—	30.00	50.00	75.00	100	—
1622P P/T	—	50.00	100	180	275	—

KM# 12a REAL

Silver **Ruler:** Philip IV **Obv. Legend:** PHILIPPVS IIII D G HISPANIARVM **Note:** .700-.931 fineness.

Date	Mintage	Good	VG	F	VF	XF
ND(1626-1648)P Date off flan	—	30.00	50.00	75.00	100	—
1626P P Rare	—	—	—	—	—	—
1628P P Rare	—	—	—	—	—	—
1628P P/T Rare	—	—	—	—	—	—
1628P T Rare	—	—	—	—	—	—
1629P T Rare	—	—	—	—	—	—
1630P T Rare	—	—	—	—	—	—
1631P T Rare	—	—	—	—	—	—
1632P T Rare	—	—	—	—	—	—
1633P T Rare	—	—	—	—	—	—
1634P T Rare	—	—	—	—	—	—
1636P T Rare	—	—	—	—	—	—
1636P TR Rare	—	—	—	—	—	—
1637P TR Rare	—	—	—	—	—	—
1638P TR Rare	—	—	—	—	—	—
1639P TR Rare	—	—	—	—	—	—
1640P FR Rare	—	—	—	—	—	—
1641P FR Rare	—	—	—	—	—	—
1642P FR Rare	—	—	—	—	—	—
1643P FR Rare	—	—	—	—	—	—
1644P FR Reported, not confirmed	—	—	—	—	—	—
1644P T Reported, not confirmed	—	—	—	—	—	—
1644P TR Rare	—	—	—	—	—	—
1645P T Rare	—	—	—	—	—	—
1646P V Rare	—	—	—	—	—	—
1647P Z Rare	—	—	—	—	—	—
1648P Z Rare	—	—	—	—	—	—
1648P Z/(tr) Reported, not confirmed	—	—	—	—	—	—

KM# 12b REAL

3.3834 g., 0.8960 Silver 0.0975 oz. ASW **Ruler:** Philip III **Obv. Legend:** PHILIPPVS IIII D G HISPANIARVM

Date	Mintage	Good	VG	F	VF	XF
ND(1649-51)P Date off flan	—	30.00	50.00	75.00	100	—
1649P (o)/Z Rare	—	—	—	—	—	—
1649P (o) Rare	—	—	—	—	—	—
1650P (o) Rare	—	—	—	—	—	—
1651P E Rare	—	—	—	—	—	—
1651P (o) Rare	—	—	—	—	—	—

KM# 13 REAL

3.3841 g., 0.9310 Silver 0.1013 oz. ASW **Ruler:** Philip IV **Obv:** Cross of Jerusalem, castles and lions in quarters **Obv. Legend:** PHILIPVS IV, D. G. HISPANIARUM REX **Rev:** Pillars and waves with 3-line inscription: Mint mark I, assayer's initial/ PLV-SVL-TRA/ date, mint mark

Date	Mintage	Good	VG	F	VF	XF
ND(1652-66)P Date off flan	—	25.00	40.00	60.00	90.00	125
1652P E I. PH. 6	—	40.00	90.00	175	300	375
1653P E PH	—	40.00	60.00	100	175	275
1654P E-PH	—	30.00	50.00	90.00	140	225
1655P E PH	—	30.00	50.00	90.00	140	225
1656P E	—	30.00	50.00	90.00	140	225
1657P E	—	30.00	50.00	80.00	125	200
1658P E	—	30.00	50.00	80.00	125	200
1659P E	—	30.00	50.00	80.00	125	200
1660P E	—	30.00	50.00	80.00	125	200
1661P E	—	30.00	50.00	80.00	125	200
1662P E	—	30.00	50.00	80.00	125	200
1663P E	—	30.00	50.00	80.00	125	200
1664P E	—	30.00	50.00	80.00	125	200
1665P E	—	30.00	50.00	80.00	125	200
1666P E	—	30.00	50.00	90.00	140	225

Obverse

Type I:
I I
• •
P E
• •

Type II:
I I
A O
P E
5 2

Reverse

Type I:
F I IIII
PLV SVL TRA
E I E

Type II:
A I O
PLV SVL TRA
E I E

Type III:
P I IIII
PLV SVL TRA
E • E

KM# A13.1 REAL

3.3834 g., 0.9310 Silver 0.1013 oz. ASW **Ruler:** Philip IV **Obv:** Castles and lions in shield **Obv. Legend:** PHILIPPVS IIII D G HISPANIARVM **Rev:** Pillars and waves **Rev. Legend:** POTOSI ANO 1652 EL PERU **Note:** Type I inscription.

Date	Mintage	Good	VG	F	VF	XF
1652P E Rare	—	—	—	—	—	—

KM# A13.2 REAL

3.3841 g., 0.9310 Silver 0.1013 oz. ASW **Ruler:** Philip IV **Obv:** Castles and lions in shield **Obv. Legend:** PHILIPPVS IIII D G HISPANIARVM **Rev:** Pillars and waves **Rev. Legend:** POTOSI ANO 1652 EL PERU **Note:** Type II inscription.

Date	Mintage	Good	VG	F	VF	XF
1652P E	—	125	200	275	375	—

KM# A13.3 REAL

3.3841 g., 0.9310 Silver 0.1013 oz. ASW **Ruler:** Philip IV **Obv:** Castles and lions in shield **Obv. Legend:** PHILIPPVS IIII D G HISPANIARVM **Rev:** Pillars and waves **Rev. Legend:** POTOSI ANO 1652 EL PERU **Note:** Type II inscription.

Date	Mintage	Good	VG	F	VF	XF
1652P E Rare	—	—	—	—	—	—

KM# 12.7 1/2 REAL

1.6921 g., 0.9310 Silver 0.0506 oz. ASW **Ruler:** Philip III **Rev. Inscription:** ...PL-V-SV above LT-R-A

Date	Mintage	Good	VG	F	VF	XF
1652P	—	100	150	250	375	—

KM# A13.4 REAL

3.3841 g., 0.9310 Silver 0.1013 oz. ASW **Ruler:** Philip IV **Obv:** Castles and lions in shield **Obv. Legend:** PHILIPPVS IIII D G HISPANIARVM **Rev:** Pillars and waves **Rev. Legend:** POTOSI ANO 1652 EL PERU **Note:** Type II obverse inscription. Type IIII reverse inscription.

Date	Mintage	Good	VG	F	VF	XF
1652P E	—	125	200	275	375	—

KM# B13.1 REAL

3.3834 g., 0.9310 Silver 0.1013 oz. ASW **Ruler:** Philip IV **Obv:** Cross of Jerusalem with castles and lions in quarters, mint mark to left, assayer's initial to right, date below **Note:** Type III reverse inscription

Date	Mintage	Good	VG	F	VF	XF
1652P E	—	100	150	225	325	—

KM# 23 REAL

3.3841 g., 0.9310 Silver 0.1013 oz. ASW **Ruler:** Charles II **Obv:** Cross of Jerusalem **Obv. Legend:** CAROLVS II

Date	Mintage	Good	VG	F	VF	XF
ND(1667-1701)P Date off flan	—	25.00	40.00	60.00	90.00	125
1667P E	—	30.00	50.00	90.00	140	225
1668P E	—	30.00	50.00	80.00	125	200
1669P E	—	30.00	50.00	80.00	125	200
1670P E	—	30.00	50.00	80.00	125	200
1671P E	—	30.00	50.00	80.00	125	200
1672/1P E Rare	—	—	—	—	—	—
1672P E	—	30.00	50.00	80.00	125	200
1672P E Dot between 7 and 2; Rare	—	—	—	—	—	—
1673/2P E Rare	—	—	—	—	—	—
1673P E	—	30.00	50.00	80.00	125	200

Date	Mintage	Good	VG	F	VF	XF
1674P E	—	30.00	50.00	80.00	125	200
1675//(17)65P E Rare	—	—	—	—	—	—
1675P E	—	30.00	50.00	80.00	125	200
1676P E	—	30.00	50.00	80.00	125	200
1677/6P E Rare	—	—	—	—	—	—
1677P E	—	30.00	50.00	80.00	125	200
1678P E	—	30.00	50.00	80.00	125	200
1678P C, E Rare	—	—	—	—	—	—
1678P C/E Rare	—	—	—	—	—	—
1678P C	—	30.00	50.00	85.00	135	210
1679P C	—	30.00	50.00	85.00	135	210
1679P C/E Reported, not confirmed	—	—	—	—	—	—
1679P V	—	30.00	50.00	85.00	135	210
1680P V	—	30.00	50.00	80.00	125	200
1680P V Rare	—	—	—	—	—	—
Note: Mint mark at upper right						
1681P V	—	30.00	50.00	80.00	125	200
1681/0P V Repoted, not confirmed	—	—	—	—	—	—
1682P V	—	30.00	50.00	80.00	125	200
1683P V	—	30.00	50.00	80.00	125	200
1684P V	—	30.00	50.00	85.00	135	210
1684P VR	—	30.00	50.00	85.00	135	210
1685P VR	—	30.00	50.00	80.00	125	200
1686P VR	—	30.00	50.00	80.00	125	200
1687P VR	—	30.00	50.00	80.00	125	200
1688P VR	—	30.00	50.00	80.00	125	200
1689P VR	—	30.00	50.00	80.00	125	200
1690P VR	—	30.00	50.00	80.00	125	200
1691P VR	—	30.00	50.00	80.00	125	200
1692P VR	—	30.00	50.00	80.00	125	200
1693P VR	—	30.00	50.00	80.00	125	200
1693P VR	—	30.00	50.00	80.00	125	200
1693P VR 1 and 3 inverted; Reported, not confirmed	—	—	—	—	—	—
1694P VR	—	30.00	50.00	80.00	125	200
1695P VR	—	30.00	50.00	80.00	125	200
1696P VR	—	30.00	50.00	80.00	125	—
1697P VR	—	35.00	65.00	95.00	150	250
1697P CH	—	70.00	90.00	150	275	—
1697P F	—	35.00	65.00	95.00	150	250
1697P F/CH Rare	—	—	—	—	—	—
1698P F	—	30.00	50.00	90.00	150	250
1699P F	—	30.00	50.00	90.00	150	250
1700P F	—	30.00	50.00	90.00	150	250

KM# 8 2 REALES

6.7682 g., 0.9310 Silver 0.2026 oz. ASW **Ruler:** Philip III **Obv. Legend:** PHILIPPVS III D. G:HISPANIARVM

Date	Mintage	Good	VG	F	VF	XF
ND(1596-1605)P B Rare	—	—	—	—	—	—
ND(1605-13)P R	—	50.00	75.00	100	150	250
Note: Curved leg R						
ND(1605-13)P RL	—	50.00	75.00	100	150	250
ND(1613-17)P Q	—	50.00	75.00	100	150	250
ND(1616-17)P M	—	50.00	75.00	100	150	250
ND(1617-21)P Date off flan	—	45.00	70.00	90.00	125	200
1617P M	—	125	180	250	375	—
1617P M/C Rare	—	—	—	—	—	—
1618P RL	—	125	200	300	400	—
1618P T	—	125	180	250	375	—
1618P T/RL Rare	—	—	—	—	—	—
1618P T/RL and T to right Rare	—	—	—	—	—	—
1619P T	—	125	180	250	375	—
1620P T	—	125	180	250	375	—
1621P T	—	125	180	250	375	—

KM# 14 2 REALES

6.7668 g., 0.9310 Silver 0.2025 oz. ASW **Ruler:** Philip IV **Obv. Legend:** PHILIPPVS IV D.G. HISPANIARVM REX **Note:** Prev. KM#14.1.

Date	Mintage	Good	VG	F	VF	XF
ND(1622-23)P Date off flan	—	45.00	70.00	90.00	125	200
1622P P Rare	—	—	—	—	—	—
16ZIIIP P Rare	—	—	—	—	—	—

KM# 14a 2 REALES

Silver .700-.931 **Ruler:** Philip IV **Obv. Legend:** PHILIPPVS IV D. G. HISPANIARVM REX **Note:** .700-.931 fineness

Date	Mintage	Good	VG	F	VF	XF
ND(1626-48)P Date off flan	—	45.00	70.00	90.00	125	200
1626P P Rare	—	—	—	—	—	—
1626P T/P Rare	—	—	—	—	—	—
1626P T Rare	—	—	—	—	—	—
1627P T Rare	—	—	—	—	—	—
1628P P Rare	—	—	—	—	—	—
1628P T Rare	—	—	—	—	—	—
1629P T Rare	—	—	—	—	—	—
1630P T Rare	—	—	—	—	—	—
1631/0P T Rare	—	—	—	—	—	—
1631P T Rare	—	—	—	—	—	—
1632P T Rare	—	—	—	—	—	—
1633P T Rare	—	—	—	—	—	—
1634P T Rare	—	—	—	—	—	—
1635P T Rare	—	—	—	—	—	—
1637P T or TR Rare	—	—	—	—	—	—
1638P TR Rare	—	—	—	—	—	—
1639P TR Rare	—	—	—	—	—	—
1640P FR Reported, not confirmed	—	—	—	—	—	—
1641P FR Rare	—	—	—	—	—	—
1642P FR Rare	—	—	—	—	—	—
1643P FR Reported, not confirmed	—	—	—	—	—	—
1644P TR Rare	—	—	—	—	—	—
1645P T/R Reported, not confirmed	—	—	—	—	—	—
1645P TR Rare	—	—	—	—	—	—
1646P P Rare	—	—	—	—	—	—
1646P V/TR Rare	—	—	—	—	—	—
1648P TR Rare	—	—	—	—	—	—
1648P Z/T Rare	—	—	—	—	—	—

KM# 14b 2 REALES

6.7668 g., 0.8590 Silver 0.1869 oz. ASW **Ruler:** Philip IV **Obv. Legend:** PHILIPPVS IV D. G. HISPANIARVM REX **Note:** Early examples exist with castles and lions transposed.

Date	Mintage	Good	VG	F	VF	XF
ND(1649-52)P Date off flan	—	45.00	70.00	90.00	125	200
1649P (o) Rare	—	—	—	—	—	—
1649P Z Rare	—	—	—	—	—	—
1650P (o) Rare	—	—	—	—	—	—
1651P E Rare	—	—	—	—	—	—
1652P E Rare	—	—	—	—	—	—

KM# 15.3 2 REALES

6.7682 g., 0.9310 Silver 0.2026 oz. ASW **Ruler:** Philip IV **Obv:** Type III **Rev:** Type II

Date	Mintage	Good	VG	F	VF	XF
1652P E	—	200	325	500	750	—

KM# A16.2 2 REALES

6.7682 g., 0.9310 Silver 0.2026 oz. ASW **Ruler:** Philip IV **Obv:** Cross of Jerusalem with castles and lions in quarters, mint mark to left, assayer's initial to right **Rev:** Type I

Date	Mintage	Good	VG	F	VF	XF
1652P E	—	200	325	500	750	—

KM# 15.1 2 REALES

6.7682 g., 0.9310 Silver 0.2026 oz. ASW **Ruler:** Philip IV **Obv:** Type I, crowned shield with castles and lions **Obv. Legend:** PHILIPPVS IIII D. G. HISPANIARVM **Rev:** Type I, pillars and waves, inscription **Rev. Legend:** POTOSI ANO 1652 EL PERV

Date	Mintage	Good	VG	F	VF	XF
1652P E	—	200	325	500	750	—

Obverse

Type I	Type II	Type III
A O	A O	A O
P E	P E	P E
2 52	2 5/2	5 2

Reverse

Type I	Type II	Type III
F 2 IIII	P H E	P 2 IIII
PLV SVL TRA	PLV SVL TRA	PLV SVL TRA
E 2 E	E 2 P	E 2 P

KM# 15.2 2 REALES

6.7682 g., 0.9310 Silver 0.2026 oz. ASW **Ruler:** Philip IV **Obv:** Type II **Rev:** Type II

Date	Mintage	Good	VG	F	VF	XF
1652	—	200	325	500	750	—

KM# A16.1 2 REALES

6.7682 g., 0.9310 Silver 0.2026 oz. ASW **Ruler:** Philip IV **Obv:** Cross of Jerusalem with castles and lions in quarters, mint mark to left, assayer's initial to right **Rev:** Type II **Note:** Prev. KM#16.1.

Date	Mintage	Good	VG	F	VF	XF
1652P E	—	200	325	500	750	—

KM# 16 2 REALES

6.7682 g., 0.9310 Silver 0.2026 oz. ASW **Ruler:** Philip III **Obv:** Cross of Jerusalem **Rev:** P. O. E **Note:** Prev. KM#16.2.

Date	Mintage	Good	VG	F	VF	XF
ND(1652-67)P Date off flan	—	45.00	70.00	90.00	125	175
1652P I-PH-6	—	65.00	110	200	300	400
1653P E-PH	—	60.00	100	200	300	400
1654P E-PH	—	60.00	100	200	300	400
1655/4P E-PH Rare	—	—	—	—	—	—
1655P E-PH	—	60.00	100	200	300	400
1656P E-PH	—	60.00	100	200	300	400
1657P E	—	60.00	80.00	125	200	400
1658P E	—	50.00	75.00	100	150	275
1659P E	—	50.00	75.00	100	150	275
1660P E	—	50.00	75.00	70.00	150	275
1661P E	—	50.00	75.00	100	150	275
1662P E	—	50.00	75.00	100	150	275
1663P E	—	50.00	75.00	100	150	275
1664P E	—	50.00	75.00	100	150	275
1665P E	—	50.00	75.00	100	150	275
1666P E	—	50.00	75.00	100	150	275
1667P E	—	50.00	75.00	100	150	275

KM# 24 2 REALES

6.7682 g., 0.9310 Silver 0.2026 oz. ASW **Ruler:** Charles II **Obv:** Cross of Jerusalem, castles and lions in quarters **Obv. Legend:** CAROLVS II **Rev:** Crowned pillars of Hercules and waves, value at top center

Date	Mintage	Good	VG	F	VF	XF
ND(1667-1701)P Date off flan	—	45.00	70.00	90.00	125	175
1667P E	—	50.00	75.00	100	150	275
1668/7P E Rare	—	—	—	—	—	—
1668P E	—	50.00	75.00	100	150	275
1669P E	—	50.00	75.00	100	150	275
1670/69P E Rare	—	—	—	—	—	—
1670P E	—	50.00	75.00	100	150	275
1671/0P E Rare	—	—	—	—	—	—
1671P E	—	50.00	75.00	100	150	275
1672P E	—	50.00	75.00	100	150	275
1673P E	—	50.00	75.00	100	150	275
1674P E	—	50.00	75.00	100	150	275
1675P E	—	50.00	75.00	100	150	275
1676P E	—	50.00	75.00	100	150	275
1677P E	—	50.00	75.00	100	150	275

Date	Mintage	Good	VG	F	VF	XF
1678P E	—	50.00	75.00	100	150	275
1679P C	—	50.00	75.00	100	150	275
1679P V	—	50.00	75.00	100	150	275
1680P V	—	50.00	75.00	100	150	275
1681/0P V Reported, not confirmed	—	—	—	—	—	—
1681P V	—	50.00	75.00	100	150	275
1682P V	—	50.00	75.00	100	150	275
1683P V	—	50.00	75.00	100	150	275
1684P V	—	50.00	75.00	100	150	275
1684P V, VR Rare	—	—	—	—	—	—
1684P VR	—	60.00	90.00	125	175	300
1685P VR	—	50.00	80.00	110	160	285
1686P VR	—	50.00	80.00	110	160	285
1687P VR	—	50.00	80.00	110	160	285
1688P VR	—	50.00	80.00	110	160	285
1689P VR	—	50.00	80.00	110	160	285
1690P VR	—	50.00	80.00	110	160	285
1691P VR	—	50.00	80.00	110	160	285
1692/1P VR Reported, not confirmed	—	—	—	—	—	—
1692P VR	—	50.00	80.00	110	160	285
1693P VR	—	50.00	80.00	110	160	285
1694P VR	—	50.00	80.00	110	160	285
1695P VR	—	50.00	80.00	110	160	285
1696P VR	—	50.00	80.00	110	160	285
1697P (c)	—	60.00	100	200	300	400
1697P F	—	50.00	80.00	110	160	285
1697P F/(c) Rare	—	—	—	—	—	—
1697P VR	—	50.00	80.00	110	160	285
1698P F	—	50.00	75.00	100	150	275
1699P F	—	50.00	75.00	100	150	275
1700P F	—	50.00	75.00	100	150	275

KM# 9 4 REALES

13.5365 g., 0.9310 Silver 0.4052 oz. ASW **Ruler:** Philip III **Obv. Legend:** PHILIPPVS III D.G. HISPANIARVM **Note:** Prev. KM#9.1.

Date	Mintage	Good	VG	F	VF	XF
ND(1596-1605)P B Rare	—	—	—	—	—	—
ND(1605-13)P R	—	75.00	120	200	350	475
Note: Curved leg R						
ND(1613-17)P Q	—	75.00	120	200	350	475
ND(1616-17)P M	—	75.00	120	200	350	475
ND(1617-21)P Date off flan	—	60.00	85.00	140	200	350
1617P M Rare	—	—	—	—	—	—
1618P PAL Rare	—	—	—	—	—	—
1618P T Rare	—	—	—	—	—	—
1620P T Rare	—	—	—	—	—	—
1621P T Rare	—	—	—	—	—	—

Note: Early examples exist with castles and lions transposed

KM# 17 4 REALES

13.5365 g., 0.9310 Silver 0.4052 oz. ASW **Ruler:** Philip IV **Obv:** Crowned arms **Obv. Legend:** PHILIPPVS IIII **Rev:** Cross of Jerusalem, lions and castles in quarters

Date	Mintage	Good	VG	F	VF	XF
ND(1622)P Date off flan	—	60.00	85.00	140	200	350
1622P P Rare	—	—	—	—	—	—

KM# 17a 4 REALES

0.7000 Silver .700-.931 fineness **Ruler:** Philip IV **Obv:** Crowned arms **Obv. Legend:** PHILIPPVS IIII **Rev:** Cross of Jerusalem, lions and castles in quarters

Date	Mintage	Good	VG	F	VF	XF
ND(1624-47)P Date off flan	—	60.00	85.00	140	200	350
1624P P or T Rare	—	—	—	—	—	—
1627P T Rare	—	—	—	—	—	—
1628P T Rare	—	—	—	—	—	—
1629P P Rare	—	—	—	—	—	—
1629P T Rare	—	—	—	—	—	—
1630P T Rare	—	—	—	—	—	—
1631P T Rare	—	—	—	—	—	—
1632P T Rare	—	—	—	—	—	—
1633P T Rare	—	—	—	—	—	—
1635P T Reported, not confirmed	—	—	—	—	—	—
1639P TR Rare	—	—	—	—	—	—
1640P FR Rare	—	—	—	—	—	—
1643P TR or FR Rare	—	—	—	—	—	—
1644P T, TR or FR Rare	—	—	—	—	—	—
1646P V/T Rare	—	—	—	—	—	—
1647P P Reported, not confirmed	—	—	—	—	—	—

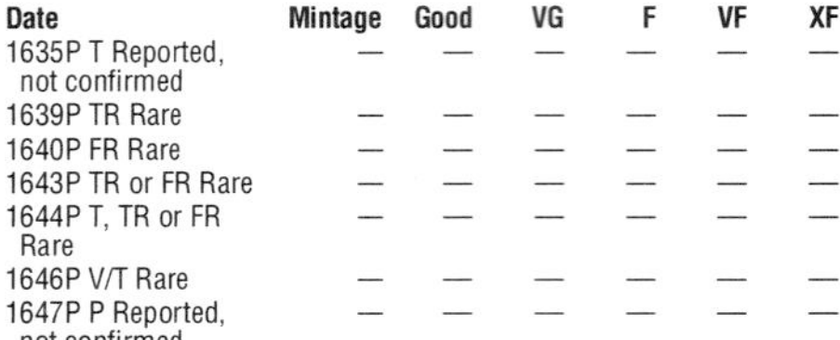

KM# 17b 4 REALES

13.5339 g., 0.8590 Silver 0.3738 oz. ASW **Ruler:** Philip IV **Obv:** Crowned arms **Obv. Legend:** PHILIPPVS IIII **Rev:** Cross of Jerusalem, lions and castles in quarters

Date	Mintage	Good	VG	F	VF	XF
ND(1649-51)P Date off flan	—	60.00	85.00	140	200	350
1649P (o)	—	175	275	375	475	575
1649P (o)/Z Rare	—	—	—	—	—	—
1649P Z Rare	—	—	—	—	—	—
1650P (o)	—	175	275	375	475	575
1651P E	—	175	275	375	475	575
1651P (o)	—	175	275	375	475	575

KM# 18 4 REALES

13.5365 g., 0.9310 Silver 0.4052 oz. ASW **Ruler:** Philip IV **Obv:** Crowned cross of Jerusalem, lions and castles in quarters **Rev:** Crowned pillars and waves, inscription includes mint mark, denomination, assayer's initial/PLV-SVL-TRA/assayer's initial; date-mint mark **Note:** Prev. KM#18.1.

Date	Mintage	Good	VG	F	VF	XF
ND(1652-66)P Date off flan	—	60.00	85.00	140	200	300
1652P E 1-PH-6 Reported, not confirmed	—	—	—	—	—	—
1653/2P E Rare	—	—	—	—	—	—
1653P E-PH	—	125	200	300	400	500
1654P E-PH	—	125	200	300	400	500
1655P E-PH	—	125	200	300	400	500
1656P E-PH	—	175	250	350	450	575
1657P E	—	125	200	300	400	500
1658P E	—	125	200	300	400	500
1659//(16)58P E Rare	—	—	—	—	—	—
1659P E	—	125	200	300	400	500
1660P E	—	125	200	300	400	500
1661P E	—	125	200	300	400	500
1662P E	—	175	250	350	450	575
1664P E	—	125	200	300	400	500
1665P E	—	125	200	300	400	500
1666P E	—	125	200	300	400	500

KM# A18 4 REALES

13.5337 g., 0.9310 Silver 0.4051 oz. ASW **Ruler:** Philip IV **Obv:** Crowned arms, lions and castles in quarters, A/P/4 at left, O/E/52 at right **Obv. Legend:** PHILIPPVS IIII D.G. HISPANIARVM **Rev:** Pillars and waves **Rev. Legend:** POTOSI ANO 1652 EL PERU **Rev. Inscription:** ... PLV - SVL - TRA/ E-4-E

Date	Mintage	Good	VG	F	VF	XF
1652P E Rare	—	—	—	—	—	—

KM# B18 4 REALES

13.5337 g., 0.9310 Silver 0.4051 oz. ASW **Ruler:** Philip IV **Obv:** Crowned cross of Jerusalem, castles and lions in quarters, mint mark to left, assayer's initial to right, date below

Date	Mintage	Good	VG	F	VF	XF
1652P E Rare	—	—	—	—	—	—

KM# 25 4 REALES

13.5365 g., 0.9310 Silver 0.4052 oz. ASW **Ruler:** Charles II **Obv:** Cross of Jerusalem, castles and lions at quarters **Rev:** Crowned pillars of Hercules and waves, value at top center

Date	Mintage	Good	VG	F	VF	XF
ND(1667-1701)P Date off flan	—	60.00	85.00	140	200	300
1667P E	—	175	250	350	450	575
1668P E	—	125	200	300	400	500
1669P E	—	125	200	300	400	500
1670P E	—	125	200	300	400	500
1671/0P E Rare	—	—	—	—	—	—
1671P E	—	175	250	350	450	575
1672P E	—	175	250	350	450	575
1673P E	—	175	250	350	450	575
1674P E	—	175	250	350	450	575
1675P E	—	175	250	350	450	575
1676P E	—	175	250	350	450	575
1677P E	—	125	200	300	400	500
1678P E	—	125	200	300	400	500
1679P C	—	125	200	300	400	500
1679P C/E Rare	—	—	—	—	—	—
1679P V	—	125	200	300	400	500
1680P V	—	125	200	300	400	500
1681P V	—	125	200	300	425	575
1682P V	—	125	200	300	425	575
1683P V	—	125	200	300	425	575
1684P V	—	125	200	300	425	575
1684P VR	—	175	250	400	575	—
1685P VR	—	125	200	300	425	575
1686P VR	—	125	200	300	425	575
1687P VR	—	125	200	300	425	575
1688P VR	—	125	200	300	425	575
1689P VR	—	125	200	300	425	575
1690P VR	—	125	200	300	425	575
1691P VR	—	125	200	300	425	575
1692P VR	—	125	200	300	425	575
1693P VR	—	125	200	300	425	575
1694P VR	—	125	200	300	425	575
1695P VR	—	125	200	300	425	575
1696P VR	—	125	200	300	425	575
1697P CH	—	175	275	400	600	—
1697P F/CH Rare	—	—	—	—	—	—
1697P F Rare	—	—	—	—	—	—
1697P VR	—	125	200	300	425	575
1698P F	—	125	200	300	425	575
1699P F	—	175	250	400	575	—
1700P F Rare	—	—	—	—	—	—

KM# 10 8 REALES

27.0674 g., 0.9310 Silver 0.8102 oz. ASW **Ruler:** Philip III **Obv. Legend:** PHILIPPVS (PHILIPVS or PHYLYPVS) III D.G. HISPANIARVM **Note:** Some examples exist with castles and lions, elements of the arms transposed.

Date	Mintage	Good	VG	F	VF	XF
ND(1596-1605)P B Rare	—	—	—	—	—	—
ND(1605-13)P R/B Curved leg R, Rare	—	—	—	—	—	—
ND(1605-13)P R Curved leg R	—	75.00	150	225	300	—

Date	Mintage	Good	VG	F	VF	XF
ND(1613-17)P Q/R Curved leg R, Rare	—	—	—	—	—	—
ND(1613-1617)P Q	—	75.00	150	225	300	—
ND(1613)P C/Q Rare	—	—	—	—	—	—
ND(1613)P C Rare	—	—	—	—	—	—
ND(1613-17)P Q/c Rare	—	—	—	—	—	—
ND(1616-17)P M/Q Rare	—	—	—	—	—	—
ND(1616-17)P M	—	75.00	150	225	300	—
ND(1617-21)P Date off flan	—	75.00	100	150	220	—
1617P M	—	250	500	750	1,000	—
1617P PAL Unique mule	—	—	—	—	—	—
1618P PAL	—	500	750	1,000	1,750	—
1618P T/PAL Rare	—	—	—	—	—	—
1618P T/PAL Rare	—	—	—	—	—	—

Note: Additional T to right

Date	Mintage	Good	VG	F	VF	XF
1619P T	—	150	200	300	400	—
1620P T	—	150	200	300	400	—
1612P T (error for 1621); Rare	—	—	—	—	—	—
1621P T	—	150	200	300	400	—

KM# 19 8 REALES

27.0703 g., 0.9310 Silver 0.8102 oz. ASW **Ruler:** Philip IV **Note:** Prev. KM#19.1.

Date	Mintage	Good	VG	F	VF	XF
ND(1622-24)P Date off flan	—	75.00	125	175	275	—
1622P T	—	150	200	300	400	—
1622P P/T Rare	—	—	—	—	—	—
1622P P	—	150	200	300	400	—
1623 (16ZIII)P T	—	200	350	500	750	—
1623(16ZIII)P P Rare	—	—	—	—	—	—
1624P T Rare	—	—	—	—	—	—
1624P P Rare	—	—	—	—	—	—

KM# 19a 8 REALES

Silver **Ruler:** Philip IV **Note:** .700-.931 fineness.

Date	Mintage	Good	VG	F	VF	XF
ND(1625-48)P Date off flan	—	75.00	125	175	275	—
1625P P Rare	—	—	—	—	—	—
1626P T Reported, not confirmed	—	—	—	—	—	—
1626P P Rare	—	—	—	—	—	—
1627P T	—	200	300	400	500	—
1628P T	—	150	200	350	475	—
1628P P/T Rare	—	—	—	—	—	—
1628P P	—	150	200	350	475	—
1629P T	—	150	200	300	400	—
1629P P Rare	—	—	—	—	—	—
1630P T	—	150	200	300	400	—
1631P T	—	150	200	300	400	—
1632P T	—	150	200	350	475	—
1633P T	—	150	200	350	475	—
1634P T	—	150	200	350	475	—
1635P T	—	150	200	350	475	—
1636P T Rare	—	—	—	—	—	—
1636P TR Rare	—	—	—	—	—	—
1637P TR Rare	—	—	—	—	—	—
1638P TR Rare	—	—	—	—	—	—
1639P TR Rare	—	—	—	—	—	—
1640P FR Rare	—	—	—	—	—	—
1640P TR Rare	—	—	—	—	—	—
1641P FR Rare	—	—	—	—	—	—
1642P FR Rare	—	—	—	—	—	—
1643P FR Rare	—	—	—	—	—	—
1643P T Rare	—	—	—	—	—	—
1643P TR Rare	—	—	—	—	—	—
1644P T Rare	—	—	—	—	—	—
1644P FR Rare	—	—	—	—	—	—
1644P TR Rare	—	—	—	—	—	—
1645/4P R Rare	—	—	—	—	—	—
1645P TR Rare	—	—	—	—	—	—
1645P T (16455); Rare	—	—	—	—	—	—
1645P T	—	150	200	350	475	—
1646P R Reported, not confirmed	—	—	—	—	—	—
1646P T Rare	—	—	—	—	—	—
1646P V/T Rare	—	—	—	—	—	—
1646P V Rare	—	—	—	—	—	—
1646P P Reported, not confirmed	—	—	—	—	—	—
1647P TR Rare	—	—	—	—	—	—
1647P P Unique	—	—	—	—	—	—
1647P T Rare	—	—	—	—	—	—
1647P Z Rare	—	—	—	—	—	—
1648P Z/R Rare	—	—	—	—	—	—
1648P Z	—	150	200	350	475	—
1648P T Rare	—	—	—	—	—	—

KM# 19b 8 REALES

27.0674 g., 0.8590 Silver 0.7475 oz. ASW **Ruler:** Philip IV **Note:** Scarce examples of coins dated 1650 and 1651 with different "5's" and some with single dot or five dot ornaments between and flanking the digits of the date exist.

Date	Mintage	Good	VG	F	VF	XF
ND(1649-52)P Date off flan	—	75.00	125	175	275	—
1649P Z	—	150	200	300	425	—
1649P (o)/Z Rare	—	—	—	—	—	—
1649P (o)	—	100	175	275	400	—
1650/49P (o) Rare	—	—	—	—	—	—
1650P (o)	—	100	175	275	400	—
1651P (o)	—	100	175	275	400	—
1651P E/(o)	—	150	200	300	450	—
1651P E	—	100	175	275	400	—
1652P E Rare	—	—	—	—	—	—

KM# 21 8 REALES

27.0703 g., 0.9310 Silver 0.8102 oz. ASW **Ruler:** Philip IV **Obv:** Crowned cross of Jerusalem, castles and lions in quarters **Obv. Legend:** PHILIPVS IIII **Rev:** Crowned pillars and waves **Rev. Legend:** POTOSI ANO....

Date	Mintage	Good	VG	F	VF	XF
1652P 1-PH-6	—	175	325	500	750	—
ND(1652-67)P Date off flan	—	75.00	125	175	225	—
1653P E-PH	—	100	200	300	420	—
1654P E-PH	—	100	200	300	420	—
1655P E-PH	—	100	200	300	420	—
1656P E-PH	—	100	200	300	420	—
1657P E-PH	—	125	250	375	525	—
1657P E	—	100	200	300	420	—
1657P E Rare	—	—	—	—	—	—

Note: (E to left of cross)

Date	Mintage	Good	VG	F	VF	XF
1658P E	—	100	200	300	420	—
1659P E	—	100	200	300	420	—
1660P E	—	100	200	300	420	—
1661/0P E Rare	—	—	—	—	—	—
1661P E	—	100	200	300	420	—
1662P E	—	100	200	300	420	—
1663P E	—	100	200	300	420	—
1664P E	—	100	200	300	420	—
1665P E	—	100	200	300	420	—
1666P E	—	125	240	325	500	—
1666P E Rare	—	—	—	—	—	—

Note: With 666 below pillars

Date	Mintage	Good	VG	F	VF	XF
1667P E Rare	—	—	—	—	—	—

Obverse

A O
P E
8 52

Reverse

F 8 IIII
PL VSVL TRA

Type I

F 8 IIII
PLV SVL TRA
E E

Type II

F 8 IIII
PLV SVL TRA
E • E

Type III

F 8 IIII
PLV SVL TRA
E 8 E

Type IV

F 8 IIII
PLV SVL TRA
E 52 E

Type V

PH
P 8 E
PLV SVL TRA
E 52 E

Type VI

PH
P 8 E
PLV SVL TRA
E 52 P

Type VII

I • PH • 6
P 8 E
PLV SVL TRA
E 52 P

Type VIII

KM# A20.1 8 REALES

27.0674 g., 0.9310 Silver 0.8102 oz. ASW **Ruler:** Philip IV **Obv:** Crowned arms, castles and lions **Obv. Legend:** PHILIPPUS IIII D.G. HISPANIARUM **Rev:** Type I. Crowned pillars and waves **Rev. Legend:** POTOSI ANO 1652 EL PERV **Note:** Prev. KM#19.3.

Date	Mintage	Good	VG	F	VF	XF
1652P E Rare	—	—	—	—	—	—

KM# A20.2 8 REALES

27.0674 g., 0.9310 Silver 0.8102 oz. ASW **Ruler:** Philip IV **Obv:** Arms **Rev:** Type II

Date	Mintage	Good	VG	F	VF	XF
1652P E Rare	—	—	—	—	—	—

KM# A20.3 8 REALES

27.0674 g., 0.9310 Silver 0.8102 oz. ASW **Ruler:** Philip IV **Obv:** Arms **Rev:** Type III **Note:** Prev. KM#19.5.

Date	Mintage	Good	VG	F	VF	XF
1652P E	—	200	500	750	1,250	—

KM# A20.4 8 REALES

27.0674 g., 0.9310 Silver 0.8102 oz. ASW **Ruler:** Philip IV **Obv:** Arms **Rev:** Type IV **Note:** Prev. KM#19.4.

Date	Mintage	Good	VG	F	VF	XF
1652P E	—	200	500	750	1,250	—

KM# A20.5 8 REALES

27.0674 g., 0.9310 Silver 0.8102 oz. ASW **Ruler:** Philip IV **Obv:** Arms **Rev:** Type V **Note:** Prev. KM#19.6.

Date	Mintage	Good	VG	F	VF	XF
1652P E	—	200	500	750	1,250	—

KM# A20.6 8 REALES
27.0674 g., 0.9310 Silver 0.8102 oz. ASW **Ruler:** Philip IV
Obv: Crowned Spanish shield with arms of Castile **Rev:** Type VI

Date	Mintage	Good	VG	F	VF	XF
1652P E Rare	—	—	—	—	—	—

KM# A20.7 8 REALES
27.0674 g., 0.9310 Silver 0.8102 oz. ASW **Ruler:** Philip IV
Obv: Arms **Rev:** Type VII

Date	Mintage	Good	VG	F	VF	XF
1652P E Rare	—	—	—	—	—	—

KM# A20.8 8 REALES
27.0674 g., 0.9310 Silver 0.8102 oz. ASW **Ruler:** Philip IV
Obv: Arms **Rev:** Type VIII **Note:** Prev. KM#20.1.

Date	Mintage	Good	VG	F	VF	XF
1652P E Rare	—	—	—	—	—	—

KM# 20.1 8 REALES
27.0703 g., 0.9310 Silver 0.8102 oz. ASW **Ruler:** Philip IV
Obv: Cross of Jerusalem, castles and lions in quarters, mint mark to left, assayer's initial to right **Rev:** Type V, crowned pillars and waves **Rev. Legend:** POTOSI ANO 1652 EL PERV **Note:** Prev. KM#20.2.

Date	Mintage	Good	VG	F	VF	XF
1652P E	—	275	450	750	1,250	—

KM# 20.2 8 REALES
27.0674 g., 0.9310 Silver 0.8102 oz. ASW **Ruler:** Philip IV
Obv: Cross of Jerusalem, castles and lions in quarters, mint mark to left, assayer's initial to right **Rev:** Type VII

Date	Mintage	Good	VG	F	VF	XF
1652P E Rare	—	—	—	—	—	—

KM# 26 8 REALES
27.0703 g., 0.9310 Silver 0.8102 oz. ASW **Ruler:** Charles II
Obv: Cross of Jerusalem, castles and lions in quarters
Obv. Legend: CAROLVS II D.G. HISPANIA **Rev:** Crowned pillars of Hercules and waves, value at top center

Date	Mintage	Good	VG	F	VF	XF
ND(1667-1701)P Date off flan	—	75.00	125	175	225	—
1667P E	—	110	220	330	450	—
1667P E King's name as CARDLVS, Rare	—	—	—	—	—	—
1668P E	—	100	200	300	420	—
1668P E Rare	—	—	—	—	—	—
Note: Mint mark to left and right						
1669/8P E Reported, not confirmed	—	—	—	—	—	—
1669P E	—	100	200	300	420	—
1669P E Small date, Rare	—	—	—	—	—	—
1670/69P E Rare	—	—	—	—	—	—
1670P E	—	100	200	300	420	—
1671/0P E Rare	—	—	—	—	—	—
1671P E	—	100	200	300	420	—
1672P E	—	100	200	300	420	—
1673P E	—	100	200	300	420	—
1674/2P E Rare	—	—	—	—	—	—
1674P E	—	100	200	300	420	—
1675P E	—	100	200	300	420	—
1676P E	—	100	200	300	420	—
1677P E	—	100	200	300	420	—
1678/7P E Rare	—	—	—	—	—	—
1678P E	—	100	200	300	420	—
1679P C/E Rare	—	—	—	—	—	—
1679P C	—	100	200	325	475	—
1679P V/C	—	150	250	350	500	—
1679P V	—	110	220	340	420	—
1680P V	—	100	200	325	475	—
1681P V	—	100	200	325	475	—
1682P V	—	100	200	325	475	—
1683P V	—	100	200	325	475	—
1684P V	—	100	200	325	475	—
1684P V, VR Rare	—	—	—	—	—	—
1684P VR	—	110	220	340	500	—
1685P VR	—	100	200	325	475	—
1686//(16)85P VR Rare	—	—	—	—	—	—
1686P VR	—	100	200	325	475	—
1687P VR	—	100	200	325	475	—
1688P VR	—	100	200	325	475	—
1689P VR	—	100	200	325	475	—
1690P VR	—	100	200	325	475	—
1691P VR	—	100	200	325	475	—
1692P VR	—	100	200	325	475	—
1693P VR	—	100	200	325	475	—
1694//(16)93P VR Reported, not confirmed	—	—	—	—	—	—
1694P VR	—	100	200	325	475	—
1695P VR	—	100	200	325	475	—
1696P VR	—	100	200	325	475	—
1697P VR	—	110	220	340	500	—
1697P F/CH Rare	—	—	—	—	—	—
1697P CH	—	150	300	550	800	—
1697P F	—	110	220	340	500	—
1698/7P F Reported, not confirmed	—	—	—	—	—	—
1698P F	—	100	200	325	475	—
1699P F	—	100	200	325	475	—
1700P F	—	100	200	325	475	—

ROYAL COINAGE

Struck on specially prepared round planchets using well centered dies in excellent condition to prove the quality of the minting to the Viceroy or even to the King

KM# R-B12 1/2 REAL
1.6917 g., 0.9310 Silver 0.0506 oz. ASW **Ruler:** Philip IV
Obv: Monogram of PHILIPVS IIII superimposed on Cross of Jerusalem **Rev:** Crowned arms

Date	Mintage	Good	VG	F	VF	XF
1655P E Rare	—	—	—	—	—	—
1662P E Rare	—	—	—	—	—	—

KM# R13 REAL
3.3834 g., 0.9310 Silver 0.1013 oz. ASW **Ruler:** Philip IV
Obv: Cross of Jerusalem, castles and lions in quarters
Obv. Legend: PHILIPVS IV **Rev:** Pillars and waves with 3-line inscription consisting of mint mark, I-assayer's initial, PLV-SVL-TRA, assayer's initial, date, mint mark

Date	Mintage	Good	VG	F	VF	XF
1654P E PH Rare	—	—	—	—	—	—

KM# R23 REAL
3.3834 g., 0.9310 Silver 0.1013 oz. ASW **Ruler:** Charles II
Obv: Cross of Jerusalem **Obv. Legend:** CAROLVS II

Date	Mintage	Good	VG	F	VF	XF
1677P E Rare	—	—	—	—	—	—
1679P C Reported, not confirmed	—	—	—	—	—	—

KM# R15.3 2 REALES
6.7668 g., 0.9310 Silver 0.2025 oz. ASW **Ruler:** Philip IV
Obv: Arms **Rev:** Type II

Date	Mintage	Good	VG	F	VF	XF
1652P E Rare	—	—	—	—	—	—

KM# R-A16.1 2 REALES
6.7668 g., 0.9310 Silver 0.2025 oz. ASW **Ruler:** Philip IV
Obv: Cross of Jerusalem with castles and lions in quarters, mint mark to left, assayers initial to right **Rev:** Pillars and waves

Date	Mintage	Good	VG	F	VF	XF
1652P E Rare	—	—	—	—	—	—

KM# R-A16.2 2 REALES
6.7668 g., 9.3100 Silver 2.0254 oz. ASW **Ruler:** Philip IV
Rev: Type I

Date	Mintage	Good	VG	F	VF	XF
1654P E Rare	—	—	—	—	—	—
1656P E Rare	—	—	—	—	—	—
1659P E Rare	—	—	—	—	—	—
1660P E Rare	—	—	—	—	—	—

KM# R24 2 REALES
6.7668 g., 0.9310 Silver 0.2025 oz. ASW **Ruler:** Charles II
Obv. Legend: CAROLVS II

Date	Mintage	Good	VG	F	VF	XF
1671P E Rare	—	—	—	—	—	—
1683P V Rare	—	—	—	—	—	—
1685P VR Rare	—	—	—	—	—	—
1686P VR Rare	—	—	—	—	—	—
1687P VR Rare	—	—	—	—	—	—
1691P VR Rare	—	—	—	—	—	—
1692P VR Rare	—	—	—	—	—	—
1696P VR Rare	—	—	—	—	—	—
1697P VR Rare	—	—	—	—	—	—

KM# R18 4 REALES
13.5337 g., 0.9310 Silver 0.4051 oz. ASW **Ruler:** Philip IV **Obv:** Crowned cross of Jerusalem, lions and castles in quarters **Rev:** Crowned pillars and waves, inscription: mint mark, denomination, assayer's initial, PVS-SVL-TRA, assayer's initial, date, mint mark

Date	Mintage	Good	VG	F	VF	XF
1656P E Rare	—	—	—	—	—	—
1659P E Rare	—	—	—	—	—	—

KM# R25 4 REALES
13.5337 g., 0.9310 Silver 0.4051 oz. ASW **Ruler:** Charles II

Date	Mintage	Good	VG	F	VF	XF
1675P E Reported, not confirmed	—	—	—	—	—	—
1677P E Rare	—	—	—	—	—	—
1678P E Rare	—	—	—	—	—	—
1679P C Rare	—	—	—	—	—	—
1697P VR Rare	—	—	—	—	—	—

KM# R19.a 8 REALES
27.0674 g., 0.9310 Silver 0.8102 oz. ASW **Ruler:** Philip IV

Date	Mintage	Good	VG	F	VF	XF
1630P T Rare	—	—	—	—	—	—
1631P T Rare	—	—	—	—	—	—
1637P TR Rare	—	—	—	—	—	—
1638P TR Rare	—	—	—	—	—	—
1639P T Rare	—	—	—	—	—	—
1639P TR Rare	—	—	—	—	—	—
1640P FR Rare	—	—	—	—	—	—
1640P TR Rare	—	—	—	—	—	—
1641P FR Rare	—	—	—	—	—	—
1643P TR Rare	—	—	—	—	—	—
1644P FR Rare	—	—	—	—	—	—
1644P TR Rare	—	—	—	—	—	—
1646P T Rare	—	—	—	—	—	—
1647P T Rare	—	—	—	—	—	—
1648P T Rare	—	—	—	—	—	—

KM# R19.b 8 REALES

27.0674 g., 0.9310 Silver 0.8102 oz. ASW **Ruler:** Philip IV

Date	Mintage	Good	VG	F	VF	XF
1649P (o) Rare	—	—	—	—	—	—
1649P Z Rare	—	—	—	—	—	—
1650P (o) Rare	—	—	—	—	—	—
1651P (o) Rare	—	—	—	—	—	—
1651P E Rare	—	—	—	—	—	—

KM# R-A20.1 8 REALES

27.0674 g., 0.9310 Silver 0.8102 oz. ASW **Ruler:** Philip IV
Obv: Crowned arms, castles and lions **Obv. Legend:** PHILIPPUS IIII D.G. HISPANIARUM **Rev:** Type I, crowned pillars and waves **Rev. Legend:** POTOSI ANO...

Date	Mintage	Good	VG	F	VF	XF
1652P E Transitional Type I, Rare	—	—	—	—	—	—

KM# R-A20.2 8 REALES

27.0674 g., 0.9310 Silver 0.8102 oz. ASW **Ruler:** Philip IV
Obv: Arms **Rev:** Type II

Date	Mintage	Good	VG	F	VF	XF
1652P E Transitional Type II, Rare	—	—	—	—	—	—

KM# R-A20.3 8 REALES

27.0674 g., 0.9310 Silver 0.8102 oz. ASW **Ruler:** Philip IV
Obv: Arms **Rev:** Type III

Date	Mintage	Good	VG	F	VF	XF
1652P E Transitional Type III, Rare	—	—	—	—	—	—

KM# R-A20.4 8 REALES

27.0674 g., 0.9310 Silver 0.8102 oz. ASW **Ruler:** Philip IV
Obv: Arms **Rev:** Type IV

Date	Mintage	Good	VG	F	VF	XF
1652P E Rare	—	—	—	—	—	—

KM# R-A20.5 8 REALES

27.0674 g., 0.9310 Silver 0.8102 oz. ASW **Ruler:** Philip IV
Obv: Arms **Rev:** Type V

Date	Mintage	Good	VG	F	VF	XF
1652P E Rare	—	—	—	—	—	—

KM# R-A20.6 8 REALES

27.0674 g., 0.9310 Silver 0.8102 oz. ASW **Ruler:** Philip IV
Obv: Arms **Rev:** Type VI

Date	Mintage	Good	VG	F	VF	XF
1652P E Rare	—	—	—	—	—	—

KM# R21 8 REALES

27.0674 g., 0.9310 Silver 0.8102 oz. ASW **Ruler:** Philip IV
Obv: Crowned cross of Jerusalem, castles and lions in quarters **Obv. Legend:** PHILIPVS IIII **Rev:** Crowned pillars and waves **Rev. Legend:** POTOSI ANO...

Date	Mintage	Good	VG	F	VF	XF
1652P E Rare	—	—	—	—	—	—
1653P E Rare	—	—	—	—	—	—
1654P E Rare	—	—	—	—	—	—
1655P E Rare	—	—	—	—	—	—
1656P E Rare	—	—	—	—	—	—
1657P E Rare	—	—	—	—	—	—
1658P E/P Reported, not confirmed	—	—	—	—	—	—
1658P E Rare	—	—	—	—	—	—
1659P E Rare	—	—	—	—	—	—
1660P E Rare	—	—	—	—	—	—
1661P E Rare	—	—	—	—	—	—
1662/1P E Rare	—	—	—	—	—	—
1662P E Rare	—	—	—	—	—	—
1663P E Rare	—	—	—	—	—	—
1664P E Rare	—	—	—	—	—	—
1665P E Rare	—	—	—	—	—	—
1666P E 666 between pillars, Rare	—	—	—	—	—	—
1666P E 66 between pillars, Rare	—	—	—	—	—	—

KM# R26 8 REALES

27.0674 g., 0.9310 Silver 0.8102 oz. ASW **Ruler:** Charles II
Obv: Cross of Jerusalem, lions and castles in quarters **Obv. Legend:** CAROLVS II D.G. HISPANIA **Rev:** Pillars of Hercules and waves, value at top center

Date	Mintage	Good	VG	F	VF	XF
1667P E Rare	—	—	—	—	—	—
1668P E Rare	—	—	—	—	—	—
1669P E Rare	—	—	—	—	—	—
1670P E Rare	—	—	—	—	—	—
1671P E Rare	—	—	—	—	—	—
1672P E Rare	—	—	—	—	—	—
1673P E Rare	—	—	—	—	—	—
1674P E Rare	—	—	—	—	—	—
1675P E Rare	—	—	—	—	—	—
1676P E Rare	—	—	—	—	—	—
1677P E Rare	—	—	—	—	—	—
1678P E Rare	—	—	—	—	—	—
1679P C Rare	—	—	—	—	—	—
1680P V Rare	—	—	—	—	—	—
1681P V Rare	—	—	—	—	—	—
1682P V Rare	—	—	—	—	—	—
1683P V Rare	—	—	—	—	—	—
1684P VR Rare	—	—	—	—	—	—
1685P VR Rare	—	—	—	—	—	—
1686P VR Rare	—	—	—	—	—	—
1687P VR Rare	—	—	—	—	—	—
1688P VR Rare	—	—	—	—	—	—
1689P VR Rare	—	—	—	—	—	—
1690P VR Rare	—	—	—	—	—	—
1691P VR Rare	—	—	—	—	—	—
1692P VR Rare	—	—	—	—	—	—
1693P VR Rare	—	—	—	—	—	—
1694P VR Rare	—	—	—	—	—	—
1695P VR Rare	—	—	—	—	—	—
1696P VR Rare	—	—	—	—	—	—
1697P VR Rare	—	—	—	—	—	—
1698P F Rare	—	—	—	—	—	—
1700P F Rare	—	—	—	—	—	—

COUNTERMARKED COINAGE

1651-1652

Problems with debasement of the coinage struck at Potosi in the 1620s-1640s prompted a visit by the Royal Inspector Don Francisco de Nestares Marin, under orders by King Philip IV of Spain, at the end of 1648. Upon completion of the investigation, the order was given in October of 1650 to recall all coinage minted at Potosi since 1625 and prior to the accession of Juan Rodriguez de Rodas (assayer O with dot in middle) to the post of assayer in 1649. All half, 1, and 2 Reales , as well as any 4 and 8 Reales that were found to be heavily debased, were ordered to be melted, with all 4 Reales devalued to 3 Reales and 8 Reales devalued to 6 Reales. To differentiate the good new coinage from 1649 until a completely new design could be implemented in 1652, various countermarks were applied on the 4 and 8 Reales to reflect their higher net values of 3-3/4 Reales and 7-1/2 Reales respectively. Most of these countermarks bear a crown at the top, with either an initial or monogram or symbol below, all contained within a beaded circle (most common) or simple circle (single line, no beads) or beaded pentagon (rare) or no border (rarest). It is believed that each different countermark was applied in a different location within the Spanish colonies, but it is not known which countermark corresponds to which locale

KM# C17.1 3-3/4 REALES

13.5337 g., 0.8590 Silver 0.3738 oz. ASW **Ruler:** Philip IV
Countermark: Crown in beaded circle **Note:** Countermark on shield side of 4 Reales, KM#17b.

CM Date	Host Date	Good	VG	F	VF	XF
ND(1651-52)	1649P o/Z	200	300	400	525	—
ND(1651-52)	1649P o	175	275	400	525	—
ND(1651-52)	1649P Z	200	375	500	675	—
ND(1651-52)	1651P E	100	175	275	375	—

KM# C17.2 3-3/4 REALES

13.5337 g., 0.8590 Silver 0.3738 oz. ASW **Ruler:** Philip IV
Countermark: Crowned •F• in beaded circle **Note:** Countermark on 4 Reales, KM#17b.

CM Date	Host Date	Good	VG	F	VF	XF
ND(1651-52)	1650P o	175	275	400	500	—
ND(1651-52)	1651P E	200	300	400	525	—

KM# C17.3 3-3/4 REALES
13.5337 g., 0.8590 Silver 0.3738 oz. ASW **Ruler:** Philip IV **Countermark:** Crowned L in beaded circle **Note:** Countermark on 4 Reales, KM#17b.

CM Date	Host Date	Good	VG	F	VF	XF
ND(1651-52)	1649P o	175	275	400	500	—
ND(1651-52)	1650P o	175	275	400	500	—
ND(1651-52)	1651P	175	275	400	500	—

KM# C17.4 3-3/4 REALES
13.5337 g., 0.8590 Silver 0.3738 oz. ASW **Ruler:** Philip IV **Countermark:** Crowned A in beaded circle **Note:** Countermark on 4 Reales, KM#17b.

CM Date	Host Date	Good	VG	F	VF	XF
ND(1651-52)	ND(1649-51)P Rare	—	—	—	—	—

KM# C17.5 3-3/4 REALES
13.5337 g., 0.8590 Silver 0.3738 oz. ASW **Ruler:** Philip IV **Countermark:** Crowned C in beaded circle **Note:** Countermark on 4 Reales, KM#17b.

CM Date	Host Date	Good	VG	F	VF	XF
ND(1651-52)	1650P o Rare	—	—	—	—	—

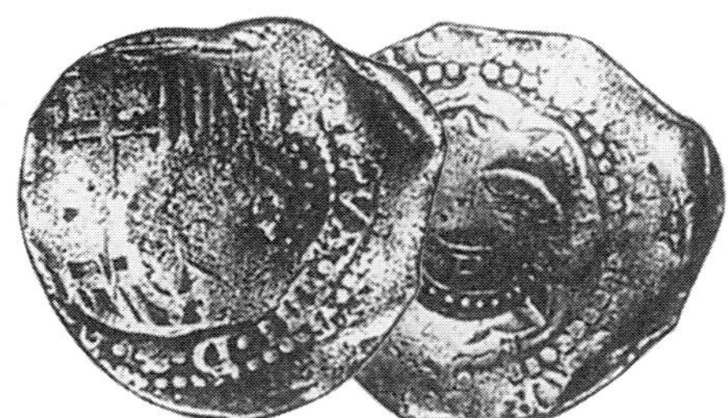

KM# C17.6 3-3/4 REALES
Silver **Ruler:** Philip IV **Countermark:** Crowned P in beaded circle **Note:** Countermark on 4 Reales, KM#17b.

CM Date	Host Date	Good	VG	F	VF	XF
ND(1651-52)	ND(1649-51)P Rare	—	—	—	—	—

KM# C17.7 3-3/4 REALES
13.5337 g., 0.8590 Silver 0.3738 oz. ASW **Ruler:** Philip IV **Countermark:** Crowned Philip IV monogram in circle **Note:** Countermark on 4 Reales, KM#17b.

CM Date	Host Date	Good	VG	F	VF	XF
ND(1651-52)	1650P o	225	375	500	600	—

KM# C17.8 3-3/4 REALES
13.5337 g., 0.8590 Silver 0.3738 oz. ASW **Ruler:** Philip IV **Countermark:** Crowned retrograde L in circle **Note:** Countermark on 4 Reales, KM#17b.

CM Date	Host Date	Good	VG	F	VF	XF
ND(1651-52)	1649-51P Rare	—	—	—	—	—

KM# C17.9 3-3/4 REALES
13.5337 g., 0.8590 Silver 0.3738 oz. ASW **Ruler:** Philip IV **Countermark:** Crowned O in beaded circle **Note:** Countermark on 4 Reales, KM#17b.

CM Date	Host Date	Good	VG	F	VF	XF
ND(1651-52)	1649-51P Rare	—	—	—	—	—

KM# C17.10 3-3/4 REALES
13.5337 g., 0.8590 Silver 0.3738 oz. ASW **Ruler:** Philip IV **Countermark:** Crowned arms, pomegranate below in beaded circle **Note:** Countermark on 4 Reales, KM#17b.

CM Date	Host Date	Good	VG	F	VF	XF
ND(1651-52)	1651P Rare	—	—	—	—	—

KM# C19.1 7-1/2 REALES
27.0674 g., 0.8590 Silver 0.7475 oz. ASW **Ruler:** Philip IV **Countermark:** Plain crown in beaded circle **Note:** Countermark on 8 Reales, KM#19b.

CM Date	Host Date	Good	VG	F	VF	XF
ND(1651-52)	1649P o	90.00	150	285	435	—
ND(1651-52)	1649P Z	100	175	300	475	—
ND(1651-52)	1650P o	90.00	150	285	435	—
ND(1651-52)	1651P E	90.00	150	285	435	—
ND(1651-52)	1651P o	90.00	150	285	435	—

KM# C19.2 7-1/2 REALES
27.0674 g., 0.8590 Silver 0.7475 oz. ASW **Ruler:** Philip IV **Countermark:** Crowned L in beaded circle **Note:** Countermark on 8 Reales, KM#19b.

CM Date	Host Date	Good	VG	F	VF	XF
ND(1651-52)	1649P o/Z	100	175	300	475	—
ND(1651-52)	1649P o	90.00	150	285	435	—
ND(1651-52)	1649P Z	100	175	300	475	—
ND(1651-52)	1650P o	90.00	150	285	435	—
ND(1651-52)	1651P o	90.00	150	285	435	—
ND(1651-52)	1651P E	90.00	150	285	435	—

KM# C19.3 7-1/2 REALES
27.0674 g., 0.8590 Silver 0.7475 oz. ASW **Ruler:** Philip IV **Countermark:** Crowned •F• in beaded circle **Note:** Countermark on 8 Reales, KM#19b.

CM Date	Host Date	Good	VG	F	VF	XF
ND(1651-52)	1649P o/Z	100	175	300	435	—
ND(1651-52)	1649P o	90.00	150	285	435	—
Note: Host coin dated 1649Z exists with c/m on obverse (crowned arms) and is considered rare.						
ND(1651-52)	1650P o	90.00	150	285	435	—
ND(1651-52)	1651P o	90.00	150	285	435	—
ND(1651-52)	1651P E	90.00	150	285	435	—
ND(1651-52)	1652P E	300	750	1,250	2,500	—

KM# C19.4 7-1/2 REALES
27.0674 g., 0.8590 Silver 0.7475 oz. ASW **Ruler:** Philip IV **Countermark:** Crowned large O in beaded circle **Note:** Countermark on 8 Reales, KM#19b.

CM Date	Host Date	Good	VG	F	VF	XF
ND(1651-52)	1649P o	125	225	375	550	—
ND(1651-52)	1649P Z	150	240	400	575	—
ND(1651-52)	1650P o	125	225	375	550	—
ND(1651-52)	1651P E/o	200	300	400	600	—
ND(1651-52)	1651P E	125	225	375	550	—
ND(1651-52)	1651P o	125	225	375	550	—

KM# C19.5 7-1/2 REALES
27.0674 g., 0.8590 Silver 0.7475 oz. ASW **Ruler:** Philip IV **Countermark:** Crowned S in beaded circle **Note:** Countermark on 8 Reales, KM#19b.

CM Date	Host Date	Good	VG	F	VF	XF
ND(1651-52)	1649P o	125	250	400	575	—
ND(1651-52)	1650P o	125	250	400	575	—
ND(1651-52)	1651P o	125	250	400	575	—

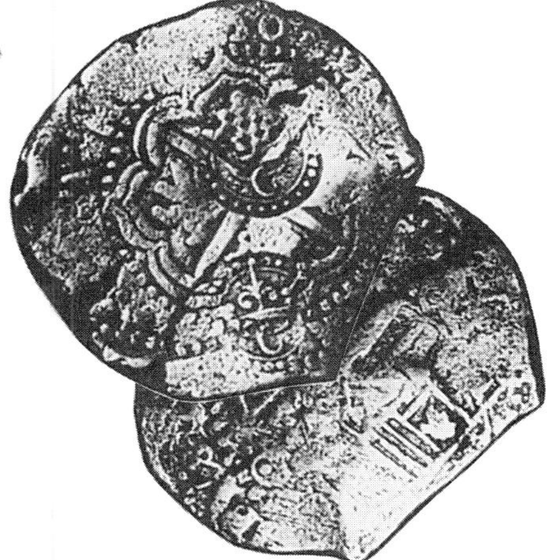

KM# C19.6 7-1/2 REALES

27.0674 g., 0.8590 Silver 0.7475 oz. ASW **Ruler:** Philip IV **Countermark:** Crowned A in beaded circle **Note:** Countermark on 8 Reales, KM#19b.

CM Date	Host Date	Good	VG	F	VF	XF
ND(1651-52)	1649-51P Rare	—	—	—	—	—

KM# C19.7 7-1/2 REALES

27.0674 g., 0.8590 Silver 0.7475 oz. ASW **Ruler:** Philip IV **Countermark:** Crowned C in beaded circle **Note:** Countermark on 8 Reales, KM#19b.

CM Date	Host Date	Good	VG	F	VF	XF
ND(1651-52)	1649P o Rare	—	—	—	—	—
ND(1651-52)	1650P o Rare	—	—	—	—	—
ND(1651-52)	1651P E Rare	—	—	—	—	—
ND(1651-52)	1651P o Rare	—	—	—	—	—

KM# C19.8 7-1/2 REALES

27.0674 g., 0.8590 Silver 0.7475 oz. ASW **Ruler:** Philip IV **Countermark:** Crowned G in beaded circle **Note:** Countermark on 8 Reales, KM#19b.

CM Date	Host Date	Good	VG	F	VF	XF
ND(1651-52)	1650P o	150	240	400	575	—
ND(1651-52)	1651P o Rare	150	240	400	575	—

KM# C19.9 7-1/2 REALES

27.0674 g., 0.8590 Silver 0.7475 oz. ASW **Ruler:** Philip IV **Countermark:** Crowned P in beaded circle **Note:** Countermark on 8 Reales, KM#19b. Two varieties of this countermark exist.

CM Date	Host Date	Good	VG	F	VF	XF
ND(1651-52)	1649P o Rare	—	—	—	—	—
ND(1651-52)	1650P o Rare	—	—	—	—	—

KM# C19.10 7-1/2 REALES

27.0674 g., 0.8590 Silver 0.7475 oz. ASW **Ruler:** Philip IV **Countermark:** Crowned Philip IV monogram in circle **Note:** Countermark on 8 Reales, KM#19b.

CM Date	Host Date	Good	VG	F	VF	XF
ND(1651-52)	1649P o	125	250	400	575	—
ND(1651-52)	1650P o	125	250	400	575	—
ND(1651-52)	1651P E	125	250	400	575	—
ND(1651-52)	1651P o	125	250	400	575	—

KM# C19.11 7-1/2 REALES

27.0674 g., 0.8590 Silver 0.7475 oz. ASW **Ruler:** Philip IV **Countermark:** Crowned T in beaded circle **Note:** Countermark on 8 Reales, KM#19b. Three varieties of this countermark exist.

CM Date	Host Date	Good	VG	F	VF	XF
ND(1651-52)	1650P o Rare	—	—	—	—	—
ND(1651-52)	1651P E Rare	—	—	—	—	—

KM# C19.12 7-1/2 REALES

27.0674 g., 0.8590 Silver 0.7475 oz. ASW **Ruler:** Philip IV **Countermark:** Crowned Z in beaded circle **Note:** Countermark on 8 Reales, KM#19b.

CM Date	Host Date	Good	VG	F	VF	XF
ND(1651-52)	ND(1649-51)P Rare	—	—	—	—	—

KM# C19.13 7-1/2 REALES

27.0674 g., 0.8590 Silver 0.7475 oz. ASW **Ruler:** Philip IV **Countermark:** Crowned 1652 in beaded pentagon **Note:** Countermark on 8 Reales, KM#19b.

CM Date	Host Date	Good	VG	F	VF	XF
ND(1651-52)	1650P o	200	300	450	675	—
ND(1651-52)	1651P E/o	125	200	285	375	—

KM# C19.14 7-1/2 REALES

27.0674 g., 0.8590 Silver 0.7475 oz. ASW **Ruler:** Philip IV **Countermark:** Crown (varieties) in beaded circle **Note:** Countermark on 8 Reales, KM# 19.b.

CM Date	Host Date	Good	VG	F	VF	XF
ND(1651-52)	1649P Rare	—	—	—	—	—
ND(1651-52)	1650P o Rare	—	—	—	—	—
ND(1651-52)	1651P E/o Rare	—	—	—	—	—
ND(1651-52)	1651P o Rare	—	—	—	—	—

KM# C19.15 7-1/2 REALES

27.0674 g., 0.8590 Silver 0.7475 oz. ASW **Ruler:** Philip IV **Countermark:** Crown in circle **Note:** Countermark on 8 Reales, KM#19b.

CM Date	Host Date	Good	VG	F	VF	XF
ND(1651-52)	1649P o Rare	—	—	—	—	—
ND(1651-52)	1649P Z Rare	—	—	—	—	—
ND(1651-52)	1650P o Rare	—	—	—	—	—
ND(1651-52)	1651P E Rare	—	—	—	—	—

KM# C19.16 7-1/2 REALES
27.0674 g., 0.8590 Silver 0.7475 oz. ASW **Ruler:** Philip IV **Countermark:** Crowned "a" in beaded circle **Note:** Countermark on 8 Reales, KM#19b.

CM Date	Host Date	Good	VG	F	VF	XF
ND(1651-52)	1649P o Rare	—	—	—	—	—
ND(1651-52)	1650P o Rare	—	—	—	—	—

KM# C19.17 7-1/2 REALES
27.0674 g., 0.8590 Silver 0.7475 oz. ASW **Ruler:** Philip IV **Countermark:** Crowned •F• with two dots above crown **Note:** Countermark on 8 Reales, KM#19b.

CM Date	Host Date	Good	VG	F	VF	XF
ND(1651-52)	1651P E/o Rare	—	—	—	—	—

KM# C19.18 7-1/2 REALES
27.0674 g., 0.8590 Silver 0.7475 oz. ASW **Ruler:** Philip IV **Countermark:** Crowned •G• in beaded circle **Note:** Countermark on 8 Reales, KM#19b.

CM Date	Host Date	Good	VG	F	VF	XF
ND(1651-52)	1650P o Rare	—	—	—	—	—

KM# C19.19 7-1/2 REALES
27.0674 g., 0.8590 Silver 0.7475 oz. ASW **Ruler:** Philip IV **Countermark:** Crowned retrograde L in beaded circle **Note:** Countermark on 8 Reales, KM#19b.

CM Date	Host Date	Good	VG	F	VF	XF
ND(1651-52)	ND(1649-51)P Rare	—	—	—	—	—

KM# C19.20 7-1/2 REALES
27.0674 g., 0.8590 Silver 0.7475 oz. ASW **Ruler:** Philip IV **Countermark:** Crowned o in beaded circle **Note:** Countermark on 8 Reales, KM#19b.

CM Date	Host Date	Good	VG	F	VF	XF
ND(1651-52)	1649P o Rare	—	—	—	—	—
ND(1651-52)	1650P o Rare	—	—	—	—	—
ND(1651-52)	1651P E Rare	—	—	—	—	—

KM# C19.21 7-1/2 REALES
27.0674 g., 0.8590 Silver 0.7475 oz. ASW **Ruler:** Philip IV **Countermark:** Crowned •T• in circle **Note:** Countermark on 8 Reales, KM#19b.

CM Date	Host Date	Good	VG	F	VF	XF
ND(1651-52)	1651P E	—	—	—	—	—

KM# C19.22 7-1/2 REALES
27.0674 g., 0.8590 Silver 0.7475 oz. ASW **Ruler:** Philip IV **Countermark:** Crowned arms, pomegranate below in circle **Note:** Countermark on 8 Reales, KM#19b.

CM Date	Host Date	Good	VG	F	VF	XF
ND(1651-52)	1649P Z	—	—	—	—	—
ND(1651-52)	1650P o	—	—	—	—	—
ND(1651-52)	1651P E/o	—	—	—	—	—
ND(1651-52)	1651P	—	—	—	—	—

KM# C19.23 7-1/2 REALES
27.0674 g., 0.8590 Silver 0.7475 oz. ASW **Ruler:** Philip IV **Countermark:** Crowned 1605 in beaded pentagon **Note:** Countermark on 8 Reales, KM#19b.

CM Date	Host Date	Good	VG	F	VF	XF
ND(1651-52)	1650P o Rare	—	—	—	—	—

KM# C19.24 7-1/2 REALES
27.0674 g., 0.8590 Silver 0.7475 oz. ASW **Ruler:** Philip IV **Countermark:** Crowned castle, BAIRES below **Note:** Countermark on 8 Reales, KM#19b. BAIRES = Buenos Aires.

CM Date	Host Date	Good	VG	F	VF	XF
ND(1651-52)	1649-51P o Rare	—	—	—	—	—

BRAZIL

Brazil, which comprises half the continent of South America and is the only Latin American country deriving its culture and language from Portugal, has an area of 3,286,488 sq. mi. (8,511,965 sq. km.

Brazil was discovered and claimed for Portugal by Admiral Pedro Alvares Cabral in 1500. Portugal established a settlement in 1532 and proclaimed the area a royal colony in 1549. During the Napoleonic Wars, Dom Joao VI established the seat of Portuguese government in Rio de Janeiro. When he returned to Portugal, his son Dom Pedro I declared Brazil's independence on Sept. 7, 1822, and became emperor of Brazil. The Empire of Brazil was maintained until 1889 when the federal republic was established. The Federative Republic was established in 1946 by terms of a constitution drawn up by a constituent assembly. Following a coup in 1964 the armed forces retained overall control under a dictatorship until civilian government was restored on March 15, 1985. The current constitution was adopted in 1988.

RULERS
Dutch Occupation, 1624-1661
Portuguese
Alfonso VI, 1656-1667
Pedro,
As Prince Regent, 1667-1683
As Pedro II, 1683-1706

MINT MARKS
B - Bahia
P - Pernambuco
R - Rio de Janeiro

MONETARY SYSTEM
(Until 1833)
120 Reis = 1 Real
6400 Reis 1 Peca (Dobra = Johannes (Joe) = 4 Escudos

PORTUGUESE COLONY

OCCUPATION COINAGE

Geotroyerde Westindishe Compangnie

The Dutch issuer was established in Brazil in 1624 remaining there until 1661.

KM# 8 10 STUIVERS
Silver **Obv:** Monogram of company with value above, date below **Note:** Uniface.

Date	Mintage	VG	F	VF	XF	Unc
1654 Rare	—	—	—	—	—	—

KM# 9 10 STUIVERS
Silver **Obv:** Monogram of company with value above, date below **Note:** Uniface.

Date	Mintage	VG	F	VF	XF	Unc
1654 Rare	—	—	—	—	—	—

KM# 10 20 STUIVERS
Silver **Obv:** Monogram of company with value above, date below **Note:** Uniface.

Date	Mintage	VG	F	VF	XF	Unc
1654 Rare	—	—	—	—	—	—

KM# 12 40 STUIVERS
Silver **Obv:** Monogram of company with value above, date below **Note:** Uniface.

Date	Mintage	VG	F	VF	XF	Unc
1654 Rare	—	—	—	—	—	—

Note: Silver emergency issues of 1654 are of questionable origin

KM# 5.1 3 FLORIN
1.8000 g., Gold **Rev:** Diamond after Brasil **Note:** Klippe.

Date	Mintage	VG	F	VF	XF	Unc
1645 Rare	—	—	—	—	—	—

KM# 5.2 3 FLORIN
1.8000 g., Gold **Obv:** Without periods **Rev:** Without periods **Note:** Klippe.

Date	Mintage	VG	F	VF	XF	Unc
1646 Rare	—	—	—	—	—	—

KM# 5.3 3 FLORIN
1.8000 g., Gold **Obv:** Period after III **Rev:** Period after Brasil **Note:** Klippe.

Date	Mintage	VG	F	VF	XF	Unc
1646 Rare	—	—	—	—	—	—

KM# 6.1 6 FLORIN
3.7000 g., Gold **Rev:** Diamond after Brasil **Note:** Klippe.

Date	Mintage	VG	F	VF	XF	Unc
1645 Rare	—	—	—	—	—	—

KM# 6.2 6 FLORIN
3.7000 g., Gold **Obv:** Without periods **Rev:** Without periods **Note:** Klippe.

Date	Mintage	VG	F	VF	XF	Unc
1646 Rare	—	—	—	—	—	—

KM# 6.3 6 FLORIN
3.7000 g., Gold **Obv:** Period after VI **Rev:** Period after Brasil **Note:** Klippe.

Date	Mintage	VG	F	VF	XF	Unc
1646 Rare	—	—	—	—	—	—

KM# 7.1 12 FLORIN
7.6000 g., Gold **Rev:** Diamond after Brasil **Note:** Klippe.

Date	Mintage	VG	F	VF	XF	Unc
1645 Rare	—	—	—	—	—	—
1646 Rare	—	—	—	—	—	—

KM# 7.2 12 FLORIN
7.6000 g., Gold **Obv:** Period after XII **Rev:** Period after Brasil **Note:** Klippe.

Date	Mintage	VG	F	VF	XF	Unc
1646 Rare	—	—	—	—	—	—

COUNTERMARKED COINAGE

Type I

c/m: Crowned 60, 120, 240, or 480 in countoured frame. Authorized by decree of February 26, 1643 on spanish

Colonial 1, 2, 4, and 8 Reales "cob" coins. Value was raised 50%

KM# 1 60 REIS
3.3800 g., Silver **Countermark:** Type I **Note:** Countermark on Spanish Colonial 1 Real.

CM Date	Host Date	Good	VG	F	VF	XF
ND(1643)	ND	27.50	48.00	70.00	180	—

KM# 2 120 REIS
6.7700 g., Silver **Countermark:** Type I **Note:** Countermark on Spanish Colonial 2 Reales.

CM Date	Host Date	Good	VG	F	VF	XF
ND(1643)	ND	30.00	60.00	90.00	200	—

KM# 3 240 REIS
13.5400 g., Silver **Countermark:** Type I **Note:** Countermark on Spanish Colonial 4 Reales.

CM Date	Host Date	Good	VG	F	VF	XF
ND(1643)	ND	36.00	70.00	120	270	—

KM# 4 480 REIS
27.0700 g., Silver **Countermark:** Type I **Note:** Countermark on Spanish Colonial 8 Reales.

CM Date	Host Date	Good	VG	F	VF	XF
ND(1643)	ND	60.00	120	210	425	—

COUNTERMARKED COINAGE

Type III

c/m: Crowned 75, 150, 300, or 600 in contoured frame. Authorized by Decree of March 22, 1663 on Spanish Colonial 1, 2, 4, and 8 Reales cob coins. Value was raised 25%.

KM# 16 75 REIS
3.3800 g., Silver **Countermark:** Type III **Note:** Countermark on Spanish Colonial 1 Real.

CM Date	Host Date	Good	VG	F	VF	XF
ND(1663)	ND	27.50	45.00	75.00	125	—

KM# 17 150 REIS
6.7700 g., Silver **Countermark:** Type III **Note:** Countermark on Spanish Colonial 2 Reales.

CM Date	Host Date	Good	VG	F	VF	XF
ND(1663)	ND	32.00	50.00	80.00	145	—

KM# 18.2 300 REIS
Silver **Countermark:** Type III **Note:** Countermark on Bolivia 4 Reales, KM#18.

CM Date	Host Date	Good	VG	F	VF	XF
ND(1663)	ND	145	240	425	650	—

KM# 18.3 300 REIS
Silver **Countermark:** Type III **Note:** Countermark on Peru Star of Lima 4 Reales, KM#17.

CM Date	Host Date	Good	VG	F	VF	XF
ND(1663)	1659 Rare	—	—	—	—	—

KM# 18.1 300 REIS
Silver **Countermark:** Type III **Note:** Countermark on Spanish Colonial 4 Reales.

CM Date	Host Date	Good	VG	F	VF	XF
ND(1663)	ND	48.00	80.00	145	240	—

KM# 19.1 600 REIS
Silver **Countermark:** Type III **Note:** Countermarked on Spanish Colonial 8 Reales.

CM Date	Host Date	Good	VG	F	VF	XF
ND(1658)	ND	60.00	120	220	425	—

KM# 19.2 600 REIS
Silver **Countermark:** Type III **Note:** Countermarked on Bolivia 8 Reales, KM#21.

CM Date	Host Date	Good	VG	F	VF	XF
ND(1663)	1658	200	325	550	850	—

KM# 19.3 600 REIS
Silver **Countermark:** Type III **Note:** Countermarked on Peru Star of Lima 8 Reales, KM#18.

CM Date	Host Date	Good	VG	F	VF	XF
ND(1663)	1659	1,600	2,700	4,200	6,000	—

COUNTERMARKED COINAGE

Type IV

c/m: Crowned 50, 60, 100, 120, 125, 200, 250, or 500 in contoured frame. Authorized by amendment on July 7, 1663 to Decree of March 22, 1663 on Portuguese coins of John IV and Alfonso VI.

KM# 21 50 REIS
Silver **Countermark:** Type IV **Note:** Countermarked on Portugal 1/2 Tostao (value 5 as S).

CM Date	Host Date	Good	VG	F	VF	XF
ND(1663)	ND	30.00	50.00	90.00	170	—

KM# 23 50 REIS
Silver **Countermark:** Type IV **Note:** Countermarked on Portugal 1/2 Tostao.

CM Date	Host Date	Good	VG	F	VF	XF
ND(1663)	ND	30.00	50.00	90.00	170	—

KM# 20 50 REIS
Silver **Countermark:** Type IV **Note:** Countermarked on Portugal 40 Reis (5 in value as S).

CM Date	Host Date	Good	VG	F	VF	XF
ND(1663)	ND	30.00	50.00	90.00	170	—

KM# 22 50 REIS
Silver **Countermark:** Type IV **Note:** Countermarked on Portugal 40 Reis, KM#34.

CM Date	Host Date	Good	VG	F	VF	XF
ND(1663)	ND	30.00	50.00	90.00	170	—

KM# 25 60 REIS
Silver **Countermark:** Type IV **Note:** Countermarked on Portugal 1/2 Tostao.

CM Date	Host Date	Good	VG	F	VF	XF
ND(1663)	ND	36.00	60.00	100	180	—

KM# 24 60 REIS
Silver **Countermark:** Type IV **Note:** Countermarked on Portugal 40 Reis.

CM Date	Host Date	Good	VG	F	VF	XF
ND(1663)	ND	36.00	60.00	100	180	—

KM# 26 75 REIS
Silver **Countermark:** Type IV **Note:** Countermarked on Portugal 1/2 Tostao.

CM Date	Host Date	Good	VG	F	VF	XF
ND(1663)	ND	35.00	55.00	95.00	175	—

KM# 28 100 REIS
Silver **Countermark:** Type IV **Note:** Countermarked on Portugal 1/2 Tostao.

CM Date	Host Date	Good	VG	F	VF	XF
ND(1663)	ND	35.00	55.00	95.00	175	—

KM# 27 100 REIS
Silver **Countermark:** Type IV **Note:** Countermarked on Portugal 80 Reis.

CM Date	Host Date	Good	VG	F	VF	XF
ND(1663)	ND	35.00	55.00	95.00	175	—

KM# 29 120 REIS
Silver **Countermark:** Type IV **Note:** Countermarked on Portugal 80 Reis.

CM Date	Host Date	Good	VG	F	VF	XF
ND(1663)	ND	42.00	65.00	115	225	—

KM# 30 125 REIS
Silver **Countermark:** Type IV **Note:** Countermarked on Portugal 1 Tostao.

CM Date	Host Date	Good	VG	F	VF	XF
ND(1663)	ND	60.00	95.00	145	300	—

KM# 31 150 REIS
Silver **Countermark:** Type IV **Note:** Countermarked on Portugal 1 Tostao.

CM Date	Host Date	Good	VG	F	VF	XF
ND(1663)	ND	36.00	60.00	100	210	—

KM# 32 200 REIS
Silver **Countermark:** Type IV **Note:** Countermarked on Portugal 1 Tostao.

CM Date	Host Date	Good	VG	F	VF	XF
ND(1663)	ND	42.00	70.00	120	270	—

KM# 33.1 250 REIS

Silver **Countermark:** Type IV **Note:** Countermarked on Portugal-Evora Mint 200 Reis, KM#51. (Value 5 as 5).

CM Date	Host Date	Good	VG	F	VF	XF
ND(1663)	ND	240	400	625	900	—

KM# 33.2 250 REIS

Silver **Countermark:** Type IV **Note:** Countermarked on Portugal-Lisbon Mint 200 Reis, KM#49.

CM Date	Host Date	Good	VG	F	VF	XF
ND(1663)	ND	300	500	800	—	—

KM# 33.3 250 REIS

Silver **Countermark:** Type IV **Note:** Countermarked on Portugal-Porto Mint 200 Reis, KM#50.

CM Date	Host Date	Good	VG	F	VF	XF
ND(1663)	ND	180	300	475	725	—

KM# 35 300 REIS

Silver **Countermark:** Type IV **Note:** Countermarked on Portual 200 Reis.

CM Date	Host Date	Good	VG	F	VF	XF
ND(1663)	ND	90.00	180	300	475	—

KM# 37 500 REIS

Silver **Countermark:** Type IV **Note:** Countermarked on Portugal 1 Cruzado.

CM Date	Host Date	Good	VG	F	VF	XF
ND(1663)	ND	250	350	750	1,200	—

KM# 36 500 REIS

Silver **Countermark:** Type IV **Note:** Countermarked on Portugal 400 Reis.

CM Date	Host Date	Good	VG	F	VF	XF
ND(1663)	ND	125	175	350	600	—

KM# 38 600 REIS

Silver **Countermark:** Type IV **Note:** Countermarked on Portugal 400 Reis.

CM Date	Host Date	Good	VG	F	VF	XF
ND(1663)	ND	145	240	500	850	—

COUNTERMARKED COINAGE

Type VI

c/m: Crowned 80, 160, 320, or 640 in contoured frame. Authorized by Provision of March 23, 1679 on Spanish Colonial 1, 2, 4, and 8 Reales cob coins.

KM# 50 80 REIS

3.3800 g., Silver **Countermark:** Type VI **Note:** Countermarked on Spanish Colonial 1 Real.

CM Date	Host Date	Good	VG	F	VF	XF
ND(1679)	ND Rare	—	—	—	—	—

KM# 51 160 REIS

6.7700 g., Silver **Countermark:** Type VI **Note:** Countermarked on Spanish Colonial 2 Reales.

CM Date	Host Date	Good	VG	F	VF	XF
ND(1679)	ND Rare	—	—	—	—	—

KM# 52 320 REIS

13.5400 g., Silver **Countermark:** Type VI **Note:** Countermarked on Spanish Colonial 4 Reales.

CM Date	Host Date	Good	VG	F	VF	XF
ND(1679)	ND Rare	—	—	—	—	—

KM# 53 640 REIS

27.0700 g., Silver **Countermark:** Type VI **Note:** Countermarked on Spanish Colonial 8 Reales.

CM Date	Host Date	Good	VG	F	VF	XF
ND(1679)	ND Rare	—	—	—	—	—

COUNTERMARKED COINAGE

Type VIII

c/m: Crowned globe. Authorized by Royal charter of March 17, 1688 on Portuguese Tostaos or Spanish Colonial 4 and 8 Reales cob coins. Often found with additional countermarks.

KM# 63.1 200 REIS

Silver **Countermark:** Type VIII **Note:** Countermarked on Portugal 1 Tostao.

CM Date	Host Date	Good	VG	F	VF	XF
ND(1688)	ND	80.00	150	150	450	—

KM# 63.2 200 REIS

Silver **Countermark:** Type VIII **Note:** Countermarked on Brazil 200 Reis, KM#32.

CM Date	Host Date	Good	VG	F	VF	XF
ND(1688)	ND	165	325	525	—	—

KM# 64.1 300 REIS

13.5400 g., Silver **Countermark:** Type VIII **Note:** Countermarked on Spanish Colonial 4 Reales.

CM Date	Host Date	Good	VG	F	VF	XF
ND(1688)	ND	100	200	325	525	—

KM# 64.2 300 REIS

13.5400 g., Silver **Countermark:** Type VIII **Note:** Countermarked on Bolivia 4 Reales, KM#18.3.

CM Date	Host Date	Good	VG	F	VF	XF
ND(1688)	1660	175	325	525	850	—

KM# 65 600 REIS

27.0700 g., Silver **Countermark:** Type VIII **Note:** Countermarked on Spanish Colonial 8 Reales.

CM Date	Host Date	Good	VG	F	VF	XF
ND(1688)	ND	200	400	650	1,100	—

MILLED COINAGE

KM# 74 20 REIS

0.5600 g., 0.9170 Silver 0.0165 oz. ASW **Obv:** Narrow crown on shield of arms

Date	Mintage	VG	F	VF	XF	Unc
ND(1695-1698)	—	120	180	450	650	—

KM# 73 20 REIS
0.5600 g., 0.9170 Silver 0.0165 oz. ASW **Obv:** Large crown on shield of arms **Obv. Legend:** PETRVS. II. D. G. P. REX. R. D **Rev:** Globe on cross, rosettes in angles **Note:** Struck at Bahia.

Date	Mintage	VG	F	VF	XF	Unc
ND(1695) Unique	—	—	—	—	—	—

KM# 85.2 20 REIS
Silver **Ruler:** Pedro As Pedro II **Obv:** Crowned arms **Rev:** Globe on cross, rosettes in angles

Date	Mintage	VG	F	VF	XF	Unc
ND(1700-1702) P	—	45.00	110	225	400	—

KM# 85.1 20 REIS
0.5600 g., 0.9170 Silver 0.0165 oz. ASW **Obv:** Crowned arms **Note:** Struck at Rio de Janeiro.

Date	Mintage	VG	F	VF	XF	Unc
ND(1699)	—	70.00	115	230	400	—

KM# 76 40 REIS
1.1200 g., 0.9170 Silver 0.0330 oz. ASW **Obv:** Wide, low crown on shield of arms

Date	Mintage	Good	VG	F	VF	XF
ND(1695-98)	—	60.00	90.00	175	300	—

KM# 75 40 REIS
1.1200 g., 0.9170 Silver 0.0330 oz. ASW **Obv:** Large high crown on shield of arms **Obv. Legend:** PETRVS. II. D. G. P. REX. R. D **Note:** Struck at Bahia.

Date	Mintage	Good	VG	F	VF	XF
ND(1695) Unique	—	—	—	—	—	—

KM# 86.2 40 REIS
Silver **Ruler:** Pedro As Pedro II **Obv:** Crowned arms **Obv. Legend:** PETRVS • II • D • G • P • R • E • B • D • **Rev:** Sash crosses globe on cross, thin straight parallels **Rev. Legend:** SIGN NATA STAB SVBQ **Note:** Varieties exist.

Date	Mintage	Good	VG	F	VF	XF
ND(1700-02)P	—	60.00	90.00	175	300	—

KM# 86.1 40 REIS
1.1200 g., 0.9170 Silver 0.0330 oz. ASW **Obv:** Crowned arms **Note:** Struck at Rio de Janeiro.

Date	Mintage	Good	VG	F	VF	XF
ND(1699)	—	60.00	90.00	175	300	—

KM# 78 80 REIS
2.2400 g., 0.9170 Silver 0.0660 oz. ASW **Obv:** Narrow crown above shield of arms

Date	Mintage	Good	VG	F	VF	XF
1695	—	25.00	36.00	60.00	90.00	—
1696	—	25.00	36.00	60.00	90.00	—
1697	—	42.00	85.00	180	400	—

KM# 77 80 REIS
2.2400 g., 0.9170 Silver 0.0660 oz. ASW **Obv:** Large crown above shield of arms, value at left, date divided near top **Obv. Legend:** PETRVS. II. D. G. PORT. REX. B. D **Rev:** Globe on cross **Note:** Struck at Bahia.

Date	Mintage	Good	VG	F	VF	XF
1695	—	35.00	70.00	140	250	—

KM# 87.1 80 REIS
2.2648 g., 0.9170 Silver 0.0668 oz. ASW **Obv:** Crowned arms divide date, value at left **Note:** Struck at Rio de Janeiro

Date	Mintage	Good	VG	F	VF	XF
1699	—	17.00	35.00	60.00	90.00	—
1700	—	22.50	45.00	115	240	—

KM# 87.2 80 REIS
2.2400 g., 0.9170 Silver 0.0660 oz. ASW **Ruler:** Pedro As Pedro II **Obv:** Crowned arms **Obv. Legend:** PETRVS • II • D • G • ... **Rev:** Globe on cross with "P" at center **Rev. Legend:** SIGN NATA STAB SVBQ **Note:** Varieties exist.

Date	Mintage	Good	VG	F	VF	XF
1700P	—	40.00	80.00	160	350	—

KM# 79.1 160 REIS
4.4800 g., 0.9170 Silver 0.1321 oz. ASW **Obv:** Large crown above shield of arms, value at left, date divided near top **Obv. Legend:** PETRVS. II. D. G. PORT. REX. E. B. D **Rev:** Globe on cross **Note:** Struck at Bahia.

Date	Mintage	Good	VG	F	VF	XF
1695	—	25.00	35.00	60.00	90.00	—

KM# 79.2 160 REIS
4.4800 g., 0.9170 Silver 0.1321 oz. ASW **Rev:** Without punctuation

Date	Mintage	Good	VG	F	VF	XF
1695	—	35.00	70.00	145	290	—

KM# 80 160 REIS
4.4800 g., 0.9170 Silver 0.1321 oz. ASW **Obv:** Narrow crown above shield of arms

Date	Mintage	Good	VG	F	VF	XF
1695	—	25.00	42.00	65.00	100	—
1696	—	25.00	42.00	65.00	100	—
1697	—	75.00	145	260	450	—

KM# 88.1 160 REIS
4.4800 g., 0.9170 Silver 0.1321 oz. ASW **Obv:** Crowned arms divide date, value at left **Note:** Struck at Rio de Janiero.

Date	Mintage	Good	VG	F	VF	XF
1699	—	25.00	42.00	60.00	100	—
1700	—	35.00	70.00	145	290	—

KM# 88.2 160 REIS
Silver **Ruler:** Pedro As Pedro II **Obv:** Crowned arms divide value at left from crosses at right **Obv. Legend:** PETRVS • II • D • G • P • R • E .... **Rev:** Globe on cross with "P" at center **Rev. Legend:** SIGN NATA STAB SVBQ **Note:** Varieties exist.

Date	Mintage	Good	VG	F	VF	XF
1700P	—	75.00	145	260	450	—

KM# 82 320 REIS
8.9600 g., 0.9170 Silver 0.2641 oz. ASW **Obv:** Narrow crown above shield of arms **Note:** Struck at Bahia, varieties exist.

Date	Mintage	VG	F	VF	XF	Unc
1695	—	22.50	42.00	80.00	150	—
1696	—	22.50	42.00	80.00	150	—
1697	—	70.00	115	230	450	—
1698	—	145	285	525	975	—

KM# 81.1 320 REIS
8.9600 g., 0.9170 Silver 0.2641 oz. ASW **Obv:** Large crown above shield of arms, value at left, date divided near top **Obv. Legend:** PETRVS. II. D. G. PORT. REX. E. BRAS. D **Rev:** Oval globe on cross **Note:** Struck at Bahia.

Date	Mintage	VG	F	VF	XF	Unc
1695	—	25.00	45.00	90.00	175	—

KM# 81.2 320 REIS
8.9600 g., 0.9170 Silver 0.2641 oz. ASW **Rev:** Round globe on cross **Note:** Struck at Bahia

Date	Mintage	VG	F	VF	XF	Unc
1695	—	22.50	45.00	90.00	185	—
1695 PETRS	—	60.00	110	215	425	—

KM# 89.1 320 REIS
8.9600 g., 0.9170 Silver 0.2641 oz. ASW **Note:** Struck at Rio de Janeiro, varieties exist.

Date	Mintage	VG	F	VF	XF	Unc
1699	—	22.50	42.00	80.00	150	—

KM# 89.2 320 REIS
8.9600 g., 0.9170 Silver 0.2641 oz. ASW **Ruler:** Pedro As Pedro II **Obv:** Crowned arms divide date, value at left **Obv. Legend:** PETRVS • II • D • G • PORT • .... **Rev:** Round globe on cross **Rev. Legend:** SIGN • NATA STAB • SVBQ

Date	Mintage	VG	F	VF	XF	Unc
1700P	—	12.00	18.00	36.00	90.00	—

KM# 84 640 REIS
17.9200 g., 0.9170 Silver 0.5283 oz. ASW **Obv:** Narrow crown above shield of arms, value at left, date divided near top **Rev:** Globe on cross **Note:** Varieties exist.

Date	Mintage	VG	F	VF	XF	Unc
1695	—	20.00	35.00	65.00	125	—
1696	—	20.00	35.00	65.00	125	—
1697	—	25.00	45.00	75.00	145	—
1698	—	25.00	45.00	75.00	145	—

KM# 83.1 640 REIS
17.9200 g., 0.9170 Silver 0.5283 oz. ASW **Obv:** Large crown above shield of arms, value at left, date divided near top **Obv. Legend:** PETRVS. II. D. G. PORT. REX. ET. BRAS. D.. **Rev:** Globe on cross

Date	Mintage	VG	F	VF	XF	Unc
1695	—	45.00	75.00	125	200	—

KM# 83.2 640 REIS
17.9200 g., 0.9170 Silver 0.5283 oz. ASW **Rev:** Without punctuation

Date	Mintage	VG	F	VF	XF	Unc
1695	—	60.00	100	200	350	—

KM# 90.1 640 REIS

17.9200 g., 0.9170 Silver 0.5283 oz. ASW **Note:** Varieties exist.

Date	Mintage	VG	F	VF	XF	Unc
1699	—	25.00	40.00	70.00	135	—
1700	—	30.00	55.00	85.00	160	—

KM# 90.2 640 REIS

17.9200 g., 0.9170 Silver 0.5283 oz. ASW **Ruler:** Pedro As Pedro II **Obv:** Crowned arms divide date above and value at left from florals at right **Obv. Legend:** PETRVS • II • D • G • PORT • REX ... **Rev:** Globe on cross, thick, curved parallels **Rev. Legend:** SIGN • NATA • STAB • SVBQ

Date	Mintage	VG	F	VF	XF	Unc
1700P	—	45.00	75.00	125	250	—

KM# 87 1000 REIS

2.0400 g., 0.9170 Gold 0.0601 oz. AGW **Obv:** Crowned arms, value at side **Rev:** Cross in quatrefoil, date above **Note:** Struck at Bahia.

Date	Mintage	VG	F	VF	XF	Unc
1696 Unique	—	—	—	—	—	—

KM# 96 1000 REIS

2.0400 g., 0.9170 Gold 0.0601 oz. AGW **Note:** Struck at Rio de Janeiro; legend varieties exist.

Date	Mintage	VG	F	VF	XF	Unc
1699	—	50.00	90.00	150	300	—
1700	—	50.00	90.00	150	300	—

KM# 88 2000 REIS

4.0800 g., 0.9170 Gold 0.1203 oz. AGW **Obv:** Smaller crown above arms

Date	Mintage	VG	F	VF	XF	Unc
1696	—	90.00	175	325	450	—
1697	—	85.00	165	300	400	—

KM# 85 2000 REIS

4.0800 g., 0.9170 Gold 0.1203 oz. AGW **Obv:** Crowned arms, value at side **Rev. Legend:** Cross in quatrefoil, date above **Note:** Struck at Bahia.

Date	Mintage	VG	F	VF	XF	Unc
1695	—	500	1,000	2,000	3,500	—

KM# 97 2000 REIS

4.0800 g., 0.9170 Gold 0.1203 oz. AGW **Note:** Legend varieties exist; Struck at Rio De Janero.

Date	Mintage	VG	F	VF	XF	Unc
1699	—	75.00	150	275	375	—
1700	—	85.00	165	300	400	—

KM# 89 4000 REIS

8.1600 g., 0.9170 Gold 0.2406 oz. AGW **Obv:** Taller crown above arms **Note:** Struck at Bahia.

Date	Mintage	VG	F	VF	XF	Unc
1696	—	150	300	500	750	—
1697	—	150	300	500	750	—
1698	—	150	300	500	750	—

KM# 86 4000 REIS

8.1600 g., 0.9170 Gold 0.2406 oz. AGW **Obv:** Crowned arms, value at side **Rev:** Cross in quatrefoil, date above **Note:** Struck at Bahia.

Date	Mintage	VG	F	VF	XF	Unc
1695	—	175	350	600	1,150	—

KM# 98 4000 REIS

8.1600 g., 0.9170 Gold 0.2406 oz. AGW **Note:** Legend and punctuation varieties exist.

Date	Mintage	VG	F	VF	XF	Unc
1699/8	—	125	175	300	550	—
1699	—	125	175	300	550	—
1700	—	125	175	300	550	—

CENTRAL ASIA

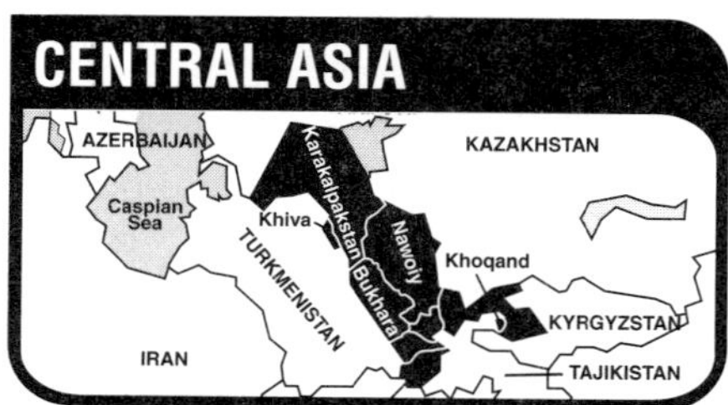

In the several centuries prior to 1500 which witnessed the breakup of the Mongol Empire and the subsequent rise of smaller successor states, no single power or dynasty was able to control the vast expanses of Western and Central Asia. The region known previously as Transoxiana, the land beyond the Oxus River (modern Amu Darya), became the domain of the Shaybanids, then the Janids. The territory ruled by these dynasties had no set borders, which rather expanded and contracted as the fortunes of the rulers ebbed and flowed. At their greatest extent, the khanate took in parts of what are now northern Iran and Afghanistan, as well as part or all of modern Turkmenistan, Uzbekistan, Kazakhstan, Tadzhikistan and Kyrgyzstan. Coins are known to have been struck by virtually every ruler, but some are quite scarce owing to short reigns or the ever-changing political and economic situation.

JANID

The Janids were the successors to the Shaybanid dynasty and they maintained coinage traditions similar to those of their predecessors. Janid silver coins are almost invariably poorly struck, rarely showing either mint or date. After about AH1090/1679AD, the alloy became increasingly debased and was mostly copper after the early AH1100s/1670s AD. By contrast, the gold coins of the Janids are found to be of high quality and alloy. The original silver tanka conformed to the 4.7 gram weight inherited from the Shaybanids, but sank to below 4 grams by the end of the dynasty. Mint names, when they are visible on the silver coins, have only been recorded for Balkh, Bukhara and Samarqand.

The dates of rule given for the Janid khans are rather tentative. The standard lists in the genealogical references to not agree with the dates found on the coins in all cases.

RULERS

Yar Muhammad Khan, ca AH1007-08/1598-99AD
Jani Muhammad Khan, AH1007-10/1598-1601AD
Baqi Muhammad Khan, AH1010-14/1601-05AD
Wali Muhammad Khan, AH1014-27/1605-18AD
Imam Quli Khan, AH1027-54/1618-44AD
Nadr Muhammad Khan, AH1054-57/1644-47AD
Occupation by Mughal Shah Jahan I, at Balkh AH1056-57/1647AD
'Abd al-'Aziz Khan, AH1057-91/1647-80AD
Subhan Quli Khan, AH1091-1114/1680-1702AD

KHANATE

Jani Muhammad Khan

AH1007-1010

HAMMERED COINAGE

Balkh

MB# 5.1 TANKA

4.6000 g., Silver

Date	Mintage	Good	VG	F	VF	XF
AH1008	—	—	30.00	50.00	80.00	125
ND(1601)	—	—	20.00	30.00	50.00	85.00

Bukhara

MB# 5.2 TANKA

4.6000 g., Silver

Date	Mintage	Good	VG	F	VF	XF
AH1009	—	—	40.00	60.00	100	150
ND(1601)	—	—	30.00	45.00	70.00	110

Samarqand

MB# 5.3 TANKA

4.6000 g., Silver

Date	Mintage	Good	VG	F	VF	XF
AH1010	—	—	40.00	60.00	100	150
ND(1601)	—	—	30.00	50.00	85.00	125

No mint

MB# 5.4 TANKA

4.6000 g., Silver

Date	Mintage	Good	VG	F	VF	XF
ND(1601)	—	—	20.00	35.00	60.00	95.00

Baqi Muhammad Khan

AH1010-1014

HAMMERED COINAGE

Balkh

KM# 7.1 TANKA

4.6000 g., Silver **Obv:** Ruler's names in cartouch, titles, mint and date around **Rev:** Kalima in cartouche

Date	Mintage	Good	VG	F	VF	XF
AH1011	—	—	35.00	50.00	85.00	125
ND	—	—	18.00	30.00	45.00	70.00

Bukhara

KM# 7.2 TANKA

4.6000 g., Silver **Obv:** Ruler's names in cartouch, titles, mint and date around **Rev:** Kalima in cartouche

Date	Mintage	Good	VG	F	VF	XF
AH1011	—	—	30.00	50.00	100	165
AH1012	—	—	30.00	50.00	100	165
AH1014	—	—	20.00	40.00	75.00	110

Samarqand

KM# 7.3 TANKA

4.6000 g., Silver **Obv:** Ruler's names in cartouch, titles, mint and date around **Rev:** Kalima in cartouche

Date	Mintage	Good	VG	F	VF	XF
AH1011	—	—	30.00	50.00	100	140
ND	—	—	20.00	40.00	70.00	110

No mint

KM# 7.4 TANKA

4.6000 g., Silver **Obv:** Ruler's names in cartouch, titles, mint and date around **Rev:** Kalima in cartouche

Date	Mintage	Good	VG	F	VF	XF
AH1011	—	—	20.00	40.00	70.00	110
AH1013	—	—	20.00	40.00	70.00	110
ND	—	—	12.00	25.00	45.00	75.00

Wali Muhammad Khan

AH1014-1027

HAMMERED COINAGE

Balkh

KM# 9.1 TANKA

4.5300 g., Silver **Obv:** Ruler's name in cartouche, titles around **Rev:** Kalima in cartouche

Date	Mintage	Good	VG	F	VF	XF
AH1014	—	—	35.00	50.00	80.00	125
ND(1618)	—	—	20.00	30.00	60.00	100

Bukhara

KM# 9.2 TANKA

4.5300 g., Silver **Obv:** Ruler's name in cartouche, titles around **Rev:** Kalima in cartouche

Date	Mintage	Good	VG	F	VF	XF
ND(1618)	—	—	17.50	35.00	60.00	100

Samarqand

KM# 9.3 TANKA

4.5300 g., Silver **Obv:** Ruler's name in cartouche, titles around **Rev:** Kalima in cartouche

Date	Mintage	Good	VG	F	VF	XF
AH1014	—	—	40.00	60.00	95.00	140
AH1015	—	—	40.00	60.00	95.00	140
AH1020	—	—	40.00	60.00	95.00	140
ND	—	—	17.50	35.00	60.00	100

No mint

KM# 9.4 TANKA

4.5300 g., Silver **Obv:** Ruler's names and titles in cartouche **Rev:** Kalima in cartouche

Date	Mintage	Good	VG	F	VF	XF
ND(1618)	—	—	20.00	30.00	60.00	100

Imam Quli Khan

AH1027-1054

HAMMERED COINAGE

Balkh

KM# 11.1 TANKA

4.2500 g., Silver **Obv:** Ruler's names in cartouche, titles, mint and date around **Rev:** Kalima in cartouche

Date	Mintage	Good	VG	F	VF	XF
ND(1644) Balkh	—	—	25.00	45.00	70.00	115

Bukhara

KM# 11.2 TANKA

4.2500 g., Silver **Obv:** Ruler's names in cartouche, titles, mint and date around **Rev:** Kalima in cartouche

Date	Mintage	Good	VG	F	VF	XF
ND(1644)	—	—	25.00	45.00	75.00	115

No mint

KM# 11.3 TANKA

4.2500 g., Silver **Obv:** Ruler's names in cartouche, titles, mint and date around **Rev:** Kalima in cartouche

Date	Mintage	Good	VG	F	VF	XF
AH1033	—	—	30.00	50.00	85.00	135
ND(1644)	—	—	12.00	25.00	45.00	70.00

Nadr Muhammad Khan

AH1054-1057

HAMMERED COINAGE

Balkh

KM# 13.1 TANKA

4.2500 g., Silver

Date	Mintage	Good	VG	F	VF	XF
AH1053	—	—	40.00	70.00	110	165
AH1055	—	—	40.00	70.00	110	165
ND(1647)	—	—	25.00	45.00	70.00	110

Bukhara

KM# 13.2 TANKA

4.2500 g., Silver

Date	Mintage	Good	VG	F	VF	XF
ND(1647)	—	—	25.00	45.00	75.00	110

No mint

KM# 12 DANGI (PUL)

Copper wt. 3.38-4.51g

Date	Mintage	Good	VG	F	VF	XF
ND(1650)	—	—	—	—	—	—

KM# 13.3 TANKA

4.2500 g., Silver

Date	Mintage	Good	VG	F	VF	XF
AH1054	—	—	25.00	45.00	70.00	110
AH1055	—	—	25.00	45.00	70.00	110
ND(1647)	—	—	20.00	30.00	50.00	85.00

Shah Jahan I (Mughal)

AH1056-1057

HAMMERED COINAGE

Balkh

KM# 18 MOHUR

Gold Wt. varies 10.8-11g **Obv:** Legend within square, with knots at corners; "Shah Jahan Bad Shah Ghazi," titles, mint and date around. **Rev:** Kalima in cartouche **Note:** Listed under Mughal India as KM# 260.16.

Date	Mintage	Good	VG	F	VF	XF
AH1056//1057	—	—	325	550	750	1,100
AH1057	—	—	325	550	750	1,100

No mint

KM# 15 TANKA

4.2500 g., Silver **Obv:** Emperor's name in cartouche **Rev:** Kalima in cartouche **Note:** All coins of this type struck at Balkh, but mintname almost never visible.

Date	Mintage	Good	VG	F	VF	XF
AH1057 Balkh	—	—	200	325	475	725
AH1057	—	—	175	250	375	600
ND(1647)	—	—	90.00	150	250	500

'Abd al-'Aziz Khan

AH1057-1091

HAMMERED COINAGE

Balkh

KM# 20.1 TANKA

4.2500 g., Silver

Date	Mintage	Good	VG	F	VF	XF
AH1060	—	—	40.00	70.00	100	165
AH1062	—	—	40.00	70.00	100	165
ND(1680)	—	—	20.00	40.00	65.00	100

Bukhara

KM# 20.2 TANKA

4.2500 g., Silver

Date	Mintage	Good	VG	F	VF	XF
ND(1680)	—	—	20.00	40.00	70.00	110

No mint

KM# 19 DANGI (PUL)

4.5000 g., Copper

Date	Mintage	Good	VG	F	VF	XF
ND(1660)	—	—	—	—	—	—

KM# 20.3 TANKA

4.2500 g., Silver

Date	Mintage	Good	VG	F	VF	XF
AH1058	—	—	17.50	35.00	60.00	100
AH1077	—	—	17.50	35.00	60.00	100
ND(1680)	—	—	12.00	25.00	45.00	70.00

KM# 22 TANKA

4.2500 g., Silver **Countermark:** 'abd al-'aziz bahadur khan **Obv:** Countermarked with name of ruler in crescent moon on earlier issues

Date	Mintage	Good	VG	F	VF	XF
ND(1680)	—	—	50.00	75.00	110	165

Subhan Quli Khan

AH1091-1114

HAMMERED COINAGE

Balkh

KM# 25 TANKA

4.2500 g., Silver **Countermark:** "balkh"

Date	Mintage	Good	VG	F	VF	XF
ND(1685)	—	—	45.00	75.00	115	175

No mint

KM# 23 DANGI (PUL)

4.1000 g., Copper

Date	Mintage	Good	VG	F	VF	XF
ND(1685)	—	—	—	—	—	—

KM# 24 TANKA

4.2500 g., Billon **Note:** All specimens lack mint in the dies.

Date	Mintage	Good	VG	F	VF	XF
ND(1685)	—	25.00	50.00	75.00	110	165

SHAYBANID

The Shaybanids, an Uzbek dynasty which ruled from Samarqand and Bukhara, derived their name from a possible genealogical connection to the early Islamic Shaybanid Arabs. Their coinage closely follows Timurid prototypes and retains the silver tanka denomination. The only gold coins produced in sufficient numbers for circulation is only found issued by 'Abd Allah II and 'Abd al-Mu'min. Only those of the former are at all common.

The earliest Shaybanid silver tankas weighted one mithqal, then reckoned as 4.78 grams. From AH913-19/1507-13AD, the tanka was 1/12 heavier and so weighted about 5.15 grams, but the mithqal weight was restored by AH924/1513AD. The mithqal fell gradually during the 10th/16th century to about 4.6 grams by the time the Janid dynasty replaced the Shaybanids.

Many of the rulers produced countermarked coins, mostly anonymously and thus not always readily assigned to an individual reign. The only listed countermarks are those which have been attributed to a ruler with any certainty.

The mint names on most Shaybanid coins are prefixed with the expression *shirmard*, roughly translatable as "lion-hearted." The term is not an epithet for the mint, but rather the name of the currency, just as *bih bud* had previously been the name of the currency of the Timurid Sultan Husayn.

Types of Shaybanid silver coins are characterized by their obverse and reverse cartouches. However, the listings here will give generic types for each reign, with various mint and date combinations noted.

LOCAL RULERS

Muhammad Ibrahim, at Balkh AH1008-09/1599-1600AD

KHANATE

Muhammad Ibrahim

Local ruler at Balkh

HAMMERED COINAGE

Balkh

MB# 61 TANKA

4.7000 g., Silver **Note:** Sometimes dated on both sides

Date	Mintage	Good	VG	F	VF	XF
AH1008	—	—	40.00	60.00	85.00	135
AH1008//1009	—	—	55.00	80.00	115	165
ND	—	—	20.00	35.00	65.00	100

CEYLON

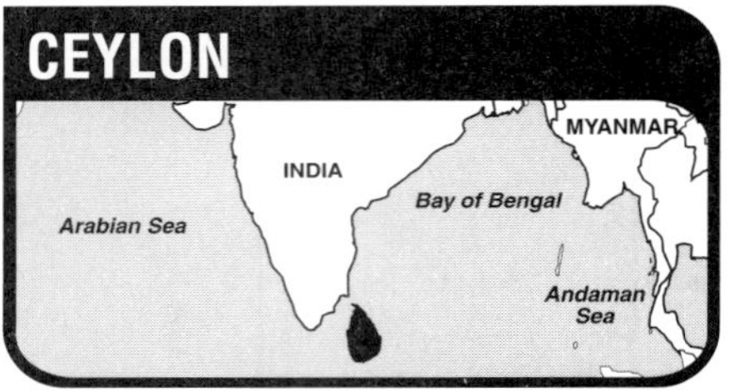

The earliest known inhabitants of Ceylon, the Veddahs, were subjugated by the Sinhalese from northern India in the 6th century B.C. Sinhalese rule was maintained until 1408, after which the island was controlled by China for 30 years. The Portuguese came to Ceylon in 1505 and maintained control of the coastal area for 150 years. The Dutch supplanted them in 1658, which were in turn supplanted by the British who seized the Dutch colonies in 1796, and made them a Crown Colony in 1802.

PORTUGUESE COLONY

Portuguese ships appeared off India in 1498. By 1505 their first governor was installed and was looking forward to settlement and trade expansion, especially the latter. Through his son he made a contact with the king of Ceylon that involved the paying of tribute to the Portuguese.

All of the early trade in Ceylon used local or the home coins of Portugal. The first coins made in Ceylon were not produced until the reign of Philip II, 1598-1621. He claimed Ceylon as a possession even though the kings of Kandy ruled the interior. Coins were made intermittently until 1645. After 1642, however, most of the silver was produced at Goa.

The last Portuguese fortress fell into Dutch hands in 1655.

OCCUPATION COINAGE

KM# 1 1/4 BAZARUCO

1.2000 g., Copper **Obv:** Cross in circle **Rev:** Globe

Date	Mintage	Good	VG	F	VF	XF
ND(1597-1655)	—	30.00	60.00	120	200	—

KM# 2 1/4 BAZARUCO

1.3000 g., Copper **Obv:** Circle in cross **Rev:** Cross - L monogram in circle

Date	Mintage	Good	VG	F	VF	XF
ND(1597-1655)	—	30.00	60.00	120	200	—

KM# 3 1/4 BAZARUCO

1.3000 g., Copper **Rev:** Cross - L monogram retrograde

Date	Mintage	Good	VG	F	VF	XF
ND(1597-1655)	—	30.00	60.00	120	200	—

KM# 4 BAZARUCO

2.7000 g., Copper **Obv:** Crowned arms in circle **Rev:** Globe

Date	Mintage	Good	VG	F	VF	XF
ND(1597-1655)	—	30.00	60.00	120	200	—

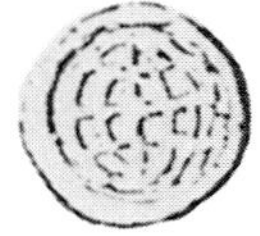

KM# 5 BAZARUCO

3.0000 g., Tin **Obv:** Globe **Rev:** Gridiron of St. Lawrence

Date	Mintage	Good	VG	F	VF	XF
ND(1621-40)	—	25.00	50.00	100	175	—

KM# 6 TANGA

2.6600 g., Silver **Obv:** Crowned arms divide D T in circle **Rev:** A over T in circle

Date	Mintage	Good	VG	F	VF	XF
ND(1598-1621)	—	60.00	120	250	400	—

KM# 7 TANGA

2.6400 g., Silver **Obv:** Crowned arms in circle **Rev:** T A monogram i circle

Date	Mintage	Good	VG	F	VF	XF
ND(1598-1621)	—	50.00	100	200	350	—

KM# 8 TANGA

2.6200 g., Silver **Rev:** Gridiron of St. Lawrence in circle

Date	Mintage	Good	VG	F	VF	XF
ND(1598-1621)	—	27.50	55.00	90.00	150	—

KM# 9.1 TANGA

2.3600 g., Silver **Obv:** Crowned arms **Rev:** Gridiron of St. Lawrence divides S-F

Date	Mintage	Good	VG	F	VF	XF
ND(1621-40)	—	25.00	50.00	80.00	125	—
1631	—	25.00	50.00	80.00	130	—

KM# 9.2 TANGA

2.3700 g., Silver **Obv:** Crowned arms divide C Lo, in circle **Rev:** Gridiron of St. Lawrence divides date, crown below

Date	Mintage	Good	VG	F	VF	XF
1640	—	35.00	65.00	135	250	—

KM# 12 TANGA

1.9600 g., Silver **Obv:** Crowned arms divide C Lo in circle

Date	Mintage	Good	VG	F	VF	XF
1644	—	120	225	450	750	—

KM# 10 TANGA

2.2000 g., Silver **Obv:** Crowned arms divide G A in circle **Rev:** TA monogram divides D S, date below

Date	Mintage	Good	VG	F	VF	XF
1642	—	12.50	25.00	50.00	90.00	—
1643	—	15.00	30.00	60.00	110	—
1647	—	13.50	27.50	55.00	100	—

KM# 11 TANGA

2.1000 g., Silver **Rev:** Gridiron of St. Lawrence divides date, crown below

Date	Mintage	Good	VG	F	VF	XF
1645	—	27.50	55.00	110	200	—
1646	—	27.50	55.00	110	200	—

KM# 13 TANGA

1.9600 g., Silver **Obv:** Crowned arms divide A G

Date	Mintage	Good	VG	F	VF	XF
1646	—	30.00	60.00	120	225	—

KM# 14 2 TANGAS

4.3700 g., Silver **Obv:** Crowned arms divide G A in circle **Rev:** T A monogram divides D S, date below

Date	Mintage	Good	VG	F	VF	XF
1642	—	35.00	65.00	135	250	—
1643	—	20.00	40.00	75.00	150	—
1644	—	22.00	45.00	80.00	165	—
1649	—	50.00	100	200	350	—

KM# 15 2 TANGAS

4.3100 g., Silver **Rev:** Gridiron of St. Lawrence divides date, crown below

Date	Mintage	Good	VG	F	VF	XF
1645	—	45.00	85.00	175	325	—

DUTCH COLONY

The Dutch first sighted Ceylon in 1602. They made a treaty with the king of Kandy for trading rights and the Dutch would have to expel the Portuguese. Between 1638 and 1658 the Dutch had accomplished their purpose. The Portuguese were gone from Ceylon.

As the Dutch trade with Ceylon prospered the coins in use were local coins and countermarked coins of the Portuguese colonies. It was not until sometime after 1660 that the Dutch began striking anonymous copper coins.

In the second third of the 1700's, copper duits of the Netherlands provinces were sent to the East and used widely there. The VOC monogram on these coins became a familiar sight to the merchants of the sub-continent and the East Indies.

Local coinage started again in 1783.

Netherlands United East India Company

MONETARY SYSTEM

4 Duiten = 1 Stuiver
4 Stuivers = 1 Fanam
4-1/2 Stuivers = 1 Shahi
9-1/2 Stuivers = 1 Larin

OCCUPATION COINAGE

KM# 16 1/8 STUIVER

Copper **Obv:** Value in wreath **Rev:** Value in wreath

Date	Mintage	Good	VG	F	VF	XF
ND(1660-1720)	—	25.00	35.00	60.00	100	—

KM# 17 1/4 STUIVER

Copper **Obv:** Value in wreath **Rev:** Value in wreath

Date	Mintage	Good	VG	F	VF	XF
ND(1660-1720)	—	20.00	25.00	45.00	70.00	—

KM# 18.1 1/2 STUIVER

Copper **Obv:** Value in wreath **Rev:** Value in wreath

Date	Mintage	Good	VG	F	VF	XF
ND(1660-1720)	—	12.00	22.00	38.00	55.00	—

KM# 18.2 1/2 STUIVER

Copper **Obv:** Small value in wreath **Rev:** Small value in wreath

Date	Mintage	Good	VG	F	VF	XF
ND(1660-1720)	—	12.00	22.00	38.00	55.00	—

KM# 19.2 STUIVER

Copper **Obv:** Value "1 St" in wreath of 2 branches **Rev:** Value "1 St" in wreath of 2 branches

Date	Mintage	Good	VG	F	VF	XF
ND(ca. 1675)	—	22.00	38.00	65.00	85.00	—

KM# 19.3 STUIVER

Copper **Obv:** Value "1 St" in wreath of small leaves (thorns) **Rev:** Value "1 St" in wreath of small leaves (thorns)

Date	Mintage	Good	VG	F	VF	XF
ND(1660-1720)	—	20.00	35.00	60.00	80.00	—

KM# 20 2 STUIVER

Copper **Obv:** Value "11 St" in wreath **Rev:** Value "11 St" in wreath

Date	Mintage	Good	VG	F	VF	XF
ND(1660-1720)	—	12.50	17.50	25.00	35.00	—

BRITISH COMMONWEALTH

COUNTERMARKED COINAGE

Type I

Type II

Type III

KM# 52 TANGA

Silver **Series:** Galle **Countermark:** G/LL **Note:** Type II countermark on Tanga of Colombo.

CM Date	Host Date	Good	VG	F	VF	XF
ND(c.1680)	1631	130	260	435	650	—

KM# 53 TANGA

Silver **Series:** Galle **Countermark:** G/LL **Note:** Type II countermark on Tanga of Malacca.

CM Date	Host Date	Good	VG	F	VF	XF
ND(c.1680)	1631	150	300	500	750	—
ND(c.1680)	1632	150	300	500	750	—

KM# 54 TANGA

Silver **Series:** Galle **Countermark:** G/LL **Note:** Type II countermark on Tanga of Colombo.

CM Date	Host Date	Good	VG	F	VF	XF
ND(c.1680)	1640	130	260	435	650	—

KM# 39 TANGA

Silver **Series:** Colombo **Countermark:** C/VOC **Note:** Type I countermark on India-Portuguese Tanga of Goa.

CM Date	Host Date	Good	VG	F	VF	XF
ND(c.1680)	164x	100	200	350	500	—

KM# 38 TANGA

Silver **Series:** Colombo **Countermark:** C/VOC **Note:** Type I countermark on India-Portuguese Tanga of Goa.

CM Date	Host Date	Good	VG	F	VF	XF
ND(c.1680)	1645	100	160	225	350	—
ND(c.1680)	1649	100	200	350	500	—

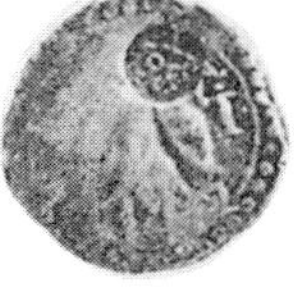

KM# 59 2 TANGAS

Silver **Series:** Jaffna **Countermark:** I/VOC **Note:** Type III countermark on India-Portuguese 2 Tangas of Goa.

CM Date	Host Date	Good	VG	F	VF	XF
ND(c.1680)	1640	150	300	500	750	—
ND(c.1680)	1642	150	300	500	750	—
ND(c.1680)	16xx	150	300	500	750	—

KM# 55 2 TANGAS

Silver **Series:** Galle **Countermark:** G/LL **Note:** Type II countermark on India-Portuguese 2 Tangas of Goa.

CM Date	Host Date	Good	VG	F	VF	XF
ND(c.1680)	164x	100	200	275	450	—
ND(c.1680)	1642	100	200	275	450	—

KM# 40 2 TANGAS

Silver **Series:** Colombo **Countermark:** C/VOC **Note:** Type I countermark on India-Portuguese 2 Tangas of Goa, KM#68.

CM Date	Host Date	Good	VG	F	VF	XF
ND(c.1680)	1642	130	260	435	650	—

KM# 60 2 TANGAS

Silver **Series:** Jaffna **Countermark:** I/VOC **Note:** Type III countermark on India-Portuguese 2 Tangas of Goa.

CM Date	Host Date	Good	VG	F	VF	XF
ND(c.1680)	1645	150	300	500	750	—

KM# 41 2 TANGAS

Silver **Series:** Colombo **Countermark:** C/VOC **Note:** Type I countermark on India-Portuguese 2 Tangas of Chaul-Bassein.

CM Date	Host Date	Good	VG	F	VF	XF
ND(c.1680)	1646	150	300	500	750	—

KM# 56 2 TANGAS

Silver **Series:** Galle **Countermark:** G/LL **Note:** Type II countermark on India-Portuguese 2 Tangas of Goa.

CM Date	Host Date	Good	VG	F	VF	XF
ND(c.1680)	1650	100	200	350	500	—
ND(c.1680)	1651	100	200	350	500	—
ND(c.1680)	1652	100	200	350	500	—

KM# 42 2 TANGAS

Silver **Series:** Colombo **Countermark:** C/VOC **Note:** Type I countermark on India-Portuguese 2 Tangas of Diu.

CM Date	Host Date	Good	VG	F	VF	XF
ND(c.1680)	1655	100	200	350	500	—

KM# 43 2 TANGAS

Silver **Series:** Colombo **Countermark:** C/VOC **Note:** Type I countermark on India-Portuguese 2 Tangas of Goa.

CM Date	Host Date	Good	VG	F	VF	XF
ND(c.1680)	1656	100	200	350	500	—

KM# 46 1/2 ABBASI (Mahmudi or 2 Shahis)

3.6900 g., Silver **Countermark:** C/VOC **Note:** Type I countermark on Iranian 1/2 Abbasi of Safi I.

CM Date	Host Date	Good	VG	F	VF	XF
ND(c.1680)	ND(AH1039-52)	35.00	60.00	100	150	—

KM# 47 1/2 ABBASI (Mahmudi or 2 Shahis)

3.6900 g., Silver **Countermark:** C/VOC **Note:** Type I countermark on Iranian 1/2 Abbasi of Abbas II.

CM Date	Host Date	Good	VG	F	VF	XF
ND(c.1680)	ND(AH1052-77)	35.00	60.00	100	150	—

KM# 48 1/2 ABBASI (Mahmudi or 2 Shahis)

3.6900 g., Silver **Countermark:** C/VOC **Note:** Type I countermark on Iranian 1/2 Abbasi of Sulaiman I.

CM Date	Host Date	Good	VG	F	VF	XF
ND(c.1680)	ND(AH1080-92) Date off flan	35.00	60.00	100	150	—
ND(c.1680)	AH1080	35.00	60.00	100	150	—
ND(c.1680)	AH1085	35.00	60.00	100	150	—
ND(c.1680)	AH1086	35.00	60.00	100	150	—
ND(c.1680)	AH1088	35.00	60.00	100	150	—
ND(c.1680)	AH1089	35.00	60.00	100	150	—
ND(c.1680)	AH1091	35.00	60.00	100	150	—
ND(c.1680)	AH1092	35.00	60.00	100	150	—

KM# 49 ABBASI (4 Shahis)

7.3900 g., Silver **Countermark:** C/VOC **Note:** Type I countermark on Iranian Abbasi of Abbas II.

CM Date	Host Date	Good	VG	F	VF	XF
ND(c.1680)	AH1065	45.00	75.00	125	200	—

KM# 50 ABBASI (4 Shahis)

7.3900 g., Silver **Countermark:** C/VOC **Note:** Type I countermark on Iranian Abbasi of Sulaiman I.

CM Date	Host Date	Good	VG	F	VF	XF
ND(c.1680)	AH1078	45.00	75.00	125	200	—
	ND(AH1080-92)//(c.1680) Date off flan	45.00	75.00	125	200	—

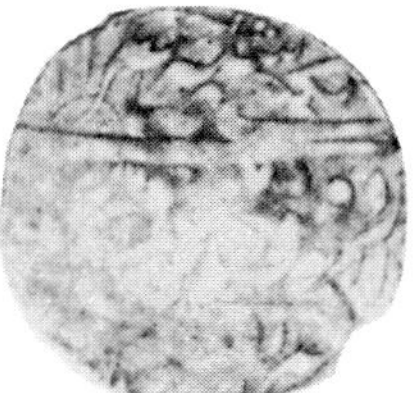

KM# 51 LARGE ABBASI (5 Shahis)

9.2300 g., Silver **Countermark:** C/VOC **Note:** Type I countermark on Iranian 5 Shahi of Abbas II.

CM Date	Host Date	Good	VG	F	VF	XF
ND(c.1680)	ND(AH1052-77)	100	160	225	300	—

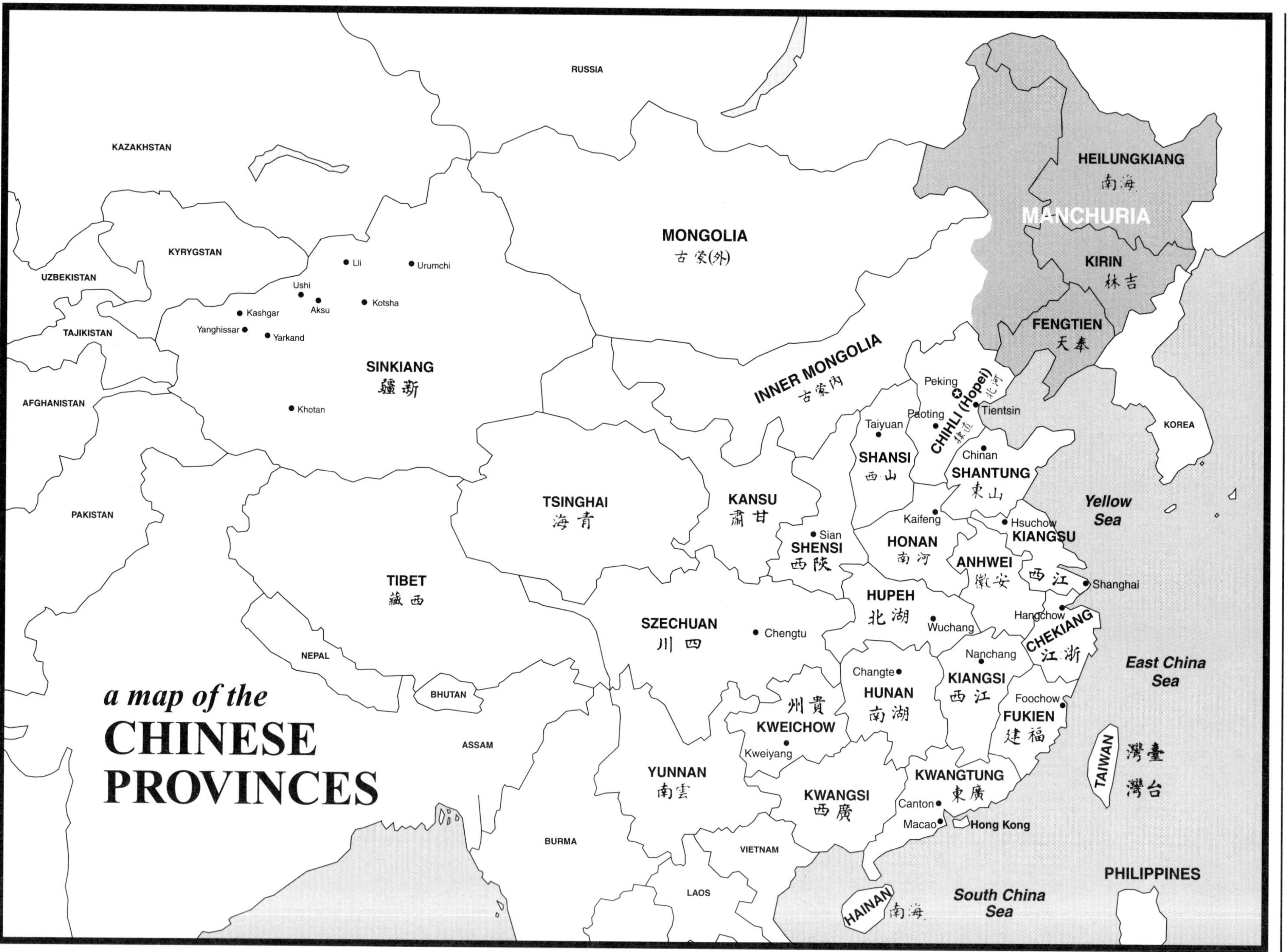
a map of the
CHINESE
PROVINCES
RUSSIA
KAZAKHSTAN
KYRYGSTAN
UZBEKISTAN
TAJIKISTAN
AFGHANISTAN
PAKISTAN
MONGOLIA
古蒙(外)
SINKIANG
疆新
Lli
Urumchi
Ushi
Aksu
Kotsha
Kashgar
Yanghissar
Yarkand
Khotan
INNER MONGOLIA
古蒙内
TSINGHAI
海青
TIBET
藏西
NEPAL
BHUTAN
ASSAM
BURMA
VIETNAM
LAOS
KANSU
肅甘
SHENSI
西陝
Sian
SHANSI
西山
Taiyuan
CHIHLI (Hopei)
Peking
Paoting
Tientsin
SHANTUNG
東山
Chinan
HONAN
南河
Kaifeng
KIANGSU
Hsuchow
ANHWEI
徽安
西江
Shanghai
HUPEH
北湖
Wuchang
SZECHUAN
川四
Chengtu
CHEKIANG
江浙
Hangchow
KIANGSI
西江
Nanchang
HUNAN
南湖
Changte
KWEICHOW
州貴
Kweiyang
FUKIEN
建福
Foochow
YUNNAN
南雲
KWANGSI
西廣
KWANGTUNG
東廣
Canton
Macao
Hong Kong
HAINAN
南海
HEILUNGKIANG
南海
MANCHURIA
KIRIN
林吉
FENGTIEN
天奉
KOREA
Yellow Sea
East China Sea
TAIWAN
灣臺
灣台
South China Sea
PHILIPPINES

CHINA

EMPIRE

EMPERORS
MING DYNASTY

During the reign of Wan-li (Shen Tsung), the Board of Revenue and Board of Works were ordered to produce the *Wan-li T'ung-pao* cash pieces in 1576AD. The reverses of these cash pieces include: dot, crescent, *Kung* (two types), *Cheng, T'ien, Fen, Li* and muled obverses. Subsequently, due to large scales of war and famine, military authorities, provinces, and private sources minted similar coins in large quantities, including 2, 5, and 10 cash, 1 Fen and 1 Tael pieces. It is interesting to note that even the palace eunuch produced small silver coins during later years of Wan-li.

萬 曆

Wan li (Shen Tsung)
1573-1619AD

萬 曆 通 寶

Wan-li T'ung-pao

泰 昌

T'ai-ch'ang (Kwang Tsung)
1620AD

泰 昌 通 寶

T'ai-ch'ang T'ung-pao

天 啓

T'ien-chi (Hsi Tsung)
1621-1627AD

天 啓 通 寶

T'ien-ch'i T'ung-pao

崇 禎

Ch'ung-chên (Chuang Lieh)
1628-1644AD

崇 禎 通 寶

Ch'ung-chên T'ung-pao

NOTE: The character *chen* is written 禎 or 禎

The minting of the Ch'ung-chên T'ung-pao pieces started in the first year of Ch'ung-chên (1628). There are many varieties in lettering on the obverse. The reverses include: mints, areas, years, worth and events.

MING-CH'ING REBEL ERA

大 明

Ta-ming (Ming Prince of Lu)

大 明 通 寶

Ta-ming T'ung-pao

弘 光　福 王

Hung-kuang (Prince of Fu; Fu King; Fu Wang)

弘 光 通 寶

Hung-kuang T'ung-pao

隆 武　唐 王

Lung-wu (Prince of T'ang, Foochow; T'ang King, T'ang Wang)

隆 武 通 寶

Lung'wu T'ung-pao

永 曆

Yung-li (Prince Yung-ming, 'Chao-ch'ing Fu', Kwangtung)
1647-1662AD

永 曆 通 寶

Yung-li T'ung-pao

永 昌　李 自 成

Yung-ch'ang (Li Tzu-ch'eng 'Hsi-an Fu')
1606-1645AD

永 昌 通 寶

Yung-ch'ang T'ung-pao

大 順　張 獻 忠

Ta-shun (Chang Hsien-chung 'Ch'eng-tu')

大 順 通 寶

Ta-shun T'ung-pao

興 朝　孫 可 望

Hsing-ch'ao (Sun K'o-wang 'Kuei-yang')

興 朝 通 寶

Hsing-chao T'ung-pao

利 用　吳 三 桂

Li-yung (Wu San-kuei)

利 用 通 寶

Li-yung T'ung-pao

昭 武　平 西 王

Chao-wu (P'ing-hsi Wang, Yunnan)

昭 武 通 寶

Chao-wu T'ung-pao

洪 化　吳 世 璠

Hung-hua (Wu Shih-fan)

洪 化 通 寶

Hung-hua T'ung-pao

裕 民　耿 精 忠

Yü-min (Keng Ching-chung)

裕 民 通 寶

Yü-min T'ung-pao

CH'ING DYNASTY

1644-1911AD

天 命

T'ien-ming (T'ai Tsu)
1616-1627AD

天 命 通 寶

T'ien-ming T'ung-pao

順 治

Shun-chih (Shih Tsu)
1644-1661AD (Peking)

順 治 通 寶

Shun-chih T'ung-pao

康 熙

K'ang-hsi (Sheng Tsu)
(Kangxi) 1662-1722AD

康 熙 通 寶

K'ang-hsi T'ung-pao

CHARACTERS

一	I, YI	士	Shih I	心	Hsin
二	Erh	合	Ho	宇	Yu
三	San	工	Kung	宙	Chou
四	Szu	主	Chu	來	Lai
五	Wu	川	Ch'uan	往	Wang
六	Liu	之	Chih	晋	Chin
七	Ch'i	正	Cheng	村	Ts'un
八	Pa	又	Yu	日	Jih
九	Chiu	山	Shan	列	Lieh
十	Shih	大	Ta	仁	Jen
主	Chung	中	Feng	手	Shang
順	Shun	云	Yun	手	Shou
天	T'ien	利	Li	穴	Kung
分	Fen				

SYCEE (INGOTS)

Prior to 1889 the general coinage issued by the Chinese government was the copper-alloy cash coin. Despite occasional short-lived experiments with silver and gold coinage, and disregarding paper money which tended to be unreliable, the government expected the people to get by solely with cash coins. This system worked well for individuals making purchases for themselves, but was unsatisfactory for trade and large business transactions, since a dollar's worth of cash coins weighed about four pounds. As a result, a private currency consisting of silver ingots, usually stamped by the firm which made them, came into use. These were the sycee ingots.

It is not known when these ingots first came into use. Some sources date them to the Yuan (Mongol) dynasty but they are certainly much older. Examples are known from as far back as the Han dynasty (206 BC - 220 AD) but prior to the Sung era (960 - 1280AD) they were used mainly for hoarding wealth. The development of commerce by the Sung dynasty, however, required the use of silver or gold to pay for large purchases. By the Mongol period (1280-1368) silver ingots and paper money had become the dominant currencies, especially for trade. The western explorers who traveled to China during this period (such as Marco Polo) mention both paper money and sycee but not a single one refers to cash coins.

During the Ming dynasty (1368-1644) trade fell off and the use of silver decreased. But toward the end of that dynasty, Dutch and British ships began a new China trade and sycee once again became common

The word sycee (pronounced "sigh - see") is a western corruption of the Chinese word hsi-szu ("fine silk") or hsi yin ("fine silver") and is first known to have appeared in the English language in the late 1600's. By the early 1700's the word appeared regularly in the records of the British East India Company. Westerners also called these ingots "boat money" or "shoe money" owing to the fact that the most common type of ingot resembles a Chinese shoe. The Chinese, however, called the ingots by a variety of names, the most common of which were yuan pao, wen-yin (fine silver) and yin-ting (silver ingot).

The ingots were cast in molds (giving them their characteristic shapes) and while the metal was still semi-liquid, the inscription was impressed. It was due to this procedure that the sides of some sycee are higher than the center. The manufacturers were usually silver firms, often referred to as lu fang's, and after the sycee was finished it was occasionally tested and marked by the kung ku (public assayer).

Sycee were not circulated as we understand it. One didn't usually carry a sycee to market and spend it. Usually the ingots were used as a means of carrying a large amount of money on trips (as we would carry $100 bills instead of $5 bills) or for storing wealth. Large transactions between merchants or banks were paid by means of crates of sycee - each containing 60 fifty tael ingots.

Sycee are known in a variety of shapes the most common of which are the shoe or boat shaped, drum shaped, and loaf shaped (rectangular or hourglass-shaped, with a generally flat surface). Other shapes include one that resembles a double headed axe (this is the oldest type known), one that is square and flat, and others that are "fancy" (in the form of fish, butterflies, leaves, etc.).

Sycee have no denominations as they were simply ingots that passed by weight. Most are in more or less standard weights, however, the most common being 1, 5, 10 and 50 taels. Other weights known include 1/10, 1/5, 1/4, 1/3, 1/2, 2/3, 72/100 (this is the weight of a dollar), 3/4, 2, 3, 4, 6, 7, 8 and 25 taels. Most of the pieces weighing less than 5 taels were used as gifts or souvenirs.

The actual weight of any given value of sycee varied considerably due to the fact that the tael was not a single weight but a general term for a wide range of local weight standards. The weight of the tael varied depending upon location and type of tael in question. For example in one town, the weight of a tael of rice, of silver and of stones may each be different. In addition, the fineness of silver also varied depending upon location and type of tael in question. It was not true, as westerners often wrote, that sycee were made of pure silver. For most purposes, a weight of 37 grams may be used for the tael.

Weights and Current Market Value of Sycee
(Weights are approximate)

1/2 Tael	17-19 grams	26.00
72/100 Tael	25-27 grams	36.00
1 Tael	35-38 grams	46.00
2 Taels	70-75 grams	70.00
3 Taels	100-140 grams	85.00
5 Taels	175-190 grams	110.00
7 Taels	240-260 grams	125.00
10 Taels	350-380 grams	250.00
25 Taels	895-925 grams	3500.
50 Taels	1790-1850 grams	2000.
50 Taels, square	1790-1850 grams	1600.

REFERENCE

Catalog reference Schjöth #: *Chinese Currency* by Fredrik Schjöth ©1965 by Virgil Hancock, published by Krause Publications, Iola, Wisconsin, U.S.A.

MING DYNASTY

1368 - 1644

Wan-li

Wanli, Shen Tsung

CAST COINAGE

KM# A4 CASH

Cast Bronze **Obv. Inscription:** "Wan-li T'ung-pao" **Rev:** "Ho" sideways above crescent at lower left **Note:** Prev. KM#4.1 Size varies: 24-26mm.

Date	Mintage	Good	VG	F	VF	XF
ND(1573-1619)	—	175	250	350	500	—

KM# 4.1 CASH

Cast Bronze **Obv. Inscription:** Wan-li T'ung-pao **Rev:** Small "T'ien" above **Note:** Size varies: 24-26mm.

Date	Mintage	Good	VG	F	VF	XF
ND(1573-1619)	—	10.00	14.00	20.00	30.00	—

KM# 4.2 CASH

Cast Bronze **Obv. Inscription:** "Wan-li T'ung-pao" **Rev:** Large "T'ien" above **Note:** Size varies: 24-26mm.

Date	Mintage	Good	VG	F	VF	XF
ND(1573-1619)	—	8.50	12.50	17.50	25.00	—

KM# 5.1 CASH

Cast Bronze **Obv. Inscription:** "Wan-li T'ung-pao" **Rev:** Small "Chêng" above **Note:** Size varies: 24-26mm. Prev. KM#5.

Date	Mintage	Good	VG	F	VF	XF
ND(1573-1619)	—	37.50	55.00	90.00	130	—

KM# 6 CASH

Cast Bronze **Obv. Inscription:** "Wan-li T'ung-pao" **Rev:** Plain **Note:** Reduced size varies: 20-22mm. Schjöth #1190.

Date	Mintage	Good	VG	F	VF	XF
ND(1573-1619)	—	1.00	2.00	3.00	4.00	—

KM# 7.1 CASH

Cast Bronze **Obv. Inscription:** "Wan-li T'ung-pao" **Rev:** "Li" at right **Note:** Schjöth #1191. "Li" = 1/1000 of a Tael. Prev. KM#7.

Date	Mintage	Good	VG	F	VF	XF
ND(1573-1619)	—	15.00	25.00	35.00	—	—

KM# 7.2 CASH

Cast Bronze **Obv. Inscription:** Wan-li T'ung-pao **Rev:** "Li" at right, "Erh" sideways at left

Date	Mintage	Good	VG	F	VF	XF
ND(1573-1619)	—	70.00	100	150	225	—

KM# 8 CASH

Cast Bronze **Obv. Inscription:** "Wan-li T'ung-pao" **Rev:** "Li" and "Ts'ai" **Note:** Size varies 24-26mm.

Date	Mintage	Good	VG	F	VF	XF
ND(1573-1619)	—	12.00	20.00	—	—	—

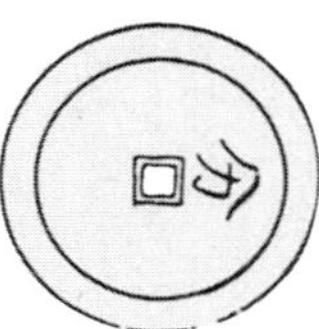

KM# 9 CASH

Cast Bronze **Obv. Inscription:** "Wan-li T'ung-pao" **Rev:** "Fen" sideways at right **Note:** Size varies: 24-26mm. Schjöth #1192.

Date	Mintage	Good	VG	F	VF	XF
ND(1573-1619)	—	6.00	8.50	12.50	18.50	—

KM# 10 CASH

Cast Bronze **Obv. Inscription:** "Wan-li T'ung-pao" **Note:** Schjöth #1198. Muled obverses, (error). Size varies: 24-26mm.

Date	Mintage	Good	VG	F	VF	XF
ND(1573-1619)	—	15.00	25.00	35.00	50.00	—

KM# 2.4 CASH

Cast Bronze **Obv. Inscription:** Wan-li T'ung-pao **Rev:** Inverted "Kung" at bottom **Mint:** Kung-pu Board of Public Works **Note:** Size varies: 24-26mm.

Date	Mintage	Good	VG	F	VF	XF
ND(1573-1619)	—	10.00	15.00	21.50	30.00	—

KM# 3.1 CASH

Cast Bronze **Obv. Inscription:** "Wan-li T'ung-pao" **Rev:** Small "Kung" above **Mint:** Kung-pu Board of Public Works **Note:** Size varies: 24-26mm. Schjöth #1189.

Date	Mintage	Good	VG	F	VF	XF
ND(1573-1619)	—	8.50	12.50	17.50	25.00	—

KM# 3.2 CASH

Cast Bronze **Obv. Inscription:** Wan-li T'ung-pao **Rev:** Medium "Kung" above **Mint:** Kung-pu Board of Public Works **Note:** Size varies: 24-26mm.

Date	Mintage	Good	VG	F	VF	XF
ND(1573-1619)	—	7.00	10.00	15.00	20.00	—

KM# 3.3 CASH

Cast Bronze **Obv. Inscription:** Wan-li T'ung-pao **Rev:** Large "Kung" above **Mint:** Kung-pu Board of Public Works **Note:** Size varies: 24-26mm.

Date	Mintage	Good	VG	F	VF	XF
ND(1573-1619)	—	14.00	20.00	30.00	42.50	—

KM# 5.2 CASH

Cast Bronze **Obv. Inscription:** Wan-li T'ung-pao **Rev:** Large "Chêng" above **Mint:** Kung-pu Board of Public Works **Note:** Size varies: 24-26mm.

Date	Mintage	Good	VG	F	VF	XF
ND(1573-1619)	—	35.00	50.00	70.00	100	—

KM# 13.1 2 CASH

Cast Bronze **Obv. Inscription:** "Wan-li T'ung-pao" **Rev:** Plain **Note:** Size varies: 27-29mm. Schjöth #1193.

Date	Mintage	Good	VG	F	VF	XF
ND(1573-1619)	—	10.00	17.50	25.00	37.50	—

KM# 13.2 2 CASH

Cast Bronze **Obv. Inscription:** "Wan-li T'ung-pao" **Rev:** Dot in crescent above **Note:** Size varies: 27-29mm.

Date	Mintage	Good	VG	F	VF	XF
ND(1573-1619)	—	20.00	30.00	45.00	62.50	—

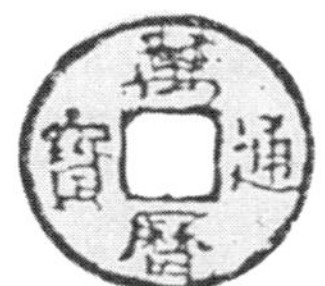

KM# 14 MACE

Cast Silver, 20 mm. **Obv. Inscription:** "Wan-li T'ung-pao" **Rev:** "K'uang-yin" **Note:** Previous number: KM#A13.

Date	Mintage	Good	VG	F	VF	XF
ND(1573-1619)	—	275	385	550	800	—

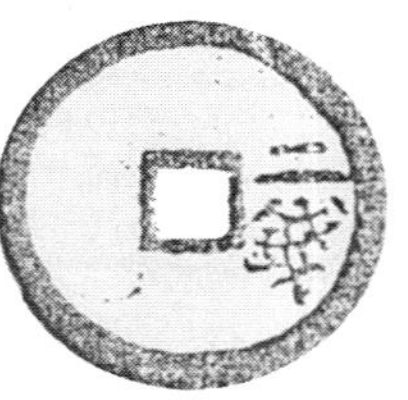

KM# 15 2 MACE

Cast Silver, 26 mm. **Obv. Inscription:** "Wan-li Nien-tsao" **Rev:** "Erh (2) Mace" at right **Note:** Previous number: KM#14.

Date	Mintage	Good	VG	F	VF	XF
ND(1573-1619)	—	1,400	2,000	3,500	5,000	—

KM# 16 4 MACE

Cast Silver, 31 mm. **Obv. Inscription:** "Wan-li T'ung-pao" **Rev. Inscription:** "K'uang-yin Szu (4)-Mace"

Date	Mintage	Good	VG	F	VF	XF
ND(1573-1619)	—	4,000	6,000	8,500	12,500	—

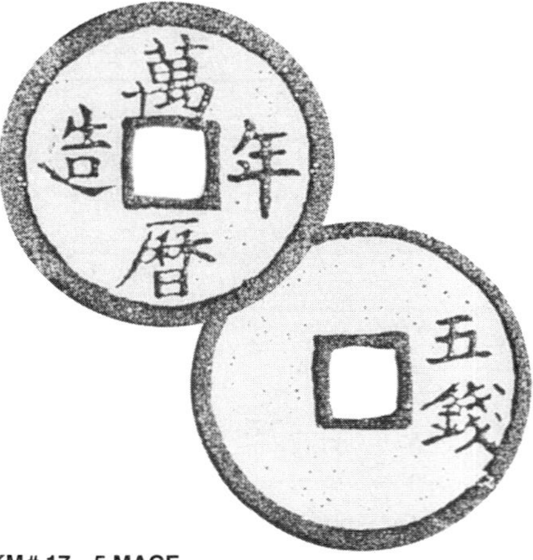

KM# 17 5 MACE

Cast Silver, 37 mm. **Obv. Inscription:** "Wan-li Nien-tsao" **Rev:** Wu (5) Mace at right

Date	Mintage	Good	VG	F	VF	XF
ND(1573-1619)	—	6,000	8,500	12,500	18,000	—

T'ai-ch'ang

Kwang Tsung

CAST COINAGE

KM# 20.1 CASH

Cast Copper **Obv. Inscription:** "Tai-ch'ang T'ung-pao" **Rev:** Plain **Note:** Schjöth #1199.

Date	Mintage	Good	VG	F	VF	XF
ND(1620)	—	6.00	10.00	15.00	22.50	—

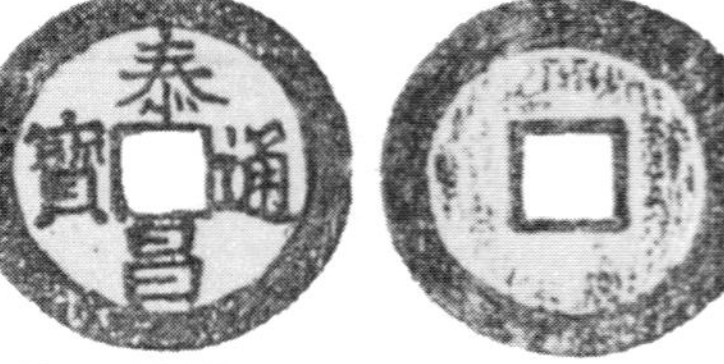

KM# 20.x CASH

Cast Copper **Obv:** Lower part of T'ai composed differently: hsin instead of shui **Note:** The "hsin-tai" is getting close to too rare to list.

Date	Mintage	Good	VG	F	VF	XF
ND(1620)	—	—	130	190	250	—

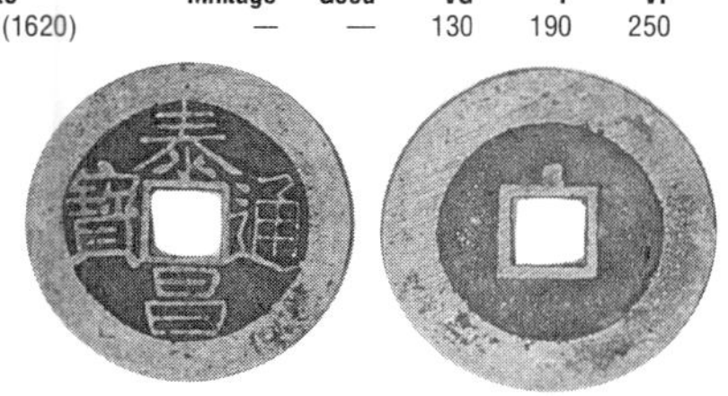

KM# 20.2 CASH
Cast Copper **Obv. Inscription:** "Tai-ch'ang T'ung-pao" **Rev:** Dot above **Note:** Schjöth #1200.

Date	Mintage	Good	VG	F	VF	XF
ND(1620)	—	8.00	14.00	20.00	28.50	—

KM# 20.3 CASH
Cast Copper **Obv. Inscription:** "Tai-ch'ang T'ung-pao" **Rev:** Crescent above

Date	Mintage	Good	VG	F	VF	XF
ND(1620)	—	15.00	25.00	35.00	50.00	—

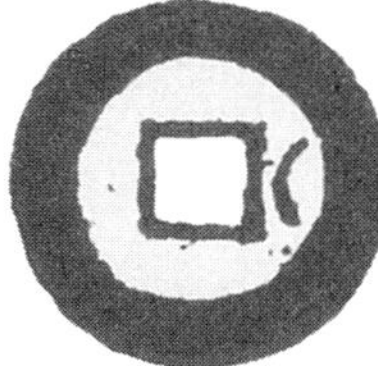

KM# 20.4 CASH
Cast Copper **Obv. Inscription:** "Tai-ch'ang T'ung-pao" **Rev:** Crescent at right

Date	Mintage	Good	VG	F	VF	XF
ND(1620)	—	15.00	25.00	35.00	50.00	—

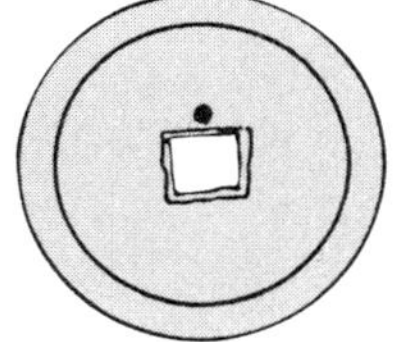

KM# 21 CASH
Cast Copper **Obv. Inscription:** "Tai-ch'ang T'ien-ch'i" **Rev:** Dot above **Note:** Schjöth #1201.

Date	Mintage	Good	VG	F	VF	XF
ND(1620)	—	25.00	40.00	60.00	85.00	—

T'ien-ch'i
Tianqi, Hsi Tsung
CAST COINAGE

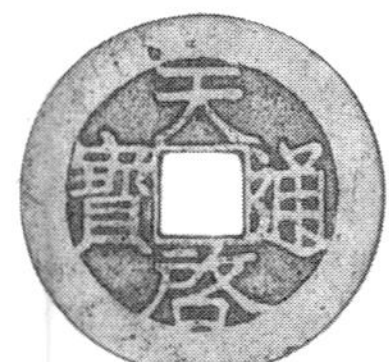
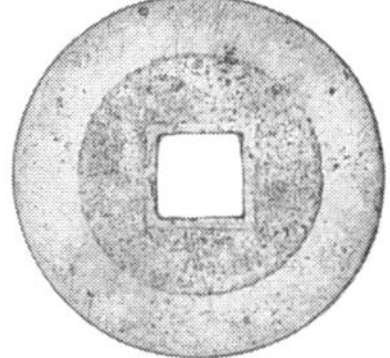

KM# 25.1 CASH
Cast Bronze **Obv. Inscription:** "T'ien-ch'i T'ung-pao" **Rev:** Plain **Note:** Schjöth #1202.

Date	Mintage	Good	VG	F	VF	XF
ND(1621-27)	—	2.25	3.75	5.50	7.50	—

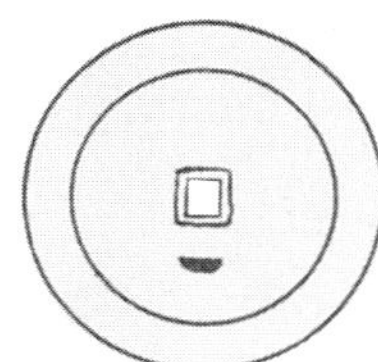

KM# 25.2 CASH
Cast Bronze **Obv. Inscription:** "T'ien-ch'i T'ung-pao" **Rev:** Crescent below **Note:** Schjöth #1203.

Date	Mintage	Good	VG	F	VF	XF
ND(1621-27)	—	2.25	3.75	5.50	7.50	—

KM# 25.3 CASH
Cast Bronze **Obv. Inscription:** "T'ien-ch'i T'ung-pao" **Rev:** Dot above

Date	Mintage	Good	VG	F	VF	XF
ND(1621-27)	—	2.25	3.75	5.50	7.50	—

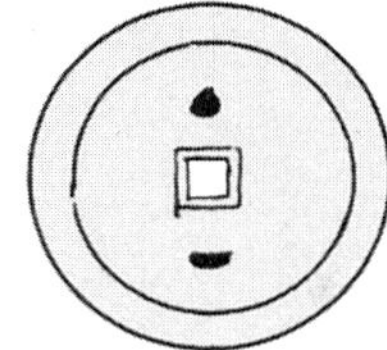

KM# 25.4 CASH
Cast Bronze **Obv. Inscription:** "T'ien-ch'i T'ung-pao" **Rev:** Dot above, crescent below **Note:** Schjöth #1204.

Date	Mintage	Good	VG	F	VF	XF
ND(1621-27)	—	6.00	10.00	15.00	20.00	—

KM# 25.5 CASH
Cast Bronze **Obv. Inscription:** "T'ien-ch'i T'ung-pao" **Rev:** Dot below **Note:** Schjöth #1205.

Date	Mintage	Good	VG	F	VF	XF
ND(1621-27)	—	2.25	3.75	5.50	7.50	—

KM# 25.6 CASH
Cast Bronze **Obv. Inscription:** "T'ien-ch'i T'ung-pao" **Rev:** Dot at right

Date	Mintage	Good	VG	F	VF	XF
ND(1621-27)	—	3.00	5.00	7.50	10.00	—

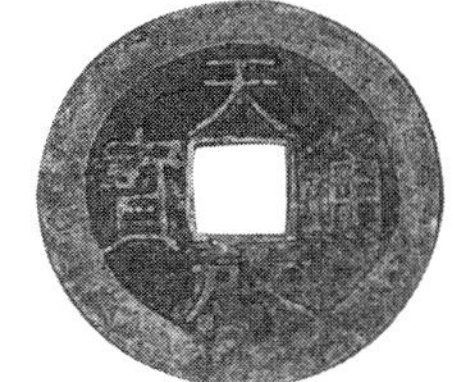

KM# 25.7 CASH
Cast Bronze **Obv. Inscription:** "T'ien-ch'i T'ung-pao" **Rev:** Circle at right **Note:** Schjöth #1206.

Date	Mintage	Good	VG	F	VF	XF
ND(1621-27)	—	2.25	3.75	5.50	7.50	—

新

KM# 31.4 CASH
Cast Bronze **Obv. Inscription:** "T'ien-ch'i T'ung-pao" **Rev:** "Hsin" above

Date	Mintage	Good	VG	F	VF	XF
ND(1621-27)	—	—	—	—	—	—

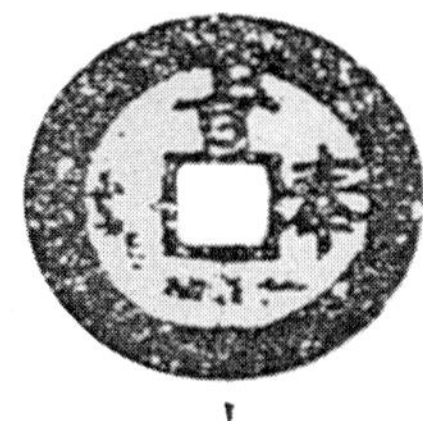

旨

KM# 31.5 CASH
Cast Bronze **Obv. Inscription:** "T'ien-ch'i T'ung-pao" **Rev:** "Chih" above and "Feng" right

Date	Mintage	Good	VG	F	VF	XF
ND(1621-27)	—	—	—	—	—	—

錢

KM# 31.6 CASH
Cast Bronze **Obv. Inscription:** "T'ien-ch'i T'ung-pao" **Rev:** "Ch'ien" left and "Yi" right

Date	Mintage	Good	VG	F	VF	XF
ND(1621-27)	—	25.00	45.00	75.00	—	—

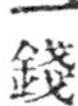

KM# 31.7 CASH
Cast Bronze **Obv. Inscription:** "T'ien-ch'i T'ung-pao" **Rev:** "Yi Ch'ien" right

Date	Mintage	Good	VG	F	VF	XF
ND(1621-27)	—	20.00	40.00	75.00	—	—

KM# 31.8 CASH
Cast Bronze **Obv. Inscription:** "T'ien-ch'i T'ung-pao" **Rev:** "Yi" above "Ch'ien" below

Date	Mintage	Good	VG	F	VF	XF
ND(1621-27)	—	—	—	—	—	—

KM# 31.9 CASH
Cast Bronze **Obv. Inscription:** "T'ien-ch'i T'ung-pao" **Rev:** "Yi Ch'ien" left

Date	Mintage	Good	VG	F	VF	XF
ND(1621-27)	—	—	—	—	—	—

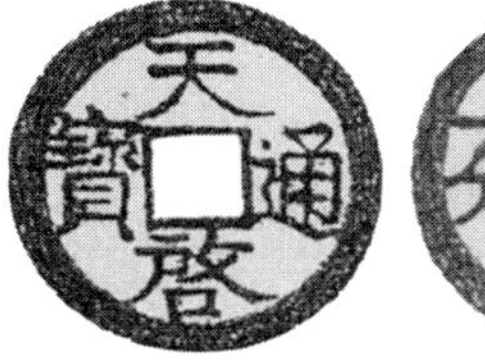
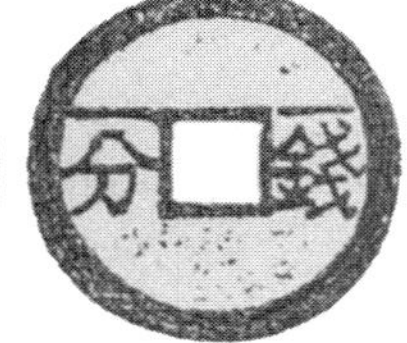
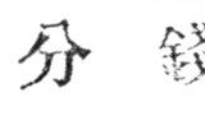

KM# 31.10 CASH
Cast Bronze **Obv. Inscription:** "T'ien-ch'i T'ung-pao" **Rev:** "Yi Fen" left, "Yi Ch'ien" right

Date	Mintage	Good	VG	F	VF	XF
ND(1621-27)	—	25.00	45.00	75.00	110	—

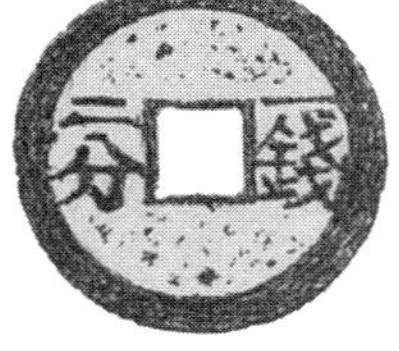
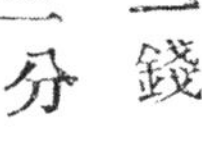

KM# 31.11 CASH
Cast Bronze **Obv. Inscription:** "T'ien-ch'i T'ung-pao" **Rev:** "Erh Fen" left, "Yi Ch'ien" right

Date	Mintage	Good	VG	F	VF	XF
ND(1621-27)	—	25.00	45.00	75.00	110	—

KM# 37.1 CASH

Cast Bronze **Obv. Inscription:** "T'ien-ch'i T'ung-pao" **Rev:** Narrow (5mm) "Yüan" above **Note:** Schjöth #1215.

Date	Mintage	Good	VG	F	VF	XF
ND(1621-27)	—	10.00	17.50	25.00	35.00	—

KM# 37.2 CASH

Cast Bronze **Obv. Inscription:** "T'ien-ch'i T'ung-pao" **Rev:** Wide (7mm) "Yüan" above **Note:** Schjöth #1215.

Date	Mintage	Good	VG	F	VF	XF
ND(1621-27)	—	10.00	17.50	25.00	35.00	—

KM# 25.8 CASH

Cast Bronze **Obv. Inscription:** T'ien-Ch'i T'ung-pao **Rev:** Circle at right, crescnet below

Date	Mintage	Good	VG	F	VF	XF
ND(1621-27)	—	2.25	3.75	5.50	7.50	—

KM# 32 CASH

Bronze, 23 mm. **Obv. Inscription:** T'ien-ch'i T'ung-pao **Rev. Inscription:** Yi Ch'ien

Date	Mintage	Good	VG	F	VF	XF
ND(1621-27)	—	3.00	7.00	12.00	26.00	—

KM# 38 CASH

Cast Bronze **Obv. Inscription:** "T'ien-ch'i T'ung-pao" **Rev:** "Yi Ch'ien" (1 Cash) **Note:** Schjöth #1216.

Date	Mintage	Good	VG	F	VF	XF
ND(1621-27)	—	13.00	21.00	30.00	40.00	—

KM# 39 CASH

Cast Bronze **Obv. Inscription:** "T'ien-ch'i T'ung-pao" **Rev:** "Chên" above

Date	Mintage	Good	VG	F	VF	XF
ND(1621-27)	—	25.00	42.50	60.00	85.00	—

KM# 35 CASH

Cast Bronze **Obv. Inscription:** "T'ien-ch'i T'ung-pao" **Rev:** "Chê" above **Mint:** Chêkiang **Note:** Schjöth #1213.

Date	Mintage	Good	VG	F	VF	XF
ND(1621-27)	—	10.00	15.00	22.50	30.00	—

Note: Also see Sch.#1213A

KM# 31.2 CASH

Cast Bronze **Obv. Inscription:** "T'ien-ch'i T'ung-pao" **Rev:** "Ching" above **Mint:** Ching

Date	Mintage	Good	VG	F	VF	XF
ND(1621-27)	—	40.00	70.00	150	225	—

KM# 26 CASH

Cast Bronze **Obv. Inscription:** "T'ien-ch'i T'ung-pao" **Rev:** "Hu" above **Mint:** Hu-pu Board of Revenue **Note:** Schjöth #1207-08.

Date	Mintage	Good	VG	F	VF	XF
ND(1621-27)	—	3.00	5.00	7.50	10.00	—

KM# 27 CASH

Cast Bronze **Obv. Inscription:** "T'ien-ch'i T'ung-pao" **Rev:** "Kung" above **Mint:** Kung-pu Board of Public Works **Note:** Schjöth #1209.

Date	Mintage	Good	VG	F	VF	XF
ND(1621-27)	—	3.00	5.00	7.50	10.00	—

Note: See also Sch.#1210

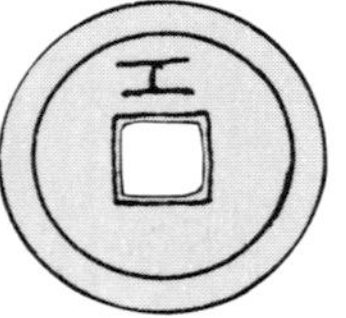

KM# 30.1 CASH

Cast Bronze **Obv. Inscription:** "T'ien-ch'i T'ung-pao" **Rev:** "Kung" above **Mint:** Kung-pu Board of Public Works **Note:** Schjöth #1210. Reduced size: 21-23mm.

Date	Mintage	Good	VG	F	VF	XF
ND(1621-27)	—	3.00	5.00	7.50	10.00	—

Note: See also Sch.#1209

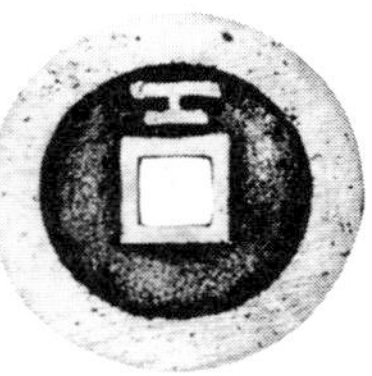

KM# 30.2 CASH

Cast Bronze **Obv. Inscription:** "T'ien-ch'i T'ung-pao" **Rev:** "Kung" below **Mint:** Kung-pu Board of Public Works **Note:** Schjöth #1211.

Date	Mintage	Good	VG	F	VF	XF
ND(1621-27)	—	3.00	5.00	7.50	12.50	—

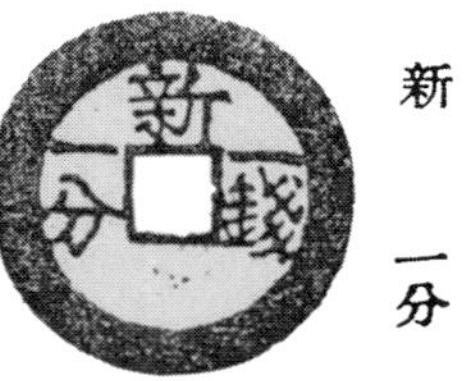

KM# 31.1 CASH

Cast Bronze **Obv. Inscription:** "T'ien-ch'i T'ung-pao" **Rev:** "Kung" below **Rev. Legend:** "Hsin yi-ch'ien yi-fen" **Mint:** Kung-pu Board of Public Works **Note:** Schjöth #1212.

Date	Mintage	Good	VG	F	VF	XF
ND(1621-27)	—	25.00	42.50	60.00	80.00	—

密

KM# 31.3 CASH

Cast Bronze **Obv. Inscription:** "T'ien-ch'i T'ung-pao" **Rev:** "Mi" above **Mint:** Miyün

Date	Mintage	Good	VG	F	VF	XF
ND(1621-27)	—	30.00	50.00	100	140	—

KM# 36 CASH

Cast Bronze **Obv. Inscription:** "T'ien-ch'i T'ung-pao" **Rev:** "Yün" above **Mint:** Yünnan Fu **Note:** Schjöth #1214.

Date	Mintage	Good	VG	F	VF	XF
ND(1621-27)	—	4.50	7.50	11.00	15.00	—

KM# 36A CASH

Cast Bronze **Obv. Inscription:** "T'ien-ch'i T'ung-pao" **Rev:** "Yün" above **Mint:** Yünnan Fu **Note:** Schjöth #1214A.

Date	Mintage	Good	VG	F	VF	XF
ND(1621-27)	—	—	—	—	—	—

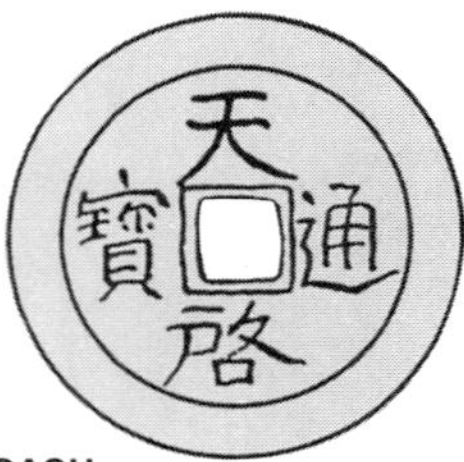

KM# 41 2 CASH

Cast Bronze **Obv. Inscription:** "T'ien-ch'i T'ung-pao" **Rev:** Blank without rim **Note:** Schjöth #1217. Size varies: 30-32mm.

Date	Mintage	Good	VG	F	VF	XF
ND(1621-27)	—	7.50	10.00	15.00	20.00	—

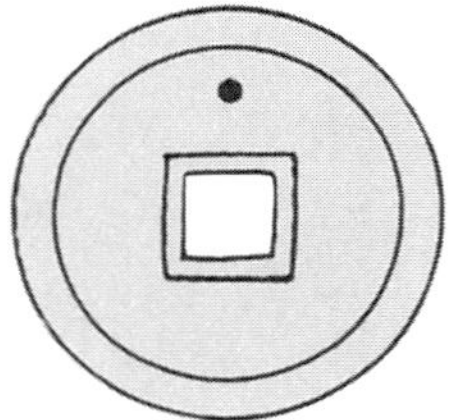

KM# 42.1 2 CASH

Cast Bronze **Obv. Inscription:** "T'ien-ch'i T'ung-pao" **Rev:** Dot above **Note:** Schjöth #1218.

Date	Mintage	Good	VG	F	VF	XF
ND(1621-27)	—	10.00	15.00	20.00	30.00	—

KM# 42.2 2 CASH

Cast Bronze **Obv. Inscription:** "T'ien-ch'i T'ung-pao" **Rev:** Dot below

Date	Mintage	Good	VG	F	VF	XF
ND(1621-27)	—	10.00	15.00	20.00	30.00	—

KM# 42.3 2 CASH

Cast Bronze **Obv. Inscription:** "T'ien-ch'i T'ung-pao" **Rev:** Dot right

Date	Mintage	Good	VG	F	VF	XF
ND(1621-27)	—	10.00	15.00	20.00	30.00	—

KM# A43 2 CASH

Cast Bronze **Obv. Inscription:** "T'ien-ch'i T'ung-pao" **Note:** Muled obverses, error. Schjöth #1219.

Date	Mintage	Good	VG	F	VF	XF
ND(1621-27)	—	—	—	—	—	—

KM# 43 2 CASH

Cast Bronze **Obv. Inscription:** "T'ien-ch'i T'ung-pao" **Rev:** "Erh" (two) above, dot below

Date	Mintage	Good	VG	F	VF	XF
ND(1621-27)	—	25.00	45.00	85.00	—	—

KM# 28 2 CASH

Cast Bronze **Obv. Inscription:** "T'ien-ch'i T'ung-pao" **Rev:** "Chê" above **Mint:** Chê **Note:** Schjöth #1213A.

Date	Mintage	Good	VG	F	VF	XF
ND(1621-27) Rare	—	—	—	—	—	—

Note: See also Schjöth #1213

KM# 45 10 CASH

Cast Brass **Obv. Inscription:** "T'ien-ch'i T'ung-pao" **Rev:** Plain **Note:** Schjöth #1220.

Date	Mintage	Good	VG	F	VF	XF
ND(1621-27)	—	10.00	15.00	22.50	30.00	—

KM# A46 10 CASH

Cast Brass **Obv. Inscription:** "T'ien-ch'i T'ung-pao" **Rev. Inscription:** "T'ien-ch'i T'ung-pao" **Note:** Mule. Two obverses of KM#45.

Date	Mintage	Good	VG	F	VF	XF
ND(1621-27)	—	—	—	—	—	—

KM# 48 10 CASH

Cast Brass **Obv. Inscription:** "T'ien-ch'i T'ung-pao" **Rev:** "Shih" (ten) below

Date	Mintage	Good	VG	F	VF	XF
ND(1621-27)	—	12.50	22.50	40.00	65.00	—

KM# 49.2 10 CASH

Cast Brass **Obv. Inscription:** "T'ien-ch'i T'ung-pao" **Rev:** "Shih" (ten) above, "Yi-liang" (one tael) right, 6 millimeter circle left, crescent below

Date	Mintage	Good	VG	F	VF	XF
ND(1621-27)	—	15.00	30.00	60.00	100	—

KM# 46 10 CASH

Cast Brass **Obv. Inscription:** "T'ien-ch'i T'ung-pao" **Rev:** "Shih" (ten) above **Mint:** Chê **Note:** Schjöth #1221.

Date	Mintage	Good	VG	F	VF	XF
ND(1621-27)	—	10.00	17.50	25.00	35.00	—

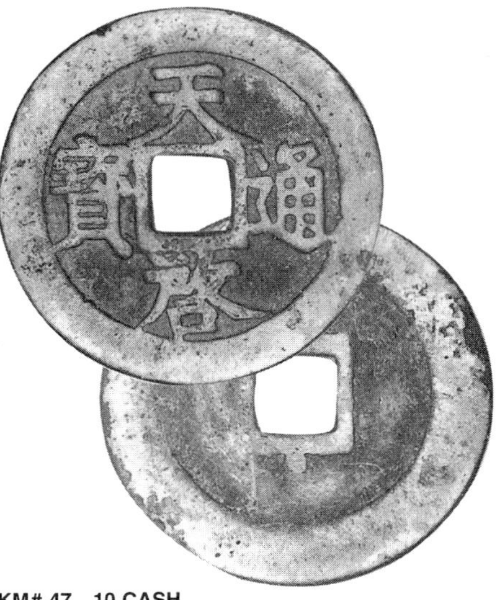

KM# 47 10 CASH

Cast Brass **Obv. Inscription:** "T'ien-ch'i T'ung-pao" **Rev:** "Shih" (ten) above, dot below **Mint:** Chê **Note:** Schjöth #1222.

Date	Mintage	Good	VG	F	VF	XF
ND(1621-27)	—	12.50	22.50	32.50	45.00	—

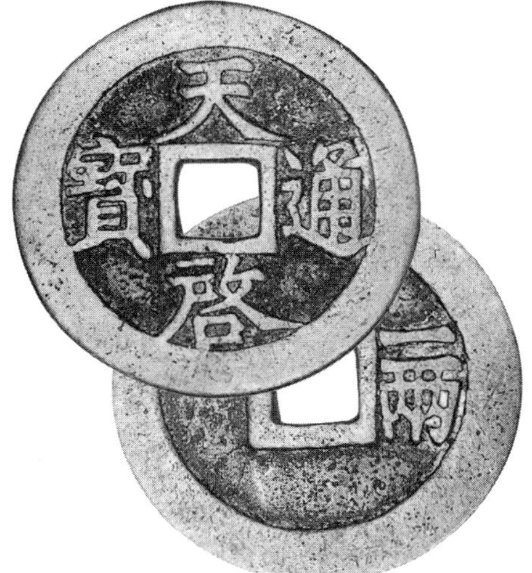

KM# 49.1 10 CASH

Cast Brass **Obv. Inscription:** "T'ien-ch'i T'ung-pao" **Rev:** "Shih" (ten) above, "Yi-liang" (one tael) at right **Mint:** Chê **Note:** Schjöth #1223. Rim size and character varieties exist.

Date	Mintage	Good	VG	F	VF	XF
ND(1621-27)	—	10.00	15.00	40.00	65.00	—

KM# 51 10 CASH

Cast Brass **Obv. Inscription:** "T'ien-ch'i T'ung-pao" **Rev:** "Chên" above, "Shih" (ten) below **Mint:** Chênting **Note:** Schjöth #1225.

Date	Mintage	Good	VG	F	VF	XF
ND(1621-27)	—	65.00	105	150	200	—

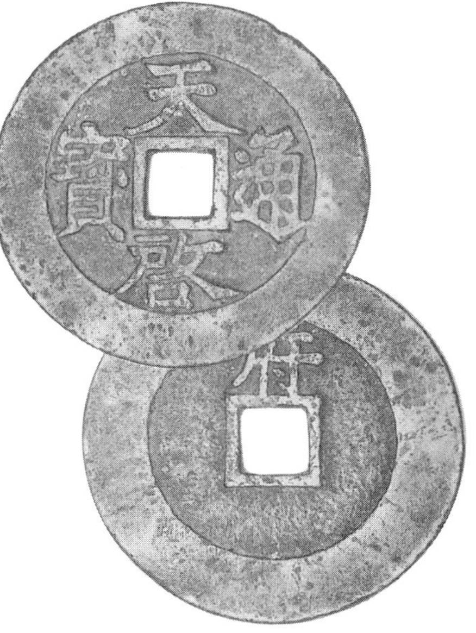

KM# 50 10 CASH

Cast Brass **Obv. Inscription:** "T'ien-ch'i T'ung-pao" **Rev:** "Fu" above **Mint:** Fu **Note:** Schjöth #1224.

Date	Mintage	Good	VG	F	VF	XF
ND(1621-27)	—	42.50	75.00	110	150	—

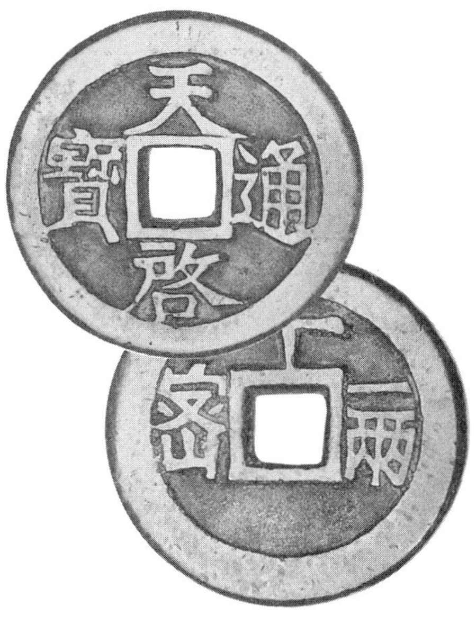

KM# 49.3 10 CASH

Cast Brass **Obv. Inscription:** "T'ien-ch'i T'ung-pao" **Rev:** "Shih" (ten) above, "Yi-liang" (one tael) at right, 6mm circle left, crescent below **Rev. Inscription:** Shih, Yi-liang, Mi **Mint:** Miyün

Date	Mintage	Good	VG	F	VF	XF
ND(1621-27)	—	75.00	100	200	—	—

Ch'ung-chên

Chongzhen, Chuang Lieh

CAST COINAGE

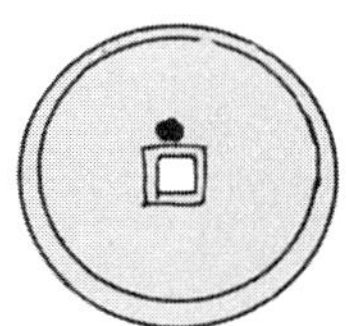

KM# 58.2 CASH

Cast Bronze **Obv. Inscription:** "Ch'ung-chên T'ung-pao" **Rev:** Dot above near square hole **Note:** Schjöth #1233.

Date	Mintage	Good	VG	F	VF	XF
ND(1628-44)	—	2.50	5.00	6.50	10.00	—

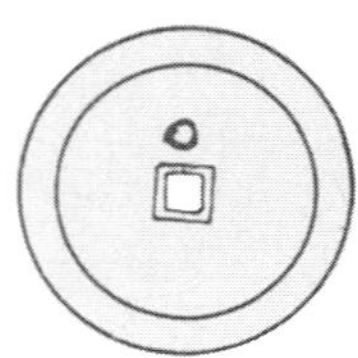

KM# 58.3 CASH
Cast Bronze **Obv. Inscription:** "Ch'ung-chên T'ung-pao"
Rev: Circle above **Note:** Schjöth #1234.

Date	Mintage	Good	VG	F	VF	XF
ND(1628-44)	—	3.00	10.00	15.00	20.00	—

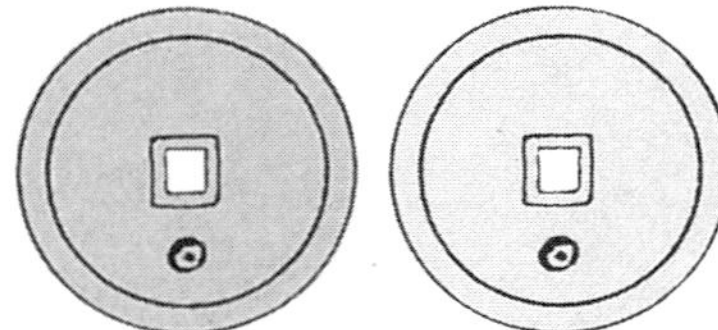

KM# 58.4 CASH
Cast Bronze **Obv. Inscription:** "Ch'ung-chên T'ung-pao"
Rev: Dot in circle below **Note:** Schjöth #1235.

Date	Mintage	Good	VG	F	VF	XF
ND(1628-44)	—	5.50	12.00	18.00	25.00	—

KM# 58.5 CASH
Cast Bronze **Obv. Inscription:** "Ch'ung-chên T'ung-pao"
Rev: Dot in circle above

Date	Mintage	Good	VG	F	VF	XF
ND(1628-44)	—	6.00	10.00	15.00	20.00	—

KM# 59 CASH
Cast Bronze **Obv. Inscription:** "Ch'ung-chên T'ung-pao"
Rev: Cyclical date "Chia" above **Note:** Schjöth #1236.

Date	Mintage	Good	VG	F	VF	XF
ND(1634-35)	—	10.00	20.00	30.00	40.00	—

KM# 60 CASH
Cast Bronze **Obv. Inscription:** "Ch'ung-chên T'ung-pao"
Rev: Cyclical date "Yi" above **Note:** Schjöth #1237.

Date	Mintage	Good	VG	F	VF	XF
ND(1636-36)	—	7.50	12.00	15.00	25.00	—

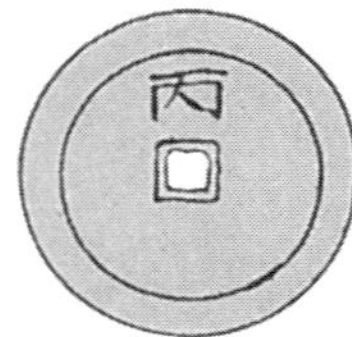

KM# 61 CASH
Cast Bronze **Obv. Inscription:** "Ch'ung-chên T'ung-pao"
Rev: Cyclical date "Ping" above **Note:** Schjöth #1238.

Date	Mintage	Good	VG	F	VF	XF
ND(1636-37)	—	15.00	25.00	35.00	50.00	—

KM# A62 CASH
Cast Bronze **Obv. Inscription:** "Ch'ung-chên T'ung-pao"
Rev: Cyclical date "Ting" above

Date	Mintage	Good	VG	F	VF	XF
ND(1637-38)	—	15.00	20.00	30.00	40.00	—

 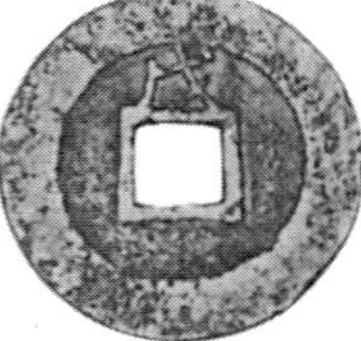

KM# 62 CASH
Cast Bronze **Obv. Inscription:** "Ch'ung-chên T'ung-pao"
Rev: Cyclical date "Wu" above **Note:** Schjöth #1239.

Date	Mintage	Good	VG	F	VF	XF
ND(1638-39)	—	10.00	20.00	30.00	40.00	—

 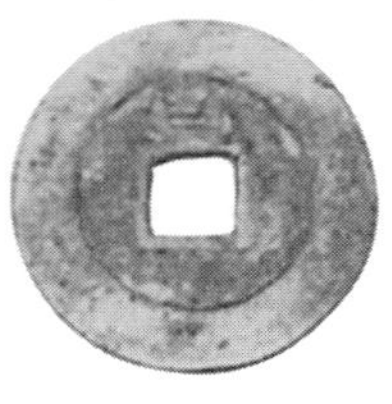

KM# 63 CASH
Cast Bronze **Obv. Inscription:** "Ch'ung-chên T'ung-pao"
Rev: Cyclical date "Chi" above **Note:** Schjöth #1240.

Date	Mintage	Good	VG	F	VF	XF
ND(1639-40)	—	15.00	20.00	30.00	40.00	—

KM# A64 CASH
Cast Bronze **Obv. Inscription:** "Ch'ung-chên T'ung-pao"
Rev: Cyclical date "Keng" above

Date	Mintage	Good	VG	F	VF	XF
ND(1640-41)	—	15.00	20.00	30.00	40.00	—

KM# 64 CASH
Cast Bronze **Obv. Inscription:** "Ch'ung-chên T'ung-pao"
Rev: "Yi" above, "Ch'ien" below **Note:** Schjöth #1241.

Date	Mintage	Good	VG	F	VF	XF
ND(1628-44)	—	10.00	17.50	25.00	35.00	—

 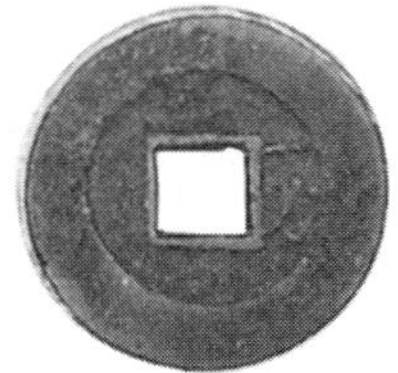

KM# 65 CASH
Cast Bronze **Obv. Inscription:** "Ch'ung-chên T'ung-pao"
Rev: "Yi-ch'ien" at right **Note:** Schjöth #1242.

Date	Mintage	Good	VG	F	VF	XF
ND(1628-44)	—	10.00	14.00	20.00	28.00	—

 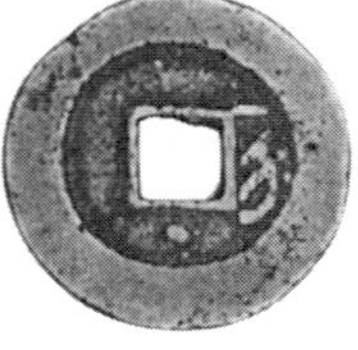

KM# 66 CASH
Cast Bronze **Obv. Inscription:** "Ch'ung-chên T'ung-pao"
Rev: "Yi Ch'ien" at right, dot below **Note:** Schjöth #1243.

Date	Mintage	Good	VG	F	VF	XF
ND(1628-44)	—	6.00	10.00	15.00	20.00	—

KM# 67 CASH
Cast Bronze **Obv. Inscription:** "Ch'ung-chên T'ung-pao"
Rev: "Pa (eight) Ch'ien" at right **Note:** Schjöth #1244.

Date	Mintage	Good	VG	F	VF	XF
ND(1628-44)	—	10.00	17.50	25.00	35.00	—

KM# 68.1 CASH
Cast Bronze **Obv. Inscription:** "Ch'ung-chên T'ung-pao"
Rev: "Pa" (eight) below **Note:** Schjöth #1245.

Date	Mintage	Good	VG	F	VF	XF
ND(1628-44)	—	6.00	10.00	15.00	20.00	—

KM# 68.2 CASH
Cast Bronze **Obv. Inscription:** "Ch'ung-chên T'ung-pao"
Rev: Dot above, "Pa" (eight) below **Note:** Schjöth #1246.

Date	Mintage	Good	VG	F	VF	XF
ND(1628-44)	—	10.00	17.50	25.00	35.00	—

KM# 74 CASH
Cast Bronze **Obv. Inscription:** "Ch'ung-chên T'ung-pao"
Rev: "Chü" above **Note:** Schjöth #1254.

Date	Mintage	Good	VG	F	VF	XF
ND(1628-44)	—	8.50	14.00	20.00	28.00	—

官

KM# 75.1 CASH
Cast Bronze **Obv. Inscription:** "Ch'ung-chên T'ung-pao"
Rev: "Kuan" above **Note:** Schjöth #1255.

Date	Mintage	Good	VG	F	VF	XF
ND(1628-44)	—	9.00	15.00	21.00	30.00	—

KM# 75.2 CASH
Cast Bronze **Obv. Inscription:** "Ch'ung-chên T'ung-pao"
Rev: "Kuan" above, crescent below **Note:** Schjöth #1256.

Date	Mintage	Good	VG	F	VF	XF
ND(1628-44)	—	9.00	15.00	21.00	30.00	—

KM# 76 CASH
Cast Bronze **Obv. Inscription:** "Ch'ung-chên T'ung-pao"
Rev: "Hsin" above **Note:** Schjöth #1257.

Date	Mintage	Good	VG	F	VF	XF
ND(1628-44)	—	8.00	13.00	16.00	26.00	—

KM# 91 CASH
Cast Bronze **Obv. Inscription:** "Ch'ung-chên T'ung-pao"
Rev: "Ch'ing" above, "Chung" below **Note:** Schjöth #1273.

Date	Mintage	Good	VG	F	VF	XF
ND(1628-44)	—	15.00	25.00	30.00	50.00	—

KM# 93 CASH

Cast Bronze **Obv. Inscription:** "Ch'ung-chên T'ung-pao" **Rev:** "Chi" below **Note:** Schjöth #1275.

Date	Mintage	Good	VG	F	VF	XF
ND(1628-44)	—	7.50	12.50	15.00	25.00	—

KM# A95 CASH

Cast Bronze **Obv. Inscription:** "Ch'ung-chên T'ung-pao" **Rev:** "Ping" (meaning unknown)

Date	Mintage	Good	VG	F	VF	XF
ND(1628-44)	—	25.00	35.00	50.00	—	—

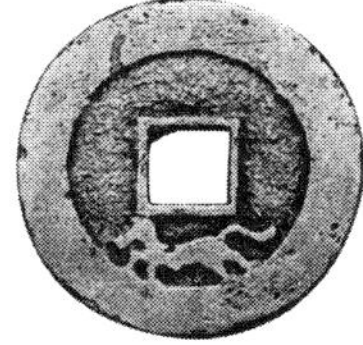

KM# 95.1 CASH

Cast Bronze, 23 mm. **Obv. Inscription:** "Ch'ung-chên T'ung-pao" **Rev:** Galloping horse below **Note:** Schjöth #1277.

Date	Mintage	Good	VG	F	VF	XF
ND(1628-44)	—	20.00	32.50	45.00	60.00	—

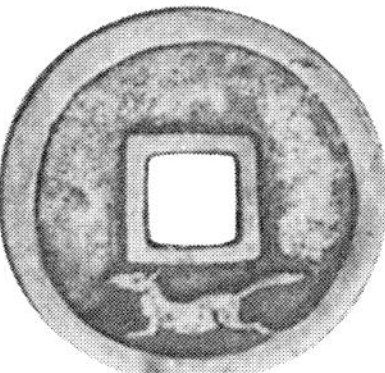

KM# 95.2 CASH

Cast Bronze, 26 mm. **Obv. Inscription:** "Ch'ung-chên T'ung-pao" **Rev:** Galloping horse left deviating in style below **Note:** Schjöth #1278. Privately made amulet.

Date	Mintage	Good	VG	F	VF	XF
ND(1628-44)	—	20.00	32.50	45.00	60.00	—

KM# 95.3 CASH

Cast Bronze **Obv. Inscription:** "Ch'ung-chên T'ung-pao" **Rev:** Horse right above and horse left below

Date	Mintage	Good	VG	F	VF	XF
ND(1628-44)	—	40.00	70.00	100	—	—

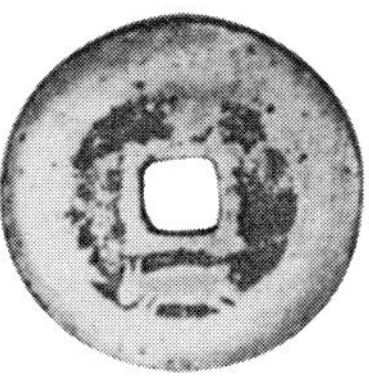

KM# 96 CASH

Cast Bronze **Obv. Inscription:** "Ch'ung-chên T'ung-pao" **Rev:** Rabbit below

Date	Mintage	Good	VG	F	VF	XF
ND(1628-44)	—	—	—	—	—	—

KM# 97 CASH

Cast Bronze **Obv. Inscription:** "Ch'ung-chên T'ung-pao" **Rev. Inscription:** Ch'ung-chên T'ung-pao **Note:** Muled obverses (error).

Date	Mintage	Good	VG	F	VF	XF
ND(1628-44)	—	32.50	52.50	75.00	100	—

KM# A98 CASH

Cast Bronze, 25 mm. **Rev. Inscription:** "Chih" above

Date	Mintage	Good	VG	F	VF	XF
ND(1628-44)	—	60.00	100	140	200	—

KM# 98 CASH

Cast Bronze, 25 mm. **Rev. Inscription:** "Tai" above, "Ping" below

Date	Mintage	Good	VG	F	VF	XF
ND(1628-44)	—	6.00	10.00	14.00	20.00	—

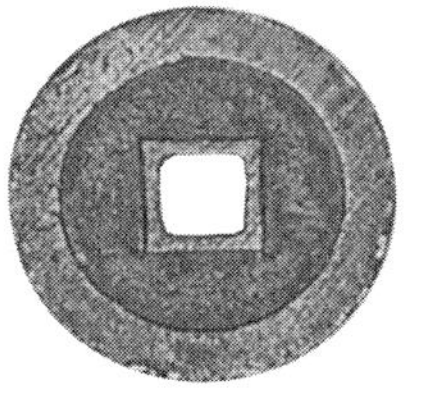

KM# 55.1 CASH

Cast Bronze **Obv:** Characters deviating in style **Obv. Inscription:** "Ch'ung-chên T'ung-pao" **Rev:** Plain **Mint:** Board of Public Works **Note:** Schjöth #1228.

Date	Mintage	Good	VG	F	VF	XF
ND(1628-44)	—	1.50	4.00	5.50	8.00	—

KM# 92 CASH

Cast Bronze **Obv. Inscription:** "Ch'ung-chên T'ung-pao" **Rev:** "Chi" above **Mint:** Board of Public Works **Note:** Schjöth #1274.

Date	Mintage	Good	VG	F	VF	XF
ND(1628-44)	—	10.00	15.00	20.00	30.00	—

KM# A94 CASH

Cast Bronze **Obv. Inscription:** Ch'ung-chên T'ung-pao **Rev:** Chiu above **Mint:** Board of Revenue **Note:** H20.268.

Date	Mintage	Good	VG	F	VF	XF
ND(1628-44)	—	40.00	80.00	135	—	—

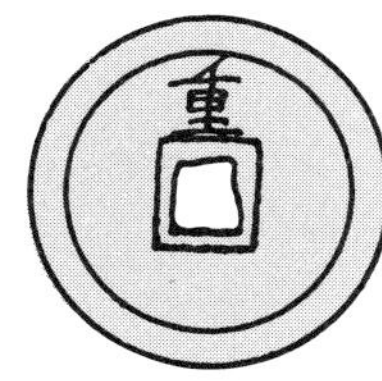

重

KM# 79.1 CASH

Cast Bronze **Obv. Inscription:** "Ch'ung-chên T'ung-pao" **Rev:** "Ch'ung" above **Mint:** Ch'ungch'ing **Note:** Schjöth #1260.

Date	Mintage	Good	VG	F	VF	XF
ND(1628-44)	—	6.00	10.00	15.00	20.00	—

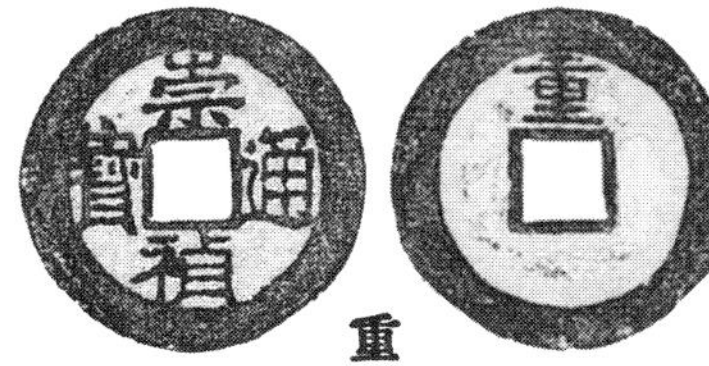

重

KM# 79.2 CASH

Cast Bronze **Obv. Inscription:** "Ch'ung-chên T'ung-pao" **Rev:** "Ch'ung" above deviating in style **Mint:** Ch'ungch'ing **Note:** Schjöth #1261.

Date	Mintage	Good	VG	F	VF	XF
ND(1628-44)	—	6.00	10.00	15.00	20.00	—

KM# 79.3 CASH

Cast Bronze **Obv. Inscription:** "Ch'ung-chên T'ung-pao" **Rev:** "Ch'ung" above, dot below **Mint:** Ch'ungch'ing

Date	Mintage	Good	VG	F	VF	XF
ND(1628-44)	—	6.00	10.00	15.00	20.00	—

KM# 79.4 CASH

Cast Bronze **Obv. Inscription:** "Ch'ung-chên T'ung-pao" **Rev:** "Ch'ung" above, crescent below **Mint:** Ch'ungch'ing

Date	Mintage	Good	VG	F	VF	XF
ND(1628-44)	—	6.00	10.00	15.00	20.00	—

KM# 79.5 CASH

Cast Bronze **Obv. Inscription:** "Ch'ung-chên T'ung-pao" **Rev:** "Ch'ung" above, "Yi-Ch'ien" right, crescent below **Mint:** Ch'ungch'ing

Date	Mintage	Good	VG	F	VF	XF
ND(1628-44)	—	10.00	15.00	25.00	—	—

KM# 77 CASH

Cast Bronze **Obv. Inscription:** "Ch'ung-chên T'ung-pao" **Rev:** "Chiang" above **Mint:** Chiangning **Note:** Schjöth #1258.

Date	Mintage	Good	VG	F	VF	XF
ND(1628-44)	—	8.00	13.00	16.00	26.00	—

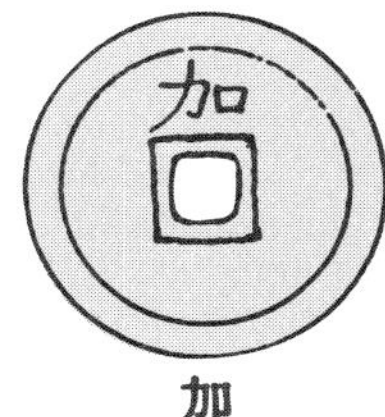

加

KM# 80.1 CASH

Cast Bronze **Obv. Inscription:** "Ch'ung-chên T'ung-pao" **Rev:** "Chia" above **Mint:** Chiating Fu **Note:** Schjöth #1262.

Date	Mintage	Good	VG	F	VF	XF
ND(1628-44)	—	8.50	14.00	20.00	28.00	—

KM# 80.2 CASH

Cast Bronze **Obv. Inscription:** "Ch'ung-chên T'ung-pao" **Rev:** Dot above, "Chia" below **Mint:** Chiating Fu

Date	Mintage	Good	VG	F	VF	XF
ND(1628-44)	—	20.00	30.00	40.00	—	—

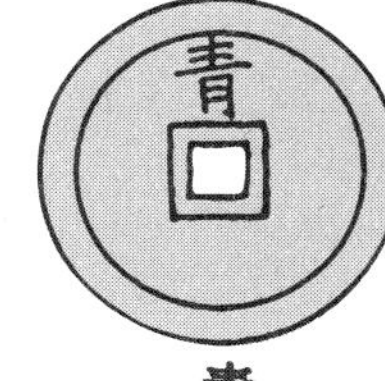

青

KM# 85 CASH

Cast Bronze **Obv. Inscription:** "Ch'ung-chên T'ung-pao" **Rev:** "Ch'ing" above **Mint:** Chingchou **Note:** Schjöth #1268.

Date	Mintage	Good	VG	F	VF	XF
ND(1628-44)	—	9.00	15.00	21.00	30.00	—

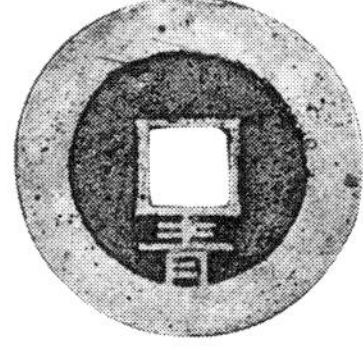

KM# 86 CASH

Cast Bronze **Obv. Inscription:** "Ch'ung-chên T'ung-pao" **Rev:** "Ch'ing" below **Mint:** Chingchou

Date	Mintage	Good	VG	F	VF	XF
ND(1628-44)	—	8.50	14.00	20.00	28.00	—

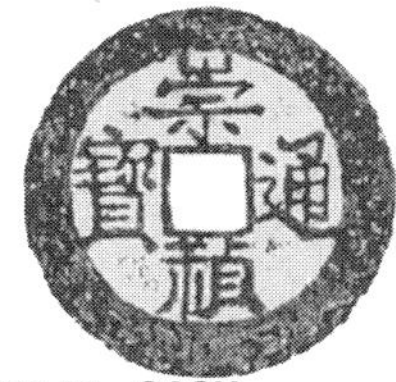

KM# 83 CASH

Cast Bronze **Obv. Inscription:** "Ch'ung-chên T'ung-pao" **Rev:** "Chung" above **Mint:** Chungchou **Note:** Schjöth #1266.

Date	Mintage	Good	VG	F	VF	XF
ND(1628-44)	—	15.00	25.00	35.00	50.00	—

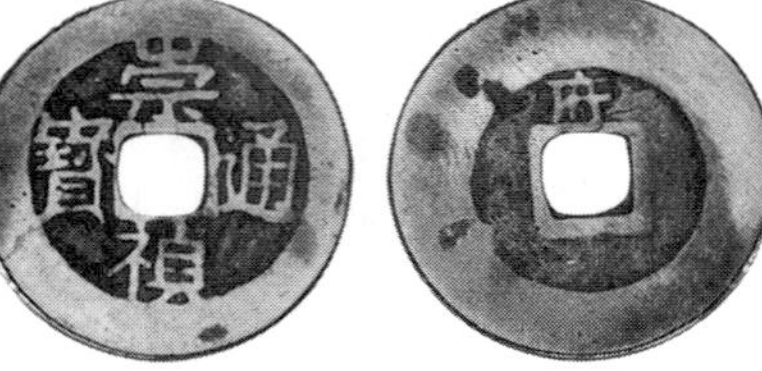

KM# 90 CASH
Cast Bronze **Obv. Inscription:** "Ch'ung-chên T'ung-pao" **Rev:** "Fu" above **Mint:** Hsüan "fu" Ch'êng **Note:** Schjöth #1272.

Date	Mintage	Good	VG	F	VF	XF
ND(1628-44)	—	10.00	15.00	20.00	30.00	—

KM# 69 CASH
Cast Bronze **Obv. Inscription:** "Ch'ung-chên T'ung-pao" **Rev:** "Hu" above **Mint:** Hu-pu Board of Revenue **Note:** Schjöth #1247-48.

Date	Mintage	Good	VG	F	VF	XF
ND(1628-44)	—	6.00	10.00	15.00	20.00	—

KM# 70 CASH
Cast Bronze **Obv. Inscription:** "Ch'ung-chên T'ung-pao" **Rev:** "Hu" below **Mint:** Hu-pu Board of Revenue **Note:** Schjöth #1249.

Date	Mintage	Good	VG	F	VF	XF
ND(1628-44)	—	5.50	9.00	13.00	18.00	—

KM# 71 CASH
Cast Bronze **Obv. Inscription:** "Ch'ung-chên T'ung-pao" **Rev:** "Hu" above, "Chiu" below **Mint:** Hu-pu Board of Revenue **Note:** Schjöth #1250.

Date	Mintage	Good	VG	F	VF	XF
ND(1628-44)	—	10.00	17.50	25.00	35.00	—

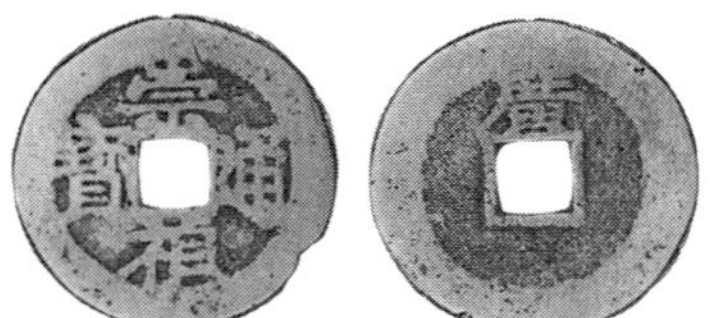

KM# 88.1 CASH
Cast Bronze **Obv. Inscription:** "Ch'ung-chên T'ung-pao" **Rev:** "Kuang" above **Mint:** Kuangchou Fu **Note:** Schjöth #1270.

Date	Mintage	Good	VG	F	VF	XF
ND(1628-44)	—	7.50	12.50	18.00	25.00	—

KM# 88.2 CASH
Cast Copper **Obv. Inscription:** "Ch'ung-chên T'ung-pao" **Rev:** Kuang below **Mint:** Kuangchou Fu **Note:** Schjöth #1270.

Date	Mintage	Good	VG	F	VF	XF
ND(1628-44)	—	20.00	35.00	50.00	70.00	—

KM# 87.1 CASH
Cast Bronze **Obv. Inscription:** "Ch'ung-chên T'ung-pao" **Rev:** "Kuei" above **Mint:** Kueichou **Note:** Schjöth #1269.

Date	Mintage	Good	VG	F	VF	XF
ND(1628-44)	—	3.25	5.50	7.50	12.00	—

KM# 87.2 CASH
Cast Bronze **Obv. Inscription:** Ch'ung-chên T'ung-pao **Rev:** Kuei above, dot below **Mint:** Kueichou **Note:** Schjöth #1269.

Date	Mintage	Good	VG	F	VF	XF
ND(1628-44)	—	10.00	20.00	35.00	50.00	—

KM# 72.1 CASH
Cast Bronze, 23 mm. **Obv. Inscription:** "Ch'ung-chên T'ung-pao" **Rev:** "Kung" above **Mint:** Kung-pu Board of Public Works **Note:** Schjöth #1251.

Date	Mintage	Good	VG	F	VF	XF
ND(1628-44)	—	6.00	10.00	15.00	20.00	—

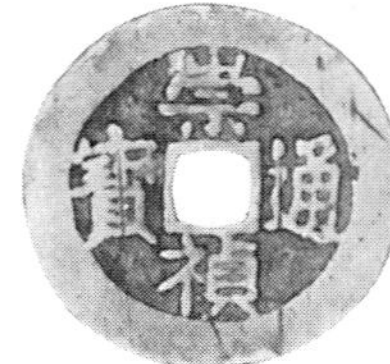
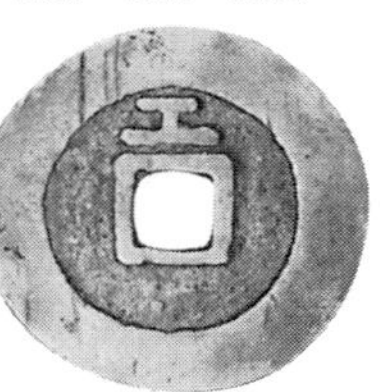

KM# 72.2 CASH
Cast Bronze, 26 mm. **Obv. Inscription:** "Ch'ung-chên T'ung-pao" **Rev:** "Kung" above **Mint:** Kung-pu Board of Public Works

Date	Mintage	Good	VG	F	VF	XF
ND(1628-44)	—	6.00	10.00	15.00	20.00	—

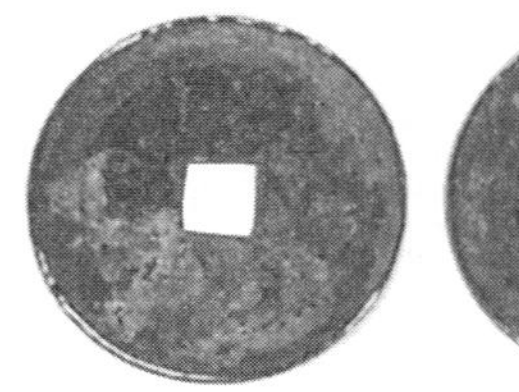

KM# 73.1 CASH
Cast Bronze **Obv. Inscription:** "Ch'ung-chên T'ung-pao" **Rev:** "Kung" below **Mint:** Kung-pu Board of Public Works **Note:** Schjöth #1252.

Date	Mintage	Good	VG	F	VF	XF
ND(1628-44)	—	6.00	10.00	15.00	20.00	—

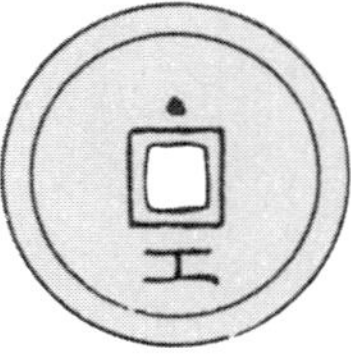

工

KM# 73.2 CASH
Cast Bronze **Obv. Inscription:** "Ch'ung-chên T'ung-pao" **Rev:** Dot above, "Kung" below **Mint:** Kung-pu Board of Public Works **Note:** Schjöth #1253.

Date	Mintage	Good	VG	F	VF	XF
ND(1628-44)	—	8.50	14.00	20.00	28.00	—

共

KM# 94 CASH
Cast Bronze **Obv. Inscription:** "Ch'ung-chên T'ung-pao" **Rev:** "Kung" below **Mint:** Kungch'êng **Note:** Schjöth #1276.

Date	Mintage	Good	VG	F	VF	XF
ND(1628-44)	—	10.00	17.50	25.00	35.00	—

KM# 81 CASH
Cast Bronze **Obv. Inscription:** "Ch'ung-chên T'ung-pao" **Rev:** "Lü" above **Mint:** Lüchou **Note:** Schjöth #1263.

Date	Mintage	Good	VG	F	VF	XF
ND(1628-44)	—	6.00	10.00	15.00	20.00	—

KM# 82.1 CASH
Cast Bronze **Obv. Inscription:** "Ch'ung-chên T'ung-pao" **Rev:** "Lü" below **Mint:** Lüchou **Note:** Schjöth #1264.

Date	Mintage	Good	VG	F	VF	XF
ND(1628-44)	—	8.50	14.00	20.00	28.00	—

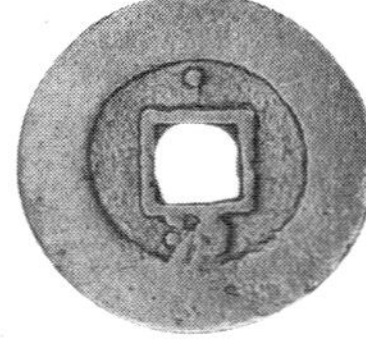

KM# 82.2 CASH
Cast Bronze **Obv. Inscription:** "Ch'ung-chên T'ung-pao" **Rev:** Dot above, "Lü" below **Mint:** Lüchou **Note:** Schjöth #1265.

Date	Mintage	Good	VG	F	VF	XF
ND(1628-44)	—	8.50	14.00	20.00	28.00	—

KM# 89 CASH
Cast Bronze **Obv. Inscription:** "Ch'ung-chên T'ung-pao" **Rev:** "T'ai" above, "P'ing" below **Mint:** T'ai-p'ing Fu **Note:** Schjöth #1271.

Date	Mintage	Good	VG	F	VF	XF
ND(1628-44)	—	10.00	15.00	20.00	30.00	—

KM# 84 CASH
Cast Bronze **Obv. Inscription:** "Ch'ung-chên T'ung-pao" **Rev:** "Ying" above **Mint:** Yingt'ien **Note:** Schjöth #1267.

Date	Mintage	Good	VG	F	VF	XF
ND(1628-44)	—	9.00	15.00	21.00	30.00	—

KM# 78 CASH
Cast Bronze **Obv. Inscription:** "Ch'ung-chên T'ung-pao" **Rev:** "Yü" above **Mint:** Yülin **Note:** Schjöth #1259.

Date	Mintage	Good	VG	F	VF	XF
ND(1628-44)	—	15.00	20.00	30.00	40.00	—

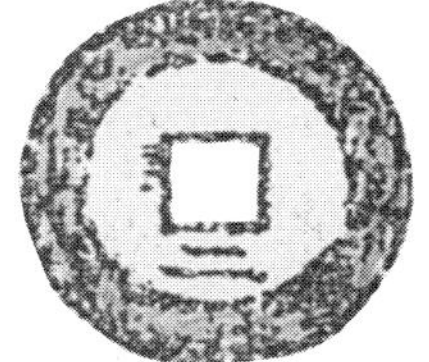

KM# A99 2 CASH
Cast Bronze, 25 mm. **Rev. Inscription:** "Erh" (two) below

Date	Mintage	Good	VG	F	VF	XF
ND(1628-44)	—	1.75	3.00	4.75	6.00	—

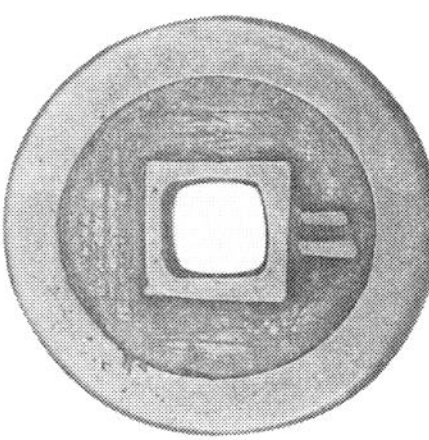

KM# 99 2 CASH
Cast Bronze **Obv. Inscription:** "Ch'ung-chên T'ung-pao" **Rev:** "Êrh" (two) at right **Note:** Schjöth #1282.

Date	Mintage	Good	VG	F	VF	XF
ND(1628-44)	—	10.00	15.00	20.00	30.00	—

KM# 100 2 CASH
Cast Bronze **Obv. Inscription:** "Ch'ung-chên T'ung-pao" **Rev:** "Êrh" (two) at right, small dot below **Note:** Schjöth #1283.

Date	Mintage	Good	VG	F	VF	XF
ND(1628-44)	—	4.00	7.00	10.00	15.00	—

Note: The illustrations for Schjöth's #1282 and 1283 were misleading while the descriptive text was correct

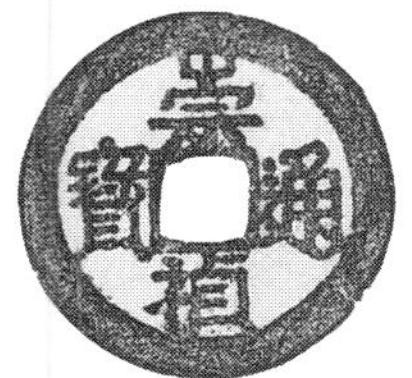

KM# A101 2 CASH
Cast Bronze **Obv. Inscription:** "Ch'ung-chên T'ung-pao" **Rev:** Dot above only

Date	Mintage	Good	VG	F	VF	XF
ND(1628-44)	—	5.00	10.00	15.00	20.00	—

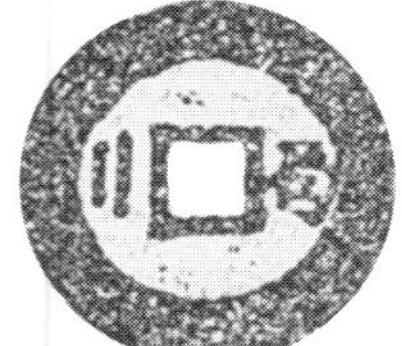

KM# A102 2 CASH
Cast Bronze **Obv. Inscription:** "Ch'ung-chên T'ung-pao" **Rev:** "Êrh" left, "Chu" right

Date	Mintage	Good	VG	F	VF	XF
ND(1628-44)	—	35.00	55.00	75.00	—	—

KM# B102 2 CASH
Cast Bronze **Obv. Inscription:** "Ch'ung-chên T'ung-pao" **Rev:** "Chih" above, "Feng" right

Date	Mintage	Good	VG	F	VF	XF
ND(1628-44)	—	22.00	37.50	50.00	—	—

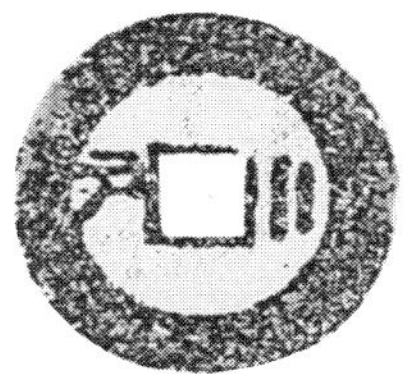

KM# A103 2 CASH
Cast Bronze, 25 mm. **Rev. Inscription:** "Erh" (two) at right, "Hu" at left

Date	Mintage	Good	VG	F	VF	XF
ND(1628-44)	—	1.50	2.50	3.50	5.00	—

KM# 105 2 CASH
Cast Bronze **Obv. Inscription:** "Ch'ung-chên T'ung-pao" **Rev:** "Chiang" above, "Êrh" (two) sideways at right

Date	Mintage	Good	VG	F	VF	XF
ND(1628-44)	—	20.00	35.00	47.50	65.00	—

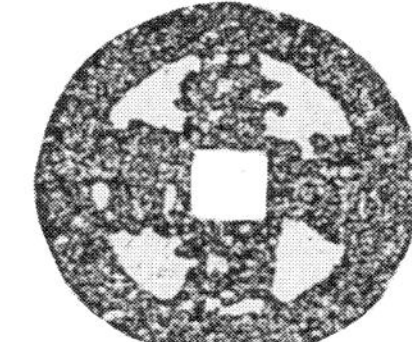

KM# 107 2 CASH
Cast Bronze, 25 mm. **Rev. Inscription:** "Chü" at right, "Chü" at left

Date	Mintage	Good	VG	F	VF	XF
ND(1628-44)	—	25.00	40.00	65.00	80.00	—

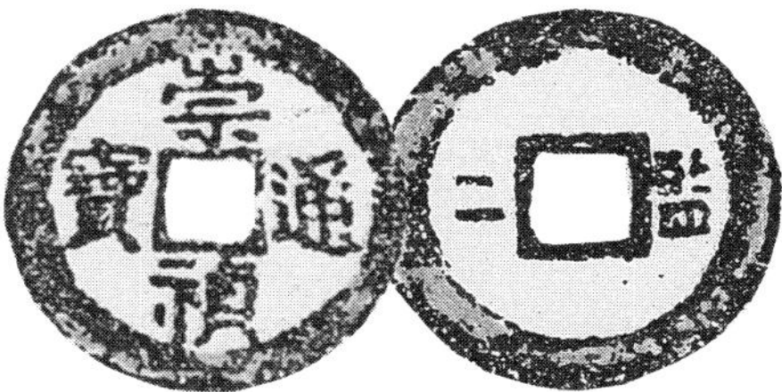

KM# 108 2 CASH
Cast Bronze, 29 mm. **Rev. Inscription:** "Chien" at right, "Erh" (two) at left

Date	Mintage	Good	VG	F	VF	XF
ND(1628-44)	—	25.00	40.00	65.00	80.00	—

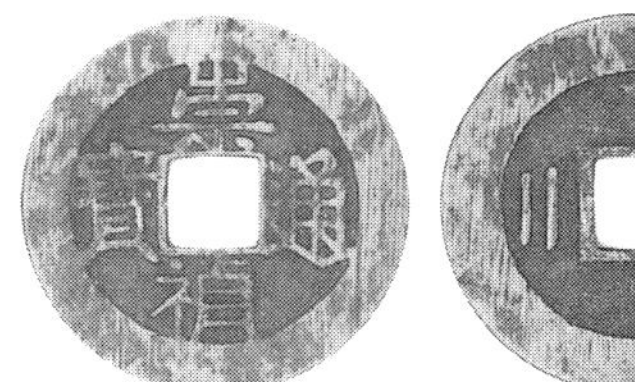

KM# 106 2 CASH
Cast Bronze **Obv. Inscription:** "Ch'ung-chên T'ung-pao" **Rev:** "Chi" at right, "Êrh" (two) at left **Mint:** Board of Public Works

Date	Mintage	Good	VG	F	VF	XF
ND(1628-44)	—	100	200	300	400	—

KM# 101 2 CASH
Cast Bronze **Obv. Inscription:** "Ch'ung-chên T'ung-pao" **Rev:** "Hu" above, "Êrh" (two) below **Mint:** Hu-pu Board of Revenue **Note:** Schjöth #1279.

Date	Mintage	Good	VG	F	VF	XF
ND(1628-44)	—	16.00	25.00	35.00	50.00	—

KM# 102 2 CASH
Cast Bronze **Obv. Inscription:** "Ch'ung-chên T'ung-pao" **Rev:** "Hu" at right, "Êrh" (two) sideways at left **Mint:** Hu-pu Board of Revenue **Note:** Schjöth #1280.

Date	Mintage	Good	VG	F	VF	XF
ND(1628-44)	—	10.00	15.00	21.50	30.00	—

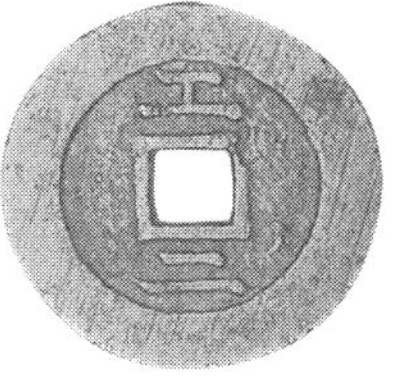

KM# 103 2 CASH
Cast Bronze **Obv. Inscription:** "Ch'ung-chên T'ung-pao" **Rev:** "Kung" above, "Êrh" (two) below **Mint:** Kung-pu Board of Public Works **Note:** Schjöth #1281.

Date	Mintage	Good	VG	F	VF	XF
ND(1628-44)	—	10.00	17.50	25.00	35.00	—

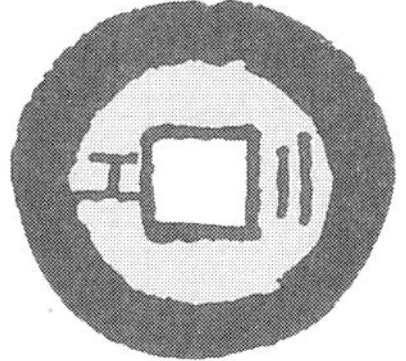

KM# 104.1 2 CASH
Cast Bronze **Obv. Inscription:** "Ch'ung-chên T'ung-pao" **Rev:** "Êrh" (two) at right, "Kung" at left **Mint:** Kung-pu Board of Public Works

Date	Mintage	Good	VG	F	VF	XF
ND(1628-44)	—	15.00	25.00	37.50	50.00	—

KM# 104.2 2 CASH
Cast Bronze **Obv:** Characters deviating in style **Obv. Inscription:** "Ch'ung-chên T'ung-pao" **Rev:** "Êrh" (two) at right, "Kung" at left **Mint:** Kung-pu Board of Public Works

Date	Mintage	Good	VG	F	VF	XF
ND(1628-44)	—	10.00	17.50	25.00	35.00	—

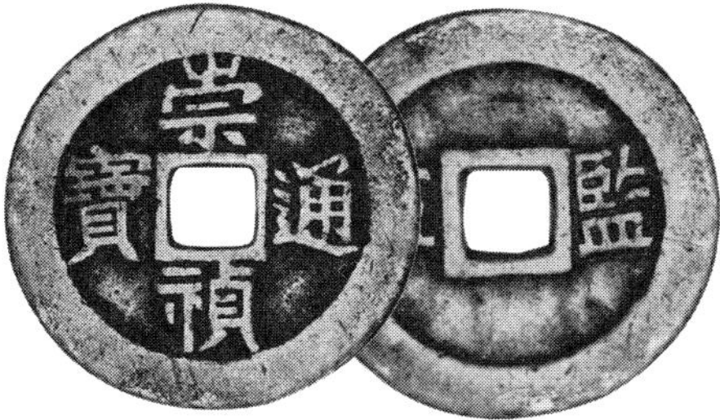

KM# 111 5 CASH
Cast Bronze **Obv. Inscription:** "Ch'ung-chên T'ung-pao" **Rev:** "Chien" at right, "Wu" (five) at left **Note:** Schjöth #1284.

Date	Mintage	Good	VG	F	VF	XF
ND(1628-44)	—	18.00	30.00	45.00	60.00	—

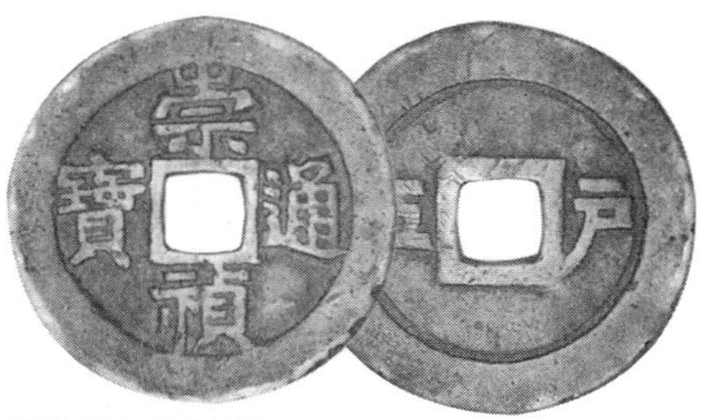

KM# 109 5 CASH
Cast Bronze **Obv. Inscription:** "Ch'ung-chên T'ung-pao" **Rev:** "Hu" at right, "Wu" (five) at left **Mint:** Hu-pu Board of Revenue

Date	Mintage	Good	VG	F	VF	XF
ND(1628-44)	—	20.00	35.00	47.50	65.00	—

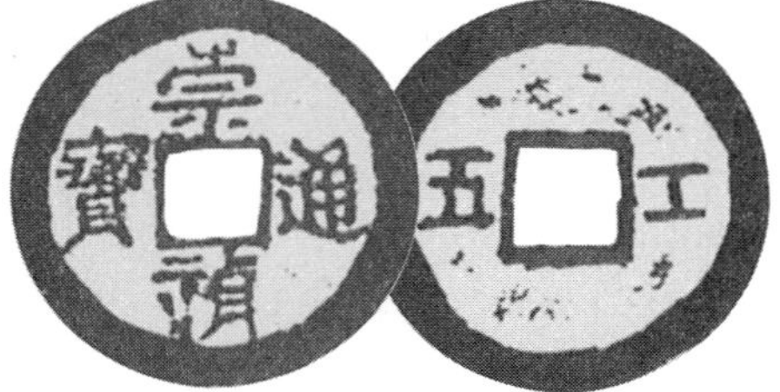

KM# 110 5 CASH
Cast Bronze **Obv. Inscription:** "Ch'ung-chên T'ung-pao" **Rev:** "Kung" at right, "Wu" (five) at left **Mint:** Kung-pu Board of Public Works

Date	Mintage	Good	VG	F	VF	XF
ND(1628-44)	—	25.00	42.50	60.00	85.00	—

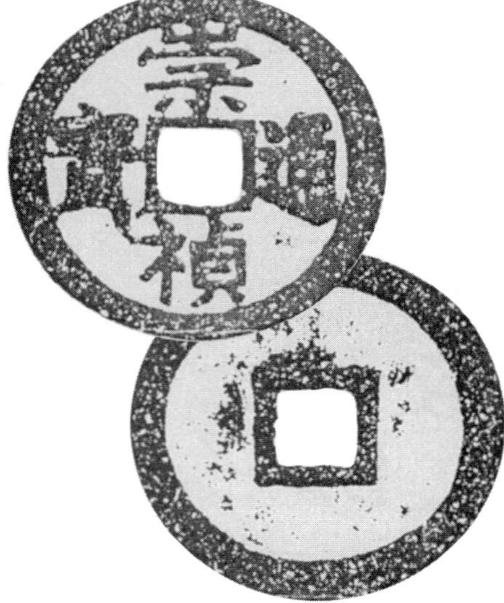

KM# 112 10 CASH
Cast Bronze **Obv. Inscription:** "Ch'ung-chên T'ung-pao"
Rev: Plain

Date	Mintage	Good	VG	F	VF	XF
ND(1628-44)	—	125	250	350	500	—

MING-CH'ING REBEL ERA

Issued during the years of the revolt to overthrow the Ming Dynasty by the Manchu's, while the Manchus (Ch'ing Dynasty) were consolidating their control over all of China. Thus classed as "rebel coinage" as issued by the Manchu's in the Ming Era.

Ta-ming
Ming Prince of Lu
CAST COINAGE

KM# 115 CASH
Cast Bronze **Obv. Inscription:** "Ta-ming T'ung-pao" **Rev:** Plain
Note: Schjöth #1285.

Date	Mintage	Good	VG	F	VF	XF
ND(1628-44)	—	20.00	30.00	45.00	60.00	—

戶

KM# 116 CASH
Cast Bronze **Rev:** "Hu" above **Note:** Schjöth #1286.

Date	Mintage	Good	VG	F	VF	XF
ND(1628-44)	—	20.00	30.00	45.00	60.00	—

KM# A117.1 CASH
Cast Bronze **Obv. Inscription:** "Ta-ming T'ung-pao"
Rev: "Shuai" above

Date	Mintage	Good	VG	F	VF	XF
ND(1628-44)	—	20.00	30.00	45.00	60.00	—

KM# A117.2 CASH
Cast Bronze **Obv. Inscription:** "Ta-ming T'ung-pao"
Rev: "Shuai" right

Date	Mintage	Good	VG	F	VF	XF
ND(1628-44)	—	20.00	30.00	45.00	60.00	—

KM# 117 CASH
Cast Bronze **Obv. Inscription:** "Ta-ming T'ung-pao"
Rev: "Kung" above

Date	Mintage	Good	VG	F	VF	XF
ND(1628-44)	—	18.00	30.00	45.00	60.00	—

Hung-kuang
Prince of Fu; Fu King; Fu Wang
CAST COINAGE

KM# 118.1 CASH
Cast Bronze **Obv. Inscription:** "Hung-kuang T'ung-pao"
Rev: Plain **Note:** Schjöth #1287.

Date	Mintage	Good	VG	F	VF	XF
ND(1644)	—	3.50	6.00	8.50	12.00	—

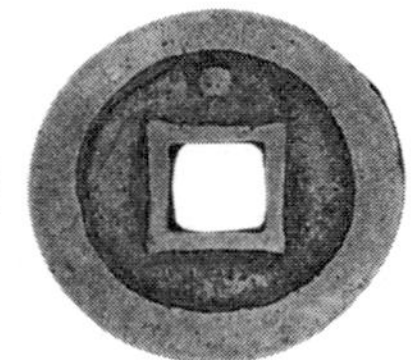

KM# 118.2 CASH
Cast Bronze **Obv. Inscription:** "Hung-kuang T'ung-pao"
Rev: Dot above **Note:** Schjöth #1288.

Date	Mintage	Good	VG	F	VF	XF
ND(1644)	—	4.50	7.50	11.00	15.00	—

KM# 119 CASH
Cast Bronze **Obv. Inscription:** "Hung-kuang T'ung-pao"
Rev: "Feng" above **Mint:** Fengyang Fu **Note:** Schjöth #1289.

Date	Mintage	Good	VG	F	VF	XF
ND(1644)	—	35.00	55.00	90.00	125	—

貳

KM# 120 2 CASH
Cast Bronze **Obv. Inscription:** "Hung-kuang T'ung-pao"
Rev: Official "Êrh" (two) at right **Note:** Schjöth #1290.

Date	Mintage	Good	VG	F	VF	XF
ND(1644)	—	30.00	60.00	120	150	—

Lung-wu
Prince of T'ang
CAST COINAGE

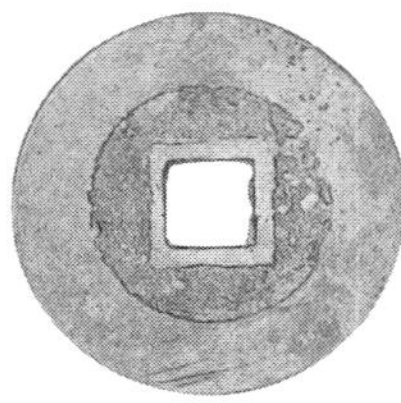

KM# 122.1 CASH
Cast Bronze **Obv. Inscription:** "Lung-wu T'ung-pao" **Rev:** Plain
Note: Size varies: 24-26 mm. Schjöth #1291.

Date	Mintage	Good	VG	F	VF	XF
ND(1645)	—	5.00	8.50	12.00	16.00	—

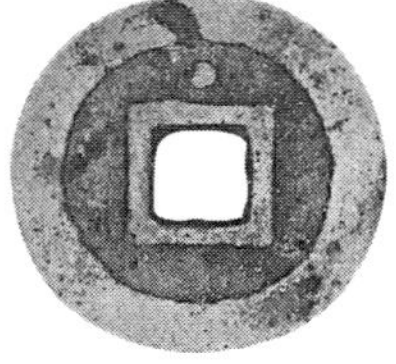

KM# 122.2 CASH
Cast Bronze **Obv. Inscription:** "Lung-wu T'ung-pao" **Rev:** Dot above **Note:** Schjöth #1292.

Date	Mintage	Good	VG	F	VF	XF
ND(1645)	—	6.00	10.00	15.00	20.00	—

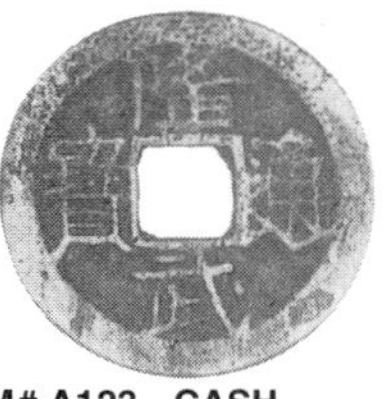

KM# A123 CASH
Cast Bronze **Obv:** Different style "lung" in legend
Obv. Legend: "Lung-wu T'ung-pao" **Rev:** Plain

Date	Mintage	Good	VG	F	VF	XF
ND(1645)	—	—	—	—	—	—

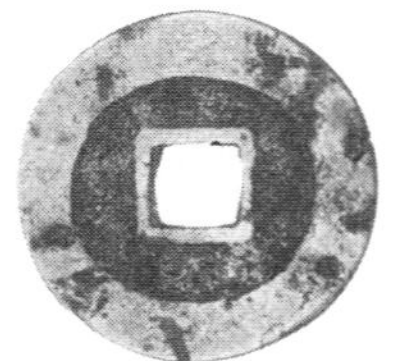

KM# B123 CASH
Cast Bronze **Obv:** Different style "lung" in legend
Obv. Legend: "Lung-wu T'ung-pao" **Rev:** Plain

Date	Mintage	Good	VG	F	VF	XF
ND(1645)	—	—	—	—	—	—

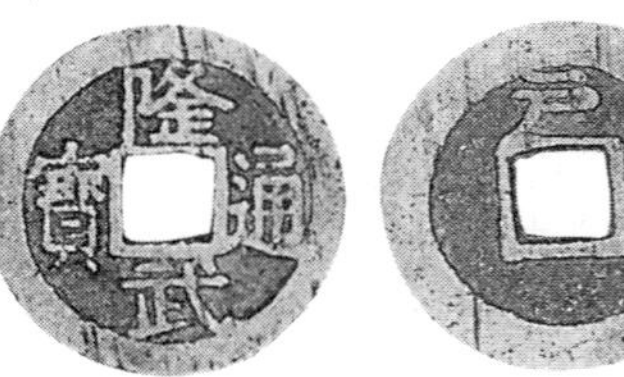

KM# 123 CASH
Cast Bronze **Obv. Inscription:** "Lung-wu T'ung-pao" **Rev:** "Hu" above **Note:** Schjöth #1293.

Date	Mintage	Good	VG	F	VF	XF
ND(1645)	—	8.00	12.00	16.00	24.00	—

KM# 124 CASH
Cast Bronze **Obv. Inscription:** "Lung-wu T'ung-pao"
Rev: "Kung" above **Note:** Schjöth #1294.

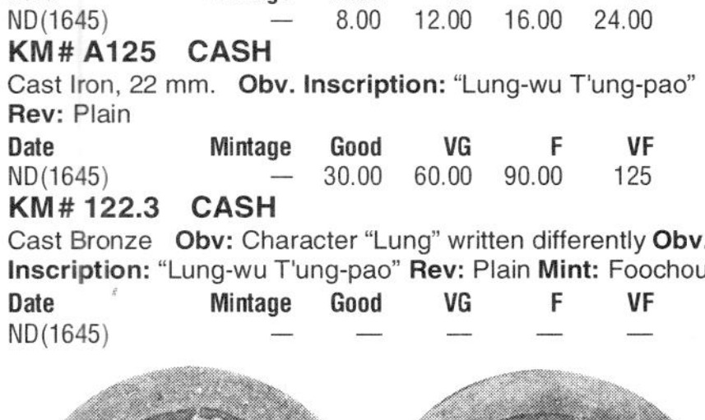

Date	Mintage	Good	VG	F	VF	XF
ND(1645)	—	8.00	12.00	16.00	24.00	—

KM# A125 CASH

Cast Iron, 22 mm. **Obv. Inscription:** "Lung-wu T'ung-pao" **Rev:** Plain

Date	Mintage	Good	VG	F	VF	XF
ND(1645)	—	30.00	60.00	90.00	125	—

KM# 122.3 CASH

Cast Bronze **Obv:** Character "Lung" written differently **Obv. Inscription:** "Lung-wu T'ung-pao" **Rev:** Plain **Mint:** Foochou

Date	Mintage	Good	VG	F	VF	XF
ND(1645)	—	—	—	—	—	—

KM# 126 2 CASH

Cast Bronze **Obv. Legend:** "Lung-wu T'ung-pao" **Rev:** Plain **Note:** Schjöth #1295.

Date	Mintage	Good	VG	F	VF	XF
ND(1645)	—	8.50	14.00	20.00	28.00	—

Yung-ch'ang

Li Tzu'ch'eng, Hsi'au Fu

CAST COINAGE

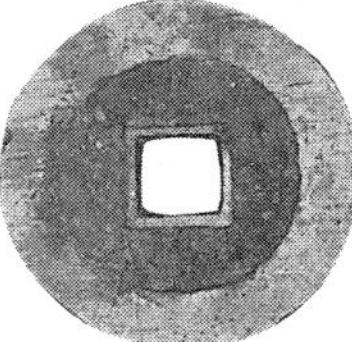

KM# 161 CASH

Cast Bronze **Obv. Inscription:** "Yung-ch'ang T'ung-pao" **Rev:** Plain **Note:** Schjöth #1323. Size varies: 23-25 mm.

Date	Mintage	Good	VG	F	VF	XF
ND(1644)	—	12.50	17.50	27.50	40.00	—

KM# 162 CASH

Cast Bronze **Obv. Inscription:** Yung-ch'ang T'ung-pao **Rev:** "Yi" above **Note:** Schjöth #1324

Date	Mintage	Good	VG	F	VF	XF
ND(1644)	—	—	—	—	—	—

KM# 165 5 CASH

Cast Bronze **Obv. Inscription:** "Yung-ch'ang T'ung-pao" **Rev:** Plain **Note:** Schjöth #1325. Size varies: 36-38 mm.

Date	Mintage	Good	VG	F	VF	XF
ND(1644)	—	12.00	21.00	30.00	45.00	—

Yung-li

Prince Yung-ming, Chao-ch'ing Fu, Kwangtung

CAST COINAGE

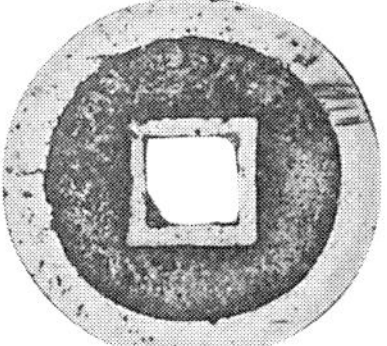

KM# 128.1 CASH

Cast Bronze **Obv. Inscription:** "Yung-li T'ung-pao" **Rev:** Plain **Note:** Schjöth #1296.

Date	Mintage	Good	VG	F	VF	XF
ND(1647-62)	—	2.00	3.50	5.00	7.50	—

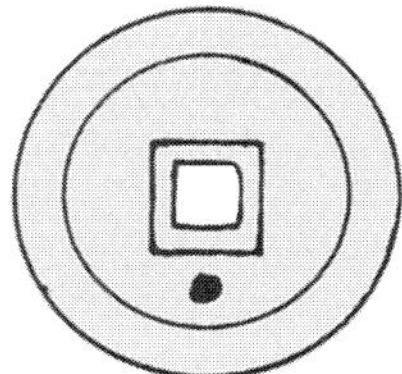

KM# 128.2 CASH

Cast Bronze **Obv. Inscription:** "Yung-li T'ung-pao" **Rev:** Dot below **Note:** Schjöth #1297.

Date	Mintage	Good	VG	F	VF	XF
ND(1647-62)	—	4.00	7.00	10.00	15.00	—

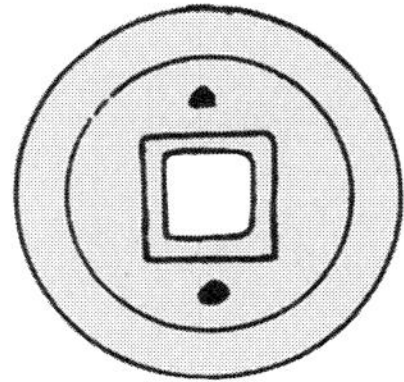

KM# 128.3 CASH

Cast Bronze **Obv. Inscription:** "Yung-li T'ung-pao" **Rev:** Dot above and below **Note:** Schjöth #1298.

Date	Mintage	Good	VG	F	VF	XF
ND(1647-62)	—	6.00	10.00	15.00	20.00	—

戶

KM# 129 CASH

Cast Bronze **Obv. Inscription:** "Yung-li T'ung-pao" **Rev:** Large "Hu" above **Note:** Schjöth #1299.

Date	Mintage	Good	VG	F	VF	XF
ND(1647-62)	—	3.00	6.00	10.00	15.00	—

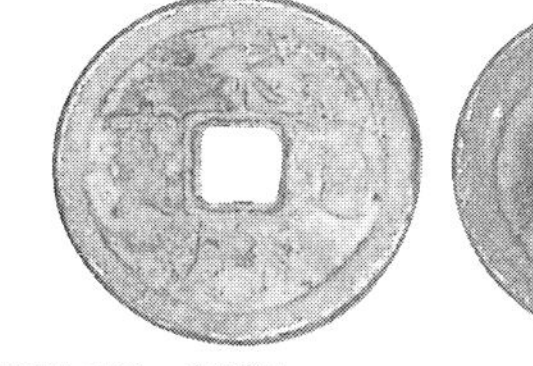

KM# 130 CASH

Cast Bronze **Obv. Inscription:** "Yung-li T'ung-pao" **Rev:** "Yu" above **Note:** Schjöth #1300.

Date	Mintage	Good	VG	F	VF	XF
ND(1647-62)	—	30.00	45.00	60.00	90.00	—

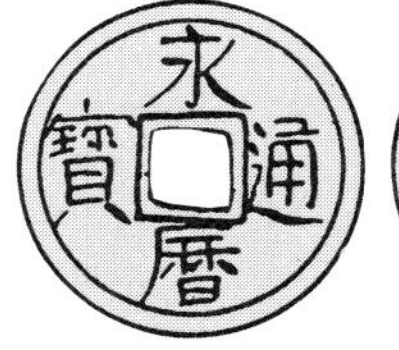

KM# 131 CASH

Cast Bronze **Obv. Inscription:** "Yung-li T'ung-pao" **Rev:** "Ch'ih" **Note:** Schjöth #1301.

Date	Mintage	Good	VG	F	VF	XF
ND(1647-62)	—	40.00	65.00	90.00	125	—

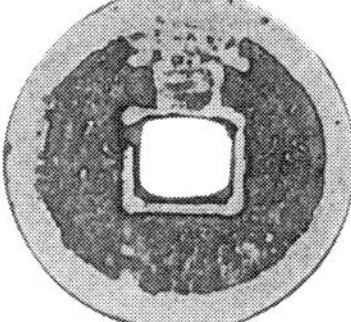

KM# 132 CASH

Cast Bronze **Obv. Inscription:** "Yung-li T'ung-pao" **Rev:** "Tu" above **Note:** Schjöth #1302-03.

Date	Mintage	Good	VG	F	VF	XF
ND(1647-62)	—	—	—	—	—	—

Note: The illustrations for Schjöth #1302 and #1303 were misleading while the descriptive text was correct

KM# 133 CASH

Cast Bronze **Obv. Inscription:** "Yung-li T'ung-pao" **Rev:** "Pu" above

Date	Mintage	Good	VG	F	VF	XF
ND(1647-62)	—	90.00	160	225	335	—

KM# 134 CASH

Cast Bronze **Obv. Inscription:** "Yung-li T'ung-pao" **Rev:** "Tao" above **Note:** Schjöth #1304.

Date	Mintage	Good	VG	F	VF	XF
ND(1647-62)	—	60.00	100	200	300	—

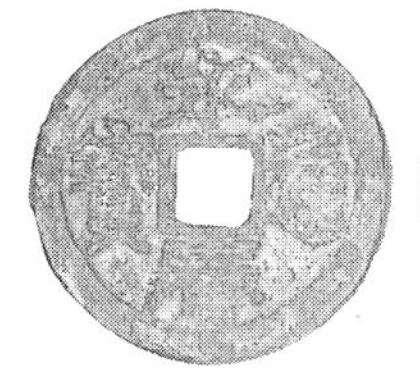

KM# 135 CASH

Cast Bronze **Obv. Inscription:** "Yung-li T'ung-pao" **Rev:** "Liu" above **Note:** Schjöth #1305.

Date	Mintage	Good	VG	F	VF	XF
ND(1647-62)	—	10.00	15.00	25.00	40.00	—

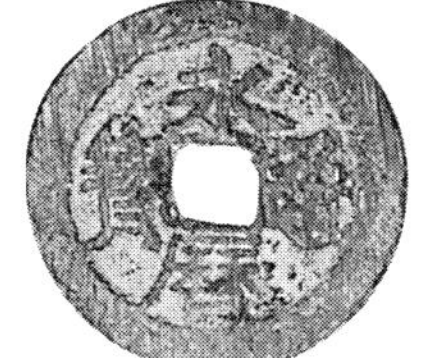

KM# 136 CASH

Cast Bronze **Obv. Inscription:** "Yung-li T'ung-pao" **Rev:** "Yüeh" **Note:** Schjöth #1306.

Date	Mintage	Good	VG	F	VF	XF
ND(1647-62)	—	16.00	28.00	40.00	50.00	—

KM# A137 CASH

Cast Bronze **Obv. Inscription:** "Yung-li T'ung-pao" **Rev:** Small "Fu" above

Date	Mintage	Good	VG	F	VF	XF
ND(1647-62)	—	10.00	15.00	25.00	40.00	—

KM# 137 CASH

Cast Bronze **Obv. Inscription:** "Yung-li T'ung-pao" **Rev:** Large "Fu" above **Note:** Schjöth #1307.

Date	Mintage	Good	VG	F	VF	XF
ND(1647-62)	—	12.00	20.00	28.00	40.00	—

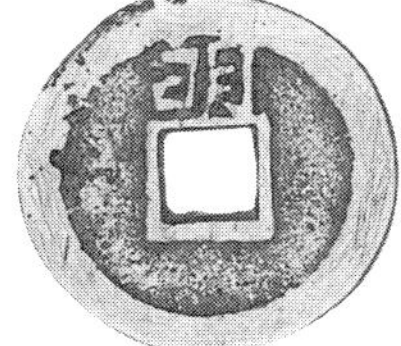

KM# 138 CASH

Cast Bronze **Obv. Inscription:** "Yung-li T'ung-pao" **Rev:** "Ming" above **Note:** Schjöth #1308.

Date	Mintage	Good	VG	F	VF	XF
ND(1647-62)	—	12.00	20.00	25.00	35.00	—

KM# A139 CASH

Cast Bronze **Obv. Inscription:** "Yung-li T'ung-pao" **Rev:** Small "T'ing" above **Note:** Schjöth #1308.

Date	Mintage	Good	VG	F	VF	XF
ND(1647-62)	1,647	150	250	500	400	—

定

KM# 139 CASH

Cast Bronze **Obv. Inscription:** "Yung-li T'ung-pao" **Rev:** "T'ing" above **Note:** Schjöth #1309.

Date	Mintage	Good	VG	F	VF	XF
ND(1647-62)	—	12.00	20.00	25.00	35.00	—

KM# 140 CASH

Cast Bronze **Obv. Inscription:** "Yung-li T'ung-pao" **Rev:** "Kuo" above **Note:** Schjöth #1310.

Date	Mintage	Good	VG	F	VF	XF
ND(1647-62)	—	12.00	20.00	25.00	35.00	—

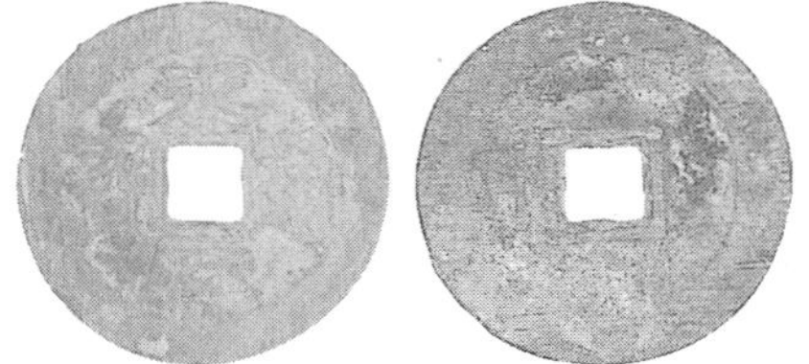

KM# 141 CASH

Cast Bronze **Obv. Inscription:** "Yung-li T'ung-pao" **Rev:** "Kung" above **Mint:** Kung-pu Board of Public Works **Note:** Schjöth #1311.

Date	Mintage	Good	VG	F	VF	XF
ND(1647-62)	—	6.00	10.00	15.00	20.00	—

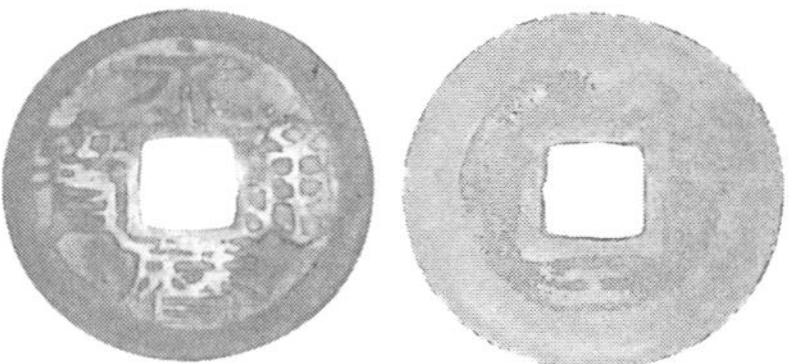

KM# 142 CASH

Cast Bronze **Obv. Inscription:** "Yung-li T'ung-pao" **Rev:** "Kung" below **Mint:** Kung-pu Board of Public Works **Note:** Schjöth #1312.

Date	Mintage	Good	VG	F	VF	XF
ND(1647-62)	—	6.00	10.00	15.00	20.00	—

二

KM# 145 2 CASH

Cast Bronze **Obv. Inscription:** Yung-li T'ung-pao **Rev:** "Erh" (two) above **Note:** Schjöth #1313.

Date	Mintage	Good	VG	F	VF	XF
ND(1647-62)	—	10.00	17.50	25.00	35.00	—

KM# 146 2 CASH

Cast Bronze **Obv. Inscription:** "Yung-li T'ung-pao" **Rev:** "Êrh" (two) above, "Li" below **Note:** Schjöth #1314.

Date	Mintage	Good	VG	F	VF	XF
ND(1647-62)	—	12.50	20.00	32.50	45.00	—

KM# 147 2 CASH

Cast Bronze **Obv:** Legend in seal script **Obv. Inscription:** "Yung-li T'ung-pao" **Note:** Schjöth #1315. Size varies: 26-28 mm.

Date	Mintage	Good	VG	F	VF	XF
ND(1647-62)	—	12.50	20.00	32.50	45.00	—

KM# 148 2 CASH

Cast Bronze **Obv:** Legend in "running hand" **Obv. Inscription:** "Yung-li T'ung-pao" **Note:** Schjöth #1316.

Date	Mintage	Good	VG	F	VF	XF
ND(1647-62)	—	12.50	20.00	32.50	45.00	—

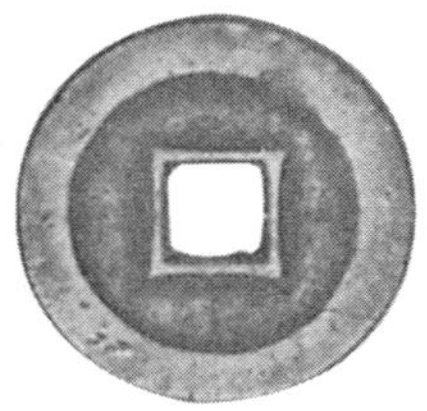

KM# 149 2 CASH

Cast Bronze **Obv:** Legend in "grass characters" **Obv. Inscription:** "Yung-li T'ung-pao" **Note:** Schjöth #1317.

Date	Mintage	Good	VG	F	VF	XF
ND(1647-62)	—	12.50	20.00	32.50	45.00	—

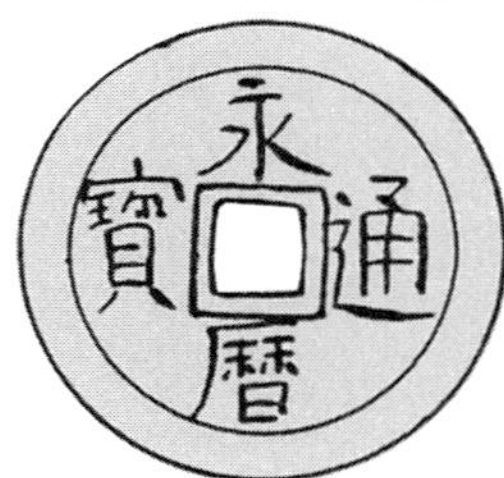

KM# 150 2 CASH

Cast Bronze **Obv. Inscription:** "Yung-li T'ung-pao" **Note:** Schjöth #1318. Size varies: 31-33 mm.

Date	Mintage	Good	VG	F	VF	XF
ND(1647-62)	—	17.50	27.50	37.50	50.00	—

KM# 153 5 CASH

Cast Bronze **Obv. Inscription:** Yung-li T'ung-pao **Rev:** "Wu" (five) above, "Li" below **Note:** Schjöth #1319. Size varies: 31-33 mm.

Date	Mintage	Good	VG	F	VF	XF
ND(1647-62)	—	12.00	20.00	28.00	40.00	—

KM# 154 5 CASH

Cast Bronze **Rev:** "Wu" (five) above, "Li" below **Note:** Schjöth #1320. Size varies: 34-36 mm.

Date	Mintage	Good	VG	F	VF	XF
ND(1647-62)	—	12.50	18.50	22.50	30.00	—

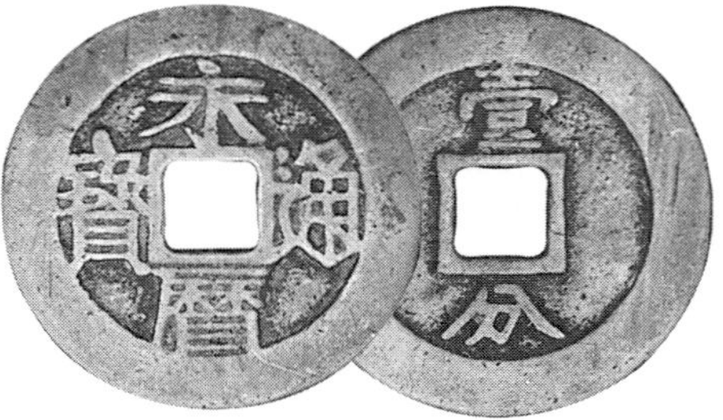

KM# 157 FEN

Cast Bronze **Obv. Inscription:** "Yung-li T'ung-pao" **Rev:** "Yi" (one) above, "Fen" (candareen) below **Note:** Schjöth #1321. Size varies: 34-36 mm.

Date	Mintage	Good	VG	F	VF	XF
ND(1647-62)	—	12.00	20.00	28.00	40.00	—

KM# 158 FEN

Cast Bronze **Obv. Inscription:** Large "Yung-li T'ung-pao" **Rev:** Large "Yi" (one) above, "Fen" (candareen) below **Note:** Schjöth #1322. Size varies: 45-47 mm.

Date	Mintage	Good	VG	F	VF	XF
ND(1647-62)	—	18.00	30.00	42.00	60.00	—

KM# 159 FEN

Cast Bronze **Obv. Inscription:** Small "Yung-li T'ung-pao" **Rev:** Small "Yi" (one) above, "Fen" (candareen) below **Note:** Size varies: 45-47mm

Date	Mintage	Good	VG	F	VF	XF
ND(1647-62)	—	18.00	30.00	42.00	60.00	—

Ta-shun
Chang Hsien-chung
CAST COINAGE

KM# 168 CASH
Cast Bronze **Obv. Inscription:** "Ta-shun T'ung-pao" **Rev:** Plain **Note:** Schjöth #1326.

Date	Mintage	Good	VG	F	VF	XF
ND(1644)	—	7.50	12.50	17.50	25.00	—

KM# 169 CASH
Cast Bronze **Obv. Inscription:** "Ta-shun T'ung-pao" **Rev:** "Hu" below **Note:** Schjöth #1327.

Date	Mintage	Good	VG	F	VF	XF
ND(1644)	—	12.00	21.00	30.00	45.00	—

KM# 170 CASH
Cast Bronze **Obv. Inscription:** "Ta-shun T'ung-pao" **Rev:** "Kung" below **Note:** Schjöth #1328.

Date	Mintage	Good	VG	F	VF	XF
ND(1644)	—	7.50	12.50	17.50	25.00	—

Hsing-ch'ao
Sun K'o-wang
CAST COINAGE

KM# 173 CASH
Cast Bronze **Obv. Inscription:** "Hsing-Ch'ao T'ung-pao" **Rev:** "Kung" below **Note:** Schjöth #1329. Size varies: 22-24 mm.

Date	Mintage	Good	VG	F	VF	XF
ND(1644)	—	12.50	17.50	27.50	40.00	—

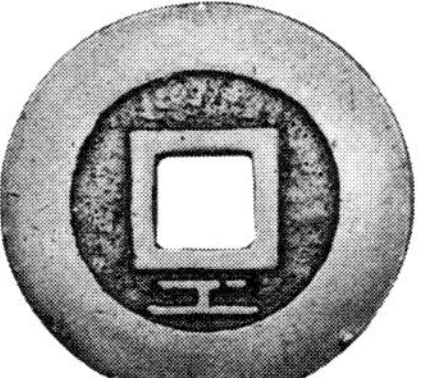

KM# 174 CASH
Cast Bronze **Obv. Inscription:** "Hsing-ch'ao T'ung-pao" **Rev:** "Kung" below **Note:** Schjöth #1330. Size varies: 26-28 mm.

Date	Mintage	Good	VG	F	VF	XF
ND(1644)	—	5.00	8.50	12.00	15.00	—

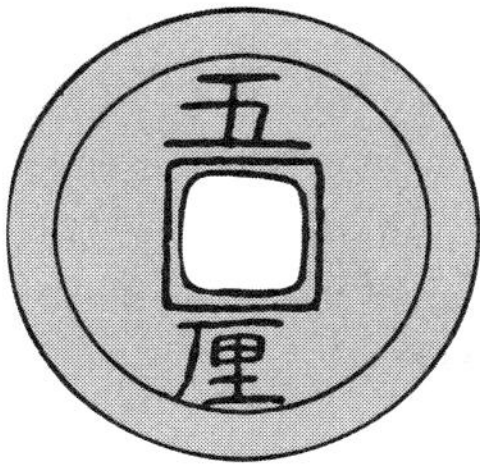

五
厘

KM# 177.1 5 CASH
Cast Bronze **Obv. Inscription:** "Hsing-ch'ao T'ung-pao" **Rev:** "Wu" (five) above, "Li" below **Note:** Schjöth #1331. Size varies: 30-32 mm.

Date	Mintage	Good	VG	F	VF	XF
ND(1644)	—	12.50	17.50	22.50	30.00	—

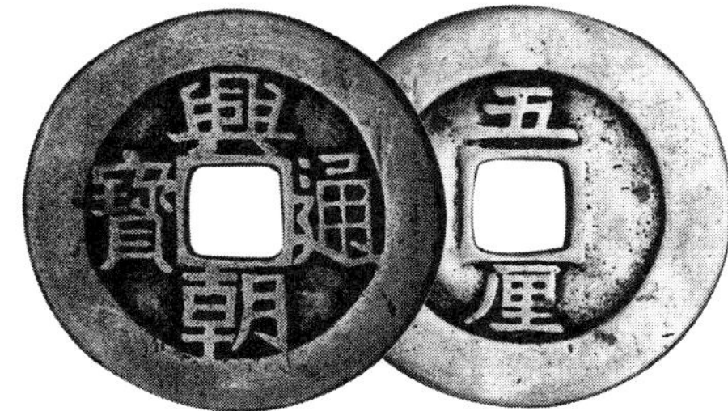

KM# 177.2 5 CASH
Cast Bronze **Obv. Inscription:** "Hsing-ch'ao T'ung-pao" **Rev:** "Wu" (five) above, "Li" below **Note:** Schjöth #1332. Size varies: 32-36 mm.

Date	Mintage	Good	VG	F	VF	XF
ND(1644)	—	10.00	15.00	20.00	25.00	—

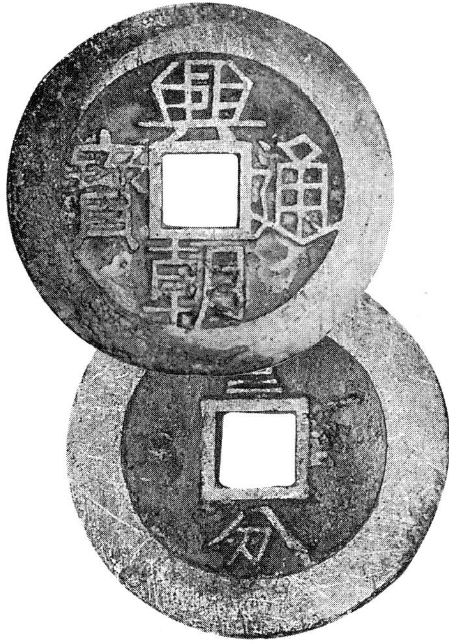

KM# 181 FEN
Cast Bronze **Obv. Inscription:** "Hsing-ch'ao T'ung-pao" **Rev:** "Yi" (one) above, "Fen" (candareen) below **Note:** Schjöth #1333. Size varies: 48-50 mm.

Date	Mintage	Good	VG	F	VF	XF
ND(1644)	—	20.00	30.00	40.00	50.00	—

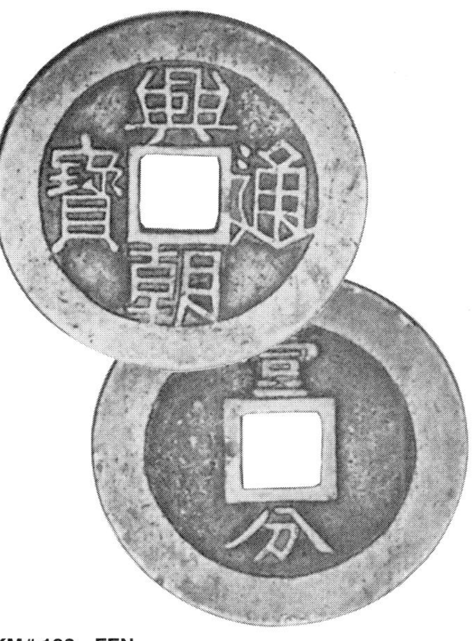

KM# 182 FEN
Cast Bronze **Obv. Inscription:** "Hsing-ch'ao T'ung-pao" **Rev:** "Yi" (one) above, "Fen" (candareen) below **Note:** Schjöth #1334. Reduced size: 44.46 mm.

Date	Mintage	Good	VG	F	VF	XF
ND(1644)	—	15.00	25.00	30.00	35.00	—

Li-yung
Wu San-kuei
CAST COINAGE

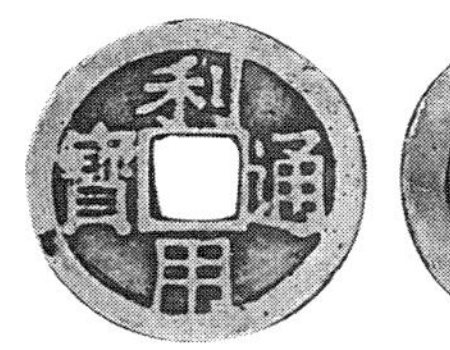
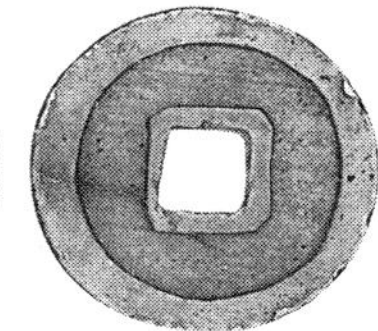

KM# 185 CASH
Cast Bronze **Obv. Inscription:** "Li-yung T'ung-pao" **Rev:** Plain **Note:** Schjöth #1335. Size varies: 22-24mm.

Date	Mintage	Good	VG	F	VF	XF
ND(1674)	—	1.50	2.50	3.50	5.00	—

KM# 186.1 CASH
Cast Bronze **Obv. Inscription:** "Li-yung T'ung-pao" **Rev:** Small-sized "Li" at right **Note:** Schjöth #1336.

Date	Mintage	Good	VG	F	VF	XF
ND(1674)	—	3.00	5.00	8.00	10.00	—

KM# 186.2 CASH
Cast Bronze **Obv. Inscription:** "Li-yung T'ung-pao" **Rev:** Small "Li" at left

Date	Mintage	Good	VG	F	VF	XF
ND(1674)	—	—	—	—	—	—

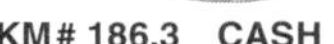

KM# 186.3 CASH

Cast Bronze **Obv. Inscription:** "Li-yung T'ung-pao" **Rev:** Large "Li" at right

Date	Mintage	Good	VG	F	VF	XF
ND(1674)	—	—	—	—	—	—

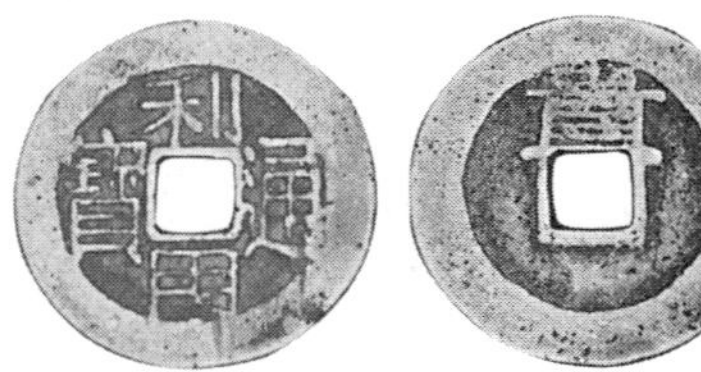

KM# 187 CASH

Cast Bronze **Obv. Inscription:** "Li-yung T'ung-pao" **Rev:** "Kuei" above **Mint:** Kueichow Fu **Note:** Schjöth #1337.

Date	Mintage	Good	VG	F	VF	XF
ND(1674)	—	3.00	5.00	8.00	10.00	—

KM# 188 CASH

Cast Bronze **Obv. Inscription:** "Li-yung T'ung-pao" **Rev:** Yün" at right **Mint:** Yünnan Fu **Note:** Schjöth #1338.

Date	Mintage	Good	VG	F	VF	XF
ND(1674)	—	5.50	9.00	14.00	18.00	—

 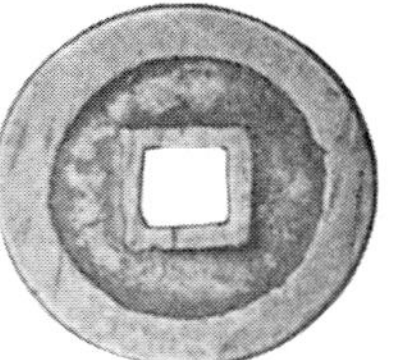

KM# 190 2 CASH

Cast Bronze **Obv. Inscription:** "Li-yung T'ung-pao" **Rev:** Plain **Note:** Size varies: 25-27 mm.

Date	Mintage	Good	VG	F	VF	XF
ND(1674)	—	5.50	9.00	14.00	18.00	—

KM# 192 2 CASH

Cast Bronze **Obv. Inscription:** "Li-yung T'ung-pao" **Rev:** "Êrh" (two) at right, "Li" at left **Note:** Schjöth #1340.

Date	Mintage	Good	VG	F	VF	XF
ND(1674)	—	5.50	9.00	14.00	18.00	—

KM# 191 2 CASH

Cast Bronze **Obv. Inscription:** "Li-yung T'ung-pao" **Rev:** Yün" at right **Mint:** Yün **Note:** Schjöth #1339.

Date	Mintage	Good	VG	F	VF	XF
ND(1674)	—	6.50	11.00	16.00	22.00	—

KM# 195 5 CASH

Cast Bronze **Obv. Inscription:** "Li-yung T'ung-pao" **Rev:** "Wu" (five) above, "Li" below **Note:** Schjöth #1341.

Date	Mintage	Good	VG	F	VF	XF
ND(1674)	—	8.00	9.00	15.00	18.00	—

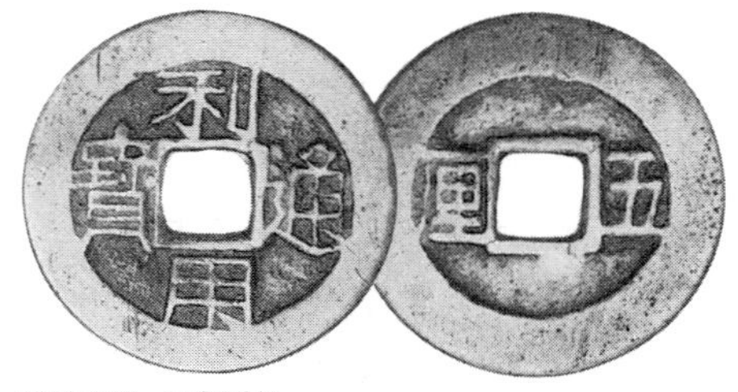

KM# 196 5 CASH

Cast Bronze **Obv. Inscription:** "Li-yung T'ung-pao" **Rev:** "Wu" (five) at right, "Li" at left

Date	Mintage	Good	VG	F	VF	XF
ND(1674)	—	9.00	12.00	18.00	25.00	—

KM# 197 FEN

Cast Bronze **Obv:** Large inscription **Obv. Inscription:** "Li-yung T'ung-pao" **Rev:** "Yi" (one) at right, "Fen" (candareen) at left **Note:** Schjöth #1342. Size varies: 39-41 mm.

Date	Mintage	Good	VG	F	VF	XF
ND(1674)	—	15.00	25.00	37.50	50.00	—

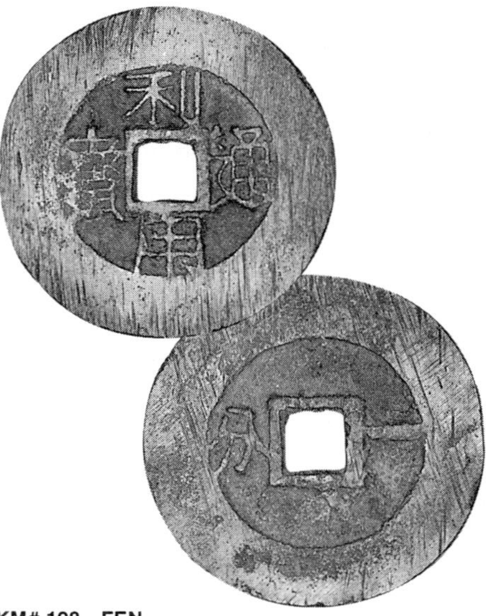

KM# 198 FEN

Cast Bronze **Obv:** Small inscription **Obv. Inscription:** "Li-yung T'ung-pao" **Rev:** Small "Yi" (one) at right, "Fen" (candareen) at left

Date	Mintage	Good	VG	F	VF	XF
ND(1674)	—	15.00	25.00	37.50	50.00	—

KM# 199 FEN

Cast Bronze **Obv:** Large inscription **Obv. Inscription:** "Li-yung T'ung-pao" **Rev:** Large "Yi" (one) above, "Fen" (candareen) below **Note:** Sch.#1343.

Date	Mintage	Good	VG	F	VF	XF
ND(1674)	—	25.00	37.50	52.50	70.00	—

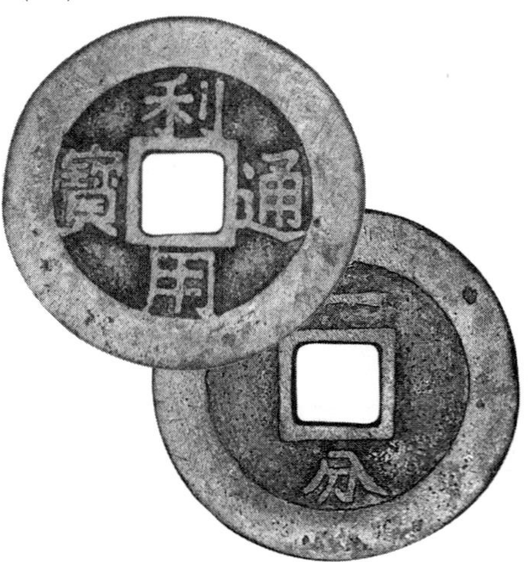

KM# 200 FEN

Cast Bronze **Obv:** Small inscription **Obv. Inscription:** "Li-yung T'ung-pao" **Rev:** Small "Yi" (one) above, "Fen" (candareen) below **Note:** Reduced size: 38-40 mm.

Date	Mintage	Good	VG	F	VF	XF
ND(1674)	—	20.00	25.00	30.00	40.00	—

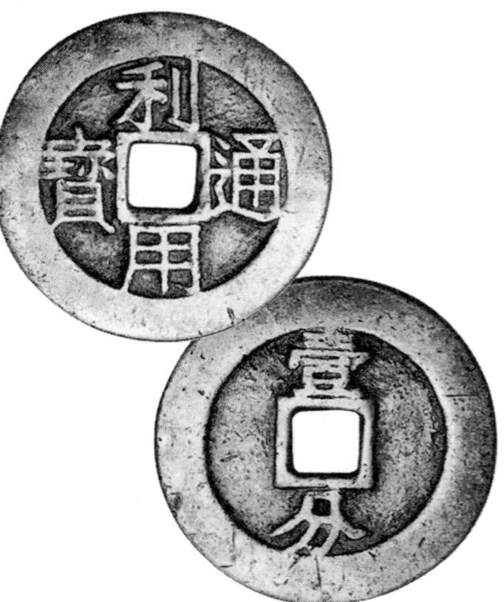

KM# 201 FEN

Cast Bronze **Obv. Inscription:** "Li-yung T'ung-pao" **Rev:** Official "Yi" (one) above, "Fen" (candareen) below

Date	Mintage	Good	VG	F	VF	XF
ND(1674)	—	30.00	45.00	60.00	85.00	—

Chao-wu

P'ing-hsi Wang

CAST COINAGE

KM# 203 CASH

Cast Bronze **Obv:** Seal script characters **Obv. Inscription:** "Chao-wu T'ung-pao" **Rev:** Plain **Note:** Size varies: 23-25 mm.

Date	Mintage	Good	VG	F	VF	XF
ND(1678)	—	15.00	25.00	35.00	50.00	—

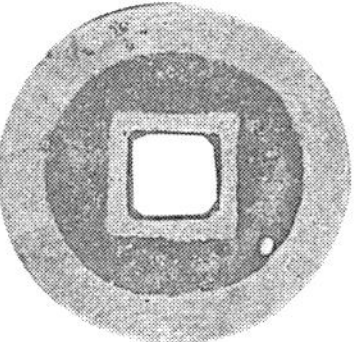

KM# 204.1 CASH

Cast Bronze **Obv:** Orthodox **Obv. Inscription:** "Chao-wu T'ung-pao" **Rev:** Plain **Note:** Schjöth #1345. Previous KM#204.

Date	Mintage	Good	VG	F	VF	XF
ND(1678)	—	0.75	1.50	3.00	5.00	—

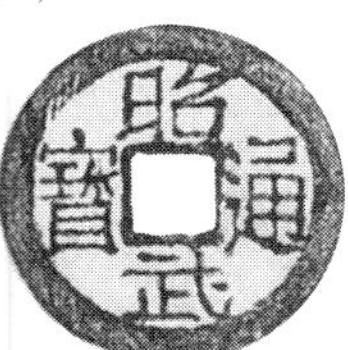
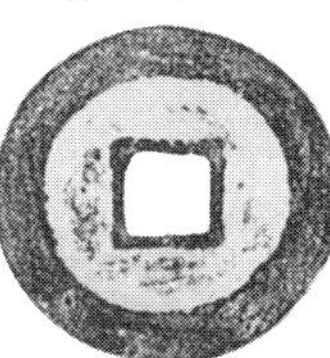

KM# 204.2 CASH

Cast Bronze **Obv:** Head of t'ung is open rectangle **Obv. Inscription:** "Chao-wu T'ung-pao" **Rev:** Plain

Date	Mintage	Good	VG	F	VF	XF
ND(1678)	—	26.50	32.50	40.00	50.00	—

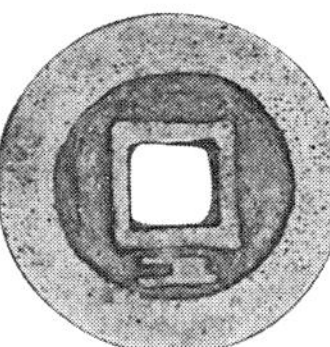

KM# 205 CASH

Cast Bronze **Obv:** Orthodox characters **Obv. Inscription:** "Chao-wu T'ung-pao" **Rev:** "Kung" below **Mint:** Kung-pu Board of Public Works **Note:** Schjöth #1346.

Date	Mintage	Good	VG	F	VF	XF
ND(1678)	—	2.00	3.00	4.50	6.00	—

KM# 208 FEN

Cast Bronze **Obv:** Seal script characters **Obv. Inscription:** "Chao-wu T'ung-pao" **Rev:** Seal script characters **Rev. Legend:** "Yi" (one), "Fen" (candareen) **Note:** Schjöth #1347.

Date	Mintage	Good	VG	F	VF	XF
ND(1678)	—	20.00	30.00	45.00	60.00	—

Hung-hua

Wu Shih-fan

CAST COINAGE

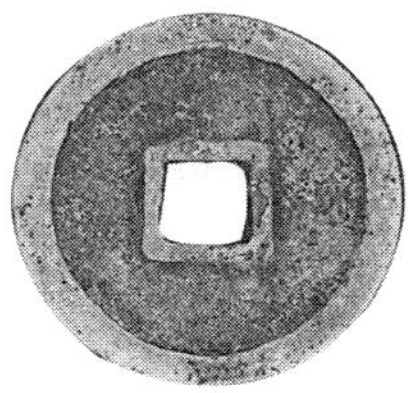

KM# 211 CASH

Cast Bronze **Obv. Inscription:** "Hung-hua T'ung-pao" **Rev:** Plain **Note:** Schjöth #1348. Size varies: 23-25 mm.

Date	Mintage	Good	VG	F	VF	XF
ND(ca.1679)	—	1.00	1.50	2.00	3.00	—

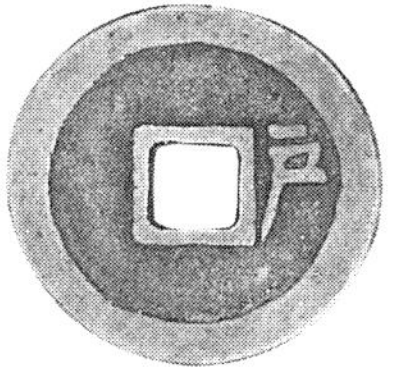

KM# 212 CASH

Cast Bronze **Obv. Inscription:** "Hung-hua T'ung-pao" **Rev:** "Hu" at right **Mint:** Hu-pu Board of Revenue **Note:** Schjöth #1349.

Date	Mintage	Good	VG	F	VF	XF
ND(ca.1679)	—	1.75	2.50	3.50	5.00	—

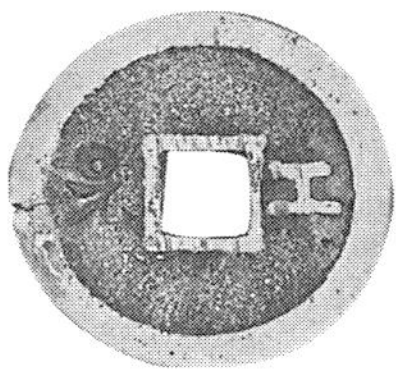

KM# 213 CASH

Cast Bronze **Obv. Inscription:** "Hung-hua T'ung-pao" **Rev:** "Kung" at right **Mint:** Kung-pu Board of Public Works **Note:** Schjöth #1350.

Date	Mintage	Good	VG	F	VF	XF
ND(ca.1679)	—	2.25	3.00	4.50	6.00	—

Yü-min

Keng Ching-chung

CAST COINAGE

KM# 217.1 CASH

Cast Bronze **Obv. Inscription:** "Yü-min T'ung-pao" **Rev:** Plain **Mint:** Fukien **Note:** Schjöth #1351. Size varies: 22-24 mm.

Date	Mintage	Good	VG	F	VF	XF
ND(1674)	—	—	—	—	—	—

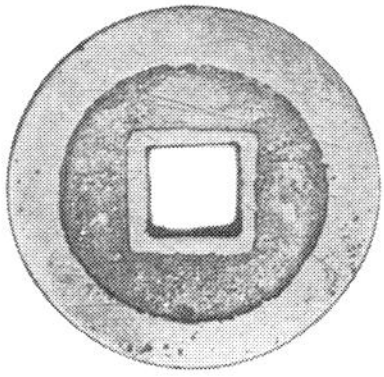

KM# 217.2 CASH

Cast Bronze **Obv:** Inscription deviating style **Obv. Inscription:** "Yü-min T'ung-pao" **Rev:** Plain **Mint:** Fukien **Note:** Schjöth #1352.

Date	Mintage	Good	VG	F	VF	XF
ND(1674)	—	6.00	10.00	15.00	20.00	—

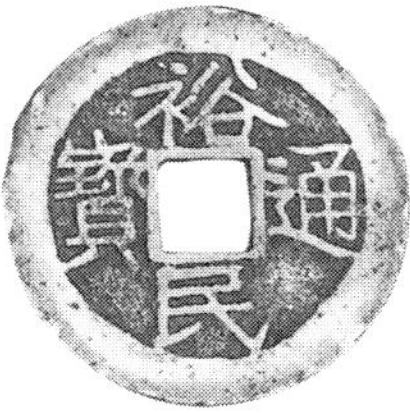

KM# 220 FEN

Cast Bronze **Obv. Inscription:** "Yü-min T'ung-pao" **Rev:** "Yi" (one) "Fen" (candareen) at right **Mint:** Fukien **Note:** Schjöth #1353. Size varies: 25-27 mm.

Date	Mintage	Good	VG	F	VF	XF
ND(1674)	—	7.50	12.50	20.00	30.00	—

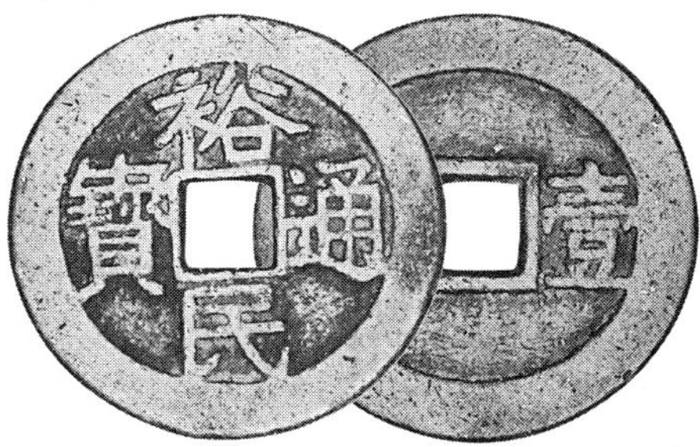

KM# 223 MACE

Cast Bronze **Obv. Inscription:** "Yü-min T'ung-pao" **Rev:** "Yi" (one) at right, "Ch'ien" (mace) at left **Mint:** Fukien **Note:** Schjöth #1354. Size varies: 37-39 mm.

Date	Mintage	Good	VG	F	VF	XF
ND(1674)	—	25.00	35.00	50.00	70.00	—

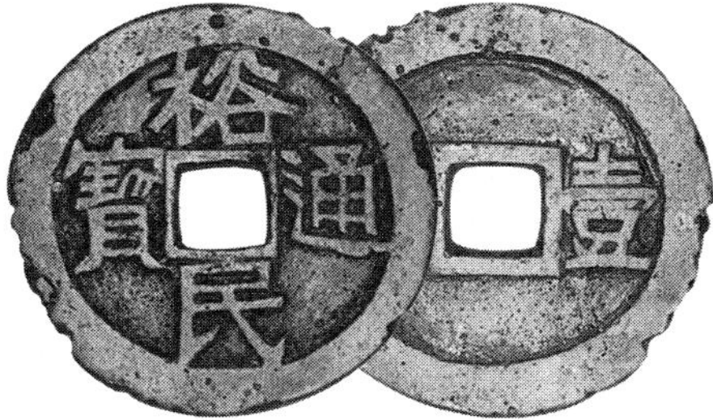

KM# 224 MACE

Cast Bronze **Obv. Inscription:** "Yü-min T'ung-pao" **Rev:** "Chê" at right, "Ch'ien" (mace) at left **Mint:** Fukien

Date	Mintage	Good	VG	F	VF	XF
ND(1674)	—	50.00	90.00	130	180	—

CH'ING DYNASTY

Manchu, 1644 - 1911

Shun-chih

Shunzhi

CAST COINAGE

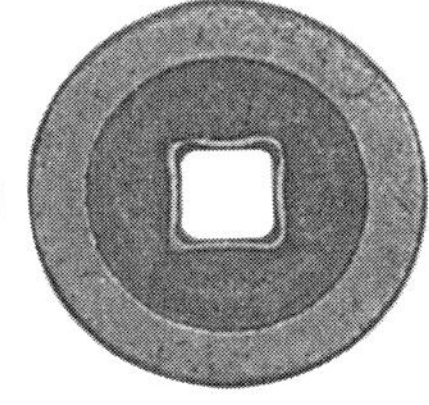

KM# 237 CASH

Cast Bronze **Obv. Inscription:** "Shun-chih T'ung-pao" **Rev:** Plain **Note:** Schjöth #1359. Size varies: 26-27mm.

Date	Mintage	Good	VG	F	VF	XF
ND(1644-61)	—	1.50	2.50	4.00	6.00	—

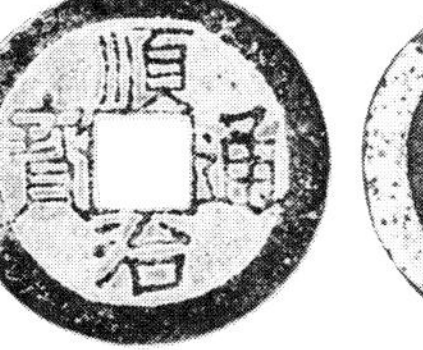
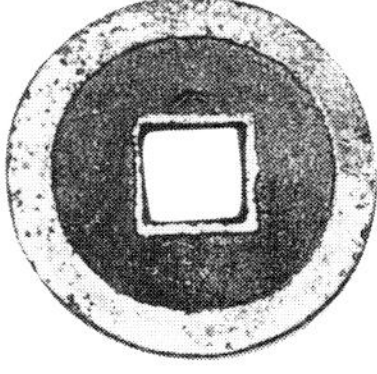

KM# 271 CASH

Cast Bronze **Obv. Inscription:** "Shun-chih T'ung-pao" **Rev:** Inverted crescent above

Date	Mintage	Good	VG	F	VF	XF
ND(1644-61)	—	5.50	9.00	15.00	25.00	—

KM# 272 CASH
Cast Bronze, 23 mm. **Obv. Inscription:** "Shun-chih T'ung-pao" **Rev:** Small circle above **Note:** Schjöth #1389. Reduced size.

Date	Mintage	Good	VG	F	VF	XF
ND(1644-61)	—	15.00	25.00	35.00	—	—

KM# 273 CASH
Cast Bronze, 26 mm. **Obv. Inscription:** "Shun-chih T'ung-pao" **Rev:** "Yi" (one) at right

Date	Mintage	Good	VG	F	VF	XF
ND(1644-61)	—	7.50	15.00	22.50	30.00	—

Note: Believed to be a trial issue

KM# 274 CASH
Cast Bronze **Obv. Inscription:** "Shun-chih T'ung-pao" **Rev:** "?rh" (two) at right

Date	Mintage	Good	VG	F	VF	XF
ND	—	40.00	80.00	120	160	—

Note: These were once found to be all circulating forgeries with 'kung' at right cut away to erh, to make a 2 cash piece. Now there are numismatic fakes being made starting with existing cash altered to make a mother cash. This will usually be a larger plain reverse piece which only needs 'erh' to be added. Above is one made from a Nurhaci large cash. No genuine 2 cash exists.

KM# 270 CASH
Cast Bronze, 25 mm. **Obv. Inscription:** "Shun-chih T'ung-pao" **Rev:** Small circle above **Note:** Schjöth #1388.

Date	Mintage	Good	VG	F	VF	XF
ND(1644)	—	5.50	9.90	15.00	22.00	—

KM# 291 CASH
Cast Bronze **Obv. Inscription:** "Shun-chih T'ung-pao" **Rev. Inscription:** "Shun-chih T'ung-pao" **Note:** Muling of 2 obverses.

Date	Mintage	Good	VG	F	VF	XF
ND(1644-61)	—	7.00	12.00	20.00	35.00	—

KM# 278 CASH
Cast Bronze **Obv. Inscription:** "Shun-chih T'ung-pao" **Rev:** "Yi (one) Li" at left, "Chê" at right **Mint:** Chêkiang **Note:** Schjöth #1393.

Date	Mintage	Good	VG	F	VF	XF
ND(1644-61)	—	8.00	10.00	15.00	20.00	—

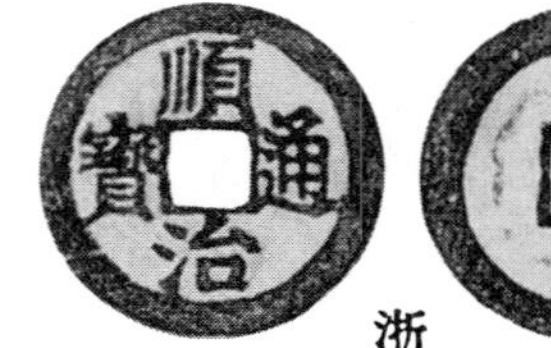

浙

KM# 258 CASH
Cast Bronze **Obv. Inscription:** "Shun-chih T'ung-pao" **Rev:** "Chê" at right **Mint:** Chêkiang **Note:** Schjöth #1378.

Date	Mintage	Good	VG	F	VF	XF
ND(1649-50)	—	1.50	3.00	6.00	—	—

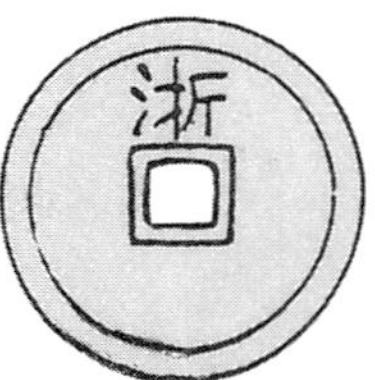

KM# 259 CASH
Cast Bronze **Obv. Inscription:** "Shun-chih T'ung-pao" **Rev:** "Chê" above **Mint:** Chêkiang **Note:** Schjöth #1379.

Date	Mintage	Good	VG	F	VF	XF
ND(1651-52)	—	2.50	5.00	10.00	—	—

KM# 296 CASH
Cast Bronze **Obv. Inscription:** "Shun-chih T'ung-pao" **Rev:** Manchu "Je" at left, Chinese "Chê" at right **Mint:** Chêkiang **Note:** Schjöth #1408.

Date	Mintage	Good	VG	F	VF	XF
ND(1644-61)	—	1.00	2.00	3.00	5.00	—

KM# 257 CASH
Cast Bronze **Obv. Inscription:** "Shun-chih T'ung-pao" **Rev:** "Ning" above **Mint:** Chiangning **Note:** Schjöth #1377.

Date	Mintage	Good	VG	F	VF	XF
ND(1644-61)	—	5.50	9.00	15.00	—	—

Note: Attributed to Ninghsia Mint by some authorities

KM# 287 CASH
Cast Bronze **Obv. Inscription:** "Shun-chih T'ung-pao" **Rev:** "Yi (one) Li" at left, "Ning" at right **Mint:** Chiangning **Note:** Schjöth #1403.

Date	Mintage	Good	VG	F	VF	XF
ND(1644-61)	—	5.50	9.00	15.00	20.00	—

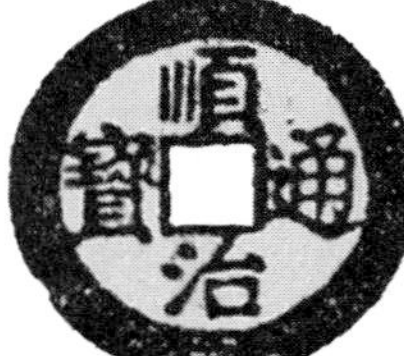

KM# 277 CASH
Cast Bronze **Obv. Inscription:** "Shun-chih T'ung-pao" **Rev:** "Yi (one) Li" at left, "Chiang" at right **Mint:** Chiangning **Note:** Schjöth #1392.

Date	Mintage	Good	VG	F	VF	XF
ND(1655-56)	—	10.00	15.00	20.00	25.00	—

KM# 295 CASH
Cast Bronze **Obv. Inscription:** "Shun-chih T'ung-pao" **Rev:** Manchu "Giyang" at left, Chinese "Chiang" at right **Mint:** Chiangning **Note:** Schjöth #1407.

Date	Mintage	Good	VG	F	VF	XF
ND(1644-61)	—	1.50	3.00	5.00	7.00	—

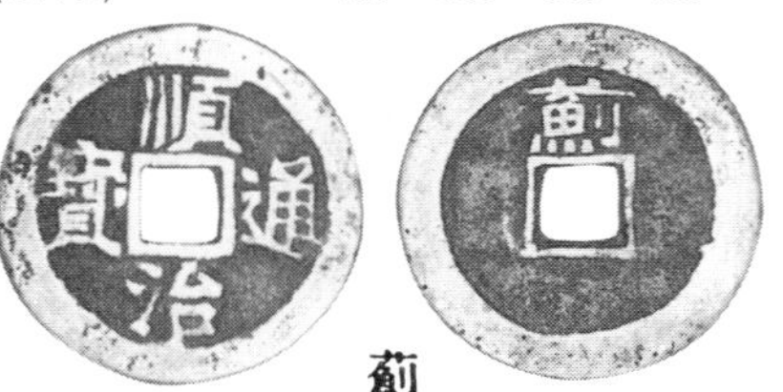

薊

KM# A249 CASH
Cast Bronze **Obv. Inscription:** "Shun-chih T'ung-pao" **Rev:** "Chi" above **Mint:** Chichou

Date	Mintage	Good	VG	F	VF	XF
ND(1644-61)	—	75.00	125	175	250	—

薊

KM# 249 CASH
Cast Bronze **Obv. Inscription:** "Shun-chih T'ung-pao" **Rev:** "Chi" at right **Mint:** Chichou **Note:** Schjöth #1369.

Date	Mintage	Good	VG	F	VF	XF
ND(1644-61)	—	22.50	35.00	50.00	75.00	—

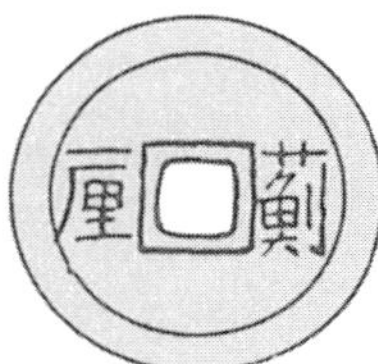

KM# 283 CASH
Cast Bronze **Obv. Inscription:** "Shun-chih T'ung-pao" **Rev:** "Yi (one) Li" at left, "Chi" at right **Mint:** Chichou **Note:** Schjöth #1399.

Date	Mintage	Good	VG	F	VF	XF
ND(1644-61)	—	5.50	9.00	15.00	20.00	—

KM# 301 CASH
Cast Bronze **Obv. Inscription:** "Shun-chih T'ung-pao" **Rev:** Manchu "Gi" at left, Chinese "Chi" at right **Mint:** Chichou **Note:** Schjöth #1413.

Date	Mintage	Good	VG	F	VF	XF
ND(1644-61)	—	1.00	2.00	3.00	5.00	—

荆

KM# 254 CASH
Cast Bronze **Obv. Inscription:** "Shun-chih T'ung-pao" **Rev:** "Ching" at right **Mint:** Chingchou **Note:** Schjöth #1374.

Date	Mintage	Good	VG	F	VF	XF
ND(1644-61)	—	75.00	125	175	250	—

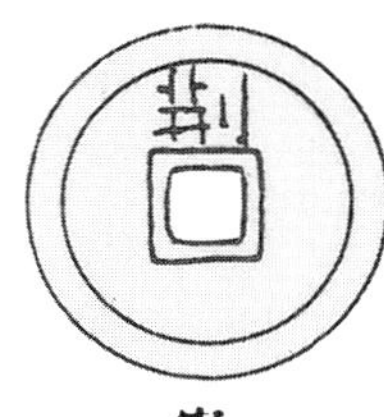

寧

KM# 255 CASH

Cast Bronze **Obv. Inscription:** "Shun-chih T'ung-pao" **Rev:** "Ching" above **Mint:** Chingchou **Note:** Schjöth #1375.

Date	Mintage	Good	VG	F	VF	XF
ND(1644-61)	—	35.00	75.00	110	150	—

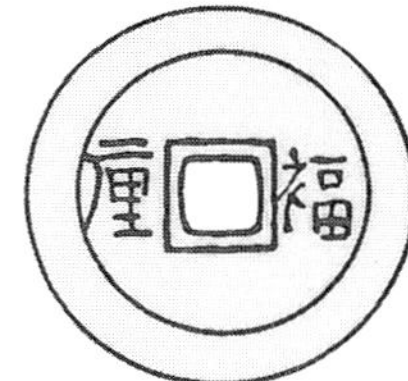

KM# 279 CASH

Cast Bronze **Obv. Inscription:** "Shun-chih T'ung-pao" **Rev:** "Yi (one) Li" at left, "Fukien" at right **Mint:** Fuchou **Note:** Schjöth #1394.

Date	Mintage	Good	VG	F	VF	XF
ND(1644-61)	—	12.00	20.00	30.00	40.00	—

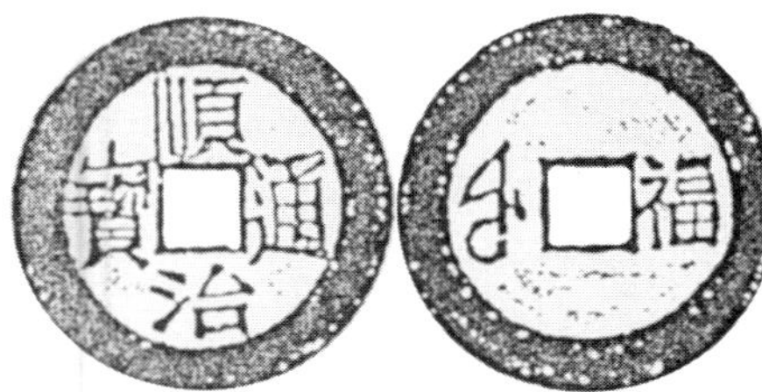

KM# 307 CASH

Cast Bronze **Obv. Inscription:** "Shun-chih T'ung-pao" **Rev:** Manchu "Fu" at left, Chinese "Fu" at right **Mint:** Fuchou

Date	Mintage	Good	VG	F	VF	XF
ND(1644-61)	—	50.00	100	150	200	—

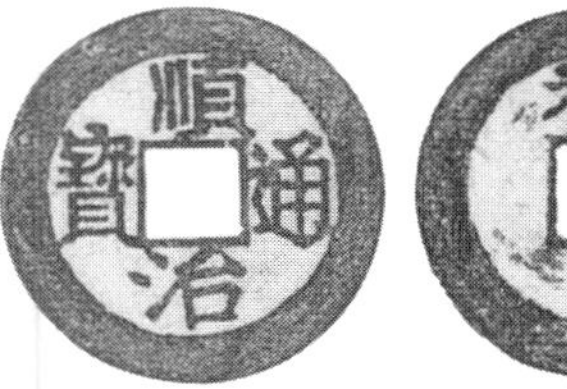

KM# 262 CASH

Cast Bronze **Obv. Inscription:** "Shun-chih T'ung-pao" **Rev:** "Fu" above **Mint:** Fuchow **Note:** Schjöth #1382.

Date	Mintage	Good	VG	F	VF	XF
ND(1651-52)	—	8.50	14.00	20.00	35.00	—

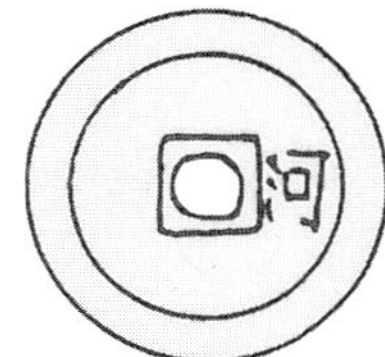

KM# 243 CASH

Cast Bronze **Obv. Inscription:** "Shun-chih T'ung-pao" **Rev:** "Ho" at right **Mint:** Honan **Note:** Schjöth #1363.

Date	Mintage	Good	VG	F	VF	XF
ND(1644-61)	—	5.00	8.00	15.00	20.00	—

KM# 244 CASH

Cast Bronze **Obv. Inscription:** "Shun-chih T'ung-pao" **Rev:** "Ho" above **Mint:** Honan **Note:** Schjöth #1364.

Date	Mintage	Good	VG	F	VF	XF
ND(1644-61)	—	5.00	8.00	15.00	20.00	—

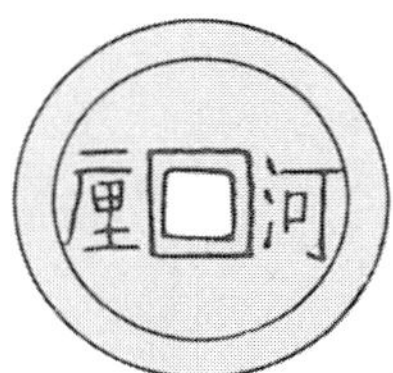

KM# 284 CASH

Cast Bronze **Obv. Inscription:** "Shun-chih T'ung-pao" **Rev:** "Yi (one) Li" at left, "Ho" at right **Mint:** Honan **Note:** Schjöth #1400.

Date	Mintage	Good	VG	F	VF	XF
ND(1644-61)	—	5.50	9.00	15.00	20.00	—

KM# 302 CASH

Cast Bronze **Obv. Inscription:** "Shun-chih T'ung-pao" **Rev:** Manchu "Ho" at left, Chinese "Ho" at right **Mint:** Honan **Note:** Schjöth #1414.

Date	Mintage	Good	VG	F	VF	XF
ND(1644-61)	—	1.00	2.00	3.00	5.00	—

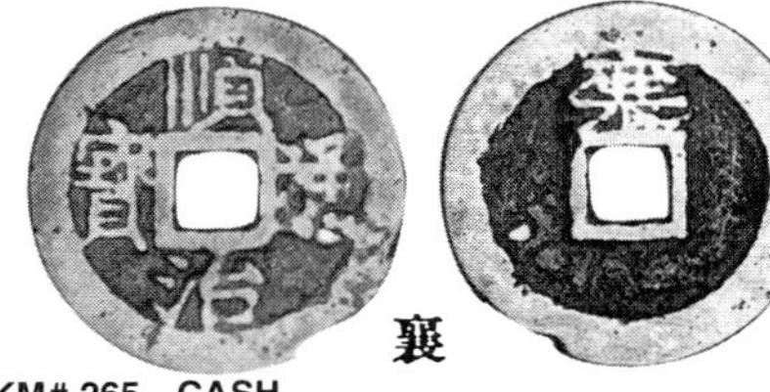

襄

KM# 265 CASH

Cast Bronze **Obv. Inscription:** "Shun-chih T'ung-pao" **Rev:** "Hsiang" above **Mint:** Hsiangyang **Note:** Schjöth #1385.

Date	Mintage	Good	VG	F	VF	XF
ND(1651)	—	20.00	35.00	75.00	150	—

Note: Records indicate some mints were to be casting in the period of single character reverse marks, but whose cash have never been found. In many works they are noted to exist regardless. In Ting Fu-pao they are even drawn in by pen, without notation of that fact. These are: shen above & right; tung & kiang above; and ning, kuang, chang, & fu at right

KM# 247 CASH

Cast Bronze **Obv. Inscription:** "Shun-chih T'ung-pao" **Rev:** "Hsüan" at right **Mint:** Hsüan Prefecture **Note:** Schjöth #1367.

Date	Mintage	Good	VG	F	VF	XF
ND(1644-61)	—	10.00	15.00	20.00	25.00	—

KM# 248 CASH

Cast Bronze **Obv. Inscription:** "Shun-chih T'ung-pao" **Rev:** "Hsüan" above **Mint:** Hsüan Prefecture **Note:** Schjöth #1368.

Date	Mintage	Good	VG	F	VF	XF
ND(1644-61)	—	100	160	225	325	—

KM# 290 CASH

Cast Bronze **Obv. Inscription:** "Shun-chih T'ung-pao" **Rev:** "Yi (one) Li" at left, "Hsüan" at right **Mint:** Hsüanfu

Date	Mintage	Good	VG	F	VF	XF
ND(1644-61)	—	4.50	7.00	11.00	15.00	—

KM# 300 CASH

Cast Bronze **Obv. Inscription:** "Shun-chih T'ung-pao" **Rev:** Manchu "Siowan" at left, Chinese "Hsüan" at right **Mint:** Hsüanfu **Note:** Schjöth #1412.

Date	Mintage	Good	VG	F	VF	XF
ND(1644-61)	—	0.75	1.25	2.00	3.00	—

KM# 241 CASH

Cast Bronze **Obv. Inscription:** "Shun-chih T'ung-pao" **Rev:** "Hu" at right **Mint:** Hu-pu Board of Revenue **Note:** Schjöth #1362.

Date	Mintage	Good	VG	F	VF	XF
ND(1644-61)	—	1.50	2.50	4.00	6.00	—

戸

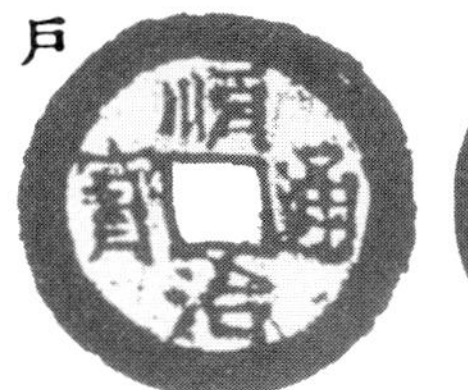

KM# 242 CASH

Cast Bronze **Obv. Inscription:** "Shun-chih T'ung-pao" **Rev:** "Hu" above **Mint:** Hu-pu Board of Revenue

Date	Mintage	Good	VG	F	VF	XF
ND(1644-61)	—	85.00	115	165	225	—

戸

KM# 275 CASH

Cast Bronze **Obv. Inscription:** "Shun-chih T'ung-pao" **Rev:** "Yi (one) Li" at left, "Hu" at right **Mint:** Hu-pu Board of Revenue **Note:** Schjöth #1390.

Date	Mintage	Good	VG	F	VF	XF
ND(1653-56)	—	1.75	3.50	5.00	7.00	—

KM# 293 CASH

Cast Bronze **Obv. Inscription:** "Shun-chih T'ung-pao" **Rev:** Manchu "Boo-Ciowan" **Mint:** Hu-pu Board of Revenue **Note:** Size varies: 26-27 mm.

Date	Mintage	Good	VG	F	VF	XF
ND(1694)	—	0.75	1.25	2.00	3.00	—

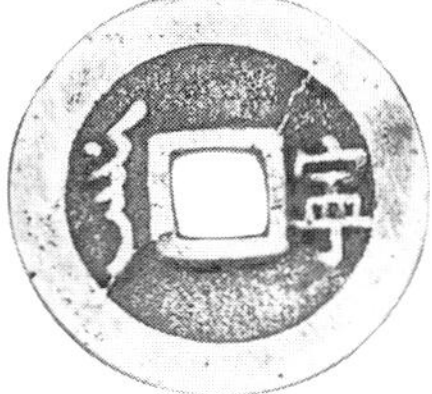

KM# 305 CASH

Cast Bronze **Rev:** Manchu "Ning"(?) at left, Chinese "Ning" at right **Rev. Inscription:** "Shun-chih T'ung-pao" **Mint:** Kiangning **Note:** Schjöth #1417.

Date	Mintage	Good	VG	F	VF	XF
ND(1644-61)	—	1.00	2.00	3.00	5.00	—

工

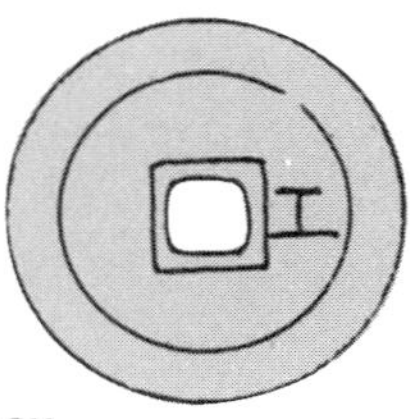

KM# 238 CASH

Cast Bronze **Obv. Inscription:** "Shun-chih T'ung-pao" **Rev:** "Kung" at right **Mint:** Kung-pu Board of Public Works **Note:** Schjöth #1360.

Date	Mintage	Good	VG	F	VF	XF
ND(1644-61)	—	2.50	4.00	6.50	8.00	—

工

KM# 239 CASH

Cast Bronze **Obv. Inscription:** "Shun-chih T'ung-pao" **Rev:** "Kung" above **Mint:** Kung-pu Board of Public Works

Date	Mintage	Good	VG	F	VF	XF
ND(1644-61)	—	50.00	85.00	150	250	—

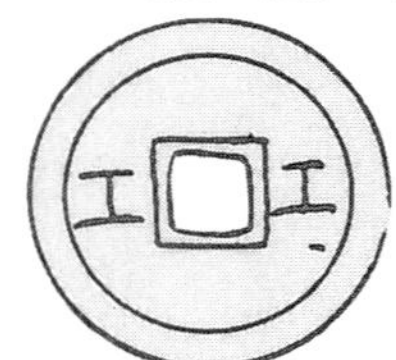

KM# 240 CASH

Cast Bronze **Obv. Inscription:** "Shun-chih T'ung-pao" **Rev:** "Kung" at left and right **Mint:** Kung-pu Board of Public Works **Note:** Schjöth #1361.

Date	Mintage	Good	VG	F	VF	XF
ND(1644-61)	—	—	—	—	—	—

KM# 276 CASH

Cast Bronze **Obv. Inscription:** "Shun-chih T'ung-pao" **Rev:** "Yi (one) Li" at left, "Kung" at right **Mint:** Kung-pu Board of Public Works **Note:** Schjöth #1391.

Date	Mintage	Good	VG	F	VF	XF
ND(1653-56)	—	1.75	3.50	5.00	7.00	—

KM# 294 CASH

Cast Bronze **Obv. Inscription:** "Shun-chih T'ung-pao" **Rev:** Manchu "Boo-yuwan" **Mint:** Kung-pu Board of Public Works **Note:** Schjöth #1406.

Date	Mintage	Good	VG	F	VF	XF
ND1644	—	0.75	1.25	2.00	3.00	—

臨

KM# 281 CASH

Cast Bronze **Obv. Inscription:** "Shun-chih T'ung-pao" **Rev:** "Yi (one) Li" at left, "Lin" at right **Mint:** Linch'ing **Note:** Schjöth #1396.

Date	Mintage	Good	VG	F	VF	XF
ND(1644-61)	—	5.50	9.00	15.00	20.00	—

KM# 298 CASH

Cast Bronze **Obv. Inscription:** "Shun-chih T'ung-pao" **Rev:** Manchu "Lin"(?) at left, Chinese "Lin" at right **Mint:** Linch'ing **Note:** Schjöth #1410.

Date	Mintage	Good	VG	F	VF	XF
ND(1644-61)	—	1.00	2.00	3.00	5.00	—

KM# 245 CASH

Cast Bronze **Obv. Inscription:** "Shun-chih T'ung-pao" **Rev:** "Lin" at right **Mint:** Linching **Note:** Schjöth #1365.

Date	Mintage	Good	VG	F	VF	XF
ND(1647-50)	—	10.00	15.00	20.00	25.00	—

臨

KM# 246 CASH

Cast Bronze **Obv. Inscription:** "Shun-chih T'ung-pao" **Rev:** "Lin" above **Mint:** Linching **Note:** Schjöth #1366.

Date	Mintage	Good	VG	F	VF	XF
ND(1651)	—	20.00	30.00	35.00	40.00	—

KM# 253 CASH

Cast Bronze **Obv. Inscription:** "Shun-chih T'ung-pao" **Rev:** "Yün" at right **Mint:** Miyün **Note:** Schjöth #1373.

Date	Mintage	Good	VG	F	VF	XF
ND(1644-61)	—	10.00	20.00	35.00	—	—

KM# 288 CASH

Cast Bronze **Obv. Inscription:** "Shun-chih T'ung-pao" **Rev:** "Yi (one) Li" at left, "Yün" at right **Mint:** Miyün **Note:** Schjöth #1404.

Date	Mintage	Good	VG	F	VF	XF
ND(1644-61)	—	5.50	9.00	15.00	20.00	—

KM# 286 CASH

Cast Bronze **Obv. Inscription:** "Shun-chih T'ung-pao" **Rev:** "Yi (one) Li" at left, "Shan" at right **Mint:** Shansi **Note:** Schjöth #1402.

Date	Mintage	Good	VG	F	VF	XF
ND(1644-61)	—	5.50	9.00	15.00	20.00	—

KM# 280 CASH

Cast Bronze **Obv. Inscription:** "Shun-chih T'ung-pao" **Rev:** "Yi (one) Li" at left, "Tung" at right **Mint:** Shantung **Note:** Schjöth #1395.

Date	Mintage	Good	VG	F	VF	XF
ND(1644-61)	—	5.00	8.00	10.00	15.00	—

東

KM# 260 CASH

Cast Bronze **Obv. Inscription:** "Shun-chih T'ung-pao" **Rev:** "Tung" at right **Mint:** Shantung **Note:** Schjöth #1380.

Date	Mintage	Good	VG	F	VF	XF
ND(1649-50)	—	1.50	3.00	6.00	—	—

KM# 261 CASH

Cast Bronze **Obv. Inscription:** "Shun-chih T'ung-pao" **Rev:** "Tung" above **Mint:** Shantung **Note:** Schjöth #1381.

Date	Mintage	Good	VG	F	VF	XF
ND(1651-52)	—	1.50	3.00	6.00	—	—

KM# 297 CASH

Cast Bronze **Obv. Inscription:** "Shun-chih T'ung-pao" **Rev:** Manchu "Dung" at left, Chinese "Tung" at right **Mint:** Shantung **Note:** Schjöth #1409.

Date	Mintage	Good	VG	F	VF	XF
ND(1644-61)	—	0.75	1.25	2.00	3.00	—

KM# 304 CASH

Cast Bronze **Obv. Inscription:** "Shun-chih T'ung-pao" **Rev:** Manchu "San" at left, Chinese "Shen" at right **Mint:** Shensi **Note:** Schjöth #1416.

Date	Mintage	Good	VG	F	VF	XF
ND(1644-61)	—	1.50	3.00	5.00	7.00	—

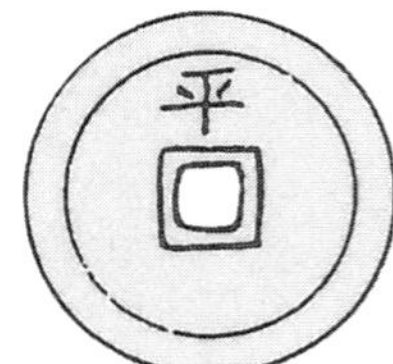

KM# 267 CASH

Cast Bronze **Obv. Inscription:** "Shun-chih T'ung-pao" **Rev:** "P'ing" above **Mint:** T'aiping Fu **Note:** Schjöth #1387.

Date	Mintage	Good	VG	F	VF	XF
ND(1644-61)	—	—	—	—	—	—

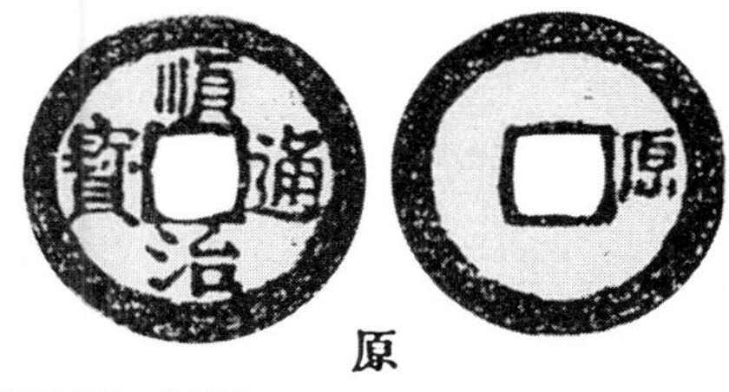

原

KM# 250 CASH
Cast Bronze **Obv. Inscription:** "Shun-chih T'ung-pao"
Rev: "Yüan" at right **Mint:** T'aiyüan Fu **Note:** Schjöth #1370.

Date	Mintage	Good	VG	F	VF	XF
ND(1644-61)	—	7.50	12.50	20.00	—	—

KM# 251 CASH
Cast Bronze **Obv. Inscription:** "Shun-chih T'ung-pao"
Rev: "Yüan" above **Mint:** T'aiyüan Fu **Note:** Schjöth #1371.

Date	Mintage	Good	VG	F	VF	XF
ND(1644-61)	—	10.00	17.50	25.00	—	—

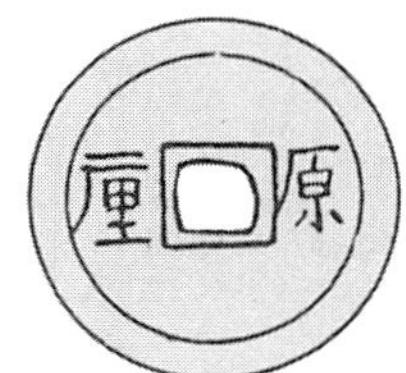

KM# A282 CASH
Cast Bronze **Obv. Inscription:** "Shun-chih T'ung-pao" **Rev:** "Yi (one) Li" at left, "Yüan" at right **Mint:** T'aiyüan Fu **Note:** Schjöth #1397. Previous number: KM#281A.

Date	Mintage	Good	VG	F	VF	XF
ND(1644-61)	—	6.00	10.00	14.00	20.00	—

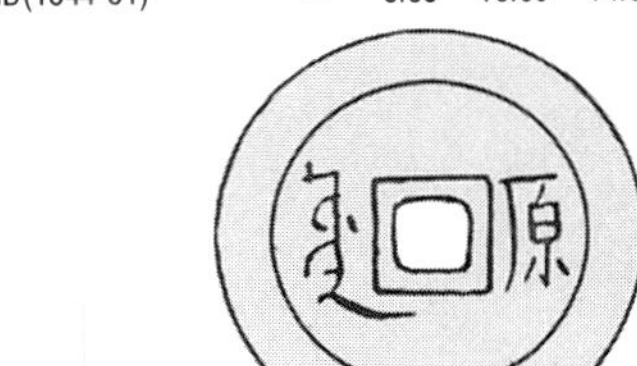

KM# 299 CASH
Cast Bronze **Obv. Inscription:** "Shun-chih T'ung-pao"
Rev: Manchu "Yuwan" at left, Chinese "Yüan" at right
Mint: T'aiyüan Fu **Note:** Schjöth #1411.

Date	Mintage	Good	VG	F	VF	XF
ND(1644-61)	—	3.00	6.00	10.00	15.00	—

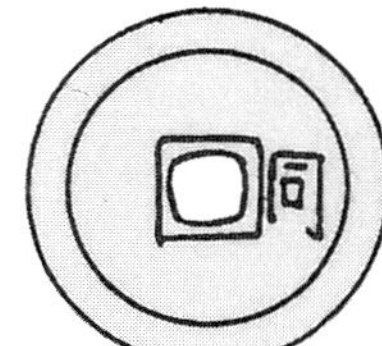

KM# 252 CASH
Cast Bronze **Obv. Inscription:** "Shun-chih T'ung-pao"
Rev: "T'ung" at right **Mint:** Tat'ung **Note:** Schjöth #1372.

Date	Mintage	Good	VG	F	VF	XF
ND(1644-61)	—	5.50	9.00	15.00	—	—

KM# 289 CASH
Cast Bronze **Obv. Inscription:** "Shun-chih T'ung-pao" **Rev:** "Yi (one) Li" at left, "T'ung" at right **Mint:** Tat'ung

Date	Mintage	Good	VG	F	VF	XF
ND(1644-61)	—	30.00	50.00	70.00	100	—

KM# 306 CASH
Cast Bronze **Obv. Inscription:** "Shun-chih T'ung-pao"
Rev: Manchu "Tung" at left, Chinese "T'ung" at right **Mint:** Tat'ung
Note: Schjöth #1418.

Date	Mintage	Good	VG	F	VF	XF
ND(1644-61)	—	1.00	2.00	3.00	5.00	—

KM# 256 CASH
Cast Bronze **Obv. Inscription:** "Shun-chih T'ung-pao"
Rev: "Ch'ang" above **Mint:** Wuch'ang **Note:** Schjöth #1376.

Date	Mintage	Good	VG	F	VF	XF
ND(1644-61)	—	5.50	9.00	15.00	—	—

KM# 285 CASH
Cast Bronze **Obv. Inscription:** "Shun-chih T'ung-pao" **Rev:** "Yi (one) Li" at left, "Ch'ang" at right **Mint:** Wuch'ang **Note:** Schjöth #1401.

Date	Mintage	Good	VG	F	VF	XF
ND(1644-61)	—	5.50	9.00	15.00	20.00	—

KM# 303 CASH
Cast Bronze **Obv. Inscription:** "Shun-chih T'ung-pao"
Rev: Manchu "Cang" at left, Chinese "Ch'ang" at right
Mint: Wuch'ang **Note:** Schjöth #1415.

Date	Mintage	Good	VG	F	VF	XF
ND(1644-61)	—	1.00	2.00	3.00	5.00	—

KM# 282 CASH
Cast Bronze **Obv. Inscription:** "Shun-chih T'ung-pao" **Rev:** "Yi (one) Li" at left, "Yang" at right **Mint:** Yangho **Note:** Schjöth #1398.

Date	Mintage	Good	VG	F	VF	XF
ND(1644-61)	—	15.00	20.00	25.00	30.00	—

陽

KM# 263 CASH
Cast Bronze **Obv. Inscription:** "Shun-chih T'ung-pao"
Rev: "Yang" at right **Mint:** Yangho **Note:** Schjöth #1383.

Date	Mintage	Good	VG	F	VF	XF
ND(1649-50)	—	10.00	25.00	50.00	100	—

KM# 264 CASH
Cast Bronze **Obv. Inscription:** "Shun-chih T'ung-pao"
Rev: "Yang" above **Mint:** Yangho **Note:** Schjöth #1384.

Date	Mintage	Good	VG	F	VF	XF
ND(1651)	—	18.00	30.00	65.00	120	—

KM# A269 CASH
Cast Bronze **Obv. Inscription:** "Shun-chih T'ung-pao"
Rev: "Yen" at top **Mint:** Yensui

Date	Mintage	Good	VG	F	VF	XF
ND(1644-61)	—	100	175	300	500	—

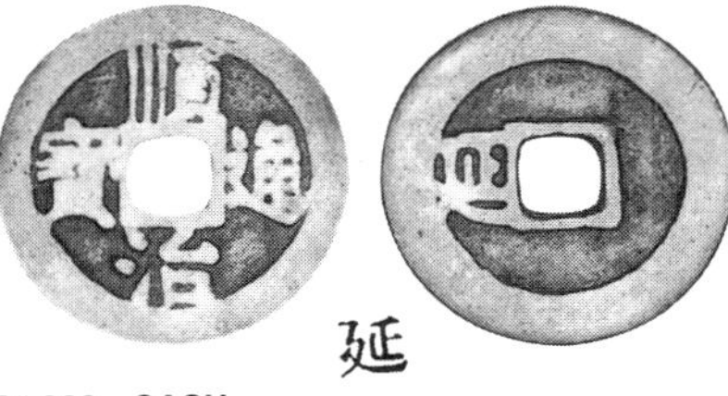

延

KM# 269 CASH
Cast Bronze **Obv. Inscription:** "Shun-chih T'ung-pao"
Rev: "Yen" at left **Mint:** Yensui

Date	Mintage	Good	VG	F	VF	XF
ND(1646)	—	45.00	75.00	150	300	—

KM# 268 CASH
Cast Bronze **Obv. Inscription:** "Shun-chih T'ung-pao"
Rev: "Yen" at right **Mint:** Yensui

Date	Mintage	Good	VG	F	VF	XF
ND(1647-48)	—	45.00	75.00	150	300	—

K'ang-hsi
1662-1722, Kangxi

K'ang-hsi T'ung-pao 

Talisman Series

Schjöth #1423-1442; KM#318-337:

The Chinese attach a talismanic virtue to these coins. If genuine and placed together, they have the power of expelling evil influences and of preventing fires. Their genuineness according to popular belief can be tested by placing them, when strung together, on the top of a chicken coop: if genuine, they will prevent the cocks from crowing in the morning!

Lo-han Series

Schjöth #1443-1445; KM#338-342:

These coins are slightly different from the preceding in the form of the character *Hsi*, which is here rendered with closed strokes instead of open strokes. They are commonly known as the "*Lo-han cash*", and are sought after by the Chinese. The word Lohan being the transcript in Chinese characters of the Sanscrit word *arhan* "venerable", the name applied to the eighteen attendants of Buddha, which are frequently seen ranged along the two sides of the principal hall in Buddhist temples. The current tradition is that while the Emperor was intimately associated with the European missionaries, he became imbued with a feeling of contempt for Buddhism and illustrated this phase in his faith by having a set of eighteen brass *Lo-han* images melted down and cast into cash. This brass is said to contain a considerable portion of gold, hence the great demand for the cash.

CAST COINAGE

KM# 355 CASH
Cast Red Copper **Obv. Inscription:** "K'ang-hsi T'ung-pao" with open "si" **Rev. Inscription:** "K'ang-hsi T'ung-pao" **Note:** Muling. Schjöth #1450.

Date	Mintage	Good	VG	F	VF	XF
ND(1662-1722)	—	17.50	25.00	35.00	50.00	—

通

KM# 312.3 CASH

Cast Bronze, 26 mm. **Obv. Inscription:** "K'ang-hsi Tung-pao" with one dot T'ung **Rev:** Manchu "Boo-Yuwan" **Note:** Wide rims.

Date	Mintage	Good	VG	F	VF	XF
ND(1662-1722)	—	3.00	6.00	10.00	17.50	—

南

KM# 330.1 CASH

Cast Bronze, 27 mm. **Series:** Talisman (Poem Cash) **Obv. Inscription:** K'ang-hsi T'ung-pao **Rev:** Manchu "Nan" at left, Chinese "Nan" at right **Mint:** Ch'angsha **Note:** Schjöth #1435.

Date	Mintage	Good	VG	F	VF	XF
ND(1662-1722)	—	12.50	17.50	25.00	35.00	—

KM# 330.2 CASH

Cast Bronze, 25 mm. **Series:** Talisman (Poem Cash) **Obv. Inscription:** "K'ang-hsi T'ung-pao" **Rev:** Manchu "Nan" at left, Chinese "Nan" at right **Mint:** Ch'angsha

Date	Mintage	Good	VG	F	VF	XF
ND(1662-1722)	—	3.00	5.00	7.00	10.00	—

Note: The larger 27mm examples were cast during later reigns

KM# 351 CASH

Cast Red Copper, 23-24 mm. **Series:** Talisman (Poem Cash) **Obv. Inscription:** "K'ang-hsi T'ung-pao" with open "hsi" **Rev:** Manchu "Nan" at left, Chinese "Nan" at right **Mint:** Ch'angsha **Note:** Size varies. Schjöth #1446.

Date	Mintage	Good	VG	F	VF	XF
ND(1662-1722)	—	12.50	17.50	25.00	35.00	—

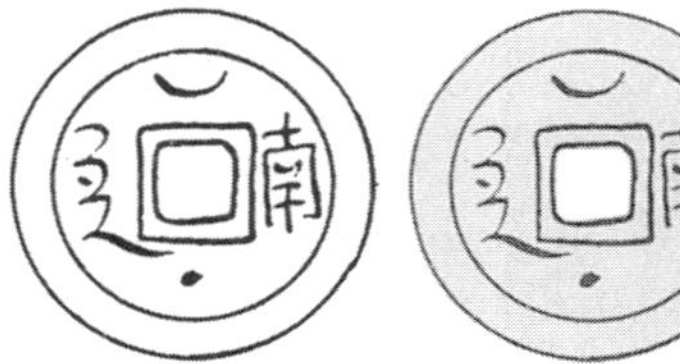
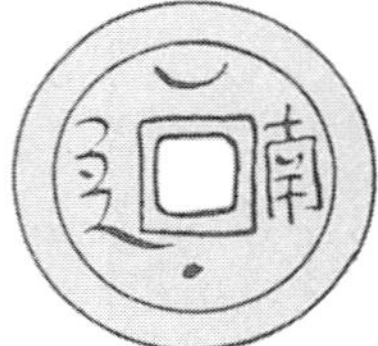

KM# 352 CASH

Cast Red Copper **Obv. Inscription:** "K'ang-hsi T'ung-pao" with open "hsi" **Rev:** Manchu "Nan" at left, Chinese "Nan" at right, crescent above, dot below **Mint:** Ch'angsha **Note:** Schjöth #1447.

Date	Mintage	Good	VG	F	VF	XF
ND(1662-1722)	—	42.50	70.00	100	150	—

KM# E340 CASH

Cast Bronze **Series:** "Lo-han" **Obv. Inscription:** K'ang-hsi T'ung-pao **Rev:** Manchu "Nan" at left, Chinese "Nan" at right **Mint:** Ch'angsha **Note:** Similar to KM#330.

Date	Mintage	Good	VG	F	VF	XF
ND(1662-1722)	—	5.00	7.00	10.00	15.00	—

漳

KM# 337 CASH

Cast Bronze **Series:** Talisman (Poem Cash) **Obv. Inscription:** "K'ang-hsi T'ung-pao" **Rev:** Manchu "Jiyang" (?) at left, Chinese "Chang" at right **Mint:** Changchou **Note:** Schjöth #1442. See also KM#342.

Date	Mintage	Good	VG	F	VF	XF
ND(1662-1722)	—	1.50	2.25	3.50	5.00	—

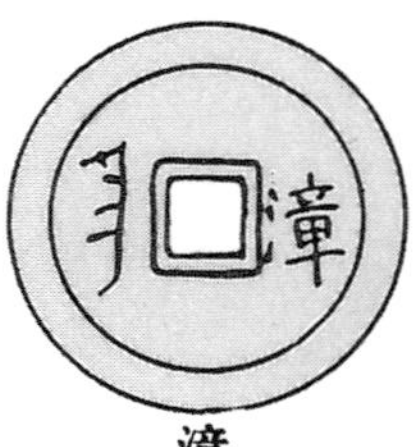

漳

KM# 342 CASH

Cast Brass **Series:** Lo-han **Obv. Inscription:** "K'ang-hsi T'ung-pao" with closed "hsi" **Rev:** Manchu "Jiyang Chang" at left, Chinese "Chang" at right **Mint:** Changchou **Note:** Schjöth #1445. See also KM#337.

Date	Mintage	Good	VG	F	VF	XF
ND(1662-1722)	—	5.00	7.00	10.00	15.00	—

浙

KM# 332 CASH

Cast Bronze, 25 mm. **Series:** Talisman (Poem Cash) **Obv. Inscription:** K'ang-hsi T'ung-pao. **Rev:** Manchu "Je" at left, Chinese "Chê" at right **Mint:** Chêkiang **Note:** Schjöth #1437.

Date	Mintage	Good	VG	F	VF	XF
ND(1662-1722)	—	1.50	2.25	3.50	5.00	—

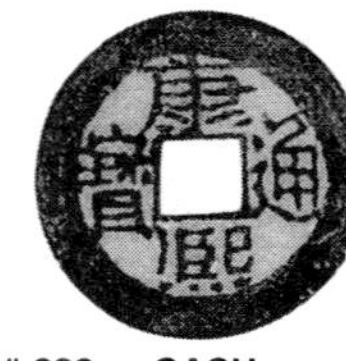

KM# 332a CASH

Cast Bronze, 22 mm. **Series:** Talisman (Poem Cash) **Obv. Inscription:** K'ang-hsi T'ung-pao **Rev:** Small Manchu "Je" at left, Chinese "Chê" at right **Mint:** Chêkiang **Note:** Schjöth #1437.

Date	Mintage	Good	VG	F	VF	XF
ND(1696-1699)	—	1.50	2.25	3.50	5.00	—

江

KM# 322 CASH

Cast Bronze **Series:** Talisman (Poem Cash) **Obv. Inscription:** K'ang-hsi T'ung-pao **Rev:** Manchu "Giyang" at left, Chinese "Chiang" at right **Mint:** Chiangning **Note:** Schjöth #1427.

Date	Mintage	Good	VG	F	VF	XF
ND(1622-1722)	—	1.50	2.25	3.50	5.00	—

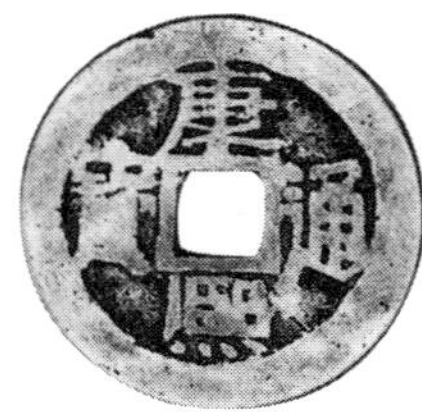

薊

KM# 326 CASH

Cast Bronze **Series:** Talisman (Poem Cash) **Obv. Inscription:** K'ang-hsi T'ung-pao **Rev:** Manchu "Gi" at left, Chinese "Chi" at right **Mint:** Chichou **Note:** Schjöth #1431.

Date	Mintage	Good	VG	F	VF	XF
ND(1662-1722)	—	1.50	2.25	3.50	5.00	—

KM# C340 CASH

Cast Bronze **Series:** "Lo-han" **Obv. Inscription:** K'ang-hsi T'ung-pao **Rev:** Manchu "Gi" at left, chinese "Chi" at right **Mint:** Chichou **Note:** Similar to KM#326.

Date	Mintage	Good	VG	F	VF	XF
ND(1662-1722)	—	5.00	7.00	10.00	15.00	—

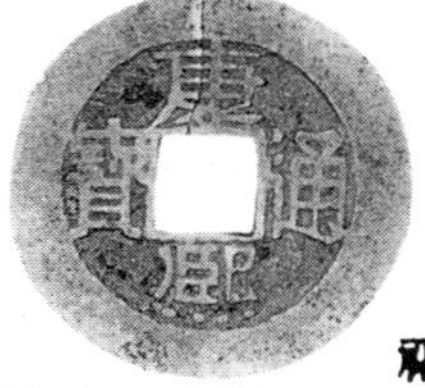
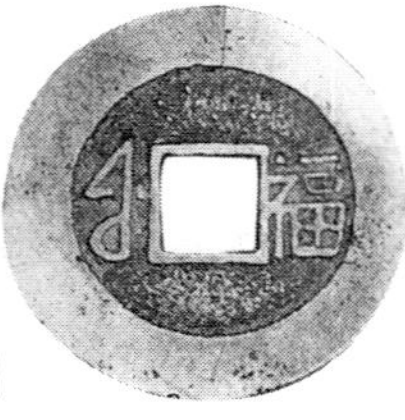

福

KM# 319 CASH

Cast Bronze **Series:** Talisman (Poem Cash) **Obv. Inscription:** K'ang-hsi T'ung-pao **Rev:** Manchu "Fu" at left, Chinese "Fu" at right **Mint:** Fuchou **Note:** Schjöth #1424.

Date	Mintage	Good	VG	F	VF	XF
ND(1662-1722)	—	1.50	2.25	3.50	5.00	—

KM# 339 CASH

Cast Bronze **Series:** "Lo-han" **Obv. Inscription:** K'ang-hsi T'ung-pao **Rev:** Manchu "Fu" at left, Chinese "Fu" at right **Mint:** Fuchou **Note:** Similar to KM#319.

Date	Mintage	Good	VG	F	VF	XF
ND(1662-1722)	—	5.00	7.00	10.00	15.00	—

KM# 347 CASH

Cast Bronze, 27 mm. **Subject:** K'ang-hsi's 60th Birthday **Obv. Inscription:** K'ang-hsi T'ung-pao with open "hsi" **Rev:** Chinese "ching" at left, "Ta" at right **Mint:** Fuchou

Date	Mintage	Good	VG	F	VF	XF
ND(1662-1722)	—	65.00	100	140	200	—

KM# 348.1 CASH

Cast Bronze, 26 mm. **Obv. Inscription:** K'ang-hsi T'ung-pao with open "hsi" **Rev:** Manchu "Fu" at left, Chinese "Fu" at right, "Tzu" (first) above **Mint:** Fuchou

Date	Mintage	Good	VG	F	VF	XF
ND(1662-1722)	—	200	400	600	800	—

KM# 348.2 CASH

Cast Bronze **Obv. Inscription:** K'ang-hsi T'ung-pao with open "hsi" **Rev:** Manchu "Fu" at left, Chinese "Fu" at right, "Chou" (2nd) above **Mint:** Fuchou

Date	Mintage	Good	VG	F	VF	XF
ND(1662-1722)	—	200	400	600	800	—

KM# 348.3 CASH

Cast Bronze **Obv. Inscription:** K'ang-hsi T'ung-pao with open "hsi" **Rev:** Manchu "Fu" at left, Chinese "Yin" (3rd) above **Mint:** Fuchou

Date	Mintage	Good	VG	F	VF	XF
ND(1662-1722)	—	200	400	600	800	—

KM# 348.4 CASH

Cast Bronze **Obv. Inscription:** K'ang-hsi T'ung-pao with open "hsi" **Rev:** Manchu "Fu" at left, Chinese "Si" (6th) above **Mint:** Fuchou

Date	Mintage	Good	VG	F	VF	XF
ND(1662-1722)	—	200	400	600	800	—

KM# 348.7 CASH

Cast Bronze **Obv. Inscription:** K'ang-hsi T'ung-pao with open "hsi" **Rev:** Manchu "Fu" at left, Chinese "Shen" (9th) above **Mint:** Fuchou

Date	Mintage	Good	VG	F	VF	XF
ND(1662-1722)	—	200	400	600	800	—

KM# 348.8 CASH

Cast Bronze **Obv. Inscription:** K'ang-hsi T'ung-pao with open "hsi" **Rev:** Manchu "Fu" at left, Chinese "Yu" (10th) above **Mint:** Fuchou

Date	Mintage	Good	VG	F	VF	XF
ND(1662-1722)	—	200	400	600	800	—

KM# 348.9 CASH

Cast Bronze **Obv. Inscription:** K'ang-hsi T'ung-pao with open "hsi" **Rev:** Manchu "Fu" at left, Chinese "Hai" (12th) above **Mint:** Fuchou

Date	Mintage	Good	VG	F	VF	XF
ND(1662-1722)	—	250	500	750	1,000	—

KM# 314 CASH

Cast Bronze, 25 mm. **Obv. Inscription:** K'ang-hsi T'ung-pao **Rev:** Manchu "Boo" at left, Chinese "Ho" (Honan) at right **Mint:** Honan

Date	Mintage	Good	VG	F	VF	XF
ND(1662-1722)	—	5.00	7.00	10.00	15.00	—

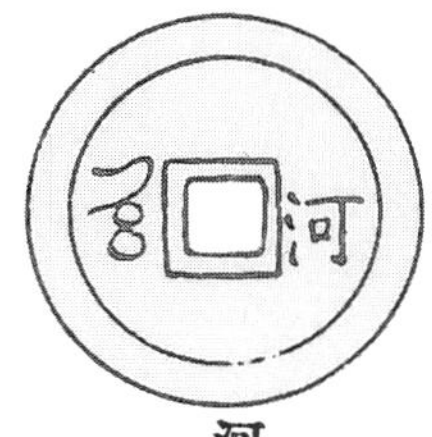

河

KM# 341 CASH

Cast Brass **Series:** Talisman (Poem Cash) **Obv. Inscription:** "K'ang-hsi T'ung-pao" with closed "hsi" **Rev:** Manchu "Ho" at left, Chinese "Ho" at right **Mint:** Honan **Note:** Schjöth #1444.

Date	Mintage	Good	VG	F	VF	XF
ND(1662-1722)	—	5.00	7.00	10.00	15.00	—

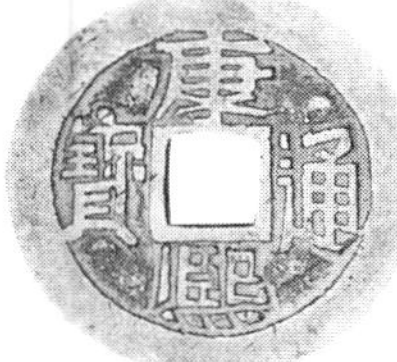
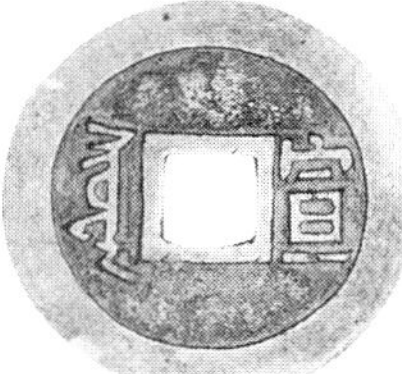

宣

KM# 323 CASH

Cast Bronze **Series:** Talisman (Poem Cash) **Obv. Inscription:** K'ang-hsi T'ung-pao **Rev:** Manchu "Siowan" at left, Chinese "Hsüan" at right **Mint:** Hsüanhua **Note:** Schjöth #1428.

Date	Mintage	Good	VG	F	VF	XF
ND(1622-1722)	—	1.50	2.25	3.50	5.00	—

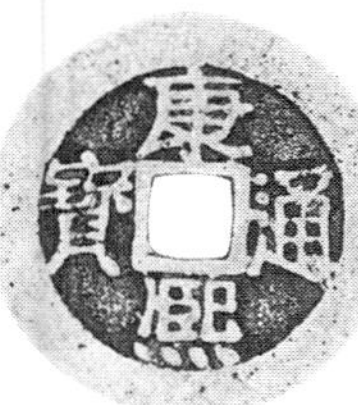

KM# 311.1 CASH

Cast Bronze, 25-27 mm. **Obv. Inscription:** "K'ang-hsi T'ung-pao" with open "hsi" **Rev:** Manchu "Boo-ciowan". **Mint:** Hu-pu Board of Revenue **Note:** Size varies. Schjöth #1419.

Date	Mintage	Good	VG	F	VF	XF
ND(1662-1722)	—	0.50	0.70	1.00	1.50	—

KM# 311.1a CASH

Cast Bronze, 25-27 mm. **Obv:** Wide rims **Obv. Inscription:** "K'ang-hsi T'ung-pao" with open "hsi" **Rev:** Manchu "Boo-ciowan" **Mint:** Hu-pu Board of Revenue **Note:** Size varies. Schjöth #1419. Prev. KM#311.1s.

Date	Mintage	Good	VG	F	VF	XF
ND(1662-1722)	—	0.50	0.70	1.00	1.50	—

KM# 311.1b CASH

Cast Bronze, 24 mm. **Obv. Inscription:** K'ang-hsi T'ung-pao. **Rev:** Manchu "Boo-ciowan". **Mint:** Hu-pu Board of Revenue **Note:** Wide rims. Prev. KM#311.2s.

Date	Mintage	Good	VG	F	VF	XF
ND(1662-1722)	—	0.50	0.70	1.00	1.50	—

KM# 311.2 CASH

Cast Bronze **Obv. Inscription:** K'ang-hsi T'ung-pao **Rev:** Manchu "Boo-ciowan" with dot above **Mint:** Hu-pu Board of Revenue **Note:** Schjöth #1420.

Date	Mintage	Good	VG	F	VF	XF
ND(1662-1722)	—	14.00	20.00	28.50	40.00	—

KM# 340 CASH

Cast Brass **Series:** Lo-han **Obv. Inscription:** "K'ang-hsi T'ung-pao" with closed "hsi" **Rev:** Manchu "Boo-ciowan" **Mint:** Hu-pu Board of Revenue **Note:** Schjöth #1443.

Date	Mintage	Good	VG	F	VF	XF
ND(1662-1722)	—	5.00	7.00	10.00	15.00	—

南

KM# 345 CASH

Cast Bronze, 28 mm. **Obv. Inscription:** K'ang-hsi T'ung-pao with open hsi **Rev:** Manchu "Nan" at left, Chinese "Nan" at right **Mint:** Hunan

Date	Mintage	Good	VG	F	VF	XF
ND(1662-1722)	—	85.00	150	220	300	—

KM# 346 CASH

Cast Bronze **Obv. Inscription:** K'ang-hsi T'ung-pao with open "hsi" **Rev:** Manchu "Si" at left, Chinese "Hsi" at right **Mint:** Jungho

Date	Mintage	Good	VG	F	VF	XF
ND(1662-1722)	—	300	600	900	1,200	—

河

KM# 329 CASH

Cast Bronze **Series:** Talisman (Poem Cash) **Obv. Inscription:** K'ang-hsi T'ung-pao **Rev:** Manchu "Ho" at left, Chinese "Ho" at right **Mint:** K'aifeng **Note:** Schjöth #1434.

Date	Mintage	Good	VG	F	VF	XF
ND(1662-1722)	—	1.50	2.25	3.50	5.50	—

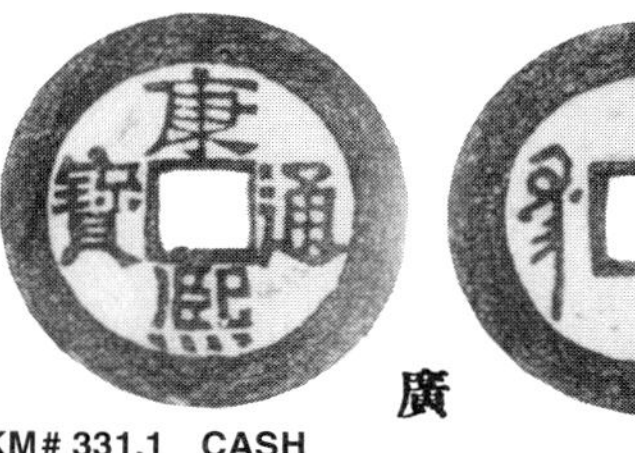

廣

KM# 331.1 CASH

Cast Bronze, 24 mm. **Series:** Talisman (Poem Cash) **Obv. Inscription:** K'ang-hsi T'ung-pao **Rev:** Manchu "Guwang" at left, Chinese "Kuang" at right **Mint:** Kuangchou **Note:** Schjöth #1436.

Date	Mintage	Good	VG	F	VF	XF
ND(1662-1722)	—	0.70	1.00	1.40	2.00	—

KM# 331.2 CASH

Cast Bronze, 27 mm. **Series:** Talisman (Poem Cash) **Obv. Inscription:** K'ang-hsi T'ung-pao **Rev:** Large Manchu "Guwang" at left, Chinese "Kuang" at right **Mint:** Kuangchou **Note:** Schjöth #1436.

Date	Mintage	Good	VG	F	VF	XF
ND(1662-1722)	—	70.00	100	140	200	—

Note: The larger 27mm examples were cast during later reigns

KM# F340 CASH

Cast Bronze **Series:** "Lo-han" **Obv. Inscription:** K'ang-hsi T'ung-pao **Rev:** Manchu "Guwang" left, Chinese "Kuang" at right **Mint:** Kuangchou **Note:** Similar to KM#331.

Date	Mintage	Good	VG	F	VF	XF
ND(1662-1722)	—	1.00	1.40	2.00	3.00	—

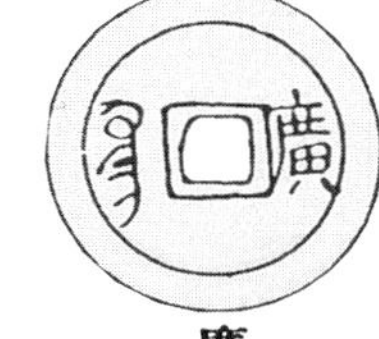

廣

KM# 354 CASH

Cast Red Copper **Obv. Inscription:** "K'ang-hsi T'ung-pao" with open "hsi" **Rev:** Rotated reverse; Manchu "Guwang" at left, Chinese "Kuang" at right **Mint:** Kuangtung **Note:** Schjöth #1449.

Date	Mintage	Good	VG	F	VF	XF
ND(1662-1722)	—	1.50	2.25	3.50	5.00	—

KM# 357 CASH

Cast Red Copper **Obv. Inscription:** K'ang-hsi T'ung-pao with open "hsi" **Rev:** Manchu "Boo-kuei" **Mint:** Kueilin **Note:** Reduced size, 19mm. Schjöth #1451.

Date	Mintage	Good	VG	F	VF	XF
ND(1662-1722)	—	1.50	2.25	3.50	5.00	—

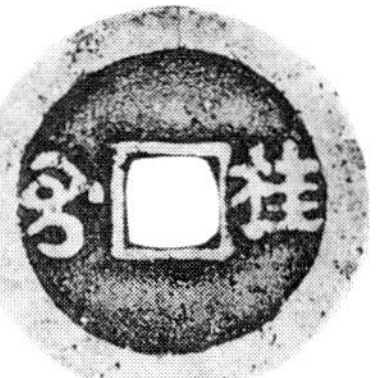

桂

KM# 334 CASH

Cast Bronze **Series:** Talisman (Poem Cash) **Obv. Inscription:** K'ang-hsi T'ung-pao **Rev:** Manchu "Guway" at left, Chinese "Kuei" at right **Mint:** Kuelin **Note:** Schjöth #1439.

Date	Mintage	Good	VG	F	VF	XF
ND(1662-1722)	—	3.00	5.00	7.00	10.00	—

KM# 312.1 CASH

Cast Bronze, 25-26 mm. **Obv:** One dot "T'ung" at right **Obv. Inscription:** K'ang-hsi T'ung-pao **Rev:** Manchu "Boo-Yuwan" **Mint:** Kung-pu Board of Public Works **Note:** Size varies. Narrow rims. Schjöth #1421.

Date	Mintage	Good	VG	F	VF	XF
ND(1662-1722)	—	0.20	0.50	0.80	2.00	—

KM# 312.2 CASH

Cast Bronze, 25-26 mm. **Obv:** 2 dot "T'ung" at right **Obv. Inscription:** K'ang-hsi T'ung-pao **Rev:** Manchu "Boo-Yuwan" **Mint:** Kung-pu Board of Public Works **Note:** Size varies. Wide rims.

Date	Mintage	Good	VG	F	VF	XF
ND(1662-1722)	—	0.20	0.50	0.80	1.50	—

KM# 312a CASH

Cast Bronze, 23-25 mm. **Obv. Inscription:** K'ang-hsi T'ung-pao **Mint:** Kung-pu Board of Public Works **Note:** Reduced size. Schjöth #1422. Prev. KM#313.

Date	Mintage	Good	VG	F	VF	XF
ND(1662-1722)	—	0.50	0.70	1.00	1.50	—

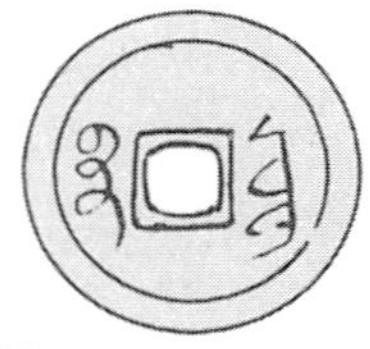

KM# 356 CASH

Cast Red Copper **Obv. Inscription:** "K'ang-hsi T'ung-pao" with open "hsi" **Rev:** Manchu "Boo-yuwan" **Mint:** Kung-pu Board of Public Works **Note:** Schjöth #1451.

Date	Mintage	Good	VG	F	VF	XF
ND(1662-1722)	—	1.50	2.25	3.50	5.00	—

KM# 312.1a CASH

Cast Bronze **Obv:** One dot "T'ung" at right **Rev. Inscription:** Manchu Boo-Yuwan **Mint:** Kung-pu Board of Public Works **Note:** Reduced size, corrupt mint product.

Date	Mintage	Good	VG	F	VF	XF
ND(1662-1722)	—	0.15	0.35	0.55	1.00	—

KM# 312.2a CASH

Cast Bronze **Obv:** 2 dot "T'ung" at right **Rev. Inscription:** Manchu Boo-Yuwan **Mint:** Kung-pu Board of Public Works **Note:** Reduced size, corrupt mint product.

Date	Mintage	Good	VG	F	VF	XF
ND(1662-1722)	—	0.15	0.35	0.55	1.00	—

KM# 315 CASH

Cast Bronze **Rev:** Manchu "Gung" at left, Chinese "Kung" **Mint:** Kungch'ang

Date	Mintage	Good	VG	F	VF	XF
ND(1670)	—	400	600	850	1,200	—

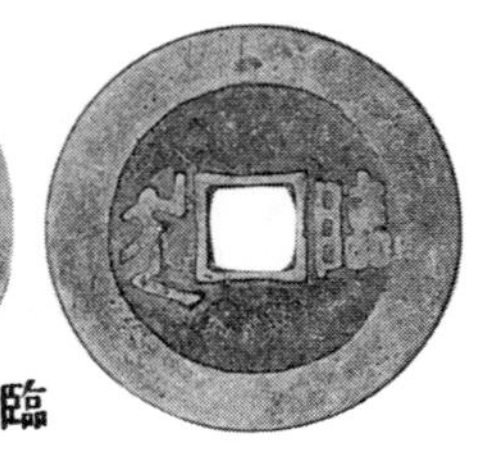

KM# 320.1 CASH

Cast Bronze **Series:** Talisman (Poem Cash) **Obv. Inscription:** K'ang-hsi T'ung-pao **Rev:** Manchu "Lin" at left, Chinese "Lin" at right **Mint:** Linch'ing **Note:** Schjöth #1425.

Date	Mintage	Good	VG	F	VF	XF
ND(1662-1722)	—	1.50	2.25	3.50	5.00	—

KM# 320.2 CASH

Cast Bronze **Series:** Talisman (Poem Cash) **Obv. Inscription:** K'ang-hsi T'ung-pao **Rev:** Manchu "Lin" at left, Chinese "Lin" at right deviating in style **Mint:** Linch'ing

Date	Mintage	Good	VG	F	VF	XF
ND(1662-1722)	—	1.50	2.25	3.50	5.00	—

寧

KM# 328 CASH

Cast Bronze **Series:** Talisman (Poem Cash) **Obv. Inscription:** K'ang-hsi T'ung-pao **Rev:** Manchu "Ning" at left, Chinese "Ning" at right **Mint:** Ningpo **Note:** Schjöth #1433.

Date	Mintage	Good	VG	F	VF	XF
ND(1662-1722)	—	1.50	2.25	3.50	5.00	—

KM# D340 CASH

Cast Bronze **Series:** "Lo-han" **Obv. Inscription:** K'ang-hsi T'ung-pao **Rev:** Manchu "Ning" at left, Chinese "Ning" at right **Mint:** Ningpo **Note:** Similar to KM#328.

Date	Mintage	Good	VG	F	VF	XF
ND(1662-1722)	—	5.00	7.00	10.00	15.00	—

東

KM# 321 CASH

Cast Bronze **Series:** Talisman (Poem Cash) **Obv. Inscription:** K'ang-hsi T'ung-pao **Rev:** Manchu "Dung" at left, Chinese "Tung" at right **Mint:** Shantung **Note:** Schjöth #1426.

Date	Mintage	Good	VG	F	VF	XF
ND(1662-1722)	—	1.50	2.25	3.50	5.00	—

陝

KM# 335.1 CASH

Cast Bronze, 27 mm. **Series:** Talisman (Poem Cash) **Obv. Inscription:** K'ang-hsi T'ung-pao with open "hsi" **Rev:** Manchu "San" at left, Chinese "Shan" at right **Mint:** Sian **Note:** Schjöth #1440.

Date	Mintage	Good	VG	F	VF	XF
ND(1662-1722)	—	1.50	2.25	3.50	5.00	—

KM# 335.2 CASH

Cast Bronze, 27 mm. **Series:** Talisman (Poem Cash) **Obv. Inscription:** K'ang-hsi T'ung-pao **Rev:** Manchu "San" at left with extra dot, Chinese "Shan" at right **Mint:** Sian **Note:** Schjöth #1440.

Date	Mintage	Good	VG	F	VF	XF
ND(1662-1722)	—	1.50	2.25	3.50	5.00	—

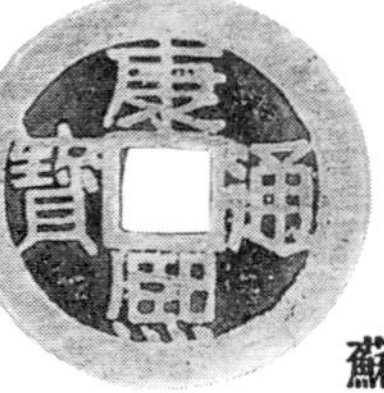

蘇

KM# 325 CASH

Cast Bronze **Series:** Talisman (Poem Cash) **Obv. Inscription:** K'ang-hsi T'ung-pao **Rev:** Manchu "Su" at left, Chinese "Su" at right **Mint:** Soochou **Note:** Schjöth #1430.

Date	Mintage	Good	VG	F	VF	XF
ND(1662-1722)	—	1.50	2.25	3.50	5.00	—

KM# B340 CASH

Cast Bronze **Series:** "Lo-han" **Obv. Inscription:** K'ang-hsi T'ung-pao **Rev:** Manchu "Su" at left, Chinese "Su" at right **Mint:** Soochou **Note:** Similar to KM#325.

Date	Mintage	Good	VG	F	VF	XF
ND(1662-1722)	—	5.00	7.00	10.00	15.00	—

KM# 333.1 CASH

Cast Bronze, 24 mm. **Series:** Talisman (Poem Cash) **Obv. Inscription:** "K'ang-hsi T'ung-pao" **Rev:** Manchu "Tai" at left, Chinese "Tai" at right **Mint:** T'aiwan **Note:** Schjöth #1438.

Date	Mintage	Good	VG	F	VF	XF
ND(1662-1722)	—	5.00	7.00	10.00	15.00	—

KM# 333.2 CASH

Cast Bronze, 27 mm. **Series:** Talisman (Poem Cash) **Obv. Inscription:** "K'ang-hsi T'ung-pao" **Rev:** Manchu "Tai" at left, Chinese "Tai" at right **Mint:** T'aiwan **Note:** Schjöth #1438. Varieties exist.

Date	Mintage	Good	VG	F	VF	XF
ND(1662-1722)	—	20.00	50.00	80.00	100	—

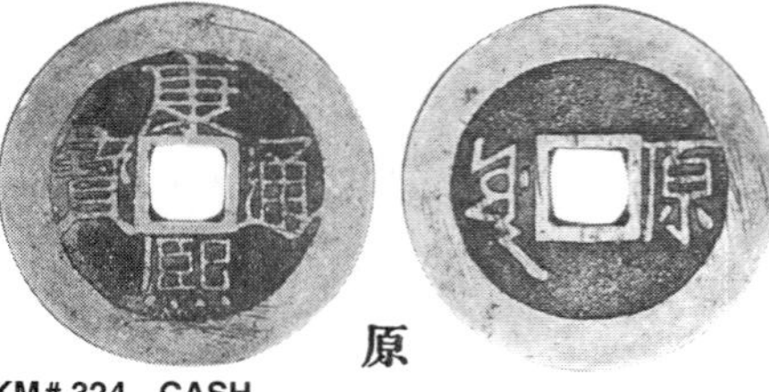

KM# 324 CASH

Cast Bronze **Series:** Talisman (Poem Cash) **Obv. Inscription:** K'ang-hsi T'ung-pao **Rev:** Manchu "Yuwan" at left, Chinese "Yuan" at right **Mint:** T'aiyüan Fu **Note:** Schjöth #1429.

Date	Mintage	Good	VG	F	VF	XF
ND(1662-1722)	—	1.50	2.25	3.50	5.00	—

KM# A340 CASH

Cast Bronze **Series:** "Lo-han" **Obv. Inscription:** K'ang-hsi T'ung-pao **Rev:** Manchu "Yuwan" at left, Chinese "Yüan" at right **Mint:** T'aiyüan-fu **Note:** Similar to KM#324.

Date	Mintage	Good	VG	F	VF	XF
ND(1662-1722)	—	5.00	7.00	10.00	15.00	—

KM# A338 CASH

Cast Bronze **Series:** Talisman (Poem Cash) **Obv. Inscription:** K'ang-hsi T'ung-pao **Rev:** Manchu "Tung" at left, Chinese "T'ung" at right **Mint:** T'ung **Note:** Schjöth #1423.

Date	Mintage	Good	VG	F	VF	XF
ND(1662-1722)	—	0.70	1.00	1.40	2.00	—

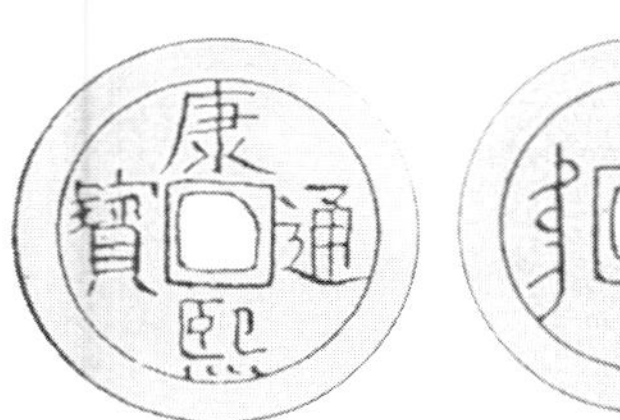

KM# 338 CASH

Cast Bronze **Series:** "Lo-han" **Obv. Inscription:** K'ang-hsi T'ung-pao **Rev:** Manchu "Tung" at left, Chinese "T'ung" at right **Mint:** T'ung **Note:** Similar to KM#318. Schjöth #1444.

Date	Mintage	Good	VG	F	VF	XF
ND(1662-1722)	—	5.00	7.00	10.00	15.00	—

同

KM# 318 CASH

Cast Bronze **Series:** Talisman (Poem Cash) **Obv. Inscription:** K'ang-hsi T'ung-pao **Rev:** Manchu "Tung" at left, Chinese "T'ung at right **Mint:** Tat'ung **Note:** Schjöth #1423.

Date	Mintage	Good	VG	F	VF	XF
ND(1662-1722)	—	1.50	2.25	3.50	5.00	—

昌

KM# 327 CASH

Cast Bronze **Series:** Talisman (Poem Cash) **Obv. Inscription:** K'ang-hsi T'ung-pao **Rev:** Manchu "Cang" at left, Chinese "Ch'ang" at right **Mint:** Wuch'ang **Note:** Schjöth #1432.

Date	Mintage	Good	VG	F	VF	XF
ND(1662-1722)	—	1.50	2.25	3.50	5.00	—

昌

KM# 353 CASH

Cast Red Copper **Obv. Inscription:** "K'ang-hsi T'ung-pao" with open "hsi" **Rev:** Manchu "Cang" at left, Chinese "Ch'ang" at right. **Mint:** Wuch'ang **Note:** Schjöth #1448.

Date	Mintage	Good	VG	F	VF	XF
ND(1662-1722)	—	1.50	2.25	3.50	5.00	—

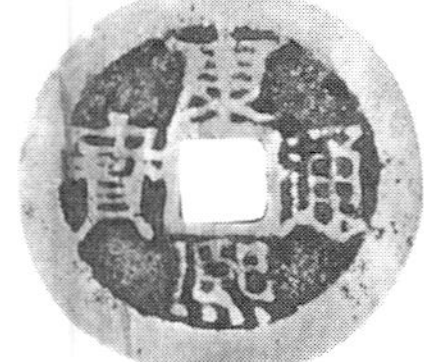

雲

KM# 336 CASH

Cast Bronze, 27 mm. **Series:** Talisman (Poem Cash) **Obv. Inscription:** "K'ang-hsi T'ung-pao" **Rev:** Manchu "Yôn" at left, Chinese "Yün" at right **Mint:** Yünnan Fu **Note:** Schjöth #1441.

Date	Mintage	Good	VG	F	VF	XF
ND(1662-1722)	—	1.50	2.25	3.50	5.00	—

T"ien-ming

T'ai Tsu

CAST COINAGE

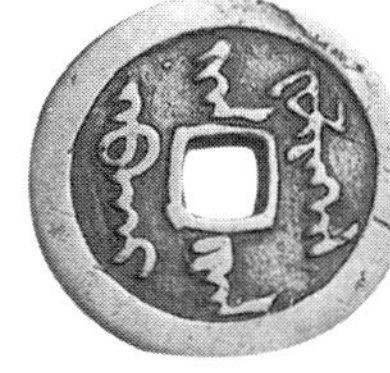
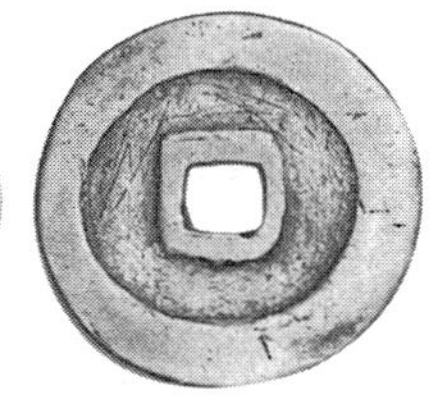

KM# 228 CASH

Cast Bronze **Obv. Inscription:** Manchu "Abkai fulingga han juha" (Imperial coin Heavenly Mandate) **Rev:** Plain **Note:** Schjöth #1355. Size varies: 25-26mm.

Date	Mintage	Good	VG	F	VF	XF
ND(1616-27)	—	9.00	15.00	22.50	35.00	—

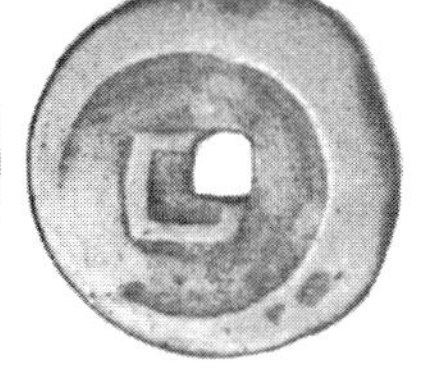

KM# 229 CASH

Cast Bronze **Obv. Inscription:** "T'ien-ming T'ung-pao" **Rev:** Plain **Note:** Schjöth #1356.

Date	Mintage	Good	VG	F	VF	XF
ND(1616-27)	—	30.00	40.00	55.00	75.00	—

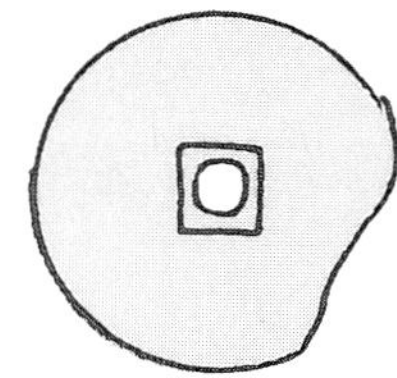

KM# 230 CASH

Cast Bronze, 23 mm. **Obv:** Inscription in different style **Obv. Inscription:** "T'ien-ming T'ung-pao" **Note:** Reduced size.

Date	Mintage	Good	VG	F	VF	XF
ND(1616-27)	—	300	600	900	1,200	—

PATTERNS

Including off metal castings

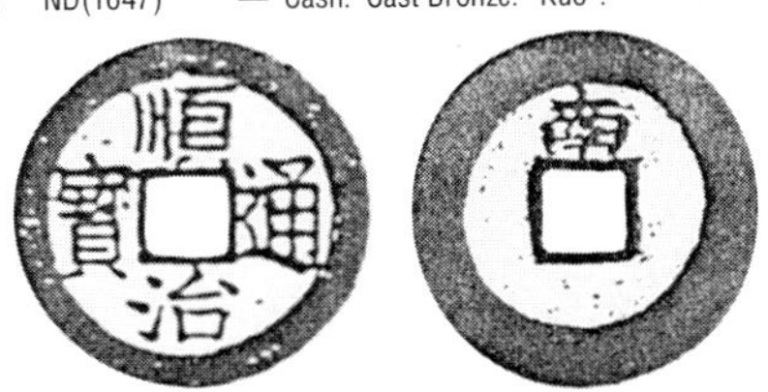

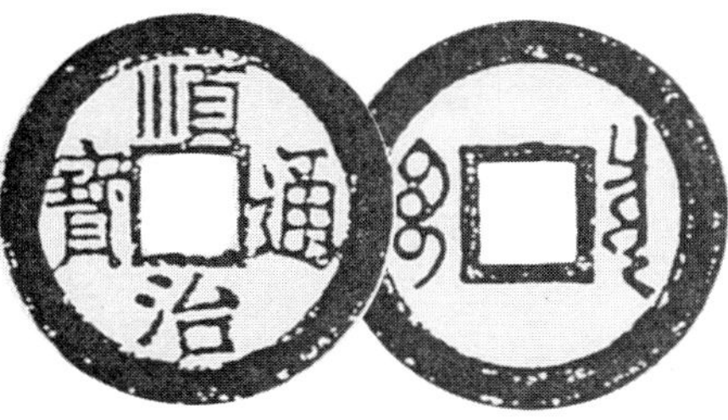

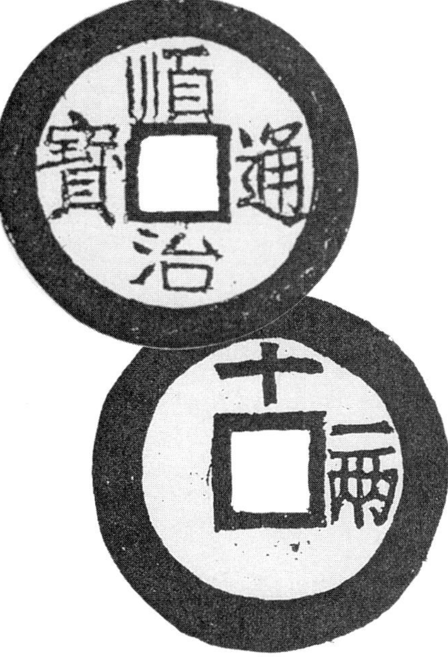

KM#	Date	Mintage	Identification	Mkt Val
Pn1	ND(1628)	—	Cash. Cast Bronze.	125
Pn2	ND(1647)	—	Cash. Cast Bronze. "Kuo".	200
Pn3	ND(1644)	—	Cash. Cast Bronze. "Nan".	2,500
Pn4	ND(1644)	—	2 Cash. Cast Bronze. "Boo-5ciowan".	1,500
Pn5	ND(1644)	—	Cash. Cast Bronze. "Boo-han".	200
Pn6	ND(1644)	—	Cash. Cast Bronze. Manchu and Chinese "Fu".	200
Pn7	ND(1644)	—	Tael. Cast Bronze. "Shih" above "Yi Tael" at right.	1,600
Pn8	ND(1662)	—	Cash. Cast Bronze. "Boo-Fu".	500
Pn9	ND(1662)	—	Cash. Cast Bronze. Manchu and Chinese "Guwang-kuang".	300

KM#	Date	Mintage	Identification	Mkt Val

Pn10	ND(1662)	—	Cash. Cast Bronze. Manchu and Chinese "Guwang-kuang".	300

Pn11	ND(1662)	—	Cash. Cast Bronze. Manchu and Chinese "Yun".	300

Pn12	ND(1662)	—	Cash. Cast Bronze. Manchu and Chinese "Tai".	300

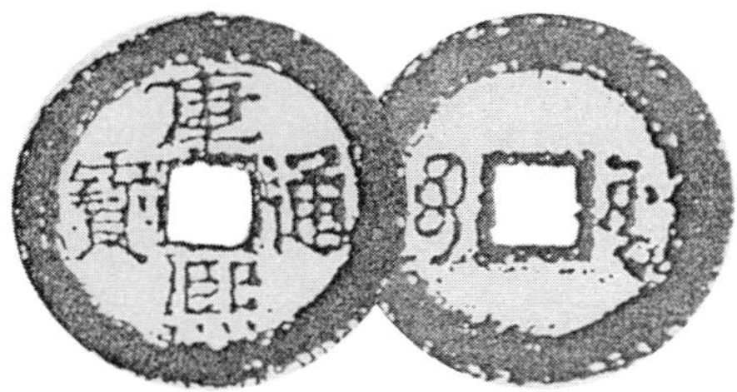

Pn13	ND(1662)	—	2 Cash. Cast Bronze. "Boo-yuwan".	2,000

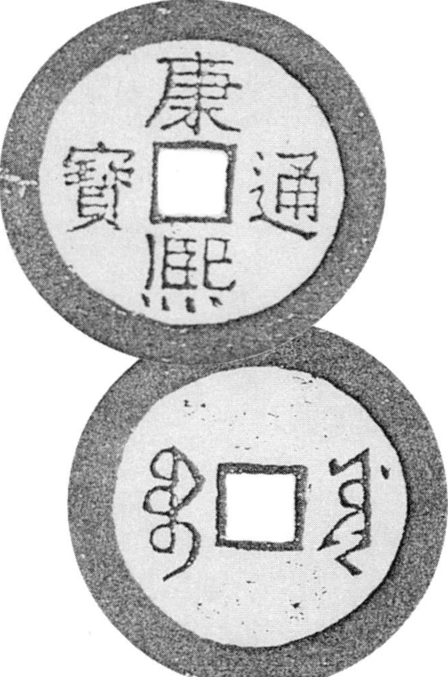

Pn14	ND(1662)	—	10 Cash. Cast Bronze. "Boo-yuwan".	1,800

SINKIANG PROVINCE

Hsinkiang, Xinjiang
"New Dominion"

An autonomous region in western China, often referred to as Chinese Turkestan. High mountains surround 2000 ft. tableland on three sides with a large desert in center of this province. Many salt lakes, mining and some farming and oil. Inhabited by early man and was referred to as the "Silk Route" to the West. Sinkiang (Xinjiang) has been historically under the control of many factions, including Genghis Khan. It became a province in 1884. China has made claim to Sinkiang (Xinjiang) for many, many years. This rule has been more nominal than actual. Sinkiang (Xinjiang) had eight imperial mints, only three of which were in operation toward the end of the reign of Kuang Hsü

MONETARY SYSTEM

2 Pul = 1 Cash
2 Cash = 5 Li
4 Cash = 10 Li = 1 Fen
25 Cash = 10 Fen = 1 Miscal = 1 Ch'ien, Mace, Tanga
10 Miscals (Mace) = 1 Liang (Tael or Sar)
20 Miscals (Tangas) = 1 Tilla

LOCAL MINT NAMES AND MARKS

MINT CHINESE MANCHU UYGHUR

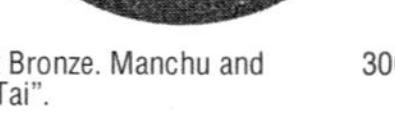

Yarkand, now Shache (Yarkant)

EMPIRE

Tsewang Arabtan
1697-1727

CAST TRIBAL COINAGE

KM# 360 PUL

Cast Copper **Obv. Inscription:** Tsewang **Rev. Inscription:** Zarb Yarkand **Mint:** Yarkand **Note:** Turki inscriptions. Prev. C36-7.1.

Date	Mintage	Good	VG	F	VF	XF
ND(1697-1727)	—	30.00	50.00	80.00	125	—

COLOMBIA

North Atlantic Ocean
VENEZUELA
North Pacific Ocean
ECUADOR
PERU
BRAZIL

The Republic of Colombia, in the northwestern corner of South America, has an area of 440,831 sq. mi. (1,138,910 sq. km

The northern coast of present Colombia was one of the first parts of the American continent to be visited by Spanish navigators. At Darien in Panama is the site of the first permanent European settlement on the American mainland in 1510. New Granada, as Colombia was known until 1861, stemmed from the settlement of Santa Marta in 1525. New Granada was established as a Spanish colony in 1549. Independence was declared in 1810, and secured in 1819 when Simon Bolivar united Colombia, Venezuela, Panama and Ecuador as the Republic of Gran Colombia. Venezuela withdrew from the Republic in 1829; Ecuador in 1830; and Panama in 1903.

RULER

Spanish, until 1819

MINT MARKS

C, NER, NR, NRE, R, RN, S - Cartagena
B, F, FS, N, NR, S, SF - Nuevo Reino (Bogota)
A, M - Medellin (capital), Antioquia (state)
(m) - Medellin, w/o mint mark
NR – Nueva Reino
P, PN, Pn, POPAYAN - Popayan
SM – Santa Marta
caduceus - Bogota
floral spray - Popayan

ASSAYERS' INITIALS

Bogota and Popayan Mints

Initials	Date	Name
A	1622-26	Inigo de Alvis
A	1632-42	Alonso de Anuncibay
A, ARC, ARCE, VA	1692-1721	Buena Ventura de Arce
G, P, PG	1678-92	Pedro Garcia de Villanueva
OLM, OLMS	1676	Jose de Olmos (silver only)
P	1627-32	Miguel Pinto Camargo
POR, PORAM, PORAMS, PORAS, PORM, PORMS, PORMOS, PORNS, PORS, PRS, R, RMS	1651-76	Pedro Ramos (pillars & waves)
R	1642-76	Pedro Ramos (Hapsburg shield)
SM	1677-78	Jose Silvestre de Soto Maldonado (gold only)
T	1627	Alonso Turrillo de Yebra

SYMBOLS

Symbol	Date	Name
(symbol)	1697	Sebastian de Chavarria
(symbol)	1649-51	Juan Rodrigues de Roas
R	1618	Baltasar Ramos Leceta
R	1636-40	Pedro Trevino
R	1640-43	Pedro Trevino
R	1643-48	Pedro Trevino
VR	1684-97	Pedro de Villar

Cartagena Mint

Initial	Date	Name
A	1622-28	Inigo de Alvis or Martin de Arbustante
E	1622	Jacobo Emayr (unconfirmed)
E	1626-35	Echeverria (unconfirmed)
H	1622	Juan de la Hera
S	1653-55	Unknown

MONETARY SYSTEM

16 Reales = 1 Escudo

COLONIAL

COB COINAGE

Note: Values given for dated cobs are representative of average strikes with the last two digits of the date discernible. The esthetic appearance, quality of strike, and presence of date, mint mark and assayer initials all have an effect on the value of cobs.

Note: Colombian cob 1/4 Reales, which are all very rare, did not bear dates in their design, but can be dated at least approximately by virtue of the fact that the castle on the obverse and the lion on the reverse match exactly with the castles and lions in the shield of the 8 Reales struck in the same year or period.

NOTE: The cob 1/2 Reales of Colombia are distinguishable from other mints cob 1/2 Reales by virtue of the fact that the P and the S of the PHILIPPVS monogram touch at the top

 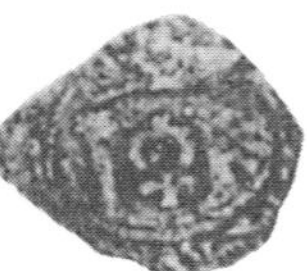

KM# 1.1 1/4 REAL

2.3000 g., Billon **Ruler:** Philip IV **Obv:** Arms **Rev:** Pomegranate between pillars, crown above **Note:** Struck at Santa Fe de Bogota. These coins were struck using one part 0.930 fine silver to four parts copper making a total silver fineness of 0.186g. Surviving examples are well under the regulatory weight. Prev. KM#1.

Date	Mintage	Good	VG	F	VF	XF
ND(1622) A Rare	—	—	—	—	—	—

KM# A7 1/4 REAL

0.8600 g., 0.9310 Silver 0.0257 oz. ASW **Obv:** Castle **Rev:** Lion **Note:** Struck at the Bogota Mint.

Date	Mintage	Good	VG	F	VF	XF
ND(1651)	—	200	250	400	650	—

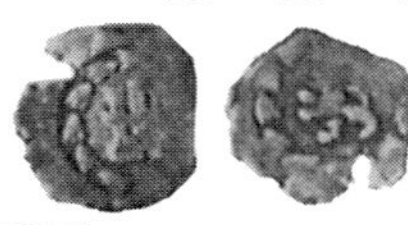

KM# B7 1/4 REAL

0.8600 g., 0.9310 Silver 0.0257 oz. ASW **Ruler:** Philip V **Obv:** Castle **Rev:** Lion

Date	Mintage	Good	VG	F	VF	XF
ND(1657) Rare	—	—	—	—	—	—

KM# 1.2 1/4 REAL

2.3000 g., Billon **Ruler:** Philip IV **Obv:** Arms **Rev:** Mintmark to left of pillars, crown above **Note:** Struck at Cartagena. These coins were struck using one part 0.930 fine silver to four parts copper making a total silver fineness of 0.186g.

Date	Mintage	Good	VG	F	VF	XF
ND(1622) RN Rare	—	—	—	—	—	—

KM# C7 1/4 REAL

0.8600 g., 0.9310 Silver 0.0257 oz. ASW **Obv:** Castle in rectangle **Rev:** Cross with castles and lions **Note:** Possibly struck at Cartagena

Date	Mintage	Good	VG	F	VF	XF
ND(1622-55) Unique	—	—	—	—	—	—

Note: Attribution tentative

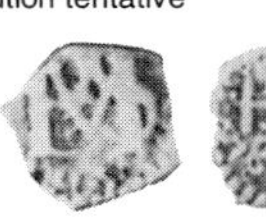

KM# 8 1/2 REAL

1.6917 g., 0.9310 Silver 0.0506 oz. ASW **Obv:** Crowned monogram **Rev:** Cross, castles, and lions in angles

Date	Mintage	Good	VG	F	VF	XF
ND(1622-66) Date off flan	—	100	140	250	350	—
1627 P Rare	—	—	—	—	—	—
1630 P Rare	—	—	—	—	—	—
1633 P Rare	—	—	—	—	—	—
1652 R Rare	—	—	—	—	—	—
1653 R Rare	—	—	—	—	—	—
1656 R Rare	—	—	—	—	—	—
1657 Rare	—	—	—	—	—	—
1658 Rare	—	—	—	—	—	—
1662 R Rare	—	—	—	—	—	—
1665 R Rare	—	—	—	—	—	—

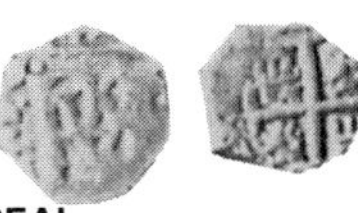

KM# A8 1/2 REAL

1.6917 g., 0.9310 Silver 0.0506 oz. ASW **Obv:** Monogram of Philip IV, legend of Charles II 1673 **Note:** Struck at the Bogota Mint.

Date	Mintage	Good	VG	F	VF	XF
ND Date off flan	—	80.00	140	220	350	—
1666 R Rare	—	—	—	—	—	—
1667/6 R Rare	—	—	—	—	—	—
1667 R Rare	—	—	—	—	—	—
1673 R	—	—	—	—	—	—

KM# D8 1/2 REAL

1.6917 g., 0.9310 Silver 0.0506 oz. ASW **Obv:** Crowned monogram **Rev:** Cross, castles, and lions in angles **Note:** Struck at the Cartagena Mint.

Date	Mintage	Good	VG	F	VF	XF
(ND) NR-E Unique	—	—	—	—	—	—
(ND) C-E Unique	—	—	—	—	—	—

KM# A9 REAL

3.3834 g., 0.9310 Silver 0.1013 oz. ASW **Obv:** Hapsburg shield **Rev:** Pillars and waves **Note:** Mule. Struck at the Bogota Mint.

Date	Mintage	Good	VG	F	VF	XF
1653 R Rare	—	—	—	—	—	—

KM# 5 REAL

3.3834 g., 0.9310 Silver 0.1013 oz. ASW **Obv:** Cross of Jerusalem, lions, and castles in quarters **Rev:** Hapsburg shield **Note:** Struck at the Bogota Mint.

Date	Mintage	Good	VG	F	VF	XF
ND(1627-50) Date off flan	—	90.00	150	250	400	—
1627 P Rare	—	—	—	—	—	—
1628 P Rare	—	—	—	—	—	—
1629 P Rare	—	—	—	—	—	—
1633 A Rare	—	—	—	—	—	—
1650 R Rare	—	—	—	—	—	—

KM# 9 REAL

3.3834 g., 0.9310 Silver 0.1013 oz. ASW **Obv:** Lions and castles **Rev:** Pillars and waves **Note:** Struck at the Bogota Mint.

Date	Mintage	Good	VG	F	VF	XF
ND(1651-53) Date off flan	—	165	275	400	575	—
1651 R	—	200	400	750	1,000	—
1652 R	—	200	400	750	1,000	—
1653 R	—	200	400	750	1,000	—

KM# 15 REAL

3.3834 g., 0.9310 Silver 0.1013 oz. ASW **Obv:** Lions and castles **Rev:** Pillars

Date	Mintage	Good	VG	F	VF	XF
ND(1666-1702) Date off flan; Rare	—	—	—	—	—	—
ND(1665-76) POR PoRS Rare	—	—	—	—	—	—
1676 OLM Rare	—	—	—	—	—	—
ND(1678-92) PG Rare	—	—	—	—	—	—
ND(1692-1702) VA Rare	—	—	—	—	—	—

KM# A5 REAL

3.3834 g., 0.9310 Silver 0.1013 oz. ASW **Obv:** Hapsburg shield **Obv. Legend:** PHILIPPVS IIII.. **Rev:** Cross of Jerusalem, lions, and castles in quarters **Note:** Struck at the Cartagena Mint.

Date	Mintage	Good	VG	F	VF	XF
162xRN H Rare	—	—	—	—	—	—
ND(1627-29)NR E Date off flan	—	100	200	300	400	—
ND(1627-29)RN E Date off flan	—	100	200	300	400	—
1633C E Rare	—	—	—	—	—	—

KM# A15 REAL

3.3834 g., 0.9310 Silver 0.1013 oz. ASW **Obv:** Castles and lions in quartered shield **Rev:** Pillars and waves **Note:** Struck at the Cartagena Mint.

Date	Mintage	Good	VG	F	VF	XF
ND(1655) S Unique	—	—	—	—	—	—

KM# 6.1 2 REALES

6.7668 g., 0.9310 Silver 0.2025 oz. ASW **Obv:** Hapsburg shield **Rev:** Castles and lions **Note:** Struck at the Bogota Mint.

Date	Mintage	Good	VG	F	VF	XF
1627 P	—	400	600	1,000	1,500	—
1628 P	—	350	550	950	1,500	—
1630 P	—	350	550	950	1,500	—
ND(1627-30) P Date off flan	—	150	250	325	500	—
ND(1632-42) A Date off flan	—	150	250	325	500	—
1647 R	—	400	600	1,000	1,500	—
ND(1647) R Date off flan	—	150	250	325	500	—

KM# 6.2 2 REALES

6.7668 g., 0.9310 Silver 0.2025 oz. ASW **Rev:** Pillars and waves **Note:** Mule. Struck at the Bogota Mint.

Date	Mintage	Good	VG	F	VF	XF
1652 R Rare	—	—	—	—	—	—

KM# 6.3 2 REALES

6.7668 g., 0.9310 Silver 0.2025 oz. ASW **Obv:** Lions and castles **Note:** Varieties in shield and denomination exist. Struck at the Bogota Mint. Prev. KM#6.2.

Date	Mintage	Good	VG	F	VF	XF
ND(1652-65) Date off flan	—	175	275	375	575	—
1652 R	—	300	500	900	1,350	—
1659 POR	—	350	550	950	1,500	—
1662 POR	—	350	550	950	1,500	—
1664 POR	—	350	550	950	1,500	—
1665 P.oS	—	350	550	950	1,500	—

KM# 16 2 REALES

6.7668 g., 0.9310 Silver 0.2025 oz. ASW **Obv:** Legend of Charles II **Rev:** Pillars and waves, PLVS VLTRA within **Note:** Struck at the Bogota Mint.

Date	Mintage	Good	VG	F	VF	XF
ND(1665-76) R	—	200	300	450	1,000	—
1676 O.L.M. Rare	—	—	—	—	—	—
1688 P Rare	—	—	—	—	—	—
1690 PG Rare	—	—	—	—	—	—
ND(1678-92) PG	—	250	350	500	1,000	—
1693 ARC	—	400	575	1,000	1,750	—

KM# A6.1 2 REALES

6.7668 g., 0.9310 Silver 0.2025 oz. ASW **Obv:** Hapsburg shield with Portuguese escutcheon, denomination right of shield **Obv. Legend:** PHILIPPVS III.. **Rev:** Castles and lions **Note:** Struck at the Cartagena Mint.

Date	Mintage	Good	VG	F	VF	XF
1622 S F	—	—	—	1,500	2,000	—

Note: No Assayer. Only two examples known

KM# A6.2 2 REALES

6.7668 g., 0.9310 Silver 0.2025 oz. ASW **Obv:** Arms without Portuguese escutcheon, without denomination right of shield **Note:** Struck at the Cartagena Mint.

Date	Mintage	Good	VG	F	VF	XF
1622 RN E	—	—	—	—	—	—

KM# A6.3 2 REALES

6.7668 g., 0.9310 Silver 0.2025 oz. ASW **Obv:** Without denomination right of shield **Obv. Legend:** PHILIPVS IIII.. **Note:** Struck at the Cartagena Mint.

Date	Mintage	Good	VG	F	VF	XF
1627 RN E	—	400	600	1,000	2,000	—
1628 RN E Rare	—	—	—	—	—	—

Date	Mintage	Good	VG	F	VF	XF
ND(1627-29) R E Date off flan	—	150	260	325	500	—
1629 RN E Rare	—	—	—	—	—	—
ND(1627-29) RN E Date off flan	—	150	250	325	500	—
ND(1627-29) NR E Date off flan	—	150	250	325	500	—
1630 CE E	—	350	550	950	1,500	—
1631 CE E	—	350	550	950	1,500	—
1632 CE E	—	350	550	950	1,500	—
1633 CE E	—	350	550	950	1,500	—
1634 CE E	—	350	550	950	1,500	—
ND(1630-34) CE E Date off flan	—	150	250	325	500	—

KM# 6.4 2 REALES

6.7668 g., 0.9310 Silver 0.2025 oz. ASW **Obv:** Lions and castles **Rev:** Pillars and waves **Note:** Struck at the Cartagena Mint. Prev. KM#6.3.

Date	Mintage	Good	VG	F	VF	XF
ND(1655) C-S Rare	—	—	—	—	—	—

KM# 2.1 4 REALES

13.5337 g., 0.9310 Silver 0.4051 oz. ASW **Obv:** Arms with Portuguese escutcheon, legend around **Rev:** Lions and castles in quarters **Note:** Struck at the Bogota Mint.

Date	Mintage	Good	VG	F	VF	XF
1622 S A Rare	—	—	—	—	—	—

KM# 2.2 4 REALES

13.5337 g., 0.9310 Silver 0.4051 oz. ASW **Obv:** Arms without Portuguese escutcheon **Note:** Struck at the Bogota Mint.

Date	Mintage	Good	VG	F	VF	XF
ND(1627-51) Date off flan	—	700	1,200	1,500	2,000	—
1627 T Rare	—	—	—	—	—	—
1627 P Rare	—	—	—	—	—	—
1628 P Rare	—	—	—	—	—	—
1631 P Rare	—	—	—	—	—	—
ND(1632-42) A Rare	—	—	—	—	—	—
1643 R Rare	—	—	—	—	—	—
1644 R Rare	—	—	—	—	—	—
1650 R Rare	—	—	—	—	—	—
1651 R Rare	—	—	—	—	—	—
ND(1628-33) R	—	700	1,200	1,500	2,000	—

KM# 10.1 4 REALES

13.5337 g., 0.9310 Silver 0.4051 oz. ASW **Obv:** Arms with lions and castles quartered, value at right **Obv. Legend:** PHILIPPVS IV.. **Rev:** Pillars, PLVS VLTRA, mint mark within, date vertical **Note:** Struck at the Bogota Mint.

Date	Mintage	Good	VG	F	VF	XF
ND(1651-65) Date off flan	—	700	1,200	1,500	2,000	—
1651 POR Rare	—	1,750	2,750	3,750	5,000	—
1653	—	1,750	2,750	3,750	5,000	—
1653 POR	—	1,750	2,750	3,750	5,000	—
1654 POR	—	1,750	2,750	3,750	5,000	—
1657 POR	—	1,750	2,750	3,750	5,000	—
1658 PRS	—	1,750	2,750	3,750	5,000	—
1661 PORS	—	1,750	2,750	3,750	5,000	—
1662 P.oR	—	1,750	2,750	3,750	5,000	—
1662 P.oRS	—	1,750	2,750	3,750	5,000	—
1662 POR	—	1,750	2,750	3,750	5,000	—
1662 PORS	—	1,750	2,750	3,750	5,000	—
1664 PoRS	—	1,750	2,750	3,750	5,000	—
1665 PoR	—	1,750	2,750	3,750	5,000	—

KM# 11 4 REALES

13.5337 g., 0.9310 Silver 0.4051 oz. ASW **Obv:** Lions and castles, legend of Charles II **Rev:** Pillars and waves, PLVS VLTRA and mint mark within **Note:** Struck at the Bogota Mint.

Date	Mintage	Good	VG	F	VF	XF
ND(1666-1701) Date off flan	—	900	1,500	2,500	3,750	—
1666 PoR Rare	—	—	—	—	—	—
1667 P. oR Rare	—	—	—	—	—	—
1669/6 PRS Rare	—	—	—	—	—	—
1668 PoRS Rare	—	—	—	—	—	—
1676 O.L.M. Rare	—	—	—	—	—	—
1680 PoGA Rare	—	—	—	—	—	—
1690 PG Rare	—	—	—	—	—	—
1693 VA Rare	—	—	—	—	—	—

KM# 2.3 4 REALES

13.5337 g., 0.9310 Silver 0.4051 oz. ASW **Obv:** Arms with Portuguese escutcheon **Note:** Struck at the Cartagena Mint.

Date	Mintage	Good	VG	F	VF	XF
ND(1622)RN A Rare	—	—	—	—	—	—
Note: Denomination below A						
ND(1662)RN A Rare	—	—	—	—	—	—
Note: Denomination above A						

KM# 2.4 4 REALES

13.5337 g., 0.9310 Silver 0.4051 oz. ASW **Obv:** Arms without Portuguese escutcheon **Note:** Struck at the Cartagena Mint.

Date	Mintage	Good	VG	F	VF	XF
ND(1628-33) Date off flan	—	700	1,200	1,500	2,000	—
1628 E Rare	—	—	—	—	—	—
1630 RN E Rare	—	—	—	—	—	—
1632 C E Rare	—	—	—	—	—	—
1633 C E Rare	—	—	—	—	—	—

KM# 10.2 4 REALES

13.5337 g., 0.9310 Silver 0.4051 oz. ASW **Obv:** Castles and lions in shield **Rev:** Pillars and waves, stars in field **Note:** Struck at the Cartagena Mint.

Date	Mintage	Good	VG	F	VF	XF
ND(1655)C S Rare	—	—	—	—	—	—

KM# 3.1 8 REALES

27.0674 g., 0.9310 Silver 0.8102 oz. ASW **Obv:** Arms with Portuguese escutcheon, legend of Philip III **Rev:** Cross with lions and castles in quarters **Note:** Struck at the Bogota Mint.

Date	Mintage	Good	VG	F	VF	XF
1622 S A Rare	—	—	—	—	—	—

KM# 3.3 8 REALES

27.0674 g., 0.9310 Silver 0.8102 oz. ASW **Obv:** Arms without Portuguese escutcheon, VIII at right **Obv. Legend:** PHILIPPVS IIII D G **Rev:** Lions and castles in quarters **Note:** Struck at the Bogota Mint.

Date	Mintage	Good	VG	F	VF	XF
1625 P Rare	—	—	—	—	—	—
1627 P Rare	—	—	—	—	—	—
1628 P	—	1,000	2,000	3,000	4,000	—
1629 P	—	1,000	2,000	3,000	4,000	—
1633 A	—	1,000	2,000	3,000	4,000	—
1634 A	—	1,000	2,000	3,000	4,000	—

KM# 7.1 8 REALES

27.0674 g., 0.9310 Silver 0.8102 oz. ASW **Obv:** Pillars and waves **Note:** Struck at the Bogota Mint.

Date	Mintage	Good	VG	F	VF	XF
ND(1651-65) Date off flan	—	700	1,000	1,250	1,500	—
1651 P. oRMS	—	1,000	2,000	3,000	4,000	—
1651 RMS	—	1,000	2,000	3,000	4,000	—
1651 PoRAM	—	1,000	2,000	3,000	4,000	—
1651 PoRAMS	—	1,000	2,000	3,000	4,000	—
1651 PoRMOS	—	1,000	2,000	3,000	4,000	—
1652 P. oRAS	—	1,000	2,000	3,000	4,000	—
1652 PoRMS	—	1,000	2,000	3,000	4,000	—
1653 P oRMS	—	1,000	2,000	3,000	4,000	—
1653 P. oMS	—	1,000	2,000	3,000	4,000	—
1654 P. oRS	—	1,000	2,000	3,000	4,000	—
1655 P. ORS	—	1,000	2,000	3,000	4,000	—
1656 P. oRS	—	1,000	2,000	3,000	4,000	—
1657 P. oRM	—	1,000	2,000	3,000	4,000	—
1657 P. oRS	—	1,000	2,000	3,000	4,000	—
1658 P. oRS	—	1,000	2,000	3,000	4,000	—
1659 P. oRS	—	1,000	2,000	3,000	4,000	—
1659 P. oRAS	—	1,000	2,000	3,000	4,000	—
166Z P. oRS	—	1,000	2,000	3,000	4,000	—
1662 PoR	—	1,000	2,000	3,000	4,000	—
1663 PoR	—	1,000	2,000	3,000	4,000	—
1663 P. oRS	—	1,000	2,000	3,000	4,000	—
1664 P. oRS	—	1,000	2,000	3,000	4,000	—
1665 P. oRS	—	1,000	2,000	3,000	4,000	—

KM# 12 8 REALES

27.0674 g., 0.9310 Silver 0.8102 oz. ASW **Ruler:** Philip V **Obv:** Arms within beaded circle, legend of Charles II **Rev:** Pillars, "PLVS VLTRA" and "MM" between

Date	Mintage	Good	VG	F	VF	XF
ND(1667-1703) Date off flan	—	1,000	1,750	2,500	3,250	—
1667 P. oRS Rare	—	—	—	—	—	—
1668 P. oRS VIII at left, Rare	—	—	—	—	—	—
1668 P. oRS VIII at right, Rare	—	—	—	—	—	—
1669 P. oRS Rare	—	—	—	—	—	—
1670 P. oRS Rare	—	—	—	—	—	—
1671 P. oRS Rare	—	—	—	—	—	—
1676 OLMS Rare	—	—	—	—	—	—
1687JEMI Unique	—	—	—	—	—	—
1688 PG Rare	—	—	—	—	—	—
1690 PG Rare	—	—	—	—	—	—
1691 PG Rare	—	—	—	—	—	—
1692 ARC Rare	—	—	—	—	—	—
1693 VA Rare	—	—	—	—	—	—

KM# 3.2 8 REALES

27.0674 g., 0.9310 Silver 0.8102 oz. ASW **Note:** Struck at the Cartagena Mint.

Date	Mintage	Good	VG	F	VF	XF
1621 RN-A Rare	—	—	—	—	—	—
1622 RN-A Rare	—	—	—	—	—	—

KM# 3.4 8 REALES

27.0674 g., 0.9310 Silver 0.8102 oz. ASW **Note:** Struck at the Cartagena Mint. Prev. KM#3.3.

Date	Mintage	Good	VG	F	VF	XF
ND(1626-34) Date off flan	—	750	1,2500	1,750	2,500	—
1626 NER Rare	—	—	—	—	—	—
1628 E Rare	—	—	—	—	—	—
1629 NRE/NER Rare	—	—	—	—	—	—
1630 RN-E	—	—	—	—	—	—
1633 RN-E Rare	—	—	—	—	—	—
1633 C-E Rare	—	—	—	—	—	—
1634 C-E Rare	—	—	—	—	—	—

Note: Cartagena 8 Reales from 1627 to 1630 show mint mark assayers as RNE, NRE, or NER. Two example is known with NER to left and small RN to right

KM# 7.2 8 REALES

27.0674 g., 0.9310 Silver 0.8102 oz. ASW **Rev:** Pillars and waves, stars in field **Note:** Struck at the Cartagena Mint.

Date	Mintage	Good	VG	F	VF	XF
1655 C-S Rare	—	—	—	—	—	—

KM# B13 ESCUDO

3.3834 g., 0.9170 Gold 0.0997 oz. AGW **Ruler:** Philip IV **Obv:** Lions and castles **Rev:** Cross of Jerusalem **Note:** Struck at the Bogota Mint.

Date	Mintage	F	VF	XF	Unc	BU
ND Unique, date off flan	—	—	—	—	—	—

KM# 13 ESCUDO

3.3834 g., 0.9170 Gold 0.0997 oz. AGW **Ruler:** Philip V **Obv:** Arms **Rev:** Cross of Jerusalem

Date	Mintage	F	VF	XF	Unc	BU
ND(1666-1715) Date off flan	—	1,750	2,000	—	—	—
1672 R Rare	—	—	—	—	—	—
1687 G Rare	—	—	—	—	—	—

KM# A13 ESCUDO

3.3834 g., 0.9170 Gold 0.0997 oz. AGW **Ruler:** Philip IV **Obv:** Arms **Rev:** Cross of Jerusalem **Note:** Struck at the Bogata Mint.

Date	Mintage	F	VF	XF	Unc	BU
ND(1627-29) NR A Rare	—	—	—	—	—	—

KM# 4.1 2 ESCUDOS

6.7668 g., 0.9170 Gold 0.1995 oz. AGW **Ruler:** Philip IV **Note:** Struck at the Bogota Mint.

Date	Mintage	F	VF	XF	Unc	BU
ND(1627-29)NR A	—	1,300	1,500	1,750	—	—
Note: This issue is distinguishable from the contemporaneous assayer A cobs of Cartagena by the inclusion of a pomegranate (dot) at the bottom and transpositions of lions and castles in the shield						
ND(1628-55) Date off flan	—	1,000	1,200	1,500	—	—
1628NR A Rare	—	1,250	1,650	2,000	—	—
1628NR P Rare	—	—	—	—	—	—
1629RN P Rare	—	—	—	—	—	—
1632NR A Rare	—	—	—	—	—	—
1633NR A	—	1,500	1,950	2,500	3,000	—
1634NR A	—	1,500	1,950	2,500	3,000	—
1635NR A	—	1,500	1,950	2,500	3,000	—
1636NR A	—	1,500	1,950	2,500	3,000	—
1637NR A Rare	—	—	—	—	—	—
1638NR A Rare	—	—	—	—	—	—
1639NR A Rare	—	—	—	—	—	—
1640NR A Rare	—	—	—	—	—	—
1641NR A Rare	—	—	—	—	—	—
1642NR R Rare	—	—	—	—	—	—
1643NR R Rare	—	—	—	—	—	—
1644NR R Rare	—	—	—	—	—	—
1645NR R Rare	—	—	—	—	—	—
1646NR R Rare	—	—	—	—	—	—
1647NR R Rare	—	—	—	—	—	—
1648NR R Rare	—	—	—	—	—	—
1649NR R Rare	—	—	—	—	—	—
1650NR R Rare	—	—	—	—	—	—
1651NR R	—	1,500	1,950	2,500	3,000	—
1652NR R	—	1,500	1,950	2,500	3,000	—
1653NR R	—	1,500	1,950	2,500	3,000	—
1654NR R	—	1,500	1,950	2,500	3,000	—
1655NR R	—	1,500	1,950	2,500	3,000	—
1656NR R Rare	—	—	—	—	—	—
1657NR R Rare	—	—	—	—	—	—
1658NR R Rare	—	—	—	—	—	—
1659NR R Rare	—	—	—	—	—	—
1660NR R Rare	—	—	—	—	—	—
1661NR R Rare	—	—	—	—	—	—
1662NR R Rare	—	—	—	—	—	—
1663NR R Rare	—	—	—	—	—	—
1664NR R Rare	—	—	—	—	—	—
1665NR R Rare	—	—	—	—	—	—

KM# 14.1 2 ESCUDOS

6.7668 g., 0.9170 Gold 0.1995 oz. AGW **Ruler:** Charles II **Obv:** Arms **Rev:** Cross of Jerusalem, lions and castles in quarters **Note:** Struck at the Bogota Mint.

Date	Mintage	F	VF	XF	Unc	BU
ND(1667-93) Date off flan	—	1,000	1,200	2,000	—	—
1667NR R Rare	—	—	—	—	—	—
1668NR R Rare	—	—	—	—	—	—
1669NR R Rare	—	—	—	—	—	—
1670NR R Rare	—	—	—	—	—	—
1671NR R Rare	—	—	—	—	—	—
1672NR R Rare	—	—	—	—	—	—
1673NR R Rare	—	—	—	—	—	—
1674NR R Rare	—	—	—	—	—	—
1675NR R Rare	—	—	—	—	—	—
1676NR R Rare	—	—	—	—	—	—
ND(1677-78)NR SM 3 known	—	—	—	—	—	—
1678NR G, P Rare	—	—	—	—	—	—
1679NR G, P Rare	—	—	—	—	—	—
1680NR G, P Rare	—	—	—	—	—	—
1681NR G, P Rare	—	—	—	—	—	—
1682NR G, P Rare	—	—	—	—	—	—
1683NR G, P Rare	—	—	—	—	—	—
1684NR G, P Rare	—	—	—	—	—	—
1685NR G, P Rare	—	—	—	—	—	—
1686NR G, P Rare	—	—	—	—	—	—
1687NR G, P Rare	—	—	—	—	—	—
1688NR G, P Rare	—	—	—	—	—	—
1689NR G, P Rare	—	—	—	—	—	—
1690NR G, P Rare	—	—	—	—	—	—
1691NR G, P Rare	—	—	—	—	—	—
1692NR G, P Rare	—	—	—	—	—	—
1692NR A	—	1,750	2,250	2,750	—	—
1693NR A	—	1,750	2,250	2,750	—	—

KM# 14.2 2 ESCUDOS

6.7682 g., 0.9170 Gold 0.1995 oz. AGW **Ruler:** Philip V **Note:** No mint mark.

Date	Mintage	F	VF	XF	Unc	BU
ND(1694-1713) Date off flan	—	1,500	2,000	2,500	3,000	—
1694 ARCE	—	1,500	2,000	2,500	3,000	—
1695 ARCE	—	1,500	2,000	2,500	3,000	—
1696 ARCE	—	1,500	2,000	2,500	3,000	—
1697 ARCE	—	1,500	2,000	2,500	3,000	—
1698 ARCE	—	1,500	2,000	2,500	3,000	—
1699 ARCE	—	1,500	2,000	2,500	3,000	—
1700 ARCE	—	1,500	2,000	2,500	3,000	—

KM# 4.3 2 ESCUDOS

6.7668 g., 0.9170 Gold 0.1995 oz. AGW **Ruler:** Ferdinand VI **Obv:** Legends of Philip III **Note:** Struck at the Cartagena Mint.

Date	Mintage	F	VF	XF	Unc	BU
1622S F Rare	—	—	—	—	—	—

Note: Swiss Bank Ortiz sale No. 27 1-91, XF realized $27,200. Spink America Norweb sale 3-97, XF realized $35,200

KM# 4.4 2 ESCUDOS

6.7668 g., 0.9170 Gold 0.1995 oz. AGW **Ruler:** Ferdinand VI **Obv:** Legends of Philip IV **Note:** Struck at the Cartagena Mint.

Date	Mintage	F	VF	XF	Unc	BU
ND(1627-29)R R or NRE or RNE Date off flan	—	1,400	1,700	2,000	—	—
1627R E Rare	—	—	—	—	—	—
1627 RN E Rare	—	—	—	—	—	—
1629R E Rare	—	—	—	—	—	—

KM# 4.6 2 ESCUDOS

6.7668 g., 0.9170 Gold 0.1995 oz. AGW **Ruler:** Ferdinand VI **Note:** Struck at the Cartagena Mint.

Date	Mintage	F	VF	XF	Unc	BU
ND(1628) Date off flan	—	1,400	1,700	2,000	—	—
ND(1630-35)C E Date off flan	—	1,300	1,650	2,000	—	—
1630C E Rare	—	—	—	—	—	—
1631C E Rare	—	—	—	—	—	—
1632C E Rare	—	—	—	—	—	—
1633C E Rare	—	—	—	—	—	—
1634C E Rare	—	—	—	—	—	—
1635C E Rare	—	—	—	—	—	—

COURLAND

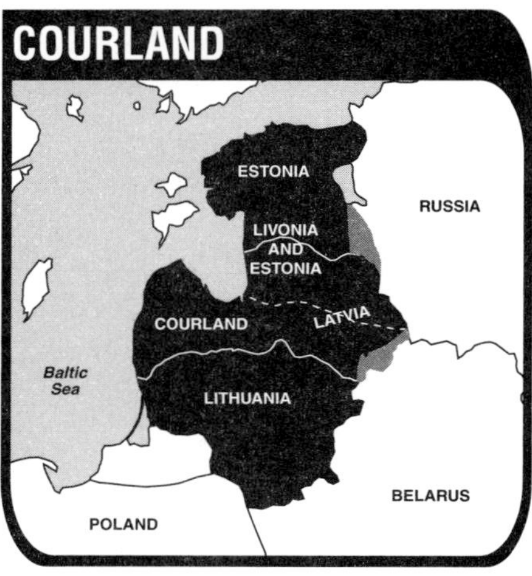

The people of Courland are of Aryan descent primarily from the German Order of Livonian Knights. They were nomadic tribesmen who settled along the Baltic prior to the 13th century. Ideally situated as a trade route and lacking a central government, they were conquered in 1561 by Poland and Sweden.

When the Livonian Order was dissolved in 1561 the then Master of the Order, Gotthard Kettler was made Duke of Courland. During the 17th century, Courland remained part of Poland, but went under Russia after Poland's division. When the Kettler line became extinct in 1737 Courland was awarded to Ernst Johann Biron, chief advisor and lover of Empress Anna of Russia. After her death he was exiled but returned in 1763. He abdicated in favor of his son Peter in 1769.

RULERS

Frederic & Guillaume Kettler, 1589-1639
Jacob Kettler, 1639-82
Friedrich Casimir Kettler, 1682-98

DUCHY

STANDARD COINAGE

KM# 3 SOLIDUS

Silver **Ruler:** Frederic & Guillaume Kettler **Obv:** S on shield below crown that divides legend **Obv. Legend:** SIGIS III D G REX POL and L - SOLIDVS DVCVM CVRLAS **Rev:** Lion of Courland within circle **Note:** Obverse legend varieties exist.

Date	Mintage	VG	F	VF	XF	Unc
1601	—	30.00	50.00	90.00	165	—
1602	—	30.00	50.00	90.00	165	—
1604	—	30.00	50.00	90.00	165	—
1605	—	30.00	50.00	90.00	165	—
1606	—	30.00	50.00	90.00	165	—
1607	—	30.00	50.00	90.00	165	—
1610	—	30.00	50.00	90.00	165	—
1611	—	30.00	50.00	90.00	165	—

KM# 6 SOLIDUS

Silver **Ruler:** Jacob Kettler **Obv:** Eagle with shield on breast within circle **Obv. Legend:** SOLIDVS D G IACOB (date) - CVRL ET SEMOE DVX **Rev:** Crowned III within circle **Note:** Obverse legend varieties exist.

Date	Mintage	VG	F	VF	XF	Unc
ND	—	30.00	50.00	90.00	165	—
1646	—	30.00	50.00	90.00	165	—
1662	—	30.00	50.00	90.00	165	—

KM# 14.1 SOLIDUS

Bronze **Ruler:** Friedrich Casimir Kettler **Obv:** Armored bust right **Obv. Legend:** FRID CASIN L C S DVX - SOLIDVS CVRLANDIAE **Rev:** Eagle with square-topped divided shield of Courland and Semgal on breast, lion and elk at bottom

Date	Mintage	VG	F	VF	XF	Unc
1696	—	20.00	40.00	75.00	145	—

KM# 14.2 SOLIDUS

Bronze **Ruler:** Friedrich Casimir Kettler **Obv:** Crowned FC monogram **Note:** Legend varieties exist.

Date	Mintage	VG	F	VF	XF	Unc
ND	—	—	—	—	—	—

KM# 9 3 POLCHER (1/2 Grosz - 1/24 Thaler)

Silver **Ruler:** Friedrich Casimir Kettler **Obv:** Square shield, divided at bottom, arms of Kettler in crown above **Rev:** 24 in orb, cross above divides legend **Note:** Legend varieties exist.

Date	Mintage	VG	F	VF	XF	Unc
1687	—	35.00	65.00	120	200	—
1689	—	35.00	65.00	120	200	—
1695	—	35.00	65.00	120	200	—

KM# 13 3 POLCHER (1/2 Grosz - 1/24 Thaler)

Silver **Ruler:** Friedrich Casimir Kettler **Obv:** Crowned divided shield within circle **Rev:** Ornate cross above orb with 24 **Note:** Legend varieties exist.

Date	Mintage	VG	F	VF	XF	Unc
1695	—	35.00	65.00	120	200	—
1696	—	35.00	65.00	120	200	—

KM# 4 3 GROSZY

Silver **Ruler:** Frederic & Guillaume Kettler **Obv:** Bust right **Rev:** III above arms dividing eagle and horse and rider, legend and date below **Note:** Legend varieties exist.

Date	Mintage	VG	F	VF	XF	Unc
1604	—	40.00	80.00	150	275	—
1606	—	40.00	80.00	150	275	—
ND	—	40.00	80.00	150	275	—

KM# 11 6 GROSZY

Silver **Ruler:** Friedrich Casimir Kettler

Date	Mintage	VG	F	VF	XF	Unc
1687	—	—	—	—	—	—
1689	—	—	—	—	—	—
1694 4CVR	—	50.00	100	185	325	—
1695	—	50.00	100	185	325	—
1696	—	50.00	100	185	325	—

KM# 12 ORT (18 Grozy - 1 Timf)

Silver **Ruler:** Friedrich Casimir Kettler

Date	Mintage	VG	F	VF	XF	Unc
1689	—	—	—	—	—	—
1694	—	35.00	70.00	140	250	—

KM# 5.1 THALER

Silver **Ruler:** Jacob Kettler **Obv:** Large ornate armor plated bust of Jacob Kettler right **Rev:** Eagle and horse and rider in geometric outline, date in legend **Note:** Dav. #4348.

Date	Mintage	VG	F	VF	XF	Unc
1643	—	—	—	—	—	—
Note: Reported, not confirmed						
1644	—	400	750	1,350	3,000	—

KM# 5.2 THALER

Silver **Ruler:** Jacob Kettler **Obv:** Small bust **Note:** Dav. #4349. Punctuation varieties exist in legends of Dav. #4348 and Dav. #4349.

Date	Mintage	VG	F	VF	XF	Unc
1645	—	400	750	1,350	3,000	—
1646 Reported, not confirmed	—	—	—	—	—	—

TRADE COINAGE

KM# 7 DUCAT

3.5000 g., 0.9860 Gold 0.1109 oz. AGW **Ruler:** Jacob Kettler **Rev:** Shield

Date	Mintage	VG	F	VF	XF	Unc
1644	—	475	1,150	2,000	3,250	—
1645	—	475	1,150	2,000	3,250	—
1646	—	475	1,150	2,000	3,250	—

KM# 10 DUCAT

3.5000 g., 0.9860 Gold 0.1109 oz. AGW **Ruler:** Friedrich Casimir Kettler **Obv:** Bust of Friedrich Casimir right **Rev:** Crowned eagle with arms of Courland and Semgal on chest, last 2 digits of date between wings and neck

Date	Mintage	VG	F	VF	XF	Unc
1689	—	325	700	1,450	2,500	—

KM# 8 10 DUCAT
35.0000 g., 0.9860 Gold 1.1095 oz. AGW **Ruler:** Jacob Kettler

Date	Mintage	VG	F	VF	XF	Unc
1644 Rare	—	—	—	—	—	—

CRIMEA (KRIM)

The Crimea (ancient Tauris or Tauric Chersonese, Turkish Kirim or Krim, Russian Krym) is a peninsula of southern Russia extending into the Black Sea southwest of the Sea of Azov.

In ancient times, The Crimea was inhabited by the Goths and Scythians, was colonized by the Greeks, and ranked, in part, as a tributary state of Rome. During the succeeding centuries, the Goths, Huns, Khazars, Byzantine Greeks, Kipchak Turks, and the Tatars of Batu Khan who founded the Tatar Khanate in Russia known as the Empire of the Golden Horde overran the Crimea. After the destruction of the Golden Horde by Tamerlane (Timur) in 1395, the Crimean Taters founded an independent khanate under Haji Ghirai, which reigned first at Solkhat (Eski Kirim or Stary Krym). The Crimean khans ruled as tributary princes of the Ottoman Empire from 1478 to 1777, when they became dependent upon Russia.

RULERS
Ghazi Giray II, AH996-1017 / 1588-1608AD
Salamat Giray I, AH1017-1019 / 1608-1610AD
Jani Beg Giray, 1st reign, AH1019-1032 / 1610-1623AD
Jani Beg Giray, 2nd reign, AH1036-1044 / 1627-1635AD
'Inayat Giray, AH1044-1046 / 1635-1637AD
Bahadur Giray, AH1046-1051 / 1637-1641AD
Islam Giray III, AH1054-1064 / 1644-1654AD
Muhammad Giray IV, 2nd reign, AH1064-1076 / 1654-1666AD
'Adil Giray, AH1076-1082 / 1666-1671AD
Selim Giray I, 1st reign, AH1082-1089 / 1671-1678AD
Murad Giray, AH1089-1094 / 1678-1683AD
Selim Giray I, 2nd reign, AH1095-1103 / 1684-1691AD
Sa'adat Giray II, AH1103 / 1691AD
Safa Giray, AH1103-1104 / 1691-1692AD
Selim Giray I, 3rd reign, AH1104-1110 / 1692-1699AD
Dawlat Giray II, 1st reign, AH1110-1114 / 1699-1702AD

MINT MARKS

Bagchih-Serai

Kaffa

MONETARY SYSTEM
3 Manghir (Agcheh, Asper) – 1 Para
2 Para = 1 Ikilik
2-1/2 Ikilik = 1 Beshlik
2 Beshlik = 1 Onlik
2 Onlik = 1 Yirmilik = 1/2 Kurus
2 Yirmilik = 1 Kurus
1-1/2 Kurus = 1 Altmishlik

Russian Names	Turkish Names
2 Polushka = 1 Denga	= 2 Akche
2 Denga = 1 Kopek	= 3 Akche
5 Kopecks = 1 Kyrmis	= 15 Akche
2 Kyrmis = 1 Ishal (Tschal)	= 25 Akche

From AH1017-1169/1608-1756AD silver coins (akeches) and copper coins were struck in the names of 24 Khanate rulers. They are all very similar to the coin illustrated as C#125, usually with the obverse showing the ruler's and his father's names and the reverse with a toughra above *duribe* and the mintname.

Ghazi Giray II

HAMMERED COINAGE

MB# 8 AKCE
Silver Or Billon Weight varies: 0.28-0.38g **Obv:** Ruler's name and titles **Rev:** Mint and date

Date	Mintage	Good	VG	F	VF	XF
AH996	—	20.00	35.00	45.00	55.00	—
ND(date missing)	—	10.00	17.00	25.00	38.00	—

Salamat Giray I

HAMMERED COINAGE

KM# 1 AKCE
Silver Weight varies: 0.28-0.30g **Obv:** Ruler's name and titles **Rev:** Mint and date

Date	Mintage	Good	VG	F	VF	XF
AH1017	—	20.00	35.00	50.00	65.00	—
ND(date missing)	—	15.00	30.00	40.00	50.00	—

Jani Beg Giray

HAMMERED COINAGE

KM# 2 AKCE
Silver Weight varies: 0.28-0.33g **Obv:** Ruler's name and titles **Rev:** Mint and date

Date	Mintage	Good	VG	F	VF	XF
AH1019	—	20.00	30.00	40.00	50.00	—
ND(date missing)	—	12.00	20.00	30.00	40.00	—

Jani Beg Giray

HAMMERED COINAGE

KM# 3.1 AKCE
Silver Weight varies: 0.28-0.33g **Obv:** Ruler's name and titles **Rev:** Mint and date

Date	Mintage	Good	VG	F	VF	XF
AH[1036]	—	20.00	35.00	45.00	55.00	—
ND(date missing)	—	15.00	25.00	35.00	45.00	—

KM# 3.2 AKCE
Silver Weight varies: 0.29-0.33g **Obv:** Ruler's name and titles **Rev:** Date

Date	Mintage	Good	VG	F	VF	XF
AH1036	—	18.00	28.00	40.00	50.00	—

'Inayat Giray

HAMMERED COINAGE

KM# 4 AKCE
0.3000 g., Silver **Obv:** Ruler's name and titles **Rev:** Tamgha in center, date below

Date	Mintage	Good	VG	F	VF	XF
AH1044	—	45.00	60.00	75.00	125	—

Bahadur Giray

HAMMERED COINAGE

KM# A5 AKCE
0.3000 g., Silver **Obv:** Ruler's name and titles **Rev:** Tamgha in center, date below

Date	Mintage	Good	VG	F	VF	XF
AH1046	—	45.00	60.00	75.00	125	—
ND(date missing)	—	35.00	45.00	60.00	90.00	—

Islam Giray III

HAMMERED COINAGE

KM# 5 AKCE
Silver Weight varies: 0.24-0.25g **Obv:** Ruler's name and titles **Rev:** Tamgha above mint and date

Date	Mintage	Good	VG	F	VF	XF
AH1054	—	30.00	45.00	60.00	75.00	—
ND(date missing)	—	15.00	25.00	35.00	50.00	—

Muhammad Giray IV

HAMMERED COINAGE

KM# 6 AKCE
0.2800 g., Silver **Obv:** "Muhammad" in circle, titles around **Rev:** Tamgha above mint and date

Date	Mintage	Good	VG	F	VF	XF
AH1064	—	25.00	40.00	50.00	60.00	—
ND(date missing)	—	20.00	35.00	45.00	55.00	—

KM# 7 BESHLIK
Silver Weight varies: 1.34-1.36g **Obv:** Ruler's name and titles **Rev:** "zarb" in cartouche, tamgha above, mint and date below

Date	Mintage	Good	VG	F	VF	XF
AH1064	—	30.00	45.00	60.00	80.00	—
ND(date missing)	—	20.00	35.00	45.00	60.00	—

'Adil Giray

HAMMERED COINAGE

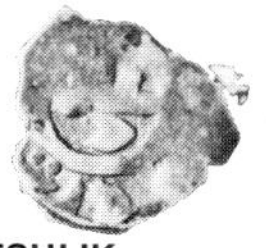

KM# 8 BESHLIK
Silver Weight varies: 1.35-1.39g **Obv:** "'Adil" in circle, titles around **Rev:** Tamgha in center, mint and date around

Date	Mintage	Good	VG	F	VF	XF
AH1076	—	30.00	45.00	60.00	80.00	—
ND(date missing)	—	20.00	35.00	45.00	60.00	—

Selim Giray I

HAMMERED COINAGE

KM# 9 BESHLIK
Silver Weight varies: 1.40-1.85g **Obv:** Ruler's name and titles **Rev:** Tamgha above mint and date

Date	Mintage	Good	VG	F	VF	XF
AH1082	—	50.00	65.00	85.00	125	—
AH1085	—	50.00	65.00	85.00	125	—
ND(date missing)	—	40.00	50.00	70.00	90.00	—

Murad Giray

HAMMERED COINAGE

KM# 10 BESHLIK
Silver Weight varies: 0.98-1.35g **Obv:** Ruler's name and titles **Rev:** Tamgha in circle, mint and date around

Date	Mintage	Good	VG	F	VF	XF
AH1089	—	50.00	65.00	85.00	125	—
ND(date missing)	—	40.00	50.00	70.00	90.00	—

Selim Giray I

HAMMERED COINAGE

KM# 11 BESHLIK
Silver Weight varies: 1.20-1.30g **Obv:** Ruler's name and titles **Rev:** Tamgha above mint and date

Date	Mintage	Good	VG	F	VF	XF
AH1095	—	50.00	65.00	85.00	110	—
ND(date missing)	—	40.00	50.00	65.00	80.00	—

KM# 11A PARA
0.6000 g., Silver **Obv:** Ruler's name and titles **Rev:** Tamgha above mint and date

Date	Mintage	Good	VG	F	VF	XF
AH1095	—	60.00	70.00	90.00	130	—
ND(date missing)	—	40.00	50.00	70.00	90.00	—

KM# 11B AKCE
0.2500 g., Silver **Obv:** Ruler's name and titles **Rev:** Tamgha above mint and date

Date	Mintage	Good	VG	F	VF	XF
AH1095	—	50.00	65.00	85.00	125	—
ND(date missing)	—	40.00	50.00	70.00	90.00	—

Sa'adat Giray II

HAMMERED COINAGE

KM# A12 BESHLIK
1.2500 g., Silver **Obv:** Ruler's name and titles **Rev:** Tamgha in center divides mintname, date below

Date	Mintage	Good	VG	F	VF	XF
AH1102 (error for 1103)	—	55.00	70.00	90.00	125	—

Safa Giray

HAMMERED COINAGE

KM# 12 BESHLIK
Silver Weight varies: 1.03-1.30g **Obv:** Ruler's name and titles **Rev:** Tamgha above mint and date

Date	Mintage	Good	VG	F	VF	XF
AH1103	—	50.00	65.00	85.00	125	—
ND(date missing)	—	40.00	50.00	70.00	90.00	—

Selim Giray I

HAMMERED COINAGE

KM# 13 BESHLIK
Silver Weight varies: 0.76-0.97g **Obv:** Ruler's name and titles **Rev:** Tamgha above mint and date

Date	Mintage	Good	VG	F	VF	XF
AH1108	—	50.00	65.00	85.00	100	—
ND(date missing)	—	40.00	50.00	70.00	90.00	—

Dawlat Giray II

HAMMERED COINAGE

KM# A14 AKCE

0.2000 g., Silver **Obv:** Ruler's name and titles **Rev:** Tamgha above mint and date

Date	Mintage	Good	VG	F	VF	XF
AH1111	—	65.00	75.00	90.00	120	—

KM# 14 BESHLIK

Silver Weight varies: 0.96-1.05g **Obv:** Ruler's name and titles **Rev:** Tamgha above mint and date

Date	Mintage	Good	VG	F	VF	XF
AH1111	—	35.00	45.00	60.00	70.00	—

DENMARK

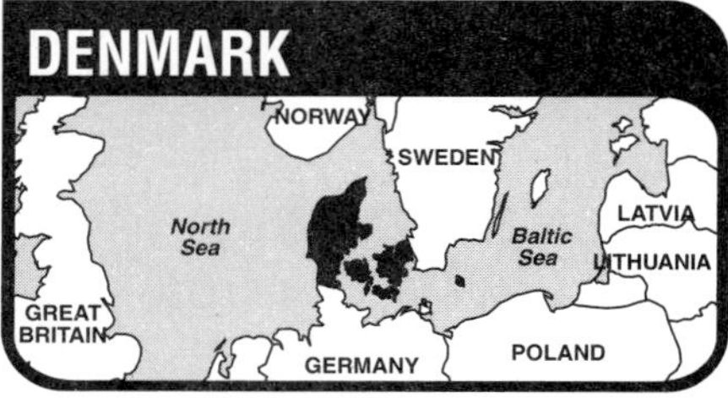

The Kingdom of Denmark (Danmark), is located at the mouth of the Baltic Sea.

Denmark, a great power during the Viking period of the 9th-11th centuries, conducted raids on western Europe and England, and in the 11th century united England, Denmark and Norway under the rule of King Canute. Despite a struggle between the crown and the nobility (13th-14th centuries) which forced the King to grant a written constitution, Queen Margaret (Margrethe) (1387-1412) succeeded in uniting Denmark, Norway, Sweden, Finland and Greenland under the Danish crown, placing all of Scandinavia under the rule of Denmark. An unwise alliance with Napoleon contributed to the dismembering of the empire and fostered a liberal movement which succeeded in making Denmark a constitutional monarchy in 1849.

RULERS

Christian IV, 1588-1648
Frederik III, 1648-1670
Christian V, 1670-1699
Frederik IV, 1699-1730

MINT MARKS

Copenhagen

Mark	Date	Name
(a)	1596-1624	Nicolaus Schwabe
NS	1624-27	Nicolaus Schwabe
BZ	1627-28	Nicolaus Schwabe
(b)	1610-14	Hans Fleming
(c)	1614-21	Johan Post
(d)	1615	Casper Fleming
(o)	1621-23	Johan Engelbrecht
(e)	1628-29	Peder Gruner
(f)	1630-43	Peder Gruner
(g)	1629	Mathias Clausen
(h)	1644	Henrik Kohler
(i)	1662-63	Johan Stichman
(j)	1663-64	Casper Herbach
(k)	1664-70	Frederik Casper Herbach
(l)	1664-70	Gottfried Kruger
GK and	1670-80	Gottfried Kruger
Heart	1690-	Christian Winnecke

Elsinore

Mark	Date	Name
(m)	1607-10	Hans Fleming

Frederiksborg

Mark	Date	Name
(n)	1621-23	Johan Engelbrecht

Gluckstadt

Mark	Date	Name
(p)	1640-43	Simon Timpf
(q)	1644-48	Jacob Schiegelt
IW	1679	Johan Woltereck
CW	1679-	Christopher Woltereck

Unknown

Mark	Date	Name
(r)	1601-1700	?
(t) single halberd	1648	?

(c) - Copenhagen (Kobenhavn), crown
(h) - Copenhagen, heart
(o) - Altona, orb, 1842-63
KM - Copenhagen
S – Rendsborg, 1716-20

NOTE: (ch) - crossed hammers - Kongsberg.

MINT OFFICIALS' INITIALS

Copenhagen

Initial	Date	Name
	1602-29	Nikolaus Schwabe
P	1614-22	Johan Post
	1620-24	Michael Wile
	1620-22	Johan Engelbrecht
BZ	1627	Balthazar Zwierner
G	1628-43	Peter Gruner
	1629	Mathius Clauesen
HK or ligate HK	1644-62	Hendrik Kohler
IS	1644-48	Jacob Schiegelt
IL	1645-46	?
IS	1662-63	Johan Stichmann
CH	1663-64	Casper Herbach
FCH	1664-71	Frederik Casper Herbach, Jr.
GK	1665-80	Gottfried Kruger
GS	1680-90	Gregorius Streseman
CW	1690-1700	Christian Winnecke, Sr.
AMB	1692-	Anton Maybusch, die-cutter

NOTE: The letter P was only used on Danish West Indies coins.

Frederiksborg

Initial	Date	Name
	1622-23	Paul Golden and Johan Engelbrecht

Gluckstadt

Initial	Date	Name
	1616-31	Albert Dionis
Feather w/ligate TS	1640-43	Simon Timpf
I, crossed halberds, W		Johan Woltereck

NOTE: This mint was temporarily closed from 1631 to 1640.

Helsinger

Initial	Date	Name
	1607-14	Hans Flemming
	1614-15	Casper Flemming

Lyngby

Initial	Date	Name
FCH	1668-70	F.C.

MONETARY SYSTEM

(Until 1813)

4 Penning = 1 Huid = 1/4 Skilling
6 Penning = 1 Sosling = 1/2 Skilling
16 Skillings = 1 Mark
64 Skilling Danske = 4 Mark = 1 Krone
96 Skilling Danske = 6 Mark = 1 Daler Specie
12 Mark = 1 Ducat
10 Ducat = 1 Portugaloser

KINGDOM

WIRE MONEY

KM# 62 DENNING

0.6000 g., 0.8850 Silver 0.0171 oz. ASW **Rev:** King's title in Russian text **Note:** Strikes with a "P" below the horse on the obverse were minted in Copenhagen. Those strikes with an "M", or no letter at all, were minted in Gluckstadt. Varieties exist. Prev. KM#62.2.

Date	Mintage	Good	VG	F	VF	XF
ND(1619) Rare	—	—	—	—	—	—

STANDARD COINAGE

Through 1813

KM# 340.2 DENNING

3.4900 g., 0.9790 Gold 0.1098 oz. AGW **Obv. Legend:** CHRISTIANVS • 5

Date	Mintage	VG	F	VF	XF	Unc
1672	—	850	1,650	3,500	—	—

KM# 6 PENNING

0.5850 g., Copper **Obv:** Date within crowned C, 1C602 **Note:** Uniface.

Date	Mintage	Good	VG	F	VF	XF
1602	—	300	600	1,200	2,000	—

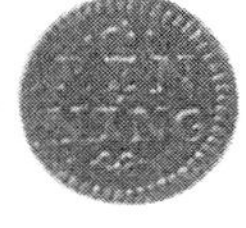

KM# 5 PENNING

0.5850 g., Copper **Obv:** Date within crowned C, 1C602 **Rev. Legend:** PEN/NING **Note:** Varieties exist with line below crown, presumably a die break.

Date	Mintage	Good	VG	F	VF	XF
1602	—	350	750	1,500	2,600	—

KM# 7 2 PENNING

0.5850 g., Copper **Obv:** Date within crowned C, 1C602 **Rev:** I*I/PEN/NING

Date	Mintage	Good	VG	F	VF	XF
1602	—	150	300	600	1,200	—

KM# 8 HVID

0.7130 g., 0.0930 Silver 0.0021 oz. ASW, 17 mm. **Obv:** Long cross on oval design divides date **Obv. Legend:** CHRISTIANVS IIII • D: G • DANI • **Rev:** Crowned C, date partially within as 1C602 **Rev. Legend:** NORVEGI: VANDA: GOT • Q • REX (clover)

Date	Mintage	Good	VG	F	VF	XF
1602	—	400	650	975	1,600	—

KM# 9 HVID

0.7130 g., 0.0930 Silver 0.0021 oz. ASW, 15 mm. **Obv:** Short cross on oval design **Obv. Legend:** CHRISTIANVS III D G DAN • **Rev:** Crowned C, date partially within as 1C602 **Rev. Legend:** NORVEGI • VANDA • GOT • Q • REX (clover)

Date	Mintage	Good	VG	F	VF	XF
1602	—	25.00	50.00	140	280	—

KM# 34 HVID

0.7130 g., 0.0930 Silver 0.0021 oz. ASW **Obv:** Crowned C within circle **Obv. Legend:** CHRISTIANVS • IIII • D: G: DAN: **Rev:** Short cross with ornaments within circle, mintmaster mark at top **Rev. Legend:** NOR: VAN: GOT: Q: REX • 1607

Date	Mintage	Good	VG	F	VF	XF
1607 Unique	—	—	—	—	—	—

KM# 54 HVID

0.7130 g., 0.0930 Silver 0.0021 oz. ASW **Obv:** Short cross on oval design **Obv. Legend:** CHRISTIAN III D G DAN • (clover) **Rev:** Crowned C, date within C **Rev. Legend:** NOR: VAN: GOT • REX

Date	Mintage	Good	VG	F	VF	XF
1613	—	400	700	1,000	—	—
1614	—	75.00	150	300	625	—

KM# 63.2 HVID

0.5640 g., 0.0930 Silver 0.0017 oz. ASW, 15 mm. **Obv:** Long cross and ornaments **Obv. Legend:** CHRISTIAN 4 D G D **Rev:** Crowned C4 **Rev. Legend:** NOR VAN GOT REX •

Date	Mintage	Good	VG	F	VF	XF
ND	—	55.00	105	275	600	—

KM# 86 HVID

Silver **Obv:** Long cross on oval shield **Rev:** Crowned C4 monogram in pellet border, legend around

Date	Mintage	Good	VG	F	VF	XF
1624	—	20.00	40.00	110	225	—
1625	—	20.00	40.00	120	250	—

KM# 175 HVID

Copper **Obv:** Crowned F3 monogram **Rev:** Date quartered by long cross

Date	Mintage	Good	VG	F	VF	XF
1651	—	30.00	60.00	150	475	—

KM# 380.1 HVID

0.5570 g., 0.1250 Silver 0.0022 oz. ASW **Obv:** Crowned C5 monogram **Rev:** Value and date, "DANSK"

Date	Mintage	Good	VG	F	VF	XF
1686	—	13.00	23.00	65.00	150	—

KM# 380.2 HVID

0.5570 g., 0.1250 Silver 0.0022 oz. ASW **Rev:** "DANS"

Date	Mintage	Good	VG	F	VF	XF
1686	—	15.00	30.00	85.00	185	—

KM# 63.1 HVID

0.5640 g., 0.0930 Silver 0.0017 oz. ASW, 13-14 mm. **Obv:** Long cross and ornaments **Obv. Legend:** CHRISTIAN 4 D G D • **Rev:** Crowned C4, date in legend **Rev. Legend:** NOR VAN GOT REX •

Date	Mintage	Good	VG	F	VF	XF
ND(a) on obverse	—	65.00	120	275	550	—
ND(a) on reverse	—	25.00	37.50	85.00	190	—
ND(c) on obverse	—	30.00	55.00	115	325	—
1619(c)	—	32.50	60.00	125	350	—

KM# 63.3 HVID

0.5640 g., 0.0930 Silver 0.0017 oz. ASW, 12 mm. **Obv:** Long cross and ornaments **Obv. Legend:** CHRISTIAN 4 DA **Rev:** Crowned C4 **Rev. Legend:** NOR • VAN • GOT • REX

Date	Mintage	Good	VG	F	VF	XF
ND(1618-19)	—	40.00	80.00	225	500	—

KM# 10 SøSLING (1/2 Skilling)

1.0630 g., 0.1250 Silver 0.0043 oz. ASW, 19 mm. **Obv:** Crowned shield with lions on forked crossarms, breaks legend at top **Obv. Legend:** CHRISTIANVS IIII D G DANI **Rev:** Crowned bust of Christian IV right within legend **Rev. Legend:** NORVEGI: VANDA: GOTH: Q · REX **Note:** Milled.

Date	Mintage	Good	VG	F	VF	XF
ND(1602)	—	100	200	380	700	—

KM# 22.1 SøSLING (1/2 Skilling)

1.0170 g., 0.1250 Silver 0.0041 oz. ASW, 17 mm. **Obv:** Crowned bust of Christian IV facing right with low collar, breaks legend at bottom **Obv. Legend:** CHRISTIAN · IIII · D: G · DAN **Rev:** Crowned shield with lions on forked crossarms, breaks legend at top **Rev. Legend:** NOR VAND GOTO REX **Note:** Milled.

Date	Mintage	Good	VG	F	VF	XF
ND(1604)	—	12.50	25.00	60.00	135	—

KM# 22.2 SøSLING (1/2 Skilling)

1.0170 g., 0.1250 Silver 0.0041 oz. ASW, 17 mm. **Obv:** Crowned bust of Christian IV facing right with low collar, breaks legend at bottom. **Obv. Legend:** CHRISTIAN · IIII · D: G · DAN **Rev:** Crowned shield with beaded border, lions on forked crossarms, breaks legend at top. **Rev. Legend:** NOR VAND GOTO REX **Note:** Similar to KM#22.1, milled.

Date	Mintage	Good	VG	F	VF	XF
ND(1604)	—	15.00	32.50	70.00	160	—

KM# 40.3 SøSLING (1/2 Skilling)

1.0170 g., 0.1250 Silver 0.0041 oz. ASW, 16.5 mm. **Obv:** Crowned bust of Christian IV facing right with high collar, breaks legend at bottom **Obv. Legend:** CHRISTIAN: IIII · D: G · DA **Rev:** Crowned shield with lions on forked crossarms, breaks legend at top **Rev. Legend:** NOR VAN GOT REX

Date	Mintage	Good	VG	F	VF	XF
ND(1607-09)	—	15.00	25.00	95.00	160	—

KM# 40.4 SøSLING (1/2 Skilling)

1.0170 g., 0.1250 Silver 0.0041 oz. ASW, 16.5 mm. **Obv:** Crowned bust of Christian IV facing right with high collar, breaks legend at top **Obv. Legend:** CHRISTIAN: IIII · D: G · DA **Rev:** Crowned shield with lions on forked crossarms, beaded border, breaks legend at top **Rev. Legend:** NOR VAN GOT REX

Date	Mintage	Good	VG	F	VF	XF
ND(1607-09)	—	22.50	45.00	150	300	—

KM# 47.1 SøSLING (1/2 Skilling)

1.0170 g., 0.1250 Silver 0.0041 oz. ASW, 16 mm. **Obv:** Crowned bust of Christian IV facing right with ruffled collar, breaks legend at top **Obv. Legend:** CHRISTIAN IIII · D G DA **Rev:** Crowned shield with lebards on forked crossarms, breaks legend at top **Rev. Legend:** NOR VAN GOT REX

Date	Mintage	Good	VG	F	VF	XF
ND(1611)	—	—	100	250	550	—

KM# 47.2 SøSLING (1/2 Skilling)

1.0170 g., 0.1250 Silver 0.0041 oz. ASW, 16 mm. **Obv:** Crowned bust of Christian IV facing right with ruffled collar, breaks legend at bottom **Obv. Legend:** CHRISTIAN IIII · D G DA **Rev:** Crowned shield with forked crossarms, breaks legend at top **Rev. Legend:** NOR VAN GOT REX

Date	Mintage	Good	VG	F	VF	XF
ND(1611) Rare	—	—	—	—	—	—

KM# 47.3 SøSLING (1/2 Skilling)

1.0170 g., 0.1250 Silver 0.0041 oz. ASW **Obv:** Crowned bust of Christian IV facing right with ruffled collar, breaks legend at top **Obv. Legend:** CHRISTIAN IIII·D G DA **Rev:** Crowned shield with hearts surrounding lebards, breaks legend at top **Rev. Legend:** NOR VAN GOT REX

Date	Mintage	Good	VG	F	VF	XF
ND(1611) Rare	—	—	—	—	—	—

KM# 48.1 SøSLING (1/2 Skilling)

1.0170 g., 0.1250 Silver 0.0041 oz. ASW, 16 mm. **Obv:** Crowned bust of Christian IV facing right with ruffled collar, breaks legend at top **Obv. Legend:** CHRISTIAN IIII D G DA **Rev:** Crowned shield with lions and hearts on crossarms with straight cut ends, breaks legend at top

Date	Mintage	Good	VG	F	VF	XF
ND(1614)(a)	—	90.00	175	380	700	—

KM# 48.2 SøSLING (1/2 Skilling)

1.0170 g., 0.1250 Silver 0.0041 oz. ASW, 16 mm. **Obv:** Crowned bust of Christian IV facing right with ruffled collar, breaks legend at top **Obv. Legend:** CHRISTIAN IIII D G DA **Rev:** Crowned shield with lions and hearts on crossarms with straight cut ends, breaks legend at top

Date	Mintage	Good	VG	F	VF	XF
ND(1614)	—	50.00	115	295	600	—

KM# 45 SøSLING (1/2 Skilling)

0.5300 g., Silver **Obv:** Crowned bust of Christian IV right, breaks legend at bottom **Obv. Legend:** CHRISTIAN 4 D G DAN **Rev:** Crowned shield on forked crossarms, breaks legend at top **Rev. Legend:** NOR VAN GOT REX

Date	Mintage	Good	VG	F	VF	XF
ND(1622)	—	55.00	110	225	500	—

KM# 176 SøSLING (1/2 Skilling)

Copper **Obv:** Crowned F3 monogram **Rev:** Value and date

Date	Mintage	Good	VG	F	VF	XF
1651	—	15.00	30.00	65.00	200	—

KM# 177 SøSLING (1/2 Skilling)

Copper **Obv:** Crowned oval shield **Rev:** Value and date within fancy border

Date	Mintage	Good	VG	F	VF	XF
1651 Unique	—	—	—	—	—	—

KM# 40.1 SøSLING (1/2 Skilling)

1.0170 g., 0.1250 Silver 0.0041 oz. ASW, 16.5 mm. **Obv:** Crowned bust of Christian IV facing right with high collar, breaks legend at bottom **Obv. Legend:** CHRISTIAN: IIII · D: G · DA **Rev:** Crowned shield with lions on forked crossarms, beaded border, breaks legend at top **Rev. Legend:** NOR VAN GOT REX

Date	Mintage	Good	VG	F	VF	XF
ND(1607-09)(a)	—	35.00	70.00	120	180	—

KM# 40.2 SøSLING (1/2 Skilling)

1.0630 g., 0.1250 Silver 0.0043 oz. ASW, 16.5 mm. **Obv:** Crowned bust of Christian IV facing right with high collar, breaks legend at bottom **Obv. Legend:** CHRISTIAN: IIII · D: G · DA **Rev:** Crowned shield with Lebards and hearts, beaded border, breaks legend at top **Rev. Legend:** NOR VAN GOT REX **Note:** Without mint mark

Date	Mintage	Good	VG	F	VF	XF
ND(1607-09)	—	25.00	50.00	90.00	120	—

KM# 87 SøSLING (1/2 Skilling)

Copper **Obv:** Crowned bust right breaks circle at bottom **Rev:** Value and date within oval shield

Date	Mintage	Good	VG	F	VF	XF
1624(a)	—	20.00	50.00	175	550	—

KM# 123 SøSLING (1/2 Skilling)

Silver **Obv:** Crowned bust right without circle **Rev:** Value and date within ornate oval shield

Date	Mintage	Good	VG	F	VF	XF
1631(a)	—	175	350	800	1,500	—

KM# 381 1/2 SKILLING

0.6680 g., 0.1560 Silver 0.0034 oz. ASW **Obv:** Crowned double C5 monogram **Rev:** Value and date

Date	Mintage	Good	VG	F	VF	XF
1686	—	15.00	30.00	65.00	250	—

KM# 421.1 1/2 SKILLING

3.6540 g., Copper **Obv:** Armored bust right **Rev:** Crown dividing value

Date	Mintage	Good	VG	F	VF	XF
1693	—	10.00	17.50	55.00	120	—
1694	—	8.00	12.50	30.00	105	—
1696	—	15.00	27.50	70.00	200	—

KM# 421.2 1/2 SKILLING

3.6540 g., Copper **Obv:** Armored bust right **Rev:** Without value

Date	Mintage	Good	VG	F	VF	XF
1693	—	1,500	2,000	2,750	3,250	—
1694 Unique	—	—	—	—	—	—

KM# A40.1 SKILLING

1.6020 g., 0.1710 Silver 0.0088 oz. ASW **Obv:** Crowned notched oval shield on long cross **Note:** Varieties exist. Previous KM#40.1.

Date	Mintage	Good	VG	F	VF	XF
1608(m)	—	20.00	37.50	60.00	160	—
1609(m)	—	20.00	37.50	60.00	160	—
1611(m)	—	15.00	30.00	40.00	100	—
1612(m)	—	15.00	30.00	65.00	155	—
1613(m)	—	15.00	30.00	50.00	110	—
1614(d)	—	22.50	45.00	72.50	170	—
1615(d)	—	20.00	37.50	60.00	160	—

KM# 67 SKILLING

0.5320 g., 0.3120 Silver 0.0053 oz. ASW **Obv:** Crowned C4 monogram **Note:** Varieties exist.

Date	Mintage	Good	VG	F	VF	XF
1619(c)	—	50.00	90.00	225	475	—
1620(a)	—	6.50	12.00	35.00	60.00	—
1620(o)	—	8.00	15.00	40.00	85.00	—
1620(r)	—	6.50	12.00	35.00	60.00	—
1621(a)	—	6.50	12.00	35.00	60.00	—
1621(o)	—	10.00	20.00	42.50	90.00	—
1621(r)	—	6.50	12.00	27.50	60.00	—
1622(a)	—	15.00	30.00	70.00	135	—
1622(o)	—	25.00	50.00	100	225	—
1622(r)	—	30.00	55.00	90.00	250	—
1623(r)	—	30.00	55.00	90.00	250	—

KM# 88 SKILLING

0.5320 g., 0.3120 Silver 0.0053 oz. ASW **Obv:** Crowned oval shield on long cross **Rev:** Value within legend and date

Date	Mintage	Good	VG	F	VF	XF
1624 closed crown	—	10.00	20.00	40.00	100	—
1624 open crown	—	30.00	60.00	150	240	—

KM# 113.1 SKILLING

0.2920 g., 0.8750 Silver 0.0082 oz. ASW **Obv:** Crowned C4 monogram dividing date, 1S **Note:** Bracteate

Date	Mintage	Good	VG	F	VF	XF
(16)29	—	75.00	125	260	700	—

KM# 113.2 SKILLING

0.2920 g., 0.8750 Silver 0.0082 oz. ASW **Obv:** Without 1S **Note:** Bracteate

Date	Mintage	Good	VG	F	VF	XF
(16)29	—	45.00	100	245	525	—

KM# 131 SKILLING

0.2920 g., 0.8750 Silver 0.0082 oz. ASW **Obv:** Crowned oval arms on long cross **Rev:** Value within legend and date

Date	Mintage	Good	VG	F	VF	XF
1644	—	12.00	25.00	75.00	130	—
1648	—	11.00	22.50	60.00	100	—

KM# 156.1 SKILLING

0.2920 g., 0.8750 Silver 0.0082 oz. ASW **Obv. Legend:** FRIDERIC • 9 • III • D • G • DAN • **Rev. Legend:** NOR • VAN • GOTO • ELEC • R •

Date	Mintage	Good	VG	F	VF	XF
1648	—	20.00	55.00	130	300	—
1648 Rare; Two knobs on shield	—	—	—	—	—	—

KM# 156.2 SKILLING

0.2920 g., 0.8750 Silver 0.0082 oz. ASW **Rev:** Legend without ELEC • R •

Date	Mintage	Good	VG	F	VF	XF
1648	—	35.00	70.00	160	325	—
1649	—	18.00	35.00	75.00	200	—
1650	—	20.00	40.00	95.00	225	—
1652 Four points on each shield side	—	18.00	35.00	70.00	175	—
1652 Three points on each shield side	—	15.00	25.00	50.00	120	—
1653 Three points on each shield side	—	18.00	35.00	75.00	175	—

KM# A157 SKILLING

0.2920 g., 0.8750 Silver 0.0082 oz. ASW **Obv:** KM#156.2, 1650 **Rev:** KM#184.1, 1655

Date	Mintage	Good	VG	F	VF	XF
1650/55	—	100	150	200	—	—

KM# 184.1 SKILLING

0.2920 g., 0.8750 Silver 0.0082 oz. ASW **Obv. Legend:** FRIDERIC • 3 • D • G • D • **Rev:** Cross arms on side of shield **Rev. Legend:** NOR • VAN • G • R •

Date	Mintage	Good	VG	F	VF	XF
1652 Convex-topped shield	—	20.00	42.50	100	250	—
1652 Rare; Round-topped shield	—	—	—	—	—	—
1653	—	20.00	42.50	100	250	—
1654 Round-topped shield	—	17.50	40.00	70.00	175	—
1654 Without cross arms	—	20.00	42.50	100	280	—
1654 Rare; Convex-topped shield	—	—	—	—	—	—
1655 Rare	—	—	—	—	—	—

KM# 184.2 SKILLING

0.2920 g., 0.8750 Silver 0.0082 oz. ASW **Obv. Legend:** FRIDERIC • III • D • G • D • **Rev. Legend:** NOR • VAN • G • REX •

Date	Mintage	Good	VG	F	VF	XF
1655 Dots flank shield	—	10.00	75.00	220	380	—
1655 Without dots; Rare	—	—	—	—	—	—

KM# 184.3 SKILLING

0.2920 g., 0.8750 Silver 0.0082 oz. ASW **Obv. Legend:** FRIDERIC • 3 D • G • DAN • **Rev. Legend:** NOR • VAN • GOT • REX •

Date	Mintage	Good	VG	F	VF	XF
1655 Second circle under shield	—	45.00	90.00	200	500	—
1655 Without second circle	—	15.00	55.00	110	275	—

KM# A185 SKILLING

0.2920 g., 0.8750 Silver 0.0082 oz. ASW **Obv:** Shield divides date **Obv. Legend:** FRIDERIC • III • D • G • DAN • **Rev. Legend:** NOR • VAN • GOT • REX •

Date	Mintage	Good	VG	F	VF	XF
1661	—	15.00	45.00	110	280	—

KM# 254 SKILLING

0.2920 g., 0.8750 Silver 0.0082 oz. ASW **Obv:** Hearts in shield **Obv. Legend:** FRIDERIC • 3 • D • G • DAN • **Rev. Legend:** NOR • VAN • GOT • REX •

Date	Mintage	Good	VG	F	VF	XF
1665(a)	—	400	800	1,250	—	—
1667(a)	—	25.00	45.00	90.00	200	—
1667(l)	—	30.00	55.00	105	250	—
1668(a) 1 known	—	—	—	1,500	—	—

KM# 357 SKILLING

0.2920 g., 0.8750 Silver 0.0082 oz. ASW **Obv:** Crowned shield, titles of Christian V **Note:** Varieties exist.

Date	Mintage	Good	VG	F	VF	XF
1676 Clover leaf mint mark	—	4.50	8.25	16.50	40.00	—
1677	—	10.00	20.00	55.00	120	—
1680	—	4.50	8.25	16.50	40.00	—
1681 GS	—	10.00	20.00	55.00	120	—

KM# 382 SKILLING

1.1140 g., 0.1870 Silver 0.0067 oz. ASW **Obv:** Crowned double C5 monogram

Date	Mintage	VG	F	VF	XF	Unc
1686	—	27.50	75.00	210	500	—

KM# 29.1 SKILLING

1.6020 g., 0.1710 Silver 0.0088 oz. ASW **Obv:** Crowned oval shield on long cross **Rev:** Value and date within central legend

Date	Mintage	Good	VG	F	VF	XF
1605(a)	—	14.00	27.50	42.50	90.00	—
1613(a)	—	200	400	875	1,100	—
1614(a)	—	17.50	32.50	47.50	120	—
1615(a)	—	17.50	32.50	47.50	125	—
1616(a)	—	22.50	45.00	85.00	210	—

KM# 29.2 SKILLING

1.6020 g., 0.1710 Silver 0.0088 oz. ASW **Rev:** Date in outer legend **Note:** Varieties exist

Date	Mintage	Good	VG	F	VF	XF
1615(c)	—	25.00	50.00	100	250	—
1617(a)	—	20.00	37.50	80.00	230	—
1618(a)	—	22.50	40.00	85.00	240	—
1619(c)	—	25.00	55.00	120	270	—
1619(a)	—	120	200	500	—	—

KM# 39 SKILLING

1.6020 g., 0.1710 Silver 0.0088 oz. ASW **Obv:** Crowned flat-topped shield on long cross **Rev:** Date in central legend

Date	Mintage	Good	VG	F	VF	XF
1608	—	100	180	400	600	—

KM# A40.2 SKILLING

1.6020 g., 0.1710 Silver 0.0088 oz. ASW **Rev:** Date in outer legend **Note:** Previous KM#40.2.

Date	Mintage	Good	VG	F	VF	XF
1615(c) Rare	—	—	—	—	—	—

KM# 65 SKILLING

0.8590 Silver **Obv:** Crowned C4 monogram **Rev:** Value above, 96 in circle dividing date

Date	Mintage	Good	VG	F	VF	XF
1619(a)	—	60.00	150	500	1,200	—
1619(c) Rare	—	—	—	—	—	—

KM# 66.1 SKILLING

0.5320 g., 0.3120 Silver 0.0053 oz. ASW **Obv:** Crown within legend **Rev:** Value and date

Date	Mintage	Good	VG	F	VF	XF
1619(a)	—	100	150	325	800	—

KM# 66.2 SKILLING

0.5320 g., 0.3120 Silver 0.0053 oz. ASW **Obv:** No inner circle **Rev:** Value and date

Date	Mintage	Good	VG	F	VF	XF
1619(a)	—	100	150	325	800	—

KM# 16.1 2 SKILLING

Silver **Obv:** Crowned shield on long cross **Rev:** Value and date within central legend **Note:** Varieties exist.

Date	Mintage	Good	VG	F	VF	XF
1603(a)	—	10.00	25.00	45.00	130	—
1604(a)	—	10.00	25.00	45.00	130	—
1605(a)	—	25.00	40.00	95.00	260	—
1607(a)	—	15.00	50.00	105	280	—
1607(m)	—	17.50	75.00	120	350	—
1608(a)	—	15.00	50.00	100	265	—
1608(m)	—	14.00	45.00	90.00	260	—
1609(a)	—	15.00	50.00	125	350	—
1611(a)	—	25.00	50.00	125	350	—
1613(a)	—	25.00	50.00	125	350	—

KM# 16.2 2 SKILLING

Silver **Rev:** Date in outer legend

Date	Mintage	Good	VG	F	VF	XF
1618(a)	—	125	200	350	600	—

KM# 68 2 SKILLING

0.7870 g., 0.8590 Silver 0.0217 oz. ASW **Obv:** Date above crown **Rev:** Value, 48 in oval, legend **Note:** Varieties exist.

Date	Mintage	Good	VG	F	VF	XF
1619(a)	—	85.00	140	375	825	—
1619(c)	—	110	225	550	950	—

KM# 69 2 SKILLING

0.5250 g., 0.8590 Silver 0.0145 oz. ASW **Obv:** Crown **Rev:** Value and date

Date	Mintage	Good	VG	F	VF	XF
1619(c)	—	50.00	100	215	525	—
1620(r)	—	40.00	85.00	200	500	—
1621(c) Rare	—	—	—	—	—	—

KM# 80.1 2 SKILLING

0.5250 g., 0.8590 Silver 0.0145 oz. ASW **Obv:** Crown within pellet circle **Rev:** Value, 72 in oval

Date	Mintage	Good	VG	F	VF	XF
1620	—	50.00	100	250	650	—

KM# 80.2 2 SKILLING

0.5250 g., 0.8590 Silver 0.0145 oz. ASW **Obv:** Without pellet circle

Date	Mintage	Good	VG	F	VF	XF
1620 Unique	—	—	—	—	—	—

KM# 89 2 SKILLING

1.2990 g., 0.2810 Silver 0.0117 oz. ASW **Obv:** Crowned shield on long cross **Rev:** Value in circle, date in legend **Note:** Varieties exist.

Date	Mintage	Good	VG	F	VF	XF
1624	—	8.00	12.00	27.50	70.00	—
1625	—	8.00	12.00	27.50	70.00	—
1626	—	15.00	27.50	45.00	120	—
1627	—	6.00	11.00	27.50	65.00	—
1629	—	12.00	25.00	45.00	120	—

KM# 120 2 SKILLING

0.5250 g., 0.8590 Silver 0.0145 oz. ASW **Obv:** Crowned shield **Rev:** Value and date

Date	Mintage	Good	VG	F	VF	XF
1630	—	20.00	40.00	90.00	250	—
1632	—	18.00	37.50	70.00	235	—

KM# 132 2 SKILLING

0.5250 g., 0.8590 Silver 0.0145 oz. ASW **Obv:** Crowned oval arms on long cross **Rev:** Value in circle, date in legend **Note:** Varieties exist.

Date	Mintage	Good	VG	F	VF	XF
1644	—	7.00	12.00	25.00	60.00	—
1645	—	7.00	12.00	25.00	60.00	—
1648	—	6.00	12.00	20.00	47.50	—

KM# 157 2 SKILLING

0.5250 g., 0.8590 Silver 0.0145 oz. ASW **Obv:** Crowned oval shield **Obv. Legend:** FRIDERIC • 9 • III • D • G • DAN • **Rev:** Value at center II/ SKIL/ DANS **Rev. Legend:** NOR • VAN • GOTO • ELEC: R:

Date	Mintage	Good	VG	F	VF	XF
1648 Date in obverse legend	—	40.00	70.00	120	250	—
1648 Shield divides date	—	17.50	35.00	70.00	120	—
1648 Shield with concave sides	—	12.00	25.00	50.00	100	—
1649	—	75.00	125	175	300	—

KM# 158 2 SKILLING

0.5250 g., 0.8590 Silver 0.0145 oz. ASW **Rev:** Value in center: II/ SKIL/ NGDA/ NSK **Rev. Legend:** NOR • VAN • GOTO • Q • REX •

Date	Mintage	Good	VG	F	VF	XF
1648 Closed notches on shield	—	6.00	12.50	30.00	65.00	—
1649	—	5.00	10.00	25.00	50.00	—
1650	—	15.00	30.00	60.00	125	—
1650 Lower notches open	—	5.00	10.00	25.00	50.00	—
1650 All notches open	—	30.00	65.00	175	360	—
1650 Without notches	—	5.00	10.00	20.00	50.00	—
1651	—	6.50	12.50	25.00	65.00	—

KM# A159 2 SKILLING

1.2990 g., 0.2810 Silver 0.0117 oz. ASW **Obv:** Obverse of KM#158, 1651 **Rev:** Reverse of KM#178, 1651, date below denomination

Date	Mintage	Good	VG	F	VF	XF
1651//1651 Rare	—	—	—	—	—	—

KM# 178 2 SKILLING

1.2990 g., 0.2810 Silver 0.0117 oz. ASW **Obv. Legend:** FRIDERIC • 9 • 3 • D • G • DAN **Rev:** Value in center: II/ SKIL/ DANS **Rev. Legend:** NOR • VAN • GOTO • Q • REX •

Date	Mintage	Good	VG	F	VF	XF
ND(1651)	—	75.00	120	200	400	—
1651 Date below denomination	—	22.50	45.00	120	325	—
1651 Date in outer legend	—	8.50	16.00	30.00	65.00	—

KM# 189.1 2 SKILLING

1.2990 g., 0.2810 Silver 0.0117 oz. ASW **Obv:** Shield on second inner circle **Obv. Legend:** NOR • V • G • REX: **Rev. Legend:** FRIDERIC • 3 • D • G • D •

Date	Mintage	Good	VG	F	VF	XF
1653	—	50.00	95.00	150	290	—

KM# 189.2 2 SKILLING

1.2990 g., 0.2810 Silver 0.0117 oz. ASW **Obv:** Without second circle **Rev. Legend:** FRIDERIC • 3 • D • G • D •

Date	Mintage	Good	VG	F	VF	XF
1653	—	5.00	8.50	20.00	40.00	—
1654	—	5.00	8.50	20.00	40.00	—
1655	—	6.50	11.00	25.00	50.00	—

KM# A190 2 SKILLING

1.2990 g., 0.2810 Silver 0.0117 oz. ASW **Obv:** Emperor's crown above shield

Date	Mintage	Good	VG	F	VF	XF
1654 Flat-topped shield	—	30.00	55.00	110	220	—
1654 Ellipse-shaped shield	—	50.00	100	180	300	—
1654 Rare; Oval-shaped shield	—	—	—	—	—	—
1655 Ellipse-shaped shield	—	50.00	100	225	350	—
1655 Oval-shaped shield	—	6.00	20.00	37.50	75.00	—

KM# 209 2 SKILLING

1.2990 g., 0.2810 Silver 0.0117 oz. ASW **Obv:** Crowned shield with ornamented sides **Obv. Legend:** FRIDERIC: III: D: G: DA **Rev. Legend:** NOR • VAN • GOT • REX •

Date	Mintage	Good	VG	F	VF	XF
1657 Rare; Long ornamentation	—	—	—	—	—	—
1657 Short ornamentation	—	10.00	17.50	37.50	75.00	—
1657 Bottom of ornamentation curls in	—	12.50	27.50	50.00	90.00	—
1658	—	12.50	27.50	50.00	90.00	—
1658 Long ornamentation	—	8.00	16.50	35.00	70.00	—
1658 Bottom of ornamentation curls out	—	30.00	55.00	110	300	—
1659 Long ornamentation	—	17.50	32.50	50.00	80.00	—
1660	—	5.50	12.00	30.00	75.00	—
1661	—	5.00	10.00	20.00	40.00	—
1662	—	6.50	12.00	25.00	45.00	—
1662(i)	—	6.00	11.00	27.50	42.50	—
1663(a)	—	17.50	35.00	70.00	125	—
1663(i)	—	5.00	10.00	22.50	27.50	—
1664(a)	—	12.00	20.00	32.50	70.00	—

KM# A210.1 2 SKILLING

1.2990 g., 0.2810 Silver 0.0117 oz. ASW **Obv:** Crowned shield in inner circle **Obv. Legend:** FRIDERIC • 3 • D • G • DAN •

Date	Mintage	Good	VG	F	VF	XF
1664(a)	—	10.00	18.00	40.00	100	—
1665(a)	—	8.00	16.00	37.50	90.00	—

KM# A210.2 2 SKILLING

1.2990 g., 0.2810 Silver 0.0117 oz. ASW **Obv:** Without inner circle **Rev. Legend:** FRIDERIC • 3 • D • G • DAN •

Date	Mintage	Good	VG	F	VF	XF
1664(a)	—	9.00	17.50	45.00	85.00	—
1665(a)	—	60.00	120	200	350	—

KM# 249.1 2 SKILLING

1.2990 g., 0.2810 Silver 0.0117 oz. ASW **Obv:** Crowned shield in inner circle with shield-like ornamentation on sides

Date	Mintage	Good	VG	F	VF	XF
1665(a)	—	7.00	12.00	27.50	60.00	—
1666(a)	—	200	400	600	—	—
1667(a)	—	100	200	300	—	—

KM# 249.2 2 SKILLING

1.2990 g., 0.2810 Silver 0.0117 oz. ASW **Obv:** Without inner circle **Note:** Varieties exist.

Date	Mintage	Good	VG	F	VF	XF
1664(a)	—	7.50	15.00	32.50	75.00	—
1665(a)	—	30.00	50.00	105	250	—
1666(a)	—	10.00	20.00	50.00	90.00	—
1667(a)	—	15.00	27.50	55.00	100	—
1667(l)	—	12.50	17.50	32.50	75.00	—

KM# 256 2 SKILLING

1.2990 g., 0.2810 Silver 0.0117 oz. ASW **Obv:** Crowned F3 monogram **Obv. Legend:** DOMINUS • PROVIDEBIT • **Rev:** Value: II/ SKILLING/ DANSKE/ 1665 **Note:** Directions of obverse legend inidcated after date.

Date	Mintage	Good	VG	F	VF	XF
1665(a) Clockwise from bottom	—	14.00	22.50	80.00	300	—
1665 GK Counterclockwise from top	—	14.00	22.50	80.00	300	—
1665 GK Clockwise from bottom	—	14.00	22.50	80.00	300	—
1665(a) Clockwise from top	—	60.00	175	425	675	—
1666(a) Clockwise from bottom	—	60.00	175	425	675	—
1666(a) Clockwise from top	—	60.00	175	425	675	—

KM# 281 2 SKILLING

1.2990 g., 0.2810 Silver 0.0117 oz. ASW **Obv:** Crowned, fancy shield **Obv. Legend:** FRIDERIC • III • D • G • DAN • **Rev:** Value: II/ SKILLI/ NGDA/ NSK **Rev. Legend:** NOR • VAN • GOT • REX •

Date	Mintage	Good	VG	F	VF	XF
1667(a) Rare; mint mark in outer legend	—	—	—	—	—	—
1667(l)	—	25.00	55.00	120	300	—
1667(l) Mintmark in center legend	—	30.00	65.00	140	350	—

KM# 282.1 2 SKILLING

1.2990 g., 0.2810 Silver 0.0117 oz. ASW **Obv. Legend:** FRIDERIC • III • D • G • DAN **Rev:** Value: II/ SKILL/ DANS after legend, date **Rev. Legend:** NOR • VAN • GOT • REX •

Date	Mintage	Good	VG	F	VF	XF
1667(l) Rare	—	—	—	—	—	—
Note: Shield bottom pointed; mint mark in outer legend						
1668(l)	—	9.00	16.00	35.00	75.00	—
Note: Mint mark in center field						
1669 GK	—	20.00	40.00	90.00	250	—
Note: Shield bottom round						

KM# 282.2 2 SKILLING

1.2990 g., 0.2810 Silver 0.0117 oz. ASW **Obv:** Shield with flat top

Date	Mintage	Good	VG	F	VF	XF
1667(l) Mint mark in center field	—	9.00	16.00	35.00	75.00	—
1667(a) Mint mark in outer legend	—	4.25	9.00	20.00	40.00	—
1667(l) Mint mark in outer legend	—	6.00	12.50	25.00	50.00	—
1668(a) Mint mark in outer legend	—	4.25	9.00	20.00	40.00	—
1668(l) Rare; Mint mark in outer legend	—	—	—	—	—	—
1669(a) Mint mark in outer legend	—	8.00	15.00	30.00	60.00	—
1670(a)	—	20.00	40.00	90.00	200	—

KM# 358 2 SKILLING

1.2990 g., 0.2810 Silver 0.0117 oz. ASW **Obv:** Titles of Christian V **Note:** Varieties exist.

Date	Mintage	Good	VG	F	VF	XF
1676	—	5.00	10.00	22.50	55.00	—
1677	—	4.00	8.00	18.00	27.50	—
1680	—	5.00	10.00	22.50	55.00	—
1681	—	3.50	60.00	12.00	27.50	—
1861 Error	—	35.00	70.00	125	380	—

KM# 383.1 2 SKILLING

1.2990 g., 0.2810 Silver 0.0117 oz. ASW **Obv:** Crowned double C5 monogram, crown 11 milimeters wide **Rev:** Value and date

Date	Mintage	Good	VG	F	VF	XF
1686 GS	—	8.50	17.50	40.00	100	—

KM# 383.2 2 SKILLING

1.2990 g., 0.2810 Silver 0.0117 oz. ASW **Obv:** Crown 13 milimeters wide

Date	Mintage	Good	VG	F	VF	XF
1686 GS	—	8.50	17.50	40.00	100	—

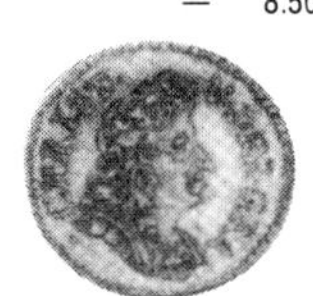

KM# 422 2 SKILLING

0.9130 g., 0.5000 Silver 0.0147 oz. ASW **Obv:** Armored bust right **Rev:** Large crown dividing value, date below

Date	Mintage	Good	VG	F	VF	XF
1693	—	25.00	55.00	140	350	—

KM# 11 4 SKILLING

1.4620 g., 0.4530 Silver 0.0213 oz. ASW **Obv:** Crowned oval shield on long cross **Rev:** Value, date in legend

Date	Mintage	Good	VG	F	VF	XF
1602(a)	—	200	250	400	800	—
1604(a)	—	70.00	110	265	550	—
1609(a) Oval shield	—	120	225	375	650	—
1609(m) Flat-topped shield	—	250	475	925	—	—

KM# 30 4 SKILLING

1.4620 g., 0.8880 Silver 0.0417 oz. ASW **Obv:** Crowned bust right **Rev:** Value above oval shield

Date	Mintage	Good	VG	F	VF	XF
1606	—	650	1,200	2,000	3,200	—
1608	—	150	300	775	1,850	—

KM# 41 4 SKILLING

1.4620 g., 0.8880 Silver 0.0417 oz. ASW **Obv:** Crowned 1/2-length figure right **Rev:** Value above square-topped shield

Date	Mintage	Good	VG	F	VF	XF
1608	—	50.00	100	260	550	—
1609	—	40.00	160	325	650	—

KM# 55.1 4 SKILLING

1.4620 g., 0.4370 Silver 0.0205 oz. ASW **Obv:** Oval shield on long cross **Rev:** Value, date in legend

Date	Mintage	Good	VG	F	VF	XF
1616(a)	—	30.00	55.00	120	285	—
1617(a)	—	75.00	175	300	550	—
1618(a)	—	30.00	55.00	120	285	—
1619(a)	—	30.00	55.00	120	285	—

KM# 55.2 4 SKILLING

1.4620 g., 0.4370 Silver 0.0205 oz. ASW **Obv:** Crowned square-topped shield on long cross **Note:** Varieties exist.

Date	Mintage	Good	VG	F	VF	XF
1616(c)	—	25.00	55.00	120	285	—
1617(c)	—	30.00	60.00	125	325	—
1618(c)	—	25.00	55.00	120	285	—
1619(c)	—	30.00	60.00	190	525	—

KM# 70.1 4 SKILLING

1.4620 g., 0.4370 Silver 0.0205 oz. ASW **Obv:** Crown intersects legend **Rev:** Value and 24 in oval, date in legend **Note:** Varieties exist.

Date	Mintage	Good	VG	F	VF	XF
1619(a)	—	50.00	100	225	500	—
Note: Mint master mark on reverse						
1619(c)	—	250	550	—	—	—

KM# 70.2 4 SKILLING

1.4620 g., 0.4370 Silver 0.0205 oz. ASW **Obv:** Date added above crown

Date	Mintage	Good	VG	F	VF	XF
1619(c) Rare; Mintmark on reverse	—	—	—	—	—	—
1619 Unique; no mintmark	—	—	—	—	—	—

KM# A71 4 SKILLING

1.4620 g., 0.4370 Silver 0.0205 oz. ASW **Obv:** 1 Skilling, KM#40.1 **Rev:** 4 Skilling, KM#70.2 **Note:** Mule.

Date	Mintage	Good	VG	F	VF	XF
1619 Unique	—	—	—	—	—	—

KM# 81 4 SKILLING

1.4620 g., 0.4370 Silver 0.0205 oz. ASW **Obv:** Crown **Rev:** Value, 36 in oval in inner circle, date in legend **Note:** Varieties exist.

Date	Mintage	Good	VG	F	VF	XF
1620(a) Mintmark on reverse	—	20.00	40.00	95.00	250	—
1620(c) Mintmark on obverse	—	250	500	1,000	—	—
1620(r)	—	30.00	60.00	165	380	—
1620(n)	—	50.00	100	225	550	—
1621(a) Mintmark on reverse	—	175	350	500	—	—
1621(r) Mintmark on obverse	—	27.50	55.00	120	275	—
1621(n)	—	50.00	100	225	550	—

KM# 121 4 SKILLING

1.1810 g., 0.8750 Silver 0.0332 oz. ASW **Obv:** Crowned bust right **Rev:** Value, date in legend

Date	Mintage	Good	VG	F	VF	XF
1630	—	14.00	27.50	65.00	175	—
1632	—	16.00	32.50	75.00	200	—

KM# 133.1 4 SKILLING

1.9490 g., 0.2500 Silver 0.0157 oz. ASW **Obv:** Crowned C4 monogram, value in legend **Rev:** Hebrew letters between IUSTUS above and IUDEX below. Date at bottom.

Date	Mintage	Good	VG	F	VF	XF
1644	—	20.00	40.00	80.00	240	—
1645	—	12.00	25.00	60.00	200	—

KM# 133.2 4 SKILLING

1.9490 g., 0.2500 Silver 0.0157 oz. ASW **Rev:** Date at top.

Date	Mintage	Good	VG	F	VF	XF
1644	—	200	—	400	600	800

KM# 257.1 4 SKILLING

1.9490 g., 0.2500 Silver 0.0157 oz. ASW **Obv:** Crowned F3 monogram, legend reads counterclockwise from top **Rev:** Value and date **Note:** Varieties exist.

Date	Mintage	Good	VG	F	VF	XF
1665	—	25.00	50.00	120	400	—

KM# 257.2 4 SKILLING

1.9490 g., 0.2500 Silver 0.0157 oz. ASW **Obv:** Legend reads clockwise from bottom **Rev:** Value and date

Date	Mintage	Good	VG	F	VF	XF
1665	—	65.00	125	235	650	—

KM# 283.1 4 SKILLING

1.9490 g., 0.2500 Silver 0.0157 oz. ASW **Obv:** Crowned shield

Date	Mintage	Good	VG	F	VF	XF
1667	—	20.00	40.00	100	350	—

KM# 283.2 4 SKILLING

1.9490 g., 0.2500 Silver 0.0157 oz. ASW **Obv:** Shield variety with pointed bottom

Date	Mintage	Good	VG	F	VF	XF
1669	—	30.00	60.00	125	400	—

KM# 440 4 SKILLING

1.9490 g., 0.2500 Silver 0.0157 oz. ASW **Obv:** Laureate bust right **Rev:** Crown divides 4S, date below

Date	Mintage	Good	VG	F	VF	XF
1696	—	300	650	1,000	1,500	—

KM# 83 6 SKILLING

Silver **Obv:** Crowned oval shield **Rev:** Crowned C4 monogram divides value, date below

Date	Mintage	Good	VG	F	VF	XF
1622	—	125	400	1,000	1,900	—

KM# 109 6 SKILLING

11.7110 g., 0.7810 Silver 0.2940 oz. ASW **Obv:** Crowned oval arms **Rev:** Value and date **Note:** Varieties exist

Date	Mintage	Good	VG	F	VF	XF
1627(a)	—	100	200	550	1,000	—
1628(a)	—	15.00	25.00	55.00	100	—
1628(e)	—	17.50	37.50	75.00	160	—
1629(e)	—	15.00	27.50	50.00	100	—

KM# 110 6 SKILLING

11.7110 g., 0.7810 Silver 0.2940 oz. ASW **Obv:** Crowned bust right **Rev:** Value and date **Note:** Varieties exist

Date	Mintage	Good	VG	F	VF	XF
1628 RD	—	17.50	35.00	70.00	125	—
1629 RD	—	75.00	150	350	500	—
1629(g)	—	10.00	32.50	60.00	115	—

KM# 31 8 SKILLING

2.9230 g., 0.8880 Silver 0.0834 oz. ASW **Obv:** Crowned oval shield on long cross **Rev:** Value and date within legend

Date	Mintage	Good	VG	F	VF	XF
1606	—	400	950	3,000	6,000	—
ND Unique	—	—	—	—	—	—

KM# 32 8 SKILLING

2.9230 g., 0.8880 Silver 0.0834 oz. ASW **Obv:** Crowned bust right, date below **Rev:** Value above oval arms

Date	Mintage	Good	VG	F	VF	XF
ND	—	100	200	600	1,000	—
1606	—	20.00	37.50	80.00	200	—
1607	—	20.00	37.50	80.00	200	—
1608	—	17.50	35.00	65.00	160	—

KM# 42 8 SKILLING

2.9230 g., 0.8880 Silver 0.0834 oz. ASW **Obv:** Crowned 1/2-length figure right **Rev:** Value above flat-topped shield

Date	Mintage	Good	VG	F	VF	XF
1608	—	25.00	42.50	110	350	—

KM# 71.1 8 SKILLING

0.8590 Silver **Obv:** Date above crown **Rev:** Date, value and 12 in oval within legend **Note:** Varieties exist.

Date	Mintage	Good	VG	F	VF	XF
1619	—	750	1,500	2,250	3,250	—

KM# 71.2 8 SKILLING

0.8590 Silver **Rev:** Without date in legend

Date	Mintage	Good	VG	F	VF	XF
1619	—	1,000	2,000	3,000	4,000	—

KM# 82 8 SKILLING

0.8590 Silver **Obv:** Crown **Rev:** Value and 18 in oval, date in legend **Note:** Varieties exist.

Date	Mintage	Good	VG	F	VF	XF
1620(a)	—	40.00	80.00	165	500	—
1620(c)	—	150	300	600	1,000	—
1620(d)	—	375	650	1,600	3,000	—
1620(n)	—	40.00	80.00	180	500	—
1620(r)	—	37.50	80.00	180	500	—
1621(a)	—	42.50	85.00	200	525	—
1621(n)	—	40.00	80.00	180	500	—
1621(r)	—	45.00	85.00	220	575	—

KM# 84 8 SKILLING

0.8880 Silver **Obv:** Crowned C4 monogram **Rev:** Value and date

Date	Mintage	Good	VG	F	VF	XF
1622	—	20.00	40.00	80.00	190	—
1623	—	25.00	45.00	95.00	210	—

KM# 90 8 SKILLING

0.8590 Silver **Obv:** Crowned C4 monogram, mint mark at right **Rev:** Value and date

Date	Mintage	Good	VG	F	VF	XF
1624 No mintmark	—	75.00	150	375	600	—
1624(a)	—	20.00	40.00	80.00	160	—
1625(a)	—	22.50	45.00	85.00	180	—

KM# 122 8 SKILLING

2.3860 g., 0.8750 Silver 0.0671 oz. ASW **Obv:** Crowned 1/2-length figure right **Rev:** Value within circle, date in legend

Date	Mintage	Good	VG	F	VF	XF
1630	—	30.00	60.00	140	425	—

KM# 305.1 8 SKILLING

2.7840 g., 0.6710 Silver 0.0601 oz. ASW, 21 mm.
Obv: Crowned and draped bust right of Frederick III **Rev:** Crown above three shields **Note:** Varieties exist.

Date	Mintage	Good	VG	F	VF	XF
1669(a)	—	75.00	150	300	750	—

KM# 305.2 8 SKILLING

2.7840 g., 0.6710 Silver 0.0601 oz. ASW, 23 mm.

Date	Mintage	Good	VG	F	VF	XF
1669 No mintmark	—	85.00	175	350	750	—

KM# 341 8 SKILLING

2.7840 g., 0.6710 Silver 0.0601 oz. ASW **Obv:** Crowned C5 monogram **Rev:** Value and date

Date	Mintage	Good	VG	F	VF	XF
1672	—	45.00	100	275	500	—

KM# 423 8 SKILLING

2.2400 g., 0.8330 Silver 0.0600 oz. ASW **Obv:** Armored bust of Christian V right **Rev:** Large crown, date below

Date	Mintage	Good	VG	F	VF	XF
1693	—	500	1,000	1,500	2,000	—

KM# 465 8 SKILLING

2.2400 g., 0.8330 Silver 0.0600 oz. ASW **Rev:** Denomination flanks crown

Date	Mintage	Good	VG	F	VF	XF
1695	—	12.50	20.00	55.00	160	—

KM# 470 8 SKILLING

3.0570 g., 0.5620 Silver 0.0552 oz. ASW **Ruler:** Frederik IV **Obv:** Armored bust right **Obv. Legend:** FERD • IIII • DEI • GRATIA • **Rev:** Large crown divides value, heart divides date in legend below **Rev. Legend:** DAN • NOR • VAN • GOT • REX •

Date	Mintage	VG	F	VF	XF	Unc
1700	—	20.00	37.50	90.00	270	—

KM# 85 12 SKILLING

3.0240 g., 0.8880 Silver 0.0863 oz. ASW **Obv:** Crowned oval shield **Rev:** Crowned C4 monogram, value below

Date	Mintage	Good	VG	F	VF	XF
1622	—	25.00	42.50	70.00	200	—
1623	—	27.50	47.50	80.00	220	—
16xx	—	10.00	20.00	40.00	60.00	—

KM# 91 12 SKILLING

3.0770 g., 0.8590 Silver 0.0850 oz. ASW **Obv:** Crowned C4 monogram **Rev:** Value and date

Date	Mintage	Good	VG	F	VF	XF
1624	—	18.00	37.50	90.00	280	—
1625	—	20.00	42.50	110	300	—

KM# 92 16 SKILLING

0.8590 Silver **Obv:** Crowned oval shield **Rev:** Value and date

Date	Mintage	Good	VG	F	VF	XF
1624(a)	—	35.00	70.00	140	300	—
1625(a)	—	40.00	85.00	180	400	—

KM# 107 16 SKILLING

0.8590 Silver **Obv:** Crowned shield w/crowned C4 monogram dividing date **Rev:** Value

Date	Mintage	Good	VG	F	VF	XF
1625(h) Unique	—	—	—	—	—	—

KM# 136.1 16 SKILLING

5.5680 g., 0.5930 Silver 0.1062 oz. ASW **Obv:** Date in legend

Date	Mintage	Good	VG	F	VF	XF
1644	—	20.00	42.50	95.00	200	—

KM# 136.2 16 SKILLING

5.5680 g., 0.5930 Silver 0.1062 oz. ASW **Rev:** Date

Date	Mintage	Good	VG	F	VF	XF
1645	—	25.00	50.00	120	300	—
1646	—	50.00	200	500	1,400	—

KM# 93 24 SKILLING

6.0500 g., Silver **Obv:** Crowned oval shield on long cross **Rev:** Value and date within legend

Date	Mintage	Good	VG	F	VF	XF
16Z4	—	100	250	550	1,000	—

KM# 12 MARK

9.4110 g., 0.5930 Silver 0.1794 oz. ASW **Obv:** Crowned oval shield on long corss **Rev:** Value and date within legend

Date	Mintage	Good	VG	F	VF	XF
1602	—	140	225	550	1,100	—
1604	—	130	210	525	950	—

KM# 12a MARK

6.1540 g., 0.8880 Silver 0.1757 oz. ASW **Obv:** Crowned oval shield on long corss **Rev:** Value and date within legend

Date	Mintage	Good	VG	F	VF	XF
1606	—	90.00	180	350	750	—

KM# 33.1 MARK

6.1540 g., 0.8880 Silver 0.1757 oz. ASW **Obv:** Crown above bust right breaking circle at bottom **Rev:** Oval arms dividing date, value above

Date	Mintage	Good	VG	F	VF	XF
1606	—	100	200	500	1,100	—

KM# 33.2 MARK

6.1540 g., 0.8880 Silver 0.1757 oz. ASW **Obv:** Crown above bust right within circle **Rev:** Oval arms dividing date, value above

Date	Mintage	Good	VG	F	VF	XF
1607	—	70.00	140	380	900	—

KM# 36 MARK

6.1540 g., 0.8880 Silver 0.1757 oz. ASW **Obv:** Crowned 1/2-length figure right **Rev:** Value above shield between branches

Date	Mintage	Good	VG	F	VF	XF
1607	—	30.00	55.00	110	280	—
Note: Coins dated 1607 exist with ornamentation						
1608	—	27.50	50.00	90.00	240	—
1609	—	60.00	120	500	1,000	—

KM# 37 MARK

9.3540 g., 0.5930 Silver 0.1783 oz. ASW **Rev:** Value above shield on long cross

Date	Mintage	Good	VG	F	VF	XF
1607 Rare	—	—	—	—	—	—
1609	—	300	500	1,100	—	—

KM# 52 MARK

8.6610 g., 0.5930 Silver 0.1651 oz. ASW **Rev:** Value above oval shield on long cross **Note:** Varieties exist

Date	Mintage	Good	VG	F	VF	XF
1612(b)	—	30.00	60.00	190	380	—
1613(b)	—	25.00	50.00	150	360	—
1614(a)	—	100	200	400	800	—
1614(b)	—	22.50	37.50	100	280	—
1614(c)	—	30.00	60.00	140	350	—
1614(d)	—	40.00	80.00	200	450	—
1615(a)	—	18.00	35.00	85.00	200	—
1615(c)	—	40.00	75.00	215	700	—
1616(a)	—	30.00	60.00	140	350	—
1616(c)	—	25.00	50.00	100	200	—
1617(a)	—	20.00	35.00	90.00	260	—
1617(c)	—	25.00	50.00	135	300	—
1618(a)	—	40.00	75.00	200	475	—
1618(c)	—	42.50	85.00	220	550	—

KM# 266 MARK
5.5680 g., 0.5930 Silver 0.1062 oz. ASW **Obv:** Draped bust of Frederik III

Date	Mintage	Good	VG	F	VF	XF
1666	—	100	160	280	600	—

KM# 297 MARK
5.5680 g., 0.5930 Silver 0.1062 oz. ASW **Obv:** Crowned F3 monogram **Rev:** Crowned shield on short cross

Date	Mintage	Good	VG	F	VF	XF
1668	—	150	300	600	1,850	—

KM# 342.1 MARK
5.5680 g., 0.6710 Silver 0.1201 oz. ASW **Obv:** Crowned C5 monogram, end of C free of 5 **Rev:** Value and date

Date	Mintage	Good	VG	F	VF	XF
1672	—	25.00	50.00	125	280	—
1676	—	40.00	75.00	175	350	—

KM# 342.2 MARK
5.5680 g., 0.6710 Silver 0.1201 oz. ASW **Obv:** End of C entwines 5 **Rev:** Value and date

Date	Mintage	Good	VG	F	VF	XF
1676	—	—	45.00	100	210	—

KM# 350 MARK
5.5680 g., 0.6710 Silver 0.1201 oz. ASW **Obv:** Crowned fancy double C5 monogram

Date	Mintage	Good	VG	F	VF	XF
1675	—	22.50	50.00	115	290	—

KM# 379 MARK
5.5680 g., 0.6710 Silver 0.1201 oz. ASW **Obv:** Crowned double C5 monogram **Rev:** Value and date on crowned shield on short cross

Date	Mintage	Good	VG	F	VF	XF
1685	—	40.00	80.00	165	375	—

KM# 404.1 MARK
5.5680 g., 0.6710 Silver 0.1201 oz. ASW **Obv:** Crowned fancy double C5 monogram, no legend **Rev:** Crowned shield divide horizontal date above 1-M **Rev. Legend:** D • G • REX • DA • NO • V • G • **Note:** Varieties exist

Date	Mintage	Good	VG	F	VF	XF
1691(g)	—	42.50	70.00	175	400	—

KM# 404.2 MARK
5.5680 g., 0.6710 Silver 0.1201 oz. ASW **Obv:** Crowned fancy double C5 monogram, no legend **Rev:** Crowned shield divide curved date above 1-M **Rev. Legend:** D • G • REX • DA • NO • V • G •

Date	Mintage	Good	VG	F	VF	XF
1691(g)	—	45.00	75.00	190	420	—

KM# 404.3 MARK
5.5680 g., 0.6710 Silver 0.1201 oz. ASW **Obv:** Crowned fancy double C5 monogram, no legend **Rev:** Crowned shield divide horizontal date, shield without value **Rev. Legend:** D • G • REX • DA • NO • V • G •

Date	Mintage	Good	VG	F	VF	XF
1691(g) Rare	—	—	—	—	—	—

KM# 404.4 MARK
5.5680 g., 0.6710 Silver 0.1201 oz. ASW **Obv:** Crowned fancy double C5 monogram, no legend **Rev:** Date in legend **Rev. Legend:** D • G • REX • DA • NO • V • G •

Date	Mintage	Good	VG	F	VF	XF
1692(g)	—	50.00	100	200	475	—

KM# 424.1 MARK
5.5680 g., 0.6710 Silver 0.1201 oz. ASW **Obv:** Armored bust right **Rev:** Large crown dividing value, date below

Date	Mintage	Good	VG	F	VF	XF
1693	—	25.00	50.00	135	325	—
1694	—	30.00	60.00	160	370	—

KM# 424.2 MARK
5.5680 g., 0.6710 Silver 0.1201 oz. ASW **Rev:** Large crown, date below, no value

Date	Mintage	Good	VG	F	VF	XF
1693	—	650	1,150	1,600	2,200	—
1696	—	600	1,000	1,500	2,000	—

KM# 23 2 MARK
16.5800 g., 0.6460 Silver 0.3443 oz. ASW **Obv:** Crowned oval arms on long cross **Obv. Legend:** CHRISTIAN IV **Rev:** Value and date within circle, legend

Date	Mintage	Good	VG	F	VF	XF
1604	—	220	700	1,400	3,200	—

KM# 137 2 MARK
11.1360 g., 0.5930 Silver 0.2123 oz. ASW

Date	Mintage	Good	VG	F	VF	XF
1644	—	30.00	60.00	120	350	—
1645	—	35.00	70.00	150	400	—
1646	—	40.00	100	250	700	—

KM# 185 2 MARK
11.1360 g., 0.6710 Silver 0.2402 oz. ASW **Obv:** Crowned F3 monogram **Rev:** Crowned shield on long cross, date in legend

Date	Mintage	Good	VG	F	VF	XF
165Z(I)	—	65.00	160	375	800	—

KM# 190 2 MARK
11.1360 g., 0.6710 Silver 0.2402 oz. ASW **Obv:** Crowned F3 monogram, date in legend **Rev:** Shield with round top

Date	Mintage	Good	VG	F	VF	XF
1653	—	150	250	425	750	—

KM# 191.1 2 MARK
11.1360 g., 0.6710 Silver 0.2402 oz. ASW **Obv:** Crowned F3 monogram **Rev:** Crowned, encircled flat-toped shield on short cross, wtihout pellets

Date	Mintage	Good	VG	F	VF	XF
1653	—	300	600	100	1,500	—

KM# 191.2 2 MARK
11.1360 g., 0.6710 Silver 0.2402 oz. ASW **Obv:** Crowned F3 monogram **Rev:** Without circle around shield

Date	Mintage	Good	VG	F	VF	XF
1653	—	150	300	500	925	—
1654	—	175	350	600	1,200	—
1655	—	140	280	475	900	—
1657	—	160	325	550	950	—

KM# A191 2 MARK
11.1360 g., 0.6710 Silver 0.2402 oz. ASW **Obv:** KM#185 **Rev:** KM#190 **Note:** Mule.

Date	Mintage	Good	VG	F	VF	XF
ND Rare	—	—	—	—	—	—

KM# 218 2 MARK
11.1360 g., 0.6710 Silver 0.2402 oz. ASW **Obv:** Crowned F3 monogram, legend, value, and date **Rev:** Crowned shield on short cross within pellet border

Date	Mintage	Good	VG	F	VF	XF
1658	—	70.00	125	250	675	—
1659	—	85.00	140	280	725	—
1660	—	100	200	350	775	—
1661	—	250	450	750	1,250	—

KM# 259.1 2 MARK
11.1360 g., 0.6710 Silver 0.2402 oz. ASW **Obv:** Laureate bust of Fredrik III right **Obv. Legend:** FRIDERICVS • III • D • G • DA • NOR • **Rev:** Crown above motto in script, date in legend **Rev. Legend:** VAN • DALORVM • GOTHORVM • QVE • REX •

Date	Mintage	Good	VG	F	VF	XF
1666	—	250	400	700	1,000	—

Date	Mintage	Good	VG	F	VF	XF
1666 GK	—	25.00	50.00	110	250	—
1667 GK	—	45.00	90.00	240	475	—

KM# 259.2 2 MARK
11.1360 g., 0.6710 Silver 0.2402 oz. ASW **Obv:** No circle around bust **Rev:** Motto in print

Date	Mintage	Good	VG	F	VF	XF
1665 GK	—	60.00	120	240	575	—
1666(a) Unique	—	—	—	—	—	—
1666 GK	—	60.00	120	240	575	—

KM# 259.3 2 MARK
11.1360 g., 0.6710 Silver 0.2402 oz. ASW **Obv:** Bust in inner circle

Date	Mintage	Good	VG	F	VF	XF
1666	—	600	1,000	—	—	—

KM# 267.1 2 MARK
11.1360 g., 0.6710 Silver 0.2402 oz. ASW **Obv:** Laureate bust of Frederik III right **Obv. Legend:** FRID • III • D • G • DAN • NOR • VAN • GO • REX • **Rev:** Date above crown **Rev. Legend:** DVS • SLESVHOLS • STORM • DITM • COM • IN • OL & DE •

Date	Mintage	Good	VG	F	VF	XF
1666	—	150	300	600	900	—

KM# 267.2 2 MARK
11.1360 g., 0.6710 Silver 0.2402 oz. ASW **Obv:** Laureate bust of Frederik III right **Obv. Legend:** FRID • III • D • G • DAN • NOR • VAN • GO • REX • **Rev:** Date below crown **Rev. Legend:** DVS • SLESVHOLS • STORM • DITM • COM • IN • OL & DE •

Date	Mintage	Good	VG	F	VF	XF
1666	—	90.00	185	375	800	—

KM# 268 2 MARK
11.1360 g., 0.6710 Silver 0.2402 oz. ASW **Obv. Legend:** FRIDERICVS • III • D • G • DAN • NORV • **Rev. Legend:** GOTHO • Q • VE • REX / II • MARCK • DANSKA • 1666

Date	Mintage	Good	VG	F	VF	XF
1666	—	190	375	600	800	—

KM# 269.1 2 MARK
11.1360 g., 0.6710 Silver 0.2402 oz. ASW **Obv. Legend:** FRIDERIC • 3 • D • G • DAN • NORVAN • GOT • REX • **Rev:** Crown 18 mm in size **Rev. Legend:** II • MARK • DANSKE • Ao • 1666

Date	Mintage	Good	VG	F	VF	XF
1666	—	200	400	750	1,000	—

KM# 269.2 2 MARK
11.1360 g., 0.6710 Silver 0.2402 oz. ASW **Obv:** Bust in inner circle **Rev:** Crown 23 mm in size

Date	Mintage	Good	VG	F	VF	XF
1666	—	75.00	175	400	900	—

KM# 284 2 MARK
11.1360 g., 0.6710 Silver 0.2402 oz. ASW **Obv:** Crowned F3 monogram **Note:** Legends face outward, counter clockwise from upper left.

Date	Mintage	Good	VG	F	VF	XF
1667	—	90.00	150	250	600	—
1668	—	70.00	135	220	550	—

KM# 298 2 MARK
11.1360 g., 0.6710 Silver 0.2402 oz. ASW **Obv:** Crowned F3 monogram. **Note:** Legends face outward, clockwise from upper right.

Date	Mintage	Good	VG	F	VF	XF
1668	—	40.00	75.00	160	380	—
1669	—	65.00	130	220	500	—

KM# 329.1 2 MARK
11.1360 g., 0.6710 Silver 0.2402 oz. ASW **Obv:** Fancy crowned C5 monogram, legends face outward

Date	Mintage	Good	VG	F	VF	XF
1671	—	80.00	155	300	675	—

KM# 329.2 2 MARK
11.1360 g., 0.6710 Silver 0.2402 oz. ASW **Obv:** Plain monogram of Christian 5

Date	Mintage	Good	VG	F	VF	XF
1671	—	90.00	170	320	700	—

KM# 369 2 MARK
11.1360 g., 0.6710 Silver 0.2402 oz. ASW **Obv:** Legends face inward **Rev:** Legends face inward

Date	Mintage	Good	VG	F	VF	XF
1681	—	75.00	150	260	500	—
1682	—	90.00	165	320	600	—

KM# 377.1 2 MARK
11.1360 g., 0.6710 Silver 0.2402 oz. ASW **Obv:** Crowned double C5 monogram **Rev:** Value and date on crowned shield on short cross

Date	Mintage	Good	VG	F	VF	XF
1684	—	50.00	100	210	525	—
1685	—	50.00	100	210	525	—

KM# 377.2 2 MARK
11.1360 g., 0.6710 Silver 0.2402 oz. ASW **Obv:** Crowned double C5 monogram **Rev:** Wider shield

Date	Mintage	Good	VG	F	VF	XF
1685	—	40.00	80.00	260	575	—

KM# 385 2 MARK
11.1360 g., 0.6710 Silver 0.2402 oz. ASW **Obv:** Crowned ornate double C5 monogram, legend around

Date	Mintage	Good	VG	F	VF	XF
1686	—	50.00	120	270	650	—

KM# 385a 2 MARK
11.1360 g., 0.5930 Silver 0.2123 oz. ASW

Date	Mintage	Good	VG	F	VF	XF
1689 GS	—	75.00	190	380	625	—

KM# 403 2 MARK
11.1360 g., 0.5930 Silver 0.2123 oz. ASW **Obv:** Half-length bust in armor right **Rev:** Crowned oval shield dividing value and date

Date	Mintage	Good	VG	F	VF	XF
1690 CW	—	100	250	625	1,300	—

KM# 406.1 2 MARK
11.1360 g., 0.5930 Silver 0.2123 oz. ASW **Obv:** Crowned double C5 monogram within legend; legend reads clockwise from top **Obv. Legend:** D • G • REX • DAN • NOR • VAN • GOT **Rev:** Crowned arms divide horizontal date above 2-M; legend reads clockwise from the top **Rev. Legend:** PIETATE ET IVSTITIA

Date	Mintage	Good	VG	F	VF	XF
1691 CW	—	—	100	225	475	—

KM# 406.2 2 MARK
11.1360 g., 0.5930 Silver 0.2123 oz. ASW **Obv:** Crowned double C5 monogram within legend; legend reads clockwise from top **Obv. Legend:** D • G • REX • DAN • NOR • VAN • GOT **Rev:** Crowned arms divide curved date above 2-M; legend reads clockwise from the top **Rev. Legend:** PIETATE ET IVSTITIA **Note:** Varieties exist.

Date	Mintage	Good	VG	F	VF	XF
1691 CW	—	—	95.00	210	450	—

KM# 406.3 2 MARK
11.1360 g., 0.5930 Silver 0.2123 oz. ASW **Obv:** Crowned double C5 monogram within legend; legend reads clockwise from top **Obv. Legend:** D • G • REX • DAN • NOR • VAN • GOT **Rev:** Date in legend **Rev. Legend:** PIETATE ET IVSTITIA

Date	Mintage	Good	VG	F	VF	XF
1692 CW	—	—	180	310	595	—

KM# 426 2 MARK
11.1360 g., 0.5930 Silver 0.2123 oz. ASW **Obv:** Armored bust right **Rev:** Large crown, value and date below **Note:** Similar to 1 Mark, KM#424, but double thickness.

Date	Mintage	Good	VG	F	VF	XF
1693 Rare	—	—	—	—	—	—
1696 Rare	—	—	—	—	—	—

KM# 427 2 MARK
11.1360 g., 0.5930 Silver 0.2123 oz. ASW **Rev:** Large crown, date below **Note:** Size of 8 Skilling, KM 423 but four times thickness. No indication of value.

Date	Mintage	Good	VG	F	VF	XF
1693	—	—	—	—	—	—

KM# 56 1/8 KRONE
2.2380 g., 0.8590 Silver 0.0618 oz. ASW **Obv:** Crowned King standing with sceptre **Obv. Legend:** CHRISTIAN IIII D G DANI **Rev:** Date above, R.F.P. below crown **Rev. Legend:** NORV: VAND: GOTO: Q: REX

Date	Mintage	Good	VG	F	VF	XF
1618	—	600	1,200	2,500	—	—

KM# 57 1/4 KRONE
4.4970 g., 0.8590 Silver 0.1242 oz. ASW **Obv:** Crowned King standing with sceptre **Obv. Legend:** CHRISTIAN IIII • D: G: DAN • **Rev:** Date above, R.F.P. below crown **Rev. Legend:** NORVE: VANDA: GOTO: REX **Note:** Varieties exist.

Date	Mintage	Good	VG	F	VF	XF
1618(a)	—	160	320	900	1,800	—
1618(c)	—	200	400	1,100	2,000	—

KM# 58 1/2 KRONE
9.3010 g., 0.8590 Silver 0.2569 oz. ASW **Obv:** Crowned king standing, sceptre upright **Obv. Legend:** CHRISTIANVS IIII • D: G • DANI **Rev:** Date above, R.F.P. below crown **Rev. Legend:** NORVEG: VANDAL: GOTO: Q • REX

Date	Mintage	Good	VG	F	VF	XF
1618(a)	—	100	200	380	775	—
1618(c)	—	125	250	500	950	—

KM# 58a 1/2 KRONE
9.4550 g., 0.8590 Silver 0.2611 oz. ASW **Note:** Varieties exist.

Date	Mintage	Good	VG	F	VF	XF
1619(a)	—	130	260	400	825	—
1619(c)	—	130	260	425	825	—
16Z0(a)	—	130	260	425	825	—
1620(c) Rare	—	—	—	—	—	—
1620(r)	—	140	300	550	1,000	—
16Z1(a)	—	150	300	600	1,200	—
1621(r)	—	140	280	550	1,100	—

KM# 94 1/2 KRONE
9.4550 g., 0.8590 Silver 0.2611 oz. ASW, 30 mm. **Obv:** Crowned king standing, sceptre horizontal **Obv. Legend:** CHRISTIAVS IIII • D: G: DANI **Rev:** Date above, R.F.P. below open crown **Rev. Legend:** NORVEG: VANDALO: GOTORU Q • REX

Date	Mintage	Good	VG	F	VF	XF
16Z4(a)	—	—	2,000	4,500	—	—

KM# 95.1 1/2 KRONE
9.4550 g., 0.8590 Silver 0.2611 oz. ASW, 26 mm. **Obv:** Crowned bust of Christian IV right, breaking legend at top and bottom **Obv. Legend:** CHRISTIAN IIII D: G **Rev:** Letters R.F.P. below large crown within circle, date in legend **Rev. Legend:** DANI • NOR • VAN • GOT • Q • REX

Date	Mintage	Good	VG	F	VF	XF
16Z4(a)	—	—	70.00	125	475	—

KM# 95.2 1/2 KRONE
9.4550 g., 0.8590 Silver 0.2611 oz. ASW **Obv:** Crowned bust of Christian IV right, breaking legend at top and bottom **Obv. Legend:** CHRISTIAN IIII D: G **Rev:** Letters R.F.P. below large crown within circle, date in legend **Rev. Legend:** DANI • NOR • VAN • GOT • Q • REX **Note:** Diameter varies 23-25mm.

Date	Mintage	Good	VG	F	VF	XF
16Z4(a)	—	—	60.00	115	400	—
16Z5(a)	—	—	70.00	165	440	—

KM# 95.3 1/2 KRONE
9.4550 g., 0.8590 Silver 0.2611 oz. ASW **Obv:** Crowned bust of Christian IV right, breaking legend at top and bottom **Obv. Legend:** CHRISTIAN IIII D: G **Rev:** Letters R.F.P. below large crown within circle, date in legend **Rev. Legend:** DANI • NOR • VAN • GOT • Q • REX **Note:** Diameter varies 23-25mm.

Date	Mintage	Good	VG	F	VF	XF
16Z4(a)	—	75.00	150	200	—	—

KM# 179 1/2 KRONE
9.4550 g., 0.8590 Silver 0.2611 oz. ASW **Obv:** Crowned bust of Frederik right dividing date **Rev:** Large crown within legend

Date	Mintage	VG	F	VF	XF	Unc
1651	—	300	650	1,400	2,500	—

KM# 258 1/2 KRONE
0.7910 Silver **Obv:** Crowned figure of Frederik III standing right **Rev:** Crown and motto within circle, date in legend

Date	Mintage	VG	F	VF	XF	Unc
1665	—	450	900	1,800	3,000	—

KM# 59 KRONE (4 Mark)
18.7660 g., 0.8590 Silver 0.5182 oz. ASW **Obv:** Crowned king standing with sceptre and orb **Obv. Legend:** CHRISTIANVS IIII D: G: DANIA • **Rev:** Date above, R.F.P. below 5-pointed crown **Note:** Dav. #3517.

Date	Mintage	Good	VG	F	VF	XF
1618(a)	—	70.00	130	325	600	—
1618(c)	—	75.00	160	325	600	—

KM# 59.1 KRONE (4 Mark)
18.7660 g., 0.8590 Silver 0.5182 oz. ASW **Obv:** Crowned king standing with sceptre and orb **Obv. Legend:** CHRISTIANVS IIII D: G: DANIA • **Rev:** Date above, R.F.P. below 3-pointed crown

Date	Mintage	Good	VG	F	VF	XF
1618(c)	—	100	200	400	800	—

KM# 59a KRONE (4 Mark)
18.9090 g., 0.8590 Silver 0.5222 oz. ASW **Obv:** Crowned king standing with sceptre and orb **Obv. Legend:** CHRISTIANVS IIII D: G: DANIA • **Rev:** Date above, R.F.P. below 5-pointed crown

Date	Mintage	Good	VG	F	VF	XF
1619(a)	—	80.00	170	350	650	—
1619(c)	—	90.00	180	380	850	—
16Z0(a)	—	80.00	170	350	650	—
1620(c)	—	200	400	600	1,050	—
1620(d)	—	90.00	190	370	850	—
1620(r) Rare	—	—	—	—	—	—
16Z1(a)	—	80.00	170	350	650	—
1621(r)	—	90.00	180	400	725	—
1622(a) Unique	—	—	—	—	—	—

KM# 96 KRONE (4 Mark)

18.9090 g., 0.8590 Silver 0.5222 oz. ASW **Obv:** Crowned standing figure of Christian IV, numerals IIII left of King's feet **Rev:** Open crown **Note:** Dav. #3519.

Date	Mintage	Good	VG	F	VF	XF
1624(a)	—	300	600	1,200	3,200	—

KM# 97 KRONE (4 Mark)

18.9090 g., 0.8590 Silver 0.5222 oz. ASW **Obv:** Numeral IIII at left of King's feet, smaller and thicker planchet **Rev:** Closed Crown **Note:** Dav. #3519A.

Date	Mintage	Good	VG	F	VF	XF
16Z4(a)	—	35.00	70.00	180	500	—
1625(a)	—	35.00	70.00	190	450	—

KM# 180 KRONE (4 Mark)

18.9090 g., 0.8590 Silver 0.5222 oz. ASW **Obv:** Crowned bust right **Rev:** Crown with DOMINUS PROVIDEBIT around bottom, reading clockwise from right **Note:** Dav. #3567.

Date	Mintage	Good	VG	F	VF	XF
1651	—	75.00	150	275	700	—
1652	—	100	200	350	800	—

KM# 181 KRONE (4 Mark)

18.9090 g., 0.8590 Silver 0.5222 oz. ASW **Rev:** Motto reading counterclockwise **Note:** Dav. #3567A.

Date	Mintage	Good	VG	F	VF	XF
1651	—	200	350	650	1,000	—

KM# 182 KRONE (4 Mark)

18.9090 g., 0.8590 Silver 0.5222 oz. ASW **Rev:** Motto DOMIN: PROVID: reading clockwise **Note:** Dav. #3567B.

Date	Mintage	Good	VG	F	VF	XF
1651	—	90.00	175	300	750	—
165Z	—	90.00	175	300	750	—

KM# 186.1 KRONE (4 Mark)

22.2720 g., 0.6710 Silver 0.4805 oz. ASW **Obv:** Crowned F3 monogram within beaded border **Rev:** Crowned shield on long cross. Hearts on sheild. No mintmaster mark. **Note:** Dav. #3569. Prev. KM#186.

Date	Mintage	Good	VG	F	VF	XF
165Z	—	45.00	70.00	150	300	—

KM# 186.2 KRONE (4 Mark)

22.2720 g., 0.6710 Silver 0.4805 oz. ASW **Obv:** Crowned F3 monogram within beaded border **Rev:** Crowned shield on long cross, beaded border. No hearts on shield. **Note:** Dav. #3569A. Prev. KM#187.

Date	Mintage	Good	VG	F	VF	XF
165Z	—	45.00	70.00	150	300	—
1653	—	120	225	350	800	—

KM# 186.3 KRONE (4 Mark)

22.2720 g., 0.6710 Silver 0.4805 oz. ASW **Ruler:** Frederik III **Rev:** Crowned shield on long cross, no beaded border. Hearts on shield, mintmaster mark to left of crown.

Date	Mintage	Good	VG	F	VF	XF
1633 error date	—	175	275	450	800	—

Note: This 1633 error date coin belongs to a group of foreign produced kroner of Frederik 3 and Christian 5 called "mysteriekroner." They are basicly copies (counterfeits) of the Danish versions with similar finess, and they circulated alongside with the Danish produced kroner, and are dificult to distinguish from these. Known dates range from 1653 (33) to 1679.

Date	Mintage	Good	VG	F	VF	XF
165Z	—	—	—	—	—	—
1653	—	40.00	60.00	125	250	—

KM# 192.1 KRONE (4 Mark)

22.2720 g., 0.6710 Silver 0.4805 oz. ASW **Obv:** Crowned F3 monogram within chain of Order of St. Michael, date in legend **Rev:** Crowned flat top shield on cross within chair of Order of St. Michael **Note:** Dav. #3570. Prev. KM#192. The Order of St. Michael is a French Order.

Date	Mintage	Good	VG	F	VF	XF
1653	—	450	900	1,400	2,500	—

KM# 192.2 KRONE (4 Mark)

22.2720 g., 0.6710 Silver 0.4805 oz. ASW **Obv:** KM#192.1 **Rev:** KM#186.3 **Note:** Mule. Prev. KM#A193

Date	Mintage	Good	VG	F	VF	XF
1653	—	300	600	900	2,250	—

KM# 192.3 KRONE (4 Mark)

22.2720 g., 0.6710 Silver 0.4805 oz. ASW **Obv:** KM#186.3 **Rev:** KM#192.1 **Note:** Mule. Prev. KM#B193.

Date	Mintage	Good	VG	F	VF	XF
1653	—	450	900	1,400	2,500	—

KM# 194.1 KRONE (4 Mark)

22.2720 g., 0.6710 Silver 0.4805 oz. ASW **Ruler:** Frederik III **Obv:** Crowned F3 monogram within beaded border, with III MARCK DANSKE (date) in legend **Rev:** Crowned flat top shield on short cross. Cross arms within rounded ends, mintmaster mark to right of crown **Rev. Legend:** DOMINVS PROVIDEBIT **Note:** Dav. #3574. Prev. KM#194.

Date	Mintage	Good	VG	F	VF	XF
1653	—	40.00	60.00	150	300	—
1654	—	60.00	90.00	180	450	—

KM# 194.1a KRONE (4 Mark)

22.2720 g., 0.6710 Silver 0.4805 oz. ASW **Ruler:** Frederik III **Rev:** As KM#194.1, mintmaster mark to left of crown **Rev. Legend:** DOMINVS PROVIDEBIT

Date	Mintage	Good	VG	F	VF	XF
1653 Rare	—	—	—	—	—	—

KM# 194.1b KRONE (4 Mark)

22.2720 g., 0.6710 Silver 0.4805 oz. ASW **Ruler:** Frederik III **Rev:** As KM#194.1 but without mintmaster mark

Date	Mintage	Good	VG	F	VF	XF
1654	—	60.00	90.00	180	450	—

KM# 194.2 KRONE (4 Mark)

22.2720 g., 0.6710 Silver 0.4805 oz. ASW **Ruler:** Frederik III **Obv:** Crowned F3 monogram within beaded border, with legend: IIII MARCK DANSKE • (date) **Rev:** Crowned flat top shield on short cross. Crossarms with forked ends, mintmarster mark to left of crown. **Rev. Legend:** DOMINVS PROVIDEBIT

Date	Mintage	Good	VG	F	VF	XF
1654	—	40.00	60.00	150	300	—
1655	—	40.00	60.00	150	300	—

KM# 194.2a KRONE (4 Mark)

22.2720 g., 0.6710 Silver 0.4805 oz. ASW **Ruler:** Frederik III **Obv:** As KM#194.2 but different style lettering **Rev:** Legend reads: DOMINVS PROUIDEBIT. No mintmaster mark

Date	Mintage	Good	VG	F	VF	XF
1655 Rare	—	—	—	—	—	—
1656	—	300	450	700	1,200	—
1657 Rare	—	—	—	—	—	—
1658	—	60.00	90.00	180	600	—

KM# 194.2b KRONE (4 Mark)

22.2720 g., 0.6710 Silver 0.4805 oz. ASW **Obv:** Crowned F3 monogram **Rev:** Shield without beaded border. Legend: DOMINVS PROVIDEBIT and mintmaster mark **Note:** Dav. #3574A. Prev. KM#203.

Date	Mintage	Good	VG	F	VF	XF
1655	—	40.00	60.00	150	300	—
1656 Rare	—	—	—	—	—	—
1657	—	70.00	120	225	600	—

KM# 194.3 KRONE (4 Mark)

22.2720 g., 0.6710 Silver 0.4805 oz. ASW **Obv:** Crowned F3 monogram within beaded border, IIII: MARCK: DANSKE • (date) in legend. **Rev:** Crowned fancy shield on short cross. Legend: DOMINUS PROVIDEBIT **Note:** Dav. #3572. Prev. KM#193.

Date	Mintage	Good	VG	F	VF	XF
1653 error date for 1657, rare	—	—	—	—	—	—
1655 error date for 1657, unique	—	—	—	—	—	—
1657	—	60.00	100	200	500	—

KM# 194.3a KRONE (4 Mark)
22.2720 g., 0.6710 Silver 0.4805 oz. ASW **Ruler:** Frederik III **Obv:** Crowned F3 monogram within beaded border, within legend: IIII MARCK DANSKE • (date) **Rev:** Crowned fancy shield on short cross within circle. Legend: DOMINUS PROVIDEBIT. Crossarms with straight sided triangular ends. Mintmaster mark to right of crown.

Date	Mintage	Good	VG	F	VF	XF
1657	—	60.00	100	220	650	—
1658	—	60.00	100	220	650	—

KM# 194.4 KRONE (4 Mark)
22.2720 g., 0.6710 Silver 0.4805 oz. ASW **Ruler:** Frederik III **Obv:** Crowned F3 monogram within beaded border, within legend: IIII MARCK DANSKE • (date) **Rev:** Crowned flat top shield on short cross within circle. Legend: DOMINUS PROVIDEBIT. Crossarms with straight sided triangular ends. Mintmaster mark to right of crown.

Date	Mintage	Good	VG	F	VF	XF
1658	—	60.00	90.00	170	350	—

KM# 194.4a KRONE (4 Mark)
22.2720 g., 0.6710 Silver 0.4805 oz. ASW **Ruler:** Frederik III **Obv:** Crowned F3 monogram within beaded border, within legend: IIII MARCK DANSKE • (date) **Rev:** Crowned flat top shield on short cross, shield breaks circle at bottom. Legend: DOMINUS PROVIDEBIT. Crossarms with straight sided triangular ends. No mintmastmark.

Date	Mintage	Good	VG	F	VF	XF
1658	—	40.00	60.00	140	290	—
1659	—	40.00	60.00	140	290	—

KM# 194.5 KRONE (4 Mark)
22.2720 g., 0.6710 Silver 0.4805 oz. ASW **Ruler:** Frederik III **Obv:** Crowned F3 monogram within beaded border, within legend: IIII MARCK DANSKE • (date) **Rev:** Crowned flat top shield on short cross. Legend: DOMINVS PROVIDEBIT. Crossarms with flat ends, no mintmaster mark

Date	Mintage	Good	VG	F	VF	XF
1659	—	40.00	60.00	140	280	—
1660	—	35.00	55.00	130	260	—
1661	—	120	250	500	1,200	—

KM# 221 KRONE (4 Mark)
0.6710 Silver **Obv:** Crowned F3 monogram, EBEN-EZER at sides, mound breaks circle **Obv. Legend:** IIII MARK DANSKE **Rev:** Arm with sword from cloud cuts hand reaching for crown **Note:** Dav. #3576.

Date	Mintage	Good	VG	F	VF	XF
1659	—	175	350	700	1,700	—

KM# 222 KRONE (4 Mark)
0.6710 Silver **Obv:** Crowned F3 monogram, mound between EBEN-EZER within circle **Obv. Legend:** IIII MARK DANSKE **Note:** Dav. #3576A.

Date	Mintage	Good	VG	F	VF	XF
1659	—	325	60.00	110	1,800	—
1660	—	400	800	1,200	2,000	—

KM# 223 KRONE (4 Mark)
0.6710 Silver **Obv:** Crowned F3 monogram - EBEN-EZER **Obv. Legend:** *DOMINVS * PROVIDEBIT * **Rev:** Small crown, hand open **Rev. Legend:** * SOLI * DEO - * GLORIA **Note:** Dav. #3578. The listing formerly 223.2 is PN15.

Date	Mintage	Good	VG	F	VF	XF
1659	—	200	425	800	1,800	—

KM# A224 KRONE (4 Mark)
0.6710 Silver **Obv:** KM#194.5, EBEN-EZER **Rev:** KM#223.1 **Note:** Mule.

Date	Mintage	Good	VG	F	VF	XF
1660 Unique	—	—	—	—	—	—

KM# 331 KRONE (4 Mark)
18.9090 g., 0.6710 Silver 0.4079 oz. ASW **Obv:** King standing **Rev:** Crown **Note:** Size of 1/2 Krone, but double thickness.

Date	Mintage	Good	VG	F	VF	XF
1665	—	300	600	950	2,750	—

KM# 270 KRONE (4 Mark)
22.2720 g., 0.6710 Silver 0.4805 oz. ASW **Obv:** Armored bust right **Rev:** Date above crown, G-K, DOMINUS PROVIDEBIT below **Note:** Dav. #3579.

Date	Mintage	Good	VG	F	VF	XF
1666 GK	—	45.00	95.00	200	400	—

KM# 271 KRONE (4 Mark)
22.2720 g., 0.6710 Silver 0.4805 oz. ASW **Obv:** King in Roman outfit **Rev:** Date above large crown **Note:** Dav. #3579A.

Date	Mintage	Good	VG	F	VF	XF
1666	—	400	800	1,100	2,000	—

KM# 272 KRONE (4 Mark)
22.2720 g., 0.6710 Silver 0.4805 oz. ASW **Obv:** Crowned F3 monogram in print **Rev:** Crowned arms divide G-K, legend reads counterclockwise from upper left **Note:** Dav. #3580.

Date	Mintage	Good	VG	F	VF	XF
1666	—	300	500	850	1,200	—

KM# 273.1 KRONE (4 Mark)
22.2720 g., 0.6710 Silver 0.4805 oz. ASW **Obv:** Crowned F3 monogram in print; legends reads clockwise from upper right **Rev:** Legends reads clockwise **Note:** Dav. #3580A.

Date	Mintage	Good	VG	F	VF	XF
1666	—	300	550	875	1,200	—

KM# 273.2 KRONE (4 Mark)
22.2720 g., 0.6710 Silver 0.4805 oz. ASW **Obv:** Crowned F3 monogram in print **Rev:** Legends reads counterclockwise from upper left

Date	Mintage	Good	VG	F	VF	XF
1667	—	500	1,000	1,500	—	—

KM# 274 KRONE (4 Mark)
22.2720 g., 0.6710 Silver 0.4805 oz. ASW **Obv:** Script monogram, legend reading left to right **Note:** Dav. #3581.

Date	Mintage	Good	VG	F	VF	XF
1666	—	40.00	80.00	200	450	—
1667	—	32.50	65.00	160	300	—
1668	—	32.50	65.00	160	300	—
1669	—	35.00	70.00	180	325	—

KM# 275 KRONE (4 Mark)

22.2720 g., 0.6710 Silver 0.4805 oz. ASW **Obv. Legend:** Legend reading right to left **Note:** Dav. #3581A.

Date	Mintage	Good	VG	F	VF	XF
1666	—	37.50	75.00	160	300	—
1668	—	200	300	400	800	—

KM# 276 KRONE (4 Mark)

22.2720 g., 0.6710 Silver 0.4805 oz. ASW **Obv. Legend:** IIII MARCK... **Rev. Legend:** DOMINUS - PROVIDEBIT **Note:** Dav. #3582.

Date	Mintage	Good	VG	F	VF	XF
1666	—	50.00	100	180	400	—
1667	—	60.00	140	260	625	—
1668	—	55.00	130	235	575	—
1669	—	55.00	120	225	550	—
1670	—	200	350	650	875	—

KM# 285 KRONE (4 Mark)

22.2720 g., 0.6710 Silver 0.4805 oz. ASW **Obv:** Crowned F3 monogram in script **Rev:** Without G-K at sides of arms, legends reading left to right **Note:** Dav. #3581B.

Date	Mintage	Good	VG	F	VF	XF
1667	—	105	210	325	750	—
1669	—	250	400	600	1,200	—

KM# 299.1 KRONE (4 Mark)

22.2720 g., 0.6710 Silver 0.4805 oz. ASW **Obv:** Legend reads right to left **Obv. Legend:** DOMINVS. PROVIDEBIT **Rev. Legend:** IIII MARCK... **Note:** Dav. #3583.

Date	Mintage	Good	VG	F	VF	XF
1668	—	60.00	120	300	650	—

KM# 299.2 KRONE (4 Mark)

22.2720 g., 0.6710 Silver 0.4805 oz. ASW **Obv:** Legend reads left to right

Date	Mintage	Good	VG	F	VF	XF
1668	—	45.00	90.00	275	625	—

KM# 306 KRONE (4 Mark)

22.2720 g., 0.6710 Silver 0.4805 oz. ASW **Obv:** Four rosettes in legend **Note:** Dav. #3584.

Date	Mintage	Good	VG	F	VF	XF
1669 Rare	—	—	—	—	—	—
1669(a)	—	125	250	275	800	—

KM# 320 KRONE (4 Mark)

22.2720 g., 0.6710 Silver 0.4805 oz. ASW **Obv:** Three crowned F3 monograms **Rev:** Three crowned shields in frame **Note:** Dav. #3585.

Date	Mintage	Good	VG	F	VF	XF
1670 Rare	—	—	3,000	5,000	7,500	10,000

KM# 330 KRONE (4 Mark)

22.2720 g., 0.6710 Silver 0.4805 oz. ASW **Obv:** Crowned ornate C5 monogram **Rev:** Crowned Danish arms **Note:** Dav. #3633.

Date	Mintage	Good	VG	F	VF	XF
1671 G-K	—	40.00	70.00	125	325	—
1672 G-K	—	40.00	70.00	140	360	—
1673 G-K Unique	—	—	—	—	—	—
1677 G-K Rare	—	—	—	—	—	—
1680 G-K Rare	—	—	—	—	—	—

KM# 343 KRONE (4 Mark)

22.2720 g., 0.6710 Silver 0.4805 oz. ASW **Obv:** Crowned plain C5 monogram **Note:** Dav. #3633A.

Date	Mintage	Good	VG	F	VF	XF
1671	—	40.00	70.00	130	310	—
1672	—	40.00	70.00	140	340	—
1674 Rare	—	—	—	—	—	—

KM# 359 KRONE (4 Mark)

22.2720 g., 0.6710 Silver 0.4805 oz. ASW **Obv:** Without inner circle **Rev:** Arms divide G-K, without inner circle **Note:** Dav. #3635.

Date	Mintage	Good	VG	F	VF	XF
1676	—	50.00	90.00	260	500	—
1677	—	150	300	500	875	—
1678 Rare	—	—	—	—	—	—

KM# 366 KRONE (4 Mark)

22.2720 g., 0.6710 Silver 0.4805 oz. ASW **Note:** Size as 1/2 Krone, but double thickness.

Date	Mintage	Good	VG	F	VF	XF
1680	—	100	190	575	1,400	—

KM# 365 KRONE (4 Mark)

22.2720 g., 0.6710 Silver 0.4805 oz. ASW **Obv:** Standing figure of king **Rev:** Crowned arms **Note:** Size as a 1/2 Krone, but double thickness

Date	Mintage	Good	VG	F	VF	XF
1680	—	180	275	675	1,500	—

KM# 367.1 KRONE (4 Mark)

22.2720 g., 0.6710 Silver 0.4805 oz. ASW **Obv:** Bust of King right on pedestal **Rev:** Crowned arms, narrow cross superimposed **Note:** Dav. #3636.

Date	Mintage	Good	VG	F	VF	XF
1680	—	150	275	750	1,350	—

KM# 367.2 KRONE (4 Mark)
22.2720 g., 0.6710 Silver 0.4805 oz. ASW **Rev:** Wide cross superimposed

Date	Mintage	Good	VG	F	VF	XF
1680	—	150	275	750	1,350	—

KM# 370 KRONE (4 Mark)
22.2720 g., 0.6710 Silver 0.4805 oz. ASW **Obv:** Crowned C5 monogram **Rev:** Crowned Danish arms on cross, G-S below **Note:** Dav. #3637.

Date	Mintage	Good	VG	F	VF	XF
1681	—	40.00	70.00	125	300	—
1682	—	40.00	70.00	125	300	—

KM# 378 KRONE (4 Mark)
22.2720 g., 0.6710 Silver 0.4805 oz. ASW **Obv:** Crowned double C5 monogram **Rev:** Crowned shield with text over cross inscription **Rev. Legend:** IIII/ MARCK/ DANSKE/ date/ G.S. **Note:** Dav. #3638. Varieties exist.

Date	Mintage	Good	VG	F	VF	XF
1684	—	70.00	125	300	550	—
1685	—	65.00	115	250	450	—

KM# 386.1 KRONE (4 Mark)
22.2720 g., 0.6710 Silver 0.4805 oz. ASW **Obv:** Small thin crowned C5 double monogram with many flourishes **Rev:** Crowned ornate arms, draped, G-S below **Note:** Dav. #3639. Varieties exist.

Date	Mintage	Good	VG	F	VF	XF
1686 GS	—	40.00	80.00	160	380	—
1689 GS	—	50.00	10.00	160	370	—

KM# 386.2 KRONE (4 Mark)
22.2720 g., 0.6710 Silver 0.4805 oz. ASW **Rev:** Undraped shield

Date	Mintage	Good	VG	F	VF	XF
1686	—	28.00	55.00	115	235	—
1689	—	32.00	67.50	110	220	—

KM# 386.3 KRONE (4 Mark)
22.2720 g., 0.6710 Silver 0.4805 oz. ASW **Obv:** Large monograms **Rev:** Draped arms, G-S below **Note:** Dav. #3639A.

Date	Mintage	Good	VG	F	VF	XF
1689 GS	—	60.00	100	225	425	—

KM# 386.4 KRONE (4 Mark)
22.2720 g., 0.6710 Silver 0.4805 oz. ASW **Rev:** Undraped shield

Date	Mintage	Good	VG	F	VF	XF
1689 GS	—	60.00	100	170	350	—

KM# 400 KRONE (4 Mark)
22.2720 g., 0.6710 Silver 0.4805 oz. ASW **Obv:** Half-length bust in armor right **Rev:** Crowned arms divide date and 4-M, C-W below **Note:** Dav. #3640.

Date	Mintage	Good	VG	F	VF	XF
1690 CW	—	150	450	775	1,450	—

KM# 401.1 KRONE (4 Mark)
22.2720 g., 0.6710 Silver 0.4805 oz. ASW **Obv:** Crowned double C5 monogram within legend, legend reads clockwise from bottom **Obv. Legend:** DEI GR REX DAN • NOR • V • G **Rev:** Crowned arms divide horizontal date and 4-M above, CW below, legend reads clockwise from top **Rev. Legend:** PIETATE ET IVSTITIA **Note:** Dav. #3642.

Date	Mintage	Good	VG	F	VF	XF
1690 CW	—	—	120	190	300	—

KM# 401.2 KRONE (4 Mark)
22.2720 g., 0.6710 Silver 0.4805 oz. ASW **Obv:** Crowned double C5 monogram within legend, legend reads clockwise from top **Obv. Legend:** D.G.REX.DAN.NOR VAN GOT **Rev:** Crowned arms divide horizontal date above 4-M, CW below, legend reads clockwise from upper right **Rev. Legend:** PIETATE ET IVSTITIA **Note:** Dav. #3643.

Date	Mintage	Good	VG	F	VF	XF
1691 CW	—	—	65.00	120	290	—
1692 CW	—	—	75.00	160	320	—

KM# 401.3 KRONE (4 Mark)
Silver **Obv:** Crowned double C5 monogram within legend, legend reads clockwise from bottom **Obv. Legend:** DEI GR REX DAN • NOR • V • G **Rev:** Crowned arms divide curved date and 4-M above, CW below, legend reads clockwise from top **Rev. Legend:** PIETATE ET IVSTITIA

Date	Mintage	Good	VG	F	VF	XF
1691 CW	—	—	75.00	140	325	—

KM# 401.4 KRONE (4 Mark)
22.2720 g., 0.6710 Silver 0.4805 oz. ASW **Obv:** Crowned double C5 monograms **Rev:** Crowned arms divide 4-M and C-W, date in legend **Rev. Legend:** PIETATE ET IVSTITIA **Note:** Dav. #3645.

Date	Mintage	VG	F	VF	XF	Unc
1692 CW	—	75.00	160	320	600	—

KM# 407 KRONE (4 Mark)
22.2720 g., 0.6710 Silver 0.4805 oz. ASW **Obv:** Bust right **Rev:** Crowned arms divide date, 4-M and C-W **Note:** Dav. #3644.

Date	Mintage	VG	F	VF	XF	Unc
1691 CW Unique	—	—	—	—	—	—

KM# 428.1 KRONE (4 Mark)
17.9880 g., 0.8330 Silver 0.4817 oz. ASW **Rev:** Crown above PIET • IVST, date divided by heart **Note:** Dav. #3648.

Date	Mintage	VG	F	VF	XF	Unc
1693	—	60.00	115	280	500	—
1694	—	60.00	115	280	500	—
1695	—	90.00	200	420	850	—
1696	—	70.00	160	375	750	—
1699	—	450	700	1,000	—	—

KM# 428.2 KRONE (4 Mark)
17.9880 g., 0.8330 Silver 0.4817 oz. ASW **Obv:** AMB. F. below bust **Note:** Dav. #3648A.

Date	Mintage	VG	F	VF	XF	Unc
1693	—	250	500	1,000	2,000	—

KM# 428.4 KRONE (4 Mark)
17.9880 g., 0.8330 Silver 0.4817 oz. ASW **Rev:** Ring around crown **Note:** Dav. #3648C.

Date	Mintage	VG	F	VF	XF	Unc
1693	—	600	1,150	1,600	2,250	—

KM# 428.5 KRONE (4 Mark)
17.9880 g., 0.8330 Silver 0.4817 oz. ASW **Obv:** Armored bust right **Rev:** Large crown **Note:** Date in Roman Numerals

Date	Mintage	VG	F	VF	XF	Unc
1693 (MDCXCIII)	—	—	—	—	—	—

KM# 448 KRONE (4 Mark)
17.9880 g., 0.8330 Silver 0.4817 oz. ASW **Ruler:** Frederik IV **Obv:** Bust right **Obv. Legend:** FRID • IIII • D • G • DAN • NOR • VA • GO • RE... **Rev:** Three crowned double "F4" monograms, arms between **Rev. Legend:** DOMINUS • MI HI • ADIUTOR • **Note:** Dav. #A1287.

Date	Mintage	VG	F	VF	XF	Unc
1699	—	375	650	1,400	2,100	—
1700	—	275	450	1,300	2,000	—

KM# 60.1 2 KRONE
37.8190 g., 0.8590 Silver 1.0444 oz. ASW **Obv:** Crowned King standing right with scepter, star in legend at left foot **Obv. Legend:** CHRISTIANUS IIII D: G • DANIA **Rev:** R.F.P. above, CORONA

DANICA below crown, within legend **Rev. Legend:** NORVEG: VANDALO: GOTOR: Q: REX **Note:** Dav. #3516 & 3516B.

Date	Mintage	Good	VG	F	VF	XF
1618(a)	—	180	375	750	1,500	—

KM# 60.2 2 KRONE

37.8190 g., 0.8590 Silver 1.0444 oz. ASW **Obv:** Crowned King standing right with scepter **Obv. Legend:** CHRISTIANUS IIII D: G • DANIA **Rev:** R.F.P. above, CORONA DANICA below crown, within legend **Rev. Legend:** NORVEG: VANDALO: GOTOR: Q: REX **Note:** Dav. #3516A.

Date	Mintage	Good	VG	F	VF	XF
1618(a)	—	180	375	750	1,500	—
1618(c)	—	250	500	900	1,750	—
1619(a)	—	250	500	900	1,750	—
1619(c)	—	250	500	900	1,750	—

KM# 60.3 2 KRONE

37.8190 g., 0.8590 Silver 1.0444 oz. ASW **Obv:** Crowned King standing right with scepter, star in legend at left foot **Obv. Legend:** CHRISTIANUS IIII D:G.DANIA **Rev:** R.F.P. missing above crown, CORONA DANICA below crown, within legend **Rev. Legend:** NORVEG:VANDALO:GOTOR:Q:REX

Date	Mintage	Good	VG	F	VF	XF
1618(a)	—	600	1,000	1,500	2,000	—

KM# 60.4 2 KRONE

37.8190 g., 0.8590 Silver 1.0444 oz. ASW **Obv:** Crowned King standing right with scepter, star in legend at left foot **Obv. Legend:** CHRISTIANZVS IIII D: G • DANIÆ **Rev:** *R*F*P* above, CORONA DANICA below crown, within legend **Rev. Legend:** NORVEG: VANDALO: GOTOR: Q: REX **Note:** Dav. #3516C.

Date	Mintage	Good	VG	F	VF	XF
1619(c)	—	250	500	900	1,750	—

KM# 61.1 2 KRONE

37.8190 g., 0.8590 Silver 1.0444 oz. ASW **Obv:** Without star in legend **Rev:** R • F • P • above crown **Note:** Dav. #3516A.

Date	Mintage	Good	VG	F	VF	XF
1618	—	90.00	185	375	800	—

KM# 61.2 2 KRONE

37.8190 g., 0.8590 Silver 1.0444 oz. ASW **Obv:** Crowned King standing right without scepter **Rev:** R. F. P. above crown **Note:** Dav. #3516B.

Date	Mintage	Good	VG	F	VF	XF
1618(c)	—	250	500	900	1,750	—

KM# 61.3 2 KRONE

37.8190 g., 0.8590 Silver 1.0444 oz. ASW **Rev:** *R * F * P * above crown **Note:** Dav. #3516C.

Date	Mintage	Good	VG	F	VF	XF
1618	—	135	270	500	860	—

KM# 99 2 KRONE

37.8190 g., 0.8590 Silver 1.0444 oz. ASW **Obv:** King with lowered scepter **Rev:** New crown **Note:** Dav. #3518.

Date	Mintage	Good	VG	F	VF	XF
1624	—	300	600	1,300	3,100	—

KM# 183 2 KRONE

37.8190 g., 0.8590 Silver 1.0444 oz. ASW **Note:** Similar to 1 Krone, KM#180, but double thickness. Dav. #3566.

Date	Mintage	Good	VG	F	VF	XF
1651	—	2,000	3,000	4,000	5,000	—

KM# 195 2 KRONE

44.5440 g., 0.6710 Silver 0.9609 oz. ASW **Note:** Similar to 1 Krone, KM#186, but double thickness. Dav. #3568.

Date	Mintage	Good	VG	F	VF	XF
1653	—	3,000	4,000	5,000	6,000	—

KM# 210 2 KRONE

44.5440 g., 0.6710 Silver 0.9609 oz. ASW **Note:** Similar to 1 Krone, KM#194, but double thickness. Dav. #3573.

Date	Mintage	Good	VG	F	VF	XF
1655	—	1,500	2,250	3,500	4,500	—

KM# 211 2 KRONE

44.5440 g., 0.6710 Silver 0.9609 oz. ASW **Note:** Similar to 1 Krone, KM#193, but double thickness. Dav. #3571.

Date	Mintage	Good	VG	F	VF	XF
1657 Rare	—	1,600	2,300	3,400	4,250	—

KM# 224 2 KRONE

44.5440 g., 0.6710 Silver 0.9609 oz. ASW **Note:** Similar to 1 Krone, KM#221, but double thickness. Dav. #3575.

Date	Mintage	Good	VG	F	VF	XF
1659 Rare	—	—	—	—	—	—

KM# 225 2 KRONE

44.5440 g., 0.6710 Silver 0.9609 oz. ASW **Note:** Dav. #3577. Similar to KM#223.1.

Date	Mintage	Good	VG	F	VF	XF
1659	—	400	750	1,200	4,500	—

KM# A226 2 KRONE

44.5440 g., 0.6710 Silver 0.9609 oz. ASW **Note:** Similar to 1 Krone, KM#270, but double thickness.

Date	Mintage	Good	VG	F	VF	XF
1666 Unique	—	—	—	—	—	—

KM# 351.1 2 KRONE

39.0020 g., 0.7670 Silver 0.9617 oz. ASW **Obv:** King on horseback **Rev:** Crowned Danish arms **Note:** Dav. #3634. 8 Mark.

Date	Mintage	Good	VG	F	VF	XF
1675	—	60.00	105	325	600	—

KM# 351.2 2 KRONE

39.0020 g., 0.7670 Silver 0.9617 oz. ASW **Obv:** Horse walking on grass **Note:** 8 Mark

Date	Mintage	Good	VG	F	VF	XF
1675	—	80.00	180	400	900	—

KM# 408 2 KRONE

44.5440 g., 0.6710 Silver 0.9609 oz. ASW **Obv:** Crowned double C5 monograms **Rev:** Crowned arms divide date and 4-M at sides, date below **Note:** Dav. #3641. Similar to KM#401.3.

Date	Mintage	VG	F	VF	XF	Unc
1691	—	—	—	7,000	12,000	—

KM# 409 2 KRONE

44.5440 g., 0.6710 Silver 0.9609 oz. ASW **Obv:** King on horseback right **Rev:** Crowned arms divide date C-W, date in legend **Note:** Dav. #A3644. 8 Mark.

Date	Mintage	VG	F	VF	XF	Unc
1691 Unique	—	—	—	—	—	—

KM# 429 2 KRONE

35.9770 g., 0.8330 Silver 0.9635 oz. ASW **Note:** Dav. #A3647. Similar to 1 Krone, KM#428.1, but double thickness.

Date	Mintage	VG	F	VF	XF	Unc
1693	—	—	1,200	2,000	3,250	—
1694	—	—	1,350	2,250	3,500	—
1695	—	—	2,000	4,000	6,000	—
1696 Unique	—	—	—	—	—	—

KM# A430 2 KRONE

35.9770 g., 0.8330 Silver 0.9635 oz. ASW **Note:** Similar to 1 Mark, KM#424, but eight times in thickness.

Date	Mintage	VG	F	VF	XF	Unc
1693	—	625	1,400	2,500	5,000	—
1696 Rare	—	—	—	—	—	—

KM# 410 3 KRONE

66.8150 g., 0.8330 Silver 1.7893 oz. ASW **Obv:** Crowned double C5 monograms **Rev:** Crowned arms divide date and 4-M, date below **Note:** Dav. #A3641. Similar to KM#401.3 but three times thickness.

Date	Mintage	VG	F	VF	XF	Unc
1691 Rare	—	—	—	—	—	—

KM# 430 3 KRONE

53.9660 g., 0.8330 Silver 1.4452 oz. ASW **Note:** Dav. #3646. Similar to KM#428.1 but three times thickness.

Date	Mintage	VG	F	VF	XF	Unc
1693	—	—	2,500	4,500	6,500	—
1694	—	—	2,000	3,500	5,500	—

Date	Mintage	VG	F	VF	XF	Unc
1695 Rare	—	—	—	—	—	—
1696 Rare	—	—	—	—	—	—

KM# 449 3 KRONE
45.2870 g., 0.9330 Silver 1.3584 oz. ASW **Subject:** Death of Christian V and Accession of Frederik IV **Note:** Dav. #A3649.

Date	Mintage	VG	F	VF	XF	Unc
1699	—	—	1,850	4,000	6,500	—

KM# 431 4 KRONE
71.9550 g., 0.8830 Silver 2.0427 oz. ASW **Note:** Dav. #3646A. Similar to 1 Krone, KM#428.1, but four times thickness.

Date	Mintage	VG	F	VF	XF	Unc
1693 Unique	—	—	—	—	—	—

KM# 432 6 KRONE
107.9320 g., 0.8830 Silver 3.0640 oz. ASW **Note:** Dav. #3646B. Similar to 1 Krone, KM#428.1, but six times thickness.

Date	Mintage	VG	F	VF	XF	Unc
1693 Unique	—	—	—	—	—	—

KM# 72 1/2 GOLD KRONE
1.4610 g., 0.9170 Gold 0.0431 oz. AGW **Obv:** Crowned arms mounted on cross in inner circle **Rev:** Large crown in circle, date in legend

Date	Mintage	VG	F	VF	XF	Unc
1619	—	2,000	3,000	4,000	5,500	—

KM# 73 GOLD KRONE
2.9730 g., 0.9170 Gold 0.0876 oz. AGW **Obv:** Crowned arms mounted on cross in inner circle **Rev:** Date above large crown in inner circle

Date	Mintage	VG	F	VF	XF	Unc
1619(a) Rare	—	—	—	—	—	—
1619(c)	—	3,000	6,000	11,000	15,000	—

KM# 278 GOLD KRONE
2.9730 g., 0.9170 Gold 0.0876 oz. AGW **Obv:** Laureate bust of Frederik III right

Date	Mintage	VG	F	VF	XF	Unc
1666	—	3,000	6,000	11,000	14,000	—

KM# 303 GOLD KRONE
2.9730 g., 0.9170 Gold 0.0876 oz. AGW **Rev:** Large crown with legend above, value: 18 MARK, date below

Date	Mintage	VG	F	VF	XF	Unc
1668 GK	—	—	4,000	7,000	9,000	—

KM# 206.1 GOLD KRONE
2.9730 g., 0.9170 Gold 0.0876 oz. AGW **Rev:** Large crown with legend below in inner circle, date at top

Date	Mintage	VG	F	VF	XF	Unc
1655	—	5,000	7,000	10,000	—	—

KM# 206.2 GOLD KRONE
2.9730 g., 0.9170 Gold 0.0876 oz. AGW **Obv:** Date below shield

Date	Mintage	VG	F	VF	XF	Unc
1655 Rare	—	—	—	—	—	—

KM# 74.1 2 GOLD KRONE
5.9960 g., 0.9170 Gold 0.1768 oz. AGW **Obv:** Crowned arms mounted on cross in inner circle **Rev:** Date above large crown in inner circle

Date	Mintage	VG	F	VF	XF	Unc
1619(c)	—	4,500	7,000	10,000	13,000	—
1621(r) Rare	—	—	—	—	—	—

KM# 74.2 2 GOLD KRONE
5.9960 g., 0.9170 Gold 0.1768 oz. AGW **Rev:** Date in legend

Date	Mintage	VG	F	VF	XF	Unc
1619(a)	—	1,800	3,000	5,000	—	—
1626(a) Rare	—	—	—	—	—	—
1628(a)	—	6,000	10,000	15,000	20,000	—
1628(o) Rare	—	—	—	—	—	—
1630(a) Rare	—	—	—	—	—	—
1633(a) Rare	—	—	—	—	—	—
1635(a) Unique	—	—	—	—	—	—
1637(a)	—	6,000	10,000	15,000	20,000	—
1648(t)	—	4,500	9,000	13,000	18,000	—

KM# 111 2 GOLD KRONE
5.9960 g., 0.9170 Gold 0.1768 oz. AGW **Obv:** Crowned bust of Christian IV right in inner circle **Rev:** Large crown in inner circle, date in legend

Date	Mintage	VG	F	VF	XF	Unc
1628	—	5,000	10,000	15,000	20,000	—
1629 Rare	—	—	—	—	—	—

KM# 279 2 GOLD KRONE
5.9960 g., 0.9170 Gold 0.1768 oz. AGW **Obv:** Laureate bust of Frederik III right **Rev:** Large crown with date above and legend below in inner circle

Date	Mintage	VG	F	VF	XF	Unc
1666 Unique	—	—	—	—	—	—

KM# 286 1/8 SPECIEDALER
3.5960 g., 0.8750 Silver 0.1012 oz. ASW **Obv:** Laureate and draped bust of Frederik III right **Rev:** Crowned shield

Date	Mintage	Good	VG	F	VF	XF
1667 Rare	—	—	—	—	—	—

KM# 13 1/4 SPECIEDALER
7.3080 g., 0.8880 Silver 0.2086 oz. ASW **Subject:** Christian IV **Obv:** Crown above oval shield on long cross, oval shield in each angle **Rev:** Cross in central oval shield, seven oval shields around

Date	Mintage	Good	VG	F	VF	XF
1602 Rare	—	—	—	—	—	—

KM# 100 1/2 SPECIEDALER
14.6160 g., 0.8810 Silver 0.4140 oz. ASW **Obv:** Crowned bust of Christian IV right **Rev:** Crown above circle of 13 oval shields, large oval shield in center

Date	Mintage	Good	VG	F	VF	XF
1624 NS	—	400	800	1,500	3,500	—
1627 NS	—	375	725	1,450	3,300	—
1628 NS	—	400	800	1,500	3,500	—
1631 PG Rare	—	—	—	—	—	—
1632 PG	—	1,500	2,500	4,000	6,000	—
1634 PG	—	1,250	2,000	3,000	5,000	—
1646 HK	—	375	725	1,450	3,300	—

KM# 260 1/2 SPECIEDALER
14.3870 g., 0.8750 Silver 0.4047 oz. ASW **Obv:** Laureate and draped bust of Frederik III right **Rev:** Crowned arms

Date	Mintage	Good	VG	F	VF	XF
1665 GK Rare	—	—	—	—	—	—

KM# 17 SPECIEDALER
29.2320 g., 0.8880 Silver 0.8345 oz. ASW **Obv:** King sitting on throne, date beside pillars **Rev:** Crowned arms **Note:** Dav. #3511.

Date	Mintage	Good	VG	F	VF	XF
1603 Rare	—	—	—	—	—	—

KM# 18 SPECIEDALER
29.2320 g., 0.8880 Silver 0.8345 oz. ASW **Obv:** King on throne, date at side of pillars **Rev:** Large cross within 2 legends in 2 circles, date in Roman numerals in inner circle. **Note:** Dav. #A3512.

Date	Mintage	Good	VG	F	VF	XF
1603 Unique	—	—	—	—	—	—

KM# 19 SPECIEDALER
29.2320 g., 0.8880 Silver 0.8345 oz. ASW **Obv:** Crowned arms **Rev:** Cross **Note:** Dav. #3512. Mule of reverses of KM#17 and 18. Date in Roman numerals.

Date	Mintage	Good	VG	F	VF	XF
1603	—	6,000	9,000	12,000	16,000	—

KM# 144 SPECIEDALER
29.2320 g., 0.8750 Silver 0.8223 oz. ASW **Note:** Similar to 2 Daler, KM#147. Dav. #3537. Breddaler.

Date	Mintage	Good	VG	F	VF	XF
ND(1607-14) Unique	—	—	—	—	—	—

KM# 145 SPECIEDALER
29.2320 g., 0.8750 Silver 0.8223 oz. ASW **Obv:** Half figure of King **Rev:** King on horseback **Note:** Dav. #3538. Breddaler.

Date	Mintage	Good	VG	F	VF	XF
ND(ca.1611) Unique	—	—	—	—	13,500	—

KM# 43 SPECIEDALER
29.2320 g., 0.8750 Silver 0.8223 oz. ASW **Obv:** Crowned King standing right with scepter, orb, and sword divides date **Rev:** Crown above arms on cross, nine shields around **Note:** Dav. #3513.

Date	Mintage	Good	VG	F	VF	XF
1608(a)	—	600	1,000	1,700	2,900	—
1609(a)	—	500	900	1,600	2,800	—

KM# 44 SPECIEDALER
29.2320 g., 0.8750 Silver 0.8223 oz. ASW **Note:** Dav. #3514.

Date	Mintage	Good	VG	F	VF	XF
1608(b) Rare	—	—	—	—	—	—
1609(b)	—	1,000	2,000	3,000	4,000	—
1610(b)	—	800	1,500	2,250	3,000	—
1618(a)	—	550	1,000	1,800	3,250	—
1619(a)	—	550	1,000	1,800	3,250	—
1620(a)	—	550	1,000	1,800	3,250	—
1621(a) Rare	—	—	—	—	—	—

KM# 53 SPECIEDALER
29.2320 g., 0.8750 Silver 0.8223 oz. ASW **Obv:** Redesigned crowned King, without scepter and orb **Rev:** Crowned oval shield at center, 13 shields around **Note:** Dav. #A3516.

Date	Mintage	Good	VG	F	VF	XF
1612 Unique	—	—	—	—	—	—

KM# 101 SPECIEDALER
29.2320 g., 0.8750 Silver 0.8223 oz. ASW **Obv:** Crowned half bust right, inscription in ornate shield, date below **Rev:** Crown above oval arms on cross, 13 shields around **Note:** Dav. #3524.

Date	Mintage	Good	VG	F	VF	XF
16Z4 NS	—	200	375	600	1,350	—
16Z5 NS	—	225	400	675	1,650	—
16Z6 NS	—	200	375	600	1,450	—
16Z7 BZ	—	500	1,000	1,600	3,500	—
16Z7 NS	—	175	300	525	1,250	—
16Z8 NS	—	175	300	525	1,250	—
1631 PG	—	400	800	1,350	2,000	—
1632 PG	—	200	375	625	1,700	—
1634 PG	—	225	400	750	1,700	—

KM# 102 SPECIEDALER

29.2320 g., 0.8750 Silver 0.8223 oz. ASW **Rev:** Fancy-shaped shields **Note:** Dav. #3526.

Date	Mintage	Good	VG	F	VF	XF
1624	—	2,500	4,000	7,500	12,000	—

KM# 103 SPECIEDALER

29.2320 g., 0.8750 Silver 0.8223 oz. ASW **Rev:** Short cross at center, flat-topped shields around **Note:** Dav. #3528.

Date	Mintage	Good	VG	F	VF	XF
1624 Unique	—	—	—	—	—	—

KM# 142 SPECIEDALER

29.2320 g., 0.8750 Silver 0.8223 oz. ASW **Obv:** New small bust of King, legend by date inside frame **Rev:** Smaller crown, larger center shield **Note:** Dav. #3536.

Date	Mintage	Good	VG	F	VF	XF
1646 *HK CHRITIANUS	—	225	450	800	1,800	—
1646 *HK	—	200	400	700	1,600	—

KM# 143 SPECIEDALER

29.2320 g., 0.8750 Silver 0.8223 oz. ASW **Obv:** New larger bust, legend ends above date **Note:** Dav. #3536A.

Date	Mintage	Good	VG	F	VF	XF
1647 H-K	—	190	375	600	1,550	—

KM# 168 SPECIEDALER

29.2320 g., 0.8750 Silver 0.8223 oz. ASW **Obv:** Crowned bust right **Rev:** Crown above center shield on cross, 11 shields around, date in legend **Note:** Dav. #3540.

Date	Mintage	Good	VG	F	VF	XF
1649	—	300	600	1,225	2,500	—
1650	—	250	550	1,000	2,250	—
1651	—	—	—	—	—	7,000

KM# 169 SPECIEDALER

29.2320 g., 0.8750 Silver 0.8223 oz. ASW **Obv:** Crowned armored bust right **Obv. Legend:** FRIDERICVS III D • G • DAN • NOR • VAN • GOT • REX **Rev:** Crown divides date, 13 shields around center shield **Rev. Legend:** DOMINUS PROVIDENT • **Note:** Dav. #3540A.

Date	Mintage	Good	VG	F	VF	XF
1649	—	400	700	1,300	3,000	—

KM# A170.1 SPECIEDALER

28.7750 g., 0.8750 Silver 0.8095 oz. ASW **Rev:** Flat-topped inner shield on small cross in inner circle

Date	Mintage	Good	VG	F	VF	XF
1653 Rare	—	—	—	—	—	—

KM# A170.2 SPECIEDALER

28.7750 g., 0.8750 Silver 0.8095 oz. ASW **Rev:** Round-top inner shield

Date	Mintage	Good	VG	F	VF	XF
1653 Unique	—	—	—	—	—	—

KM# 204 SPECIEDALER

28.7750 g., 0.8750 Silver 0.8095 oz. ASW **Obv:** Fuller large head **Rev:** Oval center arms, flat-topped shields around **Note:** Dav. #3544.

Date	Mintage	Good	VG	F	VF	XF
1655	—	550	900	1,400	3,000	—
1656	—	600	1,000	1,500	3,250	—

KM# 207 SPECIEDALER

28.7750 g., 0.8750 Silver 0.8095 oz. ASW **Rev:** Oval center arms, oval provincial shields around **Note:** Dav. #3544A.

Date	Mintage	Good	VG	F	VF	XF
1656	—	—	—	—	5,000	—

KM# 212 SPECIEDALER

28.7750 g., 0.8750 Silver 0.8095 oz. ASW **Obv:** Crowned bust right barely breaking upper inner circle **Rev:** Small crown above oblong arms, shields around **Note:** Dav. #3546.

Date	Mintage	Good	VG	F	VF	XF
1657 HK	—	400	800	1,700	3,800	—
1661 HK	—	400	800	1,700	3,800	—

KM# 238 SPECIEDALER

28.7750 g., 0.8750 Silver 0.8095 oz. ASW **Obv:** Crown separates legend at top **Note:** Dav. #3546A.

Date	Mintage	Good	VG	F	VF	XF
1661 HK	—	375	750	1,650	3,600	—
1662 IS Rare	—	—	—	—	—	—

KM# 240 SPECIEDALER

28.7750 g., 0.8750 Silver 0.8095 oz. ASW **Obv:** Crowned bust right **Rev:** Crowned arms on cross divides date and I-S **Note:** Dav. #3548.

Date	Mintage	Good	VG	F	VF	XF
1662 Unique	—	—	—	—	—	—
1663	—	—	—	10,000	15,000	—

KM# 248 SPECIEDALER

28.7750 g., 0.8750 Silver 0.8095 oz. ASW **Obv:** Crown above crossed scepter and sword, orb below **Rev:** Repeated cypher of F3 in center on cross with four crowns in angles **Note:** Dav. #3549.

Date	Mintage	VG	F	VF	XF	Unc
1663 Rare	—	—	—	—	—	—

KM# 250 SPECIEDALER

28.7750 g., 0.8750 Silver 0.8095 oz. ASW **Obv:** Crown above bust right **Rev:** Crowned arms in sprays, crown divides date **Note:** Dav. #3550.

Date	Mintage	VG	F	VF	XF	Unc
1664	—	1,000	2,000	4,000	7,000	—

KM# 251 SPECIEDALER

28.7750 g., 0.8750 Silver 0.8095 oz. ASW **Rev:** Date beside arms **Note:** Dav. #3550A.

Date	Mintage	VG	F	VF	XF	Unc
1664 Rare	—	—	—	—	—	—

KM# 261 SPECIEDALER

28.7750 g., 0.8750 Silver 0.8095 oz. ASW **Obv:** Laureate bust breaks upper legend **Rev:** Date left of crown, FCH below **Note:** Dav. #3551.

Date	Mintage	VG	F	VF	XF	Unc
1665 Rare	—	—	—	—	—	—

KM# 262 SPECIEDALER

28.7750 g., 0.8750 Silver 0.8095 oz. ASW **Obv:** Crown above smaller arms on cross, date divided at top and FC-H at bottom **Note:** Dav. #3553.

Date	Mintage	VG	F	VF	XF	Unc
1665	—	2,000	3,000	4,500	6,000	—
1666 Rare	—	—	—	—	—	—

KM# 277 SPECIEDALER

28.7750 g., 0.8750 Silver 0.8095 oz. ASW **Obv:** Laureate bust without inner circle **Rev:** Crowned arms dividing G-K, date below, without inner circle **Note:** Dav. #3554.

Date	Mintage	VG	F	VF	XF	Unc
1665 Rare	—	—	—	—	—	—

KM# 288 SPECIEDALER

28.7750 g., 0.8750 Silver 0.8095 oz. ASW **Obv:** Laureate bust in arms facing right without circle **Obv. Legend:** FRID • III • D • G • DAN • NOR • VAN • GOT • REX • **Rev:** Crowned national arms on shield with flat top, GK flanking. **Rev. Legend:** DUX • SL • HO • STO • CO • OL & DEL • **Note:** Dav. #3555.

Date	Mintage	VG	F	VF	XF	Unc
1667	—	—	—	3,000	5,000	8,000

KM# 289 SPECIEDALER

28.7750 g., 0.8750 Silver 0.8095 oz. ASW **Ruler:** Frederik III **Obv:** Laureate bust facing right, without circle. Wearing robe with a lion's head on shoulder **Obv. Legend:** FRID • III • D • G • DAN • NOR • VAN • GOT • REX • **Rev:** Crowned national arms in four sections, separated by a cross, small center shield, on shield with flat top. GK flanking. **Rev. Legend:** DUX • SL • HO • STO • CO • OL & DEL • **Note:** Dav. #3555A.

Date	Mintage	VG	F	VF	XF	Unc
1667 Rare	—	—	—	—	—	—

KM# 290 SPECIEDALER

28.7750 g., 0.8750 Silver 0.8095 oz. ASW **Obv:** Laureate bust in armor and pellet circle breaks upper legend **Obv. Legend:** FRIDERICVS • 3 • D • G • DAN • NOR • VAN • GOT • REX • **Rev:** Crowned national arms in three sections in round ornimented shield on cross, FCH below **Rev. Legend:** DOMIN NUS * PROVIDE BIT • 1667 **Note:** Dav. #3556.

Date	Mintage	VG	F	VF	XF	Unc
1667 FCH	3	—	—	7,000	10,000	—

KM# 292 SPECIEDALER

28.7750 g., 0.8750 Silver 0.8095 oz. ASW **Obv:** Laureate bust in arms facing right with lion's head on shoulder. Breaks circle at top **Obv. Legend:** FRIDERICVS • 3 • D • G • DAN • NOR • VAN • GOT • REX • **Rev:** Crowned national arms on small ornamented shield on cross, within wide bayberry branch wreath **Rev. Legend:** *DOMINUS * * PROVIDEBIT * **Note:** Dav. #3557.

Date	Mintage	VG	F	VF	XF	Unc
1667 FCH Rare	—	—	—	2,500	4,000	—
ND FCH Unique	—	—	—	—	—	—

KM# 287 SPECIEDALER

28.7750 g., 0.8750 Silver 0.8095 oz. ASW **Obv:** Laureat bust in armor right, draped with lion's head on shoulder. Breaks circle at top **Obv. Legend:** FRIDERICVS • 3 • D • G • DAN • NOR • VAN • GOT • REX • **Rev:** Crowned national arms in three sections, in small round shield in bayberry branch wreath on cross **Rev. Legend:** *DOMINUS* PROVIDEBIT* **Note:** Dav. #3553A.

Date	Mintage	VG	F	VF	XF	Unc
1667 FCH Rare	—	—	—	—	—	—

KM# 291 SPECIEDALER

28.7750 g., 0.8750 Silver 0.8095 oz. ASW **Obv:** Laureate bust breaks legend at bottom **Obv. Legend:** FRID • IIII • D • G • DAN • NOR • VAN • GOT • REX • **Rev:** Crowned national arms on round ornamented shield on cross, within wide bayberry wreath. **Rev. Legend:** *DOMINUS * PROVIDEBIT * **Note:** Dav. #A3557.

Date	Mintage	VG	F	VF	XF	Unc
1667 FCH Unique	—	—	—	—	—	—

KM# 300 SPECIEDALER

28.7750 g., 0.8750 Silver 0.8095 oz. ASW **Obv:** Laureate bust divides legend at bottom **Rev:** Crowned arms on cross, 15 shields around, date divided at sides **Note:** Dav. #3559.

Date	Mintage	VG	F	VF	XF	Unc
1668	—	900	1,800	3,000	4,500	—
1669 Rare	—	—	—	—	—	—

KM# 301 SPECIEDALER

28.7750 g., 0.8750 Silver 0.8095 oz. ASW **Obv:** Bust right without inner circle, continuous legend **Rev:** Three oval shields in center crowned, 15 shields around, date in Roman numerals on edge **Note:** Dav. #3560.

Date	Mintage	VG	F	VF	XF	Unc
1668	—	1,000	2,000	3,000	4,500	—
ND	—	1,000	2,000	3,000	4,500	—

KM# 307 SPECIEDALER

28.7750 g., 0.8750 Silver 0.8095 oz. ASW **Obv:** Laureate bust divides legend at top **Rev:** Three oval shields in center crowned, 15 shields around, date in Roman numerals on edge **Note:** Dav. #3561.

Date	Mintage	VG	F	VF	XF	Unc
1669	—	1,200	2,500	4,000	6,000	—

KM# 308 SPECIEDALER

28.7750 g., 0.8750 Silver 0.8095 oz. ASW **Obv:** Laureate bust divides legend at bottom **Rev:** Date divided at sides of arms **Rev. Legend:** DOM - INVS - PROVI - DEBIT **Note:** Dav. #3563.

Date	Mintage	VG	F	VF	XF	Unc
1669 Rare	—	—	—	—	—	—

KM# 309 SPECIEDALER

28.7750 g., 0.8750 Silver 0.8095 oz. ASW **Note:** Similar to 2 Daler, KM#311. Dav. #3565.

Date	Mintage	VG	F	VF	XF	Unc
ND	—	—	—	4,000	6,000	—

KM# 321 SPECIEDALER

28.7750 g., 0.8750 Silver 0.8095 oz. ASW **Obv:** Bust of Christian V right **Rev:** Bust of Frederik III right **Note:** Dav. #3628.

Date	Mintage	VG	F	VF	XF	Unc
ND(1670)	—	—	—	10,000	14,000	—

KM# 322 SPECIEDALER

28.7750 g., 0.8750 Silver 0.8095 oz. ASW **Rev:** Three arms crowned in wreath, 15 shields around, date on edge **Note:** Dav. #3629.

Date	Mintage	VG	F	VF	XF	Unc
ND	—	1,000	2,850	5,500	8,500	—
1670	—	1,500	3,000	6,000	9,000	—

KM# 349 SPECIEDALER

28.7750 g., 0.8750 Silver 0.8095 oz. ASW **Obv:** Date below bust **Obv. Legend:** CHRIST. V. D. G... **Note:** Dav. #3630.

Date	Mintage	VG	F	VF	XF	Unc
1674	—	1,000	2,000	4,000	6,000	8,000

KM# 352 SPECIEDALER

28.7750 g., 0.8750 Silver 0.8095 oz. ASW **Obv:** Crowned bust with scepter and globe **Rev:** Three crowned C5 monograms **Note:** Dav. #3631.

Date	Mintage	VG	F	VF	XF	Unc
1675	—	800	1,300	3,100	5,000	—

KM# 411 SPECIEDALER

28.7750 g., 0.8750 Silver 0.8095 oz. ASW **Obv:** Bust right **Rev:** Crowned arms on cross, 15 crowned shields around, date below **Note:** Dav. #3632.

Date	Mintage	VG	F	VF	XF	Unc
1691 Rare	—	—	—	—	—	—

KM# 154 1-1/2 SPECIEDALER

Silver **Note:** Similar to 2 Speciedaler, KM#147. Dav. #3537A. Breddaler.

Date	Mintage	Good	VG	F	VF	XF
ND(1607-14) Rare	—	—	—	—	—	—

KM# 155 1-1/2 SPECIEDALER

Silver **Obv:** 1/2-figure of king **Rev:** King on horseback **Note:** Dav. #3538A. Breddaler.

Date	Mintage	Good	VG	F	VF	XF
ND(ca.1611) Rare	—	—	—	—	—	—

KM# 20 2 SPECIEDALER

58.4640 g., 0.8880 Silver 1.6691 oz. ASW **Obv:** Crowned arms **Rev:** Cross **Note:** Similar to 1 Mark, KM#12. Dav. #3512A. Date in Roman numerals.

Date	Mintage	Good	VG	F	VF	XF
1603 Unique	—	—	—	—	—	—

KM# 147 2 SPECIEDALER

58.4640 g., 0.8880 Silver 1.6691 oz. ASW **Ruler:** Christian IV **Obv. Legend:** • CHRISTIANVS • - IIII • D: - G • DA: NO • VA • G: Q • REX - X • **Rev. Legend:** REGNA • FIR - MAT • ... **Note:** Dav. #3537B. Breddaler.

Date	Mintage	Good	VG	F	VF	XF
ND(1607-14)	—	1,500	3,000	7,000	11,000	—

KM# 148 2 SPECIEDALER

58.4640 g., 0.8880 Silver 1.6691 oz. ASW **Obv:** 1/2-figure of king **Rev:** King on horseback **Note:** Dav. #3538B. Breddaler.

Date	Mintage	Good	VG	F	VF	XF
ND(ca,1611)	—	2,000	4,000	10,000	17,500	—

KM# 104 2 SPECIEDALER

58.4640 g., 0.8880 Silver 1.6691 oz. ASW **Obv:** Crowned 1/2-bust above framed inscription **Rev:** Crown above oval arms on cross, 13 shields around **Note:** Dav. #3523.

Date	Mintage	Good	VG	F	VF	XF
1624 NS	—	600	1,200	1,800	4,200	—
1626 NS	—	900	1,400	2,250	4,800	—
1627 BZ	—	500	1,000	2,000	4,000	—
1627 NS	—	700	1,250	1,750	4,500	—
1628 NS	—	1,000	1,500	2,500	5,000	—
1631 PG	—	600	1,100	2,500	5,500	—
1632 PG Rare	—	—	—	—	—	—
1634 PG Rare	—	—	—	—	—	—

KM# 105 2 SPECIEDALER

58.4640 g., 0.8880 Silver 1.6691 oz. ASW **Rev:** Fancy shaped shields **Note:** Similar to 1 Speciedaler, KM#102. Dav. #3525.

Date	Mintage	Good	VG	F	VF	XF
1624	—	4,000	8,000	12,000	17,000	—

KM# 106 2 SPECIEDALER

58.4640 g., 0.8880 Silver 1.6691 oz. ASW **Obv:** Crowned 1/2-bust above framed inscription **Rev:** Crown above oval arms on cross, 13 shields around **Note:** Similar to 1 Speciedaler, KM#103. Dav. #3527.

Date	Mintage	Good	VG	F	VF	XF
1624 Rare	—	—	—	—	—	—

KM# 146 2 SPECIEDALER

58.4640 g., 0.8880 Silver 1.6691 oz. ASW **Obv:** Crowned 1/2-bust above framed inscription **Rev:** Crown above oval arms on cross, 13 shields around **Note:** Similar to 1 Speciedaler, KM#142. Dav. #3535.

Date	Mintage	Good	VG	F	VF	XF
1647 Rare	—	—	—	—	—	—

KM# 170 2 SPECIEDALER

58.4640 g., 0.8880 Silver 1.6691 oz. ASW **Note:** Similar to 1 Speciedaler, KM#168. Dav. #3539.

Date	Mintage	VG	F	VF	XF	Unc
1649	—	6,500	10,000	14,000	—	—
1650 Rare	—	—	—	—	—	—

KM# 196.1 2 SPECIEDALER

57.5500 g., 0.8750 Silver 1.6189 oz. ASW **Obv:** Large crowned head right **Rev:** Center shield with flat top **Note:** Dav. #3541.

Date	Mintage	VG	F	VF	XF	Unc
1653	—	2,500	4,000	7,000	9,500	—

KM# 196.2 2 SPECIEDALER

57.5500 g., 0.8750 Silver 1.6189 oz. ASW **Obv:** Large crowned head right **Rev:** Center shield with rounded top **Note:** Dav. #3541

Date	Mintage	Good	VG	F	VF	XF
1653 Rare	—	—	—	—	—	—

KM# 205 2 SPECIEDALER

57.5500 g., 0.8750 Silver 1.6189 oz. ASW **Obv:** Large crowned had right **Rev:** Center shield with flat top **Note:** Dav. #3543. Similar to 1 Speciedaler, KM#204.

Date	Mintage	VG	F	VF	XF	Unc
1655	—	—	3,500	5,500	8,000	—
1656	—	—	4,000	6,500	10,000	—

KM# 208 2 SPECIEDALER

57.5500 g., 0.8750 Silver 1.6189 oz. ASW **Obv:** Bust right without inner circle, legend breaks at bottom **Rev:** Oval center arms with flat-top provincial shields around **Note:** Dav. #A3545. Similar to 1 Speciedaler, KM#207.

Date	Mintage	VG	F	VF	XF	Unc
1656 Rare	—	—	—	—	—	—

KM# 213 2 SPECIEDALER

57.5500 g., 0.8750 Silver 1.6189 oz. ASW **Note:** Similar to 1 Speciedaler, KM#212. Dav. #3545.

Date	Mintage	VG	F	VF	XF	Unc
1657	—	2,750	4,500	6,750	11,000	—
1661	—	2,750	4,500	6,750	11,000	—

KM# 239 2 SPECIEDALER

57.5500 g., 0.8750 Silver 1.6189 oz. ASW **Note:** Similar to 1 Speciedaler, KM#238. Dav. #3545A.

Date	Mintage	VG	F	VF	XF	Unc
1661	—	2,000	3,000	4,250	5,500	—

KM# 241 2 SPECIEDALER

57.5500 g., 0.8750 Silver 1.6189 oz. ASW **Note:** Similar to 1 Speciedaler, KM#240. Dav. #3547.

Date	Mintage	VG	F	VF	XF	Unc
1662 IS Unique	—	—	—	—	—	—
1663 IS	—	3,000	6,000	11,000	17,500	—
1664 CH Rare	—	—	—	—	—	—

KM# 263 2 SPECIEDALER

57.5500 g., 0.8750 Silver 1.6189 oz. ASW **Obv:** Laureate bust breaks upper legend **Rev:** Crown above small arms on cross, date divided at top, FC-H at bottom **Note:** Similar to 1 Speciedaler, KM#262. Dav. #3552.

Date	Mintage	VG	F	VF	XF	Unc
1665 Rare	—	—	—	—	—	—
1666 Unique	—	—	—	—	—	—

KM# 302 2 SPECIEDALER

57.5500 g., 0.8750 Silver 1.6189 oz. ASW **Obv:** Laureate bust divides legend at bottom, circle around bust **Rev:** Crowned arms on cross, 15 shields around one center shield, date divided at sides **Note:** Similar to 1 Speciedaler, KM#300. Dav. #3558.

Date	Mintage	VG	F	VF	XF	Unc
1668 Rare	—	—	—	—	—	—
1669 Rare	—	—	—	—	—	—

KM# 310 2 SPECIEDALER

57.5500 g., 0.8750 Silver 1.6189 oz. ASW **Rev:** Date divided at sides of arms **Rev. Legend:** DOM - INVS - PROVI - DEBIT **Note:** Similar to 1 Speciedaler, KM#308. Dav. #3562.

Date	Mintage	VG	F	VF	XF	Unc
1669	—	2,000	3,500	5,000	—	—

KM# 311 2 SPECIEDALER

57.5500 g., 0.8750 Silver 1.6189 oz. ASW **Note:** Similar to 1 Speciedaler, KM#309. Dav. #3564.

Date	Mintage	VG	F	VF	XF	Unc
ND Rare	—	—	—	—	—	—
1669 Date on edge	—	1,500	2,500	4,000	6,000	—

KM# 324 2 SPECIEDALER

57.5500 g., 0.8750 Silver 1.6189 oz. ASW **Note:** Similar to 1 Speciedaler, KM#322. Dav. #3629A.

Date	Mintage	VG	F	VF	XF	Unc
ND Rare	—	—	—	—	—	—

KM# 24 3 SPECIEDALER
Gold **Obv:** Crowned bust of Christian IV right in inner circle **Rev:** Value and date in circle **Note:** Klippe.

Date	Mintage	VG	F	VF	XF	Unc
1604 Unique	61	—	—	—	—	—

KM# 77 3 SPECIEDALER
Silver **Note:** Similar to 2 Speciedaler, KM#147. Dav. #3537C. Breddaler.

Date	Mintage	VG	F	VF	XF	Unc
ND(1607-14) Rare	—	—	—	—	—	—

KM# 78 3 SPECIEDALER
Silver **Obv:** 1/2-figure of king **Rev:** King on horseback **Note:** Dav. #3538C. Breddaler.

Date	Mintage	VG	F	VF	XF	Unc
ND(ca.1611) Rare	—	—	—	—	—	—

KM# 76 3 SPECIEDALER
Silver **Rev:** Fancy shaped shields **Note:** Similar to Speciedaler, KM#102. Dav. #A3525.

Date	Mintage	VG	F	VF	XF	Unc
1624 Rare	—	—	—	—	—	—

KM# 75 3 SPECIEDALER
Silver **Note:** Similar to Speciedaler, KM#104. Dav. #3622.

Date	Mintage	VG	F	VF	XF	Unc
1624	—	6,000	10,000	15,000	—	—
1627 Unique	—	—	—	—	—	—
1628 Unique	—	—	—	—	—	—

KM# 230 3 SPECIEDALER
Silver **Note:** Similar to 1 Speciedaler, KM#212. Dav. #3545B.

Date	Mintage	VG	F	VF	XF	Unc
1661 HK	—	10,000	15,000	20,000	—	—

KM# 231 3 SPECIEDALER
Silver **Note:** Similar to 1 Speciedaler, KM#240. Dav. #A3547.

Date	Mintage	VG	F	VF	XF	Unc
1662 IS Rare	—	—	—	—	—	—

KM# 232 3 SPECIEDALER
Silver **Obv:** Laureate bust breaks upper legend **Rev:** Crown above smaller arms on cross, date divided at top, FC-H at bottom **Note:** Dav. #3552A.

Date	Mintage	VG	F	VF	XF	Unc
1665 Unique	—	—	—	—	—	—

KM# 233 3 SPECIEDALER
86.3250 g., 0.8750 Silver 2.4284 oz. ASW **Obv:** Laureate bust breaks legend at bottom **Rev:** Small crowned arms on cross, divided date above, FC-H below **Note:** Dav. #B3557.

Date	Mintage	VG	F	VF	XF	Unc
1668 Unique	—	—	—	—	—	—

KM# 25 4 SPECIEDALER
9.7440 g., 0.8330 Gold 0.2609 oz. AGW **Note:** Klippe. 21 x 21 mm.

Date	Mintage	VG	F	VF	XF	Unc
1604 Diamond	588	7,000	12,000	20,000	—	—
1604 Square; rare	Inc. above	—	—	—	—	—

KM# 115 4 SPECIEDALER
Silver **Note:** Similar to 2 Specidaler, KM#147. Dav. #3537D. Breddaler.

Date	Mintage	VG	F	VF	XF	Unc
ND(1607-14) Rare	—	—	—	—	—	—

KM# 79 4 SPECIEDALER
Silver **Note:** Dav. #3521.

Date	Mintage	VG	F	VF	XF	Unc
1624	—	13,500	21,500	30,000	—	—
1627 Unique	—	—	—	—	—	—

KM# 234 4 SPECIEDALER
115.1000 g., 0.8750 Silver 3.2378 oz. ASW **Note:** Similar to 1 Specidaler, KM#212. Dav. #3545C.

Date	Mintage	VG	F	VF	XF	Unc
1661 HK Unique	—	—	—	—	—	—

KM# 315 4 SPECIEDALER
115.1000 g., 0.8750 Silver 3.2378 oz. ASW **Note:** Similar to 1 Specidaler, KM#240. Dav. #B3547.

Date	Mintage	VG	F	VF	XF	Unc
1662 IS Unique	—	—	—	—	—	—

KM# 316 4 SPECIEDALER
115.1000 g., 0.8750 Silver 3.2378 oz. ASW **Note:** Similar to 2 Specidaler, KM#311. Dav. #3564A.

Date	Mintage	VG	F	VF	XF	Unc
ND Unique	—	—	—	—	—	—

KM# 26 6 SPECIEDALER
13.1750 g., 0.9230 Gold 0.3910 oz. AGW **Obv:** Crowned bust of Christian IV right in inner circle **Rev:** Value and date in circle **Note:** Klippe.

Date	Mintage	VG	F	VF	XF	Unc
1604 Diamond	425	—	—	37,000	—	—
1604 Square; rare	Inc. above	—	—	—	—	—

KM# 116 6 SPECIEDALER
Silver **Note:** Similar to 2 Specidaler, KM#147. Dav. #3537E.

Date	Mintage	VG	F	VF	XF	Unc
ND(1607-14) Unique	—	—	—	—	—	—

KM# 27 8 SPECIEDALER
17.6490 g., 0.9370 Gold 0.5317 oz. AGW **Obv:** Crowned bust of Christian IV right in inner circle **Rev:** Value and date in circle **Note:** Klippe.

Date	Mintage	VG	F	VF	XF	Unc
1604 Rare	409	—	—	—	—	—

KM# 50.1 1/2 ROSENOBEL
4.4970 g., 0.8330 Gold 0.1204 oz. AGW, 28 mm. **Obv:** Crowned Christian IV right in inner circle, continuous legend **Rev:** Elephant left with crowned initial on side cloth

Date	Mintage	VG	F	VF	XF	Unc
1611	—	—	—	—	50,000	—

KM# 50.2 1/2 ROSENOBEL
4.4970 g., 0.8330 Gold 0.1204 oz. AGW, 24 mm. **Obv:** Crown breaks legend

Date	Mintage	VG	F	VF	XF	Unc
1611 Rare	—	—	—	—	—	—

KM# 51 ROSENOBEL
8.9940 g., 0.8330 Gold 0.2409 oz. AGW **Obv:** Crowned Christian IV right in inner circle **Rev:** Elephant left with crowned initial on side cloth

Date	Mintage	VG	F	VF	XF	Unc
1611	—	9,000	14,000	18,000	25,000	—
1612	—	10,000	15,000	20,000	27,000	—
1613	—	—	—	25,000	32,000	—
1627	—	—	—	30,000	40,000	—
1629 Rare	—	—	—	—	—	—

KM# B45 GUILDER (Hungarian Guilder)
3.4900 g., 0.9720 Gold 0.1091 oz. AGW **Obv:** King standing **Rev:** Large shield, date in legend

Date	Mintage	VG	F	VF	XF	Unc
1607 Rare	—	—	—	—	—	—
1608 Unique	—	—	—	—	—	—

KM# A45 GUILDER (Hungarian Guilder)
3.4900 g., 0.9720 Gold 0.1091 oz. AGW **Rev:** Shield of three lions mounted on cross **Note:** Previous KM#45.

Date	Mintage	VG	F	VF	XF	Unc
1608 Rare	—	—	—	—	—	—
1611	—	3,000	4,000	5,500	8,200	—

KM# 108 GUILDER (Rhinish Guilder)
3.2490 g., 0.7600 Gold 0.0794 oz. AGW **Obv:** Crowned bust of Christian IV right in inner circle **Rev:** Crowned arms mounted on cross in inner circle **Note:** Minted for paying Danish troops during part of the "30 Years War".

Date	Mintage	Good	VG	F	VF	XF
1625	29,000	—	2,000	3,000	3,750	6,000
1627	2,168	—	1,750	2,500	3,250	5,000
1628	—	—	3,000	4,500	6,000	10,000
1632	2,570	—	2,250	3,100	4,000	6,500

KM# 46 2 GUILDER (2 Hungarian Guilder)
6.9800 g., 0.9720 Gold 0.2181 oz. AGW **Obv:** Christian IV standing right in inner circle **Rev:** Crowned arms mounted on cross in circle of 13 shields of arms

Date	Mintage	VG	F	VF	XF	Unc
1608 Rare	—	—	—	—	—	—

KM# A47 3 GUILDER (3 Hungarian Guilder/Sovereign)
Gold **Obv:** Standing King Christian IV divides date **Note:** Similar to 2 Guilder, KM#46.

Date	Mintage	VG	F	VF	XF	Unc
1608	—	—	—	—	100,000	—

KM# 114 1/4 PORTUGALOSER (2-1/2 Ducat)
8.6610 g., 0.9790 Gold 0.2726 oz. AGW **Obv:** Cross in inner circle, date at top **Rev:** Crowned heart in inner circle, radiant Jehovah in Hebrew at top

Date	Mintage	VG	F	VF	XF	Unc
1629 Unique	—	—	—	—	—	—

FR# 68 PORTUGALOSER (10 Ducat)
34.6450 g., 0.9790 Gold 1.0904 oz. AGW **Obv:** Equestrian figure of Christian IV right in cartouche **Obv. Legend:** :CHRISTIANVS: IIII: D: G: DAN: NO • VA • G • REX **Rev:** Crowned arms within legend **Rev. Legend:** DUX • SCL • HOL • ST • • DIT • COM • IN • OL • ETZ

Date	Mintage	VG	F	VF	XF	Unc
ND(1610)	—	—	—	75,000	100,000	—

FR# 68a PORTUGALOSER (10 Ducat)
Silver

Date	Mintage	VG	F	VF	XF	Unc
ND(1610) Rare	—	—	—	—	—	—

KM# 174 1/16 DUCAT
Gold **Ruler:** Frederik III **Obv:** Crowned F3 monogram within legend **Obv. Legend:** DOMINUS PROVIDEBIT **Note:** Brakteate striking

Date	Mintage	VG	F	VF	XF	Unc
ND	—	550	900	—	—	—

KM# A143 1/4 DUCAT
0.8730 g., 0.9790 Gold 0.0275 oz. AGW **Obv:** Christian IV standing right **Rev:** Three-line inscription (one in Hebrew) above date **Note:** Previous KM#143.

Date	Mintage	VG	F	VF	XF	Unc
1646	—	400	800	2,000	3,200	—
1647	—	5,000	925	2,200	3,400	—
1648 Unique	—	—	—	—	—	—

KM# 149 1/4 DUCAT
0.8730 g., 0.9790 Gold 0.0275 oz. AGW **Obv:** Crowned C4 monogram divides date **Rev:** Eyeglasses above two-line inscription **Rev. Legend:** VIDE MIRA DOMI

Date	Mintage	VG	F	VF	XF	Unc
1647 Rare	—	—	—	—	—	—

KM# 150 1/4 DUCAT
0.8730 g., 0.9790 Gold 0.0275 oz. AGW **Obv:** Christian IV standing right **Rev:** Eyeglasses above two-line inscription

Date	Mintage	VG	F	VF	XF	Unc
ND Rare	—	—	—	—	—	—

KM# 235 1/4 DUCAT
0.8730 g., 0.9790 Gold 0.0275 oz. AGW **Obv:** Frederik III **Rev:** Crowned cruciform double F monograms with 3 at center

Date	Mintage	VG	F	VF	XF	Unc
1660(t)	—	800	1,100	1,400	2,100	—
1664(a)	—	1,000	1,400	1,800	2,750	—

KM# 264.1 1/4 DUCAT
0.8730 g., 0.9790 Gold 0.0275 oz. AGW **Obv:** Crowned F3 monogram, legend reads clockwise from top **Rev:** Value and date

Date	Mintage	VG	F	VF	XF	Unc
1665(a)	—	300	600	1,050	2,100	—
1668(a)	—	350	700	1,200	2,200	—

KM# 264.2 1/4 DUCAT
0.8730 g., 0.9790 Gold 0.0275 oz. AGW **Obv:** Crowned F3 monogram, legend reads counterclockwise from top

Date	Mintage	VG	F	VF	XF	Unc
1665(a) Unique	—	—	—	—	11,000	—
1665 GK	—	—	—	6,000	9,000	—

KM# 325 1/4 DUCAT
0.8730 g., 0.9790 Gold 0.0275 oz. AGW **Obv:** Two crowned F3 monograms **Note:** 3 Mark

Date	Mintage	VG	F	VF	XF	Unc
1670 GK	—	1,500	2,000	2,500	3,200	—

KM# 353 1/4 DUCAT
0.8730 g., 0.9790 Gold 0.0275 oz. AGW **Obv:** Crowned C5 monograms **Rev:** Value and date **Note:** 3 Mark

Date	Mintage	VG	F	VF	XF	Unc
1675	—	1,000	1,500	1,850	2,500	—

KM# 360 1/4 DUCAT
0.8730 g., 0.9790 Gold 0.0275 oz. AGW **Obv:** Laureate bust of Christian V right **Note:** 3 Mark

Date	Mintage	VG	F	VF	XF	Unc
1676	—	1,350	1,800	2,400	3,000	—

KM# 436 1/4 DUCAT
0.8730 g., 0.9790 Gold 0.0275 oz. AGW **Obv:** Older bust of Christian V right **Rev:** Large crown above date **Note:** Similar to 1/2 Ducat, KM#437.

Date	Mintage	VG	F	VF	XF	Unc
1694 Unique	—	—	—	—	—	—

KM# 450 1/4 DUCAT
0.8730 g., 0.9790 Gold 0.0275 oz. AGW **Obv:** Equestrian figure of Frederik IV left **Rev:** Crowned F4 monograms

Date	Mintage	VG	F	VF	XF	Unc
ND Unique	—	—	—	—	—	—

KM# 138 1/2 DUCAT
1.7450 g., 0.9790 Gold 0.0549 oz. AGW **Obv:** Christian IV standing right in inner circle **Rev:** Three-line inscription (1 in Hebrew) above date

Date	Mintage	VG	F	VF	XF	Unc
1644	—	500	1,000	1,600	3,200	—
1645	—	600	1,100	2,200	4,100	—
1646	—	600	1,100	2,350	4,500	—

KM# 151 1/2 DUCAT
1.7450 g., 0.9790 Gold 0.0549 oz. AGW **Obv:** Crowned C4 monogram **Rev:** Eyeglasses above two-line inscription and date

Date	Mintage	VG	F	VF	XF	Unc
1647	—	5,000	10,000	15,000	20,000	—

KM# 152 1/2 DUCAT
1.7450 g., 0.9790 Gold 0.0549 oz. AGW **Obv:** Christian IV standing right in inner circle **Rev:** Eyeglasses above inscription and date

Date	Mintage	VG	F	VF	XF	Unc
1647	—	4,500	8,500	13,500	18,000	—

KM# 188 1/2 DUCAT
1.7450 g., 0.9790 Gold 0.0549 oz. AGW **Obv:** Laureate bust of Frederik III in inner circle **Rev:** Three-line inscription and date in inner circle

Date	Mintage	VG	F	VF	XF	Unc
1652(t)	—	—	—	—	5,000	—

KM# 229 1/2 DUCAT
1.7450 g., 0.9790 Gold 0.0549 oz. AGW **Obv:** Frederik III **Rev:** Crowned cruciform double F monograms with 3 at center

Date	Mintage	VG	F	VF	XF	Unc
1659	—	400	800	1,750	3,500	—
1664	—	350	600	1,400	3,850	—

KM# 312 1/2 DUCAT
1.7450 g., 0.9790 Gold 0.0549 oz. AGW **Obv:** Crowned F3 monogram in inner circle **Rev:** Value and date

Date	Mintage	VG	F	VF	XF	Unc
1669	—	1,200	2,500	4,250	—	—

KM# 354 1/2 DUCAT
1.7450 g., 0.9790 Gold 0.0549 oz. AGW **Obv:** Laureate bust of Christian V right **Rev:** Crowned C5 monograms divide date

Date	Mintage	VG	F	VF	XF	Unc
1675GK	—	—	900	1,500	2,100	—

KM# 355 1/2 DUCAT
1.7450 g., 0.9790 Gold 0.0549 oz. AGW **Obv:** Equestrian figure of Christian V right **Rev:** Three crowned C5 monograms entwined

Date	Mintage	VG	F	VF	XF	Unc
ND(1685) Rare	—	—	—	—	—	—

KM# 356 1/2 DUCAT
1.7450 g., 0.9790 Gold 0.0549 oz. AGW **Obv:** Equestrian figure left

Date	Mintage	VG	F	VF	XF	Unc
ND(1685) Unique	—	—	—	—	—	—

KM# 437 1/2 DUCAT
1.7450 g., 0.9790 Gold 0.0549 oz. AGW **Obv:** Older bust of Christian V **Rev:** Large crown, date below. **Note:** Size as 1/4 Ducat KM#436 but double thickness.

Date	Mintage	VG	F	VF	XF	Unc
1694	—	400	800	1,400	2,800	—
1696	—	600	1,100	1,600	2,900	—

KM# 441 1/2 DUCAT
1.7450 g., 0.9790 Gold 0.0549 oz. AGW **Obv:** Equestrian figure of Christian V, city view behind horse walking **Rev:** Crowned oval arms mounted above cross, date below

Date	Mintage	VG	F	VF	XF	Unc
1696	—	1,000	2,000	3,500	5,500	—

KM# 442 1/2 DUCAT
1.7450 g., 0.9790 Gold 0.0549 oz. AGW **Obv:** Equestrian figure of Christian V, horse prancing **Rev:** Crowned oval arms without drapery, mounted above cross

Date	Mintage	VG	F	VF	XF	Unc
ND	—	800	1,400	2,000	3,000	—

KM# 451 1/2 DUCAT
1.7450 g., 0.9790 Gold 0.0549 oz. AGW **Obv:** Equestrian figure of Frederik IV left **Rev:** Three crowned arms and three crowned F4 monograms alternate in circle

Date	Mintage	VG	F	VF	XF	Unc
ND Rare	—	—	—	—	—	—

KM# 452 1/2 DUCAT
1.7450 g., 0.9790 Gold 0.0549 oz. AGW **Rev:** Crowned double F4 monogram

Date	Mintage	VG	F	VF	XF	Unc
ND Rare	—	—	—	—	—	—

KM# 124 DUCAT
3.4900 g., 0.9790 Gold 0.1098 oz. AGW **Obv:** Christian IV standing right in inner circle **Rev:** Crowned arms in inner circle, date in legend

Date	Mintage	VG	F	VF	XF	Unc
1637 Rare	—	—	—	—	—	—

KM# 153 DUCAT
3.4900 g., 0.9790 Gold 0.1098 oz. AGW **Obv:** Crowned C4 monogram divides date **Rev:** Eyeglasses above two-line inscription

Date	Mintage	VG	F	VF	XF	Unc
1647 Unique	—	—	—	—	—	—

KM# 171 DUCAT
3.4900 g., 0.9790 Gold 0.1098 oz. AGW **Ruler:** Frederik III **Obv:** Laureate head of Frederik III right wtih date below in inner circle

Date	Mintage	VG	F	VF	XF	Unc
1649	—	1,500	2,000	3,500	5,000	—
1650 Rare	—	—	—	—	—	—
1651	—	1,500	2,000	3,500	5,000	—

KM# 197 DUCAT
3.4900 g., 0.9790 Gold 0.1098 oz. AGW **Obv:** Crowned bust of Frederik III right, date below **Rev:** Inscription in 3 lines in center. **Rev. Legend:** DOMINUS PROVIDEBIT

Date	Mintage	VG	F	VF	XF	Unc
1653 Rare	—	—	—	—	—	—

KM# 198 DUCAT
3.4900 g., 0.9790 Gold 0.1098 oz. AGW **Obv:** Bust, date below. No motto. **Rev:** Crowned cruciform double F monograms with 3 at center

Date	Mintage	VG	F	VF	XF	Unc
1653 Rare	—	—	—	4,000	—	—

KM# 199 DUCAT
3.4900 g., 0.9790 Gold 0.1098 oz. AGW **Rev:** Motto in script writing joins crowns of cross, within legend

Date	Mintage	VG	F	VF	XF	Unc
1653 Unique	—	—	—	—	—	—

KM# 215 DUCAT
3.4900 g., 0.9790 Gold 0.1098 oz. AGW **Obv:** Smaller crowned bust of Frederik III right with date above **Rev:** Script writing removed

Date	Mintage	VG	F	VF	XF	Unc
1657	—	1,500	3,000	5,500	8,200	—

KM# 236 DUCAT
3.4900 g., 0.9790 Gold 0.1098 oz. AGW **Obv:** Bust of Frederik III right, within legend **Rev:** Crowned cruciform double F monograms with 3 at center

Date	Mintage	VG	F	VF	XF	Unc
1660(t)	—	900	1,750	2,750	3,750	—
1661(t)	—	1,000	2,000	3,000	4,250	—
1662	—	750	1,500	2,500	3,500	—
ND(t)	—	1,200	2,150	3,100	4,000	—

KM# 242 DUCAT
3.4900 g., 0.9790 Gold 0.1098 oz. AGW **Obv:** Crowned bust extends to top edge **Rev:** Crowned cruciform double F monograms with 3 at center

Date	Mintage	VG	F	VF	XF	Unc
1662 Rare	—	—	—	—	—	—
1662(i) Rare	—	—	—	—	—	—
1663(i) Rare	—	—	—	—	—	—
1664(e)	—	800	1,400	2,250	3,000	—

KM# 252 DUCAT
3.4900 g., 0.9790 Gold 0.1098 oz. AGW **Obv:** Laureate head of Frederik III right

Date	Mintage	VG	F	VF	XF	Unc
1664 Rare	—	—	—	—	—	—

KM# 265.2 DUCAT
3.4900 g., 0.9790 Gold 0.1098 oz. AGW **Obv:** Bust, legend clockwise from lower left

Date	Mintage	VG	F	VF	XF	Unc
1665 Rare	—	—	—	—	—	—

KM# 294 DUCAT
3.4900 g., 0.9790 Gold 0.1098 oz. AGW **Obv:** Laureate bust extends to lower edge, legend clockwise from lower left

Date	Mintage	VG	F	VF	XF	Unc
1667 Rare	—	—	—	—	—	—
1667(a) Rare	—	—	—	—	—	—

KM# 304 DUCAT
3.4900 g., 0.9790 Gold 0.1098 oz. AGW **Obv:** Frederik III within circle **Rev:** Crowned arms, date below within circle

Date	Mintage	VG	F	VF	XF	Unc
1667	—	2,500	4,250	6,500	9,000	—
1668	—	2,000	4,000	6,000	8,500	—

KM# 313 DUCAT
3.4900 g., 0.9790 Gold 0.1098 oz. AGW **Obv:** Crowned bust of Frederik III right **Rev:** Crown above three arms - two above one, date divided by lower shield

Date	Mintage	VG	F	VF	XF	Unc
1669 Rare	—	—	—	—	—	—
1670	—	1,000	2,000	3,500	5,000	—

KM# 340.1 DUCAT
3.4900 g., 0.9790 Gold 0.1098 oz. AGW **Obv:** Laureate bust right **Obv. Legend:** CHRIST • 5... **Note:** Broad flan

Date	Mintage	VG	F	VF	XF	Unc
1671/69	—	700	1,400	2,000	3,000	—
1672	—	850	1,650	3,500	—	—
1674 Rare	—	—	—	—	—	—

KM# A340 DUCAT
3.4900 g., 0.9790 Gold 0.1098 oz. AGW **Obv. Legend:** CHRIST • 5...

Date	Mintage	VG	F	VF	XF	Unc
1672	—	800	1,600	3,250	—	—

KM# 445 DUCAT
3.4900 g., 0.9790 Gold 0.1098 oz. AGW **Obv:** Christian V on horseback **Rev:** Crowned monogram **Note:** Small, thick planchet

Date	Mintage	VG	F	VF	XF	Unc
ND(1675)	—	400	600	1,400	2,250	—

KM# 371 DUCAT

3.4900 g., 0.9790 Gold 0.1098 oz. AGW **Obv:** Bust of Christian V right **Rev:** Crowned arms in inner circle

Date	Mintage	VG	F	VF	XF	Unc
1681 Rare	—	—	—	—	—	—
1683	—	1,150	2,250	4,500	—	—

KM# 372 DUCAT

3.4900 g., 0.9790 Gold 0.1098 oz. AGW **Rev:** Model of Frederiksborg fortress in Guinea

Date	Mintage	VG	F	VF	XF	Unc
1682	—	2,500	5,000	7,500	10,000	—

KM# 374.1 DUCAT

3.4900 g., 0.9790 Gold 0.1098 oz. AGW **Obv:** Equestrian figure of Christian V right, baton points backwards **Rev:** Three crowned C5 monograms entwined **Note:** Small, thick planchet.

Date	Mintage	VG	F	VF	XF	Unc
ND(1685)	—	1,000	1,500	2,000	3,500	—

KM# 374.2 DUCAT

3.4900 g., 0.9790 Gold Small, thick planchet 0.1098 oz. AGW **Obv:** Equistrian figure of Christian V right, baton points forward **Rev:** Three crowned C5 monograms entwined

Date	Mintage	VG	F	VF	XF	Unc
ND(1685)	—	800	1,350	1,800	3,000	—

KM# 375 DUCAT

3.4900 g., 0.9790 Gold 0.1098 oz. AGW **Obv:** Equestrian figure of Christian V left, amongst trees **Rev:** Three entwined crowned C5 monograms **Note:** Small, thick planchet

Date	Mintage	VG	F	VF	XF	Unc
ND(1685)	—	1,000	1,500	2,000	3,500	—

KM# 376 DUCAT

3.4900 g., 0.9790 Gold 0.1098 oz. AGW **Obv:** Armored bust of Christian V right **Rev:** Three entwined crowned C5 monograms

Date	Mintage	VG	F	VF	XF	Unc
ND(1687) Unique	—	—	—	—	—	—

KM# 387 DUCAT

3.4900 g., 0.9790 Gold 0.1098 oz. AGW **Obv:** Bust within legend **Rev:** Crowned arms within elephant order, surrounded by 15 small arms, date at top, GS at bottom

Date	Mintage	VG	F	VF	XF	Unc
1687 GS	—	2,000	3,000	5,500	8,000	—
ND	—	2,000	3,000	5,500	8,000	—

KM# 394 DUCAT

3.4900 g., 0.9790 Gold 0.1098 oz. AGW **Obv:** Draped bust of Christian V right in elaborate hat **Rev:** View of Christiansborg fortress in Guinea in inner circle

Date	Mintage	VG	F	VF	XF	Unc
1688 Rare	—	4,000	6,000	8,000	12,000	—

KM# 388 DUCAT

3.4900 g., 0.9790 Gold 0.1098 oz. AGW **Obv:** Older head of Christian V right

Date	Mintage	VG	F	VF	XF	Unc
ND(1690)	—	1,250	2,500	3,750	5,000	—

KM# 389 DUCAT

3.4900 g., 0.9790 Gold 0.1098 oz. AGW **Obv:** Three crowned C5 monograms entwined

Date	Mintage	VG	F	VF	XF	Unc
ND(1690) Rare	—	—	—	—	—	—

KM# 412.1 DUCAT

3.4900 g., 0.9790 Gold 0.1098 oz. AGW **Obv:** Draped bust of Christian V right **Rev:** Crowned oval arms divide date

Date	Mintage	VG	F	VF	XF	Unc
1691 Unique	—	—	—	—	—	—

KM# 415.1 DUCAT

3.4900 g., 0.9790 Gold 0.1098 oz. AGW **Obv:** Bust of Christian V right, breaks legend at top

Date	Mintage	VG	F	VF	XF	Unc
1691	—	1,500	2,750	4,250	6,500	—
1692	—	1,000	1,750	3,250	5,000	—

KM# 415.2 DUCAT

3.4900 g., 0.9790 Gold 0.1098 oz. AGW **Obv:** Bust of Christian V right, breaks legend at bottom

Date	Mintage	VG	F	VF	XF	Unc
1693	—	900	1,400	2,250	4,500	—
1696	—	1,000	1,850	3,000	5,000	—

KM# 413 DUCAT

3.4900 g., 0.9790 Gold 0.1098 oz. AGW **Obv:** Smaller draped bust of Christian V right

Date	Mintage	VG	F	VF	XF	Unc
1691	—	2,500	5,000	7,500	10,000	—
1692 Unique	—	—	—	—	—	—

KM# 412.2 DUCAT

3.4900 g., 0.9790 Gold 0.1098 oz. AGW **Obv:** Draped bust of Christian V right **Rev:** Crowned oval arms, date in legend

Date	Mintage	VG	F	VF	XF	Unc
1692	—	1,400	2,800	5,000	7,000	—

KM# 414 DUCAT

3.4900 g., 0.9790 Gold 0.1098 oz. AGW **Obv:** Crowned double C5 monograms **Rev:** Crowned arms divide date

Date	Mintage	VG	F	VF	XF	Unc
1691	—	400	600	950	1,750	—

KM# 418 DUCAT

3.4900 g., 0.9790 Gold 0.1098 oz. AGW **Obv:** Bust of Christian V left on rearing horse

Date	Mintage	VG	F	VF	XF	Unc
1692	—	100	1,750	2,750	4,250	—

KM# A433 DUCAT

3.4900 g., 0.9790 Gold 0.1098 oz. AGW **Rev:** Crown above date **Note:** Large planchet

Date	Mintage	VG	F	VF	XF	Unc
1693	—	1,000	2,000	3,100	5,500	—

KM# 433 DUCAT

3.4900 g., 0.9790 Gold 0.1098 oz. AGW **Rev:** Crown above date **Note:** Small, thick planchet. Size as 1/4 Ducat.

Date	Mintage	VG	F	VF	XF	Unc
1694	—	750	1,200	2,000	3,900	—
1696	—	700	1,000	1,600	3,100	—

KM# 438 DUCAT

3.4900 g., 0.9790 Gold 0.1098 oz. AGW **Obv:** Christian V **Rev:** Triple monogram

Date	Mintage	VG	F	VF	XF	Unc
1694	—	600	1,000	1,500	2,500	—

KM# A445 DUCAT

3.4900 g., 0.9790 Gold 0.1098 oz. AGW **Obv:** Christian V on horseback right **Rev:** Draped crowned oval arms

Date	Mintage	VG	F	VF	XF	Unc
ND(1696)	—	1,000	1,500	2,000	3,000	—

KM# 443 DUCAT

3.4900 g., 0.9790 Gold 0.1098 oz. AGW **Obv:** Christian V on horseback facing right, city view in background **Rev:** Crowned arms **Note:** Double thick planchet, Size as 1/2 Ducat.

Date	Mintage	VG	F	VF	XF	Unc
1696	—	1,000	1,500	2,200	3,000	—

KM# 444 DUCAT

3.4900 g., 0.9790 Gold 0.1098 oz. AGW **Obv:** Christian V on rearing horse, no drapery **Rev:** Crowned arms

Date	Mintage	VG	F	VF	XF	Unc
ND(1696)	—	1,000	1,500	2,000	3,000	—

KM# B445 DUCAT

3.4900 g., 0.9790 Gold 0.1098 oz. AGW **Obv:** Christian V on horseback, left **Rev:** Crowned monogram

Date	Mintage	VG	F	VF	XF	Unc
ND(1696)	—	1,350	2,500	4,500	7,500	—

KM# 453 DUCAT

3.4900 g., 0.9790 Gold 0.1098 oz. AGW **Obv:** Bust of Christian V right **Rev:** Ship

Date	Mintage	VG	F	VF	XF	Unc
1699	—	1,400	2,500	4,000	55,000	—

KM# 454 DUCAT

3.4900 g., 0.9790 Gold 0.1098 oz. AGW **Subject:** Death of the King **Obv:** Monogram on pyramid with base, winds of heaven blowing from above **Rev:** Ships in harbor of Copenhagen, motto above

Date	Mintage	VG	F	VF	XF	Unc
ND(1699)	—	550	900	1,600	2,800	—

KM# 455 DUCAT

3.4900 g., 0.9790 Gold 0.1098 oz. AGW **Subject:** Death of the King **Obv:** Without base on pyramid **Rev:** Motto in banner above city

Date	Mintage	VG	F	VF	XF	Unc
ND(1699)	—	1,000	2,000	3,250	5,500	—

KM# 456 DUCAT

3.4900 g., 0.9790 Gold 0.1098 oz. AGW **Subject:** Coronation of King Frederik IV **Obv:** Frederik IV **Rev:** Christian V

Date	Mintage	VG	F	VF	XF	Unc
ND(1699)	—	600	1,100	2,750	4,750	—

KM# 471 DUCAT

3.4900 g., 0.9790 Gold 0.1098 oz. AGW **Rev:** Crowned double F4 monograms, date below

Date	Mintage	VG	F	VF	XF	Unc
1700	—	600	1,100	2,750	4,750	—

KM# 141 DUCAT

3.4900 g., 0.9790 Gold 0.1098 oz. AGW **Obv:** Standing figure of King with sceptre and orb **Rev:** Hebrew text in center

Date	Mintage	VG	F	VF	XF	Unc
1644	—	250	950	2,100	3,800	—

Note: Flower between King's feet

Date	Mintage	VG	F	VF	XF	Unc
1644 No flower, unique	—	—	—	—	—	—
1645	—	200	800	2,000	3,500	—
1646	—	325	1,100	2,800	4,200	—
1647	—	250	1,000	2,750	3,850	—
1648	—	325	1,100	2,900	4,400	—
1664 Unique	—	—	—	—	—	—

Note: Without flower between King's feet

KM# 265.1 DUCAT

3.4900 g., 0.9790 Gold 0.1098 oz. AGW **Obv:** Crowned bust of Frederik III right within legend clockwise from upper right **Rev:** Crowned cruciform double F monograms with 3 at center

Date	Mintage	VG	F	VF	XF	Unc
1665 Rare	—	—	—	—	—	—
1666 Rare	—	—	—	—	—	—

KM# 139 2 DUCAT

6.9800 g., 0.9790 Gold 0.2197 oz. AGW **Obv:** Christian IV standing right in inner circle **Rev:** Three-line inscription (one in Hebrew) above date in starry border

Date	Mintage	VG	F	VF	XF	Unc
1644 Rare	—	—	—	8,000	12,000	—

KM# 140 2 DUCAT

6.9800 g., 0.9790 Gold 0.2197 oz. AGW **Rev:** Without starry border

Date	Mintage	VG	F	VF	XF	Unc
1644 Unique	—	—	—	—	—	—
1645(I)	—	2,500	4,000	6,000	—	—
1646(I)	—	2,000	2,800	5,000	9,000	—
1648(I)	—	1,800	2,600	4,750	9,000	—

KM# 200 2 DUCAT

6.9800 g., 0.9790 Gold 0.2197 oz. AGW **Obv:** Crowned bust of Frederik III right, date below **Rev:** Crowned cruciform double F monograms wtih 3 at center

Date	Mintage	VG	F	VF	XF	Unc
1653 Rare	—	—	—	—	—	—

KM# 216.1 2 DUCAT

6.9800 g., 0.9790 Gold 0.2197 oz. AGW **Rev:** Sailing ship, date in exergue **Rev. Legend:** VANDALOV: GOTHER: Q: REX •.

Date	Mintage	VG	F	VF	XF	Unc
1657	—	1,500	3,000	5,500	7,500	—
1658	—	1,250	2,500	5,000	7,000	—

KM# 216.2 2 DUCAT

6.9800 g., 0.9790 Gold 0.2197 oz. AGW **Rev:** Sailing ship, date in exergue **Rev. Legend:** DOMINVS • PROVIDEBIT
Note: Varieties exist.

Date	Mintage	VG	F	VF	XF	Unc
1664	—	1,500	3,000	5,000	8,000	—
1666 Unique	—	—	—	—	—	—
1667 Unique	—	—	—	—	—	—

KM# 244 2 DUCAT

6.9800 g., 0.9790 Gold 0.2197 oz. AGW **Obv:** Crowned bust of Frederik III right in inner circle **Rev:** Crowned arms mounted on cross divides date in inner circle

Date	Mintage	VG	F	VF	XF	Unc
1662	—	1,250	2,300	4,000	5,500	—
1663	—	1,400	2,500	4,200	6,500	—

KM# 243 2 DUCAT

6.9800 g., 0.9790 Gold 0.2197 oz. AGW **Rev:** Crowned cruziform double F3 monogram, 3 in center

Date	Mintage	VG	F	VF	XF	Unc
1662 Rare	—	—	—	—	—	—

KM# 295 2 DUCAT

6.9800 g., 0.9790 Gold 0.2197 oz. AGW **Obv:** Laureate bust of Frederik III right without inner circle **Rev:** Sailing ship, date in exergue

Date	Mintage	VG	F	VF	XF	Unc
1667	—	1,400	2,800	4,500	9,000	—

KM# 326 2 DUCAT

6.9800 g., 0.9790 Gold 0.2197 oz. AGW **Obv:** Laureate head of Frederik III right **Rev:** Crowned cruciform double F3 monogram, date

Date	Mintage	VG	F	VF	XF	Unc
1670	—	1,500	3,000	6,500	10,000	—

KM# 327 2 DUCAT

6.9800 g., 0.9790 Gold 0.2197 oz. AGW **Obv:** Laureate bust of Frederik III right **Rev:** Crown above orb between sword and sceptre **Note:** Small planchet.

Date	Mintage	VG	F	VF	XF	Unc
ND	—	1,750	3,000	6,500	10,000	—

KM# 328 2 DUCAT

6.9800 g., 0.9790 Gold 0.2197 oz. AGW **Obv:** Laureate bust of Christian V right **Rev:** Crowned double C5 monogram, date in legend

Date	Mintage	VG	F	VF	XF	Unc
1670	—	—	—	—	12,000	—

KM# 346 2 DUCAT

6.9800 g., 0.9790 Gold 0.2197 oz. AGW **Obv:** Crowned C5 monogram **Rev:** Elephant **Note:** Size as 1/2 Ducat, eight times as thick

Date	Mintage	VG	F	VF	XF	Unc
1673	—	1,600	3,000	4,750	7,000	—

KM# 347 2 DUCAT

6.9800 g., 0.9790 Gold 0.2197 oz. AGW **Obv:** Christian V **Note:** Size as a 1/2 Ducat, but planchet is four times as thick.

Date	Mintage	VG	F	VF	XF	Unc
ND(1675)	—	700	1,450	2,200	3,500	—

KM# 348 2 DUCAT

6.9800 g., 0.9790 Gold 0.2197 oz. AGW **Obv:** Christian V right on reearing horse **Rev:** Three crowned C5 monograms entwined **Note:** Size as 1/2 Ducat, 4 time thickness

Date	Mintage	VG	F	VF	XF	Unc
ND(1685) Unique	—	—	—	—	—	—

KM# 390 2 DUCAT

6.9800 g., 0.9790 Gold 0.2197 oz. AGW **Obv:** Bust of Christian V right **Rev:** Crowned round arms in circle of 15 shields, date divided near top

Date	Mintage	VG	F	VF	XF	Unc
1687	—	1,500	3,000	6,000	9,000	—

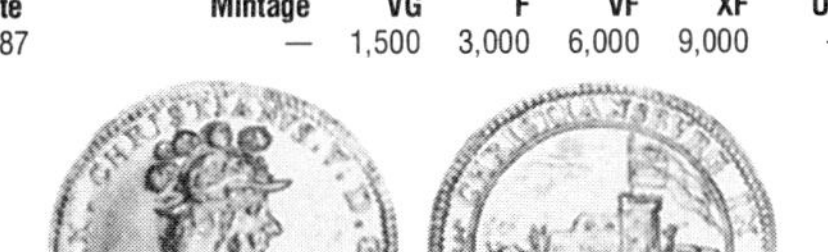

KM# 395.1 2 DUCAT

6.9800 g., 0.9790 Gold 0.2197 oz. AGW **Obv:** Draped bust of Christian V right, wearing elaborate hat **Rev:** View of Christiansborg fortress in Guinea in inner circle **Edge:** Lettered

Date	Mintage	VG	F	VF	XF	Unc
1688 Unique	—	—	—	—	—	—

KM# 395.2 2 DUCAT

6.9800 g., 0.9790 Gold 0.2197 oz. AGW **Obv:** Draped bust of Christian V right, wearing elaborate hat **Rev:** View of Christiansborg fortress in Guinea in inner circle **Edge:** Plain

Date	Mintage	VG	F	VF	XF	Unc
1688	—	2,000	4,000	6,000	8,750	—

KM# 416.1 2 DUCAT

6.9800 g., 0.9790 Gold 0.2197 oz. AGW **Obv:** Wide draped bust of Christian V right **Rev:** Crowned oval arms divide date

Date	Mintage	VG	F	VF	XF	Unc
1691	—	1,800	3,250	5,500	7,500	—

KM# 416.2 2 DUCAT

6.9800 g., 0.9790 Gold 0.2197 oz. AGW **Obv:** Slender draped bust of Christian V right **Rev:** Crowned oval arms, date in legend

Date	Mintage	VG	F	VF	XF	Unc
1691	—	200	3,500	5,500	8,500	—

KM# 419 2 DUCAT

6.9800 g., 0.9790 Gold 0.2197 oz. AGW **Obv:** Laureate bust of Christian V right **Rev:** Three crowned C5 monograms surround radiant triangle

Date	Mintage	VG	F	VF	XF	Unc
1692 Rare	—	—	—	—	—	—

KM# 439 2 DUCAT

6.9800 g., 0.9790 Gold 0.2197 oz. AGW **Obv:** Plain bust of Christian V right **Rev:** Large crown **Note:** Minted from same dies as 2 Krone, KM#429.

Date	Mintage	VG	F	VF	XF	Unc
1693 Rare	—	—	—	—	—	—

KM# 434 2 DUCAT

6.9800 g., 0.9790 Gold 0.2197 oz. AGW **Rev:** Large crown above date **Note:** Size as 1/4 Ducat, planchet eight times as thick

Date	Mintage	VG	F	VF	XF	Unc
1694	—	3,000	6,000	9,000	14,000	—
1696	—	3,000	6,000	9,000	14,000	—

KM# 446 2 DUCAT

6.9800 g., 0.9790 Gold 0.2197 oz. AGW **Obv:** Christian V right on prancing horse **Rev:** Crowned round arms mounted on cross, date divided below

Date	Mintage	VG	F	VF	XF	Unc
1696 Rare	—	—	—	—	—	—

KM# 447 2 DUCAT

6.9800 g., 0.9790 Gold 0.2197 oz. AGW **Obv:** Christian V right on rearing horse **Rev:** Crowned oval arms with drapery

Date	Mintage	VG	F	VF	XF	Unc
ND Rare	—	—	—	—	—	—

KM# A447 2 DUCAT

6.9800 g., 0.9790 Gold 0.2197 oz. AGW **Rev:** Arms without drapery **Note:** Similar to 1 Ducat, KM#A445.

Date	Mintage	VG	F	VF	XF	Unc
ND Rare	—	—	—	—	—	—

KM# 457 2 DUCAT

6.9800 g., 0.9790 Gold 0.2197 oz. AGW **Obv:** Bust of Christian V right **Rev:** Three-masted ship in harbor of Christiansborg fortress

Date	Mintage	VG	F	VF	XF	Unc
1699	—	1,750	3,250	4,500	5,750	—

KM# 458 2 DUCAT

6.9800 g., 0.9790 Gold 0.2197 oz. AGW **Subject:** Death of the King **Obv:** Monogram on pyramid with base, winds of heaven blowing from above **Rev:** Ships in harbor of Copenhagen, motto in banner above

Date	Mintage	VG	F	VF	XF	Unc
ND(1699)	—	2,250	4,500	7,500	11,000	—

KM# 459 2 DUCAT

6.9800 g., 0.9790 Gold 0.2197 oz. AGW **Subject:** Death of the King **Obv:** Without base on pyramid **Rev:** Motto above city

Date	Mintage	VG	F	VF	XF	Unc
ND(1699) Unique	—	—	—	—	—	—

KM# 460 2 DUCAT

6.9800 g., 0.9790 Gold 0.2197 oz. AGW **Obv:** Smoke and flames from center point **Rev:** Group of weapons, banner and battle trophies

Date	Mintage	VG	F	VF	XF	Unc
ND(1699)	—	—	—	3,000	5,250	—

KM# 461 2 DUCAT

6.9800 g., 0.9790 Gold 0.2197 oz. AGW **Subject:** Coronation of Frederik IV **Obv:** Bust of Frederik IV right **Rev:** Bust of Christian V right

Date	Mintage	VG	F	VF	XF	Unc
ND(1699) Rare	—	—	—	—	—	—

KM# 245 3 DUCAT

10.4710 g., 0.9790 Gold 0.3296 oz. AGW **Rev:** Crowned cruciform double F monograms with 3 at center

Date	Mintage	VG	F	VF	XF	Unc
1662 Unique	—	—	—	—	—	—

KM# 246 3 DUCAT

10.4710 g., 0.9790 Gold 0.3296 oz. AGW **Obv:** Crowned bust extends to top edge

Date	Mintage	VG	F	VF	XF	Unc
1662 Unique	—	—	—	—	—	—

KM# 280 3 DUCAT

10.4710 g., 0.9790 Gold 0.3296 oz. AGW **Obv:** Crowned bust of Frederik III right in inner circle **Rev:** Ship with date in exergue

Date	Mintage	VG	F	VF	XF	Unc
1666 Unique	—	—	—	—	—	—

KM# 296 3 DUCAT

10.4710 g., 0.9790 Gold 0.3296 oz. AGW **Obv:** Laureate bust of Frederik III right **Rev:** Ship

Date	Mintage	VG	F	VF	XF	Unc
1667 Unique	—	—	—	—	—	—

KM# 391 3 DUCAT

10.4710 g., 0.9790 Gold 0.3296 oz. AGW **Obv:** Bust of Christian V right **Rev:** Crowned round arms in circle of 15 shields, date divided near top

Date	Mintage	VG	F	VF	XF	Unc
1687 Unique	—	—	—	—	—	—

KM# 462 3 DUCAT

10.4710 g., 0.9790 Gold 0.3296 oz. AGW, 28 mm. **Subject:** Coronation of Frederik IV **Obv:** Bust of Frederik IV right **Rev:** Bust of Christian V right, A. Meibus F. below

Date	Mintage	VG	F	VF	XF	Unc
ND(1699) Unique	—	—	—	—	—	—

KM# 463 3 DUCAT

10.4710 g., 0.9790 Gold 0.3296 oz. AGW, 21 mm. **Subject:** Coronation of Frederik IV **Obv:** Bust right of Frederik IV **Rev:** Bust right of Christian V

Date	Mintage	VG	F	VF	XF	Unc
ND(1699) Rare	—	—	—	—	—	—

KM# 472 3 DUCAT

10.4710 g., 0.9790 Gold 0.3296 oz. AGW **Rev:** Crowned double F4 monograms, date below

Date	Mintage	VG	F	VF	XF	Unc
1700 Unique	—	—	—	—	—	—

KM# 217.1 4 DUCAT

13.9610 g., 0.9790 Gold 0.4394 oz. AGW **Obv:** Frederik III **Rev:** Ship **Rev. Legend:** VANDALOR: GOTHOR: Q: REX • **Note:** Size as 2 Ducat KM#216.1 but double thickness

Date	Mintage	VG	F	VF	XF	Unc
1657	—	5,000	8,500	12,500	16,500	—
1658 Unique	—	—	—	—	—	—

KM# 217.2 4 DUCAT

13.9610 g., 0.9790 Gold 0.4394 oz. AGW **Rev:** Ship **Rev. Legend:** DOMINVS • PROVIDEBIT

Date	Mintage	VG	F	VF	XF	Unc
1664 Rare	—	—	—	—	—	—

KM# 435 4 DUCAT

13.9610 g., 0.9790 Gold 0.4394 oz. AGW **Obv:** Crowned C5 monogram **Rev:** Elephant with litter on back, date in exergue

Date	Mintage	VG	F	VF	XF	Unc
1683 Unique	—	—	—	—	—	—

KM# 396 4 DUCAT

13.9610 g., 0.9790 Gold 0.4394 oz. AGW **Obv:** Draped bust of Christian V right in elaborate hat **Rev:** View of Christiansborg fortress in Guinea in inner circle

Date	Mintage	VG	F	VF	XF	Unc
1688 Rare	—	—	—	—	—	—

KM# 464 4 DUCAT

13.9610 g., 0.9790 Gold 0.4394 oz. AGW **Subject:** Coronation of Frederik IV **Obv:** Bust of Frederik IV right **Rev:** Bust of Christian V right **Note:** Similar to 1 Ducat, KM#456.

Date	Mintage	VG	F	VF	XF	Unc
ND(1699) Unique	—	—	—	—	—	—

KM# 219 5 DUCAT

17.4520 g., 0.9790 Gold 0.5493 oz. AGW **Obv:** Crowned arms divide date in inner circle **Rev:** Crowned F3 monogram above Norwegian arms in palms in inner circle

Date	Mintage	VG	F	VF	XF	Unc
1658 Unique	—	—	—	—	—	—

KM# 247 5 DUCAT

17.4520 g., 0.9790 Gold 0.5493 oz. AGW **Obv:** Crowned bust of Frederik III right in inner circle **Rev:** Crowned arms mounted on cross divides date in inner circle

Date	Mintage	VG	F	VF	XF	Unc
1662 Unique	—	—	—	—	—	—

KM# 201 5 DUCAT

17.4520 g., 0.9790 Gold 0.5493 oz. AGW **Obv:** Crowned bust extends to top edge **Note:** Similar to KM#244, but double thickness

Date	Mintage	VG	F	VF	XF	Unc
1662 Unique	—	—	—	—	—	—

KM# 253 5 DUCAT

17.4520 g., 0.9790 Gold 0.5493 oz. AGW **Obv:** Draped bust of Frederik III, right **Rev:** Crowned arms within legend and date **Note:** Similar to KM#260.

Date	Mintage	VG	F	VF	XF	Unc
1665 GK Rare	—	—	—	—	—	—

KM# 392 5 DUCAT

17.4520 g., 0.9790 Gold 0.5493 oz. AGW **Obv:** Bust of Christian V right **Rev:** Crowned round arms in circle of 15 shields, date divided near top

Date	Mintage	VG	F	VF	XF	Unc
1687 Unique	—	—	—	—	—	—

KM# 420 5 DUCAT

17.4520 g., 0.9790 Gold 0.5493 oz. AGW **Obv:** Laureate bust of Christian V right **Rev:** Three crowned C5 monograms surround radiant triangle

Date	Mintage	VG	F	VF	XF	Unc
1692 Unique	—	—	—	—	—	—

KM# 314 10 DUCAT

34.9040 g., 0.9790 Gold 1.0986 oz. AGW **Obv:** Draped and laureate bust of Federik III right **Rev:** Crown above three shields in circle of 15 shields **Edge Lettering:** DOMINVS PROVEDEBIT.ANNO.MDCLXIX

Date	Mintage	VG	F	VF	XF	Unc
1669 Unique	—	—	—	—	—	—

KM# A315 10 DUCAT

34.9040 g., 0.9790 Gold 1.0986 oz. AGW **Note:** Similar to 1 Krone, KM#428.1. Previous KM#315.

Date	Mintage	VG	F	VF	XF	Unc
1693 Unique	—	—	—	—	—	—
1696 Unique	—	—	—	—	—	—

KM# 4 LION DALER

Silver **Obv:** King standing behind arms **Rev:** Norwegian arms within legend **Note:** Dav. #3515.

Date	Mintage	VG	F	VF	XF	Unc
1608	—	—	—	—	—	—

LARGESSE COINAGE

Largesse is defined as a generous giving. It became the practice to throw coins to the people at coronations and royal funerals, while more important persons were presented with medals to commemorate the occasion.

KM# 14 4 SOLIDI (4 Skilling)

Silver **Obv:** Elephant left **Rev:** Value and date within legend

Date	Mintage	Good	VG	F	VF	XF
1603	—	125	250	550	1,450	2,100

KM# 15 8 SOLIDI (8 skilling)

Silver **Obv:** Elephant left **Rev:** Value and date within legend

Date	Mintage	Good	VG	F	VF	XF
1603	—	150	300	600	1,600	2,250

KM# 159 1/12 SPECIE DALER

0.8810 Silver **Obv:** Frederik III **Rev:** Incense vase **Note:** Klippe.

Date	Mintage	Good	VG	F	VF	XF
1648	—	35.00	70.00	200	400	—

KM# 160 1/6 SPECIEDALER

0.8810 Silver **Obv:** Laureate bust of Frederik III right **Rev:** Vase with incence **Note:** Klippe.

Date	Mintage	Good	VG	F	VF	XF
1648	—	50.00	100	300	600	—

KM# 161 1/4 SPECIEDALER

9.3080 g., Silver **Obv:** Laureate bust of Frederik III right **Obv. Legend:** Jug **Rev:** Vase with incense **Note:** Klippe.

Date	Mintage	Good	VG	F	VF	XF
1648	—	45.00	160	380	900	—

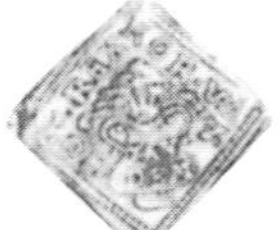

KM# 162 1/2 DUCAT

1.7450 g., 0.9790 Gold 0.0549 oz. AGW **Obv:** Frederik III **Rev:** Vase with incense **Note:** Klippe

Date	Mintage	VG	F	VF	XF	Unc
1648	—	700	1,200	2,200	4,000	—

KM# 163.1 DUCAT

3.4900 g., 0.9790 Gold 0.1098 oz. AGW **Obv:** Frederik III, small bust **Rev:** Vase with incense **Note:** Klippe

Date	Mintage	VG	F	VF	XF	Unc
1648	—	1,450	2,850	3,750	5,000	—

KM# 163.2 DUCAT

3.4900 g., 0.9790 Gold 0.1098 oz. AGW **Obv:** Frederik III, large bust **Rev:** Vase with incense **Note:** Klippe.

Date	Mintage	VG	F	VF	XF	Unc
1648	—	1,450	2,850	3,750	5,000	—

KM# 164 2 DUCAT

6.9800 g., 0.9790 Gold 0.2197 oz. AGW **Obv:** Laureate head of Frederik III right, date below **Rev:** Vase with incense **Note:** Klippe.

Date	Mintage	VG	F	VF	XF	Unc
1648	5	4,500	7,000	10,000	—	—

KM# 165 3 DUCAT

10.4710 g., 0.9790 Gold 0.3296 oz. AGW **Obv:** Laureate head of Frederik III right, date below **Rev:** Vase with incense **Note:** Klippe. Size as 2 Ducat, KM#164, but 1-1/2 times thickness.

Date	Mintage	VG	F	VF	XF	Unc
1648 Unique	5	—	—	—	—	—

KM# 166 4 DUCAT

13.9610 g., 0.9790 Gold 0.4394 oz. AGW **Obv:** Laureate head of Frederik III right, date below **Rev:** Vase with incense **Note:** Klippe. Size as 2 Ducat, KM#164, but twice thickness.

Date	Mintage	VG	F	VF	XF	Unc
1648 Unique	5	—	—	—	—	—

KM# 167 5 DUCAT

17.4520 g., 0.9790 Gold 0.5493 oz. AGW **Obv:** Laurreate head of Frederik III right, date below **Rev:** Vase with incense **Note:** Klippe. Size as 2 Ducat, KM#164. Planchet 2-1/2 times thickness.

Date	Mintage	VG	F	VF	XF	Unc
1648 Unique	5	—	—	—	—	—

TRADE COINAGE

Danish East India Co.

D.O.C. - Dansk Ostindisk Compagni

Originally formed in 1616 to develop trade and colonization in Asia and the East Indies under the protection of Christian IV. It was dissolved in 1634 and later reorganized in 1670 lasting until 1729 when it was closed due to its debts.

A few years later the company reorganized under the name, Danish Asiatic Company - D.A.C. Coins bearing these initials can be found listed under Tranquebar.

KM# 117 PIASTRE

27.1910 g., 0.9160 Silver 0.8007 oz. ASW **Obv:** Shield of arms on cross **Rev:** • R • F • P • above crown, date below

Date	Mintage	VG	F	VF	XF	Unc
1624 7 known	—	—	—	—	—	—

Note: Hoiland sale, 5-2006 realized $48,000.

KM# 317 SPECIEDALER

28.8930 g., 0.8750 Silver 0.8128 oz. ASW **Obv:** Armored bust with knot at shoulder, six laurel leaves **Rev:** Crowned C5 over crowned DOC monogram **Edge:** Plain **Note:** Dav. #409.

Date	Mintage	VG	F	VF	XF	Unc
1671 GK	—	—	2,800	4,000	6,000	—

KM# 318 SPECIEDALER

28.8930 g., 0.8750 Silver 0.8128 oz. ASW **Edge Lettering:** .PIETATE. ET. IUSTITIA. ANNO. MDCLXXI. **Note:** Dav. #409B.

Date	Mintage	VG	F	VF	XF	Unc
MDCLXXI (1671) GK 6 known	—	—	—	4,000	6,500	—

KM# 362 SPECIEDALER

28.8930 g., 0.8750 Silver 0.8128 oz. ASW **Obv:** Armored bust wearing Order of the Elephant **Note:** Dav. #410.

Date	Mintage	VG	F	VF	XF	Unc
1672 GK 10 known	—	—	—	5,500	8,000	—

KM# 319 SPECIEDALER

28.8930 g., 0.8750 Silver 0.8128 oz. ASW **Obv:** Modified armored bust with borach at shoulder, seven laurel leaves **Note:** Dav. #409A.

Date	Mintage	VG	F	VF	XF	Unc
1672 GK 5-6 known	—	—	—	5,000	7,500	—

KM# 363 2 SPECIEDALER

57.5500 g., 0.8750 Silver 1.6189 oz. ASW **Note:** Dav. #408. Similar to 1 Specidaler, KM#317.

Date	Mintage	VG	F	VF	XF	Unc
1671 Rare	—	—	—	—	—	—

PATTERNS

Including off metal strikes

KM#	Date	Mintage	Identification	Mkt Val
Pn1	ND(1606)	—	8 Skilling. Gold. 4.6500 g. off metal strike in gold	—

KM#	Date	Mintage	Identification	Mkt Val
Pn2	ND	—	Mark. Gold. 10.7500 g. off metal strike in gold	—
Pn3	ND	—	Mark. Gold. 8.0800 g. off metal strike in gold	—

KM#	Date	Mintage	Identification	Mkt Val
Pn4	ND	—	1/2 Speciedaler. Gold. 22.6400 g. off metal strike in gold	—
Pn5	1608	—	Sovereign. 10.0000 g.	—
PnA5	1619	—	Hvid. Copper. Crowned C4. Value and date within square border. Prev. Km#64.	—
Pn6	1629	—	Rosenobel. Silver. KM#51.	—
Pn7	1629	—	1/4 Portugaloser. Silver. KM#114	—
PnA8	1644	—	20 Skilling. Silver.	4,000
PnB8	1644	—	20 Skilling. Silver. Without value.	—
Pn8	ND	—	2 Ducat. Silver. KM#327	—
Pn10	1653	—	5 Ducat. Gold. 17.0000 g.	—
Pn11	1653	—	10 Ducat. Gold. 34.0000 g.	—
Pn13	1655	—	5 Ducat. Gold. 17.0000 g. KM#204	—
Pn14	1656	—	5 Ducat. Gold. 17.0000 g. KM#204	—
Pn15	1659	—	Krone. Silver.	3,200
PnA16	1659	—	3 Ducat. Gold. KM#221	—
PnB16	1659	—	3 Ducat. Gold. KM#223	—
PnC16	1659	—	4 Ducat. Gold. KM#221	—
PnD16	1659	—	4 Ducat. Gold. KM#223	—
PnE16	1659	—	6 Ducat. Gold. KM#221	—
PnF16	1659	—	6 Ducat. Gold. KM#223	—

KM#	Date	Mintage	Identification	Mkt Val
PnG16	1659	—	5 Ducat. Gold. KM#223	—
PnH16	1659	—	10 Ducat. Gold. KM#223	—
PnI16	1659	—	20 Ducat. Gold. KM#223	—
PnJ16	1659	—	5 Ducat. Gold. KM#221	—
Pn16	1664	—	1/4 Ducat. Silver. KM#235	—
PnA17	1619	—	Hvid. Copper. Like KM#64.	—
Pn17	1665	—	1/2 Ducat. Silver. 1.4700 g.	—
Pn18	1669	—	10 Ducat. Silver. KM#314	—
Pn19	ND	—	10 Ducat. Silver. KM#314	—
Pn20	1670	—	Ducat. Silver. KM#313	—
Pn21	1672	—	Ducat. Silver. KM#340	—
Pn22	ND	—	Ducat. Silver. Equestrian figure of Christian V right.	—
Pn23	ND	—	Ducat. Silver. Equestrian figure of Christian V left.	—
Pn24	1673	—	2 Ducat. Silver. KM#346	—
Pn25	ND	—	2 Ducat. Silver. KM#347	—

KM#	Date	Mintage	Identification	Mkt Val
Pn26	ND	—	Ducat. Silver. KM#445	—
Pn27	ND	—	Ducat. Silver. KM#454	—
Pn28	1683	—	4 Ducat. Silver. KM#453	—
Pn29	1687	—	2 Ducat. Silver. KM#390	—
Pn30	1689	—	Krone. Gold. 34.7000 g.	—
Pn31	1691	—	Ducat. Copper.	—
Pn32	1693	—	Krone. Silver. KM#428.2; Roman numeral date.	—
Pn33	1696	—	Ducat. Silver. KM#433	—
Pn34	1696	—	Ducat. Silver. Equestrian figure of Christian V left.	—
Pn35	ND	—	1/2 Ducat. Silver. KM#454	—
Pn36	ND(1699)	—	Ducat. Silver. KM#456	—
Pn37	ND(1699)	—	3 Ducat. Silver. KM#462	—
Pn38	1699	—	Krone. Gold. 17.0000 g. KM#448	40,000
Pn39	1699	—	Krone. Gold. 34.0000 g. KM#448	—
Pn40	1700	—	Krone. Gold. 17.0000 g. KM#448	—
Pn41	1700	—	Ducat. Silver. KM#471	—

GLUCKSTADT

DUCHY

WIRE MONEY COINAGE

Authorized by Christian IV in 1619, the denning was to be used for trade in the Petsori River region of russia by the Petsori Company. Fashioned after Russian silver wire-kopeks, dennings may have been considered counterfeits.

KM# 5.1 DENNING

0.8880 Silver **Ruler:** Christian IV **Obv:** King on horseback, M below **Rev:** Titles of czar Mikhail Fjodorovitsj Romanov **Note:** Weight varies: .470-.510 grams. Actual silver weight varies: .0134-.0146.

Date	Mintage	Good	VG	F	VF	XF
ND(1619) Rare	—	—	—	—	—	—

KM# 5.2 DENNING

0.8880 Silver **Ruler:** Christian IV **Obv:** HCPI below horse **Note:** Weight varies: .470-.510 grams. Actual silver weight varies: .0134-.0146.

Date	Mintage	Good	VG	F	VF	XF
ND(c.1620) Rare	—	—	—	—	—	—

KM# 5.3 DENNING

0.8880 Silver **Ruler:** Christian IV **Rev:** Titles of czar Vasilij Ivanovitsj Shuskij **Note:** Weight varies: .470-.510 grams. Actual silver weight varies: .0134-.0146.

Date	Mintage	Good	VG	F	VF	XF
ND(c.1620) Rare	—	—	—	—	—	—

KM# 5.4 DENNING

0.8880 Silver **Ruler:** Christian IV **Rev:** Titles of czar Boris Fjodorovitsj Gudonov **Note:** Weight varies: .470-.510 grams. Actual silver weight varies: .0134-.0146.

Date	Mintage	Good	VG	F	VF	XF
ND(c.1620) Rare	—	—	—	—	—	—

KM# 5.5 DENNING

0.8880 Silver **Ruler:** Christian IV **Rev:** Titles of (imposter) czar Dimitri Ivanovitsj **Note:** Weight varies: .470-.510 grams. Actual silver weight varies: .0134-.0146.

Date	Mintage	Good	VG	F	VF	XF
ND(c.1620) Rare	—	—	—	—	—	—

KM# 6.1 DENNING

0.8880 Silver **Ruler:** Christian IV **Obv:** King on horseback, M below **Rev:** Titles of Christian IV in German **Note:** Weight varies: .470-.510 grams. Actual silver weight varies: .0134-.0146.

Date	Mintage	Good	VG	F	VF	XF
ND(c.1620) Rare	—	—	—	—	—	—

KM# 6.2 DENNING

0.8880 Silver **Ruler:** Christian IV **Obv:** Without M below horse **Note:** Weight varies: .470-.510 grams. Actual silver weight varies: .0134-.0146.

Date	Mintage	Good	VG	F	VF	XF
ND(c.1620) Rare	—	—	—	—	—	—

KM# 7 DENNING

0.8880 Silver **Ruler:** Christian IV **Obv:** King on horseback, M below **Rev:** Titles of Christian IV in Russian **Note:** Weight varies: .470-.510 grams. Actual silver weight varies: .0134-.0146.

Date	Mintage	Good	VG	F	VF	XF
ND(c.1620) Rare	—	—	—	—	—	—

KM# 8.1 2 SKILLING LYBSK (4 Skilling Dansk)

1.0080 g., 0.8880 Silver 0.0288 oz. ASW **Ruler:** Christian IV **Obv:** King on galloping horse right, open crown; value below: IISL **Rev:** Six-line inscription **Note:** Wire money.

Date	Mintage	Good	VG	F	VF	XF
ND(1620-23)	—	30.00	60.00	165	—	—

KM# 8.2 2 SKILLING LYBSK (4 Skilling Dansk)

1.0080 g., 0.8880 Silver 0.0288 oz. ASW **Ruler:** Christian IV **Obv:** Value as: 2SL **Note:** Wire money.

Date	Mintage	Good	VG	F	VF	XF
ND(1620-23)	—	22.50	45.00	120	—	—

KM# 8.3 2 SKILLING LYBSK (4 Skilling Dansk)

1.0080 g., 0.8880 Silver 0.0288 oz. ASW **Ruler:** Christian IV **Obv:** King on jumping horse. Value as: 2SL • **Note:** Wire money.

Date	Mintage	Good	VG	F	VF	XF
ND(1620-23)	—	20.00	40.00	110	—	—

KM# 8.4 2 SKILLING LYBSK (4 Skilling Dansk)

1.0080 g., 0.8880 Silver 0.0288 oz. ASW **Ruler:** Christian IV **Obv:** Value: • 2SL **Note:** Wire money.

Date	Mintage	Good	VG	F	VF	XF
ND(1620-23)	—	50.00	100	220	—	—

KM# 8.5 2 SKILLING LYBSK (4 Skilling Dansk)

1.0080 g., 0.8880 Silver 0.0288 oz. ASW **Ruler:** Christian IV **Obv:** Hing on horseback right, no crown. Value as: 2SL: **Note:** Wire money.

Date	Mintage	Good	VG	F	VF	XF
ND(1620-23)	—	30.00	60.00	180	—	—

KM# 8.6 2 SKILLING LYBSK (4 Skilling Dansk)

1.0080 g., 0.8880 Silver 0.0288 oz. ASW **Ruler:** Christian IV **Obv:** Value: ZSL **Note:** Wire money.

Date	Mintage	Good	VG	F	VF	XF
ND(1624)	—	20.00	40.00	80.00	160	—

KM# 9.1 4 SKILLING LYBSK

2.0160 g., 0.8880 Silver 0.0576 oz. ASW **Ruler:** Christian IV **Obv:** King on horseback right, open crown, value below as: 4 SL: **Rev:** Six-line inscription **Note:** Wire money.

Date	Mintage	Good	VG	F	VF	XF
ND(1620-23)	—	50.00	100	210	—	—

KM# 9.2 4 SKILLING LYBSK

2.0160 g., 0.8880 Silver 0.0576 oz. ASW **Ruler:** Christian IV **Obv:** King on horseback, closed crown. Value: 4 SL **Note:** Wire money.

Date	Mintage	Good	VG	F	VF	XF
ND(1624-30)	—	12.00	25.00	75.00	150	—

STANDARD COINAGE

KM# 10 SøSLING LYBSK

0.0630 g., 0.3310 Silver 0.0007 oz. ASW **Ruler:** Christian IV **Obv:** Crowned C4 monogram **Rev:** Value in four lines

Date	Mintage	Good	VG	F	VF	XF
(16)23	—	25.00	50.00	75.00	110	—
(16)24	—	5.00	11.00	18.00	120	—
(16)25	—	6.00	25.00	60.00	55.00	—

KM# 25 SøSLING LYBSK

0.7040 g., 0.3120 Silver 0.0071 oz. ASW **Ruler:** Christian IV **Obv:** Crowned C4 monogram, titles of Christian IV in legend **Rev:** Value in three lines, legend, date **Rev. Legend:** G: DAN: N: V: G: Q: REX:

Date	Mintage	Good	VG	F	VF	XF
1640	—	22.00	45.00	140	375	—
1641	—	25.00	50.00	150	400	—
1642	—	25.00	50.00	150	400	—
1643	—	25.00	50.00	150	400	—
1644	—	22.50	45.00	120	350	—
1645	—	22.50	45.00	120	350	—
1646	—	16.00	35.00	90.00	225	—
1647	—	16.00	35.00	90.00	225	—
1648 Unique	—	—	—	—	—	—

KM# 41 SøSLING LYBSK

0.7040 g., 0.3120 Silver 0.0071 oz. ASW **Ruler:** Frederik III **Obv:** Crowned F3 monogram, titles of Frederic III in legend

Date	Mintage	Good	VG	F	VF	XF
1658	—	35.00	70.00	180	380	—
1659	—	25.00	50.00	120	300	—
1660	—	22.50	45.00	110	275	—

KM# 81 SKILLING DANSKE (Sosling Libsk)

0.6830 g., 0.3050 Silver 0.0067 oz. ASW **Ruler:** Christian V **Obv:** Crowned F5 monogram divides date **Rev:** Value in three lines: I/SKILLING/DANSKE

Date	Mintage	Good	VG	F	VF	XF
1694	—	40.00	80.00	270	600	—

KM# 19 2 SKILLING DANSKE (Skilling Lybsk)

1.2990 g., 0.2800 Silver 0.0117 oz. ASW **Ruler:** Christian IV **Obv:** Crowned shield, titles of Christian IV in legend **Rev:** Value in three lines: II/SKILI/DANS, date in legend

Date	Mintage	Good	VG	F	VF	XF
1627	—	150	300	700	1,200	—

KM# 71 2 SKILLING DANSKE (Skilling Lybsk)

1.2990 g., 0.2800 Silver 0.0117 oz. ASW **Obv:** Titles of Christian V in legend

Date	Mintage	Good	VG	F	VF	XF
1681	—	15.00	37.50	80.00	200	—

KM# 78 2 SKILLING DANSKE (Skilling Lybsk)

1.2240 g., 0.3430 Silver 0.0135 oz. ASW **Obv:** Crowned C5 monogram divides date **Rev:** Value in three lines: II/ SKILLING/ DANSKE

Date	Mintage	Good	VG	F	VF	XF
1693	—	9.00	16.00	50.00	120	—
1694	—	5.50	12.00	40.00	100	—

KM# 79 4 SKILLING DANSKE (2 Skilling Lybsk)

1.9510 g., 0.4370 Silver 0.0274 oz. ASW **Obv:** Crowned C5 monogram divides date **Rev:** Crowned, ornamented oval arms, value in legend: IIII • SKILLING • DANSKE •

Date	Mintage	Good	VG	F	VF	XF
1693	—	6.00	12.00	30.00	80.00	—
1694	—	6.00	18.00	37.50	90.00	—

KM# 82.1 8 SKILLING DANSKE (4 Skilling Lybsk)

3.0570 g., 0.5620 Silver 0.0552 oz. ASW **Obv:** Crowned C5 monogram, legend reads counter clockwise from top **Obv. Legend:** PIETATE IVSTITIA **Rev:** Value in three lines: VIII/ SKILLING/ DANSKE, date below

Date	Mintage	Good	VG	F	VF	XF
1694	—	100	200	300	400	—

KM# 82.2 8 SKILLING DANSKE (4 Skilling Lybsk)

3.0570 g., 0.5620 Silver 0.0552 oz. ASW **Obv:** Legend reads clockwise from top **Obv. Legend:** PIETATE IVSTITIA

Date	Mintage	Good	VG	F	VF	XF
1694	—	5.00	9.00	30.00	65.00	—
1695	—	5.00	9.00	30.00	65.00	—
1697	—	15.00	30.00	60.00	165	—

KM# 31 3 SKILLING LYBSK

1.7850 g., 0.8120 Silver 0.0466 oz. ASW **Ruler:** Christian IV **Rev:** III/SCHIL/LING/GL in circle

Date	Mintage	Good	VG	F	VF	XF
1644	—	15.00	30.00	60.00	110	—

KM# 18 6 SKILLING LYBSK

2.9230 g., 0.8880 Silver 0.0834 oz. ASW **Ruler:** Christian IV **Obv:** Crowned C4 monogram **Rev:** Value, date

Date	Mintage	Good	VG	F	VF	XF
1625	—	150	300	700	1,400	—

KM# 30.1 8 SKILLING LYBSK (Mark Dansk)

4.8720 g., 0.8120 Silver 0.1272 oz. ASW **Ruler:** Christian IV **Obv:** Crowned bust right, curved shield below **Rev:** Fortuna standing on globe with banner divides date

Date	Mintage	Good	VG	F	VF	XF
1641 (p)	—	90.00	170	400	975	—
1642 (p)	—	100	200	500	1,100	—
1645 (q)	—	400	800	1,200	1,500	—

KM# 30.2 8 SKILLING LYBSK (Mark Dansk)

4.8720 g., 0.8120 Silver 0.1272 oz. ASW **Ruler:** Christian IV **Obv:** Shield with flat top and straight sides

Date	Mintage	Good	VG	F	VF	XF
1642	—	60.00	120	380	800	—

KM# A4 MARK DANSKE (8 Skilling Lybsk)

8.3520 g., 0.5900 Silver 0.1584 oz. ASW **Obv:** 1/2 figure of Christian IV right, date in legend **Rev:** Value: • I • /MARCK/ DANSKE above shield in inner circle

Date	Mintage	Good	VG	F	VF	XF
1617 Rare	—	—	—	—	—	—
1627	—	120	225	475	1,000	—
1628	—	100	180	420	800	—
1629	—	125	400	800	1,200	—

KM# 32 2 MARK DANSKE

11.1360 g., 0.5930 Silver 0.2123 oz. ASW **Ruler:** Christian IV **Obv:** Crowned C4 monogram **Rev:** Three-line Hebrew inscription

Date	Mintage	Good	VG	F	VF	XF
1645	—	20.00	60.00	150	380	—

KM# 65 2 MARK DANSKE

11.1360 g., 0.6710 Silver 0.2402 oz. ASW **Ruler:** Christian V **Obv:** Crowned C5 monogram **Rev:** Crowned shield on cross, value and date in outer legend

Date	Mintage	Good	VG	F	VF	XF
1679	—	130	250	425	750	—
1680	—	200	400	700	1,050	—
1681	—	155	325	600	900	—
1682	—	115	225	400	650	—

KM# 80.1 2 MARK DANSKE

11.1360 g., 0.6710 Silver 0.2402 oz. ASW **Ruler:** Christian V **Obv:** Crowned double C5 monogram in palm leaves **Rev:** Crowned, ornamented oval shield on cross divides date below, value: II • MARCKE • DANSKE in legend

Date	Mintage	Good	VG	F	VF	XF
1693	—	60.00	120	220	480	—
1694	—	90.00	180	325	775	—

KM# 80.2 2 MARK DANSKE
11.1360 g., 0.6710 Silver 0.2402 oz. ASW **Ruler:** Christian V **Obv:** Smaller monogram with laurel branches

Date	Mintage	Good	VG	F	VF	XF
1694	—	80.00	160	290	520	—
1696	—	110	190	375	775	—

KM# 63 4 MARK DANSKE (Krone)
22.2720 g., 0.6710 Silver 0.4805 oz. ASW **Ruler:** Christian V **Obv:** Crowned C5 monogram, king's motto in legend **Rev:** Crowned shield on cross, date and value in legend **Note:** Dav. #3678.

Date	Mintage	Good	VG	F	VF	XF
1671	—	50.00	100	175	360	—
1672	—	35.00	65.00	120	300	—
1673	—	35.00	65.00	120	280	—
1677	—	45.00	95.00	170	350	—
1679	—	35.00	70.00	140	280	—
1680	—	40.00	85.00	165	340	—
1681	—	40.00	80.00	150	335	—
1682	—	35.00	70.00	130	330	—

KM# 77.1 4 MARK DANSKE (Krone)
22.2720 g., 0.6710 Silver 0.4805 oz. ASW **Ruler:** Christian V **Obv:** Crowned double C5 monogram in palm leaves **Rev:** Crowned, ornamented oval shield on cross with Order of the Elephant sash, value and date in legend **Note:** Dav. #3679.

Date	Mintage	Good	VG	F	VF	XF
1692	—	40.00	80.00	170	370	—
1693	—	35.00	70.00	140	265	—
1694	—	35.00	70.00	140	280	—

KM# 77.2 4 MARK DANSKE (Krone)
22.2720 g., 0.6710 Silver 0.4805 oz. ASW **Ruler:** Christian V **Rev:** Crowned, ornamented oval shield on cross with Order of the Elephant sash, date below shield

Date	Mintage	Good	VG	F	VF	XF
1693	—	35.00	70.00	160	300	—

KM# 80 4 MARK DANSKE (Krone)
22.2720 g., 0.6710 Silver 0.4805 oz. ASW **Ruler:** Christian V **Obv:** Crowned double C5 monogram in laurel branches **Rev:** Crowned, cartouched, oval shield on cross with Order of the Elephant, value and date in legend **Note:** Dav. #3680.

Date	Mintage	Good	VG	F	VF	XF
1694	—	80.00	130	300	550	—
1695	—	80.00	150	320	500	—
1696	—	90.00	130	400	625	—

KM# A43 4 MARK DANSKE (Krone)
Silver **Ruler:** Frederik III **Obv:** Crowned F3 monogram **Rev:** Crowned arms divide date

Date	Mintage	Good	VG	F	VF	XF
1659 Rare	—	—	—	—	—	—
1660	—	85.00	150	275	500	—

KM# B43 4 MARK DANSKE (Krone)
Silver **Ruler:** Frederik III **Obv:** Crowned F 3 monogram **Rev:** Crowned arms, date in legend

Date	Mintage	Good	VG	F	VF	XF
1659	—	50.00	100	170	260	—
1660	—	60.00	115	190	285	—

KM# 11 1/16 SPECIEDALER (3 Skilling Lybsk)
1.4610 g., 0.8880 Silver 0.0417 oz. ASW **Ruler:** Christian IV **Obv:** Crowned C4 monogram, 16 in cartouche **Rev:** Fortuna standing on globe, holding banner

Date	Mintage	Good	VG	F	VF	XF
ND	—	25.00	60.00	135	225	—
1623	—	10.00	20.00	42.50	120	—
1624	—	12.00	22.50	45.00	140	—
1625	—	15.00	27.50	50.00	150	—

KM# 26 1/16 SPECIEDALER (3 Skilling Lybsk)
1.7850 g., 0.8120 Silver 0.0466 oz. ASW **Ruler:** Christian IV **Obv:** Crowned bust right **Rev:** Value within legend **Rev. Legend:** MON NOV GLUCKST **Note:** Varieties exist.

Date	Mintage	Good	VG	F	VF	XF
1640 (p)	—	35.00	70.00	180	380	—
1641 (p)	—	35.00	70.00	170	360	—
1642 (p)	—	20.00	40.00	80.00	200	—
1643 (p)	—	15.00	30.00	50.00	160	—
1645 (q)	—	17.50	35.00	65.00	200	—
1646 (q)	—	20.00	40.00	75.00	220	—
1647 (q)	—	30.00	60.00	120	340	—

KM# 42.1 1/16 SPECIEDALER (3 Skilling Lybsk)
1.7850 g., 0.8120 Silver 0.0466 oz. ASW **Ruler:** Frederik III **Obv:** Elongated crowned bust right of Frederick III **Obv. Legend:** FRIDERIC • 3...

Date	Mintage	Good	VG	F	VF	XF
1658	—	25.00	50.00	100	280	—
1659	—	20.00	40.00	85.00	240	—

KM# 42.2 1/16 SPECIEDALER (3 Skilling Lybsk)
1.7850 g., 0.8120 Silver 0.0466 oz. ASW **Ruler:** Frederik III **Obv:** Wide bust, crown suspended above head

Date	Mintage	Good	VG	F	VF	XF
1658	—	25.00	55.00	120	300	—

KM# 42.3 1/16 SPECIEDALER (3 Skilling Lybsk)
1.7850 g., 0.8120 Silver 0.0466 oz. ASW **Ruler:** Frederik III **Obv:** Small bust, crown on head

Date	Mintage	Good	VG	F	VF	XF
1658	—	40.00	80.00	140	350	—

KM# 42.4 1/16 SPECIEDALER (3 Skilling Lybsk)
1.7850 g., 0.8120 Silver 0.0466 oz. ASW **Ruler:** Frederik III **Obv:** Large bust **Obv. Legend:** FRIDERIC • III •...

Date	Mintage	Good	VG	F	VF	XF
1660 Rare	—	—	—	—	—	—

KM# 54.1 1/16 SPECIEDALER (3 Skilling Lybsk)
1.7850 g., 0.8120 Silver 0.0466 oz. ASW **Obv:** Realistic crowned bust right **Rev:** Value: XVI/ E • REIC/ HS • THA

Date	Mintage	Good	VG	F	VF	XF
1665	—	15.00	32.50	62.50	150	—
1666	—	10.00	20.00	40.00	85.00	—
1667	—	15.00	37.50	90.00	240	—
1669 Rare	—	—	—	—	—	—

KM# 54.2 1/16 SPECIEDALER (3 Skilling Lybsk)
1.7850 g., 0.8120 Silver 0.0466 oz. ASW **Rev:** Value: • XVI/ • E: REIC/HS • DAL

Date	Mintage	Good	VG	F	VF	XF
1665	—	12.50	25.00	40.00	140	—

KM# 57 1/16 SPECIEDALER (3 Skilling Lybsk)
1.7850 g., 0.8120 Silver 0.0466 oz. ASW **Ruler:** Frederik III **Obv:** Armored bust of Frederic III **Rev:** Date in center legend

Date	Mintage	Good	VG	F	VF	XF
1667	—	9.00	18.50	35.00	100	—
1668	—	9.00	18.50	35.00	100	—
1669	—	12.00	22.50	50.00	120	—
1670	—	100	200	400	—	—

KM# 69 1/16 SPECIEDALER (3 Skilling Lybsk)
1.7850 g., 0.8120 Silver 0.0466 oz. ASW **Ruler:** Christian V **Obv:** Crowned bust of Christian right

Date	Mintage	Good	VG	F	VF	XF
1680	—	500	1,000	1,500	3,000	—

KM# 12 1/8 SPECIEDALER
Silver **Ruler:** Christian IV **Obv:** Crowned C4 monogram **Rev:** Fortuna standing on globe, holding banner

Date	Mintage	Good	VG	F	VF	XF
1623 Rare	—	—	—	—	—	—

KM# 55 1/8 SPECIEDALER
3.5700 g., 0.8120 Gold 0.0932 oz. AGW **Obv:** Crowned bust right **Rev:** Value: • VIII • / EINEN / REICHS / DALER • in inner circle, date below

Date	Mintage	Good	VG	F	VF	XF
1665	—	150	300	900	2,400	—

KM# 13 1/4 SPECIEDALER
Silver **Ruler:** Christian IV **Obv:** Crowned C4 monogram **Rev:** Fortuna standing on globe, holding banner

Date	Mintage	Good	VG	F	VF	XF
1623	—	1,000	1,600	3,000	5,000	—

KM# 33 1/4 SPECIEDALER
Silver **Ruler:** Christian IV **Obv:** Crowned bust right above square-topped shield **Rev:** Fortuna

Date	Mintage	Good	VG	F	VF	XF
1645	—	1,600	2,750	4,500	6,500	—

KM# 14 1/2 SPECIEDALER
0.8880 Silver **Ruler:** Christian IV **Obv:** Standing Fortuna right behind crowned shield **Rev:** Fortuna standing on globe, holding banner

Date	Mintage	Good	VG	F	VF	XF
(1)6Z3	—	400	800	1,500	3,250	—
(1)6Z5	—	1,500	2,500	3,250	4,500	—
(16)Z7 Unique	—	—	—	—	—	—

KM# 34 1/2 SPECIEDALER
0.8880 Silver **Ruler:** Christian IV **Obv:** Crowned bust right above square-topped shield

Date	Mintage	Good	VG	F	VF	XF
1645 IS	—	1,000	2,000	3,000	4,500	—
1646 IS	—	2,000	3,000	4,000	6,000	—

KM# 15 SPECIEDALER
Silver **Ruler:** Christian IV **Obv:** Lions in shield face right **Note:** Dav. #3668. Legend varieties exist.

Date	Mintage	Good	VG	F	VF	XF
16Z3	—	200	400	900	2,200	—
16Z4	—	250	500	1,050	2,350	—
16Z5	—	300	700	1,200	3,300	—
16Z7 Rare	—	—	—	—	—	—

KM# 20 SPECIEDALER
Silver **Ruler:** Christian IV **Obv:** Lions in shield face left **Note:** Dav. #3668D.

Date	Mintage	Good	VG	F	VF	XF
16Z9 Rare	—	—	—	—	—	—
1630 Unique	—	—	—	—	—	—

KM# 27 SPECIEDALER

Silver **Ruler:** Christian IV **Obv:** Crowned bust of King above Danish arms **Rev:** Fortuna with banner at left **Note:** Dav. #3670.

Date	Mintage	VG	F	VF	XF	Unc
1640 IS	—	1,000	1,900	4,750	7,000	—
1641 IS	—	1,500	2,500	5,000	7,500	—
1642 IS	—	1,000	1,900	4,750	7,000	—
1644 IS Rare	—	—	—	—	—	—
1645 IS	—	1,500	2,500	5,000	7,500	—
1646 IS	—	1,000	1,900	4,750	7,000	—
1647 IS	—	1,000	1,900	4,750	7,000	—
1648 IS Unique	—	—	—	—	—	—

KM# 43 SPECIEDALER

Silver **Ruler:** Frederik III **Obv:** King's bust divides legend at top **Rev:** Fortuna in laurel wreath **Note:** Dav. #3671.

Date	Mintage	VG	F	VF	XF	Unc
1659 Unique	—	—	—	—	—	—

KM# 44 SPECIEDALER

Silver **Ruler:** Frederik III **Obv:** Inner circle unbroken **Rev:** Inner circle unbroken **Note:** Dav. #3672.

Date	Mintage	VG	F	VF	XF	Unc
1659 Unique	—	—	—	—	—	—

KM# 45 SPECIEDALER

Silver **Ruler:** Frederik III **Obv:** Inner circle unbroken **Rev:** Fortuna in laurel wreath **Note:** Dav. #3672a.

Date	Mintage	VG	F	VF	XF	Unc
1659 Unique	—	—	—	—	—	—

KM# 51 SPECIEDALER

Silver **Ruler:** Frederik III **Obv:** Inner circle broken above and below **Rev:** Fortuna in laurel wreath **Note:** Dav. #3673.

Date	Mintage	VG	F	VF	XF	Unc
1664	—	3,750	6,250	9,500	—	—
1666 Rare	—	—	—	—	—	—

KM# 74.1 SPECIEDALER

Silver **Ruler:** Christian V **Obv:** Standing Christian V with scepter and globe **Rev:** Crowned double C5 monogram **Note:** Dav. #3676.

Date	Mintage	VG	F	VF	XF	Unc
ND(1682) Unique	—	—	—	—	—	—

KM# 74.2 SPECIEDALER

Silver **Ruler:** Christian V **Edge:** With inscription

Date	Mintage	VG	F	VF	XF	Unc
ND(1682)	—	2,000	3,500	7,000	10,000	—

KM# 73 SPECIEDALER

Silver **Ruler:** Christian V **Obv:** Bust of Christian V right **Rev:** Three crowned C5 monograms **Edge Lettering:** PIETATE-ET-JUSTITIA-ANNO-MDCLXXXIII - CW **Note:** Dav. #3677.

Date	Mintage	VG	F	VF	XF	Unc
MDCLXXXIII (1683)	—	2,000	4,000	7,000	12,000	—

KM# 16 2 SPECIEDALER

Silver **Ruler:** Christian IV **Note:** Similar to 1 Thaler, KM#15. Dav. #3667. Planchet is twice as thick.

Date	Mintage	Good	VG	F	VF	XF
1623	—	3,500	6,000	10,000	15,000	—

KM# 28 2 SPECIEDALER

Silver **Ruler:** Christian IV **Obv:** Crowned bust of King above Danish arms **Rev:** Fortuna with banner at left **Note:** Dav. #3669. Planchet is twice as thick.

Date	Mintage	Good	VG	F	VF	XF
1640 Rare	—	—	—	—	—	—
1641	—	2,000	3,500	5,000	8,000	—

KM# 17 3 SPECIEDALER

Silver **Ruler:** Christian IV **Note:** Similar to 1 Thaler, KM#15. Dav. #A3667. Planchet three times as thick.

Date	Mintage	Good	VG	F	VF	XF
1623 Unique	—	—	—	—	—	—

KM# 35 1/2 DUCAT

1.7450 g., 0.9790 Gold 0.0549 oz. AGW **Ruler:** Christian IV **Obv:** Christian IV standing right in inner circle **Rev:** Three-line inscription (one in Hebrew) above date

Date	Mintage	VG	F	VF	XF	Unc
1645 (q) Rare	—	—	—	—	—	—
1646 (q) Rare	—	—	—	—	—	—

KM# 36 DUCAT

3.5000 g., 0.9860 Gold 0.1109 oz. AGW **Ruler:** Christian IV **Rev:** Three-line inscription (one in Hebrew) above date

Date	Mintage	VG	F	VF	XF	Unc
1645 (q)	—	1,200	2,250	4,500	—	—
1646 (q) Unique	—	—	—	—	—	—

KM# 52 DUCAT

3.5000 g., 0.9860 Gold 0.1109 oz. AGW **Obv:** Crowned head of Frederic III right in inner circle **Rev:** Figure of fortune in branches, date in legend

Date	Mintage	VG	F	VF	XF	Unc
1664 Unique	—	—	—	—	—	—

KM# 64.2 DUCAT

3.5000 g., 0.9860 Gold 0.1109 oz. AGW **Obv:** Legend begins at upper right

Date	Mintage	VG	F	VF	XF	Unc
1672 Rare	—	—	—	—	—	—
1673 Rare	—	—	—	—	—	—

KM# 66 DUCAT

3.5000 g., 0.9860 Gold 0.1109 oz. AGW **Obv:** Laureate bust of Christian V right

Date	Mintage	VG	F	VF	XF	Unc
1679 Rare	—	—	—	—	—	—

KM# 70.1 DUCAT

3.5000 g., 0.9860 Gold 0.1109 oz. AGW **Obv:** Smaller, draped bust of Christian V to right

Date	Mintage	VG	F	VF	XF	Unc
1680	—	1,000	2,000	3,000	4,000	—
1685	—	1,400	2,500	3,800	5,000	—

KM# 70.2 DUCAT

3.5000 g., 0.9860 Gold 0.1109 oz. AGW **Obv:** Neck bare on draped bust

Date	Mintage	VG	F	VF	XF	Unc
1680	—	1,200	2,100	3,250	4,250	5,500

KM# 29 DUCAT

3.5000 g., 0.9860 Gold 0.1109 oz. AGW **Ruler:** Christian IV **Obv:** Christian IV standing with scepter and orb **Rev:** Four-line inscription in tablet, date below

Date	Mintage	VG	F	VF	XF	Unc
1640 Rare	—	—	—	—	—	—
1642 Unique	2,341	—	—	—	—	—
1646 IS	—	7,000	10,000	15,000	—	—

KM# 50 DUCAT

3.5000 g., 0.9860 Gold 0.1109 oz. AGW **Ruler:** Frederik III **Obv:** Laureate head of Frederik III right, date below head in inner circle **Rev:** Figure of fortune in branches **Note:** Struck at Gluckstadt Mint.

Date	Mintage	VG	F	VF	XF	Unc
1660 Rare	—	—	—	—	—	—

KM# 56 DUCAT

3.5000 g., 0.9860 Gold 0.1109 oz. AGW **Obv:** Crowned head of Frederic III right in inner circle **Rev:** Date at bottom

Date	Mintage	VG	F	VF	XF	Unc
1666 IW	—	1,100	1,900	4,000	8,200	—
1667 IW	—	2,600	4,300	5,500	9,000	—
1668 IW	—	3,250	5,500	7,500	10,000	—
1669 IW	—	2,600	4,300	5,500	9,000	—

KM# 64.1 DUCAT

3.5000 g., 0.9860 Gold 0.1109 oz. AGW **Obv:** Crowned bust of Christian V right, legend begins at lower left **Rev:** Three crowned C5 monograms entwined

Date	Mintage	VG	F	VF	XF	Unc
1672	—	1,250	2,400	3,250	5,000	—
1673	—	1,250	2,400	3,250	5,000	—
1674	—	1,000	2,000	2,800	4,000	—
1676	—	1,100	2,200	3,000	4,500	—

KM# 72 DUCAT

3.5000 g., 0.9860 Gold 0.1109 oz. AGW **Obv:** Christian V standing right **Rev:** Figure of Fortuna in branches

Date	Mintage	VG	F	VF	XF	Unc
1682	—	2,000	3,000	5,000	7,500	—

KM# 40.1 GOLD KRONE

2.9730 g., 0.9170 Gold 0.0876 oz. AGW **Ruler:** Frederik III **Obv:** Crowned, ornamented oval shield on cross, titles of Frederic III in legend **Rev:** Crown divides date in inner circle, motto: DOMINUS PROVIDEBIT below. Legend reads clockwise from lower left.

Date	Mintage	VG	F	VF	XF	Unc
1657 Rare	—	—	—	—	—	—
1659 Rare	—	—	—	—	—	—
1660	—	4,000	7,500	10,000	—	—

KM# 40.2 GOLD KRONE

2.9730 g., 0.9170 Gold 0.0876 oz. AGW **Ruler:** Frederik III **Obv:** Crowned, ornamented oval shield on cross **Rev:** Crown divides date in inner circle. Legend reads counter clockwise from upper right

Date	Mintage	VG	F	VF	XF	Unc
1660	—	2,000	5,000	8,000	—	—

PATTERNS

Including off metal strikes

KM#	Date	Mintage	Identification	Mkt Val
Pn1	1623	—	1/2 Speciedaler. Silver. 40 mm. Klippe, square.	—
Pn2	1623	—	Speciedaler. Silver. 47 mm. KM#15, square.	—
Pn3	1623	—	Speciedaler. Silver. 43 mm. KM#15, square.	—
Pn4	1624	—	Speciedaler. Silver. 48 mm. KM#15, square.	—
Pn5	1624	—	Speciedaler. Silver. 45 mm. KM#15, hexagonal.	—
Pn6	1624	—	Speciedaler. Silver. 47 mm. KM#15, hexagonal.	—
Pn7	1624	—	Speciedaler. Silver. 48 mm. KM#15, octagonal.	—

SANTO DOMINGO

(Hispaniola – Española)

The first coinage for circulation in Santo Domingo and other possessions in the New World was ordered by Fernando the Catholic on April 15, 1505 to be acquired from the Seville Mint. A second issue was acquired from the Burgos Mint.

RULERS

Ferdinand II & Elizabeth, 1479-1504
Charles & Johanna, 1516-1556
Philip II, 1556-1598
Philip III, 1598-1621
Philip IV, 1621-1665

MINT MARKS

B – Burgos
B-B – Burgos
S-S – Seville
SDo monogram – Santo Domingo

ASSAYERS' MARKS

F, oF – Francisco Rodriguez 1542-1578
X – Cristobal Medina 1578

SPANISH COLONIAL

COUNTERMARKED COINAGE

ca. 1651-52

The debasement of 4 and 8 Reales at the Potosi mint during 1625-1648 led to an investigation and the installation of new mint officials. The coinage that followed during 1649-1651 fell a little short of the required fineness and was recalled and given various countermarks, primarily done at Potosi.

KM# 1 7-1/2 REALES

27.0674 g., 0.8590 Silver 0.7475 oz. ASW **Ruler:** Philip I100 **Countermark:** Crowned S*D **Note:** Countermark in beaded circle on Potosi 8 Reales, KM#19.1b.

CM Date	Host Date	Good	VG	F	VF	XF
ND	ND(1649-51) o Rare	—	—	—	—	—

DUTCH GUIANA

Dutch Guiana, located on the north central coast of South America between Guyana and French Guiana has an area of 63,037 sq. mi. (163,270 sq. km.). The country is rich in minerals and forests, and self-sufficient in rice, the staple food crop.

Lieutenants of Amerigo Vespucci sighted the Guiana coast in 1499. Spanish explorers of the 16th century, disappointed at finding no gold, departed leaving the area to be settled by the British in 1652. The colony prospered and the Netherlands acquired it in 1667 in exchange for the Dutch rights in Nieuw Nederland (state of New York).

RULER

Dutch, until 1975

COLONY

HAMMERED COINAGE

KM# 1 DUIT

Copper **Obv:** Branch with 1 leaf above 1 **Rev:** Scroll-work above tree

Date	Mintage	Good	VG	F	VF	XF
1679	—	—	150	250	350	475

KM# 2 DUIT
Copper **Note:** Uniface.

Date	Mintage	Good	VG	F	VF	XF
1679	—	—	60.00	100	160	225

KM# 3 2 DUIT
Copper **Obv:** Parrot on branch with 2 leaves above 2 **Rev:** Ornamental tree

Date	Mintage	Good	VG	F	VF	XF
1679	—	—	75.00	115	200	300

KM# 4 2 DUIT
Copper **Note:** Uniface.

Date	Mintage	Good	VG	F	VF	XF
1679	—	—	45.00	75.00	125	200

KM# 5 4 DUIT
Copper **Obv:** Parrot on branch with 4 leaves above 4 **Rev:** Ornamental tree

Date	Mintage	Good	VG	F	VF	XF
1679	—	—	125	200	350	550

KM# 6 4 DUIT
Copper **Obv:** Branch with 3 leaves

Date	Mintage	Good	VG	F	VF	XF
1679	—	—	300	425	550	650

KM# 7 4 DUIT
Copper **Note:** Uniface.

Date	Mintage	Good	VG	F	VF	XF
1679	—	—	75.00	100	150	215

EGYPT

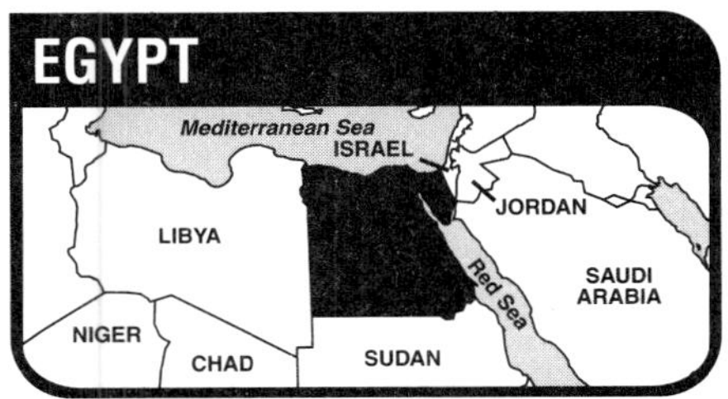

The Arab Republic of Egypt, located on the northeastern corner of Africa, has an area of 385,229 sq. mi. (1,1001,450 sq. km.). Although Egypt is an almost rainless expanse of desert, its economy is predominantly agricultural.

Egyptian history dates back to about 3000 B.C. when the empire was established by uniting the upper and lower kingdoms. Following its 'Golden Age' (16th to 13th centuries B.C.), Egypt was conquered by Persia (525 B.C.) and Alexander the Great (332 B.C.). The Ptolemies, descended from one of Alexander's generals, ruled until the suicide of Cleopatra (30 B.C.) when Egypt became the private domain of the Roman emperor, and subsequently part of the Byzantine world. Various Muslim dynasties ruled Egypt from 641 on, including Ayyubid Sultans to 1250 and Mamluks to 1517. It was then conquered by the Ottoman Turks, interrupted by the occupation of Napoleon (1798-1801). A semi-independent dynasty was founded by Muhammad Ali in 1805 which lasted until 1952

RULER
Ottoman, until 1882

MONETARY SYSTEM
40 Paras = 1 Qirsh (Piastre)

MINT MARKS
Egyptian coins issued prior to the advent of the British Protectorate series of Sultan Hussein Kamil introduced in 1916 were very similar to Turkish coins of the same period. They can best be distinguished by the presence of the Arabic word *Misr* Egypt) on the reverse, which generally appears immediately above the Muslim accession date of the ruler, which is presented in Arabic numerals. Each coin is individually dated according to the regnal years.

INITIAL LETTERS

Letters, symbols and numerals were placed on coins during the reigns of Mustafa II (1695) until Selim III (1789). They have been observed in various positions but the most common position being over *bin* in the third row of the obverse. In Egypt these letters and others used on the Paras (Medins) above the word *duribe* on the reverse during this period.

INITIAL LETTERS, NUMERALS

Alif ا i	ba ب ii	ha ح iii	ha ح iv	dal د v
ra ر vi	sin س vii	sad ص viii	(?) sm صم ix	ta ط x
tha ظ xi	'ain ع xii	(hamza) ء xiii	kaf ق xiv	mim م xv
noon ن xvi	noon w/o dot ں xvii	ha هو xviii	(?) ra ر xix	ah اح xx
es اس xxi	ba با xxii	bkr بكر xxiii	ha حا xxiv	raa را xxv
ragib راغب xxvi	sma سما xxvii	msi مسي xxviii	'aa عا xxvix	gha غا xxx
'ab عب xxxi	'abd عبد xxxii	'ad عد xxxiii	'an عن xxxiv	md مد xxxv
mr مر xxxvi	mk مط xxxvii	mdm مصر xxxviii	mha مها xxxix	ha ده xl
ya يا xli	42a ١٣٤ xlii	md6 مد٦ xliii	6md ٦مد xliv	6mdm ٦مصر xlv

REGNAL YEAR IDENTIFICATION

Misr **Accession Date**

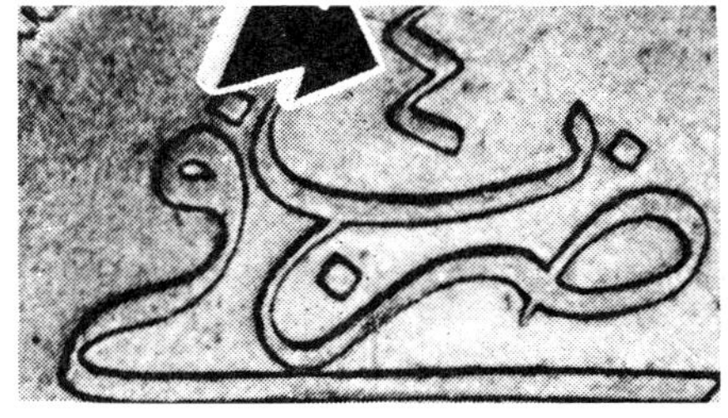

4
Duriba fi

OTTOMAN EMPIRE
1595 - 1914AD

Mehmed III
AH1003-1012/1595-1603AD

HAMMERED COINAGE

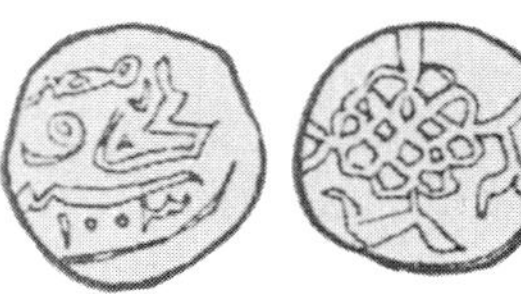

KM# 3 MANGIR
9.4000 g., Copper **Mint:** Misr

Date	Mintage	Good	VG	F	VF	XF
AH1003	—	10.00	15.00	40.00	70.00	—
AH1011 Ornament	—	—	—	—	—	—

KM# 5 AKCE
0.4500 g., Silver **Mint:** Misr

Date	Mintage	Good	VG	F	VF	XF
AH1003	—	15.00	25.00	45.00	75.00	—

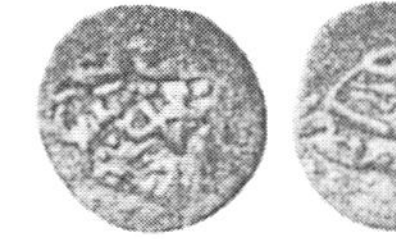

KM# 4 MEDIN
1.0000 g., Silver **Mint:** Misr

Date	Mintage	Good	VG	F	VF	XF
AH1003	—	20.00	30.00	50.00	80.00	—

KM# 6 SULTANI
3.4500 g., Gold **Mint:** Misr

Date	Mintage	VG	F	VF	XF	Unc
AH1003	—	BV	120	175	250	—

Ahmed I
AH1012-1026/1603-1617AD

HAMMERED COINAGE

KM# 8 MANGIR
Copper **Mint:** Misr

Date	Mintage	Good	VG	F	VF	XF
AH1012	—	—	—	—	—	—

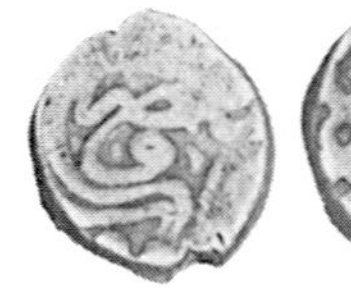
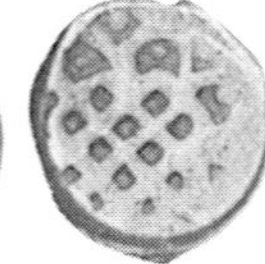

KM# 9 MANGIR
Copper **Mint:** Misr

Date	Mintage	Good	VG	F	VF	XF
AH1012	—	8.00	20.00	30.00	50.00	—
AH1013 Rare	—	—	—	—	—	—

KM# 12 AKCE
0.5000 g., Silver **Mint:** Misr

Date	Mintage	VG	F	VF	XF	Unc
AH1012	—	4.00	10.00	35.00	50.00	—

KM# 15 MEDIN
Silver **Mint:** Misr **Note:** Size varies: 14-17mm. Weight varies: 0.83-1.00 grams.

Date	Mintage	VG	F	VF	XF	Unc
AH1012	—	10.00	20.00	30.00	50.00	—

KM# 18 ALTIN
Gold **Mint:** Misr **Note:** Weight varies: 3.45-3.50 grams.

Date	Mintage	VG	F	VF	XF	Unc
AH1012	—	BV	125	200	300	—
AH1013	—	BV	125	200	300	—
AH1014	—	BV	125	200	300	—
AH1015	—	BV	125	200	300	—

Mustafa I
First Reign, AH1026-1027/1617-1618AD
HAMMERED COINAGE

KM# 28 ALTIN
Gold **Obv:** Large legend **Rev:** Large legend **Mint:** Misr **Note:** Weight varies: 3.20-3.45 grams.

Date	Mintage	VG	F	VF	XF	Unc
AH1026	—	750	1,500	3,000	5,000	—

Osman II
AH1027-1031/1618-1622AD
HAMMERED COINAGE

KM# 31 AKCE
Silver **Mint:** Misr **Note:** Weight varies: 0.28-0.36 grams.

Date	Mintage	F	VF	XF	Unc	BU
AH1027	—	25.00	45.00	75.00	—	—

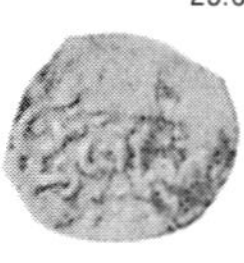

KM# 32 MEDIN
0.9200 g., Silver **Mint:** Misr

Date	Mintage	VG	F	VF	XF	Unc
AH1027	—	15.00	25.00	35.00	55.00	—

KM# 33 MEDIN
0.9200 g., Silver **Obv:** KM#32 **Rev:** KM#15 **Mint:** Misr **Note:** Weight varies: 0.80-0.98 grams. Mule.

Date	Mintage	VG	F	VF	XF	Unc
AH1012 (sic 1618)	—	15.00	25.00	35.00	55.00	—

KM# 34 ALTIN
3.5000 g., Gold **Mint:** Misr

Date	Mintage	VG	F	VF	XF	Unc
AH1027	—	300	1,000	1,500	2,000	—

Mustafa I
Second Reign, AH1031-1032/1622-1623AD
HAMMERED COINAGE

KM# 21 AKCE
0.3200 g., Silver **Mint:** Misr

Date	Mintage	VG	F	VF	XF	Unc
AH1031	—	15.00	25.00	40.00	65.00	—

KM# 26 MEDIN
Silver, 14 mm. **Mint:** Misr **Note:** Weight varies: 0.80-0.96 grams.

Date	Mintage	VG	F	VF	XF	Unc
AH1031	—	20.00	30.00	50.00	80.00	—
AH1032 (sic)	—	—	—	—	—	—

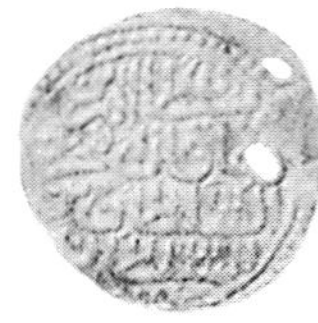

KM# 29 ALTIN
Gold **Obv:** Small legend **Rev:** Small legend **Mint:** Misr **Note:** Weight varies: 3.20-3.45 grams.

Date	Mintage	VG	F	VF	XF	Unc
AH1031	—	400	1,000	2,000	3,000	—

Murad IV
AH1032-49/1623-1640AD
HAMMERED COINAGE

KM# 36 AKCE
0.3500 g., Silver **Mint:** Misr

Date	Mintage	VG	F	VF	XF	Unc
AH1032	—	10.00	20.00	30.00	45.00	—

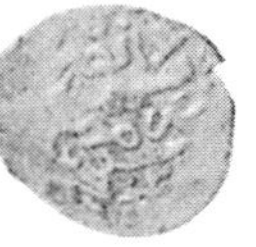

KM# 38 MEDIN
0.8500 g., Silver **Mint:** Misr

Date	Mintage	VG	F	VF	XF	Unc
AH1031 (sic)	—	—	—	—	—	—
AH1032	—	10.00	20.00	35.00	50.00	—

KM# 40 ALTIN
3.2000 g., Gold **Mint:** Misr

Date	Mintage	VG	F	VF	XF	Unc
AH1032	—	BV	200	300	400	—

Ibrahim
AH1049-1058/1640-1648AD
HAMMERED COINAGE

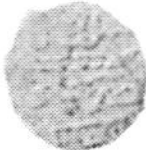

KM# 42 AKCE
Silver **Mint:** Misr **Note:** Weight varies: 0.18-0.32 grams.

Date	Mintage	VG	F	VF	XF	Unc
AH1049	—	15.00	25.00	35.00	55.00	—

KM# 48 ONLUK
2.9800 g., Silver **Mint:** Misr

Date	Mintage	VG	F	VF	XF	Unc
AH1058	—	35.00	80.00	150	250	—

KM# 43 MEDIN
2.9800 g., Silver **Mint:** Misr **Note:** Weight varies: 0.68-0.75 grams.

Date	Mintage	VG	F	VF	XF	Unc
AH1049	—	15.00	25.00	35.00	55.00	—

KM# 44 ALTIN
3.4500 g., Gold **Mint:** Misr

Date	Mintage	VG	F	VF	XF	Unc
AH1049	—	150	250	350	500	—

Mehmed IV
AH1058-1099/1648-1687AD
HAMMERED COINAGE

KM# 46 AKCE
0.3100 g., Silver, 13 mm. **Mint:** Misr

Date	Mintage	VG	F	VF	XF	Unc
AH1058	—	15.00	25.00	40.00	65.00	—

KM# 47 MEDIN
Silver **Mint:** Misr **Note:** Weight varies: 0.58-0.78 grams.

Date	Mintage	VG	F	VF	XF	Unc
AH1058	—	10.00	15.00	25.00	40.00	—

KM# 49 ALTIN
3.5000 g., Gold **Mint:** Misr

Date	Mintage	VG	F	VF	XF	Unc
AH1058	—	BV	175	300	500	—

Suleyman II
AH1099-1102/1687-1691AD
HAMMERED COINAGE

KM# 51 MEDIN
0.6900 g., Silver **Mint:** Misr

Date	Mintage	VG	F	VF	XF	Unc
AH1099	—	—	—	—	—	—

KM# 53 SHERIFI ALTIN
3.4000 g., Gold **Mint:** Misr

Date	Mintage	VG	F	VF	XF	Unc
AH1099	—	85.00	150	250	350	—

Ahmed II
AH1102-1106/1691-1695AD
HAMMERED COINAGE

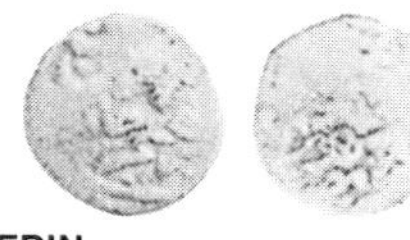

KM# 55 MEDIN
0.5700 g., Silver **Mint:** Misr

Date	Mintage	VG	F	VF	XF	Unc
AH1102	—	15.00	25.00	40.00	75.00	—

KM# 57 SHERIFI ALTIN
3.4000 g., Gold **Mint:** Misr

Date	Mintage	VG	F	VF	XF	Unc
AH1102	—	100	200	300	500	—

Mustafa II
AH1106-15/1695-1703AD
HAMMERED COINAGE

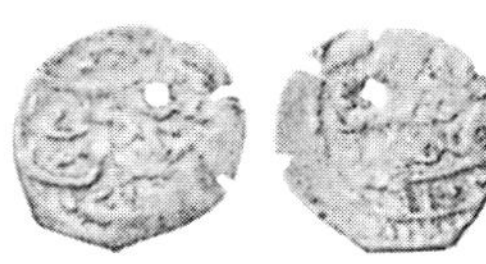

KM# 60 PARA
0.6500 g., Silver **Mint:** Misr

Date	Mintage	VG	F	VF	XF	Unc
AH1106	—	12.00	25.00	40.00	65.00	—

KM# 62 SHERIFI ALTIN
3.2000 g., Gold **Mint:** Misr

Date	Mintage	VG	F	VF	XF	Unc
AH1106	—	100	200	300	450	—

KM# 63 JEDID ESHREFI ALTIN
3.2500 g., Gold, 17-20 mm. **Obv:** Tughra **Rev:** Mint name **Mint:** Misr

Date	Mintage	VG	F	VF	XF	Unc
AH1109	—	75.00	150	250	400	—

This small and ancient Baltic state had enjoyed but two decades of independence since the 13th century until the present time. After having been conquered by the Danes, the Livonian Knights, the Teutonic Knights of Germany (who reduced the people to serfdom), the Swedes, the Poles and Russia, Estonia declared itself an independent republic on Feb. 24, 1918 but was not freed until Feb. 1919. The peace treaty was signed Feb. 2, 1920. Shortly after the start of World War II, it was again occupied by Russia and incorporated as the 16th state of the U.S.S.R Germany occupied the tiny state from 1941 to 1944, after which it was retaken by Russia. Most of the nations of the world, including the United States and Great Britain, did not recognize Estonia's incorporation into the Soviet Union.

The coinage, issued during the country's brief independence, is obsolete.

NARVA

This city was founded by the Danes in 1223. It was a center for the Livonian knights and a member of the Hanseatic League. Captured by the Swedes in 1581, and then recaptured by the Russians in 1704, it was ceded to them by the Treaty of Nystad in 1721. Narva continues to be an important industrial center.

RULERS
Swedish

MONEYERS' INITIALS

Initial	Date	Name
LN	1670-72	Lewin von Numers

SWEDISH ADMINISTRATION
STANDARD COINAGE

KM# 1 ORE
Silver **Obv:** Crowned CXI monogram in wreath **Rev:** Crowned arms divide date and value, palm branches and script LN below arms

Date	Mintage	VG	F	VF	XF	Unc
1670 LN	—	20.00	40.00	80.00	160	—
1671 LN	—	15.00	30.00	60.00	120	—

KM# 2.1 ORE
Silver **Rev:** Without palm branches below arms

Date	Mintage	VG	F	VF	XF	Unc
1670	—	20.00	40.00	80.00	160	—

KM# 2.2 ORE
Silver **Rev:** Script LN below arms

Date	Mintage	VG	F	VF	XF	Unc
1670 LN	—	15.00	30.00	60.00	120	—
1671 LN	—	15.00	30.00	60.00	120	—

KM# 2.3 ORE
Silver **Rev:** Small LN below arms

Date	Mintage	VG	F	VF	XF	Unc
1671 LN	—	15.00	30.00	60.00	120	—

KM# 2.4 ORE
Silver **Rev:** Small LN divided by arms at bottom

Date	Mintage	VG	F	VF	XF	Unc
1671 LN	—	15.00	30.00	60.00	120	—
1672 LN	—	25.00	50.00	100	200	—

KM# 3.1 2 ORE
Silver **Obv:** Crowned CRS monogram in wreath **Rev:** Crowned arms divide date and value, palm branches and script LN below arms

Date	Mintage	VG	F	VF	XF	Unc
1670 LN	—	20.00	40.00	80.00	160	—
1671 LN	—	20.00	40.00	80.00	160	—

KM# 3.2 2 ORE
Silver **Rev:** Small LN below arms

Date	Mintage	VG	F	VF	XF	Unc
1670 LN	—	25.00	50.00	100	200	—
1671 LN	—	20.00	40.00	80.00	160	—

KM# 5.1 2 ORE
Silver **Rev:** Small LN below arms, without palm branches

Date	Mintage	VG	F	VF	XF	Unc
1671 LN	—	35.00	70.00	140	285	—

KM# 5.2 2 ORE
Silver **Rev:** Arms divide LN at bottom

Date	Mintage	VG	F	VF	XF	Unc
1671 LN	—	28.00	55.00	110	225	—

KM# 4.1 4 ORE
Silver **Obv:** Crowned C in inner circle **Rev:** Crowned arms divide value in inner circle, date in legend

Date	Mintage	VG	F	VF	XF	Unc
1670	—	40.00	90.00	180	350	—
1671 Rare	—	—	—	—	—	—
1672	—	65.00	125	250	500	—

KM# 4.2 4 ORE
Silver **Rev:** Script LN mint masters initials in legend below arms

Date	Mintage	VG	F	VF	XF	Unc
1670 LN	—	30.00	60.00	120	240	—
1671 LN	—	30.00	60.00	120	240	—

KM# 4.3 4 ORE
Silver **Rev:** Arms divide value and mint masters initials

Date	Mintage	VG	F	VF	XF	Unc
1670 LN	—	50.00	100	200	400	—
1671 LN	—	25.00	50.00	100	200	—
1672 LN	—	50.00	100	200	400	—

KM# 6 4 ORE
Silver **Obv:** Without inner circle

Date	Mintage	VG	F	VF	XF	Unc
1671 LN	—	—	—	—	—	—

KM# 7 4 ORE
Silver **Rev:** Without inner circle, small LN below arms

Date	Mintage	VG	F	VF	XF	Unc
1671 LN	—	25.00	50.00	100	200	—

KM# 8 4 ORE
Silver **Obv:** Without inner circle **Rev:** Arms divide value and mint masters initials

Date	Mintage	VG	F	VF	XF	Unc
1671 LN	—	25.00	50.00	100	200	—

KM# 9.1 4 ORE
Silver **Obv:** With inner circle **Rev:** Without outer legend, small LN below arms

Date	Mintage	VG	F	VF	XF	Unc
1671 LN	—	30.00	60.00	120	240	—

KM# 9.2 4 ORE
Silver **Rev:** Script LN mint masters initials below arms

Date	Mintage	VG	F	VF	XF	Unc
1671 LN Rare	—	—	—	—	—	—

KM# 4.4 4 ORE
Silver **Rev:** Small LN below arms in legend

Date	Mintage	VG	F	VF	XF	Unc
1672 LN	—	50.00	100	200	400	—

KM# 10 DUCAT
3.5000 g., 0.9860 Gold 0.1109 oz. AGW **Obv:** Bust of Charles left **Rev:** Crowned arms, date in legend

Date	Mintage	VG	F	VF	XF	Unc
1671 LN Rare	—	—	—	—	—	—

KM# 11 DUCAT
3.5000 g., 0.9860 Gold 0.1109 oz. AGW **Obv:** Crowned C in inner circle

Date	Mintage	VG	F	VF	XF	Unc
1671 LN Rare	—	—	—	—	—	—

PATTERNS
Including off metal strikes

KM#	Date	Mintage	Identification	Mkt Val
Pn1	(1)671	—	Ducat. Silver. KM#11.	—

REVAL

This old city is the present city of Tallinn in Estonia on the Gulf of Finland. It was founded by the Danes about 1219 and became an important Baltic port and a member of the Hanseatic League. It passed to Sweden in 1561 after dissolution of the Teutonic Knights. Occupied by the Russians in 1710, it was ceded to them in 1721.

RULER
Swedish

MONEYERS' INITIALS

Initial	Date	Name
FL	1675-81	Friedrich Lembkens
GP	1648-52	Gerhard Philip
(a) Asterisk		?
(b) Crossed Battle-axes		?
(c) Crossed cannons		?
(f) Fleur de lis	1625-27	Friedrich Ulmer
(m) Maltese Cross		?
(s) Shamrock	1620-23	Cyriacus Klein
(st) Star of David		?
W/o mm	1663-75	Michael Paulsen

SWEDISH ADMINISTRATION
STANDARD COINAGE

KM# 1 ORE
Silver **Obv:** Sheaf divides G R, A above in inner circle **Obv. Legend:** MONETA (date) NOVA **Rev:** Crowned shield of 3 leopards in inner circle **Note:** Legend varieties exist.

Date	Mintage	VG	F	VF	XF	Unc
1620 Rare	—	—	—	—	—	—
1621 (s)	—	7.00	15.00	30.00	60.00	—
1621	—	7.00	15.00	30.00	60.00	—

KM# 2 ORE
Silver **Obv. Legend:** MONETA NOVA (date) **Note:** Legend varieties exist.

Date	Mintage	VG	F	VF	XF	Unc
1620 Rare	—	—	—	—	—	—
1621 Rare	—	—	—	—	—	—
1622 (s)	—	7.00	15.00	30.00	60.00	—
1622	—	10.00	20.00	40.00	80.00	—
1623 (a)	—	7.00	15.00	30.00	60.00	—
1623 (m)	—	7.00	15.00	30.00	60.00	—
1623 (s)	—	15.00	30.00	60.00	120	—
1623	—	7.00	15.00	30.00	60.00	—

Date	Mintage	VG	F	VF	XF	Unc
1624 (a)	—	7.00	15.00	30.00	60.00	—
1624 (c)	—	15.00	30.00	60.00	120	—
1624 (st)	—	7.00	15.00	30.00	60.00	—
1624	—	7.00	15.00	30.00	60.00	—
1625 (a)/(b)	—	12.00	25.00	50.00	100	—
1625 (b)	—	10.00	20.00	40.00	80.00	—
1625 (f) Rare	—	—	—	—	—	—
1625 (s + battle axe) Rare	—	—	—	—	—	—
1625 (st)	—	15.00	30.00	60.00	120	—
1626 (b) Rare	—	—	—	—	—	—
1628 (b)	—	15.00	30.00	60.00	120	—
1629	—	—	—	—	—	—

KM# 3 ORE

Silver **Note:** Klippe.

Date	Mintage	VG	F	VF	XF	Unc
1622 Rare	—	—	—	—	—	—

KM# 4 ORE

Silver **Rev:** 3 leopards in inner circle without shield

Date	Mintage	VG	F	VF	XF	Unc
1622 (s)	—	25.00	50.00	100	200	—

KM# 6 ORE

Silver **Obv:** Crowned Vasa arms divide date in inner circle **Rev:** Crowned Reval arms divide value in inner circle **Note:** Legend varieties exist.

Date	Mintage	VG	F	VF	XF	Unc
1648	—	10.00	20.00	40.00	100	—
1649	—	12.00	25.00	50.00	120	—
1650	—	12.00	25.00	50.00	120	—
1651	—	12.00	25.00	50.00	120	—

KM# 9.1 ORE

Silver **Obv:** Crowned arms (rampant lion left) divide date in inner circle **Rev:** Crowned Reval arms divide value in inner circle **Note:** Varieties exist.

Date	Mintage	VG	F	VF	XF	Unc
ND Rare	—	—	—	—	—	—
1663 Rare	—	—	—	—	—	—
1664	—	25.00	50.00	100	200	—
1665	—	10.00	20.00	40.00	80.00	—
1666	—	10.00	20.00	40.00	80.00	—
1667	—	12.00	25.00	50.00	100	—

KM# 9.2 ORE

Silver **Rev:** 1-R of value lying on side

Date	Mintage	VG	F	VF	XF	Unc
1665	—	10.00	20.00	40.00	80.00	—

KM# 9.3 ORE

Silver **Obv:** Denomination **Rev:** Date

Date	Mintage	VG	F	VF	XF	Unc
1666	—	25.00	50.00	100	200	—

KM# 10.1 ORE

Silver **Obv:** Rampant lion right in crowned arms

Date	Mintage	VG	F	VF	XF	Unc
1664	—	25.00	50.00	100	200	—

KM# 10.2 ORE

Silver **Rev:** Value 1 OR

Date	Mintage	VG	F	VF	XF	Unc
1664	—	—	50.00	100	200	—

KM# 23 ORE

Silver **Obv:** Crowned C R S **Rev:** Crowned arms in branches divide date and value

Date	Mintage	VG	F	VF	XF	Unc
1665	—	20.00	40.00	80.00	160	—

KM# 24.1 ORE

Silver **Obv:** Rampant lion left in crowned arms without inner circle

Date	Mintage	VG	F	VF	XF	Unc
1666	—	20.00	40.00	80.00	160	—

KM# 24.2 ORE

Silver **Obv:** Without inner circle **Rev:** Without inner circle

Date	Mintage	VG	F	VF	XF	Unc
1666	—	12.00	25.00	50.00	100	—
1668 Rare	—	—	—	—	—	—

KM# 27 ORE

Silver **Obv:** Crowned CXI monogram in branches **Rev:** Crowned arms divide value in inner circle

Date	Mintage	VG	F	VF	XF	Unc
ND Rare	—	—	—	—	—	—

KM# 28 ORE

Silver **Rev:** Crowned arms divide date, without branches, outer legend OR value

Date	Mintage	VG	F	VF	XF	Unc
1668	—	15.00	30.00	60.00	120	—

KM# 35 ORE

Silver **Rev:** Crowned arms in branches divide date and value

Date	Mintage	VG	F	VF	XF	Unc
1669	—	10.00	20.00	40.00	80.00	—
1670	—	10.00	20.00	40.00	80.00	—

KM# 45 ORE

Silver

Date	Mintage	VG	F	VF	XF	Unc
1672	—	12.00	25.00	50.00	100	—
1673	—	12.00	25.00	50.00	100	—
1674	—	15.00	30.00	60.00	120	—

KM# 47 ORE

Silver **Rev:** With value, without branches

Date	Mintage	VG	F	VF	XF	Unc
1673	—	12.00	25.00	50.00	100	—
1674	—	12.00	25.00	50.00	100	—

KM# 11 2 ORE

Silver **Obv:** Crowned C R S in laurel wreath **Rev:** Crowned oval arms divide date and value

Date	Mintage	VG	F	VF	XF	Unc
1664 Rare	—	—	—	—	—	—

KM# 12 2 ORE

Silver **Rev:** Crowned spade arms in branches divide date and value **Note:** Varieties exist.

Date	Mintage	VG	F	VF	XF	Unc
1664	—	15.00	30.00	60.00	120	—
1665	—	15.00	30.00	60.00	120	—
1666	—	10.00	20.00	40.00	80.00	—
1667	—	10.00	20.00	40.00	80.00	—
1668	—	10.00	20.00	40.00	80.00	—
1669	—	30.00	60.00	120	240	—

KM# A29 2 ORE

Silver **Obv:** Crowned CRS in palm branches

Date	Mintage	VG	F	VF	XF	Unc
1668	—	20.00	40.00	80.00	160	—

KM# 40 2 ORE

Silver **Obv:** Crowned CRS in laurel wreath **Rev:** Without branches below arms

Date	Mintage	VG	F	VF	XF	Unc
1671 Rare	—	—	—	—	—	—

KM# 25 4 ORE

Silver **Obv:** Crowned C in inner circle **Rev:** Crowned arms divide value, date in legend

Date	Mintage	VG	F	VF	XF	Unc
1667	—	25.00	50.00	100	200	—
667	—	15.00	30.00	60.00	120	—
668	—	15.00	30.00	60.00	120	—
1668	—	15.00	30.00	60.00	120	—
1669	—	25.00	50.00	100	200	—

KM# 30 4 ORE

Silver **Obv:** Crowned CRS in laurel wreath **Rev:** Crowned arms in branches divide date and value

Date	Mintage	VG	F	VF	XF	Unc
1668	—	18.00	35.00	70.00	140	—
1669	—	15.00	30.00	60.00	120	—
1670	—	15.00	30.00	60.00	120	—

KM# 37 4 ORE

Silver **Obv:** Crowned C in laurel wreath

Date	Mintage	VG	F	VF	XF	Unc
1670	—	20.00	40.00	80.00	160	—

KM# 41 4 ORE

Silver **Obv:** Crowned C in inner circle

Date	Mintage	VG	F	VF	XF	Unc
1671	—	15.00	30.00	60.00	120	—
1673	—	25.00	50.00	100	200	—
1674	—	30.00	60.00	120	240	—

KM# 13 MARK

Silver **Obv:** Bust of Charles XI left **Rev:** Crowned oval arms in cartouche, date in legend

Date	Mintage	VG	F	VF	XF	Unc
1664 Rare	—	—	—	—	—	—

KM# 14 2 MARK

Silver **Obv:** Draped bust of Charles XI left **Rev:** Crowned arms in cartouche, date in legend, crown divides value

Date	Mintage	VG	F	VF	XF	Unc
1664	—	700	1,350	2,250	4,500	—

KM# 15 2 MARK

Silver **Obv:** Draped bust of Charles XI right in inner circle

Date	Mintage	VG	F	VF	XF	Unc
1664 Rare	—	—	—	—	—	—

KM# 16 2 MARK

Silver **Rev:** Helmeted arms divide value in inner circle, date in legend

Date	Mintage	VG	F	VF	XF	Unc
1664 Rare	—	—	—	—	—	—

KM# 26 2 MARK

Silver **Obv:** Draped bust of Charles XI left **Rev:** Crowned spade arms divide date and value

Date	Mintage	VG	F	VF	XF	Unc
1667 Rare	—	—	—	—	—	—
1668 Unique	—	—	—	—	—	—

KM# 42 2 MARK

Silver **Obv:** Without lettering below bust

Date	Mintage	VG	F	VF	XF	Unc
1671	—	500	900	1,750	3,750	—

KM# 5.1 4 MARK

Silver **Obv:** 1/2 figure of Gustav II Adolf right with sceptre and orb in inner circle **Rev:** Crowned arms divide date in inner circle **Note:** Prev. KM#5.

Date	Mintage	VG	F	VF	XF	Unc
1623 Rare	—	—	—	—	—	—

KM# 5.2 4 MARK

Silver **Note:** 2-1/2 thickness - struck to weight of 10 mark, 47 grams. Dav. #4584.

Date	Mintage	VG	F	VF	XF	Unc
1623	—	—	—	—	—	—

KM# 5.3 4 MARK

Silver **Note:** Triple thickness - struck to weight of 12 mark, 56.4 grams. Dav. #4583.

Date	Mintage	VG	F	VF	XF	Unc
1623 Rare	—	—	—	—	—	—

KM# 17.1 4 MARK

Silver **Obv:** Draped bust of Charles XI left in inner circle **Rev:** Crowned oval arms divide value in inner circle, large cross below arms

Date	Mintage	VG	F	VF	XF	Unc
1664 Rare	—	—	—	—	—	—

KM# 17.2 4 MARK

Silver **Rev:** Small cross below arms

Date	Mintage	VG	F	VF	XF	Unc
1664	—	1,000	2,000	3,750	6,000	—

KM# 18.1 4 MARK

Silver **Rev:** Helmeted straight shield, helmet divides value, shield divides date in inner circle

Date	Mintage	VG	F	VF	XF	Unc
1664 Rare	—	—	—	—	—	—

KM# 18.2 4 MARK

Silver **Rev:** Numerals of date inverted

Date	Mintage	VG	F	VF	XF	Unc
1664	—	900	1,800	3,500	5,500	—
ND Rare	—	—	—	—	—	—

KM# 49 10 MARK

Silver **Obv:** 1/2 figure right **Rev:** Crowned arms divide date **Note:** Dav. #4584.

Date	Mintage	VG	F	VF	XF	Unc
1623 Rare	—	—	—	—	—	—

KM# 50 12 MARK

Silver **Note:** Similar to 10 Mark, KM#49.

Date	Mintage	VG	F	VF	XF	Unc
1623 Rare	—	—	—	—	—	—

KM# 8.1 RIKSDALER

Silver **Obv:** Crowned bust of Christian right in inner circle **Rev:** Crowned oval arms divide date in inner circle, GP below arms **Note:** Dav. #4585.

Date	Mintage	VG	F	VF	XF	Unc
1652 GP	—	4,500	6,500	10,000	15,000	—

KM# 8.2 RIKSDALER
Silver **Rev:** Crowned oval arms divide date in GP in inner circle **Note:** Dav. 4585A.

Date	Mintage	VG	F	VF	XF	Unc
1652 GP Rare	—	—	—	—	—	—

KM# 19 RIKSDALER
Silver **Obv:** Draped bust of Charles XI left in inner circle **Rev:** Helmeted arms in inner circle **Note:** Dav. #--.

Date	Mintage	VG	F	VF	XF	Unc
1664 Unique	—	—	—	—	—	—

TRADE COINAGE

KM# 7.1 DUCAT
3.5000 g., 0.9860 Gold 0.1109 oz. AGW **Obv:** Bust of Christina left **Rev:** GP below arms

Date	Mintage	VG	F	VF	XF	Unc
1650 GP	—	300	700	1,550	2,750	—

KM# 7.2 DUCAT
3.5000 g., 0.9860 Gold 0.1109 oz. AGW **Rev:** GP at sides of arms

Date	Mintage	VG	F	VF	XF	Unc
1650 GP	—	350	800	1,650	2,850	—

KM# 20 DUCAT
3.5000 g., 0.9860 Gold 0.1109 oz. AGW **Obv:** Laureate bust of Charles right **Rev:** Crowned arms, date in legend

Date	Mintage	VG	F	VF	XF	Unc
1664 Rare	—	—	—	—	—	—
1665 Rare	—	—	—	—	—	—
1666 Rare	—	—	—	—	—	—

KM# 31 DUCAT
3.5000 g., 0.9860 Gold 0.1109 oz. AGW **Obv:** Laureate bust of Charles left **Rev:** Crowned arms in straight sided shield divides date

Date	Mintage	VG	F	VF	XF	Unc
1668 Rare	—	—	—	—	—	—

KM# 36 DUCAT
3.5000 g., 0.9860 Gold 0.1109 oz. AGW **Rev:** Crowned arms in oval shield, date in legend

Date	Mintage	VG	F	VF	XF	Unc
1669	—	—	—	—	—	—

KM# 38 DUCAT
3.5000 g., 0.9860 Gold 0.1109 oz. AGW **Obv:** Laureate bust of Charles left with small shoulder drape **Rev:** Crowned arms in straight sided shield divides date

Date	Mintage	VG	F	VF	XF	Unc
1670 Rare	—	—	—	—	—	—
1671	—	900	1,850	3,500	6,000	—

KM# 43 DUCAT
3.5000 g., 0.9860 Gold 0.1109 oz. AGW **Rev:** Date in legend

Date	Mintage	VG	F	VF	XF	Unc
1671 Rare	—	—	—	—	—	—

KM# 48 DUCAT
3.5000 g., 0.9860 Gold 0.1109 oz. AGW **Obv:** Laureate bust of Charles right **Rev:** Crowned arms, shield with various side ornaments

Date	Mintage	VG	F	VF	XF	Unc
1675 Rare	—	—	—	—	—	—
1676 Rare	—	—	—	—	—	—
1677 Rare	—	—	—	—	—	—
1681 Rare	—	—	—	—	—	—

KM# 21 2 DUCAT
7.0000 g., 0.9860 Gold 0.2219 oz. AGW **Obv:** Large bust of Charles right **Rev:** Crwned oval arms, date in legend

Date	Mintage	VG	F	VF	XF	Unc
1664 Unique	—	—	—	—	—	—

KM# 22 2 DUCAT
7.0000 g., 0.9860 Gold 0.2219 oz. AGW **Obv:** Small bust of Charles right

Date	Mintage	VG	F	VF	XF	Unc
1664 Rare	—	—	—	—	—	—

KM# 32 2 DUCAT
7.0000 g., 0.9860 Gold 0.2219 oz. AGW **Obv:** Large bust of Charles left **Rev:** Crowned arms in straight sided shield divides date

Date	Mintage	VG	F	VF	XF	Unc
1668 Rare	—	—	—	—	—	—

KM# 39 2 DUCAT
7.0000 g., 0.9860 Gold 0.2219 oz. AGW **Obv:** Small bust of Charles left

Date	Mintage	VG	F	VF	XF	Unc
1670 Rare	—	—	—	—	—	—

KM# 44 2 DUCAT
7.0000 g., 0.9860 Gold 0.2219 oz. AGW **Rev:** Date in legend **Note:** Legend varieties exist.

Date	Mintage	VG	F	VF	XF	Unc
1671 Rare	—	—	—	—	—	—

KM# 33 4 DUCAT
14.0000 g., 0.9860 Gold 0.4438 oz. AGW **Obv:** Laureate bust of Charles left **Rev:** Crowned arms in straight sided shield divides date

Date	Mintage	VG	F	VF	XF	Unc
1668 Unique	—	—	—	—	—	—

KM# 34 5 DUCAT
17.5000 g., 0.9860 Gold 0.5547 oz. AGW **Obv:** Laureate bust of Charles left **Rev:** Crowned arms in straight sided shield divides date

Date	Mintage	VG	F	VF	XF	Unc
1668 Rare	—	—	—	—	—	—

KM# 46 5 DUCAT
17.5000 g., 0.9860 Gold 0.5547 oz. AGW **Obv:** Laureate bust of Charles left **Rev:** Crowned arms divide value, date in legend

Date	Mintage	VG	F	VF	XF	Unc
1672 Rare	—	—	—	—	—	—

PATTERNS

Including off metal strikes

KM#	Date	Mintage	Identification	Mkt Val
Pn1	1648	—	Ore. Gold. KM#6, weight of 1 Ducat.	—
Pn2	1665	—	2 Ore. Gold. KM#12.	—
Pn3	671	—	2 Ducat. Silver. KM#44.	—
Pn4	1673	—	2 Mark. Copper. KM#42.	—

FRANCE

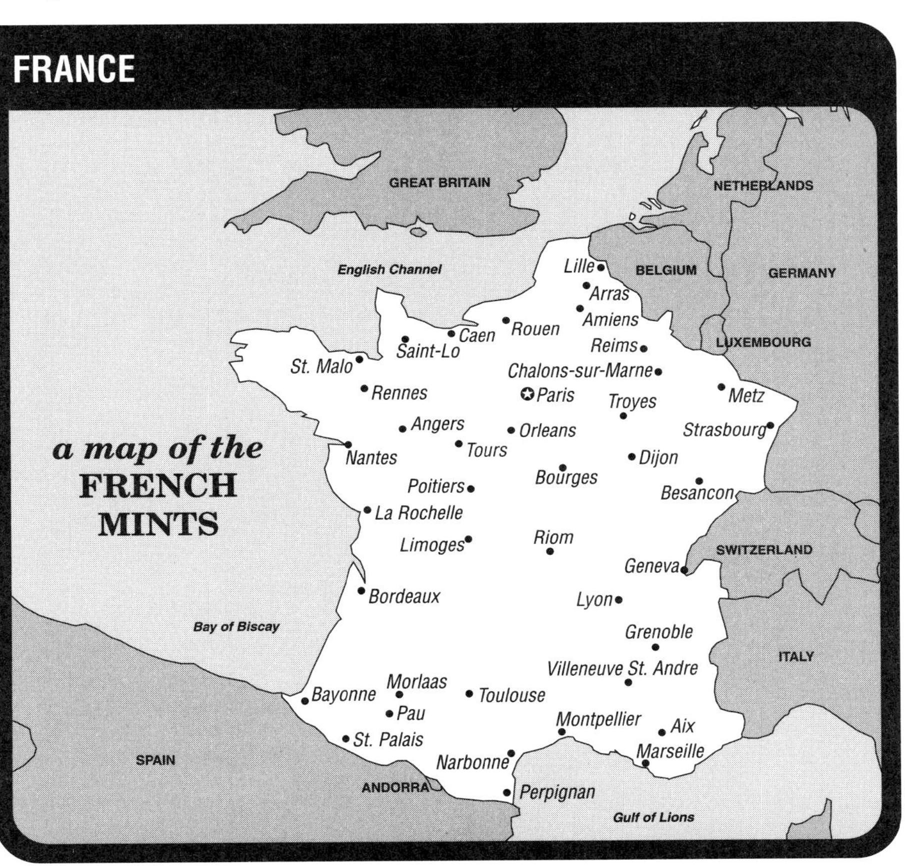

France, the Gaul of ancient times, emerged from the Renaissance as a modern centralized national state which reached its zenith during the reign of Louis XIV (1643-1715) when it became an absolute monarchy and the foremost power in Europe. Although his reign marks the golden age of French culture, the domestic abuses and extravagance of Louis XIV plunged France into a series of costly wars. This, along with a system of special privileges granted the nobility and other favored groups, weakened the monarchy and brought France to bankruptcy. This laid the way for the French Revolution of 1789-99 that shook Europe and affected the whole world.

RULERS

Henry IV, 1589-1610
Louis XIII, 1610-1643
Louis XIV, 1643-1715

MINT MARKS AND PRIVY MARKS

In addition to the date and mint mark which are customary on western civilization coinage, most coins manufactured by the French Mints contain two or three small 'Marks or Differents' as the French call them. These privy marks represent the men responsible for the dies which struck the coins. One privy mark is sometimes for the Engraver General (since 1880 the title is Chief Engraver). The other privy mark is the signature of the Mint Director of each mint; another one is the different' of the local engraver. Three other marks appeared at the end of Louis XIV's reign: one for the Director General of Mints, one for the General Engineer of Mechanical edge-marking, one identifying over struck coins in 1690-1705 and in 1715-1723. Equally amazing and unique is that sometimes the local assayer's or Judge-custody's 'different' or 'secret pellet' appears. Since 1880 this privy mark has represented the office rather than the personage of both the Administration of Coins & Medals and the Mint Director, and a standard privy mark has been used (cornucopia).

For most dates these privy marks are important though minor features for advanced collectors or local researchers. During some issue dates, however, the marks changed. To be even more accurate sometimes the marks changed when the date didn't, even though it should have. These coins can be attributed to the proper mintage report only by considering the privy marks. Previous references (before G. Sobin and F. Droulers) have by and large ignored these privy marks. It is entirely possible that unattributed varieties may exist for any privy mark transition. All transition years which may have two or three varieties or combinations of privy marks have the known attribution indicated after the date (if it has been confirmed).

MONETARY SYSTEM

1641-1689

3 Livres = 1 Silver Ecu
3-1/3 Ecus = 1 Louis d'or
1 Louis d'or = 10 Livres

1690-1725

Very unstable rates period.
1 Livre = 20 Sols
1 Sol = 12 Deniers
1 Liard = 3 Deniers

Engraver Generals' Privy Marks

Mark	Desc.	Date	Name
		1623-25	Nicolas Briot
		1625-31	Pierre Regnier
		1630-46	Johan Darmand Lorfelin
	Rose (on silver only)	1641-45	
•		1643-72	Jean Warin
	Castle tower	1662-73	Jean Baptiste du Four (assistant)
	Sun (usually or none)	1682-1703	Joseph Roettiers

Local Engravers' Privy Marks

Engraver Generals' and local engravers' privy marks may appear on coins of mints which are dated as follows:

A – Paris

Mark	Desc.	Date	Name
	4 pellets around fleur de lis	1644-48	Unknown
	Circle in triangle	1651-53	Francois Biaru
	Clover	1676	Pierre Rousseau
	Crescent	1679-93	Nicolas Aury
	Double triangle	1693-94	J. Mauger & J. Roussel
		1694-1703	Joseph Roettiers

AA – Metz

Mark	Desc.	Date	Name
	Crowned M	1690-93	Unknown
	Inflamed heart or none	1690-93	Etienne Rade
	Pierced heart	1693-94	Etienne Rade
	Hermine between 2 pellets	1694-1700	Unknown

B – Rouen

Mark	Desc.	Date	Name
	Star	1654-61	Nicolas Droux I
	Bee hive	1662-65	Nicolas Droux II
	Bee	1679-84	Nicolas Droux III
		1690-99	Nicolas Droux III
		1699-1700	Pierre Racine

BB – Strasbourg

Mark	Desc.	Date	Name
	Eagle's head	1694-99	Unknown

C – Saint Lo

Mark	Desc.	Date	Name
	Crescent	1625-28	Johan Euldes
	Star	1646-51	Israel Dubosc
	Star	1651-53	Michael Dupin
	Scallop	1653-57	Israel Dubosc

C – Caen

Mark	Desc.	Date	Name
		1693-1703	Thomas Bernard III

D – Lyon

Mark	Desc	Date	Name
	Three pellets	1643	Claude Warin
	Rose	1644-45	Jean Warin
	Star	1648-5	Claude Warin
	Eagle's head	1675-1709	Clair Jacquemin I

E - Tours

Mark	Desc.	Date	Name
	Cross	1656-80	Charles Thomas I
	Cross	1699-1722	Charles Thomas II

F – Angers

Mark	Desc.	Date	Name
	Clover	1611-32	Jean Boyoin
	Trefoil	1643-54	Unknown
	Palm	1655	Unknown
	Acorn	1656	Unknown
	Crescented cross	1658-59	Unknown
	Crossed 4 figure	1659-60	Rene Fauvel

G – Poitiers

Mark	Desc.	Date	Name
	Heart	1642-57	Rene Herpin
	Bird	1659-60	Rene Herpin
	Heart	1660	Rene Herpin
	Besant or none	1690-93	Unknown
	Heart	1693-98	Unknown

H – La Rochelle

Mark	Desc.	Date	Name
	Heart	1647-56	Abraham Desbordes
	Triangle	1658-61	Abraham Desbordes
	Rose	1690-92	Michel Brioshe
	Clover	1694-97	Gilles Nassivet I
	Acorn	1697-1704	Jacques Biollay

I – Limoges

Mark	Desc.	Date	Name
	Tear drop	1650-56	Unknown
	Rowel	1656-60	Unknown
	Tower	1660-80	Pierre Guybuert
	Carrick-bend?	1680-81	Unknown
	Tower	1690-92	Michel Briosne
	Latin cross	1693-1725	Francois Ponroy

K - Bordeaux

Mark	Desc.	Date	Name
	Nought	1620-46	
		1640-42	Pierre Prevost
		1643-44	Julien Noblet
		1645-46	Geoffrey Assore
	Fleur-de-lis	1646-47	Christophe Compuest
	Star	1660-84	Christophe Compuest
	Tower	1693-95 and 1708-09	Unknown
	Fleur-de-lis	1696-1715	Jacques Petit I

Crowned L - Lille

L - Bayonne

Mark	Desc.	Date	Name
	Cross	1652-53	Guillaume Fons
		1659-72	Leon Boisnet
	Running dog right	1672-74	Joseph Boisnet
	Star	1675-80	Jean Boisnet
	Palm	1682-94	
	Natural rose	1695-1735	Leon Mousset

M - Toulouse

Mark	Desc.	Date	Name
	Scallop	1648-53	Jean Favre I
	Flower	1691-94	Guillaume Favre III
	Scallop	1695	

Crowned M - Metz

N - Montpellier

Mark	Desc.	Date	Name
	Clover	1647-1694	Antoine Gautron
	Clover flanked by pellets	1679	
	Clover	1690-1700	Jacques Baudau

O - Riom

Mark	Desc.	Date	Name
	Rosette	1651-53	Unknown
	Clover	1691-92	Joseph Socke
	Clover	1697-1744	Jean Villa

P - Dijon

Mark	Desc.	Date	Name
	Clover	1637-1736	Guillaume Desvarennes
		1691-1738	Simon Roger

Q - Narbonne

R – Villeneuve St. André
Crowned S - Troyes

S - Reims

Mark	Desc.	Date	Name
	Rooster	1680-84	Claude Hardy
	Square	1693-1701	Pierre Delahaye

T - Nantes

Mark	Desc.	Date	Name
	Triangle	1642-56	Guillaume Langlois
	Globe	1654	
	Cross	1693-97	Pierre de la Croix
	Cross	1698-1709	Jean Beranger

V - Troyes

Mark	Desc.	Date	Name
	Double ring	1690-1710	Paul Rondot

W - Lille

Mark	Desc.	Date	Name
	Rosette	1693-1699	Claude Hardy
	Duckling	1700-02	Claude Hardy

X - Amiens

Mark	Desc.	Date	Name
	Crossed orb	1653-58	Jean Verdeloche
	Clover	1685-86	Claude Hardy
	Heart	1690-97	Michel Molard
	Star	1699-1703	Pierre-Gabriel Lemoyne

Y - Bourges

Mark	Desc.	Date	Name
	Arches	1690-92	Mathieu Malherbe des Portes
	Paddle-wheel (2 in 1703-05)	1692-1704	Francois Delobel

(2 back-to-back C's) - Besancon

Mark	Desc.	Date	Name
	Rowel	1694-99	Charles Louis Durand
	Swan	1699-1704	Bon-Anatole Nicole

& - Aix

Mark	Desc.	Date	Name
	Feather or none	1634-39	Johan Leger
	Diamond	1647-67	Jacques Cabassol I
	Diamond	1656-64	Jacques Cabassol II
	Small Diamond	1664-1708	Jean Joseph Cabassol

9 – Rennes

Mark	Desc.	Date	Name
	Acorn	1647-98	Jehan Noblet
	Crescent	1649-52	Denis Mathias
	Castle tower	1676-92	Jean Bedard
	Flower	1690-91	
	Heart	1692-1704	Rene Mathias

Legend DD or/and (cow) - Pau

Mark	Desc	Date	Name
	Intertwined olive branches	1650-51	Richard Lemy
	Various collections of pellets and stars	1651-56	Richard ?
	Dog running right	1663-83	Jacques de Soubiran
	Star	1683-91	Pierre de Loyard
	Heart	1691	Jacques de Soubiran
	Star	1692-96	Pierre de Loyard
	Heart	1696-1702	Jacques de Soubiran

Legend BD - Morlaas

Mark	Desc.	Date	Name
	1-3 stars	1637-49	Richard Lemy
	2 intertwined olive branches	1650-59	Richard Lemy
	Pellet	1660	Bertrand de Beaumont

Legend REX – Saint Palais

Mark	Desc.	Date	Name
	None	1646-49	
	Inverted heart	1650-58	Simon d'Armagnac
	Clover	1659-61	Pierre d'Armagnac
	$	1662-65	Jacques de Soubiran

Mint Directors' Privy Marks

A – Paris, Central Mint

Some modern coins struck from dies produced at the Paris Mint have the A mint mark. In the absence of a mint mark, the cornucopia privy mark serves to attribute a coin to Paris design.

Mark	Desc.	Date	Name
	Crossed palm	1630	Jean-Gabriel Fustel and Francois Ravel
	Pellet above crossed palm	1631	Francois Guibert
	Rose	1633-35	Gabriel Davin
	Forked cross	1635-42	Louis de la Croix
	Lily	1648	Jean Racle
	Marigold	1648	Jean Bouin
	Marigold	1649-53	Jean Racle
	Grape cluster	1653-55	Claude Monchallon
	Leaf	1656-57	Claude Banat
	Hermine	1657-58	Pierre Briot
	Crescent		Michel Fournier
	Lily w/stem	1662	Michel Magnier
	Lily w/stem	1662	Alexander Viollet
	Leopard right	1663	Unknown
	Inverted small heart	1663-65	Unknown
	Dove	1666	Unknown
	Sun w/human mask	1666-72	Pierre Cheval
	Cormorant	1672-74	Vincent Forher
	Laurel crown	1675-76	Jean Hindret
	Palm	1677-79	Jean Hindret
	Palm	1680-89	Pierre Batillie
	Sun	1684-85	Pierre Rouseau
	Sun	1685-88	Melchior Villain
	Sun	1688-89	Pierre Rousseau
	Sun	1689-	Jean Castagny
	Sun	1690-96	Hierosme de la Guerre
	Scallop	1699-1700	Nicolas de Saint Paul

A – Paris, Louvre Office

Mark	Desc.	Date	Name
	Rose or pellet or none (on the gold)	1640-46	Jean Warin
	Heart	1646-48	Louis Le Bicheur

A – Paris, Matignon Office

Mark	Desc.	Date	Name
	Rose between 2 pellets, 2 pellets or 1 pellet	1642-46	Isaac Briot & Jean Racle

AA - Metz

Mark	Desc.	Date	Name
	Grain ear in a crescent	1690-91	Antoine Talon
	Bomb	1692-97	Claude-Nicolas Boulard d'Ingonville
	Rose	1698-1700	Michel Rabigueau de Montelon

AR - Arras

Mark	Desc.	Date	Name
	Rat	1641-56	Artus (or Arthur) Aymond (or Emond) Jean-Jacques Morodet (1645)

B - Rouen

Mark	Desc	Date	Name
	Crown	1616-19	
	Hand	1633	
	Flower	1647-53	Pierre Cheval
	Cap	1664-65	

BB - Strasbourg

Mark	Desc.	Date	Name
	Flower	1694	

C – Saint Lo

Mark	Desc.	Date	Name
	Cross	1615	

D - Lyon

Mark	Desc.	Date	Name
	Star or none	1643-45	Jean Warin
	Crescent	1649-52	Andre Peyron
	VA monogram	1652-58	Jean Claudron
	Orb	1666-67	Isaac Estoille
	Rock pile	1669-71	Nicolas Simon
	Lion rampant or none	1681-88	Jean-Rene Dervieux
	Crescent	1690-93	Jean-Pierre Dervieux

E - Tours

Mark	Desc.	Date	Name
	Spread bird	1679	

F - Angers

Mark	Desc.	Date	Name
	Sheaf	1658-59	Matharin Haudoin
	Clover	1660	Francois de la Pierre
	Clover	1660	Nicolas Ruellan
	Torch	1660-61	Michel Garrot

G - Poitiers

Mark	Desc.	Date	Name
	Holy Spirit's dove	1647-53	Samuel Massonneau
	None	(1692-1700)	
	Latin cross	1692-1706	Gaspard Perrin

H – La Rochelle

Mark	Desc.	Date	Name
	Diamond	1647-53	Samuel Massonneau
	Diamond	1690-97	Germain and Francois Fodere
	Arrow	1697-1723	Jean Donat

I - Limoges

Mark	Desc.	Date	Name
	She-duckling	1619-22	Etienne Pinchault
	Crucifix	1650-54	Francois Malbay
	Sceptre	1679-81	Francois-Martin de la Bashide
	Kid left	1693-97	Joseph Chevreau Dumesmil
	Hound left	1697	Martin Courant
	Harp	1698-1725	Pierre David de la Vergne

K - Bordeaux

Mark	Desc.	Date	Name
	Bald head	1647	Jehan Luppe
	Bald head	1647-54	Jean de la Vaud
	Fleur-de-lis	1679-84	Jean-Baptiste Barlet
	Flower bud on stem	1694-96	Andre Langlois de Vaurain
	None	1697-1705	Bernard la Molire

L - Bayonne

Mark	Desc.	Date	Name
	LB monogram	1643-56	Martin de la Borde
	Heart	1662-66	Louis Martin
	Crown	1666-68	Joachim Gaillard
	Rose	1673-74	Etienne Verdoye
	Clover	1675-83	Michel Porchery
	Hermine	1679-83	Unknown
	Clover	1684-89	Michel Porchery

M - Toulouse

Mark	Desc.	Date	Name
	Heart	1648-49	
	Wing	1652-53	
	Fleur-de-lis	1691	

N - Montpellier

Mark	Desc.	Date	Name
	Star	1646-48	Laurent Mottry
	Tower	1666-69	Michel Porchery
	Pellets flanking star	1679-80	Francois Parent
	Lion's head (facing 1693-98)	1690-98	Pierre Berthelet

O - Clermont

O - Riom

Mark	Desc.	Date	Name
	Acorn on branch	1652	

P - Semur

P - Dijon

Mark	Desc.	Date	Name
	Fleur-de-lis	1652-53	Claude Burgat
	Arrow in quiver	1690-93	Melchior Villain
	Arrow in quiver	1693	Cezar d'Hubinet
	Arrow in quiver	1693-95	Jean-Nicolas Lancelot

Q - Narbonne

Mark	Desc.	Date	Name
	Holy spirit dove	1644-46	Tristan Brueys (1649) Claude Aubert (1645-46)
	Crescent	1650	Christophe de Jouy
	Flying angel holding crown	1650-52	Antoinne de Peyras
	Flying angel holding crown	1653	Jean Bacarisse

R – Villenueve Saint Andre

Mark	Desc.	Date	Name
	Unknown	1644-46	Charles Le Fresne
	Crescent	1660	Louis Martin
	Crescent	1661-62	Unknown

Crowned S – Troyes

(1690-93)
(See also V)

Mark	Desc.	Date	Name
	3 Cabochon's ring slantwise	1690-91	Pierre Paillot
	Heart	1691-93	Francois Boula

S - Reims

Mark	Desc.	Date	Name
	Holy Spirit dove	1680-83	Cezar Maniquet
	Clover	1690-95	Jean Hindret
	Acorn	1696-1705	Jacques Lagoille

T - Nantes

Mark	Desc.	Date	Name
	Holy Spirit dove	1646-53	Jehan Demarques
	Marigold	1653-55	Vincent Jourdain
	Hermine	1659-62	Andre Borgault

V – Troyes

(See also S)

Mark	Desc.	Date	Name
	Scallop	1694-97	Jean Baptiste de Mallerois
	Greek cross	1697-1700	Jean Sauvayre

X - Amiens

Mark	Desc.	Date	Name
	Hermine	1652-55	Nicolas Cezard
	Heart	1690-97	Louis Euldes

Y - Bourges

Mark	Desc.	Date	Name
	Sprig w/2 leaves	1694	Pierre Mace de Ballereau
	Crossed globe	1695-1700	Jules de la Planche de Coco

9 - Rennes

Mark	Desc.	Date	Name
	Rose	1651-53	Jehan Demarques
	Rose	1653-54	Vincent Jourdain
	Rose	1655	Rene Le Tellin
	Rose	1656-59	Mathieu Desrieux
	Star	1662-63	Jean Boulanger
	Star	1663-64	Claude Richard
	Star	1664-66	Jacques Nodain
	Hermine	1666-75	Marcel Memissin de Launoy
	Acorn	1673	Kin to Memissin de Launoy
	Palm	1675-77	Unknown
	Sunburst	1678-82	Marcel Memissin de Launoy
	Sunburst	1682-83	Jean-Jacques Baraly
	Orb	1684-86	Jean-Jacques Baraly
	Lion rampant	1693-1709	Jean-Jacques Baraly

& - Aix

Mark	Desc.	Date	Name
	Facing lion's head	1646-59	Laurent Motry
	Facing lion's head	1659-61	Pierre Nicolay
	Pierced star	1666-72	Pierre Desmaratz
	Olive branch	1679-84	Nicolas Simon
	Sunburst or none	1687-91	Francois Bouchaud
	None	1692-1703	Marc Pielat du Pignet

2 back to back C's - Besancon

Mark	Desc.	Date	Name
	Uprooted conifers	1694-97	Nicolas charles Nyele
	Uprooted conifers	1697-1700	Claude Francois Arbilleur

Crowned M – Metz

(1690-93 only)
From 1693, see also AA

Mark	Desc.	Date	Name
	Sprig in crescent	1690-91	Antoine Talon
	Comet	1692-97	Claude-Nicolas Boulard d'Ingonville

Legend ending NARE and/or Cow - Pau

Mark	Desc.	Date	Name
	Crossed olive	1650-51	Richard Lamy
F	Letter F alternatively w/2 or 4 stars	1651-53	Pierre Du Four
F	Letter F alternatively w/2 or 4 stars	1653-60	Robert Fisson
G	Letter G	1652	Bertrand lalande de Gayon
	Letter P	1653	Pierre de Niert
V	Letter V	1652	Etienne Du Verger
	Wood pigeon	1663-65	Reiset Du Verger
	Crescent	1663-64 and 1666-71	Louis allerie
	Blown rose	1672-75	Jean d'Azmagnan
	Clover	1673-75	
	Lily flanked by 2 pellets	1675-79	Unknown
	Orb	1685-89	Louis Allorie
	Orb	1690-95	Francois de La Serre
	Harpoon	1696-98	Rene Rousseau de Vilmor
	Hunting dog right	1698-1700 and 1708	Martin Courant

Legend ending NA, RE. DB and/or Letter M in 1652-62 only - Morlaas

Mark	Desc.	Date	Name
	Letter Z	1652-54	Bertrand La Lande de Gayon
R A	Letters A or R	1654-58	Martin d'Arretche or Robert Fisson alternatively
	Thistle flower	1659	Unknown
	Buffoon's crown	1659-60	Unknown
	She-goose	1660	Etienne Verdoya
	Buffoon's crown	1661-62	Unknown

Arms of France-Navarra – Saint Palais

Mark	Desc.	Date	Name
	W w/2 stars	1650-59	Etienne Verdoye
	2 stars under bust	1659-60	Unknown
	Tower	1665	Unknown
	Heart	1666-69	Jean d'Armagnan
		1670-72	Francois LeNoir

Feurs

Mark	Desc.	Date	Name
◦	1 pellet	1637-43	

Lay

Mark	Desc.	Date	Name
◦◦	2 pellets	1637-43	

Macon

(never open)

Mark	Desc.	Date	Name
•✱•	3 pellets	1637-43	

Maromme

Mark	Desc.	Date	Name
✣	Cross of 5 pellets	1637-43	

Roquemaure

Mark	Desc.	Date	Name
◦◦••	4 pellets	1637-43	

Troyes

Mark	Desc.	Date	Name
⁂	Starburst	1637-43	

Valence

Mark	Desc.	Date	Name
★	Star	1637-43	

KINGDOM

MILLED COINAGE

KM# 15 DENIER TOURNOIS

Copper **Ruler:** Henry IV **Obv:** Laureate bust right **Rev:** 2 fleur-de-lis, mint mark **Mint:** Paris

Date	Mintage	VG	F	VF	XF	Unc
1603A	—	12.50	25.00	50.00	90.00	—
1604A	—	12.50	25.00	50.00	90.00	—
1605/4A	—	12.50	25.00	50.00	90.00	—
1606A	—	12.50	25.00	50.00	90.00	—
1607A	—	12.50	25.00	50.00	90.00	—
1608/7A	—	12.50	25.00	50.00	90.00	—

KM# 32 DENIER TOURNOIS

Copper **Ruler:** Henry IV **Rev:** Quartered shield for France and Dauphine **Mint:** Grenoble

Date	Mintage	VG	F	VF	XF	Unc
1608Z	—	—	—	—	—	—

KM# 42.1 DENIER TOURNOIS

Copper **Ruler:** Louis XIII **Obv:** Infant bust right in shirt **Rev:** 2 fleur-de-lis, mint mark below **Mint:** Paris

Date	Mintage	VG	F	VF	XF	Unc
1611A	—	5.00	12.00	30.00	75.00	—
1612A	—	5.00	12.00	30.00	75.00	—
1613A	—	5.00	12.00	30.00	75.00	—
1614A	—	5.00	12.00	30.00	70.00	—
1615A	—	5.00	12.00	30.00	70.00	—
1616A	—	5.00	12.00	30.00	70.00	—
1617A	—	5.00	12.00	30.00	70.00	—
1618A	—	5.00	12.00	30.00	70.00	—
1620A	—	6.00	13.00	32.00	90.00	—
1621A	—	7.00	15.00	40.00	120	—

KM# 42.2 DENIER TOURNOIS

Copper **Ruler:** Louis XIII **Mint:** Lyon

Date	Mintage	VG	F	VF	XF	Unc
1611D	—	6.00	13.00	32.00	90.00	—
1613D	—	7.00	15.00	40.00	120	—
1615D	—	5.00	12.00	30.00	80.00	—
1617D	—	7.00	15.00	40.00	120	—
1618D	—	6.00	13.00	32.00	90.00	—

KM# 42.3 DENIER TOURNOIS

Copper **Ruler:** Louis XIII **Mint:** Poitiers

Date	Mintage	VG	F	VF	XF	Unc
1619G	—	7.00	15.00	40.00	120	—

KM# 42.4 DENIER TOURNOIS

Copper **Ruler:** Louis XIII **Mint:** Bordeaux

Date	Mintage	VG	F	VF	XF	Unc
1610K	—	—	—	—	—	—
1611K	—	—	—	—	—	—
1612K	—	7.00	15.00	40.00	120	—
1613K	—	—	—	—	—	—
1614K	—	—	—	—	—	—
1617K	—	—	—	—	—	—
1618K	—	7.00	15.00	40.00	120	—

KM# 42.5 DENIER TOURNOIS

Copper **Ruler:** Louis XIII **Mint:** Toulouse

Date	Mintage	VG	F	VF	XF	Unc
1611M	—	7.00	15.00	40.00	120	—
1612M	—	7.00	15.00	40.00	120	—

KM# 42.6 DENIER TOURNOIS

Copper **Ruler:** Louis XIII **Mint:** Villeneuve St. André

Date	Mintage	VG	F	VF	XF	Unc
1617R	—	9.00	18.00	45.00	135	—
1618R	—	6.00	12.00	30.00	85.00	—

KM# 42.7 DENIER TOURNOIS

Copper **Ruler:** Louis XIII **Mint:** Nantes

Date	Mintage	VG	F	VF	XF	Unc
1610T	—	7.00	15.00	40.00	120	—
1611T	—	7.00	15.00	40.00	120	—
1613T	—	7.00	15.00	40.00	120	—
1616T	—	7.00	15.00	40.00	120	—

KM# 42.8 DENIER TOURNOIS

Copper **Ruler:** Louis XIII **Mint:** Amiens

Date	Mintage	VG	F	VF	XF	Unc
1614X	—	6.00	13.00	32.00	90.00	—
1615X	—	7.00	15.00	40.00	120	—
1616X	—	7.00	15.00	40.00	120	—

KM# 70.1 DENIER TOURNOIS

Copper **Ruler:** Louis XIII **Obv:** Laureate youthful bust right in shirt **Mint:** Paris

Date	Mintage	VG	F	VF	XF	Unc
1620A	—	6.00	13.00	32.00	90.00	—
1621A	—	6.00	13.00	32.00	90.00	—
1622A	—	6.00	13.00	32.00	90.00	—
1625A	—	6.00	13.00	32.00	90.00	—
1626A	—	6.00	13.00	32.00	90.00	—
1627A	—	6.00	13.00	32.00	90.00	—
1628A	—	6.00	13.00	32.00	90.00	—
1629A	—	6.00	13.00	32.00	90.00	—

KM# 70.2 DENIER TOURNOIS

Copper **Ruler:** Louis XIII **Mint:** Lyon

Date	Mintage	VG	F	VF	XF	Unc
1624D	—	—	—	—	—	—

KM# 70.3 DENIER TOURNOIS

Copper **Ruler:** Louis XIII **Mint:** Poitiers

Date	Mintage	VG	F	VF	XF	Unc
1618G	—	—	—	—	—	—
1619G	—	6.00	13.00	32.00	90.00	—
1620G	—	6.00	13.00	32.00	90.00	—
1621G	—	6.00	13.00	32.00	90.00	—
1622G	—	6.00	13.00	32.00	90.00	—
1624G	—	6.00	13.00	32.00	90.00	—

KM# 70.4 DENIER TOURNOIS

Copper **Ruler:** Louis XIII **Mint:** La Rochelle

Date	Mintage	VG	F	VF	XF	Unc
1619H	—	—	—	—	—	—

KM# 70.5 DENIER TOURNOIS

Copper **Ruler:** Louis XIII **Mint:** Bordeaux

Date	Mintage	VG	F	VF	XF	Unc
1618K	—	6.00	13.00	32.00	90.00	—
1619K	—	—	—	—	—	—
1620K	—	—	—	—	—	—
1621K	—	—	—	—	—	—

KM# 70.6 DENIER TOURNOIS

Copper **Ruler:** Louis XIII **Mint:** Villeneuve St. André

Date	Mintage	VG	F	VF	XF	Unc
1621R	—	6.00	13.00	32.00	90.00	—
1622R	—	—	—	—	—	—
1625R	—	—	—	—	—	—

KM# 79.1 DENIER TOURNOIS

Copper **Ruler:** Louis XIII **Obv:** Older bust right in ruffled collar **Mint:** Paris

Date	Mintage	VG	F	VF	XF	Unc
1629A	—	10.00	20.00	50.00	150	—
1630A	—	10.00	20.00	50.00	150	—
1631A	—	10.00	20.00	50.00	150	—
1632A	—	10.00	20.00	50.00	150	—

KM# 79.2 DENIER TOURNOIS

Copper **Ruler:** Louis XIII **Mint:** Lyon

Date	Mintage	VG	F	VF	XF	Unc
1627D	—	10.00	20.00	50.00	150	—
1628D	—	10.00	20.00	50.00	150	—
1632D	—	10.00	20.00	50.00	150	—

KM# 79.3 DENIER TOURNOIS

Copper **Ruler:** Louis XIII **Mint:** Tours

Date	Mintage	VG	F	VF	XF	Unc
1632E	—	10.00	20.00	50.00	150	—
1633E	—	12.00	25.00	60.00	180	—
1634E	—	12.00	25.00	60.00	180	—
1635E	—	15.00	30.00	70.00	200	—

KM# 79.4 DENIER TOURNOIS

Copper **Ruler:** Louis XIII **Mint:** Poitiers

Date	Mintage	VG	F	VF	XF	Unc
1626G	—	10.00	20.00	50.00	150	—
1627G	—	10.00	20.00	50.00	150	—

KM# 79.5 DENIER TOURNOIS

Copper **Ruler:** Louis XIII **Mint:** La Rochelle

Date	Mintage	VG	F	VF	XF	Unc
1631H	—	—	—	—	—	—
1632H	—	—	—	—	—	—

KM# 79.6 DENIER TOURNOIS

Copper **Ruler:** Louis XIII **Mint:** Bordeaux

Date	Mintage	VG	F	VF	XF	Unc
1627K	—	—	—	—	—	—
1628K	—	10.00	20.00	50.00	150	—
1633K	—	10.00	20.00	50.00	150	—

KM# 79.7 DENIER TOURNOIS

Copper **Ruler:** Louis XIII **Mint:** Riom

Date	Mintage	VG	F	VF	XF	Unc
1624O	—	10.00	20.00	50.00	150	—
1625O	—	—	—	—	—	—
1626O	—	10.00	20.00	50.00	150	—

KM# 89 DENIER TOURNOIS

Copper **Ruler:** Louis XIII **Obv:** Older bust right **Rev:** 2 fleur-de-lis, shield below **Mint:** Saint Palais **Note:** Mint mark: shield.

Date	Mintage	VG	F	VF	XF	Unc
1634	—	35.00	65.00	175	420	—
1635	—	25.00	45.00	125	365	—

KM# 167 DENIER TOURNOIS

Copper **Ruler:** Louis XIV **Obv:** Laureate head right **Rev:** 2 fleur-de-lis, mint mark below **Mint:** Paris

Date	Mintage	VG	F	VF	XF	Unc
1648A	—	10.00	20.00	60.00	175	—
1649A	—	8.00	16.00	40.00	120	—

KM# 16.1 DOUBLE TOURNOIS

Copper **Ruler:** Henry IV **Obv:** Laureate, armored bust right **Mint:** Paris

Date	Mintage	VG	F	VF	XF	Unc
1603A	—	20.00	40.00	90.00	195	—
1604A	—	20.00	40.00	90.00	195	—
1605/4A	—	20.00	40.00	90.00	195	—
1606A	—	20.00	40.00	90.00	195	—
1607A	—	20.00	40.00	90.00	195	—
1608A	—	20.00	40.00	90.00	195	—
1609A	—	20.00	40.00	90.00	195	—
1610A	—	20.00	40.00	90.00	195	—

KM# 16.2 DOUBLE TOURNOIS

2.8000 g., Copper, 20.3 mm. **Ruler:** Henry IV **Subject:** Henry IV **Obv:** Portrait within legend **Rev:** Three fleur-de-lis within legend **Edge:** Plain **Mint:** Lyon

Date	Mintage	F	VF	XF	Unc	BU
1608D	—	40.00	90.00	175	—	—

KM# 33 DOUBLE TOURNOIS

Copper **Ruler:** Henry IV **Rev:** Quartered shield of France and Dauphine **Mint:** Grenoble

Date	Mintage	VG	F	VF	XF	Unc
1608Z	—	—	—	—	—	—

KM# 43.1 DOUBLE TOURNOIS

Copper **Ruler:** Louis XIII **Obv:** Juvenile bust right in shirt **Rev:** 3 fleur-de-lis **Mint:** Paris

Date	Mintage	VG	F	VF	XF	Unc
1611A	—	5.00	12.00	35.00	90.00	—
1612A	—	5.00	12.00	35.00	90.00	—
1613A	—	5.00	12.00	35.00	90.00	—
1614A	—	5.00	12.00	35.00	90.00	—
1615A	—	7.00	15.00	45.00	125	—
1616A	—	6.00	13.00	38.00	110	—
1617A	—	5.00	12.00	35.00	90.00	—
1618A	—	5.00	12.00	35.00	90.00	—

KM# 43.2 DOUBLE TOURNOIS

Copper **Ruler:** Louis XIII **Mint:** Lyon

Date	Mintage	VG	F	VF	XF	Unc
1611D	—	7.00	15.00	45.00	135	—
1613D	—	7.00	15.00	45.00	135	—
1614D	—	7.00	15.00	45.00	135	—
1615D	—	7.00	15.00	45.00	135	—
1618D	—	7.00	15.00	45.00	135	—

KM# 43.3 DOUBLE TOURNOIS

Copper **Ruler:** Louis XIII **Mint:** Poitiers

Date	Mintage	VG	F	VF	XF	Unc
1617G	—	7.00	15.00	45.00	135	—
1618G	—	7.00	15.00	45.00	135	—
1619G	—	7.00	15.00	45.00	135	—
1620G	—	5.00	12.00	35.00	90.00	—
1621G	—	6.00	13.00	38.00	110	—

KM# 43.4 DOUBLE TOURNOIS

Copper **Ruler:** Louis XIII **Mint:** Bordeaux

Date	Mintage	VG	F	VF	XF	Unc
1610K	—	8.00	17.00	50.00	150	—
1611K	—	5.00	12.00	35.00	90.00	—
1612K	—	5.00	12.00	35.00	90.00	—
1613K	—	8.00	17.00	50.00	150	—
1614K	—	8.00	17.00	50.00	150	—
1616K	—	8.00	17.00	50.00	150	—
1617K	—	8.00	17.00	50.00	150	—
1618K	—	7.00	15.00	45.00	135	—
1620K	—	8.00	17.00	50.00	150	—

KM# 43.5 DOUBLE TOURNOIS

Copper **Ruler:** Louis XIII **Mint:** Toulouse

Date	Mintage	VG	F	VF	XF	Unc
1611M	—	—	—	—	—	—
1612M	—	7.00	15.00	45.00	135	—

KM# 43.6 DOUBLE TOURNOIS

Copper **Ruler:** Louis XIII **Mint:** Villeneuve St. André

Date	Mintage	VG	F	VF	XF	Unc
1616R	—	7.00	15.00	45.00	135	—
1617R	—	7.00	15.00	45.00	135	—
1618R	—	7.00	15.00	45.00	135	—
1620R	—	10.00	20.00	65.00	190	—
1621R	—	7.00	15.00	45.00	135	—
1622R	—	8.00	17.00	50.00	150	—

KM# 43.7 DOUBLE TOURNOIS

Copper **Ruler:** Louis XIII **Mint:** Nantes

Date	Mintage	VG	F	VF	XF	Unc
1611T	—	8.00	17.00	50.00	150	—
1613T	—	7.00	15.00	45.00	135	—
1614T	—	7.00	15.00	45.00	135	—
1615T	—	7.00	15.00	45.00	135	—
1616T	—	6.00	12.00	35.00	110	—

KM# 43.8 DOUBLE TOURNOIS

Copper **Ruler:** Louis XIII **Mint:** Amiens

Date	Mintage	VG	F	VF	XF	Unc
1612X	—	7.00	15.00	45.00	135	—
1614X	—	7.00	15.00	45.00	135	—
1615X	—	6.00	12.00	40.00	120	—
1616X	—	7.00	15.00	45.00	135	—

KM# 43.9 DOUBLE TOURNOIS

Copper **Ruler:** Louis XIII **Mint:** Aix **Note:** Mint mark: Ampersand.

Date	Mintage	VG	F	VF	XF	Unc
1612	—	—	—	—	—	—
1613	—	7.00	15.00	45.00	135	—
1614	—	8.00	17.00	50.00	150	—

KM# 59.1 DOUBLE TOURNOIS

Copper **Ruler:** Louis XIII **Obv:** Laarger, youthful bust right in ruffled collar **Mint:** Paris

Date	Mintage	VG	F	VF	XF	Unc
1618A	—	10.00	20.00	60.00	180	—

KM# 59.2 DOUBLE TOURNOIS

Copper **Ruler:** Louis XIII **Mint:** Lyon

Date	Mintage	VG	F	VF	XF	Unc
1611D	—	6.00	12.00	35.00	110	—
1612D	—	8.00	17.00	50.00	150	—
1613D	—	6.00	12.00	35.00	110	—
1614D	—	10.00	20.00	60.00	180	—
1615D	—	6.00	12.00	35.00	110	—
1617D	—	7.00	15.00	45.00	135	—

KM# 59.3 DOUBLE TOURNOIS

Copper **Ruler:** Louis XIII **Mint:** Bordeaux

Date	Mintage	VG	F	VF	XF	Unc
1611K	—	7.00	15.00	45.00	135	—
1612K	—	7.00	15.00	45.00	135	—
1613K	—	8.00	17.00	50.00	150	—
1614K	—	10.00	20.00	60.00	180	—

KM# 59.4 DOUBLE TOURNOIS

Copper **Ruler:** Louis XIII **Mint:** Toulouse

Date	Mintage	VG	F	VF	XF	Unc
1611M	—	7.00	15.00	45.00	135	—
1612M	—	7.00	15.00	45.00	135	—

KM# 59.5 DOUBLE TOURNOIS

Copper **Ruler:** Louis XIII **Mint:** Nantes

Date	Mintage	VG	F	VF	XF	Unc
1610T	—	6.00	12.00	35.00	110	—
1611T	—	8.00	17.00	50.00	150	—
1612T	—	8.00	17.00	50.00	150	—
1613T	—	7.00	15.00	45.00	135	—
1614T	—	10.00	20.00	60.00	180	—
1616T	—	8.00	17.00	50.00	150	—

KM# 59.6 DOUBLE TOURNOIS

Copper **Ruler:** Louis XVII **Mint:** Aix **Note:** Mint mark: Ampersand.

Date	Mintage	VG	F	VF	XF	Unc
1612	—	7.00	15.00	45.00	135	—
1613	—	8.00	17.00	50.00	150	—
1614	—	10.00	20.00	65.00	190	—
1616	—	—	—	—	—	—

KM# 60 DOUBLE TOURNOIS

Copper **Ruler:** Louis XVII **Obv:** Large youthful mailed bust right **Mint:** Amiens

Date	Mintage	VG	F	VF	XF	Unc
1614X	—	8.00	17.00	50.00	150	—
1615X	—	7.00	15.00	45.00	135	—
1616X	—	8.00	17.00	50.00	150	—

KM# 61.1 DOUBLE TOURNOIS

Copper **Ruler:** Louis XVII **Obv:** Middle-aged laureate bust right in shirt **Mint:** Paris

Date	Mintage	VG	F	VF	XF	Unc
1620A	—	7.00	15.00	45.00	135	—
1621A	—	6.00	12.00	35.00	110	—
1622A	—	8.00	17.00	50.00	150	—
1625A	—	6.00	12.00	35.00	110	—
1626A	—	6.00	12.00	35.00	110	—
1627A	—	7.00	15.00	45.00	135	—
1628A	—	6.00	12.00	35.00	110	—
1629A	—	7.00	15.00	45.00	135	—

KM# 61.2 DOUBLE TOURNOIS

Copper **Ruler:** Louis XVII **Mint:** Lyon

Date	Mintage	VG	F	VF	XF	Unc
1624D	—	—	—	—	—	—
1625D	—	8.00	17.00	50.00	150	—
1626D	—	—	—	—	—	—
1627D	—	8.00	17.00	50.00	150	—
1628D	—	6.00	12.00	35.00	110	—
1629D	—	6.00	12.00	35.00	110	—

KM# 61.3 DOUBLE TOURNOIS

Copper **Ruler:** Louis XVII **Mint:** Poitiers

Date	Mintage	VG	F	VF	XF	Unc
1619G	1,086,000	7.00	15.00	45.00	135	—
1621G	—	10.00	20.00	60.00	180	—
1622G	—	10.00	20.00	60.00	180	—
1624G	—	—	—	—	—	—
1626G	—	8.00	17.00	50.00	150	—
1627G	—	6.00	12.00	35.00	110	—
1628G	—	10.00	20.00	60.00	180	—

KM# 61.4 DOUBLE TOURNOIS

Copper **Ruler:** Louis XVII **Mint:** La Rochelle

Date	Mintage	VG	F	VF	XF	Unc
1619H	—	—	—	—	—	—

KM# 61.5 DOUBLE TOURNOIS

Copper **Ruler:** Louis XVII **Mint:** Bordeaux

Date	Mintage	VG	F	VF	XF	Unc
1619K	—	8.00	17.00	50.00	150	—
1620K	—	7.00	15.00	45.00	135	—
1621K	—	—	—	—	—	—
1623K	—	10.00	20.00	60.00	180	—
1627K	—	7.00	15.00	45.00	135	—
1628K	—	10.00	20.00	60.00	180	—
1629K	—	8.00	17.00	50.00	150	—

KM# 61.6 DOUBLE TOURNOIS

Copper **Ruler:** Louis XVII **Mint:** Riom

Date	Mintage	VG	F	VF	XF	Unc
16220	—	—	—	—	—	—
Note: Reported, not confirmed						
16230	—	10.00	20.00	60.00	180	—
16240	—	7.00	15.00	45.00	135	—
16250	—	8.00	17.00	50.00	150	—
16260	—	8.00	17.00	50.00	150	—

KM# 61.7 DOUBLE TOURNOIS

Copper **Ruler:** Louis XVII **Mint:** Villeneuve St. André

Date	Mintage	VG	F	VF	XF	Unc
1621R	—	7.00	15.00	45.00	135	—
1622R	—	8.00	17.00	50.00	150	—
1625R	—	—	—	—	—	—
1626R	—	8.00	17.00	50.00	150	—
1627R	—	7.00	15.00	45.00	135	—

KM# 72.1 DOUBLE TOURNOIS

Copper **Ruler:** Louis XIII **Obv:** Older bust right in ruffled collar **Mint:** Paris

Date	Mintage	VG	F	VF	XF	Unc
1627A	—	7.00	15.00	45.00	135	—
1628A	—	6.00	12.00	35.00	110	—
1629A	—	6.00	12.00	35.00	110	—
1630A	—	7.00	15.00	45.00	135	—
1631A	—	8.00	17.00	50.00	150	—
1632A	—	8.00	17.00	50.00	150	—
1633A	—	8.00	17.00	50.00	150	—
1635A	—	6.00	12.00	35.00	110	—

KM# 72.2 DOUBLE TOURNOIS

Copper **Ruler:** Louis XIII **Mint:** Lyon

Date	Mintage	VG	F	VF	XF	Unc
1627D	—	8.00	17.00	50.00	150	—
1628D	—	6.00	12.00	35.00	110	—
1629D	—	6.00	12.00	35.00	110	—
1630D	—	7.00	15.00	45.00	135	—
1631D	—	6.00	12.00	35.00	110	—
1632D	—	8.00	17.00	50.00	150	—
1633D	—	6.00	12.00	35.00	110	—
1634D	—	7.00	15.00	45.00	135	—
1635D	—	8.00	17.00	50.00	150	—

KM# 72.3 DOUBLE TOURNOIS

Copper **Ruler:** Louis XIII **Mint:** Tours

Date	Mintage	VG	F	VF	XF	Unc
1629E	—	10.00	20.00	60.00	180	—
1631E	—	8.00	17.00	50.00	150	—
1632E	—	8.00	17.00	50.00	150	—
1633E	—	6.00	12.00	35.00	110	—
1634E	—	8.00	17.00	50.00	150	—
1635E	—	8.00	17.00	50.00	150	—

KM# 72.4 DOUBLE TOURNOIS

Copper **Ruler:** Louis XIII **Mint:** Poitiers

Date	Mintage	VG	F	VF	XF	Unc
1627G	—	6.00	12.00	35.00	110	—
1628G	—	10.00	20.00	60.00	180	—
1633G	—	—	—	—	—	—

KM# 72.5 DOUBLE TOURNOIS

Copper **Ruler:** Louis XIII **Mint:** La Rochelle

Date	Mintage	VG	F	VF	XF	Unc
1631H	—	7.00	15.00	45.00	135	—
1632H	—	8.00	17.00	50.00	150	—
1633H	—	8.00	17.00	50.00	150	—
1634H	—	8.00	17.00	50.00	150	—

KM# 72.6 DOUBLE TOURNOIS

Copper **Ruler:** Louis XIII **Mint:** Bordeaux

Date	Mintage	VG	F	VF	XF	Unc
1627K	—	7.00	15.00	45.00	135	—
1628K	—	10.00	20.00	60.00	180	—
1631K	—	—	—	—	—	—
1632K	—	8.00	17.00	50.00	150	—
1633K	—	8.00	17.00	50.00	150	—
1635K	—	—	—	—	—	—

KM# 72.7 DOUBLE TOURNOIS

Copper **Ruler:** Louis XIII **Mint:** Villeneuve St. André

Date	Mintage	VG	F	VF	XF	Unc
1634R	—	—	—	—	—	—

KM# 86.1 DOUBLE TOURNOIS

Copper **Ruler:** Louis XIII **Obv:** Laureate and draped large bust right **Rev:** Three fleur-de-lis **Mint:** Paris

Date	Mintage	VG	F	VF	XF	Unc
1628A	—	—	—	—	—	—
1629A	—	10.00	18.00	50.00	150	—
1630A	—	8.00	14.00	35.00	110	—
1637A	—	8.00	14.00	35.00	110	—
1638A	—	10.00	18.00	50.00	150	—

KM# 86.2 DOUBLE TOURNOIS

Copper **Ruler:** Louis XIII **Mint:** Rouen

Date	Mintage	VG	F	VF	XF	Unc
1637B	—	9.00	16.00	45.00	135	—
1638B	—	10.00	18.00	50.00	150	—
1639B	—	10.00	18.00	50.00	150	—
1640B	—	10.00	18.00	50.00	150	—

KM# 86.3 DOUBLE TOURNOIS

Copper **Ruler:** Louis XIII **Mint:** Lyon

Date	Mintage	VG	F	VF	XF	Unc
1628D	—	—	—	—	—	—
1630D	—	8.00	14.00	35.00	110	—
1631D	—	10.00	18.00	50.00	150	—
1632D	—	10.00	18.00	50.00	150	—
1637D	—	9.00	16.00	45.00	135	—
1638D	—	10.00	18.00	50.00	150	—
1639D	—	—	—	—	—	—
1640D	—	10.00	18.00	50.00	150	—

KM# 86.4 DOUBLE TOURNOIS

Copper **Ruler:** Louis XIII **Mint:** Tours

Date	Mintage	VG	F	VF	XF	Unc
1637E	—	8.00	14.00	35.00	110	—
1638E	—	10.00	18.00	50.00	150	—
1639E	—	10.00	18.00	50.00	150	—
1640E	—	10.00	18.00	50.00	150	—

KM# 86.5 DOUBLE TOURNOIS

Copper **Ruler:** Louis XIII **Mint:** La Rochelle

Date	Mintage	VG	F	VF	XF	Unc
1638H	—	10.00	18.00	50.00	150	—
1639H	—	9.00	16.00	45.00	135	—
1640H	—	9.00	16.00	45.00	135	—

KM# 86.6 DOUBLE TOURNOIS

Copper **Ruler:** Louis XIII **Mint:** Bordeaux

Date	Mintage	VG	F	VF	XF	Unc
1637K	—	8.00	14.00	35.00	110	—
1638K	—	10.00	18.00	50.00	150	—
1639K	—	9.00	16.00	45.00	135	—
1640K	—	10.00	18.00	50.00	150	—

KM# 86.7 DOUBLE TOURNOIS

Copper **Ruler:** Louis XIII **Mint:** Feurs **Note:** Strike mark: 1 pellet.

Date	Mintage	VG	F	VF	XF	Unc
1636	—	10.00	18.00	50.00	150	—
1637	—	10.00	18.00	50.00	150	—
1638	—	10.00	18.00	50.00	150	—
1639	—	10.00	18.00	50.00	150	—
1640	—	10.00	18.00	50.00	150	—

KM# 86.8 DOUBLE TOURNOIS

Copper **Ruler:** Louis XIII **Mint:** Lay **Note:** Strike mark: 2 pellets.

Date	Mintage	VG	F	VF	XF	Unc
1637	—	10.00	18.00	50.00	150	—
1638	—	10.00	18.00	50.00	150	—
1639	—	10.00	18.00	50.00	150	—
1640	—	10.00	18.00	50.00	150	—

KM# 86.9 DOUBLE TOURNOIS

Copper **Ruler:** Louis XIII **Mint:** Macon **Note:** Strike mark: 3 pellets.

Date	Mintage	VG	F	VF	XF	Unc
1637	—	10.00	18.00	50.00	150	—
1638	—	10.00	18.00	50.00	150	—
1640	—	10.00	18.00	50.00	150	—

KM# 86.10 DOUBLE TOURNOIS

Copper **Ruler:** Louis XIII **Mint:** Maromme **Note:** Strike mark: Cross of 5 pellets.

Date	Mintage	VG	F	VF	XF	Unc
1637	—	10.00	18.00	50.00	150	—
1639	—	10.00	18.00	50.00	150	—
1640	—	10.00	18.00	50.00	150	—

KM# 86.11 DOUBLE TOURNOIS

Copper **Ruler:** Louis XIII **Mint:** Roquemaure **Note:** Mint mark: 4 pellets.

Date	Mintage	VG	F	VF	XF	Unc
1637	—	10.00	18.00	50.00	150	—
1638	—	10.00	18.00	50.00	150	—
1639	—	10.00	18.00	50.00	150	—
1640	—	10.00	18.00	50.00	150	—

KM# 86.12 DOUBLE TOURNOIS

Copper **Ruler:** Louis XIII **Mint:** Troyes **Note:** Strike mark: Starburst.

Date	Mintage	VG	F	VF	XF	Unc
1637	—	10.00	18.00	50.00	150	—
1638	—	10.00	18.00	50.00	150	—

KM# 86.13 DOUBLE TOURNOIS

Copper **Ruler:** Louis XIII **Mint:** Valence **Note:** Strike mark: Star.

Date	Mintage	VG	F	VF	XF	Unc
1638	—	10.00	18.00	50.00	150	—
1639	—	10.00	18.00	50.00	150	—
1640	—	10.00	18.00	50.00	150	—

KM# 86.14 DOUBLE TOURNOIS

Copper **Ruler:** Louis XIII **Mint:** Vienne **Note:** Strike mark: Crescent.

Date	Mintage	VG	F	VF	XF	Unc
1638	—	10.00	18.00	50.00	150	—
1639	—	10.00	18.00	50.00	150	—
1640	—	10.00	18.00	50.00	150	—

KM# 85 DOUBLE TOURNOIS

Copper **Ruler:** Louis XIII **Obv:** Navarre shield below bust **Mint:** Saint Palais

Date	Mintage	VG	F	VF	XF	Unc
1632	—	20.00	40.00	125	375	—
1633	—	25.00	50.00	150	450	—
1635	—	20.00	40.00	125	375	—
1636	—	20.00	40.00	125	375	—
1638	—	25.00	50.00	150	450	—
1639	—	25.00	50.00	150	450	—
1643	—	25.00	50.00	150	450	—

KM# 127.1 DOUBLE TOURNOIS

Copper **Ruler:** Louis XIII **Obv:** Laureate head left **Obv. Legend:** LOVIS XIII R.D. FRAN ET NA... **Mint:** Paris

Date	Mintage	VG	F	VF	XF	Unc
1642A	—	6.00	12.00	35.00	110	—
1643A	—	6.00	12.00	35.00	110	—

KM# 127.2 DOUBLE TOURNOIS

Copper **Ruler:** Louis XIII **Mint:** Rouen

Date	Mintage	VG	F	VF	XF	Unc
1643B	—	9.00	18.00	50.00	150	—

KM# 127.3 DOUBLE TOURNOIS

Copper **Ruler:** Louis XIII **Mint:** Lyon

Date	Mintage	VG	F	VF	XF	Unc
1643D	—	9.00	18.00	50.00	150	—

KM# 127.4 DOUBLE TOURNOIS

Copper **Ruler:** Louis XIII **Mint:** Tours

Date	Mintage	VG	F	VF	XF	Unc
1643E	—	8.00	15.00	45.00	135	—

KM# 127.5 DOUBLE TOURNOIS

Copper **Ruler:** Louis XIII **Mint:** Angers

Date	Mintage	VG	F	VF	XF	Unc
1643F	—	8.00	15.00	45.00	135	—

KM# 127.6 DOUBLE TOURNOIS

Copper **Ruler:** Louis XIII **Mint:** La Rochelle

Date	Mintage	VG	F	VF	XF	Unc
1642H	—	8.00	12.00	35.00	110	—
1643H	—	8.00	12.00	35.00	110	—

KM# 127.7 DOUBLE TOURNOIS

Copper **Ruler:** Louis XIII **Mint:** Bordeaux

Date	Mintage	VG	F	VF	XF	Unc
1642K	—	8.00	12.00	35.00	110	—
1643K	—	8.00	12.00	35.00	110	—

KM# 127.8 DOUBLE TOURNOIS

Copper **Ruler:** Louis XIII **Mint:** Feurs **Note:** Strike mark: Pellet.

Date	Mintage	VG	F	VF	XF	Unc
1642	—	9.00	18.00	50.00	150	—
1643	—	9.00	18.00	50.00	150	—

KM# 127.9 DOUBLE TOURNOIS

Copper **Ruler:** Louis XIII **Mint:** Lay **Note:** Strike mark: 2 pellets.

Date	Mintage	VG	F	VF	XF	Unc
1642	—	9.00	18.00	50.00	150	—
1643	—	9.00	18.00	50.00	150	—

KM# 127.10 DOUBLE TOURNOIS

Copper **Ruler:** Louis XIII **Mint:** Macon **Note:** Strike mark: 3 pellets.

Date	Mintage	VG	F	VF	XF	Unc
1643	—	10.00	20.00	65.00	190	—

KM# 127.11 DOUBLE TOURNOIS

Copper **Ruler:** Louis XIII **Mint:** Roquemaure **Note:** Strike mark: 4 pellets.

Date	Mintage	VG	F	VF	XF	Unc
1643	—	12.00	20.00	75.00	200	—

KM# 127.12 DOUBLE TOURNOIS

Copper **Ruler:** Louis XIII **Mint:** Vienne **Note:** Strike mark: Crescent.

Date	Mintage	VG	F	VF	XF	Unc
1643	—	12.00	20.00	65.00	190	—

KM# 151 DOUBLE TOURNOIS

Copper **Ruler:** Louis XIV **Obv:** Laureate head right **Rev:** Crosses flanking crowned fleur-de-lis **Mint:** Paris

Date	Mintage	VG	F	VF	XF	Unc
1644A	—	100	225	350	750	—
1647A	—	125	250	400	850	—

KM# 193 DOUBLE TOURNOIS

Billon **Ruler:** Louis XIV **Obv:** Cross with fluer-de-lis at ends **Rev:** Three fleur-de-lis, crow above

Date	Mintage	VG	F	VF	XF	Unc
1656	—	25.00	50.00	170	450	—

KM# 87 DOUBLE LORRAIN

Copper **Ruler:** Louis XIII **Obv:** Laureate bust right **Rev:** Three fleur-de-lis **Mint:** Stenay

Date	Mintage	VG	F	VF	XF	Unc
1633	—	12.00	25.00	65.00	190	—
1636	—	12.00	25.00	65.00	190	—
1637	—	12.00	25.00	65.00	190	—
1638	—	12.00	25.00	65.00	190	—
1639	—	12.00	25.00	65.00	190	—
1640	—	12.00	25.00	65.00	190	—

KM# 90 DOUBLE LORRAIN

Copper **Ruler:** Louis XIII **Obv:** Bust right in shirt

Date	Mintage	VG	F	VF	XF	Unc
1635	—	15.00	30.00	75.00	200	—

KM# 91 DOUBLE LORRAIN

Copper **Ruler:** Louis XIII **Obv:** Laureate bust

Date	Mintage	VG	F	VF	XF	Unc
1635	—	20.00	40.00	125	325	—

KM# 128 DOUBLE LORRAIN

Copper **Ruler:** Louis XIII **Obv:** Laureate head

Date	Mintage	VG	F	VF	XF	Unc
1642	—	25.00	50.00	150	400	—

KM# 50 VACQUETTE

Billon **Ruler:** Louis XIII **Obv:** Quartered shield, cow and crowned L's **Rev:** Cross in quatrefoil **Mint:** Morlaas

Date	Mintage	VG	F	VF	XF	Unc
1612	—	30.00	80.00	225	575	—
1613	473,000	—	—	—	—	—
1614	291,000	—	—	—	—	—
1615	120,000	—	—	—	—	—
1619	312,000	30.00	80.00	260	600	—
1642	—	30.00	80.00	225	575	—
ND	—	25.00	70.00	200	550	—

KM# 63 DOUBLE VACQUETTE

Billon **Ruler:** Louis XIII **Obv:** Quartered shield of Bearn **Rev:** Cross in quatrefoil, date in angles **Mint:** Morlaas

Date	Mintage	VG	F	VF	XF	Unc
1619	—	65.00	125	300	750	—
1642	—	—	—	—	—	—

Note: Reported, not confirmed

KM# 78.1 SIZAIN

Billon **Ruler:** Louis XIII **Obv:** Crowned shield of France **Rev:** Cross with fleur-de-lis in angles **Mint:** Uncertain Mint

Date	Mintage	VG	F	VF	XF	Unc
1628 Rare	—	—	—	—	—	—
1629 Rare	—	—	—	—	—	—

KM# 78.2 SIZAIN

Billon **Ruler:** Louis XIII **Mint:** Paris

Date	Mintage	VG	F	VF	XF	Unc
1642A	—	100	200	400	800	—

KM# 198 SIZAIN

Billon **Ruler:** Louis XIV **Obv:** Crowned shield of France, small crowned L's at sides **Rev:** Cross with fleur-de-lis in angles

Date	Mintage	VG	F	VF	XF	Unc
1658	—	80.00	175	375	775	—

KM# 196 6 BLANCS

Billon **Ruler:** Louis XIV **Obv:** Laureate, draped and mailed bust right **Rev:** Crown above three fleur-de-lis, value in exergue **Mint:** Bordeaux

Date	Mintage	VG	F	VF	XF	Unc
1657K	—	350	750	1,450	3,000	—

KM# 58.1 DOUZAIN

Billon **Ruler:** Louis XIII **Obv:** Crowned shield of France **Rev:** Cross with crown or L's in angles **Mint:** Paris

Date	Mintage	VG	F	VF	XF	Unc
1617A	—	45.00	90.00	175	450	—
1618A	—	40.00	80.00	165	425	—

KM# 58.2 DOUZAIN

Billon **Ruler:** Louis XIII **Mint:** La Rochelle

Date	Mintage	VG	F	VF	XF	Unc
1616H	—	30.00	65.00	125	325	—
1620H	—	30.00	65.00	125	325	—
1625H	—	30.00	65.00	125	325	—
1626H	—	30.00	65.00	125	325	—
1628H	—	30.00	65.00	125	325	—

KM# 58.2a DOUZAIN

0.6000 g., 0.8780 Silver 0.0169 oz. ASW **Ruler:** Louis XIII **Rev:** Cross with crown or fleur-de-lis in angles **Mint:** Paris

Date	Mintage	VG	F	VF	XF	Unc
1625A	7,803	95.00	175	325	750	—

KM# 58.3 DOUZAIN

Billon **Ruler:** Louis XIII **Mint:** Toulouse

Date	Mintage	VG	F	VF	XF	Unc
1611M	—	50.00	100	200	500	—

KM# 58.4 DOUZAIN

Billon **Ruler:** Louis XIII **Mint:** Montpellier

Date	Mintage	VG	F	VF	XF	Unc
1621N	—	30.00	65.00	125	325	—
1622N	—	30.00	65.00	125	325	—
1628N	—	50.00	100	200	500	—
1629N	—	60.00	120	225	550	—

KM# 197 DOUZAIN

Billon **Ruler:** Louis XIV **Obv:** Crowned shield of France, small crowned L's flanking **Rev:** Cross with fleur-de-lis in angles

Date	Mintage	VG	F	VF	XF	Unc
1658	—	100	125	450	825	—

KM# 5 LIARD

Billon **Ruler:** Henry IV **Obv:** Crowned H, three fleur-de-lis around **Rev:** Short cross with fleur-de-lis at ends **Mint:** Uncertain Mint

Date	Mintage	VG	F	VF	XF	Unc
1601	—	—	—	—	—	—

KM# 34 LIARD

Billon **Ruler:** Henry IV **Obv:** Cross with cows and crowned H in angles **Rev:** Cross in quatre lobe **Mint:** Bearn

Date	Mintage	VG	F	VF	XF	Unc
1609	—	—	—	—	—	—

KM# 191.1 LIARD

Copper **Ruler:** Louis XIV **Obv:** Young bust in robe right **Rev:** Large crowned L, divide fleur-de-lis **Mint:** Paris

Date	Mintage	VG	F	VF	XF	Unc
1654A	—	100	200	325	650	—

KM# 191.2 LIARD

Copper **Ruler:** Louis XIV **Mint:** Bordeaux

Date	Mintage	VG	F	VF	XF	Unc
1656K	—	125	250	400	700	—

KM# 189 LIARD

Billon **Ruler:** Louis XIV **Obv:** Crowned shield of France **Rev:** Cross with fleur-de-lis in angles

Date	Mintage	VG	F	VF	XF	Unc
1655	—	65.00	125	250	550	—

KM# 190 LIARD

Billon **Ruler:** Louis XIV **Rev:** Maltese cross

Date	Mintage	VG	F	VF	XF	Unc
1655	—	65.00	125	250	550	—

KM# 192.1 LIARD

Copper **Ruler:** Louis XIV **Rev:** Value above three fleur-de-lis, mint mark within **Mint:** Paris

Date	Mintage	VG	F	VF	XF	Unc
1655A	—	8.00	16.00	45.00	150	—
1656A	—	10.00	18.00	50.00	160	—
1657A	—	12.00	24.00	55.00	175	—

KM# 192.2 LIARD

Copper **Ruler:** Louis XIV **Mint:** Rouen

Date	Mintage	VG	F	VF	XF	Unc
1655B	—	8.00	18.00	45.00	145	—
1656B	—	9.00	20.00	50.00	150	—
1657B	—	12.00	30.00	75.00	225	—
1658B	—	20.00	50.00	125	360	—

KM# 192.3 LIARD

Copper **Ruler:** Louis XIV **Note:** Strike mark: B*.

Date	Mintage	VG	F	VF	XF	Unc
1655	—	8.00	18.00	45.00	145	—
1656	—	10.00	25.00	60.00	180	—

KM# 192.4 LIARD

Copper **Ruler:** Louis XIV **Mint:** Saint Lô

Date	Mintage	VG	F	VF	XF	Unc
1655C	—	8.00	18.00	45.00	145	—
1656C	—	12.00	30.00	75.00	225	—
1657C	—	10.00	25.00	60.00	180	—

KM# 192.5 LIARD

Copper **Ruler:** Louis XIV **Mint:** Lyon

Date	Mintage	VG	F	VF	XF	Unc
1655D	—	7.00	16.00	45.00	150	—
1656D	—	10.00	25.00	75.00	200	—
1657D	—	8.00	18.00	55.00	160	—

KM# 192.6 LIARD

Copper **Ruler:** Louis XIV **Mint:** Tours

Date	Mintage	VG	F	VF	XF	Unc
1655E	—	9.00	20.00	50.00	160	—
1656E	—	9.00	20.00	50.00	160	—
1657E	—	9.00	20.00	50.00	160	—
1658E	—	20.00	50.00	125	360	—

KM# 192.7 LIARD

Copper **Ruler:** Louis XIV **Mint:** Poitiers

Date	Mintage	VG	F	VF	XF	Unc
1655G	—	9.00	20.00	50.00	160	—
1656G	—	25.00	60.00	150	425	—
1657G	—	12.00	30.00	75.00	225	—

KM# 192.8 LIARD

Copper **Ruler:** Louis XIV **Mint:** Poitiers

Date	Mintage	VG	F	VF	XF	Unc
1657G	—	12.00	30.00	75.00	250	—
1658G	—	17.00	40.00	100	325	—

KM# 192.9 LIARD

Copper **Ruler:** Louis XIV **Mint:** Limoges

Date	Mintage	VG	F	VF	XF	Unc
1655I	—	—	—	125	400	—
1656I	—	10.00	28.00	70.00	240	—
1657I	—	9.00	25.00	60.00	200	—
1658I	—	20.00	50.00	125	400	—

KM# 192.10 LIARD

Copper **Ruler:** Louis XIV **Mint:** Bordeaux

Date	Mintage	VG	F	VF	XF	Unc
1655K	—	12.00	30.00	75.00	250	—
1656K	—	10.00	28.00	70.00	240	—
1657K	—	12.00	30.00	75.00	250	—

KM# 192.11 LIARD

Copper **Ruler:** Louis XIV **Mint:** Villeneuve St. André

Date	Mintage	VG	F	VF	XF	Unc
1655R	—	12.00	30.00	75.00	250	—
1656R	—	10.00	28.00	70.00	240	—
1657R	—	12.00	30.00	75.00	250	—

KM# 284.1 LIARD

Copper **Ruler:** Louis XIV **Obv:** Older mailed bust right **Mint:** Paris

Date	Mintage	VG	F	VF	XF	Unc
1693A	1,291,000	9.00	25.00	60.00	200	—
1694A	—	9.00	25.00	60.00	200	—
1696A	—	9.00	25.00	60.00	200	—
1697A	—	8.00	20.00	50.00	175	—
1698A	—	8.00	20.00	50.00	175	—
1699A	—	10.00	28.00	70.00	250	—

KM# 284.2 LIARD

Copper **Ruler:** Louis XIV **Mint:** Metz

Date	Mintage	VG	F	VF	XF	Unc
1694AA	—	15.00	35.00	80.00	275	—
1697AA	—	15.00	35.00	80.00	275	—

KM# 284.3 LIARD

Copper **Ruler:** Louis XIV **Mint:** Rouen

Date	Mintage	VG	F	VF	XF	Unc
1693B	—	9.00	25.00	60.00	200	—
1694B	—	15.00	35.00	80.00	275	—
1695B	—	15.00	35.00	80.00	275	—
1697B	—	15.00	35.00	80.00	275	—
1698B	—	15.00	35.00	80.00	275	—
1699B	—	10.00	28.00	70.00	250	—
1700B	—	18.00	40.00	100	350	—

KM# 284.4 LIARD

Copper **Ruler:** Louis XIV **Mint:** Lyon

Date	Mintage	VG	F	VF	XF	Unc
1693D	2,063,000	8.00	20.00	50.00	175	—
1694D	602,000	18.00	40.00	100	350	—
1695D	2,850,000	8.00	20.00	50.00	175	—
1696D	39,000	15.00	35.00	80.00	275	—
1697D	—	—	—	—	—	—
1699D	3,876,000	9.00	25.00	60.00	200	—

KM# 284.5 LIARD

Copper **Ruler:** Louis XIV **Mint:** Tours

Date	Mintage	VG	F	VF	XF	Unc
1693E	—	15.00	35.00	80.00	275	—
1696E	317,000	—	—	—	—	—
1697E	213,000	15.00	35.00	80.00	275	—
1698E	—	10.00	28.00	70.00	250	—
1699E	—	9.00	25.00	60.00	200	—

KM# 284.6 LIARD

Copper **Ruler:** Louis XIV **Mint:** Poitiers

Date	Mintage	VG	F	VF	XF	Unc
1696G	—	10.00	28.00	70.00	250	—
1697G	—	17.00	40.00	100	350	—

KM# 284.7 LIARD

Copper **Ruler:** Louis XIV **Mint:** La Rochelle

Date	Mintage	VG	F	VF	XF	Unc
1695H	—	15.00	35.00	80.00	275	—
1696H	—	9.00	25.00	60.00	200	—
1698H	—	15.00	35.00	80.00	275	—
1699H	—	10.00	28.00	70.00	250	—

KM# 284.8 LIARD

Copper **Ruler:** Louis XIV **Mint:** Bordeaux

Date	Mintage	VG	F	VF	XF	Unc
1693K	—	10.00	28.00	70.00	250	—
1696K	—	15.00	35.00	80.00	275	—
1698K	—	10.00	28.00	70.00	250	—

KM# 284.9 LIARD

Copper **Ruler:** Louis XIV **Mint:** Bayonne

Date	Mintage	VG	F	VF	XF	Unc
1695L	—	9.00	25.00	60.00	200	—
1696L	—	15.00	35.00	80.00	275	—
1697L	—	15.00	35.00	80.00	275	—
1698L	—	15.00	35.00	80.00	275	—
1699L	—	9.00	25.00	60.00	200	—

KM# 284.10 LIARD

Copper **Ruler:** Louis XIV **Mint:** Toulouse

Date	Mintage	VG	F	VF	XF	Unc
1693	49,000	17.00	50.00	150	400	—
1694	—	—	—	—	—	—
1695	—	15.00	35.00	80.00	275	—
1697	—	10.00	28.00	70.00	250	—

KM# 284.11 LIARD

Copper **Ruler:** Louis XIV **Mint:** Montpellier

Date	Mintage	VG	F	VF	XF	Unc
1693N	768,000	15.00	35.00	80.00	275	—
1694N	—	17.00	40.00	100	350	—
1695N	—	10.00	28.00	70.00	250	—
1696N	79,000	—	—	—	—	—
1697N	3,097,000	9.00	25.00	60.00	200	—
1699N	—	15.00	35.00	80.00	275	—

KM# 284.12 LIARD

Copper **Ruler:** Louis XIV **Mint:** Riom

Date	Mintage	VG	F	VF	XF	Unc
16930	75,000	20.00	50.00	125	400	—
16950	—	15.00	35.00	80.00	275	—
16980	—	15.00	35.00	80.00	275	—
16990	—	10.00	28.00	70.00	250	—

KM# 284.13 LIARD

Copper **Ruler:** Louis XIV **Mint:** Dijon

Date	Mintage	VG	F	VF	XF	Unc
1693P	26,000	—	—	—	—	—
1695P	105,000	15.00	35.00	80.00	275	—
1697P	123,000	15.00	35.00	80.00	275	—
1698P	3,626,000	8.00	20.00	50.00	175	—

KM# 284.14 LIARD

Copper **Ruler:** Louis XIV **Mint:** Reims

Date	Mintage	VG	F	VF	XF	Unc
1693S	—	15.00	35.00	80.00	275	—
1696S	—	15.00	35.00	80.00	275	—
1697S	—	8.00	20.00	50.00	175	—
1698S	—	15.00	35.00	80.00	275	—

KM# 284.15 LIARD

Copper **Ruler:** Louis XIV **Mint:** Nantes

Date	Mintage	VG	F	VF	XF	Unc
1697T	—	9.00	25.00	60.00	200	—

KM# 284.16 LIARD

Copper **Ruler:** Louis XIV **Mint:** Troyes

Date	Mintage	VG	F	VF	XF	Unc
1693V	274,000	15.00	35.00	80.00	275	—
1695V	—	15.00	35.00	80.00	275	—
1697V	Est. 1,600,000	9.00	25.00	60.00	200	—
1698V	2,888,000	9.00	25.00	60.00	200	—

KM# 284.18 LIARD

Copper **Ruler:** Louis XIV **Mint:** Amiens

Date	Mintage	VG	F	VF	XF	Unc
1693X	—	15.00	35.00	80.00	275	—
1695X	—	15.00	35.00	80.00	275	—

Date	Mintage	VG	F	VF	XF	Unc
1696X	—	9.00	25.00	60.00	200	—
1697X	—	9.00	25.00	60.00	200	—
1698X	—	9.00	25.00	60.00	200	—
1699X	—	10.00	28.00	70.00	250	—

KM# 284.19 LIARD

Copper **Ruler:** Louis XIV **Mint:** Bourges

Date	Mintage	VG	F	VF	XF	Unc
1693Y	—	15.00	35.00	80.00	275	—
1695Y	—	15.00	35.00	80.00	275	—
1698Y	—	15.00	35.00	80.00	275	—
1699Y	—	15.00	35.00	80.00	275	—

KM# 284.20 LIARD

Copper **Ruler:** Louis XIV **Mint:** Rennes **Note:** Mint mark: Numeral 9.

Date	Mintage	VG	F	VF	XF	Unc
1693	—	15.00	35.00	80.00	275	—
1694	—	15.00	35.00	80.00	275	—
1697	—	10.00	28.00	70.00	250	—

KM# 284.21 LIARD

Copper **Ruler:** Louis XIV **Mint:** Aix **Note:** Mint mark: Ampersand.

Date	Mintage	VG	F	VF	XF	Unc
1693	—	15.00	35.00	80.00	275	—
1694	—	17.00	40.00	100	350	—
1698	—	15.00	35.00	80.00	275	—
1699	—	8.00	20.00	50.00	175	—

KM# 284.22 LIARD

Copper **Ruler:** Louis XIV **Mint:** Lille **Note:** Mint mark: Crowned L.

Date	Mintage	VG	F	VF	XF	Unc
1693	1,649,000	9.00	25.00	60.00	200	—
1694	—	15.00	35.00	80.00	275	—
1695	—	15.00	35.00	80.00	275	—
1696	2,907,000	8.00	20.00	50.00	175	—
1697	1,753,000	10.00	28.00	70.00	250	—
1698	—	10.00	28.00	70.00	250	—
1699	845,000	15.00	35.00	80.00	275	—
1700	—	17.00	40.00	100	350	—

KM# 284.23 LIARD

Copper **Ruler:** Louis XIV **Mint:** Metz **Note:** Mint mark: Crowned M.

Date	Mintage	VG	F	VF	XF	Unc
1693	—	20.00	45.00	100	350	—

KM# 284.24 LIARD

Copper **Ruler:** Louis XIV **Mint:** Troyes **Note:** Mint mark: Crowned S.

Date	Mintage	VG	F	VF	XF	Unc
1693	—	20.00	40.00	85.00	285	—
1695	—	20.00	40.00	85.00	285	—

KM# 284.25 LIARD

Copper **Ruler:** Louis XIV **Mint:** Besancon **Note:** Mint mark: Monogram of two back-to-back C's.

Date	Mintage	VG	F	VF	XF	Unc
1698	3,636,000	10.00	22.00	55.00	185	—

KM# 304 LIARD

Copper **Ruler:** Louis XIV **Obv:** Bust right **Mint:** Pau **Note:** Mint mark: Cow.

Date	Mintage	VG	F	VF	XF	Unc
1694	—	20.00	45.00	120	385	—
1695	—	20.00	45.00	120	385	—
1696	273,000	20.00	45.00	120	385	—
1697	—	20.00	45.00	120	385	—
1698	—	20.00	45.00	120	385	—

KM# 309 2 DENIERS

Copper **Ruler:** Louis XIV **Rev:** Crown above 3 fleur-de-lis **Mint:** Strasbourg

Date	Mintage	VG	F	VF	XF	Unc
1695BB	331,000	—	—	—	—	—
1696BB	—	8.00	20.00	40.00	125	—
1697BB	1,157,000	10.00	25.00	50.00	150	—
1698BB	—	8.00	20.00	40.00	125	—
1699BB	—	8.00	20.00	40.00	125	—
1700BB	—	10.00	25.00	50.00	150	—

KM# 137 3 DENIERS (Liard)

Copper **Ruler:** Louis XIV **Obv:** Laureate head right **Rev:** Crown above fleur-de-lis dividing 3D **Mint:** Paris

Date	Mintage	VG	F	VF	XF	Unc
1643A	—	60.00	125	250	475	—
1644A	—	60.00	125	250	475	—
1647A	—	60.00	125	250	475	—
1648A	—	60.00	125	250	475	—
NDA	—	60.00	125	250	475	—

KM# 170 3 DENIERS (Liard)

Copper **Ruler:** Louis XIV **Rev:** Crown above large L, dividing fleur-de-lis, denomination in exergue, 3 DENIERS **Mint:** Paris

Date	Mintage	VG	F	VF	XF	Unc
1649A	—	50.00	100	200	425	—

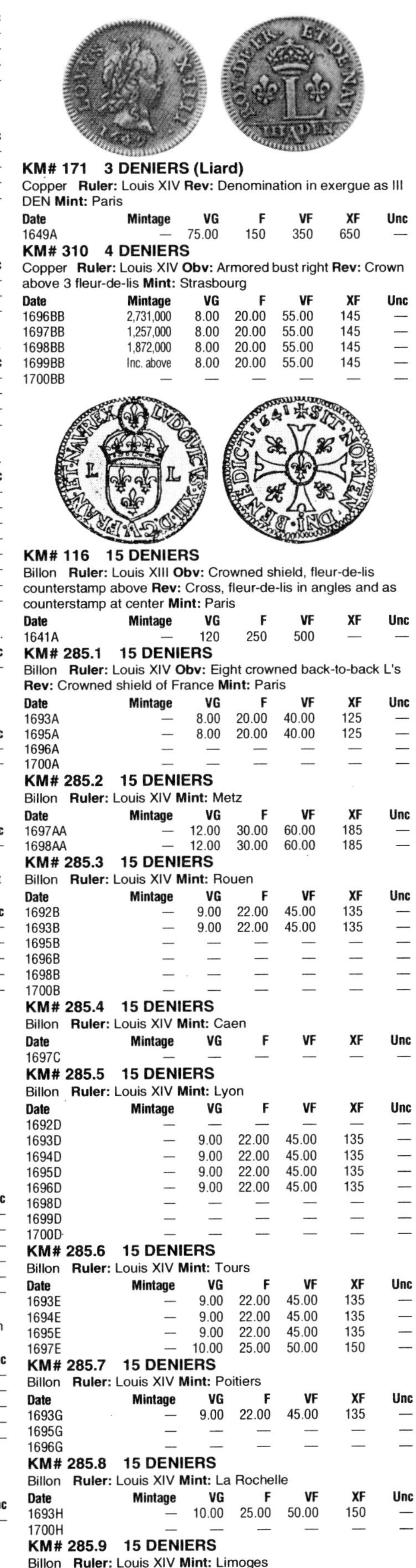

KM# 171 3 DENIERS (Liard)

Copper **Ruler:** Louis XIV **Rev:** Denomination in exergue as III DEN **Mint:** Paris

Date	Mintage	VG	F	VF	XF	Unc
1649A	—	75.00	150	350	650	—

KM# 310 4 DENIERS

Copper **Ruler:** Louis XIV **Obv:** Armored bust right **Rev:** Crown above 3 fleur-de-lis **Mint:** Strasbourg

Date	Mintage	VG	F	VF	XF	Unc
1696BB	2,731,000	8.00	20.00	55.00	145	—
1697BB	1,257,000	8.00	20.00	55.00	145	—
1698BB	1,872,000	8.00	20.00	55.00	145	—
1699BB	Inc. above	8.00	20.00	55.00	145	—
1700BB	—	—	—	—	—	—

KM# 116 15 DENIERS

Billon **Ruler:** Louis XIII **Obv:** Crowned shield, fleur-de-lis counterstamp above **Rev:** Cross, fleur-de-lis in angles and as counterstamp at center **Mint:** Paris

Date	Mintage	VG	F	VF	XF	Unc
1641A	—	120	250	500	—	—

KM# 285.1 15 DENIERS

Billon **Ruler:** Louis XIV **Obv:** Eight crowned back-to-back L's **Rev:** Crowned shield of France **Mint:** Paris

Date	Mintage	VG	F	VF	XF	Unc
1693A	—	8.00	20.00	40.00	125	—
1695A	—	8.00	20.00	40.00	125	—
1696A	—	—	—	—	—	—
1700A	—	—	—	—	—	—

KM# 285.2 15 DENIERS

Billon **Ruler:** Louis XIV **Mint:** Metz

Date	Mintage	VG	F	VF	XF	Unc
1697AA	—	12.00	30.00	60.00	185	—
1698AA	—	12.00	30.00	60.00	185	—

KM# 285.3 15 DENIERS

Billon **Ruler:** Louis XIV **Mint:** Rouen

Date	Mintage	VG	F	VF	XF	Unc
1692B	—	9.00	22.00	45.00	135	—
1693B	—	9.00	22.00	45.00	135	—
1695B	—	—	—	—	—	—
1696B	—	—	—	—	—	—
1698B	—	—	—	—	—	—
1700B	—	—	—	—	—	—

KM# 285.4 15 DENIERS

Billon **Ruler:** Louis XIV **Mint:** Caen

Date	Mintage	VG	F	VF	XF	Unc
1697C	—	—	—	—	—	—

KM# 285.5 15 DENIERS

Billon **Ruler:** Louis XIV **Mint:** Lyon

Date	Mintage	VG	F	VF	XF	Unc
1692D	—	—	—	—	—	—
1693D	—	9.00	22.00	45.00	135	—
1694D	—	9.00	22.00	45.00	135	—
1695D	—	9.00	22.00	45.00	135	—
1696D	—	9.00	22.00	45.00	135	—
1698D	—	—	—	—	—	—
1699D	—	—	—	—	—	—
1700D	—	—	—	—	—	—

KM# 285.6 15 DENIERS

Billon **Ruler:** Louis XIV **Mint:** Tours

Date	Mintage	VG	F	VF	XF	Unc
1693E	—	9.00	22.00	45.00	135	—
1694E	—	9.00	22.00	45.00	135	—
1695E	—	9.00	22.00	45.00	135	—
1697E	—	10.00	25.00	50.00	150	—

KM# 285.7 15 DENIERS

Billon **Ruler:** Louis XIV **Mint:** Poitiers

Date	Mintage	VG	F	VF	XF	Unc
1693G	—	9.00	22.00	45.00	135	—
1695G	—	—	—	—	—	—
1696G	—	—	—	—	—	—

KM# 285.8 15 DENIERS

Billon **Ruler:** Louis XIV **Mint:** La Rochelle

Date	Mintage	VG	F	VF	XF	Unc
1693H	—	10.00	25.00	50.00	150	—
1700H	—	—	—	—	—	—

KM# 285.9 15 DENIERS

Billon **Ruler:** Louis XIV **Mint:** Limoges

Date	Mintage	VG	F	VF	XF	Unc
1695I	—	—	—	—	—	—
1696I	—	—	—	—	—	—

KM# 285.10 15 DENIERS

Billon **Ruler:** Louis XIV **Mint:** Bayonne

Date	Mintage	VG	F	VF	XF	Unc
1693L	—	10.00	25.00	50.00	150	—

KM# 285.11 15 DENIERS

Billon **Ruler:** Louis XIV **Mint:** Toulouse

Date	Mintage	VG	F	VF	XF	Unc
1692M	—	9.00	22.00	45.00	135	—
1693M	—	9.00	22.00	45.00	135	—
1694M	—	—	—	—	—	—
1695M	—	—	—	—	—	—
1696M	—	—	—	—	—	—
1698M	—	—	—	—	—	—

KM# 285.12 15 DENIERS

Billon **Ruler:** Louis XIV **Mint:** Montpellier

Date	Mintage	VG	F	VF	XF	Unc
1692N	—	9.00	22.00	45.00	135	—
1693N	—	9.00	22.00	45.00	135	—
1694N	—	10.00	25.00	50.00	150	—
1695N	—	—	—	—	—	—
1696N	—	10.00	25.00	50.00	150	—
1697N	—	12.00	30.00	60.00	185	—
1698N	—	—	—	—	—	—
1700N	—	—	—	—	—	—

KM# 285.13 15 DENIERS

Billon **Ruler:** Louis XIV **Mint:** Riom

Date	Mintage	VG	F	VF	XF	Unc
16920	—	—	—	—	—	—
16930	—	—	—	—	—	—
16950	—	—	—	—	—	—
16960	—	—	—	—	—	—
16970	—	—	—	—	—	—

KM# 285.14 15 DENIERS

Billon **Ruler:** Louis XIV **Mint:** Dijon

Date	Mintage	VG	F	VF	XF	Unc
1693P	—	9.00	22.00	45.00	135	—
1694P	—	—	—	—	—	—
1695P	—	9.00	22.00	45.00	135	—
1696P	—	—	—	—	—	—
1697P	—	20.00	40.00	100	285	—
1698P	—	20.00	40.00	100	285	—

KM# 285.15 15 DENIERS

Billon **Ruler:** Louis XIV **Mint:** Reims

Date	Mintage	VG	F	VF	XF	Unc
1693S	—	—	—	—	—	—
1694S	—	9.00	22.00	45.00	135	—
1695S	—	—	—	—	—	—
1696S	—	—	—	—	—	—
1699S	—	—	—	—	—	—

KM# 285.16 15 DENIERS

Billon **Ruler:** Louis XIV **Mint:** Nantes

Date	Mintage	VG	F	VF	XF	Unc
1695T	—	9.00	22.00	45.00	135	—
1698T	—	—	—	—	—	—

KM# 285.17 15 DENIERS

Billon **Ruler:** Louis XIV **Mint:** Troyes

Date	Mintage	VG	F	VF	XF	Unc
1695V	—	12.00	30.00	60.00	185	—

KM# 285.18 15 DENIERS

Billon **Ruler:** Louis XIV **Mint:** Amiens

Date	Mintage	VG	F	VF	XF	Unc
1693X	—	—	—	—	—	—
1695X	—	—	—	—	—	—

KM# 285.19 15 DENIERS

Billon **Ruler:** Louis XIV **Mint:** Bourges

Date	Mintage	VG	F	VF	XF	Unc
1692Y	—	—	—	—	—	—
1693Y	—	—	—	—	—	—
1695Y	—	—	—	—	—	—
1698Y	—	—	—	—	—	—

KM# 285.20 15 DENIERS

Billon **Ruler:** Louis XIV **Mint:** Aix **Note:** Mint mark: Ampersand.

Date	Mintage	VG	F	VF	XF	Unc
1693	—	9.00	22.00	45.00	135	—
1694	—	9.00	22.00	45.00	135	—
1695	—	9.00	22.00	45.00	135	—
1696	—	10.00	25.00	50.00	150	—
1700	—	—	—	—	—	—

KM# 285.21 15 DENIERS

Billon **Ruler:** Louis XIV **Mint:** Rennes **Note:** Mint mark: Numeral 9.

Date	Mintage	VG	F	VF	XF	Unc
1693	—	8.00	20.00	40.00	120	—
1694	—	8.00	20.00	40.00	120	—
1697	—	10.00	25.00	50.00	150	—

KM# 285.22 15 DENIERS

Billon **Ruler:** Louis XIV **Obv:** Crowned double monograms form cross with fleur-de-lis at angles **Rev:** Crowned shield **Mint:** Lille **Note:** Mint mark: Crowned L.

Date	Mintage	VG	F	VF	XF	Unc
1693	—	—	—	—	—	—
1696	—	—	—	—	—	—
1697	—	10.00	25.00	50.00	150	—

Date	Mintage	VG	F	VF	XF	Unc
1698	—	—	—	—	—	—
1699	—	10.00	25.00	50.00	150	—
1700	—	15.00	35.00	75.00	220	—

KM# 285.23 15 DENIERS

Billon **Ruler:** Louis XIV **Mint:** Troyes **Note:** Mint mark: Crowned S.

Date	Mintage	VG	F	VF	XF	Unc
1692	—	10.00	25.00	50.00	150	—
1693	—	15.00	35.00	75.00	220	—

KM# 285.24 15 DENIERS

Billon **Ruler:** Louis XIV **Mint:** Besancon **Note:** Mint mark: Monogram of two back-to-back C's.

Date	Mintage	VG	F	VF	XF	Unc
1695	—	—	—	—	—	—
1696	—	9.00	22.00	45.00	135	—
1697	—	—	—	—	—	—
1698	—	20.00	40.00	100	285	—
1699	—	—	—	—	—	—

KM# 286.1 15 DENIERS

Billon **Ruler:** Louis XIV **Mint:** Paris **Note:** Smaller, new design overstruck on old flans.

Date	Mintage	VG	F	VF	XF	Unc
1693A	—	7.00	15.00	25.00	55.00	—

KM# 286.2 15 DENIERS

Billon **Ruler:** Louis XIV **Mint:** Lyon

Date	Mintage	VG	F	VF	XF	Unc
1693D	—	7.00	15.00	25.00	55.00	—
1694D	—	7.00	15.00	25.00	55.00	—
1695D	—	7.00	15.00	25.00	55.00	—
1696D	—	7.00	15.00	25.00	55.00	—
1698D	—	7.00	15.00	25.00	55.00	—

KM# 286.3 15 DENIERS

Billon **Ruler:** Louis XIV **Mint:** Tours

Date	Mintage	VG	F	VF	XF	Unc
1693E	—	7.00	15.00	25.00	55.00	—
1694E	—	7.00	15.00	25.00	55.00	—
1695E	—	7.00	15.00	25.00	55.00	—
1696E	—	7.00	15.00	25.00	55.00	—
1697E	—	7.00	15.00	25.00	55.00	—

KM# 286.4 15 DENIERS

Billon **Ruler:** Louis XIV **Mint:** La Rochelle

Date	Mintage	VG	F	VF	XF	Unc
1694H	—	7.00	15.00	28.00	60.00	—
1697H	—	7.00	15.00	28.00	60.00	—

KM# 286.5 15 DENIERS

Billon **Ruler:** Louis XIV **Mint:** Bayonne

Date	Mintage	VG	F	VF	XF	Unc
1695L	—	7.00	15.00	25.00	55.00	—

KM# 286.6 15 DENIERS

Billon **Ruler:** Louis XIV **Mint:** Toulouse

Date	Mintage	VG	F	VF	XF	Unc
1692M	—	7.00	15.00	25.00	55.00	—

KM# 286.7 15 DENIERS

Billon **Ruler:** Louis XIV **Mint:** Riom

Date	Mintage	VG	F	VF	XF	Unc
1695O	—	8.00	16.00	30.00	65.00	—

KM# 286.8 15 DENIERS

Billon **Ruler:** Louis XIV **Mint:** Dijon

Date	Mintage	VG	F	VF	XF	Unc
1694P	—	7.00	15.00	25.00	55.00	—
1695P	—	7.00	15.00	25.00	55.00	—

KM# 286.9 15 DENIERS

Billon **Ruler:** Louis XIV **Mint:** Rennes **Note:** Mint mark: Numeral 9.

Date	Mintage	VG	F	VF	XF	Unc
1695	—	7.00	15.00	25.00	55.00	—
1697	—	7.00	15.00	25.00	55.00	—

KM# 288 15 DENIERS

Billon **Ruler:** Louis XIV **Obv:** Eight crowned L' back-to-back **Rev:** Crowned shield of France and Navarre

Date	Mintage	VG	F	VF	XF	Unc
ND	—	65.00	135	250	—	—

KM# 289 15 DENIERS

Billon **Ruler:** Louis XIV **Rev:** Crowned shield of France, Navarre and Bearn

Date	Mintage	VG	F	VF	XF	Unc
1692	—	22.00	60.00	110	300	—
1693	—	22.00	60.00	110	300	—
1694	—	25.00	65.00	120	320	—
1695	25,000	25.00	65.00	130	340	—
1696	134,000	22.00	60.00	110	300	—
1697	—	22.00	60.00	110	300	—
1698	6,828	—	—	—	—	—
1699	3,626	25.00	65.00	120	320	—
1700	692	—	—	—	—	—

KM# 287.1 15 DENIERS

Billon **Ruler:** Louis XIV **Mint:** Lyon

Date	Mintage	VG	F	VF	XF	Unc
1693D	—	7.00	15.00	25.00	55.00	—
1694D	—	7.00	15.00	25.00	55.00	—
1696D	—	7.00	15.00	25.00	55.00	—

KM# 287.2 15 DENIERS

Billon **Ruler:** Louis XIV **Mint:** Tours **Note:** Counterstamp: Fleur-de-lis.

Date	Mintage	VG	F	VF	XF	Unc
1692E	—	7.00	15.00	25.00	55.00	—
1693E	—	7.00	15.00	25.00	55.00	—
1694E	—	7.00	15.00	25.00	55.00	—

KM# 287.3 15 DENIERS

Billon **Ruler:** Louis XIV **Mint:** La Rochelle

Date	Mintage	VG	F	VF	XF	Unc
1694H	—	7.00	15.00	25.00	55.00	—

KM# 287.4 15 DENIERS

Billon **Ruler:** Louis XIV **Mint:** Toulouse

Date	Mintage	VG	F	VF	XF	Unc
1694M	—	7.00	15.00	25.00	55.00	—

KM# 287.5 15 DENIERS

Billon **Ruler:** Louis XIV **Mint:** Montpellier

Date	Mintage	VG	F	VF	XF	Unc
1694N	—	7.00	15.00	25.00	55.00	—

KM# 287.6 15 DENIERS

Billon **Ruler:** Louis XIV **Mint:** Dijon

Date	Mintage	VG	F	VF	XF	Unc
1693P	—	7.00	15.00	25.00	55.00	—

KM# 287.7 15 DENIERS

Billon **Ruler:** Louis XIV **Mint:** Aix **Note:** Mint mark: Ampersand.

Date	Mintage	VG	F	VF	XF	Unc
1692	—	7.00	15.00	30.00	60.00	—

KM# 287.8 15 DENIERS

Billon **Ruler:** Louis XIV **Mint:** Rennes **Note:** Mint mark: Numeral 9.

Date	Mintage	VG	F	VF	XF	Unc
1697	—	7.00	15.00	25.00	55.00	—

KM# 195 5 LIARDS

Billon **Ruler:** Louis XIV **Rev:** Crown above 3 fleur-de-lis, date and value **Mint:** Bordeaux

Date	Mintage	VG	F	VF	XF	Unc
1657K	—	250	600	1,250	2,400	—

KM# 311 16 DENIERS

Billon **Ruler:** Louis XIV **Obv:** Crowned shield of France dividing value **Rev:** Fleur-de-lis at ends of outlined cross **Mint:** Strasbourg

Date	Mintage	VG	F	VF	XF	Unc
1696BB	2,084,000	9.00	22.00	45.00	135	—
1697BB	292,000	12.00	30.00	60.00	185	—
1698BB	71,000	—	—	—	—	—
1699BB	65,000	15.00	40.00	80.00	225	—
1700BB	731,000	—	—	—	—	—

KM# 13 1/4 FRANC

Billon **Ruler:** Henry IV **Obv:** Laureate, armored bust right **Rev:** Cross fleuree, H at center **Mint:** Bordeaux

Date	Mintage	VG	F	VF	XF	Unc
1602K	—	150	275	450	850	—

KM# 17.1 1/4 FRANC

Billon **Ruler:** Henry IV **Mint:** Poitiers

Date	Mintage	VG	F	VF	XF	Unc
1603G	—	150	275	450	850	—

KM# 17.2 1/4 FRANC

Billon **Ruler:** Henry IV **Obv:** Laureate, armored bust right, fleur-de-lis behind head **Mint:** Villeneuve St. André

Date	Mintage	VG	F	VF	XF	Unc
1603R	—	150	275	450	850	—

KM# 18 1/4 FRANC

Billon **Ruler:** Henry IV **Rev:** Cross fleuree, H at center, Dauphine and fleur-de-lis in angles

Date	Mintage	VG	F	VF	XF	Unc
1603	—	—	—	—	—	—

KM# 52.1 1/4 FRANC

3.5470 g., 0.8330 Silver 0.0950 oz. ASW **Ruler:** Louis XIII **Obv:** Laureate bust right in ruffled collar **Rev:** Cross fleuree with L at center **Mint:** Paris

Date	Mintage	VG	F	VF	XF	Unc
1614A	—	—	—	—	—	—
1625A	—	50.00	120	235	600	—

KM# 52.2 1/4 FRANC

3.5470 g., 0.8330 Silver 0.0950 oz. ASW **Ruler:** Louis XIII **Mint:** Rouen

Date	Mintage	VG	F	VF	XF	Unc
1612B	—	50.00	120	235	600	—
1614B	—	50.00	120	235	600	—
1615B	—	50.00	120	235	600	—

KM# 52.3 1/4 FRANC

3.5470 g., 0.8330 Silver 0.0950 oz. ASW **Ruler:** Louis XIII **Mint:** Lyon

Date	Mintage	VG	F	VF	XF	Unc
1615D	—	50.00	120	235	600	—

KM# 52.4 1/4 FRANC

3.5470 g., 0.8330 Silver 0.0950 oz. ASW **Ruler:** Louis XIII **Mint:** Toulouse

Date	Mintage	VG	F	VF	XF	Unc
1615M	—	50.00	120	235	600	—
1622M	—	50.00	120	235	600	—

KM# 52.5 1/4 FRANC

3.5470 g., 0.8330 Silver 0.0950 oz. ASW **Ruler:** Louis XIII **Mint:** Amiens

Date	Mintage	VG	F	VF	XF	Unc
1615X	—	—	—	—	—	—
1617X	—	—	—	—	—	—

KM# 53.1 1/4 FRANC

3.5470 g., 0.8330 Silver 0.0950 oz. ASW **Ruler:** Louis XIII **Obv:** Bust right in ruffled collar **Mint:** Paris

Date	Mintage	VG	F	VF	XF	Unc
1615A	—	50.00	120	235	600	—
1618A	—	—	—	—	—	—

KM# 53.2 1/4 FRANC

3.5470 g., 0.8330 Silver 0.0950 oz. ASW **Ruler:** Louis XIII **Mint:** Rouen

Date	Mintage	VG	F	VF	XF	Unc
1615B	—	50.00	120	235	600	—
1623B	—	50.00	120	235	600	—
1625B	—	50.00	120	235	600	—

KM# 53.3 1/4 FRANC

3.5470 g., 0.8330 Silver 0.0950 oz. ASW **Ruler:** Louis XIII **Mint:** Caen

Date	Mintage	VG	F	VF	XF	Unc
1617C	—	—	—	—	—	—
1625C	—	—	—	—	—	—

KM# 53.4 1/4 FRANC

3.5470 g., 0.8330 Silver 0.0950 oz. ASW **Ruler:** Louis XIII **Mint:** Reims

Date	Mintage	VG	F	VF	XF	Unc
1615S	—	50.00	120	235	600	—
1618S	4,279	50.00	120	235	600	—
1626S	5,708	50.00	120	235	600	—

KM# 93.1 1/4 FRANC

3.5470 g., 0.8330 Silver 0.0950 oz. ASW **Ruler:** Louis XIII **Obv:** Laureate bust right in shirt collar **Mint:** Bordeaux

Date	Mintage	VG	F	VF	XF	Unc
1640K	—	50.00	120	235	600	—

KM# 93.2 1/4 FRANC

3.5470 g., 0.8330 Silver 0.0950 oz. ASW **Ruler:** Louis XIII **Mint:** Bayonne

Date	Mintage	VG	F	VF	XF	Unc
1641L	—	—	—	—	—	—

KM# 93.3 1/4 FRANC

3.5470 g., 0.8330 Silver 0.0950 oz. ASW **Ruler:** Louis XIII **Mint:** Toulouse

Date	Mintage	VG	F	VF	XF	Unc
1631M	—	—	—	—	—	—
1633M	—	—	—	—	—	—
1634M	—	—	—	—	—	—
1635M	—	50.00	120	235	600	—
1636M	—	50.00	120	235	600	—
1637M	—	—	—	—	—	—
1638M	—	50.00	120	235	600	—
1639M	—	50.00	120	235	600	—
1640M	—	—	—	—	—	—
1641M	—	50.00	120	235	600	—

KM# 93.4 1/4 FRANC

3.5470 g., 0.8330 Silver 0.0950 oz. ASW **Ruler:** Louis XIII **Mint:** Montpellier

Date	Mintage	VG	F	VF	XF	Unc
1641N	—	85.00	165	300	775	—

KM# 93.5 1/4 FRANC

3.5470 g., 0.8330 Silver 0.0950 oz. ASW **Ruler:** Louis XIII **Mint:** Reims

Date	Mintage	VG	F	VF	XF	Unc
1631S	2,233	85.00	165	300	775	—
1632S	—	—	—	—	—	—
1634S	—	—	—	—	—	—
1635S	—	—	—	—	—	—

KM# 93.6 1/4 FRANC

3.5470 g., 0.8330 Silver 0.0950 oz. ASW **Ruler:** Louis XIII **Mint:** Grenoble

Date	Mintage	VG	F	VF	XF	Unc
1641Z	—	85.00	165	300	775	—

KM# 93.7 1/4 FRANC

3.5470 g., 0.8330 Silver 0.0950 oz. ASW **Ruler:** Louis XIII **Mint:** Amiens

Date	Mintage	VG	F	VF	XF	Unc
1636X	—	—	—	—	—	—

KM# 94.1 1/4 FRANC

3.5470 g., 0.8330 Silver 0.0950 oz. ASW **Ruler:** Louis XIII **Obv:** Laureate bust right in larger shirt collar **Mint:** Amiens

Date	Mintage	VG	F	VF	XF	Unc
1638	—	60.00	125	250	620	—

KM# 94.2 1/4 FRANC

3.5470 g., 0.8330 Silver 0.0950 oz. ASW **Ruler:** Louis XIII **Mint:** Montpellier

Date	Mintage	VG	F	VF	XF	Unc
1636N	—	—	—	—	—	—
1638N	—	60.00	125	250	620	—

KM# 94.3 1/4 FRANC

3.5470 g., 0.8330 Silver 0.0950 oz. ASW **Ruler:** Louis XIII **Mint:** Villeneuve St. André

Date	Mintage	VG	F	VF	XF	Unc
1638R	—	—	—	—	—	—

KM# 94.4 1/4 FRANC

3.5470 g., 0.8330 Silver 0.0950 oz. ASW **Ruler:** Louis XIII **Mint:** Aix **Note:** Mint mark: Ampersand.

Date	Mintage	VG	F	VF	XF	Unc
1636	—	—	—	—	—	—

KM# 19 1/2 FRANC

Silver **Ruler:** Henry IV **Obv:** Laureate, armored bust right, fleur-de-lis behind head **Mint:** Villeneuve St. André

Date	Mintage	VG	F	VF	XF	Unc
1602R	—	125	250	425	700	—
1603R	—	125	250	425	700	—
1607R	—	125	250	425	700	—

KM# 14.1 1/2 FRANC

Silver **Ruler:** Henry IV **Obv:** Laureate, armored bust right **Rev:** Cross fleuree, H in center **Mint:** Paris

Date	Mintage	VG	F	VF	XF	Unc
1602A	—	125	250	425	700	—

KM# 14.2 1/2 FRANC

Silver **Ruler:** Henry IV **Mint:** Lyon

Date	Mintage	VG	F	VF	XF	Unc
1602D	—	125	250	425	700	—
1603D	—	125	250	425	700	—
1604D	—	125	250	425	700	—

KM# 14.3 1/2 FRANC

Silver **Ruler:** Henry IV **Mint:** Angers

Date	Mintage	VG	F	VF	XF	Unc
1604	—	125	250	425	700	—

KM# 14.4 1/2 FRANC

Silver **Ruler:** Henry IV **Mint:** Poitiers

Date	Mintage	VG	F	VF	XF	Unc
1603G	—	125	250	425	700	—

KM# 14.5 1/2 FRANC

Silver **Ruler:** Henry IV **Mint:** Reims

Date	Mintage	VG	F	VF	XF	Unc
1600S	—	150	275	450	700	—

KM# 76 1/2 FRANC

0.8330 Silver **Ruler:** Louis XIII **Obv:** Armored laureate bust right in ruffled collar **Mint:** Toulouse

Date	Mintage	VG	F	VF	XF	Unc
1610M	—	55.00	140	310	700	—
1611M	—	40.00	100	200	500	—
1612M	—	—	—	—	—	—
1615M	—	30.00	80.00	165	425	—
1616M	—	30.00	80.00	165	425	—
1617M	—	30.00	80.00	165	425	—
1618M	—	30.00	80.00	165	425	—
1619M	—	—	—	—	—	—
1620M	—	40.00	100	200	500	—
1621M	—	40.00	100	200	500	—
1622M	—	40.00	100	200	500	—
1623M	—	40.00	100	200	500	—
1624M	—	40.00	100	200	500	—
1625M	—	30.00	80.00	165	425	—
1626M	—	30.00	80.00	165	425	—
1627M	—	30.00	80.00	165	425	—

KM# 74 1/2 FRANC

0.8330 Silver **Ruler:** Louis XIII **Obv:** Large laureate bust in ruffled collar, legend begins at 12 o'clock **Mint:** Saint Lô

Date	Mintage	VG	F	VF	XF	Unc
1611C	—	—	—	—	—	—
1614C	—	35.00	90.00	175	450	—
1615C	—	25.00	60.00	120	325	—

KM# 73.1 1/2 FRANC

Silver **Ruler:** Louis XIII **Obv:** Laureate bust right in ruffled collar, mint mark below **Rev:** Cross fleuree with L at center **Mint:** Paris

Date	Mintage	VG	F	VF	XF	Unc
1627A	—	50.00	120	235	600	—

KM# 73.2 1/2 FRANC

Silver **Ruler:** Louis XIII **Mint:** Rouen

Date	Mintage	VG	F	VF	XF	Unc
1611B	—	35.00	90.00	175	450	—
1612B	—	35.00	90.00	175	450	—
1613B	—	35.00	90.00	175	450	—
1614B	—	35.00	90.00	175	450	—
1615B	—	30.00	75.00	145	400	—
1616B	—	35.00	90.00	175	450	—
1617B	—	30.00	75.00	145	400	—
1619B	—	35.00	90.00	175	450	—
1626B	—	—	—	—	—	—
1627B	—	—	—	—	—	—

KM# 73.3 1/2 FRANC

Silver **Ruler:** Louis XIII **Mint:** Saint Lô

Date	Mintage	VG	F	VF	XF	Unc
1616C	—	35.00	90.00	175	450	—
1617C	—	35.00	90.00	175	450	—
1618C	—	—	—	—	—	—
1621C	—	—	—	—	—	—
1622C	—	—	—	—	—	—
1623C	—	—	—	—	—	—
1625C	—	—	—	—	—	—
1626C	—	—	—	—	—	—
1627C	—	—	—	—	—	—
1630C	—	—	—	—	—	—

KM# 73.4 1/2 FRANC

Silver **Ruler:** Louis XIII **Mint:** Tours

Date	Mintage	VG	F	VF	XF	Unc
1615E	—	35.00	90.00	175	450	—

KM# 73.5 1/2 FRANC

Silver **Ruler:** Louis XIII **Mint:** Angers

Date	Mintage	VG	F	VF	XF	Unc
1623F	—	35.00	90.00	185	465	—
1624F	—	—	—	—	—	—
1625F	—	35.00	90.00	185	465	—

KM# 73.6 1/2 FRANC

Silver **Ruler:** Louis XIII **Mint:** Reims

Date	Mintage	VG	F	VF	XF	Unc
1615S	—	30.00	75.00	145	400	—

KM# 75 1/2 FRANC

0.8330 Silver **Ruler:** Louis XIII **Obv:** Legend begins at 7 o'clock **Mint:** Limoges

Date	Mintage	VG	F	VF	XF	Unc
1613I	—	30.00	80.00	165	425	—
1614I	—	40.00	100	200	500	—
1615I	—	30.00	80.00	165	425	—
1620I	—	35.00	90.00	175	450	—
1621I	—	40.00	100	200	500	—
1622I	—	40.00	100	200	500	—
1626I	—	40.00	100	200	500	—
1630I	—	40.00	100	200	500	—

KM# 77.1 1/2 FRANC

0.8330 Silver **Ruler:** Louis XIII **Obv:** Large young bust right in ruffled collar **Mint:** Paris

Date	Mintage	VG	F	VF	XF	Unc
1615A	—	40.00	100	215	550	—
1616A	—	40.00	100	215	550	—
1617A	—	60.00	150	285	750	—
1618A	—	60.00	150	285	750	—
1620A	—	40.00	100	215	550	—
1622A	—	80.00	200	400	1,100	—
1623A	—	—	—	—	—	—
1624A	—	—	—	—	—	—
1625A	—	—	—	—	—	—

KM# 77.2 1/2 FRANC

0.8330 Silver **Ruler:** Louis XIII **Mint:** Saint Lô

Date	Mintage	VG	F	VF	XF	Unc
1616C	—	50.00	125	235	650	—
1617C	—	—	—	—	—	—
1618C	—	55.00	140	245	675	—
1619C	—	60.00	150	275	750	—
1620C	—	60.00	150	275	750	—
1623C	—	—	—	—	—	—

KM# 77.3 1/2 FRANC

0.8330 Silver **Ruler:** Louis XIII **Mint:** Lyon

Date	Mintage	VG	F	VF	XF	Unc
1615D	—	40.00	100	200	500	—

KM# 77.4 1/2 FRANC

0.8330 Silver **Ruler:** Louis XIII **Mint:** Tours

Date	Mintage	VG	F	VF	XF	Unc
1618E	—	55.00	140	275	675	—
1619E	—	—	—	—	—	—

KM# 77.5 1/2 FRANC

0.8330 Silver **Ruler:** Louis XIII **Mint:** Reims

Date	Mintage	VG	F	VF	XF	Unc
1611S	—	40.00	100	200	500	—
1615S	—	30.00	75.00	150	400	—
1616S	—	40.00	100	200	500	—
1617S	—	40.00	100	200	500	—
1618S	—	—	—	—	—	—
1620S	—	—	—	—	—	—
1626S	—	—	—	—	—	—

KM# 77.6 1/2 FRANC

0.8330 Silver **Ruler:** Louis XIII **Mint:** Amiens

Date	Mintage	VG	F	VF	XF	Unc
1615X	—	40.00	100	200	500	—
1616X	—	70.00	175	350	850	—
1617X	—	70.00	175	350	850	—

KM# 77.7 1/2 FRANC

0.8330 Silver **Ruler:** Louis XIII **Mint:** Rennes **Note:** Mint mark: Numeral 9.

Date	Mintage	VG	F	VF	XF	Unc
1615	—	40.00	100	200	500	—
1617	—	—	—	—	—	—
1619	—	—	—	—	—	—
1620	—	70.00	175	350	850	—

KM# 117.1 1/2 FRANC

0.8330 Silver **Ruler:** Louis XIII **Obv:** Large laureate bust right in shirt collar **Mint:** Rouen

Date	Mintage	VG	F	VF	XF	Unc
1641B	—	40.00	100	200	500	—

KM# 117.2 1/2 FRANC

0.8330 Silver **Ruler:** Louis XIII **Mint:** Saint Lô

Date	Mintage	VG	F	VF	XF	Unc
1632C	—	80.00	200	400	950	—
1636C	—	45.00	110	225	550	—
1637C	—	45.00	110	225	550	—
1640C	—	—	—	—	—	—
1641C	—	—	—	—	—	—

KM# 117.3 1/2 FRANC

0.8330 Silver **Ruler:** Louis XIII **Mint:** Lyon

Date	Mintage	VG	F	VF	XF	Unc
1632D	—	40.00	100	200	500	—
1641D	—	—	—	—	—	—

KM# 117.4 1/2 FRANC
0.8330 Silver **Ruler:** Louis XIII **Mint:** La Rochelle

Date	Mintage	VG	F	VF	XF	Unc
1641H	—	—	—	—	—	—

KM# 117.5 1/2 FRANC
0.8330 Silver **Ruler:** Louis XIII **Mint:** Limoges

Date	Mintage	VG	F	VF	XF	Unc
1630I	—	75.00	185	375	900	—
1631I	—	—	—	—	—	—
1632I	—	—	—	—	—	—

KM# 117.6 1/2 FRANC
0.8330 Silver **Ruler:** Louis XIII **Mint:** Bordeaux

Date	Mintage	VG	F	VF	XF	Unc
1638K	—	90.00	225	450	1,100	—
1639K	—	75.00	185	375	900	—

KM# 117.7 1/2 FRANC
0.8330 Silver **Ruler:** Louis XIII **Mint:** Bayonne

Date	Mintage	VG	F	VF	XF	Unc
1629L	—	40.00	100	200	500	—

KM# 117.8 1/2 FRANC
0.8330 Silver **Ruler:** Louis XIII **Mint:** Toulouse

Date	Mintage	VG	F	VF	XF	Unc
1627M	—	40.00	100	200	500	—
1628M	—	40.00	100	200	500	—
1629M	—	40.00	100	200	500	—
1630M	—	40.00	100	200	500	—
1631M	—	—	—	—	—	—
1632M	—	40.00	100	220	540	—
1633M	—	40.00	100	220	540	—
1634M	—	40.00	100	220	540	—
1635M	—	40.00	100	220	540	—
1636M	—	40.00	100	220	540	—
1637M	—	40.00	100	200	500	—
1638M	—	40.00	100	200	500	—
1639M	—	35.00	85.00	175	450	—
1640M	—	35.00	85.00	175	450	—
1641M	—	35.00	85.00	175	450	—

KM# 117.9 1/2 FRANC
0.8330 Silver **Ruler:** Louis XIII **Mint:** Dijon

Date	Mintage	VG	F	VF	XF	Unc
1637P	—	—	—	—	—	—
1638P	—	—	—	—	—	—

KM# 117.10 1/2 FRANC
0.8330 Silver **Ruler:** Louis XIII **Mint:** Reims

Date	Mintage	VG	F	VF	XF	Unc
1631S	—	75.00	185	375	900	—
1632S	—	—	—	—	—	—
1634S	—	—	—	—	—	—
1635S	—	—	—	—	—	—
1637S	—	45.00	110	225	550	—
1638S	—	45.00	110	225	550	—
1639S	—	45.00	110	225	550	—
1640S	—	—	—	—	—	—
1641S	—	—	—	—	—	—

KM# 117.11 1/2 FRANC
0.8330 Silver **Ruler:** Louis XIII **Mint:** Amiens

Date	Mintage	VG	F	VF	XF	Unc
1632X	—	—	—	—	—	—
1636X	—	90.00	225	450	1,000	—

KM# 117.12 1/2 FRANC
0.8330 Silver **Ruler:** Louis XIII **Mint:** Bourges

Date	Mintage	VG	F	VF	XF	Unc
1640Y	—	—	—	—	—	—

KM# 118.1 1/2 FRANC
0.8330 Silver **Ruler:** Louis XIII **Obv:** Tall laureate bust right in cloak **Mint:** Saint Lô

Date	Mintage	VG	F	VF	XF	Unc
1638C	—	90.00	225	450	1,000	—
1639C	—	90.00	225	450	1,000	—

KM# 118.2 1/2 FRANC
0.8330 Silver **Ruler:** Louis XIII **Mint:** Montpellier

Date	Mintage	VG	F	VF	XF	Unc
1633N	—	—	—	—	—	—
1636N	—	—	—	—	—	—
1637N	—	55.00	140	275	675	—
1638N	—	75.00	185	375	900	—
1639N	—	80.00	200	400	950	—
1640N	—	75.00	185	375	900	—
1641N	—	55.00	140	275	675	—

KM# 118.3 1/2 FRANC
0.8330 Silver **Ruler:** Louis XIII **Mint:** Aix **Note:** Mint mark: Ampersand.

Date	Mintage	VG	F	VF	XF	Unc
1635	—	70.00	175	350	850	—
1636	—	70.00	175	350	850	—
1637	—	70.00	175	350	850	—
1638	—	45.00	110	225	550	—
1639	—	75.00	185	375	900	—
1640	—	70.00	175	350	850	—
1641	—	50.00	125	250	625	—

KM# 119.1 1/2 FRANC
0.8330 Silver **Ruler:** Louis XIII **Obv:** Tall laureate draped bust right **Mint:** Arras

Date	Mintage	VG	F	VF	XF	Unc
1641AR	—	150	300	500	900	—
1642AR	—	—	—	—	—	—

KM# 119.2 1/2 FRANC
0.8330 Silver **Ruler:** Louis XIII **Mint:** Grenoble

Date	Mintage	VG	F	VF	XF	Unc
1641Z	—	275	500	850	1,600	—

KM# 245 SOL
0.5110 g., 0.8330 Silver 0.0137 oz. ASW **Ruler:** Louis XIII **Obv:** Large fleur-de-lis **Rev:** Value and date within legend **Mint:** Strasbourg

Date	Mintage	VG	F	VF	XF	Unc
1682	—	20.00	50.00	110	275	—
1683	—	25.00	60.00	125	300	—
1684	—	30.00	75.00	150	375	—
1685	—	—	—	—	—	—
1686	—	—	—	—	—	—
1687	—	—	—	—	—	—
1688	—	—	—	—	—	—

KM# 231 2 SOLS
0.8150 g., 0.7980 Silver 0.0209 oz. ASW **Ruler:** Louis XIV **Obv:** Laureate and draped bust right **Rev:** Crown above two fleur-de-lis, mint mark below

Date	Mintage	VG	F	VF	XF	Unc
1674A	—	30.00	75.00	145	350	—
1675A	—	25.00	65.00	135	325	—
1676A	—	30.00	75.00	145	350	—
1677A	—	40.00	90.00	175	420	—

KM# 246 2 SOLS
1.0220 g., 0.7980 Silver 0.0262 oz. ASW **Ruler:** Louis XIV **Obv:** Large fleur-de-lis **Rev:** Value and date within legend

Date	Mintage	VG	F	VF	XF	Unc
1682	—	15.00	35.00	95.00	200	—
1683	—	15.00	35.00	95.00	200	—
1684	—	15.00	35.00	95.00	200	—
1687	—	15.00	35.00	95.00	200	—

KM# 232.1 4 SOLS
1.8090 g., 0.7980 Silver 0.0464 oz. ASW **Ruler:** Louis XIV **Obv:** Draped bust right **Rev:** Crown above fleur-de-lis cross **Mint:** Paris

Date	Mintage	VG	F	VF	XF	Unc
1674A	—	8.00	20.00	45.00	135	—
1675A	—	7.00	18.00	40.00	120	—
1676A	—	7.00	18.00	40.00	120	—
1677A	—	7.00	18.00	40.00	120	—
1679A	—	15.00	40.00	85.00	225	—

KM# 232.2 4 SOLS
1.8090 g., 0.7980 Silver 0.0464 oz. ASW **Ruler:** Louis XIV **Mint:** Lyon

Date	Mintage	VG	F	VF	XF	Unc
1674D	Est. 370,000	8.00	20.00	45.00	135	—
1675D	Est. 3,689,000	7.00	18.00	40.00	120	—
1676D	Est. 4,186,000	7.00	18.00	40.00	120	—
1677D	Est. 4,507,000	7.00	18.00	40.00	120	—

KM# 247 4 SOLS
2.0440 g., 0.8330 Silver 0.0547 oz. ASW **Ruler:** Louis XIV **Obv:** Large fleur-de-lis **Rev:** Value and date within legend **Mint:** Strasbourg

Date	Mintage	VG	F	VF	XF	Unc
1682	91,000	70.00	150	300	600	—

KM# 281.1 4 SOLS 2 DENIERS
1.8090 g., 0.7980 Silver 0.0464 oz. ASW **Ruler:** Louis XIV **Obv:** Draped bust right **Rev:** Crowned double L monogram **Mint:** Paris

Date	Mintage	VG	F	VF	XF	Unc
1691A	—	6.00	15.00	30.00	70.00	—
1692A	—	6.00	15.00	30.00	70.00	—
1693A	—	6.00	16.00	32.00	80.00	—
1695A	—	7.00	17.00	35.00	90.00	—

KM# 281.2 4 SOLS 2 DENIERS
1.8090 g., 0.7980 Silver 0.0464 oz. ASW **Ruler:** Louis XIV **Mint:** Rouen

Date	Mintage	VG	F	VF	XF	Unc
1691B	—	6.00	16.00	32.00	80.00	—
1692B	—	7.00	17.00	35.00	90.00	—

KM# 281.3 4 SOLS 2 DENIERS
1.8090 g., 0.7980 Silver 0.0464 oz. ASW **Ruler:** Louis XIV **Mint:** Caen

Date	Mintage	VG	F	VF	XF	Unc
1696C	—	8.00	20.00	40.00	100	—
1697C	69,000	—	—	—	—	—

KM# 281.4 4 SOLS 2 DENIERS
1.8090 g., 0.7980 Silver 0.0464 oz. ASW **Ruler:** Louis XIV **Mint:** Lyon

Date	Mintage	VG	F	VF	XF	Unc
1691D	2,812,000	6.00	15.00	30.00	70.00	—
1692D	5,544,000	6.00	15.00	30.00	75.00	—
1693D	1,491,000	6.00	15.00	30.00	75.00	—
1694D	770,000	6.00	15.00	30.00	75.00	—
1695D	456,000	6.00	15.00	30.00	75.00	—
1696D	281,000	7.00	17.00	35.00	90.00	—
1697D	149,000	—	—	—	—	—
1698D	70,000	—	—	—	—	—
1699D	53,000	9.00	22.00	45.00	110	—
1700D	5,259	—	—	—	—	—

KM# 281.5 4 SOLS 2 DENIERS
1.8090 g., 0.7980 Silver 0.0464 oz. ASW **Ruler:** Louis XIV **Mint:** Tours

Date	Mintage	VG	F	VF	XF	Unc
1691E	—	6.00	15.00	30.00	75.00	—
1692E	—	6.00	15.00	30.00	75.00	—
1693E	—	7.00	17.00	35.00	90.00	—
1694E	—	7.00	17.00	35.00	90.00	—

KM# 281.6 4 SOLS 2 DENIERS
1.8090 g., 0.7980 Silver 0.0464 oz. ASW **Ruler:** Louis XIV **Mint:** La Rochelle

Date	Mintage	VG	F	VF	XF	Unc
1691H	—	6.00	15.00	30.00	75.00	—
1692H	—	8.00	20.00	40.00	100	—
1700H	—	18.00	35.00	65.00	180	—

KM# 281.7 4 SOLS 2 DENIERS
1.8090 g., 0.7980 Silver 0.0464 oz. ASW **Ruler:** Louis XIV **Mint:** Bordeaux

Date	Mintage	VG	F	VF	XF	Unc
1691K	—	6.00	16.00	32.00	80.00	—
1692K	—	6.00	15.00	30.00	75.00	—
1693K	—	6.00	16.00	32.00	80.00	—

KM# 281.8 4 SOLS 2 DENIERS
1.8090 g., 0.7980 Silver 0.0464 oz. ASW **Ruler:** Louis XIV **Mint:** Bayonne **Note:** Mint mark: Crowned L.

Date	Mintage	VG	F	VF	XF	Unc
1691	Est. 272,000	8.00	20.00	40.00	100	—
1692L	—	—	—	—	—	—

KM# 281.9 4 SOLS 2 DENIERS
1.8090 g., 0.7980 Silver 0.0464 oz. ASW **Ruler:** Louis XIV **Mint:** Toulouse

Date	Mintage	VG	F	VF	XF	Unc
1691M	—	6.00	16.00	32.00	80.00	—
1692M	—	6.00	15.00	30.00	75.00	—
1693M	—	6.00	15.00	30.00	75.00	—
1694M	—	6.00	16.00	32.00	80.00	—

KM# 281.10 4 SOLS 2 DENIERS
1.8090 g., 0.7980 Silver 0.0464 oz. ASW **Ruler:** Louis XIV
Mint: Montpellier

Date	Mintage	VG	F	VF	XF	Unc
1691N	Est. 1,084,000	6.00	15.00	30.00	75.00	—
1692N	2,113,000	6.00	15.00	30.00	70.00	—
1693N	289,000	7.00	17.00	35.00	90.00	—
1694N	196,000	—	—	—	—	—
1695N	112,000	—	—	—	—	—
1696N	63,000	8.00	20.00	40.00	100	—
1697N	40,000	—	—	—	—	—
1698N	11,000	—	—	—	—	—
1699N	17,000	—	—	—	—	—
1700N	1,000	—	—	—	—	—

KM# 281.11 4 SOLS 2 DENIERS
1.8090 g., 0.7980 Silver 0.0464 oz. ASW **Ruler:** Louis XIV
Mint: Riom

Date	Mintage	VG	F	VF	XF	Unc
1691O	—	8.00	20.00	40.00	100	—

KM# 281.12 4 SOLS 2 DENIERS
1.8090 g., 0.7980 Silver 0.0464 oz. ASW **Ruler:** Louis XIV
Mint: Dijon

Date	Mintage	VG	F	VF	XF	Unc
1691P	300,000	6.00	16.00	35.00	85.00	—
1692P	—	6.00	15.00	32.00	80.00	—
1693P	—	6.00	16.00	35.00	85.00	—

KM# 281.13 4 SOLS 2 DENIERS
1.8090 g., 0.7980 Silver 0.0464 oz. ASW **Ruler:** Louis XIV
Mint: Troyes

Date	Mintage	VG	F	VF	XF	Unc
1691S	—	7.00	17.00	35.00	90.00	—
1692S	—	6.00	16.00	32.00	80.00	—
1694S	—	8.00	20.00	40.00	100	—

KM# 281.14 4 SOLS 2 DENIERS
1.8090 g., 0.7980 Silver 0.0464 oz. ASW **Ruler:** Louis XIV
Mint: Nantes

Date	Mintage	VG	F	VF	XF	Unc
1698T	—	—	—	—	—	—

KM# 281.15 4 SOLS 2 DENIERS
1.8090 g., 0.7980 Silver 0.0464 oz. ASW **Ruler:** Louis XIV
Mint: Troyes

Date	Mintage	VG	F	VF	XF	Unc
1692V	—	7.00	17.00	35.00	90.00	—
1694V	—	—	—	—	—	—
1695V	—	—	—	—	—	—
1696V	—	—	—	—	—	—
1697V	—	—	—	—	—	—
1698V	—	—	—	—	—	—
1699V	—	—	—	—	—	—

KM# 281.16 4 SOLS 2 DENIERS
1.8090 g., 0.7980 Silver 0.0464 oz. ASW **Ruler:** Louis XIV
Mint: Lille

Date	Mintage	VG	F	VF	XF	Unc
1693W	—	6.00	16.00	32.00	80.00	—
1694W	—	6.00	16.00	32.00	80.00	—
1696W	45,000	—	—	—	—	—
1697W	45,000	—	—	—	—	—
1699W	30,000	—	—	—	—	—

KM# 281.17 4 SOLS 2 DENIERS
1.8090 g., 0.7980 Silver 0.0464 oz. ASW **Ruler:** Louis XIV
Mint: Amiens

Date	Mintage	VG	F	VF	XF	Unc
1691X	—	8.00	20.00	40.00	100	—

KM# 281.18 4 SOLS 2 DENIERS
1.8090 g., 0.7980 Silver 0.0464 oz. ASW **Ruler:** Louis XIV
Mint: Bourges

Date	Mintage	VG	F	VF	XF	Unc
1691Y	1,015,000	6.00	16.00	32.00	80.00	—
1692Y	—	7.00	17.00	35.00	90.00	—
1693Y	136,000	7.00	17.00	35.00	90.00	—
1694Y	11,000	—	—	—	—	—

KM# 281.19 4 SOLS 2 DENIERS
1.8090 g., 0.7980 Silver 0.0464 oz. ASW **Ruler:** Louis XIV
Mint: Aix **Note:** Mint mark: Ampersand.

Date	Mintage	VG	F	VF	XF	Unc
1691	—	—	—	30.00	—	—
1692	—	6.00	16.00	32.00	80.00	—
1693	—	7.00	17.00	35.00	90.00	—
1694	—	7.00	17.00	35.00	90.00	—
1696	—	7.00	17.00	40.00	90.00	—
1697	—	8.00	20.00	45.00	100	—

KM# 281.20 4 SOLS 2 DENIERS
1.8090 g., 0.7980 Silver 0.0464 oz. ASW **Ruler:** Louis XIV
Mint: Rennes **Note:** Mint mark: Numeral 9.

Date	Mintage	VG	F	VF	XF	Unc
1691	—	7.00	17.00	35.00	90.00	—
1692	—	6.00	15.00	30.00	70.00	—
1693	—	6.00	16.00	32.00	80.00	—
1694	—	7.00	17.00	35.00	90.00	—
1695	—	7.00	17.00	35.00	90.00	—

KM# 281.21 4 SOLS 2 DENIERS
1.8090 g., 0.7980 Silver 0.0464 oz. ASW **Ruler:** Louis XIV
Mint: Metz **Note:** Mint mark: Crowned M.

Date	Mintage	VG	F	VF	XF	Unc
1691	—	6.00	16.00	32.00	80.00	—

KM# 281.22 4 SOLS 2 DENIERS
1.8090 g., 0.7980 Silver 0.0464 oz. ASW **Ruler:** Louis XIV
Mint: Troyes **Note:** Mint mark: Crowned S.

Date	Mintage	VG	F	VF	XF	Unc
1691	500,000	6.00	16.00	32.00	80.00	—
1692	—	6.00	16.00	32.00	80.00	—
1693	—	6.00	16.00	32.00	80.00	—

KM# 283 4 SOLS 2 DENIERS
1.8090 g., 0.7980 Silver 0.0464 oz. ASW **Ruler:** Louis XIV
Mint: Pau

Date	Mintage	VG	F	VF	XF	Unc
1692	—	20.00	40.00	80.00	200	—
1693	—	25.00	50.00	100	250	—
1696	14,000	—	—	—	—	—
1697	7,572	—	—	—	—	—
1698	4,248	—	—	—	—	—
1699	304	—	—	—	—	—

KM# 248 10 SOLS
5.0750 g., 0.8330 Silver 0.1359 oz. ASW **Ruler:** Louis XIV
Obv: Large fleur-de-lis **Rev:** Value and date within legend
Mint: Strasbourg

Date	Mintage	VG	F	VF	XF	Unc
1682BB	—	150	300	500	900	—

KM# 249 15 SOLS (1/8 ECU)
7.6670 g., 0.8330 Silver 0.2053 oz. ASW **Ruler:** Louis XIV
Obv: Large fleur-de-lis **Rev:** Value and date within legend
Mint: Strasbourg

Date	Mintage	VG	F	VF	XF	Unc
1682	—	250	500	1,100	2,500	—
1685	—	—	—	—	—	—
1689	—	—	—	—	—	—

KM# 194 20 SOLS (Lis d'Argent)
8.0070 g., 0.9580 Silver 0.2466 oz. ASW **Ruler:** Louis XIV
Obv: Laureate and draped bust right **Rev:** Cross of 8 crowned L's back to back **Mint:** Paris

Date	Mintage	VG	F	VF	XF	Unc
1656A	—	800	1,750	3,500	6,000	—

KM# 263 30 SOLS (1/2 ECU)
15.3340 g., 0.8330 Silver 0.4107 oz. ASW **Ruler:** Louis XIV
Obv: Large fleur-de-lis **Rev:** Value and date within legend
Mint: Strasbourg

Date	Mintage	VG	F	VF	XF	Unc
1682BB	—	100	200	325	550	—
1683BB	—	125	250	400	650	—
1684BB	—	100	200	350	600	—
1685BB	—	100	200	325	550	—
1687BB	—	125	250	400	650	—
1688BB	—	100	200	325	550	—
1689BB	—	100	200	325	550	—

ECU COINAGE

KM# 130 1/48 ECU
0.5600 g., 0.9170 Silver 0.0165 oz. ASW **Ruler:** Louis XIII
Obv: Laureate and draped bust right **Rev:** Crowned shield
Mint: Paris

Date	Mintage	VG	F	VF	XF	Unc
1642A	—	350	600	1,100	—	—
1643A	—	350	600	1,100	—	—

KM# 152 1/48 ECU
0.5650 g., 0.9170 Silver 0.0167 oz. ASW **Ruler:** Louis XIV
Obv: Small laureate and draped bust right **Rev:** Crowned shield of France, long legends

Date	Mintage	VG	F	VF	XF	Unc
1644	—	300	550	950	2,000	—

KM# 153 1/48 ECU
0.5650 g., 0.9170 Silver 0.0167 oz. ASW **Ruler:** Louis XIV
Obv: Large laureate and draped bust right **Rev:** Legends are abbreviated

Date	Mintage	VG	F	VF	XF	Unc
1644A	—	85.00	180	350	700	—

KM# 139 1/24 ECU
1.1300 g., 0.9170 Silver 0.0333 oz. ASW **Ruler:** Louis XIV
Obv: Laureate, draped and mailed bust right, long legend
Rev: Crowned shield of France

Date	Mintage	VG	F	VF	XF	Unc
1643	—	200	400	700	1,450	—
1644	—	200	400	700	1,450	—

KM# 154 1/24 ECU
1.1300 g., 0.9170 Silver 0.0333 oz. ASW, 15 mm. **Ruler:** Louis XIV
Obv: Laureate and draped bust right, abbreviated legend

Date	Mintage	VG	F	VF	XF	Unc
1644A	—	125	250	425	800	—

KM# 138 1/24 ECU
1.1200 g., 0.9170 Silver 0.0330 oz. ASW **Ruler:** Louis XIV **Obv:** Laureate and draped bust right **Rev:** Crowned shield **Mint:** Paris

Date	Mintage	VG	F	VF	XF	Unc
1643A Point	—	275	500	900	1,800	—

KM# 258.1 1/16 ECU
2.3300 g., 0.8220 Silver 0.0616 oz. ASW **Ruler:** Louis XIV
Obv: Draped bust right **Rev:** Crowned quartered shield of France, Navarre, Old and New Burgundy **Mint:** Lille

Date	Mintage	VG	F	VF	XF	Unc
1686LL	—	—	—	—	—	—

KM# 258.2 1/16 ECU
2.3300 g., 0.8220 Silver 0.0616 oz. ASW **Ruler:** Louis XIV
Mint: Lille **Note:** Mint mark: Crowned L.

Date	Mintage	VG	F	VF	XF	Unc
1686	—	40.00	100	225	450	—
1687	—	50.00	125	250	500	—
1688	—	60.00	150	300	600	—

KM# 305 1/16 ECU
2.3500 g., 0.8570 Silver 0.0647 oz. ASW **Ruler:** Louis XIV
Rev: Palms at sides of crowned quartered shield **Mint:** Lille

Date	Mintage	VG	F	VF	XF	Unc
1694W	—	225	550	1,150	1,850	—
1695W	—	—	—	—	—	—
1696W	—	300	750	1,600	2,500	—
1697W	—	300	750	1,600	2,500	—
1698W	—	250	675	1,450	2,250	—
1699W	—	—	—	—	—	—

KM# 131 1/12 ECU (10 Sols)
2.2400 g., 0.9170 Silver 0.0660 oz. ASW **Ruler:** Louis XIII
Obv: Laureate, draped bust right **Rev:** Crowned shield
Mint: Paris

Date	Mintage	VG	F	VF	XF	Unc
1642A Rose	107,000	100	200	425	650	—
1642A Point	Inc. above	85.00	175	350	525	—
1642A 2 points	Inc. above	100	200	425	650	—

KM# 132.1 1/12 ECU (10 Sols)
2.2400 g., 0.9170 Silver 0.0660 oz. ASW **Ruler:** Louis XIII
Obv: Laureate, draped and mailed bust right

Date	Mintage	VG	F	VF	XF	Unc
1642 Rose	571,000	75.00	165	325	550	—
1642 Point	Inc. above	65.00	150	300	500	—
1643 Rose	13,995,000	15.00	35.00	65.00	140	—
1643 Point	31,237,000	15.00	30.00	60.00	130	—

KM# 132.2 1/12 ECU (10 Sols)
2.2400 g., 0.9170 Silver 0.0660 oz. ASW **Ruler:** Louis XIII
Mint: Lyon

Date	Mintage	VG	F	VF	XF	Unc
1643D 3 points	Est. 125,000	175	375	750	1,200	—

KM# 140.1 1/12 ECU (10 Sols)
2.2610 g., 0.9170 Silver 0.0667 oz. ASW **Ruler:** Louis XIV
Obv: Laureate, draped and mailed bust right, short hair curl before ear **Rev:** Crowned shield of France **Mint:** Paris

Date	Mintage	VG	F	VF	XF	Unc
1643A Rose	—	20.00	50.00	100	250	—
1643A Point	—	12.00	32.00	65.00	160	—
1644A Rose	—	12.00	32.00	65.00	160	—
1644A Point	—	12.00	32.00	65.00	175	—
1644A Rose and 2 points	—	16.00	40.00	80.00	200	—
1645A Rose	—	16.00	40.00	80.00	200	—
1645A Point	—	20.00	50.00	100	250	—

KM# 140.2 1/12 ECU (10 Sols)
2.2610 g., 0.9170 Silver 0.0667 oz. ASW **Ruler:** Louis XIV
Mint: Lyon

Date	Mintage	VG	F	VF	XF	Unc
1644D	—	20.00	50.00	100	250	—
1645D	—	—	—	—	—	—
1648D	—	—	—	—	—	—
1649D	—	60.00	125	225	600	—
1650D	—	—	—	—	—	—
1652D	—	—	—	—	—	—
1653D	—	—	—	—	—	—

KM# 166.1 1/12 ECU (10 Sols)
2.2610 g., 0.9170 Silver 0.0667 oz. ASW **Ruler:** Louis XIV
Obv: Larger bust, long hair curl before ear **Mint:** Paris

Date	Mintage	VG	F	VF	XF	Unc
1646A Rose	—	—	—	—	—	—
1646A Point	—	10.00	22.00	40.00	100	—
1647A	—	10.00	22.00	40.00	100	—
1648A Fleur	—	20.00	50.00	100	275	—
1648A Point	—	—	—	—	—	—
1649A	—	20.00	50.00	100	275	—
1650A	—	—	—	—	—	—
1651A	—	25.00	65.00	125	375	—
1652A	—	10.00	22.00	50.00	135	—
1653A	—	10.00	22.00	45.00	120	—
1654A	—	10.00	25.00	55.00	150	—
1655A	—	12.00	30.00	65.00	175	—
1657A	—	—	—	—	—	—
1658A	—	—	—	—	—	—

KM# 166.2 1/12 ECU (10 Sols)
2.2610 g., 0.9170 Silver 0.0667 oz. ASW **Ruler:** Louis XIV
Mint: Rouen

Date	Mintage	VG	F	VF	XF	Unc
1649B	—	—	—	—	—	—
1650B	—	—	—	—	—	—
1652B	—	—	—	—	—	—
1653B	—	10.00	22.00	45.00	120	—
1654B	—	12.00	30.00	65.00	175	—
1659B	—	20.00	50.00	110	285	—

KM# 166.3 1/12 ECU (10 Sols)
2.2610 g., 0.9170 Silver 0.0667 oz. ASW **Ruler:** Louis XIV
Mint: Saint Lô

Date	Mintage	VG	F	VF	XF	Unc
1650C	—	30.00	75.00	150	400	—
1651C	—	—	—	—	—	—
1653C	—	—	—	—	—	—
1654C	—	—	—	—	—	—

KM# 166.4 1/12 ECU (10 Sols)
2.2610 g., 0.9170 Silver 0.0667 oz. ASW **Ruler:** Louis XIV
Mint: Lyon

Date	Mintage	VG	F	VF	XF	Unc
1657D	—	35.00	85.00	165	450	—
1658D	—	10.00	20.00	55.00	150	—
1659D	—	10.00	22.00	45.00	120	—
1660D	—	10.00	22.00	40.00	100	—
1661D	—	10.00	22.00	40.00	100	—

KM# 166.5 1/12 ECU (10 Sols)
2.2610 g., 0.9170 Silver 0.0667 oz. ASW **Ruler:** Louis XIV
Mint: Tours

Date	Mintage	VG	F	VF	XF	Unc
1652E	—	35.00	85.00	165	450	—
1653E	—	—	—	—	—	—
1656E	—	40.00	100	200	550	—
1659E	—	35.00	85.00	165	450	—
1660E	—	35.00	90.00	175	465	—

KM# 166.6 1/12 ECU (10 Sols)
2.2610 g., 0.9170 Silver 0.0667 oz. ASW **Ruler:** Louis XIV
Mint: Angers

Date	Mintage	VG	F	VF	XF	Unc
1647F	—	—	—	—	—	—
1648F	—	—	—	—	—	—
1649F	—	—	—	—	—	—
1650F	—	25.00	60.00	120	325	—
1651F	—	—	—	—	—	—
1654F	—	—	—	—	—	—
1658F	—	—	—	—	—	—
1659F	—	35.00	85.00	165	450	—
1660F	—	35.00	85.00	165	450	—

KM# 166.7 1/12 ECU (10 Sols)
2.2610 g., 0.9170 Silver 0.0667 oz. ASW **Ruler:** Louis XIV
Mint: Poitiers

Date	Mintage	VG	F	VF	XF	Unc
1650G	—	—	—	—	—	—

KM# 166.8 1/12 ECU (10 Sols)
2.2610 g., 0.9170 Silver 0.0667 oz. ASW **Ruler:** Louis XIV
Mint: La Rochelle

Date	Mintage	VG	F	VF	XF	Unc
1648H	—	—	—	—	—	—
1649H	—	—	—	—	—	—
1650H	—	—	—	—	—	—
1651H	—	45.00	120	225	600	—
1652H	—	50.00	130	260	700	—
1653H	—	50.00	130	260	700	—
1654H	—	—	—	—	—	—
1655H	—	—	—	—	—	—
1656H	—	—	—	—	—	—

KM# 166.9 1/12 ECU (10 Sols)
2.2610 g., 0.9170 Silver 0.0667 oz. ASW **Ruler:** Louis XIV
Mint: Limoges

Date	Mintage	VG	F	VF	XF	Unc
1649I	—	—	—	—	—	—
1650I	—	—	—	—	—	—
1651I	—	50.00	125	250	650	—
1652I	—	—	—	—	—	—
1653I	—	—	—	—	—	—
1654I	—	—	—	—	—	—
1657I	—	35.00	85.00	165	450	—
1659I	—	30.00	75.00	150	400	—
1660I	—	30.00	75.00	150	400	—

KM# 166.10 1/12 ECU (10 Sols)
2.2610 g., 0.9170 Silver 0.0667 oz. ASW **Ruler:** Louis XIV
Mint: Bordeaux

Date	Mintage	VG	F	VF	XF	Unc
1647K	—	—	—	—	—	—
1648K	—	15.00	40.00	80.00	200	—
1649K	—	30.00	75.00	150	400	—
1650K	—	—	—	—	—	—
1651K	—	—	—	—	—	—
1652K	—	35.00	90.00	175	465	—
1653K	—	—	—	—	—	—
1654K	—	—	—	—	—	—
1655K	—	—	—	—	—	—
1656K	—	—	—	—	—	—
1657K	—	—	—	—	—	—
1658K	—	30.00	75.00	150	400	—
1659K	—	30.00	75.00	150	400	—
1660K	—	—	—	—	—	—

KM# 166.11 1/12 ECU (10 Sols)
2.2610 g., 0.9170 Silver 0.0667 oz. ASW **Ruler:** Louis XIV
Mint: Bayonne

Date	Mintage	VG	F	VF	XF	Unc
1650L	—	—	—	—	—	—
1651L	—	—	—	—	—	—
1652L	—	—	—	—	—	—
1653L	—	30.00	75.00	160	425	—
1654L	—	—	—	—	—	—
1655L	—	—	—	—	—	—
1656L	—	—	—	—	—	—
1657L	—	—	—	—	—	—
1658L	—	—	—	—	—	—
1659L	—	—	—	—	—	—
1660L	—	—	—	—	—	—

KM# 166.12 1/12 ECU (10 Sols)
2.2610 g., 0.9170 Silver 0.0667 oz. ASW **Ruler:** Louis XIV
Mint: Toulouse

Date	Mintage	VG	F	VF	XF	Unc
1647M	—	25.00	65.00	135	375	—
1648M	—	—	—	—	—	—
1649M	—	—	—	—	—	—
1650M	—	—	—	—	—	—
1653M	—	35.00	90.00	175	450	—
1655M	—	—	—	—	—	—
1658M	—	30.00	75.00	150	400	—
1659M	—	—	—	—	—	—
1661M	—	—	—	—	—	—
1662M	—	—	—	—	—	—

KM# 166.13 1/12 ECU (10 Sols)
2.2610 g., 0.9170 Silver 0.0667 oz. ASW **Ruler:** Louis XIV
Mint: Montpellier

Date	Mintage	VG	F	VF	XF	Unc
1647N	—	—	—	—	—	—
1648N	—	20.00	50.00	100	275	—
1649N	—	10.00	25.00	55.00	150	—
1650N	—	12.00	30.00	65.00	175	—
1651N	—	12.00	30.00	65.00	175	—
1652N	—	12.00	30.00	65.00	175	—
1653N	—	15.00	40.00	80.00	200	—
1658N	—	10.00	25.00	55.00	150	—
1659N	—	10.00	25.00	55.00	150	—

KM# 166.14 1/12 ECU (10 Sols)
2.2610 g., 0.9170 Silver 0.0667 oz. ASW **Ruler:** Louis XIV
Mint: Riom

Date	Mintage	VG	F	VF	XF	Unc
1652O	—	—	—	—	—	—
1653O	—	—	—	—	—	—

KM# 166.15 1/12 ECU (10 Sols)
2.2610 g., 0.9170 Silver 0.0667 oz. ASW **Ruler:** Louis XIV
Mint: Dijon

Date	Mintage	VG	F	VF	XF	Unc
1652P	—	—	—	—	—	—
1653P	—	—	—	—	—	—

KM# 166.16 1/12 ECU (10 Sols)
2.2610 g., 0.9170 Silver 0.0667 oz. ASW **Ruler:** Louis XIV
Mint: Narbonne

Date	Mintage	VG	F	VF	XF	Unc
1650Q	—	—	—	—	—	—
1651Q	—	40.00	100	220	550	—
1652Q	—	—	—	—	—	—
1653Q	—	—	—	—	—	—

KM# 166.17 1/12 ECU (10 Sols)
2.2610 g., 0.9170 Silver 0.0667 oz. ASW **Ruler:** Louis XIV
Mint: Troyes

Date	Mintage	VG	F	VF	XF	Unc
1651S	—	35.00	85.00	175	450	—
1652S	—	—	—	—	—	—
1653S	—	30.00	75.00	150	400	—
1654S	—	—	—	—	—	—

KM# 166.18 1/12 ECU (10 Sols)
2.2610 g., 0.9170 Silver 0.0667 oz. ASW **Ruler:** Louis XIV
Mint: Nantes

Date	Mintage	VG	F	VF	XF	Unc
1647T	—	—	—	—	—	—
1648T	—	—	—	—	—	—
1659T	—	—	—	—	—	—
1660T	—	—	—	—	—	—

KM# 166.19 1/12 ECU (10 Sols)
2.2610 g., 0.9170 Silver 0.0667 oz. ASW **Ruler:** Louis XIV
Mint: Amiens

Date	Mintage	VG	F	VF	XF	Unc
1653X	—	30.00	75.00	150	400	—
1655X	—	30.00	75.00	150	400	—
1658X	—	—	—	—	—	—
1660X	—	—	—	—	—	—

KM# 166.20 1/12 ECU (10 Sols)
2.2610 g., 0.9170 Silver 0.0667 oz. ASW **Ruler:** Louis XIV
Mint: Bourges

Date	Mintage	VG	F	VF	XF	Unc
1648Y	—	—	—	—	—	—
1649Y	—	—	—	—	—	—
1650Y	—	25.00	60.00	120	325	—
1653Y	—	30.00	75.00	150	400	—
1654Y	—	35.00	85.00	175	450	—
1655Y	—	30.00	75.00	150	400	—
1656Y	—	35.00	85.00	175	450	—

KM# 166.21 1/12 ECU (10 Sols)
2.2610 g., 0.9170 Silver 0.0667 oz. ASW **Ruler:** Louis XIV
Mint: Arras

Date	Mintage	VG	F	VF	XF	Unc
1652AR	—	35.00	85.00	175	450	—
1653AR	—	35.00	85.00	175	450	—

KM# 166.22 1/12 ECU (10 Sols)
2.2610 g., 0.9170 Silver 0.0667 oz. ASW **Ruler:** Louis XIV
Mint: Aix **Note:** Mint mark: Ampersand.

Date	Mintage	VG	F	VF	XF	Unc
1647	—	25.00	65.00	125	375	—
1648	—	25.00	65.00	125	375	—
1649	—	20.00	50.00	100	275	—
1651	—	35.00	85.00	175	450	—
1652	—	20.00	50.00	100	275	—
1653	—	15.00	40.00	80.00	200	—
1654	—	30.00	75.00	150	400	—
1656	—	—	—	—	—	—
1657	—	20.00	50.00	100	275	—
1658	—	12.00	30.00	65.00	175	—
1659	—	12.00	30.00	65.00	175	—
1660	—	—	—	—	—	—
1661	—	—	—	—	—	—
1663	—	35.00	85.00	175	450	—

KM# 166.23 1/12 ECU (10 Sols)
2.2610 g., 0.9170 Silver 0.0667 oz. ASW **Ruler:** Louis XIV
Mint: Rennes **Note:** Mint mark: Numeral 9.

Date	Mintage	VG	F	VF	XF	Unc
1647	—	—	—	—	—	—
1648	—	—	—	—	—	—
1649	—	—	—	—	—	—
1653	—	—	—	—	—	—
1654	—	—	—	—	—	—
1655	—	—	—	—	—	—
1657	—	—	—	—	—	—
1658	—	—	—	—	—	—
1659	—	—	—	—	—	—
1662	—	30.00	75.00	150	400	—

KM# 181 1/12 ECU (10 Sols)
2.2610 g., 0.9170 Silver 0.0667 oz. ASW **Ruler:** Louis XIV
Obv: Large laureate draped, mailed bust right **Rev:** Crowned shield of France and Navarre **Mint:** Saint Palais

Date	Mintage	VG	F	VF	XF	Unc
1651 * V *	—	200	400	750	2,000	—
1653 * V *	—	200	400	750	2,000	—
1654 * V *	—	225	450	825	2,200	—
1655 * V *	—	225	450	825	2,200	—
1656 * V *	—	250	500	900	2,400	—
1658 * V *	—	250	500	900	2,400	—
1660 * V *	—	250	500	900	2,400	—
1661 * V *	—	250	500	900	2,400	—
1663 * V *	—	—	—	—	—	—

KM# 182.1 1/12 ECU (10 Sols)
2.2610 g., 0.9170 Silver 0.0667 oz. ASW **Ruler:** Louis XIV
Rev: Crowned shield of France, Navarre and Bearn **Mint:** Pau

Date	Mintage	VG	F	VF	XF	Unc
1650 Leaves	—	175	300	650	1,500	—
1651 Leaves	—	175	300	650	1,500	—
1652 * F *	—	175	300	650	1,500	—
1653 * F *	—	175	300	650	1,500	—
1655 * F *	—	175	300	650	1,500	—
1675	—	200	400	750	1,650	—
1676	—	200	400	750	1,650	—
1679	—	200	400	750	1,650	—

KM# 182.2 1/12 ECU (10 Sols)
2.2610 g., 0.9170 Silver 0.0667 oz. ASW **Ruler:** Louis XIV
Mint: Morlaas

Date	Mintage	VG	F	VF	XF	Unc
1653 * G *	—	175	300	650	1,500	—
1660	—	175	300	650	1,500	—
1661	—	175	300	650	1,500	—

KM# 199.1 1/12 ECU (10 Sols)
2.2610 g., 0.9170 Silver 0.0667 oz. ASW **Ruler:** Louis XIV
Rev: Crowned shield of France **Mint:** Paris

Date	Mintage	VG	F	VF	XF	Unc
1658A	—	15.00	35.00	75.00	225	—
1659A	—	7.00	16.00	35.00	90.00	—
1660A	—	7.00	16.00	35.00	90.00	—
1661A	—	8.00	20.00	45.00	110	—
1662A	—	7.00	16.00	35.00	90.00	—
1663A	—	8.00	20.00	45.00	110	—
1664A	—	8.00	20.00	45.00	110	—
1665A	—	25.00	60.00	120	350	—
1667A	—	30.00	75.00	150	425	—
1669A	—	30.00	75.00	150	425	—
1670A	—	37.50	95.00	185	550	—

KM# 199.2 1/12 ECU (10 Sols)
2.2610 g., 0.9170 Silver 0.0667 oz. ASW **Ruler:** Louis XIV
Mint: Rouen

Date	Mintage	VG	F	VF	XF	Unc
1659B	—	20.00	50.00	110	300	—
1660B	—	8.00	20.00	45.00	110	—
1661B	—	30.00	75.00	150	425	—
1662B	—	16.00	40.00	85.00	250	—
1664B	—	16.00	40.00	85.00	250	—

KM# 199.3 1/12 ECU (10 Sols)
2.2610 g., 0.9170 Silver 0.0667 oz. ASW **Ruler:** Louis XIV
Mint: Lyon

Date	Mintage	VG	F	VF	XF	Unc
1660D	—	7.00	16.00	35.00	90.00	—
1661D	—	7.00	16.00	35.00	90.00	—
1662D	—	7.00	16.00	35.00	90.00	—
1663D	—	7.00	16.00	35.00	90.00	—
1664D	—	8.00	20.00	45.00	110	—
1665D	—	12.00	30.00	75.00	200	—
1666D	—	—	—	—	—	—
1668D	—	—	—	—	—	—
1669D	—	—	—	—	—	—
1670D	—	—	—	—	—	—
1671D	—	—	—	—	—	—
1673D	—	—	—	—	—	—

KM# 199.4 1/12 ECU (10 Sols)
2.2610 g., 0.9170 Silver 0.0667 oz. ASW **Ruler:** Louis XIV
Mint: La Rochelle

Date	Mintage	VG	F	VF	XF	Unc
1661H	—	30.00	75.00	150	425	—
1662H	—	—	—	—	—	—

KM# 199.5 1/12 ECU (10 Sols)
2.2610 g., 0.9170 Silver 0.0667 oz. ASW **Ruler:** Louis XIV
Mint: Limoges

Date	Mintage	VG	F	VF	XF	Unc
1659I	—	25.00	60.00	125	350	—
1660I	—	30.00	75.00	150	425	—
1661I	—	20.00	50.00	110	300	—
1662I	—	35.00	80.00	165	450	—
1663I	—	30.00	75.00	150	425	—

KM# 199.6 1/12 ECU (10 Sols)
2.2610 g., 0.9170 Silver 0.0667 oz. ASW **Ruler:** Louis XIV
Mint: Bordeaux

Date	Mintage	VG	F	VF	XF	Unc
1660K	—	30.00	75.00	150	425	—
1662K	—	30.00	75.00	150	425	—

KM# 199.7 1/12 ECU (10 Sols)
2.2610 g., 0.9170 Silver 0.0667 oz. ASW **Ruler:** Louis XIV
Mint: Bayonne

Date	Mintage	VG	F	VF	XF	Unc
1660L	—	30.00	75.00	150	425	—
1661L	—	—	—	—	—	—
1662L	—	—	—	—	—	—
1663L	—	—	—	—	—	—
1664L	—	20.00	50.00	110	300	—
1665L	—	—	—	—	—	—
1666L	—	—	—	—	—	—
1667L	—	—	—	—	—	—
1668L	—	—	—	—	—	—
1672L	—	—	—	—	—	—

KM# 199.8 1/12 ECU (10 Sols)
2.2610 g., 0.9170 Silver 0.0667 oz. ASW **Ruler:** Louis XIV
Mint: Toulouse

Date	Mintage	VG	F	VF	XF	Unc
1661M	—	15.00	35.00	80.00	225	—
1662M	—	15.00	35.00	80.00	225	—
1666M	—	—	—	—	—	—
1671M	—	—	—	—	—	—

KM# 199.9 1/12 ECU (10 Sols)
2.2610 g., 0.9170 Silver 0.0667 oz. ASW **Ruler:** Louis XIV
Mint: Montpellier

Date	Mintage	VG	F	VF	XF	Unc
1659N	—	15.00	35.00	80.00	225	—
1660N	—	20.00	50.00	110	300	—
1661N	—	20.00	50.00	110	300	—
1662N	—	25.00	60.00	125	350	—

KM# 199.10 1/12 ECU (10 Sols)
2.2610 g., 0.9170 Silver 0.0667 oz. ASW **Ruler:** Louis XIV
Mint: Dijon

Date	Mintage	VG	F	VF	XF	Unc
1661P	—	—	—	—	—	—

KM# 199.11 1/12 ECU (10 Sols)
2.2610 g., 0.9170 Silver 0.0667 oz. ASW **Ruler:** Louis XIV
Mint: Villeneuve St. André

Date	Mintage	VG	F	VF	XF	Unc
1660R	—	—	—	—	—	—
1661R	—	15.00	35.00	80.00	225	—
1662R	—	20.00	50.00	110	300	—

KM# 199.12 1/12 ECU (10 Sols)
2.2610 g., 0.9170 Silver 0.0667 oz. ASW **Ruler:** Louis XIV
Mint: Nantes

Date	Mintage	VG	F	VF	XF	Unc
1660T	—	40.00	100	200	550	—
1661T	—	8.00	20.00	45.00	110	—
1662T	—	—	—	—	—	—

KM# 199.13 1/12 ECU (10 Sols)
2.2610 g., 0.9170 Silver 0.0667 oz. ASW **Ruler:** Louis XIV
Mint: Amiens

Date	Mintage	VG	F	VF	XF	Unc
1659X	—	30.00	75.00	160	450	—
1660X	—	—	—	—	—	—

KM# 199.14 1/12 ECU (10 Sols)
2.2610 g., 0.9170 Silver 0.0667 oz. ASW **Ruler:** Louis XIV
Mint: Aix **Note:** Mint mark: Ampersand.

Date	Mintage	VG	F	VF	XF	Unc
1658	—	15.00	35.00	80.00	225	—
1659	—	12.00	30.00	70.00	200	—
1660	—	20.00	50.00	110	300	—
1661	—	15.00	35.00	80.00	225	—
1662	—	12.00	30.00	70.00	200	—
1663	—	12.00	30.00	70.00	200	—
1664	—	12.00	30.00	70.00	200	—
1665	—	12.00	30.00	70.00	200	—
1666	—	40.00	100	220	550	—
1667	—	30.00	75.00	150	425	—
1668	—	—	—	—	—	—
1669	—	35.00	80.00	165	450	—
1670	—	—	—	—	—	—
1671	—	—	—	—	—	—
1672	—	—	—	—	—	—

KM# 210 1/12 ECU (10 Sols)
2.2610 g., 0.9170 Silver 0.0667 oz. ASW **Ruler:** Louis XIV
Obv: Juvenile bust right **Rev:** Crowned quartered shield of Dauphine **Mint:** Grenoble

Date	Mintage	VG	F	VF	XF	Unc
1660Z	—	100	200	400	800	—
1661Z	—	125	250	500	1,000	—
1662Z	—	165	325	650	1,250	—

KM# 235.1 1/12 ECU (10 Sols)
2.2610 g., 0.9170 Silver 0.0667 oz. ASW **Ruler:** Louis XIV
Subject: Parliament **Obv:** Armored bust right **Rev:** Crowned shield of France **Mint:** Paris

Date	Mintage	VG	F	VF	XF	Unc
1679A	—	150	300	600	1,200	—
1680A	—	150	300	600	1,200	—
1681A	—	125	250	500	1,000	—
1682A	—	150	300	600	1,200	—
1683A	—	—	—	—	—	—

KM# 235.2 1/12 ECU (10 Sols)
2.2610 g., 0.9170 Silver 0.0667 oz. ASW **Ruler:** Louis XIV
Mint: Aix **Note:** Mint mark: Ampersand.

Date	Mintage	VG	F	VF	XF	Unc
1679	—	150	300	600	1,200	—
1680	—	150	300	600	1,200	—
1681	—	—	—	—	—	—
1682	—	175	350	700	1,500	—

KM# 282.1 1/12 ECU (10 Sols)
2.2610 g., 0.9170 Silver 0.0667 oz. ASW **Ruler:** Louis XIV
Obv: Draped bust right **Rev:** Eight crowned L's, cruciform, fleur-de-lis in angles **Mint:** Paris

Date	Mintage	VG	F	VF	XF	Unc
1691A	—	50.00	100	200	425	—

KM# 282.2 1/12 ECU (10 Sols)
2.2610 g., 0.9170 Silver 0.0667 oz. ASW **Ruler:** Louis XIV
Mint: Lille **Note:** Mint mark: Crowned L.

Date	Mintage	VG	F	VF	XF	Unc
1691	—	75.00	150	300	635	—

KM# 282.3 1/12 ECU (10 Sols)
2.2610 g., 0.9170 Silver 0.0667 oz. ASW **Ruler:** Louis XIV
Mint: Metz **Note:** Mint mark: Crowned M.

Date	Mintage	VG	F	VF	XF	Unc
1691	—	75.00	150	300	635	—

KM# 290.1 1/12 ECU (10 Sols)
2.2610 g., 0.9170 Silver 0.0667 oz. ASW **Ruler:** Louis XIV
Obv: Mailed bust right **Rev:** Palm branches below crowned circular shield of France **Mint:** Paris

Date	Mintage	VG	F	VF	XF	Unc
1693A	—	50.00	125	250	525	—
1694A	—	35.00	85.00	165	350	—
1695A	—	40.00	100	200	425	—

KM# 290.2 1/12 ECU (10 Sols)
2.2610 g., 0.9170 Silver 0.0667 oz. ASW **Ruler:** Louis XIV
Mint: Caen

Date	Mintage	VG	F	VF	XF	Unc
1694C	—	45.00	110	225	475	—
1697C	50,000	50.00	125	250	525	—

KM# 290.3 1/12 ECU (10 Sols)
2.2610 g., 0.9170 Silver 0.0667 oz. ASW **Ruler:** Louis XIV
Mint: Lyon

Date	Mintage	VG	F	VF	XF	Unc
1694D	644,000	40.00	100	200	425	—
1695D	318,000	—	—	—	—	—
1696D	181,000	55.00	130	260	550	—
1697D	72,000	60.00	140	275	575	—
1698D	24,000	—	—	—	—	—
1699D	22,000	—	—	—	—	—
1700D	3,000	—	—	—	—	—

KM# 290.4 1/12 ECU (10 Sols)
2.2610 g., 0.9170 Silver 0.0667 oz. ASW **Ruler:** Louis XIV
Mint: Tours

Date	Mintage	VG	F	VF	XF	Unc
1695E	—	50.00	125	250	525	—
1697E	—	65.00	150	300	635	—

KM# 290.5 1/12 ECU (10 Sols)
2.2610 g., 0.9170 Silver 0.0667 oz. ASW **Ruler:** Louis XIV
Mint: Poitiers

Date	Mintage	VG	F	VF	XF	Unc
1694G	—	45.00	110	225	475	—
1696G	24,000	—	—	—	—	—

KM# 290.6 1/12 ECU (10 Sols)
2.2610 g., 0.9170 Silver 0.0667 oz. ASW **Ruler:** Louis XIV
Mint: La Rochelle

Date	Mintage	VG	F	VF	XF	Unc
1694H	—	50.00	125	250	525	—
1695H	—	—	—	—	—	—
1696H	—	65.00	150	300	635	—

KM# 290.7 1/12 ECU (10 Sols)
2.2610 g., 0.9170 Silver 0.0667 oz. ASW **Ruler:** Louis XIV
Mint: Toulouse

Date	Mintage	VG	F	VF	XF	Unc
1695M	—	50.00	125	250	525	—
1697M	—	60.00	145	275	575	—

KM# 290.8 1/12 ECU (10 Sols)
2.2610 g., 0.9170 Silver 0.0667 oz. ASW **Ruler:** Louis XIV
Mint: Montpellier

Date	Mintage	VG	F	VF	XF	Unc
1694N	108,000	45.00	110	225	475	—
1695N	126,000	45.00	110	225	475	—
1696N	52,000	50.00	125	250	525	—
1697N	24,000	65.00	150	300	635	—
1698N	9,350	—	—	—	—	—
1699N	6,137	—	—	—	—	—

KM# 290.9 1/12 ECU (10 Sols)
2.2610 g., 0.9170 Silver 0.0667 oz. ASW **Ruler:** Louis XIV
Mint: Riom

Date	Mintage	VG	F	VF	XF	Unc
1694O	—	50.00	125	250	525	—

KM# 290.10 1/12 ECU (10 Sols)
2.2610 g., 0.9170 Silver 0.0667 oz. ASW **Ruler:** Louis XIV
Mint: Dijon

Date	Mintage	VG	F	VF	XF	Unc
1694P	111,000	50.00	125	250	525	—
1695P	48,000	—	—	—	—	—
1697P	5,989	—	—	—	—	—

KM# 290.11 1/12 ECU (10 Sols)
2.2610 g., 0.9170 Silver 0.0667 oz. ASW **Ruler:** Louis XIV
Mint: Reims

Date	Mintage	VG	F	VF	XF	Unc
1694S	—	50.00	125	250	525	—

KM# 290.12 1/12 ECU (10 Sols)
2.2610 g., 0.9170 Silver 0.0667 oz. ASW **Ruler:** Louis XIV
Mint: Nantes

Date	Mintage	VG	F	VF	XF	Unc
1694T	—	50.00	125	250	525	—
1698T	—	60.00	140	275	575	—

KM# 290.13 1/12 ECU (10 Sols)
2.2610 g., 0.9170 Silver 0.0667 oz. ASW **Ruler:** Louis XIV
Mint: Troyes

Date	Mintage	VG	F	VF	XF	Unc
1694V	—	—	—	—	—	—
1695V	—	—	—	—	—	—
1696V	—	—	—	—	—	—
1697V	—	60.00	140	285	625	—
1698V	—	—	—	—	—	—
1699V	—	—	—	—	—	—

KM# 290.14 1/12 ECU (10 Sols)
2.2610 g., 0.9170 Silver 0.0667 oz. ASW **Ruler:** Louis XIV
Mint: Lille

Date	Mintage	VG	F	VF	XF	Unc
1697W	12,000	—	—	—	—	—
1699W	53,000	—	—	—	—	—
1700W	—	100	200	425	875	—

KM# 290.15 1/12 ECU (10 Sols)
2.2610 g., 0.9170 Silver 0.0667 oz. ASW **Ruler:** Louis XIV
Mint: Amiens

Date	Mintage	VG	F	VF	XF	Unc
1695X	—	50.00	125	250	525	—
1697X	—	60.00	140	275	575	—

KM# 290.16 1/12 ECU (10 Sols)
2.2610 g., 0.9170 Silver 0.0667 oz. ASW **Ruler:** Louis XIV
Mint: Bourges

Date	Mintage	VG	F	VF	XF	Unc
1696Y	—	65.00	150	300	635	—

KM# 290.17 1/12 ECU (10 Sols)
2.2610 g., 0.9170 Silver 0.0667 oz. ASW **Ruler:** Louis XIV
Mint: Rennes **Note:** Mint mark: Numeral 9.

Date	Mintage	VG	F	VF	XF	Unc
1694	—	50.00	125	250	525	—
1695	—	50.00	125	250	525	—

KM# 290.18 1/12 ECU (10 Sols)
2.2610 g., 0.9170 Silver 0.0667 oz. ASW **Ruler:** Louis XIV
Mint: Aix **Note:** Mint mark: Ampersand.

Date	Mintage	VG	F	VF	XF	Unc
1694	—	50.00	125	250	525	—
1695	—	45.00	110	225	475	—

KM# 290.19 1/12 ECU (10 Sols)
2.2610 g., 0.9170 Silver 0.0667 oz. ASW **Ruler:** Louis XIV
Obv: Mailed bust right **Rev:** Palm branches below crowned circular shield of France **Mint:** Besancon **Note:** Mint mark: Back-to-back C's.

Date	Mintage	VG	F	VF	XF	Unc
1694	11,000	—	—	—	—	—
1695	5,187	—	—	—	—	—
1696	—	60.00	140	275	575	—
1697	3,516	—	—	—	—	—
1698	1,083	—	—	—	—	—
1699	759	—	—	—	—	—

KM# 291 1/12 ECU (10 Sols)
2.2610 g., 0.9170 Silver 0.0667 oz. ASW **Ruler:** Louis XIV
Rev: Palm branches below crowned circular shield of France, Navarre and Bearn **Mint:** Pau **Note:** Mint mark: Cow.

Date	Mintage	VG	F	VF	XF	Unc
1693	—	400	800	1,650	3,250	—
1694	—	400	800	1,650	3,250	—
1697	—	450	900	1,750	3,500	—
1698	912	—	—	—	—	—
1699	516	500	1,000	2,000	4,000	—

KM# 25 1/8 ECU
Silver **Ruler:** Henry IV **Obv:** Without value

Date	Mintage	VG	F	VF	XF	Unc
1601	—	25.00	60.00	150	320	—
1604	—	25.00	60.00	150	320	—

KM# 22.1 1/8 ECU
Silver **Ruler:** Henry IV **Rev:** Cross fleuree, fleur-de-lis in angle
Mint: Toulouse

Date	Mintage	VG	F	VF	XF	Unc
1602M	—	20.00	50.00	145	300	—

KM# 22.2 1/8 ECU
Silver **Ruler:** Henry IV **Mint:** Villeneuve St. André

Date	Mintage	VG	F	VF	XF	Unc
1607R	—	20.00	50.00	145	300	—

KM# 22.3 1/8 ECU
Silver **Ruler:** Henry IV **Mint:** Nantes

Date	Mintage	VG	F	VF	XF	Unc
1603T	—	20.00	50.00	145	300	—
1604T	—	20.00	50.00	145	300	—

KM# 22.4 1/8 ECU
Silver **Ruler:** Henry IV **Note:** Mint is uncertain.

Date	Mintage	VG	F	VF	XF	Unc
1603	—	20.00	50.00	145	300	—

KM# 23 1/8 ECU
Silver **Ruler:** Henry IV **Obv:** Crowned shield of Dauphine
Mint: Grenoble

Date	Mintage	VG	F	VF	XF	Unc
1603Z	—	—	—	—	—	—

KM# 24 1/8 ECU
Silver **Ruler:** Henry IV **Obv:** Fleur-de-lis cross dividing value
Rev: Crowned shield of France and Navarre **Mint:** Grenoble

Date	Mintage	VG	F	VF	XF	Unc
1604	—	30.00	75.00	145	300	—

KM# 2.1 1/8 ECU
Silver **Ruler:** Henry IV **Obv:** Fleur-de-lis cross
Obv. Legend: HENRICVS•IIII•D•G•FRANC•ET•NA(VA)•REX•BD **Rev:** Crowned arms of France, Navarre and Béarn
Rev. Legend: GRATIA•DEI•SVM•Q(•D);SVM **Mint:** Morlaas
Note: Previous KM#26.1.

Date	Mintage	Good	VG	F	VF	XF
1604	—	8.00	25.00	65.00	165	340
1607	—	—	—	—	—	—
1608	—	—	—	—	—	—
1609	—	—	—	—	—	—

KM# 2.2 1/8 ECU
Silver **Ruler:** Henry IV **Obv:** Fleur-de-lis cross **Obv. Legend:** HENRICVS•IIII (or 4)•D•G• FRANC•ET•NAVA•REX• BD
Rev: Crowned arms of France, Navarre and Béarn
Rev. Legend: GRATIA•DEI•SVM•Q•D; SVM **Mint:** Pau

Date	Mintage	Good	VG	F	VF	XF
1605	—	—	—	—	—	—
1606	—	—	—	—	—	—
1608	—	—	—	—	—	—

KM# 21 1/8 ECU
Silver **Ruler:** Henry IV **Rev:** Cross with crown at ends **Mint:** Saint Lô

Date	Mintage	VG	F	VF	XF	Unc
ND	—	20.00	50.00	145	300	—

KM# 20 1/8 ECU
Silver **Ruler:** Henry IV **Obv:** Crowned shield of France
Rev: Cross with fleur-de-lis at ends **Mint:** Paris

Date	Mintage	VG	F	VF	XF	Unc
1607A	—	20.00	50.00	145	300	—

KM# 44.1 1/8 ECU
4.7800 g., 0.9170 Silver 0.1409 oz. ASW **Ruler:** Louis XIII
Obv: Cross with fleur-de-lis at ends **Rev:** Crowned shield of France **Mint:** Paris

Date	Mintage	VG	F	VF	XF	Unc
1611A	—	—	—	—	—	—
1612A	—	—	—	—	—	—
1625A	—	—	—	—	—	—
1628A	—	—	—	—	—	—
1631A	—	—	—	—	—	—
1634A	—	—	—	—	—	—

KM# 44.2 1/8 ECU
4.7800 g., 0.9170 Silver 0.1409 oz. ASW **Ruler:** Louis XIII
Mint: Rouen

Date	Mintage	VG	F	VF	XF	Unc
1615B	—	20.00	50.00	125	325	—
1635B	—	—	—	—	—	—

KM# 44.3 1/8 ECU
4.7800 g., 0.9170 Silver 0.1409 oz. ASW **Ruler:** Louis XIII
Mint: Saint Lô

Date	Mintage	VG	F	VF	XF	Unc
1612C	—	22.00	55.00	135	345	—
1613C	—	30.00	70.00	175	425	—
1614C	—	30.00	70.00	175	425	—
1615C	—	65.00	160	400	950	—
1625C	—	—	—	—	—	—
1627C	—	—	—	—	—	—
1634C	—	—	—	—	—	—
1640C	—	45.00	120	275	675	—
1642C	—	22.00	55.00	135	345	—
1643C	—	30.00	70.00	175	425	—

KM# 44.4 1/8 ECU
4.7800 g., 0.9170 Silver 0.1409 oz. ASW **Ruler:** Louis XIII
Mint: Lyon

Date	Mintage	VG	F	VF	XF	Unc
1621D	—	—	—	—	—	—
1622D	—	—	—	—	—	—
1625D	—	—	—	—	—	—
1643D	—	—	—	—	—	—

KM# 44.5 1/8 ECU
4.7800 g., 0.9170 Silver 0.1409 oz. ASW **Ruler:** Louis XIII
Mint: Tours

Date	Mintage	VG	F	VF	XF	Unc
1618E	—	—	—	—	—	—
1643E	—	35.00	80.00	200	475	—

KM# 44.6 1/8 ECU
4.7800 g., 0.9170 Silver 0.1409 oz. ASW **Ruler:** Louis XIII
Mint: Angers

Date	Mintage	VG	F	VF	XF	Unc
1611F	—	—	—	—	—	—
1612F	—	—	—	—	—	—
1613F	—	30.00	70.00	175	425	—
1625F	—	—	—	—	—	—
1642F	—	30.00	70.00	175	425	—
1643F	—	30.00	70.00	175	425	—

KM# 44.7 1/8 ECU
4.7800 g., 0.9170 Silver 0.1409 oz. ASW **Ruler:** Louis XIII
Mint: Poitiers

Date	Mintage	VG	F	VF	XF	Unc
1643G	—	22.00	55.00	135	345	—

KM# 44.8 1/8 ECU
4.7800 g., 0.9170 Silver 0.1409 oz. ASW **Ruler:** Louis XIII
Mint: La Rochelle

Date	Mintage	VG	F	VF	XF	Unc
1616H	—	—	—	—	—	—
1617H	—	—	—	—	—	—
1618H	—	—	—	—	—	—

KM# 44.9 1/8 ECU
4.7800 g., 0.9170 Silver 0.1409 oz. ASW **Ruler:** Louis XIII
Mint: Limoges

Date	Mintage	VG	F	VF	XF	Unc
1612I	—	25.00	65.00	150	350	—
1642I	—	—	—	—	—	—

KM# 44.10 1/8 ECU
4.7800 g., 0.9170 Silver 0.1409 oz. ASW **Ruler:** Louis XIII
Mint: Bordeaux

Date	Mintage	VG	F	VF	XF	Unc
1610K	—	—	—	—	—	—
1611K	—	22.00	55.00	135	345	—
1616K	—	22.00	55.00	135	345	—
1629K	—	—	—	—	—	—
1630K	—	—	—	—	—	—
1631K	—	—	—	—	—	—
1640K	—	45.00	120	275	675	—
1642K	—	22.00	55.00	135	345	—
1643K	—	22.00	55.00	135	345	—

KM# 44.11 1/8 ECU
4.7800 g., 0.9170 Silver 0.1409 oz. ASW **Ruler:** Louis XIII
Mint: Bayonne

Date	Mintage	VG	F	VF	XF	Unc
1611L	—	22.00	55.00	135	345	—
1612L	—	—	—	—	—	—
1613L	—	—	—	—	—	—
1614L	—	22.00	55.00	135	345	—
1615L	—	—	—	—	—	—
1616L	—	22.00	55.00	135	345	—
1617L	—	—	—	—	—	—
1618L	—	22.00	55.00	135	345	—
1619L	—	22.00	55.00	135	345	—
1621L	—	—	—	—	—	—
1622L	—	35.00	80.00	200	475	—
1623L	—	—	—	—	—	—
1624L	—	—	—	—	—	—
1626L	—	35.00	80.00	200	475	—
1627L	—	30.00	70.00	175	425	—
1628L	—	30.00	70.00	175	425	—
1629L	—	30.00	70.00	175	425	—
1630L	—	35.00	80.00	200	475	—
1631L	—	—	—	—	—	—
1632L	—	—	—	—	—	—
1633L	—	—	—	—	—	—
1637L	—	—	—	—	—	—
1640L	—	—	—	—	—	—
1641L	—	—	—	—	—	—
1642L	—	22.00	55.00	135	345	—

KM# 44.12 1/8 ECU
4.7800 g., 0.9170 Silver 0.1409 oz. ASW **Ruler:** Louis XIII **Mint:** Toulouse

Date	Mintage	VG	F	VF	XF	Unc
1616M	—	22.00	55.00	135	345	—
1642M	—	—	—	—	—	—

KM# 44.13 1/8 ECU
4.7800 g., 0.9170 Silver 0.1409 oz. ASW **Ruler:** Louis XIII **Mint:** Nantes

Date	Mintage	VG	F	VF	XF	Unc
1610T	—	—	—	—	—	—
1611T	—	—	—	—	—	—
1612T	—	—	—	—	—	—
1613T	—	—	—	—	—	—
1614T	—	—	—	—	—	—
1615T	—	—	—	—	—	—
1616T	—	30.00	70.00	175	425	—
1617T	—	30.00	70.00	175	425	—
1618T	—	30.00	70.00	175	425	—
1619T	—	—	—	—	—	—
1620T	—	—	—	—	—	—
1621T	—	—	—	—	—	—
1622T	—	—	—	—	—	—
1623T	—	—	—	—	—	—
1624T	—	—	—	—	—	—
1625T	—	—	—	—	—	—
1628T	—	35.00	80.00	200	475	—
1642T	—	30.00	70.00	175	425	—
1643T	—	22.00	55.00	135	345	—

KM# 44.14 1/8 ECU
4.7800 g., 0.9170 Silver 0.1409 oz. ASW **Ruler:** Louis XIII **Mint:** Amiens

Date	Mintage	VG	F	VF	XF	Unc
1642X	—	22.00	55.00	135	345	—
1643X	—	—	—	—	—	—

KM# 44.15 1/8 ECU
4.7800 g., 0.9170 Silver 0.1409 oz. ASW **Ruler:** Louis XIII **Mint:** Bourges

Date	Mintage	VG	F	VF	XF	Unc
1640Y	—	—	—	—	—	—
1642Y	—	—	—	—	—	—
1643Y	—	—	—	—	—	—

KM# 44.16 1/8 ECU
4.7800 g., 0.9170 Silver 0.1409 oz. ASW **Ruler:** Louis XIII **Mint:** Grenoble

Date	Mintage	VG	F	VF	XF	Unc
1642Z	—	35.00	80.00	200	475	—

KM# 44.17 1/8 ECU
4.7800 g., 0.9170 Silver 0.1409 oz. ASW **Ruler:** Louis XIII **Mint:** Rennes **Note:** Mint mark: Numeral 9.

Date	Mintage	VG	F	VF	XF	Unc
1611	—	22.00	55.00	135	345	—
1612	—	22.00	55.00	135	345	—
1613	—	22.00	55.00	135	345	—
1614	—	—	—	—	—	—
1615	—	22.00	55.00	135	345	—
1616	—	22.00	55.00	135	345	—
1617	—	30.00	70.00	175	425	—
1618	—	—	—	—	—	—
1619	—	—	—	—	—	—
1620	—	—	—	—	—	—
1621	—	—	—	—	—	—
1623	—	—	—	—	—	—
1624	—	35.00	80.00	200	475	—
1625	—	—	—	—	—	—
1627	—	—	—	—	—	—
1628	—	—	—	—	—	—
1629	—	35.00	80.00	200	475	—
1642	—	30.00	70.00	175	425	—
1643	—	22.00	55.00	135	345	—

KM# 44.18 1/8 ECU
4.7800 g., 0.9170 Silver 0.1409 oz. ASW **Ruler:** Louis XIII **Mint:** Arras

Date	Mintage	VG	F	VF	XF	Unc
1641AR	—	40.00	100	250	500	—
1642AR	—	30.00	80.00	200	400	—
1646AR	—	40.00	100	250	500	—

KM# 46 1/8 ECU
4.7800 g., 0.9170 Silver 0.1409 oz. ASW **Ruler:** Louis XIII **Rev:** Crowned shield of France, Navarre and Bearne **Mint:** Pau **Note:** Mint mark: Cow.

Date	Mintage	VG	F	VF	XF	Unc
1610	—	28.00	70.00	165	375	—
1612	—	28.00	70.00	165	375	—
1613	—	28.00	70.00	165	375	—
1614	—	28.00	70.00	165	375	—
1617	—	28.00	70.00	165	375	—
1620	—	28.00	70.00	165	375	—
1623	—	28.00	70.00	165	375	—
1625	—	28.00	70.00	165	375	—
1631	—	28.00	70.00	165	375	—
1643	—	30.00	80.00	200	500	—

KM# 45 1/8 ECU
4.7800 g., 0.9170 Silver 0.1409 oz. ASW **Ruler:** Louis XIII **Rev:** Crowned shield of France and Navarre **Mint:** Saint Palais

Date	Mintage	VG	F	VF	XF	Unc
1611C	—	25.00	60.00	150	350	—
1612M	—	30.00	80.00	200	500	—
1613M	—	25.00	60.00	150	350	—
1614M	—	25.00	60.00	150	350	—
1615M	—	25.00	60.00	150	350	—
1616M	—	25.00	60.00	150	350	—
1617M	—	25.00	60.00	150	350	—
1618M	—	25.00	60.00	150	350	—
1619M	—	28.00	70.00	165	375	—
1620M	—	25.00	60.00	150	350	—
1621F	—	28.00	70.00	165	375	—
1623F	—	25.00	60.00	150	350	—
1629F	—	25.00	60.00	150	350	—

KM# 141.1 1/8 ECU
4.7800 g., 0.9170 Silver 0.1409 oz. ASW **Ruler:** Louis XIV **Obv:** Cross fleuree **Rev:** Crowned shield of France dividing value, VIII **Mint:** Paris

Date	Mintage	VG	F	VF	XF	Unc
1643A	—	20.00	50.00	125	280	—
1644A	—	—	—	—	—	—

KM# 141.2 1/8 ECU
4.7800 g., 0.9170 Silver 0.1409 oz. ASW **Ruler:** Louis XIV **Mint:** Rouen

Date	Mintage	VG	F	VF	XF	Unc
1644B	—	—	—	—	—	—

KM# 141.3 1/8 ECU
4.7800 g., 0.9170 Silver 0.1409 oz. ASW **Ruler:** Louis XIV **Mint:** Saint Lô

Date	Mintage	VG	F	VF	XF	Unc
1643C	—	30.00	75.00	165	375	—
1644C	—	30.00	75.00	165	375	—
1646C	—	30.00	75.00	165	375	—

KM# A141.3 1/8 ECU
4.7800 g., 0.9170 Silver 0.1409 oz. ASW **Ruler:** Louis XIV **Mint:** Angers

Date	Mintage	VG	F	VF	XF	Unc
1643F	—	30.00	75.00	165	375	—
1644F	—	20.00	50.00	125	280	—
1645F	—	25.00	65.00	150	350	—

KM# 141.4 1/8 ECU
4.7800 g., 0.9170 Silver 0.1409 oz. ASW **Ruler:** Louis XIV **Mint:** Poitiers

Date	Mintage	VG	F	VF	XF	Unc
1644G	—	—	—	—	—	—
1645G	—	30.00	75.00	165	375	—
1646G	2,722	35.00	90.00	200	450	—

KM# 141.5 1/8 ECU
4.7800 g., 0.9170 Silver 0.1409 oz. ASW **Ruler:** Louis XIV **Mint:** La Rochelle

Date	Mintage	VG	F	VF	XF	Unc
1644H	—	25.00	65.00	150	350	—

KM# 141.6 1/8 ECU
4.7800 g., 0.9170 Silver 0.1409 oz. ASW **Ruler:** Louis XIV **Mint:** Limoges

Date	Mintage	VG	F	VF	XF	Unc
1644I	—	—	—	—	—	—

KM# 141.7 1/8 ECU
4.7800 g., 0.9170 Silver 0.1409 oz. ASW **Ruler:** Louis XIV **Mint:** Bordeaux

Date	Mintage	VG	F	VF	XF	Unc
1644K	—	25.00	65.00	150	350	—
1645K	—	25.00	65.00	150	350	—

KM# 141.8 1/8 ECU
4.7800 g., 0.9170 Silver 0.1409 oz. ASW **Ruler:** Louis XIV **Mint:** Bayonne

Date	Mintage	VG	F	VF	XF	Unc
1645L	—	30.00	75.00	165	375	—
1646L	—	25.00	65.00	150	350	—
1647L	—	25.00	65.00	150	350	—
1648L	11,000	—	—	—	—	—
1649L	6,350	—	—	—	—	—

KM# 141.9 1/8 ECU
4.7800 g., 0.9170 Silver 0.1409 oz. ASW **Ruler:** Louis XIV **Mint:** Toulouse

Date	Mintage	VG	F	VF	XF	Unc
1644M	—	25.00	65.00	150	350	—
1645M	—	25.00	65.00	150	350	—
1647M	3,629	25.00	65.00	150	350	—

KM# 141.10 1/8 ECU
4.7800 g., 0.9170 Silver 0.1409 oz. ASW **Ruler:** Louis XIV **Mint:** Montpellier

Date	Mintage	VG	F	VF	XF	Unc
1644N	—	25.00	65.00	150	350	—
1645N	—	30.00	75.00	165	375	—

KM# 141.11 1/8 ECU
4.7800 g., 0.9170 Silver 0.1409 oz. ASW **Ruler:** Louis XIV **Mint:** Amiens

Date	Mintage	VG	F	VF	XF	Unc
1645X	—	25.00	65.00	150	350	—
1649X	—	35.00	90.00	200	450	—

KM# 141.12 1/8 ECU
4.7800 g., 0.9170 Silver 0.1409 oz. ASW **Ruler:** Louis XIV **Mint:** Bourges

Date	Mintage	VG	F	VF	XF	Unc
1648Y	—	32.00	80.00	175	400	—

KM# 141.13 1/8 ECU
4.7800 g., 0.9170 Silver 0.1409 oz. ASW **Ruler:** Louis XIV **Mint:** Aix **Note:** Mint mark: Ampersand.

Date	Mintage	VG	F	VF	XF	Unc
1646	—	—	—	—	—	—

KM# 141.14 1/8 ECU
4.7800 g., 0.9170 Silver 0.1409 oz. ASW **Ruler:** Louis XIV **Mint:** Rennes **Note:** Mint mark: Numeral 9.

Date	Mintage	VG	F	VF	XF	Unc
1645	210,000	25.00	75.00	165	375	—
1646	73,000	20.00	50.00	125	280	—
1647	3,629	30.00	75.00	165	375	—

KM# 141.15 1/8 ECU
4.7800 g., 0.9170 Silver 0.1409 oz. ASW **Ruler:** Louis XIV **Mint:** Besancon **Note:** Mint mark: Two back-to-back C's monogram.

Date	Mintage	VG	F	VF	XF	Unc
1645	—	30.00	75.00	165	375	—
1646	—	—	—	—	—	—

KM# 165 1/8 ECU
4.7800 g., 0.9170 Silver 0.1409 oz. ASW **Ruler:** Louis XIV **Mint:** Arras

Date	Mintage	VG	F	VF	XF	Unc
1644AR	—	50.00	100	200	500	—
1645AR	—	50.00	100	200	500	—
1646AR	—	50.00	100	200	500	—

KM# 168 1/8 ECU
4.7800 g., 0.9170 Silver 0.1409 oz. ASW **Ruler:** Louis XIV **Rev. Legend:** Crowned shield of France and Navarre **Mint:** Saint Palais

Date	Mintage	VG	F	VF	XF	Unc
1648	—	40.00	90.00	185	475	—
1649	—	40.00	90.00	185	475	—
1650	—	40.00	90.00	185	475	—

KM# 169 1/8 ECU
4.7800 g., 0.9170 Silver 0.1409 oz. ASW **Ruler:** Louis XIV **Rev:** Crowned shield of France, Navarre and Bearn **Mint:** Morlaas

Date	Mintage	VG	F	VF	XF	Unc
1648P B**	—	65.00	125	250	650	—

KM# 259.1 1/8 ECU
4.7000 g., 0.8570 Silver 0.1295 oz. ASW **Ruler:** Louis XIV **Obv:** Draped bust right **Rev:** Crowned quartered shield of France, Old and New Burgundy **Mint:** Lille

Date	Mintage	VG	F	VF	XF	Unc
1686LL	Est. 98,000	90.00	200	425	1,150	—

KM# 259.2 1/8 ECU
4.7000 g., 0.8570 Silver 0.1295 oz. ASW **Ruler:** Louis XIV **Mint:** Lille **Note:** Mint mark: Crowned L.

Date	Mintage	VG	F	VF	XF	Unc
1686	209,000	75.00	170	375	1,000	—
1687	77,000	90.00	200	450	1,250	—
1688	64,000	100	225	500	1,350	—

KM# 292 1/8 ECU
4.7000 g., 0.8570 Silver 0.1295 oz. ASW **Ruler:** Louis XIV **Rev:** Crowned quartered circular shield of France, Old and New Burgundy dividing palms **Mint:** Lille

Date	Mintage	VG	F	VF	XF	Unc
1693W	—	200	450	1,000	2,000	—
1694W	—	200	450	1,000	2,000	—
1695W	—	200	450	1,000	2,000	—
1696W	18,000	—	—	—	—	—
1697W	10,000	200	450	1,000	2,000	—
1698W	—	250	550	1,250	2,500	—
1699W	800	—	—	—	—	—
1700W	—	250	550	1,250	2,500	—

KM# 1.1 1/4 ECU
Silver **Ruler:** Henry IV **Obv:** Cross with lis **Obv. Legend:** HENRICVS•IIII•D•G•FRANC•ET•NA(VA)•REX• BD **Rev:** Crowned arms of France, Navarre and Béarn **Rev. Legend:** GRATIA•DEI•SVM•Q(•D) (or IDQ)•SVM **Mint:** Pau

Date	Mintage	Good	VG	F	VF	XF
1601	—	—	—	—	—	—
1602	—	—	—	—	—	—
1603	—	—	—	—	—	—
1604	—	—	—	—	—	—
1605	—	—	—	—	—	—
1606	—	—	—	—	—	—
1607	—	—	—	—	—	—
1608	—	—	—	—	—	—

Date	Mintage	Good	VG	F	VF	XF
1609	—	—	—	—	—	—
1610	—	—	—	—	—	—

KM# 1.2 1/4 ECU

Silver **Ruler:** Henry IV **Obv:** Fleur-de-lis cross **Obv. Legend:** HENRICVS•IIII•D•G•FRANC•ET • NA(VA)•REX• BD **Rev:** Crowned arms of France, Navarre and Béarn **Rev. Legend:** GRATIA•BEI•SVM•Q(•D) or (IDQ)•SVM **Mint:** Morlaas

Date	Mintage	Good	VG	F	VF	XF
1601	—	—	—	—	—	—
1602	—	—	—	—	—	—
1603	—	—	—	—	—	—
1604	—	—	—	—	—	—
1605	—	—	—	—	—	—
1606	—	—	—	—	—	—
1607	—	—	—	—	—	—
1608	—	—	—	—	—	—
1609	—	—	—	—	—	—
1610	—	—	—	—	—	—

KM# 30 1/4 ECU

Silver **Ruler:** Henry IV **Rev:** Crowned shield of Dauphine **Mint:** Grenoble

Date	Mintage	VG	F	VF	XF	Unc
1601Z	—	70.00	175	350	600	—
1603Z	—	60.00	150	300	600	—
1605Z	—	50.00	125	250	525	—

KM# 31 1/4 ECU

Silver **Ruler:** Henry IV **Rev:** Crowned shield of France and Navarre **Mint:** Saint Palais

Date	Mintage	VG	F	VF	XF	Unc
1601	—	40.00	100	250	525	—
1602	—	40.00	100	250	525	—
1603	—	40.00	100	250	525	—
1604	—	40.00	100	250	525	—
1605	—	40.00	100	250	525	—
1606	—	40.00	100	250	525	—
1607	—	40.00	100	250	525	—
1608	—	40.00	100	250	525	—
1609	—	40.00	100	250	525	—
1610F	—	40.00	100	250	525	—

KM# 27.1 1/4 ECU

Silver **Ruler:** Henry IV **Obv:** Crowned shield of France **Rev:** Cross with fleur-de-lis at ends **Mint:** Paris

Date	Mintage	VG	F	VF	XF	Unc
1607	—	35.00	90.00	225	500	—

KM# 27.3 1/4 ECU

Silver **Ruler:** Henry IV **Mint:** La Rochelle

Date	Mintage	VG	F	VF	XF	Unc
1606H	—	45.00	100	250	550	—

KM# 27.4 1/4 ECU

Silver **Ruler:** Henry IV **Mint:** Villeneuve St. André

Date	Mintage	VG	F	VF	XF	Unc
1603R	—	35.00	90.00	225	500	—

KM# 27.5 1/4 ECU

Silver **Ruler:** Henry IV

Date	Mintage	VG	F	VF	XF	Unc
1602F	—	40.00	100	250	525	—

KM# 28 1/4 ECU

Silver **Ruler:** Henry IV **Rev:** Cross with crown at ends **Mint:** Saint Lô

Date	Mintage	VG	F	VF	XF	Unc
1603C	—	35.00	90.00	225	500	—
1607C	—	35.00	90.00	225	500	—

KM# 29 1/4 ECU

Silver **Ruler:** Henry IV **Obv:** Cross fleuree **Mint:** Aix **Note:** Mint mark: Ampersand.

Date	Mintage	VG	F	VF	XF	Unc
1603	—	35.00	90.00	225	500	—

KM# A29 1/4 ECU

Silver **Ruler:** Henry IV **Obv:** Crowned shield of France divides "V" and "III" **Obv. Legend:** HENRICVS 4 D.G. **Rev:** Cross fleuree **Mint:** Bordeaux

Date	Mintage	VG	F	VF	XF	Unc
1603K	—	—	—	—	—	—

KM# 47.1 1/4 ECU

6.4400 g., 0.9170 Silver 0.1899 oz. ASW **Ruler:** Louis XIII **Obv:** Cross with fleur-de-lis at ends **Rev:** Crowned shield of France **Mint:** Paris

Date	Mintage	VG	F	VF	XF	Unc
1611A	—	—	—	—	—	—
1612A	—	—	—	—	—	—
1620A	—	—	—	—	—	—
1624A	—	—	—	—	—	—
1625A	—	40.00	100	225	500	—
1628A	—	—	—	—	—	—
1631A	—	—	—	—	—	—
1634A	—	—	—	—	—	—
1636A	—	35.00	90.00	200	450	—
1637A	—	—	—	—	—	—
1639A	—	—	—	—	—	—
1641A	—	28.00	65.00	150	325	—
1642A	—	22.00	55.00	125	275	—
1643A	—	20.00	45.00	100	225	—

KM# 47.2 1/4 ECU

6.4400 g., 0.9170 Silver 0.1899 oz. ASW **Ruler:** Louis XIII **Mint:** Rouen

Date	Mintage	VG	F	VF	XF	Unc
1611B	—	20.00	45.00	100	185	—
1614B	—	—	—	—	—	—
1615B	—	20.00	40.00	90.00	165	—
1622B	—	—	—	—	—	—
1623B	—	—	—	—	—	—
1624B	—	—	—	—	—	—
1626B	—	—	—	—	—	—
1628B	—	—	—	—	—	—
1629B	—	—	—	—	—	—
1632B	—	28.00	65.00	150	325	—
1636B	—	—	—	—	—	—
1637B	—	—	—	—	—	—
1640B	—	22.00	55.00	125	275	—
1642B	—	—	—	—	—	—

KM# 47.3 1/4 ECU

6.4400 g., 0.9170 Silver 0.1899 oz. ASW **Ruler:** Louis XIII **Mint:** Saint Lô

Date	Mintage	VG	F	VF	XF	Unc
1611C	—	—	—	—	—	—
1612C	—	22.00	50.00	110	225	—
1613C	—	22.00	50.00	110	225	—
1614C	—	22.00	50.00	110	225	—
1615C	—	22.00	50.00	110	225	—
1616C	—	28.00	65.00	160	325	—
1617C	—	35.00	90.00	200	450	—
1623C	—	—	—	—	—	—
1624C	—	35.00	90.00	200	450	—
1625C	—	—	—	—	—	—
1627C	—	90.00	200	400	900	—
1628C	—	—	—	—	—	—
1630C	—	40.00	100	225	500	—
1633C	—	—	—	—	—	—
1634C	—	40.00	100	225	500	—
1642C	—	22.00	50.00	110	225	—
1643C	—	25.00	65.00	140	300	—

KM# 47.4 1/4 ECU

6.4400 g., 0.9170 Silver 0.1899 oz. ASW **Ruler:** Louis XIII **Mint:** Lyon

Date	Mintage	VG	F	VF	XF	Unc
1621D	—	—	—	—	—	—
1622D	—	—	—	—	—	—
1624D	—	—	—	—	—	—
1625D	—	—	—	—	—	—
1633D	—	—	—	—	—	—
1642D	—	20.00	40.00	90.00	165	—
1643D	—	—	—	—	—	—

KM# 47.5 1/4 ECU

6.4400 g., 0.9170 Silver 0.1899 oz. ASW **Ruler:** Louis XIII **Mint:** Tours

Date	Mintage	VG	F	VF	XF	Unc
1617E	—	20.00	40.00	90.00	185	—
1618E	—	—	—	—	—	—
1642E	—	22.00	50.00	110	225	—
1643E	—	25.00	65.00	140	300	—

KM# 47.6 1/4 ECU

6.4400 g., 0.9170 Silver 0.1899 oz. ASW **Ruler:** Louis XIII **Mint:** Angers

Date	Mintage	VG	F	VF	XF	Unc
1611F	—	—	—	—	—	—
1612F	—	—	—	—	—	—
1613F	—	22.00	55.00	125	270	—
1614F	—	—	—	—	—	—
1615F	—	20.00	40.00	90.00	165	—
1616F	—	22.00	55.00	125	270	—
1617F	—	20.00	40.00	90.00	185	—
1618F	—	20.00	55.00	125	270	—
1621F	—	—	—	—	—	—
1623F	—	—	—	—	—	—
1625F	—	—	—	—	—	—
1642F	—	25.00	65.00	145	300	—
1643F	—	25.00	65.00	145	300	—
1644F	—	32.00	80.00	185	400	—
1645F	—	32.00	80.00	185	400	—

KM# 47.7 1/4 ECU

6.4400 g., 0.9170 Silver 0.1899 oz. ASW **Ruler:** Louis XIII **Mint:** Poitiers

Date	Mintage	VG	F	VF	XF	Unc
1642G	—	35.00	90.00	210	450	—
1643G	—	22.00	55.00	130	275	—

KM# 47.8 1/4 ECU

6.4400 g., 0.9170 Silver 0.1899 oz. ASW **Ruler:** Louis XIII **Mint:** La Rochelle

Date	Mintage	VG	F	VF	XF	Unc
1615H	—	—	—	—	—	—
1616H	—	22.00	50.00	110	225	—
1617H	—	20.00	40.00	90.00	185	—
1618H	—	—	—	—	—	—
1627H	—	35.00	90.00	200	450	—
1640H	—	35.00	90.00	200	450	—
1641H	—	—	—	—	—	—
1642H	—	28.00	65.00	150	325	—
1643H	—	—	—	—	—	—

KM# 47.9 1/4 ECU

6.4400 g., 0.9170 Silver 0.1899 oz. ASW **Ruler:** Louis XIII **Mint:** Limoges

Date	Mintage	VG	F	VF	XF	Unc
1611I	—	20.00	40.00	90.00	165	—
1612I	—	—	—	—	—	—
1613I	—	22.00	55.00	125	270	—
1615I	—	20.00	40.00	90.00	165	—
1617I	—	20.00	40.00	90.00	175	—
1642I	—	22.00	55.00	125	270	—

KM# 47.10 1/4 ECU

6.4400 g., 0.9170 Silver 0.1899 oz. ASW **Ruler:** Louis XIII **Mint:** Bordeaux

Date	Mintage	VG	F	VF	XF	Unc
1611K	—	20.00	40.00	90.00	165	—
1612K	—	22.00	50.00	110	225	—
1613K	—	—	—	—	—	—
1615K	—	22.00	55.00	125	270	—
1616K	—	22.00	55.00	125	270	—
1618K	—	—	—	—	—	—
1629K	—	—	—	—	—	—
1630K	—	—	—	—	—	—
1631K	—	—	—	—	—	—
1632K	—	—	—	—	—	—
1639K	—	35.00	90.00	200	450	—
1640K	—	22.00	55.00	125	270	—
1642K	—	22.00	50.00	110	225	—
1643K	—	22.00	50.00	110	225	—

KM# 47.11 1/4 ECU

6.4400 g., 0.9170 Silver 0.1899 oz. ASW **Ruler:** Louis XIII **Mint:** Bayonne

Date	Mintage	VG	F	VF	XF	Unc
1610L	—	—	—	—	—	—
1611L	—	20.00	40.00	90.00	175	—
1612L	—	20.00	40.00	90.00	175	—
1613L	—	20.00	40.00	90.00	175	—
1614L	—	22.00	45.00	100	185	—
1615L	—	20.00	40.00	90.00	175	—
1616L	—	22.00	45.00	100	185	—
1617L	—	22.00	45.00	100	185	—
1618L	—	22.00	45.00	100	185	—
1619L	—	30.00	65.00	150	325	—
1621L	—	22.00	45.00	100	185	—
1622L	—	22.00	45.00	100	185	—
1623L	—	22.00	45.00	100	185	—
1624L	—	22.00	50.00	110	225	—
1626L	—	22.00	50.00	110	225	—

Date	Mintage	VG	F	VF	XF	Unc
1627L	—	20.00	40.00	90.00	175	—
1628L	—	20.00	40.00	90.00	175	—
1629L	—	20.00	40.00	90.00	175	—
1630L	—	—	—	—	—	—
1631L	—	25.00	55.00	125	270	—
1632L	—	22.00	50.00	110	225	—
1633L	—	35.00	90.00	200	450	—
1637L	—	—	—	—	—	—
1640L	—	40.00	100	225	500	—
1641L	—	28.00	65.00	150	325	—
1642L	—	25.00	55.00	125	270	—
1643L	—	25.00	55.00	125	270	—

KM# 47.12 1/4 ECU

6.4400 g., 0.9170 Silver 0.1899 oz. ASW **Ruler:** Louis XIII
Mint: Toulouse

Date	Mintage	VG	F	VF	XF	Unc
1613M	—	20.00	40.00	90.00	165	—
1619M	—	25.00	55.00	125	270	—
1642M	—	35.00	90.00	200	450	—
1643M	—	20.00	40.00	90.00	165	—

KM# 47.13 1/4 ECU

6.4400 g., 0.9170 Silver 0.1899 oz. ASW **Ruler:** Louis XIII
Mint: Montpellier

Date	Mintage	VG	F	VF	XF	Unc
1642N	—	22.00	50.00	110	225	—
1643N	—	25.00	55.00	125	270	—

KM# 47.14 1/4 ECU

6.4400 g., 0.9170 Silver 0.1899 oz. ASW **Ruler:** Louis XIII
Mint: Dijon

Date	Mintage	VG	F	VF	XF	Unc
1638P	—	35.00	90.00	200	450	—
1639P	—	35.00	90.00	200	450	—
1640P	—	—	—	—	—	—

KM# 47.15 1/4 ECU

6.4400 g., 0.9170 Silver 0.1899 oz. ASW **Ruler:** Louis XIII
Mint: Perpignan

Date	Mintage	VG	F	VF	XF	Unc
1645Q	—	35.00	90.00	200	450	—

KM# 47.16 1/4 ECU

6.4400 g., 0.9170 Silver 0.1899 oz. ASW **Ruler:** Louis XIII
Mint: Nantes

Date	Mintage	VG	F	VF	XF	Unc
1610T	—	22.00	45.00	100	185	—
1611T	—	20.00	40.00	90.00	165	—
1612T	—	20.00	40.00	90.00	165	—
1613T	—	22.00	45.00	110	225	—
1614T	—	22.00	45.00	110	225	—
1615T	—	20.00	40.00	90.00	165	—
1616T	—	22.00	45.00	100	185	—
1617T	—	20.00	40.00	90.00	165	—
1618T	—	20.00	40.00	90.00	165	—
1619T	—	—	—	—	—	—
1620T	—	—	—	—	—	—
1622T	—	—	—	—	—	—
1623T	—	20.00	40.00	90.00	165	—
1624T	—	22.00	45.00	110	225	—
1625T	—	22.00	45.00	110	225	—
1626T	—	—	—	—	—	—
1642T	—	22.00	45.00	110	225	—
1643T	—	25.00	55.00	125	270	—

KM# 47.17 1/4 ECU

6.4400 g., 0.9170 Silver 0.1899 oz. ASW **Ruler:** Louis XIII
Mint: Amiens

Date	Mintage	VG	F	VF	XF	Unc
1636X	—	—	—	—	—	—
1641X	—	—	—	—	—	—
1642X	—	25.00	55.00	125	270	—
1643X	—	28.00	65.00	150	325	—

KM# 47.18 1/4 ECU

6.4400 g., 0.9170 Silver 0.1899 oz. ASW **Ruler:** Louis XIII
Mint: Bourges

Date	Mintage	VG	F	VF	XF	Unc
1640Y	—	—	—	—	—	—
1642Y	—	35.00	90.00	200	450	—

KM# 47.19 1/4 ECU

6.4400 g., 0.9170 Silver 0.1899 oz. ASW **Ruler:** Louis XIII
Mint: Grenoble

Date	Mintage	VG	F	VF	XF	Unc
1641Z	—	—	—	—	—	—
1642Z	—	28.00	65.00	150	325	—
1643Z	—	25.00	55.00	125	270	—

KM# 47.20 1/4 ECU

6.4400 g., 0.9170 Silver 0.1899 oz. ASW **Ruler:** Louis XIII
Mint: Aix **Note:** Mint mark: Ampersand.

Date	Mintage	VG	F	VF	XF	Unc
1642	—	—	—	—	—	—
1643	—	22.00	55.00	125	270	—

KM# 47.21 1/4 ECU

6.4400 g., 0.9170 Silver 0.1899 oz. ASW **Ruler:** Louis XIII
Mint: Rennes **Note:** Mint mark: Numeral 9.

Date	Mintage	VG	F	VF	XF	Unc
1611	—	20.00	40.00	90.00	165	—
1612	—	20.00	40.00	90.00	165	—
1613	—	20.00	40.00	90.00	165	—
1614	—	22.00	45.00	110	225	—
1615	—	20.00	40.00	90.00	165	—
1616	—	20.00	40.00	90.00	165	—
1617	—	20.00	40.00	90.00	165	—
1618	—	20.00	40.00	90.00	165	—
1620	—	25.00	55.00	125	270	—
1623	—	—	—	—	—	—
1624	—	20.00	40.00	90.00	165	—
1625	—	25.00	55.00	125	270	—
1642	—	—	—	—	—	—
1643	—	25.00	55.00	125	270	—

KM# 47.22 1/4 ECU

6.4400 g., 0.9170 Silver 0.1899 oz. ASW **Ruler:** Louis XIII
Mint: Arras

Date	Mintage	VG	F	VF	XF	Unc
1624AR	—	28.00	65.00	150	325	—
1641AR	1,121	70.00	175	350	750	—
1642AR	153,000	20.00	40.00	90.00	175	—
1643AR	86,000	22.00	45.00	110	225	—

KM# 48 1/4 ECU

6.4400 g., 0.9170 Silver 0.1899 oz. ASW **Ruler:** Louis XIII
Rev: Crowned shield of France and Navarre **Mint:** Saint Palais

Date	Mintage	VG	F	VF	XF	Unc
1610C	—	30.00	60.00	150	250	—
1611C	—	30.00	60.00	150	250	—
1612M	65,000	30.00	60.00	150	250	—
1613M	81,000	30.00	60.00	150	250	—
1614M	69,000	30.00	60.00	150	250	—
1615M	—	30.00	60.00	150	250	—
1616M	53,000	30.00	60.00	150	250	—
1617M	—	30.00	60.00	150	250	—
1618M	—	30.00	60.00	150	250	—
1619F	51,000	30.00	60.00	150	250	—
1619M	Inc. above	30.00	60.00	150	250	—
1620F	—	30.00	60.00	150	250	—
1620M	—	30.00	60.00	150	250	—
1621F	—	30.00	60.00	150	250	—
1623F	92,000	30.00	60.00	150	250	—
1625F	—	30.00	60.00	150	250	—
1626F	—	30.00	60.00	150	250	—
1627F	—	30.00	60.00	150	250	—
1629F	—	30.00	60.00	150	250	—
1631F	99,000	30.00	60.00	150	250	—

KM# 49.1 1/4 ECU

6.4400 g., 0.9170 Silver 0.1899 oz. ASW **Ruler:** Louis XIII
Rev: Crowned shield of France, Navarre and Bearn **Mint:** Pau

Date	Mintage	VG	F	VF	XF	Unc
1610	—	28.00	65.00	150	250	—
1612	64,000	35.00	75.00	165	275	—
1613	54,000	35.00	75.00	165	275	—
1614	42,000	35.00	75.00	165	275	—
1615	—	35.00	75.00	165	275	—
1617	—	40.00	85.00	185	300	—
1618	—	40.00	85.00	185	300	—
1619	—	35.00	75.00	165	275	—
1621	—	35.00	75.00	165	275	—
1622	64,000	40.00	85.00	185	300	—
1623	—	35.00	75.00	165	275	—
1625	—	—	—	—	—	—
1626	—	35.00	75.00	165	275	—
1627	—	35.00	75.00	165	275	—
1628	—	35.00	75.00	165	275	—
1629	—	28.00	65.00	150	250	—
1630	—	35.00	75.00	165	275	—
1631	21,000	—	—	—	—	—
1639	—	40.00	85.00	185	300	—
1643	—	40.00	85.00	185	300	—

KM# 49.2 1/4 ECU

6.4400 g., 0.9170 Silver 0.1899 oz. ASW **Ruler:** Louis XIII
Mint: Morlaas **Note:** Mint mark: Star or * and letter.

Date	Mintage	VG	F	VF	XF	Unc
1610	—	60.00	160	350	575	—
1611	—	35.00	75.00	165	275	—
1612	115,000	35.00	75.00	165	275	—
1613	72,000	35.00	75.00	165	275	—
1614	68,000	35.00	75.00	165	275	—
1615	—	40.00	85.00	185	300	—
1616	—	35.00	75.00	165	275	—
1617	—	35.00	75.00	165	275	—
1618	—	28.00	65.00	150	250	—
1619	—	35.00	75.00	165	275	—
1620	—	35.00	75.00	165	275	—
1622	—	—	—	—	—	—
1624	—	35.00	75.00	165	275	—
1625	—	35.00	75.00	165	275	—
1626	—	35.00	75.00	165	275	—
1627	—	35.00	75.00	165	275	—
1628	—	35.00	75.00	165	275	—
1629	99,000	35.00	75.00	165	275	—
1630	—	—	—	—	—	—
1631	—	35.00	75.00	165	275	—

KM# 133 1/4 ECU

6.7460 g., 0.9170 Silver 0.1989 oz. ASW **Ruler:** Louis XIII
Obv: Laureate mailed bust right **Mint:** Paris

Date	Mintage	VG	F	VF	XF	Unc
1642A Rose	625,000	125	300	625	1,000	—
1642A Point	—	110	275	575	950	—
1642A 2 points	—	110	275	575	950	—
1642A 2 points and 1 below bust	—	125	300	625	1,000	—

KM# 134.1 1/4 ECU

6.7460 g., 0.9170 Silver 0.1989 oz. ASW **Ruler:** Louis XIII
Obv: Laureate, draped and mailed bust right **Mint:** Paris

Date	Mintage	VG	F	VF	XF	Unc
1642 Rose	647,000	90.00	220	450	725	—
1642 Point	—	90.00	220	450	725	—
1642 2 points	—	90.00	220	450	725	—
1643 Rose	Est. 3,089,000	80.00	200	425	700	—
1643 Point	—	65.00	165	350	575	—
1643 2 points	Est. 4,626,000	65.00	165	350	575	—

KM# 134.2 1/4 ECU

6.7460 g., 0.9170 Silver 0.1989 oz. ASW **Ruler:** Louis XIII
Mint: Lyon

Date	Mintage	VG	F	VF	XF	Unc
1643D 3 points	Est. 17,000	175	425	825	1,350	—

KM# 142.1 1/4 ECU

6.4400 g., 0.9170 Silver 0.1899 oz. ASW **Ruler:** Louis XIII
Obv: Outlined cross with fleur-de-lis at ends **Rev:** Crowned shield of France **Mint:** Paris

Date	Mintage	VG	F	VF	XF	Unc
1643A	—	20.00	45.00	100	225	—
1644A	—	—	—	—	—	—

KM# 142.2 1/4 ECU

6.4400 g., 0.9170 Silver 0.1899 oz. ASW **Ruler:** Louis XIII
Mint: Rouen

Date	Mintage	VG	F	VF	XF	Unc
1644B	—	25.00	60.00	135	300	—
1645B	—	35.00	90.00	200	450	—

KM# 142.3 1/4 ECU

6.4400 g., 0.9170 Silver 0.1899 oz. ASW **Ruler:** Louis XIII
Mint: Saint Lô

Date	Mintage	VG	F	VF	XF	Unc
1643C	—	28.00	65.00	150	325	—
1644C	—	20.00	50.00	120	270	—
1645C	—	25.00	60.00	135	300	—
1646C	—	28.00	65.00	150	325	—
1647C	—	—	—	—	—	—

KM# 142.4 1/4 ECU

6.4400 g., 0.9170 Silver 0.1899 oz. ASW **Ruler:** Louis XIII
Mint: Tours

Date	Mintage	VG	F	VF	XF	Unc
1643E	—	32.00	80.00	175	400	—

KM# 142.5 1/4 ECU

6.4400 g., 0.9170 Silver 0.1899 oz. ASW **Ruler:** Louis XIII
Mint: Angers

Date	Mintage	VG	F	VF	XF	Unc
1643F	—	28.00	65.00	150	325	—
1644F	—	20.00	50.00	120	270	—
1645F	—	28.00	65.00	150	325	—
1646F	—	28.00	65.00	150	325	—

KM# 142.6 1/4 ECU

6.4400 g., 0.9170 Silver 0.1899 oz. ASW **Ruler:** Louis XIII
Mint: Poitiers

Date	Mintage	VG	F	VF	XF	Unc
1644G	—	35.00	90.00	200	450	—
1645G	—	35.00	90.00	200	450	—
1646G	—	35.00	90.00	200	450	—

KM# 142.7 1/4 ECU

6.4400 g., 0.9170 Silver 0.1899 oz. ASW **Ruler:** Louis XIII
Mint: La Rochelle

Date	Mintage	VG	F	VF	XF	Unc
1643H	—	—	—	—	—	—
1644H	—	32.00	80.00	175	400	—
1645H	—	35.00	90.00	200	450	—
1646H	—	—	—	—	—	—

KM# 142.8 1/4 ECU

6.4400 g., 0.9170 Silver 0.1899 oz. ASW **Ruler:** Louis XIII
Mint: Limoges

Date	Mintage	VG	F	VF	XF	Unc
1644I	—	32.00	80.00	175	400	—
1645I	—	32.00	80.00	175	400	—

KM# 142.9 1/4 ECU

6.4400 g., 0.9170 Silver 0.1899 oz. ASW **Ruler:** Louis XIII
Mint: Bordeaux

Date	Mintage	VG	F	VF	XF	Unc
1643K	—	28.00	65.00	150	325	—
1644K	—	25.00	60.00	135	300	—
1645K	—	25.00	60.00	135	300	—
1646K	—	28.00	65.00	150	325	—
1647K	—	40.00	100	225	500	—

KM# 142.10 1/4 ECU

6.4400 g., 0.9170 Silver 0.1899 oz. ASW **Ruler:** Louis XIII
Mint: Bayonne

Date	Mintage	VG	F	VF	XF	Unc
1643L	—	32.00	80.00	175	400	—
1644L	—	30.00	75.00	165	375	—
1645L	—	25.00	60.00	135	300	—
1646L	—	20.00	50.00	120	270	—
1647L	—	25.00	60.00	135	300	—
1648L	—	25.00	60.00	135	300	—
1649L	—	25.00	60.00	135	300	—

KM# 142.11 1/4 ECU

6.4400 g., 0.9170 Silver 0.1899 oz. ASW **Ruler:** Louis XIII
Mint: Toulouse

Date	Mintage	VG	F	VF	XF	Unc
1644M	—	20.00	50.00	120	270	—
1645M	—	20.00	50.00	120	270	—
1646M	—	25.00	60.00	135	300	—
1647M	17,000	—	—	—	—	—

KM# 142.12 1/4 ECU

6.4400 g., 0.9170 Silver 0.1899 oz. ASW **Ruler:** Louis XIII
Mint: Montpellier

Date	Mintage	VG	F	VF	XF	Unc
1644N	—	25.00	60.00	135	300	—
1645N	—	30.00	75.00	165	375	—
1646N	—	28.00	65.00	150	325	—

KM# 142.13 1/4 ECU

6.4400 g., 0.9170 Silver 0.1899 oz. ASW **Ruler:** Louis XIII
Mint: Narbonne

Date	Mintage	VG	F	VF	XF	Unc
1645Q	16,000	32.00	80.00	175	400	—
1646Q	—	35.00	90.00	200	450	—

KM# 142.14 1/4 ECU

6.4400 g., 0.9170 Silver 0.1899 oz. ASW **Ruler:** Louis XIII
Mint: Villeneuve St. André

Date	Mintage	VG	F	VF	XF	Unc
1643R	—	28.00	65.00	150	325	—
1644R	—	35.00	90.00	200	450	—
1645R	—	—	—	—	—	—
1646R	—	—	—	—	—	—

KM# 142.15 1/4 ECU

6.4400 g., 0.9170 Silver 0.1899 oz. ASW **Ruler:** Louis XIII
Mint: Nantes

Date	Mintage	VG	F	VF	XF	Unc
1644T	—	25.00	60.00	135	300	—
1645T	—	25.00	60.00	135	300	—
1646T	—	20.00	50.00	120	270	—
1647T	—	30.00	75.00	165	375	—

KM# 142.16 1/4 ECU

6.4400 g., 0.9170 Silver 0.1899 oz. ASW **Ruler:** Louis XIII
Mint: Amiens

Date	Mintage	VG	F	VF	XF	Unc
1644X	—	32.00	80.00	175	400	—
1645X	—	25.00	60.00	135	300	—
1646X	—	—	—	—	—	—

KM# 142.17 1/4 ECU

6.4400 g., 0.9170 Silver 0.1899 oz. ASW **Ruler:** Louis XIII
Mint: Bourges

Date	Mintage	VG	F	VF	XF	Unc
1643Y	—	32.00	80.00	175	400	—
1644Y	—	—	—	—	—	—

KM# 142.18 1/4 ECU

6.4400 g., 0.9170 Silver 0.1899 oz. ASW **Ruler:** Louis XIII
Mint: Grenoble

Date	Mintage	VG	F	VF	XF	Unc
1644Z	—	—	—	—	—	—

KM# 142.19 1/4 ECU

6.4400 g., 0.9170 Silver 0.1899 oz. ASW **Ruler:** Louis XIII
Mint: Rennes **Note:** Mint mark: Numeral 9.

Date	Mintage	VG	F	VF	XF	Unc
1644	—	20.00	50.00	120	270	—
1645	—	20.00	45.00	100	225	—
1646	—	28.00	65.00	150	325	—
1647	—	25.00	60.00	135	300	—

KM# 142.20 1/4 ECU

6.4400 g., 0.9170 Silver 0.1899 oz. ASW **Ruler:** Louis XIII
Mint: Aix **Note:** Mint mark: Ampersand.

Date	Mintage	VG	F	VF	XF	Unc
1643	—	25.00	60.00	135	300	—
1644	—	20.00	65.00	150	325	—
1645	—	—	—	—	—	—
1646	—	35.00	90.00	200	450	—

KM# 142.21 1/4 ECU

6.4400 g., 0.9170 Silver 0.1899 oz. ASW **Ruler:** Louis XIII
Mint: Besancon **Note:** Mint mark: Back-to-back C's.

Date	Mintage	VG	F	VF	XF	Unc
1644	—	32.00	80.00	175	400	—
1645	—	35.00	90.00	200	450	—
1646	—	—	—	—	—	—

KM# 161.1 1/4 ECU

6.4400 g., 0.9170 Silver 0.1899 oz. ASW **Ruler:** Louis XIII
Obv: Laureate, draped and mailed youthful bust right, short hair before ear **Rev:** Crowned shield of France **Mint:** Paris

Date	Mintage	VG	F	VF	XF	Unc
1643A Point	—	40.00	100	235	500	—
1643A Rose	—	45.00	110	250	550	—
1644A Point	—	40.00	90.00	220	450	—
1644A Rose	—	30.00	75.00	185	375	—
1644A 2 points and rose	—	50.00	135	300	675	—
1645A Point	—	40.00	90.00	220	450	—
1645A Rose	—	40.00	90.00	220	450	—
1645A 2 points and rose	—	50.00	135	300	675	—

KM# 161.2 1/4 ECU

6.4400 g., 0.9170 Silver 0.1899 oz. ASW **Ruler:** Louis XIII
Mint: Lyon

Date	Mintage	VG	F	VF	XF	Unc
1644D	—	65.00	165	345	750	—
1645D	—	65.00	165	345	750	—
1648D	—	90.00	200	420	900	—
1649D	—	90.00	200	420	900	—
1650D	—	—	—	—	—	—
1651D	—	—	—	—	—	—

KM# 143 1/4 ECU

6.4400 g., 0.9170 Silver 0.1899 oz. ASW **Ruler:** Louis XIII
Obv: Crowned shield of France **Rev:** Outlined cross, fleur-de-lis at ends **Mint:** Arras

Date	Mintage	VG	F	VF	XF	Unc
1643AR	—	30.00	75.00	165	375	—
1644AR	—	32.00	80.00	175	400	—
1645AR	—	32.00	80.00	175	400	—
1646AR	—	35.00	90.00	200	450	—

KM# 162.1 1/4 ECU

6.4400 g., 0.9170 Silver 0.1899 oz. ASW **Ruler:** Louis XIII
Obv: Long hair curl before ear **Mint:** Paris

Date	Mintage	VG	F	VF	XF	Unc
1646A	—	60.00	150	325	725	—
1647A	—	35.00	90.00	200	450	—
1648A	—	45.00	110	245	550	—
1649A	—	50.00	120	275	620	—
1650A	—	35.00	90.00	200	450	—
1651A	—	50.00	120	275	620	—
1652A	—	32.00	80.00	180	425	—
1653A	—	35.00	90.00	200	450	—
1654A	—	50.00	120	275	620	—
1655A	—	50.00	120	275	620	—
1657A	—	—	—	—	—	—

KM# 162.2 1/4 ECU

6.4400 g., 0.9170 Silver 0.1899 oz. ASW **Ruler:** Louis XIII
Mint: Arras

Date	Mintage	VG	F	VF	XF	Unc
1647AR	—	75.00	175	350	775	—
1652AR	—	50.00	120	275	620	—
1655AR	—	50.00	135	300	675	—

KM# 162.3 1/4 ECU

6.4400 g., 0.9170 Silver 0.1899 oz. ASW **Ruler:** Louis XIII
Mint: Rouen

Date	Mintage	VG	F	VF	XF	Unc
1649B	—	50.00	120	275	620	—
1650B	—	50.00	135	300	675	—
1652B	—	50.00	135	300	620	—
1653B	—	50.00	135	300	620	—
1654B	—	60.00	150	325	725	—
1655B	—	—	—	—	—	—

KM# 162.4 1/4 ECU

6.4400 g., 0.9170 Silver 0.1899 oz. ASW **Ruler:** Louis XIII
Mint: Saint Lô

Date	Mintage	VG	F	VF	XF	Unc
1649C	—	—	—	—	—	—
1650C	—	50.00	135	300	675	—
1651C	—	75.00	175	350	775	—
1652C	—	50.00	120	275	620	—
1653C	—	—	—	—	—	—
1655C	—	—	—	—	—	—

KM# 162.5 1/4 ECU

6.4400 g., 0.9170 Silver 0.1899 oz. ASW **Ruler:** Louis XIII
Mint: Lyon

Date	Mintage	VG	F	VF	XF	Unc
1652D	—	50.00	120	275	620	—
1653D	—	50.00	120	275	620	—
1654D	—	—	—	—	—	—
1657D	—	—	—	—	—	—
1658D	—	—	—	—	—	—

KM# 162.6 1/4 ECU

6.4400 g., 0.9170 Silver 0.1899 oz. ASW **Ruler:** Louis XIII
Mint: Tours

Date	Mintage	VG	F	VF	XF	Unc
1652E	—	—	—	—	—	—
1653E	—	—	—	—	—	—
1654E	—	—	—	—	—	—
1655E	—	—	—	—	—	—

KM# 162.7 1/4 ECU
6.4400 g., 0.9170 Silver 0.1899 oz. ASW **Ruler:** Louis XIII
Mint: Angers

Date	Mintage	VG	F	VF	XF	Unc
1646F	—	75.00	175	350	775	—
1647F	—	—	—	—	—	—
1648F	—	50.00	120	275	620	—
1649F	—	—	—	—	—	—
1650F	—	50.00	120	275	620	—
1651F	—	—	—	—	—	—
1652F	—	—	—	—	—	—
1653F	—	75.00	175	350	775	—
1654F	—	—	—	—	—	—
1656F	—	—	—	—	—	—

KM# 162.8 1/4 ECU
6.4400 g., 0.9170 Silver 0.1899 oz. ASW **Ruler:** Louis XIII
Mint: Poitiers

Date	Mintage	VG	F	VF	XF	Unc
1648G	—	—	—	—	—	—
1649G	—	—	—	—	—	—
1650G	—	—	—	—	—	—
1652G	—	—	—	—	—	—
1653G	—	—	—	—	—	—

KM# 162.9 1/4 ECU
6.4400 g., 0.9170 Silver 0.1899 oz. ASW **Ruler:** Louis XIII
Mint: La Rochelle

Date	Mintage	VG	F	VF	XF	Unc
1646H	—	—	—	—	—	—
1648H	—	—	—	—	—	—
1649H	—	—	—	—	—	—
1650H	—	90.00	200	400	900	—
1651H	—	—	—	—	—	—
1652H	—	—	—	—	—	—
1653H	—	—	—	—	—	—
1654H	—	—	—	—	—	—
1655H	—	—	—	—	—	—
1656H	—	—	—	—	—	—

KM# 162.10 1/4 ECU
6.4400 g., 0.9170 Silver 0.1899 oz. ASW **Ruler:** Louis XIII
Mint: Limoges

Date	Mintage	VG	F	VF	XF	Unc
1649I	—	—	—	—	—	—
1650I	—	—	—	—	—	—
1651I	—	—	—	—	—	—
1652I	—	—	—	—	—	—
1653I	—	—	—	—	—	—
1654I	—	—	—	—	—	—

KM# 162.11 1/4 ECU
6.4400 g., 0.9170 Silver 0.1899 oz. ASW **Ruler:** Louis XIII
Mint: Bordeaux

Date	Mintage	VG	F	VF	XF	Unc
1647K	—	40.00	100	225	500	—
1648K	—	50.00	120	275	620	—
1649K	—	50.00	120	275	620	—
1650K	—	50.00	120	275	620	—
1651K	—	—	—	—	—	—
1652K	—	—	—	—	—	—
1653K	—	—	—	—	—	—
1654K	—	—	—	—	—	—
1655K	—	—	—	—	—	—
1656K	—	—	—	—	—	—
1657K	—	—	—	—	—	—
1660K	—	90.00	200	400	900	—

KM# 162.12 1/4 ECU
6.4400 g., 0.9170 Silver 0.1899 oz. ASW **Ruler:** Louis XIII
Mint: Bayonne

Date	Mintage	VG	F	VF	XF	Unc
1650L	—	50.00	135	300	675	—
1651L	—	50.00	120	275	620	—
1652L	—	—	—	—	—	—
1653L	—	50.00	120	275	620	—
1654L	—	—	—	—	—	—
1655L	—	40.00	100	225	500	—
1656L	—	—	—	—	—	—
1657L	—	—	—	—	—	—
1658L	—	—	—	—	—	—
1659L	—	—	—	—	—	—
1660L	—	—	—	—	—	—
1661L	—	—	—	—	—	—

KM# 162.13 1/4 ECU
6.4400 g., 0.9170 Silver 0.1899 oz. ASW **Ruler:** Louis XIII
Mint: Toulouse

Date	Mintage	VG	F	VF	XF	Unc
1648M	—	90.00	200	400	900	—
1649M	—	50.00	120	275	620	—
1650M	—	—	—	—	—	—
1651M	—	—	—	—	—	—
1653M	—	—	—	—	—	—
1654M	—	—	—	—	—	—
1655M	—	—	—	—	—	—
1656M	—	—	—	—	—	—
1659M	—	—	—	—	—	—

KM# 162.14 1/4 ECU
6.4400 g., 0.9170 Silver 0.1899 oz. ASW **Ruler:** Louis XIII
Mint: Montpellier

Date	Mintage	VG	F	VF	XF	Unc
1646N	—	50.00	135	300	675	—
1647N	—	50.00	120	275	620	—
1648N	—	—	—	—	—	—
1649N	—	—	—	—	—	—
1650N	—	—	—	—	—	—
1651N	—	—	—	—	—	—
1652N	—	—	—	—	—	—
1653N	—	—	—	—	—	—
1659N	—	—	—	—	—	—
1660N	—	—	—	—	—	—

KM# 162.15 1/4 ECU
6.4400 g., 0.9170 Silver 0.1899 oz. ASW **Ruler:** Louis XIII
Mint: Riom

Date	Mintage	VG	F	VF	XF	Unc
1652O	—	—	—	—	—	—
1653O	—	—	—	—	—	—

KM# 162.16 1/4 ECU
6.4400 g., 0.9170 Silver 0.1899 oz. ASW **Ruler:** Louis XIII
Mint: Dijon

Date	Mintage	VG	F	VF	XF	Unc
1652P	—	—	—	—	—	—
1653P	—	50.00	135	300	675	—

KM# 162.17 1/4 ECU
6.4400 g., 0.9170 Silver 0.1899 oz. ASW **Ruler:** Louis XIII
Mint: Narbonne

Date	Mintage	VG	F	VF	XF	Unc
1650Q	—	—	—	—	—	—
1651Q	—	—	—	—	—	—
1652Q	—	—	—	—	—	—
1653Q	—	75.00	175	350	775	—

KM# 162.18 1/4 ECU
6.4400 g., 0.9170 Silver 0.1899 oz. ASW **Ruler:** Louis XIII
Mint: Troyes

Date	Mintage	VG	F	VF	XF	Unc
1650S	—	—	—	—	—	—
1651S	—	75.00	175	350	775	—
1652S	—	—	—	—	—	—
1653S	—	—	—	—	—	—
1654S	—	75.00	175	350	775	—
1655S	—	50.00	135	300	675	—
1656S	—	—	—	—	—	—

KM# 162.19 1/4 ECU
6.4400 g., 0.9170 Silver 0.1899 oz. ASW **Ruler:** Louis XIII
Mint: Nantes

Date	Mintage	VG	F	VF	XF	Unc
1647T	—	—	—	—	—	—
1648T	—	—	—	—	—	—
1649T	—	50.00	135	300	675	—
1650T	—	75.00	175	350	775	—
1653T	—	45.00	110	245	550	—
1654T	—	—	—	—	—	—
1655T	—	—	—	—	—	—
1656T	—	—	—	—	—	—
1659T	—	—	—	—	—	—
1660T	—	—	—	—	—	—

KM# 162.20 1/4 ECU
6.4400 g., 0.9170 Silver 0.1899 oz. ASW **Ruler:** Louis XIII
Mint: Amiens

Date	Mintage	VG	F	VF	XF	Unc
1652X	—	—	—	—	—	—
1653X	—	—	—	—	—	—
1655X	—	50.00	120	275	620	—

KM# 162.21 1/4 ECU
6.4400 g., 0.9170 Silver 0.1899 oz. ASW **Ruler:** Louis XIII
Mint: Bourges

Date	Mintage	VG	F	VF	XF	Unc
1648Y	—	50.00	135	300	675	—
1649Y	—	—	—	—	—	—
1650Y	—	—	—	—	—	—
1653Y	—	75.00	175	350	775	—
1654Y	—	—	—	—	—	—
1655Y	—	—	—	—	—	—

KM# 162.22 1/4 ECU
6.4400 g., 0.9170 Silver 0.1899 oz. ASW **Ruler:** Louis XIII
Mint: Aix **Note:** Mint mark: Ampersand.

Date	Mintage	VG	F	VF	XF	Unc
1646	—	50.00	120	275	620	—
1647	—	—	—	—	—	—
1648	—	—	—	—	—	—
1649	—	50.00	120	275	620	—
1651	—	—	—	—	—	—
1652	—	—	—	—	—	—
1653	—	50.00	120	275	620	—
1654	—	—	—	—	—	—
1656	—	—	—	—	—	—
1657	—	—	—	—	—	—
1658	—	—	—	—	—	—
1659	—	—	—	—	—	—
1660	—	—	—	—	—	—
1661	—	—	—	—	—	—
1662	—	—	—	—	—	—

KM# 162.23 1/4 ECU
6.4400 g., 0.9170 Silver 0.1899 oz. ASW **Ruler:** Louis XIII
Mint: Rennes **Note:** Mint mark: Numeral 9.

Date	Mintage	VG	F	VF	XF	Unc
1648	—	—	—	—	—	—
1649	—	50.00	120	275	620	—
1650	—	50.00	120	275	620	—
1651	—	40.00	100	225	500	—
1652	—	—	—	—	—	—
1653	—	40.00	100	225	500	—
1654	—	35.00	90.00	200	450	—
1655	—	40.00	100	225	500	—
1656	—	30.00	75.00	165	375	—
1657	—	—	—	—	—	—
1659	—	—	—	—	—	—

KM# 159 1/4 ECU
6.4400 g., 0.9170 Silver 0.1899 oz. ASW **Ruler:** Louis XIII
Rev: Crowned shield of Navarre and France **Mint:** Saint Palais

Date	Mintage	VG	F	VF	XF	Unc
1647	—	32.00	80.00	175	400	—
1648	—	32.00	80.00	175	400	—
1649	—	32.00	80.00	175	400	—
1650	—	32.00	80.00	175	400	—
1651	—	32.00	80.00	175	400	

KM# 160.1 1/4 ECU
6.4400 g., 0.9170 Silver 0.1899 oz. ASW **Ruler:** Louis XIII **Rev:** Crowned shield of France, Navarre and Bearn **Mint:** Morlaas

Date	Mintage	VG	F	VF	XF	Unc
1643B	—	30.00	75.00	185	350	—
1644B	—	30.00	75.00	185	350	—
1645B	—	32.00	80.00	200	400	—
1646B	—	35.00	90.00	220	450	—
1647B	—	32.00	80.00	200	400	—
1648B	—	—	—	—	—	—

KM# 160.2 1/4 ECU
6.4400 g., 0.9170 Silver 0.1899 oz. ASW **Ruler:** Louis XIII
Note: Without mint mark.

Date	Mintage	VG	F	VF	XF	Unc
1649	—	35.00	90.00	220	450	—

KM# 160.3 1/4 ECU
6.4400 g., 0.9170 Silver 0.1899 oz. ASW **Ruler:** Louis XIII
Mint: Pau **Note:** Mint mark: Crossed palms.

Date	Mintage	VG	F	VF	XF	Unc
1650	—	40.00	100	235	500	—
1652	—	40.00	100	235	500	—

KM# 187.1 1/4 ECU
6.4400 g., 0.9170 Silver 0.1899 oz. ASW **Ruler:** Louis XIII
Rev: Crowned shield of France, Navarre and Bearn **Mint:** Pau
Note: Mint mark: Crossed palms.

Date	Mintage	VG	F	VF	XF	Unc
1651	—	300	750	1,500	3,200	—

KM# 187.2 1/4 ECU
6.4400 g., 0.9170 Silver 0.1899 oz. ASW **Ruler:** Louis XIII
Mint: Pau **Note:** Mint mark: *F*.

Date	Mintage	VG	F	VF	XF	Unc
1655	—	300	750	1,500	3,200	—
1657	—	300	750	1,500	3,200	—
1658	—	300	750	1,500	3,200	—

KM# 187.3 1/4 ECU
6.4400 g., 0.9170 Silver 0.1899 oz. ASW **Ruler:** Louis XIII
Mint: Morlaas **Note:** Mint mark: *G*.

Date	Mintage	VG	F	VF	XF	Unc
1653	—	300	750	1,500	3,200	—

KM# 188 1/4 ECU

6.4400 g., 0.9170 Silver 0.1899 oz. ASW **Ruler:** Louis XIII
Rev: Crowned shield of Dauphine **Mint:** Grenoble

Date	Mintage	VG	F	VF	XF	Unc
1653Z	—	—	—	—	—	—

KM# 186.1 1/4 ECU

6.4400 g., 0.9170 Silver 0.1899 oz. ASW **Ruler:** Louis XIII
Obv: Laureate, draped and mailed bust right **Rev:** Crowned shield of France and Navarre **Mint:** Troyes

Date	Mintage	VG	F	VF	XF	Unc
1654 V*	—	250	650	1,350	2,850	—
1655 V*	—	250	650	1,350	2,850	—
1656 V*	—	250	650	1,350	2,850	—

KM# 186.2 1/4 ECU

6.4400 g., 0.9170 Silver 0.1899 oz. ASW **Ruler:** Louis XIII
Mint: Besancon **Note:** Mint mark: Back-to-back C's.

Date	Mintage	VG	F	VF	XF	Unc
1662	—	300	750	1,500	3,200	—

KM# 213.1 1/4 ECU

6.4400 g., 0.9170 Silver 0.1899 oz. ASW **Ruler:** Louis XIII
Obv: Laurreate, draped older bust right **Rev:** Crowned shield of France **Mint:** Paris

Date	Mintage	VG	F	VF	XF	Unc
1664A	—	100	250	550	1,150	—
1666A	—	80.00	200	450	950	—
1667A	—	120	300	650	1,350	—
1668A	—	120	300	650	1,350	—
1674A	—	150	350	800	1,750	—

KM# 213.2 1/4 ECU

6.4400 g., 0.9170 Silver 0.1899 oz. ASW **Ruler:** Louis XIII
Mint: Lyon

Date	Mintage	VG	F	VF	XF	Unc
1667D	—	—	—	—	—	—
1668D	—	—	—	—	—	—
1669D	—	—	—	—	—	—
1670D	—	—	—	—	—	—
1671D	—	—	—	—	—	—

KM# 213.3 1/4 ECU

6.4400 g., 0.9170 Silver 0.1899 oz. ASW **Ruler:** Louis XIII
Mint: Bayonne

Date	Mintage	VG	F	VF	XF	Unc
1663L	—	120	300	650	1,350	—
1664L	—	—	—	—	—	—
1666L	—	—	—	—	—	—
1668L	—	—	—	—	—	—
1669L	—	—	—	—	—	—
1670L	—	—	—	—	—	—
1672L	—	—	—	—	—	—

KM# 213.4 1/4 ECU

6.4400 g., 0.9170 Silver 0.1899 oz. ASW **Ruler:** Louis XIII
Mint: Toulouse

Date	Mintage	VG	F	VF	XF	Unc
1672M	—	—	—	—	—	—

KM# 213.5 1/4 ECU

6.4400 g., 0.9170 Silver 0.1899 oz. ASW **Ruler:** Louis XIII
Mint: Montpellier

Date	Mintage	VG	F	VF	XF	Unc
1666N	—	—	—	—	—	—
1667N	—	100	250	550	1,150	—
1668N	—	150	350	850	1,750	—

KM# 213.6 1/4 ECU

6.4400 g., 0.9170 Silver 0.1899 oz. ASW **Ruler:** Louis XIII
Mint: Aix **Note:** Mint mark: Ampersand.

Date	Mintage	VG	F	VF	XF	Unc
1665	—	135	325	750	1,600	—
1666	—	100	250	550	1,150	—
1667	—	135	325	750	1,600	—
1669	—	—	—	—	—	—
1670	—	135	325	750	1,600	—
1671	—	120	300	650	1,350	—
1672	—	—	—	—	—	—

KM# 213.7 1/4 ECU

6.4400 g., 0.9170 Silver 0.1899 oz. ASW **Ruler:** Louis XIII
Mint: Rennes **Note:** Mint mark: Numeral 9.

Date	Mintage	VG	F	VF	XF	Unc
1661	—	120	300	650	1,350	—
1667	—	100	250	550	1,150	—
1668	—	100	250	550	1,150	—
1669	—	—	—	—	—	—
1670	—	120	300	650	1,350	—
1671	—	—	—	—	—	—
1672	—	—	—	—	—	—
1673	—	120	300	650	1,350	—

KM# 233 1/4 ECU

6.4400 g., 0.9170 Silver 0.1899 oz. ASW **Ruler:** Louis XIII
Rev: Crowned shield of France, Navarre and Bearn **Mint:** Pau

Date	Mintage	VG	F	VF	XF	Unc
1674	—	500	1,250	2,850	5,500	—
1675	—	500	1,250	2,850	5,500	—

KM# 234.1 1/4 ECU

6.4400 g., 0.9170 Silver 0.1899 oz. ASW **Ruler:** Louis XIII
Obv: Older bust in court dress right **Rev:** Crowned shield of France **Mint:** Paris

Date	Mintage	VG	F	VF	XF	Unc
1676A	—	—	—	—	—	—
1679A	—	—	—	—	—	—
1680A	—	—	—	—	—	—
1681A	—	—	—	—	—	—
1682A	—	650	1,400	3,000	6,250	—
1683A	—	—	—	—	—	—

KM# 234.2 1/4 ECU

6.4400 g., 0.9170 Silver 0.1899 oz. ASW **Ruler:** Louis XIII
Mint: Bayonne

Date	Mintage	VG	F	VF	XF	Unc
1677L	—	—	—	—	—	—
1678L	—	—	—	—	—	—
1681L	—	—	—	—	—	—
1682L	—	—	—	—	—	—

KM# 234.3 1/4 ECU

6.4400 g., 0.9170 Silver 0.1899 oz. ASW **Ruler:** Louis XIII
Mint: Montpellier

Date	Mintage	VG	F	VF	XF	Unc
1679N	—	500	1,150	2,350	5,200	—

KM# 234.4 1/4 ECU

6.4400 g., 0.9170 Silver 0.1899 oz. ASW **Ruler:** Louis XIII
Mint: Aix **Note:** Mint mark: Ampersand.

Date	Mintage	VG	F	VF	XF	Unc
1679	—	350	850	1,800	4,200	—
1680	—	450	1,100	2,350	5,200	—
1681	—	500	1,200	2,650	5,500	—
1683	—	—	—	—	—	—

KM# 234.5 1/4 ECU

6.4400 g., 0.9170 Silver 0.1899 oz. ASW **Ruler:** Louis XIII
Mint: Rennes **Note:** Mint mark: Numeral 9.

Date	Mintage	VG	F	VF	XF	Unc
1677	—	—	—	—	—	—
1678	—	—	—	—	—	—
1679	—	—	—	—	—	—
1680	—	—	—	—	—	—
1682	—	—	—	—	—	—
1683	—	—	—	—	—	—

KM# 254 1/4 ECU

6.4400 g., 0.9170 Silver 0.1899 oz. ASW **Ruler:** Louis XIII
Obv: Modified bust

Date	Mintage	VG	F	VF	XF	Unc
1684 Rare	—	—	—	—	—	—

KM# 260.1 1/4 ECU

6.4400 g., 0.9170 Silver 0.1899 oz. ASW **Ruler:** Louis XIII
Obv: Draped bust right **Rev:** Crowned, quartered shield of France, Old and New Burgundy **Mint:** Lille

Date	Mintage	VG	F	VF	XF	Unc
1686IL	373,000	150	350	700	1,550	—

KM# 260.2 1/4 ECU

6.4400 g., 0.9170 Silver 0.1899 oz. ASW **Ruler:** Louis XIII
Mint: Lille **Note:** Mint mark: Crowned L.

Date	Mintage	VG	F	VF	XF	Unc
1686	—	165	375	750	1,650	—
1687	751,000	180	400	850	1,800	—
1688	139,000	165	375	750	1,650	—

KM# 270.1 1/4 ECU

6.4400 g., 0.9170 Silver 0.1899 oz. ASW **Ruler:** Louis XIII
Obv: Draped bust right **Rev:** Eight crowned L's back to back
Mint: Paris

Date	Mintage	VG	F	VF	XF	Unc
1690A	—	50.00	120	275	620	—
1691A	—	45.00	110	250	575	—

KM# 270.2 1/4 ECU

6.4400 g., 0.9170 Silver 0.1899 oz. ASW **Ruler:** Louis XIII
Mint: Rouen

Date	Mintage	VG	F	VF	XF	Unc
1690B	—	50.00	135	300	675	—
1691B	—	50.00	120	275	625	—

KM# 270.3 1/4 ECU

6.4400 g., 0.9170 Silver 0.1899 oz. ASW **Ruler:** Louis XIII
Mint: Lyon

Date	Mintage	VG	F	VF	XF	Unc
1690D	170,000	50.00	135	300	675	—
1691D	730,000	45.00	110	250	565	—
1692D	159,000	60.00	150	325	725	—
1693D	23,000	60.00	150	325	725	—

KM# 270.4 1/4 ECU

6.4400 g., 0.9170 Silver 0.1899 oz. ASW **Ruler:** Louis XIII
Mint: Tours

Date	Mintage	VG	F	VF	XF	Unc
1691E	—	50.00	120	275	625	—

KM# 270.5 1/4 ECU

6.4400 g., 0.9170 Silver 0.1899 oz. ASW **Ruler:** Louis XIII
Mint: Poitiers

Date	Mintage	VG	F	VF	XF	Unc
1691G	265	175	350	700	—	—

KM# 270.6 1/4 ECU

6.4400 g., 0.9170 Silver 0.1899 oz. ASW **Ruler:** Louis XIII
Mint: La Rochelle

Date	Mintage	VG	F	VF	XF	Unc
1691H	—	50.00	135	300	675	—
1693H	—	50.00	135	300	675	—

KM# 270.7 1/4 ECU

6.4400 g., 0.9170 Silver 0.1899 oz. ASW **Ruler:** Louis XIII
Mint: Limoges

Date	Mintage	VG	F	VF	XF	Unc
1691I	—	50.00	135	300	675	—
1692I	—	50.00	120	275	625	—

KM# 270.8 1/4 ECU

6.4400 g., 0.9170 Silver 0.1899 oz. ASW **Ruler:** Louis XIII
Mint: Toulouse

Date	Mintage	VG	F	VF	XF	Unc
1691M	382,000	45.00	110	250	565	—

KM# 270.9 1/4 ECU

6.4400 g., 0.9170 Silver 0.1899 oz. ASW **Ruler:** Louis XIII
Mint: Montpellier

Date	Mintage	VG	F	VF	XF	Unc
1690N	90,000	60.00	150	325	725	—
1691N	224,000	50.00	120	275	625	—
1692N	33,000	75.00	175	350	775	—
1693N	6,315	—	—	—	—	—

KM# 270.10 1/4 ECU

6.4400 g., 0.9170 Silver 0.1899 oz. ASW **Ruler:** Louis XIII
Mint: Riom

Date	Mintage	VG	F	VF	XF	Unc
1691O	16,000	—	—	—	—	—
1693O	—	—	—	—	—	—

KM# 270.11 1/4 ECU

6.4400 g., 0.9170 Silver 0.1899 oz. ASW **Ruler:** Louis XIII
Mint: Dijon

Date	Mintage	VG	F	VF	XF	Unc
1690P	7,172	50.00	135	300	675	—
1691P	—	50.00	135	300	675	—
1693P	—	—	—	—	—	—

KM# 270.12 1/4 ECU

6.4400 g., 0.9170 Silver 0.1899 oz. ASW **Ruler:** Louis XIII
Mint: Reims

Date	Mintage	VG	F	VF	XF	Unc
1691S	—	50.00	135	300	675	—
1692S	—	—	—	—	—	—

KM# 270.13 1/4 ECU

6.4400 g., 0.9170 Silver 0.1899 oz. ASW **Ruler:** Louis XIII
Mint: Amiens

Date	Mintage	VG	F	VF	XF	Unc
1690X	—	75.00	175	350	725	—
1692X	14,000	75.00	175	350	725	—

KM# 270.14 1/4 ECU

6.4400 g., 0.9170 Silver 0.1899 oz. ASW **Ruler:** Louis XIII
Mint: Bourges

Date	Mintage	VG	F	VF	XF	Unc
1691Y	37,000	50.00	120	275	625	—
1692Y	—	75.00	175	350	775	—
1693Y	8,228	—	—	—	—	—

KM# 270.15 1/4 ECU

6.4400 g., 0.9170 Silver 0.1899 oz. ASW **Ruler:** Louis XIII
Mint: Rennes **Note:** Mint mark: Numeral 9.

Date	Mintage	VG	F	VF	XF	Unc
1691	—	50.00	135	300	675	—
1692	—	80.00	185	375	800	—

KM# 270.16 1/4 ECU

6.4400 g., 0.9170 Silver 0.1899 oz. ASW **Ruler:** Louis XIII
Mint: Aix **Note:** Mint mark: Ampersand.

Date	Mintage	VG	F	VF	XF	Unc
1691	—	50.00	120	275	625	—

KM# 270.17 1/4 ECU

6.4400 g., 0.9170 Silver 0.1899 oz. ASW **Ruler:** Louis XIII
Mint: Lille **Note:** Mint mark: Crowned L.

Date	Mintage	VG	F	VF	XF	Unc
1690	—	50.00	135	300	675	—

KM# 270.18 1/4 ECU

6.4400 g., 0.9170 Silver 0.1899 oz. ASW **Ruler:** Louis XIII
Mint: Troyes **Note:** Mint mark: Crowned S.

Date	Mintage	VG	F	VF	XF	Unc
1691	—	50.00	120	275	625	—
1693	—	—	—	—	—	—

KM# 293.1 1/4 ECU
6.4400 g., 0.9170 Silver 0.1899 oz. ASW **Ruler:** Louis XIII **Obv:** Mailed bust right **Rev:** Crowned circular shield of France dividing palms **Mint:** Paris

Date	Mintage	VG	F	VF	XF	Unc
1693A	—	50.00	120	275	625	—
1694A	—	45.00	110	250	565	—
1697A	—	60.00	150	325	725	—
1698A	—	90.00	200	400	900	—

KM# 293.2 1/4 ECU
6.4400 g., 0.9170 Silver 0.1899 oz. ASW **Ruler:** Louis XIII **Mint:** Metz

Date	Mintage	VG	F	VF	XF	Unc
1693AA	—	90.00	200	400	900	—

KM# 293.3 1/4 ECU
6.4400 g., 0.9170 Silver 0.1899 oz. ASW **Ruler:** Louis XIII **Mint:** Rouen

Date	Mintage	VG	F	VF	XF	Unc
1693B	—	60.00	150	325	725	—
1694B	—	60.00	150	325	725	—
1696B	—	50.00	135	300	675	—

KM# 293.4 1/4 ECU
6.4400 g., 0.9170 Silver 0.1899 oz. ASW **Ruler:** Louis XIII **Mint:** Strasbourg

Date	Mintage	VG	F	VF	XF	Unc
1694BB	—	75.00	175	350	775	—

KM# 293.5 1/4 ECU
6.4400 g., 0.9170 Silver 0.1899 oz. ASW **Ruler:** Louis XIII **Mint:** Caen

Date	Mintage	VG	F	VF	XF	Unc
1697C	—	75.00	175	350	775	—

KM# 293.6 1/4 ECU
6.4400 g., 0.9170 Silver 0.1899 oz. ASW **Ruler:** Louis XIII **Mint:** Lyon

Date	Mintage	VG	F	VF	XF	Unc
1693D	57,000	50.00	135	300	675	—
1694D	440,000	50.00	120	275	625	—
1695D	176,000	50.00	135	300	675	—
1696D	89,000	60.00	150	325	725	—
1697D	18,000	—	—	—	—	—
1698D	6,251	75.00	175	350	775	—
1699D	6,272	—	—	—	—	—
1700D	2,020	—	—	—	—	—

KM# 293.7 1/4 ECU
6.4400 g., 0.9170 Silver 0.1899 oz. ASW **Ruler:** Louis XIII **Mint:** Tours

Date	Mintage	VG	F	VF	XF	Unc
1693E	—	50.00	120	275	625	—
1695E	—	75.00	175	350	775	—

KM# 293.8 1/4 ECU
6.4400 g., 0.9170 Silver 0.1899 oz. ASW **Ruler:** Louis XIII **Mint:** Angers

Date	Mintage	VG	F	VF	XF	Unc
1697F	3,264	—	—	—	—	—

KM# 293.9 1/4 ECU
6.4400 g., 0.9170 Silver 0.1899 oz. ASW **Ruler:** Louis XIII **Mint:** Poitiers

Date	Mintage	VG	F	VF	XF	Unc
1696G	11,000	—	—	—	—	—

KM# 293.10 1/4 ECU
6.4400 g., 0.9170 Silver 0.1899 oz. ASW **Ruler:** Louis XIII **Mint:** La Rochelle

Date	Mintage	VG	F	VF	XF	Unc
1693H	—	60.00	150	325	725	—
1694H	—	60.00	150	325	725	—

KM# 293.11 1/4 ECU
6.4400 g., 0.9170 Silver 0.1899 oz. ASW **Ruler:** Louis XIII **Mint:** Limoges

Date	Mintage	VG	F	VF	XF	Unc
1694I	—	50.00	135	325	700	—
1695I	—	50.00	135	300	675	—
1696I	—	—	—	—	—	—
1697I	—	75.00	175	350	775	—

KM# 293.12 1/4 ECU
6.4400 g., 0.9170 Silver 0.1899 oz. ASW **Ruler:** Louis XIII **Mint:** Bordeaux

Date	Mintage	VG	F	VF	XF	Unc
1694K	—	50.00	135	300	675	—
1696K	—	75.00	175	350	775	—

KM# 293.13 1/4 ECU
6.4400 g., 0.9170 Silver 0.1899 oz. ASW **Ruler:** Louis XIII **Mint:** Toulouse

Date	Mintage	VG	F	VF	XF	Unc
1693M	—	75.00	175	350	775	—
1694M	—	60.00	150	325	725	—

KM# 293.14 1/4 ECU
6.4400 g., 0.9170 Silver 0.1899 oz. ASW **Ruler:** Louis XIII **Mint:** Montpellier

Date	Mintage	VG	F	VF	XF	Unc
1693N	40,000	60.00	150	325	725	—
1694N	261,000	50.00	120	275	625	—
1695N	37,000	—	—	—	—	—
1696N	11,000	—	—	—	—	—
1697N	8,200	—	—	—	—	—
1698N	1,265	—	—	—	—	—
1699N	992	—	—	—	—	—
1700N	186	—	—	—	—	—

KM# 293.15 1/4 ECU
6.4400 g., 0.9170 Silver 0.1899 oz. ASW **Ruler:** Louis XIII **Mint:** Riom

Date	Mintage	VG	F	VF	XF	Unc
1693O	4,487	—	—	—	—	—
1694O	—	90.00	200	400	900	—
1697O	—	50.00	135	300	675	—

KM# 293.16 1/4 ECU
6.4400 g., 0.9170 Silver 0.1899 oz. ASW **Ruler:** Louis XIII **Mint:** Dijon

Date	Mintage	VG	F	VF	XF	Unc
1693P	28,000	—	—	—	—	—
1694P	247,000	50.00	120	275	625	—
1695P	24,000	—	—	—	—	—
1697P	4,373	—	—	—	—	—

KM# 293.17 1/4 ECU
6.4400 g., 0.9170 Silver 0.1899 oz. ASW **Ruler:** Louis XIII **Mint:** Reims

Date	Mintage	VG	F	VF	XF	Unc
1693S	—	75.00	175	350	775	—
1697S	—	—	—	—	—	—

KM# 293.18 1/4 ECU
6.4400 g., 0.9170 Silver 0.1899 oz. ASW **Ruler:** Louis XIII **Mint:** Nantes

Date	Mintage	VG	F	VF	XF	Unc
1694T	—	75.00	175	350	775	—
1697T	—	75.00	175	350	775	—

KM# 293.19 1/4 ECU
6.4400 g., 0.9170 Silver 0.1899 oz. ASW **Ruler:** Louis XIII **Mint:** Troyes

Date	Mintage	VG	F	VF	XF	Unc
1693V	—	—	—	—	—	—
1694V	150,000	50.00	135	300	675	—
1695V	—	—	—	—	—	—
1696V	—	75.00	175	350	775	—
1697V	—	—	—	—	—	—
1698V	—	—	—	—	—	—
1699V	—	—	—	—	—	—

KM# 293.20 1/4 ECU
6.4400 g., 0.9170 Silver 0.1899 oz. ASW **Ruler:** Louis XIII **Mint:** Lille

Date	Mintage	VG	F	VF	XF	Unc
1693W	—	60.00	150	325	725	—
1694W	—	50.00	135	300	675	—
1695W	—	75.00	175	350	775	—
1697W	6,000	—	—	—	—	—
1699W	5,400	—	—	—	—	—

KM# 293.21 1/4 ECU
6.4400 g., 0.9170 Silver 0.1899 oz. ASW **Ruler:** Louis XIII **Mint:** Amiens

Date	Mintage	VG	F	VF	XF	Unc
1693X	—	60.00	150	325	725	—
1694X	—	60.00	150	325	725	—
1695X	—	60.00	150	325	725	—

KM# 293.22 1/4 ECU
6.4400 g., 0.9170 Silver 0.1899 oz. ASW **Ruler:** Louis XIII **Mint:** Bourges

Date	Mintage	VG	F	VF	XF	Unc
1693Y	50,000	75.00	175	350	775	—
1694Y	—	60.00	150	325	725	—

KM# 293.23 1/4 ECU
6.4400 g., 0.9170 Silver 0.1899 oz. ASW **Ruler:** Louis XIII **Mint:** Aix **Note:** Mint mark: Ampersand.

Date	Mintage	VG	F	VF	XF	Unc
1693	—	75.00	175	350	775	—
1694	—	50.00	135	300	675	—
1695	—	75.00	175	350	775	—

KM# 293.24 1/4 ECU
6.4400 g., 0.9170 Silver 0.1899 oz. ASW **Ruler:** Louis XIII **Mint:** Rennes **Note:** Mint mark: Numeral 9.

Date	Mintage	VG	F	VF	XF	Unc
1693	—	—	—	—	—	—
1694	—	60.00	150	325	725	—
1695	—	50.00	135	300	675	—
1696	—	75.00	175	350	775	—

KM# 293.25 1/4 ECU
6.4400 g., 0.9170 Silver 0.1899 oz. ASW **Ruler:** Louis XIII **Mint:** Besancon **Note:** Mint mark: Two back-to-back C's monogram.

Date	Mintage	VG	F	VF	XF	Unc
1694	38,000	60.00	150	325	725	—
1695	18,000	—	—	—	—	—
1697	1,705	—	—	—	—	—
1698	908	—	—	—	—	—
1699	697	—	—	—	—	—

KM# 271 1/4 ECU
6.4400 g., 0.9170 Silver 0.1899 oz. ASW **Ruler:** Louis XIII **Obv:** Draped bust right **Rev:** Eight crowned L's back to back, fleur-de-lis in angles **Mint:** Pau

Date	Mintage	VG	F	VF	XF	Unc
1690	—	100	200	400	900	—
1691	—	100	200	400	900	—

KM# 272 1/4 ECU
6.4400 g., 0.9170 Silver 0.1899 oz. ASW **Ruler:** Louis XIII **Obv:** Laureate draped bust right **Mint:** Reims

Date	Mintage	VG	F	VF	XF	Unc
1690S	—	—	—	—	—	—

KM# 294 1/4 ECU
6.4400 g., 0.9170 Silver 0.1899 oz. ASW **Ruler:** Louis XIII **Obv:** Mailed bust right **Rev:** Crowned circular shield of France, Navarre and Bearn **Mint:** Pau

Date	Mintage	VG	F	VF	XF	Unc
1693	—	—	—	—	—	—
1694	—	750	1,500	2,750	5,000	—
1695	—	750	1,500	2,750	5,000	—
1696	1,063	—	—	—	—	—
1697	258	—	—	—	—	—
1698	476	—	—	—	—	—
1699	360	—	—	—	—	—
1700	28	—	—	—	—	—

KM# 306 1/4 ECU
6.4400 g., 0.8570 Silver 0.1774 oz. ASW **Ruler:** Louis XIII **Obv:** Mailed bust right **Rev:** Crowned circular quartered shield of France, Navarre, Old and New Burgundy **Mint:** Lille

Date	Mintage	VG	F	VF	XF	Unc
1694W	—	400	800	1,450	2,750	—
1695W	—	475	950	1,750	3,250	—
1696W	13,000	—	—	—	—	—
1697W	12,000	475	950	1,750	3,250	—
1699W	1,800	—	—	—	—	—

KM# 307 1/4 ECU
6.7460 g., 0.9170 Silver 0.1989 oz. ASW **Ruler:** Louis XIII **Obv:** Large fleur-de-lis **Rev:** Crowned circular shield of France dividing palms **Mint:** Strasbourg

Date	Mintage	VG	F	VF	XF	Unc
1694BB	—	350	750	1,400	2,500	—
1695BB	—	300	600	1,250	2,250	—
1696BB	—	350	750	1,400	2,500	—
1699BB	—	400	850	1,600	2,800	—

KM# 121 1/2 ECU
13.5440 g., 0.9170 Silver 0.3993 oz. ASW **Ruler:** Louis XIII **Obv:** Laureate and draped bust right **Rev:** Crowned shield **Mint:** Paris

Date	Mintage	VG	F	VF	XF	Unc
1641A Rose	—	600	1,000	1,700	3,000	—
1642A Rose	—	325	675	1,500	2,500	—
1642A Rose/2 points	—	300	625	1,350	2,350	—
1642A Rose/2 points	—	300	625	1,350	2,350	—

KM# 135.1 1/2 ECU
13.5440 g., 0.9170 Silver 0.3993 oz. ASW **Ruler:** Louis XIII **Obv:** Laureate, draped and mailed bust right

Date	Mintage	VG	F	VF	XF	Unc
1642 Rose	—	275	550	1,000	1,650	—
1642 1 or 2 points	—	275	550	1,000	1,650	—
1643 Rose	—	275	550	1,000	1,650	—
1643	—	300	625	1,150	2,100	—
1643 Point	—	275	550	1,000	1,650	—

KM# 135.2 1/2 ECU
13.5440 g., 0.9170 Silver 0.3993 oz. ASW **Ruler:** Louis XIII
Mint: Lyon

Date	Mintage	VG	F	VF	XF	Unc
1643D	—	400	800	1,750	3,000	—

KM# 163.1 1/2 ECU
13.5440 g., 0.9170 Silver 0.3993 oz. ASW **Ruler:** Louis XIV
Obv: Laureate, draped and mailed bust right, short hair before ear **Rev:** Crowned shield of France **Mint:** Paris

Date	Mintage	VG	F	VF	XF	Unc
1643A Point	—	60.00	150	325	725	—
1643A Rose	—	65.00	160	350	775	—
1644A Point	—	60.00	150	325	725	—
1644A Rose	—	50.00	125	275	625	—
1644A Rose and 2 points	—	50.00	125	275	625	—
1645A Point	—	45.00	110	250	575	—
1645A Rose and 2 points	—	70.00	170	375	825	—
1645A Rose	—	60.00	150	325	725	—

KM# 163.2 1/2 ECU
13.5440 g., 0.9170 Silver 0.3993 oz. ASW **Ruler:** Louis XIV
Mint: Lyon

Date	Mintage	VG	F	VF	XF	Unc
1644D	—	75.00	200	425	1,050	—
1645D	—	75.00	200	425	1,050	—
1648D	—	90.00	225	500	1,250	—
1649D	—	90.00	225	500	1,250	—
1650D	—	100	250	550	1,400	—
1651D	—	80.00	215	475	1,200	—
1652D	—	75.00	200	425	1,050	—

KM# 164.1 1/2 ECU
13.5440 g., 0.9170 Silver 0.3993 oz. ASW **Ruler:** Louis XIV
Obv: Long hair before ear **Mint:** Paris

Date	Mintage	VG	F	VF	XF	Unc
1646A	—	45.00	90.00	160	350	—
1647A	—	30.00	65.00	130	300	—
1648A	—	28.00	55.00	125	295	—
1649A	—	28.00	55.00	125	295	—
1650A	—	28.00	55.00	125	295	—
1651A	—	30.00	65.00	130	300	—
1652A	—	28.00	55.00	125	295	—
1653A	—	30.00	65.00	130	300	—
1654A	—	28.00	55.00	125	295	—
1655A	—	28.00	55.00	125	295	—
1658A	—	—	—	—	—	—
1659A	Est. 66,000	—	—	—	—	—

KM# 164.2 1/2 ECU
13.5440 g., 0.9170 Silver 0.3993 oz. ASW **Ruler:** Louis XIV
Mint: Arras

Date	Mintage	VG	F	VF	XF	Unc
1646AR	—	35.00	90.00	200	550	—
1647AR	—	50.00	120	275	750	—
1648AR	—	50.00	115	250	650	—
1649AR	—	—	—	—	—	—
1650AR	—	55.00	135	300	800	—
1651AR	—	45.00	100	225	600	—
1652AR	—	28.00	60.00	135	350	—
1653AR	—	28.00	60.00	135	350	—
1655AR	—	50.00	120	275	750	—
1656AR	—	150	325	650	—	—

KM# 164.3 1/2 ECU
13.5440 g., 0.9170 Silver 0.3993 oz. ASW **Ruler:** Louis XIV
Mint: Rouen

Date	Mintage	VG	F	VF	XF	Unc
1646B	—	28.00	60.00	140	350	—
1647B	—	25.00	55.00	125	325	—
1648B	—	25.00	55.00	125	325	—
1649B	—	25.00	50.00	120	290	—
1650B	—	25.00	55.00	125	325	—
1651B	—	25.00	50.00	120	290	—
1652B	—	25.00	50.00	120	290	—
1653B	—	25.00	50.00	120	290	—
1654B	—	35.00	75.00	165	450	—
1655B	—	25.00	50.00	120	290	—
1657B	—	—	—	—	—	—
1658B	—	75.00	175	350	925	—

KM# 164.4 1/2 ECU
13.5440 g., 0.9170 Silver 0.3993 oz. ASW **Ruler:** Louis XIV
Mint: Saint Lô

Date	Mintage	VG	F	VF	XF	Unc
1647C	—	28.00	60.00	140	350	—
1648C	—	28.00	60.00	140	350	—
1649C	—	28.00	60.00	140	350	—
1650C	—	28.00	60.00	140	350	—
1651C	—	25.00	55.00	125	325	—
1652C	—	25.00	50.00	120	290	—
1653C	—	25.00	55.00	125	325	—
1654C	—	30.00	65.00	150	400	—
1655C	—	30.00	65.00	150	400	—
1656C	—	—	—	—	—	—

KM# 164.5 1/2 ECU
13.5440 g., 0.9170 Silver 0.3993 oz. ASW **Ruler:** Louis XIV
Mint: Lyon

Date	Mintage	VG	F	VF	XF	Unc
1652D	—	40.00	95.00	200	550	—
1653D	—	25.00	55.00	125	325	—
1654D	—	35.00	75.00	165	450	—
1657D	—	45.00	100	225	600	—
1658D	—	55.00	135	300	800	—
1659D	—	40.00	95.00	200	550	—

KM# 164.6 1/2 ECU
13.5440 g., 0.9170 Silver 0.3993 oz. ASW **Ruler:** Louis XIV
Mint: Tours

Date	Mintage	VG	F	VF	XF	Unc
1649E	—	30.00	65.00	150	400	—
1651E	—	40.00	95.00	200	550	—
1652E	—	25.00	50.00	120	295	—
1653E	—	28.00	60.00	140	350	—
1654E	—	—	—	—	—	—
1656E	—	35.00	75.00	165	450	—
1657E	—	40.00	95.00	200	550	—
1658E	—	40.00	95.00	200	550	—
1659E	—	55.00	125	275	750	—
1660E	—	55.00	125	275	750	—

KM# 164.7 1/2 ECU
13.5440 g., 0.9170 Silver 0.3993 oz. ASW **Ruler:** Louis XIV
Mint: Angers

Date	Mintage	VG	F	VF	XF	Unc
1647F	—	—	—	—	—	—
1648F	—	—	—	—	—	—
1649F	—	35.00	75.00	165	450	—
1650F	—	30.00	65.00	150	400	—
1651F	—	40.00	95.00	200	550	—
1652F	—	25.00	50.00	120	290	—
1653F	—	28.00	55.00	125	300	—
1654F	—	—	—	—	—	—
1655F	—	30.00	65.00	150	400	—
1656F	—	28.00	55.00	125	325	—
1658F	—	—	—	—	—	—
1659F	—	40.00	95.00	200	550	—
1660F	—	45.00	100	225	600	—

KM# 164.8 1/2 ECU
13.5440 g., 0.9170 Silver 0.3993 oz. ASW **Ruler:** Louis XIV
Mint: Poitiers

Date	Mintage	VG	F	VF	XF	Unc
1647G	—	165	325	650	—	—
1648G	—	—	—	—	—	—
1649G	—	25.00	50.00	120	290	—
1650G	—	25.00	50.00	120	290	—
1651G	—	25.00	50.00	120	290	—
1652G	—	25.00	50.00	120	290	—
1653G	—	25.00	50.00	120	290	—
1655G	—	45.00	100	225	600	—
1656G	—	—	—	—	—	—
1657G	—	35.00	85.00	180	475	—
1659G	—	45.00	100	225	600	—
1660G	—	55.00	125	275	750	—

KM# 164.9 1/2 ECU
13.5440 g., 0.9170 Silver 0.3993 oz. ASW **Ruler:** Louis XIV
Mint: La Rochelle

Date	Mintage	VG	F	VF	XF	Unc
1646H	—	40.00	95.00	200	550	—
1647H	—	30.00	65.00	140	350	—
1648H	—	55.00	125	275	750	—
1649H	—	55.00	125	275	750	—
1650H	—	40.00	95.00	200	550	—
1651H	—	40.00	95.00	200	550	—
1652H	—	55.00	125	275	750	—
1653H	—	35.00	75.00	165	450	—
1654H	—	30.00	65.00	150	400	—
1655H	—	25.00	55.00	130	325	—
1656H	—	35.00	75.00	165	450	—
1658H	—	40.00	95.00	200	550	—
1659H	—	45.00	100	225	600	—
1660H	—	—	—	—	—	—

KM# 164.10 1/2 ECU
13.5440 g., 0.9170 Silver 0.3993 oz. ASW **Ruler:** Louis XIV
Mint: Limoges

Date	Mintage	VG	F	VF	XF	Unc
1650I	—	40.00	95.00	200	550	—
1651I	—	40.00	95.00	200	550	—
1652I	—	55.00	125	275	750	—
1653I	—	—	—	—	—	—
1654I	—	110	210	440	1,000	—
1655I	—	35.00	80.00	175	475	—
1656I	—	30.00	65.00	150	400	—
1657I	—	40.00	95.00	200	550	—
1658I	—	—	—	—	—	—
1659I	—	45.00	100	225	600	—
1660I	—	55.00	125	275	750	—

KM# 164.11 1/2 ECU
13.5440 g., 0.9170 Silver 0.3993 oz. ASW **Ruler:** Louis XIV
Mint: Bordeaux

Date	Mintage	VG	F	VF	XF	Unc
1647K	—	30.00	65.00	140	350	—
1648K	—	30.00	70.00	150	400	—
1649K	—	30.00	70.00	150	400	—

Date	Mintage	VG	F	VF	XF	Unc
1650K	—	30.00	70.00	150	400	—
1651K	—	30.00	70.00	150	400	—
1652K	—	30.00	70.00	150	400	—
1653K	—	—	—	—	—	—
1654K	—	—	—	—	—	—
1655K	—	30.00	70.00	150	400	—
1656K	—	30.00	70.00	150	400	—
1657K	—	35.00	80.00	175	475	—
1659K	—	45.00	100	225	600	—
1660K	—	40.00	95.00	200	550	—

KM# 164.12 1/2 ECU
13.5440 g., 0.9170 Silver 0.3993 oz. ASW **Ruler:** Louis XIV
Mint: Bayonne

Date	Mintage	VG	F	VF	XF	Unc
1649L	—	55.00	125	300	725	—
1650L	—	25.00	55.00	125	325	—
1651L	—	25.00	55.00	125	325	—
1652L	—	25.00	50.00	120	290	—
1653L	—	25.00	55.00	125	325	—
1654L	—	30.00	65.00	150	400	—
1655L	—	25.00	55.00	125	325	—
1656L	—	35.00	75.00	165	450	—
1657L	—	35.00	75.00	165	450	—
1658L	—	45.00	100	225	600	—
1659L	—	35.00	75.00	165	450	—
1660L	—	35.00	75.00	165	450	—

KM# 164.13 1/2 ECU
13.5440 g., 0.9170 Silver 0.3993 oz. ASW **Ruler:** Louis XIV
Mint: Toulouse

Date	Mintage	VG	F	VF	XF	Unc
1647M	—	55.00	125	275	750	—
1648M	—	35.00	75.00	165	450	—
1649M	—	40.00	95.00	200	550	—
1650M	—	30.00	65.00	140	350	—
1651M	—	30.00	65.00	140	350	—
1652M	—	30.00	65.00	140	350	—
1653M	—	45.00	100	225	600	—
1654M	—	35.00	75.00	165	450	—
1655M	—	25.00	55.00	125	325	—
1656M	—	—	—	—	—	—
1659M	—	40.00	95.00	200	550	—
1660M	—	—	—	—	—	—
1661M	—	—	—	—	—	—

KM# 164.14 1/2 ECU
13.5440 g., 0.9170 Silver 0.3993 oz. ASW **Ruler:** Louis XIV
Mint: Montpellier

Date	Mintage	VG	F	VF	XF	Unc
1646N	—	40.00	95.00	200	550	—
1647N	—	40.00	95.00	200	550	—
1648N	—	30.00	65.00	140	350	—
1649N	—	—	—	—	—	—
1650N	—	25.00	55.00	125	325	—
1651N	—	30.00	65.00	140	350	—
1652N	—	25.00	55.00	125	325	—
1653N	—	35.00	75.00	165	450	—
1656N	—	65.00	150	325	875	—
1657N	—	65.00	150	325	875	—
1658N	—	55.00	125	275	750	—
1659N	—	—	—	—	—	—

KM# 164.15 1/2 ECU
13.5440 g., 0.9170 Silver 0.3993 oz. ASW **Ruler:** Louis XIV
Mint: Riom

Date	Mintage	VG	F	VF	XF	Unc
1652O	—	55.00	125	275	750	—
1653O	—	—	—	—	—	—

KM# 164.16 1/2 ECU
13.5440 g., 0.9170 Silver 0.3993 oz. ASW **Ruler:** Louis XIV
Mint: Dijon

Date	Mintage	VG	F	VF	XF	Unc
1646P	—	—	—	—	—	—
1647P	—	—	—	—	—	—
1651P	—	—	—	—	—	—
1652P	—	25.00	55.00	125	325	—
1653P	—	25.00	55.00	125	325	—
1654P	—	—	—	—	—	—
1655P	—	45.00	100	225	600	—
1657P	—	—	—	—	—	—

KM# 164.17 1/2 ECU
13.5440 g., 0.9170 Silver 0.3993 oz. ASW **Ruler:** Louis XIV
Mint: Perpignan

Date	Mintage	VG	F	VF	XF	Unc
1650Q	—	30.00	65.00	140	350	—
1651Q	—	30.00	65.00	140	350	—
1652Q	—	35.00	75.00	165	450	—
1653Q	—	35.00	75.00	165	450	—
1654Q	—	45.00	100	225	600	—

KM# 164.18 1/2 ECU
13.5440 g., 0.9170 Silver 0.3993 oz. ASW **Ruler:** Louis XIV
Mint: Villeneuve St. André

Date	Mintage	VG	F	VF	XF	Unc
1653R	—	35.00	75.00	165	450	—
1661R	—	—	—	—	—	—
1662R	—	—	—	—	—	—

KM# 164.19 1/2 ECU
13.5440 g., 0.9170 Silver 0.3993 oz. ASW **Ruler:** Louis XIV
Mint: Troyes

Date	Mintage	VG	F	VF	XF	Unc
1649S	—	—	—	—	—	—
1650S	—	—	—	—	—	—
1651S	—	25.00	55.00	125	325	—
1652S	—	—	—	—	—	—
1653S	—	30.00	65.00	150	400	—
1654S	—	35.00	75.00	165	450	—
1655S	—	40.00	95.00	200	550	—

KM# 164.20 1/2 ECU
13.5440 g., 0.9170 Silver 0.3993 oz. ASW **Ruler:** Louis XIV
Mint: Nantes

Date	Mintage	VG	F	VF	XF	Unc
1647T	—	50.00	115	250	650	—
1648T	—	—	—	—	—	—
1649T	—	30.00	65.00	150	400	—
1650T	—	25.00	55.00	125	325	—
1651T	—	55.00	125	275	750	—
1652T	—	25.00	50.00	120	290	—
1653T	—	30.00	65.00	150	400	—
1654T	—	25.00	50.00	120	290	—
1655T	—	25.00	55.00	125	325	—
1656T	—	30.00	65.00	150	400	—
1659T	—	—	—	—	—	—

KM# 164.21 1/2 ECU
13.5440 g., 0.9170 Silver 0.3993 oz. ASW **Ruler:** Louis XIV
Mint: Bourges

Date	Mintage	VG	F	VF	XF	Unc
1648Y	—	125	275	525	—	—
1649Y	—	30.00	65.00	150	400	—
1650Y	—	40.00	95.00	200	550	—
1651Y	—	30.00	65.00	140	350	—
1652Y	—	25.00	50.00	120	290	—
1653Y	—	35.00	75.00	165	450	—
1654Y	—	35.00	75.00	165	450	—
1655Y	—	40.00	95.00	200	550	—
1656Y	—	40.00	95.00	200	550	—

KM# 164.22 1/2 ECU
13.5440 g., 0.9170 Silver 0.3993 oz. ASW **Ruler:** Louis XIV
Mint: Amiens

Date	Mintage	VG	F	VF	XF	Unc
1650X	—	—	—	—	—	—
1651X	—	—	—	—	—	—
1652X	—	25.00	55.00	125	325	—
1653X	—	25.00	50.00	120	300	—
1654X	—	30.00	65.00	150	400	—
1655X	—	25.00	50.00	120	300	—
1658X	—	—	—	—	—	—
1659X	—	—	—	—	—	—
1660X	—	—	—	—	—	—

KM# 164.23 1/2 ECU
13.5440 g., 0.9170 Silver 0.3993 oz. ASW **Ruler:** Louis XIV
Mint: Aix **Note:** Mint mark: Ampersand.

Date	Mintage	VG	F	VF	XF	Unc
1646	—	25.00	55.00	125	325	—
1647	—	25.00	50.00	120	300	—
1648	—	30.00	65.00	140	350	—
1649	—	30.00	65.00	140	350	—
1650	—	40.00	95.00	200	550	—
1651	—	30.00	65.00	150	400	—
1652	—	25.00	55.00	125	325	—
1653	—	35.00	75.00	165	450	—
1656	—	30.00	65.00	150	400	—
1657	—	30.00	65.00	140	350	—
1658	—	—	—	—	—	—
1659	—	45.00	100	225	600	—

KM# 164.24 1/2 ECU
13.5440 g., 0.9170 Silver 0.3993 oz. ASW **Ruler:** Louis XIV
Mint: Rennes **Note:** Mint mark: Numeral 9.

Date	Mintage	VG	F	VF	XF	Unc
1648	—	30.00	65.00	140	350	—
1649	—	25.00	50.00	120	300	—
1650	—	25.00	50.00	120	300	—
1651	—	25.00	50.00	120	300	—
1652	—	25.00	50.00	120	300	—
1653	—	25.00	50.00	120	300	—
1654	—	35.00	75.00	165	450	—
1655	—	25.00	55.00	125	325	—
1656	—	25.00	50.00	120	300	—
1657	—	30.00	65.00	150	400	—
1658	—	30.00	65.00	150	400	—
1659	—	45.00	100	225	600	—

KM# 183 1/2 ECU
13.5440 g., 0.9170 Silver 0.3993 oz. ASW **Ruler:** Louis XIV
Obv: Laureate draped and mailed bust right, long hair before ear
Rev: Crowned shield of France and Navarre **Mint:** Saint Palais
Note: Strike mark: * V *.

Date	Mintage	VG	F	VF	XF	Unc
1652	—	200	400	825	1,600	—
1653	—	200	400	825	1,600	—
1654	—	200	400	825	1,600	—
1655	—	200	400	825	1,600	—
1656	—	175	350	750	1,400	—
1658	—	185	375	775	1,500	—
1659 No V	—	250	500	900	1,800	—

KM# 184.2 1/2 ECU
13.5440 g., 0.9170 Silver 0.3993 oz. ASW **Ruler:** Louis XIV
Mint: Pau **Note:** Strike mark: * F *.

Date	Mintage	VG	F	VF	XF	Unc
1653	—	250	500	900	1,800	—
1654	—	250	500	900	1,800	—
1655	—	220	450	850	1,700	—
1656	—	220	450	850	1,700	—

KM# 184.3 1/2 ECU
13.5440 g., 0.9170 Silver 0.3993 oz. ASW **Ruler:** Louis XIV
Mint: Morlaas **Note:** Strike mark: * G *.

Date	Mintage	VG	F	VF	XF	Unc
1653	—	275	550	1,000	2,000	—

KM# 184.4 1/2 ECU
13.5440 g., 0.9170 Silver 0.3993 oz. ASW **Ruler:** Louis XIV
Mint: Morlaas **Note:** Strike mark: M.

Date	Mintage	VG	F	VF	XF	Unc
1662	—	275	550	1,000	2,000	—

KM# 185 1/2 ECU
13.5440 g., 0.9170 Silver 0.3993 oz. ASW **Ruler:** Louis XIV
Rev: Crowned shield of Dauphine **Mint:** Grenoble

Date	Mintage	VG	F	VF	XF	Unc
1653Z	—	—	—	—	—	—

KM# 200 1/2 ECU
13.5440 g., 0.9170 Silver 0.3993 oz. ASW **Ruler:** Louis XIV
Obv: Laureate, draped and mailed bust right **Mint:** Bourges
Note: Hybrid design.

Date	Mintage	VG	F	VF	XF	Unc
1658Y	—	200	425	825	1,650	—
1659Y	—	200	425	825	1,650	—
1660Y	—	200	425	825	1,650	—
1661Y	—	200	425	825	1,650	—
1662Y	—	200	425	825	1,650	—

KM# 202.1 1/2 ECU
13.5440 g., 0.9170 Silver 0.3993 oz. ASW **Ruler:** Louis XIV
Obv: Youthful laureate, draped and mailed bust right
Rev: Crowned French shield **Mint:** Paris

Date	Mintage	VG	F	VF	XF	Unc
1659A	—	65.00	130	325	550	—
1661A	—	—	—	—	—	—
1662A	—	60.00	125	300	525	—
1664A	—	—	—	—	—	—
1666A	—	60.00	125	300	525	—
1667A	—	55.00	115	275	475	—
1668A	—	55.00	115	275	475	—
1669A	—	60.00	125	300	525	—

KM# 202.2 1/2 ECU
13.5440 g., 0.9170 Silver 0.3993 oz. ASW **Ruler:** Louis XIV
Mint: Rouen

Date	Mintage	VG	F	VF	XF	Unc
1659B	—	100	200	485	900	—
1660B	—	—	—	—	—	—
1662B	—	50.00	110	250	425	—
1663B	—	—	—	—	—	—
1664B	—	—	—	—	—	—

KM# 202.3 1/2 ECU
13.5440 g., 0.9170 Silver 0.3993 oz. ASW **Ruler:** Louis XIV
Mint: Lyon

Date	Mintage	VG	F	VF	XF	Unc
1660D	—	85.00	175	425	750	—
1663D	—	—	—	—	—	—
1664D	—	85.00	175	425	750	—
1665D	—	60.00	125	300	525	—
1666D	—	60.00	125	300	525	—
1667D	—	60.00	125	300	525	—
1668D	—	—	—	—	—	—
1669D	—	—	—	—	—	—
1670D	—	—	—	—	—	—
1671D	—	—	—	—	—	—
1672D	—	75.00	150	375	650	—
1673D	—	75.00	150	375	650	—

KM# 202.4 1/2 ECU
13.5440 g., 0.9170 Silver 0.3993 oz. ASW **Ruler:** Louis XIV
Mint: Tours

Date	Mintage	VG	F	VF	XF	Unc
1660E	—	100	200	475	825	—
1661E	—	100	200	475	825	—
1662E	—	85.00	175	425	750	—

KM# 202.5 1/2 ECU
13.5440 g., 0.9170 Silver 0.3993 oz. ASW **Ruler:** Louis XIV
Mint: Angers

Date	Mintage	VG	F	VF	XF	Unc
1660F	—	85.00	175	425	750	—
1661F	—	—	—	—	—	—

KM# 202.6 1/2 ECU
13.5440 g., 0.9170 Silver 0.3993 oz. ASW **Ruler:** Louis XIV
Mint: La Rochelle

Date	Mintage	VG	F	VF	XF	Unc
1661H	—	85.00	175	425	750	—

KM# 202.7 1/2 ECU
13.5440 g., 0.9170 Silver 0.3993 oz. ASW **Ruler:** Louis XIV
Mint: Limoges

Date	Mintage	VG	F	VF	XF	Unc
1661I	—	85.00	175	425	750	—
1662I	—	150	300	700	1,250	—
1664I	—	85.00	175	425	750	—

KM# 202.8 1/2 ECU
13.5440 g., 0.9170 Silver 0.3993 oz. ASW **Ruler:** Louis XIV
Mint: Bordeaux

Date	Mintage	VG	F	VF	XF	Unc
1660K	—	60.00	125	300	525	—
1661K	—	85.00	175	425	750	—

KM# 202.9 1/2 ECU
13.5440 g., 0.9170 Silver 0.3993 oz. ASW **Ruler:** Louis XIV
Mint: Bayonne

Date	Mintage	VG	F	VF	XF	Unc
1659L	—	70.00	140	350	600	—
1660L	—	60.00	125	300	525	—
1661L	—	60.00	125	300	525	—
1662L	—	75.00	150	375	650	—
1663L	—	75.00	150	375	650	—
1664L	—	75.00	150	375	650	—
1665L	—	70.00	140	350	600	—
1666L	—	—	—	—	—	—
1667L	—	75.00	150	375	650	—
1668L	—	—	—	—	—	—
1669L	—	85.00	175	425	750	—
1670L	—	100	200	500	850	—
1671L	—	—	—	—	—	—
1672L	—	85.00	175	425	750	—

KM# 202.10 1/2 ECU
13.5440 g., 0.9170 Silver 0.3993 oz. ASW **Ruler:** Louis XIV
Mint: Toulouse

Date	Mintage	VG	F	VF	XF	Unc
1662M	—	—	—	—	—	—
1663M	—	75.00	145	360	625	—
1666M	—	70.00	140	350	600	—
1667M	—	70.00	140	350	600	—
1668M	—	70.00	140	350	600	—
1669M	—	—	—	—	—	—
1670M	—	—	—	—	—	—
1671M	—	85.00	175	425	750	—

KM# 202.11 1/2 ECU
13.5440 g., 0.9170 Silver 0.3993 oz. ASW **Ruler:** Louis XIV
Mint: Montpellier

Date	Mintage	VG	F	VF	XF	Unc
1660N	—	—	—	—	—	—
1661N	—	—	—	—	—	—
1662N	—	—	—	—	—	—
1666N	—	55.00	115	275	475	—
1667N	—	70.00	140	350	600	—
1668N	—	85.00	175	425	750	—

KM# 202.12 1/2 ECU
13.5440 g., 0.9170 Silver 0.3993 oz. ASW **Ruler:** Louis XIV
Mint: Riom

Date	Mintage	VG	F	VF	XF	Unc
1660O	—	100	200	500	850	—
1664O	—	85.00	175	425	750	—

KM# 202.13 1/2 ECU
13.5440 g., 0.9170 Silver 0.3993 oz. ASW **Ruler:** Louis XIV
Mint: Nantes

Date	Mintage	VG	F	VF	XF	Unc
1659T	—	85.00	175	425	750	—
1660T	—	85.00	175	425	750	—
1661T	—	—	—	—	—	—
1662T	—	60.00	125	300	525	—
1663T	—	70.00	140	350	600	—
1665T	—	70.00	140	350	600	—
1667T	—	70.00	140	350	600	—
1670T	—	85.00	175	425	750	—

KM# 202.14 1/2 ECU
13.5440 g., 0.9170 Silver 0.3993 oz. ASW **Ruler:** Louis XIV
Mint: Amiens

Date	Mintage	VG	F	VF	XF	Unc
1660X	—	—	—	—	—	—

KM# 202.15 1/2 ECU
13.5440 g., 0.9170 Silver 0.3993 oz. ASW **Ruler:** Louis XIV
Mint: Aix **Note:** Mint mark: Ampersand.

Date	Mintage	VG	F	VF	XF	Unc
1660	—	—	—	—	—	—
1661	—	—	—	—	—	—
1662	—	—	—	—	—	—
1665	—	85.00	175	425	750	—
1666	—	60.00	125	300	525	—
1667	—	70.00	140	350	600	—
1669	—	—	—	—	—	—
1670	—	100	200	500	850	—
1671	—	100	200	475	825	—
1672	—	100	200	475	825	—

KM# 202.16 1/2 ECU
13.5440 g., 0.9170 Silver 0.3993 oz. ASW **Ruler:** Louis XIV
Mint: Rennes **Note:** Mint mark: Numeral 9.

Date	Mintage	VG	F	VF	XF	Unc
1659	—	85.00	175	425	750	—
1660	—	70.00	140	350	600	—
1661	—	60.00	125	300	525	—
1662	—	50.00	115	275	475	—
1663	—	60.00	125	300	525	—
1664	—	60.00	125	300	525	—
1665	—	85.00	175	425	750	—
1667	—	65.00	130	325	550	—
1668	—	60.00	125	300	525	—
1669	—	—	—	—	—	—
1670	—	60.00	125	300	525	—
1671	—	—	—	—	—	—
1672	—	90.00	185	450	775	—

KM# 229 1/2 ECU
13.5440 g., 0.9170 Silver 0.3993 oz. ASW **Ruler:** Louis XIV
Obv: Crowned shield of Dauphine **Mint:** Grenoble

Date	Mintage	VG	F	VF	XF	Unc
1660Z Rare	642	—	—	—	—	—

KM# 228 1/2 ECU
13.5440 g., 0.9170 Silver 0.3993 oz. ASW **Ruler:** Louis XIV
Rev: Crowned shield of French, Navarre and Bearn **Mint:** Pau

Date	Mintage	VG	F	VF	XF	Unc
1667	—	300	750	1,500	3,250	—
1674	—	275	675	1,350	3,000	—
1675	—	275	675	1,350	3,000	—
1676	—	275	675	1,350	3,000	—
1677	—	275	675	1,350	3,000	—
1678	—	325	825	1,650	3,750	—
1679	—	325	825	1,650	3,750	—
1680	—	400	1,000	2,200	4,500	—

KM# 225.1 1/2 ECU
13.5440 g., 0.9170 Silver 0.3993 oz. ASW **Ruler:** Louis XIV
Obv: Laureate, draped bust right **Mint:** Paris

Date	Mintage	VG	F	VF	XF	Unc
1670A	—	60.00	125	300	625	—
1671A	—	70.00	140	350	725	—
1672A	—	55.00	115	275	575	—
1673A	—	—	—	—	—	—

KM# 225.2 1/2 ECU
13.5440 g., 0.9170 Silver 0.3993 oz. ASW **Ruler:** Louis XIV
Mint: Nantes

Date	Mintage	VG	F	VF	XF	Unc
1673T	—	100	215	550	1,000	—

KM# 225.3 1/2 ECU
13.5440 g., 0.9170 Silver 0.3993 oz. ASW **Ruler:** Louis XIV
Mint: Rennes **Note:** Mint mark: Numeral 9.

Date	Mintage	VG	F	VF	XF	Unc
1673	—	70.00	140	350	725	—
1674	—	100	200	500	1,000	—

Date	Mintage	VG	F	VF	XF	Unc
1675	—	—	—	—	—	—
1676	—	100	200	475	1,000	—
1677	—	150	300	700	1,500	—
1678	—	—	—	—	—	—
1679	—	55.00	115	275	575	—
1680	—	150	300	700	1,500	—

KM# 230.1 1/2 ECU

13.5440 g., 0.9170 Silver 0.3993 oz. ASW **Ruler:** Louis XIV **Subject:** Parliament **Obv:** Draped armored bust right **Rev:** Crowned shield of France **Mint:** Paris

Date	Mintage	VG	F	VF	XF	Unc
1674A	—	125	325	825	1,450	—
1676A	—	165	400	1,000	1,750	—
1678A	—	—	—	—	—	—
1679A	—	110	275	675	1,200	—
1680A	—	125	325	825	1,450	—
1681A	—	125	325	825	1,450	—
1682A	—	145	375	950	1,650	—
1683A	—	135	350	850	1,475	—

KM# 230.2 1/2 ECU

13.5440 g., 0.9170 Silver 0.3993 oz. ASW **Ruler:** Louis XIV **Mint:** Rouen

Date	Mintage	VG	F	VF	XF	Unc
1679B	—	125	325	825	1,450	—
1680B	—	140	365	900	1,550	—
1681B	—	165	400	1,000	1,750	—
1683B	—	—	—	—	—	—

KM# 230.3 1/2 ECU

13.5440 g., 0.9170 Silver 0.3993 oz. ASW **Ruler:** Louis XIV **Mint:** Lyon

Date	Mintage	VG	F	VF	XF	Unc
1678D	—	180	450	1,100	1,950	—
1679D	—	140	365	900	1,550	—
1680D	—	140	365	900	1,550	—
1681D	—	—	—	—	—	—
1682D	—	180	450	1,100	1,950	—

KM# 230.4 1/2 ECU

13.5440 g., 0.9170 Silver 0.3993 oz. ASW **Ruler:** Louis XIV **Mint:** La Rochelle

Date	Mintage	VG	F	VF	XF	Unc
1679H	—	140	365	900	1,550	—
1680H	—	—	—	—	—	—

KM# 230.5 1/2 ECU

13.5440 g., 0.9170 Silver 0.3993 oz. ASW **Ruler:** Louis XIV **Mint:** Bordeaux

Date	Mintage	VG	F	VF	XF	Unc
1680K	—	—	—	—	—	—
1681K	—	—	—	—	—	—
1682K	—	—	—	—	—	—
1683K	—	145	370	925	1,600	—

KM# 230.6 1/2 ECU

13.5440 g., 0.9170 Silver 0.3993 oz. ASW **Ruler:** Louis XIV **Mint:** Bayonne

Date	Mintage	VG	F	VF	XF	Unc
1673L	—	—	—	—	—	—
1674L	—	125	325	825	1,450	—
1675L	—	140	365	900	1,550	—
1676L	—	140	365	900	1,550	—
1677L	—	165	400	1,000	1,750	—
1678L	—	—	—	—	—	—
1679L	—	140	365	900	1,550	—
1680L	—	—	—	—	—	—
1681L	—	140	365	900	1,550	—
1682L	—	—	—	—	—	—
1683L	—	145	370	925	1,600	—

KM# 230.7 1/2 ECU

13.5440 g., 0.9170 Silver 0.3993 oz. ASW **Ruler:** Louis XIV **Mint:** Montpellier

Date	Mintage	VG	F	VF	XF	Unc
1679N	—	140	365	900	1,550	—
1680N	—	225	550	1,350	2,350	—

KM# 230.8 1/2 ECU

13.5440 g., 0.9170 Silver 0.3993 oz. ASW **Ruler:** Louis XIV **Mint:** Troyes

Date	Mintage	VG	F	VF	XF	Unc
1680S	—	—	—	—	—	—
1681S	—	—	—	—	—	—
1682S	—	180	450	1,100	1,950	—

KM# 230.9 1/2 ECU

13.5440 g., 0.9170 Silver 0.3993 oz. ASW **Ruler:** Louis XIV **Mint:** Aix **Note:** Mint mark: Ampersand.

Date	Mintage	VG	F	VF	XF	Unc
1679	—	140	365	900	1,550	—
1680	—	180	450	1,100	1,950	—
1681	—	—	—	—	—	—
1682	—	140	365	900	1,550	—
1683	—	—	—	—	—	—
1684	—	200	475	1,200	2,150	—

KM# 230.10 1/2 ECU

13.5440 g., 0.9170 Silver 0.3993 oz. ASW **Ruler:** Louis XIV **Mint:** Rennes **Note:** Mint mark: Numeral 9.

Date	Mintage	VG	F	VF	XF	Unc
1680	—	135	350	850	1,475	—
1681	—	—	—	—	—	—
1682	—	180	450	1,100	1,950	—
1683	—	180	450	1,100	1,950	—

KM# 251 1/2 ECU

13.5440 g., 0.9170 Silver 0.3993 oz. ASW **Ruler:** Louis XIV **Rev:** Crowned shield of France, Navarre and Bearn **Mint:** Pau

Date	Mintage	VG	F	VF	XF	Unc
1680	—	1,000	2,000	3,500	7,000	—
1681	—	1,000	2,000	3,500	7,000	—
1682	—	1,000	2,000	3,500	7,000	—
1685	—	1,000	2,000	3,500	7,000	—
1686	—	1,000	2,000	3,500	7,000	—

KM# 250.1 1/2 ECU

13.5440 g., 0.9170 Silver 0.3993 oz. ASW **Ruler:** Louis XIV **Subject:** Parliament **Obv:** Older draped bust right, palm above head **Rev:** Crowned shield of France **Mint:** Paris

Date	Mintage	VG	F	VF	XF	Unc
1683A	—	550	1,350	2,700	4,500	—
1684A	—	550	1,350	2,700	4,500	—

KM# 250.2 1/2 ECU

13.5440 g., 0.9170 Silver 0.3993 oz. ASW **Ruler:** Louis XIV **Mint:** Rouen

Date	Mintage	VG	F	VF	XF	Unc
1684B	—	—	—	—	—	—

KM# 250.3 1/2 ECU

13.5440 g., 0.9170 Silver 0.3993 oz. ASW **Ruler:** Louis XIV **Mint:** Lyon

Date	Mintage	VG	F	VF	XF	Unc
1684D	—	975	2,500	5,000	8,300	—
1685D	—	975	2,500	5,000	8,300	—

KM# 250.4 1/2 ECU

13.5440 g., 0.9170 Silver 0.3993 oz. ASW **Ruler:** Louis XIV **Mint:** Bordeaux

Date	Mintage	VG	F	VF	XF	Unc
1684K	—	975	2,500	5,000	8,300	—
1685K	—	—	—	—	—	—

KM# 250.5 1/2 ECU

13.5440 g., 0.9170 Silver 0.3993 oz. ASW **Ruler:** Louis XIV **Mint:** Bayonne

Date	Mintage	VG	F	VF	XF	Unc
1684L	—	975	2,500	5,000	8,300	—
1685L	—	—	—	—	—	—

KM# 250.6 1/2 ECU

13.5440 g., 0.9170 Silver 0.3993 oz. ASW **Ruler:** Louis XIV **Mint:** Troyes

Date	Mintage	VG	F	VF	XF	Unc
1684S	—	—	—	—	—	—

KM# 250.7 1/2 ECU

13.5440 g., 0.9170 Silver 0.3993 oz. ASW **Ruler:** Louis XIV **Mint:** Aix **Note:** Mint mark: Ampersand.

Date	Mintage	VG	F	VF	XF	Unc
1684	—	975	2,500	5,000	8,300	—
1685	—	900	2,250	5,000	7,500	—
1686	—	975	2,500	5,000	8,300	—

KM# 250.8 1/2 ECU

13.5440 g., 0.9170 Silver 0.3993 oz. ASW **Ruler:** Louis XIV **Mint:** Rennes **Note:** Mint mark: Numeral 9.

Date	Mintage	VG	F	VF	XF	Unc
1684	—	—	—	—	—	—
1685	—	—	—	—	—	—
1686	—	—	—	—	—	—

KM# 262.1 1/2 ECU

13.5440 g., 0.9170 Silver 0.3993 oz. ASW **Ruler:** Louis XIV **Obv:** Draped bust right **Rev:** Crowned quartered shield of Frand and New and Old Burgundy **Edge Lettering:** DOMINE SALVUM FAC REGEM CHRISTIANISSIMVM **Mint:** Paris

Date	Mintage	VG	F	VF	XF	Unc
1685A	—	275	675	1,350	2,250	—
1686A	—	300	750	1,500	2,500	—

KM# 262.2 1/2 ECU

13.5440 g., 0.9170 Silver 0.3993 oz. ASW **Ruler:** Louis XIV **Mint:** Lille

Date	Mintage	VG	F	VF	XF	Unc
1686IL	—	275	675	1,350	2,250	—

KM# 262.3 1/2 ECU

13.5440 g., 0.9170 Silver 0.3993 oz. ASW **Ruler:** Louis XIV **Mint:** Amiens

Date	Mintage	VG	F	VF	XF	Unc
1685X	—	300	750	1,500	2,500	—
1686X	—	300	750	1,500	2,500	—

KM# 262.4 1/2 ECU

13.5440 g., 0.9170 Silver 0.3993 oz. ASW **Ruler:** Louis XIV **Mint:** Lille **Note:** Mint mark: Crowned L.

Date	Mintage	VG	F	VF	XF	Unc
1686	—	300	750	1,500	2,500	—
1687	—	275	675	1,350	2,250	—
1688	—	325	825	1,650	2,750	—
1689	94,000	—	—	—	—	—

KM# 261.1 1/2 ECU

13.5440 g., 0.9170 Silver 0.3993 oz. ASW **Ruler:** Louis XIV **Obv:** Draped bust right **Rev:** Crowned shield of France **Edge Lettering:** DOMINE SALVUM FAC REGEM **Mint:** Paris

Date	Mintage	VG	F	VF	XF	Unc
1686A	—	2,000	4,000	8,000	12,000	—
1687A	—	2,000	4,000	8,000	12,000	—
1688A	—	—	—	—	—	—
1689A	—	—	—	—	—	—

KM# 261.2 1/2 ECU

13.5440 g., 0.9170 Silver 0.3994 oz. ASW **Ruler:** Louis XIV **Mint:** Lyon

Date	Mintage	VG	F	VF	XF	Unc
1686D	—	—	—	—	—	—
1687D	—	—	—	—	—	—
1688D	—	2,2500	4,500	8,500	12,500	—
1689D	—	—	—	—	—	—

KM# 261.3 1/2 ECU

13.5440 g., 0.9170 Silver 0.3993 oz. ASW **Ruler:** Louis XIV **Mint:** Bordeaux

Date	Mintage	VG	F	VF	XF	Unc
1686K	—	—	—	—	—	—
1687K	—	—	—	—	—	—
1688K	—	—	—	—	—	—

KM# 261.4 1/2 ECU

13.5440 g., 0.9170 Silver 0.3993 oz. ASW **Ruler:** Louis XIV **Mint:** Bayonne

Date	Mintage	VG	F	VF	XF	Unc
1686L	—	—	—	—	—	—
1687L	—	—	—	—	—	—
1688L	—	—	—	—	—	—
1689L	—	—	—	—	—	—

KM# 261.5 1/2 ECU

13.5440 g., 0.9170 Silver 0.3993 oz. ASW **Ruler:** Louis XIV **Mint:** Rennes **Note:** Mint mark: Numeral 9.

Date	Mintage	VG	F	VF	XF	Unc
1687	—	—	—	—	—	—
1688	—	—	—	—	—	—
1689	—	—	—	—	—	—

KM# 261.6 1/2 ECU

13.5440 g., 0.9170 Silver 0.3993 oz. ASW **Ruler:** Louis XIV **Mint:** Aix **Note:** Mint mark: Ampersand.

Date	Mintage	VG	F	VF	XF	Unc
1689	—	2,500	5,000	9,000	13,500	—

KM# 273.1 1/2 ECU

13.5440 g., 0.9170 Silver 0.3993 oz. ASW **Ruler:** Louis XIV **Obv:** Draped bust right **Rev:** Cruciform eight L's with crown at each end, fleur-de-lis in angles **Mint:** Paris

Date	Mintage	VG	F	VF	XF	Unc
1690A	—	35.00	90.00	200	450	—
1691A	—	35.00	90.00	200	450	—
1692A	—	50.00	135	300	675	—
1693A	—	50.00	135	300	675	—

KM# 273.2 1/2 ECU

13.5440 g., 0.9170 Silver 0.3993 oz. ASW **Ruler:** Louis XIV **Mint:** Rouen

Date	Mintage	VG	F	VF	XF	Unc
1690B	—	40.00	100	225	500	—
1691B	—	45.00	110	250	550	—

KM# 273.3 1/2 ECU

13.5440 g., 0.9170 Silver 0.3993 oz. ASW **Ruler:** Louis XIV
Mint: Lyon

Date	Mintage	VG	F	VF	XF	Unc
1690D	—	40.00	100	225	500	—
1691D	—	45.00	110	250	550	—
1692D	—	—	—	—	—	—
1693D	—	—	—	—	—	—

KM# 273.4 1/2 ECU

13.5440 g., 0.9170 Silver 0.3993 oz. ASW **Ruler:** Louis XIV
Mint: Tours

Date	Mintage	VG	F	VF	XF	Unc
1690E	—	45.00	110	250	550	—
1691E	—	45.00	110	250	550	—

KM# 273.5 1/2 ECU

13.5440 g., 0.9170 Silver 0.3993 oz. ASW **Ruler:** Louis XIV
Mint: Poitiers

Date	Mintage	VG	F	VF	XF	Unc
1690G	—	60.00	150	325	725	—
1691G	—	100	200	420	950	—
1692G	—	60.00	150	325	725	—

KM# 273.6 1/2 ECU

13.5440 g., 0.9170 Silver 0.3993 oz. ASW **Ruler:** Louis XIV
Mint: La Rochelle

Date	Mintage	VG	F	VF	XF	Unc
1690H	—	60.00	150	325	725	—
1691H	—	60.00	150	325	725	—
1692H	—	60.00	150	325	725	—

KM# 273.7 1/2 ECU

13.5440 g., 0.9170 Silver 0.3993 oz. ASW **Ruler:** Louis XIV
Mint: Limoges

Date	Mintage	VG	F	VF	XF	Unc
1690I	—	60.00	150	325	725	—
1691I	—	45.00	110	250	550	—
1693I	—	—	—	—	—	—

KM# 273.8 1/2 ECU

13.5440 g., 0.9170 Silver 0.3993 oz. ASW **Ruler:** Louis XIV
Mint: Bordeaux

Date	Mintage	VG	F	VF	XF	Unc
1690K	—	60.00	150	325	725	—
1691K	—	45.00	110	250	550	—
1692K	—	60.00	150	325	725	—

KM# 273.9 1/2 ECU

13.5440 g., 0.9170 Silver 0.3993 oz. ASW **Ruler:** Louis XIV
Mint: Bayonne

Date	Mintage	VG	F	VF	XF	Unc
1690L	—	85.00	185	385	800	—
1691L	—	60.00	150	325	725	—

KM# 273.10 1/2 ECU

13.5440 g., 0.9170 Silver 0.3993 oz. ASW **Ruler:** Louis XIV
Mint: Toulouse

Date	Mintage	VG	F	VF	XF	Unc
1690M	—	60.00	150	325	725	—
1691M	—	35.00	90.00	200	450	—
1693M	—	60.00	150	325	725	—

KM# 273.11 1/2 ECU

13.5440 g., 0.9170 Silver 0.3993 oz. ASW **Ruler:** Louis XIV
Mint: Montpellier

Date	Mintage	VG	F	VF	XF	Unc
1690N	—	50.00	135	300	675	—
1691N	—	45.00	110	250	550	—
1692N	—	60.00	150	325	725	—
1693N	—	—	—	—	—	—

KM# 273.12 1/2 ECU

13.5440 g., 0.9170 Silver 0.3993 oz. ASW **Ruler:** Louis XIV
Mint: Riom

Date	Mintage	VG	F	VF	XF	Unc
1690O	—	—	—	—	—	—
1691O	—	50.00	135	300	675	—
1692O	—	60.00	150	325	725	—
1693O	—	—	—	—	—	—

KM# 273.13 1/2 ECU

13.5440 g., 0.9170 Silver 0.3993 oz. ASW **Ruler:** Louis XIV
Mint: Dijon

Date	Mintage	VG	F	VF	XF	Unc
1690P	—	60.00	150	325	725	—
1691P	—	60.00	150	325	725	—
1692P	—	60.00	150	325	725	—
1693P	—	—	—	—	—	—

KM# 273.14 1/2 ECU

13.5440 g., 0.9170 Silver 0.3993 oz. ASW **Ruler:** Louis XIV
Mint: Troyes

Date	Mintage	VG	F	VF	XF	Unc
1690S	—	60.00	150	325	725	—
1691S	—	60.00	150	325	725	—

KM# 273.15 1/2 ECU

13.5440 g., 0.9170 Silver 0.3993 oz. ASW **Ruler:** Louis XIV
Mint: Amiens

Date	Mintage	VG	F	VF	XF	Unc
1690X	—	60.00	150	325	725	—
1691X	—	50.00	135	300	675	—
1692X	—	60.00	150	325	725	—
1693X	—	60.00	150	325	725	—

KM# 273.16 1/2 ECU

13.5440 g., 0.9170 Silver 0.3993 oz. ASW **Ruler:** Louis XIV
Mint: Bourges

Date	Mintage	VG	F	VF	XF	Unc
1690Y	—	60.00	150	325	725	—
1691Y	—	60.00	150	325	725	—
1692Y	—	—	—	—	—	—
1693Y	—	—	—	—	—	—

KM# 273.17 1/2 ECU

13.5440 g., 0.9170 Silver 0.3993 oz. ASW **Ruler:** Louis XIV
Mint: Rennes **Note:** Mint mark: Numeral 9.

Date	Mintage	VG	F	VF	XF	Unc
1690	—	50.00	135	300	675	—
1691	—	40.00	110	245	525	—
1692	—	60.00	150	325	725	—

KM# 273.18 1/2 ECU

13.5440 g., 0.9170 Silver 0.3993 oz. ASW **Ruler:** Louis XIV
Mint: Aix **Note:** Mint mark: Ampersand.

Date	Mintage	VG	F	VF	XF	Unc
1690	—	45.00	110	250	550	—
1691	—	60.00	150	325	725	—

KM# 273.19 1/2 ECU

13.5440 g., 0.9170 Silver 0.3993 oz. ASW **Ruler:** Louis XIV
Mint: Lille **Note:** Mint mark: Crowned L.

Date	Mintage	VG	F	VF	XF	Unc
1690	—	40.00	100	235	525	—
1691	—	50.00	135	300	675	—
1692	—	—	—	—	—	—
1693	—	75.00	175	350	775	—

KM# 273.20 1/2 ECU

13.5440 g., 0.9170 Silver 0.3993 oz. ASW **Ruler:** Louis XIV
Mint: Toulouse **Note:** Mint mark: Crowned M.

Date	Mintage	VG	F	VF	XF	Unc
1691	—	60.00	150	325	725	—

KM# 273.21 1/2 ECU

13.5440 g., 0.9170 Silver 0.3993 oz. ASW **Ruler:** Louis XIV
Mint: Troyes **Note:** Mint mark: Crowned S.

Date	Mintage	VG	F	VF	XF	Unc
1690	—	60.00	150	325	725	—
1691	—	45.00	110	250	550	—
1692	—	60.00	150	325	725	—
1693	—	60.00	150	325	725	—

KM# 274 1/2 ECU

13.5440 g., 0.9170 Silver 0.3993 oz. ASW **Ruler:** Louis XIV
Mint: Pau

Date	Mintage	VG	F	VF	XF	Unc
1690	—	100	225	475	1,100	—
1691	—	100	200	400	950	—
1692	—	100	200	400	950	—

KM# 295.1 1/2 ECU

13.5440 g., 0.9170 Silver 0.3993 oz. ASW **Ruler:** Louis XIV
Obv: Mailed bust right **Rev:** Crowned circular shield of France dividing palm branches **Mint:** Paris

Date	Mintage	VG	F	VF	XF	Unc
1693A	—	35.00	90.00	200	450	—
1694A	—	40.00	100	225	500	—
1695A	—	30.00	75.00	165	375	—
1696A	—	40.00	100	225	500	—
1697A	—	45.00	110	250	550	—
1698A	—	—	—	—	—	—

KM# 295.2 1/2 ECU

13.5440 g., 0.9170 Silver 0.3993 oz. ASW **Ruler:** Louis XIV
Mint: Metz

Date	Mintage	VG	F	VF	XF	Unc
1693AA	—	75.00	175	350	775	—
1694AA	—	100	215	475	1,000	—
1695AA	—	50.00	135	300	675	—
1699AA	—	100	215	475	1,000	—

KM# 295.3 1/2 ECU

13.5440 g., 0.9170 Silver 0.3993 oz. ASW **Ruler:** Louis XIV
Mint: Rouen

Date	Mintage	VG	F	VF	XF	Unc
1693B	—	45.00	110	250	550	—
1694B	—	45.00	110	250	550	—
1697B	—	50.00	135	300	675	—
1698B	—	60.00	150	325	725	—

KM# 295.4 1/2 ECU

13.5440 g., 0.9170 Silver 0.3993 oz. ASW **Ruler:** Louis XIV
Mint: Strasbourg

Date	Mintage	VG	F	VF	XF	Unc
1694BB	—	60.00	150	325	725	—
1695BB	—	60.00	150	325	725	—

KM# 295.5 1/2 ECU

13.5440 g., 0.9170 Silver 0.3993 oz. ASW **Ruler:** Louis XIV
Mint: Caen

Date	Mintage	VG	F	VF	XF	Unc
1695C	—	60.00	150	325	725	—
1697C	—	—	—	—	—	—

KM# 295.6 1/2 ECU

13.5440 g., 0.9170 Silver 0.3993 oz. ASW **Ruler:** Louis XIV
Mint: Lyon

Date	Mintage	VG	F	VF	XF	Unc
1693D	—	40.00	100	225	500	—
1694D	—	30.00	75.00	165	375	—
1695D	—	45.00	110	250	550	—
1696D	—	—	—	—	—	—
1697D	—	—	—	—	—	—
1699D	—	—	—	—	—	—
1700D	—	—	—	—	—	—

KM# 295.7 1/2 ECU

13.5440 g., 0.9170 Silver 0.3993 oz. ASW **Ruler:** Louis XIV
Mint: Tours

Date	Mintage	VG	F	VF	XF	Unc
1694E	—	40.00	100	225	500	—
1695E	—	45.00	110	250	550	—
1696E	—	45.00	110	250	550	—
1697E	—	60.00	150	325	725	—

KM# 295.8 1/2 ECU

13.5440 g., 0.9170 Silver 0.3993 oz. ASW **Ruler:** Louis XIV
Mint: Poitiers

Date	Mintage	VG	F	VF	XF	Unc
1693G	—	50.00	135	300	675	—
1694G	—	50.00	135	300	675	—
1695G	—	45.00	110	250	550	—
1696G	—	60.00	150	325	725	—
1699G	—	60.00	150	325	725	—

KM# 295.9 1/2 ECU

13.5440 g., 0.9170 Silver 0.3993 oz. ASW **Ruler:** Louis XIV
Mint: La Rochelle

Date	Mintage	VG	F	VF	XF	Unc
1693H	—	40.00	100	225	500	—
1694H	—	45.00	110	250	550	—
1695H	—	45.00	110	250	550	—
1697H	—	60.00	150	325	725	—
1698H	—	60.00	150	325	725	—

KM# 295.10 1/2 ECU

13.5440 g., 0.9170 Silver 0.3993 oz. ASW **Ruler:** Louis XIV
Mint: Limoges

Date	Mintage	VG	F	VF	XF	Unc
1694I	—	60.00	150	325	725	—
1695I	—	125	300	700	1,500	—
1696I	—	60.00	150	325	725	—

KM# 295.11 1/2 ECU

13.5440 g., 0.9170 Silver 0.3993 oz. ASW **Ruler:** Louis XIV
Mint: Bordeaux

Date	Mintage	VG	F	VF	XF	Unc
1693K	—	40.00	100	225	500	—
1694K	—	45.00	110	250	550	—
1695K	—	45.00	110	250	550	—
1697K	—	45.00	110	250	550	—
1698K	—	60.00	150	325	725	—

KM# 295.12 1/2 ECU

13.5440 g., 0.9170 Silver 0.3993 oz. ASW **Ruler:** Louis XIV
Mint: Bayonne

Date	Mintage	VG	F	VF	XF	Unc
1694L	—	50.00	135	300	675	—
1700L	—	—	—	—	—	—

KM# 295.13 1/2 ECU

13.5440 g., 0.9170 Silver 0.3993 oz. ASW **Ruler:** Louis XIV
Mint: Toulouse

Date	Mintage	VG	F	VF	XF	Unc
1694M	—	45.00	110	250	550	—
1695M	—	45.00	110	250	550	—
1696M	—	45.00	110	250	550	—

KM# 295.14 1/2 ECU

13.5440 g., 0.9170 Silver 0.3993 oz. ASW **Ruler:** Louis XIV
Mint: Montpellier

Date	Mintage	VG	F	VF	XF	Unc
1693N	—	40.00	100	225	500	—
1694N	—	40.00	100	225	500	—
1695N	—	45.00	110	250	550	—
1696N	—	—	—	—	—	—
1697N	—	—	—	—	—	—
1699N	—	—	—	—	—	—

KM# 295.15 1/2 ECU

13.5440 g., 0.9170 Silver 0.3993 oz. ASW **Ruler:** Louis XIV
Mint: Riom

Date	Mintage	VG	F	VF	XF	Unc
1693O	—	45.00	110	250	550	—
1694O	—	45.00	110	250	550	—
1697O	—	—	—	—	—	—

KM# 295.16 1/2 ECU

13.5440 g., 0.9170 Silver 0.3993 oz. ASW **Ruler:** Louis XIV
Mint: Dijon

Date	Mintage	VG	F	VF	XF	Unc
1693P	—	40.00	100	225	500	—
1694P	—	40.00	100	225	500	—
1695P	—	40.00	100	225	500	—
1697P	—	—	—	—	—	—
1700P	—	—	—	—	—	—

KM# 295.17 1/2 ECU

13.5440 g., 0.9170 Silver 0.3993 oz. ASW **Ruler:** Louis XIV
Mint: Perpignan

Date	Mintage	VG	F	VF	XF	Unc
1694Q	—	50.00	135	300	675	—

KM# 295.18 1/2 ECU

13.5440 g., 0.9170 Silver 0.3993 oz. ASW **Ruler:** Louis XIV
Mint: Troyes

Date	Mintage	VG	F	VF	XF	Unc
1693S	—	35.00	90.00	200	450	—
1694S	—	40.00	100	225	500	—
1697S	—	60.00	150	325	725	—

KM# 295.19 1/2 ECU

13.5440 g., 0.9170 Silver 0.3993 oz. ASW **Ruler:** Louis XIV
Mint: Nantes

Date	Mintage	VG	F	VF	XF	Unc
1693T	—	45.00	110	250	550	—
1694T	—	40.00	100	225	500	—
1695T	—	45.00	110	250	550	—
1696T	—	45.00	110	250	550	—
1697T	—	45.00	110	250	550	—
1698T	—	50.00	135	300	675	—

KM# 295.20 1/2 ECU
13.5440 g., 0.9170 Silver 0.3993 oz. ASW **Ruler:** Louis XIV **Mint:** Troyes

Date	Mintage	VG	F	VF	XF	Unc
1693V	—	50.00	135	300	675	—
1694V	—	40.00	100	225	500	—
1695V	—	—	—	—	—	—
1696V	—	50.00	135	300	675	—
1697V	—	60.00	150	325	725	—
1698V	—	—	—	—	—	—
1699V	—	75.00	175	350	775	—

KM# 295.21 1/2 ECU
13.5440 g., 0.9170 Silver 0.3993 oz. ASW **Ruler:** Louis XIV **Mint:** Lille

Date	Mintage	VG	F	VF	XF	Unc
1693W	—	40.00	100	225	500	—
1694W	—	40.00	100	225	500	—
1695W	—	40.00	100	225	500	—
1696W	—	—	—	—	—	—
1697W	—	—	—	—	—	—
1698W	—	—	—	—	—	—
1699W	—	60.00	150	325	725	—
1700W	—	—	—	—	—	—

KM# 295.22 1/2 ECU
13.5440 g., 0.9170 Silver 0.3993 oz. ASW **Ruler:** Louis XIV **Mint:** Amiens

Date	Mintage	VG	F	VF	XF	Unc
1693X	—	40.00	100	225	500	—
1694X	—	40.00	100	225	500	—
1695X	—	40.00	100	230	520	—
1696X	—	50.00	135	300	675	—

KM# 295.23 1/2 ECU
13.5440 g., 0.9170 Silver 0.3993 oz. ASW **Ruler:** Louis XIV **Mint:** Bourges

Date	Mintage	VG	F	VF	XF	Unc
1693Y	—	50.00	135	300	675	—
1694Y	—	50.00	135	300	675	—
1699Y	—	60.00	150	325	725	—

KM# 295.24 1/2 ECU
13.5440 g., 0.9170 Silver 0.3993 oz. ASW **Ruler:** Louis XIV **Mint:** Aix **Note:** Mint mark: Ampersand.

Date	Mintage	VG	F	VF	XF	Unc
1693	—	50.00	135	300	675	—
1694	—	40.00	100	225	500	—

KM# 295.25 1/2 ECU
13.5440 g., 0.9170 Silver 0.3993 oz. ASW **Ruler:** Louis XIV **Mint:** Rennes **Note:** Mint mark: Numeral 9.

Date	Mintage	VG	F	VF	XF	Unc
1693	—	45.00	110	250	550	—
1694	—	40.00	100	225	500	—
1695	—	35.00	90.00	200	450	—
1696	—	60.00	150	325	725	—

KM# 295.26 1/2 ECU
13.5440 g., 0.9170 Silver 0.3993 oz. ASW **Ruler:** Louis XIV **Mint:** Metz **Note:** Mint mark: Crowned M.

Date	Mintage	VG	F	VF	XF	Unc
1693	—	40.00	100	225	500	—

KM# 295.27 1/2 ECU
13.5440 g., 0.9170 Silver 0.3993 oz. ASW **Ruler:** Louis XIV **Mint:** Troyes **Note:** Mint mark: Crowned S.

Date	Mintage	VG	F	VF	XF	Unc
1693	—	100	200	450	1,000	—

KM# 295.28 1/2 ECU
13.5440 g., 0.9170 Silver 0.3993 oz. ASW **Ruler:** Louis XIV **Mint:** Besancon **Note:** Mint mark: Back-to-back C's.

Date	Mintage	VG	F	VF	XF	Unc
1694	—	45.00	110	250	550	—
1695	—	60.00	150	325	725	—
1696	—	—	—	—	—	—
1697	—	—	—	—	—	—
1698	—	—	—	—	—	—
1699	—	60.00	150	325	725	—

KM# 296 1/2 ECU
13.5440 g., 0.9170 Silver 0.3993 oz. ASW **Ruler:** Louis XIV **Rev:** Crowned circular shield of France, Navarre and Berne between palm branches **Mint:** Pau

Date	Mintage	VG	F	VF	XF	Unc
1693	—	1,050	1,900	3,150	5,600	—
1694	—	1,050	1,900	3,150	5,600	—
1695	—	1,050	1,900	3,150	5,600	—
1696	—	—	—	—	—	—
1697	—	1,050	1,900	3,150	5,600	—
1698	—	—	—	—	—	—
1700	—	—	—	—	—	—

KM# 297 1/2 ECU
13.5440 g., 0.9170 Silver 0.3993 oz. ASW **Ruler:** Louis XIV **Rev:** Crowned quartered shield of France, Navarre and Old and New Burgundy between palm branches **Mint:** Lille

Date	Mintage	VG	F	VF	XF	Unc
1693W	—	225	575	1,450	2,500	—
1694W	—	200	475	1,250	2,250	—
1695W	—	275	650	1,650	2,750	—
1696W	—	275	650	1,650	2,750	—
1697W	—	—	—	—	—	—
1699W	—	350	850	2,000	3,250	—

KM# 308 1/2 ECU
15.3340 g., 0.8330 Silver 0.4107 oz. ASW **Ruler:** Louis XIV **Obv:** Large fleur-de-lis **Rev:** Crowned quartered shield of France **Mint:** Strasbourg

Date	Mintage	VG	F	VF	XF	Unc
1694BB	—	65.00	130	325	550	—
1695BB	—	80.00	160	400	700	—
1696BB	—	85.00	175	425	750	—
1697BB	—	100	220	490	850	—

KM# 120.1 ECU
Silver **Ruler:** Louis XIII **Obv:** Bust with bare neck **Rev:** Rose above crown **Mint:** Paris **Note:** Dav. #3796.

Date	Mintage	VG	F	VF	XF	Unc
1641A	—	3,000	5,000	9,000	15,000	—
1642A	—	850	2,000	4,000	8,000	—

KM# 120.2 ECU
Silver **Ruler:** Louis XIII **Rev:** Rose flanked by points above crown

Date	Mintage	VG	F	VF	XF	Unc
1642	—	850	2,000	4,000	8,000	—

KM# 120.3 ECU
Silver **Ruler:** Louis XIII **Rev:** Point above crown

Date	Mintage	VG	F	VF	XF	Unc
1642	—	850	2,000	4,000	8,000	—

KM# 129.1 ECU
Silver **Ruler:** Louis XIII **Obv:** Draped bust **Rev:** Point above crown **Note:** Dav. #3797.

Date	Mintage	VG	F	VF	XF	Unc
1642	—	500	1,000	2,400	4,500	—
1643	—	400	800	1,900	3,500	—

KM# 129.2 ECU
Silver **Ruler:** Louis XIII **Rev:** Rose above crown

Date	Mintage	VG	F	VF	XF	Unc
1643	—	400	800	1,900	3,500	—

KM# 129.3 ECU
Silver **Ruler:** Louis XIII **Rev:** Three points above crown **Mint:** Lyon

Date	Mintage	VG	F	VF	XF	Unc
1643D	—	700	1,350	2,750	4,500	—
1643D With reverse mint mark	—	750	1,500	3,000	5,000	—

KM# 144.1 ECU
Silver **Ruler:** Louis XIV **Obv:** Bust with short curl **Rev:** Rose above crown **Mint:** Paris

Date	Mintage	VG	F	VF	XF	Unc
1643A	—	125	250	500	950	—
1644A	—	100	225	450	900	—
1645A	—	150	325	650	1,200	—

KM# 144.2 ECU
Silver **Ruler:** Louis XIV **Rev:** Rose flanked by points above crown **Mint:** Paris

Date	Mintage	VG	F	VF	XF	Unc
1644A	—	125	250	500	950	—
1645A	—	135	275	550	1,000	—

KM# 144.3 ECU
Silver **Ruler:** Louis XIV **Rev:** Point above crown **Mint:** Paris

Date	Mintage	VG	F	VF	XF	Unc
1643A	—	135	275	550	1,000	—
1644A	—	125	250	500	950	—
1645A	—	100	200	400	850	—

KM# 144.4 ECU
Silver **Ruler:** Louis XIV **Mint:** Lyon

Date	Mintage	VG	F	VF	XF	Unc
1643D	—	—	—	—	—	—
1644D	—	225	450	850	1,600	—
1645D	—	250	500	950	1,750	—

KM# 155.1 ECU
Silver **Ruler:** Louis XIV **Obv:** Bust with long curl **Mint:** Paris **Note:** Dav. #3799.

Date	Mintage	VG	F	VF	XF	Unc
1646A	—	75.00	150	300	725	—
1647A	—	250	450	800	1,800	—
1648A	—	200	350	650	1,500	—
1649A	—	60.00	125	250	575	—
1651A	—	50.00	100	200	450	—
1652A	—	40.00	80.00	165	400	—
1653A	—	50.00	100	200	450	—

KM# 155.2 ECU
Silver **Ruler:** Louis XIV **Mint:** Rouen

Date	Mintage	VG	F	VF	XF	Unc
1646B	—	65.00	135	275	625	—
1647B	—	60.00	125	250	575	—
1648B	—	55.00	115	225	500	—
1651B	—	50.00	100	200	450	—
1652B	—	50.00	100	200	450	—
1653B	—	60.00	125	250	575	—

KM# 155.3 ECU
Silver **Ruler:** Louis XIV **Mint:** Saint Lô

Date	Mintage	VG	F	VF	XF	Unc
1648C Rare	—	—	—	—	—	—
1651C Rare	—	—	—	—	—	—

KM# 155.4 ECU
Silver **Ruler:** Louis XIV **Mint:** Lyon

Date	Mintage	VG	F	VF	XF	Unc
1652D	—	65.00	135	275	625	—

KM# 155.5 ECU
Silver **Ruler:** Louis XIV **Mint:** Angers

Date	Mintage	VG	F	VF	XF	Unc
1647F	—	85.00	175	350	775	—
1648F	—	65.00	135	275	625	—
1649F	—	275	500	1,100	2,150	—
1653F	—	180	325	625	1,450	—

KM# 155.6 ECU
Silver **Ruler:** Louis XIV **Mint:** Poitiers

Date	Mintage	VG	F	VF	XF	Unc
1647G	—	85.00	175	350	725	—
1648G	—	85.00	175	350	725	—
1649G	—	85.00	175	350	725	—
1650G	—	85.00	175	350	725	—

KM# 155.7 ECU
Silver **Ruler:** Louis XIV **Mint:** La Rochelle

Date	Mintage	VG	F	VF	XF	Unc
1646H	—	85.00	175	350	750	—
1647H	—	65.00	135	275	625	—
1648H	—	85.00	175	350	750	—
1649H	—	65.00	135	275	625	—

KM# 155.8 ECU
Silver **Ruler:** Louis XIV **Mint:** Limoges

Date	Mintage	VG	F	VF	XF	Unc
1652I	—	65.00	135	275	625	—
1653I	—	65.00	135	275	625	—

KM# 155.9 ECU
Silver **Ruler:** Louis XIV **Mint:** Bordeaux

Date	Mintage	VG	F	VF	XF	Unc
1647K	—	65.00	135	275	625	—
1648K	—	75.00	150	300	700	—
1649K	—	65.00	135	275	625	—
1650K	—	250	450	800	1,800	—
1651K	—	85.00	175	350	750	—
1652K	—	65.00	135	275	625	—
1653K	—	90.00	185	375	850	—
1654K	—	250	450	800	1,800	—

KM# 155.10 ECU
Silver **Ruler:** Louis XIV **Mint:** Bayonne

Date	Mintage	VG	F	VF	XF	Unc
1652L	—	65.00	135	275	625	—
1653L	—	65.00	135	275	625	—
1654L	—	200	375	675	1,600	—
1659L	—	85.00	175	350	750	—

KM# 155.11 ECU
Silver **Ruler:** Louis XIV **Mint:** Toulouse

Date	Mintage	VG	F	VF	XF	Unc
1647M	—	65.00	135	275	625	—
1648M	—	60.00	125	250	575	—
1649M	—	250	450	825	1,850	—
1651M	—	250	450	800	1,800	—
1652M	—	65.00	135	275	625	—
1653M	—	65.00	135	275	625	—
1654M	—	250	450	825	1,850	—

KM# 155.12 ECU
Silver **Ruler:** Louis XIV **Mint:** Montpellier

Date	Mintage	VG	F	VF	XF	Unc
1647	—	180	325	750	1,450	—
1648	—	65.00	135	275	650	—
1649	—	65.00	135	275	650	—
1650	—	250	450	800	1,800	—
1651	—	—	—	—	—	—
1652	—	—	—	—	—	—
1652	—	90.00	185	375	850	—

KM# 155.13 ECU
Silver **Ruler:** Louis XIV **Mint:** Riom

Date	Mintage	VG	F	VF	XF	Unc
1652O	—	250	450	800	1,800	—
1653O	—	250	450	800	1,800	—

KM# 155.14 ECU
Silver **Ruler:** Louis XIV **Mint:** Dijon

Date	Mintage	VG	F	VF	XF	Unc
1651P	—	275	500	900	2,100	—
1652P	—	60.00	125	250	575	—
1653P	—	85.00	175	350	750	—

KM# 155.15 ECU
Silver **Ruler:** Louis XIV **Mint:** Troyes

Date	Mintage	VG	F	VF	XF	Unc
1651S	—	85.00	175	350	750	—
1652S	—	60.00	125	250	575	—
1653S	—	65.00	135	275	625	—

KM# 155.16 ECU
Silver **Ruler:** Louis XIV **Mint:** Nantes

Date	Mintage	VG	F	VF	XF	Unc
1647T	—	85.00	175	350	750	—
1648T	—	65.00	135	275	625	—
1649T	—	60.00	125	250	575	—
1650T	—	550	950	1,800	3,800	—
1651T	—	—	—	—	—	—
1652T	—	65.00	135	275	625	—
1653T	—	85.00	175	350	750	—

KM# 155.17 ECU
Silver **Ruler:** Louis XIV **Mint:** Amiens

Date	Mintage	VG	F	VF	XF	Unc
1652X	—	60.00	125	250	575	—
1653X	—	65.00	135	275	625	—

KM# 155.18 ECU
Silver **Ruler:** Louis XIV **Mint:** Aix **Note:** Mint mark: Ampersand.

Date	Mintage	VG	F	VF	XF	Unc
1647	—	250	450	800	1,800	—
1648	—	65.00	135	275	625	—
1649	—	65.00	135	275	625	—
1652	—	65.00	135	275	625	—
1653	—	65.00	135	275	625	—
1654	—	—	—	—	—	—

KM# 155.19 ECU
Silver **Ruler:** Louis XIV **Mint:** Rennes **Note:** Mint mark: Numeral 9.

Date	Mintage	VG	F	VF	XF	Unc
1648	—	65.00	135	275	625	—
1652	—	60.00	125	250	575	—
1653	—	55.00	120	225	475	—

KM# 180 ECU
Silver **Ruler:** Louis XIV **Rev:** Crowned arms of France and Navarre **Mint:** Saint Palais **Note:** Issued for Navarre. Dav. #3800.

Date	Mintage	VG	F	VF	XF	Unc
1652	—	270	475	850	1,600	—
1653	—	270	475	850	1,600	—
1654	—	300	500	900	1,750	—
1655	—	270	475	850	1,600	—
1656	—	300	500	900	1,750	—
1657	—	270	475	850	1,600	—
1658	—	300	500	900	1,750	—
1659	—	325	550	950	1,850	—
1660	—	300	500	900	1,750	—
1661	—	300	500	900	1,750	—
1662	—	350	600	1,000	2,000	—
1663	—	—	—	—	—	—

KM# 181.1 ECU
Silver **Ruler:** Louis XIV **Rev:** Crowned arms of France, Navarre and Bearn **Mint:** Pau **Note:** Dav. #3801.

Date	Mintage	VG	F	VF	XF	Unc
1650	—	225	400	700	1,350	—
1651	—	225	400	700	1,350	—
1652	—	225	400	700	1,350	—
1653	—	225	400	700	1,350	—
1654	—	275	475	850	1,650	—
1655	—	275	475	850	1,650	—
1656	—	275	475	850	1,650	—
1657	—	300	500	900	1,750	—
1658	—	300	500	900	1,750	—
1660	—	275	475	850	1,650	—
1662	—	300	500	900	1,750	—

KM# 181.2 ECU
Silver **Ruler:** Louis XIV **Mint:** Saint Palais

Date	Mintage	VG	F	VF	XF	Unc
1652	—	300	500	1,100	2,250	—

KM# 181.3 ECU
Silver **Ruler:** Louis XIV **Mint:** Toulouse

Date	Mintage	VG	F	VF	XF	Unc
1652M	—	275	425	950	1,950	—
1653M	—	275	425	950	1,950	—
1654M	—	275	475	1,000	2,050	—
1655M	—	275	425	950	1,950	—
1656M	—	250	425	900	1,800	—
1657M	—	275	425	950	1,950	—
1658M	—	275	475	1,000	2,050	—
1659M	—	275	425	950	1,950	—
1660M	—	275	425	950	1,950	—

Date	Mintage	VG	F	VF	XF	Unc
1661M	—	275	425	950	1,950	—
1662M	—	275	425	950	1,950	—

KM# 211.1 ECU

Silver **Ruler:** Louis XIV **Obv:** Draped bust **Rev:** Crowned arms of France **Mint:** Paris **Note:** Dav. #3802.

Date	Mintage	VG	F	VF	XF	Unc
1662A	—	155	295	575	1,050	—
1663A	—	130	260	525	975	—
1664A	—	155	295	575	1,050	—
1665A	—	—	—	—	—	—
1666A	—	130	260	525	975	—
1670A	—	130	260	525	975	—
1672A	—	130	260	525	975	—

KM# 211.2 ECU

Silver **Ruler:** Louis XIV **Mint:** Rouen

Date	Mintage	VG	F	VF	XF	Unc
1664B	—	145	270	550	1,050	—

KM# 211.3 ECU

Silver **Ruler:** Louis XIV **Mint:** Bayonne

Date	Mintage	VG	F	VF	XF	Unc
1663L	—	120	240	475	975	—
1664L	—	120	240	475	975	—

KM# 211.4 ECU

Silver **Ruler:** Louis XIV **Mint:** Nantes

Date	Mintage	VG	F	VF	XF	Unc
1663T	—	150	300	600	1,150	—

KM# 211.5 ECU

Silver **Ruler:** Louis XIV **Mint:** Rennes **Note:** Mint marl: Numeral 9.

Date	Mintage	VG	F	VF	XF	Unc
1663	—	185	350	650	1,250	—
1664	—	90.00	185	375	650	—
1665	—	120	225	450	800	—

KM# 216 ECU

Silver **Ruler:** Louis XIV **Rev:** Crowned arms of France, Navarre and Bearn **Mint:** Pau **Note:** Dav. #3804.

Date	Mintage	VG	F	VF	XF	Unc
1663	—	300	525	975	1,750	—
1664	—	265	450	825	1,500	—
1665	—	265	450	825	1,500	—
1666	—	300	525	975	1,750	—
1667	—	225	425	750	1,350	—
1668	—	300	525	975	1,750	—
1669	—	300	525	975	1,750	—
1670	—	425	675	1,200	2,350	—
1671	—	425	675	1,200	2,350	—
1672	—	425	675	1,200	2,350	—
1673	—	375	650	1,150	2,200	—
1674	—	225	425	750	1,350	—
1675	—	225	425	750	1,350	—
1676	—	350	600	1,050	2,050	—
1679	—	265	450	825	1,500	—
1680	—	425	675	1,200	2,350	—

KM# 215 ECU

Silver **Ruler:** Louis XIV **Rev:** Crowned arms of France and Navarre **Mint:** Saint Palais **Note:** Dav. #3803.

Date	Mintage	VG	F	VF	XF	Unc
1664	—	650	1,100	1,950	3,750	—
1665	—	650	1,000	1,800	3,550	—
1666	—	650	1,100	1,950	3,750	—
1667	—	575	975	1,750	3,300	—
1668	—	650	1,100	1,950	3,750	—
1670	—	650	1,000	1,800	3,550	—
1671	—	650	1,000	1,800	3,550	—

KM# 214.1 ECU

Silver **Ruler:** Louis XIV **Obv:** Modified draped bust **Mint:** Rouen **Note:** Dav. #3802A.

Date	Mintage	VG	F	VF	XF	Unc
1665B	—	125	250	500	900	—

KM# 214.2 ECU

Silver **Ruler:** Louis XIV **Mint:** Bayonne

Date	Mintage	VG	F	VF	XF	Unc
1665L	—	90.00	185	375	650	—
1666L	—	100	200	400	750	—
1667L	—	100	200	400	750	—
1668L	—	100	200	400	750	—
1669L	—	100	200	400	750	—
1670L	—	100	200	400	750	—
1671L	—	120	225	450	800	—
1672L	—	90.00	185	375	650	—

KM# 214.3 ECU

Silver **Ruler:** Louis XIV **Mint:** Aix **Note:** Mint mark: Ampersand.

Date	Mintage	VG	F	VF	XF	Unc
1666	—	120	225	450	800	—
1667	—	90.00	185	375	650	—
1668	—	120	225	475	850	—
1669	—	90.00	185	375	650	—
1670	—	120	225	450	800	—
1671	—	125	250	500	900	—
1672	—	180	325	625	1,150	—

KM# 214.4 ECU

Silver **Ruler:** Louis XIV **Mint:** Rennes **Note:** Mint mark: Numeral 9.

Date	Mintage	VG	F	VF	XF	Unc
1665	—	90.00	185	375	650	—
1666	—	120	225	450	800	—
1667	—	100	200	400	750	—
1668	—	75.00	150	300	550	—
1669	—	120	225	450	800	—
1670	—	75.00	150	300	550	—
1671	—	90.00	185	375	650	—
1672	—	120	225	450	800	—
1673	—	150	275	500	900	—
1674	—	—	—	—	—	—
1675	—	—	—	—	—	—
1676	—	180	325	625	1,150	—

KM# 227 ECU

Silver **Ruler:** Louis XIV **Obv:** "Parliamentary" bust in armor **Rev:** Crowned arms of France and Navarre **Mint:** Saint Palais **Note:** Dav. #3806.

Date	Mintage	VG	F	VF	XF	Unc
1672 Rare	—	—	—	20,000	30,000	—

KM# 226.1 ECU

Silver **Ruler:** Louis XIV **Obv:** "Parliamentary" bust in armor **Rev:** Crowned arms of France **Mint:** Paris **Note:** Dav. #3805.

Date	Mintage	VG	F	VF	XF	Unc
1672A	—	250	450	800	1,950	—
1673A	—	100	200	400	1,000	—
1674A	—	—	—	—	—	—
1675A	—	225	400	700	1,550	—
1676A	—	180	325	625	1,450	—
1677A	—	250	450	800	1,950	—
1678A	—	250	450	800	1,950	—
1679A	—	100	200	400	1,000	—
1680A	—	180	325	625	1,450	—
1682A	—	180	325	625	1,450	—
1683A	—	250	450	800	1,950	—

KM# 226.2 ECU

Silver **Ruler:** Louis XIV **Mint:** Rouen

Date	Mintage	VG	F	VF	XF	Unc
1679B	—	250	425	750	1,800	—
1680B	—	225	400	700	1,650	—
1682B	—	—	—	—	—	—
1683B	—	275	500	900	2,200	—

KM# 226.3 ECU

Silver **Ruler:** Louis XIV **Mint:** Lyon

Date	Mintage	VG	F	VF	XF	Unc
1676D	—	—	—	—	—	—
1681D	—	300	525	950	2,300	—

KM# 226.4 ECU

Silver **Ruler:** Louis XIV **Mint:** Tours

Date	Mintage	VG	F	VF	XF	Unc
1679E	—	180	325	625	1,450	—
1680E	—	225	400	700	1,650	—

KM# 226.5 ECU

Silver **Ruler:** Louis XIV **Mint:** La Rochelle

Date	Mintage	VG	F	VF	XF	Unc
1680H	—	225	400	700	1,750	—

KM# 226.6 ECU

Silver **Ruler:** Louis XIV **Mint:** Limoges

Date	Mintage	VG	F	VF	XF	Unc
1679I	—	225	400	700	1,650	—
1680I	—	250	450	800	1,950	—
1681I	—	250	450	800	1,950	—

KM# 226.7 ECU

Silver **Ruler:** Louis XIV **Mint:** Bordeaux

Date	Mintage	VG	F	VF	XF	Unc
1679K	—	180	325	625	1,450	—
1680K	—	225	400	700	1,650	—
1681K	—	225	400	700	1,650	—
1682K	—	225	400	700	1,650	—
1683K	—	180	325	625	1,450	—

KM# 226.8 ECU

Silver **Ruler:** Louis XIV **Mint:** Bayonne

Date	Mintage	VG	F	VF	XF	Unc
1673L	—	180	325	625	1,450	—
1674L	—	250	450	800	1,950	—
1675L	—	225	400	700	1,650	—
1676L	—	180	325	625	1,450	—
1677L	—	250	425	750	1,750	—
1678L	—	225	400	700	1,650	—
1679L	—	135	275	550	1,250	—
1680L	—	135	275	550	1,250	—
1681L	—	135	275	550	1,250	—
1682L	—	135	275	550	1,250	—
1683L	—	135	275	550	1,250	—
1684L	—	225	400	700	1,650	—

KM# 226.9 ECU

Silver **Ruler:** Louis XIV **Mint:** Montpellier

Date	Mintage	VG	F	VF	XF	Unc
1680N	—	250	450	850	2,150	—

KM# 226.10 ECU

Silver **Ruler:** Louis XIV **Mint:** Reims

Date	Mintage	VG	F	VF	XF	Unc
1680S	—	250	450	800	1,950	—
1681S	—	225	400	700	1,650	—
1682S	—	—	—	—	—	—
1683S	—	250	450	800	1,950	—

KM# 226.11 ECU

Silver **Ruler:** Louis XIV **Mint:** Amiens

Date	Mintage	VG	F	VF	XF	Unc
1679X	—	180	325	625	1,450	—
1680X	—	225	400	700	1,700	—
1681X	—	135	275	550	1,250	—
1682X	—	300	625	1,150	2,700	—
1683X	—	—	—	—	—	—

KM# 226.12 ECU

Silver **Ruler:** Louis XIV **Mint:** Aix **Note:** Mint mark: Ampersand.

Date	Mintage	VG	F	VF	XF	Unc
1679	—	180	325	625	1,450	—
1680	—	180	325	625	1,450	—
1681	—	225	400	700	1,650	—
1683	—	225	400	700	1,650	—

KM# 226.13 ECU

Silver **Ruler:** Louis XIV **Mint:** Rennes **Note:** Mint mark: Numeral 9.

Date	Mintage	VG	F	VF	XF	Unc
1673	—	135	275	550	1,250	—
1677	—	—	—	—	—	—
1679	—	135	275	550	1,250	—
1680	—	135	275	550	1,250	—
1681	—	225	400	700	1,650	—
1682	—	125	250	500	1,150	—
1683	—	135	275	550	1,250	—

KM# 252 ECU

Silver **Ruler:** Louis XIV **Obv:** Older bust **Rev:** Crowned arms of France, Navarre and Bearn **Mint:** Pau **Note:** Dav. #3807.

Date	Mintage	VG	F	VF	XF	Unc
1680	—	500	950	3,500	9,000	—
1681	—	450	850	3,250	9,000	—
1682	—	450	850	3,250	9,000	—
1683	—	500	950	3,500	10,000	—
1684	—	800	1,500	5,000	12,000	—
1685	—	800	1,500	5,000	12,000	—
1686	—	550	1,000	4,500	11,000	—

KM# 253.1 ECU

Silver **Ruler:** Louis XIV **Obv:** Older, heavier bust right **Rev:** Crowned French arms **Mint:** Paris **Note:** Dav. #3808.

Date	Mintage	VG	F	VF	XF	Unc
1683A	—	350	775	1,500	3,200	—
1684A	—	450	1,000	1,850	3,900	—

KM# 253.2 ECU

Silver **Ruler:** Louis XIV **Mint:** Lyon

Date	Mintage	VG	F	VF	XF	Unc
1684D	—	450	1,000	1,850	3,900	—

KM# 253.3 ECU

Silver **Ruler:** Louis XIV **Mint:** Bordeaux

Date	Mintage	VG	F	VF	XF	Unc
1684K	—	—	—	—	—	—

KM# 253.4 ECU

Silver **Ruler:** Louis XIV **Mint:** Aix **Note:** Mint mark: Ampersand.

Date	Mintage	VG	F	VF	XF	Unc
1684	—	—	—	—	—	—

KM# 253.5 ECU

Silver **Ruler:** Louis XIV **Mint:** Rennes **Note:** Mint mark: Numeral 9.

Date	Mintage	VG	F	VF	XF	Unc
1683	—	350	775	1,500	3,200	—
1684	—	350	775	1,500	3,200	—
1685	—	400	900	1,700	3,600	—

KM# 255.1 ECU

Silver **Ruler:** Louis XIV **Obv:** Bust right with open throat and less draping **Mint:** Paris **Note:** Dav. #3809.

Date	Mintage	VG	F	VF	XF	Unc
1684A	—	1,050	1,950	3,600	6,200	—
1685A	—	975	1,750	3,300	5,500	—
1686A	—	725	1,300	2,600	4,900	—
1687A	—	1,050	1,950	3,600	6,200	—
1688A	—	1,300	2,600	4,600	7,500	—
1689A	—	1,050	1,950	3,600	6,200	—

KM# 255.2 ECU

Silver **Ruler:** Louis XIV **Mint:** Lyon

Date	Mintage	VG	F	VF	XF	Unc
1689D	—	1,150	2,150	4,100	6,800	—

KM# 255.3 ECU

Silver **Ruler:** Louis XIV **Mint:** Bordeaux

Date	Mintage	VG	F	VF	XF	Unc
1685K	—	—	—	—	—	—
1686K	—	—	—	—	—	—
1687K	—	—	—	—	—	—
1688K	—	1,150	2,150	4,100	6,800	—

KM# 255.4 ECU

Silver **Ruler:** Louis XIV **Mint:** Bayonne

Date	Mintage	VG	F	VF	XF	Unc
1685L	—	725	1,300	2,600	4,900	—
1686L	—	1,050	1,950	3,600	6,200	—
1687L	—	—	—	—	—	—
1688L	—	—	—	—	—	—
1689L	—	1,050	1,950	3,600	6,200	—

KM# 255.5 ECU

Silver **Ruler:** Louis XIV **Mint:** Amiens

Date	Mintage	VG	F	VF	XF	Unc
1685X	—	1,300	2,600	4,900	7,800	—

KM# 255.6 ECU

Silver **Ruler:** Louis XIV **Mint:** Aix **Note:** Mint mark: Ampersand.

Date	Mintage	VG	F	VF	XF	Unc
1687	—	—	—	—	—	—
1688	—	—	—	—	—	—
1689	—	1,350	2,550	4,700	8,100	—

KM# 255.7 ECU

Silver **Ruler:** Louis XIV **Mint:** Rennes **Note:** Mint mark: Numeral 9.

Date	Mintage	VG	F	VF	XF	Unc
1685	—	1,150	2,150	4,100	6,800	—
1686	—	1,050	1,950	3,600	6,200	—
1687	—	725	1,300	2,600	4,900	—
1688	—	—	—	—	—	—
1689	—	1,050	1,950	3,600	6,200	—

KM# 257.1 ECU

Silver **Ruler:** Louis XIV **Rev:** Crowned shield with arms of France and Old and New Burgundy **Mint:** Paris **Note:** Dav. #3810.

Date	Mintage	VG	F	VF	XF	Unc
1685A	—	650	1,250	2,500	5,000	—

KM# 257.2 ECU

Silver **Ruler:** Louis XIV **Mint:** Lille

Date	Mintage	VG	F	VF	XF	Unc
1686IL	—	650	1,250	2,500	5,000	—

KM# 257.3 ECU

Silver **Ruler:** Louis XIV **Mint:** Amiens

Date	Mintage	VG	F	VF	XF	Unc
1685X	—	1,000	2,000	3,000	5,500	—

KM# 275.1 ECU

Silver **Ruler:** Louis XIV **Obv:** Date below bust **Rev:** PD in center **Mint:** Paris **Note:** Values given for the Dav. #3811 issues are for examples struck over recalled Ecus. Clear examples of the new planchets command an average 20-30% premium. Dav. #3811.

Date	Mintage	VG	F	VF	XF	Unc
1690A	—	50.00	100	200	450	—
1691A	—	50.00	100	200	450	—
1692A	—	60.00	125	250	575	—
1693A	—	55.00	115	225	500	—

KM# 275.2 ECU

Silver **Ruler:** Louis XIV **Mint:** Rouen

Date	Mintage	VG	F	VF	XF	Unc
1690B	—	75.00	150	300	700	—
1691B	—	60.00	125	250	575	—
1692B	—	75.00	150	300	700	—
1693B	—	90.00	185	375	825	—

KM# 275.3 ECU

Silver **Ruler:** Louis XIV **Mint:** Lyon

Date	Mintage	VG	F	VF	XF	Unc
1690D	—	75.00	150	300	700	—
1691D	—	55.00	115	225	500	—
1692D	—	60.00	125	250	575	—
1693D	—	80.00	160	325	725	—

KM# 275.4 ECU

Silver **Ruler:** Louis XIV **Mint:** Tours

Date	Mintage	VG	F	VF	XF	Unc
1690E	—	55.00	115	225	425	—
1691E	—	60.00	125	250	475	—
1692E	—	75.00	150	300	575	—
1693E	—	—	—	—	—	—

KM# 275.5 ECU

Silver **Ruler:** Louis XIV **Mint:** Poitiers

Date	Mintage	VG	F	VF	XF	Unc
1690G	—	90.00	185	375	825	—
1691G	—	60.00	125	250	575	—
1692G	—	90.00	190	385	875	—

KM# 275.6 ECU

Silver **Ruler:** Louis XIV **Mint:** La Rochelle

Date	Mintage	VG	F	VF	XF	Unc
1690H	—	90.00	185	375	825	—
1691H	—	60.00	125	250	575	—
1692H	—	65.00	135	275	625	—
1693H	—	75.00	150	300	700	—

KM# 275.7 ECU

Silver **Ruler:** Louis XIV **Mint:** Limoges

Date	Mintage	VG	F	VF	XF	Unc
1690I	—	90.00	190	385	875	—
1691I	—	75.00	150	300	700	—
1692I	—	60.00	125	250	575	—
1693I	—	—	—	—	—	—

KM# 275.8 ECU

Silver **Ruler:** Louis XIV **Mint:** Bordeaux

Date	Mintage	VG	F	VF	XF	Unc
1690K	—	60.00	125	250	575	—
1691K	—	75.00	150	300	700	—
1692K	—	65.00	135	275	625	—
1693K	—	80.00	160	325	725	—

KM# 275.9 ECU

Silver **Ruler:** Louis XIV **Mint:** Bayonne

Date	Mintage	VG	F	VF	XF	Unc
1690L	—	60.00	125	250	575	—
1691L	—	75.00	150	300	700	—
1692L	—	90.00	190	385	875	—

KM# 275.10 ECU

Silver **Ruler:** Louis XIV **Mint:** Toulouse

Date	Mintage	VG	F	VF	XF	Unc
1690M	—	65.00	135	275	625	—
1691M	—	60.00	125	250	575	—
1692M	—	80.00	160	325	725	—
1693M	—	75.00	150	300	700	—

KM# 275.11 ECU

Silver **Ruler:** Louis XIV **Mint:** Montpellier

Date	Mintage	VG	F	VF	XF	Unc
1690N	—	60.00	125	250	575	—
1691N	—	55.00	115	225	500	—
1692N	—	75.00	150	300	700	—
1693N	—	90.00	190	385	875	—

KM# 275.12 ECU

Silver **Ruler:** Louis XIV **Mint:** Riom

Date	Mintage	VG	F	VF	XF	Unc
1691O	—	—	—	—	—	—
1692O	—	80.00	160	325	725	—
1693O	—	—	—	—	—	—

KM# 275.13 ECU

Silver **Ruler:** Louis XIV **Mint:** Dijon

Date	Mintage	VG	F	VF	XF	Unc
1690P	—	75.00	150	300	700	—
1691P	—	60.00	125	250	575	—
1692P	—	75.00	150	300	700	—
1693P	—	90.00	190	350	875	—

KM# 275.14 ECU

Silver **Ruler:** Louis XIV **Mint:** Reims

Date	Mintage	VG	F	VF	XF	Unc
1690S	—	55.00	115	225	500	—
1691S	—	55.00	115	225	500	—
1692S	—	75.00	150	300	700	—
1693S	—	—	—	—	—	—

KM# 275.15 ECU

Silver **Ruler:** Louis XIV **Mint:** Amiens

Date	Mintage	VG	F	VF	XF	Unc
1690X	—	50.00	100	200	450	—
1691X	—	55.00	115	225	500	—
1692X	—	65.00	135	275	625	—
1693X	—	75.00	150	300	700	—

KM# 275.16 ECU

Silver **Ruler:** Louis XIV **Mint:** Bourges

Date	Mintage	VG	F	VF	XF	Unc
1690Y	—	65.00	135	275	625	—
1691Y	—	75.00	150	300	700	—
1692Y	—	60.00	125	250	575	—
1693Y	—	75.00	150	300	700	—

KM# 275.17 ECU

Silver **Ruler:** Louis XIV **Mint:** Bayonne **Note:** Mint mark: Crowned L.

Date	Mintage	VG	F	VF	XF	Unc
1690	—	65.00	135	275	625	—
1691	—	65.00	135	275	625	—
1692	—	90.00	190	385	875	—

KM# 275.18 ECU

Silver **Ruler:** Louis XIV **Mint:** Metz **Note:** Mint mark: Crowned M.

Date	Mintage	VG	F	VF	XF	Unc
1690	—	65.00	135	275	625	—
1691	—	60.00	125	250	575	—
1693	—	90.00	190	385	875	—

KM# 275.19 ECU

Silver **Ruler:** Louis XIV **Mint:** Troyes **Note:** Mint mark: Crowned S.

Date	Mintage	VG	F	VF	XF	Unc
1690	—	60.00	125	250	575	—
1691	—	75.00	150	300	700	—

KM# 275.20 ECU

Silver **Ruler:** Louis XIV **Mint:** Aix **Note:** Mint mark: Ampersand.

Date	Mintage	VG	F	VF	XF	Unc
1690	—	60.00	125	250	575	—
1691	—	60.00	125	250	575	—
1692	—	65.00	135	275	625	—
1693	—	80.00	160	325	725	—

KM# 275.21 ECU

Silver **Ruler:** Louis XIV **Mint:** Rennes **Note:** Mint mark: Numeral 9.

Date	Mintage	VG	F	VF	XF	Unc
1690	—	55.00	115	225	500	—
1691	—	50.00	100	200	450	—
1692	—	60.00	125	250	575	—

KM# 276 ECU

Silver **Ruler:** Louis XIV **Mint:** Pau **Note:** Dav. #3812.

Date	Mintage	VG	F	VF	XF	Unc
1690	—	100	225	400	700	—
1691	—	125	250	450	800	—

KM# 298.1 ECU

Silver **Ruler:** Louis XIV **Obv:** Bust with square neckline **Rev:** Crowned round arms in palm sprays **Mint:** Paris

Note: Values given for the KM#298 issues are for examples struck over recalled ECU. Clear examples struck on new planchets command an average 20-30% premium. Dav. #3813.

Date	Mintage	VG	F	VF	XF	Unc
1693A	—	45.00	90.00	175	375	—
1694A	—	45.00	90.00	175	375	—
1695A	—	45.00	90.00	175	375	—
1696A	—	75.00	150	300	700	—
1697A	—	50.00	100	200	450	—
1698A	—	55.00	115	225	500	—
1699A	—	—	—	—	—	—
1700A	—	—	—	—	—	—

KM# 298.2 ECU

Silver **Ruler:** Louis XIV **Mint:** Metz

Date	Mintage	VG	F	VF	XF	Unc
1693AA	—	75.00	150	300	700	—
1694AA	—	55.00	115	225	500	—
1695AA	—	75.00	150	300	700	—
1696AA	—	—	—	—	—	—
1697AA	—	100	200	375	825	—
1699AA	—	—	—	—	—	—

KM# 298.3 ECU

Silver **Ruler:** Louis XIV **Mint:** Rouen

Date	Mintage	VG	F	VF	XF	Unc
1693B	—	75.00	150	300	700	—
1694B	—	55.00	115	225	500	—
1695B	—	75.00	150	300	700	—
1696B	—	75.00	150	300	700	—
1697B	—	90.00	185	375	825	—
1698B	—	65.00	135	275	625	—
1699B	—	75.00	150	300	700	—
1700B	—	—	—	—	—	—

KM# 298.4 ECU

Silver **Ruler:** Louis XIV **Mint:** Strasbourg

Date	Mintage	VG	F	VF	XF	Unc
1694BB	—	65.00	135	275	625	—
1695BB	—	90.00	185	375	825	—
1697BB	—	—	—	—	—	—

KM# 298.5 ECU

Silver **Ruler:** Louis XIV **Mint:** Caen

Date	Mintage	VG	F	VF	XF	Unc
1694C	—	75.00	150	300	875	—
1695C	—	100	225	425	1,200	—
1696C	—	—	—	—	—	—
1697C	—	75.00	150	300	875	—
1700C	—	—	—	—	—	—

KM# 298.7 ECU

Silver **Ruler:** Louis XIV **Mint:** Tours

Date	Mintage	VG	F	VF	XF	Unc
1693E	—	90.00	185	375	775	—
1694E	—	60.00	125	250	550	—
1695E	—	90.00	185	375	775	—
1696E	—	90.00	190	385	850	—
1698E	—	—	—	—	—	—
1699E	—	150	275	450	950	—

KM# 298.8 ECU

Silver **Ruler:** Louis XIV **Mint:** Poitiers

Date	Mintage	VG	F	VF	XF	Unc
1693G	—	75.00	150	300	700	—
1694G	—	75.00	150	300	700	—
1695G	—	90.00	185	375	825	—
1696G	—	75.00	150	300	700	—
1697G	—	175	325	550	1,150	—
1698G	—	125	250	450	1,000	—

KM# 298.10 ECU

Silver **Ruler:** Louis XIV **Mint:** Limoges

Date	Mintage	VG	F	VF	XF	Unc
1693I	—	65.00	135	275	625	—
1694I	—	75.00	150	300	700	—
1695I	—	75.00	150	300	700	—
1696I	—	125	250	450	1,000	—
1697I	—	—	—	—	—	—
1698I	—	90.00	190	385	875	—
1699I	—	—	—	—	—	—

KM# 298.11 ECU

Silver **Ruler:** Louis XIV **Mint:** Bordeaux

Date	Mintage	VG	F	VF	XF	Unc
1693K	—	75.00	150	300	700	—
1694K	—	55.00	115	225	500	—
1695K	—	75.00	150	300	700	—
1696K	—	90.00	185	375	825	—
1697K	—	100	225	425	950	—
1698K	—	55.00	115	225	500	—
1699K	—	90.00	190	385	875	—

KM# 298.14 ECU

Silver **Ruler:** Louis XIV **Mint:** Montpellier

Date	Mintage	VG	F	VF	XF	Unc
1693N	—	55.00	115	225	500	—
1694N	—	50.00	100	200	450	—
1695N	—	65.00	135	275	625	—
1696N	—	75.00	150	300	700	—
1697N	—	90.00	185	375	825	—
1698N	—	—	—	—	—	—
1699N	—	—	—	—	—	—

KM# 298.15 ECU

Silver **Ruler:** Louis XIV **Mint:** Riom

Date	Mintage	VG	F	VF	XF	Unc
1693O	—	65.00	135	275	625	—
1694O	—	75.00	150	300	700	—
1695O	—	90.00	185	375	825	—
1696O	—	90.00	190	385	875	—
1697O	—	125	250	450	1,000	—
1698O	—	—	—	—	—	—
1700O	—	—	—	—	—	—

KM# 298.16 ECU

Silver **Ruler:** Louis XIV **Mint:** Dijon

Date	Mintage	VG	F	VF	XF	Unc
1693P	—	60.00	125	250	575	—
1694P	—	60.00	125	250	575	—
1695P	—	90.00	185	375	825	—
1696P	—	—	—	—	—	—
1697P	—	90.00	190	385	875	—
1698P	—	—	—	—	—	—
1699P	—	—	—	—	—	—

KM# 298.17 ECU

Silver **Ruler:** Louis XIV **Mint:** Troyes

Date	Mintage	VG	F	VF	XF	Unc
1693S	—	60.00	125	250	575	—
1694S	—	65.00	135	275	625	—
1695S	—	90.00	185	375	825	—
1696S	—	100	225	425	950	—
1697S	—	—	—	—	—	—
1698S	—	—	—	—	—	—
1699S	—	—	—	—	—	—

KM# 298.18 ECU

Silver **Ruler:** Louis XIV **Mint:** Nantes

Date	Mintage	VG	F	VF	XF	Unc
1693T	—	—	—	—	—	—
1694T	—	65.00	135	275	625	—
1695T	—	75.00	150	300	700	—
1696T	—	100	225	425	950	—
1697T	—	90.00	185	375	825	—
1698T	—	65.00	135	275	625	—
1699T	—	125	250	450	1,000	—

KM# 298.19 ECU

Silver **Ruler:** Louis XIV **Mint:** Troyes

Date	Mintage	VG	F	VF	XF	Unc
1693V	—	65.00	135	275	625	—
1694V	—	60.00	125	250	575	—
1695V	—	90.00	185	375	825	—
1696V	—	90.00	185	375	825	—

KM# 298.20 ECU

Silver **Ruler:** Louis XIV **Mint:** Lille

Date	Mintage	VG	F	VF	XF	Unc
1693W	—	60.00	125	250	575	—
1694W	—	55.00	115	225	500	—
1695W	—	65.00	135	275	625	—
1696W	—	75.00	150	300	700	—
1697W	—	75.00	150	300	700	—
1698W	—	90.00	190	385	875	—
1699W	—	90.00	190	385	875	—

KM# 298.21 ECU

Silver **Ruler:** Louis XIV **Mint:** Amiens

Date	Mintage	VG	F	VF	XF	Unc
1693X	—	75.00	150	300	700	—
1694X	—	65.00	135	275	625	—
1695X	—	60.00	125	250	575	—
1696X	—	90.00	185	375	825	—
1697X	—	90.00	185	375	825	—
1698X	—	—	—	—	—	—
1699X	—	125	250	450	1,000	—
1700X	—	—	—	—	—	—

KM# 298.22 ECU

Silver **Ruler:** Louis XIV **Mint:** Bourges

Date	Mintage	VG	F	VF	XF	Unc
1693Y	—	65.00	135	275	625	—
1694Y	—	75.00	150	300	700	—
1695Y	—	90.00	190	385	875	—
1696Y	—	90.00	185	375	825	—

Date	Mintage	VG	F	VF	XF	Unc
1697Y	—	—	—	—	—	—
1698Y	—	—	—	—	—	—
1699Y	—	—	—	—	—	—

KM# 298.24 ECU
Silver **Ruler:** Louis XIV **Mint:** Rennes **Note:** Mint mark: Numeral 9.

Date	Mintage	VG	F	VF	XF	Unc
1693	—	60.00	125	250	575	—
1694	—	55.00	115	225	500	—
1695	—	60.00	125	250	575	—
1696	—	65.00	135	275	625	—
1697	—	60.00	125	250	575	—
1698	—	65.00	135	275	625	—
1699	—	—	—	—	—	—
1700	—	—	—	—	—	—

KM# 298.25 ECU
Silver **Ruler:** Louis XIV **Mint:** Metz **Note:** Mint mark: Crowned M.

Date	Mintage	VG	F	VF	XF	Unc
1693	—	90.00	185	375	825	—

KM# 298.26 ECU
Silver **Ruler:** Louis XIV **Mint:** Besancon **Note:** Mint mark: Back-to-back C's.

Date	Mintage	VG	F	VF	XF	Unc
1694	—	60.00	125	250	450	—
1695	—	90.00	190	385	700	—
1696	—	90.00	185	375	650	—
1697	—	90.00	190	385	700	—
1698	—	—	—	—	—	—
1699	—	—	—	—	—	—

KM# 299 ECU
Silver **Ruler:** Louis XIV **Rev:** Crowned round arms of France, Navarre and Bearn in palm sprays **Mint:** Pau **Note:** Dav. #3814.

Date	Mintage	VG	F	VF	XF	Unc
1693	—	900	2,000	5,500	10,000	—
1694	—	900	2,000	5,500	10,000	—
1695	—	1,200	2,600	6,000	11,500	—
1696	—	1,350	3,000	6,500	12,500	—
1697	—	—	—	—	—	—
1698	—	—	—	—	—	—
1699	—	—	—	—	—	—
1700	—	—	—	—	—	—

KM# 300 ECU
Silver **Ruler:** Louis XIV **Rev:** Crowned round arms of France, Navarre and Old and New Burgundy **Mint:** Lille **Note:** Dav. #3815.

Date	Mintage	VG	F	VF	XF	Unc
1693W	—	900	1,650	2,750	—	—
1694W	—	800	1,500	2,500	—	—
1695W	—	1,200	2,250	3,750	—	—
1696W	—	1,500	2,750	4,500	—	—
1697W	—	1,650	3,000	5,000	—	—
1698W	—	2,000	3,500	5,500	—	—
1699W	—	2,250	4,000	6,500	—	—
1700W	—	2,500	4,250	7,000	—	—

KM# 6 1/2 ECU D'OR
1.6700 g., 0.9580 Gold 0.0514 oz. AGW **Ruler:** Henry IV
Obv: Legend around crowned arms in beaded circle
Obv. Legend: HENRICVX... **Rev:** H's and two fleur-de-lis in angles of cross fleuree **Note:** Various mint marks.

Date	Mintage	VG	F	VF	XF	Unc
1601-03 Rare	—	—	—	—	—	—

KM# 6.2 1/2 ECU D'OR
1.6750 g., 0.9580 Gold 0.0516 oz. AGW **Ruler:** Henry IV **Obv:** Crowned arms within inner beaded circle **Obv. Legend:** HENRICVS • IIII • D : G • FRAN • ET • NAVA • REX **Rev:** Cross fleuree in inner beaded circle **Rev. Legend:** + CHRS • VINCIT• CHRS • REGNAT • CHRS • IMP • **Edge:** Plain **Mint:** Saint Lô **Note:** Fr. #397.

Date	Mintage	Good	VG	F	VF	XF
1601C Rare	—	—	—	—	—	—
1603C Rare	—	—	—	—	—	—

KM# 7 1/2 ECU D'OR
1.6700 g., 0.9580 Gold 0.0514 oz. AGW **Ruler:** Henry IV
Obv: Legend around crowned arms **Obv. Legend:** HENRICVS...
Rev: Cross fleuree with H below each fleur-de-lis

Date	Mintage	VG	F	VF	XF	Unc
1601-03	—	600	1,100	1,600	4,500	—

KM# 7.4 1/2 ECU D'OR
1.6750 g., 0.9580 Gold 0.0516 oz. AGW **Ruler:** Henry IV
Obv: Crowned arms; legend begins at upper right **Obv. Legend:** * HENRICVS • IIII • D • G • FRAM • ET • NA • REX **Rev:** Cross fleuree with H below each lis **Rev. Legend:** + CHRISTVS • REGNAT • VINCIT • ET • IMPERAT • **Edge:** Plain **Mint:** Troyes

Date	Mintage	Good	VG	F	VF	XF
1603V	—	—	—	—	—	—

Note: Reported, not confirmed

KM# 7.5 1/2 ECU D'OR
1.6750 g., 0.9580 Gold 0.0516 oz. AGW **Ruler:** Henry IV
Obv: Crowned arms; legend begins at upper right **Obv. Legend:** * HENRICVS • IIII • D • G • FRAM • ET • NA • REX **Rev:** Cross fleuree with H below each lis **Rev. Legend:** Latin cross CHRISTVS • REGNAT • VINCIT • ET • IMPERAT • **Edge:** Plain **Mint:** Rennes **Note:** Mint mark is "9".

Date	Mintage	Good	VG	F	VF	XF
1601	—	—	600	1,100	1,800	5,000
1602	—	—	600	1,100	1,800	5,000
1603	—	—	600	1,100	1,800	5,000

KM# 8 1/2 ECU D'OR
1.6700 g., 0.9580 Gold 0.0514 oz. AGW **Ruler:** Henry IV
Obv: Crowned arms with legend around **Obv. Legend:** HENRICVS... **Rev:** Lobed and cross fleuree

Date	Mintage	VG	F	VF	XF	Unc
1601-10	—	600	1,000	1,500	3,200	—

KM# 8.1 1/2 ECU D'OR
1.6750 g., 0.9580 Gold 0.0516 oz. AGW **Ruler:** Henry IV
Obv: Crowned arms; legend begins at lower left **Obv. Legend:** * HENRICVS • IIII • D • G • FRAN • ET • NA • REX **Rev:** Lobed, floriated cross **Rev. Legend:** + CHRISTVS • REGNAT • VINCIT • ET • IMPERAT • **Edge:** Plain **Mint:** Paris

Date	Mintage	Good	VG	F	VF	XF
1601A	—	—	600	1,000	1,500	3,200
1602A	—	—	600	1,000	1,500	3,200
1603A	—	—	600	1,000	1,500	3,200
1604A	—	—	600	1,000	1,500	3,200
1605A	—	—	600	1,000	1,500	3,200
1606A	—	—	600	1,000	1,500	3,200
1607A	—	—	600	1,000	1,500	3,200
1608A	—	—	600	1,000	1,500	3,200
1609A	—	—	600	1,000	1,500	3,200
1610A	—	—	600	1,000	1,500	3,200

KM# 8.2 1/2 ECU D'OR
1.6750 g., 0.9580 Gold 0.0516 oz. AGW **Ruler:** Henry IV
Obv: Crowned arms; legend begins at lower left **Obv. Legend:** * HENRICVS • IIII • D • G • FRAN • ET • NA • REX **Rev:** Lobed, floriated cross **Rev. Legend:** + CHRISTVS • REGNAT • VINCIT • ET • IMPERAT • **Edge:** Plain **Mint:** Rouen

Date	Mintage	Good	VG	F	VF	XF
1607B	—	—	600	1,000	1,500	3,200
1608B	—	—	600	1,000	1,500	3,200
1609B	—	—	600	1,000	1,500	3,200
1610B	—	—	600	1,000	1,500	3,200

KM# 8.5 1/2 ECU D'OR
1.6750 g., 0.9580 Gold 0.0516 oz. AGW **Ruler:** Henry IV
Obv: Crowned arms; legend begins at lower left **Obv. Legend:** * HENRICVS • IIII • D • G • FRAN • ET • NA • REX **Rev:** Lobed, floriated cross **Rev. Legend:** + CHRISTVS • REGNAT • VINCIT • ET • IMPERAT • **Edge:** Plain **Mint:** La Rochelle

Date	Mintage	Good	VG	F	VF	XF
1605H	—	—	600	1,000	1,500	3,200

KM# 8.6 1/2 ECU D'OR
1.6750 g., 0.9580 Gold 0.0516 oz. AGW **Ruler:** Henry IV
Obv: Crowned arms; legend begins at lower left **Obv. Legend:** * HENRICVS • IIII • D • G • FRAN • ET • NA • REX **Rev:** Lobed, floriated cross **Rev. Legend:** Latin cross CHRISTVS • REGNAT • VINCIT • ET • IMPERAT • **Edge:** Plain **Mint:** Bordeaux

Date	Mintage	Good	VG	F	VF	XF
1607K	—	—	—	—	—	—

KM# 8.10 1/2 ECU D'OR
1.6750 g., 0.9580 Gold 0.0516 oz. AGW **Ruler:** Henry IV
Obv: Crowned arms; legend begins at lower left **Obv. Legend:** * HENRICVS • IIII • D • G • FRAN • ET • NA • REX **Rev:** Lobed, floriated cross **Rev. Legend:** + CHRISTVS • REGNAT • VINCIT • ET • IMPERAT • **Edge:** Plain **Mint:** Amiens

Date	Mintage	Good	VG	F	VF	XF
1604X	—	—	600	1,000	1,500	3,200

KM# 40.1 1/2 ECU D'OR
1.6700 g., 0.9580 Gold 0.0514 oz. AGW **Ruler:** Louis XIII
Obv: Legend around border, starting at upper right
Obv. Legend: LVDOVICVS XIII... **Mint:** Paris

Date	Mintage	VG	F	VF	XF	Unc
1610A	—	—	—	—	—	—
1611A	—	—	—	—	—	—
1613A	—	300	550	1,000	2,100	—
1614A	—	275	450	950	2,100	—
1615A	—	275	450	950	2,100	—
1618A	—	—	—	—	—	—
1619A	—	300	550	1,000	2,100	—
1620A	—	300	550	1,000	2,100	—
1621A	—	300	550	1,000	2,100	—
1622A	—	300	550	1,000	2,100	—
1623A	—	300	550	1,000	2,100	—
1624A	—	300	550	1,000	2,100	—
1625A	—	300	550	1,000	2,100	—
1626A	—	300	550	1,000	2,100	—
1627A	—	300	550	1,000	2,100	—
1628A	—	300	550	1,000	2,100	—
1629A	—	300	550	1,000	2,100	—
1630A	—	300	550	1,000	2,100	—
1631A	—	—	—	—	—	—
1632A	—	—	—	—	—	—
1633A	—	300	550	1,000	2,100	—
1634A	—	—	—	—	—	—
1635A	—	—	—	—	—	—
1636A	—	—	—	—	—	—
1637A	—	—	—	—	—	—
1638A	—	300	550	1,000	2,100	—
1643A	—	—	—	—	—	—

KM# 40.2 1/2 ECU D'OR
1.6700 g., 0.9580 Gold 0.0514 oz. AGW **Ruler:** Louis XIII
Mint: Arras

Date	Mintage	VG	F	VF	XF	Unc
1641AR Rare	—	—	—	—	—	—
1642AR Rare	—	—	—	—	—	—
1643AR Rare	—	—	—	—	—	—

KM# 40.3 1/2 ECU D'OR
1.6700 g., 0.9580 Gold 0.0514 oz. AGW **Ruler:** Louis XIII
Mint: Rouen

Date	Mintage	VG	F	VF	XF	Unc
1612B Rare	—	—	—	—	—	—
1613B Rare	—	—	—	—	—	—
1614B Rare	—	—	—	—	—	—
1615B	—	275	450	950	2,000	—
1616B	—	300	550	1,000	2,000	—
1619B Rare	—	—	—	—	—	—
1624B Rare	—	—	—	—	—	—
1627B Rare	—	—	—	—	—	—
1628B Rare	—	—	—	—	—	—
1632B	—	300	550	1,000	2,000	—
1634B Rare	—	—	—	—	—	—
1635B Rare	—	—	—	—	—	—

KM# 40.4 1/2 ECU D'OR
1.6700 g., 0.9580 Gold 0.0514 oz. AGW **Ruler:** Louis XIII
Mint: Saint Lô

Date	Mintage	VG	F	VF	XF	Unc
1615C Rare	—	—	—	—	—	—
1616C Rare	—	—	—	—	—	—
1628C Rare	—	—	—	—	—	—
1635C Rare	—	—	—	—	—	—

KM# 40.5 1/2 ECU D'OR
1.6700 g., 0.9580 Gold 0.0514 oz. AGW **Ruler:** Louis XIII
Mint: Lyon

Date	Mintage	VG	F	VF	XF	Unc
1625D Rare	—	—	—	—	—	—
1629D	—	300	550	1,000	2,000	—
1630D	—	300	550	1,000	2,000	—
1632D Rare	—	—	—	—	—	—
1638D Rare	—	—	—	—	—	—

KM# 40.6 1/2 ECU D'OR
1.6700 g., 0.9580 Gold 0.0514 oz. AGW **Ruler:** Louis XIII
Mint: Tours

Date	Mintage	VG	F	VF	XF	Unc
1616E	—	300	550	1,000	2,000	—

KM# 40.7 1/2 ECU D'OR
1.6700 g., 0.9580 Gold 0.0514 oz. AGW **Ruler:** Louis XIII
Mint: Angers

Date	Mintage	VG	F	VF	XF	Unc
1631F Rare	—	—	—	—	—	—

KM# 40.8 1/2 ECU D'OR
1.6700 g., 0.9580 Gold 0.0514 oz. AGW **Ruler:** Louis XIII
Mint: La Rochelle

Date	Mintage	VG	F	VF	XF	Unc
1633H	—	300	550	1,000	2,000	—
1637H	—	300	550	1,000	2,000	—

KM# 40.9 1/2 ECU D'OR
1.6700 g., 0.9580 Gold 0.0514 oz. AGW **Ruler:** Louis XIII
Mint: Limoges

Date	Mintage	VG	F	VF	XF	Unc
1632I Rare	—	—	—	—	—	—
1642I Rare	—	—	—	—	—	—

KM# 40.10 1/2 ECU D'OR
1.6700 g., 0.9580 Gold 0.0514 oz. AGW **Ruler:** Louis XIII
Mint: Bordeaux

Date	Mintage	VG	F	VF	XF	Unc
1611K	—	300	550	1,000	2,000	—
1629K Rare	—	—	—	—	—	—
1630K	—	300	550	1,000	2,000	—
Note: 1630 dates exist with inner circle on both sides						
1633K Rare	—	—	—	—	—	—
1638K Rare	—	—	—	—	—	—

KM# 40.11 1/2 ECU D'OR
1.6700 g., 0.9580 Gold 0.0514 oz. AGW **Ruler:** Louis XIII
Mint: Toulouse

Date	Mintage	VG	F	VF	XF	Unc
1614M	—	300	550	1,000	2,000	—
1632M Rare	—	—	—	—	—	—
1633M	—	300	550	1,000	2,000	—
1634M Rare	—	—	—	—	—	—
1635M Rare	—	—	—	—	—	—
1636M Rare	—	—	—	—	—	—
1637M Rare	—	—	—	—	—	—
1640M Rare	—	—	—	—	—	—
1642M Rare	—	—	—	—	—	—
1643M	—	300	550	1,000	2,000	—

KM# 40.12 1/2 ECU D'OR
1.6700 g., 0.9580 Gold 0.0514 oz. AGW **Ruler:** Louis XIII
Mint: Montpellier

Date	Mintage	VG	F	VF	XF	Unc
1636N	—	300	550	1,000	2,000	—
1639N	—	300	550	1,000	2,000	—
1640N Rare	—	—	—	—	—	—

KM# 40.13 1/2 ECU D'OR
1.6700 g., 0.9580 Gold 0.0514 oz. AGW **Ruler:** Louis XIII
Mint: Dijon

Date	Mintage	VG	F	VF	XF	Unc
1637P Rare	—	—	—	—	—	—
1639P Rare	—	—	—	—	—	—
1640P Rare	—	—	—	—	—	—

KM# 40.14 1/2 ECU D'OR
1.6700 g., 0.9580 Gold 0.0514 oz. AGW **Ruler:** Louis XIII
Mint: Troyes

Date	Mintage	VG	F	VF	XF	Unc
1613S	—	300	550	1,000	2,000	—
1615S	—	300	550	1,000	2,000	—
1631S	—	300	550	1,000	2,000	—
1635S	—	300	550	1,000	2,000	—

KM# 40.15 1/2 ECU D'OR
1.6700 g., 0.9580 Gold 0.0514 oz. AGW **Ruler:** Louis XIII
Mint: Amiens

Date	Mintage	VG	F	VF	XF	Unc
1615X	—	300	550	1,000	2,000	—
1631X Rare	—	—	—	—	—	—
1633X	—	300	550	1,000	2,000	—
1634X	—	300	550	1,000	2,000	—
1635X	—	275	450	950	2,000	—
1636X	—	300	550	1,000	2,000	—
1637X	—	275	450	950	2,000	—
1638X	—	300	550	1,000	2,000	—
1640X	—	300	550	1,000	2,000	—
1641X	—	300	550	1,000	2,000	—
1642X Rare	—	—	—	—	—	—
1643X Rare	—	—	—	—	—	—

KM# 40.16 1/2 ECU D'OR
1.6700 g., 0.9580 Gold 0.0514 oz. AGW **Ruler:** Louis XIII
Mint: Aix **Note:** Mint mark: Ampersand.

Date	Mintage	VG	F	VF	XF	Unc
1637 Rare	—	—	—	—	—	—
1638 Rare	—	—	—	—	—	—

KM# 54 1/2 ECU D'OR
1.6700 g., 0.9580 Gold 0.0514 oz. AGW **Ruler:** Louis XIII
Obv: Legend begins at lower left **Mint:** Rouen **Note:** Inner beaded circle on both sides

Date	Mintage	VG	F	VF	XF	Unc
1615B	—	—	—	—	—	—

KM# 56 1/2 ECU D'OR
1.6700 g., 0.9580 Gold 0.0514 oz. AGW **Ruler:** Louis XIII
Obv: Legend begins at lower left **Mint:** Paris

Date	Mintage	VG	F	VF	XF	Unc
1616A	—	300	550	1,000	2,000	—

KM# 62 1/2 ECU D'OR
1.6700 g., 0.9580 Gold 0.0514 oz. AGW **Ruler:** Louis XIII **Obv:** Mint mark below arms **Rev:** Dot at center of cross **Mint:** Amiens

Date	Mintage	VG	F	VF	XF	Unc
1618X	—	300	550	1,000	2,000	—

KM# 122 1/2 ECU D'OR
1.6700 g., 0.9580 Gold 0.0514 oz. AGW **Ruler:** Louis XIII **Obv:** Arms of France and Dauphine in inner circle **Note:** Mint mark: Anchor.

Date	Mintage	VG	F	VF	XF	Unc
1641	—	2,500	5,000	8,500	15,000	—

KM# 145.1 1/2 ECU D'OR
1.6700 g., 0.9580 Gold 0.0514 oz. AGW **Ruler:** Louis XIII
Obv: Crowned arms around border starting at upper right
Obv. Legend: LVDOVICVS XIIII... **Rev:** Ornamented and lobed cross, mint mark at center, legend around border **Mint:** Paris

Date	Mintage	VG	F	VF	XF	Unc
1643A	—	2,000	3,500	4,500	8,000	—
1645A	—	2,000	3,500	4,500	8,000	—
1647A Rare	—	—	—	—	—	—
1648A Rare	—	—	—	—	—	—
1650A Rare	—	—	—	—	—	—
1654A Rare	—	—	—	—	—	—

KM# 145.2 1/2 ECU D'OR
1.6700 g., 0.9580 Gold 0.0514 oz. AGW **Ruler:** Louis XIII
Mint: Arras

Date	Mintage	VG	F	VF	XF	Unc
1644AR Rare	—	—	—	—	—	—

KM# 145.3 1/2 ECU D'OR
1.6700 g., 0.9580 Gold 0.0514 oz. AGW **Ruler:** Louis XIII
Mint: Bordeaux

Date	Mintage	VG	F	VF	XF	Unc
1644K Rare	—	—	—	—	—	—
1645K Rare	—	—	—	—	—	—

KM# 145.4 1/2 ECU D'OR
1.6700 g., 0.9580 Gold 0.0514 oz. AGW **Ruler:** Louis XIII
Mint: Toulouse

Date	Mintage	VG	F	VF	XF	Unc
1644M Rare	—	—	—	—	—	—
1646M Rare	—	—	—	—	—	—

KM# 145.5 1/2 ECU D'OR
1.6700 g., 0.9580 Gold 0.0514 oz. AGW **Ruler:** Louis XIII
Mint: Amiens

Date	Mintage	VG	F	VF	XF	Unc
1644X Rare	—	—	—	—	—	—
1645X Rare	—	—	—	—	—	—
1647X	—	1,500	3,100	3,700	6,800	—

KM# 9.2 ECU D'OR
3.3500 g., 0.9580 Gold 0.1032 oz. AGW **Ruler:** Henry IV **Obv:** Crowned arms within inner beaded circle **Obv. Legend:** HENRICVS • IIII • D : G • FRAN • ET • NAVA • REX **Rev:** Cross fleuree in inner beaded circle **Rev. Legend:** + CHRS • VINCIT • CHRS • REGNAT • CHRS • IMP • **Edge:** Plain **Mint:** Saint Lô **Note:** Fr. #396.

Date	Mintage	Good	VG	F	VF	XF
1601C	—	—	1,500	2,800	4,500	7,500
1602C	—	—	1,500	2,800	4,500	7,500
1603C	—	—	1,500	2,800	4,500	7,500
1610C	—	—	1,500	2,800	4,500	7,500

KM# 9.3 ECU D'OR
3.3500 g., 0.9580 Gold 0.1032 oz. AGW **Ruler:** Henry IV
Obv: Legend around crowned arms in beaded circle
Obv. Legend: HENRICVS... **Rev:** H's and two lis in angles of cross fleuree **Note:** Various mint marks.

Date	Mintage	VG	F	VF	XF	Unc
1601-03	—	1,500	2,800	4,500	7,500	—

KM# 10.2 ECU D'OR
3.3500 g., 0.9580 Gold 0.1032 oz. AGW **Ruler:** Henry IV
Obv: Crowned arms; legend begins at upper right **Obv. Legend:** * HENRICVS • IIII • D • G • FRAN • ET • NA • REX **Rev:** Cross fleuree with H below each lis **Rev. Legend:** + CHRISTVS • REGNAT • VINCIT • ET • IMPERAT • **Edge:** Plain **Mint:** Tours

Date	Mintage	Good	VG	F	VF	XF
1602E	—	—	900	1,650	3,000	5,300
1604E	—	—	900	1,650	3,000	5,300

KM# 10.4 ECU D'OR
3.3500 g., 0.9580 Gold 0.1032 oz. AGW **Ruler:** Henry IV
Obv: Crowned arms; legend begins at upper right **Obv. Legend:** * HENRICVS • IIII • D • G • FRAN • ET • NA • REX **Rev:** Cross fleuree with H below each lis **Rev. Legend:** + CHRISTVS • REGNAT • VINCIT • ET • IMPERAT • **Edge:** Plain **Mint:** Troyes

Date	Mintage	Good	VG	F	VF	XF
1601V	—	—	900	1,650	3,000	4,800
1602V	—	—	900	1,650	3,000	4,800
1603V	—	—	900	1,650	3,000	4,800

KM# 10.5 ECU D'OR
3.3500 g., 0.9580 Gold 0.1032 oz. AGW **Ruler:** Henry IV
Obv: Crowned arms; legend begins at upper right **Obv. Legend:** * HENRICVS • IIII • D • G • FRAN • ET • NA • REX **Rev:** Cross fleuree with H below each lis **Rev. Legend:** + CHRISTVS • REGNAT • VINCIT • ET • IMPERAT • **Edge:** Plain **Mint:** Rennes
Note: Mint mark "9" (for Rennes mint).

Date	Mintage	Good	VG	F	VF	XF
16009	—	—	900	1,650	3,000	5,300
1601	—	—	900	1,650	3,000	5,300
1602	—	—	900	1,650	3,000	5,300
1603	—	—	900	1,650	3,000	5,300

KM# 10.6 ECU D'OR
3.3500 g., 0.9580 Gold 0.1032 oz. AGW **Ruler:** Henry IV
Obv: Legend around crowned arms **Obv. Legend:** HENRICVS...
Rev: Cross fleuree with H below each lis

Date	Mintage	VG	F	VF	XF	Unc
1601-03	—	900	1,650	3,000	4,800	—

KM# 11 ECU D'OR
3.3500 g., 0.9580 Gold 0.1032 oz. AGW **Ruler:** Louis XIII
Obv: Legend around crowned arms at lower left **Obv. Legend:** HENRICVS... **Rev:** Lobed and cross fleuree

Date	Mintage	VG	F	VF	XF	Unc
1601-10	—	550	900	1,400	2,800	—

KM# 11.1 ECU D'OR
3.3500 g., 0.9580 Gold 0.1032 oz. AGW **Ruler:** Henry IV **Obv:** Crowned arms; legend begins at lower left **Obv. Legend:** * HENRICVS • IIII • D • G • FRAN • ET • NA • REX **Rev:** Lobed, floriated cross **Rev. Legend:** + CHRISTVS • REGNAT • VINCIT • ET • IMPERAT • **Edge:** Plain **Mint:** Paris **Note:** Fr. #392.

Date	Mintage	Good	VG	F	VF	XF
1601A	—	—	825	1,350	2,100	4,200
1602A	—	—	825	1,350	2,100	4,200
1603A	—	—	825	1,350	2,100	4,200
1604A	—	—	825	1,350	2,100	4,200
1605A	—	—	825	1,350	2,100	4,200
1606A	—	—	825	1,350	2,100	4,200
1607A	—	—	825	1,350	2,100	4,200
1608A	—	—	825	1,350	2,100	4,200
1609A	—	—	825	1,350	2,100	4,200
1610A	—	—	825	1,350	2,100	4,200

KM# 11.2 ECU D'OR
3.3500 g., 0.9580 Gold 0.1032 oz. AGW **Ruler:** Henry IV
Obv: Crowned arms; legend begins at lower left **Obv. Legend:** * HENRICVS • IIII • D • G • FRAN • ET • NA • REX **Rev:** Lobed, floriated cross **Rev. Legend:** + CHRISTVS • REGNAT • VINCIT • ET • IMPERAT • **Edge:** Plain **Mint:** Rouen

Date	Mintage	Good	VG	F	VF	XF
1607B	—	—	825	1,350	2,100	4,200
1608B	—	—	825	1,350	2,100	4,200
1609B	—	—	825	1,350	2,100	4,200
1610B	—	—	825	1,350	2,100	4,200

KM# 11.5 ECU D'OR
3.3500 g., 0.9580 Gold 0.1032 oz. AGW **Ruler:** Henry IV
Obv: Crowned arms; legend begins at lower left **Obv. Legend:** * HENRICVS • IIII • D • G • FRAN • ET • NA • REX **Rev:** Lobed, floriated cross **Rev. Legend:** + CHRISTVS • REGNAT • VINCIT • ET • IMPERAT • **Edge:** Plain **Mint:** La Rochelle

Date	Mintage	Good	VG	F	VF	XF
1601H	—	—	825	1,350	2,100	4,200
1605H	—	—	825	1,350	2,100	4,200

KM# 11.7 ECU D'OR
3.3500 g., 0.9580 Gold 0.1032 oz. AGW **Ruler:** Henry IV
Obv: Crowned arms; legend begins at lower left **Obv. Legend:** * HENRICVS • IIII • D • G • FRAN • ET • NA • REX **Rev:** Lobed, floriated cross **Rev. Legend:** + CHRISTVS • REGNAT • VINCIT • ET • IMPERAT • **Edge:** Plain **Mint:** Bordeaux

Date	Mintage	Good	VG	F	VF	XF
1602K	—	—	825	1,350	2,100	4,200
1607K	—	—	825	1,350	2,100	4,200

KM# 11.11 ECU D'OR
3.3500 g., 0.9580 Gold 0.1032 oz. AGW **Ruler:** Henry IV
Obv: Crowned arms; legend begins at lower left **Obv. Legend:** * HENRICVS • IIII • D • G • FRAN • ET • NA • REX **Rev:** Lobed, floriated cross **Rev. Legend:** + CHRISTVS • REGNAT • VINCIT • ET • IMPERAT • **Edge:** Plain **Mint:** Amiens

Date	Mintage	Good	VG	F	VF	XF
1604X	—	—	825	1,350	2,100	4,200

KM# 12 ECU D'OR
3.3500 g., 0.9580 Gold 0.1032 oz. AGW **Ruler:** Louis XIII
Obv: Legend at upper right **Obv. Legend:** HENRICVS...

Date	Mintage	VG	F	VF	XF	Unc
1601-10	—	825	1,350	2,100	4,200	—

KM# 41.1 ECU D'OR
3.3500 g., 0.9580 Gold 0.1032 oz. AGW **Ruler:** Louis XIII **Obv:** Legend at upper right **Obv. Legend:** LVDOVICVS XIII... **Mint:** Paris

Date	Mintage	VG	F	VF	XF	Unc
1610A	—	300	525	675	1,350	—
1611A	—	300	525	675	1,350	—
1612A	—	300	525	675	1,350	—
1613A	—	300	525	675	1,350	—
1614A	—	300	525	675	1,350	—
1615A	—	300	525	675	1,350	—
1616A	—	300	525	675	1,350	—
1617A	—	300	525	675	1,350	—
1618A Rare	—	—	—	—	—	—
1619A Rare	—	—	—	—	—	—
1620A Rare	—	—	—	—	—	—
1621A	—	325	550	725	1,400	—
1622A Rare	—	—	—	—	—	—
1623A	—	300	525	675	1,350	—
1624A Rare	—	—	—	—	—	—
1625A	—	300	525	675	1,350	—
1626A	—	300	525	675	1,350	—
1627A	—	300	525	675	1,350	—
1628A	—	300	525	675	1,350	—
1629A	—	300	525	675	1,350	—
1630A	—	300	525	675	1,350	—
1631A	—	300	525	675	1,350	—
1632A Rare	—	—	—	—	—	—
1633A	—	300	525	675	1,350	—
1634A	—	300	525	675	1,350	—
1635A	—	300	525	675	1,350	—
1636A	—	300	525	675	1,350	—
1637A	—	300	525	675	1,350	—
1638A	—	300	525	675	1,350	—
1639A	—	300	525	675	1,350	—
1640A	—	350	600	825	1,450	—
1641A	—	350	600	825	1,450	—
1642A	—	300	525	675	1,350	—
1643A	—	300	525	675	1,350	—

KM# 41.2 ECU D'OR
3.3500 g., 0.9580 Gold 0.1032 oz. AGW **Ruler:** Louis XIII
Mint: Arras

Date	Mintage	VG	F	VF	XF	Unc
1641AR	—	375	650	1,150	1,950	—
1642AR Rare	—	—	—	—	—	—
1643AR Rare	—	—	—	—	—	—
1644AR engraving error	—	450	725	1,300	2,100	—
1645AR engraving error	—	450	725	1,300	2,100	—

KM# 41.3 ECU D'OR
3.3500 g., 0.9580 Gold 0.1032 oz. AGW **Ruler:** Louis XIII
Mint: Saint Lô

Date	Mintage	VG	F	VF	XF	Unc
1610C Rare	—	—	—	—	—	—
1612C Rare	—	—	—	—	—	—
1613C Rare	—	—	—	—	—	—
1615C	—	425	600	900	1,500	—
1616C Rare	—	—	—	—	—	—
1618C Rare	—	—	—	—	—	—
1620C Rare	—	—	—	—	—	—
1628C Rare	—	—	—	—	—	—
1632C Rare	—	—	—	—	—	—
1633C Rare	—	—	—	—	—	—
1634C Rare	—	—	—	—	—	—
1635C	—	350	600	825	1,450	—
1636C Rare	—	—	—	—	—	—
1637C	—	300	525	675	1,350	—
1638C	—	300	525	675	1,350	—
1639C Rare	—	—	—	—	—	—
1640C Rare	—	—	—	—	—	—
1641C	—	350	600	825	1,450	—
1642C Rare	—	—	—	—	—	—
1643C Rare	—	—	—	—	—	—

KM# 41.4 ECU D'OR
3.3500 g., 0.9580 Gold 0.1032 oz. AGW **Ruler:** Louis XIII
Mint: Lyon

Date	Mintage	VG	F	VF	XF	Unc
1616D	—	300	525	675	1,350	—
1624D Rare	—	—	—	—	—	—
1627D Rare	—	—	—	—	—	—
1629D	—	300	525	675	1,350	—
1630D Rare	—	—	—	—	—	—
1631D Rare	—	—	—	—	—	—
1632D Rare	—	—	—	—	—	—
1633D Rare	—	—	—	—	—	—
1635D Rare	—	—	—	—	—	—
1636D Rare	—	—	—	—	—	—
1637D	—	300	525	675	1,350	—
1638D	—	300	525	675	1,350	—
1639D	—	300	525	675	1,350	—
1640D	—	300	525	675	1,350	—
1641D	—	300	525	725	1,450	—
1642D Rare	—	—	—	—	—	—
1643D Rare	—	—	—	—	—	—

KM# 41.5 ECU D'OR
3.3500 g., 0.9580 Gold 0.1032 oz. AGW **Ruler:** Louis XIII
Mint: Tours

Date	Mintage	VG	F	VF	XF	Unc
1615E Rare	4,078	—	—	—	—	—
1618E Rare	—	—	—	—	—	—
1619E Rare	—	—	—	—	—	—
1641E Rare	—	—	—	—	—	—
1642E Rare	—	—	—	—	—	—
1643E Rare	—	—	—	—	—	—

KM# 41.6 ECU D'OR
3.3500 g., 0.9580 Gold 0.1032 oz. AGW **Ruler:** Louis XIII
Mint: Angers

Date	Mintage	VG	F	VF	XF	Unc
1631F Rare	—	—	—	—	—	—
1632F Rare	—	—	—	—	—	—
1641F Rare	—	—	—	—	—	—
1642F Rare	—	—	—	—	—	—
1643F Rare	—	—	—	—	—	—

KM# 41.7 ECU D'OR
3.3500 g., 0.9580 Gold 0.1032 oz. AGW **Ruler:** Louis XIII
Mint: Poitiers

Date	Mintage	VG	F	VF	XF	Unc
1642G	—	350	600	825	1,450	—
1643G Rare	—	—	—	—	—	—

KM# 41.8 ECU D'OR
3.3500 g., 0.9580 Gold 0.1032 oz. AGW **Ruler:** Louis XIII
Mint: La Rochelle

Date	Mintage	VG	F	VF	XF	Unc
1641H	—	350	600	825	1,450	—
1642H Rare	—	—	—	—	—	—
1643H Rare	—	—	—	—	—	—

KM# 41.9 ECU D'OR
3.3500 g., 0.9580 Gold 0.1032 oz. AGW **Ruler:** Louis XIII
Mint: Limoges

Date	Mintage	VG	F	VF	XF	Unc
1630I Rare	—	—	—	—	—	—
1631I	—	375	650	900	1,500	—
1632I Rare	—	—	—	—	—	—
1641I Rare	—	—	—	—	—	—
1642I Rare	—	—	—	—	—	—
1643I Rare	—	—	—	—	—	—

KM# 41.10 ECU D'OR
3.3500 g., 0.9580 Gold 0.1032 oz. AGW **Ruler:** Louis XIII
Mint: Bordeaux

Date	Mintage	VG	F	VF	XF	Unc
1611	—	—	—	—	—	—
1630	—	—	—	—	—	—
1631K Rare	—	—	—	—	—	—
1632K Rare	1,500	—	—	—	—	—
1633K Rare	—	—	—	—	—	—
1638K Rare	—	—	—	—	—	—
1639K	—	300	575	750	1,450	—
1640K	—	300	525	675	1,350	—
1642K	—	350	600	825	1,450	—
1643K	—	350	600	825	1,450	—

KM# 41.11 ECU D'OR
3.3500 g., 0.9580 Gold 0.1032 oz. AGW **Ruler:** Louis XIII
Mint: Bayonne

Date	Mintage	VG	F	VF	XF	Unc
1632L	—	450	725	975	1,650	—
1633L	—	350	600	825	1,450	—
1635L Rare	—	—	—	—	—	—
1636L Rare	—	—	—	—	—	—
1637L	—	300	525	675	1,350	—
1642L Rare	—	—	—	—	—	—
1643L Rare	—	—	—	—	—	—

KM# 41.12 ECU D'OR
3.3500 g., 0.9580 Gold 0.1032 oz. AGW **Ruler:** Louis XIII
Mint: Toulouse

Date	Mintage	VG	F	VF	XF	Unc
1632M	—	—	—	—	—	—
1633M	—	—	—	—	—	—
1634M	—	300	525	675	1,350	—
1635M	—	—	—	—	—	—
1636M Rare	—	—	—	—	—	—
1637M Rare	—	—	—	—	—	—
1638M Rare	—	—	—	—	—	—
1639M Rare	—	—	—	—	—	—
1640M Rare	—	—	—	—	—	—
1641M	—	350	600	825	1,450	—
1642M Rare	—	—	—	—	—	—
1643M	—	350	600	825	1,450	—

KM# 41.13 ECU D'OR
3.3500 g., 0.9580 Gold 0.1032 oz. AGW **Ruler:** Louis XIII
Mint: Montpellier

Date	Mintage	VG	F	VF	XF	Unc
1629N	—	350	600	825	1,450	—
1635N	—	350	600	825	1,450	—
1636N Rare	—	—	—	—	—	—
1637N Rare	—	—	—	—	—	—
Note: 1637 dates exist with inner circle on both sides						
1638N Rare	—	—	—	—	—	—
1639N Rare	—	—	—	—	—	—
1640N	—	300	525	675	1,350	—
1641N	—	300	525	675	1,350	—
1642N Rare	—	—	—	—	—	—
1643N	—	350	600	825	1,450	—

KM# 41.14 ECU D'OR
3.3500 g., 0.9580 Gold 0.1032 oz. AGW **Ruler:** Louis XIII
Mint: Dijon

Date	Mintage	VG	F	VF	XF	Unc
1615P	—	300	525	675	1,350	—
1637P Rare	—	—	—	—	—	—
1638P Rare	—	—	—	—	—	—
1639P Rare	—	—	—	—	—	—
1640P Rare	—	—	—	—	—	—

KM# 41.15 ECU D'OR
3.3500 g., 0.9580 Gold 0.1032 oz. AGW **Ruler:** Louis XIII
Mint: Troyes

Date	Mintage	VG	F	VF	XF	Unc
1615S	—	300	525	675	1,350	—
1631S	—	350	600	825	1,450	—
1632S Rare	—	—	—	—	—	—
1634S	—	375	675	975	1,800	—
1635S	—	350	600	825	1,450	—
1637S	—	300	525	675	1,350	—
1638S	—	300	525	675	1,350	—
1639S	—	300	525	675	1,350	—
1640S Rare	—	—	—	—	—	—
1641S Rare	—	—	—	—	—	—

KM# 41.16 ECU D'OR
3.3500 g., 0.9580 Gold 0.1032 oz. AGW **Ruler:** Louis XIII
Mint: Nantes

Date	Mintage	VG	F	VF	XF	Unc
1615T	—	300	525	675	1,350	—
1616T	—	350	600	825	1,450	—
1617T	—	300	525	675	1,350	—
1625T	—	350	600	825	1,450	—
1642T	—	350	600	825	1,450	—
1643T Rare	—	—	—	—	—	—

KM# 41.17 ECU D'OR
3.3500 g., 0.9580 Gold 0.1032 oz. AGW **Ruler:** Louis XIII
Mint: Amiens

Date	Mintage	VG	F	VF	XF	Unc
1615X Rare	—	—	—	—	—	—
1616X	—	300	525	675	1,350	—
1617X Rare	—	—	—	—	—	—
1631X	—	300	525	675	1,350	—
1632X Rare	—	—	—	—	—	—
1633X Rare	—	—	—	—	—	—
1634X	—	375	600	750	1,500	—
1635X	—	300	525	675	1,350	—
1636X	—	300	525	675	1,350	—
1637X	—	300	525	675	1,350	—
1638X	—	300	525	675	1,350	—
1639X	—	300	525	675	1,350	—
1640X	—	300	525	675	1,350	—
1641X	—	300	525	675	1,350	—
1642X	—	300	525	675	1,350	—
1643X Rare	—	—	—	—	—	—

KM# 41.18 ECU D'OR
3.3500 g., 0.9580 Gold 0.1032 oz. AGW **Ruler:** Louis XIII
Mint: Bourges

Date	Mintage	VG	F	VF	XF	Unc
1627Y Rare	—	—	—	—	—	—
1628Y Rare	—	—	—	—	—	—

Date	Mintage	VG	F	VF	XF	Unc
1629Y Rare	—	—	—	—	—	—
1639Y	—	375	650	900	1,500	—
1640Y Rare	—	—	—	—	—	—
1641Y	—	350	600	825	1,450	—
1642Y Rare	—	—	—	—	—	—
1643Y	—	350	600	825	1,450	—

KM# 41.19 ECU D'OR

3.3500 g., 0.9580 Gold 0.1032 oz. AGW **Ruler:** Louis XIII
Mint: Rennes **Note:** Mint mark: Numeral 9.

Date	Mintage	VG	F	VF	XF	Unc
1614 Rare	—	—	—	—	—	—
1642 Rare	—	—	—	—	—	—
1643 Rare	—	—	—	—	—	—

KM# 41.20 ECU D'OR

3.3500 g., 0.9580 Gold 0.1032 oz. AGW **Ruler:** Louis XIII
Mint: Aix **Note:** Mint mark: Ampersand.

Date	Mintage	VG	F	VF	XF	Unc
1634 Rare	—	—	—	—	—	—
1635	—	300	525	675	1,350	—
1637	—	300	525	675	1,350	—
1638 Rare	—	—	—	—	—	—
1639	—	350	600	825	1,450	—
1640	—	300	525	675	1,350	—
1641	—	300	525	675	1,350	—
1642	—	350	675	1,050	1,500	—
1643 Rare	—	—	—	—	—	—

KM# 51 ECU D'OR

3.3500 g., 0.9580 Gold 0.1032 oz. AGW **Ruler:** Louis XIII
Obv: Legend begins at lower left **Mint:** Rouen

Date	Mintage	VG	F	VF	XF	Unc
1612B	—	350	600	825	1,450	—
1616B	—	350	600	825	1,450	—
1617B	—	350	600	825	1,450	—
1619B	—	350	600	825	1,450	—
1626B	—	350	600	825	1,450	—
1632B	—	300	525	675	1,350	—
1633B	—	300	525	675	1,350	—
1634B	—	300	525	675	1,350	—
1635B	—	300	525	675	1,350	—
1636B	—	300	525	675	1,350	—
1637B	—	300	525	675	1,350	—
1638B	—	300	525	675	1,350	—
1641B Rare	—	—	—	—	—	—
1642B	—	—	—	—	—	—
1643B	—	350	600	825	1,450	—

KM# 55 ECU D'OR

3.3500 g., 0.9580 Gold 0.1032 oz. AGW **Ruler:** Louis XIII
Obv: Crowned arms in denticled inner circle, date in legend
Rev: Cross fleuree in denticled circle **Mint:** Saint Lô

Date	Mintage	VG	F	VF	XF	Unc
1615C	—	250	400	550	1,000	—

KM# 57 ECU D'OR

3.3500 g., 0.9580 Gold 0.1032 oz. AGW **Ruler:** Louis XIII
Obv: Crowned arms in inner circle, date in legend
Rev: Ornamented and lobed cross in inner circle, mint mark at center **Mint:** Lyon

Date	Mintage	VG	F	VF	XF	Unc
1616D	—	300	450	650	1,100	—

KM# 88 ECU D'OR

3.3500 g., 0.9580 Gold 0.1032 oz. AGW **Ruler:** Louis XIII
Obv: Legend begins at lower left **Mint:** Rouen

Date	Mintage	VG	F	VF	XF	Unc
1633B	—	250	400	550	1,000	—

KM# 92 ECU D'OR

3.3500 g., 0.9580 Gold 0.1032 oz. AGW **Ruler:** Louis XIII
Obv: Mint mark below arms **Rev:** Dot at center of cross
Mint: Amiens

Date	Mintage	VG	F	VF	XF	Unc
1638X	—	250	400	550	950	—

KM# 100 ECU D'OR

3.3500 g., 0.9580 Gold 0.1032 oz. AGW **Ruler:** Louis XIII
Obv: Plain inner circle surrounds major devices, legend begins at lower left **Rev:** Plain inner circle surrounds major devices
Mint: Montpellier

Date	Mintage	VG	F	VF	XF	Unc
1640N	—	250	400	550	1,000	—

KM# 123 ECU D'OR

3.3500 g., 0.9580 Gold 0.1032 oz. AGW **Ruler:** Louis XIII
Mint: Paris **Note:** Reduced size, finer style.

Date	Mintage	VG	F	VF	XF	Unc
1641A	—	400	650	1,100	2,000	—

KM# 124 ECU D'OR

3.3500 g., 0.9580 Gold 0.1032 oz. AGW **Ruler:** Louis XIII
Obv: Arms of France and Dauphine **Mint:** Grenoble

Date	Mintage	VG	F	VF	XF	Unc
1641Z	—	1,500	3,000	5,000	10,000	—
1642Z	—	1,500	3,000	5,000	10,000	—

KM# 146.1 ECU D'OR

3.3500 g., 0.9580 Gold 0.1032 oz. AGW **Ruler:** Louis XIV
Obv: Legend at upper right **Obv. Legend:** LVDOVICVS XIIII...
Mint: Paris

Date	Mintage	VG	F	VF	XF	Unc
1643A	—	250	450	650	1,000	—
1644A	—	250	450	650	1,000	—
1645A	—	250	450	650	1,000	—
1646A	—	250	450	650	1,000	—
1647A	—	250	450	650	1,000	—
1648A Rare	—	—	—	—	—	—
1649A	—	250	450	650	1,000	—
1650A Rare	—	—	—	—	—	—
1651A	—	—	—	—	—	—
1652A	—	400	700	1,000	1,600	—
1653A Rare	—	—	—	—	—	—
1654A Rare	—	—	—	—	—	—

KM# 146.2 ECU D'OR

3.3500 g., 0.9580 Gold 0.1032 oz. AGW **Ruler:** Louis XIV
Mint: Arras

Date	Mintage	VG	F	VF	XF	Unc
1644AR	—	400	700	1,000	1,600	—
1645AR Rare	—	—	—	—	—	—
1646AR Rare	—	—	—	—	—	—

KM# 146.3 ECU D'OR

3.3500 g., 0.9580 Gold 0.1032 oz. AGW **Ruler:** Louis XIV
Mint: Rouen

Date	Mintage	VG	F	VF	XF	Unc
1644B	—	250	450	650	1,000	—
1645B Rare	—	—	—	—	—	—

KM# 146.4 ECU D'OR

3.3500 g., 0.9580 Gold 0.1032 oz. AGW **Ruler:** Louis XIV
Mint: Saint Lô

Date	Mintage	VG	F	VF	XF	Unc
1643C Rare	—	—	—	—	—	—
1644C	—	400	700	1,000	1,600	—
1645C Rare	—	—	—	—	—	—
1646C Rare	—	—	—	—	—	—
1647C Rare	—	—	—	—	—	—

KM# 146.5 ECU D'OR

3.3500 g., 0.9580 Gold 0.1032 oz. AGW **Ruler:** Louis XIV
Mint: Lyon

Date	Mintage	VG	F	VF	XF	Unc
1643D Rare	—	—	—	—	—	—
1644D Rare	—	—	—	—	—	—
1645D	—	250	450	650	1,100	—

KM# 146.6 ECU D'OR

3.3500 g., 0.9580 Gold 0.1032 oz. AGW **Ruler:** Louis XIV
Mint: La Rochelle

Date	Mintage	VG	F	VF	XF	Unc
1644H Rare	—	—	—	—	—	—
1645H	—	400	700	1,000	1,600	—
1646H Rare	—	—	—	—	—	—

KM# 146.7 ECU D'OR

3.3500 g., 0.9580 Gold 0.1032 oz. AGW **Ruler:** Louis XIV
Mint: Limoges

Date	Mintage	VG	F	VF	XF	Unc
1644I Rare	—	—	—	—	—	—
1645I	—	400	700	1,000	1,600	—
1646I Rare	—	—	—	—	—	—
1647I	—	400	700	1,000	1,600	—
1648I Rare	—	—	—	—	—	—

KM# 146.8 ECU D'OR

3.3500 g., 0.9580 Gold 0.1032 oz. AGW **Ruler:** Louis XIV
Mint: Bordeaux

Date	Mintage	VG	F	VF	XF	Unc
1644K Rare	—	—	—	—	—	—
1645K	—	500	800	1,100	1,600	—
1646K Rare	—	—	—	—	—	—

KM# 146.9 ECU D'OR

3.3500 g., 0.9580 Gold 0.1032 oz. AGW **Ruler:** Louis XIV
Mint: Toulouse

Date	Mintage	VG	F	VF	XF	Unc
1644M Rare	—	—	—	—	—	—
1645M Rare	—	—	—	—	—	—
1646M Rare	—	—	—	—	—	—

KM# 146.10 ECU D'OR

3.3500 g., 0.9580 Gold 0.1032 oz. AGW **Ruler:** Louis XIV
Mint: Montpellier

Date	Mintage	VG	F	VF	XF	Unc
1644N Rare	—	—	—	—	—	—
1646N Rare	—	—	—	—	—	—
1647N Rare	—	—	—	—	—	—

KM# 146.11 ECU D'OR

3.3500 g., 0.9580 Gold 0.1032 oz. AGW **Ruler:** Louis XIV
Mint: Narbonne

Date	Mintage	VG	F	VF	XF	Unc
1645Q Rare	—	—	—	—	—	—
1646Q Rare	—	—	—	—	—	—

KM# 146.12 ECU D'OR

3.3500 g., 0.9580 Gold 0.1032 oz. AGW **Ruler:** Louis XIV
Mint: Nantes

Date	Mintage	VG	F	VF	XF	Unc
1644T Rare	—	—	—	—	—	—
1645T Rare	—	—	—	—	—	—
1646T Rare	—	—	—	—	—	—

KM# 146.13 ECU D'OR

3.3500 g., 0.9580 Gold 0.1032 oz. AGW **Ruler:** Louis XIV
Mint: Amiens

Date	Mintage	VG	F	VF	XF	Unc
1643X	—	250	450	650	1,000	—
1644X	—	250	450	650	1,000	—
1645X	—	250	450	650	1,000	—
1646X	—	250	450	650	1,000	—
1647X	—	250	450	650	1,000	—
1648X	—	250	450	650	1,000	—

KM# 146.14 ECU D'OR

3.3500 g., 0.9580 Gold 0.1032 oz. AGW **Ruler:** Louis XIV
Mint: Aix **Note:** Mint mark: Ampersand.

Date	Mintage	VG	F	VF	XF	Unc
1643	—	250	450	650	1,100	—
1644	—	250	450	650	1,100	—
1645 Rare	—	—	—	—	—	—
1646	—	400	700	1,000	1,750	—

KM# 146.15 ECU D'OR

3.3500 g., 0.9580 Gold 0.1032 oz. AGW **Ruler:** Louis XIV
Note: Mint mark: MA monogram.

Date	Mintage	VG	F	VF	XF	Unc
1644	—	400	700	1,000	1,600	—
1645 Rare	—	—	—	—	—	—
1646 Rare	—	—	—	—	—	—

KM# 217 LIS D'OR

3.9800 g., 0.9580 Gold 0.1226 oz. AGW **Ruler:** Louis XIV
Mint: Paris

Date	Mintage	VG	F	VF	XF	Unc
1656A	—	1,000	2,500	4,500	8,500	—
1657A	—	2,000	3,500	7,000	11,000	—

KM# 101 1/2 LOUIS D'OR

3.3400 g., 0.9170 Gold 0.0985 oz. AGW **Ruler:** Louis XIII
Obv: Loius XIII **Rev. Legend:** • CHRS • REGN • • VINC • • IMP • **Mint:** Paris

Date	Mintage	VG	F	VF	XF	Unc
1640A	—	200	400	700	1,250	—
1641A	—	200	400	700	1,250	—
1642A	—	200	400	700	1,250	—
1643A	—	200	400	700	1,250	—

KM# 102 1/2 LOUIS D'OR
3.3400 g., 0.9170 Gold 0.0985 oz. AGW **Ruler:** Louis XIII
Obv: Large head of Loius XIII right, D • G • in legend at right of head **Mint:** Paris

Date	Mintage	VG	F	VF	XF	Unc
1640A	—	600	1,000	2,000	3,000	—

KM# 103 1/2 LOUIS D'OR
3.3400 g., 0.9170 Gold 0.0985 oz. AGW **Ruler:** Louis XIII
Obv. Legend: • LVDO • XIII • D • G •... **Mint:** Paris

Date	Mintage	VG	F	VF	XF	Unc
1640A	—	450	800	1,400	2,500	—

KM# 125 1/2 LOUIS D'OR
3.3400 g., 0.9170 Gold 0.0985 oz. AGW **Ruler:** Louis XIII
Obv: Long curl on Louis XIII **Rev:** Star after legend **Mint:** Paris

Date	Mintage	VG	F	VF	XF	Unc
1641A	—	200	350	650	1,100	—
1642A	—	200	350	650	1,100	—
1643A	—	200	350	650	1,100	—

KM# 126 1/2 LOUIS D'OR
3.3400 g., 0.9170 Gold 0.0985 oz. AGW **Ruler:** Louis XIII
Obv: Large head **Rev:** Cross after legend **Mint:** Paris

Date	Mintage	VG	F	VF	XF	Unc
1641A	—	1,000	1,500	3,250	5,500	—

KM# 147 1/2 LOUIS D'OR
3.3400 g., 0.9170 Gold 0.0985 oz. AGW **Ruler:** Louis XIII
Obv. Legend: • LUD • XIII • D • G •... **Mint:** Lyon

Date	Mintage	VG	F	VF	XF	Unc
1643D	—	400	750	1,250	2,250	—

KM# 148.1 1/2 LOUIS D'OR
3.3500 g., 0.9170 Gold 0.0988 oz. AGW **Ruler:** Louis XIV
Obv: Laureate child head of Louis XIV, with short curl at right
Rev: Eight L's cruciform with crown at end of each arm, mint mark at center **Mint:** Paris

Date	Mintage	VG	F	VF	XF	Unc
1643A	—	900	1,800	2,400	3,600	—
1644A	—	650	1,300	1,900	2,700	—
1645A	—	650	1,300	1,900	2,700	—

KM# 148.2 1/2 LOUIS D'OR
3.3500 g., 0.9170 Gold 0.0988 oz. AGW **Ruler:** Louis XIV
Mint: Lyon

Date	Mintage	VG	F	VF	XF	Unc
1643D	—	900	1,800	2,400	3,600	—
1644D	—	650	1,300	2,150	3,000	—
1645D	—	900	1,800	2,400	3,600	—
1646D Rare	—	—	—	—	—	—
1649D	—	1,000	2,050	2,700	3,900	—
1650D	—	1,000	2,050	2,700	3,900	—
1652D Rare	—	—	—	—	—	—

KM# 156.1 1/2 LOUIS D'OR
3.3500 g., 0.9170 Gold 0.0988 oz. AGW **Ruler:** Louis XIV
Obv: Laureate child head of Louis XIV, with long curl at right
Mint: Paris

Date	Mintage	VG	F	VF	XF	Unc
1646A	—	350	650	1,200	2,400	—
1647	—	350	650	1,200	2,400	—
1648A	—	400	725	1,300	2,500	—
1649A Rare	—	—	—	—	—	—
1650A	—	400	725	1,300	2,500	—
1651A	—	425	775	1,450	2,650	—
1652A	—	350	650	1,200	2,400	—
1653A	—	425	775	1,450	2,750	—
1654A Rare	—	—	—	—	—	—
1657A Rare	—	—	—	—	—	—

KM# 156.2 1/2 LOUIS D'OR
3.3500 g., 0.9170 Gold 0.0988 oz. AGW **Ruler:** Louis XIV
Mint: Arras

Date	Mintage	VG	F	VF	XF	Unc
1652AR	—	425	775	1,450	2,650	—

KM# 156.3 1/2 LOUIS D'OR
3.3500 g., 0.9170 Gold 0.0988 oz. AGW **Ruler:** Louis XIV
Mint: Saint Lô

Date	Mintage	VG	F	VF	XF	Unc
1649C Rare	—	—	—	—	—	—

KM# 156.4 1/2 LOUIS D'OR
3.3500 g., 0.9170 Gold 0.0988 oz. AGW **Ruler:** Louis XIV
Mint: Lyon

Date	Mintage	VG	F	VF	XF	Unc
1653D Rare	—	—	—	—	—	—
1659D Rare	—	—	—	—	—	—
1661D Rare	—	—	—	—	—	—

KM# 156.5 1/2 LOUIS D'OR
3.3500 g., 0.9170 Gold 0.0988 oz. AGW **Ruler:** Louis XIV
Mint: Angers

Date	Mintage	VG	F	VF	XF	Unc
1648F Rare	—	—	—	—	—	—
1650F Rare	—	—	—	—	—	—

KM# 156.6 1/2 LOUIS D'OR
3.3500 g., 0.9170 Gold 0.0988 oz. AGW **Ruler:** Louis XIV
Mint: La Rochelle

Date	Mintage	VG	F	VF	XF	Unc
1648H Rare	—	—	—	—	—	—
1649H Rare	—	—	—	—	—	—
1650H Rare	—	—	—	—	—	—
1651H Rare	—	—	—	—	—	—
1652H	—	600	1,200	1,800	3,000	—
1653H Rare	—	—	—	—	—	—
1654H Rare	—	—	—	—	—	—

KM# 156.7 1/2 LOUIS D'OR
3.3500 g., 0.9170 Gold 0.0988 oz. AGW **Ruler:** Louis XIV
Mint: Limoges

Date	Mintage	VG	F	VF	XF	Unc
1652I Rare	—	—	—	—	—	—
1653I Rare	—	—	—	—	—	—
1655I Rare	—	—	—	—	—	—

KM# 156.8 1/2 LOUIS D'OR
3.3500 g., 0.9170 Gold 0.0988 oz. AGW **Ruler:** Louis XIV
Mint: Bordeaux

Date	Mintage	VG	F	VF	XF	Unc
1648K Rare	—	—	—	—	—	—

KM# 156.9 1/2 LOUIS D'OR
3.3500 g., 0.9170 Gold 0.0988 oz. AGW **Ruler:** Louis XIV
Mint: Toulouse

Date	Mintage	VG	F	VF	XF	Unc
1648M Rare	—	—	—	—	—	—

KM# 156.10 1/2 LOUIS D'OR
3.3500 g., 0.9170 Gold 0.0988 oz. AGW **Ruler:** Louis XIV
Mint: Montpellier

Date	Mintage	VG	F	VF	XF	Unc
1646N Rare	—	—	—	—	—	—
1647N Rare	—	—	—	—	—	—
1652N Rare	—	—	—	—	—	—
1653N Rare	—	—	—	—	—	—

KM# 156.11 1/2 LOUIS D'OR
3.3500 g., 0.9170 Gold 0.0988 oz. AGW **Ruler:** Louis XIV
Mint: Riom

Date	Mintage	VG	F	VF	XF	Unc
1651O Rare	—	—	—	—	—	—
1652O Rare	—	—	—	—	—	—
1653O Rare	—	—	—	—	—	—

KM# 156.12 1/2 LOUIS D'OR
3.3500 g., 0.9170 Gold 0.0988 oz. AGW **Ruler:** Louis XIV
Mint: Dijon

Date	Mintage	VG	F	VF	XF	Unc
1652P Rare	—	—	—	—	—	—

KM# 156.13 1/2 LOUIS D'OR
3.3500 g., 0.9170 Gold 0.0988 oz. AGW **Ruler:** Louis XIV
Mint: Nantes

Date	Mintage	VG	F	VF	XF	Unc
1649T Rare	—	—	—	—	—	—

KM# 156.14 1/2 LOUIS D'OR
3.3500 g., 0.9170 Gold 0.0988 oz. AGW **Ruler:** Louis XIV
Mint: Bourges

Date	Mintage	VG	F	VF	XF	Unc
1648Y Rare	—	—	—	—	—	—
1650Y Rare	—	—	—	—	—	—

KM# 212 1/2 LOUIS D'OR
3.3500 g., 0.9170 Gold 0.0988 oz. AGW **Ruler:** Louis XIV
Obv: Laureate juvenile bust of Louis XIV right, date below
Mint: Paris

Date	Mintage	VG	F	VF	XF	Unc
1661A	—	—	—	—	—	—
Note: Reported, not confirmed						
1663A	—	—	—	—	—	—
Note: Reported, not confirmed						
1668A	—	—	—	—	—	—
Note: Reported, not confirmed						

KM# 218.1 1/2 LOUIS D'OR
3.3500 g., 0.9170 Gold 0.0988 oz. AGW **Ruler:** Louis XIV **Obv:** New juvenile head of Louis XIV right, date below **Mint:** Paris

Date	Mintage	VG	F	VF	XF	Unc
1668A	—	1,450	2,700	4,250	7,800	—
1669A	—	1,450	2,700	4,250	7,800	—
1670A	—	1,450	2,700	4,250	7,800	—
1671A Rare	—	—	—	—	—	—
1674A Rare	—	—	—	—	—	—
1677A	—	1,450	2,700	4,250	7,800	—
1678A Rare	—	—	—	—	—	—
1679A	—	1,450	2,700	4,250	7,800	—
1680A Rare	—	—	—	—	—	—
1682A Rare	—	—	—	—	—	—
1683A Rare	—	—	—	—	—	—
1684A	400	1,450	2,700	4,250	7,800	—

KM# 218.2 1/2 LOUIS D'OR
3.3500 g., 0.9170 Gold 0.0988 oz. AGW **Ruler:** Louis XIV
Mint: Rennes **Note:** Mint mark: Numeral 9.

Date	Mintage	VG	F	VF	XF	Unc
1679 Rare	—	—	—	—	—	—
1680 Rare	—	—	—	—	—	—
1681 Rare	—	—	—	—	—	—

KM# 264 1/2 LOUIS D'OR
3.3500 g., 0.9170 Gold 0.0988 oz. AGW **Ruler:** Louis XIV **Obv:** Laureate juvenile head of Louis XIV right, date below **Mint:** Lyon

Date	Mintage	VG	F	VF	XF	Unc
1687D Rare	—	—	—	—	—	—
1688D Rare	—	—	—	—	—	—
1689D Rare	—	—	—	—	—	—

KM# 277.1 1/2 LOUIS D'OR
3.3500 g., 0.9170 Gold 0.0988 oz. AGW **Ruler:** Louis XIV
Obv: Older laureate head of Louis XIV right **Rev:** Crowned arms, mint mark above, date in legend **Mint:** Paris

Date	Mintage	VG	F	VF	XF	Unc
1690A	—	300	500	750	1,450	—
1691A	—	300	500	750	1,450	—
1693A	—	300	500	750	1,450	—

KM# 277.2 1/2 LOUIS D'OR
3.3500 g., 0.9170 Gold 0.0988 oz. AGW **Ruler:** Louis XIV
Mint: Rouen

Date	Mintage	VG	F	VF	XF	Unc
1690B	—	300	500	750	1,500	—
1691B	—	300	500	750	1,500	—
1692B	—	300	500	750	1,500	—

KM# 277.3 1/2 LOUIS D'OR
3.3500 g., 0.9170 Gold 0.0988 oz. AGW **Ruler:** Louis XIV
Mint: Lyon

Date	Mintage	VG	F	VF	XF	Unc
1690D	—	300	500	750	1,450	—
1691D	—	300	500	750	1,450	—
1692D Rare	—	—	—	—	—	—

KM# 277.4 1/2 LOUIS D'OR
3.3500 g., 0.9170 Gold 0.0988 oz. AGW **Ruler:** Louis XIV
Mint: Tours

Date	Mintage	VG	F	VF	XF	Unc
1691E	—	300	500	750	1,450	—
1692E	—	300	500	750	1,450	—
1693E	—	300	500	750	1,450	—

KM# 277.5 1/2 LOUIS D'OR
3.3500 g., 0.9170 Gold 0.0988 oz. AGW **Ruler:** Louis XIV
Mint: Poitiers

Date	Mintage	VG	F	VF	XF	Unc
1690G	—	350	600	900	1,700	—
1691G	—	325	550	800	1,500	—
1692G Rare	—	—	—	—	—	—

KM# 277.6 1/2 LOUIS D'OR
3.3500 g., 0.9170 Gold 0.0988 oz. AGW **Ruler:** Louis XIV
Mint: La Rochelle

Date	Mintage	VG	F	VF	XF	Unc
1693H	—	300	500	750	1,200	—

KM# 277.7 1/2 LOUIS D'OR
3.3500 g., 0.9170 Gold 0.0988 oz. AGW **Ruler:** Louis XIV
Mint: Limoges

Date	Mintage	VG	F	VF	XF	Unc
1690I	—	300	500	750	1,200	—
1691I	—	300	500	750	1,200	—
1692I Rare	—	—	—	—	—	—

KM# 277.8 1/2 LOUIS D'OR
3.3500 g., 0.9170 Gold 0.0988 oz. AGW **Ruler:** Louis XIV
Mint: Bordeaux

Date	Mintage	VG	F	VF	XF	Unc
1690K	—	300	500	750	1,450	—

KM# 277.9 1/2 LOUIS D'OR
3.3500 g., 0.9170 Gold 0.0988 oz. AGW **Ruler:** Louis XIV
Mint: Bayonne

Date	Mintage	VG	F	VF	XF	Unc
1690L	—	550	750	1,200	2,800	—
1691L	—	300	550	800	1,400	—

KM# 277.10 1/2 LOUIS D'OR
3.3500 g., 0.9170 Gold 0.0988 oz. AGW **Ruler:** Louis XIV
Mint: Toulouse

Date	Mintage	VG	F	VF	XF	Unc
1690M	—	300	500	750	1,750	—
1691M	—	300	500	750	1,750	—

KM# 277.11 1/2 LOUIS D'OR
3.3500 g., 0.9170 Gold 0.0988 oz. AGW **Ruler:** Louis XIV
Mint: Montpellier

Date	Mintage	VG	F	VF	XF	Unc
1690N Rare	—	—	—	—	—	—
1691N Rare	—	—	—	—	—	—

KM# 277.12 1/2 LOUIS D'OR
3.3500 g., 0.9170 Gold 0.0988 oz. AGW **Ruler:** Louis XIV
Mint: Riom

Date	Mintage	VG	F	VF	XF	Unc
1691O	—	300	500	750	1,450	—
1693O Rare	—	—	—	—	—	—

KM# 277.13 1/2 LOUIS D'OR
3.3500 g., 0.9170 Gold 0.0988 oz. AGW **Ruler:** Louis XIV
Mint: Dijon

Date	Mintage	VG	F	VF	XF	Unc
1690P	—	300	500	750	1,450	—
1691P	—	250	400	550	1,200	—
1692P	—	300	500	750	1,450	—
1693P Rare	—	—	—	—	—	—

KM# 277.14 1/2 LOUIS D'OR
3.3500 g., 0.9170 Gold 0.0988 oz. AGW **Ruler:** Louis XIV
Mint: Amiens

Date	Mintage	VG	F	VF	XF	Unc
1691X	—	325	550	800	1,700	—

KM# 277.15 1/2 LOUIS D'OR
3.3500 g., 0.9170 Gold 0.0988 oz. AGW **Ruler:** Louis XIV
Mint: Bourges

Date	Mintage	VG	F	VF	XF	Unc
1691Y	4,596	300	500	750	1,500	—
1692Y Rare	—	—	—	—	—	—

KM# 277.16 1/2 LOUIS D'OR
3.3500 g., 0.9170 Gold 0.0988 oz. AGW **Ruler:** Louis XIV
Mint: Aix **Note:** Mint mark: Ampersand.

Date	Mintage	VG	F	VF	XF	Unc
1690	—	300	500	750	1,450	—
1692	—	300	500	750	1,450	—

KM# 277.17 1/2 LOUIS D'OR
3.3500 g., 0.9170 Gold 0.0988 oz. AGW **Ruler:** Louis XIV
Mint: Rennes **Note:** Mint mark: Numeral 9.

Date	Mintage	VG	F	VF	XF	Unc
1690	—	300	500	750	1,450	—
1691	—	300	500	750	1,450	—

KM# 277.18 1/2 LOUIS D'OR
3.3500 g., 0.9170 Gold 0.0988 oz. AGW **Ruler:** Louis XIV
Mint: Bayonne **Note:** Mint mark: Crowned L.

Date	Mintage	VG	F	VF	XF	Unc
1690	—	300	500	750	1,200	—
1691	—	300	500	750	1,200	—
1692	—	300	500	750	1,200	—

KM# 301.1 1/2 LOUIS D'OR
3.3500 g., 0.9170 Gold 0.0988 oz. AGW **Ruler:** Louis XIV
Obv: Older laureate head of Louis XIV **Mint:** Paris

Date	Mintage	VG	F	VF	XF	Unc
1693A	—	250	400	600	1,200	—
1694A	—	250	400	600	1,200	—
1695A	—	250	400	600	1,200	—
1697A	—	250	400	600	1,200	—
1700A	—	400	600	900	1,900	—

KM# 301.2 1/2 LOUIS D'OR
3.3500 g., 0.9170 Gold 0.0988 oz. AGW **Ruler:** Louis XIV
Mint: Rouen

Date	Mintage	VG	F	VF	XF	Unc
1694B	—	250	400	600	1,200	—
1695B	—	350	500	800	1,800	—

KM# 301.3 1/2 LOUIS D'OR
3.3500 g., 0.9170 Gold 0.0988 oz. AGW **Ruler:** Louis XIV
Mint: Strasbourg

Date	Mintage	VG	F	VF	XF	Unc
1694BB	—	250	400	600	1,450	—
1695BB	—	250	400	600	1,450	—

KM# 301.4 1/2 LOUIS D'OR
3.3500 g., 0.9170 Gold 0.0988 oz. AGW **Ruler:** Louis XIV
Mint: Caen

Date	Mintage	VG	F	VF	XF	Unc
1694C	—	250	400	600	1,200	—
1696C	—	250	400	600	1,200	—

KM# 301.5 1/2 LOUIS D'OR
3.3500 g., 0.9170 Gold 0.0988 oz. AGW **Ruler:** Louis XIV
Mint: Lyon

Date	Mintage	VG	F	VF	XF	Unc
1693D Rare	—	—	—	—	—	—
1694D	—	225	375	500	1,100	—
1695D	—	250	400	600	1,200	—
1696D	—	250	400	600	1,200	—
1697D	—	300	450	700	1,300	—
1698D Rare	—	—	—	—	—	—

KM# 301.6 1/2 LOUIS D'OR
3.3500 g., 0.9170 Gold 0.0988 oz. AGW **Ruler:** Louis XIV
Mint: Tours

Date	Mintage	VG	F	VF	XF	Unc
1694E	—	250	400	600	1,200	—
1696E	—	250	400	600	1,200	—

KM# 301.7 1/2 LOUIS D'OR
3.3500 g., 0.9170 Gold 0.0988 oz. AGW **Ruler:** Louis XIV
Mint: Poitiers

Date	Mintage	VG	F	VF	XF	Unc
1694G	—	250	400	600	1,200	—

KM# 301.8 1/2 LOUIS D'OR
3.3500 g., 0.9170 Gold 0.0988 oz. AGW **Ruler:** Louis XIV
Mint: La Rochelle

Date	Mintage	VG	F	VF	XF	Unc
1693H	—	250	400	600	1,200	—
1694H	—	300	450	700	1,300	—

KM# 301.9 1/2 LOUIS D'OR
3.3500 g., 0.9170 Gold 0.0988 oz. AGW **Ruler:** Louis XIV
Mint: Limoges

Date	Mintage	VG	F	VF	XF	Unc
1693I	—	250	400	600	1,200	—
1694I	—	250	400	600	1,200	—
1696I	—	250	400	600	1,200	—

KM# 301.10 1/2 LOUIS D'OR
3.3500 g., 0.9170 Gold 0.0988 oz. AGW **Ruler:** Louis XIV
Mint: Bayonne

Date	Mintage	VG	F	VF	XF	Unc
1694L	—	250	400	600	1,200	—

KM# 301.11 1/2 LOUIS D'OR
3.3500 g., 0.9170 Gold 0.0988 oz. AGW **Ruler:** Louis XIV
Mint: Toulouse

Date	Mintage	VG	F	VF	XF	Unc
1693M	—	250	400	600	1,200	—
1694M	—	250	400	600	1,200	—
1695M	—	250	400	600	1,200	—

KM# 301.12 1/2 LOUIS D'OR
3.3500 g., 0.9170 Gold 0.0988 oz. AGW **Ruler:** Louis XIV
Mint: Montpellier

Date	Mintage	VG	F	VF	XF	Unc
1693N	—	250	400	600	1,200	—
1694N	—	250	400	600	1,200	—
1695N	—	250	400	600	1,200	—
1696N Rare	—	—	—	—	—	—
1697N Rare	—	—	—	—	—	—
1698N Rare	—	—	—	—	—	—

KM# 301.13 1/2 LOUIS D'OR
3.3500 g., 0.9170 Gold 0.0988 oz. AGW **Ruler:** Louis XIV
Mint: Riom

Date	Mintage	VG	F	VF	XF	Unc
1693O Rare	—	—	—	—	—	—
1694O	—	250	400	600	1,200	—
1695O	—	250	400	600	1,200	—
1697O Rare	—	—	—	—	—	—

KM# 301.14 1/2 LOUIS D'OR
3.3500 g., 0.9170 Gold 0.0988 oz. AGW **Ruler:** Louis XIV
Mint: Dijon

Date	Mintage	VG	F	VF	XF	Unc
1693P	—	250	400	600	1,200	—
1694P Rare	—	—	—	—	—	—
1697P Rare	—	—	—	—	—	—
1698P Rare	—	—	—	—	—	—

KM# 301.15 1/2 LOUIS D'OR
3.3500 g., 0.9170 Gold 0.0988 oz. AGW **Ruler:** Louis XIV
Mint: Reims

Date	Mintage	VG	F	VF	XF	Unc
1693S	—	250	400	600	1,200	—
1698S Rare	—	—	—	—	—	—

KM# 301.16 1/2 LOUIS D'OR
3.3500 g., 0.9170 Gold 0.0988 oz. AGW **Ruler:** Louis XIV
Mint: Troyes

Date	Mintage	VG	F	VF	XF	Unc
1694V	—	350	550	800	1,450	—
1700V	—	400	600	900	1,900	—

KM# 301.17 1/2 LOUIS D'OR
3.3500 g., 0.9170 Gold 0.0988 oz. AGW **Ruler:** Louis XIV
Mint: Lille

Date	Mintage	VG	F	VF	XF	Unc
1693W	—	250	400	600	1,200	—
1694W	—	250	400	600	1,200	—

KM# 301.18 1/2 LOUIS D'OR
3.3500 g., 0.9170 Gold 0.0988 oz. AGW **Ruler:** Louis XIV
Mint: Amiens

Date	Mintage	VG	F	VF	XF	Unc
1695X	—	250	400	600	1,200	—

KM# 301.19 1/2 LOUIS D'OR
3.3500 g., 0.9170 Gold 0.0988 oz. AGW **Ruler:** Louis XIV
Mint: Bourges

Date	Mintage	VG	F	VF	XF	Unc
1694Y	—	250	400	600	1,200	—
1698Y Rare	—	—	—	—	—	—

M# 301.20 1/2 LOUIS D'OR
3.3500 g., 0.9170 Gold 0.0988 oz. AGW **Ruler:** Louis XIV
Mint: Aix **Note:** Mint mark: Ampersand.

Date	Mintage	VG	F	VF	XF	Unc
1694	—	250	400	600	1,200	—

KM# 301.21 1/2 LOUIS D'OR
3.3500 g., 0.9170 Gold 0.0988 oz. AGW **Ruler:** Louis XIV
Mint: Rennes **Note:** Mint mark: Numeral 9.

Date	Mintage	VG	F	VF	XF	Unc
1694 Rare	—	—	—	—	—	—

KM# 301.22 1/2 LOUIS D'OR
3.3500 g., 0.9170 Gold 0.0988 oz. AGW **Ruler:** Louis XIV
Mint: Pau **Note:** Mint mark: Cow.

Date	Mintage	VG	F	VF	XF	Unc
1694	—	250	400	600	1,200	—
1696 Rare	—	—	—	—	—	—
1698 Rare	—	—	—	—	—	—

KM# 104 LOUIS D'OR
6.6900 g., 0.9170 Gold 0.1972 oz. AGW **Ruler:** Louis XIII
Obv: Laureate head with long curl **Rev. Legend:** • CHRS • • REGN • • VINC • • IMP • **Mint:** Paris

Date	Mintage	VG	F	VF	XF	Unc
1640A	—	300	600	900	1,400	—
1641A	—	300	600	900	1,400	—
1642A	—	300	600	900	1,400	—
1643A	—	300	600	950	1,550	—

KM# 105 LOUIS D'OR
6.6900 g., 0.9170 Gold 0.1972 oz. AGW **Ruler:** Louis XIII
Obv: Laureate head with short curl

Date	Mintage	VG	F	VF	XF	Unc
1640A	—	300	600	1,200	2,000	—
1641A	—	300	600	1,000	1,750	—

KM# 106 LOUIS D'OR
6.6900 g., 0.9170 Gold 0.1972 oz. AGW **Ruler:** Louis XIII
Obv: Large head **Rev:** Legend begins in lower right quarter and ends... • IMPE •

Date	Mintage	VG	F	VF	XF	Unc
1640A	—	1,000	1,750	3,000	5,500	—

KM# 107 LOUIS D'OR
6.6900 g., 0.9170 Gold 0.1972 oz. AGW **Ruler:** Louis XIII
Obv: Large head with legend **Obv. Legend:** • LVDO • XIII • D • G •... **Rev. Legend:** ...• IMPE •

Date	Mintage	VG	F	VF	XF	Unc
1640A	—	1,250	2,000	3,500	5,000	—

KM# 136.1 LOUIS D'OR
6.6900 g., 0.9170 Gold 0.1972 oz. AGW **Ruler:** Louis XIII
Obv: Older head **Rev:** Legend begins in upper left quarter

Date	Mintage	VG	F	VF	XF	Unc
1642A	—	300	600	1,100	2,000	—
1643A	—	320	625	1,100	2,000	—

KM# 136.2 LOUIS D'OR
6.6900 g., 0.9170 Gold 0.1972 oz. AGW **Ruler:** Louis XIII
Mint: Lyon

Date	Mintage	VG	F	VF	XF	Unc
1643D	—	650	1,250	2,000	3,000	—

KM# 149.1 LOUIS D'OR
6.6900 g., 0.9170 Gold 0.1972 oz. AGW **Ruler:** Louis XIV
Obv: Laureate child head of Louis XIV, with short curl **Mint:** Paris

Date	Mintage	VG	F	VF	XF	Unc
1643A	—	350	600	1,000	1,800	—
1644A	—	350	600	1,000	1,800	—
1645A	—	350	600	1,000	1,800	—
1646A Rare	—	—	—	—	—	—

KM# 149.2 LOUIS D'OR
6.6900 g., 0.9170 Gold 0.1972 oz. AGW **Ruler:** Louis XIV
Mint: Lyon

Date	Mintage	VG	F	VF	XF	Unc
1644D	—	350	600	950	1,750	—
1645D	—	350	650	1,000	1,800	—
1648D	—	350	650	1,000	1,800	—
1649D	—	350	650	1,000	1,800	—
1650D	—	425	850	1,200	2,150	—
1651D	—	350	650	1,000	1,800	—
1652D Tower	—	425	850	1,200	2,150	—
1652D Crescent	—	425	850	1,200	2,150	—
1656D	—	475	950	1,500	2,400	—

KM# 157.1 LOUIS D'OR
6.6900 g., 0.9170 Gold 0.1972 oz. AGW **Ruler:** Louis XIV
Obv: Head with long curl **Mint:** Paris

Date	Mintage	VG	F	VF	XF	Unc
1646A	—	240	475	725	1,100	—
1647A	—	240	475	725	1,100	—
1648A	—	240	475	725	1,100	—
1649A	—	240	475	725	1,100	—
1650A	—	240	475	725	1,100	—
1651A	—	240	475	725	1,100	—
1652A	—	240	475	725	1,100	—
1653A	—	240	475	725	1,100	—
1654A	—	240	475	725	1,100	—
1655A	—	240	475	725	1,100	—
1657A	—	240	475	725	1,100	—
1658A Rare	—	—	—	—	—	—
1659A	600,000	300	550	850	1,200	—

KM# 157.2 LOUIS D'OR
6.6900 g., 0.9170 Gold 0.1972 oz. AGW **Ruler:** Louis XIV
Mint: Arras

Date	Mintage	VG	F	VF	XF	Unc
1646AR	200	550	1,100	1,500	3,000	—
1648AR	—	350	600	950	1,450	—
1649AR Rare	—	—	—	—	—	—
1650AR	—	350	600	950	1,450	—
1651AR	—	350	600	950	1,450	—
1652AR	—	350	600	950	1,450	—
1653AR	—	350	600	950	1,450	—
1655AR	—	350	600	950	1,450	—
1656AR	—	350	600	950	1,450	—
1657AR	—	350	600	950	1,450	—

KM# 157.3 LOUIS D'OR
6.6900 g., 0.9170 Gold 0.1972 oz. AGW **Ruler:** Louis XIV
Mint: Rouen

Date	Mintage	VG	F	VF	XF	Unc
1646B	—	350	600	950	1,450	—
1647B	—	350	600	950	1,450	—
1648B Rare	—	—	—	—	—	—
1649B Rare	—	—	—	—	—	—
1650B	—	350	600	950	1,450	—
1651B	—	350	600	950	1,450	—
1652B	—	350	600	950	1,450	—
1653B	—	350	600	950	1,450	—
1655B Rare	—	—	—	—	—	—
1657B Rare	—	—	—	—	—	—
1658B	200	425	850	1,200	2,200	—
1659B Rare	—	—	—	—	—	—

KM# 157.4 LOUIS D'OR
6.6900 g., 0.9170 Gold 0.1972 oz. AGW **Ruler:** Louis XIV
Mint: Saint Lô

Date	Mintage	VG	F	VF	XF	Unc
1647C	—	350	600	950	1,450	—
1648C	—	350	600	950	1,450	—
1649C	—	350	600	950	1,450	—
1650C	—	350	600	950	1,450	—
1651C	—	350	600	950	1,450	—
1652C	—	350	600	950	1,450	—
1653C	2,049	350	600	950	1,450	—
1654C	—	350	600	950	1,450	—
1655C Rare	—	—	—	—	—	—

KM# 157.5 LOUIS D'OR
6.6900 g., 0.9170 Gold 0.1972 oz. AGW **Ruler:** Louis XIV
Mint: Lyon

Date	Mintage	VG	F	VF	XF	Unc
1652D	—	240	475	725	1,100	—
1653D	—	240	475	725	1,100	—
1654D Rare	—	—	—	—	—	—
1657D	—	350	600	950	1,450	—
1658D	—	350	600	950	1,450	—
1659D Rare	—	—	—	—	—	—

KM# 157.6 LOUIS D'OR
6.6900 g., 0.9170 Gold 0.1972 oz. AGW **Ruler:** Louis XIV
Mint: Tours

Date	Mintage	VG	F	VF	XF	Unc
1652E	—	300	550	850	1,200	—
1653E	—	240	475	725	1,100	—
1654E Rare	—	—	—	—	—	—

KM# 157.7 LOUIS D'OR
6.6900 g., 0.9170 Gold 0.1972 oz. AGW **Ruler:** Louis XIV
Mint: Angers

Date	Mintage	VG	F	VF	XF	Unc
1647F Rare	—	—	—	—	—	—
1648F	—	350	600	950	1,450	—
1649F	—	350	600	950	1,450	—
1650F	—	350	600	950	1,450	—
1651F	—	475	950	1,450	2,050	—
1652F	—	350	600	950	1,450	—
1653F Rare	—	—	—	—	—	—
1654F	—	350	600	950	1,450	—
1655F Rare	—	—	—	—	—	—
1656F Rare	—	—	—	—	—	—

KM# 157.8 LOUIS D'OR
6.6900 g., 0.9170 Gold 0.1972 oz. AGW **Ruler:** Louis XIV
Mint: Poitiers

Date	Mintage	VG	F	VF	XF	Unc
1650G Rare	—	—	—	—	—	—

KM# 157.9 LOUIS D'OR
6.6900 g., 0.9170 Gold 0.1972 oz. AGW **Ruler:** Louis XIV
Mint: La Rochelle

Date	Mintage	VG	F	VF	XF	Unc
1646H	—	350	600	950	1,450	—
1647H Rare	—	—	—	—	—	—
1648H Rare	—	—	—	—	—	—
1649H	—	350	600	950	1,450	—
1650H	—	350	600	950	1,450	—
1651H	—	350	600	950	1,450	—
1652H Rare	—	—	—	—	—	—
1653H	—	350	600	950	1,450	—
1654H Rare	—	—	—	—	—	—
1655H Rare	—	—	—	—	—	—

KM# 157.10 LOUIS D'OR
6.6900 g., 0.9170 Gold 0.1972 oz. AGW **Ruler:** Louis XIV
Mint: Limoges

Date	Mintage	VG	F	VF	XF	Unc
1648I Rare	—	—	—	—	—	—
1650I Rare	—	—	—	—	—	—
1651I	2,377	350	600	950	1,450	—
1652I	—	300	550	850	1,200	—
1653I	—	300	550	850	1,200	—
1654I Rare	—	—	—	—	—	—
1655I Rare	—	—	—	—	—	—
1656I Rare	—	—	—	—	—	—
1657I Rare	—	—	—	—	—	—
1659I	—	350	600	950	1,450	—

KM# 157.11 LOUIS D'OR
6.6900 g., 0.9170 Gold 0.1972 oz. AGW **Ruler:** Louis XIV
Mint: Bordeaux

Date	Mintage	VG	F	VF	XF	Unc
1647K Rare	—	—	—	—	—	—
1648K Rare	—	—	—	—	—	—
1649K Rare	—	—	—	—	—	—
1650K	1,858	350	600	950	1,450	—
1651K Rare	—	—	—	—	—	—
1652K Rare	—	—	—	—	—	—
1653K Rare	—	—	—	—	—	—
1654K Rare	—	—	—	—	—	—
1655K Rare	—	—	—	—	—	—
1656K	—	300	550	850	1,200	—
1657K Rare	—	—	—	—	—	—

KM# 157.12 LOUIS D'OR
6.6900 g., 0.9170 Gold 0.1972 oz. AGW **Ruler:** Louis XIV
Mint: Toulouse

Date	Mintage	VG	F	VF	XF	Unc
1647M	—	350	600	950	1,450	—
1648M Rare	—	—	—	—	—	—
1651M Rare	—	—	—	—	—	—
1652M	—	300	550	850	1,200	—
1653M	—	300	550	850	1,200	—
1654M Rare	—	—	—	—	—	—
1655M Rare	—	—	—	—	—	—
1656M Rare	—	—	—	—	—	—
1659M Rare	—	—	—	—	—	—

KM# 157.13 LOUIS D'OR
6.6900 g., 0.9170 Gold 0.1972 oz. AGW **Ruler:** Louis XIV
Mint: Montpellier

Date	Mintage	VG	F	VF	XF	Unc
1646N Rare	—	—	—	—	—	—
1647N Rare	—	—	—	—	—	—
1648N Rare	—	—	—	—	—	—
1649N	—	240	475	725	1,100	—
1650N	—	240	475	725	1,100	—
1651N	—	240	475	725	1,100	—
1652N	—	240	475	725	1,100	—
1653N Rare	—	—	—	—	—	—
1656N	—	240	475	725	1,100	—
1657N	—	240	475	725	1,100	—
1658N Rare	—	—	—	—	—	—
1659N Rare	—	—	—	—	—	—

KM# 157.14 LOUIS D'OR
6.6900 g., 0.9170 Gold 0.1972 oz. AGW **Ruler:** Louis XIV
Mint: Riom

Date	Mintage	VG	F	VF	XF	Unc
1652O Rare	—	—	—	—	—	—
1653O	—	300	550	850	1,200	—

KM# 157.15 LOUIS D'OR
6.6900 g., 0.9170 Gold 0.1972 oz. AGW **Ruler:** Louis XIV
Mint: Dijon

Date	Mintage	VG	F	VF	XF	Unc
1646P	—	350	600	950	1,450	—
1650P Rare	—	—	—	—	—	—
1651P	775	425	700	1,100	1,700	—
1653P	—	350	600	950	1,450	—

KM# 157.16 LOUIS D'OR
6.6900 g., 0.9170 Gold 0.1972 oz. AGW **Ruler:** Louis XIV
Mint: Narbonne

Date	Mintage	VG	F	VF	XF	Unc
1651Q	—	300	550	850	1,200	—
1652Q	—	350	600	950	1,450	—
1653Q Rare	—	—	—	—	—	—

KM# 157.17 LOUIS D'OR
6.6900 g., 0.9170 Gold 0.1972 oz. AGW **Ruler:** Louis XIV
Mint: Villeneuve St. André

Date	Mintage	VG	F	VF	XF	Unc
1651R	—	300	550	850	1,200	—

KM# 157.18 LOUIS D'OR
6.6900 g., 0.9170 Gold 0.1972 oz. AGW **Ruler:** Louis XIV
Mint: Troyes

Date	Mintage	VG	F	VF	XF	Unc
1651S	—	300	550	850	1,200	—
1652S	—	300	550	850	1,200	—
1653S	—	300	550	850	1,200	—
1654S Rare	—	—	—	—	—	—
1655S Rare	—	—	—	—	—	—

KM# 157.19 LOUIS D'OR
6.6900 g., 0.9170 Gold 0.1972 oz. AGW **Ruler:** Louis XIV
Mint: Nantes

Date	Mintage	VG	F	VF	XF	Unc
1647T Rare	—	—	—	—	—	—
1649T Rare	—	—	—	—	—	—
1650T	—	350	600	950	1,450	—
1651T	—	350	600	950	1,450	—
1652T	—	350	600	950	1,450	—
1653T Rare	—	—	—	—	—	—
1654T	—	350	600	950	1,450	—
1655T Rare	—	—	—	—	—	—
1656T Rare	—	—	—	—	—	—

KM# 157.20 LOUIS D'OR
6.6900 g., 0.9170 Gold 0.1972 oz. AGW **Ruler:** Louis XIV
Mint: Amiens

Date	Mintage	VG	F	VF	XF	Unc
1648X Rare	—	—	—	—	—	—
1649X Rare	—	—	—	—	—	—
1650X	—	240	475	725	1,100	—
1651X	—	240	475	725	1,100	—
1652X	—	240	475	725	1,100	—
1653X	—	240	475	725	1,100	—
1654X Rare	—	—	—	—	—	—
1655X Rare	—	—	—	—	—	—
1659X Rare	—	—	—	—	—	—

KM# 157.21 LOUIS D'OR
6.6900 g., 0.9170 Gold 0.1972 oz. AGW **Ruler:** Louis XIV
Mint: Bourges

Date	Mintage	VG	F	VF	XF	Unc
1653Y	—	300	550	850	1,200	—
1654Y	—	300	550	850	1,200	—

Date	Mintage	VG	F	VF	XF	Unc
1655Y	—	350	600	950	1,450	—
1656Y Rare	—	—	—	—	—	—

KM# 157.22 LOUIS D'OR
6.6900 g., 0.9170 Gold 0.1972 oz. AGW **Ruler:** Louis XIV
Mint: Aix **Note:** Mint mark: Ampersand.

Date	Mintage	VG	F	VF	XF	Unc
1646 Rare	—	—	—	—	—	—
1647 Rare	—	—	—	—	—	—
1648	—	240	475	725	1,100	—
1649 Rare	—	—	—	—	—	—
1651	—	240	475	725	1,100	—
1652	—	240	475	725	1,100	—
1653	—	240	475	725	1,100	—
1654	—	240	475	725	1,100	—
1656 Rare	—	—	—	—	—	—
1657 Rare	—	—	—	—	—	—
1658 Rare	—	—	—	—	—	—
1659 Rare	—	—	—	—	—	—

KM# 200.1 LOUIS D'OR
6.6900 g., 0.9170 Gold 0.1972 oz. AGW **Ruler:** Louis XIV
Obv: Laureate juvenile head of Louis XIV **Mint:** Paris

Date	Mintage	VG	F	VF	XF	Unc
1658A	—	300	550	850	1,500	—
1659A	—	300	550	850	1,500	—
1660A	—	300	550	850	1,500	—
1661A	—	300	550	850	1,500	—
1662A	—	300	550	850	1,500	—
1663A	—	300	550	850	1,500	—
1664A	—	300	550	850	1,500	—
1665A	—	300	550	850	1,500	—
1666A	—	300	550	850	1,500	—
1667A	—	300	550	850	1,500	—
1668A	—	300	550	850	1,500	—

KM# 200.2 LOUIS D'OR
6.6900 g., 0.9170 Gold 0.1972 oz. AGW **Ruler:** Louis XIV
Mint: Rouen

Date	Mintage	VG	F	VF	XF	Unc
1660B	—	350	600	1,000	1,750	—
1661B Rare	—	—	—	—	—	—
1662B	—	350	600	1,000	1,750	—

KM# 200.3 LOUIS D'OR
6.6900 g., 0.9170 Gold 0.1972 oz. AGW **Ruler:** Louis XIV
Mint: Lyon

Date	Mintage	VG	F	VF	XF	Unc
1661D	—	300	550	950	1,700	—
1662D	—	300	550	950	1,700	—
1663D	—	300	550	950	1,700	—
1664D	—	300	550	950	1,700	—
1665D	—	300	550	950	1,700	—
1666D Rare	—	—	—	—	—	—
1667D Rare	—	—	—	—	—	—
1668D	—	300	550	950	1,700	—
1669D	—	300	550	950	1,700	—
1670D	—	300	550	950	1,700	—

KM# 200.4 LOUIS D'OR
6.6900 g., 0.9170 Gold 0.1972 oz. AGW **Ruler:** Louis XIV
Mint: Limoges

Date	Mintage	VG	F	VF	XF	Unc
1662I	—	350	600	1,000	1,750	—

KM# 200.5 LOUIS D'OR
6.6900 g., 0.9170 Gold 0.1972 oz. AGW **Ruler:** Louis XIV
Mint: Bordeaux

Date	Mintage	VG	F	VF	XF	Unc
1660K	9,091	300	550	900	1,600	—
1661K Rare	—	—	—	—	—	—

KM# 200.6 LOUIS D'OR
6.6900 g., 0.9170 Gold 0.1972 oz. AGW **Ruler:** Louis XIV
Mint: Bayonne

Date	Mintage	VG	F	VF	XF	Unc
1662L Rare	—	—	—	—	—	—
1663L	—	350	600	1,000	1,750	—
1664L Rare	—	—	—	—	—	—
1668L	—	300	550	900	1,600	—
1669L	—	300	550	900	1,600	—
1670L	—	300	550	850	1,550	—
1671L	—	300	550	850	1,550	—
1672L	—	300	550	850	1,550	—

KM# 200.7 LOUIS D'OR
6.6900 g., 0.9170 Gold 0.1972 oz. AGW **Ruler:** Louis XIV
Mint: Montpellier

Date	Mintage	VG	F	VF	XF	Unc
1660N	1,600	350	600	1,000	1,750	—
1662N	—	350	600	1,000	1,750	—
1666N Rare	—	—	—	—	—	—
1667N	—	300	550	850	1,500	—
1668N Rare	—	—	—	—	—	—

KM# 200.8 LOUIS D'OR
6.6900 g., 0.9170 Gold 0.1972 oz. AGW **Ruler:** Louis XIV
Mint: Amiens

Date	Mintage	VG	F	VF	XF	Unc
1659X	—	300	550	850	1,500	—
1660X Rare	—	—	—	—	—	—
1661X	1,000	—	—	—	—	—

KM# 200.9 LOUIS D'OR
6.6900 g., 0.9170 Gold 0.1972 oz. AGW **Ruler:** Louis XIV
Mint: Bourges

Date	Mintage	VG	F	VF	XF	Unc
1660Y	219	600	1,100	1,500	3,000	—

KM# 200.10 LOUIS D'OR
6.6900 g., 0.9170 Gold 0.1972 oz. AGW **Ruler:** Louis XIV
Mint: Aix **Note:** Mint mark: Ampersand.

Date	Mintage	VG	F	VF	XF	Unc
1660	1,124	350	600	1,000	1,750	—
1661	1,740	350	600	1,000	1,750	—
1662	—	350	600	1,000	1,750	—
1663 Rare	—	—	—	—	—	—
1664 Rare	—	—	—	—	—	—
1665 Rare	—	—	—	—	—	—
1666 Rare	—	—	—	—	—	—
1667	—	350	600	1,000	1,750	—
1668 Rare	—	—	—	—	—	—
1669	—	—	—	—	—	—
1670 Rare	—	—	—	—	—	—
1671 Rare	—	—	—	—	—	—
1672	—	350	600	1,000	1,750	—

KM# 200.11 LOUIS D'OR
6.6900 g., 0.9170 Gold 0.1972 oz. AGW **Ruler:** Louis XIV
Mint: Pau **Note:** Mint mark: Cow.

Date	Mintage	VG	F	VF	XF	Unc
1665	—	1,200	2,700	3,900	7,200	—
1674	—	1,200	2,700	3,900	7,200	—
1679	—	1,200	2,700	3,900	7,200	—

KM# 219.1 LOUIS D'OR
6.6900 g., 0.9170 Gold 0.1972 oz. AGW **Ruler:** Louis XIV
Obv: New juvenile head of Louis XIV **Mint:** Paris

Date	Mintage	VG	F	VF	XF	Unc
1668A	—	300	550	850	1,200	—
1669A	—	300	550	850	1,200	—
1670A	—	300	550	850	1,200	—
1671A	—	300	550	850	1,200	—
1672A	—	300	550	850	1,200	—
1673A	—	300	550	850	1,200	—
1674A	—	300	550	850	1,200	—
1675A	—	300	550	850	1,200	—
1676A	—	300	550	850	1,200	—
1677A	—	300	550	850	1,200	—
1678A	—	300	550	850	1,200	—

KM# 219.2 LOUIS D'OR
6.6900 g., 0.9170 Gold 0.1972 oz. AGW **Ruler:** Louis XIV
Mint: Rouen

Date	Mintage	VG	F	VF	XF	Unc
1679B Rare	—	—	—	—	—	—
1680B	—	350	600	950	1,300	—

KM# 219.3 LOUIS D'OR
6.6900 g., 0.9170 Gold 0.1972 oz. AGW **Ruler:** Louis XIV
Mint: Lyon

Date	Mintage	VG	F	VF	XF	Unc
1669D	—	350	600	950	1,300	—
1670D	—	350	600	950	1,300	—
1671D	—	350	600	950	1,300	—
1672D	—	350	600	950	1,300	—
1673D	—	350	600	950	1,300	—
1674D	—	350	600	950	1,300	—
1675D	—	350	600	1,000	1,450	—
1677D	—	350	600	1,000	1,450	—
1678D Rare	—	—	—	—	—	—

Date	Mintage	VG	F	VF	XF	Unc
1679D	—	350	600	950	1,300	—
1680D	—	350	600	950	1,300	—
1681D	—	350	600	950	1,300	—
1682D	—	350	600	950	1,300	—
1683D	—	350	600	950	1,300	—

KM# 219.4 LOUIS D'OR
6.6900 g., 0.9170 Gold 0.1972 oz. AGW **Ruler:** Louis XIV
Mint: Tours

Date	Mintage	VG	F	VF	XF	Unc
1680E	—	—	—	—	—	—

Note: Rare

KM# 219.5 LOUIS D'OR
6.6900 g., 0.9170 Gold 0.1972 oz. AGW **Ruler:** Louis XIV
Mint: Limoges

Date	Mintage	VG	F	VF	XF	Unc
1679I Rare	—	—	—	—	—	—
1680I	—	350	600	950	1,300	—

KM# 219.6 LOUIS D'OR
6.6900 g., 0.9170 Gold 0.1972 oz. AGW **Ruler:** Louis XIV
Mint: Bordeaux

Date	Mintage	VG	F	VF	XF	Unc
1679K Rare	—	—	—	—	—	—

KM# 219.7 LOUIS D'OR
6.6900 g., 0.9170 Gold 0.1972 oz. AGW **Ruler:** Louis XIV
Mint: Bayonne

Date	Mintage	VG	F	VF	XF	Unc
1672L	—	300	550	850	1,200	—
1673L	—	300	550	850	1,200	—
1674L	—	300	550	850	1,200	—
1675L Rare	—	—	—	—	—	—
1676L	220,000	300	550	850	1,200	—
1677L Rare	—	—	—	—	—	—
1678L Rare	—	—	—	—	—	—
1679L	—	300	550	850	1,200	—
1680L	—	300	550	850	1,200	—
1681L	—	300	550	850	1,200	—
1682L	—	300	550	850	1,200	—
1683L Rare	—	—	—	—	—	—
1684L Rare	—	—	—	—	—	—

KM# 219.8 LOUIS D'OR
6.6900 g., 0.9170 Gold 0.1972 oz. AGW **Ruler:** Louis XIV
Mint: Montpellier

Date	Mintage	VG	F	VF	XF	Unc
1679N Rare	—	—	—	—	—	—
1680N Rare	—	—	—	—	—	—

KM# 219.9 LOUIS D'OR
6.6900 g., 0.9170 Gold 0.1972 oz. AGW **Ruler:** Louis XIV
Mint: Troyes

Date	Mintage	VG	F	VF	XF	Unc
1680S Rare	—	—	—	—	—	—
1681S Rare	—	—	—	—	—	—
1682S	—	350	600	1,000	1,450	—
1683S Rare	—	—	—	—	—	—
1684S Rare	—	—	—	—	—	—

KM# 219.10 LOUIS D'OR
6.6900 g., 0.9170 Gold 0.1972 oz. AGW **Ruler:** Louis XIV
Mint: Amiens

Date	Mintage	VG	F	VF	XF	Unc
1679X Rare	—	—	—	—	—	—
1681X Rare	—	—	—	—	—	—

KM# 219.11 LOUIS D'OR
6.6900 g., 0.9170 Gold 0.1972 oz. AGW **Ruler:** Louis XIV
Mint: Aix **Note:** Mint mark: Ampersand.

Date	Mintage	VG	F	VF	XF	Unc
1679 Rare	—	—	—	—	—	—
1680 Rare	—	—	—	—	—	—

KM# 219.12 LOUIS D'OR
6.6900 g., 0.9170 Gold 0.1972 oz. AGW **Ruler:** Louis XIV
Mint: Rennes **Note:** Mint mark: Numeral 9.

Date	Mintage	VG	F	VF	XF	Unc
1679 Rare	—	—	—	—	—	—
1680 Rare	—	—	—	—	—	—
1681 Rare	—	—	—	—	—	—
1682 Rare	—	—	—	—	—	—
1683 Rare	—	—	—	—	—	—

KM# 236.1 LOUIS D'OR
6.6900 g., 0.9170 Gold 0.1972 oz. AGW **Ruler:** Louis XIV
Obv: Older head of Louis XIV **Mint:** Paris

Date	Mintage	VG	F	VF	XF	Unc
1679A	—	400	750	1,750	3,000	—
1680A	—	400	750	1,750	3,000	—
1681A	—	400	750	1,750	3,000	—
1682A	—	400	750	1,750	3,000	—
1683A	470,000	400	750	1,750	3,000	—

KM# 236.2 LOUIS D'OR
6.6900 g., 0.9170 Gold 0.1972 oz. AGW **Ruler:** Louis XIV
Mint: Rouen

Date	Mintage	VG	F	VF	XF	Unc
1681B	—	425	775	1,750	3,000	—
1682B Rare	—	—	—	—	—	—
1683B Rare	—	—	—	—	—	—
1684B Rare	—	—	—	—	—	—

KM# 236.3 LOUIS D'OR
6.6900 g., 0.9170 Gold 0.1972 oz. AGW **Ruler:** Louis XIV
Mint: Bordeaux

Date	Mintage	VG	F	VF	XF	Unc
1680K	—	450	825	1,400	2,000	—
1682K Rare	—	—	—	—	—	—
1683K Rare	—	—	—	—	—	—
1684K Rare	—	—	—	—	—	—

KM# 236.4 LOUIS D'OR
6.6900 g., 0.9170 Gold 0.1972 oz. AGW **Ruler:** Louis XIV
Mint: Amiens

Date	Mintage	VG	F	VF	XF	Unc
1679X	—	425	775	1,800	3,100	—
1680X	—	425	775	1,800	3,100	—
1681X Rare	—	—	—	—	—	—

KM# 236.5 LOUIS D'OR
6.6900 g., 0.9170 Gold 0.1972 oz. AGW **Ruler:** Louis XIV
Mint: Aix **Note:** Mint mark: Ampersand.

Date	Mintage	VG	F	VF	XF	Unc
1681 Rare	—	—	—	—	—	—
1682	—	425	775	1,750	3,000	—
1683	—	425	775	1,750	3,000	—

KM# 236.6 LOUIS D'OR
6.6900 g., 0.9170 Gold 0.1972 oz. AGW **Ruler:** Louis XIV
Mint: Pau **Note:** Mint mark: Cow.

Date	Mintage	VG	F	VF	XF	Unc
1681	—	1,000	2,000	3,500	5,500	—
1683	—	1,000	2,000	3,500	5,500	—
1687 Rare	—	—	—	—	—	—
1688	—	1,000	2,000	3,500	5,500	—

KM# 256.1 LOUIS D'OR
6.6900 g., 0.9170 Gold 0.1972 oz. AGW **Ruler:** Louis XIV
Obv: Large laureate head of Louis XIV **Mint:** Paris

Date	Mintage	VG	F	VF	XF	Unc
1684A	—	725	1,150	1,700	2,950	—
1685A	—	725	1,150	1,700	2,950	—
1686A	—	725	1,150	1,700	2,950	—
1687A	—	725	1,150	1,700	2,950	—
1688A	—	725	1,150	1,700	2,950	—
1689A	—	725	1,150	1,700	2,950	—

KM# 256.2 LOUIS D'OR
6.6900 g., 0.9170 Gold 0.1972 oz. AGW **Ruler:** Louis XIV
Mint: Lyon

Date	Mintage	VG	F	VF	XF	Unc
1683D	—	725	1,150	1,700	2,950	—
1684D	—	725	1,150	1,700	2,950	—
1685D	—	725	1,150	1,700	2,950	—
1686D	—	725	1,150	1,700	2,950	—
1687D	—	725	1,150	1,700	2,950	—
1688D	—	725	1,150	1,700	2,950	—
1689D	—	725	1,150	1,700	2,950	—

KM# 256.3 LOUIS D'OR
6.6900 g., 0.9170 Gold 0.1972 oz. AGW **Ruler:** Louis XIV
Mint: Bordeaux

Date	Mintage	VG	F	VF	XF	Unc
1685K	—	675	1,150	1,650	2,800	—
1686K Rare	—	—	—	—	—	—
1687K	—	675	1,150	1,650	2,800	—
1688K Rare	—	—	—	—	—	—

KM# 256.4 LOUIS D'OR
6.6900 g., 0.9170 Gold 0.1972 oz. AGW **Ruler:** Louis XIV
Mint: Bayonne

Date	Mintage	VG	F	VF	XF	Unc
1685L Rare	—	—	—	—	—	—
1686L Rare	—	—	—	—	—	—
1687L	—	775	1,300	1,950	3,750	—
1688L Rare	—	—	—	—	—	—
1689L Rare	—	—	—	—	—	—

KM# 256.5 LOUIS D'OR
6.6900 g., 0.9170 Gold 0.1972 oz. AGW **Ruler:** Louis XIV
Mint: Troyes **Note:** Mint mark: Crowned S.

Date	Mintage	VG	F	VF	XF	Unc
1685 Rare	—	—	—	—	—	—
1686 Rare	—	—	—	—	—	—

KM# 256.6 LOUIS D'OR
6.6900 g., 0.9170 Gold 0.1972 oz. AGW **Ruler:** Louis XIV
Mint: Amiens

Date	Mintage	VG	F	VF	XF	Unc
1685X Rare	—	—	—	—	—	—

KM# 256.7 LOUIS D'OR
6.6900 g., 0.9170 Gold 0.1972 oz. AGW **Ruler:** Louis XIV
Mint: Aix **Note:** Mint mark: Ampersand.

Date	Mintage	VG	F	VF	XF	Unc
1684	—	725	1,150	1,700	2,950	—
1685 Rare	—	—	—	—	—	—
1686 Rare	—	—	—	—	—	—
1687	—	725	1,150	1,700	2,950	—
1688 Rare	—	—	—	—	—	—
1689	5,851	725	1,150	1,700	2,950	—

KM# 256.8 LOUIS D'OR
6.6900 g., 0.9170 Gold 0.1972 oz. AGW **Ruler:** Louis XIV
Mint: Rennes **Note:** Mint mark: Numeral 9.

Date	Mintage	VG	F	VF	XF	Unc
1684	—	725	1,150	1,700	2,950	—
1685 Rare	—	—	—	—	—	—
1686 Rare	—	—	—	—	—	—
1687 Rare	—	—	—	—	—	—
1688 Rare	—	—	—	—	—	—
1689 Rare	—	—	—	—	—	—

KM# 256.9 LOUIS D'OR
6.6900 g., 0.9170 Gold 0.1972 oz. AGW **Ruler:** Louis XIV
Mint: Lille **Note:** Mint mark: Crowned L.

Date	Mintage	VG	F	VF	XF	Unc
1686 Rare	—	—	—	—	—	—
1687	—	725	1,150	1,950	3,250	—
1688 Rare	—	—	—	—	—	—
1689 Rare	—	—	—	—	—	—

KM# 278.1 LOUIS D'OR
6.6900 g., 0.9170 Gold 0.1972 oz. AGW **Ruler:** Louis XIV
Obv: Old laureate head of Louis XIV **Mint:** Paris

Date	Mintage	VG	F	VF	XF	Unc
1690A	—	250	450	700	1,200	—
1691A	—	250	450	700	1,200	—
1692A	—	300	500	800	1,450	—
1693A	—	300	500	800	1,450	—

KM# 278.2 LOUIS D'OR
6.6900 g., 0.9170 Gold 0.1972 oz. AGW **Ruler:** Louis XIV
Mint: Rouen

Date	Mintage	VG	F	VF	XF	Unc
1690B	—	250	450	700	1,200	—
1691B	—	250	450	700	1,200	—

KM# 278.3 LOUIS D'OR
6.6900 g., 0.9170 Gold 0.1972 oz. AGW **Ruler:** Louis XIV
Mint: Lyon

Date	Mintage	VG	F	VF	XF	Unc
1690D	—	250	450	700	1,200	—
1691D	—	250	450	700	1,200	—
1692D	—	200	400	800	1,700	—
1693D Rare	—	—	—	—	—	—

KM# 278.4 LOUIS D'OR
6.6900 g., 0.9170 Gold 0.1972 oz. AGW **Ruler:** Louis XIV
Mint: Tours

Date	Mintage	VG	F	VF	XF	Unc
1691E	—	300	500	800	1,300	—
1692E	—	300	500	850	1,450	—
1693E Rare	—	—	—	—	—	—

KM# 278.5 LOUIS D'OR
6.6900 g., 0.9170 Gold 0.1972 oz. AGW **Ruler:** Louis XIV
Mint: Poitiers

Date	Mintage	VG	F	VF	XF	Unc
1690G	—	300	500	850	1,450	—
1691G	—	250	450	800	1,300	—
1692G Rare	—	—	—	—	—	—

KM# 278.6 LOUIS D'OR
6.6900 g., 0.9170 Gold 0.1972 oz. AGW **Ruler:** Louis XIV
Mint: La Rochelle

Date	Mintage	VG	F	VF	XF	Unc
1692H Rare	—	—	—	—	—	—
1693H Rare	—	—	—	—	—	—

KM# 278.7 LOUIS D'OR
6.6900 g., 0.9170 Gold 0.1972 oz. AGW **Ruler:** Louis XIV
Mint: Limoges

Date	Mintage	VG	F	VF	XF	Unc
1690I	—	250	450	700	1,200	—
1691I	—	250	450	700	1,200	—
1692I Rare	—	—	—	—	—	—
1693I Rare	—	—	—	—	—	—

KM# 278.8 LOUIS D'OR
6.6900 g., 0.9170 Gold 0.1972 oz. AGW **Ruler:** Louis XIV
Mint: Bordeaux

Date	Mintage	VG	F	VF	XF	Unc
1690K	—	250	450	700	1,200	—
1691K	—	250	450	700	1,200	—
1692K	—	250	450	700	1,200	—

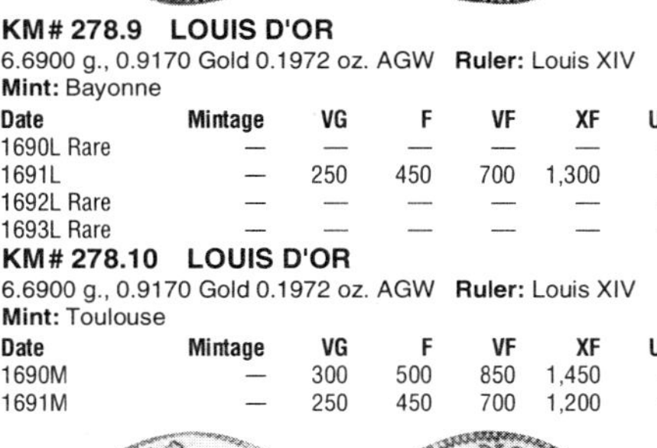

KM# 278.9 LOUIS D'OR
6.6900 g., 0.9170 Gold 0.1972 oz. AGW **Ruler:** Louis XIV
Mint: Bayonne

Date	Mintage	VG	F	VF	XF	Unc
1690L Rare	—	—	—	—	—	—
1691L	—	250	450	700	1,300	—
1692L Rare	—	—	—	—	—	—
1693L Rare	—	—	—	—	—	—

KM# 278.10 LOUIS D'OR
6.6900 g., 0.9170 Gold 0.1972 oz. AGW **Ruler:** Louis XIV
Mint: Toulouse

Date	Mintage	VG	F	VF	XF	Unc
1690M	—	300	500	850	1,450	—
1691M	—	250	450	700	1,200	—

KM# 278.11 LOUIS D'OR
6.6900 g., 0.9170 Gold 0.1972 oz. AGW **Ruler:** Louis XIV
Mint: Montpellier

Date	Mintage	VG	F	VF	XF	Unc
1690N	—	250	450	700	1,200	—
1691N	—	250	450	700	1,200	—
1693N Rare	—	—	—	—	—	—

KM# 278.12 LOUIS D'OR
6.6900 g., 0.9170 Gold 0.1972 oz. AGW **Ruler:** Louis XIV
Mint: Riom

Date	Mintage	VG	F	VF	XF	Unc
1690O	—	300	500	800	1,450	—
1691O Rare	—	—	—	—	—	—
1692O	—	300	500	800	1,450	—
1693O Rare	—	—	—	—	—	—

KM# 278.13 LOUIS D'OR
6.6900 g., 0.9170 Gold 0.1972 oz. AGW **Ruler:** Louis XIV
Mint: Dijon

Date	Mintage	VG	F	VF	XF	Unc
1690P	—	250	450	700	1,200	—
1691P	—	250	450	700	1,200	—
1692P Rare	—	—	—	—	—	—
1693P	—	300	500	900	1,550	—

KM# 278.14 LOUIS D'OR
6.6900 g., 0.9170 Gold 0.1972 oz. AGW **Ruler:** Louis XIV
Mint: Villeneuve St. André

Date	Mintage	VG	F	VF	XF	Unc
1691R Rare	—	—	—	—	—	—

KM# 278.15 LOUIS D'OR
6.6900 g., 0.9170 Gold 0.1972 oz. AGW **Ruler:** Louis XIV
Mint: Reims

Date	Mintage	VG	F	VF	XF	Unc
1690S	—	250	450	700	1,200	—
1691S	—	250	450	700	1,200	—
1692S Rare	—	—	—	—	—	—
1693S	—	300	500	800	1,400	—

KM# 278.16 LOUIS D'OR
6.6900 g., 0.9170 Gold 0.1972 oz. AGW **Ruler:** Louis XIV
Mint: Amiens

Date	Mintage	VG	F	VF	XF	Unc
1690X	—	300	500	800	1,400	—
1691X Rare	—	—	—	—	—	—

Date	Mintage	VG	F	VF	XF	Unc
1692X	—	300	500	900	1,550	—
1693X Rare	—	—	—	—	—	—

KM# 278.17 LOUIS D'OR
6.6900 g., 0.9170 Gold 0.1972 oz. AGW **Ruler:** Louis XIV
Mint: Bourges

Date	Mintage	VG	F	VF	XF	Unc
1690Y	—	250	450	700	1,200	—
1691Y	—	300	500	800	1,450	—
1692Y	—	300	500	800	1,450	—
1693Y Rare	—	—	—	—	—	—

KM# 278.18 LOUIS D'OR
6.6900 g., 0.9170 Gold 0.1972 oz. AGW **Ruler:** Louis XIV
Mint: Aix **Note:** Mint mark: Ampersand.

Date	Mintage	VG	F	VF	XF	Unc
1690	—	250	450	700	1,200	—
1691 Rare	—	—	—	—	—	—

KM# 278.19 LOUIS D'OR
6.6900 g., 0.9170 Gold 0.1972 oz. AGW **Ruler:** Louis XIV
Mint: Rennes **Note:** Mint mark: Numeral 9.

Date	Mintage	VG	F	VF	XF	Unc
1690	—	250	450	700	1,200	—
1691	—	300	500	800	1,300	—
1692	—	300	500	800	1,300	—
1693	—	300	500	850	1,450	—

KM# 278.20 LOUIS D'OR
6.6900 g., 0.9170 Gold 0.1972 oz. AGW **Ruler:** Louis XIV
Mint: Lille **Note:** Mint mark: Crowned L.

Date	Mintage	VG	F	VF	XF	Unc
1690	—	250	450	700	1,300	—
1691 Rare	—	—	—	—	—	—
1692 Rare	—	—	—	—	—	—
1693 Rare	—	—	—	—	—	—

KM# 278.21 LOUIS D'OR
6.6900 g., 0.9170 Gold 0.1972 oz. AGW **Ruler:** Louis XIV
Mint: Metz **Note:** Mint mark: Crowned M.

Date	Mintage	VG	F	VF	XF	Unc
1690	—	250	450	700	1,200	—
1691	—	250	450	700	1,200	—

KM# 278.22 LOUIS D'OR
6.6900 g., 0.9170 Gold 0.1972 oz. AGW **Ruler:** Louis XIV
Mint: Troyes **Note:** Mint mark: Crowned S.

Date	Mintage	VG	F	VF	XF	Unc
1690	—	300	500	850	1,300	—
1691 Rare	—	—	—	—	—	—
1692 Rare	—	—	—	—	—	—

KM# 279 LOUIS D'OR
6.6900 g., 0.9170 Gold 0.1972 oz. AGW **Ruler:** Louis XIV
Rev: Arms of France and Navarre Bearn **Mint:** Pau

Date	Mintage	VG	F	VF	XF	Unc
1690	—	1,500	3,000	4,000	7,500	—
1691	—	1,750	3,750	5,500	9,000	—
1692	—	2,500	4,250	6,500	11,000	—
1693	—	3,500	6,000	9,000	14,000	—

KM# 302.1 LOUIS D'OR
6.6900 g., 0.9170 Gold 0.1972 oz. AGW **Ruler:** Louis XIV
Obv: Old laureate head of Louis XIV **Mint:** Paris

Date	Mintage	VG	F	VF	XF	Unc
1693A	—	240	350	600	1,450	—
1694A	—	240	350	600	1,450	—
1695A	—	240	350	600	1,450	—
1696A	—	240	350	600	1,450	—
1697A	—	240	350	600	1,450	—
1698A	—	240	350	600	1,450	—
1699A	—	240	350	600	1,450	—
1700A	—	240	350	600	1,450	—

KM# 302.2 LOUIS D'OR
6.6900 g., 0.9170 Gold 0.1972 oz. AGW **Ruler:** Louis XIV
Mint: Metz

Date	Mintage	VG	F	VF	XF	Unc
1693AA Rare	—	—	—	—	—	—
1694AA	—	240	350	600	1,450	—
1695AA	—	240	350	600	1,450	—
1696AA	—	240	350	600	1,450	—
1699AA Rare	—	—	—	—	—	—

KM# 302.3 LOUIS D'OR
6.6900 g., 0.9170 Gold 0.1972 oz. AGW **Ruler:** Louis XIV
Mint: Rouen

Date	Mintage	VG	F	VF	XF	Unc
1693B	—	240	350	600	1,450	—
1694B	—	240	350	600	1,450	—
1695B	—	240	350	600	1,450	—
1696B	—	240	350	600	1,450	—
1699B Rare	—	—	—	—	—	—
1700B Rare	—	—	—	—	—	—

KM# 302.4 LOUIS D'OR
6.6900 g., 0.9170 Gold 0.1972 oz. AGW **Ruler:** Louis XIV
Obv: Older laureate head of Lois XIV **Rev:** 4 L's around mint mark **Mint:** Strasbourg

Date	Mintage	VG	F	VF	XF	Unc
1694BB	—	240	350	600	1,450	—
1695BB	—	240	350	600	1,450	—
1696BB	—	240	350	600	1,450	—
1697BB	—	240	350	600	1,450	—
1700BB Rare	—	—	—	—	—	—

KM# 302.5 LOUIS D'OR
6.6900 g., 0.9170 Gold 0.1972 oz. AGW **Ruler:** Louis XIV
Mint: Caen

Date	Mintage	VG	F	VF	XF	Unc
1694C	—	240	350	600	1,450	—
1695C	—	240	350	600	1,450	—
1696C	—	240	350	600	1,450	—
1697C Rare	—	—	—	—	—	—

KM# 302.6 LOUIS D'OR
6.6900 g., 0.9170 Gold 0.1972 oz. AGW **Ruler:** Louis XIV
Mint: Lyon

Date	Mintage	VG	F	VF	XF	Unc
1693D	—	300	475	725	1,550	—
1694D	—	240	350	600	1,450	—
1695D	—	240	350	600	1,450	—
1696D	—	240	350	600	1,450	—
1697D	—	240	350	600	1,450	—
1698D Rare	—	—	—	—	—	—
1699D Rare	—	—	—	—	—	—
1700D	—	240	350	600	1,450	—

KM# 302.7 LOUIS D'OR
6.6900 g., 0.9170 Gold 0.1972 oz. AGW **Ruler:** Louis XIV
Mint: Tours

Date	Mintage	VG	F	VF	XF	Unc
1693E	—	240	350	600	1,200	—
1694E	—	240	350	600	1,200	—
1695E Rare	—	—	—	—	—	—
1696E Rare	—	—	—	—	—	—
1697E	—	240	350	600	1,200	—
1698E Rare	—	—	—	—	—	—
1699E Rare	—	—	—	—	—	—

KM# 302.8 LOUIS D'OR
6.6900 g., 0.9170 Gold 0.1972 oz. AGW **Ruler:** Louis XIV
Mint: Poitiers

Date	Mintage	VG	F	VF	XF	Unc
1693G	—	240	350	600	1,450	—
1694G	—	240	350	600	1,450	—
1695G	—	240	350	600	1,450	—
1697G Rare	—	—	—	—	—	—
1699G Rare	—	—	—	—	—	—

KM# 302.9 LOUIS D'OR
6.6900 g., 0.9170 Gold 0.1972 oz. AGW **Ruler:** Louis XIV
Mint: La Rochelle

Date	Mintage	VG	F	VF	XF	Unc
1693H Rare	—	—	—	—	—	—
1694H	—	240	350	600	1,450	—
1695H	—	240	350	600	1,450	—
1698H	—	300	475	725	1,550	—
1699H	—	240	350	600	1,450	—
1700H Rare	—	—	—	—	—	—

KM# 302.10 LOUIS D'OR
6.6900 g., 0.9170 Gold 0.1972 oz. AGW **Ruler:** Louis XIV
Mint: Limoges

Date	Mintage	VG	F	VF	XF	Unc
1693I	—	300	475	800	1,550	—
1694I	—	300	475	800	1,550	—
1696I	—	300	475	800	1,550	—

KM# 302.11 LOUIS D'OR
6.6900 g., 0.9170 Gold 0.1972 oz. AGW **Ruler:** Louis XIV
Mint: Bordeaux

Date	Mintage	VG	F	VF	XF	Unc
1693K	—	240	350	600	1,450	—
1694K Rare	—	—	—	—	—	—
1695K	—	240	350	600	1,450	—
1696K	—	240	350	600	1,450	—
1698K Rare	—	—	—	—	—	—
1699K Rare	—	—	—	—	—	—
1700K Rare	—	—	—	—	—	—

KM# 302.12 LOUIS D'OR
6.6900 g., 0.9170 Gold 0.1972 oz. AGW **Ruler:** Louis XIV
Mint: Bayonne

Date	Mintage	VG	F	VF	XF	Unc
1693L Rare	—	—	—	—	—	—
1694L	—	240	350	600	1,450	—
1696L	—	240	350	600	1,450	—
1700L Rare	—	—	—	—	—	—

KM# 302.13 LOUIS D'OR
6.6900 g., 0.9170 Gold 0.1972 oz. AGW **Ruler:** Louis XIV
Mint: Toulouse

Date	Mintage	VG	F	VF	XF	Unc
1693M	—	240	350	600	1,450	—
1694M	—	240	350	600	1,450	—
1695M	—	240	350	600	1,450	—
1696M	—	300	475	725	1,550	—

KM# 302.14 LOUIS D'OR
6.6900 g., 0.9170 Gold 0.1972 oz. AGW **Ruler:** Louis XIV
Mint: Montpellier

Date	Mintage	VG	F	VF	XF	Unc
1693N	—	240	350	600	1,450	—
1694N	—	240	350	600	1,450	—
1695N Rare	—	—	—	—	—	—
1696N Rare	—	—	—	—	—	—
1697N Rare	—	—	—	—	—	—
1698N Rare	—	—	—	—	—	—
1699N Rare	—	—	—	—	—	—
1700N Rare	—	—	—	—	—	—

KM# 302.15 LOUIS D'OR
6.6900 g., 0.9170 Gold 0.1972 oz. AGW **Ruler:** Louis XIV
Mint: Riom

Date	Mintage	VG	F	VF	XF	Unc
16930	—	240	350	600	1,450	—
16940	—	240	350	600	1,450	—
16950	—	240	350	600	1,450	—
16960	—	240	350	600	1,450	—
16970 Rare	—	—	—	—	—	—
16980 Rare	—	—	—	—	—	—
17000 Rare	—	—	—	—	—	—

KM# 302.16 LOUIS D'OR
6.6900 g., 0.9170 Gold 0.1972 oz. AGW **Ruler:** Louis XIV
Mint: Dijon

Date	Mintage	VG	F	VF	XF	Unc
1693P	—	240	350	600	1,200	—
1694P	—	240	350	600	1,200	—
1695P Rare	—	—	—	—	—	—
1697P Rare	—	—	—	—	—	—
1698P	—	240	350	600	1,200	—
1700P Rare	—	—	—	—	—	—

KM# 302.17 LOUIS D'OR
6.6900 g., 0.9170 Gold 0.1972 oz. AGW **Ruler:** Louis XIV
Mint: Reims

Date	Mintage	VG	F	VF	XF	Unc
1693S	—	250	400	600	1,300	—
1695S	—	200	300	500	1,200	—
1696S	—	200	300	500	1,200	—
1697S Rare	—	—	—	—	—	—
1699S Rare	—	—	—	—	—	—
1700S Rare	—	—	—	—	—	—

KM# 302.18 LOUIS D'OR
6.6900 g., 0.9170 Gold 0.1972 oz. AGW **Ruler:** Louis XIV
Mint: Nantes

Date	Mintage	VG	F	VF	XF	Unc
1693T	—	240	350	600	1,450	—
1694T	—	240	350	600	1,450	—
1695T	—	240	350	600	1,450	—
1696T	—	240	350	600	1,450	—
1698T	—	300	475	725	1,550	—
1699T	—	240	350	600	1,450	—

KM# 302.19 LOUIS D'OR
6.6900 g., 0.9170 Gold 0.1972 oz. AGW **Ruler:** Louis XIV
Mint: Troyes

Date	Mintage	VG	F	VF	XF	Unc
1693V Rare	—	—	—	—	—	—
1694V	—	240	350	600	1,450	—
1697V	—	300	475	725	1,550	—
1699V Rare	—	—	—	—	—	—

KM# 302.20 LOUIS D'OR
6.6900 g., 0.9170 Gold 0.1972 oz. AGW **Ruler:** Louis XIV
Mint: Lille

Date	Mintage	VG	F	VF	XF	Unc
1693W	—	240	350	600	1,450	—
1694W	—	240	350	600	1,450	—
1695W	—	240	350	600	1,450	—
1696W	—	240	350	600	1,450	—
1697W Rare	—	—	—	—	—	—
1698W Rare	—	—	—	—	—	—
1699W	—	240	350	600	1,450	—
1700W	—	240	350	600	1,450	—

KM# 302.21 LOUIS D'OR
6.6900 g., 0.9170 Gold 0.1972 oz. AGW **Ruler:** Louis XIV
Mint: Amiens

Date	Mintage	VG	F	VF	XF	Unc
1693X Rare	—	—	—	—	—	—
1694X	—	240	350	600	1,450	—
1695X	—	240	350	600	1,450	—
1696X	—	240	350	600	1,450	—
1697X Rare	—	—	—	—	—	—

KM# 302.22 LOUIS D'OR

6.6900 g., 0.9170 Gold 0.1972 oz. AGW **Ruler:** Louis XIV **Mint:** Bourges

Date	Mintage	VG	F	VF	XF	Unc
1693Y	—	240	350	600	1,450	—
1694Y	—	300	475	725	1,550	—
1696Y	—	240	350	600	1,450	—
1698Y Rare	—	—	—	—	—	—

KM# 302.23 LOUIS D'OR

6.6900 g., 0.9170 Gold 0.1972 oz. AGW **Ruler:** Louis XIV **Mint:** Aix **Note:** Mint mark: Ampersand.

Date	Mintage	VG	F	VF	XF	Unc
1693	—	240	350	600	1,450	—
1694	—	240	350	600	1,450	—
1695	—	240	350	600	1,450	—
1696 Rare	—	—	—	—	—	—
1698 Rare	—	—	—	—	—	—
1700 Rare	—	—	—	—	—	—

KM# 302.24 LOUIS D'OR

6.6900 g., 0.9170 Gold 0.1972 oz. AGW **Ruler:** Louis XIV **Mint:** Rennes **Note:** Mint mark: 9.

Date	Mintage	VG	F	VF	XF	Unc
1693	—	240	350	600	1,450	—
1694	—	240	350	600	1,450	—
1695	—	240	350	600	1,450	—
1696	—	300	475	725	1,550	—
1697	—	300	475	725	1,550	—
1700	—	240	350	600	1,450	—

KM# 302.25 LOUIS D'OR

6.6900 g., 0.9170 Gold 0.1972 oz. AGW **Ruler:** Louis XIV **Mint:** Pau **Note:** Mint mark: Cow.

Date	Mintage	VG	F	VF	XF	Unc
1693	—	425	650	1,100	2,150	—
1694	—	425	650	1,100	2,150	—
1695	—	425	650	1,100	2,150	—
1696 Rare	—	—	—	—	—	—
1697	—	425	650	1,150	2,300	—
1698 Rare	—	—	—	—	—	—
1699 Rare	—	—	—	—	—	—
1700 Rare	—	—	—	—	—	—

KM# 302.26 LOUIS D'OR

6.6900 g., 0.9170 Gold 0.1972 oz. AGW **Ruler:** Louis XIV **Mint:** Besancon **Note:** Mint mark: Back-to-back C's.

Date	Mintage	VG	F	VF	XF	Unc
1694	—	300	550	900	1,800	—
1695	—	300	550	900	1,800	—
1697 Rare	—	—	—	—	—	—
1698 Rare	—	—	—	—	—	—
1699 Rare	—	—	—	—	—	—

KM# 334.1 LOUIS D'OR

6.6900 g., 0.9170 Gold 0.1972 oz. AGW **Ruler:** Louis XIV **Obv:** Laureate head right **Obv. Legend:** LVD • XIIII • D • G FR • ET • NAV • REX • **Rev:** Crowned back to back L's, Hand of Justice and sceptre cross at center **Rev. Legend:** CHRS • REGN • VINC • IMP **Mint:** Paris

Date	Mintage	VG	F	VF	XF	Unc
1700A	—	240	400	650	1,350	—

KM# 108 2 LOUIS D'OR

13.3900 g., 0.9170 Gold 0.3948 oz. AGW **Ruler:** Louis XIII **Rev. Legend:** • CHRS • • REGN • • VINC • • IMP • **Mint:** Paris

Date	Mintage	VG	F	VF	XF	Unc
1640A	432,000	1,000	2,500	4,250	7,500	—
1641A	72,000	1,500	3,250	5,500	9,500	—
1642A Rare	894	—	—	—	—	—
1643A Rare	—	—	—	—	—	—

KM# 109 2 LOUIS D'OR

13.3900 g., 0.9170 Gold 0.3948 oz. AGW **Ruler:** Louis XIII **Obv:** Large head **Obv. Legend:** • LVDO • XIII • D • G •... **Rev. Legend:** ...IMPE •

Date	Mintage	VG	F	VF	XF	Unc
1640	—	2,000	3,500	6,750	11,000	—

KM# 110.1 2 LOUIS D'OR

13.3900 g., 0.9170 Gold 0.3948 oz. AGW **Ruler:** Louis XIII **Rev:** Cross at end of legend **Mint:** Paris

Date	Mintage	VG	F	VF	XF	Unc
1640	—	2,500	4,500	9,500	15,000	—
1641	—	2,500	4,500	9,500	15,000	—

KM# 110.2 2 LOUIS D'OR

13.3900 g., 0.9170 Gold 0.3948 oz. AGW **Ruler:** Louis XIII **Mint:** Lyon

Date	Mintage	VG	F	VF	XF	Unc
1643D	13,000	2,000	4,000	7,500	10,000	—

KM# 150.1 2 LOUIS D'OR

13.3900 g., 0.9170 Gold 0.3948 oz. AGW **Ruler:** Louis XIV **Obv:** Laureate child head of Louis XIV right with short curl **Mint:** Paris

Date	Mintage	VG	F	VF	XF	Unc
1643A Rare	200	—	—	—	—	—
1644A	—	4,500	7,500	12,500	25,000	—

KM# 150.2 2 LOUIS D'OR

13.3900 g., 0.9170 Gold 0.3948 oz. AGW **Ruler:** Louis XIV **Mint:** Lyon

Date	Mintage	VG	F	VF	XF	Unc
1644D Rare	7,000	—	—	—	—	—
1645D Rare	1,160	—	—	—	—	—
1648D	1,582	5,000	9,500	15,000	30,000	—

KM# 158.1 2 LOUIS D'OR

13.3900 g., 0.9170 Gold 0.3948 oz. AGW **Ruler:** Louis XIV **Obv:** Head with long curl **Mint:** Paris

Date	Mintage	VG	F	VF	XF	Unc
1646A Rare	—	—	—	—	—	—
1650A Rare	13,000	—	—	—	—	—

KM# 158.2 2 LOUIS D'OR

13.3900 g., 0.9170 Gold 0.3948 oz. AGW **Ruler:** Louis XIV **Mint:** Rouen

Date	Mintage	VG	F	VF	XF	Unc
1647B Rare	—	—	—	—	—	—

KM# 158.3 2 LOUIS D'OR

13.3900 g., 0.9170 Gold 0.3948 oz. AGW **Ruler:** Louis XIV **Mint:** Angers

Date	Mintage	VG	F	VF	XF	Unc
1647F	362	2,100	4,900	8,400	14,000	—
1648F Rare	725	—	—	—	—	—

KM# 158.4 2 LOUIS D'OR

13.3900 g., 0.9170 Gold 0.3948 oz. AGW **Ruler:** Louis XIV **Mint:** La Rochelle

Date	Mintage	VG	F	VF	XF	Unc
1646H Rare	—	—	—	—	—	—
1647H	2,400	1,250	3,100	7,000	14,000	—
1648H	120	2,400	5,600	9,100	17,000	—
1649H	—	1,250	3,100	7,000	14,000	—

KM# 158.5 2 LOUIS D'OR

13.3900 g., 0.9170 Gold 0.3948 oz. AGW **Ruler:** Louis XIV **Mint:** Bordeaux

Date	Mintage	VG	F	VF	XF	Unc
1648K	1,522	1,400	3,500	7,000	14,000	—
1649K	—	1,400	3,500	7,000	14,000	—
1650K Rare	600	—	—	—	—	—

KM# 158.6 2 LOUIS D'OR

13.3900 g., 0.9170 Gold 0.3948 oz. AGW **Ruler:** Louis XIV **Mint:** Toulouse

Date	Mintage	VG	F	VF	XF	Unc
1647M	600	1,400	3,500	7,000	14,000	—
1648M	1,112	1,400	3,500	7,000	14,000	—

KM# 158.7 2 LOUIS D'OR

13.3900 g., 0.9170 Gold 0.3948 oz. AGW **Ruler:** Louis XIV **Mint:** Montpellier

Date	Mintage	VG	F	VF	XF	Unc
1646N Rare	—	—	—	—	—	—
1647N Rare	471	—	—	—	—	—
1648N	526	2,000	4,250	8,500	15,000	—
1649N Rare	363	—	—	—	—	—
1651N Rare	892	—	—	—	—	—
1652N Rare	1,319	—	—	—	—	—

KM# 158.8 2 LOUIS D'OR

13.3900 g., 0.9170 Gold 0.3948 oz. AGW **Ruler:** Louis XIV **Mint:** Dijon

Date	Mintage	VG	F	VF	XF	Unc
1646P	120	—	—	8,400	17,000	—
1651P Rare	1,660	—	—	—	—	—
1652P	2,127	1,050	2,800	6,300	12,500	—

KM# 158.9 2 LOUIS D'OR

13.3900 g., 0.9170 Gold 0.3948 oz. AGW **Ruler:** Louis XIV **Mint:** Aix **Note:** Mint mark: Ampersand.

Date	Mintage	VG	F	VF	XF	Unc
1646 Rare	—	—	—	—	—	—
1647 Rare	—	—	—	—	—	—

KM# 280.1 2 LOUIS D'OR

13.3900 g., 0.9170 Gold 0.3948 oz. AGW **Ruler:** Louis XIV **Obv:** Laureate older head of Louis XIV **Mint:** Paris

Date	Mintage	VG	F	VF	XF	Unc
1690A	—	600	1,150	2,350	4,750	—
1691A	—	900	1,500	2,950	6,000	—
1692A	—	900	1,500	2,950	6,000	—

KM# 280.2 2 LOUIS D'OR

13.3900 g., 0.9170 Gold 0.3948 oz. AGW **Ruler:** Louis XIV **Mint:** Rouen

Date	Mintage	VG	F	VF	XF	Unc
1690B	—	900	1,500	2,950	6,000	—
1691B Rare	—	—	—	—	—	—
1692B	—	900	1,500	2,950	6,000	—
1693B Rare	—	—	—	—	—	—

KM# 280.3 2 LOUIS D'OR

13.3900 g., 0.9170 Gold 0.3948 oz. AGW **Ruler:** Louis XIV **Mint:** Lyon

Date	Mintage	VG	F	VF	XF	Unc
1690D	295,000	900	1,500	2,950	6,000	—
1691D Rare	—	—	—	—	—	—
1692D Rare	—	—	—	—	—	—

KM# 280.4 2 LOUIS D'OR

13.3900 g., 0.9170 Gold 0.3948 oz. AGW **Ruler:** Louis XIV **Mint:** Tours

Date	Mintage	VG	F	VF	XF	Unc
1690E	—	900	1,500	2,950	6,000	—

KM# 280.5 2 LOUIS D'OR

13.3900 g., 0.9170 Gold 0.3948 oz. AGW **Ruler:** Louis XIV **Mint:** Poitiers

Date	Mintage	VG	F	VF	XF	Unc
1690G	—	900	1,650	3,250	6,800	—
1691G	—	900	1,500	2,950	6,000	—
1692G Rare	—	—	—	—	—	—
1693G Rare	—	—	—	—	—	—

KM# 280.6 2 LOUIS D'OR

13.3900 g., 0.9170 Gold 0.3948 oz. AGW **Ruler:** Louis XIV **Mint:** La Rochelle

Date	Mintage	VG	F	VF	XF	Unc
1691H	—	900	1,500	2,950	6,000	—
1692H Rare	—	—	—	—	—	—

KM# 280.7 2 LOUIS D'OR

13.3900 g., 0.9170 Gold 0.3948 oz. AGW **Ruler:** Louis XIV **Mint:** Limoges

Date	Mintage	VG	F	VF	XF	Unc
1690I Rare	—	—	—	—	—	—
1692I Rare	—	—	—	—	—	—
1693I Rare	—	—	—	—	—	—

KM# 280.8 2 LOUIS D'OR

13.3900 g., 0.9170 Gold 0.3948 oz. AGW **Ruler:** Louis XIV **Mint:** Bordeaux

Date	Mintage	VG	F	VF	XF	Unc
1690K	—	900	1,650	3,250	6,800	—

KM# 280.9 2 LOUIS D'OR

13.3900 g., 0.9170 Gold 0.3948 oz. AGW **Ruler:** Louis XIV **Mint:** Toulouse

Date	Mintage	VG	F	VF	XF	Unc
1691M	—	900	1,500	2,950	6,000	—
1692M Rare	—	—	—	—	—	—
1693M Rare	—	—	—	—	—	—

KM# 280.10 2 LOUIS D'OR

13.3900 g., 0.9170 Gold 0.3948 oz. AGW **Ruler:** Louis XIV **Mint:** Montpellier

Date	Mintage	VG	F	VF	XF	Unc
1690N	1,235	1,200	1,750	3,600	7,500	—

KM# 280.11 2 LOUIS D'OR
13.3900 g., 0.9170 Gold 0.3948 oz. AGW **Ruler:** Louis XIV
Mint: Riom

Date	Mintage	VG	F	VF	XF	Unc
16910 Rare	—	—	—	—	—	—

KM# 280.12 2 LOUIS D'OR
13.3900 g., 0.9170 Gold 0.3948 oz. AGW **Ruler:** Louis XIV
Mint: Dijon

Date	Mintage	VG	F	VF	XF	Unc
1691P	3,145	1,200	1,750	3,600	7,500	—
1693P Rare	—	—	—	—	—	—

KM# 280.13 2 LOUIS D'OR
13.3900 g., 0.9170 Gold 0.3948 oz. AGW **Ruler:** Louis XIV
Mint: Amiens

Date	Mintage	VG	F	VF	XF	Unc
1690X	5,200	1,200	1,750	3,600	7,500	—
1691X	—	900	1,500	2,950	6,000	—
1692X Rare	—	—	—	—	—	—

KM# 280.14 2 LOUIS D'OR
13.3900 g., 0.9170 Gold 0.3948 oz. AGW **Ruler:** Louis XIV
Mint: Bourges

Date	Mintage	VG	F	VF	XF	Unc
1690Y Rare	—	—	—	—	—	—
1691Y Rare	—	—	—	—	—	—
1692Y Rare	—	—	—	—	—	—
1693Y Rare	—	—	—	—	—	—

KM# 280.15 2 LOUIS D'OR
13.3900 g., 0.9170 Gold 0.3948 oz. AGW **Ruler:** Louis XIV
Mint: Aix **Note:** Mint mark: Ampersand.

Date	Mintage	VG	F	VF	XF	Unc
1690	—	900	1,500	2,950	6,000	—
1691 Rare	—	—	—	—	—	—
1692 Rare	—	—	—	—	—	—

KM# 280.16 2 LOUIS D'OR
13.3900 g., 0.9170 Gold 0.3948 oz. AGW **Ruler:** Louis XIV
Mint: Rennes **Note:** Mint mark: Numeral 9.

Date	Mintage	VG	F	VF	XF	Unc
1690	—	900	1,500	2,950	6,000	—
1691	—	900	1,500	2,950	6,000	—
1692 Rare	—	—	—	—	—	—
1693 Rare	—	—	—	—	—	—

KM# 280.17 2 LOUIS D'OR
13.3900 g., 0.9170 Gold 0.3948 oz. AGW **Ruler:** Louis XIV
Mint: Lille **Note:** Mint mark: Crowned L.

Date	Mintage	VG	F	VF	XF	Unc
1692 Rare	—	—	—	—	—	—

KM# 280.18 2 LOUIS D'OR
13.3900 g., 0.9170 Gold 0.3948 oz. AGW **Ruler:** Louis XIV
Mint: Metz **Note:** Mint mark: Crowned M.

Date	Mintage	VG	F	VF	XF	Unc
1691	—	900	1,650	3,250	6,800	—

KM# 280.19 2 LOUIS D'OR
13.3900 g., 0.9170 Gold 0.3948 oz. AGW **Ruler:** Louis XIV
Mint: Troyes **Note:** Mint mark: Crowned S.

Date	Mintage	VG	F	VF	XF	Unc
1690	—	1,200	1,750	3,600	7,500	—
1691 Rare	—	—	—	—	—	—
1692 Rare	—	—	—	—	—	—

KM# 303.1 2 LOUIS D'OR
13.3900 g., 0.9170 Gold 0.3948 oz. AGW **Ruler:** Louis XIV
Obv: Older laureate head of Louis XIV **Mint:** Paris

Date	Mintage	VG	F	VF	XF	Unc
1693A	—	550	1,100	2,400	3,900	—
1694A	—	550	1,100	2,400	3,900	—
1695A	—	550	1,100	2,400	3,900	—
1696A	—	550	1,100	2,400	3,900	—
1697A	—	550	1,100	2,400	3,900	—
1698A	—	550	1,100	2,400	3,900	—
1699A	—	550	1,100	2,400	3,900	—
1700A	—	550	1,100	2,400	3,900	—

KM# 303.2 2 LOUIS D'OR
13.3900 g., 0.9170 Gold 0.3948 oz. AGW **Ruler:** Louis XIV
Mint: Metz

Date	Mintage	VG	F	VF	XF	Unc
1693AA Rare	—	—	—	—	—	—
1694AA	—	550	1,100	2,400	3,900	—
1695AA	—	550	1,100	2,400	3,900	—
1696AA Rare	—	—	—	—	—	—
1697AA	—	550	1,100	2,400	3,900	—
1699AA	—	550	1,100	2,400	3,900	—

KM# 303.3 2 LOUIS D'OR
13.3900 g., 0.9170 Gold 0.3948 oz. AGW **Ruler:** Louis XIV
Mint: Rouen

Date	Mintage	VG	F	VF	XF	Unc
1693B	—	550	1,200	2,700	4,600	—
1694B Rare	—	—	—	—	—	—
1695B Rare	—	—	—	—	—	—
1696B Rare	—	—	—	—	—	—
1697B Rare	—	—	—	—	—	—
1698B Rare	—	—	—	—	—	—
1700B Rare	—	—	—	—	—	—

KM# 303.4 2 LOUIS D'OR
13.3900 g., 0.9170 Gold 0.3948 oz. AGW **Ruler:** Louis XIV
Mint: Strasbourg

Date	Mintage	VG	F	VF	XF	Unc
1694BB	—	550	1,100	2,400	4,200	—
1695BB	—	550	1,100	2,400	4,200	—
1696BB	—	550	1,100	2,400	4,200	—
1697BB Rare	—	—	—	—	—	—
1698BB Rare	—	—	—	—	—	—
1699BB Rare	—	—	—	—	—	—
1700BB	—	550	1,100	2,400	4,200	—

KM# 303.5 2 LOUIS D'OR
13.3900 g., 0.9170 Gold 0.3948 oz. AGW **Ruler:** Louis XIV
Mint: Caen

Date	Mintage	VG	F	VF	XF	Unc
1695C	—	550	1,100	2,400	4,200	—
1696C Rare	—	—	—	—	—	—
1697C Rare	—	—	—	—	—	—
1700C Rare	—	—	—	—	—	—

KM# 303.6 2 LOUIS D'OR
13.3900 g., 0.9170 Gold 0.3948 oz. AGW **Ruler:** Louis XIV
Mint: Lyon

Date	Mintage	VG	F	VF	XF	Unc
1693D	—	550	1,200	2,700	4,600	—
1694D	—	550	1,200	2,700	4,600	—
1695D	—	550	1,200	2,700	4,600	—
1696D Rare	—	—	—	—	—	—
1697D Rare	—	—	—	—	—	—
1698D Rare	—	—	—	—	—	—
1699D Rare	—	—	—	—	—	—
1700D Rare	—	—	—	—	—	—

KM# 303.7 2 LOUIS D'OR
13.3900 g., 0.9170 Gold 0.3948 oz. AGW **Ruler:** Louis XIV
Mint: Tours

Date	Mintage	VG	F	VF	XF	Unc
1696E	—	550	1,100	2,400	4,200	—

KM# 303.8 2 LOUIS D'OR
13.3900 g., 0.9170 Gold 0.3948 oz. AGW **Ruler:** Louis XIV
Mint: Angers

Date	Mintage	VG	F	VF	XF	Unc
1697F Rare	—	—	—	—	—	—

KM# 303.9 2 LOUIS D'OR
13.3900 g., 0.9170 Gold 0.3948 oz. AGW **Ruler:** Louis XIV
Mint: Poitiers

Date	Mintage	VG	F	VF	XF	Unc
1694G Rare	—	—	—	—	—	—
1695G Rare	—	—	—	—	—	—
1696G	—	725	1,300	2,950	6,000	—
1697G Rare	—	—	—	—	—	—
1698G Rare	—	—	—	—	—	—

KM# 303.10 2 LOUIS D'OR
13.3900 g., 0.9170 Gold 0.3948 oz. AGW **Ruler:** Louis XIV
Mint: La Rochelle

Date	Mintage	VG	F	VF	XF	Unc
1694H	—	600	1,150	2,650	5,500	—
1695H Rare	—	—	—	—	—	—
1696H	—	550	1,100	2,400	4,200	—
1697H Rare	—	—	—	—	—	—
1698H Rare	—	—	—	—	—	—
1699H Rare	—	—	—	—	—	—
1700H Rare	—	—	—	—	—	—

KM# 303.11 2 LOUIS D'OR
13.3900 g., 0.9170 Gold 0.3948 oz. AGW **Ruler:** Louis XIV
Mint: Limoges

Date	Mintage	VG	F	VF	XF	Unc
1694I Rare	—	—	—	—	—	—
1695I Rare	—	—	—	—	—	—
1696I	—	550	1,100	2,400	4,200	—
1697I	—	775	2,150	4,200	6,000	—
1699I Rare	—	—	—	—	—	—

KM# 303.12 2 LOUIS D'OR
13.3900 g., 0.9170 Gold 0.3948 oz. AGW **Ruler:** Louis XIV
Mint: Bordeaux

Date	Mintage	VG	F	VF	XF	Unc
1697K Rare	—	—	—	—	—	—
1698K Rare	—	—	—	—	—	—
1699K Rare	—	—	—	—	—	—

KM# 303.13 2 LOUIS D'OR
13.3900 g., 0.9170 Gold 0.3948 oz. AGW **Ruler:** Louis XIV
Mint: Bayonne

Date	Mintage	VG	F	VF	XF	Unc
1694L Rare	—	—	—	—	—	—
1695L	—	550	1,100	2,400	4,200	—
1696L	—	550	1,100	2,400	4,200	—
1697L	—	550	1,100	2,400	4,200	—
1698L Rare	—	—	—	—	—	—
1699L Rare	—	—	—	—	—	—
1700L Rare	—	—	—	—	—	—

KM# 303.14 2 LOUIS D'OR
13.3900 g., 0.9170 Gold 0.3948 oz. AGW **Ruler:** Louis XIV
Mint: Toulouse

Date	Mintage	VG	F	VF	XF	Unc
1694M	—	550	1,100	2,400	4,200	—
1695M	—	600	1,200	2,700	4,200	—
1696M Rare	—	—	—	—	—	—
1697M	—	550	1,100	2,400	4,200	—
1698M Rare	—	—	—	—	—	—
1699M Rare	—	—	—	—	—	—
1700M Rare	—	—	—	—	—	—

KM# 303.15 2 LOUIS D'OR
13.3900 g., 0.9170 Gold 0.3948 oz. AGW **Ruler:** Louis XIV
Mint: Montpellier

Date	Mintage	VG	F	VF	XF	Unc
1693N Rare	—	—	—	—	—	—
1694N Rare	—	—	—	—	—	—
1695N Rare	—	—	—	—	—	—
1696N	—	775	2,100	4,800	7,800	—
1697N Rare	—	—	—	—	—	—
1698N Rare	—	—	—	—	—	—
1699N Rare	—	—	—	—	—	—
1700N Rare	—	—	—	—	—	—

KM# 303.16 2 LOUIS D'OR
13.3900 g., 0.9170 Gold 0.3948 oz. AGW **Ruler:** Louis XIV
Mint: Riom

Date	Mintage	VG	F	VF	XF	Unc
16930 Rare	—	—	—	—	—	—
16940 Rare	—	—	—	—	—	—
16950 Rare	—	—	—	—	—	—
16960	—	600	1,200	3,000	5,400	—
16980 Rare	—	—	—	—	—	—

KM# 303.17 2 LOUIS D'OR
13.3900 g., 0.9170 Gold 0.3948 oz. AGW **Ruler:** Louis XIV
Mint: Dijon

Date	Mintage	VG	F	VF	XF	Unc
1693P	6,025	600	1,200	3,000	5,400	—
1694P	7,917	600	1,200	3,000	5,400	—
1695P Rare	—	—	—	—	—	—
1696P	—	600	1,200	3,000	5,400	—
1697P Rare	—	—	—	—	—	—
1698P Rare	—	—	—	—	—	—
1699P	—	600	1,200	3,000	5,400	—
1700P Rare	—	—	—	—	—	—

KM# 303.18 2 LOUIS D'OR
13.3900 g., 0.9170 Gold 0.3948 oz. AGW **Ruler:** Louis XIV
Mint: Reims

Date	Mintage	VG	F	VF	XF	Unc
1695S	—	550	1,100	2,400	4,200	—
1696S Rare	—	—	—	—	—	—
1697S Rare	—	—	—	—	—	—

KM# 303.19 2 LOUIS D'OR
13.3900 g., 0.9170 Gold 0.3948 oz. AGW **Ruler:** Louis XIV
Mint: Nantes

Date	Mintage	VG	F	VF	XF	Unc
1695T	—	550	1,100	2,400	4,200	—
1696T Rare	—	—	—	—	—	—
1697T Rare	—	—	—	—	—	—
1698T Rare	—	—	—	—	—	—
1699T	—	600	1,200	2,700	4,600	—

KM# 303.20 2 LOUIS D'OR
13.3900 g., 0.9170 Gold 0.3948 oz. AGW **Ruler:** Louis XIV
Mint: Troyes

Date	Mintage	VG	F	VF	XF	Unc
1694V Rare	—	—	—	—	—	—
1695V Rare	—	—	—	—	—	—
1696V Rare	—	—	—	—	—	—
1699V Rare	—	—	—	—	—	—

KM# 303.21 2 LOUIS D'OR
13.3900 g., 0.9170 Gold 0.3948 oz. AGW **Ruler:** Louis XIV
Mint: Lille

Date	Mintage	VG	F	VF	XF	Unc
1693W	—	550	1,100	2,400	4,200	—
1699W Rare	—	—	—	—	—	—

KM# 303.22 2 LOUIS D'OR
13.3900 g., 0.9170 Gold 0.3948 oz. AGW **Ruler:** Louis XIV
Mint: Amiens

Date	Mintage	VG	F	VF	XF	Unc
1698X Rare	—	—	—	—	—	—
1699X Rare	—	—	—	—	—	—

KM# 303.23 2 LOUIS D'OR
13.3900 g., 0.9170 Gold 0.3948 oz. AGW **Ruler:** Louis XIV
Mint: Bourges

Date	Mintage	VG	F	VF	XF	Unc
1694Y	—	600	1,200	2,700	5,000	—
1695Y Rare	—	—	—	—	—	—
1696Y Rare	—	—	—	—	—	—
1697Y	—	600	1,200	2,700	5,000	—
1698Y Rare	—	—	—	—	—	—

KM# 303.24 2 LOUIS D'OR
13.3900 g., 0.9170 Gold 0.3948 oz. AGW **Ruler:** Louis XIV
Mint: Rennes **Note:** Mint mark: Numeral 9.

Date	Mintage	VG	F	VF	XF	Unc
1693	—	550	1,100	2,400	4,200	—
1695 Rare	—	—	—	—	—	—

Date	Mintage	VG	F	VF	XF	Unc
1696 Rare	—	—	—	—	—	—
1697 Rare	—	—	—	—	—	—
1698 Rare	—	—	—	—	—	—
1699 Rare	—	—	—	—	—	—

KM# 303.25 2 LOUIS D'OR

13.3900 g., 0.9170 Gold 0.3948 oz. AGW **Ruler:** Louis XIV **Mint:** Aix **Note:** Mint mark: Ampersand.

Date	Mintage	VG	F	VF	XF	Unc
1694 Rare	—	—	—	—	—	—
1695 Rare	—	—	—	—	—	—
1696 Rare	—	—	—	—	—	—
1699 Rare	—	—	—	—	—	—

KM# 303.26 2 LOUIS D'OR

13.3900 g., 0.9170 Gold 0.3948 oz. AGW **Ruler:** Louis XIV **Mint:** Besancon **Note:** Mint mark: Back-to-back C's.

Date	Mintage	VG	F	VF	XF	Unc
1694 Rare	—	—	—	—	—	—
1695	—	550	1,100	2,400	4,200	—
1696	—	600	1,200	3,000	4,700	—
1697 Rare	—	—	—	—	—	—
1698 Rare	—	—	—	—	—	—
1699 Rare	—	—	—	—	—	—

KM# 303.27 2 LOUIS D'OR

13.3900 g., 0.9170 Gold 0.3948 oz. AGW **Ruler:** Louis XIV **Mint:** Pau **Note:** Mint mark: Cow.

Date	Mintage	VG	F	VF	XF	Unc
1695	—	750	1,500	3,000	5,500	—
1696 Rare	—	—	—	—	—	—
1697	—	750	1,500	3,000	5,500	—
1698 Rare	—	—	—	—	—	—
1699 Rare	—	—	—	—	—	—

KM# 335.1 2 LOUIS D'OR

13.3900 g., 0.9170 Gold 0.3948 oz. AGW **Ruler:** Louis XIV **Obv:** Laureate head right **Obv. Legend:** LVD • XIIII • D • G FR • ET • NAV • REX **Rev:** Crowned back to back L's with sceptre and hand of Justice crossed at center behind circle **Rev. Legend:** CHRS REGN VINC IMP **Mint:** Paris

Date	Mintage	VG	F	VF	XF	Unc
1700A	—	700	1,400	2,500	4,750	—

KM# 111 4 LOUIS D'OR

26.7700 g., 0.9170 Gold 0.7892 oz. AGW **Ruler:** Louis XIII **Obv:** Laureate head of Louis XIII right, date below **Rev:** Eight L's back-to-back forming cross with crown at end of each arm, mint mark at center **Mint:** Paris

Date	Mintage	VG	F	VF	XF	Unc
1640A	—	—	35,000	75,000	125,000	—

KM# 112 8 LOUIS D'OR

53.5400 g., 0.9170 Gold 1.5784 oz. AGW **Ruler:** Louis XIII **Obv:** Laureate head of Louis XIII right, date below **Rev:** Eight L's back-to-back forming cross with crown at end of each arm, mint mark at center **Rev. Legend:** CHRISTUS • REGNAT • VINCIT • ET • IMPERAT **Mint:** Paris

Date	Mintage	VG	F	VF	XF	Unc
1640A	—	—	30,000	55,000	100,000	—

KM# 113 8 LOUIS D'OR

53.5400 g., 0.9170 Gold 1.5784 oz. AGW **Ruler:** Louis XIII **Rev. Legend:** CHRS • REGN • VINC • IMP •

Date	Mintage	VG	F	VF	XF	Unc
1640	—	—	32,000	60,000	110,000	—

KM# 114 10 LOUIS D'OR

66.9200 g., 0.9170 Gold 1.9729 oz. AGW **Ruler:** Louis XIII **Mint:** Paris

Date	Mintage	VG	F	VF	XF	Unc
1640A	—	—	—	65,000	120,000	—

KM# 115 10 LOUIS D'OR

66.9200 g., 0.9170 Gold 1.9729 oz. AGW **Ruler:** Louis XIII **Obv:** Laureate and draped bust of Louis XIII right

Date	Mintage	VG	F	VF	XF	Unc
1640 Rare	—	—	—	—	—	—

ESSAIS

Standard metals unless otherwise noted

KM#	Date	Mintage	Identification	Mkt Val
E1	1634	—	1/2 Ecu D'Or. Gold. 1.3500 g.	5,000

KM#	Date	Mintage	Identification	Mkt Val
E2	1634	—	Ecu D'Or. Gold.	7,000
AE3	1642	—	Sizain. Gold. 4.5700 g.	—

PATTERNS

Including off metal strikes

KM#	Date	Mintage	Identification	Mkt Val
Pn1	1602	—	4 Sols.	—
Pn2	1602	—	6 Sols.	—
Pn3	1604A	—	Double Tournois. Silver. Ciani #1579	1,000
Pn4	1607A	—	Douzain.	1,000
Pn5	1607A	—	1/4 Franc. Silver. Ciani #1552	4,000
Pn6	1607A	—	1/2 Franc. Silver.	4,000
Pn7	1607A	—	Franc. Silver.	6,000
Pn8	ND	—	Liard. Silver. of Bearn	—
Pn9	1613D	—	Denier Tournois. Silver.	1,150
Pn10	1616A NB	—	Franc. 0.8330 Silver. 14.1880 g. Nicolas Briot	1,200

KM#	Date	Mintage	Identification	Mkt Val
PnA11	1618A	—	1/4 Franc. Silver.	4,500
Pn11	1618A	—	Franc. Silver.	—

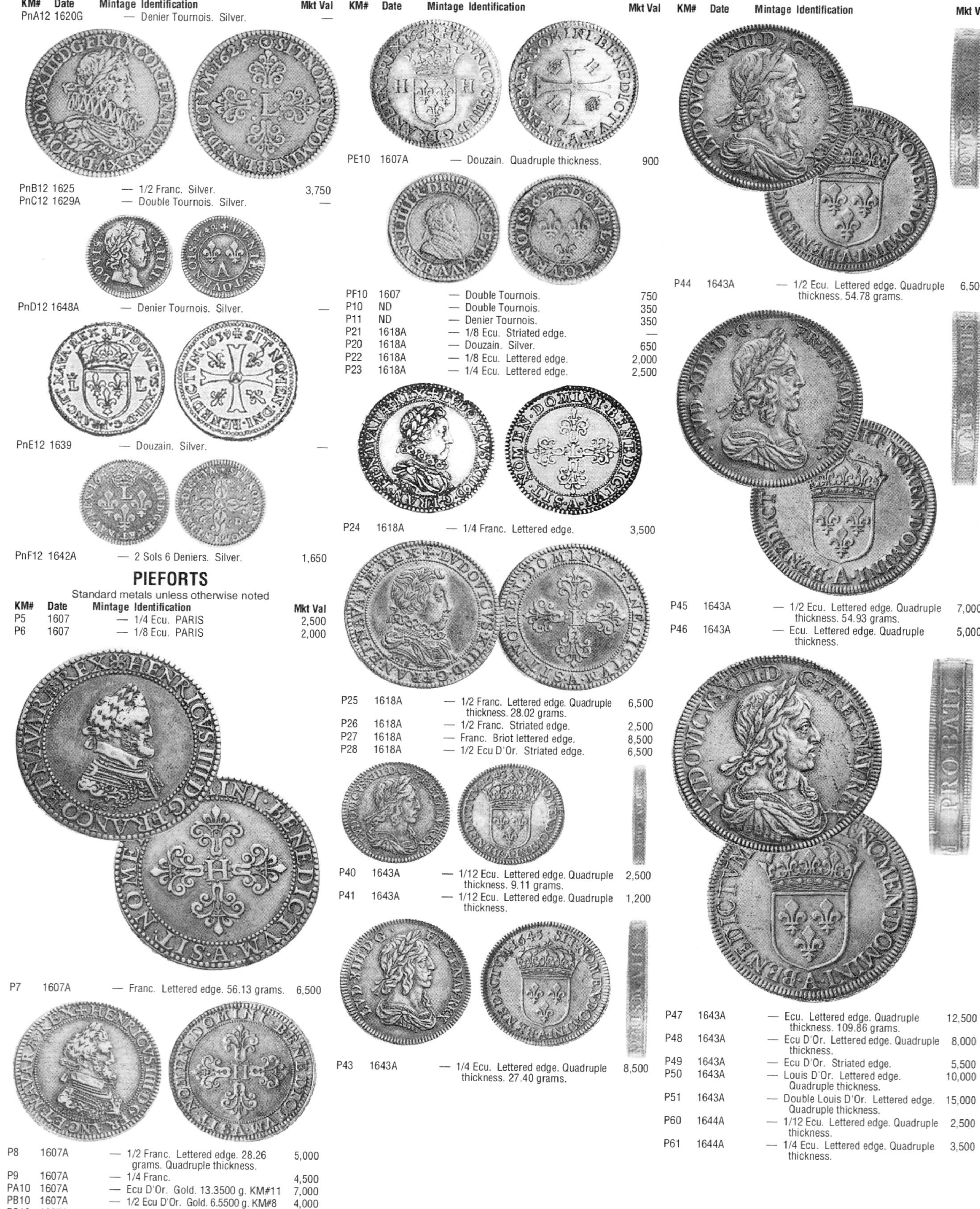

KM#	Date	Mintage	Identification	Mkt Val
PnA12	1620G	—	Denier Tournois. Silver.	—
PnB12	1625	—	1/2 Franc. Silver.	3,750
PnC12	1629A	—	Double Tournois. Silver.	—
PnD12	1648A	—	Denier Tournois. Silver.	—
PnE12	1639	—	Douzain. Silver.	—
PnF12	1642A	—	2 Sols 6 Deniers. Silver.	1,650

PIEFORTS

Standard metals unless otherwise noted

KM#	Date	Mintage	Identification	Mkt Val
P5	1607	—	1/4 Ecu. PARIS	2,500
P6	1607	—	1/8 Ecu. PARIS	2,000
P7	1607A	—	Franc. Lettered edge. 56.13 grams.	6,500
P8	1607A	—	1/2 Franc. Lettered edge. 28.26 grams. Quadruple thickness.	5,000
P9	1607A	—	1/4 Franc.	4,500
PA10	1607A	—	Ecu D'Or. Gold. 13.3500 g. KM#11	7,000
PB10	1607A	—	1/2 Ecu D'Or. Gold. 6.5500 g. KM#8	4,000
PC10	1607A	—	Ecu D'Or. Gold. KM#11. Weight varies: 5.70-6.75 grams.	—
PD10	1607A	—	1/2 Ecu D'Or. Gold. 3.2700 g. KM#8	—
PE10	1607A	—	Douzain. Quadruple thickness.	900
PF10	1607	—	Double Tournois.	750
P10	ND	—	Double Tournois.	350
P11	ND	—	Denier Tournois.	350
P21	1618A	—	1/8 Ecu. Striated edge.	—
P20	1618A	—	Douzain. Silver.	650
P22	1618A	—	1/8 Ecu. Lettered edge.	2,000
P23	1618A	—	1/4 Ecu. Lettered edge.	2,500
P24	1618A	—	1/4 Franc. Lettered edge.	3,500
P25	1618A	—	1/2 Franc. Lettered edge. Quadruple thickness. 28.02 grams.	6,500
P26	1618A	—	1/2 Franc. Striated edge.	2,500
P27	1618A	—	Franc. Briot lettered edge.	8,500
P28	1618A	—	1/2 Ecu D'Or. Striated edge.	6,500
P40	1643A	—	1/12 Ecu. Lettered edge. Quadruple thickness. 9.11 grams.	2,500
P41	1643A	—	1/12 Ecu. Lettered edge. Quadruple thickness.	1,200
P43	1643A	—	1/4 Ecu. Lettered edge. Quadruple thickness. 27.40 grams.	8,500
P44	1643A	—	1/2 Ecu. Lettered edge. Quadruple thickness. 54.78 grams.	6,500
P45	1643A	—	1/2 Ecu. Lettered edge. Quadruple thickness. 54.93 grams.	7,000
P46	1643A	—	Ecu. Lettered edge. Quadruple thickness.	5,000
P47	1643A	—	Ecu. Lettered edge. Quadruple thickness. 109.86 grams.	12,500
P48	1643A	—	Ecu D'Or. Lettered edge. Quadruple thickness.	8,000
P49	1643A	—	Ecu D'Or. Striated edge.	5,500
P50	1643A	—	Louis D'Or. Lettered edge. Quadruple thickness.	10,000
P51	1643A	—	Double Louis D'Or. Lettered edge. Quadruple thickness.	15,000
P60	1644A	—	1/12 Ecu. Lettered edge. Quadruple thickness.	2,500
P61	1644A	—	1/4 Ecu. Lettered edge. Quadruple thickness.	3,500

KM#	Date	Mintage	Identification	Mkt Val

P62	1644A	—	1/2 Ecu. Lettered edge. Quadruple thickness. 5474 grams.	4,500

P63	1644A	—	Ecu. Lettered edge. Quadruple thickness. 109.77 grams.	10,000

P64	1644A	—	1/2 Louis D'Or. Lettered edge. Quadruple thickness. 13.43 grams.	13,500

FRENCH STATES

AIRE

(Aire-sur-la-lys, Artois)

A town in north France on the Lys, lies in a low and marshy area at the junction of 3. canals

In the middle ages, Aire belonged to the counts of Flanders and a charter of 1188 is still extant. It was given to France by the Peace of Utrecht in 1713. In World War I, it was one of the headquarters of the British Army Expeditionary Forces.

NOTE: See also Spanish Netherlands-Artois.

COUNTY

SIEGE COINAGE

1641

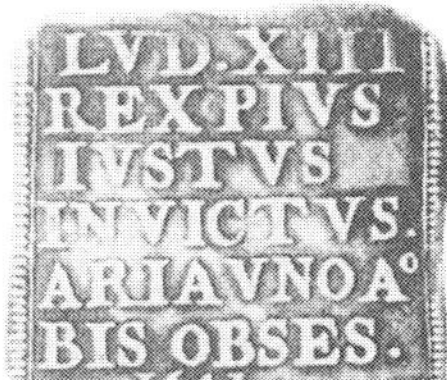

KM# 13 4 GRAMMES 70

Silver **Obv:** Legend in seven lines - LVD XIII/REX PIVS/JVSTYS/INVICTVS/ARIA ANO A /BIS OBES/1641 **Note:** Uniface.

Date	Mintage	VG	F	VF	XF	Unc
1641	—	375	675	1,250	2,000	—

KM# 14 9 GRAMMES 80

Silver **Obv:** Legend in seven lines - LVD XIII/REX PIVS/JVSTYS/INVICTVS/ARIA ANO A /BIS OBES/1641 **Note:** Uniface.

Date	Mintage	VG	F	VF	XF	Unc
1641	—	375	675	1,250	2,000	—

BOISBELLE & HENRICHEMONT

A principality located 22 miles east of Vierzon, Cher Department, northwest of Bourges.

RULERS

Maximilian I of Bethune, 1597-1641
Maximilian III, 1641-1661

PRINCIPALITY

STANDARD COINAGE

KM# 3 DOUBLE TOURNOIS

Copper **Obv. Legend:** MAX • D • BETHVNE • P • S • DENRIC **Rev:** Lis around shield **Rev. Legend:** DOVBLE • TOVRNOIS

Date	Mintage	VG	F	VF	XF	Unc
1636	—	18.00	35.00	75.00	150	—

KM# 4 DOUBLE TOURNOIS

Copper **Obv. Legend:** MAXI. P. BET. P. S. DENRIC ET BB

Date	Mintage	VG	F	VF	XF	Unc
1636	—	18.00	40.00	90.00	175	—

KM# 5 DOUBLE TOURNOIS

2.7700 g., Copper, 20.6 mm. **Ruler:** Maximilien I of Bethune **Obv:** Bust right **Obv. Legend:** MAX. D. BETH. NE. P. S. DHENRIC. **Rev:** Arms in circle of fleur-de-liis **Rev. Legend:** DOVBLE TOVRNOIS 1637L **Edge:** Plain

Date	Mintage	F	VF	XF	Unc	BU
1637L	—	50.00	100	200	—	—

KM# 6 DOUBLE TOURNOIS

Copper **Obv. Legend:** MAX D BETHVNE P S DHEN

Date	Mintage	VG	F	VF	XF	Unc
1641	—	18.00	40.00	90.00	175	—

KM# 15 DOUBLE TOURNOIS

Copper **Obv:** Bust **Obv. Legend:** M. D. BETHVNE P. S. DENRICHE.

Date	Mintage	VG	F	VF	XF	Unc
1642 H	—	20.00	45.00	100	200	—

KM# 10 1/2 FRANC

7.0800 g., Silver **Obv. Legend:** MAXI. D BETHVNE. P. S... **Rev:** M on floral cross

Date	Mintage	VG	F	VF	XF	Unc
1637	—	650	1,250	2,000	3,000	—

PATTERNS

Including off metal strikes

KM#	Date	Mintage	Identification	Mkt Val

Pn1	1636	—	Double Tournois. Silver. 2.6000 g.	650

PIEFORTS

KM#	Date	Mintage	Identification	Mkt Val
P1	1637	—	1/2 Franc. Silver. 14.0000 g.	1,200

BOUILLON & SEDAN

Small duchy located in the southeastern Province of Luxembourg in Belgium and also in the Sedan of northern France. Sold by Godfrey V in 1098 to Bishopric of Liege to finance his activities in the crusades. It came under the French in 1678 and later became a part of the Netherlands in 1815.

RULERS

Henri de la Tour, 1591-1623
Frederick Maurice, 1623-1652
Geoffrey Maurice, 1652-1671

MONETARY SYSTEM

3 Deniers = 1 Liard
4 Liards = 1 Sol
20 Sols = 1 Livre
6 Livres = 1 Ecu

DUCHY

STANDARD COINAGE

KM# 9 2 TOURNOIS

Copper **Obv:** Henri de la Tour **Rev:** Crowned arms **Rev. Legend:** DOVBLE TOVRNOIS

Date	Mintage	Good	VG	F	VF	XF
1614	—	5.00	10.00	20.00	40.00	—

KM# 14.1 2 TOURNOIS

Copper **Obv:** Bust right **Obv. Legend:** F. MAVRICE. DE. LATOVR. P. S. D. S. **Rev:** Tower with fleur-de-lis **Rev. Legend:** DOVBLE TOVRNOIS

Date	Mintage	Good	VG	F	VF	XF
1632	—	5.00	10.00	20.00	40.00	—
1633	—	5.00	10.00	20.00	40.00	—

KM# 14.2 2 TOURNOIS

Copper **Obv:** Bust right **Obv. Legend:** F. M. D. L. TOVR. DVC. D. BVILLON **Rev:** Tower with fleur-de-lis, and date **Rev. Legend:** DOVBLE. DE. SEDAN

Date	Mintage	Good	VG	F	VF	XF
1635	—	5.00	10.00	20.00	40.00	—
1636	—	5.00	10.00	20.00	40.00	—
1637	—	5.00	10.00	20.00	40.00	—
1638	—	5.00	10.00	20.00	40.00	—

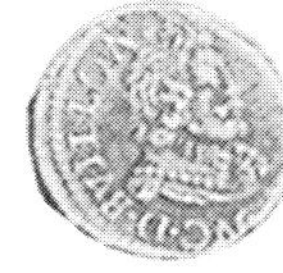

KM# 14.3 2 TOURNOIS

Copper **Obv:** Bust right **Obv. Legend:** F. M. D. L. TOVR. DVC. D. BVILLON **Rev:** Three fleur-de-lis around tower **Rev. Legend:** DOVBLE. DE. SEDAN

Date	Mintage	Good	VG	F	VF	XF
1641	—	6.00	12.00	25.00	45.00	—
1642	—	6.00	12.00	25.00	45.00	—
1643	—	6.00	12.50	25.00	45.00	—

KM# 5 LIARD

Copper **Rev:** Fleur-de-lis **Rev. Legend:** LIARD TOVRNOIS

Date	Mintage	Good	VG	F	VF	XF
1614	—	70.00	150	300	550	—

KM# 40 LIARD

Copper **Obv:** Frederic Maurice **Rev:** Fleur-de-lis

Date	Mintage	Good	VG	F	VF	XF
1642	—	8.00	12.00	25.00	50.00	—

KM# 42 LIARD

Copper **Obv:** Crowned arms **Obv. Legend:** GODF. F. MAV. D. G. DVX. BVLLIONEVS. **Rev:** LIARD DE BOVILLON 1681, with fleur-de-lis between towers

Date	Mintage	Good	VG	F	VF	XF
1681	—	5.00	10.00	20.00	40.00	—

KM# 12.1 2 LIARDS

Copper **Obv. Legend:** HENR•DE•LA•TPVR•D•BVLLIONAEVS **Rev:** Crowned arms **Rev. Legend:** ...SEDANENSIS

Date	Mintage	Good	VG	F	VF	XF
1613	—	6.50	12.50	25.00	55.00	—
1614	—	6.50	12.50	25.00	50.00	—

KM# 12.2 2 LIARDS

Copper **Rev. Legend:** ...BVLLIONEVS

Date	Mintage	Good	VG	F	VF	XF
1613	—	7.00	13.50	27.50	60.00	—

KM# 12.3 2 LIARDS

Copper **Rev. Legend:** ...SEDANI ET RAV

Date	Mintage	Good	VG	F	VF	XF
1614	—	5.00	10.00	22.00	50.00	—

KM# 12.4 2 LIARDS

Copper **Rev. Legend:** ...SEDANI ET RAVC

Date	Mintage	Good	VG	F	VF	XF
1614	—	5.00	10.00	22.00	50.00	—

KM# 13 2 LIARDS

Copper **Obv:** Large bust

Date	Mintage	Good	VG	F	VF	XF
ND	—	6.00	12.50	30.00	60.00	—

KM# 43 2 LIARDS

3.5500 g., Copper, 23.9 mm. **Ruler:** Geoffrey Maurice **Obv:** Bust right **Obv. Legend:** BVLLIONEUS. GOD. EF. FD. G. DUX **Rev:** DOVBLE DE BOVILLON in three lines above a fleur-de-lis between two towers **Edge:** Plain

Date	Mintage	F	VF	XF	Unc	BU
ND(circa 1681)	—	35.00	70.00	—	—	—

KM# 15 5 SOLS

Copper **Obv. Legend:** HENR DE L D BVLLINAEVS **Rev:** Crowned arms **Rev. Legend:** MONET. ARC. NOVA. SEDAN.

Date	Mintage	Good	VG	F	VF	XF
ND	—	275	550	875	—	—

KM# 45 5 SOLS

Copper **Obv:** Geoffrey Maurice **Rev:** Crowned arms

Date	Mintage	Good	VG	F	VF	XF
1684	—	—	—	40.00	65.00	—

Note: Restrike c.1845-60

KM# 16 1/2 ECU

9.9500 g., Silver **Obv:** Date at lower left, value "XV" at lower right below eagle's talons **Obv. Legend:** HENRICVS. DE... **Rev:** Crowned arms

Date	Mintage	Good	VG	F	VF	XF
1613	—	350	700	1,250	2,150	—
1614	—	350	700	1,250	2,150	—

KM# 19 ECU (30 Sous)

Silver **Obv:** Date at left, XXX at right below eagle's talons **Obv. Legend:** * HENRICVS. DE. LA. TOVR. **Note:** Dav. #3816.

Date	Mintage	VG	F	VF	XF	Unc
1613	—	95.00	180	325	550	—
1614	—	95.00	180	325	550	—

KM# 21 ECU (30 Sous)

Silver **Rev:** Similar to KM#19 with Bouillon arms in fourth quarter **Note:** Dav. #3817.

Date	Mintage	VG	F	VF	XF	Unc
1613	—	115	230	400	700	—
1614	—	115	230	400	700	—

KM# 22 ECU (30 Sous)

Silver **Obv:** Similar to KM#19 with date at lower right, value "XXX" at lower left below eagle's talons **Rev:** Similar to KM#19 with Turenne arms in second and third quarters **Note:** Dav. #3818.

Date	Mintage	VG	F	VF	XF	Unc
1613 Rare	—	—	—	—	—	—
1614 Rare	—	—	—	—	—	—

KM# 24 ECU (45 Sous)

Silver **Obv:** Legend around bust with .XLV. below **Obv. Legend:** * HENRICVS. DE. LA.- TOVR. DVX. BVLLIONII **Note:** Dav. #3819.

Date	Mintage	VG	F	VF	XF	Unc
1614 Rare	—	—	—	—	—	—

KM# 25 ECU (45 Sous)
Silver **Obv:** Similar to KM#24 with legend beginning at lower left **Rev:** Modified frame for arms **Note:** Dav. #3820.

Date	Mintage	VG	F	VF	XF	Unc
1614	—	775	1,550	2,650	4,500	—

KM# 28 ECU (45 Sous)
Silver **Obv:** Similar to KM#27 with date below smaller bust **Rev. Legend:** SVPREMVS. PRINCEPS. SEDANI... **Note:** Dav. #3821.

Date	Mintage	VG	F	VF	XF	Unc
1614 Rare	—	—	—	—	—	—

KM# 26 ECU (45 Sous)
Silver **Obv:** Similar to KM#25 without • XLV • below bust **Rev:** Similar to KM#25 **Note:** Dav. #A3821.

Date	Mintage	VG	F	VF	XF	Unc
1614 Rare	—	—	—	—	—	—

KM# 27 ECU (45 Sous)
Silver **Obv:** Date below bust **Note:** Dav. #B3821.

Date	Mintage	VG	F	VF	XF	Unc
1614 Rare	—	—	—	—	—	—

KM# 29 ECU (45 Sous)
Silver **Obv. Legend:** *HENRICVS + DE + LA * TOVR... **Rev. Legend:** SVP. PRINCEPS. SEDANI. ET RAVCVRT. **Note:** Dav. #3822.

Date	Mintage	VG	F	VF	XF	Unc
1615	—	775	1,550	2,650	4,500	—
1616	—	775	1,550	2,650	4,500	—

KM# 35 ECU (45 Sous)
Silver **Obv:** Legend around cuirassed knight over lion arms **Obv. Legend:** * FRED. MAVRIT * - * D. G. PRIN. AVR * **Rev:** Rampant lion left **Rev. Legend:** * CONFIDENS * DNO * NON * MOVETVR * 1634 **Note:** Dav. #3823.

Date	Mintage	VG	F	VF	XF	Unc
1634	—	800	1,650	2,850	4,750	—

KM# 3 ECU D'OR
3.3600 g., 0.9520 Gold 0.1028 oz. AGW **Obv:** Crowned arms in inner circle **Rev:** Cross in inner circle

Date	Mintage	VG	F	VF	XF	Unc
1610	—	325	725	1,200	2,000	—
ND	—	325	725	1,200	2,000	—

KM# 30 ECU D'OR
3.3600 g., 0.9520 Gold 0.1028 oz. AGW **Obv:** Bust of Henri right in inner circle **Rev:** Crowned arms

Date	Mintage	VG	F	VF	XF	Unc
1614	—	750	1,650	3,000	5,500	—

KM# 4 2 ECU D'OR
6.7200 g., 0.9520 Gold 0.2057 oz. AGW **Obv:** Crowned arms in inner circle **Rev:** Cross in inner circle

Date	Mintage	VG	F	VF	XF	Unc
1610	—	925	1,950	3,250	5,200	—
1614	—	1,350	2,850	5,500	7,500	—
ND	—	925	1,950	3,250	5,200	—

BURGUNDY

(Dole)

City in eastern France 25 miles southeast of Dijon. Roman ruins show early settlement in the area. Later used as a Burgundian mint by the Spanish kings.

RULER
Spanish

POSSESSION
(of Spain)
STANDARD COINAGE

DAV# 4472 PATAGON
Silver **Ruler:** Philip IV **Obv:** Burgundian cross divides date, crown above **Obv. Legend:** ✠ • PHIL • IIII • D • G • REX • HISP • INDIAR **Rev:** Crowned Spanish arms in Order chain **Rev. Legend:** ARCHID • AVST(RIE) • (DVX) • ET • COM • BVRG • Zc

Date	Mintage	Good	VG	F	VF	XF
1622(c)	—	45.00	90.00	165	285	450
1622(r)	—	45.00	90.00	165	285	450
1623(r)	—	45.00	90.00	165	285	450
1624(r)	—	45.00	90.00	165	285	450
1625(r)	—	45.00	90.00	165	285	450
1625(s)	—	45.00	90.00	165	285	450
1626(r)	—	45.00	90.00	165	285	450
1626(s)	—	45.00	90.00	165	285	450
1627(s)	—	45.00	90.00	165	285	450
1628(s)	—	45.00	90.00	165	285	450
1634(s)	—	45.00	90.00	165	285	450
1635(s)	—	45.00	90.00	165	285	450
1636(s)	—	45.00	90.00	165	285	450
1639(s)	—	45.00	90.00	165	285	450

DAV# 4471 2 PATAGON
Silver **Ruler:** Philip IV **Obv:** Burgundian cross divides date, crown above **Obv. Legend:** ✠ • PHIL • IIII • D • G • REX • HISP • INDIAR **Rev:** Crowned Spanish arms in Order chain **Rev. Legend:** ARCHID • AVST(RIE) • (DVX) • ET • COM • BVRG • Zc

Date	Mintage	Good	VG	F	VF	XF
1622 Rare	—	—	—	—	—	—
1633(s) Rare	—	—	—	—	—	—

TRADE COINAGE

FR# 118 CORONA
3.3800 g., 0.9170 Gold 0.0996 oz. AGW **Ruler:** Philip IV **Obv:** Floreate cross in inner circle, date in legend **Rev:** Crowned Spanish arms between two crowned steels

Date	Mintage	VG	F	VF	XF	Unc
1632 Rare	—	—	—	—	—	—

CHATEAU-RENAUD

A small city in northern France near the Belgian border. Francois de Bourbon, Prince Conti acquired the city when he married Louise Marguerite of Lorraine in 1605. After his death in 1614 Louise Marguerite ruled until she ceded the property to Louis XIII of France in 1629.

RULERS
Francois and Louise Marguerite, 1605-1614
Louise Marguerite, alone 1614-1631

PRINCIPALITY
STANDARD COINAGE

KM# 5 2 DENIERS (Tournois)
Copper **Obv:** Bust **Obv. Legend:** F • DE • BOVRBON • P • DE • CONTI **Rev:** Fleur-de-lis **Rev. Legend:** DOVBLE TOVRNOIS **Note:** Varieties exist.

Date	Mintage	VG	F	VF	XF	Unc
ND(1603-05)	—	7.00	15.00	30.00	60.00	—

KM# 25 LIARD
Copper **Obv:** Bust **Obv. Legend:** FRANCOIS DE BOYRBON **Rev:** Crowned arms **Rev. Legend:** PRINCE. DE. CONTI. SOVER.

Date	Mintage	VG	F	VF	XF	Unc
1613	—	10.00	20.00	40.00	80.00	—

KM# 26.1 LIARD
Copper **Obv:** Large bust right **Obv. Legend:** FRANCOIS. DE. BOVRBON. **Rev:** Crowned arms **Rev. Legend:** P. DE. CONTI. S. DE. CH. RENAV.

Date	Mintage	VG	F	VF	XF	Unc
1613	—	10.00	15.00	40.00	80.00	—
1614	—	10.00	18.00	45.00	85.00	—

KM# 26.2 LIARD
Copper **Obv:** Small bust right **Obv. Legend:** FRANCOIS. DE. BOVRBON. **Rev:** Crowned arms **Rev. Legend:** P. DE. CONTI. S. DE. CH. RENAV.

Date	Mintage	VG	F	VF	XF	Unc
1613	—	8.00	14.00	35.00	75.00	—
1614	—	8.00	16.00	40.00	85.00	—

KM# 7 2 KREUTZERS (Douzain)
Billon **Obv:** Crowned arms **Rev:** Cross with two crowns and two lis in angles

Date	Mintage	VG	F	VF	XF	Unc
ND(1605-14)	—	125	225	450	750	—

KM# 30 2 KREUTZERS (Douzain)
Billon **Obv:** Crowned arms **Obv. Legend:** MONETA NOVA ARGEN. CH. **Rev:** Eagle **Rev. Legend:** SVB. VMBRA ALARVM TVARVM

Date	Mintage	VG	F	VF	XF	Unc
1619	—	125	225	450	750	—

KM# 35.1 GROS
Billon **Obv:** Crowned arms **Obv. Legend:** LVDOVICA. MARGAR. LOT **Rev:** Crowned eagle **Rev. Legend:** IN. OMNEM. TERR. SONVS. EOR.

Date	Mintage	VG	F	VF	XF	Unc
ND(1614)	—	100	200	375	675	—

KM# 35.2 GROS
Billon **Obv:** Crowned arms **Obv. Legend:** LVD MARGARETA A LO **Rev. Legend:** IN OMNEM. TER. SONVS EOR.

Date	Mintage	VG	F	VF	XF	Unc
ND(1614-31)	—	125	250	475	750	—

KM# 39 ESCALIN

Silver **Ruler:** Louise Marguerite, alone **Obv:** Ornate crowned arms **Obv. Legend:** MONETA ⁜ NOVA ⁜ ARGENT ⁜ L **Rev:** Crowned imperial eagle with orb on chest

Date	Mintage	Good	VG	F	VF	XF
ND(1614-29)	—	65.00	125	200	350	—

KM# 37 ESCALIN

4.9000 g., Silver **Obv:** Crowned arms **Obv. Legend:** MARG. A. LOTH. D. G... **Rev:** Crowned St. Andrew's cross **Rev. Legend:** MONETA ARGENTEA. CASTRO. REGINAL. CV.

Date	Mintage	VG	F	VF	XF	Unc
ND(1614-31)	—	250	450	800	—	—

KM# 38 ESCALIN

4.9000 g., Silver **Obv:** Crowned arms **Obv. Legend:** With: LVD

Date	Mintage	VG	F	VF	XF	Unc
ND(1614-31)	—	250	450	800	—	—

KM# 40 ESCALIN

4.9000 g., Silver **Obv:** Crowned arms on St. Andrew's cross **Obv. Legend:** MONETA NOVA ARGENT-IA CHA **Rev:** Crowned imperial eagle **Rev. Legend:** SIT • NOMEN • DOMINI • BENEDICTVM

Date	Mintage	VG	F	VF	XF	Unc
ND(1614-31)	—	150	300	550	850	—

KM# 41 ESCALIN

4.9000 g., Silver **Obv:** Date in legend

Date	Mintage	VG	F	VF	XF	Unc
1617	—	175	350	600	900	—

KM# 59 ESCALIN

4.9000 g., Silver **Obv:** Crowned and feathered arms **Obv. Legend:** MONE • NOVA • ARGENTCHA **Rev:** Crowned imperial eagle **Rev. Legend:** DA. PACEM. DOMINE. IN. DIEBVS. NOS. **Note:** Imitation of 5 Stuber from East Friesland.

Date	Mintage	VG	F	VF	XF	Unc
ND(1625)	—	150	300	550	850	—

KM# 45 1/4 ECU

Silver **Obv:** Crowned arms **Obv. Legend:** F. BOVRB. LVD MARGAR. LOT. **Rev:** Cross, fleur-de-lis **Rev. Legend:** IN OMNEM. TERRAM.

Date	Mintage	VG	F	VF	XF	Unc
ND(1605-14)	—	750	1,250	1,850	2,750	—

KM# 52 ECU (30 Sous)

Silver **Obv:** Legend around chateau surmounted by three towers with lion above **Obv. Legend:** MONETA. NOVA. ARGENTIA * PRINCIP: CHA. R. **Rev:** Legend around crowned double eagle **Rev. Legend:** DILIGITE. IVSTICIA. QUI. IVDICATIS. TERRAM **Note:** Dav. #A3828.

Date	Mintage	VG	F	VF	XF	Unc
1612 (7?) Rare	—	—	—	—	—	—

KM# 50 ECU (30 Sous)

Silver **Obv. Legend:** * F. BOVRBONIVS. L. MARGARETA. A. LOTARINGIA. **Rev. Legend:** IN. OMNEM. TERRAM. SONVS. EORVM. **Note:** Dav. #3824.

Date	Mintage	VG	F	VF	XF	Unc
1614	—	2,000	3,500	6,500	—	—

KM# 51 ECU (30 Sous)

Silver **Obv:** Legend around bust **Obv. Legend:** .FR. BOVRBONIVS. LVD. MARGARETA. A LOTHARIN **Rev:** Similar to KM#50 **Note:** Dav. #3825.

Date	Mintage	VG	F	VF	XF	Unc
ND	—	2,150	4,000	7,000	—	—

KM# 53 PATAGON

Silver **Obv. Legend:** LVD MARG. A LODH. D G. SVP. PR. C. REGI. **Rev. Legend:** ...CAS. TRO. REGINALDI. **Note:** Dav. #3826.

Date	Mintage	VG	F	VF	XF	Unc
ND CV Rare	—	—	—	—	—	—

KM# 56 PATAGON

Silver **Rev. Legend:** ...CAST. REGI. CVSA + **Note:** Dav. #3827.

Date	Mintage	VG	F	VF	XF	Unc
ND Rare	—	—	—	—	—	—

KM# 63 PATAGON

Silver **Obv:** Similar to KM#53 **Obv. Legend:** DEI. GR. **Rev:** Eagle arms in center and below **Rev. Legend:** MON. NOVA. ARGENTEA. CAST. REG. CVSA **Note:** Dav. #3828.

Date	Mintage	VG	F	VF	XF	Unc
1626 Rare	—	—	—	—	—	—

KM# 64 PATAGON

Silver **Obv:** Similar to KM#53 **Rev:** Similar to KM#53 but date divided by cross **Note:** Dav. #3829.

Date	Mintage	VG	F	VF	XF	Unc
1628 Rare	—	—	—	—	—	—

KM# 17 FLORIN D'OR

3.5000 g., 0.9860 Gold 0.1109 oz. AGW **Obv:** Bust of Francois, legend begins at lower left **Rev:** Crowned arms with cross of Lorraine on each side **Note:** Fr.#114.

Date	Mintage	VG	F	VF	XF	Unc
ND	—	475	950	1,500	2,350	—

KM# 18 FLORIN D'OR

3.5000 g., 0.9860 Gold 0.1109 oz. AGW **Rev:** Without crosses of Lorraine

Date	Mintage	VG	F	VF	XF	Unc
ND	—	400	875	1,450	2,150	—

KM# 19 FLORIN D'OR

3.5000 g., 0.9860 Gold 0.1109 oz. AGW **Rev:** Legend begins at lower left

Date	Mintage	VG	F	VF	XF	Unc
ND	—	400	875	1,450	2,150	—

KM# 20 FLORIN D'OR

3.5000 g., 0.9860 Gold 0.1109 oz. AGW

Date	Mintage	VG	F	VF	XF	Unc
ND	—	400	875	1,450	2,150	—

KM# 70 ECU D'OR

3.3600 g., 0.9520 Gold 0.1028 oz. AGW **Obv:** Crowned arms with Jerusalem cross on each side **Rev:** Cross **Note:** Fr.#115.

Date	Mintage	VG	F	VF	XF	Unc
ND	—	800	1,750	3,000	4,250	—

DOMBES

Region in eastern France near the Swiss border. Purchased by the Duke of Bourbon in 1402. Briefly in the royal domains from 1527 to 1560. Granted at that time to the Duke of Bourbon-Montpensier. The brother of Louis XIII married a Dombes heiress in 1626. After the death of their daughter, Dombes was once again annexed to France.

RULERS
Henri II de Montpensier, 1592-1608
Marie de Montpensier, 1608-1626
Gaston de Orleans and Marie, 1626-1627
Gaston de Orleans, 1627-1650
Anne Marie Louise de Orleans, 1650-1693

DUCHY

STANDARD COINAGE

KM# 16 LIARD
Billon **Ruler:** Henri II de Montpensier **Obv:** Crowned H within three fleur-de-lis **Obv. Legend:** H. P. DOMBAR. D. MONTISP. M. **Rev:** Cross of the Order of Saint-Esprit **Rev. Legend:** DNS. ADIVTOR. MEVS.

Date	Mintage	VG	F	VF	XF	Unc
1606	—	10.00	20.00	42.00	85.00	—
1609	—	10.00	20.00	42.00	85.00	—

KM# A22 LIARD
Billon **Obv:** Crowned M within 3 fleur-de-lis, legend around **Obv. Legend:** MAR... BARD • MONTISP... **Rev:** Maltese cross **Rev. Legend:** DNS • ADIVTOR....

Date	Mintage	VG	F	VF	XF	Unc
1615	—	10.00	20.00	42.00	85.00	—

KM# 25 LIARD
Billon **Ruler:** Gaston de Orleans and Marie **Obv:** Crowned GM monogram within 3 fleur-de-lis **Obv. Legend:** GAST.ET.M. SOVV.D.D.DOMB **Rev:** Cross of the Order of Saint-Esprit **Rev. Legend:** DNS.ADIVTOR.MEVS.

Date	Mintage	VG	F	VF	XF	Unc
ND	—	18.00	36.00	70.00	120	—
1628	—	18.00	36.00	70.00	120	—
1629	—	18.00	36.00	70.00	120	—

KM# 26 LIARD
Billon **Ruler:** Gaston de Orleans **Obv:** Crowned G within three fleur-de-lis **Obv. Legend:** GASTON. VS. D. L. SOV. DOMB. **Rev:** Cross fo the Order of Saint-Esprit, date **Rev. Legend:** DNS. ADIVTOR. MEVS.

Date	Mintage	VG	F	VF	XF	Unc
1639	—	8.00	18.00	37.50	80.00	—

KM# 22 DENIER TOURNOIS
Copper **Ruler:** Marie de Montpensier **Obv:** Bust left **Obv. Legend:** MARIE. SOVVE. DE. DOMBES **Rev:** M with two fleur-de-lis above, date **Rev. Legend:** DENIER TOVRNOIS

Date	Mintage	VG	F	VF	XF	Unc
1624	—	15.00	30.00	55.00	110	—

KM# 28 DENIER TOURNOIS
Copper **Ruler:** Gaston de Orleans **Obv:** Bust right **Obv. Legend:** GAST. PAT. R. VSVFR. PR. DOM **Rev:** Three fleur-de-lis, date **Rev. Legend:** DENIER. TOVRNOIS.

Date	Mintage	VG	F	VF	XF	Unc
1644	—	12.00	25.00	48.00	95.00	—
1649	—	12.00	25.00	48.00	95.00	—

KM# 29 DENIER TOURNOIS
Copper **Ruler:** Gaston de Orleans **Obv:** Bust right **Obv. Legend:** GASTON. V. F. P. D. **Rev:** Two fleur-de-lis, date **Rev. Legend:** DENIER. TOVRNOIS.

Date	Mintage	VG	F	VF	XF	Unc
1649 Small bust	—	12.00	25.00	48.00	95.00	—
1650A	—	12.00	25.00	48.00	95.00	—
1651A Large bust	—	12.00	25.00	48.00	95.00	—
1652	—	12.00	25.00	48.00	95.00	—
1654A	—	12.00	25.00	48.00	95.00	—

KM# 24 DOUBLE TOURNOIS
Copper **Ruler:** Marie de Montpensier **Obv:** Bust left **Obv. Legend:** MARIE. SOVVER. DE. DOMBES. B. **Rev:** Three fleur-de-lis, date **Rev. Legend:** DOVBLE. TOVRNOIS.

Date	Mintage	VG	F	VF	XF	Unc
1621	—	12.00	27.50	50.00	100	—
1622	—	12.00	25.00	48.00	95.00	—
1624	—	12.00	25.00	48.00	95.00	—
1626	—	12.00	25.00	48.00	95.00	—
1627	—	12.00	27.50	50.00	100	—

KM# 32 DOUBLE TOURNOIS
Copper, 22.5 mm. **Ruler:** Gaston de Orleans **Obv:** Bust right **Obv. Legend:** GASTON. VSV. F. DE. LA. SOV. DOM. **Rev:** Three fleur-de-lis, date **Rev. Legend:** DOVBLE. TOVRNOIS.

Date	Mintage	VG	F	VF	XF	Unc
1629	—	12.00	25.00	48.00	95.00	—
1635	—	12.00	25.00	48.00	95.00	—
1636	—	12.00	25.00	48.00	95.00	—
Note: Minor legend varieties exist						
1642	—	12.00	25.00	48.00	95.00	—
1643	—	12.00	25.00	48.00	95.00	—

KM# 34 DOUBLE TOURNOIS
Copper **Obv:** Bust right **Obv. Legend:** GASTON. VSV. D. LA. SOV. DOM. G. **Rev:** Three fleur-de-lis, date **Rev. Legend:** DOVBLE. TOVRNOIS.

Date	Mintage	VG	F	VF	XF	Unc
1640	—	12.00	25.00	48.00	95.00	—
1641	—	12.00	25.00	48.00	95.00	—
1643	—	12.00	25.00	48.00	95.00	—

KM# 40 1/12 ECU
13.5500 g., Silver **Ruler:** Anne Marie Louise de Orleans **Obv:** Bust right **Obv. Legend:** AN • MA • LOV • PRINC • SOVV • DE • DOM **Rev:** Crowned arms divides date **Rev. Legend:** DNS • ADIVTOR • ET • REDEM • MEVS

Date	Mintage	Good	VG	F	VF	XF
1664	—	25.00	65.00	125	250	450
1665	—	25.00	65.00	125	250	450

KM# 41 1/12 ECU
13.5500 g., Silver, 21 mm. **Ruler:** Anne Marie Louise de Orleans **Obv:** Bust right **Obv. Legend:** AN • MA • LOV • DE • BOVRBON **Rev:** Crowned arms divides date **Rev. Legend:** PRINC + SOVV DE + DOMBES

Date	Mintage	Good	VG	F	VF	XF
1668	—	25.00	65.00	125	250	450

KM# 18 1/2 TESTON
4.6800 g., Silver **Ruler:** Henri II de Montpensier **Obv:** Bust left, date **Obv. Legend:** HENRIC. P. DOMBAR. D. MONTISP. R. **Rev:** Crowned arms between crowned H's, date **Rev. Legend:** DNS. ADIVTOR. ET. REDEM. MEVS.

Date	Mintage	Good	VG	F	VF	XF
16xx	—	35.00	75.00	145	275	450

KM# 20 TESTON
8.1600 g., Silver **Ruler:** Henri II de Montpensier **Obv:** Bust right **Obv. Legend:** HENRIC. P. DOMBAR. D. MONTISP. R. **Rev:** Crowned arms between crowned H's, date **Rev. Legend:** DNS. ADIVTOR. ET. REDEM. MEVS.

Date	Mintage	Good	VG	F	VF	XF
1605	—	18.00	42.00	80.00	160	285
1606	—	18.00	42.00	80.00	160	285

KM# 21 TESTON
8.1600 g., Silver **Ruler:** Henri II de Montpensier **Obv:** Bust of Henry II left **Obv. Legend:** ✠ HENRIC • P • DOMBAR • D • MONTISP • R **Rev:** Crowned arms between crowned H's **Rev. Legend:** ✠ DNS • ADIVTOR • ET • REDEM • MEVS •

Date	Mintage	Good	VG	F	VF	XF
1606/5	—	20.00	45.00	100	165	300

KM# 45 1/2 ECU (30 Sols)
13.5500 g., Silver **Ruler:** Anne Marie Louise de Orleans **Obv:** Bust right **Obv. Legend:** AN • MA • LVD • PRINC • SVPRE • DOMBA **Rev:** Crowned arms **Rev. Legend:** * DOMINVS * ADIVTOR • • ET REDE • MEVS **Note:** Prev. KM#39.

Date	Mintage	Good	VG	F	VF	XF
1673A	—	650	1,250	2,500	4,500	7,500

DAV# 3830 ECU
Silver **Ruler:** Gaston de Orleans **Obv:** Armored bust right **Obv. Legend:** GASTON • VS • P DOMBARVM **Rev:** Crowned arms **Rev. Legend:** DOMINVS. ADIVTOR. ET. REDE. MEVS.

Date	Mintage	VG	F	VF	XF	Unc
1652	—	1,450	2,850	4,800	7,800	—

DAV# 3831 ECU

Silver **Ruler:** Anne Marie Louise de Orleans **Obv:** Bust right **Obv. Legend:** AN. MA. LVD. PRIN. SVPRE. DOMBAR. **Rev:** Crowned arms **Rev. Legend:** DOMINVS * ADVITOR * * ET • REDE • MEVS

Date	Mintage	VG	F	VF	XF	Unc
1673A	—	1,500	3,000	5,000	8,500	—

FR# 126 1/2 ECU D'OR

1.7100 g., 0.9520 Gold 0.0523 oz. AGW **Ruler:** Marie de Montpensier **Obv:** Crowned arms **Rev:** Ornamental cross, date in legend

Date	Mintage	VG	F	VF	XF	Unc
1614 Unique	—	—	—	—	—	—

FR# 125 ECU D'OR

3.3600 g., 0.9520 Gold 0.1028 oz. AGW **Ruler:** Marie de Montpensier **Obv:** Crowned arms **Rev:** Ornamental cross of palms, date in legend

Date	Mintage	VG	F	VF	XF	Unc
1618 Unique	—	—	—	—	—	—

FR# 127 ECU D'OR

3.2700 g., 0.9520 Gold 0.1001 oz. AGW **Ruler:** Gaston de Orleans and Marie **Obv:** Crowned arms **Rev:** Ornamental lobed cross with fleurs de lis at end of each arm, date in legend

Date	Mintage	VG	F	VF	XF	Unc
1627 Unique	—	—	—	—	—	—

FR# 129 ECU D'OR

3.3600 g., 0.9520 Gold 0.1028 oz. AGW **Ruler:** Gaston de Orleans **Obv:** Crowned arms **Rev:** Ornamental lobed cross with fleurs de lis at end of each arm, date in legend

Date	Mintage	VG	F	VF	XF	Unc
1639 Unique	—	—	—	—	—	—
1640	—	850	1,700	2,800	5,000	—
1641	—	850	1,700	2,800	5,000	—

FR# 128 2 ECU D'OR

6.6000 g., 0.9520 Gold 0.2020 oz. AGW **Ruler:** Gaston de Orleans **Obv:** Crowned arms **Rev:** Ornamental lobed cross with lis at end of each arm, date in legend

Date	Mintage	VG	F	VF	XF	Unc
1640	—	1,150	2,200	4,500	7,500	—
1641	—	1,150	2,200	4,500	7,500	—
1642	—	1,150	2,200	4,500	7,500	—

FR# 131 LOUIS D'OR

6.7100 g., 0.9170 Gold 0.1978 oz. AGW **Ruler:** Gaston de Orleans **Obv:** Laureate bust right, date below **Rev:** Cross of eight L's with crown at end of each arm, fleur de lis in angles **Note:** Posthumous issue.

Date	Mintage	VG	F	VF	XF	Unc
1652	—	4,500	6,000	8,000	12,000	—

FR# 130 2 LOUIS D'OR

13.3800 g., 0.9170 Gold 0.3945 oz. AGW **Ruler:** Gaston de Orleans **Obv:** Laureate bust of Gaston right, date below **Rev:** Cross of 8 L's with crown at end of each arm, fleur de lis in angles **Note:** Posthumous issue.

Date	Mintage	VG	F	VF	XF	Unc
1652A	—	6,000	7,500	11,500	17,000	—

TRADE COINAGE

FR# 132 DUCAT

3.5000 g., 0.9860 Gold 0.1109 oz. AGW **Ruler:** Anne Marie Louise de Orleans **Obv:** Ruler by standing saint **Rev:** Standing figure of Christ

Date	Mintage	VG	F	VF	XF	Unc
ND	—	550	1,100	2,200	3,850	—

PATTERNS

Including off metal strikes

KM#	Date	Mintage	Identification	Mkt Val
Pn1	1620	—	Liard. Silver.	—

NEVERS & RETHEL

The county of Nevers, located in central France, and the duchy of Rethel established in 1581 located in northern France near the Belgian border were united when a Rethel heiress married the son of the Duke of Mantua, Louis Gonzaga. Their great-grandson, Charles III (1637-1665) was active as Duke of Mantua and sold Rethel and all the rest of his French possessions to Cardinal Mazarin in 1663.

RULERS

Charles of Gonzaga, 1601-1637
Charles II of Gonzaga, 1637-1659

DUCHY

STANDARD COINAGE

KM# 9 DENIER TOURNOIS

Copper **Ruler:** Charles of Gonzaga **Obv:** Charles **Rev:** Crowned arms

Date	Mintage	VG	F	VF	XF	Unc
1609	—	25.00	45.00	85.00	175	—

KM# 47 DENIER TOURNOIS

Copper **Rev:** Two fluer-de-lis **Note:** Varieties exist.

Date	Mintage	VG	F	VF	XF	Unc
1652A	—	9.00	18.00	35.00	75.00	—
1653	—	—	—	—	—	—
1653A	—	9.00	18.00	35.00	75.00	—

KM# 1 DOUBLE TOURNOIS

Copper **Obv:** Bust right **Obv. Legend:** CH. D. GONZ. D. DE. NEVERS. **Rev:** Crowned arms **Rev. Legend:** DOUBLE. TOVRNOIS.

Date	Mintage	VG	F	VF	XF	Unc
1608	—	10.00	20.00	40.00	80.00	—
1610	—	10.00	20.00	40.00	80.00	—
1611	—	10.00	20.00	40.00	80.00	—

KM# 3 DOUBLE TOURNOIS

Copper **Ruler:** Charles of Gonzaga **Obv:** Bust **Rev:** Fleur-de-lis **Rev. Legend:** DOVBLE TOURNOIS **Note:** Varieties exist.

Date	Mintage	VG	F	VF	XF	Unc
1634	—	20.00	35.00	70.00	150	—

KM# 5 DOUBLE TOURNOIS

Copper **Obv:** Charles I, like KM-3 **Rev. Legend:** like KM-50 **Note:** Similar to KM#3.

Date	Mintage	VG	F	VF	XF	Unc
1635	—	10.00	20.00	40.00	85.00	—
1636	—	10.00	20.00	40.00	85.00	—
1637	—	10.00	20.00	40.00	85.00	—

KM# 50 DOUBLE TOURNOIS

Copper **Obv:** Bust right Charles II **Obv. Legend:** CHARLES. II. BVC. D. MANT. S. DAR. **Rev:** Three fleur-de-lis and date **Rev. Legend:** DOVBLE D. LA. SOV. DAR.

Date	Mintage	VG	F	VF	XF	Unc
1639	—	9.00	18.00	35.00	75.00	—
1640	—	9.00	18.00	35.00	75.00	—
1642	—	9.00	18.00	35.00	75.00	—
1645	—	9.00	18.00	35.00	75.00	—

KM# 2 LIARD

Copper **Ruler:** Charles of Gonzaga **Obv:** Crowned bust of Charles left **Obv. Legend:** KARO • DVX • NIV • ET • RETH • S • PR • ARCH **Rev:** Crowned five-fold arms between K's **Rev. Legend:** * MEI • DEVS • SIGNACVLVM • CORDIS

Date	Mintage	Good	VG	F	VF	XF
1607	—	20.00	42.50	75.00	125	200

KM# 53 LIARD

Copper **Obv:** Charles II **Obv. Legend:** CHARLES II: D. D. MANOV. **Rev:** Three lis **Rev. Legend:** LIARD DE FRANC • C • **Note:** Struck in imitation of liards of Louis XIV.

Date	Mintage	VG	F	VF	XF	Unc
1655A	—	10.00	20.00	40.00	85.00	—

KM# 12.1 2 LIARD

Copper **Obv:** Bust **Obv. Legend:** CAR • GONZ • D • NIV • ET • RETH **Rev:** Crowned arms **Rev. Legend:** SVP • PRINCEPS • ARCHENSIS

Date	Mintage	VG	F	VF	XF	Unc
1608	—	12.00	25.00	48.00	100	—
1609	—	12.00	25.00	48.00	100	—
1610	—	12.00	25.00	48.00	100	—
1611	—	12.00	25.00	48.00	100	—
1613	—	12.00	25.00	48.00	100	—

KM# 12.2 2 LIARD

Copper **Obv:** Bust right **Rev:** Crowned arms **Rev. Legend:** SVP•PRINCEPS•ARCHENSIS **Note:** Variation in obverse legend.

Date	Mintage	VG	F	VF	XF	Unc
1614	—	12.00	25.00	48.00	100	—

KM# 15 1/2 ESCALIN

Silver **Obv:** Floral cross **Obv. Legend:** CAROLVS • GONZ • D • NIVERN • ET • RETH **Rev:** Crowned arms **Rev. Legend:** SVP • PRINCEPS • ARCHENSIS

Date	Mintage	VG	F	VF	XF	Unc
1609	—	275	450	700	1,150	—

KM# 21 1/2 ECU

Silver **Obv:** Crowned arms **Obv. Legend:** CAROLVS • I • D.G. • MAN • MONF • NIV • MA • I • RET • DVX... **Rev:** St. Louis of Gonzaque

Date	Mintage	VG	F	VF	XF	Unc
ND	—	950	1,500	—	—	—

KM# 28 ECU OF 30 SOUS

Silver **Obv:** Without value **Obv. Legend:** CAROLVS • DVX •... **Note:** Dav. #3834.

Date	Mintage	VG	F	VF	XF	Unc
ND Rare	—	—	—	—	—	—

KM# 24 ECU OF 30 SOUS

Silver **Obv:** Date at left, "XXX" at right below eagle's talons **Obv. Legend:** CAROLVS. GONZAGA. DVX. NIVERN. ET. RETH. **Note:** Dav. #3832.

Date	Mintage	VG	F	VF	XF	Unc
1610	—	120	240	425	725	—

KM# 25 ECU OF 30 SOUS

Silver **Obv:** With • XXX • at left, date at right below eagle's talons **Note:** Dav. #3832A.

Date	Mintage	VG	F	VF	XF	Unc
1611	—	120	240	425	725	—

KM# 26 ECU OF 30 SOUS

Silver **Obv:** With XXX at left, date at right below eagle's talons **Obv. Legend:** CAROLVS • DVX • NIVERNENS (IS) • RETHELENSIS **Note:** Dav. #3833.

Date	Mintage	VG	F	VF	XF	Unc
1613	—	120	240	425	725	—

KM# 27 ECU OF 30 SOUS

Silver **Obv:** With date at left, XXX at right below eagle's talons **Note:** Dav. #3833A.

Date	Mintage	VG	F	VF	XF	Unc
1614	—	140	275	465	775	—

KM# 31 ECU

Silver **Obv. Legend:** CAR. GONZ. D. NIV. ET. RET. DEI. GRA. ... **Note:** Dav. #3837.

Date	Mintage	VG	F	VF	XF	Unc
ND	—	1,650	2,750	4,200	—	—

KM# 32 ECU

Silver **Obv. Legend:** S • IMP • PRINC **Note:** Dav. #3838.

Date	Mintage	VG	F	VF	XF	Unc
ND	—	1,650	2,750	4,200	—	—

KM# 33 ECU

Silver **Obv. Legend:** CAROLVS. I. DE. G. DVX. MANTVAE. VIII. ET. MON. FER. VI. **Note:** Dav. #3839.

Date	Mintage	VG	F	VF	XF	Unc
ND	—	1,650	2,750	4,200	6,250	—

KM# 34 ECU

Silver **Obv. Legend:** ...DEI. GRATIA. DVX. MANTVAE. BIII. ET. **Rev. Legend:** .MONTIS * FERRATI. VI * SVP. PRIN... **Note:** Dav. #3840.

Date	Mintage	VG	F	VF	XF	Unc
ND	—	1,650	2,750	4,200	—	—

KM# 29 ECU

Silver **Obv. Legend:** .CAR. GONZ. ET. CLEVEN. D. NIV. ET. RETH **Note:** Dav. #3835.

Date	Mintage	VG	F	VF	XF	Unc
1611 Rare	—	—	—	—	—	—

KM# 30 ECU

Silver **Obv. Legend:** CAROLVS. DVX. NIVERNENSIS... **Note:** Dav. #3836.

Date	Mintage	VG	F	VF	XF	Unc
1614	—	650	1,250	2,500	4,500	—

KM# 38 GOLD ECU

3.3600 g., 0.9520 Gold 0.1028 oz. AGW **Obv:** Bust of Charles of Gonzaga right, date below **Rev:** Crowned arms in inner circle

Date	Mintage	VG	F	VF	XF	Unc
1608	—	2,500	4,500	7,000	10,000	—

KM# 60 PATAGON

Silver **Obv:** Legend around crowned arms in order collar **Obv. Legend:** .CAROLVS. II. D. G. DVX. MANT. MONT. ET. AR. P. **Rev:** Legend around crowned Burgundian cross with crowned monograms at side, mint mark below **Rev. Legend:** .SIT. NOMEN. DOMINI. BENEDICTVM. **Note:** Dav. #3841.

Date	Mintage	VG	F	VF	XF	Unc
ND(1637-59) Rare	—	—	—	—	—	—

KM# 39 FLORIN

3.5000 g., 0.9860 Gold 0.1109 oz. AGW **Obv:** Charles of Gonzaga standing in nner circle **Rev:** Crowned arms in inner circle

Date	Mintage	VG	F	VF	XF	Unc
ND(1601-37)	—	600	1,200	2,000	3,000	—

KM# 40 FLORIN

3.5000 g., 0.9860 Gold 0.1109 oz. AGW **Obv:** Legend in cartouche

Date	Mintage	VG	F	VF	XF	Unc
ND(1601-37)	—	500	1,000	1,800	2,750	—

KM# 42 FLORIN

3.5000 g., 0.9860 Gold 0.1109 oz. AGW **Obv:** Arms in inner circle **Rev:** Crowned imperial eagle in inner circle

Date	Mintage	VG	F	VF	XF	Unc
ND Rare	—	—	—	—	—	—

KM# 43 FLORIN

3.5000 g., 0.9860 Gold 0.1109 oz. AGW **Obv:** Crowned arms in inner circle **Rev:** Jerusalem cross in inner circle

Date	Mintage	VG	F	VF	XF	Unc
1608 Rare	—	—	—	—	—	—

ORANGE

Principality in south-central France, with the town of Orange being 18 miles north of Avignon. Originally became of importance during the time of Charlemagne. Passed through the houses of Baux and Chalon. In 1530 Rene of Nassau (1530-1544) became the ruler and then William the Silent (1544-1584), regarded as the founder of the Dutch Republic. William III (1650-1702) was the last ruler of Orange. William's attention was drawn to the Netherlands and in 1672 the troops of Louis XIV occupied Orange and it was incorporated into France (though actual title did not pass until 1713). William became King of England in 1689.

RULERS

Philip William, 1584-1618
Maurice, 1618-1625
Frederick Henry, 1625-1647
William IX of Nassau, 1647-1650
William Henry of Nassau, 1650-1702

MONETARY SYSTEM

3 Deniers = 1 Liard
4 Liards = 1 Sol
20 Sols = 1 Livre
6 Livres = 1 Ecu
4 Ecus = 1 D'or

PRINCIPALITY

STANDARD COINAGE

KM# 54 OBOL

Billon **Note:** Similar to 1 Denier, KM#58.

Date	Mintage	VG	F	VF	XF	Unc
ND(1625-47)	—	25.00	50.00	100	—	—

KM# 58 DENIER TOURNOIS

Billon **Obv:** Cornet divides F-H

Date	Mintage	VG	F	VF	XF	Unc
ND(1625-47)	—	15.00	30.00	60.00	125	—

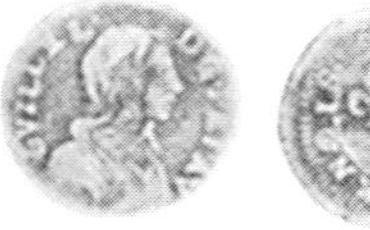

KM# 81 DENIER TOURNOIS

Copper **Obv:** Bust **Obv. Legend:** GVILLEM. D. G. PRI. AVR **Rev:** Three lis **Rev. Legend:** DENIER TOURNOIS

Date	Mintage	VG	F	VF	XF	Unc
1650	—	12.50	25.00	50.00	100	—

KM# 109 DENIER TOURNOIS

Copper **Obv:** Similar to KM#107 **Rev:** Cornet and three lis

Date	Mintage	VG	F	VF	XF	Unc
ND(1650-1702)	—	12.50	25.00	50.00	100	—

KM# 111 DENIER TOURNOIS

Copper **Obv:** Later bust

Date	Mintage	VG	F	VF	XF	Unc
ND(1650-1702)	—	12.50	25.00	50.00	100	—

KM# 107 DENIER TOURNOIS

Copper **Obv:** Bust **Rev:** Three lis

Date	Mintage	VG	F	VF	XF	Unc
1651	—	12.50	25.00	50.00	100	—
1652	—	12.50	25.00	50.00	100	—
1653/2	—	12.50	25.00	50.00	100	—
1653	—	12.50	25.00	50.00	100	—
1654	—	12.50	25.00	50.00	100	—

KM# 38 LIARD

Billon **Obv:** Crowned M **Rev:** Cross

Date	Mintage	VG	F	VF	XF	Unc
ND(1618-25)	—	12.50	25.00	50.00	100	—

KM# 59 DOUBLE TOURNOIS

Copper **Ruler:** Frederick Henry **Obv:** Bust **Rev:** 3 lis

Date	Mintage	VG	F	VF	XF	Unc
ND	—	12.50	25.00	55.00	110	—
1637	—	12.50	25.00	55.00	110	—
1640	—	12.50	25.00	55.00	110	—
1641	—	12.50	25.00	55.00	110	—
1642	—	12.50	25.00	55.00	110	—

KM# 112 DOUBLE TOURNOIS

Copper **Ruler:** William Henry of Nassau **Obv:** Bust **Rev:** 3 lis

Date	Mintage	VG	F	VF	XF	Unc
1659	—	15.00	30.00	65.00	125	—

KM# 5 DOUZAIN

Billon **Obv:** Arms **Obv. Legend:** PH. GVILL. IIII D. G. PRINC. AVRAICE **Rev:** Cross, two cornets, two crowns **Rev. Legend:** MANC TENEBO...

Date	Mintage	VG	F	VF	XF	Unc
ND(1584-1618)	—	10.00	20.00	40.00	85.00	—

KM# 10 GROS

Billon **Obv:** Crowned G, two cornets **Obv. Legend:** GVILEL... **Rev:** Cross with fleur-de-lis

Date	Mintage	VG	F	VF	XF	Unc
ND(1584-1618)	—	15.00	32.00	70.00	145	—

KM# 86 1/12 ECU (5 Sols)

2.2500 g., Silver **Obv:** Small long bust **Obv. Legend:** GVILLEMVS. D. G. PRIN. AVR. **Rev:** Crowned arms **Rev. Legend:** SOLI • DEO • HONOR...

Date	Mintage	VG	F	VF	XF	Unc
1650	—	35.00	75.00	145	250	—

KM# 115 1/12 ECU (5 Sols)

2.2500 g., Silver **Obv:** Young bust **Obv. Legend:** GVIL. HNR. D. G. PRI. AV. **Rev:** Crowned arms, three lis

Date	Mintage	VG	F	VF	XF	Unc
1661	—	35.00	75.00	145	250	—

KM# 118 1/12 ECU (5 Sols)

2.2500 g., Silver **Obv:** Young bust **Obv. Legend:** GVIL. HNR. D. G. PRI. AVR. **Rev:** Lions in crowned arms **Rev. Legend:** SOLI. DEO. HONOR. ET. GLO.

Date	Mintage	VG	F	VF	XF	Unc
1667	—	35.00	75.00	145	250	—

KM# 90 1/12 ECU (5 Sols)

2.2500 g., Silver **Obv:** Large bust **Obv. Legend:** GVIL. HNR. D. G. PRI. AV. **Rev:** Crowned arms, date divided by crown

Date	Mintage	VG	F	VF	XF	Unc
1657	—	35.00	75.00	145	250	—
1661	—	35.00	75.00	145	250	—
1665	—	35.00	75.00	145	250	—

KM# 20 1/2 FRANC

6.8700 g., Silver **Obv:** Bust of Philip William **Obv. Legend:** PHIL. G. I. D. G. PRIN. AVR. COM. NAS. **Rev:** Floral cross with fleur-de-lis

Date	Mintage	VG	F	VF	XF	Unc
1617	—	75.00	150	325	450	—

KM# 43.1 1/2 FRANC

6.8700 g., Silver **Ruler:** Maurice **Obv:** Bust of Maurice right **Rev:** Floreate cross **Note:** Prev. KM#43.

Date	Mintage	VG	F	VF	XF	Unc
1619	—	60.00	120	250	375	—
1621	—	60.00	120	250	375	—

KM# 43.2 1/2 FRANC

6.8700 g., Silver **Ruler:** Maurice **Obv:** Bust of Maurice right in inner circle

Date	Mintage	VG	F	VF	XF	Unc
1621	—	60.00	120	250	375	—

KM# 63.1 1/2 FRANC

6.8700 g., Silver **Obv:** Bust of Frederick Henry **Obv. Legend:** ...CO. NAS. **Rev:** H in floral cross

Date	Mintage	VG	F	VF	XF	Unc
1641	—	50.00	100	225	350	—

KM# 63.2 1/2 FRANC

6.8700 g., Silver **Obv. Legend:** ...COM. NASS.

Date	Mintage	VG	F	VF	XF	Unc
1642	—	50.00	100	225	350	—

KM# 15 TESTON

9.2700 g., Silver **Obv:** Bust of Philip William **Obv. Legend:** PHILIP. G. I. D. G... **Rev:** Crowned arms

Date	Mintage	VG	F	VF	XF	Unc
1607	—	75.00	150	325	450	—

KM# 68 TESTON
9.2700 g., Silver **Obv:** Bust of Frederick Henry right
Rev: Crowned arms within inner circle

Date	Mintage	VG	F	VF	XF	Unc
ND(1625-47)	—	45.00	90.00	200	300	—

KM# 69 TESTON
9.2700 g., Silver **Obv:** Bust of Frederick Henry **Rev:** Crowned arms separate legend

Date	Mintage	VG	F	VF	XF	Unc
ND(1625-47)	—	60.00	120	225	350	—

KM# 95 1/2 ECU
13.5900 g., Silver **Obv:** Bust **Obv. Legend:** GVILLELMVS. D. G. PRINC. AVR. **Rev:** Crowned arms

Date	Mintage	VG	F	VF	XF	Unc
1649	—	200	375	650	1,000	—

KM# 25 ECU
Silver **Obv. Legend:** MAVRITIVS. I. D. G. PRIN. ABR. COM. NA(SS). **Rev:** Legend around **Rev. Legend:** SOLI DEO. HONOR. ET. GLORI **Note:** Dav. #3843.

Date	Mintage	VG	F	VF	XF	Unc
1618	—	1,400	2,800	4,500	6,500	—
1622	—	1,400	2,800	4,500	6,500	—

KM# 98 ECU
Silver **Ruler:** William IX of Nassau **Note:** Dav. #3844.

Date	Mintage	VG	F	VF	XF	Unc
1649	—	1,750	3,500	5,500	—	—
1650	—	1,750	3,500	5,500	—	—

KM# 99 ECU
Silver **Ruler:** William Henry of Nassau **Note:** Dav. #3845.

Date	Mintage	VG	F	VF	XF	Unc
1652 Retrograde 2; rare	—	—	—	—	—	—

KM# 30 1/2 PISTOLE
3.3500 g., Gold **Obv:** Bust of Philip William right **Rev:** Crowned arms

Date	Mintage	VG	F	VF	XF	Unc
1617 Rare	—	—	—	—	—	—

KM# 32 PISTOLE
6.6200 g., Gold **Obv:** Bust of Philip William right **Rev:** Crowned arms

Date	Mintage	VG	F	VF	XF	Unc
ND	—	1,750	3,500	5,500	9,500	—
1617	—	1,750	3,500	5,500	9,500	—

KM# 72 PISTOLE
6.6200 g., Gold **Obv:** Bust of Frederick Henry right in inner circle **Rev:** Crowned arms in inner circle, date in legend

Date	Mintage	VG	F	VF	XF	Unc
ND	—	750	1,650	3,250	5,500	—
1640	—	750	1,650	3,250	5,500	—

KM# 75 PISTOLE
6.6200 g., Gold **Obv:** Old bust of Frederick Henry

Date	Mintage	VG	F	VF	XF	Unc
1643	—	750	1,650	2,750	5,000	—

KM# 101 PISTOLE
6.6200 g., Gold **Obv:** Armored bust of William right
Rev: Crowned arms, date in legend

Date	Mintage	VG	F	VF	XF	Unc
1649 Rare	—	—	—	—	—	—

KM# 34 2 PISTOLE
13.0900 g., Gold **Obv:** Bust of Philip William right **Rev:** Crowned arms, date above crown

Date	Mintage	VG	F	VF	XF	Unc
1616	—	2,000	4,000	7,000	11,500	—

KM# 49 2 PISTOLE
13.0900 g., Gold **Obv:** Bust of Maurice right **Rev:** Crowned arms in inner circle

Date	Mintage	VG	F	VF	XF	Unc
1618 Rare	—	—	—	—	—	—
1619 Rare	—	—	—	—	—	—

KM# 73 2 PISTOLE
13.0900 g., Gold **Obv:** Frederick Henry **Rev:** Crowned arms in inner circle, date in legend

Date	Mintage	VG	F	VF	XF	Unc
ND	—	850	1,850	3,500	5,500	—
1641	—	850	1,850	3,500	5,500	—

KM# 76 2 PISTOLE
13.0900 g., Gold **Obv:** Old bust of Frederick Henry

Date	Mintage	VG	F	VF	XF	Unc
1645	—	725	1,550	2,750	5,000	—

KM# 102 2 PISTOLE
13.0900 g., Gold **Obv:** Armored bust of William right
Rev: Crowned arms, date in legend

Date	Mintage	VG	F	VF	XF	Unc
1649 Rare	—	—	—	—	—	—

TRADE COINAGE

KM# 74 DUCAT
3.5000 g., 0.9860 Gold 0.1109 oz. AGW

Date	Mintage	VG	F	VF	XF	Unc
1645	—	450	1,000	2,000	3,250	—

KM# 125 ZECCHINO
3.5000 g., 0.9860 Gold 0.1109 oz. AGW **Obv:** Prince kneeling before Christ **Rev:** Madonna in oval shield

Date	Mintage	VG	F	VF	XF	Unc
ND(1650-1702)	—	450	1,000	1,850	3,000	—

VERDUN

(Verdun-sur-Meuse)

Town, dating to Roman times, in northeastern France 35 miles west of Metz. A bishopric founded here in the 3rd century. City destroyed during Barbarian invasions and took until the end of the 5th century to recover. Site of signing of famous treaty in 843. Part of German empire until taken by Henry II of France in 1552 and officially recognized by the Treaty of Westphalia in 1648. Pivotal locale during the Franco-Prussian War and in World War I.

RULERS
Eric of Lorraine-Vaudemont, 1593-1611
Charles of Lorraine-Chaligny, 1611-1622

BISHOPRIC

STANDARD COINAGE

KM# 13 GROS
Billon **Ruler:** Charles **Obv:** Crowned eagle **Obv. Legend:** CAROLVS. A. LOTHARINGIA. EPIS. **Rev:** Crowned paired shields **Rev. Legend:** ET. COMES. VIR. JVS. PRS. IMPE.

Date	Mintage	VG	F	VF	XF	Unc
ND(1611-22)	—	85.00	165	300	550	—

KM# 5 1/8 TESTON
Billon **Ruler:** Eric **Obv:** Bust **Obv. Legend:** ERRIC. A. LOTH. EPS. ET. CO. VIR. **Rev:** Crowned arms of Lorraine, mitre

Date	Mintage	VG	F	VF	XF	Unc
1608	—	900	1,750	—	—	—

KM# 17 1/8 TESTON
Billon **Ruler:** Eric **Obv:** Bust **Obv. Legend:** CAROLVS... **Rev:** Crowned arms, mitre **Rev. Legend:** MONET. NO. AN.

Date	Mintage	VG	F	VF	XF	Unc
1610	—	800	1,650	—	—	—

KM# 8 TESTON
8.3800 g., Silver **Ruler:** Eric **Obv:** Eric left **Rev:** Crowned arms

Date	Mintage	VG	F	VF	XF	Unc
1608	—	800	1,500	—	—	—

KM# 20 TESTON
8.3800 g., Silver **Ruler:** Charles **Obv:** Charles right **Rev:** Crowned arms

Date	Mintage	VG	F	VF	XF	Unc
ND(1617)	—	700	1,150	—	—	—

KM# 24 THALER
Silver **Ruler:** Charles **Rev. Legend:** ...VIRDVNENSIS. PRS. IMP. -* **Note:** Dav. #5911.

Date	Mintage	VG	F	VF	XF	Unc
ND	—	1,650	2,750	4,500	—	—

KM# 25 THALER
Silver **Ruler:** Charles **Rev:** Crowned arms decorated **Rev. Legend:** ...PRS. STI. IMPErii **Note:** Dav. #5912.

Date	Mintage	VG	F	VF	XF	Unc
ND	—	1,650	2,750	4,500	—	—

KM# 26 THALER
Silver **Ruler:** Charles **Rev:** Crowned arms **Rev. Legend:** ...PRS. SRI. IMPERIi (IMPERIii) **Note:** Dav. #5913

Date	Mintage	VG	F	VF	XF	Unc
ND	—	1,250	2,250	4,000	—	—

KM# 11 FLORIN D'OR
3.5000 g., 0.9860 Gold 0.1109 oz. AGW **Ruler:** Eric

Date	Mintage	VG	F	VF	XF	Unc
1608	—	750	1,650	3,200	5,500	—
1610	—	750	1,650	3,200	5,500	—
1611	—	750	1,650	3,200	5,500	—

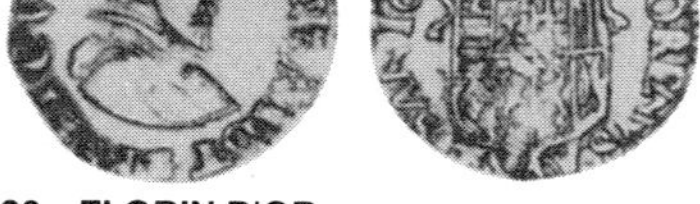

KM# 30 FLORIN D'OR
3.5000 g., 0.9860 Gold 0.1109 oz. AGW **Ruler:** Charles

Date	Mintage	VG	F	VF	XF	Unc
1612	—	650	1,450	3,000	5,000	—

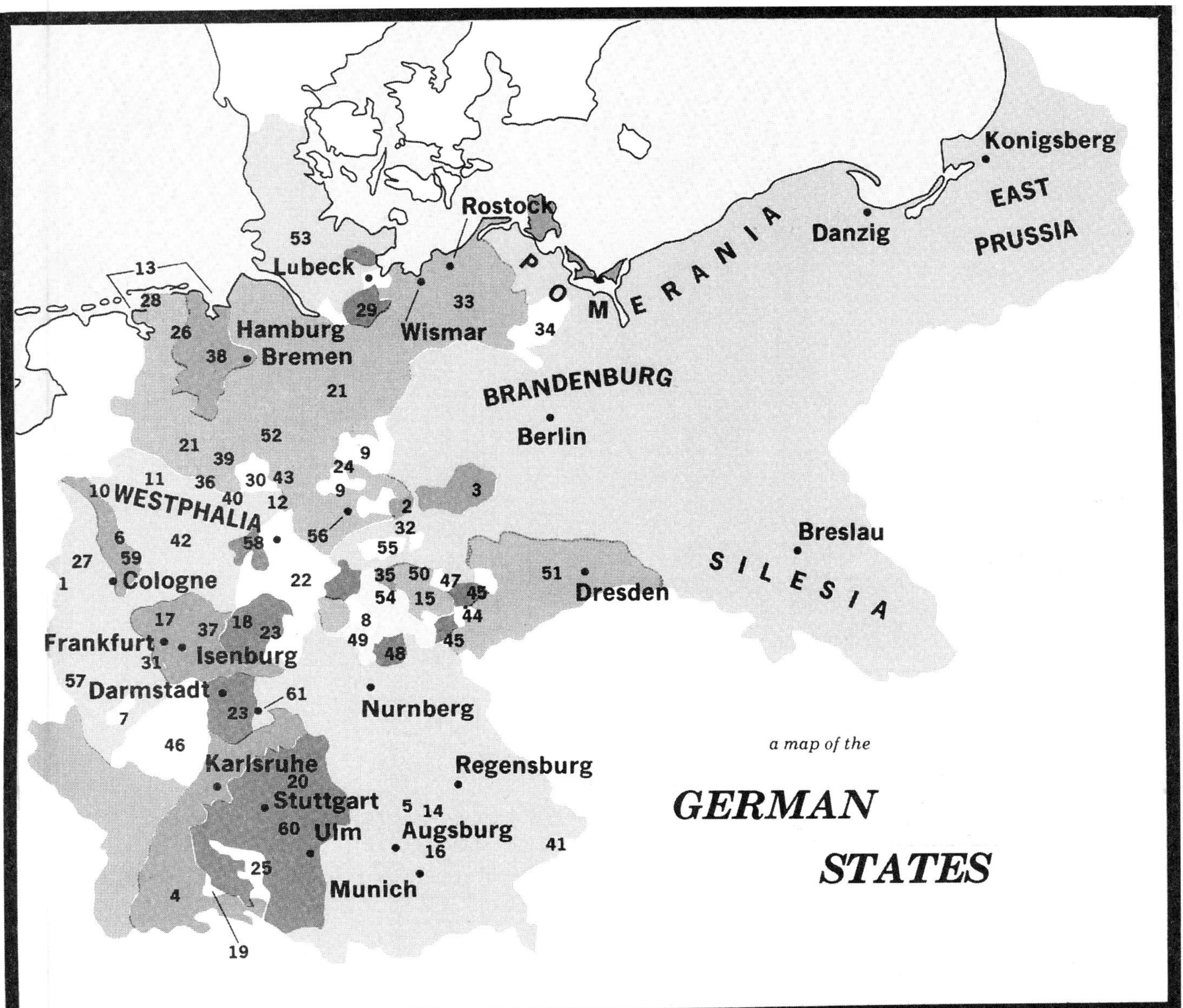

1 Aachen
2 Anhalt-Bernburg
3 Anhalt-Dessau
4 Baden
5 Bavaria
6 Berg
7 Birkenfeld
8 Brandenburg-Ansbach Bayreuth
9 Brunswick-Luneburg & Wolfenbuttel
10 Cleve
11 Coesfeld
12 Corvey
13 East Friesland
14 Eichstadt
15 Erfurt
16 Freising
17 Friedberg
18 Fulda
19 Furstenberg
20 Halle
21 Hannover
22 Hesse-Cassel
23 Hesse-Darmstadt
24 Hildesheim
25 Hohenzollern
26 Jever
27 Julich
28 Knyphausen
29 Lauenburg
30 Lippe-Detmold
31 Mainz
32 Mansfeld
33 Mecklenburg-Schwerin
34 Mecklenburg-Strelitz
35 Muhlhausen
36 Munster
37 Nassau
38 Oldenburg
39 Osnabruck
40 Paderborn
41 Passau
42 Prussia
43 Pyrmont
44 Reuss-Greiz
45 Reuss-Schleiz
46 Rhein-Pfalz
47 Saxe-Altenburg
48 Saxe-Coburg-Gotha
49 Saxe-Meiningen
50 Saxe-Weimar-Eisenach
51 Saxony
52 Schaumberg-Hessen & Lippe
53 Schleswig-Holstein
54 Schwarzburg-Rudolstadt
55 Schwarzburg Sonderhausen
56 Stolberg-Wernigerode
57 Trier
58 Wallmoden-Pyrmont
59 Wallmoden-Gimborn
60 Wurttemberg
61 Wurzburg

GERMAN STATES

Although the origin of the German Empire can be traced to the Treaty of Verdun that ceded Charlemagne's lands east of the Rhine to German Prince Louis, it was for centuries little more than a geographic expression, consisting of hundreds of effectively autonomous big and little states. Nominally the states owed their allegiance to the Holy Roman Emperor, who was also a German king, but as the Emperors exhibited less and less concern for Germany the actual power devolved on the lords of the individual states. The fragmentation of the empire climaxed with the tragic denouement of the Thirty Years War, 1618-48, which devastated much of Germany, destroyed its agriculture and medieval commercial eminence and ended the attempt of the Hapsburgs to unify Germany. Deprived of administrative capacity by a lack of resources, the imperial authority became utterly powerless. At this time Germany contained an estimated 1,800 individual states, some with a population of as little as 300. The German Empire of recent history (the creation of Bismarck) was formed on April 14, 1871, when the king of Prussia became German Emperor William I. The new empire comprised 4 kingdoms, 6 grand duchies, 12 duchies and principalities, 3 free cities and the non-autonomous province of Alsace-Lorraine. The states had the right to issue gold and silver coins of higher value than 1 Mark; coins of 1 Mark and under were general issues of the empire.

MONETARY SYSTEM

Until 1871 the Mark (Marck) was a measure of weight.

North German States until 1837

2 Heller = 1 Pfennig
8 Pfennige = 1 Mariengroschen
12 Pfennige = 1 Groschen
24 Groschen = 1 Thaler
2 Gulden = 1-1/3 Reichsthaler
1 Speciesthaler (before 1753)

South German States until 1837

8 Heller = 4 Pfennige = 1 Kreuzer
24 Kreuzer Landmunze = 20 Kreuzer Convention Munze
120 Convention Kreuzer = 2 Convention Gulden = 1 Convention Thaler

AACHEN

(Achen, Urbs Aquensis, Aquis Grani)

FREE CITY

STANDARD COINAGE

KM# 1 HELLER

Copper **Obv:** Eagle **Rev:** Value "I" divides date in wreath

Date	Mintage	Good	VG	F	VF	XF
(1)604	15,000	55.00	100	150	275	600

KM# 4 2 HELLER

Copper **Obv:** Eagle in shield divides date **Rev:** Value "II" in center

Date	Mintage	Good	VG	F	VF	XF
(1)6(0)5	20,000	40.00	90.00	135	240	450

KM# 14 2 HELLER

Copper **Obv:** Eagle, date divided by tail **Rev:** Value in center

Date	Mintage	Good	VG	F	VF	XF
(16)22	—	35.00	50.00	100	150	—
(16)38	—	35.00	50.00	100	150	—

KM# 2 3 HELLER

Copper **Obv:** Eagle **Rev:** Value "III" in center

Date	Mintage	Good	VG	F	VF	XF
(1604/5) Rare	—	—	—	—	—	—

KM# 3 4 HELLER

Copper **Obv:** Eagle divides date **Rev:** Value "III" in center

Date	Mintage	Good	VG	F	VF	XF
1604	30,000	35.00	60.00	125	200	—
(1)605	30,000	35.00	60.00	125	200	—
1619	80,000	12.00	25.00	50.00	100	—
1621	40,000	20.00	40.00	70.00	125	—
1624	40,000	20.00	40.00	70.00	125	—
1625	—	—	—	—	—	—
Note: Reported, not confirmed						
1634	140,000	5.00	9.00	20.00	40.00	—
(16)38	600,000	5.00	9.00	20.00	40.00	—
(16)43	200,000	5.00	9.00	20.00	40.00	—
(16)55	200,000	5.00	9.00	20.00	40.00	—
(16)6- Rare	—	—	—	—	—	—

KM# 5 4 HELLER

Copper **Obv:** Eagle divides date, legend around **Rev:** Value "IIII" in wreath

Date	Mintage	Good	VG	F	VF	XF
1614	60,000	27.00	55.00	100	150	—
1615	60,000	27.00	55.00	100	150	—
1616	100,000	27.00	55.00	100	150	—

KM# 30 4 HELLER

Copper **Obv:** Eagle divides date **Rev. Legend:** AQVIS / GRANVM / IIII

Date	Mintage	Good	VG	F	VF	XF
(16)56	—	—	—	—	—	—
Note: Reported, not confirmed						
(16)58	500,000	5.00	9.00	20.00	40.00	—

KM# 31 4 HELLER

Copper **Obv:** Arms divide date **Rev:** Legend above value **Rev. Legend:** REICHS / STAT.ACH / IIII

Date	Mintage	VG	F	VF	XF	Unc
(16)70	150,000	7.00	13.00	27.00	60.00	—
(16)71	80,000	7.00	13.00	27.00	60.00	—
(16)74	—	7.00	13.00	27.00	60.00	—
(16)76	150,000	7.00	13.00	27.00	60.00	—
(16)78	60,000	7.00	13.00	27.00	60.00	—
(16)81	60,000	7.00	13.00	27.00	60.00	—
(16)85	100,000	7.00	13.00	27.00	60.00	—
(16)86	60,000	7.00	13.00	27.00	60.00	—
(16)87	20,000	7.00	13.00	27.00	60.00	—
(16)88	200,000	7.00	13.00	27.00	60.00	—
(16)90	50,000	7.00	13.00	27.00	60.00	—
(16)91	30,000	7.00	13.00	27.00	60.00	—
(16)93	—	7.00	13.00	27.00	60.00	—
(16)96	—	7.00	13.00	27.00	60.00	—

KM# 7 MARCK

Silver **Obv:** Imperial eagle, titles of Matthias **Rev:** 1/2 length figure of Charlemagne above arms, date

Date	Mintage	VG	F	VF	XF	Unc
1616	—	110	175	250	350	—

KM# 10 MARCK

Silver **Obv:** 1/2-length figure of Charlemagne above arms **Rev:** Value, date in center, legend **Note:** Kipper Marck.

Date	Mintage	VG	F	VF	XF	Unc
1619	—	40.00	75.00	125	200	—
1620	—	40.00	75.00	125	200	—

KM# 16 MARCK

Silver **Obv:** 1/2-length figure of Charlemagne above arms, date **Rev:** Imperial eagle, titles of Ferdinand II

Date	Mintage	VG	F	VF	XF	Unc
1631	—	85.00	140	200	275	—
(16)31	—	85.00	140	200	275	—
1633	—	85.00	140	200	275	—

KM# 23 MARCK

Silver **Obv:** 1/2-length figure of Charlemagne above arms **Rev:** Value, date

Date	Mintage	VG	F	VF	XF	Unc
1643 Rare	—	—	—	—	—	—

KM# 6 2 MARCK

Silver **Obv:** 1/2-length figure of Charlemagne above arms, date **Rev:** Imperial eagle, titles of Matthias

Date	Mintage	VG	F	VF	XF	Unc
1615 Rare	—	—	—	—	—	—
1616 Rare	—	—	—	—	—	—

KM# 19 2 MARCK

Silver **Rev:** Imperial eagle with 2 on breast, titles of Ferdinand III

Date	Mintage	VG	F	VF	XF	Unc
(16)39	—	45.00	100	160	300	—
(16)46	—	45.00	100	160	300	—
ND	—	45.00	100	160	300	—

KM# 29 2 MARCK

Silver **Rev:** Value **Rev. Legend:** II/MARCK/ACH

Date	Mintage	VG	F	VF	XF	Unc
1649 Rare	—	—	—	—	—	—

KM# 11 3 MARCK

Silver **Obv:** 1/2-length figure of Charlemagne above arms **Rev:** Value, date in center, inscription around **Note:** Kipper 3 Marck.

Date	Mintage	VG	F	VF	XF	Unc
1619	—	75.00	140	200	350	—

KM# 15 3 MARCK

Silver **Obv:** 1/2-length figure of Charlemagne, date **Rev:** Value in center, titles of Ferdinand II

Date	Mintage	VG	F	VF	XF	Unc
(16)26	—	60.00	120	200	300	—
(16)31	—	60.00	120	200	300	—
(16)34	—	60.00	120	200	300	—

KM# 20 3 MARCK

Silver **Rev:** Titles of Ferdinand III

Date	Mintage	VG	F	VF	XF	Unc
(16)39	—	60.00	120	200	300	—
(16)40	—	60.00	120	200	300	—
(16)41	—	60.00	120	200	300	—

KM# 21 4 MARCK

Silver **Obv:** 1/2-length figure of Charlemagne divides date **Rev:** Value in rhombus, titles of Ferdinand III

Date	Mintage	VG	F	VF	XF	Unc
(16)3-	—	35.00	80.00	170	275	—
(16)42	—	35.00	80.00	170	275	—
(16)44	—	35.00	80.00	170	275	—
(16)45	—	35.00	80.00	170	275	—
(16)46	—	35.00	80.00	170	274	—

KM# 26 4 MARCK

Silver **Rev:** Value in baroque frame, date in legend

Date	Mintage	VG	F	VF	XF	Unc
1646	—	35.00	80.00	170	275	—
1647	—	35.00	80.00	170	275	—
1648	—	35.00	80.00	170	275	—

KM# 27 4 MARCK

Silver **Obv:** KM#21 **Rev:** KM#26 **Note:** Mule.

Date	Mintage	VG	F	VF	XF	Unc
1646/1647	—	35.00	80.00	170	275	—

KM# 12 6 MARCK

Silver **Obv:** 1/2-length figure of Charlemagne above arms **Rev:** Value, date in center, inscription around **Note:** Kipper 6 Marck.

Date	Mintage	VG	F	VF	XF	Unc
1619	—	60.00	120	175	300	—
1620	—	60.00	120	175	300	—
1621	—	125	225	325	500	—

KM# 13 6 MARCK

Silver **Rev:** Value and date in cartouche

Date	Mintage	VG	F	VF	XF	Unc
1620	—	60.00	120	175	300	—

KM# 8 THALER

Silver **Obv:** Imperial eagle, titles of Matthias **Rev:** Charlemagne seated above city arms, divides date **Note:** Dav. #5002.

Date	Mintage	VG	F	VF	XF	Unc
1616 Rare	—	—	—	—	—	—

KM# 24 THALER

Silver **Obv:** Titles of Ferdinand III **Rev:** Smaller figure of Charlemagne **Rev. Legend:** MON. NOVA. REGIAE.. **Note:** Dav. #5004

Date	Mintage	VG	F	VF	XF	Unc
1643 Rare	—	—	—	—	—	—

KM# 40 THALER

Silver **Rev. Legend:** MON. NOVA. REGNE.. **Note:** Dav. #5005.

Date	Mintage	VG	F	VF	XF	Unc
1644 Rare	—	—	—	—	—	—

KM# 53 THALER

Silver **Note:** Similar to 2 Thaler, KM#54. Dav. #5007.

Date	Mintage	VG	F	VF	XF	Unc
ND Rare	—	—	—	—	—	—

KM# 9 2 THALER

Silver **Obv:** Imperial eagle, titles of Matthias **Rev:** Charlemagne seated above city arms divides date **Note:** Thick flan. Dav. #5001.

Date	Mintage	VG	F	VF	XF	Unc
1616 Rare	—	—	—	—	—	—

KM# 25 2 THALER

Silver **Obv:** Titles of Ferdinand III **Rev:** Smaller figure of CHarlemagne **Note:** Dav. #5003.

Date	Mintage	VG	F	VF	XF	Unc
1643 Rare	—	—	—	—	—	—

KM# 54 2 THALER

Silver **Rev:** Wildman with crowned helmet, surmounted by eagle holding flags, standing behind city arms **Note:** Dav. #5006.

Date	Mintage	VG	F	VF	XF	Unc
ND Rare	—	—	—	—	—	—

TRADE COINAGE

KM# 18 GOLDGULDEN

3.5000 g., 0.9860 Gold 0.1109 oz. AGW **Note:** Klippe. Fr. #7.

Date	Mintage	VG	F	VF	XF	Unc
1634 Rare	—	—	—	—	—	—

KM# 17 GOLDGULDEN

3.5000 g., 0.9860 Gold 0.1109 oz. AGW **Obv:** Charlemagne seated facing **Rev:** Imperial eagle, titles of Ferdinand II **Note:** Fr. #6.

Date	Mintage	VG	F	VF	XF	Unc
1634	—	2,000	4,000	7,000	10,000	—

KM# 46 DUCAT
3.5000 g., 0.9860 Gold 0.1109 oz. AGW **Obv:** Madonna standing **Rev:** Value in tablet

Date	Mintage	VG	F	VF	XF	Unc
ND(1640) Unique	—	—	—	10,000	—	—

KM# 22 DUCAT
3.5000 g., 0.9860 Gold 0.1109 oz. AGW **Obv:** Ferdinand III standing **Rev:** Bust of Charlemagne **Note:** Fr. #8.

Date	Mintage	VG	F	VF	XF	Unc
1641	—	1,600	3,200	6,000	9,000	—
1643	—	1,600	3,200	6,000	9,000	—
1645	—	1,600	3,200	6,000	9,000	—

KM# 28 DUCAT
3.5000 g., 0.9860 Gold 0.1109 oz. AGW **Obv:** Ferdinand III standing **Rev:** Value and date in tablet **Note:** Fr. #9.

Date	Mintage	VG	F	VF	XF	Unc
1646	—	500	1,250	2,250	3,500	—

KM# 45 DUCAT
3.5000 g., 0.9860 Gold 0.1109 oz. AGW **Obv:** Bust of Charlemagne **Rev:** Madonna standing **Note:** Fr. #10.

Date	Mintage	VG	F	VF	XF	Unc
ND Rare	—	—	—	—	—	—

AHLEN

(Alen)

A city in Westphalia, 18 miles southeast of Munster, the center for the manufacture of shoes and enamelware. Coal mining is also done in the area. Issued copper coins in 1584, 1610 and 1616.

Arms:
Crowned and winged eel

CROSS REFERENCE:
F = Gisela Förschner, ***Deutsche Münzen Mittelalter bis Neuzeit***, v. 1 – ***Aachen bis Augsburg***, Melsungen, 1984.

CITY

REGULAR COINAGE

KM# 1 2 PFENNINGE
Copper **Obv:** Arms in center, legend, date **Obv. Legend:** STADT ALEN **Rev:** Value: II in center

Date	Mintage	Good	VG	F	VF	XF
1610	—	50.00	80.00	125	220	—

KM# 2 3 PFENNINGE
Copper **Obv:** Arms in center, legend, date **Obv. Legend:** STADT ALEN **Rev:** Value: III in center

Date	Mintage	Good	VG	F	VF	XF
1610	—	50.00	80.00	125	220	—

KM# 3 6 PFENNINGE
Copper **Obv:** Arms in center, legend, date **Obv. Legend:** STADT ALEN **Rev:** Value: VI in center

Date	Mintage	Good	VG	F	VF	XF
1610	—	90.00	150	250	450	—

KM# 4 12 PFENNINGE
Copper **Obv:** Arms in center, legend, date **Obv. Legend:** STADT ALEN **Rev:** Value: XII in center

Date	Mintage	Good	VG	F	VF	XF
1610	—	125	225	375	625	—
1616 Rare	—	—	—	—	—	—

ALSACE

An old German area located in northeastern France between the Rhine River and Vosges Mountains which later became a French province.

Ruled by Rome, gradually being penetrated by the Germanic peoples. Belonged to the Holy Roman Empire 870-1648 while being united to the duchy of Swabia in 925. Later broken up into feudal principalities controlled chiefly by the Bishop of Strasbourg and Hapsburg family in the 14th century. Upper Alsace was given to Burgundy in 1469, but soon broke free. Occupied by French in Thirty Years' War and linked with France by means of Louis XIV's "Chambers of Reunion" 1680. Ceded to Germany by the Treaty of Frankfurt 1871 and under the German Empire 1871-1918. It was subject to unsuccessful attempts to Germanize between 1880-1910 and was restored to France by the Treaty of Versailles in 1919. In World War II held by Germany 1940-44; retaken by French and American armies and again restored to France.

RULERS
Rudolf II, 1603-1612
Maximilian, 1613-1618
Ferdinand II, 1619-1623
Leopold of Austria,
As Bishop of Strasbourg, 1620-
As Landgrave of Alsace, -1632

ENSISHEIM MINT

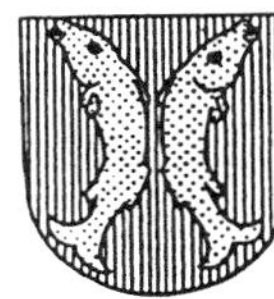

Coat of arms usually at bottom left or right section of extensive crowned arms or in legend.

MINT OFFICIALS' INITIALS

Initials	Date	Name
B, PB	1601-29	Peter Balde

MONETARY SYSTEM
8 Heller = 4 Pfennig = 1 Kreuzer
60 Kreuzer = 1 Florin Gulden
120 Kreuzer = 1 Thaler

LANDGRAVIATE

County

STANDARD COINAGE

KM# 275 4 HELLER
Silver **Ruler:** Maximilian, Erzherzog 1612-1619 **Obv:** Coat of arms **Rev:** Cruciform

Date	Mintage	VG	F	VF	XF	Unc
ND(1612-18)	—	100	200	400	600	—

KM# 238 4 HELLER
Silver **Ruler:** Rudolf II von Habsburg 1602-1612 **Obv:** Crowned pointed-top oval arms **Rev:** Cross **Mint:** Ensisheim

Date	Mintage	VG	F	VF	XF	Unc
ND(1602-12)	—	—	—	—	—	—

KM# 239 4 HELLER
Silver **Ruler:** Rudolf II von Habsburg 1602-1612 **Obv:** Crowned square-topped arms **Mint:** Ensisheim

Date	Mintage	VG	F	VF	XF	Unc
ND(1602-12)	—	—	—	—	—	—

KM# 282 3 KREUZER
Silver **Ruler:** Ferdinand I von Habsburg 1556-1564

Date	Mintage	VG	F	VF	XF	Unc
ND(1590-1619)	—	28.00	55.00	110	200	—

KM# 240 3 KREUZER
Silver **Ruler:** Rudolf II von Habsburg 1602-1612 **Obv:** Bust of Rudolph right **Rev:** Three shields **Mint:** Ensisheim

Date	Mintage	VG	F	VF	XF	Unc
1602	—	28.00	65.00	125	240	—
1603	—	28.00	65.00	125	240	—
1604	—	28.00	65.00	125	240	—
1605	—	28.00	65.00	125	240	—
1606	—	28.00	65.00	125	240	—
1607	—	28.00	65.00	125	240	—
ND	—	28.00	65.00	125	240	—

KM# 241 6 KREUZER
Silver **Ruler:** Rudolf II von Habsburg 1602-1612 **Obv:** Bust of Rudolph right **Rev:** Crowned arms **Mint:** Ensisheim

Date	Mintage	VG	F	VF	XF	Unc
ND(1602-12)	—	60.00	125	200	350	—

KM# 276 10 KREUZER
Silver **Ruler:** Maximilian, Erzherzog 1612-1619 **Obv:** Bust right

Date	Mintage	VG	F	VF	XF	Unc
ND(1612)	—	120	190	340	550	—

KM# 242 10 KREUZER
Silver **Ruler:** Rudolf II von Habsburg 1602-1612 **Obv:** Bust of Rudolph II right **Rev:** Crowned arms in Order chain **Mint:** Ensisheim

Date	Mintage	VG	F	VF	XF	Unc
ND(1602-12)	—	65.00	130	240	450	—

KM# 250 VIERER
Silver **Obv:** Crowned arms **Rev:** Round cruciform

Date	Mintage	VG	F	VF	XF	Unc
ND(1619)	—	20.00	40.00	75.00	140	—
1623	—	20.00	40.00	75.00	140	—
1624	—	20.00	40.00	75.00	140	—

KM# 251 PLAPPERT (Schilling)
Silver **Obv:** Crowned arms **Rev:** Short cross

Date	Mintage	VG	F	VF	XF	Unc
ND(1619)	—	35.00	70.00	120	200	—
1623	—	35.00	70.00	120	200	—
1624	—	35.00	70.00	120	200	—

KM# 252 DUPLEX (Schilling)
Silver **Ruler:** Leopold V, Erzherzog 1619-1634 **Obv:** Crowned arms **Rev:** Short cross **Mint:** Ensisheim

Date	Mintage	VG	F	VF	XF	Unc
ND(1621-25)	—	50.00	95.00	150	350	—

KM# 262 DUPLEX (Schilling)
Silver **Ruler:** Leopold V, Erzherzog 1619-1634 **Obv:** Crowned ornate arms **Rev:** Short cross **Mint:** Ensisheim

Date	Mintage	VG	F	VF	XF	Unc
1623	—	40.00	90.00	140	250	—
1624	—	40.00	90.00	140	250	—

KM# A282 DUPLEX (2 Schilling)
Silver **Ruler:** Leopold V, Erzherzog 1619-1634 **Obv:** Crowned two-fold arms of Alsace and Pfirt, date divided at top **Obv. Legend:** Titles of Archduke Leopold **Rev:** Floriated cross, "2" in circle in center **Rev. Legend:** Titles continued **Mint:** Ensisheim

Date	Mintage	VG	F	VF	XF	Unc
1634	—	—	—	—	—	—

KM# 253 24 KREUZER (Sechsbätzner)
Silver **Obv:** Crowned armored bust of Leopold holding scepter right **Rev:** Crowned circular arms

Date	Mintage	VG	F	VF	XF	Unc
ND(1630-32)	—	100	200	350	500	—

KM# 277 1/4 THALER
Silver **Ruler:** Maximilian, Erzherzog 1612-1619 **Note:** Similar to 1/4 Thaler, KM#243.

Date	Mintage	VG	F	VF	XF	Unc
ND(1612)	—	65.00	150	250	400	—

KM# 243 1/4 THALER
Silver **Ruler:** Rudolf II von Habsburg 1602-1612 **Obv:** Bust of Rudolph II right **Rev:** Crowned arms in Order chain **Mint:** Ensisheim

Date	Mintage	VG	F	VF	XF	Unc
ND(1602-12)	—	65.00	130	240	450	—

KM# 254.1 1/4 THALER
Silver **Ruler:** Leopold V, Erzherzog 1619-1634 **Obv:** Draped bust of Leopold right **Rev:** Crowned arms **Mint:** Ensisheim

Date	Mintage	VG	F	VF	XF	Unc
ND(1630-32)	—	65.00	150	250	400	—

KM# 254.2 1/4 THALER
Silver **Ruler:** Leopold V, Erzherzog 1619-1634 **Obv:** Crowned half-length bust of Leopold in plain armor holding scepter right **Rev:** Crowned arms **Mint:** Ensisheim

Date	Mintage	VG	F	VF	XF	Unc
ND(1619)	—	65.00	150	250	400	—

KM# 254.3 1/4 THALER
Silver **Ruler:** Leopold V, Erzherzog 1619-1634 **Obv:** Crowned half-length bust of Leopold in ornate armor holding scepter right **Rev:** Crowned arms **Mint:** Ensisheim

Date	Mintage	VG	F	VF	XF	Unc
ND(1627-30)	—	65.00	150	250	400	—

KM# 278 1/2 THALER
Silver **Ruler:** Maximilian, Erzherzog 1612-1619 **Obv:** Similar to 2 Thaler, KM#280

Date	Mintage	VG	F	VF	XF	Unc
ND(1612)	—	50.00	110	200	375	—

KM# 244 1/2 THALER
Silver **Ruler:** Rudolf II von Habsburg 1602-1612 **Obv:** Bust of Rudolph II right **Rev:** Crowned arms in Order chain **Mint:** Ensisheim

Date	Mintage	VG	F	VF	XF	Unc
ND(1602-12)	—	50.00	110	200	375	—

KM# 259 1/2 THALER
Silver **Ruler:** Leopold V, Erzherzog 1619-1634 **Obv:** Draped bust of Leopold right **Rev:** Crowned arms **Mint:** Ensisheim

Date	Mintage	VG	F	VF	XF	Unc
ND(1621-25)	—	50.00	110	200	375	—

KM# 264 1/2 THALER
Silver **Ruler:** Leopold V, Erzherzog 1619-1634 **Obv:** Crowned half-length bust of Leopold in plain armor holding scepter right **Rev:** Crowned arms **Mint:** Ensisheim

Date	Mintage	VG	F	VF	XF	Unc
ND(1625-26)	—	50.00	110	200	375	—

KM# 266 1/2 THALER
Silver **Ruler:** Leopold V, Erzherzog 1619-1634 **Obv:** Crowned half-length bust of Leopold in ornate armor holding scepter right **Rev:** Crowned arms **Mint:** Ensisheim

Date	Mintage	VG	F	VF	XF	Unc
ND(1627-30)	—	50.00	110	200	375	—

KM# 269 1/2 THALER
Silver **Ruler:** Leopold V, Erzherzog 1619-1634 **Obv:** Bust of Leopold right **Rev:** Crowned arms **Mint:** Ensisheim

Date	Mintage	VG	F	VF	XF	Unc
ND(1631)	—	50.00	110	200	375	—

KM# 270 1/2 THALER
Silver **Ruler:** Leopold V, Erzherzog 1619-1634 **Mint:** Ensisheim **Note:** Klippe

Date	Mintage	VG	F	VF	XF	Unc
ND(1631) Rare	—	—	—	—	—	—

KM# 245 THALER
Silver **Ruler:** Rudolf II von Habsburg 1602-1612 **Obv:** Small bust of Rudolph II right with lion's head on shoulder **Obv. Legend:** + RVDOLPHVS•II•D:G•RO•... **Rev:** Crowned arms in Order chain **Rev. Legend:** NEC NON ARCHIDVCES... **Mint:** Ensisheim **Note:** Dav. #A3033.

Date	Mintage	VG	F	VF	XF	Unc
1603	—	100	200	325	550	—
1606	—	100	200	325	550	—

KM# 246.1 THALER
Silver **Ruler:** Rudolf II von Habsburg 1602-1612 **Obv:** Large bust of Rudolf II right **Obv. Legend:** RVDOLPHVS. II. D. G. RO: IM. SEM. AVG. HVN. BO(H). REX **Rev. Legend:** NEC NON ARCHIDVCES. AVS. D. BVR. LANDG. ALS CO FE(R). **Mint:** Ensisheim **Note:** Dav. #3032.

Date	Mintage	VG	F	VF	XF	Unc
ND	—	100	200	325	550	—

KM# 246.2 THALER
Silver **Ruler:** Rudolf II von Habsburg 1602-1612 **Obv:** Date below shoulder **Mint:** Ensisheim **Note:** Dav. #3033.

Date	Mintage	VG	F	VF	XF	Unc
1603	—	100	200	325	550	—
1603 PB	—	100	200	325	550	—
1605	—	100	200	325	550	—
1608	—	100	200	325	550	—

KM# 246.3 THALER

Silver **Ruler:** Rudolf II von Habsburg 1602-1612 **Obv:** Date below shoulder **Rev:** Crown divides legend, larger arms in Order chain **Mint:** Ensisheim **Note:** Dav. #3034.

Date	Mintage	VG	F	VF	XF	Unc
1603 B	—	100	200	325	550	—
1605 B	—	100	200	325	550	—
1606	—	100	200	325	550	—
1610	—	100	200	325	550	—

KM# 246.4 THALER

Silver **Ruler:** Rudolf II von Habsburg 1602-1612 **Obv:** Date in field behind collar **Mint:** Ensisheim

Date	Mintage	VG	F	VF	XF	Unc
1607	—	125	250	385	650	—

KM# 247.1 THALER

Silver **Ruler:** Rudolf II von Habsburg 1602-1612 **Obv:** Large bust of Rudolph II right, lion's head on shoulder, date reads inward **Mint:** Ensisheim **Note:** Dav. #3035.

Date	Mintage	VG	F	VF	XF	Unc
1606	—	125	250	385	650	—

KM# 247.2 THALER

Silver **Ruler:** Rudolf II von Habsburg 1602-1612 **Obv:** Small bust of Rudolf II right **Mint:** Ensisheim **Note:** Dav. #A3035.

Date	Mintage	VG	F	VF	XF	Unc
1606	—	125	250	385	650	—

KM# 247.3 THALER

Silver **Ruler:** Rudolf II von Habsburg 1602-1612 **Obv:** Without lion's head on shoulder, date reads outward **Mint:** Ensisheim **Note:** Dav. #B3035. Varieties exist.

Date	Mintage	VG	F	VF	XF	Unc
1608	—	125	250	385	650	—
1609	—	125	250	385	650	—
1610	—	125	250	385	650	—
1611	—	125	250	385	650	—
1612	—	125	250	385	650	—

KM# 247.4 THALER

Silver **Ruler:** Rudolf II von Habsburg 1602-1612 **Obv:** With lion's head on shoulder, date reads outward **Mint:** Ensisheim

Date	Mintage	VG	F	VF	XF	Unc
1609	—	125	250	385	650	—

KM# 247.5 THALER

Silver **Ruler:** Rudolf II von Habsburg 1602-1612 **Rev. Legend:** NEC NON ARCHDUSES... **Mint:** Ensisheim **Note:** Dav. #3035A.

Date	Mintage	VG	F	VF	XF	Unc
1612	—	—	—	—	—	—
1613	—	125	250	385	650	—

KM# 256.1 THALER

Silver **Ruler:** Leopold V, Erzherzog 1619-1634 **Obv:** Bust of Leopold right, date in front **Rev:** Crowned arms with two shields at left and right **Rev. Legend:** ET - STIR.CARIN: - CARN:LAND: - ALS **Mint:** Ensisheim **Note:** Dav. #3340.

Date	Mintage	VG	F	VF	XF	Unc
16Z0	—	45.00	90.00	175	250	—

KM# 256.2 THALER

Silver **Ruler:** Leopold V, Erzherzog 1619-1634 **Obv:** Bust of Leopold right, date below bust **Obv. Legend:** D: G: LEOPOL:... **Mint:** Ensisheim **Note:** Dav. #3341.

Date	Mintage	VG	F	VF	XF	Unc
16Z0	—	45.00	90.00	175	250	—

KM# 256.3 THALER

Silver **Ruler:** Leopold V, Erzherzog 1619-1634 **Obv. Legend:** LEOPOLDVS. D: G. ET... **Mint:** Ensisheim **Note:** Dav. #3342.

Date	Mintage	VG	F	VF	XF	Unc
16Z0	—	45.00	90.00	175	250	—

KM# 256.4 THALER

Silver **Ruler:** Leopold V, Erzherzog 1619-1634 **Obv. Legend:** LEOPOLD: D: G: ET •... **Mint:** Ensisheim **Note:** Dav. #3343.

Date	Mintage	VG	F	VF	XF	Unc
16Z0	—	45.00	90.00	175	250	—

KM# 256.5 THALER

Silver **Ruler:** Leopold V, Erzherzog 1619-1634 **Obv:** Bust divides date **Obv. Legend:** + LEOPOL: D: G: ET. AR - CHIDVCES... **Mint:** Ensisheim **Note:** Dav. #3344.

Date	Mintage	VG	F	VF	XF	Unc
16Z0	—	45.00	90.00	175	250	—

KM# 279.1 THALER

Silver **Ruler:** Maximilian, Erzherzog 1612-1619 **Obv:** Draped bust, date in front **Note:** Dav. #3326.

Date	Mintage	VG	F	VF	XF	Unc
ND(1612)	—	100	200	325	550	—
1614	—	100	200	325	550	—
1615	—	100	200	325	550	—

KM# 279.2 THALER

Silver **Ruler:** Maximilian, Erzherzog 1612-1619 **Obv:** Armored bust with lion's face in shoulder drapery, date in front

Date	Mintage	VG	F	VF	XF	Unc
1616	—	100	200	325	550	—
1617	—	100	200	325	550	—

KM# 279.3 THALER

Silver **Ruler:** Maximilian, Erzherzog 1612-1619 **Obv:** Armored bust with lion's face sideways in shoulder drapery, date below **Note:** Dav. #3327.

Date	Mintage	VG	F	VF	XF	Unc
1617	—	120	240	375	600	—
1618	—	120	240	375	600	—

KM# 279.4 THALER

Silver **Ruler:** Maximilian, Erzherzog 1612-1619 **Obv:** Bust barely touches legend at "G" **Rev:** Without inner circle **Note:** Dav. #3327A.

Date	Mintage	VG	F	VF	XF	Unc
1618	—	60.00	120	200	350	—

KM# 279.5 THALER

Silver **Ruler:** Maximilian, Erzherzog 1612-1619 **Obv:** Similar to KM#279.3 but date in front **Note:** Dav. #3327B. Struck posthumously.

Date	Mintage	VG	F	VF	XF	Unc
1619	—	60.00	120	200	350	—

KM# A257 THALER

27.9200 g., Silver **Ruler:** Ferdinand II 1619-1632 **Obv:** Date before bust **Note:** Dav. #3168.

Date	Mintage	VG	F	VF	XF	Unc
1621	—	75.00	150	250	400	—

KM# B257.1 THALER

Silver **Ruler:** Ferdinand II 1619-1632 **Obv:** Date behind bust with straight ruffled collar **Note:** Dav. #3169.

Date	Mintage	VG	F	VF	XF	Unc
1621	—	75.00	150	250	400	—

KM# A270 THALER

Silver **Ruler:** Ferdinand II 1619-1632 **Obv:** Date below bust **Note:** Dav. #3170.

Date	Mintage	VG	F	VF	XF	Unc
1621	—	75.00	150	250	400	—
1623	—	75.00	150	250	400	—

KM# B257.2 THALER

Silver **Ruler:** Ferdinand II 1619-1632 **Obv:** Date behind bust with curved ruffled collar

Date	Mintage	VG	F	VF	XF	Unc
1622	—	75.00	150	250	400	—

KM# A265 THALER

Silver **Ruler:** Ferdinand II 1619-1632 **Note:** Dav. #3170A. Klippe.

Date	Mintage	VG	F	VF	XF	Unc
1623 Rare	—	—	—	—	—	—

KM# 257.1 THALER

Silver **Ruler:** Leopold V, Erzherzog 1619-1634 **Obv:** Bust of Leopold right **Obv. Legend:** + LEOPOLD: D: G. ARCHIDVX:... **Rev:** Crowned arms **Rev. Legend:** + RELIZ: ARCHID: GVBERNAT: PLEN: ET. COM: TIR: LAND. ALS **Mint:** Ensisheim **Note:** Varieties exist. Dav. #3345.

Date	Mintage	VG	F	VF	XF	Unc
1621	—	35.00	80.00	135	240	—
1622	—	35.00	80.00	135	240	—
1623	—	35.00	80.00	135	240	—
1624	—	35.00	80.00	135	240	—

KM# 257.2 THALER

Silver **Ruler:** Leopold V, Erzherzog 1619-1634 **Obv:** Bust divides date **Mint:** Ensisheim **Note:** Varieties exist. Dav. #3346.

Date	Mintage	VG	F	VF	XF	Unc
1621	—	35.00	80.00	135	240	—
1624	—	35.00	80.00	135	240	—

KM# 257.3 THALER

Silver **Ruler:** Leopold V, Erzherzog 1619-1634 **Obv. Legend:** LEOPOLDVS. AVS... **Mint:** Ensisheim **Note:** Varieties exist. Dav. #3346A.

Date	Mintage	VG	F	VF	XF	Unc
1625	—	35.00	70.00	110	185	—

KM# 260 THALER

Silver **Ruler:** Leopold V, Erzherzog 1619-1634 **Obv:** Date behind bust **Mint:** Ensisheim **Note:** Dav. #3347.

Date	Mintage	VG	F	VF	XF	Unc
16ZZ	—	45.00	90.00	170	285	—

KM# 261 THALER

Silver **Ruler:** Leopold V, Erzherzog 1619-1634 **Obv:** Date in front of bust **Mint:** Ensisheim **Note:** Dav. #3348.

Date	Mintage	VG	F	VF	XF	Unc
16Z3	—	40.00	85.00	150	250	—
16ZZ	—	40.00	85.00	150	250	—

KM# 265.1 THALER

Silver **Ruler:** Leopold V, Erzherzog 1619-1634 **Obv:** 1/2-length bust right with sceptre, date in front **Rev:** Crowned arms with Alsace as central arms **Mint:** Ensisheim **Note:** Dav. #3350.

Date	Mintage	VG	F	VF	XF	Unc
1626	—	50.00	100	180	300	—

KM# 265.2 THALER

Silver **Ruler:** Leopold V, Erzherzog 1619-1634 **Obv:** Thinner modified bust **Mint:** Ensisheim **Note:** Dav. #3350A.

Date	Mintage	VG	F	VF	XF	Unc
1626	—	50.00	100	180	300	—

KM# 267.1 THALER

Silver **Ruler:** Leopold V, Erzherzog 1619-1634 **Obv:** Bust breaking legend at bottom **Mint:** Ensisheim **Note:** Dav. #3351.

Date	Mintage	VG	F	VF	XF	Unc
1627	—	50.00	100	180	300	—

KM# 267.2 THALER

Silver **Ruler:** Leopold V, Erzherzog 1619-1634 **Obv:** Small bust with cloak over left shoulder **Mint:** Ensisheim **Note:** Dav. #3352.

Date	Mintage	VG	F	VF	XF	Unc
1627	—	80.00	150	275	450	—

KM# 267.3 THALER

Silver **Ruler:** Leopold V, Erzherzog 1619-1634 **Obv:** Large bust with cloak over left shoulder **Mint:** Ensisheim **Note:** Dav. #3352.

Date	Mintage	VG	F	VF	XF	Unc
1627	—	80.00	150	275	450	—

KM# 267.4 THALER

Silver **Ruler:** Leopold V, Erzherzog 1619-1634 **Obv:** Bust right with date in front **Mint:** Ensisheim **Note:** Varieties exist. Dav. #3353.

Date	Mintage	VG	F	VF	XF	Unc
1627	—	50.00	100	185	275	—
1628	—	50.00	100	185	275	—
1629	—	50.00	100	185	275	—
1630	—	50.00	100	185	275	—

KM# 268 THALER

Silver **Ruler:** Leopold V, Erzherzog 1619-1634 **Mint:** Ensisheim **Note:** Klippe. Dav. #3353A.

Date	Mintage	VG	F	VF	XF	Unc
1630 Rare	—	—	—	—	—	—

KM# 272 THALER

Silver **Ruler:** Leopold V, Erzherzog 1619-1634 **Obv:** Bust without cloak **Rev:** Crowned arms in order chain with two small shields at sides **Mint:** Ensisheim **Note:** Dav. #3355.

Date	Mintage	VG	F	VF	XF	Unc
1631	—	50.00	100	180	265	—
1632	—	50.00	100	180	265	—

KM# 273 THALER

Silver **Ruler:** Leopold V, Erzherzog 1619-1634 **Mint:** Ensisheim **Note:** Klippe. Dav. #3355A.

Date	Mintage	VG	F	VF	XF	Unc
1632 Rare	—	—	—	—	—	—
ND Rare	—	—	—	—	—	—

KM# 280 2 THALER

Silver **Ruler:** Maximilian, Erzherzog 1612-1619 **Obv:** Armored bust of Maximilian right **Obv. Legend:** + MAXIMILIANVS D: G ++ ARCH: AVST: DVX: BVR: STIR: CARIN(T) **Rev:** Crowned arms with shields at left and right **Rev. Legend:** (:)ET: CARN: MAG: PRVSS: ADML: LAND: ALS: COM: FER. **Note:** Dav. #3325.

Date	Mintage	VG	F	VF	XF	Unc
1614	—	400	750	1,250	2,000	—
1619	—	400	750	1,250	2,000	—

KM# 281 2 THALER

Silver

Date	Mintage	VG	F	VF	XF	Unc
1617	—	500	900	1,500	2,200	—

KM# 284 2 THALER

Silver **Ruler:** Leopold of Austria as Bishop of Strasbourg

Date	Mintage	VG	F	VF	XF	Unc
ND(1620)	—	350	700	1,350	2,250	—

KM# 248 2 THALER

Silver **Ruler:** Rudolf II von Habsburg 1602-1612 **Obv:** Bust of Rudolf II right **Obv. Legend:** + RVDOLPHVS: II: DG: ROM: IM: SE: AV: GE: HV: BO: REX **Rev:** Crowned ornate rounded arms **Rev. Legend:** NEC NON ARCHIDVCESA... **Mint:** Ensisheim **Note:** Dav. #3031.

Date	Mintage	VG	F	VF	XF	Unc
1603	—	700	1,200	1,850	3,000	—
1604	—	700	1,200	1,850	3,000	—
1607	—	700	1,200	1,850	3,000	—
1609	—	700	1,200	1,850	3,000	—

KM# 258 2 THALER

Silver **Ruler:** Leopold V, Erzherzog 1619-1634 **Obv:** Bust of Leopold right, legend **Obv. Legend:** LEOPOLDVS D G... **Rev:** Crowned arms shield at left and right **Rev. Legend:** .STIRIAE. CARINT - CARN: LAND: ALS **Mint:** Ensisheim **Note:** Dav. #3339.

Date	Mintage	VG	F	VF	XF	Unc
ND(1621)	—	550	1,100	1,800	3,000	—

KM# 271 2 THALER

Silver **Ruler:** Leopold V, Erzherzog 1619-1634 **Obv:** Crowned half-length bust of Leopold with scepter **Rev:** Crowned arms **Rev. Legend:** SAC: CAES: MA: ANTER: PROVINC. PLEN. GVB. **Mint:** Ensisheim **Note:** Dav. #3349.

Date	Mintage	VG	F	VF	XF	Unc
ND(1627)	—	350	750	1,250	2,000	—

KM# 274 2 THALER

Silver **Ruler:** Leopold V, Erzherzog 1619-1634 **Rev:** Crowned arms in Order chain with shields at left and right **Rev. Legend:** DVX. - DURG. LAND, ALS. - FER. **Mint:** Ensisheim **Note:** Dav. #3354.

Date	Mintage	VG	F	VF	XF	Unc
ND(1631) Rare	—	—	—	—	—	—

TRADE COINAGE

KM# 283 DUCAT

3.5000 g., 0.9860 Gold 0.1109 oz. AGW **Ruler:** Leopold V, Erzherzog 1619-1634 **Obv:** Arms of Alsace in order chain within circle, legend surrounds **Obv. Legend:** LEOPOLDVS. D-G:... **Rev:** St. Leopold standing facing with banner, holding church model in left hand **Mint:** Ensisheim **Note:** Posthumous issue. Fr. #119a.

Date	Mintage	VG	F	VF	XF	Unc
ND(1631-34) Rare	—	—	—	—	—	—

KM# A276 6-1/2 DUCAT

22.7500 g., 0.9860 Gold 0.7212 oz. AGW **Ruler:** Rudolf II von Habsburg 1602-1612 **Obv:** Laureate bust of Rudolph II right **Rev:** Crowned arms **Mint:** Ensisheim **Note:** Struck with 1 Thaler dies, KM#247.3.

Date	Mintage	VG	F	VF	XF	Unc
1611 Rare	—	—	—	—	—	—

ANHALT

The Principality of Anhalt in Central Germany, surrounded by Brandenburg, Brunswick and Saxony, had its origins in the same Ascanian family from which descended the margraves of Brandenburg and the dukes of Saxony. The nucleus of the Anhalt domains was the countship of Ballenstädt, whose first recorded ruler, Albrecht I, was in control there during the late 10th century. Albrecht's great-great-grandson, Albrecht III the Bear, ruled in Anhalt until 1170 and was also the margrave of Brandenburg until his death, as well as duke of Saxony until 1153. The patrimony was divided in 1170 and Albrecht III's third son, Bernhard, ruled in Anhalt and began a line of descendants, which lasted into the 20th century.

Various divisions occurred during the ensuing centuries, but the ruling princes often struck joint coinages. At the death of Georg I of Dessau and Köthen in 1474, his five surviving sons ruled together. Only two of them had any male children and they ruled separately in Dessau and Köthen until the latter fell extinct in 1566, at which time that branch reverted to Dessau. Meanwhile, Dessau had been divided in 1516 into Dessau, Plötzkau and Zerbst, but all reverted to Zerbst after a generation. One of the Zerbst princes succeeded in reuniting all the Anhalt lands in 1570 and his sons ruled jointly until the great division of 1603.

RULERS

After the division of 1603, the princes of Anhalt continued to issue joint coinage in many denominations. As some members of one generation died, their places were taken by their sons and various combinations of brothers, uncles, nephews and cousins are represented on the coins, either with their full or abbreviated names or simply as "brothers and fathers - princes of Anhalt". There are 4 distinct periods of joint coinage, 3 of which follow one upon the other and a later period separated from the first 3 by forty years.

Period I, 1603-1618

Johann Georg I von Dessau
Christian I von Bernburg
Augustus von Plötzkau
Rudolf von Zerbst
Ludwig von Köthen

Period II, 1618-1621

Christian I von Bernburg
Augustus von Plötzkau
Rudolf von Zerbst
Ludwig von Köthen
Johann Kasimir von Dessau
Georg Aribert von Dessau

Period III, 1621-1630

Christian I von Bernburg
Augustus von Plötzkau
Ludwig von Köthen
Johann Kasimir von Dessau
Georg Aribert von Dessau
Johann von Zerbst

Period IV, 1670-1693

Johann Georg II von Dessau (d.1693)
Victor Amadeus von Bernburg (d.1718)
Wilhelm von Harzgerode (d.1709)
Carl Wilhelm von Zerbst (d.1718)
Emanuel Lebrecht von Köthen (d. 1704)

MINT OFFICIALS' INITIALS

Initials	Date	Name
CP	1674-90	Christoph Pflug
DH		?
EI		Erik Jäger
GK		?
HB		?
HF		?
HI, II	1614-18	Johann (Hans) Jakob
HS	1622-24	Heinrich Schultze
IA	1666-76	Johann Arendsberg der Jünger in Zerbst and Reinstein
IS		?
IW		?
K		?
SK		?
SV		?

ARMS:

Anhalt – two-fold divided vertically, ½ eagle on left, 8 (or more) horizontal bars on right, alternately shaded, sometimes with opened crown laid across diagonally (ducal Saxony). The two sides are often reversed in early issues.

Ascanian dynasty – crowned bear standing (early), crowned bear on wall (later).

Aschersleben – checkerboard.

CROSS REFERENCE:

M = **Julius Mann,** *Anhaltische Münzen und Medaillen vom Ende des XV. Jahrhunderts bis 1906*, **Hannover, 1907.**

PRINCIPALITY

JOINT COINAGE

KM# 15 HELLER

Copper Or Billon **Note:** Uniface. Two-fold arms separate two-digit date or date above. Varieties exist.

Date	Mintage	Good	VG	F	VF	XF
1619	—	20.00	40.00	65.00	100	200
(16)20	—	20.00	40.00	65.00	100	200
1621	—	20.00	40.00	65.00	100	200
(16)21	—	20.00	40.00	65.00	100	200
(16)22	—	20.00	40.00	65.00	100	200
ND	—	20.00	40.00	65.00	100	200

KM# 21 HELLER

Copper Or Billon **Obv:** Two-fold arms **Rev:** Date **Note:** Uniface. Varieties exist.

Date	Mintage	Good	VG	F	VF	XF
1621	—	20.00	35.00	60.00	100	175

KM# 20 HELLER

Copper Or Billon **Obv:** Two-fold arms, date above **Rev:** Two-fold arms

Date	Mintage	Good	VG	F	VF	XF
(16)21	—	20.00	35.00	60.00	100	175

KM# 22 HELLER

Copper Or Billon **Obv:** Two-fold arms, one above **Rev:** Imperial orb divides date

Date	Mintage	Good	VG	F	VF	XF
1621	—	27.00	45.00	65.00	110	190
(16)21	—	27.00	45.00	65.00	110	190

KM# 23 HELLER

Copper Or Billon **Obv:** Two-fold arms **Rev:** Bear right on wall

Date	Mintage	Good	VG	F	VF	XF
ND	—	35.00	60.00	95.00	140	250

KM# 19 HELLER

Copper Or Billon **Note:** Bear on wall with gate.

Date	Mintage	Good	VG	F	VF	XF
ND Rare	—	—	—	—	—	—

KM# 25 PFENNIG

Copper Or Billon **Rev:** Gate with three towers divides date

Date	Mintage	Good	VG	F	VF	XF
1621 Rare	—	—	—	—	—	—

KM# 24 PFENNIG

Copper Or Billon **Obv:** Two-fold arms **Rev:** Bear right on wall, date in legend **Note:** Kipper Pfennig.

Date	Mintage	Good	VG	F	VF	XF
1621 Rare	—	—	—	—	—	—

KM# 26 2 PFENNIG

Billon **Obv:** Two-fold arms, date above **Rev:** II/PFEN/GE **Note:** Kipper 2 Pfennig.

Date	Mintage	Good	VG	F	VF	XF
(16)21 Rare	—	—	—	—	—	—

KM# 27 3 PFENNIG (Dreier)

Billon **Obv:** Two-fold arms, date above **Rev:** Imperial orb with 3 **Note:** Kipper 3 Pfennig. Varieties exist.

Date	Mintage	Good	VG	F	VF	XF
1621 GK	—	9.00	16.00	22.00	45.00	80.00
1621 SK	—	9.00	16.00	22.00	45.00	80.00
(16)21	—	9.00	16.00	22.00	45.00	80.00

KM# 28 3 PFENNIG (Dreier)

Billon **Rev:** Heart-shaped shield and date **Note:** Varieties exist.

Date	Mintage	Good	VG	F	VF	XF
(16)21	—	12.00	20.00	30.00	55.00	100

KM# 29 3 PFENNIG (Dreier)

Billon **Rev:** Imperial orb in rhombus

Date	Mintage	Good	VG	F	VF	XF
1621	—	12.00	20.00	35.00	60.00	110
(16)21	—	12.00	20.00	35.00	60.00	110

KM# 30 3 PFENNIG (Dreier)

Billon **Obv:** Oval shield

Date	Mintage	Good	VG	F	VF	XF
(16)21	—	12.00	20.00	35.00	60.00	110

KM# 53 3 PFENNIG (Dreier)

Silver **Obv:** Two-fold arms, date above **Rev:** Imperial orb with 3 in lower half divides date

Date	Mintage	Good	VG	F	VF	XF
(16)22	—	14.00	27.00	60.00	90.00	150

KM# 48 3 PFENNIG (Dreier)

Billon **Obv:** Two-fold arms in round or oval shield **Rev:** Imperial orb with 3 in lower half divides date **Note:** Varieties exist.

Date	Mintage	Good	VG	F	VF	XF
(16)22	—	9.00	14.00	25.00	40.00	75.00
ND	—	9.00	14.00	25.00	40.00	75.00
ND V	—	9.00	14.00	25.00	40.00	75.00
ND SV	—	9.00	14.00	25.00	40.00	75.00

KM# 49 3 PFENNIG (Dreier)

Billon **Obv:** Square or rectangular shield, pointed or rounded bottom **Note:** Varieties exist.

Date	Mintage	Good	VG	F	VF	XF
(16)22	—	9.00	14.00	25.00	40.00	75.00
ND	—	—	—	—	—	—

KM# 50 3 PFENNIG (Dreier)

Billon **Obv:** Heart-shaped shield **Rev:** Orb in rhombus **Note:** Varieties exist.

Date	Mintage	Good	VG	F	VF	XF
(16)22	—	12.00	20.00	30.00	50.00	90.00

KM# 51 3 PFENNIG (Dreier)

Billon **Obv:** Large B **Rev:** Lion left, value III above **Note:** Varieties exist.

Date	Mintage	Good	VG	F	VF	XF
ND Rare	—	—	—	—	—	—

KM# 52 3 PFENNIG (Dreier)

Billon **Obv:** Large B between two flowers **Rev:** 3 in heart-shaped cartouche **Note:** Varieties exist.

Date	Mintage	Good	VG	F	VF	XF
ND Rare	—	—	—	—	—	—

KM# 54 3 PFENNIG (Dreier)

Silver **Obv:** Two-fold arms in square or rectangular shield **Note:** Varieties exist.

Date	Mintage	Good	VG	F	VF	XF
1622 HB	—	14.00	27.00	60.00	95.00	175
1622 SV	—	14.00	27.00	60.00	95.00	175

Date	Mintage	Good	VG	F	VF	XF
1622	—	14.00	27.00	60.00	95.00	175
(16)22	—	14.00	27.00	60.00	95.00	175

KM# 55 3 PFENNIG (Dreier)
Silver **Obv:** Two-fold arms in round or oval shield **Note:** Varieties exist.

Date	Mintage	Good	VG	F	VF	XF
(16)22	—	10.00	20.00	40.00	60.00	120
ND SV	—	10.00	20.00	40.00	60.00	120

KM# 57 4 PFENNIG
Silver **Obv:** Date added

Date	Mintage	Good	VG	F	VF	XF
1622 Rare	—	—	—	—	—	—

KM# 56 4 PFENNIG
Silver **Obv:** Two-fold arms in oval shield **Rev:** Square with value IIII, date **Note:** Kipper 4 Pfennig. Varieties exist.

Date	Mintage	Good	VG	F	VF	XF
1622	—	20.00	40.00	65.00	100	175

KM# 18 2 SCHILLING
Silver **Obv:** Crowned two-fold arms **Rev:** DS monogram, date either split above and below or all below **Note:** Kipper 2 Schilling. Varieties exist.

Date	Mintage	VG	F	VF	XF	Unc
1620	—	20.00	40.00	70.00	125	175
1621	—	20.00	40.00	70.00	125	175
ND	—	20.00	40.00	70.00	125	175

KM# 42 12 KREUZER
Silver **Obv:** Angel above two-fold arms **Rev:** Imperial eagle with value 12 on breast **Note:** Kipper 12 Kreuzer. Varieties exist.

Date	Mintage	VG	F	VF	XF	Unc
ND Rare	—	—	—	—	—	—

KM# 43 12 KREUZER
Silver **Rev:** Three shields, one above two, value 12 in legend at bottom **Note:** Varieties exist.

Date	Mintage	VG	F	VF	XF	Unc
ND HW Rare	—	—	—	—	—	—

KM# 44 12 KREUZER
Silver **Obv:** Crowned two-fold arms **Rev:** Three shields, two above one, one below divides date **Note:** Varieties exist.

Date	Mintage	VG	F	VF	XF	Unc
1621	—	55.00	150	250	400	—
1621 DH	—	55.00	150	250	400	—

KM# 73 12 KREUZER
Silver **Obv:** Small angel's head above heart-shaped two-fold arms **Rev:** Imperial eagle with value 12 on breast, date

Date	Mintage	VG	F	VF	XF	Unc
1622 IW	—	55.00	150	250	400	—

KM# 45 24 KREUZER
Silver **Obv:** Angel above two-fold arms, date **Rev:** Imperial eagle with value 24 on breast **Note:** Kipper 24 Kreuzer. Varieties exist.

Date	Mintage	VG	F	VF	XF	Unc
1621	—	70.00	140	225	400	—
ND	—	70.00	140	225	400	—

KM# 46 24 KREUZER
Silver **Obv:** Two-fold arms

Date	Mintage	VG	F	VF	XF	Unc
1621 DH	—	70.00	140	225	400	—
ND	—	70.00	140	225	400	—

KM# 47 24 KREUZER
Silver **Obv:** Crowned two-fold arms **Rev:** One shield above divides date, two shields below, value 24 in legend at bottom **Note:** Varieties exist.

Date	Mintage	VG	F	VF	XF	Unc
ND K	—	70.00	140	225	400	—
ND	—	70.00	140	225	400	—

KM# 74 24 KREUZER
Silver **Obv:** Angel above two-fold arms, date **Rev:** Imperial eagle with 24 on breast, date

Date	Mintage	VG	F	VF	XF	Unc
1622	—	70.00	140	225	400	—

KM# 11 4 GROSCHEN
Silver **Obv:** Heart-shaped two-fold arms, date **Rev:** Three shields, one above, two below; value 4 in lower legend

Date	Mintage	VG	F	VF	XF	Unc
1616 Rare	—	—	—	—	—	—

KM# 38 4 GROSCHEN
Silver **Rev:** Without date **Note:** Varieties exist.

Date	Mintage	VG	F	VF	XF	Unc
1620	—	50.00	85.00	130	200	—
1621	—	50.00	85.00	130	200	—
ND	—	50.00	85.00	130	200	—

KM# 39 4 GROSCHEN
Silver **Obv:** Crowned two-fold arms **Rev:** Three shields, one above divides date, two below without value **Note:** Varieties exist.

Date	Mintage	VG	F	VF	XF	Unc
1621	—	45.00	80.00	125	190	—
1621 HW	—	50.00	85.00	140	225	—
ND	—	45.00	80.00	125	190	—

KM# 33 4 GROSCHEN
Silver **Obv:** Angel aboe two-fold arms **Rev:** Three shields, two above, one below divides date, value 4 in center **Note:** Kipper 4 Groschen.

Date	Mintage	VG	F	VF	XF	Unc
1621	—	55.00	95.00	140	225	—

KM# 34 4 GROSCHEN
Silver **Rev:** One shield above, two below, value 4 between lower two **Note:** Varieties exist.

Date	Mintage	VG	F	VF	XF	Unc
ND	—	55.00	95.00	140	225	—

KM# 35 4 GROSCHEN
Silver **Obv:** Two-fold arms **Rev:** 4 in circle at bottom **Note:** Varieties exist.

Date	Mintage	VG	F	VF	XF	Unc
1621	—	50.00	95.00	135	200	—
ND	—	50.00	95.00	135	200	—

KM# 36 4 GROSCHEN
Silver **Obv:** Crowned two-fold arms **Rev:** One shield above divides date, two shields below, value 4 in circle in lower legend **Note:** Varieties exist.

Date	Mintage	VG	F	VF	XF	Unc
(16)21	—	55.00	95.00	140	225	—

KM# 37 4 GROSCHEN
Silver **Obv:** Two-fold arms **Rev:** Three shields, two above, one below divides date, value IIII in circle at bottom **Note:** Varieties exist.

Date	Mintage	VG	F	VF	XF	Unc
ND	—	55.00	95.00	140	225	—

KM# 40 8 GROSCHEN
Silver **Obv:** Angel above two-fold arms **Rev:** Three shields, two above, one below divides date, value 8 in legend at bottom **Note:** Kipper 8 Groschen.

Date	Mintage	VG	F	VF	XF	Unc
1621	—	60.00	100	170	250	—
ND HW	—	60.00	100	170	250	—

KM# 41 8 GROSCHEN
Silver **Obv:** Crowned two-fold arms **Rev:** Three shields, one above divides date, two below **Note:** Varieties exist.

Date	Mintage	VG	F	VF	XF	Unc
1621	—	55.00	95.00	140	225	—
(16)21	—	55.00	95.00	140	225	—
ND	—	55.00	95.00	140	225	—
ND K	—	55.00	95.00	140	225	—

KM# 83 8 GROSCHEN
Silver **Obv:** Crowned nine-fold arms **Rev:** Value, date **Note:** Gute 8 Groschen. Varieties exist.

Date	Mintage	VG	F	VF	XF	Unc
1669	—	35.00	65.00	120	175	—

KM# 90 8 GROSCHEN
Silver **Obv:** Crowned nine-fold arms in wreath

Date	Mintage	VG	F	VF	XF	Unc
1689 CP	—	35.00	65.00	120	175	—

KM# 88 16 GROSCHEN
Silver **Note:** Varieties exist.

Date	Mintage	VG	F	VF	XF	Unc
1683 CP	—	50.00	95.00	140	200	—
1684 CP	—	50.00	95.00	140	200	—
1685 CP	—	50.00	95.00	140	200	—
1686 CP	—	50.00	95.00	140	200	—
1689 CP	—	50.00	95.00	140	200	—

KM# 59 1/84 THALER (6 Pfennig - Kortling)
Billon **Obv:** Two-fold arms **Rev:** Orb in rhombus

Date	Mintage	Good	VG	F	VF	XF
1622	—	15.00	35.00	60.00	96.00	150

KM# 60 1/84 THALER (6 Pfennig - Kortling)
Billon **Obv:** Arms of Aschersleben (checkerboard) **Rev:** Imperial orb with value 84 divides date

Date	Mintage	Good	VG	F	VF	XF
(16)22 Rare	—	—	—	—	—	—

KM# 58 1/84 THALER (6 Pfennig - Kortling)
Billon **Obv:** Two-fold arms in ornate frame **Rev:** Imperial orb with value 84 divides date **Note:** Kipper 1/84 Thaler. Varieties exist.

Date	Mintage	Good	VG	F	VF	XF
1622	—	13.00	27.00	50.00	95.00	150

KM# 1 1/24 THALER (Groschen)
Silver **Obv:** Four-fold arms in heart-shaped shield, legend **Rev:** Imperial orb with 24 divides date, legend **Note:** Varieties exist.

Date	Mintage	VG	F	VF	XF	Unc
1614 II	—	13.00	24.00	45.00	70.00	—
1615	—	13.00	24.00	45.00	70.00	—
1615 II	—	13.00	24.00	45.00	70.00	—

KM# 7 1/24 THALER (Groschen)
Silver **Rev:** Crowned two-fold arms in oval shield, date **Note:** Varieties exist.

Date	Mintage	VG	F	VF	XF	Unc
1615	—	13.00	24.00	45.00	70.00	—
1616	—	13.00	24.00	45.00	70.00	—
1617	—	13.00	24.00	45.00	70.00	—

KM# 8 1/24 THALER (Groschen)
Silver **Note:** Klippe. Varieties exist.

Date	Mintage	VG	F	VF	XF	Unc
1615	—	35.00	60.00	100	170	—
1617	—	25.00	45.00	75.00	125	—

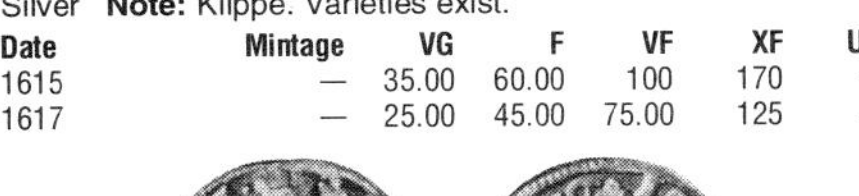

KM# 14 1/24 THALER (Groschen)
Silver **Obv:** Square shield, rounded at bottom **Note:** Varieties exist.

Date	Mintage	VG	F	VF	XF	Unc
1617	—	13.00	20.00	45.00	75.00	—
1618	—	12.00	20.00	45.00	75.00	—

KM# 16 1/24 THALER (Groschen)
Silver **Obv:** Crowned two-fold arms **Rev:** Imperial orb with 24, date in legend. **Note:** Kipper 1/24 Thaler. Varieties exist.

Date	Mintage	VG	F	VF	XF	Unc
1619	—	12.00	20.00	45.00	75.00	—
1620	—	12.00	20.00	45.00	75.00	—
(16)20	—	12.00	20.00	45.00	75.00	—
1621	—	12.00	20.00	45.00	75.00	—
ND	—	12.00	20.00	45.00	75.00	—

KM# 17 1/24 THALER (Groschen)
Silver **Note:** Klippe.

Date	Mintage	VG	F	VF	XF	Unc
1619	—	35.00	70.00	100	170	—
1620	—	35.00	70.00	100	170	—

KM# 31 1/24 THALER (Groschen)
Silver **Obv:** Bear right on wall **Rev:** Imperial orb with 24, date

Date	Mintage	VG	F	VF	XF	Unc
1621 Rare	—	—	—	—	—	—

KM# 32 1/24 THALER (Groschen)
Copper Or Billon **Obv:** Crowned two-fold arms **Rev:** Imperial orb with 24, date in legend

Date	Mintage	VG	F	VF	XF	Unc
1621	—	12.00	20.00	45.00	75.00	—

KM# 63 1/24 THALER (Groschen)
Silver **Rev:** Small orb with 24 above two shields, date

Date	Mintage	VG	F	VF	XF	Unc
1622 HB	—	14.00	27.00	50.00	90.00	—

KM# 72 1/24 THALER (Groschen)
Silver **Obv:** Four-fold arms **Rev:** Imperial orb with 24, date **Note:** Klippe.

Date	Mintage	VG	F	VF	XF	Unc
1622 IS Rare	—	—	—	—	—	—

KM# 61 1/24 THALER (Groschen)
Silver **Obv:** Helmeted two-fold arms **Rev:** Imperial orb with 24, date **Note:** Size varies: 22-24 milimeters. Varieties exist.

Date	Mintage	VG	F	VF	XF	Unc
1622	—	12.00	20.00	45.00	75.00	—
1623	—	12.00	20.00	45.00	75.00	—

KM# 64 1/24 THALER (Groschen)
Silver **Obv:** Oval two-fold arms **Rev:** Imperial orb with 24, date **Note:** Size varies: 14-17 milimeters. Varieties exist.

Date	Mintage	VG	F	VF	XF	Unc
1622	—	12.00	22.00	45.00	75.00	—
1622 HB	—	12.00	22.00	45.00	75.00	—
ND	—	12.00	22.00	45.00	75.00	—

KM# 65 1/24 THALER (Groschen)
Silver **Note:** Klippe. Varieties exist.

Date	Mintage	VG	F	VF	XF	Unc
ND	—	27.00	50.00	95.00	140	—

KM# 66 1/24 THALER (Groschen)
Silver **Obv:** Bear on wall right

Date	Mintage	VG	F	VF	XF	Unc
(16)22 Rare	—	—	—	—	—	—

KM# 67 1/24 THALER (Groschen)
Silver **Obv:** Two-fold arms with straight-sided shield with pointed or rounded bottom **Note:** Varieties exist.

Date	Mintage	VG	F	VF	XF	Unc
ND	—	16.00	35.00	60.00	100	—

KM# 68 1/24 THALER (Groschen)
Silver **Obv:** Two shields above one shield **Rev:** Imperial orb with 24

Date	Mintage	VG	F	VF	XF	Unc
ND	—	16.00	35.00	60.00	100	—

KM# 69 1/24 THALER (Groschen)
Silver **Obv:** Bear on wall right

Date	Mintage	VG	F	VF	XF	Unc
ND	—	16.00	35.00	60.00	100	—

KM# 70 1/24 THALER (Groschen)
Silver **Obv:** Arms of Aschersleben (checkerborad)

Date	Mintage	VG	F	VF	XF	Unc
ND	—	20.00	35.00	65.00	120	—

KM# 71 1/24 THALER (Groschen)
Silver **Obv:** Angel's head and wings above two-fold arms **Note:** Size varies: 22-24 milimeters.

Date	Mintage	VG	F	VF	XF	Unc
ND	—	20.00	35.00	65.00	110	—

KM# 62 1/24 THALER (Groschen)
Silver **Note:** Klippe.

Date	Mintage	VG	F	VF	XF	Unc
1623	—	35.00	60.00	95.00	150	—

KM# 87 1/24 THALER (Groschen)
Silver **Obv:** Crowned nine-fold arms in wreath **Rev:** Value: 24 EINEN..., date **Note:** Varieties exist.

Date	Mintage	VG	F	VF	XF	Unc
1683 CP	—	20.00	35.00	65.00	110	—
1684 CP	—	20.00	35.00	65.00	110	—

KM# 89 1/12 THALER
Silver **Obv:** Crowned nine-fold arms in wreath **Rev:** Value: 12 EINEN... **Note:** Varieties exist.

Date	Mintage	VG	F	VF	XF	Unc
1684 CP	—	16.00	35.00	75.00	120	—
1686 CP	—	16.00	35.00	75.00	120	—
1688 CP	—	16.00	35.00	75.00	120	—
1689 CP	—	16.00	35.00	75.00	120	—

KM# 79 1/4 THALER
Silver **Obv:** Helmeted nine-fold arms **Rev:** Crowned imperial eagle with orb and VI on breast, date

Date	Mintage	VG	F	VF	XF	Unc
1624 HS Rare	—	—	—	—	—	—

KM# 84 1/3 THALER
Silver **Obv:** Crowned nine-fold arms **Rev:** Crowned, erect bear walking left, value, date **Note:** Varieties exist.

Date	Mintage	VG	F	VF	XF	Unc
1669 IA	—	60.00	100	190	350	—
1670 IA	—	60.00	100	190	350	—

KM# 85 1/3 THALER
Silver **Obv:** Value below arms

Date	Mintage	VG	F	VF	XF	Unc
1670 IA	—	65.00	110	200	400	—

KM# 2 1/2 THALER
Silver **Note:** Similar to 1 thaler, KM#3.

Date	Mintage	VG	F	VF	XF	Unc
1614 II Rare	—	—	—	—	—	—

KM# 75 1/2 THALER
Silver **Obv:** Nine-fold arms **Rev:** Crowned imperial eagle with orb and 12 on breast, date

Date	Mintage	VG	F	VF	XF	Unc
1622 HS Rare	—	—	—	—	—	—

KM# 78 1/2 THALER
Silver **Note:** Klippe.

Date	Mintage	VG	F	VF	XF	Unc
1623 HS Rare	—	—	—	—	—	—

KM# 77 1/2 THALER
Silver **Note:** Similar to 1 Thaler, KM#76.

Date	Mintage	VG	F	VF	XF	Unc
1623 HS	—	600	1,000	1,500	2,200	—
1624 HS	—	600	1,000	1,500	2,200	—

KM# 80 1/2 THALER
Silver **Note:** Similar to 1 Thaler, KM#81. Varieties exist.

Date	Mintage	VG	F	VF	XF	Unc
1624 Rare	—	—	—	—	—	—
1625 EI Rare	—	—	—	—	—	—

KM# 86.1 2/3 THALER
Silver **Obv:** Capped nine-fold arms **Obv. Legend:** MONETA • NOVA • PRINC • ANHALT **Rev:** Crowned, erect bear left, value below divides date **Note:** Varieties exist.

Date	Mintage	VG	F	VF	XF	Unc
1670	—	90.00	145	250	400	—
1670 IA	—	90.00	145	250	400	—

KM# 86.2 2/3 THALER
Silver **Obv:** Capped 9-fold arms in inner circle **Obv. Legend:** *MONETA • NOVA • PRINC • ANHALTINOR **Rev:** Crowned erect bear left in inner circle, date at right of value below **Rev. Legend:** IN • DOMINO • FIDUCIA • NOSTRA

Date	Mintage	VG	F	VF	XF	Unc
1670 IA	—	90.00	145	250	400	—

KM# 3 THALER
Silver **Note:** Dav. #6002.

Date	Mintage	VG	F	VF	XF	Unc
1614 II	—	300	550	950	1,500	—
1615 HI	—	300	550	950	1,500	—
1616 HI	—	300	550	950	1,500	—
1617 HI	—	300	550	950	1,500	—
1618 HI	—	300	550	950	1,500	—

KM# 9 THALER
Silver **Note:** Klippe. Dav. #6002A.

Date	Mintage	VG	F	VF	XF	Unc
1615 HI Rare	—	—	—	—	—	—
1616 HI Rare	—	—	—	—	—	—

KM# 76.1 THALER
Silver **Note:** Dav. #6003A.

Date	Mintage	VG	F	VF	XF	Unc
1622	—	200	325	550	900	—

KM# 76.2 THALER
Silver **Rev:** Date divided by crown **Note:** Varieties exist. Dav. #6003.

Date	Mintage	VG	F	VF	XF	Unc
1622 HS	—	175	300	500	800	—
1623 HS	—	175	300	500	800	—
1624 HS	—	175	300	500	800	—

KM# 81 THALER
Silver **Note:** Varieties exist. Dav. #6005.

Date	Mintage	VG	F	VF	XF	Unc
1624	—	175	300	500	800	—
1624 EI	—	175	300	500	800	—
1625 EI	—	175	300	500	800	—

KM# 4 2 THALER
60.0000 g., Silver **Note:** Similar to 1 Thaler, KM#3, thick flan. Dav. #6001.

Date	Mintage	VG	F	VF	XF	Unc
1614 II Rare	—	—	—	—	—	—
1615 HI Rare	—	—	—	—	—	—
1618 HI Rare	—	—	—	—	—	—

KM# 82 2 THALER
70.0000 g., Silver **Note:** Similar to 1 Thaler, KM#81. Thick flan. Varieties exist. Dav. #6004.

Date	Mintage	VG	F	VF	XF	Unc
1624 EI Rare	—	—	—	—	—	—
1624 EI/HS Rare	—	—	—	—	—	—
1625 EI Rare	—	—	—	—	—	—

TRADE COINAGE

KM# 12 1/2 DUCAT
1.7500 g., 0.9860 Gold 0.0555 oz. AGW **Obv:** Three tournament helmets **Rev:** Helmeted arms

Date	Mintage	VG	F	VF	XF	Unc
1616	—	450	1,150	2,250	4,500	—
1618	—	450	1,150	2,250	4,500	—

KM# 13 1/2 DUCAT
1.7500 g., 0.9860 Gold 0.0555 oz. AGW **Obv:** Crowned arms **Rev:** Crowned imperial eagle **Note:** Klippe.

Date	Mintage	VG	F	VF	XF	Unc
1616 Rare	—	—	—	—	—	—

KM# 10 DUCAT
3.5000 g., 0.9860 Gold 0.1109 oz. AGW **Obv:** Three tournament helmets **Rev:** Crowned arms

Date	Mintage	VG	F	VF	XF	Unc
1615	—	625	1,250	2,550	5,500	—
1616	—	625	1,250	2,550	5,500	—
1617	—	625	1,250	2,550	5,500	—
1618	—	625	1,250	2,550	5,500	—
ND	—	625	1,250	2,550	5,500	—

KM# 5 3 DUCAT
10.5000 g., 0.9860 Gold 0.3328 oz. AGW **Obv:** Facing busts of Johann Georg and Christian in inner circle **Rev:** Busts of August and Rudolf facing Ludwig in inner circle

Date	Mintage	VG	F	VF	XF	Unc
1614 II Rare	—	—	—	—	—	—
1616 HI Rare	—	—	—	—	—	—

KM# 6 4 DUCAT
14.0000 g., 0.9860 Gold 0.4438 oz. AGW **Obv:** Facing busts of Johann Georg and Christian in inner circle **Rev:** Busts of August and Rudolf facing Ludwig in inner circle

Date	Mintage	VG	F	VF	XF	Unc
1614 Rare	—	—	—	—	—	—

PATTERNS

Including off metal strikes

KM#	Date	Mintage	Identification	Mkt Val
Pn1	1615 HI	—	3 Ducat. Silver. KM#5	—
Pn2	1615 HI	—	3 Ducat. Silver. 17.1200 g. Klippe, KM#5.	—

ANHALT-BERNBURG

Located in north-central Germany. Appeared as part of the patrimony of Albrecht the Bear of Brandenburg in 1170. Bracteates were first made in the 12th century. It was originally in the inheritance of Heinrich the Fat in 1252 and became extinct in 1468. The division of 1603, among the sons of Joachim Ernst, revitalized Anhalt-Bernburg. Bernburg passed to Dessau after the death of Alexander Carl in 1863.

RULERS
Christian I, 1603-1630
Christian II, 1630-1656
Viktor I Amadeus, 1656-1718

DUCHY

REGULAR COINAGE

KM# 1 THALER
Silver **Ruler:** Christian II **Obv:** Bust of Christian II right divides date **Obv. Legend:** D:G:CHRISTIANVS.PR.ANHALD... **Rev:** Crowned imperial eagle **Rev. Legend:** FERDINANDVS. II.D:G: ROMANORVM... **Note:** Dav. #6006.

Date	Mintage	VG	F	VF	XF	Unc
1635	—	575	800	1,100	1,750	—

KM# 2 THALER
Silver **Ruler:** Christian II **Obv:** Similar to KM#1 **Rev:** Helmeted arms **Rev. Legend:** *ASTRA PETIT VIRTVS **Note:** Dav. #6007.

Date	Mintage	VG	F	VF	XF	Unc
1636	—	125	275	550	950	—
1640	—	125	275	550	950	—
1643	—	125	275	550	950	—
1644	—	125	275	550	950	—
1645	—	125	275	550	950	—

ANHALT-DESSAU

Dessau was part of the 1252 division that included Zerbst and Cothen. In 1396 Zerbst divided into Zerbst and Dessau. In 1508 Zerbst was absorbed into Dessau. Dessau was given to the eldest son of Joachim Ernst in the division of 1603. As other lines became extinct, they fell to Dessau, which united all branches in 1863.

RULERS
Johann Georg I, 1603-1618
Johann Kasimir, 1618-1660
Johann Georg II, 1660-1693
Leopold I, 1693-1747

MINT OFFICIALS' INITIALS

Initials	Date	Name
AB	1657-64	Adrian Becker, warden in Berlin
ABK-APK	1667-80	Anton Bernhard Koburger in Mansfeld-Eisleben
CM	1693-94	Christoph Muller
FCV	1674-76	Franc Carl Uhle
IEG	1692-93	Johann Ernst Graul

DUCHY

REGULAR COINAGE

KM# 1 GROSCHEN
Silver **Subject:** Death of Johann Kasimir **Obv:** Crowned 9-fold arms **Rev:** 12-line inscription **Note:** Varieties exist.

Date	Mintage	VG	F	VF	XF	Unc
MDCLX (1660) AB	—	35.00	75.00	125	190	—

KM# 8 1/12 THALER
Silver **Obv:** Crowned 2-fold arms **Rev:** Value, date **Note:** Varieties exist.

Date	Mintage	VG	F	VF	XF	Unc
1693 IEG	—	30.00	65.00	110	175	—

KM# 4 1/3 THALER
Silver **Note:** Similar to 2/3 Thaler, KM#5. Varieties exist.

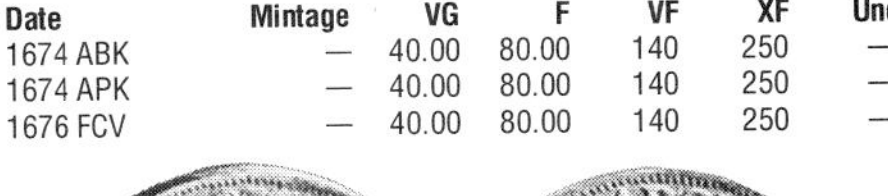

Date	Mintage	VG	F	VF	XF	Unc
1674 ABK	—	40.00	80.00	140	250	—
1674 APK	—	40.00	80.00	140	250	—
1676 FCV	—	40.00	80.00	140	250	—

KM# 9 1/3 THALER
Silver **Note:** Similar to 2/3 Thaler, KM#5. Varieties exist.

Date	Mintage	VG	F	VF	XF	Unc
1693 IEG	—	45.00	85.00	150	275	—

KM# 10 1/3 THALER
Silver **Obv:** Similar to 2/3 Thaler, KM#6 but bust left
Note: Varieties exist.

Date	Mintage	VG	F	VF	XF	Unc
1693 Rare	—	—	—	—	—	—

KM# 2 2/3 THALER
Silver **Subject:** Death of Johann Kasimir **Obv:** Helmeted 9-fold arms **Rev:** 12-line inscription

Date	Mintage	VG	F	VF	XF	Unc
MDCLX (1660) AB	—	—	200	375	700	—

KM# 5.1 2/3 THALER
Silver **Obv:** Bust of Johann George II right **Rev:** Large date in legend at 10 o'clock; crowned arms

Date	Mintage	VG	F	VF	XF	Unc
1674 APK	—	40.00	65.00	120	250	—
1674 ABK	—	55.00	90.00	170	325	—

KM# 5.2 2/3 THALER
Silver **Rev:** Small date in a legend at 10 o'clock

Date	Mintage	VG	F	VF	XF	Unc
1674 APK	—	55.00	90.00	170	325	—
1675	—	55.00	90.00	170	325	—
1675 FCV	—	55.00	90.00	170	325	—
1676 FCV	—	55.00	90.00	170	325	—

KM# 5.3 2/3 THALER
Silver **Rev:** Oval arms within palm branches

Date	Mintage	VG	F	VF	XF	Unc
1674	—	55.00	90.00	170	325	—
1674 APK	—	55.00	90.00	170	325	—
1675 FCV	—	55.00	90.00	170	325	—
1676 FCV	—	55.00	90.00	170	325	—

KM# 5.4 2/3 THALER
Silver **Rev:** Date divided by denomination at bottom **Note:** Varieties exist.

Date	Mintage	VG	F	VF	XF	Unc
1676 FCV	—	55.00	90.00	170	325	—

KM# 6.1 2/3 THALER
Silver **Obv:** Bust of Johann George II right **Rev:** Crowned arms in sprays

Date	Mintage	VG	F	VF	XF	Unc
1692 IEG	—	140	275	450	850	—
1693 IEG	—	140	275	450	850	—

KM# 6.2 2/3 THALER
Silver **Rev:** Arms divide IE-G, shorter palm branches **Note:** Varieties exist.

Date	Mintage	VG	F	VF	XF	Unc
1692 IEG	—	14.00	275	450	850	—
1693 IEG	—	100	200	325	600	—

KM# 12 2/3 THALER
Silver **Note:** Similar to KM#6.

Date	Mintage	VG	F	VF	XF	Unc
1694 CM Rare	—	—	—	—	—	—

KM# 3 THALER
Silver **Subject:** Death of Johann Kasimir **Obv:** Helmeted 9-fold arms **Obv. Legend:** D. G. IOHAN: CASIMER: PRINCEPS ANHALT:... **Rev:** 12-line inscription **Note:** Varieties exist. Dav. #6008.

Date	Mintage	VG	F	VF	XF	Unc
MDCLX (1660) AB	—	175	300	550	850	—

KM# 7.1 THALER
Silver **Obv:** Bust of Johann George II right **Obv. Legend:** IOH.GEORG.D. - G.PR.ANHALT **Rev:** Crowned arms divide date

Date	Mintage	VG	F	VF	XF	Unc
1692	—	350	650	1,100	1,750	—

KM# 7.2 THALER
Silver **Rev:** Crowned arms divide date and I.E. - G. **Note:** Dav. #6010. Varieties exist.

Date	Mintage	VG	F	VF	XF	Unc
1692 IEG	—	350	650	1,100	1,750	—
1693 IEG	—	350	650	1,100	1,750	—

KM# 11 THALER
Silver **Subject:** Death of Johann Georg II **Obv:** Bust of Johann Georg II right **Obv. Legend:** IOH. GEORG. D-G. PR. ANHALT **Rev:** 18-line inscription, date **Note:** Dav. #6011. Varieties exist.

Date	Mintage	VG	F	VF	XF	Unc
1693 Rare	—	—	—	—	—	—

PATTERNS

Including off metal strikes

KM#	Date	Mintage	Identification	Mkt Val
PnA1	1660 AB	—	Groschen. Gold. KM1.	5,000
PnB1	1660 AB	—	2/3 Thaler. Gold. KM2.	—
PnC1	1863A	—	Thaler. Copper. KM15.	1,250
Pn1	1901A	—	2 Mark. Silver. KM23.	3,500
Pn2	1901A	—	5 Mark. Silver. KM24.	5,000
Pn3	1914	—	3 Mark. Silver. Wreath around rim. KM30.	—
Pn4	1914	—	3 Mark. Brass.	—
Pn5	1914	—	5 Mark. Silver. Pn6. KM31.	2,500
Pn6	1914	—	5 Mark. Silver. Lettered edge.	2,000
Pn7	1914	—	5 Mark. Silver. Plain edge.	2,000

ANHALT-HARZGERODE

Established as a colateral line from Anhalt-Bernburg in 1630. When it became extinct in 1709, title reverted to Bernburg.

RULERS
Friedrich, 1630-1670
Wilhelm, 1670-1709

MINT OFFICIALS' INITIALS

Initials	Date	Name
AF	?	
BA	1679-80	Bastian Altmann in Plotzkau
CF	1678-86	Christoph Fischer in Dresden
CP	1674-90	Christoph Pflug in Zerbst
E	?	
HF	?	
SD	1675-76, 1669-75, 1678-80	Simon (Siegmund) Dannes in Reuss-Schleiz
TF	1695-96	Thomas Fischer

PRINCIPALITY

REGULAR COINAGE

KM# 2 6 PFENNIG
Silver **Obv:** Crowned W **Rev:** Value, date

Date	Mintage	VG	F	VF	XF	Unc
1694	—	35.00	60.00	100	175	—

KM# 1.1 2/3 THALER
Silver **Obv:** Legend above portrait with loose hair curls

Date	Mintage	VG	F	VF	XF	Unc
ND	—	60.00	100	175	275	—
ND BA	—	60.00	100	175	275	—
1675 SD	—	60.00	100	175	275	—
1675 CP	—	60.00	100	175	275	—
1676 SD	—	60.00	100	175	275	—
1679 BA Date above initials	—	60.00	100	175	275	—
1679 BA Date below initials	—	60.00	100	175	275	—
1679	—	60.00	100	175	275	—

KM# 1.2 2/3 THALER
Silver **Rev:** Vertical date divided by arms

Date	Mintage	VG	F	VF	XF	Unc
1675	—	60.00	100	175	275	—

KM# 1.3 2/3 THALER
Silver **Obv:** Small portrait with loose curls

Date	Mintage	VG	F	VF	XF	Unc
1675 CP	—	60.00	100	175	275	—

KM# 1.4 2/3 THALER
Silver **Obv:** Crude portrait, tight curls, unbroken legend above

Date	Mintage	VG	F	VF	XF	Unc
1676 AF	—	60.00	100	175	275	—
1676 SD	—	60.00	100	175	275	—
1677 AF	—	60.00	100	175	275	—
1679 SD	—	60.00	100	175	275	—

KM# 1.5 2/3 THALER
Silver **Obv:** Tight curls break legend at top

Date	Mintage	VG	F	VF	XF	Unc
1676 AF	—	60.00	100	175	275	—

KM# 1.6 2/3 THALER
Silver **Obv:** Refined older portrait **Note:** Varieties exist.

Date	Mintage	VG	F	VF	XF	Unc
1695 TF	—	60.00	100	175	275	—
1696 TF	—	60.00	100	175	275	—

KM# 5 2/3 THALER
Silver **Rev:** Value divides date **Rev. Legend:** NACH/DEN/ LEIPZIGER/FUS

Date	Mintage	VG	F	VF	XF	Unc
1695	—	90.00	150	250	350	—

KM# 3 THALER
Silver **Obv:** Helmeted ornate arms **Rev:** Five-line inscription with date **Note:** Dav. #6012.

Date	Mintage	VG	F	VF	XF	Unc
1694 Rare	—	—	—	—	—	—

KM# 4 THALER
Silver **Obv:** Half-length bust right **Rev:** Five-line inscription with date in circle **Note:** Dav. #6013.

Date	Mintage	VG	F	VF	XF	Unc
1694 E	—	575	950	1,600	2,250	—

KM# 6 THALER
Silver **Rev:** Helmeted arms, date **Note:** Dav. #6014.

Date	Mintage	VG	F	VF	XF	Unc
1695 TF	—	550	900	1,500	2,200	—
1696 TF	—	550	900	1,500	2,200	—

KM# 7 THALER
Silver **Obv:** Three-line inscription AUS/BEU. THE/THAL surrounded by mining tools **Rev:** Fourteen-line inscription with date **Note:** Mining Thaler. Dav. #6015.

Date	Mintage	VG	F	VF	XF	Unc
1698 Rare	—	—	—	—	—	—

ANHALT-KOTHEN

Köthen has a checkered history after the patrimony of Heinrich the Fat in 1252. It was often ruled with other segments of the House of Anhalt. Founded as a separate line in 1603, became extinct in 1665 and passed to Plötzkau which changed the name to Köthen. It passed to Dessau after the death of Heinrich in 1847.

RULERS
Ludwig, 1603-1650
Wilhelm Ludwig, 1650-1665
Lebrecht von Plötzkau, 1665-1669
Emanuel von Plötzkau, 1669-1670
Emanuel Lebrecht, 1671-1704

DUCHY

REGULAR COINAGE

KM# 15 1/8 THALER
Silver **Subject:** Death of Ludwig Wilhelm **Obv:** Helmeted 9-fold arms, date **Obv. Legend:** 9-line inscription

Date	Mintage	VG	F	VF	XF	Unc
1665 HPK	—	—	450	950	1,400	—

KM# 1 1/3 THALER
Silver **Subject:** Death of Ludwig's Son, Ludwig **Obv:** Crowned 9-fold arms **Obv. Legend:** 9-line inscription, date in Roman numerals

Date	Mintage	VG	F	VF	XF	Unc
1624	—	400	650	1,400	2,300	—

KM# 7 1/3 THALER
Silver **Subject:** Death of Ludwig's Daughter, Louise Amona **Obv:** 9-fold arms **Obv. Legend:** 12-line inscription

Date	Mintage	VG	F	VF	XF	Unc
1625 AK	—	400	650	1,400	2,300	—

KM# 12 1/3 THALER
Silver **Subject:** Death of Ludwig **Obv:** Helmeted 9-fold arms **Obv. Legend:** 7-line inscription, date in Roman numerals

Date	Mintage	VG	F	VF	XF	Unc
1650 HPK	—	375	600	1,200	2,000	—

KM# 16 1/3 THALER
Silver **Subject:** Death of Wilhelm Ludwig **Obv:** Helmeted 9-fold arms, date **Obv. Legend:** 9-line inscription

Date	Mintage	VG	F	VF	XF	Unc
1665 HPK	—	400	650	1,400	2,300	—

KM# A13 1/2 THALER
14.4100 g., Silver **Subject:** Death of Ludwig **Obv:** Helmeted 9-fold arms **Rev:** 9-line inscription

Date	Mintage	VG	F	VF	XF	Unc
MDCL (1650) HPK	—	—	—	—	—	—

KM# 17 1/2 THALER
Silver **Subject:** Death of Wilhelm Ludwig **Note:** Similar to 1 Thaler, KM#19.

Date	Mintage	VG	F	VF	XF	Unc
1665 HPK	—	700	1,200	2,000	3,000	—

KM# 2 2/3 THALER
Silver **Subject:** Death of Ludwig's Son, Ludwig **Obv:** Helmeted 9-fold arms, date below **Obv. Legend:** 10-line inscription

Date	Mintage	VG	F	VF	XF	Unc
1624 Rare	—	—	—	—	—	—

KM# 3 2/3 THALER
Silver **Obv. Legend:** Imperial eagle with 12 in orb on breast, date

Date	Mintage	VG	F	VF	XF	Unc
1624 HS Rare	—	—	—	—	—	—

KM# 8 2/3 THALER
Silver **Subject:** Death of Ludwig's Daughter, Louise Amona **Obv:** Helmeted 9-fold arms **Obv. Legend:** 12-line inscription

Date	Mintage	VG	F	VF	XF	Unc
MDCXXV (1625) AK Rare	—	—	—	—	—	—

KM# 9 2/3 THALER
Silver **Subject:** Death of Ludwig's Wife, Amona Amalia von Bentheim **Obv:** Crowned arms of Bentheim-Tecklenburg and Anhalt **Obv. Legend:** 13-line inscription

Date	Mintage	VG	F	VF	XF	Unc
MDCXXV (1625) Rare	—	—	—	—	—	—

KM# 13 2/3 THALER
Silver **Subject:** Death of Ludwig **Note:** Similar to 1 Thaler, KM#14. Varieties exist.

Date	Mintage	VG	F	VF	XF	Unc
1650 HPK Rare	—	—	—	—	—	—

KM# 18 2/3 THALER
Silver **Subject:** Death of Wilhelm Ludwig **Obv:** Crowned supported arms **Obv. Legend:** D. G. AVGVSTVS LVDOVICVS PRINCEPS ANHALT **Rev:** Bear holding shield **Note:** Similar to 1 Thaler, KM#19.

Date	Mintage	VG	F	VF	XF	Unc
1665 HPK Rare	—	—	—	—	—	—

KM# 4 THALER
Silver **Subject:** Death of Ludwig's Son, Ludwig **Obv:** Helmeted nine-fold arms **Obv. Legend:** • MEIN • END • UND • LEBEN • **Rev. Inscription:** ...HO • XVI • REQIE • IN/SP(E)RE • MOR • **Note:** Dav. #6016. Varieties exist.

Date	Mintage	VG	F	VF	XF	Unc
1624	—	150	300	600	900	—

KM# 6 THALER
Silver **Obv:** Similar to KM#4 **Rev:** Crowned imperial eagle with 24 in orb on breast, date **Note:** Dav. #6017.

Date	Mintage	VG	F	VF	XF	Unc
1624 HS Rare	—	—	—	—	—	—

KM# 5 THALER
Silver **Note:** Klippe. Dav. #6016A.

Date	Mintage	VG	F	VF	XF	Unc
1624 Rare	—	—	—	—	—	—

KM# 10 THALER
Silver **Subject:** Death of Ludwig's Daughter, Louise Amona **Obv:** Helmeted 9-fold arms **Rev:** 12-line inscription **Note:** Dav. #6018. Varieties exist.

Date	Mintage	VG	F	VF	XF	Unc
MDCXXV (1625) AK Rare	—	—	—	—	—	—

KM# 11 THALER
Silver **Subject:** Death of Ludwig's Wife, Amona Amalia von Bentheim **Obv:** Crowned arms of Bentheim-Tecklenburg and Anhalt **Rev:** 13-line inscription **Note:** Dav. #6019. Varieties exist.

Date	Mintage	VG	F	VF	XF	Unc
MDCXXV (1625)	—	175	350	650	1,100	—

KM# 14 THALER
Silver **Subject:** Death of Ludwig **Obv:** Helmeted ornate nine-fold arms **Obv. Legend:** AUF DEINEN WEGEN LEIT;... **Rev. Inscription:** LUDOVICUS • / SENIOR • D G : PRIN/... **Note:** Dav. #6020. Varieties exist.

Date	Mintage	VG	F	VF	XF	Unc
MDCL (1650) HPK	—	150	300	600	1,000	—

KM# 19 THALER
Silver **Subject:** Death of Wilhelm Ludwig **Obv:** Helmeted ornate nine-fold arms **Obv. Legend:** LEHRE MICH DEIN WORT MEINER... **Rev. Inscription:** WILHELMUS/LUDOVICVS DG • PRIN/... **Note:** Dav. #6022.

Date	Mintage	VG	F	VF	XF	Unc
1665 HPK	—	250	650	1,000	1,700	—

KM# 21 THALER
Silver **Subject:** Founding of the Lutheran Church **Obv:** Bust right wtih two-fold arms below **Rev:** Leaping horse right **Note:** Dav. #6024. Varieties exist.

Date	Mintage	VG	F	VF	XF	Unc
1694	—	450	850	1,200	1,850	—

KM# 20 2 THALER
Silver **Subject:** Death of Wilhelm Ludwig **Obv:** Helmeted ornate nine-fold arms **Obv. Legend:** LEHRE MICH DEIN WORT MEINER... **Rev. Inscription:** WILHELMUS/LUDOVICVS D G • PRIN/... **Note:** Dav. #6021. Varieties exist.

Date	Mintage	VG	F	VF	XF	Unc
1665 HPK	—	900	1,500	2,500	4,000	—

KM# 22 2 THALER
Silver **Subject:** Founding of the Lutheran Church **Obv:** Bust right with two-fold arms below **Rev:** Leaping horse right **Note:** Dav. #6023.

Date	Mintage	VG	F	VF	XF	Unc
1694 Rare	—	—	—	—	—	—

PATTERNS

Including off metal strikes

KM#	Date	Mintage	Identification	Mkt Val
Pn1	1650 HPK	—	1/3 Thaler. Gold. KM#12.	—

ANHALT-PLOTZKAU

Main Plötzkau line founded during the new division of the Anhalt properties in 1603. Continued until 1665 when it inherited Köthen. Hereafter this branch known as Anhalt-Köthen.

RULERS
August, 1603-1653
Lebrecht, 1653-1665

MINT OFFICIALS' INITIALS

Initials	Date	Name
PS	1622	Peter Schroder

PRINCIPALITY

REGULAR COINAGE

KM# 4 DREIER (3 Pfennig)
Silver **Obv:** Helmet **Rev:** Imperial orb with value 3 divides date **Note:** Kipper Dreier. Varieties exist.

Date	Mintage	VG	F	VF	XF	Unc
1622 PS	—	30.00	75.00	150	250	—

KM# 5 GULDEN (2/3 Thaler)
Silver **Obv:** Half-length bust right **Rev:** Helmeted nine-fold arms, date

Date	Mintage	VG	F	VF	XF	Unc
1625 Rare	—	—	—	—	—	—
ND Rare	—	—	—	—	—	—

KM# 1 GOLDGULDEN
3.5000 g., 0.9860 Gold 0.1109 oz. AGW **Obv:** Phoenix rising from altar **Rev:** Fountain

Date	Mintage	VG	F	VF	XF	Unc
1615	—	650	1,250	2,550	4,500	—
1617	—	650	1,250	2,550	4,500	—
1620	—	650	1,250	2,550	4,500	—

KM# 2 2 GOLDGULDEN
7.0000 g., 0.9860 Gold 0.2219 oz. AGW **Obv:** Phoenix rising from altar **Rev:** Fountain

Date	Mintage	VG	F	VF	XF	Unc
1620 Rare	—	—	—	—	—	—

KM# 3 3 GOLDGULDEN
10.5000 g., 0.9860 Gold 0.3328 oz. AGW **Obv:** Phoenix rising from altar **Rev:** Fountain below portico, lamb with banner

Date	Mintage	VG	F	VF	XF	Unc
1620 Rare	—	—	—	—	—	—

PATTERNS

Including off metal strikes

KM#	Date	Mintage	Identification	Mkt Val
Pn1	1625	—	Gulden. Gold. KM#5	—
Pn2	ND	—	Gulden. Gold. KM#5	—

ANHALT-ZERBST

Zerbst was one of the major parts of the division of 1252. It was divided into Zerbst and Dessau in 1396 and absorbed Bernburg in 1486. Zerbst ceded to Dessau in 1508 and was given to the 4th son of Joachim Ernst in the division of 1603. It became extinct in 1793 and was divided between Dessau, Bernburg and Cothen.

RULERS
Rudolf III, 1603-1621
Johann VI, 1621-1667
Carl Wilhelm, 1667-1718

MINT OFFICIALS' INITIALS

Initials	Date	Name
AF	?	
CP	1674-90	Christoph Pflug
GW	1701	
IB	Ca.1664	Johann Bostelmann
IO	1663	Johann Otto
PS	1622	Peter Schroder in Köthen
SD	1675-76	Simon (Siegmund) Dannes in Harzgerode

DUCHY

REGULAR COINAGE

KM# 9 PFENNING
Silver **Ruler:** Johann VI **Note:** Uniface. 2-fold arms, date above. Varieties exist.

Date	Mintage	Good	VG	F	VF	XF
1663 IO	—	20.00	35.00	60.00	110	200

KM# 10 3 PFENNIG (Dreier)
Silver **Ruler:** Johann VI **Obv:** Helmet **Rev:** Imperial orb with 3 divides date **Note:** Varieties exist.

Date	Mintage	Good	VG	F	VF	XF
1663 IO	—	16.00	35.00	55.00	95.00	175

KM# 24 3 PFENNIG (Dreier)
Silver **Ruler:** Carl Wilhelm **Rev:** Imperial orb with 3 divides date

Date	Mintage	VG	F	VF	XF	Unc
1676 AF	—	16.00	35.00	60.00	100	—
1676 CP	—	16.00	35.00	60.00	100	—

KM# 23 3 PFENNIG (Dreier)
Silver **Ruler:** Carl Wilhelm **Obv:** Oval 2-fold arms **Rev:** 2 branches form wreath with 3 that divides date **Note:** Varieties exist.

Date	Mintage	VG	F	VF	XF	Unc
1676 SD	—	20.00	40.00	65.00	110	—

KM# 5 GROSCHEN
Silver **Ruler:** Johann VI **Subject:** Under Regency of August von Plotzkau **Obv:** Helmeted 2-fold arms **Rev:** Imperial orb with 24, date **Note:** Kipper Groschen. Varieties exist.

Date	Mintage	VG	F	VF	XF	Unc
1622 PS	—	13.00	27.00	55.00	100	—

KM# 11 GROSCHEN
Silver **Ruler:** Johann VI **Obv:** Helmeted 2-fold arms **Rev:** Imperial orb with 24, date **Note:** Varieties exist.

Date	Mintage	VG	F	VF	XF	Unc
1663 IO	—	13.00	27.00	55.00	100	—
1664 IB	—	13.00	27.00	55.00	100	—

KM# 12 GROSCHEN
Silver **Ruler:** Johann VI **Subject:** Death of Johann **Obv:** Bust right **Rev:** Crowned arms, date **Note:** Varieties exist.

Date	Mintage	VG	F	VF	XF	Unc
1667	—	—	—	—	—	—

KM# 22 GROSCHEN
Silver **Ruler:** Carl Wilhelm **Obv:** Crowned arms **Rev:** Imperial orb with 3 divides date **Note:** Varieties exist.

Date	Mintage	VG	F	VF	XF	Unc
1675 CP	—	16.00	35.00	75.00	115	—
1676 CP	—	16.00	35.00	75.00	115	—
1676 SD	—	16.00	35.00	75.00	115	—
1677 CP	—	16.00	35.00	75.00	115	—
1677 SD	—	16.00	35.00	75.00	115	—

KM# 2 1/2 GULDEN (1/3 Thaler)
Silver **Ruler:** Rudolf III **Subject:** Death of Rudolf **Obv:** Angel holding crowned heart-shaped 2-fold arms **Rev:** 10-line inscription

Date	Mintage	VG	F	VF	XF	Unc
MDCXXI (1621) Rare	—	—	—	—	—	—

KM# 6 1/2 GULDEN (1/3 Thaler)
Silver **Ruler:** Johann VI **Subject:** Death of Johann's sister, Elisabeth **Obv:** 8-line inscription **Rev:** 8-line inscription, date in Roman numerals

Date	Mintage	VG	F	VF	XF	Unc
1639 Rare	—	—	—	—	—	—

KM# 28 GULDEN (2/3 Thaler)
Silver **Ruler:** Carl Wilhelm **Subject:** Death of Karl Wilhelm's mother, Sophie Auguste von Holstein-Gottorp **Note:** Similar to 1 Thaler, KM#29 but 10 line inscription. Varieties exist.

Date	Mintage	VG	F	VF	XF	Unc
1680 Rare	—	—	—	—	—	—

KM# 26 1/192 THALER
Silver **Ruler:** Carl Wilhelm **Obv:** 2-fold arms **Rev:** Value 192 in center, date

Date	Mintage	VG	F	VF	XF	Unc
(16)77	—	—	—	—	—	—

KM# 20 1/16 THALER
Silver **Ruler:** Carl Wilhelm **Obv:** Bust right in circle **Obv. Legend:** CARL WIL.P.A.C.A.D.S.B.I&K. **Rev:** Denomination in circle **Rev. Legend:** IN.DOMIN:FIDUCIA.HOSTRA. **Note:** Varieties exist.

Date	Mintage	VG	F	VF	XF	Unc
ND	—	65.00	125	200	—	—

KM# 13 1/4 THALER
Silver **Ruler:** Johann VI **Subject:** Death of Johann **Obv:** 1/2-length bust right **Rev:** Crowned arms, date

Date	Mintage	VG	F	VF	XF	Unc
1667	—	—	—	—	—	—

KM# 17 1/3 THALER
Silver **Ruler:** Carl Wilhelm **Note:** Varieties exist.

Date	Mintage	VG	F	VF	XF	Unc
1674 CP	—	400	650	1,300	2,500	—
1675 CP	—	400	650	1,300	2,500	—

KM# 14 1/2 THALER
Silver **Ruler:** Carl Wilhelm **Obv:** 1/2-length bust right **Rev:** Crowned arms, date

Date	Mintage	VG	F	VF	XF	Unc
1667 CP	—	—	—	—	—	—

KM# 18 2/3 THALER
Silver **Ruler:** Carl Wilhelm **Obv:** Bust right within inner circle, legend around **Rev:** Crowned 12-fold arms divide date, value below in circle, legend around

Date	Mintage	VG	F	VF	XF	Unc
1674 CP	—	55.00	95.00	165	300	—
1675 CP	—	55.00	95.00	165	300	—

KM# 19.1 2/3 THALER
Silver **Ruler:** Carl Wilhelm **Obv:** Portrait in inner circle **Rev:** Vertical date divided by arms

Date	Mintage	VG	F	VF	XF	Unc
1674 CP	—	—	—	—	—	—

KM# 19.2 2/3 THALER
Silver **Ruler:** Carl Wilhelm **Rev:** Date in legend divided by crown

Date	Mintage	VG	F	VF	XF	Unc
1674 CP	—	—	—	—	—	—

KM# 19.3 2/3 THALER
Silver **Ruler:** Carl Wilhelm **Obv:** Portrait divides legend at bottom, without inner circle, date in legend at 10 o'clock

Date	Mintage	VG	F	VF	XF	Unc
1675 CP	—	50.00	80.00	140	275	—

KM# 19.4 2/3 THALER
Silver **Ruler:** Carl Wilhelm **Rev:** Misaligned date divided by arms

Date	Mintage	VG	F	VF	XF	Unc
1676 CP	—	60.00	100	170	325	—

KM# 19.5 2/3 THALER
Silver **Ruler:** Carl Wilhelm **Rev:** Horizontal date divided by straight sided arms

Date	Mintage	VG	F	VF	XF	Unc
1676 CP	—	60.00	100	170	325	—

KM# 19.6 2/3 THALER
Silver **Ruler:** Carl Wilhelm **Rev:** Horizontal date divided by concave sided arms

Date	Mintage	VG	F	VF	XF	Unc
1677 CP	—	60.00	100	170	325	—
1678 CP	—	40.00	75.00	140	275	—
1679 CP	—	40.00	75.00	140	275	—

KM# 19.7 2/3 THALER
Silver **Ruler:** Carl Wilhelm **Rev:** Date divided by ornamented coat of arms **Note:** Varieties exist.

Date	Mintage	VG	F	VF	XF	Unc
1678 CP	—	40.00	75.00	140	275	—

KM# 1 THALER
Silver **Ruler:** Rudolf III **Obv:** Bust right **Rev:** Crowned 9-fold arms, date **Note:** Dav. #6025.

Date	Mintage	VG	F	VF	XF	Unc
1605 Rare	—	—	—	—	—	—

KM# 4 THALER
Silver **Ruler:** Rudolf III **Rev. Inscription:** ...DI / MID **Note:** Dav. #6027.

Date	Mintage	VG	F	VF	XF	Unc
1621	—	250	450	750	1,250	—

KM# 3 THALER
Silver **Ruler:** Rudolf III **Subject:** Death of Rudolf **Note:** Similar to KM#4 but inscription ends: HOR: 13 1/2, date. Dav. #6026.

Date	Mintage	VG	F	VF	XF	Unc
1621	—	450	750	1,250	2,000	—

KM# 7 THALER
Silver **Ruler:** Johann VI **Subject:** Death of Johann's sister, Elisabeth **Obv:** 8-line inscription **Rev:** 8-line inscription **Note:** Dav. #6029.

Date	Mintage	VG	F	VF	XF	Unc
MDCXXXIX (1639) Rare	—	—	—	—	—	—

KM# 15 THALER
Silver **Ruler:** Johann VI **Subject:** Death of Johann **Note:** Dav. #6031. Varieties exist.

Date	Mintage	VG	F	VF	XF	Unc
MDCLXVII (1667)	—	285	550	950	1,600	—

KM# 25 THALER
Silver **Ruler:** Carl Wilhelm **Note:** Dav. #6032.

Date	Mintage	VG	F	VF	XF	Unc
1676 CP	—	550	950	1,800	2,750	—
ND Rare	—	—	—	—	—	—

KM# 27 THALER
Silver **Ruler:** Carl Wilhelm **Note:** Dav. #6033. Varieties exist.

Date	Mintage	VG	F	VF	XF	Unc
1677 CP	—	550	950	1,800	2,750	—
1678 CP	—	550	950	1,800	2,750	—

KM# 29 THALER
Silver **Ruler:** Carl Wilhelm **Subject:** Death of Karl Wilhelm's mother, Sophie Auguste von Holstein-Gottorp **Note:** Dav. #A6035. Varieties exist.

Date	Mintage	VG	F	VF	XF	Unc
1680	—	285	550	950	1,600	—

KM# 8 2 THALER
Silver **Ruler:** Johann VI **Subject:** Death of Johann's sister, Elisabeth **Obv:** 8-line inscription **Rev:** 8-line inscription **Note:** Dav. #6028.

Date	Mintage	VG	F	VF	XF	Unc
MDCXXXIX (1639) Rare	—	—	—	—	—	—

KM# 16 2 THALER
Silver **Ruler:** Johann VI **Subject:** Death of Johann **Note:** Similar to 1 Thaler, KM#15. Dav. #6030.

Date	Mintage	VG	F	VF	XF	Unc
1667	—	500	900	1,700	2,500	—

TRADE COINAGE

KM# A21 4 DUCAT
14.0000 g., 0.9860 Gold 0.4438 oz. AGW **Ruler:** Carl Wilhelm **Obv:** Bust of Carl Wilhelm right **Rev:** Crowned arms divide date **Note:** Struck with 1/3 Thaler dies.

Date	Mintage	F	VF	XF	Unc	BU
1676 CP Rare	—	—	—	—	—	—

PATTERNS

Including off metal strikes

KM#	Date	Mintage	Identification	Mkt Val
Pn1	1667	—	Groschen. Gold. KM#12.	—
Pn2	1667	—	1/2 Thaler. Gold. KM#14.	—
Pn3	1674 CP	—	2/3 Thaler. Tin. KM#18.	300

ANHOLT

A town in Westphalia, Anholt is 7 miles (12km) west of Bocholt and very near the border with the Netherlands. It had early been the seat of a lordship, later a county, which passed into the possession of the Bronkhorst-Batenburg dynasty. A few coins were struck for local use in the late 16th century and again about the time of the Peace of Westphalia (1648-50).

RULERS
Dietrick V von Bronckhorst-Batenburg, 1585-1637
Leopold Philipp von Salm, 1637-1663

LORDSHIP

REGULAR COINAGE

KM# 2 STUBER
Copper **Ruler:** Leopold Philipp **Obv:** Crowned eight-fold arms divide value 6-S, titles of Leopold Philipp **Rev:** Rampant lion left holding sword and shield with Anholt arms (crowned column)

Date	Mintage	Good	VG	F	VF	XF
ND	—	—	—	—	—	—

KM# 1 STUBER
Copper **Ruler:** Leopold Philipp **Obv:** Crowned four-fold arms divide value 1-S, titles of Leopold Philipp **Rev:** Ornate cross **Note:** Varieties exist.

Date	Mintage	Good	VG	F	VF	XF
ND	—	40.00	80.00	175	300	500

TOWN

The town of Anholt in the lordship issued some coppers in the early 17th century.

REGULAR COINAGE

KM# 6 1/4 STUBER
Copper **Ruler:** Leopold Philipp **Obv:** Crowned rampant lion left in crowned shield between branches **Rev:** CI/VITAS/ANH in wreath

Date	Mintage	Good	VG	F	VF	XF
ND	—	27.00	55.00	120	200	350

KM# 7 1/4 STUBER
Copper **Ruler:** Leopold Philipp **Obv:** Lion right **Rev:** CVS/ANH in wreath

Date	Mintage	Good	VG	F	VF	XF
ND	—	27.00	55.00	120	200	350

PATTERNS

Including off metal strikes

KM#	Date	Mintage	Identification	Mkt Val
Pn1	ND	—	Stuber. Silver. KM#1	—

ANKLAM

Anklam was a town in the duchy of Pomerania (Pommern) situated on the Peene River, 5 miles (8 kilometers) from the Baltic Sea coast and 27 miles (45 kilometers) northeast of Neubrandenburg. It was founded as a fortress by the Slavs, but gained rights as an important town and became a member of the Hanseatic League. Anklam bought the right to produce its own coinage from the duke in 1325 and began striking a series of small silver coins. After the dissolution of the Pomeranian provincial diet in 1622, during the Kipper Period of the Thirty Years' War, Anklam countermarked the minor silver coinage which circulated from other nearby states in its local region. The town came under Swedish rule in 1648, but was taken by Brandenburg-Prussia in 1676. Except for a short period in the early 18th century, it remained part of Prussia.

ARMS:
Arrowhead pointing upwards

REFERENCE:
F = Gisela Föschner, ***Deutsche Münzen: Mittelalter bis Neuzeit, vol. I,*** Melsungen, 1984.

PROVINCIAL TOWN

COUNTERMARKED COINAGE

Countermark types:

Countermark #1: Arrowhead (city arms) divides 'A - 3' (=3 sundische Schilling)

Countermark #2: Arrowhead (city arms) only

KM# 5 3 SCHILLING (Suncische)
Silver **Note:** Countermark 1 on Pomerania-Wolgast 2 Schilling, KM#5. F#8.

CM Date	Host Date	Good	VG	F	VF	XF
ND(1622)	1609	35.00	70.00	125	245	—
ND(1622)	1610	35.00	70.00	125	245	—
ND(1622)	1611	35.00	70.00	125	245	—
ND(1622)	161Z	35.00	70.00	125	245	—
ND(1622)	1613	35.00	70.00	125	245	—
ND(1622)	1614	35.00	70.00	125	245	—
ND(1622)	1615	35.00	70.00	125	245	—
ND(1622)	1616	35.00	70.00	125	245	—
ND(1622)	1617	35.00	70.00	125	245	—
ND(1622)	1618	35.00	70.00	125	245	—
ND(1622)	1619	35.00	70.00	125	245	—
ND(1622)	16Z0	35.00	70.00	125	245	—
ND(1622)	16Z1	35.00	70.00	125	245	—

KM# 4 3 SCHILLING (Suncische)
Silver **Note:** Countermark 1 on Pomerania-Stettin 2 Schilling, KM#6.

CM Date	Host Date	Good	VG	F	VF	XF
ND(1622)	1618	40.00	80.00	150	250	—
ND(1622)	1619	40.00	80.00	150	250	—
ND(1622)	16Z0	40.00	80.00	150	250	—

KM# 1 3 SCHILLING (Suncische)
Silver **Note:** Countermark 1 on Brunswick-Hargurg 1/16 Thaler, KM#14.1. F#9. Known also with additional countermark of Hamburg (city).

CM Date	Host Date	Good	VG	F	VF	XF
ND(1622)	16Z0	45.00	95.00	175	275	—
ND(1622)	16Z1	45.00	95.00	175	275	—
ND(1622)	ND(1620-1)	45.00	95.00	175	275	—

KM# 2 3 SCHILLING (Suncische)
Silver **Note:** Countermark 1 on Pomerania-Stettin 2 Schilling, KM#95. F#6.

CM Date	Host Date	Good	VG	F	VF	XF
ND(1622)	16Z1	40.00	80.00	150	250	—
ND(1622)	16ZZ	40.00	80.00	150	250	—
ND(1622)	16Z3	40.00	80.00	150	250	—
ND(1622)	16Z4	40.00	80.00	150	250	—
ND(1622)	16Z5	40.00	80.00	150	250	—
ND(1622)	16Z8	40.00	80.00	150	250	—
ND(1622)	16Z9	40.00	80.00	150	250	—

ARENBERG

A small principality with lands between the present-day Belgian border and the Rhine, west of Koblenz. The earliest lords of Arenberg are mentioned in the 12th century. The title and lands passed in marriage to the countship of Mark from where a new line of Arenberg lords began in the 14th century. At the end of the 15th century branch lines were founded in Sedan, Lumain and Roche-- fort. The male line of Arenberg became extinct in 1541 and passed by marriage to Ligne-Barbancon in 1547. The new line was raised to the rank of count in 1549, to prince in 1576 and to that of duke in 1644. The right to mint coins was granted in 1570. Philipp Franz issued Arenberg's only 17th century thaler. The lands on the left bank of the Rhine were lost to France in 1801 and the remaining possessions were mediatized in 1810.

RULERS
Karl, 1568-1616, prince 1576
Philipp Karl, 1616-1640
Philipp Franz, 1640-1674, duke 1644
Karl Eugen, 1674-1681
Philipp Karl Franz, 1681-1691
Leopold Philipp Karl, 1691-1754
Under regency of Maria Henrietta, 1691-1706
Alone, 1706-1754

MINTOFFICIALS' INITIALS

Initials	Date	Name
NL	Ca. 1668-80	Nikolaus Longerich in Dortmund

PRINCIPALITY

REGULAR COINAGE

KM# 4 8 HELLER

Silver **Ruler:** Karl Eugen **Obv:** Crowned arms **Rev:** Value in center, date in legend

Date	Mintage	VG	F	VF	XF	Unc
1676 NL	—	275	400	600	900	—

KM# 5 2 ALBUS

Silver **Ruler:** Karl Eugen **Obv:** Crowned arms **R ev:** 2/ALBVS/COLSCH/date **Note:** Varieties exist.

Date	Mintage	VG	F	VF	XF	Unc
1676	—	55.00	125	200	350	600
1676 NL	—	55.00	125	200	350	600
1677 NL	—	55.00	125	200	350	600

KM# 1 1/20 THALER

Silver **Ruler:** Karl **Obv:** Arms in ornately-shaped shield **Rev:** Christchild with imperial orb within sun with wavy rays, date between rays

Date	Mintage	VG	F	VF	XF	Unc
1601 Rare	—	—	—	—	—	—

KM# 3.1 2/3 THALER

Silver **Ruler:** Philipp Franz **Obv:** Crowned supported arms with value 2/3 below **Rev:** Eagle standing on rocks with wings spread looking over left wing at sun, date

Date	Mintage	VG	F	VF	XF	Unc
1670	—	—	—	—	—	—
Note: Reported, not confirmed						
1676 NL	—	350	700	1,200	1,800	—

KM# 3.2 2/3 THALER

Silver **Ruler:** Karl Eugen **Obv:** Value 60 below arms

Date	Mintage	VG	F	VF	XF	Unc
1676 NL Rare	—	—	—	—	—	—

KM# 6 2/3 THALER

Silver **Ruler:** Karl Eugen **Obv:** Bust right **Rev:** Crowned and supported arms, value 2/3 below, date

Date	Mintage	VG	F	VF	XF	Unc
1676 NL	—	350	700	1,200	1,800	—

KM# 2 THALER

Silver **Ruler:** Philipp Franz **Obv:** Crowned, helmeted and supported arms with date divided above **Rev:** Christchild seated with imperial orb in sun with rays **Note:** Dav. #6035.

Date	Mintage	VG	F	VF	XF	Unc
1641 Rare	—	—	—	—	—	—

AUGSBURG

BISHOPRIC

Founded in the late 9th century in the city of Augsburg, the bishopric eventually extended as far as the Bavarian frontier on the north and east, to Tyrol on the south and to Upper Swabia on the west. The earliest episcopal coinage dates from the mid-10th century and issues continued through each of the next eight and one-half centuries. The bishopric was secularized in 1803 and was absorbed by Bavaria.

RULERS

Heinrich V von Knöringen, 1598-1646
Gustavus Adolphus, King of Sweden, 1632-1634
Sigmund Franz, Grossherzog von Österreich, 1646-1665
Johann Christof von Freiberg, 1665-1690
Alexander Sigismund von Pfalz-Neuburg, 1690-1737

MINT OFFICIALS' INITIALS

Initial	Date	Name
M	1494-1515	Hieronymus Müller, mintmaster
M	1717-41	Christian Ernst Muller
PHM	d.1718	Philipp Heinrich Muller, die-cutter and medailleur
2 horseshoes	1668-97	Johann Christoph Holeisen

Reference:

F = Gisela Förschner, ***Deutsche Münzen Mittelalter bis Neuzeit, v. 1 – Aachen bis Augsburg***, Melsungen, 1984.

REGULAR COINAGE

KM# 7 1/2 KREUTZER

Silver **Note:** Kipper 1/2 Kreutzer. Uniface. Arms in braoque frame divide date, value 240 (1/240th Thaler) above.

Date	Mintage	VG	F	VF	XF	Unc
1623	—	125	200	300	500	—

KM# 2 KREUTZER

Copper **Note:** Arms divide date, HEA above. Varieties exist.

Date	Mintage	Good	VG	F	VF	XF
1621	—	20.00	50.00	75.00	120	200
1622	—	20.00	50.00	75.00	120	200

KM# A1 KREUTZER

Copper **Note:** Kipper Kreutzer. Uniface. Monogram HAE above arms divides value 1-20, (1/120th Thaler), date above.

Date	Mintage	Good	VG	F	VF	XF
1621	—	20.00	50.00	75.00	120	200

KM# 4 KREUTZER

Copper **Obv:** Ornately-shaped arms, date above **Rev:** I/KREIT/ZER **Note:** Varieties exist.

Date	Mintage	Good	VG	F	VF	XF
1622	—	16.00	35.00	60.00	90.00	—

KM# 3 KREUTZER

Copper **Obv:** Round arms wtih date above, all in wreath **Rev:** I/KREIT/ZER in wreath

Date	Mintage	Good	VG	F	VF	XF
1622	—	16.00	35.00	60.00	90.00	—

KM# 10 2 KREUTZER

Silver **Obv:** Two oval arms in baroque frame, date above **Rev:** Imperial eagle, orb with 2 on breast

Date	Mintage	VG	F	VF	XF	Unc
1681	—	—	—	—	—	—

KM# 12 2 KREUTZER

Silver **Obv:** Crowned arms **Rev:** Oval shield with 2 in center, mitre above divides date

Date	Mintage	VG	F	VF	XF	Unc
1694	—	—	—	—	—	—

KM# 5 24 KREUTZER

Silver **Obv:** Arms in baroque frame, date **Rev:** Imperial eagle with 24 on breast **Note:** Kipper 24 Kreutzer.

Date	Mintage	VG	F	VF	XF	Unc
1622	—	200	300	500	750	—

KM# 13 1/2 THALER

Silver **Obv:** Bust right **Rev:** Crowned double oval arms in baroque frame, date below

Date	Mintage	VG	F	VF	XF	Unc
1694 PHM	—	400	650	1,200	2,000	—

KM# 6 THALER

Silver **Obv:** Madonna and child above arms, date **Rev:** Crowned imperial eagle with arms on breast **Note:** Dav. #5008.

Date	Mintage	VG	F	VF	XF	Unc
1622 Rare	—	—	—	—	—	—

KM# 11 THALER

Silver **Obv:** Mitred and supported arms divide date **Rev:** Madonna and child on crescent, surrounded by flames **Note:** Dav. #5009.

Date	Mintage	VG	F	VF	XF	Unc
1681 PHM Rare	—	—	—	—	—	—

KM# 14 THALER

Silver **Note:** Dav. #5010.

Date	Mintage	VG	F	VF	XF	Unc
1694 PHM	—	150	300	550	900	—

FREE CITY

Founded by the Romans about 15B.C. and named Augusta Vindelicorum in honor of the Emperor Augustus, the city was the site of a German imperial mint for several centuries from about the year 1000. In 1276, Augsburg was made a free imperial city, but did not receive the right to strike its own coins until 1521. Earlier date issues were produced under the office of the Imperial Chamberlain, as listed above. Augsburg's coinage came to an end in 1805 and the city followed the bishopric into Bavarian envelopment in the following year.

MINT OFFICIALS' INITIALS

Initials	Date	Name
B	1731-56	Konrad Borer, die-cutter
BS, or 3 corn ears	1630-38	Balthasar Schmidt
CM, M	1714-41	Christian Ernst Muller, die-cutter
FH, F(A)H	1761-66	Frings, mint warden and Johann Christian Holeisen
FT	1758	Frings, mint warden and Thiebaud, die-cutter
PHM, M or *	1677-1718	Philipp Heinrich Muller, die-cutter
T, IT	1740-69	Jonas Peter Thiebaud, die-cutter
* or **	1775-82	Peter Neuss

1 horseshoe	1638-68	Johann Bartholomaus Holeisen the Elder
2 horseshoes	1668-97	Johann Christoph Holeisen
3 horseshoes	1639-68	Johann Bartholomaus Holeisen the Younger, assistant mintmaster

ARMS:
Pinecone

Reference:
F = Albert von Forster, ***Die Erzeugnisse der Stempelschneidekunst in ugsburg und Ph. H. Müller's nach meiner Sammlung beschrieben Und die Augsburger Stadtmünzen,*** Leipzig, 1910.

REGULAR COINAGE

KM# 1 HELLER

Copper **Obv:** Pine cone divides date within wreath **Rev:** CCCC/XX (1/420th of a gulden) **Note:** Varieties exist.

Date	Mintage	Good	VG	F	VF	XF
1608	—	10.00	20.00	35.00	60.00	—
1609	—	10.00	20.00	35.00	60.00	—
1610	—	10.00	20.00	35.00	60.00	—
1612	—	10.00	20.00	35.00	60.00	—
1614	—	10.00	20.00	35.00	60.00	—
1615	—	10.00	20.00	35.00	60.00	—
1617	—	10.00	20.00	35.00	60.00	—
1620	—	10.00	20.00	35.00	60.00	—
1621	—	10.00	20.00	35.00	60.00	—
1622	—	10.00	20.00	35.00	60.00	—

KM# A23 HELLER

Copper **Obv:** Pine cone in cartouche divides date **Rev:** Cross in quatrefoil **Note:** Struck on rhomboid flan. Varieties exist.

Date	Mintage	VG	F	VF	XF	Unc
1624	—	6.00	20.00	35.00	60.00	—
1626	—	6.00	20.00	35.00	60.00	—
1629	—	6.00	20.00	35.00	60.00	—
1630	—	6.00	20.00	35.00	60.00	—
1631	—	6.00	20.00	35.00	60.00	—
1632	—	6.00	20.00	35.00	60.00	—
1633	—	6.00	20.00	35.00	60.00	—
1636	—	6.00	20.00	35.00	60.00	—
1645	—	6.00	20.00	35.00	60.00	—
1659	—	6.00	20.00	35.00	60.00	—
1660	—	6.00	20.00	35.00	60.00	—
1661	—	6.00	20.00	35.00	60.00	—
1664	—	6.00	20.00	35.00	60.00	—
1665	—	6.00	20.00	35.00	60.00	—
1666	—	6.00	20.00	35.00	60.00	—
1668	—	6.00	20.00	35.00	60.00	—
1669	—	6.00	20.00	35.00	60.00	—
1670	—	6.00	20.00	35.00	60.00	—
1671	—	6.00	20.00	35.00	60.00	—
1672	—	6.00	20.00	35.00	60.00	—
1673	—	6.00	20.00	35.00	60.00	—
1674	—	6.00	20.00	35.00	60.00	—
1676	—	6.00	20.00	35.00	60.00	—
1677	—	6.00	20.00	35.00	60.00	—
1678	—	6.00	20.00	35.00	60.00	—
1680	—	6.00	20.00	35.00	60.00	—
1681	—	6.00	20.00	35.00	60.00	—
1682	—	6.00	20.00	35.00	60.00	—
1683	—	6.00	20.00	35.00	60.00	—
1684	—	6.00	20.00	35.00	60.00	—
1685	—	6.00	20.00	35.00	60.00	—
1686	—	6.00	20.00	35.00	60.00	—
1687	—	6.00	20.00	35.00	60.00	—
1689	—	6.00	20.00	35.00	60.00	—
1690	—	6.00	20.00	35.00	60.00	—
1691	—	6.00	20.00	35.00	60.00	—
1692	—	6.00	20.00	35.00	60.00	—
1693	—	6.00	20.00	35.00	60.00	—
1694	—	6.00	20.00	35.00	60.00	—
1695	—	6.00	20.00	35.00	60.00	—
1697	—	6.00	20.00	35.00	60.00	—
1699	—	6.00	20.00	35.00	60.00	—
1700	—	6.00	20.00	35.00	60.00	—

KM# A7 2 HELLER

Copper **Obv:** Large A divides date within circle **Rev:** CC/X (1/210th of a gulden) in circle **Note:** Struck on square flan.

Date	Mintage	Good	VG	F	VF	XF
1621	—	9.00	16.00	35.00	55.00	100
1622	—	9.00	16.00	35.00	55.00	100

MB# 84 PFENNING

Silver **Ruler:** Markwart II von Berg **Obv:** 'A' in circle **Rev:** Date in circle **Note:** F#85, 86, 89. Varieties exist.

Date	Mintage	VG	F	VF	XF	Unc
1582	—	—	—	—	—	—

KM# A14 PFENNING

Silver **Obv:** Letter A in circle **Rev:** Date in circle **Note:** Struck on square flan.

Date	Mintage	Good	VG	F	VF	XF
1623	—	10.00	18.00	35.00	60.00	100

KM# A24 PFENNING

Silver **Obv:** Letter A in circle **Rev:** Date in clover-shape **Note:** Klippe.

Date	Mintage	Good	VG	F	VF	XF
1624	—	14.00	24.00	45.00	100	175

KM# 9 1/2 KREUZER

Copper **Rev:** HALB/KREITZER in wreath

Date	Mintage	Good	VG	F	VF	XF
1621	—	9.00	16.00	35.00	60.00	100

KM# 8 1/2 KREUZER

Copper **Obv:** Pinecone divides date within wreath **Rev:** HALB/KREITZ/ER in wreath **Note:** Kipper 1/2 Kreutzer. Varieties exist.

Date	Mintage	Good	VG	F	VF	XF
1621	—	9.00	16.00	35.00	60.00	—

KM# A25 1/2 KREUTZER

Silver **Note:** Uniface. Pinecone divides 1/2-K in trefoil, date divided by upper lboe of trefoil.

Date	Mintage	Good	VG	F	VF	XF
(16)24	—	9.00	16.00	35.00	60.00	—
(16)25	—	9.00	16.00	35.00	60.00	—

KM# 81 1/2 KREUTZER

Silver **Rev:** Pine cone divides date within ornamented trefoil **Note:** Varieties exist.

Date	Mintage	Good	VG	F	VF	XF
1643	—	9.00	16.00	35.00	60.00	100
1644	—	12.00	20.00	40.00	75.00	125
1651	—	9.00	16.00	35.00	60.00	100
1677	—	9.00	16.00	35.00	60.00	100
1696	—	9.00	16.00	35.00	60.00	100

KM# 111 1/2 KREUTZER

Silver **Rev:** Pine cone divides date, branch on either side

Date	Mintage	Good	VG	F	VF	XF
1697	—	9.00	16.00	35.00	60.00	—

KM# A10 KREUTZER

Silver **Obv:** Pinecone divides date within wreath **Rev:** I/KREI/ZER in wreath

Date	Mintage	Good	VG	F	VF	XF
1622	—	12.00	20.00	35.00	65.00	—

KM# A15 KREUTZER

Copper **Obv:** Crowned imperial eagle with 1 in orb on breast, titles of Ferdinand II **Rev:** Pinecone divides date within circle **Note:** Varieties exist.

Date	Mintage	Good	VG	F	VF	XF
1623	—	8.00	12.00	35.00	55.00	—
1624	—	8.00	12.00	35.00	55.00	—
1625	—	8.00	12.00	35.00	55.00	—

KM# 78 KREUTZER

Copper **Obv:** Titles of Ferdinand III **Note:** Varieties exist.

Date	Mintage	Good	VG	F	VF	XF
1640	—	12.00	20.00	35.00	60.00	—
1641	—	12.00	20.00	35.00	60.00	—
1642	—	12.00	20.00	35.00	60.00	—
1643	—	12.00	20.00	35.00	60.00	—
1644	—	12.00	20.00	35.00	60.00	—
1645	—	12.00	20.00	35.00	60.00	—
1651	—	12.00	20.00	35.00	60.00	—

KM# 109 KREUTZER

Silver **Obv:** Crowned imperial eagle with 1 in orb circle, titles of Leopold **Rev:** Pine cone divides date within circle **Note:** Varieties exist.

Date	Mintage	VG	F	VF	XF	Unc
1695	—	12.00	20.00	35.00	60.00	—
1696	—	12.00	20.00	35.00	60.00	—
1697	—	12.00	20.00	35.00	60.00	—

KM# A5 2 KREUTZER (1/2 Batzen)

Silver **Obv:** Crowned imperial eagle with II in orb on breast, titles of Fedinand II **Rev:** Pine cone divides date within circle

Date	Mintage	VG	F	VF	XF	Unc
1620	—	—	—	—	—	—

KM# A16 2 KREUTZER (1/2 Batzen)

Silver **Obv:** Value 2 in orb **Note:** Varieties exist.

Date	Mintage	Good	VG	F	VF	XF
1623	—	14.00	28.00	40.00	85.00	—
1624	—	14.00	28.00	40.00	85.00	—
1625	—	14.00	28.00	40.00	85.00	—
1635	—	14.00	28.00	40.00	85.00	—
1636	—	14.00	28.00	40.00	85.00	—
1637	—	14.00	28.00	40.00	85.00	—

KM# A28 2 KREUTZER (1/2 Batzen)

Silver **Rev:** Pine cone in cartouche divides date within circle

Date	Mintage	VG	F	VF	XF	Unc
1625	—	16.00	35.00	55.00	95.00	—

KM# 72 2 KREUTZER (1/2 Batzen)

Silver **Rev:** Titles of Ferdinand III

Date	Mintage	VG	F	VF	XF	Unc
1637	—	—	—	—	—	—

KM# 88 2 KREUTZER (1/2 Batzen)

Silver **Obv:** Titles of Leopold **Note:** Varieties exist.

Date	Mintage	VG	F	VF	XF	Unc
1660	—	16.00	30.00	50.00	100	—
1661	—	16.00	30.00	50.00	100	—
1665	—	16.00	30.00	50.00	100	—
1680	—	16.00	30.00	50.00	100	—
1681	—	16.00	30.00	50.00	100	—
1692	—	16.00	30.00	50.00	100	—
1694	—	16.00	30.00	50.00	100	—
1695	—	16.00	30.00	50.00	100	—

KM# 95 2 KREUTZER (1/2 Batzen)

Silver **Obv:** Pine cone in oval shield **Rev:** STADT/MINTZ/date in circle

Date	Mintage	VG	F	VF	XF	Unc
1687	—	—	—	—	—	—

KM# 102 4 KREUTZER (Batzen)

Silver **Obv:** Crowned imperial eagle, 4 in orb on breast, titles of Leopold **Rev:** Pine cone in oval baroque frame, date above **Note:** Varieties exist.

Date	Mintage	VG	F	VF	XF	Unc
1694	—	16.00	28.00	55.00	110	—
1695	—	27.00	50.00	100	200	—

KM# A6 6 KREUTZER

Silver **Obv:** Crowned imperial eagle, VI in orb on breast, titles of Ferdinand II **Rev:** Pine cone between two branches within circle, date in Roman numerals **Note:** Kipper 6 Kreutzer.

Date	Mintage	VG	F	VF	XF	Unc
1620	—	—	—	—	—	—

KM# 11.1 6 KREUTZER

Silver **Obv:** Pine cone in oval baroque frame divides date **Rev:** VI/STADT/MINTZ

Date	Mintage	VG	F	VF	XF	Unc
1622	—	—	—	—	—	—

KM# 11.2 6 KREUTZER

Silver **Rev:** VI:K/STADT/MINTZ

Date	Mintage	VG	F	VF	XF	Unc
1622	—	70.00	140	275	500	—

KM# 12.2 15 KREUTZER

Silver **Rev:** XV:K/STADT/MINTZ

Date	Mintage	VG	F	VF	XF	Unc
1622	—	—	—	—	—	—

KM# 12.1 15 KREUTZER

Silver **Obv:** Pine cone divides date within oval baroque frame **Rev:** XV/STADT/MINTZ **Note:** Kipper 15 Kreutzer.

Date	Mintage	VG	F	VF	XF	Unc
1622	—	—	—	—	—	—

KM# A13 30 KREUTZER

Silver **Obv:** Pine cone divides date within oval baroque frame **Rev:** XXX/STADT/MINTZ

Date	Mintage	VG	F	VF	XF	Unc
1622	—	—	—	—	—	—

KM# A17 1/9 THALER

Silver **Obv:** Crowned imperial eagle, 1/9 in shield on breast, titles of Ferdinand II **Rev:** Pine cone in cartouche, date in Roman numerals in margin **Note:** Varieties exist.

Date	Mintage	Good	VG	F	VF	XF
1623	—	50.00	100	200	400	—
1624	—	50.00	100	200	400	—
1625	—	50.00	100	200	400	—

KM# 35 1/9 THALER

Silver **Obv:** Crowned eagle with wings spread, perched on shield with 1/9 **Rev:** Pine cone in oval baroque frame, date above

Date	Mintage	VG	F	VF	XF	Unc
1626	—	120	200	350,600	350	—

KM# 46 1/9 THALER
Silver

Date	Mintage	VG	F	VF	XF	Unc
MDCXXVII (1627)	—	50.00	100	200	350	—

KM# 57 1/9 THALER
Silver **Note:** Similar to 1/6 Thaler, KM#58 but 1/9 on reverse.

Date	Mintage	VG	F	VF	XF	Unc
1628	—	75.00	150	225	400	—

KM# A18 1/6 THALER
Silver **Note:** Varieties exist.

Date	Mintage	VG	F	VF	XF	Unc
1623	—	90.00	175	350	—	—
1624	—	90.00	175	350	—	—
1625	—	90.00	175	350	—	—

KM# 36 1/6 THALER
Silver **Obv:** Crowned imperial eagle with wings spread, perched on shield with value 1/6, titles of Ferdinand II **Rev:** Pine cone in oval baroque frame, date above

Date	Mintage	VG	F	VF	XF	Unc
1626	—	—	—	—	—	—

KM# 47 1/6 THALER
Silver **Note:** Similar to 1/3 Thaler, KM#37, but value 1/6 on reverse.

Date	Mintage	VG	F	VF	XF	Unc
1627	—	60.00	125	250	500	—

KM# 58 1/6 THALER
Silver

Date	Mintage	VG	F	VF	XF	Unc
MDCXXVIII (1628)	—	60.00	125	200	400	—

KM# 59 1/6 THALER
Silver **Obv:** Pine cone within wreath held by hand above, rays from clouds, date

Date	Mintage	VG	F	VF	XF	Unc
1628	—	150	225	350	600	—

KM# A19 1/4 THALER
Silver **Obv:** Crowned imperial eagle with 1/4 in shield on breast, titles of Ferdinand II **Rev:** Pine cone in baroque frame, date in legend **Note:** Varieties exist.

Date	Mintage	VG	F	VF	XF	Unc
MDCXXIII (1623)	—	—	—	—	—	—

KM# 103 1/4 THALER
Silver **Obv:** Titles of Leopold

Date	Mintage	VG	F	VF	XF	Unc
MDCXCIV (1694)	—	60.00	125	250	400	—

KM# 112 1/4 THALER
Silver **Obv:** Bust of Leopold right **Rev:** Pine cone on pedestal between two river gods, date below

Date	Mintage	VG	F	VF	XF	Unc
1700	—	—	—	—	—	—

KM# 37 1/3 THALER
Silver **Obv:** Titles of Ferdinand II

Date	Mintage	VG	F	VF	XF	Unc
MDCXXVI (1626)	—	100	175	275	425	—

KM# 38 1/3 THALER
Silver

Date	Mintage	VG	F	VF	XF	Unc
MDCXXVI (1626)	—	300	550	1,000	4,500	—

KM# 60 1/3 THALER
Silver

Date	Mintage	VG	F	VF	XF	Unc
MDCXXVIII (1628)	—	—	—	—	—	—

KM# 82 1/3 THALER
Silver **Obv:** 1/3 in shield **Rev:** Date in Arabic numerals

Date	Mintage	VG	F	VF	XF	Unc
1643	—	90.00	150	225	450	—

KM# A20 1/2 THALER
Silver **Obv:** Bust of Ferdinand II left above eagle **Rev:** Pine cone between two river gods, date below

Date	Mintage	VG	F	VF	XF	Unc
MDCXXIII (1623)	—	500	900	1,500	2,250	—

KM# 48 1/2 THALER
Silver **Obv:** Crowned eagle, titles of Ferdinand II **Rev:** Pine cone held by angels above city view, date below

Date	Mintage	VG	F	VF	XF	Unc
MDCXXVII (1627)	—	200	325	500	850	—

KM# 64 1/2 THALER
Silver **Obv:** Date divided by crown at top **Rev:** Pine cone within wreath held by hand above, rays from clouds

Date	Mintage	VG	F	VF	XF	Unc
1629	—	—	—	—	—	—

KM# 79 1/2 THALER
Silver

Date	Mintage	VG	F	VF	XF	Unc
1640	—	125	200	300	500	—
1641	—	125	200	300	500	—
1643	—	60.00	100	175	285	—

KM# 104 1/2 THALER
Silver **Obv:** Crowned imperial eagle, titles of Leopold **Rev:** Pine cone in oval baroque frame, date above

Date	Mintage	VG	F	VF	XF	Unc
MDCLXXXXIV (1694)	—	100	200	325	550	—

KM# 39 2/3 THALER
Silver **Obv:** Crowned eagle with 2/3 in shield on breast, titles of Ferdinand II **Rev:** Pine cone in oval baroque frame, date above

Date	Mintage	VG	F	VF	XF	Unc
1626	—	—	—	—	—	—

KM# 40 2/3 THALER
Silver **Rev:** Date in Roman numerals

Date	Mintage	VG	F	VF	XF	Unc
1626	—	—	—	—	—	—
1627	—	—	—	—	—	—
1628	—	—	—	—	—	—

KM# 49 2/3 THALER
Silver **Rev:** City view, pine cone above, date below

Date	Mintage	VG	F	VF	XF	Unc
MDCXXVII (1627)	—	200	350	600	1,200	—

KM# A21 THALER
Silver **Obv:** Bust of Ferdinand II facing left above eagle **Note:** Varieties exist. Dav. #5011.

Date	Mintage	VG	F	VF	XF	Unc
MDCXXIII (1623)	—	450	850	1,350	—	—
MDCXXIV (1624)	—	450	850	1,350	—	—

KM# 26.1 THALER

Silver **Obv:** Eagle holding imperial orb and scepter, titles of Ferdinand II **Rev:** Enthroned Augusta holding pine cone and lance, date below **Note:** Varieties exist. Dav. #5012.

Date	Mintage	VG	F	VF	XF	Unc
MDCXXIV (1624)	—	150	300	500	900	—

KM# 26.2 THALER

Silver **Obv:** Eagle with tail closed **Note:** Dav. #5013.

Date	Mintage	VG	F	VF	XF	Unc
1624	—	150	300	500	900	—

KM# 27.1 THALER

Silver **Rev:** Pine cone held by angels above city view **Note:** Dav. #5014.

Date	Mintage	VG	F	VF	XF	Unc
MDCXXIV (1624)	—	80.00	165	350	600	—
MDCXXV (1625)	—	80.00	165	350	600	—

KM# 27.2 THALER

Silver **Rev:** Flower garlands below angels, three grain heads in frame **Note:** Dav. #5024.

Date	Mintage	VG	F	VF	XF	Unc
MDCXXVI (1626)	—	85.00	175	375	650	1,750

KM# 27.3 THALER

Silver **Rev:** Without flower garlands below angels **Note:** Dav. #5024A.

Date	Mintage	VG	F	VF	XF	Unc
MDCXXVI (1626)	—	85.00	175	375	650	1,750

KM# 27.4 THALER

Silver **Rev:** Without inner circle **Note:** Dav. #5026.

Date	Mintage	VG	F	VF	XF	Unc
MDCXXVII (1627)	—	100	200	450	750	—

KM# 29 THALER

Silver **Rev:** Larger city view, smaller pine cone **Note:** Dav. #5017.

Date	Mintage	VG	F	VF	XF	Unc
1625 Rare	—	—	—	—	—	—

KM# 30.1 THALER

Silver **Rev:** St. Ulrich behind pine cone in oval baroque frame dividing date **Note:** Dav. #5019.

Date	Mintage	VG	F	VF	XF	Unc
1625	—	85.00	175	350	600	—

KM# 30.2 THALER

Silver **Rev:** Crozier breaking legend ANV - S **Note:** Dav. #5019A.

Date	Mintage	VG	F	VF	XF	Unc
1625	—	85.00	175	350	600	—

KM# 41 THALER

Silver **Obv:** Crowned eagle **Rev:** Pine cone in oval baroque frame, date above **Note:** Dav. #5021.

Date	Mintage	VG	F	VF	XF	Unc
1626	—	75.00	150	300	500	—

KM# 50 THALER

Silver **Rev:** Pine cone held by angels above city view **Note:** Dav. #5028.

Date	Mintage	VG	F	VF	XF	Unc
MDCXXVII (1627)	—	90.00	180	400	700	—
1628	—	90.00	180	400	700	—

KM# 51 THALER

Silver **Rev:** Pine cone in baroque frame, date above **Note:** Dav. #5029.

Date	Mintage	VG	F	VF	XF	Unc
MDCXXVII (1627)	—	100	220	475	800	—

KM# 52 THALER

Silver **Obv:** Crowned imperial eagle, orb on breast **Note:** Dav. #5031.

Date	Mintage	VG	F	VF	XF	Unc
MDCXXVII (1627)	—	100	220	475	800	—

KM# 61 THALER

Silver **Note:** Varieties exist. Dav. #5035.

Date	Mintage	VG	F	VF	XF	Unc
1628	—	75.00	150	400	1,000	2,000
1629	—	75.00	150	400	1,000	2,000
1635	—	75.00	150	400	1,000	2,000

KM# A68 THALER

Silver **Ruler:** Gustavus Adolphus Sweden **Note:** Swedish occupation. Varieties exist. Dav. #4543.

Date	Mintage	VG	F	VF	XF	Unc
1632	—	175	325	550	950	—

KM# 74 THALER

Silver **Obv:** Titles of Ferdinand III **Note:** Dav. #5037.

Date	Mintage	VG	F	VF	XF	Unc
1638	—	150	300	500	900	—

KM# 76 THALER

Silver **Obv:** Bust of Ferdinand III 3/4 right **Rev:** City view with pine cone in center, base dividing date **Note:** Dav. #5038.

Date	Mintage	VG	F	VF	XF	Unc
1639	—	200	400	600	1,000	—

KM# 77 THALER

Silver **Note:** Dav. #5039.

Date	Mintage	VG	F	VF	XF	Unc
1639	—	65.00	125	250	450	900
1640	—	65.00	125	250	450	900
1641	—	65.00	125	250	450	900
1642	—	65.00	125	250	450	900
1643	—	65.00	125	250	450	900
1645	—	65.00	125	250	450	900

KM# 86 THALER

Silver **Obv:** Bust of Leopold right in circle **Note:** Dav. #5040.

Date	Mintage	VG	F	VF	XF	Unc
1658	—	400	700	1,200	2,000	—

KM# 91.1 THALER

Silver **Obv:** Bust of Leopold right **Rev:** Crowned imperial eagle, orb above shield on breast, small pine cone below, date left of crown **Note:** Dav. #5041.

Date	Mintage	VG	F	VF	XF	Unc
1676	—	700	1,200	2,000	3,500	—

KM# 91.2 THALER

Silver **Rev:** Crown divides date at top **Rev. Legend:** AVGVSTA - VINDELICORVM **Note:** Dav. #5042.

Date	Mintage	VG	F	VF	XF	Unc
1676 Rare	—	—	—	—	—	—

KM# 91.3 THALER

Silver **Obv:** Fuller bust **Note:** Dav. #5044.

Date	Mintage	VG	F	VF	XF	Unc
1681 Rare	—	—	—	—	—	—

KM# 96 THALER

Silver **Obv:** Bust of Leopold right in double circle **Rev:** Pine cone on pedestal between palm and laurel branches, rays shining down, date above **Note:** Dav. #5045.

Date	Mintage	VG	F	VF	XF	Unc
1689 Rare	—	—	—	—	—	—

KM# 105.1 THALER

Silver **Obv:** Titles of Leopold **Note:** Dav. #5047.

Date	Mintage	VG	F	VF	XF	Unc
MDCXCIV (1694)	—	100	200	425	750	—

KM# 105.2 THALER

Silver **Obv:** Smaller lettering **Rev:** River gods reversed, smaller lettering **Note:** Varieties exist. Dav. #5048.

Date	Mintage	VG	F	VF	XF	Unc
1694	—	100	200	425	750	—

KM# 106 THALER

Silver **Rev:** Pine cone in oval baroque frame, date above **Note:** Dav. #5049.

Date	Mintage	VG	F	VF	XF	Unc
1694	—	100	200	425	750	—

KM# 107 THALER

Silver **Rev:** Pine cone between two laurel sprays **Note:** Dav. #5050.

Date	Mintage	VG	F	VF	XF	Unc
1694 Rare	—	—	—	—	—	—

KM# 31 2 THALER

Silver **Obv:** Crowned eagle, titles of Ferdinand II **Rev:** Pine cone held by angels above city view, date below **Note:** Dav. #5016.

Date	Mintage	VG	F	VF	XF	Unc
MDCXXV (1625) Rare	—	—	—	—	—	—
MDCXXVI (1626) Rare	—	—	—	—	—	—

KM# 32.1 2 THALER

Silver **Rev:** Larger city view, smaller pine cone **Note:** Dav. #5018.

Date	Mintage	VG	F	VF	XF	Unc
1625	—	1,650	2,750	3,750	6,500	—

KM# 32.2 2 THALER

Silver **Rev:** Left angel holding lightning bolt, right angel holding halo **Note:** Dav. #A5023.

Date	Mintage	VG	F	VF	XF	Unc
1626	—	1,650	2,750	3,750	6,500	—

KM# 32.3 2 THALER

Silver **Rev:** Without inner circle **Note:** Dav. #A5025.

Date	Mintage	VG	F	VF	XF	Unc
1627 Rare	—	—	—	—	—	—

KM# 42 2 THALER

Silver **Rev:** Pine cone in oval baroque frame, date above **Note:** Dav. #A5020.

Date	Mintage	VG	F	VF	XF	Unc
1626	—	1,500	2,500	3,500	6,000	—

KM# 53 2 THALER

Silver **Obv:** Crowned imperial eagle **Rev:** Pine cone held by angels above city view, date below **Note:** Dav. #5027.

Date	Mintage	VG	F	VF	XF	Unc
MDCXXVII (1627)	—	1,500	2,500	3,500	6,000	—

KM# 54 2 THALER

Silver **Rev:** Pine cone in baroque frame **Note:** Dav. #5030.

Date	Mintage	VG	F	VF	XF	Unc
1627	—	1,500	2,500	3,500	6,000	—

KM# 62 2 THALER

Silver **Obv:** Imperial eagle not in circle, without orb **Rev:** Pine cone held by angels above city view, date below **Note:** Dav. #5032.

Date	Mintage	VG	F	VF	XF	Unc
MDCXXVIII (1628) Rare	—	—	—	—	—	—

KM# 63 2 THALER

Silver **Rev:** Roman numeral date **Note:** Dav. #5034.

Date	Mintage	VG	F	VF	XF	Unc
1628	—	1,000	1,750	2,750	4,500	—
1629	—	1,000	1,750	2,750	4,500	—

KM# B68 2 THALER

Silver **Obv:** Bust of Gustav Adolph II right **Rev:** Similar to 1 thaler, KM#A68 **Note:** Swedish issue. Dav. #4542.

Date	Mintage	VG	F	VF	XF	Unc
1632 Unique	—	—	—	—	—	—

KM# 94 2 THALER

Silver **Obv:** Bust of Leopold right **Rev:** Crowned imperial eagle, orb above shield on breast, small pine cone below, crown divides date at top **Note:** Dav. #5043.

Date	Mintage	VG	F	VF	XF	Unc
1681 Rare	—	—	—	—	—	—

KM# 108 2 THALER

Silver **Obv:** Crowned imperial eagle, titles of Leopold **Rev:** Pine cone on pedestal supported by river gods, date below **Note:** Dav. #5046.

Date	Mintage	VG	F	VF	XF	Unc
MDCXCIV (1694) Rare	—	—	—	—	—	—

KM# 33 3 THALER

Silver **Obv:** Crowned eagle, titles of Ferdinand II **Rev:** Small pine cone held by angels above large city view, date below **Note:** Dav. #A5015.

Date	Mintage	VG	F	VF	XF	Unc
MDCXXV (1625) Rare	—	—	—	—	—	—

KM# 43 3 THALER

Silver **Rev:** Pine cone in oval baroque frame, date above **Note:** Dav. #5020.

Date	Mintage	VG	F	VF	XF	Unc
1626 Rare	—	—	—	—	—	—

KM# 55 3 THALER

Silver **Rev:** Larger pine cone held by angels above smaller city view, date below **Note:** Dav. #5025.

Date	Mintage	VG	F	VF	XF	Unc
MDCXXVII (1627) Rare	—	—	—	—	—	—

KM# 65 3 THALER

Silver **Obv:** Crowned imperial eagle, orb on breast **Rev:** Pine cone in baroque frame, date **Note:** Dav. #5033.

Date	Mintage	VG	F	VF	XF	Unc
MDCXXIX (1629) Rare	—	—	—	—	—	—

KM# C68 3 THALER

Silver **Obv:** Bust of Gustav Adolph II right **Rev:** Similar to 1 Thaler, KM#A68

Date	Mintage	VG	F	VF	XF	Unc
1632 Unique	—	—	—	—	—	—

KM# 34 4 THALER

Silver **Obv:** Crowned eagle, titles of Ferdinand II **Rev:** Small pine cone held by angels above large city view, date below **Note:** Dav. #5015.

Date	Mintage	VG	F	VF	XF	Unc
MDCXXV (1625) Rare	—	—	—	—	—	—
MDCXXVI (1626) Rare	—	—	—	—	—	—

KM# 44 4 THALER

Silver **Rev:** Larger pine cone and small city view **Note:** Dav. #5023.

Date	Mintage	VG	F	VF	XF	Unc
1626 Rare	—	—	—	—	—	—

TRADE COINAGE

KM# A2 GOLDGULDEN

3.5000 g., 0.9860 Gold 0.1109 oz. AGW **Obv:** Crowned imperial eagle in inner circle, titles of Rudolf II **Rev:** Pine cone on pedestal in inner circle, date in exergue

Date	Mintage	VG	F	VF	XF	Unc
MDCIX (1609)	—	1,250	2,500	4,500	7,500	—

KM# A3 GOLDGULDEN

3.5000 g., 0.9860 Gold 0.1109 oz. AGW **Obv:** Pine cone in cartouche, titles of Matthias **Rev:** Seated female figure left

Date	Mintage	VG	F	VF	XF	Unc
1613	—	375	700	1,350	2,750	—

KM# A4 GOLDGULDEN

3.5000 g., 0.9860 Gold 0.1109 oz. AGW **Obv:** Bust of Ferdinand II right

Date	Mintage	VG	F	VF	XF	Unc
1619	—	700	1,500	3,500	6,500	—

KM# A22 GOLDGULDEN

3.5000 g., 0.9860 Gold 0.1109 oz. AGW **Obv:** Crowned imperial eagle in inner circle, titles of Ferdinand II **Rev:** Pine cone in cartouche

Date	Mintage	VG	F	VF	XF	Unc
1623	—	600	1,200	2,500	4,500	—
1628	—	600	1,200	2,500	4,500	—

KM# 56 GOLDGULDEN

3.5000 g., 0.9860 Gold 0.1109 oz. AGW **Obv:** St. Afra and St. Ulric standing

Date	Mintage	VG	F	VF	XF	Unc
1627	—	1,200	2,500	4,500	7,500	—
1628	—	1,200	2,500	4,500	7,500	—

KM# 66 DUCAT

3.5000 g., 0.9860 Gold 0.1109 oz. AGW **Obv:** Crowned imperial eagle in inner circle, titles of Ferdinand II **Rev:** St. Afra with pine cone

Date	Mintage	VG	F	VF	XF	Unc
1629	—	175	275	600	1,350	—
1630 BS	—	175	275	600	1,350	—
1631	—	175	275	600	1,350	—
1634	—	175	275	600	1,350	—
1635 BS	—	175	275	600	1,350	—
1636 BS	—	175	275	600	1,350	—
1637 BS	—	175	275	600	1,350	—

KM# 68 DUCAT

3.5000 g., 0.9860 Gold 0.1109 oz. AGW **Obv:** Gustavus Adolphus

Date	Mintage	VG	F	VF	XF	Unc
1632	—	200	300	650	1,450	—
1633	—	200	300	650	1,450	—

KM# 71 DUCAT

3.5000 g., 0.9860 Gold 0.1109 oz. AGW **Obv:** Bust of Gustavus Adolphus right

Date	Mintage	VG	F	VF	XF	Unc
1634	—	200	300	650	1,450	—
1635	—	200	300	650	1,450	—

KM# 73 DUCAT

3.5000 g., 0.9860 Gold 0.1109 oz. AGW **Obv:** Ferdinand III

Date	Mintage	VG	F	VF	XF	Unc
1637	—	200	300	650	1,450	—
1638	—	200	300	650	1,450	—

Date	Mintage	VG	F	VF	XF	Unc
1639	—	200	300	650	1,450	—
1640	—	200	300	650	1,450	—
1641	—	200	300	650	1,450	—
1642	—	200	300	650	1,450	—
1643	—	200	300	650	1,450	—

KM# 75 DUCAT

3.5000 g., 0.9860 Gold 0.1109 oz. AGW

Date	Mintage	VG	F	VF	XF	Unc
1637	—	250	350	700	1,500	—
1638	—	250	350	700	1,500	—
1639	—	250	350	700	1,500	—
1642	—	250	350	700	1,500	—

KM# 83 DUCAT

3.5000 g., 0.9860 Gold 0.1109 oz. AGW **Obv:** Ferdinand III

Date	Mintage	VG	F	VF	XF	Unc
1645	—	200	300	550	1,150	2,000
1646	—	200	300	550	1,150	2,000
1647	—	200	300	550	1,150	2,000
1648	—	200	300	550	1,150	2,000
1649	—	200	300	550	1,150	2,000
1650	—	200	300	550	1,150	2,000
1651	—	200	300	550	1,150	2,000
1652	—	200	300	550	1,150	2,000
1653	—	200	300	550	1,150	2,000
1654	—	200	300	550	1,150	2,000
1655	—	200	300	550	1,150	2,000
1656	—	200	300	550	1,150	2,000
1657	—	200	300	550	1,150	2,000

KM# 84 DUCAT

3.5000 g., 0.9860 Gold 0.1109 oz. AGW **Subject:** Coronation of Ferdinand IV as King of the Romans (Holy Roman Emperor) **Obv:** Eight-line inscription with date in wreath **Rev:** Crowned imperial eagle on column, trophies below

Date	Mintage	VG	F	VF	XF	Unc
1653	—	300	500	800	1,650	—

KM# 87 DUCAT

3.5000 g., 0.9860 Gold 0.1109 oz. AGW **Obv:** Leopold

Date	Mintage	VG	F	VF	XF	Unc
1658	—	250	350	650	1,450	—
1659	—	250	350	650	1,450	—
1660	—	250	350	650	1,450	—
1661	—	250	350	650	1,450	—
1662	—	250	350	650	1,450	—
1663	—	250	350	650	1,450	—
1664	—	250	350	650	1,450	—
1667	—	250	350	650	1,450	—
1669	—	250	350	650	1,450	—
1671	—	250	350	650	1,450	—
1672	—	250	350	650	1,450	—
1673	—	250	350	650	1,450	—
1675	—	250	350	650	1,450	—
1677	—	250	350	650	1,450	—

KM# 92 DUCAT

3.5000 g., 0.9860 Gold 0.1109 oz. AGW **Rev:** Pine cone on pedestal in wreath, date at top

Date	Mintage	VG	F	VF	XF	Unc
1677	—	300	500	800	1,600	—
1681	—	300	500	800	1,600	—
1682	—	300	500	800	1,600	—
1684	—	300	500	800	1,600	—
1685	—	300	500	800	1,600	—
1686	—	300	500	800	1,600	—
1687	—	300	500	800	1,600	—
1688	—	300	500	800	1,600	—
1689	—	300	500	800	1,600	—
1691	—	300	500	800	1,600	—
1692	—	300	500	800	1,600	—

KM# 97 DUCAT

3.5000 g., 0.9860 Gold 0.1109 oz. AGW **Obv:** Bust of Leopold right **Rev:** Bust of Eleonora Magdalene left

Date	Mintage	VG	F	VF	XF	Unc
1689	—	250	350	650	1,450	—

KM# 98 DUCAT

3.5000 g., 0.9860 Gold 0.1109 oz. AGW **Rev:** Eleonora Magdalene

Date	Mintage	VG	F	VF	XF	Unc
1690	—	250	350	650	1,450	—

KM# 99 DUCAT

3.5000 g., 0.9860 Gold 0.1109 oz. AGW **Subject:** Coronation of Josef (I) as King of Hungary (Holy Roman Emperor) **Obv:** Bust 3/4 right **Rev:** Crown above three-line inscription with date in Roman numerals within wreath

Date	Mintage	VG	F	VF	XF	Unc
1690	—	350	550	850	1,750	—

KM# 110 DUCAT

3.5000 g., 0.9860 Gold 0.1109 oz. AGW **Obv:** Pine cone between river gods **Rev:** Bust of Leopold right

Date	Mintage	VG	F	VF	XF	Unc
1695	—	300	500	900	1,850	—
1697	—	300	500	900	1,850	—
1699	—	300	500	900	1,850	—

KM# 45 2 DUCAT

7.0000 g., 0.9860 Gold 0.2219 oz. AGW **Obv:** St. Afra and St. Ulric standing **Rev:** Crowned imperial eagle in inner circle, titles of Ferdinand II

Date	Mintage	VG	F	VF	XF	Unc
1626	—	1,000	2,000	4,500	8,500	—

KM# 69 2 DUCAT

7.0000 g., 0.9860 Gold 0.2219 oz. AGW **Obv:** Conjoined busts of Gustavus Adolphus and Maria Eleonora right

Date	Mintage	VG	F	VF	XF	Unc
1632	—	950	1,850	4,000	8,000	—

KM# 80 2 DUCAT

7.0000 g., 0.9860 Gold 0.2219 oz. AGW **Obv:** Facing laureate bust of Ferdinand III **Rev:** Pine cone in cartouche

Date	Mintage	VG	F	VF	XF	Unc
1641	—	750	1,800	3,450	6,500	—
1643	—	750	1,800	3,450	6,500	—

KM# 85 2 DUCAT

7.0000 g., 0.9860 Gold 0.2219 oz. AGW **Obv:** Conjoined busts of Ferdinand III and Eleanor right

Date	Mintage	VG	F	VF	XF	Unc
1657	—	700	1,500	2,750	5,000	—

KM# 89 2 DUCAT

7.0000 g., 0.9860 Gold 0.2219 oz. AGW **Obv:** Conjoined busts of Leopold and Margaret left

Date	Mintage	VG	F	VF	XF	Unc
1672	—	650	1,250	2,500	4,500	7,750

KM# 100 2 DUCAT

7.0000 g., 0.9860 Gold 0.2219 oz. AGW **Obv:** Conjoined busts of Leopold and Eleanore right

Date	Mintage	VG	F	VF	XF	Unc
1691	—	1,000	2,000	3,500	6,500	—

KM# 113 2 DUCAT

7.0000 g., 0.9860 Gold 0.2219 oz. AGW **Obv:** Laureate bust of Leopold right **Rev:** Pine cone between river gods

Date	Mintage	VG	F	VF	XF	Unc
1700 Rare	—	—	—	—	—	—

KM# 70 3 DUCAT

10.5000 g., 0.9860 Gold 0.3328 oz. AGW **Obv:** Conjoined busts of Gustav Adolphus and Maria Eleanore right

Date	Mintage	VG	F	VF	XF	Unc
1632 Rare	—	—	—	—	—	—

KM# 90 3 DUCAT

10.5000 g., 0.9860 Gold 0.3328 oz. AGW **Obv:** Conjoined busts of Leopold and Margaret right **Rev:** Pine cone in cartouche

Date	Mintage	VG	F	VF	XF	Unc
1672	—	1,400	2,800	5,200	9,000	—

KM# 101 3 DUCAT

10.5000 g., 0.9860 Gold 0.3328 oz. AGW **Obv:** Conjoined busts of Leopold and Eleanore right

Date	Mintage	VG	F	VF	XF	Unc
1691	—	1,600	3,200	6,000	10,000	—

KM# 67 4 DUCAT

14.0000 g., 0.9860 Gold 0.4438 oz. AGW **Obv:** Crowned imperial eagle, titles of Ferdinand II **Rev:** St. Afra standing between pyre and pine cone

Date	Mintage	VG	F	VF	XF	Unc
1630 Rare	—	—	—	—	—	—

KM# A33 10 DUCAT

35.0000 g., 0.9860 Gold 1.1095 oz. AGW **Obv:** Crowned eagle with sword and sceptre **Rev:** Ctiy view

Date	Mintage	VG	F	VF	XF	Unc
1625 Rare	—	—	—	—	—	—

KM# A64 10 DUCAT

35.0000 g., 0.9860 Gold 1.1095 oz. AGW **Note:** Struck with 1 Thaler dies, KM#61.

Date	Mintage	VG	F	VF	XF	Unc
1629 Rare	—	—	—	—	—	—

PATTERNS

Including off metal strikes

KM#	Date	Mintage	Identification	Mkt Val
PnA1	1608	—	Heller. Silver. KM#1	—
Pn2	1608	—	Heller. Gold. KM#1	—
Pn3	1609	—	Heller. Silver. KM#1	—
Pn4	1615	—	Heller. Silver. KM#1	—
Pn5	1621	—	2 Heller. Silver. KM#7	—
Pn6	1653	—	Ducat. Silver. KM#84	—
Pn7	1690	—	Ducat. Silver. KM#99	—

BADEN

The earliest rulers of Baden, in the southwestern part of Germany along the Rhine, descended from the dukes of Zähringen in the late 11th century. The first division of the territory occurred in 1190, when separate lines of margraves were established in Baden and in Hachberg. Immediately prior to its extinction in 1418, Hachberg was sold back to Baden, which underwent several minor divisions itself during the next century. Baden acquired most of the Countship of Sponheim from Electoral Pfalz near the end of the 15th century. In 1515, the most significant division of the patrimony took place, in which the Baden-Baden and Baden-(Pforzheim) Durlach lines were established.

BADEN-BADEN LINE

Established in 1515 by Christoph I's eldest son, Bernhard III. This branch was often at odds with the rulers of the younger Baden-Durlach line because of religious differences resulting from the Protestant Reformation. When Baden-Baden finally became extinct in 1771, all lands and titles reverted to Baden-Durlach and all of Baden was reunited after a split of more than 250 years.

RULERS

Wilhelm, 1622-1677
Ludwig Wilhelm, 1677-1707
Ludwig Georg, 1707-1761

ARMS

Baden – diagonal bar from upper left to lower right
The usual arrangement is shield of 4-fold arms of Baden quartered with Sponheim

MINT OFFICIALS' INITIALS

Initials	Date	Name
GC	1624-29	Georg Cramer
IPB	Ca.1704	Johann Peter Bischof in Würzburg

REGULAR COINAGE

KM# 2 PFENNIG
Silver **Note:** Uniface. Four-fold arms divide W-M, date above. Varieties exist.

Date	Mintage	Good	VG	F	VF	XF
1624	—	45.00	90.00	175	250	—
1626	—	45.00	90.00	175	250	—

KM# 9 PFENNIG
Silver **Note:** Four-fold arms, WM above date.

Date	Mintage	Good	VG	F	VF	XF
ND	—	45.00	90.00	175	250	—

KM# 17 PFENNIG
Silver **Note:** Klippe. Four-fold arms divide W-M, date above.

Date	Mintage	Good	VG	F	VF	XF
1676 Rare	—	—	—	—	—	—

KM# 5 ALBUS
Silver **Obv:** Four-fold arms in baroque frame **Rev:** Crowned imperial eagle with 2 in orb on breast, date **Note:** Varieties exist.

Date	Mintage	Good	VG	F	VF	XF
1625	—	60.00	110	190	275	—
1636	—	60.00	110	190	275	—
1637	—	60.00	110	190	275	—

KM# 4 12 KREUZER (3 Batzen)
Silver **Obv:** Bust with wide collar right **Rev:** Manifold arms, date above, value XII at top **Note:** Varieties exist.

Date	Mintage	Good	VG	F	VF	XF
1624	—	65.00	130	200	300	—
1625	—	65.00	130	200	300	—
1626	—	65.00	130	200	300	—

KM# 7 12 KREUZER (3 Batzen)
Silver **Note:** Klippe.

Date	Mintage	Good	VG	F	VF	XF
1626 Rare	—	—	—	—	—	—

KM# 3 GROSCHEN
Silver **Obv:** Four-fold arms, date above **Rev:** Crowned imperial eagle with 3 in orb on breast **Note:** Varieties exist.

Date	Mintage	Good	VG	F	VF	XF
1624	—	55.00	125	200	325	—

KM# 14 1/18 THALER
Silver **Obv:** Half-length bust in mantle right **Rev:** Manifold arms in baroque frame, date above, value 18.ST.FVR. 1/.R. DALER below

Date	Mintage	VG	F	VF	XF	Unc
1638	—	—	—	—	—	—

KM# 15 1/6 THALER
Silver **Obv:** Half-length bust in mantle right **Rev:** Manifold arms in baroque frame, date above, value 6.ST.FVR. 1.R. THALER

Date	Mintage	VG	F	VF	XF	Unc
1638	—	—	—	—	—	—

KM# 10 1/2 THALER
Silver **Obv:** Half-length bust right **Rev:** Eight shields around central shield which divides date

Date	Mintage	VG	F	VF	XF	Unc
1629 GC	—	—	—	—	—	—

KM# 6.1 THALER
Silver **Obv. Legend:** GVILHELM'D+G+MAR+BAD+ET+HACH: **Note:** Dav. #6036.

Date	Mintage	VG	F	VF	XF	Unc
1624	—	550	900	1,600	2,750	—

KM# 6.2 THALER
Silver **Obv:** Different bust from KM#6.1 **Obv. Legend:** GVILHELMVS. D. G. MARCHIO... **Note:** Dav. #6038.

Date	Mintage	VG	F	VF	XF	Unc
1625	—	325	550	950	1,450	—
1626	—	325	550	950	1,450	—
1627	—	325	550	950	1,450	—

KM# 11 THALER
Silver **Obv:** Half-length bust right **Rev:** Eight shields around central shield **Note:** Dav. #6040.

Date	Mintage	VG	F	VF	XF	Unc
ND(1629) GC	—	1,250	2,250	4,000	6,000	—

KM# 8 2 THALER
Silver **Note:** Similar to 1 Thaler, KM#6.2. Dav. #6037.

Date	Mintage	VG	F	VF	XF	Unc
1627 Rare	—	—	—	—	—	—

KM# 12 2 THALER
Silver **Obv:** Half-length bust right **Rev:** Eight shields around central shield **Note:** Dav. #6039.

Date	Mintage	VG	F	VF	XF	Unc
ND(1629) GC Rare	—	—	—	—	—	—

TRADE COINAGE

KM# 13 3 GOLDGULDEN
10.5000 g., 0.9860 Gold 0.3328 oz. AGW **Obv:** St. George and the dragon in inner circle **Rev:** Eight shields in a circle with Baden shield in center of inner circle

Date	Mintage	VG	F	VF	XF	Unc
ND(1629) GC Rare	—	—	—	—	—	—

KM# 16 DUCAT
3.5000 g., 0.9860 Gold 0.1109 oz. AGW **Obv:** Wilhelm

Date	Mintage	VG	F	VF	XF	Unc
1674	—	—	—	7,500	11,500	—

TOKEN COINAGE

Property of St. Blasien Monastery

Used to pay workers at Gutenburg Mint.

KM# Tn1 3 KREUZER
1.5400 g., Copper **Ruler:** Ludwig Wilhelm

Date	Mintage	VG	F	VF	XF	Unc
1694	—	—	—	—	—	—

KM# Tn2 15 KREUZER
4.2200 g., Copper **Ruler:** Ludwig Wilhelm

Date	Mintage	VG	F	VF	XF	Unc
1694	—	—	—	—	—	—

KM# Tn3 GULDEN
11.4100 g., Copper **Ruler:** Ludwig Wilhelm

Date	Mintage	VG	F	VF	XF	Unc
1694	—	—	—	—	—	—

BADEN-DURLACH LINE

Grand Duchy

Although Baden-Durlach was founded upon the division of Baden in 1515, the youngest son of Christoph I did not begin ruling in his own right until the demise of his father. This part of Baden was called Pforzheim until 1565, when the margrave moved his seat from the former to Durlach, located to the west and nearer the Rhine. After the male line of Baden-Baden failed in 1771 and the two parts of Baden were reunited, the fortunes of the margraviate continued to grow. Karlsruhe, near Durlach, was developed into a well-planned capital city. The ruler was given the rank of elector in 1803, only to be raised to grand duke three years later. The monarchy came to an end in 1918, but had by this time become one of the largest states in Germany.

RULERS

Georg Friedrich, 1604-1622
Friedrich V, 1622-1659
Friedrich VI, 1659-1677
Friedrich VII Magnus, 1677-1709

REGULAR COINAGE

KM# A9 PFENNIG
Silver **Note:** Uniface. Schussel type. Arms divide Z-B, GFM above. Prev. KM#9.

Date	Mintage	Good	VG	F	VF	XF
ND(1610)	—	30.00	60.00	100	150	—

KM# A12 PFENNIG
Silver **Note:** Arms divide date. GFM above, D below. Prev. KM#12.

Date	Mintage	Good	VG	F	VF	XF
1621 D	—	30.00	60.00	100	150	—

KM# 29 PFENNIG
Silver **Note:** Schussel type. Arms divide Z-B, FM above, date below.

Date	Mintage	Good	VG	F	VF	XF
1623	—	30.00	60.00	100	150	—
1624	—	30.00	60.00	100	150	—

KM# A5 2 PFENNIGE (1/84 Gulden)
Silver **Obv:** Ornately-shaped arms divide Z-B, GFM above **Rev:** Imperial orb with 84 divides date **Note:** Klippe. Prev. KM#5.

Date	Mintage	Good	VG	F	VF	XF
1609	—	35.00	65.00	110	160	—
1610	—	35.00	65.00	110	160	—

KM# A10 6 PFENNIGE (1/28 Gulden)
Silver **Obv:** Four-fold arms with central shield, value 6 at top **Rev:** Imperial orb with 28, cross on top divides date **Note:** Klippe. Prev. KM#10.

Date	Mintage	Good	VG	F	VF	XF
1610	—	45.00	90.00	150	225	—

KM# A18 8 PFENNIGE
Silver **Obv:** Bust of Georg Friedrich right **Rev:** Eight-fold arms with VIII above, date in legend **Note:** Prev. KM#18.

Date	Mintage	Good	VG	F	VF	XF
1622	—	45.00	80.00	140	200	—

KM# A20 8 PFENNIGE
Silver **Obv:** Bust of Friedrich V right **Rev:** Eight-fold arms with VIII above **Note:** Prev. KM#20.

Date	Mintage	Good	VG	F	VF	XF
ND(1622-23)	—	45.00	80.00	140	200	—

KM# A19 8 PFENNIGE
Silver **Obv:** Helmeted and mantled triangular arms, titles of Friedrich V **Rev:** Value VIII in center, date in legend **Note:** Varieties exist. Prev. KM#19.

Date	Mintage	Good	VG	F	VF	XF
1622	—	45.00	80.00	140	200	—

KM# 30 KREUZER

Silver **Obv:** Bust of Friedrich V right **Rev:** Arms with value (1) above, date in legend

Date	Mintage	Good	VG	F	VF	XF
1623	—	45.00	80.00	140	200	—

KM# 31 KREUZER

Silver **Obv:** Value (1) below bust **Note:** Varieties exist.

Date	Mintage	Good	VG	F	VF	XF
1623	—	45.00	80.00	140	200	—
1624	—	45.00	80.00	140	200	—

KM# 32 2 KREUZER (1/2 Batzen)

Silver **Obv:** Bust right, value (2) below **Rev:** Eight-fold arms, date in legend

Date	Mintage	Good	VG	F	VF	XF
1623	—	60.00	100	175	240	—
1624	—	60.00	100	175	240	—

KM# 57 2 KREUZER (1/2 Batzen)

Silver **Obv:** Eight-fold arms **Rev:** Imperial orb with 2, date divided at top

Date	Mintage	Good	VG	F	VF	XF
1633	—	40.00	80.00	150	225	—
1634	—	40.00	80.00	150	225	—
1637	—	45.00	85.00	160	250	—

KM# 58 2 KREUZER (1/2 Batzen)

Silver **Obv:** Crown with horns above mantled arms, titles of Friedrich VII **Rev:** Three shields, two slanted above one, value below

Date	Mintage	Good	VG	F	VF	XF
ND	—	35.00	65.00	140	200	—

KM# 59 3 KREUZER (1 Groschen)

Silver **Obv:** Bust of Friedrich VII right **Rev:** Crowned arms between two branches, value 3 below

Date	Mintage	VG	F	VF	XF	Unc
ND	—	—	—	—	—	—

KM# 47 6 KREUZER (1/15 Thaler)

Silver **Obv:** Half-length armored figure right, value 1/15 in oval below **Rev:** Eight-fold arms, value 6.K above. date in legend

Date	Mintage	Good	VG	F	VF	XF
1626	—	60.00	110	190	275	—

KM# 60 6 KREUZER (1/15 Thaler)

Silver **Obv:** Bust of Friedrich VII right **Rev:** Crowned arms between two branches, value 6 below

Date	Mintage	Good	VG	F	VF	XF
ND	—	40.00	80.00	140	200	—

KM# A13 12 KREUZER (3 Batzen)

Silver **Obv:** Bust right **Rev:** Eight-fold arms divide date, value (12) above **Note:** Prev. KM#13.

Date	Mintage	Good	VG	F	VF	XF
1621	—	60.00	110	190	275	—

KM# 21 12 KREUZER (Kipper)

Silver **Obv:** Bust of Friedrich V right divides date **Rev:** Eight-fold arms with value 12 above

Date	Mintage	Good	VG	F	VF	XF
1622	—	60.00	110	190	275	—

KM# 33 12 KREUZER (Kipper)

Silver **Obv:** Bust of Friedrich V right **Rev:** Eight-fold arms, date above, without value

Date	Mintage	Good	VG	F	VF	XF
1623	—	60.00	110	190	275	—

KM# 61 12 KREUZER (Kipper)

Silver **Obv:** Bust of Friedrich VII right **Rev:** Crowned eight-fold arms, value (12) above

Date	Mintage	Good	VG	F	VF	XF
ND	—	40.00	80.00	140	200	—

KM# A15 24 KREUZER (6 Batzen)

Silver **Rev:** 10-fold arms and vlaue (24) below **Note:** Klippe. Prev. KM#15.

Date	Mintage	VG	F	VF	XF	Unc
1621 Rare	—	—	—	—	—	—

KM# A14 24 KREUZER (6 Batzen)

Silver **Obv:** Bust right **Rev:** Eight-fold arms divide date, value (24) above **Note:** Prev. KM#14.

Date	Mintage	VG	F	VF	XF	Unc
1621	—	—	—	—	—	—

KM# A17 24 KREUZER (Kipper)

Silver **Obv:** 1/2-length figure of Georg Friedrich right, date divided by head **Rev:** Eight-fold arms, without value **Note:** Varieties exist. Prev. KM#17.

Date	Mintage	Good	VG	F	VF	XF
1621	—	65.00	125	200	350	—
1622	—	65.00	125	200	350	—
1622 D-PI	—	65.00	125	200	350	—
ND	—	65.00	125	200	350	—
ND D	—	65.00	125	200	350	—
ND D-PI	—	65.00	125	200	350	—
ND IPL	—	65.00	125	200	350	—
ND PI	—	65.00	125	200	350	—

KM# A16 24 KREUZER (Kipper)

Silver **Obv:** Bust of Georg Friedrich right **Rev:** Eight-fold arms, date above, without value **Note:** Varieties exist. Prev. KM#16.

Date	Mintage	VG	F	VF	XF	Unc
1621	—	—	—	—	—	—

KM# 23 24 KREUZER (Kipper)

Silver **Obv:** Bust of Friedrich V right, head divides date **Rev:** Eight-fold arms, value 24 above

Date	Mintage	Good	VG	F	VF	XF
1622	—	—	—	—	—	—
1623	—	—	—	—	—	—

KM# 22 24 KREUZER (Kipper)

Silver **Note:** Klippe. Varieties exist.

Date	Mintage	Good	VG	F	VF	XF
1622 D	—	—	—	—	—	—
ND D	—	—	—	—	—	—

KM# 35 24 KREUZER (Kipper)

Silver **Obv:** Bust of Friedrich V right **Rev:** Eight-fold arms, without value **Note:** Varieties exist.

Date	Mintage	Good	VG	F	VF	XF
ND	—	—	—	—	—	—
ND PI	—	—	—	—	—	—

KM# 36 24 KREUZER (Kipper)

Silver **Obv:** 1/2-length figure of Friedrich V right **Note:** Varieties exist.

Date	Mintage	Good	VG	F	VF	XF
ND	—	50.00	100	200	300	—
ND PI	—	50.00	100	200	300	—

KM# 34 24 KREUZER (Kipper)

Silver **Note:** Klippe.

Date	Mintage	Good	VG	F	VF	XF
1623 Rare	—	—	—	—	—	—

KM# 37 24 KREUZER (Kipper)

Silver **Note:** Klippe.

Date	Mintage	Good	VG	F	VF	XF
ND Rare	—	—	—	—	—	—

KM# 39 1/4 THALER

Silver **Obv:** 1/2-length figure right, value (1/4) below **Rev:** Eight-fold arms in ornate frame, date above

Date	Mintage	Good	VG	F	VF	XF
1624	—	—	—	—	—	—

KM# 40 1/4 THALER

Silver **Note:** Klippe.

Date	Mintage	Good	VG	F	VF	XF
1624 Rare	—	—	—	—	—	—

KM# 49 1/4 THALER

Silver **Rev:** Ornamented square arms with curved bottom, without value, floral ornaments in each corner **Note:** Klippe.

Date	Mintage	Good	VG	F	VF	XF
1626 Rare	—	—	—	—	—	—

KM# 48 1/4 THALER

Silver **Obv:** 1/2-length figure right **Rev:** Eight-fold arms in oval baroque frame, surmounted by angel's head, value (1/4) above, date divided below

Date	Mintage	Good	VG	F	VF	XF
1626 I	—	—	—	—	—	—

KM# 41 1/2 THALER

Silver **Obv:** 1/2-length figure right, value (1/2) below **Rev:** Eight-fold arms in ornate frame, date above

Date	Mintage	Good	VG	F	VF	XF
1624	—	—	—	—	—	—

KM# 42 1/2 THALER

Silver **Note:** Klippe.

Date	Mintage	Good	VG	F	VF	XF
1624 Rare	—	—	—	—	—	—

KM# 50 1/2 THALER

Silver **Obv:** 1/2-length figure right **Rev:** Ornamented square arms with curved bottom, without value, floral ornaments in each corner **Note:** Klippe.

Date	Mintage	Good	VG	F	VF	XF
1626 Rare	—	—	—	—	—	—

KM# 53 1/2 THALER

Silver **Rev:** Oval eight-fold arms in baroque frame, date in legend

Date	Mintage	Good	VG	F	VF	XF
1628 MS-I	—	—	—	—	—	—

KM# 54 1/2 THALER

Silver **Rev:** Date divided below arms

Date	Mintage	Good	VG	F	VF	XF
1629 P	—	—	—	—	—	—

KM# A6.1 THALER

Silver **Note:** Similar to KM#6.2 but arms at top in V-shape. Prev. KM#6.1. Dav. 6042.

Date	Mintage	VG	F	VF	XF	Unc
1609	—	725	1,250	2,150	3,250	—

KM# A6.2 THALER

Silver **Note:** Prev. KM#6.2. Dav. 6043.

Date	Mintage	VG	F	VF	XF	Unc
1610	—	900	1,600	2,500	4,000	—

KM# 25 THALER

Silver **Note:** Klippe. Dav. #6045A.

Date	Mintage	VG	F	VF	XF	Unc
1622 Rare	—	—	—	—	—	—

KM# 24 THALER

Silver **Obv:** Georg Friedrich **Note:** Dav. #6045.

Date	Mintage	VG	F	VF	XF	Unc
1622	—	350	650	1,100	1,750	—

KM# 26 THALER

Silver **Note:** Dav. #6046.

Date	Mintage	VG	F	VF	XF	Unc
1622	—	350	650	1,100	1,750	—

KM# 38.1 THALER
Silver **Note:** Similar to KM#43 but date divided above arms, P-I below. Dav. #6047.

Date	Mintage	VG	F	VF	XF	Unc
1623 PI	—	450	850	1,600	2,500	—

KM# 38.2 THALER
Silver **Rev:** Date above arms, P-I divided below **Note:** Dav. #6053.

Date	Mintage	VG	F	VF	XF	Unc
1626 PI	—	300	550	950	1,450	—

KM# 44 THALER
Silver **Note:** Klippe. Dav. #6048A.

Date	Mintage	VG	F	VF	XF	Unc
1624 Rare	—	—	—	—	—	—

KM# 43 THALER
Silver **Note:** Dav. #6048.

Date	Mintage	VG	F	VF	XF	Unc
1624	—	265	450	750	1,200	—

KM# 45 THALER
Silver **Rev:** Date arranged differently **Note:** Dav. #6049.

Date	Mintage	VG	F	VF	XF	Unc
1624	—	265	450	750	1,200	—
1625	—	265	450	750	1,200	—

KM# 46 THALER
Silver **Rev:** Date below arms **Note:** Dav. #6050.

Date	Mintage	VG	F	VF	XF	Unc
1625	—	265	450	750	1,200	—

KM# 51.1 THALER
Silver **Note:** Dav. #6052.

Date	Mintage	VG	F	VF	XF	Unc
1626 I	—	350	725	1,250	2,000	—
1627 I	—	350	725	1,250	2,000	—

KM# 51.2 THALER
Silver **Obv. Legend:** ...MAR. Z. BAD. V. H. A. L. Z. S. G. Z. SP. **Note:** Dav. #6055.

Date	Mintage	VG	F	VF	XF	Unc
1628 I	—	350	725	1,250	2,000	—

KM# 55.1 THALER
Silver **Rev:** Date divided 16-29 by lower half of arms, P below **Note:** Dav. #6056.

Date	Mintage	VG	F	VF	XF	Unc
1629 P	—	375	650	1,150	1,750	—

KM# 55.2 THALER
Silver **Obv. Legend:** ...M. Z: BA. V: HA: L. Z. SAV... **Note:** Dav. #6058.

Date	Mintage	VG	F	VF	XF	Unc
1634 P Rare	—	—	—	—	—	—

KM# 56 THALER
Silver **Ruler:** Friedrich V **Rev:** Helmeted arms, date above **Note:** Dav. #6057.

Date	Mintage	VG	F	VF	XF	Unc
1629 P	—	750	1,350	2,250	3,750	—

KM# 62 THALER
Silver **Obv:** Bust right **Rev:** Eight-fold arms, crown above divides date **Note:** Dav. #6059.

Date	Mintage	VG	F	VF	XF	Unc
1681 Rare	—	—	—	—	—	—

KM# A7 2 THALER
28.6000 g., 0.8330 Silver 0.7659 oz. ASW **Note:** Similar to 1 Thaler, KM#6.1. Prev. KM#7. Dav. 6041.

Date	Mintage	VG	F	VF	XF	Unc
1609 Rare	—	—	—	—	—	—

KM# 27 2 THALER
Silver **Note:** Klippe. Similar to 1 Thaler, KM#24. Dav. #6044.

Date	Mintage	VG	F	VF	XF	Unc
1622 Rare	—	—	—	—	—	—

KM# 52.1 2 THALER
Silver **Note:** Similar to 1 Thaler, KM#51.1. Dav. #6051.

Date	Mintage	VG	F	VF	XF	Unc
1626 Rare	—	—	—	—	—	—

KM# 52.2 2 THALER
Silver **Obv. Legend:** MAR • Z • BAD. V. H. L. Z. S. G. Z. SP. **Note:** Dav. #6054.

Date	Mintage	VG	F	VF	XF	Unc
1628 I Rare	—	—	—	—	—	—

TRADE COINAGE

KM# A8 GOLDGULDEN
3.5000 g., 0.9860 Gold 0.1109 oz. AGW **Obv:** Bust of Georg Friedrich right divides date in inner circle **Rev:** Ornate cross with arms in angles, Baden shield at center in inner circle

Date	Mintage	VG	F	VF	XF	Unc
1609 Rare	—	—	—	—	—	—

KM# 28 DUCAT
3.5000 g., 0.9860 Gold 0.1109 oz. AGW **Obv:** Georg Friedrich standing right divides date in inner circle **Rev:** Square arms within inner circle

Date	Mintage	VG	F	VF	XF	Unc
1622	—	—	—	—	—	—

KM# A11 2 DUCAT
7.0000 g., 0.9860 Gold 0.2219 oz. AGW **Obv:** Large bust of Georg Friedrich right divides date in inner circle **Rev:** Ornate cross with arms in angles, Baden shield in center of inner circle

Date	Mintage	VG	F	VF	XF	Unc
1610 Rare	—	—	—	—	—	—

KM# B12 6 DUCAT
21.0000 g., 0.9860 Gold 0.6657 oz. AGW **Obv:** 1/2-length bust Georg Friedrich right divides date in inner circle **Note:** Struck with 1 Thaler dies, KM#6.2.

Date	Mintage	VG	F	VF	XF	Unc
1610 Rare	—	—	—	—	—	—

LOCAL COINAGE

KM# B10 RAPPEN

Silver **Issuer:** Hachberg, Struck on Swiss Standard
Note: Uniface. Plain arms in circle within circle of pellets. Varieties exist. Prev. KM#10.

Date	Mintage	VG	F	VF	XF	Unc
ND	—	—	—	—	—	—

KM# A6 2 PFENNIG (Kipper)

Silver **Obv:** Arms in circle of pellets, value and date in legend **Rev:** Arms of Usenberg (wings), around H. LANDSWEHRUNG **Note:** Prev. KM#6.

Date	Mintage	VG	F	VF	XF	Unc
1622	—	50.00	100	200	350	550

KM# B11 2 PFENNIG (Kipper)

Silver **Obv:** Value around arms within wreath **Note:** Prev. KM#11.

Date	Mintage	VG	F	VF	XF	Unc
ND	—	—	—	—	—	—

KM# C12 2 PFENNIG (Kipper)

Silver **Obv:** Arms in circle of dots, value around **Rev:** Three small shields, one above two **Rev. Legend:** H. LANDSWEHRVNG **Note:** Prev. KM#12.

Date	Mintage	VG	F	VF	XF	Unc
ND	—	15.00	25.00	50.00	100	—

KM# B13 2 PFENNIG (Kipper)

Silver **Rev:** Arms of Usenberg **Rev. Legend:** H. LANDSWEHRUNG **Note:** Prev. KM#13.

Date	Mintage	VG	F	VF	XF	Unc
ND	—	15.00	25.00	50.00	100	—

KM# B14 4 PFENNIG

Silver **Obv:** Arms in circle of dots, value IIII around **Rev:** Three small shields, one above two **Rev. Legend:** H. LANDSWEHRVNG **Note:** Prev. KM#14.

Date	Mintage	VG	F	VF	XF	Unc
ND	—	30.00	60.00	100	150	—

KM# B15 5 PFENNIG

Silver **Obv:** Arms in notched shield between two rosettes **Rev:** Usenberg arms, around V. PF. HACB. L. WEHRUNG **Note:** Prev. KM#15.

Date	Mintage	VG	F	VF	XF	Unc
ND	—	—	—	—	—	—

KM# B7 8 PFENNIG (Kipper)

Silver **Obv:** Arms, date **Rev:** Usenberg arms **Rev. Legend:** HACHBERGENSIS **Note:** Prev. KM#7.

Date	Mintage	VG	F	VF	XF	Unc
1622	—	—	—	—	—	—
1623	—	—	—	—	—	—

KM# B16 9 KREUZER (1/12 Thaler)

Silver **Obv:** Arms, titles of Friedrich VII **Rev:** Usenberg arms, IX above, 1/12 in oval cartouche below **Note:** Prev. KM#16.

Date	Mintage	VG	F	VF	XF	Unc
ND	—	—	—	—	—	—

KM# B17 12 KREUZER (3 Batzen)

Silver **Obv:** Crown with horns above mantles arms, titles of Friedrich VII **Rev:** Three shields, one above two, crown above, value XII in legend at top **Note:** Prev. KM#17.

Date	Mintage	VG	F	VF	XF	Unc
ND	—	100	200	350	650	—

KM# B8 12 KREUZER (3 Batzen)

Silver **Obv:** Bust of Groeg Friedrich right **Rev:** Four-fold arms (Baden and Usenberg), value 12 above, date in legend **Note:** Prev. KM#8.

Date	Mintage	VG	F	VF	XF	Unc
1622	—	—	—	—	—	—

KM# B5 24 KREUZER (6 Batzen)

Silver **Obv:** Bust of Georg Friedrich right **Rev:** Four-fold arms(Baden and Usenberg), value 24 above, date in legend **Note:** Varieties exist. Prev. KM#5.

Date	Mintage	VG	F	VF	XF	Unc
16Z1	—	250	500	900	1,350	—
16ZZ	—	250	500	900	1,350	—

KM# B18 15 BATZEN (60 Kreuzer)

Silver **Obv:** Bust of Friedrich VII right **Rev:** Value in four lines **Note:** Prev. KM#18.

Date	Mintage	VG	F	VF	XF	Unc
ND	—	—	—	—	—	—

KM# B18a 15 BATZEN (60 Kreuzer)

Lead **Note:** Prev. KM#18a.

Date	Mintage	VG	F	VF	XF	Unc
ND	—	—	—	—	—	—

KM# B19 15 BATZEN (60 Kreuzer)

Silver **Rev:** Three shields, one above two, crown above, value XV BAZEN in legend at top **Note:** Prev. KM#19.

Date	Mintage	VG	F	VF	XF	Unc
ND	—	—	—	—	—	—

KM# B20 16 BATZEN

Silver **Obv:** Bust of Friedrich VII right **Rev:** Value XVI. BZ. **Note:** Prev. KM#20.

Date	Mintage	VG	F	VF	XF	Unc
ND	—	—	—	—	—	—

KM# A21 GULDEN

Silver **Obv:** Crowned and supported arms, titles of Friedrich VII **Rev:** Three shields, one above two, value LX. K. above **Note:** Prev. KM#21.

Date	Mintage	VG	F	VF	XF	Unc
ND	—	—	—	—	—	—

PATTERNS

Including off metal strikes

KM#	Date	Mintage	Identification	Mkt Val
Pn1	1624	—	Thaler. Lead. KM#6.	—
PnA2	1610	—	2 Ducat. Silver. KM#11.	—
Pn2	1627	—	Thaler. Lead. KM#6.	—
PnA3	1622	—	Thaler. Lead. KM#24.	—

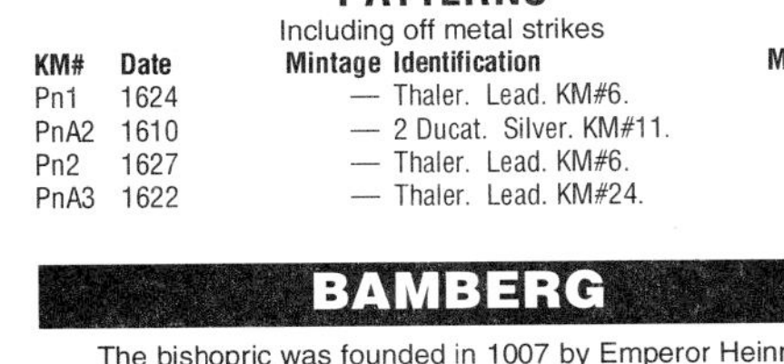

BAMBERG

The bishopric was founded in 1007 by Emperor Heinrich II (1002-24) in the town of Bamberg, 32 miles (53 kilometers) north-northwest of Nürnberg. The bishops began issuing their own coinage almost from the beginning and were given the rank of Prince of the Empire by the emperor about 1250. The bishopric was secularized in 1801 and was incorporated into Bavaria the following year.

RULERS

Johann Philipp von Gebsattel, 1599-1609
Johann Gottfried von Aschhausen, 1609-1622
Johann Georg II, Fuchs von Dornheim, 1622-1633
Franz, Graf von Hatzfeld, 1633-1642
Melchior Otto, Voigt von Salzburg, 1642-1653
Philipp Valentin, Voigt von Rieneck, 1653-1672
Peter Philipp von Dernbach, 1672-1683
Marquard Sebastian, Schenk von Staufenberg, 1683-1693
Lothar Franz, Freiherr von Schönborn, 1693-1729

ARMS: Lion rampant left over which superimposed a diagonal band from upper left to lower right.

MINT MARKS

B - Bamberg Mint
F - Fürth Mint

MINT OFFICIALS' INITIALS

Initials	Date	Name
A		
AL	1678-83	Adam Longerich in Koblenz
CB	1683-96	Conrad Bechtmann in Aschaffenburg
CS	1622-54	Conrad Stutz, die-cutter in Fürth and mintmaster of the Franconian Circle
GFN or +	1682-1724	Georg Friedrich Nurnberger, die-cutter and mintmaster in Nurnberg
MF	1681-82	Jakob Merkel, die-cutter in Bamberg
VBW	1685, 1695-1729	Ulrich Buckhard Wildering in Mainz

BISHOPRIC

REGULAR COINAGE

KM# 11 HELLER

Copper **Note:** Uniface. Arms of Bamberg divide date, value I above.

Date	Mintage	Good	VG	F	VF	XF
1622	—	13.00	27.00	45.00	65.00	—

KM# 12 2 HELLER

Copper **Note:** Uniface. Arms of Bamberg divide date, value II above.

Date	Mintage	Good	VG	F	VF	XF
1622	—	13.00	27.00	45.00	65.00	—

KM# 13 3 HELLER

Copper **Obv:** Arms with date divided by B above **Rev:** Value III in wreath

Date	Mintage	Good	VG	F	VF	XF
1622 B	—	13.00	27.00	45.00	66.00	—
ND B	—	13.00	27.00	45.00	66.00	—

KM# 25 3 HELLER

Billon **Note:** Uniface. Two shields with arms of Bamberg and Dornheim divide date, value III above.

Date	Mintage	Good	VG	F	VF	XF
1629 F	—	16.00	24.00	45.00	70.00	—

KM# 34 3 HELLER

Copper **Obv:** Arms with date divided by B above **Rev:** Value III in wreath

Date	Mintage	Good	VG	F	VF	XF
1649	—	16.00	24.00	45.00	70.00	—

KM# 35 3 HELLER

Billon **Obv:** Two shields with arms, crown above divides date, value III h1 below **Rev:** Value III h1

Date	Mintage	Good	VG	F	VF	XF
1649	—	16.00	24.00	45.00	70.00	—

KM# 53 3 HELLER

Billon **Note:** Uniface. Crowned triple arms in trefoil, date above.

Date	Mintage	Good	VG	F	VF	XF
1676	—	13.00	20.00	40.00	65.00	120
1677	—	13.00	20.00	40.00	65.00	120
1681	—	13.00	20.00	40.00	65.00	120
1683	—	13.00	20.00	40.00	65.00	120
ND	—	13.00	20.00	40.00	65.00	120

KM# 70 3 HELLER

Copper **Obv:** Crowned double arms, date **Rev:** Value III h1. in wreath

Date	Mintage	VG	F	VF	XF	Unc
1683 AL	—	16.00	30.00	45.00	90.00	—
1685 ++	—	16.00	30.00	45.00	90.00	—
1686 ++	—	16.00	30.00	45.00	90.00	—
1687 ++	—	16.00	30.00	45.00	90.00	—
1688 ++	—	16.00	30.00	45.00	90.00	—
1689 ++	—	16.00	30.00	45.00	90.00	—
1690 ++	—	16.00	30.00	45.00	90.00	—

KM# 10 PFENNIG

Silver **Note:** Uniface. Two shields with arms of Bamberg and Dornheim

Date	Mintage	VG	F	VF	XF	Unc
1620 F	—	20.00	40.00	65.00	100	—
1627 F	—	20.00	40.00	65.00	100	—
1629 F	—	20.00	40.00	65.00	100	—

KM# 19 PFENNIG

Silver **Note:** Hohlpfennig. Bamberg arms divide date.

Date	Mintage	VG	F	VF	XF	Unc
1624	—	13.00	27.00	45.00	75.00	—

KM# 18 PFENNIG

Silver **Note:** Arms with date above.

Date	Mintage	VG	F	VF	XF	Unc
1624	—	13.00	27.00	45.00	75.00	—

KM# 36 PFENNIG

Silver **Note:** Arms divide date.

Date	Mintage	VG	F	VF	XF	Unc
1649	—	13.00	27.00	45.00	75.00	—

KM# 37 PFENNIG

Silver **Note:** Two shields with arms, crown divides date above, value 1 below.

Date	Mintage	VG	F	VF	XF	Unc
1649	—	13.00	27.00	45.00	75.00	—

KM# 56 PFENNIG

Silver **Note:** Crowned triple arms in trefoil, date above, value 1 below.

Date	Mintage	VG	F	VF	XF	Unc
1677	—	13.00	27.00	45.00	75.00	—

KM# 57 PFENNIG

Silver **Note:** Without date or value.

Date	Mintage	VG	F	VF	XF	Unc
ND	—	13.00	27.00	45.00	75.00	—

KM# 77 PFENNIG

Silver **Note:** Crowned double arms of Bamberg and Staufenberg, date above.

Date	Mintage	VG	F	VF	XF	Unc
1685	—	10.00	20.00	35.00	55.00	—
1687	—	10.00	20.00	35.00	55.00	—
1690	—	10.00	20.00	35.00	55.00	—
ND	—	10.00	20.00	35.00	55.00	—

KM# 97 PFENNIG

Silver **Ruler:** Luther Franz **Obv:** Three shields of arms, lower one divides date, value 1 above **Note:** Uniface.

Date	Mintage	VG	F	VF	XF	Unc
1700	—	7.00	15.00	30.00	48.00	—

KM# 14 KREUZER

Copper

Date	Mintage	Good	VG	F	VF	XF
1622 B	—	13.00	27.00	45.00	75.00	—

KM# 22 2 KREUZER (1/2 Batzen)

Silver **Obv:** Crowned arms, date above **Rev:** Bust of St. Heinrich holding scepter and imperial orb with value 2

Date	Mintage	Good	VG	F	VF	XF
1627 F	—	13.00	27.00	45.00	75.00	—
1629 F	—	13.00	27.00	45.00	75.00	—
ND	—	13.00	27.00	45.00	75.00	—

KM# 39 2 KREUZER (1/2 Batzen)

Silver **Obv:** Crowned double arms, date below

Date	Mintage	Good	VG	F	VF	XF
1649	—	13.00	27.00	45.00	75.00	—

KM# 51 2 KREUZER (1/2 Batzen)

Silver **Obv:** Crowned triple arms in trefoil **Rev:** Bust of Heinrich holding orb with 2, date divided to either side

Date	Mintage	VG	F	VF	XF	Unc
1673	—	13.00	27.00	45.00	75.00	—
1676	—	13.00	27.00	45.00	75.00	—
1677	—	13.00	27.00	45.00	75.00	—
1678	—	13.00	27.00	45.00	75.00	—
1683	—	13.00	27.00	45.00	75.00	—

KM# 52 2 KREUZER (1/2 Batzen)

Silver **Obv:** Triple arms with rose in center

Date	Mintage	VG	F	VF	XF	Unc
ND	—	13.00	27.00	45.00	75.00	—

KM# 88 2 KREUZER (1/2 Batzen)

Silver **Note:** Similar to 4 Kreuzer, KM#85 but with value 2.

Date	Mintage	VG	F	VF	XF	Unc
1696 GFN	756,000	13.00	27.00	45.00	75.00	—

KM# 42 3 KREUZER

Silver **Subject:** Death of Melchior Otto **Obv:** Crowned four-fold arms **Rev:** Seven-line inscription with date, imperial orb with 3

Date	Mintage	VG	F	VF	XF	Unc
1653	2,440	—	120	200	350	—

KM# 47 3 KREUZER

Silver **Subject:** Death of Philipp Valentin

Date	Mintage	VG	F	VF	XF	Unc
1672	4,000	—	100	185	300	—

KM# 81 3 KREUZER

Silver **Subject:** Death of Marquard Sebastian **Obv:** Crowned double arms, supported by two lions, between branches **Rev:** Eight-line inscription with date, imperial orb with 3 below

Date	Mintage	VG	F	VF	XF	Unc
1693 GFN	—	—	100	175	285	—

KM# 23 4 KREUZER (Batzen)

Silver **Obv:** Crowned arms, date above **Rev:** Bust of St. Heinrich holding scepter and imperial orb with value 4

Date	Mintage	VG	F	VF	XF	Unc
1627 F	—	20.00	40.00	60.00	120	—
1628 F	—	20.00	40.00	60.00	120	—
1629 F	—	20.00	40.00	60.00	120	—
1630 F	—	20.00	40.00	60.00	120	—

KM# 31 4 KREUZER (Batzen)

Silver **Obv:** Crowned triple arms in form of trefoil, date below **Rev:** Bust of St. Heinrich holding imperial orb with value 4

Date	Mintage	VG	F	VF	XF	Unc
1635	—	20.00	40.00	60.00	120	250

KM# 40 4 KREUZER (Batzen)

Silver **Obv:** Crowned double arms, date above

Date	Mintage	VG	F	VF	XF	Unc
1649	—	20.00	40.00	60.00	120	—

KM# 59 4 KREUZER (Batzen)

Silver **Obv:** Crowned tirple arms in trefoil **Rev:** Date divided to either side

Date	Mintage	VG	F	VF	XF	Unc
1680	—	20.00	40.00	60.00	120	—

KM# 60 4 KREUZER (Batzen)

Silver **Obv:** Crowned four-fold arms, central shield of Dernbach arms **Note:** Varieties exist.

Date	Mintage	VG	F	VF	XF	Unc
1680	—	45.00	90.00	150	250	—

KM# 85 4 KREUZER (Batzen)

Silver **Ruler:** Luther Franz **Rev:** St. Heinrich

Date	Mintage	VG	F	VF	XF	Unc
1696 GFN	891,000	16.00	35.00	60.00	120	—
1698 GFN	1,382,000	16.00	35.00	60.00	120	—
1700 GFN	1,093,000	16.00	35.00	60.00	120	—

KM# 61 6 KREUZER

Silver **Obv:** Four-fold arms with central shield of Dernbach arms divide date, value VI:K: above **Rev:** Bust of bishop

Date	Mintage	VG	F	VF	XF	Unc
1680 Rare	—	—	—	—	—	—

KM# 15 GROSCHEN (3 Kreuzer)

Silver **Subject:** Death of Johann Gottfried **Obv:** Crowned and helmeted arms **Rev:** Inscription with date above imperial orb with B

Date	Mintage	VG	F	VF	XF	Unc
1622	—	—	—	—	—	—

KM# 29 GROSCHEN (3 Kreuzer)

Silver **Subject:** Death of Franz von Hatzfeld **Obv:** Crowned and helmeted four-fold arms with central shield of Hatzfeld **Rev:** Six-line inscription with dates, small imperial orb below, B at bottom

Date	Mintage	VG	F	VF	XF	Unc
1642	—	—	—	—	—	—

KM# 20 1/84 THALER (3 Pfennig)

Silver **Obv:** Two shields with arms of Bamberg and Dornheim, date above **Rev:** Imperial orb with 84

Date	Mintage	Good	VG	F	VF	XF
1624	—	12.00	20.00	35.00	55.00	100

KM# 30 1/84 THALER (3 Pfennig)

Silver **Obv:** Three arms in form of trefoil, date below

Date	Mintage	Good	VG	F	VF	XF
1635	—	12.00	20.00	35.00	55.00	—

KM# 38 1/84 THALER (3 Pfennig)

Silver **Obv:** Crowned double arms, date below

Date	Mintage	Good	VG	F	VF	XF
1649	—	10.00	16.00	27.00	45.00	—
1652	—	10.00	16.00	27.00	45.00	—

KM# 54 1/84 THALER (3 Pfennig)

Silver **Obv:** Triple arms **Rev:** Imperial orb with 84 divides date

Date	Mintage	Good	VG	F	VF	XF
1676	—	10.00	16.00	27.00	45.00	—
1678	—	10.00	16.00	27.00	45.00	—
1680	—	10.00	16.00	27.00	45.00	—
1681	—	10.00	16.00	27.00	45.00	—
1682	—	10.00	16.00	27.00	45.00	—

KM# 55 1/84 THALER (3 Pfennig)

Silver **Obv:** Triple arms, F in center, date below **Rev:** Imperial orb with 84

Date	Mintage	Good	VG	F	VF	XF
1676 F	—	10.00	16.00	27.00	45.00	—
1677 F	—	10.00	16.00	27.00	45.00	—
1682 F	—	10.00	16.00	27.00	45.00	—
ND F	—	10.00	16.00	27.00	45.00	—

KM# 58 1/84 THALER (3 Pfennig)

Silver **Obv:** Triple arms in trefoil divide date

Date	Mintage	Good	VG	F	VF	XF
1679	—	10.00	16.00	27.00	45.00	—

KM# 75 1/84 THALER (3 Pfennig)

Silver **Obv:** Crowned double arms with A between **Rev:** Imperial orb with 84 divides date

Date	Mintage	VG	F	VF	XF	Unc
1684 A	—	10.00	16.00	27.00	45.00	—
1685 A	—	10.00	16.00	27.00	45.00	—
1686 A	—	10.00	16.00	27.00	45.00	—
1687 A	—	10.00	16.00	27.00	45.00	—
1690 A	—	10.00	16.00	27.00	45.00	—
1691 A	—	10.00	16.00	27.00	45.00	—

KM# 5 1/48 THALER (1/2 Groschen)

Silver **Obv:** Two shields with arms of Bamberg and Gebsattel (horsehead), crown above **Rev:** Imperial orb with 48 in cartouche divides date

Date	Mintage	VG	F	VF	XF	Unc
1600 Rare	—	—	—	—	—	—

KM# 69 1/24 THALER (Groschen)

Silver **Obv:** Triple arms in trefoil **Rev:** Imperial orb with 24, date divided above

Date	Mintage	VG	F	VF	XF	Unc
1682 MF	—	—	—	—	—	—

KM# 72 1/24 THALER (Groschen)

Silver **Subject:** Death of Peter Philipp **Obv:** Crowned four-fold arms, central shield of Dernbach arms

Date	Mintage	VG	F	VF	XF	Unc
1683	—	35.00	85.00	175	300	—

KM# 71 1/24 THALER (Groschen)

Silver **Obv:** Crowned triple arms **Note:** Varieties exist.

Date	Mintage	VG	F	VF	XF	Unc
1683 AL	—	12.00	20.00	40.00	80.00	—
1683 MF	—	12.00	20.00	40.00	80.00	—

KM# 76 1/24 THALER (Groschen)

Silver **Obv:** Crowned double arms **Rev:** Imperial orb with 24 divides date

Date	Mintage	VG	F	VF	XF	Unc
1684 AL	—	13.00	27.00	55.00	90.00	—
1684 VBW	—	13.00	27.00	55.00	90.00	—
1685 VBW	—	13.00	27.00	55.00	90.00	—
1685	—	13.00	27.00	55.00	90.00	—

KM# 62 1/4 THALER

Silver **Obv:** Bust of bishop **Rev:** Crowned four-fold arms, central shield of Dernbach arms, value 1/4 below divides date

Date	Mintage	VG	F	VF	XF	Unc
1680 Rare	—	—	—	—	—	—

KM# 63 1/4 THALER

Silver **Obv:** Bust right, value 1/2 below **Rev:** Crowned four-fold arms, central shield of Dernbach arms, date above

Date	Mintage	VG	F	VF	XF	Unc
1680 Rare	—	—	—	—	—	—

KM# 66 1/4 THALER

Silver **Rev:** Date below arms

Date	Mintage	VG	F	VF	XF	Unc
1681 Rare	—	—	—	—	—	—

KM# 86 1/4 THALER

Silver **Obv:** Bust right **Rev:** Crowned and helmeted four-fold arms, date below

Date	Mintage	VG	F	VF	XF	Unc
1694 GFN	640	—	—	—	—	—

KM# 8 THALER

Silver **Obv:** Facing bust, four arms in legend with IOANNES. CHRISTOPH.NEVSTETTER.D.STVRMER. **Rev:** Crown in clouds above figure of man, PRAEPOS. ET. SEN. BAMB. CVSTOS. MOGVNT. CAN. HERB. P. S. C. M. A. CO. **Note:** Issued by Johann Christoph Neustaedter, Provost of the Cathedral, 1610-38.

Date	Mintage	VG	F	VF	XF	Unc
ND(ca.1610) Rare	—	—	—	—	—	—

KM# 26 THALER

Silver **Obv:** Crowned four-fold arms with arms of Hatzfeld in center **Rev:** Crowned imperial eagle with orb on breast, titles of Ferdinand II **Note:** Dav. #5053.

Date	Mintage	VG	F	VF	XF	Unc
ND(1632) Rare	—	—	—	—	—	—

KM# 41 THALER

Silver **Note:** Dav. #5054.

Date	Mintage	VG	F	VF	XF	Unc
1649	—	850	1,750	3,500	6,500	—

KM# 45 THALER

Silver **Note:** Dav. #5055.

Date	Mintage	VG	F	VF	XF	Unc
1657	—	1,200	2,250	4,500	7,250	—

KM# 64.1 THALER

Silver **Obv:** Bust right **Obv. Legend:** PETRVS... **Rev:** Crowned four-fold arms, central shield of Dernbach arms, all in baroque frame, date divided to lower left and right **Note:** Dav. #5056.

Date	Mintage	VG	F	VF	XF	Unc
1680	—	2,500	4,500	7,000	10,000	—

KM# 65 THALER

Silver **Rev:** Date divided at top **Note:** Dav. #5058.

Date	Mintage	VG	F	VF	XF	Unc
1680	—	2,500	4,500	7,000	10,000	—

KM# 64.2 THALER

Silver **Obv. Legend:** PETR... **Note:** Varieties exist. Dav. #5057.

Date	Mintage	VG	F	VF	XF	Unc
1680	—	2,500	4,500	7,000	10,000	—

KM# 67.1 THALER

Silver **Rev:** Smaller arms between two branches, date at bottom **Note:** Dav. #5059.

Date	Mintage	VG	F	VF	XF	Unc
1681	—	2,500	4,500	7,000	10,000	—

KM# 67.2 THALER

Silver **Rev:** Crowned arms divide date **Note:** Dav. #5060.

Date	Mintage	VG	F	VF	XF	Unc
1681	—	2,500	4,500	7,000	10,000	—

KM# 68 THALER

Silver **Rev:** Four-fold arms, central shield of Dernbach arms, supported by two lions, all between two branches **Note:** Dav. #5061.

Date	Mintage	VG	F	VF	XF	Unc
ND	—	—	—	—	—	—

KM# 78 THALER

Silver **Rev:** Crowned four-fold arms in baroque frame, date above **Note:** Dav. #5062.

Date	Mintage	VG	F	VF	XF	Unc
1687	—	2,000	3,500	6,000	9,000	—

KM# 80 THALER

Silver **Obv:** Sts. Heinrich and Kunigunda **Rev:** Madonna **Note:** Dav. #5063.

Date	Mintage	VG	F	VF	XF	Unc
1690 GFN	—	200	350	600	1,000	—
1691	—	200	350	600	1,000	—

KM# 82 THALER

Silver **Rev:** Emperor Heinrich II **Note:** Sede Vacante. Dav. #5064.

Date	Mintage	VG	F	VF	XF	Unc
1693 GFN	—	250	500	1,250	2,500	—

KM# 87 THALER

Silver **Ruler:** Luther Franz **Obv:** Bust right **Obv. Legend:** LOTHAR•FRANC•D.G.•EPIS-BAMB•S•R•I•PRINC• **Rev:** Crowned and helmeted four-fold arms, date below **Note:** Dav. #5065.

Date	Mintage	VG	F	VF	XF	Unc
1694 GFN	13,000	175	350	650	1,000	—

KM# 89 THALER
Silver **Note:** Dav. #5066.

Date	Mintage	VG	F	VF	XF	Unc
1696 GFN	53,000	175	350	650	1,000	4,000
1696 CB	Inc. above	175	350	650	1,000	—

KM# 95 THALER
Silver **Obv:** Oval arms, angel's head and wings below **Note:** Dav. #5067.

Date	Mintage	VG	F	VF	XF	Unc
1697 GFN	Inc. above	240	425	725	1,200	—

KM# 27 2 THALER
Silver **Obv:** Crowned four-fold arms with arms of Hatzfeld in center **Rev:** Crowned imperial eagle with orb on breast, titles of Ferdinand II **Note:** Dav. #5052.

Date	Mintage	VG	F	VF	XF	Unc
ND(1632) Rare	—	—	—	—	—	—

KM# 96 3 THALER
Silver **Note:** Similar to 1 Thaler, KM#89, but oval arms, angel head, wings below arms. Dav. #A5057.

Date	Mintage	VG	F	VF	XF	Unc
1697 GFN Rare	—	—	—	—	—	—

TRADE COINAGE

KM# 17 GOLDGULDEN
3.5000 g., 0.9860 Gold 0.1109 oz. AGW **Subject:** Death of the Bishop **Obv:** Crowned arms **Rev:** Inscription

Date	Mintage	VG	F	VF	XF	Unc
1622	—	—	—	—	—	—

KM# 21 GOLDGULDEN
3.5000 g., 0.9860 Gold 0.1109 oz. AGW **Obv:** Bust of Johann Gerorg facing 1/2 right in inner circle **Rev:** Two saints holding church, two shields of arms below

Date	Mintage	VG	F	VF	XF	Unc
1624	—	2,000	4,000	7,000	15,000	—
1628	—	750	1,500	2,750	4,500	—

KM# 6 DUCAT
3.5000 g., 0.9860 Gold 0.1109 oz. AGW **Obv:** Two saints holding church, arms below in inner circle **Rev:** Two shields of arms below crown in inner circle

Date	Mintage	VG	F	VF	XF	Unc
1601	—	1,250	2,500	5,500	9,000	—
1602	—	1,250	2,500	5,500	9,000	—

KM# 24 DUCAT
3.5000 g., 0.9860 Gold 0.1109 oz. AGW **Obv:** Bust of Johann Georg facing 1/2 right in inner circle **Rev:** Two saints holding church, two shields of arms below

Date	Mintage	VG	F	VF	XF	Unc
1628 CS	—	1,150	2,400	5,000	8,000	—
1631 CS	—	1,150	2,400	5,000	8,000	—

KM# 32 DUCAT
3.5000 g., 0.9860 Gold 0.1109 oz. AGW

Date	Mintage	VG	F	VF	XF	Unc
1635	—	300	650	1,100	1,750	—
1637	—	300	650	1,100	1,750	—
1638	—	300	650	1,100	1,750	—
1640	—	300	650	1,100	1,750	—

KM# 33 DUCAT
3.5000 g., 0.9860 Gold 0.1109 oz. AGW **Obv:** Bust of Melchoir Otto right **Rev:** Crowned arms divide date

Date	Mintage	VG	F	VF	XF	Unc
1647	—	800	1,800	3,000	5,000	—

KM# 46 DUCAT
3.5000 g., 0.9860 Gold 0.1109 oz. AGW **Obv:** Bust of Philip Valentin right **Rev:** Two shields of arms below crown, date below

Date	Mintage	VG	F	VF	XF	Unc
1657	—	700	1,650	2,750	4,750	—

KM# 79 DUCAT
3.5000 g., 0.9860 Gold 0.1109 oz. AGW **Obv:** Bust right **Rev:** Crowned four-fold arms in baroque frame, date above

Date	Mintage	VG	F	VF	XF	Unc
1687 Rare	—	—	—	—	—	—

KM# 90 DUCAT
3.5000 g., 0.9860 Gold 0.1109 oz. AGW **Subject:** Peace of Ryswick **Obv:** Crowned and mantled six-fold arms, date below **Rev:** Altar divides EIN-DVC

Date	Mintage	VG	F	VF	XF	Unc
1696 GFN	—	—	—	—	—	—

KM# 91 DUCAT
3.5000 g., 0.9860 Gold 0.1109 oz. AGW **Rev:** Minerva standing with olive branch and shield, FAVENTE NVMINE

Date	Mintage	VG	F	VF	XF	Unc
1696 GFN	—	—	—	—	—	—

KM# 92 DUCAT
3.5000 g., 0.9860 Gold 0.1109 oz. AGW **Rev:** Concordia seated female left, CONCORDIA below

Date	Mintage	VG	F	VF	XF	Unc
ND(1696) GFN	—	—	450	750	1,600	—

KM# 7 2 DUCAT
7.0000 g., 0.9860 Gold 0.2219 oz. AGW **Obv:** Two saints holding church, arms below in inner circle **Rev:** Two shield of arms below crown in inner circle

Date	Mintage	VG	F	VF	XF	Unc
1601 Rare	—	—	—	—	—	—

KM# 93 2 DUCAT
7.0000 g., 0.9860 Gold 0.2219 oz. AGW **Obv:** Crowned and mantled six-fold arms, date below **Rev:** Altar divides Ein-Duc **Note:** Struck with Ducat dies but double in weight.

Date	Mintage	VG	F	VF	XF	Unc
1696 Rare	838	—	—	—	—	—

KM# 94 2 DUCAT
7.0000 g., 0.9860 Gold 0.2219 oz. AGW **Rev:** Minerva standing with olive branch and shield, FAVENTE NVMINE.

Date	Mintage	VG	F	VF	XF	Unc
1696 Rare	1,441	—	—	—	—	—

KM# A47 5 DUCAT
17.5000 g., 0.9860 Gold 0.5547 oz. AGW **Obv:** Bust of Philipp Valentin right **Rev:** Two ornate shields below crown

Date	Mintage	F	VF	XF	Unc	BU
1657 Rare	—	—	—	—	—	—

KM# A97 5 DUCAT
17.5000 g., 0.9860 Gold 0.5547 oz. AGW **Obv:** Bust of Lothar Franz right **Rev:** Arms

Date	Mintage	F	VF	XF	Unc	BU
1697 Rare	—	—	—	—	—	—

KM# A80 10 DUCAT
35.0000 g., 0.9860 Gold 1.1095 oz. AGW **Note:** Struck with 1 Thaler dies, KM#78.

Date	Mintage	F	VF	XF	Unc	BU
1687 Rare	—	—	—	—	—	—

KM# B97 10 DUCAT
35.0000 g., 0.9860 Gold 1.1095 oz. AGW **Note:** Struck with 1 Thaler dies, KM#95.

Date	Mintage	F	VF	XF	Unc	BU
1697 GFN Rare	—	—	—	—	—	—

PATTERNS

Including off metal strikes

KM#	Date	Mintage	Identification	Mkt Val
Pn2	1698 GFN	—	4 Kreuzers. Copper. KM#85	—
Pn3	1700 GFN	—	4 Kreuzers. Copper. KM#85	—

BARBY

A small lordship located near the junction of the Elbe and Saale rivers, about midway between Magdeburg and Dessau, founded in the early 13th century. The lord of Barby was a vassal of Saxony and was raised to the rank of count in 1497. The countship was divided in 1565, but only the main line of Barby and its successor in 1617, Barby-Mühlingen, issued any coinage. Barby became extinct in 1659 and its lands passed to Anhalt and Saxe-Weissenfels.

RULERS

Wolfgang II, 1565-1615
Wolfgang Friedrich, 1615-1617
Albrecht Friedrich, 1617-1641
August Ludwig, 1641-1659

MINT OFFICIALS' INITIALS

Initials	Date	Name
HM	1611-15	Heinrich Meyer

LORDSHIP

REGULAR COINAGE

KM# 19 FLITTER
Copper **Note:** Uniface. Crowned arms (rose) divide date. Kipper Flitter.

Date	Mintage	Good	VG	F	VF	XF
(16)21	—	10.00	20.00	35.00	55.00	—

KM# 21 3 FLITTER
Copper **Ruler:** Albrecht Friedrich **Obv:** Crowned four-fold arms **Rev:** III/FLITT/REN/date

Date	Mintage	Good	VG	F	VF	XF
1621	—	30.00	65.00	125	225	—

KM# 20 3 FLITTER
Copper **Ruler:** Albrecht Friedrich **Obv:** Crowned four-fold arms **Rev:** Value 3, date in ornamented rhombus **Note:** Kipper 3 Flitter.

Date	Mintage	Good	VG	F	VF	XF
1621	—	25.00	50.00	100	200	—

KM# 5 1/24 THALER (Groschen)
Silver **Ruler:** Wolfgang II **Obv:** Four-fold arms **Rev:** Imperial orb with 24, cross on top divides date, titles of Rudolf II

Date	Mintage	VG	F	VF	XF	Unc
1611	—	30.00	50.00	90.00	160	—
1612	—	30.00	50.00	90.00	160	—

KM# 6 1/24 THALER (Groschen)
Silver **Ruler:** Wolfgang II **Rev:** Titles of Matthias

Date	Mintage	VG	F	VF	XF	Unc
1612	—	25.00	50.00	100	175	—
1613 HM	—	25.00	50.00	100	175	—
1614 HM	—	25.00	50.00	100	175	—
1615 HM	—	25.00	50.00	100	175	—
1616	—	25.00	50.00	100	175	—
1617	—	25.00	50.00	100	175	—

KM# 15 1/24 THALER (Groschen)
Silver **Ruler:** Albrecht Friedrich **Obv:** Crowned four-fold arms **Rev:** Imperial orb with 24, date divided at top, titles of Matthias

Date	Mintage	VG	F	VF	XF	Unc
1617	—	25.00	40.00	80.00	130	—
1618	—	25.00	40.00	80.00	130	—
1619	—	25.00	40.00	80.00	130	—

KM# 16 1/24 THALER (Groschen)
Silver **Obv:** Crowned four-fold arms pointed at top **Rev:** Titles of Ferdinand II

Date	Mintage	VG	F	VF	XF	Unc
ND	—	15.00	25.00	45.00	85.00	—

KM# 17 2 SCHILLING (1/16 Thaler)
Silver **Ruler:** Albrecht Friedrich **Obv:** Crowned four-fold arms in ornately-shaped shield, titles of Albrecht Friedrich **Rev:** DS monogram

Date	Mintage	VG	F	VF	XF	Unc
ND(1617)	—	—	—	—	—	—

KM# 18 2 SCHILLING (1/16 Thaler)
Silver **Obv:** Round arms **Note:** Kipper 2 Schilling.

Date	Mintage	VG	F	VF	XF	Unc
ND(1617)	—	—	—	—	—	—

KM# 10 THALER
Silver **Obv:** Helmeted four-fold arms, date divided 1-6 above and 1-5 below **Rev:** Half-length bust right, legend divided by four small shields **Note:** Dav. #6060.

Date	Mintage	VG	F	VF	XF	Unc
1615 Rare	—	—	—	—	—	—

KM# 11 THALER
Silver **Subject:** Death of Wolfgang **Rev:** Nine-line inscription, date in Roman numerals **Note:** Dav. #6062.

Date	Mintage	VG	F	VF	XF	Unc
1615 HM	—	450	850	1,500	3,000	—

KM# 12 2 THALER
Silver **Subject:** Death of Wolfgang **Obv:** Helmeted four-fold arms, date divided 1-6 above and 1-5 below **Rev:** Nine-line inscription, date in Roman numerals **Note:** Dav. #6061.

Date	Mintage	VG	F	VF	XF	Unc
1615 Rare	—	—	—	—	—	—

BAVARIA

(Bayern)

One of the largest states in Germany, Bavaria was a duchy from earliest times, ruled by the Agilholfingen dynasty from 553 until it was suppressed by Charlemagne in 788. Bavaria remained a territory of the Carolingian Empire from that time until 911, when the son of the Count of Scheyern was made duke and began a new line of rulers there. A number of dukes during the next century and a half were elected emperor, but when the mail line became extinct, Empress Agnes gave Bavaria to the Counts of Nordheim in 1061. His descendant, Heinrich XII the Lion, fell out of favor with the emperor and was deposed. The duchy was then entrusted to Otto VI von Wittelsbach, Count of Scheyern and descendant of the counts who had ruled from the early 10th century. Duke Otto I, as he was known from 1180 on, was the ancestor of the dynasty which ruled in Bavaria until 1918 and, from the late 13th century, in the Rhine Palatinate as well (see Electoral Pfalz). The first of several divisions took place in 1255 when lines in Upper and Lower Bavaria were established. The line in Lower Bavaria became extinct in 1340 and the territory reverted to Upper Bavaria. Meanwhile, the division of Upper Bavaria and the Palatinate took place and was confirmed by treaty in 1329, although the electoral vote residing with the Wittelsbachs was to be held jointly by the two branches. In 1347, Bavaria and all other holdings of the family in Brandenburg, the Tyrol and Holland were divided among six brothers. Munich had become the chief city of the duchy by this time. In 1475, Duke Stephen I, who had reunited most of the family's holdings in Bavaria, died and left three sons who promptly divided their patrimony once again. The lines of Ingolstadt, Landshut and Munich were founded, but as the other lines died out, the one seated in Munich regained control of all of Bavaria. Duke Albrecht IV instituted primogeniture in 1506 and from that time on, Bavaria remained united. When Elector Friedrich V of the Palatinate (Pfalz) was elected King of Bohemia in 1618, an event which helped precipitate the Thirty Years' War, Duke Maximilian I of Bavaria sided with the emperor against his kinsman. The electoral dignity had been given to the Pfalz branch of the Wittelsbachs by the Golden Bull of 1356, a fact which was a source of contention with the Bavarian branch of the family. With the ouster of Friedrich V, Maximilian I obtained the electoral right and control of the Palatinate in 1623, then also ruled over the Upper Palatinate (Oberpfalz) from 1628 until the conclusion of the war and the Peace of Westphalia. The Bavarian Wittelsbachs became extinct in 1777 and the line in Electoral Pfalz acquired Bavaria, thus uniting the two main territories of the dynasty under a single ruler for the first time since the early 14th century. When Napoleon abolished the Holy Roman Empire in 1806, bringing an end to the electoral system, the ruler of Bavaria was raised to the rank of king. The 19th century saw tragedy upon tragedy visit the royal family. Because of his opposition to the parliamentary reform movement, Ludwig I was forced to abdicate in 1848. His grandson, Ludwig II, inspired by his upbringing to spend his fortune building the fairy tale castle of Neuschwanstein, was forcibly removed by court nobles and died under mysterious circumstances in 1886. His younger brother, Otto, was declared insane and the kingdom was ruled by his uncle, the beloved Prince Luitpold, as prince regent. Ludwig II, the last King of Bavaria, was forced to abdicate at the end of World War I.

RULERS

Maximilian I, 1598-1651
Ferdinand Maria, 1651-1679
Maximilian II, Emanuel, 1679-1726

MINT OFFICIALS' INITIALS

Amberg Mint

Initials or marks	Date	Name
(a)= ☿	1621-22	Nicholas Fischer, mintmaster
NF		
(b)= ☾	1621-22	Johann Rentsch and Jonas Riedl, mintmasters
(c)= ♀ and/or	1622	Georg Kellner and Neuberger, mintmasters
(d)= ✳	1622-23	Christoph Hegner, mintmaster and Georg Kellner
	1622-23	Michael Liedl, mintmaster
	1623	Barthel Simon, warden
(e)= ☾ or G	1624-26	Hans Christoph Geissler
	1624-26	Georg Thomas Paur, die-cutter
	1626-27	Claus Oppermann, mintmaster
	1627	Johann Weber, warden

Heidelberg Mint

Initials or mark	Date	Name
	1620-24	Johann Ludwig Eichelstein, mintmaster
GC	1624-28	Georg Crämer, mint director

Kemnath Mint

Initial or mark	Date	Name
(f)= ✳	1623	Andreas Liebholz (Liebholdt) aand Georg Kellner, mintmasters

Munich Mint

Initials	Date	Name
	1586-1615	Kaspar Lechner, die-cutter
	1596-1620	Balthasar Hitschler (Hutschler), warden
	1596-1601	Paulus van Vianen, goldsmith
	1600-34	Eberl Christoph Ulrich, die-cutter and medailleur
	Ca. 1618-23	Hans Pernegger, warden
	Ca. 1618-20	Hans Georg Vollmann, goldsmith and die-cutter
	1618-26	Isaak Zeggin, goldsmith
	1620-25	Paul Krieger, mint director
	Ca. 1620	Maximilian Jungholzer, warden
	1620	Zacharias Hülz, comptroller
	Ca. 1620	Andreas Pfundtmaier, comptroller
	1621	Saulus Beringer, mint director
	Ca. 1623-66	Paul Zeggin, medailleur
	1625	Martin Ziegler, mint contractor
	1625-32	Martin Hollmayr, warden
	Ca. 1631	Hans Jakob Perschl, die-cutter
	Ca. 1631	Georg Schultes, die-cutter in Augsburg
	Ca. 1632-35	Martin Holmayr, mintmaster
	Ca. 1635-65	Philipp Paul, mint contractor
	1637	Christoph Früchtinger, warden
	1641	Christoph Fichner, warden
	1642-50	Balthasar Müller, goldsmith
	1647-69	Johann Schändl, warden
	1651	Hans Diener, warden
	1651-62	Christoph Wascher, goldsmith
	1652-61	Johann Benno Hözer, die-cutter
	Ca. 1654	Georg Jungholzer, warden
	1661	Johann Jakob Hözer, die-cutter
	Ca. 1665-68	Franz Friesshamer, mint inspector
CZ	1666-1713	Kaspar Zeggin, die-cutter
	1669	Kaspar Preiss, goldsmith
	1673	Christian Sayler, goldsmith
	1675	Albrecht Johann Philipp Jakob Oberleitner, warden
	1677-1705	Moritz Angermayr, warden
MB	Ca. 1680-1725	Martin Brunner, medailleur in Nürnberg
	1681-82	Sebastian Wendl, goldsmith
	1681-1702	Hans Georg Schmidt, goldsmith
	1682	Johann Karl Renner, die-cutter
	Ca. 1687-1718	Johann Christoph Packhenreiter, mint director
	1690	Johann Jakob Langebein, die-cutter
	1691-1700	Johann Gottlieb Stotz, warden
	1692	Franz Karl Angermayr, warden
	1697	Johann Strobl, goldsmith

Neumarkt Mint

Initial	Date	Name
(g)= or	1623-26	Hans Zissler, mintmaster

ARMS

Wittelsbach and Bavaria – field of lozenges (diamond shapes); Pfalz – rampant lion, usually to the left

MINT MARKS

A – Amberg, 1763-95
M - Munich

DUCHY

REGULAR COINAGE

KM# 5 PFENNIG

Copper **Obv:** Bavarian arms in circle **Rev:** M below date in circle **Shape:** Rectangular **Mint:** Munich

Date	Mintage	VG	F	VF	XF	Unc
1606	—	8.00	13.00	27.00	55.00	—
1607	—	8.00	13.00	27.00	55.00	—
1608	—	8.00	13.00	27.00	55.00	—
1609	—	8.00	13.00	27.00	55.00	—
1610	—	8.00	13.00	27.00	55.00	—
1611	—	8.00	13.00	27.00	55.00	—
1612	—	8.00	13.00	27.00	55.00	—
1613	—	8.00	13.00	27.00	55.00	—
1614	—	8.00	13.00	27.00	55.00	—
1615	—	8.00	13.00	27.00	55.00	—
1616	—	8.00	13.00	27.00	55.00	—
1617	—	8.00	13.00	27.00	55.00	—
1618	—	8.00	13.00	27.00	55.00	—
1620	—	8.00	13.00	27.00	55.00	—
1621	—	8.00	13.00	27.00	55.00	—
1623	—	8.00	13.00	27.00	55.00	—
1624	—	8.00	13.00	27.00	55.00	—
1625	—	8.00	13.00	27.00	55.00	—
1626	—	8.00	13.00	27.00	55.00	—
1627	—	8.00	13.00	27.00	55.00	—
1631	—	8.00	13.00	27.00	55.00	—

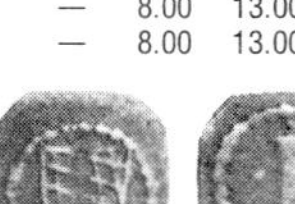

KM# 12 PFENNIG

Copper **Rev:** Value in circle **Shape:** Octagonal **Note:** Kipper. Prev. KM#6.

Date	Mintage	VG	F	VF	XF	Unc
ND	—	10.00	27.00	55.00	100	—

KM# 107 PFENNIG

Silver **Ruler:** Maximilian I **Obv:** 3-fold arms of Pfalz, Bavaria and imperial orb, legend above **Obv. Legend:** M.P.C. **Mint:** Kemnath **Note:** Uniface. Ref. #G116. Prev. Pfalz-Simmern KM#8. Oberpfalz issue.

Date	Mintage	VG	F	VF	XF	Unc
ND	—	14.00	28.00	50.00	100	—

KM# 108 PFENNIG

Silver **Ruler:** Maximilian I **Obv:** 3-fold arms, legend above **Obv. Legend:** M.D.E. **Mint:** Kemnath **Note:** Uniface. Ref. #G123-124. Prev. Pfalz-Simmern KM#7. Oberpfalz issue.

Date	Mintage	VG	F	VF	XF	Unc
ND	—	14.00	28.00	50.00	100	—
ND (f)	—	14.00	28.00	50.00	100	—

KM# 242 PFENNIG

Billon **Obv:** Bavarian arms divide date, C above **Note:** Uniface. Prev. KM#51.

Date	Mintage	VG	F	VF	XF	Unc
1630	—	7.00	10.00	20.00	40.00	—
1631	187,000	7.00	10.00	20.00	40.00	—
1632	—	7.00	10.00	20.00	40.00	—
1633	—	7.00	10.00	20.00	40.00	—
1634	—	7.00	10.00	20.00	40.00	—
1635	—	7.00	10.00	20.00	40.00	—
1638	—	7.00	10.00	20.00	40.00	—
1639	—	7.00	10.00	20.00	40.00	—
1640	—	7.00	10.00	20.00	40.00	—
1642	—	7.00	10.00	20.00	40.00	—
1643	—	7.00	10.00	20.00	40.00	—
1644	—	7.00	10.00	20.00	40.00	—
1645	—	7.00	10.00	20.00	40.00	—
1646	—	7.00	10.00	20.00	40.00	—
1647	—	7.00	10.00	20.00	40.00	—
1648	—	7.00	10.00	20.00	40.00	—
1649	—	7.00	10.00	20.00	40.00	—

KM# 251 PFENNIG

Billon **Obv:** C divides date above Bavarian arms **Note:** Uniface. Prev. KM#54.

Date	Mintage	VG	F	VF	XF	Unc
1634	—	7.00	10.00	20.00	40.00	—

KM# 286 PFENNIG

Billon **Obv:** Bavarian arms divide date, C above **Note:** Uniface. Prev. KM#77.

Date	Mintage	VG	F	VF	XF	Unc
1653	—	7.00	10.00	20.00	40.00	—
1654	—	7.00	10.00	20.00	40.00	—
1655	—	7.00	10.00	20.00	40.00	—
1660	—	7.00	10.00	20.00	40.00	—
1661	—	7.00	10.00	20.00	40.00	—
1662	—	7.00	10.00	20.00	40.00	—
1663	—	7.00	10.00	20.00	40.00	—
1664	—	7.00	10.00	20.00	40.00	—
1665	—	7.00	10.00	20.00	40.00	—
1666	—	7.00	10.00	20.00	40.00	—
1667	—	7.00	10.00	20.00	40.00	—
1672	—	7.00	10.00	20.00	40.00	—
1675	—	7.00	10.00	20.00	40.00	—

KM# 331 PFENNIG

Billon **Obv:** C divides date above Bavarian arms **Note:** Uniface. Prev. KM#104.

Date	Mintage	VG	F	VF	XF	Unc
1677	—	7.00	10.00	20.00	40.00	—
1678	—	7.00	10.00	20.00	40.00	—
1679	—	7.00	10.00	20.00	40.00	—
1699	—	7.00	10.00	20.00	40.00	—

KM# 335 PFENNIG

Billon **Ruler:** Maximilian II, Emanuel **Obv:** C divides date above Bavarian arms in branches **Note:** Uniface. Prev. KM#112.

Date	Mintage	VG	F	VF	XF	Unc
1680	—	7.00	13.00	27.00	55.00	—
1681	—	7.00	13.00	27.00	55.00	—
1682	—	7.00	13.00	27.00	55.00	—
1683	—	7.00	13.00	27.00	55.00	—
1684	—	7.00	13.00	27.00	55.00	—
1685	—	7.00	13.00	27.00	55.00	—
1686	—	7.00	13.00	27.00	55.00	—
1688	—	7.00	13.00	27.00	55.00	—
1690	—	7.00	13.00	27.00	55.00	—
1693	—	7.00	13.00	27.00	55.00	—
1695	—	7.00	13.00	27.00	55.00	—
1696	—	7.00	13.00	27.00	55.00	—
1697	—	7.00	13.00	27.00	55.00	—
1699	—	7.00	13.00	27.00	55.00	—
1700	—	7.00	13.00	27.00	55.00	—

KM# 48 PFENNIG (Kipper)

Copper **Ruler:** Maximilian I **Obv:** Crowned Pfalz lion left holding imperial orb, 'P' at left **Mint:** Amberg **Note:** Uniface. Ref. G#96. Oberpfalz issue.

Date	Mintage	VG	F	VF	XF	Unc
ND(1621-23)	—	—	—	—	—	—

KM# 49 PFENNIG (Kipper)

Copper **Ruler:** Maximilian I **Obv:** Crowned Pfalz lion right, 'P' at left **Mint:** Amberg **Note:** Uniface. Ref. G#97. Oberpfalz issue.

Date	Mintage	VG	F	VF	XF	Unc
ND(1621-23)	—	—	—	—	—	—

KM# 8 2 PFENNIG

Copper **Obv:** Bavarian arms in circle **Rev:** Value in circle **Mint:** Munich **Note:** Kipper. Prev. KM#23.

Date	Mintage	VG	F	VF	XF	Unc
ND	—	12.00	27.00	55.00	100	—

KM# 15 2 PFENNIG

Copper **Shape:** Square **Note:** Prev. KM#24.

Date	Mintage	VG	F	VF	XF	Unc
ND	—	12.00	27.00	55.00	100	—

KM# 110 2 PFENNIG

Silver **Ruler:** Maximilian I **Obv:** 3 small shields of arms, 2 above 1, in trefoil, value II above, date divided by lower arms **Note:** Uniface. Ref. #G122. Prev. Pfalz-Simmern KM#57.

Date	Mintage	VG	F	VF	XF	Unc
1623	—	15.00	30.00	55.00	110	—

KM# 114 3 PFENNIG

Silver **Ruler:** Maximilian I **Obv:** 3-fold arms of Pfalz, Bavaria and imperial orb, legend above **Obv. Legend:** • M • D • E • **Rev:** Imperial orb with III divides date **Mint:** Kemnath **Note:** Ref. #G115, 121. Prev. Pfalz-Simmern KM#58. Oberpfalz Issue. Varieties exist.

Date	Mintage	VG	F	VF	XF	Unc
1623 (f)	—	—	—	—	—	—
1623	—	20.00	40.00	75.00	135	—

KM# 17 4 PFENNIG (Kipper)

Copper **Obv:** Bavarian arms in circle **Rev:** K in circle **Note:** Octagonal planchet. Prev. KM#27.

Date	Mintage	VG	F	VF	XF	Unc
ND	—	12.00	27.00	55.00	100	—

KM# 18 4 PFENNIG (Kipper)

Copper **Rev:** Cross in circle **Note:** Prev. KM#28.

Date	Mintage	VG	F	VF	XF	Unc
ND	—	12.00	27.00	55.00	100	—

KM# 51 4 PFENNIG (Kipper)

Silver **Ruler:** Maximilian I **Obv:** 2 ornate adjacent shields of arms, Pfalz at left and Bavaria at right, imperial orb below **Rev:** Inscription in laurel wreath **Rev. Inscription:** • IIII • / • PFE • **Mint:** Amberg **Note:** Ref. G#94. Oberpfalz issue.

Date	Mintage	VG	F	VF	XF	Unc
ND(1621-23)	—	—	—	—	—	—

KM# 10 4 PFENNIG (Kipper)

Copper **Obv:** Bavarian arms in wreath **Rev:** Value in wreath **Mint:** Munich **Note:** Prev. KM#26.

Date	Mintage	VG	F	VF	XF	Unc
ND(1621-22)	—	8.00	10.00	20.00	45.00	—

KM# 338 5 PFENNIG

Silver **Note:** Prev. KM#110.

Date	Mintage	VG	F	VF	XF	Unc
1683	—	30.00	55.00	120	225	—
1684	—	30.00	55.00	120	225	—

KM# 336 10 PFENNIG (2-1/2 Kreuzer)

Silver **Obv:** Capped Bavarian arms in branches **Note:** Varieties exist. Prev. KM#113.

Date	Mintage	VG	F	VF	XF	Unc
1681	—	7.00	13.00	27.00	55.00	—
1682	—	7.00	13.00	27.00	55.00	—
1683	—	7.00	13.00	27.00	55.00	—
1684	—	7.00	13.00	27.00	55.00	—
1685	—	7.00	13.00	27.00	55.00	—
1686	—	7.00	13.00	27.00	55.00	—
1687	—	7.00	13.00	27.00	55.00	—
1688	—	7.00	13.00	27.00	55.00	—
1689	—	7.00	13.00	27.00	55.00	—
1690	—	7.00	13.00	27.00	55.00	—

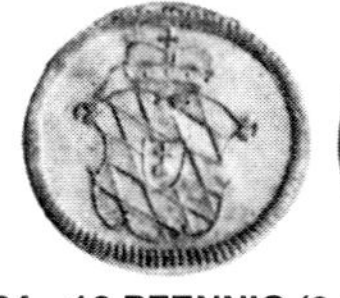

KM# 334 10 PFENNIG (2-1/2 Kreuzer)

Silver **Obv:** Capped Bavarian arms **Rev:** Two-line inscription and date **Mint:** Munich **Note:** Prev. KM#111.

Date	Mintage	VG	F	VF	XF	Unc
1679	—	7.00	13.00	27.00	55.00	—
1680	—	7.00	13.00	27.00	55.00	—
1681	—	7.00	13.00	27.00	55.00	—

KM# 117 1/2 KREUZER

Silver **Obv:** Value divides date above Bavarian arms **Note:** Uniface. Prev. KM#25.

Date	Mintage	VG	F	VF	XF	Unc
1623	—	7.00	13.00	27.00	55.00	—
1624	—	7.00	13.00	27.00	55.00	—
1625	—	7.00	13.00	27.00	55.00	—
1626	—	7.00	13.00	27.00	55.00	—
1627	—	7.00	13.00	27.00	55.00	—

KM# 220 1/2 KREUZER

Silver **Obv:** Bavarian arms divide date, value above **Note:** Uniface. Prev. KM#47.

Date	Mintage	VG	F	VF	XF	Unc
1627	—	7.00	12.00	24.00	55.00	—
1631	—	7.00	12.00	24.00	55.00	—
1632	—	7.00	12.00	24.00	55.00	—
1635	—	7.00	12.00	24.00	55.00	—
1638	—	7.00	12.00	24.00	55.00	—
1639	—	7.00	12.00	24.00	55.00	—
1640	—	7.00	12.00	24.00	55.00	—
1642	—	7.00	12.00	24.00	55.00	—
1646	—	7.00	12.00	24.00	55.00	—
1647	—	7.00	12.00	24.00	55.00	—
1649	—	7.00	12.00	24.00	55.00	—
1651	—	7.00	12.00	24.00	55.00	—

KM# 283 1/2 KREUZER

Silver **Note:** Uniface. Prev. KM#75.

Date	Mintage	VG	F	VF	XF	Unc
1652	—	7.00	12.00	24.00	55.00	—
1661	—	7.00	12.00	24.00	55.00	—
1666	—	7.00	12.00	24.00	55.00	—
1668	—	7.00	12.00	24.00	55.00	—
1671	—	7.00	12.00	24.00	55.00	—

KM# 327 1/2 KREUZER

Silver **Obv:** Value divides date above Bavarian arms **Note:** Uniface. Prev. KM#101.

Date	Mintage	VG	F	VF	XF	Unc
1676	—	7.00	12.00	24.00	55.00	—

KM# 120 KREUZER

Silver **Obv:** Bavarian arms **Note:** Prev. KM#29.

Date	Mintage	VG	F	VF	XF	Unc
1623	—	7.00	16.00	30.00	60.00	—
1624	—	7.00	16.00	30.00	60.00	—
1625	—	7.00	16.00	30.00	60.00	—
1630	—	7.00	16.00	30.00	60.00	—
1631	—	7.00	16.00	30.00	60.00	—
1635	—	7.00	16.00	30.00	60.00	—
1638	—	7.00	16.00	30.00	60.00	—
1640	—	7.00	16.00	30.00	60.00	—
1644	—	7.00	16.00	30.00	60.00	—
1646	—	7.00	16.00	30.00	60.00	—
1648	—	7.00	16.00	30.00	60.00	—
1650	—	7.00	16.00	30.00	60.00	—
1651	—	7.00	16.00	30.00	60.00	—
1652	—	7.00	16.00	30.00	60.00	—
1653	—	7.00	16.00	30.00	60.00	—
1654	—	7.00	16.00	30.00	60.00	—

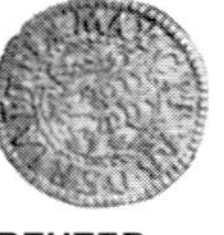

KM# 121 KREUZER

Silver **Ruler:** Maximilian I **Obv:** 3-fold arms of Pfalz, Bavaria and imperial orb, electoral hat above, titles of Maximilian I **Rev:** Crowned imperial eagle, I in orb on breast, titles of Ferdinand II **Mint:** Amberg **Note:** Ref. G#101. Prev. Pfalz-Simmern KM#59. Oberpfalz issue.

Date	Mintage	VG	F	VF	XF	Unc
ND (d)	—	22.00	45.00	80.00	150	—

KM# 123 KREUZER

Silver **Ruler:** Maximilian I **Obv:** Imperial orb with 'I' divides date, titles of Maximilian I **Rev:** Crowned imperial eagle, titles of Ferdinand II **Mint:** Kemnath **Note:** Ref. G#120. Prev. Pfalz-Simmern KM#60. Oberpfalz issue.

Date	Mintage	VG	F	VF	XF	Unc
1623	—	22.00	45.00	80.00	150	—

KM# 288 KREUZER

Silver **Obv:** Titles of Ferdinand Maria **Note:** Prev. KM#78.

Date	Mintage	VG	F	VF	XF	Unc
1653	—	13.00	27.00	55.00	120	—
1654	—	20.00	40.00	80.00	170	—
1656	—	20.00	40.00	80.00	170	—

KM# 352 KREUZER

Silver **Ruler:** Maximilian II, Emanuel **Obv:** Head right **Rev:** Crowned double-headed imperial eagle with arms on breast **Note:** First reign. Prev. KM#120.

Date	Mintage	VG	F	VF	XF	Unc
1692	—	10.00	20.00	35.00	55.00	—
1695	—	10.00	20.00	35.00	55.00	—
1696	—	10.00	20.00	35.00	55.00	—
1697	—	10.00	20.00	35.00	55.00	—
1698	—	10.00	20.00	35.00	55.00	—
1699	—	10.00	20.00	35.00	55.00	—
1700	—	10.00	20.00	35.00	55.00	—

KM# 81 KREUZER (Kipper)

Silver **Ruler:** Maximilian I **Obv:** 2 ornate adjacent shields of arms, Pfalz on left, Bavaria on right, imperial orb below **Rev:** Inscription, date **Rev. Inscription:** (flower) I (flower) / KREVT / • ZER • **Mint:** Amberg **Note:** Ref. G#95. Oberpfalz issue.

Date	Mintage	VG	F	VF	XF	Unc
1622	—	—	—	—	—	—

KM# 82 KREUZER (Kipper)

Silver **Ruler:** Maximilian I **Obv:** 2 ornate adjacent shields of arms, Pfalz on left, Bavaria on right, imperial orb below **Rev:** Inscription, date **Rev. Inscription:** KREUTZ / ? ER ? **Mint:** Amberg **Note:** Ref. G#95. Oberpfalz issue.

Date	Mintage	VG	F	VF	XF	Unc
1622	—	—	—	—	—	—

KM# 20 2 KREUZER (1/2 Batzen)

Silver **Obv:** Spade-shaped Bavarian arms in inner circle **Rev:** Orb with 2 at bottom in inner circle **Note:** Prev. KM#30.

Date	Mintage	VG	F	VF	XF	Unc
ND	—	8.00	16.00	30.00	60.00	—

KM# 128 2 KREUZER (1/2 Batzen)

Silver **Ruler:** Maximilian IV, Josef as Elector **Note:** Prev. KM#31.

Date	Mintage	VG	F	VF	XF	Unc
1623	—	8.00	16.00	30.00	60.00	—
1624	—	8.00	16.00	30.00	60.00	—
1625	—	8.00	16.00	30.00	60.00	—
1626	—	8.00	16.00	30.00	60.00	—
1628	—	8.00	16.00	30.00	60.00	—
1629	—	8.00	16.00	30.00	60.00	—
1630	—	8.00	16.00	30.00	60.00	—
1631	20,000	8.00	16.00	30.00	60.00	—
1632	—	8.00	16.00	30.00	60.00	—
1635	—	8.00	16.00	30.00	60.00	—
1636	—	8.00	16.00	30.00	60.00	—
1637	—	8.00	16.00	30.00	60.00	—

KM# 244.1 2 KREUZER (1/2 Batzen)

Silver **Obv:** Crown above arms and without inner circle on both sides **Note:** Prev. KM#52.1.

Date	Mintage	VG	F	VF	XF	Unc
1632	—	10.00	20.00	45.00	90.00	—

KM# 244.2 2 KREUZER (1/2 Batzen)

Silver **Obv:** Inflated shield without crown in inner circle **Note:** Prev. KM#52.2.

Date	Mintage	VG	F	VF	XF	Unc
1635	—	10.00	20.00	45.00	90.00	—

KM# 304 2 KREUZER (1/2 Batzen)

Silver **Obv:** Large arms in circle **Note:** Prev. KM#88.

Date	Mintage	VG	F	VF	XF	Unc
1660	—	10.00	20.00	45.00	90.00	—

KM# 308 2 KREUZER (1/2 Batzen)

Silver **Obv:** Capped small arms in inner circle **Note:** Prev. KM#90.

Date	Mintage	VG	F	VF	XF	Unc
1661	—	10.00	20.00	45.00	90.00	—
1665	—	10.00	20.00	45.00	90.00	—
1666	—	10.00	20.00	45.00	90.00	—
1667	—	10.00	20.00	45.00	90.00	—
1669	—	10.00	20.00	45.00	90.00	—
1671	—	10.00	20.00	45.00	90.00	—
1672	—	10.00	20.00	45.00	90.00	—
1676	—	10.00	20.00	45.00	90.00	—

KM# 129 2 KREUZER (GROSCHL)

Silver **Ruler:** Maximilian I **Obv:** 3-fold arms of Pfalz, Bavaria and imperial orb, electoral hat above, titles of Maximilian I **Rev:** Crowned imperial eagle, '2' in orb on breast, titles of Ferdinand II **Mint:** Amberg **Note:** Ref. G#100. Oberpfalz issue.

Date	Mintage	VG	F	VF	XF	Unc
ND(1623) (d)	—	—	—	—	—	—

KM# 130 2 KREUZER (GROSCHL)

Silver **Ruler:** Maximilian I **Obv:** Imperial orb with Z or 2, titles of Maximilian I **Rev:** Crowned imperial eagle, titles of Ferdinand II **Mint:** Kemnath **Note:** Ref. G#117. Oberpfalz issue.

Date	Mintage	VG	F	VF	XF	Unc
ND(1623) (f)	—	—	—	—	—	—

KM# 131 2 KREUZER (GROSCHL)

Silver **Ruler:** Maximilian I **Obv:** Imperial orb with Z or 2 divides date, titles of Maximilian I **Rev:** Crowned imperial eagle, titles of Ferdinand II **Mint:** Kemnath **Note:** Ref. G#118-19. Oberpfalz issue. Varieties exist.

Date	Mintage	VG	F	VF	XF	Unc
1623 (f)	—	—	—	—	—	—

KM# 132 2 KREUZER (GROSCHL)

Silver **Ruler:** Maximilian I **Obv:** Imperial orb with Z or 2, titles of Maximilian I **Rev:** Crowned imperial eagle, titles of Ferdinand II **Mint:** Neumarkt **Note:** Ref. G#172. Oberpfalz issue.

Date	Mintage	VG	F	VF	XF	Unc
ND(1623-26) (g)	—	—	—	—	—	—

KM# 347 3 KREUZER (Groschen)

Silver **Obv:** Maximilian II Emanuel **Note:** Prev. KM#117.

Date	Mintage	VG	F	VF	XF	Unc
1690 GZ	—	12.00	25.00	55.00	100	—
1691	—	12.00	25.00	55.00	100	—
1692	—	12.00	25.00	55.00	100	—
1693	—	12.00	25.00	55.00	100	—
1694	—	12.00	25.00	55.00	100	—
1695	—	12.00	25.00	55.00	100	—
1696	—	12.00	25.00	55.00	100	—
1697	—	12.00	25.00	55.00	100	—
1698	—	12.00	25.00	55.00	100	—

KM# 366 3 KREUZER (Groschen)

Silver **Obv:** Bust within circle **Rev:** Arms within circle **Note:** Prev. KM#128.

KM# 38 3 KREUZER (Groschen)

Silver **Obv:** Bavarian arms in inner circle **Rev:** Rampant lion in inner circle, value below **Mint:** Munich **Note:** Prev. KM#116.

Date	Mintage	VG	F	VF	XF	Unc
ND(1620)	290,000	75.00	150	300	450	—

KM# 84 6 KREUZER

Silver **Obv:** Bavarian arms in inner circle **Rev:** Date and value **Note:** Prev. KM#17.

Date	Mintage	VG	F	VF	XF	Unc
1622	—	13.00	27.00	40.00	70.00	—

KM# 348 15 KREUZER

Silver **Obv:** Maximilian II Emanuel **Note:** First reign. Prev. KM#118.

Date	Mintage	VG	F	VF	XF	Unc
1691	—	25.00	40.00	90.00	175	—
1691 CZ	—	25.00	40.00	90.00	175	—
1692	—	27.00	55.00	90.00	200	—
1692 CZ	—	27.00	55.00	90.00	200	—
1692 CZ Retrograde Z	—	27.00	55.00	90.00	200	—

KM# 353.1 15 KREUZER

Silver **Obv:** Maximilian II Emanuel **Rev:** Crowned arms **Note:** Prev. KM#121.1.

Date	Mintage	VG	F	VF	XF	Unc
1692	—	27.00	45.00	90.00	200	—
1692 CZ	—	27.00	45.00	90.00	200	—
1692 +C+Z+	—	27.00	45.00	90.00	200	—
1692 C+Z	—	27.00	45.00	90.00	200	—
1693 C+Z	—	27.00	45.00	90.00	200	—
1693 +C+Z+	—	27.00	45.00	90.00	200	—

KM# 353.2 15 KREUZER

Silver **Obv:** Altered portrait **Note:** Prev. KM#121.2.

Date	Mintage	VG	F	VF	XF	Unc
1694	—	30.00	55.00	100	200	—
1695	—	30.00	55.00	100	200	—
1696	—	30.00	55.00	100	200	—

KM# 369.1 15 KREUZER

Silver **Obv:** Portrait and arms within circle **Rev:** Portrait and arms within circle **Note:** Prev. KM#129.1.

Date	Mintage	VG	F	VF	XF	Unc
1696	—	30.00	55.00	90.00	175	—
1697	—	30.00	55.00	90.00	175	—

KM# 369.2 15 KREUZER

Silver **Ruler:** Maximilian II, Emanuel **Obv:** Bust right within beaded circle **Rev:** Crowned arms within beaded circle, value below **Note:** Prev. KM#129.2.

Date	Mintage	VG	F	VF	XF	Unc
1697	—	30.00	55.00	100	200	—
1698	—	30.00	55.00	100	200	—
1699	—	30.00	55.00	100	200	—
1700	—	30.00	55.00	100	200	—

KM# 86 15 KREUZER

Silver **Mint:** Munich **Note:** Prev. KM#18.

Date	Mintage	VG	F	VF	XF	Unc
1622	—	30.00	55.00	110	200	—

KM# 40 24 KREUZER (Kipper)

Silver **Subject:** Maximilian I as Duke **Mint:** Munich **Note:** Prev. KM#11.

Date	Mintage	VG	F	VF	XF	Unc
ND(1620)	1,013,000	100	225	450	700	—

KM# 53.1 24 KREUZER (Kipper)

Silver **Ruler:** Maximilian I **Obv:** Ornate 3-fold arms of Pfalz, Bavaria and imperial orb, electoral hat above **Obv. Legend:** ★ MONET ★ ARGE ★ SVPERI ★ PALA ★ BAVAR (or variant) **Rev:** Crowned Pfalz lion to left in baroque frame, value (24) at top **Rev. Legend:** ADIVTOR ★ NOST ★ IN ★ NOMIN ★ DOMI (or variant) **Mint:** Amberg **Note:** Ref. G#66. Prev. Pfalz-Simmern KM#45. Oberpfalz issue.

Date	Mintage	VG	F	VF	XF	Unc
ND	—	—	—	—	—	—

KM# 53.2 24 KREUZER (Kipper)

Silver **Ruler:** Maximilian I **Obv:** Ornate 3-fold arms of Pfalz, Bavaria and imperial orb, electoral hat above, date at end of legend **Obv. Legend:** ★ MONET ★ ARGE ★ SVPERI ★ PALA ★ BAVAR (or variant) **Rev:** Crowned Pfalz lion to left in baroque frame, value (24) at top **Rev. Legend:** ADIVTOR ★ NOST ★ IN ★ NOMIN ★ DOMI (or variant) **Mint:** Amberg **Note:** Ref. G#72. Prev. Pfalz-Simmern KM#45. Oberpfalz issue.

Date	Mintage	VG	F	VF	XF	Unc
1621 (a)	—	—	—	—	—	—

KM# 53.3 24 KREUZER (Kipper)

Silver **Ruler:** Maximilian I **Obv:** Ornate 3-fold arms of Pfalz, Bavaria and imperial orb, electoral hat and value above, date at end of legend **Obv. Legend:** ★ MONET ★ ARGE ★ SVPERI ★ PALA ★ BAVAR (or variant) **Rev:** Crowned Pfalz lion to left in baroque frame **Rev. Legend:** ADIVTOR ★ NOST ★ IN ★ NOMIN ★ DOMI (or variant) **Mint:** Amberg **Note:** Ref. G#75. Prev. Pfalz-Simmern KM#45. Oberpfalz issue.

Date	Mintage	VG	F	VF	XF	Unc
1621 (a) NF	—	—	—	—	—	—

KM# 53.4 24 KREUZER (Kipper)

Silver **Ruler:** Maximilian I **Obv:** Ornate 3-fold arms of Pfalz, Bavaria and imperial orb, electoral hat and value above **Obv. Legend:** ★ MONET ★ ARGE ★ SVPERI ★ PALA ★ BAVAR (or variant) **Rev:** Crowned Pfalz lion to left in baroque frame, date at end of legend **Rev. Legend:** ADIVTOR ★ NOST ★ IN ★ NOMIN ★ DOMI (or variant) **Mint:** Amberg **Note:** Ref. G#82-83. Prev. Pfalz-Simmern KM#45. Oberpfalz issue. Varieties exist.

Date	Mintage	VG	F	VF	XF	Unc
1622 (c)	—	—	—	—	—	—

KM# 57.1 24 KREUZER (Kipper)

Silver **Ruler:** Maximilian I **Obv:** Ornate 3-fold arms of Pfalz, Bavaria and imperial orb, electoral hat above **Obv. Legend:** ★ MONET ★ ARGE ★ SVPERI ★ PALA ★ BAVAR (or variant) **Rev:** Bust right in circle, date at end of legend **Rev. Legend:** ADIVTOR ★ NOST ★ IN ★ NOMIN ★ DOMI (or variant) **Mint:** Amberg **Note:** Ref. G#67. Prev. Pfalz-Simmern KM#45. Oberpfalz issue.

Date	Mintage	VG	F	VF	XF	Unc
1621 (a)	—	—	—	—	—	—

KM# 57.2 24 KREUZER (Kipper)

Silver **Ruler:** Maximilian I **Obv:** Ornate 3-fold arms of Pfalz, Bavaria and imperial orb, electoral hat and value (24) at top **Obv. Legend:** ★ MONET ★ ARGE ★ SVPERI ★ PALA ★ BAVAR (or variant) **Rev:** Bust right in circle, date at end of legend **Rev. Legend:** ADIVTOR ★ NOST ★ IN ★ NOMIN ★ DOMI (or variant) **Mint:** Amberg **Note:** Ref. G#69-70. Prev. Pfalz-Simmern KM#45. Oberpfalz issue.

Date	Mintage	VG	F	VF	XF	Unc
1621	—	—	—	—	—	—

KM# 54.1 24 KREUZER (Kipper)

Ruler: Maximilian I **Obv:** Crowned Pfalz lion to left in baroque frame **Obv. Legend:** MONET • ARGE ★ SVPERI ★PALA • BAVAR • 24 **Rev:** Ornate 3-fold arms of Pfalz, Bavaria and imperial orb, electoral hat above, date at end of legend **Rev. Legend:** • ADIVTOR ★ NOST ★ IN ★ NOMIN • DOMIN **Mint:** Amberg **Note:** Ref. G#71, 73, 76, 78-80. Prev. Pfalz-Simmern KM#45. Oberpfalz issue. Varieties exist.

Date	Mintage	VG	F	VF	XF	Unc
1621 (a)	—	—	—	—	—	—
1621 (b)	—	—	—	—	—	—
1622 (b)	—	—	—	—	—	—

KM# 54.2 24 KREUZER (Kipper)

Ruler: Maximilian I **Obv:** Crowned Pfalz lion to left in baroque frame, date at end of legend **Obv. Legend:** MONET ? ARGE ★ SVPERI ★ PALA ? BAVAR ? 24 **Rev:** Ornate 3-fold arms of Pfalz, Bavaria and imperial orb, electoral hat and value (24) above **Rev. Legend:** ? ADIVTOR ★ NOST ★ IN ★ NOMIN ? DOMIN **Mint:** Amberg **Note:** Ref. G#74.

Date	Mintage	VG	F	VF	XF	Unc
1621 (a)	—	—	—	—	—	—

KM# 54.3 24 KREUZER (Kipper)

Silver **Ruler:** Maximilian I **Obv:** Crowned Pfalz lion to left in baroque frame, value (24) in imperial orb at top **Obv. Legend:** MONET • ARGE ★ SVPERI ★PALA • BAVAR • 24 **Rev:** Ornate 3-fold arms of Pfalz, Bavaria and imperial orb, electoral hat above **Rev. Legend:** • ADIVTOR ★ NOST ★ IN ★ NOMIN • DOMIN **Mint:** Amberg **Note:** Ref. G#77. Prev. Pfalz-Simmern KM#45. Oberpfalz issue.

Date	Mintage	VG	F	VF	XF	Unc
1621 (b)	—	—	—	—	—	—

KM# 55 24 KREUZER (Kipper)

Silver **Ruler:** Maximilian I **Obv:** Crowned Pfalz lion to left in baroque frame **Rev:** 2 ornate adjacent shields of arms, Pfalz at left, Bavaria at right, imperial orb between 2 arms below, electoral hat above **Mint:** Amberg **Note:** Ref. G#81, 86. Prev. Pfalz-Simmern KM#45. Oberpfalz issue. Varieties exist.

Date	Mintage	VG	F	VF	XF	Unc
1622	—	—	—	—	—	—

KM# 56.1 24 KREUZER (Kipper)

Silver **Ruler:** Maximilian I **Obv:** Ornate 3-fold arms of Pfalz, Bavaria and imperial orb, electoral hat and date above **Obv. Legend:** ★ MONET ★ ARGE ★ SVPERI ★ PALA ★ BAVAR (or variant) **Rev:** 2 adjacent shields of arms with imperial orb between and below **Rev. Legend:** ADIVTOR ★ NOST ★ IN ★ NOMIN ★ DOMI (or variant) **Mint:** Amberg **Note:** Ref. G#84. Prev. Pfalz-Simmern KM#45. Oberpfalz issue.

Date	Mintage	VG	F	VF	XF	Unc
1622 (c)	—	—	—	—	—	—

KM# 56.2 24 KREUZER (Kipper)

Silver **Ruler:** Maximilian I **Obv:** 2 adjacent shields of arms, imperial orb below, value (24) at top **Obv. Legend:** ★ MONET ★ ARGE ★ SVPERI ★ PALA ★ BAVAR (or variant) **Rev:** Crowned Pfalz lion to left in baroque frame, date at end of legend **Rev. Legend:** ADIVTOR ★ NOST ★ IN ★ NOMIN ★ DOMI (or variant) **Mint:** Amberg **Note:** Ref. G#85, 87, 88-93. Prev. Pfalz-Simmern KM#45. Oberpfalz issue. Varieties exist.

Date	Mintage	VG	F	VF	XF	Unc
1622	—	—	—	—	—	—
1622 (d)	—	—	—	—	—	—
1623 (d)	—	—	—	—	—	—

KM# 56.3 24 KREUZER (Kipper)

Silver **Ruler:** Maximilian I **Obv:** 2 adjacent shields of arms, imperial orb below, electoral hat and value (24) at top **Obv. Legend:** ★ MONET ★ ARGE ★ SVPERI ★ PALA ★ BAVAR (or variant) **Rev:** Crowned Pfalz lion to left in baroque frame, date at end of legend **Rev. Legend:** ADIVTOR ★ NOST ★ IN ★ NOMIN ★ DOMI (or variant) **Mint:** Kemnath **Note:** Ref. G#111. Prev. Pfalz-Simmern KM#45. Oberpfalz issue.

Date	Mintage	VG	F	VF	XF	Unc
1623 (f)	—	—	—	—	—	—

KM# 356 30 KREUZER

Silver **Obv:** Small bust of Maximilian II Emanuel **Note:** Prev. KM#123.

Date	Mintage	VG	F	VF	XF	Unc
1692 +C+Z+	—	35.00	80.00	125	250	—
1693 +C+Z+	—	35.00	80.00	125	250	—

KM# 355 30 KREUZER

Silver **Obv:** Maximilian II Emanuel **Mint:** Munich **Note:** First reign. Prev. KM#122.

Date	Mintage	VG	F	VF	XF	Unc
1692 +C+Z+	—	35.00	80.00	120	200	—

KM# 96 30 KREUZER (Kipper)

Silver **Obv:** Capped arms in Order collar in inner circle **Rev:** Facing crouched lion behind cross with value, date divided near bottom, all in inner circle **Mint:** Munich **Note:** Prev. KM#20.

Date	Mintage	VG	F	VF	XF	Unc
1622	—	40.00	100	175	275	—

KM# 95 30 KREUZER (1/4 Thaler)

Silver **Obv:** Bavarian arms in inner circle **Rev:** Value in cartouche, date above **Mint:** Munich **Note:** Prev. KM#19.

Date	Mintage	VG	F	VF	XF	Unc
1622	—	40.00	100	175	275	—

KM# 65.1 48 KREUZER (Kipper)
Silver **Mint:** Munich **Note:** Prev. KM#152.1.

Date	Mintage	VG	F	VF	XF	Unc
ND(1621-23)	—	70.00	125	400	600	—

KM# 65.2 48 KREUZER
Silver **Obv:** Single inner circles **Rev:** Single inner circles **Note:** Prev. KM#152.2.

Date	Mintage	VG	F	VF	XF	Unc
ND(1621-23)	—	70.00	125	400	600	—

KM# 69.1 60 KREUZER
Silver **Obv:** Double inner circle around arms with flat-topped shield **Note:** Prev. KM#13.1.

Date	Mintage	VG	F	VF	XF	Unc
1621	—	170	325	550	900	—

KM# 69.2 60 KREUZER
Silver **Obv:** Single inner circle **Rev:** Single inner circle **Note:** Prev. KM#13.2.

Date	Mintage	VG	F	VF	XF	Unc
1623	—	170	325	550	900	—

KM# 44.1 60 KREUZER (Kipper)
Silver **Obv:** Oval arms in Order collar in double inner circles **Rev:** Facing crouched lion behind cross with value, date divided near bottom, all in double inner circles **Mint:** Munich **Note:** Prev. KM#12.1.

Date	Mintage	VG	F	VF	XF	Unc
ND	—	170	325	550	900	—
1621	—	170	325	550	900	—
1622	—	170	325	550	900	—
1623	—	170	325	550	900	—

KM# 44.2 60 KREUZER
Silver **Obv:** Single inner circles **Rev:** Single inner circles **Note:** Prev. KM#12.2.

Date	Mintage	VG	F	VF	XF	Unc
1621	—	170	325	550	900	—
1622	—	170	325	550	900	—
1623	—	170	325	550	900	—

KM# 74 120 KREUZER
Silver **Rev:** Date divided near bottom of inner circle **Note:** Prev. KM#16.

Date	Mintage	VG	F	VF	XF	Unc
1621	—	325	650	1,250	2,500	—
1622	—	325	650	1,250	2,500	—

KM# 73 120 KREUZER (Kipper)
Silver **Obv:** Capped oval arms **Note:** Prev. KM#15.

Date	Mintage	VG	F	VF	XF	Unc
1621	—	225	475	875	1,250	—

KM# 142 1/24 THALER (GROSCHEN)
Silver **Ruler:** Maximilian I **Obv:** 4-fold arms of Bavaria and Pfalz with central shield of imperial orb, surrounded by Order of the Golden Fleece, electoral hat above, titles of Maximilian I **Rev:** Imperial orb with 24 divides date, titles of Ferdinand II **Mint:** Kemnath **Note:** Ref. G#113. Oberpfalz issue.

Date	Mintage	VG	F	VF	XF	Unc
1623	—	—	—	—	—	—

KM# 145 1/9 THALER
Silver **Rev:** Date arched above Madonna's shoulders **Note:** Prev. KM#33.

Date	Mintage	VG	F	VF	XF	Unc
1623	—	20.00	35.00	70.00	130	—
1640	—	20.00	35.00	70.00	130	—

KM# 254 1/9 THALER
Silver **Obv:** Date above elector's cap **Note:** Prev. KM#55.

Date	Mintage	VG	F	VF	XF	Unc
1638	—	20.00	35.00	70.00	135	—
1640	—	20.00	35.00	70.00	135	—

KM# 144 1/9 THALER
Silver **Mint:** Munich **Note:** Prev. KM#32.

Date	Mintage	VG	F	VF	XF	Unc
ND(1623)	—	35.00	70.00	165	300	—

KM# 293 1/9 THALER
Silver **Obv:** Capped arms in inner circle, date divided near bottom, value at bottom **Rev:** Radiant Madonna and child in inner circle **Note:** Vicariat issue. Prev. KM#81.

Date	Mintage	VG	F	VF	XF	Unc
1657	—	200	400	800	1,600	—

KM# 294 1/9 THALER
Silver **Obv:** Without inner circle, date at sides **Note:** Vicariat issue. Prev. KM#82.

Date	Mintage	VG	F	VF	XF	Unc
1657	—	200	400	800	1,600	—

KM# 147 1/6 THALER
Silver **Rev:** Date arched above Madonna's shoulders **Note:** Prev. KM#35.

Date	Mintage	VG	F	VF	XF	Unc
1623	—	40.00	80.00	160	300	—
1624	—	40.00	80.00	160	300	—

KM# 190 1/6 THALER
Silver **Obv:** Date above elector's cap **Note:** Prev. KM#38.

Date	Mintage	VG	F	VF	XF	Unc
1625	—	35.00	70.00	140	225	—

Date	Mintage	VG	F	VF	XF	Unc
1626	—	35.00	70.00	140	225	—
1638	—	35.00	70.00	140	225	—

KM# 295 1/6 THALER
Silver **Obv:** Capped arms in inner circle, date divided near bottom, value at bottom **Rev:** Radiant Madonna and child in inner circle **Note:** Vicariat issue. Prev. KM#83.

Date	Mintage	VG	F	VF	XF	Unc
1657	—	275	700	1,250	2,000	—

KM# 98 1/6 THALER
Silver **Mint:** Munich **Note:** Prev. KM#34.

Date	Mintage	VG	F	VF	XF	Unc
ND	—	40.00	75.00	150	300	—

KM# 149 1/4 THALER
Silver **Obv:** Capped arms in Order collar in inner circle, date above cap **Rev:** Radiant Madonna and child in inner circle **Note:** Prev. KM#36.

Date	Mintage	VG	F	VF	XF	Unc
1623	—	40.00	100	200	275	—

KM# 261 1/3 THALER
Silver **Obv:** Capped arms in order collar in inner circle, value at bottom **Rev:** Madonna and child in inner circle **Mint:** Munich **Note:** Prev. KM#59.

Date	Mintage	VG	F	VF	XF	Unc
ND	—	400	800	1,600	2,500	—

KM# 264 1/3 THALER
Silver **Obv:** Capped arms in Order collar, date near top in inner circle, value at bottom **Note:** Prev. KM#60.

Date	Mintage	VG	F	VF	XF	Unc
1640	—	275	700	1,300	2,000	—

KM# 297 1/3 THALER
Silver **Obv:** Without inner circle, arms divide date **Note:** Vicariat issue. Prev. KM#84.

Date	Mintage	VG	F	VF	XF	Unc
1657	—	400	800	1,600	2,500	—

KM# 100 1/2 THALER
Silver **Subject:** Maximilian as Duke **Obv:** Capped arms with lion supporters, date in panel below in inner circle **Rev:** Radiant Madonna and child in inner circle **Note:** Prev. KM#21.

Date	Mintage	VG	F	VF	XF	Unc
1622	—	120	275	550	950	—

KM# 223 1/2 THALER
Silver **Subject:** Maximilian as Elector **Obv:** Date below arms without panel **Note:** Prev. KM#48.

Date	Mintage	VG	F	VF	XF	Unc
1627	—	130	275	550	950	—
1627/3	—	270	550	1,100	1,600	—

KM# 224 1/2 THALER
Silver **Note:** Prev. KM#49.

Date	Mintage	VG	F	VF	XF	Unc
1627	—	100	200	400	750	—
1638	—	100	200	400	750	—

KM# 360 1/2 THALER
Silver **Note:** Prev. KM#124.

Date	Mintage	VG	F	VF	XF	Unc
1694	—	275	550	1,100	1,600	—

KM# 361 1/2 THALER
Silver **Obv:** Maximilian II Emanuel **Note:** Prev. KM#125.

Date	Mintage	VG	F	VF	XF	Unc
1694	—	275	550	1,100	1,600	—

KM# 30 THALER
Silver **Obv:** Long, narrow oval arms **Rev:** Crowned imperial eagle **Note:** Dav. #6063.

Date	Mintage	VG	F	VF	XF	Unc
MDCVIII (1618)	—	250	450	750	1,250	—

KM# 31.1 THALER
Silver **Obv:** Wider arms, notched at top **Note:** Dav. #6064. Prev. KM#9.1.

Date	Mintage	VG	F	VF	XF	Unc
MDCXVIII (1618)	—	150	275	500	800	—
MDCXX (1620)	41,000	150	275	500	800	—

KM# 31.2 THALER

Silver **Obv:** Arabic date in legend at top **Note:** Dav. #6065. Prev. KM#9.2.

Date	Mintage	VG	F	VF	XF	Unc
1622	—	195	375	725	—	—

KM# 31.3 THALER

Silver **Obv:** Date in cartouche below crowned and supported arms **Note:** Dav. #6066. Prev. KM#9.3.

Date	Mintage	VG	F	VF	XF	Unc
1623	—	100	200	350	550	—

KM# 156 THALER

Silver **Obv:** Crowns break inner circle **Rev:** Crowns break inner circle **Note:** Dav. #6067. Prev. KM#37.

Date	Mintage	VG	F	VF	XF	Unc
1623	—	85.00	150	275	450	—
1624	—	85.00	150	275	450	—

KM# 157 THALER

Silver **Ruler:** Maximilian I **Obv:** Bavarian arms **Obv. Legend:** MAX: COM: P: RHE ... **Rev:** Crowned imperial eagle in inner circle, legend around **Rev. Legend:** FERDINANDVS • II • ROMANORVM • IMPERATOR * **Mint:** Amberg **Note:** Dav. #6083. Prev. Pfalz-Simmern KM#49. Oberpfalz issue.

Date	Mintage	VG	F	VF	XF	Unc
ND(1623) (d)	—	—	—	—	—	—

KM# 158 THALER

Silver **Ruler:** Maximilian I **Obv:** Capped, lion supported Bavarian arms **Rev:** Crowned double eagle **Mint:** Kemnath **Note:** Dav. #6084. Prev. Pfalz-Simmern KM#50. Oberpfalz issue.

Date	Mintage	VG	F	VF	XF	Unc
ND(1623)	—	—	—	—	—	—

KM# 159 THALER

Silver **Ruler:** Maximilian I **Obv:** Capped square-topped arms in Order chain **Obv. Legend:** MAXIMIL • DG • COMP AL • RH • V • BDS • RIA • ET • ... **Rev:** Crowned double-headed eagle **Rev. Legend:** FERDINANDVS • II • ROMANORVM • IMPERATOR **Mint:** Neumarkt **Note:** Dav. #6086. Prev. Pfalz-Simmern KM#51. Oberpfalz issue.

Date	Mintage	VG	F	VF	XF	Unc
ND(1623-26) (g)	—	—	—	—	—	—

KM# 194 THALER

Silver **Obv:** Crowned arms in Order chain, date at sides of arms **Rev:** Madonna within circle **Note:** Dav. #6069. Prev. KM#39.

Date	Mintage	VG	F	VF	XF	Unc
1625	—	85.00	150	275	450	—

KM# 195 THALER

Silver **Obv:** Date divided near top of arms **Note:** Dav. #6070. Prev. KM#40.

Date	Mintage	VG	F	VF	XF	Unc
16Z5	—	85.00	150	275	450	—
1626	—	85.00	150	275	450	—

KM# 196 THALER

Silver **Obv:** Crowned oval arms in Order collar with lion supporters, date in bracket at bottom, all in inner circle **Note:** Dav. #6071. Prev. KM#41.

Date	Mintage	VG	F	VF	XF	Unc
1625	—	85.00	150	275	450	—

KM# 197 THALER

Silver **Obv:** Madonna facing half left **Note:** Dav. #6071A. Prev. KM#42.

Date	Mintage	VG	F	VF	XF	Unc
1625	—	90.00	165	300	500	—

KM# 208 THALER

Silver **Obv:** Without inner circle **Note:** Dav. #6073. Prev. KM#45.

Date	Mintage	VG	F	VF	XF	Unc
1626	—	85.00	150	275	450	—
1627/6	—	85.00	150	275	450	—
1627	—	85.00	150	275	450	—

KM# 209 THALER

Silver **Obv:** Date divided in two cartouches below arms **Rev:** Child at left, radiant beams behind **Note:** Dav. #6074. Prev. KM#A50.

Date	Mintage	VG	F	VF	XF	Unc
1626	—	85.00	150	275	450	—
1627	—	85.00	150	275	450	—

KM# 227.1 THALER

Silver **Obv:** Date in one cartouche **Rev:** Without inner circle **Note:** Dav. #6075. Prev. KM#50.1.

Date	Mintage	VG	F	VF	XF	Unc
1627	—	85.00	150	275	450	—
1628/7	—	85.00	150	275	450	—
1628	—	85.00	150	275	450	—
1629	—	85.00	150	275	450	—
1631	1,352	85.00	150	275	450	—
1637	—	85.00	150	275	450	—

KM# 227.2 THALER

Silver **Obv:** Cable border around arms **Rev:** Madonna and child in thin cable border **Note:** Dav. #6076. Prev. KM#50.2.

Date	Mintage	VG	F	VF	XF	Unc
1632 Rare	—	—	—	—	—	—

KM# 227.3 THALER

Silver **Rev:** Without inner circle **Note:** Dav. #6078. Prev. KM#50.3.

Date	Mintage	VG	F	VF	XF	Unc
MDCXXXVIII (1638)	—	100	200	350	550	—

KM# 263.1 THALER

Silver **Obv:** Date divided in one cartouche **Rev:** Radiant Madonna and child in beaded inner circle **Note:** Dav. #6079. Prev. KM#58.1.

Date	Mintage	VG	F	VF	XF	Unc
1639 Rare	—	—	—	—	—	—

KM# 263.2 THALER

Silver **Note:** Dav. #6080. Prev. KM#58.2.

Date	Mintage	VG	F	VF	XF	Unc
MDCXL (1640)	—	100	200	350	550	—

KM# 263.3 THALER

Silver **Obv:** Date in Arabic numerals **Note:** Dav. #6081. Prev. KM#58.3.

Date	Mintage	VG	F	VF	XF	Unc
1641	—	100	200	350	550	—

KM# 276 THALER

Silver **Note:** Dav. #6082. Prev. KM#65.

Date	Mintage	VG	F	VF	XF	Unc
1643	—	500	1,000	2,000	3,250	—

KM# 300 THALER

Silver **Obv:** Elector kneeling before Madonna and child, crowned arms divide date at bottom **Rev:** 10-line inscription **Note:** Vicariat issue. Dav. #6097. Prev. KM#86.

Date	Mintage	VG	F	VF	XF	Unc
1657	—	700	1,600	3,000	5,000	—

KM# 299 THALER

Silver **Obv:** Crowned arms in garlands, cap divides date **Note:** Vicariat issue. Dav. #6098. Prev. KM#85.

Date	Mintage	VG	F	VF	XF	Unc
1657	—	650	1,550	3,000	5,000	—

KM# 363.1 THALER

Silver **Obv:** Maximilian II Emanuel **Rev:** Madonna looking right **Note:** Dav. #6099. Prev. KM#126.1.

Date	Mintage	VG	F	VF	XF	Unc
1694	—	75.00	150	275	450	—

KM# 363.2 THALER

Silver **Obv:** Different hair style **Note:** Dav. #6099A. Prev. KM#126.2.

Date	Mintage	VG	F	VF	XF	Unc
1694	—	75.00	150	275	450	—

KM# 365.1 THALER

Silver **Rev:** Madonna looking left **Note:** Dav. #6100. Prev. KM#127.1.

Date	Mintage	VG	F	VF	XF	Unc
1694	—	75.00	150	275	450	—

KM# 365.2 THALER

Silver **Obv:** Larger lettering **Rev:** Madonna looking right, larger lettering **Note:** Dav. #6101. Prev. KM#127.2.

Date	Mintage	VG	F	VF	XF	Unc
1695	—	75.00	150	275	450	—

KM# 200 2 THALER

Silver **Obv:** Capped arms in Order collar in inner circle, date at sides of arms **Rev:** Radiant Madonna and child in inner circle **Mint:** Munich **Note:** Dav. #6068. Prev. KM#43.

Date	Mintage	VG	F	VF	XF	Unc
1625	—	300	600	1,750	2,500	—

KM# 215 2 THALER

Silver **Note:** Dav. #6072. Prev. KM#46.

Date	Mintage	VG	F	VF	XF	Unc
1626	—	200	500	1,500	2,250	—

KM# 257 2 THALER

Silver **Obv:** Without inner circles **Rev:** Without inner circles **Note:** Dav. #6077. Prev. KM#56.

Date	Mintage	VG	F	VF	XF	Unc
1638	—	200	500	1,500	2,250	—

TRADE COINAGE

KM# 325 GOLDGULDEN

3.5000 g., 0.9860 Gold 0.1109 oz. AGW **Obv:** Armored bust of Ferdinand Maria right **Rev:** Madonna and child above crowned arms divide date **Note:** Fr. #210. Prev. KM#100.

Date	Mintage	VG	F	VF	XF	Unc
1674CZ	—	200	400	800	1,200	—
1675CZ	—	150	250	400	750	—
1676CZ	—	150	300	500	900	—
1677CZ	—	200	350	600	1,000	—
1678CZ	—	200	400	800	1,200	—
1679CZ	—	150	300	500	900	—

KM# 350 GOLDGULDEN

3.5000 g., 0.9860 Gold 0.1109 oz. AGW **Ruler:** Maximilian III, Josef **Obv:** Draped bust right **Rev:** Date divided by Madonna and child above and arms below **Note:** First reign. Fr. #219/220. Prev. KM#119.

Date	Mintage	VG	F	VF	XF	Unc
1691	—	500	900	1,600	2,400	—
1697	—	400	800	1,200	2,000	—
1698	—	400	800	1,200	2,000	—
1699	—	400	800	1,200	2,000	—
1700	—	400	800	1,200	2,000	—

KM# 202 GOLDGULDEN

3.5000 g., 0.9860 Gold 0.1109 oz. AGW **Obv:** Crowned arms with lion supporters in inner circle **Rev:** Radiant Madonna and child in inner circle **Mint:** Munich **Note:** Prev. KM#44.

Date	Mintage	VG	F	VF	XF	Unc
(16)25	—	600	1,200	2,250	3,750	—

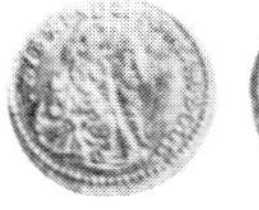

KM# 317 1/4 DUCAT

0.8750 g., 0.9860 Gold 0.0277 oz. AGW **Obv:** Bust of Ferdinand Maria right, continuous legend **Rev:** Capped arms, value below, cap divides date without legend **Mint:** Munich **Note:** Vicariat issue. Fr. #212. Prev. KM#96.

Date	Mintage	VG	F	VF	XF	Unc
1672	—	225	600	1,000	1,500	—

KM# 321 1/4 DUCAT

0.8750 g., 0.9860 Gold 0.0277 oz. AGW **Obv:** Divided legend **Rev:** Continuous legend **Note:** Fr. #212. Prev. KM#98.

Date	Mintage	VG	F	VF	XF	Unc
1673	—	225	600	1,000	1,500	—

KM# 329 1/4 DUCAT

0.8750 g., 0.9860 Gold 0.0277 oz. AGW **Obv:** Bust of Ferdinand Maria right in inner circle **Rev:** Capped arms in inner circle, value below, cap divides date **Note:** Fr. #212. Prev. KM#102.

Date	Mintage	VG	F	VF	XF	Unc
1676	—	225	600	1,000	1,500	—

KM# 309 1/2 DUCAT

1.7500 g., 0.9860 Gold 0.0555 oz. AGW **Subject:** Birth of Maximilian Emanuel **Obv:** Crowned arms **Rev:** Madonna and child seated facing **Note:** Fr. #204. Prev. KM#91.

Date	Mintage	VG	F	VF	XF	Unc
1662	—	425	1,100	1,800	2,700	—

KM# 319 1/2 DUCAT

1.7500 g., 0.9860 Gold 0.0555 oz. AGW **Obv:** Bust of Ferdinand Maria right in inner circle **Rev:** Crowned arms in inner circle, value below **Mint:** Munich **Note:** Fr. #211. Prev. KM#97.

Date	Mintage	VG	F	VF	XF	Unc
1672	—	450	1,000	2,000	3,500	—
1678	—	450	1,000	2,000	3,500	—

KM# 259 DUCAT

3.4900 g., 0.9860 Gold 0.1106 oz. AGW **Obv:** Elector kneeling before Madonna and child in inner circle **Note:** Fr. #195. Prev. KM#57.

Date	Mintage	VG	F	VF	XF	Unc
1638	—	300	650	1,250	2,200	—

KM# 274 DUCAT

3.4900 g., 0.9860 Gold 0.1106 oz. AGW **Obv:** Without inner circle **Note:** Fr. #195. Prev. KM#63.

Date	Mintage	VG	F	VF	XF	Unc
1642	—	250	600	1,200	2,000	—
1643	—	250	600	1,200	2,000	—
1644	—	250	600	1,200	2,000	—
1645	—	250	600	1,200	2,000	—
1646	—	450	1,000	1,600	2,400	—
1647	—	250	600	1,200	2,000	—

KM# 277 DUCAT

3.4900 g., 0.9860 Gold 0.1106 oz. AGW **Obv:** Elector standing facing 1/2 right **Rev:** Madonna and child seated facing **Note:** Fr. #199. Prev. KM#66.

Date	Mintage	VG	F	VF	XF	Unc
1644	—	600	1,500	3,000	5,000	—
1645	—	600	1,500	3,000	5,000	—
1646	—	600	1,500	3,000	5,000	—

KM# 278 DUCAT

3.4900 g., 0.9860 Gold 0.1106 oz. AGW **Obv:** Elector standing facing 1/2 right, pedestal with arms on front holds orb **Rev:** City view of Munich **Note:** Fr. #197. Prev. KM#67.

Date	Mintage	VG	F	VF	XF	Unc
1645	—	500	1,150	2,250	4,500	—

KM# 279 DUCAT

3.4900 g., 0.9860 Gold 0.1106 oz. AGW **Obv:** Without arms on side of table **Note:** Prev. KM#68.

Date	Mintage	VG	F	VF	XF	Unc
1645	—	500	1,150	2,250	4,500	—

KM# 290 DUCAT

3.4900 g., 0.9860 Gold 0.1106 oz. AGW **Obv:** Elector Ferdinand Maria standing near table at right which holds an orb
Rev: Madonna and child above capped arms, date divided at sides **Note:** Prev. KM#79.

Date	Mintage	VG	F	VF	XF	Unc
1655	—	750	1,850	3,250	5,500	—

KM# 291 DUCAT

3.4900 g., 0.9860 Gold 0.1106 oz. AGW **Obv:** Elector standing facing with left hand on helmet on pedestal **Rev:** Madonna and child with shield of arms **Note:** Fr. #202. Prev. KM#80.

Date	Mintage	VG	F	VF	XF	Unc
1655	—	625	1,650	2,850	4,500	—
1660	—	625	1,650	2,850	4,500	—
1667	—	625	1,650	2,850	4,500	—
1671	—	625	1,650	2,850	4,500	—

KM# 302 DUCAT

3.4900 g., 0.9860 Gold 0.1106 oz. AGW **Note:** Vicariat issue. Fr. #201. Prev. KM#87.

Date	Mintage	VG	F	VF	XF	Unc
1657	—	750	1,800	3,750	5,250	—

KM# 306 DUCAT

3.4900 g., 0.9860 Gold 0.1106 oz. AGW **Obv:** Bust of Ferdinand Maria right **Note:** Prev. KM#89.

Date	Mintage	VG	F	VF	XF	Unc
1660 Rare	—	—	—	—	—	—
1678 Rare	—	—	—	—	—	—

KM# 311 DUCAT

3.4900 g., 0.9860 Gold 0.1106 oz. AGW **Subject:** Birth of Princess Louise **Obv:** Bust of Adelaide facing 1/2 right **Rev:** Arms in cartouche divides date **Note:** Fr. #205. Prev. KM#92.

Date	Mintage	VG	F	VF	XF	Unc
1663	—	750	1,500	2,500	3,750	—

KM# 316 DUCAT

3.4900 g., 0.9860 Gold 0.1106 oz. AGW **Subject:** Birth of Joseph Clemens **Obv:** Arms topped by three cherubs divides date **Rev:** St. Nicholas seated facing **Note:** Fr. #208. Prev. KM#95.

Date	Mintage	VG	F	VF	XF	Unc
1671	—	725	1,600	2,850	4,500	—

KM# 330 DUCAT

3.4900 g., 0.9860 Gold 0.1106 oz. AGW **Obv:** Elector standing facing with left hand on helmet on pedestal **Rev:** Madonna and child with angels above view of Munich in inner circle **Note:** Fr. #213. Prev. KM#103.

Date	Mintage	VG	F	VF	XF	Unc
1676	—	1,000	2,400	4,200	6,000	—
1677	—	1,000	2,400	4,200	6,000	—
1678	—	1,000	2,400	4,200	6,000	—

KM# 345 DUCAT

3.4900 g., 0.9860 Gold 0.1106 oz. AGW **Obv:** Maximilian Emanuel **Note:** Fr. #217. Prev. KM#115.

Date	Mintage	VG	F	VF	XF	Unc
1687	—	800	1,800	3,200	5,000	—
1697	—	800	1,800	3,200	5,000	—

KM# 246 DUCAT

3.4900 g., 0.9860 Gold 0.1106 oz. AGW **Obv:** Capped arms in Order collar, cap divides date **Rev:** Radiant Madonna and child **Mint:** Munich **Note:** Fr. #193. Prev. KM#53.

Date	Mintage	VG	F	VF	XF	Unc
1632	—	400	1,000	1,800	2,800	—
1640	—	400	1,000	1,800	2,800	—

KM# 275 2 DUCAT

7.0000 g., 0.9860 Gold 0.2219 oz. AGW **Subject:** Maximilian I as Elector **Obv:** Elector kneeling before Madonna and child **Note:** Fr. #194. Prev. KM#64.

Date	Mintage	VG	F	VF	XF	Unc
1642	—	350	700	1,500	2,500	—
1644	—	350	700	1,500	2,500	—
1645	—	350	700	1,500	2,500	—
1647	—	350	700	1,500	2,500	—

KM# 281 2 DUCAT

7.0000 g., 0.9860 Gold 0.2219 oz. AGW **Note:** Fr. #198. Prev. KM#69.

Date	Mintage	VG	F	VF	XF	Unc
1645	—	900	1,850	3,700	6,000	—

KM# 314 2 DUCAT

7.0000 g., 0.9860 Gold 0.2219 oz. AGW **Subject:** Birth of Prince Cajetan Maria **Obv:** Sun and moon above globe **Rev:** Three shields of arms **Note:** Fr. #207. Prev. KM#94.

Date	Mintage	VG	F	VF	XF	Unc
1670	—	1,500	3,000	5,500	8,500	—

KM# 323 2 DUCAT

7.0000 g., 0.9860 Gold 0.2219 oz. AGW **Subject:** Birth of Princess Violanta Beatrix **Obv:** Crowned and mantled arms, two above one, date below **Rev:** Column with orb on top in inner circle **Note:** Fr. #209. Prev. KM#99.

Date	Mintage	VG	F	VF	XF	Unc
1673	—	1,150	2,250	3,750	7,500	—

KM# 339 2 DUCAT

7.0000 g., 0.9860 Gold 0.2219 oz. AGW **Obv:** Armored bust of Maximilian Emanuel, date below **Rev:** Madonna standing with crowned shield of arms **Note:** Fr. #216. Prev. KM#114.

Date	Mintage	VG	F	VF	XF	Unc
1685	—	1,400	2,800	5,300	8,500	—
1687	—	1,400	2,800	5,300	8,500	—

KM# 371 2 DUCAT

7.0000 g., 0.9860 Gold 0.2219 oz. AGW **Subject:** Birth of Prince Karl Albert **Note:** Fr. #221. Prev. KM#130.

Date	Mintage	VG	F	VF	XF	Unc
1697	—	600	1,200	2,250	4,000	—

KM# 372 2 DUCAT

7.0000 g., 0.9860 Gold 0.2219 oz. AGW **Subject:** Birth of Prince Ferdinand Maria **Note:** Fr. #222. Prev. KM#131.

Date	Mintage	VG	F	VF	XF	Unc
1699	—	400	900	1,750	3,500	—

KM# 33 2 DUCAT

7.0000 g., 0.9860 Gold 0.2219 oz. AGW **Subject:** Maximilian I as Duke **Mint:** Munich **Note:** Fr. #191. Prev. KM#10.

Date	Mintage	VG	F	VF	XF	Unc
MDCXVIII (1618)	—	350	775	1,400	2,650	—

KM# 285 3 DUCAT

10.5000 g., 0.9860 Gold 0.3328 oz. AGW **Subject:** Wedding of Ferdinand Maria and Adelaide **Obv:** Ferdinand Maria and Adelaide **Note:** Fr. #200. Prev. KM#76.

Date	Mintage	VG	F	VF	XF	Unc
1652	—	2,200	4,500	7,000	11,500	—

KM# 27 4 DUCAT

14.0000 g., 0.9860 Gold 0.4438 oz. AGW **Obv:** Elector standing facing 1-2 right, pedestal with arms on front holds orb **Rev:** Madonna and Child with angels over view of Munich **Note:** Fr.#189. Prev. KM#7.

Date	Mintage	VG	F	VF	XF	Unc
1610 Rare	—	—	—	—	—	—

KM# 312 4 DUCAT

14.0000 g., 0.9860 Gold 0.4438 oz. AGW **Subject:** Birth of Prince Louis Amadeus **Obv:** Crowned double shield with initialled medallions at sides **Rev:** Family kneeling before new prince, angel with palm and wreath above **Note:** Fr. #206. Prev. KM#93.

Date	Mintage	VG	F	VF	XF	Unc
1665	—	3,250	5,500	8,500	15,000	—

KM# 268 5 DUCAT

17.5000 g., 0.9860 Gold 0.5547 oz. AGW **Rev:** New fortifications of Munich, date at top **Note:** Fr.#196. Prev. KM#61.

Date	Mintage	VG	F	VF	XF	Unc
1640	—	—	1,250	2,500	4,750	—

KM# 269 5 DUCAT

17.5000 g., 0.9860 Gold 0.5547 oz. AGW **Rev:** New fortifications of Munich, date divided by city view **Note:** Fr.#196. Prev. KM#62.

Date	Mintage	VG	F	VF	XF	Unc
1640	—	—	1,750	3,250	6,500	—

ELECTORATE

REGULAR COINAGE

KM# 163 PFENNIG

Copper **Ruler:** Maximilian I **Obv:** Bavaria arms in Spanish shield within circle of pellets **Mint:** Heidelberg **Note:** Uniface hohl-type. Ref. B#1008. Rheinpfalz issue.

Date	Mintage	VG	F	VF	XF	Unc
ND(ca.1624-28)	—	—	—	—	—	—

KM# 122 KREUZER

Silver **Ruler:** Maximilian I **Obv:** 3 small shields of arms, 2 above 1, value 'I' between 2 upper arms, lower shield divides date, legend above **Obv. Legend:** • M • D • E • **Rev:** Maltese cross in circle of pellets, titles of Ferdinand II **Mint:** Amberg **Note:** Ref. G#102, 103. Prev. Pfalz-Simmern KM#61. Oberpfalz issue.

Date	Mintage	VG	F	VF	XF	Unc
1623 (d)	—	22.00	45.00	80.00	150	—
1624 (d)	—	22.00	45.00	80.00	150	—

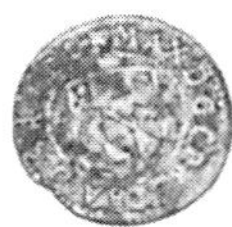

KM# 165 KREUZER

Silver **Ruler:** Maximilian I **Obv:** Bavaria arms in Spanish shield, titles of Maximilian I **Obv. Legend:** MAX • D • G • C ... **Rev:** Imperial orb with 'I' divides date, titles of Ferdinand II **Rev. Legend:** FER • II • ROM • IMP ... **Mint:** Heidelberg **Note:** Ref. B#1004-06. Prev. Pfalz-Simmern KM#63. Rheinpfalz issue. Legend varieties exist.

Date	Mintage	VG	F	VF	XF	Unc
1624	—	22.00	45.00	80.00	150	—
1625	—	22.00	45.00	80.00	150	—

KM# 248 KREUZER

Silver **Ruler:** Maximilian I **Obv:** Shield w/Bavarian lozenges **Obv. Legend:** MAX • D • G • C • **Rev:** Orb, value **Rev. Legend:** FER • II • ROM • IMP • **Mint:** Heidelberg **Note:** Klippe. Ref. B#1007. Prev. Pfalz-Simmern KM#85. Rheinpfalz issue.

Date	Mintage	VG	F	VF	XF	Unc
1633	—	—	—	—	—	—

KM# 170.1 2 KREUZER (1/2 Batzen)

Billon **Ruler:** Maximilian I **Obv:** Bavaria arms in ornamented Spanish shield, date above, titles of Maximilian I **Rev:** Imperial orb with Z, titles of Ferdinand II **Mint:** Heidelberg **Note:** Ref. B#998. Prev. Pfalz-Simmern KM#64. Rheinpfalz issue.

Date	Mintage	VG	F	VF	XF	Unc
1624	—	25.00	50.00	100	175	—

KM# 170.2 2 KREUZER (1/2 Batzen)

Billon **Ruler:** Maximilian I **Obv:** Bavaria arms in ornamented Spanish shield, titles of Maximilian I **Obv. Legend:** MAX • D • G • CO • ... **Rev:** Imperial orb divides date, titles of Ferdinand II **Rev. Legend:** FERD • II • ROM • IMP • SEMP • AVG • **Mint:** Heidelberg **Note:** Ref. B#999-1003. Prev. Pfalz-Simmern KM#64. Rheinpfalz issue. Varieties exist.

Date	Mintage	VG	F	VF	XF	Unc
1624	—	25.00	50.00	100	175	—
1625	—	25.00	50.00	100	175	—
1626	—	25.00	50.00	100	175	—
1632	—	25.00	50.00	100	175	—
1633	—	25.00	50.00	100	175	—

KM# 170.3 2 KREUZER (1/2 Batzen)

Billon **Ruler:** Maximilian I **Obv:** With lion countermark **Mint:** Heidelberg **Note:** Ref. B#1000. Prev. Pfalz-Simmern KM#70. Rheinpfalz issue.

Date	Mintage	VG	F	VF	XF	Unc
1625	—	—	—	—	—	—

KM# 133 2 KREUZER (GROSCHL)

Silver **Ruler:** Maximilian I **Obv:** Imperial orb with Z or 2 divides date, titles of Maximilian I **Rev:** Crowned imperial eagle, titles of Ferdinand II **Mint:** Amberg **Note:** Ref. G#174. Oberpfalz issue.

Date	Mintage	VG	F	VF	XF	Unc
1623 (g)	—	—	—	—	—	—

KM# 168 2 KREUZER (GROSCHL)

Silver **Ruler:** Maximilian I **Obv:** Imperial orb with Z or 2, titles of Maximilian I **Rev:** Crowned imperial eagle, titles of Ferdinand II **Mint:** Amberg **Note:** Ref. G#104-105. Oberpfalz issue.

Date	Mintage	VG	F	VF	XF	Unc
ND(1624-26) (e)	—	—	—	—	—	—
ND(1624-26) G	—	—	—	—	—	—

KM# 169 2 KREUZER (GROSCHL)

Silver **Ruler:** Maximilian I **Obv:** Imperial orb with Z or 2 divides date, titles of Maximilian I **Rev:** Crowned imperial eagle, titles of Ferdinand II **Mint:** Amberg **Note:** Ref. G#106-09. Oberpfalz issue. Varieties exist.

Date	Mintage	VG	F	VF	XF	Unc
1624	—	—	—	—	—	—
1624 (e)	—	—	—	—	—	—
1625	—	—	—	—	—	—
1625 (e)	—	—	—	—	—	—

KM# 205 2 KREUZER (GROSCHL)

Silver **Ruler:** Maximilian I **Obv:** Imperial orb with Z or 2, cross at top of orb divides date, titles of Maximilian I **Rev:** Crowned imperial eagle, titles of Ferdinand II **Mint:** Amberg **Note:** Ref. G#110. Oberpfalz issue.

Date	Mintage	VG	F	VF	XF	Unc
1626 (e)	—	—	—	—	—	—

KM# 134 3 KREUZER (Groschen)

Billon **Ruler:** Maximilian I **Obv:** Oval 4-fold arms of Bavaria and Pfalz surrounded by Order of Golden Fleece, electoral hat at top, titles of Maximilian I **Rev:** Imperial orb with 3 divides date, titles of Ferdinand II **Mint:** Kemnath **Note:** Ref. G#114. Prev. Pfalz-Simmern KM#62. Oberpfalz issue.

Date	Mintage	VG	F	VF	XF	Unc
1623	—	—	—	—	—	—

KM# 150 1/4 THALER

Silver **Ruler:** Maximilian I **Obv:** 2 ornately shaped shield of arms of Pfalz on left and Bavaria on right, small Spanish shield of imperial orb between, electoral hat above, Order of Golden Fleece underneath all, titles of Maximilian I **Rev:** Crowned imperial eagle, titles of Ferdinand II **Mint:** Neumarkt **Note:** Ref. G#171. Prev. Pfalz-Simmern KM#27. Oberpfalz issue.

Date	Mintage	VG	F	VF	XF	Unc
ND(1623-26) (g)	—	—	—	—	—	—

KM# 151 1/4 THALER

Silver **Ruler:** Maximilian I **Obv:** 2 ornately shaped shield of arms of Pfalz on left and Bavaria on right, small Spanish shield of imperial orb between divides date, electoral hat above, Order of Golden Fleece underneath all, titles of Maximilian I **Rev:** Crowned imperial eagle, titles of Ferdinand II **Mint:** Neumarkt **Note:** Ref. G#173. Oberpfalz issue.

Date	Mintage	VG	F	VF	XF	Unc
(16)23 (g)	—	—	—	—	—	—

KM# 225 1/2 THALER

Silver **Ruler:** Maximilian I **Obv:** Oval 4-fold arms of Bavaria and Pfalz in baroque frame, electoral hat above, Order of Golden Fleece below, titles of Maximilian I **Rev:** Crowned imperial eagle, date divided below, titles of Ferdinand II **Mint:** Heidelberg **Note:** Ref. B#997. Rheinpfalz issue.

Date	Mintage	VG	F	VF	XF	Unc
(16)27 GC	—	—	—	—	—	—

KM# 178 THALER
Silver **Ruler:** Maximilian I **Obv:** Capped oval arms in Order chain **Obv. Legend:** • MAXI: D:G: COM: P: RH: V ... BA: DVX: ... **Rev:** Crowned double-headed eagle **Rev. Legend:** FERDINAND: II • D:G: ROMA: IMPER: SEMP: AVGV • **Mint:** Heidelberg **Note:** Dav. #6090. Prev. Pfalz-Simmern KM#66.1. Rheinpfalz issue.

Date	Mintage	VG	F	VF	XF	Unc
1624 Rare	—	—	—	—	—	—
1626 Rare	—	—	—	—	—	—

KM# 210 THALER
Silver **Ruler:** Maximilian I **Mint:** Heidelberg **Note:** Dav. #6092. Prev. Pfalz-Simmern KM#72. Rheinpfalz issue.

Date	Mintage	VG	F	VF	XF	Unc
1626 GC Rare	—	—	—	—	—	—

KM# 228 THALER
Silver **Ruler:** Maximilian I **Obv:** Date divided above, G-C divided below **Mint:** Heidelberg **Note:** Dav. #6093. Prev. Pfalz-Simmern KM#75. Rheinpfalz issue. Varieties exist.

Date	Mintage	VG	F	VF	XF	Unc
1627 GC Rare	—	—	—	—	—	—

KM# 229 THALER
Silver **Ruler:** Maximilian I **Obv:** Bust of Maximilian right **Obv. Legend:** MAXIMILIANVS: D:G: COM: PAL: RHENI... TRI: BAVARIA • DVX • **Rev:** Helmeted and supported arms in Order chain **Rev. Legend:** SACRI • ROM • IMP • ARCHIDA ... **Mint:** Heidelberg **Note:** Dav. #6096. Prev. Pfalz-Simmern KM#76. Rheinpfalz issue.

Date	Mintage	VG	F	VF	XF	Unc
1627 GC Rare	—	—	—	—	—	—

KM# 176 THALER
Silver **Ruler:** Maximilian I **Obv:** 4-fold Bavarian arms **Obv. Legend:** MAXIMIL • DG • ... **Rev:** Crowned double-headed eagle, large date divided by bottom of tail **Rev. Legend:** FERDINANDVS • II • ROMANORVM ... **Mint:** Neumarkt **Note:** Oberpfalz issue.

Date	Mintage	VG	F	VF	XF	Unc
1624	—	—	—	—	—	—

KM# 177 THALER
Ruler: Maximilian I **Obv:** 4-fold Bavarian arms **Obv. Legend:** MAXIMIL • DG • ... **Rev:** Crowned double-headed eagle, small date below eagle's legs **Rev. Legend:** FERDINANDVS • II • ROMANORVM ... **Mint:** Neumarkt **Note:** Oberpfalz issue.

Date	Mintage	VG	F	VF	XF	Unc
1624 (g)	—	—	—	—	—	—

KM# 175.1 THALER
Silver **Ruler:** Maximilian I **Obv:** 4-fold Bavarian arms **Obv. Legend:** MAXIMIL • DG • • **Rev:** Crowned double-headed eagle, eagle's legs divide date above **Rev. Legend:** FERDINANDVS • II • ROMANORVM • **Mint:** Neumarkt **Note:** Dav. #6089. Prev. Pfalz-Simmern KM#65. Oberpfalz issue.

Date	Mintage	VG	F	VF	XF	Unc
1624 (g)	—	650	1,250	2,500	—	—

KM# 175.2 THALER
Silver **Ruler:** Maximilian I **Obv:** 4-fold Bavarian arms **Obv. Legend:** MAXIMIL • DG • ... **Rev:** Crowned double-headed eagle. Eagle's legs divide date below **Rev. Legend:** FERDINANDVS • II • ROMANORVM ... **Mint:** Neumarkt **Note:** Dav. #6089. Prev. Pfalz-Simmern KM#65. Oberpfalz issue.

Date	Mintage	VG	F	VF	XF	Unc
1624 (g)	—	650	1,250	2,500	—	—

KM# 161 2 THALER
Silver **Ruler:** Maximilian I **Obv:** 4-fold arms, titles of Maximilian I. **Obv. Legend:** MAXIMIL • DG • COM • P... AL • RH • V • BD • S • **Rev:** Crowned imperial eagle, titles of Ferdinand II. **Rev. Legend:** FERDINAND • II • ROMANORVM • IMPERATOR • **Mint:** Neumarkt **Note:** Dav. #6085. Prev. Pfalz-Simmern KM#30. Oberpfalz issue.

Date	Mintage	VG	F	VF	XF	Unc
ND(1623-26) (g) Rare	—	—	—	—	—	—

KM# 216 2 THALER
Silver **Ruler:** Maximilian I **Obv:** Capped square-topped arms divide date in Order chain **Obv. Legend:** MAXIMIL • DG • COM • P - AL • RH. • V •B • D • S • R • I • A • ET • E • **Rev:** Crowned imperial eagle, titles of Ferdinand II **Rev. Legend:** FERDINAN • II • ROMANORVM • IMPERATOR • ... **Mint:** Heidelberg **Note:** Dav. #A6090. Prev. Pfalz-Simmern KM#73. Rheinpfalz issue.

Date	Mintage	VG	F	VF	XF	Unc
1626 Rare	—	—	—	—	—	—

KM# 217 2 THALER
Silver **Ruler:** Maximilian I **Obv:** Shield of arms in Order chain **Rev:** Crowned imperial eagle **Mint:** Heidelberg **Note:** Dav. 6091. Prev. Pfalz-Simmern KM#74. Rheinpfalz issue.

Date	Mintage	VG	F	VF	XF	Unc
1626 GC Rare	—	—	—	—	—	—

KM# 236 2 THALER
Silver **Ruler:** Maximilian I **Obv:** Bust right, titles of Maximilian **Obv. Legend:** MAXIMILIANVS • D:G: COM: PAL: RHENI. VTRI: BAVARI • DVX **Rev:** Helmeted round arms with supporters **Rev. Legend:** FERDINAND: II • D:G: ROMA: **Mint:** Heidelberg **Note:** Dav. #6094. Prev. Pfalz-Simmern KM#78. Rheinpfalz issue.

Date	Mintage	VG	F	VF	XF	Unc
1627 GC Rare	—	—	—	—	—	—

KM# 183 2 THALER
Silver **Ruler:** Maximilian I **Obv:** Oval arms, titles of Maximilian I **Obv. Legend:** MAXIMIL • DG COMP ... **Rev:** Crowned imperial eagle, legs divide date, titles of Ferdinand II **Rev. Legend:** FERDINANDVS II ROMANORVM • IMPERATOR • **Mint:** Neumarkt **Note:** Dav. #6087. Prev. Pfalz-Simmern KM#68. Oberpfalz issue.

Date	Mintage	VG	F	VF	XF	Unc
1624 (g) Rare	—	—	—	—	—	—

KM# 184 2 THALER
Silver **Ruler:** Maximilian I **Obv:** Oval shield of arms, titles of Maximilian **Rev:** Crowned imperial eagle, date above or below legs, titles of Ferdinand II **Mint:** Neumarkt **Note:** Dav. #6088. Prev. Pfalz-Simmern KM#69. Oberpfalz issue.

Date	Mintage	VG	F	VF	XF	Unc
1624 (g) Rare	—	—	—	—	—	—
1626 (g) Rare	—	—	—	—	—	—

TRADE COINAGE

KM# 326 GOLDGULDEN
Gold **Ruler:** Maximilian I **Obv:** Oval 4-fold arms of Bavaria and Pfalz with central shield of imperial orb, Order of Golden Fleece around, titles of Maximilian I **Rev:** Crowned imperial eagle, date divided near feet, titles of Maximilian **Mint:** Heidelberg **Note:** Fr. #192. Rheinpfalz issue. Prev. Pfalz-Simmern KM#71.

Date	Mintage	VG	F	VF	XF	Unc
1625	—	—	—	—	—	—

KM# 307 5 DUCAT
Gold **Ruler:** Ferdinand Maria **Subject:** Birth of Princess Maria Anna **Obv:** Busts of Ferdinand Maria and Henriette Adelheid to right, titles of Ferdinand Maria **Rev:** Ornamented shield of Bavaria arms, angel head and wings above, legend with date in chronogram **Note:** Fr. #203. Coinage for Rheinpfalz. Prev. KM#A90.

Date	Mintage	VG	F	VF	XF	Unc
1660	—	2,000	4,000	6,000	10,000	—

KM# 342 5 DUCAT

Gold **Ruler:** Maximilian II, Emanuel **Subject:** Homage of Cities for Marriage of Maximilian II Emanuel and Maria Antonie von Habsburg **Obv:** 2 busts to right **Obv. Legend:** A DEO PACIS BELLIQUE ... **Rev:** Shield of Bavaria arms hanging from garland, arms of Munich, Landshut, Burghausen and Straubing around, angel above **Rev. Legend:** ITA VOVENTIBVS VTRIVSQVE ... **Note:** Fr. #215. Rheinpfalz issue. Prev. KM#B115.

Date	Mintage	VG	F	VF	XF	Unc
ND(1685)	—	—	3,500	6,000	9,000	—

KM# 341 5 DUCAT

Gold **Ruler:** Maximilian II, Emanuel **Subject:** Marriage of Maximilian II Emanuel and Maria Antonie von Habsburg **Obv:** 2 busts facing one another within palm and laurel branches **Obv. Legend:** QVOS DEVS CONIVNXIT ... **Rev:** 2 adjacent oval shields, crowned arms of Austria on left, 4-fold arms of Bavaria and Pfalz with central shield of imperial orb, electoral hat above, on right, all within palm and laurel branches **Rev. Legend:** VT VIDEANT ... **Note:** Fr.#214. Rheinpfalz issue. Prev. KM#A115.

Date	Mintage	VG	F	VF	XF	Unc
ND(1685) CZ	—	—	3,500	6,000	9,000	—

KM# 357 5 DUCAT

Gold **Ruler:** Maximilian II, Emanuel **Subject:** Birth of Prince Josef Ferdinand **Obv:** Young prince among arms of Austria and Bavaria, imperial orb on pedestal on which 3-line inscription with date **Rev:** Imperial orb on globe, above triangle with Eye of God, rays streaming down **Rev. Legend:** EX PARVO SPES ... **Note:** Fr. #218. Rheinpfalz issue. Prev. KM#A124.

Date	Mintage	VG	F	VF	XF	Unc
1692	—	2,000	5,000	8,000	—	—

KM# 240 5 DUCAT

Gold **Ruler:** Maximilian I **Subject:** Maximilian I as Duke **Obv:** Crowned arms **Rev:** Madonna with child **Mint:** Heidelberg **Note:** Fr. #190. Rheinpfalz issue. Prev. KM#A11.

Date	Mintage	VG	F	VF	XF	Unc
1627 Rare	—	—	—	—	—	—

BECKUM

A small provincial city in Westphalia located about 20 miles southeast of Munster, founded in 1139. It had a local copper coinage in the late 16th and early 17th centuries.

PROVINCIAL CITY

REGULAR COINAGE

KM# 7 2 PFENNIG

Copper **Obv:** Arms (three wavy bends), STADT BE-KEM **Rev:** Value II and date in ornamented square

Date	Mintage	Good	VG	F	VF	XF
1622 Rare	—	—	—	—	—	—

KM# 8 3 PFENNIG

Copper **Obv:** Arms, STADT BEKEM **Rev:** Value interspersed with date 1I6I2I2 in ornamented square

Date	Mintage	Good	VG	F	VF	XF
1622	—	45.00	90.00	135	190	—

KM# 5 6 PFENNIG

Copper **Obv:** Arms, STADT BEKEM, date **Rev:** Value VI in ornamented square

Date	Mintage	Good	VG	F	VF	XF
1609	—	45.00	90.00	150	225	—

KM# 9 6 PFENNIG

Copper **Obv:** Arms, STADT BEKEM **Rev:** Value interspersed with date 1 212

Date	Mintage	Good	VG	F	VF	XF
1622	—	45.00	90.00	150	225	—

KM# 6 12 PFENNIG

Copper **Obv:** Arms, STADT BEKEM **Rev:** Date interspersed with value XII

Date	Mintage	Good	VG	F	VF	XF
1609	—	150	225	250	375	—
1622	—	135	200	225	350	—

BEESKOW

A provincial town on the River Spree in Brandenburg-Prussia, about 43 miles southeast of Berlin. Beeskow is mentioned as early as 1185 and came under the control of the lords of Strele in the second half of the 13th century. It passed through the possession of several local noble families before its final acquisition by Brandenburg in 1571. The Elector of Brandenburg permitted a local copper coinage during the inflationary period at the beginning of the Thirty Years' War.

PROVINCIAL TOWN

REGULAR COINAGE

KM# 1 PFENNIG

Copper **Note:** Kipper Pfenning. Arms of Biberstein (stag antler) and Strele (three scythe blades), date above, letter B below.

Date	Mintage	Good	VG	F	VF	XF
1621	—	27.00	45.00	90.00	150	—

BENTHEIM-BENTHEIM

The countship of Bentheim was located on both sides of the Vechte River along the border between the Netherlands and Westphalia. The lords of Bentheim were descended from an eleventh-century marriage alliance of the countships of Holland and Nordheim. Tecklenburg was obtained through marriage in the middle of the 13th century with a separate line being founded in 1269. In 1454, Bentheim was divided into the lines of Bentheim-Bentheim and Bentheim-Steinfurt. The latter was a territory located about midway between the county of Bentheim and the city of Münster in Westphalia. The various divisions were reunited by marriage during the 16th century only to be divided again into five lines in 1606. By family agreement (1691), the heirs to the two lines of Bentheim-Bentheim and Bentheim-Steinfurt exchanged their counties and titles in 1693. Bentheim-Bentheim became extinct in 1803, when the last count died, but he had already ceded Bentheim to Hannover in 1753. It passed to Berg in 1806 and then to Prussia in 1813. Bentheim-Steinfurt was mediatized in 1806, but the count was raised to the rank of prince in 1817. The counts of Bentheim-Steinfurt did not issue any coinage, rather allowing that of Bentheim-Bentheim to circulate in their territory.

RULERS

Arnold Jobst, 1606-1643
Ernst Wilhelm, 1643-1693
Arnold Moritz Wilhelm, 1693-1701
Hermann Friedrich, 1701-1731
Friedrich Karl Philipp, 1731-1753 – (1803)

MINT OFFICIALS' INITIALS

Initials	Date	Name
JO	1692-96	Johann Odendahl in Munster
LK	Ca. 1659-64	Johann Longerich, warden
	1659-62	Engelbert Kettler, mintmaster

COUNTY

REGULAR COINAGE

KM# 2.1 DEUT (2 Pfennig - 1/8 Stüber)

Copper **Ruler:** Ernest Wilhelm **Obv:** Crowned double EC monogram between two branches **Rev:** Between two branches DVTT/PENT/HEIM/date

Date	Mintage	Good	VG	F	VF	XF
1654	—	10.00	20.00	35.00	60.00	—

KM# 2.2 DEUT (2 Pfennig - 1/8 Stüber)

Copper **Ruler:** Ernest Wilhelm **Obv:** Crowned double EC monogram between 2 laurel branches. **Rev:** DVTT/BENT/HEIM

Date	Mintage	Good	VG	F	VF	XF
1662	—	27.00	60.00	120	200	—
1664	—	27.00	60.00	120	200	—

KM# 16 DEUT (2 Pfennig - 1/8 Stüber)

Copper **Ruler:** Ernest Wilhelm **Obv:** Without branches

Date	Mintage	Good	VG	F	VF	XF
1662	—	35.00	70.00	130	220	—

KM# 17 STUBER

Silver **Ruler:** Ernest Wilhelm **Obv:** Bentheim arms in baroque frame, date above in margin. **Rev:** Crowned imperial eagle, value 'I' in circle on breast. **Note:** Kennepohl 15.

Date	Mintage	VG	F	VF	XF	Unc
1662	—	25.00	45.00	90.00	175	—

KM# 15 2 STUBER

Silver **Ruler:** Ernest Wilhelm **Obv:** Bentheim arms, date above **Rev:** Crowned imperial eagle with 2 on breast

Date	Mintage	VG	F	VF	XF	Unc
1660	—	25.00	45.00	90.00	175	—
1662	—	25.00	45.00	90.00	175	—
1663	—	25.00	45.00	90.00	175	—

KM# 3 6 STUBER (Blamüser)

Silver **Ruler:** Ernest Wilhelm **Obv:** Crowned manifold arms in baroque frame, date divided above **Rev:** Crowned imperial eagle

Date	Mintage	VG	F	VF	XF	Unc
1659 LK	—	27.00	55.00	100	170	—
1662 LK	—	27.00	55.00	100	170	—

KM# 20 1/8 THALER

Silver **Ruler:** Ernest Wilhelm **Obv:** Crowned arms between two branches **Rev:** VIII/EINEN/REICHES/THALER in center, date in legend

Date	Mintage	VG	F	VF	XF	Unc
1673	—	—	—	—	—	—

KM# 25 1/2 THALER

Silver **Ruler:** Arnold Moritz Wilhelm **Obv:** Bust right **Rev:** Helmeted arms, date

Date	Mintage	VG	F	VF	XF	Unc
1695 JO	—	—	—	—	—	—

KM# 4 THALER

Silver **Ruler:** Ernest Wilhelm **Note:** Dav. #6104.

Date	Mintage	VG	F	VF	XF	Unc
1659 LK	—	1,000	1,700	2,750	4,500	—
1660 LK	—	1,000	1,700	2,750	4,500	—

KM# 26 THALER

Silver **Ruler:** Arnold Moritz Wilhelm **Obv:** Bust right **Rev:** Helmeted arms, date **Note:** Dav. #6105.

Date	Mintage	VG	F	VF	XF	Unc
1696 JO Rare	—	—	—	—	—	—

KM# 5 1-1/2 THALER

Silver **Ruler:** Ernest Wilhelm **Note:** Dav. #6103.

Date	Mintage	VG	F	VF	XF	Unc
1659 LK Rare	—	—	—	—	—	—

KM# 6 2 THALER

Silver **Ruler:** Ernest Wilhelm **Note:** Similar to 1 Thaler, KM#4. Dav. #6102.

Date	Mintage	VG	F	VF	XF	Unc
1659 LK Rare	—	—	—	—	—	—
1660 LK Rare	—	—	—	—	—	—

TRADE COINAGE

KM# 7 DUCAT

3.5000 g., 0.9860 Gold 0.1109 oz. AGW **Ruler:** Ernest Wilhelm **Obv:** Crowned arms **Rev:** Three-line inscription with date below

Date	Mintage	VG	F	VF	XF	Unc
1659 LK	—	3,500	5,500	9,000	14,500	—

KM# 8 2 DUCAT

7.0000 g., 0.9860 Gold 0.2219 oz. AGW **Ruler:** Ernest Wilhelm **Obv:** Crowned arms **Rev:** Three-line inscription with date below

Date	Mintage	VG	F	VF	XF	Unc
1659 LK Rare	—	—	—	—	—	—

KM# 9 2 DUCAT

7.0000 g., 0.9860 Gold 0.2219 oz. AGW **Ruler:** Ernest Wilhelm **Note:** Klippe.

Date	Mintage	VG	F	VF	XF	Unc
1659 LK Rare	—	—	—	—	—	—

LOCAL COINAGE

Helfenstein

Coinage struck for the Lordship of Helfenstein (Helpenstein)

KM# 32 GROSCHEN (1/24 Thaler)

Silver **Ruler:** Arnold Moritz Wilhelm **Obv:** Lion right, ARNO: DO: IN: HELFEN: **Rev:** Imperial eagle with 24 on breast, titles of Ferdinand II **Note:** Kipper Groschen.

Date	Mintage	VG	F	VF	XF	Unc
ND Rare	—	—	—	—	—	—

BENTHEIM-TECKLENBURG-RHEDA

The county of Tecklenburg was located about halfway between the cities of Münster and Osnabrück in Westpha- lia and was acquired by Bentheim through marriage during the first half of the 13th century and the separate line of Bentheim-Tecklenburg was founded in 1269. The lordship of Rheda, to the southeast of Tecklenburg, was acquired by marriage in the mid-14th century. After the reunification of the 16th century, a new line of Bentheim-Tecklenburg-Rheda was founded in 1606. The county of Tecklenburg was lost to Solms in 1696, then sold to Prussia in 1707. Rheda was mediatized in 1805.

RULERS

Adolf, 1606-1623
Moritz, 1623-1674
Johann Adolf, 1674-1701

MINT OFFICIALS' INITIALS

Initials	Date	Name
ILC		Johann Schitzkey of Liegnitz, die-cutter for Cologne, initials read "Johann Liegnitz Coloniensis"
IS, JS		Johann (Wilhelm) Salter

COUNTY / LORDSHIP

REGULAR COINAGE

KM# 106 PFENNIG

Copper **Obv:** 4-fold arms with central shield of Rheda arms between two branches, date above **Rev:** I/G. T. P. between two branches

Date	Mintage	VG	F	VF	XF	Unc
1685	—	13.00	27.00	40.00	75.00	—

Note: G.T.P. = Graflich Tecklenburgische Pfennige

KM# 107 1-1/2 PFENNIG

Copper **Obv:** 4-fold arms with central shield of Rheda arms between two branches, date above **Rev:** Value between two branches

Date	Mintage	VG	F	VF	XF	Unc
1685	—	13.00	27.00	40.00	75.00	—

KM# 108 2 PFENNIG

Copper **Obv:** 4-fold arms with central shield of Rheda arms between two branches, date above **Rev:** Value I.I. between two branches

Date	Mintage	VG	F	VF	XF	Unc
1685	—	13.00	27.00	40.00	75.00	—

KM# 32 3 PFENNING

Copper **Obv:** 4-fold arms, TEKELNBVRGK in legend **Rev:** Value III surrounded by ornaments within circle, outer border of 16 lilies **Note:** Kipper 3 Pfennig.

Date	Mintage	Good	VG	F	VF	XF
ND(1622-23)	—	13.00	27.00	45.00	80.00	—

KM# 34 3 PFENNING (Dreier)

Billon **Obv:** Crowned arms of Tecklenburg and Rheda in heart-shaped shield, divide ADO-G. Z. B.

Date	Mintage	VG	F	VF	XF	Unc
1622	—	—	—	—	—	—

KM# 35 3 PFENNING (Dreier)

Billon **Ruler:** Adolf **Obv:** Helmeted arms of Hoya divide inscription. **Obv. Legend:** ADOL - G. Z. B. T. **Rev:** Imperial orb with '3' divides date.

Date	Mintage	VG	F	VF	XF	Unc
16ZZ	—	—	—	—	—	—

KM# 36 3 PFENNING (Dreier)

Billon **Obv:** Helmeted arms of Linden divide ADOLF. G.- Z. B. V. TEC.

Date	Mintage	VG	F	VF	XF	Unc
1622	—	—	—	—	—	—

Note: Hoya and Lingen were counties belonging to Bentheim

KM# 33 3 PFENNING (Dreier)

Billon **Obv:** 4-fold arms, central shield of Rheda arms, all in ornamented shield **Rev:** Imperial orb with 3 divides date **Note:** Kipper 3 Pfennig

Date	Mintage	VG	F	VF	XF	Unc
1622	—	—	—	—	—	—

KM# 109 3 PFENNING (Dreier)

Copper **Obv:** 4-fold arms with central shield of Rheda arms between two branches, date above **Rev:** Value I. I. I. between two branches

Date	Mintage	VG	F	VF	XF	Unc
1685	—	13.00	27.00	40.00	80.00	—

KM# 110 4 PFENNIG

Copper **Ruler:** Johann Adolf **Obv:** 4-fold arms with central shield of Rheda arms between two branches, date above. **Rev:** 2-line inscription with value between 2 branches. **Rev. Inscription:** IIII/G.T.P. **Mint:** Tecklenburg **Note:** Kennepohl 130.

Date	Mintage	VG	F	VF	XF	Unc
1685	—	16.00	33.00	55.00	100	—

KM# 89 4-1/2 PFENNIG

Copper **Obv:** 4-fold arms, central shield of Rheda arms, date above **Rev:** 4 1/2/PFENN/TECL

Date	Mintage	VG	F	VF	XF	Unc
1674	—	40.00	80.00	175	300	—

KM# 90 5 PFENNIG

Billon **Obv:** Helmet in wreath **Rev:** Date/V/G.T.P.

Date	Mintage	VG	F	VF	XF	Unc
1674	—	60.00	100	170	200	—

KM# 95 5 PFENNIG

Billon **Obv:** Helmet between two palm branches

Date	Mintage	VG	F	VF	XF	Unc
1677	—	60.00	100	170	300	—

KM# 91 6 PFENNING (1/42 Thaler)

Billon **Ruler:** Moritz **Obv:** Crowned M in wreath **Rev:** 4-line inscription with date, value '42' in oval below. **Rev. Inscription:** 1674/VI/PFENN/TECL. **Mint:** Kirchstapel **Note:** Kennepohl 117.

Date	Mintage	VG	F	VF	XF	Unc
1674	—	16.00	33.00	60.00	110	—

KM# 96 6 PFENNING (1/42 Thaler)

Billon **Obv:** Crowned 4-fold arms, central shield of Rheda arms date divided to either side **Rev:** VI/PFENN/TECL/42

Date	Mintage	VG	F	VF	XF	Unc
1677	—	25.00	50.00	100	200	—

KM# 105 6 PFENNING (1/42 Thaler)

Billon **Obv:** Crowned JA monogram between two palm branches **Rev:** Date/VI/PFENNI/TECLB/42

Date	Mintage	VG	F	VF	XF	Unc
1683	—	25.00	50.00	100	200	—

KM# 16 8 PFENNIG (Fürstengroschen)

Silver **Obv:** 4-fold arms, central shield of Rheda arms **Obv. Legend:** TECKELNB.LANDMVNTZ **Rev:** Crowned imperial eagle, orb on breast **Rev. Legend:** VIII SVVER PFENNINGE **Note:** Kipper 8 Pfennig. Valued at 8 heavy Pfennig, the standard for the Furstengroschen was usually 9 heavy Pfennig in Westphalia.

Date	Mintage	VG	F	VF	XF	Unc
ND(1620)	—	60.00	120	250	450	—

KM# 37 MARIENGROSCHEN (1/36 Thaler)

Billon **Obv:** 4-fold arms, central shield of Rheda arms in ornamented shield, ADOL. C. B... around **Rev:** Madonna, MARIA.-GROSS., date

Date	Mintage	VG	F	VF	XF	Unc
1622	—	—	—	—	—	—

KM# 44 MARIENGROSCHEN (1/36 Thaler)

Billon **Obv:** Crowned lion left (Rheda) holding Tecklenburg arms, date in legend **Rev:** Madonna with rays on either side

Date	Mintage	VG	F	VF	XF	Unc
1623	—	—	—	—	—	—

Note: These mariengroschen were struck to the equivalent of a Tecklenburger half-schilling

KM# 56 2 MARIENGROSCHEN

Silver **Obv:** Crowned 4-fold arms **Rev:** II/MARI/GRO, date in legend

Date	Mintage	VG	F	VF	XF	Unc
1656	—	—	—	—	—	—

KM# 57 4 MARIENGROSCHEN

Silver **Obv:** Crowned 4-fold arms **Rev:** IIII/MARIE/GRO, date in legend

Date	Mintage	VG	F	VF	XF	Unc
1656	—	—	—	—	—	—

KM# 82 6 MARIENGROSCHEN

Silver **Obv:** Crowned 4-fold arms, central shield of Rheda arms **Rev:** VI/MARIE/GROS, date in legend

Date	Mintage	VG	F	VF	XF	Unc
1671	—	65.00	125	225	400	—

KM# 86 6 MARIENGROSCHEN

Silver **Obv:** Helmeted arms, date in legend

Date	Mintage	VG	F	VF	XF	Unc
1672	—	60.00	100	200	350	—

KM# 87 6 MARIENGROSCHEN

Silver **Rev:** Date below value in center

Date	Mintage	VG	F	VF	XF	Unc
1672	—	45.00	90.00	180	350	—
1673	—	45.00	90.00	180	350	—

KM# 81 12 MARIENGROSCHEN (1/3 Thaler)

Silver **Ruler:** Moritz **Obv:** Crowned 4-fold arms with central shield in circle. **Obv. Legend:** MAUR. C. I. B. TEC. S. ET L. D. I. R. W. HL. AH. **Rev:** 3-line inscription in circle, date at end of legend. **Rev. Legend:** VON FEINEM SILBER. **Rev. Inscription:** XII/MARIEN/GROS. **Note:** Varieties exist.

Date	Mintage	VG	F	VF	XF	Unc
1670	—	60.00	125	200	350	—
1671 MAVRITZ	—	90.00	175	350	600	—
1671 MAUR	—	45.00	90.00	150	300	—
1672	—	60.00	125	200	350	—

KM# 92 12 MARIENGROSCHEN (1/3 Thaler)

Silver **Note:** Similar to KM#81.

Date	Mintage	VG	F	VF	XF	Unc
1675	—	65.00	125	200	350	—

KM# 94 12 MARIENGROSCHEN (1/3 Thaler)

Silver **Obv:** Helmet above arms

Date	Mintage	VG	F	VF	XF	Unc
1676	—	65.00	125	200	350	—

KM# 93 24 MARIENGROSCHEN (2/3 Thaler)

Silver **Ruler:** Johann Adolf **Obv:** Ornate helmet. **Obv. Legend:** I. ADOLF. C. I. B. TEC. SI. ET L. D. I. R. W. HL. A. H. **Rev:** 3-line inscription in circle, date at end of legend. **Rev. Legend:** MONETA NOVA ARGENTEA. **Rev. Inscription:** XXIIII/MARIEN/GROS. **Note:** Dav. #1019. Varieties exist.

Date	Mintage	VG	F	VF	XF	Unc
1675	—	90.00	175	350	550	—
1676	—	90.00	175	350	550	—
1677	—	90.00	175	350	550	—

KM# 19 12 KREUZER (Schreckenberger)

Silver **Rev:** Helmeted 4-fold arms, central shield of Rheda

Date	Mintage	VG	F	VF	XF	Unc
ND(1620-22)	—	50.00	90.00	150	250	—

KM# 20 12 KREUZER (Schreckenberger)

Silver **Ruler:** Adolf **Rev:** Helmeted Tecklenburg arms, A. G. Z...

Date	Mintage	VG	F	VF	XF	Unc
ND(1620-22)	—	50.00	90.00	150	250	—

KM# 21 12 KREUZER (Schreckenberger)

Silver **Rev:** Helmeted Rheda arms

Date	Mintage	VG	F	VF	XF	Unc
ND(1620-22)	—	50.00	90.00	150	250	—

KM# 18 12 KREUZER (Schreckenberger)

Silver **Ruler:** Adolf **Obv:** Helmeted 4-fold arms without central shield. **Obv. Legend:** ADOLF. COM. TECKLENBVRG. **Rev:** Crowned imperial eagle, '1Z' in circle on breast. **Rev. Legend:** FERDINAN. II. D. G. R. I. S. AV. **Mint:** Freudenberg **Note:** Kennepohl 50a.

Date	Mintage	VG	F	VF	XF	Unc
ND(1620-22)	—	50.00	90.00	150	250	—

KM# 17 12 KREUZER (Schreckenberger)

Silver **Obv:** 4-fold arms, central shield of Rheda arms **Obv. Legend:** TECKELNB.LANDMUNTZ **Rev:** Crowned imperial eagle, orb on breast with 12, titles of Ferdinand II **Note:** Kipper 12 Kreuzer.

Date	Mintage	VG	F	VF	XF	Unc
ND(1620-22)	—	50.00	90.00	150	250	—

KM# 27 12 KREUZER (Schreckenberger)

Silver **Rev:** Helmet divides date

Date	Mintage	VG	F	VF	XF	Unc
1621	—	50.00	90.00	150	250	—

KM# 11 5 STUBER

Silver **Rev:** Helmeted arms with central shield of Rheda arms

Date	Mintage	VG	F	VF	XF	Unc
ND(1619-22)	—	45.00	125	225	400	—

KM# 8 5 STUBER

Silver **Obv:** Crowned imperial eagle, titles of Matthias **Rev:** Helmeted arms of Rheda (lion left) **Rev. Legend:** PIETATE. ET. IUSTICIA. U. S. **Note:** Kipper 5 Stuber.

Date	Mintage	VG	F	VF	XF	Unc
ND(1619)	—	45.00	125	225	400	—

KM# 13 5 STUBER

Silver **Ruler:** Adolf **Obv:** Ornate helmet above 4-fold arms with central shield. **Obv. Legend:** MO. NO. ADOLF. CO. ET DO. TECKLEBVR. **Rev:** Crowned imperial eagle in circle. **Rev. Legend:** PIETATE. ET. IVSTITIA. V. B. **Mint:** Freudenberg **Note:** Kipper 6 Stüber. Varieties exist.

Date	Mintage	VG	F	VF	XF	Unc
ND(1619-22)	—	45.00	125	225	400	—

KM# 10 5 STUBER

Silver **Note:** Klippe.

Date	Mintage	VG	F	VF	XF	Unc
ND(1619-22) Rare	—	—	—	—	—	—

KM# 12 5 STUBER

Silver **Note:** Klippe.

Date	Mintage	VG	F	VF	XF	Unc
ND(1619-22) Rare	—	—	—	—	—	—

KM# 14 5 STUBER

Silver **Note:** Klippe.

Date	Mintage	VG	F	VF	XF	Unc
ND(1619-22) Rare	—	—	—	—	—	—

KM# 9 5 STUBER

Silver **Obv. Legend:** DEVS. PROVIDEBIT. V. ST. **Rev:** Helmeted 4-fold arms **Note:** Varieties exist.

Date	Mintage	VG	F	VF	XF	Unc
ND(1619-22)	—	45.00	125	225	400	—

KM# 15 6 STUBER

Silver **Ruler:** Adolf **Obv:** Crowned 6-fold arms in circle. **Obv. Legend:** MO. NO. ADOLF. CO. ET DO. TECLEBVRG. **Rev:** Crowned imperial eagle in circle. **Rev. Legend:** MATH. D.G. EL. RO. IMP. SEM. AVG. **Note:** Kipper 6 Stüber. Varieties exist.

Date	Mintage	VG	F	VF	XF	Unc
ND(1619)	—	70.00	150	300	450	—

KM# 58 1/28 THALER (Fürstengroschen)

Silver **Obv:** Crowned imperial eagle, orb on breast with 28, titles of Ferdinand III **Rev:** Crowned 4-fold arms, central shield of Rheda arms, date in legend

Date	Mintage	VG	F	VF	XF	Unc
1656	—	—	—	—	—	—
1657	—	—	—	—	—	—

KM# 59 1/28 THALER (Fürstengroschen)

Silver **Obv:** Value (28) at bottom

Date	Mintage	VG	F	VF	XF	Unc
1656	—	—	—	—	—	—

KM# 5 1/24 THALER (1 Groschen)

Silver **Obv:** Imperial orb with 24, date divided at top, titles of Matthias **Rev:** Helmeted 4-fold arms, central shield of Rheda arms **Note:** Varieties exist.

Date	Mintage	VG	F	VF	XF	Unc
1618	—	40.00	75.00	150	300	—
1619	—	40.00	75.00	150	300	—

KM# 24 1/24 THALER (1 Groschen)

Silver **Obv:** Imperial orb with 24, date in legend, titles of Ferdinand II **Rev:** Helmeted 4-fold arms **Note:** Small module. Varieties exist.

Date	Mintage	VG	F	VF	XF	Unc
(1)620	—	—	—	—	—	—
(16)20	—	—	—	—	—	—
(16)02 Error for 1620	—	—	—	—	—	—

KM# 38 1/24 THALER (1 Groschen)

Silver **Obv:** Imperial orb with 24, date divided at top, titles of Ferdinand II **Rev:** Helmeted 4-fold arms, central shield of Rheda arms

Date	Mintage	VG	F	VF	XF	Unc
1622	—	—	—	—	—	—

KM# 39 1/24 THALER (1 Groschen)

Silver **Obv:** Date divided by orb **Rev:** Crowned 4-fold arms

Date	Mintage	VG	F	VF	XF	Unc
1622	—	—	—	—	—	—

KM# 22 1/21 THALER (1 Schilling)

Silver **Obv:** Crowned imperial eagle, orb on breast, titles of Ferdinand II **Rev:** 4-fold arms, central shield of Rheda arms, LANTMVNTZ XXI. ZVM. DALER

Date	Mintage	VG	F	VF	XF	Unc
ND(1620)	—	—	—	—	—	—

KM# 23 1/21 THALER (1 Schilling)

Silver **Obv:** Helmeted 4-fold arms, MO. NO. ADOL... **Rev:** Crowned imperial eagle, 21 in orb on breast, LANDT. MVNTZ XXI. Z. THATL. date **Note:** This Tecklenburg schilling equalled 1-1/2 schilling on the Westphalian standard.

Date	Mintage	VG	F	VF	XF	Unc
1620	—	125	275	450	700	—
(1)620	—	125	275	450	700	—
1621	—	125	275	450	700	—
(1)621	—	125	275	450	700	—
(16)21	—	125	275	450	700	—

KM# 6 1/16 THALER (2 Schilling)

Silver **Obv:** Crowned imperial eagle, orb with 16 on breast, titles of Matthias and date in legend **Rev:** 4-fold arms, three helmets above

Date	Mintage	VG	F	VF	XF	Unc
1618	—	175	350	600	—	—
1619	—	175	350	600	—	—

KM# 25 1/16 THALER (2 Schilling)

Silver **Obv:** Eagle's tail divides value 1-6, titles of Ferdinand II **Rev:** Single helmet

Date	Mintage	VG	F	VF	XF	Unc
1620	—	—	—	—	—	—

KM# 98 1/16 THALER (2 Schilling)

Silver **Obv:** Crowned 4-fold arms, central shield of Rheda arms

Date	Mintage	VG	F	VF	XF	Unc
1677	—	40.00	90.00	170	275	—

KM# 97 1/16 THALER (2 Schilling)

Silver **Ruler:** Johann Adolf **Obv:** Bust right in circle. **Obv. Legend:** ADOLF. C. I. B. TEC. Si. E. L. **Rev:** 4-line inscription with date in circle. **Rev. Legend:** MONETA. NOVA. ARGENTEA. **Rev. Inscription:** XVI/REICHS/THAL/1677. **Mint:** Kirchstapel **Note:** Kennepohl 125.

Date	Mintage	VG	F	VF	XF	Unc
1677	—	65.00	145	325	500	—

KM# 60 1/14 THALER (2 Fürstengroschen)

Silver **Obv:** Crowned imperial eagle, 14 in orb on breast, titles of Ferdinand III, date in legend **Rev:** Helmeted 4-fold arms, central shield of Rheda arms

Date	Mintage	VG	F	VF	XF	Unc
1656	—	—	—	—	—	—

KM# 84 1/14 THALER (2 Fürstengroschen)
Silver **Rev:** Crowned arms

Date	Mintage	VG	F	VF	XF	Unc
1671	—	75.00	150	300	500	—

KM# 83 1/14 THALER (2 Fürstengroschen)
Silver **Obv:** Titles of Leopold **Rev:** Date in legend **Note:** Varieties exist.

Date	Mintage	VG	F	VF	XF	Unc
1671	—	70.00	125	250	400	—
1672	—	70.00	125	250	400	—
1673	—	70.00	125	250	400	—

KM# 85 1/8 THALER (Blamüser)
Silver **Ruler:** Moritz **Obv:** Crowned 4-fold arms in ornamented frame with central shield. **Obv. Legend:** M. C. IN B. TEC. SI. ET L. D. R. WH. A. H. **Rev:** 4-line inscription in circle, small imperial orb at bottom, date at end of legend. **Rev. Legend:** MONETA NOVA - ARGENTEA. **Rev. Inscription:** VIII/EINEN/REICHS/THAL. **Note:** Kennepohl 111. Varieties exist.

Date	Mintage	VG	F	VF	XF	Unc
1671	—	65.00	125	250	400	—
1672	—	65.00	125	250	400	—
1673	—	65.00	125	250	400	—

KM# 26 1/2 THALER
Silver **Obv:** Arms with three helmets above **Rev:** Helmeted arms of Nassau **Note:** Klippe.

Date	Mintage	VG	F	VF	XF	Unc
ND(1621) Rare	—	—	—	—	—	—

KM# 88 2/3 THALER
Silver **Obv:** Crowned 4-fold arms, central shield of Rheda arms, branch on each side, value in oval below, date in legend **Rev:** Helmet of Tecklenburg

Date	Mintage	VG	F	VF	XF	Unc
1673	—	—	—	—	—	—

KM# 7 THALER
Silver **Obv:** Crowned imperial eagle divides date, titles of Matthias II **Rev:** Bust of Adolf right **Note:** Dav. #7801.

Date	Mintage	VG	F	VF	XF	Unc
1618 Rare	—	—	—	—	—	—
ND Rare	—	—	—	—	—	—

KM# 62 THALER
Silver **Note:** Klippe. Dav. #7801A.

Date	Mintage	VG	F	VF	XF	Unc
ND Rare	—	—	—	—	—	—

KM# 63 THALER
Silver **Note:** Similar to KM#64. Dav. #7803.

Date	Mintage	VG	F	VF	XF	Unc
ND Rare	—	—	—	—	—	—

KM# 64 THALER
Silver **Note:** Dav. #7804.

Date	Mintage	VG	F	VF	XF	Unc
1657 ILC	—	1,250	3,000	5,500	7,500	—

KM# 66 1-1/2 THALER
Silver **Obv:** Crowned imperial eagle, titles of Matthias II **Rev:** Bust of Adolf right **Note:** Klippe.

Date	Mintage	VG	F	VF	XF	Unc
ND Rare	—	—	—	—	—	—

KM# 30 3 THALER
Silver **Obv:** Crowned imperial eagle divides date left and right of heads and feet, titles of Ferdinand II **Rev:** Arms with three helmets above **Note:** Dav. #7802.

Date	Mintage	VG	F	VF	XF	Unc
1621 Rare	—	—	—	—	—	—

TRADE COINAGE

KM# 31 GOLDGULDEN
Gold **Obv:** Tecklenburg arms with helmet of Limburg above **Rev:** Nassau arms and helmet

Date	Mintage	VG	F	VF	XF	Unc
ND(1621) Rare	—	—	—	—	—	—

KM# 61 DUCAT
3.5000 g., 0.9860 Gold 0.1109 oz. AGW **Obv:** Bust of Moritz right **Rev:** Crowned arms

Date	Mintage	VG	F	VF	XF	Unc
1656	—	3,500	5,500	9,000	14,500	—

KM# 65 DUCAT
3.5000 g., 0.9860 Gold 0.1109 oz. AGW **Obv:** Without circles **Rev:** Without circles

Date	Mintage	VG	F	VF	XF	Unc
1657	—	—	—	—	—	—

LOCAL COINAGE

Rheda

Special Coinage for the Lordship of Rheda

KM# 40 HELLER
Copper **Obv:** Crowned rampant lion left (Rheda arms), REDE in legend **Rev:** 1 in circle, border of 12 lilies

Date	Mintage	Good	VG	F	VF	XF
ND(pre-1623)	—	55.00	100	200	325	—

KM# 41.1 PFENNIG
Copper **Obv:** Crowned rampant lion left, REDE in legend **Rev:** I in circle, border of 12 lilies

Date	Mintage	Good	VG	F	VF	XF
ND(pre-1623)	—	45.00	85.00	160	300	—

KM# 41.2 PFENNIG
Copper **Obv:** RHEDA in legend

Date	Mintage	Good	VG	F	VF	XF
ND(pre-1623)	—	45.00	85.00	160	300	—

KM# 52 PFENNIG
Copper **Obv:** Similar to 5 Pfennig, KM#69 **Note:** Varieties exist.

Date	Mintage	Good	VG	F	VF	XF
1655	—	40.00	65.00	100	185	—
1659	—	45.00	70.00	110	200	—

KM# 51 1-1/2 PFENNIG
Copper **Obv:** Similar to 5 Pfennig, KM#69 **Rev:** I I **Note:** Varieties exist.

Date	Mintage	Good	VG	F	VF	XF
ND	—	35.00	55.00	90.00	165	—
1655	—	35.00	55.00	90.00	165	—
1659	—	35.00	55.00	90.00	165	—

KM# 53 2 PFENNIG
Copper **Obv:** Similar to 5 Pfennig, KM#69 **Rev:** II in circle of 12 lilies **Note:** Varieties exist.

Date	Mintage	Good	VG	F	VF	XF
1655	—	20.00	30.00	60.00	125	—
1659	—	25.00	40.00	75.00	150	—

KM# 42 3 PFENNIG
Copper **Obv:** Rheda arms **Rev:** III in ornamented square

Date	Mintage	Good	VG	F	VF	XF
ND(pre-1623)	—	90.00	175	300	500	—

KM# 43 3 PFENNIG
Copper **Obv:** Crowned rampant lion left, REDE in legend **Rev:** Value III in ornamented circle

Date	Mintage	Good	VG	F	VF	XF
ND(pre-1623)	—	70.00	140	275	450	—

KM# 54 3 PFENNIG
Copper **Ruler:** Moritz **Note:** Kennepohl 95. Varieties exist.

Date	Mintage	Good	VG	F	VF	XF
1655	—	25.00	45.00	90.00	150	—
1659	—	15.00	30.00	50.00	90.00	350

KM# 67 3 PFENNIG
Copper **Obv:** Lion right

Date	Mintage	Good	VG	F	VF	XF
1659	—	60.00	120	200	350	—

KM# 55.1 4 PFENNIG
Copper **Obv:** Similar to 5 Pfennig, KM#69. **Rev:** IIII in circle, border of 12 lilies

Date	Mintage	Good	VG	F	VF	XF
1655	—	20.00	40.00	80.00	150	—
1659	—	10.00	25.00	40.00	80.00	—

KM# 68 4 PFENNIG
Copper **Obv:** Lion right

Date	Mintage	Good	VG	F	VF	XF
1659	—	25.00	50.00	100	200	—

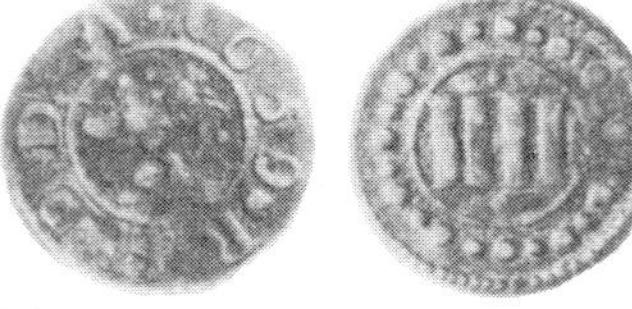

KM# 55.2 4 PFENNIG
Copper **Ruler:** Moritz **Rev:** Border of dots **Note:** Kennepohl 93. Additional varieties exist.

Date	Mintage	Good	VG	F	VF	XF
1659	—	10.00	25.00	40.00	80.00	—

KM# 71 5 PFENNIG
Copper **Obv:** DE/RANG/D in circle

Date	Mintage	Good	VG	F	VF	XF
1659 Rare	—	—	—	—	—	—

KM# 69 5 PFENNIG
Copper **Ruler:** Moritz **Note:** Varieties exist.

Date	Mintage	Good	VG	F	VF	XF
1659	—	15.00	30.00	45.00	100	—
1669	—	15.00	30.00	45.00	100	—

KM# 70 5 PFENNIG
Copper **Obv:** Lion right **Note:** Varieties exist.

Date	Mintage	Good	VG	F	VF	XF
1659	—	40.00	80.00	165	300	—

KM# 72 6 PFENNIG
Copper **Obv:** Similar to 5 Pfennig, KM#69. **Rev:** Value VI **Note:** Varieties exist.

Date	Mintage	Good	VG	F	VF	XF
1659	—	18.00	36.00	55.00	120	—

BERLIN

Located on the River Spree, Berlin was settled in the 12th century. It grew to become a major city and the capital of the margraviate and electorate of Brandenburg (see). It later was capital of the Kingdom of Prussia and finally, of the German Empire of 1871-1918 and the German Republic until 1945. Local coinage was struck for Berlin in the early period of the Thirty Years' War.

CITY

REGULAR COINAGE

KM# 1 SCHERF (1/2 Pfennig)
Copper **Note:** 1/2 Pfennig kipper. Uniface. Bear left in oval frame, date curved.

Date	Mintage	Good	VG	F	VF	XF
1621	—	15.00	30.00	60.00	120	—

KM# 3 SCHERF (1/2 Pfennig)
Copper **Note:** Date divided by frame, 1-6 above 2-1.

Date	Mintage	Good	VG	F	VF	XF
1621	—	15.00	30.00	60.00	120	—

KM# 2 SCHERF (1/2 Pfennig)
Copper **Note:** Date in straight line.

Date	Mintage	Good	VG	F	VF	XF
1621	—	15.00	30.00	60.00	120	—

BERLIN & KOLLN

During the early part of the Thirty Years' War, a joint coinage was issued for Berlin and Kolln, a city on the Spree just southeast of Berlin. Kolln was also the site of a mint for the electors of Brandenburg.

CITY

REGULAR COINAGE

KM# 3 PFENNIG
Copper **Note:** Frames connected by loop at top.

Date	Mintage	Good	VG	F	VF	XF
1621	—	16.00	35.00	70.00	130	—

KM# 1 PFENNIG
Copper **Note:** Kipper Pfennig. Uniface. Arms of Berlin (bear left) and Kolln (eagle) in adjoining oval frames, date below.

Date	Mintage	Good	VG	F	VF	XF
1621	—	16.00	35.00	70.00	130	—

KM# 2 PFENNIG
Copper **Note:** Oval frames connected by arch at top.

Date	Mintage	Good	VG	F	VF	XF
1621	—	16.00	35.00	70.00	130	—

BESANCON

Besançon is located in Franche-Comté, 70 miles (116 kilometers) southwest of Mühlhausen in Alsace and almost the same distance west-northwest of Bern, Switzerland. This city was well known in Roman times as Vesontio and was first occupied by Julius Caesar in 58 B.C. An archbishopric was founded here in the 2nd century. The archbishops became princes of the empire ca.1288.

The city became a free imperial city in 1184 and soon came under the influence of the dukes of Burgundy, then of the imperial Hapsburgs and later within the Spanish sphere of influence after the abdication of Emperor Charles V in 1556. In 1678 it was formally ceded to France by the Peace of Nijmegen.

The normal devices employed on the city coinage are the city arms and a bust or figure of Emperor Charles V, even long after his death, because it was he who gave Besançon the mint right in 1526 and renewed it in 1534.

ARMS
Eagle, head to left, between two columns.

FREE CITY

STANDARD COINAGE

KM# 10 CAROLUS
Billon **Obv:** Arms **Obv. Legend:** MONE.CIVI.BISVNTINAE **Rev:** Bust left divides date **Rev. Legend:** CAROLVS:V:IMPERATOR

Date	Mintage	VG	F	VF	XF	Unc
1622	—	20.00	40.00	75.00	150	—

KM# 15 GROSCHEN
Billon **Obv:** Crowned B between columns divides date **Obv. Legend:** MONETA.CIV.IMP.BISONT.B **Rev:** Bust left **Rev. Legend:** CAROLVS.V.IMPERATOR

Date	Mintage	VG	F	VF	XF	Unc
1622	—	30.00	60.00	120	250	—

KM# 20 2 GROSCHEN (1/4 Teston)
Billon **Obv:** Eagle between pillars **Obv. Legend:** MONETA.VIC.IMP.BISONT **Rev:** Bust left divides date **Rev. Legend:** CAROLVS.V.IMPERATOR

Date	Mintage	VG	F	VF	XF	Unc
1624	—	55.00	110	200	400	—

KM# 25 8 GROS (Teston)
Silver **Ruler:** Charles V **Obv:** Laureate bust of Charles V left **Obv. Legend:** + CAROLVS • V (8) IMPERATOR **Rev:** Date above shield **Rev. Legend:** + MONETA • CIV • IMP • BISONT

Date	Mintage	Good	VG	F	VF	XF
1623	—	25.00	50.00	125	275	450
1624	—	25.00	50.00	125	275	450

KM# 28 1/2 THALER (16 Gros)
Silver **Ruler:** Charles V **Obv:** Laureate bust of Charles V left **Obv. Legend:** CAROLVS * V * IMPERATOR **Rev:** Eagle, wings spread behind columns **Rev. Legend:** + MONETA : CIVI : IMP : BISVNTINÆ

Date	Mintage	Good	VG	F	VF	XF
1642	—	—	—	—	—	—
1643	—	200	400	750	1,250	—
1644	—	250	450	850	—	—

DAV# 5068 THALER (32 Gros)
Silver **Obv:** Legend around eagle holding columns **Obv. Legend:** + MONETA: CIVI: IMP: BISVNTINAD: **Rev:** Legend around bust left with outlined 32 below **Rev. Legend:** + CAROLVS:V: (32): IMPERATOR

Date	Mintage	VG	F	VF	XF	Unc
1624	—	425	850	1,450	2,400	—
1625	—	425	850	1,450	2,400	—

DAV# 5069 THALER (32 Gros)
Silver **Obv:** Without outlined "32" below bust **Note:** Similar to Dav. #5068.

Date	Mintage	VG	F	VF	XF	Unc
1640	—	450	900	1,550	2,750	—
1641	—	450	900	1,550	2,750	—

DAV# 5070 THALER (32 Gros)
Silver **Rev:** Charles V standing in armor holding orb

Date	Mintage	VG	F	VF	XF	Unc
1658	—	70.00	150	350	600	—
1659	—	70.00	150	350	600	—
1660	—	70.00	150	350	600	—
1661	—	70.00	150	350	600	—
1663	—	70.00	150	350	600	—
1664	—	70.00	150	350	600	—
1666	—	70.00	150	350	600	—
1667	—	70.00	150	350	600	—

FR# 76 2 PISTOLET
Gold **Rev:** Charles V

Date	Mintage	VG	F	VF	XF	Unc
1662	—	1,000	2,500	4,250	7,000	—
1664	—	1,000	2,500	4,250	7,000	—

FR# 74 2 PISTOLET
Gold

Date	Mintage	VG	F	VF	XF	Unc
1667	—	950	2,250	3,750	6,000	—
1673	—	950	2,250	3,750	6,000	—

FR# 80 4 PISTOLET
Gold **Obv:** 3-line inscription, date in chronogram **Rev:** Laureate bust of Philip IV of Spain right

Date	Mintage	VG	F	VF	XF	Unc
1664 Rare	—	—	—	—	—	—

TRADE COINAGE

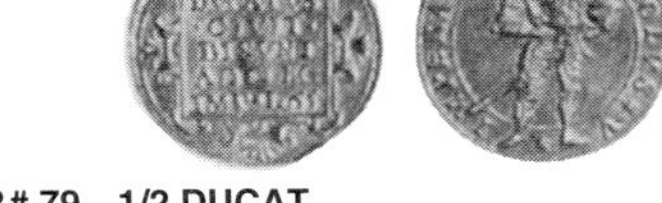

FR# 79 1/2 DUCAT
1.7500 g., 0.9860 Gold 0.0555 oz. AGW **Obv:** Five-line inscription and date in tablet **Rev:** Charles V standing

Date	Mintage	VG	F	VF	XF	Unc
1655	—	300	500	1,000	1,650	—

FR# 78 DUCAT
3.5000 g., 0.9860 Gold 0.1109 oz. AGW **Note:** Similar to 1/2 Ducat, FR#79.

Date	Mintage	VG	F	VF	XF	Unc
1655 Rare	—	—	—	—	—	—

FR# 77 2 DUCAT

7.0000 g., 0.9860 Gold 0.2219 oz. AGW **Note:** Similar to 1/2 Ducat, FR#79.

Date	Mintage	VG	F	VF	XF	Unc
1642	—	—	—	—	—	—
1654	—	—	—	—	—	—

BIBERACH

Located in Württemberg 22 miles to the southwest of Ulm, Biberach became a free imperial city in 1312. The city came under the control of Baden in 1803 and then of Württemberg in 1806.

FREE CITY

REGULAR COINAGE

KM# 5 1/2 BATZEN (2 Kreuzer)

Silver **Obv:** Crowned beaver (arms) right **Rev:** Crowned imperial eagle, titles of Ferdinand II **Note:** Kipper 1/2 Batzen.

Date	Mintage	VG	F	VF	XF	Unc
ND(1619-22) Rare	—	—	—	—	—	—

KM# 7 3 BATZEN (12 Kreuzer)

Silver **Countermark:** Crowned beaver left in oval, 12 below **Note:** Countermark on Pfalz-Neuburg 6 Batzen.

Date	Mintage	VG	F	VF	XF	Unc
ND(1619-22) Rare	—	—	—	—	—	—

KM# 6 3 BATZEN (12 Kreuzer)

Silver **Obv:** Crowned beaver right **Rev:** Crowned imperial eagle with 12 on breast **Note:** Kipper 3 Batzen.

Date	Mintage	VG	F	VF	XF	Unc
ND(1619-22) Rare	—	—	—	—	—	—

BOCHOLT

This provincial town in the bishopric of Munster is located near the Dutch border. It had a local copper coinage from 1615-1762. Bocholt passed to Salm-Salm in 1803 and later went to Prussia.

MONETARY SYSTEM

21 Heller = 6 Pfennig = 1/60 Thaler

PROVINCIAL TOWN

REGULAR COINAGE

KM# 5 10-1/2 HELLER

Copper **Obv:** City arms, STADT BOCHOLT, date **Rev:** Value X in ornamented border **Note:** Varieities exist.

Date	Mintage	VG	F	VF	XF
1616	—	16.00	33.00	60.00	120	—
1690	—	16.00	33.00	60.00	120	—

KM# 6.1 15-1/2 HELLER

Copper **Obv:** City arms, STADT BOCHOLT, date **Rev:** Value X.V. in ornamented border

Date	Mintage	Good	VG	F	VF	XF
1616	—	20.00	40.00	65.00	125	—

KM# 6.2 15-1/2 HELLER

Copper **Rev:** Value X.V.

Date	Mintage	Good	VG	F	VF	XF
1689	—	16.00	33.00	60.00	120	—

KM# 7 21 HELLER

Copper **Obv:** City arms, STADT BOCHOLT, date **Rev:** Value XXI in ornamented border

Date	Mintage	Good	VG	F	VF	XF
1616	—	25.00	40.00	75.00	135	—

KM# 15 21 HELLER

Copper **Rev:** Angel head and wings above value in center, 60 EININ REICHSTALER in legend

Date	Mintage	Good	VG	F	VF	XF
1670	—	20.00	40.00	65.00	125	—

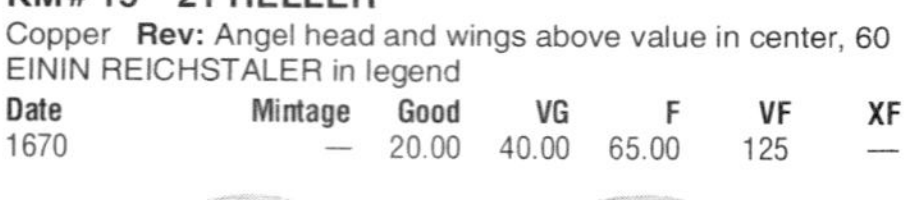

KM# 20 21 HELLER

Copper **Rev:** Angel head and wings above city arms, arms dividing I-S (1Stuber) **Note:** Varieties exist.

Date	Mintage	VG	F	VF	XF	Unc
1689	—	16.00	33.00	55.00	110	—
1690	—	16.00	33.00	55.00	110	—

KM# 8 2 PFENNIG

Copper **Obv:** City arms, STADT BOCHOLT, date **Rev:** Value II in ornamented border

Date	Mintage	Good	VG	F	VF	XF
1616 Rare	—	—	—	—	—	—

KM# 9 3 PFENNIG

Copper **Obv:** City arms, STADT BOCHOLT, date **Rev:** Value III in ornamented border

Date	Mintage	Good	VG	F	VF	XF
1616	—	20.00	40.00	65.00	130	—

KM# 10 4 PFENNIG

Copper **Obv:** City arms, STADT BOCHOLT, date **Rev:** Value IIII in ornamented border

Date	Mintage	Good	VG	F	VF	XF
1616	—	20.00	40.00	65.00	130	—

KM# 11 12 PFENNIG

Copper **Obv:** City arms, STADT BOCHOLT, date **Rev:** Value XII in ornamented square

Date	Mintage	Good	VG	F	VF	XF
1617	—	27.00	45.00	75.00	135	—

BRANDENBURG CITY ISSUES

A city in the old margraviate of Brandenburg, originally the capital of the local pre-Christian Slavic tribe of the area. It is located on the Havel River 35 miles west-southwest of Berlin. It was the capital of the margraviate prior to Berlin. Some copper coins were issued during the early part of the Thirty Years' War for the Altstadt and Neustadt (old and new divisions of the city).

ALSTADT

STANDARD COINAGE

KM# 1 SCHERF (1/2 Pfennig)

Copper **Obv:** City gate, ASB above (Alt-Stadt-Brandenburg) **Note:** Kipper. Uniface.

Date	Mintage	Good	VG	F	VF	XF
ND(1621)	—	27.00	55.00	100	175	—

NEUSTADT

STANDARD COINAGE

KM# 2 SCHERF (1/2 Pfennig)

Copper **Obv:** Knight w/eagle shield in arch of city gate, date above **Note:** Kipper. Uniface.

Date	Mintage	Good	VG	F	VF	XF
(1)621	—	27.00	55.00	100	175	—
1621	—	27.00	55.00	100	175	—

KM# 3 PFENNIG

Copper **Obv:** Knight w/eagle shield in arch of city gate, NSB above (Neu-Stadt Brandenburg) **Note:** Kipper. Uniface.

Date	Mintage	Good	VG	F	VF	XF
ND(1621)	—	33.00	65.00	140	250	—

KM# 4 PFENNIG

Copper **Obv:** Knight w/eagle shield in arch of city gate, date above **Note:** Kipper. Uniface.

Date	Mintage	Good	VG	F	VF	XF
1621	—	33.00	65.00	140	250	—

BRANDENBURG

(Brandenburg-Prussia)

The territory which was to become Brandenburg was inhabited by various Slavic tribes in the early Middle Ages. Charlemagne managed to diminish their power to some extent, but they regained their control after his passing. The Slav capital at Brennibor was captured by Emperor Heinrich I (918-36) and from that place Brandenburg takes its name. A series of margraves more or less continued to press the Slav tribes, but some were so ineffectual that the Slavs regained much of their former domains, especially after the death of Emperor Otto I (973). The early 12th century saw the return to active warfare against the Slavs. In 1134, the conquered lands were divided into the Altmark (Old or North Mark), west of the Elbe River, the Mittelmark (Middle Mark), between the Elbe and the Oder, and the Neumark (New Mark), east of the Oder River. Duke Lothar of Saxony appointed Albrecht the Bear of Ballenstädt as Margrave of the Nordmark (Altmark) and his long reign until 1170 brought stability to the lands under his control. The Ascanian rulers consolidated their power in Brandenburg and eventually obtained the electoral dignity in the 13th century. When the dynasty in Brandenburg became extinct, title passed to Emperor Ludwig III of Bavaria (1314-47), who made his eldest son ruler there. The margraviate continued to be ruled by members of the various imperial families or their appointees until the early 15th century. The Hohenzollerns of Swabia, who had been hereditary burgraves of Nürnberg since the late 12th century, acquired a mortgage on Brandenburg from the perpetually impecunious Emperor. In a stroke, Friedrich VI of Nürnberg became Elector Friedrich I of Brandenburg in 1415, thus placing the family into position to become rulers of the future most powerful state of the Empire.

Several of the Electors' sons ruled in the Hohenzollern possessions of Franconia (see Brandenburg in Franconia) and two founded the lines of Brandenburg-Ansbach and Brandenburg-Bayreuth (which see). Elector Johann Sigismund inherited the Duchy of Prussia in 1618 and the electorate was known henceforth as Brandenburg-Prussia. The Electorate sided with the Protestant cause during the Thirty Years' War, having submitted to the Reformation in 1539. The lessons of the war brought about the build-up of military power and territorial expansion under Friedrich Wilhelm, the Great Elector, which formed the basis of the Hohenzollerns' rise as a leading power in Europe. Johann Sigismund's great grandson assumed the title of King in Prussia in 1701 and the old margraviate of Brandenburg became just a province of the Kingdom. See Prussia for subsequent history and coin issues.

RULERS

Joachim Friedrich, 1598-1608
Johann Sigismund, 1608-1619
Georg Wilhelm, 1619-1640
Friedrich Wilhelm, 1640-1688
Friedrich III, 1688-1701

MINT OFFICIALS' INITIALS

Berlin/Kölln

Initial	Date	Name
AB	1642-44	Adrian Berlin
AB	1658-64	Andreas Becker, warden
CS	1675-1701	Christoph Stricker, warden
CT	1645-58	Carl Thauer, as mintmaster and warden
GL	1667-83	Gottfried Leygebe, die-cutter
IBS, IS, S	1681-97	Johann Bernhard Schultz, die-cutter
IL	1664-75	Jobst Liebmann, warden
IP	1625-27	Jacob Panckaert
LCS	1682-1701	Lorenz Christoph Schneider
LM, M	1620-42	Liborius Müller
RF	1688-1703	Raimund Faltz, die-cutter

Driesen

Initial	Date	Name
HL	1607-15	Heinrich Laffert

Emmerich

See Cleves listings.

Halberstadt

Initial	Date	Name
LCS	1679-82	Lorenz Christoph Schneider

Kölln an der Spree

Initial	Date	Name
HVR (swan)	1584-1604	Heinrich von Rehnen
MH	1589-1604	Melchior Hoffman as warden
	1604-20	As mintmaster

Konigsberg

Initial	Date	Name
BA	1685-87	Bastian Altmann
CG, G	1664-78	Caspar Geelhaar, the Elder as warden
CG	1699-1728	Caspar Geelhaar, the Younger
CM	1646-60	Christoph Melchior as warden
(q) = Cross on heart	1619-39	Ernst Pfaler as warden
CV	1672-74	Christoph Varenhorst
DK	1627-51, 56	David Koch
DS	1667-91	David Schirmer as warden
GR	1684	Unknown die-cutter
HM, HM monogram	1660-63	Hans Muller
HS	1674-77, 79-85, 87-94	Heinrich Sievertz
MK	1624-27	Marcus Koch
NB	1624-59	Noah Brettschneider, die-cutter
SD	1695-99	Siegmund Dannies
SI	?-1624	Simon Jansen
TT	1669-72	Thomas Timpf
(e)= UM with 3 stars	1653-60	Jonas Kasimir von Eulenburg

Krossen

Initial	Date	Name
GF	1668-74	Gottfried Frommholdt
IPE	1667-68	Julius Philipp Eisendracht

Magdeburg

Initial	Date	Name
HFH	1698-1719	Heinrich Friedrich Halter
ICS	1683-90	Johann Christoph Seehie, as warden
	1690-95	As mintmaster
IE	1683-90	Johann Ehlers

Minden

Initial	Date	Name
AVH	1674-79	Arnold Vahrenholtz
AVH	1674-79	August von Hakeberg as warden
BH	1682-1713	Bastian Hille
GDZ	1674-78	Georg David Ziegenhorn
GM	1689-1711	Gottfried Metelles as die-cutter
HB	1652, 69-73	Heinrich Bonhorst
IW	1671-73	Johann Willemsen
SD	1682-85	Siegmund Dannies

Regenstein

Initial	Date	Name
IA	1674-77	Johann Arendsburg

Stargard

Initial	Date	Name
SD	1689-92	Siegmund Dannies

NOTE: All issues of Joachim Friedrich were struck in Kölln.

References: B = Emil Bahrfeldt, ***Das Münzwesen der Mark Brandenburg unter den Hohenzollern bis zum grossen Kurfürsten, von 1415 bis 1640***, Berlin 1895.

D = Kurt Dost, ***Münzen im Preussenland – Herzogtum Preussen und Provinz Ostpreussen im Königreich 1525-1821***, Essen, 1990.

N = Erich Neumann, ***Münzeprägungen des Kurfürstentums Brandenburg und des Königreichs Preussen,*** 1. Band, ***Hohenzollern 1415-1701, Cologne, 1998. Die Münzen des Kurfürstentums Brandenburg unter der Herrschaft der Hozenzollern 1415-1701***, Cologne, 1998.

ELECTORATE

REGULAR COINAGE

KM# 481 MATTHIER

Silver **Obv:** Crowned scepter divides date **Rev:** EIN / MATIER / MIND. **Mint:** Minden

Date	Mintage	VG	F	VF	XF	Unc
1679	—	—	—	—	—	—

KM# 514 MATTHIER

Silver **Rev:** Date moved to fourth line

Date	Mintage	VG	F	VF	XF	Unc
1684	—	—	—	—	—	—

KM# 5 PFENNIG

Silver **Obv:** Scepter arms divides date **Rev:** XV/VMB.I./S.GR.

Date	Mintage	VG	F	VF	XF	Unc
(15)98	218,000	40.00	80.00	150	250	—
(15)99	Inc. above	40.00	80.00	150	250	—

KM# 15 PFENNIG

Silver **Obv:** Scepter arms **Rev:** XV/VMB.I/S:GRO:/date

Date	Mintage	VG	F	VF	XF	Unc
1600	—	40.00	80.00	150	250	—

KM# 260 PFENNIG

Silver **Obv:** Inscription, date **Obv. Inscription:** I/PF.BR/ LANDES/MVNZ **Mint:** Kolln **Note:** Uniface. Varieties exist.

Date	Mintage	VG	F	VF	XF	Unc
1653	117,000	40.00	80.00	160	350	—
1657	Inc. above	40.00	80.00	160	350	—
ND	Inc. above	40.00	80.00	160	350	—
1663	—	40.00	80.00	160	350	—

KM# 321 PFENNIG

Silver **Obv:** Crowned scepter divides date turned on side and mintmaster's initials **Note:** Uniface.

Date	Mintage	VG	F	VF	XF	Unc
1662 AB	163,000	40.00	100	200	400	—

KM# 384 PFENNIG

Silver **Obv:** Crowned scepter divides 1 - PF and date, palm branches below **Mint:** Berlin **Note:** Uniface.

Date	Mintage	VG	F	VF	XF	Unc
1669	—	40.00	100	200	400	—

KM# 405 PFENNIG

Silver **Note:** Crowned scepter, three small leaves on both sides.

Date	Mintage	VG	F	VF	XF	Unc
ND(1670)	—	40.00	90.00	175	300	—

KM# 438 PFENNIG

Silver **Obv:** Crowned scepter arms divide mintmaster's initials **Rev:** 1/PFEN/date

Date	Mintage	VG	F	VF	XF	Unc
1675 IL	—	40.00	100	200	400	—

KM# 439 PFENNIG

Silver **Obv:** Ornamented oval arms

Date	Mintage	VG	F	VF	XF	Unc
1675 CS	—	40.00	100	200	400	—

KM# 462 PFENNIG

Silver **Obv:** Crowned scepter divides date **Rev:** I/PF: BR / LANDT / MVNZ / C.S.

Date	Mintage	VG	F	VF	XF	Unc
1676 CS	—	40.00	100	200	400	—
1679 CS	—	40.00	100	200	400	—

KM# 463 PFENNIG

Silver **Obv:** Crowned scepter arms **Rev:** I / PF. BR / LAND.M / date / C.S.

Date	Mintage	VG	F	VF	XF	Unc
1676 CS	—	55.00	120	200	350	—

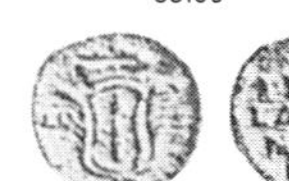
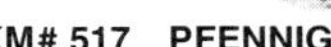

KM# 517 PFENNIG

Silver **Obv:** Crowned scepter arms between two palm branches **Rev:** I / PF. BR / LANDT / MVNZ / date

Date	Mintage	VG	F	VF	XF	Unc
1685 LCS	—	40.00	100	200	350	—

KM# 537 PFENNIG

Silver **Mint:** Minden

Date	Mintage	VG	F	VF	XF	Unc
ND(1688-1701) BH	—	40.00	100	200	350	—

KM# 536 PFENNIG

Silver **Note:** Uniface. Scepter between palm branches.

Date	Mintage	VG	F	VF	XF	Unc
ND(1688-1701)	—	40.00	80.00	160	300	—

KM# 565 PFENNIG

Silver **Obv:** Crowned scepter arms between two palm branches **Rev:** 1 / PF.BR / LANDT / MVNZ / date **Mint:** Stargard **Note:** Varieties exist.

Date	Mintage	VG	F	VF	XF	Unc
1690 SD	—	40.00	100	200	350	—
1692 SD	—	40.00	100	200	350	—

KM# 597 PFENNIG

Silver **Obv:** Inscription, date **Obv. Inscription:** I / PF:BR / L:MVNZ **Mint:** Berlin **Note:** Uniface.

Date	Mintage	VG	F	VF	XF	Unc
1695 LCS	1,062,000	40.00	80.00	160	300	—

KM# 239 2 PFENNIG

Silver **Obv:** Crowned oval scepter arms divide date **Rev. Inscription:** II/PF.BR/LANDES/MUNZ (or MVNZ) **Mint:** Kolln **Note:** Varieties exist.

Date	Mintage	VG	F	VF	XF	Unc
1651	749,000	40.00	100	200	400	—
1653	Inc. above	40.00	100	200	400	—
1654	Inc. above	40.00	100	200	400	—
1656	Inc. above	40.00	100	200	400	—
1657	Inc. above	40.00	100	200	400	—
1658	Inc. above	40.00	100	200	400	—
1659	Inc. above	40.00	100	200	400	—
1660	Inc. above	40.00	100	200	400	—
1666	—	40.00	100	200	400	—

KM# 261 2 PFENNIG

Silver **Rev:** Date also at bottom

Date	Mintage	VG	F	VF	XF	Unc
1653	Inc. above	40.00	100	200	400	—

KM# 367 2 PFENNIG

Silver **Obv:** Crowned scepter arms between palm branches **Rev:** Inscription in cartouche, date above **Rev. Inscription:** II/PFEN **Mint:** Berlin

Date	Mintage	VG	F	VF	XF	Unc
1668 IL	—	40.00	100	200	400	—

KM# 428 2 PFENNIG

Silver **Rev:** Without cartouche, leaf on each side of II

Date	Mintage	VG	F	VF	XF	Unc
1674 IL	—	40.00	100	200	400	—

KM# 464 2 PFENNIG

Silver **Obv:** Crowned scepter arms divide date **Rev. Inscription:** II / PF.BR / LANDT / MVNZ

Date	Mintage	VG	F	VF	XF	Unc
1676 CS	—	40.00	100	200	400	—
1684 LCS	—	40.00	100	200	400	—
1685 LCS	—	40.00	100	200	400	—

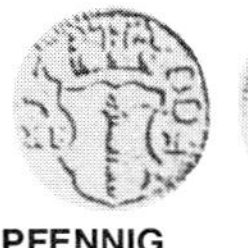

KM# 566 2 PFENNIG

Silver **Mint:** Magdeburg

Date	Mintage	VG	F	VF	XF	Unc
1690 ICS	—	40.00	90.00	180	300	—
1692 ICS	—	40.00	90.00	180	300	—
1700 HFH	—	40.00	90.00	180	300	—

KM# 567 2 PFENNIG

Silver **Obv:** Crowned scepter arms divide date **Rev. Inscription:** II / PF.BR / LANDT / MVNZ **Mint:** Stargard

Date	Mintage	VG	F	VF	XF	Unc
1690 SD	—	40.00	90.00	180	300	—
1692 SD	—	40.00	90.00	180	300	—

KM# 598 2 PFENNIG

Silver **Mint:** Berlin

Date	Mintage	VG	F	VF	XF	Unc
1695 LCS	636,000	27.00	55.00	130	250	—
1700 LCS	—	27.00	55.00	130	250	—

KM# 599 2 PFENNIG

Silver **Mint:** Minden

Date	Mintage	VG	F	VF	XF	Unc
1695 BH	—	40.00	100	200	400	—
ND BH	—	40.00	100	200	400	—

KM# 7 3 PFENNIG (Dreier)

Silver **Ruler:** Joachim Friedrich **Obv:** 4-fold arms with scepter shield in center **Mint:** Kolln **Note:** Ref. B#519-521.

Date	Mintage	VG	F	VF	XF	Unc
1601 (e)	—	125	240	400	650	—

KM# 60 3 PFENNIG (Dreier)

Silver **Obv:** Eagle arms **Rev:** Scepter divides date **Mint:** Berlin **Note:** Kipper. Varieties exist.

Date	Mintage	VG	F	VF	XF	Unc
16Z0	—	16.00	35.00	55.00	95.00	—

KM# 82 3 PFENNIG (Dreier)

Silver **Obv:** Eagle's head in shield **Note:** Varieties exist.

Date	Mintage	VG	F	VF	XF	Unc
16Z1	—	16.00	35.00	55.00	95.00	—
16ZZ	—	16.00	35.00	55.00	95.00	—

KM# 81 3 PFENNIG (Dreier)

Silver **Obv:** Eagle not in shield

Date	Mintage	VG	F	VF	XF	Unc
16Z1	—	16.00	35.00	55.00	95.00	—

KM# 83 3 PFENNIG (Dreier)

Silver **Obv:** Imperial orb with value 3 in circle **Rev:** Scepter divides date in circle

Date	Mintage	VG	F	VF	XF	Unc
16Z1	—	16.00	35.00	55.00	95.00	—

KM# 262 3 PFENNIG (Dreier)

Silver **Obv:** Crowned eagle, scepter arms on breast **Rev:** Inscription, date **Rev. Inscription:** 3/PF.BR/LANDES/ MUNZ/ **Mint:** Kolln

Date	Mintage	VG	F	VF	XF	Unc
1653	898,000	13.00	27.00	45.00	80.00	—
1654	Inc. above	13.00	27.00	45.00	80.00	—
1657	Inc. above	13.00	27.00	45.00	80.00	—
1658	Inc. above	13.00	27.00	45.00	80.00	—
1659	Inc. above	13.00	27.00	45.00	80.00	—
1660	Inc. above	13.00	27.00	45.00	80.00	—

KM# 326 3 PFENNIG (Dreier)

Silver **Obv:** Crowned eagle with scepter arms **Rev:** Imperial orb with value 3 divides date **Mint:** Berlin

Date	Mintage	VG	F	VF	XF	Unc
1663 AB	40,000	16.00	33.00	55.00	100	—

KM# 368 3 PFENNIG (Dreier)

Silver **Obv:** Two arms above one, crown above **Rev:** Value 3/date in shield

Date	Mintage	VG	F	VF	XF	Unc
1668	—	20.00	40.00	60.00	100	—

KM# 369 3 PFENNIG (Dreier)

Silver **Rev:** Value and date in ornamented oval shield

Date	Mintage	VG	F	VF	XF	Unc
1668	—	20.00	40.00	60.00	100	—

KM# 370 3 PFENNIG (Dreier)

Silver **Obv:** Crowned 4-fold arms **Rev:** 3/PFEN in two palm branches, date above

Date	Mintage	VG	F	VF	XF	Unc
1668 IL	—	20.00	40.00	60.00	100	—

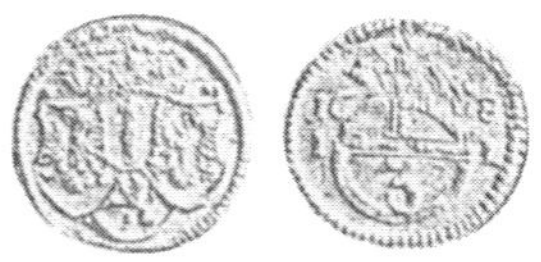

KM# 371 3 PFENNIG (Dreier)

Silver **Rev:** Imperial orb with 3 divides date **Note:** Varieties exist.

Date	Mintage	VG	F	VF	XF	Unc
1668 IL	—	20.00	40.00	60.00	100	—
1669 IL	—	20.00	40.00	60.00	100	—
1669	—	20.00	40.00	60.00	100	—
1673 IL	—	20.00	40.00	60.00	100	—
1675 CS	—	20.00	40.00	60.00	100	—

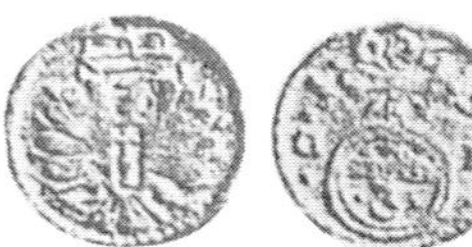

KM# 385 3 PFENNIG (Dreier)

Silver **Obv:** Crowned eagle, scepter arms on breast **Rev:** Imperial orb with 3 divides date **Mint:** Krossen

Date	Mintage	VG	F	VF	XF	Unc
1669 GF	—	20.00	40.00	65.00	120	—
1670 GF	—	20.00	40.00	65.00	120	—

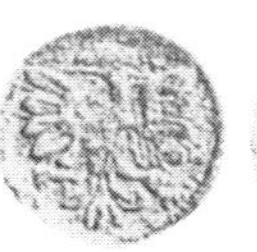

KM# 418 3 PFENNIG (Dreier)

Silver **Obv:** Without scepter on eagle's breast **Rev:** Inscription, date **Rev. Inscription:** 3/PF.BR/LANDES/MVNZ/ **Mint:** Minden

Date	Mintage	VG	F	VF	XF	Unc
1671 IW	—	20.00	40.00	65.00	120	—

KM# 465 3 PFENNIG (Dreier)

Silver **Obv:** Scepter on eagle's breast **Mint:** Berlin **Note:** Varieties exist.

Date	Mintage	VG	F	VF	XF	Unc
1676 CS	—	8.00	16.00	35.00	60.00	—
1679 CS	—	8.00	16.00	35.00	60.00	—
1683 LCS	—	8.00	16.00	35.00	60.00	—
1684 LCS	—	8.00	16.00	35.00	60.00	—
1685 LCS	—	8.00	16.00	35.00	60.00	—
1686 LCS	—	8.00	16.00	35.00	60.00	—
1687 LCS	357,000	8.00	16.00	35.00	60.00	—

KM# 547 3 PFENNIG (Dreier)

Silver **Mint:** Stargard **Note:** Varieties exist.

Date	Mintage	VG	F	VF	XF	Unc
1689 SD	—	10.00	20.00	40.00	75.00	—
1690 SD	—	10.00	20.00	40.00	75.00	—
1691 SD	—	10.00	20.00	40.00	75.00	—
1692 SD	—	10.00	20.00	40.00	75.00	—

KM# 546 3 PFENNIG (Dreier)

Silver **Rev. Inscription:** LANDT/MVNTZ **Mint:** Magdeburg

Date	Mintage	VG	F	VF	XF	Unc
1689 IE	—	8.00	16.00	35.00	60.00	—
1690 ICS	—	8.00	16.00	35.00	60.00	—
1691 ICS	—	8.00	16.00	35.00	60.00	—
1692 ICS	—	8.00	16.00	35.00	60.00	—
1695 ICS	—	8.00	16.00	35.00	60.00	—
1700 HFH	—	8.00	16.00	35.00	60.00	—

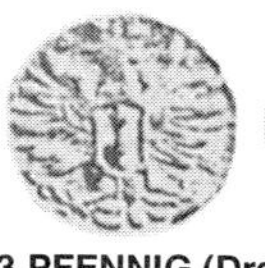

KM# 600 3 PFENNIG (Dreier)

Silver **Rev. Inscription:** LANDT/MVNZ **Mint:** Berlin

Date	Mintage	VG	F	VF	XF	Unc
1695 LCS	651,000	8.00	16.00	35.00	60.00	—

KM# 601 3 PFENNIG (Dreier)

Silver **Rev. Inscription:** LANDT/MVNTZ **Mint:** Minden

Date	Mintage	VG	F	VF	XF	Unc
1695 BH	—	27.00	45.00	75.00	135	—

KM# 625 3 PFENNIG (Dreier)

Silver **Obv:** Crowned 4-fold arms **Rev:** Imperial orb with 3 divides date **Mint:** Berlin

Date	Mintage	VG	F	VF	XF	Unc
1700 LCS	—	8.00	16.00	35.00	60.00	—

KM# 466 4 PFENNIG

Silver **Obv:** Crowned oval scepter arms **Rev:** Inscription, date **Rev. Inscription:** IIII/PFEN. BRA/DEB. LAND/MVNTZ/ **Mint:** Berlin **Note:** Varieties exist.

Date	Mintage	VG	F	VF	XF	Unc
1676 CS	—	13.00	27.00	55.00	100	—
1684 LCS	—	13.00	27.00	55.00	100	—
1685 LCS	—	13.00	27.00	55.00	100	—
1686 LCS	—	13.00	27.00	55.00	100	—
1687 LCS	144,000	13.00	27.00	55.00	100	—

KM# 548 4 PFENNIG

Silver **Obv:** Oval arms in baroque cartouche **Mint:** Stargard **Note:** Varieties exist.

Date	Mintage	VG	F	VF	XF	Unc
1689 SD	—	20.00	40.00	75.00	140	—
1690 SD	—	20.00	40.00	75.00	140	—
1691 SD	—	20.00	40.00	75.00	140	—
1692 SD	—	20.00	40.00	75.00	140	—

KM# 626 4 PFENNIG

Silver **Mint:** Berlin

Date	Mintage	VG	F	VF	XF	Unc
1700 LCS	—	27.00	60.00	100	190	—

KM# 627 4 PFENNIG

Silver **Obv:** Different cartouche and small crown **Mint:** Magdeburg

Date	Mintage	VG	F	VF	XF	Unc
1700 HFH	—	27.00	60.00	100	190	—

KM# 240 6 PFENNIG

Silver **Obv:** Crowned oval scepter arms **Rev:** Inscription, date **Rev. Inscription:** 6/PFENN (or PFENNIG)/BRANDENB/ LANDES/MUNZ (or MVNZ)/ **Mint:** Kolln **Note:** Varieties exist.

Date	Mintage	VG	F	VF	XF	Unc
1651	486,000	16.00	33.00	55.00	100	—
1652	Inc. above	16.00	33.00	55.00	100	—
1653	Inc. above	16.00	33.00	55.00	100	—
1656	Inc. above	16.00	33.00	55.00	100	—
1657	Inc. above	16.00	33.00	55.00	100	—
1658	Inc. above	16.00	33.00	55.00	100	—
1659	Inc. above	16.00	33.00	55.00	100	—

KM# 406 6 PFENNIG

Silver **Obv:** Crowned scepter arms between palm branches **Rev:** Inscription, date **Mint:** Berlin

Date	Mintage	VG	F	VF	XF	Unc
1670 IL	—	25.00	45.00	80.00	150	—

KM# 467 6 PFENNIG

Silver **Note:** Varieties exist.

Date	Mintage	VG	F	VF	XF	Unc
1676 CS	—	9.00	16.00	33.00	65.00	—
1678 CS	—	8.00	13.00	27.00	60.00	—
1682 LCS	—	8.00	13.00	27.00	60.00	—
1683 LCS	—	8.00	13.00	27.00	60.00	—
1684 LCS	—	8.00	13.00	27.00	60.00	—
1685 LCS	—	8.00	13.00	27.00	60.00	—
1686 LCS	—	8.00	13.00	27.00	60.00	—
1687 LCS	—	8.00	13.00	27.00	60.00	—

KM# 513 6 PFENNIG

Silver **Rev. Inscription:** 6/PF.BRAN/DEB... **Mint:** Magdeburg **Note:** Varieties exist.

Date	Mintage	VG	F	VF	XF	Unc
1684 IE	—	9.00	16.00	33.00	65.00	—
1685 IE	—	9.00	16.00	33.00	65.00	—
1686 IE	—	9.00	16.00	33.00	65.00	—
1687 IE	—	9.00	16.00	33.00	65.00	—
1688 ICS	—	9.00	16.00	33.00	65.00	—

KM# 569 6 PFENNIG

Silver **Mint:** Minden **Note:** Varieties exist.

Date	Mintage	VG	F	VF	XF	Unc
1690 BH	—	9.00	16.00	33.00	65.00	—
1693 BH	—	9.00	16.00	33.00	65.00	—
1695 BH	—	9.00	16.00	33.00	65.00	—

KM# 568 6 PFENNIG

Silver **Mint:** Magdeburg

Date	Mintage	VG	F	VF	XF	Unc
1690 IE	—	9.00	16.00	33.00	65.00	—
1691 ICS	—	8.00	13.00	27.00	60.00	—
1692 ICS	—	8.00	13.00	27.00	60.00	—
1693 ICS	—	8.00	13.00	27.00	60.00	—
1694 ICS	—	8.00	13.00	27.00	60.00	—
1695 ICS	—	8.00	13.00	27.00	60.00	—
1700 HFH	—	9.00	16.00	33.00	65.00	—

KM# 592 6 PFENNIG
Silver **Mint:** Berlin

Date	Mintage	VG	F	VF	XF	Unc
1694 LCS	1,048,000	8.00	13.00	27.00	60.00	—
1700 LCS	—	8.00	13.00	27.00	60.00	—

KM# 84 8 PFENNIG
Silver **Obv:** Scepter arms, date above **Rev:** Inscription in circle **Mint:** Berlin

Date	Mintage	VG	F	VF	XF	Unc
16Z0 Rare	—	—	—	—	—	—

KM# 338 24 PFENNIG
Silver **Obv:** Bust right **Rev:** Silesian eagle, value (XXIIII) below, date in legend **Mint:** Krossen

Date	Mintage	VG	F	VF	XF	Unc
1665	—	—	—	—	—	—

KM# 386 KORTLING (1/84 Taler)
Silver **Obv:** 6-fold arms **Rev:** Imperial orb with 6 **Mint:** Minden

Date	Mintage	VG	F	VF	XF	Unc
ND(ca.1669-73)	—	12.00	25.00	45.00	75.00	—

KM# 343 KREUZER
Silver **Obv:** Bust right, value (1) below **Rev:** Silesian eagle, date in legend **Mint:** Krossen

Date	Mintage	VG	F	VF	XF	Unc
1666	—	—	—	—	—	—

KM# 40 3 KREUZER
Silver **Obv:** Crowned eagle with shield on breast divides date **Rev:** Six shields surround Hohenzollern arms **Mint:** Kolln

Date	Mintage	VG	F	VF	XF	Unc
1611	—	—	—	—	—	—
161Z Rare	—	—	—	—	—	—
ND(1612) Rare	—	—	—	—	—	—

KM# 344 3 KREUZER
Silver **Obv:** Bust right, value (3) below **Rev:** Silesian eagle, date in legend **Mint:** Krossen

Date	Mintage	VG	F	VF	XF	Unc
1666	—	—	—	—	—	—
1667	—	—	—	—	—	—

KM# 345 6 KREUZER
Silver **Obv:** Crowned bust right **Rev:** Crowned triple arms, date in legend **Mint:** Krossen

Date	Mintage	VG	F	VF	XF	Unc
1666	—	—	—	—	—	—
(16)66	—	—	—	—	—	—

KM# 339 15 KREUZER (1/6 Taler)
Silver **Obv:** Bust right, value XV below **Rev:** Silesian eagle (crescent and cross on breast), date in legend **Mint:** Krossen

Date	Mintage	VG	F	VF	XF	Unc
1665	—	—	—	—	—	—

KM# 531 15 KREUZER (1/6 Taler)
Silver **Mint:** Berlin **Note:** Coinage for District of Krossen.

Date	Mintage	VG	F	VF	XF	Unc
1687 LCS	255,000	30.00	65.00	125	175	—

KM# 92 24 KREUZER
Silver **Obv:** Bust right, balue 24 below **Rev:** Crowned eagle with scepter arms on breast **Mint:** Krossen **Note:** Kipper.

Date	Mintage	VG	F	VF	XF	Unc
ND(1622)	3,734	—	—	—	—	—

KM# 113 SOLIDUS (Schilling)
Silver **Mint:** Konigsberg

Date	Mintage	VG	F	VF	XF	Unc
1623 (a)	—	16.00	33.00	60.00	100	—
1624 (a)	44,000	16.00	33.00	60.00	100	—
1625 (a)	2,093,000	10.00	20.00	35.00	65.00	—
1626 (a)	1,120,000	10.00	20.00	35.00	65.00	—
1627 (a)	6,970,000	10.00	20.00	35.00	65.00	—
1628 (a)	4,990,000	10.00	20.00	35.00	65.00	—
1629 (a)	8,586,000	10.00	20.00	35.00	65.00	—
1630 (a)	6,000,000	10.00	20.00	35.00	65.00	—
1631 (a)	—	10.00	20.00	35.00	65.00	—
1633 (a)	—	10.00	20.00	35.00	65.00	—

KM# 56.1 DREIPOLKER
Silver **Mint:** Konigsberg

Date	Mintage	VG	F	VF	XF	Unc
1619	3,373,000	9.00	20.00	33.00	50.00	—
1620	4,796,000	9.00	20.00	33.00	50.00	—
1621	2,560,000	9.00	20.00	33.00	50.00	—
1622	5,198,000	9.00	20.00	33.00	50.00	—
1623	4,452,000	9.00	20.00	33.00	50.00	—
1624	1,084,000	9.00	20.00	33.00	50.00	—
1624 MK	6,479,000	9.00	20.00	33.00	50.00	—
1625	5,459,000	9.00	20.00	33.00	50.00	—
1626	10,901,000	9.00	20.00	33.00	50.00	—
1627	2,380,000	9.00	20.00	33.00	50.00	—
1628	258,000	9.00	20.00	33.00	50.00	—
1633	151,000	9.00	20.00	33.00	50.00	—
1634	157,000	9.00	20.00	33.00	50.00	—
1635	Inc. above	9.00	20.00	33.00	50.00	—

KM# 56.2 DREIPOLKER
Silver **Ruler:** Georg Wilhelm **Obv:** Imperial orb with Z4 divides date, titles of Johann Sigismund **Rev:** Electoral hat above three-fold arms, value "3" in frame at bottom **Rev. Legend:** PRO LEGE & PR. GREGE **Mint:** Konigsberg **Note:** Ref. D#300-11.

Date	Mintage	VG	F	VF	XF	Unc
(16)19 (q)	3,373,000	—	—	—	—	—
(16)Z0 (q)	4,796,000	—	—	—	—	—

KM# 56.3 DREIPOLKER
Silver **Ruler:** Georg Wilhelm **Obv:** Imperial orb with 24 divides date, titles of Georg Wilhelm **Rev:** Crowned 4-fold arms with scepter shield in center, value "3" below **Rev. Legend:** DIEV & MON. DROICT **Mint:** Konigsberg **Note:** Ref. N#10.110. Varieties exist.

Date	Mintage	VG	F	VF	XF	Unc
(16)1Z (q) Error	Inc. above	—	—	—	—	—
(16)Z1 (q)	2,560,000	—	—	—	—	—
(16)ZZ (q)	5,198,000	—	—	—	—	—
(16)22 (q)	Inc. above	—	—	—	—	—
(16)23 (q)	4,452,000	—	—	—	—	—
1624 (q)	1,084,000	—	—	—	—	—

KM# 56.4 DREIPOLKER
Silver **Ruler:** Georg Wilhelm **Mint:** Konigsberg **Note:** Ref. N#10.110a. Similar to KM#56.2 but titles of Georg Wilhelm on both sides. Varieties exist.

Date	Mintage	VG	F	VF	XF	Unc
(16)24 (q)	Inc. above	—	—	—	—	—

KM# 56.5 DREIPOLKER
Silver **Ruler:** Georg Wilhelm **Obv:** Crowned 4-fold arms with scepter shield in center, value (3) below, titles of Georg Wilhelm **Rev:** Imperial orb with 24 divides date **Rev. Legend:** MONE. NOVA. DVC. PRVS. **Mint:** Konigsberg **Note:** Ref. N#10.111, 10.112. Varieties exist.

Date	Mintage	VG	F	VF	XF	Unc
(16)24 (q)	6,479,000	—	—	—	—	—
(16)25 (q)	5,459,000	—	—	—	—	—
(16)26 (q)	10,901,000	—	—	—	—	—
(16)Z7 (q)	2,380,000	—	—	—	—	—
(16)Z8 (q)	258,000	—	—	—	—	—
(16)33 (q)	151,000	—	—	—	—	—

KM# 515 DREIPOLKER
Silver **Mint:** Berlin **Note:** Coinage for Province of Russia.

Date	Mintage	VG	F	VF	XF	Unc
1684	480,000	—	—	—	—	—

KM# 518 DREIPOLKER
Silver **Obv:** 5-fold arms, value 3 below **Rev:** Imperial orb with 24 divides date to upper left and right **Mint:** Konigsberg

Date	Mintage	VG	F	VF	XF	Unc
(16)85	480,000	—	—	—	—	—

KM# 8 1/2 SCHILLING (1/64 Thaler)
Silver **Obv:** Eagle **Rev:** Hohenzollern arms divide date

Date	Mintage	VG	F	VF	XF	Unc
(15)99	13,000	—	—	—	—	—

KM# 263 SCHILLING (1/32 Thaler)
Silver **Obv:** Crowned eagle, value 1 on breast **Rev:** FW monogram, date in legend

Date	Mintage	VG	F	VF	XF	Unc
1653	3,783,000	10.00	20.00	40.00	70.00	—
1654	5,595,000	10.00	20.00	40.00	70.00	—
1655	1,693,000	10.00	20.00	40.00	70.00	—

KM# 288 SCHILLING (1/32 Thaler)
Silver **Obv:** FWC monogram divides date **Rev:** Value in three lines

Date	Mintage	VG	F	VF	XF	Unc
1657	1,080,000	13.00	27.00	45.00	70.00	—
1657	Inc. above	13.00	27.00	45.00	70.00	—
1658	—	13.00	27.00	45.00	70.00	—
1658	Inc. above	13.00	27.00	45.00	70.00	—
1659	—	—	—	—	—	—
1659	47,000	13.00	27.00	45.00	70.00	—

KM# 330 SCHILLING (1/32 Thaler)
Silver **Obv:** FWC monogram behind scepter
Rev. Inscription: NU / MUS. PRUS / SIAE / date

Date	Mintage	VG	F	VF	XF	Unc
1664	997,000	27.00	55.00	100	170	—
1665	Inc. above	27.00	55.00	100	170	—

KM# 387 SCHILLING (1/32 Thaler)
Silver **Obv:** Crowned FWC monogram **Rev:** Value, date in four lines

Date	Mintage	VG	F	VF	XF	Unc
1669	2,141,000	10.00	20.00	40.00	80.00	—
1670	7,830,000	10.00	20.00	40.00	80.00	—
1671	Inc. above	10.00	20.00	40.00	80.00	—

KM# 590 SCHILLING (1/32 Thaler)
Silver **Obv:** Crowned FC III monogram **Rev:** Value, date in four lines

Date	Mintage	VG	F	VF	XF	Unc
1693 HS	4,340,000	8.00	13.00	33.00	65.00	—
1694 HS	761,000	8.00	13.00	33.00	65.00	—
1695 SD	612,000	8.00	13.00	33.00	65.00	—
1697 SD	737,000	8.00	13.00	33.00	65.00	—
1698 SD	1,473,000	8.00	13.00	33.00	65.00	—
1699 SD	737,000	8.00	13.00	33.00	65.00	—
1700 CG	300,000	10.00	20.00	40.00	65.00	—

KM# 9 2 SCHILLING (1/16 Thaler)
Silver **Obv:** 7-fold arms **Rev:** Imperial orb with 16 divides date, all in baroque frame

Date	Mintage	VG	F	VF	XF	Unc
(15)99 Swan	11,000	175	300	500	—	—

KM# 16 2 SCHILLING (1/16 Thaler)
Silver **Obv:** 5-fold arms **Rev:** Inscription in oval baroque frame
Rev. Inscription: II / SCHIL / LING / date

Date	Mintage	VG	F	VF	XF	Unc
1600 Swan	20,000	—	300	500	—	—

KM# A56 2 SCHILLING (1/16 Thaler)
Silver **Ruler:** Georg Wilhelm **Obv:** Eagle, scepter shield on breast, titles of Georg Wilhelm **Rev:** Intertwined "DS", date below, titles continuous **Mint:** Berlin **Note:** Ref. B#612-13. Kipper 2 Schilling.

Date	Mintage	VG	F	VF	XF	Unc
16Z1 LM	—	—	—	—	—	—
16Z1	—	—	—	—	—	—

KM# 93 2 SCHILLING (1/16 Thaler)
Silver **Obv:** Eagle, scepter arms on breast **Rev:** Imperial orb without value **Mint:** Berlin

Date	Mintage	VG	F	VF	XF	Unc
1622	—	—	—	—	—	—

KM# A119 GROSCHEN (1/24 Thaler)
Silver **Ruler:** Georg Wilhelm **Obv:** Crowned bust right, titles of Georg Wilhelm **Rev:** Eagle with "S" on breast in circle, date in legend **Rev. Legend:** GROSS. DUC. PRVSSIAE **Mint:** Konigsberg **Note:** Ref. N#10.108.

Date	Mintage	VG	F	VF	XF	Unc
1625 (q)	35,000	—	—	—	—	—

KM# A150 GROSCHEN (1/24 Thaler)
Silver **Ruler:** Georg Wilhelm **Obv:** Scepter shield, titles of Georg Wilhelm **Rev:** Eagle with crowend "GV" on breast, small shield of Hohenzollern arms below, date in legend **Mint:** Konigsberg **Note:** Ref. N#10.109.

Date	Mintage	VG	F	VF	XF	Unc
1633 (q)	—	—	—	—	—	—

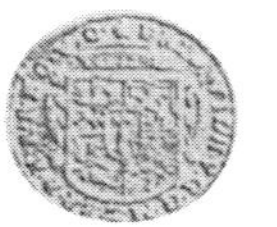

KM# 241 GROSCHEN (1/24 Thaler)
Silver **Ruler:** Friedrich Wilhelm **Obv:** Crowned 5-fold arms **Rev. Inscription:** I / GROSCH / BRANDENB / LANDES / MUNZ / date **Mint:** Berlin **Note:** Varieties exist.

Date	Mintage	VG	F	VF	XF	Unc
1651	1,884,000	13.00	27.00	45.00	70.00	—
1652	Inc. above	13.00	27.00	45.00	70.00	—
1653	Inc. above	13.00	27.00	45.00	70.00	—
1659	Inc. above	13.00	27.00	45.00	70.00	—

KM# 616 GROSCHEN (1/24 Thaler)
Silver **Obv:** Crowned scepter arms between palm branches, date divided above **Rev:** Value in four lines **Mint:** Konigsberg

Date	Mintage	VG	F	VF	XF	Unc
1699 SD	150,000	25.00	40.00	75.00	140	—

KM# 628 GROSCHEN (1/24 Thaler)
Silver **Rev:** Date at bottom

Date	Mintage	VG	F	VF	XF	Unc
1700 CG	100,000	25.00	40.00	75.00	140	—

KM# 94 2 GROSCHEN (1/12 Thaler)
Silver **Obv:** Bust right, value 2 below **Rev:** Oval scepter arms in baroque frame **Mint:** Krossen

Date	Mintage	VG	F	VF	XF	Unc
ND(1622/23)	9,880	—	—	—	—	—

KM# 95 2 GROSCHEN (1/12 Thaler)
Silver **Obv:** Value II

Date	Mintage	VG	F	VF	XF	Unc
ND(1622/23)	Inc. above	—	—	—	—	—

KM# 149 2 GROSCHEN (1/12 Thaler)
Silver **Mint:** Konigsberg

Date	Mintage	VG	F	VF	XF	Unc
1634	—	—	—	—	—	—

KM# 242 2 GROSCHEN (1/12 Thaler)
Silver **Obv:** Crowned 5-fold arms **Rev. Inscription:** II / GROSCH / BRANDENB / LANDES / MUNZ / date **Mint:** Kolln **Note:** Varieties exist.

Date	Mintage	VG	F	VF	XF	Unc
1651	16,051,000	20.00	33.00	55.00	125	—
1652	Inc. above	20.00	33.00	55.00	125	—
1653	Inc. above	20.00	33.00	55.00	125	—
1654	Inc. above	20.00	33.00	55.00	125	—
1655	Inc. above	20.00	33.00	55.00	125	—
1656	Inc. above	20.00	33.00	55.00	125	—
1657	Inc. above	20.00	33.00	55.00	125	—
1658	Inc. above	20.00	33.00	55.00	125	—
1659	Inc. above	20.00	33.00	55.00	125	—
1660	Inc. above	20.00	33.00	55.00	125	—

KM# 617 2 GROSCHEN (1/12 Thaler)
Silver **Obv:** Crowned eagle **Rev:** Value, date in six lines **Mint:** Konigsberg

Date	Mintage	VG	F	VF	XF	Unc
1699 SD	75,000	13.00	27.00	45.00	80.00	—
1700 CG	50,000	13.00	27.00	45.00	80.00	—

KM# 97 3 GROSCHEN
Silver **Obv:** Bust right, value III below **Rev:** Crowned eagle with scepter arms on breast divides date **Mint:** Krossen

Date	Mintage	VG	F	VF	XF	Unc
1622	97,000	25.00	45.00	75.00	150	—

KM# 98 3 GROSCHEN
Silver **Obv:** Without crown above eagle

Date	Mintage	VG	F	VF	XF	Unc
1622	Inc. above	20.00	40.00	65.00	125	—
(16)22	Inc. above	20.00	40.00	65.00	125	—
1623	2,851,000	20.00	40.00	65.00	125	—

KM# 96 3 GROSCHEN
Silver **Obv:** Eagle with scepter arms on breast **Rev:** Imperial orb with value 3 G **Mint:** Kolln **Note:** Kipper 3 Groschen.

Date	Mintage	VG	F	VF	XF	Unc
ND(1622/23)	—	20.00	40.00	65.00	125	—

KM# 602 3 GROSCHEN
Silver **Mint:** Konigsberg **Note:** Varieties exist.

Date	Mintage	VG	F	VF	XF	Unc
1695 SD	1,384,000	10.00	20.00	40.00	80.00	—
1696 SD	2,800,000	10.00	20.00	40.00	80.00	—
1697 SD	650,000	10.00	20.00	40.00	80.00	—
1698 SD	750,000	10.00	20.00	40.00	80.00	—
1699 SD	—	10.00	20.00	40.00	80.00	—
1700 CG	360,000	10.00	20.00	40.00	80.00	—

KM# 61 4 GROSCHEN
Silver **Obv:** Bust right **Rev:** Four oval arms in cartouche, one at top divides date, value IIII/GROS in center **Mint:** Berlin

Date	Mintage	VG	F	VF	XF	Unc
16Z0 LM	—	25.00	45.00	80.00	140	—

KM# 62 4 GROSCHEN
Silver **Rev:** Value in center IIII only

Date	Mintage	VG	F	VF	XF	Unc
16Z0 LM	—	25.00	45.00	80.00	140	—
16Z1 LM	—	25.00	45.00	80.00	140	—

KM# 63 6 GROSCHEN
Silver **Obv:** Bust right **Rev:** Eagle with scepter shield on breast divides date, VI below in legend **Mint:** Berlin **Note:** Kipper 6 Groschen.

Date	Mintage	VG	F	VF	XF	Unc
1620 LM	—	20.00	40.00	65.00	125	—
1621	—	20.00	40.00	65.00	125	—
1621 LM	—	20.00	40.00	65.00	125	—

KM# 99 6 GROSCHEN
Silver **Obv:** Eagle with scepter arms on breast **Rev:** Imperial orb with 6 G **Mint:** Kolln **Note:** Kipper 6 Groschen.

Date	Mintage	VG	F	VF	XF	Unc
ND(1622/23)	—	16.00	33.00	55.00	85.00	—

KM# 100 6 GROSCHEN
Silver **Obv:** Bust right, value VI below **Rev:** Oval scepter arms in baroque frame, imperial orb with 6 above divides date **Mint:** Krossen **Note:** Kipper 6 Groschen.

Date	Mintage	VG	F	VF	XF	Unc
1622	151,000	27.00	45.00	75.00	140	—

KM# 101 6 GROSCHEN
Silver **Rev:** Date divided below arms

Date	Mintage	VG	F	VF	XF	Unc
1622	Inc. above	35.00	65.00	120	200	—
1623	129,000	35.00	65.00	120	200	—

KM# 297 6 GROSCHEN
Silver **Obv:** Crowned bust right **Mint:** Konigsberg

Date	Mintage	VG	F	VF	XF	Unc
1658 (r)	288,000	20.00	40.00	65.00	125	—
1659 (r)	288,000	20.00	40.00	65.00	125	—

KM# 429 6 GROSCHEN
Silver **Note:** Varieties exist.

Date	Mintage	VG	F	VF	XF	Unc
1674 CV	104,000	30.00	55.00	75.00	140	—
1679 HS	1,114,000	16.00	33.00	55.00	85.00	—
1680 HS	Inc. above	16.00	33.00	55.00	85.00	—
1681 HS	1,650,000	16.00	33.00	55.00	85.00	—
1682 HS	4,400,000	16.00	33.00	55.00	85.00	—
1683 HS	3,367,000	16.00	33.00	55.00	85.00	—
1684 HS	4,193,000	16.00	33.00	55.00	85.00	—
1685 HS	1,043,000	16.00	33.00	55.00	85.00	—
1685 BA	Inc. above	16.00	33.00	55.00	85.00	—
1686 BA	Inc. above	16.00	33.00	55.00	85.00	—
1687 HS	480,000	16.00	33.00	55.00	85.00	—
1688 HS	Inc. above	16.00	33.00	55.00	85.00	—

KM# 519 6 GROSCHEN
Silver **Obv:** Laureate bust right **Rev:** Crowned triple arms, date divided below, value VI **Mint:** Berlin **Note:** Coinage for Province of Prussia.

Date	Mintage	VG	F	VF	XF	Unc
1685 LCS	866,000	20.00	40.00	65.00	125	—

KM# 610 6 GROSCHEN
Silver **Note:** Varieties exist.

Date	Mintage	VG	F	VF	XF	Unc
1698 SD	1,529,000	16.00	33.00	55.00	85.00	—
1699 SD	Inc. above	16.00	33.00	55.00	85.00	—
1700 CG	274,000	16.00	33.00	55.00	85.00	—

KM# 64 8 GROSCHEN
Silver **Obv:** Bust right **Rev:** Scepter arms in ornamented frame divide date, value VIII below in legend **Mint:** Berlin **Note:** Varieties exist.

Date	Mintage	VG	F	VF	XF	Unc
1620 LM	—	65.00	130	250	400	—
16Z1 LM	—	65.00	130	250	400	—
16Z1	—	65.00	130	250	400	—
162Z	—	65.00	130	250	400	—

KM# 85 12 GROSCHEN
Silver **Obv:** Eagle with scepter arms on breast divides date, value XII below **Rev:** Imperial orb and seven small shields around center in which value "1Z G" appears **Mint:** Berlin

Date	Mintage	VG	F	VF	XF	Unc
1621	—	—	—	—	—	—

KM# 102 12 GROSCHEN
Silver **Obv:** Bust right, value XII below **Rev:** Eagle with scepter arms on breast, date divided below **Mint:** Krossen **Note:** Kipper 12 Groschen.

Date	Mintage	VG	F	VF	XF	Unc
1622	33,000	40.00	65.00	125	200	—

KM# 103 12 GROSCHEN
Silver **Rev:** Crown above eagle **Note:** Kipper 12 Groschen.

Date	Mintage	VG	F	VF	XF	Unc
1622	Inc. above	55.00	100	175	300	—
1623	12,000	55.00	100	175	300	—
ND	Inc. above	55.00	100	175	300	—

KM# 243 18 GROSCHEN (1/5 Thaler)
Silver **Obv:** Crowned half-length figure right **Rev:** 5-fold arms divide 18 and mintmaster's initials (or only 18 and initials), crown above dvides date **Mint:** Konigsberg

Date	Mintage	VG	F	VF	XF	Unc
1651 CM	53,000	27.00	55.00	100	200	—
1652 CM	27,000	45.00	80.00	170	275	—
1655 CM	80,000	25.00	45.00	75.00	175	—
1656	Inc. above	25.00	45.00	75.00	175	—
1656 CM	318,000	25.00	45.00	75.00	175	—
1656 DK	Inc. above	25.00	45.00	75.00	175	—

Date	Mintage	VG	F	VF	XF	Unc
1657 CM	—	25.00	45.00	75.00	175	—
1657 DK	265,000	25.00	45.00	75.00	175	—
1657 NB	Inc. above	25.00	45.00	75.00	175	—
1658 NB	53,000	27.00	55.00	100	200	—

KM# 311 18 GROSCHEN (1/5 Thaler)

Silver **Obv:** Bust right **Rev:** Eagle divides value 1-8

Date	Mintage	VG	F	VF	XF	Unc
MDCLX (1660) HM	163,000	27.00	45.00	80.00	160	—

KM# 318 18 GROSCHEN (1/5 Thaler)

Silver **Ruler:** Friedrich Wilhelm **Rev:** Arabic date

Date	Mintage	VG	F	VF	XF	Unc
1661 HM	149,000	27.00	45.00	80.00	160	—
1662 HM	144,000	27.00	45.00	80.00	160	—
1663 HM	96,000	27.00	45.00	80.00	160	—

KM# 331 18 GROSCHEN (1/5 Thaler)

Silver **Rev:** Without value, date in legend

Date	Mintage	VG	F	VF	XF	Unc
1664	27,000	27.00	45.00	80.00	160	—

KM# 336 18 GROSCHEN (1/5 Thaler)

Silver **Rev:** Arms divide value 1-8

Date	Mintage	VG	F	VF	XF	Unc
1665	122,000	27.00	45.00	80.00	160	—
1666	69,000	27.00	50.00	100	170	—
1667	30,000	27.00	50.00	100	170	—

KM# 431 18 GROSCHEN (1/5 Thaler)

Silver **Obv:** Head right **Rev:** Crowned 5-fold arms divide 1-8, date in legend

Date	Mintage	VG	F	VF	XF	Unc
1674 CV	30,000	27.00	50.00	100	170	—
1674 HS	369,000	27.00	50.00	100	170	—

KM# 440 18 GROSCHEN (1/5 Thaler)

Silver **Ruler:** Friedrich Wilhelm **Obv:** Laureate bust right

Date	Mintage	VG	F	VF	XF	Unc
1675 HS	106,000	27.00	45.00	80.00	160	—

KM# 441 18 GROSCHEN (1/5 Thaler)

Silver **Obv:** Crowned bust right **Rev:** Crowned eagle divides 1-8

Date	Mintage	VG	F	VF	XF	Unc
MDCLXXV (1675) HS	Inc. above	27.00	45.00	80.00	160	—
MDCLXXVI (1676) HS	158,000	27.00	45.00	80.00	160	—

KM# 468 18 GROSCHEN (1/5 Thaler)

Silver

Date	Mintage	VG	F	VF	XF	Unc
1676 HS	Inc. above	16.00	30.00	55.00	120	—
1679 HS	120,000	16.00	30.00	55.00	120	—
1680 HS	Inc. above	16.00	30.00	55.00	120	—
1681 HS	178,000	16.00	30.00	55.00	120	—
1682 HS	474,000	16.00	30.00	55.00	120	—
1683 HS	364,000	16.00	30.00	55.00	120	—
1684 HS	1,109,000	16.00	30.00	55.00	120	—
1685 HS	3,316,000	16.00	30.00	55.00	120	—
1685 BA	337,000	16.00	30.00	55.00	120	—
1686 BA	Inc. above	16.00	30.00	55.00	120	—
1687 BA	—	16.00	30.00	55.00	120	—
1687 HS	41,000	27.00	55.00	100	155	—
1688 AB	—	16.00	30.00	55.00	120	—
1689 HS	—	16.00	30.00	55.00	120	—

KM# 520 18 GROSCHEN (1/5 Thaler)

Silver **Obv:** Laureate bust right **Rev:** Crowned oval 5-fold arms divide value 1 - 8, date in legend **Mint:** Berlin **Note:** Coinage for the Province of Prussia.

Date	Mintage	VG	F	VF	XF	Unc
1685 LCS	69,000	20.00	40.00	80.00	160	—
1686 LCS	—	20.00	40.00	80.00	160	—

KM# 611 18 GROSCHEN (1/5 Thaler)

Silver, 28.6 mm. **Ruler:** Friedrich III **Obv:** Crowned bust with sword right **Rev:** Crowned imperial eagle **Mint:** Konigsberg **Note:** Varieties exist.

Date	Mintage	VG	F	VF	XF	Unc
1698 SD	5,904,000	16.00	35.00	55.00	120	—
1699 SD	Inc. above	16.00	35.00	55.00	120	—
1700 CG	84,000	20.00	40.00	80.00	150	—

KM# 108 1/96 THALER

Silver **Obv:** Eagle with scepter arms in baroque frame **Rev:** Imperial orb with 96, date above, all in shield frame **Mint:** Kolln **Note:** Dreier 1/96 Thaler.

Date	Mintage	VG	F	VF	XF	Unc
1623 LM	—	13.00	27.00	55.00	120	—

KM# 114 1/96 THALER

Silver **Obv:** Eagle in squared shield frame **Rev:** Date divided outside frame

Date	Mintage	VG	F	VF	XF	Unc
1624 LM	1,275,000	8.00	16.00	33.00	60.00	—

KM# 118 1/96 THALER

Silver **Obv:** Eagle not enclosed in frame **Rev:** Imperial orb with 96, not enclosed in frame **Note:** Varieties exist.

Date	Mintage	VG	F	VF	XF	Unc
1625	480,000	13.00	27.00	55.00	125	—

KM# 407 1/48 THALER (1/2 Groschen)

Billon **Obv:** Crowned 5-fold arms **Rev. Inscription:** 48 / EINEN / REICHS / THALER / date **Mint:** Berlin

Date	Mintage	VG	F	VF	XF	Unc
1670 IL	—	25.00	45.00	80.00	140	—

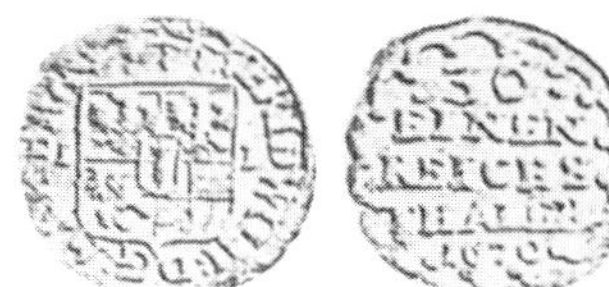

KM# 408 1/36 THALER

Silver **Obv:** Crowned 5-fold arms **Rev. Inscription:** 36 / EINEN / REICHS / THALER / date

Date	Mintage	VG	F	VF	XF	Unc
1670 IL	—	—	—	—	—	—

KM# 6 1/24 THALER

Silver **Ruler:** Joachim Friedrich **Obv:** Ornate 4-fold arms with scepter shield in center, titles of Joachim Friedrich **Rev:** Imperial orb with 24 in baroque frame, date in legend **Mint:** Kolln **Note:** Ref. B#522-525. Varieties exist.

Date	Mintage	VG	F	VF	XF	Unc
1601 (e)	—	—	—	—	—	—

KM# 20 1/24 THALER

Silver **Ruler:** Joachim Friedrich **Rev:** Imperial orb with 24 in baroque frame divides date **Mint:** Kolln **Note:** Ref. B#526-27. Similar to KM#6.

Date	Mintage	VG	F	VF	XF	Unc
1604 MH	22,000	—	—	—	—	—
1606 MH	—	—	—	—	—	—
1607	—	—	—	—	—	—

KM# A43 1/24 THALER

Silver **Ruler:** Johann Sigismund **Mint:** Kolln **Note:** Ref. B#593, 595. Klippe.

Date	Mintage	VG	F	VF	XF	Unc
161Z HL	—	—	—	—	—	—
1614 HL	—	—	—	—	—	—

KM# 42 1/24 THALER

Silver **Obv:** Imperial orb with 24 divides date **Rev:** 5-fold arms **Mint:** Driesen **Note:** Varieties exist.

Date	Mintage	VG	F	VF	XF	Unc
161Z HL	—	20.00	45.00	55.00	120	—
1613 HL	—	20.00	45.00	55.00	120	—
1614 HL	—	20.00	45.00	55.00	120	—
1615 HL	—	20.00	45.00	55.00	120	—
ND HL	—	20.00	45.00	55.00	120	—

KM# 41 1/24 THALER

Silver **Obv:** Eagle with arms on breast **Rev:** Imperial orb with 24 divides date **Mint:** Kolln

Date	Mintage	VG	F	VF	XF	Unc
1612 MH	530,000	16.00	33.00	45.00	90.00	—
1613 MH	Inc. above	16.00	33.00	45.00	90.00	—
1614 MH	325,000	16.00	33.00	45.00	90.00	—
1615 MH	Inc. above	16.00	33.00	45.00	90.00	—
1616 MH	466,000	16.00	33.00	45.00	90.00	—
1617 MH	Inc. above	16.00	33.00	45.00	90.00	—
1618 MH	—	16.00	33.00	45.00	90.00	—
1619 MH	—	16.00	33.00	45.00	90.00	—

KM# 65 1/24 THALER

Silver **Obv:** Imperial orb with 24 **Rev:** 4-fold arms in cruciform **Mint:** Berlin **Note:** Kipper 1/24 Thaler.

Date	Mintage	VG	F	VF	XF	Unc
ND(ca.1620) LM	—	25.00	45.00	65.00	125	—

KM# 104 1/24 THALER

Silver **Rev:** Crowned scepter arms **Mint:** Kolln **Note:** Kipper 1/24 Thaler.

Date	Mintage	VG	F	VF	XF	Unc
ND(1622/23)	—	25.00	40.00	60.00	125	—

KM# 106 1/24 THALER

Silver **Obv:** Imperial orb with 24 divides date **Rev:** Crowned scepter arms **Mint:** Krossen **Note:** Kipper 1/24 Thaler.

Date	Mintage	VG	F	VF	XF	Unc
1622	317,000	20.00	40.00	60.00	120	—
1623	131,000	20.00	40.00	60.00	120	—
ND	—	—	—	—	—	—

KM# 105 1/24 THALER

Silver **Obv:** Crowned scepter arms **Rev:** Imperial orb with 24

Date	Mintage	VG	F	VF	XF	Unc
ND(1622/23)	—	20.00	40.00	60.00	125	—

KM# 109 1/24 THALER

Silver **Obv:** Five small arms around scepter arms in center **Rev:** Imperial orb with 24, cross divides date, all in shield frame **Mint:** Kolln

Date	Mintage	VG	F	VF	XF	Unc
1623 LM	—	27.00	60.00	100	175	—

KM# 110 1/24 THALER

Silver **Rev:** Orb in oval frame divides date

Date	Mintage	VG	F	VF	XF	Unc
1623 LM	—	20.00	40.00	85.00	160	—

KM# 111 1/24 THALER

Silver **Obv:** 5-fold arms **Rev:** Imperial orb with 24, cross divides date, all in shield frame

Date	Mintage	VG	F	VF	XF	Unc
16Z3 LM	—	16.00	33.00	60.00	120	—

KM# 115 1/24 THALER

Silver **Rev:** Date divied outside shield frame

Date	Mintage	VG	F	VF	XF	Unc
1624 LM	423,000	13.00	27.00	45.00	80.00	—
1628 LM	79,000	13.00	27.00	45.00	80.00	—
1631 LM	—	13.00	27.00	45.00	80.00	—

KM# 116.1 1/24 THALER

Silver **Mint:** Konigsberg

Date	Mintage	VG	F	VF	XF	Unc
1624	35,000	16.00	33.00	60.00	120	—

Date	Mintage	VG	F	VF	XF	Unc
1625	—	16.00	33.00	60.00	120	—
1626	—	16.00	33.00	60.00	120	—

KM# 119 1/24 THALER

Silver **Mint:** Kolln

Date	Mintage	VG	F	VF	XF	Unc
1625 IP	480,000	16.00	33.00	60.00	120	—
1627 IP	117,000	20.00	40.00	80.00	160	—

KM# 140 1/24 THALER

Silver **Obv:** Imperial orb with 24 **Rev:** 5-fold arms, date above

Date	Mintage	VG	F	VF	XF	Unc
1631 LM	—	16.00	33.00	65.00	140	—
1632 LM	—	16.00	33.00	65.00	140	—
1633 LM	—	16.00	33.00	65.00	140	—
1634 LM	—	16.00	33.00	65.00	140	—
1635 LM	—	16.00	33.00	65.00	140	—
1636 LM	—	16.00	33.00	65.00	140	—

KM# 116.2 1/24 THALER

Silver

Date	Mintage	VG	F	VF	XF	Unc
1634	33,000	16.00	33.00	60.00	120	—
1635	Inc. above	—	—	—	—	—

KM# 244 1/24 THALER

Silver **Obv:** Bust with large head right **Rev:** Scepter arms in baroque frame, value Z-4 in two ovals below divide date **Mint:** Halberstadt

Date	Mintage	VG	F	VF	XF	Unc
1651	101,000	20.00	40.00	80.00	160	—

KM# 245 1/24 THALER

Silver **Obv:** Smaller head **Rev:** Value 24 in oval divides date **Note:** Varieties exist.

Date	Mintage	VG	F	VF	XF	Unc
1651	Inc. above	16.00	33.00	65.00	130	—
1656	1,246,000	16.00	33.00	65.00	130	—
1657	1,134,000	16.00	33.00	65.00	130	—
1658	908,000	16.00	33.00	65.00	130	—
1659	958,000	16.00	33.00	65.00	130	—
1660	367,000	16.00	33.00	65.00	130	—

KM# 246 1/24 THALER

Silver **Rev:** Date above arms **Note:** Varieties exist.

Date	Mintage	VG	F	VF	XF	Unc
1651	Inc. above	16.00	33.00	65.00	130	—
1652	—	16.00	33.00	65.00	130	—
1653	300,000	16.00	33.00	65.00	130	—

KM# 264 1/24 THALER

Silver **Rev:** Date divided below value **Note:** Varieties exist.

Date	Mintage	VG	F	VF	XF	Unc
1653	Inc. above	9.00	16.00	33.00	85.00	—
1654	450,000	9.00	16.00	33.00	85.00	—
1655	600,000	9.00	16.00	33.00	85.00	—
1656	Inc. above	9.00	16.00	33.00	85.00	—
1658	Inc. above	9.00	16.00	33.00	85.00	—
1659	Inc. above	9.00	16.00	33.00	85.00	—
1660	Inc. above	9.00	16.00	33.00	85.00	—
1661	119,000	9.00	16.00	33.00	85.00	—

KM# 265 1/24 THALER

Silver **Obv:** Eagle with oval scepter arms on breast **Rev:** Inscription, date in legend **Rev. Inscription:** HALBER / STETISCHE / LANDMVNZ / Z4

Date	Mintage	VG	F	VF	XF	Unc
1653	Inc. above	—	—	—	—	—

KM# 319 1/24 THALER

Silver **Obv:** Eagle, scepter arms on breast **Rev:** Imperial orb with 24 divides date **Mint:** Berlin

Date	Mintage	VG	F	VF	XF	Unc
1661 AB	372,000	13.00	27.00	45.00	85.00	—
1662 AB	672,000	13.00	27.00	45.00	85.00	—
1663 AB	124,000	13.00	27.00	45.00	85.00	—
1664 AB	83,000	13.00	27.00	45.00	85.00	—

KM# 337 1/24 THALER

Silver **Obv:** Bust right **Rev:** Eagle, scepter arms on breast, divides date at bottom

Date	Mintage	VG	F	VF	XF	Unc
1665	—	13.00	27.00	45.00	85.00	—
1666	—	13.00	27.00	45.00	85.00	—

KM# 346 1/24 THALER

Silver **Rev:** 24 on eagle's breast

Date	Mintage	VG	F	VF	XF	Unc
1666	—	12.00	24.00	40.00	80.00	—
1666 IL	—	12.00	24.00	40.00	80.00	—
1667 IL	—	12.00	24.00	40.00	80.00	—

KM# 349 1/24 THALER

Silver **Obv:** Crowned 5-fold arms **Rev. Inscription:** 24/EINEN/ REICHS/THALER/date

Date	Mintage	VG	F	VF	XF	Unc
1667 IL	—	9.00	16.00	33.00	65.00	—
1668 IL	—	9.00	16.00	33.00	65.00	—

KM# 350 1/24 THALER

Silver **Obv:** Date divided by crown at top

Date	Mintage	VG	F	VF	XF	Unc
1667 IL	—	9.00	16.00	33.00	65.00	—

KM# 351 1/24 THALER

Silver **Rev:** Date also at bottom **Note:** Varieties exist.

Date	Mintage	VG	F	VF	XF	Unc
1667 IL	—	9.00	16.00	33.00	65.00	—
1667/8 IL	—	9.00	16.00	33.00	65.00	—
1668 IL	—	9.00	16.00	33.00	65.00	—

KM# 352 1/24 THALER

Silver **Obv:** Crowned 5-fold arms, crown divides date **Mint:** Krossen **Note:** Varieties exist.

Date	Mintage	VG	F	VF	XF	Unc
1667 IPE	—	9.00	16.00	33.00	65.00	—
1667 GF	—	9.00	16.00	33.00	65.00	—
1668 GF	—	9.00	16.00	33.00	65.00	—

KM# 372 1/24 THALER

Silver **Obv:** Crowned 5-fold arms **Rev:** Imperial orb with 24 divides date at top **Note:** Varieties exist.

Date	Mintage	VG	F	VF	XF	Unc
1668 GF	—	9.00	16.00	33.00	65.00	—
1669 GF	—	9.00	16.00	33.00	65.00	—
1670 GF	—	9.00	16.00	33.00	65.00	—
1671 GF	—	9.00	16.00	33.00	65.00	—
1672 GF	—	9.00	16.00	33.00	65.00	—
1674 GF	—	9.00	16.00	33.00	65.00	—

KM# 374 1/24 THALER

Silver **Rev:** Imperial orb with 24 divides date **Note:** Varieties exist.

Date	Mintage	VG	F	VF	XF	Unc
1668 IL	—	9.00	16.00	33.00	65.00	—
1669 IL	—	9.00	16.00	33.00	65.00	—
1670 IL	—	9.00	16.00	33.00	65.00	—
1671 IL	—	9.00	16.00	33.00	65.00	—
1672 IL	—	9.00	16.00	33.00	65.00	—

Date	Mintage	VG	F	VF	XF	Unc
1673 IL	—	9.00	16.00	33.00	65.00	—
1674 IL	—	9.00	16.00	33.00	65.00	—
1675 CS	—	9.00	16.00	33.00	65.00	—

KM# 373 1/24 THALER

Silver **Rev. Inscription:** 24 / 1.R / THAL / date **Mint:** Berlin

Date	Mintage	VG	F	VF	XF	Unc
1668 IL	—	27.00	55.00	100	175	—

KM# 388 1/24 THALER

Silver **Rev. Inscription:** 24 / 1.R. / THALER / date

Date	Mintage	VG	F	VF	XF	Unc
1668 IL	—	27.00	55.00	100	175	—
1669 IL	—	27.00	55.00	100	175	—

KM# 389 1/24 THALER

Silver **Obv:** Arms **Rev:** Value **Mint:** Minden

Date	Mintage	VG	F	VF	XF	Unc
1669 HB	—	13.00	27.00	55.00	100	—
1670 HB	—	13.00	27.00	55.00	100	—
1671 IW	—	13.00	27.00	55.00	100	—
1672 IW	—	13.00	27.00	55.00	100	—
1679 AVH	—	13.00	27.00	55.00	100	—
1683 BH	—	13.00	27.00	55.00	100	—

KM# 442 1/24 THALER

Silver **Obv:** Imperial orb with 24, date in legend **Mint:** Berlin **Note:** Struck at Berlin Mint.

Date	Mintage	VG	F	VF	XF	Unc
1675 CS	—	13.00	27.00	55.00	90.00	—

KM# 482 1/24 THALER

Silver **Rev. Inscription:** 24 / EINEN / REICHS / THALER / date **Note:** Varieties exist.

Date	Mintage	VG	F	VF	XF	Unc
1679 CS	—	9.00	16.00	33.00	65.00	—
1684 LCS	—	9.00	16.00	33.00	65.00	—
1685 LCS	—	9.00	16.00	33.00	65.00	—

KM# 485 1/24 THALER

Silver **Obv:** Crowned 5-fold arms **Rev:** Imperial orb with 24 **Note:** Varieties exist.

Date	Mintage	VG	F	VF	XF	Unc
1679	—	13.00	27.00	55.00	100	—
1679 AVH	—	13.00	27.00	55.00	100	—
1683 BH	—	13.00	27.00	55.00	100	—

KM# 483 1/24 THALER

Silver **Mint:** Halberstadt

Date	Mintage	VG	F	VF	XF	Unc
1679 LCS	—	10.00	20.00	40.00	75.00	—

KM# 484 1/24 THALER

Silver **Obv:** Bust **Rev:** Value **Mint:** Minden

Date	Mintage	VG	F	VF	XF	Unc
1679 AVH	—	16.00	33.00	65.00	130	—

KM# 503 1/24 THALER

Silver **Obv:** Date in legend **Mint:** Berlin **Note:** Varieties exist.

Date	Mintage	VG	F	VF	XF	Unc
1682 LCS	—	9.00	16.00	33.00	65.00	—
1683 LCS	—	9.00	16.00	33.00	65.00	—

KM# 505 1/24 THALER

Silver **Obv:** Crowned 5-fold arms **Rev. Inscription:** 24 / EINEN / REICHS / THALER / date **Mint:** Magdeburg **Note:** Varieties exist.

Date	Mintage	VG	F	VF	XF	Unc
1683 IE	—	—	—	—	—	—
1685 IE	—	—	—	—	—	—
1687 IE	—	—	—	—	—	—

KM# 549 1/24 THALER

Silver **Obv:** Arms divide date **Mint:** Berlin **Note:** Varieties exist.

Date	Mintage	VG	F	VF	XF	Unc
1689 LCS	103,000	16.00	33.00	65.00	125	—

KM# A9 1/16 THALER

Silver **Obv:** 7-fold arms **Rev:** Imperial orb with 16 divides date, all in baroque frame

Date	Mintage	VG	F	VF	XF	Unc
(15)99 Swan	11,000	—	—	—	—	—

KM# 87 1/16 THALER

Silver **Obv:** Eagle, scepter arms on breast **Rev:** DS (= Doppelschilling), imperial orb with 16 above, date below **Mint:** Berlin

Date	Mintage	VG	F	VF	XF	Unc
1621 Rare	—	—	—	—	—	—

KM# B149 1/12 THALER

Silver **Ruler:** Georg Wilhelm **Obv:** Crowned bust right, titles of Georg Wilhellm **Rev. Inscription:** MONE: / NOVA • ARG: / DVC • PRVSSIAE / +XII+ / EINEN • REICHS / • THALER • / • date• **Mint:** Konigsberg **Note:** Ref. D#603.

Date	Mintage	VG	F	VF	XF	Unc
1634	—	—	—	—	—	—

Note: The above two coins are possibly patterns

KM# 486 1/12 THALER

Silver **Mint:** Berlin **Note:** Varieties exist.

Date	Mintage	VG	F	VF	XF	Unc
1679 CS	—	16.00	33.00	60.00	115	—
1683 IL	—	16.00	33.00	60.00	115	—
1683 LCS	—	16.00	33.00	60.00	115	—
1684 LCS	—	16.00	33.00	60.00	115	—
1685 LCS	—	16.00	33.00	60.00	115	—
1686 LCS	—	16.00	33.00	60.00	115	—
1687 LCS	2,674,000	16.00	33.00	60.00	115	—
1688 LCS	Inc. above	16.00	33.00	60.00	115	—

KM# 487 1/12 THALER

Silver **Obv:** Crowned 5-fold arms **Rev. Inscription:** 12 / EINEN / REICHS / THALER / date **Mint:** Halberstadt

Date	Mintage	VG	F	VF	XF	Unc
1679 LCS	—	—	—	—	—	—

KM# 507 1/12 THALER

Silver **Mint:** Minden

Date	Mintage	VG	F	VF	XF	Unc
1683 BH	—	13.00	27.00	55.00	100	—
1684 BH	—	13.00	27.00	55.00	100	—
1685 BH	—	13.00	27.00	55.00	100	—
1686 SD	—	13.00	27.00	55.00	100	—

KM# 506 1/12 THALER

Silver **Mint:** Magdeburg **Note:** Varieties exist.

Date	Mintage	VG	F	VF	XF	Unc
1683 IE	—	20.00	33.00	60.00	120	—
1684 IE	—	20.00	33.00	60.00	120	—
1685 IE	—	20.00	33.00	60.00	120	—
1686 IE	—	20.00	33.00	60.00	120	—
1687 IE	—	20.00	33.00	60.00	120	—
1689 IE	—	20.00	33.00	60.00	120	—

KM# 533 1/12 THALER

Silver **Rev:** 5-line inscription **Rev. Inscription:** 12 / EINEN / REICHS / THAL / date **Note:** Varieties exist.

Date	Mintage	VG	F	VF	XF	Unc
1687 IE	—	25.00	40.00	65.00	130	—
1688 IE	—	25.00	40.00	65.00	130	—
1688 ICS	—	25.00	40.00	65.00	130	—

KM# 532 1/12 THALER

Copper **Note:** Klippe.

Date	Mintage	VG	F	VF	XF	Unc
1687 IS	—	—	100	175	300	—

KM# 550 1/12 THALER

Silver **Mint:** Berlin **Note:** Varieties exist.

Date	Mintage	VG	F	VF	XF	Unc
1689 LCS	681,000	16.00	33.00	60.00	120	—
1692 LCS	Inc. above	16.00	33.00	60.00	120	—

KM# 551 1/12 THALER

Silver **Obv:** Arms divide date **Note:** Varieties exist.

Date	Mintage	VG	F	VF	XF	Unc
1689 LCS	Inc. above	16.00	33.00	60.00	120	—
1690 LCS	2,653,000	16.00	33.00	60.00	120	—
1691 LCS	4,903,000	16.00	33.00	60.00	120	—
1692 LCS	Inc. above	16.00	33.00	60.00	120	—

KM# 552 1/12 THALER

Silver **Mint:** Stargard

Date	Mintage	VG	F	VF	XF	Unc
1689 SD	—	13.00	27.00	45.00	90.00	—
1690 SD	—	13.00	27.00	45.00	90.00	—
1691 SD	—	13.00	27.00	45.00	90.00	—

KM# 553 1/12 THALER

Silver **Obv:** Crowned oval arms **Rev. Inscription:** 12 / EINEN / REICHS / THALE / date **Mint:** Minden

Date	Mintage	VG	F	VF	XF	Unc
1689 BH	—	13.00	27.00	45.00	90.00	—
1690 BH	—	13.00	27.00	45.00	90.00	—
1691 BH	—	13.00	27.00	45.00	90.00	—
1693 BH	—	13.00	27.00	45.00	90.00	—
1695 BH	—	13.00	27.00	45.00	90.00	—

KM# 571 1/12 THALER

Silver **Mint:** Magdeburg

Date	Mintage	VG	F	VF	XF	Unc
1690 IE	—	13.00	27.00	45.00	90.00	—
1691 ICS	—	13.00	27.00	45.00	90.00	—
1692 ICS	—	13.00	27.00	45.00	90.00	—
1693 ICS	—	13.00	27.00	45.00	90.00	—
1699 HFH	—	13.00	27.00	45.00	90.00	—
1700 HFH	—	13.00	27.00	45.00	90.00	—

KM# 572 1/12 THALER

Silver **Mint:** Stargard

Date	Mintage	VG	F	VF	XF	Unc
1690 SD	—	13.00	27.00	45.00	90.00	—

KM# 580 1/12 THALER

Silver **Mint:** Berlin

Date	Mintage	VG	F	VF	XF	Unc
1692 LCS	Inc. above	13.00	27.00	45.00	90.00	—
1693 LCS	5,489,000	13.00	27.00	45.00	90.00	—
1699 LCS	204,000	13.00	27.00	45.00	90.00	—
1700 LCS	993,000	13.00	27.00	45.00	90.00	—

KM# 581 1/12 THALER

Silver **Mint:** Stargard

Date	Mintage	VG	F	VF	XF	Unc
1692 SD	—	—	—	—	—	—

KM# 582 1/12 THALER

Silver **Mint:** Magdeburg

Date	Mintage	VG	F	VF	XF	Unc
1692 ICS	—	13.00	27.00	45.00	90.00	—
1693 ICS	—	13.00	27.00	45.00	90.00	—
1698 HFH	—	13.00	27.00	45.00	90.00	—
1699 HFH	—	13.00	27.00	45.00	90.00	—
1700 HFH	—	13.00	27.00	45.00	90.00	—

KM# 209 1/8 THALER (Blamüser)

Silver **Mint:** Berlin

Date	Mintage	VG	F	VF	XF	Unc
1643 AB	—	—	—	—	—	—
1648 CT	—	—	—	—	—	—

KM# 274 1/8 THALER (Blamüser)

Silver **Subject:** Birthday of Friedrich Wilhelm and Birth of Prince Karl Emil **Obv:** Crowned 1/2-length facing bust **Rev:** 7-line inscription, date

Date	Mintage	VG	F	VF	XF	Unc
1655	—	—	—	—	—	—

KM# 275 1/8 THALER (Blamüser)

Silver **Obv:** Uncrowned bust

Date	Mintage	VG	F	VF	XF	Unc
1655	—	—	—	—	—	—

KM# 276 1/8 THALER (Blamüser)

Silver **Ruler:** Friedrich Wilhelm **Obv:** 7-line inscription, floral decoration above

Date	Mintage	VG	F	VF	XF	Unc
1655 CT	—	—	—	—	—	—

KM# 353 1/8 THALER (Blamüser)

Silver **Ruler:** Friedrich Wilhelm **Subject:** Death of Friedrich Wilhelm's Wife, Luise Henriette von Nassau-Oranien **Obv:** Crowned CL monogram **Rev:** 7-line inscription with date

Date	Mintage	VG	F	VF	XF	Unc
1667 IL	—	—	—	—	—	—

KM# 354 1/8 THALER (Blamüser)

Silver **Ruler:** Friedrich Wilhelm **Obv:** Crowned arms **Rev:** 7-line inscription with date, laurel spray above

Date	Mintage	VG	F	VF	XF	Unc
1667 IL	—	33.00	75.00	125	200	—

KM# 355 1/8 THALER (Blamüser)
Silver **Rev:** Eight-line inscription with date, without spray above

Date	Mintage	VG	F	VF	XF	Unc
1667 IL	—	33.00	75.00	125	200	—

KM# 409 1/8 THALER (Blamüser)
Silver **Obv:** Head right **Rev:** 10-fold arms, crown above divides date, value 1/8 below **Mint:** Minden

Date	Mintage	VG	F	VF	XF	Unc
1670 HB	—	60.00	100	200	300	—

KM# 419 1/8 THALER (Blamüser)
Silver

Date	Mintage	VG	F	VF	XF	Unc
1670 HB	—	60.00	120	200	300	—
1671 HB	—	60.00	120	200	300	—
1671 IW	—	60.00	120	200	300	—
1672 IW	—	70.00	125	225	350	—
1676 GDZ	—	60.00	120	200	300	—
1676 AVH	—	60.00	120	200	300	—

KM# 302 1/6 THALER (1/4 Gulden)
Silver **Subject:** Death of Princess Anna Sophie **Obv:** Crowned arms in wreath **Rev:** 11-line inscription with date, value 1/6 in circle below **Mint:** Berlin

Date	Mintage	VG	F	VF	XF	Unc
1659 AB	—	—	—	—	—	—

KM# 312 1/6 THALER (1/4 Gulden)
Silver **Subject:** Death of Friedrich Wilhelm's Mother, Elisabet Charlotte **Obv:** 17-line inscription **Rev:** 12-line inscription with date

Date	Mintage	VG	F	VF	XF	Unc
1660 AB	—	—	—	—	—	—

KM# 322 1/6 THALER (1/4 Gulden)
Silver **Obv:** Crowned FWC monogram **Rev. Inscription:** VI / EINEN REICHS / THALER / Ao date

Date	Mintage	VG	F	VF	XF	Unc
1662 AB	—	55.00	120	200	375	—
1663 AB	—	55.00	120	200	375	—
1664 AB	—	55.00	120	200	375	—

KM# 356 1/6 THALER (1/4 Gulden)
Silver **Obv:** Bust right **Rev:** Crowned arms divide date, value (1/6) below

Date	Mintage	VG	F	VF	XF	Unc
1667 IL	—	—	—	—	—	—
1668 IL	—	—	—	—	—	—

KM# 375 1/6 THALER (1/4 Gulden)
Silver **Obv:** Bust right **Rev:** Crowned ornate 5-fold arms, value 1/6 below **Note:** Varieties exist.

Date	Mintage	VG	F	VF	XF	Unc
1668 IL	—	40.00	90.00	170	275	—
1669 IL	—	40.00	90.00	170	275	—
1673 IL	—	40.00	90.00	170	275	—
1674 IL	—	40.00	90.00	170	275	—

KM# 430 1/6 THALER (1/4 Gulden)
Silver **Rev:** Date in legend

Date	Mintage	VG	F	VF	XF	Unc
1674 IL	—	40.00	90.00	170	275	—
1675 IL	—	40.00	90.00	170	275	—

KM# 17 1/4 THALER
Silver **Obv:** 1/2-length bust right **Rev:** 7-fold arms, date in legend

Date	Mintage	VG	F	VF	XF	Unc
1602 (e)	—	—	—	—	—	—

KM# 21 1/4 THALER
Silver **Rev:** 7-fold arms divide date

Date	Mintage	VG	F	VF	XF	Unc
1604 MH	—	—	—	—	—	—

KM# 43 1/4 THALER
Silver **Ruler:** Johann Sigismund **Obv:** 1/2-length bust right, date below **Rev:** 12-fold arms

Date	Mintage	VG	F	VF	XF	Unc
1612 MH	—	—	—	—	—	—

KM# 86.1 1/4 THALER
Silver **Obv:** 1/2-length armored figure right, scepter on shoulder, divides date, titles of Georg Wilhelm **Rev:** Crowned 4-fold arms, scepter shield in center, all in baroque frame, titles continuous **Mint:** Konigsberg **Note:** Ref. N#95.

Date	Mintage	VG	F	VF	XF	Unc
16Z1 (q)	584,000	27.00	45.00	75.00	160	—

KM# 86.2 1/4 THALER
Silver **Ruler:** Georg Wilhelm **Obv:** 1/2-length armored figure right, scepter on shoulder, date to right of figure, titles of Georg Wilhelm **Rev:** Crowned 4-fold arms, scepter shield in center, all in baroque frame, titles continuous **Mint:** Konigsberg **Note:** Ref. N#96.

Date	Mintage	VG	F	VF	XF	Unc
16Z1 (q)	Inc. above	—	—	—	—	—

KM# 86.3 1/4 THALER
Silver **Ruler:** Georg Wilhelm **Obv:** 1/2-length armored figure right, scepter on shoulder, date below figure and helmet to right, titles of Georg Wilhelm **Rev:** Crowned 4-fold arms, scepter shield in center, all in baroque frame, titles continuous **Mint:** Konigsberg **Note:** Ref. N#97. Varieties exist.

Date	Mintage	VG	F	VF	XF	Unc
16Z1	Inc. above	25.00	40.00	70.00	150	—
16Z1 (q)	Inc. above	25.00	40.00	70.00	150	—

Date	Mintage	VG	F	VF	XF	Unc
16ZZ (q)	1,589,000	25.00	40.00	70.00	150	—
16ZZ	Inc. above	25.00	40.00	70.00	150	—

KM# 86.4 1/4 THALER
Silver **Ruler:** Georg Wilhelm **Obv:** 1/2-length armored figure right, scepter on shoulder, titles of Georg Wilhelm **Rev:** Date divided by arms **Mint:** Konigsberg **Note:** Ref. N#98.

Date	Mintage	VG	F	VF	XF	Unc
16ZZ (q)	Inc. above	27.00	45.00	75.00	160	—
(16)ZZ (q)	Inc. above	27.00	45.00	75.00	160	—

KM# 86.5 1/4 THALER
Silver **Ruler:** Georg Wilhelm **Obv:** 1/2-length figure with large ruffled collar right, scepter on shoulder, titles of Georg Wilhelm **Rev:** Crowned 4-fold arms, scepter shield in center, all in baroque frame **Mint:** Konigsberg **Note:** Ref. N#99.

Date	Mintage	VG	F	VF	XF	Unc
(16)ZZ (q)	—	27.00	45.00	75.00	160	—

KM# 86.6 1/4 THALER
Silver **Ruler:** Georg Wilhelm **Obv:** 1/2-length figure with crown and no helmet right, titles of Georg Wilhelm **Rev:** Crowned 4-fold arms, scepter shield in center, all in baroque frame **Mint:** Konigsberg **Note:** Ref. N#100.

Date	Mintage	VG	F	VF	XF	Unc
(16)ZZ (q)	Inc. above	—	—	—	—	—

KM# 86.7 1/4 THALER
Silver **Obv:** 1/2-length figure in electoral robe right, scepter on shoulder, titles of Georg Wilhelm **Rev:** Crowned 4-fold arms, scepter shield in center, all in baroque frame **Note:** Ref. N#101. Varieties exist. Prev. KM#86.2.

Date	Mintage	VG	F	VF	XF	Unc
(16)ZZ (q)	Inc. above	—	—	—	—	—
(16)22 (q)	Inc. above	—	—	—	—	—
(16)24 (q)	1,055,000	—	—	—	—	—
(16)24 (q)	2,334,000	—	—	—	—	—

KM# 86a 1/4 THALER
Silver **Ruler:** Georg Wilhelm **Obv:** 1/2-length figure wears ermine robe, scepter on shoulder, titles of Georg Wilhelm **Rev:** Crowned 4-fold arms, scepter shield in center, all in baroque frame **Mint:** Konigsberg **Note:** Ref. N#102. Kipper 1/4 Thaler. Similar 86.7 but approximate weight: 3.5 grams.

Date	Mintage	VG	F	VF	XF	Unc
(16)23 (q)	—	27.00	45.00	75.00	160	—

KM# 86.8 1/4 THALER
Silver, 30.2 mm. **Ruler:** Georg Wilhelm **Obv:** Crowned bust right **Rev:** Large crown above arms and "S" on breast of eagle in upper left quarter **Mint:** Konigsberg **Note:** Ref. N#103.

Date	Mintage	VG	F	VF	XF	Unc
(16)24 (q)	Inc. above	—	—	—	—	—

KM# 86.9 1/4 THALER
Silver **Ruler:** Georg Wilhelm **Obv:** 1/2-length uncrowned figure right, scepter on shoulder, titles of Georg Wilhelm **Rev:** Crowned 4-fold arms divide date **Mint:** Konigsberg **Note:** Ref. N#104.

Date	Mintage	VG	F	VF	XF	Unc
(16)24 (q)	Inc. above	—	—	—	—	—
16Z4 (q)	Inc. above	—	—	—	—	—

KM# 86.10 1/4 THALER
Silver **Ruler:** Georg Wilhelm **Obv:** Eagle with "S" on breast in circle **Obv. Legend:** MONETA. NOVA. **Rev:** Shield of Hohenzollern arms in baroque frame, date **Rev. Legend:** DVCIS IN BORVSSIA • • A • **Mint:** Konigsberg **Note:** Ref. D#600. Possibly a pattern.

Date	Mintage	VG	F	VF	XF	Unc
16Z4	—	—	—	—	—	—

KM# 86.11 1/4 THALER
Silver **Ruler:** Georg Wilhelm **Obv:** Eagle with 'S' on breast in circle **Obv. Legend:** MONETA. NOVA. **Rev:** ANNI/date in circle **Rev. Legend:** DVCIS. IN . BORVSSIA. **Mint:** Konigsberg **Note:** Ref. D#601. Possibly a pattern.

Date	Mintage	VG	F	VF	XF	Unc
16Z4	—	—	—	—	—	—

KM# 86.12 1/4 THALER
Silver **Ruler:** Georg Wilhelm **Obv:** 1/2-length figure wears ermine robe, scepter on shoulder, titles of Georg Wilhelm **Rev:** Large crown above arms without 'S' on breast of eagle in upper left quarter **Mint:** Konigsberg **Note:** Ref. N#105.

Date	Mintage	VG	F	VF	XF	Unc
(16)25/4 (q)	—	—	—	—	—	—

KM# 86.13 1/4 THALER
Silver **Ruler:** Georg Wilhelm **Obv:** 1/2-length figure right, scepter on shoulder, titles of Georg Wilhelm **Rev:** Large crown above arms, 'S' on breast of eagle in lower right quarter **Mint:** Konigsberg **Note:** Ref. N#106.

Date	Mintage	VG	F	VF	XF	Unc
(16)25 (q)	353,000	—	—	—	—	—

KM# 86.14 1/4 THALER
Silver **Obv:** 1/2-length figure right, scepter on shoulder, titles of Georg Wilhelm **Obv. Legend:** GEORGWILHD • G • MARCHIO

• BRAND **Rev:** Mintmaster's symbol in cartouche below arms **Note:** Ref. N#107.

Date	Mintage	VG	F	VF	XF	Unc
(16)25 (q)	Inc. above	27.00	45.00	75.00	160	—
(16)26 (q)	56,000	—	—	—	—	—

KM# 86.15 1/4 THALER

Silver **Ruler:** Georg Wilhelm **Obv:** 1/2-length figure right, scepter on shoulder, titles of Georg Wilhelm **Rev:** 11-fold arms with scepter shield in center, date above, titles continuous in legend **Mint:** Kolln **Note:** Ref. N#40.

Date	Mintage	VG	F	VF	XF	Unc
1633 LM Rare	—	—	—	—	—	—

KM# 124.2 1/4 THALER

Silver **Ruler:** Georg Wilhelm **Obv:** 1/2-length armored figure to right, scepter over shoulder, titles of Georg Wilhelm **Rev:** 7-fold arms with central shield, electoral hat above, date divided at top **Rev. Legend:** ANFANG BEDENCK DAS END (or variant) **Mint:** Konigsberg **Note:** Ref. N#38b.

Date	Mintage	VG	F	VF	XF	Unc
1634 (q)	—	—	—	—	—	—

KM# 175 1/4 THALER

Silver **Subject:** Death of Georg Wilhelm **Obv:** In ornamented shield with electoral hat above, 8-fold arms with scepter shield in center, titles of Georg Wilhelm **Rev:** 6-line inscription with R.N. dates **Mint:** Konigsberg **Note:** Ref. D#619.

Date	Mintage	VG	F	VF	XF	Unc
1640 (MDCXL) DK	—	—	—	—	—	—

KM# 182 1/4 THALER

Silver **Obv:** Crowned and robed elector holding scepter on horse rearing to right **Rev:** Scepter arms in center of large rose, 23 small oval arms around

Date	Mintage	VG	F	VF	XF	Unc
ND(1641/3)	—	—	—	—	—	—

KM# 210 1/4 THALER

Silver **Ruler:** Friedrich Wilhelm **Obv:** Crowned and robed half-length figure right **Rev:** 5-fold arms, date above **Mint:** Berlin

Date	Mintage	VG	F	VF	XF	Unc
1643 AB	—	—	—	—	—	—
1648 CT	—	—	—	—	—	—

KM# 277 1/4 THALER

Silver **Subject:** Birthday of Friedrich Wilhelm and Birth of Prince Karl Emil

Date	Mintage	VG	F	VF	XF	Unc
1655 AB	—	—	—	—	—	—
1655 CT	—	275	525	900	—	—

KM# 303 1/4 THALER

Silver **Ruler:** Friedrich Wilhelm **Subject:** Death of Princess Anna Sophia **Obv:** Crowned arms in wreath **Rev:** 11-line inscription with date in circle below

Date	Mintage	VG	F	VF	XF	Unc
1659 AB	—	—	—	—	—	—

KM# 313 1/4 THALER

Silver **Subject:** Death of Friedrich Wilhelm's Mother, Elisabet Charlotte **Obv:** 14-line inscription **Rev:** 14-line inscription with date

Date	Mintage	VG	F	VF	XF	Unc
1660 AB	—	—	—	—	—	—

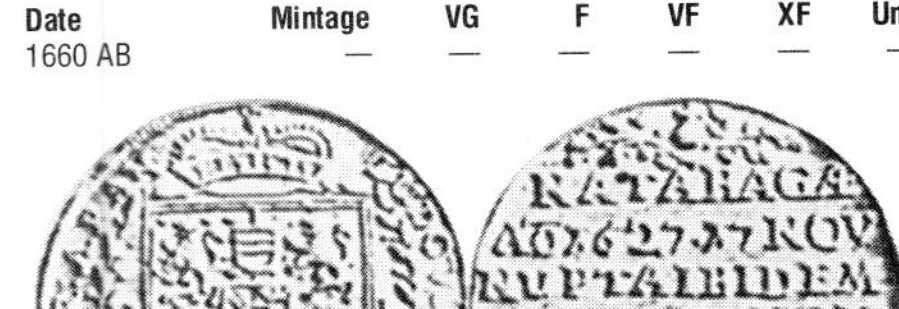

KM# 357 1/4 THALER

Silver **Subject:** Death of Friedrich Wilhelm's Wife, Luise Henriette von Nassau-Oranien **Obv:** Crowned arms in laurel wreath **Rev:** Seven-line inscription with date, imperial orb in laurel spray above

Date	Mintage	VG	F	VF	XF	Unc
1667 IL	—	—	—	—	—	—

KM# 358 1/4 THALER

Silver **Obv:** Crowned CL monogram, figure of Genius holding a live branch at right **Rev:** Seven-line inscription with date in frame, imperial orb between two laurel sprays above

Date	Mintage	VG	F	VF	XF	Unc
1667 IL-GL	—	—	—	—	—	—

KM# A509 1/4 THALER

Silver **Subject:** Death of Wilhelm (III)'s wife, Elisabeth Henriette von Hessen-Kassel **Obv:** Bust right **Rev:** Crowned tablet with 8-line inscrption and dates, skull and crossbones below

Date	Mintage	VG	F	VF	XF	Unc
1683	—	—	—	—	—	—

KM# 538 1/4 THALER

Silver **Subject:** Homage of County of Mark

Date	Mintage	VG	F	VF	XF	Unc
1688	—	33.00	80.00	135	250	—

KM# 539 1/4 THALER

Silver **Subject:** Death of Friedrich Wilhelm **Obv:** Bust right, two legend inscription around **Rev:** Eagle on palm tree above trophies

Date	Mintage	VG	F	VF	XF	Unc
1688 Schultz	—	—	—	—	—	—

KM# 323 1/3 THALER (1/2 Gulden)

Silver **Ruler:** Friedrich Wilhelm **Obv:** Crowned FWC monogram **Rev. Inscription:** III / EINEN REICHS / THALER / Ao date **Mint:** Berlin

Date	Mintage	VG	F	VF	XF	Unc
1662 AB	—	100	200	375	550	—
1664 AB	—	175	325	475	700	—

KM# 359 1/3 THALER (1/2 Gulden)

Silver **Obv:** Bust right **Rev:** Crowned arms divide date, value (1/3) below

Date	Mintage	VG	F	VF	XF	Unc
1667 IL	—	33.00	60.00	110	200	—
1668 IL	—	33.00	60.00	110	200	—

KM# 360.2 1/3 THALER (1/2 Gulden)

Silver **Obv:** Inner circle, modified designs **Rev:** Inner circle, modified designs

Date	Mintage	VG	F	VF	XF	Unc
1667 GF	—	45.00	85.00	160	290	—

KM# 360.1 1/3 THALER (1/2 Gulden)

Silver **Ruler:** Friedrich Wilhelm **Obv:** without inner circle **Rev:** without inner circle **Mint:** Krossen **Note:** Varieties exist.

Date	Mintage	VG	F	VF	XF	Unc
1667 IPE	—	45.00	85.00	160	275	—
1667 GF	—	45.00	85.00	160	275	—
1668 GF	—	45.00	85.00	160	275	—
1669 GF	—	45.00	85.00	160	275	—
1670 GF	—	45.00	85.00	160	275	—

KM# 376.1 1/3 THALER (1/2 Gulden)

Silver **Ruler:** Friedrich Wilhelm **Obv:** Bust right, date below bust **Rev:** Value below crowned arms **Mint:** Berlin **Note:** Varieties exist.

Date	Mintage	VG	F	VF	XF	Unc
1668 IL	—	33.00	65.00	120	200	—
1669 IL	—	33.00	65.00	120	200	—
1670 IL	—	33.00	65.00	120	200	—
1671 IL	—	33.00	65.00	120	200	—
1672 IL	—	33.00	65.00	120	200	—
1673 IL	—	33.00	65.00	120	200	—
1674 IL	—	33.00	65.00	120	200	—
1675 IL	—	33.00	65.00	120	200	—

KM# 377 1/3 THALER (1/2 Gulden)

Silver **Rev:** Arms between two palm branches **Note:** Varieties exist.

Date	Mintage	VG	F	VF	XF	Unc
1668 IL	—	33.00	60.00	110	200	—
1669 IL	—	33.00	60.00	110	200	—

KM# 378 1/3 THALER (1/2 Gulden)

Silver **Ruler:** Friedrich Wilhelm **Mint:** Krossen **Note:** Varieties exist.

Date	Mintage	VG	F	VF	XF	Unc
1668 GF	—	33.00	65.00	120	200	—
1670 GF	—	33.00	65.00	120	200	—
1671 GF	—	33.00	65.00	120	200	—
1672 GF	—	33.00	65.00	120	200	—
1673 GF	—	33.00	65.00	120	200	—
1674 GF	—	33.00	65.00	120	200	—
ND(1675) GF	—	33.00	65.00	120	200	—

KM# 379 1/3 THALER (1/2 Gulden)

Silver **Mint:** Konigsberg **Note:** Varieties exist.

Date	Mintage	VG	F	VF	XF	Unc
1668 G-DS	100,000	—	—	—	—	—
1668 CG-DS	Inc. above	—	—	—	—	—
ND1669 CG-SD	150,000	—	—	—	—	—
1669 TT	278,000	55.00	100	165	300	—
1670 TT	1,055,000	40.00	75.00	125	200	—

Date	Mintage	VG	F	VF	XF	Unc
1671 TT	833,000	40.00	80.00	190	275	—
1672 TT	865,000	40.00	80.00	190	275	—
1672 CV	Inc. above	40.00	80.00	190	275	—
1673 CV	638,000	55.00	100	165	300	—
1674 CV	736,000	55.00	100	165	300	—
1675 HS	1,407,000	33.00	60.00	100	175	—

KM# 390 1/3 THALER (1/2 Gulden)
Silver **Obv:** Laureate head

Date	Mintage	VG	F	VF	XF	Unc
ND1669 CG-DS	Inc. above	55.00	100	165	300	—
ND1669 TT-DS	Inc. above	55.00	100	165	300	—
1674 HS	Inc. above	55.00	100	165	300	—

KM# 391 1/3 THALER (1/2 Gulden)
Silver **Rev:** Complete date left of crown

Date	Mintage	VG	F	VF	XF	Unc
1669 DS-TT	Inc. above	55.00	100	200	300	—
1669 TT	Inc. above	55.00	100	200	300	—
1670 TT	Inc. above	55.00	100	200	300	—
1675 HS	Inc. above	55.00	100	200	300	—
1676 HS	17,000	55.00	100	200	300	—

KM# 392 1/3 THALER (1/2 Gulden)
Silver **Ruler:** Friedrich Wilhelm **Mint:** Minden

Date	Mintage	VG	F	VF	XF	Unc
1669 HB	—	175	375	700	1,200	—
1670 HB	—	175	375	700	1,200	—

KM# 410 1/3 THALER (1/2 Gulden)
Silver **Obv:** 1/3 on label at shoulder

Date	Mintage	VG	F	VF	XF	Unc
1670 HB	—	100	200	375	600	—
1671 HB	—	100	200	375	600	—
1671 IW	—	65.00	130	275	525	—
1672 IW	—	65.00	130	275	525	—
1673 IW	—	55.00	110	250	425	—

KM# 421 1/3 THALER (1/2 Gulden)
Silver **Ruler:** Friedrich Wilhelm **Obv:** Bust right, value 1/3 below **Rev:** Crowned arms, 1/3 below **Mint:** Berlin

Date	Mintage	VG	F	VF	XF	Unc
ND(1672) IL	—	45.00	75.00	140	200	—

KM# 433 1/3 THALER (1/2 Gulden)
Silver **Ruler:** Friedrich Wilhelm **Obv:** Bust right **Rev:** 10-fold arms, crown above divides date, value 1/3 below **Mint:** Regenstein

Date	Mintage	VG	F	VF	XF	Unc
1674 IA	—	65.00	130	260	525	—
1675 IA	—	65.00	130	260	525	—

KM# 434 1/3 THALER (1/2 Gulden)
Silver **Rev:** Complete date left of crown

Date	Mintage	VG	F	VF	XF	Unc
1674 GDZ	—	45.00	80.00	150	250	—
1674 AVH	—	45.00	80.00	150	250	—
1675 GDZ	—	45.00	80.00	150	250	—
1679 AVH	—	45.00	80.00	150	250	—
1683 BH	—	45.00	80.00	150	250	—

KM# 432 1/3 THALER (1/2 Gulden)
Silver **Ruler:** Friedrich Wilhelm **Obv:** Bust right **Rev:** Value below crowned arms, date in legend **Mint:** Berlin **Note:** Varieties exist.

Date	Mintage	VG	F	VF	XF	Unc
1674 IL	—	40.00	65.00	120	200	—
1675 IL	—	40.00	65.00	120	200	—
1687 LCS	—	40.00	65.00	120	200	—
1688 LCS	—	40.00	65.00	120	200	—

KM# 376.2 1/3 THALER (1/2 Gulden)
Silver **Obv:** CS below bust **Rev:** Date in legend **Note:** Varieties exist.

Date	Mintage	VG	F	VF	XF	Unc
1675 CS	—	33.00	65.00	120	200	—

KM# 469 1/3 THALER (1/2 Gulden)
Silver **Obv:** Date in legend divided by bust

Date	Mintage	VG	F	VF	XF	Unc
1676 IA	—	65.00	130	260	525	—

KM# 470 1/3 THALER (1/2 Gulden)
Silver **Obv:** KM#469 **Rev:** KM#433

Date	Mintage	VG	F	VF	XF	Unc
1676/1675 IA	—	65.00	130	260	525	—

KM# 508 1/3 THALER (1/2 Gulden)
Silver **Ruler:** Friedrich Wilhelm **Obv:** Bust right **Rev:** 10-fold arms, crown above divides date, value 1/3 below **Mint:** Magdeburg

Date	Mintage	VG	F	VF	XF	Unc
1683 IE	—	80.00	160	320	600	—
1686 IE	—	80.00	160	320	600	—

KM# 524 1/3 THALER (1/2 Gulden)
Silver **Ruler:** Friedrich Wilhelm **Mint:** Berlin

Date	Mintage	VG	F	VF	XF	Unc
1686 LCS	—	45.00	65.00	120	200	—

KM# 554 1/3 THALER (1/2 Gulden)
Silver **Ruler:** Friedrich III **Mint:** Stargard **Note:** Similar to KM#573.

Date	Mintage	VG	F	VF	XF	Unc
1689 SD	—	110	200	400	750	—
1690 SD	—	110	200	400	750	—

KM# 573 1/3 THALER (1/2 Gulden)
Silver **Ruler:** Friedrich III **Mint:** Berlin **Note:** Varieties exist.

Date	Mintage	VG	F	VF	XF	Unc
1690 LCS	—	40.00	85.00	170	300	—
1691 LCS	—	80.00	175	350	600	—
1692 LCS	—	80.00	175	350	600	—
1693 LCS	—	80.00	175	350	600	—
1698 LCS	19,000	80.00	175	350	600	—
1699 LCS	18,000	80.00	175	350	600	—
1700 LCS	8,000	110	200	400	750	—

KM# 583 1/3 THALER (1/2 Gulden)
Silver **Ruler:** Friedrich III **Obv:** Bust right **Rev:** Arms **Mint:** Minden

Date	Mintage	VG	F	VF	XF	Unc
1692 BH	—	125	200	375	650	—
1693 BH	—	125	200	375	650	—

KM# 593 1/3 THALER (1/2 Gulden)
Silver **Ruler:** Friedrich III **Mint:** Magdeburg **Note:** Similar to KM#573.

Date	Mintage	VG	F	VF	XF	Unc
1694 ICS	—	125	250	400	725	—
1695 ICS	—	135	275	475	900	—
1700 HFH	—	115	200	375	650	—

KM# 18 1/2 THALER
Silver **Obv:** Half-length bust right divides date **Rev:** 7-fold arms

Date	Mintage	VG	F	VF	XF	Unc
1602 (e)	—	—	—	—	—	—

KM# 22 1/2 THALER
Silver **Rev:** Date in legend

Date	Mintage	VG	F	VF	XF	Unc
1604 MH	—	—	—	—	—	—
1605 MH	—	—	—	—	—	—

KM# 44 1/2 THALER
Silver **Obv:** Half-length bust right, date below **Rev:** 12-fold arms

Date	Mintage	VG	F	VF	XF	Unc
1612 MH	—	2,000	3,250	5,000	7,000	—

KM# 66 1/2 THALER
Silver **Ruler:** Georg Wilhelm **Obv:** 3/4-length figure right, holding baton and helmet **Rev:** Crowned 12-fold arms in baroque frame **Mint:** Berlin

Date	Mintage	VG	F	VF	XF	Unc
ND(1620/21) LM	—	—	—	—	—	—

KM# 124.1 1/2 THALER
Silver **Obv:** 1/2-length armored figure to right, scepter over shoulder, titles of Georg Wilhelm **Rev:** 23-fold arms with scepter shield in center, electoral hat above, date divided at top **Rev. Legend:** ANFANG BEDENCK DAS END (or variant) **Mint:** Konigsberg **Note:** Ref. N#38a. Prev. KM#124.

Date	Mintage	VG	F	VF	XF	Unc
16Z7 (q)	2,179	325	600	1,000	1,500	—
16Z8 (q)	5,425	325	600	1,000	1,500	—
16Z9 (q)	11,000	325	600	1,000	1,500	—
1634 (q)	—	—	—	—	—	—

KM# 127 1/2 THALER

Silver **Ruler:** Georg Wilhelm **Rev:** Crowned 12-fold arms, date in legend **Mint:** Kolln

Date	Mintage	VG	F	VF	XF	Unc
1628 LM	—	200	400	775	1,100	—
1631 LM	—	200	400	775	1,100	—
1636 LM	—	200	400	775	1,100	—
1637 LM	—	200	400	775	1,100	—

KM# 150.2 1/2 THALER

Silver **Obv:** 1/2-length armored figure to right, scepter over shoulder, titles of Georg Wilhelm **Rev:** 7-fold arms with central shield, legend and date above crown **Rev. Legend:** MONETA. NOVA. ARGENTEA DVCIS PRVSSIÆ **Mint:** Konigsberg **Note:** Ref. N#39. Varieties exist.

Date	Mintage	VG	F	VF	XF	Unc
1635 DK (q)	—	—	—	—	—	—
1636 DK (q)	—	—	—	—	—	—
1637 DK (q)	—	—	—	—	—	—
1638 DK (q)	—	—	—	—	—	—

KM# 150.1 1/2 THALER

Silver **Obv:** 1/2-length figure right with helmet **Rev:** 8-fold arms with scepter shield in center, electoral hat above, date divided at top **Mint:** Konigsberg **Note:** Ref. N#38c. Prev. KM#150.

Date	Mintage	VG	F	VF	XF	Unc
1636 DK (q)	—	—	—	—	—	—
1639 DK	—	—	—	—	—	—

Note: Some coins dated 1639 were struck from Thaler dies of KM#160.2 on thin, broad flans

KM# 162 1/2 THALER

Silver **Ruler:** Georg Wilhelm **Obv:** Crowned half-length bust right **Mint:** Kolln

Date	Mintage	VG	F	VF	XF	Unc
1637 LM	—	—	—	—	—	—
1638 LM	—	—	—	—	—	—
1639 LM	—	—	—	—	—	—

KM# 176 1/2 THALER

Silver **Rev:** Without crown above arms, only date

Date	Mintage	VG	F	VF	XF	Unc
1640 LM	—	—	—	—	—	—

KM# 183 1/2 THALER

Silver **Ruler:** Friedrich Wilhelm **Obv:** Crowned and robed half-length figure **Rev:** Arms in rhombus divides date at top **Mint:** Berlin

Date	Mintage	VG	F	VF	XF	Unc
1641 LM	—	—	—	—	—	—

KM# 186 1/2 THALER

Silver **Obv:** Bust entirely within circle

Date	Mintage	VG	F	VF	XF	Unc
ND(1641/3) DK	—	—	—	—	—	—

KM# 184 1/2 THALER

Silver **Obv:** Crowned and robed half-length figure in wreath **Rev:** Arms in wreath, date in legend **Note:** Varieties exist.

Date	Mintage	VG	F	VF	XF	Unc
1641 LM	—	—	—	—	—	—
1642 LM	—	—	—	—	—	—

KM# 185 1/2 THALER

Silver **Ruler:** Friedrich Wilhelm **Obv:** Half-length bust 3/4 right breaks circle at top **Rev:** Plumed helmet, ARMAT ET ORNAT on band below, surrounded by 23 small oval arms **Mint:** Konigsberg **Note:** Varieties exist.

Date	Mintage	VG	F	VF	XF	Unc
ND(1641/3) DK	—	—	—	—	—	—

KM# 204 1/2 THALER

Silver **Obv:** Half-length figure right with helmet **Rev:** Crowned ornate 9-fold arms, date divided in upper left and right

Date	Mintage	VG	F	VF	XF	Unc
1642 DK	—	—	—	—	—	—

KM# 211 1/2 THALER

Silver **Ruler:** Friedrich Wilhelm **Obv:** 1/2-length figure with cap right **Rev:** Arms with 12 fields **Mint:** Berlin

Date	Mintage	VG	F	VF	XF	Unc
1643 AB	—	—	—	—	—	—
1644 AB	—	—	—	—	—	—
1647 CT	—	—	—	—	—	—

KM# 247 1/2 THALER

Silver **Ruler:** Friedrich Wilhelm **Obv:** Bust right in circle **Rev:** Helmeted arms **Mint:** Konigsberg

Date	Mintage	VG	F	VF	XF	Unc
ND(1651-6) CM Rare	—	—	—	—	—	—

KM# 279 1/2 THALER

Silver **Obv:** Elector standing 3/4 right, helmet on table at right **Rev:** Square arms, crown above divides date

Date	Mintage	VG	F	VF	XF	Unc
1655 CT	—	—	—	—	—	—
1657 CT	—	—	—	—	—	—

KM# 278 1/2 THALER

Silver **Subject:** Birthday of Friedrich Wilhelm and Birth of Prince Karl Emil **Obv:** Facing half-length bust **Rev:** Crowned six-line inscription, date **Mint:** Berlin **Note:** Struck on thick flan with 1/4 Thaler dies.

Date	Mintage	VG	F	VF	XF	Unc
1655 AB	—	—	—	—	—	—
1655 CT	—	—	—	—	—	—

KM# 298 1/2 THALER

Silver **Subject:** Attainment of Sovereignty over East Prussia **Obv:** Elector on horse galloping right, town below hoofs, date at bottom **Rev:** Eight-line inscription

Date	Mintage	VG	F	VF	XF	Unc
1658 CT	—	550	1,100	2,000	3,400	—

KM# 299 1/2 THALER

Silver **Rev:** Nine-line inscription

Date	Mintage	VG	F	VF	XF	Unc
1658 AB	—	550	1,100	2,000	3,400	—

KM# 314 1/2 THALER

Silver **Subject:** Death of Friedrich Wilhelm's Mother, Elisabet Charlotte **Obv:** 17-line inscription **Rev:** 12-line inscription with date

Date	Mintage	VG	F	VF	XF	Unc
1660 AB	—	—	—	—	—	—

KM# 332 1/2 THALER

Silver **Obv:** Elector standing 3/4 right, helmet on table at right **Rev:** Crowned arms divide date

Date	Mintage	VG	F	VF	XF	Unc
1664 AB	425	—	—	—	—	—

KM# 361 1/2 THALER

Silver **Ruler:** Friedrich Wilhelm **Subject:** Death of Friedrich Wilhelm's Wife, Luise Henriette von Nassau-Oranien **Obv:** Facing bust of Luise Henriette **Rev:** Nine-line inscription, date

Date	Mintage	VG	F	VF	XF	Unc
1667	—	700	1,350	2,500	4,000	—

KM# 362 1/2 THALER

Silver **Obv:** Bust of Luise Henriette left **Rev:** Six-line inscription with date in ornamented square

Date	Mintage	VG	F	VF	XF	Unc
1667 GL-IL	—	650	1,250	2,250	—	—

KM# 584 1/2 THALER

Silver **Ruler:** Friedrich III **Mint:** Minden

Date	Mintage	VG	F	VF	XF	Unc
1692 BH	—	—	—	—	—	—

KM# 420 2/3 THALER (Gulden)

Silver **Ruler:** Friedrich Wilhelm **Obv:** Laureate bust right **Rev:** Crowned ornate arms, value 2/3 below, date in legend **Mint:** Konigsberg

Date	Mintage	VG	F	VF	XF	Unc
1671 TT	56,000	135	250	400	675	—
1672 TT	56,000	135	250	400	675	—
1675 HS	54,000	135	250	400	675	—
1676 HS	25,000	135	250	400	675	—

KM# 422 2/3 THALER (Gulden)

Silver **Ruler:** Friedrich Wilhelm **Rev:** Arms between palm branches **Mint:** Berlin

Date	Mintage	VG	F	VF	XF	Unc
1672 IL	—	100	200	300	525	—
1673 IL	—	100	200	300	525	—

KM# 423 2/3 THALER (Gulden)

Silver **Ruler:** Friedrich Wilhelm **Rev:** 2/3 below arms, date divided at top **Mint:** Minden

Date	Mintage	VG	F	VF	XF	Unc
1672 IW	—	200	425	675	1,000	—

KM# 437 2/3 THALER (Gulden)

Silver **Ruler:** Friedrich Wilhelm **Rev:** Date divided at top by crown **Mint:** Regenstein

Date	Mintage	VG	F	VF	XF	Unc
1674 IA	—	80.00	140	250	375	—
1647 IA Rare; error	—	—	—	—	—	—

KM# 435 2/3 THALER (Gulden)

Silver **Ruler:** Friedrich Wilhelm **Obv:** Bust right, date below **Obv. Legend:** FRID: WILH: D:G: M ? BR ? S ? R ? I ? ARCH(1C): & EL(EC) ? **Rev:** Crowned arms, value below **Rev. Legend:** MONETA NOVA - ARGENTIA **Mint:** Berlin **Note:** Dav.#244.

Date	Mintage	VG	F	VF	XF	Unc
1674 IL	—	80.00	160	275	475	—
1675 IL	—	80.00	160	275	475	—
ND IL	—	80.00	160	275	475	—
1675 CS	—	80.00	160	275	475	—

KM# 436 2/3 THALER (Gulden)

Silver **Ruler:** Friedrich Wilhelm **Obv. Legend:** FRID: WILH: D:G: M ? BR ? S ? R ? I ? ... **Rev:** Crowned arms, date at upper left, value below **Rev. Legend:** MONETA NOVA - ARGENT: **Mint:** Berlin **Note:** Dav. #245.

Date	Mintage	VG	F	VF	XF	Unc
1674 IL	—	90.00	165	275	475	—
1675 IL	—	90.00	165	275	475	—

KM# 445.1 2/3 THALER (Gulden)

Silver **Ruler:** Friedrich Wilhelm **Obv:** Bust right, value 2/3 on shoulder **Obv. Legend:** FRID: WILH: D ? G ? M ? BR: & ELEC **Rev:** Crowned arms, crown divides date, arms divide initials. **Rev. Legend:** MONETA ? NOVA ? ARGENTEA ? **Mint:** Minden **Note:** Varieties exist. Dav.#261A.

Date	Mintage	VG	F	VF	XF	Unc
1675 GD-Z	—	80.00	140	250	400	—
1676 GD-Z	—	80.00	140	250	400	—

KM# 443 2/3 THALER (Gulden)

Silver **Ruler:** Friedrich Wilhelm **Obv:** Bust right, CS below **Obv. Legend:** FRID: WILH: D:G: M: BR ? SRI ARC & EL(E) ? **Rev:** Crowned arms, date at upper left, value below **Rev. Legend:** MONETA ? NOVA - ARGENT: **Mint:** Berlin **Note:** Dav.#246.

Date	Mintage	VG	F	VF	XF	Unc
1675 CS	—	45.00	100	175	275	—
1676 CS	—	45.00	100	175	275	—

KM# 444 2/3 THALER (Gulden)

Silver **Obv:** Bust of Friedrich Wilhelm right **Obv. Legend:** FRID. WILH. D.G.M. BR. & ELEC. **Rev:** Crowned arms with intials above, value 2/3 below **Rev. Legend:** 1.6.75. MONETA NO. (VA). ARGENTIA **Mint:** Minden **Note:** Dav.#260.

Date	Mintage	VG	F	VF	XF	Unc
1.6.75. GD-Z	—	110	200	350	500	—

KM# 445.2 2/3 THALER (Gulden)

Silver **Mint:** Minden **Note:** Dav.#261B.

Date	Mintage	VG	F	VF	XF	Unc
1675 A-VH	—	80.00	140	250	400	—
1676 A-VH	—	80.00	140	250	400	—

KM# 445.3 2/3 THALER (Gulden)

Silver **Rev:** Date at upper left **Mint:** Minden **Note:** Dav.#261C.

Date	Mintage	VG	F	VF	XF	Unc
1675 GD-Z	—	80.00	140	250	400	—
1676 GD-Z	—	80.00	140	250	400	—
1678 GD-Z	—	80.00	140	250	400	—
1679 GD-Z	—	80.00	140	250	400	—

KM# 447 2/3 THALER (Gulden)

Silver **Ruler:** Friedrich Wilhelm **Obv:** Bust right divides date at bottom **Obv. Legend:** FRID: WILH: D: G: M: B: ELEC **Rev:** Crowned arms, value below **Rev. Legend:** MONETA ? NO ? ARG: REINS **Mint:** Regenstein **Note:** Varieties exist. Dav.#267.

Date	Mintage	VG	F	VF	XF	Unc
1675 IA	—	55.00	110	200	375	—
1676 IA	—	55.00	110	200	375	—
1677 IA	—	55.00	110	200	375	—

KM# 445.4 2/3 THALER (Gulden)

Silver **Rev:** Two sets of initials **Mint:** Minden **Note:** Dav.#261D.

Date	Mintage	VG	F	VF	XF	Unc
1676 GD-Z/A-VH	—	80.00	140	250	400	—

KM# 480 2/3 THALER (Gulden)

Silver **Ruler:** Friedrich Wilhelm **Obv:** Value 2/3 below bust **Mint:** Berlin

Date	Mintage	VG	F	VF	XF	Unc
1678 CS	—	100	200	300	500	—
1679 CS	—	100	200	300	500	—
1680 CS	—	100	200	300	500	—
1682 LCS	—	100	200	300	500	—

KM# 488 2/3 THALER (Gulden)

Silver **Ruler:** Friedrich Wilhelm **Obv:** Bust right in circle, date divided below **Rev:** Crowned arms in circle, value 2/3 below **Mint:** Halberstadt

Date	Mintage	VG	F	VF	XF	Unc
1679 LCS	—	125	250	450	725	—

KM# 509.1 2/3 THALER (Gulden)

Silver **Ruler:** Friedrich Wilhelm **Mint:** Berlin

Date	Mintage	VG	F	VF	XF	Unc
1683 LCS	—	100	200	300	550	—
1685 LCS	—	100	200	300	550	—

KM# 509.2 2/3 THALER (Gulden)

Silver

Date	Mintage	VG	F	VF	XF	Unc
1683 LCS	—	100	200	300	525	—

KM# 510 2/3 THALER (Gulden)

Silver **Ruler:** Friedrich Wilhelm **Rev:** Crowned arms, value 2/3 below, date divided in legend at top **Mint:** Magdeburg

Date	Mintage	VG	F	VF	XF	Unc
1683 IE	—	45.00	100	200	300	—

KM# 445.5 2/3 THALER (Gulden)

Silver **Mint:** Minden **Note:** Dav.#261E.

Date	Mintage	VG	F	VF	XF	Unc
1683 B H	—	80.00	140	250	400	—

KM# A446 2/3 THALER (Gulden)

Silver **Rev:** Crowned arms divide date. **Mint:** Minden **Note:** Dav.#262.

Date	Mintage	VG	F	VF	XF	Unc
1683 B H	—	80.00	140	250	400	—

KM# 446 2/3 THALER (Gulden)
Silver **Rev:** Large crowned arms, date in legend at upper left, arms divide initials **Mint:** Minden **Note:** Varieties exist. Dav.#263.

Date	Mintage	VG	F	VF	XF	Unc
1683 B-H	—	175	375	600	875	—

KM# 511 2/3 THALER (Gulden)
Silver **Mint:** Minden **Note:** Varieties exist.

Date	Mintage	VG	F	VF	XF	Unc
1683 BH	—	55.00	125	200	375	—
1684 BH	—	55.00	125	200	375	—

KM# 525 2/3 THALER (Gulden)
Silver **Ruler:** Friedrich Wilhelm **Obv:** Bust right in circle **Rev:** Crowned arms, date above, value below **Mint:** Berlin

Date	Mintage	VG	F	VF	XF	Unc
1686 LCS	—	100	200	300	550	—

KM# 526 2/3 THALER (Gulden)
Silver **Rev:** Arms between two palm branches and date in legend **Mint:** Berlin

Date	Mintage	VG	F	VF	XF	Unc
1686 LCS	—	100	200	300	550	—
1687 LCS	1,459,000	100	200	300	550	—

KM# 534.1 2/3 THALER (Gulden)
Silver **Rev:** Crowned arms divide mintmaster's initials, date in legend, value 2/3 below **Mint:** Berlin **Note:** Varieties exist.

Date	Mintage	VG	F	VF	XF	Unc
1687 LCS	Inc. above	27.00	45.00	100	200	—
1688 LCS	Inc. above	27.00	45.00	100	200	—

KM# A541 2/3 THALER (Gulden)
Silver **Ruler:** Friedrich Wilhelm **Obv:** Bust of Friedrich Wilhelm right in inner circle **Obv. Legend:** FRID. WILH: D:G. M. B. S. R. I. ARC & EL **Rev:** Crown arms, value 2/3 below **Rev. Legend:** CHVRF. BRAND LANDMVNZ **Mint:** Berlin **Note:** Dav. #252.

Date	Mintage	VG	F	VF	XF	Unc
1688 LCS	—	45.00	85.00	150	275	—

KM# B541 2/3 THALER (Gulden)
Silver **Ruler:** Friedrich Wilhelm **Obv:** Bust of Friedrich Wilhelm right in inner circle **Obv. Legend:** FRID. WILH: D:G. M. B. S. R. I. ARC & EL **Rev:** Crowned arms in inner circle, value 2/3 below **Rev. Legend:** CHVRF: BRAND LANDMVNZ **Mint:** Berlin **Note:** Dav. #253.

Date	Mintage	VG	F	VF	XF	Unc
1688 LCS	—	45.00	85.00	150	275	—

KM# 534.2 2/3 THALER (Gulden)
Silver

Date	Mintage	VG	F	VF	XF	Unc
1688 LCS	Inc. above	27.00	45.00	100	200	—

KM# 540 2/3 THALER (Gulden)
Silver **Ruler:** Friedrich Wilhelm **Mint:** Magdeburg

Date	Mintage	VG	F	VF	XF	Unc
1688 ICS	—	80.00	140	250	400	—

KM# 555 2/3 THALER (Gulden)
Silver **Ruler:** Friedrich III **Rev:** Crowned arms divide date **Mint:** Berlin

Date	Mintage	VG	F	VF	XF	Unc
1689 LCS	2,216,000	45.00	85.00	155	275	—

KM# 557 2/3 THALER (Gulden)
Silver **Ruler:** Friedrich III **Mint:** Magdeburg

Date	Mintage	VG	F	VF	XF	Unc
1689 IE	—	33.00	55.00	130	250	—
1690 IE	—	33.00	55.00	130	250	—
1690 ICS	—	33.00	55.00	130	250	—
1691 ICS	—	33.00	55.00	130	250	—
1692 ICS	—	33.00	55.00	130	250	—
1693 ICS	—	33.00	55.00	130	250	—
1694 ICS	—	33.00	55.00	130	250	—
1695 ICS	—	33.00	55.00	130	250	—

KM# 558 2/3 THALER (Gulden)
Silver **Ruler:** Friedrich Wilhelm **Mint:** Minden

Date	Mintage	VG	F	VF	XF	Unc
1689	—	55.00	110	240	350	—
1690	—	55.00	110	240	350	—
1690 BH	—	55.00	110	240	350	—
1691 BH	—	55.00	110	240	350	—
1693 BH	—	55.00	110	240	350	—
1694 BH	—	55.00	110	240	350	—

KM# 559 2/3 THALER (Gulden)
Silver **Mint:** Minden

Date	Mintage	VG	F	VF	XF	Unc
1689 BH	—	65.00	140	250	375	—
1689 BH-GM	—	65.00	140	250	375	—

KM# 560 2/3 THALER (Gulden)
Silver **Ruler:** Friedrich III **Mint:** Stargard **Note:** Varieties exist.

Date	Mintage	VG	F	VF	XF	Unc
1689 SD	—	80.00	140	250	375	—
1690 SD	—	55.00	100	200	350	—
1691 SD	—	55.00	100	200	350	—

KM# 556 2/3 THALER (Gulden)
Silver **Mint:** Berlin **Note:** Many varieties exist.

Date	Mintage	VG	F	VF	XF	Unc
1689 LCS	Inc. above	33.00	55.00	135	250	—
1690 LCS	4,743,000	33.00	55.00	135	250	—
1691 LCS	2,101,000	33.00	55.00	135	250	—
1692 LCS	Inc. above	33.00	55.00	135	250	—
1693 LCS	1,472,000	33.00	55.00	135	250	—
1695 LCS	Inc. above	33.00	55.00	135	250	—

KM# 576 2/3 THALER (Gulden)
Silver **Mint:** Minden **Note:** Varieties exist.

Date	Mintage	VG	F	VF	XF	Unc
1691 BH	—	45.00	100	200	325	—
1692 BH	—	45.00	100	200	325	—
1693 BH	—	45.00	100	200	325	—
1694 BH	—	45.00	100	200	325	—

KM# 594 2/3 THALER (Gulden)
Silver **Ruler:** Friedrich III **Mint:** Magdeburg

Date	Mintage	VG	F	VF	XF	Unc
1694 ICS	—	65.00	135	275	475	—
1695 ICS	—	65.00	135	275	475	—

KM# 612 2/3 THALER (Gulden)
Silver **Ruler:** Friedrich III **Rev:** Shield more ornately shaped **Mint:** Berlin

Date	Mintage	VG	F	VF	XF	Unc
1698 LCS	240,000	65.00	135	275	475	—
1699 LCS	168,000	65.00	135	275	475	—
1700 LCS	75,000	65.00	135	275	475	—

KM# 613 2/3 THALER (Gulden)
Silver **Ruler:** Friedrich III **Mint:** Magdeburg

Date	Mintage	VG	F	VF	XF	Unc
1698 HFH	—	65.00	135	275	475	—
1699 HFH	—	65.00	135	275	475	—
1700 HFH	—	65.00	135	275	475	—

KM# 618 2/3 THALER (Gulden)
Silver

Date	Mintage	VG	F	VF	XF	Unc
1699 HFH	—	65.00	135	275	475	—
1700 HFH	—	65.00	135	275	475	—

KM# 448 3/4 THALER
Silver **Ruler:** Friedrich Wilhelm **Subject:** Victory at Battle of Fehrbellin **Obv:** Elector on horse galloping right **Rev:** 14-line inscription with date **Mint:** Berlin

Date	Mintage	VG	F	VF	XF	Unc
1675	—	—	—	—	—	—

KM# 19 THALER
Silver **Ruler:** Joachim Friedrich **Obv:** Half-length bust right divides date **Rev:** Helmeted 16-fold arms **Mint:** Kolln **Note:** Dav. #6112.

Date	Mintage	VG	F	VF	XF	Unc
1602 (e)	1,355	1,500	2,500	4,000	6,350	—
1604 MH	—	1,500	2,500	4,000	6,350	—

KM# 23 THALER
Silver **Rev:** 17-fold arms **Note:** Dav. #6113.

Date	Mintage	VG	F	VF	XF	Unc
1604	—	1,450	2,400	4,000	6,000	—

KM# 25 THALER
Silver **Rev:** Date in legend **Note:** Dav. #6114.

Date	Mintage	VG	F	VF	XF	Unc
1605 MH Rare	—	—	—	—	—	—

KM# 26.1 THALER
Silver **Rev:** Arms divide date **Rev. Legend:** IMP: ARCHI. CA... **Note:** Dav. #6116.

Date	Mintage	VG	F	VF	XF	Unc
1605 MH Rare	—	—	—	—	—	—

KM# 26.2 THALER
Silver **Rev. Legend:** ROM. IMP. ARC... **Note:** Dav. #6117.

Date	Mintage	VG	F	VF	XF	Unc
ND MH Rare	—	—	—	—	—	—

KM# 35.1 THALER
Silver **Obv:** Half-length bust, date below **Obv. Legend:** IOH. SIGISM... **Rev:** Helmeted manifold arms **Note:** Dav. #6119.

Date	Mintage	VG	F	VF	XF	Unc
1611	—	1,200	2,100	3,300	5,000	—
1611 MH	—	1,200	2,100	3,300	5,000	—
1614 MH	—	1,200	2,100	3,300	5,000	—

KM# 35.2 THALER
Silver **Obv. Legend:** IOH. SIGIS... **Note:** Dav. #6124.

Date	Mintage	VG	F	VF	XF	Unc
1615 MH Rare	—	—	—	—	—	—

KM# 36 THALER
Silver **Obv:** Facing half-length bust, date below **Rev:** Cross, arms in center and in border at end of each arm **Note:** Dav. #6120.

Date	Mintage	VG	F	VF	XF	Unc
1611	—	1,500	2,400	4,200	6,500	—

KM# 45 THALER
Silver **Rev:** Helmeted manifold arms **Note:** Dav. #6121.

Date	Mintage	VG	F	VF	XF	Unc
ND MH	—	1,250	2,000	3,500	5,500	—
1612 MH	—	1,250	2,000	3,500	5,500	—

KM# 47 THALER
Silver **Ruler:** Johann Sigismund **Mint:** Kolln **Note:** Dav. #6123.

Date	Mintage	VG	F	VF	XF	Unc
ND(1612/13) MH	—	1,500	2,500	4,500	7,000	—

KM# 35.3 THALER
Silver **Obv. Legend:** IOH. SIGISM...ROM...E. E. L. **Note:** Dav. #6125.

Date	Mintage	VG	F	VF	XF	Unc
1617 MH	—	1,450	2,400	4,200	—	—
1617 HL	—	1,450	2,400	4,200	—	—
ND HL	—	1,450	2,400	4,200	—	—

KM# 54 THALER
Silver **Rev:** Arms divide date

Date	Mintage	VG	F	VF	XF	Unc
1617 MH Rare	—	—	—	—	—	—

KM# 46 THALER
Silver **Ruler:** Johann Sigismund **Mint:** Driesen **Note:** Dav. #6122.

Date	Mintage	VG	F	VF	XF	Unc
ND(1619)	—	1,500	2,400	4,200	6,500	—

KM# 67 THALER
Silver **Ruler:** Georg Wilhelm **Subject:** Union of Brandenburg With Prussia **Obv:** 3/4-length figure right **Rev:** Eagle, heart-shaped shield with SA on breast divides date **Mint:** Berlin **Note:** Dav. #6126.

Date	Mintage	VG	F	VF	XF	Unc
1620 LM	—	450	750	1,250	2,000	—

KM# 68 THALER
Silver **Obv:** Similar to KM#64 **Note:** Dav. #6127.

Date	Mintage	VG	F	VF	XF	Unc
1620 LM	—	450	750	1,250	2,000	—

KM# 69 THALER
Silver **Note:** Dav. #6128.

Date	Mintage	VG	F	VF	XF	Unc
1620 LM	—	450	750	1,250	2,000	—

KM# 70 THALER
Silver **Obv:** Similar to KM#69 but without helmet in front of figure **Note:** Dav. #6129.

Date	Mintage	VG	F	VF	XF	Unc
1620 LM	—	550	900	1,550	2,500	—

KM# 71 THALER
Silver **Obv:** Similar to KM#69 **Rev:** Helmeted 25-fold arms, date divided at top by initials **Note:** Dav. #6130.

Date	Mintage	VG	F	VF	XF	Unc
1620 LM	—	550	900	1,550	2,500	—

KM# 72 THALER

Silver **Rev:** Date divides initials at top **Note:** Dav. #6131.

Date	Mintage	VG	F	VF	XF	Unc
1620 LM	—	550	900	1,550	2,500	—

KM# 74 THALER

Silver **Note:** Dav. #6134.

Date	Mintage	VG	F	VF	XF	Unc
1620 LM	—	550	900	1,550	2,500	—

KM# 73 THALER

Silver **Note:** Similar to KM#69 but without arms on eagle's wings. Dav. #6132.

Date	Mintage	VG	F	VF	XF	Unc
1620 LM	—	550	900	1,550	2,500	—

KM# 89 THALER

Silver **Ruler:** Georg Wilhelm **Rev:** Mint mark of Ernst Pfaler at end inscription **Mint:** Konigsberg **Note:** Similar to KM#88.

Date	Mintage	VG	F	VF	XF	Unc
1621 (a) Rare	—	—	—	—	—	—

KM# 88 THALER

Silver **Obv:** Half-length figure right, date below **Rev:** Arms **Note:** Dav. #6135.

Date	Mintage	VG	F	VF	XF	Unc
1621 Rare	—	—	—	—	—	—

KM# 117 THALER

Silver **Ruler:** Georg Wilhelm **Obv:** Crowned bust right **Rev:** Arms, crown above divides date **Mint:** Kolln **Note:** Dav. #6138.

Date	Mintage	VG	F	VF	XF	Unc
1624 LM Rare	—	—	—	—	—	—

KM# 125 THALER

Silver **Ruler:** Georg Wilhelm **Mint:** Konigsberg **Note:** Dav. #6141.

Date	Mintage	VG	F	VF	XF	Unc
16Z7 (a)	7,318	350	600	1,000	1,650	—
16Z8 (a)	11,000	350	600	1,000	1,650	—
16Z9 (a)	15,000	350	600	1,000	1,650	—
1630 (a)	20,000	350	600	1,000	1,650	—
1631 (a)	4,000	350	600	1,000	1,650	—
1632 (a)	—	350	600	1,000	1,650	—
1633 (a)	34,000	350	600	1,000	1,650	—
1634 (a)	Inc. above	350	600	1,000	1,650	—
1635 (a)	Inc. above	350	600	1,000	1,650	—

KM# 128 THALER

Silver **Ruler:** Georg Wilhelm **Obv:** Half-length figure right **Rev:** Helmeted arms, date above **Mint:** Kolln **Note:** Dav. #6143.

Date	Mintage	VG	F	VF	XF	Unc
1628 LM	—	850	1,450	2,400	3,600	—
1631 LM	—	850	1,450	2,400	3,600	—
1632 LM	—	850	1,450	2,400	3,600	—
1633 LM	—	850	1,450	2,400	3,600	—

KM# A143 THALER

Silver **Obv:** 1/2-length figure of Georg Wilhelm right, scepter on shoulder **Rev:** Shield of arms **Mint:** Konigsberg **Note:** Ref. Dost #608-11. Struck from 2 Thaler dies, KM#143.

Date	Mintage	VG	F	VF	XF	Unc
1630 (q)	—	—	—	—	—	—
1631	—	—	—	—	—	—

KM# 141.1 THALER

Silver **Rev:** Different arms divide L-M **Note:** Dav. #6146.

Date	Mintage	VG	F	VF	XF	Unc
1631 LM	—	600	1,150	1,850	3,000	—
1633 LM	—	600	1,150	1,850	3,000	—

KM# 145.1 THALER

Silver **Rev:** Mintmaster's initials and date in legend **Note:** Dav. #6147.

Date	Mintage	VG	F	VF	XF	Unc
1632 LM	—	750	1,200	2,100	3,300	—
1633 LM	—	750	1,200	2,100	3,300	—
1635 LM	—	750	1,200	2,100	3,300	—

KM# 145.2 THALER

Silver **Rev:** Larger cap on arms **Note:** Dav. #6149.

Date	Mintage	VG	F	VF	XF	Unc
1633 LM	—	750	1,200	2,100	3,300	—
1636 LM	—	750	1,200	2,100	3,300	—

KM# 146 THALER

Silver **Rev:** Cap above arms divides mintmaster's initials **Note:** Dav. #6150.

Date	Mintage	VG	F	VF	XF	Unc
1633 LM	—	300	500	850	1,300	—

KM# 147.1 THALER

Silver **Obv. Legend:** GEORG. WILH... **Rev:** Arms divide mintmaster's initials, **Rev. Legend:** PRVS. IVL... **Note:** Dav. #6154.

Date	Mintage	VG	F	VF	XF	Unc
1633 LM	—	1,200	2,000	3,000	4,200	—
1637 LM	—	1,200	2,000	3,000	4,200	—

KM# 147.2 THALER

Silver **Obv. Legend:** GEORG. WILHEL... **Rev. Legend:** ET. EL. PR... **Note:** Dav. #6156.

Date	Mintage	VG	F	VF	XF	Unc
1639 LM	—	1,200	2,000	3,000	4,200	—

KM# 156 THALER

Silver **Ruler:** Georg Wilhelm **Mint:** Konigsberg **Note:** Dav. #6151.

Date	Mintage	VG	F	VF	XF	Unc
1635 DK (a)	Inc. above	325	525	875	1,400	—
1636 DK (a)	17,000	325	525	875	1,400	—

Date	Mintage	VG	F	VF	XF	Unc
1637 DK (a)	3,428	325	525	875	1,400	—
1638 DK (a)	5,556	325	525	875	1,400	—
1639 DK	3,000	325	525	875	1,400	—

KM# 160.1 THALER

Silver **Ruler:** Georg Wilhelm **Obv:** Heavier figure **Rev:** Date divided by large crown **Rev. Legend:** ANFANG ... **Note:** Dav. #6152.

Date	Mintage	VG	F	VF	XF	Unc
1636 DK (a)	Inc. above	425	725	1,200	2,000	—

KM# 163 THALER

Silver **Ruler:** Georg Wilhelm **Mint:** Berlin **Note:** Similar to KM#146 but smaller crown above arms. Dav. #6155.

Date	Mintage	VG	F	VF	XF	Unc
1637 LM	—	1,200	2,000	3,000	4,200	—
1638 LM	—	1,200	2,000	3,000	4,200	—
1639 LM	—	1,200	2,000	3,000	4,200	—

KM# 166.1 THALER

Silver **Rev. Legend:** PRVS. IVL... **Note:** Similar to KM#166.3. Dav. #6157.

Date	Mintage	VG	F	VF	XF	Unc
1639 LM Rare	—	—	—	—	—	—

KM# 166.2 THALER

Silver **Rev. Legend:** EL. PRV. GV. CL... **Note:** Similar to KM#166.3. Dav. #6159.

Date	Mintage	VG	F	VF	XF	Unc
1639 Rare	—	—	—	—	—	—

KM# 167 THALER

Silver **Ruler:** Georg Wilhelm **Obv:** Similar to KM#156, but half-length figure 3/4 to left. **Mint:** Konigsberg **Note:** Dav. #6158.

Date	Mintage	VG	F	VF	XF	Unc
1639 DK Rare	Inc. above	—	—	—	—	—

KM# 160.2 THALER

Silver **Obv:** Different bust with short wig **Rev. Legend:** ANFANCK...ENDE. **Note:** Dav. #6160. Varieties exist.

Date	Mintage	VG	F	VF	XF	Unc
1639 DK	Inc. above	850	1,450	2,400	3,600	—

KM# 166.3 THALER

Silver **Note:** Dav. #6161.

Date	Mintage	VG	F	VF	XF	Unc
1640 LM	—	600	1,150	1,850	3,000	—

KM# 141.2 THALER

Silver **Note:** Dav. #6163.

Date	Mintage	VG	F	VF	XF	Unc
1640 LM	—	600	1,150	1,850	3,000	—

KM# 177 THALER

Silver **Ruler:** Friedrich Wilhelm **Rev:** Similar to KM#166, but date divided below arms **Mint:** Berlin **Note:** Dav. #6165.

Date	Mintage	VG	F	VF	XF	Unc
1640 LM	—	600	1,150	1,850	3,000	—

KM# 178 THALER

Silver **Ruler:** Friedrich Wilhelm **Subject:** Death of Georg Wilhelm **Obv:** Facing bust, two circular inscriptions **Rev:** 11-line inscription with R.N. date in border of 24 small arms **Mint:** Konigsberg **Note:** Dav. #6166.

Date	Mintage	VG	F	VF	XF	Unc
MDCXL (1640) DK	3,000	1,200	2,000	3,000	4,500	—

KM# A181 THALER

Silver **Mint:** Konigsberg **Note:** Ref. Dost #556. Similar to 2 Thaler, KM#181.

Date	Mintage	VG	F	VF	XF	Unc
1640 DK	—	—	—	—	—	—

KM# 192 THALER

Silver **Rev:** Scepter arms in center of large rose, 23 small oval arms around

Date	Mintage	VG	F	VF	XF	Unc
ND(1641/3)	—	—	—	—	—	—

KM# 187 THALER

Silver **Ruler:** Friedrich Wilhelm **Mint:** Berlin **Note:** Dav. #6167.

Date	Mintage	VG	F	VF	XF	Unc
1641 LM	—	750	1,200	2,100	3,300	—

KM# 188 THALER

Silver **Obv:** Larger figure lower on die **Note:** Dav. #6168.

Date	Mintage	VG	F	VF	XF	Unc
1641 LM	—	750	1,200	2,100	3,300	—

KM# 189 THALER

Silver **Obv:** Larger figure extends to lower edge of flan **Note:** Dav. #6169.

Date	Mintage	VG	F	VF	XF	Unc
1641 LM	—	600	1,150	1,850	3,000	—
1642 LM	—	600	1,150	1,850	3,000	—
1642	—	600	1,150	1,850	3,000	—

KM# 190 THALER

Silver **Ruler:** Friedrich Wilhelm **Obv:** Crowned bust right **Rev:** Crowned arms **Mint:** Konigsberg **Note:** Dav. #6171.

Date	Mintage	VG	F	VF	XF	Unc
ND(1641) Rare	—	—	—	—	—	—

KM# 191 THALER

Silver **Note:** Dav. #6172.

Date	Mintage	VG	F	VF	XF	Unc
1641 DK	—	475	775	1,250	2,000	—

KM# 206 THALER

Silver **Note:** Dav. #6173.

Date	Mintage	VG	F	VF	XF	Unc
1642 DK	—	900	1,600	2,700	4,200	—

KM# 205 THALER

Silver **Rev:** Without wreath **Note:** Dav. #6170.

Date	Mintage	VG	F	VF	XF	Unc
ND(1642/3)	—	600	1,150	1,850	3,000	—

KM# 212.1 THALER

Silver **Ruler:** Friedrich Wilhelm **Rev:** Similar to KM#212.2 but different shield decorations. **Mint:** Berlin **Note:** Dav. #6174.

Date	Mintage	VG	F	VF	XF	Unc
1643 AB Rare	—	—	—	—	—	—

KM# 212.2 THALER

Silver **Note:** Dav. #6178.

Date	Mintage	VG	F	VF	XF	Unc
1643 AB	—	725	1,200	2,000	3,150	—
1644 AB	—	725	1,200	2,000	3,150	—
1645 CT	—	725	1,200	2,000	3,150	—

KM# 212.3 THALER

Silver **Obv:** Broader bust **Rev:** Date above complicated arms **Note:** Varieties exist. Dav. #6180.

Date	Mintage	VG	F	VF	XF	Unc
1645 CT	—	475	775	1,350	2,150	—
1647 CT	—	475	775	1,350	2,150	—

KM# 220 THALER

Silver **Ruler:** Friedrich Wilhelm **Note:** Dav. #6182.

Date	Mintage	VG	F	VF	XF	Unc
1645 CT	—	475	775	1,350	2,150	—
1646 CT	—	475	775	1,350	2,150	—
1647 CT	—	475	775	1,350	2,150	—
1648 CT	—	475	775	1,350	2,150	—
1649 CT	—	475	775	1,350	2,150	—
1650 CT	—	475	775	1,350	2,150	—

KM# 235.1 THALER

Silver **Rev:** Helmeted and supported arms **Rev. Legend:** MADG. PR... **Note:** Dav. #6183.

Date	Mintage	VG	F	VF	XF	Unc
1650 CT	—	475	775	1,350	2,150	—

KM# 235.2 THALER

Silver **Rev. Legend:** C. U. I. N. S. C. C... **Note:** Dav. #6184.

Date	Mintage	VG	F	VF	XF	Unc
ND(1651)	—	550	950	1,700	2,700	—

KM# 249 THALER

Silver **Obv. Legend:** BR.S.-R. I. ARCHIC. ET. ELECT. **Note:** Dav. #6185.

Date	Mintage	VG	F	VF	XF	Unc
1651 CT	—	1,300	2,200	3,600	5,750	—
1653 CT	—	1,300	2,200	3,600	5,750	—

KM# 248 THALER

Silver **Obv:** Elector standing 3/4 to right **Obv. Legend:** BR:-SAC. R. I. ARC: C. ET EL :. **Rev:** Date divided left and right **Note:** Dav. #6185A.

Date	Mintage	VG	F	VF	XF	Unc
1651 CT Rare	—	—	—	—	—	—

KM# 250 THALER

Silver **Ruler:** Friedrich Wilhelm **Obv:** Bust right in circle **Rev:** Helmeted arms **Mint:** Konigsberg **Note:** Struck from 1/2 Thaler dies.

Date	Mintage	VG	F	VF	XF	Unc
ND(1651-6) CM Rare	—	—	—	—	—	—

KM# 257 THALER

Silver **Obv:** Half-length figure 3/4 to right **Rev:** Helmeted and supported amrs, date divided below **Note:** Dav. #6186.

Date	Mintage	VG	F	VF	XF	Unc
1652 CM	—	1,300	2,200	3,600	5,750	—

KM# 290 THALER

Silver **Obv:** Eagle below forelegs of horse **Note:** Dav. #6187.

Date	Mintage	VG	F	VF	XF	Unc
1657 AB	—	400	700	1,200	2,000	—
1657 CT	—	400	700	1,200	2,000	—

KM# 289 THALER

Silver **Ruler:** Friedrich Wilhelm **Subject:** Attainment of Sovereignty over East Prussia **Obv:** Similar to KM#290 but town below hoofs. **Mint:** Berlin **Note:** Similar to KM#290 but town below hoofs. Dav. #6188.

Date	Mintage	VG	F	VF	XF	Unc
1657 CT	—	450	750	1,250	2,000	—

KM# 315 THALER

Silver **Subject:** Death of Friedrich Wilhelm's Mother, Elisabet Charlotte **Note:** Dav. #6191.

Date	Mintage	VG	F	VF	XF	Unc
1660 AB	—	200	350	575	950	—

KM# 324 THALER

Silver **Ruler:** Friedrich Wilhelm **Obv:** Half-length bust right **Rev:** Helmeted and supported arms divide date **Mint:** Berlin **Note:** Dav. #6192.

Date	Mintage	VG	F	VF	XF	Unc
1662 AB	940	1,400	2,350	4,000	6,000	—

KM# 327 THALER

Silver **Obv:** Similar to KM#328 but round **Note:** Dav. #6193.

Date	Mintage	VG	F	VF	XF	Unc
1663 AB	2,193	600	1,150	1,850	3,000	—

KM# 328 THALER

Silver **Note:** Klippe. Dav. #A6193.

Date	Mintage	VG	F	VF	XF	Unc
1663 AB Rare	Inc. above	—	—	—	—	—

KM# 333 THALER

Silver **Ruler:** Friedrich Wilhelm **Note:** Dav. #6194.

Date	Mintage	VG	F	VF	XF	Unc
1664 AB	2,972	550	1,100	1,800	3,000	—
1664 IL	Inc. above	550	1,100	1,800	3,000	—
1665 IL	Inc. above	550	1,100	1,800	3,000	—

KM# 363 THALER

Silver **Subject:** Death of Friedrich Wilhelm's Wife, Luise Henriette von Nassau-Oranien **Obv:** Facing bust of Luise Henriette **Rev:** Ten-line inscription with date **Note:** Dav. #6195.

Date	Mintage	VG	F	VF	XF	Unc
1667 IL	—	1,250	2,500	4,500	7,500	—

KM# 364 THALER

Silver **Rev:** Crowned frame with five-line inscription **Note:** Dav. #6196.

Date	Mintage	VG	F	VF	XF	Unc
1667 IL-GL	—	2,000	4,000	6,500	10,000	—

KM# 365 THALER

Silver **Obv:** Bust of Luise Henriette left **Note:** Dav. #6197.

Date	Mintage	VG	F	VF	XF	Unc
1667 IL-GL	—	2,000	4,000	6,500	10,000	—

KM# 411 THALER

Silver **Obv:** Bust right, date below **Rev:** Crowned arms between two palm branches **Note:** Dav. #6198.

Date	Mintage	VG	F	VF	XF	Unc
1670 IL Rare	—	—	—	—	—	—
1673 IL Rare	—	—	—	—	—	—

KM# 424 THALER

Silver **Ruler:** Friedrich Wilhelm **Obv:** Laureate bust right **Rev:** Helmeted and supported arms, date in legend **Mint:** Konigsberg **Note:** Dav. #6199.

Date	Mintage	VG	F	VF	XF	Unc
1672 TT	5,400	1,400	2,350	3,850	6,000	—
1677 HS	1,000	1,400	2,350	3,850	6,000	—

KM# 449 THALER

Silver **Ruler:** Friedrich Wilhelm **Subject:** Victory at Battle of Fehrbellin **Mint:** Berlin **Note:** Dav. #6200.

Date	Mintage	VG	F	VF	XF	Unc
1675	—	425	650	1,150	1,850	—

KM# 452 THALER

Silver **Rev:** LINVM. 18 IVN, date below figure **Note:** Dav. #6201.

Date	Mintage	VG	F	VF	XF	Unc
1675	—	550	900	1,600	2,700	—

KM# 451 THALER

Silver **Ruler:** Friedrich Wilhelm **Rev:** Inscription, date below figure **Rev. Inscription:** F. BELLIN VM. 18 IVN/ **Note:** Dav. #6201A.

Date	Mintage	VG	F	VF	XF	Unc
1675	—	475	775	1,450	2,400	—

KM# 453 THALER

Silver **Rev:** Figure without helmet looking right **Note:** Dav. #6201B.

Date	Mintage	VG	F	VF	XF	Unc
1675	—	500	1,000	1,800	3,000	—

KM# 454 THALER

Silver **Obv:** Elector on horse galloping left **Note:** Dav. #6202.

Date	Mintage	VG	F	VF	XF	Unc
1675	—	750	1,200	2,100	3,300	—

KM# 450 THALER

Silver **Rev:** 14-line inscription

Date	Mintage	VG	F	VF	XF	Unc
1675	—	425	650	1,150	1,850	—

KM# 472 THALER

Silver **Obv:** Half-length figure right with helmet, date in lower left **Rev:** Crowned eagle, scepter arms on breast, 25 small shields on wings **Note:** Dav. #6203.

Date	Mintage	VG	F	VF	XF	Unc
1677 CS Rare	—	—	—	—	—	—

KM# 473.1 THALER

Silver **Note:** Dav. #6204.

Date	Mintage	VG	F	VF	XF	Unc
1677 CS	—	1,300	2,200	3,600	5,700	—
1678 CS	—	1,300	2,200	3,600	5,700	—

KM# 473.2 THALER

Silver **Rev:** Shield different shape **Note:** Dav. #6206.

Date	Mintage	VG	F	VF	XF	Unc
1678 CS	—	1,300	2,200	3,600	5,700	—
1679 CS	—	1,300	2,200	3,600	5,700	—

KM# 473.3 THALER

Silver **Ruler:** Friedrich Wilhelm **Obv. Legend:** ... A. RC. & EL & **Note:** Varieties exist. Dav. #6209.

Date	Mintage	VG	F	VF	XF	Unc
1680 CS	—	950	1,600	2,700	4,200	—

KM# 474 THALER

Silver **Rev:** Date divided by arms **Note:** Dav. #6205.

Date	Mintage	VG	F	VF	XF	Unc
1677 CS	—	1,100	1,850	3,000	4,750	—
1678 CS	—	1,100	1,850	3,000	4,750	—

KM# 489 THALER

Silver **Subject:** Victory Against Sweden for Pomerania **Obv:** Elector on horse galloping right, date below **Rev:** Helmeted and supported arms **Note:** Dav. #6207.

Date	Mintage	VG	F	VF	XF	Unc
1679 CS-GL Rare	—	—	—	—	—	—

KM# 490 THALER

Silver **Note:** Dav. #6208.

Date	Mintage	VG	F	VF	XF	Unc
1679 CS	—	1,100	1,800	3,000	4,750	—

KM# 500 THALER

Silver **Ruler:** Friedrich Wilhelm **Obv:** Bust right, date divided to lower sides **Rev:** Helmeted arms divide mintmaster's initials **Mint:** Halberstadt **Note:** Dav. #6210.

Date	Mintage	VG	F	VF	XF	Unc
1680 LCS	—	2,000	3,500	6,000	9,000	—

KM# 501 THALER

Silver **Ruler:** Friedrich Wilhelm **Subject:** Homage of the City of Madgeburg, 30 May 1681 **Obv:** Bust of elector right in oval frame linked to clouds and to city of Madgeburg by three chains **Rev:** Maiden kneeling right in landscape, sun, eagle and cornucopia in clouds above, date below **Mint:** Magdeburg

Date	Mintage	VG	F	VF	XF	Unc
1681 IE Rare	—	—	—	—	—	—

KM# 516 THALER

Silver **Note:** Dav. #6211.

Date	Mintage	VG	F	VF	XF	Unc
1684 IE	—	1,700	2,800	4,700	7,200	—
1686 IE	—	1,700	2,800	4,700	7,200	—

KM# 521 THALER

Silver **Ruler:** Friedrich Wilhelm **Obv:** Bust right in circle **Rev:** Crowned eagle, scepter arms on breast, eight shields on wings, date divided at lower left and right **Mint:** Berlin **Note:** Dav. #6212.

Date	Mintage	VG	F	VF	XF	Unc
1685 LCS	—	1,250	2,000	3,200	5,000	—

KM# 527 THALER

Silver **Note:** Dav. #6213.

Date	Mintage	VG	F	VF	XF	Unc
1686 LCS	—	1,300	2,200	3,600	5,700	—

KM# 577 THALER

Silver **Ruler:** Friedrich III **Obv:** Bust right **Rev:** Large crowned ornate arms, date divided to lower left and right **Mint:** Magdeburg **Note:** Dav. #6214.

Date	Mintage	VG	F	VF	XF	Unc
1691 ICS	—	1,100	1,800	3,000	4,550	—

KM# 585 THALER

Silver **Ruler:** Friedrich III **Rev:** Arms divide date **Mint:** Minden **Note:** Dav. #6215.

Date	Mintage	VG	F	VF	XF	Unc
1692 BH Rare	—	—	—	—	—	—

KM# 586.1 THALER

Silver **Ruler:** Friedrich III **Mint:** Berlin **Note:** Dav. #6217.

Date	Mintage	VG	F	VF	XF	Unc
1692 LCS-IBS	500,000	1,400	2,400	4,000	6,000	—

KM# 586.2 THALER

Silver **Obv:** Side and back view of bust **Note:** Varieties exist. Dav. #6218.

Date	Mintage	VG	F	VF	XF	Unc
1692 LCS-IBS	Inc. above	1,300	2,300	3,850	5,800	—

KM# 591 THALER

Silver **Rev:** Crown divides date **Note:** Dav. #6219.

Date	Mintage	VG	F	VF	XF	Unc
1693 LCS-IBS	Inc. above	1,300	2,300	3,850	5,800	—

KM# 603 THALER

Silver **Rev:** Larger crown and arms **Note:** Dav. #6220.

Date	Mintage	VG	F	VF	XF	Unc
ND1695 LCS-IBS	—	1,300	2,300	3,850	5,800	—

KM# 605.1 THALER

Silver **Rev. Legend:** Without legend **Note:** Dav. #6222.

Date	Mintage	VG	F	VF	XF	Unc
1695 LCS Rare	—	—	—	—	—	—

KM# 604.2 THALER

Silver **Ruler:** Friedrich Wilhelm **Mint:** Magdeburg

Date	Mintage	VG	F	VF	XF	Unc
1695 ICS	—	200	350	575	900	—

KM# 605.2 THALER

Silver **Ruler:** Friedrich III **Mint:** Magdeburg

Date	Mintage	VG	F	VF	XF	Unc
1695 ICS Rare	—	—	—	—	—	—

KM# 604.1 THALER

Silver **Ruler:** Friedrich Wilhelm **Note:** Albertus Thaler. Dav. #6221.

Date	Mintage	VG	F	VF	XF	Unc
1695 LCS	—	200	350	575	900	—
1696 LCS	—	200	350	575	900	—

KM# 604.3 THALER

Silver **Ruler:** Friedrich III **Mint:** Minden

Date	Mintage	VG	F	VF	XF	Unc
1696 BH	—	200	350	575	900	—

KM# 10 2 THALER

Silver **Ruler:** Joachim Friedrich **Obv:** Half-length bust right **Rev:** Helmeted 15-fold arms, date in legend **Mint:** Kolln **Note:** Dav. #6111.

Date	Mintage	VG	F	VF	XF	Unc
1599 (e) Rare	—	—	—	—	—	—
1602/0 (e) Rare	—	—	—	—	—	—

KM# 27 2 THALER

Silver **Obv:** Half-length bust of Joachim right divides date **Rev:** Helmeted 16-fold arms divide date **Note:** Dav. #6115.

Date	Mintage	VG	F	VF	XF	Unc
1605 MH Rare	—	—	—	—	—	—

KM# 37 2 THALER

Silver **Obv:** Half-length bust of Johann, date below **Rev:** Helmeted mani-fold arms **Note:** Dav. #6118.

Date	Mintage	VG	F	VF	XF	Unc
1611	—	2,000	3,300	5,500	8,500	—
1611 MH	—	2,000	3,300	5,500	8,500	—
1614 MH	—	2,000	3,300	5,500	8,500	—

KM# 75 2 THALER

Silver **Ruler:** Georg Wilhelm **Mint:** Berlin **Note:** Dav. #6133.

Date	Mintage	VG	F	VF	XF	Unc
1620 LM Rare	—	—	—	—	—	—

KM# 112.1 2 THALER

Silver **Ruler:** Georg Wilhelm **Obv:** Crowned half-length figure right **Obv. Legend:** GEORG: WILHELM :V:: G: G: **Rev:** Helmeted arms, date above **Mint:** Konigsberg **Note:** Dav. #6136.

Date	Mintage	VG	F	VF	XF	Unc
1623	300	1,450	2,400	4,000	6,500	—

KM# 112.2 2 THALER

Silver **Obv. Legend:** GEORG. WILHEL: V: G: G: MARC... **Note:** Dav. #6137.

Date	Mintage	VG	F	VF	XF	Unc
1623	Inc. above	1,450	2,400	4,000	6,500	—

KM# 133 2 THALER

Silver **Note:** Dav. #6140.

Date	Mintage	VG	F	VF	XF	Unc
1629	—	1,300	2,200	3,600	5,700	—
1630	3,000	1,300	2,200	3,600	5,700	—
1635	—	1,300	2,200	3,600	5,700	—

KM# 143 2 THALER

Silver **Mint:** Konigsberg **Note:** Dav. #6144.

Date	Mintage	VG	F	VF	XF	Unc
1630 (a)	—	1,300	2,200	3,600	5,700	—
1631	—	1,300	2,200	3,600	5,700	—

KM# 142 2 THALER

Silver **Ruler:** Georg Wilhelm **Obv:** Half-length figure right **Rev:** Helmeted arms, date above **Mint:** Berlin **Note:** Dav. #6142.

Date	Mintage	VG	F	VF	XF	Unc
1631 LM	—	1,550	2,500	4,500	7,000	—

KM# 164 2 THALER

Silver **Note:** Similar to 1 Thaler, KM#147. Dav. #6153.

Date	Mintage	VG	F	VF	XF	Unc
1633 LM Rare	—	—	—	—	—	—
1635 LM Rare	—	—	—	—	—	—
1636 LM Rare	—	—	—	—	—	—
1637 LM Rare	—	—	—	—	—	—

KM# 151 2 THALER

Silver **Ruler:** Georg Wilhelm **Rev:** Similar to 1 Thaler, KM#146 but date and mintmaster's initials in legend **Mint:** Berlin **Note:** Dav. #6148.

Date	Mintage	VG	F	VF	XF	Unc
1634 LM Rare	—	—	—	—	—	—
1635 LM Rare	—	—	—	—	—	—
1636 LM Rare	—	—	—	—	—	—

KM# 180 2 THALER

Silver **Rev:** Date divided below arms **Note:** Dav. #6164.

Date	Mintage	VG	F	VF	XF	Unc
1640 LM Rare	—	—	—	—	—	—

KM# 181 2 THALER

Silver **Ruler:** Georg Wilhelm **Mint:** Konigsberg **Note:** Dav. #LS256.

Date	Mintage	VG	F	VF	XF	Unc
1640 DK	—	2,000	3,500	5,750	9,000	—

KM# 179 2 THALER

Silver **Note:** Similar to 1 Thaler, KM#166. Dav. #6162.

Date	Mintage	VG	F	VF	XF	Unc
1640 LM Rare	—	—	—	—	—	—

KM# 193 2 THALER

Silver **Rev:** Scepter arms in center of large rose, 23 interlinked small oval arms around **Note:** Dav. #LS258.

Date	Mintage	VG	F	VF	XF	Unc
ND(1641/3)	—	1,550	2,500	4,500	7,000	—

KM# 213 2 THALER

Silver **Ruler:** Friedrich Wilhelm **Mint:** Berlin **Note:** Dav. #6177.

Date	Mintage	VG	F	VF	XF	Unc
1643 AB	—	1,250	2,150	3,600	5,700	—
1644 AB	—	1,250	2,150	3,600	5,700	—
1645 CT	—	1,250	2,150	3,600	5,700	—

KM# 221 2 THALER

Silver **Note:** Similar to 1 Thaler, KM#220. Dav. #6181.

Date	Mintage	VG	F	VF	XF	Unc
1645 CT	—	1,250	2,150	3,500	5,500	—
1646 CT	—	1,250	2,150	3,500	5,500	—
1648 CT	—	1,250	2,150	3,500	5,500	—

KM# 236 2 THALER

Silver **Note:** Similar to 1 Thaler, KM#235. Dav. #A6183.

Date	Mintage	VG	F	VF	XF	Unc
1650 CT	—	1,300	2,200	3,600	5,700	—

KM# 266 2 THALER

Silver **Note:** Similar to 1 Thaler, KM#249.

Date	Mintage	VG	F	VF	XF	Unc
1653 CT	—	1,500	2,400	4,200	6,650	—

KM# 267 2 THALER

Silver **Ruler:** Friedrich Wilhelm **Mint:** Konigsberg **Note:** Dav. #LS260.

Date	Mintage	VG	F	VF	XF	Unc
1653 CM	—	2,000	3,500	5,750	9,000	—

KM# 292 2 THALER

Silver **Ruler:** Friedrich Wilhelm **Subject:** Attainment of Sovereignty over East Prussia **Obv:** Town below hoofs **Mint:** Berlin

Date	Mintage	VG	F	VF	XF	Unc
1657 CT	—	1,450	2,400	4,000	6,500	—

KM# 455 2 THALER

Silver **Subject:** Victory at Battle of Fehrbellin **Note:** Similar to 1 Thaler, KM#449.

Date	Mintage	VG	F	VF	XF	Unc
1675	—	1,300	2,200	3,600	5,700	—

KM# 456 2 THALER

Silver **Note:** Similar to 1 Thaler, KM#451.

Date	Mintage	VG	F	VF	XF	Unc
1675	—	1,300	2,200	3,600	5,700	—

KM# 587 2 THALER

Silver **Note:** Similar to 1 Thaler, KM#586. Dav. #6216.

Date	Mintage	VG	F	VF	XF	Unc
ND1692 LCS-IBS Rare	—	—	—	—	—	—

KM# 11 3 THALER

Silver **Obv:** Half-length bust right **Rev:** Helmeted 15-fold arms, date in legend

Date	Mintage	VG	F	VF	XF	Unc
1599 Swan	—	—	—	—	—	—

Note: Rare

KM# A118 3 THALER

Silver **Ruler:** Georg Wilhelm **Obv:** Armored bust right, wide band with 19 small shields of arms around **Rev:** 4-fold arms with scepter shield in center, within ornamented shield, date divided near bottom, electoral hat above, all in circle, three circles of legends with name and titles of Georg Wilhelm **Mint:** Konigsberg **Note:** Ref. Dost #604.

Date	Mintage	VG	F	VF	XF	Unc
1624 MK-NB	—	—	—	—	—	—

KM# 217 3 THALER

Silver **Ruler:** Friedrich Wilhelm **Mint:** Berlin **Note:** Similar to 1 Thaler, KM#212. Dav. #6176.

Date	Mintage	VG	F	VF	XF	Unc
1644 AB Rare	—	—	—	—	—	—

KM# 222 3 THALER

Silver **Note:** Similar to 1 Thaler, KM#220.

Date	Mintage	VG	F	VF	XF	Unc
1645 CT Rare	—	—	—	—	—	—

KM# 457 3 THALER

Silver **Subject:** Victory at Battle of Fehrbellin **Note:** Similar to 1 Thaler, KM#449

Date	Mintage	VG	F	VF	XF	Unc
1675 Rare	—	—	—	—	—	—

KM# 129 4 THALER

Silver **Ruler:** Georg Wilhelm **Mint:** Konigsberg **Note:** Similar to 1 Thaler, KM#125. Dav. #6139.

Date	Mintage	VG	F	VF	XF	Unc
1628 (a) Rare	—	—	—	—	—	—

KM# A139 4 THALER

Silver **Ruler:** Georg Wilhelm **Obv:** 1/2-length bust of Georg Wilhelm right, scepter on shoulder **Rev:** Shield of arms **Mint:** Konigsberg **Note:** Ref. Dost #607. Struck from 2 Thaler dies, KM#143.

Date	Mintage	VG	F	VF	XF	Unc
1630 (q)	—	—	—	—	—	—

KM# 218 4 THALER

Silver **Ruler:** Friedrich Wilhelm **Mint:** Berlin **Note:** Similar to 1 Thaler, KM#212. Dav. #6175.

Date	Mintage	VG	F	VF	XF	Unc
1644 AB Rare	—	—	—	—	—	—

KM# 223 4 THALER

Silver **Note:** Similar to 1 Thaler, KM#220. Dav. #6179.

Date	Mintage	VG	F	VF	XF	Unc
1645 CT Rare	—	—	—	—	—	—

TRADE COINAGE

KM# 51 GOLDGULDEN

3.5000 g., 0.9860 Gold 0.1109 oz. AGW **Obv:** Facing bust of Johann Sigismund **Rev:** Crowned arms in inner circle **Mint:** Kolln **Note:** Fr.#2145.

Date	Mintage	VG	F	VF	XF	Unc
1614	1,314	750	1,650	3,300	5,500	—
1615	Inc. above	750	1,650	3,300	5,500	—
1617	1,296	750	1,650	3,300	5,500	—

KM# 52 GOLDGULDEN

3.5000 g., 0.9860 Gold 0.1109 oz. AGW **Obv:** Bust of Johann Sigismund to right **Note:** Fr.#2144.

Date	Mintage	VG	F	VF	XF	Unc
1615	Inc. above	1,400	3,000	5,700	8,500	—

KM# 55 GOLDGULDEN

3.5000 g., 0.9860 Gold 0.1109 oz. AGW **Obv:** Half figure of Johann Sigismund right **Note:** Fr.#2146.

Date	Mintage	VG	F	VF	XF	Unc
1617	Inc. above	1,000	2,250	4,300	6,500	—

KM# 76 GOLDGULDEN

3.5000 g., 0.9860 Gold 0.1109 oz. AGW **Ruler:** Georg Wilhelm **Obv:** Bust of George Wilhelm right **Rev:** Crowned sceptre shield in inner circle **Mint:** Berlin

Date	Mintage	VG	F	VF	XF	Unc
1620 LM Rare	—	—	—	—	—	—

KM# 107 GOLDGULDEN

3.5000 g., 0.9860 Gold 0.1109 oz. AGW **Obv:** Laureate bust right, titles of Georg Wilhelm **Rev:** 6-fold arms with scepter shield in center, date above, titles continuous **Note:** Fr. #2155.

Date	Mintage	VG	F	VF	XF	Unc
16ZZ	—	1,750	3,500	6,500	10,000	—

KM# 130 GOLDGULDEN

3.5000 g., 0.9860 Gold 0.1109 oz. AGW **Ruler:** Georg Wilhelm **Obv:** Armored bust of George Wilhelm right holding scepter **Rev:** Crowned arms in inner circle **Mint:** Kolln

Date	Mintage	VG	F	VF	XF	Unc
1628 LM	—	750	1,650	3,300	5,500	—

KM# 131 GOLDGULDEN

3.5000 g., 0.9860 Gold 0.1109 oz. AGW **Obv:** Bust of Georg Wilhelm right in elector's atire

Date	Mintage	VG	F	VF	XF	Unc
1628 LM	—	1,000	2,250	4,300	6,500	—

KM# 90 2 GOLDGULDEN

7.0000 g., 0.9860 Gold 0.2219 oz. AGW **Ruler:** Georg Wilhelm **Obv:** Bust of Georg Wilhelm right **Rev:** Twelve-fold arms in inner circle **Mint:** Berlin

Date	Mintage	VG	F	VF	XF	Unc
1621 Rare	—	—	—	—	—	—

KM# 132.2 2 GOLDGULDEN

Silver **Obv:** Bust of Georg Wilhelm right in elector's costume holding scepter **Rev:** 12-fold arms **Mint:** Kolln **Note:** Fr. #2159.

Date	Mintage	VG	F	VF	XF	Unc
ND LM	—	1,500	3,000	5,500	9,000	—

KM# 132.1 2 GOLDGULDEN

7.0000 g., 0.9860 Gold 0.2219 oz. AGW **Ruler:** Georg Wilhelm **Obv:** Bust of Georg Wilhelm right in elector's attire holding scepter **Rev:** Twelve-fold arms topped by elector's cap **Mint:** Kolln **Note:** Prev. KM#132.

Date	Mintage	VG	F	VF	XF	Unc
1628 LM Rare	—	—	—	—	—	—

KM# 380 1/4 DUCAT

0.8750 g., 0.9860 Gold 0.0277 oz. AGW **Ruler:** Friedrich Wilhelm **Obv:** Bust of Friedrich Wilhelm right in laureated helmet **Rev:** Crown above displayed eagle **Mint:** Berlin

Date	Mintage	VG	F	VF	XF	Unc
1668 IL	—	400	950	1,800	2,800	—

KM# 458 1/4 DUCAT

0.8750 g., 0.9860 Gold 0.0277 oz. AGW **Obv:** Bust of Friedrich Wilhelm right

Date	Mintage	VG	F	VF	XF	Unc
1675 IL	—	400	950	1,800	2,800	—

KM# 273 1/2 DUCAT

0.8750 g., 0.9860 Gold 0.0277 oz. AGW **Obv:** Bust of Friedrich Wilhelm right in elector's atire in inner circle **Rev:** Crowned scepter shield in palm branches **Mint:** Berlin

Date	Mintage	VG	F	VF	XF	Unc
ND	—	550	1,350	2,600	4,300	—

KM# 281 1/2 DUCAT

0.8750 g., 0.9860 Gold 0.0277 oz. AGW **Rev:** Capped complex arms in inner circle, arms divide date

Date	Mintage	VG	F	VF	XF	Unc
1655 CT	—	350	800	1,550	2,700	—

KM# 381 1/2 DUCAT

0.8750 g., 0.9860 Gold 0.0277 oz. AGW **Obv:** Bust of Friedrich Wilhelm to right in laureated helmet **Rev:** Crown above displayed eagle

Date	Mintage	VG	F	VF	XF	Unc
1668 IL	—	400	900	1,700	3,000	—

KM# 412 1/2 DUCAT

0.8750 g., 0.9860 Gold 0.0277 oz. AGW **Obv:** Laureate bust of Friedrich Wilhelm right **Rev:** Crowned displayed eagle divides date **Mint:** Konigsberg **Note:** Varieties exist.

Date	Mintage	VG	F	VF	XF	Unc
1670 TT	—	250	475	850	1,450	—
1671 TT	—	250	475	850	1,450	—
1685 HS	400	250	475	850	1,450	—

KM# 475 1/2 DUCAT

0.8750 g., 0.9860 Gold 0.0277 oz. AGW **Subject:** The Conquest of Stettin **Obv:** Equestrian figure of Friedrich Wilhelm right **Rev:** Five-line inscription **Mint:** Berlin **Note:** Varieties exist.

Date	Mintage	VG	F	VF	XF	Unc
1677	—	300	675	1,200	2,000	—

KM# 606 1/2 DUCAT

0.8750 g., 0.9860 Gold 0.0277 oz. AGW **Obv:** Laureate bust of Friedrich III **Rev:** Crowned scepter shield **Mint:** Minden

Date	Mintage	VG	F	VF	XF	Unc
1695 BH	—	1,150	1,950	3,750	7,500	—

KM# 629 1/2 DUCAT

0.8750 g., 0.9860 Gold 0.0277 oz. AGW **Ruler:** Friedrich III **Obv:** Laureate head of Friedrich III right **Rev:** Crowned displayed eagle with date at bottom **Mint:** Konigsberg

Date	Mintage	VG	F	VF	XF	Unc
1700 CG	400	450	975	1,800	3,000	—

KM# 286 3/4 DUCAT

2.6250 g., 0.9860 Gold 0.0832 oz. AGW **Ruler:** Friedrich Wilhelm **Obv:** Facing bust of Friedrich Wilhelm in elector's costume in inner circle **Rev:** Capped scepter shield divides date with value below in inner circle **Mint:** Berlin

Date	Mintage	VG	F	VF	XF	Unc
1656 CT	—	1,000	2,600	5,000	9,000	—

KM# 28 DUCAT

3.5000 g., 0.9860 Gold 0.1109 oz. AGW **Obv:** Joachim Friedrich standing in inner circle **Rev:** Eagle in inner circle, arms on breast **Mint:** Kolln **Note:** Fr. #2142.

Date	Mintage	VG	F	VF	XF	Unc
1605	—	1,000	2,200	4,200	6,500	—
1606	—	1,000	2,200	4,200	6,500	—

KM# 31 DUCAT

3.5000 g., 0.9860 Gold 0.1109 oz. AGW **Obv:** Bust of Johann Sigismund right in inner circle **Rev:** Crowned arms in inner circle **Note:** Fr. #2147.

Date	Mintage	VG	F	VF	XF	Unc
ND	—	2,000	4,500	8,500	12,500	—

KM# 38 DUCAT

3.5000 g., 0.9860 Gold 0.1109 oz. AGW **Obv:** Johann Sigismund standing in inner circle **Rev:** Eagle in inner circle **Note:** Fr. #2148.

Date	Mintage	VG	F	VF	XF	Unc
1610	—	1,200	2,400	4,500	7,500	—
1611	—	1,200	2,400	4,500	7,500	—
1612	—	1,200	2,400	4,500	7,500	—
1614	1,206	1,200	2,400	4,500	7,500	—

KM# 77 DUCAT

3.5000 g., 0.9860 Gold 0.1109 oz. AGW **Obv:** George Wilhelm standing beside table holding helmet **Rev:** Five shields of arms

Date	Mintage	VG	F	VF	XF	Unc
1620 LM Rare	—	—	—	—	—	—

KM# 121 DUCAT

3.5000 g., 0.9860 Gold 0.1109 oz. AGW **Obv:** Bust of George Wilhelm right in elector's atire **Rev:** Twelve-fold arms in inner circle **Mint:** Kolln

Date	Mintage	VG	F	VF	XF	Unc
1626 IP	—	600	1,300	2,350	4,000	—

KM# 126 DUCAT

3.5000 g., 0.9860 Gold 0.1109 oz. AGW **Ruler:** Georg Wilhelm **Obv:** Full-length armored figure to right, titles of Georg Wilhelm **Rev:** 12-fold arms, date **Rev. Legend:** MONE. NOVA. AVREA. DVCA. PRVSSIAE **Mint:** Konigsberg **Note:** Fr. #2179.

Date	Mintage	VG	F	VF	XF	Unc
1627 (q)	—	600	1,300	2,350	4,000	—

KM# 144 DUCAT

3.5000 g., 0.9860 Gold 0.1109 oz. AGW **Ruler:** Georg Wilhelm **Obv:** Full-length armored figure right, titles of Georg Wilhelm **Rev:** Electoral hat above 12-fold arms **Rev. Legend:** MONE. NOVA. AVREA. DVCA. PRVSSI? **Mint:** Konigsberg **Note:** Fr. #2180.

Date	Mintage	VG	F	VF	XF	Unc
1631	—	600	1,300	2,350	4,000	—
1632	—	600	1,300	2,350	4,000	—

KM# 148 DUCAT

3.5000 g., 0.9860 Gold 0.1109 oz. AGW **Ruler:** Georg Wilhelm **Obv:** Crowned bust right, titles of Georg Wilhelm **Rev:** 4-fold arms with scepter shield in center divide date, electoral hat above **Rev. Legend:** MONE. NOVA ? **Mint:** Konigsberg **Note:** Fr. #2182, 2183.

Date	Mintage	VG	F	VF	XF	Unc
1632	—	600	1,200	2,250	3,750	—
1633 DK	—	600	1,200	2,250	3,750	—
1634 DK (q)	—	600	1,200	2,250	3,750	—
1635 DK	—	600	1,200	2,250	3,750	—
1635 DK (q)	—	600	1,200	2,250	3,750	—
1636 DK (q)	—	600	1,200	2,250	3,750	—
1637 DK (q)	—	600	1,200	2,250	3,750	—
1638 DK	—	600	1,200	2,250	3,750	—
1638 DK (q)	—	600	1,200	2,250	3,750	—
1639 DK	—	600	1,200	2,250	3,750	—
1640 DK	—	600	1,200	2,250	3,750	—

KM# A148 DUCAT

Gold **Ruler:** Georg Wilhelm **Obv:** Full-length armored figure right, titles of Georg Wilhelm **Rev:** 4-fold arms with scepter shield in center divide date, electoral hat above **Rev. Legend:** MONE. NOVA ... **Mint:** Konigsberg **Note:** Ref. Dost #569, Neumann #10.13.

Date	Mintage	VG	F	VF	XF	Unc
1633 (q)	—	—	—	—	—	—

KM# 158 DUCAT

3.5000 g., 0.9860 Gold 0.1109 oz. AGW **Ruler:** Georg Wilhelm **Obv:** Bust of Georg Wilhelm facing right, in elector's cap **Rev:** Capped arms of 5 fiefs divides date in inner circle **Mint:** Konigsberg

Date	Mintage	VG	F	VF	XF	Unc
1635 DK	—	350	850	1,500	2,350	—
1637 DK	—	350	850	1,500	2,350	—
1639 DK	—	350	850	1,500	2,350	—
1640 DK	—	350	850	1,500	2,350	—

KM# 157 DUCAT

3.5000 g., 0.9860 Gold 0.1109 oz. AGW **Ruler:** Georg Wilhelm **Obv:** Crowned bust right, titles of Georg Wilhelm **Rev:** 8-fold arms with central shield divide date **Mint:** Konigsberg **Note:** Fr. #2185.

Date	Mintage	VG	F	VF	XF	Unc
1635 DK (q)	3,898	350	850	1,500	2,350	—
1638 DK (q)	2,947	350	850	1,500	2,350	—
1639 DK	—	350	850	1,500	2,350	—

KM# A166 DUCAT

3.5000 g., 0.9860 Gold 0.1109 oz. AGW **Ruler:** Georg Wilhelm **Obv:** Bust right, titles of Georg Wilhelm **Rev:** 8-fold arms with central shield divide date **Mint:** Konigsberg **Note:** Fr. #2186.

Date	Mintage	VG	F	VF	XF	Unc
1639 DK	—	—	—	—	—	—

KM# 168 DUCAT

3.5000 g., 0.9860 Gold 0.1109 oz. AGW **Obv:** Georg Wilhelm standing in inner circle **Rev:** Scepter wtihin circle of shields of arms in inner circle **Mint:** Kolln

Date	Mintage	VG	F	VF	XF	Unc
1639 LM	—	350	850	1,500	2,350	—

KM# 169 DUCAT

3.5000 g., 0.9860 Gold 0.1109 oz. AGW **Obv:** Bust of Georg Wilhelm right in inner circle **Rev:** Capped arms of nine fiefs in inner circle **Mint:** Konigsberg

Date	Mintage	VG	F	VF	XF	Unc
1639 DK	—	350	850	1,500	2,350	—

KM# 194 DUCAT

3.5000 g., 0.9860 Gold 0.1109 oz. AGW **Obv:** Friedrich Wilhelm standing to right by table **Rev:** Scepter withing circle of six shields of arms in inner circle **Mint:** Berlin

Date	Mintage	VG	F	VF	XF	Unc
1641 LM	—	400	1,000	1,800	2,850	—

KM# 195 DUCAT

3.5000 g., 0.9860 Gold 0.1109 oz. AGW **Rev:** Elaborate arms of nine fiefs

Date	Mintage	VG	F	VF	XF	Unc
1641 LM	—	400	900	1,750	2,750	—

KM# 196 DUCAT

3.5000 g., 0.9860 Gold 0.1109 oz. AGW **Obv:** Crowned bust of Friedrich Wilhelm right in inner circle **Rev:** Capped arms divides date in inner circle **Mint:** Konigsberg

Date	Mintage	VG	F	VF	XF	Unc
1641 DK	—	300	750	1,400	2,250	—
1648 DK	—	300	750	1,400	2,250	—
1649 DK	—	300	750	1,400	2,250	—

KM# 214 DUCAT

3.5000 g., 0.9860 Gold 0.1109 oz. AGW **Obv:** Friedrich Wilhelm standing to right by table in inner circle **Rev:** Elaborate arms of twelve fiefs, date bove in inner circle **Mint:** Berlin

Date	Mintage	VG	F	VF	XF	Unc
1643 AB	—	400	900	1,700	2,650	—

KM# 215 DUCAT

3.5000 g., 0.9860 Gold 0.1109 oz. AGW **Obv:** Facing bust of Friedrich wilhelm in inner circle **Rev:** Capped arms divide date in inner circle **Mint:** Konigsberg

Date	Mintage	VG	F	VF	XF	Unc
1643 DK	—	400	900	1,700	2,650	—

KM# 224 DUCAT

3.5000 g., 0.9860 Gold 0.1109 oz. AGW **Ruler:** Friedrich Wilhelm **Subject:** For Prussia **Obv:** Bust of Friedrich Wilhelm right in elector's attire in inner circle **Mint:** Berlin

Date	Mintage	VG	F	VF	XF	Unc
1646 CT	—	400	900	1,750	2,650	—

KM# 229 DUCAT

3.5000 g., 0.9860 Gold 0.1109 oz. AGW **Obv:** Bust of Friedrich Wilhelm right in elector's costume in inner circle **Rev:** Capped arms of six fiefs in inner circle **Mint:** Bielefeld

Date	Mintage	VG	F	VF	XF	Unc
1648	—	500	1,100	2,100	3,000	—

KM# 251 DUCAT

3.5000 g., 0.9860 Gold 0.1109 oz. AGW **Obv:** Bust of Friedrich Wilhelm standing facing in inner circle **Rev:** Capped arms in inner circle, cap divides date **Mint:** Berlin

Date	Mintage	VG	F	VF	XF	Unc
1651 CT	—	500	1,100	2,100	3,000	—

KM# 252 DUCAT

3.5000 g., 0.9860 Gold 0.1109 oz. AGW **Obv:** Bust of Friedrich Wilhelm right in inner circle **Rev:** Capped arms divide date in inner circle **Mint:** Konigsberg

Date	Mintage	VG	F	VF	XF	Unc
1651 CM	—	300	750	1,400	2,250	—
1657 DK	2,400	300	750	1,400	2,250	—
1660/57 DK	—	300	750	1,400	2,250	—

KM# 258 DUCAT

3.5000 g., 0.9860 Gold 0.1109 oz. AGW **Obv:** Small bust of Friedrich Wilhelm right in elector's attire in crenellated circle **Rev:** Capped arms 26 fiefs, date at bottom **Mint:** Minden

Date	Mintage	VG	F	VF	XF	Unc
1652 HB	—	500	1,100	2,100	3,000	—

KM# 270 DUCAT

3.5000 g., 0.9860 Gold 0.1109 oz. AGW **Obv:** 3/4 figure of Friedrich Wilhelm right in inner circle **Rev:** Capped arms in inner circle **Mint:** Berlin

Date	Mintage	VG	F	VF	XF	Unc
1654 CT	—	400	900	1,700	2,650	—
1656 CT	—	400	900	1,700	2,650	—

KM# 293 DUCAT

3.5000 g., 0.9860 Gold 0.1109 oz. AGW **Obv:** Friedrich Wilhelm **Mint:** Konigsberg

Date	Mintage	VG	F	VF	XF	Unc
1657 NB	—	600	1,200	2,250	3,750	—
1658	3,600	600	1,200	2,250	3,750	—

KM# 320 DUCAT

3.5000 g., 0.9860 Gold 0.1109 oz. AGW **Mint:** Konigsberg

Date	Mintage	VG	F	VF	XF	Unc
1661 HM	14,000	600	1,300	2,350	4,000	—
1662 HM	Inc. above	600	1,300	2,350	4,000	—
1663 HM	Inc. above	600	1,300	2,350	4,000	—

KM# 325 DUCAT

3.5000 g., 0.9860 Gold 0.1109 oz. AGW **Obv:** Friedrich Wilhelm **Mint:** Berlin

Date	Mintage	VG	F	VF	XF	Unc
1662 AB	456	500	1,100	2,100	3,000	—
1665 IL	—	500	1,100	2,100	3,000	—
1666 IL	—	500	1,100	2,100	3,000	—

KM# 335 DUCAT

3.5000 g., 0.9860 Gold 0.1109 oz. AGW **Mint:** Konigsberg **Note:** Varieties exist.

Date	Mintage	VG	F	VF	XF	Unc
1664	6,781	500	1,100	2,100	3,000	—
1665	Inc. above	500	1,100	2,100	3,000	—
1666	3,626	500	1,100	2,100	3,000	—
1667 CG	3,500	500	1,100	2,100	3,000	—

KM# 340 DUCAT

3.5000 g., 0.9860 Gold 0.1109 oz. AGW **Obv:** 3/4 figure of Friedrich Wilhelm right in inner circle **Rev:** Crowned arms divide date in inner circle **Mint:** Berlin **Note:** For Prussia.

Date	Mintage	VG	F	VF	XF	Unc
1665 IL	—	750	1,650	3,250	5,000	—

KM# 341 DUCAT

3.5000 g., 0.9860 Gold 0.1109 oz. AGW **Obv:** Bust of Friedrich Wilhelm right in inner circle

Date	Mintage	VG	F	VF	XF	Unc
1665 IL	—	1,600	3,500	7,000	11,000	—

KM# A366 DUCAT

3.5000 g., 0.9860 Gold 0.1109 oz. AGW **Obv:** Half-length bust Friedrich Wilhelm right holding sword **Rev:** Five-fold arms, on ornamented shield

Date	Mintage	VG	F	VF	XF	Unc
1666	—	1,250	2,750	5,300	7,500	—

KM# 366 DUCAT

3.5000 g., 0.9860 Gold 0.1109 oz. AGW **Rev:** Small capped scepter shield and date surrounded by 13 shields of arms

Date	Mintage	VG	F	VF	XF	Unc
1667 IL	—	500	1,100	2,100	3,000	—

KM# 382 DUCAT

3.5000 g., 0.9860 Gold 0.1109 oz. AGW **Obv:** Laureate bust of Friedrich Wilhelm right **Rev:** Crowned displayed eagle, crown divides date **Mint:** Konigsberg

Date	Mintage	VG	F	VF	XF	Unc
1668 CG	4,500	500	1,100	2,100	3,000	—
1668 DS	Inc. above	500	1,100	2,100	3,000	—
1673 CV	—	500	1,100	2,100	3,000	—
1674 CV	—	500	1,100	2,100	3,000	—

KM# 383 DUCAT

3.5000 g., 0.9860 Gold 0.1109 oz. AGW **Obv:** Bust of Friedrich Wilhelm right **Rev:** Crowned scepter shield in garter oval in palm branches, date **Mint:** Berlin

Date	Mintage	VG	F	VF	XF	Unc
1668 IL	—	400	1,000	1,800	2,850	—
1673 IL	—	400	1,000	1,800	2,850	—
1674 IL	—	400	1,000	1,800	2,850	—
1675 CS	—	400	1,000	1,800	2,850	—
1677 CS	—	400	1,000	1,800	2,850	—

KM# 393 DUCAT

3.5000 g., 0.9860 Gold 0.1109 oz. AGW **Obv:** Friedrich Wilhelm **Mint:** Konigsberg

Date	Mintage	VG	F	VF	XF	Unc
1669 CG/DS	—	500	1,100	2,150	3,200	—

KM# 394 DUCAT

3.5000 g., 0.9860 Gold 0.1109 oz. AGW **Obv:** Bust of Friedrich Wilhelm right, date below **Rev:** Crown scepter shield in garter oval in branches **Mint:** Berlin

Date	Mintage	VG	F	VF	XF	Unc
1669 IL	—	400	1,000	1,800	2,850	—
1670 IL	—	400	1,000	1,800	2,850	—
1671 IL	—	400	1,000	1,800	2,850	—
1672 IL	—	400	1,000	1,800	2,850	—

KM# 413 DUCAT

3.5000 g., 0.9860 Gold 0.1109 oz. AGW **Obv:** Bust of Friedrich Wilhelm right **Rev:** Crowned arms, crown divides date **Mint:** Minden

Date	Mintage	VG	F	VF	XF	Unc
1670 HB	—	900	1,850	3,750	6,000	—

KM# 414 DUCAT

3.5000 g., 0.9860 Gold 0.1109 oz. AGW **Ruler:** Friedrich Wilhelm **Obv:** Laureate bust of Friedrich Wilhelm right **Mint:** Konigsberg

Date	Mintage	VG	F	VF	XF	Unc
1670 TT	—	600	1,300	2,500	4,500	—
1671 TT	—	600	1,300	2,500	4,500	—
1672 TT	—	600	1,300	2,500	4,500	—
1679 HS	400	600	1,300	2,500	4,500	—
1681 HS	—	600	1,300	2,500	4,500	—
1682 HS	200	600	1,300	2,500	4,500	—

KM# 471 DUCAT

3.5000 g., 0.9860 Gold 0.1109 oz. AGW **Rev:** Crowned round arms, crown divides date

Date	Mintage	VG	F	VF	XF	Unc
1676 HS	200	600	1,300	2,500	4,500	—
1683 HS	200	600	1,300	2,500	4,500	—
1684 HS	600	600	1,300	2,500	4,500	—
1686 BA	1,000	600	1,300	2,500	4,500	—

KM# 491 DUCAT

3.5000 g., 0.9860 Gold 0.1109 oz. AGW **Obv:** Bust of Friedrich Wilhelm right in inner circle, date below **Rev:** Scepter in branches in inner circle **Mint:** Halberstadt

Date	Mintage	VG	F	VF	XF	Unc
1679 LCS	—	1,350	2,850	5,000	8,000	—

KM# 492 DUCAT

3.5000 g., 0.9860 Gold 0.1109 oz. AGW **Obv:** Bust of Friedrich Wilhelm right **Rev:** Crowned scepter shield in garter oval in palm branches **Mint:** Berlin

Date	Mintage	VG	F	VF	XF	Unc
1679 CS	—	500	1,100	2,150	3,200	—
1680 CS	—	500	1,100	2,150	3,200	—
1681 CS	—	500	1,100	2,150	3,200	—
1682 CS	—	500	1,100	2,150	3,200	—
1683 LCS	—	500	1,100	2,150	3,200	—
1684 LCS	—	500	1,100	2,150	3,200	—
1685 LCS	—	500	1,100	2,150	3,200	—
1686 LCS	—	500	1,100	2,150	3,200	—

KM# 504 DUCAT

3.5000 g., 0.9860 Gold 0.1109 oz. AGW **Obv:** Friedrich Wilhelm **Note:** Trade coin for the Guinea Coast of Africa.

Date	Mintage	VG	F	VF	XF	Unc
1682 CS	—	775	1,750	3,400	6,200	—
1682 LCS	—	775	1,750	3,400	6,200	—
1683 LCS	—	775	1,750	3,400	6,200	—
1685 LCS	—	775	1,750	3,400	6,200	—
1686 LCS	—	775	1,750	3,400	6,200	—

KM# 522.1 DUCAT

3.5000 g., 0.9860 Gold 0.1109 oz. AGW **Rev:** Crowned round scepter shield in garter in palm branches

Date	Mintage	VG	F	VF	XF	Unc
1685 LCS	—	750	1,650	3,300	6,400	—

KM# 522.2 DUCAT

3.5000 g., 0.9860 Gold 0.1109 oz. AGW **Obv:** Different armor

Date	Mintage	VG	F	VF	XF	Unc
1686 LCS	—	750	1,650	3,300	6,400	—

KM# 528 DUCAT

3.5000 g., 0.9860 Gold 0.1109 oz. AGW **Obv:** Half figure of Friedrich Wilhelm right

Date	Mintage	VG	F	VF	XF	Unc
1686 LCS	—	775	1,750	3,450	6,200	—
1687 LCS	—	775	1,750	3,450	6,200	—
1688 LCS	—	775	1,750	3,450	6,200	—

KM# 529 DUCAT

3.5000 g., 0.9860 Gold 0.1109 oz. AGW **Ruler:** Friedrich Wilhelm **Obv:** Armored half figure of Friedrich Wilhelm **Rev:** Sailing ship right, date in legend **Note:** Trade coin for the Guinea Coast of Africa.

Date	Mintage	VG	F	VF	XF	Unc
1686 LCS	—	775	1,750	3,450	6,200	—
1687 LCS	—	775	1,750	3,450	6,200	—
1688 LCS	—	775	1,750	3,450	6,200	—

KM# 535 DUCAT

3.5000 g., 0.9860 Gold 0.1109 oz. AGW **Obv:** Laureate bust of Friedrich Wilhelm **Rev:** Crowned round arms, crown divides date **Mint:** Konigsberg

Date	Mintage	VG	F	VF	XF	Unc
1687 HS	200	500	1,100	2,200	4,250	—

KM# 541 DUCAT

3.5000 g., 0.9860 Gold 0.1109 oz. AGW **Obv:** Bust of Friedrich III **Rev:** Cruciform crowned F III monogram **Mint:** Berlin

Date	Mintage	VG	F	VF	XF	Unc
1688	—	600	1,350	2,650	4,750	—

KM# 543 DUCAT

3.5000 g., 0.9860 Gold 0.1109 oz. AGW **Rev:** Brandenburg flag at stern

Date	Mintage	VG	F	VF	XF	Unc
1688 LCS	—	775	1,750	3,450	6,200	—
1690 LCS	—	775	1,750	3,450	6,200	—

KM# 542 DUCAT

3.5000 g., 0.9860 Gold 0.1109 oz. AGW **Obv:** Draped bust of Friedrich III right **Rev:** Sailing ship right, date in legend **Note:** Trade coin for the Guinea Coast of Africa.

Date	Mintage	VG	F	VF	XF	Unc
1688 LCS	—	775	1,750	3,450	6,200	—

KM# 561 DUCAT

3.5000 g., 0.9860 Gold 0.1109 oz. AGW **Obv:** Bust of Friedrich III right **Rev:** Crowned oval scepter shield in palm branches **Note:** Varieties exist.

Date	Mintage	VG	F	VF	XF	Unc
1689 LCS	—	775	1,700	3,300	5,800	—
1690 LCS	—	775	1,700	3,300	5,800	—

KM# 574 DUCAT

3.5000 g., 0.9860 Gold 0.1109 oz. AGW **Subject:** Homage

Date	Mintage	VG	F	VF	XF	Unc
1690	—	—	—	—	—	—

KM# 578 DUCAT

3.5000 g., 0.9860 Gold 0.1109 oz. AGW **Rev:** Crowned arms divide date **Mint:** Minden

Date	Mintage	VG	F	VF	XF	Unc
1691 BH	—	750	1,650	3,250	5,500	—

KM# 579 DUCAT

3.5000 g., 0.9860 Gold 0.1109 oz. AGW **Obv:** Laureate and draped bust of Friedrich III right **Rev:** Crowned oval arms in cartouche, crown divides date **Mint:** Konigsberg

Date	Mintage	VG	F	VF	XF	Unc
1691 HS	400	550	1,150	2,250	4,500	—
1693 HS	200	550	1,150	2,250	4,500	—
1695 SD	200	550	1,150	2,250	4,500	—
1697 SD	200	550	1,150	2,250	4,500	—
1700 CG	—	550	1,500	2,250	4,500	—

KM# 588 DUCAT

3.5000 g., 0.9860 Gold 0.1109 oz. AGW **Obv:** Bust of Friedrich III right **Rev:** Crowned scepter shield **Mint:** Magdeburg

Date	Mintage	VG	F	VF	XF	Unc
1692 ICS	—	750	1,650	3,250	5,500	—

KM# 589 DUCAT

3.5000 g., 0.9860 Gold 0.1109 oz. AGW **Ruler:** Friedrich III **Obv:** Bust right **Obv. Legend:** FRID. III. D.G. M. B. S. R. I. A. C. E **Rev:** Sailing ship divides date **Rev. Legend:** DEO DUCE **Mint:** Berlin

Date	Mintage	VG	F	VF	XF	Unc
169Z S//LCS	—	700	1,500	3,000	5,000	—
1694 S//LCS	—	700	1,500	3,000	5,000	—
1695 S//LCS	—	700	1,500	3,000	5,000	—
1696 S//LCS	—	700	1,500	3,000	5,000	—

KM# 595 DUCAT

3.5000 g., 0.9860 Gold 0.1109 oz. AGW **Subject:** Founding of University of Halle an der Saale

Date	Mintage	VG	F	VF	XF	Unc
1694	—	—	—	—	—	—

KM# 607 DUCAT

3.5000 g., 0.9860 Gold 0.1109 oz. AGW **Rev:** Crowned eagle above arms divides date **Mint:** Minden

Date	Mintage	VG	F	VF	XF	Unc
1695 BH	—	750	1,650	3,250	5,500	—

KM# 608 DUCAT

3.5000 g., 0.9860 Gold 0.1109 oz. AGW **Obv:** Draped bust of Friedrich III right **Rev:** Crowned scepter shield in garter in palm branches **Mint:** Berlin

Date	Mintage	VG	F	VF	XF	Unc
1696 LCS	—	550	1,150	2,250	4,500	—

KM# 609 DUCAT

3.5000 g., 0.9860 Gold 0.1109 oz. AGW **Rev:** Scepter shield in garter within cruciform crowned F III monograms, date at top

Date	Mintage	VG	F	VF	XF	Unc
1697 RF//LCS	—	600	1,300	2,600	5,000	—

KM# 614.1 DUCAT

3.5000 g., 0.9860 Gold 0.1109 oz. AGW **Obv:** Small head of Friedrich III

Date	Mintage	VG	F	VF	XF	Unc
1697 FR//LCS	—	600	1,300	2,600	5,000	—

KM# 614.2 DUCAT

3.5000 g., 0.9860 Gold 0.1109 oz. AGW **Obv:** Large head of Friedrich III

Date	Mintage	VG	F	VF	XF	Unc
1698 RF//LCS	—	450	1,000	2,100	3,750	—
1699 RF//LCS	—	450	1,000	2,100	3,750	—

KM# 24 2 DUCAT

7.0000 g., 0.9860 Gold 0.2219 oz. AGW **Obv:** Half-length bust right **Rev:** 7-fold arms, date in legend **Mint:** Kolln

Date	Mintage	VG	F	VF	XF	Unc
1604 MH Rare	—	—	—	—	—	—

KM# 30 2 DUCAT

7.0000 g., 0.9860 Gold 0.2219 oz. AGW **Obv:** Joachim Friedrich standing in inner circle **Rev:** Eagle in inner circle, arms on breast **Note:** Fr.#2141.

Date	Mintage	VG	F	VF	XF	Unc
1606	—	2,500	4,500	6,500	9,500	—

KM# 48 2 DUCAT

7.0000 g., 0.9860 Gold 0.2219 oz. AGW **Obv:** Half-length bust right, date below **Rev:** Arms in ornamented shield

Date	Mintage	VG	F	VF	XF	Unc
1612 MH Rare	—	—	—	—	—	—

KM# 53 2 DUCAT

7.0000 g., 0.9860 Gold 0.2219 oz. AGW **Obv:** Johann Sigismund standing in inner circle **Rev:** Crowned arms in inner circle **Note:** Fr.#2149.

Date	Mintage	VG	F	VF	XF	Unc
1615	—	2,000	3,500	5,500	8,500	—

KM# 78 2 DUCAT

7.0000 g., 0.9860 Gold 0.2219 oz. AGW **Obv:** George Wilhelm standing by table with helmet **Rev:** Scepter surrounded by eight shields of arms **Mint:** Berlin

Date	Mintage	VG	F	VF	XF	Unc
1620 LM	—	1,000	2,000	3,500	5,500	—

KM# 79 2 DUCAT

7.0000 g., 0.9860 Gold 0.2219 oz. AGW **Rev:** Crowned arms in inner circle

Date	Mintage	VG	F	VF	XF	Unc
ND(1620-21) LM	—	1,200	2,500	4,500	6,500	—

KM# B56 2 DUCAT

7.0000 g., 0.9860 Gold 0.2219 oz. AGW **Ruler:** Georg Wilhelm **Mint:** Berlin **Note:** Struck with 12 Gröscher dies, KM#85. Ref. Neumann #10.41.

Date	Mintage	VG	F	VF	XF	Unc
16Z1	—	—	—	—	—	—

KM# 122 2 DUCAT

7.0000 g., 0.9860 Gold 0.2219 oz. AGW **Obv:** Bust of Georg Wilhelm right in elector's costume **Rev:** Crowned arms of 12 fiefs in inner circle **Mint:** Kolln **Note:** Struck from Ducat dies.

Date	Mintage	VG	F	VF	XF	Unc
1626 IP Rare	—	—	—	—	—	—

KM# 152 2 DUCAT

7.0000 g., 0.9860 Gold 0.2219 oz. AGW **Obv:** Bust of Georg Wilhelm right with elector's cap **Rev:** Capped arms of five fiefs **Mint:** Konigsberg **Note:** Fr. #2181.

Date	Mintage	VG	F	VF	XF	Unc
1634 DK (a)	—	1,200	2,500	4,500	6,500	—

KM# 153 2 DUCAT

7.0000 g., 0.9860 Gold 0.2219 oz. AGW **Obv:** Georg Wilhelm standing by table with helmet **Rev:** Twelve-fold arms in inner circle **Mint:** Kolln

Date	Mintage	VG	F	VF	XF	Unc
1634 LM	—	1,000	2,000	3,500	5,500	—
1636 LM	—	900	2,000	3,500	—	—

KM# 159 2 DUCAT

7.0000 g., 0.9860 Gold 0.2219 oz. AGW **Rev:** Crowned oval arms in inner circle

Date	Mintage	VG	F	VF	XF	Unc
1635 LM	—	1,000	2,000	3,750	5,750	—

KM# 165 2 DUCAT

7.0000 g., 0.9860 Gold 0.2219 oz. AGW **Rev:** Crowned eagle with 12 small shields of arms on breast and wings

Date	Mintage	VG	F	VF	XF	Unc
1637 LM	—	1,000	2,000	3,500	5,000	—
1638 LM	—	1,000	2,000	3,500	5,000	—
1640 LM	—	1,000	2,000	3,500	5,000	—

KM# 197 2 DUCAT

7.0000 g., 0.9860 Gold 0.2219 oz. AGW **Ruler:** Friedrich Wilhelm **Mint:** Berlin

Date	Mintage	VG	F	VF	XF	Unc
1641 LM	—	1,000	2,300	4,000	6,000	—

KM# 198 2 DUCAT

7.0000 g., 0.9860 Gold 0.2219 oz. AGW **Obv:** Friedrich Wilhelm standing in floral arch, date below **Rev:** Arms in floral wreath

Date	Mintage	VG	F	VF	XF	Unc
1641	—	1,000	2,300	4,000	6,000	—
1641 LM	—	1,000	2,300	4,000	6,000	—

KM# 199 2 DUCAT

7.0000 g., 0.9860 Gold 0.2219 oz. AGW **Obv:** Crowned and robed elector holding scepter on horse rearing to right **Rev:** Scepter arms in center of large rose, 23 small oval arms around **Mint:** Konigsberg

Date	Mintage	VG	F	VF	XF	Unc
ND(1641-3)	—	1,200	2,500	4,500	6,500	—

KM# 216 2 DUCAT

7.0000 g., 0.9860 Gold 0.2219 oz. AGW **Obv:** Friedrich Wilehlm standing with left hand and helmet on table **Rev:** Elaborate arms in inner circle **Mint:** Berlin

Date	Mintage	VG	F	VF	XF	Unc
1643 AB	—	1,000	2,000	3,500	5,500	—
1644 AB	—	1,000	2,000	3,500	5,500	—
1646 CT	—	1,000	2,000	3,500	5,500	—

KM# 237 2 DUCAT

7.0000 g., 0.9860 Gold 0.2219 oz. AGW **Rev:** Crowned arms in inner circle, date above crown

Date	Mintage	VG	F	VF	XF	Unc
1650 CT	—	1,200	2,500	4,500	6,500	—
1654 CT	—	1,200	2,500	4,500	6,500	—

KM# 271 2 DUCAT

7.0000 g., 0.9860 Gold 0.2219 oz. AGW **Obv:** Armored bust of Friedrich Wilhelm in inner circle **Rev:** Crowned arms in inner circle, crown divides date

Date	Mintage	VG	F	VF	XF	Unc
1654 CT	—	1,500	3,500	5,500	8,500	—
1665 IL	—	1,500	3,500	5,500	8,500	—

KM# 282 2 DUCAT
7.0000 g., 0.9860 Gold 0.2219 oz. AGW **Ruler:** Friedrich Wilhelm **Subject:** 35th Birthday of Friedrich Wilhelm and Birth of Prince Karl Emil

Date	Mintage	VG	F	VF	XF	Unc
1655	—	1,000	2,000	3,500	5,000	—

KM# 283 2 DUCAT
7.0000 g., 0.9860 Gold 0.2219 oz. AGW **Rev:** Cap above inscription

Date	Mintage	VG	F	VF	XF	Unc
1655	—	1,000	2,000	3,500	5,000	—

KM# 287 2 DUCAT
7.0000 g., 0.9860 Gold 0.2219 oz. AGW **Obv:** 3/4 figure of Friedrich Wilhelm right in inner circle **Rev:** Capped arms in inner circle **Note:** Struck from 1 Ducat dies, KM#270.

Date	Mintage	VG	F	VF	XF	Unc
1656 CT	—	1,500	3,500	5,500	8,500	—

KM# 342 2 DUCAT
7.0000 g., 0.9860 Gold 0.2219 oz. AGW **Obv:** Half-length figure to right **Rev:** Crown above square 25-fold arms divides date

Date	Mintage	VG	F	VF	XF	Unc
1665 IL	—	1,500	3,500	5,500	8,500	—

KM# 395 2 DUCAT
7.0000 g., 0.9860 Gold 0.2219 oz. AGW **Ruler:** Friedrich III **Obv:** Draped bust of Friedrich Wilhelm **Rev:** Crowned arms in palm branches

Date	Mintage	VG	F	VF	XF	Unc
1669	—	1,500	3,500	5,500	8,500	—

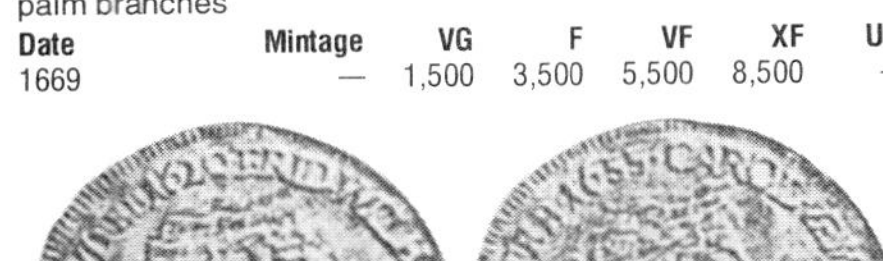

KM# 396 2 DUCAT
7.0000 g., 0.9860 Gold 0.2219 oz. AGW **Subject:** 14th Birthday of Prince Karl Emil **Obv:** Friedrich Wilhelm **Rev:** Prince Karl Emil **Mint:** Konigsberg

Date	Mintage	VG	F	VF	XF	Unc
1669 CG	—	1,750	3,750	5,750	9,000	—

KM# 415 2 DUCAT
7.0000 g., 0.9860 Gold 0.2219 oz. AGW **Obv:** Bust of Friedrich Wilhelm right in elector's cap and atire **Rev:** Crowned arms in palm branches **Mint:** Berlin

Date	Mintage	VG	F	VF	XF	Unc
1670	—	1,500	3,500	5,500	8,500	—

KM# 416.1 2 DUCAT
7.0000 g., 0.9860 Gold 0.2219 oz. AGW **Ruler:** Friedrich Wilhelm **Obv:** Laureate bust of Friedrich Wilhelm right **Mint:** Konigsberg

Date	Mintage	VG	F	VF	XF	Unc
1670 TT	—	1,000	2,250	4,500	7,500	—
1671 TT	—	1,000	2,250	4,500	7,500	—
1672 TT	—	1,000	2,250	4,500	7,500	—
1673 CV	—	1,000	2,250	4,500	7,500	—
1674 CV	—	1,000	2,250	4,500	7,500	—

KM# 416.2 2 DUCAT
7.0000 g., 0.9860 Gold 0.2219 oz. AGW **Rev:** Florals at sides of arms

Date	Mintage	VG	F	VF	XF	Unc
1675 HS	—	1,000	2,250	4,500	7,500	—
1679 HS	—	1,000	2,250	4,500	7,500	—
1682 HS	—	1,000	2,250	4,500	7,500	—
1683 HS	—	1,000	2,250	4,500	7,500	—
1684 HS	—	1,000	2,250	4,500	7,500	—
1686 BA	—	1,000	2,250	4,500	7,500	—

KM# 476.2 2 DUCAT
7.0000 g., 0.9860 Gold 0.2219 oz. AGW **Note:** Finer style than 476.1.

Date	Mintage	VG	F	VF	XF	Unc
1677 IH	—	1,000	2,000	3,500	5,000	—

KM# 476.1 2 DUCAT
7.0000 g., 0.9860 Gold 0.2219 oz. AGW **Subject:** Conquest of Stettin **Obv:** Laureate bust right **Rev:** Eagle and griffin holding scepter above city view

Date	Mintage	VG	F	VF	XF	Unc
1677 CS	—	1,000	2,000	3,500	5,000	—

KM# 477 2 DUCAT
7.0000 g., 0.9860 Gold 0.2219 oz. AGW **Rev:** City view with sun shining at right

Date	Mintage	VG	F	VF	XF	Unc
1677 CS	—	1,000	2,000	3,500	5,000	—

KM# 478.1 2 DUCAT
7.0000 g., 0.9860 Gold 0.2219 oz. AGW **Rev:** Sun shining at left

Date	Mintage	VG	F	VF	XF	Unc
1677 IH	—	1,000	2,000	3,500	5,000	—

KM# 478.2 2 DUCAT
7.0000 g., 0.9860 Gold 0.2219 oz. AGW **Ruler:** Friedrich Wilhelm **Rev:** Modified city view, face in sun

Date	Mintage	VG	F	VF	XF	Unc
1677 CS	—	1,000	2,000	3,500	5,000	—

KM# B509 2 DUCAT
7.0000 g., 0.9860 Gold 0.2219 oz. AGW **Subject:** Death of Wilhelm (III)'s wife, Elisabeth Henriette von Hessen-Kassel **Obv:** Bust right **Rev:** Crowned tablet with 8-line inscription and dates, skull and crossbones below **Note:** Struck with 1/4 Thaler dies, KM#A509.

Date	Mintage	VG	F	VF	XF	Unc
1683	—	—	—	—	—	—

KM# 544 2 DUCAT
7.0000 g., 0.9860 Gold 0.2219 oz. AGW **Subject:** Homage of County of Mark

Date	Mintage	VG	F	VF	XF	Unc
1688	—	—	—	—	—	—

KM# 575 2 DUCAT
7.0000 g., 0.9860 Gold 0.2219 oz. AGW **Subject:** Homage

Date	Mintage	VG	F	VF	XF	Unc
1690	—	—	—	—	—	—

KM# 615 2 DUCAT
7.0000 g., 0.9860 Gold 0.2219 oz. AGW **Obv:** Head of Friedrich III right **Rev:** Scepter shield in garter within cruciform crowned F III monogram, date at top **Mint:** Berlin

Date	Mintage	VG	F	VF	XF	Unc
1698 RF/LCS	—	1,500	3,500	5,500	8,500	—
1699 RF/LCS	—	1,500	3,500	5,500	8,500	—
1700 RF/LCS	—	1,500	3,500	5,500	8,500	—

KM# A160 3 DUCAT
10.5000 g., 0.9860 Gold 0.3328 oz. AGW **Ruler:** Georg Wilhelm **Obv:** 1/2-length armored figure to right, scepter over shoulder, helmet at right, titles of Georg Wilhelm **Rev:** 8-fold arms with scepter shield in center within ornamented frame, electoral hat above divides date **Rev. Legend:** ANFANCK. BEDENCK... **Mint:** Konigsberg **Note:** Fr. #2177.

Date	Mintage	VG	F	VF	XF	Unc
1635 DK (q)	—	—	—	—	—	—

KM# 200 3 DUCAT
10.5000 g., 0.9860 Gold 0.3328 oz. AGW **Obv:** Crowned and robed elector holding scepter on horse rearing to right **Rev:** Scepter arms in center of large rose, 23 small oval arms around **Mint:** Konigsberg **Note:** Struck from 1/4 Thaler dies.

Date	Mintage	VG	F	VF	XF	Unc
ND(1641/3)	—	—	—	6,500	10,000	—

KM# 284 3 DUCAT
10.5000 g., 0.9860 Gold 0.3328 oz. AGW **Subject:** Birthday of Friedrich Wilhelm and Birth of Prince Karl Emil **Mint:** Berlin **Note:** Similar to 2 Ducat, KM#282, but crowned six-line inscription on reverse. Struck from 1/4 Thaler dies.

Date	Mintage	VG	F	VF	XF	Unc
1655 CT Rare	—	—	—	—	—	—

KM# 329 3 DUCAT
10.5000 g., 0.9860 Gold 0.3328 oz. AGW **Subject:** Homage of Konigsberg

Date	Mintage	VG	F	VF	XF	Unc
1663	—	—	—	3,500	5,000	—

KM# 417 3 DUCAT
10.5000 g., 0.9860 Gold 0.3328 oz. AGW **Obv:** Bust right, date below **Rev:** Crowned arms above crossed palm branches

Date	Mintage	VG	F	VF	XF	Unc
1670	—	—	—	—	—	—

KM# 545 3 DUCAT
10.5000 g., 0.9860 Gold 0.3328 oz. AGW **Subject:** Death of Friedrich Wilhelm **Obv:** Bust right, two legends around **Rev:** Eagle on palm tree above trophies

Date	Mintage	VG	F	VF	XF	Unc
1688	—	—	—	—	—	—

KM# 596 3 DUCAT
10.5000 g., 0.9860 Gold 0.3328 oz. AGW **Subject:** Founding of University of Halle an der Saale

Date	Mintage	VG	F	VF	XF	Unc
1694	—	—	—	—	—	—

KM# 123 4 DUCAT
14.0000 g., 0.9860 Gold 0.4438 oz. AGW **Obv:** Bust of Georg Wilhelm right in elector's costume **Rev:** Crowned twelve-fold arms in inner circle **Mint:** Kolln

Date	Mintage	VG	F	VF	XF	Unc
1626 IP Rare	4	—	—	—	—	—

KM# 225 4 DUCAT
14.0000 g., 0.9860 Gold 0.4438 oz. AGW **Mint:** Berlin **Note:** Similar to 1/2 Thaler, KM#211a. Struck with 1/2 Thaler dies.

Date	Mintage	VG	F	VF	XF	Unc
1647 CT Rare	—	—	—	—	—	—

KM# 285 4 DUCAT
14.0000 g., 0.9860 Gold 0.4438 oz. AGW **Subject:** Birthday of Friedrich Wilhelm and Birth of Prince Karl Friedrich **Rev:** Crowned six-line inscription and value 4 punched in

Date	Mintage	VG	F	VF	XF	Unc
1655 AB Rare	—	—	—	—	—	—

KM# 294 4 DUCAT
14.0000 g., 0.9860 Gold 0.4438 oz. AGW **Obv:** Bust of Friedrich Wilhelm right in inner circle **Rev:** Capped arms in inner circle **Mint:** Konigsberg

Date	Mintage	VG	F	VF	XF	Unc
ND(1657) Rare	—	—	—	—	—	—

KM# 347 4 DUCAT
14.0000 g., 0.9860 Gold 0.4438 oz. AGW **Obv:** Elector standing 3/4 right, helmet on table at right **Rev:** Crowned arms divide altered date

Date	Mintage	VG	F	VF	XF	Unc
1666/64 IL/AB Rare	—	—	—	—	—	—

KM# 39 5 DUCAT (1/2 Portugalöser)
14.0000 g., 0.9860 Gold 0.4438 oz. AGW **Obv:** Bust right **Rev:** Cross, arms in center, shield at end of each arm **Mint:** Kolln **Note:** Fr. #2151.

Date	Mintage	VG	F	VF	XF	Unc
ND(1611)	—	—	—	—	—	—
1613	—	—	—	—	—	—
1614	—	—	—	—	—	—

KM# 49 5 DUCAT (1/2 Portugalöser)
14.0000 g., 0.9860 Gold 0.4438 oz. AGW **Obv:** Half-length bust right, date below **Rev:** Arms in ornamented shield

Date	Mintage	VG	F	VF	XF	Unc
1612 MH	—	—	—	—	—	—

KM# A127 5 DUCAT (1/2 Portugalöser)
17.5000 g., 0.9860 Gold 0.5547 oz. AGW **Obv:** 1/2-length armored figure to right, titles of Georg Wilhelm **Rev:** 12-fold arms in ornamented frame, electoral hat above divides date, titles continuous **Mint:** Konigsberg **Note:** Struck from dies intended for 1/2 Thaler.

Date	Mintage	VG	F	VF	XF	Unc
1627 (q)	—	—	—	—	—	—

KM# B143 5 DUCAT (1/2 Portugalöser)
17.5000 g., 0.9860 Gold 0.5547 oz. AGW **Obv:** 1/2-length figure right, scepter on shoulder **Rev:** Crowned shield of arms **Mint:** Konigsberg **Note:** Struck from Thaler dies, KM#125.

Date	Mintage	VG	F	VF	XF	Unc
1630 (q)	—	—	—	—	—	—

KM# 154 5 DUCAT (1/2 Portugalöser)
14.0000 g., 0.9860 Gold 0.4438 oz. AGW **Obv:** Elector on horse rearing to right **Rev:** Eagle with arms on breast and small shields on wings, date divided by legs below **Mint:** Berlin

Date	Mintage	VG	F	VF	XF	Unc
1634 LM Rare	—	—	—	—	—	—

KM# 161 5 DUCAT (1/2 Portugalöser)
14.0000 g., 0.9860 Gold 0.4438 oz. AGW **Obv:** Half-length figure right with helmet **Rev:** Crowned arms, date divided above **Mint:** Konigsberg **Note:** Struck with 1/2 Thaler dies, KM#150.1. Fr. #2176.

Date	Mintage	VG	F	VF	XF	Unc
1636 DK Rare	—	—	—	—	—	—

KM# 201 5 DUCAT (1/2 Portugalöser)
14.0000 g., 0.9860 Gold 0.4438 oz. AGW **Obv:** Half-length bust 3/4 right breaks circle at top **Rev:** Plumed helmet, ARMAT ET ORNAT on band below, surrounded by 23 small oval arms **Note:** Struck with 1/2 Thaler dies.

Date	Mintage	VG	F	VF	XF	Unc
ND (1641-43)	—	—	—	—	—	—

KM# 219 5 DUCAT (1/2 Portugalöser)
14.0000 g., 0.9860 Gold 0.4438 oz. AGW **Mint:** Berlin **Note:** Struck with 1/2 Thaler dies.

Date	Mintage	VG	F	VF	XF	Unc
1644 AB	—	—	—	—	—	—

KM# 226 5 DUCAT (1/2 Portugalöser)
14.0000 g., 0.9860 Gold 0.4438 oz. AGW **Note:** Similar to 1 Thaler, KM#235 with 1 Thaler dies.

Date	Mintage	VG	F	VF	XF	Unc
1647 CT	—	—	—	—	—	—

KM# 238 5 DUCAT (1/2 Portugalöser)
14.0000 g., 0.9860 Gold 0.4438 oz. AGW **Obv:** Half figure of Friedrich Wilhelm right in elector's costume in inner circle **Rev:** Capped arms in inner circle, date in legend

Date	Mintage	VG	F	VF	XF	Unc
1650 CT	—	1,500	3,500	7,000	10,000	—

KM# 253 5 DUCAT (1/2 Portugalöser)
14.0000 g., 0.9860 Gold 0.4438 oz. AGW **Note:** Similar to 1 Thaler, KM#235. Struck with 1 Thaler dies, KM#235.

Date	Mintage	VG	F	VF	XF	Unc
ND(1651)	—	—	—	—	—	—

KM# 254 5 DUCAT (1/2 Portugalöser)
14.0000 g., 0.9860 Gold 0.4438 oz. AGW **Obv:** Bust right in circle **Rev:** Helmeted arms **Mint:** Konigsberg **Note:** Struck with 1/2 Thaler dies, KM#247.

Date	Mintage	VG	F	VF	XF	Unc
ND(1651-61) CM Rare	—	—	—	—	—	—

KM# 259 5 DUCAT (1/2 Portugalöser)
14.0000 g., 0.9860 Gold 0.4438 oz. AGW **Obv:** Friedrich Wilhelm standing by table with helmet **Rev:** Capped arms in inner circle, date divided at top **Mint:** Berlin

Date	Mintage	VG	F	VF	XF	Unc
1652 CT	—	1,300	2,600	5,500	8,500	—
1653 CT	—	1,300	2,600	5,500	8,500	—
1655 CT	—	1,300	2,600	5,500	8,500	—
1657 CT	—	1,300	2,600	5,500	8,500	—

KM# 268 5 DUCAT (1/2 Portugalöser)
14.0000 g., 0.9860 Gold 0.4438 oz. AGW **Obv:** Friedrich Wilhelm

Date	Mintage	VG	F	VF	XF	Unc
1653 CT	—	1,800	3,800	6,500	10,000	—

KM# 272 5 DUCAT (1/2 Portugalöser)
14.0000 g., 0.9860 Gold 0.4438 oz. AGW **Obv:** 3/4 figure of Friedrich Wilhelm right in inner circle **Rev:** Capped arms in inner circle **Note:** Thick planchet, from Ducat dies, KM#270.

Date	Mintage	VG	F	VF	XF	Unc
1654	—	2,500	4,500	8,500	12,000	—

KM# 295 5 DUCAT (1/2 Portugalöser)
14.0000 g., 0.9860 Gold 0.4438 oz. AGW **Obv:** Bust of Friedrich Wilhelm right in inner circle **Mint:** Konigsberg

Date	Mintage	VG	F	VF	XF	Unc
ND(1657) Rare	—	—	—	—	—	—

KM# 300 5 DUCAT (1/2 Portugalöser)
14.0000 g., 0.9860 Gold 0.4438 oz. AGW **Subject:** Attainment of Sovereignty over East Prussia **Obv:** Elector on horse galloping right, town below hoofs, date at bottom **Rev:** Eight-line inscription **Mint:** Berlin

Date	Mintage	VG	F	VF	XF	Unc
1658 CT	—	—	—	—	—	—

KM# 301 5 DUCAT (1/2 Portugalöser)
14.0000 g., 0.9860 Gold 0.4438 oz. AGW **Rev:** Nine-line inscription

Date	Mintage	VG	F	VF	XF	Unc
1658 AB	—	—	—	—	—	—

KM# 348 5 DUCAT (1/2 Portugalöser)
14.0000 g., 0.9860 Gold 0.4438 oz. AGW **Rev:** Crowned arms divide date in inner circle

Date	Mintage	VG	F	VF	XF	Unc
1664 AB	—	—	—	—	—	—
1666/64 IL/AB Rare	—	—	—	—	—	—

KM# 425 5 DUCAT (1/2 Portugalöser)
14.0000 g., 0.9860 Gold 0.4438 oz. AGW **Obv:** Laureate bust right **Rev:** Helmeted and supported arms, date in legend **Mint:** Konigsberg **Note:** Struck with 1 Thaler dies.

Date	Mintage	VG	F	VF	XF	Unc
1672 TT	—	—	—	—	—	—

KM# 493 5 DUCAT (1/2 Portugalöser)
14.0000 g., 0.9860 Gold 0.4438 oz. AGW **Mint:** Berlin **Note:** Struck at Berlin Mint with 1 Thaler dies KM#490. Similar to 1 Thaler, KM#490.

Date	Mintage	VG	F	VF	XF	Unc
1679 CS	—	—	—	—	—	—

KM# 512 5 DUCAT (1/2 Portugalöser)
14.0000 g., 0.9860 Gold 0.4438 oz. AGW **Obv:** Armored bust of Friedrich Wilhelm right, date in legend **Rev:** Capped arms **Mint:** Magdeburg

Date	Mintage	VG	F	VF	XF	Unc
1683 IE Rare	—	—	—	—	—	—

KM# 523 5 DUCAT (1/2 Portugalöser)
14.0000 g., 0.9860 Gold 0.4438 oz. AGW **Obv:** Bust right in circle **Rev:** Crowned eagle, scepter arms on breast, eight shields on wings, date divided at lower left and right **Mint:** Berlin **Note:** Struck with 1 Thaler dies, KM#521.

Date	Mintage	VG	F	VF	XF	Unc
1685 LCS	—	—	—	—	—	—

KM# 91 6 DUCAT
21.0000 g., 0.9860 Gold 0.6657 oz. AGW **Mint:** Konigsberg **Note:** Struck at Konigsberg Mint. Similar to 1 Thaler, KM#88, but mint mark of Ernst Pfaler at end of reverse legend inscription.

Date	Mintage	VG	F	VF	XF	Unc
1621 (a) Unique	—	—	—	—	—	—

KM# 227 6 DUCAT
21.0000 g., 0.9860 Gold 0.6657 oz. AGW **Obv:** Half-length figure with cap right **Rev:** Arms with 12 fields **Mint:** Berlin **Note:** Struck with 1/2 Thaler dies, KM#211.

Date	Mintage	VG	F	VF	XF	Unc
1647 CT Rare	—	—	—	—	—	—

KM# 479 6 DUCAT
21.0000 g., 0.9860 Gold 0.6657 oz. AGW **Obv:** Laureate bust right **Rev:** Helmeted and supported arms, date in legend **Mint:** Konigsberg **Note:** Struck with 1 Thaler dies.

Date	Mintage	VG	F	VF	XF	Unc
1677 HS	—	—	—	—	—	—

KM# 530 6 DUCAT
21.0000 g., 0.9860 Gold 0.6657 oz. AGW **Mint:** Berlin **Note:** Struck with 1 Thaler dies, similar to KM#527.

Date	Mintage	VG	F	VF	XF	Unc
1686 LCS Rare	—	—	—	—	—	—

KM# B127 8 DUCAT
28.0000 g., 0.9860 Gold 0.8876 oz. AGW **Ruler:** Georg Wilhelm **Obv:** 1/2-length figure right **Rev:** Crowned shield of arms **Mint:** Konigsberg **Note:** Fr. #2175.Struck from Thaler dies, KM#125.

Date	Mintage	VG	F	VF	XF	Unc
16Z7 (q)	—	—	—	—	—	—

KM# 459 8 DUCAT
28.0000 g., 0.9860 Gold 0.8876 oz. AGW **Subject:** Victory at Battle of Fehrbellin **Mint:** Berlin **Note:** Struck with 1 Thaler dies, KM#449.

Date	Mintage	VG	F	VF	XF	Unc
1675 Rare	—	—	—	—	—	—

Note: Tempelhofer Auction 2-83 XF realized $19,500

KM# 29 10 DUCAT (Portugalöser)
35.0000 g., 0.9860 Gold 1.1095 oz. AGW **Obv:** Half-length bust right holding scepter and helmet **Rev:** Ornate cross, date at bottom arm, surrounded by 17 small shields **Mint:** Kolln **Note:** Fr. #2143.

Date	Mintage	VG	F	VF	XF	Unc
1605 Rare	—	—	—	—	—	—

KM# 50 10 DUCAT (Portugalöser)
35.0000 g., 0.9860 Gold 1.1095 oz. AGW **Obv:** Bust right **Rev:** Cross, arms in center, shield at end of each arm **Note:** Fr. #2150.

Date	Mintage	VG	F	VF	XF	Unc
ND(1611) Rare	—	—	—	—	—	—
1612 Rare	—	—	—	—	—	—
1613 Rare	—	—	—	—	—	—
1614 Rare	—	—	—	—	—	—

KM# 80 10 DUCAT (Portugalöser)
35.0000 g., 0.9860 Gold 1.1095 oz. AGW **Obv:** Elector on horse galloping right **Rev:** Similar to 1 Thaler, KM#74 **Mint:** Berlin **Note:** Struck with 1 Thaler dies, KM#74.

Date	Mintage	VG	F	VF	XF	Unc
1620 LM Rare	—	—	—	—	—	—

KM# A100 10 DUCAT (Portugalöser)
35.0000 g., 0.9860 Gold 1.1095 oz. AGW **Ruler:** Georg Wilhelm **Obv:** Crowned 1/2-length figure right **Obv. Legend:** GEORG: WILHELM: V: G: G: **Rev:** Helmeted arms, date above **Mint:** Konigsberg **Note:** Struck from 1 Thaler dies, KM#112.1. Ref. Dost #558.

Date	Mintage	VG	F	VF	XF	Unc
1623	—	—	—	—	—	—

KM# C143 10 DUCAT (Portugalöser)
35.0000 g., 0.9860 Gold 1.1095 oz. AGW **Ruler:** Georg Wilhelm **Obv:** 1/2-length figure right, scepter on shoulder **Rev:** Shield of arms **Mint:** Konigsberg **Note:** Fr. #2174. Struck from 2 Thaler dies, KM#143.

Date	Mintage	VG	F	VF	XF	Unc
1630 (q)	—	—	—	—	—	—

KM# 155 10 DUCAT (Portugalöser)
35.0000 g., 0.9860 Gold 1.1095 oz. AGW **Obv:** Elector on horse rearing to right **Rev:** Eagle with arms on breast and small shields on wings, date divided by legs below **Note:** Struck with 5 Ducat dies, KM#154.

Date	Mintage	VG	F	VF	XF	Unc
1634 LM Rare	—	—	—	—	—	—

KM# 202 10 DUCAT (Portugalöser)
35.0000 g., 0.9860 Gold 1.1095 oz. AGW **Obv:** Crowned and robed half-length figure right **Rev:** Scepter arms in center of large rose, 23 small oval arms around **Mint:** Konigsberg

Date	Mintage	VG	F	VF	XF	Unc
ND(1641-3) Rare	—	—	—	—	—	—

KM# 208 10 DUCAT (Portugalöser)
35.0000 g., 0.9860 Gold 1.1095 oz. AGW **Obv:** Bust right, helmet at right **Rev:** Helmeted arms divide date **Note:** Struck with 1 Thaler dies, KM#206.

Date	Mintage	VG	F	VF	XF	Unc
1642 DK	—	—	—	—	—	—

KM# 255 10 DUCAT (Portugalöser)
35.0000 g., 0.9860 Gold 1.1095 oz. AGW **Obv:** Friedrich Wilhelm standing in ornamental inner circle **Rev:** Seven helmeted arms with knight supporters, date divided near center **Mint:** Berlin

Date	Mintage	VG	F	VF	XF	Unc
1651 CT Rare	—	—	—	—	—	—

KM# 256 10 DUCAT (Portugalöser)
35.0000 g., 0.9860 Gold 1.1095 oz. AGW **Obv:** Capped bust right with sword and sceptre **Rev:** Helmeted and supported arms **Note:** Struck with 1 Thaler dies, KM#235.

Date	Mintage	VG	F	VF	XF	Unc
ND(1651) Unique	—	—	—	—	—	—

Note: Hess Auction 3-83 XF realized $25,000

KM# 269 10 DUCAT (Portugalöser)
35.0000 g., 0.9860 Gold 1.1095 oz. AGW **Obv:** Elector standing 3.4 to right **Obv. Legend:** BR. S.-R. I. ARCHIC. ET. ELECT. **Rev:** Helmeted arms **Note:** Struck with 1 Thaler dies, KM#249.

Date	Mintage	VG	F	VF	XF	Unc
1653 CT	—	—	—	—	—	—

KM# 296 10 DUCAT (Portugalöser)
35.0000 g., 0.9860 Gold 1.1095 oz. AGW **Subject:** Attainment of Sovereignty over East Prussia **Obv:** Town below hoofs **Note:** Struck with 1 Thaler dies, KM#249.

Date	Mintage	VG	F	VF	XF	Unc
1657 CT	—	—	—	—	—	—

KM# 397 10 DUCAT (Portugalöser)
35.0000 g., 0.9860 Gold 1.1095 oz. AGW **Subject:** Return of Elector to Prussia in 1669 **Obv:** Crowned and robed figure of elector holding scepter on horse rearing right on carpet, date below **Rev:** Figure of Brandenburgia in landscape with child on knee, eagle with laruel wreath in beak above

Date	Mintage	VG	F	VF	XF	Unc
1669 GL	—	—	—	—	—	—

KM# 426 10 DUCAT (Portugalöser)
35.0000 g., 0.9860 Gold 1.1095 oz. AGW **Obv:** Laureate bust right **Rev:** Helmeted and supported arms, date in legend **Mint:** Konigsberg **Note:** Struck with 1 Thaler dies, KM#424.

Date	Mintage	VG	F	VF	XF	Unc
1672 TT	—	—	—	—	—	—

KM# 460 10 DUCAT (Portugalöser)
35.0000 g., 0.9860 Gold 1.1095 oz. AGW **Subject:** Victory at Battle of Fehrbellin **Mint:** Berlin **Note:** Struck with 1 Thaler dies, similar to KM#449.

Date	Mintage	VG	F	VF	XF	Unc
1675 Rare	—	—	—	—	—	—

KM# 502 10 DUCAT (Portugalöser)
35.0000 g., 0.9860 Gold 1.1095 oz. AGW **Subject:** Homage of the City of Magdeburg, 30 May 1681 **Obv:** Bust of elector right in oval frame linked to clouds and to city of Magdeburg by three chains **Rev:** Maiden kneeling right in landscape, sun, eagle and cornucopia in clouds above, date below **Mint:** Magdeburg **Note:** Struck with 1 Thaler dies, KM#501.

Date	Mintage	VG	F	VF	XF	Unc
1681 IE Rare	—	—	—	—	—	—

KM# B100 15 DUCAT
52.5000 g., 0.9860 Gold 1.6642 oz. AGW **Ruler:** Georg Wilhelm **Obv:** Crowned 1/2-length figure right **Obv. Legend:** GEORG: WILHELM: V: G: G **Rev:** Helmeted arms, date above **Mint:** Konigsberg **Note:** Struck from 2 Thaler dies, KM#112.1.

Date	Mintage	VG	F	VF	XF	Unc
1623	—	—	—	—	—	—

KM# 203 15 DUCAT
52.5000 g., 0.9860 Gold 1.6642 oz. AGW **Obv:** Half-length bust 3/4 to right **Rev:** Scepter arms in center of large rose, 23 small oval arms around **Mint:** Konigsberg **Note:** Struck with 1 Thaler dies, KM#192.

Date	Mintage	VG	F	VF	XF	Unc
ND(1641-3)	—	—	—	—	—	—

KM# 461 20 DUCAT
70.0000 g., 0.9860 Gold 2.2190 oz. AGW **Subject:** Victory at Battle of Fehrbellin **Mint:** Berlin **Note:** Struck with 1 Thaler dies, KM#449.

Date	Mintage	VG	F	VF	XF	Unc
1675 Rare	—	—	—	—	—	—

KM# B119 50 DUCAT
175.0000 g., 0.9860 Gold 5.5474 oz. AGW **Ruler:** Georg Wilhelm **Obv:** Armored bust right, wide band with 19 small shields of arms around **Rev:** 4-fold arms with scepter shield in center, within ornamented shield, date divided near bottom, electoral hat above, all in circle, 3 circles of legends with name and titles of Georg Wilhelm **Mint:** Konigsberg **Note:** Fr. #2173. Struck from 3 Thaler dies, KM#A118.

Date	Mintage	VG	F	VF	XF	Unc
1624 MK-NB	—	—	—	—	—	—

PATTERNS

Including off metal strikes

KM#	Date	Mintage	Identification	Mkt Val
Pn1	1668 IL	—	Ducat. Silver. KM#394	125
PnA2	1677 CS	—	2 Ducat. Silver. KM#476.1	250
Pn2	1677 CS	—	2 Ducat. Silver. KM#477	200
PnA3	1677 CS	—	2 Ducat. Silver. KM#478.2	250
Pn3	1688	—	2 Ducat. Silver. KM#544. County of Mark.	135
Pn4	1690	—	Ducat. Silver. KM#574. Homage.	150
Pn5	1690	—	2 Ducat. Silver. KM#575. Homage.	200
Pn6	1694	—	Ducat. Silver. KM#595. University of Halle an der Salle.	175
Pn7	1694	—	3 Ducat. Silver. KM#596. University of Halle an der Salle.	120
Pn8	1699 RF/LCS	—	2 Ducat. Silver. KM#619. Struck on octagonal flan.	—

BRANDENBURG-ANSBACH

Located in northern Bavaria. The first coins appeared ca. 1150. This area was given and sold to many individuals, usually with some relationship to the elector of Brandenburg. It was sold to Prussia in 1791 and was ceded to Bavaria in 1806.

RULERS
Joachim Ernst, 1603-1625
Friedrich II, Albrecht and Christian, 1625-1634
Albrecht III, 1634-1667
Johann Friedrich, 1667-1686
Christian Albrecht, 1686-1692
Georg Friedrich II, 1692-1703

MINT MARKS
(c) - Crailsheim, pot hook
(d) - Dachsbach, lily
F - Furth
(f) - Furth, cloverleaf
(k) - Kitzingen, crenellated tower top
O - Onolzbach (Ansbach)
(r) - Roth, rosette
R - Roth
(s) - Schwabach, four-petaled flower
S - Schwabach

MINT OFFICIALS' INITIALS

Initial	Date	Name
(a) 2 horseshoes	1668-97	Johann Christoph Holeisen in Augsburgi
CG	Ca. 1622-25	Christian Goebel
CS	1622-54	Conrad Stutz, die-cutter in Furth, mintmaster of the Franconian Circle
GH	1683-1711	Georg Hautsch, die-cutter in Nürnberg
GL	1621-22	Georg Lesse in Roth
IR	Ca. 1624	Unknown
PG		Unknown

DUCHY

Margraviate

REGULAR COINAGE

KM# 130 HELLER
Copper **Ruler:** Georg Friedrich II **Obv:** Crowned arms **Rev:** 1/HEL/LER/date

Date	Mintage	VG	F	VF	XF	Unc
1699	—	9.00	16.00	27.00	45.00	—
1700	—	9.00	16.00	27.00	45.00	—

KM# 18 PFENNING
Copper **Note:** Kipper Pfennig. Uniface. Arms divide I-E, value above.

Date	Mintage	VG	F	VF	XF	Unc
1622	—	27.00	55.00	80.00	140	—

KM# 55 PFENNING
Copper **Note:** Hohenzollern arms, B. O. above.

Date	Mintage	VG	F	VF	XF	Unc
ND(1639-67)	—	—	—	—	—	—

KM# 129 PFENNING
Billon **Note:** Uniface. Noe description available.

Date	Mintage	VG	F	VF	XF	Unc
1698	—	—	—	—	—	—
1700	—	—	—	—	—	—

KM# 19 2 PFENNING
Copper **Note:** Kipper Pfenning. Uniface. Arms divide value II and date.

Date	Mintage	VG	F	VF	XF	Unc
1622	—	27.00	55.00	100	150	—

KM# 34 2 PFENNING
Billon **Obv:** Two arms, IEMB above, F below **Rev:** Value, date in four lines

Date	Mintage	VG	F	VF	XF	Unc
1623 F	—	—	—	—	—	—

KM# 20 3 PFENNIG
Copper **Obv:** Arms divide date, I.E.M.Z.B. above **Rev:** FC (Frankisher Creis) above 3 **Note:** Kipper 2 Pfennig.

Date	Mintage	VG	F	VF	XF	Unc
1622	—	25.00	45.00	80.00	140	—

KM# 21 3 PFENNIG (Dreier)
Billon **Obv:** Eagle **Rev:** Imperial orb with value 3, date

Date	Mintage	VG	F	VF	XF	Unc
1622	—	—	—	—	—	—

KM# 22 4 PFENNING
Copper **Note:** Kipper 4 Pfenning.

Date	Mintage	VG	F	VF	XF	Unc
1622	—	16.00	40.00	65.00	125	—

KM# 23 KREUZER (4 Pfennig)
Silver **Obv:** Arms **Rev:** Value

Date	Mintage	VG	F	VF	XF	Unc
1622 F	—	10.00	20.00	33.00	60.00	—
1623 F	—	10.00	20.00	33.00	60.00	—

KM# 35 KREUZER (4 Pfennig)
Silver **Obv:** Three arms

Date	Mintage	VG	F	VF	XF	Unc
1623	—	—	—	—	—	—

KM# 43 KREUZER (4 Pfennig)
Silver **Obv:** Oval arms, IEMZB above **Rev:** Value, date in four lines

Date	Mintage	VG	F	VF	XF	Unc
1624 R	—	75.00	150	275	450	—

KM# 100 KREUZER (4 Pfennig)
Silver

Date	Mintage	VG	F	VF	XF	Unc
1683	—	12.00	25.00	45.00	75.00	—
1685	—	12.00	25.00	45.00	75.00	—

KM# 105 KREUZER (4 Pfennig)
Silver **Obv:** Bust right **Rev:** Crowned eagle with I on breast, date divided above

Date	Mintage	VG	F	VF	XF	Unc
1686	—	16.00	33.00	65.00	125	—

KM# 115 KREUZER (4 Pfennig)
Silver **Obv:** Monogram **Rev:** Arms, date

Date	Mintage	VG	F	VF	XF	Unc
1693	—	13.00	27.00	60.00	100	—

KM# 116 KREUZER (4 Pfennig)
Silver **Ruler:** Georg Friedrich II **Obv:** Bust right **Rev:** Crowned eagle with I on breast, date divided above **Note:** Similar to KM#136.

Date	Mintage	VG	F	VF	XF	Unc
1693	—	10.00	20.00	40.00	60.00	—
1694	—	10.00	20.00	40.00	60.00	—
1695	—	10.00	20.00	40.00	60.00	—

Date	Mintage	VG	F	VF	XF	Unc
1696	—	10.00	20.00	40.00	60.00	—
1697	—	10.00	20.00	40.00	60.00	—
1698	—	10.00	20.00	40.00	60.00	—
1699	—	10.00	20.00	40.00	60.00	—
1700	—	10.00	20.00	40.00	60.00	—

KM# A23 2 KREUZER (1/2 Batzen)
Silver **Obv:** Eagle **Rev:** Imperial orb with value 2, date

Date	Mintage	VG	F	VF	XF	Unc
1622 R	—	27.00	55.00	80.00	140	—

KM# 36 2 KREUZER (1/2 Batzen)
Silver **Obv:** Two arms, value II above, F below **Rev:** Eagle

Date	Mintage	VG	F	VF	XF	Unc
1623 F	—	27.00	55.00	80.00	140	—

KM# 101 2 KREUZER (1/2 Batzen)
Silver **Obv:** Bust right **Rev:** Imperial orb with value 2, date

Date	Mintage	VG	F	VF	XF	Unc
1683	—	27.00	55.00	80.00	140	—
1686	—	27.00	55.00	80.00	140	—

KM# 117 2 KREUZER (1/2 Batzen)
Silver **Note:** Similar to KM#101.

Date	Mintage	VG	F	VF	XF	Unc
1693	—	27.00	55.00	80.00	140	—
1694	—	27.00	55.00	80.00	140	—
1695	—	27.00	55.00	80.00	140	—
1696	—	27.00	55.00	80.00	140	—

KM# 118 2 KREUZER (1/2 Batzen)
Silver **Obv:** Four arms **Rev:** Imperial orb with vlaue 2, date

Date	Mintage	VG	F	VF	XF	Unc
1694	—	20.00	40.00	60.00	100	—

KM# 27 3 KREUZER (Groschen)
Silver **Obv:** Eagle with arms on breast, date in legend **Rev:** Imperial orb with value 3

Date	Mintage	VG	F	VF	XF	Unc
1622	—	13.00	27.00	45.00	75.00	—
1623	—	13.00	27.00	45.00	75.00	—
1624	—	13.00	27.00	45.00	75.00	—
1625	—	13.00	27.00	45.00	75.00	—

KM# 44 3 KREUZER (Groschen)
Silver **Note:** Klippe.

Date	Mintage	VG	F	VF	XF	Unc
1624	—	80.00	175	275	425	—

KM# 61 3 KREUZER (Groschen)
Silver **Obv:** Arms **Rev:** Imperial orb with value 3, date

Date	Mintage	VG	F	VF	XF	Unc
1652	—	—	—	—	—	—

KM# 24 4 KREUZER (Batzen)
Silver **Obv:** Two arms, value IIII K above, F below, date in legend **Rev:** Eagle **Note:** Varieties exist.

Date	Mintage	VG	F	VF	XF	Unc
1622 F	—	15.00	30.00	60.00	120	—
1623 F	—	15.00	30.00	60.00	120	—
1624 F	—	15.00	30.00	60.00	120	—
1625 F	—	15.00	30.00	60.00	120	—

KM# 102 4 KREUZER (Batzen)
Silver **Obv:** Arms **Rev:** Value, date

Date	Mintage	VG	F	VF	XF	Unc
1683	—	75.00	125	200	350	—

KM# 124 4 KREUZER (Batzen)
Silver

Date	Mintage	VG	F	VF	XF	Unc
1695	—	10.00	25.00	40.00	80.00	—
1696	—	10.00	25.00	40.00	80.00	—

KM# 37 6 KREUZER
Silver **Obv:** Two arms, value VI K above, F below **Rev:** Eagle, date

Date	Mintage	VG	F	VF	XF	Unc
1623 F	—	60.00	120	240	325	—

KM# 45 6 KREUZER
Silver **Subject:** Death of Joachim Ernst **Obv:** Bust **Rev:** Inscription with date, value below VI. K.

Date	Mintage	VG	F	VF	XF	Unc
1625 F	—	45.00	120	200	275	—

KM# 46 6 KREUZER
Silver **Rev:** Without inidcation of value

Date	Mintage	VG	F	VF	XF	Unc
1625	—	55.00	115	200	300	—

KM# 83 6 KREUZER
Silver **Obv:** Bust, value 6 below **Rev:** Arms, date

Date	Mintage	VG	F	VF	XF	Unc
1677	—	55.00	115	200	300	—
1678	—	55.00	115	200	300	—

KM# 103 6 KREUZER
Silver **Obv:** Two arms, value above **Rev:** Eagle, date

Date	Mintage	VG	F	VF	XF	Unc
1683	—	55.00	115	200	300	—
1684	—	55.00	115	200	300	—

KM# 16 24 KREUZER
Silver **Obv:** Facing bust **Rev:** Value 24 between shields

Date	Mintage	VG	F	VF	XF	Unc
1621 CS	—	80.00	140	275	525	—

KM# 13 24 KREUZER
Silver **Obv:** Bust right, date in legend **Rev:** Eagle with 24 in orb on breast **Note:** Kipper 24 Kreuzer. Varieties exist.

Date	Mintage	VG	F	VF	XF	Unc
1621	—	65.00	120	225	450	—
1621 (f)	—	65.00	120	225	450	—
1621 (k)	—	65.00	120	225	450	—
1622	—	65.00	120	225	450	—
1622 (d)	—	65.00	120	225	450	—
1622 (f)	—	65.00	120	225	450	—
1622 (k)	—	65.00	110	220	450	—
1622 0	—	65.00	110	220	450	—
1622 (r)	—	65.00	110	220	450	—
1622 (s)	—	65.00	110	220	450	—

KM# 14 24 KREUZER
Silver **Note:** Klippe.

Date	Mintage	VG	F	VF	XF	Unc
1621 (k)	—	—	—	—	—	—

KM# 15 24 KREUZER
Silver **Obv:** 4-fold arms, central shield of Nuremberg burgraviate (lion rampant left), date **Note:** Varieties exist.

Date	Mintage	VG	F	VF	XF	Unc
1621	—	65.00	110	220	450	—
1621 (d)	—	65.00	110	220	450	—
1621 GL	—	65.00	110	220	450	—
1622 (f)	—	65.00	110	220	450	—

KM# 25.1 24 KREUZER
Silver **Obv:** Bust right divides date **Rev:** Eagle with 24 in orb on breast

Date	Mintage	VG	F	VF	XF	Unc
1622 (c)	—	80.00	140	275	525	—

KM# 25.2 24 KREUZER
Silver **Obv:** Bust right, date in legend

Date	Mintage	VG	F	VF	XF	Unc
1622 (c)	—	80.00	140	275	525	—

KM# 26 48 KREUZER (Kippergulden)
Silver **Obv:** Bust 3/4 to right, date in legend **Rev:** Eagle wtih 48 in orb on breast **Note:** Kipper 48 Kreuzer.

Date	Mintage	VG	F	VF	XF	Unc
1622 (d)	—	250	425	675	1,000	—

KM# 67 GROSCHEN (1/24 Thaler)
Silver **Obv:** Facing bust **Rev:** Inscription with date **Note:** Kipper Groschen.

Date	Mintage	VG	F	VF	XF	Unc
1667	—	—	—	—	—	—

KM# 99 GROSCHEN (1/24 Thaler)
Silver **Obv:** Arms **Rev:** Value as GG(Guter Groschen), date

Date	Mintage	VG	F	VF	XF	Unc
1682	—	—	—	—	—	—

KM# 106 GROSCHEN (1/24 Thaler)
Silver **Subject:** Death of Johann Friedrich **Obv:** Bust right **Rev:** Inscription with date

Date	Mintage	VG	F	VF	XF	Unc
1686	—	—	—	—	—	—

KM# 107 2 GROSCHEN (1/12 Thaler)
Silver **Subject:** Death of Johann Friedrich **Obv:** Bust right **Rev:** Inscription with date

Date	Mintage	VG	F	VF	XF	Unc
1686	—	—	—	—	—	—

KM# 17 1/24 THALER (Groschen)
Silver **Obv:** Eagle, date in legend **Rev:** Imperial orb with value 24

Date	Mintage	VG	F	VF	XF	Unc
1621	—	16.00	33.00	60.00	100	—

KM# 81 1/24 THALER (Groschen)
Silver **Rev:** Imperial orb with value 24, date

Date	Mintage	VG	F	VF	XF	Unc
1676	—	10.00	25.00	45.00	75.00	—
1682	—	10.00	25.00	45.00	75.00	—
1683	—	10.00	25.00	45.00	75.00	—
1684	—	10.00	25.00	45.00	75.00	—

KM# 28 1/8 THALER
Silver **Obv:** Bust 3/4 right divides date **Rev:** 4-fold arms in baroque frame

Date	Mintage	VG	F	VF	XF	Unc
1622	—	—	—	—	—	—

KM# 68 1/8 THALER
Silver **Subject:** Death of Albrecht **Obv:** Facing bust **Rev:** Inscription with date

Date	Mintage	VG	F	VF	XF	Unc
1667	—	—	—	—	—	—

KM# 38 1/6 THALER (1/4 Gulden)
Silver **Obv:** Eagle with 6 on breast **Rev:** Three arms in cartouche, one above 2 with top one dividing date

Date	Mintage	VG	F	VF	XF	Unc
1623 F	—	—	—	—	—	—

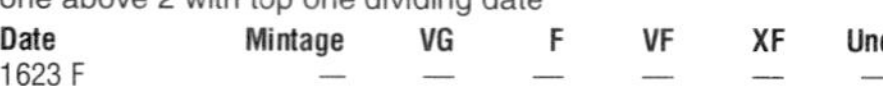

KM# 82 1/6 THALER (1/4 Gulden)
Silver

Date	Mintage	VG	F	VF	XF	Unc
1676	—	16.00	30.00	60.00	115	—
1677	—	16.00	30.00	60.00	115	—
1678	—	20.00	35.00	65.00	125	—
1679	—	16.00	30.00	60.00	115	—

KM# 84 1/6 THALER (1/4 Gulden)
Silver **Obv:** Bust right **Rev:** Piety and Justice standing

Date	Mintage	VG	F	VF	XF	Unc
1679	—	—	—	—	—	—

KM# 56 1/3 THALER (1/2 Gulden)
Silver **Obv:** Bust right **Rev:** Crowned arms between palm branches, date divides value below

Date	Mintage	VG	F	VF	XF	Unc
1676	—	275	550	900	1,500	—

KM# 29 1/2 THALER
Silver

Date	Mintage	VG	F	VF	XF	Unc
1622	—	—	—	—	—	—

KM# 39 1/2 THALER
Silver **Obv:** Half-length bust 3/4 right **Rev:** 4-fold arms, central shield of Nuremberg burgraviate, divide date

Date	Mintage	VG	F	VF	XF	Unc
1623 CS	—	—	—	—	—	—

KM# 47 1/2 THALER
Silver **Subject:** Death of Joachim Ernst **Rev:** 7-line inscription, date

Date	Mintage	VG	F	VF	XF	Unc
1625	—	—	—	—	—	—

KM# 51 1/2 THALER
Silver

Date	Mintage	VG	F	VF	XF	Unc
1628	—	—	—	—	—	—
1629	—	—	—	—	—	—

KM# 108 1/2 THALER
Silver **Subject:** Death of Johann Friedrich

Date	Mintage	VG	F	VF	XF	Unc
1686	—	375	750	1,500	2,400	—

KM# 79 2/3 THALER (Gulden)
Silver

Date	Mintage	VG	F	VF	XF	Unc
1675	—	55.00	110	185	350	—
1676	—	55.00	110	185	350	—
1677	—	55.00	110	185	350	—
1679	—	55.00	110	185	350	—

KM# 80 2/3 THALER (Gulden)
Silver **Rev:** Arms between palm sprays

Date	Mintage	VG	F	VF	XF	Unc
1675	—	55.00	110	185	350	—
1676	—	55.00	110	185	350	—
1677	—	55.00	110	185	350	—
1679	—	55.00	110	185	350	—

KM# 85 2/3 THALER (Gulden)
Silver **Obv:** Crowned oval arms in baroque frame, value divides date below **Rev:** Arm from clouds holds crown above heart on altar

Date	Mintage	VG	F	VF	XF	Unc
1679	—	—	—	—	—	—

KM# 86 2/3 THALER (Gulden)
Silver **Obv:** Bust right **Rev:** Table with cross, scales, branches, value divides date below

Date	Mintage	VG	F	VF	XF	Unc
1679	—	—	—	—	—	—

KM# 87 2/3 THALER (Gulden)
Silver **Obv:** Bust right **Rev:** Piety and Justice, value divides date

Date	Mintage	VG	F	VF	XF	Unc
1679	—	—	—	—	—	—

KM# 5 THALER
Silver **Note:** Dav. #6226.

Date	Mintage	VG	F	VF	XF	Unc
1609	—	600	1,200	2,000	3,500	—
1619	—	170	300	500	800	—
1620	—	170	300	500	800	—

KM# 11 THALER

Silver **Note:** Dav. #6227.

Date	Mintage	VG	F	VF	XF	Unc
1620	—	175	325	650	1,250	—

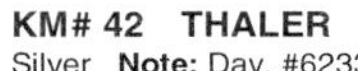

KM# 12 THALER

Silver **Obv:** Smaller bust holding baton **Note:** Dav. #6228.

Date	Mintage	VG	F	VF	XF	Unc
1620	—	200	375	600	1,000	—
1621	—	250	500	1,000	1,750	—

KM# 30 THALER

Silver **Obv:** Bust 3/4 to left **Rev:** Squared 12-fold arms in baroque frame, date divided above **Note:** Dav. #6229.

Date	Mintage	VG	F	VF	XF	Unc
1622 Rare	—	—	—	—	—	—

KM# 31 THALER

Silver **Note:** Dav. #6230.

Date	Mintage	VG	F	VF	XF	Unc
1622 CG	—	200	400	700	1,250	—
1625 CG	—	200	400	700	1,250	—

KM# 40 THALER

Silver **Obv:** Similar to KM#41 **Rev:** Oval 4-fold arms, central shield of Nuremberg lion, all in baroque frame whtich divides date **Note:** Dav. #6231.

Date	Mintage	VG	F	VF	XF	Unc
1623 CS	—	300	600	1,200	2,000	—

KM# 41 THALER

Silver **Note:** Dav. #6232.

Date	Mintage	VG	F	VF	XF	Unc
1623 CS	—	250	500	950	1,650	4,000

KM# 42 THALER

Silver **Note:** Dav. #6233.

Date	Mintage	VG	F	VF	XF	Unc
1623	—	375	750	1,250	2,000	7,250

KM# 48.1 THALER

Silver **Subject:** Death of Joachim Ernst **Obv:** Similar to KM#41 **Rev:** As KM#48.2 **Note:** Dav. #6234.

Date	Mintage	VG	F	VF	XF	Unc
1625	—	450	900	1,600	2,500	—

KM# 48.2 THALER

Silver **Subject:** Death of Joachim Ernst **Obv:** Facing bust holding baton and helmet **Note:** Varieties exist. Dav. #6235.

Date	Mintage	VG	F	VF	XF	Unc
1625	—	500	1,000	1,750	3,000	—

KM# 50.1 THALER

Silver **Obv:** Three facing half figure, shield dividing date below **Rev:** Helmeted arms **Note:** Dav. #6236.

Date	Mintage	VG	F	VF	XF	Unc
1626	—	75.00	150	300	550	—

KM# 50.2 THALER

Silver **Obv:** Slightly changed design **Rev:** Longer shield **Note:** Dav. #6237.

Date	Mintage	VG	F	VF	XF	Unc
1627	—	50.00	100	200	375	1,150
1628/7	—	60.00	125	250	450	—
1628	—	50.00	100	200	375	—
1629/8	—	60.00	125	250	450	—

KM# 50.3 THALER

Silver **Obv:** Ornate oval shield below figures **Note:** Varieties exist. Dav. #6238.

Date	Mintage	VG	F	VF	XF	Unc
1629	—	60.00	120	200	375	1,150
1630	—	65.00	125	300	750	1,500
1631	—	75.00	150	350	900	2,250

KM# 69.1 THALER

Silver **Subject:** Death of Albrecht **Obv:** Facing bust **Obv. Legend:** ALBERTVS. MARCH. BRAN. **Rev:** 7-line inscription, VAND. IN. SILES. CROS. ET. TAG. **Note:** Dav. #6239.

Date	Mintage	VG	F	VF	XF	Unc
1667	—	1,200	1,850	3,250	6,000	—

KM# 69.2 THALER

Silver **Subject:** Death of Albrecht **Obv. Legend:** ALBERT. MRCH: BRAND... **Rev. Legend:** VAND: IN SIL: CROS: & IAGER... **Note:** Dav. #6240.

Date	Mintage	VG	F	VF	XF	Unc
1667	—	850	1,350	3,000	5,500	—

KM# 88 THALER

Silver **Obv:** Helmeted arms, date divided below **Rev:** Three standing figures, column at right, value on edge **Note:** Dav. #6242.

Date	Mintage	VG	F	VF	XF	Unc
1679 Rare	—	—	—	—	—	—

KM# 95 THALER

Silver **Obv:** Oval arms **Note:** Dav. #6243.

Date	Mintage	VG	F	VF	XF	Unc
1680 Rare	—	—	—	—	—	—

KM# 96 THALER

Silver **Note:** Dav. #6245.

Date	Mintage	VG	F	VF	XF	Unc
1680	—	1,200	2,000	4,000	6,500	—
1684	—	1,500	2,500	4,500	7,000	—
1685	—	1,500	2,500	4,500	7,000	—

KM# 109.1 THALER

Silver **Subject:** Death of Johann Friedrich **Note:** Dav. #6246.

Date	Mintage	VG	F	VF	XF	Unc
1686	—	1,500	2,500	4,250	6,800	—

KM# 109.2 THALER

Silver **Subject:** Death of Johann Friedrich **Rev. Legend:** STET. POM. VAND. I. SIL... **Note:** Dav. #6247.

Date	Mintage	VG	F	VF	XF	Unc
1686	—	1,500	2,500	4,250	6,800	—

KM# 119 THALER

Silver **Note:** Dav. #6249.

Date	Mintage	VG	F	VF	XF	Unc
1694	—	1,650	2,750	4,750	7,500	—

KM# 121 THALER

Silver **Rev:** Arms flanked by palm branches **Note:** Dav. #6251.

Date	Mintage	VG	F	VF	XF	Unc
1694 GH	—	1,750	3,000	5,000	8,500	—

KM# 122 THALER

Silver **Obv:** Bust right **Rev:** Crowned arms, date divided below **Note:** Dav. #6252.

Date	Mintage	VG	F	VF	XF	Unc
1694	—	1,750	3,000	5,000	8,500	—

KM# 120.2 THALER

Silver **Note:** Dav. #6253.

Date	Mintage	VG	F	VF	XF	Unc
1694 PHM-(a)	—	525	900	1,500	2,400	—
1695 PHM	—	525	900	1,500	2,400	—
1695 PHM-PG	—	525	900	1,500	2,400	—

KM# 120.1 THALER

Silver **Note:** Similar to KM#120.2 but without initials below bust. Dav. #6250.

Date	Mintage	VG	F	VF	XF	Unc
1694	—	825	1,350	2,250	3,750	—
1695	—	825	1,350	2,250	3,750	—

KM# 125 THALER

Silver **Obv:** Bust right **Rev:** Similar to KM#126 obverse **Note:** Dav. #6255.

Date	Mintage	VG	F	VF	XF	Unc
1696 Rare	—	—	—	—	—	—

KM# 127 THALER

Silver **Note:** Dav. #6257.

Date	Mintage	VG	F	VF	XF	Unc
1696 PHM-PG	—	1,000	2,000	3,750	6,500	—

KM# 126 THALER

Silver **Obv:** Reverse of KM#125 **Rev:** Reverse of KM#119 **Note:** Mule. Dav. #6256.

Date	Mintage	VG	F	VF	XF	Unc
1696//1694 Rare	—	—	—	—	—	—

KM# 89 2 THALER

Silver **Obv:** Helmeted ornate arms, date divided below **Rev:** Three standing figures, column at right, value on edge **Note:** Dav. #6241.

Date	Mintage	VG	F	VF	XF	Unc
1679 Rare	—	—	—	—	—	—

KM# 97 2 THALER

Silver **Obv:** Bust right **Rev:** Helmeted ornate arms, date divided below **Note:** Dav. #6244.

Date	Mintage	VG	F	VF	XF	Unc
1680 Rare	—	—	—	—	—	—

KM# 123 2 THALER

Silver **Note:** Similar to 1 Thaler, KM#119. Dav. #6248.

Date	Mintage	VG	F	VF	XF	Unc
1694 Rare	—	—	—	—	—	—

KM# 128 2 THALER

Silver **Note:** Dav. #6254.

Date	Mintage	VG	F	VF	XF	Unc
1696 PHM Rare	—	—	—	—	—	—

TRADE COINAGE

KM# 10 GOLDGULDEN

3.5000 g., 0.9860 Gold 0.1109 oz. AGW **Obv:** Facing armored half figure of Joachim Ernst

Date	Mintage	VG	F	VF	XF	Unc
1610	—	200	500	900	1,650	—
1611	—	200	500	900	1,650	—

Date	Mintage	VG	F	VF	XF	Unc
1619	—	200	500	900	1,650	2,250
1620	—	200	500	900	1,650	—
1621	—	200	500	900	1,650	—
1623	—	200	500	900	1,650	—
1624	—	200	500	900	1,650	—

KM# 75 CAROLIN

10.5000 g., 0.9860 Gold 0.3328 oz. AGW **Obv:** Bust of Johann Friedrich right in inner circle **Rev:** Arms in inner circle

Date	Mintage	VG	F	VF	XF	Unc
1672 Rare	—	—	—	—	—	—

KM# 98 1/4 DUCAT

0.8750 g., 0.9860 Gold 0.0277 oz. AGW **Rev:** Figures of Piety and Justice

Date	Mintage	VG	F	VF	XF	Unc
1680	—	100	175	300	600	—
1684	—	100	175	300	600	1,000

KM# 6 DUCAT

3.5000 g., 0.9860 Gold 0.1109 oz. AGW **Obv:** Joachim Ernst standing facing in inner circle **Rev:** Complex arms divide date in inner circle

Date	Mintage	VG	F	VF	XF	Unc
1609	—	200	325	650	1,350	—
1619	—	200	325	650	1,350	—
1620	—	200	325	650	1,350	—
1623	—	200	325	650	1,350	—
1624	—	200	325	650	1,350	—

KM# 49 DUCAT

3.5000 g., 0.9860 Gold 0.1109 oz. AGW **Obv:** Friedrich, Albrecht, and Christian

Date	Mintage	VG	F	VF	XF	Unc
1625	—	200	300	600	1,200	—
1626	—	200	300	600	1,200	—
1627	—	200	300	600	1,200	—
1628	—	200	300	600	1,200	—
1629	—	200	300	600	1,200	—
1630	—	200	300	600	1,200	—
1632	—	200	300	600	1,200	—

KM# 60 DUCAT

3.5000 g., 0.9860 Gold 0.1109 oz. AGW **Obv:** Albrecht

Date	Mintage	VG	F	VF	XF	Unc
1651	—	275	600	1,200	2,250	—
1652	—	275	600	1,200	2,250	—
1663	—	350	750	1,500	2,500	—

KM# 66 DUCAT

3.5000 g., 0.9860 Gold 0.1109 oz. AGW **Obv:** Bust of Johann Friedrich right **Rev:** Cruciform monogram

Date	Mintage	VG	F	VF	XF	Unc
1664 Rare	—	—	—	—	—	—

KM# 76.1 DUCAT

3.5000 g., 0.9860 Gold 0.1109 oz. AGW **Obv:** Johann Friedrich **Note:** Fr. #333.

Date	Mintage	VG	F	VF	XF	Unc
1672	—	750	1,650	3,200	5,500	—

KM# 76.2 DUCAT

3.5000 g., 0.9860 Gold 0.1109 oz. AGW **Obv:** Bust of Johann Friedrich right **Rev:** Ornate capped arms **Rev. Legend:** PIETATE ET IVSTITIA **Note:** Fr. #334.

Date	Mintage	VG	F	VF	XF	Unc
1680	—	700	1,450	2,500	4,750	—
1683	—	700	1,450	2,500	4,750	—

KM# 78 1-1/4 DUCAT

4.3750 g., 0.9860 Gold 0.1387 oz. AGW **Obv:** Crowned arms **Rev:** Piety and Justice standing

Date	Mintage	VG	F	VF	XF	Unc
1674	—	200	400	800	1,250	—

KM# 32 2 DUCAT

7.0000 g., 0.9860 Gold 0.2219 oz. AGW **Obv:** Joachim Ernst standing facing in inner circle **Rev:** Complex arms divide date in inner circle

Date	Mintage	VG	F	VF	XF	Unc
1622 Rare	—	—	—	—	—	—

KM# 65 2 DUCAT

7.0000 g., 0.9860 Gold 0.2219 oz. AGW **Obv:** Bust of Albrecht right in inner circle **Rev:** Arms in inner circle

Date	Mintage	VG	F	VF	XF	Unc
1660 Rare	—	—	—	—	—	—

KM# 77 2 DUCAT

7.0000 g., 0.9860 Gold 0.2219 oz. AGW **Obv:** Bust of Johann Friedrich right in inner circle

Date	Mintage	VG	F	VF	XF	Unc
1672	—	650	1,450	3,000	6,000	—
1677	—	650	1,450	3,000	6,000	—
1683	—	650	1,450	3,000	6,000	—

KM# 104 2 DUCAT

7.0000 g., 0.9860 Gold 0.2219 oz. AGW **Obv:** Crowned arms **Rev:** Piety and Justice standing

Date	Mintage	VG	F	VF	XF	Unc
1683 Rare	—	—	—	—	—	—

KM# 54 3 DUCAT

10.5000 g., 0.9860 Gold 0.3328 oz. AGW **Note:** Similar to 1 Ducat, KM#49.

Date	Mintage	VG	F	VF	XF	Unc
1630 Rare	—	—	—	—	—	—

KM# A77 3 DUCAT

10.5000 g., 0.9860 Gold 0.3328 oz. AGW

Date	Mintage	VG	F	VF	XF	Unc
1672 Rare	—	—	—	—	—	—

KM# 33 4 DUCAT

14.0000 g., 0.9860 Gold 0.4438 oz. AGW **Obv:** Joachim Ernst standing facing in inner circle **Rev:** Complex arms divide date in inner circle

Date	Mintage	VG	F	VF	XF	Unc
1622 Rare	—	—	—	—	—	—

KM# A50 4 DUCAT

14.0000 g., 0.9860 Gold 0.4438 oz. AGW **Note:** Similar to 1 Ducat, KM#49.

Date	Mintage	VG	F	VF	XF	Unc
1626 Rare	—	—	—	—	—	—
1628 Rare	—	—	—	—	—	—
1629 Rare	—	—	—	—	—	—

KM# A55 5 DUCAT (1/2 Portugalöser)

17.5000 g., 0.9860 Gold 0.5547 oz. AGW **Note:** Similar to 1 Ducat, KM#49.

Date	Mintage	VG	F	VF	XF	Unc
1631 Rare	—	—	—	—	—	—

KM# 53 6 DUCAT

21.0000 g., 0.9860 Gold 0.6657 oz. AGW **Note:** Similar to 1 Ducat, KM#49.

Date	Mintage	VG	F	VF	XF	Unc
1629 Rare	—	—	—	—	—	—

KM# 52 10 DUCAT (Portugalöser)

35.0000 g., 0.9860 Gold 1.1095 oz. AGW **Note:** Struck with 1 Thaler dies, KM#50.2.

Date	Mintage	VG	F	VF	XF	Unc
1628 Rare	—	—	—	—	—	—

PATTERNS

Including off metal strikes

KM#	Date	Mintage	Identification	Mkt Val
Pn1	1675	—	2/3 Thaler. Lead. KM#79	—

BRANDENBURG-BAYREUTH

Located in northern Bavaria. Became the property of the first Hohenzollern Elector of Brandenburg, Friedrich I. Bayreuth, passed to several individuals and became extinct in 1769 with the lands passing to Ansbach.

RULERS

Christian, 1603-1655
Christian Ernst, 1655-1712

MINT MARKS

B - Bayersdorf
(b) - Bayreuth
C,(c), (cu) - heart, (K) - Kulmbach
(cr) urn - Creussen
(d) bee - Dachsbach
(e) half-moon - Erlangen
F - Furth

MINT OFFICIALS' INITIALS

Initial	Date	Name
(ba) arrow	1622	Christoph Niedermann in Bayreuth
CA	1622	Christof Arnold in Kulmbach
CO	1613-23	Claus Oppermann in Bayreuth
CS	1622-54	Conrad Stutz, die-cutter in Furth and mintmaster of the Franconian Circle
(el) cross	1621	Johann Creitz in Hof
(er) flower	1621	Heinrich Oppermann in Hof
GFN	1682-1724	Georg Friedrich Nurnberger, die-cutter and mintmaster in Nüremberg
	1682-1710	Mintmaster of the Franconian Circle
H	1622	Michael Junghannss in Hof
HDE	1614-24	Hans David Emmert in Kulmbach
HR	1621	Hans Rentsch in Neustadt/Aisch
HR-IR	1621	Hans Rentsch and Jonas Ruedel, joint mintmasters in Kulmbach
HS	1622-23	Heinrich Straub in Nüremberg
HZ		Unknown
IAP		Unknown
ICF		Unknown
IR	1621	Jonas Ruedel in Bayreuth
L, LS	1622	Hans Luders in Pegnitz
(n) acorn	1622	Stefan Peckstein in Neustadt/Culm
(S) (s) letter s in stirrup	1622	Joachim Freundt in Schauenstein
SK		Unknown
SS	1622	Peter Steininger in Wunsiedel
VW	1622	Valentin Wolffram in Schauenstein
(w) millwheel	1622	Andreas Muller in Weissenstadt
(wu)	1622	H. Preussinger and D. Zetzner, mintmasters in Wunsiedel

DUCHY

Margraviate

REGULAR COINAGE

KM# 58 HELLER

Silver **Note:** Uniface. Four arms in cruciform, in angles value I and divided date.

Date	Mintage	VG	F	VF	XF	Unc
1637 Rare	—	—	—	—	—	—

KM# 100 HELLER

Silver **Obv:** Crowned CE monogram between branches **Rev:** Arms, date above, value in legend

Date	Mintage	VG	F	VF	XF	Unc
1693	—	9.00	16.00	33.00	60.00	—
1696	—	9.00	16.00	33.00	60.00	—
ND	—	9.00	16.00	33.00	60.00	—

KM# 108 HELLER

Silver **Obv:** Crowned CE monogram divides date **Rev:** BAY/REUTH/ER HEL/LER

Date	Mintage	VG	F	VF	XF	Unc
1697	—	9.00	16.00	33.00	60.00	—
1698	—	9.00	16.00	33.00	60.00	—

KM# 109 HELLER

Copper **Obv:** Crowned oval Hohenzollern arms in baroque frame **Rev:** 1/HEL/LER/date

Date	Mintage	VG	F	VF	XF	Unc
1698	—	9.00	16.00	33.00	60.00	—
1699	—	9.00	16.00	33.00	60.00	—
1700	—	9.00	16.00	33.00	60.00	—

KM# 44 3 HELLER (1-1/2 Pfennig)

Silver **Obv:** Eagle **Rev:** ++/III h1/date

Date	Mintage	VG	F	VF	XF	Unc
1624	—	27.00	60.00	100	140	—

KM# 19 PFENNIG

Billon **Note:** Kipper Pfennig. Two arms, date above, HZ below.

Date	Mintage	VG	F	VF	XF	Unc
1622	—	20.00	40.00	75.00	125	—

KM# 36 PFENNIG

Billon **Obv:** 3 arms, HS below **Note:** Uniface.

Date	Mintage	VG	F	VF	XF	Unc
1623	—	27.00	55.00	100	175	—

KM# 37 PFENNIG
Billon **Note:** Hohl type. Two arms, date above, HS below.

Date	Mintage	VG	F	VF	XF	Unc
1623	—	20.00	40.00	75.00	125	—

KM# 45 PFENNIG
Billon **Obv:** Three arms, date

Date	Mintage	VG	F	VF	XF	Unc
1624	—	20.00	40.00	80.00	150	—
1625	—	20.00	40.00	80.00	150	—

KM# 66 PFENNIG
Billon **Note:** Hohenzollern arms, date divided above.

Date	Mintage	VG	F	VF	XF	Unc
1650	—	13.00	27.00	45.00	90.00	—

KM# 101 PFENNIG
Billon **Obv:** Crowned and mantled arms **Rev:** Crowned eagle divides date

Date	Mintage	VG	F	VF	XF	Unc
1693	—	10.00	20.00	35.00	65.00	—

KM# 13 3 PFENNIG (Dreier)
Billon **Obv:** Eagle, value 3 on breast **Rev:** Nuremberg burgraviate arms, date above **Note:** Kipper 3 Pfennig.

Date	Mintage	VG	F	VF	XF	Unc
1621 (e)	—	—	—	—	—	—

KM# 20 3 PFENNIG (Dreier)
Billon **Obv:** Imperial orb with value 3 **Rev:** Hohenzollern arms, date in legend **Note:** Kipper 3 Pfennig.

Date	Mintage	VG	F	VF	XF	Unc
1622	—	13.00	27.00	55.00	100	—
1623	—	13.00	27.00	55.00	100	—

KM# 83 3 PFENNIG (Dreier)
Billon **Rev:** Arms

Date	Mintage	VG	F	VF	XF	Unc
1678	—	13.00	27.00	55.00	100	—
1686	—	13.00	27.00	55.00	100	—

KM# 95 6 PFENNIG
Silver **Obv:** Imperial orb with value 6 **Rev:** Arms

Date	Mintage	VG	F	VF	XF	Unc
1688	—	16.00	33.00	60.00	120	—
1689	—	16.00	33.00	60.00	120	—
1690	—	16.00	33.00	60.00	120	—
1691	—	16.00	33.00	60.00	120	—
1695	—	16.00	33.00	60.00	120	—
1696	—	16.00	33.00	60.00	120	—

KM# 22 KREUZER
Copper **Obv:** Nuremberg burgraviate arms in ornamented shield **Rev:** Value, date in four lines

Date	Mintage	VG	F	VF	XF	Unc
1622 C	—	27.00	40.00	70.00	125	—

KM# 21 KREUZER
Copper **Obv:** Eagle **Rev:** Value **Note:** Kipper Kreuzer.

Date	Mintage	VG	F	VF	XF	Unc
1622	—	—	—	—	—	—

KM# 38 KREUZER
Copper **Obv:** Eagle **Rev:** Imperial orb with value I, date

Date	Mintage	VG	F	VF	XF	Unc
1623	—	27.00	40.00	75.00	125	—

KM# 59 KREUZER
Copper **Obv:** Four arms in cruciform date **Rev:** Double cross (*)

Date	Mintage	VG	F	VF	XF	Unc
1637	—	27.00	40.00	75.00	125	—

KM# 67 KREUZER
Copper **Obv:** Hohenzollern arms **Rev:** Eagle with value 1 on breast, date

Date	Mintage	VG	F	VF	XF	Unc
1650	—	27.00	40.00	75.00	125	—

KM# 115 KREUZER
Silver **Ruler:** Christian Ernst **Obv:** Bust right **Obv. Legend:** EINEN CREVZER **Rev:** Crowned eagle, Hohenzollern arms on breast, date in legend

Date	Mintage	VG	F	VF	XF	Unc
1697	—	16.00	27.00	55.00	100	—
1700	—	13.00	25.00	45.00	100	—

KM# 46 2 KREUZER (1/2 Batzen)
Silver

Date	Mintage	VG	F	VF	XF	Unc
1624	—	10.00	20.00	30.00	50.00	—
1637	—	10.00	20.00	30.00	50.00	—
1651	—	10.00	20.00	30.00	50.00	—

KM# 56 2 KREUZER (1/2 Batzen)
Silver

Date	Mintage	VG	F	VF	XF	Unc
1631	—	13.00	27.00	40.00	65.00	—
1650	—	13.00	27.00	40.00	65.00	—

KM# 75 3 KREUZER
Silver **Obv:** Arms **Rev:** Imperial orb with value 3

Date	Mintage	VG	F	VF	XF	Unc
1662	—	15.00	30.00	55.00	90.00	—

KM# 39 4 KREUZER (Batzen)
Silver

Date	Mintage	VG	F	VF	XF	Unc
1623 (b)	—	20.00	40.00	75.00	130	—
1623 (k)	—	20.00	40.00	75.00	130	—
1624 (k)	—	20.00	40.00	75.00	130	—
1630	—	20.00	40.00	75.00	130	—
1630 F	—	20.00	40.00	75.00	130	—
1632 F	—	20.00	40.00	75.00	130	—
1633 F	—	20.00	40.00	75.00	130	—

KM# 47 4 KREUZER (Batzen)
Silver **Obv:** Arms **Rev:** Value

Date	Mintage	VG	F	VF	XF	Unc
1624	—	—	—	—	—	—

KM# 51 4 KREUZER (Batzen)
Silver **Obv:** Four arms in cruciform, date **Rev:** Crowned imperial eagle

Date	Mintage	VG	F	VF	XF	Unc
1625	—	—	—	—	—	—

KM# 10 12 KREUZER
Silver **Obv:** 4-fold arms with central shield divide C-O, date above **Rev:** Eagle, orb with 12 on breast **Note:** Kipper 12 Kreuzer.

Date	Mintage	VG	F	VF	XF	Unc
1620 CO	—	—	—	—	—	—
1620	—	—	—	—	—	—

KM# 107 15 KREUZER
Silver **Ruler:** Alexander **Obv:** Bust right, value XV below **Rev:** Crowned eagle, Hohenzollern arms on breast, neck divides date

Date	Mintage	VG	F	VF	XF	Unc
1696	—	—	—	—	—	—

KM# 11 24 KREUZER (6 Batzen)
Silver **Obv:** Arms of Nuremberg burgraviate in ornamented frame, date above **Rev:** Eagle, value (24) above **Note:** Kipper 24 Kreuzer.

Date	Mintage	VG	F	VF	XF	Unc
1620 (b)	—	80.00	125	220	325	—
1621	—	80.00	125	220	325	—

KM# 14 24 KREUZER (6 Batzen)
Silver **Note:** Varieties exist.

Date	Mintage	VG	F	VF	XF	Unc
1621 (b)	—	65.00	100	175	250	—
1621 (e)	—	65.00	100	175	250	—
1621 (el)	—	65.00	100	175	250	—
1621 (er)	—	65.00	100	175	250	—
1621 IR	—	65.00	100	175	250	—

KM# 17 24 KREUZER (6 Batzen)
Silver **Obv:** Eagle, orb with 24 on breast, tail divides date **Rev:** Similar to KM#14 **Note:** Varieties exist.

Date	Mintage	VG	F	VF	XF	Unc
1621	—	65.00	100	175	250	—
1622 (ba)	—	65.00	100	175	250	—
1622 CA	—	65.00	100	175	250	—
1622 (cu)	—	65.00	100	175	250	—
1622 H	—	65.00	100	175	250	—
1622 (w)	—	65.00	100	175	250	—
ND	—	65.00	100	175	250	—
ND (d)	—	65.00	100	175	250	—
ND (e)	—	65.00	100	175	250	—
ND (w)	—	65.00	100	175	250	—

KM# 15 24 KREUZER (6 Batzen)
Silver **Obv:** Eagle **Rev:** Date divided above arms **Note:** Varieties exist.

Date	Mintage	VG	F	VF	XF	Unc
1621 HR	—	85.00	140	225	350	—

KM# 16 24 KREUZER (6 Batzen)
Silver **Obv:** 4-fold arms, date above **Rev:** Eagle, orb with 24 on breast

Date	Mintage	VG	F	VF	XF	Unc
1621 (c)	—	80.00	135	200	300	—
1621 HR-IR	—	80.00	135	200	300	—

KM# 24 24 KREUZER (6 Batzen)
Silver **Obv:** Bust right, date in legend **Rev:** Eagle, orb with 24 on breast

Date	Mintage	VG	F	VF	XF	Unc
1622 (cr)	—	85.00	140	225	350	—

KM# 25 24 KREUZER (6 Batzen)
Silver **Rev:** Date in legend

Date	Mintage	VG	F	VF	XF	Unc
1622	—	65.00	100	165	250	—

KM# 26 24 KREUZER (6 Batzen)
Silver **Rev:** Eagle's tail divides date

Date	Mintage	VG	F	VF	XF	Unc
1622 (e)	—	85.00	140	225	350	—

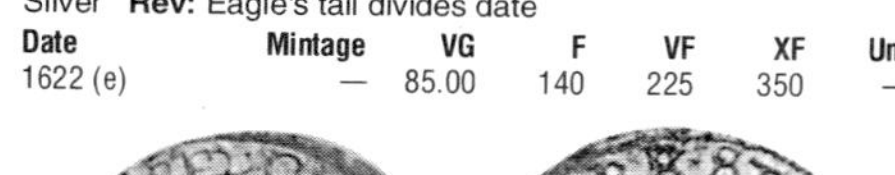

KM# 27 24 KREUZER (6 Batzen)
Silver **Obv:** Ealge, orb with 24 on breast, tail divides date **Rev:** Arms of Nuremberg burgraviate in ornamented frame

Date	Mintage	VG	F	VF	XF	Unc
1622 (n)	—	65.00	100	165	250	—

KM# 28 24 KREUZER (6 Batzen)
Silver **Obv:** Ealge, orb with 24 on breast **Rev:** Oval arms of Nuremberg in baroque frame, date divided above

Date	Mintage	VG	F	VF	XF	Unc
1622 L	—	75.00	125	190	275	—
1622 LS	—	75.00	125	190	275	—
ND (S)	—	75.00	125	190	275	—

KM# 29 24 KREUZER (6 Batzen)
Silver **Obv:** Date in legend **Rev:** Arms of Nuremberg burgraviate in ornamented frame

Date	Mintage	VG	F	VF	XF	Unc
1622	—	100	200	375	625	—
ND (S)	—	100	200	375	625	—

KM# 30 24 KREUZER (6 Batzen)
Silver **Obv:** Oval arms of Nuremberg in baroque frame, date in legend **Rev:** Eagle, orb with 24 on breast

Date	Mintage	VG	F	VF	XF	Unc
1622 VW-(s)	—	75.00	125	190	275	—
1622 (S)	—	75.00	125	190	275	—
1622 SS	—	75.00	125	190	275	—

KM# 31 24 KREUZER (6 Batzen)
Silver **Obv:** Eagle, orb with 24 on breast, tail divides date **Rev:** Arms of Nuremberg burgraviate in ornamented frame

Date	Mintage	VG	F	VF	XF	Unc
1622 (wu)	—	80.00	120	200	300	—

KM# 32 24 KREUZER (6 Batzen)
Silver **Rev:** Tail of eagle divides date, orb with 24 on breast

Date	Mintage	VG	F	VF	XF	Unc
1622	—	80.00	120	200	300	—

KM# 23 24 KREUZER (6 Batzen)
Silver **Note:** Klippe.

Date	Mintage	VG	F	VF	XF	Unc
1622 (w)	—	100	200	375	625	—

KM# A29 24 KREUZER (6 Batzen)
Silver **Ruler:** Christian **Obv:** Displayed eagle, '24' in orb on breast, mint symbol at top in margin **Obv. Legend:** CHRISTIAN • D.G. MAR • BRAN • PRVSSI • **Rev:** Arms of Nuremberg burgraviate in baroque frame, date at end of legend **Rev. Legend:** ST•PO•CA•V•CR•IAD• BVRG:I•NV• P.R. **Mint:** Schauenstein **Note:** Klipper coinage.

Date	Mintage	F	VF	XF	Unc	BU
16ZZ (s)	—	—	—	—	—	—

KM# 48 SCHILLING (1/28 Gulden)
Silver **Obv:** Four arms in cruciform date **Rev:** Crowned imperial eagle, value 28 in orb on breast

Date	Mintage	VG	F	VF	XF	Unc
1624 Rare	—	—	—	—	—	—

KM# 69 GROSCHEN (1/24 Thaler)
Silver **Subject:** Death of Christian **Obv:** Bust right **Rev:** Inscription with date **Note:** Kipper Groschen.

Date	Mintage	VG	F	VF	XF	Unc
1655	—	40.00	85.00	150	220	—

KM# 81 GROSCHEN (1/24 Thaler)
Silver **Obv:** Bust right **Rev:** Arms

Date	Mintage	VG	F	VF	XF	Unc
1676	—	—	—	—	—	—

KM# 34 1/24 THALER (Groschen)
Silver **Rev:** Nuremberg burgraviatre arms **Note:** Large module.

Date	Mintage	VG	F	VF	XF	Unc
ND(1622)	—	—	—	—	—	—

KM# 35 1/24 THALER (Groschen)
Silver **Note:** Similar to KM#33.

Date	Mintage	VG	F	VF	XF	Unc
1622	—	11.00	25.00	40.00	75.00	—
1623	—	11.00	25.00	40.00	75.00	—
1624	—	11.00	25.00	40.00	75.00	—
1650	—	11.00	25.00	40.00	75.00	—

KM# 33 1/24 THALER (Groschen)
Silver **Obv:** Imperial orb with value 24 **Rev:** Hohenzollern arms, date **Note:** small module.

Date	Mintage	VG	F	VF	XF	Unc
1622	—	13.00	27.00	45.00	80.00	—

KM# 90 1/24 THALER (Groschen)
Silver **Ruler:** Alexander **Obv:** Orb with value within inner circle, legend surrounds **Rev:** Eagle with shield on breast within inner circle **Note:** Similar to KM#125.

Date	Mintage	VG	F	VF	XF	Unc
1680	—	13.00	27.00	50.00	100	—
1684	—	13.00	27.00	50.00	100	—
1695	—	13.00	27.00	50.00	100	—
1696	—	13.00	27.00	50.00	100	—

KM# 91 1/12 THALER (2 Groschen)
Silver **Obv:** Imperial orb with value 12 **Rev:** Crowned arms

Date	Mintage	VG	F	VF	XF	Unc
1680	—	16.00	33.00	60.00	100	—
1685	—	16.00	33.00	60.00	100	—

KM# 103 1/12 THALER (2 Groschen)
Silver **Ruler:** Christian Ernst **Obv:** Crowned two oval arms in baroque frame **Rev:** 12/EINEN/THAL/ date

Date	Mintage	VG	F	VF	XF	Unc
1695	—	16.00	33.00	60.00	100	—
1696	—	16.00	33.00	60.00	100	—

KM# 70 1/4 THALER
Silver **Subject:** Death of Christian

Date	Mintage	VG	F	VF	XF	Unc
1655	—	250	400	800	1,200	—

KM# 104 1/4 THALER
Silver **Obv:** Bust right **Rev:** Crowned oval arms in baroque frame divide date, value 1/4 below

Date	Mintage	VG	F	VF	XF	Unc
1695 IAP	—	—	—	—	—	—

KM# 49 1/2 THALER
Silver

Date	Mintage	VG	F	VF	XF	Unc
1624 HDE	—	—	—	—	—	—
1624/7	—	—	—	—	—	—

KM# 93 1/2 THALER
Silver **Obv:** Bust right **Rev:** Crowned oval arms between two branches, date below

Date	Mintage	VG	F	VF	XF	Unc
1683	—	—	—	—	—	—

KM# 5 2/3 THALER (Gulden)
Silver **Obv:** Bust right, small Nuremberg burgraviate arms below **Rev:** Oval arms divide date **Note:** Dav. #6258.

Date	Mintage	VG	F	VF	XF	Unc
1609	—	800	1,250	2,400	3,500	—

KM# 12 2/3 THALER (Gulden)
Silver **Rev:** Date in legend **Note:** Klippe. Dav. #6259.

Date	Mintage	VG	F	VF	XF	Unc
1620 Rare	—	—	—	—	—	—

KM# 18 2/3 THALER (Gulden)
Silver **Obv:** Date in legend **Rev:** Helmeted arms **Note:** Dav. #6260.

Date	Mintage	VG	F	VF	XF	Unc
1621 CO	—	800	1,250	2,400	3,500	—

KM# 40 2/3 THALER (Gulden)
Silver **Obv:** Margrave on horse rearing right **Rev:** Oval 4-fold arms with central shield divides date **Note:** Dav. #6261.

Date	Mintage	VG	F	VF	XF	Unc
1623 CO Rare	—	—	—	—	—	—

KM# 41 2/3 THALER (Gulden)
Silver **Obv:** Similar to KM#42 **Rev:** Arms, date above **Rev. Legend:** VA. CR. I. DUX. BUR. IN. NUR. **Note:** Dav. #6262.

Date	Mintage	VG	F	VF	XF	Unc
1623 HS Rare	—	—	—	—	—	—

KM# 42.1 2/3 THALER (Gulden)
Silver **Note:** Dav. #6263.

Date	Mintage	VG	F	VF	XF	Unc
1623 Rare	—	—	—	—	—	—

KM# 42.2 2/3 THALER (Gulden)
Silver **Note:** Dav. #6265.

Date	Mintage	VG	F	VF	XF	Unc
1623 HDE	—	325	575	950	1,400	—
1624 HDE	—	325	575	950	1,400	—

KM# 50 2/3 THALER (Gulden)
Silver **Obv:** Bust right, small Nuremberg burgraviate arms below **Rev:** Helmeted complex arms in baroque frame, date in legend **Note:** Dav. #6266.

Date	Mintage	VG	F	VF	XF	Unc
1624 CS	—	325	575	950	1,400	—

KM# 52.1 2/3 THALER (Gulden)
Silver **Obv. Legend:** CHRISTIAN... **Rev:** Similar to KM#42, but date in legend **Note:** Dav. #6267.

Date	Mintage	VG	F	VF	XF	Unc
1627	—	325	575	950	1,400	—
1630	—	325	575	950	1,400	—

KM# 53 2/3 THALER (Gulden)
Silver **Obv:** Bust right, small arms below **Obv. Legend:** CHRISTIANUS... **Rev:** Date divided by lower part of shield **Note:** Dav. #6268.

Date	Mintage	VG	F	VF	XF	Unc
1628	—	325	575	950	1,400	—
1629	—	325	575	950	1,400	—

KM# 55 2/3 THALER (Gulden)
Silver **Obv:** Bust 3/4 rigjt, small shield below **Rev:** Similar to KM#42 but date in reverse legend **Note:** Dav. #6269.

Date	Mintage	VG	F	VF	XF	Unc
1630 Rare	—	—	—	—	—	—

KM# 52.2 2/3 THALER (Gulden)
Silver **Rev:** Date above helmets **Note:** Dav. #6267A.

Date	Mintage	VG	F	VF	XF	Unc
1636	—	325	575	950	1,400	—
1638	—	325	575	950	1,400	—
1641	—	325	575	950	1,400	—
1644	—	325	575	950	1,400	—

KM# 71 2/3 THALER (Gulden)
Silver **Subject:** Death of Christian **Note:** Dav. #6270.

Date	Mintage	VG	F	VF	XF	Unc
1655	—	650	1,150	1,800	3,000	—

KM# 77 2/3 THALER (Gulden)
Silver **Note:** Dav. #6271.

Date	Mintage	VG	F	VF	XF	Unc
1662	—	500	750	1,250	2,000	—

KM# 78 2/3 THALER (Gulden)
Silver **Subject:** Election of Christian Ernst as Captain of Franconian Circle **Note:** Dav. #6272.

Date	Mintage	VG	F	VF	XF	Unc
1664	—	400	700	1,100	1,900	3,000

KM# 80 2/3 THALER (Gulden)
Silver **Subject:** Marriage of Christian Ernst to Sophie Luisa von Wurttemberg **Note:** Dav. #6273.

Date	Mintage	F	VF	XF	Unc	BU
1671	—	525	800	1,500	2,500	—

KM# 82 2/3 THALER (Gulden)
Silver

Date	Mintage	VG	F	VF	XF	Unc
1677	—	—	—	—	—	—

KM# 84 2/3 THALER (Gulden)
Silver **Subject:** Christian Ernst's Name Day **Note:** Dav. #6274.

Date	Mintage	F	VF	XF	Unc	BU
1679 Rare	—	—	—	—	—	—

KM# 85 2/3 THALER (Gulden)
Silver **Subject:** Birth of Prince Georg Wilhelm **Note:** Dav. #6275.

Date	Mintage	F	VF	XF	Unc	BU
1679 Rare	—	—	—	—	—	—

KM# 87 2/3 THALER (Gulden)
Silver **Rev:** Without four words next to tree **Note:** Dav. #6276A.

Date	Mintage	F	VF	XF	Unc	BU
1679	—	600	1,000	1,800	2,800	—

KM# 86 2/3 THALER (Gulden)
Silver **Subject:** Pregnancy of Sophie Luisa **Obv:** Crowned column in garden **Rev:** Palm tree, sun above, crowned hearts on either side, date **Note:** Dav. #6276.

Date	Mintage	VG	F	VF	XF	Unc
1679	—	—	600	1,000	1,800	2,800

KM# 92 2/3 THALER (Gulden)
Silver **Note:** Dav. #6277.

Date	Mintage	VG	F	VF	XF	Unc
1680 Rare	—	—	—	—	—	—
1681 Rare	—	—	—	—	—	—
1683 Rare	—	—	—	—	—	—

KM# 102 2/3 THALER (Gulden)
Silver **Obv:** Bust right **Rev:** Helmeted arms between crossed palm branches, date in legend **Note:** Dav. #6278.

Date	Mintage	VG	F	VF	XF	Unc
1693 ICF Rare	—	—	—	—	—	—

KM# 105 2/3 THALER (Gulden)
Silver **Note:** Similar to KM#102 but date and IAP below crossed palm branches. Dav. #6279.

Date	Mintage	VG	F	VF	XF	Unc
1695 IAP Rare	—	—	—	—	—	—

KM# 43 2 THALER
Silver **Note:** Similar to 1 Thaler, KM#42. Dav. #6264.

Date	Mintage	VG	F	VF	XF	Unc
1623 HDE Rare	—	—	—	—	—	—
1624 HDE Rare	—	—	—	—	—	—

TRADE COINAGE

KM# 94 1/2 DUCAT
1.7500 g., 0.9860 Gold 0.0555 oz. AGW **Obv:** Bust of Christian Ernst right **Rev:** Arms

Date	Mintage	VG	F	VF	XF	Unc
1685	—	200	400	850	1,450	—

KM# 6 DUCAT

3.5000 g., 0.9860 Gold 0.1109 oz. AGW **Obv:** Christian standing in inner circle **Rev:** Arms in inner circle

Date	Mintage	VG	F	VF	XF	Unc
1609	—	175	325	750	1,200	—
1628	—	175	325	750	1,200	—
1629	—	175	325	750	1,200	—
1630	—	175	325	750	1,200	—
1631	—	175	325	750	1,200	—
1632	—	175	325	750	1,200	—

KM# 57 DUCAT

3.5000 g., 0.9860 Gold 0.1109 oz. AGW **Obv:** Bust of Christian right **Rev:** Arms in inner circle, date divided at top of arms

Date	Mintage	VG	F	VF	XF	Unc
1631	—	150	300	650	1,000	—
1641	—	150	300	650	1,000	—
1642	—	150	300	650	1,000	—
1644	—	150	300	650	1,000	—
ND	—	150	300	650	1,000	—

KM# 68 DUCAT

3.5000 g., 0.9860 Gold 0.1109 oz. AGW **Subject:** 50th Year of Reign

Date	Mintage	VG	F	VF	XF	Unc
1653 Rare	—	—	—	—	—	—

KM# 72 DUCAT

3.5000 g., 0.9860 Gold 0.1109 oz. AGW **Ruler:** Christian Ernst **Obv:** Bust right **Rev:** Arms in inner circle

Date	Mintage	VG	F	VF	XF	Unc
1659	—	200	450	900	1,500	—
1662	—	200	450	900	1,500	—
1677	—	200	450	900	1,500	—
1694	—	200	450	900	1,500	—

KM# 7 2 DUCAT

7.0000 g., 0.9860 Gold 0.2219 oz. AGW **Obv:** Christian standing in inner circle **Rev:** Arms in inner circle

Date	Mintage	VG	F	VF	XF	Unc
1609	—	1,200	2,400	4,200	6,750	—

KM# 106 2 DUCAT

7.0000 g., 0.9860 Gold 0.2219 oz. AGW **Obv:** Conjoined busts of Christian Ernst and Louisa right, date below **Rev:** View of Cronach mine with sun chariot in sky above

Date	Mintage	VG	F	VF	XF	Unc
1695 Rare	—	—	—	—	—	—

KM# 8 4 DUCAT

14.0000 g., 0.9860 Gold 0.4438 oz. AGW **Obv:** Christian standing in inner circle **Rev:** Arms in inner circle

Date	Mintage	VG	F	VF	XF	Unc
1609	—	2,500	4,500	6,500	10,000	—

KM# A81 5 DUCAT (1/2 Portugalöser)

17.5000 g., 0.9860 Gold 0.5547 oz. AGW **Subject:** Marriage of Christian Ernst to Sophia Luisa von Wurttemberg **Note:** Similar to 1 Thaler, KM#80.

Date	Mintage	VG	F	VF	XF	Unc
1671 Rare	—	—	—	—	—	—

KM# A79 6 DUCAT

21.0000 g., 0.9860 Gold 0.6657 oz. AGW **Subject:** Election of Christian Ernst as Captain of Franconian Circle **Note:** Similar to 1 Thaler, KM#78.

Date	Mintage	VG	F	VF	XF	Unc
1664 Rare	—	—	—	—	—	—

KM# A72 8 DUCAT

28.0000 g., 0.9860 Gold 0.8876 oz. AGW **Subject:** Death of Christian **Note:** Struck with 1 Thaler dies, KM#71.

Date	Mintage	VG	F	VF	XF	Unc
1655 Rare	—	—	—	—	—	—

KM# A56 10 DUCAT (Portugalöser)

35.0000 g., 0.9860 Gold 1.1095 oz. AGW **Note:** Struck with 1 Thaler dies, KM#55.

Date	Mintage	VG	F	VF	XF	Unc
1630 Rare	—	—	—	—	—	—

PATTERNS

Including off metal strikes

KM#	Date	Mintage	Identification	Mkt Val
Pn1	1630	—	4 Kreuzer. Tin. KM#39	—
Pn2	1676	—	Groschen. Lead. KM#81	—
Pn3	1691	—	6 Pfennig. Copper. KM#95	—

BRANDENBURG-FRANCONIA

(Brandenburg in Franken)

The Hohenzollerns of Swabia established their power as Burgraves of Nürnberg in the early 13th century. They soon acquired first Ansbach, then Bayreuth through marriage, becoming the most influential family in East Franconia, territories which extended from southwest to northeast between Swabia and Meissen. Various sons of the Brandenburg electors ruled portions of the Franconian holdings during the 15th century. Friedrich I, the younger brother of Elector Johann II Cicero (1486-99) established a permanent presence in Franconia in the late 15th century, becoming sole ruler there when Sigmund of Bayreuth and Kulmbach died in 1495. Friedrich I's descendants ruled jointly or separately during all of the 16th century, as well as supplying the Dukes of Prussia for much of the same period. When Friedrich I's grandson, Georg Friedrich, died childless in 1603, two younger sons of Elector Johann Georg were sent to rule as Margraves of Brandenburg-Ansbach and Brandenburg-Bayreuth. Georg Friedrich was Duke of Jägerndorf from 1543 and Administrator of Prussia from 1578. Coinage in his name for those places are listed therein.

RULERS

Georg Friedrich I, 1543-1603

DISTRICT

REGULAR COINAGE

KM# 5 1/8 THALER

Silver **Subject:** Death of Georg Friedrich I **Obv:** Half-length armored figure to right, titles of Georg Friedrich I **Rev:** Five-line inscription with date, IST GOTT MIT VNS... **Mint:** Nurnberg

Date	Mintage	VG	F	VF	XF	Unc
1603	—	100	175	300	500	—

KM# 16 1/8 THALER

Silver **Subject:** Death of Georg Friedrich I's Wife, Sophia of Brunswick-Lüneburg **Obv:** Two adjacent oval shields of arms, four-fold of Brandenburg on left, five-fold of Brunswick on right, crown above, titles of Sophia **Rev:** Ten-line inscription with dates **Mint:** Nurnberg

Date	Mintage	VG	F	VF	XF	Unc
1639	—	—	—	—	—	—

KM# 6 1/4 THALER

Silver **Subject:** Death of Georg Friedrich I **Obv:** Similar to MB#42 **Rev:** Five-line inscription with dates, IST GOTT MIT VNS... **Mint:** Nurnberg

Date	Mintage	VG	F	VF	XF	Unc
1603	—	—	250	350	450	—

KM# 7 1/2 THALER

Silver **Subject:** Death of Georg Friedrich I **Obv:** Similar to 1/4 Thaler, KM#6 **Rev:** Seven-line inscription with dates **Mint:** Nurnberg

Date	Mintage	VG	F	VF	XF	Unc
1603	—	—	—	—	—	—

KM# 17 1/2 THALER

Silver **Subject:** Death of Georg Friedrich I's Wife, Sophia of Brunswick-Lüneburg **Obv:** Similar to 1/8 Thaler, KM#6 **Mint:** Nurnberg

Date	Mintage	VG	F	VF	XF	Unc
1639	—	—	—	—	—	—

KM# 8 THALER

Silver **Subject:** Death of Georg Friedrich **Obv:** Half figure right **Rev:** Seven-line inscription **Note:** Dav.#6224.

Date	Mintage	VG	F	VF	XF	Unc
1603	—	575	950	1,550	2,500	—

KM# 18 THALER

Silver **Subject:** Death of Georg Friedrich I's Wife, Sophia of Brunswick-Lüneburg **Obv:** Similar to 1/8 Thaler, KM#16 **Mint:** Schwabach

Date	Mintage	VG	F	VF	XF	Unc
1639	—	—	—	—	—	—

KM# 9 2 THALER

Silver **Subject:** Death of Georg Friedrich **Note:** Similar to 1 Thaler, KM#8. Dav.#6223.

Date	Mintage	VG	F	VF	XF	Unc
1603 Rare	—	—	—	—	—	—

JOINT COINAGE

KM# 12 THALER

Silver **Obv:** Facing busts of Christian and Joachim, date below **Rev:** Oval arms **Note:** Dav.#6225.

Date	Mintage	VG	F	VF	XF	Unc
1609	—	650	1,150	1,850	3,000	—

TRADE COINAGE

KM# 19 2 DUCAT

7.0000 g., 0.9860 Gold 0.2219 oz. AGW **Subject:** Death of Georg Friedrich I's Wife, Sophia of Brunswick-Lüneburg **Note:** Struck with 1/2 Thaler dies, KM#16.

Date	Mintage	VG	F	VF	XF	Unc
1639	—	—	—	—	—	—

KM# 13 10 DUCAT (Portugalöser)

35.0000 g., 0.9860 Gold 1.1095 oz. AGW **Note:** Struck with 1 Thaler dies, KM#12. Fr. #316.

Date	Mintage	VG	F	VF	XF	Unc
1609 Rare	—	—	—	—	—	—

BREISACH

(Breysach, Brisach)

The city of Breisach, located on the Rhine about 12.5 miles (21km) west-northwest of Freiburg, has been an inhabited place since ancient times. It was a Roman fortified town and was of such importance that the surrounding territory became known as the Breisgau. Acquired by Emperor Otto I in 939, Breisach was later the site of an imperial mint and became an imperial town in 1275. Breisach issued its own coinage from about the mid-14th until the late 16th centuries. However, a series of emergency coins were struck during the Thirty Years' War, when the imperial garrison was besieged by the Swedish army in 1633. The French ended up in possession of Breisach at the end of the war in 1648 and it was taken and retaken by them all during the latter half of the 17th century. The city was reunited to the Empire in 1697 and so remained until 1801, when Breisach and all of the Breisgau were acquired by the Duke of Modena. Breisach finally passed to Baden in 1805.

ARMS

Six hills arranged in two rows of three each, one behind the other, sometimes with cross above.

REFERENCES

S = Hugo Frhr. Von Saurma-Jeltsch, ***Die Saurmasche Münzsammlung deutscher, schweizerischer und polnischer Gepräge von etwa dem Beginn der Groschenzeit bis zur Kipperperiode***, Berlin, 1892.

Sch = Wolfgang Schulten, ***Deutsche Münzen aus der Zeit Karls V.***, Frankfurt am Main, 1974.

CITY

SIEGE COINAGE

1633

KM# 1 KREUZER

3.6200 g., Silver **Note:** Klippe.

Date	Mintage	VG	F	VF	XF	Unc
1633	—	140	275	400	750	—

KM# 2 24 KREUZER (Sechsbätzner)

8.0000 g., Silver **Rev:** Date above 3 shields, lower shield divides value: XX-IIII **Note:** Klippe.

Date	Mintage	VG	F	VF	XF	Unc
1633	—	250	375	550	900	—

KM# 3.1 48 KREUZER (Zwolfbätzner)

16.4000 g., Silver **Rev:** Date above 3 shields, lower shield divides value: XL-VIII **Note:** Klippe.

Date	Mintage	VG	F	VF	XF	Unc
1633	—	250	375	600	1,000	—

KM# 3.2 48 KREUZER (Zwolfbätzner)

16.4000 g., Silver **Obv:** Legend **Rev:** Date above three ornate arms

Date	Mintage	F	VF	XF	Unc	BU
1633	—	375	600	1,000	—	—

KM# 5 THALER

Silver **Note:** Klippe.

Date	Mintage	VG	F	VF	XF	Unc
1633	—	275	425	750	1,150	—

KM# 4 DUCAT

3.5000 g., 0.9860 Gold 0.1109 oz. AGW **Note:** Klippe.

Date	Mintage	VG	F	VF	XF	Unc
1633	—	2,000	3,500	5,000	7,500	—

TRADE COINAGE

KM# 6 DUCAT

3.5000 g., 0.9860 Gold 0.1109 oz. AGW **Subject:** Capitulation of City to French and Protestant Forces **Obv:** City arms **Rev:** 6-line inscription with date

Date	Mintage	VG	F	VF	XF	Unc
1638	—	3,000	5,000	7,000	10,000	—

BREMEN

ARCHBISHOPRIC

A bishopric was established at the present site of Bremen by St. Wilhad in 787. When the Norse destroyed Hamburg in 848, the archbishop of that city transferred his see to Bremen. Eventually, the connection between the two waned and Bremen remained the seat of an archbishop, which obtained the mint right as early as 888. during the 11th century, this right was extended to allow mints to be established in various towns under Bremen's control. The Protestant Reformation overtook Bremen in 1522, although Catholic episcopal princes attempted to maintain Rome's influence there. At the start of the Thirty Years' War in 1618, however, Protestantism was firmly entrenched in Bremen. The last archbishop was driven from his see by the Swedes in 1644 and Bremen was joined to Verden as a secular duchy (see Bremen and Verden). This arrangement was confirmed by the Peace of Westphalia in 1648.

RULERS

Johann III Rode von Wale, 1496-1511
Christoph, Herzog von Braunschweig-Lüneburg, 1511-1558, Administrator, 1511-1514
Georg, Herzog von Braunschweig-Lüneburg, 1558-1566
Heinrich III, Herzog von Sachsen-Lauenburg, 1567-1585
Johann Adolf, Herzog von Holstein-Gottorp, 1585-1596
Johann Friedrich, Herzog von Holstein-Gottorp, 1585-1634
Friedrich II, Prince of Denmark, 1634-44 (1648)

MINT MASTERS' INITIALS

Initial	Date	Name
HR	1615-18	Hans Rücke
PT	1641-43	Peter Timpf

ARMS

Key at angle to upper left or right, sometimes 2 crossed keys (representing dual sees of Bremen and Hamburg.

TRADE COINAGE

KM# 21 GOLDGULDEN

3.5000 g., 0.9860 Gold 0.1109 oz. AGW **Ruler:** Johann Friedrich of Holstein-Gottorp **Obv:** Arms topped by 3 helmets **Rev:** St. Peter standing holding key and book, date in exergue

Date	Mintage	VG	F	VF	XF	Unc
1612	—	1,500	2,500	3,500	5,500	—

KM# 23 GOLDGULDEN

3.5000 g., 0.9860 Gold 0.1109 oz. AGW **Ruler:** Johann Friedrich of Holstein-Gottorp **Obv:** Arms of Holstein joined with those of Bremen

Date	Mintage	VG	F	VF	XF	Unc
1618	—	1,500	2,500	3,500	5,500	—

KM# 10 10 DUCAT (Portugalöser)

Gold **Obv:** Bust right, margin of 8 small oval arms **Rev:** Cross in center, 3 circular legends

Date	Mintage	VG	F	VF	XF	Unc
ND Rare	—	—	—	—	—	—

FREE CITY

Established at about the same time as the bishopric in 787, Bremen was under the control of the bishops and archbishops until joining the Hanseatic League in 1276. Archbishop Albrecht II granted the mint right to the city in 1369, but this was not formalized by imperial decree until 1541. In 1646, Bremen was raised to free imperial status and continued to strike its own coins into the early 20th century. The city lost its free imperial status in 1803 and was controlled by France from 1806 until 1813. Regaining it independence in 1815, Bremen joined the North German Confederation in 1867 and the German Empire in 1871. Since 1369, there was practically continuous coinage until 1907.

MINT OFFICIALS' INITIALS

Initial or marks	Date	Name
	1572-1604	Alrich Koldewehr
	1603-28	Heinrich (Johann?) Klamp, warden
	1613-16	Ippo Ritzema
	1617-24	Johann Wientjes
	1624-34	Gerhard (Gerdt) Dreyer
	1634-69	Thomas Isenbein
	1634	Johann Caulitz, warden
	1674-84	Ernst Krulle, warden and mintmaster
	1687-97	Otto Krulle

ARMS

Key, often in shield

REGULAR COINAGE

KM# 145 SCHWAREN

Billon **Obv:** Key in circle **Rev:** St. Peter in circle

Date	Mintage	VG	F	VF	XF	Unc
ND(1671) HL	103,000	33.00	60.00	125	175	—

KM# 151 SCHWAREN

Billon **Obv:** Key divides date in circle

Date	Mintage	VG	F	VF	XF	Unc
1676	143,000	20.00	33.00	60.00	125	—

KM# 155 SCHWAREN

Billon **Obv:** Key with date in legend **Rev:** St. Peter in circle

Date	Mintage	VG	F	VF	XF	Unc
1687	144,000	10.00	20.00	35.00	85.00	—
1690	—	10.00	20.00	35.00	85.00	—
1697	180,000	10.00	20.00	35.00	85.00	—

KM# 50 1/2 GROTE

Billon **Obv:** Key in shield in circle **Rev:** Cross in circle

Date	Mintage	VG	F	VF	XF	Unc
ND(ca.1602-13)	—	16.00	33.00	60.00	120	—

KM# 82 1/2 GROTE

Billon **Obv:** Key in circle

Date	Mintage	VG	F	VF	XF	Unc
ND(ca.1624-34)	36,000	13.00	27.00	45.00	90.00	—

KM# 100.1 1/2 GROTE

Billon **Obv:** Key divides date in circle **Rev:** Cross in circle **Note:** Varieties exist.

Date	Mintage	VG	F	VF	XF	Unc
1640	90,000	10.00	20.00	33.00	60.00	—
1659	17,000	10.00	20.00	33.00	60.00	—
1672	—	10.00	20.00	33.00	60.00	—
1688	—	10.00	20.00	33.00	60.00	—

KM# 64 GROTEN

Silver **Obv:** Key in shield within pointed trilobe, date in legend **Rev:** Imperial eagle, titles of Matthias

Date	Mintage	VG	F	VF	XF	Unc
1614	—	—	—	—	—	—

KM# 78 GROTEN

Silver **Obv:** Imperial eagle, titles of Ferdinand II **Rev:** Key in shield in circle, date in legend

Date	Mintage	VG	F	VF	XF	Unc
1623	2,448,000	10.00	20.00	33.00	75.00	—
1626	—	10.00	20.00	33.00	75.00	—
1627	—	10.00	20.00	33.00	75.00	—

KM# 150 GROTEN

Silver **Obv:** Crowned imperial eagle, titles of Leopold

Date	Mintage	VG	F	VF	XF	Unc
1674	376,000	16.00	33.00	60.00	120	—

KM# 53 2 GROTE / 1/27 THALER

Silver **Obv:** Arms in ornamented oval shield, date in legend **Rev:** Crowned imperial eagle, 27 on breast, titles of Rudolf II

Date	Mintage	VG	F	VF	XF	Unc
1603	—	—	—	—	—	—

KM# 86 2 GROTE / 1/27 THALER

Silver **Obv:** Imperial eagle, titles of Ferdinand II **Rev:** Key in circle, date in legend

Date	Mintage	VG	F	VF	XF	Unc
1625	—	—	—	—	—	—

KM# 106 2 GROTE / 1/36 THALER

Silver **Obv:** Key divides date in circle, 2 in circle in legend **Rev:** Imperial eagle, 36 in circle above

Date	Mintage	VG	F	VF	XF	Unc
1641	114,000	12.00	25.00	45.00	90.00	—
1642	86,000	12.00	25.00	45.00	90.00	—
1646	290,000	12.00	25.00	45.00	90.00	—

KM# 110 2 GROTE / 1/36 THALER

Silver **Rev:** 36 not in circle above

Date	Mintage	VG	F	VF	XF	Unc
1646	Inc. above	12.00	25.00	45.00	90.00	—

KM# 130 2 GROTE / 1/36 THALER

Silver **Obv:** Key divides date in circle **Rev:** Crowned imperial eagle, 36 on breast, titles of Leopold

Date	Mintage	VG	F	VF	XF	Unc
1660	—	13.00	27.00	45.00	90.00	—
1671	199,000	13.00	27.00	45.00	90.00	—

KM# 54 3 GROTE / 1/18 THALER (2 Schilling)

Silver **Obv:** Arms in ornamented oval shield, date in legend **Rev:** Crowned imperial eagle, 18 on breast, titles of Rudolf II

Date	Mintage	VG	F	VF	XF	Unc
1603	—	—	—	—	—	—
1608	—	—	—	—	—	—

KM# 65 3 GROTE / 1/18 THALER (2 Schilling)

Silver **Rev:** Titles of Matthias

Date	Mintage	VG	F	VF	XF	Unc
1614	—	33.00	55.00	100	175	—
1615	—	33.00	55.00	100	175	—

KM# 88 3 GROTE / 1/24 THALER

Silver **Obv:** Arms, date divided partly inside and outside shield **Rev:** Crowned imperial eagle, 24 in orb on breast, titles of Ferdinand II

Date	Mintage	VG	F	VF	XF	Unc
1629	—	25.00	40.00	80.00	140	—

KM# 90 3 GROTE / 1/24 THALER

Silver **Obv:** Without value in orb **Rev:** Arms divide date in ornamented shield

Date	Mintage	VG	F	VF	XF	Unc
1634	61,000	10.00	20.00	40.00	85.00	—
1635	90,000	10.00	20.00	40.00	85.00	—
1636	101,000	10.00	20.00	40.00	85.00	—
1637	101,000	10.00	20.00	40.00	85.00	—

KM# 147 3 GROTE / 1/24 THALER

Silver **Obv:** Crowned arms in baroque shield divide date, value III GROT below **Rev:** Crowned imperial eagle, 24 in orb on breast, titles of Leopold

Date	Mintage	VG	F	VF	XF	Unc
1672 HL	—	13.00	27.00	55.00	110	—

KM# 108 4 GROTE (Flinderken)

Silver **Rev:** Crowned imperial eagle, titles of Ferdinand III

Date	Mintage	VG	F	VF	XF	Unc
1646	48,000	13.00	27.00	60.00	120	—
1647	12,000	13.00	27.00	60.00	120	—
1649	197,000	13.00	27.00	60.00	120	—

KM# 131 4 GROTE (Flinderken)

Silver **Rev:** Crowned imperial eagle, titles of Leopold

Date	Mintage	VG	F	VF	XF	Unc
1660	66,000	12.00	25.00	45.00	100	—

KM# 146 4 GROTE (Flinderken)

Silver **Rev:** 18 in orb on breast

Date	Mintage	VG	F	VF	XF	Unc
1671	22,000	16.00	30.00	55.00	120	—

KM# 148 6 GROTE / 1/12 THALER

Silver

Date	Mintage	VG	F	VF	XF	Unc
1672 HL	—	16.00	30.00	55.00	120	—

KM# 68 12 GROTE (1/6 Thaler)

Silver **Obv:** Supported oval arms in shield, crown above **Rev:** Crowned imperial eagle, date and titles of Matthias in legend

Date	Mintage	VG	F	VF	XF	Unc
1617	—	—	—	—	—	—

KM# 79 12 GROTE (1/6 Thaler)

Silver **Obv:** Helmeted and supported arms **Rev:** Crowned imperial eagle, date divided above, titles of Ferdinand II

Date	Mintage	VG	F	VF	XF	Unc
16Z3	—	40.00	80.00	140	250	—

KM# 121 12 GROTE (1/6 Thaler)

Silver **Obv:** Crowned oval arms divide date in baroque frame, value (XII) below in legend **Rev:** Crowned imperial eagle, titles of Ferdinand III

Date	Mintage	VG	F	VF	XF	Unc
1653	15,000	25.00	45.00	75.00	140	—

KM# 122 12 GROTE (1/6 Thaler)

Silver

Date	Mintage	VG	F	VF	XF	Unc
1654	127,000	16.00	33.00	60.00	120	—
1657	141,000	16.00	33.00	60.00	120	—

KM# 123 12 GROTE (1/6 Thaler)

Silver **Rev:** Titles of Leopold **Note:** Varieties exist.

Date	Mintage	VG	F	VF	XF	Unc
1658	140,000	13.00	30.00	55.00	110	—
1659	411,000	13.00	30.00	55.00	110	—
1664	69,000	13.00	30.00	55.00	110	—
1666	88,000	13.00	30.00	55.00	110	—
1667	145,000	13.00	30.00	55.00	110	—
1672 HL	—	13.00	30.00	55.00	110	—

KM# 124.1 24 GROTE (1/3 Thaler)

Silver **Obv:** Vertical date divided by arms **Note:** Varieties exist.

Date	Mintage	VG	F	VF	XF	Unc
1658	35,000	40.00	80.00	150	275	—
1659	54,000	40.00	80.00	150	275	—
1660	34,000	40.00	80.00	150	275	—
1664	9,000	40.00	80.00	150	275	—
1666	39,000	40.00	80.00	150	275	—
1672	—	40.00	80.00	150	275	—

KM# 124.2 24 GROTE (1/3 Thaler)

Silver **Obv:** Horizontal date divided by arms

Date	Mintage	VG	F	VF	XF	Unc
1672 HL	—	45.00	90.00	180	300	—

KM# 66 32 GROTE / MARK

Silver **Obv:** Supported oval arms, 1 MARCK below, date in legend **Rev:** Crowned imperial eagle, 32 in orb on breast, titles of Matthias

Date	Mintage	VG	F	VF	XF	Unc
1614	—	—	1,250	2,000	3,500	—

KM# 69 32 GROTE / MARK

Silver **Obv:** Crown above supported oval arms in ornamented shield, date above crown

Date	Mintage	VG	F	VF	XF	Unc
1617	—	—	850	1,500	2,250	—

KM# 70 32 GROTE / MARK

Silver **Note:** Klippe.

Date	Mintage	VG	F	VF	XF	Unc
1617 Rare	—	—	—	—	—	—

KM# 135 48 GROTE (2/3 Thaler)
Silver **Obv:** Crowned arms divide date 48 GROT in border **Rev:** Crowned imperial eagle, titles of Leopold

Date	Mintage	VG	F	VF	XF	Unc
1666	—	—	—	—	—	—

KM# 67 GROSCHEN / 1/24 THALER
Silver **Obv:** Arms in oval baroque frame **Rev:** Imperial orb with 24 divides date, titles of Matthias

Date	Mintage	VG	F	VF	XF	Unc
1616	—	27.00	55.00	100	160	—

KM# 60 GROSCHEN / 1/24 THALER
Silver **Obv:** Helmeted and supported oval arms **Rev:** Imperial orb with 24, titles of Matthias

Date	Mintage	VG	F	VF	XF	Unc
ND(1617-19)	—	—	—	—	—	—

KM# 71 1/16 THALER (Dütchen)
Silver **Obv:** Helmeted and supported oval arms **Rev:** Crowned imperial eagle, value 16 in orb on breast, date and titlews of Matthias in legend

Date	Mintage	VG	F	VF	XF	Unc
ND(1617-19)	—	—	—	—	—	—

Note: Some pieces exist with a key countermark (VF $250)

KM# 72 1/16 THALER (Dütchen)
Silver **Note:** Klippe.

Date	Mintage	VG	F	VF	XF	Unc
1617	—	—	—	—	—	—

KM# 55 1/4 THALER
Silver **Obv:** Supported arms in oval baroque frame, date divided above **Rev:** Crowned imperial eagle, titles of Rudolf II

Date	Mintage	VG	F	VF	XF	Unc
1603	—	—	—	—	—	—

KM# 119 1/4 THALER
Silver **Obv:** Crowned and supported oval arms, date below, 1/4 in orb above **Rev:** Titles of Ferdinand III

Date	Mintage	VG	F	VF	XF	Unc
1651 TI NOVA.	732	200	350	500	850	—
1651 TI NOVA:	—	225	375	550	1,000	—

KM# 51 1/2 THALER
Silver **Obv:** Supported oval arms, date above **Rev:** Titles of Rudolf II

Date	Mintage	VG	F	VF	XF	Unc
1602	—	900	1,600	2,700	4,500	—

KM# 107 1/2 THALER
Silver

Date	Mintage	VG	F	VF	XF	Unc
1643 TI	—	425	675	1,000	1,650	—

KM# 115 1/2 THALER
Silver **Obv:** Crown above arms, date below

Date	Mintage	VG	F	VF	XF	Unc
1650 TI	—	500	825	1,350	2,400	—

KM# 134 1/2 THALER
Silver **Rev:** Titles of Leopold

Date	Mintage	VG	F	VF	XF	Unc
1661 TI	—	250	400	650	950	—

KM# 136 1/2 THALER
Silver **Obv:** Crowned and supported oval arms **Rev:** 1/2-length figure of Leopold left, holding orb and sword

Date	Mintage	VG	F	VF	XF	Unc
ND(1666)	—	—	—	—	—	—

KM# 137 1/2 THALER
Silver **Rev:** Crowned imperial eagle, titles of Leopold

Date	Mintage	VG	F	VF	XF	Unc
ND(1666)	—	—	—	—	—	—

KM# 52.1 THALER
Silver **Obv:** Supported oval arms, date divided above **Rev:** Crowned imperial eagle, titles of Rudolf II **Note:** Dav. #5080.

Date	Mintage	VG	F	VF	XF	Unc
1602	—	1,000	1,650	2,750	4,500	—
1603	—	1,000	1,650	2,750	4,500	—

KM# 52.2 THALER
Silver **Note:** Thick flan. Dav. #5080A.

Date	Mintage	VG	F	VF	XF	Unc
1602 Rare	—	—	—	—	—	—

KM# 61 THALER
Silver **Rev:** Titles of Matthias **Note:** Dav. #5082.

Date	Mintage	VG	F	VF	XF	Unc
1613 Rare	—	—	—	—	—	—

KM# 73 THALER
Silver **Obv:** Supported oval arms in larger shield with ornate helmet above, date divided above **Note:** Dav. #5084.

Date	Mintage	VG	F	VF	XF	Unc
1617	—	3,000	5,000	7,500	—	—

KM# 76 THALER
Silver **Obv:** Helmeted and supported arms **Rev:** Titles of Ferdinand II and date in legend **Note:** Dav. #5086.

Date	Mintage	VG	F	VF	XF	Unc
1621	—	850	1,450	2,500	4,000	—
1622	—	850	1,450	2,500	4,000	—

KM# 80 THALER
Silver **Rev:** Date divided by eagle's tail **Note:** Dav. #5089.

Date	Mintage	VG	F	VF	XF	Unc
1623	—	850	1,450	2,500	4,000	—
1624	49,000	850	1,450	2,500	4,000	—

KM# 83 THALER
Silver **Obv:** Large key, date in legend **Note:** Dav. #5090.

Date	Mintage	VG	F	VF	XF	Unc
1624	Inc. above	350	650	1,350	3,000	—

KM# 84 THALER
Silver **Obv:** Lion supported oval arms in ornamented frame, date divided above **Note:** Dav. #5091.

Date	Mintage	VG	F	VF	XF	Unc
1624	Inc. above	850	1,450	2,500	4,000	—

KM# 91.1 THALER
Silver **Obv:** Supported arms in ornately-shaped frame, date **Note:** Dav. #5093.

Date	Mintage	VG	F	VF	XF	Unc
1634 TI	2,988	300	500	800	1,300	—

KM# 91.2 THALER
Silver **Obv:** T - I separated by support arms **Note:** Dav. #5094.

Date	Mintage	VG	F	VF	XF	Unc
1634 TI	Inc. above	300	500	800	1,300	—

KM# 91.3 THALER
Silver **Obv:** T - I divided below by bottom of frame **Note:** Varieties exist. Dav. #5096.

Date	Mintage	VG	F	VF	XF	Unc
1635 TI	748	400	650	1,100	1,700	—

KM# 101.1 THALER
Silver **Obv. Legend:** MON. NOVA... **Note:** Similar to KM#101.2. Dav. #5098.

Date	Mintage	VG	F	VF	XF	Unc
1640 TI	946	300	500	800	1,650	—

KM# 101.2 THALER
Silver **Note:** Varieties exist. Dav. #5100.

Date	Mintage	VG	F	VF	XF	Unc
1641 TI	Inc. above	400	650	1,150	1,850	—
1642 TI	—	400	650	1,150	1,850	—
1644 TI	—	400	650	1,150	1,850	—

KM# 116.1 THALER
Silver **Note:** Dav. #5102.

Date	Mintage	VG	F	VF	XF	Unc
1650 TI	1,627	450	800	1,350	2,250	—

KM# 116.2 THALER
Silver **Obv:** Lion supporters looking outward **Note:** Dav. #5104.

Date	Mintage	VG	F	VF	XF	Unc
1657 TI	378	700	1,200	2,000	3,000	—

KM# 116.3 THALER
Silver **Obv:** Different lions **Obv. Legend:** MON: NOVA: ARG. **Note:** Varieties exist. Dav. #5105.

Date	Mintage	VG	F	VF	XF	Unc
1657 TI	Inc. above	—	—	2,250	3,500	—

KM# 132.2 THALER
Silver **Rev. Legend:** ...AUGUS: **Note:** Dav. #5107.

Date	Mintage	VG	F	VF	XF	Unc
1660 TI	3,942	300	500	800	1,300	—
1666 TI	—	300	500	800	1,300	—

KM# 132.1 THALER
Silver **Rev. Legend:** ...AUGUST: **Note:** Dav. #5107A.

Date	Mintage	VG	F	VF	XF	Unc
1660 TI	—	400	600	1,000	1,700	—

KM# 132.3 THALER
Silver **Obv. Legend:** MONETA NOVA REIPUBLICAE... **Note:** Varieties exist. Dav. #5110.

Date	Mintage	VG	F	VF	XF	Unc
1668	—	300	500	800	1,300	—

KM# 77 THALER (Vereins)
Silver **Obv:** Helmeted and supported arms **Rev:** Crowned imperial eagle, titles of Ferdinand II, date in legend **Note:** Klippe. Dav. #5085.

Date	Mintage	F	VF	XF	Unc	BU
1621 Rare	—	—	—	—	—	—

KM# 81 THALER (Vereins)
Silver **Rev:** Date divided by eagle's tail **Note:** Klippe. Dav. #5085.

Date	Mintage	F	VF	XF	Unc	BU
1623 Rare	—	—	—	—	—	—
1624 Rare	—	—	—	—	—	—

KM# 56 2 THALER
Silver **Obv:** Supported oval arms, date divided above **Rev:** Crowned imperial eagle, titles of Rudolf II **Note:** Dav. #5079.

Date	Mintage	F	VF	XF	Unc	BU
1603 Rare	—	—	—	—	—	—

KM# 62 2 THALER
Silver **Rev:** Titles of Matthias **Note:** Dav. #5081.

Date	Mintage	F	VF	XF	Unc	BU
1613 Rare	—	—	—	—	—	—

KM# 74 2 THALER
Silver **Obv:** Supported oval arms in larger shield with ornate helnet above, date divided above **Note:** Dav. #5083.

Date	Mintage	VG	F	VF	XF	Unc
1617 Rare	—	—	—	—	—	—

KM# 85 2 THALER
Silver **Obv:** Helmeted and supported arms **Rev:** Titles of Ferdinand II, date divided by eagle's tail **Note:** Dav. #5087.

Date	Mintage	VG	F	VF	XF	Unc
1624 Rare	—	—	—	—	—	—

KM# 92.1 2 THALER
Silver **Obv:** Supported arms in ornately-shaped frame, date above, .T. .I. below **Note:** Dav. #5092.

Date	Mintage	VG	F	VF	XF	Unc
1634 TI Rare	—	—	—	—	—	—

KM# 92.2 2 THALER
Silver **Obv:** .T. .I. divided below by bottom of frame **Note:** Varieties exist. Dav. #5095.

Date	Mintage	VG	F	VF	XF	Unc
1635 TI Rare	—	—	—	—	—	—

KM# 102.1 2 THALER
Silver **Obv. Legend:** .MON. NOVA. ARG... **Note:** Similar to KM#102.2 but different obverse legend. Dav. #5097.

Date	Mintage	VG	F	VF	XF	Unc
1640 TI Rare	—	—	—	—	—	—

KM# 102.2 2 THALER

Silver **Note:** Varieties exist. Dav. #5099.

Date	Mintage	VG	F	VF	XF	Unc
1641 TI Rare	—	—	—	—	—	—

Note: Westfälische Auktionsgesellschaft, Auction 46, 2-08, XF+ realized approximately $22,108.

Date	Mintage	VG	F	VF	XF	Unc
164Z TI Rare	—	—	—	—	—	—

KM# 117.1 2 THALER

Silver **Note:** Dav. #5101A.

Date	Mintage	VG	F	VF	XF	Unc
1650 TI	—	1,200	2,000	3,500	6,000	—

KM# 117.2 2 THALER

Silver **Obv:** Lion supporters looking outward **Note:** Dav. #5103.

Date	Mintage	VG	F	VF	XF	Unc
1657 TI	—	1,500	3,000	6,000	10,500	—

KM# 133.1 2 THALER

Silver **Obv:** Lion supporters looking inward **Rev. Legend:** LEOPOLD: D: G:... **Note:** Dav. #5106.

Date	Mintage	VG	F	VF	XF	Unc
1660 TI Rare	—	—	—	—	—	—
1666 TI Rare	—	—	—	—	—	—

KM# 133.2 2 THALER

Silver **Obv:** Lion supporters looking outward **Note:** Dav. #5109.

Date	Mintage	VG	F	VF	XF	Unc
1666	—	750	1,500	2,750	4,500	—
1668	—	750	1,500	2,750	4,500	—

KM# 133.3 2 THALER

Silver **Rev. Legend:** LEOPOLDUS... **Note:** Dav. #5109A.

Date	Mintage	VG	F	VF	XF	Unc
1666	—	750	1,500	2,750	4,500	—
1668	—	750	1,500	2,750	4,500	—

KM# 118 3 THALER

Silver **Note:** Similar to 1 Thaler KM#116. Dav. #5101.

Date	Mintage	VG	F	VF	XF	Unc
1650 TI	—	1,350	2,250	3,750	6,500	—

KM# 138 3 THALER

Silver **Note:** Similar to 1 Thaler KM#132. Dav. #A5108.

Date	Mintage	VG	F	VF	XF	Unc
1668 Rare	—	—	—	—	—	—

KM# 139 4 THALER

Silver **Note:** Similar to 1 Thaler KM#132. Dav. #5108.

Date	Mintage	VG	F	VF	XF	Unc
1668 Rare	—	—	—	—	—	—

COUNTERMARKED COINAGE

1620-1621

A countermark of the city arms - a key - was used to identify some coins which circulated in the city. The precise reason for the use of this countermark in not known, but it is interesting to note that it occurs on double-schilling type coins during the very early period of the Thirty Years' War. It's use may be related to a new monetary ordinance agreed to among the cities of Bremen, Hamburg, Lubeck, and the duchies of Mecklenburg-Schwerin and Mecklenburg-Strelitz dated 20 April 1620.

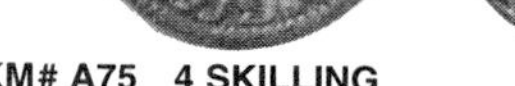

KM# A75 4 SKILLING

Silver **Countermark:** Key **Note:** Countermark on Denmark 4 Skilling, KM#55.2.

CM Date	Host Date	Good	VG	F	VF	XF
ND(c.1620-21)	1616 (c)	28.50	47.50	95.00	175	—
ND(ca.1620-21)	1617 (c)	28.50	47.50	95.00	175	—
ND(ca.1620-21)	1618 (c)	28.50	47.50	95.00	175	—
ND(ca.1620-21)	1619 (c)	28.50	47.50	95.00	175	—

KM# C75.6 2 SCHILLING

Silver **Countermark:** Key **Note:** Countermark on Mecklenburg-Schwerin 2 Schilling, KM#22.

CM Date	Host Date	Good	VG	F	VF	XF
ND(ca.1620-21)	1612	27.50	45.00	90.00	165	—
ND(ca.1620-21)	1614 (b)	27.50	45.00	90.00	165	—

CM Date	Host Date	Good	VG	F	VF	XF
ND(ca.1620-21)	1615 (b)	27.50	45.00	90.00	165	—
ND(ca.1620-21)	(16)15 (b)	27.50	45.00	90.00	165	—
ND(ca.1620-21)	1616 (b)	27.50	45.00	90.00	165	—

KM# C75.4 2 SCHILLING

Silver **Countermark:** Key **Note:** Countermark on Mecklenburg-Schwerin 2 Schilling, KM#19.

CM Date	Host Date	Good	VG	F	VF	XF
ND(ca.1620-21)	1613 (b)	45.00	75.00	150	260	—
ND(ca.1620-21)	(16)15 (b)	45.00	75.00	150	260	—

KM# C75.5 2 SCHILLING

Silver **Countermark:** Key **Note:** Countermark on Mecklenburg-Schwerin 2 Schilling, KM#20.

CM Date	Host Date	Good	VG	F	VF	XF
ND(ca.1620-21)	1613 (b)	40.00	65.00	130	240	—
ND(ca.1620-21)	(1)613 (b)	40.00	65.00	130	240	—
ND(ca.1620-21)	1614 (b)	40.00	65.00	130	240	—
ND(ca.1620-21)	(1)614 (b)	40.00	65.00	130	240	—
ND(ca.1620-21)	(16)14 (b)	40.00	65.00	130	240	—
ND(ca.1620-21)	(16)15 (b)	40.00	65.00	130	240	—

KM# C75.3 2 SCHILLING

Silver **Countermark:** Key **Note:** Countermark on Mecklenburg-Güstrow 2 Schilling, KM#20.

CM Date	Host Date	Good	VG	F	VF	XF
ND(ca.1620-21)	1614	40.00	65.00	130	240	—
ND(ca.1620-21)	1615 (b)	40.00	65.00	130	240	—
ND(ca.1620-21)	1615	40.00	65.00	130	240	—
ND(ca.1620-21)	1616 (b)	40.00	65.00	130	240	—
ND(ca.1620-21)	1616	40.00	65.00	130	240	—
ND(ca.1620-21)	1617 (b)	40.00	65.00	130	240	—
ND(ca.1620-21)	1617	40.00	65.00	130	240	—
ND(ca.1620-21)	1618	40.00	65.00	130	240	—
ND(ca.1620-21)	ND(1614-18) (b)	40.00	65.00	130	240	—

KM# C75.8 2 SCHILLING

Silver **Countermark:** Key **Note:** Countermark on Pomerania-Wolgast 2 Schilling.

CM Date	Host Date	Good	VG	F	VF	XF
ND(ca.1620-21)	1615	20.00	32.50	65.00	115	—

KM# C75.1 2 SCHILLING

Silver **Countermark:** Key **Note:** Countermark on Holstein-Gottorp 2 Schilling.

CM Date	Host Date	Good	VG	F	VF	XF
ND(ca.1620-21)	1615	32.50	55.00	110	195	—

KM# C75.7 2 SCHILLING

Silver **Countermark:** Key **Note:** Countermark on Mecklenburg-Schwerin 2 Schilling, KM#33.

CM Date	Host Date	Good	VG	F	VF	XF
ND(ca.1620-21)	1616 (b)	27.50	45.00	90.00	165	—
ND(ca.1620-21)	(16)16 (b)	27.50	45.00	90.00	165	—
ND(ca.1620-21)	1617 (b)	27.50	45.00	90.00	165	—
ND(ca.1620-21)	(1)6(1)7 (b)	27.50	45.00	90.00	165	—
ND(ca.1620-21)	ND(1618) (b)	27.50	45.00	90.00	165	—

KM# C75.2 2 SCHILLING

Silver **Countermark:** Key **Note:** Countermark on Holstein-Gottorp 2 Schilling.

CM Date	Host Date	Good	VG	F	VF	XF
ND(ca.1620-21)	1617	32.50	55.00	110	195	—
ND(ca.1620-21)	1618	32.50	55.00	110	195	—

KM# B75 1/18-1/2 THALER

Silver **Countermark:** Key **Note:** Countermark on Schaumburg-Pinneberg 1/18-1/2 Thaler, KM#72.

CM Date	Host Date	Good	VG	F	VF	XF
ND(ca.1620-21)	(1)613 (q)	40.00	65.00	130	230	—
ND(ca.1620-21)	(1)614 (q)	40.00	65.00	130	230	—
ND(ca.1620-21)	(1)615 (q)	40.00	65.00	130	230	—
ND(ca.1620-21)	(1)616 (q)	40.00	65.00	130	230	—

KM# 75.1 1/16 THALER

Silver **Countermark:** Key **Note:** Countermark on Bentheim-Tecklenburg-Rheda 1/16 Thaler, KM#6.

CM Date	Host Date	Good	VG	F	VF	XF
ND(ca.1620-21)	1618	75.00	125	240	450	—
ND(ca.1620-21)	1619	75.00	125	240	450	—

KM# 75.2 1/16 THALER

Silver **Countermark:** Key **Note:** Countermark on Bremen and Verden 1/16 Thaler, KM#18.

CM Date	Host Date	Good	VG	F	VF	XF
ND(ca.1620-21)	161Z	16.50	27.50	55.00	100	—
ND(ca.1620-21)	1613	16.50	27.50	55.00	100	—
ND(ca.1620-21)	1614	16.50	27.50	55.00	100	—
ND(ca.1620-21)	1615	16.50	27.50	55.00	100	—
ND(ca.1620-21)	1616	16.50	27.50	55.00	100	—

KM# 75.3 1/16 THALER

Silver **Countermark:** Key **Note:** Countermark on Bremen and Verden 1/16 Thaler, KM#22.

CM Date	Host Date	Good	VG	F	VF	XF
ND(ca.1620-21)	1613	16.50	27.50	55.00	100	—
ND(ca.1620-21)	1614	16.50	27.50	55.00	100	—
ND(ca.1620-21)	1615 HR	16.50	27.50	55.00	100	—
ND(ca.1620-21)	1616	16.50	27.50	55.00	100	—
ND(ca.1620-21)	1616 HR	16.50	27.50	55.00	100	—
ND(ca.1620-21)	1617	16.50	27.50	55.00	100	—
ND(ca.1620-21)	1618	16.50	27.50	55.00	100	—
ND(ca.1620-21)	1619	16.50	27.50	55.00	100	—

KM# 75.12 1/16 THALER

Silver **Countermark:** Key **Note:** Countermark on Wismar 1/16 Thaler.

CM Date	Host Date	Good	VG	F	VF	XF
ND(ca.1620-21)	1613	30.00	50.00	100	180	—
ND(ca.1620-21)	1614	30.00	50.00	100	180	—
ND(ca.1620-21)	1615	30.00	50.00	100	180	—
ND(ca.1620-21)	1616	30.00	50.00	100	180	—
ND(ca.1620-21)	1617	30.00	50.00	100	180	—
ND(ca.1620-21)	1618	30.00	50.00	100	180	—
ND(ca.1620-21)	1619	30.00	50.00	100	180	—

KM# 75.5 1/16 THALER

Silver **Countermark:** Key **Note:** Countermark on Hamburg-City 1/16 Thaler, KM#29.

CM Date	Host Date	Good	VG	F	VF	XF
ND(ca.1620-21)	1614	37.50	65.00	120	225	—
ND(ca.1620-21)	1615	37.50	65.00	120	225	—
ND(ca.1620-21)	1616	37.50	65.00	120	225	—
ND(ca.1620-21)	1617	37.50	65.00	120	225	—

KM# 75.11 1/16 THALER

Silver **Countermark:** Key **Note:** Countermark on Stade 1/16 Thaler.

CM Date	Host Date	Good	VG	F	VF	XF
ND(ca.1620-21)	1615	32.50	55.00	110	195	—
ND(ca.1620-21)	1616	32.50	55.00	110	195	—
ND(ca.1620-21)	1617	32.50	55.00	110	195	—
ND(ca.1620-21)	1618	32.50	55.00	110	195	—
ND(ca.1620-21)	1619	32.50	55.00	110	195	—

KM# 75.4 1/16 THALER

Silver **Countermark:** Key **Note:** Countermark on Brunswick-Lüneburg-Harburg 1/16 Thaler, KM#7.

CM Date	Host Date	Good	VG	F	VF	XF
ND(ca.1620-21)	1616	60.00	100	200	350	—
ND(ca.1620-21)	1617	60.00	100	200	350	—
ND(ca.1620-21)	1618	60.00	100	200	350	—
ND(ca.1620-21)	1619	60.00	100	200	350	—
ND(ca.1620-21)	ND(1616-19)	60.00	100	200	350	—

KM# 75.7 1/16 THALER

Silver **Countermark:** Key **Note:** Countermark on Schaumburg-Pinneberg 1/16 Thaler, KM#77. Also found with countermark of Hamburg.

CM Date	Host Date	Good	VG	F	VF	XF
ND(ca.1620-21)	(1)616 (f)	37.50	62.50	120	230	—
ND(ca.1620-21)	(1)617 (f)	37.50	62.50	120	230	—
ND(ca.1620-21)	(1)617 (q)	37.50	62.50	120	230	—
ND(ca.1620-21)	(1)618 (t)	37.50	62.50	120	230	—
ND(ca.1620-21)	(1)619 (t)	37.50	62.50	120	230	—
ND(ca.1620-21)	(1)6Z0 (t)	37.50	62.50	120	230	—

KM# 75.6 1/16 THALER

Silver **Countermark:** Key **Note:** Countermark on Ratzeburg 1/16 Thaler.

CM Date	Host Date	Good	VG	F	VF	XF
ND(ca.1620-21)	1617	30.00	50.00	100	180	—
ND(ca.1620-21)	1618	30.00	50.00	100	180	—

KM# 75.8 1/16 THALER

Silver **Countermark:** Key **Note:** Countermark on Schaumburg-Pinneberg 1/16 Thaler, KM#100.

CM Date	Host Date	Good	VG	F	VF	XF
ND(ca.1620-21)	(1)6Z0	30.00	50.00	100	180	—
ND(ca.1620-21)	(1)6Z0 (b)	30.00	50.00	100	180	—
ND(ca.1620-21)	(1)6Z1 (i)	30.00	50.00	100	180	—

KM# 75.9 1/16 THALER

Silver **Countermark:** Key **Note:** Countermark on Schaumburg-Pinneberg 1/16 Thaler, KM#118.

CM Date	Host Date	Good	VG	F	VF	XF
ND(ca.1620-21)	16Z1(p)//16Z1 (h)	30.00	50.00	100	180	—

KM# 75.10 1/16 THALER

Silver **Countermark:** Key **Note:** Countermark on Schaumberg-Pinneberg 1/16 Thaler, KM#122.

CM Date	Host Date	Good	VG	F	VF	XF
ND(ca.1620-21)	16Z1 (h)	27.50	45.00	90.00	165	—
ND(ca.1620-21)	ND(1621) (h)	27.50	45.00	90.00	165	—

TRADE COINAGE

KM# 63 GOLDGULDEN

3.5000 g., 0.9860 Gold 0.1109 oz. AGW **Obv:** Bremen arms, date divided at bottom in inner circle **Rev:** Crowned imperial eagle in inner circle, titles of Matthias

Date	Mintage	F	VF	XF	Unc
1613	—	1,400	2,800	5,600	9,300	—

KM# 87 GOLDGULDEN

3.5000 g., 0.9860 Gold 0.1109 oz. AGW **Obv:** Bremen arms in inner circle, date in legend **Rev:** Crowned imperial eagle in inner circle, titles of Ferdinand II **Note:** Varieties exist.

Date	Mintage	VG	F	VF	XF	Unc
1627	—	650	1,250	2,500	4,500	—
1635 TI	1,121	650	1,250	2,500	4,500	—

KM# 93 GOLDGULDEN

3.5000 g., 0.9860 Gold 0.1109 oz. AGW **Obv:** Bremen arms with supporters, date above in inner circle **Note:** Varieties exist.

Date	Mintage	VG	F	VF	XF	Unc
1635	Inc. above	650	1,250	2,500	4,500	—
1637	—	650	1,250	2,500	4,500	—

KM# 94 GOLDGULDEN

3.5000 g., 0.9860 Gold 0.1109 oz. AGW **Obv:** Date divided below arms

Date	Mintage	VG	F	VF	XF	Unc
1637	—	—	—	—	—	—

KM# 103 GOLDGULDEN

3.5000 g., 0.9860 Gold 0.1109 oz. AGW **Rev:** Crowned imperial eagle in inner circle, titles of Ferdinand III

Date	Mintage	VG	F	VF	XF	Unc
1640	—	750	1,500	3,000	5,000	—

KM# 109 2 GOLDGULDEN

7.0000 g., 0.9860 Gold 0.2219 oz. AGW **Obv:** Bremen arms with lion supporters, date above in inner circle **Rev:** Crowned imperial eagle in inner circle, titles of Ferdinand III

Date	Mintage	VG	F	VF	XF	Unc
1649 Rare	—	—	—	—	—	—

KM# 104 DUCAT

3.5000 g., 0.9860 Gold 0.1109 oz. AGW **Obv:** Ferdinand II standing divides date in inner circle **Rev:** Bremen arms with lion supporters in inner circle

Date	Mintage	VG	F	VF	XF	Unc
1640	116	400	900	1,650	3,200	—
1640 TI	Inc. above	400	900	1,650	3,200	—
1641	Inc. above	400	900	1,650	3,200	—
1641 TI	Inc. above	400	900	1,650	3,200	—
1642 TI	—	400	900	1,650	3,200	—
1652 TI	—	600	1,200	2,250	4,000	—

KM# 125 DUCAT

3.5000 g., 0.9860 Gold 0.1109 oz. AGW **Obv:** Leopold standing divides date in inner circle **Rev:** Crowned arms with lion supporters in inner circle

Date	Mintage	VG	F	VF	XF	Unc
1659 TI	—	600	1,200	2,250	4,000	—
1667 TI	—	600	1,200	2,250	4,000	—

KM# 149 DUCAT

3.5000 g., 0.9860 Gold 0.1109 oz. AGW

Date	Mintage	VG	F	VF	XF	Unc
167Z HL	—	650	1,500	2,500	4,250	—

KM# 105 2 DUCAT

7.0000 g., 0.9860 Gold 0.2219 oz. AGW **Obv:** Ferdinand III standing divides date in inner circle **Rev:** Crowned arms with lion supporters in inner circle

Date	Mintage	VG	F	VF	XF	Unc
1640 TI	—	2,000	4,250	8,000	12,500	—
1652 TI	—	2,000	4,000	7,500	11,500	—

KM# 126 2 DUCAT
7.0000 g., 0.9860 Gold 0.2219 oz. AGW **Obv:** Leopold standing divides date in inner circle

Date	Mintage	VG	F	VF	XF	Unc
1659 TI	—	1,500	3,000	6,000	9,000	—
1667 TI	—	1,500	3,000	6,000	9,000	—

KM# 120 3 DUCAT
10.5000 g., 0.9860 Gold 0.3328 oz. AGW **Obv:** Ferdinand III standing divides date in inner circle **Rev:** Crowned arms with lion supporters in inner circle

Date	Mintage	VG	F	VF	XF	Unc
1659 TI Rare	—	—	—	—	—	—

PATTERNS

Including off metal strikes

KM#	Date	Mintage	Identification	Mkt Val
Pn1	1613	—	Thaler. Gold. KM#61	—
Pn2	1614	—	3 Grote / 1/18 Thaler. Gold. KM#65	—
Pn3	1617	—	12 Grote. Gold. KM#68	—
Pn4	1666	—	48 Grote. Gold. KM#135	—
Pn5	ND(1666)	—	1/12 Thaler. Gold. KM#136	—
Pn6	ND(1666)	—	1/12 Thaler. Gold. KM#137	—
Pn7	1666 TI	—	Thaler. Gold. KM#132	—
Pn8	1668	—	Thaler. Gold. KM#132	—
Pn9	ND(1671) HL	—	Schwaren. Gold. KM#145	—
Pn10	1671	—	2 Grote / 1/36 Thaler. Gold. KM#130	—
Pn11	1671 HL	—	4 Grote. Gold. KM#146	—
Pn12	1697	—	Schwaren. Gold. KM#155	1,000

BREMEN & VERDEN

The Archbishopric of Bremen and the Bishopric of Verden (which see) were taken by Sweden during the Thirty Years' War and joined together as a secular duchy. This action by Sweden was confirmed as part of the Peace of Westphalia which brought an end to the war in 1648. The King of Sweden was also entitled as Duke of Bremen and Verden. Except for a brief period of Danish rule (1702-04), Sweden continued its rule over the duchy until 1719, at which time it was transferred to the Electorate of Hannover.

RULERS
Johann Friedrich of Holstein-Gottorp, 1596-1634

SWEDISH RULERS
Queen Christina, 1648-54
Karl X Gustaf, 1654-60
Karl XI, 1660-97
Karl XII, 1697-1718

MINT OFFICIALS' INITIALS

Initial	Date	Name
AH	1670-76	Andreas Hille
HR	1615-18	Hans Rucke
ICA	1691-93	Julius Christian Arensburg
IS	1680-85	Jacob Schroeder
LM	1695-98	Lambert Marinus
MM	1659-60, 1666-70	Michael Moller
PT	1641-43, 49-50	Peter Timpf

ARCHBISHOPRIC

REGULAR COINAGE

KM# 35 SECHSLING (1/2 Schilling; 1/96 Thaler)
0.7040 g., 0.3120 Silver 0.0071 oz. ASW **Ruler:** Frederik **Obv:** Two crossed keys (arms) **Obv. Legend:** FRID:D:G:A:E:EP: BRE:E:VER: **Rev:** Denomination in center: I/SECH/S.LIN **Rev. Legend:** C:H:H:N:D:S:H:S:D:C:O:E:D:1641 **Mint:** Bremervörde

Date	Mintage	VG	F	VF	XF	Unc
1641 PT	—	80.00	200	400	700	—

KM# A40 1/2 REICHSORT (1/8 Thaler; 6 Schilling)
Silver **Ruler:** Frederik **Obv:** Bust of Frederik III right, titles in legend **Obv. Legend:** FRID.D:G:A:E:EP:BR:E:V. **Rev:** Denomination in center within legend **Rev. Legend:** C:H:H:N:D: S:H:S:D:C:O:E:D:1642:PT around: I/HALB/REICHS/ORT **Mint:** Bremervörde

Date	Mintage	VG	F	VF	XF	Unc
1642 PT Unique	—	—	—	—	—	—

Note: Westfalische Munzauktion No.13, 9-98, VF realized $8300

KM# 16 2 GROTEN
Silver **Obv:** Helmeted 8-fold arms **Rev:** Crossed keys in ornately shaped shield, date in legend

Date	Mintage	VG	F	VF	XF	Unc
1611	—	—	—	—	—	—

KM# 7 4 GROSCHEN
Silver **Obv:** Bust right **Rev:** 8-fold arms

Date	Mintage	VG	F	VF	XF	Unc
ND	—	250	425	850	1,350	—

KM# 8 4 GROSCHEN
Silver **Rev:** 4 GROS above arms

Date	Mintage	VG	F	VF	XF	Unc
ND	—	250	425	850	1,350	—

KM# 4 2 SCHILLING / 1/16 THALER (Dütchen)
Silver **Obv:** Horseman right, crossed keys at upper right, Holstein arms (nettle) upper left, value 2 SL below **Rev:** Five-line inscription with titles of Johann Freidrich **Note:** In style of Russian wire Kopek.

Date	Mintage	VG	F	VF	XF	Unc
ND	—	27.00	45.00	80.00	140	—

KM# 36 2 SCHILLING / 1/16 THALER (Dütchen)
Silver **Obv:** Crossed keys **Rev:** Date in legend **Rev. Legend:** II/SCHIL/LING

Date	Mintage	VG	F	VF	XF	Unc
1641 PT	—	350	600	1,150	1,600	—
1643 PT	—	—	—	—	—	—

KM# 5 4 SCHILLING
Silver **Obv:** Horseman right, crossed keys at upper right, Holstein arms (nettle) upper left, value 4 SL below **Rev:** Five-line inscription with titles of Johann Friedrich **Note:** In style of Russian wire kopeks.

Date	Mintage	VG	F	VF	XF	Unc
ND	—	33.00	75.00	150	250	—

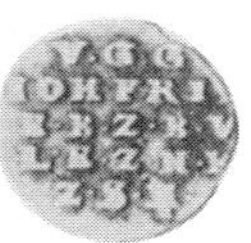

KM# 6 4 SCHILLING
Silver **Obv:** Horseman left

Date	Mintage	VG	F	VF	XF	Unc
ND	—	40.00	80.00	160	260	—

KM# 25 1/24 THALER (Groschen; 2 Schilling)
Silver **Note:** Klippe.

Date	Mintage	VG	F	VF	XF	Unc
(16)19 Rare	—	—	—	—	—	—

KM# 24 1/24 THALER (Groschen; 2 Schilling)
Silver **Obv:** Imperial orb with 24 divides date, titles of Matthias **Rev:** 8-fold arms

Date	Mintage	VG	F	VF	XF	Unc
(1)619	—	40.00	85.00	150	250	—
(1)619	—	40.00	85.00	150	250	—

KM# 31 1/24 THALER (Groschen; 2 Schilling)
Silver **Obv:** Imperial orb with 24, date in legend, titles of Ferdinand II **Rev:** 3-fold arms **Note:** Small module.

Date	Mintage	VG	F	VF	XF	Unc
(1)621	—	45.00	100	160	275	—
(16)21	—	45.00	100	160	275	—

KM# 15 1/16 THALER (Dütchen; 3 Schilling)
Silver **Obv:** Helmeted 8-fold arms **Rev:** Crowned Imperial Eagle, crossed keyes on breast, necks divide value 1-6, date in legend, titles of Rudolf II **Note:** Normal Style.

Date	Mintage	VG	F	VF	XF	Unc
1611	—	33.00	60.00	100	180	—

KM# 18 1/16 THALER (Dütchen; 3 Schilling)
Silver **Obv:** 8-fold arms **Rev:** Three helmets, value 1-6 below, date in legend

Date	Mintage	VG	F	VF	XF	Unc
1612	—	25.00	45.00	85.00	170	—
1613	—	25.00	45.00	85.00	170	—
1614	—	25.00	45.00	85.00	170	—
1615	—	25.00	45.00	85.00	170	—
1616	—	25.00	45.00	85.00	170	—

KM# 22 1/16 THALER (Dütchen; 3 Schilling)
Silver **Obv:** Helmeted 8-fold arms **Rev:** Crowned Imperial Eagle, crossed keys on breast, necks divide value 1-6, date in legend, titles of Mathias **Note:** Varieties exist.

Date	Mintage	VG	F	VF	XF	Unc
1613	—	25.00	45.00	85.00	170	—
1614	—	25.00	45.00	85.00	170	—
1615 HR	—	25.00	45.00	85.00	170	—
1616	—	25.00	45.00	85.00	170	—
1616 HR	—	25.00	45.00	85.00	170	—
1617	—	25.00	45.00	85.00	170	—
1618	—	25.00	45.00	85.00	170	—
1619	—	25.00	45.00	85.00	170	—

KM# 30 1/16 THALER (Dütchen; 3 Schilling)
Silver **Obv:** Titles of Ferdinand II, without indication of value **Note:** Kipper.

Date	Mintage	VG	F	VF	XF	Unc
1620	—	40.00	80.00	160	235	—

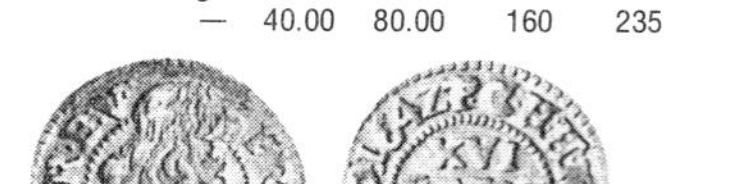

KM# 37.1 1/16 THALER (Dütchen; 3 Schilling)
1.7850 g., 0.8120 Silver 0.0466 oz. ASW **Ruler:** Frederik **Obv:** Bust right **Obv. Legend:** FRID:D:G:A:E:EP:BR:E:VE: **Rev:** Denomination in center: XVI/E. REIC/HS DA. Date in legend **Rev. Legend:** C:H:H:N:D:S:H:S:D:C:O:E:D: **Mint:** Bremervörde **Note:** Varieties exist.

Date	Mintage	VG	F	VF	XF	Unc
1641	—	20.00	40.00	80.00	160	—
1642	—	20.00	40.00	80.00	160	—
1643	—	20.00	40.00	80.00	160	—

KM# 37.2 1/16 THALER (Dütchen; 3 Schilling)
1.7850 g., 0.8120 Silver 0.0466 oz. ASW **Ruler:** Frederik **Obv:** Bust of Archbishop Frederik within inner circle **Obv. Legend:** FREDERICVS.D.G.A.EP.BR.E.VERD: **Rev:** Denomination in center: XVI E: REIC HS.DA: Date in legend. **Rev. Legend:** C.H.H.N.D.S.H.S.D.C.O.E.D. **Mint:** Bremervörde **Note:** Kipper. Legend varieties exist.

Date	Mintage	VG	F	VF	XF	Unc
1642	—	55.00	160	380	550	—
1643 Unique	—	—	—	—	—	—

KM# 17 MARK (32 Grote)
Silver **Obv:** Helmeted 8-fold arms **Rev:** Crossed keys divide 32 GRO, MARCK and date in legend

Date	Mintage	VG	F	VF	XF	Unc
1611	—	—	—	—	—	—

KM# 40 1/2 THALER
14.6160 g., 0.8880 Silver 0.4173 oz. ASW **Obv:** Bust of Archbishop Frederik and motto within inner circle and legend. **Obv. Legend:** FRIDERICVS:D:G.ARCH:EPISC:BREM: VERDEN: **Rev:** Crowned arms, date divided below **Rev. Legend:** .C.HALB.HAE.NOR.D SLE HOLS.STO.DIT.C.O.E.D.

Date	Mintage	VG	F	VF	XF	Unc
1642 PT Rare	—	—	—	—	—	—

KM# 9 THALER
29.2320 g., 0.8880 Silver 0.8345 oz. ASW **Obv:** Bust right **Rev:** Helmeted arms **Note:** Dav.#5071.

Date	Mintage	VG	F	VF	XF	Unc
ND(1611) Rare	—	—	—	—	—	—

KM# 19.1 THALER
29.2320 g., 0.8880 Silver 0.8345 oz. ASW **Rev:** Helmeted 8-fold arms, legend and date **Rev. Legend:** HER: NORW...

Date	Mintage	VG	F	VF	XF	Unc
1612 Rare	—	—	—	—	—	—

KM# 19.2 THALER
29.2320 g., 0.8880 Silver 0.8345 oz. ASW **Rev. Legend:** HER: NORWEG: DVX: SLES: **Note:** Dav.#5074.

Date	Mintage	VG	F	VF	XF	Unc
1616 HR Rare	—	—	—	—	—	—

KM# 19.3 THALER
29.2320 g., 0.8880 Silver 0.8345 oz. ASW **Rev. Legend:** HER: NORWEG: DVX: SLESW: ET: HOL: **Note:** Dav.#5075.

Date	Mintage	VG	F	VF	XF	Unc
1618 Rare	—	—	—	—	—	—

KM# 19.4 THALER
29.2320 g., 0.8880 Silver 0.8345 oz. ASW **Rev. Legend:** HER: NOR: DUX - SLES: E: HOL: **Note:** Dav.#5076; varieties exist.

Date	Mintage	VG	F	VF	XF	Unc
1622	—	800	1,350	2,250	3,750	—

KM# 38 THALER
29.2320 g., 0.8880 Silver 0.8345 oz. ASW **Ruler:** Frederik **Obv:** Bust of Archbishop Frederik and motto withtin inner circle and legend **Obv. Legend:** FRIDERICVS:D:G:ARCH:&.EPISC: BREM:&.VERDEN: **Rev:** Crowned oval arms, date divided above **Rev. Legend:** C:HALB:HÆ:NOR:D:SLE:HOLS:STO:DIT: C:O:E:D: **Mint:** Bremervörde **Note:** Dav.#5078.

Date	Mintage	VG	F	VF	XF	Unc
1641 PT	—	2,000	3,500	6,000	9,500	—

KM# 20 2 THALER
58.4640 g., 0.8880 Silver 1.6691 oz. ASW **Obv:** Bust right **Rev:** Helmeted 8-fold arms, date in legend **Note:** Dav.#5072.

Date	Mintage	VG	F	VF	XF	Unc
1612 Rare	—	—	—	—	—	—

KM# 39 2 THALER
58.4640 g., 0.8880 Silver 1.6691 oz. ASW **Ruler:** Frederik **Obv:** Bust of Archbishop Frederik and motto within inner circle and legend. **Obv. Legend:** FRIDERICUS:D:G.ARCH:&EPISC: BREM:&.VERDEN: **Rev:** Crowned oval arms, date divided above **Rev. Legend:** C:HALB:HÆ:NOR:D:SLE:HOLS:STO:DIT: C:O:E:D: **Mint:** Bremervörde **Note:** Dav.#5077.

Date	Mintage	VG	F	VF	XF	Unc
1641 PT	—	3,500	5,500	9,000	12,000	—

TRADE COINAGE

KM# 21 GOLDGULDEN
3.5000 g., 0.9860 Gold 0.1109 oz. AGW **Obv:** Arms topped by 3 helmets **Rev:** St. Peter standing, holding key and book, date in exergue

Date	Mintage	VG	F	VF	XF	Unc
1612 Rare	—	—	—	—	—	—

KM# 23 GOLDGULDEN
3.5000 g., 0.9860 Gold 0.1109 oz. AGW **Obv:** Arms of Holstein joined with those of Bremen

Date	Mintage	VG	F	VF	XF	Unc
1618 Rare	—	—	—	—	—	—

KM# 10 10 DUCAT (Portugalöser)
Gold **Obv:** Bust right, margin of 8 small oval arms **Rev:** Cross in center, 3 circular legends

Date	Mintage	VG	F	VF	XF	Unc
ND Rare	—	—	—	—	—	—

DUCHY

REGULAR COINAGE

KM# 84 SECHSLING (1/2 Schilling; 1/96 Thaler)
Silver

Date	Mintage	VG	F	VF	XF	Unc
1674 AH	—	9.00	16.00	33.00	75.00	—
1675 AH	—	9.00	16.00	33.00	75.00	—
1676 AH	—	9.00	16.00	33.00	75.00	—
1680 IS	288,000	9.00	16.00	33.00	75.00	—
1681 IS	336,000	9.00	16.00	33.00	75.00	—
1682 IS	288,000	9.00	16.00	33.00	75.00	—
1683 IS	576,000	9.00	16.00	33.00	75.00	—
1684 IS	288,000	9.00	16.00	33.00	75.00	—
1685 IS	48,000	9.00	16.00	33.00	75.00	—

KM# 110 SECHSLING (1/2 Schilling; 1/96 Thaler)
Silver

Date	Mintage	VG	F	VF	XF	Unc
1691 ICS	82,000	10.00	20.00	40.00	80.00	—
1696 LM	145,000	10.00	20.00	40.00	80.00	—
1697 LM	177,000	10.00	20.00	40.00	80.00	—

KM# 50 2 SCHILLING
Silver **Obv:** Crossed keys above cross (arms of Bremen & Verden) **Rev:** II/SCHIL/LING/date

Date	Mintage	VG	F	VF	XF	Unc
(1)650 PT	3,000	45.00	90.00	165	250	—

KM# 75 1/48 THALER (Schilling)
Silver **Obv:** Crowned arms **Rev:** 48/REICHS/DALER/date

Date	Mintage	VG	F	VF	XF	Unc
1670	—	16.00	33.00	65.00	100	—
1671	—	16.00	33.00	65.00	100	—
1672	—	16.00	33.00	65.00	100	—

KM# 90 1/48 THALER (Schilling)
Silver **Note:** Similar to 1/24 Thaler (KM#38) but 48/REICHS/ DALER.

Date	Mintage	VG	F	VF	XF	Unc
1676 AH	—	13.00	27.00	45.00	90.00	—
1685 IS	48,000	13.00	27.00	45.00	90.00	—

KM# 111 1/48 THALER (Schilling)
Silver **Note:** Similar to 1/24 Thaler (KM#47) but 48/EIN/REICHS/ THAL.

Date	Mintage	VG	F	VF	XF	Unc
1691 ICA	73,000	13.00	27.00	45.00	90.00	—

KM# 114 1/48 THALER (Schilling)
Silver **Note:** Similar to 1/24 Thaler (KM#50) but 48 EIN. R.D.

Date	Mintage	VG	F	VF	XF	Unc
1696 LM	83,000	13.00	27.00	45.00	90.00	—
1697 LM	144,000	13.00	27.00	45.00	90.00	—

KM# 60 1/24 THALER (Groschen; 2 Schilling)
Silver **Obv:** Crowned arms **Rev:** 24/E. REICHS/DALER/date

Date	Mintage	VG	F	VF	XF	Unc
1660 MM	—	33.00	65.00	100	175	—
1666 MM	—	33.00	65.00	100	175	—
1667 MM	—	33.00	65.00	100	175	—

KM# 65 1/24 THALER (Groschen; 2 Schilling)
Silver **Rev:** 24/I REICH/S DALER

Date	Mintage	VG	F	VF	XF	Unc
1668 MM	—	33.00	65.00	100	175	—

KM# 66 1/24 THALER (Groschen; 2 Schilling)
Silver **Rev:** 24/I REICH/S TALER

Date	Mintage	VG	F	VF	XF	Unc
1668 MM	—	33.00	65.00	100	175	—
1669 MM	—	33.00	65.00	100	175	—

KM# 76 1/24 THALER (Groschen; 2 Schilling)
Silver **Rev:** 24/I REICH/S DALER **Note:** Varieties exist.

Date	Mintage	VG	F	VF	XF	Unc
1670 AH	—	33.00	65.00	100	175	—
1671 AH	—	33.00	65.00	100	175	—
1672 AH	—	33.00	65.00	100	175	—
1673 AH	—	33.00	65.00	100	175	—

KM# 80 1/24 THALER (Groschen; 2 Schilling)
Silver **Obv:** Crowned script CRS monogram in circle **Rev:** 24/E RT/date

Date	Mintage	VG	F	VF	XF	Unc
1673 AH	—	—	—	—	—	—

KM# 81 1/24 THALER (Groschen; 2 Schilling)
Silver **Obv:** Monogram not in circle

Date	Mintage	VG	F	VF	XF	Unc
1673 AH	—	—	—	—	—	—

KM# 91 1/24 THALER (Groschen; 2 Schilling)
Silver

Date	Mintage	VG	F	VF	XF	Unc
1676 AH	—	13.00	27.00	45.00	90.00	—
1682 IS	60,000	13.00	27.00	45.00	90.00	—
1683 IS	48,000	13.00	27.00	45.00	90.00	—
1684 IS	60,000	13.00	27.00	45.00	90.00	—

KM# 100 1/24 THALER (Groschen; 2 Schilling)
Silver **Obv:** Crowned C monogram **Rev:** 3 sections - arms of Bremen, arms of Verden and value, and IS

Date	Mintage	VG	F	VF	XF	Unc
1682 IS Rare	—	—	—	—	—	—

KM# 112 1/24 THALER (Groschen; 2 Schilling)
Silver

Date	Mintage	VG	F	VF	XF	Unc
1691 ICA	89,000	10.00	20.00	35.00	65.00	—
1692 ICA	94,000	10.00	20.00	35.00	65.00	—

KM# 115 1/24 THALER (Groschen; 2 Schilling)
Silver

Date	Mintage	VG	F	VF	XF	Unc
1696 LM	149,000	10.00	20.00	40.00	80.00	—
1697 LM	124,000	10.00	20.00	40.00	80.00	—

KM# 41 1/16 THALER (Dütchen; 3 Schilling)
Silver **Obv:** Laureate bust of Queen Christina right **Rev:** XVI/I REICH/DALER/date **Note:** Varieties exist.

Date	Mintage	VG	F	VF	XF	Unc
(1)649 PT	96,000	40.00	65.00	100	185	—
(1)650 PT	Inc. above	40.00	65.00	100	185	—

KM# 51 1/16 THALER (Dütchen; 3 Schilling)
Silver **Obv:** Small bust

Date	Mintage	VG	F	VF	XF	Unc
1650 PT	—	27.00	55.00	100	185	—

KM# 62 1/16 THALER (Dütchen; 3 Schilling)
Silver **Obv:** Laureate bust of Karl XI right **Rev:** XVI/I REIC/HS DA/date

Date	Mintage	VG	F	VF	XF	Unc
1666 MM	—	33.00	60.00	100	175	—

KM# 63 1/16 THALER (Dütchen; 3 Schilling)
Silver

Date	Mintage	VG	F	VF	XF	Unc
1666 MM	—	33.00	60.00	100	175	—
1667 MM	—	33.00	60.00	100	175	—
1668 MM	—	33.00	60.00	100	175	—
1669 MM	—	33.00	60.00	100	175	—

KM# 67 1/16 THALER (Dütchen; 3 Schilling)
Silver **Obv:** Plain bust

Date	Mintage	VG	F	VF	XF	Unc
1668 MM Rare	—	—	—	—	—	—

KM# 77 1/16 THALER (Dütchen; 3 Schilling)
Silver

Date	Mintage	VG	F	VF	XF	Unc
1670 AH	—	33.00	60.00	100	175	—

KM# 82 1/16 THALER (Dütchen; 3 Schilling)
Silver **Obv:** Crowned script CRS monogram **Rev:** 16/E R T/date **Note:** Varieties exist.

Date	Mintage	VG	F	VF	XF	Unc
1673 AH	—	—	—	—	—	—

KM# 101 1/12 THALER (4 Schilling)
Silver

Date	Mintage	VG	F	VF	XF	Unc
1682 IS	12,000	13.00	27.00	45.00	90.00	—

KM# 102 1/12 THALER (4 Schilling)
Silver **Note:** Klippe. Weight of 1/2 Thaler.

Date	Mintage	VG	F	VF	XF	Unc
1682 IS Rare	—	—	—	—	—	—

KM# 116 1/12 THALER (4 Schilling)
Silver **Note:** Similar to 1/24 Thaler (KM#50) but 12/EIN R D.

Date	Mintage	VG	F	VF	XF	Unc
1696 LM	49,000	12.00	25.00	40.00	80.00	—
1697 LM	25,000	12.00	25.00	40.00	80.00	—

KM# 85 1/6 THALER (4 Groschen; 1/2 Mark)
Silver **Obv:** Karl XI

Date	Mintage	VG	F	VF	XF	Unc
1674 AH	—	—	—	—	—	—
1675 AH	—	—	—	—	—	—

KM# 117 1/6 THALER (4 Groschen; 1/2 Mark)
Silver

Date	Mintage	VG	F	VF	XF	Unc
1697 LM	9,194	—	—	—	—	—

KM# 86 1/3 THALER (1/2 Gulden; Mark)
Silver

Date	Mintage	VG	F	VF	XF	Unc
1674 AH	—	400	600	1,100	1,700	—
1675 AH	—	300	450	700	1,100	—

KM# 118 1/3 THALER (1/2 Gulden; Mark)
Silver **Obv:** Older, larger bust

Date	Mintage	VG	F	VF	XF	Unc
1697 LM	5,000	—	—	—	—	—

KM# 119 1/3 THALER (1/2 Gulden; Mark)
Silver **Note:** Similar to 2/3 Thaler (KM#56).

Date	Mintage	VG	F	VF	XF	Unc
1697 LM	Inc. above	525	1,000	1,600	2,750	—

KM# 68 2 MARK
Silver **Obv:** Bust within inner circle **Rev:** Small crown

Date	Mintage	VG	F	VF	XF	Unc
1668	—	165	375	675	1,150	—

KM# 69 2 MARK
Silver **Obv:** Similar to 4 Marks (KM#23)

Date	Mintage	VG	F	VF	XF	Unc
1668 MM	—	165	375	675	1,150	—
1670 AH	—	165	375	675	1,150	—

KM# 78 2 MARK
Silver **Note:** Similar to 4 Marks (KM#79).

Date	Mintage	VG	F	VF	XF	Unc
1670 (c)	—	325	675	1,350	2,300	—

KM# 87 2/3 THALER (Gulden; 2 Mark)
Silver

Date	Mintage	VG	F	VF	XF	Unc
1674 AH	—	90.00	175	300	650	—
1675 AH	—	90.00	175	300	650	—

KM# 89 2/3 THALER (Gulden; 2 Mark)
Silver **Obv:** Bust without drapery

Date	Mintage	VG	F	VF	XF	Unc
1675 AH	—	150	250	350	650	—

KM# 120 2/3 THALER (Gulden; 2 Mark)
Silver **Obv:** Older, larger bust

Date	Mintage	VG	F	VF	XF	Unc
1697 LM	—	180	300	500	800	—

KM# 121 2/3 THALER (Gulden; 2 Mark)
Silver

Date	Mintage	VG	F	VF	XF	Unc
1697 LM	5,000	325	425	700	1,200	—
1698/7 LM	30,000	200	325	550	900	—

KM# 42 THALER
Silver **Obv:** Laureate bust of Christina right **Rev:** Crowned and supported arms, date divided below **Note:** Dav. #6280.

Date	Mintage	VG	F	VF	XF	Unc
1649 PT Unique	—	—	—	—	—	—

KM# 83 THALER
Silver **Note:** Dav. #6282.

Date	Mintage	VG	F	VF	XF	Unc
1673 AH	—	850	1,600	3,200	5,500	—
1674 AH	—	850	1,600	3,200	5,500	—

KM# 113 THALER
Silver **Obv:** Bust right **Rev:** Crowned and supported arms, date in legend **Note:** Dav. #6283.

Date	Mintage	VG	F	VF	XF	Unc
1692 ICA	6,111	900	1,700	3,350	5,750	—

KM# 61 4 MARK
Silver **Obv:** Script CGRS monogram **Note:** Varieties exist.

Date	Mintage	VG	F	VF	XF	Unc
1660 MM	—	250	500	850	1,250	—

KM# 64 4 MARK
Silver

Date	Mintage	VG	F	VF	XF	Unc
1666 MM	—	—	—	—	—	—
1667 MM	—	600	1,200	2,000	3,500	—
ND MM	—	600	1,200	2,000	3,500	—

KM# 70 4 MARK
Silver

Date	Mintage	VG	F	VF	XF	Unc
1668 MM	—	200	450	800	1,150	—

KM# 79 4 MARK
Silver **Obv:** Bust within inner circle

Date	Mintage	VG	F	VF	XF	Unc
1670 AH	—	200	450	800	1,150	—

KM# 88 2 THALER
Silver **Note:** Similar to Thaler, KM#31. Dav. #6281.

Date	Mintage	VG	F	VF	XF	Unc
1674 AH Rare	—	—	—	—	—	—

TRADE COINAGE

KM# 92 DUCAT
3.5000 g., 0.9860 Gold 0.1109 oz. AGW **Obv:** Laureate head of Charles right **Rev:** Entwined C's with date above

Date	Mintage	VG	F	VF	XF	Unc
1676 AH Rare	—	—	—	—	—	—

KM# 52 5 DUCAT (1/2 Portugalöser)
17.5000 g., 0.9860 Gold 0.5547 oz. AGW **Obv:** Laureate bust of Christina right in inner circle **Rev:** Crowned arms in inner circle, date below

Date	Mintage	VG	F	VF	XF	Unc
1650 PT Rare	—	—	—	—	—	—

KM# 53 10 DUCAT (Portugalöser)
35.0000 g., 0.9860 Gold 1.1095 oz. AGW **Obv:** Laureate bust of Christina right in inner circle **Rev:** Crowned arms in inner circle, date below

Date	Mintage	VG	F	VF	XF	Unc
1650 PT Rare	—	—	—	—	—	—

BRESLAU

One of the chief cities of Silesia, Breslau is the present day Wroclaw in Poland, 135 miles (225 kilometers) east of Dresden and 200 miles (330 kilometers) southwest of Warsaw. The site was settled in the early 10th century and a bishopric was soon established in close proximity to the town. The bishop was made a Prince of the Empire in 1290 and he obtained the right to coin money at the same time. The fortunes of the bishopric closely followed those of the city. The portion of territory which came into the possession of Prussia was secularized in 1810.

RULERS
Johann VI of Sitsch, 1600-1608
Karl, Erzherzog of Österreich, 1608-1624
Karl Ferdinand, Prinz von Polen, 1625-1655
Leopold Wilhelm, Erzherzog of Österreich, 1655-1662
Karl Josef, Erzherzog of Österreich, 1662-1664
Sebastian of Rostock, 1664-1671
Friedrich, Landgraf of Hessen-Darmstadt, 1671-1682
Wolfgang Georg of Pfalz, elected 1682, not seated
Franz Ludwig, Pfalzgraf of Neuburg, 1683-1732

MINT OFFICIALS' INITIALS

Initial or marks	Date	Name
(a)=	1614-?	Valentin Jahn (Janus)
HR	1612-53	Jans Rieger (Johann Rüger) der Ältere,
(b)= and/or		warden and die-cutter
HR	1653-60	Han Rieger der Jüngere, warden
(c)=	1618-20	Unknown
BZ	1620-24	Balthasar Zwirner (Zwürner), contractor
(d)=	1621-36	Johann Hans Riedel
(e)= HH	1624-27	Johann Jakob Huser, contractor
(f)=		
LPH/ЯH =	1678-1701	Leonhard Paul Haller, warden and mintmaster
(g)=	Ca. 1693	Unknown

ARMS
Breslau/Neisse – one to six lilies
Austria – horizontal shaded bar across middle of shield
Silesia – eagle, crescent moon on breast

NOTE: The arms of Neisse, a principality acquired by the bishops, are usually found on the episcopal coinage of Breslau, being practically identical one with the other.

REFERENCES
F/S = Ferdinand Friedensburg and Hans Seger, ***Schlesiens Münzen und Medaillen der neueren Zeit***, Breslau, 1901 (reprint Frankfurt/Main, 1976.

J/M = Norbert Jaschke and Fritz P. Maercker, ***Schlesische Münzen und Medaillen,*** Ihringen, 1985.

S = Hugo Frhr. Von Saurma-Jeltsch, ***Die Saurmasche Münzsammlung Deutscher, Schweizeerischer und Polnischer Gepräge von etwa dem Beginn der Groschenzeit bis zur Kipperperiode***, Berlin, 1892.

S/S = Hugo Frhr. Von Saurma-Jeltsch, ***Schlesische Münzen und Medaillen***, Breslau, 1883.

Sch = Wolfgangg Schulten, ***Deutsche Münzen aus der Zeit Karls V***, Frankfurt am Main, 1974.

BISHOPRIC

REGULAR COINAGE

KM# 401 15 KREUZER
5.6600 g., Silver, 29.9 mm. **Ruler:** Friedrich von Hessen **Obv:** Portrait above denomination **Rev:** Coat of arms **Edge:** Plain

Date	Mintage	F	VF	XF	Unc	BU
1679	—	30.00	75.00	150	—	—

DAV# 5121 THALER
Silver **Obv:** Capped bust right **Obv. Legend:** FRIDERICVS. S. R. E. CARD... **Rev:** Capped arms **Rev. Legend:** *PRO*DEO*ET*ECCLES...

Date	Mintage	VG	F	VF	XF	Unc
MDCXXIX	—	425	825	1,500	2,650	7,000
MDCXXX	—	425	825	1,500	2,650	7,000

DAV# 5114 THALER
Silver **Obv:** 3/4 facing bust **Obv. Legend:** KAR+FERD+PP+... **Rev:** Two oval shields with crossed Bishop's rod and staff, eiy of God above **Rev. Legend:** OMNIS POTESTAS...

Date	Mintage	VG	F	VF	XF	Unc
1639	—	425	825	1,500	2,650	—

DAV# 5114A THALER
Silver **Note:** Octagonal klippe.

Date	Mintage	VG	F	VF	XF	Unc
1639 Rare	—	—	—	—	—	—

DAV# 5114B THALER
Silver **Note:** Oval flan.

Date	Mintage	VG	F	VF	XF	Unc
1639 Rare	—	—	—	—	—	—

DAV# 5116 THALER
Silver **Obv:** Bust right **Obv. Legend:** CAROLVS • FERDINAN: D: G:... **Rev:** Similar to Dav. #5114

Date	Mintage	VG	F	VF	XF	Unc
1642	—	500	975	1,800	3,000	—

DAV# 5118 THALER
Silver **Obv:** Bust left **Obv. Legend:** CAROLVS FERDINANDVS... **Rev:** Crowned oval arms **Rev. Legend:** EPIS: WRATIS:ET.PLO...

Date	Mintage	VG	F	VF	XF	Unc
1653 Rare	—	—	—	—	—	—

DAV# 5119 THALER
Silver **Obv:** Bust right **Obv. Legend:** CAROLUS FERDINANDUS... **Rev:** Similar to Dav. #5118

Date	Mintage	VG	F	VF	XF	Unc
1654 Rare	—	—	—	—	—	—

DAV# 5119A THALER
Silver **Note:** Klippe.

Date	Mintage	VG	F	VF	XF	Unc
1654 Rare	—	—	—	—	—	—

DAV# 5119B THALER
Silver **Note:** Octagonal klippe.

Date	Mintage	VG	F	VF	XF	Unc
1654 Rare	—	—	—	—	—	—

DAV# 5120 THALER
Silver **Obv:** Mitered ornamented shield **Obv. Legend:** SEBASTIANVS... **Rev:** St. John standing divides date **Rev. Legend:** MVNVS. CAESAR: - MAXIMILIANI. I: **Note:** Ausbeute Thaler.

Date	Mintage	VG	F	VF	XF	Unc
1667	—	500	975	1,800	3,000	—

DAV# 5122 THALER
Silver **Obv:** Bust right **Obv. Legend:** FRANC. LUDOV. D. G... **Rev:** Capped ornamental shield **Rev. Legend:** COM.PALAT .RHENI...

Date	Mintage	VG	F	VF	XF	Unc
1694	—	525	1,050	1,950	3,250	—

DAV# 5111 2 THALER
Silver **Obv:** Bust of Karl right, date below **Obv. Legend:** CAR • FERD • P • P • ET • S • EPS • WRAT **Rev:** Bishop's hat above arms in cartouche **Rev. Legend:** A • IOVA • PRINCIPIVM

Date	Mintage	VG	F	VF	XF	Unc
1631	—	3,000	5,300	9,000	—	—

DAV# 5113A 2 THALER
Silver **Note:** Octagonal klippe. Similar to 1 Thaler, Dav. #5114.

Date	Mintage	VG	F	VF	XF	Unc
1639 Rare	—	—	—	—	—	—

DAV# 5113 2 THALER
Silver **Note:** Similar to 1 Thaler, Dav. #5114.

Date	Mintage	VG	F	VF	XF	Unc
1639	—	1,500	2,700	4,500	7,500	—

DAV# 5115 2 THALER
Silver **Note:** Similar to 1 Thaler, Dav. #5116.

Date	Mintage	VG	F	VF	XF	Unc
1642	—	2,500	4,250	7,000	—	—

DAV# 5115A 2 THALER
Silver **Note:** Oval flan.

Date	Mintage	VG	F	VF	XF	Unc
1642 Rare	—	—	—	—	—	—

DAV# 5115B 2 THALER
Silver **Note:** Hexagonal flan.

Date	Mintage	VG	F	VF	XF	Unc
1642 Rare	—	—	—	—	—	—

DAV# 5115C 2 THALER
Silver **Note:** Octagonal flan.

Date	Mintage	VG	F	VF	XF	Unc
1642 Rare	—	—	—	—	—	—

DAV# 5117 2 THALER
Silver **Note:** Similar to 1 Thaler, Dav. #5118.

Date	Mintage	VG	F	VF	XF	Unc
1653 Rare	—	—	—	—	—	—

DAV# 5115E 2-1/2 THALER
Silver **Note:** Hexagonal klippe.

Date	Mintage	VG	F	VF	XF	Unc
1642 Rare	—	—	—	—	—	—

DAV# 5115D 2-1/2 THALER
Silver **Note:** Similar to 2 Thaler, Dav. #5115A.

Date	Mintage	VG	F	VF	XF	Unc
1642 Rare	—	—	—	—	—	—

DAV# 5113B 3 THALER
Silver **Note:** Similar to 1 Thaler, Dav. #5114.

Date	Mintage	VG	F	VF	XF	Unc
1639 Rare	—	—	—	—	—	—

DAV# 5113C 4 THALER
Silver **Note:** Similar to 1 Thaler, Dav. #5114.

Date	Mintage	VG	F	VF	XF	Unc
1639 Rare	—	—	—	—	—	—

TRADE COINAGE

FR# 526 1/6 DUCAT
0.5833 g., 0.9860 Gold 0.0185 oz. AGW **Obv:** Bust of Franz Ludwig right **Rev:** Arms

Date	Mintage	VG	F	VF	XF	Unc
ND	—	150	300	600	1,000	—

FR# 498 1/2 DUCAT
1.7500 g., 0.9860 Gold 0.0555 oz. AGW **Obv:** Bust of Karl right **Rev:** Crowned arms

Date	Mintage	VG	F	VF	XF	Unc
1618	—	400	800	1400	2800	—

FR# 484 DUCAT
3.5000 g., 0.9860 Gold 0.1109 oz. AGW **Obv:** St. John standing facing **Rev:** Arms topped by mitre

Date	Mintage	VG	F	VF	XF	Unc
ND	—	400	900	1,400	2,500	—

FR# 486 DUCAT
3.5000 g., 0.9860 Gold 0.1109 oz. AGW **Obv:** Bust of Karl right **Rev:** Two shields of arms topped by crown and mitre

Date	Mintage	VG	F	VF	XF	Unc
1611	—	500	1000	1600	3000	—
1612	—	500	1000	1600	3000	—

FR# 489 DUCAT
3.5000 g., 0.9860 Gold 0.1109 oz. AGW **Subject:** Shooting Festival **Obv:** Two shields of arms topped by crown and mitre **Rev:** Five-line inscription with date above

Date	Mintage	VG	F	VF	XF	Unc
1612	—	450	900	1,400	2,750	—

FR# 496 DUCAT
3.5000 g., 0.9860 Gold 0.1109 oz. AGW **Obv:** Bust of Karl right **Rev:** Three shields abreast

Date	Mintage	VG	F	VF	XF	Unc
1614	—	450	950	1,500	2,900	—

FR# 497 DUCAT
3.5000 g., 0.9860 Gold 0.1109 oz. AGW **Rev:** Arms

Date	Mintage	VG	F	VF	XF	Unc
1618 Rare	—	—	—	—	—	—

FR# 512b DUCAT
3.5000 g., 0.9860 Gold 0.1109 oz. AGW **Obv:** Karl Ferdinand **Rev:** Crowned arms

Date	Mintage	VG	F	VF	XF	Unc
1653 Rare	—	—	—	—	—	—

FR# 515 DUCAT

3.5000 g., 0.9860 Gold 0.1109 oz. AGW **Obv:** Bust of Sebastian right **Rev:** Arms

Date	Mintage	VG	F	VF	XF	Unc
1665 Rare	—	—	—	—	—	—

FR# 518 DUCAT

3.5000 g., 0.9860 Gold 0.1109 oz. AGW **Obv:** Bust of Frederich right **Rev:** Arms with cherub head above

Date	Mintage	VG	F	VF	XF	Unc
1679	—	400	900	1,500	2,900	—
1680	—	400	900	1,500	2,900	—
1681	—	400	900	1,500	2,900	—
1682	—	400	900	1,500	2,900	—

FR# 523 DUCAT

3.5000 g., 0.9860 Gold 0.1109 oz. AGW **Obv:** Bust of Franz Ludwig right **Rev:** Elaborate arms topped by mitre dividing date

Date	Mintage	VG	F	VF	XF	Unc
1686	—	400	900	1,500	2,900	—
1688	—	400	900	1,500	2,900	—
1691	—	400	900	1,500	2,900	—
1696	—	400	900	1,500	2,900	—
1700	—	400	900	1,500	2,900	—

FR# 483a 2 DUCAT

7.0000 g., 0.9860 Gold 0.2219 oz. AGW **Obv:** Arms topped by mitre **Rev:** St. John standing

Date	Mintage	VG	F	VF	XF	Unc
1603	—	1,100	2,200	4,500	8,000	—

FR# 483 2 DUCAT

7.0000 g., 0.9860 Gold 0.2219 oz. AGW **Note:** Klippe.

Date	Mintage	VG	F	VF	XF	Unc
1603 Rare	—	—	—	—	—	—

FR# 488 2 DUCAT

7.0000 g., 0.9860 Gold 0.2219 oz. AGW **Subject:** Shooting Festival **Obv:** Two shields of armor topped by crown and mitre **Rev:** Five-line inscription with date above

Date	Mintage	VG	F	VF	XF	Unc
1612	—	400	800	1,650	3,250	—

KM# 50 2 DUCAT

7.0000 g., 0.9860 Gold 0.2219 oz. AGW **Obv:** Bust of Karl right **Rev:** Three shields abreast in inner circle

Date	Mintage	VG	F	VF	XF	Unc
ND	—	1,000	2,000	4,000	7,000	—

FR# 511 2 DUCAT

7.0000 g., 0.9860 Gold 0.2219 oz. AGW **Obv:** Bust of Karl Ferdinand right **Rev:** Two shields of arms topped by mitre

Date	Mintage	VG	F	VF	XF	Unc
1632	—	1,000	2,000	4,000	7,000	—

FR# 512 2 DUCAT

7.0000 g., 0.9860 Gold 0.2219 oz. AGW **Note:** Octagonal klippe.

Date	Mintage	VG	F	VF	XF	Unc
1632 Rare	—	—	—	—	—	—

FR# 512a 2 DUCAT

7.0000 g., 0.9860 Gold 0.2219 oz. AGW **Note:** Octagonal klippe.

Date	Mintage	VG	F	VF	XF	Unc
1653 Rare	—	—	—	—	—	—

FR# 511a 2 DUCAT

7.0000 g., 0.9860 Gold 0.2219 oz. AGW **Rev:** Crowned arms

Date	Mintage	VG	F	VF	XF	Unc
1653 Rare	—	—	—	—	—	—

FR# 514 2 DUCAT

7.0000 g., 0.9860 Gold 0.2219 oz. AGW **Obv:** Bust of Sebastian right **Rev:** Arms

Date	Mintage	VG	F	VF	XF	Unc
1665 Rare	—	—	—	—	—	—

FR# 515a 2 DUCAT

7.0000 g., 0.9860 Gold 0.2219 oz. AGW **Obv:** Arms topped by mitre **Rev:** St. John standing **Rev. Legend:** MUNUS CAESAR MAXIMILIANI I

Date	Mintage	VG	F	VF	XF	Unc
1665	—	1,300	2,700	5,400	9,600	—

FR# 517 2 DUCAT

7.0000 g., 0.9860 Gold 0.2219 oz. AGW **Subject:** Bishop Freidrich

Date	Mintage	VG	F	VF	XF	Unc
1679 Rare	—	—	—	—	—	—

FR# 517a 2 DUCAT

7.0000 g., 0.9860 Gold 0.2219 oz. AGW **Subject:** Freidrich

Date	Mintage	VG	F	VF	XF	Unc
1680 Rare	—	—	—	—	—	—

FR# 522 2 DUCAT

7.0000 g., 0.9860 Gold 0.2219 oz. AGW **Obv:** Bust of Franz Ludwig right **Rev:** Elaborate arms topped by mitre dividing date

Date	Mintage	VG	F	VF	XF	Unc
1690	—	450	1,000	2,000	3,500	—
1693	—	450	1,000	2,000	3,500	—

FR# 482 3 DUCAT

10.5000 g., 0.9860 Gold 0.3328 oz. AGW **Obv:** St. John standing **Rev:** Arms topped by mitre **Note:** Klippe.

Date	Mintage	VG	F	VF	XF	Unc
1603 Rare	—	—	—	—	—	—

FR# 487 3 DUCAT

10.5000 g., 0.9860 Gold 0.3328 oz. AGW **Subject:** Shooting Festival **Obv:** Two shields of arms topped by crown and mitre **Rev:** Five-line inscription with date above

Date	Mintage	VG	F	VF	XF	Unc
1612 Rare	—	—	—	—	—	—

FR# 495 3 DUCAT

10.5000 g., 0.9860 Gold 0.3328 oz. AGW **Obv:** Bust of Karl right **Rev:** Three shields abreast

Date	Mintage	VG	F	VF	XF	Unc
1614 Rare	—	—	—	—	—	—
1618 Rare	—	—	—	—	—	—

FR# 509 3 DUCAT

10.5000 g., 0.9860 Gold 0.3328 oz. AGW **Obv:** Bust of Karl Ferdinand right **Rev:** Two shields of arms topped by mitre

Date	Mintage	VG	F	VF	XF	Unc
1632	—	900	1,800	3,600	6,000	—

FR# 510 3 DUCAT

10.5000 g., 0.9860 Gold 0.3328 oz. AGW **Note:** Octagonal klippe.

Date	Mintage	VG	F	VF	XF	Unc
1632 Rare	—	—	—	—	—	—

FR# 510a 3 DUCAT

10.5000 g., 0.9860 Gold 0.3328 oz. AGW **Note:** Octagonal klippe.

Date	Mintage	VG	F	VF	XF	Unc
1653 Rare	—	—	—	—	—	—

FR# 509a 3 DUCAT

10.5000 g., 0.9860 Gold 0.3328 oz. AGW **Note:** Struck with 1 Ducat dies, Fr. #512b.

Date	Mintage	VG	F	VF	XF	Unc
1653	—	900	1,800	3,600	6,000	—

FR# 516 3 DUCAT

10.5000 g., 0.9860 Gold 0.3328 oz. AGW **Obv:** Bust of Friedrich right **Rev:** Arms with cherub head above

Date	Mintage	VG	F	VF	XF	Unc
1674 Rare	—	—	—	—	—	—

FR# 494 4 DUCAT

14.0000 g., 0.9860 Gold 0.4438 oz. AGW **Obv:** Bust of Karl right **Rev:** Three shields abreast in inner circle

Date	Mintage	VG	F	VF	XF	Unc
1618 Rare	—	—	—	—	—	—

FR# 508 4 DUCAT

14.0000 g., 0.9860 Gold 0.4438 oz. AGW **Obv:** Bust of Karl Ferdinand right **Rev:** Crowned arms

Date	Mintage	VG	F	VF	XF	Unc
1632 Rare	—	—	—	—	—	—

FR# 506 5 DUCAT (1/2 Portugalöser)

17.5000 g., 0.9860 Gold 0.5547 oz. AGW **Obv:** Bust of Carl Ferdinand right **Rev:** Crowned arms

Date	Mintage	VG	F	VF	XF	Unc
1632 Rare	—	—	—	—	—	—
1639 Rare	—	—	—	—	—	—

FR# 507 5 DUCAT (1/2 Portugalöser)

17.5000 g., 0.9860 Gold 0.5547 oz. AGW **Note:** Klippe.

Date	Mintage	VG	F	VF	XF	Unc
1632 Rare	—	—	—	—	—	—

FR# 504 6 DUCAT

21.0000 g., 0.9860 Gold 0.6657 oz. AGW **Obv:** Bust of Carl Ferdinand right

Date	Mintage	VG	F	VF	XF	Unc
1632 Rare	—	—	—	—	—	—
1639 Rare	—	—	—	—	—	—

FR# 505 6 DUCAT

21.0000 g., 0.9860 Gold 0.6657 oz. AGW **Note:** Klippe.

Date	Mintage	VG	F	VF	XF	Unc
1632 Rare	—	—	—	—	—	—

FR# 503 10 DUCAT (Portugalöser)

35.0000 g., 0.9860 Gold 1.1095 oz. AGW **Obv:** Bust of Karl Ferdinand right **Rev:** Arms

Date	Mintage	VG	F	VF	XF	Unc
1631 Rare	—	—	—	—	—	—
1638 Rare	—	—	—	—	—	—

FR# 503a 10 DUCAT (Portugalöser)

35.0000 g., 0.9860 Gold 1.1095 oz. AGW **Note:** Struck with 1 Thaler dies, Dav. #5114.

Date	Mintage	VG	F	VF	XF	Unc
1639 Rare	—	—	—	—	—	—

FR# 503b 10 DUCAT (Portugalöser)

35.0000 g., 0.9860 Gold 1.1095 oz. AGW **Note:** Struck with 1 Thaler dies, Dav. #5116.

Date	Mintage	VG	F	VF	XF	Unc
1642 Rare	—	—	—	—	—	—

FR# 513 10 DUCAT (Portugalöser)

35.0000 g., 0.9860 Gold 1.1095 oz. AGW **Note:** Struck with 1 Thaler dies, Dav. #5120.

Date	Mintage	VG	F	VF	XF	Unc
1667 Rare	—	—	—	—	—	—

FR# 502 15 DUCAT

52.5000 g., 0.9860 Gold 1.6642 oz. AGW **Obv:** Bust of Karl Ferdinand right **Rev:** Crowned arms

Date	Mintage	VG	F	VF	XF	Unc
1631 Rare	—	—	—	—	—	—
1632 Rare	—	—	—	—	—	—

CITY

After its founding in the early 10th century, Breslau was subject to Poland until it became the capital of the Duchy of Middle Silesia in 1163. Duke Heinrich VI gave the already semi-autonomous city the mint right in 1318. Breslau came under the rule of Bohemia in 1360 and for most of the time up until 1526 maintained some semblance of independence. In that year, all of Bohemia and Silesia became Habsburg domains, but as a result of a war with Prussia, Breslau was ceded to the latter in 1741. A city coinage was struck until about the early 18th century, and a Prussian mint operated in Breslau from about 1750 until the late 19th century.

MINT OFFICIALS' INITIALS

Initial	Date	Name
HR (sometimes in ligature)	1622-36	Hans Riedel (Rüdel)

REGULAR COINAGE

DAV# 5123 THALER

Silver **Obv:** Bust right **Obv. Legend:** FERDINA • D: G • RO... **Rev:** Helmeted arms **Rev. Legend:** MONETA • S • P. Q. WRATISLAVIENS

Date	Mintage	VG	F	VF	XF	Unc
16ZZ	—	425	825	1,500	2,650	—

DAV# 5124 THALER

Silver **Obv:** Bust right **Obv. Legend:** LEOPOLD. D. G. R... **Rev:** Helmeted arms **Rev. Legend:** MON. NOV... WRATISLAV

Date	Mintage	VG	F	VF	XF	Unc
1662	—	350	675	1,300	2,250	—

TRADE COINAGE

FR# 469 1/2 DUCAT

1.7500 g., 0.9860 Gold 0.0555 oz. AGW **Obv:** Crowned bust of Ferdinand II right **Rev:** Crowned arms

Date	Mintage	VG	F	VF	XF	Unc
1622	—	190	375	750	1,350	—

KM# 95 1/2 DUCAT

1.7500 g., 0.9860 Gold 0.0555 oz. AGW **Subject:** Ferdinand III

Date	Mintage	VG	F	VF	XF	Unc
1642	—	225	450	900	1,650	—

FR# 457 DUCAT

3.5000 g., 0.9860 Gold 0.1109 oz. AGW **Obv:** Crowned bust of Matthias II right **Rev:** Arms in inner circle

Date	Mintage	VG	F	VF	XF	Unc
1611	—	240	475	900	1,600	—
1612	—	240	475	900	1,600	—
1613	—	240	475	900	1,600	—

FR# 461 DUCAT

3.5000 g., 0.9860 Gold 0.1109 oz. AGW **Subject:** Shooting Festival

Date	Mintage	VG	F	VF	XF	Unc
1614	—	325	575	1,150	2,300	—

FR# 464 DUCAT

3.5000 g., 0.9860 Gold 0.1109 oz. AGW

Date	Mintage	VG	F	VF	XF	Unc
1617	—	265	525	975	1,800	—

FR# 466 DUCAT

3.5000 g., 0.9860 Gold 0.1109 oz. AGW

Date	Mintage	VG	F	VF	XF	Unc
1620 Rare	—	—	—	—	—	—

Note: Fritz Rudolf Künker Münzenhandlung Auction 140, 6-08, nearly XF realized approximately $17,050.

FR# 468 DUCAT

3.5000 g., 0.9860 Gold 0.1109 oz. AGW **Obv:** Crowned bust of Ferdinand II right **Rev:** Crowned arms

Date	Mintage	VG	F	VF	XF	Unc
1622	—	295	550	1,050	2,100	—

FR# 471 DUCAT

3.5000 g., 0.9860 Gold 0.1109 oz. AGW **Rev:** Christ on cross, balance scale over date divided by arms

Date	Mintage	VG	F	VF	XF	Unc
1630	—	210	425	775	1,450	—

KM# 110 DUCAT

3.5000 g., 0.9860 Gold 0.1109 oz. AGW **Obv:** Crowned bust of Ferdinand III right **Rev:** Crowned arms

Date	Mintage	VG	F	VF	XF	Unc
1646	—	375	750	1,450	2,800	—

FR# 455.1 2 DUCAT

7.0000 g., 0.9860 Gold 0.2219 oz. AGW **Obv:** Large crowned bust of Matthias II right **Rev:** Helmeted arms

Date	Mintage	VG	F	VF	XF	Unc
1611	—	400	800	1,800	3,400	—

FR# 455.2 2 DUCAT

7.0000 g., 0.9860 Gold 0.2219 oz. AGW **Obv:** Small crowned bust of Matthias II right

Date	Mintage	VG	F	VF	XF	Unc
1612	—	600	1,200	2,400	5,000	—

FR# 456 2 DUCAT

7.0000 g., 0.9860 Gold 0.2219 oz. AGW **Note:** Klippe. Struck with 1 Ducat dies, Fr.#457.

Date	Mintage	VG	F	VF	XF	Unc
1612 Rare	—	—	—	—	—	—

FR# 460 2 DUCAT

7.0000 g., 0.9860 Gold 0.2219 oz. AGW **Subject:** Shooting Festival **Obv:** Helmeted arms of Breslau **Rev:** Five-line inscription with date above

Date	Mintage	VG	F	VF	XF	Unc
1614	—	600	1,200	2,400	4,200	—

FR# 463 2 DUCAT

7.0000 g., 0.9860 Gold 0.2219 oz. AGW **Note:** Klippe. Struck with 1 Ducat dies, Fr.#464.

Date	Mintage	VG	F	VF	XF	Unc
1617	—	375	900	1,800	3,600	—

FR# 462 2 DUCAT

7.0000 g., 0.9860 Gold 0.2219 oz. AGW **Obv:** Crowned bust of Matthias II right **Rev:** Crowned F, inscription over arms

Date	Mintage	VG	F	VF	XF	Unc
1617	—	240	550	1,150	2,200	—

FR# 465 2 DUCAT

7.0000 g., 0.9860 Gold 0.2219 oz. AGW **Obv:** Crowned bust of Freidrich V inside double circle **Rev:** Helmeted arms of Breslau, date divided by helmet

Date	Mintage	VG	F	VF	XF	Unc
1620 Rare	—	—	—	—	—	—

Note: Fritz Rudolf Künker Münzenhandlung Auction 140, 6-08, VF realized approximately $17,050.

FR# 470 2 DUCAT

7.0000 g., 0.9860 Gold 0.2219 oz. AGW **Subject:** Ferdinand II **Rev:** Christ on cross, balance scale over date divided by arms

Date	Mintage	VG	F	VF	XF	Unc
1630	—	260	575	1,250	2,400	—

FR# 453 3 DUCAT

10.5000 g., 0.9860 Gold 0.3328 oz. AGW **Obv:** Crowned bust of Matthias II right **Rev:** Arms in inner circle

Date	Mintage	VG	F	VF	XF	Unc
1612	—	750	1,400	2,850	5,000	—

FR# 454 3 DUCAT

10.5000 g., 0.9860 Gold 0.3328 oz. AGW **Note:** Klippe.

Date	Mintage	VG	F	VF	XF	Unc
1612	—	775	1,500	3,200	5,700	—

FR# 459 3 DUCAT

10.5000 g., 0.9860 Gold 0.3328 oz. AGW **Note:** Klippe.

Date	Mintage	VG	F	VF	XF	Unc
1614 Rare	—	—	—	—	—	—

FR# 458 3 DUCAT

10.5000 g., 0.9860 Gold 0.3328 oz. AGW **Subject:** Shooting Festival **Obv:** Helmeted arms of Breslau **Rev:** Five-line inscription with date above

Date	Mintage	VG	F	VF	XF	Unc
1614 Rare	—	—	—	—	—	—

FR# 467 3 DUCAT

10.5000 g., 0.9860 Gold 0.3328 oz. AGW **Obv:** Crowned bust of Ferdinand II right **Rev:** Crowned arms **Note:** Klippe.

Date	Mintage	VG	F	VF	XF	Unc
1622	—	500	1,000	2,200	4,500	—

FR# 452 4 DUCAT

14.0000 g., 0.9860 Gold 0.4438 oz. AGW **Obv:** Crowned bust of Matthias II right **Rev:** Helmeted arms

Date	Mintage	VG	F	VF	XF	Unc
1612 Rare	—	—	—	—	—	—

FR# 450 5 DUCAT (1/2 Portugalöser)

17.5000 g., 0.9860 Gold 0.5547 oz. AGW **Obv:** Crowned bust of Matthias II right **Rev:** Helmeted arms

Date	Mintage	VG	F	VF	XF	Unc
1612 Rare	—	—	—	—	—	—

FR# 451 5 DUCAT (1/2 Portugalöser)

17.5000 g., 0.9860 Gold 0.5547 oz. AGW **Note:** Klippe.

Date	Mintage	VG	F	VF	XF	Unc
1612 Rare	—	—	—	—	—	—

BRUNSWICK

FREE CITY

The city of Brunswick (German: Braunschweig) is located on the Oker River in northern Germany, 37 miles (62 kilometers) southeast of Hannover and 53 miles (88 kilometers) northwest of Magdeburg. Founded about 861 by Bruno of Saxony, the town became an important place in the late Middle Ages and was an early member of the Hanseatic League. The dukes of Brunswick made the city their early capital and never relinquished their control completely. The city was granted the right to produce its own coins, however, first in 1296 and reiterated in 1345. The municipal coinage was produced in considerable quantities during the 16th and most of the 17th centuries. Brunswick became a Protestant enclave during the Reformation and suffered during the Thirty Years' War. It was included in the Kingdom of Westphalia from 1807 until 1813. In 1834, Brunswick gained its independence from the duke and enjoyed self-rule from that point onwards into the modern age.

MINT OFFICIALS' MARKS & INITIALS

Mark	Desc.	Date	Name
(b) = or		1599-1600, 1606-09	Peter Schrader (or Schröder)
		1620-48	Paul Becker
(c) = or HB		1648-67	Hans Becker
	B/IGB	1675-85	Johann Georg Breuer
	BH	1675-76	Bastian Hille

ARMS

Rampant lion to left

Patron saint – St. Author

REGULAR COINAGE

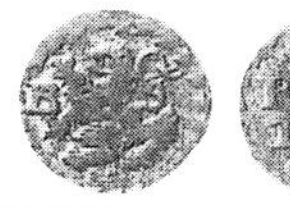

KM# 15.1 FLITTER

Copper **Obv:** Rampant lion left, B between forepaws, in wreath **Rev:** Date in wreath **Rev. Legend:** I/FLIT/TER **Note:** Kipper Flitter.

Date	Mintage	VG	F	VF	XF	Unc
(1)6Z0	—	20.00	35.00	60.00	120	—
(1)6Z1	—	20.00	35.00	60.00	120	—
ND	—	20.00	35.00	60.00	120	—

KM# 15.2 FLITTER

Copper **Obv:** Without B between paws

Date	Mintage	VG	F	VF	XF	Unc
16Z0	—	20.00	35.00	60.00	120	—
(1)6Z1	—	20.00	35.00	60.00	120	—
ND	—	20.00	35.00	60.00	120	—

KM# 16 3 FLITTER

Copper **Obv:** Large 'B' between 4 annulets **Rev:** City arms without shield, value III above **Note:** Kipper.

Date	Mintage	VG	F	VF	XF	Unc
ND(1620-21)	—	—	—	—	—	—

KM# A17 3 FLITTER

Copper **Obv:** Rampant lion right **Rev. Legend:** III/FLIT/TER/16Z1

Date	Mintage	VG	F	VF	XF	Unc
1621	—	20.00	40.00	75.00	140	—

KM# 47 MATTHIER

Silver **Obv:** Rampant lion left **Rev:** Date in legend **Rev. Legend:** I/MAT/TIR **Note:** Weight varies: 1.06-1.17g.

Date	Mintage	VG	F	VF	XF	Unc
1647 (b)	—	—	—	—	—	—

KM# 32 PFENNIG

Silver **Note:** Uniface. Klippe. Rampant lion left, B below, date divided anbove 1-62-5.

Date	Mintage	VG	F	VF	XF	Unc
1625	—	—	—	—	—	—

KM# 34 PFENNIG

Silver **Note:** Uniface hohlpfennig type. Rampant lion left in cup-shape, date below on rim.

Date	Mintage	VG	F	VF	XF	Unc
1627	—	9.00	20.00	40.00	80.00	—
1632	—	9.00	20.00	40.00	80.00	—
1635	—	9.00	20.00	40.00	80.00	—
1637	—	9.00	20.00	40.00	80.00	—
1638	—	9.00	20.00	40.00	80.00	—
1641	—	9.00	20.00	40.00	80.00	—
1644	—	9.00	20.00	40.00	80.00	—
1650	—	9.00	20.00	40.00	80.00	—

Date	Mintage	VG	F	VF	XF	Unc
1653	—	9.00	20.00	40.00	80.00	—
1657	—	9.00	20.00	40.00	80.00	—

KM# 36 PFENNIG

Silver **Note:** Uniface, round flan. Rampant lion left, B divides date below.

Date	Mintage	VG	F	VF	XF	Unc
1628	—	8.00	16.00	35.00	65.00	—
1629	—	8.00	16.00	35.00	65.00	—
1630	—	8.00	16.00	35.00	65.00	—
1631	—	8.00	16.00	35.00	65.00	—
1633	—	8.00	16.00	35.00	65.00	—
1634	—	8.00	16.00	35.00	65.00	—
1635	—	8.00	16.00	35.00	65.00	—
1637	—	8.00	16.00	35.00	65.00	—
1638	—	8.00	16.00	35.00	65.00	—
1640	—	8.00	16.00	35.00	65.00	—
1641	—	8.00	16.00	35.00	65.00	—
1642	—	8.00	16.00	35.00	65.00	—
1644	—	8.00	16.00	35.00	65.00	—
1645	—	8.00	16.00	35.00	65.00	—
1646	—	8.00	16.00	35.00	65.00	—
1647	—	8.00	16.00	35.00	65.00	—
1648	—	8.00	16.00	35.00	65.00	—
1649	—	8.00	16.00	35.00	65.00	—
1652	—	8.00	16.00	35.00	65.00	—
1653	—	8.00	16.00	35.00	65.00	—
1657	—	8.00	16.00	35.00	65.00	—
1659	—	8.00	16.00	35.00	65.00	—
1678	—	8.00	16.00	35.00	65.00	—

KM# 70 2 PFENNIG

Silver **Obv:** 2/PENN/date/B **Rev. Legend:** BR/STAT/GEL

Date	Mintage	VG	F	VF	XF	Unc
1676 B	—	27.00	55.00	85.00	165	—

KM# 5 3 PFENNIG (Dreier)

Silver **Obv:** Rampant lion left, B between forepaws

Date	Mintage	VG	F	VF	XF	Unc
(1)600	—	20.00	35.00	60.00	120	—

KM# 11 3 PFENNIG (Dreier)

Silver **Obv:** Rampant lion left in ornamented shield **Rev:** Imperial orb with 3 divides date **Note:** Varieties exist.

Date	Mintage	VG	F	VF	XF	Unc
1608	—	20.00	33.00	60.00	120	—
1623	—	20.00	33.00	60.00	120	—

KM# 22 3 PFENNIG (Dreier)

Silver **Obv:** MO NO BRUN above shield

Date	Mintage	VG	F	VF	XF	Unc
16ZZ (b)	—	16.00	30.00	55.00	85.00	—
1623 (b)	—	16.00	30.00	55.00	85.00	—
1633 (b)	—	16.00	30.00	55.00	85.00	—
1634 (b)	—	16.00	30.00	55.00	85.00	—
1635 (b)	—	16.00	30.00	55.00	85.00	—
1637 (b)	—	16.00	30.00	55.00	85.00	—
1638 (b)	—	16.00	30.00	55.00	85.00	—
1641 (b)	—	16.00	30.00	55.00	85.00	—
1642 (b)	—	16.00	30.00	55.00	85.00	—
1644 (b)	—	16.00	30.00	55.00	85.00	—
1645 (b)	—	16.00	30.00	55.00	85.00	—
1646 (b)	—	16.00	30.00	55.00	85.00	—

KM# 71 3 PFENNIG (Dreier)

Silver **Obv:** Crowned script B divides STAT-GELT

Date	Mintage	VG	F	VF	XF	Unc
1676 B	—	33.00	60.00	100	200	—

KM# 72 3 PFENNIG (Dreier)

Silver **Obv:** Crowned rampant lion left, BR. ST-GELT

Date	Mintage	VG	F	VF	XF	Unc
1676 B	—	27.00	55.00	90.00	170	—

KM# 73 4 PFENNIG

Silver **Obv:** Crowned rampant lion left **Rev:** Date **Rev. Inscription:** IIII/GVTE/PENN **Note:** Gute 4 Pfennig. Varieties exist.

Date	Mintage	VG	F	VF	XF	Unc
1676 B	—	27.00	55.00	100	200	—
ND B	—	27.00	55.00	100	200	—

KM# 80 4-1/2 PFENNIG

Silver **Obv:** Rampant lion left in circle **Rev:** Date in legend **Rev. Legend:** 4 1/2 • PENN

Date	Mintage	VG	F	VF	XF	Unc
1680	—	—	—	—	—	—

KM# 10 GROSCHEN (1/24 Thaler)

Silver **Note:** Klippe.

Date	Mintage	VG	F	VF	XF	Unc
1606	—	—	—	—	—	—

KM# 8 GROSCHEN (1/24 Thaler)

Silver **Obv:** Rampant lion left in circle **Rev:** Imperial orb divides date, titles of Rudolf II

Date	Mintage	VG	F	VF	XF	Unc
1606	—	—	—	—	—	—

KM# 9 GROSCHEN (1/24 Thaler)

Silver **Obv:** Date in legend at top

Date	Mintage	VG	F	VF	XF	Unc
1606	—	—	—	—	—	—

KM# 18 GROSCHEN (1/24 Thaler)

Silver **Obv:** Helmeted oval arms (rampant lion left) **Rev:** Imperial orb with 24, date divided at top in legend, titles of Ferdinand II **Note:** Kipper Groschen. Small module.

Date	Mintage	VG	F	VF	XF	Unc
1620	—	20.00	40.00	65.00	120	—

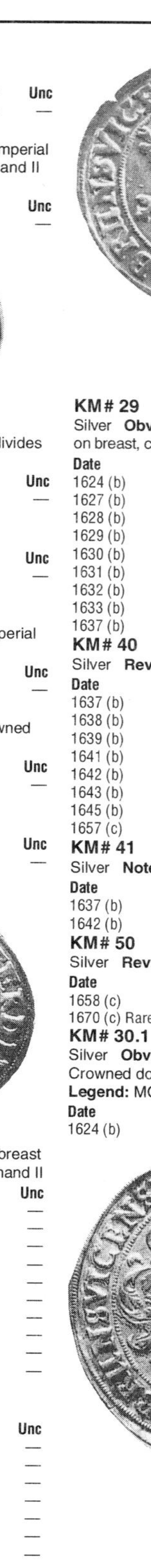

KM# 23 GROSCHEN (1/24 Thaler)

Silver **Obv:** Helmeted arms **Rev:** Imperial orb wtih 24 divides date, titles of Ferdinand II

Date	Mintage	VG	F	VF	XF	Unc
1622 (b)	—	20.00	40.00	65.00	120	—

KM# 46 GROSCHEN (1/24 Thaler)

Silver **Rev:** Titles of Ferdinand III

Date	Mintage	VG	F	VF	XF	Unc
1642 (b)	—	—	—	—	—	—

Note: Reported, not confirmed

KM# 74 GROSCHEN (1/24 Thaler)

Silver **Obv:** Crowned arms divide BRVN-SVIC **Rev:** Imperial orb with 24, date in legend

Date	Mintage	VG	F	VF	XF	Unc
1676	—	20.00	33.00	60.00	120	—

KM# 27 3 GROSCHEN

Silver **Obv:** Rampant lion left, date in legend **Rev:** Crowned imperial eagle, orb on breast with 3, titles of Ferdinand II

Date	Mintage	VG	F	VF	XF	Unc
1624 (b)	—	—	—	—	—	—

KM# 43 3 GROSCHEN

Silver **Rev:** Titles of Ferdinand III

Date	Mintage	VG	F	VF	XF	Unc
1638 (b)	—	—	—	—	—	—

Note: Reported, not confirmed

KM# 28 6 GROSCHEN (1/4 Thaler)

Silver **Obv:** Rampant lion left **Rev:** Imperial eagle, orb on breast with 6, crown above divides date in legend, titles of Ferdinand II

Date	Mintage	VG	F	VF	XF	Unc
1624 (b)	—	250	500	850	1,500	—
1625 (b)	—	250	500	850	1,500	—
1627 (b)	—	250	500	850	1,500	—
1628 (b)	—	250	500	850	1,500	—
1629 (b)	—	250	500	850	1,500	—
1630 (b)	—	250	500	850	1,500	—
1631 (b)	—	250	500	850	1,500	—
1632 (b)	—	250	500	850	1,500	—
1633 (b)	—	250	500	850	1,500	—
1636 (b)	—	250	500	850	1,500	—

KM# 44 6 GROSCHEN (1/4 Thaler)

Silver **Rev:** Titles of Ferdinand III

Date	Mintage	VG	F	VF	XF	Unc
1638 (b)	—	250	500	850	1,500	—
1639 (b)	—	250	500	850	1,500	—
1641 (b)	—	250	500	850	1,500	—
1643 (b)	—	250	500	850	1,500	—
1646 (b)	—	250	500	850	1,500	—
1647 (b)	—	250	500	850	1,500	—
1648 (b)	—	250	500	850	1,500	—
1657 (c)	—	250	500	850	1,500	—

KM# 45 6 GROSCHEN (1/4 Thaler)

Silver **Note:** Klippe.

Date	Mintage	VG	F	VF	XF	Unc
1641 (b)	—	—	—	—	—	—

KM# 60 6 GROSCHEN (1/4 Thaler)

Silver **Rev:** Titles of Leopold

Date	Mintage	VG	F	VF	XF	Unc
1670 (b) Rare	—	—	—	—	—	—

KM# 29 12 GROSCHEN (1/2 Thaler)

Silver **Obv:** Rampant lion left **Rev:** Imperial eagle with 12 in orb on breast, crown above divides date in legend, titles of Ferdinand II

Date	Mintage	VG	F	VF	XF	Unc
1624 (b)	—	150	275	500	850	—
1627 (b)	—	150	275	500	850	—
1628 (b)	—	150	275	500	850	—
1629 (b)	—	150	275	500	850	—
1630 (b)	—	150	275	500	850	—
1631 (b)	—	150	275	500	850	—
1632 (b)	—	150	275	500	850	—
1633 (b)	—	150	275	500	850	—
1637 (b)	—	150	275	500	850	—

KM# 40 12 GROSCHEN (1/2 Thaler)

Silver **Rev:** Titles of Ferdinand III

Date	Mintage	VG	F	VF	XF	Unc
1637 (b)	—	150	275	500	850	—
1638 (b)	—	150	275	500	850	—
1639 (b)	—	150	275	500	850	—
1641 (b)	—	150	275	500	850	—
1642 (b)	—	150	275	500	850	—
1643 (b)	—	150	275	500	850	—
1645 (b)	—	150	275	500	850	—
1657 (c)	—	150	275	500	850	—

KM# 41 12 GROSCHEN (1/2 Thaler)

Silver **Note:** Klippe.

Date	Mintage	VG	F	VF	XF	Unc
1637 (b)	—	—	—	—	—	—
1642 (b)	—	—	—	—	—	—

KM# 50 12 GROSCHEN (1/2 Thaler)

Silver **Rev:** Titles of Leopold

Date	Mintage	VG	F	VF	XF	Unc
1658 (c)	—	—	—	—	—	—
1670 (c) Rare	—	—	—	—	—	—

KM# 30.1 24 GROSCHEN (Thaler)

Silver **Obv:** Helmeted arms with small shield above **Rev:** Crowned double eagle with orb and 24 on breast, 1.6.2.4 **Rev. Legend:** MONETA **Note:** Dav. #5125.

Date	Mintage	VG	F	VF	XF	Unc
1624 (b)	—	95.00	180	350	650	—

KM# 30.2 24 GROSCHEN (Thaler)

Silver **Obv. Legend:** X. MON. NOV REIP BRU NSV ICENS **Note:** Dav. #5127.

Date	Mintage	VG	F	VF	XF	Unc
1624 (b)	—	95.00	180	350	650	—
1625 (b)	—	95.00	180	350	650	—
1626 (b)	—	95.00	180	350	650	—
1627 (b)	—	95.00	180	350	650	—
1628 (b)	—	95.00	180	350	650	—
1629 (b)	—	95.00	180	350	650	—
1630 (b)	—	95.00	180	350	650	—
1633 (b)	—	95.00	180	350	650	—

KM# 30.3 24 GROSCHEN (Thaler)

Silver **Rev. Legend:** MONE NOVA REIP... **Note:** Dav. #5128.

Date	Mintage	VG	F	VF	XF	Unc
1631 (b)	—	95.00	180	350	650	—
1632 (b)	—	95.00	180	350	650	—
1633 (b)	—	95.00	180	350	650	—
1634 (b)	—	95.00	180	350	650	—
1635 (b)	—	95.00	180	350	650	—
1636 (b)	—	95.00	180	350	650	—

KM# 42 24 GROSCHEN (Thaler)

Silver **Rev:** Titles of Ferdinand III **Note:** Dav. #5129.

Date	Mintage	VG	F	VF	XF	Unc
1637 (b)	—	140	270	525	900	—
1638 (b)	—	140	270	525	900	—
1639 (b)	—	140	270	525	900	—
1640 (b)	—	140	270	525	900	—
1641 (b)	—	140	270	525	900	—
1642 (b)	—	140	270	525	900	—
1643 (b)	—	140	270	525	900	—
1644 (b)	—	140	270	525	900	—
1645 (b)	—	140	270	525	900	—
1646 (b)	—	140	270	525	900	—
1647 (b)	—	140	270	525	900	—
1648 (b)	—	140	270	525	900	—
1651 (b)	—	140	270	525	900	—
1653 (c)	—	140	270	525	900	—
1655 (c)	—	140	270	525	900	—
1657 (c)	—	140	270	525	900	—

KM# 51 24 GROSCHEN (Thaler)

Silver **Note:** Dav. #5130.

Date	Mintage	VG	F	VF	XF	Unc
1658 (c)	—	180	350	725	1,250	—
1659 (c)	—	180	350	725	1,250	—
1660 (c)	—	180	350	725	1,250	—
1670 (c)	—	180	350	725	1,250	—

KM# 25 MARIENGROSCHEN (1/36 Thaler)

Silver **Note:** Klippe, 4.65-4.95g. Weight of 1/6 Thaler.

Date	Mintage	VG	F	VF	XF	Unc
1622 (b)	—	100	140	275	450	—

KM# 24 MARIENGROSCHEN (1/36 Thaler)

Silver **Obv:** Rampant lion left, date in legend **Rev:** Madonna surrounded by flames **Note:** Varieties exist.

Date	Mintage	VG	F	VF	XF	Unc
1622 (b)	—	20.00	33.00	60.00	120	—
1623 (b)	—	20.00	33.00	60.00	120	—
1625 (b)	—	20.00	33.00	60.00	120	—
1627 (b)	—	20.00	33.00	60.00	120	—
1653 HB	—	20.00	33.00	60.00	120	—

KM# 55 6 MARIENGROSCHEN (1/4 Gulden)

Silver **Obv:** Rampant lion left **Rev:** Value in 3 lines, date in legend

Date	Mintage	VG	F	VF	XF	Unc
1669	—	33.00	60.00	100	200	—
1671	—	33.00	60.00	100	200	—
1671/69	—	33.00	60.00	100	200	—

KM# 61 6 MARIENGROSCHEN (1/4 Gulden)

Silver **Obv:** Value, date in 4 lines **Rev:** Bust of Duke Rudolf August right

Date	Mintage	VG	F	VF	XF	Unc
1675 B	—	33.00	60.00	100	200	—

KM# 56 12 MARIENGROSCHEN (1/2 Gulden)

Silver **Obv:** Rampant lion left **Rev:** Value in 4 lines, date in legend

Date	Mintage	VG	F	VF	XF	Unc
1669	—	60.00	100	175	350	—
1671	—	60.00	100	175	350	—

KM# 62 12 MARIENGROSCHEN (1/2 Gulden)

Silver **Obv:** Value, date in 4 lines **Rev:** Bust of Duke Rudolf August right

Date	Mintage	VG	F	VF	XF	Unc
1675 B	—	60.00	100	175	350	—

KM# 63 12 MARIENGROSCHEN (1/2 Gulden)

Silver **Rev:** Crowned rampant lion left

Date	Mintage	VG	F	VF	XF	Unc
1675 B	—	60.00	100	175	350	—

KM# 64 24 MARIENGROSCHEN (Gulden)

Silver **Obv:** Crowned oval arms, value above and vidied on eithe rside, date divided below **Rev:** Bust of Duke Rudolf August right

Date	Mintage	VG	F	VF	XF	Unc
1675 B	—	100	175	275	500	—

KM# 75 24 MARIENGROSCHEN (Gulden)

Silver **Obv:** Value in 3 lines, date below

Date	Mintage	VG	F	VF	XF	Unc
1676 B	—	100	175	275	500	—

KM# 77 24 MARIENGROSCHEN (Gulden)

Silver **Obv:** Date at top

Date	Mintage	VG	F	VF	XF	Unc
1677	—	100	175	275	500	—

KM# 20.1 12 KREUZER

Silver **Obv:** Helmeted arms **Rev:** Crowned imperial eagle, orb with 1Z on breast, date in legend, titles of Ferdinand II **Note:** Kipper 12 Kreuzer.

Date	Mintage	VG	F	VF	XF	Unc
(16)Z1	—	80.00	140	250	400	—

KM# 20.2 12 KREUZER

5.5000 g., Silver **Note:** Klippe.

Date	Mintage	VG	F	VF	XF	Unc
(16)Z1	—	—	—	—	—	—

KM# 21 12 KREUZER

Silver **Rev:** Date divided by crown at top **Note:** Klippe. Finer style.

Date	Mintage	VG	F	VF	XF	Unc
1621 Rare	—	—	—	—	—	—

KM# 76 1/96 THALER

Silver **Obv:** Rampant lion left **Rev:** 96 in center, date in legend

Date	Mintage	VG	F	VF	XF	Unc
1676 B	—	33.00	60.00	100	200	—

KM# 33 1/64 THALER

Silver **Obv:** Rampant lion left **Rev:** Imperial orb with 64, date in legend **Note:** Weight varies: 0.85-1.04g.

Date	Mintage	VG	F	VF	XF	Unc
1625 (b)	—	—	—	—	—	—
1644 (b)	—	—	—	—	—	—
1645 (b)	—	—	—	—	—	—

KM# 19 2 SCHILLING (1/16 Thaler or Dütchen)

Silver **Obv:** Rampant lion left in ornamented shield **Rev:** Crowned imperial eagle, orb with 16 on breast, date in legend, titles of Ferdinand II

Date	Mintage	VG	F	VF	XF	Unc
(1)620 (a)	—	—	—	—	—	—

KM# 65 2 SCHILLING (1/16 Thaler or Dütchen)

Silver **Obv:** Date in legend **Rev:** Bust of Duke Rudolf August right **Rev. Legend:** XVI/REICHS/THALE/GB

Date	Mintage	VG	F	VF	XF	Unc
1675 GB	—	35.00	75.00	125	225	—
1676 GB	—	35.00	75.00	125	225	—
1676	—	35.00	75.00	125	225	—

KM# 78 2 SCHILLING (1/16 Thaler or Dütchen)

Silver **Rev:** Date **Rev. Legend:** XVI/RECH/TALE

Date	Mintage	VG	F	VF	XF	Unc
1677	—	—	—	—	—	—

MB# 81 1/2 THALER

14.4800 g., Silver **Obv:** Date in margin **Rev:** Titles of Rudolf II **Note:** Similar to MB#66. (12 groschen)

Date	Mintage	VG	F	VF	XF	Unc
(15)91	—	—	—	—	—	—

KM# 68 2/3 THALER (Gulden)

Silver

Date	Mintage	VG	F	VF	XF	Unc
1675 BH	—	100	160	275	475	—
1675	—	100	160	275	475	—

KM# 69 2/3 THALER (Gulden)

Silver **Obv:** Crowned arms, value 2/3 divides date below **Rev:** Bust of Duke Rudolf August right

Date	Mintage	VG	F	VF	XF	Unc
1675 BH	—	90.00	150	250	450	—

KM# 67 2/3 THALER (Gulden)

Silver **Note:** Date divided above lion.

Date	Mintage	VG	F	VF	XF	Unc
1675 IGB	—	100	160	275	475	—

KM# 66 2/3 THALER (Gulden)

Silver **Note:** Varieties exist.

Date	Mintage	VG	F	VF	XF	Unc
1675 IGB	—	80.00	140	200	425	—
1675 B	—	80.00	140	200	425	—
1676 IGB	—	80.00	140	200	425	—
1676 B	—	80.00	140	200	425	—
1676	—	80.00	140	200	425	—

MB# 84 THALER

Silver **Rev:** Z4 in orb on eagle's breast **Note:** Dav.#9105. Similar to MB#81. (24 groschen)

Date	Mintage	VG	F	VF	XF	Unc
(15)91	—	—	—	—	—	—

MB# 85 THALER

Silver **Obv:** Ornate helmet above shield of city arms, date divided near top **Rev:** Similar to MB#84 **Note:** Dav.#9107. (24 groschen)

Date	Mintage	VG	F	VF	XF	Unc
(15)91	—	—	—	—	—	—

KM# 52 1-1/4 THALER

35.4000 g., Silver **Note:** Dav. #LS265.

Date	Mintage	VG	F	VF	XF	Unc
1659 (c)	—	550	900	1,450	2,000	—

KM# 53 1-1/2 THALER

43.4000 g., Silver **Note:** Dav. #LS264.

Date	Mintage	VG	F	VF	XF	Unc
1659 (c)	—	650	1,100	1,750	2,500	—

MB# 88 2 THALER

Silver **Note:** Dav.#9106. Similar to Thaler, MB#85.

Date	Mintage	VG	F	VF	XF	Unc
(15)91	—	—	—	—	—	—

KM# 31 2 THALER

Silver **Note:** Similar to 1 Thaler, KM#29. Dav. #5126.

Date	Mintage	VG	F	VF	XF	Unc
1624 Rare	—	—	—	—	—	—
1628 Rare	—	—	—	—	—	—

KM# 54 2-1/4 THALER

Silver **Note:** Similar to 1-1/4 Thaler, KM#52. Dav. #5263.

Date	Mintage	VG	F	VF	XF	Unc
1659 (c) Rare	—	—	—	—	—	—

MB# 90 2-1/2 THALER

Silver **Note:** Dav.#A9106. Similar to Thaler, KM#85.

Date	Mintage	VG	F	VF	XF	Unc
(15)91	—	—	—	—	—	—

TRADE COINAGE

KM# 26 GOLDGULDEN

3.5000 g., 0.9860 Gold 0.1109 oz. AGW **Obv:** Crowned imperial eagle **Rev:** Lion of Brunswick

Date	Mintage	VG	F	VF	XF	Unc
1622 (b)	—	625	1,500	2,200	4,000	—
1627 (b)	—	625	1,500	2,200	4,000	—
1628 (b)	—	625	1,500	2,200	4,000	—
1629 (b)	—	625	1,500	2,200	4,000	—
1630 (b)	—	625	1,500	2,200	4,000	—
1631 (b)	—	625	1,500	2,200	4,000	—
1632 (b)	—	625	1,500	2,200	4,000	—
1633 (b)	—	625	1,500	2,200	4,000	—
1634 (b)	—	625	1,500	2,200	4,000	—
1635 (b)	—	625	1,500	2,200	4,000	—
1636 (b)	—	625	1,500	2,200	4,000	—

KM# 35 DUCAT

3.5000 g., 0.9860 Gold 0.1109 oz. AGW

Date	Mintage	VG	F	VF	XF	Unc
1638 (b)	—	575	1,250	1,900	3,500	—
1639 (b)	—	575	1,250	1,900	3,500	—
1640 (b)	—	575	1,250	1,900	3,500	—
1641 (b)	—	575	1,250	1,900	3,500	—
1642 (b)	—	575	1,250	1,900	3,500	—
1643 (b)	—	575	1,250	1,900	3,500	—
1646 (b)	—	575	1,250	1,900	3,500	—
1648 HB	—	575	1,250	1,900	3,500	—
1649 HB	—	575	1,250	1,900	3,500	—
1650 HB	—	575	1,250	1,900	3,500	—
1654 HB	—	575	1,250	1,900	3,500	—
1656 HB	—	575	1,250	1,900	3,500	—
1658 HB	—	575	1,250	1,900	3,500	—
1659 HB	—	575	1,250	1,900	3,500	—
1660 HB	—	575	1,250	1,900	3,500	—
ND HB	—	575	1,250	1,900	3,500	—

BRUNSWICK DUCHIES

Braunschweig

The earliest rulers of Brunswick, in north-central Germany, were the Brunon dukes of Saxony, who controlled the territory from about 1000AD. By 1137, the dynasty died out in the male line and Brunswick passed in marriage to the Welf Duke of Bavaria, Heinrich I the Proud (1136-39). His son, Heinrich II the Lion (1139-95), ruled all of Bavaria, Saxony and Brunswick, but lost control of all his territories except Brunswick in 1180. This, then was the beginning of the rule of the Welf dynasty over the lands of Brunswick which would last until 1918. Over the centuries, many acquisitions and divisions of territory took place and one branch of the dynasty even became kings of Great Britain.

ARMS

Brunswick – 2 leopards passant left, one above the other

Lüneburg – lion rampant left, often surrounded by many small hearts

Unter-Diepholz – heraldic eagle, head left, wings spread

NOTE: Additionally, the symbol for all Welf lands, invoking the memory of the dynasty's rule over Lower Saxony, was the leaping Saxon horse, usually found as a crest above helmets and shields of arms.

REFERENCE:

W = Gerhard Welter, ***Die Münzen der Welfen seit Heinrich dem Löwen***, 3 v., Braunschweig: Klinkhardt & Biermann, 1971-78.

BRUNSWICK-BEVERN

Branch of the house of Brunswick founded in 1666 by Ferdinand Albrecht I, son of August II of Brunswick-Dannenberg. At the death of Ferdinand Albrecht II in 1735, his eldest son maintained the Wolfenbüttel line and a younger son maintained the Bevern line. After 1735 Bevern was closely associated with Prussian policy. With the extinction of the line in 1809 properties reverted to Brunswick-Wolfenbüttel.

RULERS

Ferdinand Albrecht I, 1666-1687

MINT OFFICIALS' INITIALS

Initial	Date	Name
RB	1676-1711	Rudolf Bornemann in Zellerfeld

DUCHY

REGULAR COINAGE

KM# 7 THALER

Silver **Subject:** Death of Ferdinand Albrecht **Obv. Legend:** Helmeted 11-fold arms **Rev. Legend:** 12-line inscription, Roman numeral date **Note:** Dav. #6399.

Date	Mintage	VG	F	VF	XF	Unc
1687 RB	—	650	1,150	1,850	3,000	—

TRADE COINAGE

KM# 6 DUCAT

3.5000 g., 0.9860 Gold 0.1109 oz. AGW **Obv:** Facing bust of Ferdinand Albrecht in laurel wreath **Obv. Legend:** Crowned arms in branches, date below

Date	Mintage	VG	F	VF	XF	Unc
1680	—	1,200	2,400	4,200	7,800	—

KM# 5 2 DUCAT

7.0000 g., 0.9860 Gold 0.2219 oz. AGW **Obv:** Facing bust of Ferdinand Albrecht in laurel wreath **Obv. Legend:** Crowned arms in branches, date below

Date	Mintage	VG	F	VF	XF	Unc
1678	—	1,800	3,600	6,000	10,000	—

PATTERNS

Including off metal strikes

KM#	Date	Mintage	Identification	Mkt Val
Pn1	1680	—	Ducat. Silver. KM#6.	650

BRUNSWICK-DANNENBERG

Established upon the division of Brunswick-Lüneburg-Celle in 1559, but only remained a separate entity for two generations. Upon the death of Julius Ernst in 1636, it was joined by his son with the domains of Hitzacker and Wolfenbüttel to form a much enlarged Brunswick-Wolfenbüttel.

RULERS

Julius Ernst, 1598-1636
August II the Younger, in district of Hitzacker, 1604-1635

MINT OFFICIALS' MARKS & INITIALS

Mark or Initial	Date	Name
HL	1617	Henning Loehr mintmaster in Osterode
(d)=	1617-21	Georg Krukenberg, mintmaster in Hitzacker
(a)=	1619-25	Bartold Bartels in Dannenberg
	1623-25	In Scharnebeck
(b)=	Ca.1623	Unknown in Scharnebeck
HGM	1619-21	Hans Georg Meinhard in Winseln
	1622-?	In Moisburg
(c)=	Ca.1623	Unknown in Scharnebeck
HMG	Ca.1623	Unknown in Scharnebeck
HKW or W	Ca.1624	Unknown in Scharnebeck

DUCHY

REGULAR COINAGE

KM# 22 6 PFENNIG

Copper **Obv:** Brunswick arms **Rev:** Value and date in four lines **Note:** W#717.

Date	Mintage	VG	F	VF	XF	Unc
1621	—	—	—	—	—	—

KM# 13 3 KREUZER (Groschen)

Silver **Obv:** 4-fold arms **Obv. Legend:** ORA.ET.L[ABO]RA. **Rev:** Crowned imperial eagle, 3 in circle on breast, legend, date **Rev. Legend:** MA-R... **Note:** W#716. Kipper.

Date	Mintage	VG	F	VF	XF	Unc
16Z0	—	—	—	—	—	—

KM# 14 4 GROSCHEN

Silver **Obv:** Crowned 4-fold arms **Obv. Legend:** CONVERTE. ME. DOMINE. **Rev:** Crowned imperial eagle, orb with 4G on breast, titles of Ferdinand **Note:** W#715. Kipper.

Date	Mintage	VG	F	VF	XF	Unc
ND	—	—	—	—	—	—

KM# 7 DOPPELSCHILLING (1/16 Thaler)

Silver **Obv:** 4-fold arms, titles of Julius Ernst **Rev:** Intertwined DS, small imperial orb above, titles of Matthias **Note:** W#711, 712C. Varieties exist. Kipper.

Date	Mintage	VG	F	VF	XF	Unc
ND (a)	—	65.00	120	200	300	—

KM# 8 DOPPELSCHILLING (1/16 Thaler)

Silver **Obv:** 4-fold arms, 3 helmets above, titles of Julius Ernst **Rev:** Intertwined DS, small imperial orb above **Rev. Legend:** DUX.BRUNS... **Note:** W#712A.

Date	Mintage	VG	F	VF	XF	Unc
ND	—	65.00	120	200	300	—

KM# 16 DOPPELSCHILLING (1/16 Thaler)

Silver **Obv:** Without helmets above arms **Rev. Legend:** D. G. DUX. BRVNS... **Note:** W#712B. Similar to KM#7. Varieties exist.

Date	Mintage	VG	F	VF	XF	Unc
1620 (a)	—	65.00	120	200	300	—
ND (a)	—	65.00	120	200	300	—

KM# 28 DOPPELSCHILLING (1/16 Thaler)

Silver **Obv:** 4-fold arms **Rev:** Value II SCHILLING... in four lines with date **Rev. Legend:** REICHS.SCHROT.U.KORN. **Note:** W#713.

Date	Mintage	VG	F	VF	XF	Unc
1624 (a)	—	—	—	—	—	—

KM# 18 1/2 REICHSORT (= 1/8 Thaler)

Silver **Subject:** Death of Julius Ernst's Mother, Ursula of Saxe-Lauenburg **Obv:** Bust of Julius Ernst right **Rev:** Six-line inscription with date

Date	Mintage	VG	F	VF	XF	Unc
1620 (b)	—	—	—	—	—	—

KM# 24 1/2 REICHSORT (= 1/8 Thaler)

Silver **Obv:** Bust right, titles of Julius Ernst, date in legend **Rev:** Inscription, date **Rev. Inscription:** I/HALBER/REICHES/ORDT/ **Note:** W#708.

Date	Mintage	VG	F	VF	XF	Unc
(1)6Z3//16Z3 HMG	—	90.00	150	250	450	—

KM# 29 1/2 REICHSORT (= 1/8 Thaler)

Silver **Obv:** Bust right **Rev:** Value in four lines, date in legend **Note:** W#709. Similar to KM#24.

Date	Mintage	VG	F	VF	XF	Unc
16Z4 (a)	—	90.00	150	250	450	—

KM# 15 1/24 THALER (Groschen)

Silver **Obv:** Arms of Unter-Diepholz, legend **Obv. Legend:** DURAT-VIRTVS **Rev:** Imperial orb with Z4, titles of Ferdinand II **Note:** W#714.

Date	Mintage	VG	F	VF	XF	Unc
ND (a)	—	—	—	—	—	—

KM# 6 1/16 THALER

Silver **Obv:** 4-fold arms, 3 helmets above, titles of Julius Ernst **Rev:** Crowned imperial eagle, 16 in orb on breast, titles of Matthias **Note:** W#712D. Kipper.

Date	Mintage	VG	F	VF	XF	Unc
1619	—	—	—	—	—	—

KM# 17 1/16 THALER

Silver **Obv:** 8-fold arms **Rev:** Date at end of legend **Note:** W#710. Similar to KM#6.

Date	Mintage	VG	F	VF	XF	Unc
ND (a)	—	—	—	—	—	—

KM# 25 1/4 THALER

Silver **Obv:** Armored bust right, titles of Julius Ernst, date **Rev:** 8-fold arms **Rev. Legend:** TIME. DEUM. HONORA. CE-S. **Note:** W#707A.

Date	Mintage	VG	F	VF	XF	Unc
16Z3 (b)	—	75.00	150	225	325	—
16Z3 HMG	—	75.00	150	225	325	—

KM# 30 1/4 THALER

Silver **Obv:** Bust right, date in legend **Rev:** 3 helmets above arms **Note:** W#707. Similar to KM#25.

Date	Mintage	VG	F	VF	XF	Unc
(1)6Z4 (a)	—	75.00	150	225	325	—
(1)6Z4 WHK	—	75.00	150	225	350	—

KM# 19 1/2 THALER

Silver **Subject:** Death of Julius Ernst's Mother, Ursula of Saxe-Lauenburg **Obv:** Bust of Julius Ernst right **Rev:** Seven-line inscription with date

Date	Mintage	VG	F	VF	XF	Unc
16Z0 (a)	—	—	—	—	—	—

KM# 31 1/2 THALER

Silver **Obv:** Bust right, titles of Julius Ernst **Obv. Legend:** V:G:G:IULIUS... **Rev:** 8-fold arms, 3 helmets above, date divided among helmets **Rev. Legend:** TIM. DEU. - HON. CÆS. **Note:** W#706. Varieties exist.

Date	Mintage	VG	F	VF	XF	Unc
16Z3 (c)	—	450	900	1,500	2,750	—
16Z4 (a)	—	450	900	1,500	2,750	—
16Z5 (a)	—	450	900	1,500	2,750	—

KM# 20 1/2 THALER

Silver **Obv:** Bust right **Obv. Legend:** IULIUS.ERNESTUS. D. G. ... **Rev:** Helmeted eight-fold arms, helmets divide date **Note:** W#705. Similar to KM#31.

Date	Mintage	VG	F	VF	XF	Unc
ND	—	425	825	1,400	2,250	—
ND W	—	425	825	1,400	2,250	—

KM# 5.1 THALER

Silver **Obv:** Two busts facing each other **Rev:** Helmeted eight-fold arms, date in legend **Note:** Dav. #6415.

Date	Mintage	VG	F	VF	XF	Unc
1617 HL Rare	—	—	—	—	—	—

KM# 5.2 THALER

Silver **Rev:** Orb and mintmark at sides of arms **Note:** Dav. #6416.

Date	Mintage	VG	F	VF	XF	Unc
1617 (d) Rare	—	—	—	—	—	—

KM# 9 THALER

Silver **Obv:** Bust right **Obv. Legend:** IULIUS. ERNESTUS. D: G: DUX. B: ET: LUNAEB **Rev:** Date divided between helmets **Rev. Legend:** RECTE. FACIENDO.-NEMINEM.TIMEAS. **Note:** Dav. #6418.

Date	Mintage	VG	F	VF	XF	Unc
1619 (a)	—	375	750	1,200	2,000	—
1620 (a)	—	375	750	1,200	2,000	—

KM# 10 THALER

Silver **Obv:** Crowned imperial eagle, 32 in orb on breast, titles of Ferdinand II **Note:** Dav. #6419.

Date	Mintage	VG	F	VF	XF	Unc
ND (a)	—	350	700	1,100	1,850	—

KM# 21 THALER

Silver **Subject:** Death of Julius Ernst's Mother, Ursula of Saxe-Lauenburg **Rev:** Eight-line inscription with date **Note:** Dav. #6428.

Date	Mintage	VG	F	VF	XF	Unc
16Z0 (a) Rare	—	—	—	—	—	—

KM# 23.1 THALER

Silver **Obv. Legend:** IULIUS. ERNESTUS... **Rev:** Helmeted eight-fold arms, date in legend at top **Rev. Legend:** TIME. DEUM.-HONO. CAESA. **Note:** Dav. #6420.

Date	Mintage	VG	F	VF	XF	Unc
1622 (a)	—	375	750	1,200	2,000	—
1623 (a)	—	375	750	1,200	2,000	—

KM# 23.2 THALER

Silver **Rev. Legend:** HO-N-ORA.CAESAR. **Note:** Varieties exist. Dav. #6423.

Date	Mintage	VG	F	VF	XF	Unc
1624 (a)	—	300	600	975	1,600	—

KM# 26.1 THALER

Silver **Obv. Legend:** ...DUX. B: ET: LUNAEB. **Rev:** Date divided between helmets **Rev. Legend:** ...HONO. CAESA. **Note:** Dav. #6421.

Date	Mintage	VG	F	VF	XF	Unc
1623 (c)	—	300	600	975	1,650	—

KM# 26.2 THALER

Silver **Obv. Legend:** ...BRUN:U:LUN. **Rev. Legend:** ...HON-ORA.CAESAREM. **Note:** Dav. #6424.

Date	Mintage	VG	F	VF	XF	Unc
1624	—	300	600	950	1,600	—

KM# 27.1 THALER

Silver **Obv. Legend:** Begins: V. or U.G.G.IULIUS... **Rev. Legend:** HM-G:HONO.CAESA. **Note:** Dav. #6422.

Date	Mintage	VG	F	VF	XF	Unc
1623 HMG	—	300	600	975	1,650	—

KM# 27.2 THALER

Silver **Rev:** Legend without HM-G, different shield decorations **Note:** Dav. #6422A.

Date	Mintage	VG	F	VF	XF	Unc
1623 (c)	—	300	500	825	1,350	—

KM# 27.3 THALER

Silver **Obv. Legend:** W.V.G. IVLIVS... **Note:** Dav. #6425.

Date	Mintage	VG	F	VF	XF	Unc
1624 HKW	—	300	600	975	1,650	—

KM# 27.4 THALER

Silver **Obv. Legend:** V:G:G:IULIUS... **Rev. Legend:** ...HO-NORA. CAESAREM. **Note:** Dav. #6426.

Date	Mintage	VG	F	VF	XF	Unc
1624 (a)	—	280	550	900	1,450	—
1625 (a)	—	280	550	900	1,450	—

KM# 27.5 THALER

Silver **Obv:** Different bust **Rev. Legend:** ...HONO.CAESA. **Note:** Dav. #6426A.

Date	Mintage	VG	F	VF	XF	Unc
1624 (a)	—	275	475	825	1,350	—

KM# 27.6 THALER

Silver **Rev. Legend:** ...CAESAR. **Note:** Varieties exist. Dav. #6426B.

Date	Mintage	VG	F	VF	XF	Unc
1625 (a)	—	275	425	750	1,250	—

KM# 32 THALER

Silver **Rev:** Date divided at top **Note:** Dav. #6427.

Date	Mintage	VG	F	VF	XF	Unc
1624 (a)	—	280	550	900	1,450	—
1625 (a)	—	280	550	900	1,450	—

KM# 11 2 THALER

Silver **Obv:** Bust right **Rev:** Helmeted eight-fold arms divide date **Note:** Dav. #6417.

Date	Mintage	VG	F	VF	XF	Unc
1619 (a)	—	4,500	7,500	12,500	—	—

TRADE COINAGE

KM# 12 GOLDGULDEN

3.5000 g., 0.9860 Gold 0.1109 oz. AGW **Obv:** Bust right **Obv. Legend:** IVLIUS... **Rev:** Helmeted eight-fold arms, date in legend **Note:** Fr. #539.

Date	Mintage	VG	F	VF	XF	Unc
619 (a) Rare	—	—	—	—	—	—

KM# 33 DUCAT

3.5000 g., 0.9860 Gold 0.1109 oz. AGW **Obv:** Bust right **Obv. Legend:** V.G.G.IUL... **Rev:** Helmeted eight-fold arms, date in legend **Note:** Fr. #540.

Date	Mintage	VG	F	VF	XF	Unc
1625 (a) Rare	—	—	—	—	—	—

BRUNSWICK-HARBURG

Harburg, a city on the Elbe just south of Hamburg and about 22 miles northwest of the city of Lüneburg, was the seat of a branch line of dukes founded from Brunswick-Lüneburg in 1521. This line became extinct and the territory went to Brunswick-Lüneburg-Celle in 1642.

RULERS

Otto I der Ältere, 1521-1549
Otto II der Jüngere, 1549-1603
Christoph, 1603-1606
Otto III, 1603-41
Johann Friedrich, 1603-1619
Wilhelm VI August, 1603-1642

MINT OFFICIALS' INITIALS

Initial	Date	Name
(t)=	1615-19	Thomas Timpf the Elder
(h)=	1618-24	Thomas Timpf the Younger
(b)=	1619-25	Barthold Bartels in Dannenberg
	1625	In Scharnebeck
	1630-31	In Harburg
GM=	1622	Hans Georg Meinhard in Moisburg
HS	1622-40	Henning Schreiber in Clausthal
HR	1622-27	Hans Rücke in Harburg
	1622-26	In Moisburg
CH	1625-26	Lazarus Christian Hopfgarten in Harburg
(q)=	1627-29	Wilhelm Quensel in Harburg and Moisburg

DUCHY

REGULAR COINAGE

KM# 6 PFENNIG

Silver **Ruler:** Wilhelm VI August **Note:** 4-fold arms. Varieties exist.

Date	Mintage	VG	F	VF	XF	Unc
ND(ca-1610)	—	75.00	150	300	600	—

KM# 5 PFENNIG

Silver **Ruler:** Wilhelm VI August **Note:** Uniface. Hohlpfennig type. 6-fold arms, W above, no legend.

Date	Mintage	VG	F	VF	XF	Unc
ND(ca-1610)	—	75.00	150	300	600	—

KM# 20 3 PFENNIG

Silver **Ruler:** Wilhelm VI August **Obv:** Brunswick helmet with horse **Rev:** Imperial orb with 3

Date	Mintage	VG	F	VF	XF	Unc
1622	—	—	—	—	—	—

KM# A20 3 PFENNIG

Silver **Obv:** Ornamented shield of Lüneburg arms, W.D.B.E.L. above **Rev:** Value in 4 lines

Date	Mintage	VG	F	VF	XF	Unc
ND(1622-23)	—	—	—	—	—	—

KM# 27 3 PFENNIG

Copper **Ruler:** Wilhelm VI August **Obv:** Lion rampant left **Rev:** Value, date in 4 lines

Date	Mintage	VG	F	VF	XF	Unc
1623	—	—	—	—	—	—

KM# A23 3 PFENNIG

Silver **Obv:** Lüneburg arms in oval shield (lion with 8 hearts around) **Rev:** Value and date in 4 lines

Date	Mintage	VG	F	VF	XF	Unc
16Z3	—	—	—	—	—	—

KM# A21 WITTEN (1/96 Thaler)

Silver, 16 mm. **Obv:** Lüneburg arms **Rev:** Cross divides value 9 - 6 **Note:** W#742B.

Date	Mintage	VG	F	VF	XF	Unc
16ZZ	—	—	—	—	—	—

KM# 18 12 KREUZER

Silver **Ruler:** Wilhelm VI August **Obv:** Crowned imperial eagle, 12 in orb on breast, titles of Ferdinand II **Rev:** Crowned 12-fold arms **Note:** Kipper 12 Kreuzer.

Date	Mintage	VG	F	VF	XF	Unc
(1621/2)	—	40.00	75.00	150	250	—

KM# 42 2 MARIENGROSCHEN

Silver **Ruler:** Wilhelm VI August **Obv:** Brunswick helmet with horse **Rev:** Value II, date in 4 lines

Date	Mintage	VG	F	VF	XF	Unc
1638 HS	—	30.00	60.00	100	175	—
1639 HS	—	30.00	60.00	100	175	—
1640 HS	—	30.00	60.00	100	175	—
1642 HS	—	30.00	60.00	100	175	—
ND HS	—	30.00	60.00	100	175	—

KM# 19 4 GROSCHEN

Silver **Ruler:** Wilhelm VI August **Obv:** Crowned imperial eagle, 4G in orb on breast, titles of Ferdinand II **Rev:** Crowned 6-fold arms **Note:** Kipper 4 Groschen.

Date	Mintage	VG	F	VF	XF	Unc
1621	—	—	—	—	—	—

KM# 11 1/24 THALER

Silver **Ruler:** Wilhelm VI August **Obv:** Imperial orb with 24, titles of Matthias **Rev:** Ornamented 4-fold arms **Note:** Varieties exist.

Date	Mintage	VG	F	VF	XF	Unc
1618	—	15.00	30.00	50.00	90.00	—
1619	—	15.00	30.00	50.00	90.00	—

KM# B12 1/24 THALER

Silver **Ruler:** Wilhelm VI August **Obv:** Imperial orb with 24, titles of Matthias **Rev:** Helmet above 2 shields with 2 leopards and lion rampant left between hearts **Note:** Prev. KM#51.

Date	Mintage	VG	F	VF	XF	Unc
1619	—	150	300	525	900	—

KM# 13 1/24 THALER

Silver **Ruler:** Wilhelm VI August **Obv:** Titles of Ferdinand II

Date	Mintage	VG	F	VF	XF	Unc
1620	—	18.00	40.00	60.00	110	—
1621	—	18.00	40.00	60.00	110	—
ND	—	18.00	40.00	60.00	110	—

KM# 23 1/24 THALER

Silver **Ruler:** Wilhelm VI August **Rev:** Brunswick helmet with horse

Date	Mintage	VG	F	VF	XF	Unc
1622	—	18.00	40.00	60.00	110	—

KM# 7 1/16 THALER

Silver **Ruler:** Wilhelm VI August **Obv:** Crowned imperial eagle, 16 in orb on breast, date in legend, titles of Matthias **Rev:** Helmeted 6-fold arms

Date	Mintage	VG	F	VF	XF	Unc
1616	—	30.00	50.00	100	180	—
1617	—	30.00	50.00	100	180	—
1618	—	30.00	50.00	100	180	—
1619	—	30.00	50.00	100	180	—
ND	—	30.00	50.00	100	180	—

KM# 12 1/16 THALER

Silver **Ruler:** Wilhelm VI August **Rev:** Crowned 6-fold arms

Date	Mintage	VG	F	VF	XF	Unc
1619	—	30.00	55.00	100	200	—

KM# 14.1 1/16 THALER

Silver **Ruler:** Wilhelm VI August **Obv:** Titles of Ferdinand II

Date	Mintage	VG	F	VF	XF	Unc
1620	—	55.00	110	180	300	—
1621	—	55.00	110	180	300	—
ND	—	55.00	110	180	300	—

KM# 14.2 1/16 THALER

Silver **Ruler:** Wilhelm VI August **Obv:** 4-fold arms with 3 helmets above

Date	Mintage	VG	F	VF	XF	Unc
16Z0	—	55.00	110	180	300	—

KM# 22 1/2 REICHSORT (= 1/8 Thaler)

Silver **Ruler:** Wilhelm VI August **Note:** Klippe.

Date	Mintage	VG	F	VF	XF	Unc
1622(h) HR	—	—	—	—	—	—

KM# 21 1/2 REICHSORT (= 1/8 Thaler)

Silver **Ruler:** Wilhelm VI August **Note:** Varieties exist.

Date	Mintage	VG	F	VF	XF	Unc
1622	—	75.00	150	275	375	—
1622 (h)	—	75.00	150	275	375	—
1622 HR	—	75.00	150	275	375	—
1623 (h)	—	75.00	150	275	375	—
1624 (h)	—	75.00	150	275	375	—
1627 HR	—	75.00	150	275	375	—

KM# 24 1/8 THALER

Silver **Ruler:** Wilhelm VI August **Obv:** Bust right **Rev:** Helmeted 6-fold arms

Date	Mintage	VG	F	VF	XF	Unc
1622	—	200	400	600	—	—

KM# 30 1/8 THALER

Silver **Ruler:** Wilhelm VI August **Rev:** Value in 4 lines

Date	Mintage	VG	F	VF	XF	Unc
1625 CH	—	200	400	600	—	—

KM# 31 1/8 THALER

Silver **Ruler:** Wilhelm VI August **Obv:** 6-fold arms, small imperial orb **Rev. Legend:** VIII/EINEN/REICHS/DALER

Date	Mintage	VG	F	VF	XF	Unc
1625 CH	—	200	400	600	—	—

KM# 32 1/8 THALER

Silver **Ruler:** Wilhelm VI August **Subject:** Death of Wilhelm August's 7th Son, Johannes **Note:** Similar to 1 Thaler, KM#35.

Date	Mintage	VG	F	VF	XF	Unc
1628 HS	—	95.00	180	300	525	—

KM# 36 1/8 THALER

Silver **Ruler:** Wilhelm VI August **Subject:** Death of Wilhelm August's 5th Son, Magnus **Obv:** Crowned 7-fold arms **Rev:** Crown above 7-line inscription with date

Date	Mintage	VG	F	VF	XF	Unc
1632 HS	—	95.00	180	300	525	—

KM# 43 1/8 THALER

Silver **Ruler:** Wilhelm VI August **Subject:** Death of Wilhelm August **Obv:** Crowned 11-fold arms **Rev:** 9-line inscription with date

Date	Mintage	VG	F	VF	XF	Unc
1642 HS	—	95.00	180	300	525	—

KM# 25 1/4 THALER

Silver **Ruler:** Wilhelm VI August **Obv:** Bust right **Rev:** Helmeted oval 6-fold arms, date divided at top **Note:** Varieties exist.

Date	Mintage	VG	F	VF	XF	Unc
1622 HR	—	325	675	1,200	1,850	—
1623	—	650	1,250	2,500	—	—
1624 HR	—	325	675	1,200	1,850	—
1627 HR	—	325	675	1,200	1,850	—
1630	—	325	675	1,200	1,850	—
1630 (b)	—	325	675	1,200	1,850	—
1631 (b)	—	325	675	1,200	1,850	—
ND (h)	—	325	675	1,200	1,850	—
ND HR	—	325	675	1,200	1,850	—

KM# 33 1/4 THALER

Silver **Ruler:** Wilhelm VI August **Subject:** Death of Wilhelm August's 7th Son, Johannes **Note:** Similar to 1 Thaler, KM#35.

Date	Mintage	VG	F	VF	XF	Unc
1628 HS	—	150	300	525	850	—

KM# 37 1/4 THALER

Silver **Ruler:** Wilhelm VI August **Subject:** Death of Wilhelm August's 5th Son, Magnus **Note:** Similar to 1/8 Thaler, KM#36.

Date	Mintage	VG	F	VF	XF	Unc
1632 HS	—	150	300	525	850	—

KM# 44 1/4 THALER

Silver **Ruler:** Wilhelm VI August **Subject:** Death of Wilhelm August **Obv:** Crowned 11-fold arms **Rev:** 9-line inscription with date

Date	Mintage	VG	F	VF	XF	Unc
1642 HS	—	150	300	525	850	—

KM# 47 1/4 THALER

Silver **Ruler:** Wilhelm VI August **Subject:** Death of Wilhelm August's Sister, Catherine Sophie, Countess of Schaumburg-Saxonhagen **Obv:** Crowned 12-fold arms **Rev:** 8-line inscription with date

Date	Mintage	VG	F	VF	XF	Unc
1665	—	150	300	525	850	—

KM# 15 1/2 THALER

Silver **Ruler:** Wilhelm VI August **Obv:** Bust right **Rev:** Helmeted oval 6-fold arms, date divided at top **Note:** Varieties exist.

Date	Mintage	VG	F	VF	XF	Unc
1620 (h)	—	525	1,100	1,850	—	—
1622 HR	—	525	1,100	1,850	—	—
1622	—	525	1,100	1,850	—	—
1623 (h)	—	525	1,100	1,850	—	—
1623	—	525	1,100	1,850	—	—
1624 HR	—	525	1,100	1,850	—	—
1625 CH	—	525	1,100	1,850	—	—
1627	—	525	1,100	1,850	—	—
1630 (b)	—	525	1,100	1,850	—	—

KM# 34 1/2 THALER

Silver **Ruler:** Wilhelm VI August **Subject:** Death of Wilhelm August's 7th Son, Johannes **Note:** Similar to 1 Thaler, KM#35.

Date	Mintage	VG	F	VF	XF	Unc
1628 HS	—	275	475	750	1,250	—

KM# 38 1/2 THALER

Silver **Ruler:** Wilhelm VI August **Subject:** Death of Wilhelm August's 5th Son, Magnus **Note:** Similar to 1/8 Thaler, KM#36.

Date	Mintage	VG	F	VF	XF	Unc
1632 HS	—	275	475	750	1,250	—

KM# 45 1/2 THALER

Silver **Ruler:** Wilhelm VI August **Subject:** Death of Wilhelm August **Obv:** Facing bust **Rev:** 9-line inscription with date

Date	Mintage	VG	F	VF	XF	Unc
1642 HS	—	275	475	750	1,250	—

KM# 48 1/2 THALER

Silver **Ruler:** Wilhelm VI August **Subject:** Death of Wilhelm August's Sister, Catherine Sophie, Countess of Schaumburg-Saxonhagen **Obv:** Crowned 12-fold arms **Rev:** 8-line inscription with date

Date	Mintage	VG	F	VF	XF	Unc
1665	—	275	475	750	1,250	—

KM# 8 THALER

Silver **Ruler:** Wilhelm VI August **Obv:** Bust right, date in field to right **Rev:** Triple-helmeted 6-fold arms **Note:** Dav. #6402.

Date	Mintage	VG	F	VF	XF	Unc
1617	—	300	525	825	1,350	—

KM# 9 THALER

Silver **Ruler:** Wilhelm VI August **Obv:** Similar to KM#16 **Rev:** Date at top **Note:** Dav. #6403.

Date	Mintage	VG	F	VF	XF	Unc
1617	—	300	525	825	1,350	—

KM# 16 THALER

Silver **Ruler:** Wilhelm VI August **Obv:** Bust right **Rev:** Triple-helmeted 6-fold arms, date divided at top **Note:** Varieties exist. Dav. #6405.

Date	Mintage	VG	F	VF	XF	Unc
1620 (h)	—	150	300	500	950	—
1622 (h)	—	150	300	500	950	—
1622 HR	—	150	300	500	950	—
1622	—	150	300	500	950	—
1623 (h)	—	150	300	500	950	—
1623 HR	—	150	300	500	950	—
1623	—	150	300	500	950	—
1624 (h)	—	150	300	500	950	—
1624 HR	—	150	300	500	950	—
1625 CH	—	150	300	500	950	—
1625 HR	—	150	300	500	950	—
1627 HR	—	150	300	500	950	—
1627 (q)	—	150	300	500	950	—
1630 (b)	—	150	300	500	950	—
1631 (b)	—	150	300	500	950	—
ND HR	—	150	300	500	950	—

KM# 26 THALER

Silver **Ruler:** Wilhelm VI August **Note:** Klippe. Dav. #6405A.

Date	Mintage	VG	F	VF	XF	Unc
1622 (h) GM Rare	—	—	—	—	—	—
1624 (h) Rare	—	—	—	—	—	—

KM# 28 THALER

Silver **Ruler:** Wilhelm VI August **Rev:** Date divided below arms **Note:** Dav. #6406.

Date	Mintage	VG	F	VF	XF	Unc
1623 HR	—	300	525	825	1,350	—

KM# 29 THALER

Silver **Ruler:** Wilhelm VI August **Rev:** Date divided between helmets **Note:** Dav. #6406A.

Date	Mintage	VG	F	VF	XF	Unc
1623 HR	—	300	525	825	1,350	—

KM# 35 THALER

Silver **Ruler:** Wilhelm VI August **Subject:** Death of Wilhelm August's 7th Son, Johannes **Note:** Dav. #6656.

Date	Mintage	VG	F	VF	XF	Unc
16Z8 HS	—	300	600	1,150	2,150	—

KM# 39 THALER

Silver **Ruler:** Wilhelm VI August **Subject:** Death of Wilhelm August's 5th Son, Magnus **Note:** Similar to 1/2 Thaler, KM#38. Dav. #6657.

Date	Mintage	VG	F	VF	XF	Unc
1632 HS	—	300	600	1,150	2,150	—

KM# 40.1 THALER

Silver **Ruler:** Wilhelm VI August **Obv:** Facing 1/2-length figure **Obv. Legend:** WILHELMUS.D:G. DUX.BRUNS.ET.LUNEB **Rev:** 5 helmets above 11-fold arms, date in legend **Note:** Dav. #6407.

Date	Mintage	VG	F	VF	XF	Unc
1636 HS	—	150	300	525	825	—

KM# 40.2 THALER

Silver **Ruler:** Wilhelm VI August **Obv. Legend:** BRUNSUIC.ET. LUNEB **Note:** Dav. #6408.

Date	Mintage	VG	F	VF	XF	Unc
1637 HS	—	150	300	525	825	—
1638 HS	—	150	300	525	825	—

KM# 40.3 THALER

Silver **Ruler:** Wilhelm VI August **Rev:** Date right of plume above helmets **Note:** Dav. #6409.

Date	Mintage	VG	F	VF	XF	Unc
1638 HS	—	150	300	525	825	—

KM# 40.4 THALER

Silver **Ruler:** Wilhelm VI August **Obv. Legend:** ...LUNE **Rev:** Date **Rev. Legend:** ...PROUI--DEBIT-ANO **Note:** Varieties exist. Dav. #6410.

Date	Mintage	VG	F	VF	XF	Unc
1639 HS	—	125	265	425	675	—

KM# 40.5 THALER

Silver **Ruler:** Wilhelm VI August **Obv:** Head to outer edge **Rev:** Helmeted arms to edge at top **Note:** Dav. #6411.

Date	Mintage	VG	F	VF	XF	Unc
1639 HS	—	125	265	425	675	—

KM# 40.6 THALER

Silver **Ruler:** Wilhelm VI August **Rev:** Legend without ANO or AO **Note:** Varieties exist. Dav. #6412.

Date	Mintage	VG	F	VF	XF	Unc
1640 HS	—	125	265	425	675	—
1641 HS	—	125	265	425	675	—
1642 HS	—	125	265	425	675	—

KM# 46 THALER

Silver **Ruler:** Wilhelm VI August **Subject:** Death of Wilhelm August **Obv:** Facing 1/2-length figure **Rev:** 10-line inscription with date **Note:** Dav. #6413.

Date	Mintage	VG	F	VF	XF	Unc
1642 HS	—	150	300	525	825	—

KM# 49 THALER

Silver **Subject:** Death of Wilhelm August's Sister, Catherine Sophie, Countess of Schaumburg-Saxonhagen **Obv:** Crowned 12-fold arms **Rev:** 9-line inscription with date **Note:** Dav. #6414.

Date	Mintage	VG	F	VF	XF	Unc
1665 Rare	—	—	—	—	—	—

KM# A12 1-1/2 THALER

44.7000 g., Silver **Ruler:** Wilhelm VI August **Obv:** 1/2-length figure towards helmet on table right **Rev:** Triple-helmeted 6-fold arms **Note:** Dav. #LS248. Prev. KM#50.

Date	Mintage	VG	F	VF	XF	Unc
ND(ca.l1618) Rare	—	—	—	—	—	—

KM# 10 2 THALER

Silver **Ruler:** Wilhelm VI August **Obv:** Bust right, date in field to right **Rev:** Triple-helmeted 6-fold arms **Note:** Dav. #6401.

Date	Mintage	VG	F	VF	XF	Unc
1617 Rare	—	—	—	—	—	—

KM# 17 2 THALER

Silver **Ruler:** Wilhelm VI August **Obv:** Bust right **Rev:** Triple-helmeted 6-fold arms, date divided at top **Note:** Dav. #6404.

Date	Mintage	VG	F	VF	XF	Unc
1620 (h) Rare	—	—	—	—	—	—

BRUNSWICK-HITZACKER

This subdivision of Brunswick-Dannenberg, centered on the town of the same name located on the Elbe Riveer just 4 miles (7 km) north-northwest of Dannenberg, was administered separately by one ruler in the early 17th century. It returned to the general governance of Dannenberg a year before the latter was united to Brunswick-Wolfenbüttel.

RULER

August II der Jüngere, 1604-1635

DUCHY

REGULAR COINAGE

KM# 54 1/96 THALER (Sechsling)

Silver **Ruler:** August II der Jungere **Obv:** Imperial orb with 96, titles of Ferdinand II, date in legend **Rev:** Lion rampant left

Date	Mintage	VG	F	VF	XF	Unc
1622	—	—	—	—	—	—

KM# 46 1/24 THALER (Groschen)

Silver **Ruler:** August II der Jungere **Obv:** 2-fold arms divided vertically, Brunswick on left, Luneburg on right, titles of August II **Rev:** Imperial orb with Z4, titles of Ferdinand II, date in margin **Note:** W#761.

Date	Mintage	VG	F	VF	XF	Unc
1620	—	165	300	500	800	—
1621	—	165	300	500	800	—
16ZZ	—	165	300	500	800	—

KM# 40 1/16 THALER (Doppelschilling)

Silver **Ruler:** August II der Jungere **Obv:** Five-fold arms, titles of August II **Rev:** DS in imperial orb, date in margin **Note:** W#757A.

Date	Mintage	VG	F	VF	XF	Unc
(1)618	—	—	—	—	—	—

KM# 42.2 1/16 THALER (Doppelschilling)

Silver **Ruler:** August II der Jungere **Obv:** Crowned arms of lion rampant right, surrounded by small hearts (Luneburg) **Rev:** Similar to KM#41

Date	Mintage	VG	F	VF	XF	Unc
1619	—	—	—	—	—	—

KM# 41 1/16 THALER (Doppelschilling)

Silver **Ruler:** August II der Jungere **Obv:** Lion rampant to right, date in margin **Rev:** DS in circle **Note:** Kipper. W#755.

Date	Mintage	VG	F	VF	XF	Unc
1619	—	—	—	—	—	—
ND	—	—	—	—	—	—

KM# 42.1 1/16 THALER (Doppelschilling)

Silver **Ruler:** August II der Jungere **Rev:** Date in margin **Note:** Similar to KM#41. W#755.

Date	Mintage	VG	F	VF	XF	Unc
1619	—	—	—	—	—	—

KM# 49 1/16 THALER (Doppelschilling)

Silver **Ruler:** August II der Jungere **Obv:** H.Z. BRUN. U LUN. in margin, date **Note:** Similar to KM#48. W#757.

Date	Mintage	VG	F	VF	XF	Unc
1619	—	65.00	140	250	375	—
16Z0	—	65.00	140	250	375	—

KM# 42.3 1/16 THALER (Doppelschilling)

Silver **Ruler:** August II der Jungere **Rev:** DS in Spanish shield **Note:** W#755B.

Date	Mintage	VG	F	VF	XF	Unc
1619	—	—	—	—	—	—

KM# 43 1/16 THALER (Doppelschilling)

Silver **Ruler:** August II der Jungere **Obv:** Four-fold arms, titles of August II **Rev:** DS in circle, small imperial orb above, date in margin **Note:** W#756.

Date	Mintage	VG	F	VF	XF	Unc
1619	—	65.00	140	250	375	—
16Z0	—	65.00	140	250	375	—

KM# 48 1/16 THALER (Doppelschilling)

Silver **Ruler:** August II der Jungere **Obv:** DS in circle, date in margin **Rev:** Crowned imperial eagle, 16 in orb on breast, titles of Ferdinand II **Note:** W#757.

Date	Mintage	VG	F	VF	XF	Unc
(16)Z0	—	65.00	140	250	375	—

KM# 50 1/16 THALER (Doppelschilling)

Silver **Ruler:** August II der Jungere **Obv:** Four-fold arms, AUGUSTUS... **Rev:** DS is circle, margin AUGUSTUS..., date **Note:** W#759.

Date	Mintage	VG	F	VF	XF	Unc
(16)Z0	—	—	—	—	—	—

KM# 51 1/16 THALER (Doppelschilling)

Silver **Ruler:** August II der Jungere **Obv:** DS in circle **Rev:** Imperial eagle, 16 in orb on breast **Note:** W#760.

Date	Mintage	VG	F	VF	XF	Unc
16Z0	—	65.00	140	250	350	—

KM# 55 1/4 THALER

Silver **Ruler:** August II der Jungere **Note:** W#754.

Date	Mintage	VG	F	VF	XF	Unc
16ZZ	—	—	—	—	—	—
1623 (t)	—	—	—	—	—	—

KM# 56 1/2 THALER

Silver **Ruler:** August II der Jungere **Note:** W#753.

Date	Mintage	VG	F	VF	XF	Unc
ND (h)	—	2,000	3,250	5,250	—	—

KM# 57 1/2 THALER

Silver **Ruler:** August II der Jungere **Subject:** Death of August's First Wife, Clara Maria von Pommern **Obv:** Eleven-fold arms **Rev:** Six-line inscription with date

Date	Mintage	VG	F	VF	XF	Unc
1623	—	—	—	—	—	—

KM# 45 THALER

Silver **Ruler:** August II der Jungere **Note:** Dav. #6329. Klippe.

Date	Mintage	VG	F	VF	XF	Unc
1619 Rare	—	—	—	—	—	—

KM# 44.1 THALER

Silver **Ruler:** August II der Jungere **Obv:** Bust right **Rev:** Helmeted eleven-fold arms, date divided above **Note:** Dav. #6332.

Date	Mintage	VG	F	VF	XF	Unc
1619 Rare	—	—	—	—	—	—
1623 Rare	—	—	—	—	—	—
1624 Rare	—	—	—	—	—	—

KM# 52 THALER

Silver **Ruler:** August II der Jungere **Obv:** Helmeted eleven-fold arms **Rev:** Arm from cloud holding trowel above unfinished pyramid, date in legend **Note:** Dav. #6331.

Date	Mintage	VG	F	VF	XF	Unc
1621 Rare	—	—	—	—	—	—

KM# 53 THALER

Silver **Ruler:** August II der Jungere **Obv:** Crowned imperial eagle, titles of Ferdinand II **Note:** Dav. #6334. Kipper.

Date	Mintage	VG	F	VF	XF	Unc
ND Rare	—	—	—	—	—	—

KM# 44.2 THALER

Silver **Ruler:** August II der Jungere **Rev:** Without date **Note:** Dav. #6330.

Date	Mintage	VG	F	VF	XF	Unc
ND	—	—	—	—	—	—

KM# 58 THALER

Silver **Ruler:** August II der Jungere **Subject:** Death of August's First Wife, Clara Maria von Pommern **Obv:** Seven-line inscription with date, baroque scroll above and below **Rev:** Panel with five-line inscription in center, skull and hourglass above, dates in legend **Note:** Dav. #6333. Kipper.

Date	Mintage	VG	F	VF	XF	Unc
1623	—	1,500	2,500	4,500	7,000	—

BRUNSWICK-LUNEBURG-CALENBERG

The duchy of Brunswick-Lüneburg-Calenberg was established as a division of Brunswick-New-Lüneburg in 1636. It was further divided into Brunswick-Lüneburg-Calenberg and Brunswick-Lüneburg-Celle in 1648. In 1692 the duke was raised to the rank of elector and the principality became known as the Electorate of Brunswick-Lüneburg-Calenberg-Hannover. After the Napoleonic Wars, Hannover became a kingdom in 1814 and passed to Prussia in 1866.

RULERS

Georg I, 1636-1641
Christian Ludwig, 1641-1648
Georg II Wilhelm, 1648-1665
Johann Friedrich, 1665-1679
Ernst August, 1679-1698

MINT OFFICIALS' INITIALS

Initial	Date	Name
CH	-	?
HB	1675-1711	Heinrich Bonhorst in Clausthal
HIF	Ca.1678	?
HS (w/ or w/o crossed keys)	1626-72	Henning Schluter in Goslar and Zellerfeld
IES	1676-84	Johann Erich Schidt in Hannover
IH	Ca.1638	Unknown die-cutter
IPE	1672-75	Julius Philipp Eisendrath in Goslar and Zellerfeld
LW	1640-75	Lippold Weber (Weffer, Wepper) in Clausthal
RB	1673-76	Rudolf Bornemann in Hannover
	1676-1711	In Zellerfeld
	1685-1704	In Goslar
(b) ligate backward B and H		Bastian Hille

DUCHY

REGULAR COINAGE

KM# 43 PFENNIG

Silver **Note:** Uniface. Hohlpfennig type. Crowned CL monogram, date.

Date	Mintage	VG	F	VF	XF	Unc
1642 LW	—	45.00	80.00	140	250	—
1647	—	45.00	80.00	140	250	—
1648	—	45.00	80.00	140	250	—

KM# 59 PFENNIG

Silver **Obv:** Crowned GW monogram divides date **Note:** Uniface, Hohlpfennig type.

Date	Mintage	VG	F	VF	XF	Unc
1659	—	45.00	80.00	140	250	—
1663 HS	—	45.00	80.00	140	250	—
ND	—	45.00	80.00	140	250	—

KM# 86 PFENNIG

Silver **Note:** Crowned script JF monogram, date.

Date	Mintage	VG	F	VF	XF	Unc
1665 HS	—	40.00	75.00	125	220	—
1667 HS	—	40.00	75.00	125	220	—
1668 HS	—	40.00	75.00	125	220	—
1669 HS	—	40.00	75.00	125	220	—
1671 HS	—	40.00	75.00	125	220	—
1672 HS	—	40.00	75.00	125	220	—
1672 IPE	—	40.00	75.00	125	220	—
1675 IPE	—	40.00	75.00	125	220	—
1677 RB	—	40.00	75.00	125	220	—
1678 RB	—	40.00	75.00	125	220	—
1679 RB	—	40.00	75.00	125	220	—

KM# 91 PFENNIG

Silver **Obv:** Crowned JF monogram, date. **Note:** Hohlpfennig type.

Date	Mintage	VG	F	VF	XF	Unc
1666 LW	—	35.00	70.00	110	200	—
1667 LW	—	35.00	70.00	110	200	—
1668 LW	—	35.00	70.00	110	200	—
1670 LW	—	35.00	70.00	110	200	—
1671 LW	—	35.00	70.00	110	200	—
1672 LW	—	35.00	70.00	110	200	—
1673 LW	—	35.00	70.00	110	200	—
1675	—	35.00	70.00	110	200	—
1677	—	35.00	70.00	110	200	—
1679	—	35.00	70.00	110	200	—

KM# 92 PFENNIG

Silver **Note:** St. Andrew with cross divides date.

Date	Mintage	VG	F	VF	XF	Unc
1666 LW	—	—	—	—	—	—
1667 LW	—	—	—	—	—	—

KM# 193 PFENNIG

Silver **Obv:** Crowned script JF monogram **Rev:** */EX/DURIS/GLORIA/*

Date	Mintage	VG	F	VF	XF	Unc
1677	—	—	—	—	—	—

KM# 255 PFENNIG

Silver **Note:** Uniface hohlpfennig type. Crowned EA monogram divides date. Varieties exist.

Date	Mintage	VG	F	VF	XF	Unc
1680 RB	—	30.00	45.00	80.00	140	—
1681 RB	—	30.00	45.00	80.00	140	—
1684 RB	—	30.00	45.00	80.00	140	—
1685 RB	—	30.00	45.00	80.00	140	—
1687 RB	—	30.00	45.00	80.00	140	—
1690 RB	—	30.00	45.00	80.00	140	—
1693 RB	—	30.00	45.00	80.00	140	—
1694 RB	—	30.00	45.00	80.00	140	—
1697 RB	—	30.00	45.00	80.00	140	—

KM# 289 PFENNIG

Silver **Mint:** Clausthal **Note:** Without mintmaster's initials. Varieties exist.

Date	Mintage	VG	F	VF	XF	Unc
1682	—	20.00	35.00	60.00	100	—
1683	—	20.00	35.00	60.00	100	—
1690	—	20.00	35.00	60.00	100	—

KM# 352 PFENNIG

Copper **Obv:** Crowned script EA monogram **Rev:** Value, date

Date	Mintage	VG	F	VF	XF	Unc
1691	—	10.00	20.00	40.00	75.00	—
1692	—	10.00	20.00	40.00	75.00	—

KM# 386 PFENNIG

Copper **Obv:** Plain script monogram

Date	Mintage	VG	F	VF	XF	Unc
1694	—	10.00	20.00	40.00	75.00	—

KM# 387 PFENNIG

Silver **Note:** Uniface. Hohlpfennig type. Horse leaping left, date below.

Date	Mintage	VG	F	VF	XF	Unc
1694	—	—	—	—	—	—
1697	—	—	—	—	—	—
1698	—	—	—	—	—	—

KM# 296 1-1/2 PFENNIG

Silver **Obv:** Crowned EA monogram **Rev:** Value, date in two lines

Date	Mintage	VG	F	VF	XF	Unc
1680	—	—	—	—	—	—
1683	—	—	—	—	—	—
1686	—	—	—	—	—	—

KM# 297 1-1/2 PFENNIG

Silver **Rev:** Value, date in three lines **Note:** Gute 1-1/2 Pfennig.

Date	Mintage	VG	F	VF	XF	Unc
1683	—	—	—	—	—	—

KM# 353 1-1/2 PFENNIG

Copper **Obv:** Crowned script EA monogram **Rev:** Value, date in five lines

Date	Mintage	VG	F	VF	XF	Unc
1691	—	—	—	—	—	—

KM# 178 2 PFENNIG

Silver **Obv:** Crowned script JF monogram dividing date **Rev:** Value in four lines

Date	Mintage	VG	F	VF	XF	Unc
1676	—	—	—	—	—	—
1679	—	—	—	—	—	—

KM# 298 2 PFENNIG

Silver **Obv:** Crowned intertwined script EA monogram **Rev:** Value

Date	Mintage	VG	F	VF	XF	Unc
1683	—	—	—	—	—	—

KM# 307 2 PFENNIG

Silver **Obv:** Monogram in block letters

Date	Mintage	VG	F	VF	XF	Unc
1684	—	—	—	—	—	—

KM# 58 3 PFENNIG

Silver **Obv:** Crowned GW monogram divides date **Rev:** Imperial orb with 3 **Note:** Dreier 3 Pfennig.

Date	Mintage	VG	F	VF	XF	Unc
1657 HS	—	20.00	40.00	70.00	125	—
1662 HS	—	20.00	40.00	70.00	125	—
1665 HS	—	20.00	40.00	70.00	125	—

KM# 93 3 PFENNIG

Silver **Obv:** Crowned script JF monogram

Date	Mintage	VG	F	VF	XF	Unc
1666 LW	—	13.00	30.00	60.00	120	—
1667 LW	—	13.00	30.00	60.00	120	—
1668 LW	—	13.00	30.00	60.00	120	—
1670 LW	—	13.00	30.00	60.00	120	—
1671 HS	—	13.00	30.00	60.00	120	—
1673 IPE	—	27.00	55.00	100	165	—
1675	—	13.00	30.00	60.00	120	—
1677 RB	—	13.00	30.00	60.00	120	—
1678 RB	—	13.00	30.00	60.00	120	—

KM# 103 3 PFENNIG

Silver **Obv:** St. Andrew with cross

Date	Mintage	VG	F	VF	XF	Unc
1667 LW	—	20.00	40.00	65.00	125	—
1673 LW	—	20.00	40.00	65.00	125	—
1674 LW	—	20.00	40.00	65.00	125	—

KM# 274 3 PFENNIG

Silver **Obv:** Crowned script EA monogram divides date **Note:** Varieties exist.

Date	Mintage	VG	F	VF	XF	Unc
1681 HB	—	13.00	30.00	60.00	125	—
1682 HB	—	13.00	30.00	60.00	125	—
1683 HB	—	13.00	30.00	60.00	125	—
1683	—	13.00	30.00	60.00	125	—
1684	—	13.00	30.00	60.00	125	—
1692 RB	—	13.00	30.00	60.00	125	—

KM# 308 3 PFENNIG

Silver **Obv:** Intertwined monogram

Date	Mintage	VG	F	VF	XF	Unc
1684 HB	—	—	—	—	—	—

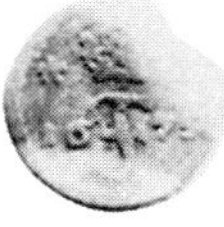

KM# 160 4 PFENNIG

Silver **Obv:** Crowned script JF monogram **Rev:** Value in three or four lines

Date	Mintage	VG	F	VF	XF	Unc
1675	—	20.00	33.00	60.00	125	—
1677	—	20.00	33.00	60.00	125	—

KM# 161 4 PFENNIG

Silver **Obv:** Crowned monogram **Rev:** Value 4 **Note:** Gute 4 Pfennig.

Date	Mintage	VG	F	VF	XF	Unc
1675	—	20.00	33.00	60.00	125	—
1677 RB	—	20.00	33.00	60.00	125	—
1678	—	20.00	33.00	60.00	125	—
1679	—	20.00	33.00	60.00	125	—

KM# 162 MATTIER (= 4 Pfennig)

Silver **Obv:** Crowned JF monogram **Rev:** Value in three lines

Date	Mintage	VG	F	VF	XF	Unc
1675	—	—	—	—	—	—
1676	—	—	—	—	—	—

KM# 194 4 PFENNIG

Silver **Rev:** Value IIII in three lines **Note:** Gute 4 Pfennig.

Date	Mintage	VG	F	VF	XF	Unc
1677	—	20.00	33.00	60.00	125	—
1679	—	20.00	33.00	60.00	125	—

KM# 275 4 PFENNIG

Silver **Obv:** Crowned EA monogram divides date **Rev:** Value 4 **Note:** Gute 4 Pfennig.

Date	Mintage	VG	F	VF	XF	Unc
1681 RB	—	27.00	45.00	85.00	140	—
1682 RB	—	27.00	45.00	85.00	140	—

KM# 290 4 PFENNIG

Silver **Obv:** Crowned script EA monogram **Rev:** Value IIII, date

Date	Mintage	VG	F	VF	XF	Unc
1682 HB	—	27.00	45.00	85.00	140	—
1687 HB	—	27.00	45.00	85.00	140	—

KM# 299 4 PFENNIG

Silver **Obv:** Crowned EA monogram divides date **Rev:** Value IIII **Note:** Gute 4 Pfennig.

Date	Mintage	VG	F	VF	XF	Unc
1683	—	27.00	45.00	85.00	140	—

KM# 309 4 PFENNIG
Silver **Obv:** EA monogram, SOLA BOMA... in legend **Rev:** Value IIII, date

Date	Mintage	VG	F	VF	XF	Unc
1684	—	27.00	45.00	85.00	140	—

KM# 330 4 PFENNIG
Silver **Obv:** Crowned EA monogram divides date **Rev:** Value IIII LANDMUNTZ... **Note:** Varieties exist.

Date	Mintage	VG	F	VF	XF	Unc
1686 HB	—	27.00	45.00	85.00	140	—
1688 HB	—	27.00	45.00	85.00	140	—

KM# 332 4 PFENNIG
Silver **Obv:** Crowned script EA monogram divides date **Rev:** Value IIII, date

Date	Mintage	VG	F	VF	XF	Unc
1688 HB	—	27.00	45.00	85.00	140	—

KM# 354 4 PFENNIG
Silver **Note:** Date on obverse only.

Date	Mintage	VG	F	VF	XF	Unc
1691	—	27.00	45.00	85.00	140	—

KM# 361 4 PFENNIG
Silver **Obv:** Crowned EA monogram divides mintmaster's initials **Rev:** Value 4 in center, date in legend **Note:** Gute 4 Pfennig.

Date	Mintage	VG	F	VF	XF	Unc
1692 RB	—	27.00	45.00	85.00	140	—

KM# 371 4 PFENNIG
Silver **Obv:** Crowned script monogram **Rev:** Value IIII, date in four lines

Date	Mintage	VG	F	VF	XF	Unc
1693	—	27.00	45.00	85.00	140	—
1694	—	27.00	45.00	85.00	140	—
1695	—	27.00	45.00	85.00	140	—
1697	—	27.00	45.00	85.00	140	—

KM# 301 4-1/2 PFENNIG
Silver **Rev:** Value without GUTE

Date	Mintage	VG	F	VF	XF	Unc
1683	—	—	—	—	—	—

KM# 300 4-1/2 PFENNIG
Silver **Obv:** Crowned EA monogram **Rev:** Value, date **Note:** Gute 4-1/2 Pfennig.

Date	Mintage	VG	F	VF	XF	Unc
1683	—	—	—	—	—	—

KM# 302 6 PFENNIG
Silver **Obv:** Crowned EA monogram divides date **Rev:** Imperial orb with 6

Date	Mintage	VG	F	VF	XF	Unc
1683	—	—	—	—	—	—
1684	—	—	—	—	—	—
1685	—	—	—	—	—	—

KM# 17 MARIENGROSCHEN (1/36 Thaler)
Silver **Obv:** Helmet with horse **Rev:** Value in three lines

Date	Mintage	VG	F	VF	XF	Unc
ND(ca.1636) HS	—	8.00	16.00	30.00	60.00	—

KM# 56 MARIENGROSCHEN (1/36 Thaler)
Silver **Obv:** Crowned GW monogram

Date	Mintage	VG	F	VF	XF	Unc
1652	—	13.00	26.00	45.00	100	—
1655	—	13.00	26.00	45.00	100	—
1656	—	13.00	26.00	45.00	100	—
1657	—	13.00	26.00	45.00	100	—

KM# 104 MARIENGROSCHEN (1/36 Thaler)
Silver **Obv:** Crowned script JF monogram, date in legend

Date	Mintage	VG	F	VF	XF	Unc
1667	—	13.00	26.00	45.00	100	—
1673	—	13.00	26.00	45.00	100	—

KM# 141 MARIENGROSCHEN (1/36 Thaler)
Silver **Obv:** Wildman, tree in right hand

Date	Mintage	VG	F	VF	XF	Unc
1673	—	13.00	26.00	45.00	100	—
1674	—	13.00	26.00	45.00	100	—
1675	—	13.00	26.00	45.00	100	—
1676	—	13.00	26.00	45.00	100	—
1677	—	13.00	26.00	45.00	100	—
1678	—	13.00	26.00	45.00	100	—
1679	—	13.00	26.00	45.00	100	—

KM# 163 MARIENGROSCHEN (1/36 Thaler)
Silver **Obv:** Horse leaping left **Rev:** Madonna, value in legend

Date	Mintage	VG	F	VF	XF	Unc
1675	—	16.00	35.00	55.00	110	—

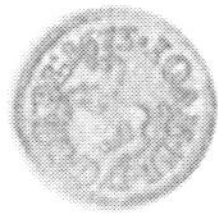

KM# 164 MARIENGROSCHEN (1/36 Thaler)
Silver **Rev:** Value in three lines

Date	Mintage	VG	F	VF	XF	Unc
1675	—	13.00	27.00	45.00	100	—

KM# 165 MARIENGROSCHEN (1/36 Thaler)
Silver **Obv:** Crowned script JF monogram **Rev:** Madonna

Date	Mintage	VG	F	VF	XF	Unc
1675	—	10.00	20.00	40.00	80.00	—
1679	—	10.00	20.00	40.00	80.00	—

KM# 166 MARIENGROSCHEN (1/36 Thaler)
Silver **Obv:** Value in three lines

Date	Mintage	VG	F	VF	XF	Unc
ND(ca.1675)	—	10.00	20.00	40.00	80.00	—

KM# 291 MARIENGROSCHEN (1/36 Thaler)
Silver **Obv:** Widlman, tree in right hand **Rev:** Value, date

Date	Mintage	VG	F	VF	XF	Unc
1682	—	10.00	20.00	40.00	80.00	—
1683	—	10.00	20.00	40.00	80.00	—
1684	—	10.00	20.00	40.00	80.00	—
1685	—	10.00	20.00	40.00	80.00	—
1686	—	10.00	20.00	40.00	80.00	—
1687	—	10.00	20.00	40.00	80.00	—
1688	—	10.00	20.00	40.00	80.00	—

KM# 292 MARIENGROSCHEN (1/36 Thaler)
Silver **Obv:** Value in three lines **Rev:** Madonna divides date

Date	Mintage	VG	F	VF	XF	Unc
1682	—	10.00	18.00	35.00	75.00	—
1683 HB	—	10.00	18.00	35.00	75.00	—

KM# 303 MARIENGROSCHEN (1/36 Thaler)
Silver **Obv:** Crowned script EA monogram **Rev:** Value, date

Date	Mintage	VG	F	VF	XF	Unc
1683	—	20.00	33.00	60.00	120	—
1684	—	20.00	33.00	60.00	120	—
1685	—	20.00	33.00	60.00	120	—
1691 HB	—	20.00	33.00	60.00	120	—

KM# 310 MARIENGROSCHEN (1/36 Thaler)
Silver **Obv:** Intertwined script EA monogram

Date	Mintage	VG	F	VF	XF	Unc
1684	—	20.00	33.00	60.00	120	—

KM# 333 MARIENGROSCHEN (1/36 Thaler)
Silver **Obv:** KM#291 **Rev:** Type of Rudolf august, with REMIGIO ALTISSIMI UNI, date **Note:** Mule.

Date	Mintage	VG	F	VF	XF	Unc
1688	—	—	—	—	—	—

KM# 355 MARIENGROSCHEN (1/36 Thaler)
Silver **Obv:** Value, date in four lines **Obv. Legend:** FURSTL... **Rev:** Madonna

Date	Mintage	VG	F	VF	XF	Unc
1691 HB	—	—	—	—	—	—
1697 HB	—	—	—	—	—	—

KM# 356 MARIENGROSCHEN (1/36 Thaler)
Silver **Obv. Legend:** ERNEST: AUG:

Date	Mintage	VG	F	VF	XF	Unc
1691	—	—	—	—	—	—

KM# 357 MARIENGROSCHEN (1/36 Thaler)
Silver **Obv. Legend:** FR. BR. LUNE...

Date	Mintage	VG	F	VF	XF	Unc
1691 HB	—	—	—	—	—	—
1692 HB	—	—	—	—	—	—
1695 HB	—	—	—	—	—	—
1697 HB	—	—	—	—	—	—

KM# 372 MARIENGROSCHEN (1/36 Thaler)
Silver **Obv. Legend:** C. B. LVNEB...

Date	Mintage	VG	F	VF	XF	Unc
1693 HB	—	—	—	—	—	—
1695 HB	—	—	—	—	—	—
1697 HB	—	—	—	—	—	—

KM# 23.2 2 MARIENGROSCHEN
1.3200 g., Silver, 19.7 mm. **Ruler:** Georg I **Obv:** Horse ornamented helmet **Rev:** Denomination as "MARIE GROS" and radiant sun at top **Edge:** Plain

Date	Mintage	F	VF	XF	Unc	BU
1638HS	—	—	—	—	—	—

KM# 23 2 MARIENGROSCHEN
Silver **Obv:** Helmet with horse **Rev:** Value in three lines, date divided by II

Date	Mintage	VG	F	VF	XF	Unc
1638 HS	—	13.00	27.00	45.00	85.00	—
1639 HS	—	13.00	27.00	45.00	85.00	—
1640 HS	—	13.00	27.00	45.00	85.00	—
1641 HS	—	13.00	27.00	45.00	85.00	—
1642 HS Error	—	13.00	27.00	45.00	85.00	—
ND	—	13.00	27.00	45.00	85.00	—

KM# 44 2 MARIENGROSCHEN
Silver

Date	Mintage	VG	F	VF	XF	Unc
1642 HS	—	10.00	20.00	33.00	65.00	—
1643 HS	—	10.00	20.00	33.00	65.00	—
1644 HS	—	10.00	20.00	33.00	65.00	—
1645 HS	—	10.00	20.00	33.00	65.00	—
1646 HS	—	10.00	20.00	33.00	65.00	—

KM# 45 2 MARIENGROSCHEN
Silver **Obv:** Crowned CL monogram **Rev:** Value in three lines

Date	Mintage	VG	F	VF	XF	Unc
1642	—	10.00	20.00	33.00	65.00	—
1645	—	10.00	20.00	33.00	65.00	—
1646	—	10.00	20.00	33.00	65.00	—
1647	—	10.00	20.00	33.00	65.00	—
1648	—	10.00	20.00	33.00	65.00	—

KM# 51 2 MARIENGROSCHEN
Silver **Obv:** Crowned GW monogram

Date	Mintage	VG	F	VF	XF	Unc
1649	—	10.00	20.00	33.00	65.00	—
1650	—	10.00	20.00	33.00	65.00	—
1651	—	10.00	20.00	33.00	65.00	—
1652	—	10.00	20.00	33.00	65.00	—
1653	—	10.00	20.00	33.00	65.00	—
1654	—	10.00	20.00	33.00	65.00	—
1655	—	10.00	20.00	33.00	65.00	—
1656	—	10.00	20.00	33.00	65.00	—
1657	—	10.00	20.00	33.00	65.00	—
1659	—	10.00	20.00	33.00	65.00	—
1661	—	10.00	20.00	33.00	65.00	—

KM# 105 2 MARIENGROSCHEN
Silver **Obv:** Wildman, tree in right hand

Date	Mintage	VG	F	VF	XF	Unc
1667	—	8.00	13.00	30.00	60.00	—
1673	—	8.00	13.00	30.00	60.00	—
1675	—	8.00	13.00	30.00	60.00	—
1676 GROS	—	8.00	13.00	30.00	60.00	—
1677 GORS Error	—	8.00	13.00	30.00	60.00	—
1678	—	8.00	13.00	30.00	60.00	—
1679	—	8.00	13.00	30.00	60.00	—

KM# 107 2 MARIENGROSCHEN
Silver **Obv:** Crowned IF monogram, date in legend

Date	Mintage	VG	F	VF	XF	Unc
1667	—	13.00	27.00	45.00	80.00	—

KM# 106 2 MARIENGROSCHEN
Silver **Obv:** Horse leaping left **Note:** Varieties exist.

Date	Mintage	VG	F	VF	XF	Unc
1667	—	—	—	—	—	—
1673	—	—	—	—	—	—
1675	—	—	—	—	—	—

KM# 179 2 MARIENGROSCHEN
Silver **Obv:** Value in three lines **Rev:** Madonna

Date	Mintage	VG	F	VF	XF	Unc
1676	—	—	—	—	—	—

KM# 256 2 MARIENGROSCHEN

Silver **Obv:** Wildman, tree in right hand, title as duke **Rev:** Value in three lines, date in legend

Date	Mintage	VG	F	VF	XF	Unc
1680	—	8.00	20.00	45.00	80.00	—
1682	—	8.00	20.00	45.00	80.00	—
1683	—	8.00	20.00	45.00	80.00	—
1684	—	8.00	20.00	45.00	80.00	—
1688 BEL Error	—	8.00	20.00	45.00	80.00	—
1689 B & L	—	8.00	20.00	45.00	80.00	—
1690 BEL Error	—	8.00	20.00	45.00	80.00	—

KM# 257 2 MARIENGROSCHEN

Silver **Obv:** Value, date in four lines **Rev:** Horse leaping left

Date	Mintage	VG	F	VF	XF	Unc
1680 HB	—	—	—	—	—	—

KM# 276 2 MARIENGROSCHEN

Silver **Obv:** Date in legend

Date	Mintage	VG	F	VF	XF	Unc
1681 HB	—	8.00	20.00	40.00	75.00	—
1684 HB	—	8.00	20.00	40.00	75.00	—
1685 HB	—	8.00	20.00	40.00	75.00	—
1688	—	8.00	20.00	40.00	75.00	—

KM# 311 2 MARIENGROSCHEN

Silver **Obv:** Value in three line, date in legends **Rev:** St. Andrew with cross

Date	Mintage	VG	F	VF	XF	Unc
1684 HB	—	—	—	—	—	—

KM# 336 2 MARIENGROSCHEN

Silver **Obv:** Crowned script EA monogram **Rev:** Value in three lines, date in legend

Date	Mintage	VG	F	VF	XF	Unc
1689 HB	—	—	—	—	—	—
1697 HB	—	—	—	—	—	—

KM# 362 2 MARIENGROSCHEN

Silver **Obv:** Date divided by monogram

Date	Mintage	VG	F	VF	XF	Unc
1692 HB	—	7.00	16.00	27.00	55.00	—
1693 HB	—	7.00	16.00	27.00	55.00	—

KM# 373 2 MARIENGROSCHEN

Silver **Obv:** Wildman, tree in right hand, title as elector **Rev:** Value in three lines, date in legend

Date	Mintage	VG	F	VF	XF	Unc
1693	—	—	—	—	—	—
1694	—	—	—	—	—	—
1695	—	—	—	—	—	—
1696	—	—	—	—	—	—
1697	—	—	—	—	—	—

KM# 363 3 MARIENGROSCHEN (= 1/12 Thaler)

Silver **Obv:** Value in four lines **Rev:** Horse leaping left

Date	Mintage	VG	F	VF	XF	Unc
1692	—	—	—	—	—	—

KM# 87 4 MARIENGROSCHEN

Silver **Obv:** Horse leaping left **Rev:** Value in four lines **Note:** Varieties exist.

Date	Mintage	VG	F	VF	XF	Unc
1665	—	9.00	13.00	30.00	60.00	—
1667	—	9.00	13.00	30.00	60.00	—
1668	—	9.00	13.00	30.00	60.00	—
1669	—	9.00	13.00	30.00	60.00	—
1670	—	9.00	13.00	30.00	60.00	—
1671	—	9.00	13.00	30.00	60.00	—
1672	—	9.00	13.00	30.00	60.00	—
1673	—	9.00	13.00	30.00	60.00	—

KM# 108 4 MARIENGROSCHEN

Silver **Obv:** Wildman, tree in right hand **Rev:** Value in three lines, date in legend

Date	Mintage	VG	F	VF	XF	Unc
1667	—	9.00	13.00	30.00	60.00	—
1668	—	9.00	13.00	30.00	60.00	—
1669	—	9.00	13.00	30.00	60.00	—
1673	—	9.00	13.00	30.00	60.00	—

KM# 109 4 MARIENGROSCHEN

Silver **Obv:** Crowned script JF monogram, date in legend **Rev:** Value in four lines

Date	Mintage	VG	F	VF	XF	Unc
1667	—	10.00	20.00	35.00	70.00	—

KM# 142 4 MARIENGROSCHEN

Silver **Obv:** Horse leaping left **Rev:** St. Andrew with cross

Date	Mintage	VG	F	VF	XF	Unc
1673	—	12.00	25.00	45.00	80.00	—

KM# 143 4 MARIENGROSCHEN

Silver **Obv:** Value in five lines **Rev:** St. Andrew with cross, date in legend **Rev. Legend:** S. ANDREASBERG * ANNO

Date	Mintage	VG	F	VF	XF	Unc
1673	—	12.00	25.00	45.00	80.00	—

KM# 154 4 MARIENGROSCHEN

Silver **Obv:** Wildman with tree in right hand, 4 at right **Rev:** Value in three lines, date in legend

Date	Mintage	VG	F	VF	XF	Unc
1674	—	10.00	20.00	40.00	75.00	—
1675	—	10.00	20.00	40.00	75.00	—
1676	—	10.00	20.00	40.00	75.00	—
1677	—	10.00	20.00	40.00	75.00	—
1678	—	10.00	20.00	40.00	75.00	—
1679	—	10.00	20.00	40.00	75.00	—

KM# 180 4 MARIENGROSCHEN

Silver

Date	Mintage	VG	F	VF	XF	Unc
1676	—	20.00	40.00	80.00	135	—

KM# 210 4 MARIENGROSCHEN

Silver **Obv:** Value in five lines **Rev:** St. Andrew with cross **Rev. Legend:** ST. ANDREAS * REVIVISCENS

Date	Mintage	VG	F	VF	XF	Unc
1679	—	12.00	25.00	45.00	80.00	—

KM# 277 4 MARIENGROSCHEN

Silver **Rev:** Horse leaping left, date at bottom

Date	Mintage	VG	F	VF	XF	Unc
1681 HB	—	9.00	16.00	33.00	65.00	—
1686 HB	—	9.00	16.00	33.00	65.00	—

KM# 304 4 MARIENGROSCHEN

Silver **Obv:** Wildman with tree in right hand, title as duke **Rev:** Value in three lines, date in legend

Date	Mintage	VG	F	VF	XF	Unc
1683	—	9.00	16.00	33.00	70.00	—
1687	—	9.00	16.00	33.00	70.00	—
1688	—	9.00	16.00	33.00	70.00	—
1689	—	9.00	16.00	33.00	70.00	—

KM# 338 4 MARIENGROSCHEN

Silver **Rev:** Arabic date at bottom

Date	Mintage	VG	F	VF	XF	Unc
1689 HB	—	9.00	13.00	30.00	60.00	—
1690 HB	—	9.00	13.00	30.00	60.00	—
1692	—	9.00	13.00	30.00	60.00	—

KM# 337 4 MARIENGROSCHEN

Silver **Note:** Similar to KM#338 but Roman numeral date.

Date	Mintage	VG	F	VF	XF	Unc
1689 HB	—	—	—	—	—	—

KM# 364 4 MARIENGROSCHEN

Silver

Date	Mintage	VG	F	VF	XF	Unc
1692 HB	—	9.00	13.00	30.00	60.00	—
1694 HB	—	9.00	13.00	30.00	60.00	—
1696 HB	—	9.00	13.00	30.00	60.00	—

KM# 374 4 MARIENGROSCHEN

Silver **Obv:** Wildman with tree in right hand, title as elector **Rev:** Value in three lines, date in legend

Date	Mintage	VG	F	VF	XF	Unc
1693	—	9.00	13.00	30.00	60.00	—
1694	—	9.00	13.00	30.00	60.00	—
1695	—	9.00	13.00	30.00	60.00	—
1697	—	9.00	13.00	30.00	60.00	—

KM# 120.1 6 MARIENGROSCHEN (= 1/6 Thaler)

Silver **Obv:** Wildman with tree in right hand, 6 at right **Rev:** Value in three lines

Date	Mintage	VG	F	VF	XF	Unc
1668	—	13.00	27.00	45.00	100	—
1669	—	13.00	27.00	45.00	100	—
1671	—	13.00	27.00	45.00	100	—
1673	—	13.00	27.00	45.00	100	—
1674	—	13.00	27.00	45.00	100	—
1675	—	13.00	27.00	45.00	100	—
1676	—	13.00	27.00	45.00	100	—
1677	—	13.00	27.00	45.00	100	—
1678	—	13.00	27.00	45.00	100	—
1679	—	13.00	27.00	45.00	100	—

KM# 120.2 6 MARIENGROSCHEN (= 1/6 Thaler)

Silver **Obv:** Without 6 at right of wildman

Date	Mintage	VG	F	VF	XF	Unc
1668	—	—	—	—	—	—

KM# 121 6 MARIENGROSCHEN (= 1/6 Thaler)

Silver **Obv:** Horse leaping left **Rev:** Value in four lines

Date	Mintage	VG	F	VF	XF	Unc
1668	—	13.00	27.00	55.00	110	—

KM# 258 6 MARIENGROSCHEN (= 1/6 Thaler)

Silver **Obv:** Wildman with tree in right hand, title as duke **Rev:** Value in three lines, date in legend

Date	Mintage	VG	F	VF	XF	Unc
1680	—	13.00	27.00	45.00	100	—
1681	—	13.00	27.00	45.00	100	—
1682	—	13.00	27.00	45.00	100	—
1683	—	13.00	27.00	45.00	100	—
1687	—	13.00	27.00	45.00	100	—
1688	—	13.00	27.00	45.00	100	—
1689	—	13.00	27.00	45.00	100	—

KM# 334 6 MARIENGROSCHEN (= 1/6 Thaler)

Silver **Obv:** Title as duke

Date	Mintage	VG	F	VF	XF	Unc
1688 HB	—	10.00	20.00	40.00	80.00	—
1689 HB	—	10.00	20.00	40.00	80.00	—
1690 HB	—	10.00	20.00	40.00	80.00	—
1692 HB	—	10.00	20.00	40.00	80.00	—

KM# 375 6 MARIENGROSCHEN (= 1/6 Thaler)

Silver **Obv:** Wildman with tree in right hand, title as elector **Rev:** Value in three lines, date in legend

Date	Mintage	VG	F	VF	XF	Unc
1693	—	13.00	27.00	45.00	100	—
1694	—	13.00	27.00	45.00	100	—
1695	—	13.00	27.00	45.00	100	—
1696	—	13.00	27.00	45.00	100	—

Date	Mintage	VG	F	VF	XF	Unc
1697	—	13.00	27.00	45.00	100	—
1698	—	13.00	27.00	45.00	100	—

KM# 376 6 MARIENGROSCHEN (= 1/6 Thaler)
Silver **Obv:** Value, date in four lines, titles as elector **Rev:** Horse leaping left

Date	Mintage	VG	F	VF	XF	Unc
1693 HB	—	10.00	20.00	40.00	85.00	—
1694 HB	—	10.00	20.00	40.00	85.00	—
1696 HB	—	10.00	20.00	40.00	85.00	—
1697 HB	—	10.00	20.00	40.00	85.00	—

KM# 122 12 MARIENGROSCHEN (= 1/3 Thaler)
Silver **Note:** Similar to KM#136 but without 12 at right of wildman.

Date	Mintage	VG	F	VF	XF	Unc
1668	—	20.00	33.00	60.00	125	—
1669	—	20.00	33.00	60.00	125	—
1670	—	20.00	33.00	60.00	125	—
1673	—	20.00	33.00	60.00	125	—
1674	—	20.00	33.00	60.00	125	—

KM# 123 12 MARIENGROSCHEN (= 1/3 Thaler)
Silver **Note:** Varieties exist.

Date	Mintage	VG	F	VF	XF	Unc
1668	—	20.00	33.00	60.00	130	—
1669	—	20.00	33.00	60.00	130	—
1670	—	20.00	33.00	60.00	130	—
1671	—	20.00	33.00	60.00	130	—
1672	—	20.00	33.00	60.00	130	—
1673	—	20.00	33.00	60.00	130	—

KM# 136 12 MARIENGROSCHEN (= 1/3 Thaler)
Silver

Date	Mintage	VG	F	VF	XF	Unc
1669	—	—	—	—	—	—
1671	—	20.00	33.00	60.00	125	—
1672	—	20.00	33.00	60.00	125	—
1627 Error, 27 instead of 72	—	—	—	—	—	—
1675	—	20.00	33.00	60.00	125	—
1676	—	20.00	33.00	60.00	125	—
1677	—	20.00	33.00	60.00	125	—
1678	—	20.00	33.00	60.00	125	—
1679	—	20.00	33.00	60.00	125	—
1970 date error	—	—	—	—	—	—

KM# 137 12 MARIENGROSCHEN (= 1/3 Thaler)
Silver **Obv:** Similar to KM#123 **Rev:** St. Andrew with cross

Date	Mintage	VG	F	VF	XF	Unc
1672	—	—	—	—	—	—

KM# 138 12 MARIENGROSCHEN (= 1/3 Thaler)
Silver **Obv:** Value in five lines

Date	Mintage	VG	F	VF	XF	Unc
1672	—	—	—	—	—	—

KM# 167 12 MARIENGROSCHEN (= 1/3 Thaler)
Silver **Note:** Similar to KM#123 but struck on smaller, thicker flan (27mm).

Date	Mintage	VG	F	VF	XF	Unc
1675	—	40.00	65.00	120	240	—

KM# 259 12 MARIENGROSCHEN (= 1/3 Thaler)
Silver **Obv:** Title as Duke

Date	Mintage	VG	F	VF	XF	Unc
1680	—	20.00	33.00	60.00	120	—
1681	—	20.00	33.00	60.00	120	—
1682	—	20.00	33.00	60.00	120	—
1683	—	—	—	—	—	—
1684	—	20.00	33.00	60.00	120	—
1686	—	20.00	33.00	60.00	120	—
1687	—	20.00	33.00	60.00	120	—
1688	—	20.00	33.00	60.00	120	—
1689	—	20.00	33.00	60.00	120	—
1690	—	20.00	33.00	60.00	120	—
1691	—	20.00	33.00	60.00	120	—
1692	—	20.00	33.00	60.00	120	—

KM# 377 12 MARIENGROSCHEN (= 1/3 Thaler)
Silver **Obv:** Title as elector

Date	Mintage	VG	F	VF	XF	Unc
1693	—	20.00	40.00	80.00	150	—
1694	—	20.00	40.00	80.00	150	—
1695	—	20.00	40.00	80.00	150	—
1696	—	20.00	40.00	80.00	150	—
1697	—	20.00	40.00	80.00	150	—
1698	—	20.00	40.00	80.00	150	—

KM# 139 24 MARIENGROSCHEN (= 2/3 Thaler)
Silver, 36 mm. **Obv:** Horse leaping left **Rev:** Value 24, date in four lines

Date	Mintage	VG	F	VF	XF	Unc
1672	—	25.00	40.00	85.00	175	—
1673	—	25.00	40.00	85.00	175	—
1674	—	25.00	40.00	85.00	175	—

KM# 140 24 MARIENGROSCHEN (= 2/3 Thaler)
Silver **Obv:** Value (XXIIII), date in four lines **Rev:** St. Andrew with cross **Note:** Thick flan (30mm).

Date	Mintage	VG	F	VF	XF	Unc
1672	—	100	200	300	450	—
1675	—	100	200	300	450	—

KM# 158 24 MARIENGROSCHEN (= 2/3 Thaler)
Silver **Note:** Smaller, thicker flan (30mm), value XXIIII.

Date	Mintage	VG	F	VF	XF	Unc
1674	—	100	175	250	350	—
1675	—	100	175	250	350	—

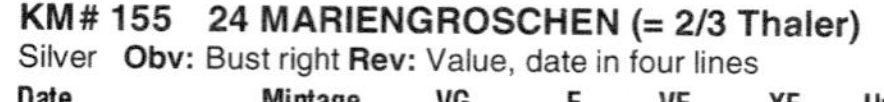

KM# 155 24 MARIENGROSCHEN (= 2/3 Thaler)
Silver **Obv:** Bust right **Rev:** Value, date in four lines

Date	Mintage	VG	F	VF	XF	Unc
1674	—	—	—	—	—	—
1676	—	—	—	—	—	—

KM# 156 24 MARIENGROSCHEN (= 2/3 Thaler)
Silver **Obv:** Wildman, tree in right hand, 24 at right **Rev:** Value in three lines, date in legend

Date	Mintage	VG	F	VF	XF	Unc
1674	—	—	—	—	—	—

KM# 157 24 MARIENGROSCHEN (= 2/3 Thaler)
Silver **Obv:** Horse leaping left **Rev:** Value and date in six lines

Date	Mintage	VG	F	VF	XF	Unc
1674	—	25.00	40.00	80.00	160	—
1675	—	25.00	40.00	80.00	160	—
1676	—	25.00	40.00	80.00	160	—

KM# 168 24 MARIENGROSCHEN (= 2/3 Thaler)
Silver

Date	Mintage	VG	F	VF	XF	Unc
1675 RB	—	55.00	110	180	300	—

KM# 169 24 MARIENGROSCHEN (= 2/3 Thaler)
Silver **Rev:** Large ship right of palm

Date	Mintage	VG	F	VF	XF	Unc
1675 RB	—	55.00	110	180	300	—

KM# 195 24 MARIENGROSCHEN (= 2/3 Thaler)
Silver **Obv:** Wildman with tree in right hand, 24 at right **Rev:** Value in four lines with V. FEIN. SILB.

Date	Mintage	VG	F	VF	XF	Unc
1677	—	40.00	80.00	150	275	—
1678	—	40.00	80.00	150	275	—
1679	—	40.00	80.00	150	275	—
1680	—	40.00	80.00	150	275	—

KM# 260 24 MARIENGROSCHEN (= 2/3 Thaler)
Silver **Obv:** Crowned 12-fold arms, date above **Rev:** Horse leaping left, value in legend

Date	Mintage	VG	F	VF	XF	Unc
1680 IES	—	—	—	—	—	—

KM# 378 24 MARIENGROSCHEN (= 2/3 Thaler)
Silver **Note:** Similar to 12 Mariengroschen KM#377, but 24 at right of wildman on obverse, value in four lines on reverse.

Date	Mintage	VG	F	VF	XF	Unc
1693	—	40.00	65.00	145	275	—
1694	—	40.00	65.00	145	275	—
1695	—	40.00	65.00	145	275	—
1696	—	40.00	65.00	145	275	—
1697	—	40.00	65.00	145	275	—
1698	—	40.00	65.00	145	275	—

KM# 5 1/28 THALER
Silver **Obv:** Crowned 4-fold arms **Rev:** Crowned imperial eagle, orb on breast with 28, titles of Ferdinand II

Date	Mintage	VG	F	VF	XF	Unc
ND(1619)	—	—	—	—	—	—

KM# 13 1/24 THALER (Groschen)
Silver **Obv:** Helmet with horse above shield with lion left **Rev:** Imperial orb with 24, date divided by cross above

Date	Mintage	VG	F	VF	XF	Unc
1635 CH	—	10.00	20.00	33.00	65.00	—
1636 CH	—	10.00	20.00	33.00	65.00	—
1637 CH	—	10.00	20.00	33.00	65.00	—

KM# 94 1/24 THALER (Groschen)
Silver **Obv:** Imperial orb with 24 **Rev:** St. Andrew with cross

Date	Mintage	VG	F	VF	XF	Unc
1666 LW	—	33.00	60.00	110	200	—
1667 LW	—	33.00	60.00	110	200	—

KM# 95 1/24 THALER (Groschen)
Silver **Rev:** Horse leaping left

Date	Mintage	VG	F	VF	XF	Unc
1666 LW	—	33.00	60.00	110	200	—

KM# 211 1/24 THALER (Groschen)
Silver **Obv:** Crowned script JF monogram, date in legend **Rev:** Imperial orb with 24

Date	Mintage	VG	F	VF	XF	Unc
1679	—	—	—	—	—	—

KM# 212 1/24 THALER (Groschen)
Silver **Subject:** Death of Johann Friedrich **Rev:** 11-line inscription

Date	Mintage	VG	F	VF	XF	Unc
1679 RB	—	33.00	55.00	90.00	170	—

KM# 213 1/24 THALER (Groschen)
Silver **Rev:** 12-line inscription

Date	Mintage	VG	F	VF	XF	Unc
1679 HB	—	33.00	55.00	90.00	170	—

KM# 181 1/16 THALER
Silver **Obv:** Bust left **Rev:** Value in four lines, date in legend **Note:** Varieties exist.

Date	Mintage	VG	F	VF	XF	Unc
1676	—	—	—	—	—	—
1676 TAHL Error	—	—	—	—	—	—
1677	—	—	—	—	—	—

KM# 214 1/16 THALER
Silver **Subject:** Death of Johann Friedrich **Obv:** Imperial orb with 1/16 **Rev:** 11-line inscription with date

Date	Mintage	VG	F	VF	XF	Unc
1679 RB	—	33.00	65.00	120	200	—

KM# 215 1/16 THALER
Silver **Rev:** 12-line inscription with date

Date	Mintage	VG	F	VF	XF	Unc
1679 HB	—	33.00	65.00	120	200	—

KM# 35 1/8 THALER
Silver **Obv:** Crowned 11-fold arms **Rev:** Wildman, tree in right hand, date

Date	Mintage	VG	F	VF	XF	Unc
1640 HS	—	—	—	—	—	—
1641 HS	—	—	—	—	—	—

KM# 36 1/8 THALER
Silver **Subject:** Death of Georg **Obv:** Bust left **Rev:** 12-line inscription

Date	Mintage	VG	F	VF	XF	Unc
MDCXXXXI (1641)	—	—	—	—	—	—

KM# 37 1/8 THALER
Silver **Rev:** 13-line inscription

Date	Mintage	VG	F	VF	XF	Unc
1641 HS	—	—	—	—	—	—

KM# 60 1/8 THALER
3.5000 g., Silver **Subject:** Death of Ann Eleonora, Wife of Georg **Note:** Similar to 1 Thaler, KM#64.

Date	Mintage	VG	F	VF	XF	Unc
1659 HS	—	250	400	600	1,000	—

KM# 80 1/8 THALER
Silver **Obv:** Crowned 12-fold arms **Rev:** Wildman, tree in right hand

Date	Mintage	VG	F	VF	XF	Unc
1664 HS	—	—	—	—	—	—

KM# 96.1 1/8 THALER
Silver **Rev:** St. Andrew with cross, date in legend

Date	Mintage	VG	F	VF	XF	Unc
1666 LW	—	—	—	—	—	—

KM# 96.2 1/8 THALER
Silver **Ruler:** Johann Friedrich **Obv:** Crowned 12-fold arms, titles of Johann Friedrich in German **Rev:** Wildman holding tree branch in his right hand

Date	Mintage	VG	F	VF	XF	Unc
1667	—	—	—	—	—	—

KM# 217 1/8 THALER
Silver **Note:** Similar to KM#216 but 25.8mm.

Date	Mintage	VG	F	VF	XF	Unc
1679 HB	—	70.00	120	200	325	—

KM# 216 1/8 THALER
Silver, 29 mm. **Subject:** Death of Johann Friedrich

Date	Mintage	VG	F	VF	XF	Unc
MDCLXXIX (1679) RB	—	75.00	150	250	400	—

KM# A365 1/8 THALER
Silver **Obv:** Helmeted 12-fold arms **Rev:** Wildman with tree in right hand

Date	Mintage	VG	F	VF	XF	Unc
1692	—	—	—	—	—	—

KM# 365 1/8 THALER
Silver **Obv:** Bust right **Rev:** Crowned 12-fold arms

Date	Mintage	VG	F	VF	XF	Unc
1692 HB	—	65.00	125	200	325	—

KM# 408 1/8 THALER
Silver **Subject:** Death of Ernest August **Rev:** Nine-line inscription with date

Date	Mintage	VG	F	VF	XF	Unc
1698	—	80.00	140	200	325	—

KM# 24 1/4 THALER
Silver **Obv:** Crowned 11-fold arms **Rev:** Wildman, tree in right hand, date

Date	Mintage	VG	F	VF	XF	Unc
1638 HS	—	—	—	—	—	—

KM# 38 1/4 THALER
Silver **Subject:** Death of Georg **Obv:** Crowned 11-fold arms **Rev:** 11-line inscription, date in roman numerals

Date	Mintage	VG	F	VF	XF	Unc
1641 HS	—	60.00	115	170	325	—

KM# 48 1/4 THALER
Silver **Obv:** Bust right **Rev:** Crowned 12-fold arms, date in legend

Date	Mintage	VG	F	VF	XF	Unc
1646 HS	—	—	—	—	—	—

KM# 55 1/4 THALER
Silver **Obv:** Crowned 12-fold arms **Rev:** Wildman, tree in right hand, date in legend

Date	Mintage	VG	F	VF	XF	Unc
1650 HS	—	27.00	55.00	100	200	—
1651 HS	—	27.00	55.00	100	200	—
1653 HS	—	27.00	55.00	100	200	—

KM# 61 1/4 THALER
Silver **Subject:** Death of Ann Eleanora, Wife of Georg **Note:** Similar to 1 Thaler, KM#64.

Date	Mintage	VG	F	VF	XF	Unc
1659 HS	—	—	—	—	—	—

KM# 81 1/4 THALER
Silver **Obv:** Similar to KM#97 **Rev:** Wildman, tree in both hands on right side

Date	Mintage	VG	F	VF	XF	Unc
1664 HS	—	—	—	—	—	—

KM# 97 1/4 THALER
Silver

Date	Mintage	VG	F	VF	XF	Unc
1666 LW	—	140	300	525	825	—
1671 LW	—	140	300	525	825	—

KM# 110 1/4 THALER
Silver **Obv:** Title: DUX **Rev:** Wildman, tree in right hand, date in legend

Date	Mintage	VG	F	VF	XF	Unc
1667 HS	—	—	—	—	—	—

KM# 111 1/4 THALER
Silver **Obv:** Title: HERTZOG

Date	Mintage	VG	F	VF	XF	Unc
1667 HS	—	—	—	—	—	—

KM# 130 1/4 THALER
Silver **Obv:** Horse leaping left **Rev:** Palm tree on stone

Date	Mintage	VG	F	VF	XF	Unc
1670	—	—	—	—	—	—

KM# 145 1/4 THALER
Silver **Obv:** Head right

Date	Mintage	VG	F	VF	XF	Unc
1673	—	—	—	—	—	—

KM# 144 1/4 THALER
Silver **Note:** Similar to 1/3 Thaler, KM#146.

Date	Mintage	VG	F	VF	XF	Unc
1673	—	—	—	—	—	—

KM# 182 1/4 THALER
Silver **Obv:** Bust right **Rev:** Crowned 12-fold arms

Date	Mintage	VG	F	VF	XF	Unc
1676 HB	—	—	—	—	—	—

KM# 218 1/4 THALER
Silver, 30 mm. **Subject:** Death of Johann Friedrich **Obv:** Helmeted 12-fold arms **Rev:** 13-line inscription with date **Note:** Varieties exist.

Date	Mintage	VG	F	VF	XF	Unc
1679 RB	—	85.00	160	275	450	—
1679 HB	—	85.00	160	275	450	—

KM# 261 1/4 THALER
Silver **Obv:** Crowned 12-fold arms **Rev:** Horse leaping left **Note:** Posthumous issue for Johann Friedrich.

Date	Mintage	VG	F	VF	XF	Unc
1680 HB	—	—	—	—	—	—

KM# 331 1/4 THALER
Silver **Obv:** Helmeted 12-fold arms

Date	Mintage	VG	F	VF	XF	Unc
1686 HB	—	525	850	1,350	2,000	—

KM# 345 1/4 THALER
Silver **Obv:** Crowned 12-fold arms **Rev:** St. Andrew with cross

Date	Mintage	VG	F	VF	XF	Unc
1690 HB	—	—	—	—	—	—

KM# 366 1/4 THALER
Silver **Obv:** Bust right **Rev:** Helmeted 12-fold arms

Date	Mintage	VG	F	VF	XF	Unc
1692 HB	—	—	—	—	—	—

KM# 367 1/4 THALER
Silver **Obv:** Crowned 12-fold arms **Rev:** Wildman, tree in right hand

Date	Mintage	VG	F	VF	XF	Unc
1692 RB	—	—	—	—	—	—

KM# 409 1/4 THALER
Silver **Subject:** Death of Ernest August **Obv:** Bust right **Rev:** 11-line inscription with date

Date	Mintage	VG	F	VF	XF	Unc
1698	—	—	—	—	—	—

KM# 146 1/3 THALER
Silver

Date	Mintage	VG	F	VF	XF	Unc
1673	—	55.00	90.00	150	275	—

KM# 147.1 1/3 THALER
Silver

Date	Mintage	VG	F	VF	XF	Unc
1673	—	40.00	80.00	130	210	—

KM# 147.2 1/3 THALER
7.2000 g., Silver **Obv:** Wide portrait and cloak **Rev:** FEIN SILB and Arabic date in exergue

Date	Mintage	VG	F	VF	XF	Unc
1676	—	40.00	80.00	130	210	—

KM# 147.3 1/3 THALER
Silver **Obv:** Thin portrait and cloak

Date	Mintage	VG	F	VF	XF	Unc
1679 HB	—	40.00	80.00	120	200	—

KM# 183 1/3 THALER
Silver, 28 mm. **Obv:** Bust left

Date	Mintage	VG	F	VF	XF	Unc
1676	—	60.00	110	175	350	—
ND	—	60.00	110	175	350	—

KM# 184 1/3 THALER
Silver **Obv:** Horse leaping left, value divided date below **Rev:** St. Andrew with cross

Date	Mintage	VG	F	VF	XF	Unc
1676	—	125	200	300	475	—
1677	—	125	200	300	475	—
1678	—	125	200	300	475	—

KM# 185 1/3 THALER
Silver

Date	Mintage	VG	F	VF	XF	Unc
ND(1678)	—	100	200	300	400	—

KM# 219 1/3 THALER
Silver

Date	Mintage	VG	F	VF	XF	Unc
MDCLXXIX (1679) HB	—	65.00	120	200	375	—

KM# 220 1/3 THALER
7.2000 g., Silver **Subject:** Death of Johann Friedrich

Date	Mintage	VG	F	VF	XF	Unc
1679 RB	—	—	—	—	—	—

KM# 278 1/3 THALER
Silver **Obv:** Crowned 12-fold arms **Rev:** Horse leaping left, value 1/3 below divides date **Note:** Varieties exist.

Date	Mintage	VG	F	VF	XF	Unc
1681 HB	—	—	—	—	—	—
1684 HB	—	—	—	—	—	—
1686 HB	—	—	—	—	—	—

KM# 305 1/3 THALER
Silver **Note:** Varieties exist.

Date	Mintage	VG	F	VF	XF	Unc
MDCLXXXIII (1683) HB	—	55.00	120	160	325	—
MDCLXXXVI (1686) HB	—	55.00	120	160	325	—
MDCLXXXVII (1687) HB	—	55.00	120	160	325	—
MDCLXXXVIII (1688) HB	—	55.00	120	160	325	—

KM# 346 1/3 THALER
Silver **Rev:** St. Andrew with cross, date in legend

Date	Mintage	VG	F	VF	XF	Unc
1690 HB	—	20.00	40.00	80.00	160	—
1692 HB	—	20.00	40.00	80.00	160	—

KM# 388 1/3 THALER
Silver **Obv:** Crowned script EA monogram **Rev:** St. Andrew with cross

Date	Mintage	VG	F	VF	XF	Unc
MDCXCIV (1694) HB	—	27.00	60.00	100	200	—
MDCVC (1695) HB	—	27.00	60.00	100	200	—

KM# 393 1/3 THALER
Silver **Obv:** KM#388 **Rev:** KM#392 **Note:** Mule.

Date	Mintage	VG	F	VF	XF	Unc
1694/1695 HB	—	55.00	100	200	375	—

KM# 392 1/3 THALER
Silver **Rev:** Arabic year divided near bottom

Date	Mintage	VG	F	VF	XF	Unc
1695 HB	—	27.00	60.00	110	200	—

KM# 404 1/3 THALER
Silver **Obv:** Arabic date divided by monogram

Date	Mintage	VG	F	VF	XF	Unc
1696 HB	—	20.00	45.00	90.00	180	—
1697 HB	—	20.00	45.00	90.00	180	—

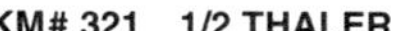

KM# 19 1/2 THALER
Silver **Obv:** Half-length figure left **Rev:** Crowned 11-fold arms, date in legend

Date	Mintage	VG	F	VF	XF	Unc
1637 HS	—	60.00	120	200	350	—
1638 HS	—	60.00	120	200	350	—
1639 HS	—	60.00	120	200	350	—
1640 HS	—	60.00	120	200	350	—
1641 HS	—	60.00	120	200	350	—

KM# 39 1/2 THALER
Silver **Subject:** Death of George **Rev:** 13-line inscription

Date	Mintage	VG	F	VF	XF	Unc
MDCXLI (1641) HS	—	—	—	—	—	—

KM# 50 1/2 THALER
Silver **Obv:** Crowned 12-fold arms **Rev:** Wildman, tree in right hand

Date	Mintage	VG	F	VF	XF	Unc
1647 HS	—	—	—	—	—	—

KM# 62 1/2 THALER
Silver **Obv:** Crowned 12-fold arms **Rev:** Wildman, tree in both hands on right side

Date	Mintage	VG	F	VF	XF	Unc
1659 HS	—	—	—	—	—	—
1660 HS	—	—	—	—	—	—

KM# 63 1/2 THALER
Silver **Subject:** Death of Anna Eleonora, Wife of Georg **Note:** Similar to 1 thaler, KM#64.

Date	Mintage	VG	F	VF	XF	Unc
1659 HS	—	—	—	—	—	—

KM# 100 1/2 THALER
Silver **Note:** Varieties exist.

Date	Mintage	VG	F	VF	XF	Unc
1666 HS	—	—	—	—	—	—
1667 HS	—	—	—	—	—	—
1679 RB	—	—	—	—	—	—

KM# 99 1/2 THALER
Silver **Note:** Klippe.

Date	Mintage	VG	F	VF	XF	Unc
1666 LW	—	—	—	—	—	—

KM# 98 1/2 THALER
Silver

Date	Mintage	VG	F	VF	XF	Unc
1666 LW	—	85.00	170	275	375	—
1671 LW	—	85.00	170	275	375	—

KM# 186 1/2 THALER
Silver **Obv:** Bust right **Rev:** Crowned 12-fold arms

Date	Mintage	VG	F	VF	XF	Unc
1676 HB	—	—	—	—	—	—

KM# 201 1/2 THALER
Silver **Obv:** Helmeted 12-fold arms **Rev:** 13-line inscription with date

Date	Mintage	VG	F	VF	XF	Unc
1678 HB	—	—	—	—	—	—

KM# 221 1/2 THALER
Silver **Rev:** Roman numeral date in legend

Date	Mintage	VG	F	VF	XF	Unc
1679 HB	—	—	—	—	—	—

KM# 222 1/2 THALER
Silver **Obv:** Bust right **Rev:** Horse leaping left

Date	Mintage	VG	F	VF	XF	Unc
1679	—	—	—	—	—	—

KM# 223 1/2 THALER
Silver **Subject:** Death of Johann Friedrich **Obv:** Helmeted 12-fold arms **Rev:** 13-line inscription

Date	Mintage	VG	F	VF	XF	Unc
MDCXXIX (1679) HB	—	—	—	—	—	—
MDCXXIX (1679) RB	—	—	—	—	—	—
MDCXXIX (1679)	—	—	—	—	—	—

KM# 321 1/2 THALER
Silver **Obv:** Bust right **Rev:** Helmeted 12-fold arms

Date	Mintage	VG	F	VF	XF	Unc
MDCLXXXV (1685)	—	—	—	—	—	—

KM# 339 1/2 THALER
Silver **Rev:** Arabic date in legend

Date	Mintage	VG	F	VF	XF	Unc
1689 HB	—	—	—	—	—	—

KM# 368 1/2 THALER
Silver **Rev:** Value as R.T. (Reichstaler)

Date	Mintage	VG	F	VF	XF	Unc
1692 HB	—	—	—	—	—	—

KM# 410 1/2 THALER
Silver **Subject:** Death of Ernst August **Rev:** 12-line inscription with date

Date	Mintage	VG	F	VF	XF	Unc
1698	—	150	200	300	450	—

KM# 148 2/3 THALER
Silver **Note:** Similar to KM#187 but without V. FEIN SILB.

Date	Mintage	VG	F	VF	XF	Unc
1673	—	60.00	110	200	375	—
1674	—	60.00	110	200	375	—
1676	—	60.00	110	200	375	—
1677	—	60.00	110	200	375	—
1678	—	60.00	110	200	375	—

KM# 170 2/3 THALER
Silver **Rev:** Large 2/3, date in legend

Date	Mintage	VG	F	VF	XF	Unc
1675 RB	—	200	400	6,560	1,100	—

KM# 171 2/3 THALER
Silver

Date	Mintage	VG	F	VF	XF	Unc
1675 RB	—	45.00	75.00	175	300	—
1676 RB	—	45.00	75.00	175	300	—

KM# 172 2/3 THALER
Silver

Date	Mintage	VG	F	VF	XF	Unc
1675 RB	—	40.00	65.00	160	280	—
1676	—	40.00	65.00	160	280	—
1676 RB	—	40.00	65.00	160	280	—
1677	—	40.00	65.00	160	280	—
1678	—	40.00	65.00	160	280	—
ND	—	40.00	65.00	160	280	—

KM# 188.1 2/3 THALER
Silver

Date	Mintage	VG	F	VF	XF	Unc
1676	—	45.00	80.00	170	300	—

KM# 187 2/3 THALER
Silver **Note:** Varieties exist.

Date	Mintage	VG	F	VF	XF	Unc
1676	—	40.00	65.00	160	285	—
1677	—	40.00	65.00	160	285	—
1678	—	40.00	65.00	160	285	—
1679 HB	—	40.00	65.00	160	285	—

KM# 188.2 2/3 THALER
Silver

Date	Mintage	VG	F	VF	XF	Unc
1677	—	75.00	150	300	550	—

KM# 188.3 2/3 THALER
Silver

Date	Mintage	VG	F	VF	XF	Unc
1678	—	60.00	125	260	450	—

KM# 202 2/3 THALER
Silver

Date	Mintage	VG	F	VF	XF	Unc
1678	—	100	200	300	500	—

KM# 204 2/3 THALER
Silver, 30.5 mm.

Date	Mintage	VG	F	VF	XF	Unc
ND	—	55.00	100	200	375	—

KM# 203 2/3 THALER
Silver **Note:** Similar to KM#204 but 34mm and value in wreath.

Date	Mintage	VG	F	VF	XF	Unc
ND	—	—	—	—	—	—

KM# A224 2/3 THALER
Silver **Obv:** Bust right **Rev:** Two ships "keeling" left, flanking island palm

Date	Mintage	VG	F	VF	XF	Unc
1677	—	75.00	150	300	550	—

KM# B224 2/3 THALER
Silver **Rev:** Ships upright

Date	Mintage	VG	F	VF	XF	Unc
1677	—	65.00	140	285	500	—

KM# C224 2/3 THALER
Silver **Rev:** Island with four rocks

Date	Mintage	VG	F	VF	XF	Unc
1679 HB	—	65.00	140	285	500	—

KM# D224 2/3 THALER
Silver **Rev:** Island with six rocks

Date	Mintage	VG	F	VF	XF	Unc
1679 HB	—	65.00	140	285	500	—

KM# E224 2/3 THALER
Silver **Rev:** Island rock cluster

Date	Mintage	VG	F	VF	XF	Unc
1679 HB	—	65.00	140	285	500	—

KM# F224 2/3 THALER
14.5000 g., Silver, 34 mm. **Rev:** Roman numeral date in legend

Date	Mintage	VG	F	VF	XF	Unc
1679 HB	—	60.00	125	260	450	—

KM# 224 2/3 THALER
Silver

Date	Mintage	VG	F	VF	XF	Unc
1679 HB	—	60.00	125	260	450	—

KM# 225 2/3 THALER
Silver **Subject:** Death of Johann Friedrich

Date	Mintage	VG	F	VF	XF	Unc
1679 RB	—	—	—	—	—	—

KM# 262.1 2/3 THALER
Silver **Rev:** Trees behind wildman

Date	Mintage	VG	F	VF	XF	Unc
1680	—	33.00	65.00	120	275	—
1681	—	33.00	65.00	120	275	—
1682	—	33.00	65.00	120	275	—
1683	—	33.00	65.00	120	275	—
1684	—	33.00	65.00	120	275	—
1685	—	33.00	65.00	120	275	—
1686	—	33.00	65.00	120	275	—
1687	—	33.00	65.00	120	275	—
1688	—	33.00	65.00	120	275	—
1689	—	33.00	65.00	120	275	—
1690	—	33.00	65.00	120	275	—
1691	—	33.00	65.00	120	275	—
1692	—	33.00	65.00	120	275	—
1693	—	33.00	65.00	120	275	—
1693 RB	—	38.00	80.00	130	300	—

KM# 262.2 2/3 THALER
Silver **Obv:** Stars above date **Rev:** Grass under wildman

Date	Mintage	VG	F	VF	XF	Unc
1690	—	33.00	65.00	130	275	—
1693	—	33.00	65.00	130	275	—

KM# 263 2/3 THALER
Silver **Rev:** Horse leaping left in circle, value 2/3 below **Note:** Varieties exist.

Date	Mintage	VG	F	VF	XF	Unc
1680 HB	—	40.00	80.00	160	300	—
1681 HB	—	40.00	80.00	160	300	—
1682 HB	—	40.00	80.00	160	300	—
1683 HB	—	40.00	80.00	160	300	—
1683 IES	—	40.00	80.00	160	300	—
1684 HB	—	40.00	80.00	160	300	—

KM# A264 2/3 THALER
Silver **Obv:** Date above crowned shield **Rev:** Leaping horse

Date	Mintage	VG	F	VF	XF	Unc
1680 IES	—	—	—	—	—	—

KM# B264 2/3 THALER
Silver **Obv:** Crowned shield divides date and initials **Rev:** Value below horse

Date	Mintage	VG	F	VF	XF	Unc
1680 HB	—	—	—	—	—	—
1681 HB	—	—	—	—	—	—
1682 HB	—	—	—	—	—	—
1683 HB	—	—	—	—	—	—

KM# 264 2/3 THALER
Silver **Obv:** Larger arms with sprays **Rev:** Date divided by value at bottom

Date	Mintage	VG	F	VF	XF	Unc
1680 IES	—	—	—	—	—	—

KM# A312 2/3 THALER
16.8000 g., Silver, 37 mm. **Rev:** Initials

Date	Mintage	VG	F	VF	XF	Unc
1683 IES	—	—	—	—	—	—

KM# B312 2/3 THALER
16.5000 g., Silver **Obv:** Initials

Date	Mintage	VG	F	VF	XF	Unc
MDCLXXXIII (1683) IES	—	—	—	—	—	—
MDCLXXXIV (1684) IES	—	—	—	—	—	—

KM# 312 2/3 THALER
16.5000 g., Silver **Obv:** Helmeted 12-fold arms divide date **Rev:** Horse leaping left

Date	Mintage	VG	F	VF	XF	Unc
1684 HB	—	—	—	—	—	—

KM# 314 2/3 THALER
Silver **Rev:** Horse in wreath

Date	Mintage	VG	F	VF	XF	Unc
1684 IES	—	—	—	—	—	—

KM# 313 2/3 THALER
Silver **Note:** Similar to KM#315 but 2/3 divides date below.

Date	Mintage	VG	F	VF	XF	Unc
1684 IES	—	—	—	—	—	—

KM# 315 2/3 THALER
Silver **Note:** Varieties exist.

Date	Mintage	VG	F	VF	XF	Unc
MDCLXXXV (1685) HB	—	55.00	100	220	350	—
MDCLXXXVI (1686) HB	—	55.00	100	220	350	—
MDCLXXXVII (1687) HB	—	55.00	110	220	350	—
MDCLXXXVII (1687) HB Error "DUAE"	—	55.00	100	220	350	—
MDCLXXXVIII (1688) HB	—	55.00	110	220	350	—

KM# 340 2/3 THALER
Silver **Rev:** 2/3 below divides date and FEIN-SILB

Date	Mintage	VG	F	VF	XF	Unc
1689 HB	—	40.00	80.00	150	225	—
1690 HB	—	40.00	80.00	150	225	—

Date	Mintage	VG	F	VF	XF	Unc
1691 HB	—	40.00	80.00	150	225	—
1692 HB	—	40.00	80.00	150	225	—
1693 HB	—	40.00	80.00	150	225	—

KM# 347 2/3 THALER

Silver **Rev:** Without wreath and without FEIN-SILB

Date	Mintage	VG	F	VF	XF	Unc
1690 IES	—	37.00	60.00	100	160	—
1690 Stars	—	37.00	60.00	100	160	—
1691 Stars	—	37.00	60.00	100	160	—
1692 Stars	—	37.00	60.00	100	160	—

KM# 348 2/3 THALER

Silver **Rev:** FEIN-SILB divided by value

Date	Mintage	VG	F	VF	XF	Unc
1690	—	40.00	80.00	135	200	—
1692	—	40.00	80.00	135	200	—

KM# 269 2/3 THALER

15.4000 g., Silver, 34.8 mm. **Ruler:** Ernst August **Obv:** Crowned arms in center circle divide stars **Rev:** Horse jumping left in inner circle above denomination which divides the date in the legend **Edge:** Plain

Date	Mintage	F	VF	XF	Unc	BU
1690	—	—	—	—	—	—

KM# 379 2/3 THALER

Silver

Date	Mintage	VG	F	VF	XF	Unc
1693	—	40.00	80.00	150	275	—
1694	—	40.00	80.00	150	275	—

KM# 380 2/3 THALER

Silver **Rev:** Large crown above horse leaping left, value 2/3 below, date in legend

Date	Mintage	VG	F	VF	XF	Unc
1693	—	—	—	—	—	—

KM# 10 THALER

Silver **Obv:** Half-length figure right, date **Rev:** Female figure of Concord between figures of four dukes

Date	Mintage	VG	F	VF	XF	Unc
1634 HS	—	—	—	—	—	—

KM# 14 THALER

Silver **Obv:** Bust right **Rev:** Helmeted arms, date in legend **Note:** Dav. #6502.

Date	Mintage	VG	F	VF	XF	Unc
1635	—	400	800	1,500	2,400	—
1636	—	400	800	1,500	2,400	—

KM# 18 THALER

Silver **Rev:** Date divided at top in legend **Note:** Dav. #6503.

Date	Mintage	VG	F	VF	XF	Unc
1636	—	400	800	1,500	2,400	—

KM# 20 THALER

Silver **Rev:** Similar to KM#21 but larger arms, date in upper right legend **Note:** Dav. #6504.

Date	Mintage	VG	F	VF	XF	Unc
1637 HS	—	130	250	450	700	—
1638 HS	—	130	250	450	700	—

KM# 21 THALER

Silver **Note:** Dav. #6505.

Date	Mintage	VG	F	VF	XF	Unc
1637 HS	—	130	250	450	700	—
1638 HS	—	130	250	450	700	—
1639 HS	—	130	250	450	700	—

KM# 22.1 THALER

Silver **Rev:** Wildman facing forward, legend, date **Rev. Legend:** TRAWE ICH ANNO **Note:** Dav. #6507.

Date	Mintage	VG	F	VF	XF	Unc
1637 HS	—	90.00	170	300	500	—
1638 HS	—	90.00	170	300	500	—
1639 HS	—	90.00	170	300	500	—

KM# 22.2 THALER

Silver **Note:** Varieties exist. Dav. #6508.

Date	Mintage	VG	F	VF	XF	Unc
1639 HS	—	90.00	170	300	500	—
1640 HS	—	90.00	170	300	500	—
1641 HS	—	90.00	170	300	500	—
1642 HS	—	90.00	170	300	500	—

KM# 30 THALER

Silver **Note:** Dav. #6506.

Date	Mintage	VG	F	VF	XF	Unc
1639 HS	—	130	250	450	700	—
1640 HS	—	130	250	450	700	—
1641 HS	—	130	250	450	700	—
1642 HS	—	130	250	450	700	—

KM# 40 THALER

Silver **Subject:** Death of Georg **Obv:** Half-length figure left **Rev:** 11-line inscription **Note:** Dav. #6510.

Date	Mintage	VG	F	VF	XF	Unc
1641 HS	—	400	650	1,100	1,700	—

KM# 41 THALER

Silver **Obv:** Half-length figure left **Rev:** 10-line inscription, date in Roman numerals **Note:** Dav. #6510A.

Date	Mintage	VG	F	VF	XF	Unc
1641 HS	—	400	650	1,100	1,700	—

KM# 47.1 THALER

Silver **Obv:** Helmeted 12-fold arms dividing H S **Obv. Legend:** C RIS: LUD: HERTZ. Z. G: L. **Rev:** Wildman with tree in right hand **Note:** Dav. #6515.

Date	Mintage	VG	F	VF	XF	Unc
1643 HS	—	90.00	170	300	500	—

KM# 47.2 THALER

Silver **Obv. Legend:** CHRISTI: LUD: D. G. DUX. BR: E: L: **Note:** Dav. #6516.

Date	Mintage	VG	F	VF	XF	Unc
1643 HS	—	90.00	170	300	500	—

KM# 47.3 THALER

Silver **Obv. Legend:** CHRISTI: LUD: H. Z: B: L: **Note:** Dav. #6517.

Date	Mintage	VG	F	VF	XF	Unc
1643 HS	—	90.00	170	300	500	—
1646 HS	—	90.00	170	300	500	—
1648	—	90.00	170	300	500	—
1648 HS	—	90.00	170	300	500	—
1649	—	90.00	170	300	500	—
1649 HS	—	90.00	170	300	500	—
1650	—	90.00	170	300	500	—
1650 HS	—	90.00	170	300	500	—
1652	—	90.00	170	300	500	—
1652 HS	—	90.00	170	300	500	—

KM# 47.4 THALER

Silver **Rev:** H mint mark, S in legend **Note:** Dav. #6517B.

Date	Mintage	VG	F	VF	XF	Unc
1643	—	90.00	170	300	500	—
1648	—	90.00	170	300	500	—
1652	—	90.00	170	300	500	—
1653	—	90.00	170	300	500	—
1655	—	90.00	170	300	500	—
1657	—	90.00	170	300	500	—
1663	—	90.00	170	300	500	—
1664	—	90.00	170	300	500	—
1665	—	90.00	170	300	500	—

KM# 46.1 THALER

Silver **Obv:** 3/4-length bust right, baton in left hand **Rev:** Helmeted 12-fold arms, date in legend **Note:** Dav. #6512.

Date	Mintage	VG	F	VF	XF	Unc
1643 HS	—	240	450	800	1,300	—
1644	—	240	450	800	1,300	—
1645	—	240	450	800	1,300	—

KM# 46.2 THALER

Silver **Obv:** 3/4-length bust right, baton in right hand **Note:** Dav. #6513.

Date	Mintage	VG	F	VF	XF	Unc
1645	—	240	450	800	1,300	—
1645 HS	—	240	450	800	1,300	—
1646	—	240	450	800	1,300	—
1646 HS	—	240	450	800	1,300	—
1647	—	240	450	800	1,300	—
1647 HS	—	240	450	800	1,300	—

KM# 46.3 THALER

Silver **Obv:** 3/4-length bust right, raised baton in left hand **Note:** Dav. #6514.

Date	Mintage	VG	F	VF	XF	Unc
1647	—	240	450	800	1,300	—
1648 HS	—	240	450	800	1,300	—
1649	—	240	450	800	1,300	—

KM# 52.1 THALER

Silver **Obv. Legend:** V. G. G. GEORG. WILH: HERTZ:... **Note:** Dav. #6526.

Date	Mintage	VG	F	VF	XF	Unc
1649	—	90.00	170	300	500	—

KM# 52.2 THALER

Silver **Note:** Dav. #6527.

Date	Mintage	VG	F	VF	XF	Unc
1649 HS	—	90.00	170	300	500	—
1650 HS	—	90.00	170	300	500	—
1651 HS	—	90.00	170	300	500	—
1652	—	90.00	170	300	500	—
1652 HS	—	90.00	170	300	500	—
1653 HS	—	90.00	170	300	500	—

KM# 57.1 THALER

Silver **Note:** Dav. #6528.

Date	Mintage	VG	F	VF	XF	Unc
1654 HS	—	90.00	170	300	500	—
1655 HS	—	90.00	170	300	500	—
1656 HS	—	90.00	170	300	500	—
1657 HS	—	90.00	170	300	500	—
1658 HS	—	90.00	170	300	500	—
1659 HS	—	90.00	170	300	500	—
1660 HS	—	90.00	170	300	500	—
1661 HS	—	90.00	170	300	500	—
1662 HS	—	90.00	170	300	500	—
1663 HS	—	90.00	170	300	500	—
1664 HS	—	90.00	170	300	500	—

KM# 57.2 THALER

Silver **Obv:** Legend continuous from left to right **Note:** Dav. #6529.

Date	Mintage	VG	F	VF	XF	Unc
1664 HS	—	90.00	170	300	500	—
1665 HS	—	90.00	170	300	500	—
1666 HS	—	90.00	170	300	500	—

KM# 64 THALER

Silver **Subject:** Death of Eleanora, Wife of Georg **Note:** Dav. #6511.

Date	Mintage	VG	F	VF	XF	Unc
1659 HS Rare	—	—	—	—	—	—

KM# 73 THALER

Silver **Obv:** Bust right in circle of fourteen small shields, date divided below **Rev:** Figures of Piety and Justice below tree, arm from heaven with wreath **Note:** Dav. #6532.

Date	Mintage	VG	F	VF	XF	Unc
1661 HS	—	350	600	1,000	1,600	—
1662 HS	—	350	600	1,000	1,600	—

KM# 79 THALER

Silver **Obv:** Bust right **Rev:** Helmeted 12-fold arms, date in legend **Note:** Dav. #6535.

Date	Mintage	VG	F	VF	XF	Unc
1662	—	500	700	1,200	1,800	—
1664 HS	—	500	700	1,200	1,800	—
1665	—	500	700	1,200	1,800	—

KM# 88 THALER

Silver **Obv:** Bust left **Rev:** Helmeted 12-fold arms, date in legend **Note:** Dav. #6536.

Date	Mintage	VG	F	VF	XF	Unc
1664 LW	—	90.00	170	300	500	—
1665 Rare	—	—	—	—	—	—
1665 HS Rare	—	—	—	—	—	—

KM# 89 THALER
Silver **Note:** Dav. #6544.

Date	Mintage	VG	F	VF	XF	Unc
1665 HS	—	90.00	170	300	1,000	—
1666 HS	—	90.00	170	300	1,000	—
1667 HS	—	90.00	170	300	1,000	—

KM# 82 THALER
Silver **Rev:** Date, prancing horse left **Rev. Legend:** ANNO **Note:** Dav. #6549.

Date	Mintage	VG	F	VF	XF	Unc
1665 LW	—	90.00	170	300	500	—
1667 LW	—	90.00	170	300	500	—
1668 LW	—	90.00	170	300	500	—
1669 LW	—	90.00	170	300	500	—
1670 LW	—	90.00	170	300	500	—
1671 LW	—	90.00	170	300	500	—
1672 LW	—	90.00	170	300	500	—
1673 LW	—	90.00	170	300	500	—

KM# 101 THALER
Silver **Obv:** Similar to KM#216 **Rev:** St. Andrew with cross, date in legend **Note:** Dav. #6557.

Date	Mintage	VG	F	VF	XF	Unc
1666 LW	—	240	450	800	1,300	—
1667 LW	—	240	450	800	1,300	—
1669 LW	—	240	450	800	1,300	—

KM# 102 THALER
Silver **Note:** Dav. #6569.

Date	Mintage	VG	F	VF	XF	Unc
1666	—	400	650	1,100	1,700	—
1667	—	400	650	1,100	1,700	—
1668	—	400	650	1,100	1,700	—
1669	—	400	650	1,100	1,700	—
1670	—	400	650	1,100	1,700	—
1671	—	400	650	1,100	1,700	—

KM# 114 THALER
Silver **Rev:** Legend, date, prancing horse left **Rev. Legend:** EX DURIS GLORIA * ANNO * **Note:** Dav. #6550.

Date	Mintage	VG	F	VF	XF	Unc
1667 LW	—	90.00	170	300	500	—
1673 LW	—	90.00	170	300	500	—

KM# 115 THALER
Silver **Note:** Dav. #6551.

Date	Mintage	VG	F	VF	XF	Unc
1667 LW	—	200	400	700	1,100	—
1668 LW	—	200	400	700	1,100	—
1669 LW	—	200	400	700	1,100	—
1670 LW	—	200	400	700	1,100	—
1671 LW	—	200	400	700	1,100	—
1673 LW	—	200	400	700	1,100	—
1674 LW	—	200	400	700	1,100	—
1675 HB	—	200	400	700	1,100	—

KM# 113.1 THALER
Silver **Obv. Legend:** IOHAN FRIEDRICH: D: G DUX BR: ET LUNEB **Note:** Dav. #6546.

Date	Mintage	VG	F	VF	XF	Unc
1667 HS	—	90.00	170	300	500	—
1668 HS	—	90.00	170	300	500	—
1669 HS	—	90.00	170	300	500	—

KM# 113.2 THALER
Silver **Obv. Legend:** ...BRUNS: ET LUN: **Rev:** Initials by tree **Note:** Dav. #6547.

Date	Mintage	VG	F	VF	XF	Unc
1670 HS	—	90.00	170	300	500	—
1671 HS	—	90.00	170	300	500	—
1672 HS	—	90.00	170	300	500	—
1673 IPE	—	90.00	170	300	500	—
1675 IPE	—	90.00	170	300	500	—

KM# 113.3 THALER
Silver **Obv. Legend:** ...FRIDER...LUNAE **Note:** Dav. #6548.

Date	Mintage	VG	F	VF	XF	Unc
1677 RB	—	180	350	600	1,000	—
1678 RB	—	180	350	600	1,000	—
1679 RB	—	180	350	600	1,000	—

KM# 116 THALER
Silver **Obv:** Bust left **Rev:** Horse leaping left in empty field

Date	Mintage	VG	F	VF	XF	Unc
1667	—	—	—	—	—	—
1670	—	—	—	—	—	—

KM# 112 THALER

Silver **Note:** Similar to KM#89 but EX DVRIS GLORIA added to reverse legend. Dav. #6545.

Date	Mintage	VG	F	VF	XF	Unc
1667 HS	—	90.00	170	300	500	—

KM# 124.1 THALER

Silver **Rev:** Helmeted 12-fold arms, date in legend **Note:** Dav. #6578.

Date	Mintage	VG	F	VF	XF	Unc
1668 LW Rare	—	—	—	—	—	—

KM# 124.2 THALER

Silver **Rev:** Legend, date **Rev. Legend:** EX DVRIS GLORIA ANNO **Note:** Dav. #6579.

Date	Mintage	VG	F	VF	XF	Unc
1669	—	500	900	1,400	2,200	—
1670	—	500	900	1,400	2,200	—
1671	—	500	900	1,400	2,200	—

KM# 124.3 THALER

Silver **Obv:** C below bust **Note:** Dav. #6579A.

Date	Mintage	VG	F	VF	XF	Unc
1670 C	—	500	900	1,400	2,200	—

KM# 149.1 THALER

Silver **Obv:** Bust right with short hair **Note:** Dav. #6570.

Date	Mintage	VG	F	VF	XF	Unc
1673	—	600	1,000	1,700	2,700	—

KM# 149.2 THALER

Silver **Obv:** Bust right with long hair **Note:** Dav. #6573.

Date	Mintage	VG	F	VF	XF	Unc
1675	—	400	650	1,100	1,700	—
1676	—	400	650	1,100	1,700	—

KM# 150 THALER

Silver **Note:** Helmeted 12-fold arms, date divided near bottom. Dav. #6580.

Date	Mintage	VG	F	VF	XF	Unc
1673 HB Rare	—	—	—	—	—	—
1676 HB Rare	—	—	—	—	—	—
1677 HB Rare	—	—	—	—	—	—

KM# 159 THALER

Silver **Note:** Dav. #6558.

Date	Mintage	VG	F	VF	XF	Unc
1674	—	700	1,100	1,800	2,800	—

KM# 173 THALER

Silver **Rev:** Horse on hilly ground **Note:** Dav. #6552.

Date	Mintage	VG	F	VF	XF	Unc
1675 HB Rare	—	—	—	—	—	—
1677 HB Rare	—	—	—	—	—	—

KM# 174 THALER

Silver **Note:** Similar to KM#227. Dav. #6560.

Date	Mintage	VG	F	VF	XF	Unc
1675 HB	—	500	900	1,400	2,200	—
1678 HB	—	500	900	1,400	2,200	—
1679 HB	—	500	900	1,400	2,200	—

KM# 189 THALER

Silver **Subject:** 100th Anniversary - University of Helmstedt **Obv:** 16-line inscription **Rev:** Fountain between two palm trees **Note:** Dav. #6588.

Date	Mintage	VG	F	VF	XF	Unc
1676 HB	—	1,900	3,100	5,200	8,000	—

KM# 206.1 THALER

Silver **Note:** Similar to KM#115, but date at reverse bottom. Dav. #6554.

Date	Mintage	VG	F	VF	XF	Unc
1678 HB Rare	—	—	—	—	—	—

KM# 206.2 THALER

Silver **Obv:** Taller shield **Obv. Legend:** DUX BR. EL. **Note:** Dav. #6555.

Date	Mintage	VG	F	VF	XF	Unc
1678 HB Rare	—	—	—	—	—	—

KM# 205 THALER

Silver **Note:** Similar to KM#115, but date divided by arms. Dav. #6553.

Date	Mintage	VG	F	VF	XF	Unc
1678 HB Rare	—	—	—	—	—	—

KM# 207 THALER

Silver **Note:** Hybrid Thaler. Similar to KM#227. Dav. #6561.

Date	Mintage	VG	F	VF	XF	Unc
1678 HB	—	500	900	1,400	2,200	—

KM# 226 THALER

Silver **Note:** Similar to KM#115, but horse in circle. Dav. #6556.

Date	Mintage	VG	F	VF	XF	Unc
MDCLXXIX (1679) HB Rare	—	—	—	—	—	—

KM# 232 THALER

Silver **Obv:** Small bust right in laurel wreath **Rev:** Helmeted 12-fold arms, date divided near top **Note:** Dav. #6582.

Date	Mintage	VG	F	VF	XF	Unc
1679 HB Rare	—	—	—	—	—	—

KM# 233 THALER

Silver **Note:** Dav. #6583.

Date	Mintage	VG	F	VF	XF	Unc
1679 HB Rare	—	—	—	—	—	—

KM# 208.1 THALER

Silver **Obv:** Small bust right **Rev:** Helmeted 12-fold arms, divided near top **Note:** Dav. #6581.

Date	Mintage	VG	F	VF	XF	Unc
1678 HB Rare	—	—	—	—	—	—

KM# 208.2 THALER

Silver **Rev:** Date divided at top, arms dividing H-B **Note:** Dav. #6584.

Date	Mintage	VG	F	VF	XF	Unc
1679 HB Rare	—	—	—	—	—	—

KM# 229 THALER

Silver **Note:** Dav. #6575.

Date	Mintage	VG	F	VF	XF	Unc
1679 RB	—	400	650	1,100	1,700	—

KM# 230 THALER

Silver **Note:** Dav. #6576.

Date	Mintage	VG	F	VF	XF	Unc
1679 RB	—	400	650	1,100	1,700	—

KM# 231 THALER

Silver **Rev:** Sea and ships added **Note:** Dav. #6577.

Date	Mintage	VG	F	VF	XF	Unc
1679 RB Rare	—	—	—	—	—	—

KM# 234 THALER

Silver **Subject:** Death of Joahnn Friedrich **Note:** Dav. #6589.

Date	Mintage	VG	F	VF	XF	Unc
1679	—	350	600	1,000	1,600	—

KM# 235 THALER

Silver **Note:** Dav. #6590.

Date	Mintage	VG	F	VF	XF	Unc
1679 HB	—	300	550	900	1,400	—

KM# 227.1 THALER

Silver **Rev:** Date in Roman numerals **Note:** Dav. #6562.

Date	Mintage	VG	F	VF	XF	Unc
1679 HB	—	500	900	1,400	2,200	—

KM# 227.2 THALER

Silver **Obv. Legend:** IOANNES. FRIDER-ICVS... **Note:** Dav. #6564.

Date	Mintage	VG	F	VF	XF	Unc
1679 Rare	—	—	—	—	—	—

KM# 227.3 THALER

Silver **Obv:** Helmeted arms divide HB **Obv. Legend:** IOAN. FRIDER-D. G. **Note:** Dav. #6565.

Date	Mintage	VG	F	VF	XF	Unc
1679 HB Rare	—	—	—	—	—	—

KM# 228 THALER

Silver **Obv:** Date in top legend **Note:** Dav. #6563.

Date	Mintage	VG	F	VF	XF	Unc
1679 HB Rare	—	—	—	—	—	—

KM# 265.1 THALER

Silver **Obv:** Titles of Ernst August **Note:** Dav. #6591.

Date	Mintage	VG	F	VF	XF	Unc
1680 RB	—	100	200	350	550	—
1681 RB	—	100	200	350	550	—
1683 RB	—	100	200	350	550	—
1686 RB	—	100	200	350	550	—
1687 RB	—	100	200	350	550	—

KM# 265.2 THALER

Silver **Obv. Legend:** ERNEST: AVG: D: G. EPISC OSN: DVX BR: +LU **Note:** Dav. #6594.

Date	Mintage	VG	F	VF	XF	Unc
1689 RB	—	100	200	350	550	—
1692 RB	—	100	200	350	550	—

KM# 265.3 THALER

Silver **Obv. Legend:** ...AUG:...DUX BR: +LUN: **Note:** Dav. #6595.

Date	Mintage	VG	F	VF	XF	Unc
1691 RB	—	100	200	350	550	—

KM# 266 THALER

Silver **Rev:** Horse leaping left in circle, date in legend **Note:** Dav. #6602.

Date	Mintage	VG	F	VF	XF	Unc
1680 HB	—	200	400	700	1,050	—

KM# 267.1 THALER

Silver **Obv. Legend:** ERNEST: AUG: D. G. -EP: OSN: DUX+.L. **Note:** Dav. #6603.

Date	Mintage	VG	F	VF	XF	Unc
MDCLXXX (1680) HB	—	200	400	700	1,050	—

KM# 267.2 THALER

Silver **Obv. Legend:** ...D: G: EPISC. -OSN: DUX BR: ET LUN: **Note:** Dav. #6604.

Date	Mintage	VG	F	VF	XF	Unc
1680 HB	—	200	400	700	1,050	—
1681 HB	—	200	400	700	1,050	—

KM# 267.3 THALER

Silver **Obv. Legend:** ERN: AUG: D. G. EP: O. D. B. +L. **Note:** Dav. #6605.

Date	Mintage	VG	F	VF	XF	Unc
1682 HB Rare	—	—	—	—	—	—

KM# 267.4 THALER

Silver **Obv. Legend:** ...E. O. D. BR. +LUN: **Note:** Dav. #6606.

Date	Mintage	VG	F	VF	XF	Unc
1683 HB Rare	—	—	—	—	—	—

KM# 267.5 THALER

Silver **Obv:** Legend on band **Obv. Legend:** ERNEST: AUG: D. G. EP. EP. OSN. D. B. ++L **Note:** Dav. #6607.

Date	Mintage	VG	F	VF	XF	Unc
1684 HB Rare	—	—	—	—	—	—

KM# 279 THALER

Silver **Note:** Dav. #6592.

Date	Mintage	VG	F	VF	XF	Unc
1681 RB	—	100	200	350	575	—
1686 RB	—	100	200	350	575	—
1687 RB	—	100	200	350	575	—

KM# 280 THALER

Silver **Note:** Similar to KM#293 but arms divide date. Dav. #6629.

Date	Mintage	VG	F	VF	XF	Unc
1681 HB	—	400	700	1,200	1,900	—
1682 HB	—	400	700	1,200	1,900	—

KM# 293 THALER

Silver **Note:** Dav. #6630.

Date	Mintage	VG	F	VF	XF	Unc
1682 RB	—	400	700	1,200	1,900	—
1685 RB	—	400	700	1,200	1,900	—
1687 RB	—	400	700	1,200	1,900	—

KM# 294 THALER

Silver **Ruler:** Ernst August **Obv:** Bust of Ernst facing 3/4 right **Note:** Dav. #6631.

Date	Mintage	VG	F	VF	XF	Unc
1682 HB	—	500	900	1,400	2,300	—

KM# A294 THALER

Silver **Note:** Dav. #A6631.

Date	Mintage	VG	F	VF	XF	Unc
1682 HB	—	500	900	1,400	2,300	—

KM# 295 THALER

Silver **Obv:** Bust right within full circle continuous legend **Rev:** Helmeted arms divide date near bottom **Note:** Dav. #A6632.

Date	Mintage	VG	F	VF	XF	Unc
1682 HB	—	500	900	1,400	2,300	—

KM# 306 THALER

Silver **Note:** Dav. #6612.

Date	Mintage	VG	F	VF	XF	Unc
1683 HB	—	350	600	1,000	1,600	—
1685 HB	—	350	600	1,000	1,600	—
1686 HB	—	350	600	1,000	1,600	—
1687 HB	—	350	600	1,000	1,600	—

KM# 316 THALER

Silver **Note:** Dav. #6593.

Date	Mintage	VG	F	VF	XF	Unc
1684 RB	—	100	180	350	550	—
1685 RB	—	100	180	350	550	—

KM# 318 THALER

Silver **Obv:** Bust right splits circle at top and bottom **Rev:** Helmeted arms divide date near top **Note:** Dav. #6632.

Date	Mintage	VG	F	VF	XF	Unc
1684 HB	—	450	800	1,300	2,000	—

KM# 319 THALER

Silver **Obv:** Bust right **Rev:** Horse leaping left **Note:** Dav. #6634.

Date	Mintage	VG	F	VF	XF	Unc
MDCLXXXIV (1684)	—	450	800	1,300	2,000	—

KM# 320.1 THALER

Silver **Rev:** Arabic date **Note:** Dav. #6633.

Date	Mintage	VG	F	VF	XF	Unc
1684 HB	—	450	800	1,300	2,000	—

KM# 320.2 THALER

Silver **Obv:** Without inner circle **Rev:** Inner circle at top **Note:** Dav. #6640.

Date	Mintage	VG	F	VF	XF	Unc
1687 HB	—	450	800	1,300	2,000	—
1688 HB	—	350	600	1,000	1,600	—
1689 HB	—	350	600	1,000	1,600	—

KM# 320.3 THALER

Silver **Rev:** Large legends, small date **Note:** Dav. #6642.

Date	Mintage	VG	F	VF	XF	Unc
1690 HB	—	350	600	1,000	1,600	—

KM# 320.4 THALER

Silver **Note:** Dav. #6645.

Date	Mintage	VG	F	VF	XF	Unc
1691 HB	—	350	600	1,000	1,600	—

KM# 317.1 THALER

Silver **Rev:** Horse leaping left in laurel wreath **Note:** Dav. #6608.

Date	Mintage	VG	F	VF	XF	Unc
1684 HB Rare	—	—	—	—	—	—

KM# 317.2 THALER

Silver **Obv. Legend:** ERNESTUS. AUGUSTUS.-...+LUNB. **Note:** Dav. #6610.

Date	Mintage	VG	F	VF	XF	Unc
1685 HB	—	550	950	1,500	2,500	—
1686 HB	—	550	950	1,500	2,500	—

KM# 317.3 THALER

Silver **Obv. Legend:** Ends:...ET. L. **Note:** Dav. #6611.

Date	Mintage	VG	F	VF	XF	Unc
1686 HB	—	550	950	1,500	2,500	—

KM# 323 THALER
Silver **Obv:** Bust left **Rev:** Helmeted arms, date in legend **Note:** Dav. #6635.

Date	Mintage	VG	F	VF	XF	Unc
1685 RB Rare	—	—	—	—	—	—

KM# 324 THALER
Silver **Note:** Similar to KM#320 but date divided above. Dav. #6636.

Date	Mintage	VG	F	VF	XF	Unc
1685 HB	—	450	800	1,300	2,000	—

KM# 322 THALER
Silver **Obv:** Helmeted 12-fold arms **Rev:** Horse leaping left in laurel wreath, edge inscription **Note:** Mining Thaler. Dav. #6609.

Date	Mintage	VG	F	VF	XF	Unc
1685 HB	—	550	950	1,500	2,500	—
1686 HB Rare	—	—	—	—	—	—

KM# 325.1 THALER
Silver **Note:** Similar to KM#320 but Roman numeral in legend. Dav. #6637.

Date	Mintage	VG	F	VF	XF	Unc
MDCLXXXV (1685) HB	—	350	600	1,000	1,600	—
MDCLXXXVI (1686) HB	—	350	600	1,000	1,600	—

KM# 325.2 THALER
Silver **Obv. Legend:** ERN. AUG. D. G.-EP. OSN. D. BR. ET LUN. **Rev. Legend:** ...HO-NESTA. ANNO... **Note:** Dav. #6638.

Date	Mintage	VG	F	VF	XF	Unc
1687 HB	—	350	600	1,000	1,600	—

KM# 325.3 THALER
Silver **Obv. Legend:** ERNST: AUG:-D. G. EP. O. D. B. ET L. **Note:** Dav. #6641.

Date	Mintage	VG	F	VF	XF	Unc
1690 HB	—	350	600	1,000	1,600	—

KM# 325.4 THALER
Silver **Obv. Legend:** ERNST: AUGUST:-D. G. EP. OSN: D. BR: +LU: **Note:** Dav. #6643.

Date	Mintage	VG	F	VF	XF	Unc
1690 HB	—	350	600	1,000	1,600	—

KM# 325.5 THALER
Silver **Obv. Legend:** ERN: AUG: D. G.-EP: O. D. B. ET LU: **Note:** Dav. #6644.

Date	Mintage	VG	F	VF	XF	Unc
1691 HB	—	350	600	1,000	1,600	—

KM# 325.6 THALER
Silver **Obv. Legend:** ERN: AUG:-D. G... **Note:** Dav. #6646.

Date	Mintage	VG	F	VF	XF	Unc
1692 HB	—	350	600	1,000	1,600	—

KM# 325.7 THALER
Silver **Obv. Legend:** ERNEST: AUG:... **Note:** Dav. #6647.

Date	Mintage	F	VF	XF	Unc	BU
1692 HB	—	350	600	1,000	1,600	—

KM# 335.1 THALER
Silver **Obv:** Helmeted arms **Rev:** St. Andrew with cross **Note:** Dav. #6621.

Date	Mintage	VG	F	VF	XF	Unc
MDCLXXXVIII (1688) HB	—	200	400	700	1,100	—

KM# 335.2 THALER
Silver **Obv:** Without inner circle **Note:** Dav. #6623.

Date	Mintage	VG	F	VF	XF	Unc
MDCLXXXVIII (1688) HB	—	200	400	700	1,100	—

KM# 351.1 THALER
Silver **Obv:** Helmeted plain shield **Note:** Dav. #6624.

Date	Mintage	VG	F	VF	XF	Unc
1690 HB	—	180	350	600	1,000	—

KM# 349 THALER
Silver **Obv:** Helmeted 12-fold arms divide date **Rev:** Horse leaping left in open field **Note:** Dav. #6613.

Date	Mintage	VG	F	VF	XF	Unc
1690 HB	—	350	600	1,000	1,600	—

KM# 350 THALER
Silver **Note:** With edge inscription. Mining Thaler. Dav. #6615.

Date	Mintage	VG	F	VF	XF	Unc
1690 HB	—	350	600	1,000	1,600	—
1692 HB	—	350	600	1,000	1,600	—

KM# 359 THALER
Silver **Note:** Similar to KM#351 but date in legend. Dav. #6625.

Date	Mintage	VG	F	VF	XF	Unc
1691 HB	—	180	350	600	1,000	—

KM# 360 THALER
Silver **Obv:** Bust right **Rev:** Roman arms and trophies **Rev. Legend:** EN. LABOR... **Note:** Dav. #6650.

Date	Mintage	VG	F	VF	XF	Unc
ND(1691-92)	—	700	1,200	2,000	3,200	—

KM# 358 THALER
Silver **Obv:** Helmeted 12-fold arms, date in legend **Rev:** Horse leaping left in open field **Note:** Dav. #6614.

Date	Mintage	VG	F	VF	XF	Unc
1691 HB	—	350	600	1,000	1,600	—

KM# 351.2 THALER
Silver **Obv:** Helmeted curved shield **Note:** Dav. #6626.

Date	Mintage	VG	F	VF	XF	Unc
1692 HB	—	180	350	600	1,000	—

KM# 370 THALER
Silver **Note:** Similar to KM#320, but date is on edge. Dav. #6648.

Date	Mintage	VG	F	VF	XF	Unc
1692 HB Rare	—	—	—	—	—	—

KM# 369 THALER
Silver **Note:** Similar to KM#265, but arms divide date on obverse. Dav. #6596.

Date	Mintage	VG	F	VF	XF	Unc
1692 RB	—	120	220	400	700	—
1693 RB	—	—	—	—	—	—

KM# 385 THALER
Silver **Obv:** KM#384 reverse **Rev:** KM#383 **Note:** Mule.

Date	Mintage	VG	F	VF	XF	Unc
1693 HB-H Rare	—	—	—	—	—	—

KM# 384 THALER
Silver **Note:** Varieties exist. Dav. #6649.

Date	Mintage	VG	F	VF	XF	Unc
1693 HB	—	260	450	800	1,200	—
1694 HB	—	260	450	800	1,200	—
1695 HB	—	260	450	800	1,200	—
1696 HB	—	260	450	800	1,200	—
1697 HB	—	260	450	800	1,200	—

KM# 383 THALER
Silver **Obv:** Crowned 15-fold arms **Rev:** Horse leaping left above Roman numeral date **Note:** Dav. #6616.

Date	Mintage	VG	F	VF	XF	Unc
1693 HB	—	450	800	1,300	2,000	—

KM# 382.1 THALER
Silver **Note:** Similar to KM#382.2, but different scrollwork below wildman. Dav. #6597.

Date	Mintage	VG	F	VF	XF	Unc
1693 RB	—	120	220	400	700	—

KM# 382.2 THALER
Silver **Note:** Dav. #6598.

Date	Mintage	VG	F	VF	XF	Unc
1694 RB	—	120	220	400	700	—
1695 RB	—	120	220	400	700	—
1696 RB	—	120	220	400	700	—

KM# 382.3 THALER

Silver **Rev:** Without scrollwork below wildman, R. B at right **Note:** Dav. #6599.

Date	Mintage	VG	F	VF	XF	Unc
1696 RB	—	120	220	400	700	—

KM# 382.4 THALER

Silver **Obv:** Very small date **Note:** Dav. #6600.

Date	Mintage	VG	F	VF	XF	Unc
1696 RB	—	120	220	400	700	—

KM# 382.5 THALER

Silver **Obv:** Smaller letters, different cartouche **Note:** Dav. #6601.

Date	Mintage	VG	F	VF	XF	Unc
1697 RB	—	120	220	400	700	—
1698 RB	—	120	220	400	700	—

KM# 394.1 THALER

Silver **Note:** Dav. #6627.

Date	Mintage	VG	F	VF	XF	Unc
1695 HB	—	130	250	450	700	—
1697 HB	—	130	250	450	700	—

KM# 394.2 THALER

Silver **Obv:** Crowned arms rounded at top **Note:** Dav. #6628.

Date	Mintage	VG	F	VF	XF	Unc
1697	—	180	350	600	1,000	—

KM# 405.1 THALER

Silver **Obv:** Crowned 15-fold arms **Obv. Legend:** ...EL: EP: O: **Rev:** Horse leaping left above Arabic date **Note:** Dav. #6617.

Date	Mintage	VG	F	VF	XF	Unc
1696 HB	—	450	800	1,300	2,000	—
1697 HB	—	450	800	1,300	2,000	—

KM# 405.2 THALER

Silver **Obv. Legend:** ...ELECT: EP: OSN: **Note:** Dav. #6618.

Date	Mintage	VG	F	VF	XF	Unc
1696 HB	—	450	800	1,300	2,000	—

KM# 406 THALER

Silver **Obv:** Arms divide date **Note:** Dav. #6620.

Date	Mintage	VG	F	VF	XF	Unc
1697 HB	—	450	800	1,300	2,000	—

KM# 411 THALER

Silver **Subject:** Death of Earnest August **Obv:** Bust right **Rev:** 12-line inscription with Roman numeral date **Note:** Dav. #6651.

Date	Mintage	VG	F	VF	XF	Unc
1698	—	300	550	900	1,400	—

KM# 75 1-1/4 THALER

35.8000 g., Silver **Rev:** Without value stamped in **Note:** Dav. #6531B.

Date	Mintage	VG	F	VF	XF	Unc
1661 HS	—	375	675	1,300	2,400	—

KM# 74.1 1-1/4 THALER

35.8000 g., Silver **Rev:** Stamped with value 1-1/4 **Note:** Dav. #6531. Illustration reduced.

Date	Mintage	VG	F	VF	XF	Unc
1661 HS	—	325	600	1,150	2,250	—
1662 HS	—	325	600	1,150	2,250	—

KM# 74.2 1-1/4 THALER

35.8000 g., Silver **Rev:** Stamped with value 5/4 **Note:** Dav. #6531A.

Date	Mintage	VG	F	VF	XF	Unc
1661 HS	—	375	675	1,300	2,400	—
1662 HS	—	375	675	1,300	2,400	—

KM# 83 1-1/4 THALER

35.8000 g., Silver **Note:** Dav. #6534.

Date	Mintage	VG	F	VF	XF	Unc
1664 HS	—	350	600	1,150	2,100	—

KM# 117 1-1/4 THALER

35.8000 g., Silver **Note:** Similar to 1 Thaler, KM#102, but 1-1/4 stamped in. Dav. #6568.

Date	Mintage	VG	F	VF	XF	Unc
1667	—	325	600	1,150	2,100	—
1668	—	325	600	1,150	2,100	—
1669	—	325	600	1,150	2,100	—
1671	—	325	600	1,150	2,100	—

KM# 175 1-1/4 THALER

35.8000 g., Silver **Note:** Similar to 1 Thaler, KM#149. Dav. #6572.

Date	Mintage	VG	F	VF	XF	Unc
1675	—	325	600	1,150	2,100	—

KM# 236 1-1/4 THALER

35.8000 g., Silver **Note:** Similar to 1 Thaler, KM#229. Dav. #6574.

Date	Mintage	VG	F	VF	XF	Unc
1679 RB	—	325	600	1,150	2,100	—

KM# 268 1-1/4 THALER

36.1000 g., Silver **Obv:** Helmeted arms **Rev:** Wildman, tree in right hand, date in legend, value in oval at bottom in die **Note:** Dav. #LS235.

Date	Mintage	VG	F	VF	XF	Unc
1680	—	1,300	2,250	4,150	7,300	—

KM# 11 1-1/2 THALER

Silver **Obv:** Half-length figure right, date **Rev:** Female figure of Concord between figures of four dukes **Note:** Dav. #LS137.

Date	Mintage	VG	F	VF	XF	Unc
1634 HS	—	2,650	4,500	7,100	—	—

KM# 84 1-1/2 THALER

Silver **Note:** Similar to 1-1/4 Thaler, KM#83, but 1-1/2 stamped in. Dav. #6533.

Date	Mintage	VG	F	VF	XF	Unc
1664 HS	—	325	600	1,150	2,100	—

KM# 131.1 1-1/2 THALER

42.0000 g., Silver **Obv:** Crowned script JF monogram surrounded by 14 small shields, date in legend, 1-1/2 stamped in **Rev:** Horse leaping left above mining scene **Note:** Dav. #LS202.

Date	Mintage	VG	F	VF	XF	Unc
1670 LW	—	525	900	1,500	2,350	—

KM# 131.2 1-1/2 THALER

42.0000 g., Silver **Note:** Dav. #LS204.

Date	Mintage	VG	F	VF	XF	Unc
1671 LW	—	525	900	1,500	2,350	—

KM# 131.3 1-1/2 THALER

42.0000 g., Silver **Note:** Dav. #LS206.

Date	Mintage	VG	F	VF	XF	Unc
1672 LW	—	525	900	1,500	2,350	—

KM# 131.4 1-1/2 THALER

42.0000 g., Silver **Note:** Dav. #LS208. Illustration reduced.

Date	Mintage	VG	F	VF	XF	Unc
1672 RB	—	525	900	1,500	2,350	—

KM# 176 1-1/2 THALER

Silver **Note:** Varieties exist. Similar to 1 Thaler, KM#227, but 1-1/2 stamped in. Dav. #6559.

Date	Mintage	VG	F	VF	XF	Unc
1675 HB	—	525	975	1,800	3,000	—

KM# 190 1-1/2 THALER

Silver **Subject:** 100th Anniversary - University of Helmstedt **Obv:** 16-line inscription **Rev:** Fountain between two palm trees **Note:** Dav. #6587.

Date	Mintage	VG	F	VF	XF	Unc
1676 Rare	—	—	—	—	—	—

KM# 237 1-1/2 THALER

42.8000 g., Silver, 64 mm. **Subject:** Death of Johann Friedrich **Note:** Dav. #LS223. Illustration reduced.

Date	Mintage	VG	F	VF	XF	Unc
1679 RB	—	525	1,050	1,950	3,400	—

KM# 281.1 1-1/2 THALER

42.0000 g., Silver, 63 mm. **Note:** Illustration reduced. Dav. #LS240.

Date	Mintage	VG	F	VF	XF	Unc
1681 RB	—	650	1,300	2,350	3,900	—

KM# 281.2 1-1/2 THALER

43.4000 g., Silver **Note:** Dav. #LS245. Illustration reduced.

Date	Mintage	VG	F	VF	XF	Unc
1688 RB	—	500	975	1,800	3,000	—

KM# 196 1-3/4 THALER

50.0000 g., Silver **Obv:** Crowned script JF monogram surrounded by 14 small shields, date in legend **Rev:** Horse leaping left above mining scene

Date	Mintage	VG	F	VF	XF	Unc
1677 HB	—	—	—	—	—	—

KM# 407 1-3/4 THALER

52.0000 g., Silver **Obv:** Bust right **Rev:** Crowned oval 15-fold arms, without value stated

Date	Mintage	VG	F	VF	XF	Unc
1697 HB	—	—	—	—	—	—

KM# 12 2 THALER

Silver **Obv:** Half-lentgh figure right, date **Rev:** Female figure of Concord between figures of four ducks **Note:** Dav. #LS136.

Date	Mintage	VG	F	VF	XF	Unc
1634 HS	—	4,550	6,500	9,100	—	—

KM# 42 2 THALER

Silver **Subject:** Death of Georg **Obv:** Half-length figure left **Rev:** 10-line inscription **Note:** Dav. #6509.

Date	Mintage	VG	F	VF	XF	Unc
MDCXLI (1641) HS Rare	—	—	—	—	—	—

KM# 76 2 THALER

Silver **Obv:** Bust right in circle of 14 small shields, date divided below **Rev:** Figures of Piety and Justice below tree, arm from heaven with wreath, 2 punched in **Note:** Dav. #6530.

Date	Mintage	VG	F	VF	XF	Unc
1661 HS	—	650	1,250	2,300	3,600	—

KM# 118 2 THALER

Silver **Note:** Similar to 1 Thaler, KM#102. Dav. #6567.

Date	Mintage	VG	F	VF	XF	Unc
1667	—	525	975	1,750	2,950	—
1669	—	525	975	1,750	2,950	—
1670	—	525	975	1,750	2,950	—

KM# 132.1 2 THALER
57.3000 g., Silver, 66 mm. **Note:** Illustration reduced. Dav. #LS201.

Date	Mintage	VG	F	VF	XF	Unc
1670 LW	—	575	1,100	1,950	3,250	—

KM# 132.2 2 THALER
57.3000 g., Silver **Note:** Dav. #LS203. Illustration reduced.

Date	Mintage	VG	F	VF	XF	Unc
1671 LW	—	575	1,100	1,950	3,250	—

KM# 132.3 2 THALER
57.3000 g., Silver **Note:** Dav. #LS205.

Date	Mintage	VG	F	VF	XF	Unc
1672 LW	—	575	1,100	1,950	3,250	—

KM# 132.4 2 THALER
57.3000 g., Silver **Note:** Dav. #LS207.

Date	Mintage	VG	F	VF	XF	Unc
1672 RB	—	575	1,100	1,950	3,250	—

KM# 132.5 2 THALER
57.3000 g., Silver **Note:** Dav. #LS213.

Date	Mintage	VG	F	VF	XF	Unc
1677 RB	—	575	1,100	1,950	3,250	—
1677 HB	—	575	1,100	1,950	3,250	—

KM# 192 2 THALER
Silver **Subject:** 100th Anniversary of the University of Helmstedt **Obv:** 16-line inscription **Rev:** Fountain between two palm trees **Note:** Dav. #6586.

Date	Mintage	VG	F	VF	XF	Unc
1676 Rare	—	—	—	—	—	—

KM# 191 2 THALER
Silver **Note:** Similar to 1 Thaler, KM#149. Dav. #6571.

Date	Mintage	VG	F	VF	XF	Unc
1676	—	525	975	1,750	2,950	—

KM# 209 2 THALER
Silver **Obv:** Bust right in circle **Rev:** Mining scene, Roman numeral date in legend **Note:** Mining Thaler. Dav. #6585.

Date	Mintage	VG	F	VF	XF	Unc
1678 HIF	—	850	1,650	2,950	4,900	—

KM# 239 2 THALER
50.6000 g., Silver, 64 mm. **Obv:** Crowned script JF monogram in wreath, 2 punched in at bottom **Rev:** 20-line inscription **Note:** Illustration reduced. Dav.#LS226.

Date	Mintage	VG	F	VF	XF	Unc
1679	—	5,200	8,500	11,500	—	—

KM# 238 2 THALER
56.6000 g., Silver, 64 mm. **Subject:** Death of Friedrich **Note:** Dav. #LS222. Illustration reduced.

Date	Mintage	VG	F	VF	XF	Unc
1679	—	650	1,300	2,450	4,350	—

KM# A269 2 THALER
52.3000 g., Silver, 65 mm. **Note:** Illustration reduced. Dav. #LS233.

Date	Mintage	VG	F	VF	XF	Unc
1680 RB	—	—	775	1,300	—	—

KM# 282.1 2 THALER
57.0000 g., Silver **Note:** Similar to 1-1/2 thalers, KM#281. Dav. #LS239.

Date	Mintage	VG	F	VF	XF	Unc
1681 RB	—	975	1,950	3,600	5,900	—

KM# 282.2 2 THALER
59.3000 g., Silver **Note:** Dav. #LS244. Illustration reduced.

Date	Mintage	VG	F	VF	XF	Unc
1688 RB	—	725	1,450	2,600	4,250	—

KM# 326 2 THALER
59.3000 g., Silver **Obv:** Helmeted arms, date at bottom, value punched in at left **Rev:** Lute player standing on snail, panoramic view of countryside behind **Note:** Dav.#LS243.

Date	Mintage	VG	F	VF	XF	Unc
1685 RB	—	1,300	2,300	3,600	5,200	—

KM# 197 2-1/4 THALER
67.5000 g., Silver **Obv:** Crowned script JF monogram surrounded by 14 small shields, date in legend **Rev:** Horse leaping left above mining scene **Note:** Dav. #LS210A.

Date	Mintage	VG	F	VF	XF	Unc
1677 HB	—	—	—	—	—	—

KM# 283 2-1/2 THALER
Silver **Obv:** Intertwined crowned script EA monogram in wreath surrounded by 15 small crowned arms, date at lower right in legend, 2-1/2 punched in at bottom **Rev:** Horse leaping left above mining scene **Note:** Dav. #LS239.

Date	Mintage	VG	F	VF	XF	Unc
1681 RB	—	—	—	—	—	—

KM# 119 3 THALER
Silver **Note:** Similar to 1 Thaler, KM#102. Dav. #6566.

Date	Mintage	VG	F	VF	XF	Unc
1667 Rare	—	—	—	—	—	—

KM# 133.1 3 THALER
86.2000 g., Silver, 73 mm. **Obv:** Crowned script JF monogram surrounded by 14 small shields, date in legend, 3 punched in **Note:** Illustration reduced. Dav. #LS200.

Date	Mintage	VG	F	VF	XF	Unc
1670 LW	—	775	1,450	2,600	4,550	—

KM# 133.2 3 THALER
86.2000 g., Silver **Note:** Dav. #LS212.

Date	Mintage	VG	F	VF	XF	Unc
1677 RB	—	775	1,450	2,600	4,550	—

KM# 240 3 THALER
83.7000 g., Silver, 78 mm. **Subject:** Death of Johann Friedrich **Obv:** 3 punched in **Rev:** 21-line inscription **Note:** Dav. #LS221. Illustration reduced.

Date	Mintage	VG	F	VF	XF	Unc
1679	—	1,300	2,600	4,900	8,500	—

KM# 270 3 THALER

Silver **Obv:** Bust right in circle **Rev:** Arms of Osnabruck in lower foreground, palm tree at left, sailing ship in background, rock at right, sun above, date below **Note:** Dav. #LS232. Illustration reduced.

Date	Mintage	VG	F	VF	XF	Unc
1680 RB Rare	—	—	—	—	—	—

KM# 271 3 THALER

86.6000 g., Silver **Obv:** Helmeted arms **Rev:** Wildman, tree in right hand, date in legend, 3 punched in over die-struck 1-1/4 **Note:** Dav. #LS234.

Date	Mintage	VG	F	VF	XF	Unc
1680	—	2,600	4,550	7,800	—	—

KM# 284 3 THALER

86.6000 g., Silver **Obv:** Intertwined crowned script EA monogram in wreath surrounded by 15 small crowned arms, date at lower right in legend, 3 punched in at bottom **Rev:** Horse leaping left above mining scene **Note:** Dav. #LS238. Illustration reduced.

Date	Mintage	VG	F	VF	XF	Unc
1681 RB	—	650	1,300	2,450	4,350	—

KM# 327 3 THALER

77.7000 g., Silver, 75 mm. **Obv:** Hlemeted arms, date divided at bottom, 3 punched in at left **Rev:** Lute player standing on snail, panoramic view of countryside behind **Note:** Illustration reduced. Dav. #LS242.

Date	Mintage	VG	F	VF	XF	Unc
1685 RB	—	1,750	2,950	4,550	6,500	—

KM# 328 3-1/2 THALER

103.5000 g., Silver, 72 mm. **Obv:** Helmeted arms, date divided at bottom **Rev:** Lute player standing on snail, panoramic view of countryside behing **Note:** Dav. #LS241A.

Date	Mintage	VG	F	VF	XF	Unc
1685 RB Rare	—	—	—	—	—	—

KM# 25 4 THALER

Silver **Obv:** Duke on horse left **Rev:** Helmeted 12-fold arms, supported by two wildmen, date in Roman numerals **Note:** Varieties exist. Dav. #LS242.

Date	Mintage	VG	F	VF	XF	Unc
1638 HS-IH Rare	—	—	—	—	—	—

KM# 70 4 THALER

Silver, 87 mm. **Note:** Illustration reduced. Dav. #LS195.

Date	Mintage	VG	F	VF	XF	Unc
1660 HS	—	900	1,750	3,250	5,200	—

KM# 77 4 THALER

Silver **Note:** Similar to KM#70, but bust right and 4 punched in. Dav. #LS196.

Date	Mintage	VG	F	VF	XF	Unc
1661 HS	—	—	—	—	—	—

KM# 134 4 THALER

115.2000 g., Silver **Obv:** Crowned script JF monogram surrounded by 14 small shields, date in legend, 4 punched in **Rev:** Horse leaping left above mining scene **Note:** Dav. #LS199. Illustration reduced.

Date	Mintage	VG	F	VF	XF	Unc
1670 LW	—	1,550	2,600	4,550	7,800	—

KM# 198 4 THALER

Silver **Obv:** 4 punched in or omitted **Note:** Dav. #LS211

Date	Mintage	VG	F	VF	XF	Unc
1677 RB	—	1,950	3,250	5,200	8,500	—

KM# 242 4 THALER

Silver **Obv:** Crowned script JF monogram in laurel wreath, 4 punched in **Rev:** Death cutting numbered branches off palm tree, four-line inscription **Note:** Dav. #LS218.

Date	Mintage	VG	F	VF	XF	Unc
1679	—	1,950	3,250	5,200	8,500	—

KM# 241 4 THALER

Silver **Subject:** Death of Johann Friedrich **Note:** Similar to 1 Thaler, KM#235, but 4 punched in. Dav. #LS220

Date	Mintage	VG	F	VF	XF	Unc
1679	—	900	1,750	3,250	5,200	—

KM# 272 4 THALER

Silver **Obv:** Bust right in circle, 4 punched in below bust **Rev:** Arms of Osnabruck in lower foreground, palm tree at left, sailing ship in background, rock at right, sun above, date below **Note:** Dav. #LS231.

Date	Mintage	VG	F	VF	XF	Unc
1680 RB	—	1,950	3,250	5,200	8,500	—

KM# 285 4 THALER

Silver **Obv:** Intertwined crowned script EA monogram in wreath, surrounded by 15 small crowned arms, date at lower right in legend, 4 punched at bottom **Rev:** Horse leaping left above mining scene **Note:** Dav. #LS237. Illustration reduced.

Date	Mintage	VG	F	VF	XF	Unc
1681 RB	—	1,950	3,250	5,200	8,500	—

KM# 329 4 THALER

101.6000 g., Silver, 75 mm. **Obv:** Helmeted arms, date divided at bottom, 4 punched in at left **Rev:** Lute player, standing on snail, panoramic view of countryside behind **Note:** Illustration reduced. Dav. #LS241.

Date	Mintage	VG	F	VF	XF	Unc
1685 RB	—	2,350	3,900	5,900	8,500	—

KM# 26 5 THALER

Silver, 87 mm. **Obv:** Duke on horse left **Rev:** Helmeted 12-fold arms, supported by two wildmen, date in Roman numerals **Note:** Varieties exist. Dav. #LS141.

Date	Mintage	VG	F	VF	XF	Unc
1638 HS-IH Rare	—	—	—	—	—	—

Note: Spink Taisei Zurich Milas sale 4-92 XF realized $15,075

KM# 71 5 THALER

143.5000 g., Silver, 82 mm. **Ruler:** Georg II Wilhelm **Note:** Sumilar to 4 Thalers, KM#70, but 5 punched in. Dav. #LS194.

Date	Mintage	VG	F	VF	XF	Unc
1660 HS Rare	—	—	—	—	—	—

Note: Spink Taisei Zurich Milas sale 4-92 XF realized $12,060

KM# 78 5 THALER

Silver **Note:** Sumilar to KM#71, but bust right. Dav. #LS196.

Date	Mintage	VG	F	VF	XF	Unc
1661 HS Rare	—	—	—	—	—	—

KM# 135 5 THALER

Silver **Obv:** Crowned script JF monogram surrounded by 14 small shields, date in margin, 5 punched in **Rev:** Horse leaping left above mining scene **Note:** Dav. #LS198.

Date	Mintage	VG	F	VF	XF	Unc
1670 LW Rare	—	—	—	—	—	—

KM# 199.1 5 THALER

Silver **Obv:** Without value shown **Note:** Dav. #LS209.

Date	Mintage	VG	F	VF	XF	Unc
1677 RB Rare	—	—	—	—	—	—

KM# 199.2 5 THALER

Silver **Note:** Dav. #LS210.

Date	Mintage	VG	F	VF	XF	Unc
1677 HB Rare	—	—	—	—	—	—

KM# 243 5 THALER

Silver **Subject:** Death of Johann Friedrich **Note:** Similar to 1 Thaler, KM#235, but 5 punched in. Dav. #LS219.

Date	Mintage	VG	F	VF	XF	Unc
1679 Rare	—	—	—	—	—	—

KM# 286 5 THALER

Silver **Obv:** Intertwined crowned script EA monogram in wreath, surrounded by 15 small crowned arms, date at lower right in legend, 5 punched in at bottom **Rev:** Horse leaping left above mining scene **Note:** Dav. #LS236.

Date	Mintage	VG	F	VF	XF	Unc
1681 RB Rare	—	—	—	—	—	—

KM# 27 6 THALER

Silver **Obv:** Duke on horse left **Rev:** Helmeted 12-fold arms, supported by two wildmen, date in Roman numerals **Note:** Dav. #LS140.

Date	Mintage	VG	F	VF	XF	Unc
1638 HS-IH Rare	—	—	—	—	—	—

KM# 72 6 THALER

172.5000 g., Silver, 85 mm. **Obv:** Bust 3/4 left in circle of 14 small shields, date divided below, 6 punched in **Rev:** Figures of Piety and Justice below tree, arm from heaven with wreath **Note:** Illustration reduced. Dav. #LS193.

Date	Mintage	VG	F	VF	XF	Unc
1660 HS Rare	—	—	—	—	—	—

Note: Spink Taisei Zurich Milas sale 4-92 VF-XF realized $12,060

KM# 200 6 THALER

Silver **Obv:** Crowned script JF monogram surrounded by 14 small shields, date in legend, 6 punched in **Rev:** Horse leaping left above mining scene **Note:** Dav. #LS210B.

Date	Mintage	VG	F	VF	XF	Unc
1677 RB Rare	—	—	—	—	—	—

KM# 246 6 THALER

Silver **Rev:** Dates in Arabic numerals

Date	Mintage	VG	F	VF	XF	Unc
1679 Rare	—	—	—	—	—	—

KM# 244 6 THALER

Silver **Subject:** Death of Johann Friedrich **Obv:** Crowned script JF monogram in laurel wreath, 6 punched in **Rev:** Death, cutting numbered branches off palm tree, four-line inscription **Note:** Dav. #LS217.

Date	Mintage	VG	F	VF	XF	Unc
1679 Rare	—	—	—	—	—	—

KM# 245 6 THALER

Silver **Rev:** 18-line inscription with Roman numeral dates **Note:** Dav. #LS225.

Date	Mintage	VG	F	VF	XF	Unc
1679 Rare	—	—	—	—	—	—

KM# 28 8 THALER

Silver, 91 mm. **Note:** Illustration reduced. Dav. #LS139.

Date	Mintage	VG	F	VF	XF	Unc
1638 HS-IH Rare	—	—	—	—	—	—

KM# 248 8 THALER

Silver **Rev:** 18-line inscription

Date	Mintage	VG	F	VF	XF	Unc
MDCXXIX (1679) Rare	—	—	—	—	—	—

KM# 247 8 THALER

Silver **Subject:** Death of Johann Friedrich **Obv:** Crowned script JF monogram in laurel wreath, 8 punched in **Rev:** Death cutting numbered branches off palm tree, four-line inscription **Note:** Dav. #LS216.

Date	Mintage	VG	F	VF	XF	Unc
1679 Rare	—	—	—	—	—	—

KM# 29 10 THALER

Silver **Obv:** Duke on horse left **Rev:** Helmeted 12-fold arms supported by two wildmen **Note:** Dav. #LS138.

Date	Mintage	VG	F	VF	XF	Unc
MDCXXXVIII (1638) HS-IH Rare	—	—	—	—	—	—

KM# 249 10 THALER

Silver **Subject:** Death of Johann Friedrich **Obv:** Crowned script JF monogram in laurel wreath, 10 punched in **Rev:** Death cutting numbered branches off palm tree, four-line inscription **Note:** Dav. #LS215.

Date	Mintage	VG	F	VF	XF	Unc
1679 Rare	—	—	—	—	—	—

KM# 250 10 THALER

Silver **Rev:** 18-line inscription with Roman numeral dates **Note:** Dav. #LS224.

Date	Mintage	VG	F	VF	XF	Unc
1679 Rare	—	—	—	—	—	—

KM# 251 12 THALER
Silver **Obv:** Crowned script JF monogram in laurel wreath, 12 punched in **Rev:** Death cutting numbered branches off palm tree, four-line inscription **Note:** Dav. #LS214. Illustration reduced.

Date	Mintage	VG	F	VF	XF	Unc
1679 Rare	—	—	—	—	—	—

TRADE COINAGE

KM# 15 GOLDGULDEN
3.5000 g., 0.9860 Gold 0.1109 oz. AGW **Obv:** Crowned arms in inner circle **Rev:** Orb in inner circle

Date	Mintage	VG	F	VF	XF	Unc
1635	—	800	1,800	3,500	5,500	—

KM# 395 1/4 DUCAT
0.8750 g., 0.9860 Gold 0.0277 oz. AGW **Obv:** Bust right, value 1/4 below **Rev:** Horse leaping left

Date	Mintage	VG	F	VF	XF	Unc
1695	—	125	190	500	1,000	—

KM# 396 1/4 DUCAT
0.8750 g., 0.9860 Gold 0.0277 oz. AGW **Obv:** Ernst August

Date	Mintage	VG	F	VF	XF	Unc
1695	—	—	—	—	—	—

KM# 397 1/2 DUCAT
1.7500 g., 0.9860 Gold 0.0555 oz. AGW **Obv:** Bust right, value 1/2 below **Rev:** Horse leaping left

Date	Mintage	VG	F	VF	XF	Unc
1695	—	150	300	650	1,300	—

KM# 398 1/2 DUCAT
1.7500 g., 0.9860 Gold 0.0555 oz. AGW **Obv:** Bust of Ernst August right

Date	Mintage	VG	F	VF	XF	Unc
1695	—	—	—	—	—	—

KM# 16 DUCAT
3.5000 g., 0.9860 Gold 0.1109 oz. AGW **Obv:** Armored bust of Georg left holding scepter in inner circle **Rev:** Crowned arms in inner circle

Date	Mintage	VG	F	VF	XF	Unc
1635 HS	—	450	1,050	1,900	3,250	—
1636 HS	—	450	1,050	1,900	3,250	—
1637 HS	—	450	1,050	1,900	3,250	—
1638 HS	—	450	1,050	1,900	3,250	—
ND HS	—	450	1,050	1,900	3,250	—

KM# 49 DUCAT
3.5000 g., 0.9860 Gold 0.1109 oz. AGW **Obv:** Bust of Christian Ludwig right in inner circle

Date	Mintage	VG	F	VF	XF	Unc
1646 HS	—	600	1,350	2,650	4,150	—

KM# 85 DUCAT
3.5000 g., 0.9860 Gold 0.1109 oz. AGW **Obv:** Bust right **Rev:** Crowned 12-fold arms, date in legend

Date	Mintage	VG	F	VF	XF	Unc
1664 HS	—	525	1,200	2,100	3,550	—

KM# 125 DUCAT
3.5000 g., 0.9860 Gold 0.1109 oz. AGW **Rev:** Palm on rock in sea

Date	Mintage	VG	F	VF	XF	Unc
1668	—	425	950	1,700	2,800	—

KM# 126 DUCAT
3.5000 g., 0.9860 Gold 0.1109 oz. AGW **Obv:** Bust left **Rev:** Crowned 12-fold arms

Date	Mintage	VG	F	VF	XF	Unc
1669 HB	—	425	950	1,700	2,800	—
ND LW	—	425	950	1,700	2,800	—

KM# 151 DUCAT
3.5000 g., 0.9860 Gold 0.1109 oz. AGW **Rev:** Palm tree on rockyisland, ships at sides in inner circle, Roman numeral date

Date	Mintage	VG	F	VF	XF	Unc
1673	—	350	850	1,500	2,600	—
1679 HB	—	350	850	1,500	2,600	—

KM# 177 DUCAT
3.5000 g., 0.9860 Gold 0.1109 oz. AGW **Obv:** Bust of Johann Friedrich right

Date	Mintage	VG	F	VF	XF	Unc
1675	—	350	850	1,500	2,600	—

KM# 287 DUCAT
3.5000 g., 0.9860 Gold 0.1109 oz. AGW **Obv:** Bust of Ernst August right **Rev:** Crowned arms divide date

Date	Mintage	VG	F	VF	XF	Unc
1681 RB	—	600	1,200	2,650	3,850	—
1685	—	600	1,200	2,650	3,850	—
1694 HB	—	600	1,200	2,650	3,850	—
1698 HB	—	600	1,200	2,650	3,850	—

KM# 389 DUCAT
3.5000 g., 0.9860 Gold 0.1109 oz. AGW **Obv:** Capped arms divides date

Date	Mintage	VG	F	VF	XF	Unc
1694	—	375	825	1,500	3,000	—
1698	—	375	825	1,500	3,000	—

KM# 399 DUCAT
3.5000 g., 0.9860 Gold 0.1109 oz. AGW **Obv:** Bust right **Rev:** Horse leaping left

Date	Mintage	VG	F	VF	XF	Unc
1695	—	700	1,350	2,750	5,000	—

KM# 400 DUCAT
3.5000 g., 0.9860 Gold 0.1109 oz. AGW **Rev:** Rearing horse, date in exergue

Date	Mintage	VG	F	VF	XF	Unc
1695	—	500	1,100	2,000	4,000	—
1698	—	500	1,100	2,000	4,000	—

KM# 412 DUCAT
3.5000 g., 0.9860 Gold 0.1109 oz. AGW **Subject:** Death of the Duke

Date	Mintage	VG	F	VF	XF	Unc
1698	—	350	850	1,700	2,800	—

KM# 152 2 DUCAT
7.0000 g., 0.9860 Gold 0.2219 oz. AGW **Obv:** Johann Friedrich

Date	Mintage	VG	F	VF	XF	Unc
1673	—	2,000	4,000	7,000	13,000	—

KM# 390 2 DUCAT
7.0000 g., 0.9860 Gold 0.2219 oz. AGW **Obv:** Bust right **Rev:** Crowned 15-fold arms, date below

Date	Mintage	VG	F	VF	XF	Unc
1694 HB	—	1,300	2,900	5,500	9,000	—

KM# 391 2 DUCAT
7.0000 g., 0.9860 Gold 0.2219 oz. AGW **Obv:** Bust of Ernst August right **Rev:** Capped arms divides date

Date	Mintage	VG	F	VF	XF	Unc
1694	—	1,300	2,900	5,500	9,000	—
1695	—	1,300	2,900	5,500	9,000	—

KM# 401 2 DUCAT
7.0000 g., 0.9860 Gold 0.2219 oz. AGW **Rev:** Horse leaping left

Date	Mintage	VG	F	VF	XF	Unc
1695	—	1,000	2,200	5,000	8,500	—

KM# 402 2 DUCAT
7.0000 g., 0.9860 Gold 0.2219 oz. AGW **Rev:** Rearing horse, date in exergue

Date	Mintage	VG	F	VF	XF	Unc
1695	—	1,300	2,400	5,500	9,000	—

KM# 153 4 DUCAT
14.0000 g., 0.9860 Gold 0.4438 oz. AGW **Obv:** Bust of Johann Friedrich right **Rev:** Palm tree on rocky island, ships at sides in inner circle

Date	Mintage	VG	F	VF	XF	Unc
1673 Rare	—	—	—	—	—	—

KM# 90 10 DUCAT (Portugalöser)
35.0000 g., 0.9860 Gold 1.1095 oz. AGW **Obv:** Bust left **Rev:** Helmeted 12-fold arms, date in legend **Note:** Struck with 1 Thaler dies, KM#88.

Date	Mintage	VG	F	VF	XF	Unc
1665 Rare	—	—	—	—	—	—

KM# 129 10 DUCAT (Portugalöser)
33.6900 g., 0.9860 Gold 1.0679 oz. AGW

Date	Mintage	VG	F	VF	XF	Unc
1670 Unique	—	—	—	—	—	—

Note: Bowers and Merena Guia sale 3-88, XF realized $16,500

KM# 288 10 DUCAT (Portugalöser)
35.0000 g., 0.9860 Gold 1.1095 oz. AGW **Obv:** Bust right in circle **Rev:** Crowned arms divide date **Note:** Similar to 1 thaler, KM#293 but arms divide date.

Date	Mintage	VG	F	VF	XF	Unc
1681 HB Rare	—	—	—	—	—	—

KM# A333 10 DUCAT (Portugalöser)
35.0000 g., 0.9860 Gold 1.1095 oz. AGW **Obv:** Bust of Ernst August **Rev:** Arms

Date	Mintage	VG	F	VF	XF	Unc
1685 Rare	—	—	—	—	—	—

KM# 403 10 DUCAT (Portugalöser)
35.0000 g., 0.9860 Gold 1.1095 oz. AGW **Note:** Similar to 1 Thaler, KM#394.

Date	Mintage	VG	F	VF	XF	Unc
1695 HB Rare	—	—	—	—	—	—

KM# 273 20 DUCAT (Doppelportugalöser)
70.0000 g., 0.9860 Gold 2.2190 oz. AGW **Obv:** Bust right **Rev:** Arms of Osnabruck (wheel) in front of seascape

Date	Mintage	VG	F	VF	XF	Unc
1680 RB Rare	—	—	—	—	—	—

BRUNSWICK-LUNEBURG-CALENBERG-HANNOVER

Located in north-central Germany. The first duke began his rule in 1235. The first coinage appeared c. 1175. There was considerable shuffling of territory until 1692 when Ernst August became the elector of Hannover. George Ludwig became George I of England in 1714. There was separate coinage for Luneburg until during the reign of George III. The name was changed to Hannover in 1814.

RULERS
Georg Ludwig (George I of England), 1698-1727

BRUNSWICK MINTS AND MINT OFFICIALS' INITIALS

Celle Mint

Initial	Date	Name
III	1687-1705	Jobst Jakob Janisch

Clausthal Mint

Initial	Date	Name
HB	1675-1711	Heinrich Bonhorst

Zellerfeld Mint

Initial	Date	Name
RB	1676-1711	Rudolf Bornemann
***	1698-1715	Used instead of initials during this period

ELECTORATE

REGULAR COINAGE

KM# 5 PFENNING
Silver **Ruler:** George Ludwig **Obv:** Horse leaping left, date below **Note:** Uniface. Hohlpfennig type.

Date	Mintage	VG	F	VF	XF	Unc
1698	—	5.00	8.00	14.00	25.00	—
1700	—	5.00	8.00	14.00	25.00	—

KM# 24 PFENNING

Copper **Ruler:** George Ludwig **Obv:** Crowned GLC monogram **Rev:** Value, date

Date	Mintage	VG	F	VF	XF	Unc
1699	—	10.00	16.00	30.00	55.00	—

KM# 30 PFENNING

Silver **Ruler:** George Ludwig **Obv:** Crowned monogram, date **Note:** Uniface. Hohlpfennig type.

Date	Mintage	VG	F	VF	XF	Unc
1700 RB	—	5.00	10.00	20.00	40.00	—

KM# 25 4 PFENNING

Billon **Ruler:** George Ludwig **Obv:** Horse leaping left **Rev:** Value, date **Note:** Varieties exist.

Date	Mintage	VG	F	VF	XF	Unc
1699	—	10.00	20.00	33.00	55.00	—
1700 HB	—	10.00	20.00	33.00	55.00	—

KM# 26 MARIENGROSCHEN

Silver **Ruler:** George Ludwig **Obv:** Value, date in 4 lines **Rev:** Madonna and child

Date	Mintage	VG	F	VF	XF	Unc
1699 HB	—	7.00	13.00	20.00	40.00	—
1700 HB	—	7.00	13.00	20.00	40.00	—

KM# 6 2 MARIENGROSCHEN

Silver **Ruler:** George Ludwig **Obv:** Value in 3 lines, date in legend **Rev:** Wildman, tree in right hand

Date	Mintage	VG	F	VF	XF	Unc
1698 ***	—	7.00	13.00	22.00	45.00	—
1700 ***	—	7.00	13.00	22.00	45.00	—

KM# 7 2 MARIENGROSCHEN

Silver **Ruler:** George Ludwig **Obv:** Wildman, tree in right hand **Rev:** Value, date

Date	Mintage	VG	F	VF	XF	Unc
1698 ***	—	8.00	16.00	27.00	55.00	—
1699 ***	—	8.00	16.00	27.00	55.00	—

KM# 31 2 MARIENGROSCHEN

Silver **Ruler:** George Ludwig **Obv:** Value and date within inner circle **Rev:** Horse leaping left within inner circle

Date	Mintage	VG	F	VF	XF	Unc
1700	—	7.00	12.00	25.00	45.00	—

KM# 8 4 MARIENGROSCHEN

Silver **Obv:** Crowned GLC monogram **Rev:** Value, date

Date	Mintage	VG	F	VF	XF	Unc
1698 HB	—	10.00	20.00	40.00	80.00	—

KM# 9 4 MARIENGROSCHEN

Silver **Obv:** Wildman, tree in right hand **Rev:** Value, date

Date	Mintage	VG	F	VF	XF	Unc
1698 ***	—	13.00	27.00	45.00	85.00	—

KM# 33 4 MARIENGROSCHEN

2.0600 g., Silver Clausthal Mint - 1705, Zellerfeld Mint 1712-14., 21.17 mm. **Ruler:** George Ludwig **Obv:** Value in 4 lines **Obv. Legend:** GEORG: LVD: D•G•D•B•&•L•S•R•I•A•T•&•E* **Rev:** Horse leaping left, date below **Rev. Legend:** IN RECTO DECUS **Edge:** Plain **Note:** Varieties exist.

Date	Mintage	VG	F	VF	XF	Unc
1700	—	6.00	12.00	25.00	45.00	—

KM# 32 4 MARIENGROSCHEN

Silver **Ruler:** George Ludwig **Obv:** Value in 3 lines, date in legend **Rev:** Wildman, tree in right hand

Date	Mintage	VG	F	VF	XF	Unc
1700 ***	—	8.00	16.00	33.00	60.00	—

KM# 10 6 MARIENGROSCHEN

Silver **Obv:** Wildman, tree in right hand **Rev:** Value, date

Date	Mintage	VG	F	VF	XF	Unc
1698 ***	—	13.00	27.00	45.00	85.00	—
1699 ***	—	13.00	27.00	45.00	85.00	—

KM# 11 6 MARIENGROSCHEN

Silver **Ruler:** George Ludwig **Obv:** Value, date **Rev:** Wildman, tree in right hand

Date	Mintage	VG	F	VF	XF	Unc
1699 ***	—	13.00	27.00	45.00	85.00	—
1700 ***	—	13.00	27.00	45.00	85.00	—

KM# 12 6 MARIENGROSCHEN (1/6 Thaler)

Silver **Ruler:** George Ludwig **Obv:** Value VI..., date in circle **Rev:** Horse leaping left, value Y6 below in circle

Date	Mintage	VG	F	VF	XF	Unc
1698 HB	—	13.00	30.00	55.00	90.00	—
1700 HB	—	13.00	30.00	55.00	90.00	—

KM# 13 12 MARIENGROSCHEN

Silver **Obv:** Similar to 24 Mariengroschen, KM#14 but 12 to right **Rev:** XII... in three lines, date in legend

Date	Mintage	VG	F	VF	XF	Unc
1698 ***	—	20.00	45.00	85.00	150	—

KM# 34 12 MARIENGROSCHEN

Silver **Ruler:** George Ludwig **Obv:** Value XII... in 3 lines, date in legend **Obv. Legend:** * GEORG: LUD: D: G: D: BR: & L: S: R: I: EL: **Rev:** Wildman, tree in right hand, 12 to right **Rev. Legend:** IN RECTO DECUS.

Date	Mintage	VG	F	VF	XF	Unc
1700 ***	—	16.00	33.00	60.00	120	—

KM# 15 24 MARIENGROSCHEN (Gulden)

Silver **Ruler:** George Ludwig **Obv:** Value, date in legend **Obv. Legend:** GEORG: LUD: D: G: D: BR: & L: S: R: I: ELECT: **Rev:** Wildman with tree in right hand, 24 at right **Rev. Legend:** IN RECTO DECUS

Date	Mintage	VG	F	VF	XF	Unc
1698 ***	—	33.00	55.00	85.00	250	—
1699 ***	—	33.00	55.00	85.00	250	—
1700 ***	—	33.00	55.00	85.00	250	—

KM# 14 24 MARIENGROSCHEN (Gulden)

Silver

Date	Mintage	VG	F	VF	XF	Unc
1698 ***	—	33.00	65.00	100	175	—
1699 ***	—	33.00	65.00	100	175	—

KM# 27 1/3 THALER

Silver

Date	Mintage	VG	F	VF	XF	Unc
1699 HB	—	45.00	100	150	250	—
1700 HB	—	45.00	100	150	250	—

KM# A17 2/3 THALER (Gulden)

Silver **Ruler:** Ernst August **Obv:** Bust right **Rev:** Leaping horse left, value divides date below **Note:** Prev. Bruns.-Lune-Calenberg 2/3 Thaler, KM#381.

Date	Mintage	VG	F	VF	XF	Unc
1693	—	40.00	80.00	165	300	—
1693 HB	—	40.00	80.00	165	300	—
1694 HB	—	40.00	80.00	165	300	—
1695 HB	—	40.00	80.00	165	300	—
1696 HB	—	40.00	80.00	165	300	—
1697 HB	—	40.00	80.00	165	300	—

KM# 17 2/3 THALER (Gulden)

Silver **Ruler:** George Ludwig **Obv:** Crowned complex arms divide date **Rev:** Horse leaping left, value below

Date	Mintage	VG	F	VF	XF	Unc
1698 HB	—	33.00	80.00	125	175	—
1699 HB	—	33.00	80.00	125	175	—
1700 HB	—	33.00	80.00	125	175	—

KM# 16 2/3 THALER (Gulden)

Silver **Obv:** Crowned arms divide date **Rev:** Column, 2/3 on base, IN RECTO DECUS on band behind

Date	Mintage	VG	F	VF	XF	Unc
1698 HB	—	70.00	160	275	500	—

KM# 18 THALER

Silver **Obv:** Crowned arms divide date to lower left and right **Rev:** Wildman, tree in right hand **Note:** Dav. #6652.

Date	Mintage	F	VF	XF	Unc	BU
1698 RB	—	150	265	425	—	—
1699 RB	—	150	265	425	—	—

KM# 19 THALER

Silver **Ruler:** George Ludwig **Note:** Dav. #6654 and #2057.

Date	Mintage	F	VF	XF	Unc	BU
1698 HB	—	125	225	350	750	—
1699 HB	—	125	225	350	750	—
1700 HB	—	125	225	350	750	—

KM# 20 THALER

Silver **Ruler:** George Ludwig **Note:** Dav. #6655 and #2061.

Date	Mintage	F	VF	XF	Unc	BU
1698 HB	—	125	225	375	800	—
1699 HB	—	125	225	375	800	—
1700 HB	—	125	225	375	800	—

KM# 35 THALER

Silver **Ruler:** George Ludwig **Obv:** Crowned complex arms within ornate frame **Obv. Legend:** GEORG: LUD: D: G: D: BR: & L: S: R: I: EL **Rev:** Wildman with tree in right hand, RB at right **Rev. Legend:** IN RECTO DECUS **Note:** Dav. #6653 and #2065.

Date	Mintage	F	VF	XF	Unc	BU
1700 RB	—	80.00	150	275	675	—

TRADE COINAGE

KM# 21 DUCAT

3.5000 g., 0.9860 Gold 0.1109 oz. AGW **Ruler:** George Ludwig **Obv:** Crowned arms **Rev:** Horse leaping left

Date	Mintage	VG	F	VF	XF	Unc
1698	—	600	1,050	2,000	3,500	—
1700	—	600	1,050	2,000	3,500	—

KM# 22 2 DUCAT

7.0000 g., 0.9860 Gold 0.2219 oz. AGW **Obv:** Laureate bust of George I left **Rev:** Capped arms, date in legend

Date	Mintage	VG	F	VF	XF	Unc
1698 HB	—	1,000	2,500	5,600	8,800	—

BRUNSWICK-LUNEBURG-CELLE

When Heinrich (VII) der Mittlere abdicated in 1520, his three sons soon divided the duchy, establishing the lines of Brunswick-Lüneburg-Celle, Brunswick-Gifhorn and Brunswick-Harburg. Celle was further divided in 1559 into Brunswick-Lüneburg-Celle and Brunswick-Dannenberg, but had been effectively ruled as two separate territories from 1546. The seat of the duchy was the town of Celle (Zelle), located about 20 miles (33 kilometers) northeast of Hannover. When the line fell extinct in 1705, Celle passed to Brunswick-Lüneburg-Calenberg-Hannover.

RULERS

Ernst V, 1592-1611
Christian, 1611-1633
August I the Elder, 1633-1636
Friedrich V, 1636-1648
Christian Ludwig, 1648-1665
Georg II Wilhelm, 1665-1705

MINT MARKS

N - Nienburg Mint
- Zellerfeld Mint, 1698-1715

MINT OFFICIALS' INITIALS

Initial	Date	Name
CD	1622	Cord Delbruge die-cutter in Celle
GM/HGM	1619-21	Hans Georg Meinhard
(h)	1622	Henning Hans in Winsen
HB	1675-1711	Heinrich Bonhorst in Clausthal
HHO	1625	Henning Oppermann in Catlenburg
HL	1617	Heinrich Leohr in Clausthal and Hitzacker
HL	1622-25	Henning Loehr in Goslar, Osterode and Zellerfeld
HP	1623-29	Heinrich Pechstein in andreasberg
HR	Ca.1647	Unknown die-cutter
HS (usually w/ingot hook)	1622-40	Henning Schreiber in Clausthal
	1621-24	In Lauterberg
	1619-21	In Osterode
HS(w/ or w/o crossed keys)	1626-72	Henning Schluter in Goslar and Zellerfeld
HVE	1619	Hans von Ecke in Andreasberg
	1621-23	In Catlenburg
	1622-25	In Osterode
Iii/III/JJJ	1687-1705	Jobst Jakob Janisch in Celle
IR	-	Unknown
(k) or variant	1617-21	Georg Krukenberg in Clausthal
LW	1640-75	Lippold Weber (Wefer) in Clausthal
+M+	Ca.1635	Unknown
NZ	Ca.1635	Unknown
RD	1673-86	Rudolf Dornstrauch in Celle
VF	1623-24	Urban Feigenhauer in Catlenburg
(w)	1622	Hans Heine in Winsen

DUCHY

REGULAR COINAGE

KM# 20 PFENNIG

Copper **Obv:** Lion rampant left **Rev:** Value, date in 4 lines

Date	Mintage	VG	F	VF	XF	Unc
1620	—	20.00	33.00	60.00	130	—

KM# 22 PFENNIG

Copper **Rev:** Value in 2 lines

Date	Mintage	VG	F	VF	XF	Unc
ND(1620/1)	—	27.00	55.00	100	175	—

KM# 21 PFENNIG

Copper **Rev:** GUTER added to value **Note:** Guter PFennig.

Date	Mintage	VG	F	VF	XF	Unc
1620	—	20.00	33.00	60.00	130	—
1621	—	20.00	33.00	60.00	130	—

KM# 59 PFENNIG

Silver **Note:** Hohlpfennig type. Crowned initials C, date.

Date	Mintage	VG	F	VF	XF	Unc
1623 VF	—	33.00	55.00	80.00	150	—
1624 VF	—	33.00	55.00	80.00	150	—
1624 HS	—	33.00	55.00	80.00	150	—
1625 VF	—	33.00	55.00	80.00	150	—
1633 HSA	—	33.00	55.00	80.00	150	—

KM# 58 PFENNIG

Silver **Note:** Uniface. St. Andrew with cross, date.

Date	Mintage	VG	F	VF	XF	Unc
1623 HP	—	—	—	—	—	—

KM# 148 PFENNIG

Silver **Note:** Hohlpfennig type. Crowned F monogram, date.

Date	Mintage	VG	F	VF	XF	Unc
1638 HS	—	33.00	55.00	80.00	150	—
1642 LW	—	33.00	55.00	80.00	150	—
1647 LW	—	33.00	55.00	80.00	150	—
1648 LW	—	33.00	55.00	80.00	150	—

KM# 214 PFENNIG

Silver **Obv:** Crowned CL monogram, date **Note:** Uniface. Hohlpfennig type.

Date	Mintage	VG	F	VF	XF	Unc
1650 LW	—	27.00	45.00	80.00	135	—
1651 LW	—	27.00	45.00	80.00	135	—
1655 LW	—	27.00	45.00	80.00	135	—
1656 LW	—	27.00	45.00	80.00	135	—
1657 LW	—	27.00	45.00	80.00	135	—
1657 SW Error	—	27.00	45.00	80.00	135	—
1659 LW	—	27.00	45.00	80.00	135	—
1660 LW	—	27.00	45.00	80.00	135	—
1663 HST	—	27.00	45.00	80.00	135	—
1663 LW	—	27.00	45.00	80.00	135	—
1664 LW	—	27.00	45.00	80.00	135	—
1665 LW	—	27.00	45.00	80.00	135	—
1665 HS	—	27.00	45.00	80.00	135	—

KM# 318 PFENNIG

Copper

Date	Mintage	VG	F	VF	XF	Unc
1686	—	7.00	13.00	30.00	60.00	—
1687/6	—	9.00	18.00	40.00	80.00	—
1687	—	8.00	16.00	35.00	75.00	—

KM# 320 PFENNIG

Copper

Date	Mintage	VG	F	VF	XF	Unc
1687	—	3.00	8.00	25.00	50.00	—
1688	—	3.00	8.00	25.00	50.00	—
1689	—	3.00	8.00	25.00	50.00	—

KM# 319 PFENNIG

Copper **Note:** Similar to 1-1/2 Pfennig, KM#321.

Date	Mintage	VG	F	VF	XF	Unc
1687	—	3.00	8.00	25.00	50.00	—

KM# 336 PFENNIG

Copper

Date	Mintage	VG	F	VF	XF	Unc
1691 GW	—	3.00	6.00	20.00	45.00	—
1694	—	3.00	6.00	20.00	45.00	—
1695	—	3.00	6.00	20.00	45.00	—
1696	—	3.00	6.00	20.00	45.00	—
1697	—	3.00	6.00	20.00	45.00	—
1698	—	3.00	6.00	20.00	45.00	—
1699	—	3.00	6.00	20.00	45.00	—

KM# 351 PFENNIG

Silver **Note:** Uniface. Horse leaping left, date below.

Date	Mintage	VG	F	VF	XF	Unc
1694	—	—	—	—	—	—

KM# 353 PFENNIG

Copper **Note:** Similar to 1-1/2 Pfennig, KM#354.

Date	Mintage	VG	F	VF	XF	Unc
1698	—	3.00	6.00	20.00	45.00	—

KM# 321 1-1/2 PFENNIG

Copper **Obv:** Horse leaping left, monogram above, date below **Rev:** Value

Date	Mintage	VG	F	VF	XF	Unc
1687	—	5.00	13.00	25.00	50.00	—
1688	—	5.00	13.00	25.00	50.00	—
1689	—	5.00	13.00	25.00	50.00	—

KM# 337 1-1/2 PFENNIG

Copper

Date	Mintage	VG	F	VF	XF	Unc
1691	—	4.00	10.00	20.00	45.00	—
1699	—	4.00	10.00	20.00	45.00	—
ND	—	4.00	10.00	20.00	45.00	—

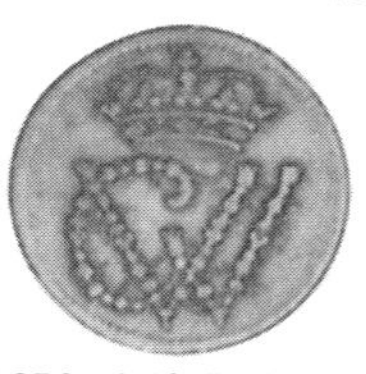

KM# 354 1-1/2 PFENNIG

Copper

Date	Mintage	VG	F	VF	XF	Unc
1698	—	4.00	10.00	20.00	45.00	—
1699	—	4.00	10.00	20.00	45.00	—
ND	—	4.00	10.00	20.00	45.00	—

KM# 23 2 GUTE PFENNIG

Copper **Obv:** Lion rampant left **Rev:** Value with GUTE and date in 2 or 3 lines

Date	Mintage	VG	F	VF	XF	Unc
1620	—	13.00	27.00	55.00	110	—
1620 GM	—	13.00	27.00	55.00	110	—
1621 GM	—	13.00	27.00	55.00	110	—
ND CD	—	13.00	27.00	55.00	110	—

KM# 186 2 GUTE PFENNIG

Silver **Obv:** Crowned F monogram **Rev:** Value, date in 3 lines

Date	Mintage	VG	F	VF	XF	Unc
1648 LW	—	—	—	—	—	—

KM# 215 2 GUTE PFENNIG

Silver **Obv:** Crowned CL monogram **Rev:** Value in 3 lines

Date	Mintage	VG	F	VF	XF	Unc
1650 LW	—	—	—	—	—	—
1653 LW	—	—	—	—	—	—
1654 LW	—	—	—	—	—	—

KM# 25.1 3 PFENNIG

Copper **Obv:** Lion rampant left **Rev:** Value GUTER III **Note:** Gute 3 Pfennig.

Date	Mintage	VG	F	VF	XF	Unc
1620 GM	—	16.00	33.00	60.00	120	—
1621 GM	—	16.00	33.00	60.00	120	—
1622 (h)	—	16.00	33.00	60.00	120	—
1622 GM	—	—	—	—	—	—

KM# 25.2 3 PFENNIG

Copper **Rev:** Value III GP

Date	Mintage	VG	F	VF	XF	Unc
ND CD	—	13.00	33.00	60.00	110	—

KM# 30 3 PFENNIG

Copper **Rev:** Without GUTER **Note:** Varieties exist.

Date	Mintage	VG	F	VF	XF	Unc
1621	—	10.00	27.00	55.00	90.00	—

KM# 31 3 PFENNIG

Copper **Obv:** Lion rampant left **Rev:** Imperial orb with 3

Date	Mintage	VG	F	VF	XF	Unc
1621	—	16.00	33.00	60.00	110	—
1622	—	16.00	33.00	60.00	110	—

KM# 51 3 PFENNIG

Copper **Obv:** Titles in 4 lines, crown above **Rev:** Imperial orb with 3

Date	Mintage	VG	F	VF	XF	Unc
1622	—	16.00	33.00	60.00	110	—

KM# 52 3 PFENNIG

Copper **Rev:** Orb in rhombus

Date	Mintage	VG	F	VF	XF	Unc
1622	—	16.00	33.00	60.00	110	—

KM# 53 3 PFENNIG

Copper **Obv:** Lion rampant left in shield **Rev:** Value with GUTE in 2 lines

Date	Mintage	VG	F	VF	XF	Unc
1622	—	16.00	33.00	60.00	110	—

KM# 60 3 PFENNIG

Silver **Obv:** St. Andrew with cross **Rev:** Imperial orb with 3 **Note:** Dreier 3 Pfennig.

Date	Mintage	VG	F	VF	XF	Unc
1623 HP	—	—	—	—	—	—

KM# 96 3 PFENNIG

Silver **Obv:** Lion rampant left **Rev:** Value with GUTE in 3 lines, date in legend **Note:** Gute 3 Pfennig.

Date	Mintage	VG	F	VF	XF	Unc
1630 HS	—	16.00	33.00	60.00	110	—

KM# 140 3 PFENNIG

Silver **Rev:** Imperial orb with 3

Date	Mintage	VG	F	VF	XF	Unc
1637 HS	—	16.00	33.00	60.00	110	—
1638 HS	—	16.00	33.00	60.00	110	—
1639 HS	—	16.00	33.00	60.00	110	—
1642 LW	—	16.00	33.00	60.00	110	—
1643 LW	—	16.00	33.00	60.00	110	—
1644 LW	—	16.00	33.00	60.00	110	—
1645 LW	—	16.00	33.00	60.00	110	—
1646 LW	—	16.00	33.00	60.00	110	—
1647 LW	—	16.00	33.00	60.00	110	—
1648 LW	—	16.00	33.00	60.00	110	—

KM# 201 3 PFENNIG

Silver **Obv:** Crowned CL monogram

Date	Mintage	VG	F	VF	XF	Unc
1649 HS	—	—	—	—	—	—
1650 HS	—	—	—	—	—	—

KM# 216 3 PFENNIG

Silver **Obv:** Crowned CL monogram

Date	Mintage	VG	F	VF	XF	Unc
1650 LW	—	16.00	33.00	60.00	110	—
1653 LW	—	16.00	33.00	60.00	110	—
1656 LW	—	16.00	33.00	60.00	110	—

KM# 239 3 PFENNIG

Silver **Rev. Legend:** H.Z. - M.B

Date	Mintage	VG	F	VF	XF	Unc
1656	—	16.00	33.00	60.00	110	—

KM# 275 3 PFENNIG

Silver **Obv:** Crowned GW monogram, date in legend **Rev:** Imperial orb with 3

Date	Mintage	VG	F	VF	XF	Unc
1673 RD	—	13.00	27.00	55.00	100	—
1674 RD	—	13.00	27.00	55.00	100	—
1675 RD	—	13.00	27.00	55.00	100	—
1677 RD	—	13.00	27.00	55.00	100	—

KM# 276 3 PFENNIG

Silver **Obv:** Crowned GW monogram **Rev:** Value in 3 lines, date in legend

Date	Mintage	VG	F	VF	XF	Unc
1673 RD	—	13.00	27.00	55.00	100	—

KM# 307 3 PFENNIG

Silver **Obv:** Crowned GW monogram **Rev:** Imperial orb with 3, date

Date	Mintage	VG	F	VF	XF	Unc
1683 III	—	13.00	27.00	55.00	110	—
1696 iii	—	13.00	27.00	55.00	110	—

KM# 329 3 PFENNIG

Silver **Ruler:** Georg II Wilhelm **Obv:** Crowned GW monogram divides date **Rev:** Imperial orb with 3

Date	Mintage	VG	F	VF	XF	Unc
1690 iii	—	10.00	20.00	40.00	75.00	—

KM# 26 WITTEN (4 Pfennig)

Copper **Obv:** Lion rampant left **Rev:** Value in 3 lines

Date	Mintage	VG	F	VF	XF	Unc
1620 GM	—	—	—	—	—	—
1621 GM	—	—	—	—	—	—

KM# 187 4 GUTE PFENNIG

Silver **Obv:** Crowned F monogram **Rev:** Value in 3 lines

Date	Mintage	VG	F	VF	XF	Unc
1648 LW	—	33.00	60.00	110	170	—

KM# 217 4 GUTE PFENNIG

Silver **Obv:** Crowned CL monogram

Date	Mintage	VG	F	VF	XF	Unc
1650 LW	—	33.00	60.00	110	170	—
1653 LW	—	33.00	60.00	110	170	—
1656 LW	—	33.00	60.00	110	170	—

KM# 277 4 GUTE PFENNIG

Silver **Obv:** Crowned GW monogram, date in legend **Rev:** Value in 4 lines

Date	Mintage	VG	F	VF	XF	Unc
1673 RD	—	27.00	55.00	90.00	170	—
1677 RD	—	27.00	55.00	90.00	170	—

KM# 171 6 PFENNIG

Silver **Obv:** Lion rampant left in circle of hearts **Rev:** Imperial orb with 6

Date	Mintage	VG	F	VF	XF	Unc
1645 LW	—	—	—	—	—	—
1647 LW	—	—	—	—	—	—

KM# 218 6 PFENNIG

Silver **Obv:** Lion rampant left in circle **Rev:** Imperial orb with 6 divides date

Date	Mintage	VG	F	VF	XF	Unc
1650 LW	—	—	—	—	—	—
1653 LW	—	—	—	—	—	—
1655 LW	—	—	—	—	—	—

KM# 308 6 PFENNIG

Silver **Obv:** Crowned GW monogram **Rev:** Imperial orb with 6

Date	Mintage	VG	F	VF	XF	Unc
1684	—	—	—	—	—	—
1685	—	—	—	—	—	—

KM# 27 SESLING (6 Pfennig)

Copper **Obv:** Lion rampant left **Rev:** Value in 4 lines

Date	Mintage	VG	F	VF	XF	Unc
(1)620 GM	—	—	—	—	—	—

KM# 32 1/2 SILBERGROSCHEN

Silver **Obv:** 4-fold arms with central shield of Minden arms (crossed keys) **Rev:** Value in 4 lines, small imperial orb below with value 48

Date	Mintage	VG	F	VF	XF	Unc
1621	—	—	—	—	—	—

KM# 33 SILBERGROSCHEN

Silver **Obv:** Lion rampant right in circle of hearts **Rev:** Value in 4 lines

Date	Mintage	VG	F	VF	XF	Unc
1621	—	—	—	—	—	—

KM# 34 SILBERGROSCHEN

Silver **Obv:** 4-fold arms **Rev:** Value in 4 lines

Date	Mintage	VG	F	VF	XF	Unc
1621	—	—	—	—	—	—

KM# 35 SILBERGROSCHEN

Silver **Rev:** Small imperial orb with 24 at bottom

Date	Mintage	VG	F	VF	XF	Unc
1621	—	—	—	—	—	—

KM# 36 SILBERGROSCHEN

Silver **Rev:** Arms in circle and 32 in orb

Date	Mintage	VG	F	VF	XF	Unc
1621	—	—	—	—	—	—

KM# 120 MARIENGROSCHEN

Silver **Obv:** Brunswick helmet with horse **Rev:** Value, date in 4 lines

Date	Mintage	VG	F	VF	XF	Unc
ND(1636-40) HS	—	—	—	—	—	—

KM# 188 MARIENGROSCHEN

Silver **Note:** Similar to 2 Mariengroschen, KM#202.

Date	Mintage	VG	F	VF	XF	Unc
1648	—	9.00	18.00	40.00	80.00	—
1653	—	9.00	18.00	40.00	80.00	—
1662	—	9.00	18.00	40.00	80.00	—

KM# 278 MARIENGROSCHEN

Silver **Obv:** Crowned GW monogram, date in legend **Rev:** Value in 4 lines **Rev. Legend:** VON REICHSTAL.SILB

Date	Mintage	VG	F	VF	XF	Unc
1673 RB	—	—	—	—	—	—

KM# 279 MARIENGROSCHEN

Silver **Rev. Legend:** N.REICHS.SCHROUT U.KORN

Date	Mintage	VG	F	VF	XF	Unc
1673 RD	—	—	—	—	—	—

KM# 292 MARIENGROSCHEN

Silver **Rev:** Value in 4 lines

Date	Mintage	VG	F	VF	XF	Unc
1675 RD	—	—	—	—	—	—

KM# 299 MARIENGROSCHEN

Silver **Obv:** Value, date in 4 lines **Rev:** Madonna and child

Date	Mintage	VG	F	VF	XF	Unc
1676	—	7.00	16.00	40.00	80.00	—
1683	—	7.00	16.00	40.00	80.00	—
1684	—	7.00	16.00	40.00	80.00	—
1685	—	7.00	16.00	40.00	80.00	—

KM# 304 MARIENGROSCHEN

Silver **Obv:** Date in legend

Date	Mintage	VG	F	VF	XF	Unc
1677	—	8.00	18.00	45.00	90.00	—
1680	—	8.00	18.00	45.00	90.00	—

KM# 339 MARIENGROSCHEN

Silver **Obv:** Value, date in 4 lines **Obv. Legend:** FURST:BR: LUN:LANDTMUNTZ

Date	Mintage	VG	F	VF	XF	Unc
1691	—	13.00	30.00	55.00	90.00	—
1697 iii	—	13.00	30.00	55.00	90.00	—

KM# 338.1 MARIENGROSCHEN

Silver **Ruler:** Georg II Wilhelm **Obv:** Value in 4 lines, date **Obv. Legend:** F: BR: L: LANDTMUNTZ **Rev:** Madonna and child

Date	Mintage	VG	F	VF	XF	Unc
1691 RD	—	10.00	30.00	55.00	90.00	—
1697 JJJ	—	10.00	30.00	55.00	90.00	—

KM# 141 2 MARIENGROSCHEN

Silver **Obv:** Brunswick helmet with horse **Rev:** Value, date in 4 lines

Date	Mintage	VG	F	VF	XF	Unc
1637 HS	—	13.00	27.00	55.00	100	—
1638 HS	—	13.00	27.00	55.00	100	—
1639 HS	—	13.00	27.00	55.00	100	—
1640 HS	—	13.00	27.00	55.00	100	—
ND HS	—	13.00	27.00	55.00	100	—
1647 HS	—	13.00	27.00	55.00	100	—

KM# 202 2 MARIENGROSCHEN

Silver

Date	Mintage	VG	F	VF	XF	Unc
1649	—	10.00	20.00	40.00	80.00	—
1650	—	10.00	20.00	40.00	80.00	—
1651	—	10.00	20.00	40.00	80.00	—
1652	—	10.00	20.00	40.00	80.00	—
1653	—	10.00	20.00	40.00	80.00	—
1654	—	10.00	20.00	40.00	80.00	—
1655	—	10.00	20.00	40.00	80.00	—
1656	—	10.00	20.00	40.00	80.00	—
1659	—	10.00	20.00	40.00	80.00	—

KM# 271 2 MARIENGROSCHEN

Silver **Obv:** Crowned GW monogram **Rev:** Value in 3 lines

Date	Mintage	VG	F	VF	XF	Unc
1667	—	13.00	30.00	55.00	90.00	—
1680	—	13.00	30.00	55.00	90.00	—
1681	—	13.00	30.00	55.00	90.00	—
1681/71	—	13.00	30.00	55.00	90.00	—

KM# 280 2 MARIENGROSCHEN

Silver **Obv:** Crowned GW monogram, date in legend

Date	Mintage	VG	F	VF	XF	Unc
1673 RD	—	—	—	—	—	—

KM# 322 2 MARIENGROSCHEN

Silver **Ruler:** Georg II Wilhelm **Obv:** Crowned GW monogram, date in legend **Rev:** Value in 4 lines

Date	Mintage	VG	F	VF	XF	Unc
1687	—	13.00	30.00	55.00	90.00	—
1687 ***	—	13.00	30.00	55.00	90.00	—
1687 III	—	13.00	30.00	55.00	90.00	—
1697 JJJ	—	13.00	30.00	55.00	90.00	—
1698 JJJ	—	13.00	30.00	55.00	90.00	—

KM# 355 2 MARIENGROSCHEN

Silver **Obv:** Monogram in ornate letters

Date	Mintage	VG	F	VF	XF	Unc
1698 JJJ	—	16.00	33.00	60.00	110	—

KM# 37 4 GROSCHEN

Silver **Obv:** Crowned 4-fold arms **Rev:** Crowned imperial eagle, value 4 G in orb on breast, titles of Ferdinand II **Note:** Kipper 4 Groschen.

Date	Mintage	VG	F	VF	XF	Unc
ND(1621/2)	—	—	—	—	—	—

KM# 270 4 MARIENGROSCHEN

Silver **Obv:** Crowned GW monogram, date in legend **Rev:** Value in 3 lines

Date	Mintage	VG	F	VF	XF	Unc
1666 JJJ	—	13.00	30.00	55.00	90.00	—
1667	—	13.00	30.00	55.00	90.00	—

KM# 327 6 MARIENGROSCHEN

Silver **Obv:** Value in 4 lines **Rev:** Horse leaping left

Date	Mintage	VG	F	VF	XF	Unc
1689 JJJ	—	16.00	33.00	60.00	110	—

KM# 352 8 GUTE GROSCHEN (1/3 Thaler)

Silver **Note:** Similar to 16 Gute Groschen, KM#347 but value VIII.

Date	Mintage	VG	F	VF	XF	Unc
1694 JJJ	—	33.00	65.00	110	170	—
1698 JJJ	—	33.00	65.00	110	170	—

KM# 347.1 16 GUTE GROSCHEN (2/3 Thaler)

Silver

Date	Mintage	VG	F	VF	XF	Unc
1693 JJJ	—	40.00	85.00	125	200	—
1694 JJJ	—	40.00	85.00	125	200	—

KM# 347.2 16 GUTE GROSCHEN (2/3 Thaler)

Silver

Date	Mintage	VG	F	VF	XF	Unc
1698 JJJ	—	60.00	125	200	325	—

KM# 288 24 MARIENGROSCHEN (2/3 Thaler)

Silver **Obv:** Date in circle **Obv. Legend:** 24/MARIEN/GROSCH **Rev:** Horse leaping left

Date	Mintage	VG	F	VF	XF	Unc
1674	—	40.00	80.00	130	210	—
1674 RD	—	40.00	80.00	130	210	—
1675	—	40.00	80.00	130	210	—
1675 RD	—	40.00	80.00	130	210	—
1676	—	40.00	80.00	130	210	—
1676 RD	—	40.00	80.00	130	210	—

KM# 293 24 MARIENGROSCHEN (2/3 Thaler)

Silver **Obv:** XXIIII, date in wreath

Date	Mintage	VG	F	VF	XF	Unc
1675 RD	—	45.00	85.00	140	225	—
1677	—	45.00	85.00	140	225	—

KM# 300 24 MARIENGROSCHEN (2/3 Thaler)

Silver **Obv:** Bust right, value 60 below **Rev:** XXIIII and date without wreath

Date	Mintage	VG	F	VF	XF	Unc
1676	—	—	—	—	—	—

KM# 330 24 MARIENGROSCHEN (2/3 Thaler)

Silver **Obv:** Value in 3 lines **Rev:** Horse leaping left, date below

Date	Mintage	VG	F	VF	XF	Unc
1690 JJJ	—	27.00	55.00	100	170	—
1691 JJJ	—	27.00	55.00	100	170	—

KM# 12 2 SCHILLING

Silver **Obv:** 4-fold arms **Rev:** Intertwined DS, date in legend

Date	Mintage	VG	F	VF	XF	Unc
1619 GM	—	—	—	—	—	—
1621 GM	—	—	—	—	—	—
ND GM	—	—	—	—	—	—

KM# 13 2 SCHILLING

Silver **Obv:** Helmeted 4-fold arms

Date	Mintage	VG	F	VF	XF	Unc
1619 GM	—	—	—	—	—	—
1620 GM	—	—	—	—	—	—
ND GM	—	—	—	—	—	—

KM# 14 2 SCHILLING

Silver **Rev:** Date 1-9 divided by DS, 16 below

Date	Mintage	VG	F	VF	XF	Unc
1619 GM	—	—	—	—	—	—

KM# 38 2 SCHILLING

Silver **Obv:** 5-line inscription **Rev:** Helmet with horse, value Z S below

Date	Mintage	VG	F	VF	XF	Unc
1621	—	—	—	—	—	—

KM# 54 2 SCHILLING
Silver **Obv:** Four-fold arms **Rev:** Value in four lines **Note:** Varieties exist.

Date	Mintage	VG	F	VF	XF	Unc
(1)6ZZ	—	33.00	55.00	135	220	—
(1)6Z3	—	33.00	55.00	135	220	—

KM# 19 12 KREUZER (Dreibätzner; Schreckenberger)
Silver **Obv:** Crowned Luneburg lion rampant left **Obv. Legend:** IN MANV... **Rev:** Crowned imperial eagle, 12 in orb on breast, titles of Ferdinand II, date in legend **Note:** Kipper 12 Kreuzer.

Date	Mintage	VG	F	VF	XF	Unc
1621	—	85.00	200	375	550	—

KM# 39 12 KREUZER (Dreibätzner; Schreckenberger)
Silver **Obv:** Crowned arms of Luttenberg, lion left above 6 bars **Obv. Legend:** MONETA DVCAT.GRVBENHA **Rev:** Crowned imperial eagle with 12 in orb on breast, titles of Ferdinand II **Note:** Kipper Coinage for Grubenhagen.

Date	Mintage	VG	F	VF	XF	Unc
1621	—	85.00	200	375	550	—

KM# 24 12 KREUZER (Dreibätzner; Schreckenberger)
Silver **Obv:** Crowned Luneburg lion rampant right, titles of Christian **Rev:** Crowned imperial eagle, 1Z in orb on breast, titles of Ferdinand II, date in legend **Note:** Varieties exist.

Date	Mintage	VG	F	VF	XF	Unc
16Z1	—	85.00	200	375	550	—

KM# 40 24 KREUZER
Silver **Obv:** Crowned lion rampant right **Rev:** Crowned imperial eagle, 24 in orb on breast, titles of Ferdinand II **Note:** Kipper 24 Kreuzer.

Date	Mintage	VG	F	VF	XF	Unc
1621	—	135	325	525	825	—

KM# 43 HALB ORT HALB (1/4 Ort; 1/16 Thaler)
Silver **Obv:** Crowned imperial eagle wtih 16 in orb on breast, titles of Ferdinand II **Rev:** 4-fold arms with central shield of Minden (crossed keys) **Note:** Kipper Halb Ort Halb.

Date	Mintage	VG	F	VF	XF	Unc
1621	—	—	—	—	—	—

KM# 56 HALB ORT HALB (1/4 Ort; 1/16 Thaler)
Silver **Obv:** Bust right **Rev:** Value in 4 lines **Note:** Kipper Halb Ort Halb.

Date	Mintage	VG	F	VF	XF	Unc
1622	—	—	—	—	—	—

KM# 70 HALB ORT HALB (1/4 Ort; 1/16 Thaler)
Silver **Obv:** Crowned 8-fold arms **Rev:** Value in 4 lines **Rev. Legend:** IN.SPE.ET.SILENTIO

Date	Mintage	VG	F	VF	XF	Unc
1624 HS	—	27.00	60.00	120	200	—
1627 HS	—	27.00	60.00	120	200	—

KM# 84 HALB ORT HALB (1/4 Ort; 1/16 Thaler)
Silver **Obv:** Crowned 9-fold arms **Rev. Legend:** DANTE.DEO.VIRTUTE.DUCE

Date	Mintage	VG	F	VF	XF	Unc
1626 HS	—	27.00	60.00	120	200	—
1627 HS	—	27.00	60.00	120	200	—

KM# 85 HALB ORT HALB (1/4 Ort; 1/16 Thaler)
Silver **Obv:** Ornamented 9-fold arms **Rev:** Value in 5 lines

Date	Mintage	VG	F	VF	XF	Unc
1626 HS	—	—	—	—	—	—

KM# 118 HALB ORT HALB (1/4 Ort; 1/16 Thaler)
Silver **Obv:** Crowned 7-fold arms with central shield of Ratzeburg arms (mitre above castle tower) **Rev:** Date in legend **Rev. Legend:** I/HALB/ORT/HALB

Date	Mintage	VG	F	VF	XF	Unc
1635 HS	—	—	—	—	—	—

KM# 175 HALB ORT HALB (1/4 Ort; 1/16 Thaler)
Silver **Obv:** Crowned F monogram **Rev:** Value in 5 lines

Date	Mintage	VG	F	VF	XF	Unc
1647 LW	—	27.00	60.00	100	170	—
1648 LW	—	27.00	60.00	100	170	—

KM# 248 HALB ORT HALB (1/4 Ort; 1/16 Thaler)
Silver **Obv:** Crowned CL monogram above date in laurel wreath **Rev:** Horse leaping left, 16 in field

Date	Mintage	VG	F	VF	XF	Unc
1659 LW	—	20.00	33.00	60.00	120	—
1661 LW	—	20.00	33.00	60.00	120	—
1663 LW	—	20.00	33.00	60.00	120	—
1665 LW	—	20.00	33.00	60.00	120	—

KM# 47 HALB REICHSORT (1/8 Thaler)
Silver

Date	Mintage	VG	F	VF	XF	Unc
1621	—	45.00	85.00	160	300	—
1624 HS	—	45.00	85.00	160	300	—
1625 HS	—	45.00	85.00	160	300	—
1626 HS	—	45.00	85.00	160	300	—
1627 HS	—	45.00	85.00	160	300	—
1628 HS	—	45.00	85.00	160	300	—

KM# 71 HALB REICHSORT (1/8 Thaler)
Silver **Obv:** Value in 3 lines **Rev:** 10-fold arms

Date	Mintage	VG	F	VF	XF	Unc
1624	—	45.00	85.00	160	300	—

KM# 72 HALB REICHSORT (1/8 Thaler)
Silver **Obv:** St. Andrew with cross **Rev:** Crowned 8-fold arms, date divided at bottom

Date	Mintage	VG	F	VF	XF	Unc
1624 HP	—	—	—	—	—	—

KM# 88 HALB REICHSORT (1/8 Thaler)
Silver **Obv:** Crowned 9-fold arms **Rev:** Value in 5 lines

Date	Mintage	VG	F	VF	XF	Unc
1629 HS	—	80.00	170	275	475	—
1630 HS	—	80.00	170	275	475	—
1631 HS	—	80.00	170	275	475	—
1632 HS	—	80.00	170	275	475	—
1633 HS	—	80.00	170	275	475	—

KM# 103 HALB REICHSORT (1/8 Thaler)
Silver **Obv:** St. Andrew with cross **Rev:** Crowned 9-fold arms, divided at bottom

Date	Mintage	VG	F	VF	XF	Unc
1633 HS	—	—	—	—	—	—

KM# 104 HALB REICHSORT (1/8 Thaler)
Silver **Subject:** Death of Christian **Obv:** Crowned 9-fold arms **Rev:** 9-line inscription with date

Date	Mintage	VG	F	VF	XF	Unc
1633	—	—	—	—	—	—

KM# 113 HALB REICHSORT (1/8 Thaler)
Silver **Obv:** Crowned 9-fold arms with central shield of Ratzeburg arms **Rev:** Date in legend **Rev. Legend:** I/HALB/REICHS/ORT

Date	Mintage	VG	F	VF	XF	Unc
1634 HS	—	100	175	300	525	—
1635 HS	—	100	175	300	525	—
1636 HS	—	100	175	300	525	—

KM# 123 HALB REICHSORT (1/8 Thaler)
Silver **Obv:** Crowned 11-fold arms with central shield **Rev:** Wildman, tree in right hand

Date	Mintage	VG	F	VF	XF	Unc
1636 HS	—	—	—	—	—	—

KM# 124 HALB REICHSORT (1/8 Thaler)
Silver **Subject:** Death of August I **Rev:** 9-line inscription with date

Date	Mintage	VG	F	VF	XF	Unc
1636 HS	—	—	—	—	—	—

KM# 125 HALB REICHSORT (1/8 Thaler)
Silver **Obv:** Crowned 7-fold arms with central shield

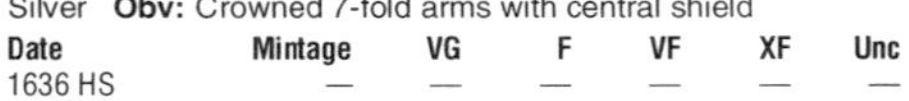

Date	Mintage	VG	F	VF	XF	Unc
1636 HS	—	—	—	—	—	—

KM# 149 HALB REICHSORT (1/8 Thaler)
Silver **Obv:** Crowned 11-fold arms

Date	Mintage	VG	F	VF	XF	Unc
1638 HS	—	25.00	50.00	85.00	140	—
1639 HS	—	25.00	50.00	85.00	140	—
1640 HS	—	25.00	50.00	85.00	140	—
1640 LW	—	25.00	50.00	85.00	140	—
1642 LW	—	25.00	50.00	85.00	140	—

KM# 162 HALB REICHSORT (1/8 Thaler)
Silver **Subject:** Death of Friedrich's Sister, Margarethe, Wife of Johann Casimir of Saxe-Coburg **Obv:** Helmeted 12-fold arms **Rev:** 10-line inscription with date

Date	Mintage	VG	F	VF	XF	Unc
1643 LW	—	—	—	—	—	—

KM# 161 HALB REICHSORT (1/8 Thaler)
Silver **Obv:** Crowned 12-fold arms **Note:** Varieties exist.

Date	Mintage	VG	F	VF	XF	Unc
1643 LW	—	55.00	110	175	250	—
1644 LW	—	55.00	110	175	250	—
1645 LW	—	55.00	110	175	250	—
ND LW	—	55.00	110	175	250	—

KM# 172.1 HALB REICHSORT (1/8 Thaler)
Silver **Note:** Varieties exist with and without bow at shoulder.

Date	Mintage	VG	F	VF	XF	Unc
1645 LW	—	55.00	110	175	250	—
1646 LW	—	55.00	110	175	250	—
1647 LW	—	55.00	110	175	250	—
1648 LW	—	55.00	110	175	250	—

KM# 173 HALB REICHSORT (1/8 Thaler)
Silver **Rev:** Similar to KM#149

Date	Mintage	VG	F	VF	XF	Unc
1646	—	—	—	—	—	—

KM# 189 HALB REICHSORT (1/8 Thaler)
Silver **Subject:** Death of Friedrich V **Rev:** 9-line inscription with date

Date	Mintage	VG	F	VF	XF	Unc
1648 LW	—	—	—	—	—	—

KM# 204 HALB REICHSORT (1/8 Thaler)
Silver **Obv:** 12-fold arms in circle, date divided 1-6/4-8, titles of Friedrich V **Rev:** Horse leaping left in circle, date **Rev. Legend:** *SINCERE **Note:** Mule.

Date	Mintage	VG	F	VF	XF	Unc
1648/1649 LW Rare	—	—	—	—	—	—

KM# 172.2 HALB REICHSORT (1/8 Thaler)
Silver

Date	Mintage	VG	F	VF	XF	Unc
ND LW	—	55.00	110	175	250	—

KM# 203 HALB REICHSORT (1/8 Thaler)
Silver **Obv:** 12-fold arms, small crown in legend **Rev:** Horse leaping left

Date	Mintage	VG	F	VF	XF	Unc
1649 LW	—	55.00	110	175	250	—
1650 LW	—	55.00	110	175	250	—

KM# 220 HALB REICHSORT (1/8 Thaler)
Silver **Obv:** Large crown above arms

Date	Mintage	VG	F	VF	XF	Unc
1650 LW	—	55.00	110	175	250	—
1653 LW	—	55.00	110	175	250	—
1654 LW	—	55.00	110	175	250	—
1655 LW	—	55.00	110	175	250	—
1657 LW	—	55.00	110	175	250	—
1659 LW	—	55.00	110	175	250	—
1660 LW	—	55.00	110	175	250	—
1662 LW	—	55.00	110	175	250	—
1663 LW	—	55.00	110	175	250	—
1664 LW	—	55.00	110	175	250	—
1665 LW	—	55.00	110	175	250	—

KM# 265 HALB REICHSORT (1/8 Thaler)
Silver **Subject:** Death of Christian Ludwig **Obv:** 12-fold arms, small crown in legend **Rev:** 10-line inscription with date

Date	Mintage	VG	F	VF	XF	Unc
1665 LW	—	—	—	—	—	—

KM# 282 HALB REICHSORT (1/8 Thaler)
Silver **Obv:** Horse leaping left **Rev:** Crowned 12-fold arms

Date	Mintage	VG	F	VF	XF	Unc
1673 RD	—	—	—	—	—	—

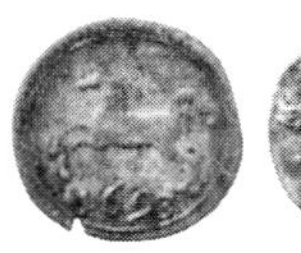

KM# 348 1/96 THALER
Silver **Obv:** Value 96 in palm wreath **Rev:** Horse leaping left

Date	Mintage	VG	F	VF	XF	Unc
1693 iii	—	27.00	45.00	80.00	145	—

KM# 323 1/48 THALER (1/2 Groschen)
Silver **Ruler:** Georg II Wilhelm **Obv:** Crowned GW monogram **Rev:** Value, date **Rev. Legend:** F. BR. LANTMUNTZ

Date	Mintage	VG	F	VF	XF	Unc
1687 III	—	9.00	20.00	40.00	70.00	—
1688 III	—	9.00	20.00	40.00	70.00	—
1688 iii	—	9.00	20.00	40.00	70.00	—
1690 III	—	9.00	20.00	40.00	70.00	—
1690 iii	—	9.00	20.00	40.00	70.00	—
1691 iii	—	9.00	20.00	40.00	70.00	—
1694 iii	—	9.00	20.00	40.00	70.00	—
1695 III	—	9.00	20.00	40.00	70.00	—
1695 iii	—	9.00	20.00	40.00	70.00	—
1696 iii	—	9.00	20.00	40.00	70.00	—
1699 III	—	9.00	20.00	40.00	70.00	—

KM# 356 1/48 THALER (1/2 Groschen)
Silver **Ruler:** Georg II Wilhelm **Obv:** Monogram of ornate letters **Rev:** Value within orb

Date	Mintage	VG	F	VF	XF	Unc
1698 III	—	9.00	20.00	40.00	70.00	—

KM# 5 1/24 THALER (Groschen)
Silver **Obv:** Imperial orb with 24, titles of Matthias **Rev:** Helmeted 4-fold arms

Date	Mintage	VG	F	VF	XF	Unc
1617	—	20.00	33.00	60.00	110	—
1619	—	20.00	33.00	60.00	110	—

KM# 10 1/24 THALER (Groschen)
Silver **Obv:** Lion rampant right **Rev:** Imperial orb wtih 24

Date	Mintage	VG	F	VF	XF	Unc
1618 (k)	—	27.00	55.00	100	125	—

KM# 11 1/24 THALER (Groschen)
Silver **Obv:** Lion rampant left **Rev:** Imperial orb with 24 **Rev. Legend:** IUSTITIA.ET.CONCOR

Date	Mintage	VG	F	VF	XF	Unc
1618 (k)	—	20.00	40.00	65.00	130	—
1619 (k)	—	20.00	40.00	65.00	130	—

KM# 15 1/24 THALER (Groschen)
Silver **Obv:** Lion rampant right

Date	Mintage	VG	F	VF	XF	Unc
1619 (k)	—	27.00	55.00	100	170	—

KM# 41 1/24 THALER (Groschen)
Silver **Obv:** Lion rampant left **Obv. Legend:** C. D. G. E. E. M. D BEL **Rev:** Imperial orb with 24 **Rev. Legend:** NACH. R. SCHROT. V. KORN

Date	Mintage	VG	F	VF	XF	Unc
1621	—	27.00	55.00	100	170	—

KM# 42 1/24 THALER (Groschen)
Silver **Subject:** Coinage for Grubenhagen **Obv:** Imperial orb with 24, titles of Ferdinand II **Rev:** Round Lutterberg arms (lion left above 6 bars) **Rev. Legend:** MONE-DVC.GRVBENH

Date	Mintage	VG	F	VF	XF	Unc
1621	—	—	—	—	—	—

KM# 55 1/24 THALER (Groschen)
Silver **Obv:** Arms of Lutterberg **Rev:** Imperial orb with 24 **Rev. Legend:** NACH.R.SCHROT.V.KORN

Date	Mintage	VG	F	VF	XF	Unc
1622 HS	—	10.00	20.00	40.00	80.00	—
1623 HS	—	10.00	20.00	40.00	80.00	—
1624 HS	—	10.00	20.00	40.00	80.00	—
1628 HS	—	10.00	20.00	40.00	80.00	—
1629 HS	—	10.00	20.00	40.00	80.00	—
1631 HS	—	10.00	20.00	40.00	80.00	—
1632 HS	—	10.00	20.00	40.00	80.00	—
1633 HS	—	10.00	20.00	40.00	80.00	—

KM# 61 1/24 THALER (Groschen)
Silver **Obv:** St. Andrew with cross divides date

Date	Mintage	VG	F	VF	XF	Unc
1623 HP	—	—	—	—	—	—
1624 HP	—	—	—	—	—	—

KM# 63 1/24 THALER (Groschen)
Silver **Rev. Legend:** NACH.A.SCHROT.V.K.16.23

Date	Mintage	VG	F	VF	XF	Unc
1623 HP	—	—	—	—	—	—

KM# 64 1/24 THALER (Groschen)
Silver **Obv:** Crowned arms **Rev:** St. Andrew with cross

Date	Mintage	VG	F	VF	XF	Unc
1623 HP	—	—	—	—	—	—

KM# 65 1/24 THALER (Groschen)
Silver **Obv:** Imperial orb with 24

Date	Mintage	VG	F	VF	XF	Unc
1623	—	13.00	27.00	55.00	110	—
1624	—	13.00	27.00	55.00	110	—
1624 HP	—	13.00	27.00	55.00	110	—

KM# 62 1/24 THALER (Groschen)
Silver **Note:** Klippe.

Date	Mintage	VG	F	VF	XF	Unc
1623 HP	—	—	—	—	—	—

KM# 68 1/24 THALER (Groschen)
Silver **Obv. Legend:** CHRIST.D.G **Rev. Legend:** CHRISTIAN D.G

Date	Mintage	VG	F	VF	XF	Unc
1624	—	—	—	—	—	—

KM# 69 1/24 THALER (Groschen)
Silver **Obv:** Crowned 8-fold arms **Rev:** Imperial orb with 24 **Rev. Legend:** NACH.R.SCHROT.V K 16-24

Date	Mintage	VG	F	VF	XF	Unc
1624 HS	—	33.00	55.00	100	170	—

KM# 112 1/24 THALER (Groschen)
Silver **Obv:** Lutterberg arms **Rev:** Imperial orb with 24

Date	Mintage	VG	F	VF	XF	Unc
1634 HS	—	13.00	27.00	55.00	110	—
1635 HS	—	13.00	27.00	55.00	110	—
1636 HS	—	13.00	27.00	55.00	110	—

KM# 122 1/24 THALER (Groschen)
Silver **Obv:** Crowned Lutterberg-Scharzfeld arms

Date	Mintage	VG	F	VF	XF	Unc
1635 HS Error	—	20.00	40.00	80.00	150	—
1637 HS	—	20.00	40.00	80.00	150	—
1638 HS	—	20.00	40.00	80.00	150	—
1641 LW	—	20.00	40.00	80.00	150	—
1642 LW	—	20.00	40.00	80.00	150	—
1643 LW	—	20.00	40.00	80.00	150	—
1644 LW	—	20.00	40.00	80.00	150	—
1647 LW	—	20.00	40.00	80.00	150	—
1648 LW	—	20.00	40.00	80.00	150	—

KM# 121 1/24 THALER (Groschen)
Silver **Obv:** Brunswick helmet with horse **Note:** Varieties exist (mintmasters initials on either obverse or reverse).

Date	Mintage	VG	F	VF	XF	Unc
1636 HS	—	—	—	—	—	—

KM# 219 1/24 THALER (Groschen)
Silver **Obv:** Crowned Lutterberg arms (wtih 5 bars)

Date	Mintage	VG	F	VF	XF	Unc
1650 LW	—	20.00	40.00	80.00	150	—
1651 LW	—	20.00	40.00	80.00	150	—
1655 LW	—	20.00	40.00	80.00	150	—
1657 LW	—	20.00	40.00	80.00	150	—

KM# 228 1/24 THALER (Groschen)
Silver **Subject:** Death of Sybilla, 2nd Wife of Julius Ernst zu Dannenberg **Obv:** Crowned 12-fold arms, value 24 sideways on left **Rev:** 9-line inscription with date

Date	Mintage	VG	F	VF	XF	Unc
1652	—	—	—	—	—	—

KM# 246 1/24 THALER (Groschen)
Silver **Subject:** Death of Christian Ernst's Aunt Clara **Obv:** Horse leaping left, 24 in oval below **Rev:** 10-line inscription with date

Date	Mintage	VG	F	VF	XF	Unc
1658 LW	—	27.00	55.00	85.00	140	—

KM# 255 1/24 THALER (Groschen)
Silver **Obv:** Imperial orb wtih 24 in circle **Rev:** Horse leaping left in circle

Date	Mintage	VG	F	VF	XF	Unc
1661 LW	—	13.00	27.00	45.00	90.00	—
1662 LW	—	13.00	27.00	45.00	90.00	—
1663 LW	—	13.00	27.00	45.00	90.00	—
1665 LW	—	13.00	27.00	45.00	90.00	—

KM# 264 1/24 THALER (Groschen)
Silver **Subject:** Death of Christian Ludwig

Date	Mintage	VG	F	VF	XF	Unc
1665 LW	—	40.00	80.00	130	175	—

KM# 281 1/24 THALER (Groschen)
Silver **Obv:** Crowned GW monogram, date in legend **Rev:** Imperial orb with 24 **Rev. Legend:** REICHSTHALER SILBER

Date	Mintage	VG	F	VF	XF	Unc
1673 RD	—	20.00	40.00	80.00	140	—

KM# A279 1/24 THALER (Groschen)
Silver **Rev. Legend:** F.BR.LUNEB.LANDTMUNTZ

Date	Mintage	VG	F	VF	XF	Unc
1674 RD	—	13.00	30.00	60.00	120	—
1675 RD	—	13.00	30.00	60.00	120	—
1688 iii	—	13.00	30.00	60.00	120	—
1690 iii	—	13.00	30.00	60.00	120	—
1691 iii	—	13.00	30.00	60.00	120	—

KM# 301 1/24 THALER (Groschen)
Silver **Obv:** Horse leaping left, German titles **Rev:** Imperial orb with 24, date

Date	Mintage	VG	F	VF	XF	Unc
1676 RD	—	13.00	27.00	45.00	90.00	—
1677 RD	—	13.00	27.00	45.00	90.00	—
1678 RD	—	13.00	27.00	45.00	90.00	—
1680 RD	—	13.00	27.00	45.00	90.00	—

KM# 309 1/24 THALER (Groschen)
Silver **Rev. Legend:** MONETA NOVA ARGENTEA

Date	Mintage	VG	F	VF	XF	Unc
1684 IT	—	13.00	27.00	45.00	90.00	—

KM# 324 1/24 THALER (Groschen)
Silver **Obv:** GW monogram above horse

Date	Mintage	VG	F	VF	XF	Unc
1687 III	—	13.00	27.00	45.00	90.00	—
1688 III	—	13.00	27.00	45.00	90.00	—

KM# 349 1/24 THALER (Groschen)
Silver **Ruler:** Georg II Wilhelm **Obv:** Latin titles and date below horse **Rev:** Imperial orb with 24

Date	Mintage	VG	F	VF	XF	Unc
1693 III	—	8.00	20.00	40.00	80.00	—
1693 iii	—	8.00	20.00	40.00	80.00	—
1694 III	—	8.00	20.00	40.00	80.00	—
1694 iii	—	8.00	20.00	40.00	80.00	—
1695 III	—	8.00	20.00	40.00	80.00	—
1695 iii	—	8.00	20.00	40.00	80.00	—
1696 III	—	8.00	20.00	40.00	80.00	—
1696 iii	—	8.00	20.00	40.00	80.00	—

KM# 236 1/16 THALER
Silver **Obv:** Crowned CL monogram in wreath **Rev:** Value XVI... in 4 lines

Date	Mintage	VG	F	VF	XF	Unc
1655 LW	—	33.00	65.00	125	225	—
1656 LW	—	33.00	65.00	125	225	—
1657 LW	—	33.00	65.00	125	225	—
1658 LW	—	33.00	65.00	125	225	—

KM# 44 1/12 THALER
Silver **Obv:** Crowned imperial eagle with 12 in orb on breast, date in legend, titles of Ferdinand II **Rev:** Crowned lion rampant right

Date	Mintage	VG	F	VF	XF	Unc
1621	—	60.00	120	240	400	—

KM# 45 1/12 THALER
Silver **Obv:** N below lion

Date	Mintage	VG	F	VF	XF	Unc
1621 N Rare	—	—	—	—	—	—

KM# 46 1/12 THALER
Silver **Obv:** Crowned lion rampant left **Obv. Legend:** IN.MANV.DEI.SORTES.MEAE

Date	Mintage	VG	F	VF	XF	Unc
1621	—	60.00	120	240	400	—

KM# 86 1/12 THALER
Silver **Obv:** St. Andrew with cross **Obv. Legend:** RECTE. FACIEN.NEM.IMT

Date	Mintage	VG	F	VF	XF	Unc
1626	—	—	—	—	—	—

KM# 6 1/4 THALER
Silver **Note:** Similar to KM#66.

Date	Mintage	VG	F	VF	XF	Unc
1617	—	80.00	160	275	425	—
1617 (k)	—	80.00	160	275	425	—
1618 (k)	—	80.00	160	275	425	—
1620 (k)	—	80.00	160	275	425	—
1623 HS	—	80.00	160	275	425	—
1624 HS	—	80.00	160	275	425	—

KM# 16 1/4 THALER
Silver **Rev:** Helmeted 8-fold arms

Date	Mintage	VG	F	VF	XF	Unc
1619 (k)	—	—	—	—	—	—

KM# 28 1/4 THALER
Silver **Note:** Struck on octagonal flan.

Date	Mintage	VG	F	VF	XF	Unc
1620 GM Rare	—	—	—	—	—	—

KM# 57 1/4 THALER
Silver **Rev. Legend:** DUX:BR.-ET.LU

Date	Mintage	VG	F	VF	XF	Unc
1622 (w)	—	—	—	—	—	—

KM# 66 1/4 THALER
Silver

Date	Mintage	VG	F	VF	XF	Unc
1623 HP	—	55.00	115	225	400	—
1624 HP	—	55.00	115	225	400	—
1625 HP	—	55.00	115	225	400	—

KM# 79 1/4 THALER
Silver **Rev:** 9-fold arms

Date	Mintage	VG	F	VF	XF	Unc
1625 HS	—	55.00	115	210	325	—
1627 HS	—	55.00	15.00	210	325	—

KM# 89 1/4 THALER
Silver **Rev. Legend:** IN*SPE*ET*-SILENTIO*H.S

Date	Mintage	VG	F	VF	XF	Unc
1629 HS	—	55.00	115	220	325	—
1630 HS	—	55.00	115	220	325	—
1631 HS	—	55.00	115	220	325	—

KM# 97 1/4 THALER
Silver **Obv:** Similar to KM#65 **Rev:** Crowned 9-fold arms

Date	Mintage	VG	F	VF	XF	Unc
1630 HS	—	—	—	—	—	—

KM# 105 1/4 THALER
Silver **Subject:** Death of Christian **Obv:** Ornamented 9-fold arms **Rev:** 10-line inscription with date

Date	Mintage	VG	F	VF	XF	Unc
1633	—	—	—	—	—	—
1633 HS	—	—	—	—	—	—

KM# 119 1/4 THALER
Silver **Obv:** Bust right **Rev:** Crowned 9-fold arms with central shield

Date	Mintage	VG	F	VF	XF	Unc
1635 HS	—	—	—	—	—	—
1636 HS	—	—	—	—	—	—

KM# 126 1/4 THALER
Silver **Obv:** Crowned 11-fold arms with central shield **Rev:** Wildman, tree in right hand, date in legend

Date	Mintage	VG	F	VF	XF	Unc
1636 HS	—	325	600	1,000	1,700	—

KM# 127 1/4 THALER
Silver **Subject:** Death of August I **Rev:** 10-line inscription

Date	Mintage	VG	F	VF	XF	Unc
1636 HS	—	135	275	450	675	—

KM# 128 1/4 THALER
Silver **Obv:** Crowned 7-fold arms with central shield

Date	Mintage	VG	F	VF	XF	Unc
1636 HS	—	200	375	600	1,000	—

KM# 142 1/4 THALER
Silver **Rev:** Crowned 11-fold arms

Date	Mintage	VG	F	VF	XF	Unc
1637 HS	—	125	240	400	650	—
1638 HS	—	125	240	400	650	—
1639 HS	—	125	240	400	650	—
1641 LW	—	125	240	400	650	—
1642 LW	—	125	240	400	650	—
1643 LW	—	125	240	400	650	—
1644 LW	—	125	240	400	650	—

KM# 163 1/4 THALER
Silver **Rev:** 12-fold arms

Date	Mintage	VG	F	VF	XF	Unc
1643 LW	—	85.00	175	300	500	—
1644 LW	—	85.00	175	300	500	—
1645 LW	—	85.00	175	300	500	—
1646 LW	—	85.00	175	300	500	—
1647 LW	—	85.00	175	300	500	—
1648 LW	—	85.00	175	300	500	—

KM# 176 1/4 THALER
Silver **Obv:** Without COADI.D.STIFT.RATZ

Date	Mintage	VG	F	VF	XF	Unc
1647 LW Rare	—	—	—	—	—	—

KM# 190 1/4 THALER
Silver **Subject:** Death of Friedrich V **Rev:** 10-line inscription

Date	Mintage	VG	F	VF	XF	Unc
1648 LW	—	—	—	—	—	—

KM# 205 1/4 THALER
Silver **Rev:** Crowned 12-fold arms, date in legend

Date	Mintage	VG	F	VF	XF	Unc
1649 HS	—	—	—	—	—	—

KM# 206 1/4 THALER
Silver **Obv:** Crowned 12-fold arms **Rev:** Horse leaping left

Date	Mintage	VG	F	VF	XF	Unc
1649 LW	—	90.00	175	350	650	—
1650 LW	—	90.00	175	350	650	—
1653 LW	—	90.00	175	350	650	—
1654 LW	—	90.00	175	350	650	—
1656 LW	—	90.00	175	350	650	—
1658 LW	—	90.00	175	350	650	—
1659 LW	—	90.00	175	350	650	—
1661 LW	—	90.00	175	350	650	—
1662 LW	—	90.00	175	350	650	—
1664 LW	—	90.00	175	350	650	—
1665 LW	—	90.00	175	350	650	—

KM# 266 1/4 THALER
Silver **Subject:** Death of Christian Ludwig

Date	Mintage	VG	F	VF	XF	Unc
1665 LW	—	100	200	375	625	—

KM# 283 1/4 THALER
Silver **Obv:** Horse leaping left **Rev:** Crowned 12-fold arms

Date	Mintage	VG	F	VF	XF	Unc
1673 RD	—	—	—	—	—	—

KM# 340 1/4 THALER

Silver **Obv:** Crowned 12-fold arms **Rev:** Horse leaping left, 1/4 in oval divides date below

Date	Mintage	VG	F	VF	XF	Unc
1691 III	—	40.00	80.00	150	225	—

KM# 290 1/3 THALER

Silver

Date	Mintage	VG	F	VF	XF	Unc
1674	—	65.00	140	225	400	—

KM# 291 1/3 THALER

Silver **Obv:** Denomination **Rev:** Horse leaping left

Date	Mintage	VG	F	VF	XF	Unc
1674	—	65.00	140	225	400	—
1675	—	65.00	140	225	400	—
1676	—	65.00	140	225	400	—

KM# 344 1/3 THALER

Silver

Date	Mintage	VG	F	VF	XF	Unc
1692 JJJ	—	40.00	75.00	150	270	—
1693 JJJ	—	40.00	75.00	150	270	—

KM# 7 1/2 THALER

Silver

Date	Mintage	VG	F	VF	XF	Unc
1617 (k)	—	90.00	175	300	475	—
1618 (k)	—	90.00	175	300	475	—
1620 (k)	—	90.00	175	300	475	—
1622 HS	—	90.00	175	300	475	—
1623	—	90.00	175	300	475	—
1623 HP	—	90.00	175	300	475	—
1623 HS	—	90.00	175	300	475	—
1624 HS	—	90.00	175	300	475	—
1625 HS	—	90.00	175	300	475	—

KM# 67 1/2 THALER

Silver **Note:** Similar to 1/4 Thaler, KM#66.

Date	Mintage	VG	F	VF	XF	Unc
1623 HP	—	85.00	170	300	475	—
1624 HP	—	85.00	170	300	475	—

KM# 73 1/2 THALER

Silver **Rev:** 9-fold arms

Date	Mintage	VG	F	VF	XF	Unc
1624 HS	—	100	200	330	600	—
1625 HS	—	100	200	330	600	—
1626 HS	—	100	200	330	600	—
1627 HS	—	100	200	330	600	—
1629 HS	—	100	200	330	600	—

KM# 74 1/2 THALER

Silver **Rev:** 10-fold arms

Date	Mintage	VG	F	VF	XF	Unc
1624 HVE	—	140	275	450	725	—

KM# 98 1/2 THALER

Silver

Date	Mintage	VG	F	VF	XF	Unc
1630 HS	—	100	190	325	625	—
1631 HS	—	100	190	325	625	—
1632 HS	—	100	190	325	625	—
1633 HS	—	100	190	325	625	—

KM# 102 1/2 THALER

Silver **Obv:** Similar to 1/4 Thaler, KM#66

Date	Mintage	VG	F	VF	XF	Unc
1632 HS	—	140	225	425	625	—
1633 HS	—	140	225	425	625	—

KM# 106 1/2 THALER

Silver **Subject:** Death of Christian **Obv:** Ornamented 9-fold arms **Rev:** 10-line inscription with date

Date	Mintage	VG	F	VF	XF	Unc
1633 HS	—	—	—	—	—	—

KM# 114 1/2 THALER

Silver **Obv:** Bust right **Rev:** Crowned 9-fold arms with central shield

Date	Mintage	VG	F	VF	XF	Unc
1634 HS	—	140	280	475	775	—
1635 HS	—	140	280	475	775	—
1636 HS	—	140	280	475	775	—

KM# 129 1/2 THALER

Silver **Obv:** Crowned 11-fold arms with central shield **Rev:** Wildman, tree in right hand divides date

Date	Mintage	VG	F	VF	XF	Unc
1636 HS	—	—	—	—	—	—

KM# 130 1/2 THALER

Silver **Subject:** Death of August I **Rev:** 13-line inscription

Date	Mintage	VG	F	VF	XF	Unc
1636 HS	—	180	350	550	875	—

KM# 131 1/2 THALER

Silver **Obv:** Crowned 7-fold arms with central shield **Rev:** 10-line inscription

Date	Mintage	VG	F	VF	XF	Unc
1636 HS	—	180	350	550	875	—

KM# 143 1/2 THALER

Silver **Rev:** Helmeted 11-fold arms divide date, Gothic letters

Date	Mintage	VG	F	VF	XF	Unc
1637 HS	—	85.00	175	325	500	—
1638 HS	—	85.00	175	325	500	—
1639 HS	—	85.00	175	325	500	—
1640 HS	—	85.00	175	325	500	—
1641 LW	—	85.00	175	325	500	—
1642 LW	—	85.00	175	325	500	—
1643 LW	—	85.00	175	325	500	—

KM# 144 1/2 THALER

Silver **Note:** Latin letters.

Date	Mintage	VG	F	VF	XF	Unc
1637 HS	—	75.00	150	275	450	—

KM# 164 1/2 THALER

Silver **Rev:** Crowned 12-fold arms

Date	Mintage	VG	F	VF	XF	Unc
1643 LW	—	65.00	130	250	375	—
1644 LW	—	65.00	130	250	375	—
1645 LW	—	65.00	130	250	375	—
1646 LW	—	65.00	130	250	375	—
1647 LW	—	65.00	130	250	375	—
1648 LW	—	65.00	130	250	375	—

KM# 165 1/2 THALER

Silver **Subject:** Death of Friedrich's Sister, Margarethe, Wife of Johann Casimir of Saxe-Coburg **Obv:** Helmeted 12-fold arms **Rev:** 10-line inscription with date

Date	Mintage	VG	F	VF	XF	Unc
1643 LW	—	—	—	—	—	—

KM# 191 1/2 THALER

Silver **Subject:** Death of Friedrich V **Obv:** Bust right

Date	Mintage	VG	F	VF	XF	Unc
1648 LW	—	—	—	—	—	—

KM# 207 1/2 THALER

Silver **Obv:** Crowned 12-fold arms **Rev:** Horse leaping left

Date	Mintage	VG	F	VF	XF	Unc
1649 LW	—	165	325	500	750	—
1651 LW	—	165	325	500	750	—
1653 LW	—	165	325	500	750	—
1655 LW	—	165	325	500	750	—
1656 LW	—	165	325	500	750	—
1658 LW	—	165	325	500	750	—
1659 LW	—	165	325	500	750	—
1660 LW	—	165	325	500	750	—
1662 LW	—	165	325	500	750	—
1665 LW	—	165	325	500	750	—

KM# 240 1/2 THALER

Silver **Rev:** Wildman, tree in right hand

Date	Mintage	VG	F	VF	XF	Unc
1657 HS	—	—	—	—	—	—

KM# 258 1/2 THALER

Silver **Note:** Klippe.

Date	Mintage	VG	F	VF	XF	Unc
1664 LW	—	—	—	—	—	—

KM# 267 1/2 THALER

Silver **Subject:** Death of Christian Ludwig **Obv:** 12-fold arms, small crown in legend **Rev:** 11-line inscription with date

Date	Mintage	VG	F	VF	XF	Unc
1665 LW	—	85.00	145	275	500	—
1665 HS	—	85.00	145	275	500	—

KM# 284 1/2 THALER

Silver **Obv:** Horse leaping left **Rev:** Crowned 12-fold arms

Date	Mintage	VG	F	VF	XF	Unc
1673 RD	—	—	—	—	—	—

KM# 341 1/2 THALER

Silver **Obv:** Bust right, date below **Rev:** Halmeted 12-fold arms

Date	Mintage	VG	F	VF	XF	Unc
1691 iii	—	—	—	—	—	—

KM# 328 2/3 THALER

Silver **Obv:** Bust right **Rev:** Horse leaping left in circle, 2/3 in oval divides date below

Date	Mintage	VG	F	VF	XF	Unc
1689 JJJ	—	—	—	—	—	—

KM# 331 2/3 THALER

Silver

Date	Mintage	VG	F	VF	XF	Unc
1690 JJJ	—	40.00	75.00	130	225	—

KM# 345.1 2/3 THALER

Silver **Obv:** Similar to KM#341 but arms break circle at bottom

Date	Mintage	VG	F	VF	XF	Unc
1691 JJJ	—	80.00	140	225	300	—
1692 JJJ	—	80.00	140	225	300	—
1693 JJJ	—	80.00	140	225	300	—
1694 JJJ	—	80.00	140	225	300	—

KM# 345.2 2/3 THALER

Silver **Ruler:** Georg II Wilhelm **Rev:** FEIN.SILB added above date

Date	Mintage	VG	F	VF	XF	Unc
1694 JJJ	—	80.00	140	220	300	—

KM# 346.1 2/3 THALER

Silver

Date	Mintage	VG	F	VF	XF	Unc
1692 JJJ	—	40.00	85.00	140	250	—
1693 JJJ	—	40.00	85.00	140	250	—
1694 JJJ	—	40.00	85.00	140	250	—

KM# 346.2 2/3 THALER

Silver **Rev:** REIN. SILB added above date

Date	Mintage	VG	F	VF	XF	Unc
1697 JJJ	—	40.00	85.00	140	220	—

KM# 8 THALER

Silver **Note:** Friendship Thaler. Dav. #6429.

Date	Mintage	VG	F	VF	XF	Unc
1617 HL	—	450	775	1,300	2,150	—

KM# 9.1 THALER

Silver **Obv. Legend:** CHRISTIANUS.D:G:EL:EP:MIND:DUX.BR: ET:LU* **Rev:** Triple-helmeted 8-fold arms divide H-L **Rev. Legend:** IUSTITIA.-ET.CONCORDIA*ANNO.1617 **Note:** Dav.#6430.

Date	Mintage	VG	F	VF	XF	Unc
1617 H-L	—	65.00	130	230	350	—

KM# 9.2 THALER

Silver **Rev:** Helmeted arms divide H-S

Date	Mintage	VG	F	VF	XF	Unc
1617 H-L	—	65.00	130	230	350	—

KM# 9.3 THALER

Silver **Obv. Legend:** CHRISTIAN **Rev:** Arms divide half moon-* **Note:** Dav.#6431.

Date	Mintage	VG	F	VF	XF	Unc
1617 (k)	—	65.00	130	230	350	—

KM# 9.4 THALER

Silver **Obv:** Large rosette at top **Rev:** Legend begins at 9 o'clock, divided at top **Note:** Dav. #6432.

Date	Mintage	VG	F	VF	XF	Unc
1618 (k)	—	65.00	130	230	350	—

KM# 9.5 THALER

Silver **Obv:** Different bust, large collar **Note:** Dav. #A6433.

Date	Mintage	VG	F	VF	XF	Unc
1619 HGM	—	65.00	130	230	350	—

KM# 9.6 THALER

Silver **Obv:** Squatter bust, more ornate collar **Note:** Dav. #6435.

Date	Mintage	VG	F	VF	XF	Unc
1619 (k)	—	65.00	130	230	350	—

KM# 9.7 THALER

Silver **Obv:** Changed armor with spiked edge on collar **Note:** Dav. #6436.

Date	Mintage	VG	F	VF	XF	Unc
1620 (k)	—	65.00	130	230	350	—
1621 (k)	—	65.00	130	230	350	—

KM# 9.8 THALER

Silver **Obv:** Larger bust **Obv. Legend:** BRUN.ET.LU.H/S **Note:** Dav. #6437.

Date	Mintage	VG	F	VF	XF	Unc
1622 H-S	—	65.00	130	230	350	—

KM# 9.9 THALER

Silver **Obv. Legend:** BRU.ET.LU* **Note:** Dav. #6438.

Date	Mintage	VG	F	VF	XF	Unc
1622 (w)	—	65.00	130	230	350	—

KM# 9.10 THALER

Silver **Obv:** Half moon mint mark above bust, drapery with lined sleeves **Rev:** Ornament divides legend **Note:** Dav. #6439.

Date	Mintage	VG	F	VF	XF	Unc
1622 (k)	—	65.00	130	230	350	—

KM# 9.11 THALER

Silver **Obv:** Mint mark S **Obv. Legend:** BRUN ET LUN H **Rev. Legend:** IUSTITIA.-ET.CONCORDIA **Note:** Dav. #6440.

Date	Mintage	VG	F	VF	XF	Unc
16ZZ H-S	—	65.00	130	230	350	—
1623 H-S	—	65.00	130	230	350	—

KM# 9.12 THALER

Silver **Rev. Legend:** ETCON-CORDIA **Note:** Dav. #6440A.

Date	Mintage	VG	F	VF	XF	Unc
1623 H-S	—	65.00	130	230	350	—

KM# 9.13 THALER

Silver **Note:** Similar to KM#9.14 but date at left bottom. Dav. #A6440.

Date	Mintage	VG	F	VF	XF	Unc
1622	—	65.00	130	230	350	—

KM# 9.14 THALER

Silver **Rev. Legend:** ET CON-CORDIA **Note:** Dav. #6441.

Date	Mintage	VG	F	VF	XF	Unc
1622	—	65.00	130	230	350	—
1623	—	65.00	130	230	350	—

KM# 9.15 THALER

Silver **Rev. Legend:** ET CO-NCORDIA **Note:** Dav. #6441A.

Date	Mintage	VG	F	VF	XF	Unc
1623	—	65.00	130	230	350	—

KM# 9.16 THALER

Silver **Obv:** Bust right in circle of stars **Note:** Dav. #6442.

Date	Mintage	VG	F	VF	XF	Unc
1623	—	65.00	130	230	350	—

KM# 9.17 THALER

Silver **Obv:** Bust right without circle of stars **Rev:** Date divided at top by helmeted arms **Note:** Dav. #6456.

Date	Mintage	VG	F	VF	XF	Unc
1624	—	65.00	130	230	350	—

KM# 9.18 THALER

Silver **Rev:** Date in legend at upper left **Note:** Dav. #6457.

Date	Mintage	VG	F	VF	XF	Unc
1624 LB	—	65.00	130	230	350	—

KM# 9.19 THALER

Silver **Obv:** Orb above bust right, legend begins at right **Rev:** Date divided at top by arms **Note:** Dav. #6467.

Date	Mintage	VG	F	VF	XF	Unc
1625	—	65.00	130	230	350	—

KM# 29.1 THALER

Silver **Obv:** Bust right **Obv. Legend:** CHRISTIANUS+ +D:G:EL.EP.MIND:DUX.B.ET.L **Rev:** 5 helmets above arms, legend ending with orb **Note:** Dav. #6444.

Date	Mintage	VG	F	VF	XF	Unc
1620 H-S	—	65.00	130	230	350	—
1624 H-S	—	65.00	130	230	350	—

KM# 29.2 THALER

Silver **Obv:** Orb **Obv. Legend:** CHRISTIANVS.D.G.. **Rev:** Arms divide VF-H **Note:** Dav. #6445.

Date	Mintage	VG	F	VF	XF	Unc
1624 VF-H	—	65.00	130	230	350	—

KM# 17.1 THALER

Silver **Obv:** St. Andrew standing with cross in border of lilies **Rev:** Tri-helmeted arms, date at 8 o'clock **Note:** Dav. #6476.

Date	Mintage	VG	F	VF	XF	Unc
1619	—	80.00	155	295	450	—
1620	—	80.00	155	295	450	—
1621	—	80.00	155	295	450	—
1622	—	80.00	155	295	450	—

KM# 17.2 THALER

Silver **Obv:** Without border of lilies **Note:** Dav. #6476A.

Date	Mintage	VG	F	VF	XF	Unc
1622	—	80.00	155	295	450	—

KM# 17.3 THALER

Silver **Rev:** Legend unbroken by shield at bottom **Note:** Dav. #6477.

Date	Mintage	VG	F	VF	XF	Unc
1619 (k)	—	80.00	155	295	450	—
1622 (k)	—	80.00	155	295	450	—

KM# 17.4 THALER

Silver **Obv:** St. Andrew and cross breaking legend at top **Rev:** Arms breaking legend at bottom, date at top left **Note:** Dav. #6478.

Date	Mintage	VG	F	VF	XF	Unc
1623 H-P	—	80.00	155	295	450	—

KM# 17.5 THALER

Silver **Rev:** Date divided at top, arms divide H-P **Note:** Dav. #6479.

Date	Mintage	VG	F	VF	XF	Unc
1624 H-P	—	80.00	155	295	450	—

KM# 75.1 THALER

Silver **Obv:** Bust right, legend begins at 10 o'clock **Rev:** 9-fold arms with center shield, 3 helmets above, date divided at top **Note:** Dav. #6443.

Date	Mintage	VG	F	VF	XF	Unc
1624	—	65.00	130	230	350	—

KM# 75.2 THALER

Silver **Obv:** Bust right with different drapery, legend begins at top **Rev:** Date at left of plume which divides HV-E **Note:** Dav. #6448.

Date	Mintage	VG	F	VF	XF	Unc
1624 HV-E	—	65.00	130	230	350	—

KM# 75.3 THALER

Silver **Obv:** Different bust, legend begins at 10 o'clock **Rev:** Date left of plume, arms divide HV-E **Note:** Dav. #6449.

Date	Mintage	VG	F	VF	XF	Unc
1624 HV-E	—	65.00	130	230	350	—

KM# 75.4 THALER

Silver **Rev:** Arms divide HU-E **Note:** Dav. #6449A.

Date	Mintage	VG	F	VF	XF	Unc
1624 HU-E	—	65.00	130	230	350	—

KM# 75.5 THALER

Silver **Rev:** Plume above helmeted arms divide date **Note:** Dav. #6450.

Date	Mintage	VG	F	VF	XF	Unc
1624 HV-E	—	65.00	130	230	350	—

KM# 75.6 THALER

Silver **Obv. Legend:** ...DUX.BR.ET.LUN **Rev:** Arms divide L-B **Note:** Dav. #6452.

Date	Mintage	VG	F	VF	XF	Unc
1624 L-B	—	65.00	130	230	350	—

KM# 75.7 THALER

Silver **Obv. Legend:** ...DVX.B.ET.LVNE **Rev:** Arms divide date above and L-B below **Note:** Dav. #6453.

Date	Mintage	VG	F	VF	XF	Unc
1624 L-B	—	65.00	130	230	350	—

KM# 76.1 THALER

Silver **Obv:** Bust right **Rev:** Helmeted arms supported by 2 lions divide HV16-24E at bottom **Note:** Dav. #6446.

Date	Mintage	VG	F	VF	XF	Unc
1624 HV-E	—	65.00	130	230	350	—

KM# 76.2 THALER

Silver **Rev:** Date divided at top, HV-E below **Note:** Dav. #6447.

Date	Mintage	VG	F	VF	XF	Unc
1624 HV-E	—	65.00	130	230	350	—

KM# 76.3 THALER

Silver **Obv. Legend:** CHRISTIANUS **Rev:** Supported arms divide VF-H below **Note:** Dav. #6459.

Date	Mintage	VG	F	VF	XF	Unc
1624 VF-H	—	65.00	130	230	350	—

KM# 29.3 THALER

Silver **Obv:** Large buttons on drapery **Obv. Legend:** MIN.DUX.B.E.L **Note:** Dav. #A6458.

Date	Mintage	VG	F	VF	XF	Unc
1624	—	65.00	130	230	350	—

KM# 29.4 THALER

Silver **Obv:** Small buttons on drapery **Obv. Legend:** MIND.DUX.B.ET.L **Note:** Dav. #6458.

Date	Mintage	VG	F	VF	XF	Unc
1624	—	65.00	130	230	350	—

KM# 29.5 THALER

Silver **Obv. Legend:** ...BR.ET.LU **Rev:** Arms divide HH-O **Note:** Dav. #6460.

Date	Mintage	VG	F	VF	XF	Unc
1624 HH-O	—	65.00	130	230	350	—
1625 HH-O	—	65.00	130	230	350	—

KM# 29.6 THALER

Silver **Obv:** Orb, flowers at edge of collar **Obv. Legend:** ...DUX.:B:E:L **Rev:** Date divided below arms **Note:** Dav. #6461.

Date	Mintage	VG	F	VF	XF	Unc
1625	—	65.00	130	230	350	—

KM# 29.7 THALER

Silver **Obv:** H mm S below bust **Obv. Legend:** ...DUX:B.ET.L **Rev:** Date divided by arms within circle **Note:** Dav. #6464.

Date	Mintage	VG	F	VF	XF	Unc
1625 H-S	—	65.00	130	230	350	—

KM# 29.8 THALER

Silver **Obv:** Without mint mark **Note:** Dav. #6464A.

Date	Mintage	VG	F	VF	XF	Unc
1625	—	65.00	130	230	350	—

KM# 29.9 THALER

Silver **Obv. Legend:** ...DUX.B.E.L **Rev:** Date above in helmets **Note:** Dav. #A6465.

Date	Mintage	VG	F	VF	XF	Unc
1625	—	65.00	130	230	350	—

KM# 29.10 THALER

Silver **Obv. Legend:** ...DUX.B.ET.LU **Rev:** Date below **Note:** Dav. #6465.

Date	Mintage	VG	F	VF	XF	Unc
1625	—	65.00	130	230	350	—

KM# 29.11 THALER

Silver **Obv. Legend:** D:G:EL++H mm S++EP **Rev:** Date divided above arms **Note:** Dav. #6468.

Date	Mintage	VG	F	VF	XF	Unc
1626 H-S	—	65.00	130	230	350	—

KM# 29.12 THALER

Silver **Obv:** Different bust **Rev:** Date divided by curved arms at bottom **Note:** Dav. #6469.

Date	Mintage	VG	F	VF	XF	Unc
1626	—	65.00	130	230	350	—

KM# 29.13 THALER

Silver **Obv. Legend:** ...LU **Rev:** Arms divide date in straight line **Note:** Dav. #6470.

Date	Mintage	VG	F	VF	XF	Unc
1626	—	65.00	130	230	350	—

KM# 29.14 THALER

Silver **Obv:** Different bust **Obv. Legend:** CHRISTIANUS. D: G: EL. H mm S EP. MIND. DUX. B. ET .LU **Rev:** Helmeted oval arms, date divided at top **Rev. Legend:** JUSTITIA. ET. - CONCORDIA **Note:** Dav. #6471. Legend varieties exist.

Date	Mintage	VG	F	VF	XF	Unc
1627 H-S	—	65.00	130	230	350	—
1628 H-S	—	65.00	130	230	350	—
1629 H-S	—	65.00	130	230	350	—

KM# 29.15 THALER

Silver **Rev. Legend:** ET.CO.-.NCORDIA **Note:** Dav. #6471A.

Date	Mintage	VG	F	VF	XF	Unc
1627	—	65.00	130	230	350	—

KM# 29.16 THALER

Silver **Obv. Legend:** MIND.DUX.B.ET.L **Rev:** Square topped arms **Note:** Dav. #6473.

Date	Mintage	VG	F	VF	XF	Unc
1629	—	65.00	130	230	350	—

KM# 90 THALER

Silver **Note:** Varieties exist. Dav. #6475.

Date	Mintage	VG	F	VF	XF	Unc
1629 H-S	—	65.00	130	230	350	—
1630 H-S	—	65.00	130	230	350	—
1631 H-S	—	65.00	130	230	350	—
1632 H-S	—	65.00	130	230	350	—
1633 H-S	—	65.00	130	230	350	—

KM# A90 THALER

Silver **Subject:** Death of Wilhelm V's Son, Johann **Obv:** 10-fold arms in ornamented shield **Rev:** 8-line inscription with dates, mintmaster's initials, symbol below **Note:** Dav. #6656.

Date	Mintage	VG	F	VF	XF	Unc
16Z8 HS	—	450	850	1,250	—	—

KM# 100 THALER

Silver **Note:** Similar to KM#17, but 5-helmeted 9-fold arms. Dav. #6480.

Date	Mintage	VG	F	VF	XF	Unc
1631 H-S	—	80.00	155	295	450	—
1632 H-S	—	80.00	155	295	450	—
1633 H-S	—	80.00	155	295	450	—

KM# A107 THALER

Silver **Subject:** Death of Wilhelm V's Son, Magnus **Obv:** 10-fold arms in ornamented shield, titles of Magnus **Rev:** Ornament above 6-line inscription with dates, mintmaster's initials, symbol below **Note:** Dav. #6657.

Date	Mintage	VG	F	VF	XF	Unc
1632 HS	—	450	850	1,250	—	—

KM# 107 THALER

Silver **Subject:** Death of Christian **Note:** Dav. #6482.

Date	Mintage	VG	F	VF	XF	Unc
1633 HS	—	155	260	650	—	—

KM# 134.1 THALER

Silver **Subject:** Joint coinage of August I with Friedrich V and Georg of Calenberg **Obv:** Half-length figure of August 3/4 to right **Rev:** Half-length figures of Friedrich and Georg facing each other, date below **Note:** Dav. #6484.

Date	Mintage	VG	F	VF	XF	Unc
1636 HS	—	650	1,100	1,800	2,950	—

KM# 134.2 THALER

Silver **Obv:** Smaller busts **Obv. Legend:** FRIDERIC: ET. GEORG: DUCES. BRUNSVIC. ET. LUN **Note:** Dav. #6485.

Date	Mintage	VG	F	VF	XF	Unc
1636 HS	—	650	1,100	1,800	2,950	—

KM# 145.1 THALER

Silver **Obv:** Bust left breaks circle **Rev:** Helmeted 11-fold arms, date divided below **Note:** Dav. #6491.

Date	Mintage	VG	F	VF	XF	Unc
1637 HS	—	260	425	675	1,100	—

KM# 145.2 THALER

Silver **Obv:** Bust left within circle **Note:** Dav. #6491A.

Date	Mintage	VG	F	VF	XF	Unc
1637 HS	—	295	500	775	1,250	—

KM# 146.1 THALER

Silver **Obv:** Bust right in ornate circle, script legend **Obv. Legend:** FRIDERICH HERTZOG. ZU. BR. UND. LUNEB. THUMPROBST DES ERTZSTIF BREM. **Rev:** Helmeted arms, H mintmark S, dividing date below **Note:** Dav. #6492.

Date	Mintage	VG	F	VF	XF	Unc
1637 H-S	—	65.00	130	240	400	—
1638 H-S	—	65.00	130	240	400	—

KM# 146.2 THALER

Silver **Obv. Legend:** FRIDER(ICH) HERT(Z). ZU. B. U. L. COADI. DS STIF(T)RATZB. THUM(P). D. E(RTZST). B(R) (E) (M) (E). **Note:** Dav. #6494.

Date	Mintage	VG	F	VF	XF	Unc
1637 HS	—	65.00	130	240	400	—
1638 HS	—	65.00	130	240	400	—
1639 HS	—	65.00	130	240	400	—
1640 HS	—	65.00	130	240	400	—
1640 LW	—	65.00	130	240	400	—
1641 LW	—	65.00	130	240	400	—
1642 LW	—	65.00	130	240	400	—
1643 LW	—	65.00	130	240	400	—

KM# 155.1 THALER

Silver **Obv:** Friedrich V **Note:** Dav. #6488.

Date	Mintage	VG	F	VF	XF	Unc
1641 HS	—	105	195	350	550	—
1643 HS	—	105	195	350	550	—
1645 HS	—	105	195	350	550	—
1648 HS	—	105	195	350	550	—
1649 HS Error	—	105	195	350	550	—
ND HS	—	105	195	350	550	—

KM# 155.2 THALER

Silver **Obv:** Baton in right hand **Note:** Dav. #6489.

Date	Mintage	VG	F	VF	XF	Unc
ND(1651)	—	260	450	775	1,150	—

KM# 156 THALER

Silver **Obv:** Title:...HERTZOG... **Note:** Dav. #6490.

Date	Mintage	VG	F	VF	XF	Unc
ND(1651) HS	—	105	195	325	525	—

KM# 168 THALER

Silver **Subject:** Death of Friedrich's sister, Margarethe, Wife of Johann Casimir of Saxe-Coburg **Obv:** Helmeted 12-fold arms **Rev:** 12-line inscription with date **Note:** Dav. #6501.

Date	Mintage	VG	F	VF	XF	Unc
1643 LW	—	295	500	775	1,150	—

KM# 166 THALER

Silver **Obv:** Similar to KM#169.1 **Rev:** Similar to KM#169.1 but date at lower right **Note:** Dav. #6495.

Date	Mintage	VG	F	VF	XF	Unc
1643 LW	—	65.00	130	240	400	—

KM# 167 THALER

Silver **Note:** Varieties exist. Dav. #6487.

Date	Mintage	VG	F	VF	XF	Unc
1643 HS	—	65.00	130	230	350	—
1644 HS	—	65.00	130	230	350	—
1645 HS	—	65.00	130	230	350	—
ND HS	—	65.00	130	230	350	—
ND	—	65.00	130	230	350	—

KM# 169.1 THALER

Silver **Note:** Dav. #6497.

Date	Mintage	VG	F	VF	XF	Unc
1644 LW	—	65.00	130	240	400	—
1645 LW	—	65.00	130	240	400	—
1646 LW	—	65.00	130	240	400	—
1647 LW	—	65.00	130	240	400	—

KM# 169.2 THALER

Silver **Rev:** Date horizontal or slanting right of arms **Note:** Dav. #6498.

Date	Mintage	VG	F	VF	XF	Unc
1647 LW	—	65.00	130	240	400	—
1648 LW	—	65.00	130	240	400	—

KM# 170 THALER

Silver **Note:** Dav. #6486.

Date	Mintage	VG	F	VF	XF	Unc
1644 HS	—	65.00	130	230	350	—
ND	—	65.00	130	230	350	—

KM# 192 THALER

Silver **Subject:** Death of Friedrich V **Note:** Dav. #6500.

Date	Mintage	VG	F	VF	XF	Unc
1648 LW	—	130	230	400	575	—

KM# 209 THALER

Silver **Obv:** KM#208 **Rev:** Similar to KM#210, but date divided by wildman **Note:** Mule.

Date	Mintage	VG	F	VF	XF	Unc
1648/49 HS Rare	—	—	—	—	—	—

KM# 211 THALER

Silver **Obv:** Helmeted arms **Obv. Legend:** CHRISTIAN: LUDOVI: CUS D.G. DUX BR: ET LUNEBERG **Rev:** Rearing horse left **Rev. Legend:** SINCERE ET CONSTANTOR ANNO **Note:** Dav. #6521.

Date	Mintage	VG	F	VF	XF	Unc
1649 LW	—	65.00	130	230	350	—
1650 LW	—	65.00	130	230	350	—
1651 LW	—	65.00	130	230	350	—
1652 LW	—	65.00	130	230	350	—
1653 LW	—	65.00	130	230	350	—
1654 LW	—	65.00	130	230	350	—
1655 LW	—	65.00	130	230	350	—
1656 LW	—	65.00	130	230	350	—
1657 LW	—	65.00	130	230	350	—
1658 LW	—	65.00	130	230	350	—
1659 LW	—	65.00	130	230	350	—
1660 LW	—	65.00	130	230	350	—
1661 LW	—	65.00	130	230	350	—
1662 LW	—	65.00	130	230	350	—
1663 LW	—	65.00	130	230	350	—
1664 LW	—	65.00	130	230	350	—
1665 LW	—	65.00	130	230	350	—

KM# 208 THALER

Silver **Obv:** 3/4-length bust right **Rev:** Helmeted 12-fold arms, date in legend **Note:** Dav. #6514.

Date	Mintage	VG	F	VF	XF	Unc
1649 HS	—	155	295	525	850	—

KM# 229 THALER

Silver **Subject:** Death of Sybilla, Second Wife of Julius Ernst zu Dannenberg **Obv:** Helmeted 12-fold arms **Rev:** 9-line inscription with date **Note:** Dav. #6523.

Date	Mintage	VG	F	VF	XF	Unc
1652 LW Rare	—	—	—	—	—	—

KM# 237 THALER

Silver **Rev:** Tree in left hand **Note:** Dav. #6518.

Date	Mintage	VG	F	VF	XF	Unc
1654 HS	—	65.00	130	230	350	—
1655 HS	—	65.00	130	230	350	—
1658 HS	—	65.00	130	230	350	—
1659 HS	—	65.00	130	230	350	—
1660 HS	—	65.00	130	230	350	—
1661 HS	—	65.00	130	230	350	—
1662 HS	—	65.00	130	230	350	—
1665 HS	—	65.00	130	230	350	—

KM# 238 THALER

Silver **Rev:** Tree in both hands **Note:** Dav. #6517A.

Date	Mintage	VG	F	VF	XF	Unc
1655 HS	—	65.00	130	230	350	—

KM# 241 THALER

Silver **Obv:** Helmeted 12-fold arms **Rev:** Wildman, PIETATE..., date in legend (die of Georg Wilhelm) **Note:** Mule. Dav. #6522.

Date	Mintage	VG	F	VF	XF	Unc
1657 HS	—	65.00	130	230	350	—
1662 HS	—	65.00	130	230	350	—

KM# 247 THALER

Silver **Subject:** Death of Christian Ludwig's Aunt Clara **Obv:** Horse leaping left in laurel wreath **Rev:** 9-line inscription with date **Note:** Dav. #6524.

Date	Mintage	VG	F	VF	XF	Unc
1658 LW	—	195	350	575	900	—

KM# 210 THALER

Silver **Note:** Dav. #6519.

Date	Mintage	VG	F	VF	XF	Unc
1663 HS	—	65.00	130	230	350	—
1664 HS	—	65.00	130	230	350	—
1665 HS	—	65.00	130	230	350	—

KM# 268 THALER

Silver **Subject:** Death of Christian Ludwig **Note:** Dav. #6525.

Date	Mintage	VG	F	VF	XF	Unc
1665 LW	—	130	260	425	725	—
1665 HS	—	130	260	425	725	—

KM# 285 THALER

Silver **Obv:** Bust left **Rev:** Horse leaping left, date in legend **Note:** Dav. #6537.

Date	Mintage	VG	F	VF	XF	Unc
1673 RD Rare	—	—	—	—	—	—

KM# 286 THALER

Silver **Obv:** Horse leaping left **Rev:** Helmeted 12-fold arms, date in legend **Note:** Dav. #6538.

Date	Mintage	VG	F	VF	XF	Unc
1673 RD Rare	—	—	—	—	—	—
1674 RD Rare	—	—	—	—	—	—

KM# 287 THALER

Silver **Obv:** Bust left

Date	Mintage	VG	F	VF	XF	Unc
1673 RD Rare	—	—	—	—	—	—

KM# 302 THALER

Silver **Subject:** 100th Anniversary of the University of Helmstedt **Obv:** Samson wrestling lion in cartouche **Note:** Dav. #6543.

Date	Mintage	VG	F	VF	XF	Unc
1676	—	260	450	775	1,150	—

KM# 332 THALER

Silver **Obv:** Bust right **Rev:** Horse leaping left in circle broken by ground below which divides date **Note:** Dav. #6539.

Date	Mintage	VG	F	VF	XF	Unc
1690 JJJ Rare	—	—	—	—	—	—

KM# 342 THALER

Silver **Obv:** Helmeted 12-fold arms **Rev:** Horse leaping left, date below **Note:** Dav. #6540.

Date	Mintage	VG	F	VF	XF	Unc
1691 Rare	—	—	—	—	—	—
1691 iii Rare	—	—	—	—	—	—

KM# 343 THALER

Silver **Obv:** Bust right **Rev:** Helmeted 12-fold arms, date in legend **Note:** Dav. #6541.

Date	Mintage	VG	F	VF	XF	Unc
1691 iii	—	450	775	1,300	2,150	—

KM# 249 1-1/2 THALER

43.1300 g., Silver, 59 mm. **Obv:** Triple-helmeted 8-fold arms with central shield **Rev:** Rider on rearing horse to right, without value **Note:** Illustration reduced. Dav. #LS125.

Date	Mintage	VG	F	VF	XF	Unc
ND(1622 W)	—	3,000	4,700	6,800	—	—

KM# 250 1-1/2 THALER

42.8000 g., Silver, 62 mm. **Obv:** Crowned CL monogram in laurel wreath surrounded by 14 small shields, date in legend, 1-1/2 punched in **Rev:** Horse leaping left above mining scene, head turned up towards wreath held by arms from clouds **Note:** Illustration reduced. Dav. #LS166.

Date	Mintage	VG	F	VF	XF	Unc
1659 L-W	—	600	1,000	1,700	3,000	—

KM# 251.1 1-1/2 THALER

Silver **Rev:** Horse looking ahead, wreath held in arm from clouds above head **Note:** Dav. #LS164.

Date	Mintage	VG	F	VF	XF	Unc
1659 L-W	—	350	600	1,000	1,600	—

KM# 251.2 1-1/2 THALER

Silver **Note:** Dav. #LS170.

Date	Mintage	VG	F	VF	XF	Unc
1661 L-W	—	350	600	1,000	1,600	—

KM# 251.3 1-1/2 THALER

Silver **Note:** Dav. #LS175. Illustration reduced.

Date	Mintage	VG	F	VF	XF	Unc
1662 L-W	—	350	600	1,000	1,600	—

KM# 251.4 1-1/2 THALER

Silver **Note:** Dav. #LS179.

Date	Mintage	VG	F	VF	XF	Unc
1663 L-W	—	350	600	1,000	1,600	—

KM# 251.5 1-1/2 THALER

Silver, 62 mm. **Note:** Illustration reduced. Dav. #LS190. Varieties exist.

Date	Mintage	VG	F	VF	XF	Unc
1664 L-W	—	350	600	1,000	1,600	—

KM# 303 1-1/2 THALER

Silver **Subject:** 100th Anniversary of the University of Helmstedt **Note:** Similar to 1 Thaler, KM#302. Dav. #6542.

Date	Mintage	VG	F	VF	XF	Unc
1676 Rare	—	—	—	—	—	—

KM# 18 2 THALER

Silver **Note:** Similar to 1 Thaler, KM#9. Dav. #6533. Varieties exist.

Date	Mintage	VG	F	VF	XF	Unc
1619 HGM Rare	—	—	—	—	—	—
1624 H-S Rare	—	—	—	—	—	—
1625 Rare	—	—	—	—	—	—

KM# 77.1 2 THALER

Silver **Obv:** Bust right, H-S below **Obv. Legend:** CHRISTIANUS D: G. EL. EP MIND.-DUX. B. ET. L. **Rev:** Helmeted arms divide date above **Rev. Legend:** IUSTITIA ET CO.-.NCORDIA. ANNO. **Note:** Dav. #6554.

Date	Mintage	VG	F	VF	XF	Unc
1624 H-S Rare	—	—	—	—	—	—

KM# 77.2 2 THALER

Silver **Obv. Legend:** ...+D. G. EL. EP: M + DUX. B. EL. **Note:** Dav. #6555.

Date	Mintage	VG	F	VF	XF	Unc
1624 Rare	—	—	—	—	—	—

KM# 77.3 2 THALER

Silver **Obv. Legend:** ...D: G*H (mm). S*EL. EP. MIND. DUX. B. L. **Rev. Legend:** ...ET-CONCORDIA **Note:** Dav. #6562.

Date	Mintage	VG	F	VF	XF	Unc
1625 H-S Rare	—	—	—	—	—	—

KM# 77.4 2 THALER

Silver **Rev:** Arms divided date below **Note:** Dav. #6563.

Date	Mintage	VG	F	VF	XF	Unc
1625 H-S Rare	—	—	—	—	—	—

KM# 77.5 2 THALER

Silver **Obv. Legend:** Ends: DUX. B. E. L. **Rev:** Date divided at top by plume, shorter and wider shield **Note:** Dav. #6572.

Date	Mintage	VG	F	VF	XF	Unc
1629 H-S Rare	—	—	—	—	—	—

KM# 77.6 2 THALER

Silver **Rev:** Square-topped arms **Note:** Dav. #6573.

Date	Mintage	VG	F	VF	XF	Unc
1629 H-S Rare	—	—	—	—	—	—

KM# 101 2 THALER

Silver **Note:** Dav. #6574. Similar to 1 Thaler, KM#90.

Date	Mintage	VG	F	VF	XF	Unc
1631 HS Rare	—	—	—	—	—	—

KM# 108 2 THALER

Silver **Subject:** Death of Christian **Note:** Dav. #6581. Similar to 1 Thaler, KM#107.

Date	Mintage	VG	F	VF	XF	Unc
1633 HS Rare	—	—	—	—	—	—

KM# 109 2 THALER

65.5000 g., Silver **Obv:** Duke August on horse to right **Rev:** Fortune with sail in hands, battle scene in background without value **Note:** Dav. #LS127.

Date	Mintage	VG	F	VF	XF	Unc
ND +M+ Rare	—	—	—	—	—	—

KM# 137 2 THALER

Silver **Obv:** Half-length figure of August 3/4 right **Rev:** Half-length figures of Friedrich and Georg facing each other, date below **Note:** Joint Coinage of August I with Friedrich V and Georg of Calenberg. Dav. #6483.

Date	Mintage	VG	F	VF	XF	Unc
1636 HS Rare	—	—	—	—	—	—

KM# 157 2 THALER

Silver **Note:** Similar to 1 Thaler, KM#146. Dav. #6493.

Date	Mintage	VG	F	VF	XF	Unc
1641 LW Rare	—	—	—	—	—	—

KM# 174.1 2 THALER

Silver **Obv:** Different bust **Obv. Legend:** ...BR. U. LUN. P. C. D. S. R. E. D. P. D. E. B. **Rev:** Date slanted left of arms **Note:** Dav. #6496.

Date	Mintage	VG	F	VF	XF	Unc
1646 LW	—	850	1,450	2,400	3,850	—

KM# 174.2 2 THALER

Silver **Obv. Legend:** ...BR: LUNBURG. **Rev:** Date slanted left of arms **Note:** Dav. #A6498.

Date	Mintage	VG	F	VF	XF	Unc
1648 LW	—	850	1,450	2,400	3,850	—

KM# 193 2 THALER

Silver **Subject:** Death of Friedrich V **Note:** Similar to 1 Thaler, KM#192. Dav. #6499.

Date	Mintage	VG	F	VF	XF	Unc
1648 LW Rare	—	—	—	—	—	—

KM# 221 2 THALER

Silver **Note:** Similar to 1 Thaler, KM#211. Dav. #6520.

Date	Mintage	VG	F	VF	XF	Unc
1650 LW Rare	—	—	—	—	—	—

KM# 242.1 2 THALER

Silver **Obv:** Crowned CL monogram in laurel wreath surrounded by 14 small shields, date in legend, 2 punched in **Rev:** Horse leaping left above mining scene, head turned up towards wreath held by arm from clouds **Note:** Dav. #LS162. Illustration reduced.

Date	Mintage	VG	F	VF	XF	Unc
1657 LW	—	500	850	1,350	2,150	—

KM# 242.2 2 THALER

Silver **Note:** Dav. #LS165. Illustration reduced.

Date	Mintage	VG	F	VF	XF	Unc
1659 LW	—	500	850	1,350	2,150	—

KM# 252.1 2 THALER

Silver **Note:** Similar to 1-1/2 Thaler, KM#251 but 2 punched in. Dav. #LS163. Illustration reduced.

Date	Mintage	VG	F	VF	XF	Unc
1659 LW	—	500	850	1,350	2,150	—

KM# 252.2 2 THALER

Silver **Note:** Dav. #LS169.

Date	Mintage	VG	F	VF	XF	Unc
1661 LW	—	500	850	1,350	2,150	—

KM# 252.3 2 THALER

Silver **Note:** Dav. #LS174. Illustration reduced.

Date	Mintage	VG	F	VF	XF	Unc
1662 LW	—	500	850	1,350	2,150	—

KM# 252.4 2 THALER

Silver **Note:** Dav. #LS178.

Date	Mintage	VG	F	VF	XF	Unc
1663 LW	—	500	850	1,350	2,150	—

KM# 252.5 2 THALER

Silver, 64 mm. **Ruler:** Christian Ludwig **Note:** Dav. #LS189. Illustration reduced.

Date	Mintage	VG	F	VF	XF	Unc
1664 LW	—	500	850	1,350	2,150	—

KM# 194 2-1/2 THALER

78.0000 g., Silver **Ruler:** Christian Ludwig **Obv:** Duke on rearing horse right **Rev:** Helmeted 12-fold arms, date in legend **Note:** Dav. #LS147A.

Date	Mintage	VG	F	VF	XF	Unc
1648 HS Rare	—	—	—	—	—	—

KM# 80 3 THALER

Silver **Obv:** 3/4-length figure 3/4 to right, helmet on table at right **Rev:** Helmeted and supported 9-fold arms with central shield, Roman numeral date in legend, 3 punched in **Note:** Dav. #LS119.

Date	Mintage	VG	F	VF	XF	Unc
1625 HB Rare	—	—	—	—	—	—

KM# 91 3 THALER
Silver **Rev:** Arabic date divided at top **Note:** Dav. #LS123.

Date	Mintage	VG	F	VF	XF	Unc
1629 HL-HS Rare	—	—	—	—	—	—

KM# 110 3 THALER
85.0000 g., Silver **Subject:** Death of Christian **Note:** Similar to 1 Thaler, KM#107.

Date	Mintage	VG	F	VF	XF	Unc
1633 HS Rare	—	—	—	—	—	—

KM# 151 3 THALER
86.6000 g., Silver, 81 mm. **Rev:** 3 punched in **Note:** Illustration reduced. Dav. #LS131.

Date	Mintage	VG	F	VF	XF	Unc
1639 HS	—	1,550	2,600	4,250	5,900	—

KM# 177 3 THALER
Silver, 80 mm. **Obv:** Bust right in wreath surrounded by 14 small shields **Rev:** Mining scene, date in legend, 3 punched in **Note:** Illustration reduced. Dav. #LS135.

Date	Mintage	VG	F	VF	XF	Unc
1647 LW	—	1,300	2,400	3,900	5,500	—

KM# 178 3 THALER
Silver **Obv:** Inscription instead of wreath around bust **Note:** Dav. #LS-A135.

Date	Mintage	VG	F	VF	XF	Unc
1647 HR-LW Rare	—	—	—	—	—	—

KM# 195 3 THALER
Silver, 71 mm. **Ruler:** Christian Ludwig **Rev:** 84 g or 3 punched in **Note:** Illustration reduced. Dav. #LS146.

Date	Mintage	VG	F	VF	XF	Unc
1648 HS	—	900	1,650	2,950	5,200	—

KM# 222.1 3 THALER
Silver **Obv:** Similar to 1-1/2 Thaler, KM#251 but ca. 85 g or 3 punched in **Note:** Dav. #LS150.

Date	Mintage	VG	F	VF	XF	Unc
1650 LW	—	900	1,650	2,950	5,200	—

KM# 222.2 3 THALER
Silver **Note:** Dav. #LS159.

Date	Mintage	VG	F	VF	XF	Unc
1657 LW	—	900	1,650	2,950	5,200	—

KM# 222.3 3 THALER
Silver **Note:** Dav. #LS173.

Date	Mintage	VG	F	VF	XF	Unc
1662 LW	—	900	1,650	2,950	5,200	—

KM# 222.4 3 THALER
Silver **Note:** Dav. #LS177.

Date	Mintage	VG	F	VF	XF	Unc
1663 LW	—	900	1,650	2,950	5,200	—

KM# 222.5 3 THALER
Silver **Note:** Dav. #LS188.

Date	Mintage	VG	F	VF	XF	Unc
1664 LW	—	900	1,650	2,950	5,200	—

KM# 230 3 THALER
Silver **Note:** Dav. #LS156.

Date	Mintage	VG	F	VF	XF	Unc
1654 LW	—	650	1,150	2,150	3,600	—

KM# 243 3 THALER

Silver, 72 mm. **Note:** Illustration reduced. Dav. #LS161.

Date	Mintage	VG	F	VF	XF	Unc
1657 LW	—	575	1,100	1,950	3,250	—

KM# 256.1 3 THALER

Silver, 80 mm. **Obv:** 3 punched in at bottom **Note:** Illustration reduced. Dav. #LS181.

Date	Mintage	VG	F	VF	XF	Unc
1663 HS Rare	—	—	—	—	—	—

KM# 256.2 3 THALER

Silver **Note:** Dav. #LS192. Illustration reduced.

Date	Mintage	VG	F	VF	XF	Unc
1665 HS	—	2,600	4,550	7,200	10,000	—

KM# 196 3-1/2 THALER

Silver **Obv:** Duke on rearing horse right **Rev:** Helmeted 12-fold arms, date in legend **Note:** Dav. #LS146b. Approximate weight: 99.00 grams.

Date	Mintage	VG	F	VF	XF	Unc
1648 HS Rare	—	—	—	—	—	—

KM# 81 4 THALER

116.0000 g., Silver **Obv:** 3/4-length figure 3/4 to right, helmet on table at right **Rev:** Helmeted and supproted 9-fold arms with central shield, roman numeral date in legend, without value **Note:** Dav. #LS118.

Date	Mintage	VG	F	VF	XF	Unc
1625 NZ	—	3,900	5,900	8,500	12,500	—

KM# 93 4 THALER

116.0000 g., Silver **Rev:** Arabic date divided at top **Note:** Dav. #LS122.

Date	Mintage	VG	F	VF	XF	Unc
1629 HL-HS Rare	—	—	—	—	—	—

KM# 147 4 THALER

116.0000 g., Silver **Obv:** Facing bust, inscription, date in tablet below, two legends **Rev:** Brunswick helmet surrounded by 14 small shields **Note:** Dav. #LS128.

Date	Mintage	VG	F	VF	XF	Unc
1637 HS	—	—	—	—	—	—

KM# 152 4 THALER

116.0000 g., Silver **Ruler:** Friedrich V **Note:** Similar to 3 Thaler, KM#151 but 4 punched in. Dav. #LS130. Illustration reduced.

Date	Mintage	VG	F	VF	XF	Unc
1639 HS	—	2,300	3,600	5,200	—	—

KM# 179 4 THALER

116.0000 g., Silver, 86 mm. **Note:** Illustration reduced. Dav. #LS134.

Date	Mintage	VG	F	VF	XF	Unc
1647 LW Rare	—	—	—	—	—	—

KM# 180 4 THALER

115.4000 g., Silver, 80 mm. **Obv:** Inscription instead of wreath around bust **Rev:** 4 punched in **Note:** Illustration reduced. Dav. #LS134a.

Date	Mintage	VG	F	VF	XF	Unc
1647 HR-LW	—	—	—	—	—	—

Note: Spink Taisei Zurich Milas sale 4-92 XF realized $12,730

KM# 197 4 THALER

114.9000 g., Silver, 70 mm. **Ruler:** Christian Ludwig **Note:** Similar to 3 Thaler, KM#195. Dav. #LS145. Illustration reduced.

Date	Mintage	VG	F	VF	XF	Unc
1648 HS	—	1,950	3,250	4,900	—	—

KM# 223.1 4 THALER

Silver, 79 mm. **Ruler:** Christian Ludwig **Obv:** Ca. 115 g or 4 punched in **Note:** Similar to 1-1/2 Thaler, KM#251. Dav. #LS149.

Date	Mintage	VG	F	VF	XF	Unc
1650 LW	—	1,750	2,950	4,550	6,500	—

KM# 231 4 THALER

115.3000 g., Silver, 72 mm. **Note:** Illustration reduced. Dav. #LS155.

Date	Mintage	VG	F	VF	XF	Unc
1654 LW	—	1,300	2,200	3,450	—	—

KM# 223.2 4 THALER

Silver **Note:** Dav. #LS158. Illustration reduced.

Date	Mintage	VG	F	VF	XF	Unc
1657 LW	—	1,750	2,950	4,550	6,500	—

KM# 223.3 4 THALER

Silver **Note:** Dav. #LS172.

Date	Mintage	VG	F	VF	XF	Unc
1662 LW	—	1,750	2,950	4,550	6,500	—

KM# 223.4 4 THALER

Silver **Note:** Dav. #LS176.

Date	Mintage	VG	F	VF	XF	Unc
1663 LW	—	1,750	2,950	4,550	6,500	—

KM# 223.5 4 THALER

Silver **Note:** Dav. #LS187. Illustration reduced.

Date	Mintage	VG	F	VF	XF	Unc
1664 LW	—	1,750	2,950	4,550	6,500	—

KM# 244 4 THALER

115.3000 g., Silver **Rev:** Horse leaping left above mining scene, head turned up towards wreath held by arm from clouds **Note:** Dav. #LS160. Illustration reduced.

Date	Mintage	VG	F	VF	XF	Unc
1657 LW	—	1,550	2,600	4,250	—	—

KM# 257.1 4 THALER

115.1000 g., Silver, 75 mm. **Obv:** 4 punched in at bottom **Rev:** Wildman, tree in right hand, mining scene, in background, date in legend **Note:** Dav. #LS180.

Date	Mintage	VG	F	VF	XF	Unc
1663 HS	—	3,900	6,200	8,800	—	—

KM# 257.2 4 THALER

Silver **Rev:** Periods separate legend **Note:** Dav. #LS191.

Date	Mintage	VG	F	VF	XF	Unc
1665 HS	—	3,900	6,200	8,800	—	—

KM# 82 5 THALER

150.0000 g., Silver **Obv:** 3/4-length figure 3/4 to right, helmet on table at right **Rev:** Helmeted and supported 9-fold arms with central shield, Roman numeral date in legend, without value **Note:** Dav. #LS117.

Date	Mintage	VG	F	VF	XF	Unc
1625 NZ Rare	—	—	—	—	—	—

KM# 94 5 THALER

Silver **Rev:** Arabic date divided at top, 5 punched in **Note:** Dav. #LS121.

Date	Mintage	VG	F	VF	XF	Unc
1629 HL-HS Rare	—	—	—	—	—	—

KM# 26.1 5 THALER
Silver **Obv:** Duke **Obv. Legend:** ...GEORG HERTZOG ZU... **Rev:** Helmeted and supported arms **Note:** Dav. #LS141.

Date	Mintage	VG	F	VF	XF	Unc
1638	—	2,350	3,900	6,500	9,100	—

KM# 26.2 5 THALER
Silver **Obv. Legend:** GEORG HIERTZOG ZU... **Note:** Dav. #LS141a. Illustration reduced.

Date	Mintage	VG	F	VF	XF	Unc
1638	—	2,350	3,900	6,500	9,100	—

KM# 153 5 THALER
Silver **Ruler:** Friedrich V **Obv:** Facing bust in baroque frame **Rev:** Helmeted 12-fold arms, date divided at top, 5 punched in **Note:** Dav. #LS129. Illustration reduced.

Date	Mintage	VG	F	VF	XF	Unc
1639 HS	—	4,250	6,500	9,800	13,000	—

KM# 182 5 THALER
Silver **Obv:** Inscription instead of wreath around bust **Note:** Dav. #LS133a.

Date	Mintage	VG	F	VF	XF	Unc
1647 HR-LW Rare	—	—	—	—	—	—

KM# 181 5 THALER
Silver **Rev:** 5 punched in **Note:** Similar to 4 Thaler, KM#179. Dav. #LS133. Illustration reduced.

Date	Mintage	VG	F	VF	XF	Unc
1647 LW	—	3,600	5,500	8,100	11,000	—

KM# 198 5 THALER
144.7000 g., Silver **Obv:** Duke on rearing horse right **Rev:** Helmeted 12-fold arms, date in legend **Note:** Dav. #LS144.

Date	Mintage	VG	F	VF	XF	Unc
1648 HS	—	3,250	5,200	7,800	—	—

KM# 232 5 THALER
Silver **Rev:** Horse above city view of Celle **Note:** Similar to 4 Thaler, KM#231. Dav. #LS186.

Date	Mintage	VG	F	VF	XF	Unc
1654 LW Rare	—	—	—	—	—	—

KM# 245 5 THALER
144.0000 g., Silver **Note:** Similar to 3 Thaler, KM#243. Dav. #LS-A160.

Date	Mintage	VG	F	VF	XF	Unc
1657 LW Rare	—	—	—	—	—	—

KM# 224.1 5 THALER
Silver **Obv:** 5 punched in **Note:** Similar to 1-1/2 Thaler, KM#251. Dav. #LS148. Illustration reduced.

Date	Mintage	VG	F	VF	XF	Unc
1650 LW	—	2,950	4,900	7,500	9,800	—

KM# 224.2 5 THALER
Silver **Note:** Dav. #LS157.

Date	Mintage	VG	F	VF	XF	Unc
1657 LW	—	2,950	4,900	7,500	9,800	—

KM# 224.3 5 THALER
Silver **Note:** Dav. #LS171.

Date	Mintage	VG	F	VF	XF	Unc
1662 LW	—	2,950	4,900	7,500	9,800	—

KM# 224.4 5 THALER
Silver **Note:** Dav. #LS186.

Date	Mintage	VG	F	VF	XF	Unc
1664 LW	—	2,950	4,900	7,500	9,800	—

KM# 83 6 THALER
174.0000 g., Silver **Obv:** 3/4-length figure 3/4 to right, helmet on table at right **Rev:** Helmeted and supported 9-fold arms with central shield, Roman numeral date in legend, without value **Note:** Dav. #LS116. Illustration reduced.

Date	Mintage	VG	F	VF	XF	Unc
1625 NZ Rare	—	—	—	—	—	—

KM# 183 6 THALER
Silver **Obv:** Bust right in inscription surrounded by 14 small shields **Rev:** Mining scene, date in legend; 6 punched in **Note:** Dav. #LS-A133.

Date	Mintage	VG	F	VF	XF	Unc
1647 HR-LW Rare	—	—	—	—	—	—

KM# 199 6 THALER
Silver **Obv:** Duke on rearing horse right **Rev:** Helmeted 12-fold arms, date in legend **Note:** Dav. #LS143.

Date	Mintage	VG	F	VF	XF	Unc
1648 HS Rare	—	—	—	—	—	—

KM# 233.1 6 THALER
Silver **Obv:** Crowned CL monogram in laurel wreath surrounded by 14 small shields, date in legend, 6 punched in **Rev:** Horse leaping left above city view of Celle, head turned up towards wreath held by arm from clouds **Note:** Dav. #LS153.

Date	Mintage	VG	F	VF	XF	Unc
1654 LW Rare	—	—	—	—	—	—

KM# 233.2 6 THALER
Silver **Note:** Dav. #LS168.

Date	Mintage	VG	F	VF	XF	Unc
1660 LW Rare	—	—	—	—	—	—

KM# 259 6 THALER

Silver **Note:** Similar to 1-1/2 Thaler, KM#251. Dav. #LS185. Illustration reduced.

Date	Mintage	VG	F	VF	XF	Unc
1664 LW	—	4,550	6,500	9,100	12,500	—

KM# 234 8 THALER

Silver **Obv:** Crowned CL monogram in laurel wreath surrounded by 14 small shields, date in legend, 8 punched in **Rev:** Horse leaping left above city view of Celle, head turned up towards wreath held by arms from clouds **Note:** Dav. #LS152. Illustration reduced.

Date	Mintage	VG	F	VF	XF	Unc
1654 LW Rare	—	—	—	—	—	—

Note: Spink Taisei Zurich Milas sale 4-92 XF realized $14,750

KM# 260 8 THALER

Silver **Rev:** Horse looking ahead, wreath held in arm from clouds above head **Note:** Dav. #LS184.

Date	Mintage	VG	F	VF	XF	Unc
1664 LW Rare	—	—	—	—	—	—

KM# 76 10 THALER

289.2000 g., Silver, 75 mm. **Note:** Illustration reduced. Dav. #LS-A116.

Date	Mintage	VG	F	VF	XF	Unc
1625 NZ Rare	—	—	—	—	—	—

Note: Spink Taisei Zurich Milas sale 4-92 VF realized $26,800

KM# 184 10 THALER

Silver **Obv:** Bust right in wreath surrounded by 14 small shields **Rev:** Mining scene, date in legend, 10 punched in **Note:** Dav. #LS132.

Date	Mintage	VG	F	VF	XF	Unc
1647 LW Rare	—	—	—	—	—	—

KM# 225 10 THALER

Silver **Obv:** Crowned CL monogram in laurel wreath surrounded by 14 small shields, date in legend, 10 punched in **Rev:** Horse leaping left above mining scene, head turned up towards wreath held by arm from clouds **Note:** Dav. #LS147.

Date	Mintage	VG	F	VF	XF	Unc
1650 LW Rare	—	—	—	—	—	—

KM# 235.1 10 THALER

Silver **Rev:** Horse above city view of Celle **Note:** Dav. #LS151.

Date	Mintage	VG	F	VF	XF	Unc
1654 LW Rare	—	—	—	—	—	—

KM# 235.2 10 THALER

Silver **Note:** Dav. #LS167.

Date	Mintage	VG	F	VF	XF	Unc
1660 LW Rare	—	—	—	—	—	—

KM# 261 10 THALER

Silver **Note:** Similar to 1-1/2 Thaler, KM#251. Dav. #LS183. Illustration reduced.

Date	Mintage	VG	F	VF	XF	Unc
1664 LW Rare	—	—	—	—	—	—

Note: Spink Taisei Zurich Milas sale 4-92 XF realized $28,810

KM# 262 12 THALER

Silver **Obv:** Crowned CL monogram in laurel wreath surrounded by 14 small shields, date in legend, 12 punched in **Rev:** Horse leaping left above mining scene, head turned up towards wreath held by arm from clouds **Note:** Dav. #LS182.

Date	Mintage	VG	F	VF	XF	Unc
1664 LW Rare	—	—	—	—	—	—

TRADE COINAGE

KM# 48 GOLDGULDEN

3.5000 g., 0.9860 Gold 0.1109 oz. AGW **Obv:** Bust of Christian right in inner circle **Rev:** Crowned arms in inner circle, date at top

Date	Mintage	VG	F	VF	XF	Unc
1621	—	500	1,200	2,400	4,000	—
1624	—	500	1,200	2,400	4,000	—
1628	—	500	1,200	2,400	4,000	—
1630	—	500	1,200	2,400	4,000	—
1631	—	500	1,200	2,400	4,000	—
1633	—	500	1,200	2,400	4,000	—

KM# 78 GOLDGULDEN

3.5000 g., 0.9860 Gold 0.1109 oz. AGW **Subject:** Gold from St. Andreas Mine **Obv:** St. Andrew standing **Rev:** Crowned arms in inner circle

Date	Mintage	VG	F	VF	XF	Unc
1624	—	700	1,500	3,000	6,000	—
1629	—	700	1,500	3,000	6,000	—

KM# 333 1/4 DUCAT

0.8750 g., 0.9860 Gold 0.0277 oz. AGW **Obv:** Georg Wilhelm

Date	Mintage	VG	F	VF	XF	Unc
1690	—	100	200	500	1,200	—

KM# 312 1/2 DUCAT

1.7500 g., 0.9860 Gold 0.0555 oz. AGW **Obv:** Helmeted 12-fold arms, date **Rev:** Horse leaping left, sun above

Date	Mintage	VG	F	VF	XF	Unc
1685 RD	—	225	375	600	1,450	—

KM# 313 1/2 DUCAT

1.7500 g., 0.9860 Gold 0.0555 oz. AGW **Obv:** Bust of George Wilhelm right **Rev:** Rearing horse, date in exergue

Date	Mintage	VG	F	VF	XF	Unc
1685	—	225	375	650	1,500	—
1690	—	225	375	650	1,500	—

KM# 314 1/2 DUCAT

1.7500 g., 0.9860 Gold 0.0555 oz. AGW **Obv:** Crowned arms in order collar

Date	Mintage	VG	F	VF	XF	Unc
1685	—	225	350	575	1,350	—
1688	—	225	350	575	1,350	—
1690	—	225	350	575	1,350	—

KM# 334 1/2 DUCAT

1.7500 g., 0.9860 Gold 0.0555 oz. AGW **Obv:** Bust right

Date	Mintage	VG	F	VF	XF	Unc
1690	—	265	425	675	1,650	—

KM# 49 DUCAT

3.5000 g., 0.9860 Gold 0.1109 oz. AGW **Obv:** Bust right **Rev:** Helmeted 8-fold arms with central shield

Date	Mintage	VG	F	VF	XF	Unc
1621 GM	—	500	900	1,800	3,500	—

KM# 50 DUCAT

3.5000 g., 0.9860 Gold 0.1109 oz. AGW **Obv:** Bust right, date in legend **Rev:** Crowned 8-fold arms with central shield

Date	Mintage	VG	F	VF	XF	Unc
(16)21 GM	—	500	900	1,800	3,500	—

KM# 87 DUCAT

3.5000 g., 0.9860 Gold 0.1109 oz. AGW **Rev:** 9-fold arms

Date	Mintage	VG	F	VF	XF	Unc
1628 HS	—	500	900	1,800	3,500	—
1629 HS	—	500	900	1,800	3,500	—

KM# 95 DUCAT

3.5000 g., 0.9860 Gold 0.1109 oz. AGW **Obv:** Crowned 7-fold arms with central shield **Rev:** St. Andrew with cross

Date	Mintage	VG	F	VF	XF	Unc
1629 HP	—	500	900	1,800	3,500	—
ND HP	—	500	900	1,800	3,500	—

KM# 99 DUCAT

3.5000 g., 0.9860 Gold 0.1109 oz. AGW **Rev:** Date in legend

Date	Mintage	VG	F	VF	XF	Unc
1630 HS	—	500	900	1,800	3,500	—
1632 HS	—	500	900	1,800	3,500	—
1633 HS	—	500	900	1,800	3,500	—

KM# 117 DUCAT

3.5000 g., 0.9860 Gold 0.1109 oz. AGW **Obv:** Bust right **Rev:** Crowned 8-fold arms with central shield of Ratzeburg

Date	Mintage	VG	F	VF	XF	Unc
1634 HS	—	875	1,600	3,150	6,100	—

KM# 139 DUCAT

3.5000 g., 0.9860 Gold 0.1109 oz. AGW **Obv:** Standing figure of Friedrich right in inner circle **Rev:** Crowned arms in inner circle

Date	Mintage	VG	F	VF	XF	Unc
1636	—	400	800	1,700	3,300	—
1638	—	400	800	1,700	3,300	—
1639	—	400	800	1,700	3,300	—
1641	—	400	800	1,700	3,300	—
1644	—	400	800	1,700	3,300	—
1647	—	400	800	1,700	3,300	—
1648	—	400	800	1,700	3,300	—
ND	—	400	800	1,700	3,300	—

KM# 150 DUCAT

3.5000 g., 0.9860 Gold 0.1109 oz. AGW **Obv:** Standing figure of duke, head turned right **Rev:** Crowned oval 11-fold arms, date above crown

Date	Mintage	VG	F	VF	XF	Unc
1638 HS	—	500	900	1,800	3,500	—
1641 LW	—	500	900	1,800	3,500	—

KM# 158 DUCAT

3.5000 g., 0.9860 Gold 0.1109 oz. AGW **Obv:** Duke's head turned to left

Date	Mintage	VG	F	VF	XF	Unc
1642 LW	—	500	900	1,800	3,500	—

KM# 159 DUCAT

3.5000 g., 0.9860 Gold 0.1109 oz. AGW **Obv:** Duke turned half right

Date	Mintage	VG	F	VF	XF	Unc
ND LW	—	500	900	1,800	3,500	—

KM# 160 DUCAT

3.5000 g., 0.9860 Gold 0.1109 oz. AGW **Rev:** 12-fold arms

Date	Mintage	VG	F	VF	XF	Unc
ND	—	500	900	1,800	3,500	—

KM# 185 DUCAT

3.5000 g., 0.9860 Gold 0.1109 oz. AGW **Obv:** Armored bust of Friedrich right in inner circle **Rev:** Crowned arms in inner circle

Date	Mintage	VG	F	VF	XF	Unc
1647	—	400	800	1,700	3,300	—
1648	—	400	800	1,700	3,300	—
ND	—	400	800	1,700	3,300	—

KM# 200 DUCAT

3.5000 g., 0.9860 Gold 0.1109 oz. AGW **Obv:** Bust right **Rev:** Crowned 12-fold arms divide date 1-6/4-8

Date	Mintage	VG	F	VF	XF	Unc
1648 LW	—	400	800	1,700	3,300	—

KM# 226 DUCAT

3.5000 g., 0.9860 Gold 0.1109 oz. AGW

Date	Mintage	VG	F	VF	XF	Unc
1650	—	350	650	1,500	3,100	—
1661	—	350	650	1,500	3,100	—

KM# 227 DUCAT

3.5000 g., 0.9860 Gold 0.1109 oz. AGW **Obv:** Crowned 12-fold arms **Rev:** Horse leaping left in wreath, date in legend

Date	Mintage	VG	F	VF	XF	Unc
1650 LW	—	350	650	1,500	3,100	—
1661 LW	—	350	650	1,500	3,100	—

KM# 263 DUCAT

3.5000 g., 0.9860 Gold 0.1109 oz. AGW **Obv:** Bust of Georg Wilhelm right **Rev:** Crowned arms in inner circle

Date	Mintage	VG	F	VF	XF	Unc
1664	—	700	1,300	2,400	4,400	—
1675	—	700	1,300	2,400	4,400	—

KM# 294 DUCAT

3.5000 g., 0.9860 Gold 0.1109 oz. AGW **Obv:** Bust right **Rev:** Crowned 12-fold arms, date in legend

Date	Mintage	VG	F	VF	XF	Unc
1675 RD	—	700	1,300	2,400	4,400	—

KM# 310 DUCAT

3.5000 g., 0.9860 Gold 0.1109 oz. AGW **Obv:** Helmeted 12-fold arms, date **Rev:** Horse leaping left, sun above

Date	Mintage	VG	F	VF	XF	Unc
1684	—	150	275	650	1,450	—
1685 RD	—	150	275	650	1,450	—
ND III	—	150	275	650	1,450	—

KM# 311 DUCAT

3.5000 g., 0.9860 Gold 0.1109 oz. AGW **Obv:** Crowned arms in garter

Date	Mintage	VG	F	VF	XF	Unc
1684	—	150	275	650	1,450	—
1687	—	150	275	650	1,450	—
1689	—	150	275	650	1,450	—
1691	—	150	275	650	1,450	—
1694	—	150	275	650	1,450	—
1697	—	150	275	650	1,450	—
ND	—	150	275	650	1,450	—

KM# 315 DUCAT

3.5000 g., 0.9860 Gold 0.1109 oz. AGW **Rev:** Rearing horse, date in exergue

Date	Mintage	VG	F	VF	XF	Unc
1685	—	300	500	1,150	2,350	—
1690	—	300	500	1,150	2,350	—

KM# 325 DUCAT

3.5000 g., 0.9860 Gold 0.1109 oz. AGW **Rev:** Date added

Date	Mintage	VG	F	VF	XF	Unc
1688 JJJ	—	300	500	1,150	2,350	—

KM# 335 DUCAT

3.5000 g., 0.9860 Gold 0.1109 oz. AGW **Obv:** Bust right

Date	Mintage	VG	F	VF	XF	Unc
1690 JJJ	—	—	—	—	—	—

Note: Reported, not confirmed

KM# 350 DUCAT

3.5000 g., 0.9860 Gold 0.1109 oz. AGW **Obv:** Helmeted 12-fold arms in Order of the Garter **Rev:** Horse leaping left

Date	Mintage	VG	F	VF	XF	Unc
1693	—	200	325	750	1,550	—
1697	—	200	325	750	1,550	—

KM# 295 2 DUCAT

7.0000 g., 0.9860 Gold 0.2219 oz. AGW **Obv:** Bust right **Rev:** Crowned 12-fold arms, date in legend

Date	Mintage	VG	F	VF	XF	Unc
1675 RD	—	800	2,000	4,200	7,500	—

KM# 296 2 DUCAT

7.0000 g., 0.9860 Gold 0.2219 oz. AGW **Obv:** Horse leaping left **Rev:** Crowned 12-fold arms

Date	Mintage	VG	F	VF	XF	Unc
1675 RD	—	800	2,000	4,200	7,500	—

KM# 297 2 DUCAT

7.0000 g., 0.9860 Gold 0.2219 oz. AGW **Obv:** Bust of Georg Wilhelm right **Rev:** Crowned arms

Date	Mintage	VG	F	VF	XF	Unc
1675	—	800	2,000	4,200	7,500	—
1699	—	800	2,000	4,200	7,500	—

KM# 298 2 DUCAT

7.0000 g., 0.9860 Gold 0.2219 oz. AGW

Date	Mintage	VG	F	VF	XF	Unc
1675	—	800	2,000	4,200	7,500	—
1699	—	800	2,000	4,200	7,500	—
1700	—	800	2,000	4,200	7,500	—

KM# 316 2 DUCAT

7.0000 g., 0.9860 Gold 0.2219 oz. AGW **Obv:** Bust right **Rev:** Horse leaping left, sun above

Date	Mintage	VG	F	VF	XF	Unc
1685 RD	—	1,000	2,250	4,950	8,100	—
1688 RD	—	1,000	2,250	4,950	8,100	—

KM# 317 2 DUCAT

7.0000 g., 0.9860 Gold 0.2219 oz. AGW **Obv:** Bust of George Wilhelm right

Date	Mintage	VG	F	VF	XF	Unc
1685	—	1,000	2,250	4,950	8,100	—
1688	—	1,000	2,250	4,950	8,100	—
1690	—	1,000	2,250	4,950	8,100	—
1699	—	1,000	2,250	4,950	8,100	—

KM# 357 2 DUCAT

7.0000 g., 0.9860 Gold 0.2219 oz. AGW **Rev:** Horse leaping left

Date	Mintage	VG	F	VF	XF	Unc
1699 III	—	1,350	3,150	6,800	9,000	—

KM# 358 2 DUCAT

7.0000 g., 0.9860 Gold 0.2219 oz. AGW **Obv:** Crowned 12-fold arms in Order of the Garter

Date	Mintage	VG	F	VF	XF	Unc
1699 III	—	1,000	2,250	4,950	8,100	—
1700 III	—	1,000	2,250	4,950	8,100	—

KM# 305 4 DUCAT

14.0000 g., 0.9860 Gold 0.4438 oz. AGW **Obv:** Bust right **Rev:** Horse leaping left

Date	Mintage	VG	F	VF	XF	Unc
1681 Rare	—	—	—	—	—	—
1688 JJJ Rare	—	—	—	—	—	—

KM# 306 4 DUCAT

14.0000 g., 0.9860 Gold 0.4438 oz. AGW **Obv:** Crowned arms **Rev:** Rearing horse, date in exergue

Date	Mintage	VG	F	VF	XF	Unc
1681 Rare	—	—	—	—	—	—

KM# 326 4 DUCAT

14.0000 g., 0.9860 Gold 0.4438 oz. AGW **Obv:** Bust of Georg Wilhelm right

Date	Mintage	VG	F	VF	XF	Unc
1688 Rare	—	—	—	—	—	—

PATTERNS

Including off metal strikes

KM#	Date	Mintage	Identification	Mkt Val
Pn1	ND	—	2 Pfennig. Gold. II/GVD/PEN.	—
Pn2	1690	—	1/2 Ducat. Silver. KM#334	300
Pn3	1690 JJ	—	Ducat. Silver. KM#335	350

BRUNSWICK-WOLFENBUTTEL

(Braunschweig-Wolfenbüttel)

Located in north-central Germany. Wolfenbüttel was annexed to Brunswick in 1257. One of the five surviving sons of Albrecht II founded the first line in Wolfenbüttel in 1318. A further division in Wolfenbüttel and Lüneburg was undertaken in 1373. Another division occurred in 1495, but the Wolfenbüttel duchy survived in the younger line. Heinrich IX was forced out of his territory during the religious wars of the mid-sixteenth century by Duke Johann Friedrich I of Saxony and Landgrave Philipp of Hessen in 1542, but was restored to his possessions in 1547. Duke Friedrich Ulrich was forced to cede the Grubenhagen lands, which had been acquired by Wolfenbüttel in 1596, to Lüneburg in 1617. When the succession died out in 1634, the lands and titles fell to the cadet line in Dannenberg. The line became extinct once again and passed to Brunswick-Bevern in 1735 from which a new succession of Wolfenbüttel dukes descended. The ducal family was beset by continual personal and political tragedy during the nineteenth century. Two of the dukes were killed in battles with Napoleon, the territories were occupied by the French and became part of the Kingdom of Westphalia, another duke was forced out by a revolt in 1823. From 1884 until 1913, Brunswick-Wolfenbüttel was governed by Prussia and then turned over to a younger prince of Brunswick who married a daughter of Kaiser Wilhelm II. His reign was short, however, as he was forced to abdicate at the end of World War I.

RULERS

Heinrich VIII der Ältere, 1495-1514
Heinrich IX der Jüngere, 1514-1568
Julius, 1568-1589

...Note: For joint issues of Heinrich IX with Erich II von Calenberg, 1551-1556, see under Brunswick-Calenberg.

Heinrich Julius, 1589-1613
Friedrich Ulrich, 1613-1634
August II, 1634-1666
Rudolf August, 1666-1704
Anton Ulrich, as joint ruler, 1685-1704
alone, 1704-1714

MINT OFFICIALS' INITIALS

Andreasberg Mint

Initial	Date	Name
(d)	1594-1611	Heinrich Depsern, mintmaster
HP	1623-1629	Heinrich Pechstein, mintmaster

Brunswick Mint

Initial	Date	Name
GB/B	1675-1684	Johann Georg Breuer, mintmaster
HCH	1689-1729	Heinrich Christoph Hille, mintmaster

Catlenburg Mint

Initial	Date	Name
VF (ligature), sometimes with H	1623-1624	Urban Felgenhauer

Clausthal Mint

Initial	Date	Name
HS (often with ingot hook	1622-1640	Henning Schreiber
HB	1675-1711	Heinrich Bonhorst

Goslar Mint

Initial	Date	Name
	1543-47	Gregor Ainkhüren, mintmaster
(aa)=	Before 1550	Unknown
(bb)=	1551-55	Unknown
(cc)=	1556-57, 1561	Unknown
(dd)=	1557-58	Unknown
(ee)=	1558-62, 65-70	Hans Küne
(ff)=Stag leaping left	1559	Unknown
	1563	Lazarus Erkel, mintmaster
(gg)=	1563-64	Samuel Salwar
(hh)=	1570-96, 97-99	Andreas Küne
(ii)= or	1596-97	Commission
(d)=	1599-1612	Heinrich Depsern
(o)= or or	1613-1618	Heinrich Oeckeler
(c)	1619-1625	Hans Laffers
HL	1622-1625	Henning Loehr
(k)= S	?-1625	Hermann Schlanbusch
HS (sometimes with crossed keys)	1626-1672	Henning Schlüter
IPE	1672	Julius Philipp Eisendrath
RB	1685-1704	Rudolf Bornemann

Hannover Mint

Initial	Date	Name
RB	1673-1676	Rudolf Bornemann

Heinrichsstadt Mint

Initial	Date	Name
	1574-85	Heinrich Veeber (Veever), mintmaster

Helmstedt Mint

Initial	Date	Name
	1510-1512	Bartold Lücken, mintmaster

Lauterberg Mint

Initial	Date	Name
HS	1621-1624	Henning Schreiber

Moritzburg Mint

Initial	Date	Name
CH/ch	1622-1625	Lazarus Christian Hopfgarten

Osterode Mint

Initial	Date	Name
	1619-1622	Henning Schreiber
HL	1622-1625	Henning Loehr

Riechenberg Mint

Initial	Date	Name
(jj)=	1531-32	Valentin von Stoghem, mintmaster
(kk)=	1534-35	Beghart Utz, mintmaster
(ll)= or	1535-40	Hans Khöne, mintmaster
(mm)=	1539-40, 42	Vacant
(nn)= stag rampant left holding ingot hook and	1540	Unknown
(oo)=	1540-43	Andreas Blankenhagen, mintmaster
(pp)=	1545	Unknown
(qq)=	1547-48	Johann Dankwerts, mintmaster
(rr)=stag rampant left holding ingot hook	1548-51	Martin Huxter, mintmaster

Wolfenbüttel Mint

Initial	Date	Name
(ss)=	1587-89	Dietrich Ockeler, mintmaster
ICB/ICP	1693-1697	Johann Christoph Bähr
DF	1697	Damian Fritsch

Zellerfeld Mint

Initial	Date	Name
(o)	1601-1618	Heinrich Oeckeler
(c)=	1619-1625	Hans Laffers
HL	1622-1625	Henniing Loehr
HS (sometimes with crossed keys	1626-1672	Henning Schlüter
RB	1676-1711	Rudolf Bornemann
***	1698-1715	Used in place of mintmasters' initials

MISCELLANEOUS MINT OFFICIALS' INITIALS

Initial	Date	Name
(a) = acorn	ca.1620	Unknown
(b) = or	ca.1620	possibly Henning Schreiber
LB	ca.1620	Lewin Brockmann
WQ	ca.1620	Unknown
HH	1620-1621	Hardeg Hardegen in Weende bei Göttingen
CV	ca.1621	Unknown
HLM	ca.1621	Unknown
IB	ca.1621	Unknown
ID	ca.1621	Unknown
IL	ca.1621	Unknown
CL	ca.1622	Unknown
GL	ca.1622	Unknown
PHM	1650-1718	Philipp Heinrich Müller), goldsmith, die-cutter, medailleur In Nürnberg and Augsburg
GFN	1682-1724	Georg Friedrich Nürnberger, die-cutter and mintmaster In Nürnberg

DUCHY

REGULAR COINAGE

KM# 64 PFENNIG

Copper **Ruler:** Frederich Ulrich **Note:** Similar to KM#130.

Date	Mintage	VG	F	VF	XF	Unc
1617	—	16.00	33.00	60.00	110	—

KM# 130 PFENNIG

Copper **Ruler:** Frederich Ulrich **Obv:** Brunswick helmet with horse **Rev:** Value, date in 4 lines **Note:** Kipper Pfennig.

Date	Mintage	VG	F	VF	XF	Unc
1620	—	16.00	33.00	60.00	110	—
1621	—	16.00	33.00	60.00	110	—

KM# 230 PFENNIG

Copper **Ruler:** Frederich Ulrich **Obv:** Lion rampant left

Date	Mintage	VG	F	VF	XF	Unc
1621	—	10.00	20.00	40.00	80.00	—

KM# 231 PFENNIG

Copper **Ruler:** Frederich Ulrich **Obv:** Lion in shield **Rev:** 3 helmets

Date	Mintage	VG	F	VF	XF	Unc
ND	—	10.00	20.00	40.00	80.00	—

KM# 405 PFENNIG

Silver **Ruler:** August II **Note:** Uniface. Crowned FV monogram divides date.

Date	Mintage	VG	F	VF	XF	Unc
(16)39	—	—	—	—	—	—
(16)39	—	—	—	—	—	—

KM# 432 PFENNIG

Silver **Ruler:** August II **Note:** Crowned A, date.

Date	Mintage	VG	F	VF	XF	Unc
1647	—	10.00	20.00	40.00	75.00	—
1657	—	10.00	20.00	40.00	75.00	—
1661	—	10.00	20.00	40.00	75.00	—
1664 (s)	—	10.00	20.00	40.00	75.00	—
1666 (s)	—	10.00	20.00	40.00	75.00	—
1667 (s) (error)	—	10.00	20.00	40.00	75.00	—

KM# 466 PFENNIG

Silver **Ruler:** August II **Subject:** 83rd Birthday of August II **Note:** Crowned A, 10 APRIL _ 1661.

Date	Mintage	VG	F	VF	XF	Unc
1661	—	—	—	—	—	—

KM# 496 PFENNIG

Silver **Ruler:** Rudolf August **Note:** Uniface.Guter-Pfennig. Crowned cursive RA monogram, date.

Date	Mintage	VG	F	VF	XF	Unc
1667 (s)	—	10.00	20.00	40.00	75.00	—
1668 (s)	—	10.00	20.00	40.00	75.00	—
1669 (s)	—	10.00	20.00	40.00	75.00	—
1672 IPE	—	10.00	20.00	40.00	75.00	—
1675 IPE	—	10.00	20.00	40.00	75.00	—
1676 IPE	—	10.00	20.00	40.00	75.00	—
1677 RB	—	10.00	20.00	40.00	75.00	—
1679 RB	—	10.00	20.00	40.00	75.00	—
1680 RB	—	10.00	20.00	40.00	75.00	—
1681 RB	—	10.00	20.00	40.00	75.00	—
1682 RB	—	10.00	20.00	40.00	75.00	—
1684 RB	—	10.00	20.00	40.00	75.00	—

KM# 556 PFENNIG

Silver **Ruler:** Rudolf August **Note:** Guter-Pfennig. Intertwined cursive RAV monogram, date.

Date	Mintage	VG	F	VF	XF	Unc
1685 RB	—	10.00	20.00	40.00	75.00	—
1686 RB	—	10.00	20.00	40.00	75.00	—
1688 RB	—	10.00	20.00	40.00	75.00	—
1693 RB	—	10.00	20.00	40.00	75.00	—

KM# 545 1-1/2 PFENNIGE

Silver **Ruler:** Rudolf August **Obv:** Crowned RA monogram **Rev:** Value, date

Date	Mintage	VG	F	VF	XF	Unc
1680	—	9.00	20.00	40.00	80.00	—

KM# 65 2 PFENNIGE

Copper **Ruler:** Frederich Ulrich **Obv:** Brunswick helmet with horse **Rev:** Value, date in 4 lines

Date	Mintage	VG	F	VF	XF	Unc
1617	—	13.00	27.00	55.00	110	—

KM# 131 2 PFENNIGE

Copper **Ruler:** Frederich Ulrich **Note:** Similar to KM#65.

Date	Mintage	VG	F	VF	XF	Unc
1620	—	13.00	27.00	55.00	110	—

KM# 232 2 PFENNIGE

Copper **Ruler:** Frederich Ulrich **Obv:** Lion rampant right **Rev:** Value, date in 4 lines **Note:** Kipper.

Date	Mintage	VG	F	VF	XF	Unc
1621	—	10.00	20.00	40.00	80.00	—

KM# 133 3 PFENNIG

Copper **Ruler:** Frederich Ulrich **Rev:** Value date in 4 lines

Date	Mintage	VG	F	VF	XF	Unc
1620	—	13.00	27.00	45.00	80.00	—
1621	—	13.00	27.00	45.00	80.00	—

KM# 233 3 PFENNIG

Copper **Ruler:** Frederich Ulrich **Obv:** Arms divided horizontally, lion rampant left above, 3 bars below **Rev:** Imperial orb with 3 **Rev. Legend:** MAT D G

Date	Mintage	VG	F	VF	XF	Unc
ND	—	20.00	40.00	65.00	120	—

KM# 234 3 PFENNIG

Copper **Ruler:** Frederich Ulrich **Rev:** Orb divides date

Date	Mintage	VG	F	VF	XF	Unc
1621	—	20.00	40.00	65.00	120	—

KM# 235 3 PFENNIG

Copper **Ruler:** Frederich Ulrich **Obv:** Lion walking left **Rev:** Imperial orb with 3

Date	Mintage	VG	F	VF	XF	Unc
ND	—	20.00	40.00	65.00	120	—

KM# 236 3 PFENNIG

Copper **Ruler:** Frederich Ulrich **Obv:** Lion rampant right **Rev:** Value III. . ., date in 4 lines

Date	Mintage	VG	F	VF	XF	Unc
1621	—	20.00	40.00	65.00	120	—

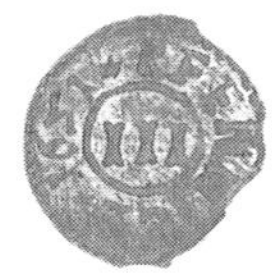

KM# 237 3 PFENNIG
Copper **Ruler:** Frederich Ulrich **Obv:** Crowned 'R' between two stars **Rev:** Value 'III' in circle, date in legend **Rev. Legend:** PFENNIGE (date) **Note:** Issued for Regenstein.

Date	Mintage	VG	F	VF	XF	Unc
1621	—	20.00	40.00	65.00	120	—

KM# 238 3 PFENNIG
Silver **Ruler:** Frederich Ulrich **Obv:** Arms with lion leaping left over 2 sheaves **Rev:** Imperial orb with 3 divides date **Note:** Kipper-3 Pfennig.

Date	Mintage	VG	F	VF	XF	Unc
1621	—	20.00	40.00	65.00	120	—

KM# 333 3 PFENNIG
Silver **Ruler:** Frederich Ulrich **Note:** Uniface. Crowned FV monogram divides 3 to left, mintmasters initials to right.

Date	Mintage	VG	F	VF	XF	Unc
ND ch	—	—	—	—	—	—

KM# 330 3 PFENNIG
Silver **Ruler:** Frederich Ulrich **Obv:** Lion rampant right **Rev:** Imperial orb with 3 divides date

Date	Mintage	VG	F	VF	XF	Unc
1622	—	20.00	40.00	65.00	120	—

KM# 331 3 PFENNIG
Silver **Ruler:** Frederich Ulrich **Obv:** Lion rampant right **Rev:** Imperial orbe with 3

Date	Mintage	VG	F	VF	XF	Unc
1622	—	20.00	40.00	65.00	120	—

KM# 332 3 PFENNIG
Silver **Ruler:** Frederich Ulrich **Obv:** Brunswick helmet with horse

Date	Mintage	VG	F	VF	XF	Unc
16ZZ GL	—	20.00	40.00	65.00	120	—
1622	—	20.00	40.00	65.00	120	—
1622 CL	—	20.00	40.00	65.00	120	—
1622 G	—	20.00	40.00	65.00	120	—
1623 GL	—	20.00	40.00	65.00	120	—

KM# 458 3 PFENNIG
Silver **Ruler:** August II **Obv:** Crowned A **Rev:** Imprial orb with 3 divides mintmasters initials

Date	Mintage	VG	F	VF	XF	Unc
1659 (s)	—	16.00	33.00	55.00	95.00	—
1664 (s)	—	16.00	33.00	55.00	95.00	—

KM# 467 3 PFENNIG
Silver **Ruler:** August II **Subject:** 83rd Birthday of August II **Obv. Legend:** 10 APRIL - 1661

Date	Mintage	VG	F	VF	XF	Unc
1661 (s)	—	—	—	—	—	—

KM# 517 3 PFENNIG
Silver **Ruler:** Rudolf August **Obv:** Crowned RA monogram **Rev:** Imperial orb with 3

Date	Mintage	VG	F	VF	XF	Unc
1675 IPE	—	16.00	33.00	55.00	95.00	—
1677 RB	—	16.00	33.00	55.00	95.00	—
1678 RB	—	16.00	33.00	55.00	95.00	—

KM# 547 3 PFENNIG
Silver **Ruler:** Rudolf August **Obv. Legend:** F. B. LU. L. MUN.

Date	Mintage	VG	F	VF	XF	Unc
1684	—	20.00	40.00	65.00	120	—

KM# 557 3 PFENNIG
Silver **Ruler:** Rudolf August **Obv:** Crowned intertwined cursive RAV **Rev:** Imperial orb with 3 divides date

Date	Mintage	VG	F	VF	XF	Unc
1685 RB	—	13.00	27.00	45.00	85.00	—
1692 HCH	—	13.00	27.00	45.00	85.00	—

KM# 596 3 PFENNIG
Silver **Ruler:** Rudolf August **Obv:** Date

Date	Mintage	VG	F	VF	XF	Unc
1692 HCH	—	13.00	27.00	45.00	85.00	—

KM# 603 3 PFENNIG
Silver **Ruler:** Rudolf August **Obv:** Horse leaping left **Rev:** Imperial orb with 3 divides date

Date	Mintage	VG	F	VF	XF	Unc
1693	—	13.00	27.00	45.00	85.00	—

KM# 66 4 PFENNIGE
Copper **Ruler:** Frederich Ulrich **Obv:** Brunswick helmet with horse **Rev:** Value, IIII, date in 4 lines

Date	Mintage	VG	F	VF	XF	Unc
1617	—	20.00	40.00	65.00	120	—

KM# 528 4 PFENNIGE
Silver **Ruler:** Rudolf August **Obv:** Crowned RA monogram **Rev:** Value 4..., date

Date	Mintage	VG	F	VF	XF	Unc
1677 RB	—	20.00	40.00	70.00	125	—
1684 RB	—	20.00	40.00	70.00	125	—

KM# 548 4 PFENNIGE
Silver **Ruler:** Rudolf August **Obv:** Crowned cursive RA monogram **Rev:** Value IIII. . ., date

Date	Mintage	VG	F	VF	XF	Unc
1684 B	—	20.00	40.00	70.00	125	—

KM# 558 4 PFENNIGE
Silver **Obv:** Crowned intertwined cursive RAV monogram, date in legend **Rev:** Value 4. . . in 3 lines **Note:** Gute.

Date	Mintage	VG	F	VF	XF	Unc
1685	—	20.00	40.00	70.00	125	—
1691	—	20.00	40.00	70.00	125	—
1692	—	20.00	40.00	70.00	125	—

KM# 588 4 PFENNIGE
Silver **Rev:** Value IIII...

Date	Mintage	VG	F	VF	XF	Unc
1691 RB	—	20.00	40.00	70.00	125	—
1694 RB	—	20.00	40.00	70.00	125	—

KM# 589 4-1/2 PFENNIG
Silver **Obv:** Crowned intertwined cursive RAV monogram, date in legend **Rev:** Value 4-1/2. . . in 3 lines **Note:** Gute-4 1/2 Pfennig.

Date	Mintage	VG	F	VF	XF	Unc
1691	—	27.00	55.00	95.00	175	—

KM# 597 5 PFENNIG
Silver **Obv:** Crowned intertwined cursive RAAV monogram **Rev:** Value V..., date in 4 lines

Date	Mintage	VG	F	VF	XF	Unc
1692 HCH	—	27.00	55.00	95.00	175	—

KM# 598 5 PFENNIG
Silver **Obv:** Monogram doubled with backwards: RAAVAA

Date	Mintage	VG	F	VF	XF	Unc
1692 HCH	—	27.00	55.00	95.00	175	—

KM# 599 5 PFENNIG
Silver **Obv:** Simple RAV monogram

Date	Mintage	VG	F	VF	XF	Unc
1692 HCH	—	27.00	55.00	95.00	175	—

KM# 549 6 PFENNIGE
Silver **Obv:** RA monogram **Rev:** Imperial orb with 6, date

Date	Mintage	VG	F	VF	XF	Unc
1684	—	16.00	33.00	55.00	110	—

KM# 590 6 PFENNIGE
Silver **Obv:** Crowned intertwined cursive RAV monogram **Rev:** Imperial orb with 6, divides date

Date	Mintage	VG	F	VF	XF	Unc
1691 HCH	—	16.00	33.00	55.00	120	—
1692 HCH	—	16.00	33.00	55.00	120	—

KM# 604 6 PFENNIGE
Silver **Obv:** Horse leaping left

Date	Mintage	VG	F	VF	XF	Unc
1693	—	13.00	27.00	45.00	90.00	—

KM# 240 FLITTER (2 Pfennig)
Copper **Obv:** Lion rampant left, + below **Rev:** Value in 4 lines

Date	Mintage	VG	F	VF	XF	Unc
ND	—	20.00	33.00	60.00	120	—

KM# 241 FLITTER (2 Pfennig)
Copper **Obv:** Lion walking left, +++ below **Rev:** Value in 3 lines

Date	Mintage	VG	F	VF	XF	Unc
ND	—	20.00	33.00	60.00	120	—

KM# 242 FLITTER (2 Pfennig)
Copper **Obv:** Brunswick helmet with horse **Rev:** Value, date in 4 lines

Date	Mintage	VG	F	VF	XF	Unc
1621	—	20.00	33.00	60.00	120	—
ND	—	20.00	33.00	60.00	120	—

KM# 239 FLITTER (2 Pfennig)
Copper **Obv:** Lion rampant right **Rev:** Value, date in 4 lines **Note:** Kipper-Flitter.

Date	Mintage	VG	F	VF	XF	Unc
1621	—	20.00	33.00	60.00	120	—

KM# 243 FLITTER (2 Pfennig)
Copper **Note:** Uniface. Lion rampant right in cord circle.

Date	Mintage	VG	F	VF	XF	Unc
ND	—	16.00	27.00	55.00	110	—

KM# 245 2 FLITTER
Copper **Obv:** Brunswick helmet with horse

Date	Mintage	VG	F	VF	XF	Unc
1621	—	10.00	20.00	33.00	65.00	—

KM# 244 2 FLITTER
Copper **Obv:** Lion rampant right **Rev:** Value, date in 4 lines **Note:** Kipper-2 Flitter.

Date	Mintage	VG	F	VF	XF	Unc
1621	—	10.00	20.00	33.00	65.00	—

KM# 247 3 FLITTER
Copper **Obv:** Lion rampant left in shield **Rev:** Value, date in 4 lines

Date	Mintage	VG	F	VF	XF	Unc
1621	—	12.00	25.00	45.00	80.00	—

KM# 248 3 FLITTER
Copper **Rev:** Value only in 3 lines

Date	Mintage	VG	F	VF	XF	Unc
ND	—	12.00	25.00	45.00	80.00	—

KM# 249 3 FLITTER
Copper **Obv:** Crowned lion rampant left **Rev:** Similar to KM#251

Date	Mintage	VG	F	VF	XF	Unc
1621	—	12.00	25.00	45.00	80.00	—

KM# 250 3 FLITTER
Copper **Obv:** Lion walking left in shield **Rev:** Value in 3 lines

Date	Mintage	VG	F	VF	XF	Unc
ND	—	12.00	25.00	45.00	80.00	—

KM# 251 3 FLITTER
Copper **Obv:** Lion rampant right

Date	Mintage	VG	F	VF	XF	Unc
1621	—	12.00	25.00	45.00	80.00	—

KM# 252 3 FLITTER
Copper **Rev:** Value, date in 5 lines

Date	Mintage	VG	F	VF	XF	Unc
1621	—	9.00	16.00	33.00	65.00	—
1612 (error)	—	13.00	27.00	55.00	80.00	—

KM# 253 3 FLITTER
Copper **Rev:** Value, date in 4 lines

Date	Mintage	VG	F	VF	XF	Unc
ND	—	9.00	16.00	33.00	65.00	—

KM# 254 3 FLITTER
Copper **Obv:** 2 leopards to left **Rev:** III in imperial orb **Rev. Legend:** FLITTERN

Date	Mintage	VG	F	VF	XF	Unc
ND	—	12.00	25.00	45.00	70.00	—

KM# 255 3 FLITTER
Copper **Rev:** III in circle **Rev. Legend:** FLITTER 1621

Date	Mintage	VG	F	VF	XF	Unc
1621	—	9.00	16.00	33.00	65.00	—

KM# 256 3 FLITTER
Copper **Rev. Legend:** FLITTER with orb, without date

Date	Mintage	VG	F	VF	XF	Unc
1621	—	9.00	16.00	33.00	65.00	—
ND	—	9.00	16.00	33.00	65.00	—

KM# 257 3 FLITTER
Copper **Obv:** Arms divided horizontally, lion walking left above, * * below **Rev:** Value in 3 lines

Date	Mintage	VG	F	VF	XF	Unc
ND	—	9.00	16.00	33.00	65.00	—

KM# 258 3 FLITTER
Copper **Obv:** Brunswick helmet with horse **Rev:** Ornamented III in circle **Rev. Legend:** FLITTERN. 1621 and ornament

Date	Mintage	VG	F	VF	XF	Unc
1621	—	9.00	16.00	33.00	65.00	—
ND	—	9.00	16.00	33.00	65.00	—

KM# 259 3 FLITTER

Copper **Rev:** Value, date in 4 lines

Date	Mintage	VG	F	VF	XF	Unc
1621	—	9.00	16.00	33.00	65.00	—
1621 HH	—	10.00	20.00	40.00	75.00	—
ND	—	9.00	16.00	33.00	65.00	—

KM# 260 3 FLITTER

Copper **Rev:** 3 in imperial orb **Rev. Legend:** FLITTER **

Date	Mintage	VG	F	VF	XF	Unc
ND	—	9.00	16.00	33.00	65.00	—

KM# 246 3 FLITTER

Copper **Obv:** Lion rampant left **Rev:** Value in 3 lines in circle **Note:** Kipper-3 Flitter.

Date	Mintage	VG	F	VF	XF	Unc
ND	—	12.00	25.00	45.00	75.00	—

KM# 262 3 FLITTER

Copper **Note:** Uniface. III/FLIT/TERN/1621 in 4-part circle.

Date	Mintage	VG	F	VF	XF	Unc
1621	—	13.00	27.00	45.00	85.00	—

KM# 261 3 FLITTER

Copper **Note:** Uniface. Lion rampant left in ornamented oval shield, value III above.

Date	Mintage	VG	F	VF	XF	Unc
ND	—	13.00	27.00	45.00	85.00	—

KM# 334 3 FLITTER

Copper **Obv:** Similar to KM#251 **Rev:** III in imprial orb **Rev. Legend:** 1622 FLITTER

Date	Mintage	VG	F	VF	XF	Unc
1622	—	13.00	27.00	45.00	85.00	—

KM# 335 3 FLITTER

Copper **Obv:** 2 leopards left **Rev:** 3 in imprial orb **Rev. Legend:** FLITTER

Date	Mintage	VG	F	VF	XF	Unc
1622	—	13.00	27.00	45.00	85.00	—

KM# 263 6 FLITTER

Copper **Obv:** 2 leopards to left **Rev:** VI in imperial orb **Rev. Legend:** FLITTER 1621 **Note:** Kipper-6 Flitter.

Date	Mintage	VG	F	VF	XF	Unc
1621	—	13.00	27.00	45.00	85.00	—
ND	—	8.00	16.00	32.00	60.00	—

KM# 343 MATTIER (4 Pfennig)

Silver **Obv:** Crowned FV monogram **Rev:** Value in 4 lines

Date	Mintage	VG	F	VF	XF	Unc
1624	—	16.00	27.00	55.00	100	—
1629	—	16.00	27.00	55.00	100	—

KM# 344 MATTIER (4 Pfennig)

Silver **Note:** Uniface. Crowned FV monogram.

Date	Mintage	VG	F	VF	XF	Unc
1624	—	10.00	20.00	40.00	70.00	—

KM# 134 MARIENGROSCHEN

Silver **Obv:** Cronwed FV monogram **Rev:** Value I. . . in 3 lines

Date	Mintage	VG	F	VF	XF	Unc
1620	—	10.00	20.00	40.00	80.00	—
1623	—	10.00	20.00	40.00	80.00	—
1624	—	10.00	20.00	40.00	80.00	—
1625	—	10.00	20.00	40.00	80.00	—
1626	—	10.00	20.00	40.00	80.00	—
1627	—	10.00	20.00	40.00	80.00	—
1628	—	10.00	20.00	40.00	80.00	—
1629	—	10.00	20.00	40.00	80.00	—
1631	—	10.00	20.00	40.00	80.00	—
1634	—	10.00	20.00	40.00	80.00	—
ND	—	10.00	20.00	40.00	80.00	—

KM# 433 MARIENGROSCHEN

Silver **Obv:** Cronwed A **Rev:** Value, date

Date	Mintage	VG	F	VF	XF	Unc
1647	—	10.00	20.00	40.00	80.00	—
1652	—	10.00	20.00	40.00	80.00	—
1656	—	10.00	20.00	40.00	80.00	—
1657	—	10.00	20.00	40.00	80.00	—

KM# 434 MARIENGROSCHEN

Silver **Obv:** Brunswick helmet

Date	Mintage	VG	F	VF	XF	Unc
ND (s)	—	—	—	—	—	—

KM# 497 MARIENGROSCHEN

Silver **Obv:** Wildman holding tree with both hands to left

Date	Mintage	VG	F	VF	XF	Unc
1667	—	13.00	27.00	55.00	100	—
1673	—	13.00	27.00	55.00	100	—
1674	—	13.00	27.00	55.00	100	—
1675	—	13.00	27.00	55.00	100	—
1676	—	13.00	27.00	55.00	100	—
1677	—	13.00	27.00	55.00	100	—
1678	—	13.00	27.00	55.00	100	—
1679	—	13.00	27.00	55.00	100	—
1680	—	13.00	27.00	55.00	100	—
1681	—	13.00	27.00	55.00	100	—
1682	—	13.00	27.00	55.00	100	—
1683	—	13.00	27.00	55.00	100	—
1684	—	13.00	27.00	55.00	100	—

KM# 550 MARIENGROSCHEN

Silver **Obv:** Crowned RA monogram **Obv. Legend:** HERZ. ZU. BR. U. LUN

Date	Mintage	VG	F	VF	XF	Unc
1684	—	10.00	20.00	40.00	80.00	—
1684 B	—	10.00	20.00	40.00	80.00	—

KM# 567 MARIENGROSCHEN

Silver **Ruler:** Anton Ulrich as Joint ruler **Obv:** Wildman holding tree with both hands to left **Rev:** Value I...in 3 lines, date in legend

Date	Mintage	VG	F	VF	XF	Unc
1686	—	13.00	27.00	55.00	100	—
1687	—	13.00	27.00	55.00	100	—
1688	—	13.00	27.00	55.00	100	—
1689	—	13.00	27.00	55.00	100	—

KM# 264 2 MARIENGROSCHEN

Silver

Date	Mintage	VG	F	VF	XF	Unc
1621	—	9.00	16.00	33.00	75.00	—
1623	—	9.00	16.00	33.00	75.00	—
1624	—	9.00	16.00	33.00	75.00	—
1625	—	9.00	16.00	33.00	75.00	—
1626	—	9.00	16.00	33.00	75.00	—
1627	—	9.00	16.00	33.00	75.00	—
1627 (h)	—	9.00	16.00	33.00	75.00	—
1628	—	9.00	16.00	33.00	75.00	—
1628 (h)	—	9.00	16.00	33.00	75.00	—
1629	—	9.00	16.00	33.00	75.00	—
1629 (h)	—	9.00	16.00	33.00	75.00	—
1631	—	9.00	16.00	33.00	75.00	—
1632	—	9.00	16.00	33.00	75.00	—
1633	—	9.00	16.00	33.00	75.00	—
1634	—	9.00	16.00	33.00	75.00	—
1635 (error)	—	9.00	16.00	33.00	75.00	—

KM# 397 2 MARIENGROSCHEN

Silver

Date	Mintage	VG	F	VF	XF	Unc
1638 (s)	—	9.00	16.00	33.00	75.00	—
1639 (s)	—	9.00	16.00	33.00	75.00	—
1640 (s)	—	9.00	16.00	33.00	75.00	—
1641 (s)	—	9.00	16.00	33.00	75.00	—
1642 (s)	—	9.00	16.00	33.00	75.00	—
1643 (s)	—	9.00	16.00	33.00	75.00	—
1644 (s)	—	9.00	16.00	33.00	75.00	—
1645 (s)	—	9.00	16.00	33.00	75.00	—
1646 (s)	—	9.00	16.00	33.00	75.00	—
1647 (s)	—	9.00	16.00	33.00	75.00	—
1648 (s)	—	9.00	16.00	33.00	75.00	—
1649 (s)	—	9.00	16.00	33.00	75.00	—
1659 (s)	—	9.00	16.00	33.00	75.00	—
ND (s)	—	9.00	16.00	33.00	75.00	—

KM# 431 2 MARIENGROSCHEN

Silver

Date	Mintage	VG	F	VF	XF	Unc
1645	—	10.00	20.00	40.00	80.00	—
1647	—	10.00	20.00	40.00	80.00	—
1648	—	10.00	20.00	40.00	80.00	—
1649	—	10.00	20.00	40.00	80.00	—
1650	—	10.00	20.00	40.00	80.00	—
1651	—	10.00	20.00	40.00	80.00	—
1652	—	10.00	20.00	40.00	80.00	—
1653	—	10.00	20.00	40.00	80.00	—
1654	—	10.00	20.00	40.00	80.00	—
1655	—	10.00	20.00	40.00	80.00	—
1656	—	10.00	20.00	40.00	80.00	—
1659	—	10.00	20.00	40.00	80.00	—

KM# 443 2 MARIENGROSCHEN

Silver **Obv:** Crowned AW monogram

Date	Mintage	VG	F	VF	XF	Unc
1654	—	10.00	20.00	40.00	80.00	—
1655	—	10.00	20.00	40.00	80.00	—

KM# 498 2 MARIENGROSCHEN

Silver **Note:** Similar to 1 Mariengroschen, KM#497.

Date	Mintage	VG	F	VF	XF	Unc
1667	—	9.00	16.00	33.00	70.00	—
1673	—	9.00	16.00	33.00	70.00	—
1674	—	9.00	16.00	33.00	70.00	—
1675	—	9.00	16.00	33.00	70.00	—
1676	—	9.00	16.00	33.00	70.00	—
1677	—	9.00	16.00	33.00	70.00	—
1679	—	9.00	16.00	33.00	70.00	—
1680	—	9.00	16.00	33.00	70.00	—
1681	—	9.00	16.00	33.00	70.00	—
1682	—	9.00	16.00	33.00	70.00	—
1683	—	9.00	16.00	33.00	70.00	—
1684	—	9.00	16.00	33.00	70.00	—

KM# 568 2 MARIENGROSCHEN

Silver **Ruler:** Anton Ulrich as Joint ruler **Obv:** Wildman holding tree with both hands to left **Rev:** Value II. . . in 3 lines, date in legend

Date	Mintage	VG	F	VF	XF	Unc
1686	—	16.00	33.00	60.00	100	—
1687	—	16.00	33.00	60.00	100	—
1688	—	16.00	33.00	60.00	100	—
1689	—	16.00	33.00	60.00	100	—
1690	—	16.00	33.00	60.00	100	—
1691	—	16.00	33.00	60.00	100	—
1692	—	16.00	33.00	60.00	100	—
1693	—	16.00	33.00	60.00	100	—
1697	—	16.00	33.00	60.00	100	—
1698	—	16.00	33.00	60.00	100	—
1699	—	16.00	33.00	60.00	100	—

KM# 551 3 MARIENGROSCHEN

Silver **Obv:** Horse leaping left, date below **Rev:** Value III. . .

Date	Mintage	VG	F	VF	XF	Unc
1684 GFN	—	—	—	—	—	—

KM# 552 3 MARIENGROSCHEN

Silver **Obv:** Horse leaping right, date below

Date	Mintage	VG	F	VF	XF	Unc
1684 B	—	—	—	—	—	—

KM# 345 4 MARIENGROSCHEN

Silver **Obv:** Crowned FV monogram **Rev:** Value IIII. . . in 4 lines

Date	Mintage	VG	F	VF	XF	Unc
1624 HS	—	25.00	40.00	80.00	160	—
1625 (b)	—	10.00	20.00	40.00	80.00	—

KM# 499 4 MARIENGROSCHEN

Silver **Obv:** Wildman holding tree at right, with both hands, DG after duke's name **Rev:** Value IIII. . . in 3 lines, date in legend

Date	Mintage	VG	F	VF	XF	Unc
1667	—	—	—	—	—	—

KM# 500 4 MARIENGROSCHEN

Silver **Obv:** D. G. before duke's name

Date	Mintage	VG	F	VF	XF	Unc
1667	—	10.00	27.00	45.00	85.00	—
1668	—	10.00	27.00	45.00	85.00	—
1669	—	10.00	27.00	45.00	85.00	—
1671	—	10.00	27.00	45.00	85.00	—
1672	—	10.00	27.00	45.00	85.00	—
1673	—	10.00	27.00	45.00	85.00	—
1674	—	10.00	27.00	45.00	85.00	—

KM# 518 4 MARIENGROSCHEN

Silver **Obv:** 4 added next to wildman

Date	Mintage	VG	F	VF	XF	Unc
1675	—	10.00	27.00	45.00	85.00	—
1676	—	10.00	27.00	45.00	85.00	—
1677	—	10.00	27.00	45.00	85.00	—
1678	—	10.00	27.00	45.00	85.00	—
1679	—	10.00	27.00	45.00	85.00	—
1681	—	10.00	27.00	45.00	85.00	—
1683	—	10.00	27.00	45.00	85.00	—

KM# 574 4 MARIENGROSCHEN

Silver

Date	Mintage	VG	F	VF	XF	Unc
1687	—	10.00	27.00	45.00	85.00	—
1688	—	10.00	27.00	45.00	85.00	—
1689	—	10.00	27.00	45.00	85.00	—
1691	—	10.00	27.00	45.00	85.00	—
1697	—	10.00	27.00	45.00	85.00	—

KM# 503 6 MARIENGROSCHEN

Silver **Obv:** Wildman holding tree with both hands to left, 6 added next to wildman, D.G. after duke's name **Rev:** Value VI. . . in 3 lines, date in legend

Date	Mintage	VG	F	VF	XF	Unc
1668	—	25.00	45.00	80.00	140	—
1671	—	25.00	45.00	80.00	140	—
1673	—	25.00	45.00	80.00	140	—
1674	—	25.00	45.00	80.00	140	—
1675	—	25.00	45.00	80.00	140	—
1676	—	25.00	45.00	80.00	140	—
1677	—	25.00	45.00	80.00	140	—
1678	—	25.00	45.00	80.00	140	—

KM# 505 6 MARIENGROSCHEN

Silver **Obv:** Without 6 next go wildman

Date	Mintage	VG	F	VF	XF	Unc
1669	—	16.00	33.00	65.00	130	—
1679	—	16.00	33.00	65.00	130	—
1682	—	16.00	33.00	65.00	130	—

KM# 519 6 MARIENGROSCHEN

Silver **Obv:** Bust right **Rev:** Value VI. . ., date in 4 lines

Date	Mintage	VG	F	VF	XF	Unc
1675	—	—	—	—	—	—

KM# 569 6 MARIENGROSCHEN

Silver

Date	Mintage	VG	F	VF	XF	Unc
1686	—	25.00	45.00	80.00	140	—
1687	—	25.00	45.00	80.00	140	—
1688	—	25.00	45.00	80.00	140	—
1689	—	25.00	45.00	80.00	140	—
1690	—	25.00	45.00	80.00	140	—
1691	—	25.00	45.00	80.00	140	—
1692	—	25.00	45.00	80.00	140	—
1693	—	25.00	45.00	80.00	140	—
1694	—	25.00	45.00	80.00	140	—
1695	—	25.00	45.00	80.00	140	—
1696	—	25.00	45.00	80.00	140	—
1697	—	25.00	45.00	80.00	140	—
1698	—	25.00	45.00	80.00	140	—
1699	—	25.00	45.00	80.00	140	—
1700	—	25.00	45.00	80.00	140	—

KM# 578 6 MARIENGROSCHEN (1/6 Thaler)

Silver **Obv:** Horse leaping left, value 1/6 in oval below **Rev:** VI...in 3 lines **Rev. Legend:** REMIGIO ALTISSIMI UNI, date

Date	Mintage	VG	F	VF	XF	Unc
1689	—	25.00	45.00	80.00	140	—

KM# 605 6 MARIENGROSCHEN (1/6 Thaler)

Silver **Rev. Legend:** MONETA NOVA BRUNS. & LV:, date

Date	Mintage	VG	F	VF	XF	Unc
1693 HCH	—	25.00	45.00	80.00	140	—

KM# 606 6 MARIENGROSCHEN (1/6 Thaler)

Silver **Rev. Legend:** NACH DEM LEIP. FUSS

Date	Mintage	VG	F	VF	XF	Unc
1693 HCH	—	16.00	33.00	60.00	110	—
1695 HCH	—	16.00	33.00	60.00	110	—
1696 HCH	—	16.00	33.00	60.00	110	—
1697 HCH	—	16.00	33.00	60.00	110	—

KM# 614 6 MARIENGROSCHEN (1/6 Thaler)

Silver **Rev. Legend:** FURSTL. BRUNS. LUNEB. MUNTZ, date

Date	Mintage	VG	F	VF	XF	Unc
1694 HCH	—	16.00	33.00	60.00	110	—

KM# 622 6 MARIENGROSCHEN (1/6 Thaler)

Silver **Obv:** Value VI. . . in 4 lines

Date	Mintage	VG	F	VF	XF	Unc
1696 ICP	—	20.00	40.00	70.00	120	—
1696 ICB	—	20.00	40.00	70.00	120	—
1697 ICP	—	20.00	40.00	70.00	120	—
1697 ICB	—	20.00	40.00	70.00	120	—

Note: Varieties exist

KM# 346 10 MARIENGROSCHEN

Silver **Obv:** Crowned VF monogram, date in legend **Rev:** Value X...in 3 lines

Date	Mintage	VG	F	VF	XF	Unc
1624	—	—	—	—	—	—

KM# 504 12 MARIENGROSCHEN (1/3 Thaler)

Silver

Date	Mintage	VG	F	VF	XF	Unc
1668	—	33.00	65.00	100	160	—
1669	—	33.00	65.00	100	160	—
1670	—	33.00	65.00	100	160	—
1671	—	33.00	65.00	100	160	—
1672	—	33.00	65.00	100	160	—
1673	—	33.00	65.00	100	160	—
1674	—	33.00	65.00	100	160	—
1675	—	33.00	65.00	100	160	—
1676	—	33.00	65.00	100	160	—
1677	—	33.00	65.00	100	160	—
1678	—	33.00	65.00	100	160	—
1679	—	33.00	65.00	100	160	—
1680	—	33.00	65.00	100	160	—
1681	—	33.00	65.00	100	160	—
1682	—	33.00	65.00	100	160	—
1683	—	33.00	65.00	100	160	—
1684	—	33.00	65.00	100	160	—

KM# 570 12 MARIENGROSCHEN (1/3 Thaler)

Silver **Ruler:** Anton Ulrich as Joint ruler **Obv:** Wildman holding tree with two hands at left, 12 at left of wildman **Rev:** Value XII...in 3 lines, date in legend

Date	Mintage	VG	F	VF	XF	Unc
1686	—	25.00	45.00	75.00	140	—
1687	—	25.00	45.00	75.00	140	—
1688	—	25.00	45.00	75.00	140	—
1690	—	25.00	45.00	75.00	140	—
1691	—	25.00	45.00	75.00	140	—
1692	—	25.00	45.00	75.00	140	—
1694	—	25.00	45.00	75.00	140	—
1695	—	25.00	45.00	75.00	140	—
1696	—	25.00	45.00	75.00	140	—
1697	—	25.00	45.00	75.00	140	—
1698	—	25.00	45.00	75.00	140	—
1699	—	25.00	45.00	75.00	140	—
1700	—	25.00	45.00	75.00	140	—

KM# 585 12 MARIENGROSCHEN (1/3 Thaler)

Silver **Obv:** Horse leaping left **Rev:** Value XII. . . in 3 lines, date in legend

Date	Mintage	VG	F	VF	XF	Unc
1690 HCH	—	—	—	—	—	—
1691 HCH	—	—	—	—	—	—

KM# 516 24 MARIENGROSCHEN (2/3 Thaler)

Silver

Date	Mintage	VG	F	VF	XF	Unc
1674	—	45.00	85.00	155	230	—
1675	—	45.00	85.00	155	230	—
1676	—	45.00	85.00	155	230	—
1677	—	45.00	85.00	155	230	—
1679	—	45.00	85.00	155	230	—

KM# 521 24 MARIENGROSCHEN (2/3 Thaler)

Silver **Obv:** Bust right **Rev:** Value, date

Date	Mintage	VG	F	VF	XF	Unc
1676 B	—	120	200	325	475	—

KM# 529 24 MARIENGROSCHEN (2/3 Thaler)

Silver **Note:** Similar to KM#516, but V. FEIN. SILB: added below value.

Date	Mintage	VG	F	VF	XF	Unc
1677	—	35.00	75.00	120	225	—
1678	—	35.00	75.00	120	225	—
1679	—	35.00	75.00	120	225	—
1680	—	35.00	75.00	120	225	—
1681	—	35.00	75.00	120	225	—
1682	—	35.00	75.00	120	225	—
1683	—	35.00	75.00	120	225	—
1684	—	35.00	75.00	120	225	—
1685	—	35.00	75.00	120	225	—

KM# 559 24 MARIENGROSCHEN (2/3 Thaler)

Silver **Ruler:** Anton Ulrich as Joint ruler **Obv:** Wildman with tree in both hands at right, value at left **Rev:** Value within inner circle, date in legend

Date	Mintage	VG	F	VF	XF	Unc
1685	—	33.00	65.00	100	200	—
1686	—	33.00	65.00	100	200	—
1687	—	33.00	65.00	100	200	—
1688	—	33.00	65.00	100	200	—
1689	—	33.00	65.00	100	200	—
1690	—	33.00	65.00	100	200	—
1691	—	33.00	65.00	100	200	—
1692	—	33.00	65.00	100	200	—
1693	—	33.00	65.00	100	200	—
1694	—	33.00	65.00	100	200	—
1695	—	33.00	65.00	100	200	—
1696	—	33.00	65.00	100	200	—
1697	—	33.00	65.00	100	200	—
1698	—	33.00	65.00	100	200	—
1699	—	33.00	65.00	100	200	—
1700	—	33.00	65.00	100	200	—

KM# 586 24 MARIENGROSCHEN (2/3 Thaler)
Silver

Date	Mintage	VG	F	VF	XF	Unc
1690	—	35.00	75.00	125	225	—
1690 HCH	—	35.00	75.00	125	225	—
1691 HCH	—	35.00	75.00	125	225	—
1692 HCH	—	35.00	75.00	125	225	—
1693 HCH	—	35.00	75.00	125	225	—

KM# 607 24 MARIENGROSCHEN (2/3 Thaler)
Silver **Rev:** Value XXIIII. . .

Date	Mintage	VG	F	VF	XF	Unc
1693 HCH	—	40.00	85.00	160	275	—

KM# 608 24 MARIENGROSCHEN (2/3 Thaler)
Silver **Rev. Legend:** NACH DEN...

Date	Mintage	VG	F	VF	XF	Unc
1693 HCH	—	40.00	85.00	160	275	—
1694 HCH	—	40.00	85.00	160	275	—

KM# 615 24 MARIENGROSCHEN (2/3 Thaler)
Silver **Ruler:** Anton Ulrich as Joint ruler **Obv:** Horse leaping left, 2/3 in oval below

Date	Mintage	VG	F	VF	XF	Unc
1694 HCH	—	40.00	85.00	160	275	—
1695 HCH	—	40.00	85.00	160	275	—
1696 HCH	—	40.00	85.00	160	275	—
1697 HCH	—	40.00	85.00	160	275	—
1698 HCH	—	40.00	85.00	160	275	—
1699 HCH	—	40.00	85.00	160	275	—
1700 HCH	—	40.00	85.00	160	275	—

KM# 347 1/2 MARIENGULDEN (1/3 Thaler)
Silver **Obv:** Similar to 1 Mariengulden, KM#342 **Rev:** I/HALBE/MARIE/GULD **Rev. Legend:** BRAUN. MUNTZ...

Date	Mintage	VG	F	VF	XF	Unc
1624	—	85.00	165	360	525	—

KM# 342 MARIENGULDEN (2/3 Thaler)
Silver

Date	Mintage	VG	F	VF	XF	Unc
1623	—	90.00	175	275	475	—
1624	—	90.00	175	275	475	—

KM# 136 3 KREUZER (Groschen)
Silver **Rev. Legend:** IN FOEL. C. N. INVI

Date	Mintage	VG	F	VF	XF	Unc
ND	—	20.00	40.00	65.00	120	—

KM# 137 3 KREUZER (Groschen)
Silver **Rev. Legend:** LABORE. CONSUMIN.

Date	Mintage	VG	F	VF	XF	Unc
ND	—	20.00	40.00	65.00	120	—

KM# 138 3 KREUZER (Groschen)
Silver **Rev. Legend:** M. G. V. K. K. V. G. M.

Date	Mintage	VG	F	VF	XF	Unc
1620	—	20.00	40.00	65.00	120	—

KM# 140 3 KREUZER (Groschen)
Silver **Rev. Legend:** SI. DE9 PRO. N. Q. C. N.

Date	Mintage	VG	F	VF	XF	Unc
16Z0	—	20.00	40.00	65.00	120	—

KM# 141 3 KREUZER (Groschen)
Silver **Rev. Legend:** SOLI. DEO. GLORIA.

Date	Mintage	VG	F	VF	XF	Unc
ND	—	20.00	40.00	65.00	120	—

KM# 142 3 KREUZER (Groschen)
Silver **Obv. Legend:** Titles of Ferdinand II **Rev. Legend:** SEMPER. PRO. PATRIA.

Date	Mintage	VG	F	VF	XF	Unc
ND (b)	—	20.00	40.00	65.00	120	—

KM# 143 3 KREUZER (Groschen)
Silver **Obv:** Titles of Matthias **Rev:** Arms divided horizontally, lion above, chessboard below **Rev. Legend:** DEUS. EST. UINDEX.

Date	Mintage	VG	F	VF	XF	Unc
1620	—	20.00	40.00	65.00	120	—

KM# 144 3 KREUZER (Groschen)
Silver **Obv:** Imperial eagle, 3 on breast, Z.O.N.H.T.D.G. **Rev:** Crown with horse above **Rev. Legend:** W.G.W.V.F.L.

Date	Mintage	VG	F	VF	XF	Unc
1620	—	20.00	40.00	65.00	120	—

KM# 145 3 KREUZER (Groschen)
Silver **Obv:** Lion left **Obv. Legend:** AGENDO. CONANDO.

Date	Mintage	VG	F	VF	XF	Unc
ND	—	20.00	40.00	65.00	120	—

KM# 146 3 KREUZER (Groschen)
Silver **Obv:** Lion rampant left **Obv. Legend:** FID. B. DESER. DEUS. **Rev:** Titles of Ferdinand II

Date	Mintage	VG	F	VF	XF	Unc
ND	—	20.00	40.00	650	120	—

KM# 147 3 KREUZER (Groschen)
Silver **Obv. Legend:** PAR. PR. NO. IR. L.

Date	Mintage	VG	F	VF	XF	Unc
ND	—	20.00	40.00	65.00	120	—

KM# 148 3 KREUZER (Groschen)
Silver **Obv:** Tower to side of lion **Obv. Legend:** TIME. DEVM. ET. DVCE. M.

Date	Mintage	VG	F	VF	XF	Unc
ND	—	20.00	40.00	65.00	120	—

KM# 149 3 KREUZER (Groschen)
Silver **Obv:** Lion rampant left in 3-turretted tower **Obv. Legend:** GOT. D. E. S. N. M. **Rev:** Titles of Matthias

Date	Mintage	VG	F	VF	XF	Unc
ND	—	20.00	40.00	65.00	120	—

KM# 150 3 KREUZER (Groschen)
Silver **Obv:** Deear antlers **Obv. Legend:** ORA. ET. LABORA **Rev:** Titles of Ferdinand II

Date	Mintage	VG	F	VF	XF	Unc
1620	—	20.00	40.00	65.00	120	—

KM# 151 3 KREUZER (Groschen)
Silver **Obv. Legend:** PRO PATRIA, date

Date	Mintage	VG	F	VF	XF	Unc
1620	—	20.00	40.00	65.00	120	—

KM# 152 3 KREUZER (Groschen)
Silver **Obv:** Large rose **Obv. Legend:** SI. DE. PRO. N. Q. C. N. **Rev:** Titles of Matthias

Date	Mintage	VG	F	VF	XF	Unc
1620	—	20.00	40.00	65.00	120	—

KM# 135 3 KREUZER (Groschen)
Silver **Obv:** Imperial eagle, 3 on breast, titles of Matthias **Rev:** 4-fold arms, H below, **Rev. Legend:** GOT. DI. EH... **Note:** Kipper-3 Kreuzer.

Date	Mintage	VG	F	VF	XF	Unc
ND	—	20.00	4.00	65.00	120	—
1620	—	20.00	40.00	65.00	120	—

KM# 139 3 KREUZER (Groschen)
Silver **Rev. Legend:** ORA. ET. LABORA. **Note:** Varieties exist.

Date	Mintage	VG	F	VF	XF	Unc
1620	—	20.00	40.00	65.00	120	—

KM# 265 3 KREUZER (Groschen)
Silver **Obv:** Crowned 4-fold arms **Rev:** Crowned imprial eagle, 3 on breast

Date	Mintage	VG	F	VF	XF	Unc
1621	—	20.00	40.00	65.00	120	—

KM# 171 12 KREUZER (1/12 Thaler)
Silver **Obv:** Crowned 3-fold arms **Obv. Legend:** SOLI. DEO. GLORIA. **Rev:** Titles of Matthias

Date	Mintage	VG	F	VF	XF	Unc
ND	—	33.00	65.00	110	200	—

KM# 89 12 KREUZER (1/12 Thaler)
Silver **Obv. Legend:** IS. AL. NO. SIT. QU. SUI. P.

Date	Mintage	VG	F	VF	XF	Unc
1619	—	33.00	65.00	110	200	—

KM# 88 12 KREUZER (1/12 Thaler)
Silver **Obv:** Crowned imperial eagle, 12 in orb on breast, titles of Matthias **Rev:** Crowned 4-fold arms **Rev. Legend:** D. ME. SP. IS. EIN. GRE. V. G., date **Note:** Kipper 12 Kreuzer.

Date	Mintage	VG	F	VF	XF	Unc
1619	—	33.00	65.00	110	200	—
1620	—	33.00	65.00	110	200	—

Note: Varieties exist

KM# 90 12 KREUZER (1/12 Thaler)
Silver **Obv. Legend:** ORA. ET. LABORA, date **Note:** Varieties exist.

Date	Mintage	VG	F	VF	XF	Unc
(1)619	—	33.00	65.00	110	200	—
(1)619	—	33.00	65.00	110	200	—

Note: Varieties exist

KM# 154 12 KREUZER (1/12 Thaler)
Silver **Obv:** Brunswick helmet with horse **Rev:** Date in legend **Note:** Varieties exist.

Date	Mintage	VG	F	VF	XF	Unc
1620	—	27.00	55.00	95.00	180	—
1621	—	27.00	55.00	95.00	180	—
ND	—	27.00	55.00	95.00	180	—

KM# 155 12 KREUZER (1/12 Thaler)
Silver **Note:** Varieties exist.

Date	Mintage	VG	F	VF	XF	Unc
1620	—	27.00	45.00	85.00	170	—
1621	—	27.00	45.00	85.00	170	—

KM# 157 12 KREUZER (1/12 Thaler)
Silver **Obv:** Oval 4-fold arms **Rev:** Date in legend **Note:** Varieties exist.

Date	Mintage	VG	F	VF	XF	Unc
1620	—	27.00	55.00	90.00	170	—
1620 (b)	—	27.00	55.00	90.00	170	—
(1)621 (b)	—	27.00	55.00	90.00	170	—

KM# 170 12 KREUZER (1/12 Thaler)
Silver **Obv. Legend:** SOLI. DEO. GLORIA. **Note:** Varieties exist.

Date	Mintage	VG	F	VF	XF	Unc
1620	—	27.00	55.00	90.00	170	—
ND	—	27.00	55.00	90.00	170	—

KM# 168 12 KREUZER (1/12 Thaler)
Silver **Rev. Legend:** ORA. ET. LABORA. **Note:** Kipper.

Date	Mintage	VG	F	VF	XF	Unc
1620	—	27.00	55.00	90.00	170	—

KM# 165 12 KREUZER (1/12 Thaler)
Silver **Note:** Klippe-12 Kreuzer.

Date	Mintage	VG	F	VF	XF	Unc
ND	—	—	—	—	—	—

KM# 153 12 KREUZER (1/12 Thaler)
Silver **Obv:** Imperial eagle, 12 in orb on breast, titles of Ferdinand II **Rev:** Wildman, tree in right hand **Rev. Legend:** MONE. NO AR. D. B. E. L.

Date	Mintage	VG	F	VF	XF	Unc
1620 CH	—	27.00	45.00	85.00	165	—
1620 HH	—	27.00	45.00	85.00	165	—
1620 LB	—	27.00	45.00	85.00	165	—
1620 WG	—	27.00	45.00	85.00	165	—
1621	—	27.00	45.00	85.00	165	—
1621 CV	—	27.00	45.00	85.00	165	—
1621 IL	—	27.00	45.00	85.00	165	—
ND	—	27.00	45.00	85.00	165	—
16ZZ	—	27.00	45.00	85.00	165	—

KM# 156 12 KREUZER (1/12 Thaler)
Silver **Obv:** Crowned arms with horse in front of column

Date	Mintage	VG	F	VF	XF	Unc
1620	—	27.00	55.00	100	185	—

KM# 158 12 KREUZER (1/12 Thaler)
Silver **Obv:** 9-fold arms divide date

Date	Mintage	VG	F	VF	XF	Unc
1620	—	33.00	65.00	110	200	—
1621	—	33.00	65.00	110	200	—

KM# 159 12 KREUZER (1/12 Thaler)
Silver **Obv:** Crowned imperial eagle, 12 in orb on breast, titles of Matthias **Rev:** Crowned 4-fold arms **Rev. Legend:** ADIVVANTE DEO, date

Date	Mintage	VG	F	VF	XF	Unc
1620	—	27.00	55.00	110	200	—

KM# 160 12 KREUZER (1/12 Thaler)
Silver **Rev. Legend:** LABORE. CONSUMIMUR

Date	Mintage	VG	F	VF	XF	Unc
1620	—	27.00	55.00	110	200	—
ND	—	27.00	55.00	110	200	—

Note: Varieties exist

KM# 161 12 KREUZER (1/12 Thaler)
Silver **Obv. Legend:** SIT NOM: BENEDICTIVM.

Date	Mintage	VG	F	VF	XF	Unc
ND	—	27.00	55.00	110	200	—

Note: Varieties exist

KM# 162 12 KREUZER (1/12 Thaler)
Silver **Obv. Legend:** SOLI. DEO. GLORIA.

Date	Mintage	VG	F	VF	XF	Unc
ND	—	27.00	55.00	110	200	—

Note: Varieties exist.

KM# 163 12 KREUZER (1/12 Thaler)
Silver **Obv:** Central shield with pellet in arms

Date	Mintage	VG	F	VF	XF	Unc
ND	—	27.00	55.00	110	200	—

KM# 164 12 KREUZER (1/12 Thaler)
Silver **Obv:** Titles of Ferdinand II **Rev. Legend:** CONVERTE. ME. DOMINE.

Date	Mintage	VG	F	VF	XF	Unc
ND	—	27.00	55.00	110	200	—

KM# 166 12 KREUZER (1/12 Thaler)
Silver **Rev. Legend:** D. ME. SP. IS. EIN. GRE. V. G.

Date	Mintage	VG	F	VF	XF	Unc
1620	—	27.00	55.00	110	200	—

KM# 167 12 KREUZER (1/12 Thaler)
Silver **Obv:** Titles of Ferdinan II **Rev. Legend:** LABORE. CONSUMIMUR.

Date	Mintage	VG	F	VF	XF	Unc
1620	—	27.00	55.00	110	200	—

KM# 169 12 KREUZER (1/12 Thaler)
Silver **Obv. Legend:** SIT NOM: DOM: BENEDICTUM.

Date	Mintage	VG	F	VF	XF	Unc
ND	—	27.00	55.00	110	200	—

KM# 172 12 KREUZER (1/12 Thaler)
Silver **Obv:** Shield with bars **Obv. Legend:** DURA. PATI-S **Rev:** Titles of Ferdinand II

Date	Mintage	VG	F	VF	XF	Unc
1620	—	33.00	65.00	120	225	—

KM# 266 12 KREUZER (1/12 Thaler)
Silver **Obv:** Crowned imperial eagle, 12 in orb on breast, titles of Ferdinand II **Rev:** Facing bust of St. Jacob

Date	Mintage	VG	F	VF	XF	Unc
1621	—	—	—	—	—	—

KM# 267 12 KREUZER (1/12 Thaler)
Silver **Obv:** Crowned imperial eagle, 12 on breast, titles of Ferdinand II **Rev:** Wildman, tree in right hand

Date	Mintage	VG	F	VF	XF	Unc
1621	—	27.00	45.00	85.00	160	—
ND	—	27.00	45.00	85.00	160	—

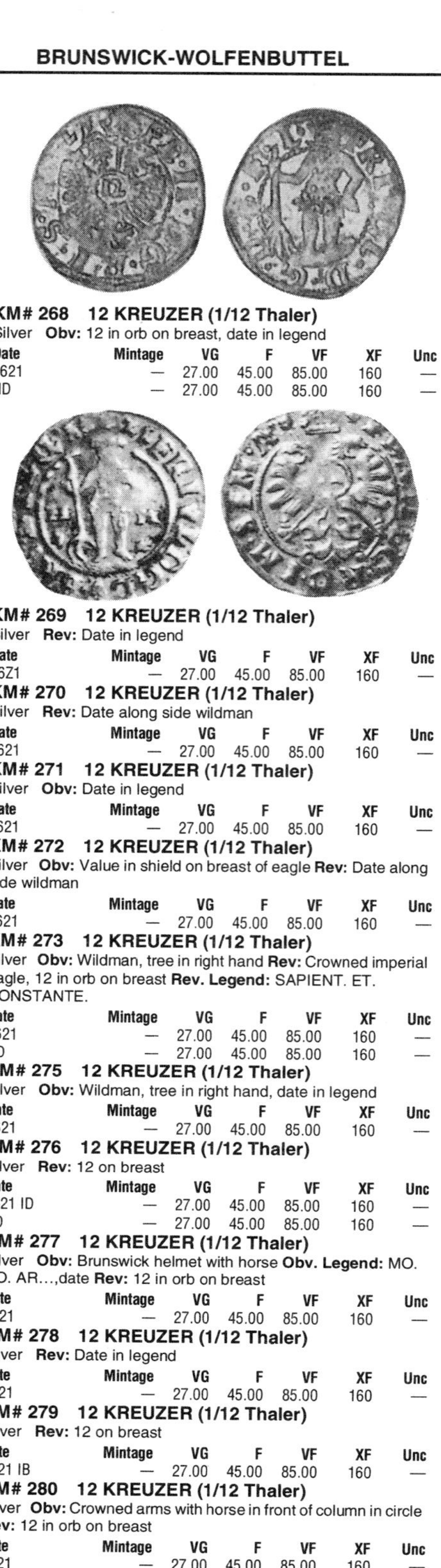

KM# 268 12 KREUZER (1/12 Thaler)
Silver **Obv:** 12 in orb on breast, date in legend

Date	Mintage	VG	F	VF	XF	Unc
1621	—	27.00	45.00	85.00	160	—
ND	—	27.00	45.00	85.00	160	—

KM# 269 12 KREUZER (1/12 Thaler)
Silver **Rev:** Date in legend

Date	Mintage	VG	F	VF	XF	Unc
16Z1	—	27.00	45.00	85.00	160	—

KM# 270 12 KREUZER (1/12 Thaler)
Silver **Rev:** Date along side wildman

Date	Mintage	VG	F	VF	XF	Unc
1621	—	27.00	45.00	85.00	160	—

KM# 271 12 KREUZER (1/12 Thaler)
Silver **Obv:** Date in legend

Date	Mintage	VG	F	VF	XF	Unc
1621	—	27.00	45.00	85.00	160	—

KM# 272 12 KREUZER (1/12 Thaler)
Silver **Obv:** Value in shield on breast of eagle **Rev:** Date along side wildman

Date	Mintage	VG	F	VF	XF	Unc
1621	—	27.00	45.00	85.00	160	—

KM# 273 12 KREUZER (1/12 Thaler)
Silver **Obv:** Wildman, tree in right hand **Rev:** Crowned imperial eagle, 12 in orb on breast **Rev. Legend:** SAPIENT. ET. CONSTANTE.

Date	Mintage	VG	F	VF	XF	Unc
1621	—	27.00	45.00	85.00	160	—
ND	—	27.00	45.00	85.00	160	—

KM# 275 12 KREUZER (1/12 Thaler)
Silver **Obv:** Wildman, tree in right hand, date in legend

Date	Mintage	VG	F	VF	XF	Unc
1621	—	27.00	45.00	85.00	160	—

KM# 276 12 KREUZER (1/12 Thaler)
Silver **Rev:** 12 on breast

Date	Mintage	VG	F	VF	XF	Unc
1621 ID	—	27.00	45.00	85.00	160	—
ND	—	27.00	45.00	85.00	160	—

KM# 277 12 KREUZER (1/12 Thaler)
Silver **Obv:** Brunswick helmet with horse **Obv. Legend:** MO. NO. AR...,date **Rev:** 12 in orb on breast

Date	Mintage	VG	F	VF	XF	Unc
1621	—	27.00	45.00	85.00	160	—

KM# 278 12 KREUZER (1/12 Thaler)
Silver **Rev:** Date in legend

Date	Mintage	VG	F	VF	XF	Unc
1621	—	27.00	45.00	85.00	160	—

KM# 279 12 KREUZER (1/12 Thaler)
Silver **Rev:** 12 on breast

Date	Mintage	VG	F	VF	XF	Unc
1621 IB	—	27.00	45.00	85.00	160	—

KM# 280 12 KREUZER (1/12 Thaler)
Silver **Obv:** Crowned arms with horse in front of column in circle **Rev:** 12 in orb on breast

Date	Mintage	VG	F	VF	XF	Unc
1621	—	27.00	45.00	85.00	160	—

KM# 281 12 KREUZER (1/12 Thaler)
Silver **Obv:** Crown lion rampant left **Rev:** Date in legend

Date	Mintage	VG	F	VF	XF	Unc
1621	—	27.00	45.00	85.00	160	—

KM# 282 12 KREUZER (1/12 Thaler)
Silver **Obv:** Lion striding left above ornamented base

Date	Mintage	VG	F	VF	XF	Unc
1621	—	27.00	55.00	100	200	—

KM# 283 12 KREUZER (1/12 Thaler)
Silver **Obv:** Date in legend

Date	Mintage	VG	F	VF	XF	Unc
1621	—	27.00	55.00	100	200	—

KM# 284 12 KREUZER (1/12 Thaler)
Silver **Obv:** Lion rampant left **Rev:** Wildman, tree in right hand **Rev. Legend:** SAPIENTER. . .

Date	Mintage	VG	F	VF	XF	Unc
1621	—	27.00	55.00	100	200	—

KM# 285 12 KREUZER (1/12 Thaler)
Silver **Obv:** Crown imperial eagle, 12 in orb on breast, titles of Ferdinand II **Rev:** Lion rampant right

Date	Mintage	VG	F	VF	XF	Unc
1621	—	27.00	55.00	100	200	—

KM# 286 12 KREUZER (1/12 Thaler)
Silver **Rev. Legend:** SAPIENTER. . .

Date	Mintage	VG	F	VF	XF	Unc
1621	—	27.00	55.00	100	200	—
ND	—	27.00	55.00	100	200	—

KM# 287 12 KREUZER (1/12 Thaler)
Silver **Obv:** Oval 4-fold arms **Obv. Legend:** MON. NOVA. DVCA. . .

Date	Mintage	VG	F	VF	XF	Unc
1621	—	27.00	55.00	100	200	—

KM# 288 12 KREUZER (1/12 Thaler)
Silver **Obv:** St. Andrew with cross **Obv. Legend:** RECTE FACIEN: NEM. TIMEA.

Date	Mintage	VG	F	VF	XF	Unc
1621	—	27.00	55.00	100	200	—
1622	—	27.00	55.00	100	200	—

KM# 289 12 KREUZER (1/12 Thaler)
Silver **Obv:** Wildman, tree in right hand **Obv. Legend:** PRO LEGE ET GREGE, date

Date	Mintage	VG	F	VF	XF	Unc
1621	—	27.00	55.00	100	200	—

KM# 290 12 KREUZER (1/12 Thaler)
Silver **Obv. Legend:** MONE NO B. E. L.

Date	Mintage	VG	F	VF	XF	Unc
ND	—	27.00	55.00	100	200	—

KM# 291 12 KREUZER (1/12 Thaler)
Silver **Obv. Legend:** SAPIENTER. ET: CONSTANTER.

Date	Mintage	VG	F	VF	XF	Unc
1621	—	27.00	45.00	90.00	175	—

KM# 292 12 KREUZER (1/12 Thaler)
Silver **Obv:** Cowned 2-fold arms, lion rampant left above bars **Obv. Legend:** DEVS ** DO ** MEA. **Rev:** Titles

Date	Mintage	VG	F	VF	XF	Unc
1621	—	27.00	55.00	100	200	—

KM# 293 12 KREUZER (1/12 Thaler)
Silver **Obv:** Lion walking left **Obv. Legend:** CONSILIO. ET. ARMIS.

Date	Mintage	VG	F	VF	XF	Unc
ND	—	27.00	55.00	100	200	—

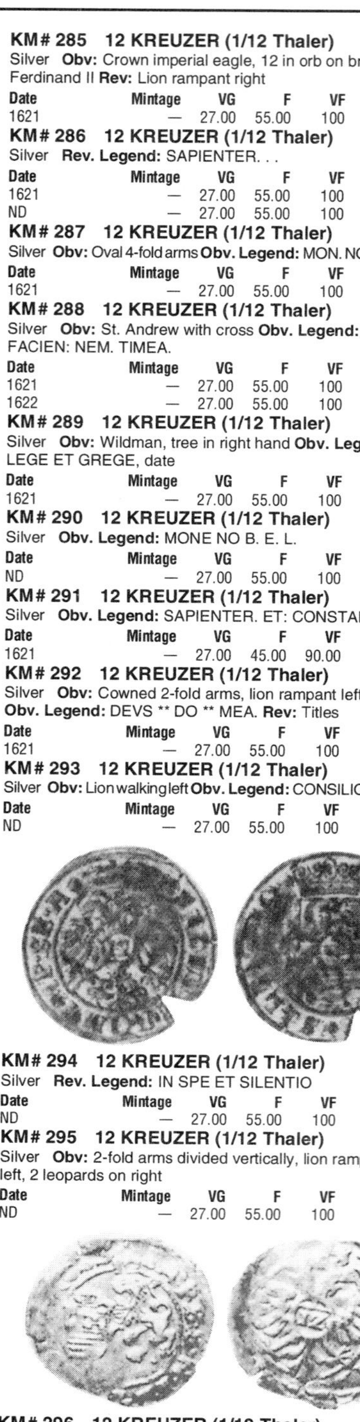

KM# 294 12 KREUZER (1/12 Thaler)
Silver **Rev. Legend:** IN SPE ET SILENTIO

Date	Mintage	VG	F	VF	XF	Unc
ND	—	27.00	55.00	100	200	—

KM# 295 12 KREUZER (1/12 Thaler)
Silver **Obv:** 2-fold arms divided vertically, lion rampant left on left, 2 leopards on right

Date	Mintage	VG	F	VF	XF	Unc
ND	—	27.00	55.00	100	200	—

KM# 296 12 KREUZER (1/12 Thaler)
Silver **Obv:** Crowned lion rampant left, holding arms **Obv. Legend:** GVDE. GROS.

Date	Mintage	VG	F	VF	XF	Unc
ND	—	27.00	55.00	100	200	—

KM# 297 12 KREUZER (1/12 Thaler)
Silver **Obv:** Lion rampant left **Rev:** SPES. NON. CONFVNDIT, date

Date	Mintage	VG	F	VF	XF	Unc
1621	—	27.00	55.00	100	200	—

KM# 299 12 KREUZER (1/12 Thaler)
Silver **Obv:** Lion rampant right **Obv. Legend:** ALLES STHET BEI GLVC. V. ZEIT.

Date	Mintage	VG	F	VF	XF	Unc
1621	—	27.00	55.00	100	200	—
ND	—	27.00	55.00	100	200	—

KM# 300 12 KREUZER (1/12 Thaler)
Silver **Obv:** Lion passant right

Date	Mintage	VG	F	VF	XF	Unc
1621	—	27.00	55.00	100	200	—

KM# 301 12 KREUZER (1/12 Thaler)
Silver **Obv:** Lion right, tower at side **Obv. Legend:** PRO. LEGE. ET. GREGE, date

Date	Mintage	VG	F	VF	XF	Unc
1621	—	27.00	55.00	100	200	—

KM# 302 12 KREUZER (1/12 Thaler)
Silver **Obv:** 2 leopards **Obv. Legend:** AVDCES OR IVVAT

Date	Mintage	VG	F	VF	XF	Unc
ND	—	27.00	55.00	100	200	—

KM# 303 12 KREUZER (1/12 Thaler)
Silver **Obv. Legend:** NEG. S. -G: MI-date

Date	Mintage	VG	F	VF	XF	Unc
1621	—	27.00	55.00	100	200	—

KM# 304 12 KREUZER (1/12 Thaler)
Silver **Obv:** Old Brunswick helmet with horse **Obv. Legend:** FIDEM. AES: DE. DEI.

Date	Mintage	VG	F	VF	XF	Unc
ND	—	27.00	45.00	90.00	180	—

KM# 305 12 KREUZER (1/12 Thaler)
Silver **Obv. Legend:** IN. TE. DOMI. SPERA. NON. CON. F.

Date	Mintage	VG	F	VF	XF	Unc
1621	—	27.00	45.00	90.00	180	—

KM# 306 12 KREUZER (1/12 Thaler)
Silver **Obv:** Helmet with 2 bear paws **Obv. Legend:** IN. DEO. VIRT. FACIEMUS.

Date	Mintage	VG	F	VF	XF	Unc
1621	—	27.00	45.00	90.00	180	—
ND	—	27.00	45.00	90.00	180	—

KM# 307 12 KREUZER (1/12 Thaler)
Silver **Obv:** Horse in front of column **Obv. Legend:** PRO. LEGE. ET. GREGE.

Date	Mintage	VG	F	VF	XF	Unc
ND	—	27.00	55.00	100	200	—

KM# 308 12 KREUZER (1/12 Thaler)
Silver **Obv:** 2 bear paws in shield **Obv. Legend:** ARMIS. ET. LEGIBUS.

Date	Mintage	VG	F	VF	XF	Unc
ND	—	27.00	45.00	90.00	180	—

KM# 274 12 KREUZER (1/12 Thaler)
Silver **Obv:** Brunswick helmet with horse **Rev:** Crowned imperial eagle, 12 in orb on breast, date in legend **Note:** Klippe.

Date	Mintage	VG	F	VF	XF	Unc
1621	—	—	—	—	—	—

KM# 298 12 KREUZER (1/12 Thaler)
Silver **Rev:** Lion rampant right in shield **Rev. Legend:** CONSILIO. ET. ARMIS **Note:** Varieties exist.

Date	Mintage	VG	F	VF	XF	Unc
1621	—	27.00	55.00	100	200	—
ND (b)	—	27.00	55.00	100	200	—
ND	—	27.00	55.00	100	200	—

KM# 310 24 KREUZER (1/6 Thaler)
Silver **Obv:** Crowned imperial eagle, 24 in orb on breast, titles of Ferdinand II, date in legend **Rev:** Brunswick helmet with horse

Date	Mintage	VG	F	VF	XF	Unc
1621	—	60.00	120	225	350	—

KM# 311 24 KREUZER (1/6 Thaler)
Silver **Obv:** 2-fold arms, lion right above bars below **Obv. Legend:** DEV. TI-TVDO ** MEA.

Date	Mintage	VG	F	VF	XF	Unc
1621	—	60.00	120	225	350	—

KM# 309 24 KREUZER (1/6 Thaler)
Silver **Obv:** Crown above Brunswick helmet with horse, 3 arms below **Rev:** Angel standing behind shield with deer left, date in legend **Note:** Kipper-24 Kreuzer.

Date	Mintage	VG	F	VF	XF	Unc
1621	—	60.00	120	225	350	—

KM# 23 1/96 THALER (Körtling)
Silver **Obv:** Brunswick helmet with horse **Rev:** Imperial orb with 96 divides date

Date	Mintage	VG	F	VF	XF	Unc
1605	—	—	—	—	—	—

KM# 35 1/28 THALER
Silver **Obv:** Brunswick helmet with horse **Rev:** Wildman, tree branch in right hand, 28 below

Date	Mintage	VG	F	VF	XF	Unc
1610 (o)	—	—	—	—	—	—

KM# 4 1/24 THALER (Groschen)
Silver **Obv:** Brunswick helmet with horse **Rev:** Imperial orb with 24

Date	Mintage	VG	F	VF	XF	Unc
1599	—	25.00	45.00	85.00	170	—
1599 (d)	—	25.00	45.00	85.00	170	—
1600 (d)	—	25.00	45.00	85.00	170	—
1602	—	25.00	45.00	85.00	170	—
1603	—	25.00	45.00	85.00	170	—
1605	—	25.00	45.00	85.00	170	—

KM# 40 1/24 THALER (Groschen)
Silver **Rev:** Wildman, imperial orb with 24 in right hand, date in legend

Date	Mintage	VG	F	VF	XF	Unc
1613 (o)	—	25.00	45.00	85.00	170	—
1614 (o)	—	25.00	45.00	85.00	170	—
1615 (o)	—	25.00	45.00	85.00	170	—

KM# 67 1/24 THALER (Groschen)
Silver **Obv:** Imperial orb with 24, titles of Matthias, date **Rev:** Rampant lion left **Rev. Legend:** AN. GOT. SE. I. AL. GE.

Date	Mintage	VG	F	VF	XF	Unc
1617	—	13.00	27.00	45.00	100	—
1618	—	13.00	27.00	45.00	100	—

KM# 68 1/24 THALER (Groschen)
Silver **Note:** Klipper-1/24 Thaler, 5.50 g.

Date	Mintage	VG	F	VF	XF	Unc
1617	—	—	—	—	—	—

KM# 69 1/24 THALER (Groschen)
Silver **Obv:** Imperial orb with 24, titles of Matthias **Rev:** LIon rampant right **Rev. Legend:** AGENDO CONANDO **Note:** Varieties exist.

Date	Mintage	VG	F	VF	XF	Unc
1617	—	13.00	27.00	45.00	100	—
1619	—	13.00	27.00	45.00	100	—
ND	—	13.00	27.00	45.00	100	—

KM# 80 1/24 THALER (Groschen)
Silver **Obv:** Imperial orb with 24, titles of Matthias **Rev:** Arms with 2 bear claws (Hoya) **Rev. Legend:** D. MENSCHEN. G. I. V. S. **Note:** Varieties exist.

Date	Mintage	VG	F	VF	XF	Unc
1618	—	16.00	33.00	60.00	110	—
1619	—	16.00	33.00	60.00	110	—

KM# 75 1/24 THALER (Groschen)
Silver **Obv:** 4-fold arms **Obv. Legend:** DOMI. PROVIDEBIT, date

Date	Mintage	VG	F	VF	XF	Unc
1618	—	16.00	33.00	60.00	110	—
1619	—	16.00	33.00	60.00	110	—

KM# 76 1/24 THALER (Groschen)
Silver **Obv:** 2-fold arms divided vertically **Obv. Legend:** BI. GO. IST. RHAT. V. THA. R.

Date	Mintage	VG	F	VF	XF	Unc
1618	—	16.00	33.00	60.00	110	—
1619	—	16.00	33.00	60.00	110	—

KM# 77 1/24 THALER (Groschen)
Silver **Obv:** Rampant lion left **Obv. Legend:** B. GOT. I. RADT. V. DHAD.

Date	Mintage	VG	F	VF	XF	Unc
1618	—	16.00	27.00	45.00	100	—

KM# 78 1/24 THALER (Groschen)
Silver **Obv:** Lion holding key **Obv. Leg.:** GOTT. GI: WE. ER. WIL.

Date	Mintage	VG	F	VF	XF	Unc
1618	—	12.00	25.00	40.00	80.00	—
1619	—	12.00	25.00	40.00	80.00	—

KM# 79 1/24 THALER (Groschen)
Silver **Obv:** Stag antlers **Obv. Legend:** B. E. GOT. I. RAHT.

Date	Mintage	VG	F	VF	XF	Unc
1618	—	20.00	40.00	65.00	125	—

KM# 92 1/24 THALER (Groschen)
Silver **Obv. Legend:** SOLI. DEO. G.

Date	Mintage	VG	F	VF	XF	Unc
ND	—	16.00	33.00	60.00	100	—

KM# 95 1/24 THALER (Groschen)
Silver **Obv. Legend:** GOTT. BI. WE. ER. WIL.

Date	Mintage	VG	F	VF	XF	Unc
1619	—	13.00	27.00	45.00	90.00	—

KM# 97 1/24 THALER (Groschen)
Silver **Obv:** Lion rampant left **Obv. Legend:** AGENDO: CONANDO

Date	Mintage	VG	F	VF	XF	Unc
1619	—	13.00	27.00	45.00	90.00	—
ND	—	13.00	27.00	45.00	90.00	—

KM# 98 1/24 THALER (Groschen)
Silver **Obv. Legend:** I. A. N. S. Q. S. E. P., date

Date	Mintage	VG	F	VF	XF	Unc
1619	—	13.00	27.00	45.00	90.00	—

KM# 99 1/24 THALER (Groschen)
Silver **Obv. Legend:** SI. D. P. N. Q. C. N.

Date	Mintage	VG	F	VF	XF	Unc
1619	—	13.00	27.00	45.00	90.00	—

KM# 100 1/24 THALER (Groschen)
Silver **Obv:** Lion left below crowned band **Obv. Legend:** A DIVVANTE DEO

Date	Mintage	VG	F	VF	XF	Unc
ND	—	12.00	25.00	40.00	80.00	—

KM# 101 1/24 THALER (Groschen)
Silver **Obv. Legend:** AGENDO: CONANDO

Date	Mintage	VG	F	VF	XF	Unc
1619	—	12.00	25.00	40.00	80.00	—

KM# 102 1/24 THALER (Groschen)
Silver **Obv:** Lion rampant left in shield **Obv. Legend:** I. A. N. S. Q. S. E. P.

Date	Mintage	VG	F	VF	XF	Unc
1619	—	12.00	25.00	40.00	80.00	—

KM# 103 1/24 THALER (Groschen)
Silver **Obv:** Crowned lion in gatehouse **Obv. Legend:** FID. N. DE. DEV.

Date	Mintage	VG	F	VF	XF	Unc
ND	—	12.00	25.00	40.00	80.00	—

KM# 104 1/24 THALER (Groschen)
Silver **Obv:** Lion rampant left in 3-towered gatehouse

Date	Mintage	VG	F	VF	XF	Unc
1619	—	10.00	20.00	40.00	75.00	—

KM# 105 1/24 THALER (Groschen)
Silver **Obv. Legend:** GOT. DI. EH. S. . M.

Date	Mintage	VG	F	VF	XF	Unc
1619	—	10.00	20.00	40.00	75.00	—
1620	—	10.00	20.00	40.00	75.00	—

KM# 106 1/24 THALER (Groschen)
Silver **Obv. Legend:** M. G. C. K.

Date	Mintage	VG	F	VF	XF	Unc
1619	—	10.00	20.00	40.00	75.00	—

KM# 107 1/24 THALER (Groschen)
Silver **Obv:** Lion walking left **Obv. Legend:** ORA. ET. LABORA.

Date	Mintage	VG	F	VF	XF	Unc
1619	—	9.00	20.00	33.00	65.00	—
1620	—	9.00	20.00	33.00	65.00	—

KM# 108 1/24 THALER (Groschen)
Silver **Obv:** Lion rampant right **Obv. Legend:** DEUS. PROVIDEBIT.

Date	Mintage	VG	F	VF	XF	Unc
1619	—	12.00	25.00	40.00	80.00	—
ND	—	12.00	25.00	40.00	80.00	—

KM# A109 1/24 THALER (Groschen)
Silver **Obv. Legend:** DURANT MODERATA

Date	Mintage	VG	F	VF	XF	Unc
ND	—	13.00	27.00	45.00	85.00	—

KM# 110 1/24 THALER (Groschen)
Silver **Obv. Legend:** IN CRIMEN. COELITS

Date	Mintage	VG	F	VF	XF	Unc
1619	—	12.00	25.00	40.00	80.00	—
1620	—	12.00	25.00	40.00	80.00	—

KM# 111 1/24 THALER (Groschen)
Silver **Obv:** Titles of Ferdinand II

Date	Mintage	VG	F	VF	XF	Unc
ND	—	12.00	25.00	40.00	80.00	—

KM# 112 1/24 THALER (Groschen)
Silver **Rev. Legend:** IUSTIT. ET. CONCOR., date

Date	Mintage	VG	F	VF	XF	Unc
1619	—	12.00	25.00	40.00	80.00	—

KM# 113 1/24 THALER (Groschen)
Silver **Obv:** Titles of Ferdinand II

Date	Mintage	VG	F	VF	XF	Unc
ND	—	12.00	25.00	40.00	80.00	—

KM# 116 1/24 THALER (Groschen)
Silver **Obv:** 2 small towers in front of lion, without church

Date	Mintage	VG	F	VF	XF	Unc
1619 (b)	—	12.00	27.00	45.00	85.00	—

KM# 117 1/24 THALER (Groschen)
Silver **Obv:** Lion rampant right in castle gate with 2 towers **Obv. Legend:** G. V. KR. K. V. G. M.

Date	Mintage	VG	F	VF	XF	Unc
1619 (b)	—	13.00	27.00	45.00	85.00	—

KM# 118 1/24 THALER (Groschen)
Silver **Obv:** Titles of Ferdinand II **Rev:** Lion waling right **Rev. Legend:** MON: NOV: ARGEN

Date	Mintage	VG	F	VF	XF	Unc
ND	—	13.00	27.00	45.00	85.00	—

KM# 91 1/24 THALER (Groschen)
Silver **Obv:** 4-fold arms **Obv. Legend:** SI. D. P. N. Q, C. N, date **Note:** Varieties exist.

Date	Mintage	VG	F	VF	XF	Unc
1619	—	16.00	33.00	60.00	100	—

KM# 93 1/24 THALER (Groschen)
Silver **Obv:** 2-fold arms divided horizontally **Obv. Legend:** BI GOTT. IST. RA. V. T. **Note:** Varieties exist.

Date	Mintage	VG	F	VF	XF	Unc
1619	—	13.00	27.00	45.00	85.00	—
1620	—	13.00	27.00	45.00	85.00	—

KM# 94 1/24 THALER (Groschen)
Silver **Obv. Legend:** SI. D. P. N. Q. C. N. **Note:** Varieties exist.

Date	Mintage	VG	F	VF	XF	Unc
1619	—	13.00	27.00	45.00	85.00	—
1620	—	13.00	27.00	45.00	85.00	—

KM# 96 1/24 THALER (Groschen)
Silver **Obv:** 2 lions on gate with towers **Obv. Legend:** BI. GO. IS. R. V. T. **Note:** Varieties exist.

Date	Mintage	VG	F	VF	XF	Unc
1619	—	13.00	27.00	45.00	85.00	—

KM# 114 1/24 THALER (Groschen)
Silver **Obv:** Imperial orb with 24, titles of Matthias **Rev:** Lion rampant right, holding up model of church **Rev. Legend:** PRO LEGE. ET. GREGE. **Note:** Varieties exist.

Date	Mintage	VG	F	VF	XF	Unc
1619	—	13.00	27.00	45.00	85.00	—

KM# 119 1/24 THALER (Groschen)
Silver **Obv:** Titles of Matthias **Rev:** 2 leopards left in circle **Rev. Legend:** GOT: GI: GOT: NIM. **Note:** Varieties exist.

Date	Mintage	VG	F	VF	XF	Unc
1619 (b)	—	13.00	27.00	45.00	85.00	—
1619	—	13.00	27.00	45.00	85.00	—
1620	—	13.00	27.00	45.00	85.00	—

KM# 125 1/24 THALER (Groschen)
Silver **Obv:** Helmeted arms with 2 keys **Obv. Legend:** SOLI. DEO. GLORIA **Note:** Varieties exist.

Date	Mintage	VG	F	VF	XF	Unc
1619	—	12.00	25.00	40.00	80.00	—
1620	—	12.00	25.00	40.00	80.00	—
ND	—	12.00	25.00	40.00	80.00	—
ND	—	12.00	25.00	40.00	80.00	—

Note: Varieties exist

KM# 115 1/24 THALER (Groschen)
Silver **Note:** Klippe-1/24 Thaler.

Date	Mintage	VG	F	VF	XF	Unc
1619 (b)	—	—	—	—	—	—

KM# 124 1/24 THALER (Groschen)
Silver **Obv:** Arms with 2 bear claws **Obv. Legend:** D. MENSCHEN. G. I. V. S. **Note:** Klippe-1/24 Thaler.

Date	Mintage	VG	F	VF	XF	Unc
1619	—	—	—	—	—	—

KM# 121 1/24 THALER (Groschen)
Silver **Obv:** Stag left **Obv. Legend:** ORA. ET. LABORA.

Date	Mintage	VG	F	VF	XF	Unc
1619	—	20.00	40.00	85.00	120	—

KM# 122 1/24 THALER (Groschen)
Silver **Obv:** Stag antlers **Obv. Legend:** PRO PATRIA, date

Date	Mintage	VG	F	VF	XF	Unc
619 (b)	—	20.00	40.00	85.00	120	—
620 (b)	—	20.00	40.00	85.00	120	—

KM# 123 1/24 THALER (Groschen)
Silver **Obv. Legend:** I. A. N. S. Q. S. E. P. 16-19

Date	Mintage	VG	F	VF	XF	Unc
1619	—	20.00	40.00	85.00	120	—

KM# 126 1/24 THALER (Groschen)
Silver **Obv:** Small tree with 7 branches in circle **Obv. Legend:** ME. G. L. V. KR. K. V. G. M.

Date	Mintage	VG	F	VF	XF	Unc
1619 (b)	—	20.00	40.00	85.00	120	—

KM# 173 1/24 THALER (Groschen)
Silver **Obv:** Imperial orb with 24, titles of Ferdinand II **Rev:** Crowned shield with lion rampant left, value 3 below

Date	Mintage	VG	F	VF	XF	Unc
1620	—	13.00	27.00	45.00	80.00	—

KM# 174 1/24 THALER (Groschen)
Silver **Rev:** Without 3

Date	Mintage	VG	F	VF	XF	Unc
1620	—	13.00	27.00	45.00	80.00	—

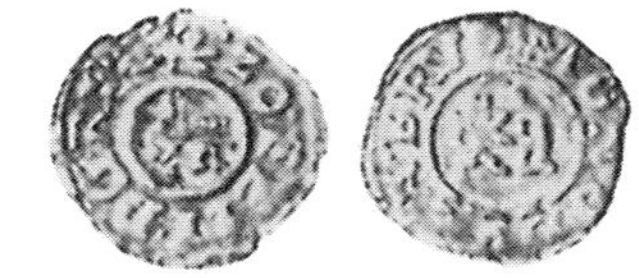

KM# 175 1/24 THALER (Groschen)
Silver **Rev:** Lion rampant right holding tower

Date	Mintage	VG	F	VF	XF	Unc
1620	—	13.00	27.00	45.00	80.00	—
1621	—	13.00	27.00	45.00	80.00	—
ND	—	13.00	27.00	45.00	80.00	—

KM# 177 1/24 THALER (Groschen)
Silver **Obv:** Arms of Hoya (2 bear claws)

Date	Mintage	VG	F	VF	XF	Unc
1620	—	16.00	33.00	60.00	100	—
ND	—	16.00	33.00	60.00	100	—

KM# 178 1/24 THALER (Groschen)
Silver **Obv:** 2-fold arms, lion left, tower right

Date	Mintage	VG	F	VF	XF	Unc
1620 (a)	—	16.00	33.00	60.00	100	—

KM# 179 1/24 THALER (Groschen)
Silver **Obv:** 4-fold arms

Date	Mintage	VG	F	VF	XF	Unc
1620 (b)	—	16.00	33.00	60.00	100	—

KM# 180 1/24 THALER (Groschen)
Silver **Obv:** Crowned 4-fold arms **Obv. Legend:** ADIVVANTE **Rev:** Imperial orb with 24

Date	Mintage	VG	F	VF	XF	Unc
ND	—	16.00	33.00	60.00	100	—

KM# 181 1/24 THALER (Groschen)
Silver **Obv:** Imperial orb with 24, title of Matthias **Rev. Legend:** GOT. DE. E. S. N. M.

Date	Mintage	VG	F	VF	XF	Unc
ND	—	16.00	33.00	60.00	100	—

KM# 182 1/24 THALER (Groschen)
Silver **Obv:** Titles of Ferdinand II

Date	Mintage	VG	F	VF	XF	Unc
ND	—	16.00	33.00	60.00	100	—

KM# 183 1/24 THALER (Groschen)
Silver **Obv:** Titles of Matthias **Rev:** 4-fold arms **Rev. Legend:** D. M. S. I. E. G. V. G., date

Date	Mintage	VG	F	VF	XF	Unc
1620 (b)	—	16.00	33.00	60.00	100	—

KM# 184 1/24 THALER (Groschen)
Silver **Obv:** Titles of Ferdinand II **Rev. Legend:** IN FOE LC. N. IN.VI.

Date	Mintage	VG	F	VF	XF	Unc
1620	—	16.00	33.00	60.00	100	—
ND	—	16.00	33.00	60.00	100	—

KM# 185 1/24 THALER (Groschen)
Silver **Obv:** Heart-shaped arms **Obv. Legend:** IN. F. O. E. L. C. N. I. N. V.*

Date	Mintage	VG	F	VF	XF	Unc
1620	—	16.00	33.00	60.00	100	—

KM# 188 1/24 THALER (Groschen)
Silver **Obv. Legend:** ORA. ET. LABORA. **Rev:** Without legend

Date	Mintage	VG	F	VF	XF	Unc
ND	—	16.00	33.00	60.00	100	—

KM# 189 1/24 THALER (Groschen)
Silver **Obv. Legend:** SEMPER. PRO. PATRIA.

Date	Mintage	VG	F	VF	XF	Unc
1620 (b)	—	16.00	33.00	60.00	100	—

KM# 190 1/24 THALER (Groschen)
Silver **Obv. Legend:** TIME DEV ET. DVCEM.

Date	Mintage	VG	F	VF	XF	Unc
1620	—	16.00	33.00	60.00	100	—

KM# 191 1/24 THALER (Groschen)
Silver **Obv:** Titles of Ferdinand II **Rev:** 2-fold arms divided horizontally **Rev. Legend:** BI GOTT. IST. RA. V. T.

Date	Mintage	VG	F	VF	XF	Unc
1620	—	16.00	33.00	60.00	100	—

KM# 192 1/24 THALER (Groschen)
Silver **Obv. Legend:** FID. DES. DE., date

Date	Mintage	VG	F	VF	XF	Unc
(16)20	—	16.00	33.00	60.00	100	—

KM# 193 1/24 THALER (Groschen)
Silver **Obv. Legend:** OMNI. CR. DE.

Date	Mintage	VG	F	VF	XF	Unc
1620	—	16.00	33.00	60.00	100	—

KM# 194 1/24 THALER (Groschen)
Silver **Obv. Legend:** ORA. ET. LABORA. *20*

Date	Mintage	VG	F	VF	XF	Unc
(16)20	—	16.00	33.00	60.00	100	—

KM# 195 1/24 THALER (Groschen)
Silver **Obv:** Titles of Ferdinand II **Rev:** 2-fold arms divided vertically **Rev. Legend:** TIME. DEV. ET. DUCEM.

Date	Mintage	VG	F	VF	XF	Unc
ND	—	16.00	33.00	60.00	100	—

KM# 196 1/24 THALER (Groschen)
Silver **Obv:** Imperial orb with 24, titles of Matthias, date **Rev:** Horse leaping left in circle **Rev. Legend:** M. G. V. KR. K. V. G. M.

Date	Mintage	VG	F	VF	XF	Unc
1620 (b)	—	27.00	55.00	100	175	—

KM# 197 1/24 THALER (Groschen)
Silver **Obv:** Imperial orb with 24, titles of Ferdinand II **Rev:** 2 lions holding up 2 towers **Rev. Legend:** PRO LEGE ET GREGE

Date	Mintage	VG	F	VF	XF	Unc
1620 (b)	—	16.00	33.00	60.00	100	—

KM# 199 1/24 THALER (Groschen)
Silver **Obv:** Lion rampant left **Obv. Legend:** SI.DE9.PRO.N.Q. C.N.

Date	Mintage	VG	F	VF	XF	Unc
1620	—	13.00	27.00	45.00	85.00	—

KM# 200 1/24 THALER (Groschen)
Silver **Obv:** Titles of FerdinandII **Rev. Legend:** AGENDO: CONANDO

Date	Mintage	VG	F	VF	XF	Unc
1620	—	13.00	27.00	45.00	85.00	—
1621	—	13.00	27.00	45.00	85.00	—

KM# 201 1/24 THALER (Groschen)
Silver **Obv. Legend:** DEUS. (or DEVS) PROVIDER

Date	Mintage	VG	F	VF	XF	Unc
1620	—	13.00	27.00	45.00	85.00	—
1621 (b)	—	13.00	27.00	45.00	85.00	—
ND	—	13.00	27.00	45.00	85.00	—

KM# 202 1/24 THALER (Groschen)
Silver **Obv. Legend:** FIDE. N. DESER. DEUS.

Date	Mintage	VG	F	VF	XF	Unc
ND	—	13.00	27.00	45.00	85.00	—

KM# 203 1/24 THALER (Groschen)
Silver **Obv. Legend:** I. A. N. S. Q. S. E. P., date

Date	Mintage	VG	F	VF	XF	Unc
ND	—	13.00	27.00	45.00	85.00	—

KM# 204 1/24 THALER (Groschen)
Silver **Obv. Legend:** PAR. PRO. S. N. IRA. L. 2. 0.

Date	Mintage	VG	F	VF	XF	Unc
(16)20	—	13.00	27.00	45.00	85.00	—
ND	—	13.00	27.00	45.00	85.00	—

KM# 205 1/24 THALER (Groschen)
Silver **Obv:** Crowned lion rampant left **Obv. Legend:** PAR. PRO. S. N. IRA. L.

Date	Mintage	VG	F	VF	XF	Unc
1620	—	13.00	27.00	45.00	85.00	—
ND	—	13.00	27.00	45.00	85.00	—

KM# 206 1/24 THALER (Groschen)
Silver **Obv. Legend:** PRO. ARIS. ET. FO.

Date	Mintage	VG	F	VF	XF	Unc
ND	—	13.00	27.00	45.00	85.00	—

KM# 207 1/24 THALER (Groschen)
Silver **Obv:** Lion left below crowned band **Obv. Legend:** A DIVVANTE DEO

Date	Mintage	VG	F	VF	XF	Unc
1620	—	13.00	27.00	45.00	85.00	—
1621	—	13.00	27.00	45.00	85.00	—

KM# 208 1/24 THALER (Groschen)
Silver **Obv:** Imperial orb with 24, titles of Matthias **Rev:** Lion rampant left, tower to side **Rev. Legend:** TIME. DEV. ET. DVCE.

Date	Mintage	VG	F	VF	XF	Unc
1620	—	13.00	27.00	45.00	85.00	—

KM# 209 1/24 THALER (Groschen)
Silver **Obv:** Titles of Ferdinand II **Rev:** Lion rampant left in 3-towered gatehouse

Date	Mintage	VG	F	VF	XF	Unc
ND	—	13.00	27.00	45.00	85.00	—
1620	—	13.00	27.00	45.00	85.00	—

KM# 210 1/24 THALER (Groschen)
Silver **Obv. Legend:** FID. N. DE. DEUS.

Date	Mintage	VG	F	VF	XF	Unc
ND	—	13.00	27.00	45.00	85.00	—

KM# 212 1/24 THALER (Groschen)

Silver **Obv:** Lion rampant left, gate with 1 tower **Obv. Legend:** M. GL. V. KR. K. V. G. M.

Date	Mintage	VG	F	VF	XF	Unc
1620 (b)	—	13.00	27.00	45.00	85.00	—

KM# 213 1/24 THALER (Groschen)

Silver **Obv:** Titles of Ferdinand II **Rev:** Gate with 2 towers **Rev. Legend:** NERVI RERVM

Date	Mintage	VG	F	VF	XF	Unc
1620	—	13.00	27.00	45.00	85.00	—

KM# 214 1/24 THALER (Groschen)

Silver **Obv:** Lion to left below cloverleaf in gate with 2 towers **Obv. Legend:** NERVI. RERUM. **Rev:** Imperial orb with 24

Date	Mintage	VG	F	VF	XF	Unc
1620	—	13.00	27.00	45.00	85.00	—

KM# 215 1/24 THALER (Groschen)

Silver **Obv:** Lion rampant right **Obv. Legend:** COELITUS. IN GREME

Date	Mintage	VG	F	VF	XF	Unc
1620	—	13.00	27.00	45.00	85.00	—

KM# 216 1/24 THALER (Groschen)

Silver **Obv. Legend:** NON. PROCRASTIND

Date	Mintage	VG	F	VF	XF	Unc
1620	—	13.00	27.00	45.00	85.00	—
ND	—	13.00	27.00	45.00	85.00	—

KM# 217 1/24 THALER (Groschen)

Silver **Obv:** Tower to side of lion **Obv. Legend:** PRO LEGE

Date	Mintage	VG	F	VF	XF	Unc
1620 (b)	—	13.00	27.00	45.00	85.00	—

KM# 218 1/24 THALER (Groschen)

Silver **Obv. Legend:** TIME. DEV. ET. DVC.

Date	Mintage	VG	F	VF	XF	Unc
1620	—	13.00	27.00	45.00	85.00	—

KM# 219 1/24 THALER (Groschen)

Silver **Obv:** 2 small towers in front of lion, without church

Date	Mintage	VG	F	VF	XF	Unc
1620 (b)	—	13.00	27.00	45.00	85.00	—

KM# 220 1/24 THALER (Groschen)

Silver **Obv:** Imperial orb with 24 **Obv. Legend:** M. D. G. R. I. S. A 6-19

Date	Mintage	VG	F	VF	XF	Unc
1620/(1)619	—	—	—	—	—	—

KM# 221 1/24 THALER (Groschen)

Silver **Obv:** Titles of Ferdinand II, date in legend **Rev:** Stag antlers

Date	Mintage	VG	F	VF	XF	Unc
1620	—	20.00	40.00	65.00	125	—
1621	—	20.00	40.00	65.00	125	—

KM# 223 1/24 THALER (Groschen)

Silver **Obv:** Date in legend

Date	Mintage	VG	F	VF	XF	Unc
1620	—	20.00	40.00	65.00	125	—

KM# 224 1/24 THALER (Groschen)

Silver **Obv:** Titles of Ferdinand II **Rev:** Helmeted arms with 2 keys

Date	Mintage	VG	F	VF	XF	Unc
1620	—	16.00	33.00	60.00	100	—

KM# 225 1/24 THALER (Groschen)

Silver **Obv:** Heart-shaped arms with bars **Obv. Legend:** OM. CREAVI. DEVS.

Date	Mintage	VG	F	VF	XF	Unc
1620	—	16.00	33.00	60.00	100	—

KM# 176 1/24 THALER (Groschen)

Silver **Obv:** Brunswick helmet with horse **Note:** Varieties exist.

Date	Mintage	VG	F	VF	XF	Unc
1620	—	12.00	25.00	40.00	80.00	—
1622	—	12.00	25.00	40.00	80.00	—
1622 CL	—	12.00	25.00	40.00	80.00	—
1623 GL	—	12.00	25.00	40.00	80.00	—

KM# 187 1/24 THALER (Groschen)

Silver **Obv:** 4-fold arms **Obv. Legend:** OMNIA. CREAV. DEVS. **Note:** 1/24 Thaler-Klippe.

Date	Mintage	VG	F	VF	XF	Unc
1620	—	16.00	33.00	60.00	100	—

KM# 198 1/24 THALER (Groschen)

Silver **Note:** 1/24 Thaler-Klippe.

Date	Mintage	VG	F	VF	XF	Unc
1620 (b)	—	—	—	—	—	—

KM# 211 1/24 THALER (Groschen)

Silver **Note:** 1/24 Thaler-Klippe.

Date	Mintage	VG	F	VF	XF	Unc
ND	—	—	—	—	—	—

KM# 222 1/24 THALER (Groschen)

Silver **Rev. Legend:** F. E. I. I. D. G. R. I. 6-20 **Note:** 1/24-Klippe.

Date	Mintage	VG	F	VF	XF	Unc
1620	—	—	—	—	—	—

KM# 109 1/24 THALER (Groschen)

Silver **Obv. Legend:** DURANT MODERATA **Note:** Klippe, 4.20 G.

Date	Mintage	VG	F	VF	XF	Unc
ND	—	—	—	—	—	—

KM# 120 1/24 THALER (Groschen)

Silver **Obv. Legend:** LABOR. CONSUMIMU.

Date	Mintage	VG	F	VF	XF	Unc
ND	—	12.00	25.00	40.00	80.00	—

KM# 313 1/24 THALER (Groschen)

Silver **Note:** 1/14 Thaler-Klippe.

Date	Mintage	VG	F	VF	XF	Unc
(16)21	—	—	—	—	—	—

KM# 312 1/24 THALER (Groschen)

Silver **Obv:** Imperial orb with 24, titles of Ferdinand II **Rev:** Wildman, tree in right hand **Note:** Kipper coinage.

Date	Mintage	VG	F	VF	XF	Unc
(16)21	—	—	—	—	—	—
ND	—	—	—	—	—	—

KM# 318 1/24 THALER (Groschen)

Silver **Note:** 1/24 Thaler-Klippe.

Date	Mintage	VG	F	VF	XF	Unc
1621	—	—	—	—	—	—

KM# 320 1/24 THALER (Groschen)

Silver **Obv:** Arms of Hoya (2 bear claws) **Note:** 1/24 Thaler-Klippe.

Date	Mintage	VG	F	VF	XF	Unc
1621	—	—	—	—	—	—

KM# 316 1/24 THALER (Groschen)

Silver **Obv:** Brunswick helmet with horse **Note:** 1/24 Thaler/Klippe.

Date	Mintage	VG	F	VF	XF	Unc
1621 ID	—	—	—	—	—	—

KM# 317 1/24 THALER (Groschen)

Silver **Obv:** Horse in front of column, value 3 in legend **Note:** Varieties exist.

Date	Mintage	VG	F	VF	XF	Unc
1621	—	—	—	—	—	—

KM# 314 1/24 THALER (Groschen)

Silver **Obv:** Lion rampant left in ornamented shield

Date	Mintage	VG	F	VF	XF	Unc
1621	—	13.00	27.00	45.00	85.00	—

KM# 315 1/24 THALER (Groschen)

Silver **Obv:** Lion rampant right holding 2 towers

Date	Mintage	VG	F	VF	XF	Unc
1621	—	13.00	27.00	45.00	85.00	—

KM# 319 1/24 THALER (Groschen)

Silver **Obv:** Without 3 in legend

Date	Mintage	VG	F	VF	XF	Unc
1621	—	—	—	—	—	—
ND	—	—	—	—	—	—

KM# 321 1/24 THALER (Groschen)

Silver **Obv:** Lion rampant left **Obv. Legend:** SOLI. DEO. GLORIA.

Date	Mintage	VG	F	VF	XF	Unc
1621	—	13.00	27.00	45.00	85.00	—

KM# 322 1/24 THALER (Groschen)

Silver **Obv. Legend:** MIT. RAT. VNT. THAT.

Date	Mintage	VG	F	VF	XF	Unc
1621	—	13.00	27.00	45.00	85.00	—

KM# 323 1/24 THALER (Groschen)

Silver **Obv:** Lion rampant right, S at each side **Obv. Legend:** MONE: NOVA, ARGENT

Date	Mintage	VG	F	VF	XF	Unc
1621	—	13.00	27.00	45.00	85.00	—

KM# 324 1/24 THALER (Groschen)

Silver **Obv. Legend:** CONSILIO. ET. ARM.

Date	Mintage	VG	F	VF	XF	Unc
1621	—	13.00	27.00	45.00	85.00	—

KM# 325 1/24 THALER (Groschen)

Silver **Obv:** Titles of Matthias **Rev:** Brunswick helmet **Rev. Legend:** ORA. ET. LABORA

Date	Mintage	VG	F	VF	XF	Unc
ND	—	16.00	33.00	60.00	100	—

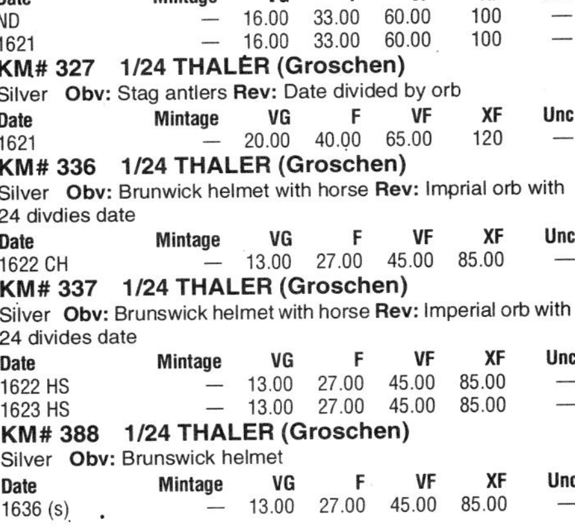

KM# 326 1/24 THALER (Groschen)

Silver **Obv:** Titles of Ferdinand II **Rev. Legend:** FI. N. DE. DEI.

Date	Mintage	VG	F	VF	XF	Unc
ND	—	16.00	33.00	60.00	100	—
1621	—	16.00	33.00	60.00	100	—

KM# 327 1/24 THALER (Groschen)

Silver **Obv:** Stag antlers **Rev:** Date divided by orb

Date	Mintage	VG	F	VF	XF	Unc
1621	—	20.00	40.00	65.00	120	—

KM# 336 1/24 THALER (Groschen)

Silver **Obv:** Brunwick helmet with horse **Rev:** Imprial orb with 24 divdies date

Date	Mintage	VG	F	VF	XF	Unc
1622 CH	—	13.00	27.00	45.00	85.00	—

KM# 337 1/24 THALER (Groschen)

Silver **Obv:** Brunswick helmet with horse **Rev:** Imperial orb with 24 divides date

Date	Mintage	VG	F	VF	XF	Unc
1622 HS	—	13.00	27.00	45.00	85.00	—
1623 HS	—	13.00	27.00	45.00	85.00	—

KM# 388 1/24 THALER (Groschen)

Silver **Obv:** Brunswick helmet

Date	Mintage	VG	F	VF	XF	Unc
1636 (s)	—	13.00	27.00	45.00	85.00	—

KM# 553 1/24 THALER (Groschen)

Silver **Obv:** Horse leaping left **Rev:** Imperial orb with 24

Date	Mintage	VG	F	VF	XF	Unc
1684	—	13.00	27.00	45.00	85.00	—

KM# 591 1/24 THALER (Groschen)

Silver **Obv:** Crowned intertwined cursive RAV monogram, date in legend

Date	Mintage	VG	F	VF	XF	Unc
1691 HCH	—	16.00	33.00	60.00	100	—
1692 HCH	—	16.00	33.00	60.00	100	—
1693 HCH	—	16.00	33.00	60.00	100	—

KM# 609 1/24 THALER (Groschen)

Silver **Rev. Legend:** NACH DEN. . .

Date	Mintage	VG	F	VF	XF	Unc
1693 HCH	—	16.00	33.00	60.00	100	—

KM# 610 1/24 THALER (Groschen)

Silver **Obv:** Horse leaping left **Rev:** Imperial orb with 24

Date	Mintage	VG	F	VF	XF	Unc
1693 HCH	—	16.00	33.00	60.00	100	—

KM# 26 1/16 THALER

Silver **Obv:** Brunswick helmet with horse **Rev:** Wildman, tree branch in right hand, date in legend, 16 at top

Date	Mintage	VG	F	VF	XF	Unc
1605	—	—	—	—	—	—
1606	—	—	—	—	—	—

KM# 329 1/16 THALER

Silver **Obv:** Imperial eagle, 16 in orb on breast, titles of Ferdinand II, date in legend **Rev:** DS in circle

Date	Mintage	VG	F	VF	XF	Unc
(1)621	—	45.00	100	175	275	—
ERR(1)612 (error)	—	45.00	100	175	275	—

KM# 328 1/16 THALER

Silver **Obv:** Lion rampant left **Rev:** DS **Rev. Legend:** PAX. AL. PRO. BELLO. **Note:** Kipper 1/16 Thaler.

Date	Mintage	VG	F	VF	XF	Unc
ND	—	60.00	120	210	350	—

KM# 510 1/16 THALER

Silver **Obv:** Bust right **Rev:** XVI EININ REICHSTHALER..., date in legend

Date	Mintage	VG	F	VF	XF	Unc
1671 GB	—	33.00	65.00	120	200	—
1675 GB	—	33.00	65.00	120	200	—
1676 GB	—	33.00	65.00	120	200	—
1678 GB	—	33.00	65.00	120	200	—

KM# 522 1/16 THALER

Silver **Rev:** Date below value

Date	Mintage	VG	F	VF	XF	Unc
1676 R	—	33.00	65.00	120	200	—
1677 R	—	—	—	—	—	—

KM# 36 1/14 THALER

Silver **Obv:** Brunswick helmet with horse **Rev:** Wildman, tree branch in right hand, 14 in legend

Date	Mintage	VG	F	VF	XF	Unc
1610 (d)	—	27.00	55.00	100	200	—
1610 (o)	—	27.00	55.00	100	200	—

KM# 554 1/12 THALER (2 Groschen)

Silver **Obv:** Horse leaping left, date below **Rev:** 12/EINEN/EEICHS/TAL

Date	Mintage	VG	F	VF	XF	Unc
1684	—	—	—	—	—	—

KM# 600 1/12 THALER (2 Groschen)

Silver **Obv:** Horse leaping left **Rev:** Value 12. . ., LANDMUNTZ in 5 lines **Note:** Varieties exist.

Date	Mintage	VG	F	VF	XF	Unc
1692 HCH	—	13.00	27.00	55.00	100	—
1693 HCH	—	13.00	27.00	55.00	100	—
1695 HCH	—	13.00	27.00	55.00	100	—
1695 ICB	—	13.00	27.00	55.00	100	—
1697 DF	—	13.00	27.00	55.00	100	—

KM# 616 1/12 THALER (2 Groschen)

Silver **Ruler:** Anton Ulrich as Joint ruler **Obv. Legend:** NACH DEN..., Horse leaping left, date below horse **Rev:** Value 12. . ., LANDMUNTZ IN 5 lines

Date	Mintage	VG	F	VF	XF	Unc
1694	—	16.00	33.00	65.00	120	—
1695	—	16.00	33.00	65.00	120	—
1697	—	16.00	33.00	65.00	120	—

KM# 626 1/12 THALER (2 Groschen)

Silver **Ruler:** Anton Ulrich as Joint ruler **Rev:** Date below value

Date	Mintage	VG	F	VF	XF	Unc
1699 HCH	—	16.00	33.00	65.00	120	—
1700 HCH	—	16.00	33.00	65.00	120	—

KM# 15 1/8 THALER

Silver **Subject:** DEath of Heinrich Juluis' Mother, Hedwig von Brandenburg **Obv:** 11-fold arms **Rev:** 10-line inscription with date

Date	Mintage	VG	F	VF	XF	Unc
1602 (o)	—	—	—	—	—	—

KM# 27 1/8 THALER

Silver **Obv:** 11-fold arms with central shield of Halberstadt arms **Rev:** Wildman, tree branch in right hand

Date	Mintage	VG	F	VF	XF	Unc
1606 (o)	—	—	—	—	—	—

KM# 41 1/8 THALER

Silver **Subject:** Death of Heinrich Julius **Rev:** 9-line inscription with date

Date	Mintage	VG	F	VF	XF	Unc
1613 (o)	—	33.00	80.00	145	250	—

KM# 49 1/8 THALER

Silver **Obv:** 11-fold arms **Obv. Legend:** Without D. G. in titles **Rev:** Wildman, tree in right hand, date in legend

Date	Mintage	VG	F	VF	XF	Unc
1614 (o)	—	33.00	80.00	145	250	—

KM# 127 1/8 THALER

Silver **Obv. Legend:** D. G. in titles

Date	Mintage	VG	F	VF	XF	Unc
1619 (c)	—	27.00	70.00	135	240	—
1620 (c)	—	27.00	70.00	135	240	—
1621 (c)	—	27.00	70.00	135	240	—
1623 HS	—	27.00	70.00	135	240	—
1624 (b)	—	27.00	70.00	135	240	—

KM# 362 1/8 THALER

Silver **Subject:** Death of Friedrich Ulrich's Mother, Elisabeth of Denmark **Obv:** Arms of 2 lions on left facing 3 leopards on right, double legend inscriptions **Rev:** 13-line inscription with date

Date	Mintage	VG	F	VF	XF	Unc
1626 (s)	—	—	—	—	—	—

KM# 367 1/8 THALER

Silver **Obv:** Crowned 11-fold arms **Rev:** Wildman, tree in right hand, date in legend

Date	Mintage	VG	F	VF	XF	Unc
1629 HS	—	33.00	80.00	145	250	—
1634 HS	—	33.00	80.00	145	250	—

KM# 389 1/8 THALER

Silver **Obv:** Crowned 11-fold arms, titles in Latin **Rev:** Wildman, tree in right hand

Date	Mintage	VG	F	VF	XF	Unc
1636 (s)	—	33.00	80.00	145	250	—

KM# 394 1/8 THALER

Silver **Obv:** Titles in German

Date	Mintage	VG	F	VF	XF	Unc
1637 (s)	—	27.00	70.00	135	240	—
1639 (s)	—	27.00	70.00	135	240	—
1641 (s)	—	27.00	70.00	135	240	—
1647 (s)	—	27.00	70.00	135	240	—

KM# 459 1/8 THALER

Silver **Rev:** Wildman holds tree with both hands to his left

Date	Mintage	VG	F	VF	XF	Unc
1659 (s)	—	—	—	—	—	—
1664 (s)	—	—	—	—	—	—

KM# 460 1/8 THALER

Silver **Rev:** Wildman holds tree across in front of him, date in legend

Date	Mintage	VG	F	VF	XF	Unc
1659 (s)	—	—	—	—	—	—

KM# 474 1/8 THALER

Silver **Subject:** Death of August II **Obv:** 11-line inscription with date **Rev:** Withered tree with skull at base

Date	Mintage	VG	F	VF	XF	Unc
1666	—	75.00	150	225	300	—

KM# 520 1/8 THALER

Silver **Obv:** Crowned 11-fold arms **Rev:** Wildman holding tree with both hands to his left, date in legend

Date	Mintage	VG	F	VF	XF	Unc
1675 IPE	—	—	—	—	—	—

KM# 601 1/8 THALER

Silver **Obv:** Helmeted 11-fold arms divide date **Rev:** Wildman holding tree with both hands to his left

Date	Mintage	VG	F	VF	XF	Unc
1692 RB	—	—	—	—	—	—

KM# 618 1/8 THALER

Silver **Subject:** Death of August Wilhelm's Wife, Christine Sophie **Obv:** Eagle above globe, inscription on ribbon above **Rev:** 13-line inscription

Date	Mintage	VG	F	VF	XF	Unc
MDCVC (1695) ICB	—	33.00	65.00	120	225	—

KM# 611 1/6 THALER

Silver **Obv:** Crowned 12-fold arms **Rev:** Horse leaping left, 1/6 below

Date	Mintage	VG	F	VF	XF	Unc
1693 ICB	—	33.00	60.00	120	200	—
1696 ICB	—	33.00	6.00	120	200	—

KM# 617 1/6 THALER

Silver **Obv:** Horse leaping left **Rev:** Crowned 11-fold arms divide date, 1/6 below

Date	Mintage	VG	F	VF	XF	Unc
1694 ICB	—	33.00	70.00	140	240	—
1695 ICB	—	33.00	70.00	140	240	—

KM# 5 1/4 THALER

Silver **Obv:** 11-fold arms with central shield of Halberstadt arms

Date	Mintage	VG	F	VF	XF	Unc
1601 (d)	—	60.00	120	200	300	—
1601 (o)	—	60.00	120	200	300	—
160Z (d)	—	—	—	—	—	—
160Z (o)	—	—	—	—	—	—
1603 (d)	—	60.00	120	200	300	—
1603 (o)	—	60.00	120	200	300	—
1604 (d)	—	—	—	—	—	—
1604 (o)	—	60.00	120	200	300	—
1605 (o)	—	—	—	—	—	—
1605 (d)	—	60.00	120	200	300	—
1606 (d)	—	—	—	—	—	—
1606 (o)	—	60.00	120	200	300	—
1607 (d)	—	60.00	120	20.00	300	—
1607 (o)	—	60.00	120	200	300	—
1608 (d)	—	60.00	120	200	300	—
1608 (o)	—	60.00	120	200	300	—
1609 (d)	—	60.00	120	200	300	—
1609 (o)	—	60.00	120	200	300	—
1610 (d)	—	6.00	120	200	300	—
1610 (o)	—	60.00	120	200	300	—
1611 (d)	—	60.00	120	200	300	—
1611 (o)	—	60.00	120	200	300	—
1612 (o)	—	60.00	120	200	300	—
1613 (o)	—	60.00	120	200	300	—

KM# 8 1/4 THALER

Silver **Rev:** St. Andrew with cross, date in legend

Date	Mintage	VG	F	VF	XF	Unc
1601 (d)	—	45.00	100	175	300	—
1602 (d)	—	45.00	100	175	300	—
1604 (d)	—	45.00	100	175	300	—
1605 (d)	—	45.00	100	175	300	—
1606 (d)	—	45.00	100	175	300	—
1609 (d)	—	45.00	100	175	300	—
1610 (d)	—	45.00	100	175	300	—
1612 (d)	—	45.00	100	175	300	—

KM# 16 1/4 THALER

Silver **Subject:** Death of Heinrich Julius' Mother, Hedwig von Brandenburg **Note:** Similar to 1 Thaler, KM#18.

Date	Mintage	VG	F	VF	XF	Unc
1602 (o)	—	—	—	—	—	—

KM# 42 1/4 THALER

Silver **Subject:** Death of Heinrich Julius **Note:** Similar to 1 Thaler, KM#46.

Date	Mintage	VG	F	VF	XF	Unc
1613	—	85.00	165	300	500	—
1613 (o)	—	85.00	165	300	500	—

KM# 43 1/4 THALER

Silver **Note:** Similar to 1 Thaler, KM#47.

Date	Mintage	VG	F	VF	XF	Unc
1613 (o)	—	45.00	100	200	325	—
1614 (o)	—	45.00	100	200	325	—

KM# 50 1/4 THALER

Silver

Date	Mintage	VG	F	VF	XF	Unc
1614 (o)	—	45.00	110	225	330	—
1614/3 (o)	—	—	—	—	—	—
1615 (o)	—	45.00	110	225	330	—
1616 (o)	—	45.00	110	225	330	—
1617 (o)	—	45.00	110	225	330	—
1618	—	45.00	110	225	330	—
1619	—	45.00	110	225	330	—
1619 (c)	—	45.00	110	225	330	—
1620 (c)	—	45.00	110	225	330	—
1621 (c)	—	45.00	110	225	330	—
1622 (c)	—	45.00	110	225	330	—
1624 (c)	—	45.00	110	225	330	—
1624 HL	—	45.00	110	225	330	—
1624 HS	—	45.00	110	225	330	—
1625 (s)	—	45.00	110	225	330	—
1625 HL	—	45.00	110	225	330	—
1626 (s)	—	45.00	110	225	330	—
1627 (s)	—	45.00	110	225	330	—
1628 (s)	—	45.00	110	225	330	—
1629 (s)	—	45.00	110	225	330	—

KM# 59 1/4 THALER

Silver **Obv:** 11-fold arms **Rev:** St. Andrew with cross

Date	Mintage	VG	F	VF	XF	Unc
1616 (o)	—	—	—	—	—	—

KM# 363 1/4 THALER

Silver **Subject:** Death of Friedrich Ulrich's Mother, Elisabeth of Denmark **Note:** Similar to 1 Thaler, KM#365.

Date	Mintage	VG	F	VF	XF	Unc
1626 (s)	—	—	—	—	—	—

KM# 376 1/4 THALER

Silver **Obv:** Crowned 11-fold arms **Rev:** Wildman, tree in right hand, date in legend

Date	Mintage	VG	F	VF	XF	Unc
1631 (s)	—	45.00	100	225	330	—
1632 (s)	—	45.00	100	225	330	—
1634 (s)	—	45.00	100	225	330	—

KM# 377 1/4 THALER

Silver **Obv:** Crowned 11-fold arms **Rev:** St. Jacob, staff in right hand

Date	Mintage	VG	F	VF	XF	Unc
1633 (s)	—	—	—	—	—	—

KM# 390 1/4 THALER

Silver **Note:** Similar to KM#395 but titles in Latin.

Date	Mintage	VG	F	VF	XF	Unc
1636 (s)	—	40.00	100	170	275	—

KM# 395 1/4 THALER

Silver **Obv:** Titles in German

Date	Mintage	VG	F	VF	XF	Unc
1637 (s)	—	33.00	60.00	110	220	—
1638 (s)	—	33.00	60.00	110	220	—
1639 (s)	—	33.00	60.00	110	220	—
1642 (s)	—	33.00	60.00	110	220	—
1654 (s)	—	33.00	60.00	110	220	—
1655 (s)	—	33.00	60.00	110	220	—

KM# 411 1/4 THALER

Silver **Note:** 1/4 2nd Bell Thaler.

Date	Mintage	VG	F	VF	XF	Unc
1643 (s)	—	60.00	120	240	440	—

KM# 435 1/4 THALER

Silver **Obv:** Bust left **Rev:** Crowned 11-fold arms, date in legend

Date	Mintage	VG	F	VF	XF	Unc
1647 (s)	—	—	—	—	—	—

KM# 461 1/4 THALER

Silver **Note:** Similar to KM#395 but wildman holds tree across in front of him.

Date	Mintage	VG	F	VF	XF	Unc
1659 (s)	—	40.00	80.00	140	250	—
1660 (s)	—	40.00	80.00	140	250	—
1665 (s)	—	40.00	80.00	140	250	—

KM# 465 1/4 THALER

Silver

Date	Mintage	VG	F	VF	XF	Unc
1660 (s)	—	60.00	120	240	440	—
1663 (s)	—	60.00	120	240	440	—
1664 (s)	—	60.00	120	240	440	—

KM# 475 1/4 THALER

Silver **Subject:** Death of August II

Date	Mintage	VG	F	VF	XF	Unc
1666	—	160	275	375	500	—

KM# 515 1/4 THALER

Silver **Note:** Similar to KM#395 but wildman holding tree with both hands to his left.

Date	Mintage	VG	F	VF	XF	Unc
1673 IPE	—	40.00	80.00	140	240	—
1684 RD	—	40.00	80.00	140	240	—

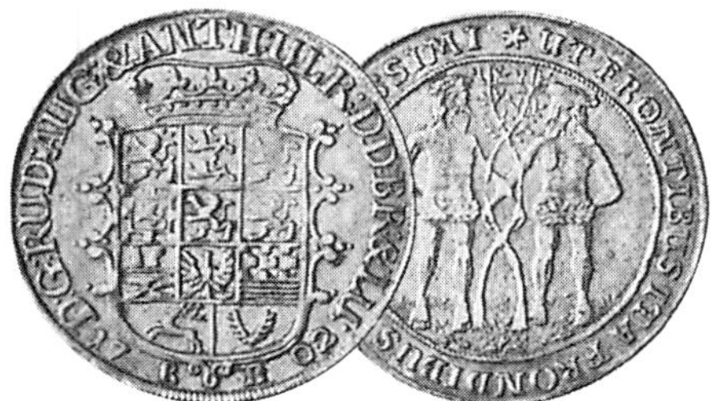

KM# 592 1/4 THALER

Silver **Ruler:** Anton Ulrich as Joint ruler **Mint:** Zellerfeld

Date	Mintage	VG	F	VF	XF	Unc
1691 RB	—	40.00	80.00	160	275	—

KM# 619 1/4 THALER

Silver **Subject:** Death of August Wilhelm's wife, Christine Sophia **Note:** Similar to 1 Thaler, KM#621.

Date	Mintage	VG	F	VF	XF	Unc
1695 ICB	—	—	—	—	—	—

KM# 612 1/3 THALER

Silver **Obv:** Horse leaping left **Rev:** Crowned 11-fold arms, value 1/3 below

Date	Mintage	VG	F	VF	XF	Unc
1693 ICB	—	—	—	—	—	—
1694 ICB	—	—	—	—	—	—

KM# 6 1/2 THALER

Silver **Obv:** Helmeted 11-fold arms with central shield of Halberstadt arms **Rev:** Wildman, tree branch in right hand

Date	Mintage	VG	F	VF	XF	Unc
1601 (o)	—	85.00	160	250	350	—
1602 (d)	—	85.00	160	250	350	—
1602 (o)	—	85.00	160	250	350	—
1603 (d)	—	85.00	160	250	350	—
1603 (o)	—	85.00	160	250	350	—
1603/Z (o)	—	—	—	—	—	—
1604	—	85.00	160	250	350	—
1604 (o)	—	85.00	160	250	350	—

KM# 9 1/2 THALER

Silver **Rev:** St. Andrew with cross, date in legend

Date	Mintage	VG	F	VF	XF	Unc
1601 (d)	—	250	400	675	1,000	—
1602 (d)	—	250	400	675	1,000	—
1604 (d)	—	250	400	675	1,000	—
1605 (d)	—	250	400	675	1,000	—

KM# 10 1/2 THALER

Silver **Note:** Klippe 1/2 Thaler.

Date	Mintage	VG	F	VF	XF	Unc
1601 (d)	—	—	—	—	—	—

KM# 17 1/2 THALER

Silver **Subject:** Death of Heinrich Julius' Mother, Hedwig von Brandenburg **Note:** Similar to 1 Thaler, KM#18.

Date	Mintage	VG	F	VF	XF	Unc
1602 (o)	—	—	—	—	—	—

KM# 22 1/2 THALER

Silver **Obv:** Without helmets above arms

Date	Mintage	VG	F	VF	XF	Unc
1604 (o)	—	70.00	140	220	325	—
1605 (o)	—	70.00	140	220	325	—
1605 (d)	—	—	—	—	—	—
1606 (o)	—	70.00	140	220	325	—
1607 (o)	—	70.00	140	220	325	—
1608 (o)	—	70.00	140	220	325	—
1609 (o)	—	70.00	140	220	325	—
1610 (o)	—	70.00	140	220	325	—
1611 (o)	—	70.00	140	220	325	—
1611 (d)	—	70.00	140	220	325	—
1612 (o)	—	70.00	140	220	325	—
1613 (o)	—	70.00	140	220	325	—

KM# 28 1/2 THALER

Silver **Rev:** St. Andrew with cross, date in legend

Date	Mintage	VG	F	VF	XF	Unc
1608 (d)	—	—	—	—	—	—
1610 (d)	—	—	—	—	—	—
1612 (d)	—	—	—	—	—	—

KM# 44 1/2 THALER

Silver **Subject:** Death of Heinrich Julius **Note:** Similar to 1 Thaler, KM#46.

Date	Mintage	VG	F	VF	XF	Unc
1613 (o)	—	120	250	375	575	—

KM# 45 1/2 THALER

Silver **Note:** Similar to 1 Thaler, KM#47.

Date	Mintage	VG	F	VF	XF	Unc
1613 (o)	—	—	—	—	—	—
1614 (o)	—	—	—	—	—	—

KM# 51 1/2 THALER

Silver **Note:** Similar to 1 Thaler, KM#52.

Date	Mintage	VG	F	VF	XF	Unc
1614 (o)	—	55.00	110	175	275	—
1615 (o)	—	55.00	110	175	275	—
1616 (o)	—	55.00	110	175	275	—
1617 (o)	—	55.00	110	175	275	—
1618	—	55.00	110	175	275	—
1619	—	55.00	110	175	275	—
1621 (c)	—	55.00	110	175	275	—
1622 (c)	—	55.00	110	175	275	—
1622 HL	—	55.00	110	175	275	—
1623 (h)	—	55.00	110	175	275	—
1624 (h)	—	55.00	110	175	275	—
1625 (h)	—	55.00	110	175	275	—
1625 HL	—	55.00	110	175	275	—
1626 (s)	—	55.00	110	175	275	—
1627 (s)	—	55.00	110	175	275	—
1628 (s)	—	55.00	110	175	275	—
1629 (h)	—	55.00	110	175	275	—
1632 (s)	—	55.00	110	175	275	—

KM# 70 1/2 THALER

Silver **Obv:** Angel's head and wings above 11-fold arms **Rev:** Wildman, tree in right hand, date in legend

Date	Mintage	VG	F	VF	XF	Unc
1617	—	—	—	—	—	—
1618	—	—	—	—	—	—
1624	—	—	—	—	—	—

KM# 364 1/2 THALER

Silver **Subject:** Death of Friedrich Ulrich's Mother, Elisabeth of Denmark **Note:** Similar to 1 Thaler, KM#365.

Date	Mintage	VG	F	VF	XF	Unc
1626 (h)	—	—	—	—	—	—
1626 (s)	—	—	—	—	—	—

KM# 368 1/2 THALER

Silver **Obv:** Crowned 11-fold arms **Rev:** Wildman, tree in right hand

Date	Mintage	VG	F	VF	XF	Unc
1628 HS	—	—	—	—	—	—
1629 HS	—	—	—	—	—	—
1631 HS	—	—	—	—	—	—
1633 HS	—	—	—	—	—	—
1634 HS	—	—	—	—	—	—

KM# 378 1/2 THALER

Silver **Obv:** Similar to 1 Thaler, KM#365 **Rev:** St. Jacob with staff in right hand

Date	Mintage	VG	F	VF	XF	Unc
1633 (s)	—	—	—	—	—	—

KM# 382 1/2 THALER

Silver **Obv:** Helmeted 11-fold arms **Rev:** Wildman, tree in right hand, date in legend **Note:** August II.

Date	Mintage	VG	F	VF	XF	Unc
1634 (s)	—	—	—	—	—	—

KM# 391 1/2 THALER

Silver **Note:** Similar to 1/4 Thaler, KM#395.

Date	Mintage	VG	F	VF	XF	Unc
1636 (s)	—	120	200	300	450	—
1637 (s)	—	120	200	300	450	—
1639 (s)	—	120	200	300	450	—
1653 (s)	—	120	200	300	450	—
1655 (s)	—	120	200	300	450	—
1656 (s)	—	120	200	300	450	—

KM# 410 1/2 THALER

Silver

Date	Mintage	VG	F	VF	XF	Unc
1641 (s)	—	—	—	—	—	—
1642 (s)	—	—	—	—	—	—

KM# 412 1/2 THALER

Silver **Note:** 1/2 1st Bell Thaler. Similar to 1 Thaler, KM#418.

Date	Mintage	VG	F	VF	XF	Unc
1643	—	60.00	120	200	300	—

KM# 413 1/2 THALER

Silver **Note:** 1/2 2nd Bell Thaler. Similar to 1 Thaler, KM#419.

Date	Mintage	VG	F	VF	XF	Unc
1643 (s)	—	60.00	120	200	300	—

KM# 414 1/2 THALER

Silver **Note:** 1/2 3rd Bell Thaler.

Date	Mintage	VG	F	VF	XF	Unc
1643	—	80.00	160	300	500	—

KM# 415 1/2 THALER

Silver **Note:** 1/2 4th Bell Thaler.

Date	Mintage	VG	F	VF	XF	Unc
1643	—	70.00	140	250	350	—

KM# 416 1/2 THALER

Silver **Note:** 1/2 5th Bell Thaler.

Date	Mintage	VG	F	VF	XF	Unc
1643 (s)	—	60.00	120	200	300	—

KM# 417 1/2 THALER

Silver **Note:** 1/2 6th Bell Thaler.

Date	Mintage	VG	F	VF	XF	Unc
1643 (s)	—	60.00	120	200	300	—

KM# 454 1/2 THALER

Silver

Date	Mintage	VG	F	VF	XF	Unc
1656 (s)	—	55.00	110	175	275	—
1663 (s)	—	55.00	110	175	275	—
1664 (s)	—	55.00	110	175	275	—
1665 (s)	—	55.00	110	175	275	—

KM# 468 1/2 THALER

Silver **Rev:** Wildman holds tree across in front of him

Date	Mintage	VG	F	VF	XF	Unc
1661 (s)	—	70.00	140	250	375	—

KM# 476 1/2 THALER

Silver **Subject:** Death of August II **Note:** Similar to 1 Thaler, KM#477.

Date	Mintage	VG	F	VF	XF	Unc
1666	—	135	240	375	500	—

KM# 575 1/2 THALER

Silver **Ruler:** Anton Ulrich as Joint ruler **Obv:** Crowned 11-fold arms, date divided below **Rev:** 2 wildman holding 2 interwined trees **Note:** Similar to 1 Thaler, KM#571.

Date	Mintage	VG	F	VF	XF	Unc
1687 RB	—	55.00	110	175	300	—
1691 RB	—	55.00	110	175	300	—
1697 RB	—	55.00	110	175	300	—

KM# A620 1/2 THALER

Silver **Subject:** Death of August Wilhelm's Wife, Christine Sophie **Note:** Similar to 1 Thaler, KM#621.

Date	Mintage	VG	F	VF	XF	Unc
1695 ICB	—	—	—	—	—	—

KM# 620 1/2 THALER

Silver **Obv:** Crowned 11-fold arms **Rev:** Wildman holding tree with both hands to his left, date in legend

Date	Mintage	VG	F	VF	XF	Unc
1695 ICB	—	—	—	—	—	—

KM# 635 1/2 THALER

Silver **Ruler:** Anton Ulrich as Joint ruler **Obv:** Crowned 11-fold arms **Rev:** Wildman holding tree to his left with 2 hands, date in legend

Date	Mintage	VG	F	VF	XF	Unc
1700 RB	—	70.00	140	200	325	—

KM# 587 2/3 THALER

Silver **Obv:** Horse leaping left **Rev:** Crowned 11-fold arms divide date, REMIGIO... in legend, value below

Date	Mintage	VG	F	VF	XF	Unc
1690 ICB	—	40.00	85.00	140	250	—
1693 ICB	—	40.00	85.00	140	250	—
1694 ICB	—	40.00	85.00	140	250	—
1695 ICB	—	40.00	85.00	140	250	—

KM# 613 2/3 THALER

Silver **Rev. Legend:** LAND. MUNTZ...

Date	Mintage	VG	F	VF	XF	Unc
1693	—	45.00	100	170	290	—

KM# 623 2/3 THALER

Silver **Obv:** Crowned 12-fold arms **Rev:** Horse leaping left, 2/3 divide date below

Date	Mintage	VG	F	VF	XF	Unc
1696 ICB	—	33.00	70.00	110	220	—
1697 ICB	—	33.00	70.00	110	220	—

KM# 624 2/3 THALER

Silver **Obv:** Crowned 11-fold arms, value 2/3 below **Rev:** Horse leaping left, date below **Note:** Varieties exist.

Date	Mintage	VG	F	VF	XF	Unc
1697 DF	—	45.00	100	170	200	—

KM# 627 2/3 THALER

Silver **Ruler:** Anton Ulrich as Joint ruler **Obv:** Crowned 14-fold arms divide date **Rev:** Horse leaping left, value 2/3 below

Date	Mintage	VG	F	VF	XF	Unc
1699 HCH	—	70.00	140	220	350	—
1700 HCH	—	70.00	140	220	350	—

KM# 636 2/3 THALER

Silver **Ruler:** Anton Ulrich as Joint ruler **Rev:** Date divided by value below horse

Date	Mintage	VG	F	VF	XF	Unc
1700 HCH	—	25.00	55.00	90.00	175	—

KM# 7 THALER

Silver **Subject:** Heinrich Julius **Obv:** Helmeted 11-fold arms with central shield of Halberstadt arms **Rev:** Wildman, tree trunk in right hand, date in legend **Note:** Dav.#6285.

Date	Mintage	VG	F	VF	XF	Unc
1601 (d)	—	65.00	145	230	350	—
1601 (d)	—	65.00	145	230	350	—
1601 (o)	—	65.00	145	230	350	—
1602 (d)	—	65.00	145	230	350	—
1602 (o)	—	65.00	145	230	350	—
1603 (d)	—	65.00	145	230	350	—
1603 (o)	—	65.00	145	230	350	—
1604 (d)	—	65.00	145	230	350	—
1604 (o)	—	65.00	145	230	350	—
1605 (d)	—	65.00	145	230	350	—
1605 (o)	—	65.00	145	230	350	—
1606 (d)	—	—	—	—	—	—
1606 (o)	—	65.00	145	230	350	—
1607 (d)	—	—	—	—	—	—
1607 (o)	—	65.00	145	230	350	—
1608 (d)	—	65.00	145	230	350	—
1608 (o)	—	65.00	145	230	350	—
1609 (d)	—	—	—	—	—	—
1609 (o)	—	65.00	145	230	350	—
1610 (d)	—	65.00	145	230	350	—
1610 (o)	—	65.00	145	230	350	—
1611 (d)	—	65.00	145	230	350	—
1611 (o)	—	65.00	145	230	350	—
1612 (d)	—	—	—	—	—	—
1612 (o)	—	65.00	145	230	350	—
1613 (o)	—	65.00	145	230	350	—

KM# 11 THALER

Silver **Rev:** Cross below right arm **Note:** Dav. #6288.

Date	Mintage	VG	F	VF	XF	Unc
1601 (d)	—	100	180	325	525	—

KM# 12.1 THALER

Silver **Rev:** St. Andrew holding cross **Note:** Dav.#6290.

Date	Mintage	VG	F	VF	XF	Unc
1601 (d)	—	100	180	325	525	—
1602 (d)	—	100	180	325	525	—
1603 (d)	—	100	180	325	525	—
1604 (d)	—	100	180	325	525	—
1605 (d)	—	100	180	325	525	—
1606 (d)	—	100	180	325	525	—
1607 (d)	—	100	180	325	525	—
1608 (d)	—	100	180	325	525	—
1609 (d)	—	100	180	325	525	—
1610 (d)	—	100	180	325	525	—
1611 (d)	—	100	180	325	525	—

KM# 12.2 THALER

Silver **Rev:** Left hand over joint of cross **Note:** Dav. #6292.

Date	Mintage	VG	F	VF	XF	Unc
1602 (d)	—	100	180	325	525	—
1603 (d)	—	100	180	325	525	—

KM# 18 THALER

Silver **Subject:** Death of Heinrich Julius' Mother, Hedwig von Brandenburg **Note:** Central shield of Halberstadt arms. Dav. #6296.

Date	Mintage	VG	F	VF	XF	Unc
1602 (o)	—	145	275	500	800	—

KM# 12.3 THALER

Silver **Rev:** St. Andrew within circle of arabesques **Note:** Dav. #6293.

Date	Mintage	VG	F	VF	XF	Unc
1604 (d)	—	100	180	325	525	—
1605 (d)	—	100	180	325	525	—

KM# 24 THALER

Silver **Obv:** Helmeted 11-fold arms with central shield of Halberstadt arms, thick flan **Rev:** St. Andrew with cross, date in legend **Note:** Dav. #6286A.

Date	Mintage	VG	F	VF	XF	Unc
1605 (d)	—	—	—	—	—	—

KM# 46 THALER

Silver **Subject:** Death of Heinrich Julius **Note:** Dav. #6298.

Date	Mintage	VG	F	VF	XF	Unc
1613 (o)	—	145	275	500	800	—

KM# 47 THALER

Silver **Obv:** Helmeted 11-fold arms, without D. G. in titles **Note:** Dav. #A6303.

Date	Mintage	VG	F	VF	XF	Unc
1613 (o)	—	65.00	145	230	350	—
1614 (o)	—	65.00	145	230	350	—
1615 (o)	—	65.00	145	230	350	—

KM# 52.1 THALER

Silver **Obv:** With D.G. in titles **Note:** Dav.#6303.

Date	Mintage	VG	F	VF	XF	Unc
1613 (o)	—	65.00	145	230	350	—
1614 (o)	—	65.00	145	230	350	—
1615 (o)	—	65.00	145	230	350	—
1616 (o)	—	65.00	145	230	350	—
1617 (o)	—	65.00	145	230	350	—
1618 (o)	—	65.00	145	230	350	—
1619 (o)	—	65.00	145	230	350	—
1619 (c)	—	65.00	145	230	350	—
1620 (c)	—	65.00	145	230	350	—
1621 (c)	—	65.00	145	230	350	—
1622 (c)	—	65.00	145	230	350	—
1622 HL-(c)	—	65.00	145	230	350	—
1623 HL-(c)	—	65.00	145	230	350	—
1623 HL	—	65.00	145	230	350	—
1624 HL	—	65.00	145	230	350	—
1625 HL	—	65.00	145	230	350	—
1625	—	65.00	145	230	350	—
1626 (s)	—	65.00	145	230	350	—
1627 (s)	—	65.00	145	230	350	—
1628 (s)	—	65.00	145	230	350	—

KM# 52.2 THALER

Silver **Rev:** Border of crosses **Note:** Dav. #6303A.

Date	Mintage	VG	F	VF	XF	Unc
1615	—	65.00	145	230	350	—

KM# 52.3 THALER

Silver **Rev:** Top on tree **Note:** Dav. #6303B.

Date	Mintage	VG	F	VF	XF	Unc
1615	—	65.00	145	230	350	—

KM# 52.4 THALER

Silver **Rev:** With mintmaster initials HS **Note:** Dav. #6306.

Date	Mintage	VG	F	VF	XF	Unc
1622 (h)	—	65.00	145	230	350	—
1623 (h)	—	65.00	145	230	350	—
1624 (h)	—	65.00	145	230	350	—
1625 (h)	—	65.00	145	230	350	—
1626 (h)	—	65.00	145	230	350	—
1627 (h)	—	65.00	145	230	350	—
1628 (h)	—	65.00	145	230	350	—
1629 (h)	—	65.00	145	230	350	—

KM# 52.5 THALER

Silver **Rev:** Inner pearl border and flowers **Note:** Dav. #6307.

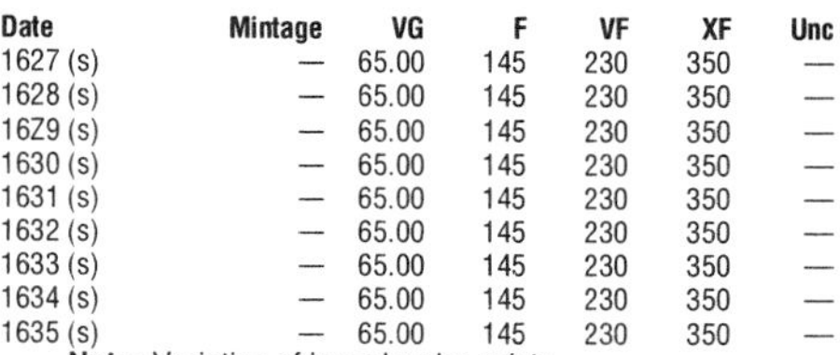

Date	Mintage	VG	F	VF	XF	Unc
1627 (s)	—	65.00	145	230	350	—
1628 (s)	—	65.00	145	230	350	—
16Z9 (s)	—	65.00	145	230	350	—
1630 (s)	—	65.00	145	230	350	—
1631 (s)	—	65.00	145	230	350	—
1632 (s)	—	65.00	145	230	350	—
1633 (s)	—	65.00	145	230	350	—
1634 (s)	—	65.00	145	230	350	—
1635 (s)	—	65.00	145	230	350	—

Note: Varieties of inner border exists

KM# 60 THALER

Silver **Rev:** St. Andrew with cross, date in legend **Note:** Dav. #6305.

Date	Mintage	VG	F	VF	XF	Unc
1616 (o)	—	130	260	450	725	—

KM# 365 THALER

Silver **Subject:** Death of Friedrich Ulrich's Mother, Elisabeth of Denmark **Note:** Dav. #6299.

Date	Mintage	VG	F	VF	XF	Unc
1626 (h)	—	150	285	525	850	—
1626 (s)	—	150	285	525	850	—

KM# 366 THALER

Silver **Rev:** 12-line inscription with month of death as IULI instead of IUNI **Note:** Dav. #6300.

Date	Mintage	VG	F	VF	XF	Unc
1626 (h)	—	130	260	450	725	—

KM# 380 THALER

Silver **Rev:** St. Jacob divides LAVTEN-TAHL, SI-date **Note:** Dav. #6309.

Date	Mintage	VG	F	VF	XF	Unc
1633 (s)	—	575	975	1,700	2,600	—

KM# 381 THALER

Silver **Rev:** St. Jacob divides 16-33 and S-I in 2 lines **Note:** Dav. #6310.

Date	Mintage	VG	F	VF	XF	Unc
1633 (s)	—	575	975	1,700	2,600	—

KM# 379 THALER

Silver **Rev:** Date at left of St. Jacob **Note:** Lauthenthal Mining Thalers. Dav. #6308.

Date	Mintage	VG	F	VF	XF	Unc
1633 (s)	—	525	900	1,550	2,350	—
1634 (s)	—	525	900	1,550	2,350	—

KM# 449 THALER

Silver **Obv:** Capped bust 3/4 to left **Note:** Dav. #6361.

Date	Mintage	VG	F	VF	XF	Unc
ND	—	295	525	900	1,500	—

KM# 447.1 THALER

Silver **Obv. Legend:** ...LUNEB:. **Note:** Dav. #6362.

Date	Mintage	VG	F	VF	XF	Unc
ND (s)	—	130	260	525	850	—

KM# 447.2 THALER

Silver **Rev:** Mint mark on shore nearer ship **Note:** Dav. #6362A.

Date	Mintage	VG	F	VF	XF	Unc
ND (s)	—	130	260	525	850	—

KM# 447.3 THALER

Silver **Obv. Legend:** ...U*LUNE:. **Note:** Dav. #6362B.

Date	Mintage	VG	F	VF	XF	Unc
ND (s)	—	130	260	525	850	—

KM# 447.4 THALER

Silver **Rev. Legend:** Larger boat farther from land with mm below, more clouds above **Note:** Dav. #6362C.

Date	Mintage	VG	F	VF	XF	Unc
ND (s)	—	130	260	525	850	—

KM# 448 THALER

Silver **Note:** Similar to KM#446 but capped bust and 1 large ship on reverse. Dav. #6360.

Date	Mintage	VG	F	VF	XF	Unc
ND	—	295	525	900	1,500	—

KM# 446 THALER

Silver **Note:** Reisse Thaler. Varieties exist. Dav. #6357.

Date	Mintage	VG	F	VF	XF	Unc
ND	—	130	260	525	850	—
ND (s)	—	130	260	525	850	—

KM# 392.1 THALER

Silver **Obv:** Helmeted 11-fold arms, titles in Latin **Rev:** Wildman, tree in right hand, date in legend **Note:** Dav. #6335.

Date	Mintage	VG	F	VF	XF	Unc
1636 (s)	—	65.00	145	230	350	—

KM# 392.2 THALER

Silver **Obv. Legend:** AUGUST' IUNI. D. -G: -DUX... **Note:** Dav. #6336.

Date	Mintage	VG	F	VF	XF	Unc
1636 (s)	—	65.00	145	230	350	—

KM# 393.1 THALER

Silver **Obv:** Titles in German, AUGUS: HERTZOB--ZU. BR: UND: L. **Note:** Dav. #6337.

Date	Mintage	VG	F	VF	XF	Unc
1636 (s)	—	65.00	145	230	350	—
1637 (s)	—	65.00	145	230	350	—
1638 (s)	—	65.00	145	230	350	—
1639 (s)	—	65.00	145	230	350	—

KM# 396 THALER

Silver **Note:** Similar to KM#444, but wildman holds tree with only his left hand

Date	Mintage	VG	F	VF	XF	Unc
1637	—	—	—	—	—	—

KM# 398.1 THALER

Silver **Obv:** 1/2-length figure left **Obv. Legend:** AUGUSTUS HERTOZOG. ZU. BRAUNS. UND. LUN. **Rev:** Helmeted 11-fold arms, date in legend **Note:** Dav. #6346.

Date	Mintage	VG	F	VF	XF	Unc
1638 (s)	—	65.00	145	240	400	—
1639 (s)	—	65.00	145	240	400	—

KM# 398.2 THALER

Silver **Rev:** Legend unbroken by arms at bottom **Note:** Dav. #6347.

Date	Mintage	VG	F	VF	XF	Unc
1639 (s)	—	65.00	145	240	400	—
1640 (s)	—	65.00	145	240	400	—
1641 (s)	—	65.00	145	240	400	—
1642 (s)	—	65.00	145	240	400	—
1643 (s)	—	65.00	145	240	400	—
1644 (s)	—	65.00	145	240	400	—
1644	—	65.00	145	240	400	—
1645 (s)	—	65.00	145	240	400	—
1646	—	65.00	145	240	400	—

KM# 398.3 THALER

Silver **Note:** Dav. #6348.

Date	Mintage	VG	F	VF	XF	Unc
1647 (s)	—	65.00	145	240	400	—
1648 (s)	—	65.00	145	240	400	—
1649 (s)	—	65.00	145	240	400	—
1650 (s)	—	65.00	145	240	400	—

KM# 393.2 THALER

Silver **Obv. Legend:** AUGUS. HERTZ. ZU. BR. U. LUN. **Note:** Dav. #6338.

Date	Mintage	VG	F	VF	XF	Unc
1639	—	65.00	145	230	350	—
1640 (s)	—	65.00	145	230	350	—
1641 (s)	—	65.00	145	230	350	—
1642 (s)	—	65.00	145	230	350	—
1643 (s)	—	65.00	145	230	350	—
1644 (s)	—	65.00	145	230	350	—
1645 (s)	—	65.00	145	230	350	—
1646 (s)	—	65.00	145	230	350	—
1647	—	65.00	145	230	350	—
1647 (s)	—	65.00	145	230	350	—
1648 (s)	—	65.00	145	230	350	—

KM# 393.3 THALER

Silver **Obv. Legend:** AUGUSTUS. HERTZUG... **Note:** Dav. #6340.

Date	Mintage	VG	F	VF	XF	Unc
1650 (s)	—	65.00	145	230	350	—
1651 (s)	—	65.00	145	230	350	—
1652 (s)	—	65.00	145	230	350	—
1653 (s)	—	65.00	145	230	350	—
ND	—	65.00	145	230	350	—

KM# 418.1 THALER

Silver **Rev. Legend:** ALLES*MIT BEDACHT*ANNO, date **Note:** 1st Bell Thaler. Dav. #6363.

Date	Mintage	VG	F	VF	XF	Unc
1643	—	130	230	425	650	—

KM# 418.2 THALER

Silver **Rev. Legend:** ...BEDACHT. mm.-ANO., date **Note:** Dav. #6364.

Date	Mintage	VG	F	VF	XF	Unc
1643 (s)	—	130	230	425	650	—

KM# 419.1 THALER

Silver **Obv:** Small 3/4 length armored figure of August II left. **Obv. Legend:** • AUGUSTUS • HERTZOG • ZU **Rev:** Bell with *UTI * SIC * NISI * below **Rev. Legend:** * ALLES * MIT * BEDACHT * ANNO **Note:** 2nd Bell Thaler. Dav. #6366. Prev. KM#419. Varieties exist.

Date	Mintage	VG	F	VF	XF	Unc
1643	—	130	230	425	650	—
1643 (s)	—	130	230	425	650	—

KM# 419.2 THALER

Silver **Obv:** Small 3/4 length armored figure of August II left **Note:** Dav. #6366A.

Date	Mintage	VG	F	VF	XF	Unc
1643 HS	—	130	230	425	650	—

KM# 419.3 THALER

Silver **Obv:** Large 3/4 length armored figure of August II left **Note:** Dav. #6366B.

Date	Mintage	VG	F	VF	XF	Unc
1643	—	130	230	425	650	—

Note: 1643 (s) is error.

KM# 422 THALER

Silver **Note:** 3rd Bell Thaler. Dav. #6368.

Date	Mintage	VG	F	VF	XF	Unc
1643	—	165	295	550	850	—
1643 (s)	—	165	295	550	850	—

KM# 425 THALER

Silver **Rev:** Clapper style bell with stone block **Note:** 4th Bell Thaler. Dav. #6371.

Date	Mintage	VG	F	VF	XF	Unc
1643	—	130	230	425	650	—

KM# 427 THALER

Silver **Note:** 5th Bell Thaler. Dav. #6373.

Date	Mintage	VG	F	VF	XF	Unc
1643 (s)	—	130	230	425	650	—

KM# 428 THALER

Silver **Note:** 6th Bell Thaler. Dav. #6374.

Date	Mintage	VG	F	VF	XF	Unc
1643 (s)	—	130	230	425	650	—

Note: Varieties exist

KM# 429 THALER

Silver **Rev:** Sun above city scene **Note:** 7th Bell Thaler. Dav. #6375. Varieties exist.

Date	Mintage	VG	F	VF	XF	Unc
1643	—	85.00	165	350	525	—
1643 (s)	—	85.00	165	350	525	—

KM# 420 THALER

Silver **Obv:** Helmeted 11-fold arms **Note:** Dav. #6367.

Date	Mintage	VG	F	VF	XF	Unc
1643 (s)	—	130	230	425	650	—

KM# 423 THALER

Silver **Rev:** UTI SIC NISI below bell **Note:** Dav. #6369.

Date	Mintage	VG	F	VF	XF	Unc
1643	—	165	295	550	850	—
1643 (s)	—	165	295	550	850	—

KM# 424 THALER

Silver **Obv:** Helmeted 11-fold arms **Note:** Dav. #6370.

Date	Mintage	VG	F	VF	XF	Unc
1643	—	165	295	550	850	—

KM# 426 THALER

Silver **Obv:** Helmeted 11-fold arms **Note:** Dav. #6372.

Date	Mintage	VG	F	VF	XF	Unc
1643	—	130	230	425	650	—

KM# 436 THALER

Silver **Obv:** KM#393 **Rev:** Die of Christian Ludwig von Calenberg, KM#47. **Note:** Mule. Dav. #6339.

Date	Mintage	VG	F	VF	XF	Unc
1648 (s)	—	—	—	—	—	—
1652 (s)	—	—	—	—	—	—

KM# 440.1 THALER

Silver **Obv:** Bust 3/4 to right **Rev:** Similar to KM#441 **Note:** Dav. #6349.

Date	Mintage	VG	F	VF	XF	Unc
1650 (s)	—	105	195	350	550	—
1651 (s)	—	105	195	350	550	—
1651	—	105	195	350	550	—

KM# 440.2 THALER

Silver **Rev. Legend:** ANNO, date **Note:** Dav. #6350. Varieties exist.

Date	Mintage	VG	F	VF	XF	Unc
1652 (s)	—	105	195	350	550	—
1653 (s)	—	105	195	350	550	—

KM# 441 THALER

Silver **Note:** Dav. #6351.

Date	Mintage	VG	F	VF	XF	Unc
1652 (s)	—	115	215	400	650	—
1653 (s)	—	115	215	400	650	—
1654 (s)	—	115	215	400	650	—
1655 (s)	—	115	215	400	650	—

KM# 442.1 THALER

Silver **Obv:** Legend reads right to left **Note:** Dav. #6341.

Date	Mintage	VG	F	VF	XF	Unc
1653 (s)	—	65.00	145	230	350	—
1655 (s)	—	65.00	145	230	350	—
1656 (s)	—	65.00	145	230	350	—
1657 (s)	—	65.00	145	230	350	—
1658 (s)	—	65.00	145	230	350	—
1659 (s)	—	65.00	145	230	350	—

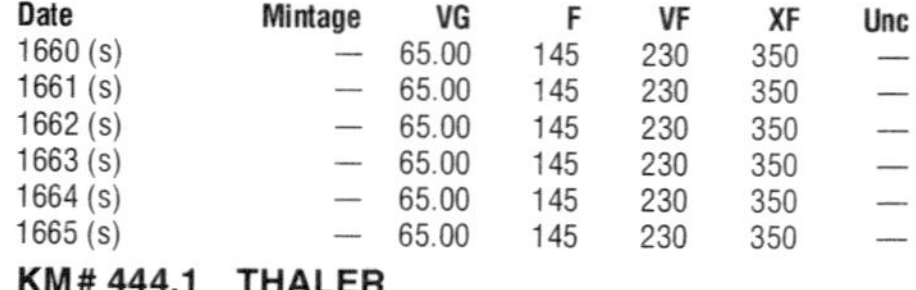

Date	Mintage	VG	F	VF	XF	Unc
1660 (s)	—	65.00	145	230	350	—
1661 (s)	—	65.00	145	230	350	—
1662 (s)	—	65.00	145	230	350	—
1663 (s)	—	65.00	145	230	350	—
1664 (s)	—	65.00	145	230	350	—
1665 (s)	—	65.00	145	230	350	—

KM# 444.1 THALER

Silver **Obv:** Similar to KM#442.1 **Rev:** Similar to KM#444.2 **Note:** Dav. #6343.

Date	Mintage	VG	F	VF	XF	Unc
1655 (s)	—	65.00	145	230	350	—
1657 (s)	—	65.00	145	230	350	—
1658 (s)	—	65.00	145	230	350	—
1659 (s)	—	65.00	145	230	350	—
1660 (s)	—	65.00	145	230	350	—
1661 (s)	—	65.00	145	230	350	—
1662 (s)	—	65.00	145	230	350	—
1663 (s)	—	65.00	145	230	350	—
1664 (s)	—	65.00	145	230	350	—
1665 (s)	—	65.00	145	230	350	—

KM# 444.2 THALER

Silver **Note:** Dav. #6344.

Date	Mintage	VG	F	VF	XF	Unc
1662	—	65.00	145	230	350	—
1664	—	65.00	145	230	350	—
1665	—	65.00	145	230	350	—
1666 (s)	—	65.00	145	230	350	—
1667 (s)	—	65.00	145	230	350	—

KM# 455 THALER

Silver **Obv:** Bust left, legend on both sides on ribbons spiraled around laurel wreaths **Note:** Dav. #6352.

Date	Mintage	VG	F	VF	XF	Unc
1656	—	165	295	550	850	—

KM# 456 THALER

Silver **Note:** Dav. #6353.

Date	Mintage	VG	F	VF	XF	Unc
1656	—	115	215	400	650	—
1657	—	115	215	400	650	—
1658	—	115	215	400	650	—
1659	—	115	215	400	650	—
1661	—	115	215	400	650	—
1664	—	115	215	400	650	—

KM# 469 THALER

Silver **Obv:** KM#393 **Rev:** Die of George Wilhelm von Calenberg, KM#57 **Note:** Mule. Dav. #6345.

Date	Mintage	VG	F	VF	XF	Unc
1662 (s)	—	50.00	105	195	325	—

KM# 470 THALER

Silver **Note:** Dav. #6354.

Date	Mintage	VG	F	VF	XF	Unc
1664	—	175	350	750	1,200	—
1665	—	175	350	750	1,200	—
1665 (s)	—	175	350	750	1,200	—

KM# 442.2 THALER

Silver **Obv:** Legend reads left to right **Note:** Dav. #6342.

Date	Mintage	VG	F	VF	XF	Unc
1664 (s)	—	65.00	145	230	350	—
1665 (s)	—	65.00	145	230	350	—
1666 (s)	—	65.00	145	230	350	—

KM# 445 THALER

Silver **Note:** Dav. #6355.

Date	Mintage	VG	F	VF	XF	Unc
1665	—	145	275	550	875	—
1665 (s)	—	145	275	550	875	—
1666	—	145	275	550	875	—
1666 (s)	—	145	275	550	875	—

KM# 478 THALER

Silver **Obv:** D. G. after duke's name **Note:** Dav. #6378.

Date	Mintage	VG	F	VF	XF	Unc
1666 HS	—	65.00	145	240	400	—
1667 HS	—	65.00	145	240	400	—

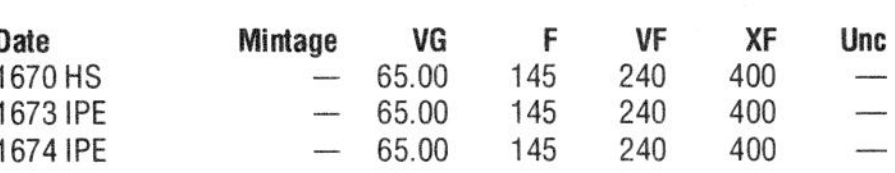

Date	Mintage	VG	F	VF	XF	Unc
1670 HS	—	65.00	145	240	400	—
1673 IPE	—	65.00	145	240	400	—
1674 IPE	—	65.00	145	240	400	—

KM# 477 THALER

Silver **Subject:** Death of August II **Note:** Dav. #6376.

Date	Mintage	VG	F	VF	XF	Unc
1666	—	145	275	550	875	—

KM# 502 THALER

Silver **Obv:** D. G. before duke's name **Note:** Varieties exist. Dav. #6379.

Date	Mintage	VG	F	VF	XF	Unc
1667 HS	—	65.00	145	240	400	—
1668 HS	—	65.00	145	240	400	—
1669 HS	—	65.00	145	240	400	—
1670 HS	—	65.00	145	240	400	—
1671 HS	—	65.00	145	240	400	—
1672 IPE	—	65.00	145	240	400	—
1673 IPE	—	65.00	145	240	400	—
1674 IPE	—	65.00	145	240	400	—
1675 IPE	—	65.00	145	240	400	—
1676 RB	—	65.00	145	240	400	—
1678 RB	—	65.00	145	240	400	—
1679 RB	—	65.00	145	240	400	—
1680 RB	—	65.00	145	240	400	—
1681 RB	—	65.00	145	240	400	—
1682 RB	—	65.00	145	240	400	—
1683 RB	—	65.00	145	240	400	—

KM# 511 THALER

Silver **Subject:** Capture of the city of Brunswick **Note:** Dav. #6381.

Date	Mintage	VG	F	VF	XF	Unc
1671 RB	—	230	400	725	1,300	—

KM# 512 THALER
Silver **Obv:** Top of bust breaks legend **Note:** Dav. #6382.

Date	Mintage	VG	F	VF	XF	Unc
1671	—	230	400	725	1,300	—
1671 RB	—	230	400	725	1,300	—

KM# 513.1 THALER
Silver **Note:** Dav. #6383.

Date	Mintage	VG	F	VF	XF	Unc
1671	—	175	350	700	1,350	—

Note: Varieties exist

KM# 513.2 THALER
Silver **Note:** Dav. #6384. Varieties exist.

Date	Mintage	VG	F	VF	XF	Unc
1671 RB	—	175	350	700	1,350	—

KM# 514 THALER
Silver **Obv:** Bust enclosed in circle **Note:** Dav. #6385.

Date	Mintage	VG	F	VF	XF	Unc
1671	—	175	350	700	1,350	—

KM# 524 THALER
Silver **Subject:** Death of August II's 3rd Wife, Sophie Elisabeth von Mecklenburg-Gustrow **Obv:** 2 angels holding crowned heart, 2 hands from clouds above **Rev:** 13-line inscription with Roman numeral date **Note:** Dav. #6377.

Date	Mintage	VG	F	VF	XF	Unc
1676	—	200	400	850	1,500	—

KM# 523 THALER
Silver **Subject:** Death of August Friedrich, Eldest Son of Anton Ulrich **Note:** Dav. #6398.

Date	Mintage	VG	F	VF	XF	Unc
1676	—	450	750	1,250	2,000	—

KM# 555 THALER
Silver **Note:** Dav. #6380.

Date	Mintage	VG	F	VF	XF	Unc
1684 RB	—	65.00	145	240	400	—
1685 RB	—	65.00	145	240	400	—

KM# 560 THALER
Silver **Obv:** Bust left enclosed in circle **Rev:** Helmeted 11-fold arms, date in legend **Note:** Dav. #6386.

Date	Mintage	VG	F	VF	XF	Unc
1685	—	400	700	1,200	1,850	—
1686 RB	—	400	700	1,200	1,850	—

KM# 561 THALER
Silver **Obv:** Intertwined cursive mirror-image RAVA monogram **Note:** Dav. #6387.

Date	Mintage	VG	F	VF	XF	Unc
ND	—	1,200	2,000	3,500	5,500	—

KM# 562 THALER
Silver **Obv:** Helmeted 11-fold arms divide date **Rev:** Wildman holding tree with both hands to his left in circle **Note:** Dav. #6388.

Date	Mintage	VG	F	VF	XF	Unc
1685 RB	—	65.00	145	230	350	—

KM# 571 THALER
Silver **Note:** Dav. #6392.

Date	Mintage	VG	F	VF	XF	Unc
1686 RB	—	80.00	165	260	400	—
1687 RB	—	80.00	165	260	400	—

KM# 572.1 THALER
Silver **Obv:** Small shield with round base, **Obv. Legend:** with U's **Note:** Dav. #6393.

Date	Mintage	VG	F	VF	XF	Unc
1686 RB	—	80.00	165	260	400	—
1687 RB	—	80.00	165	260	400	—

KM# 572.2 THALER
Silver **Obv:** Large shield with scalloped base **Obv. Legend:** W/V's **Note:** Dav. #6393A.

Date	Mintage	VG	F	VF	XF	Unc
1688 RB	—	80.00	165	260	400	—
1689 RB	—	80.00	165	260	400	—

Date	Mintage	VG	F	VF	XF	Unc
1690 RB	—	80.00	165	260	400	—
1691 RB	—	80.00	165	260	400	—
1692 RB	—	80.00	165	260	400	—

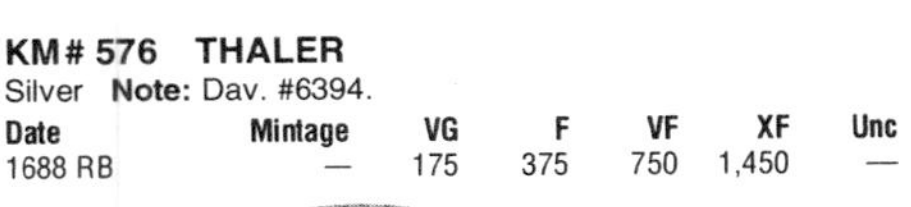

KM# 576 THALER

Silver **Note:** Dav. #6394.

Date	Mintage	VG	F	VF	XF	Unc
1688 RB	—	175	375	750	1,450	—

KM# 577 THALER

Silver **Obv:** Bust of 2 dukes right within inner circle **Note:** Dav. #6395.

Date	Mintage	F	VF	XF	Unc	BU
1688 RB	—	150	250	485	875	1,650
1689 RB	—	150	250	485	875	1,650
1690 RB	—	150	250	485	875	1,650
1691 RB	—	150	250	485	875	1,650
1692 RB	—	150	250	485	875	1,650
1693 RB	—	150	250	485	875	1,650
1694 RB	—	150	250	485	875	1,650
1695 RB	—	150	250	485	875	1,650
1696 RB	—	150	250	485	875	1,650
1697 RB	—	150	250	485	875	1,650
1698 RB	—	150	250	485	875	1,650
1699 RB	—	150	250	485	875	1,650
1700 RB	—	150	250	485	875	1,650

KM# 593 THALER

Silver **Note:** Dav. #6389.

Date	Mintage	F	VF	XF	Unc	BU
1691 RB	—	145	230	400	825	—
1692 RB	—	145	230	400	825	—
1693 RB	—	145	230	400	825	—
1694 RB	—	145	230	400	825	—
1695 RB	—	145	230	400	825	—
1696 RB	—	145	230	400	825	—
1697 RB	—	145	230	400	825	—
1698 RB	—	145	230	400	825	—
1699 RB	—	145	230	400	825	—

KM# 602.1 THALER

Silver **Note:** Varieties exist. Dav. #6396.

Date	Mintage	F	VF	XF	Unc	BU
1692 RB	—	525	900	1,500	2,600	—
1693 RB	—	525	900	1,500	2,600	—

KM# 602.2 THALER

Silver **Obv:** Armored bust right **Rev:** Larger bust **Note:** Varieties exist. Dav. #6397.

Date	Mintage	F	VF	XF	Unc	BU
1694 RB	—	525	900	1,500	2,600	—
1695 RB	—	525	900	1,500	2,600	—

KM# 621 THALER

Silver **Subject:** Death of August Wilhelm's wife, Christine Sophie **Note:** Dav. #6400.

Date	Mintage	F	VF	XF	Unc	BU
1695	—	450	775	1,150	1,950	—

KM# 628 THALER

Silver **Note:** Similar to KM#637 but small date divided. Dav. #6390.

Date	Mintage	F	VF	XF	Unc	BU
1699 RB	—	145	230	400	825	—

KM# 637 THALER

Silver **Ruler:** Anton Ulrich as Joint ruler **Obv:** Helmeted 11-fold arms, date in legend **Rev:** Wildman holding tree with both hands to his left **Note:** Dav. #6391.

Date	Mintage	F	VF	XF	Unc	BU
1700 RB	—	145	230	400	825	—

KM# 341 1-1/4 THALER

Silver **Note:** Similar to KM#338 but Fortuna divides date on obverse and a different scene upper left on reverse. Dav. #6315.

Date	Mintage	VG	F	VF	XF	Unc
1622	—	850	1,450	2,150	3,600	—

KM# 19 1-1/2 THALER

Silver **Subject:** Death of Heinrich JUlius' Mother, Hedwig von Brandenburg **Note:** Similar to 1 Thaler, KM#18. Dav. #6295.

Date	Mintage	VG	F	VF	XF	Unc
1602 (o) Rare	—	—	—	—	—	—

KM# 37 1-1/2 THALER

43.0000 g., Silver, 63 mm. **Ruler:** Heinrich Julius **Note:** Similar to 3 Thaler, KM#29. Varieties with and without denomination. Dav. #LS33.

Date	Mintage	VG	F	VF	XF	Unc
1612 (o)	—	475	850	1,500	2,400	—

KM# 81 1-1/2 THALER
43.0000 g., Silver, 71 mm. **Note:** Illustration reduced. Dav. #LS42.

Date	Mintage	VG	F	VF	XF	Unc
1618 (o)	—	650	1,000	1,800	3,000	—

KM# 356 1-1/2 THALER
43.3000 g., Silver **Note:** Similar to 3 Thaler, KM#359 but without denomination shown. Dav. #LS57. Illustration reduced.

Date	Mintage	VG	F	VF	XF	Unc
1625 HS	—	900	1,600	3,000	5,100	—

KM# 450.1 1-1/2 THALER
43.0000 g., Silver **Note:** Similar to 2 Thaler, KM#451, but without denomination value punched in. Dav. #LS71. Illustration reduced.

Date	Mintage	VG	F	VF	XF	Unc
1655 (s)	—	300	550	1,000	1,750	—

KM# 450.2 1-1/2 THALER
43.0000 g., Silver **Note:** Similar to 2 Thaler, KM#451.2, with value 1-1/2. Dav. #LS73.

Date	Mintage	VG	F	VF	XF	Unc
1660 (s)	—	300	550	1,000	1,750	—

KM# 450.3 1-1/2 THALER
43.0000 g., Silver, 63 mm. **Ruler:** August II **Note:** Similar to 2 Thaler, KM#451.3. Dav. #LS75. Illustration reduced.

Date	Mintage	VG	F	VF	XF	Unc
1662 (s)	—	300	550	1,000	1,750	—

KM# 450.4 1-1/2 THALER
43.0000 g., Silver, 62 mm. **Ruler:** August II **Obv:** August II mounted right with plumed hat, value stamped below **Rev:** Helmeted arms **Note:** Dav. #LS77. Illustration reduced.

Date	Mintage	VG	F	VF	XF	Unc
1664 (s)	—	300	550	1,000	1,750	—

KM# 464 1-1/2 THALER
43.0000 g., Silver **Subject:** Death of Princess Anna Sophie **Obv:** Crowned arms in wreath **Rev:** 11-line inscription with date **Note:** Dav. #6317.

Date	Mintage	VG	F	VF	XF	Unc
1659 Rare	—	—	—	—	—	—

KM# 479.1 1-1/2 THALER
43.0000 g., Silver **Subject:** 88th Birthday of August II **Note:** Similar to 2 Thaler, KM#482 with or without value. Dav. #LS88.

Date	Mintage	VG	F	VF	XF	Unc
1666 (s)	—	600	850	1,200	1,900	—

KM# 479.2 1-1/2 THALER
43.0000 g., Silver **Note:** Dav. #LS88a.

Date	Mintage	VG	F	VF	XF	Unc
1666 IPE	—	270	475	900	1,400	—

Note: IPE mintmasters initials indicate later restrike

KM# 479.3 1-1/2 THALER
43.0000 g., Silver **Note:** Dav. #LS88b.

Date	Mintage	VG	F	VF	XF	Unc
1666 RB	—	650	1,000	1,800	3,000	—

KM# 480 1-1/2 THALER
43.0000 g., Silver **Subject:** Death of August II **Note:** Similar to 1 Thaler, KM#477 but denomination 1-1/2 punched in. Dav. #LS94.

Date	Mintage	VG	F	VF	XF	Unc
1666 Rare	—	—	—	—	—	—

KM# 530.1 1-1/2 THALER
43.0000 g., Silver, 64 mm. **Note:** Illustration reduced. Dav. #LS106.

Date	Mintage	VG	F	VF	XF	Unc
1679 RB	—	270	475	900	1,400	—

KM# 530.2 1-1/2 THALER
43.0000 g., Silver **Note:** Dav. #LS108.

Date	Mintage	VG	F	VF	XF	Unc
1683 RB	—	270	475	900	1,400	—

KM# 530.3 1-1/2 THALER
43.0000 g., Silver **Ruler:** Rudolf August **Note:** Dav. #LS115.

Date	Mintage	VG	F	VF	XF	Unc
1686 RB	—	270	475	900	1,400	—

KM# 14 2 THALER
Silver **Note:** Similar to 1 Thaler, KM#12 but with cross below right arm. Dav. #6287.

Date	Mintage	VG	F	VF	XF	Unc
1601 (d) Rare	—	—	—	—	—	—

KM# 13 2 THALER
Silver **Obv:** Helmeted 11-fold arms with central shield of Halberstadt arms **Rev:** Wildman, tree trunk in right hand, date in legend **Note:** Dav. #6284.

Date	Mintage	VG	F	VF	XF	Unc
1601 (o)	—	900	1,450	2,200	—	—
1604 (o)	—	900	1,450	2,200	—	—
1605 (o)	—	900	1,450	2,200	—	—

KM# 20 2 THALER
Silver **Subject:** Death of Heinrich Julius' Mother, Hedwig von Brandenburg **Note:** Similar to 1 Thaler, KM#18. Dav. #6294.

Date	Mintage	VG	F	VF	XF	Unc
1602 (o) Rare	—	—	—	—	—	—

KM# 21.1 2 THALER
Silver **Note:** Similar to 1 Thaler, KM#12. Dav. #6291.

Date	Mintage	VG	F	VF	XF	Unc
1603 (d) Rare	—	—	—	—	—	—

KM# 21.2 2 THALER
Silver **Note:** Dav. #6289.

Date	Mintage	VG	F	VF	XF	Unc
1607 (d) Rare	—	—	—	—	—	—
1611 (d) Rare	—	—	—	—	—	—

KM# 25.1 2 THALER
Silver **Obv:** Helmeted 11-fold arms with central shield of Halberstadt arms **Obv. Legend:** HENRICVS. IVLIVS. . . BRVNSVIC. ET. L. **Rev:** Wildman, tree trunk in right hand, date in legend **Note:** Dav. #6286.

Date	Mintage	VG	F	VF	XF	Unc
1605 (o)	—	300	550	900	1,600	—

KM# 25.2 2 THALER
Silver **Obv. Legend:** Ends: ...BRUNSVI. ET. LU. **Note:** Dav. #6286A.

Date	Mintage	VG	F	VF	XF	Unc
1605 (o)	—	300	550	900	1,600	—

KM# 25.3 2 THALER
Silver **Obv. Legend:** HENRICUS.IULIUS...BRUNSVI.ET.LU. **Note:** Dav. #6286B.

Date	Mintage	VG	F	VF	XF	Unc
1605 (o)	—	300	550	900	1,600	—

KM# 38 2 THALER
57.2000 g., Silver **Note:** Similar to 3 Thaler, KM#29. Dav. #LS32. Illustration reduced.

Date	Mintage	VG	F	VF	XF	Unc
1612 (o)	—	650	1,150	2,000	3,300	—

Note: Struck with 1-1/2 Thaler dies. Varieties with and without denomination

KM# 48 2 THALER
57.2000 g., Silver **Subject:** Death of Heinrich Julius **Note:** Struck from 1 Thaler dies on thick flan. Similar to 1 Thaler, KM#46. Dav. #6297.

Date	Mintage	VG	F	VF	XF	Unc
1613 (o) Rare	—	—	—	—	—	—

KM# 62 2 THALER
57.2000 g., Silver **Obv:** KM#61 **Rev:** KM#25 **Note:** Mule. Dav. #6301.

Date	Mintage	VG	F	VF	XF	Unc
(1616)/1605 (o)	—	1,100	1,800	2,700	—	—

KM# 61 2 THALER
57.2000 g., Silver **Note:** Dav. #6302.

Date	Mintage	VG	F	VF	XF	Unc
1616 (o)	—	1,150	1,900	3,000	—	—
1621 (c)	—	1,150	1,900	3,000	—	—

KM# 63 2 THALER
57.2000 g., Silver **Obv:** Similar to 1 Thaler, KM#52 **Rev:** St. Andrew with cross, date in legend **Note:** Dav. #6304.

Date	Mintage	VG	F	VF	XF	Unc
1616 (o) Rare	—	—	—	—	—	—

KM# 82 2 THALER
57.0000 g., Silver **Note:** 2 Glucks Thaler. Similar to 1-1/4 Thaler, KM#339, but without value shown. Dav. #6312.

Date	Mintage	VG	F	VF	XF	Unc
ND	—	1,150	1,900	3,000	—	—

KM# 83 2 THALER
57.0000 g., Silver **Note:** Similar to 1-1/2 Thaler, KM#81, but 2 punched in. Dav. #LS41.

Date	Mintage	VG	F	VF	XF	Unc
1618 (o)	—	900	1,500	2,400	—	—

Note: Varieties with and without denomination.

KM# 357 2 THALER
57.5300 g., Silver **Note:** Similar to 3 Thaler, KM#359, but 2 punched in. Dav. #LS56.

Date	Mintage	VG	F	VF	XF	Unc
1625 HS	—	900	1,600	3,000	5,100	—

KM# 430 2 THALER

57.5300 g., Silver **Note:** 2nd Bell Thaler. Similar to 1 Thaler, KM#419. Dav. #6365.

Date	Mintage	VG	F	VF	XF	Unc
1643 Rare	—	—	—	—	—	—

KM# 451.1 2 THALER

58.0000 g., Silver, 63 mm. **Obv:** Without 2 punched in **Note:** Illustration reduced. Dav. #LS570

Date	Mintage	VG	F	VF	XF	Unc
1655 (s)	—	325	575	1,100	2,000	—

KM# 451.2 2 THALER

58.0000 g., Silver **Obv:** With 2 punched in **Note:** Dav. #LS72. Illustration reduced.

Date	Mintage	VG	F	VF	XF	Unc
1660 (s)	—	325	575	1,100	2,000	—

KM# 451.3 2 THALER

46.9400 g., Silver, 61 mm. **Note:** Illustration reduced. Dav. #LS74.

Date	Mintage	VG	F	VF	XF	Unc
1662 (s)	—	325	575	1,100	2,000	—

KM# 451.4 2 THALER

57.4000 g., Silver, 62 mm. **Rev:** No inner circle **Note:** Illustration reduced. Dav. #LS76.

Date	Mintage	VG	F	VF	XF	Unc
1664 (s)	—	325	575	1,100	2,000	—

KM# 482.1 2 THALER

Silver **Note:** Similar to KM#482.2. Dav. #LS87. Illustration reduced.

Date	Mintage	VG	F	VF	XF	Unc
1666 (s)	—	325	575	1,100	2,000	—

KM# 482.2 2 THALER

Silver, 66 mm. **Note:** Illustration reduced. Dav. #LS87A.

Date	Mintage	VG	F	VF	XF	Unc
1666 IPE	—	300	550	950	1,700	—

KM# 482.3 2 THALER

Silver **Note:** Dav. #LS87B.

Date	Mintage	VG	F	VF	XF	Unc
1666 RB	—	600	1,200	2,400	3,900	—

Note: The above with mintmaster's initials other than (s) are later restrikes

KM# 481 2 THALER

Silver **Subject:** 88th Birthday of August II **Note:** With 2 punched in. Dav. #LS97C.

Date	Mintage	VG	F	VF	XF	Unc
1666 (s)	—	300	550	900	1,600	—

KM# 483 2 THALER

Silver **Subject:** Death of August II **Note:** Similar to 1 Thaler, KM#477 but 2 punched in. Dav. #LS93.

Date	Mintage	VG	F	VF	XF	Unc
1666 Rare	—	—	—	—	—	—

KM# 531.1 2 THALER
Silver **Note:** Similar to 1-1/2 Thaler, KM#530 but 2 punched in. Dav. #LS105.

Date	Mintage	VG	F	VF	XF	Unc
1679 RB	—	350	650	1,200	2,200	—

KM# 531.2 2 THALER
Silver **Note:** Dav. #LS107.

Date	Mintage	VG	F	VF	XF	Unc
1683 RB	—	350	650	1,200	2,200	—

KM# 531.3 2 THALER
Silver **Ruler:** Rudolf August **Note:** Dav. #LS114.

Date	Mintage	VG	F	VF	XF	Unc
1686 RB	—	350	650	1,200	2,200	—

KM# 563 2 THALER
Silver **Note:** Similar to 3 Thaler, KM#564. Dav. #LS112.

Date	Mintage	VG	F	VF	XF	Unc
1685 RB Rare	—	—	—	—	—	—

KM# 39 2-1/2 THALER
72.0000 g., Silver **Note:** Struck from 1-1/2 Thaler dies. Similar to 3 Thaler, KM#29. Dav. #LS-A32.

Date	Mintage	VG	F	VF	XF	Unc
1612 Rare	—	—	—	—	—	—

KM# 484 2-1/2 THALER
Silver **Note:** Similar to 1-1/2 Thaler, KM#479, 2-1/2 punched in. Dav. #LS86.

Date	Mintage	VG	F	VF	XF	Unc
1666 (s) Rare	—	—	—	—	—	—

KM# 29.1 3 THALER
Silver **Note:** Similar to 5 Thaler, KM#31.1. Dav.#LS26. Illustration reduced.

Date	Mintage	VG	F	VF	XF	Unc
1608 (o)	—	450	900	1,650	2,600	—
1609 (o)	—	—	—	—	—	—

KM# 29.2 3 THALER
Silver **Note:** Similar to 5 Thaler, KM#31.1. Dav.#LS29.

Date	Mintage	VG	F	VF	XF	Unc
1610 (o)	—	575	1,150	2,150	3,600	—

KM# 29.3 3 THALER
86.0000 g., Silver, 65 mm. **Note:** Illustration reduced. Varieties exist with differences in background on obverse and ornamentation around arms on reverse. Dav. #LS31.

Date	Mintage	VG	F	VF	XF	Unc
1612 (o)	—	550	1,100	1,950	3,250	—

KM# 72 3 THALER
Silver, 69 mm. **Obv:** Non-marred die **Note:** Illustration reduced. Dav. #LS38.

Date	Mintage	VG	F	VF	XF	Unc
1617 (o)	—	650	1,300	2,600	4,550	—

KM# 71 3 THALER
Silver, 73 mm. **Obv:** Marred die **Rev:** Small horse and shield, 3 stamped in cartouche at bottom **Note:** Illustration reduced. Dav. #LS38a.

Date	Mintage	VG	F	VF	XF	Unc
1617 (o)	—	575	1,150	2,150	3,600	—

KM# 85.1 3 THALER
Silver, 72 mm. **Obv:** KM#71. **Rev:** KM#84. **Note:** Illustration reduced. Dav. #LS38b.

Date	Mintage	VG	F	VF	XF	Unc
1618 (o)	—	575	1,150	2,150	3,600	—

KM# 85.2 3 THALER
Silver **Obv:** KM#712 **Rev:** KM#84. **Note:** Dav. #LS38c.

Date	Mintage	VG	F	VF	XF	Unc
1618 (o)	—	575	1,150	2,150	3,600	—

KM# 84 3 THALER
Silver, 69 mm. **Note:** Illustration reduced. Dav. #LS40.

Date	Mintage	VG	F	VF	XF	Unc
1618 (o)	—	550	1,100	1,950	3,250	—

KM# 349 3 THALER
Silver **Note:** Similar to 1-1/4 Thaler, KM#338, but 3 on globe. Dav. #LS53.

Date	Mintage	VG	F	VF	XF	Unc
1624 Rare	—	—	—	—	—	—

KM# 359 3 THALER
Silver, 68 mm. **Rev:** With or without 3 punched in **Note:** Illustration reduced. Dav. #LS55.

Date	Mintage	VG	F	VF	XF	Unc
1625 HS Rare	—	—	—	—	—	—

KM# A452 3 THALER
Silver **Note:** Similar to 2 Thaler, KM#451.1. Dav. #LS-A70.

Date	Mintage	VG	F	VF	XF	Unc
1655 (s)	—	650	1,150	2,150	3,600	—

KM# 452 3 THALER
Silver **Note:** With or without 3 punched in. Dav. #LS69. Illustration reduced.

Date	Mintage	VG	F	VF	XF	Unc
1655 (s)	—	550	1,100	1,950	3,250	—

KM# 471 3 THALER
Silver **Obv:** Date 1665 in ground below horse **Rev:** With or without 3 punched in **Note:** Similar to 4 Thaler, KM#453. Dav. #LS80.

Date	Mintage	VG	F	VF	XF	Unc
1665/1655 (s)	—	550	1,100	1,950	3,250	—

KM# 485 3 THALER
Silver **Subject:** 88th Birthday of August II **Note:** Similar to 4 Thaler, KM#488 but 3 punched in. Dav. #LS85C.

Date	Mintage	VG	F	VF	XF	Unc
1666 (s) Rare	—	—	—	—	—	—

KM# 486.1 3 THALER
87.0000 g., Silver **Note:** Similar to 2 Thaler, KM#482, but without value shown. Dav. #LS85.

Date	Mintage	VG	F	VF	XF	Unc
1666 (s) Rare	—	—	—	—	—	—

KM# 486.2 3 THALER
87.0000 g., Silver **Note:** Dav. #LS85A.

Date	Mintage	VG	F	VF	XF	Unc
1666 IPE Rare	—	—	—	—	—	—

KM# 486.3 3 THALER
87.0000 g., Silver **Note:** Dav. #LS85B.

Date	Mintage	VG	F	VF	XF	Unc
1666 RB Rare	—	—	—	—	—	—

Note: Mintmaster's initials other than (s) indicate later restrikes

KM# 348 3 THALER
87.0000 g., Silver, 82 mm. **Rev:** With or without 3 punched in **Note:** Illustration reduced. Dav. #LS51.

Date	Mintage	VG	F	VF	XF	Unc
1624 HS	—	625	1,250	2,450	4,250	—

KM# 487 3 THALER
85.0000 g., Silver **Subject:** Death of August II **Note:** Similar to 1 Thaler, KM#477, but without value shown.

Date	Mintage	VG	F	VF	XF	Unc
1666	—	—	—	—	—	—

KM# 525 3 THALER
83.7000 g., Silver, 79 mm. **Subject:** Death of August Friedrich, Eldest Son of Anton Ulrich **Obv:** With or without 3 punched in **Note:** Illustration reduced. Dav. #LS97.

Date	Mintage	VG	F	VF	XF	Unc
1676	—	1,300	2,600	4,550	7,800	—

KM# 533 3 THALER
Silver **Obv:** Altered bust not in circle **Note:** Dav. #LS104.

Date	Mintage	VG	F	VF	XF	Unc
1679 Rare	—	—	—	—	—	—

KM# 532 3 THALER
Silver **Note:** Similar to 5 Thaler, KM#536, but 3 punched in. Dav. #LS101. Illustration reduced.

Date	Mintage	VG	F	VF	XF	Unc
1679	—	1,750	3,250	5,900	9,100	—

KM# 564 3 THALER

78.0000 g., Silver, 76 mm. **Ruler:** Rudolf August **Note:** Illustration reduced. With or without 3 punched in. Dav. #LS111.

Date	Mintage	VG	F	VF	XF	Unc
1685 RB	—	650	1,150	2,150	3,600	—
1685 HH/RB	—	650	1,150	2,150	3,600	—

KM# 30.1 4 THALER

117.0000 g., Silver **Note:** Struck from 1-1/2 Thaler dies in each year. Similar to 3 Thaler, KM#29, but 4 punched in. Dav. #LS25.

Date	Mintage	VG	F	VF	XF	Unc
1608 (o)	—	1,050	1,950	3,500	5,900	—

KM# 30.2 4 THALER

Silver **Note:** Similar to 3 Thaler, KM#29.3. Dav. #LS30.

Date	Mintage	VG	F	VF	XF	Unc
1612 (o)	—	1,150	2,150	3,900	6,500	—

KM# 74 4 THALER

Silver **Obv:** Marred die **Note:** Dav. #LS37a.

Date	Mintage	VG	F	VF	XF	Unc
1617 (o)	—	1,050	1,950	3,500	5,900	—

KM# 73 4 THALER

Silver **Note:** Similar to 3 Thaler, KM#71, but 4 punched in. Dav. #LS37.

Date	Mintage	VG	F	VF	XF	Unc
1617 (o)	—	1,050	1,950	3,500	5,900	—

KM# 86.1 4 THALER

Silver **Note:** Similar to 1-1/2 Thaler, KM#81, but 4 punched in. Dav. #LS39.

Date	Mintage	VG	F	VF	XF	Unc
1618 (o)	—	1,150	2,150	3,900	6,500	—

KM# 86.2 4 THALER

Silver **Obv. Legend:** Error FRIIDERICUS **Note:** Dav. #LS39a.

Date	Mintage	VG	F	VF	XF	Unc
1618 (o)	—	1,300	2,300	4,250	7,200	—

KM# 87 4 THALER

Silver **Obv:** KM#74 **Rev:** KM#86 **Note:** Mule. Dav. #LS37b.

Date	Mintage	VG	F	VF	XF	Unc
1618 (o)	—	1,150	2,150	3,900	6,500	—

KM# 226 4 THALER

Silver, 81 mm. **Rev:** 4 punched in cartouche at bottom **Note:** Illustration reduced. Dav. #LS46.

Date	Mintage	VG	F	VF	XF	Unc
1620 (c) Rare	—	—	—	—	—	—

KM# 352 4 THALER

117.0000 g., Silver **Rev:** 4 on globe **Note:** Dav. #52a.

Date	Mintage	VG	F	VF	XF	Unc
1624 Rare	—	—	—	—	—	—

KM# 351 4 THALER

117.0000 g., Silver **Note:** Similar to 1-1/4 Thaler, KM#339, but without value shown. Dav. #52.

Date	Mintage	VG	F	VF	XF	Unc
1624 HP Rare	—	—	—	—	—	—

KM# 350 4 THALER

114.9000 g., Silver **Note:** Similar to 3 Thaler, KM#348 but with or without 4 punched in. Dav. #LS50. Illustration reduced.

Date	Mintage	VG	F	VF	XF	Unc
1624 (h)	—	1,150	2,150	3,900	6,500	—

KM# 360 4 THALER

Silver **Note:** Similar to 3 Thaler, KM#359, but 4 punched in. Dav. #LS54.

Date	Mintage	VG	F	VF	XF	Unc
1625 HS Rare	—	—	—	—	—	—

KM# 399 4 THALER

116.0000 g., Silver **Obv:** Similar to 2 Thaler, KM#451 **Rev:** Helmeted 11-fold arms, 2 lions as supporters, Roman numeral date in legend, without value shown **Note:** Dav. #LS65.

Date	Mintage	VG	F	VF	XF	Unc
1638 (s) Rare	—	—	—	—	—	—

KM# 400 4 THALER

114.9000 g., Silver **Obv:** Duke without hat on horse right, TANDEM behind head **Note:** Dav. #LS66.

Date	Mintage	VG	F	VF	XF	Unc
1638 (s) Rare	—	—	—	—	—	—

KM# 453 4 THALER

115.3000 g., Silver, 85 mm. **Ruler:** August II **Note:** Illustration reduced. With or without 4 punched in. Dav. #LS68.

Date	Mintage	VG	F	VF	XF	Unc
1655 HS	—	1,100	1,950	3,600	5,900	—

KM# 472 4 THALER

Silver **Obv:** Date 1665 in ground below horse **Rev:** 4 punched in **Note:** Dav. #LS79.

Date	Mintage	VG	F	VF	XF	Unc
1665/55 (s)	—	1,100	1,950	3,600	5,900	—

KM# 489 4 THALER

Silver, 87 mm. **Subject:** Death of August II **Note:** Illustration reduced. Similar to 1 Thaler, KM#477, but 4 punched in. Dav. #LS92.

Date	Mintage	VG	F	VF	XF	Unc
1666 Rare	—	—	—	—	—	—

Note: Spink Taisei Zurich Milas sale 4-92 XF realized $12,060

KM# 488 4 THALER

114.0500 g., Silver, 87 mm. **Subject:** 88th Birthday of August II **Note:** Illustration reduced. With or without 4 punched in. Dav. #LS84.

Date	Mintage	VG	F	VF	XF	Unc
1666 HS	—	1,150	2,150	3,900	6,500	—

KM# 526 4 THALER

Silver **Subject:** Death of August Friedrich, Eldest Son of Anton Ulrich **Note:** Similar to 3 Thaler, KM#525, but 4 punched in. Dav. #LS96.

Date	Mintage	VG	F	VF	XF	Unc
1676 Rare	—	—	—	—	—	—

KM# 535 4 THALER

Silver **Obv:** Altered bust not in circle **Note:** Dav. #LS103.

Date	Mintage	VG	F	VF	XF	Unc
1679 Rare	—	—	—	—	—	—

KM# 534 4 THALER

Silver **Note:** Similar to 5 Thaler, KM#536, but 4 punched in. Dav. #LS100. Illustration reduced.

Date	Mintage	VG	F	VF	XF	Unc
1679	—	3,250	5,200	7,800	11,000	—

KM# 565 4 THALER

Silver **Note:** Similar to 3 Thaler, KM#564, but 4 punched in. Dav. #LS110.

Date	Mintage	VG	F	VF	XF	Unc
1685 RB	—	1,300	2,300	4,250	7,200	—
1685 HH/RB	—	1,300	2,300	4,250	7,200	—

KM# 31.1 5 THALER

145.6000 g., Silver, 65 mm. **Note:** Illustration reduced. Struck from 3 Thaler dies, 5 punched in. Dav. #LS24.

Date	Mintage	VG	F	VF	XF	Unc
1608 (o)	—	1,950	3,250	4,550	6,500	—

KM# 31.2 5 THALER

144.2000 g., Silver, 81 mm. **Note:** Illustration reduced. Dav. #LS28.

Date	Mintage	VG	F	VF	XF	Unc
1609 (o)	—	2,600	4,550	7,200	10,500	—

KM# 31.3 5 THALER

144.2000 g., Silver **Note:** Dav. #LS-A29. Varieties exist with differences in background on obverse and ornamentation around arms on reverse.

Date	Mintage	VG	F	VF	XF	Unc
1610 (o)	—	2,600	4,550	7,200	11,000	—

KM# 31.4 5 THALER

Silver **Note:** Stamped 5 but having weight of only 3-1/4 Thaler. Dav. #LS28A.

Date	Mintage	VG	F	VF	XF	Unc
1609 (o)	—	2,600	4,550	7,200	11,000	—

KM# 53 5 THALER

Silver **Obv:** Helmeted 11-fold arms, 5 punched in **Rev:** Duke fully armored on horse left **Note:** Dav. #LS-A35.

Date	Mintage	VG	F	VF	XF	Unc
MDCXIV (1614) (o) Rare	—	—	—	—	—	—

KM# 54 5 THALER

Silver, 88 mm. **Rev:** 5 punched in cartouche at bottom **Note:** Illustration reduced. Dav. #LS36.

Date	Mintage	VG	F	VF	XF	Unc
1614 (o)	—	2,600	4,550	7,200	10,500	—

KM# 227 5 THALER

Silver, 82 mm. **Ruler:** Frederich Ulrich **Note:** Similar to 4 Thaler, KM#226, but 5 punched in. Dav. #LS45. Illustration reduced.

Date	Mintage	VG	F	VF	XF	Unc
1620 (c)	—	1,950	3,250	5,200	7,800	—

KM# 353 5 THALER

144.8000 g., Silver, 84 mm. **Note:** Illustration reduced. Similar to 3 Thaler, KM#348, but with or without 5 punched in. Dav. #LS49.

Date	Mintage	VG	F	VF	XF	Unc
1624 (h)	—	3,250	5,200	7,800	11,500	—

KM# 401 5 THALER

144.2000 g., Silver **Obv:** Duke without hat on horse right, TANDEM behind head **Rev:** Helmeted 4-fold arms, 2 lions as supporters, without value shown **Note:** Dav. #LS65.

Date	Mintage	VG	F	VF	XF	Unc
MDCXXXVIII (1638) (s) Rare	—	—	—	—	—	—

KM# 402 5 THALER

Silver **Note:** Similar to 4 Thaler, KM#453, but 5 punched in. Dav. #LS67.

Date	Mintage	VG	F	VF	XF	Unc
1655 (s) Rare	—	—	—	—	—	—

KM# 473 5 THALER

Silver **Obv:** Date 1665 in ground below horse **Rev:** 5 punched in **Note:** Dav. #LS78.

Date	Mintage	VG	F	VF	XF	Unc
1665/1655 (s) Rare	—	—	—	—	—	—

KM# 490 5 THALER

Silver **Subject:** 88th Birthday of August II **Note:** Similar to 4 Thaler, KM#488, but with or without 5 punched in. Dav. #LS83.

Date	Mintage	VG	F	VF	XF	Unc
1666 (s)	—	1,950	3,250	5,200	7,800	—

KM# 491 5 THALER

Silver **Subject:** Death of August II **Note:** Similar to 1 Thaler, KM#477, but 5 punched in. Dav. #LS91.

Date	Mintage	VG	F	VF	XF	Unc
1666 Rare	—	—	—	—	—	—

KM# 527 5 THALER

Silver **Subject:** Death of August Friedrich, Eldest Son of Anton Ulrich **Note:** Similar to 3 Thaler, KM#525, but 5 punched in. Dav. #LS95.

Date	Mintage	VG	F	VF	XF	Unc
1676 Rare	—	—	—	—	—	—

KM# 537 5 THALER

Silver **Obv:** Altered bust not in circle **Note:** Dav. #LS102.

Date	Mintage	VG	F	VF	XF	Unc
1679 Rare	—	—	—	—	—	—

KM# 536 5 THALER

Silver, 79 mm. **Rev:** 5 punched in **Note:** Illustration reduced. Dav. #LS99.

Date	Mintage	VG	F	VF	XF	Unc
1679 Rare	—	—	—	—	—	—

Note: Spink Taisei Zurich Milas sale 4-92 XF realized $10,050

KM# 566 5 THALER

Silver **Note:** Similar to 3 Thaler, KM#564, but 5 punched in. Dav. #LS109. Illustration reduced.

Date	Mintage	VG	F	VF	XF	Unc
1685 RB Rare	—	—	—	—	—	—

KM# 228 6 THALER

170.9000 g., Silver, 85 mm. **Note:** Illustration reduced. Similar to 4 Thaler, KM#226, but with or without 6 punched in. Dav. #LS44.

Date	Mintage	VG	F	VF	XF	Unc
1620 (c)	—	3,600	5,900	8,500	11,500	—

KM# 354 6 THALER

172.6000 g., Silver **Note:** Similar to 3 Thaler, KM#348, but with or without 6 punched in. Dav. #LS48.

Date	Mintage	VG	F	VF	XF	Unc
1624 (h)	—	2,600	4,250	6,500	9,800	—

KM# 383 6 THALER

171.0000 g., Silver **Note:** Similar to 10 Thaler, KM#385, but with or without 6 punched in. Dav. #LS61.

Date	Mintage	VG	F	VF	XF	Unc
1634 (s)	—	2,850	4,550	7,200	10,500	—

KM# 492 6 THALER

173.1000 g., Silver **Subject:** 88th Birthday of August II **Note:** Similar to 4 Thaler, KM#488, but with or without 6 punched in. Dav. #LS82.

Date	Mintage	VG	F	VF	XF	Unc
1666 (s) Rare	—	—	—	—	—	—

Note: Spink Taisei Zurich Milas sale 4-92 XF realized $11,055

KM# 493 6 THALER

173.1000 g., Silver **Subject:** Death of August II **Note:** Similar to 1 Thaler, KM#477, but 6 punched in. Dav. #LS90.

Date	Mintage	VG	F	VF	XF	Unc
1666 Rare	—	—	—	—	—	—

KM# 538 6 THALER

173.1000 g., Silver **Note:** Similar to 5 Thaler, KM#536, but 6 punched in. Dav. #LS98.

Date	Mintage	VG	F	VF	XF	Unc
1679 Rare	—	—	—	—	—	—

KM# 573 7 THALER

Silver **Note:** Similar to 1-1/2 Thaler, KM#530, but 7 punched in. Dav. #LS113.

Date	Mintage	VG	F	VF	XF	Unc
1686 RB Rare	—	—	—	—	—	—

MB# 235 8 THALER

233.0000 g., Silver **Rev:** Value 8 punched over 5 (TALER) **Note:** Schauthaler. Dav.#LS21. Similar to 2 Thaler MB#222.

Date	Mintage	VG	F	VF	XF	Unc
1588	—	—	—	—	—	—

KM# 384 8 THALER

230.0000 g., Silver **Note:** Similar to 10 Thaler, KM#385, but with or without 8 punched in. Dav. #LS60.

Date	Mintage	VG	F	VF	XF	Unc
1634 (s) Rare	—	—	—	—	—	—

KM# 494 8 THALER

230.0000 g., Silver **Subject:** Death of August II **Note:** Similar to 1 Thaler, KM#477, but 8 punched in. Dav. #LS89.

Date	Mintage	VG	F	VF	XF	Unc
1666 Rare	—	—	—	—	—	—

MB# 196 10 THALER

Silver **Rev:** Value X (THA) punched over 5 **Note:** Schauthaler. Dav.#LS12. Similar to 2 Thaler MB#222. Weight varies: 290-293g.

Date	Mintage	VG	F	VF	XF	Unc
(15)83	—	—	—	—	—	—

KM# 32 10 THALER

292.5000 g., Silver **Note:** Struck from 5 Thaler dies. Similar to 3 Thaler, KM#29, but with 10 in cartouche at bottom reverse. Dav. #LS27.

Date	Mintage	VG	F	VF	XF	Unc
1609 (o) Rare	—	—	—	—	—	—

Note: Spink Taisei Zurich Milas sale 4-92 XF realized $18,760

KM# 56 10 THALER

292.5000 g., Silver **Note:** Similar to 5 Thaler, KM#54, but 10 punched in. Dav. #LS35.

Date	Mintage	VG	F	VF	XF	Unc
1614 (o) Rare	—	—	—	—	—	—

KM# 55 10 THALER

292.5000 g., Silver **Obv:** Helmeted 11-fold arms, value 10 punched in **Rev:** Duke fully armored on horse left, Roman numeral date in legend **Note:** Dav. #LS34.

Date	Mintage	VG	F	VF	XF	Unc
1614 (o) Rare	—	—	—	—	—	—

KM# 229 10 THALER

289.9000 g., Silver **Note:** Similar to 4 Thaler, KM#226, but 10 punched in or omitted. Dav. #LS43.

Date	Mintage	VG	F	VF	XF	Unc
1620 (c) Rare	—	—	—	—	—	—

Note: Spink Taisei Zurich Milas sale 4-92 XF realized $15,400

KM# 355 10 THALER

290.0000 g., Silver **Note:** Similar to 3 Thaler, KM#348, but without value shown. Dav. #LS47.

Date	Mintage	VG	F	VF	XF	Unc
1624 (h) Rare	—	—	—	—	—	—

KM# 386 10 THALER

284.8000 g., Silver **Note:** Altered features, especially sun without face. Dav. #LS62.

Date	Mintage	VG	F	VF	XF	Unc
1634 (s) Rare	—	—	—	—	—	—

KM# 385 10 THALER
284.8000 g., Silver, 100 mm. **Note:** Illustration reduced. With or without 10 punched in. Dav. #LS59.

Date	Mintage	VG	F	VF	XF	Unc
1634 (s) Rare	—	—	—	—	—	—

Note: Spink Taisei Zurich Milas sale 4-92 XF realized $37,520

KM# 403 10 THALER
284.0000 g., Silver **Obv:** Duke without hat on horse right, TANDEN behind head **Rev:** Helmeted 11-fold arms, 2 lions as supporters, Roman numeral date in legend, without value shown **Note:** Dav. #LS63.

Date	Mintage	VG	F	VF	XF	Unc
1638 (s) Rare	—	—	—	—	—	—

KM# 495 10 THALER
284.0000 g., Silver **Subject:** 88th Birthday of August II **Note:** Similar to 4 Thaler, KM#488, but 10 punched in. Dav. #LS81.

Date	Mintage	VG	F	VF	XF	Unc
1666 (s) Rare	—	—	—	—	—	—

KM# 387 12 THALER
349.0000 g., Silver **Note:** Similar to 10 Thaler, KM#385, but without value shown. Dav. #LS58.

Date	Mintage	VG	F	VF	XF	Unc
1634 (s) Rare	—	—	—	—	—	—

TRADE COINAGE

KM# 57 DUCAT
3.5000 g., 0.9860 Gold 0.1109 oz. AGW **Obv:** Crowned arms in inner circle **Rev:** Wildman holding tree

Date	Mintage	VG	F	VF	XF	Unc
1615 (o)	—	500	1,100	2,400	4,400	—
1617	—	500	1,100	2,400	4,400	—
1618 (o)	—	500	1,100	2,400	4,400	—
1620	—	500	1,100	2,400	4,400	—
1621	—	500	1,100	2,400	4,400	—
1624	—	500	1,100	2,400	4,400	—
1629 (h)	—	500	1,100	2,400	4,400	—
1631 (s)	—	500	1,100	2,400	4,400	—

KM# 361 DUCAT
3.5000 g., 0.9860 Gold 0.1109 oz. AGW **Obv:** Bust of Friedrich Ulrich right in inner circle **Rev:** Crowned arms in inner circle

Date	Mintage	VG	F	VF	XF	Unc
1625 HS	—	600	1,300	3,000	4,800	—
1626 HS	—	600	1,300	3,000	4,800	—

KM# 375 DUCAT
3.5000 g., 0.9860 Gold 0.1109 oz. AGW **Obv:** Friedrich Ulrich standing in inner circle

Date	Mintage	VG	F	VF	XF	Unc
1630 HS	—	425	850	1,850	3,000	—

KM# 404 DUCAT
3.5000 g., 0.9860 Gold 0.1109 oz. AGW **Obv:** Bust of August right in inner circle **Rev:** Crowned arms in inner circle

Date	Mintage	VG	F	VF	XF	Unc
1638 (s)	--	350	725	1,500	2,700	—

KM# 406 DUCAT
3.5000 g., 0.9860 Gold 0.1109 oz. AGW **Obv:** August **Rev:** Date in legend

Date	Mintage	VG	F	VF	XF	Unc
1639 (s)	—	350	725	1,500	2,700	—

KM# 457 DUCAT
3.5000 g., 0.9860 Gold 0.1109 oz. AGW **Obv:** Facing bust of August in hat

Date	Mintage	VG	F	VF	XF	Unc
1658 (s)	—	300	600	1,250	2,250	—

KM# 506 DUCAT
3.5000 g., 0.9860 Gold 0.1109 oz. AGW **Obv:** Crowned arms in inner circle **Rev:** Rearing horse, date in exergue

Date	Mintage	VG	F	VF	XF	Unc
1669	—	450	900	1,900	3,400	—

KM# 546 DUCAT
3.5000 g., 0.9860 Gold 0.1109 oz. AGW **Obv:** Rudolf August **Rev:** War galley at sea, "Jehovah" (in Hebrew) above

Date	Mintage	VG	F	VF	XF	Unc
1680 RB	—	1,000	2,150	4,150	7,100	—

KM# 594 DUCAT
3.5000 g., 0.9860 Gold 0.1109 oz. AGW **Obv:** Bust of 2 dukes right **Rev:** Crowned 11-fold arms, date in legend

Date	Mintage	VG	F	VF	XF	Unc
1691 HCH	—	550	1,100	2,400	4,300	—

KM# 625 DUCAT
3.5000 g., 0.9860 Gold 0.1109 oz. AGW **Ruler:** Anton Ulrich as Joint ruler **Obv:** Bust of Rudolf August right **Rev:** Bust of Anton Ulrich right **Note:** Varieties exist.

Date	Mintage	VG	F	VF	XF	Unc
1698 HCH	—	900	2,000	4,600	8,000	—

KM# 595 DUCAT
3.5000 g., 0.9860 Gold 0.1109 oz. AGW **Obv:** Conjoined busts of Rudolf August and Anton Ulrich right **Rev:** Crowned 15-fold arms divide date

Date	Mintage	VG	F	VF	XF	Unc
1699 HCH	—	500	1,000	2,300	4,000	—

KM# 507 2 DUCAT
7.0000 g., 0.9860 Gold 0.2219 oz. AGW **Obv:** Crowned arms in inner circle **Rev:** Rearing horse, date in exergue

Date	Mintage	VG	F	VF	XF	Unc
1669 (S)	—	975	1,800	3,750	6,800	—

KM# 58 10 DUCAT (Portugalöser)
35.0000 g., 0.9860 Gold 1.1095 oz. AGW **Obv:** 1/2 length figure right **Rev:** Helmeted 11-fold arms, wildman to left, date in legend **Note:** Struck with 1 Thaler dies, KM#7.

Date	Mintage	VG	F	VF	XF	Unc
1615 (o) Rare	—	—	—	—	—	—

PATTERNS

Including off metal strikes

KM#	Date	Mintage	Identification	Mkt Val
Pn1	1608 (d)	—	1/4 Thaler. Gold. KM#8.	—
PnA2	1625 HS	—	2 Thaler. Gold. KM#357.	—
Pn2	1643 (s)	—	1/4 Thaler. Gold. KM#411.	—
Pn3	1643 (s)	—	Thaler. Gold. 6th bell thaler, KM#428.	—
Pn4	1643 (s)	—	Thaler. Gold. 7th bell thaler, KM#429.	—
Pn5	1687	—	Thaler. Silver. KM#576.	—

BUCHEIM

The Bucheim house were hereditary cupbearers to the archdukes of Austria. Johann Christof III (1619-1657) was the only issuer of coins.

RULERS
Johann Christian, 1619-1657

LORDSHIP

TRADE COINAGE

KM# 1 DUCAT
3.5000 g., 0.9860 Gold 0.1109 oz. AGW **Obv:** Bust of Johann Christian right

Date	Mintage	VG	F	VF	XF	Unc
1650 Rare	—	—	—	—	—	—

BURGMILCHLING

(Wilhermsdorf)

A knight named Heinrich Hartmann Schutzpar, who descended from the late 13th century Hartmann von Schutzpeer (= Schüttle den Speer, same meaning as Shakespeare in English), lived with the nickname Milchling (milkman). Heinrich Hartmann bought the ruined castle of Wilhermsdorf, 15 miles (25km) west of Nüremberg, and its surrounding territory. When he had restored the castle, he renamed it Burgmilchling and was given the title of free baron in 1569. His son succeeded him in 1591 and struck a few coins.

RULERS
Heinrich Hermann, 1591-1649

BARONY

REGULAR COINAGE

KM# 10 THALER
Silver **Obv:** Helmeted four fold arms **Obv. Legend:** + HENR: HERM: L: B: INBVRGMILCHLING ET. WILHERMSDORF **Rev:** 3/4 length laureate bust of Rudolf II with sceptre and orb facing 3/4 right **Rev. Legend:** RVDOLPH • II • ROM: IMP:... **Note:** Dav. #6659.

Date	Mintage	VG	F	VF	XF	Unc
1605	—	1,450	2,500	4,500	7,200	—
1606	434	1,200	2,100	3,750	6,000	—
1608	—	1,450	2,500	4,500	7,200	—
1610	—	1,200	2,100	3,750	6,000	—
1611	—	1,200	2,100	3,750	6,000	—

CAMENZ

(Kamenz)

A provincial town in Saxony, some 20 miles northeast of Dresden, founded about the year 1200. First owned by Brandenburg, then Bohemia, it passed to Saxony in 1635.

TOWN

REGULAR COINAGE

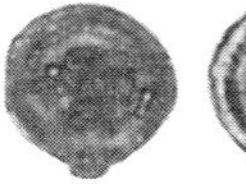

KM# 1 PFENNIG
Copper **Note:** Kipper Pfennig. Uniface. Arms (angel's wing, three pellets left), value 1 to right.

Date	Mintage	VG	F	VF	XF	Unc
ND(1622)	—	10.00	20.00	30.00	60.00	125
1622	—	10.00	20.00	30.00	60.00	125

KM# 2 2 PFENNIG
Copper **Note:** Kipper 2 Pfennig.

Date	Mintage	VG	F	VF	XF	Unc
1622	—	13.00	25.00	40.00	80.00	150

KM# 3 3 PFENNIG (Dreier)
Copper **Obv:** Arms, value 3 PF below **Rev:** BONO/PVBL./CAM./date **Note:** Kipper 3 Pfennig.

Date	Mintage	VG	F	VF	XF	Unc
1622	—	20.00	40.00	60.00	100	225

PATTERNS

Including off metal strikes

KM#	Date	Mintage	Identification	Mkt Val
Pn1	ND(1622)	—	Pfennig. Silver. KM#1	—

CAMMIN

BISHOPRIC

The town of Cammin in Pomerania (see, near the Baltic coast some 20 miles north-northeast of Stettin), was the seat of a bishopric founded by Adalbert (1139-62). The first Protestant bishop ruled from 1544, but in the next decade, Cammin came under the control of the dukes of Pomerania. From that time until the end of the Thirty Years' War in 1648-50, members of the ducal house were Bishops of Cammin. The part of Pomerania in which Cammin is situated passed with it to Brandenburg-Prussia in 1650. Except for some denars of the 13th century, no coins were struck for the bishopric until the 17th century.

RULERS

Kasimir VII Herzog, of Pomerania, 1574-1602
Franz of Pomerania, 1602-1618
Ulrich of Pomerania, 1618-1622
Bogislaus II (XIV) of Pomerania, 1622-1637
Ernst Bogislaus of Croy, 1637-1650

NOTE: Coinage for Cammin was interchangeable with that of Pomerania, which see for additional pieces that circulated freely in the bishopric.

MINTMASTERS' INITIALS

Initial	Date	Name
GT, sometimes in legature	Ca. 1628-37, 54	Gottfried Tabbert, die-cutter in Stettin
HS	1612-19	Johann (Hans) Schampan in Stettin
(z)=	1628-30	Unknown
VB	1633-63	Ulrich Butkau in Stettin

ARMS

Bishopric – Cross
Pomerania – Griffen, usually rampant to left

REGULAR COINAGE

KM# 1 DREIER (3 Pfennig)

Silver **Obv:** Shield of Pomeranian griffin left, ornate helmet above, over all F.I.D.-S.P.O. **Rev:** Imperial orb in baroque shield divides date **Note:** Prev. KM#5. Hildisch #242.

Date	Mintage	VG	F	VF	XF	Unc
(16)15	—	16.00	33.00	65.00	135	—

KM# 2 DREIER (3 Pfennig)

Silver **Obv:** III / F.H.Z. / S.P. / date **Rev:** Griffin rampant left **Note:** Hildisch #243.

Date	Mintage	VG	F	VF	XF	Unc
1616	—	—	—	—	—	—

KM# 21 DREIER (3 Pfennig)

0.6600 g., Silver **Obv:** Ornate helmet over shield of Pomeranian arms, bishop's cap above divides V.I.D - S. POM **Rev:** Ornate helmet over shield of Pomeranian arms divides date **Note:** Hildisch #253.

Date	Mintage	VG	F	VF	XF	Unc
16Z1	—	—	—	—	—	—

KM# 25 DREIER (3 Pfennig)

Silver **Obv:** Ornate helmet, feathers at top divide V.H.Z.-S.P. **Rev:** Shield with concave sides, griffin left, date above

Date	Mintage	VG	F	VF	XF	Unc
16ZZ	—	—	—	—	—	—

KM# 26 DREIER (3 Pfennig)

Silver **Obv:** Ornate helmet divided date, feathers at top divide V.H.Z.-S.P. **Rev:** Shield with concave sides, griffin left, date above

Date	Mintage	VG	F	VF	XF	Unc
(16)ZZ//16ZZ	—	—	—	—	—	—

KM# 27 1/4 SCHILLING (Dreiling; 1/128 Thaler)

0.7800 g., Silver **Obv:** Crowned griffin to left in circle, titles of Ulrich begin VLRIC9 **Rev:** Large "1Z8" in circle, legend, date **Rev. Legend:** DEVS. PROTECTOR. MEV.

Date	Mintage	VG	F	VF	XF	Unc
(16)ZZ	—	—	—	—	—	—

KM# 18 WITTEN (4 Pfennig)

0.5400 g., Silver **Obv:** Crowned griffin left in circle, titles of Ulrich begin VLRIC9 **Rev:** Cross, arms divide A-O (Anno)/Z-0 **Rev. Legend:** DEVS. PROTECTOR. MEV. **Note:** Prev. KM#15.

Date	Mintage	VG	F	VF	XF	Unc
(16)Z0	—	13.00	27.00	55.00	110	—

KM# 28 WITTEN (4 Pfennig)

0.5400 g., Silver **Obv:** Crowned griffin to left in circle, titles of Ulrich begin VLRIC9 **Rev:** Short cross in circle, date in angles **Rev. Legend:** DEVS. PROTECTOR. MEV.

Date	Mintage	VG	F	VF	XF	Unc
16ZZ	—	—	—	—	—	—

KM# 29 1/2 SCHILLING (1/64 Thaler)

Silver **Obv:** Crowned griffin left in circle **Rev:** Large 6•4 in field, date **Rev. Legend:** DEVS.PROTECTOR.MEV. **Note:** Prev. KM#19.

Date	Mintage	VG	F	VF	XF	Unc
(16)22	—	—	—	—	—	—

KM# 30 SCHILLING (1/32 Thaler)

1.5700 g., Silver **Obv:** Crowned griffin left in circle, titles of Ulrich begin VLRIC9 **Rev:** Large 3•Z in field, date **Rev. Legend:** DEVS.PROTECTOR.MEV. **Note:** Prev. KM#22.

Date	Mintage	VG	F	VF	XF	Unc
(16)22	—	—	—	—	—	—

KM# 3 2 SCHILLING (Doppelschilling)

Silver **Obv:** Crowned griffin to left in circle, titles of Franz **Rev:** Intertwined "DS" in circle, legend, date **Rev. Legend:** ADSIT. AB. ALTO.

Date	Mintage	VG	F	VF	XF	Unc
1616 HS	—	—	—	—	—	—
1617	—	—	—	—	—	—

KM# 10 2 SCHILLING (Doppelschilling)

1.3200 g., Silver **Obv:** Crowned griffin to left in circle, titles of Ulrich begin VLRIC9 **Rev:** Intertwined "DS" in circle **Rev. Legend:** DEVS.PROTECTOR.MEV9.

Date	Mintage	VG	F	VF	XF	Unc
ND(1618-22)	—	—	—	—	—	—

KM# 11 2 SCHILLING (Doppelschilling)

1.3200 g., Silver **Obv:** Crowned griffin to left in circle, titles of Ulrich begin VLDARIC9 **Rev:** Intertwined "DS" in circle **Rev. Legend:** DEVS.PROTECTOR.MEV9.

Date	Mintage	VG	F	VF	XF	Unc
ND(1618-22)	—	—	—	—	—	—

Note: Reported, not confirmed

KM# 15 2 SCHILLING (Doppelschilling)

1.3200 g., Silver **Obv:** Crowned griffin to left in circle, titles of Ulrich begin VLDARIC9 **Rev:** Intertwined "DS" in circle divides date **Rev. Legend:** DEVS.PROTECTOR.MEVS.

Date	Mintage	VG	F	VF	XF	Unc
(16)19	—	—	—	—	—	—
(16)Z0	—	—	—	—	—	—

KM# 16 2 SCHILLING (Doppelschilling)

1.3200 g., Silver **Obv:** Crowned griffin to left in circle, titles of Ulrich begin VLDARIC9 **Rev:** Intertwined "DS" in circle, legend, date **Rev. Legend:** DEVS.PROTECTOR.MEVS.

Date	Mintage	VG	F	VF	XF	Unc
(16)19	—	—	—	—	—	—

KM# 17 2 SCHILLING (Doppelschilling)

1.3200 g., Silver **Obv:** Crowned griffin to left in circle, titles of Ulrich begin VLRIC9 **Rev:** Intertwined "DS" in circle, date below **Rev. Legend:** DEVS.PROTECTOR.MEVS. **Note:** Varieties exist.

Date	Mintage	VG	F	VF	XF	Unc
(16)19	—	16.00	40.00	75.00	120	—
(16)Z0	—	16.00	40.00	75.00	120	—
(16)Z1	—	16.00	40.00	75.00	120	—
(16)ZZ	—	16.00	40.00	75.00	120	—

KM# 22 2 SCHILLING (Doppelschilling)

1.3200 g., Silver **Obv:** Crowned griffin to left in circle, titles of Ulrich begin VLRIC9 **Rev:** Intertwined "DS" in circle divides date **Rev. Legend:** DEVS.PROTECTOR.MEVS.

Date	Mintage	VG	F	VF	XF	Unc
(16)Z1	—	—	—	—	—	—
(16)ZZ	—	—	—	—	—	—

KM# 31 2 SCHILLING (Doppelschilling)

1.3200 g., Silver **Obv:** Crowned griffin to left in circle, titles of Ulrich begin VLRIC9 **Rev:** Intertwined "DS" in circle divides date **Rev. Legend:** DEVS.PROTECTOR.MEVS.

Date	Mintage	VG	F	VF	XF	Unc
16ZZ	—	—	—	—	—	—

KM# 19 DOPPEL-SCHILLING (1/16 Thaler)

Silver **Obv:** Griffin left in oval baroque frame **Rev:** Date **Rev. Legend:** II/SCHIL/LING/POM/date DEVS.PROTECTOR.MEVS. **Note:** Prev. KM#17.

Date	Mintage	VG	F	VF	XF	Unc
(16)Z0	—	—	—	—	—	—

KM# 32 DOPPEL-SCHILLING (1/16 Thaler)

Silver **Obv:** Crowned griffin left in circle **Rev:** Large Gothic "1•6" in field, date **Rev. Legend:** DEVS.PROTECTOR.MEVS. **Note:** Prev. KM#24.

Date	Mintage	VG	F	VF	XF	Unc
16ZZ	—	—	—	—	—	—

KM# 7 1/24 THALER (Groschen)

Silver **Obv:** Smaller bust right breaks circle at top, titles of Franz **Rev:** Imperial orb with 24 divides date **Rev. Legend:** ADSIT. AB. ALTO.

Date	Mintage	VG	F	VF	XF	Unc
1616	—	10.00	27.00	55.00	100	—
1617	—	10.00	27.00	55.00	100	—

KM# 14 1/24 THALER (Groschen)

1.2800 g., Silver **Obv:** Crowned griffin left, "3" in oval below, titles of Ulrich begin VLDARIC9 **Rev:** Imperial orb with "Z4" divides date **Rev. Legend:** DEVS.PROTECTOR.MEVS. **Note:** Prev. KM#11.

Date	Mintage	VG	F	VF	XF	Unc
(16)18	—	20.00	40.00	80.00	160	—
1618	—	20.00	40.00	80.00	160	—
(16)19	—	20.00	40.00	80.00	160	—
(16)Z0	—	20.00	40.00	80.00	160	—

KM# A2 1/24 THALER (Reichsgroschen)

Silver **Obv:** Large bust right breaks circle at top, titles of Franz **Rev:** ADSIT. AB. ALTO.

Date	Mintage	VG	F	VF	XF	Unc
1615 HS	—	60.00	120	220	400	—
1616 HS	—	60.00	120	220	400	—

KM# 4 1/24 THALER (Reichsgroschen)

Silver **Obv:** Large bust right breaks circle at top, titles of Franz **Rev:** Imperial orb with "Z4" in circle, date at top divided by cross **Rev. Legend:** ADSIT.AB.ALTO.

Date	Mintage	VG	F	VF	XF	Unc
1616 HS	—	60.00	120	220	400	—
1616	—	60.00	120	220	400	—

KM# 5 1/24 THALER (Reichsgroschen)

Silver **Obv:** Large bust right breaks circle at top, titles of Franz **Rev:** Imperial orb with "24" in circle, date divided by base of cross on orb **Rev. Legend:** ADSIT.AB.ALTO.

Date	Mintage	VG	F	VF	XF	Unc
1616 HS	—	45.00	100	200	350	—

KM# 6 1/24 THALER (Dreipölker)

Silver **Obv:** Smaller head right breaks circle at top, titles of Franz **Rev:** Imperial orb with "Z4" in circle, legend, date **Rev. Legend:** ADSIT.AB.ALTO.

Date	Mintage	VG	F	VF	XF	Unc
1616	—	—	—	—	—	—

KM# 8 1/24 THALER (Dreipölker)

Silver **Obv:** Smaller head right breaks circle at top, value "3" in oval below shoulder, titles of Franz **Rev:** Imperial orb with "Z4" in circle, date divided by cross on top **Rev. Legend:** ADSIT.AB.ALTO.

Date	Mintage	VG	F	VF	XF	Unc
1616	—	—	—	—	—	—
1618	—	—	—	—	—	—

KM# 9 1/24 THALER (Dreipölker)

Silver **Obv:** Crowned griffin left, value "3" in oval below, titles of Franz **Rev:** Imperial orb with "Z4" in circle, date divided by cross on top **Rev. Legend:** ADSIT.AB.ALTO.

Date	Mintage	VG	F	VF	XF	Unc
1617	—	—	—	—	—	—

KM# 12 1/24 THALER (Dreipölker)

Silver **Obv:** Crowned griffin to left, value "3" in oval below, titles of Franz **Rev:** Imperial orb with "Z4" in circle, date divided by cross on top **Rev. Legend:** ADSIT.AB.ALTO.

Date	Mintage	VG	F	VF	XF	Unc
1618	—	—	—	—	—	—

KM# 13 1/24 THALER (Dreipölker)

Silver **Obv:** Crowned griffin left, titles of Franz **Rev:** Imperial orb with "24" in circle, date divided by base of cross on orb **Rev. Legend:** ADSIT.AB.ALTO.

Date	Mintage	VG	F	VF	XF	Unc
1618	—	—	—	—	—	—

KM# 20 1/24 THALER (Dreipölker)

1.2800 g., Silver **Obv:** Crowned griffin left, "3" in oval below, titles of Ulrich begin VLRIC9 **Rev:** Imperial orb with "Z4" divides date **Rev. Legend:** DEVS.PROTECTOR.MEVS.

Date	Mintage	VG	F	VF	XF	Unc
(16)Z0	—	—	—	—	—	—

KM# 23 1/24 THALER (Dreipölker)

0.9000 g., Silver **Obv:** 4-fold arms with central shield of bishopric (cross), titles of Ulrich begin VLRIC9 **Rev:** Imperial orb with "Z4" divides date **Rev. Legend:** DEVS. PROTECTOR. MEVS.

Date	Mintage	VG	F	VF	XF	Unc
(16)Z1	—	—	—	—	—	—
(16)ZZ	—	—	—	—	—	—

KM# 24 1/24 THALER (Dreipölker)

0.9000 g., Silver **Obv:** Four-fold arms with central shield of bishopric (cross), crown above, "3" below, titles of Ulrich begin VLRIC9 **Rev:** Imperial orb with "Z4" divides date **Rev. Legend:** DEVS.PROTECTOR.MEVS.

Date	Mintage	VG	F	VF	XF	Unc
(16)Z1	—	—	—	—	—	—

KM# 33 1/8 THALER (Halber Reichsort)

3.4100 g., Silver **Subject:** Death of Ulrich **Obv:** Bust left breaks circle at top, titles of Ulrich, date **Rev:** Fierce storm from upper right breaks branch from tree in lower left **Rev. Legend:** +DEO.ASPIRANTE. VIRESCIT.

Date	Mintage	VG	F	VF	XF	Unc
16ZZ	—	—	—	—	—	—

KM# 90 1/8 THALER (Halber Reichsort)

3.4100 g., Silver **Subject:** Entombment of Hedwig von Braunschweig-Wolfenbüttel, Widow of Ulrich **Obv:** Seven-line inscription around titles of Hedwig **Rev:** Ten-line inscription with R.N. dates

Date	Mintage	VG	F	VF	XF	Unc
1654 (MIDCLIV)	—	—	—	—	—	—

KM# 34 1/4 THALER (Reichsort)

6.5700 g., Silver **Subject:** Death of Ulrich **Obv:** Bust left, date in legend **Rev:** Rays from sun in upper right through clouds to tree **Rev. Legend:** DEO.ASPIRANTE.VIRESCIT. **Note:** Prev. KM#30.

Date	Mintage	VG	F	VF	XF	Unc
1622	—	—	—	—	—	—

KM# 35 1/2 THALER

Silver Weight varies, 13.54-13.67g **Ruler:** Ulrich, Herzog von Pommern **Subject:** Death of Ulrich **Obv:** Armored bust to left, date divided in margin at top **Obv. Legend:** VLRICVS. D.G. D: POM. EPISCOP. CAMMIN. **Rev:** Fierce storm from upper right breaks branch from tree in lower left **Rev. Legend:** +DEO.ASPIRANTE.VIRESCIT. **Note:** Hildisch 274.

Date	Mintage	VG	F	VF	XF	Unc
16ZZ	—	—	—	—	—	—

KM# 75 1/2 THALER

13.6700 g., Silver **Obv:** Bust right breaks circle at top, titles of Bogislaw **Rev:** Oval ten-fold arms in baroque frame, ducal cap above divides date in legend **Note:** Varieties exist.

Date	Mintage	VG	F	VF	XF	Unc
1633	—	475	1,000	1,600	—	—

KM# 76 1/2 THALER

Silver **Obv:** Bust right breaks circle at top, titles of Bogislaw **Rev:** Squarish ten-fold arms with rounded corners in baroque frame, date divided above, ducal cap at top over all, titles continuous **Note:** Varieties exist. Prev. KM#90.

Date	Mintage	VG	F	VF	XF	Unc
1633	—	475	1,000	1,600	—	—
1634	—	475	1,000	1,600	—	—

KM# 85 1/2 THALER

13.6700 g., Silver **Obv:** Bust right breaks circle at top, titles of Bogislaw **Rev:** Oval ten-fold arms in baroque frame, date divided to either side near top of arms, ducal cap above all, titles continuous

Date	Mintage	VG	F	VF	XF	Unc
1635	—	475	1,000	1,600	—	—

KM# 37 THALER

Silver **Subject:** Death of Ulrich **Obv:** Bust left breaks circle at top, date above head, titles of Ulrich **Rev:** Nine-line inscription with dates **Note:** Dav. #7243. Prev. KM#36.

Date	Mintage	VG	F	VF	XF	Unc
16ZZ	—	1,200	2,250	3,750	6,500	—

KM# 36 THALER

Silver **Obv:** Bust left breaks circle at top, date above head, titles of Ulrich **Rev:** Bust of Philipp II right in ornamented circle, titles of Phillip II of Pomerania-Stettin **Note:** Mule. Dav. #7240. Prev. KM#35.

Date	Mintage	VG	F	VF	XF	Unc
16ZZ Rare	—	—	—	—	—	—

KM# 44 THALER

Silver **Obv:** Bust right in circle, bow on shoulder, titles of Bogislaw **Rev:** Crowned griffin left holding sword and book in baroque frame, ducal cap above divides date, titles continuous **Rev. Legend:** ...ET. BV. DOM.

Date	Mintage	VG	F	VF	XF	Unc
16Z8 (z)	—	—	—	—	—	—
16Z9 (z)	—	—	—	—	—	—

KM# 46 THALER

Silver **Obv:** Bust right in circle, titles of Bogislaw **Obv. Legend:** ...PR:RV: **Rev:** Ornate helmet over nine-fold arms supported by two wildmen wearing helmets, titles continuous, date **Rev. Legend:** ...DO.

Date	Mintage	VG	F	VF	XF	Unc
1628	—	—	—	—	—	—

KM# 42 THALER

Silver **Obv:** Bust right **Obv. Legend:** BOGISLAVS. XIV: D: G: DVS. STET. POM. CASSVB. ET. VAN: X **Rev:** Crowned griffin to left holding sword and book in baroque frame, ducal cap above divides date, titles continuous **Note:** Dav. #7262. Prev. KM#48.1.

Date	Mintage	VG	F	VF	XF	Unc
16Z8 GT(z)	—	300	600	1,200	2,000	—

KM# 43 THALER

Silver **Obv:** Bust right with bowknot on shoulder, titles of Bogislaw **Obv. Legend:** BOGISLAVS.XIV.D:G:DVS.STE.PO:CAS:E: V:P:RVG **Rev:** Helmeted and supported arms, date **Rev. Legend:** X EP:CAM:CO:GVT ZK:TER:LEOB:E:BV:DO **Note:** Dav. #7263. Prev. KM#50.1.

Date	Mintage	VG	F	VF	XF	Unc
16Z8 (z)	—	300	600	1,200	2,000	—

KM# 45 THALER

Silver **Obv:** Without bowknot **Obv. Legend:** Ends...PR:RV: **Rev:** Ornate helmet over nine-fold arms supported by wildmen with helmets, titles continuous ending with DO:, date **Note:** Dav. #7264. Prev. KM#50.2.

Date	Mintage	VG	F	VF	XF	Unc
16Z8 (z)	—	300	600	1,200	2,000	—

KM# 47 THALER

Silver **Obv:** Bust right in circle, titles of Bogilsaw **Obv. Legend:** ...PR:RV: **Rev:** Ornate helmet over large nine-fold arms supported by two wildmen wearing helmets, date **Rev. Legend:** ...BV:DO **Note:** Dav. #7265. Prev. KM#50.3.

Date	Mintage	VG	F	VF	XF	Unc
16Z8	—	300	600	1,200	2,000	—

KM# 48 THALER

Silver **Obv:** Bust right in circle, titles of Bogislaw **Obv. Legend:** PR:RVG* **Rev:** Crowned griffin left holding sword and book in baroque frame, ducal cap above divides date, titles contiuous **Rev. Legend:** ...ET.BV.DOM. **Note:** Dav. #7266. Prev. KM#50.4.

Date	Mintage	VG	F	VF	XF	Unc
16Z8 GT	—	300	600	1,200	2,000	—

KM# 51 THALER

Silver **Obv:** Bust right in circle, titles of Bogislaw **Obv. Legend:** STE:PO:CAS:E:V:P:RV **Rev:** Crowned griffin left holding sword and book in baroque frame, ducal cap above divides date, titles continuous **Rev. Legend:** ...ET.BV.DOM. **Note:** Dav. #7267. Prev. KM#48.2.

Date	Mintage	VG	F	VF	XF	Unc
1629 (z)	—	375	675	1,350	2,250	—

KM# 55 THALER

Silver **Obv:** Half-length armored figure right with baton, helmet before **Obv. Legend:** ...E.V.P.RV **Rev:** Crowned griffin to left holding sword and book in baroque frame, ducal cap divides date, titles continuous **Rev. Legend:** ...GVTZK. TER. LEOB. ET. BV. DO. **Note:** Dav. #7268. Prev. KM#64.1.

Date	Mintage	VG	F	VF	XF	Unc
16Z9 (z)	—	875	1,400	2,250	3,750	—

KM# 59 THALER

Silver **Obv. Legend:** E:V:P:R: **Rev:** Ornate helmeted arms supported by two wildmen wearing helmets, titles continuous, legend, date **Rev. Legend:** ...BV:D: **Note:** Dav. #7269. Prev. KM#64.2.

Date	Mintage	VG	F	VF	XF	Unc
1629 GT(z)	—	875	1,400	2,250	3,750	—

KM# 52 THALER

Silver **Obv:** Bust right in circle, titles of Bogislaw **Obv. Legend:** ...E: V: P: R **Rev:** Crowned griffin left holding sword and book in baroque frame, ducal cap above divides date, titles continuous **Rev. Legend:** ...ET. BV. DOM.

Date	Mintage	VG	F	VF	XF	Unc
16Z9 (z)	—	500	900	1,500	2,750	—

KM# 53 THALER

Silver **Obv:** Bust right in circle, titles of Bogislaw **Obv. Legend:** ...E: V: P: RVG **Rev:** Crowned griffin left holding sword and book in baroque frame, ducal cap above divides date, titles continuous **Rev. Legend:** ...ET. BV. DOM.

Date	Mintage	VG	F	VF	XF	Unc
16Z9 (z)	—	500	900	1,500	2,750	—

KM# 54 THALER

Silver **Obv:** Half-length armored figure right holding baton, helmet at right, titles of Bogilsaw **Obv. Legend:** ...E: V: P: RV **Rev:** Ten-fold arms in baroque frame, ducal cap above divides date, titles continuous **Rev. Legend:** ...BV. DOM.

Date	Mintage	VG	F	VF	XF	Unc
16Z9 GT(z)	—	500	900	1,500	2,750	—

KM# 56 THALER

Silver **Obv:** Half-length armored figure right holding baton, helmet at right, titles of Bogilsaw **Obv. Legend:** ...E: V: P: RV **Rev:** Crowned griffin to left holding sword and book in baroque frame, ducal cap above divides date, titles continuous **Rev. Legend:** ...GVTZ. TER. LEOB. ET. BV. DOM.

Date	Mintage	VG	F	VF	XF	Unc
16Z9 (z)	—	500	900	1,500	2,750	—

KM# 57 THALER

Silver **Obv:** Half-length armored figure right holding baton, helmet at right, titles of Bogilsaw **Obv. Legend:** ...E. V. P. RV. **Rev:** Crowned griffin to left holding sword and book in baroque frame, ducal cap above divides date, mintmaster's initials below arms, titles continuous **Rev. Legend:** ...GVTZK. TER. LEOB. ET. BV. DO.

Date	Mintage	VG	F	VF	XF	Unc
16Z9 GT	—	500	900	1,500	2,750	—

KM# 58 THALER

Silver **Obv:** Half-length armored figure right holding baton, helmet at right, titles of Bogilsaw **Obv. Legend:** ...E. V. P. RV. **Rev:** Crowned griffin left holding sword and book in baroque frame, ducal cap above divides date, mintmaster's initials below arms, titles continuous **Rev. Legend:** ...GVTZK. TER. LEOB. ET. BV. DOM.

Date	Mintage	VG	F	VF	XF	Unc
16Z9 (z)	—	500	900	1,500	2,750	—

KM# 60 THALER

Silver **Obv:** Half-length armored figure right holding baton, helmet at right, titles of Bogislaw **Obv. Legend:** ...E:V:P:RV **Rev:** Ornate helmet over nine-fold arms supported by two wildmen wearing helmets, titles continuous, legend, date **Rev. Legend:** ...BV:D:

Date	Mintage	VG	F	VF	XF	Unc
16Z9 (z)	—	500	900	1,500	2,750	—

KM# 61 THALER

Silver **Obv:** Half-length armored figure right holding baton, helmet at right, titles of Bogislaw **Obv. Legend:** ...E:V:P:R **Rev:** Ornate helmet over nine-fold arms supported by two wildmen wearing helmets, date in legend **Rev. Legend:** ...BV.DO.

Date	Mintage	VG	F	VF	XF	Unc
16Z9 (z)	—	500	900	1,500	2,750	—

KM# 62 THALER

Silver **Obv:** Half-length armored figure right holding baton, helmet at right, titles of Bogislaw **Obv. Legend:** ...E.V.P.RV. **Rev:** Crowned griffin left holding sword and book in baroque frame, ducal cap above divides date in legend **Rev. Legend:** ...BV.DOM.

Date	Mintage	VG	F	VF	XF	Unc
16Z9 (z)	—	500	900	1,500	2,750	—

KM# 63 THALER

Silver **Obv:** Armored bust right in circle, titles of Bogislaw **Obv. Legend:** ...CASE.E.V.P.R **Rev:** Crowned griffin to left holding sword and book in baroque frame, date in legend **Rev. Legend:** ...GVTZK. TER. LEOB. ET. BV. DOM. **Note:** Dav. #7271. Prev. KM#48.3.

Date	Mintage	VG	F	VF	XF	Unc
1630 (z)	—	400	800	1,350	2,250	—

KM# 65 THALER

Silver **Obv:** Half-length armored figure right holding baton, helmet at right, titles of Bogislaw **Obv. Legend:** ...E.V.P.RV. **Rev:** Crowned griffin left holding sword and book in baroque frame, ducal cap above divides date, titles continuous **Rev. Legend:** LEOB.E.B.D. **Note:** Dav. #7272. Prev. KM#64.3.

Date	Mintage	VG	F	VF	XF	Unc
1631	—	400	800	1,350	2,250	—

KM# 66 THALER

Silver **Obv:** Armored bust right in circle, titles of Bogislaw **Obv. Legend:** CAS.EV.PR* **Rev:** Crowned griffin left holding book and sword in baroque frame, ducal cap above divides date, titles continuous **Rev. Legend:** ...LEOB. E. B.D. **Note:** Dav. #7273. Prev. KM#48.4.

Date	Mintage	VG	F	VF	XF	Unc
1631	—	400	800	1,350	2,250	—

KM# 67 THALER

Silver **Obv:** Bust right **Obv. Legend:** PO:C.E.T.V.P.R **Rev:** Helmeted and supported arms divide date above **Rev. Legend:** EP: CAM:... **Note:** Dav. #7274. Prev. KM#71.1. Varieties exist.

Date	Mintage	VG	F	VF	XF	Unc
1631 GT	—	400	800	1,350	2,250	—

KM# 68 THALER

Silver **Obv:** Bust right in circle, titles of Bogislaw **Obv. Legend:** ...E.V.P.R. **Rev:** Ornate helmet over ten-fold arms supported by two wildmen wearing helmets, titles continuous **Rev. Legend:** EP: CAM:... **Note:** Dav. #7275. Prev. KM#71.2.

Date	Mintage	VG	F	VF	XF	Unc
1631 GT	—	400	800	1,350	2,250	—

KM# 69 THALER

Silver **Obv:** Bust off center to right, hand breaks through legend **Rev:** Ornate helmet over ten-fold arms supported by two wildmen wearing helmets, date in legend **Rev. Legend:** EP: CAM:... **Note:** Dav. #7276. Prev. KM#71.3.

Date	Mintage	VG	F	VF	XF	Unc
1631 GT	—	750	1,250	2,250	3,750	—

KM# 72 THALER

Silver **Obv:** Large bust right **Obv. Legend:** ...DVX.STE.P.C.E. V.P.R **Rev:** Large arms, date **Rev. Legend:** EP.CAM.CO. GVTZK.TER.LEOB.ET.BV.DOM **Note:** Dav. #7279. Prev. KM#82.1.

Date	Mintage	VG	F	VF	XF	Unc
163Z	—	400	800	1,350	2,250	—

KM# 73 THALER

Silver **Obv:** Bust right divides date in legend at top **Rev:** Ornate helmet over ten-fold arms, supported by two wildmen wearing helmets, date in legend **Note:** Dav. #7280. Prev. KM#82.2.

Date	Mintage	VG	F	VF	XF	Unc
1632	—	400	800	1,350	2,250	—

KM# 71 THALER

Silver **Obv:** Bust right in circle, titles of Bogislaw **Obv. Legend:** ...E. V. P. R. **Rev:** Ornate helmet over nine-fold arms supported by two wildmen wearing helmets, date in legend **Note:** Dav.#7277. Prev. KM#50.5.

Date	Mintage	VG	F	VF	XF	Unc
163Z	—	400	800	1,350	2,250	—

Note: The "3" and "2" in date are engraved backwards

KM# 78 THALER

Silver **Obv:** Large bust right breaks circle at top, titles with BOGISLAVS **Obv. Legend:** ...E.V.P.R. **Rev:** Ornate helmet over ten-fold arms supported by two wildmen wearing helmets, date in legend **Rev. Legend:** EP: CAM:...

Date	Mintage	VG	F	VF	XF	Unc
1633	—	400	800	1,350	2,250	—

KM# 79 THALER

Silver **Obv:** Broad bust to right breaks circle at top, titles with BOISLAVS **Obv. Legend:** ...ET.V.P.R. **Rev:** Ornate helmet over ten-fold arms supported by two wildmen wearing helmets, date in legend **Rev. Legend:** EP: CAM:...

Date	Mintage	VG	F	VF	XF	Unc
1633	—	400	800	1,350	2,250	—

KM# A77 THALER

Silver **Obv:** Date in legend above large bust; titles with BOGISLAVS **Obv. Legend:** ...ET.V.P.R. **Rev:** Helmeted and supported ten-fold arms, date in legend **Rev. Legend:** EP: CAM:... **Note:** Dav. #7282. Prev. KM#82.3.

Date	Mintage	VG	F	VF	XF	Unc
1633	—	400	800	1,350	2,250	—
1634	—	400	800	1,350	2,250	—

KM# 83 THALER

Silver **Obv:** Large bust right **Obv. Legend:** DVX:S*P*C*ET *V*P*R* **Rev:** Large arms, date divided by feathers on helmet below legend **Rev. Legend:** TER*LEOB*E*BV **Note:** Dav. #7283. Prev. KM#71.4.

Date	Mintage	VG	F	VF	XF	Unc
1634	—	400	800	1,350	2,250	—

KM# 84 THALER

Silver **Obv:** Large bust right breaks circle, titles of Bogislaw **Obv. Legend:** DVX.STE.PO.CAS.E.V.P.R **Rev:** Ornate helmet over nine-fold arms supported by two wildmen wearing helmets, date divided by feathers on helmet at top in legend **Rev. Legend:** TER:LEOB:ETBU:DO **Note:** Dav. #7284. Prev. KM#71.5.

Date	Mintage	VG	F	VF	XF	Unc
1634	—	400	800	1,350	2,250	—

KM# 82 THALER

Silver **Obv:** Large bust right breaks circle at top, titles with BOFILAVS **Obv. Legend:** ...ET.V.P.R. **Rev:** Ornate helmet over ten-fold arms supported by two wildmen wearing helmets, date in legend **Rev. Legend:** EP: CAM:...

Date	Mintage	VG	F	VF	XF	Unc
1634	—	400	800	1,350	2,250	—

KM# A88 THALER

Silver **Obv:** Different bust **Obv. Legend:** EOB:ET:BV: **Note:** Dav.#7287. Prev. KM#.71.8.

Date	Mintage	VG	F	VF	XF	Unc
1635	—	400	800	1,350	2,250	—

KM# 86 THALER

Silver **Obv:** Large bust right breaks circle, titles of Bogislaw **Obv. Legend:** DVX.S.P.C.E.P.R **Rev:** Ornate helmet over ten-fold arms supported by two wildmen wearing helmets, date divided by featehrs on helmet below legend **Rev. Legend:** EP - *CAM*CO*GVTZK *TER*LEOB*E*BV* - DO **Note:** Dav. #7285. Prev. KM#71.6.

Date	Mintage	VG	F	VF	XF	Unc
1635	—	400	800	1,350	2,250	—

KM# 87 THALER

Silver **Obv:** Large bust right breaks circle, titles of Bogislaw **Rev:** Ornate helmet over ten-fold arms supported by two wildmen wearing helmets, date divided by feathers on helmet below legend, date in legend **Rev. Legend:** E - *CAM*CO*GV - TZK*TER*L--EOB*E*BV* - D - O* **Note:** Dav. #7286. Prev. KM#71.7.

Date	Mintage	VG	F	VF	XF	Unc
1635	—	400	800	1,350	2,250	—

KM# 88 THALER

Silver **Obv:** Large bust right breaks circle, titles of Bogislaw **Obv.**

Legend: S.P.C.E.V.P.R **Rev:** Ornate helmet over ten-fold arms supported by two wildmen wearing helmets, date divided by helmet above arms **Rev. Legend:** EP:CAM:... **Note:** Dav. #7288. Prev. KM#71.9.

Date	Mintage	VG	F	VF	XF	Unc
1636 Rare	—	—	—	—	—	—

KM# 89 THALER

Silver **Obv:** Large different bust right breaks circle, titles of Bogislaw **Rev:** Ornate helmet over ten-fold arms supported by two wildmen wearing helmets to either side, date divided by helmet above arms **Rev. Legend:** EP - *CAM*CO*G - V - TZK*TER - *LEOB*ET*B - DO* **Note:** Dav. #7289. Prev. KM#71.10.

Date	Mintage	VG	F	VF	XF	Unc
1637 Rare	—	—	—	—	—	—

KM# 91 THALER

Silver **Subject:** Entombment of Hedwig von Braunschsweig-Wolfenbüttel, Widow of Ulrich **Obv:** Seven-line inscription around titles of Hedwig **Rev:** Ten-line inscription with R.N. dates

Date	Mintage	VG	F	VF	XF	Unc
1654(MIDCLIV)	—	—	—	—	—	—

KM# 38 1-1/2 THALER

Silver **Subject:** Death of Ulrich **Obv:** Bust left breaks circle at top, date above head, titles of Ulrich **Rev:** Nine-line inscription with dates **Note:** Dav. #A7243.

Date	Mintage	VG	F	VF	XF	Unc
16ZZ Rare	—	—	—	—	—	—

KM# 39 2 THALER

Silver **Subject:** Death of Ulrich **Obv:** Bust left breaks circle at top, date above head, titles of Ulrich **Rev:** Nine-line inscription with dates **Note:** Dav. #7242. Prev. KM#40.

Date	Mintage	VG	F	VF	XF	Unc
16ZZ Rare	—	—	—	—	—	—

KM# 74 2 THALER

Silver **Obv:** Large bust to right breaks circle at top, titles of Bosislaw end with small date **Rev:** Ornate helmet over ten-fold arms supported by two wildmen wearing helmets to either side, date in legend **Note:** Similar to 1 Thaler, KM#73. Dav. #7278. Prev. KM#83.

Date	Mintage	VG	F	VF	XF	Unc
163Z Rare	—	—	—	—	—	—

KM# 80 2 THALER

Silver **Obv:** Large bust right breaks circle at top, titles with BOGISLAVS **Obv. Legend:** E.V.P.R. **Rev:** Ornate helmet over ten-fold arms supported by two wildmen wearing helmets, date in legend **Note:** Similar to 1 Thaler, KM#A77. Prev. KM#84.

Date	Mintage	VG	F	VF	XF	Unc
1633 Rare	—	—	—	—	—	—

KM# 40 2-1/2 THALER

Silver **Subject:** Death of Ulrich **Obv:** Bust left breaks circle at top, date above head, titles of Ulrich **Rev:** Nine-line inscription with dates

Date	Mintage	VG	F	VF	XF	Unc
16ZZ Rare	—	—	—	—	—	—

KM# 41 3 THALER

Silver **Subject:** Death of Ulrich **Obv:** Bust left breaks circle at top, date above head, titles of Ulrich **Rev:** Nine-line inscription with dates **Note:** Similar to 1 Thaler, KM#36. Dav. #7241. Prev. KM#45.

Date	Mintage	VG	F	VF	XF	Unc
1622	—	4,500	7,500	12,000	—	—

TRADE COINAGE

KM# 49 GOLDGULDEN

3.5000 g., 0.9860 Gold 0.1109 oz. AGW **Obv:** Bust right in circle, titles of Bogislaw **Rev:** Ornamented shield fo four-folds arms, date above, titles continuous **Rev. Legend:** PL R: EP. CA...

Date	Mintage	VG	F	VF	XF	Unc
16Z8	—	1,150	2,250	4,150	6,800	—

KM# 50 GOLDGULDEN

3.5000 g., 0.9860 Gold 0.1109 oz. AGW **Obv:** Large bust right in circle, titles of Bogislaw **Rev:** Narroew four-fold arms divide date at sides and above 1-6Z-8 **Rev. Legend:** EP: CA:... **Note:** Prev. KM#60.

Date	Mintage	VG	F	VF	XF	Unc
1628	—	1,150	2,250	4,150	6,800	—

KM# 64 DUCAT

3.5000 g., 0.9860 Gold 0.1109 oz. AGW **Obv:** Full-length figure facing right, titles of Bogislaw **Rev:** Ten-fold arms in shield within circle, date in legend

Date	Mintage	VG	F	VF	XF	Unc
ND(1630-35)	—	750	1,500	2,650	4,500	—

KM# 70 DUCAT

3.5000 g., 0.9860 Gold 0.1109 oz. AGW **Obv:** Full-length figure facing right, head divides date, titles of Bogislaw **Rev:** Ten-fold arms in shield within circle, date in legend

Date	Mintage	VG	F	VF	XF	Unc
1631	—	750	1,500	2,650	4,500	—

KM# 81 DUCAT

3.5000 g., 0.9860 Gold 0.1109 oz. AGW **Obv:** Full-length figure facing right, head divides mintmaster's initials, titles of Bogislaw **Rev:** Ten-fold arms in shield within circle, date in legend **Note:** Varieties exist.

Date	Mintage	VG	F	VF	XF	Unc
1633 VB	—	750	1,500	2,650	4,500	—
1634 VB	—	750	1,500	2,650	4,500	—
1635 VB	—	750	1,500	2,650	4,500	—
1636 VB	—	750	1,500	2,650	4,500	—
ND VB	—	750	1,500	2,650	4,500	—

CLEVES

(Cleve, Kleve)

The county, later duchy, of Cleves, located on both sides of the Rhine at the Dutch Border, had its beginnings in the early 11th century. It passed in marriage to the counts of Mark in 1368, who were raised to the rank of duke in 1417. In 1511 Jülich, Berg and Ravensburg were obtained by marriage. The last duke died in 1609 without a male heir, causing a great struggle for the various territories between Pfalz-Neuburg, Brandenburg-Prussia and Saxony. (See Jülich-Cleves-Berg for coinage to 1609). Eventually, the first two won out and made a pact to divide the territories between them. Brandenburg-Prussia obtained Cleves, Mark and Ravensberg, while Pfalz-Neuburg received Jülich and Berg. Saxony refused to give up its claims and, though never managing to obtain any territory, the dukes continued to place the arms of Cleves on their coinage throughout the rest of the 17th century. The rulers of Brandenburg-Prussia and Pfalz-Neuburg struck a joint coinage in the disputed territories until the formal division in 1624. The joint coinage struck in Cleves is listed here. That of Jülich-Berg is listed under that name. The special coinage of Brandenburg-Prussia for Mark and Ravensberg are included under those place names.

RULERS

Johann II, 1485-1521
Johann III, 1521-1539
Joint Coinage, 1609-1624
Georg Wilhelm of Brandenburg-Prussia, 1624-1640
Friedrich Wilhelm of Brandenburg-Prussia, 1640-1688

MINT MARKS

C - Cleves

MINT OFFICIALS' INITIALS

Initial	Date	Name
(h)	1603-15	Conrad Hoyer in Emmerich
WH	1689-94	Seger Wendel, warden and ? Hoyer, mintmaster in Emmerich
	1615-	Anton Hoyer in Emmerich
	-1618	Arnold Rath, warden in Emmerich
	1618-	Johann Von Wannere, warden in Emmerich

ARMS

Cleves – 8 rods (scepters) with lilies at tip, arranged as spokes in a wheel, small shield in center
Mark – Horizontal band of checkerboard design across center

MONETARY SYSTEM

8 Duit = 1 Stuber
60 Stuber = 1 Reichsthaler
5 Reichsthalers = 1 Friedrich D'or

References:

Sch = Wolfgang Schulten, ***Deutsche Münzen aus der Zeit Karls V.***, Frankfurt am Main, 1974
S = Hugo Frhr. Von Saurma-Jeltsch, ***Die Saurmasche Münzsammlung deutscher, schweizerischer und polnischer Gepräge von etwa dem Beginn der Groschenzeit bis zur Kipperperiode***, Berlin, 1892.

DUCHY

REGULAR COINAGE

KM# 5 3 HELLER

Copper **Obv:** Crowned 6-fold arms **Rev:** III in wreath **Rev. Legend:** NVMMVS. CLIVENSIS

Date	Mintage	VG	F	VF	XF	Unc
ND(1609-15) (h)	—	16.00	33.00	60.00	120	—

KM# 20 3 HELLER

Copper **Rev:** DV/CLI/VIAE in wreath, without indication of value **Note:** Varieties exist.

Date	Mintage	VG	F	VF	XF	Unc
ND(ca.1618)	—	16.00	33.00	60.00	120	—

KM# 25.1 DUIT

Copper **Ruler:** Friedrich Wilhelm **Obv:** Crowned scepter divides date within wreath **Rev:** DU/CLI/VIAE in wreath

Date	Mintage	VG	F	VF	XF	Unc
1669	—	9.00	25.00	45.00	90.00	—
1670	—	9.00	25.00	45.00	90.00	—

KM# 25.2 DUIT

Copper **Ruler:** Friedrich Wilhelm **Rev. Legend:** DU/CLIV/IAE

Date	Mintage	VG	F	VF	XF	Unc
1677	—	9.00	25.00	45.00	90.00	—
1678	—	9.00	25.00	45.00	90.00	—
1679	—	9.00	25.00	45.00	90.00	—
1680	—	9.00	25.00	45.00	90.00	—

KM# 32 DUIT

Copper **Ruler:** Friedrich III **Obv:** Scepter in crowned oval shield with lion supporters **Rev. Legend:** EEN/DUIT

Date	Mintage	VG	F	VF	XF	Unc
ND(1688-1701)	—	8.00	17.00	35.00	70.00	—

KM# 37 DUIT

Copper **Ruler:** Friedrich III

Date	Mintage	VG	F	VF	XF	Unc
1692	—	7.00	20.00	40.00	70.00	—
1693	—	7.00	20.00	40.00	70.00	—
1694	—	7.00	20.00	40.00	70.00	—
1695	—	7.00	20.00	40.00	70.00	—
1696	—	7.00	20.00	40.00	70.00	—
1697	—	7.00	20.00	40.00	70.00	—
1698	—	7.00	20.00	40.00	70.00	—

KM# 6 1/2 STUBER (10 Heller)

Silver **Obv:** Large X in center divides date **Obv. Legend:** NVMMVS. CLIVENSIS **Rev:** XCII in center **Rev. Legend:** CVSVS. EMBRICAE **Note:** Struck at Emmerich Mint.

Date	Mintage	VG	F	VF	XF	Unc
(1)6(0)9 (h)	—	20.00	40.00	70.00	125	—

KM# 7 1/2 STUBER (10 Heller)

Silver **Obv:** Crowned 6-fold arms divide X-O **Rev:** Ornate cross divides X - CII at top and date below **Note:** Varieties exist.

Date	Mintage	VG	F	VF	XF	Unc
(1)609	—	20.00	40.00	70.00	125	—
(1)609 (h)	—	20.00	40.00	70.00	125	—

KM# 8 1/2 STUBER (10-1/2 Heller)

Silver **Rev:** Value XCI

Date	Mintage	VG	F	VF	XF	Unc
(1)609	—	20.00	40.00	70.00	125	—

KM# 15 1/2 STUBER (10-1/2 Heller)

Silver **Rev:** Without indiciation of value

Date	Mintage	VG	F	VF	XF	Unc
ND(ca.1612)	—	20.00	40.00	70.00	125	—

KM# 16 STUBER (21 Heller)

Silver **Obv:** Crowned 6-fold arms divide I-S **Obv. Legend:** NVMMVS. CLIVENSIS **Rev:** Ornate cross **Rev. Legend:** MO. AR. CVSVS. EMBRIC **Note:** Struck at Emmerich Mint. Varieties exist.

Date	Mintage	VG	F	VF	XF	Unc
ND(ca.1612) (h)	—	20.00	40.00	70.00	125	—

KM# 19 STUBER (21 Heller)

Silver **Rev. Legend:** MON. ARG. CVS. EMB **Note:** Varieties exist.

Date	Mintage	VG	F	VF	XF	Unc
ND(ca.1616-1624)	—	20.00	40.00	70.00	125	—

KM# 30 STUBER (21 Heller)

Silver **Ruler:** Friedrich Wilhelm **Rev. Legend:** MON. ARG. CVS. CLI

Date	Mintage	VG	F	VF	XF	Unc
1668	—	10.00	25.00	40.00	85.00	—
1669	—	10.00	25.00	40.00	85.00	—
1670	—	10.00	25.00	40.00	85.00	—

KM# 21 3 STUBER

Silver **Obv:** Crowned imperial eagle, **Obv. Legend:** III. ST **Rev:** Crowned 6-fold arms **Note:** Kipper 3 Stuber. Struck at Emmerich Mint. Varieties exist.

Date	Mintage	VG	F	VF	XF	Unc
ND(1619-22)	—	—	—	—	—	—

KM# 9 SCHILLING

Silver **Obv:** Crowned imperial eagle, titles of Rudolf II **Rev:** Crowned 6-fold arms **Note:** Varieties exist.

Date	Mintage	VG	F	VF	XF	Unc
ND(1609-12)	—	20.00	40.00	70.00	125	—
ND(1609-12) (h)	—	20.00	40.00	70.00	125	—

KM# 17 SCHILLING

Silver **Obv:** Titles of Matthias **Note:** Varieties exist.

Date	Mintage	VG	F	VF	XF	Unc
ND(1612-15) (h)	—	20.00	40.00	70.00	125	—

KM# 18 SCHILLING

9.8400 g., Silver **Note:** Klippe.

Date	Mintage	VG	F	VF	XF	Unc
ND(1612-15) (h)	—	—	—	—	—	—

KM# 35 1/12 THALER (2 Groschen)

Silver **Ruler:** Friedrich III **Obv:** Crowned ornate 6-fold arms **Rev:** Date **Rev. Legend:** 12/EINEN/REICHS/THALER

Date	Mintage	VG	F	VF	XF	Unc
1690 WH	—	16.00	30.00	55.00	100	—
1691 WH	—	16.00	30.00	55.00	100	—
1692 WH	—	16.00	30.00	55.00	100	—
1693 WH	—	16.00	30.00	55.00	100	—

KM# 38 1/3 THALER (1/2 Gulden)

Silver **Ruler:** Friedrich III **Obv:** Bust right **Rev:** Crowned 10-fold arms, value (1/3) below, date in legend

Date	Mintage	VG	F	VF	XF	Unc
1693 WH	—	—	—	—	—	—

KM# 36.1 2/3 THALER

Silver **Ruler:** Friedrich III **Obv:** Undivided legend at top **Note:** Struck at Emmerich Mint. Varieties exist.

Date	Mintage	VG	F	VF	XF	Unc
1690 WH	—	65.00	130	250	450	—
1691 WH	—	65.00	130	250	450	—
1692 WH	—	65.00	130	250	450	—

KM# 36.2 2/3 THALER

Silver **Ruler:** Friedrich III **Obv:** Portrait divides legend at top **Note:** Varieties exist.

Date	Mintage	VG	F	VF	XF	Unc
1692 WH	—	65.00	130	265	475	—
1693 WH	—	65.00	130	265	475	—
1694 WH	—	65.00	130	265	475	—
1695 WH	—	65.00	130	265	475	—
1696 WH	—	65.00	130	265	475	—
1696/5 WH	—	65.00	130	265	475	—

KM# 11 THALER

Silver **Rev:** Crowned arms dividing date in inner circle **Note:** Dav. #6665.

Date	Mintage	VG	F	VF	XF	Unc
1604 Rare	—	—	—	—	—	—
1608 Rare	—	—	—	—	—	—
1609 Rare	—	—	—	—	—	—

KM# 10 THALER

Silver **Ruler:** Friedrich III **Obv:** Bust right **Rev:** Helmeted arms **Note:** Dav. #6661.

Date	Mintage	VG	F	VF	XF	Unc
ND Rare	—	—	—	—	—	—

KM# 39 THALER (Albertus)

Silver **Ruler:** Friedrich III **Obv:** Ornate arms, crown above divides date **Rev:** 4 crowned double-F monograms alternating wioth 4 III's, scepter arms in center, inscription between crowns **Note:** Dav. #6221.

Date	Mintage	VG	F	VF	XF	Unc
1695 WH	—	250	500	900	1,400	—

KM# 40 THALER (Albertus)

Silver **Ruler:** Friedrich III **Rev:** Without inscription between crowns **Note:** Dav. #6222.

Date	Mintage	VG	F	VF	XF	Unc
1695 WH Rare	—	—	—	—	—	—

KM# 12 1-1/2 THALER

Silver **Obv:** Bust right **Rev:** Crowned arms dividing date in inner circle **Note:** Klippe. Dav. #6664. illustration reduced.

Date	Mintage	VG	F	VF	XF	Unc
1608 Rare	—	—	—	—	—	—
1609 Rare	—	—	—	—	—	—

KM# 14 2 THALER

Silver **Rev:** Crowned arms divide date in inner circle **Note:** Dav. #6663.

Date	Mintage	VG	F	VF	XF	Unc
1604 Rare	—	—	—	—	—	—
1608 Rare	—	—	—	—	—	—

KM# 22 2 THALER

Silver **Note:** Klippe. Dav. #6663A.

Date	Mintage	VG	F	VF	XF	Unc
1608 Rare	—	—	—	—	—	—

KM# 13 2 THALER

Silver **Obv:** Bust right **Rev:** Helmeted arms **Note:** Dav. #6660.

Date	Mintage	VG	F	VF	XF	Unc
ND Rare	—	—	—	—	—	—

KM# 23 3 THALER

Silver **Obv:** Bust right **Rev:** Crowned arms divide date in inner circle **Note:** Klippe. Dav. #6662.

Date	Mintage	VG	F	VF	XF	Unc
1609 Rare	—	—	—	—	—	—

COESFELD

The town of Coesfeld in Westphalia is located on the Berkel River some 19 miles (32 kilometers) west of Münster. Although Coesfeld belonged to the bishops of Münster, it was permitted to issue a local minor coinage from the late 16th century until 1763. When the bishopric was secularized in 1802, Coesfeld was acquired by the Rhinegraves of Salm. The latter's territories were soon mediatized in 1806 and became a part of Joachim Murat's grand duchy of Berg. Coesfeld finally passed to Prussia along with the rest of Berg at the conclusion of the Napoleonic Wars.

Reference:
H = Wolf Holtmann,"Beschreibung der Coesfelder Kupfermün", in ***Geschichtsblätter des Kreises Coesfeld***, 1 (1979)

CITY

REGULAR COINAGE

KM# 12 HELLER

Copper **Obv:** Crowned steer's head in circle, date **Obv. Legend:** STADT. COSVELT **Rev:** In ornamented square

Date	Mintage	VG	F	VF	XF	Unc
1627	—	13.00	27.00	45.00	85.00	—

MB# 2 PFENNIG

Copper **Rev:** I in circle on reverse **Note:** H#7, 8. Similar to Heller, MB1.

Date	Mintage	Good	VG	F	VF	XF
ND(ca. 1590)	—	—	—	—	—	—

KM# 11 PFENNIG

Copper **Obv:** Crowned bull's head within circle **Obv. Legend:** STADT. COSVELT **Rev:** Value within box **Note:** Varieties exist.

Date	Mintage	VG	F	VF	XF	Unc
1617	—	8.00	16.00	33.00	65.00	—
1627	—	8.00	16.00	33.00	65.00	—
1644	—	8.00	16.00	33.00	65.00	—
1694	—	8.00	16.00	33.00	65.00	—

KM# 5 2 PFENNIG

Copper **Obv:** Crowned bull's head within shield, circle surrounds **Rev:** Value within square **Note:** Varieties exist.

Date	Mintage	VG	F	VF	XF	Unc
1608	—	9.00	20.00	35.00	75.00	—
1609	—	9.00	20.00	35.00	75.00	—
1617	—	9.00	20.00	35.00	75.00	—
1644	—	9.00	20.00	35.00	75.00	—
1694	—	9.00	20.00	35.00	75.00	—

KM# 6 3 PFENNIG

Copper **Note:** Similar to 4 Pfennig, KM#7 but III on reverse. Varieties exist.

Date	Mintage	VG	F	VF	XF	Unc
1609	—	13.00	27.00	45.00	90.00	—
1617	—	13.00	27.00	45.00	90.00	—
1644	—	13.00	27.00	45.00	90.00	—
1650	—	13.00	27.00	45.00	90.00	—
1699	—	13.00	27.00	45.00	90.00	—

KM# 7 4 PFENNIG

Copper **Obv:** Crowned bull's head within shield, circle surrounds **Rev:** Value within square **Note:** Varieties exist.

Date	Mintage	VG	F	VF	XF	Unc
1609	—	8.00	16.00	40.00	70.00	—
1617	—	8.00	16.00	40.00	70.00	—
1634	—	8.00	16.00	40.00	70.00	—
1644	—	8.00	16.00	40.00	70.00	—
1650	—	8.00	16.00	40.00	70.00	—
1673 Reported, not confirmed	—	—	—	—	—	—
1693	—	8.00	16.00	40.00	70.00	—

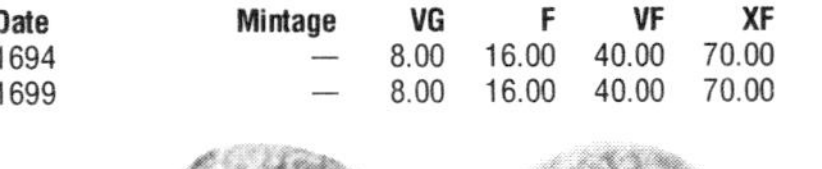

Date	Mintage	VG	F	VF	XF	Unc
1694	—	8.00	16.00	40.00	70.00	—
1699	—	8.00	16.00	40.00	70.00	—

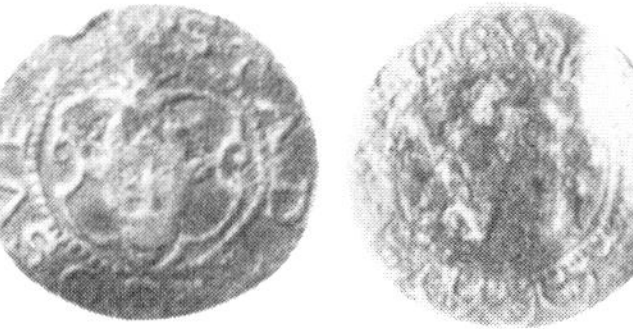

KM# 8 6 PFENNIG

Copper **Rev:** Value VI in inner circle **Note:** Similar to 4 Pfennig, KM#7. Varieties exist.

Date	Mintage	VG	F	VF	XF	Unc
1609	—	16.00	33.00	60.00	110	—
1617	—	16.00	33.00	60.00	110	—

KM# 9 8 PFENNIG

Copper **Obv:** Crowned bull's head within shield, circle surrounds **Rev:** Value within square **Note:** Varieties exist.

Date	Mintage	VG	F	VF	XF	Unc
1609	—	10.00	25.00	45.00	85.00	—
1617	—	10.00	25.00	45.00	85.00	—
1634	—	10.00	25.00	45.00	85.00	—
1636 Rare	—	—	—	—	—	—
1691	—	10.00	25.00	45.00	85.00	—
1694	—	10.00	25.00	45.00	85.00	—

KM# 10 12 PFENNIG

Copper **Note:** Similar to 8 Pfennig, KM#9, but XII on reverse. Varieties exist.

Date	Mintage	VG	F	VF	XF	Unc
1616 Reported, not confirmed	—	—	—	—	—	—
1617	—	20.00	45.00	85.00	145	—
1636	—	20.00	45.00	85.00	145	—
1663 Error for 1636; Rare	—	—	—	—	—	—

COLMAR

A city in central Alsace, about 37 miles west of Freiburg in Breisgau, known to exist as early as 823. Colmar became a free imperial city in 1226. It was captured by Swedish forces in 1632, then by the French in 1635 during the Thirty Years' War. It regained its free status in 1649, but was taken back in 1673 and finally annexed by France in 1681.

MONETARY SYSTEM

2 Staber = Rappen (Pfennig)
Plappart = 42 Rappen = 7 Schilling
Dicken = 5 Plappart = 210 Rappen
2 Heller = 1 Pfennig
4 (Vierer) Pfennig = 1 Kreuzer

ARMS

A mace, usually tilted to the left

CITY

REGULAR COINAGE

KM# 6 DOPPELVIERER

Silver **Obv:** Eagle in circle **Obv. Legend:** MONET = N - O + COLMA **Rev:** Similar to KM#5

Date	Mintage	VG	F	VF	XF	Unc
ND(c.1660)	—	—	—	—	—	—

KM# 7 DOPPELVIERER

Silver **Note:** Klippe.

Date	Mintage	VG	F	VF	XF	Unc
ND(c.1660) Rare	—	—	—	—	—	—

KM# 4 DOPPELVIERER

Silver **Obv:** Crowned imperial eagle, arms of city (mace)on breast **Obv. Legend:** MON: NO: CIVIT: IM: COLMAR: **Rev:** Long cross dividing legend **Rev. Legend:** S:MA-RTIN-VS. PA-TRON **Note:** Prev. KM#5.

Date	Mintage	VG	F	VF	XF	Unc
ND(c.1660)	—	25.00	45.00	90.00	150	—

KM# 5 DOPPELVIERER

Silver **Rev. Legend:** GLOR-IA. IN.E-XCE-L'DEO **Note:** Varieties exist. Prev. KM#6.

Date	Mintage	VG	F	VF	XF	Unc
ND(c.1660)	—	—	—	—	—	—

Note: Four pieces known

KM# 9 2 KREUZER

Silver **Note:** Klippe.

Date	Mintage	VG	F	VF	XF	Unc
ND(c.1576-1612)	—	—	—	—	—	—

KM# 16 4 KREUZER (Batzen)

Silver **Obv:** City arms (mace), date above **Rev:** Imperial eagle in inner circle **Note:** Similar to 12 Kreuzer, KM#17.

Date	Mintage	VG	F	VF	XF	Unc
1666	—	40.00	85.00	150	220	—
1667	—	40.00	85.00	150	220	—
1669	—	40.00	85.00	150	220	—

KM# 15 12 KREUZER (Zwölfer)

Silver **Obv:** Crowned imperial eagle **Rev:** Oval city arms (mace) in baroque frame, value XII.K above

Date	Mintage	VG	F	VF	XF	Unc
ND(c.1660)	—	80.00	160	300	525	—

KM# 17 12 KREUZER (Zwölfer)

Silver **Obv:** Crowned imperial eagle **Rev:** City arms (mace)

Date	Mintage	VG	F	VF	XF	Unc
1666	—	115	225	400	675	—
1669	—	115	225	400	675	—

KM# 20 30 KREUZER (1/2 Gulden)

Silver **Obv:** Crowned imperial eagle **Rev:** City arms in baroque frame divide date, 30 in oval at bottom

Date	Mintage	VG	F	VF	XF	Unc
1670	—	—	—	—	—	—

Note: Three pieces known

KM# 22 60 KREUZER (Gulden)

Silver **Rev:** Different shield and incorporating value "60" at bottom, within circle **Note:** Dav. #462.

Date	Mintage	VG	F	VF	XF	Unc
ND	—	275	575	1,150	2,000	—

KM# 21 60 KREUZER (Gulden)

Silver **Obv:** Similar to 12 Kreuzer, KM#17 **Rev:** City arms in baroque frame divides date **Note:** Dav. #461.

Date	Mintage	VG	F	VF	XF	Unc
1670	—	400	850	1,400	2,400	—

KM# 18 THALER

Silver **Obv:** Crowned imperial eagle **Obv. Legend:** LEOPOLD: DG:... **Rev:** City view with COLLMAR on banner above, angel's head above two shields below **Note:** Dav# 5131.

Date	Mintage	VG	F	VF	XF	Unc
1666 Rare	—	—	—	—	—	—

KM# 23 THALER

Silver **Obv:** Small crown and square topped shield **Rev:** "COLMAR" on banner **Note:** Dav# 5133.

Date	Mintage	VG	F	VF	XF	Unc
1670 Rare	—	—	—	—	—	—

Note: Moller Auction 10-92 VF/XF realized $15,750

KM# 24 2 THALER

Silver **Obv:** City view with COLMAR" on banner above, angel's head above two shields below **Obv. Legend:** LEOPOLD: DG:... **Rev:** Crowned double-headed imperial eagle with city arms on breast **Note:** Dav# 5132.

Date	Mintage	VG	F	VF	XF	Unc
1670 Rare	—	—	—	—	—	—

COLOGNE

(Köln)

A bishopric was established in the city of Roman foundation in 313 and transformed into an archbishopric by Charlemagne in 785. Joint issues of coinage by the archbishops and the emperors began in the mid-10th century and the first independent ecclesiastic issues appeared in the late 11th century. Upon the breakup of the old duchy of Saxony in 1180, the archbishop obtained the duchy of Westphalia. The archbishops became Electors of the Empire by the Gold Bull of 1356 and continued to gain power and territory during the ensuing centuries. In 1801, Cologne was secularized and its lands west of the Rhine were taken by France. Several principalities divided Cologne's territories east of the Rhine, the largest portions having been taken by Hesse-Darmstadt and Nassau.

RULERS

Hermann IV, Landgraf von Hessen, 1480-1508
Philipp II, Graf von Dhaun-Oberstein, 1508-1515
Hermann V, Graf von Wied, 1515-1546
Adolf III, Graf von Schaumburg-Pinneberg, 1547-1556
Anton, Graf von Schaumburg-Pinneberg, 1556-1558
Johann Gebhard (I), Graf von Mansfeld-Vorderort, 1558-1562
Friedrich IV, Graf von Wied, 1562-1567
Salentin, Graf von Isenburg-Grenzau, 1567-1577
Gebhard (II), Truchsess von Waldburg-Trauchburg, 1577-1583
Ernst, Herzog von Bayern, 1583-1612
Ferdinand, Herzog von Bayern, 1612-1650
Maximilian Heinrich, Herzog von Bayern, 1650-1688
Josef Clemens, Herzog von Bayern, 1688-1723

ARMS

Archbishopric – Cross

EARLY MINT OFFICIALS

Deutz Mint

Date	Name
1547-57	Dietrich Grünwalt, mintmaster
	Jürgen Bornheim, warden
1558-65	Johann Bitter von Raesfeld, mintmaster
1565-72	Peter Bitter von Raesfeld, mintmaster
1565-69	Tilman Wickerath, warden
1569-84	Gabriel Phinoir, warden
1572-79	Reiner Budels, mintmaster
1580	Heinrich Rörichs
1581-1584	Gilles von Siburg, mintmaster
1583-1601	Reiner Budels, mintmaster
1600-	Ulrich von Wernberg, warden
1615-17	Heinrich Lambertz, mintmaster
1617-?	Johann Gerhardt, warden

MINT OFFICIALS' INITIALS

Initials	Date	Name
BS	1641-42	Benedikt Stephani in Bonn
C		Commission, Committee
FE	1638-39	Franz Engels in bonn
FL	Ca.1657	Unknown in Bonn
FW	1693	Friedrich Wendels in Deutz
	1698-1728	In Bonn
IPL/PL	1681-88	Johann Peter Longerich in Bonn
NK	1663-64	Unknown
NL	1693-94	Nikolaus Longerich in Deutz
NR	1672-1725	Norbert Roettiers, die-cutter in Bruxelles
PL	1609-12	Paul Lachentriess in Deutz, die-cutter in Cleves
VFH	1630	Urban Felgenhauer in Marsberg
	1631-50	In Arnsberg
(w)	Ca.1608-12	Werl mint, unknown mintmaster

REFERENCES

N = Alfred Noss, ***Die Münzen und Medaillen von Köln, v. 3, Die Münzen der Erzbischöfe von Köln, 1547-1794***. Cologne, 1926.
Sch = Wolfgang Schulten, ***Deutsche Münzen aus der Zeit Karls V.*** Frankfurt am Main, 1974.

ARCHBISHOPRIC

REGULAR COINAGE

KM# 18 HELLER (1/2 Pfennig)

Silver **Ruler:** Ferdinand von Bayern **Note:** C above arms.

Date	Mintage	VG	F	VF	XF	Unc
ND(ca.1612-20)	—	7.00	13.00	27.00	45.00	—

KM# 17 HELLER (1/2 Pfennig)

Silver **Ruler:** Ferdinand von Bayern **Note:** Uniface. 4-fold arms of Cologne.

Date	Mintage	VG	F	VF	XF	Unc
ND(ca.1612-20)	—	7.00	13.00	27.00	45.00	—

KM# 65 HELLER (1/2 Pfennig)

Silver **Ruler:** Maximilian Heinrich von Bayern **Note:** Hohl-type. Arms of Cologne (cross).

Date	Mintage	VG	F	VF	XF	Unc
ND(ca.1680)	—	—	—	—	—	—

KM# 80 2 HELLER (Pfennig)

Silver **Ruler:** Josef Clemens von Bayern **Obv:** Crowned 4-fold arms of Bavaria-Pfalz divide 2-H

Date	Mintage	VG	F	VF	XF	Unc
1698 FW	—	27.00	55.00	100	150	—

KM# 51 4 HELLER

Silver **Ruler:** Maximilian Heinrich von Bayern **Obv:** Round arms of Cologne (cross) **Rev:** IIII in center, date in legend

Date	Mintage	VG	F	VF	XF	Unc
1659	—	16.00	33.00	60.00	110	—
1662	—	16.00	33.00	60.00	110	—
1663	—	16.00	33.00	60.00	110	—

KM# 60 4 HELLER

Silver **Ruler:** Maximilian Heinrich von Bayern **Obv:** Arms of Bavaria **Rev:** IIII in center, date in legend

Date	Mintage	VG	F	VF	XF	Unc
1679	—	—	—	—	—	—

KM# 5 8 HELLER (4 Pfennig)

Silver **Ruler:** Ernst von Bayern **Obv:** 4-fold arms of Bavaria-Pfalz, value 8 in legend **Rev:** 4-fold arms of Cologne, 74 in legend **Note:** Varieties exist.

Date	Mintage	VG	F	VF	XF	Unc
ND(1609-12) PL	—	10.00	20.00	40.00	80.00	—

KM# 10 8 HELLER (4 Pfennig)

Silver **Ruler:** Ernst von Bayern **Obv:** 2 arms of Pfalz and Bavaria above VIII **Rev:** 4-fold arms of Cologne **Note:** Varieties exist.

Date	Mintage	VG	F	VF	XF	Unc
ND(ca.1610) (w)	—	—	—	—	—	—

KM# 11 8 HELLER (4 Pfennig)

Silver **Ruler:** Ernst von Bayern **Obv:** 4-fold arms of Bavaria-Pfalz **Rev:** VIII above arms of Werl **Rev. Legend:** WERL... **Note:** Varieties exist.

Date	Mintage	VG	F	VF	XF	Unc
ND(ca.1610) (w)	—	—	—	—	—	—

KM# 12 8 HELLER (4 Pfennig)

Silver **Ruler:** Ernst von Bayern **Rev:** Without value

Date	Mintage	VG	F	VF	XF	Unc
ND(ca.1610) (w)	—	—	—	—	—	—

KM# 13 8 HELLER (4 Pfennig)

Silver **Ruler:** Ernst von Bayern **Obv:** 4-fold arms of Cologne **Rev:** VIII above arms of Werl **Rev. Legend:** WERL...

Date	Mintage	VG	F	VF	XF	Unc
ND(ca.1610) (w)	—	—	—	—	—	—

KM# 19 8 HELLER (4 Pfennig)

Silver **Ruler:** Ferdinand von Bayern **Obv:** 4-fold arms **Obv. Legend:** FERD.D:G... **Rev:** Crowned imperial eagle, 8 HE or HEL in legend at bottom, titles of Matthias

Date	Mintage	VG	F	VF	XF	Unc
ND(1612-19)	—	33.00	65.00	120	220	—

KM# 25 8 HELLER (4 Pfennig)

Silver **Ruler:** Ferdinand von Bayern **Obv:** Arms of Bavaria, date in legend **Rev:** Arms of Cologne (cross) **Note:** Varieties exist.

Date	Mintage	VG	F	VF	XF	Unc
1630	—	8.00	16.00	33.00	60.00	—
1631	—	8.00	16.00	33.00	60.00	—
1632	—	8.00	16.00	33.00	60.00	—
1633	—	8.00	16.00	33.00	60.00	—
1634	—	8.00	16.00	33.00	60.00	—
1636	—	8.00	16.00	33.00	60.00	—
1637	—	8.00	16.00	33.00	60.00	—
1649	—	8.00	16.00	33.00	60.00	—

KM# 28 8 HELLER (4 Pfennig)

Silver **Obv:** 4-fold arms of Cologne **Rev:** 4-fold arms of Bavaria-Pfalz, date in legend

Date	Mintage	VG	F	VF	XF	Unc
1638 FE	—	8.00	16.00	33.00	60.00	—
1639	—	8.00	16.00	33.00	60.00	—
1640	—	8.00	16.00	33.00	60.00	—
1641 BS	—	8.00	16.00	33.00	60.00	—

KM# 35 8 HELLER (4 Pfennig)

Silver **Ruler:** Ferdinand von Bayern **Obv:** 4-fold arms of Cologne, date above **Rev:** 4-fold arms of Bavaria-Pfalz between 2 laurel sprigs

Date	Mintage	VG	F	VF	XF	Unc
1642	—	12.00	25.00	40.00	75.00	—

KM# 40 8 HELLER (4 Pfennig)

Silver **Ruler:** Maximilian Heinrich von Bayern **Obv:** Arms of Bavaria in small, ornamented shields, date in legend **Rev:** Arms of Cologne (cross) in small, ornamented shields

Date	Mintage	VG	F	VF	XF	Unc
1650	—	10.00	20.00	35.00	65.00	—

KM# 41 8 HELLER (4 Pfennig)

Silver **Ruler:** Maximilian Heinrich von Bayern **Obv:** KM#40 **Rev:** Similar to KM#40 but with posthumous dates in legend **Note:** Mule.

Date	Mintage	VG	F	VF	XF	Unc
1650/51	—	—	—	—	—	—
1650/52	—	—	—	—	—	—

KM# 42 8 HELLER (4 Pfennig)

Silver **Ruler:** Maximilian Heinrich von Bayern **Obv:** Arms of Bavaria in small, ornamented shields **Rev:** Arms of Cologne, (cross) in small, ornamented shields, date in legend **Note:** Varieties exist.

Date	Mintage	VG	F	VF	XF	Unc
1651	—	8.00	16.00	33.00	60.00	—
1652	—	8.00	16.00	33.00	60.00	—
1653	—	8.00	16.00	33.00	60.00	—
1654	—	8.00	16.00	33.00	60.00	—
1655	—	8.00	16.00	33.00	60.00	—
1656	—	8.00	16.00	33.00	60.00	—
1657	—	8.00	16.00	33.00	60.00	—

Date	Mintage	VG	F	VF	XF	Unc
1658	—	8.00	16.00	33.00	60.00	—
1659	—	8.00	16.00	33.00	60.00	—

KM# 43 8 HELLER (4 Pfennig)

Silver **Ruler:** Maximilian Heinrich von Bayern **Obv:** Large 8 in shield

Date	Mintage	VG	F	VF	XF	Unc
1654	—	8.00	16.00	33.00	60.00	—
1655	—	8.00	16.00	33.00	60.00	—

KM# 48 8 HELLER (4 Pfennig)

Silver **Ruler:** Maximilian Heinrich von Bayern **Obv:** Date divided by arms of Bavaria

Date	Mintage	VG	F	VF	XF	Unc
1658	—	—	—	—	—	—

KM# 49 8 HELLER (4 Pfennig)

Silver **Ruler:** Maximilian Heinrich von Bayern **Obv:** KM#48 **Rev:** Similar to KM#42 but date also in reverse legend **Note:** Mule.

Date	Mintage	VG	F	VF	XF	Unc
1658	—	—	—	—	—	—

KM# 52 8 HELLER (4 Pfennig)

Silver **Ruler:** Maximilian Heinrich von Bayern **Obv:** Date divided by arms of Bavaria **Rev:** Arms of Cologne (cross) in small, ornamented shield

Date	Mintage	VG	F	VF	XF	Unc
1659	—	—	—	—	—	—

KM# 61 8 HELLER (4 Pfennig)

Silver **Ruler:** Maximilian Heinrich von Bayern **Obv:** Arms of Bavaria **Rev:** VIII in center, date in legend

Date	Mintage	VG	F	VF	XF	Unc
1679	—	8.00	16.00	33.00	60.00	—
1680	—	8.00	16.00	33.00	60.00	—

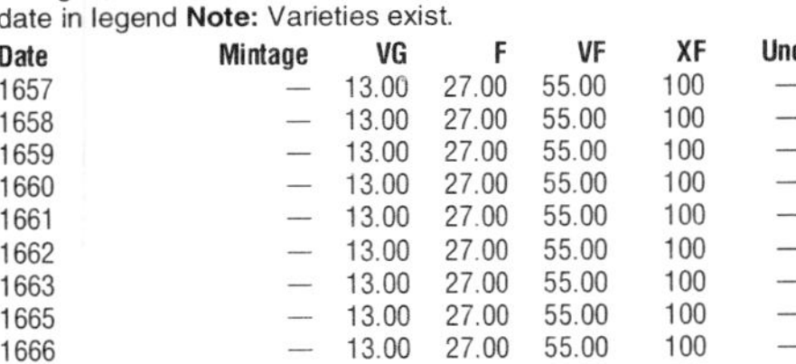

KM# 66 8 HELLER (4 Pfennig)

Silver **Ruler:** Maximilian Heinrich von Bayern **Obv:** Arms of Cologne **Rev:** Arms of Bavaria, date in legend **Note:** Varieties exist.

Date	Mintage	VG	F	VF	XF	Unc
1681 PL	—	8.00	16.00	33.00	60.00	—
1684 IPL	—	8.00	16.00	33.00	60.00	—
1688 IPL	—	8.00	16.00	33.00	60.00	—

KM# 83 8 HELLER (4 Pfennig)

Silver **Ruler:** Josef Clemens von Bayern **Obv:** Arms of Bavaria in circle **Rev:** Arms of Cologne (cross) in circle, date at top in legend

Date	Mintage	VG	F	VF	XF	Unc
1699 FW	—	9.00	18.00	35.00	60.00	—
1700 FW	—	9.00	18.00	35.00	60.00	—

KM# 6 PFENNIG

Silver **Ruler:** Ernst von Bayern **Note:** Uniface. Schussel-type. 4-fold arms with C above.

Date	Mintage	VG	F	VF	XF	Unc
ND(ca.1609)	—	20.00	40.00	80.00	140	—

KM# 7 ALBUS (12 Heller)

Silver **Ruler:** Ernst von Bayern **Obv:** 4-fold arms of Bavaria-Pfalz **Rev:** Arms of Mainz, Trier, Cologne and Bavaria in cruciform

Date	Mintage	VG	F	VF	XF	Unc
ND(1609-12) PL	—	—	—	—	—	—

KM# 55.1 ALBUS (12 Heller)

Silver **Ruler:** Maximilian Heinrich von Bayern **Obv:** Round arms of Cologne (cross) **Rev. Legend:** IALBVS/COLS/CH

Date	Mintage	VG	F	VF	XF	Unc
ND(ca.1662/3)	—	10.00	20.00	40.00	80.00	—

KM# 55.2 ALBUS (12 Heller)

Silver **Ruler:** Maximilian Heinrich von Bayern **Rev. Legend:** I/ALBVS/COLSCH

Date	Mintage	VG	F	VF	XF	Unc
ND(ca.1662/3)	—	10.00	20.00	40.00	80.00	—

KM# 55.3 ALBUS (12 Heller)

Silver **Ruler:** Maximilian Heinrich von Bayern **Rev. Legend:** I/ALBVS/COLN/CH

Date	Mintage	VG	F	VF	XF	Unc
ND(ca.1662/3)	—	10.00	20.00	40.00	80.00	—

KM# 55.4 ALBUS (12 Heller)

Silver **Ruler:** Maximilian Heinrich von Bayern **Rev. Legend:** COLN/ISCHER/ALBVS

Date	Mintage	VG	F	VF	XF	Unc
ND(ca.1662/3)	—	10.00	20.00	40.00	80.00	—

KM# 44 2 ALBUS

Silver **Ruler:** Maximilian Heinrich von Bayern **Obv:** Arms of Cologne, 2 AL or ALB below in legend **Rev:** Arms of Bavaria, date in legend **Note:** Varieties exist.

Date	Mintage	VG	F	VF	XF	Unc
1657	—	13.00	27.00	55.00	100	—
1658	—	13.00	27.00	55.00	100	—
1659	—	13.00	27.00	55.00	100	—
1660	—	13.00	27.00	55.00	100	—
1661	—	13.00	27.00	55.00	100	—
1662	—	13.00	27.00	55.00	100	—
1663	—	13.00	27.00	55.00	100	—
1665	—	13.00	27.00	55.00	100	—
1666	—	13.00	27.00	55.00	100	—
1667	—	13.00	27.00	55.00	100	—
1671	—	13.00	27.00	55.00	100	—
1672	—	13.00	27.00	55.00	100	—
1673	—	13.00	27.00	55.00	100	—
1681 PL	—	13.00	27.00	55.00	100	—
1687 IPL	—	13.00	27.00	55.00	100	—

KM# 45 2 ALBUS

Silver **Ruler:** Maximilian Heinrich von Bayern **Rev:** Date divided by arms **Note:** Varieties exist.

Date	Mintage	VG	F	VF	XF	Unc
1657	—	13.00	27.00	55.00	100	—
1658	—	13.00	27.00	55.00	100	—
1659	—	13.00	27.00	55.00	100	—

KM# 62 2 ALBUS

Silver **Ruler:** Maximilian Heinrich von Bayern **Obv:** Date divided by arms

Date	Mintage	VG	F	VF	XF	Unc
1679	—	—	—	—	—	—

KM# 27 4 ALBUS (Blaffert)

Silver **Ruler:** Ferdinand von Bayern **Obv:** Crowned 4-fold arms of Bavaria-Pfalz **Rev:** Arms of Cologne, date in legend

Date	Mintage	VG	F	VF	XF	Unc
1633	—	33.00	65.00	120	200	—
1635	—	33.00	65.00	120	200	—

KM# 29 4 ALBUS (Blaffert)

Silver **Ruler:** Ferdinand von Bayern **Obv:** Crowned oval 4-fold arms of Cologne with central shield of Bavaria-Pfalz **Rev:** IIII/ALBVS in square, date in legend

Date	Mintage	VG	F	VF	XF	Unc
1638 FE	—	—	—	—	—	—

KM# 36 4 ALBUS (Blaffert)

Silver **Ruler:** Ferdinand von Bayern **Obv:** 4-fold arms of Cologne, date in legend **Rev:** Crowned 4-fold arms of Bavaria-Pfalz between 2 laurel sprigs

Date	Mintage	VG	F	VF	XF	Unc
1642 BS	—	27.00	55.00	100	175	—

KM# 70 4 ALBUS (Blaffert)

Silver **Ruler:** Josef Clemens von Bayern **Obv:** Crowned 4-fold arms of Bavaria-Pfalz **Rev:** Date above arms of Cologne

Date	Mintage	VG	F	VF	XF	Unc
1693 FW	—	25.00	45.00	90.00	160	—

KM# 14 MARIENGROSCHEN

Silver **Ruler:** Ernst von Bayern **Obv:** Bust of St. Peter above 4-fold arms of Bavaria-Pfalz **Rev:** Madonna and child, date in legend

Date	Mintage	VG	F	VF	XF	Unc
1610	—	25.00	50.00	85.00	135	—

KM# A27 MARIENGROSCHEN

1.3500 g., Silver, 20 mm. **Ruler:** Ferdinand von Bayern **Obv:** City arms (Cologne cross) above "36" **Obv. Legend:** FERDIN • D • G • ARCH CO • **Rev:** Bavarian arms **Rev. Legend:** S • R • I • P • ELEC • BAV • DVX *

Date	Mintage	VG	F	VF	XF	Unc
1631 VH	—	—	—	—	—	—

KM# A29 MARIENGROSCHEN

1.3500 g., Silver, 20 mm. **Ruler:** Ferdinand von Bayern **Obv:** Three-line denomination in center *I*/MARI/GRO above "36" **Rev:** Bavarian arms on the Cologne cross above VF **Rev. Legend:** S • R • I • P • ELEC • BAVA • ET • W • DVX • * •

Date	Mintage	VG	F	VF	XF	Unc
1638 VF	—	65.00	135	275	450	—

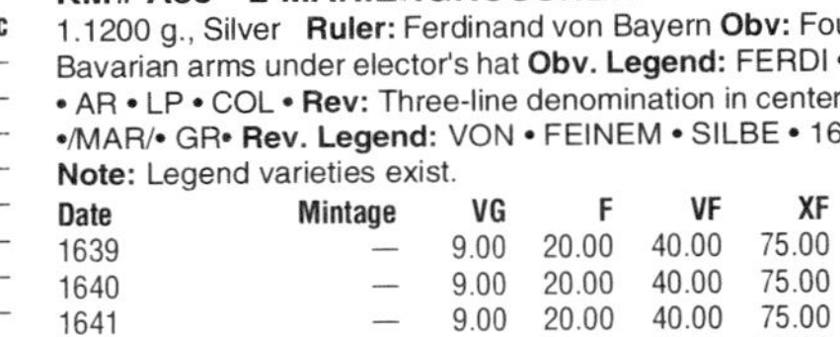

KM# A33 2 MARIENGROSCHEN

1.1200 g., Silver **Ruler:** Ferdinand von Bayern **Obv:** Four-part Bavarian arms under elector's hat **Obv. Legend:** FERDI • D • G • AR • LP • COL • **Rev:** Three-line denomination in center as • II •/MAR/• GR• **Rev. Legend:** VON • FEINEM • SILBE • 16*39 • **Note:** Legend varieties exist.

Date	Mintage	VG	F	VF	XF	Unc
1639	—	9.00	20.00	40.00	75.00	—
1640	—	9.00	20.00	40.00	75.00	—
1641	—	9.00	20.00	40.00	75.00	—
1642	—	9.00	20.00	40.00	75.00	—
1643	—	9.00	20.00	40.00	75.00	—
1644	—	9.00	20.00	40.00	75.00	—
1645	—	9.00	20.00	40.00	75.00	—
1649	—	9.00	20.00	40.00	75.00	—
1650	—	9.00	20.00	40.00	75.00	—

KM# 50 MARK

Silver **Ruler:** Maximilian Heinrich von Bayern **Obv:** Crowned arms of Bavaria-Pfalz quartered by cross, arms extending out of shield **Rev:** Date **Rev. Legend:** I/MARCK/COLSCH

Date	Mintage	VG	F	VF	XF	Unc
1658	—	—	—	—	—	—
1659	—	—	—	—	—	—

KM# 8 1/24 THALER (Groschen)

Silver **Ruler:** Ernst von Bayern **Obv:** Imperial orb with 24, date divided above orb by cross, titles of Rudolf II **Rev:** 4-fold arms of Bavaria-Pfalz **Note:** Varieties exist.

Date	Mintage	VG	F	VF	XF	Unc
1609	—	40.00	85.00	140	230	—

KM# 15 1/24 THALER (Groschen)

Silver **Ruler:** Ernst von Bayern **Rev:** Crowned 4-fold arms of Bavaria-Pfalz

Date	Mintage	VG	F	VF	XF	Unc
1610 PL	—	13.00	27.00	45.00	75.00	—
1611 PL	—	13.00	27.00	45.00	75.00	—

KM# 16 1/24 THALER (Groschen)

Silver **Ruler:** Ernst von Bayern **Obv:** 1/2 length figure of St. Peter above arms of Cologne **Note:** Klippe.

Date	Mintage	VG	F	VF	XF	Unc
1611 Rare	—	—	—	—	—	—

KM# 71 1/6 THALER (1/4 Gulden)

Silver **Ruler:** Josef Clemens von Bayern **Obv:** Bust right in circle **Rev:** Crowned 7-fold arms with central shield of 4-fold arms of Bavaria-Pfalz divide date, 1/6 in oval at bottom

Date	Mintage	VG	F	VF	XF	Unc
1693 FW	—	33.00	75.00	140	235	—

KM# 72 1/6 THALER (1/4 Gulden)

Silver **Ruler:** Josef Clemens von Bayern **Obv:** Bust breaks circle at bottom

Date	Mintage	VG	F	VF	XF	Unc
1693 FW	—	33.00	75.00	140	235	—

KM# 73 1/3 THALER (1/2 Gulden)

Silver **Ruler:** Josef Clemens von Bayern **Obv:** Bust right in circle **Rev:** Crowned 7-fold arms with central shield of 4-fold arms of Bavaria-Pfalz dividing date, 1/3 in oval at bottom

Date	Mintage	VG	F	VF	XF	Unc
1693 FW	—	—	—	—	—	—

KM# 85 1/3 THALER (1/2 Gulden)

Silver **Ruler:** Josef Clemens von Bayern **Subject:** Consecration of the Palace Chapel in Bonn **Obv:** Crowned IEC monogram between branches **Rev:** 15-line inscription with date

Date	Mintage	VG	F	VF	XF	Unc
1700	—	300	600	1,100	1,750	—

KM# 74 2/3 THALER (Gulden)

Silver **Ruler:** Josef Clemens von Bayern **Obv:** Bust right in circle broken at bottom **Rev:** Crowned 7-fold arms with central shield of 4-fold arms of Bavaria-Pfalz divide date, 2/3 in oval at bottom

Date	Mintage	VG	F	VF	XF	Unc
1693 FW	—	—	—	—	—	—

KM# 75 2/3 THALER (Gulden)

Silver **Ruler:** Josef Clemens von Bayern **Note:** Varieties exist in arrangement of date.

Date	Mintage	VG	F	VF	XF	Unc
1693 NL	—	60.00	120	190	300	—
1694 NL	—	60.00	120	190	300	—

KM# 76 2/3 THALER (Gulden)

Silver **Ruler:** Josef Clemens von Bayern

Date	Mintage	VG	F	VF	XF	Unc
1694 NL	—	60.00	120	200	325	—

KM# 86 2/3 THALER (Gulden)

Silver **Ruler:** Josef Clemens von Bayern **Rev:** 12-fold arms

Date	Mintage	VG	F	VF	XF	Unc
1700 FW	—	—	—	—	—	—

KM# 20.1 THALER

Silver **Ruler:** Ferdinand von Bayern **Obv:** Helmeted 4-fold arms with central shield of Bavaria-Pfalz **Rev:** Figure of St. Peter divides date **Note:** Dav.#5134.

Date	Mintage	VG	F	VF	XF	Unc
1616 Rare	—	—	—	—	—	—

KM# 20.2 THALER

Silver **Ruler:** Ferdinand von Bayern **Rev:** Circle of laurel around St. Peter **Note:** Dav.#5136. Varieties exist.

Date	Mintage	VG	F	VF	XF	Unc
1617 Rare	—	—	—	—	—	—

KM# 26 THALER

Silver **Ruler:** Ferdinand von Bayern **Obv:** 1/2 length facing figure of st. Peter **Rev:** Crowned 4-fold arms of Bavaria-Pfalz divide date **Note:** Dav.#5137.

Date	Mintage	VG	F	VF	XF	Unc
1630 Rare	—	—	—	—	—	—

KM# 30 THALER

Silver **Ruler:** Ferdinand von Bayern **Obv:** Bust right **Rev:** Crowned oval 4-fold arms of Cologne with central shield of Bavaria-Pfalz, date at left of crown in legend **Note:** Dav.#5142.

Date	Mintage	VG	F	VF	XF	Unc
1638 FE	—	500	1,000	1,750	2,700	—

KM# 31 THALER

Silver **Ruler:** Ferdinand von Bayern **Obv:** Bust 3/4 to right **Rev:** Crown replaced by mitre **Note:** Dav.#5143.

Date	Mintage	VG	F	VF	XF	Unc
1638 FE Rare	—	—	—	—	—	—

KM# 33 THALER

Silver **Ruler:** Ferdinand von Bayern **Obv:** Bust right, 2 legend inscriptions, inner broken by top of bust **Rev:** Crowned oval 4-fold arms of Bavaria-Pfalz supported by 2 lions, surrounded by circle of 17 small shields, date divided by crown **Note:** Dav.#5144.

Date	Mintage	VG	F	VF	XF	Unc
1639 FE Rare	—	—	—	—	—	—

KM# 46.1 THALER

Silver **Ruler:** Maximilian Heinrich von Bayern **Obv:** Bust right in circle **Rev:** Crowned oval 4-fold arms of Cologne with central shield of Bavaria-Pfalz **Rev. Legend:** V.- BA. WE. AN. BV. DVX. MA. FR. CO. PIVM. LOS. LO. H-OR **Note:** Dav.#5146.

Date	Mintage	VG	F	VF	XF	Unc
ND(ca.1657) FL	—	1,000	2,200	4,000	6,500	—

KM# 46.2 THALER

Silver **Ruler:** Maximilian Heinrich von Bayern **Rev. Legend:** V.-BAV: WE: AN: BVL: DVX: LANDG: LEVCH: MAR: - FRA: **Note:** Dav.#5147.

Date	Mintage	VG	F	VF	XF	Unc
ND(ca.1657)	—	1,000	2,200	4,000	6,500	—

Note: Slight differences in arms and inscription on reverse

KM# 53 THALER

Silver **Ruler:** Maximilian Heinrich von Bayern **Obv:** Bust right in mantle **Obv. Legend:** ... COL.PR.EL.EP.LEOD.HILD.ADM. BERCH. **Rev:** Capped arms divide date **Rev. Legend:** VTR. BAV.WEST:ANG...COM.PAL.RHE.LAND.LEV. **Note:** Dav.#5149.

Date	Mintage	VG	F	VF	XF	Unc
1657 Rare	—	—	—	—	—	—

KM# 54 THALER

Silver **Ruler:** Maximilian Heinrich von Bayern **Rev. Legend:** ...BVL.COM.PAL.RHE.LAN:L. **Note:** Dav.#5150.

Date	Mintage	VG	F	VF	XF	Unc
1657 Rare	—	—	—	—	—	—

KM# 58 THALER

Silver **Ruler:** Maximilian Heinrich von Bayern **Obv. Legend:** ...EP:HIL:LEOD:A:BER: **Rev. Legend:** LAND:LEV:VTR:BA: WEST:AN:B:DVX:CO:PA.RHE: **Note:** Dav.#5151.

Date	Mintage	VG	F	VF	XF	Unc
1657 Rare	—	—	—	—	—	—

KM# 68 THALER

Silver **Ruler:** Sede Vacante **Obv:** St. Peter **Rev:** Nativity **Note:** Dav.#5153.

Date	Mintage	VG	F	VF	XF	Unc
1688	—	250	400	750	1,250	—

KM# 67 THALER

Silver **Ruler:** Sede Vacante **Obv:** St. Peter **Rev:** Nativity **Note:** Sede Vacante issue. Dav.#5152.

Date	Mintage	VG	F	VF	XF	Unc
1688	—	400	750	1,250	2,200	—

KM# 77 THALER

Silver **Ruler:** Josef Clemens von Bayern **Subject:** Joseph Clemens **Note:** Dav.#5154.

Date	Mintage	F	VF	XF	Unc	BU
1694 NL	—	750	1,350	2,250	3,750	—

KM# 81 THALER

Silver **Ruler:** Josef Clemens von Bayern **Obv:** Bust right **Rev:** Crowned II's in cruciform, date above crown at top, double C in angles, round Bavarian arms in center **Note:** Dav.#5155.

Date	Mintage	F	VF	XF	Unc	BU
1698 FW	—	1,000	1,750	3,250	5,500	—

KM# 21 2 THALER

Silver **Ruler:** Ferdinand von Bayern **Obv:** Helmeted 4-fold arms with central shield of Bavaria-Pfalz **Rev:** St. Peter divides date **Note:** Dav.#5135.

Date	Mintage	F	VF	XF	Unc	BU
1617 Rare	—	—	—	—	—	—

KM# 59 2 THALER

Silver **Ruler:** Maximilian Heinrich von Bayern **Obv:** Bust of Maximillian right **Rev:** Capped arms divide date **Note:** Dav.#5148.

Date	Mintage	VG	F	VF	XF	Unc
1657	—	—	—	—	—	—

MB# 325 2-1/2 THALER

Silver **Ruler:** Gebhard (II), Truchsess von Waldburg-Trauchburg **Note:** Dav.#A9134. Similar to 1 Thaler, MB#312.

Date	Mintage	VG	F	VF	XF	Unc
(15)81	—	—	—	—	—	—

TRADE COINAGE

KM# 32 DUCAT

3.5000 g., 0.9860 Gold 0.1109 oz. AGW **Ruler:** Ferdinand von Bayern **Obv:** Radiant Madonna and child in inner circle **Rev:** Crowned arms in inner circle

Date	Mintage	VG	F	VF	XF	Unc
ND(1638)	—	450	875	2,000	3,850	—

KM# 47 DUCAT

3.5000 g., 0.9860 Gold 0.1109 oz. AGW **Ruler:** Maximilian Heinrich von Bayern **Obv:** Bust right in circle **Rev:** Crowned 4-fold arms of Cologne with central shield of Bavaria-Pfalz, DVCAT at bottom in legend

Date	Mintage	VG	F	VF	XF	Unc
ND(ca.1657)	—	525	975	2,300	4,300	—

KM# 56 DUCAT

3.5000 g., 0.9860 Gold 0.1109 oz. AGW **Ruler:** Maximilian Heinrich von Bayern **Obv:** Bust 3/4 to right, legend broken by top of head **Rev:** Crowned 4-fold arms of Cologne, central shield of Bavaria-Pfalz, date below

Date	Mintage	VG	F	VF	XF	Unc
1664	—	400	800	1,800	3,500	—

KM# 57 DUCAT

3.5000 g., 0.9860 Gold 0.1109 oz. AGW **Ruler:** Maximilian Heinrich von Bayern **Obv:** Bust right breaks top of circle

Date	Mintage	VG	F	VF	XF	Unc
1665 NK	—	500	900	2,150	4,000	—

KM# 78 DUCAT

3.5000 g., 0.9860 Gold 0.1109 oz. AGW **Ruler:** Josef Clemens von Bayern **Rev:** Crowned arms in inner circle

Date	Mintage	VG	F	VF	XF	Unc
1694 NL	—	700	1,400	2,600	5,000	—

KM# 82 DUCAT

3.5000 g., 0.9860 Gold 0.1109 oz. AGW **Ruler:** Josef Clemens von Bayern **Obv:** Bust of Josef Clemens right **Rev:** Seated Madonna and child with crowned arms at right

Date	Mintage	VG	F	VF	XF	Unc
1698 FW	—	1,400	2,800	5,200	10,000	—
1699 FW	—	1,400	2,800	5,200	10,000	—

KM# 79 3 DUCAT

10.5000 g., 0.9860 Gold 0.3328 oz. AGW **Ruler:** Josef Clemens von Bayern

Date	Mintage	VG	F	VF	XF	Unc
1696 FW	—	4,500	7,500	13,000	20,500	—
1696	—	4,500	7,500	13,000	20,500	—

KM# 69 10 DUCAT (Portugalöser)

35.0000 g., 0.9860 Gold 1.1095 oz. AGW **Ruler:** Sede Vacante **Obv:** St. Peter standing with shield **Note:** Sede Vacante Issue.

Date	Mintage	VG	F	VF	XF	Unc
1688 Rare	—	—	—	—	—	—

FREE CITY

(Köln)
CITY

One of the oldest cities in Europe, Cologne on the Rhine was founded as the Roman colony of Colonia Agrippinensis in 50 A.D. The town grew in importance after becoming the site of a bishopric and later an archbishopric. For two centuries beginning about the mid-10th century, Cologne contained an imperial mint. The archbishops had nominal control of the city until the 12th century. In 1201, Cologne joined the Hanseatic League and gained the right to govern itself in 1288. As the commercial importance of Cologne rose through membership in the League, it finally gained the mint right in 1474 and was soon striking its own coinage. The city remained in the Catholic fold after the Reformation, but its importance as a commercial center waned during the next several centuries. The French occupied Cologne in 1794 and annexed it three years later. At the end of the Napoleonic Wars in 1815, it was acquired by Prussia.

MINT OFFICIALS' INITIALS & MARKS

LETTER	DATE	NAME
	1506-11	Heinrich von Coisfeld, warden
	1511-14	Mintmaster
	1511-14	Arnt von Hamant, warden
	1515-18	Heinrich von Lynnar, mintmaster
	1515-18	Severin von Myle, warden
	1518-?	Johann von Eltmer, mintmaster
	1519-31	Kaspar Rave, warden
	1547-74	Ludwig Gronwalt, mintmaster
	1565-1608	Johann von Worringen, warden
	Ca. 1575	Meister Daniel, die-cutter?
	1567-1602	Jacob Lamberts, die-cutter
	1574-1602	Herbert Gronwalt
	Ca. 1575-79	Heinrich Attendahr, die-cutter
	1602-05	Reiner Gronwalt
	1602-08	Johann Lamberts, die-cutter
	1605-29	Johann Reess

	1608-43	Konrad Duisberg, warden
	1608-25	Peter Schlebusch, die-cutter
	1626-59	Hans Schwertzge, die-cutter
	1629-52	Hermann Cramer
	1642-?	Heinrich Mittweg, die-cutter
	1643-44	Johann Duisberg, warden
	1644-85	Friedrich Rodorff, warden
	1652-80	Kaspar Cramer
	1658-?	Georg Hartmann Plappert, die-cutter
	1659-1700	Jacob Leer, die-cutter
TB	1678-1717	Tobias Bernard, die-cutter in Paris
PN	1680-1698	Peter Newers, mintmaster
P	1685-1702	Johann Post, warden
NL	1699-1700	Nikolaus Longerich, mintmaster

ARMS

Divided horizontally, 3 crowns in upper half, lower half shaded, usually with cross-hatching, but sometimes with other devices.

REFERENCES

N = Alfred Noss, ***Die Münzen und Medaillen von Köln, v. 4, Die Münzen der Städte Köln und Neuss 1474-1794.*** Cologne, 1926

Sch = Wolfgang Schulten, ***Deutsche Münzen aus der Zeit Karls V.*** Frankfurt am Main, 1974.

REGULAR COINAGE

KM# 313 HELLER

Silver **Note:** Uniface. Hohl-type. City arms (3 crowns above arabesques) in shield, divide date where present.

Date	Mintage	VG	F	VF	XF	Unc
ND(1604-11)	10,340,000	5.00	10.00	25.00	45.00	—
1611	2,396,000	5.00	10.00	25.00	45.00	—

KM# 339 HELLER

Silver **Note:** Intertwined arabesques below crowns.

Date	Mintage	VG	F	VF	XF	Unc
ND(1635-52)	2,761,000	—	—	—	—	—

KM# 356 HELLER

Silver **Note:** Arms not in shield.

Date	Mintage	VG	F	VF	XF	Unc
ND(1653-64)	705,000	5.00	10.00	25.00	45.00	—

KM# 376 HELLER

Silver **Note:** Uniface. 2 spirals below crowns, separated by 2 parallel lines.

Date	Mintage	VG	F	VF	XF	Unc
ND(1676-77)	313,000	6.00	13.00	30.00	45.00	—

KM# 395 HELLER

Silver **Note:** Spirals separated from crowns by single line.

Date	Mintage	VG	F	VF	XF	Unc
ND(1692-94)	—	6.00	13.00	30.00	45.00	—

KM# 330 2 HELLER

Silver **Note:** Uniface. Hohl-type. City arms (3 crowns above arabesques.

Date	Mintage	VG	F	VF	XF	Unc
ND(ca.1625)	—	—	—	—	—	—

KM# 360 4 HELLER

Silver **Obv:** City arms (3 crowns above cross-hatch pattern) **Rev:** IIII in center, HELLER.COLON, date in legend

Date	Mintage	VG	F	VF	XF	Unc
1661	—	16.00	33.00	55.00	100	—
1662	16,000	10.00	16.00	33.00	65.00	—
1663	—	10.00	16.00	33.00	65.00	—
1681	—	10.00	16.00	33.00	65.00	—

KM# 361 4 HELLER

Silver **Rev:** 4 in center

Date	Mintage	VG	F	VF	XF	Unc
1662	—	13.00	27.00	45.00	80.00	—

KM# 314 8 HELLER (Fettmännchen)

Silver **Obv:** VIII in circle **Obv. Legend:** NVMMVS: COLONIENSIS **Rev:** Value LXX/IIII in circles, date **Rev. Legend:** CVSVS. COLONIAE **Note:** Legend varieties exist.

Date	Mintage	VG	F	VF	XF	Unc
1604	25,000	8.00	16.00	27.00	55.00	—
1605	318,000	8.00	16.00	27.00	55.00	—
1606	250,000	8.00	16.00	27.00	55.00	—
1608	122,000	8.00	16.00	27.00	55.00	—
1609	286,000	8.00	16.00	27.00	55.00	—
1610	213,000	8.00	16.00	27.00	55.00	—
1611	49,000	8.00	16.00	27.00	55.00	—

KM# 315 8 HELLER (Fettmännchen)

Silver **Obv:** KM#314 **Rev:** From die of Mulheim mint **Note:** Mule.

Date	Mintage	VG	F	VF	XF	Unc
1605	Inc. above	—	—	—	—	—
1608	Inc. above	—	—	—	—	—
1609	Inc. above	—	—	—	—	—

KM# 317 8 HELLER (Fettmännchen)

Silver **Obv:** From die of Julich **Rev:** KM#314 **Note:** Mule.

Date	Mintage	VG	F	VF	XF	Unc
1609	Inc. above	—	—	—	—	—
1610	Inc. above	—	—	—	—	—

KM# 320 8 HELLER (Fettmännchen)

Silver **Note:** Klippe.

Date	Mintage	VG	F	VF	XF	Unc
1610	—	—	—	—	—	—

KM# 328 8 HELLER (Fettmännchen)

Silver **Rev. Legend:** LXX/VIIII

Date	Mintage	VG	F	VF	XF	Unc
ND	—	6.00	13.00	25.00	50.00	—
1624	23,000	6.00	13.00	25.00	50.00	—
1625	182,000	6.00	13.00	25.00	50.00	—
1626	177,000	6.00	13.00	25.00	50.00	—
1627	104,000	6.00	13.00	25.00	50.00	—
1628	46,000	6.00	13.00	25.00	50.00	—
1629	111,000	6.00	13.00	25.00	50.00	—
1630	40,000	6.00	13.00	25.00	50.00	—
1631	44,000	6.00	13.00	25.00	50.00	—
1633	—	6.00	13.00	25.00	50.00	—
1649	42,000	6.00	13.00	25.00	50.00	—

KM# 375 2 ALBUS

Silver **Obv:** City arms (3 crowns above 2 intertwined arabesques) in ornate shield, date above 2.ALB in legend below **Rev:** Titles of Leopold I

Date	Mintage	VG	F	VF	XF	Unc
1674	—	6.50	13.00	30.00	60.00	—
1675	—	6.50	13.00	30.00	60.00	—
1676	122,000	6.50	13.00	30.00	60.00	—
1677	77,000	6.50	13.00	30.00	60.00	—
1678	177,000	6.50	13.00	30.00	60.00	—
1681 PN	—	6.50	13.00	30.00	60.00	—
1682 PN	—	6.50	13.00	30.00	60.00	—
1683 PN	—	6.50	13.00	30.00	60.00	—
1684 PN	—	6.50	13.00	30.00	60.00	—
1685 PN	31,000	6.50	13.00	30.00	60.00	—

KM# 332 4 ALBUS (Blaffert)

Silver **Obv:** Oval city arms (3 crowns above 11 flames) in baroque frame, date in legend, 4 below arms **Rev:** Crowned imperial eagle, orb on breast, titles of Ferdinand II

Date	Mintage	VG	F	VF	XF	Unc
1627	20,000	16.00	33.00	60.00	110	—

KM# 334 4 ALBUS (Blaffert)

Silver **Obv:** City arms (3 crowns above 2 intertwined arabesques) in ornate shield, date above, value in legend below

Date	Mintage	VG	F	VF	XF	Unc
1628	97,000	12.00	22.00	38.00	65.00	—
1629	55,000	12.00	22.00	38.00	65.00	—
1630	191,000	12.00	22.00	38.00	65.00	—
1631	56,000	12.00	22.00	38.00	65.00	—
1632	61,000	12.00	22.00	38.00	65.00	—
1633	79,000	12.00	22.00	38.00	65.00	—
1634	67,000	12.00	22.00	38.00	65.00	—
1635	39,000	12.00	22.00	38.00	65.00	—
1636	—	12.00	22.00	38.00	65.00	—

KM# 341 4 ALBUS (Blaffert)

Silver **Rev:** 11 flames in lower 1/2 of arms

Date	Mintage	VG	F	VF	XF	Unc
1636	—	13.00	25.00	40.00	75.00	—

KM# 346 4 ALBUS (Blaffert)

Silver **Obv:** 2 intertwined arabesques in lower 1/2 of arms **Rev:** Titles of Ferdinand III

Date	Mintage	VG	F	VF	XF	Unc
1638	19,000	13.00	25.00	40.00	75.00	—
1644	—	13.00	25.00	40.00	75.00	—
1645	—	13.00	25.00	40.00	75.00	—
1646	15,000	13.00	25.00	40.00	75.00	—
1647	12,000	13.00	25.00	40.00	75.00	—
1648/6	—	13.00	25.00	40.00	75.00	—
1651	6,000	13.00	25.00	40.00	75.00	—
1656	12,000	13.00	25.00	40.00	75.00	—
1657	10,000	13.00	25.00	40.00	75.00	—
1658	12,000	13.00	25.00	40.00	75.00	—

KM# 357 4 ALBUS (Blaffert)

Silver **Obv:** Titles of Leopold I

Date	Mintage	VG	F	VF	XF	Unc
1658	Inc. above	16.00	27.00	45.00	85.00	—
1659	28,000	16.00	27.00	45.00	85.00	—
1682 PN	—	16.00	27.00	45.00	85.00	—

KM# 335 8 ALBUS

Silver **Obv:** Crowned imperial eagle, orb on breast, titles of Ferdinand II **Rev:** Large, ornate plumed helmet, 8.ALB in legend below

Date	Mintage	VG	F	VF	XF	Unc
ND(ca.1631)	6,000	40.00	80.00	150	220	—

KM# 336 8 ALBUS

Silver **Obv:** Crowned imperial eagle, 8 in orb on breast, VIII/ALB above **Rev:** City arms (similar to KM#340) divide date, titles of Ferdinand II

Date	Mintage	VG	F	VF	XF	Unc
1633	1,404	33.00	65.00	120	200	—

KM# 340 8 ALBUS

Silver

Date	Mintage	VG	F	VF	XF	Unc
1635	12,000	27.00	45.00	80.00	140	—
1636	15,000	27.00	45.00	80.00	140	—
1637	6,000	27.00	45.00	80.00	140	—

KM# 342 8 ALBUS

Silver **Obv:** KM#344 **Rev:** KM#340 **Note:** Mule.

Date	Mintage	VG	F	VF	XF	Unc
1636	Inc. above	33.00	60.00	100	175	—

KM# 344 8 ALBUS

Silver **Obv:** Titles of Ferdinand III

Date	Mintage	VG	F	VF	XF	Unc
1637	Inc. above	27.00	45.00	80.00	140	—
1639	—	27.00	45.00	80.00	140	—
1641	37,000	27.00	45.00	80.00	140	—
1644	10,000	27.00	45.00	80.00	140	—

KM# 345 8 ALBUS

Silver **Obv:** 8/ALBUS/COLS in ornamented rhombus

Date	Mintage	VG	F	VF	XF	Unc
1637	Inc. above	27.00	45.00	80.00	140	—
1641	Inc. above	27.00	45.00	80.00	140	—
1644	Inc. above	27.00	45.00	80.00	140	—

KM# 370 1/16 THALER

Silver **Obv:** Similar to KM#371. **Rev:** Crowned imperial eagle, orb on breast, titles of Leopold I

Date	Mintage	VG	F	VF	XF	Unc
1670	—	30.00	55.00	90.00	170	—

KM# 371 1/16 THALER

Silver **Note:** Varieties exist.

Date	Mintage	VG	F	VF	XF	Unc
1670	—	27.00	45.00	80.00	140	—
1671	—	27.00	45.00	80.00	140	—

KM# 373 1/8 THALER

Silver

Date	Mintage	VG	F	VF	XF	Unc
1673	—	35.00	75.00	125	225	—
1674	—	50.00	90.00	155	300	—

KM# 374 1/8 THALER

Silver

Date	Mintage	VG	F	VF	XF	Unc
1673	—	45.00	80.00	140	275	—

KM# 386 1/4 THALER

Silver **Obv:** City arms (3 crowns above 2 intertwined arabesques), date above, all in square punched into square flan **Note:** Uniface. Klippe.

Date	Mintage	VG	F	VF	XF	Unc
1683 Rare	—	—	—	—	—	—

KM# 309 1/2 THALER

Silver **Obv:** Helmeted arms (3 crowns above arabesques), supported by lion and griffin, date in legend **Rev:** Crowned imperial eagle, orb on breast, titles of Rudolf II

Date	Mintage	VG	F	VF	XF	Unc
1602	—	—	—	—	—	—

KM# 326 1/2 THALER

Silver **Note:** Similar to 1 Thaler, KM#325.

Date	Mintage	VG	F	VF	XF	Unc
1621	—	—	—	—	—	—
1627	—	—	—	—	—	—

KM# 350 1/2 THALER

Silver **Subject:** Titles of Ferdinand III

Date	Mintage	VG	F	VF	XF	Unc
1641	—	—	—	—	—	—

KM# 387 1/2 THALER

Silver **Note:** Klippe. Similar to 1/4 Thaler, KM#386, but weight of 1/2 Thaler.

Date	Mintage	VG	F	VF	XF	Unc
1683 Rare	—	—	—	—	—	—

KM# 397 1/2 THALER

Silver **Note:** Similar to 1 Thaler, KM#398, BVRG 31/36 FVES below arms. Struck to Burgundian standard of fineness.

Date	Mintage	VG	F	VF	XF	Unc
1699 NL	—	—	—	—	—	—

KM# 396 2/3 THALER (Gulden)

Silver **Obv:** Supported arms in inner circle **Rev:** Crowned imperial eagle, orb on breast in inner circle **Note:** Varieties exist.

Date	Mintage	VG	F	VF	XF	Unc
1693 PN	—	65.00	135	250	475	—
1694 PN	—	65.00	135	250	475	—

Date	Mintage	VG	F	VF	XF	Unc
1695 PN	—	65.00	135	250	475	—
1700 IAL	—	65.00	135	250	475	—

KM# 401 2/3 THALER (Gulden)

Silver **Obv:** Arms surrounded by 2 laurel branches **Rev:** Crowned imperial eagle

Date	Mintage	VG	F	VF	XF	Unc
1700 IAL	—	100	185	350	575	—

KM# 400 2/3 THALER (Gulden)

Silver **Rev:** Arms flanked by 2 small palm branches **Note:** Known overstruck on 2/3 Thaler of Anhalt (1677), East Frisia (1694), Hanau (1694) and Saxe-Lauenburg (ca.1680). Some of the under types may show traces of the Franconian Circle countermark of 1693-5.

Date	Mintage	VG	F	VF	XF	Unc
1700 IAL	—	65.00	135	250	475	—

KM# 305.1 THALER

Silver **Obv:** Helmeted arms supported by a lion and griffin **Obv. Legend:** MO. NO. ARGEN. CIV. COLONIE **Rev:** Crowned double eagle w/orb on breast **Rev. Legend:** RVDOLP. II. IMP. AVG. P. F. DECRETO **Note:** Varieties exist. Dav.#5157.

Date	Mintage	VG	F	VF	XF	Unc
1602	2,000	300	500	850	1,450	—
1611	13,000	300	500	850	1,450	—

KM# 305.2 THALER

Silver **Note:** Klippe. Dav.#5157A.

Date	Mintage	VG	F	VF	XF	Unc
1601 Rare	5,000	—	—	—	—	—
1602 Rare	—	—	—	—	—	—
1611 Rare	—	—	—	—	—	—

KM# 306.1 THALER

Silver **Obv. Legend:** ROM . IMP . SEMP . AVGVST **Note:** Dav.#5160.

Date	Mintage	VG	F	VF	XF	Unc
1602	Inc. above	300	500	850	1,500	—

KM# 306.2 THALER

Silver **Note:** Klippe. Dav.#5160A.

Date	Mintage	VG	F	VF	XF	Unc
1603 Rare	8,000	—	—	—	—	—
1609 Rare	3,000	—	—	—	—	—
1610 Rare	5,000	—	—	—	—	—
1611 Rare	—	—	—	—	—	—

KM# 306.3 THALER

Silver **Rev. Legend:** ...COLONIAE **Note:** Varieties exist.

Date	Mintage	VG	F	VF	XF	Unc
1611 Rare	—	—	—	—	—	—

KM# 322.1 THALER

Silver **Obv. Legend:** FERDENANT. II. D.G. EL. RO. IM. SEM. AVG. **Note:** Similar to KM#322.2. Dav.#5161.

Date	Mintage	VG	F	VF	XF	Unc
1619	—	300	500	900	—	—

KM# 322.2 THALER

Silver **Note:** Dav.#5162.

Date	Mintage	VG	F	VF	XF	Unc
1619	—	350	600	1,000	—	—

KM# 325.1 THALER

Silver **Rev:** New shield **Note:** Dav.#5163.

Date	Mintage	VG	F	VF	XF	Unc
1620	—	300	500	800	—	—

KM# 325.2 THALER

Silver **Note:** Dav.#5166.

Date	Mintage	VG	F	VF	XF	Unc
1621	1,040	550	950	1,700	—	—
1622	6,000	500	850	1,500	—	—
1623	6,000	500	850	1,500	—	—
1624	9,000	500	850	1,500	—	—
1626	7,000	500	850	1,500	—	—
1627	11,000	500	850	1,500	—	—

KM# 325.3 THALER

Silver **Obv. Legend:** MO. NO-ARG. CIVI. COL **Rev. Legend:** ...AVGVS **Note:** Dav.#5167.

Date	Mintage	VG	F	VF	XF	Unc
1631	11,000	500	850	1,500	—	—

KM# 325.4 THALER

Silver **Rev. Legend:** ...AVG **Note:** Dav.#5168.

Date	Mintage	VG	F	VF	XF	Unc
1636/3	5,000	500	850	1,500	—	—
1636	Inc. above	500	850	1,500	—	—
1637	9,000	500	850	1,500	—	—

KM# 333 THALER

Silver **Note:** Klippe. Struck on flan of thaler weight from same dies.

Date	Mintage	VG	F	VF	XF	Unc
1627 Rare	Inc. above	—	—	—	—	—

KM# 343 THALER

Silver **Obv:** KM#325.2 **Rev:** KM#355 **Note:** Mule. Dav.#5169.

Date	Mintage	VG	F	VF	XF	Unc
1636	Inc. above	500	850	1,500	—	—

KM# 348 THALER

Silver **Rev:** Titles of Ferdinand III and without inner circles. **Note:** Similar to KM#325.2. Dav.#5171.

Date	Mintage	VG	F	VF	XF	Unc
1638	Inc. above	500	850	1,500	—	—
1643	6,000	500	850	1,500	—	—
1644	4,000	500	850	1,500	—	—
1645	23,000	500	850	1,500	—	—

KM# 347 THALER

Silver **Obv:** KM#325.2 **Rev:** KM#348 **Note:** Mule. Dav.#5168.

Date	Mintage	VG	F	VF	XF	Unc
1638	33,000	500	850	1,500	—	—

KM# 355 THALER

Silver **Note:** Similar to KM#325.2, but titles of Ferdinand III. Dav.#5169.

Date	Mintage	VG	F	VF	XF	Unc
1650	3,000	500	850	1,500	2,250	—

KM# 362 THALER

Silver **Obv:** 1/2 length crowned figure right holding orb and scepter **Note:** Dav.#5172.

Date	Mintage	VG	F	VF	XF	Unc
1663 Rare	—	—	—	—	—	—

KM# 363 THALER

Silver **Obv:** The Three Kings standing behind oval city arms in baroque frame, date below **Rev:** 3 persons on ship, other figures behind on dock

Date	Mintage	VG	F	VF	XF	Unc
1668 Rare	—	—	—	—	—	—

KM# 398 THALER

Silver **Obv:** Crowned imperial eagle with orb on breast divide date **Rev:** Helmeted arms supported by lion and griffin **Note:** Dav. #5173. Varieties exist.

Date	Mintage	F	VF	XF	Unc	BU
1699 NL	—	350	700	1,200	2,000	—
1700 NL	—	350	700	1,200	2,000	—
1700 IAL	—	350	700	1,200	2,000	—

KM# 310.1 2 THALER

Silver **Obv:** Helmeted arms supported by lion and griffon, Titles of Rudolf II **Rev:** Crowned imperial eagle with orb on breast **Note:** Dav.#A5156.

Date	Mintage	F	VF	XF	Unc	BU
1602 Rare	—	—	—	—	—	—

KM# 310.2 2 THALER

Silver **Note:** Klippe.

Date	Mintage	F	VF	XF	Unc	BU
1611 Rare	—	—	—	—	—	—

KM# 311 2 THALER

Silver **Obv. Legend:** ROM.IMP.SEMP.AVGVST **Note:** Klippe. Dav.#5159.

Date	Mintage	F	VF	XF	Unc	BU
1610 Rare	—	—	—	—	—	—

KM# 327 2 THALER

Silver **Note:** Similar to 1 Thaler, KM#325.2. Dav.#5165.

Date	Mintage	F	VF	XF	Unc	BU
1621 Rare	—	—	—	—	—	—
1622 Rare	—	—	—	—	—	—

KM# 351 2 THALER

Silver **Note:** Similar to 1 Thaler, KM#325.2, but titles of Ferdinand III and without inner circles. Dav.#5170.

Date	Mintage	F	VF	XF	Unc	BU
1643 Rare	—	—	—	—	—	—
1645 Rare	—	—	—	—	—	—

KM# 353 2 THALER

Silver **Note:** Klippe. Dav.#5170A.

Date	Mintage	F	VF	XF	Unc	BU
1645 Rare	—	—	—	—	—	—

KM# 364 2 THALER

Silver **Obv:** The Three King's standing behind oval city arms in baroque frame, date below **Rev:** 3 people in ship, other figures behind on dock

Date	Mintage	F	VF	XF	Unc	BU
1668 Rare	—	—	—	—	—	—
ND Rare	—	—	—	—	—	—

KM# 307.1 3 THALER

Silver **Obv:** Helmeted arms supported by lion and griffon **Rev:** Crowned double eagle w/orb on breast **Note:** Dav.#5156.

Date	Mintage	F	VF	XF	Unc	BU
1601 Rare	—	—	—	—	—	—

KM# 307.2 3 THALER

Silver **Obv. Legend:** ROM. IMP. SEMP. AVGVST **Note:** Klippe. Dav.#5158.

Date	Mintage	F	VF	XF	Unc	BU
1609 Rare	—	—	—	—	—	—
1611 Rare	—	—	—	—	—	—

KM# 331 3 THALER

Silver **Note:** Klippe. Similar to 1 Thaler, KM#325.2. Dav.#5164.

Date	Mintage	F	VF	XF	Unc	BU
1626 Rare	—	—	—	—	—	—

COUNTERMARKED COINAGE

KM# 377 36 ALBUS
Silver **Countermark:** 3 crowns above 36, small P (post) below **Note:** Countermark on Sayn-Wittgenstein 16 Gute Groschen.

CM Date	Host Date	Good	VG	F	VF	XF
ND	ND(ca.1695)	—	—	—	—	—

KM# 385 36 ALBUS
Silver **Countermark:** 3 crowns above 36, small P (post) below **Note:** Countermark on Sayn-Wittgenstein 2/3 Thaler.

CM Date	Host Date	Good	VG	F	VF	XF
ND	ND(ca.1695)	—	—	—	—	—

KM# 380 42 ALBUS
Silver **Countermark:** 3 crowns above 42, small P below **Note:** Countermark on Saxe-Gotha 2/3 Thaler.

CM Date	Host Date	Good	VG	F	VF	XF
ND	ND(ca.1695)	—	—	—	—	—

KM# 378 42 ALBUS
Silver **Countermark:** 3 crowns above 42, small P below **Note:** Countermark on Sayn-Wittgenstein 2/3 Thaler.

CM Date	Host Date	Good	VG	F	VF	XF
ND	ND(ca.1695)	—	—	—	—	—

KM# 390 44 ALBUS
Silver **Countermark:** 3 crowns above 44, small P below **Note:** Countermark on Saxe-Romhild 2/3 Thaler.

CM Date	Host Date	Good	VG	F	VF	XF
ND	ND(ca.1695)	—	—	—	—	—

KM# 389 46 ALBUS
Silver **Countermark:** 3 crowns above 46, small P below **Note:** Countermark on Mecklenburg-Gustrow 2/3 Thaler, KM#110.

CM Date	Host Date	Good	VG	F	VF	XF
ND	ND(ca.1695)	—	—	—	—	—

KM# 379 50 ALBUS
Silver **Countermark:** 3 crowns above 50, small P below **Note:** Countermark on Lübeck 2/3 Thaler.

CM Date	Host Date	Good	VG	F	VF	XF
ND	ND(ca.1695)	—	—	—	—	—

TRADE COINAGE

KM# 312 GOLDGULDEN
3.5000 g., 0.9860 Gold 0.1109 oz. AGW **Subject:** Titles of Rudolf II **Obv:** City arms with four shields in quatrefoil **Rev:** Crowned imperial eagle **Rev. Legend:** Titles of Rudolf II

Date	Mintage	VG	F	VF	XF	Unc
1603	1,069	220	450	875	1,550	—
1604	2,605	220	450	875	1,550	—
1605 2 known	3,000	—	—	—	—	—
1607	735	220	450	875	1,550	—
1608	1,069	220	450	875	1,550	—
1609 2 known	3,000	—	—	—	—	—
1610	3,000	220	450	875	1,550	—
1611	2,000	220	450	875	1,550	—

KM# 316 GOLDGULDEN
6.5300 g., 0.9860 Gold 0.2070 oz. AGW **Note:** Klippe.

Date	Mintage	VG	F	VF	XF	Unc
1605 Rare	—	—	—	—	—	—

KM# 323 GOLDGULDEN
3.5000 g., 0.9860 Gold 0.1109 oz. AGW **Subject:** Titles of Ferdinand II

Date	Mintage	VG	F	VF	XF	Unc
1619	—	300	600	1,200	2,250	—
1621	401	300	600	1,200	2,250	—
1622	8,000	300	600	1,200	2,250	—

KM# 329 GOLDGULDEN
3.5000 g., 0.9860 Gold 0.1109 oz. AGW

Date	Mintage	VG	F	VF	XF	Unc
1624	1,737	350	700	1,400	2,750	—
1625	9,000	350	700	1,400	2,750	—
1628	9,000	350	700	1,400	2,750	—
1631	4,000	350	700	1,400	2,750	—
1633	4,000	350	700	1,400	2,750	—
1634	534	350	700	1,400	2,750	—

KM# 388 1/2 DUCAT
1.7500 g., 0.9860 Gold 0.0555 oz. AGW **Note:** Klippe. Similar to 1/4 Thaler, KM#386.

Date	Mintage	VG	F	VF	XF	Unc
1683 Rare	—	—	—	—	—	—

KM# 337 DUCAT
3.5000 g., 0.9860 Gold 0.1109 oz. AGW **Obv:** Arms in inner circle **Rev:** Value in tablet

Date	Mintage	VG	F	VF	XF	Unc
1634	—	1,600	3,150	6,500	11,500	—

KM# 338 DUCAT
3.5000 g., 0.9860 Gold 0.1109 oz. AGW **Subject:** Titles of Ferdinand II

Date	Mintage	VG	F	VF	XF	Unc
1634	—	180	300	650	1,200	—
1635	2,664	180	300	650	1,200	—
1636	12,000	180	300	650	1,200	—

KM# 352 DUCAT
3.5000 g., 0.9860 Gold 0.1109 oz. AGW **Subject:** Titles of Ferdinand III

Date	Mintage	VG	F	VF	XF	Unc
1643	2,806	150	250	550	1,000	—
1644	13,000	150	250	550	1,000	—
Note: Orb in right hand						
1650	5,155	150	250	550	1,000	—
1652	802	—	—	—	—	—
1653	802	—	—	—	—	—
1654	1,670	—	—	—	—	—
1655	4,609	150	250	550	1,000	—
1657	1,202	150	250	550	1,000	—

KM# 358 DUCAT
3.5000 g., 0.9860 Gold 0.1109 oz. AGW **Subject:** Titles of Leopold

Date	Mintage	VG	F	VF	XF	Unc
1659/7	400	1,000	1,750	2,500	3,250	—
1661	—	200	400	750	1,250	—
1662	802	300	600	1,000	1,800	—
1664	2,338	200	400	750	1,250	—
1668	2,271	200	400	750	1,250	—
1672	—	200	400	750	1,250	—

KM# 372 DUCAT
3.5000 g., 0.9860 Gold 0.1109 oz. AGW **Obv:** Laureate bust of Leopold right **Rev:** Similar to KM#352

Date	Mintage	VG	F	VF	XF	Unc
1671	—	280	550	1,200	2,250	—

KM# 365 DUCAT
3.5000 g., 0.9860 Gold 0.1109 oz. AGW **Subject:** Titles of Leopold

Date	Mintage	VG	F	VF	XF	Unc
1681	—	300	600	1,350	2,500	—
1689 PN	—	300	600	1,350	2,500	—
1693 PN	—	300	600	1,350	2,500	—

KM# 321 4 DUCAT
14.0000 g., 0.9860 Gold 0.4438 oz. AGW **Obv:** The Three Wise Men **Rev:** St. Ursula in medieval ship

Date	Mintage	VG	F	VF	XF	Unc
1612 Rare	—	—	—	—	—	—

KM# 308 6 DUCAT
21.0000 g., 0.9860 Gold 0.6657 oz. AGW **Obv:** The Three Wise Men **Rev:** St. Ursula in medieval ship

Date	Mintage	VG	F	VF	XF	Unc
ND(ca.1601) Rare	—	—	—	—	—	—

KM# A309 7 DUCAT
24.5000 g., 0.9860 Gold 0.7766 oz. AGW **Note:** Similar to 6 Ducat, KM#308.

Date	Mintage	VG	F	VF	XF	Unc
ND(ca.1601) Rare	—	—	—	—	—	—

PATTERNS

Including off metal strikes

KM#	Date	Mintage	Identification	Mkt Val
Pn1	1698 FW	—	Ducat. Silver. KM#82.	—
Pn2	1699 FW	—	8 Heller. Gold. KM#83.	—
Pn3	1700	—	1/3 Thaler. Copper. KM#85.	—
Pn10	ND(1604-11)	—	Heller. Gold. KM#313.	550
Pn11	1610	—	8 Heller. Gold. KM#314.	—
Pn12	1610	—	8 Heller. Gold. KM#317.	—
PnA13	1624	—	8 Heller. Gold. KM#328.	—
Pn13	ND(ca.1625)	—	2 Heller. Gold. KM#330.	—
Pn14	1627	—	8 Heller. Gold. KM#328.	—
Pn15	ND(1635-52)	—	Heller. Gold. KM#339.	—
Pn16	1641	—	8 Albus. Gold. KM#345.	—
Pn17	ND(1653-64)	—	Heller. Gold. KM#356.	—
Pn18	1663	—	4 Heller. Gold. KM#360.	—
Pn19	ND(1676-77)	—	Heller. Gold. KM#376.	—
Pn20	ND(1692-94)	—	Heller. Gold. KM#395.	—

CONSTANCE

(Konstanz, Kostnitz, Costnitz)

This bishopric, which is centered on the city of the same name, was transferred to that location from Vindinissa in Aargau late in the 6th century. The first episcopal coinage was produced at the end of the 9th century and minting continued intermittently during the next 850 years. By the time of the Protestant Reformation, the bishop had become a Prince of the Empire and ruled over a large expanse of territory encompassing much of what is now southwest Germany and northern Switzerland. In 1527, Bishop Hugo refused to submit to the Reformation and was forced to flee the city. He went to Meersburg, across the lake on the north shore, and it became the bishop's residence until the diocese was secularized in 1802. It was acquired by Baden along with the city at that time.

RULERS

Hugo von Hohenlandenberg, 1st reign, 1496-1529
Balthasar Merklin (Merkler), 1529-1531
Hugo, 2nd reign, 1531-1532
Johann II, Graf von Lupfen, 1532-1537
Johann III von Welza (Weza), 1537-1548
Christoph Metzler von Andelberg, 1548-1561
Marcus Sittich, Graf von Hohenembs, 1561-1589
Andreas, Grossherzog von Österreich, 1589-1600
Johann Georg von Hallwyl, 1601-1604
Jacob, Graf von Fugger-Weissenhorn, 1604-1626
Sixtus Werner von Prassberg, 1626-1627
Johann IV, Truchsess von Waldburg, 1628-1644
Johann Franz I von Prassberg, 1644-1689
Markwart Rudolf von Rodt, 1689-1704

ARMS

Plain cross

MINT MARKS

G = Günzburg Mint

REFERENCES

SCH = Wolfgang Schulten, ***Deutsche Münzen aus der Zeit Karls V.*** Frankfurt am Main, 1974
S = Hugo Frhr. Von Saurma-Jeltsch, ***Schlesische Münzen Und Medaillen***, Breslau, 1883.

BISHOPRIC

REGULAR COINAGE

KM# 5 4 HELLER
Copper **Ruler:** Johann Georg von Hallwyl **Obv:** Oval arms (cross) in baroque, G. 4. E. above (Georgius Episcopus), all in laurel wreath **Note:** Uniface.

Date	Mintage	VG	F	VF	XF	Unc
ND(1601-1604)	—	16.00	33.00	55.00	90.00	—

KM# 6 4 HELLER
Copper **Note:** Only 4 above arms.

Date	Mintage	VG	F	VF	XF	Unc
ND(1604-1626)	—	16.00	33.00	55.00	90.00	—

FREE CITY

Located at the western end of the Bodensee (Lake Constance) and on the German-Swiss border, Constance stands on the site of the late Roman fortress of Constantia. When the bishopric in Aargau was transferred to the place shortly before 600, the town began to grow in importance. An Imperial mint was established in Constance at the beginning of the 11th century and it functioned until about 1250. Constance became an imperial free city in either 1192 or 1255, but the bishop controlled most of its affairs at least until the Protestant Reformation. The city joined the League of Schmalkalden in 1530, but was the lone Protestant holdout in the region after 1547. Karl V took Constance in 1548 and incorporated it into his Austrian realm. The city retained its coinage rights, however, and continued minting until about 1733. Constance became part of Baden in 1803.

MINT OFFICIALS' INITIALS

Initial	Date	Name
	1620	Martin Stoff
	1621-22	Martin Näf and Johann Rudolf Wegerich
	1642	Marx Stütz, warden
	1652-56	Franz Änzinger
	1652-56	Jakob Weingartner, warden
	1676-80	Franz Staiffel
	1676-86	Hans Konrad Betzerin, warden

ARMS

Cross, horizontal bar usually shaded, often a single-headed eagle above

REFERENCE

N = Elisabeth Nau, ***Die Münzen und Medaillen des oberschwäbischen Städte***. Freiburg im Breisgau, 1964

REGULAR COINAGE

KM# 163 PFENNIG

Billon **Obv:** City arms, 6-pointed star above **Note:** Uniface.

Date	Mintage	VG	F	VF	XF	Unc
ND(1653-55)	—	9.00	20.00	33.00	60.00	—

KM# 175 PFENNIG

Copper **Obv:** City arms, C above **Note:** Uniface.

Date	Mintage	VG	F	VF	XF	Unc
ND(1671-1674)	—	9.00	20.00	33.00	60.00	—

KM# 176 PFENNIG

Copper **Obv:** City arms, date above. **Note:** Varieties exist.

Date	Mintage	VG	F	VF	XF	Unc
1675	—	8.00	16.00	27.00	50.00	—
1676	—	8.00	16.00	27.00	50.00	—
1677	—	8.00	16.00	27.00	50.00	—
1678	—	8.00	16.00	27.00	50.00	—
1679	—	8.00	16.00	27.00	50.00	—
1680	—	8.00	16.00	27.00	50.00	—
1681	—	8.00	16.00	27.00	50.00	—
1684	—	8.00	16.00	27.00	50.00	—
1686	—	8.00	16.00	27.00	50.00	—
1687	—	8.00	16.00	27.00	50.00	—
1688	—	8.00	16.00	27.00	50.00	—
1689	—	8.00	16.00	27.00	50.00	—
1690	—	8.00	16.00	27.00	50.00	—
1691	—	8.00	16.00	27.00	50.00	—

Note: NOTE: Varieties exist.</p>

KM# 190 PFENNIG

Billon **Note:** Uniface. City arms in cartouche, date divided by C above.

Date	Mintage	VG	F	VF	XF	Unc
1700	—	20.00	40.00	70.00	125	—

KM# 110 2 PFENNIG (Zweier)

Silver **Obv:** City arms in quatrefoil, C above **Note:** Uniface.

Date	Mintage	VG	F	VF	XF	Unc
ND(1622)	—	—	—	—	—	—

KM# 111 4 PFENNIG (Kreuzer)

Silver **Obv:** Oval city arms, 4 above, all in wreath **Note:** Uniface.

Date	Mintage	VG	F	VF	XF	Unc
ND(ca.1622)	—	—	—	—	—	—

KM# 134 6 PFENNIG (Sechser)

Silver **Obv:** City arms in quatrefoil **Rev:** Eagle with oval shield on breast divides date and value V-I

Date	Mintage	VG	F	VF	XF	Unc
(16)26	—	60.00	120	240	375	—

KM# 137 6 PFENNIG (Sechser)

Silver **Rev:** Value VI below eagle

Date	Mintage	VG	F	VF	XF	Unc
(16)27	—	60.00	120	240	375	—

KM# 166 KREUZER

Billon **Obv:** City arms with double-cross behind **Rev:** Eagle with arms on breast **Note:** Varieties exist.

Date	Mintage	VG	F	VF	XF	Unc
ND(1657-1705)	—	10.00	20.00	35.00	75.00	—

KM# 165 KREUZER

Silver **Obv:** City arms with double-cross (*), value 1 below **Rev:** Crowned imperial eagle, titles of Leopold I

Date	Mintage	VG	F	VF	XF	Unc
ND	—	9.00	20.00	40.00	85.00	—

KM# 130 1/2 BATZEN (2 Kreuzer)

Silver **Obv:** City arms divide date **Rev:** Imperial eagle, 2 in orb on breast, titles of Ferdinand II

Date	Mintage	VG	F	VF	XF	Unc
(16)24	—	27.00	55.00	100	180	—
(16)25	—	27.00	55.00	100	180	—

KM# 131 1/2 BATZEN (2 Kreuzer)

Silver **Note:** Klippe.

Date	Mintage	VG	F	VF	XF	Unc
(16)24	—	—	—	—	—	—
(16)25	—	—	—	—	—	—

KM# 133 1/2 BATZEN (2 Kreuzer)

Silver **Note:** Klippe.

Date	Mintage	VG	F	VF	XF	Unc
(16)25	—	—	—	—	—	—

KM# 132 1/2 BATZEN (2 Kreuzer)

Silver **Rev:** Crowned imperial eagle

Date	Mintage	VG	F	VF	XF	Unc
(16)25	—	27.00	55.00	100	175	—
(16)26	—	27.00	55.00	100	175	—

KM# 160 1/2 BATZEN (2 Kreuzer)

Silver **Obv:** Date above arms **Rev:** Value 2 below eagle, titles of Ferdinand III

Date	Mintage	VG	F	VF	XF	Unc
1652	—	25.00	45.00	90.00	165	—
1653	—	25.00	45.00	90.00	165	—

KM# 164 1/2 BATZEN (2 Kreuzer)

Silver **Obv:** Date divided by arms

Date	Mintage	VG	F	VF	XF	Unc
1654	—	25.00	45.00	90.00	180	—

KM# 118 3 KREUZER (Groschen)

Silver **Obv:** Crowned imperial eagle, shield on breast, value 3 below, titles of Ferdinand II **Rev:** City arms in quatrefoil **Note:** Varieties exist.

Date	Mintage	VG	F	VF	XF	Unc
ND	—	27.00	55.00	100	170	—

KM# 150 3 KREUZER (Groschen)

Silver **Obv:** Titles of Ferdinand III **Rev:** City arms in ornate shield

Date	Mintage	VG	F	VF	XF	Unc
ND	—	33.00	65.00	120	200	—

KM# 154 3 KREUZER (Groschen)

Silver **Obv:** Crowned shield divides 1-6 above 2 shields, with 39 below **Rev:** 3 in orb on breast

Date	Mintage	VG	F	VF	XF	Unc
1639	—	25.00	45.00	80.00	150	—

KM# 180 3 KREUZER (Groschen)

Silver **Obv:** Titles of Leopold I

Date	Mintage	VG	F	VF	XF	Unc
1680	—	25.00	45.00	80.00	150	—

KM# 185 3 KREUZER (Groschen)

Silver **Obv:** City arms in ornate shield, date in legend **Rev:** Titles of Leopold I

Date	Mintage	VG	F	VF	XF	Unc
1694	—	20.00	40.00	70.00	120	—

KM# 151 10 KREUZER

Silver **Obv:** Titles of Ferdinand III **Rev:** Ornate city arms

Date	Mintage	VG	F	VF	XF	Unc
ND	—	—	—	—	—	—

KM# 119 10 KREUZER

Silver **Obv:** City arms in quatrefoil, date in legend **Rev:** Crowned imperial eagle, value 10 below, titles of Ferdinand II **Note:** Varieties exist.

Date	Mintage	VG	F	VF	XF	Unc
(16)23	—	16.00	33.00	60.00	120	—
ND	—	16.00	33.00	60.00	120	—

KM# 115 3 BATZEN (Dreibätzener)

Silver **Obv:** City arms, date in legend **Rev:** Imperial eagle, value 3 below, titles of Ferdinand II

Date	Mintage	VG	F	VF	XF	Unc
1622	—	40.00	80.00	145	240	—
ND	—	40.00	80.00	145	240	—

KM# 116 3 BATZEN (Dreibätzener)

Silver **Obv:** Arms divide date

Date	Mintage	VG	F	VF	XF	Unc
1622	—	40.00	80.00	145	240	—
1623	—	40.00	80.00	145	240	—
1624	—	40.00	80.00	145	240	—

KM# 120 3 BATZEN (Dreibätzener)

Silver **Note:** Klippe.

Date	Mintage	VG	F	VF	XF	Unc
1623	—	—	—	1,500	2,500	—
1624	—	—	—	1,500	2,500	—

KM# 135 3 BATZEN (12 Kreuzer)

Silver **Rev:** Crowned imperial eagle, value XII below

Date	Mintage	VG	F	VF	XF	Unc
1626	—	40.00	80.00	150	250	—
ND(1626)	—	40.00	80.00	150	250	—

KM# 138 3 BATZEN (12 Kreuzer)

Silver **Obv:** Date above arms **Rev:** Without indication of value

Date	Mintage	VG	F	VF	XF	Unc
1628	—	—	—	—	—	—

KM# 139 3 BATZEN (12 Kreuzer)

Silver **Obv:** City arms in quatrefoil **Rev:** Crowned imperial eagle, value below

Date	Mintage	VG	F	VF	XF	Unc
ND	—	45.00	90.00	170	275	—

KM# 140 3 BATZEN (12 Kreuzer)
Silver **Rev:** 3 arms (1 above 2) between branches

Date	Mintage	VG	F	VF	XF	Unc
ND	—	45.00	90.00	170	275	—

KM# 141 3 BATZEN (12 Kreuzer)
Silver **Obv:** Without branches

Date	Mintage	VG	F	VF	XF	Unc
ND	—	45.00	90.00	170	275	—

KM# 112 15 KREUZER
Silver **Obv:** Saints Pelagius and Conrad behind city arms **Rev:** Crowned imperial eagle, 15 on breast, titles of Ferdinand II

Date	Mintage	VG	F	VF	XF	Unc
ND(1622)	—	110	220	400	675	—

KM# 113 15 KREUZER
7.4300 g., Silver **Note:** Klippe.

Date	Mintage	VG	F	VF	XF	Unc
ND	—	—	400	750	1,200	—

KM# 114 15 KREUZER
5.3600 g., Silver **Note:** Octagonal Klippe.

Date	Mintage	VG	F	VF	XF	Unc
ND(1622)	—	—	425	800	1,250	—

KM# 152 15 KREUZER
Silver **Obv:** Oval arms with date below

Date	Mintage	VG	F	VF	XF	Unc
1636	—	45.00	100	180	300	—

KM# 153 15 KREUZER
Silver **Obv:** Titles of Ferdinand III

Date	Mintage	VG	F	VF	XF	Unc
ND	—	—	—	—	—	—

KM# 177 15 KREUZER
Silver **Obv:** Titles of Leopold I

Date	Mintage	VG	F	VF	XF	Unc
1679	—	55.00	115	200	350	—

KM# 136 6 BATZEN (24 Kreuzer)
Silver **Obv:** City arms in quatrefoil **Rev:** Crowned imperial eagle, date below, titles of Ferdinand II

Date	Mintage	VG	F	VF	XF	Unc
1626	—	55.00	115	210	275	—
1627	—	55.00	115	210	275	—
1630	—	55.00	115	210	275	—
1633/0	—	55.00	115	210	275	—
1633	—	55.00	115	210	275	—

KM# 181 6 BATZEN (24 Kreuzer)
Silver **Obv:** Titles of Leopold I

Date	Mintage	VG	F	VF	XF	Unc
1681	—	—	—	—	—	—

KM# 181.1 6 BATZEN (24 Kreuzer)
Silver **Obv:** Large city shield in quadralobe **Obv. Legend:** *MO: NO: CIVI: CONSTANTIEN **Rev:** Crowned imperial eagle, date in exergue **Rev. Legend:** LEOPOLDVS•D•G•R•I•S•A•G•H•B•R

Date	Mintage	VG	F	VF	XF	Unc
1681	—	165	325	525	925	1,700

KM# 181.2 6 BATZEN (24 Kreuzer)
Silver **Obv:** Small city shield in more ornate quadralobe **Obv. Legend:** *MONETA: NOVA: CIVITATIS: CONSTANTIENSIS **Rev:** Crowned imperial eagle, date in exergue **Rev. Legend:** LEOPOLDVS . D . G . I . S . A . G . H . ET . B . REX

Date	Mintage	VG	F	VF	XF	Unc
1681	—	200	400	700	1,100	1,850

KM# 121 1/2 THALER
Silver **Obv:** Saints Pelagius and Conrad standing behind city arms **Rev:** Crowned imperial eagle, titles of Ferdinand II

Date	Mintage	VG	F	VF	XF	Unc
ND(1622)	—	450	850	1,600	3,000	—

KM# 122 1/2 THALER
Silver **Note:** Klippe.

Date	Mintage	VG	F	VF	XF	Unc
ND(1622)	—	—	—	—	—	—

KM# 123 1/2 THALER
Silver **Obv:** City arms divide date

Date	Mintage	VG	F	VF	XF	Unc
16Z3	—	200	400	750	1,250	—

KM# 105 THALER
Silver **Obv:** Saints Pelagius and Conrad standing behind city arms **Rev:** Crowned imperial eagle, titles of Ferdinand II **Note:** Struck on thick flan. Dav. #5174.

Date	Mintage	F	VF	XF	Unc	BU
ND(1619-1637)	—	3,500	5,500	8,500	—	—

KM# 124 THALER
Silver **Note:** Regiments Thaler. Similar to 2 Thaler, KM#128. Dav. #5176.

Date	Mintage	F	VF	XF	Unc	BU
1623	—	1,000	1,800	2,750	—	—

KM# 125.1 THALER
Silver **Obv:** Large city shield divides date **Obv. Legend:** MON: NO: CIVITAT: CONSTANTIENSIS **Rev:** Titles of Ferdinand II **Rev. Legend:** FERD: II: D: G: ROM: IMP: ... **Note:** Dav. #5177.

Date	Mintage	F	VF	XF	Unc	BU
16Z3	—	165	300	500	—	—
16Z4	—	165	300	500	—	—
16Z5	—	165	300	500	—	—
16Z6	—	165	300	500	—	—

KM# 126 THALER
28.8600 g., Silver **Note:** Klippe. Struck on square flan with 1/2 thaler dies, KM#123.

Date	Mintage	F	VF	XF	Unc	BU
16Z3	—	2,500	4,500	7,500	—	—

KM# 125.2 THALER
Silver **Obv:** Sprays around shield **Note:** Dav. #5178. Varieties exist.

Date	Mintage	F	VF	XF	Unc	BU
16Z8	—	300	500	800	—	—

KM# 142 THALER
Silver **Obv:** City view, CONSTANTIA in exergue **Rev:** Five shields in center surrounded by 22 shields **Note:** Regiments Thaler. Dav. #5179.

Date	Mintage	F	VF	XF	Unc	BU
1629	—	900	1,500	2,500	—	—

KM# 127 1-1/2 THALER
Silver **Note:** Regiments 1-1/2 Thaler. Klippe. Similar to 2 Thaler, KM#128. Dav. #5175B.

Date	Mintage	F	VF	XF	Unc	BU
16Z3	—	1,500	2,500	3,750	—	—

KM# 128 2 THALER
Silver **Note:** Regiments 2 Thaler. Dav. #5171A.

Date	Mintage	F	VF	XF	Unc	BU
16Z3	—	2,000	3,500	5,500	—	—

KM# A130 2 THALER
56.2900 g., Silver **Note:** Similar to 1 Thaler, KM#125.1. Dav. #A5177.

Date	Mintage	F	VF	XF	Unc	BU
16Z3	—	4,000	7,000	12,000	—	—

KM# A126 2 THALER

Silver **Obv:** Large city shield divides date **Obv. Legend:** MON: NO: CIVITAT: CONSTANTIENSIS **Rev:** Crowned imperial eagle **Rev. Legend:** FERD: II: D: G: ROM: IMP: ... **Note:** Dav. #A5177.

Date	Mintage	VG	F	VF	XF	Unc
16Z3	—	—	1,000	2,000	3,250	5,500

KM# 129 2-1/2 THALER

Silver **Note:** Regiments 2-1/2 Thaler. Klippe. Similar to 2 Thaler, KM#128. Dav. #5175.

Date	Mintage	F	VF	XF	Unc	BU
16Z3 Rare	—	—	—	—	—	—

TRADE COINAGE

KM# 143 GOLDGULDEN

3.5000 g., 0.9860 Gold 0.1109 oz. AGW **Obv:** Arms of Constance **Rev:** Eagle, titles of Ferdinand II, date **Note:** Fr.#843.

Date	Mintage	VG	F	VF	XF	Unc
1629	—	1,050	2,100	5,300	9,100	—

KM# 161 DUCAT

3.5000 g., 0.9860 Gold 0.1109 oz. AGW **Obv:** Oval city arms, date above **Obv. Legend:** DVCATVS • NOVVS • CIVI • CONSTANTENS **Rev:** Crowned imperial eagle, titles of Ferdinand III **Rev. Legend:** FERDINAND: III • D • G • ROM • IMP • S • AVG • **Note:** Fr. #844.

Date	Mintage	VG	F	VF	XF	Unc
1652	—	850	1,750	4,000	6,500	—
1654	—	850	1,750	4,000	6,500	—
ND	—	850	1,750	4,000	6,500	—

KM# 162 DUCAT

3.5000 g., 0.9860 Gold 0.1109 oz. AGW **Note:** Klippe.

Date	Mintage	VG	F	VF	XF	Unc
ND	—	—	—	—	—	—

KM# 117 2 DUCAT

7.0000 g., 0.9860 Gold 0.2219 oz. AGW **Obv:** Arms of Constance, date in legend **Rev:** Crowned imperial eagle, titles of Ferdinand II

Date	Mintage	VG	F	VF	XF	Unc
1622 Rare	—	—	—	—	—	—

KM# 155 2 DUCAT

7.0000 g., 0.9860 Gold 0.2219 oz. AGW **Subject:** Titles of Ferdinand III **Note:** Klippe. Fr.#842. (ND1600's).

Date	Mintage	VG	F	VF	XF	Unc
ND(1601) Rare	—	—	—	—	—	—

CORVEY

(Corvei-Corbie-Corbey-Curbei)

Located on the Weser River just east of Höxter in Westphalia, the Benedictine abbey of Corvey was founded in 820 at the instigation of Emperor Ludwig the Pious (814-40) by monks from the monastery of Corbei in Picardy. Not long after it was established, the new abbey received the mint right as stated in the surviving document dated 1 June 833. Over the next several decades, Corvey also received the right to mint coins in several nearby towns including Marsberg and Meppen. Except for a long period between about 1370 and 1500, Corvey produced a long series of coinage. In 1793, the abbey was transformed into a bishopric, but did not long remain an independent entity. Corvey was secularized in 1803 and its territory was acquired by Nassau-Dietz the same year. After having been incorporated into the Kingdom of Westphalia (1807-13) during the Napoleonic Wars, Corvey was absorbed by Prussia in 1813. Corvey struck some joint issues with Höxter and these are included here.

RULERS

Hermann III von Bömmelberg, 1479-1504
Franz von Ketteler, 1504-1547
Kaspar I von Hörsel, 1547-1555
Reinhard II von Bocholz, 1555-1585
Dietrich IV von Beringhausen, 1585-1616
Heinrich V von Aschenbrok, 1616-1624
Johann Christoph von Brambach, 1624-1638
Arnold IV von Waldois, 1638-1661
Christof Bernhard von Galen, 1661-1678
Christof von Bellinghausen, 1678-1696
Florenz von der Velde, 1696-1714

MINT OFFICIALS' INITIALS

Initial	Date	Name
	1552-58?	Johann von Köln, mintmaster
	Ca. 1558-69?	Anna, widow of Johann, mintmistress
	1561-64	Johann von Geismar, warden
	1606-09	Jakob Pfaler, mintmaster in Marsberg
	1610-19	In Corvey
GB	1683-88	Beorg Binnenbose in Höxter
GIH	Ca.1686	Unknown
GK	1646	Georg Kruckenberg in Höxter
(h)	Ca.1631-32	Unknown
HC	Ca.1649	Unknown
HCH	1689-1729	Heinrich Christoph Hille in Brunswick
HK	1612-13	Unknown
HL	1607-11	Hans Laschentweiss in Moritzburg bei Hildesheim
HO/HLO	1698-1706	Heinrich Laurenz Odendahl in Westphalia
IO	1689-99	Johann Odendahl in Höxter
VF/VFH	1655-57, 1659-?	Urban Felgenhauer in Höxter

ARMS

2-fold divided horizontally, lower half usually shaded by various devices.

REFERENCES

W = Joseph Weingärtner, ***Die Gold = und Silber = Münzen der Abtei Corvey***, Münster, 1883.
Sch = Wolfgang Schulten, ***Deutsche Münzen aus der Zeit Karls V.*** Frankfurt am Main, 1974.

BENEDICTINE ABBEY

REGULAR COINAGE

KM# 33 PFENNIG

Copper **Ruler:** Johann Christoph **Obv:** Arms of Brambach (comb and diagonal bar) **Obv. Legend:** IO. CH. ABB. COR **Rev:** I in center, date **Rev. Legend:** S. VITVS

Date	Mintage	VG	F	VF	XF	Unc
1638	—	40.00	70.00	130	230	—

KM# 34 PFENNIG

Copper **Ruler:** Arnold IV **Obv:** Large A in center **Obv. Legend:** D. G. ABBAS. COR **Rev:** I in center **Rev. Legend:** LANT: MVNT

Date	Mintage	VG	F	VF	XF	Unc
ND(1638-1661)	—	45.00	95.00	175	300	—

KM# 35 PFENNIG

Silver **Ruler:** Arnold IV **Obv:** 4-fold arms **Rev:** Imperial orb with 2 **Rev. Legend:** ABBAS. CORBEINEN

Date	Mintage	VG	F	VF	XF	Unc
ND(1638-1661)	—	120	200	325	—	—

KM# 40 PFENNIG

Copper **Ruler:** Arnold IV **Obv:** Arms of Waldois (ox-head) **Obv. Legend:** ARNOLD **Rev:** I in center, date **Rev. Legend:** S. VITVS **Note:** Varieties exist.

Date	Mintage	VG	F	VF	XF	Unc
1640	—	40.00	80.00	145	235	—
1641	—	40.00	80.00	145	235	—
1642	—	40.00	80.00	145	235	—
1644	—	40.00	80.00	145	235	—
1646	—	40.00	80.00	145	235	—

KM# 83 PFENNIG

Silver **Ruler:** Christof **Note:** Uniface. Hohl-type. Crowned C divides date.

Date	Mintage	VG	F	VF	XF	Unc
1683	—	135	270	400	600	—

KM# 19 3 PFENNIG (Dreier)

Silver **Ruler:** Heinrich V **Obv:** Arms of abbey divide M.N.-A.C **Rev:** Imperial orb with 3 divides date **Note:** Varieties exist.

Date	Mintage	VG	F	VF	XF	Unc
1621	—	25.00	45.00	80.00	140	—
1622	—	25.00	45.00	80.00	140	—
1623	—	25.00	45.00	80.00	140	—

KM# 36 3 PFENNIG (Dreier)

Copper **Ruler:** Johann Christoph **Obv:** Arms of Brambach (comb and diagonal bar) **Obv. Legend:** IO. CH. ABB. COR **Rev:** III in center, date **Rev. Legend:** S VITVS

Date	Mintage	VG	F	VF	XF	Unc
1638	—	40.00	65.00	120	200	—

KM# 41 3 PFENNIG (Dreier)

Copper **Ruler:** Arnold IV **Obv:** Arms of Waldois (ox-head) **Obv. Legend:** ARNOLD

Date	Mintage	VG	F	VF	XF	Unc
1641	—	40.00	65.00	120	200	—
1642	—	40.00	65.00	120	200	—
1649	—	40.00	65.00	120	200	—

KM# 84 3 PFENNIG (Dreier)

Silver **Ruler:** Christof **Obv:** 4-fold arms in ornate shield **Obv. Legend:** F. C. L. M **Rev:** Imperial orb with 3 divides date

Date	Mintage	VG	F	VF	XF	Unc
1683	—	20.00	40.00	70.00	125	—

KM# 44 4 PFENNIG

Copper **Ruler:** Arnold IV **Obv:** Large A in center **Obv. Legend:** D. G. ABBAS. COR **Rev:** IIII in center, date in legend **Rev. Legend:** LANT: MVNT

Date	Mintage	VG	F	VF	XF	Unc
1648	—	27.00	55.00	110	200	—

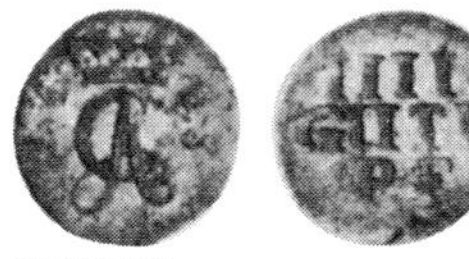

KM# 85 4 PFENNIG

Silver **Ruler:** Christof **Obv:** 4-fold arms **Obv. Legend:** F. C. L. M **Rev:** IIII/GUTE/PF divides date **Note:** Gute 4 Pfennig.

Date	Mintage	VG	F	VF	XF	Unc
1683	—	45.00	80.00	145	250	—

KM# 30 MATTIER

Silver **Ruler:** Johann Christoph **Obv:** 4-fold arms **Rev:** Date below **Rev. Legend:** I/MATTI/ER

Date	Mintage	VG	F	VF	XF	Unc
1631 (h)	—	—	—	—	—	—
(16)32	—	—	—	—	—	—

KM# 15 12 KREUZER

Silver **Ruler:** Heinrich V **Obv:** Oval 4-fold arms, mitre above, date in legend at top **Rev:** Crowned imperial eagle, 12 in orb on breast, titles of Ferdinand II **Note:** Kipper 12 Kreuzer.

Date	Mintage	VG	F	VF	XF	Unc
1620	—	40.00	70.00	125	200	—
ND	—	40.00	70.00	125	200	—

KM# 16 12 KREUZER

Silver **Ruler:** Heinrich V **Obv:** Oval 4-fold arms of Corvey, mitre above, MO. NO and date in legend **Note:** Varieties exist.

Date	Mintage	VG	F	VF	XF	Unc
(16)20	—	40.00	80.00	140	250	—
(16)21	—	40.00	80.00	140	250	—
1621	—	40.00	80.00	140	250	—

KM# 20 12 KREUZER

Silver **Ruler:** Heinrich V **Rev. Legend:** LANTMVN. DA. ST. 12. SW: PE **Note:** Varieties exist.

Date	Mintage	VG	F	VF	XF	Unc
(16)21	—	27.00	60.00	80.00	125	—
1621	—	27.00	60.00	80.00	125	—

KM# 23 MARIENGROSCHEN

Silver **Ruler:** Heinrich V **Obv:** Arms of Corvey, date in legend at top **Rev:** Madonna and child

Date	Mintage	VG	F	VF	XF	Unc
1622	—	—	—	—	—	—

KM# 31 MARIENGROSCHEN

Silver **Ruler:** Johann Christoph **Obv:** Oval 4-fold arms **Rev:** Date **Rev. Legend:** I/MARI/GROS

Date	Mintage	VG	F	VF	XF	Unc
1631 (h)	—	33.00	55.00	100	175	—

KM# 45 MARIENGROSCHEN

Silver **Ruler:** Arnold IV **Obv:** 4-fold arms **Rev:** Madonna and child, date in legend

Date	Mintage	VG	F	VF	XF	Unc
1649	—	—	—	—	—	—

KM# 55 MARIENGROSCHEN

Silver **Ruler:** Arnold IV **Obv. Legend:** I/MARI/GRO **Rev:** Madonna and child divide date **Note:** Denomination abbreviations vary.

Date	Mintage	VG	F	VF	XF	Unc
1653	—	40.00	65.00	120	200	—
1654	—	40.00	65.00	120	200	—

KM# A86 MARIENGROSCHEN

Silver **Ruler:** Christof von Bellinghausen **Obv:** Crowned arms **Obv. Legend:** CHRISTO • II • G • AB • COR • IMP **Rev. Legend:** SACRI • ROM • IMP • PR **Mint:** Hoxter

Date	Mintage	Good	VG	F	VF	XF
1683	—	—	—	—	—	—

KM# B86 MARIENGROSCHEN

Silver **Ruler:** Christof von Bellinghausen **Obv:** Corvey arms within inner circle **Rev. Inscription:** I / MARI / GROS **Mint:** Hoxter

Date	Mintage	VG	F	VF	XF	Unc
1683	—	40.00	75.00	150	240	—

KM# 43 2 MARIENGROSCHEN

Silver **Ruler:** Arnold IV **Obv:** Large A, mitre above, divides date **Rev. Legend:** II/MAR/GR **Note:** Varieties exist.

Date	Mintage	VG	F	VF	XF	Unc
1645	—	13.00	27.00	55.00	110	—
1646 GK	—	13.00	27.00	55.00	110	—
1649	—	13.00	27.00	55.00	110	—
1649 HC	—	13.00	27.00	55.00	110	—
1650	—	13.00	27.00	55.00	110	—
1651	—	13.00	27.00	55.00	110	—
1652	—	13.00	27.00	55.00	110	—
1653	—	13.00	27.00	55.00	110	—
1654	—	13.00	27.00	55.00	110	—

KM# 56 2 MARIENGROSCHEN

Silver **Ruler:** Arnold IV **Rev:** Date in legend

Date	Mintage	VG	F	VF	XF	Unc
1655	—	16.00	33.00	60.00	120	—
1655 VF	—	16.00	33.00	60.00	120	—
1656 VF	—	16.00	33.00	60.00	120	—

KM# 86 6 MARIENGROSCHEN

Silver **Ruler:** Christof **Obv:** Crowned imperial eagle, titles of Leopold I **Rev:** Value, date **Rev. Legend:** VI/MARIEN/GROS

Date	Mintage	VG	F	VF	XF	Unc
1683	—	80.00	170	240	300	—

KM# 65 16 GUTE GROSCHEN (2/3 Thaler)

Silver **Ruler:** Christof **Obv:** Crowned 4-fold arms in palm sprigs **Rev:** 16/GUTE GR/OSCHEN, date **Rev. Legend:** CANDORE

Date	Mintage	VG	F	VF	XF	Unc
1682	—	175	350	525	800	—

KM# 66 16 GUTE GROSCHEN (2/3 Thaler)

Silver **Ruler:** Christof **Rev:** Value inscription **Rev. Legend:** IN DOMINO **Rev. Inscription:** 16 / GUTE / GROSCH / EN

Date	Mintage	VG	F	VF	XF	Unc
1682	—	175	325	500	800	—

KM# 67 16 GUTE GROSCHEN (2/3 Thaler)

Silver **Ruler:** Christof **Obv:** Crowned CACC in palm sprigs **Rev:** 16/GUTE GR/OSCHEN, date **Rev. Legend:** CANDORE

Date	Mintage	VG	F	VF	XF	Unc
1682	—	—	—	—	—	—

KM# 68 16 GUTE GROSCHEN (2/3 Thaler)

Silver **Ruler:** Christof **Rev. Legend:** CANDORE..

Date	Mintage	VG	F	VF	XF	Unc
1682	—	—	—	—	—	—

KM# 94 16 GUTE GROSCHEN (2/3 Thaler)

Silver **Ruler:** Christof **Obv:** Crowned CACC **Rev:** Date **Rev. Legend:** CANDORE

Date	Mintage	VG	F	VF	XF	Unc
1684	—	—	—	—	—	—

KM# 95 16 GUTE GROSCHEN (2/3 Thaler)

Silver **Ruler:** Christof **Obv:** Bust right

Date	Mintage	VG	F	VF	XF	Unc
1684	—	200	400	675	1,150	—

KM# 96 16 GUTE GROSCHEN (2/3 Thaler)

Silver **Ruler:** Christof **Obv:** Crowned arms

Date	Mintage	VG	F	VF	XF	Unc
1684	—	—	—	—	—	—

KM# 69 24 MARIENGROSCHEN (2/3 Thaler)

Silver **Ruler:** Christof **Obv:** Bust left **Rev. Legend:** XXIIII/MARIEN/GROSCH CANDORE.. **Note:** Varieties exist.

Date	Mintage	VG	F	VF	XF	Unc
ND	—	—	—	—	—	—

KM# 70 24 MARIENGROSCHEN (2/3 Thaler)

Silver **Ruler:** Christof **Obv:** Crowned CACC in palm sprays **Note:** Varieties exist.

Date	Mintage	VG	F	VF	XF	Unc
ND	—	—	—	—	—	—
1682	—	—	—	—	—	—

KM# 71 24 MARIENGROSCHEN (2/3 Thaler)

Silver **Ruler:** Christof **Rev:** Value **Rev. Legend:** 24/MARIEN **Note:** Varieties exist.

Date	Mintage	VG	F	VF	XF	Unc
1682	—	—	—	—	—	—
1684	—	—	—	—	—	—

KM# 72 24 MARIENGROSCHEN (2/3 Thaler)

Silver **Ruler:** Christof **Obv:** Crowned 4-fold arms in palm sprays **Rev:** Date **Rev. Legend:** XXIIII/MARIEN/GROSCH, CANDORE..

Date	Mintage	VG	F	VF	XF	Unc
1682	—	—	—	—	—	—
1684	—	—	—	—	—	—

KM# 73 24 MARIENGROSCHEN (2/3 Thaler)

Silver **Ruler:** Christof **Obv:** Crowned imperial eagle, titles of Leopold I **Rev:** Date **Rev. Legend:** 24/MARIEN/GROSCH

Date	Mintage	VG	F	VF	XF	Unc
1682	—	—	—	—	—	—

KM# 74 24 MARIENGROSCHEN (2/3 Thaler)

Silver **Ruler:** Christof **Rev:** Date **Rev. Legend:** XXIIII/MARIEN..

Date	Mintage	VG	F	VF	XF	Unc
1682	—	—	—	—	—	—
1683	—	—	—	—	—	—

KM# 75 24 MARIENGROSCHEN (2/3 Thaler)

Silver **Ruler:** Christof **Obv:** Mule **Obv. Legend:** XXIIII/MARIEN/GROSCHEN/*** **Rev:** Large 2/3 in center, both sides with name, titles of Abbot Christof

Date	Mintage	VG	F	VF	XF	Unc
ND	—	325	575	900	1,400	—

KM# 5 1/24 THALER (Groschen)

Silver **Ruler:** Dietrich IV **Obv:** Imperial orb with 24, date divided in legend at top by cross, titles of Rudolf II **Rev:** 4-fold arms **Note:** Varieties exist.

Date	Mintage	VG	F	VF	XF	Unc
1607	—	20.00	35.00	60.00	120	—
1607 HL	—	20.00	35.00	60.00	120	—
1612	—	20.00	35.00	60.00	120	—
1612 HK	—	20.00	35.00	60.00	120	—
ND	—	20.00	35.00	60.00	120	—

KM# 12 1/24 THALER (Groschen)

Silver **Ruler:** Dietrich IV **Obv:** Titles of Matthias **Note:** Varieties exist.

Date	Mintage	VG	F	VF	XF	Unc
1613 HK	—	20.00	35.00	60.00	120	—
1614	—	20.00	35.00	60.00	120	—
1615	—	20.00	35.00	60.00	120	—
1616	—	20.00	35.00	60.00	120	—

KM# 13 1/24 THALER (Groschen)

Silver **Ruler:** Heinrich V **Obv:** 2 ornately-shaped arms, mitre above **Note:** Kipper 1/24 Thaler.

Date	Mintage	VG	F	VF	XF	Unc
1619	—	20.00	40.00	70.00	125	—
1620	—	20.00	40.00	70.00	125	—

KM# 87 1/24 THALER (Groschen)

Silver **Ruler:** Christof **Obv:** Crowned 4-fold arms **Rev:** Imperial orb with 24, date in legend **Note:** Varieties exist.

Date	Mintage	VG	F	VF	XF	Unc
1683	—	20.00	40.00	70.00	125	—

KM# 22 1/21 THALER (1-1/2 Schilling)

Silver **Ruler:** Heinrich V **Rev:** Value 21 or Z1 in legend

Date	Mintage	VG	F	VF	XF	Unc
(16)21	—	25.00	45.00	80.00	140	—

KM# 21 1/21 THALER (1-1/2 Schilling)

Silver **Ruler:** Heinrich V **Obv:** 4-fold arms, mitre above, date in legend **Rev:** Crowned imperial eagle, 21 in orb on breast **Rev. Legend:** LANDMVNZ. XXI. ZVM. R. DA **Note:** Kipper 1/21 Thaler. Varieties exist.

Date	Mintage	VG	F	VF	XF	Unc
1621	—	25.00	45.00	80.00	140	—

KM# 17 1/8 THALER

Silver **Ruler:** Heinrich V **Obv:** Arms, date **Rev:** Crowned imperial eagle, titles of Ferdinand II

Date	Mintage	VG	F	VF	XF	Unc
1620	—	—	—	—	—	—

KM# 59 1/4 THALER

Silver **Ruler:** Arnold IV **Obv:** 4-fold arms divide date, mitre and 4 above **Rev:** Full-length standing figure of St. Vitus

Date	Mintage	VG	F	VF	XF	Unc
1657 VFH	—	—	—	—	—	—

KM# 51 1/2 THALER

Silver **Ruler:** Arnold IV **Obv:** Full-length standing figure of St. Vitus divides date **Rev:** Crucifix **Rev. Legend:** DOMINI MANET

Date	Mintage	VG	F	VF	XF	Unc
1652	—	—	—	—	—	—

KM# 60 1/2 THALER

Silver **Ruler:** Arnold IV **Obv:** Ornate 4-fold arms divide date, mitre above **Rev:** Full-length standing figure of St. Vitus

Date	Mintage	VG	F	VF	XF	Unc
1657 VFH	—	—	—	—	—	—

KM# 88 1/2 THALER

Silver **Ruler:** Christof **Obv:** Bust left **Rev:** Crowned 4-fold arms, date **Rev. Legend:** CANDORE

Date	Mintage	VG	F	VF	XF	Unc
1683	—	—	—	—	—	—

KM# 61 2/3 THALER (Gulden)

Silver **Ruler:** Arnold IV **Obv:** Ornate 4-fold arms divide date, mitre above **Rev:** Full-length standing figure of St. Vitus

Date	Mintage	VG	F	VF	XF	Unc
1657 VFH	—	—	—	—	—	—

KM# 76 2/3 THALER (Gulden)
Silver **Ruler:** Christof **Obv:** Bust right **Rev:** Large 2/3 in wreath, date at top **Rev. Legend:** CANDORE

Date	Mintage	VG	F	VF	XF	Unc
1682	—	165	325	500	800	—
1683	—	165	325	500	800	—

KM# 77 2/3 THALER (Gulden)
Silver **Ruler:** Christof **Rev:** Large 2/3 in circle

Date	Mintage	VG	F	VF	XF	Unc
1682	—	165	325	500	800	—

KM# 78 2/3 THALER (Gulden)
Silver **Ruler:** Christof **Obv:** Bust left

Date	Mintage	VG	F	VF	XF	Unc
ND	—	500	875	1,200	1,800	—

KM# 80 2/3 THALER (Gulden)
Silver **Ruler:** Christof **Obv:** Crowned script CACC in palm sprays **Rev:** Large 2/3, date in legend

Date	Mintage	VG	F	VF	XF	Unc
1682	—	—	—	—	—	—

KM# 81 2/3 THALER (Gulden)
Silver **Ruler:** Christof **Obv:** Crowned script CACC **Rev:** Large 2/3

Date	Mintage	VG	F	VF	XF	Unc
ND	—	—	—	—	—	—

KM# 82 2/3 THALER (Gulden)
Silver **Ruler:** Christof **Obv:** Crowned 4-fold arms **Rev:** Large 2/3, date in legend

Date	Mintage	VG	F	VF	XF	Unc
1682	—	—	—	—	—	—

KM# 79 2/3 THALER (Gulden)
Silver **Ruler:** Christof **Obv:** Bust right **Rev:** Crowned 4-fold arms, date in legend, 2/3 in oval below **Note:** Varieties exist.

Date	Mintage	VG	F	VF	XF	Unc
1682	—	165	325	500	800	—
1683	—	165	325	500	800	—

KM# 89 2/3 THALER (Gulden)
Silver **Ruler:** Christof **Obv:** Bust right **Rev:** Large 2/3 divides date 1-6 - 8-3

Date	Mintage	VG	F	VF	XF	Unc
1683	—	165	325	500	800	—

KM# 90 2/3 THALER (Gulden)
Silver **Ruler:** Christof **Obv:** Date in legend

Date	Mintage	VG	F	VF	XF	Unc
1683	—	—	—	—	—	—

KM# 91 2/3 THALER (Gulden)
Silver **Ruler:** Christof **Obv:** Large 2/3, 4 small crosses around **Rev:** Crowned 4-fold arms, date **Rev. Legend:** CANDORE

Date	Mintage	VG	F	VF	XF	Unc
1683	—	—	—	—	—	—

KM# 97 2/3 THALER (Gulden)
Silver **Ruler:** Christof **Obv:** Bust left **Rev:** Crowned 4-fold arms, date in legend, 2/3 in oval below

Date	Mintage	VG	F	VF	XF	Unc
1684	—	200	400	675	1,150	—

KM# 98 2/3 THALER (Gulden)
Silver **Ruler:** Christof **Obv:** Crowned script CAGDC **Rev:** Large 2/3, date in legend

Date	Mintage	VG	F	VF	XF	Unc
1684	—	—	—	—	—	—

KM# 99 2/3 THALER (Gulden)
Silver **Ruler:** Christof **Obv:** Crowned oval 4-fold arms

Date	Mintage	VG	F	VF	XF	Unc
1684	—	—	—	—	—	—

KM# 105 2/3 THALER (Gulden)
Silver **Ruler:** Christof **Obv:** Crowned script CACC in palm sprays **Rev:** Large 2/3, date **Rev. Legend:** IN DOMINO

Date	Mintage	VG	F	VF	XF	Unc
1690	—	—	—	—	—	—

KM# 6 THALER
Silver **Ruler:** Dietrich IV **Obv:** Crowned imperial eagle, 24 in orb on breast, titles of Rudolf II **Rev:** Full-length standing figure of St. Vitus divides S-V and 2 small arms, date divided at top **Note:** Dav. #5182.

Date	Mintage	VG	F	VF	XF	Unc
1607 Rare	—	—	—	—	—	—

KM# 10 THALER
Silver **Ruler:** Dietrich IV **Obv:** Crowned imperial eagle, crown divides titles of Matthias **Rev:** Without S-V **Note:** Dav. #5184.

Date	Mintage	VG	F	VF	XF	Unc
1612 Rare	—	—	—	—	—	—

KM# 18 THALER
Silver **Ruler:** Heinrich V **Obv:** Titles of Ferdinand II **Rev:** 4-fold arms, mitre above **Rev. Legend:** HENRICVS.. **Note:** Dav. #5185.

Date	Mintage	VG	F	VF	XF	Unc
1620 Rare	—	—	—	—	—	—

KM# 24 THALER
Silver **Ruler:** Heinrich V **Obv. Legend:** D. G. IOAN. CHRISTOP **Note:** Dav. #5186.

Date	Mintage	VG	F	VF	XF	Unc
1624 Rare	—	—	—	—	—	—

KM# 32.1 THALER
Silver **Ruler:** Johann Christoph **Obv:** Similar to KM#57 but mitre above divides date **Note:** Dav. #5187.

Date	Mintage	VG	F	VF	XF	Unc
1631	—	900	1,850	3,250	5,500	—
1632	—	900	1,850	3,250	5,500	—

KM# 32.2 THALER
Silver **Ruler:** Johann Christoph **Obv. Legend:** IOAN: CHRISTOP: D: G: ABB: CORBEIENS **Note:** Dav. #5188.

Date	Mintage	VG	F	VF	XF	Unc
1631	—	900	1,850	3,250	5,500	—

KM# 50 THALER
Silver **Ruler:** Arnold IV **Obv:** Triple-helmeted oval 4-fold arms **Rev:** Date in legend **Note:** Dav. #5190.

Date	Mintage	VG	F	VF	XF	Unc
1650 Rare	—	—	—	—	—	—

KM# 52 THALER
Silver **Ruler:** Arnold IV **Obv:** Single helmet above arms **Note:** Dav. #5192.

Date	Mintage	VG	F	VF	XF	Unc
1652	—	1,750	3,750	6,000	9,000	—

KM# 57.1 THALER
Silver **Ruler:** Arnold IV **Obv. Legend:** ARNOLDVS... CONFIR: AB: CORB **Note:** Dav. #5194.

Date	Mintage	VG	F	VF	XF	Unc
1656 VFH	—	750	1,450	2,400	3,750	—

KM# 57.2 THALER
Silver **Ruler:** Arnold IV **Obv. Legend:** ... CON: AB: CORB **Note:** Dav. #5195.

Date	Mintage	VG	F	VF	XF	Unc
1657 VFH	—	750	1,450	2,400	3,750	—

KM# 92.1 THALER
Silver **Ruler:** Christof **Rev:** St. Vitus with falcon **Note:** Dav. #5197.

Date	Mintage	VG	F	VF	XF	Unc
1683 GB	—	300	600	1,150	1,650	—

KM# 92.2 THALER
Silver **Ruler:** Christof **Obv:** Altered frame for arms **Rev:** Lion's head added in front of St. VItus **Note:** Dav. #5198.

Date	Mintage	VG	F	VF	XF	Unc
1686	—	300	600	1,150	1,650	—

KM# 92.3 THALER
Silver **Ruler:** Christof **Obv:** G.I.-H. added below arms **Note:** Dav. #5198A.

Date	Mintage	VG	F	VF	XF	Unc
1686 GIH	—	300	600	1,150	1,650	—

KM# 100.1 THALER
Silver **Ruler:** Christof **Obv:** Capped bust right, 2 legends outer with titles of Leopold I **Rev:** Helmeted 4-fold arms, St. Vitus and mitre above, date in legend **Note:** Dav. #5199.

Date	Mintage	VG	F	VF	XF	Unc
1688 GB Rare	—	—	—	—	—	—

KM# 100.2 THALER
Silver **Ruler:** Christof **Note:** Dav. #5202.

Date	Mintage	VG	F	VF	XF	Unc
1690 IO Rare	—	—	—	—	—	—

KM# 101.1 THALER
Silver **Ruler:** Christof **Obv:** Helmeted 4-fold arms, St. Vitus and mitre above, date divided by arms below, large letters **Rev:** Laureate bust of Leopold I right **Note:** Dav. #5200.

Date	Mintage	VG	F	VF	XF	Unc
1688 GB	—	1,250	2,500	4,500	7,750	—

KM# 101.2 THALER
Silver **Ruler:** Christof **Obv:** Date in legend, IO divided near top **Note:** Dav. #5201.

Date	Mintage	VG	F	VF	XF	Unc
1690 IO	—	1,250	2,500	4,500	7,750	—

KM# 107 THALER
Silver **Ruler:** Christof **Obv:** Larger mitre above helmets replaces saint, date divided by arms **Note:** Dav. #5203.

Date	Mintage	VG	F	VF	XF	Unc
1694 IO Rare	—	—	—	—	—	—
ND IO Rare	—	—	—	—	—	—

KM# 106 THALER
Silver **Ruler:** Christof **Obv:** Not in circle, date in obverse legend **Rev:** Not in circle, date in obverse legend **Note:** Dav. #5204.

Date	Mintage	VG	F	VF	XF	Unc
1694 IO Rare	—	—	—	—	—	—

KM# 108 THALER
Silver **Ruler:** Florenz **Obv:** Helmeted ornate oval 4-fold arms, mitre above **Rev:** St. Vitus with lion and falcon, date in legend **Note:** Dav. #5205.

Date	Mintage	VG	F	VF	XF	Unc
1698 HLO	—	400	750	1,350	2,550	—

KM# 11 2 THALER
Silver **Ruler:** Dietrich IV **Obv:** Crowned imperial eagle crown divides date, titles of Matthias **Rev:** Full-length standing figure of St. Vitus divides 2 small arms, date divided at top **Note:** Dav. #5183.

Date	Mintage	VG	F	VF	XF	Unc
1612 Rare	—	—	—	—	—	—
1616	—	—	—	—	—	—

Note: Reported, not confirmed

KM# 53 2 THALER
Silver **Ruler:** Arnold IV **Obv:** Full-length standing figure of St. Vitus divides date **Rev:** Crucivix **Rev. Legend:** DOMINI MANET **Note:** Dav. #5183.

Date	Mintage	VG	F	VF	XF	Unc
1652 Rare	—	—	—	—	—	—

KM# 58 2 THALER
Silver **Ruler:** Arnold IV **Note:** Similar to 1 Thaler, KM#57. Dav. #5193.

Date	Mintage	VG	F	VF	XF	Unc
1656 VFH Rare	—	—	—	—	—	—

KM# 93 2 THALER
Silver **Ruler:** Christof **Note:** Similar to 1 Thaler, KM#92. Dav. #5196.

Date	Mintage	VG	F	VF	XF	Unc
1683 GB Rare	—	—	—	—	—	—

TRADE COINAGE

KM# 42 DUCAT
3.5000 g., 0.9860 Gold 0.1109 oz. AGW **Ruler:** Arnold IV **Obv:** 4-fold arms, date in legend **Rev:** Full-length figure of St. Vitus

Date	Mintage	VG	F	VF	XF	Unc
1642	—	1,200	2,400	4,800	8,400	—

KM# 54 DUCAT
3.5000 g., 0.9860 Gold 0.1109 oz. AGW **Ruler:** Arnold IV **Obv:** Ornate oval 4-fold arms, mitre above **Rev:** DVCA to left of saint

Date	Mintage	VG	F	VF	XF	Unc
1652	—	1,200	2,400	4,800	8,400	—

PATTERNS

Including off metal strikes

KM#	Date	Mintage	Identification	Mkt Val
Pn1	1632	—	Thaler. Tin. KM#32.1.	125
Pn2	1683	—	Thaler. Tin. KM#92.1.	125

COTTBUS

A provincial town about 70 miles southeast of Berlin. There was a mint for Brandenburg located in it during the 13th century. Cottbus and the surrounding territory belonged to Brandenburg from 1462 except 1807-13 when it was controlled by Saxony. Coins were issued during the Kipper Period.

TOWN

REGULAR COINAGE

KM# 1 PFENNIG
Copper **Note:** Uniface. Kipper Pfennig. Crayfish, head at top.

Date	Mintage	VG	F	VF	XF	Unc
ND(1622)	—	16.00	30.00	55.00	100	—

KM# 2 PFENNIG
Copper **Note:** S-C at lower left and right (Stadt Cottbus). Varieties exist.

Date	Mintage	VG	F	VF	XF	Unc
ND(1622)	—	13.00	27.00	55.00	100	—

DORTMUND

(Tremoniensis)

Dortmund is located in Westphalia, 50 miles east of Düsseldorf. It was the site of an imperial mint from the 10th to early 16th century and later had its own city coinage, dated pieces being known from 1553 to 1760. In 1803 Dortmund was annexed to Nassau-Dillenburg and passed to Prussia in 1815.

MINT OFFICIALS' INITIALS

Initials	Date	Name
NL	1688-95	Nikolaus Longerich
(t)	1631-50	Simon Textor
	1650-88	Ernst Textor

ARMS

Eagle with wings spread, head usually turned to left.

CITY

REGULAR COINAGE

KM# 5 1/8 SCHILLING (1-1/2 Pfennig)

Silver **Note:** Uniface. Eagle, head left, in circle.

Date	Mintage	VG	F	VF	XF	Unc
ND(ca.1625/30)	—	—	—	—	—	—

KM# 6 1/8 SCHILLING (1-1/2 Pfennig)

Silver **Note:** Eagle not in circle and D below.

Date	Mintage	VG	F	VF	XF	Unc
ND(ca.1630/35)	—	—	—	—	—	—

KM# 71 1/8 SCHILLING (1-1/2 Pfennig)

Silver **Note:** Eagle, head right, in circle of pellets, NL below.

Date	Mintage	VG	F	VF	XF	Unc
ND(1688-95) NL	—	—	—	—	—	—

KM# 70 3 PFENNIG

Silver **Obv:** Eagle, head right, divides TRE-MON **Rev:** III/PFEN/NING

Date	Mintage	VG	F	VF	XF	Unc
ND(ca.1680) (t)	—	—	—	—	—	—

KM# 67 8 HELLER

Billon **Obv:** Eagle, head right **Obv. Legend:** TREMONIENSIS **Rev:** VIII in center, date in legend

Date	Mintage	VG	F	VF	XF	Unc
1676 (t)	—	—	—	—	—	—

KM# 7 6 PFENNING (1/2 Schilling)

Silver **Obv:** Eagle, head left, in circle **Obv. Legend:** TREMONIENSIS **Rev:** VI/PFENN/ING/ date in circle

Date	Mintage	VG	F	VF	XF	Unc
1631 (t)	—	35.00	70.00	125	—	—

KM# 8 6 PFENNING (1/2 Schilling)

Silver **Obv:** Eagle, not in circle

Date	Mintage	VG	F	VF	XF	Unc
1631	—	35.00	70.00	125	—	—

KM# 45 6 PFENNING (1/2 Schilling)

Silver **Obv:** Date in legend **Rev:** VI/PFEN/NING

Date	Mintage	VG	F	VF	XF	Unc
1651	—	33.00	65.00	120	170	—

KM# 46 6 PFENNING (1/2 Schilling)

Silver **Rev:** VI/PFEN/NING/ date

Date	Mintage	VG	F	VF	XF	Unc
1651	—	33.00	65.00	120	170	—

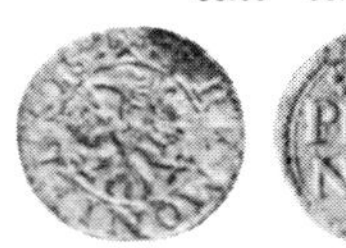

KM# 49 6 PFENNING (1/2 Schilling)

Silver **Rev:** VI/PFEN/NING **Note:** Varieties exist.

Date	Mintage	VG	F	VF	XF	Unc
ND(1658-88)	—	9.00	20.00	40.00	80.00	—
ND(1658-88) (t)	—	9.00	20.00	40.00	80.00	—

KM# 9 SCHILLING

Silver **Obv:** Eagle, head left, in circle, titles of Ferdinand II **Rev:** 1/SCHIL/LING/ date **Note:** These are also known with countermarks of arms of the county of Mark (checkerboard).

Date	Mintage	VG	F	VF	XF	Unc
1631 (t)	—	20.00	40.00	70.00	125	—
1632 (t)	—	20.00	40.00	70.00	125	—
1633 (t)	—	20.00	40.00	70.00	125	—
1635 (t)	—	20.00	40.00	70.00	125	—
1640 (t)	—	20.00	40.00	70.00	125	—

KM# 36 SCHILLING

Silver **Obv:** Eagle's head to right

Date	Mintage	VG	F	VF	XF	Unc
1641 (t)	—	20.00	40.00	70.00	125	—

KM# 35 SCHILLING

Silver **Obv:** Titles of Ferdinand III **Note:** Often found with countermark of Mark arms.

Date	Mintage	VG	F	VF	XF	Unc
1641 (t)	—	20.00	40.00	70.00	125	—
1643 (t)	—	20.00	40.00	70.00	125	—
1644 (t)	—	20.00	40.00	70.00	125	—
1646 (t)	—	20.00	40.00	70.00	125	—
1647 (t)	—	20.00	40.00	70.00	125	—
1653 (t)	—	20.00	40.00	70.00	125	—
1655 (t)	—	20.00	40.00	70.00	125	—
1656 (t)	—	20.00	40.00	70.00	125	—

KM# 10 1/52 THALER (Schilling)

Silver **Obv:** Eagle, head left, in circle, titles of Ferdinand II **Rev:** Imperial orb with 52 divides date

Date	Mintage	VG	F	VF	XF	Unc
1631 (t)	—	60.00	120	200	—	—

KM# 14 1/16 THALER (Halber Blamüser)

Silver **Obv:** Titles of Ferdinand II, value 16 in legend at bottom **Rev:** Eagle, head left, in circle, date in legend

Date	Mintage	VG	F	VF	XF	Unc
1632 (t)	—	85.00	170	300	475	—
1633 (t)	—	85.00	170	300	475	—
1637 (t)	—	85.00	170	300	475	—

KM# 25 1/16 THALER (Halber Blamüser)

Silver **Rev:** Eagle's head right

Date	Mintage	VG	F	VF	XF	Unc
1637 (t)	—	85.00	170	300	475	—

KM# 29 1/16 THALER (Halber Blamüser)

Silver **Obv:** Titles of Ferdinand III, value 16 bottom

Date	Mintage	VG	F	VF	XF	Unc
1639 (t)	—	150	250	350	550	—
1640 (t)	—	150	250	350	550	—
1642 (t)	—	150	250	350	550	—
1645 (t)	—	150	250	350	550	—
1646 (t)	—	150	250	350	550	—
1647 (t)	—	150	250	350	550	—
1648 (t)	—	150	250	350	550	—
1650 (t)	—	150	250	350	550	—

KM# 47 1/16 THALER (Halber Blamüser)

Silver **Obv:** Value 16 in legend above bust

Date	Mintage	VG	F	VF	XF	Unc
1656 (t)	—	65.00	140	275	450	—
1658 (t)	—	65.00	140	275	450	—

KM# 65 1/16 THALER (Dütchen)

Silver **Obv:** Titles of Leopold I

Date	Mintage	VG	F	VF	XF	Unc
1670 (t)	—	16.00	33.00	60.00	100	—
1671 (t)	—	16.00	33.00	60.00	100	—
1672 (t)	—	16.00	33.00	60.00	100	—

KM# 50 1/13 THALER (4 Stüber)

Silver **Obv:** Titles of Leopold I, value 13 above in legend

Date	Mintage	VG	F	VF	XF	Unc
1659 (t)	—	45.00	80.00	140	225	—
1660 (t)	—	45.00	80.00	140	225	—

KM# 17 1/4 THALER

Silver **Obv:** Crowned 1/2-length bust of emperor right, titles of Ferdinand II **Rev:** Eagle, head left, in circle, date in legend

Date	Mintage	VG	F	VF	XF	Unc
1634 (t)	—	—	—	—	—	—
1637 (t)	—	—	—	—	—	—

KM# 38 1/4 THALER

Silver **Obv:** Bust of emperor right, titles of Ferdinand III **Rev:** Eagle, head left, in circle, double legend, date in outer legend

Date	Mintage	VG	F	VF	XF	Unc
1646 (t)	—	—	—	—	—	—

KM# 72 2/3 THALER (Gulden)

Silver **Obv:** Laureate bust right, titles of Leopold I **Rev:** Eagle, head left, value 2/3 in oval below, date in legend

Date	Mintage	VG	F	VF	XF	Unc
1688 NL	—	—	—	—	—	—

Note: The few known specimens have countermark on obverse of leaping horse left, IP on flank, for monetary warden-general of the Lower Rhine-Westphalian imperial circle, Johann Post (1682-1702)

KM# 11.1 THALER

Silver **Note:** Similar to KM#18 but date in reverse legend.

Date	Mintage	VG	F	VF	XF	Unc
16Z1 Rare	—	—	—	—	—	—

KM# 11.2 THALER

Silver **Obv:** Crowned half figure with scepter right **Obv. Legend:** FERDINANDVS. II. DG. RO. IMP. SEM. AVGB.--S. **Rev:** Legend, eagle, date **Rev. Legend:** MON. NO. CIVIT. IMP. TREMONIENSIS **Note:** Dav. #5207.

Date	Mintage	VG	F	VF	XF	Unc
1631 (t) Rare	—	—	—	—	—	—

KM# 11.3 THALER

Silver **Note:** Klippe. Dav. #5207A.

Date	Mintage	VG	F	VF	XF	Unc
1631 (t) Rare	—	—	—	—	—	—

KM# 11.4 THALER

Silver **Obv. Legend:** MONE. NOV... **Note:** Dav. #5209.

Date	Mintage	VG	F	VF	XF	Unc
163Z (t) Rare	—	—	—	—	—	—

KM# 11.5 THALER

Silver **Note:** Klippe. Dav. #5209A.

Date	Mintage	VG	F	VF	XF	Unc
163Z (t) Rare	—	—	—	—	—	—

KM# 18.1 THALER

Silver **Obv:** Date in field before bust **Obv. Legend:** FERDI. , II. DG: ROM: IMPERIA: SEMP. AVG-X. **Rev. Legend:** MONETA: NOV: CIVIT: IMPERIA: TREMONIENS. **Note:** Dav. #5210.

Date	Mintage	VG	F	VF	XF	Unc
1634 (t) Rare	—	—	—	—	—	—

KM# 18.2 THALER

Silver **Note:** Dav. #5212.

Date	Mintage	VG	F	VF	XF	Unc
1635 (t)	—	600	1,200	2,000	3,500	—

KM# 18.3 THALER

Silver **Note:** Dav. #5213.

Date	Mintage	VG	F	VF	XF	Unc
1636 (t) Rare	—	—	—	—	—	—

KM# 27.1 THALER

Silver **Obv:** Bust of emperor right, titles of Ferdinand III **Rev:** Eagle, head left, in circle, double legend, date divided by eagle's legs **Note:** Dav. #5215.

Date	Mintage	VG	F	VF	XF	Unc
ND(1637-48) Rare	—	—	—	—	—	—

Note: Fritz Rudolf Künker Münzenhandlung Auction 98, 3-05, VF realized approximately $46,000.

KM# 27.2 THALER

Silver **Obv. Legend:** ...ROM. IMP. SEMP. AVGVSTVS. **Note:** Dav. #5216.

Date	Mintage	VG	F	VF	XF	Unc
ND(1637-48) Rare	—	—	—	—	—	—

KM# 27.3 THALER

Silver **Note:** Klippe. Dav. #5216A.

Date	Mintage	VG	F	VF	XF	Unc
ND(1637-48) Rare	—	—	—	—	—	—

KM# 27.4 THALER

Silver **Rev:** Date divided by eagle **Note:** Dav. #5217.

Date	Mintage	VG	F	VF	XF	Unc
1638 Rare	—	—	—	—	—	—
1640 Rare	—	—	—	—	—	—

KM# 27.5 THALER

Silver **Obv:** Harnessed bust right **Note:** Dav. #5218.

Date	Mintage	VG	F	VF	XF	Unc
1646 Rare	—	—	—	—	—	—

KM# 27.6 THALER

Silver **Obv:** Different bust **Note:** Dav. #5220.

Date	Mintage	VG	F	VF	XF	Unc
1647 Rare	—	—	—	—	—	—

KM# 27.7 THALER

Silver

Date	Mintage	VG	F	VF	XF	Unc
1650 Rare	—	—	—	—	—	—

KM# 48 THALER

Silver **Rev:** Date in outer legend **Note:** Dav. #5221.

Date	Mintage	VG	F	VF	XF	Unc
1657 (t) Rare	—	—	—	—	—	—

Note: Bank Leu Auction 46 5-88 VF realized $14,000

KM# 55.1 THALER

Silver **Note:** Dav. #5223.

Date	Mintage	VG	F	VF	XF	Unc
1660 (t)	—	1,250	2,500	6,250	—	—
1668 (t)	—	1,250	2,500	6,250	—	—

KM# 55.2 THALER

Silver **Note:** Klippe. Dav. #5223A.

Date	Mintage	VG	F	VF	XF	Unc
1668 (t) Rare	—	—	—	—	—	—

KM# 55.3 THALER

Silver **Obv:** Different bust with longer hair and softer looking drapings **Note:** Dav. #5224.

Date	Mintage	VG	F	VF	XF	Unc
1683 Rare	—	—	—	—	—	—

Note: Swiss Bank sale 19 1-88 VF/XF realized $23,400

KM# 55.4 THALER

Silver **Note:** Klippe. Dav. #5224A.

Date	Mintage	VG	F	VF	XF	Unc
1683 Rare	—	—	—	—	—	—

Note: Bank Leu Auction 46 5-88 VF realized $18,000

KM# 55.5 THALER

Silver **Obv:** Larger letters in wider legend **Note:** Dav. #5225.

Date	Mintage	VG	F	VF	XF	Unc
1688 NL Rare	—	—	—	—	—	—

KM# 75 THALER

Silver **Obv:** Large bust not in circle **Rev:** Double legend broken at top by eagle, head of which divides mintmaster's initials from date **Note:** Dav. #5226.

Date	Mintage	VG	F	VF	XF	Unc
1695 NL Rare	—	—	—	—	—	—

Note: Bank Leu Auction 46 5-88 VF realized $26,000

KM# 77 THALER

Silver **Note:** Dav. #5227.

Date	Mintage	VG	F	VF	XF	Unc
1698 Rare	—	—	—	—	—	—

Note: Bank Leu Auction 46 5-88 VF-XF realized $35,000

KM# 39 1-1/2 THALER

Silver **Obv:** Bust of emperor right, titles of Ferdinand III **Rev:** Eagle, head left, in circle, double legend, date divided by legs

Date	Mintage	VG	F	VF	XF	Unc
1647 Rare	—	—	—	—	—	—

Note: May be a 2 Thaler. Similar to KM#40.3, listed as a 2 Thaler

KM# 12.1 2 THALER

Silver **Note:** Similar to 1 Thaler, KM#18 but date in reverse legend. Dav. #5206.

Date	Mintage	VG	F	VF	XF	Unc
1631 (t) Rare	—	—	—	—	—	—

KM# 12.2 2 THALER

Silver **Obv. Legend:** MONE. NOV... **Note:** Dav. #5208.

Date	Mintage	VG	F	VF	XF	Unc
163Z (t) Rare	—	—	—	—	—	—

KM# 13 2 THALER

Silver **Note:** Klippe. Dav. #5208A.

Date	Mintage	VG	F	VF	XF	Unc
163Z (t) Rare	—	—	—	—	—	—

KM# 20 2 THALER

Silver **Note:** Klippe. Dav. #5211A.

Date	Mintage	VG	F	VF	XF	Unc
1635 (t) Rare	—	—	—	—	—	—

KM# 19 2 THALER

Silver **Note:** Similar to 1 Thaler, KM#18. Dav. #5211.

Date	Mintage	VG	F	VF	XF	Unc
1635 (t) Rare	—	—	—	—	—	—

KM# 40.1 2 THALER

Silver **Obv:** Bust of emperor right, titles of Ferdinand III **Rev:** Eagle, head left, in circle, double legend **Note:** Dav. #5214.

Date	Mintage	VG	F	VF	XF	Unc
ND(1637-48) Rare	—	—	—	—	—	—

KM# 40.2 2 THALER

Silver **Note:** Dav. #5214A.

Date	Mintage	VG	F	VF	XF	Unc
ND(1637-48) Rare	—	—	—	—	—	—

KM# 40.3 2 THALER

Silver **Rev:** Date divided by eagle's legs **Note:** Dav. #5219.

Date	Mintage	VG	F	VF	XF	Unc
1647 Rare	—	—	—	—	—	—

Note: 1647 may actually be 1-1/2 Thaler as KM#39

KM# 40.4 2 THALER

Silver **Note:** Klippe. Dav. #5219A.

Date	Mintage	VG	F	VF	XF	Unc
1647 Rare	—	—	—	—	—	—

KM# 56.1 2 THALER

Silver **Note:** Dav. #5222.

Date	Mintage	VG	F	VF	XF	Unc
1660 (t) Rare	—	—	—	—	—	—

Note: Bank Leu Auction 46 5-88 XF realized $22,000

Date	Mintage	VG	F	VF	XF	Unc
1668 (t) Rare	—	—	—	—	—	—

KM# 56.2 2 THALER

Silver **Note:** Klippe. Dav. #5222A.

Date	Mintage	VG	F	VF	XF	Unc
1660 (t) Rare	—	—	—	—	—	—

KM# 56.3 2 THALER

Silver **Obv:** Large letters in wide legend **Note:** Dav. #A5225.

Date	Mintage	VG	F	VF	XF	Unc
1688 NL Rare	—	—	—	—	—	—

KM# 56.4 2 THALER

Silver **Note:** Klippe. Dav. #A5225A.

Date	Mintage	VG	F	VF	XF	Unc
1688 NL Rare	—	—	—	—	—	—

KM# 76 2 THALER

Silver **Obv:** Large bust not in circle **Rev:** Double legend broken at top by eagle, head of which divides mintmasters initials from date **Note:** Dav. #A5226.

Date	Mintage	VG	F	VF	XF	Unc
1695 NL Rare	—	—	—	—	—	—

TRADE COINAGE

KM# 15 GOLDGULDEN

3.5000 g., 0.9860 Gold 0.1109 oz. AGW **Obv:** Ferdinand II standing in inner circle **Rev:** Large orb in center circle

Date	Mintage	VG	F	VF	XF	Unc
1632 Rare	—	—	—	—	—	—

KM# 16 GOLDGULDEN

3.5000 g., 0.9860 Gold 0.1109 oz. AGW **Rev:** Imperial orb in hexalobe

Date	Mintage	VG	F	VF	XF	Unc
1633	—	750	1,500	3,300	6,000	—
1635/3	—	750	1,500	3,300	6,000	—

KM# 22 DUCAT

3.5000 g., 0.9860 Gold 0.1109 oz. AGW **Obv:** Full-length facing standing figure of emperor, titles of Ferdinand II in legend **Rev:** Eagle, head left, divides date above four-line inscription

Date	Mintage	VG	F	VF	XF	Unc
1635	—	1,500	3,600	7,500	13,500	—

KM# 24 DUCAT

3.5000 g., 0.9860 Gold 0.1109 oz. AGW **Rev:** Eagle, head right, date in legend

Date	Mintage	VG	F	VF	XF	Unc
1636	—	750	1,800	3,750	6,800	—

KM# 26 DUCAT

3.5000 g., 0.9860 Gold 0.1109 oz. AGW **Rev:** Eagle's head to left

Date	Mintage	VG	F	VF	XF	Unc
1637	—	750	1,800	3,750	6,800	—

KM# 30 DUCAT

3.5000 g., 0.9860 Gold 0.1109 oz. AGW **Rev:** Three-line inscription with posthumous date, titles of Ferdinand II

Date	Mintage	VG	F	VF	XF	Unc
1639	—	1,000	2,400	5,000	9,000	—

KM# 37 DUCAT

3.5000 g., 0.9860 Gold 0.1109 oz. AGW **Obv:** Figure of emperor divides date, titles of Ferdinand III **Rev:** Eagle, head left

Date	Mintage	VG	F	VF	XF	Unc
1644 (t)	—	750	1,800	3,750	6,800	—
1655 (t)	—	750	1,800	3,750	6,800	—

KM# 58 DUCAT

3.5000 g., 0.9860 Gold 0.1109 oz. AGW **Obv:** Leopold standing in inner circle **Rev:** Displayed eagle in inner circle

Date	Mintage	VG	F	VF	XF	Unc
1660	—	2,500	4,500	9,000	15,000	—

KM# 59 DUCAT

3.5000 g., 0.9860 Gold 0.1109 oz. AGW **Rev:** Date divided by eagle's head

Date	Mintage	VG	F	VF	XF	Unc
1663 (t)	—	2,500	4,500	9,000	15,000	—

KM# 66 DUCAT

3.5000 g., 0.9860 Gold 0.1109 oz. AGW **Obv:** Laureate bust of emperor right, titles of Leopold I **Rev:** Eagle, head left, date in legend

Date	Mintage	VG	F	VF	XF	Unc
1670 (t) Rare	—	—	—	—	—	—

DROSSEN

A town in Brandenburg and mint site in the 13th century. Drossen received the right to coin Pfennigs in 1369. Local coinage was also struck during the Kipper Period.

TOWN

REGULAR COINAGE

KM# 1 PFENNIG

Copper **Note:** Kipper Pfennig. Uniface. Eagle in shield divides sideways date, D below.

Date	Mintage	VG	F	VF	XF	Unc
16ZZ	—	13.00	30.00	45.00	100	—

KM# 2 PFENNIG

Copper **Note:** Eagle in shield, date above divided by D.

Date	Mintage	VG	F	VF	XF	Unc
16ZZ	—	13.00	30.00	45.00	100	—

KM# 3 PFENNIG

Copper **Note:** Eagle, head left, D below.

Date	Mintage	VG	F	VF	XF	Unc
ND(1622)	—	13.00	30.00	45.00	100	—

DULMEN

A town in Westphalia some 18 miles southwest of Munster. Between 1590 and 1625 a series of copper coins were struck for local use.

TOWN

REGULAR COINAGE

KM# 1 PFENNIG

Copper **Obv:** Arms, (cross in shield), legend, date around **Obv. Legend:** STADT DVLMEN **Rev:** Value I in circle with ornaments around

Date	Mintage	Good	VG	F	VF	XF
ND(c.1609)	—	65.00	120	200	325	—
1625	—	65.00	120	200	325	—

KM# 2 2 PFENNIG

Copper **Obv:** Arms, legend, date around **Obv. Legend:** STADT DVLMEN **Rev:** Value II in circle with ornaments around

Date	Mintage	Good	VG	F	VF	XF
1609	—	65.00	120	200	325	—

KM# 3 3 PFENNIG

Copper **Obv:** Arms, legend, date around **Obv. Legend:** STADT DVLMEN **Rev:** Value III in circle with ornaments around

Date	Mintage	Good	VG	F	VF	XF
1609	—	65.00	120	200	325	—
1625	—	65.00	120	200	325	—

KM# 4 4 PFENNIG

Copper **Obv:** Arms, legend, date around **Obv. Legend:** STADT DVLMEN **Rev:** Value IIII in circle with ornaments around

Date	Mintage	Good	VG	F	VF	XF
1609	—	65.00	120	200	325	—

KM# 5 6 PFENNIG

Copper **Obv:** Arms, legend, date around **Obv. Legend:** STADT DVLMEN **Rev:** Value VI in circle with ornaments around

Date	Mintage	Good	VG	F	VF	XF
1609	—	40.00	85.00	160	275	—
1622	—	40.00	85.00	160	275	—

EAST FRIESLAND

The countship, and later principality, of East Friesland was located along the North Sea coast between the Rivers Ems and Weser. By the late 14th and early 15th centuries, several powerful families controlled various areas of what was to become the countship. The Cirksena family of Greetsyl managed to emerge during this period as a leading force in the region through astute marriages and sometimes by armed might. Ulrich I Cirksena was created the first count of East Friesland in 1454. This confirmed his line as the ruling dynasty with the capital at Aurich. In 1654, the count was raised to the rank of prince. In 1744, the Cirksenas became extinct and East Friesland passed to Prussia, which maintained the mint at Aurich for the new province. East Friesland became part of Hannover at the end of the Napoleonic Wars in 1815, but returned to Prussian control when Hannover itself was absorbed by Prussia in 1866.

RULERS
Enno III, 1599-1625
Rudolph Christian, 1625-1628
Ulrich II, 1628-1648
Enno IV Ludwig, 1648-1660
Georg Christian, 1660-1665
Christine Charlotte, regent, 1665-1690
Christian Eberhard, 1665-1708

MINT MARKS
A - Berlin
B - Breslau
D - Aurich
F - Magdeburg
Star - Dresden

MINT OFFICIALS' INITIALS

Initial	Date	Name
	1519-26	Uko Hessena, warden in Emden
(a)=	ca. 1528	Johann?, mintmaster
(b)=	ca. 1529-32	Hinrich, mintmaster
(c)=	1532-39	Martin Nycamer, mintmaster
	1533-40	Hinrich Scrapper, warden
(d)=	1558-63	Heinrich Meinerts, mintmaster
(e)=	1563-74?	Dirk Iden Kruitkremer, mintmaster
(f)=	1574-82	Johann Iden, mintmaster
	1577-99	Franz Munting, die-cutter
(g)=	1582-1602	Joest Janssen van Strijp, mintmaster
(h)=	1602-11	Franz Munting in Emden
(i)=	1611-13	Meinhard Caspars in Emden
(j)=	1614-17	Jacob Stalpert in Emden
(k)=	1617-24	Johann von Romunde in Emden
HS	1626-72	Henning Schlüter in Zellerfeld
(l)=	1629-32	Unknown
(m)= or, or with or without BH	1660-65	Unknown
(n)=	Ca.1690	Unknown at Esens
FBP	Ca.1693-1700	Unknown

MONETARY SYSTEM
Witte = 4 Hohlpfennig = 1/3 Schilling = 1/20 Schaf = 1/10 Stuber
Ciffert = 6 Witten
Stuber = 10 Witten = 1/30 Reichstaler
Schaf = 20 Witten = 2 Stuber
Flindrich = 3 Stuber
Schilling = 6 Stuber
288 Pfennige = 54 Stuber = 36 Mariengroschen = 1 Reichsthaler

COUNTSHIP

REGULAR COINAGE

KM# 10 WITTE (1/10 Stüber)
Silver **Obv:** Harpy facing (arms of Cirksena family) **Rev:** Date across center, imperial orb above, 1/Z0 below

Date	Mintage	VG	F	VF	XF	Unc
1603 (h)	—	—	—	—	—	—
1604 (h)	—	—	—	—	—	—

KM# 46 WITTE (1/10 Stüber)
Silver **Note:** Uniface. Schussel type. Shield with harpy divides date, mintmaster's symbol above.

Date	Mintage	VG	F	VF	XF	Unc
1621 (k)	—	—	—	—	—	—

KM# 34 3 WITTEN
Silver **Obv:** Harpy, titles of Enno III **Rev:** Value 3 in imperial orb **Rev. Legend:** DA. PAC...

Date	Mintage	VG	F	VF	XF	Unc
ND(ca.1617-20)	—	—	—	—	—	—

KM# 15 CIFFERT (1/2 Stüber)
Silver **Obv:** Crowned harpy arms divid H-S (Halb Stuber), date above crown **Rev:** Ornate cross, O-F/H-S in angles **Rev. Legend:** DA. PA...

Date	Mintage	VG	F	VF	XF	Unc
1612 (i)	77,000	13.00	27.00	55.00	100	—
ND	—	13.00	27.00	55.00	100	—

KM# 18 CIFFERT (1/2 Stüber)
Silver **Rev:** Date in angles of cross instead of letters

Date	Mintage	VG	F	VF	XF	Unc
1612 (i)	Inc. above	16.00	33.00	65.00	120	—

KM# 16 CIFFERT (1/2 Stüber)
Silver **Note:** Klippe.

Date	Mintage	VG	F	VF	XF	Unc
ND (i)	—	—	—	—	—	—

KM# 17 CIFFERT (1/2 Stüber)
Silver **Obv:** Arms divide date, without H-S **Note:** Klippe.

Date	Mintage	VG	F	VF	XF	Unc
(16)12 (i)	Inc. above	16.00	33.00	65.00	120	—

KM# 95 CIFFERT (1/2 Stüber)
Silver **Obv:** Arms divide H-S, date above crown **Rev:** O-F/H-S in angles of cross

Date	Mintage	VG	F	VF	XF	Unc
1660	—	16.00	33.00	65.00	120	—

KM# 106 CIFFERT (1/2 Stüber)
Silver **Obv:** Crowned harpy arms, titles of Christian Eberhard

Date	Mintage	VG	F	VF	XF	Unc
ND (n)	—	16.00	33.00	65.00	120	—

KM# 35 1/4 STUBER (2-1/2 Witten)
Silver **Obv:** Harpy, titles of Enno III **Rev:** Imperial orb **Rev. Legend:** DA. PAC...

Date	Mintage	VG	F	VF	XF	Unc
ND(ca.1617-20)	—	10.00	20.00	40.00	80.00	—

KM# 107 1/4 STUBER (2-1/2 Witten)
Billon **Obv:** Titles of Christian Eberhard **Rev. Legend:** IN. DEO...

Date	Mintage	VG	F	VF	XF	Unc
ND(ca.1665-1708)	—	10.00	20.00	40.00	80.00	—

KM# 19 STUBER
Silver **Obv:** Crowned harpy arms divide I-S (1 Stuber), date above crown **Rev:** Ornate cross in quatrefoil, DA. PA... around

Date	Mintage	VG	F	VF	XF	Unc
1612 (i)	123,000	10.00	27.00	65.00	120	—
ND	231,000	10.00	27.00	65.00	120	—

KM# 21 STUBER
Silver **Obv:** S-I divided by date

Date	Mintage	VG	F	VF	XF	Unc
ND	Inc. above	10.00	27.00	65.00	120	—

KM# 20 STUBER
Silver **Note:** Klippe.

Date	Mintage	VG	F	VF	XF	Unc
ND (i)	—	—	—	—	—	—

KM# 47 STUBER
Silver **Obv:** Crowned harpy arms divide I-S **Rev:** Ornate cross

Date	Mintage	VG	F	VF	XF	Unc
ND(1628-48)	—	27.00	45.00	90.00	210	—

KM# 96 STUBER
Silver

Date	Mintage	VG	F	VF	XF	Unc
1660	—	27.00	60.00	110	175	—
ND	—	27.00	60.00	110	175	—

KM# 130 STUBER
Silver

Date	Mintage	VG	F	VF	XF	Unc
ND(1690-1708)	—	27.00	60.00	110	175	—

KM# 23 SCHAF (2 Stüber)
Silver **Obv:** Crowned harpy arms divide 2-S, date above crown **Rev:** Ornate cross **Rev. Legend:** DA. PACEM...

Date	Mintage	VG	F	VF	XF	Unc
1612 (i)	72,000	13.00	27.00	55.00	100	—
ND (j)	180,000	13.00	27.00	55.00	100	—
ND (k)	46,000	13.00	27.00	55.00	100	—

KM# 24 SCHAF (2 Stüber)
Silver **Note:** Klippe.

Date	Mintage	VG	F	VF	XF	Unc
ND	—	—	—	—	—	—

KM# 55 SCHAF (2 Stüber)
Silver **Obv:** Crowned harpy arms divide 2-S, date above crowne **Rev:** Ornate cross

Date	Mintage	VG	F	VF	XF	Unc
1632	—	33.00	65.00	135	250	—
1633	—	33.00	65.00	135	250	—
ND	—	33.00	65.00	135	250	—

KM# 66 SCHAF (2 Stüber)
Silver **Obv:** Crowned harpy arms, titles of Enno Ludwig **Rev:** Ornate cross **Rev. Legend:** DA. PACEM...

Date	Mintage	VG	F	VF	XF	Unc
ND	—	13.00	27.00	55.00	100	—

KM# 99 SCHAF (2 Stüber)
Silver **Obv:** Titles of Georg Christian

Date	Mintage	VG	F	VF	XF	Unc
ND	—	16.00	33.00	65.00	120	—

KM# 109 SCHAF (2 Stüber)
Silver **Obv:** Titles of Christian Eberhard **Rev. Legend:** LAND. MUNTZ.

Date	Mintage	VG	F	VF	XF	Unc
ND	—	13.00	27.00	55.00	100	—

KM# 67 FLINDRICH (3 Stüber)
Silver **Obv:** Crowned harpy arms, ENNO... **Rev:** Crowned imperial eagle, orb on breast, titles of Ferdinand II

Date	Mintage	VG	F	VF	XF	Unc
ND	—	40.00	80.00	125	210	—
ND (k)	—	40.00	80.00	125	210	—

KM# 132 FLINDRICH (3 Stüber)
Silver **Obv:** Crowned harpy arms **Rev:** Value, date

Date	Mintage	VG	F	VF	XF	Unc
1697	—	13.00	27.00	55.00	100	—
1698	—	13.00	27.00	55.00	100	—

KM# 97 4 STUBER
Silver **Obv:** Bust of Enno Ludwig right **Rev:** Crowned harpy shield, date in legend

Date	Mintage	VG	F	VF	XF	Unc
1660	—	—	—	—	—	—

KM# 22 5 STUBER
Silver **Obv:** Small harpy arms divide date, crowned helmet above **Rev:** Crowned imperial eagle, 1/10 in orb on breast **Rev. Legend:** DA. PACEM...

Date	Mintage	VG	F	VF	XF	Unc
1612 (i)	130,000	40.00	85.00	150	220	—
ND (k)	140,000	40.00	85.00	150	220	—
ND	176,000	40.00	85.00	150	220	—

KM# 65 28 STUBER (Gulden)
Silver **Obv:** Crowned imperial eagle, orb with 28 on breast, titles of Leopold I **Rev:** Crowned four-fold arms, titles of Enno Ludwig

Date	Mintage	VG	F	VF	XF	Unc
ND	—	675	975	1,350	2,200	—

KM# 98 28 STUBER (Gulden)
Silver **Obv:** Titles of Georg Christian

Date	Mintage	VG	F	VF	XF	Unc
ND	—	—	—	—	—	—

KM# 108 30 STUBER (Gulden)
Silver **Obv:** 30 in orb on breast of eagle **Rev:** Crowned six-fold arms divide 30-ST, titles of Christian Eberhard

Date	Mintage	VG	F	VF	XF	Unc
ND (m)	—	160	300	525	875	—

KM# 45 SCHILLING (6 Stüber)
Silver **Obv:** Crowned imperial eagle, orb on breast, titles of Ferdinand II **Rev:** Crowned harpy arms **Note:** Kipper Schilling.

Date	Mintage	VG	F	VF	XF	Unc
ND(1620/1)	—	40.00	80.00	125	225	—

KM# 57 SCHILLING (6 Stüber)
Silver **Obv:** Crowned six-fold arms

Date	Mintage	VG	F	VF	XF	Unc
1633 (l)	—	—	—	—	—	—

KM# 72 SCHILLING (6 Stüber)
Silver **Obv:** Titles of Leopold I **Rev:** Titles of Enno Ludwig

Date	Mintage	VG	F	VF	XF	Unc
ND	—	—	—	—	—	—

KM# 71 SCHILLING (6 Stüber)
Silver **Note:** Klippe.

Date	Mintage	VG	F	VF	XF	Unc
ND (j)	—	—	—	—	—	—
ND (k)	—	—	—	—	—	—

KM# 69 SCHILLING (6 Stüber)
Silver **Obv:** Crowned imperial eagle, titles of Rudolf II **Rev:** Crowned six-fold arms, MO-NO. ENN...

Date	Mintage	VG	F	VF	XF	Unc
ND (i)	236,000	33.00	65.00	120	180	—

KM# 70 SCHILLING (6 Stüber)
Silver **Obv:** Titles of Matthias

Date	Mintage	VG	F	VF	XF	Unc
ND (j)	1,815,000	33.00	65.00	120	180	—
ND (k)	73,000	33.00	65.00	120	180	—

KM# 100 SCHILLING (6 Stüber)
Silver **Obv:** Titles of Georg Christian

Date	Mintage	VG	F	VF	XF	Unc
ND (m)	—	—	—	—	—	—

KM# 110 SCHILLING (6 Stüber)
Silver **Rev:** Titles of Christian Eberhard

Date	Mintage	VG	F	VF	XF	Unc
ND	—	27.00	60.00	110	220	—
1693 FBP	—	27.00	60.00	110	220	—
1694 FBP	—	27.00	60.00	110	220	—
1696 FBP	—	27.00	60.00	110	220	—
1697 FBP	—	27.00	60.00	110	220	—
1700 FBP	—	27.00	60.00	110	220	—

KM# 104 1/24 THALER
Silver **Obv:** Bust right **Rev:** Crowned imperial eagle, 24 in orb on breast, titles of Leopold I

Date	Mintage	VG	F	VF	XF	Unc
ND (z) Rare	—	—	—	—	—	—

KM# 85 1/16 THALER (2 Schilling)
Silver **Subject:** Death of Juliane of Hesse-Darmstadt, Wife of Ulrich II

Date	Mintage	VG	F	VF	XF	Unc
1659 HS	—	55.00	110	185	275	—

KM# 105 1/12 THALER (2 Groschen)
Silver **Obv:** Bust right **Rev:** Crowned harpy arms, date in legend

Date	Mintage	VG	F	VF	XF	Unc
1661	—	—	—	—	—	—

KM# 86 1/8 THALER
Silver **Subject:** Death of Juliane of Hesse-Darmstadt, Wife of Ulrich II **Note:** Similar to 1 Thaler, KM#89.

Date	Mintage	VG	F	VF	XF	Unc
1659 HS	—	115	200	375	600	—

KM# 87 1/4 THALER
Silver **Subject:** Death of Juliane of Hesse-Darmstadt, Wife of Ulrich II **Note:** Similar to 1 Thaler, KM#89.

Date	Mintage	VG	F	VF	XF	Unc
1659 HS	—	300	500	675	1,075	—

KM# 134 1/4 THALER
Silver **Subject:** Death of Christine Charlotte of Wurttemberg, Wife of Georg Christian **Obv:** Crowned momogram **Rev:** Inscription with date, loveknot below

Date	Mintage	VG	F	VF	XF	Unc
1699	—	165	375	525	825	—

KM# 135 1/4 THALER
Silver **Obv:** Arms of East Friesland and Wurttemberg

Date	Mintage	VG	F	VF	XF	Unc
1699	—	—	—	—	—	—

KM# 145 1/4 THALER
Silver **Subject:** Death of Eberhardine Sophie of Ottingen, Wife of Christian Eberhard

Date	Mintage	VG	F	VF	XF	Unc
1700	—	240	450	850	1,400	—

KM# 101 1/3 THALER
Silver **Obv:** Crowned imperial eagle, titles of Leopold I **Rev:** Crowned six-fold arms, value 3.EIN.RT, below, titles of Georg Christian **Note:** Varieties exist.

Date	Mintage	VG	F	VF	XF	Unc
ND (m)	—	80.00	140	240	400	—

KM# 111 1/3 THALER
Silver **Obv:** Crowned four-fold arms of Wurttemberg, central shield of harpy arms, titles of Christine Charlotte **Rev:** Crowned six-fold arms, value 3.EIN.RT, below, titles of Christian Eberhard

Date	Mintage	VG	F	VF	XF	Unc
ND	—	—	—	—	—	—

KM# 112 1/3 THALER
Silver **Obv:** Crowned imperial eagle, titles of Leopold I **Rev:** Crowned six-fold arms, value 3.EIN.RT. below, titles of Christian Eberhard

Date	Mintage	VG	F	VF	XF	Unc
ND (m)	—	45.00	90.00	180	325	—

KM# 26 1/2 THALER
Silver **Note:** Klippe.

Date	Mintage	VG	F	VF	XF	Unc
1614 (j)	—	—	—	—	—	—

KM# 32 1/2 THALER
Silver **Note:** Similar to 1 thaler, KM#27.

Date	Mintage	VG	F	VF	XF	Unc
1616 (j)	—	—	—	—	—	—

KM# 88 1/2 THALER
Silver **Subject:** Death of Juliane of Hesse-Darmstadt, Wife of Ulrich II **Note:** Similar to 1 Thaler, KM#89.

Date	Mintage	VG	F	VF	XF	Unc
1659 HS	—	260	300	500	800	—

KM# 131 2/3 THALER (Gulden)
Silver **Obv:** Bust right **Rev:** Crowned six-fold arms, value 2/3 in oval below divides date **Note:** Varieties exist.

Date	Mintage	VG	F	VF	XF	Unc
1694	—	—	—	—	—	—
1694 FBP	—	—	—	—	—	—

KM# 27.1 THALER
Silver **Subject:** Enno III **Note:** Varieties exist. Dav. #7122.

Date	Mintage	VG	F	VF	XF	Unc
1614 (j)	26,000	325	525	850	1,300	—
1615 (j)	12,000	325	525	850	1,300	—
1616 (j)	Inc. above	500	800	1,250	2,000	—
1617 (k)	4,000	500	800	1,250	2,000	—
1619 (k)	Inc. above	500	800	1,250	2,000	—
1622 (k)	—	325	525	850	1,300	—

KM# 27.2 THALER
Silver **Note:** Similar to KM#27.1 but without date on obverse. Dav. #7123.

Date	Mintage	VG	F	VF	XF	Unc
ND (j)	—	325	525	850	1,300	—

KM# 28 THALER
Silver **Note:** Klippe. Dav. #7122A.

Date	Mintage	VG	F	VF	XF	Unc
1615 (j) Rare	—	—	—	—	—	—
1616 (j) Rare	—	—	—	—	—	—
1617 (k) Rare	—	—	—	—	—	—

KM# 48 THALER
Silver **Obv:** Facing bust, harpy arms below **Rev:** Crowned imperial eagle, orb on breast, date in legend **Note:** Dav. #7125.

Date	Mintage	VG	F	VF	XF	Unc
1629 (l) Rare	—	—	—	—	—	—

KM# 56 THALER
Silver **Rev:** Date divided to lower left and right of eagle **Note:** Dav. #7126.

Date	Mintage	VG	F	VF	XF	Unc
1632 (l) Rare	—	—	—	—	—	—

KM# 89 THALER
Silver **Subject:** Death of Juliane of Hesse-Darmstadt, Wife of Ulrich II **Note:** Dav. #7127.

Date	Mintage	VG	F	VF	XF	Unc
1659 HS	—	575	975	1,650	2,400	—

KM# 102.1 THALER
Silver **Note:** Dav. #7128.

Date	Mintage	VG	F	VF	XF	Unc
ND (m) Rare	—	—	—	—	—	—

KM# 102.2 THALER
28.7700 g., Silver **Obv:** Different bust with longer hair **Obv. Legend:** ... ET. W. **Note:** Dav. #7129.

Date	Mintage	VG	F	VF	XF	Unc
ND (m) Rare	—	—	—	—	—	—

Note: Fritz Rudolf Künker Münzenhandlung Auction 127, 6-07, VF realized approximately $21,470.

KM# 103 THALER
Silver **Obv:** Facing bust **Note:** Dav. #7130.

Date	Mintage	VG	F	VF	XF	Unc
ND (m) Rare	—	—	—	—	—	—

KM# 120 THALER
28.8300 g., Silver **Subject:** 20th Anniversary of Regency of Christine Charlotte of Wurttemburg **Obv:** Facing bust **Rev:** Crowned joined oval arms of East Freisland and Wurttemberg, date in inner of two legends **Note:** Dav. #7132.

Date	Mintage	VG	F	VF	XF	Unc
1685 BH (m) Rare	—	—	—	—	—	—

Note: Fritz Rudolf Künker Münzenhandlung Auction 90, 3-03, near XF realized approximately $23,215.

KM# 121.1 THALER
Silver **Obv:** Bust of Christian Eberhard right **Rev:** Crowned six-fold arms divide date, two legends **Rev. Legend:** Outer: DA PAC...; inner: CHARITATE & CANDORE ERIGIMUR **Note:** Dav. #7133.

Date	Mintage	VG	F	VF	XF	Unc
1685 BH (m) Rare	—	—	—	—	—	—

KM# 121.2 THALER
Silver **Note:** Dav. #7134.

Date	Mintage	VG	F	VF	XF	Unc
1686	—	—	—	—	—	—

Note: Reported, not confirmed

KM# A134 THALER
Silver **Obv:** Bust right **Rev:** Ornate helmeted six-fold arms, date below **Note:** Dav. #7135.

Date	Mintage	VG	F	VF	XF	Unc
1698 FBP Rare	—	—	—	—	—	—

KM# 36 1-1/2 THALER
Silver **Subject:** Enno III **Note:** Klippe. Similar to 1 Thaler, KM#27. Dav. #7121.

Date	Mintage	VG	F	VF	XF	Unc
1617 (k) Rare	—	—	—	—	—	—
1619 (k) Rare	—	—	—	—	—	—
1622 (k) Rare	—	—	—	—	—	—

KM# 37 1-1/2 THALER
Silver **Obv:** Count on horse leaping right over landscape with town, ship, etc., legend quartered by four small shields **Obv. Legend:** DEO. CONFID... **Rev:** Female figure of Peace sitting, background of town, harbor with ship, etc. **Rev. Legend:** DA. PACEM... **Note:** Dav. #LS366.

Date	Mintage	VG	F	VF	XF	Unc
ND Rare	—	—	—	—	—	—

KM# A102 1-1/2 THALER
43.4700 g., Silver **Ruler:** Georg Christian **Obv:** Bust with long hair, right **Rev:** Three crowned helmets above six fold arms **Note:** As Dav. #7129

Date	Mintage	VG	F	VF	XF	Unc
ND (m) Rare	—	—	—	—	—	—

Note: Fritz Rudolf Künker Münzenhandlung Auction 93, 6-04, VF-XF realized approximately $67,700.

KM# 30 2 THALER

Silver **Note:** Klippe. Dav. #A7120.

Date	Mintage	VG	F	VF	XF	Unc
1614 (j) Rare	—	—	—	—	—	—
1615 (j) Rare	—	—	—	—	—	—
1617 (k) Rare	—	—	—	—	—	—
1619 (k) Rare	—	—	—	—	—	—

KM# 29 2 THALER

Silver **Subject:** Enno III **Note:** Similar to 1 Thaler, KM#27. Dav. #A7120.

Date	Mintage	VG	F	VF	XF	Unc
1614 (j) Rare	—	—	—	—	—	—

KM# 38 2 THALER

Silver **Obv:** Count on horse leaping right over landscape with town, etc., legend quartered by four small shields **Obv. Legend:** DEO. CONFID... **Rev:** Female figure of Peace sitting, background of town, harbor with ship, etc. **Rev. Legend:** DA. PACEM... **Note:** Dav. #LS365.

Date	Mintage	VG	F	VF	XF	Unc
ND Rare	—	—	—	—	—	—

KM# 49 2 THALER

Silver **Obv:** Crowned imperial eagle, orb on breast, date in legend **Rev:** Facing bust of Ulrich II, harpy arms below **Note:** Dav. #7124.

Date	Mintage	VG	F	VF	XF	Unc
1629 (l) Rare	—	—	—	—	—	—
1632 (l) Rare	—	—	—	—	—	—

KM# 122 2 THALER

Silver **Subject:** 20th Anniversary of Regency of Christine Charlotte of Wurttemberg **Obv:** Facing bust **Rev:** Crowned joined oval arms of East Friesland and Wurttemberg, date in inner of two legends **Note:** Dav. #7131.

Date	Mintage	VG	F	VF	XF	Unc
1685 BH (m) Rare	—	—	—	—	—	—

TRADE COINAGE

KM# 31 GOLDGULDEN

3.5000 g., 0.9860 Gold 0.1109 oz. AGW **Obv:** Bust of Enno right, date in legend **Rev:** Four shields in cruciform separated by arms of cross

Date	Mintage	VG	F	VF	XF	Unc
1615	576	625	1,350	3,600	6,300	—

KM# 33 GOLDGULDEN

3.5000 g., 0.9860 Gold 0.1109 oz. AGW **Note:** Klippe.

Date	Mintage	VG	F	VF	XF	Unc
1616	—	1,450	2,800	5,600	8,000	—

KM# 73 GOLDGULDEN

3.5000 g., 0.9860 Gold 0.1109 oz. AGW **Obv:** Crowned imperial eagle, orb on breast **Obv. Legend:** DA. PACEM... **Rev:** Titles of Enno

Date	Mintage	VG	F	VF	XF	Unc
ND	324	750	1,650	4,000	7,000	—

KM# 74 GOLDGULDEN

3.5000 g., 0.9860 Gold 0.1109 oz. AGW **Obv:** Christ standing **Rev:** Crowned arms

Date	Mintage	VG	F	VF	XF	Unc
ND	—	525	1,150	3,000	5,300	—

KM# 75 1/2 DUCAT

1.7500 g., 0.9860 Gold 0.0555 oz. AGW **Obv:** Crowned arms **Rev:** Cross in circle

Date	Mintage	VG	F	VF	XF	Unc
ND	—	265	525	1,050	1,800	—

KM# 25 DUCAT

3.5000 g., 0.9860 Gold 0.1109 oz. AGW **Obv:** Five-line inscription in ornamented square MON. AVE/ENN... **Rev:** Full-length figure of knight standing to right with sword and shield divides date

Date	Mintage	VG	F	VF	XF	Unc
1612	2,035	800	1,600	3,850	6,800	—

PATTERNS

Including off metal strikes

KM#	Date	Mintage	Identification	Mkt Val
Pn1	ND (i)	—	Ciffert. Gold And Silver. Klippe. KM#16.	—
Pn2	ND (k)	—	Flindrich. Gold. KM#67.	—
Pn3	1659 HS	—	Thaler. Lead. KM#89.	—

EICHSTATT

(Eichstadt)

A Bishopric in central Bavaria, which was founded in 745. The Imperial Mint was founded c. 908 and Episcopal coinage began in the 11th century. Eichstatt was secularized in 1802 and given to Salzburg. It passed to Bavaria in 1805.

RULERS

Johann Conrad von Gemmingen, 1595-1612
Johann Christoph von Westerstetten, 1612-1636
Marquard II, Schenk von Castell, 1636-1685
Johann Eucharius, Schenk von Castell, 1685-1697
Johann Martin von Eyb, 1697-1704

MINT OFFICIALS' INITIALS

Initial	Date	Name
(c), GFN	1682-1724	Georg Friedrich Nurnberger, mintmaster and die-cutter in Nüremberg
(d)	Ca.1606	Paulus Biether in Nüremberg
(h) 2 horshoes	1626-28	Bartholomaus Holeisen in Augsburg
IB	Ca.1634-37	Unknown

BISHOPRIC

REGULAR COINAGE

KM# 16 PFENNIG

Copper **Note:** Kipper Pfennig. Uniface. Oval Eichstatt arms divide date, I above.

Date	Mintage	VG	F	VF	XF	Unc
1621	—	33.00	65.00	120	185	—

KM# 17 PFENNIG

Copper **Note:** Shield is flat on top, pointed bottom.

Date	Mintage	VG	F	VF	XF	Unc
1621	—	55.00	130	275	450	—

KM# 18 1/2 KREUZER

Copper **Note:** Kipper 1/2 Kreuzer. Uniface. Bishop's staff between two crosses.

Date	Mintage	VG	F	VF	XF	Unc
ND(1621/2)	—	25.00	40.00	65.00	120	—

KM# 26 1/2 KREUZER

Silver **Obv:** Two shields of Eichstatt and Westerstetten arms, date above **Rev:** Imperial orb with 1/2

Date	Mintage	VG	F	VF	XF	Unc
1623	—	65.00	130	220	290	—
1624	—	65.00	130	220	290	—

KM# 19 KREUZER

Copper **Obv:** Bishop's staff **Rev:** I/KREI/ZER **Note:** Kipper Kreuzer. Varieties exist.

Date	Mintage	VG	F	VF	XF	Unc
ND(1621/2)	—	20.00	40.00	70.00	120	—

KM# 20 KREUZER

Copper **Rev:** KREIZER/I **Note:** Varieties exist.

Date	Mintage	VG	F	VF	XF	Unc
ND(1621/2)	—	20.00	40.00	70.00	120	—

KM# 31 KREUZER

Silver **Obv:** Bishop's mitre above two shilds of Eichstatt and Westerstetten arms, date below **Rev:** Horseshoes above legend, pine cone of Augsburg below **Rev. Legend:** CONFIRMET/ET/CONSERVET/DEVS

Date	Mintage	VG	F	VF	XF	Unc
1628 (h)	—	27.00	60.00	120	175	—

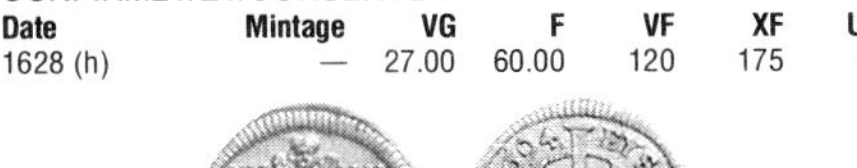

KM# 40 KREUZER

Silver **Obv:** Two shields of Eichstsattt and Castell arms, angel's head above divides I.E.-E.E. **Rev:** Double cross forming star, value I in central circle, date in legend

Date	Mintage	VG	F	VF	XF	Unc
1694 (c)	—	16.00	33.00	65.00	120	—

KM# 28 2 KREUZER (1/2 Batzen)

Silver **Obv:** Crowned imperial eagle, two in orb on breast, titles of Ferdinand II **Rev:** Four-fold arms of Eichstatt and Westerstetten in circle, date above in legend

Date	Mintage	VG	F	VF	XF	Unc
1623	—	27.00	45.00	80.00	135	—

KM# 29 2 KREUZER (1/2 Batzen)

Silver **Obv:** Two in orb **Rev:** Date above shields **Note:** Varieties exist.

Date	Mintage	VG	F	VF	XF	Unc
1623	—	16.00	33.00	60.00	125	—
1624	—	16.00	33.00	60.00	125	—
1634	—	16.00	33.00	60.00	125	—
1634 IB	—	16.00	33.00	60.00	125	—

KM# 38 2 KREUZER (1/2 Batzen)

Silver **Rev:** Two oval arms, date in legend

Date	Mintage	VG	F	VF	XF	Unc
1636 IB	—	16.00	33.00	60.00	120	—

KM# 39 2 KREUZER (1/2 Batzen)

Silver **Obv:** Titles of Ferdinand III

Date	Mintage	VG	F	VF	XF	Unc
1637 IB	—	16.00	33.00	60.00	120	—

KM# 41 2 KREUZER (1/2 Batzen)

Silver **Obv:** Crowned imperial eagle, value 2 in shield on breast, date and titles of Leopold I in legend **Rev:** Four-fold arms of cathedral chapter and Castell arms, with central shield of Eichstatt arms

Date	Mintage	VG	F	VF	XF	Unc
1694 (c)	282,000	16.00	33.00	65.00	115	—

KM# 23 3 KREUZER (Groschen)

Silver **Obv:** Crowned imperial eagle, 3 in orb on breast, titles of Ferdinand II **Rev:** Four-fold arms of Eichstatt and Westerstetten, date in legend at top **Note:** Varieties exist.

Date	Mintage	VG	F	VF	XF	Unc
1622	—	40.00	85.00	140	220	—
1623	—	40.00	85.00	140	220	—

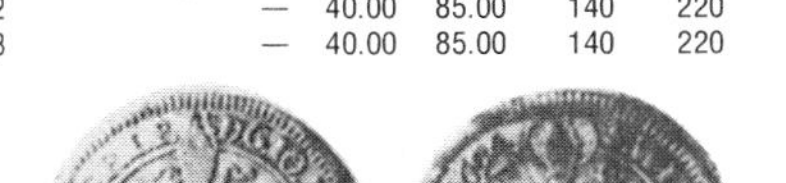

KM# 42 4 KREUZER (Batzen)

Silver **Obv:** Four-fold arms of cathedral chapter and Castell between palm branches, angel's head with mitre above **Rev:** St. Willibald standing, value (4) below

Date	Mintage	VG	F	VF	XF	Unc
1694 GFN	135,000	40.00	75.00	140	240	—

KM# 35 10 KREUZER

Silver **Obv:** Crowned imperial eagle, X.K. in shield on breast, titles of Ferdinand II **Rev:** Two oval arms of Eichstatt and Westerstetten in baroque frame, date in legend

Date	Mintage	VG	F	VF	XF	Unc
1634 IB	—	275	425	575	800	—

KM# 36 10 KREUZER

Silver **Rev:** Value 10 in shield on eagle's breast **Note:** Varieties exist.

Date	Mintage	VG	F	VF	XF	Unc
1635 IB	—	200	300	425	750	—
1636 IB	—	200	300	425	750	—
1637 IB	—	200	300	425	750	—

KM# 21 24 KREUZER

Silver **Obv:** Westerstetten arms in baroque frame **Obv. Legend:** MONETA. NOVA... **Rev:** Eichstatt arms in baroque frame, (24) in legend at top **Note:** Kipper 24 Kreuzer.

Date	Mintage	VG	F	VF	XF	Unc
ND(1621)	—	—	—	—	—	—

KM# 22 24 KREUZER

Silver **Rev:** Value in field above arms **Note:** Varieties exist.

Date	Mintage	VG	F	VF	XF	Unc
ND(1621)	—	—	—	—	—	—

KM# 15 1/4 THALER (24 Kreuzer)

Silver **Obv:** Three leopards left (cathedral chapter arms) **Obv. Legend:** MONETA. NOVA... **Rev:** Eichstatt arms in baroque frame divide date

Date	Mintage	VG	F	VF	XF	Unc
1620 Rare	—	—	—	—	—	—

KM# 7 1/2 THALER

Silver **Obv:** Crowned imperial eagle, titles of Rudolf II **Rev:** Four-fold arms of Eichstatt and Gemmingen, angel's head and wings above, date divided below

Date	Mintage	VG	F	VF	XF	Unc
1606 (d)	500	—	—	—	—	—

KM# 5 1/2 THALER

Silver **Note:** Similar to 1 Thaler, KM#8.

Date	Mintage	VG	F	VF	XF	Unc
1606 (d)	500	525	850	1,500	2,750	—

KM# 6 1/2 THALER

Silver **Note:** Similar to 1 Thaler, KM#9.

Date	Mintage	VG	F	VF	XF	Unc
1606 (d)	500	—	—	—	—	—

KM# 43 1/2 THALER

Silver **Note:** Similar to 1 Thaler, KM#45.

Date	Mintage	VG	F	VF	XF	Unc
1694 GFN Rare	192	—	—	—	—	—

KM# 44 1/2 THALER

Silver **Note:** Similar to 1 Thaler, KM#46.

Date	Mintage	VG	F	VF	XF	Unc
1694 GFN	3,392	275	500	800	1,250	—

KM# 8 THALER

Silver **Rev:** Madonna and child **Note:** Dav. #5228.

Date	Mintage	VG	F	VF	XF	Unc
1606 (d) Rare	1,000	—	—	—	—	—

Note: Dr. Busso Peus Nachfolger Auction 390, 5-07, XF-VF realized approximately $27,200.

KM# 9 THALER

Silver **Rev:** St. Wilibaldus seated **Note:** Dav. #5229.

Date	Mintage	VG	F	VF	XF	Unc
1606 (d) Rare	999	—	—	—	—	—

Note: Dr. Busso Peus Nachfolger Auction 390, 5-07, XF-VF realized approximately $11,550.

KM# 10 THALER

Silver **Obv:** Crowned imperial eagle, titles of Rudolf II **Rev:** Four-fold arms of Eichstatt and Gemmingen, angel's head and wings above, date divided below **Note:** Dav. #5230.

Date	Mintage	VG	F	VF	XF	Unc
1606 (d) Rare	1,002	—	—	—	—	—

KM# 24.1 THALER

Silver **Obv:** Crowned imperial eagle, orb on breast, titles of Ferdinand II **Rev:** Two oval arms of Eichstatt and Westerstetten in baroque frame, angel's head above, date below **Note:** Dav. #5231.

Date	Mintage	VG	F	VF	XF	Unc
1622 Rare	—	—	—	—	—	—

KM# 24.2 THALER

Silver **Obv:** Two pointed arms and cherub face in cartouche, date in frame below **Note:** Varieties exist. Dav. #5232.

Date	Mintage	VG	F	VF	XF	Unc
1622 Rare	—	—	—	—	—	—

KM# 25 THALER

Silver **Obv:** Floral spray instead of angel's head **Note:** Dav. #5233.

Date	Mintage	VG	F	VF	XF	Unc
1622 Rare	—	—	—	—	—	—

KM# 30 THALER

Silver **Subject:** Johann Christoph **Obv:** Four-fold arms of Eichstatt and Westerstetten, two helmets and mitre above, date in legend at top **Note:** Dav. #5234.

Date	Mintage	VG	F	VF	XF	Unc
1626 Rare	—	—	—	—	—	—

KM# 45 THALER

Silver **Subject:** Johann Eucharius **Note:** Dav. #5235.

Date	Mintage	VG	F	VF	XF	Unc
1694 GFN	2,208	375	750	1,250	2,500	7,000

KM# 46 THALER

Silver **Rev:** St. Wilibaldus standing **Note:** Dav. #5236.

Date	Mintage	VG	F	VF	XF	Unc
1694 GFN	24,000	125	250	400	850	1,750

KM# 47 2 THALER

Silver **Note:** Similar to 1 Thaler, KM#46. Dav. #5236A.

Date	Mintage	VG	F	VF	XF	Unc
1694 GFN Rare	—	—	—	—	—	—

TRADE COINAGE

KM# 32 GOLDGULDEN

3.2300 g., 0.9860 Gold 0.1024 oz. AGW **Obv:** Two coats of arms in inner circle **Rev:** St. Walburga standing behind arms divides date

Date	Mintage	VG	F	VF	XF	Unc
1633	—	775	1,650	3,850	6,600	—

KM# 33 GOLDGULDEN

3.1800 g., 0.9860 Gold 0.1008 oz. AGW **Rev:** St. Willibald standing behind arms divides date

Date	Mintage	VG	F	VF	XF	Unc
1633	—	775	1,650	3,850	6,600	—
1634	—	775	1,650	3,850	6,600	—
1635 IB	—	775	1,650	3,850	6,600	—

KM# 34 GOLDGULDEN

3.2000 g., 0.9860 Gold 0.1014 oz. AGW **Rev:** Date angled at sides of shield

Date	Mintage	VG	F	VF	XF	Unc
1633	—	775	1,650	3,850	6,600	—

KM# 37 DUCAT

3.4700 g., 0.9860 Gold 0.1100 oz. AGW **Obv:** Imperial eagle in inner circle, date in legend **Rev:** St. Willibald behind shield of arms

Date	Mintage	VG	F	VF	XF	Unc
1635 IB	—	1,000	2,100	4,800	8,400	—

KM# A45 5 DUCAT

17.5000 g., 0.9860 Gold 0.5547 oz. AGW **Note:** Struck with 1/2 Thaler dies, KM#44.

Date	Mintage	VG	F	VF	XF	Unc
1694 GFN Rare	—	—	—	—	—	—

KM# A46 10 DUCAT (Portugalöser)

0.9860 Gold **Note:** Struck with 1 Thaler dies, KM#45.

Date	Mintage	VG	F	VF	XF	Unc
1694 GFN Rare	—	—	—	—	—	—

EINBECK

(Eimbeck)

The town of Einbeck, near the confluence of the Leine and Ilme Rivers, 38 miles (65 kilometers) south of Hannover, was associated early on with the nearby monastery of St. Alexander which was founded about 1080. Its first mention as a town came in 1274 and soon thereafter it was the location of a mint for the dukes of Brunswick-Grubenhagen. At some point during the 15th century, Einbeck obtained the mint right and began striking its own local coinage in 1498. By an edict of Johann Friedrich, Duke of Brunswick-Lüneburg-Calenberg (1665-79) in 1674, the minting of silver coinage was halted, but the town continued striking undated copper pfennigs until 1717.

MINT OFFICIALS' INITIALS

Initial	Date	Name
(a)shield with half of seal ring in top, bottom shaded	1616-18	Heindrich von der Ecke
AS	1668-71	Andreas Schele
(b)same as (a)	1623-25	Hans von der Ecke der Jungere
(c) crossed halberds	1628	Georg Krukenberg
HE (combined in oval)	1604-05	Hans von der Ecke der Alter
HE (combined in oval)	1606-18	Heinrich von der Ecke
HH (sometimes in ligature)	1672-74	Hans Hallensen
IK or (d) halberd	1629	Unknown
VF (sometimes in ligature)	1659	Urban Felgenhauer

Arms:

Large Gothic 'E', later in 17th century, a Latin 'E'

Reference:

B = Heinrich Buck, ***Die Münzen der Stadt Einbeck.*** Hildeshiem and Leipzig, 1939.

CITY

REGULAR COINAGE

KM# 15 FLITTER (1/2 Pfennig)

Copper **Obv:** Crowned Gothic E **Rev:** Date **Rev. Legend:** I/FLIT/TER **Note:** Klipper Flitter.

Date	Mintage	VG	F	VF	XF	Unc
(1)620	—	16.00	33.00	65.00	130	—

KM# 16 FLITTER (1/2 Pfennig)

Copper **Obv:** Similar to KM#15 **Rev:** I in circle, date **Rev. Legend:** FLITTER **Note:** Varieties exist.

Date	Mintage	VG	F	VF	XF	Unc
1620	—	16.00	33.00	65.00	130	—
1621	—	16.00	33.00	65.00	130	—
1612 Error	—	16.00	33.00	65.00	130	—

KM# 19 3 FLITTER

Copper **Obv:** Crowned Gothie C **Rev:** III in circle, date **Rev. Legend:** FLITTER **Note:** Klipper 3 Flitter. Varieties exist.

Date	Mintage	VG	F	VF	XF	Unc
16Z1	—	16.00	33.00	65.00	130	—
1Z61 Error	—	16.00	33.00	65.00	130	—
1621	—	16.00	33.00	65.00	130	—

KM# 22 PFENNIG

Silver **Note:** Uniface. Schüssel type. Gothic E, date above, in shield surrounded by circle of pellets. Varieties exist.

Date	Mintage	VG	F	VF	XF	Unc
16Z3	—	16.00	33.00	60.00	110	—
16Z4	—	16.00	33.00	60.00	110	—
ND(1623/4)	—	16.00	33.00	60.00	110	—

KM# 32 PFENNIG

Silver **Note:** Crowned Gothic E divides date in circle of pellets. Varieties exist.

Date	Mintage	VG	F	VF	XF	Unc
16Z9	—	16.00	33.00	60.00	110	—
1660	—	16.00	33.00	60.00	110	—

KM# 35 PFENNIG

Silver **Note:** Crowned Roman E divides date in circle of pellets. Varieties exist.

Date	Mintage	VG	F	VF	XF	Unc
1631	—	16.00	33.00	60.00	110	—
1632	—	16.00	33.00	60.00	110	—
1634	—	16.00	33.00	60.00	110	—
1635	—	16.00	33.00	60.00	110	—
1638	—	16.00	33.00	60.00	110	—
1641	—	16.00	33.00	60.00	110	—

KM# 40 PFENNIG

Copper **Obv:** EINBECK around **Rev:** Value **Note:** Varieties exist.

Date	Mintage	VG	F	VF	XF	Unc
ND(1647-1717)	—	13.00	30.00	45.00	80.00	—

KM# 41 PFENNIG

Copper **Obv:** With rosette **Note:** Varieties exist.

Date	Mintage	VG	F	VF	XF	Unc
ND(1647-1717)	—	13.00	30.00	45.00	80.00	—

KM# 51 PFENNIG

Silver **Note:** Uniface. Crowned Gothic E divides date.

Date	Mintage	VG	F	VF	XF	Unc
1668	—	13.00	33.00	55.00	95.00	—
1668 AS	—	13.00	33.00	55.00	95.00	—

KM# 67 PFENNIG

Silver **Note:** Schussel type. Crowned Roman E divides date and mintmasters initials.

Date	Mintage	VG	F	VF	XF	Unc
1673 HH	—	13.00	33.00	55.00	95.00	—

KM# 20 3 PFENNIG (1/96 Thaler)

Silver **Obv:** Crowned Gothic E **Rev:** Imperial orb with 3 divides date

Date	Mintage	VG	F	VF	XF	Unc
1622	—	20.00	40.00	70.00	125	—
1635	—	20.00	40.00	70.00	125	—

KM# 21 3 PFENNIG (1/96 Thaler)

Silver **Obv:** Smaller E **Rev:** Smaller imperial orb on ornamented rhombus

Date	Mintage	VG	F	VF	XF	Unc
1622	—	20.00	40.00	70.00	125	—

KM# 52 3 PFENNIG (1/96 Thaler)
Silver **Obv:** Crowned Gothic E, EINBECK, date **Rev:** Imperial orb with 3

Date	Mintage	VG	F	VF	XF	Unc
1668 AS	—	10.00	20.00	40.00	80.00	—
1669 AS	—	10.00	20.00	40.00	80.00	—
1670 AS	—	10.00	20.00	40.00	80.00	—

KM# 53 3 PFENNIG (1/96 Thaler)
Silver **Obv. Legend:** EIMBEC

Date	Mintage	VG	F	VF	XF	Unc
1668 AS	—	13.00	27.00	45.00	95.00	—

KM# 60 3 PFENNIG (1/96 Thaler)
Silver **Obv. Legend:** EINBEC

Date	Mintage	VG	F	VF	XF	Unc
1670 AS	—	13.00	27.00	45.00	95.00	—
1672 HH	—	13.00	27.00	45.00	95.00	—
1673 HH	—	13.00	27.00	45.00	95.00	—

KM# 54 4 PFENNIG (Gute)
Silver **Obv:** Crowned Gothic E, MO. NO. EINBECIC, date around **Rev. Legend:** IIII/GUTE/PF

Date	Mintage	VG	F	VF	XF	Unc
1668 AS	—	16.00	33.00	60.00	120	—
1669 AS	—	16.00	33.00	60.00	120	—

KM# 68 4 PFENNIG (Gute)
Silver **Obv. Legend:** EINBEC

Date	Mintage	VG	F	VF	XF	Unc
1673 HH	—	16.00	33.00	60.00	120	—

KM# 23 MARIENGROSCHEN
Silver **Obv:** Crowned Gothic E, date in legend **Rev:** Madonna and child **Note:** Varieties exist.

Date	Mintage	VG	F	VF	XF	Unc
16Z3	—	16.00	35.00	70.00	140	—
16Z4	—	16.00	35.00	70.00	140	—
1659 VF	—	16.00	35.00	70.00	140	—
1668 AS	—	16.00	35.00	70.00	140	—
1669 AS	—	16.00	35.00	70.00	140	—
1670 AS	—	16.00	35.00	70.00	140	—
1673 HH	—	16.00	35.00	70.00	140	—
1674 HH	—	16.00	35.00	70.00	140	—

KM# 61 2 MARIENGROSCHEN
Silver **Obv:** Crowned Gothic E, date in legend **Rev. Legend:** II/MARI/GR

Date	Mintage	VG	F	VF	XF	Unc
1671 AS	—	—	—	—	—	—

KM# 62 4 MARIENGROSCHEN
Silver **Obv:** Crowned Gothic E, date in legend **Rev. Legend:** IIII/MARIEN/GROS

Date	Mintage	VG	F	VF	XF	Unc
1671 AS	—	45.00	85.00	170	275	—

KM# 55 6 MARIENGROSCHEN
Silver **Obv:** Crowned Gothic E **Rev:** Date in legend **Rev. Legend:** VI/MARIEN/GROS

Date	Mintage	VG	F	VF	XF	Unc
1669 AS	—	40.00	85.00	140	250	—
1671 AS	—	40.00	85.00	140	250	—
1673 HH	—	40.00	85.00	140	250	—
1674 HH	—	40.00	85.00	140	250	—

KM# 63 6 MARIENGROSCHEN
Silver **Rev:** Date **Rev. Legend:** VI/MARIEN/GROSCH

Date	Mintage	VG	F	VF	XF	Unc
1671 AS	—	60.00	115	185	300	—

KM# 64 12 MARIENGROSCHEN
Silver **Obv:** Crowned Gothic E **Rev:** Date **Rev. Legend:** XII/MARIEN/GROSCH

Date	Mintage	VG	F	VF	XF	Unc
1671 AS	—	—	—	—	—	—

KM# 65 24 MARIENGROSCHEN (2/3 Thaler)
Silver **Obv:** Crowned Gothic E, date in legend **Rev. Legend:** XXIIII/MARIEN/GROS **Note:** Dav. #502.

Date	Mintage	VG	F	VF	XF	Unc
1671	—	—	—	—	—	—

Note: Reported, not confirmed

KM# 66 24 MARIENGROSCHEN (2/3 Thaler)
Silver **Obv:** Crowned Gothic E **Rev:** Value, date **Rev. Legend:** XXIIII **Note:** Dav. #503.

Date	Mintage	VG	F	VF	XF	Unc
1671 AS	—	—	—	—	—	—

Note: Reported, not confirmed

KM# 17 12 KREUZER (Schreckenberger)
Silver **Obv:** Crowned imperial eagle, 12 in orb on breast, titles of Ferdinand II **Rev:** Crowned Gothic E in shield **Note:** Kipper 12 Kreuzer.

Date	Mintage	VG	F	VF	XF	Unc
ND(1620-21)	—	—	—	—	—	—

KM# 5 1/96 THALER (3 Pfennig)
Silver **Obv:** Crowned Gothic E **Rev:** Imperial orb with 96 divides date

Date	Mintage	VG	F	VF	XF	Unc
1604	—	55.00	120	200	350	—
1604 HE	—	55.00	120	200	350	—
1605 HE	—	55.00	120	200	350	—
ND	—	55.00	120	200	350	—

KM# 7 1/24 THALER (Groschen)
Silver **Note:** Klippe.

Date	Mintage	VG	F	VF	XF	Unc
1604 HE Rare	—	—	—	—	—	—

KM# 6 1/24 THALER (Groschen)
Silver **Obv:** Imperial orb with 24, cross divides date, titles of Rudolf II **Rev:** Crowned Gothic E **Note:** Varieties exist.

Date	Mintage	VG	F	VF	XF	Unc
1604 HE	—	16.00	33.00	65.00	120	—
1605 HE	—	16.00	33.00	65.00	120	—
1606 HE	—	16.00	33.00	65.00	120	—
1607 HE	—	16.00	33.00	65.00	120	—

KM# 10 1/24 THALER (Groschen)
Silver **Obv:** Titles of Matthias **Note:** Varieties exist.

Date	Mintage	VG	F	VF	XF	Unc
1614	—	16.00	33.00	60.00	110	—
1615	—	16.00	33.00	60.00	110	—
1616	—	16.00	33.00	60.00	110	—
1616 (a)	—	16.00	33.00	60.00	110	—
1617	—	16.00	33.00	60.00	110	—
1617 (a)	—	16.00	33.00	60.00	110	—

KM# 11 1/24 THALER (Groschen)
Silver **Rev:** Date divided at top **Note:** Kipper 1/24 Thaler. Varieties exist.

Date	Mintage	VG	F	VF	XF	Unc
1618	—	16.00	33.00	60.00	120	—
1619	—	16.00	33.00	60.00	120	—
1602 Error	—	16.00	33.00	60.00	120	—

KM# 18 1/24 THALER (Groschen)
Silver **Obv:** Titles of Ferdinand II

Date	Mintage	VG	F	VF	XF	Unc
1620	—	16.00	33.00	60.00	120	—

KM# 56 1/24 THALER (Groschen)
Silver **Obv:** Imperial orb with 24, titles of Leopold I **Rev:** Crowned Gothic E, date in legend

Date	Mintage	VG	F	VF	XF	Unc
1669 AS	—	16.00	33.00	60.00	120	—
1670 AS	—	16.00	33.00	60.00	120	—
1671 AS	—	16.00	33.00	60.00	120	—

KM# 29 1/2 REICHSORT (1/8 Thaler)
Silver **Obv:** EIN/HALB/REICHS/ORT, cross on imperial orb above divides date in legend, titles of Ferdinand II **Rev:** Crowned Gothic E

Date	Mintage	VG	F	VF	XF	Unc
1628	—	—	—	—	—	—

KM# 24 1/4 THALER
Silver **Obv:** Crowned imperial eagle, orb on breast, titles of Ferdinand II **Rev:** Crowned Gothic E, date in legend **Note:** Varieties exist.

Date	Mintage	VG	F	VF	XF	Unc
1624 (b)	—	500	925	1,400	2,200	—
1625 (b)	—	500	925	1,400	2,200	—
1628 (c)	—	500	925	1,400	2,200	—

KM# 25 1/2 THALER
Silver **Obv:** Crowned imperial eagle, orb on breast, titles of Ferdinand II **Rev:** Crowned Gothic E in ornamented shield, date in legend **Note:** Varieties exist.

Date	Mintage	VG	F	VF	XF	Unc
1624 (b)	—	600	1,250	2,000	2,750	—
1625 (b)	—	600	1,250	2,000	2,750	—
1627	—	600	1,250	2,000	2,750	—

KM# 12 THALER
Silver **Obv:** Crowned imperial eagle, orb on breast, titles of Matthias **Rev:** Crowned Gothic E in ornamented shield, date in legend **Note:** Dav. #5237.

Date	Mintage	VG	F	VF	XF	Unc
1618 (a) Rare	—	—	—	—	—	—

KM# 26 THALER
Silver **Obv:** Titles of Ferdinand II **Rev:** Angel's head above Gothic E **Note:** Dav. #5238.

Date	Mintage	VG	F	VF	XF	Unc
1624	—	1,200	2,200	4,500	7,000	—

KM# 27 THALER
Silver **Obv:** Titles of Ferdinand II **Note:** Dav. #5239.

Date	Mintage	VG	F	VF	XF	Unc
1624 (b)	—	900	1,900	3,500	5,600	—

KM# 28 THALER
Silver **Note:** Dav. #5241.

Date	Mintage	VG	F	VF	XF	Unc
1624 (b)	—	700	1,400	2,500	4,200	—
1625 (b)	—	700	1,400	2,500	4,200	—
1627	—	700	1,400	2,500	4,200	—
1628 (c)	—	700	1,400	2,500	4,200	—
1631	—	700	1,400	2,500	4,200	—

KM# 45 THALER
Silver **Note:** Dav. #5242.

Date	Mintage	VG	F	VF	XF	Unc
1659 VF Rare	—	—	—	—	—	—

KM# 30 2 THALER
Silver **Note:** Struck from KM#28 dies. Dav. #5240.

Date	Mintage	VG	F	VF	XF	Unc
1628 (c) Rare	—	—	—	—	—	—

KM# 50 2 THALER
Silver **Note:** Struck from KM#36 dies. Dav. #5243.

Date	Mintage	VG	F	VF	XF	Unc
1660 VF Rare	—	—	—	—	—	—

TRADE COINAGE

KM# 13 GOLDGULDEN
3.5000 g., 0.9860 Gold 0.1109 oz. AGW **Obv:** Imperial eagle, orb on breast, titles of Ferdinand II **Rev:** Crowned Gothic E, date in legend

Date	Mintage	VG	F	VF	XF	Unc
1619 Rare	—	—	—	—	—	—

KM# 31 GOLDGULDEN
3.5000 g., 0.9860 Gold 0.1109 oz. AGW **Obv:** Crowned imperial eagle, orb on breast, titles of Ferdinand II **Rev:** Crowned Gothic E in city gate with 2 towers which divides date, lion left above gate

Date	Mintage	VG	F	VF	XF	Unc
1628 Rare	—	—	—	—	—	—

KM# 33 GOLDGULDEN
3.5000 g., 0.9860 Gold 0.1109 oz. AGW **Rev:** Gothic E in city gate with 2 towers

Date	Mintage	VG	F	VF	XF	Unc
1629	—	1,200	2,400	4,200	7,200	—
1629 IK Rare	—	—	—	—	—	—
1629 (d) Rare	—	—	—	—	—	—

PATTERNS

Including off metal strikes

KM#	Date	Mintage	Identification	Mkt Val
Pn1	1633	—	Thaler. Copper. KM#28.	—

TRIAL STRIKES

KM#	Date	Mintage	Identification	Mkt Val
TS1	1636	—	Thaler. Silver. Klippe, obverse, KM#36.	—

ELLWANGEN

Founded as a Benedictine Abbey about 764 but not recognized as a town until about 1229, Ellwangen is located in northern Württemberg about 18 miles northwest of Nordlingen. The Abbey was reorganized as a college in 1460. The mint right was obtained in 1555. The town was mediatized and the properties given to Württemberg in 1803.

RULERS
Wolfgang von Hausen, 1584-1603
Johann Christoph I von Westerstetten, 1603-1613
Johann Christoph II von Freyberg-Eisenberg, 1613-1620
Johann Jakob Blarer von Wartensee, 1621-1654
Johann Rudolf von Rechberg, 1654-1660
Johann Christoph III von Freyberg-Eisenberg, 1660-1674
Johann Christoph IV Adelmann von Adelmannsfelden, 1674-1687
Heinrich Christoph von Wolfframsdorf, 1687-1689
Ludwig Anton, Pfalzgraf bei Rhein und zu Neuburg, 1689-1694
Franz Ludwig von der Pfalz, 1694-1732

MINT OFFICIALS' INITIALS

Initial	Date	Name
(a) horseshoe	Ca.1620-68	Johann Bartholomaus Holesen der Altere in Augsburg
(b) horseshoe	1668-97	Johann Christoph Holeisen in Augsburg
CIL	1683-1707	Christoph Jakob Leherr, die-cutter in Augsburg
GFN	1682-1704	George Friedrich Nurnberger in Nüremberg

PROVOSTSHIP

Abbey

REGULAR COINAGE

KM# 5 PFENNIG

Copper **Ruler:** Johann Jakob Blarer **Obv:** Mitre with cross above divides date 1 - 6/Z - 1 **Rev. Legend:** I/PFEN/NING/++

Date	Mintage	VG	F	VF	XF	Unc
16Z1	—	—	—	—	—	—

KM# 6 2 KREUZER (1/2 Batzen)

Silver **Ruler:** Johann Jakob Blarer **Obv:** Crowned imperial eagle, Z in orb on breast, titles of Ferdinand II **Rev:** 2 oval arms, angel's head above, date below **Note:** Varieties exist.

Date	Mintage	VG	F	VF	XF	Unc
(16)24 (a)	—	20.00	40.00	65.00	120	—
(16)25 (a)	—	20.00	40.00	65.00	120	—
(16)26 (a)	—	20.00	40.00	65.00	120	—

KM# 15 3 KREUZER (Groschen)

Silver **Ruler:** Ludwig Anton **Subject:** Death of Ludwig Anton **Obv:** Crowned oval 4-fold arms in baroque frame **Rev:** 7-line inscription with date, value 3 in imperial orb below

Date	Mintage	VG	F	VF	XF	Unc
1694 Rare	—	—	—	—	—	—

KM# 16 1/4 THALER

Silver **Ruler:** Ludwig Anton **Subject:** Death of Ludwig Anton **Obv:** Crowned oval 4-fold arms in baroque frame **Rev:** 6-line inscription with date, value in imperial orb below

Date	Mintage	VG	F	VF	XF	Unc
1694 GFN Rare	—	—	—	—	—	—

KM# 7 THALER

Silver **Ruler:** Johann Jakob Blarer **Obv:** Oval 4-fold arms, angel's head and wings above, date in cartouche below **Rev:** Crowned imperial eagle, orb on breast, arms (pinecone) of Augsburg below, titles of Ferdinand II **Note:** Dav. #5244.

Date	Mintage	VG	F	VF	XF	Unc
1624 (a)	—	2,000	3,500	5,500	8,500	—

KM# 10 THALER

Silver **Ruler:** Heinrich Christoph **Obv:** Bust right **Rev:** Helmeted and mitred oval 4-fold arms, date below divided by small Augsburg arms **Note:** Dav. #5245.

Date	Mintage	VG	F	VF	XF	Unc
1689 CIL-(b) Rare	—	—	—	—	—	—

KM# 11 THALER

Silver **Ruler:** Heinrich Christoph **Obv:** Bust right **Rev:** Romulus and Remus with wolf in landscape, ornate 4-fold arms above divide date **Note:** Dav. #5246.

Date	Mintage	VG	F	VF	XF	Unc
1689 CIL Rare	—	—	—	—	—	—

EMDEN

A seaport on the Ems River adjoining the North Sea was founded in the 9th century and became a pirate lair in the 14th century. It was taken by Hamburg and East Friesland in 1431. Hamburg sold its local holdings to East Friesland in 1453. Emden became a Free City of the Empire in 1595, was transferred to Prussia in 1744, then became a Free Port in 1751. It was passed to Holland in 1806, Hannover in 1815 and Prussia in 1866.

MINT OFFICIALS' INITIALS

Initial	Date	Name
IG, G	Pre-1603	Jonas Georgens
CP	Ca.1619	Unknown
CP	1673-74	Christian Pfahler
IS	1648-50	Jacob Schweiger
JR	Ca.1681	Unknown

ARMS:

Upper half of crowned harpy (because of the association with East Friesland) above a stone wall, waves below.

Reference:

K = ***Nachtrag zum Münz- und Medaillen – Kabinet des Grafen Karl zu Inn- und Knyphausen.*** Hannover, 1877.

FREE CITY

REGULAR COINAGE

KM# 3 2 STUBER

Silver, 24 mm. **Obv:** Shield of city arms **Obv. Legend:** CIVITAT. EMBDENSIS. **Rev:** Floriated cross in circle **Rev. Legend:** BENEDICTVS. DOMINVS. DEVS. **Note:** Ref. K#9656.

Date	Mintage	VG	F	VF	XF	Unc
ND(17th c)	—	—	—	—	—	—

KM# 4.1 6 STUBER

Silver **Obv:** Shield of city arms **Obv. Legend:** CIVIT. EMBDEN. **Rev:** Crowned imperial eagle, orb on breast **Rev. Legend:** FERD. II. D. G. ? **Note:** Ref. K#9653. 29-30mm.

Date	Mintage	VG	F	VF	XF	Unc
ND(1619-37)	—	—	—	—	—	—

KM# 4.3 6 STUBER

Silver **Obv:** Shield of city arms **Obv. Legend:** MONNO - CIV + - EMBD. **Rev:** Crowned imperial eagle, orb on breast **Rev. Legend:** FERD. II D G ROM IMP. SEM. AVG. **Note:** Ref. K#9655. 29-30mm.

Date	Mintage	VG	F	VF	XF	Unc
ND(1619-37)	—	—	—	—	—	—

KM# 27 6 STUBER

Silver **Obv:** Crowned shield of city arms **Obv. Legend:** DA: PACEM. DOMINE. **Rev:** Crowned imperial eagle **Rev. Legend:** LEOP: I. D. G. ROM. - IMP. SEM. AUG. **Note:** Ref. K#9652. 29-30mm.

Date	Mintage	VG	F	VF	XF	Unc
ND(1680-90)	—	—	—	—	—	—

KM# 10.1 28 STUBER (2/3 Thaler - Gulden)

Silver

Date	Mintage	VG	F	VF	XF	Unc
ND(1624-37)	—	45.00	85.00	160	300	—

KM# 16 28 STUBER (2/3 Thaler - Gulden)

Silver **Obv:** Titles of Ferdinand III

Date	Mintage	VG	F	VF	XF	Unc
ND(1624-57)	—	55.00	100	170	300	—

KM# 10.2 28 STUBER (2/3 Thaler - Gulden)

Silver **Obv:** Crowned arms with modified ornamentation **Note:** Dav. #508.

Date	Mintage	VG	F	VF	XF	Unc
ND(1624-37)	—	45.00	85.00	160	300	—

KM# 11 28 STUBER (2/3 Thaler - Gulden)

Silver **Note:** Klippe.

Date	Mintage	VG	F	VF	XF	Unc
ND(1624-37) Rare	—	—	—	—	—	—

KM# 28 1/3 THALER

Silver **Obv:** Crowned shield of city arms, palm fronds at each side **Obv. Legend:** DA. PACEM. - DOMINE. **Rev:** Crowned imperial eagle **Rev. Legend:** LEOP. I. D. G. ROM. IMP. SEM. AVG. **Note:** 30-31mm.

Date	Mintage	VG	F	VF	XF	Unc
ND(1680-1700)	—	—	—	—	—	—

KM# 30 2/3 THALER (Gulden)

Silver **Obv:** Value 2/3 below crossing of branches **Note:** Varieties exist.

Date	Mintage	VG	F	VF	XF	Unc
1684	—	35.00	100	170	275	—
1688	—	35.00	100	170	275	—
1689	—	35.00	100	170	275	—
1690	—	35.00	100	170	275	—
1691	—	35.00	100	170	275	—

KM# 31 2/3 THALER (Gulden)

Silver **Rev:** Crowned arms of Emden (harpy on wall above waves) divide date, value 2/3 in oval below

Date	Mintage	VG	F	VF	XF	Unc
1687	—	80.00	160	275	450	—

KM# 32 2/3 THALER (Gulden)

Silver **Rev:** Smaller arms within palm branches

Date	Mintage	VG	F	VF	XF	Unc
1687	—	65.00	130	240	375	—

KM# 33 2/3 THALER (Gulden)

Silver **Note:** Date divided above crown, value divided by crossing of branches.

Date	Mintage	VG	F	VF	XF	Unc
1688	—	65.00	130	240	375	—

KM# 5.1 THALER

Silver **Obv:** Crowned double eagle with orb on breast, titles of Ferdinand Ii **Rev:** Crowned arms with CP between crown and arms. **Note:** Dav. #5247.

Date	Mintage	VG	F	VF	XF	Unc
ND(1619-37) CP	—	250	450	750	1,200	—

KM# 5.2 THALER

Silver **Obv:** Crowned imperial eagle, orb on breast **Rev:** Crowned city arms in ornate frame **Note:** Varieties exist. Dav. #5248.

Date	Mintage	VG	F	VF	XF	Unc
ND(1624-37)	—	250	450	750	1,200	—

KM# 20 THALER

Silver **Note:** Similar to KM#21. Dav. #5249.

Date	Mintage	VG	F	VF	XF	Unc
ND(1673-74) CP	—	3,000	5,000	8,500	—	—

KM# 22 THALER

Silver **Obv:** Crowned imperial eagle with orb on breast **Note:** Dav. #5250.

Date	Mintage	VG	F	VF	XF	Unc
1674 CP Rare	—	—	—	—	—	—

KM# 21 THALER

27.9700 g., Silver **Rev:** Arms above city divide date **Note:** Dav. #5251.

Date	Mintage	VG	F	VF	XF	Unc
1674 Rare	—	—	—	—	—	—

Note: Fritz Rudolf Künker Münzenhandlung Auction 127, 6-07, nearly XF realized approximately $28,180.

KM# 23.1 THALER

Silver **Note:** Dav. #5252.

Date	Mintage	VG	F	VF	XF	Unc
1674 CP	—	950	1,500	2,500	4,000	—

KM# 23.2 THALER

Silver **Obv:** Narrow legend **Rev:** Without inner circle **Note:** Varieties exist. Dav. #5255.

Date	Mintage	VG	F	VF	XF	Unc
1689 JR	—	750	1,450	2,750	5,000	—

KM# 24 THALER

Silver **Obv:** Rampant lion left, 40 S and date in legend **Rev:** Knight standing behind shield of arms, imperial eagle above harpy **Note:** Dav. #5253.

Date	Mintage	VG	F	VF	XF	Unc
1675	—	1,200	2,200	3,500	5,750	—

KM# 25 THALER

Silver **Obv:** Rampant lion left holding city arms, 40 in legend below **Rev:** Shield of imperial eagle only **Note:** Dav. #5254.

Date	Mintage	VG	F	VF	XF	Unc
ND(ca.1675)	—	300	700	1,350	2,500	—

KM# A21 2 THALER

57.9800 g., Silver, 57 mm. **Obv:** City view, crowned shield of city arms above, supported by 2 angels in clouds, divides curved legend **Obv. Legend:** MO: NO: - CI: EMB: **Rev:** Crowned imperial eagle, orb on breast, date at end of legend **Rev. Legend:** LEOPOLDUS I. DEI GR: ROMA: IMP: SEM: AUGUS: **Note:** Dav. #A5251

Date	Mintage	VG	F	VF	XF	Unc
1674CP Rare	—	—	—	—	—	—

TRADE COINAGE

Formerly listed 18th Century 2, 2-1/4, 3-1/4, and 4 Ducat issues are considered medals by leading authorities. Currently unlisted in the Standard Catalog series.

KM# 15 DUCAT

3.5000 g., 0.9860 Gold 0.1109 oz. AGW

Date	Mintage	VG	F	VF	XF	Unc
1635	—	550	1,200	2,400	4,200	—
1644	—	550	1,200	2,400	4,200	—
1651	—	550	1,200	2,400	4,200	—
1663	—	550	1,200	2,400	4,200	—
1668	—	550	1,200	2,400	4,200	—
1676	—	550	1,200	2,400	4,200	—
1681	—	550	1,200	2,400	4,200	—
1687	—	550	1,200	2,400	4,200	—
1689	—	700	1,500	3,000	5,000	—
1698	—	550	1,200	2,400	4,200	—
ND	—	550	1,200	2,400	4,200	—

KM# 35 2 DUCAT

7.0000 g., 0.9860 Gold 0.2219 oz. AGW **Obv:** Knight standing in inner circle **Rev:** Four line inscription in ornamental tablet

Date	Mintage	VG	F	VF	XF	Unc
1694	—	3,000	5,000	8,500	14,000	—

ERBACH

The lords of Erbach, located in the Odenwalde about 20 miles to the southeast of Darmstadt, are known from the early 12th century. Beginning in the early 13th century and lasting until 1806, the rulers of Erbach held the office of hereditary cupbearer to the elector-counts palatine of the Rhine. The rank of count was obtained from the emperor in 1532. The countship was divided by the four sons of Georg IV in 1605, although they struck a joint coinage. The family patrimony was further divided during the later 17th and early 18th centuries. Only some rulers of the several branches struck coins. Erbach was mediatized and its lands went to Hesse-Darmstadt in 1806.

RULERS

George IV, 1564-1605
Friedrich Magnus von Erbach-Reichenberg--Furstenau, 1605-1618
Ludwig II von Erbach, 1605-1643
Johann Kasimir von Erbach-Wildenstein--Breuberg, 1605-1627
Georg Albrecht I von Erbach, 1605-1647
Erbach
Georg Ludwig I, 1647-1693
Philipp Ludwig, 1693-1720

MINT OFFICIALS' INITIALS

Initial	Date	Name
ID	1691-92	Johann Ditmar in Darmstadt
ILI	1675-78	Jurgen Lippoldt Jaster in Breuberg
PPP	1675	Peter Paul Peckstein in Breuberg

COUNTY

REGULAR COINAGE

KM# 7 PFENNIG

Silver **Note:** Uniface. E above 4-fold arms, all in circle of pellets.

Date	Mintage	VG	F	VF	XF	Unc
ND(1623)	—	60.00	120	240	400	—

KM# 9 2 KREUZER (1/2 Batzen)

Silver **Rev:** Date Z - 3 divided by orb

Date	Mintage	VG	F	VF	XF	Unc
(16)Z3	Inc. above	45.00	100	200	375	—

KM# 8 2 KREUZER (1/2 Batzen)

Silver **Obv:** Imperial orb with Z, titles of Ferdinand II **Rev:** 4-fold arms divide Z - 3 **Rev. Legend:** MON: COM: IN: ERPACH **Note:** Varieties exist.

Date	Mintage	VG	F	VF	XF	Unc
(16)Z3	109,000	45.00	100	200	375	—

KM# 5 3 KREUZER (Groschen)

Silver **Obv:** Crowned imperial eagle, 3 in orb on breast, titles of Ferdinand II **Rev:** 4-fold arms **Note:** Varieties exist.

Date	Mintage	VG	F	VF	XF	Unc
ND(1622)	—	65.00	130	260	475	—

KM# 10 4 KREUZER (Batzen)

Silver **Obv:** Crowned imperial eagle, 4 in orb on breast, titles of Ferdinand II **Rev:** 4-fold arms

Date	Mintage	VG	F	VF	XF	Unc
1623 Reported, not confirmed	—	—	—	—	—	—

KM# 6 12 KREUZER (6 Albus)

Silver **Obv:** Crowned imperial eagle, 12 in orb on breast, titles of Ferdinand II and date in legend **Rev:** Crowned 4-fold arms **Rev. Legend:** IO CAS. E. GEORG. ALB. C. I. ERB. D. I. BRE

Date	Mintage	VG	F	VF	XF	Unc
1622	—	80.00	165	300	525	—

KM# 15 60 KREUZER (2/3 Thaler)

Silver **Note:** Varieties exist.

Date	Mintage	VG	F	VF	XF	Unc
1675 PPP	38,000	160	275	400	775	—
1675 ILI	—	160	275	400	775	—
1675 ILP	—	160	275	400	775	—
1675	—	160	275	400	775	—

KM# 11 THALER

Silver **Obv:** Titles of Ferdinand II **Note:** Dav. #6666. Varieties exist.

Date	Mintage	VG	F	VF	XF	Unc
1623	157,000	100	200	350	650	—
1624	—	100	200	350	650	—

KM# 12 THALER

Silver **Rev:** Date in legend **Note:** Dav. #6667.

Date	Mintage	VG	F	VF	XF	Unc
1624	Inc. above	125	250	400	700	—

KM# 16 THALER

Silver **Obv:** 4-fold arms **Obv. Legend:** MONETA NOVA ARGENTEA **Rev:** Similar to 60 Kreuzer, KM#15

Date	Mintage	VG	F	VF	XF	Unc
1675	—	—	—	—	—	—

Note: Reported, not confirmed

KM# 13 GOLDGULDEN

3.5000 g., 0.9860 Gold 0.1109 oz. AGW **Obv:** Crowned imperial eagle, titles of Ferdinand II **Rev:** 4-fold arms, date above

Date	Mintage	VG	F	VF	XF	Unc
1624	—	—	—	—	—	—

Note: Reported, not confirmed

ERBACH-BREUBERG

RULER

George VI, 1647-1678

DUCHY

REGULAR COINAGE

KM# 5 GULDEN (2/3 Thaler)

Silver **Obv:** Bust left, titles of George VI **Rev:** Crowned 4-fold arms, legend, date **Rev. Legend:** PRO DEO ET PATRIA

Date	Mintage	VG	F	VF	XF	Unc
1675	—	450	850	1,350	2,100	—

ERBACH-FURSTENAU

RULER

Georg Albrecht II, 1647-1717

DUCHY

REGULAR COINAGE

KM# 15 2 ALBUS (4 Kreuzer)

Silver

Date	Mintage	VG	F	VF	XF	Unc
1691 ID	—	40.00	85.00	140	240	—

KM# 17 1/12 THALER (2 Groschen)

Silver **Obv:** Similar to 2 Albus, KM#15 **Rev:** 12/EINEN/REICHS/THALER/date in wreath

Date	Mintage	VG	F	VF	XF	Unc
1691 ID Rare	—	—	—	—	—	—

KM# 16 15 KREUZER (1/4 Gulden - 1/6 Thaler)

Silver

Date	Mintage	VG	F	VF	XF	Unc
1691 ID	—	75.00	140	190	290	—

KM# 5 30 KREUZER (1/2 Gulden - 1/3 Thaler)

Silver **Note:** Similar to 60 Kreuzer, KM#9 but 30 in bottom legend.

Date	Mintage	VG	F	VF	XF	Unc
1675 PPP	—	—	—	—	—	—
1676 ILI	—	—	—	—	—	—

Note: Reported, not confirmed

KM# 7 30 KREUZER (1/2 Gulden - 1/3 Thaler)

38.5000 g., Silver **Note:** Klippe. Struck on square flan.

Date	Mintage	VG	F	VF	XF	Unc
1676 ILI Rare	—	—	—	—	—	—

KM# 6 60 KREUZER (2/3 Thaler - 1 Gulden)

Silver **Obv:** Facing bust with long wig, 60 below in oval **Rev:** Similar to 60 Kreuzer, KM#9 **Note:** Varieties exist.

Date	Mintage	VG	F	VF	XF	Unc
1675	—	160	265	400	775	—
1676	—	160	265	400	775	—

KM# 8 60 KREUZER (2/3 Thaler - 1 Gulden)

Silver **Rev:** Date in legend

Date	Mintage	VG	F	VF	XF	Unc
1676 ILI Rare	—	—	—	—	—	—

KM# 9 60 KREUZER (2/3 Thaler - 1 Gulden)

Silver

Date	Mintage	VG	F	VF	XF	Unc
1676 ILI	—	160	265	400	775	—

KM# 10 60 KREUZER (2/3 Thaler - 1 Gulden)

Silver **Obv:** Bust left

Date	Mintage	VG	F	VF	XF	Unc
1676 ILI	—	160	265	400	775	—

ERFURT

The city of Erfurt is located in northern Thuringia (Thüringen), about 12.5 miles (21 kilometers) west of Weimar. It was a place of some importance as early as 741 when it became a branch bishopric of Mainz. The archbishops of the latter city remained very much involved in the affairs of Erfurt throughout the High Middle Ages and even located one of their mints there from the 11th through the 13th centuries. An imperial mint also produced coinage in Erfurt during the 12th century. By the mid-13th century, however, the town gained enough power to force the archbishop to grant it self-governing rights. Erfurt was given the right to mint its own coins in 1341 and 1354, and a long series of coins began which lasted until the beginning of the 19th century. Having joined the Hanseatic League during the early 15th century, Erfurt was at the height of its power and prestige, but events began to cause the decline of the city. Saxony managed to wrest control of Erfurt away from Mainz in 1483. During the Thirty Years' War, the city was seized and occupied by Swedish forces in 1631. The treaties which ended the war in 1648 gave control of Erfurt back to Mainz, but the good citizens refused to submit. The city held out until 1664 when it was captured by the archbishop's forces. It remained under Mainz until 1803, when the archbishopric was secularized, and then passed to Prussia.

Free City, 1601-1631

Swedish Occupation, 1631-1648

MINT OFFICIALS' INITIALS

Initial	Date	Name
(a)=	ca. 1548	Unknown
(b)=	ca. 1562	Unknown
FG	ca. 1561-62	Unknown
HL (in ligature)	1592-99	Hans Liphard, mintmaster
	1597-?	Hans Weber, warden
FG/G	1599-1607	Florian Gruber
(c)= or HG/G	1607-09	Hieronymus Kronberger (Gronberger)
AW	1617-24	Asmus Wagner
IS	1624-35	Johann Schneider (known as Weissmantel)
	1625	Jakob Zeuner of Freiburg
EW	Ca.1632	Unknown
CZ	1650-59	Christof Ziegler
ICD	1673-76	Johann Christoph Dürr
	Ca.1675	Johann Georg Philipp Reipp, warden
MW	Ca.1676-81	Marcus Weissmantel
D	Ca.1683	Unknown
GFS	1689	Georg Friedrich Staude
ICS	1690-91	Johann Christoph Staude

ARMS

6-spoked wheel of Mainz, sometimes in 2-fold shield, half of which is 3 vertical bars (Capellendorf).

CITY

REGULAR COINAGE

KM# 27 2 SCHERF (Pfennig)

Copper **Obv:** 2-fold arms, wheel left, pales right, BPE above **Rev:** II/S/date **Note:** Kipper 2 Scherf.

Date	Mintage	VG	F	VF	XF	Unc
16Z1	—	9.00	20.00	33.00	60.00	—

KM# 2 PFENNIG

Silver **Note:** Uniface. Two arms side-by-side, wheel left, six pales right, date divided by E above, mintmaster's initial below. Prev. KM#5.

Date	Mintage	VG	F	VF	XF	Unc
1600 FG	—	8.00	16.00	30.00	60.00	—
1602 G	—	8.00	16.00	30.00	60.00	—
1603 G	—	8.00	16.00	30.00	60.00	—
1603	—	8.00	16.00	30.00	60.00	—
1605 G	—	8.00	16.00	30.00	60.00	—
1607 HG	—	8.00	16.00	30.00	60.00	—
1609 HG	—	8.00	16.00	30.00	60.00	—
1609 (c)	—	8.00	16.00	30.00	60.00	—

KM# 25 PFENNIG

Silver **Note:** Kipper Pfennig. Wheel arms in cartouche, date divided by E above.

Date	Mintage	VG	F	VF	XF	Unc
1620	—	13.00	27.00	45.00	80.00	—
1622	—	13.00	27.00	45.00	80.00	—

KM# 33 PFENNIG

Silver **Note:** Wheel arms divide date, + E + above.

Date	Mintage	VG	F	VF	XF	Unc
1622	—	13.00	27.00	45.00	80.00	—

KM# 28 3 SCHERF (1-1/2 Pfennig)

Copper **Obv:** 2-fold arms, wheel left, pales right, BPE above **Rev. Legend:** III/S **Note:** Kipper 3 Scherf. Varieties exist.

Date	Mintage	VG	F	VF	XF	Unc
16Z1	—	9.00	20.00	33.00	60.00	—

KM# 38 3 SCHERF (1-1/2 Pfennig)

Copper **Rev:** Date **Rev. Legend:** III/SCHERF

Date	Mintage	VG	F	VF	XF	Unc
1622	—	9.00	20.00	33.00	60.00	—

KM# 29 6 SCHERF (3 Pfennig)

Copper **Obv:** Wheel arms **Obv. Legend:** +ERFVRTENSIVM **Rev:** VI/S/date **Rev. Legend:** BONO PVBLICO **Note:** Kipper 6 Scherf. Varieties exist.

Date	Mintage	VG	F	VF	XF	Unc
16Z1	—	13.00	27.00	45.00	75.00	—

KM# 39 6 SCHERF (3 Pfennig)

Copper **Rev:** Date **Rev. Legend:** VI/SCHERF

Date	Mintage	VG	F	VF	XF	Unc
1622	—	13.00	27.00	45.00	75.00	—

KM# 8 3 PFENNIG (Dreier)

Silver **Obv:** Helmeted shield with wheel arms **Rev:** Helmeted shield with pales, date above, FG below

Date	Mintage	VG	F	VF	XF	Unc
1604 FG	—	13.00	27.00	45.00	80.00	—

KM# 15 3 PFENNIG (Dreier)

Silver **Obv:** Wheel arms in cartouche **Rev:** Helmeted wheel arms divide date

Date	Mintage	VG	F	VF	XF	Unc
1613	—	13.00	27.00	45.00	80.00	—

KM# 34 3 PFENNIG (Dreier)

Silver **Obv:** Ornamented wheel **Note:** Kipper 3 Pfennig.

Date	Mintage	VG	F	VF	XF	Unc
1622	—	8.00	16.00	30.00	60.00	—

KM# 35 3 PFENNIG (Dreier)

Copper **Note:** Kipper 3 Pfennig. Similar to KM#34. Varieties exist.

Date	Mintage	VG	F	VF	XF	Unc
1622	—	8.00	16.00	30.00	60.00	—

KM# 36 3 PFENNIG (Dreier)

Silver Or Billon **Rev:** Date divided near bottom **Note:** Kipper 3 Pfennig. Varieties exist.

Date	Mintage	VG	F	VF	XF	Unc
16ZZ	—	8.00	16.00	30.00	60.00	—

KM# 44 3 PFENNIG (Dreier)
Silver **Obv:** Wheel arms in cartouche **Rev:** Helmeted wheel arms, date divided above **Note:** Varieties exist.

Date	Mintage	VG	F	VF	XF	Unc
1623	—	8.00	16.00	30.00	60.00	—
1623 AW	—	8.00	16.00	30.00	60.00	—
1624	—	8.00	16.00	30.00	60.00	—
1625	—	8.00	16.00	30.00	60.00	—
1650	—	8.00	16.00	30.00	60.00	—
1655	—	8.00	16.00	30.00	60.00	—
1656	—	8.00	16.00	30.00	60.00	—

KM# 30 12 SCHERF (6 Pfennig)
Copper **Obv:** Wheels arms, date **Obv. Legend:** ERFVRTENSIVM **Rev. Legend:** XII/SCHERF **Note:** Kipper 12 Scherf. Varieties exist.

Date	Mintage	VG	F	VF	XF	Unc
16Z1	—	27.00	55.00	80.00	125	—
16ZZ	—	27.00	55.00	80.00	125	—

KM# 37 12 PFENNIG
Copper **Obv:** Wheel arms in ornamented shield **Rev:** Date **Rev. Legend:** 12/PFENNI/GE **Note:** Kipper 3 Kreuzer or 1/24 Thaler. Varieties exist. Previously Mainz, KM #31.

Date	Mintage	VG	F	VF	XF	Unc
16ZZ	—	10.00	20.00	40.00	75.00	—

KM# 41 1/24 THALER (Groschen)
Copper **Note:** Kipper Groschen. Similar to KM#40. Varieties exist.

Date	Mintage	VG	F	VF	XF	Unc
(16)22	—	16.00	33.00	60.00	120	—
1623	—	16.00	33.00	60.00	120	—
11623 Error	—	16.00	33.00	60.00	120	—

KM# 40 1/24 THALER (Groschen)
Silver **Obv:** Helmeted wheel arms, another wheel above helmet, date in legend **Rev:** Wheel arms in ornamented shield, Z4 above **Note:** Varieties exist.

Date	Mintage	VG	F	VF	XF	Unc
16ZZ	—	16.00	33.00	60.00	120	—
1622	—	16.00	33.00	60.00	120	—
1623 AW	—	16.00	33.00	60.00	120	—
1623 IS	—	16.00	33.00	60.00	120	—
1623	—	16.00	33.00	60.00	120	—

KM# 97 1/24 THALER (Groschen)
Silver **Subject:** Peace of Westphalia **Obv:** Inscription ending GRATIAR/MONIMENT.F.F./ANNO 1650/8 SEPT **Rev:** Jehovah in Hebrew above, rays streaming down, hand from clouds below holding palm and laurel branches with wheel, in band above SUPER HIS SERVATA QVIESCO

Date	Mintage	VG	F	VF	XF	Unc
1650	—	—	—	—	—	—

KM# 17 1/3 THALER (1/2 Gulden)
Silver **Note:** Similar to 1 Thaler, KM#16.

Date	Mintage	VG	F	VF	XF	Unc
1617	—	—	—	—	—	—
1618	—	—	—	—	—	—

KM# 31 1/3 THALER (1/2 Gulden)
Silver **Rev:** 5-fold arms, date in legend

Date	Mintage	VG	F	VF	XF	Unc
1621	—	325	625	1,000	1,700	—

KM# 98 30 KREUZER (1/2 Gulden)
Silver **Subject:** Peace of Westphalia **Obv. Inscription:** Ends: GRATIARUM/MONIMENT/FIERIFECIT/Ao 1650. 8. SEPT. **Note:** Similar to Groschen, KM#97.

Date	Mintage	VG	F	VF	XF	Unc
1650	—	—	—	—	—	—

KM# 42 1/2 THALER
Silver **Obv:** Oval wheel arms in baroque frame, date in legend **Rev:** Ornamented 5-fold arms, value 21 gl (groschen) below

Date	Mintage	VG	F	VF	XF	Unc
1622	—	—	—	—	—	—

KM# 18 2/3 THALER (Gulden)
Silver **Note:** Similar to 1 Thaler, KM#16 but date divided above arms on obverse.

Date	Mintage	VG	F	VF	XF	Unc
1617	—	—	—	—	—	—

KM# 5 60 KREUZER (Gulden)
Silver **Obv:** Helmeted city arms, wildman and wildwoman as supporters, wheel of Mainz above, MON.REIPVBLIC... **Rev:** Two angels suspended holding wreath in center in which date, small shield below with "60", legend divided by four small shields of arms, AVF. IEDES. SCHIS. - EN. MEIN. R. DIS IAR - ZV. VORN. 100. 60. 40. - GEBEN. WAR. 29. AVG. & 5. SEPT.

Date	Mintage	VG	F	VF	XF	Unc
1603 FG	—	350	650	1,250	2,500	—

KM# 99 60 KREUZER (Gulden)
Silver **Subject:** Peace of Westphalia **Note:** Similar to 30 Kreuzer, KM#98.

Date	Mintage	VG	F	VF	XF	Unc
1650	—	—	—	—	—	—

KM# 6 THALER
Silver **Obv:** Similar to KM#5 **Rev:** Arms divide date **Note:** Dav. #5256.

Date	Mintage	VG	F	VF	XF	Unc
1603	—	400	700	1,350	2,750	—

KM# 16.1 THALER
Silver **Obv:** Supported arms **Rev:** Arms with angel head above, date divided below, 16-13 **Note:** Dav. #5257.

Date	Mintage	VG	F	VF	XF	Unc
1613	—	200	400	750	1,250	—

KM# 16.2 THALER
Silver **Obv. Legend:** MON...ERFFORDI **Rev:** Date divided below, 1.6-1.7 **Note:** Dav. #5258.

Date	Mintage	VG	F	VF	XF	Unc
1617	—	100	200	400	650	—

KM# 16.3 THALER
Silver **Rev:** Squares with dots at sides of arms, symbols before and after date **Note:** Dav. #5259.

Date	Mintage	VG	F	VF	XF	Unc
1617	—	100	200	400	650	—

KM# 16.4 THALER
Silver **Obv. Legend:** MO:...EFFFORD **Rev:** Alchemy symbols at sides **Note:** Dav. #5260.

Date	Mintage	VG	F	VF	XF	Unc
1617	—	120	240	475	800	—

KM# 16.5 THALER
Silver **Obv. Legend:** MON:...ERFFORDENSIS **Rev:** Alchemy symbols at sides **Note:** Dav. #5274.

Date	Mintage	VG	F	VF	XF	Unc
1637	—	235	475	950	1,750	—

KM# 16.6 THALER
Silver **Obv. Legend:** MON...ERFFORDENSIS **Rev:** Alchemy symbols at sides **Note:** Dav. #A5259.

Date	Mintage	VG	F	VF	XF	Unc
1617	—	—	—	—	—	—

KM# 19.1 THALER
Silver **Rev:** Date above arms instead on angel's head **Note:** Dav. #5262.

Date	Mintage	VG	F	VF	XF	Unc
1617 AW	—	135	265	475	800	—
1618 AW	—	135	265	475	800	—

KM# 19.2 THALER
Silver **Rev:** AW. IS below shield **Note:** Dav. #5262A.

Date	Mintage	VG	F	VF	XF	Unc
1617 AW-IS	—	135	265	475	800	—

KM# 32 THALER
Silver **Obv:** Ornamented oval wheel arms, date in legend **Rev:** 4-fold arms with central shield, 24 below **Note:** Kipper Thaler. Varieties exist.

Date	Mintage	VG	F	VF	XF	Unc
16Z1	—	250	450	700	1,050	—
16ZZ	—	250	450	700	1,050	—

KM# 19.3 THALER
Silver **Obv:** Helmeted and supported oval shield **Rev:** AW below shield **Note:** Dav. #5263.

Date	Mintage	VG	F	VF	XF	Unc
1621 AW	—	400	900	1,850	3,000	—

KM# 19.4 THALER
Silver **Rev:** Date above shield, I-S at sides and E-W below **Note:** Dav. #5268.

Date	Mintage	VG	F	VF	XF	Unc
1632 IS-EW	—	135	265	500	850	—

KM# 101 THALER
Silver **Obv:** Angel putting sword in sheath, treading on dead bodies, nearby a tablet surmounted by skull **Obv. Legend:** MORS IVGLANS CEDIT VITA SAL VSQ. REDIT. **Obv. Inscription:** A. 1683. SVMMA MORTV/ORVM/9437 **Rev:** Inscription at top **Rev. Inscription:** HOC REDEVNTE PERIT CONTAGIOSA LVES; ERPHORDIA A PESTE LIBERA ANNO 1683. EXEVNTE in exergue **Note:** Leitzmann #811.

Date	Mintage	VG	F	VF	XF	Unc
1683 D	—	—	—	—	—	—

KM# 102 THALER
Silver **Obv:** Without skull on tablet **Obv. Inscription:** SUM. D.A. 1683. ZV. ERFF. ERSTORB. PERSON. 9437. **Note:** Plague Double Thaler. Similar to KM#101. Leitzmann #812.

Date	Mintage	VG	F	VF	XF	Unc
1683 D	—	—	—	—	—	—

KM# 7 2 THALER
Silver **Note:** Similar to 1 Thaler, KM#6. Dav. #A5256.

Date	Mintage	VG	F	VF	XF	Unc
1603 Rare	—	—	—	—	—	—

KM# 20 2 THALER
Silver **Note:** Similar to 1 Thaler, KM#19. Dav. #5261.

Date	Mintage	VG	F	VF	XF	Unc
1617 AW Rare	—	—	—	—	—	—

KM# 43 2 THALER
Silver **Obv:** Ornamented oval wheel arms, date in legend **Rev:** 4-fold arms with central shield, 48 below **Note:** Kipper 2 Thaler.

Date	Mintage	VG	F	VF	XF	Unc
16ZZ Rare	—	—	—	—	—	—

TRADE COINAGE

KM# 26 GOLDGULDEN
3.5000 g., 0.9860 Gold 0.1109 oz. AGW **Obv:** Helmeted arms divide date in inner circle **Rev:** Arms in inner circle **Note:** Fr.#916.

Date	Mintage	VG	F	VF	XF	Unc
1620	—	900	1,750	3,400	7,500	—
1622	—	900	1,750	3,400	7,500	—
1670	—	900	1,750	3,400	7,500	—
	—	900	1,750	3,400	7,500	—

KM# 100 DUCAT
3.5000 g., 0.9860 Gold 0.1109 oz. AGW **Obv:** Wheel arms divide date **Rev:** 5-fold arms

Date	Mintage	VG	F	VF	XF	Unc
1670 Rare	—	—	—	—	—	—

OCCUPATION COINAGE

Issued by Swedish forces 1631-48

KM# 69 1/4 THALER
Silver **Subject:** Death of Gustavus Adolphus **Obv:** Crowned 4-fold arms with central shield, 2 inscriptions around, date divided by crown **Rev:** Grapevine growing out of skull resting on ground, 2 inscriptions around with date

Date	Mintage	VG	F	VF	XF	Unc
1633	—	65.00	125	260	425	—

KM# 50 1/2 THALER
Silver **Obv:** "Jehovah" in Hebrew in rayed oval above, A. DOMINO/FACTVM. EST/ISTVD, below fronds on E **Rev:** 11-line inscription with Roman numeral date

Date	Mintage	VG	F	VF	XF	Unc
1631 Rare	—	—	—	—	—	—

KM# 58 1/2 THALER
Silver **Obv:** Bust of Gustavus II Adolphus 3/4 to right **Rev:** Crowned oval 4-fold arms with central shield in baroque frame, wheel below divides date

Date	Mintage	VG	F	VF	XF	Unc
1632 Rare	—	—	—	—	—	—

KM# 57 1/2 THALER
Silver **Note:** Similar to 1 Thaler, KM#59.

Date	Mintage	VG	F	VF	XF	Unc
1632 Rare	—	—	—	—	—	—

KM# A70 1/2 THALER
Silver **Obv:** King laying in state, battle in background **Obv. Legend:** GUSTAVUS ADOLPHUS MAGNUS... **Rev:** King in triumphant chariot, crowned by Religion and Justice, crushing his enemies below

Date	Mintage	VG	F	VF	XF	Unc
1633	—	—	—	—	—	—

KM# 86 1/2 THALER
Silver **Note:** Similar to 1 Thaler, KM#87.

Date	Mintage	VG	F	VF	XF	Unc
1645	—	600	1,000	1,600	—	—
1648 Rare	—	—	—	—	—	—

KM# 49 THALER
Silver **Obv:** 2 branches below inscription

Date	Mintage	VG	F	VF	XF	Unc
1631 Unique	—	—	—	—	—	—

KM# 51 THALER
Silver **Obv:** 11-line inscription with Roman numeral date **Rev:** "Jehovah" in Hebrew in rayed oval above, A. DOMINO./ FACTVM. EST/ISTVD, below fronds on E **Note:** Dav. #4544.

Date	Mintage	VG	F	VF	XF	Unc
1631	—	300	600	1,250	2,000	—

KM# 53 THALER
Silver **Obv:** Arabic numeral date below 12-line inscription **Note:** Dav. #4545.

Date	Mintage	VG	F	VF	XF	Unc
1631	—	350	700	1,450	2,250	—

KM# 52 THALER
Silver **Note:** Klippe. Dav. #4545A.

Date	Mintage	VG	F	VF	XF	Unc
1631 Rare	—	—	—	—	—	—

KM# 61 THALER
Silver **Rev:** Without small wheel below arms **Note:** Swedish issue. Dav. #4547.

Date	Mintage	VG	F	VF	XF	Unc
1632 Rare	—	—	—	—	—	—

KM# 59 THALER
Silver **Subject:** 2nd Anniversary of Victory at Leipzig **Note:** Dav. #4546.

Date	Mintage	VG	F	VF	XF	Unc
1632	—	200	500	1,150	1,850	—

KM# 60 THALER
Silver **Obv:** Bust of Gustavus II Adolphus 3/4 to right **Rev:** Crowned oval 4-fold arms with central shield in baroque frame, wheel below divides date **Note:** Dav. #4548.

Date	Mintage	VG	F	VF	XF	Unc
1632 Rare	—	—	—	—	—	—

KM# 62 THALER
Silver **Subject:** Death of Gustavus Adolphus **Obv:** Grapevine growing out of skull resting on ground, 2 inscriptions around with date **Rev:** Crowned 4-fold arms with central shield, 2 inscriptions around, date divided by crown

Date	Mintage	VG	F	VF	XF	Unc
1632 Rare	—	—	—	—	—	—

KM# 77 THALER
Silver **Obv:** King lying in state, battle in background **Obv. Legend:** GUSTAVUS ADOLPHUS MAGNUS... **Rev:** King in triumphant chariot, crowned by Religion and Justice, crushing his enemies below **Rev. Legend:** DUX FLORIOS : PRINC : PIUS:... **Note:** Dav. #5272.

Date	Mintage	Good	VG	F	VF	XF
1633	—	200	450	1,000	2,250	4,000

KM# 70 THALER
Silver **Obv:** Helmeted and supported arms, wheel above divides date **Rev:** Angels holding "Jehovah" in Hebrew in oval above city view, all in wreath divided by 4 small arms **Note:** Dav. #5270.

Date	Mintage	VG	F	VF	XF	Unc
1633	—	1,200	2,250	4,750	7,500	—

KM# 71 THALER
Silver **Obv:** Gustavus Adolphus lying in state with battle in background **Rev:** King in chariot crushing enemies below **Note:** Dav. #5272.

Date	Mintage	VG	F	VF	XF	Unc
1634	—	550	1,150	2,250	4,000	—

KM# 87 THALER
Silver **Subject:** Christina **Note:** Dav. #4570.

Date	Mintage	F	VF	XF	Unc	BU
1645	—	375	800	1,500	2,500	—
1648	—	650	1,250	2,250	3,250	—

KM# 72 1-1/2 THALER
Silver **Obv:** Helmeted and supported arms, wheel above divides date **Rev:** Angels holding "Jehovah" in Hebrew in oval above city view, all in wreath divided by 4 small arms **Note:** Dav. #5269A.

Date	Mintage	VG	F	VF	XF	Unc
1603 Rare	—	—	—	—	—	—
1633 Rare	—	—	—	—	—	—

KM# A78 1-1/2 THALER
Silver **Obv:** King lying in state, battle in background **Obv. Legend:** GUSTAVUS ADOLPHUS MAGNUS... **Rev:** King in triumphant chariot, crowned by Religion and Justice, crushing his enemies below **Rev. Legend:** DUX FLORIOS : PRINC : PIUS:... **Note:** Dav. #5271, 275.

Date	Mintage	Good	VG	F	VF	XF
1633	—	—	—	—	—	—

KM# 73 2 THALER
Silver **Obv:** Helmeted and supported arms, wheel above divides date **Rev:** Angels holding "Jehovah" in Hebrew in oval above city view, all in wreath divided by 4 small arms **Note:** Dav. #5269.

Date	Mintage	VG	F	VF	XF	Unc
1633 Rare	—	—	—	—	—	—

KM# 78 2 THALER
59.7000 g., Silver **Obv:** King lying in state, battle in background **Obv. Legend:** GUSTAVUS ADOLPHUS MAGNUS... **Rev:** King in triumphant chariot, crowned by Religion and Justice, crushing his enemies below **Rev. Legend:** DUX FLORIOS : PRINC : PIUS:... **Note:** Dav. #5271A, 274.

Date	Mintage	VG	F	VF	XF	Unc
1633	—	725	1,200	2,000	3,200	—

KM# 76 2 THALER

Silver **Obv:** Gustavus Adolphus seated in chariot left, raising sword to clouds in heaven, date divided by small ornate oval arms below **Rev:** King lying in state, angels with Jehovah above, 8 inscribed ovals around, 7 of which have baldachini above them in legend **Note:** Dav. #5273.

Date	Mintage	VG	F	VF	XF	Unc
1634 Rare	—	—	—	—	—	—

KM# 79 3 THALER

83.7000 g., Silver **Obv:** King lying in state, battle in background **Obv. Legend:** GUSTAVUS ADOLPHUS MAGNUS... **Rev:** King in triumphant chariot, crowned by Religion and Justice, crushing his enemies below **Rev. Legend:** DUX GLORIOS : PRINC : PIUS:... **Note:** Dav. #5271B, 273.

Date	Mintage	VG	F	VF	XF	Unc
1633	—	950	1,650	2,750	4,500	—

KM# 80 4 THALER

116.0000 g., Silver **Obv:** King lying in state, battle in background **Obv. Legend:** GUSTAVUS ADOLPHUS MAGNUS... **Rev:** King in triumphant chariot, crowned by Religion and Justice, crushing his enemies below **Rev. Legend:** DUX FLORIOS : PRINC : PIUS:... **Note:** Dav. #5271C, 272.

Date	Mintage	VG	F	VF	XF	Unc
1633	—	1,350	2,250	3,750	6,000	—

KM# A81 5 THALER

Silver **Obv:** King lying in state, battle in background **Obv. Legend:** GUSTAVUS ADOLPHUS MAGNUS... **Rev:** King in triumphant chariot, crowned by Religion and Justice, crushing his enemies below **Rev. Legend:** DUX FLORIOS : PRINC : PIUS:... **Note:** Dav. #275A. Weight varies: 139.00-152.00 grams.

Date	Mintage	Good	VG	F	VF	XF
1634	—	—	—	—	—	—

KM# 64 DUCAT

3.5000 g., 0.9860 Gold 0.1109 oz. AGW **Rev:** Date in outer legend

Date	Mintage	VG	F	VF	XF	Unc
1631 Rare	—	—	—	—	—	—
1632 Rare	—	—	—	—	—	—

KM# 54 DUCAT

3.5000 g., 0.9860 Gold 0.1109 oz. AGW **Obv:** Gustavus Adolphus **Note:** Fr.#923.

Date	Mintage	VG	F	VF	XF	Unc
1631 Unique	—	—	—	—	—	—
1632 Rare	—	—	—	—	—	—
1634	—	300	600	1,200	2,400	—

KM# 63 DUCAT

3.5000 g., 0.9860 Gold 0.1109 oz. AGW **Rev:** Crown above inscription in inner circle **Note:** Fr.#919.

Date	Mintage	VG	F	VF	XF	Unc
1632	—	150	325	600	1,150	—
1633	—	150	325	600	1,150	—
1634	—	150	325	600	1,150	—

KM# 74 DUCAT

3.5000 g., 0.9860 Gold 0.1109 oz. AGW **Rev:** Date below shield

Date	Mintage	VG	F	VF	XF	Unc
1633 Rare	—	—	—	—	—	—
1634	—	300	600	1,200	2,400	—

KM# 81 DUCAT

3.5000 g., 0.9860 Gold 0.1109 oz. AGW **Rev:** Shield divides date **Note:** Prev. KM#77.

Date	Mintage	VG	F	VF	XF	Unc
1634	—	300	600	1,200	2,400	—

KM# 82 DUCAT

3.5000 g., 0.9860 Gold 0.1109 oz. AGW **Rev:** Date above crown **Note:** Prev. KM#78.

Date	Mintage	VG	F	VF	XF	Unc
1634	—	300	600	1,200	2,400	—

KM# 85 DUCAT

3.5000 g., 0.9860 Gold 0.1109 oz. AGW **Obv:** Bust of Christina facing 1/2 left in inner circle **Rev:** Crowned arms in inner circle

Date	Mintage	VG	F	VF	XF	Unc
1644 Rare	—	—	—	—	—	—
1645	—	260	525	1,100	2,150	—

KM# 88 DUCAT

3.5000 g., 0.9860 Gold 0.1109 oz. AGW **Rev:** Crowned arms without inner circle **Note:** Fr.#929.

Date	Mintage	VG	F	VF	XF	Unc
1645	—	260	525	1,100	2,150	—
1646 Rare	—	—	—	—	—	—
1647	—	260	525	1,100	2,150	—
1648	—	260	525	1,100	2,150	—

KM# 91 DUCAT

3.5000 g., 0.9860 Gold 0.1109 oz. AGW **Obv:** Bust of Christina right in inner circle **Rev:** Crowned arms with ornamentation **Note:** Fr.#930.

Date	Mintage	VG	F	VF	XF	Unc
1646 Rare	—	—	—	—	—	—
1647 Rare	—	—	—	—	—	—
1648	—	550	1,100	2,200	4,200	—

KM# 93 DUCAT

3.5000 g., 0.9860 Gold 0.1109 oz. AGW **Rev:** Small crown above arms

Date	Mintage	VG	F	VF	XF	Unc
1648	—	260	525	1,100	2,150	—

KM# 94 DUCAT

3.5000 g., 0.9860 Gold 0.1109 oz. AGW **Obv:** Bust of Christina right without inner circle **Rev:** Crowned arms without ornamentation

Date	Mintage	VG	F	VF	XF	Unc
1648 Unique	—	—	—	—	—	—

KM# 75 2 DUCAT

7.0000 g., 0.9860 Gold 0.2219 oz. AGW **Obv:** Skull below grape vine in inner circle **Rev:** Crowned arms in inner circle **Note:** Fr.#923a.

Date	Mintage	VG	F	VF	XF	Unc
1633 Rare	—	—	—	—	—	—

KM# 92 2 DUCAT

7.0000 g., 0.9860 Gold 0.2219 oz. AGW **Obv:** Christina with radiant "Jehovah" in Hebrew **Rev:** Crowned ornate arms **Note:** Fr.#928.

Date	Mintage	VG	F	VF	XF	Unc
1646	—	1,000	2,000	3,600	6,000	—

KM# A55 3 DUCAT

10.5000 g., 0.9860 Gold 0.3328 oz. AGW **Subject:** Victory **Obv:** Radiant "Jehovah" in Hebrew above legend and ornamentation **Rev:** 11 line inscription with date below **Note:** Fr.#918.

Date	Mintage	VG	F	VF	XF	Unc
1631 Rare	—	—	—	—	—	—

KM# 55 4 DUCAT

14.0000 g., 0.9860 Gold 0.4438 oz. AGW **Obv:** Radiant "Jehovah" in Hebrew above legend and ornamentation **Rev:** 11 line inscription with date below

Date	Mintage	VG	F	VF	XF	Unc
1631 Rare	—	—	—	—	—	—

KM# 84 4 DUCAT

14.0000 g., 0.9860 Gold 0.4438 oz. AGW **Obv:** Crowned king lying in state, battlefield in background **Obv. Legend:** GUSTAVUS ADOLPHUS MAGNUS... **Rev:** King in chariot between two angels running over his enemies **Rev. Legend:** DUX GLORIOW • PRINC : PIUS • HEROS... **Note:** Prev. KM#80. Fr.#923.

Date	Mintage	VG	F	VF	XF	Unc
1634	—	3,600	5,400	7,800	11,500	—

KM# 65 5 DUCAT (1/2 Portugalöser)

17.5000 g., 0.9860 Gold 0.5547 oz. AGW **Obv:** Laureate bust of Gustavus Adolphus in inner circle **Rev:** Crowned arms in inner circle, date in legend **Note:** Fr.#922.

Date	Mintage	VG	F	VF	XF	Unc
1632 Rare	—	—	—	—	—	—

KM# 89 5 DUCAT (1/2 Portugalöser)

17.5000 g., 0.9860 Gold 0.5547 oz. AGW **Obv:** Bust of Christina in inner circle **Rev:** Crowned arms in inner circle, crown divides date **Note:** Fr.#927.

Date	Mintage	VG	F	VF	XF	Unc
1645 Rare	—	—	—	—	—	—
1648 Rare	—	—	—	—	—	—

KM# 66 8 DUCAT

28.0000 g., 0.9860 Gold 0.8876 oz. AGW **Obv:** Laureate bust of Gustavus Adolphus in inner circle **Rev:** Crowned arms in inner circle, date in legend **Note:** Fr.#921.

Date	Mintage	VG	F	VF	XF	Unc
1632 Rare	—	—	—	—	—	—

KM# 56 10 DUCAT (Portugalöser)

35.0000 g., 0.9860 Gold 1.1095 oz. AGW **Subject:** Victory **Obv:** Radiant "Jehovah" in Hebrew above legend and ornamentation **Rev:** 10-line legend with Roman numeral date below **Note:** Fr.#917.

Date	Mintage	VG	F	VF	XF	Unc
1631 Rare	—	—	—	—	—	—

KM# 67 10 DUCAT (Portugalöser)

35.0000 g., 0.9860 Gold 1.1095 oz. AGW **Obv:** Within inner circle **Rev:** Within inner circle **Note:** Fr.#920.

Date	Mintage	VG	F	VF	XF	Unc
1632 Rare	—	—	—	—	—	—

KM# 68 10 DUCAT (Portugalöser)

35.0000 g., 0.9860 Gold 1.1095 oz. AGW **Obv:** Laureate bust of Gustavus Adolphus in inner circle **Rev:** Crowned arms in inner circle, date in legend

Date	Mintage	VG	F	VF	XF	Unc
1632 Rare	—	—	—	—	—	—

KM# 83 10 DUCAT (Portugalöser)

35.0000 g., 0.9860 Gold 1.1095 oz. AGW **Obv:** Gustavus Adolphus lying in state **Rev:** King riding triumphantly in chariot **Note:** Prev. KM#79. Fr.#924.

Date	Mintage	VG	F	VF	XF	Unc
1634 Rare	—	—	—	—	—	—

KM# 90 10 DUCAT (Portugalöser)

35.0000 g., 0.9860 Gold 1.1095 oz. AGW **Note:** Fr.#926.

Date	Mintage	VG	F	VF	XF	Unc
1645 Rare	—	—	—	—	—	—
1648 Unique	—	—	—	—	33,000	—

PATTERNS

Including off metal strikes

KM#	Date	Mintage	Identification	Mkt Val
Pn1	1631	—	2 Thaler. Silver. A Domino.	—
Pn2	1631	—	2 Thaler. Silver. A Domino, Klippe.	—
Pn3	1631	—	3 Thaler. Silver. A Domino, Klippe.	—
Pn4	1632	—	Ducat. Silver. KM#63.	—
Pn5	1632	—	10 Ducat. Silver. KM#68, weight of 1/2 Thaler.	—
Pn6	1646	—	2 Ducat. Silver. KM#92, weight of 1/2 Thaler.	—

TRIAL STRIKES

KM#	Date	Mintage	Identification	Mkt Val
TS1	1618	—	2/3 Thaler. Lead. 4-fold arms with central shield, date in legend.	—

ESSEN

The city of Essen lies in the Ruhr Valley, about 18 miles (30 kilometers) northeast of Düsseldorf and about the same distance west of Dortmund. A Benedictine abbey for women was founded in the place during the first half of the 9th century and the town of Essen grew up around the religious institution. The earliest coinage was of the imperial type pfennigs dating from the first half of the 11th century. The abbess attained the distinction as a princess of the Empire in 1275 and it is from that time that coinage of the abbesses themselves first dates. In the general secularization of the Empire in 1802-03, Essen was given to Prussia, but passed to Berg in 1806. Prussia regained possession of the monastery and city at the end of the Napoleonic Wars in 1815. There was no coinage during the 16th century.

RULERS

Margaretha Elisabeth, Grafin von Manderscheid-Geroldstein, 1598-1604
Elisabeth IX von Berg, 1604-1614
Maria Clara, Grafin von Spaur, 1614-1644
Anna Eleonora, Grafin von Stauffen, 1645-1646
Anna Salome I, Grafin von Salm-Reifferscheidt, 1646-1688
Anna Salome II, Grafin von Manderscheid-Blankenheim, 1689-1691
Bernhardine Sophie, Grafin von Ostfriesland-Ritberg, 1691-1726

MINT OFFICIALS' INITIALS

Initial	Date	Name
CBH	1660-72	Christian Bornhorst
N(crossed swords)L	1686-99	Nikolaus Longerich, mintmaster in Bonn

Reference:

K = Heinz Josef Kramer, ***Das Stift Essen Münzen und Medaillen***. Münster, 1993.

ABBEY

REGULAR COINAGE

KM# 5 8 HELLER (1/120 Thaler)

Silver **Ruler:** Anne Salome I **Obv:** Arms of Salm (2 fish), date **Obv. Legend:** MONETA. NOVA **Rev:** VIII in center **Rev. Legend:** NVMMVS.ESSENSIS **Note:** Varieties exist.

Date	Mintage	VG	F	VF	XF	Unc
1656	—	20.00	40.00	75.00	125	—
1657	—	20.00	40.00	75.00	125	—
(1)657	—	20.00	40.00	75.00	125	—

KM# 30 8 HELLER (1/120 Thaler)
Silver **Ruler:** Anna Salome II **Obv:** 4-fold arms, date above **Rev:** VIII **Rev. Legend:** MONE.NOVA.ESSENDIS

Date	Mintage	VG	F	VF	XF	Unc
1691 NL	—	16.00	33.00	70.00	120	—

KM# 15 1/120 THALER
Silver **Ruler:** Anne Salome I **Obv:** Arms of Salm **Obv. Legend:** SINGULA. COLL: IUVAT **Rev:** Inscription, date **Rev. Legend:** NUMMUS. ESSEND **Rev. Inscription:** 120 / I.REIC / HSTHA / LER **Note:** Varieties exist. Ref. K#54.

Date	Mintage	VG	F	VF	XF	Unc
1671	79,000	16.00	33.00	70.00	120	—
1672 Rare	—	—	—	—	—	—

KM# 11 ALBUS (1/104 Thaler)
Silver **Ruler:** Anne Salome I **Obv:** Crowned 4-fold arms **Rev:** I/ALBVS/ESSEN/date **Rev. Legend:** (104) EINNER REICHSTAHLER

Date	Mintage	VG	F	VF	XF	Unc
1662	30,000	27.00	55.00	85.00	150	—

KM# 19 1/40 THALER (2 Albus)
Silver **Ruler:** Anne Salome I **Obv:** Crowned Salm arms, date in legend **Rev:** Value 40/I.REIC/HSTHA/LER **Note:** Varieties exist.

Date	Mintage	VG	F	VF	XF	Unc
1674	15,000	33.00	75.00	125	180	—
1675	Inc. above	33.00	75.00	125	180	—

KM# 12 MARK (1/26 Thaler)
Silver **Ruler:** Anne Salome I **Obv:** 4-fold arms with central shield divide date **Rev:** I/MARCK/ESSEN/DISCH **Rev. Legend:** (26) EINEN REICHS THALER

Date	Mintage	VG	F	VF	XF	Unc
1662	6,000	135	240	375	525	—

KM# 16 1/16 THALER (5 Albus)
Silver **Ruler:** Anne Salome I **Obv:** 4-fold arms with central shield **Rev:** Date in legend **Rev. Legend:** XVI/I.REICH/HSTHA/LER

Date	Mintage	VG	F	VF	XF	Unc
1671	—	45.00	110	165	250	—

KM# 31 1/6 THALER
Silver **Ruler:** Anna Salome II **Obv:** Crowned 4-fold arms, (1/6) below in legend **Rev:** Madonna and child surrounded by flames, date in legend

Date	Mintage	VG	F	VF	XF	Unc
1691 NL	—	165	290	400	625	—

KM# 9 1/2 THALER
Silver **Ruler:** Anne Salome I **Obv:** Crowned 5-fold arms divides ANNO - date **Rev:** Madonna holding child standing on crescent surrounded by flames **Note:** Ref. K#44.

Date	Mintage	VG	F	VF	XF	Unc
1672 CBH Rare	—	—	—	—	—	—

Note: Only one example of this coin is known, in Vienna; Described as a gulden but same diameter as thaler, most likely struck with thaler dies

KM# 10 THALER
Silver **Ruler:** Anne Salome I **Obv:** Bust of Anna Salome I facing 3/4 left **Obv. Legend:** ANN:SLAO:V.G.:G.FVRSTIN.ZV.ESS. GEBORN: GRAFIN.Z.S:* **Rev:** Crowned five-fold arms divides date **Rev. Legend:** OVI-LITEM.AVFFERT... **Note:** Dav. #5276.

Date	Mintage	VG	F	VF	XF	Unc
1660 Rare	—	—	—	—	—	—

KM# 17 THALER
Silver **Ruler:** Anne Salome I **Obv:** Crowned 5-fold arms divides ANNO - date **Obv. Legend:** ANNA SALOME. D:G:PRIN: ESEND:COMITISSA SALMEN: **Rev:** Madonna holding child standing on crescent surrounded by flames **Rev. Legend:** SUBTUUM PRAESIDIUM CONFUGIMUS **Note:** Dav. #5277.

Date	Mintage	VG	F	VF	XF	Unc
1672 CBH Rare	—	—	—	—	—	—

KM# 25 THALER
Silver **Ruler:** Anne Salome I **Obv:** Crowned five-fold arms divides date **Rev:** City view in lower 1/2, battle scene in upper half with saint in clouds above, date in chronogram in legend **Note:** Dav. #5278.

Date	Mintage	VG	F	VF	XF	Unc
1680 Rare	—	—	—	—	—	—

KM# 26 THALER
Silver **Ruler:** Anne Salome I **Obv:** Bust left, titles of Leopold I **Note:** Dav. #5279.

Date	Mintage	VG	F	VF	XF	Unc
1680 Rare	—	—	—	—	—	—

TRADE COINAGE

KM# 18 DUCAT
3.5000 g., 0.9860 Gold 0.1109 oz. AGW **Ruler:** Anne Salome I **Obv:** Crowned 4-fold arms, dividing date **Rev:** Madonna standing holding child **Note:** Fr. 932.

Date	Mintage	VG	F	VF	XF	Unc
1672 CBH Rare	—	—	—	—	—	—

PATTERNS

Including off metal strikes

KM#	Date	Mintage	Identification	Mkt Val
Pn1	1660	—	Thaler. Tin. KM#10.	350

FINSTINGEN

(Fenestrange, Fenetrange)

A city located 28 miles south of Saarbrucken in France, Moselle Department. To Lorraine in 1665.

RULER
Diana

FREE CITY

REGULAR COINAGE

KM# 10 1/4 ECU
Silver **Obv:** Crowned arms **Obv. Legend:** DIANA. PRINC: : S: IMP: MARCH LE HAVRE. **Rev:** St. Maurice on horseback **Rev. Legend:** SANCTVS MAVRITIVS. PATRONVS. VINSTIN.

Date	Mintage	VG	F	VF	XF	Unc
ND(CA.1613) Rare	—	—	—	—	—	—

FRANCONIA

(Franken)

Franconia became a territorial part of the empire established by Charlemagne and remained a division of Germany until early modern times. It was situated north of Bavaria between the Palatinate and the Upper Palatinate and formed the basis for the Franconian Circle (see) of the Empire from the 16th century. During the Thirty Years' War Bernhard of Saxe-Weimar took control of the area and proclaimed himself Duke of Franconia, having coins struck with his name and titles thus stylized, a circumstance which did not outlive him.

RULER
Bernhard of Saxe-Weimar, 1633-1639

MINT OFFICIALS' INITIALS

Initial	Date	Name
CS	1622-54	Conrad Stutz, Franconian Circle, die-cutter in Furth

DUCHY

REGULAR COINAGE

KM# 5 1/2 BATZEN (2 Kreuzer)
Silver **Obv:** Arms **Rev:** Christ

Date	Mintage	VG	F	VF	XF	Unc
1633	—	33.00	60.00	120	200	—

KM# 6.1 BATZEN (4 Kreuzer)
Silver **Ruler:** Bernhard of Saxe-Weimar **Obv:** Crowned squarish shield of ducal Saxony arms in baroque frame, value IIII K in oval above **Obv. Legend:** BERNHARD. D.G. DVX. SAXONI. IVL. C. E. M. **Rev:** Full-length standing figure of Christ facing divides date **Rev. Legend:** SALVATOR. MV - NDI. ADIUVANOS

Date	Mintage	VG	F	VF	XF	Unc
1633	—	20.00	40.00	85.00	150	—

KM# 6.2 BATZEN (4 Kreuzer)
Silver **Ruler:** Bernhard of Saxe-Weimar **Obv:** Crowned oval shield of ducal Saxony arms in baroque frame, value IIII K above in oval **Obv. Legend:** BERNHARD. D.G. DVX. SAX. IVL. CL. E. MO. **Rev:** Full-length facing figure of Christ divides date **Rev. Legend:** SALVATOR. MV - NDI. ADIVUAN.

Date	Mintage	VG	F	VF	XF	Unc
1633	—	20.00	40.00	85.00	150	—
1634	—	20.00	40.00	85.00	150	—

KM# 10 1/28 THALER (1 Schilling)
Silver **Obv:** Crowned oval arms, 28 in oval above **Rev:** Full-lentgh standing figure of Christ facing divides date

Date	Mintage	VG	F	VF	XF	Unc
1633	—	—	—	—	—	—

KM# 7 THALER
Silver **Obv:** Facing bust of Gustav Adolf, arms below **Rev:** Christ standing facing with orb **Note:** Dav. #A6670.

Date	Mintage	VG	F	VF	XF	Unc
1632 Rare	—	—	—	—	—	—

KM# 8 THALER
Silver **Obv:** Facing bust of Axel Oxensteirna, arms below **Rev:** Lion left with sword and crown **Note:** Dav. #B6670.

Date	Mintage	VG	F	VF	XF	Unc
ND Rare	—	—	—	—	—	—

Note: Dr. Busso Peus Nachfolger Auction 390, 5-07, XF-Unc realized approximately $16,995.

KM# 9 THALER
Silver **Obv:** Facing 1/2-length bust, crowned arms of Saxony below **Rev:** "Jehovah" in Hebrew in oval with rays, hand extending from heaven with wreath, small oval arms in baroque frame divide date **Note:** Dav. #C6670.

Date	Mintage	VG	F	VF	XF	Unc
1634 CS Rare	—	—	—	—	—	—

FRANCONIAN CIRCLE

(Frankischer Kreis)

The Holy Roman Empire was divided into six administrative circles in 1500, the number being raised to ten in 1512. The Franconian Circle was one of these and comprised about the same territory as the ancient division of Franconia, north of Bavaria. Under the imperial coinage reforms of 1559 and 1566, the Franconian Circle was permitted to have only four mints at Nüremberg, Schwabach, Wertheim and Würzburg, although others were opened at various times. During the 17th and 18th centuries a sporadic coinage of the Franconian Circle was produced at one or another of these mints. The circle also counterstamped coins from other territories entering its jurisdiction.

MINT MARKS
F - Furth Mint
N - Nüremberg Mint
S - Schwabach Mint

MINT OFFICIALS' INITIALS

Initials	Date	Name
GFN	1682-1710	Georg Friedrich Nurnberger

NOTE: The usual design of most coins of the Franconian Circle incorporates the four arms of Bamberg, Brandenburg-Ansbach, Brandenburg-Bayreuth and Nuremberg.

IMPERIAL CIRCLE

REGULAR COINAGE

KM# 5 3 HELLER
Silver **Obv:** Four arms, date divided to left and right, F below **Rev:** III/HELL/ER **Mint:** Furth

Date	Mintage	VG	F	VF	XF	Unc
1624F	—	—	—	—	—	—

KM# 15 KREUZER
Silver **Obv:** Four arms divided date, star below **Rev:** Cross and St. Andrew's cross above and below 8-spoked wheel

Date	Mintage	VG	F	VF	XF	Unc
1637	—	—	—	—	—	—

KM# 6 2 KREUZER (1/2 Batzen)
Silver **Obv:** Imperial orb with 2 divides date, titles of Ferdinand II **Rev:** Four arms, F below **Rev. Legend:** AD LEG: IM... **Mint:** Furth

Date	Mintage	VG	F	VF	XF	Unc
1624F	—	25.00	40.00	65.00	120	—

KM# 7 2 KREUZER (1/2 Batzen)
Silver **Obv:** Cross at top divides date **Rev:** Four arms in cruciform, F between 2 at lower right **Rev. Legend:** AD LEG: IM... **Mint:** Furth

Date	Mintage	VG	F	VF	XF	Unc
1624F	—	27.00	45.00	85.00	180	—

KM# 16 2 KREUZER (1/2 Batzen)
Silver **Obv:** Imperial orb with 2 divides date **Rev:** Similar to 4 Kreuzer, KM#10

Date	Mintage	VG	F	VF	XF	Unc
1637	—	33.00	60.00	120	175	—

KM# 17 2 KREUZER (1/2 Batzen)
Silver **Obv:** Imperial eagle, 2 in orb on breast, titles of Ferdinand III

Date	Mintage	VG	F	VF	XF	Unc
1637	—	55.00	110	175	260	—

KM# 8 4 KREUZER (1 Batzen)
Silver **Obv:** Similar to KM#10 but date in legend **Rev:** Four arms in cruciform, F between 2 at lower right **Rev. Legend:** AD LEG: IMP...

Date	Mintage	VG	F	VF	XF	Unc
1624	—	—	—	—	—	—

KM# 10 4 KREUZER (1 Batzen)
Silver **Mint:** Furth

Date	Mintage	VG	F	VF	XF	Unc
1625F	—	40.00	85.00	145	225	—

KM# 12 1/28 THALER (1 Schilling)
Silver **Obv:** Crowned imperial eagle, Z8 in orb on breast, titles of Ferdinand II **Rev:** Four arms **Mint:** Furth

Date	Mintage	VG	F	VF	XF	Unc
16Z4F	—	—	—	—	—	—

KM# 20 1/3 THALER (1/2 Gulden)
Silver **Note:** Similar to 2/3 Thaler, KM#21.

Date	Mintage	VG	F	VF	XF	Unc
1693 GFN	—	—	—	—	—	—

KM# 21 2/3 THALER (Gulden)
Silver, 37.4 mm.

Date	Mintage	VG	F	VF	XF	Unc
1693 GFN	—	65.00	120	200	280	—

KM# 9 THALER
Silver **Obv:** Crowned imperial eagle, orb on breast, titles of Ferdinand II **Rev:** Four oval arms in baroque frames in form of X, palm sprays around, date in legend **Note:** Dav. #6668.

Date	Mintage	VG	F	VF	XF	Unc
1624 CS Rare	—	—	—	—	—	—

KM# 13 THALER
36.0000 g., Silver **Note:** Klippe. Dav. #6668A.

Date	Mintage	VG	F	VF	XF	Unc
1624 CS Rare	—	—	—	—	—	—

KM# 11 THALER
Silver **Obv:** Facing heads of four rulers in oval frames in cruciform, smaller arms in cruciform in center **Rev:** Female allegorical figures of Justice and Peace seated on bench, two angels above, "JEHOVAH" in Hebrew with rays at top, Roman numeral date in legend **Note:** Dav. #6669.

Date	Mintage	VG	F	VF	XF	Unc
1625 CS Rare	—	—	—	—	—	—

Note: Leu Numismatik AG Auction 85, 10-02, good XF realized approximately $11,975.

COUNTERMARKED COINAGE

1693-1695

KM# 31.15 60 KREUZER (Gulden)
Silver **Countermark:** 60 K/FC monogram **Note:** Countermarked on Sayn-Wittgenstein-Hohnstein 2/3 Thaler, KM#52.

CM Date	Host Date	Good	VG	F	VF	XF
ND(1693-5)	1674 IZW	—	—	—	—	—

KM# 30.1 60 KREUZER (Gulden)
Silver **Countermark:** 60K/FC monogram **Note:** Countermark on Montfort 2/3 Thaler, KM#45.

CM Date	Host Date	Good	VG	F	VF	XF
ND(1693-5)	1675	—	120	200	375	600

KM# 30.2 60 KREUZER (Gulden)
Silver **Countermark:** 60K/FC monogram **Note:** Countermark on Montfort 60 Kreuzer, KM#61.

CM Date	Host Date	Good	VG	F	VF	XF
ND(1693-5)	1679	—	120	200	375	600

KM# 30.3 60 KREUZER (Gulden)
Silver **Countermark:** 60K/FC monogram **Note:** Countermark on Montfort 60 Kreuzer, KM#76.

CM Date	Host Date	Good	VG	F	VF	XF
ND(1693-5)	1690 FIG	—	120	200	375	600

KM# 30.4 60 KREUZER (Gulden)
Silver **Countermark:** 60K/FC monogram **Note:** Countermark on Montfort 60 Kreuzer, KM#78.

CM Date	Host Date	Good	VG	F	VF	XF
ND(1693-5)	1690 FIG	—	120	200	375	600

KM# 30.5 60 KREUZER (Gulden)
Silver **Countermark:** 60K/FC monogram **Note:** Countermark on Montfort 60 Kreuzer, KM#78.

CM Date	Host Date	Good	VG	F	VF	XF
ND(1693-95)	1690	—	85.00	150	275	450

KM# 31.1 60 KREUZER (Gulden)
Silver **Countermark:** 60K/FC monogram **Note:** Countermark on Anhalt-Desau 2/3 Thaler, KM#6.2.

CM Date	Host Date	Good	VG	F	VF	XF
ND(1693-5)	1693 IEG	—	55.00	100	190	300

KM# 31.2 60 KREUZER (Gulden)
Silver **Countermark:** 60K/FC monogram **Note:** Countermark on Anhalt-Harzegerode 2/3 Thaler, KM#1.1.

CM Date	Host Date	Good	VG	F	VF	XF
ND(1693-5)	ND1675-79	—	55.00	100	190	300

KM# 31.3 60 KREUZER (Gulden)
Silver **Countermark:** 60K/FC monogram **Note:** Countermark on Anhalt-Harzegerode 2/3 Thaler, KM#1.4.

CM Date	Host Date	Good	VG	F	VF	XF
ND(1693-5)	1679 SD	—	55.00	100	190	300

KM# 31.4 60 KREUZER (Gulden)
Silver **Countermark:** 60K/FC monogram **Note:** Countermark on Anhalt-Harzegerode 2.3 Thaler, KM#1.4.

CM Date	Host Date	Good	VG	F	VF	XF
ND(1693-5)	1676 CP	—	55.00	100	190	300

KM# 31.5 60 KREUZER (Gulden)
Silver **Countermark:** 60K/FC monogram **Note:** Countermark on Anhalt-Zerbst 2/3 Thaler, KM#19.6.

CM Date	Host Date	Good	VG	F	VF	XF
ND(1693-5)	1679 CP	—	55.00	100	190	300

KM# 31.6 60 KREUZER (Gulden)
Silver **Countermark:** 60K/FC monogram **Note:** Countermark on Emden 2/3 thaler, KM#30.

CM Date	Host Date	Good	VG	F	VF	XF
ND(1693-5)	1688	—	55.00	100	190	300

KM# 31.7 60 KREUZER (Gulden)
Silver **Countermark:** 60K/FC m onogram **Note:** Countermark on Henneberg-Ilmenau 2/3 Thaler, KM#10.

CM Date	Host Date	Good	VG	F	VF	XF
ND(1693-5)	1692-93 BA	—	55.00	100	190	300

KM# 31.8 60 KREUZER (Gulden)
Silver **Countermark:** 60K/FC monogram **Note:** Countermark on Lauenberg 2/3 Thaler.

CM Date	Host Date	Good	VG	F	VF	XF
ND(1693-5)	1678	—	55.00	100	190	300

KM# 31.9 60 KREUZER (Gulden)
Silver **Countermark:** 60K/FC monogram **Note:** Countermark on Lubeck 2/3 Thaler, KM#62.

CM Date	Host Date	Good	VG	F	VF	XF
ND(1693-5)	1678	—	55.00	100	190	300

KM# 31.10 60 KREUZER (Gulden)
Silver **Countermark:** 60K/FC monogram **Note:** Countermark on Münster 24 Mariengroschen, KM#101.

CM Date	Host Date	Good	VG	F	VF	XF
ND(1693-5)	1693 JO	—	55.00	100	190	300

KM# 31.11 60 KREUZER (Gulden)
Silver **Countermark:** 60K/FC monogram **Note:** Countermark on Pfalz-Sulzbach Gulden.

CM Date	Host Date	Good	VG	F	VF	XF
ND(1693-5)	1690-91	—	55.00	100	190	300

KM# 31.12 60 KREUZER (Gulden)
Silver **Countermark:** 60K/FC monogram **Note:** Countermark on Saxe-Weimar Gulden.

CM Date	Host Date	Good	VG	F	VF	XF
ND(1693-5)	1677-78	—	55.00	100	190	300

KM# 31.13 60 KREUZER (Gulden)
Silver **Countermark:** 60K/FC monogram **Note:** Countermark on Sayn-Wittgenstein-Wittgenstein 2/3 Thaler, KM#79.

CM Date	Host Date	Good	VG	F	VF	XF
ND(1693-5)	1676	—	55.00	100	190	300

KM# 31.14 60 KREUZER (Gulden)
Silver **Countermark:** 60K/FC monogram **Note:** Countermark on Henneberg-Ilmenau 2/3 Thaler, KM#9. Prev. KM#31.

CM Date	Host Date	Good	VG	F	VF	XF
ND(1693-5)	1692 BA	—	120	200	375	600

TRADE COINAGE

KM# A13 4 DUCAT
14.0000 g., 0.9860 Gold 0.4438 oz. AGW

Date	Mintage	VG	F	VF	XF	Unc
1625 CS Rare	—	—	—	—	—	—

Note: Similar to 1 Thaler, KM#11, struck from same dies.

FRANKENTHAL

Located about 6 miles northwest of Mannheim, Frankenthal was besieged by the Spaniards during the Thirty Years' War and forced to strike obsidional coinage.

NOTE: The horizontal line below VII represents 1/2.

TOWN

SIEGE COINAGE

Frankenthal was besieged by the Spaniards during the Thirty Years War and forced to strike obsidional coinage.

KM# 1 7-1/2 BATZEN
4.5000 g., Silver **Note:** Uniface. Klippe. City arms above denom: BATZ/VII. Legends FRANCKENTHALER: NOTH•M•16•23. The horizontal line below VII represents 1/2.

Date	Mintage	VG	F	VF	XF	Unc
1623	—	1,150	1,600	2,300	3,000	—

KM# 3.2 15 BATZEN
8.7000 g., Silver **Note:** Legend: FRANCKEN•NOTHM•1623.

Date	Mintage	VG	F	VF	XF	Unc
1623	—	—	—	—	—	—

Note: Reported, not confirmed

KM# 3.1 15 BATZEN
8.7000 g., Silver **Note:** Uniface. Klippe. Town arms above denom: BATZ/XV. Legend FRANCKENTHALER•NOTH•M•16•23.

Date	Mintage	VG	F	VF	XF	Unc
1623	—	400	675	925	1,400	—

KM# 4.1 GULDEN
7.1000 g., Silver **Note:** Uniface. Klippe. Town arms with F below divide date, legend GOTT•IST•VNSER•ECKSTEIN, value 1 punched in below outside legend.

Date	Mintage	VG	F	VF	XF	Unc
1623	—	400	675	925	1,400	—

KM# 4.2 GULDEN
7.1000 g., Silver **Note:** Without value punch.

Date	Mintage	VG	F	VF	XF	Unc
1623	—	400	675	925	1,400	—

KM# 9.4 2 GULDEN
Silver **Note:** City arms surrounded by six arcs, forming one circle. Legend DEVS•PETRA•NOSTRA•ANGVLARIS•1623.

Date	Mintage	VG	F	VF	XF	Unc
1623 Rare	—	—	—	—	—	—

KM# 9.1 2 GULDEN
Silver **Note:** F between two stars, legend GOTT•IST•VNSER• ECKSTEIN, value 2 in round indent.

Date	Mintage	VG	F	VF	XF	Unc
1623	—	325	675	1,200	2,000	—

KM# 6 2 GULDEN
Silver **Note:** Legend: GOTT•IST•VNSER•EKSTEIN.

Date	Mintage	VG	F	VF	XF	Unc
1623	—	325	675	1,200	2,000	—

KM# 9.2 2 GULDEN
Silver **Note:** Value 2 punched in all four corners.

Date	Mintage	VG	F	VF	XF	Unc
1623	—	400	725	1,300	2,250	—

KM# 5 2 GULDEN
Silver **Note:** Weight varies 14.0-14.3 grams. Uniface. Klippe. Town arms with F below divide date, legend DEVS•PETRA• NOSTRA•ANGVLARIS, value 2 punched in below outside lgend.

Date	Mintage	VG	F	VF	XF	Unc
1623	—	450	850	1,500	2,400	—

KM# 9.3 2 GULDEN
Silver **Note:** Without value punch.

Date	Mintage	VG	F	VF	XF	Unc
1623	—	325	675	1,200	2,000	—

KM# 8 4 GULDEN
Silver **Note:** Legend GOTT•IST•VNSER•ECKSTEIN, value 4 punched in below outside legend.

Date	Mintage	VG	F	VF	XF	Unc
1623	—	325	675	1,200	2,000	—

KM# 7.1 4 GULDEN
Silver **Obv:** Town arms with F below divide date, value 4 punched in below outside legend. **Obv. Legend:** DEVS•PETRA•NOSTRA• ANGVLARIS **Note:** Weight varies 28.0-28.5 g. Uniface. Klippe.

Date	Mintage	VG	F	VF	XF	Unc
1623	—	450	850	1,500	2,400	—

KM# 7.2 4 GULDEN
Silver **Note:** Without F below town arms.

Date	Mintage	VG	F	VF	XF	Unc
1623	—	525	1,000	1,650	2,750	—

TRADE COINAGE

KM# 11 DUCAT
3.5000 g., 0.9860 Gold 0.1109 oz. AGW **Obv:** Town arms with F below divide date, legend, no value shown **Obv. Legend:** GOTT • IST • VNSER • ECKSTEIN **Note:** Klippe, uniface.

Date	Mintage	VG	F	VF	XF	Unc
1623 Rare	—	—	—	—	—	—

KM# 12 2 DUCAT
6.6800 g., Gold **Obv:** Town arms with F below divide date, legend, no value shown. **Obv. Legend:** GOTT • IST • VNSER • ECKSTEIN **Note:** Uniface.

Date	Mintage	VG	F	VF	XF	Unc
1623 Rare	—	—	—	—	—	—

KM# 13 2 DUCAT
6.6800 g., Gold **Obv:** Town arms encircled by three storm clouds, legend **Obv. Legend:** DEVS • PETRA • NOSTRA • ANGVLARIS • 1623 F

Date	Mintage	VG	F	VF	XF	Unc
1623 Rare	—	—	—	—	—	—

FRANKFURT AM MAIN

One of the largest cities of modern Germany, Frankfurt is located on the north bank of the Main River about 25 miles (42 kilometers) upstream from where it joins the Rhine at Mainz. It was the site of a Roman camp in the first century. Frankfurt was a commercial center from the early Middle Ages and became a favored location for imperial councils during the Carolingian period because of its central location. An imperial mint operated from early times and had a large production during the 12th to 14th centuries. Local issues were produced from at least the mid-14th century, but it was not until 1428 that the city was officially granted the right to coin its own money. In establishing the seven permanent electors of the Empire in 1356, the Golden Bull also made Frankfurt the site of those elections and increased the prestige of the city even further. Frankfurt remained a free city until 1806 and then was the capital of the Grand Duchy of Frankfurt from 1810 until 1814, only to regain its free status in 1815. The city chose the wrong side in the Austro-Prussian War of 1866 and thus was absorbed by victorious Prussia in the latter year.

MINT MARKS
F = Frankfurt

MINT OFFICIALS' INITIALS

Initial	Date	Name
PM	1567-1603	Philipp Mussler, warden
LS	1611-30	Lorenz Schilling, diecutter
(a) or or or AE or C AE	1618-25, 27-36	Caspar Ayrer
HE, HS	1625-27	Hans Schmidt
GN	1644-45	George Nurnberger der Jungere
AM	1637-44	Johann Anselm Munch
(h) (3 acorns)	1646-66	Johann Ludwig Hallaicher
(f) and/or MR	1666-89	Michael Faber
IF, IIF	1690-1737	Johann Jeremias Freytag

NOTE: In some instances old dies were used with initials beyond the date range of the man that held the position.

FREE CITY

REGULAR COINAGE

KM# 16 PFENNIG

Silver **Obv. Legend:** Crowned eagle left in circle **Note:** Schussel type. Uniface.

Date	Mintage	VG	F	VF	XF	Unc
ND(1606)	—	20.00	40.00	80.00	150	—

KM# 24 PFENNIG

Silver **Note:** Uniface. Schussel type. Crowned eagle, head left in circle, around FRANCFVRTI, date. Varieties exist.

Date	Mintage	VG	F	VF	XF	Unc
1609	—	18.00	40.00	65.00	140	—
1610	—	18.00	40.00	65.00	140	—

KM# 68 PFENNIG

Silver **Note:** Shield with crowned eagle, head left, divides date, F above.

Date	Mintage	VG	F	VF	XF	Unc
16Z1	—	15.00	33.00	65.00	120	—

KM# 73 PFENNIG

Silver **Note:** Shield with crowned eagle, head left, date above divided by F.

Date	Mintage	VG	F	VF	XF	Unc
16ZZ	—	15.00	33.00	65.00	120	—

KM# 69 DREIER (3 Pfennig)

Silver **Obv:** Crowned eagle, head left, in shield, divides date, F above **Rev:** Imperial orb with 3 **Note:** Kipper Dreier.

Date	Mintage	VG	F	VF	XF	Unc
1621	—	—	—	—	—	—

Note: Reported, not confirmed

KM# A20 ENGLISH (7 Heller)

Silver **Obv:** 4-fold shield, Frankfurt crowned eagle in each quadrant **Obv. Legend:** MON ETA NOV **Rev:** Ornate floriated cross in circle **Rev. Legend:** ANGLIE FRANCF

Date	Mintage	VG	F	VF	XF	Unc
1601	—	—	—	—	—	—

Note: Orignally issued in the late Middle Ages to facilitate exchange with English sterling or pennies which circulated widely in continental Europe.

KM# 99 1/4 KREUZER

Silver **Note:** Uniface. Schussel type. Crowned eagle, head left, divides date in circle of pellets, 1/4 below.

Date	Mintage	VG	F	VF	XF	Unc
1647	—	—	—	—	—	—

Note: Reported, not confirmed

KM# 60 KREUZER

Silver **Obv:** Crowned eagle, head left, in shield, F above, all within wreath **Rev:** Date **Rev. Legend:** I/KREVTZ/ER **Note:** Kipper Kreuzer. Varieties exist.

Date	Mintage	VG	F	VF	XF	Unc
1620	—	33.00	65.00	120	240	—
16Z0	—	33.00	65.00	120	240	—
1622	—	33.00	65.00	120	240	—
16ZZ	—	33.00	65.00	120	240	—

KM# 74 KREUZER

Silver **Obv:** Eagle, head left, in shield, F above, all in laurel wreath **Note:** Kipper Kreuzer. Varieties exist.

Date	Mintage	VG	F	VF	XF	Unc
16ZZ	—	15.00	45.00	90.00	175	—
16Z3	—	20.00	50.00	100	200	—

KM# 77 KREUZER

Silver **Obv:** Eagle's head to right

Date	Mintage	VG	F	VF	XF	Unc
16Z3	—	20.00	50.00	90.00	175	—

KM# 135 KREUZER

Silver **Obv:** Eagle head right **Rev:** Date divided by F/ KREU/ TZER, in laurel wreath

Date	Mintage	VG	F	VF	XF	Unc
1666 MF	—	27.00	60.00	120	240	—

KM# 139 KREUZER

Silver **Obv:** Eagle's head left

Date	Mintage	VG	F	VF	XF	Unc
1668 MF	—	27.00	60.00	120	240	—
1669 MF	—	27.00	60.00	120	240	—
1676 MF	—	20.00	55.00	110	200	—

KM# 151 KREUZER

Silver **Rev:** Date divided by F/ KREV/ TZER in circle **Rev. Legend:** NACH • DEM • SCHLUS • DER • V • STAND

Date	Mintage	VG	F	VF	XF	Unc
1693 IIF	—	20.00	55.00	110	200	—
1695 IIF	—	20.00	55.00	110	200	—

KM# 158 KREUZER

Silver **Obv:** Floral design above FRANC/ FURT **Rev. Legend:** I/ KREU/ ZER

Date	Mintage	VG	F	VF	XF	Unc
ND(ca.1695) 1 known; Rare	—	—	—	—	—	—

KM# 61 2 KREUZER (1/2 Halbbatzen)

Silver **Obv:** Crowned eagle, head left, in shield **Rev:** Date **Rev. Legend:** II/KREVTZ/ER **Note:** Varieties exist.

Date	Mintage	VG	F	VF	XF	Unc
16Z0 Rare	—	—	—	—	—	—

KM# 25 ALBUS (8 Heller)

Silver **Obv:** Crowned eagle, head left, date in legend **Rev:** Cross divides 8 **Rev. Legend:** NOVVS • ALBVS

Date	Mintage	VG	F	VF	XF	Unc
1609	—	65.00	120	210	300	—

KM# 31.1 ALBUS (8 Heller)

Silver **Obv:** Crowned eagle, head left **Obv. Legend:** NO • ALBVS • FRANCOFVRTENSIS **Rev:** VIII/ ++/ date in laurel wreath **Note:** Varieties exist.

Date	Mintage	VG	F	VF	XF	Unc
1610	—	33.00	65.00	120	175	—
1612	—	33.00	65.00	120	175	—

KM# 31.2 ALBUS (8 Heller)

Silver **Obv. Legend:** ...FRANCOFVRTENS **Rev:** ALB/ +/ 1610 within laurel wreath

Date	Mintage	VG	F	VF	XF	Unc
1610	—	33.00	65.00	120	190	—

KM# 31.3 ALBUS (8 Heller)

Silver **Obv. Legend:** NO • ALB • FRANCOFVRTENS[IS] **Rev:** VIII/ */ date within laurel wreath

Date	Mintage	VG	F	VF	XF	Unc
1610	—	33.00	65.00	130	175	—
1611	—	33.00	65.00	130	175	—

KM# 32 ALBUS (8 Heller)

Silver **Note:** Klippe.

Date	Mintage	VG	F	VF	XF	Unc
1610	—	—	—	—	—	—

KM# 33 ALBUS (8 Heller)

Silver **Rev:** ALB/+/date

Date	Mintage	VG	F	VF	XF	Unc
1610	—	90.00	200	350	500	—

KM# 87.1 ALBUS (8 Heller)

Silver **Obv:** Crowned eagle, in inner circle, head left **Obv. Legend:** REIP • FRANCOFVRT **Rev:** ALBVS/+/date in laurel wreath and inner circle

Date	Mintage	VG	F	VF	XF	Unc
1637	—	16.00	27.00	50.00	100	—
1637 AM	—	16.00	27.00	50.00	100	—
1638 AM	—	16.00	27.00	50.00	100	—
1639 AM	—	16.00	27.00	50.00	100	—
1640 AM	—	16.00	27.00	50.00	100	—
1642 (h)	—	—	—	—	—	—

Note: Reported, not confirmed

Date	Mintage	VG	F	VF	XF	Unc
1647 (a)	—	16.00	27.00	50.00	100	—
1647 (h)	—	16.00	27.00	50.00	100	—
1654 (h)	—	16.00	27.00	50.00	100	—
1655 (h)	—	16.00	27.00	50.00	100	—

KM# 87.2 ALBUS (8 Heller)

Silver **Obv:** Without inner circles **Obv. Legend:** ...REIPVB **Rev:** Without inner circles **Rev. Legend:** ALBVS / + / date

Date	Mintage	VG	F	VF	XF	Unc
1647 (h)	—	16.00	27.00	50.00	100	—
1648 (h)	—	16.00	27.00	50.00	100	—

KM# 87.3 ALBUS (8 Heller)

Silver **Obv. Legend:** REIP...

Date	Mintage	VG	F	VF	XF	Unc
1648 (h)	—	16.00	27.00	45.00	90.00	—

KM# 105 ALBUS (8 Heller)

Silver **Rev:** Date/++/ALBVS

Date	Mintage	VG	F	VF	XF	Unc
1648 (h)	—	20.00	40.00	100	180	—

KM# 107.1 ALBUS (8 Heller)

Silver **Obv:** Eagle head left **Rev:** I/ ALBVS/ date divided by cross below, in laurel wreath **Note:** Varieties exist.

Date	Mintage	VG	F	VF	XF	Unc
1649 (h)	—	13.00	27.00	60.00	110	—
1650 (h)	—	13.00	27.00	60.00	110	—
1651 (h)	—	13.00	27.00	60.00	110	—
1652 (h)	—	13.00	27.00	60.00	110	—
1653	—	13.00	27.00	60.00	110	—
1657	—	13.00	27.00	60.00	110	—

KM# 107.2 ALBUS (8 Heller)

Silver **Obv:** Eagle head right **Rev:** I/ ALBVS/ date divided by cross below, in laurel wreath

Date	Mintage	VG	F	VF	XF	Unc
1651 (h)	—	13.00	30.00	65.00	125	—
1652 (h)	—	13.00	30.00	65.00	125	—
1653 (h)	—	13.00	30.00	65.00	125	—
1653	—	13.00	30.00	65.00	125	—
1654	—	13.00	30.00	65.00	125	—

KM# 108.1 ALBUS (8 Heller)

Silver **Obv. Legend:** REIPUB: FRANCOFURT **Rev:** ALBVS/ date divided by cross below, in laurel wreath

Date	Mintage	VG	F	VF	XF	Unc
1649 (h)	—	27.00	55.00	90.00	150	—
1651 (h)	—	27.00	55.00	90.00	150	—
1652 (h)	—	27.00	55.00	90.00	150	—

KM# 136 ALBUS (8 Heller)

Silver **Obv:** Eagle head right, without inner circle

Date	Mintage	VG	F	VF	XF	Unc
1651 (h)	—	27.00	55.00	110	220	—

KM# A108 ALBUS (8 Heller)

Silver **Obv:** Smaller eagle, head left **Rev:** ALBVS around, date intact

Date	Mintage	VG	F	VF	XF	Unc
1655	—	27.00	65.00	150	250	—

KM# 108.2 ALBUS (8 Heller)

Silver **Obv:** Eagle left in inner circle **Rev:** ALBUS above cross, date flanking, within inner circle **Rev. Legend:** REIPVB FRANCOFURT **Note:** Varieties exist.

Date	Mintage	VG	F	VF	XF	Unc
1655 (h)	—	27.00	40.00	70.00	125	—
1655	—	27.00	40.00	70.00	125	—
1656 (h)	—	27.00	40.00	70.00	125	—
1656	—	27.00	40.00	70.00	125	—
1657 (h)	—	27.00	40.00	70.00	125	—
1657	—	27.00	40.00	70.00	125	—
1666 (f)	—	27.00	40.00	70.00	125	—
1667 (f)	—	27.00	40.00	70.00	125	—
1668 (f)	—	27.00	40.00	70.00	125	—
1669 (f)	—	27.00	40.00	70.00	125	—
1670 (f)	—	27.00	40.00	70.00	125	—
1671 (f)	—	27.00	40.00	70.00	125	—
1680 (f)	—	27.00	40.00	70.00	125	—
1681 (f)	—	27.00	40.00	70.00	125	—

KM# 152.1 ALBUS (8 Heller)

Silver **Rev:** I/ ALBUS/ date and mintmasters initials divided by cross **Rev. Legend:** NACH • DEM • SCHLUS • DER • V • STaND

Date	Mintage	VG	F	VF	XF	Unc
1693 IIF	—	27.00	55.00	100	170	—
1695 IIF	—	27.00	55.00	100	170	—

KM# 152.2 ALBUS (8 Heller)

Silver **Rev. Legend:** ...V • STAEND

Date	Mintage	VG	F	VF	XF	Unc
1693 IIF	—	27.00	55.00	100	170	—
1695 IIF	—	27.00	55.00	100	170	—

KM# 152.3 ALBUS (8 Heller)
Silver **Rev. Legend:** ...V • STEND

Date	Mintage	VG	F	VF	XF	Unc
1693 IIF	—	27.00	55.00	100	170	—
1695 IIF	—	27.00	55.00	100	170	—

KM# 153 2 ALBUS
Silver **Obv:** Similar to 1 Albus, KM#108 **Rev:** II/ ALBUS/ date and mintmasters initials divided by cross **Note:** Varities exist.

Date	Mintage	VG	F	VF	XF	Unc
1693 IIF	—	25.00	50.00	85.00	155	—
1694 IIF	—	27.00	55.00	90.00	180	—

KM# 62 6 KREUZER
Silver **Obv:** Crowned eagle, head left, F on breast **Rev:** Date in laurel wreath **Rev. Legend:** VI/ KREVTZ/ ER **Note:** Varieties exist.

Date	Mintage	VG	F	VF	XF	Unc
16Z0 (a)	—	80.00	200	450	800	—
16Z0 (a) AE	—	80.00	200	450	800	—

KM# 30 12 KREUZER (Zwölfer)
Silver **Obv:** Crowned eagle, head left, F in heart-shaped shield on breast **Rev:** Crowned imperial eagle, (12) in orb on breast, titles of Rudolf II, date in legend **Note:** Varieties exist.

Date	Mintage	VG	F	VF	XF	Unc
1610 With 12 in orb	—	65.00	130	300	475	—
1611	—	65.00	130	300	475	—
161Z	—	65.00	130	300	475	—
1612	—	65.00	130	300	475	—

KM# 37 12 KREUZER (Zwölfer)
Silver **Obv:** Titles of Matthias

Date	Mintage	VG	F	VF	XF	Unc
1612	—	80.00	170	350	650	—

KM# 63 12 KREUZER (Zwölfer)
Silver **Obv:** Crowned imperial eagle, 1Z in orb on breast, titles of Ferdinand II **Rev:** Crowned eagle, head left, in shield divides date **Note:** Varieties exist.

Date	Mintage	VG	F	VF	XF	Unc
16Z0 (a)	—	110	240	550	1,100	—
16Z1	—	110	240	550	1,100	—

KM# 70 12 KREUZER (Zwölfer)
Silver **Obv:** Eagle with F on breast

Date	Mintage	VG	F	VF	XF	Unc
ND(1621/2) 2 known; Rare	—	—	—	—	—	—

KM# 154 6 ALBUS (12 Kreuzer)
Silver **Obv:** Similar to 1 Albus, KM#108 **Rev:** VI/ ALBUS/ date and mintmasters initials divided by cross

Date	Mintage	VG	F	VF	XF	Unc
1693 IIF	—	27.00	55.00	110	220	—

KM# 146 60 KREUZER (2/3 Thaler)
Silver **Obv. Legend:** MONETA • NOVA... **Note:** Varieties exist.

Date	Mintage	VG	F	VF	XF	Unc
1672 MF	—	45.00	100	200	300	—
1673 MF	—	45.00	100	200	300	—
1674 MF	—	45.00	100	200	300	—
1675 MF	—	45.00	100	200	300	—

KM# 150 60 KREUZER (2/3 Thaler)
Silver **Obv. Legend:** FRANCFVRTER • STADT • MUNTZ **Note:** Varieties exist.

Date	Mintage	VG	F	VF	XF	Unc
1690 IIF	—	45.00	100	200	325	—
1691 IIF	—	45.00	100	200	325	—
1693 IIF	—	45.00	100	200	325	—
1695 IIF	—	45.00	100	200	325	—

KM# 155 60 KREUZER (2/3 Thaler)
Silver **Obv:** Eagle not in circle

Date	Mintage	VG	F	VF	XF	Unc
1694 IIF	—	65.00	130	275	450	—

KM# 14 TURNOSGROSHEN
Silver **Obv:** W/o CIVIT **Rev:** Small cross, circle with 5 bows around **Note:** Klippe.

Date	Mintage	VG	F	VF	XF	Unc
1601	—	—	—	—	—	—
1606	—	—	—	—	—	—

KM# 15.3 TURNOSGROSHEN
Silver **Obv. Legend:** FRANCOFVRDI

Date	Mintage	VG	F	VF	XF	Unc
1606	—	40.00	85.00	150	300	—

KM# 13.2 TURNOSGROSHEN
Silver **Obv:** Crowned eagle, head left, date **Obv. Legend:** TVRONVS • FRANCOFVRDI **Rev:** Small cross in circle, surrounded by circle of none fleur-de-lis in arches **Rev. Legend:** SIT • NOMEN • DOMINI • BENEDICTVM

Date	Mintage	VG	F	VF	XF	Unc
1606	—	55.00	110	210	350	—

KM# 13.3 TURNOSGROSHEN
Silver **Obv. Legend:** TVRONVS CIVIT • FRANCOFVRDI:

Date	Mintage	VG	F	VF	XF	Unc
1606	—	55.00	110	210	350	—

KM# 15.1 TURNOSGROSHEN
Silver **Obv. Legend:** TVRONVS: CIVIT • FRANCOFVRTENSIS **Rev:** Cross in quatrilobe

Date	Mintage	VG	F	VF	XF	Unc
1606	—	40.00	85.00	150	300	—

KM# 15.2 TURNOSGROSHEN
Silver **Obv. Legend:** FRANCOFVRTENS

Date	Mintage	VG	F	VF	XF	Unc
1606	—	40.00	85.00	150	300	—

KM# 17.1 TURNOSGROSHEN
Silver **Obv. Legend:** TVRONVS • CIVIT • FRANCFVRTEN[S] **Rev:** Large cross with flourishes in angles

Date	Mintage	VG	F	VF	XF	Unc
1606	—	40.00	85.00	145	275	—
ND	—	85.00	200	400	800	—

KM# 17.2 TURNOSGROSHEN
Silver **Obv. Legend:** FRANCFVRTENSIS

Date	Mintage	VG	F	VF	XF	Unc
1606	—	60.00	160	400	525	—

KM# 17.3 TURNOSGROSHEN
Silver **Obv:** Eagle's head divides date **Obv. Legend:** FRANCOFVRTENS **Rev:** Flourishes around cross

Date	Mintage	VG	F	VF	XF	Unc
1606	—	65.00	165	325	600	—

KM# 18.1 TURNOSGROSHEN
Silver **Obv:** Crowned eagle, date **Obv. Legend:** CIVIT FRANCOFVRT[EN] **Rev:** Short ornamented cross without flourishes in angles

Date	Mintage	F	VF	XF	Unc	BU
1606	—	55.00	110	200	300	—

KM# 18.2 TURNOSGROSHEN
Silver **Obv. Legend:** TVRONVS • CIVIT • FRANCFVRTEN **Rev:** Short cross without flourishes and ornaments

Date	Mintage	F	VF	XF	Unc	BU
1606	—	55.00	110	200	300	—

KM# 19 TURNOSGROSHEN
Silver **Obv:** With CIVIT **Rev:** Cross with ornaments in three angles **Note:** Klippe.

Date	Mintage	VG	F	VF	XF	Unc
1606	—	—	—	—	—	—

KM# 137.1 TURNOSGROSHEN
Silver **Rev:** Large cross without flourishes

Date	Mintage	VG	F	VF	XF	Unc
1666 (f)	—	40.00	85.00	200	350	—

KM# 137.2 TURNOSGROSHEN
Silver **Rev:** Large cross with flourishes

Date	Mintage	VG	F	VF	XF	Unc
1680 MF	—	40.00	85.00	200	350	—
1689/0 MF	—	40.00	85.00	200	350	—
1689 MF-IF	—	40.00	85.00	200	350	—

KM# 75 1/8 THALER
Silver **Note:** Similar to 1 Thaler, KM#72 but 1/8 in orb on breast.

Date	Mintage	VG	F	VF	XF	Unc
16Z2 AE Rare	—	—	—	—	—	—
16Z2 (a) Rare	—	—	—	—	—	—

KM# 45 1/6 THALER (1/4 Gulden)
Silver, 25 mm. **Subject:** Centenary of Reformation **Note:** Weight varies 4.25-4.40 grams. Same dies as a goldgulden.

Date	Mintage	VG	F	VF	XF	Unc
1617	—	80.00	140	275	400	—

KM# 20 1/4 THALER
Silver **Note:** Similar to 1 Thaler, KM#22.

Date	Mintage	VG	F	VF	XF	Unc
1606	—	—	—	—	—	—

KM# 29 1/4 THALER
7.0000 g., Silver, 29 mm. **Subject:** Centenary of Reformation

Date	Mintage	VG	F	VF	XF	Unc
1617	—	—	—	—	—	—

KM# 53 1/4 THALER
7.0000 g., Silver **Obv:** Large cross with eagle in a small center shield

Date	Mintage	VG	F	VF	XF	Unc
1619 AE	—	450	825	1,300	2,500	—
Note: Strikes dated 1619 have a mint mark on either the obverse or reverse side						
1620 AE	—	450	825	1,300	2,500	—

KM# 71 1/4 THALER
7.0000 g., Silver **Rev:** 1/4 in orb, date in legend

Date	Mintage	VG	F	VF	XF	Unc
16Z1 (a)	—	—	—	—	—	—
16ZZ (a) AE	—	—	—	—	—	—

KM# 156 1/4 THALER
7.0000 g., Silver **Note:** Similar to 1/2 Thaler, KM#157.

Date	Mintage	VG	F	VF	XF	Unc
1694 IIF	—	625	1,150	2,000	3,000	—

KM# 159 1/4 THALER
7.0000 g., Silver **Obv:** Without angels **Rev:** Without circle around eagle

Date	Mintage	VG	F	VF	XF	Unc
1695 IIF	—	900	1,500	2,600	5,500	—

KM# 117 1/3 THALER (1/2 Gulden)
Silver **Subject:** Coronation of Leopold I **Obv:** Laureate bust of Leopold right, date in legend **Rev:** Crowned imperial eagle, F in heart-shaped shield on breast

Date	Mintage	VG	F	VF	XF	Unc
1658	—	500	875	1,500	3,000	—

KM# 21 1/2 THALER
Silver **Note:** Similar to 1 Thaler KM#45, titles of Rudolf II.

Date	Mintage	VG	F	VF	XF	Unc
1606 Rare	—	—	—	—	—	—
1610 Rare	—	—	—	—	—	—
1611 Rare	—	—	—	—	—	—

KM# 50 1/2 THALER
Silver **Obv:** Titles of Matthias **Note:** Klippe.

Date	Mintage	VG	F	VF	XF	Unc
1618 AE	—	—	—	—	—	—

Note: Reported, not confirmed

KM# 64 1/2 THALER
Silver **Note:** Similar to Thaler KM#65, titles of Ferdinand II.

Date	Mintage	VG	F	VF	XF	Unc
1620 AE Rare	—	—	—	—	—	—

KM# 76 1/2 THALER
Silver **Note:** Similar to 1 Thaler, KM#72.

Date	Mintage	VG	F	VF	XF	Unc
16ZZ AE Rare	—	—	—	—	—	—

KM# 106 1/2 THALER
Silver **Subject:** End of Thirty Years' War **Obv:** City view, FRANCOFVRT in cartouche below **Rev:** Crowned eagle, head left, date above **Rev. Legend:** NOMEN • DOMINI • TVRRIS • FORTISSIMA

Date	Mintage	VG	F	VF	XF	Unc
1648 (h)	—	1,750	3,400	4,500	6,500	—

KM# 145 1/2 THALER
Silver **Obv:** Cross **Rev:** Eagle **Note:** Varieties exist.

Date	Mintage	VG	F	VF	XF	Unc
1670 MF	—	1,000	1,850	3,000	6,000	—
1671 MF	—	800	1,500	3,000	6,000	—

KM# 157 1/2 THALER
Silver **Obv:** City view **Rev:** Eagle

Date	Mintage	VG	F	VF	XF	Unc
1694 IIF	—	1,350	2,400	4,000	7,800	—

KM# 160 1/2 THALER
Silver **Obv:** Revised imperial eagle **Rev:** Alternate city view **Note:** Varieties exist.

Date	Mintage	VG	F	VF	XF	Unc
1695 IIF rare	—	—	—	—	—	—
1696 IIF rare	—	—	—	—	—	—

KM# 162 1/2 THALER
Silver **Note:** Similar to 1/2 Thaler, KM#145 but value 1/2 added below eagle on reverse.

Date	Mintage	VG	F	VF	XF	Unc
1696 IIF rare	—	—	—	—	—	—

KM# 22 THALER
Silver **Obv:** Cross **Rev:** Titles of Rudolph II, eagle **Note:** Dav.#5281. Varieties exist.

Date	Mintage	VG	F	VF	XF	Unc
1606 rare	—	—	—	—	—	—

Note: Aucttion Peus #394, 2007 VF realized $15,500

KM# 34 THALER
Silver **Obv:** Eagle in baroque ornament on plain cross **Rev:** Titles of Rudolf II **Note:** Dav.#5283. Varieties exist.

Date	Mintage	VG	F	VF	XF	Unc
1610 rare	—	—	—	—	—	—
1611 rare	—	—	—	—	—	—

KM# 46 THALER
Silver **Rev:** Titles of Matthias **Note:** Dav.#5285.

Date	Mintage	VG	F	VF	XF	Unc
1617	—	900	1,800	3,500	6,800	—
1618 AE	—	900	1,800	3,500	6,800	—

KM# 61.1 THALER
Silver **Obv:** Eagle in oval shield on cross **Rev:** Titles of Ferdinand II, crowned imperial eagle **Note:** Dav.#5287. Prev. KM#65.1.

Date	Mintage	VG	F	VF	XF	Unc
16Z0 AE	—	—	—	—	—	—
ND AE	—	—	—	—	—	—

KM# 61.2 THALER
Silver **Obv:** Eagle in shield on cross within double circle **Rev:** Crowned imperial eagle **Note:** Dav.#5287C. Prev. KM#65.2.

Date	Mintage	VG	F	VF	XF	Unc
16Z0 AE	—	—	—	—	—	—

KM# 65.1 THALER
Silver **Obv:** Eagle in oval shield at center of cross, angel heads at ends, small letters **Rev:** Crowned double-headed imperial eagle, small letters **Note:** Dav.#5290. Prev. KM65.3. Both dates exist with the date on either side

Date	Mintage	VG	F	VF	XF	Unc
16Z3 AE	—	75.00	160	320	650	—
16Z4 AE	—	85.00	200	400	800	—

KM# 65.3 THALER
Silver **Obv:** Eagle in oval shield on cross,large letters **Rev:** Crowned imperial eagle, large letters **Note:** Prev. KM#65.4. Year on either side.

Date	Mintage	VG	F	VF	XF	Unc
16Z3 AE	—	100	250	500	1,000	—

KM# 72.1 THALER

Silver **Obv:** Eagle on shield at center of cross, legends in small letters **Rev:** Crowned imperial eagle, legends in small letters **Note:** Both dates exist with the year on the reverse side, 1620 exists with the year on the obverse as well. 16Z1 AE strikes have inverted N's in their legends. Dav.#5289.

Date	Mintage	VG	F	VF	XF	Unc
16Z0 AE	—	65.00	140	280	600	—
16Z1 AE	—	65.00	140	280	600	—

KM# 72.3 THALER

Silver **Obv:** Eagle in shield at center of cross, legends in large letters **Rev:** Crowned imperial eagle, legends in large letters **Note:** Both dates exist with the year on either the obverse or reverse. Dav.#5289.

Date	Mintage	VG	F	VF	XF	Unc
16Z1 AE	—	65.00	140	280	600	—
16ZZ AE	—	65.00	140	280	600	—
1622 AE	—	70.00	170	350	700	—

KM# 72.4 THALER

Silver **Obv:** Eagle on shield at center of cross, large letters **Rev:** Crowned imperial eagle, large letters

Date	Mintage	VG	F	VF	XF	Unc
16Z1 AE	—	65.00	140	280	600	—
16ZZ AE	—	65.00	140	280	600	—

KM# 88.1 THALER

Silver **Rev:** Eagle faces right on cross **Note:** Dav.#5291. Prev. KM#65.6.

Date	Mintage	VG	F	VF	XF	Unc
16Z4 AE	—	50.00	100	200	385	—
16Z5 HS	—	50.00	100	200	385	—
16Z6 HS	—	50.00	100	200	385	—

Note: 16Z6 dates exist with the year on either obverse and reverse 1626 on reverse exists

KM# 88.2 THALER

Silver **Obv:** Eagle on roundeded shield in center of cross within circle **Rev:** Crowned double-headed imperial eagle within circle **Note:** Dav.#5293. Prev. KM#65.5.

Date	Mintage	VG	F	VF	XF	Unc
16Z5 AE	—	100	250	500	1,000	—
16Z5 HS	—	80.00	180	360	720	—
16Z6 HS	—	80.00	180	360	720	—
1627 HS	—	80.00	180	360	720	—
1627 AE	—	100	250	500	1,000	—

Date	Mintage	VG	F	VF	XF	Unc
163Z AE	—	100	250	500	1,000	—
1634 AE	—	80.00	180	360	720	—
1635 AE	—	80.00	180	360	720	—
1636 AM	—	100	250	500	1,000	—
1637 AM	—	100	250	500	1,000	—

KM# 78 THALER

Silver **Obv:** Crowned eagle, head left, in laurel wreath, date divided below tail **Rev:** City view, FRANCOFORDIA above, FROTECTORE DEO in band at top

Date	Mintage	VG	F	VF	XF	Unc
16Z5 LS	—	—	5,000	8,000	11,000	—

KM# 88.3 THALER

Silver **Obv:** Crowned eagle on shield in center of cross within circle **Rev:** Titles of Ferdinand III **Note:** Dav.#5294. Prev. KM#88. Varieties exist. Legends in small letters in both obverse and reverse.

Date	Mintage	VG	F	VF	XF	Unc
1638 AM	—	100	250	500	1,000	—
1639 AM	—	100	250	500	1,000	—
1641 AM	—	120	300	600	1,200	—
1642 AM	—	120	300	600	1,200	—
1643 AM	—	140	350	750	1,500	—
1644 GN Unique	—	—	—	—	—	—

KM# 95 THALER

Silver **Obv:** Crowned eagle on shield in center of designed cross within circle **Rev:** Date divided by crown at top **Note:** Dav.#5295. Varieties exist. Legends in small letters in both obverse and reverse.

Date	Mintage	VG	F	VF	XF	Unc
1644 GN	—	—	2,500	5,000	10,000	—
1645 GN	—	—	2,500	5,000	10,000	—
1646 (h)	—	—	750	1,500	3,000	—
1647 (h)	—	—	—	—	—	—

Note: Reported, not confirmed

KM# 100 THALER

Silver **Obv:** Without circle around imperial eagle **Note:** Dav.#5296.

Date	Mintage	VG	F	VF	XF	Unc
1647 (h)	—	—	750	1,500	3,000	—

KM# 101 THALER

Silver **Obv:** Crowned eagle on shield in center of cross within circle **Rev:** Date in legend **Note:** Dav.#5297. Legends in small letters in both obverse and reverse.

Date	Mintage	VG	F	VF	XF	Unc
1647 (h)	—	—	750	150	3,000	—
1650 (h)	—	—	1,000	2,000	4,000	—
1651 (h)	—	—	1,200	2,500	5,500	—
1652 (h)	—	—	1,200	2,500	5,500	—
1655 (h)	—	—	1,200	2,500	5,500	—

KM# 115 THALER

Silver **Obv:** KM#101 **Rev:** KM#78

Date	Mintage	VG	F	VF	XF	Unc
1650 (h) Unique	—	—	—	—	—	—

KM# 123 THALER

Silver **Note:** Similar to KM#101 but titles of Leopold I. Dav.#5298.

Date	Mintage	VG	F	VF	XF	Unc
1658 (h) rare	—	—	—	—	—	—

KM# 138 THALER

Silver **Obv:** Crowned eagle on shield in center of designed cross within circle **Rev:** Titles of Leopold I **Note:** Dav.#5299. Varieties exist. Legends in small letters on both sides.

Date	Mintage	VG	F	VF	XF	Unc
1667 MF	—	—	1,500	4,000	8,000	—
1669 MF	—	—	1,500	4,000	8,000	—
1671 MF	—	—	1,500	4,000	8,000	—
1674 MF	—	—	1,500	4,000	8,000	—
1694 IIF	—	—	2,000	4,500	10,000	—

KM# 161 THALER

Silver **Obv:** Heraldic angel above city view, within circle **Rev:** Crowned double-headed imperial eagle **Note:** Dav.#5300. Legends in small letters on both sides.

Date	Mintage	VG	F	VF	XF	Unc
1695 IIF	—	1,800	3,600	7,000	14,000	—
1696 IIF	—	1,800	3,600	7,000	14,000	—

KM# 23 2 THALER

Silver **Obv:** Crowned eagle on shield in center of cross within designed circle **Rev:** Titles of Rudolph II **Note:** Dav.#5280. Varieties exist.

Date	Mintage	VG	F	VF	XF	Unc
1606 Rare	—	—	—	—	15,000	—

KM# 35 2 THALER

Silver **Note:** Struck with 1 Thaler dies, thick flan. Titles of Rudolf II. Varieties exist. Dav.#5282.

Date	Mintage	VG	F	VF	XF	Unc
1610 Rare	—	—	—	—	11,000	—

KM# 51 2 THALER

Silver **Note:** Similar to 1 Thaler, KM#46. Dav.#5284.

Date	Mintage	VG	F	VF	XF	Unc
1618 AE	—	—	—	—	—	—

Note: Reported, not confirmed

KM# 66.1 2 THALER

Silver **Note:** Similar to 1 Thaler, KM#65.1. Dav.#5286.

Date	Mintage	VG	F	VF	XF	Unc
16Z0 AE Rare	—	—	—	—	—	—

KM# 66.2 2 THALER

Silver **Note:** Similar to 1 Thaler, KM#88. Varieties exist. Dav.#5292.

Date	Mintage	VG	F	VF	XF	Unc
1637 AM Unique	—	—	—	—	—	—

KM# 102 2 THALER

Silver **Note:** Similar to 1 Thaler, KM#100. Dav.#A5296.

Date	Mintage	VG	F	VF	XF	Unc
1647 (h) Rare	—	—	—	—	—	—

KM# 103 2 THALER

Silver **Note:** Similar to 1 Thaler, KM#101. Dav.#A5297.

Date	Mintage	VG	F	VF	XF	Unc
1647 (h) Rare	—	—	—	—	—	—

TRADE COINAGE

KM# 36 GOLDGULDEN

3.5000 g., 0.9860 Gold 0.1109 oz. AGW **Obv:** St. John standing in inner circle, arms at bottom **Rev:** Crowned imperial eagle in inner circle, date in legend, titles of Rudolf II

Date	Mintage	VG	F	VF	XF	Unc
1611	—	300	900	1,800	3,500	—

KM# 38 GOLDGULDEN

3.5000 g., 0.9860 Gold 0.1109 oz. AGW **Obv:** Enthroned king in center panel flanked by angels **Rev:** Angel blowing trumpet, eagle preparing to place wreath on angel's head

Date	Mintage	VG	F	VF	XF	Unc
1612	—	1,600	3,500	6,000	11,000	—

KM# 39.1 GOLDGULDEN

3.5000 g., 0.9860 Gold 0.1109 oz. AGW **Subject:** Coronation of Matthias

Date	Mintage	VG	F	VF	XF	Unc
1612	—	350	800	1,500	2,800	—

KM# 39.2 GOLDGULDEN

3.5000 g., 0.9860 Gold 0.1109 oz. AGW **Rev:** Without inner circle

Date	Mintage	VG	F	VF	XF	Unc
1612	—	350	850	1,700	3,500	—

KM# 47 GOLDGULDEN

3.8000 g., 0.9860 Gold 0.1205 oz. AGW **Subject:** Centennial of the Reformation **Rev:** Angel inside double circle of legend

Date	Mintage	VG	F	VF	XF	Unc
1617	—	—	3,500	6,000	10,000	—

KM# 48 GOLDGULDEN

3.5000 g., 0.9860 Gold 0.1109 oz. AGW **Note:** Klippe.

Date	Mintage	VG	F	VF	XF	Unc
1617 Rare	—	—	—	—	—	—

KM# 49.1 GOLDGULDEN

3.5000 g., 0.9860 Gold 0.1109 oz. AGW **Obv:** St. John standing **Rev:** Titles of Matthias

Date	Mintage	VG	F	VF	XF	Unc
1617	—	150	250	450	750	—

KM# 49.2 GOLDGULDEN

3.5000 g., 0.9860 Gold 0.1109 oz. AGW **Obv:** St. John standing with small shield, mm in legend **Rev:** Titles of Matthias

Date	Mintage	VG	F	VF	XF	Unc
1618 AE	—	150	200	450	750	—

KM# 54 GOLDGULDEN

3.5000 g., 0.9860 Gold 0.1109 oz. AGW **Obv:** St. John standing right with oval shield **Rev:** Titles of Matthias

Date	Mintage	VG	F	VF	XF	Unc
1619 AE	—	150	350	700	1,200	—

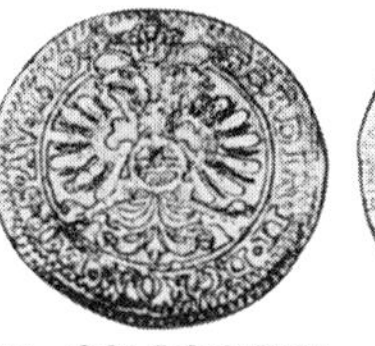

KM# 55 GOLDGULDEN

3.5000 g., 0.9860 Gold 0.1109 oz. AGW **Obv:** St. John standing right **Rev:** Crowned imperial eagle, titles of Ferdinand II

Date	Mintage	VG	F	VF	XF	Unc
1619 AE	—	—	—	—	—	—

KM# 56 GOLDGULDEN

3.5000 g., 0.9860 Gold 0.1109 oz. AGW **Subject:** Coronation of Ferdinand II **Obv:** Crown, small eagle divides circle below **Rev:** Seated figure facing within circle, titles of Ferdinand II

Date	Mintage	VG	F	VF	XF	Unc
1619	—	250	500	1,200	2,400	—

KM# 67 GOLDGULDEN

3.5000 g., 0.9860 Gold 0.1109 oz. AGW **Obv:** St. John standing right **Rev:** Orb in trefoil within inner circle

Date	Mintage	VG	F	VF	XF	Unc
16Z0	—	150	300	600	1,000	—
16Z1	—	150	300	600	1,000	—
16Z1 (a)	—	150	300	600	1,000	—
16ZZ (a)	—	150	300	600	1,000	—
16Z4 (a)	—	250	550	1,000	2,000	—
16Z5	—	150	400	800	1,500	—

KM# 40.1 2 GOLDGULDEN

7.0000 g., 0.9860 Gold 0.2219 oz. AGW **Subject:** Coronation of Matthias II **Obv:** Laureate bust of Matthias right in inner circle **Rev:** Large crown in inner circle between sun and moon **Note:** Prev. KM#40.

Date	Mintage	VG	F	VF	XF	Unc
1612	—	800	2,000	4,000	7,000	—

KM# 40.2 2 GOLDGULDEN

7.0000 g., 0.9860 Gold 0.2219 oz. AGW **Rev:** Similar to 1 Goldgulden, KM#39.1, with inner circle

Date	Mintage	VG	F	VF	XF	Unc
1612 Rare	—	—	—	—	—	—

KM# 40.3 2 GOLDGULDEN

7.0000 g., 0.9860 Gold 0.2219 oz. AGW **Obv:** Laureate bust without inner circle **Rev:** Similar to 1 Goldgulden, KM#39.2, without inner circle **Note:** Prev. KM#41.

Date	Mintage	VG	F	VF	XF	Unc
1612	—	800	2,000	4,000	7,000	—

KM# 42 2 GOLDGULDEN

7.0000 g., 0.9860 Gold 0.2219 oz. AGW **Obv:** Enthroned king in center panel flanked by angels **Rev:** Angel blowing trumpet, eagle preparing to pace wreath on angel's head

Date	Mintage	VG	F	VF	XF	Unc
1612 Rare	—	—	—	—	—	—

KM# 58 1/2 DUCAT

1.7500 g., 0.9860 Gold 0.0555 oz. AGW **Subject:** Coronation of Ferdinand II **Obv:** Crowned F above II, crossed palm and laurel branches, behind crown **Rev:** Crown with crossed palm and laurel branches behind, all above 5-line inscription with date

Date	Mintage	VG	F	VF	XF	Unc
1619	—	300	700	1,500	2,800	—

KM# 59 1/2 DUCAT

1.7500 g., 0.9860 Gold 0.0555 oz. AGW **Note:** Klippe.

Date	Mintage	VG	F	VF	XF	Unc
1619	—	400	900	2,000	3,500	—

KM# 124 1/2 DUCAT

1.7500 g., 0.9860 Gold 0.0555 oz. AGW **Subject:** Coronation of Leopold I **Obv:** Crown above 5-line inscription and date **Rev:** Crowned globe with hand holding scepter at left, arm holding sword at right

Date	Mintage	VG	F	VF	XF	Unc
1658	—	130	280	550	1,100	—

KM# 125 1/2 DUCAT

1.7500 g., 0.9860 Gold 0.0555 oz. AGW **Obv:** Leopold I

Date	Mintage	VG	F	VF	XF	Unc
ND(1658)	—	130	280	550	1,100	—

KM# 52 DUCAT

3.5000 g., 0.9860 Gold 0.1109 oz. AGW **Subject:** Sighting of a Comet **Obv:** Comet passing from right to left in laurel wreath **Rev:** Hands in prayer at center, flaming altar at right, stalks at left **Note:** Klippe.

Date	Mintage	VG	F	VF	XF	Unc
1618 Rare	—	—	—	—	—	—

KM# A70 DUCAT

3.5000 g., 0.9860 Gold 0.1109 oz. AGW **Subject:** Coronation of Ferdinand II **Obv:** Hand from clouds extended right, holding crown, inscription on ribbon winding in-and-out, all in laurel wreath **Rev:** Arabesque above 6-line inscription, date in Roman numerals

Date	Mintage	VG	F	VF	XF	Unc
MCCXIX (1619)	—	—	600	1,300	2,500	4,800

KM# 79 DUCAT

3.5000 g., 0.9860 Gold 0.1109 oz. AGW **Obv:** Bust in circle, titles of Ferdinand II **Rev:** Imperial crown above crossed sword and sceptre, crossed palm and laurel branches behind **Note:** Klippe.

Date	Mintage	VG	F	VF	XF	Unc
ND(1619) Rare	—	—	—	—	—	—

Note: Auction Peus #390 2007 XF realized $8500.

KM# 80 DUCAT

3.5000 g., 0.9860 Gold 0.1109 oz. AGW **Note:** Similar to KM#79 except reverse has hands from clouds holding royal crown above imperial crown.

Date	Mintage	VG	F	VF	XF	Unc
ND(1619) Rare	—	—	—	—	—	—

KM# 85 DUCAT

3.5000 g., 0.9860 Gold 0.1109 oz. AGW **Obv:** Eagle in oval shield **Rev:** Inscription within square

Date	Mintage	VG	F	VF	XF	Unc
1633 AE (a)	—	200	330	500	850	—
1634 AE (a)	—	150	260	480	750	—
1635 AE (a)	—	150	260	480	750	—
1636 AE (a)	—	150	260	480	750	—
1637 AM (a)	—	150	260	480	750	—
1638 AM (a)	—	150	260	480	750	—
1639 AM (a)	—	150	260	480	750	—
1640 AM (a)	—	150	260	480	750	—
1641 AM (a)	—	150	260	480	750	—
1642 AM (a)	—	150	260	480	750	—
1643 AM (a)	—	150	260	480	750	—
1644 AM (a)	—	150	260	480	750	—

KM# 96.1 DUCAT

3.5000 g., 0.9860 Gold 0.1109 oz. AGW **Obv:** Angel holding shield of arms **Obv. Legend:** ...NOMEN **Rev:** 4-line legend in cartouche, angel head above, date flanking

Date	Mintage	VG	F	VF	XF	Unc
1644 GN (a)	—	200	500	900	1,600	—

KM# 96.2 DUCAT

3.5000 g., 0.9860 Gold 0.1109 oz. AGW **Obv:** N's in NOMEN are inverted **Rev:** 4-line legend and date in cartouche, angel head and wings above

Date	Mintage	VG	F	VF	XF	Unc
1645 GN	—	200	500	900	1,600	—

Note: N of mint mark is inverted

KM# 97.1 DUCAT

3.5000 g., 0.9860 Gold 0.1109 oz. AGW **Obv:** Crowned eagle with head to left, date divided below tail as 1-6-4-6 in inner circle **Rev:** 5-line legend in ornamental cartouche

Date	Mintage	VG	F	VF	XF	Unc
1646 (h)	—	180	300	520	900	—

KM# 97.2 DUCAT

3.5000 g., 0.9860 Gold 0.1109 oz. AGW **Obv:** Without inner circle, mintmark

Date	Mintage	VG	F	VF	XF	Unc
1646	—	180	320	550	1,000	—
1646 (h)	—	180	320	550	1,000	—

KM# 97.3 DUCAT

3.5000 g., 0.9860 Gold 0.1109 oz. AGW **Obv:** Legend ends with date

Date	Mintage	VG	F	VF	XF	Unc
1646 (h)	—	200	350	700	1,200	—

KM# 104.1 DUCAT

3.5000 g., 0.9860 Gold 0.1109 oz. AGW **Obv:** With eagle's head to left **Rev:** Mintmark

Date	Mintage	VG	F	VF	XF	Unc
1647 (h)	—	180	320	550	1,000	—
1648 (h)	—	180	320	550	1,000	—
1649 (h)	—	180	320	550	1,000	—
1652 (h)	—	180	320	550	1,000	—
1654 (h)	—	180	320	550	1,000	—

KM# 104.2 DUCAT

3.5000 g., 0.9860 Gold 0.1109 oz. AGW **Obv:** With eagle's head to right

Date	Mintage	VG	F	VF	XF	Unc
ND	—	200	360	600	1,200	—
1649 (h)	—	180	320	550	1,000	—
1650 (h)	—	180	320	550	1,000	—
1651 (h)	—	180	320	550	1,000	—
1652 (h)	—	180	320	550	1,000	—
1653 (h)	—	180	320	550	1,000	—
1654 (h)	—	180	320	550	1,000	—
1655 (h)	—	180	320	550	1,000	—
1656 (h)	—	180	320	550	1,000	—
1657 (h)	—	180	320	550	1,000	—
1658 (h)	—	180	320	550	1,000	—
1660 (h)	—	180	320	550	1,000	—
1661 (h)	—	180	320	550	1,000	—
1666 (h)	—	180	320	550	1,000	—

KM# 126 DUCAT

3.5000 g., 0.9860 Gold 0.1109 oz. AGW **Subject:** Coronation of Leopold I **Obv:** Crown above 5-line inscription and Roman numeral date **Rev:** Crowned glove with hand holding scepter at left, arm holding sword at right

Date	Mintage	VG	F	VF	XF	Unc
MDCLVIII (1658)	—	200	450	800	1,400	—

KM# 57 2 DUCAT

7.0000 g., 0.9860 Gold 0.2219 oz. AGW **Subject:** Coronation of Ferdinand II **Obv:** Laureate bust of Ferdinand II right in inner circle **Rev:** Crown above crossed sword and scepter, laurel wreath above in inner circle **Note:** Klippe.

Date	Mintage	VG	F	VF	XF	Unc
MDCXIX (1619) Unique	—	—	—	—	—	—

KM# 81 2 DUCAT

7.0000 g., 0.9860 Gold 0.2219 oz. AGW **Subject:** Coronation of Ferdinand II **Obv:** Head from clouds extended right, holding crown, inscription on ribbon winding in-and-out, all in laurel wreath **Rev:** Arabesque above 6-line inscription, date in Roman numerals **Note:** Similar to 1 Ducat, KM#70.

Date	Mintage	VG	F	VF	XF	Unc
MDCXIX (1619)	—	950	2,200	4,400	8,000	—

KM# 86 2 DUCAT

7.0000 g., 0.9860 Gold 0.2219 oz. AGW

Date	Mintage	VG	F	VF	XF	Unc
1633 AE	—	400	900	1,800	3,000	—
1634 AE	—	400	900	1,800	3,000	—
1635 AE	—	400	900	1,800	3,000	—
1637 AE	—	400	900	1,800	3,000	—

KM# 127 2 DUCAT

7.0000 g., 0.9860 Gold 0.2219 oz. AGW **Subject:** Coronation of Leopold I **Obv:** Crown above 5-line inscription, Roman numeral date **Rev:** Crowned globe with hand holding scepter at left and arm holding sword at right

Date	Mintage	VG	F	VF	XF	Unc
1658	—	500	1,000	2,000	4,000	—

KM# 43 3 DUCAT
10.5000 g., 0.9860 Gold 0.3328 oz. AGW **Subject:** Coronation of Matthias **Obv:** Matthias on rearing horse right, city in background **Rev:** Crowned imperial eagle surrounded by 7 shields of arms

Date	Mintage	VG	F	VF	XF	Unc
ND(1612) Rare	—	—	—	—	—	—

KM# A128 3 DUCAT
Gold **Subject:** Coronation of Leopold I **Obv:** Crown above 5-line inscription and Roman numeral date **Rev:** Crowned globe w/hand holding scepter at left, arms holding sword at right

Date	Mintage	VG	F	VF	XF	Unc
1658 Rare	—	—	—	—	—	—

Note: Auction Peus 390 2007 XF/Unc realized $8600.

KM# 128 4 DUCAT
14.0000 g., 0.9860 Gold 0.4438 oz. AGW **Subject:** Coronation of Leopold I **Obv:** Crown above 5-line inscription, Roman numeral date **Rev:** Crowned globe with hand holding scepter at left, arm holding sword at right

Date	Mintage	VG	F	VF	XF	Unc
MDCLVIII (1658) Rare	—	—	—	—	—	—

KM# A23 5 DUCAT (1/2 Portugalöser)
17.5000 g., 0.9860 Gold 0.5547 oz. AGW **Note:** Struck with 1/2 Thaler dies, KM#21.

Date	Mintage	VG	F	VF	XF	Unc
1606 Rare	—	—	—	—	—	—

KM# 44 5 DUCAT (1/2 Portugalöser)
17.5000 g., 0.9860 Gold 0.5547 oz. AGW **Subject:** Coronation of Matthias **Obv:** Matthias on rearing horse right, city in background **Rev:** Crowned imperial eagle surrounded by 7 shields of arms

Date	Mintage	VG	F	VF	XF	Unc
ND(1612) Rare	—	—	—	—	—	—

KM# B108 5 DUCAT (1/2 Portugalöser)
17.5000 g., 0.9860 Gold 0.5547 oz. AGW **Note:** Struck with 1/2 Thaler dies, KM#106.

Date	Mintage	VG	F	VF	XF	Unc
1648 (h) Rare	—	—	—	—	—	—

KM# 82 5 DUCAT (1/2 Portugalöser)
17.5000 g., 0.9860 Gold 0.5547 oz. AGW **Subject:** Coronation of Leopold I **Obv:** Imperial crown with 2 angel supporters above 6-line inscription, Roman numeral date **Rev:** Similar to 4 Ducat, KM#128

Date	Mintage	VG	F	VF	XF	Unc
NDMDCLVIII (1658) Rare	—	—	—	—	—	—

KM# B23 10 DUCAT (Portugalöser)
35.0000 g., 0.9860 Gold 1.1095 oz. AGW

Date	Mintage	VG	F	VF	XF	Unc
1606 Rare	—	—	—	—	—	—

Note: Struck with 1 Thaler dies, KM#22

PATTERNS

Including off metal strikes

KM#	Date	Mintage	Identification	Mkt Val
Pn2	1606	—	Turnosgroshen. Gold. Klippe, KM#19.	—
Pn3	1606	—	1/4 Thaler. Gold. KM#20.	—

KM#	Date	Mintage	Identification	Mkt Val
PnA5	1612	—	2 Goldgulden. Silver. KM#40.	220
Pn5	ND(1612)	—	3 Ducat. Silver. Matthias, KM#43.	250
Pn6	ND(1612)	—	5 Ducat. Silver. Matthias, KM#44.	450
PnA7	1617	—	1/6 Thaler. Silver. 12.0000 g. Klippe, KM#45.	—

KM#	Date	Mintage	Identification	Mkt Val
PnB7	1617	—	Goldgulden. Silver. KM#47.	—
PnC7	1617	—	Goldgulden. Silver. Klippe, KM#48.	—

KM#	Date	Mintage	Identification	Mkt Val
PnD7	1618	—	Ducat. Silver. Klippe, KM#52.	200
Pn7	1618	—	Ducat. Silver. Comet, KM#52.	90.00

KM#	Date	Mintage	Identification	Mkt Val
PnA8	1619	—	1/2 Ducat. Silver. Ferdinand II, KM#58.	100

KM#	Date	Mintage	Identification	Mkt Val
PnB8	1619	—	1/2 Ducat. Silver. Klippe, Ferdinand II, KM#59.	135
PnC8	1619	—	Ducat. Silver. KM#70.	200
PnD8	ND(1619)	—	Ducat. Copper. Klippe, KM#79.	100
PnE8	ND(1619)	—	Ducat. Silver. Klippe, Ferdinand II, KM#79.	250
PnF8	ND(1619)	—	Ducat. Silver. Klippe, KM#80.	250
Pn8	ND(1619)	—	2 Ducat. Silver. Ferdinand II, KM#57.	175
Pn9	ND(1619)	—	2 Ducat. Bronze. KM#57.	60.00
PnA11	1619	—	2 Ducat. Silver. Ferdinand II, KM#81.	250
Pn11	1651 (h)	—	Albus. Gold. KM#108.	—

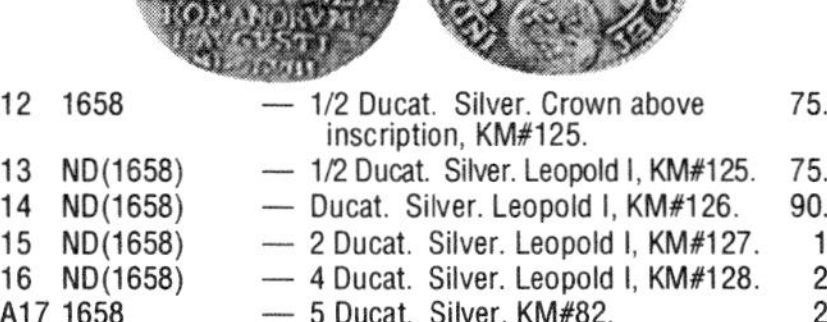

KM#	Date	Mintage	Identification	Mkt Val
Pn12	1658	—	1/2 Ducat. Silver. Crown above inscription, KM#125.	75.00
Pn13	ND(1658)	—	1/2 Ducat. Silver. Leopold I, KM#125.	75.00
Pn14	ND(1658)	—	Ducat. Silver. Leopold I, KM#126.	90.00
Pn15	ND(1658)	—	2 Ducat. Silver. Leopold I, KM#127.	175
Pn16	ND(1658)	—	4 Ducat. Silver. Leopold I, KM#128.	250
PnA17	1658	—	5 Ducat. Silver. KM#82.	275
Pn17	1667 (f)	—	Albus. Gold. KM#136.	—
Pn18	1695 IIF	—	1/4 Thaler. Gold. KM#159.	—

FRANKFURT AM ODER

A provincial city in Brandenburg, established on the Oder River about 50 miles east of Berlin in the 13th century. Local copper coins were struck during the Kipper Period. Today, the river Oder creates a natural boundary line between Germany and Poland.

CITY

REGULAR COINAGE

KM# 1 PFENNIG
Copper **Obv:** Two joined arms, helmet left, hen facing left on right, F below, ornamentation above. Varieties exist. **Note:** Kipper Pfennig. Uniface.

Date	Mintage	VG	F	VF	XF	Unc
ND(1621)	—	20.00	40.00	70.00	100	—

KM# 2 PFENNIG
Copper **Obv:** Two joined arms, helmet left, hen facing left on right, date above **Note:** Varieties exist.

Date	Mintage	VG	F	VF	XF	Unc
1622	—	27.00	45.00	80.00	125	—
16ZZ	—	27.00	45.00	80.00	125	—

FREIBURG IM BREISGAU

Located in Baden about 35 miles north of Basel and east of the Rhine, Freiburg was a free city in the early 12th century. A century later the city lost its free status when it fell to the counts of Urach. In 1368, Freiburg became a Hapsburg possession and it remained so until 1803. In 1805 the city was united to Baden. Freiburg struck coins from the 14th century until 1739. As a member of the Rappenmünzbund from 1387 until 1584, Freiburg struck coins in accordance with the provisions of that monetary union of South German and Swiss entities.

ARMS

Raven's head, usually turned to the left.

CITY

REGULAR COINAGE

KM# 40 KREUZER
Silver **Obv:** Raven's head left in shield, date in legend **Rev:** Cross in shield **Rev. Legend:** SALVE...

Date	Mintage	VG	F	VF	XF	Unc
1624	—	27.00	45.00	90.00	175	—

KM# 45 3 KREUZER (Groschen)
Silver **Obv:** Raven's head left in shield, date in legend **Rev:** Cross in shield, 3 above **Rev. Legend:** SALVE...

Date	Mintage	VG	F	VF	XF	Unc
ND(ca. 1625)	—	—	—	—	—	—

KM# 5 10 KREUZER
Silver **Obv:** Raven's head left divides date, 10 in legend below **Rev:** Madonna seated on throne

Date	Mintage	VG	F	VF	XF	Unc
16Z0	—	—	—	—	—	—

KM# 10 12 KREUZER
Silver **Obv:** Raven's head left divides date, 1Z in legend at bottom **Rev:** Cross in ornamented shield **Rev. Legend:** DOMINE...

Date	Mintage	VG	F	VF	XF	Unc
16Z0	—	—	—	—	—	—

KM# 15 1/4 THALER
Silver **Obv:** Similar to 1 Thaler, KM#25 **Rev:** Eagle, head left **Rev. Legend:** SI.DEVS...

Date	Mintage	VG	F	VF	XF	Unc
16Z0 Rare	—	—	—	—	—	—

KM# 20 1/2 THALER
Silver **Obv:** Similar to 1 Thaler, KM#25 **Rev:** Eagle with head left **Rev. Legend:** SI.DEVS...

Date	Mintage	VG	F	VF	XF	Unc
16Z0 Rare	—	—	—	—	—	—

KM# 25 THALER
Silver **Rev. Legend:** DOMINE... **Note:** Dav. #5302.

Date	Mintage	VG	F	VF	XF	Unc
16Z0	—	1,200	2,200	3,900	6,600	—

KM# 27 THALER
Silver **Obv:** Different head and smaller letters **Rev:** Smaller eagle and letters **Note:** Dav. #5302A.

Date	Mintage	VG	F	VF	XF	Unc
16Z0 Rare	—	—	—	—	—	—

KM# 26 THALER

Silver **Obv:** Raven's head left in ornamented shield, date above **Note:** Dav. #5303.

Date	Mintage	VG	F	VF	XF	Unc
16Z0 Rare	—	—	—	—	—	—

KM# 50 THALER

Silver **Note:** Dav. #5304.

Date	Mintage	VG	F	VF	XF	Unc
1626	—	1,150	2,100	3,600	6,000	—
1627	—	1,150	2,100	3,600	6,000	—
1628	—	1,150	2,100	3,600	6,000	—
1629	—	1,150	2,100	3,600	6,000	—

KM# 51 THALER

Silver **Note:** Klippe. Dav. #5304A.

Date	Mintage	VG	F	VF	XF	Unc
1627 Rare	—	—	—	—	—	—
1628 Rare	—	—	—	—	—	—

KM# 30 2 THALER

Silver **Note:** Similar to 1 Thaler, KM#25. Dav. #5201.

Date	Mintage	VG	F	VF	XF	Unc
16Z0 Rare	—	—	—	—	—	—

TRADE COINAGE

KM# 35 GOLDGULDEN

3.5000 g., 0.9860 Gold 0.1109 oz. AGW **Obv:** Madonna and child facing **Rev:** 4-fold arms of Freiburg, date in legend

Date	Mintage	VG	F	VF	XF	Unc
1622 Rare	—	—	—	—	—	—

FREISING

A Bishopric located in central Bavaria, was founded in 724. It became the site of an imperial mint in the 11th century. Bracteates of the bishops appeared c. 1150. The bishops were made princes of the empire in the 17th century. It became secularized in 1802 with part of the territories going to Bavaria and the rest to Salzburg.

RULERS

Ernst, Herzog von Bayern, 1566-1612
Stephan von Siboldsdorf, 1612-1618
Veit Adam von Gebeck, 1618-1651
Albert Sigismund, Herzog von Bayern, 1652-1685
Joseph Clemens, Herzog von Bayern, 1685-1694
Johann Franz Eckher Freiherr von Kapfing, 1695-1727

MINT OFFICIALS' INITIALS

Initial	Date	Name
*, PHM	Ca.1685-1719	Philipp Heinrich Muller, medailleur in Augsburg

BISHOPRIC

REGULAR COINAGE

KM# 5 HELLER

Silver **Obv:** Freising and Gebeck family arms in adjoining shield, date above, F below. **Note:** Kipper Heller. Uniface. Hohl type.

Date	Mintage	VG	F	VF	XF	Unc
1622	—	—	—	—	—	—

KM# 6 HELLER

Silver **Obv:** Band connecting both arms at top replaces date. **Note:** Uniface.

Date	Mintage	VG	F	VF	XF	Unc
ND(ca.1622)	—	—	—	—	—	—

KM# 7 2 HELLER (Pfennig)

Copper **Obv:** Joined VA monogram in wreath **Rev:** Crowned head left in circle

Date	Mintage	VG	F	VF	XF	Unc
ND(ca.1622)	—	30.00	60.00	120	200	—

KM# 8 2 HELLER (Pfennig)

Copper **Obv:** Feather crown on head left in circle **Rev:** Large Z (2 Heller) in wreath

Date	Mintage	VG	F	VF	XF	Unc
ND(ca.1622)	—	22.00	45.00	85.00	145	—

KM# 9 4 HELLER (1/2 Kreuzer)

Copper **Obv:** Crowned head left in wreath **Rev:** Value 4 in wreath **Note:** Kipper 4 Heller.

Date	Mintage	VG	F	VF	XF	Unc
ND(ca.1622)	—	27.00	55.00	100	180	—

KM# 10 KREUZER

Copper **Obv:** Feather crown on head left in wreath **Rev:** Script K in wreath **Note:** Kipper Kreuzer

Date	Mintage	VG	F	VF	XF	Unc
ND(ca.1622)	—	—	—	—	—	—

KM# 11 24 KREUZER (Sechsbätzner)

Billon **Obv:** Crowned imperial eagle, 24 in orb on breast, titles of Ferdinand II **Rev:** Crowned head left in oval cartouche, date in legend **Note:** Kipper 24 Kreuzer

Date	Mintage	VG	F	VF	XF	Unc
1622	—	70.00	120	200	—	—

FRIEDBERG

The fortified town of Friedberg, located in Hesse about 14 miles north of Frankfurt am Main, dates from Roman times. It attained free status in 1211 and was the site of an imperial mint until the mid-13th century. In 1349 Friedberg passed to the countship of Schwarzburg, losing its free status shortly thereafter. Local nobles began electing one among themselves to the office of burgrave-for-life. The burgraves obtained the mint right in 1541 and recognized only the emperor as overlord. In 1802 Friedberg passed in fief to Hesse-Darmstadt and was mediatized in 1818.

RULERS

Johann Eberhard von Cronberg, 1577-1617
Konrad Low von Steinfurt, 1617-1632
Wolf Adolf von Karben, 1632-1671
Johann Eitel I von Diede zu Furstenstein, 1671-1685
Phillipp Adolf Rau von Holzhausen, 1685-1692
Johann IV Schiltz von Gortz, 1692-1699
Adolf Johann Karl von Bettendorf, 1700-1705

MINT OFFICIALS' INITIALS

Initial	Date	Name
AL	1674-76	Adam Longerich
CB	1688-90	Conrad Bethmann
HS	1625-72	Henning Schluter in Zellerfeld
(r) and/or R, HR	1618-22	Hans Ruck
RA	1679-88	Johann Reinhard Arnold
VBW	1684-88, 1702-14	Ulrich Burkhard Willerding in Mainz

BURGRAVESHIP

REGULAR COINAGE

KM# 32 PFENNIG

Silver **Ruler:** Konrad **Note:** 4-fold arms divide date in circle of pellets.

Date	Mintage	VG	F	VF	XF	Unc
16Z3	—	—	—	—	—	—

KM# 47 KREUZER

Silver **Ruler:** Johann Eitel I **Obv:** Crowned 2-fold arms in laurel wreath **Rev:** I/ KREV/ TZER/ date/ mintmasters initials in laureal wreath **Note:** Varieties exist.

Date	Mintage	VG	F	VF	XF	Unc
1679 RA	—	13.00	27.00	60.00	120	—
1680 RA	—	13.00	27.00	60.00	120	—
1680	—	13.00	27.00	60.00	120	—
1682	—	13.00	27.00	60.00	120	—
1683	—	13.00	27.00	60.00	120	—
1684	—	13.00	27.00	60.00	120	—

KM# 56 KREUZER

Silver **Ruler:** Phillipp Adolf Ray

Date	Mintage	VG	F	VF	XF	Unc
1685	—	10.00	25.00	45.00	85.00	—
1686	—	10.00	25.00	45.00	85.00	—

KM# 41 2 KREUZER

Silver **Ruler:** Wolf Adolf **Rev:** Without Z in orb

Date	Mintage	VG	F	VF	XF	Unc
1657 HS	—	27.00	60.00	110	170	—

KM# 40 2 KREUZER

Silver **Ruler:** Wolf Adolf **Obv:** Crowned rampant lion left with bend superimposed (Kraichen arms) in laurel wreath **Note:** Varieties exist.

Date	Mintage	VG	F	VF	XF	Unc
1657 HS	—	27.00	60.00	110	170	—
1658 HS	—	27.00	60.00	110	170	—

KM# 55 ALBUS

Silver **Ruler:** Johann Eitel I **Obv:** Ornamented 4-fold arms divide mintmasters initials **Rev:** Date in laurel wreath **Rev. Legend:** I/ ALBVS

Date	Mintage	VG	F	VF	XF	Unc
1683 RA	—	80.00	160	280	400	—

KM# 10 3 KREUZER (Groschen)

Silver **Ruler:** Konrad **Obv:** Crowned imperial eagle, 3 in orb on breast, titles of Matthias and date in legend **Rev:** 4-fold arms **Rev. Legend:** CASTR • IMP **Note:** Varieties exist.

Date	Mintage	VG	F	VF	XF	Unc
ND(1618) (r)	96,000	20.00	40.00	85.00	150	—
1618 (R)	Inc. above	20.00	40.00	85.00	150	—
1619 (r)	43,000	20.00	40.00	85.00	150	—

KM# 20 3 KREUZER (Groschen)

Silver **Ruler:** Konrad **Obv:** Titles of Ferdinand II

Date	Mintage	VG	F	VF	XF	Unc
16Z0 (r)	28,000	27.00	60.00	100	170	—
1623	—	27.00	60.00	100	170	—

KM# 27 3 KREUZER (Groschen)

Silver **Ruler:** Konrad **Obv:** Date in legend

Date	Mintage	VG	F	VF	XF	Unc
16Z1	—	20.00	40.00	85.00	150	—

KM# 26 3 KREUZER (Groschen)

Silver **Ruler:** Konrad **Obv:** Arms divide date **Note:** Kipper 3 Kreuzer.

Date	Mintage	VG	F	VF	XF	Unc
16Z1 (r)	—	20.00	40.00	85.00	150	—
16ZZ (r)	—	20.00	40.00	85.00	150	—
16ZZ (r)	—	20.00	40.00	85.00	150	—

KM# 48 3 KREUZER (Groschen)

Silver **Ruler:** Johann Eitel I **Note:** Similar to KM#49 but date in legend.

Date	Mintage	VG	F	VF	XF	Unc
1679	—	27.00	60.00	100	170	—

KM# 49 3 KREUZER (Groschen)

Silver **Ruler:** Johann Eitel I **Obv:** Crowned double-headed imperial eagle **Rev:** Date divided by crown

Date	Mintage	VG	F	VF	XF	Unc
1679	—	27.00	60.00	100	170	—

KM# 57 6 KREUZER

Silver **Ruler:** Johann Eitel I **Obv:** Phillipp Adolf Rau **Rev:** Crown divides cirle and date above **Note:** Varieties exist.

Date	Mintage	VG	F	VF	XF	Unc
1688 RA	—	45.00	85.00	165	275	—
1688	—	45.00	85.00	165	275	—
1688 VBW	—	45.00	85.00	165	275	—

KM# 21 12 KREUZER (Zwölfer)

Silver **Ruler:** Konrad **Obv:** Crowned imperial eagle, 1Z in orb on breast, titles of Ferdinand II and date in legend **Rev:** 4-fold arms **Rev. Legend:** CASTR.IMP...

Date	Mintage	VG	F	VF	XF	Unc
16Z0	—	—	—	—	—	—

KM# 28 12 KREUZER (Zwölfer)
Silver **Ruler:** Konrad **Obv:** Date in legend

Date	Mintage	VG	F	VF	XF	Unc
16Z1	—	—	—	—	—	—

KM# 50 15 KREUZER (1/4 Gulden)
Silver **Ruler:** Johann Eitel I **Obv:** Church façade within circle, legend around border **Rev:** Date in legend **Note:** Varieties exist.

Date	Mintage	VG	F	VF	XF	Unc
1679 RA	—	40.00	80.00	150	260	—

KM# 45 30 KREUZER (1/3 Thaler)
Silver **Ruler:** Johann Eitel I

Date	Mintage	VG	F	VF	XF	Unc
1674 AL	—	85.00	180	350	550	—

KM# 46 60 KREUZER (2/3 Thaler)
Silver **Ruler:** Johann Eitel I **Note:** Varieties exist.

Date	Mintage	VG	F	VF	XF	Unc
1674 AL	—	72.00	125	200	375	—
1675 AL	—	72.00	125	200	375	—
1676 AL	—	72.00	125	200	375	—

KM# 11 1/4 THALER (Teston)
Silver **Ruler:** Konrad **Obv:** Oval 4-fold arms in baroque frame **Rev:** Crowned imperial eagle, arms of Austria on breast date separated by eagle's neck, titles of Matthias

Date	Mintage	VG	F	VF	XF	Unc
1618 (r) Reported, not confirmed	3,201	—	—	—	—	—
1619 (r)	19,000	—	—	—	—	—

KM# 22 1/4 THALER (Teston)
Silver **Ruler:** Konrad **Rev:** Titles of Ferdinand II

Date	Mintage	VG	F	VF	XF	Unc
1620 (r)	2,852	—	—	—	—	—

Note: Reported, not confirmed

KM# 29 1/4 THALER (Teston)
Silver **Ruler:** Konrad **Note:** Similar to 1/2 Thaler, KM#30 but orb on breast of eagle.

Date	Mintage	VG	F	VF	XF	Unc
ND(1622) HB	—	—	—	—	—	—

KM# 30 1/2 THALER
Silver **Ruler:** Konrad **Obv:** Standing armored figure **Rev:** Austrian arms on eagle's breast

Date	Mintage	VG	F	VF	XF	Unc
ND(1622) R	—	325	525	900	—	—

KM# 33 1/2 THALER
Silver **Ruler:** Konrad **Obv:** Standing armored figure **Rev:** Date in legend

Date	Mintage	VG	F	VF	XF	Unc
1623 R	—	450	800	1,400	—	—

KM# 12 THALER
Silver **Ruler:** Konrad **Obv:** St. George and dragon with shields in legend **Rev:** Crowned double eagle with Austrian arms on breast, date divided by neck, 2 arms below, titles of Rudolph II **Note:** Dav. #5308.

Date	Mintage	VG	F	VF	XF	Unc
1618 Reported, not confirmed	198	—	—	—	—	—
1619 (r)	505	700	1,500	3,000	5,000	—

KM# 23 THALER
Silver **Ruler:** Konrad **Rev:** Date divided above claws of eagle. **Note:** Similar to KM#34. Dav. #5309.

Date	Mintage	VG	F	VF	XF	Unc
1620 Reported, not confirmed	630	—	—	—	—	—
16ZZ R	—	600	1,200	2,500	4,500	—

KM# 34 THALER
Silver **Ruler:** Konrad **Obv:** Standing armored figure **Rev:** Titles of Ferdinand II **Note:** Dav. #5310.

Date	Mintage	VG	F	VF	XF	Unc
16Z3	—	500	1,000	2,250	4,250	—

KM# 58 THALER
Silver **Ruler:** Phillipp Adolf Ray **Obv:** Armored equestrian, left, above date, flanked by shields **Rev:** Titles of Leopold I **Note:** Dav. #5311.

Date	Mintage	VG	F	VF	XF	Unc
1688 CB	—	1,200	2,200	3,600	5,500	—

KM# 60 THALER
Silver **Ruler:** Phillipp Adolf Ray **Obv:** Armored equestrian, right, flanked by shields **Rev:** Titles of Leopold I **Note:** Dav. #5312.

Date	Mintage	VG	F	VF	XF	Unc
1690 CB	—	1,200	2,200	3,600	5,500	—

KM# 14 2 THALER
Silver **Ruler:** Konrad **Obv:** St. George and dragon with shields in legend **Rev:** Crowned double eagle with Austrian arms on breast, date divided by neck, 2 arms below, titles of Rudolph II **Note:** Dav. #5307.

Date	Mintage	VG	F	VF	XF	Unc
1619 (r) Rare	110	—	—	—	—	—

TRADE COINAGE

KM# 7 GOLDGULDEN
3.5000 g., 0.9860 Gold 0.1109 oz. AGW **Ruler:** Konrad **Obv:** 4-fold arms **Rev:** Crowned imperial eagle, titles of Rudolf II

Date	Mintage	VG	F	VF	XF	Unc
ND Rare	5,101	—	—	—	—	—

KM# 13 GOLDGULDEN
3.5000 g., 0.9860 Gold 0.1109 oz. AGW **Ruler:** Konrad **Obv:** Crowned imperial eagle, Austrian arms on breast, titles of Matthias and date in legend **Rev:** 4-fold arms, family arms to left and right in legend

Date	Mintage	VG	F	VF	XF	Unc
1618 (r) Rare	1,359	—	—	—	—	—

KM# 15 GOLDGULDEN
3.5000 g., 0.9860 Gold 0.1109 oz. AGW **Ruler:** Konrad **Obv:** Date divided by eagle's neck

Date	Mintage	VG	F	VF	XF	Unc
1619 (r) Rare	2,529	—	—	—	—	—

KM# 24 GOLDGULDEN
3.5000 g., 0.9860 Gold 0.1109 oz. AGW **Ruler:** Konrad **Obv:** Titles of Ferdinand II and date in legend

Date	Mintage	VG	F	VF	XF	Unc
16Z0 (r) Rare	2,673	—	—	—	—	—

KM# 25 GOLDGULDEN
3.5000 g., 0.9860 Gold 0.1109 oz. AGW **Ruler:** Konrad **Note:** Klippe.

Date	Mintage	VG	F	VF	XF	Unc
16Z0 (r) Unique	—	—	—	—	—	—

KM# 31 GOLDGULDEN
3.5000 g., 0.9860 Gold 0.1109 oz. AGW **Ruler:** Konrad **Obv:** Date in legend **Rev:** Crowned double-headed imperial eagle

Date	Mintage	VG	F	VF	XF	Unc
16ZZ R	—	3,000	5,000	9,000	15,000	—

PATTERNS

Including off metal strikes

KM#	Date	Mintage	Identification	Mkt Val
Pn1	16ZZ RA	—	Thaler. Gold. KM#23.	—

FUGGER

A wealthy banking and commercial family of Augsburg, which first came into prominence about 1370 and became the bankers of the Hapsburgs by 1475. In 1500 they were given the county of Kirchberg and the lordship of Weissenborn (in Swabia) as security for a loan. The emperor made them hereditary counts of these areas and gave them the mint right in 1534. There was a complicated succession with many lines and few coin issuers. The land was mediatized to Bavaria and Württemberg in 1806.

FAMILY ARMS
2 lilies on adjacent fields

References:
K = Johann Veit Kull, Die Münzen des gräflichen und fürstlichen Hauses Fugger, ***Mitteilungen der Bayerischen Numismatischen Gesellschaft 8 (1889)***, pp. 1-96.
Sch = Wolfgang Schulten, ***Deutsche Münzen aus der Zeit Karls V.*** Frankfurt am Main, 1974.

FUGGER-BABENHAUSEN

RULERS
(Issuers of Coinage Only)
Maximilian II zu Babenhausen, 1598-1629
Johann III zu Babenhausen, 1598-1633
Sebastian zu Kirchheim-Worth, guardian of Sigmund Joseph and Johann Rudolf zu Babenhausen, 1668-1677
Sigmund Joseph zu Babenhausen, 1685-1696
Johann Rudolf zu Babenhausen, 1685-1693

DUCHY

REGULAR COINAGE

KM# 11 HELLER (1/420 Gulden)
Copper **Obv:** Arms in wreath **Rev:** MAX divides date in frame, C CC C above, X X below **Note:** Kipper Heller.

Date	Mintage	VG	F	VF	XF	Unc
1621	—	—	—	—	—	—

KM# 12 PFENNIG (1/210 Gulden)
Copper **Obv:** MAX divides date in frame, C C above, X below **Rev:** Arms in wreath **Note:** Kipper Pfennig.

Date	Mintage	VG	F	VF	XF	Unc
1621	—	45.00	85.00	145	210	—
1622	—	45.00	85.00	145	210	—

KM# 13 1/2 KREUZER (1/20 Gulden)
Copper **Obv:** Arms in wreath **Rev:** MAX divides date in frame, 120 below **Note:** Kipper 1/2 Kreuzer.

Date	Mintage	VG	F	VF	XF	Unc
1621	—	25.00	40.00	75.00	125	—

KM# 20 1/2 KREUZER (1/20 Gulden)
Copper **Rev:** IF monogram in frame, date above, 120 below

Date	Mintage	VG	F	VF	XF	Unc
1622	—	27.00	45.00	80.00	125	—

KM# 21 KREUZER (1/60 Gulden)
Copper **Obv:** Arms in wreath **Rev:** K in ornamented round shield divides date, MAX. F above, 60 below **Note:** Kipper Kreuzer.

Date	Mintage	VG	F	VF	XF	Unc
1622	—	22.00	35.00	60.00	100	—

KM# 22 KREUZER (1/60 Gulden)
Copper **Note:** Uniface. Arms in wreath divides date, MAX above, K below.

Date	Mintage	VG	F	VF	XF	Unc
1622	—	22.00	35.00	60.00	100	—

KM# 23 KREUZER (1/60 Gulden)
Copper **Obv:** MAX • F, date above, 60 below.

Date	Mintage	VG	F	VF	XF	Unc
1622	—	22.00	35.00	60.00	100	—

KM# 24 KREUZER (1/60 Gulden)
Copper **Note:** Similar to KM#23 but MAX.

Date	Mintage	VG	F	VF	XF	Unc
1622	—	15.00	25.00	45.00	75.00	—

KM# 25 KREUZER (1/60 Gulden)
Silver **Obv:** Arms in heart-shaped shield **Obv. Legend:** MAX • F • L... **Rev:** Eight-armed cross, I in center, K-R-E-I-Z-E-R-++ in angles of cross

Date	Mintage	VG	F	VF	XF	Unc
ND	—	25.00	40.00	65.00	120	—

KM# 5 2 KREUZER (1/2 Batzen)
Silver **Obv:** Arms **Obv. Legend:** MAX • FVG... **Rev:** Imperial orb with 2 **Rev. Legend:** GLO • ET • HO...

Date	Mintage	VG	F	VF	XF	Unc
ND(ca.1620)	—	40.00	70.00	125	175	—

KM# 6 2 KREUZER (1/2 Batzen)
Silver **Rev. Legend:** PAX • ET • VERIT...

Date	Mintage	VG	F	VF	XF	Unc
ND(ca.1620)	—	40.00	70.00	125	175	—

KM# 7 2 KREUZER (1/2 Batzen)
Silver **Rev. Legend:** NON EST PAX...

Date	Mintage	VG	F	VF	XF	Unc
ND(ca.1620)	—	40.00	70.00	125	175	—

KM# 8 2 KREUZER (1/2 Batzen)
Silver **Rev. Legend:** PAX ET HONOS...

Date	Mintage	VG	F	VF	XF	Unc
ND(ca.1620)	—	40.00	70.00	125	175	—

KM# 9 2 KREUZER (1/2 Batzen)
Silver **Obv:** Crowned imperial eagle, 2 in orb on breast, titles of Ferdinand II

Date	Mintage	VG	F	VF	XF	Unc
ND(ca.1620)	—	40.00	70.00	125	175	—

KM# 30 6 KREUZER
Silver **Obv:** Crowned four-fold arms, F-S above, date divided in points of crown **Rev:** Crowned intertwined cipher, two palm branches below, 6 in frame

Date	Mintage	VG	F	VF	XF	Unc
1676	2,470	—	—	—	—	—

KM# 35 6 KREUZER
Silver **Obv:** Bust right, VI below **Rev:** Crowned four-fold arms, date in legend

Date	Mintage	VG	F	VF	XF	Unc
1684	—	—	—	—	—	—

KM# 14 12 KREUZER (Zwölfer)
Silver **Obv:** Crowned imperial eagle, 12 in orb on breast, titles of Ferdinand II **Rev:** Oval four-fold arms, date divided below **Note:** Kipper 12 Kreuzer.

Date	Mintage	VG	F	VF	XF	Unc
1621	—	—	—	—	—	—

KM# 31 15 KREUZER (1/4 Gulden)
Silver

Date	Mintage	VG	F	VF	XF	Unc
1676	941,000	45.00	100	220	375	—
1677	Inc. above	45.00	100	220	375	—

KM# 36 15 KREUZER (1/4 Gulden)
Silver **Obv:** Bust right, XV below **Rev:** Crowned four-fold arms, date in legend divided by crown

Date	Mintage	VG	F	VF	XF	Unc
1684	—	80.00	135	25.00	350	—

KM# 32 60 KREUZER (2/3 Thaler - Gulden)
Silver **Obv:** Crowned four-fold arms divide F-S, date above **Rev:** Intertwined cipher, 60 in frame below with palm branches

Date	Mintage	VG	F	VF	XF	Unc
1676	858	—	—	—	—	—

KM# 10 1/24 THALER (Groschen)
Silver **Obv:** Arms **Obv. Legend:** MAX: FVGGER... **Rev:** 24/ AVF • EIN/ REICHS/ TALER in frame

Date	Mintage	VG	F	VF	XF	Unc
ND(ca.1620)	—	—	—	—	—	—

KM# 37 2/3 THALER (60 Kreuzer - Gulden)
Silver **Obv:** Bust right **Rev:** 2/3 in wreath, date below

Date	Mintage	VG	F	VF	XF	Unc
1684	—	—	—	—	—	—

KM# 15 THALER (120 Kreuzer)
Silver **Obv:** Crowned imperial eagle, 120 in frame below, titles of Ferdinand II **Rev:** Four-fold arms divide date

Date	Mintage	VG	F	VF	XF	Unc
1621	—	450	900	1,500	2,400	—

KM# 16 THALER (120 Kreuzer)
Silver **Obv:** Ornate shield within circle **Rev:** Crown above double-headed imperial eagle within circle **Note:** Dav. #6672. Varieties exist.

Date	Mintage	VG	F	VF	XF	Unc
1621	—	450	800	1,300	2,000	—

KM# 17 THALER (120 Kreuzer)
Silver **Obv:** Ornate shield divides date within circle **Rev:** Crown above double-headed imperial eagle **Note:** Dav. #6673.

Date	Mintage	VG	F	VF	XF	Unc
1621	—	175	325	600	1,250	2,000
1623	—	175	325	600	1,250	2,000

KM# 27 THALER (120 Kreuzer)
Silver **Rev:** Titles of Ferdinand II **Note:** Dav. #6674.

Date	Mintage	VG	F	VF	XF	Unc
1624	—	350	650	1,100	1,800	—

TRADE COINAGE

KM# 18 GOLDGULDEN
3.5000 g., 0.9860 Gold 0.1109 oz. AGW

Date	Mintage	VG	F	VF	XF	Unc
ND	—	800	1,600	2,900	4,500	—

KM# 26 DUCAT
3.5000 g., 0.9860 Gold 0.1109 oz. AGW **Obv:** 3 Oval shields within circle **Rev:** Crown above double-headed imperial eagle within circle

Date	Mintage	VG	F	VF	XF	Unc
1622	—	725	1,500	2,800	4,400	—

KM# 19 4 DUCAT

14.0000 g., 0.9860 Gold 0.4438 oz. AGW **Obv:** Crowned imperial eagle, titles of Ferdinand II **Rev:** Four-fold arms, date divided below

Date	Mintage	VG	F	VF	XF	Unc
1621 Rare	—	—	—	—	—	—

KM# A28 6 DUCAT

21.0000 g., 0.9860 Gold 0.6657 oz. AGW **Note:** Struck with 1 Thaler dies, KM#17.

Date	Mintage	VG	F	VF	XF	Unc
1621 Rare	—	—	—	—	—	—

KM# B28 8 DUCAT

27.0000 g., 0.9860 Gold 0.8559 oz. AGW **Note:** Struck with 1 Thaler dies, KM#17.

Date	Mintage	VG	F	VF	XF	Unc
1621 Rare	—	—	—	—	—	—

KM# C28 10 DUCAT (Portugalöser)

35.0000 g., 0.9860 Gold 1.1095 oz. AGW **Note:** Struck with 1 Thaler dies, KM#17.

Date	Mintage	VG	F	VF	XF	Unc
1621	—	—	—	12,000	22,500	—

KM# 28 11 DUCAT

38.5000 g., 0.9860 Gold 1.2204 oz. AGW **Note:** Struck with 1 Thaler dies, KM#17.

Date	Mintage	VG	F	VF	XF	Unc
1621 Rare	—	—	—	—	—	—

KM# A29 12 DUCAT

42.0000 g., 0.9860 Gold 1.3314 oz. AGW **Note:** Struck with 1 Thaler dies, KM#17.

Date	Mintage	VG	F	VF	XF	Unc
1621 Rare	—	—	—	—	—	—

KM# B29 13 DUCAT

45.0000 g., 0.9860 Gold 1.4265 oz. AGW **Note:** Struck with 1 Thaler dies, KM#17.

Date	Mintage	VG	F	VF	XF	Unc
1621 Rare	—	—	—	—	—	—

KM# 29 15 DUCAT

52.5000 g., 0.9860 Gold 1.6642 oz. AGW **Note:** Struck with 1 Thaler dies, KM#17.

Date	Mintage	VG	F	VF	XF	Unc
1621 Rare	—	—	—	—	—	—

FUGGER-BABENHAUSEN-WELLENBURG

RULERS

(Issuers of Coinage Only)

Georg IV zu Babenhausen-Wellenburg, 1598-1643

DUCHY

REGULAR COINAGE

KM# 7 KREUZER

Copper **Obv:** Similar to KM#5, but G-F above and L-F below arms.

Date	Mintage	VG	F	VF	XF	Unc
1622	—	33.00	55.00	100	175	—

KM# 5 KREUZER

Copper **Note:** Kipper Kreuzer. Varieties exist.

Date	Mintage	VG	F	VF	XF	Unc
1622	—	33.00	55.00	100	175	—

KM# 6 KREUZER

Copper **Obv:** Square arms **Rev:** Date below value **Note:** Varieties exist.

Date	Mintage	VG	F	VF	XF	Unc
1622	—	33.00	55.00	100	175	—

KM# 11 2 KREUZER (1/2 Batzen)

Silver **Obv:** Ornate shield within circle **Rev:** Crown above double-headed imperial eagle within circle **Note:** Varieties exist.

Date	Mintage	VG	F	VF	XF	Unc
1624	—	27.00	45.00	65.00	120	—

KM# 9 12 KREUZER (Zwölfer)

Silver **Obv:** Half-length bust right divides date

Date	Mintage	VG	F	VF	XF	Unc
1622	—	120	200	375	525	—

KM# 8 12 KREUZER (Zwölfer)

Silver **Obv:** Crowned bust holding orb and scepter **Rev:** Crowned imperial eagle, 12 on breast, titles of Ferdinand II **Note:** Kipper 12 Kreuzer. Struck at Wasserburg Mint.

Date	Mintage	VG	F	VF	XF	Unc
ND	—	90.00	135	250	350	—

KM# 10 THALER

Silver **Obv:** Armored equestrian, left, 4-fold arms below divides circle **Rev:** Titles of Ferdinand II **Note:** Kipper Thaler. Struck at Wasserburg Mint. Dav. #6671.

Date	Mintage	VG	F	VF	XF	Unc
1622	—	250	400	1,200	2,250	—

FUGGER-GLOTT

RULERS

(Issuers of Coinage Only)

Franz Ernst zu Glott, 1673-1711

DUCHY

REGULAR COINAGE

KM# 5 THALER

Silver **Obv:** Crowned ornate shield **Rev:** Titles of Leopold I **Note:** Dav. #6675.

Date	Mintage	F	VF	XF	Unc	BU
1694	—	450	850	1,350	2,250	—

FUGGER-NORDENDORF

RULERS

(Issuers of Coinage Only)

Marquard zu Nordendorf, 1601-1624

Nikolaus zu Nordendorf, 1611-1676

DUCHY

REGULAR COINAGE

KM# 5 PFENNIG (1/210 Gulden)

Copper **Obv:** Arms in wreath **Rev:** NF monogram in frame, CXC below **Note:** Kipper Pfennig. Klippe.

Date	Mintage	VG	F	VF	XF	Unc
ND(c.1622)	—	—	—	—	—	—

KM# 7 1/2 KREUZER (1/120 Gulden)

Copper **Obv:** Arms in wreath, NF monogram above **Rev. Legend:** HALB/ KREIC/ ER/ date **Note:** Kipper 1/2 Kreuzer.

Date	Mintage	VG	F	VF	XF	Unc
1622	—	25.00	40.00	70.00	125	—

KM# 6 1/120 GULDEN (1/2 Kreuzer)

Copper **Obv:** Oval ornamented arms in wreath **Rev:** NF monogram, date above, 120 below **Note:** Varieties exist.

Date	Mintage	VG	F	VF	XF	Unc
1622	—	22.00	33.00	60.00	120	—

KM# 8 1/60 GULDEN (Kreuzer)

Copper **Obv:** Ornamented oval arms in wreath **Rev:** MQF monogram, date divided above, 60 below **Note:** Kipper 1/60 Gulden. Varieties exist.

Date	Mintage	VG	F	VF	XF	Unc
1622	—	25.00	40.00	70.00	125	—

KM# 9 1/60 GULDEN (Kreuzer)

Copper **Obv:** Arms in wreath **Rev:** MQF monogram, date divided above and 60 below, cloverleaf to left

Date	Mintage	VG	F	VF	XF	Unc
1622	—	25.00	40.00	70.00	125	—

KM# 10 1/60 GULDEN (Kreuzer)

Copper **Obv:** MQF monogram, date divided above and 60 below, cloverleaf at left. **Note:** Uniface.

Date	Mintage	VG	F	VF	XF	Unc
1622	—	20.00	33.00	60.00	120	—

KM# 11 1/60 GULDEN (Kreuzer)

Copper **Obv:** Ornamental oval arms in wreath **Rev:** NF monogram between two rosettes, date above, 60 below **Note:** Varieties exist.

Date	Mintage	VG	F	VF	XF	Unc
1622	—	20.00	33.00	60.00	120	—

KM# 12 THALER

Silver **Obv:** Ornate oval arms within circle **Obv. Legend:** * MARQUARDT • FVGGE(R) • F:H:V... **Rev:** Crowned imperial eagle, titles of Ferdinand II **Note:** Dav. #6670.

Date	Mintage	VG	F	VF	XF	Unc
1623	—	450	850	1,450	2,500	—

FUGGER-PFIRT

RULERS

(Issuers of Coinage Only)

Wilhelm zu Pfirt, 1601-1659

DUCHY

REGULAR COINAGE

KM# 5 4 PFENNIG

Copper **Obv:** Lily arms in wreath, 4 above, W below. **Note:** Uniface. Kipper 4 Pfennig.

Date	Mintage	VG	F	VF	XF	Unc
ND(c.1621/22)	—	35.00	75.00	140	225	—

FULDA

Located in central Germany, the abbey was founded in 744. The abbot became prince of the empire in the late 10th century. The first coins were struck in the 11th century. It became a bishopric in 1752 and in 1803, Fulda was secularized and passed successively to Orange-Nassau, Westphalia, Hesse-Cassel and Prussia.

RULERS

Balthasar von Dernbach, 1570-1606
 under control of the Teutonic Order, 1576-1602

Johann Friedrich von Schwalbach, 1606-1622

Johann Bernhard, Schenk von Schweinsberg, 1623-1632

Johann Adolf von Hoheneck, 1633-1635

Hermann Georg von Neuhof, 1635-1644

Joachim von Graveneck, 1644-1671

Bernhard Gustav Adolf, Markgraf von Baden, 1671-1677

Placidus von Droste zu Erwite, 1678-1700

Adalbert I von Schleifras, 1700-1714

MINT OFFICIALS' INITIALS

Initial	Date	Name
OS	Ca.1600	Unknown
PHM	Ca.1688	P.H. Müller

ABBEY

REGULAR COINAGE

KM# 5 PFENNIG

Silver **Ruler:** Balthasar **Obv:** 4-fold arms of Fulda and Dernbach, B above. **Note:** Uniface. Schussel-type.

Date	Mintage	VG	F	VF	XF	Unc
ND(ca.1602-06)	—	33.00	65.00	120	200	—

KM# 22 ALBUS

Silver **Ruler:** Placidus

Date	Mintage	VG	F	VF	XF	Unc
1679	—	65.00	150	250	325	—

KM# 6 3 KREUZER (Groschen)

Silver **Ruler:** Balthasar **Obv:** 4-fold arms in Fulda and Dernbach in oval baroque frame **Rev:** Crowned imperial eagle, 3 in orb on breast, titles of Rudolf II

Date	Mintage	VG	F	VF	XF	Unc
ND(ca.1602-06) OS	—	55.00	120	225	350	—

KM# 7 3 KREUZER (Groschen)
Silver **Ruler:** Balthasar **Rev:** Square 4-fold arms

Date	Mintage	VG	F	VF	XF	Unc
ND(ca.1602-06)	—	55.00	120	225	350	—

KM# 15 1/8 THALER
Silver **Ruler:** Bernhard Gustav Adolf **Obv:** Legend with Roman numeral date **Rev:** Arms

Date	Mintage	VG	F	VF	XF	Unc
MDCLXXII (1672)	—	95.00	200	325	450	—

KM# 16 THALER
Silver **Ruler:** Bernhard Gustav Adolf **Note:** Dav. #5315.

Date	Mintage	VG	F	VF	XF	Unc
1672	—	375	750	1,500	2,750	—

KM# 17 THALER
Silver **Ruler:** Bernhard Gustav Adolf **Note:** Dav. #5316.

Date	Mintage	VG	F	VF	XF	Unc
1672	—	450	950	1,850	3,000	—

KM# 25 THALER
Silver **Ruler:** Placidus **Obv:** Bust of Placidus right **Rev:** Mitered and helmeted 4-fold arms with cross above, date in legend **Note:** Dav. #5318.

Date	Mintage	VG	F	VF	XF	Unc
1687	—	600	1,200	2,250	3,500	—

KM# 26 THALER
Silver **Ruler:** Placidus **Note:** Klippe. Dav. #5318A.

Date	Mintage	VG	F	VF	XF	Unc
1687	—	—	—	—	—	—

Note: Reported, not confirmed

KM# 29 THALER
Silver **Ruler:** Placidus **Note:** Dav. #5996.

Date	Mintage	VG	F	VF	XF	Unc
1688	—	250	450	1,000	2,500	—

KM# 30 1-1/4 THALER
Silver **Ruler:** Placidus **Note:** Similar to 1 Thaler, KM#29. Dav. #--.

Date	Mintage	VG	F	VF	XF	Unc
1688	—	550	950	1,850	3,000	—

KM# 8 2 THALER
Silver **Ruler:** Balthasar **Obv:** Crowned imperial eagle, titles of Rudolf II and date in legend **Rev:** Helmeted 4-fold arms **Note:** Klippe. Dav. #5313.

Date	Mintage	VG	F	VF	XF	Unc
1605 Rare	—	—	—	—	—	—

KM# 10 2 THALER
Silver **Ruler:** Balthasar **Note:** Klippe. Dav. #5314A.

Date	Mintage	VG	F	VF	XF	Unc
1606 Rare	—	—	—	—	—	—

KM# 9 2 THALER
Silver **Ruler:** Balthasar **Rev:** Orb on breast of eagle **Note:** Dav. #5314.

Date	Mintage	VG	F	VF	XF	Unc
1606 Rare	—	—	—	—	—	—

KM# 27 2 THALER
Silver **Ruler:** Placidus **Obv:** Bust right **Rev:** Mitered and helmeted 4-fold arms with cross above, date in legend **Note:** Dav. #5317.

Date	Mintage	VG	F	VF	XF	Unc
1687 Rare	—	—	—	—	—	—

KM# 28 2 THALER
Silver **Ruler:** Placidus **Note:** Klippe. Dav. #5317A.

Date	Mintage	VG	F	VF	XF	Unc
1687 Rare	—	—	—	—	—	—

TRADE COINAGE

KM# 18 1/4 DUCAT
0.8750 g., 0.9860 Gold 0.0277 oz. AGW **Ruler:** Bernhard Gustav Adolf **Obv:** St. Boniface **Rev:** AFBG monogram

Date	Mintage	VG	F	VF	XF	Unc
1672	—	265	575	1,200	2,200	—

KM# 19 1/2 DUCAT
1.7500 g., 0.9860 Gold 0.0555 oz. AGW **Ruler:** Bernhard Gustav Adolf **Obv:** St. Boniface **Rev:** AFBG monogram

Date	Mintage	VG	F	VF	XF	Unc
1672	—	375	975	1,900	3,400	—

KM# 20 DUCAT
3.5000 g., 0.9860 Gold 0.1109 oz. AGW **Ruler:** Bernhard Gustav Adolf **Obv:** St. Boniface above shield of arms **Rev:** AFBG monogram

Date	Mintage	VG	F	VF	XF	Unc
1672	—	600	1,450	3,000	5,300	—

KM# 35 DUCAT
3.5000 g., 0.9860 Gold 0.1109 oz. AGW **Ruler:** Placidus **Obv:** Bust of Placidus right **Rev:** Helmeted arms

Date	Mintage	VG	F	VF	XF	Unc
1692	—	1,500	3,050	6,100	10,500	—

KM# 21 2 DUCAT
7.0000 g., 0.9860 Gold 0.2219 oz. AGW **Ruler:** Bernhard Gustav Adolf **Obv:** St. Boniface above shield of arms **Rev:** AFBG monogram

Date	Mintage	VG	F	VF	XF	Unc
1672 Rare	—	—	—	—	—	—

KM# 36 2 DUCAT
7.0000 g., 0.9860 Gold 0.2219 oz. AGW **Ruler:** Placidus **Obv:** Bust of Placidus right **Rev:** Helmeted arms

Date	Mintage	VG	F	VF	XF	Unc
1692 Rare	—	—	—	—	—	—

KM# A30 7 DUCAT
24.5000 g., 0.9860 Gold 0.7766 oz. AGW **Ruler:** Placidus

Date	Mintage	VG	F	VF	XF	Unc
1688 Rare	—	—	—	—	—	—

Note: Struck with 1 Thaler dies, KM#29

KM# A31 7 DUCAT
24.5000 g., 0.9860 Gold 0.7766 oz. AGW **Ruler:** Placidus **Note:** Struck with 1 Thaler dies, KM#29.

Date	Mintage	VG	F	VF	XF	Unc
1688 Rare	—	—	—	—	—	—

KM# 31 8 DUCAT
28.0000 g., 0.9860 Gold 0.8876 oz. AGW **Ruler:** Placidus **Note:** Struck with 1 Thaler dies, KM#29.

Date	Mintage	VG	F	VF	XF	Unc
1688 Rare	—	—	—	—	—	—

KM# 32 10 DUCAT (Portugalöser)
35.0000 g., 0.9860 Gold 1.1095 oz. AGW **Ruler:** Placidus **Note:** Struck with 1 Thaler dies, KM#29.

Date	Mintage	VG	F	VF	XF	Unc
1688 Rare	—	—	—	—	—	—

FURSTENBERG

A noble family with holdings in Baden and Württemberg. The lord of Fürstenberg assumed the title of Count in the 13th century, which was raised to the rank of Prince in 1664. The Fürstenberg possessions were mediatized in 1806.

FURSTENBERG-HEILIGENBERG

RULERS
Friedrich IV, 1598-1617
Wilhelm II, 1617-1618
Egon VIII, 1618-1635
Hermann Egon, 1635-1674
Anton Egon, 1674-1716

DUCHY

REGULAR COINAGE

KM# 5 KREUZER
Copper **Obv:** 4-fold arms of Heiligenberg and Werdeenberg, HB aboe in wreath **Rev:** I/CREI/ZER in wreath **Note:** Kipper Kreuzer. Varieties exist.

Date	Mintage	VG	F	VF	XF	Unc
ND(c.1621/2)	—	—	—	—	—	—

KM# 6 3 KREUZER (Groschen)
Silver **Obv:** Bust right **Rev:** Crowned imperial eagle, 3 in orb on breast, titles of Ferdinand II and date in legend

Date	Mintage	VG	F	VF	XF	Unc
1623	—	—	—	—	—	—

KM# 7 6 KREUZER
Silver **Obv:** Crowned imperial eagle, 6 in orb on breast, titles of Ferdinand II **Rev:** Ornamented helmet

Date	Mintage	VG	F	VF	XF	Unc
ND(1623)	—	—	—	—	—	—

KM# 8 12 KREUZER (Dreibätzner)
Silver **Obv:** Crowned imperial eagle, 1Z in orb on breast, titles of Ferdinand II **Rev:** Crowned arms in ornamented shield

Date	Mintage	VG	F	VF	XF	Unc
ND(1623)	—	—	—	—	—	—

KM# 9 THALER
Silver **Obv:** Crowned imperial eagle, titles of Ferdinand II **Rev:** Crowned oval arms in ornamented frame **Note:** Dav. #6677.

Date	Mintage	F	VF	XF	Unc	BU
ND(1623) Rare	—	—	—	—	—	—

KM# 16 THALER
Silver **Obv:** Bust right **Rev:** Crowned Furstenberg arms, spread eagle, 4-fold arms in small shield on breast, date in legend **Note:** Dav. #6678. Varieties exist.

Date	Mintage	F	VF	XF	Unc	BU
1670 Rare	—	—	—	—	—	—

KM# 10 2 THALER
Silver **Obv:** Crowned imperial eagle, titles **Rev:** Crowned oval arms in ornamented frame **Note:** Dav. #6676.

Date	Mintage	F	VF	XF	Unc	BU
ND(1623) Rare	—	—	—	—	—	—

FURSTENWALDE

The provincial town of Furstenwalde in Prussia is located on the River Spree some 30 miles east-southeast of central Berlin. A local kipper coinage was struck during the Thirty Years' War.

TOWN

REGULAR COINAGE

KM# 3 PFENNIG

Copper **Obv:** Tree in oval shield, date above, F • W below. **Note:** Uniface.

Date	Mintage	VG	F	VF	XF	Unc
16Z1	—	20.00	33.00	45.00	85.00	—
1621	—	20.00	33.00	45.00	85.00	—
1622	—	20.00	33.00	45.00	85.00	—

KM# 1 PFENNIG

Copper **Obv:** Two adjoining oval arms, eagle in left, tree in right, date above, FW below. **Note:** Kipper Pfennig. Uniface. Varieties exist.

Date	Mintage	VG	F	VF	XF	Unc
1621	—	20.00	33.00	45.00	85.00	—
16Z1	—	20.00	33.00	45.00	85.00	—
16ZZ	—	20.00	33.00	45.00	85.00	—

KM# 4 PFENNIG

Copper **Obv:** Tree in ornately-shaped shield divides FW, date above. Varieties exist. **Note:** Uniface.

Date	Mintage	VG	F	VF	XF	Unc
1621	—	20.00	33.00	45.00	85.00	—
16Z1	—	20.00	33.00	45.00	85.00	—

KM# 5 PFENNIG

Copper **Obv:** Tree dividing FW in ornately-shaped shield, date above. **Note:** Uniface.

Date	Mintage	VG	F	VF	XF	Unc
1621	—	20.00	33.00	45.00	85.00	—
16Z1	—	20.00	33.00	45.00	85.00	—

KM# 6 PFENNIG

Copper **Obv:** Tree in ornamented oval arms divide FW near bottom, date above. **Note:** Uniface.

Date	Mintage	VG	F	VF	XF	Unc
1621	—	20.00	33.00	45.00	85.00	—
16Z1	—	20.00	33.00	45.00	85.00	—

KM# 7 PFENNIG

Copper **Obv:** Oval tree arms in baroque frame, date divided above, F-W divided below. **Note:** Uniface.

Date	Mintage	VG	F	VF	XF	Unc
1621	—	20.00	33.00	45.00	85.00	—

KM# 8 PFENNIG

Copper **Obv:** F-W divided above and date divided below arms. **Note:** Uniface.

Date	Mintage	VG	F	VF	XF	Unc
1621	—	20.00	33.00	45.00	85.00	—

KM# 9 PFENNIG

Copper **Obv:** Tree between two eagles, date divided above, F-W divided below. **Note:** Uniface.

Date	Mintage	VG	F	VF	XF	Unc
1621	—	20.00	33.00	45.00	85.00	—

KM# 10 PFENNIG

Copper **Note:** Tree divides F-W in oval baroque frame, date divided above.

Date	Mintage	VG	F	VF	XF	Unc
1622	—	15.00	25.00	35.00	60.00	—

KM# 2 PFENNIG

Copper **Note:** FW above, date below arms.

Date	Mintage	VG	F	VF	XF	Unc
16ZZ	—	15.00	25.00	35.00	60.00	—

FURTH

City 5 miles northwest of Nürnberg. Originally a Franconian settlement dating from the 8th century. Mentioned in 1007 when village was given to Bishopric of Bamberg. Claimed by Ansbach and Nürnberg in late medieval period. Captured briefly by Gustavus II Adolphus in 1632 during the 30 Years War. Town passed to Bavaria in 1806 and was chartered in 1808.

RULERS

Swedish

MONEYERS' INITIALS

Initial	Date	Name
CS	1632	Conrad Stutz

SWEDISH ADMINISTRATION

REGULAR COINAGE

KM# 3 PFENNIG

Silver **Obv:** "JEHOVAH" in Hebrew, rays streaming down on GA monogram dividing date, value I below. **Note:** Uniface.

Date	Mintage	VG	F	VF	XF	Unc
1632	—	45.00	100	175	275	—

KM# 4 1/28 GULDEN

Silver **Obv:** Crowned 4-fold arms with central shield, (28) above **Rev:** Figure of Christ holding orb divides date

Date	Mintage	VG	F	VF	XF	Unc
1632 CS Unique	—	—	—	—	—	—

KM# 5 4 KREUZER (Batzen)

Silver **Obv:** Half-length bust of Gustavus Adolphus 3/4 right holding sword over shoulder **Rev:** Crown above 4-fold arms with central shield divides date, value at top (IIII.K.)

Date	Mintage	VG	F	VF	XF	Unc
1632 CS	—	120	250	400	600	—

KM# 6 4 KREUZER (Batzen)

Silver **Obv:** Crown above 4-fold arms supported by two lions, value at top (IIII. K.) **Rev:** Figure of Christ holding orb divides date **Note:** Varieties exist.

Date	Mintage	VG	F	VF	XF	Unc
1632	—	27.00	50.00	110	175	—

KM# 7 4 KREUZER (Batzen)

Silver **Obv:** Arms and lions within inner circle

Date	Mintage	VG	F	VF	XF	Unc
1632	—	27.00	55.00	110	175	—

KM# 8 4 KREUZER (Batzen)

Silver **Obv:** Crowned shield

Date	Mintage	VG	F	VF	XF	Unc
1632	—	27.00	50.00	110	175	—

KM# 9 THALER

Silver **Obv:** Gustabus Adolphus **Rev:** Christ wtih orb, "JEHOVAH" in Hebrew above **Note:** Dav. #4549.

Date	Mintage	F	VF	XF	Unc	BU
1632 CS Rare	—	—	—	—	—	—

Note: Dr. Busso Peus Nachfolger Auction 390, 5-07, XF realized approximately $19,035.

TRADE COINAGE

KM# 10 DUCAT

3.5000 g., 0.9860 Gold 0.1109 oz. AGW **Obv:** Gustabus Adolphus standing right, divides date **Rev:** Crowned arms

Date	Mintage	VG	F	VF	XF	Unc
1632 CS Rare	—	—	—	—	—	—

PATTERNS

Including off metal strikes

KM#	Date	Mintage	Identification	Mkt Val
Pn1	1632 CS	—	Ducat. Silver. KM#10	—

GLOGAU

A city on the Oder River in Silesia (present-day Poland), about 105 miles northeast of Dresden, Glogau was the seat of a duchy, which passed successively to Poland in 1476, to Austria in 1526 and to Prussia in 1740. A rather scarce city coinage was struck during the early part of the Thirty Years' War.

MINT OFFICIALS' INITIALS

Initial	Date	Name
PN1	1621	Mathes Jachtmann
IC	1622	Johann Curtz aus Haynau
IH	1623	Johann Jacob Huser
	1624	Balthasar Zwirner
	1624	Peter Geldner, coinage leaseholder
	1624	Peter John
	1624	Jeremias Reinwaldt
	1625	Jacob Jamniter, coinage leaseholder

AUSTRIAN ADMINISTRATION

REGULAR COINAGE

KM# 1 KREUZER

Silver **Obv:** Silesian eagle, titles of Ferdinand II **Rev:** 4-fold arms divide date **Note:** Kipper Kreuzer.

Date	Mintage	VG	F	VF	XF	Unc
(16)ZZ	—	20.00	40.00	85.00	150	—

KM# 2 3 KREUZER (Groschen)

Silver **Note:** Kipper 3 Kreuzer. Varieties exist.

Date	Mintage	VG	F	VF	XF	Unc
1622 IC	—	27.00	55.00	100	170	—

KM# 3 3 KREUZER (Groschen)

Silver **Obv:** Laureate bust right, titles of Ferdinand II, date in legend **Rev:** Silesian eagle, value 3 below, date in legend

Date	Mintage	VG	F	VF	XF	Unc
1622 IC	—	—	—	—	—	—

KM# 4 3 KREUZER (Groschen)

Silver **Obv:** Silesian eagle, titles of Ferdinand II **Rev:** Two shields above value 3 in oval

Date	Mintage	VG	F	VF	XF	Unc
1622 IC	—	27.00	55.00	100	170	—

KM# 5 3 KREUZER (Groschen)

Silver **Obv:** Silesian eagle, value 3 below, titles of Ferdinand II, date in legend **Rev:** Madonna and child **Note:** Klippe.

Date	Mintage	VG	F	VF	XF	Unc
1622	—	—	—	—	—	—

KM# 6 3 KREUZER (Groschen)

Silver **Obv:** Silesian eagle, value 3 below, titles of Ferdinand II **Rev:** Ornate gothic G, date in legend

Date	Mintage	VG	F	VF	XF	Unc
16ZZ IH	—	—	—	—	—	—

KM# 7 24 KREUZER

Silver **Obv:** Similar to KM#8, titles of Ferdinand II **Rev:** Silesian eagle **Note:** Kipper 24 Kreuzer

Date	Mintage	VG	F	VF	XF	Unc
1622 IC	—	90.00	170	300	475	—

KM# 8 24 KREUZER

Silver

Date	Mintage	VG	F	VF	XF	Unc
1622 IC	—	90.00	170	300	475	—
1622 IH	—	90.00	170	300	475	—

KM# 9 1/4 THALER

Silver **Note:** Similar to 24 Kreuzer KM#8, but 1/4 below bust and without date.

Date	Mintage	VG	F	VF	XF	Unc
ND(1622) IC	—	—	—	—	—	—

GOLDBERG

A provincial town in Silesia founded in 1211 at the site of a gold mine. A local coinage was struck during the Kipper period of the Thirty Years' War.

MINT OFFICIALS' INITIALS

Initial	Date	Name
GH	1612-23	Georg Heinecke
HB	Ca.1623	Unknown
MH	1604-20	Uncertain, perhaps Melchior Hoffmann in Kolln an der Spree

TOWN

REGULAR COINAGE

KM# 1 HELLER

Copper **Obv:** Silesian eagle above three mounds, value I below. **Note:** Uniface.

Date	Mintage	VG	F	VF	XF	Unc
ND(1621-22)	—	—	—	—	—	—

KM# 2 HELLER

Copper **Obv:** Silesian eagle above straight line, value I below divides mintmaster's initials. **Note:** Uniface.

Date	Mintage	VG	F	VF	XF	Unc
ND(1621-22) GH	—	—	—	—	—	—

KM# 3 HELLER

Copper **Obv:** Three circles with an eagle, GB and date. **Note:** Uniface.

Date	Mintage	VG	F	VF	XF	Unc
(16)23	—	—	—	—	—	—

KM# 4 2 HELLER

Copper **Obv:** Silesian eagle above three mounds, vlaue II below. **Note:** Uniface. Kipper 2 Heller.

Date	Mintage	VG	F	VF	XF	Unc
ND(1621-22)	—	—	—	—	—	—

KM# 5 3 HELLER

Copper **Obv:** Silesian eagle above three mounds, value III below. **Note:** Uniface. Kipper 3 Heller.

Date	Mintage	VG	F	VF	XF	Unc
ND(1621/2)	—	—	—	—	—	—

KM# 6 3 HELLER

Copper **Obv:** Smaller eagle dividing G-B. **Note:** Uniface.

Date	Mintage	VG	F	VF	XF	Unc
ND(1621-22)	—	—	—	—	—	—

KM# 7 3 HELLER

Copper **Obv:** H before III below eagle. **Note:** Uniface.

Date	Mintage	VG	F	VF	XF	Unc
ND(1621-22)	—	—	—	—	—	—

KM# 11 3 HELLER

Copper **Obv:** Silesian eagle above three mounds divides date 1-6/2-2 and G-B, ++III++ below **Note:** Uniface.

Date	Mintage	VG	F	VF	XF	Unc
16ZZ	—	40.00	80.00	160	275	—
16Z3	—	40.00	80.00	160	275	—

KM# 8 3 HELLER

Copper **Obv:** Silesian eagle above three mounds in circle, around +16. G. III. B. 22+ **Note:** Uniface.

Date	Mintage	VG	F	VF	XF	Unc
1622	—	40.00	80.00	160	275	—

KM# 9 3 HELLER

Copper **Obv:** Silesian eagle above three mounds divides date and G-B, value III below. **Note:** Uniface.

Date	Mintage	VG	F	VF	XF	Unc
16ZZ	—	40.00	80.00	160	275	—
ZZ61 MH Error date	—	40.00	80.00	160	275	—

KM# 10 3 HELLER

Copper **Obv:** H before III below **Note:** Uniface.

Date	Mintage	VG	F	VF	XF	Unc
16ZZ	—	40.00	80.00	160	275	—

KM# 12 3 HELLER

Copper **Obv:** Three circles, eagle in top circle divides 1-6, bottom two circles have GB and III, 22 below. **Note:** Uniface.

Date	Mintage	VG	F	VF	XF	Unc
1622	—	33.00	65.00	135	225	—

KM# 14 3 HELLER

Copper **Obv:** Silesian eagle above three mounds divides date 1-6/2-3, G III B below **Note:** Uniface.

Date	Mintage	VG	F	VF	XF	Unc
1623	—	33.00	65.00	135	225	—

KM# 15 3 HELLER

Copper **Obv:** G-B separated by mounds, G III H below **Note:** Uniface.

Date	Mintage	VG	F	VF	XF	Unc
1623 GH	—	40.00	80.00	160	275	—

KM# 16 3 HELLER

Copper **Obv:** Silesian eagle above three mounds, GB and III, date divided near top in trefoil. **Note:** Uniface.

Date	Mintage	VG	F	VF	XF	Unc
(16)23	—	33.00	65.00	135	225	—
(16)23 HB	—	33.00	65.00	135	225	—

KM# 17 3 HELLER

Copper **Obv:** Three mounds, GB and III, date in center trefoil **Note:** Uniface.

Date	Mintage	VG	F	VF	XF	Unc
(16)23	—	40.00	80.00	160	275	—

KM# 18 3 HELLER

Copper **Obv:** Date 16/23 above, GB and III below, three mounds in center in trefoil. **Note:** Uniface.

Date	Mintage	VG	F	VF	XF	Unc
1623	—	40.00	80.00	160	275	—

KM# 19 3 HELLER

Copper **Obv:** Three mounds above, 16-23 below, GB III in center in trefoil **Note:** Uniface.

Date	Mintage	VG	F	VF	XF	Unc
1623	—	40.00	80.00	160	275	—

KM# 20 3 HELLER

Copper **Obv:** GB above, III and 23 below, three mounds in center in trefoil **Note:** Uniface.

Date	Mintage	VG	F	VF	XF	Unc
(16)23	—	40.00	80.00	160	275	—

KM# 21 3 HELLER

Copper **Obv:** III above, GB and 23 below in trefoil **Note:** Uniface.

Date	Mintage	VG	F	VF	XF	Unc
(16)23	—	40.00	80.00	160	275	—

KM# 22 3 HELLER

Copper **Obv:** Three circles, eagle in top circle divides date, GB and III in lower circles **Note:** Uniface.

Date	Mintage	VG	F	VF	XF	Unc
(16)23	—	40.00	80.00	160	275	—

KM# 23 3 HELLER

Copper **Obv:** Three circles, 23 in top, GB and III in lower circles **Note:** Uniface.

Date	Mintage	VG	F	VF	XF	Unc
(16)23	—	40.00	80.00	160	275	—

KM# 24 3 HELLER

Copper **Obv:** Three mounds replace 23 in top circle which divides date **Note:** Uniface.

Date	Mintage	VG	F	VF	XF	Unc
(16)23	—	40.00	80.00	160	275	—
(16)23 GH	—	40.00	80.00	160	275	—

KM# 25 3 HELLER

Copper **Obv:** Circle divided into four segments, Silesian eagle top left, GB top right, three mounds above 2 bottom left, III above 3 bottom right. **Note:** Uniface.

Date	Mintage	VG	F	VF	XF	Unc
(16)23	—	45.00	100	200	350	—

GORLITZ

A provincial city located about 60 miles east of Dresden on the Neisse River in Upper Lusatia (Oberlausitz). Görlitz received the mint right in 1330. Kipper coins were issued there during the early part of the Thirty Years' War. The city passed to Prussia in 1815.

REFERENCES:

Sch = Wolfgang Schulten, ***Deutsche Münzen aus der Zeit Karls V.***, Frankfurt am Main, 1976.

S = Hugo Frhr. Von Saurma-Jeltsch, **Die Saurmasche Münzsammlung deutscher, schweizerischer und polnischer Gepräge von etwa dem Beginn der Groschenzeit bis zur Kipperperiode**, Berlin, 1892.

PROVINCIAL CITY

REGULAR COINAGE

KM# 1 PFENNIG

Copper **Obv:** Large crown above G divides date. **Note:** Kipper Pfennig. Uniface.

Date	Mintage	VG	F	VF	XF	Unc
ND(1621-22)	—	13.00	25.00	40.00	70.00	—
16Z1	—	13.00	25.00	40.00	70.00	—

KM# 2 PFENNIG

Copper **Obv:** GOR, crown above, date below. **Note:** Uniface.

Date	Mintage	VG	F	VF	XF	Unc
1622	—	—	—	—	—	—

KM# 3 DREIER (3 Pfennig)

Copper **Obv:** Three arms (crown, lion, eagle) arranged in clover leaf, value 3 in center, G-O-R between shields around **Note:** Uniface.

Date	Mintage	VG	F	VF	XF	Unc
ND(1621-22)	—	—	—	—	—	—
1622	—	—	—	—	—	—

KM# 4 3 KREUZER (Groschen)

Copper Or Billon **Obv:** Lion rampant left, date in legend **Rev:** Crowned imperial eagle, 3 in orb on breast, titles of Ferdinand II **Note:** Kipper 3 Kreuzer. Varieties exist.

Date	Mintage	VG	F	VF	XF	Unc
ND(1621-22)	—	55.00	110	170	350	—
16ZZ	—	55.00	110	170	350	—
1622	—	55.00	110	170	350	—
1623	—	55.00	110	170	350	—

GORZE

A monastery located within the city of Gorze southeast of Metz in Lorraine, was founded in 745 by Bishop Chrodegang. In 1543 it and the city were captured from the duke of Guise and taken possession of by the French. It was secularized in 1580 but remained a cloister until 1752.

RULER

Karl von Remoncourt, 1607-1645

ABBEY

REGULAR COINAGE

KM# 10 TESTON

Silver **Obv. Legend:** CAR • A LOTH • D • A • ETS • S • A • G • SVP • DNS • GORZ • AB **Rev. Legend:** MONETA NOVA GORZIAE CVSA

Date	Mintage	VG	F	VF	XF	Unc
ND(1607-30)	—	—	—	—	—	—

KM# 20 THALER

Silver **Obv:** Bust of Karl right **Obv. Legend:** Ends: ...GORZ * AB* **Rev:** Crowned ornamented arms **Note:** Dav. #5319

Date	Mintage	VG	F	VF	XF	Unc
ND Rare	—	—	—	—	—	—

KM# 21 THALER

Silver **Obv. Legend:** Ends: ...GORZIENS • AB **Note:** Dav. #5320.

Date	Mintage	VG	F	VF	XF	Unc
ND Rare	—	—	—	—	—	—

KM# 22 THALER

Silver **Obv:** Date divided by bust **Note:** Dav. #5321.

Date	Mintage	VG	F	VF	XF	Unc
1630 Rare	—	—	—	—	—	—

KM# 35 THALER

Silver **Obv:** Partial date end of legend above bust **Note:** Dav. #5321A.

Date	Mintage	VG	F	VF	XF	Unc
(1640) Rare	—	—	—	—	—	—

TRADE COINAGE

KM# 30 2 DUCAT

7.0000 g., 0.9860 Gold 0.2219 oz. AGW **Obv:** Bust of Karl right **Obv. Legend:** CAR • A • LOTH • D • S • S • A • G • SVP • DNS • GO • AB • **Rev:** Crowned arms **Rev. Legend:** MONETA • AVREA • GORZ • CVSA •

Date	Mintage	VG	F	VF	XF	Unc
ND(1607-30) Rare	—	—	—	—	—	—

GOSLAR

The small city of Goslar is located on the northern flank of the Harz Mountains, about 26 miles (44 kilometers) west of Halberstadt. It was founded as a free city by Emperor Heinrich I (918-936) about the year 920 and was later a royal residence, as well as the site of an imperial mint. Goslar was ideally situated close to mines in the Harz Mountains which produced an abundance of metals including copper and silver among others. The growing town became a member of the Hanseatic League in the mid-14th century and was soon producing its own coinage. The free imperial status of Goslar came to an end in 1802 when it passed to the rule of Prussia. It became a part of the Kingdom of Westphalia from 1807 until 1813, after which it was returned to Prussia for a short time. It was then assigned to Hannover in the peace which ended the Napoleonic Wars in 1815. When Hannover was annexed by Prussia in 1866, Goslar was once again in the Prussian fold.

MINT OFFICIALS' INITIALS

Initials	Date	Name
CHS	1674-75	Christoph Heinrich Schluter
GK	Ca.1619-28	Georg Kruckenberg
ICB	1663-68	Johann Christoph Bahr
IW	Ca.1671	Unknown, possibly Julius Wefer

ARMS

Crowned eagle

REFERENCES:

C = Heinrich Philipp Cappe, **Beschreibung der Münzen von Goslar**, Dresden, 1860.

Sch = Wolfgang Schulten, ***Deutsche Münzen aus der Zeit Karls V.***, Frankfurt am Main, 1976.

S = Hugo Frhr. Von Saurma-Jeltsch, **Die Saurmasche Münzsammlung deutscher, schweizerischer und polnischer Gepräge von etwa dem Beginn der Groschenzeit bis zur Kipperperiode**, Berlin, 1892.

FREE CITY

REGULAR COINAGE

KM# 20 FLITTER

Copper **Obv:** Eagle with G on breast **Rev:** I/ FLIT/ TER/ date **Note:** Kipper Flitter.

Date	Mintage	VG	F	VF	XF	Unc
(1)6Z0	—	10.00	25.00	40.00	70.00	—

KM# 21 FLITTER

Copper **Rev:** I/ FLITTER/ date

Date	Mintage	VG	F	VF	XF	Unc
(1)6Z0	—	10.00	25.00	40.00	70.00	—

KM# 42 PFENNIG

Billon **Obv:** GOS/ date. **Note:** Hohl type.

Date	Mintage	VG	F	VF	XF	Unc
16Z8	—	33.00	55.00	100	170	—
1633	—	33.00	55.00	100	170	—
1638	—	33.00	55.00	100	170	—
164Z	—	33.00	55.00	100	170	—

KM# 41 PFENNIG

Billon **Obv:** Eagle in ornately-shaped shield, GOS (or GOSL) above divides date **Note:** Hohl type. Varieties exist.

Date	Mintage	VG	F	VF	XF	Unc
1628	—	33.00	55.00	100	170	—
1629	—	33.00	55.00	100	170	—
1630	—	33.00	55.00	100	170	—
1676	—	33.00	55.00	100	170	—
1677	—	33.00	55.00	100	170	—
1693	—	33.00	55.00	100	170	—

KM# 50 PFENNIG

Billon **Obv:** Crowned G divides date.

Date	Mintage	VG	F	VF	XF	Unc
1634	—	33.00	65.00	120	180	—

KM# 61 PFENNIG

Billon **Obv:** GOS/ date **Note:** Uniface. Varieties exist.

Date	Mintage	VG	F	VF	XF	Unc
1664	—	33.00	60.00	110	175	—
1668	—	33.00	60.00	110	175	—

KM# 12 3 PFENNIG (Dreier)

Silver **Obv:** Eagle in ornamented shield **Rev:** Imperial orb with 3 divides date above

Date	Mintage	VG	F	VF	XF	Unc
1615	—	—	—	—	—	—

KM# 13 3 PFENNIG (Dreier)

Silver **Obv:** Eagle

Date	Mintage	VG	F	VF	XF	Unc
1616	—	—	—	—	—	—

KM# 32 3 PFENNIG (Dreier)

Silver **Obv:** Eagle in ornately-shaped shield, GOSLAR above **Note:** Kipper 3 Pfennig.

Date	Mintage	VG	F	VF	XF	Unc
1622	—	33.00	65.00	130	200	—

KM# 33 3 PFENNIG (Dreier)

Silver **Obv:** Eagle arms in baroque frame

Date	Mintage	VG	F	VF	XF	Unc
1622	—	33.00	65.00	130	200	—

KM# 34 3 PFENNIG (Dreier)

Silver, 18 mm. **Obv:** Eagle, head left, G on breast **Rev:** Imperial orb with 3 divides date, all in rhombus

Date	Mintage	Good	VG	F	VF	XF
1622	—	—	33.00	65.00	130	200

KM# 65 3 PFENNIG (Dreier)

Silver **Rev:** Without rhombus

Date	Mintage	VG	F	VF	XF	Unc
1671 IW	—	20.00	40.00	65.00	125	—

KM# 70 3 PFENNIG (Dreier)

Silver **Obv:** GOS/ LAR/ date **Rev:** Imperial orb with 3

Date	Mintage	VG	F	VF	XF	Unc
1676	—	20.00	40.00	65.00	125	—

KM# 71 3 PFENNIG (Dreier)

Silver **Obv:** GOS/ date

Date	Mintage	VG	F	VF	XF	Unc
1676	—	20.00	40.00	65.00	125	—

KM# 60 4 PFENNIG (Gute)

Silver **Obv:** Eagle **Rev:** IIII/ GUTE/ 16PF63/ mintmaster's initials (if present)

Date	Mintage	VG	F	VF	XF	Unc
1663 ICB	—	16.00	40.00	65.00	125	—
1668 ICB	—	16.00	40.00	65.00	125	—
1676	—	16.00	40.00	65.00	125	—

KM# 39 6 PFENNIG

Silver **Obv:** Crowned imperial eagle, 6 in orb on breast, titles of Ferdinand II **Rev:** Madonna and child, date in legend

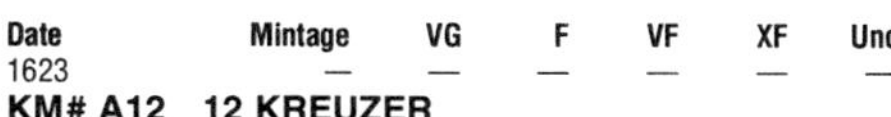

Date	Mintage	VG	F	VF	XF	Unc
1623	—	—	—	—	—	—

KM# A12 12 KREUZER

Silver **Obv:** Crowned imperial eagle, 12 in orb on breast, titles of Ferdinand II and date (where present) in legend **Rev:** Eagle in circle

Date	Mintage	VG	F	VF	XF	Unc
1620	—	33.00	75.00	120	190	—
ND(1620/1)	—	33.00	75.00	120	190	—

KM# 28 12 KREUZER

Silver **Rev:** Date in legend **Note:** Varieties exist.

Date	Mintage	VG	F	VF	XF	Unc
1621	—	33.00	75.00	120	190	—

KM# 23 24 KREUZER

Silver **Obv:** Crowned imperial eagle, 24 in orb on breast, titles of Ferdinand II **Rev:** Eagle in circle

Date	Mintage	VG	F	VF	XF	Unc
ND(1620/21)	—	45.00	100	175	275	—

KM# 29 MARIENGROSCHEN

Silver **Obv:** Madonna and child surrounded by flames **Rev:** Eagle, date in legend

Date	Mintage	VG	F	VF	XF	Unc
16Z1	—	—	—	—	—	—

KM# 62 MARIENGROSCHEN

Silver **Note:** Similar to KM#29

Date	Mintage	VG	F	VF	XF	Unc
1668 ICB	—	40.00	80.00	130	200	—
1671 ICB	—	30.00	60.00	90.00	150	—

KM# 69 24 MARIENGROSCHEN (2/3 Thaler)

Silver **Obv:** Helmeted arms with plumes **Rev:** Value and date within inner circle **Note:** Similar to KM#99.

Date	Mintage	VG	F	VF	XF	Unc
1675 CHS	—	80.00	135	225	400	—
1676 CHS	—	80.00	135	225	400	—

KM# 67 16 GUTE GROSCHEN (2/3 Thaler)

Silver **Obv:** 2/3 added below eagle **Rev:** Value XVI...

Date	Mintage	VG	F	VF	XF	Unc
1674 CHS	—	100	170	275	540	—
1675 CHS	—	100	170	275	540	—

KM# 66 16 GUTE GROSCHEN (2/3 Thaler)

Silver **Obv:** Eagle **Rev:** 16/ GUTE/ GROSCH/ EN/ date

Date	Mintage	VG	F	VF	XF	Unc
1674 CHS	—	100	175	275	540	—

KM# 43 1/36 THALER

Silver **Obv:** Madonna and child surrounded by flames **Rev:** Eagle, date divided below, 36 in imperial orb above

Date	Mintage	VG	F	VF	XF	Unc
1628 GK	—	—	—	—	—	—

KM# 5 1/24 THALER (Groschen)

Silver **Obv:** Eagle head left **Rev:** Imperial orb with 24 divides date, titles of Rudolf II

Date	Mintage	VG	F	VF	XF	Unc
1605	—	—	—	—	—	—

KM# 14 1/24 THALER (Groschen)

Silver **Rev:** Titles of Matthias

Date	Mintage	VG	F	VF	XF	Unc
1615	—	20.00	33.00	60.00	120	—
1618	—	20.00	33.00	60.00	120	—
1619	—	20.00	33.00	60.00	120	—
1620	—	20.00	33.00	60.00	120	—

KM# 24 1/24 THALER (Groschen)

Silver **Obv:** Titles of Ferdinand II **Note:** Kipper 1/24 Thaler.

Date	Mintage	VG	F	VF	XF	Unc
ND	—	27.00	45.00	70.00	125	—

KM# 30 1/24 THALER (Groschen)

Silver **Obv:** Imperial orb with 24, titles of Ferdinand II, date in legend **Rev:** Eagle

Date	Mintage	VG	F	VF	XF	Unc
(16)21	—	27.00	45.00	70.00	125	—

KM# 35 1/24 THALER (Groschen)

Silver **Obv:** Crowned imperial eagle, 24 in orb on breast, titles of Ferdinand II **Rev:** Helmeted eagle arms

Date	Mintage	VG	F	VF	XF	Unc
1622	—	27.00	45.00	75.00	125	—

KM# 40 1/24 THALER (Groschen)

Silver **Obv:** Imperial orb with 24 divides date above, titles of Ferdinand II

Date	Mintage	VG	F	VF	XF	Unc
16Z3 GK	—	27.00	45.00	75.00	125	—

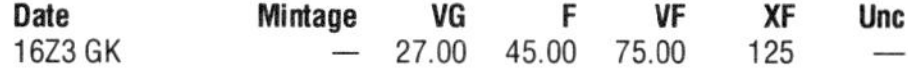

KM# 31 1/6 THALER (4 Groschen)

Silver **Obv:** Madonna and child, date in legend **Rev:** Crowned imperial eagle, 4 in orb on breast, titles of Ferdinand II **Note:** Kipper 1/6 Thaler.

Date	Mintage	VG	F	VF	XF	Unc
(16)21	—	70.00	140	230	375	—

KM# 68 1/6 THALER (4 Groschen)

Silver **Obv:** Eagle, value 1/6 below **Rev:** IIII/ GVTE/ GROSCH/ EN/ date **Note:** 4 Gute Groschen 1/6 Thaler.

Date	Mintage	VG	F	VF	XF	Unc
1674 CHS	—	—	—	—	—	—

KM# 56 1/4 THALER (6 Groschen)

Silver **Obv:** Madonna and child surrounded by flames, eagle in shield below **Rev:** Crowned imperial eagle, 6 in orb on breast, date divides above claws, titles of Leopold I

Date	Mintage	VG	F	VF	XF	Unc
1659	—	—	—	—	—	—

KM# 10.1 1/2 THALER (12 Groschen)

Silver **Obv:** Madonna and child surrounded by flames, eagle in shield below **Rev:** Titles of Rudolf II **Note:** Dav. #5322.

Date	Mintage	VG	F	VF	XF	Unc
1610	—	450	900	1,600	2,400	—

KM# 10.2 1/2 THALER (12 Groschen)

Silver **Rev. Legend:** RUDOL * II * ROM * IMPER * SEMP * AU **Note:** Dav. #5323.

Date	Mintage	F	VF	XF	Unc	BU
1611	—	450	900	1,600	2,400	—

KM# 11 1/2 THALER (12 Groschen)

Silver **Rev:** 24 in orb on eagle's breast

Date	Mintage	VG	F	VF	XF	Unc
1610	—	—	—	—	—	—

KM# 36 1/2 THALER (12 Groschen)

Silver **Obv:** Crowned imperial eagle, 1Z in orb on breast, titles of Ferdinand II **Rev:** Madonna and child surrounded by flames, eagle in shield below, date in legend

Date	Mintage	VG	F	VF	XF	Unc
16ZZ GK	—	—	—	—	—	—

KM# 37 1/2 THALER (12 Groschen)

Silver **Obv:** Titles of Ferdinand II **Note:** Dav. #5324.

Date	Mintage	VG	F	VF	XF	Unc
16ZZ	—	525	1,050	1,750	2,600	—
16ZZ GK	—	525	1,050	1,750	2,600	—
16Z3	—	525	1,050	1,750	2,600	—
16Z8	—	525	1,050	1,750	2,600	—

KM# 38 1/2 THALER (12 Groschen)

Silver **Obv:** Z4 in orb on eagle's breast

Date	Mintage	VG	F	VF	XF	Unc
16ZZ	—	675	1,250	2,000	3,300	—

KM# 44.1 1/2 THALER (12 Groschen)
Silver **Obv:** Date at bottom **Note:** Dav. #5325.

Date	Mintage	VG	F	VF	XF	Unc
16Z8	—	525	1,050	1,750	2,600	—
16Z8 GK	—	525	1,050	1,750	2,600	—

KM# 44.2 1/2 THALER (12 Groschen)
Silver **Obv. Legend:** ...D: G: ROM: IMP: SEMP • AU • **Note:** Dav. #5326.

Date	Mintage	VG	F	VF	XF	Unc
16Z9 GK	—	525	1,050	1,750	2,600	—

KM# 51 1/2 THALER (12 Groschen)
Silver **Rev:** Date divided by eagle's claws, titles of Ferdinand III **Note:** Dav. #5327.

Date	Mintage	VG	F	VF	XF	Unc
1637	—	525	1,050	1,750	2,600	—

Note: Dates 1638 and 1642 probably do not exist; listing in Davenport due to misreading of Cappe

KM# 57 1/2 THALER (12 Groschen)
Silver **Note:** Similar to KM#75 but titles of Leopold I.

Date	Mintage	VG	F	VF	XF	Unc
1659	—	—	—	—	—	—

KM# 55.1 1/2 THALER (12 Groschen)
Silver **Note:** Similar to KM# 63. Dav. #5328.

Date	Mintage	VG	F	VF	XF	Unc
1650 Error of 1659	—	525	1,050	1,750	2,600	—

KM# 55.2 1/2 THALER (12 Groschen)
Silver **Obv:** Date divided above eagle's claws, titles of Leopold I **Note:** Dav. #5329.

Date	Mintage	VG	F	VF	XF	Unc
1659	—	525	1,050	1,750	2,600	—

TRADE COINAGE

KM# 45 GOLDGULDEN
3.5000 g., 0.9860 Gold 0.1109 oz. AGW **Obv:** Helmeted arms in inner circle **Rev:** Crowned imperial eagle in inner circle

Date	Mintage	VG	F	VF	XF	Unc
1628	—	950	2,000	4,000	7,200	—
ND	—	950	2,000	4,000	7,200	—

KM# 6 DUCAT
3.5000 g., 0.9860 Gold 0.1109 oz. AGW **Obv:** Imperial orb in trefoil, titles of Rudolf II and date in legend **Rev:** Eagle, head left **Note:** Fr.#1072.

Date	Mintage	VG	F	VF	XF	Unc
1605	—	1,300	2,450	6,000	10,000	—

KM# 25 DUCAT
3.5000 g., 0.9860 Gold 0.1109 oz. AGW **Obv:** Crowned imperial eagle, orb on breast, titles of Ferdinand II **Rev:** Helmeted city arms

Date	Mintage	VG	F	VF	XF	Unc
ND GK	—	1,250	2,350	4,800	8,300	—

KM# 26 DUCAT
3.5000 g., 0.9860 Gold 0.1109 oz. AGW **Obv:** Bust of Ferdinand II right **Rev:** Shield of arms **Note:** Fr.#1070.

Date	Mintage	VG	F	VF	XF	Unc
ND	—	1,150	2,200	4,650	7,400	—

KM# 27 DUCAT
3.5000 g., 0.9860 Gold 0.1109 oz. AGW **Obv:** Ferdinand II in inner circle **Note:** Fr.#1071.

Date	Mintage	VG	F	VF	XF	Unc
ND	—	900	1,800	3,750	6,000	—

GOTTINGEN

The provincial city of Göttingen is located in present-day Niedersachsen, 12 miles (20 km) south of Northeim and about 60 miles (100 km) south of Hannover. Göttingen is first mentioned in a document of 953 and received some limited self-governing rights in 1210. It was a seat of the Brunswick dukes from 1286 until 1442. By the 14th century, Göttingen was one of the foremost members of the Hanseatic League and obtained the mint right from the duke of Brunswick in 1351 and again in 1368. The earliest coinage of Göttingen consists of bracteates from the beginning of the 13th century, but dated coins begin in 1410 and continue intermittently until 1664. Coins of the Göttingen type with dates after 1664 are spurious issues of Count Gustav von Sayn-Wittgenstein. The town passed along with the rest of Brunswick-Hannover to Prussia in 1866.

MINT OFFICIALS' INITIALS

Initial	Date	Name
H, HL	1601-06	Hans Liphart
(e)=	1601-07	Hans Lachentries, mintmaster
	1601-20, 1622	Hardege Hardege, warden
	1613	Andreas Laffert, mintmaster
(h)= or or (i)=	1614, 1624-25	Valentin Block, mintmaster
(f)=	1614-17	Hans Schlessewigk, mintmaster
	1618-19	Heinrich von der Ecke, mintmaster
(g)=	1619-20, 1622	Steffen Ulmer, mintmaster
	1620-22	Hans Rukop, mintmaster
	1622	Steffen Ulmer, 2nd time
	1622	Hardege Ardege, mintmaster
	1623-24	Levin Brockmann, mintmaster
	1624-26?	Franz Helfte, mintmaster
WN	1625-64	Wilhelm Nordmeier, warden
VB	1624-25	Valentin Block, warden
(j)= or (k)=	1626-29	Jacob Eisenvalet, mintmaster
+IE/IEV	1634-35, 1637-38, 1641	Heinrich Eichenberg, mintmaster
PL	1655-64	Peter (Heinrich) Lohr, mintmaster

PROVINCIAL CITY

REGULAR COINAGE

KM# 15 3 FLITTER
Copper **Obv:** Gothic G between rosettes **Rev:** III/ FLITTER/ date **Note:** Kipper 3 Flitter.

Date	Mintage	VG	F	VF	XF	Unc
1620	—	27.00	45.00	75.00	125	—
1621	—	27.00	45.00	75.00	125	—

KM# 16 PFENNIG
Copper **Obv:** Crowned gothic G **Rev:** I, date above **Note:** Kipper Pfennig.

Date	Mintage	VG	F	VF	XF	Unc
1621	—	27.00	45.00	75.00	125	—

KM# 26 PFENNIG
Copper **Obv:** Crowned gothic G divides date, where present. **Note:** Uniface. Schussel type.

Date	Mintage	VG	F	VF	XF	Unc
ND(ca.1623-64)	—	20.00	40.00	70.00	125	—
(16)33 IE	—	20.00	40.00	70.00	125	—
1634	—	20.00	40.00	70.00	125	—
1635	—	20.00	40.00	70.00	125	—
1637	—	20.00	40.00	70.00	125	—
1638	—	20.00	40.00	70.00	125	—
1641	—	20.00	40.00	70.00	125	—
1656	—	20.00	40.00	70.00	125	—
1656 WN	—	20.00	40.00	70.00	125	—
1658	—	20.00	40.00	70.00	125	—
1659	—	20.00	40.00	70.00	125	—
1660	—	20.00	40.00	70.00	125	—
1661	—	20.00	40.00	70.00	125	—
1664	—	20.00	40.00	70.00	125	—

KM# 17 2 PFENNIG
Copper **Obv:** Crowned Gothic G **Rev:** II, date above **Note:** Kipper 2 Pfennig.

Date	Mintage	VG	F	VF	XF	Unc
1621	—	27.00	45.00	75.00	130	—

KM# 18 2 PFENNIG
Copper **Rev:** Date divided above and below II in quatrefoil

Date	Mintage	VG	F	VF	XF	Unc
1621	—	27.00	45.00	75.00	130	—

KM# 6 3 PFENNIG (Dreier)
Silver **Obv:** Crowned Gothic G **Rev:** Imperial orb with 3 divides date

Date	Mintage	VG	F	VF	XF	Unc
1601	—	27.00	55.00	100	170	—
1602	—	27.00	55.00	100	170	—

KM# 7 3 PFENNIG (Dreier)
Silver **Obv:** Crowned Gothic G in shield **Rev:** Imperial orb with 3 divides date in quatrefoil

Date	Mintage	VG	F	VF	XF	Unc
1602	—	33.00	65.00	120	200	—
1603	—	33.00	65.00	120	200	—

KM# A8 3 PFENNIG (Dreier)
Silver **Obv:** Crowned "G" in ornate shield **Rev:** Imperial orb with 3 in oval, cross on orb divides date, arabesque ornaments around oval

Date	Mintage	VG	F	VF	XF	Unc
160Z	—	35.00	75.00	140	225	—

KM# 19 3 PFENNIG (Dreier)
Silver **Obv:** Crowned Gothic G **Rev:** III, date above

Date	Mintage	VG	F	VF	XF	Unc
16Z1	—	25.00	40.00	65.00	120	—

KM# 20 3 PFENNIG (Dreier)
Silver **Note:** Varieties exist.

Date	Mintage	VG	F	VF	XF	Unc
16Z1	—	16.00	30.00	55.00	120	—

KM# 25 3 PFENNIG (Dreier)
Silver **Obv:** Crowned Gothic G **Rev:** Imperial orb with 3 divides date **Note:** Kipper 3 Pfennig.

Date	Mintage	VG	F	VF	XF	Unc
16ZZ	—	25.00	40.00	65.00	120	—
1623	—	25.00	40.00	65.00	120	—

KM# A30 3 PFENNIG (Dreier)
Silver **Obv:** Crowned ornate "G" **Rev:** Imperial orb with 3 divides date

Date	Mintage	VG	F	VF	XF	Unc
1635	—	33.00	60.00	120	200	—

KM# 35 3 PFENNIG (Dreier)
Silver **Obv:** Crowned Gothic G between two stars **Note:** Varieties exist.

Date	Mintage	VG	F	VF	XF	Unc
1657	—	27.00	55.00	100	175	—
1658	—	27.00	55.00	100	175	—
1659	—	27.00	55.00	100	175	—
1674	—	27.00	55.00	100	175	—
1675	—	27.00	55.00	100	175	—
1684 ILA	—	27.00	55.00	100	175	—

KM# 36 3 PFENNIG (Dreier)
Silver **Obv:** Crowned Gothic G, GOTTINGEN above

Date	Mintage	VG	F	VF	XF	Unc
1658	—	—	—	—	—	—

KM# 55 3 PFENNIG (Dreier)
Silver **Obv:** Crowned Gothic G divides date **Rev:** Imperial orb with 3 between two stars

Date	Mintage	VG	F	VF	XF	Unc
1672	—	—	—	—	—	—

KM# 21 4 PFENNIG
Copper **Obv:** Crowned Gothic G **Rev:** IIII, date above **Note:** Kipper 4 Pfennig.

Date	Mintage	VG	F	VF	XF	Unc
16Z1	—	20.00	40.00	70.00	125	—

KM# 22 4 PFENNIG
Copper **Note:** Similar to 3 Pfennig, KM#20 but IIII.

Date	Mintage	VG	F	VF	XF	Unc
16Z1	—	16.00	30.00	55.00	110	—

KM# 23 4 PFENNIG
Copper **Rev:** IIII, date above

Date	Mintage	VG	F	VF	XF	Unc
16Z1	—	20.00	40.00	70.00	125	—

KM# 24 4 PFENNIG
Copper **Rev:** Value 4

Date	Mintage	VG	F	VF	XF	Unc
16Z1	—	—	—	—	—	—

KM# 45 4 PFENNIG
Silver **Obv:** Crowned Gothic G divides date **Rev:** IIII/G.PEN. (or PENI)

Date	Mintage	VG	F	VF	XF	Unc
1660	—	—	—	—	—	—
1664	—	—	—	—	—	—

KM# 39 MARIENGROSCHEN
Silver **Obv:** Crowned Gothic 'G', date **Obv. Legend:** MO • NO • GOTTIN • **Rev:** Madonna and child with rays around

Date	Mintage	VG	F	VF	XF	Unc
16ZZ	—	45.00	75.00	140	220	—

KM# 37 MARIENGROSCHEN
Silver **Obv:** Crowned Gothic G, date in legend **Rev:** Madonna and child

Date	Mintage	VG	F	VF	XF	Unc
1658	—	33.00	60.00	120	200	—
1659	—	33.00	60.00	120	200	—
1660	—	33.00	60.00	120	200	—

KM# 5 1/24 THALER (Groschen)
Silver **Obv:** Crowned Gothic G **Rev:** Imperial orb with 24 divides date, titles of Rudolf II

Date	Mintage	VG	F	VF	XF	Unc
1601	—	20.00	40.00	70.00	120	—
1601-7	—	20.00	40.00	70.00	120	—
1602	—	20.00	40.00	70.00	120	—
1603	—	20.00	40.00	70.00	120	—
1605	—	20.00	40.00	70.00	120	—
1606 HL	—	20.00	40.00	70.00	120	—
1606	—	20.00	40.00	70.00	120	—

KM# 8 1/24 THALER (Groschen)
Silver **Note:** Klippe.

Date	Mintage	VG	F	VF	XF	Unc
1603 Rare	—	—	—	—	—	—
1605	—	—	—	—	—	—
1606	—	—	—	—	—	—

KM# A9 1/24 THALER (Groschen)
Silver **Rev:** Without value Z4 in imperial orb **Note:** The dies for this coin may have been intended to strike goldgulden, but only known in silver.

Date	Mintage	VG	F	VF	XF	Unc
1606	—	20.00	40.00	75.00	130	—

KM# 11 1/24 THALER (Groschen)
Silver **Obv:** Imperial orb with 24 divides date, titles of Rudolf II **Rev:** Crowned Gothic G, but without value Z4 in imperial orb **Note:** Dies for this coin may have been intended to strike goldgulden, but only known in silver.

Date	Mintage	VG	F	VF	XF	Unc
1606	—	20.00	40.00	70.00	120	—

KM# 10 1/24 THALER (Groschen)
Silver **Rev:** Titles of Matthias **Note:** Varieties exist.

Date	Mintage	VG	F	VF	XF	Unc
1610	—	25.00	50.00	70.00	125	—
1614	553,000	25.00	50.00	70.00	125	—
1615	1,307,000	25.00	50.00	70.00	125	—
1615	Inc. above	25.00	50.00	70.00	125	—
1616	2,094,000	25.00	50.00	70.00	125	—
1617	1,676,000	25.00	50.00	70.00	125	—
1618	1,751,000	25.00	50.00	70.00	125	—
1619	1,368,000	25.00	50.00	70.00	125	—
1619	Inc. above	25.00	50.00	70.00	125	—
1620	1,912,000	25.00	50.00	70.00	125	—
ND	—	25.00	50.00	70.00	125	—

KM# 12 1/24 THALER (Groschen)
Silver **Note:** Klippe.

Date	Mintage	VG	F	VF	XF	Unc
1614	—	—	—	—	—	—
1617	—	—	—	—	—	—

KM# 14 1/8 THALER (1/2 Reichsort)
Silver **Obv:** Crowned ornate 'G' superimposed on cross in circle **Obv. Legend:** MONETA • NOVA GOTTINGENSIS • **Rev:** Date, titles of Ferdinand II

Date	Mintage	VG	F	VF	XF	Unc
16Z4	—	—	—	—	—	—

KM# 29 1/4 THALER
Silver **Obv:** Small crowned Gothic G in ornamented frame divides date 1-6/Z-6 **Rev:** Crowned imperial eagle, orb on breast, titles of Ferdinand II

Date	Mintage	VG	F	VF	XF	Unc
1626 IEV	—	—	—	—	—	—

KM# 30 1/4 THALER
Silver **Obv:** Crowned Gothic G, date in legend

Date	Mintage	VG	F	VF	XF	Unc
1627 IE	—	—	—	—	—	—

KM# 43 1/2 THALER
Silver **Obv:** City arms in ornamented shield within circle, mintmaster's symbol and date **Obv. Legend:** MONETA • NOVA • GOTTINGENSIS **Rev:** Crowned imperial eagle, orb on breast, titles of Ferdinand II

Date	Mintage	VG	F	VF	XF	Unc
16Z4 (i)	—	—	—	—	—	—

KM# 44 1/2 THALER
Silver **Obv:** Large crowned 'G' superimposed on cross in circle, date **Obv. Legend:** MONET • NOVA GOTT **Rev:** Crowned imperial eagle, orb on breast, titles of Ferdinand II

Date	Mintage	VG	F	VF	XF	Unc
16Z8 IE(k)	—	—	—	—	—	—

KM# 46 1/2 THALER
Silver **Obv:** Crowned imperial eagle, orb on breast, titles of Leopold I **Rev:** Helmeted arms, crowned Gothic G above divides date

Date	Mintage	VG	F	VF	XF	Unc
1660 PL Rare	—	—	—	—	—	—

KM# 47 2/3 THALER (Gulden)
Silver **Obv:** Crowned imperial eagle, orb on breast, titles of Leopold I **Rev:** Helmeted arms, Gothic G above divides date

Date	Mintage	VG	F	VF	XF	Unc
1660 PL Rare	—	—	—	—	—	—

KM# 27 THALER
Silver **Obv:** Crowned imperial eagle, orb on breast, titles of Ferdinand II **Rev:** Helmeted arms, date in legend **Note:** Dav. #5330.

Date	Mintage	F	VF	XF	Unc	BU
1624 VB Rare	—	—	—	—	—	—

KM# 28 THALER
Silver **Obv:** Crowned Gothic G in ornate frame, date in legend **Note:** Dav. #5331.

Date	Mintage	F	VF	XF	Unc	BU
1625 VB Rare	—	—	—	—	—	—

KM# 38 THALER
Silver **Obv:** Crowned imperial eagle, 24 in orb on breast, titles of Leopold I **Rev:** Helmeted arms, Gothic G above divides date **Note:** Dav. #5332.

Date	Mintage	F	VF	XF	Unc	BU
1659 PL Rare	—	—	—	—	—	—

KM# 40 2 THALER
Silver **Obv:** Crowned Imperial Eagle, 24 in orb on breast, titles of Leopold I **Rev:** Helmeted arms, Gothis 'G' above divides date **Note:** Struck from same dies as KM#38.

Date	Mintage	VG	F	VF	XF	Unc
1659 PL Rare	—	—	—	—	—	—

TRADE COINAGE

KM# A48 3 DUCAT
10.1900 g., 0.9860 Gold 0.3230 oz. AGW **Obv:** Shield of arms in inner circle **Rev:** Crowned Imperial Eagle in inner circle

Date	Mintage	VG	F	VF	XF	Unc
1660 PL Rare	—	—	—	—	—	—

KM# 48 4 DUCAT
14.0000 g., 0.9860 Gold 0.4438 oz. AGW **Obv:** Shield of arms in inner circle **Rev:** Crowned imperial eagle in inner circle **Note:** Fr.#1073.

Date	Mintage	VG	F	VF	XF	Unc
1660 Rare	—	—	—	—	—	—

PATTERNS

Including off metal strikes

KM#	Date	Mintage	Identification	Mkt Val
Pn1	1660 PL	—	2/3 Thaler. Lead. KM#47.	—

GREIFSWALD

Located near the Baltic coast about 18 miles (30 kilometers) southeast of Stralsund, Greifswald was an important trading center in Pomerania. Originally founded by merchants and traders from Holland about 1240, the town obtained civic rights from the duke of Pomerania some ten years later. In 1270, Greifswald allied itself with the Hanseatic League and obtained the mint right in 1398. Issues of silver small denominations continued into the 16th century. The city was besieged by the Swedes in 1631 and the Imperial Colonel Franz Ludwig Perusi, who commanded the defending garrison, had emergency coinage struck. After the capitulation of the imperial forces, Sweden held the city for most of the time between 1631 and 1715, then Denmark obtained it for a short while until 1721. After the Danish interlude, Greifswald returned to Swedish control until 1815, when all of Pomerania still held by Sweden was taken by Prussia.

ARMS

Field of cross-hatching divided by horizontal bar with a pellet in center.

REFERENCES

Sch = Wolfgang Schulten, ***Deutsche Münzen aus der Zeit Karls V.***, Frankfurt am Main, 1976.

S = Hugo Frhr. Von Saurma-Jeltsch, **Die Saurmasche Münzsammlung deutscher, schweizerischer und polnischer Gepräge von etwa dem Beginn der Groschenzeit bis zur Kipperperiode**, Berlin, 1892.

Friedrich Wiegand, "Das Notgeld der Stadt Greifswald vom Jahre 1631," **Berlineer Münzblätter** 33 (1912), pp. 275-80.

NOTE: All siege coinage of Greifswald is rare.

CITY

OBSIDIONAL COINAGE

KM# 1 SCHILLING
29.0700 g., Lead/Tin, 36-37 mm. **Obv:** Griffin left, front foot on tree stump, divides date, value 'I' above, all in pointillate circle **Obv. Legend:** NECESSITAS. GRYPSWALDENSIS. **Rev:** Crowned imperial eagle, shield of city arms on breast, in pointillate circle **Rev. Legend:** FERD. II. ROM. IMPF. SEMP. AVGVST &c.

Date	Mintage	VG	F	VF	XF	Unc
1631	—	650	900	1,250	1,500	—

KM# 2 SCHILLING
Lead Or Pewter **Note:** Uniface. Griffin rampant left on tree stump with new branches divides date, value 1 above, GRYPSWALDENSIS in legend, smaller module.

Date	Mintage	VG	F	VF	XF	Unc
1631 Rare	—	—	—	—	—	—

KM# 3 2 SCHILLING
Lead/Tin, 33 mm. **Obv:** Griffin left, front foot on tree stump, divides date, value 'II' above, all in pointillate circle **Obv. Legend:** NECESSITAS. GRYPSWALDENSIS. **Rev:** Crowned imperial eagle, shield of city arms on breast, in pointillate circle **Rev. Legend:** FERD. II. ROM. IMPF. SEMP. AVGVST &c.

Date	Mintage	VG	F	VF	XF	Unc
1631 Rare	—	—	—	—	—	—

KM# 4 3 SCHILLING
Lead/Tin, 40 mm. **Obv:** Griffin left, front foot on tree stump, divides date, value 'III' above, in pointillate circle **Obv. Legend:** NECESSITAS. GRYPESWALDIÆ. **Rev:** Crowned imperial eagle, shield of city arms on breast, in pointillate circle. **Rev. Legend:** FERD. II. ROM. IMPF. SEMP. AVGVST &c.

Date	Mintage	VG	F	VF	XF	Unc
1631 Rare	—	—	—	—	—	—

KM# 5 4 SCHILLING
Lead/Tin, 37 mm. **Obv:** Griffin left, front foot on tree stump, divides date, value 'IIII' above, all in pointillate circle **Obv. Legend:** NECESSITAS. GRYPSWALDIÆ. **Rev:** Crowned imperial eagle, shield of city arms on breast, in pointillate circle **Rev. Legend:** FERD. II. ROM. IMPF. SEMP. AVGVST &c. **Note:** Also known in single example struck in silver.

Date	Mintage	VG	F	VF	XF	Unc
1631 Rare	—	—	—	—	—	—

GRONSFELD

(Gronsveld, Gronsvelt)

The free barony of Gronsfeld was located southeast of Maastricht, near the Netherlands – German border. It was acquired by the countship of Bronkhorst-Batenburg by marriage in 1432. The lordship of Alpen was added by marriage in 1450. The rank of count was granted by the emperor in either 1585 or 1588. The ruling line became extinct in 1719 and Gronsfeld was divided among several heirs. A portion went to Diepenbroich, centered on Empel, near the Rhine in Westphalia. The other part was inherited by the countship of Töring, which was vassal to Limburg-Styrum.

RULERS

Johann II, 1588-1617
Jobst Maximilian, 1617-1662
Johann Franz, 1662-1719

MINT OFFICIALS' INITIALS

Initials	Date	Name
PN	1680-98	Peter Newers, mintmaster in Cologne

ARMS

Batenburg – crowned rampant lion left
Gronsfeld – 3 globes or spheres, usually arranged in triangular shape

REFERENCE.

P.J.A.M. van Daalen, ***De Munten van het Graafschap Gronsveld.*** Gronsveld, 1964.

COUNTY

STANDARD COINAGE

KM# 13 4 MYTE
Copper **Obv:** Eagle, date **Rev:** Value: IIII

Date	Mintage	Good	VG	F	VF	XF
(16)38	—	20.00	40.00	85.00	—	—

KM# 3 DUIT
Copper **Obv:** Bust right **Obv. Legend:** IOES • COMES • D • BRONE • **Rev:** Crowned four-fold arms with central shield **Rev. Legend:** IN • GRON • BAR D BE •

Date	Mintage	Good	VG	F	VF	XF
ND(1588-1617)	—	25.00	45.00	100	170	—

KM# 4 DUIT
Copper **Obv:** Bust left **Obv. Legend:** IOES • COMES • D • BRONCE • **Rev:** Crowned four-fold arms with central shield **Rev. Legend:** IN • GRON • BARO • D • BAT • I •

Date	Mintage	Good	VG	F	VF	XF
ND(1588-1617)	—	25.00	45.00	100	170	—

KM# 8 DUIT
Copper **Obv:** Crowned shield of Batenburg lion in wreath **Rev:** Inscription in wreath, small shield of Gronsfeld arms at top **Rev. Inscription:** CO/ METAT/ GRON

Date	Mintage	Good	VG	F	VF	XF
ND(1617-62)	—	27.00	55.00	115	180	—

KM# 11 DUIT
Copper **Obv:** Crowned shield of Batenburg arms divides date in wreath **Rev:** Inscription in wreath, small Gronsfeld arms at bottom **Rev. Inscription:** IN/ GRON/ CVS

Date	Mintage	Good	VG	F	VF	XF
1636	—	27.00	55.00	115	180	—

KM# 5 OORD (1/4 Stuiver = 2 Duit)
Copper **Obv:** Crowned four-fold arms with central shield **Obv. Legend:** Titles of Johann II **Rev:** Three small shield of arms, two above one, small crown over all, titles continuous

Date	Mintage	Good	VG	F	VF	XF
ND(1588-1617)	—	27.00	65.00	120	200	—

KM# 9 OORD (1/4 Stuiver = 2 Duit)
Copper **Obv:** Crowned B-E over G in circle **Obv. Legend:** Titles of Jobst Maximilian **Rev:** Crowned four-fold arms with central shield in circle, titles continuous

Date	Mintage	Good	VG	F	VF	XF
ND(1617-62)	—	22.00	45.00	90.00	170	—

KM# 10 OORD (1/4 Stuiver = 2 Duit)
Copper **Obv:** Crowned four-fold arms with central shield **Obv. Legend:** Titles of Jobst Maximilian **Rev:** Four small shields of arms below large crown

Date	Mintage	Good	VG	F	VF	XF
ND(1617-62)	—	22.00	45.00	90.00	170	—

KM# 12 OORD (1/4 Stuiver = 2 Duit)
Copper **Obv:** Crowned bust left **Obv. Legend:** Titles of Jobst Maximilian **Rev:** Crowned four-fold arms with central shield **Rev. Legend:** Titles of Ferdinand III

Date	Mintage	Good	VG	F	VF	XF
ND(1637-62)	—	16.00	40.00	85.00	160	—

KM# 18 1/3 THALER (1/2 Gulden)
Silver **Obv:** Crowned arms **Obv. Legend:** Titles of Johann Franz **Rev:** Value 1/3 divides date **Rev. Legend:** Titles continuous

Date	Mintage	Good	VG	F	VF	XF
1688 PN	—	135	275	600	—	—
1692 PN	—	135	275	600	—	—
1693 PN	—	135	275	600	—	—

KM# 19 2/3 THALER (Gulden)
Silver **Obv:** Crowned arms **Obv. Legend:** Titles of Johann Franz **Rev:** Value 2/3 divides date **Rev. Legend:** Titles continuous

Date	Mintage	Good	VG	F	VF	XF
1688 PN	—	260	400	850	—	—
1692 PN	—	260	400	850	—	—
1693 PN	—	260	400	850	—	—

KM# 20 2/3 THALER (Gulden)
Silver **Obv:** Crowned eight-fold arms, left four have central shield of Gronsfeld, date **Obv. Legend:** Titles of Johann Franz **Rev:** Crowned script CBE monogram with palm fronds on either side, value 2/3 in oval below

Date	Mintage	Good	VG	F	VF	XF
1692 PN	—	200	400	850	—	—
1693 PN	—	200	400	850	—	—
ND PN	—	200	400	850	—	—

KM# 21 2/3 THALER (Gulden)
Silver **Obv:** Bust left **Obv. Legend:** Titles of Johann Franz **Rev:** Crowned manifold arms divide date and mintmaster's initials

Date	Mintage	Good	VG	F	VF	XF
1693 PN	—	200	400	850	—	—
1694 PN	—	200	400	850	—	—

KM# 16 THALER
Silver **Ruler:** Jobst Maximilian **Obv:** 4-line inscription, "Jehovah" in Hebrew above, ornament below **Rev:** Crowned arms in double legend **Note:** Dav. #4502. Prev. KM#10.

Date	Mintage	VG	F	VF	XF	Unc
ND(1658)	—	550	900	1,500	2,500	—

KM# 17 THALER
Silver **Ruler:** Jobst Maximilian **Obv:** Date below inscription **Rev:** Large crowned arms within single legend **Note:** Dav. #4503. Prev. KM#11.

Date	Mintage	VG	F	VF	XF	Unc
1658	—	1,000	2,000	4,000	6,500	—

KM# 15 2 THALER
57.9000 g., Silver, 56 mm. **Ruler:** Jobst Maximilian **Obv:** 4-line inscription, "Jehovah" in Hebrew above dividing date, ornament below **Rev:** Crowned arms in double legend **Note:** Klippe. Dav. #4501. Prev. KM#5.

Date	Mintage	VG	F	VF	XF	Unc
1642 Rare	—	—	—	—	—	—

Note: Hess-Divo AG Auction 300, 10-04, VF realized approximately $65,840.

TRADE COINAGE

KM# 14 DUCAT
3.4140 g., 0.9860 Gold 0.1082 oz. AGW **Ruler:** Jobst Maximilian **Obv:** Crowned four-fold arms with central shield **Obv. Legend:** MO • NO • AV • IVST • MAX • C • A • BR • IN • GR • **Rev:** Inscription in circle **Rev. Legend:** Titles continuous **Rev. Inscription:** date/ IVSTVS/ VI PALMA/ FLORE/ BIT **Note:** Prev. Fr. #153.

Date	Mintage	VG	F	VF	XF	Unc
ND	—	700	1,400	2,500	4,050	—
1641	—	700	1,400	2,500	4,050	—
1642	—	700	1,400	2,500	4,050	—
1657	—	700	1,400	2,500	4,050	—
1664	—	700	1,400	2,500	4,050	—

GUBEN

A provincial town located about 25 miles south-southwest of Frankfurt am Oder. Guben passed to Brandenburg in about 1311 and then to Bohemia in 1368. Local coins were struck there during the Kipper Period of the Thirty Years' War. The town belonged to Saxony from 1635 until 1815 when it reverted to Prussia.

Initial	Date	Name
ZL	Ca.1622	Unknown

TOWN

REGULAR COINAGE

KM# 3 PFENNIG
Copper **Obv:** Pfennig symbol in G **Note:** Uniface. Varieties exist.

Date	Mintage	VG	F	VF	XF	Unc
16Z1	—	25.00	45.00	85.00	145	—
1621	—	25.00	45.00	85.00	145	—
16ZZ	—	25.00	45.00	85.00	145	—
1622	—	25.00	45.00	85.00	145	—

KM# 1 PFENNIG
Copper **Obv:** Large crown above G divides date **Note:** Kipper Pfennig. Uniface. Varieties exist.

Date	Mintage	VG	F	VF	XF	Unc
16Z1	—	25.00	45.00	85.00	145	—
1621	—	25.00	45.00	85.00	145	—

Note: Above are possibly issues of Gorlitz

KM# 2 PFENNIG
Copper **Obv:** Small crown above large G divides date, dot in center **Note:** Uniface.

Date	Mintage	VG	F	VF	XF	Unc
16Z1	—	25.00	45.00	85.00	145	—
1621	—	25.00	45.00	85.00	145	—

KM# 4 3 KREUZER (Groschen)
Silver **Obv:** Crowned imperial eagle, 3 in orb on breast, titles of Ferdinand II **Rev:** Crown above triple-turreated gate, date in legend **Note:** Kipper 3 Kreuzer.

Date	Mintage	VG	F	VF	XF	Unc
1621	—	—	—	—	—	—
1622	—	—	—	—	—	—

KM# 5 3 KREUZER (Groschen)
Silver **Obv:** Bust right, titles of Ferdinand II **Rev:** Crowned triple-turreted gate, wtih G, 3 in oval below

Date	Mintage	VG	F	VF	XF	Unc
(1)622 ZL Rare	—	—	—	—	—	—

KM# 6 1/24 THALER (Groschen)
Silver **Obv:** Imperial orb with 24, titles of Ferdinand II **Rev:** Gothic G in circle, crown above divides date **Note:** Kipper 1/24 Thaler. Varieties exist.

Date	Mintage	VG	F	VF	XF	Unc
1622	—	33.00	65.00	120	200	—

GUTENBURG

Iron mine and smelter in Baden operated by the Benedictine Abbey of St. Blasien. With the backing of the House of Schwarzenberg in 1694, 600 gulden worth of copper coins in the denominations of 1, 3, 15 Creuzer and 1 Gulden were minted to pay the workers.

ABBEY

REGULAR COINAGE

KM# 1 CREUZER
Copper

Date	Mintage	VG	F	VF	XF	Unc
1694	—	650	1,200	3,000	—	—

KM# 2 III (3) CREUZER
1.5400 g., Copper

Date	Mintage	VG	F	VF	XF	Unc
1694	—	100	200	400	750	—

KM# 3 XV (15) CREUZER
4.2200 g., Copper

Date	Mintage	VG	F	VF	XF	Unc
1694	—	75.00	175	375	850	—

KM# 4 GULDEN
11.4100 g., Copper

Date	Mintage	VG	F	VF	XF	Unc
1694	—	175	450	950	1,750	—

HAGENAU

A city located in Alsace north of Strasburg, emerged in the 12th century. In 1257 it became a free imperial city but did not obtain the mint right until the 16th century. Although it went with other parts of Alsace to France in 1648, coins continued to be minted in the emperor's name. In 1679 it was completely absorbed into France.

MINT OFFICIALS' INITIALS

Initial	Date	Name
	1600-1624	Philipp Wulvesheim, Mint Superintendant
	1600-1603 (d.1604)	Jakob Dietrich
	1600-1622	Hans Zaberer, Warden
	1603-1606	Ernst Knorr
	1606-1625	Hans Caspar Mock, Mintmaster
	1625-1634 (d.1636)	Mint Superintendant
	1622-ca.1630	Jakob Zeck, Warden
	1625-1630	Andreas Welland
	1630-1634	Johann Modersdorfer
	1634-1636	Johann Christian Herrmann, Mint Superintendant
(p) or GHP	1664-1673	Georg Hartmann Plappert

FREE IMPERIAL CITY

REGULAR COINAGE

KM# 5 HELLER
Silver **Obv:** Rose **Rev:** Rose

Date	Mintage	VG	F	VF	XF	Unc
ND Rare	—	—	—	—	—	—

KM# 14 PFENNIG
Silver **Note:** Uniface. Schussel type. City arms, H above.

Date	Mintage	VG	F	VF	XF	Unc
ND(ca.1603/5)	754,000	20.00	35.00	65.00	120	—

KM# 15 PFENNIG
Silver **Note:** Schussel type. Rose with H in center.

Date	Mintage	VG	F	VF	XF	Unc
ND(ca.1603/5)	Inc. above	16.00	33.00	60.00	100	—

KM# 18 PFENNIG
Silver **Obv:** Rose **Rev:** Rose

Date	Mintage	VG	F	VF	XF	Unc
ND(ca.1608/14)	523,000	16.00	33.00	60.00	100	—

KM# 40 PFENNIG
Silver **Note:** Uniface.

Date	Mintage	VG	F	VF	XF	Unc
ND(ca.1625/6)	226,000	13.00	27.00	40.00	65.00	—

KM# 17 KREUZER
Silver **Obv:** City arms, date above **Rev:** Crowned imperial eagle, 1 in orb on breast, titles of Rudolf II

Date	Mintage	VG	F	VF	XF	Unc
1604 3 known	—	—	—	—	—	—

KM# 50 KREUZER
Silver **Rev:** Titles of Leopold I

Date	Mintage	VG	F	VF	XF	Unc
1664	—	13.00	27.00	45.00	90.00	—
1668	—	13.00	27.00	45.00	90.00	—
1669	—	13.00	27.00	45.00	90.00	—
1670	—	13.00	27.00	45.00	90.00	—
1671	—	13.00	27.00	45.00	90.00	—

KM# 41 2 KREUZER (1/2 Batzen)
Silver **Obv:** Similar to KM#51 **Rev:** Value II/KREUTZ/ER, titles of Ferdinand II

Date	Mintage	VG	F	VF	XF	Unc
1625	—	10.00	25.00	45.00	90.00	—
ND	—	9.00	22.00	40.00	85.00	—

KM# 51 2 KREUZER (1/2 Batzen)
Silver **Rev:** Crowned imperial eagle, value 2 in orb on breast, titles of Leopold I

Date	Mintage	VG	F	VF	XF	Unc
1664 (p)	—	10.00	25.00	45.00	90.00	—
1665 (p)	—	10.00	25.00	45.00	90.00	—
1666 (p)	—	10.00	25.00	45.00	90.00	—
1667 (p)	524,000	10.00	25.00	45.00	90.00	—
1668 (p)	—	10.00	25.00	45.00	90.00	—

KM# 6 3 KREUZER (Groschen)
Silver **Rev:** Crowned imperial eagle, value 3 in orb on breast, titles of Rudolf II

Date	Mintage	VG	F	VF	XF	Unc
1601	172,000	16.00	33.00	55.00	100	—
1602	144,000	16.00	33.00	55.00	100	—
1603	67,000	16.00	33.00	55.00	100	—
1604	115,000	16.00	33.00	55.00	100	—
1607	84,000	16.00	33.00	55.00	100	—
1608	44,000	16.00	33.00	55.00	100	—
1610	—	16.00	33.00	55.00	100	—
ND	—	16.00	33.00	55.00	100	—

KM# 16 3 KREUZER (Groschen)
Silver **Note:** Klippe.

Date	Mintage	VG	F	VF	XF	Unc
1603 Rare	—	—	—	—	—	—
1604 Rare	—	—	—	—	—	—

KM# 25 3 KREUZER (Groschen)
Silver **Rev:** Titles of Matthias

Date	Mintage	VG	F	VF	XF	Unc
ND(1612-19) Rare	—	—	—	—	—	—

KM# 11 4 KREUZER (Batzen)

Silver **Obv:** City arms, date above **Rev:** Crowned imperial eagle, 4 in orb on breast, titles of Rudolf II

Date	Mintage	VG	F	VF	XF	Unc
1601	—	40.00	85.00	145	220	—
1602	—	40.00	85.00	145	220	—
1603	—	40.00	85.00	145	220	—
1604	—	40.00	85.00	145	220	—
1607	—	40.00	85.00	145	220	—
1608	—	40.00	85.00	145	220	—
1609	—	40.00	85.00	145	220	—

KM# 12 4 KREUZER (Batzen)

Silver **Obv:** Shield ornately-shaped, no date

Date	Mintage	VG	F	VF	XF	Unc
ND 3 known	—	—	—	—	—	—

KM# 36 4 KREUZER (Batzen)

Silver **Obv:** City arms **Rev:** RAHTS/GELT, titles of Ferdinand II in legend

Date	Mintage	VG	F	VF	XF	Unc
ND	7,000	100	175	350	475	—

KM# 55 4 KREUZER (Batzen)

Silver **Obv:** City arms, date above **Rev:** RAHTS/GELT/date, titles of Leopold I

Date	Mintage	VG	F	VF	XF	Unc
1666	—	100	175	350	475	—
1667	—	100	175	350	475	—

KM# 37 12 KREUZER (Zwölfer = Dreibätzner/3 Batzen)

4.2200 g., Silver **Obv:** City arms, date above **Rev:** Crowned imperial eagle, orb with value "IZ" on breast, titles of Ferdinand II **Note:** Kipper 12 Kreuzer.

Date	Mintage	VG	F	VF	XF	Unc
1621	—	120	260	425	625	—
ND(1621/2)	—	85.00	170	350	500	—

KM# 39 12 KREUZER (Zwölfer = Dreibätzner/3 Batzen)

4.2200 g., Silver **Rev. Legend:** IVSTITIA MAMET IN AETER

Date	Mintage	VG	F	VF	XF	Unc
1623 Rare	—	—	—	—	—	—

KM# 42 12 KREUZER (Zwölfer = Dreibätzner/3 Batzen)

4.2200 g., Silver

Date	Mintage	VG	F	VF	XF	Unc
1625	71,000	55.00	115	220	325	—
1626	Inc. above	55.00	115	220	325	—

KM# 53 12 KREUZER (Zwölfer = Dreibätzner/3 Batzen)

4.2200 g., Silver **Obv:** Date in legend

Date	Mintage	VG	F	VF	XF	Unc
1665	—	45.00	90.00	175	245	—

KM# 58 12 KREUZER (Zwölfer = Dreibätzner/3 Batzen)

4.2200 g., Silver **Obv:** Similar to KM#53 but plain arms without ornaments

Date	Mintage	VG	F	VF	XF	Unc
ND	—	60.00	115	200	375	—

KM# 52 12 KREUZER (Zwölfer = Dreibätzner/3 Batzen)

4.2200 g., Silver **Obv:** Similar to KM#53 but date above city arms **Rev:** Titles of Leopold I **Note:** Varieties exist.

Date	Mintage	VG	F	VF	XF	Unc
1665	—	45.00	100	175	250	—
1666	—	45.00	100	175	250	—
1667	10,000	45.00	100	175	250	—
1668	10,000	45.00	100	175	250	—
1669	—	45.00	100	175	250	—

KM# 28.1 18 KREUZER (1/4 Thaler = Dicken)

Silver **Obv:** Ornate city arms **Obv. Legend:** HAGENOIA * IMPERII * CANERA **Rev:** Crowned imperial eagle, orb on breast **Rev. Legend:** IVSTITIA.MANET

Date	Mintage	VG	F	VF	XF	Unc
ND(c.1614)	38,000	55.00	120	200	350	—

KM# 29 18 KREUZER (1/4 Thaler = Dicken)

Silver **Note:** Klippe.

Date	Mintage	VG	F	VF	XF	Unc
ND Rare	—	—	—	—	—	—

KM# 28.2 18 KREUZER (1/4 Thaler = Dicken)

Silver **Obv:** Plain city arms **Obv. Legend:** IVSTITIA. MANET... **Rev:** Crowned imperial eagle, orb on breast **Note:** Prev. KM#28.

Date	Mintage	VG	F	VF	XF	Unc
1614	501,000	40.00	85.00	145	250	—

KM# 38 18 KREUZER (1/4 Thaler = Dicken)

Silver **Note:** Kipper 18 Kreuzer.

Date	Mintage	VG	F	VF	XF	Unc
1621	—	115	200	300	425	—

KM# 56 30 KREUZER (1/2 Gulden)

Silver

Date	Mintage	VG	F	VF	XF	Unc
1668	4,000	200	300	425	600	—
1669	—	200	300	425	600	—
1671	4,000	200	300	425	600	—

KM# 65 30 KREUZER (1/2 Gulden)

Silver **Obv:** Not enclosed in circles **Rev:** Not enclosed in circles

Date	Mintage	VG	F	VF	XF	Unc
1673 2 known	—	—	—	—	—	—

KM# 35 60 KREUZER (Guldentaler)

Silver **Obv:** City arms in ornate shield **Rev:** Date divided by eagle's tail, titles of Ferdinand II

Date	Mintage	F	VF	XF	Unc	BU
1620 2 known	—	—	—	—	—	—

KM# 66 60 KREUZER (Guldentaler)

Silver **Obv:** Without inner circles **Rev:** Without inner circles

Date	Mintage	VG	F	VF	XF	Unc
1673	—	425	800	1,400	2,400	—

KM# 57 60 KREUZER (Gulden = 2/3 Thaler)

Silver **Note:** Similar to 30 Kreuzer, KM#56.

Date	Mintage	VG	F	VF	XF	Unc
1668	2,000	450	900	1,500	2,500	—
1669	—	450	900	1,500	2,500	—

KM# 46 THALER

Silver **Obv:** City arms in ornate frame **Obv. Legend:** FERDINANDVS.II.D:G:... **Rev:** Crowned imperial eagle **Note:** Dav. #5333.

Date	Mintage	VG	F	VF	XF	Unc
1635 Rare	—	—	—	—	—	—

KM# 54 THALER

Silver **Obv:** City arms on shield **Obv. Legend:** LEOPOLDVS: I:D:G:... **Rev:** Crowned imperial eagle **Note:** Dav. #5334.

Date	Mintage	VG	F	VF	XF	Unc
1665 GH-P Rare	—	—	—	—	—	—

KM# 59 THALER

Silver **Obv:** City arms **Obv. Legend:** LEOPOLDVS:I:D:G:... **Rev:** Crowned imperial eagle **Rev. Legend:** Ends: ...HGEN **Note:** Dav. #5335.

Date	Mintage	VG	F	VF	XF	Unc
1668 GH-P Rare	—	—	—	—	—	—

TRADE COINAGE

KM# 13 GOLDGULDEN

3.5000 g., 0.9860 Gold 0.1109 oz. AGW **Obv:** Arms of Hagenau with date above in inner circle **Rev:** Crowned imperial eagle in inner circle, titles of Rudolf II

Date	Mintage	VG	F	VF	XF	Unc
1601	2,613	2,100	4,900	8,400	13,500	—
1604	1,474	2,100	4,900	8,400	13,500	—
1608	1,407	2,100	4,900	8,400	13,500	—
1609	670	2,100	4,900	8,400	13,500	—
1610	2,077	2,100	4,900	8,400	13,500	—
1611	1,608	2,100	4,900	8,400	13,500	—

KM# 26 GOLDGULDEN

3.5000 g., 0.9860 Gold 0.1109 oz. AGW **Obv:** St. John standing **Rev:** Imperial eagle, titles of Rudolf II

Date	Mintage	VG	F	VF	XF	Unc
ND	8,308	1,200	2,500	4,500	7,500	—

KM# 27 GOLDGULDEN

3.5000 g., 0.9860 Gold 0.1109 oz. AGW **Rev:** Titles of Matthias

Date	Mintage	VG	F	VF	XF	Unc
ND	5,025	—	—	—	—	—

KM# 45 GOLDGULDEN

3.5000 g., 0.9860 Gold 0.1109 oz. AGW **Rev:** Titles of Ferdinand II

Date	Mintage	VG	F	VF	XF	Unc
1634	1,340	—	—	—	—	—

HALBERSTADT

Bishopric transferred to Halberstadt, about 30 miles southwest of Magdeburg, in 820. Bishops were given the coin right in 989. The town received its charter in 998, and its coin right in 1363. The bishopric was assigned to Brandenburg as a secular principality in 1648. Dated city coinage was struck from 1519-1691.

RULERS

Heinrich Julius of Brunswick-Wolfenbuttel, 1566-1613
Heinrich Karl of Brunswick-Wolfenbuttel, 1613-1615
Rudolf III of Brunswick-Wolfenbuttel, 1615-1616
Christian of Brunswick-Wolfenbuttel, 1616-1624
Christian Wilhelm of Brandenburg-Prussia, 1625-1627
Leopold Wilhelm of Austria, 1627-1648

MINT OFFICIALS' INITIALS

Initial	Date	Name
CZ	1628-31	Christoph Ziegenhorn
HS	1626-72	Henning Schluter in Zellerfeld
HS	1614-26	Henning Schreiber
IA	1653-65	Johann Arendsburg
ICS	1690-95	Johann Christoph Seehte in Magdeburg
(b)	1633-34	Unknown
(c)	1663	Unknown

ARMS

2-fold divided vertically, right half usually shaded.

REFERENCES:

T = Otto Tornau, **Die Halberstädter Münzen der neueren Zeit**, Halberstadt, n.d.

Sch = Wolfgang Schulten, ***Deutsche Münzen aus der Zeit Karls V.***, Frankfurt am Main, 1976.

S = **Hugo Frhr. Von Saurma-Jeltsch**, Die Saurmasche Münzsammlung deutscher, schweizerischer und polnischer Gepräge von etwa dem Beginn der Groschenzeit bis zur Kipperperiode, **Berlin, 1892.**

BISHOPRIC

REGULAR COINAGE

KM# 6 1/24 THALER (Groschen)

Silver **Obv:** Date divided by cross below legend

Date	Mintage	VG	F	VF	XF	Unc
1614	—	16.00	30.00	45.00	75.00	—
1615 (a)	—	16.00	30.00	45.00	75.00	—

KM# 5 1/24 THALER (Groschen)

Silver **Obv:** Ornate helmet above arms **Rev:** Imperial orb with Z4, date divided in legend above, titles of Matthias **Note:** Varieties exist.

Date	Mintage	VG	F	VF	XF	Unc
1614	—	16.00	30.00	45.00	75.00	—
1614 (a)	—	16.00	30.00	45.00	75.00	—
1615 (a)	—	16.00	30.00	45.00	75.00	—
1615	—	16.00	30.00	45.00	75.00	—

KM# 7 1/24 THALER (Groschen)

Silver **Obv:** Value 24 **Note:** Varieties exist.

Date	Mintage	VG	F	VF	XF	Unc
1614	—	16.00	30.00	45.00	75.00	—
1615	—	16.00	30.00	45.00	75.00	—

KM# 9 1/24 THALER (Groschen)

Silver **Obv:** Ornate helmet above arms **Rev:** Imperial orb within circle **Note:** Varieties exist.

Date	Mintage	VG	F	VF	XF	Unc
1616	—	13.00	27.00	45.00	75.00	—
1617	—	13.00	27.00	45.00	75.00	—
1617 (a)	—	13.00	27.00	45.00	75.00	—
1618 (a)	—	13.00	27.00	45.00	75.00	—
1618 HS	—	13.00	27.00	45.00	75.00	—
1618	—	13.00	27.00	45.00	75.00	—
1619	—	13.00	27.00	45.00	75.00	—

KM# 10 1/24 THALER (Groschen)

Silver **Obv:** Value 24

Date	Mintage	VG	F	VF	XF	Unc
1616	—	16.00	30.00	45.00	75.00	—
1619	—	16.00	30.00	45.00	75.00	—

KM# 13 1/24 THALER (Groschen)

Silver **Obv:** Date divided by cross below legend

Date	Mintage	VG	F	VF	XF	Unc
1618	—	16.00	30.00	45.00	75.00	—

KM# 22 1/24 THALER (Groschen)

Silver **Obv:** Titles of Ferdinand II

Date	Mintage	VG	F	VF	XF	Unc
16ZZ	—	16.00	33.00	55.00	80.00	—
16Z3	—	16.00	33.00	55.00	80.00	—

KM# 55 1/24 THALER (Groschen)

Silver **Obv:** Helmeted oval arms **Rev:** Imperial orb with 4Z (error), date divided in legend at top

Date	Mintage	VG	F	VF	XF	Unc
1628 CZ	—	16.00	33.00	55.00	80.00	—

KM# 51 1/8 THALER

Silver **Subject:** Death of Christian **Obv:** Crowned 11-fold arms, double legends around **Rev:** 10-line inscription with Roman numeral date

Date	Mintage	VG	F	VF	XF	Unc
MDCXXVII (1627) HS Error	—	—	—	—	—	—

KM# 41 1/2 REICHSORT (1/8 Thaler)

Silver **Obv:** Oval arms in baroque frame below divide date **Obv. Legend:** EIN./HALB.REIC./ORT **Rev:** St. Stephen standing

Date	Mintage	VG	F	VF	XF	Unc
16Z5	—	—	—	—	—	—

KM# 46 1/4 THALER

Silver **Subject:** Death of Christian **Obv:** Crowned 11-fold arms, double legends around **Rev:** 8-line inscription with Roman numeral date

Date	Mintage	VG	F	VF	XF	Unc
1626 HS	—	—	—	—	—	—

KM# 59 1/4 THALER

Silver **Obv:** Oval arms in baroque frame **Rev:** St. Stephen standing divides date **Note:** Varieties exist.

Date	Mintage	VG	F	VF	XF	Unc
1629 CZ	—	60.00	120	225	375	—
1631 CZ	—	60.00	120	225	375	—

KM# 69 1/4 THALER

Silver **Obv:** Helmeted oval arms

Date	Mintage	VG	F	VF	XF	Unc
1631 CZ	—	65.00	140	240	400	—

KM# 42 REICHSORT (1/4 Thaler)

Silver **Obv:** Oval arms in baroque frame below divide date **Obv. Legend:** EIN.ORTS.THA/LER **Rev:** St. Stephen standing

Date	Mintage	VG	F	VF	XF	Unc
16Z5 (a)	—	—	—	—	—	—

KM# 52 REICHSORT (1/4 Thaler)

Silver **Obv:** Oval arms in baroque frame **Rev:** Date **Rev. Legend:** EIN./REICHS./ORTH./

Date	Mintage	VG	F	VF	XF	Unc
16Z8 CZ	—	—	—	—	—	—

KM# 47 1/2 THALER

Silver **Subject:** Death of Christian **Obv:** Crowned 11-fold arms, double legends around **Rev:** 9-line inscription around

Date	Mintage	VG	F	VF	XF	Unc
1626 HS	—	—	—	—	—	—

KM# 45 GULDEN (1/2 Reichsthaler)

Silver **Obv:** Oval arms in baroque frame **Rev:** St. Stephen standing divides date

Date	Mintage	VG	F	VF	XF	Unc
16Z5 HS	—	65.00	135	240	400	—

KM# 53 GULDEN (1/2 Reichsthaler)

Silver **Obv:** Ornately-helmeted oval arms **Note:** Varieties exist.

Date	Mintage	VG	F	VF	XF	Unc
16Z8 CZ	—	55.00	120	200	300	—
1628 CZ	—	55.00	120	200	300	—
16Z9 CZ	—	55.00	120	200	300	—
1629 CZ	—	55.00	120	200	300	—
ND CZ	—	55.00	120	200	300	—

KM# 65 GULDEN (1/2 Reichsthaler)

Silver **Obv:** Date in legend

Date	Mintage	VG	F	VF	XF	Unc
1630 CZ	—	85.00	175	350	550	—
1631 CZ	—	85.00	175	350	550	—

KM# 26 THALER

Silver **Obv:** Titles of Christian around legend **Obv. Legend:** GOTTES/FREVNDT/DER PFAFFEN/FEINDT **Rev:** Arm from cloud on right holding sword upright, date **Rev. Legend:** TOVT.AVEC.DIEV **Note:** Dav.#6320.

Date	Mintage	VG	F	VF	XF	Unc
1622	—	300	650	1,350	2,250	—
16ZZ	—	350	700	1,500	2,500	—

KM# 27 THALER

Silver **Obv. Legend:** FREINDT (error) **Note:** Dav.#6320A.

Date	Mintage	VG	F	VF	XF	Unc
1622	—	400	800	1,650	2,750	—

KM# 28 THALER

Silver **Rev:** Jesuit cap on point of sword **Note:** Dav.#6322.

Date	Mintage	VG	F	VF	XF	Unc
1622	—	500	900	1,750	3,500	—

KM# 29 THALER

Silver **Rev:** Crown on point of sword **Note:** Dav.#6323.

Date	Mintage	VG	F	VF	XF	Unc
1622	—	600	1,200	2,000	4,000	—

KM# 38 THALER

Silver **Obv:** 5 helmets above 11-fold arms, titles of Christian **Rev:** Wildman, tree trunk in right hand **Rev. Legend:** HONESTUM.PRO.PATRIA.ANNO. date HS **Note:** Dav.#6324.

Date	Mintage	VG	F	VF	XF	Unc
1623 HS	—	650	1,250	2,300	4,500	—

KM# 39 THALER

Silver **Rev. Legend:** DEO.ET.PATRIAE.ANNO. date HS **Note:** Dav.#6325.

Date	Mintage	VG	F	VF	XF	Unc
1623 HS	—	650	1,250	2,300	4,500	—

KM# 40 THALER

Silver **Obv:** Ornately-helmeted oval arms **Rev:** St. Stephen standing divides date **Note:** Dav.#5339.

Date	Mintage	VG	F	VF	XF	Unc
16Z3	—	150	300	475	775	—

KM# 43 THALER

Silver **Obv:** Helmeted shield **Note:** Dav.#5343.

Date	Mintage	VG	F	VF	XF	Unc
16Z5	—	250	500	800	1,300	—

KM# 48 THALER

Silver **Rev:** Symbol of Mercury below left 1/2 of date **Note:** Dav.#5345.

Date	Mintage	VG	F	VF	XF	Unc
1626 HS	—	250	450	950	1,700	—

KM# 49.1 THALER

Silver **Subject:** Death of Christian **Obv:** Crowned 11-fold arms, double legends broken by crown **Rev:** 10-line inscription with Roman numeral date **Note:** Dav.#6327.

Date	Mintage	VG	F	VF	XF	Unc
1626 HS	—	300	500	1,000	1,850	—

KM# 49.2 THALER

Silver **Obv:** Crown breaks outer legend only **Note:** Dav.#6328. Varieties exist.

Date	Mintage	VG	F	VF	XF	Unc
1626	—	300	600	1,200	2,000	—

KM# 56.1 THALER

Silver **Note:** Similar to KM#56.2. Dav.#5346.

Date	Mintage	VG	F	VF	XF	Unc
16Z8 CZ	—	225	450	750	1,350	—

KM# 56.2 THALER
Silver **Note:** Dav.#5348. Varieties exist.

Date	Mintage	VG	F	VF	XF	Unc
16Z9 CZ	—	95.00	185	325	600	—

KM# 60 THALER
Silver **Obv:** Date divided by helmet **Note:** Dav.#5347.

Date	Mintage	VG	F	VF	XF	Unc
16Z9 CZ	—	125	250	400	650	—

KM# 61 THALER
Silver **Note:** Klippe. Dav.#5347A.

Date	Mintage	VG	F	VF	XF	Unc
16Z9 CZ Rare	—	—	—	—	—	—

KM# 66.1 THALER
Silver **Obv:** Date in legend **Note:** Dav.#5349.

Date	Mintage	VG	F	VF	XF	Unc
1630 CZ	—	175	350	750	1,250	—

KM# 66.2 THALER
Silver **Obv:** Dots between date in outer legend **Note:** Dav.#5351. Varieties exist.

Date	Mintage	VG	F	VF	XF	Unc
1631 CZ	—	175	350	750	1,250	—

KM# 30 1-1/4 THALER
36.0000 g., Silver **Note:** Similar to 1 Thaler, KM#26 with value punched in. Dav.#6322A.

Date	Mintage	VG	F	VF	XF	Unc
16ZZ Rare	—	—	—	—	—	—

KM# 31 1-1/2 THALER
44.0000 g., Silver **Note:** Similar to 1 Thaler, KM#26 with value punched in. Dav.#6322A.

Date	Mintage	VG	F	VF	XF	Unc
16ZZ Rare	—	—	—	—	—	—

KM# 12 2 THALER
Silver **Obv:** Ornately-helmeted pointed oval arms, date divided in legend at top **Rev:** St. Stephen standing **Note:** Dav.#5337.

Date	Mintage	VG	F	VF	XF	Unc
1617 HS Rare	—	—	—	—	—	—

KM# 14 2 THALER
Silver **Obv:** Ornately-helmeted oval arms, date divided by plumes near top **Rev:** St. Stephen standing **Note:** Dav.#5338.

Date	Mintage	VG	F	VF	XF	Unc
1618 Rare	—	—	—	—	—	—
16Z8 CZ Rare	—	—	—	—	—	—

KM# 50 2 THALER
Silver **Subject:** Death of Christian **Obv:** Similar to reverse of 1 Thaler, KM#39 but with date 1620 **Rev:** 8-line inscription with Roman Numeral date **Note:** Mule. Dav.#6326.

Date	Mintage	VG	F	VF	XF	Unc
1620/1626 HS Rare	—	—	—	—	—	—

KM# 33 2 THALER
Silver **Note:** Similar to 1 Thaler, KM#26, but Jesuit cap on point of sword. Dav.#6321.

Date	Mintage	VG	F	VF	XF	Unc
1622 Rare	—	—	—	—	—	—

KM# 32 2 THALER
Silver **Note:** Similar to 1 Thaler, KM#26. Dav.#6319.

Date	Mintage	VG	F	VF	XF	Unc
1622 Rare	—	—	—	—	—	—

KM# 44.1 2 THALER
Silver **Note:** Similar to 1 Thaler, KM#56.

Date	Mintage	VG	F	VF	XF	Unc
16Z5 Rare	—	—	—	—	—	—

KM# 44.2 2 THALER
Silver **Note:** Similar to 1 Thaler, KM#56.2.

Date	Mintage	VG	F	VF	XF	Unc
1626 HS Rare	—	—	—	—	—	—

KM# 70 2 THALER
Silver **Note:** Dav.#5350.

Date	Mintage	VG	F	VF	XF	Unc
1631 CZ Rare	—	—	—	—	—	—

KM# 11 3 THALER
Silver **Obv:** Ornately-helmeted pointed oval arms, date divided in legend at top **Rev:** St. Stephen standing **Note:** Dav.#5336.

Date	Mintage	VG	F	VF	XF	Unc
1617 HS Rare	—	—	—	—	—	—

TRADE COINAGE

KM# 8 GOLDGULDEN
3.5000 g., 0.9860 Gold 0.1109 oz. AGW **Obv:** Arms divide date in inner circle **Rev:** St. Stephen standing in inner circle

Date	Mintage	VG	F	VF	XF	Unc
1615 1 known	1,165	—	—	—	—	—
1616 Rare	1,353	—	—	—	—	—
1617 Rare	594	—	—	—	—	—

KM# 54 GOLDGULDEN
3.5000 g., 0.9860 Gold 0.1109 oz. AGW **Obv:** Helmeted arms in inner circle **Rev:** St. Stephen standing divides date and moneyers initials

Date	Mintage	VG	F	VF	XF	Unc
1628 CZ	—	650	1,250	2,500	4,500	—
ND(1628) CZ	—	650	1,250	2,500	4,500	—

KM# 58 GOLDGULDEN
3.5000 g., 0.9860 Gold 0.1109 oz. AGW **Rev:** Date divided by St. Stephen standing

Date	Mintage	VG	F	VF	XF	Unc
1629	—	650	1,250	2,500	4,500	—
ND(1631)	—	650	1,250	2,500	4,500	—

KM# 34 DUCAT
3.5000 g., 0.9860 Gold 0.1109 oz. AGW **Obv. Inscription:** GOTTES / FREINT / VND / DER PAFFE / FEINT **Note:** Similar to 1 Thaler, KM#26.

Date	Mintage	VG	F	VF	XF	Unc
1622 Rare	—	—	—	—	—	—

KM# 35 2 DUCAT
7.0000 g., 0.9860 Gold 0.2219 oz. AGW **Note:** Similar to 1 Thaler, KM#26.

Date	Mintage	VG	F	VF	XF	Unc
1622 Rare	—	—	—	—	—	—

KM# 36 2 DUCAT
7.0000 g., 0.9860 Gold 0.2219 oz. AGW **Rev:** Jesuit cap on point of sword

Date	Mintage	VG	F	VF	XF	Unc
1622 Rare	—	—	—	—	—	—

KM# 37 10 DUCAT (Portugalöser)
35.0000 g., 0.9860 Gold 1.1095 oz. AGW **Note:** Similar to 1 Thaler, KM#26.

Date	Mintage	VG	F	VF	XF	Unc
1622 Rare	—	—	—	—	—	—

CITY

The city mint functioned from 1651 as a mint for Brandenburg-Prussia.

ARMS
Wolf trap superimposed on episcopal arms

REGULAR COINAGE

KM# 75 PFENNIG
Silver **Note:** Uniface. Schussel-type. City arms, date.

Date	Mintage	VG	F	VF	XF	Unc
1633	—	—	—	—	—	—

KM# 76 3 PFENNIG (Dreier)
Silver **Obv:** City arms **Rev:** Imperial orb with 3

Date	Mintage	VG	F	VF	XF	Unc
1633	—	16.00	33.00	60.00	120	—

KM# 77 1/24 THALER (Groschen)
Silver **Obv:** Helmeted city arms **Obv. Legend:** NACH.REICHS. SCHR:V:KOR **Rev:** Imperial orb with Z4 **Rev. Legend:** MON.NOVA...

Date	Mintage	VG	F	VF	XF	Unc
1633 (b)	—	20.00	40.00	70.00	125	—
1634 (b)	—	20.00	40.00	70.00	125	—

KM# 78.1 THALER
Silver **Obv:** Capped and helmeted small oval arms **Obv. Legend:** MON:NOU:CIU:... **Rev:** St. Stephan standing **Note:** Dav.#5352.

Date	Mintage	VG	F	VF	XF	Unc
1633 (b) Rare	—	—	—	—	—	—

KM# 78.2 THALER
Silver **Obv. Legend:** MONETA.NOVA.ARG:... **Rev:** St. Stephen standing divides date **Note:** Dav.#5355.

Date	Mintage	VG	F	VF	XF	Unc
1663 (c) Rare	—	—	—	—	—	—

KM# 80 THALER
Silver **Rev:** Date in legend **Note:** Dav.#5354.

Date	Mintage	VG	F	VF	XF	Unc
1663	—	650	1,250	2,750	4,750	—

KM# 81 1-1/2 THALER
Silver **Note:** Similar to 1 Thaler, KM#80, with value punched in on reverse. Dav.#5353A.

Date	Mintage	VG	F	VF	XF	Unc
1663 Rare	—	—	—	—	—	—

KM# 82 2 THALER
Silver **Note:** Similar to 1 Thaler, KM#80, with value punched in on reverse. Dav.#5353.

Date	Mintage	VG	F	VF	XF	Unc
1663 Rare	—	—	—	—	—	—

TRADE COINAGE

FR# 79 GOLDGULDEN
3.5000 g., 0.9860 Gold 0.1109 oz. AGW **Obv:** Crowned and helmeted arms in inner circle **Rev:** St. Stephen standing divides date

Date	Mintage	VG	F	VF	XF	Unc
1633	—	650	1,250	2,500	4,500	—

JOINT COINAGE

KM# 20 3 PFENNIG (Dreier)
Billon **Obv:** Helmeted episcopal arms divide date **Rev:** City arms, 3 in circle above

Date	Mintage	VG	F	VF	XF	Unc
1622	—	13.00	27.00	55.00	90.00	—
ND	—	13.00	27.00	55.00	90.00	—

KM# 21 3 PFENNIG (Dreier)
Billon **Obv:** St. Stephen standing above episcopal arms **Rev:** City arms, 3 in circle below

Date	Mintage	VG	F	VF	XF	Unc
ND	—	13.00	27.00	55.00	90.00	—

KM# 24 1/24 THALER (Groschen)
Silver **Obv:** Oval episcopal arms, date divided above helmet **Rev. Legend:** MONETA NO...

Date	Mintage	VG	F	VF	XF	Unc
16ZZ	—	16.00	33.00	60.00	120	—

KM# 23 1/24 THALER (Groschen)

Silver **Obv:** Imperial orb with 24 above city arms, titles of Ferdinand II **Rev:** Helmeted episcopal arms, date divided in legend at top **Note:** Kipper 1/24 Thaler.

Date	Mintage	VG	F	VF	XF	Unc
16ZZ	—	16.00	33.00	60.00	120	—

KM# 25 1/24 THALER (Groschen)

Silver **Note:** Klippe.

Date	Mintage	VG	F	VF	XF	Unc
16ZZ	—	—	—	—	—	—

KM# 85 THALER

Silver **Obv:** Helmeted city arms **Rev:** St. Stephan **Note:** Dav.#5356.

Date	Mintage	VG	F	VF	XF	Unc
1691 IC-S	—	125	250	500	900	1,500

PATTERNS

Including off metal strikes

KM#	Date	Mintage	Identification	Mkt Val
Pn1	1622	—	Ducat. Silver. KM#34.	—
Pn2	1628 CZ	—	Gulden. Gold. KM#53.	—
Pn3	ND CZ	—	Gulden. Gold. KM#53.	—
Pn4	1630 CZ	—	Thaler. Gold. KM#66.	—
Pn5	1631 CZ	—	1/4 Thaler. Gold. Arms in frame. KM#59.	5,000
Pn6	1631 CZ	—	1/4 Thaler. Gold. Helmeted arms. KM#69.	5,000

HALL

(Schwabisch Hall)
(Hall am Kocher)

This city in Swabia, situated on the River Kocher 34 miles (56 kilometers) northeast of Stüttgart, was founded at an early date, probably because of the presence of natural salt in the area. Small silver coins struck beginning in the second half of the 12th century and called *haller* were the origin of both the denomination and its name which has come down over the centuries as *heller*. Hall was made a free imperial city in 1276 and was given the right to strike its own coins in 1396. The city soon began to mint hellers with an open hand on the obverse and a cross on the reverse. These coins became known as *handelshellers* and the hand became the symbol of the city. Hall produced some coins during each of the following centuries, but total mintages were never very high. Most coins issued during the 18th century were commemorative in nature and usually only struck in a single year. The last city coins were produced in 1798. Württemberg annexed the city in 1803 as part of Napoleon's consolidation plans for Germany.

MINT OFFICIAL'S INITIALS

Initials	Date	Name
MB	1659-1725	Martin Brunner

ARMS

Usually 2-fold, but also found in separate shields, Open-palmed hand with fingers pointed upwards or a cross.

REFERENCE:

R = Albert Raff, **Die Münzen und Medaillen der Stadt Schwäbisch Hall**, Freiburg im Breisgau, 1986.

FREE CITY

REGULAR COINAGE

KM# 5 PFENNIG

Silver **Note:** Uniface. 2 joined shields, cross in left, open hand in right, rising eagle above, date below.

Date	Mintage	VG	F	VF	XF	Unc
1664	—	7.00	16.00	33.00	65.00	—
1675	—	7.00	16.00	33.00	65.00	—
1681	—	7.00	16.00	33.00	65.00	—
1697	—	7.00	16.00	33.00	65.00	—

KM# 7 PFENNIG

Silver **Obv:** Imperial eagle rising above arms **Note:** Uniface

Date	Mintage	VG	F	VF	XF	Unc
1696	—	5.00	13.00	30.00	65.00	—

KM# 6 1/2 KREUZER

Silver **Note:** Uniface. 2 joined shields, cross in left, open hand in right, rising eagle above divides date, value 1/2 below.

Date	Mintage	VG	F	VF	XF	Unc
1664	—	10.00	20.00	40.00	75.00	—

PATTERNS

Including off metal strikes

KM#	Date	Mintage	Identification	Mkt Val
Pn1	1681	—	Pfennig. Gold. KM#5.	—

HALTERN

A provincial town located about 25 miles southwest of Münster in Westphalia. Two series of copper coins were struck for local use in 1595 and 1624.

ARMS

A halter, as for a horse.

PROVINCIAL TOWN

REGULAR COINAGE

KM# 1 3 PFENNIG

Copper **Obv:** Arms in ornamented shield, STADT. HALTEREN, date around **Rev:** Value III in ornamented rectangle

Date	Mintage	VG	F	VF	XF	Unc
1624	—	20.00	40.00	80.00	145	—

KM# 2 6 PFENNIG

Copper **Obv:** Arms in ornamented shield, STADT. HALTEREN, date around **Rev:** Value VI in ornamented rectangle

Date	Mintage	VG	F	VF	XF	Unc
1624	—	20.00	40.00	80.00	145	—

KM# 3 9 PFENNIG

Copper **Obv:** Arms in ornamented shield, STADT. HALTEREN, date around **Rev:** Value VIIII in ornamented rectangle

Date	Mintage	VG	F	VF	XF	Unc
1624	—	20.00	40.00	80.00	145	—

HAMBURG

The city of Hamburg is located on the Elbe River about 75 miles from the North Sea. It was founded by Charlemagne in the 9th century. In 1241 it joined Lubeck to form the Hanseatic League. The mint right was leased to the citizens in 1292. However, the first local halfpennies had been struck almost 50 years earlier. In 1510 Hamburg was formally made a Free City, though, in fact, it had been free for about 250 years. It was occupied by the French during the Napoleonic period. In 1866 it joined the North German Confederation and became a part of the German Empire in 1871. The Hamburg coinage is almost continuous up to the time of World War I.

MINT OFFICIALS' INITIALS

Initial	Date	Name
	1592-1606	Matthias Mörsch, warden
(f)=	1599-1605	Claus Flegel
(g)=monk's head left	1606-1619	Matthias Mörsch, (Moors)
(h)= or	1618-19	Jacob Stoer, warden
	1619-20	Henning Hanses
(i)= or	1620-34	Christoff Fuessel (Feustal)
(j)= or with or without MF	1635-68	Matthias Freude der Altere
(k)= with or without MF	1635-?	Jacob Stoer, warden (2nd)
	1668-73	Matthias Freude der Jungere
HL	1673-92	Hermann Luders
	1691-1718	Jacob Schroeder, warden
IR	1692-1724	Jochim Rustmeyer

FREE CITY

REGULAR COINAGE

KM# 6 PFENNIG

Silver **Obv:** Two joined shields, imperial orb in left, city arms in right NSP (Neuer Stadt-Pfennig) above, cross below. **Note:** Uniface.

Date	Mintage	VG	F	VF	XF	Unc
ND(1599-1605) (f)	—	20.00	33.00	70.00	130	—

KM# 52 PFENNIG

Copper **Obv:** City arms **Rev:** Inscription, date **Rev. Inscription:** I / PEN / NING /

Date	Mintage	VG	F	VF	XF	Unc
1621	—	—	—	—	—	—

KM# 65 3 PFENNIG

Silver **Obv:** Date; HAMB: / STADT/ GELD in octagonal frame **Rev:** 3P. in octagonal frame

Date	Mintage	VG	F	VF	XF	Unc
1632	—	—	—	—	—	—

KM# 53 SECHSLING (6 Pfennig)

Silver **Obv:** City arms in circle **Rev:** Inscription, date **Rev. Inscription:** I / SOES / LIN(G) **Note:** Varieties exist.

Date	Mintage	VG	F	VF	XF	Unc
(1)621 (i)	—	16.00	33.00	60.00	100	—
1624 (i)	—	16.00	33.00	60.00	100	—
1635 (i)	—	16.00	33.00	60.00	100	—
1636 (j)	—	16.00	33.00	60.00	100	—
1641 (j)	—	16.00	33.00	60.00	100	—
1646 (j)	—	16.00	33.00	60.00	100	—
1648 (j)	—	16.00	33.00	60.00	100	—
1659 (j)	—	16.00	33.00	60.00	100	—
1660 (j)	—	16.00	33.00	60.00	100	—
1669 (k)	—	16.00	33.00	60.00	100	—
1670 (k)	—	16.00	33.00	60.00	100	—

KM# 40 1/2 SCHILLING (6 Pfennig)

Silver **Obv:** Crowned imperial eagle, 1/2 on breast, titles of Ferdinand II **Rev:** City arms in circle **Note:** Kipper.

Date	Mintage	VG	F	VF	XF	Unc
ND(1620/21) (i)	—	33.00	65.00	135	240	—

KM# 41 SCHILLING (12 Pfennig)

Silver **Obv:** City arms within circle **Rev:** Crowned imperial eagle, I on breast, titles of Ferdinand II **Note:** Kipper. Varieties exist.

Date	Mintage	VG	F	VF	XF	Unc
ND(1620/21) (i)	—	33.00	65.00	135	240	—

KM# 88 SCHILLING (12 Pfennig)

Silver **Rev:** Inscription, date **Rev. Inscription:** I / SCHIL / LING

Date	Mintage	VG	F	VF	XF	Unc
1669 (k)	—	12.00	25.00	45.00	80.00	—
1670 (k)	—	12.00	25.00	45.00	80.00	—

KM# 7.2 SCHERF

Copper **Obv:** City arms **Rev:** Lily/I.S/cross

Date	Mintage	Good	VG	F	VF	XF
ND(1572-1605)	—	—	13.00	27.00	60.00	90.00

KM# 7.1 SCHERF

Copper **Obv:** City arms **Rev:** I.S, blank field or rosette above, ornaments below **Note:** Varieties exist.

Date	Mintage	VG	F	VF	XF	Unc
ND(1572-1605)	—	13.00	27.00	60.00	90.00	—

KM# 42 2 SCHILLING (1/16 Thaler)

Silver **Obv:** City arms in circle **Rev:** Crowned imperial eagle, Z in orb on breast, titles of Ferdinand II **Note:** Kipper

Date	Mintage	VG	F	VF	XF	Unc
ND(1620/21) (i)	—	20.00	40.00	65.00	120	—

KM# 58 2 SCHILLING (1/16 Thaler)

Silver **Rev:** Inscription, date **Rev. Inscription:** II / SCHIL / LING /

Date	Mintage	VG	F	VF	XF	Unc
(1)623 (i)	—	16.00	33.00	60.00	120	—
(1)624 (i)	—	16.00	33.00	60.00	120	—

KM# 59 2 SCHILLING (1/16 Thaler)

Silver **Rev:** Inscription, date **Rev. Inscription:** II / SCHIL / LING **Note:** Varieties exist.

Date	Mintage	VG	F	VF	XF	Unc
1624 (i)	—	13.00	27.00	55.00	100	—
1627 (i)	—	13.00	27.00	55.00	100	—
1628 (i)	—	13.00	27.00	55.00	100	—
ND(1631) (i)	—	13.00	27.00	55.00	100	—
1636 (j)	—	13.00	27.00	55.00	100	—
1637 (j)	—	13.00	27.00	55.00	100	—
1639 (j)	—	13.00	27.00	55.00	100	—
1641 (j)	—	13.00	27.00	55.00	100	—
1646 (j)	—	13.00	27.00	55.00	100	—
1647 (j)	—	13.00	27.00	55.00	100	—
1659 (j)	—	13.00	27.00	55.00	100	—
1660 (j)	—	13.00	27.00	55.00	100	—
1669 (k)	—	13.00	27.00	55.00	100	—
1670 (k)	—	13.00	27.00	55.00	100	—
(1)672	—	13.00	27.00	55.00	100	—

KM# 98 2 SCHILLING (1/16 Thaler)

Silver **Obv:** Crowned imperial eagle, 2/S on breast, date in legend **Rev:** Madonna and child, small oval city arms below resting on crescent

Date	Mintage	VG	F	VF	XF	Unc
1673 MF	—	20.00	40.00	75.00	125	—

KM# 102 2 SCHILLING (1/16 Thaler)

Silver **Obv:** Madonna with scepter and child **Rev:** 2 on eagle's breast **Note:** Varieties exist.

Date	Mintage	VG	F	VF	XF	Unc
1674 HL	—	20.00	45.00	80.00	140	—
1675 HL	—	20.00	45.00	80.00	140	—
1677 HL	—	20.00	45.00	80.00	140	—
1678 HL	—	20.00	45.00	80.00	140	—
1687 HL	—	20.00	45.00	80.00	140	—
1688 HL	—	20.00	45.00	80.00	140	—
1689 HL	—	20.00	45.00	80.00	140	—

KM# 125 2 SCHILLING (1/16 Thaler)
Silver **Obv:** City arms between palm branches **Rev:** Value on breast of double-headed imperial eagle

Date	Mintage	VG	F	VF	XF	Unc
1692 IR	—	13.00	27.00	55.00	90.00	—
1693 IR	—	13.00	27.00	55.00	90.00	—
1695 IR	—	13.00	27.00	55.00	90.00	—

KM# 43 4 SCHILLING (1/4 Mark)
Silver **Obv:** City arms, date divided among towers **Rev:** Crowned imperial eagle, IIII in rhombus on breast, titles of Ferdinand II

Date	Mintage	VG	F	VF	XF	Unc
1620 (g)	—	85.00	160	300	475	—

KM# 89 4 SCHILLING (1/4 Mark)
Silver **Obv:** City arms within circle **Rev:** Inscription, date, titles of Leopold I **Rev. Inscription:** IIII / SCHIL / LING

Date	Mintage	VG	F	VF	XF	Unc
1669 (k)	—	40.00	80.00	140	240	—

KM# 54 4 SCHILLING (1/8 Thaler)
Silver **Obv:** City arms in circle, date divided by towers **Rev:** Crowned imperial eagle, 4 in orb on breast, titles of Ferdinand II and date inlegend

Date	Mintage	VG	F	VF	XF	Unc
1621 (i)	—	60.00	120	240	375	—

KM# 57 4 SCHILLING (1/8 Thaler)
Silver **Obv:** Towered building facade within beaded circle **Rev:** Date only in legend

Date	Mintage	VG	F	VF	XF	Unc
(1)6ZZ (i)	—	60.00	120	240	375	—
(1)623 (i)	—	60.00	120	240	375	—

KM# 75 4 SCHILLING (1/8 Thaler)
Silver **Rev:** Titles of Ferdinand III

Date	Mintage	VG	F	VF	XF	Unc
1642 (j)	—	60.00	120	240	375	—

KM# 12 8 SCHILLING (1/4 Thaler)
Silver **Obv:** Crowned imperial eagle, 8 in orb on breast, titles f Rudolf II and date in legend **Rev:** City arms in circle **Note:** Varieties exist.

Date	Mintage	VG	F	VF	XF	Unc
(1)602 (f)	—	55.00	120	200	350	—
(1)606 (g)	—	55.00	120	200	350	—
1607 (g)	—	55.00	120	200	350	—
(1)608 (g)	—	55.00	120	200	350	—
1608 (g)	—	55.00	120	200	350	—
ND (g)	—	55.00	120	200	350	—

KM# 44 8 SCHILLING (1/4 Thaler)
Silver **Obv:** Towered building facade within beaded circle **Rev:** Titles of Ferdinand II **Note:** Varieties exist.

Date	Mintage	VG	F	VF	XF	Unc
(1)620 (i)	—	45.00	110	200	325	—
(1)621 (i)	—	45.00	110	200	325	—
(1)622 (i)	—	45.00	110	200	325	—
1622 (i)	—	45.00	110	200	325	—

KM# 45 8 SCHILLING (1/4 Thaler)
Silver **Obv:** Date divided by towers within beaded circle **Rev:** Value on breast of double-headed eagle within beaded circle

Date	Mintage	VG	F	VF	XF	Unc
1620 (i)	—	45.00	110	200	325	—
1622 (i)	—	45.00	110	200	325	—

KM# 55 8 SCHILLING (1/2 Mark)
Silver **Obv:** City arms, date divided among towers **Rev:** Crowned imperial eagle, value VIII in rhombus on breast, titles of Ferdinand II

Date	Mintage	VG	F	VF	XF	Unc
16Z1 (i)	—	—	—	—	—	—
1631 (i)	—	—	—	—	—	—

KM# 80 8 SCHILLING (1/2 Mark)
Silver **Obv:** City arms in circle, date in legend **Rev:** 8 in orb on breast, titles of Ferdinand III

Date	Mintage	VG	F	VF	XF	Unc
1653 (j)	—	—	—	—	—	—

KM# 81 8 SCHILLING (1/2 Mark)
Silver **Obv:** Titles of Leopold I

Date	Mintage	VG	F	VF	XF	Unc
1659 (j)	—	—	—	—	—	—
1667 (j)	—	—	—	—	—	—

KM# 85 8 SCHILLING (1/2 Mark)
Silver, 60 mm. **Obv:** Date in legend **Note:** Illustration reduced.

Date	Mintage	VG	F	VF	XF	Unc
1668 (k)	—	135	350	650	875	—

KM# 90 8 SCHILLING (1/2 Mark)
Silver **Obv:** City arms in circle **Rev:** Value inscription, date at end, titles of Leopold I **Rev. Inscription:** VIII / SCHIL / LING

Date	Mintage	VG	F	VF	XF	Unc
1669 (k)	—	—	—	—	—	—

KM# 95 8 SCHILLING (1/2 Mark)
Silver **Obv:** Towered building facade within beaded circle **Rev:** Value on breast of double-headed imperial eagle within beaded circle

Date	Mintage	VG	F	VF	XF	Unc
1672 (k)	—	65.00	135	240	400	—

KM# 127 1/2 MARK (8 Schilling)
Silver **Obv:** City arms in baroque shield, date below **Rev:** Crowned imperial eagle, 1/2 in orb on breast, titles of Leopold I

Date	Mintage	VG	F	VF	XF	Unc
1694 IR	—	80.00	175	350	500	—

KM# 13 16 SCHILLING (1/2 Thaler)
Silver **Note:** Similar to KM#15 but date in obverse legend.

Date	Mintage	VG	F	VF	XF	Unc
1602 (f)	—	—	—	—	—	—

KM# 15 16 SCHILLING (1/2 Thaler)
Silver **Obv:** Towered building facade within beaded circle **Rev:** Value on breast of double-headed imperial eagle within beaded circle **Note:** Varieties exist.

Date	Mintage	VG	F	VF	XF	Unc
1605 (f)	—	55.00	110	200	350	—
(1)607 (g)	—	55.00	110	200	350	—
(1)608 (g)	—	55.00	110	200	350	—
1610 (g)	—	55.00	110	200	350	—
ND (f)	—	55.00	110	200	350	—

KM# 26 16 SCHILLING (1/2 Thaler)
Silver **Rev:** Date divided among towers

Date	Mintage	VG	F	VF	XF	Unc
1611 (g)	—	—	—	—	—	—

KM# 33 16 SCHILLING (1/2 Thaler)
Silver **Obv:** Titles of Matthias

Date	Mintage	VG	F	VF	XF	Unc
1619 (h)	—	—	—	—	—	—

KM# 46 16 SCHILLING (1/2 Thaler)
Silver **Obv:** Date divided by towers within beaded circle **Rev:** Titles of Ferdinand II **Note:** Varieties exist.

Date	Mintage	VG	F	VF	XF	Unc
1620 (g)	—	80.00	175	300	450	—
16Z1 (i)	—	80.00	175	300	450	—
1629 (i)	—	80.00	175	300	450	—

KM# 56 16 SCHILLING (1/2 Thaler)
Silver **Obv:** Towered building facade within beaded circle **Rev:** Value on breast of double-headed imperial eagle within beaded circle **Note:** Varieties exist.

Date	Mintage	VG	F	VF	XF	Unc
(1)6Z1 (i)	—	55.00	115	250	375	—
(1)6ZZ (i)	—	55.00	115	250	375	—
(1)6Z3 (i)	—	55.00	115	250	375	—
1624 (i)	—	55.00	115	250	375	—
(1)625 (i)	—	55.00	115	250	375	—
1629 (i)	—	55.00	115	250	375	—
1632 (i)	—	55.00	115	250	375	—
1634 (j)	—	55.00	115	250	375	—
1636 (j)	—	55.00	115	250	375	—

KM# 70 16 SCHILLING (1/2 Thaler)
Silver **Obv:** Titles of Ferdinand III **Note:** Varieties exist.

Date	Mintage	VG	F	VF	XF	Unc
1638 (j)	—	55.00	115	250	375	—
1640 (j)	—	55.00	115	250	375	—
1641 (j)	—	55.00	115	250	375	—
1642 (j)	—	55.00	115	250	375	—
1644 (j)	—	55.00	115	250	375	—
1645 (j)	—	55.00	115	250	375	—

KM# 99 16 SCHILLING (1/2 Thaler)
Silver **Obv:** Titles of Leopold I

Date	Mintage	VG	F	VF	XF	Unc
1673 MF (k)	—	120	275	450	750	—

KM# 92 16 SCHILLING (Mark)
Silver **Rev:** Value inscription, titles of Leopold I and date in legend **Rev. Inscription:** XVI / SCHIL / LING

Date	Mintage	VG	F	VF	XF	Unc
1669 (k)	—	—	—	—	—	—

KM# 96 16 SCHILLING (Mark)
Silver **Obv:** City arms within inner circle **Rev:** Double-headed eagle with 16 S in orb on breast

Date	Mintage	VG	F	VF	XF	Unc
1672 (k)	—	65.00	135	275	450	—

KM# 128 MARK

Silver **Obv:** City arms in baroque shield, date below **Obv. Legend:** HAMBURGER-STADT GELDT **Rev:** Crowned imperial eagle, 1 in orb on breast, titles of Leopold I **Rev. Legend:** LEOPOLDUS DG: ROMA: IMP: SEM: AU

Date	Mintage	VG	F	VF	XF	Unc
1694 IR	—	110	200	375	600	—

KM# 97 32 SCHILLING (2 Mark)

Silver **Obv:** City arms within inner circle **Rev:** Double-headed eagle in inner circle, date at end of legend

Date	Mintage	VG	F	VF	XF	Unc
1672 (k)	—	200	400	650	1,050	—

KM# 100 32 SCHILLING (2 Mark)

Silver **Note:** Similar to KM#101 but 39 millimeters.

Date	Mintage	VG	F	VF	XF	Unc
1673 MF (k)	—	—	—	—	—	—

KM# 14 32 SCHILLING (Thaler)

Silver **Rev:** Titles of Rudolf II and date in reverse legend. **Note:** Varieties exist. Similar to KM#17. Dav. #5357.

Date	Mintage	VG	F	VF	XF	Unc
1603 (f)	—	165	325	525	875	—
1604 (f)	—	165	325	525	875	—
1605 (f)	—	165	325	525	875	—
(1)607 (g)	—	165	325	525	875	—
1608 (g)	—	165	325	525	875	—
(1)608 (g)	—	80.00	160	275	450	—

KM# 16.1 32 SCHILLING (Thaler)

Silver **Note:** Similar to KM#16.2 but with straight wall. Dav. #5358.

Date	Mintage	VG	F	VF	XF	Unc
1606 (g)	—	165	325	525	875	—
(1)606 (g)	—	165	325	525	875	—
1607 (g)	—	165	325	525	875	—

KM# 17 32 SCHILLING (Thaler)

Silver **Obv:** City arms within inner circle **Rev:** Crowned double-headed imperial eagle **Note:** Varieties exist. Date in both obverse and reverse legend. Dav. #5359.

Date	Mintage	VG	F	VF	XF	Unc
1606/1607 (g)	—	110	225	400	650	—
1606/(1)607 (g)	—	110	225	400	650	—
(1)606/(1)606 (g)	—	110	225	400	650	—
(1)607/(1)606 (g)	—	110	225	400	650	—
(1)607/(1)607 (g)	—	110	225	400	650	—
(1)608/1608 (g)	—	110	225	400	650	—
(1)608/(1)608 (g)	—	110	225	400	650	—

KM# 16.2 32 SCHILLING (Thaler)

Silver **Obv:** City arms within inner circle **Rev:** Crowned imperial eagle with 3Z in orb on breast **Note:** Varieties exist. Dav. #5361.

Date	Mintage	VG	F	VF	XF	Unc
(1)607 (g)	—	100	200	350	700	—
(1)608 (g)	—	100	200	350	700	—
1608 (g)	—	100	200	350	700	—
1610 (g)	—	100	200	350	700	—
ND (g)	—	100	200	350	700	—

KM# 20 32 SCHILLING (Thaler)

Silver **Obv:** City arms' towers divide date 1 (tower) 6 (tower) 1 (tower) 0 **Rev:** Crowned double-headed imperial eagle with 3Z in orb on breast **Note:** Varieties exist. Dav. #5360.

Date	Mintage	VG	F	VF	XF	Unc
1608 (g)	—	100	200	350	700	—
1610 (g)	—	100	200	350	700	—
1611 (g)	—	100	200	350	700	—
161Z (g)	—	100	200	350	700	—

KM# 27.1 32 SCHILLING (Thaler)

Silver **Rev:** Titles of Matthias **Note:** Dav. #5362.

Date	Mintage	VG	F	VF	XF	Unc
1613 (g)	—	675	1,300	2,000	3,000	—
1616 (g)	—	675	1,300	2,000	3,000	—

KM# 27.2 32 SCHILLING (Thaler)

Silver **Obv:** City arms' towers divide date numerals **Obv. Legend:** MONETA. NOVA CIVITATIS HAMBURGENSIS **Rev:** Crowned imperial eagle with 3Z in orb on breast, titles of Matthias **Rev. Legend:** MATTHIAS ? D:G:ROMA IMPE: SEM: AUGU: **Note:** Varieties exist. Dav. #5363.

Date	Mintage	VG	F	VF	XF	Unc
1619 (h)	—	675	1,300	2,000	3,000	—

KM# 34 32 SCHILLING (Thaler)

Silver **Obv:** City arms' towers divide date numerals **Rev:** Crowned imperial eagle with 3Z in orb on breast, titles of Ferdinand II **Note:** Varieties exist. Dav. #5364.

Date	Mintage	VG	F	VF	XF	Unc
1619 (h)	—	60.00	120	240	475	—
1620 (i)	—	60.00	120	240	475	—
1620 (g)	—	—	—	—	—	—
1621 (i)	—	60.00	120	240	475	—
1622 (i)	—	60.00	120	240	475	—
1625 (i)	—	60.00	120	240	475	—

KM# 47 32 SCHILLING (Thaler)

Silver **Note:** Varieties exist. Dav. #5365.

Date	Mintage	VG	F	VF	XF	Unc
1620 (i)	—	90.00	175	300	525	—
1621 (i)	—	90.00	175	300	525	—
(1)621 (i)	—	90.00	175	300	525	—
(16)21 (i)	—	90.00	175	300	525	—
(1)622 (i)	—	90.00	175	300	525	—
1623 (i)	—	90.00	175	300	525	—
(1)623 (i)	—	90.00	175	300	525	—
(16)23 (i)	—	90.00	175	300	525	—
1624 (i)	—	90.00	175	300	525	—
(1)624 (i)	—	90.00	175	300	525	—
(1)625 (i)	—	90.00	175	300	525	—
1626 (i)	—	90.00	175	300	525	—
1628 (i)	—	90.00	175	300	525	—
1629 (i)	—	90.00	175	300	525	—
1630 (i)	—	90.00	175	300	525	—
1631 (i)	—	90.00	175	300	525	—
1632 (i)	—	90.00	175	300	525	—
1634 (i)	—	90.00	175	300	525	—
1635 (j)	—	90.00	175	300	525	—
1636 (j)	—	90.00	175	300	525	—
1636 MF (j)	—	90.00	175	300	525	—
1637 (j)	—	90.00	175	300	525	—
ND (j)	—	90.00	175	300	525	—

KM# 67.1 32 SCHILLING (Thaler)

Silver **Rev:** Titles of Ferdinand III **Note:** Dav. #5366.

Date	Mintage	VG	F	VF	XF	Unc
1637 (j)	—	135	275	450	725	—
1638 (j)	—	135	275	450	725	—
1640 (j)	—	135	275	450	725	—
1641 (j)	—	135	275	450	725	—
1642 (j)	—	135	275	450	725	—
1644 (j)	—	135	275	450	725	—

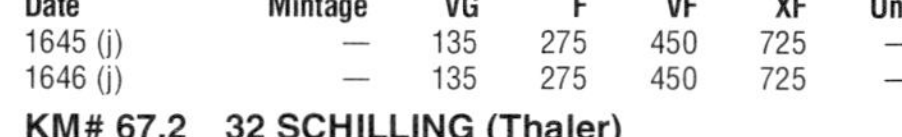

Date	Mintage	VG	F	VF	XF	Unc
1645 (j)	—	135	275	450	725	—
1646 (j)	—	135	275	450	725	—

KM# 67.2 32 SCHILLING (Thaler)

Silver **Obv:** City arms in inner circle, date divided at top **Rev:** Double-headed imperial eagle, titles of Ferdinand II **Note:** Varieties exist. Dav. #5367.

Date	Mintage	VG	F	VF	XF	Unc
1643 (j)	—	165	340	525	950	—
1645 (j)	—	165	340	525	950	—
1647 (j)	—	165	340	525	950	—
1648 (j)	—	165	340	525	950	—
1649 (j)	—	165	340	525	950	—
1650 (j)	—	165	340	525	950	—
1651 (j)	—	165	340	525	950	—
1652 (j)	—	165	340	525	950	—
1653 (j)	—	165	340	525	950	—

KM# 101 32 SCHILLING (Thaler)

Silver **Note:** Dav. #5368.

Date	Mintage	VG	F	VF	XF	Unc
1673 MF (k)	—	275	525	850	1,400	—

KM# 115 48 SCHILLING (Thaler)

Silver **Subject:** Peace of Nymwegan **Note:** Dav. #5370.

Date	Mintage	VG	F	VF	XF	Unc
1680 HL	—	750	1,400	2,400	3,500	—

KM# 119 48 SCHILLING (Thaler)

Silver **Obv:** Crowned imperial eagle, orb on breast, titles of Leopold I **Rev:** City arms, date divided to left and right of towers, all in palm wreath **Note:** Dav. #5372.

Date	Mintage	VG	F	VF	XF	Unc
1687 HL	—	1,350	2,400	4,000	6,250	—

KM# 129 2 MARK

Silver **Obv:** City arms in baroque shield, date below **Rev:** Crowned imperial eagle, 2 in orb on breast, titles of Leopold I

Date	Mintage	VG	F	VF	XF	Unc
1694 IR	—	220	450	825	1,300	—

KM# 10 1/128 THALER (3 Pfennig)

Silver **Obv:** City arms in circle **Rev:** Imperial orb with 128, titles of Rudolf II **Note:** Varieties exist.

Date	Mintage	VG	F	VF	XF	Unc
1601	—	27.00	55.00	100	175	—

KM# 1 1/128 THALER (3 Pfennig)

Silver **Obv:** City arms **Obv. Legend:** MO. NOV. CIVI. HAMBVRG **Rev:** Imperial orb with 1Z8 , titles of Rudolf II in legend

Date	Mintage	VG	F	VF	XF	Unc
ND(1602-05)	—	20.00	40.00	80.00	150	—

KM# 48 1/96 THALER

Silver **Obv:** City arms in circle, date in legend **Rev:** Imperial orb with titles of Ferdinand II and date in legend

Date	Mintage	VG	F	VF	XF	Unc
(1)6Z0 (g)	—	25.00	45.00	80.00	140	—

KM# 103 1/96 THALER

Silver **Obv:** City arms between palm branches **Rev:** 96 between palm branches, date in legend

Date	Mintage	VG	F	VF	XF	Unc
1675 HL	—	20.00	40.00	65.00	110	—

KM# 8 1/64 THALER (6 Pfennig)

Silver **Obv:** City arms in inner circle **Rev:** Imperial eagle, orb with 64, date in legend

Date	Mintage	VG	F	VF	XF	Unc
(1)601 (f)	—	20.00	45.00	85.00	140	—
(1)602 (f)	—	20.00	45.00	85.00	140	—
(1)603 (f)	—	20.00	45.00	85.00	140	—
(1)605 (f)	—	20.00	45.00	85.00	140	—

KM# 71 1/48 THALER (Schilling)

Silver **Obv:** City arms in circle **Rev:** 48 in shield, date in legned **Note:** Varieties exist.

Date	Mintage	VG	F	VF	XF	Unc
1639 (j)	—	33.00	60.00	120	200	—
1641 (j)	—	33.00	60.00	120	200	—
1646 (j)	—	33.00	60.00	120	200	—
1659 (j)	—	33.00	60.00	120	200	—
1660 (j)	—	33.00	60.00	120	200	—

KM# 104 1/48 THALER (Schilling)

Silver **Obv:** City arms between palm branches **Rev:** 48 between palm branches, date in legend **Note:** Varieties exist.

Date	Mintage	VG	F	VF	XF	Unc
1675 HL	—	27.00	55.00	110	175	—
1676 HL	—	27.00	55.00	110	175	—
1680 HL	—	27.00	55.00	110	175	—
1687 HL	—	27.00	55.00	110	175	—

KM# 126 1/48 THALER (Schilling)

Silver **Rev:** 48/REICHS/DALER, date in legend

Date	Mintage	VG	F	VF	XF	Unc
1693 IR	—	—	—	—	—	—

KM# 32 1/20 THALER

Silver **Obv:** Two interlocking shields of Lübeck and Hamburg arms above DALER-A-20.STVC and below 24, all in a circle, date at end of legend **Obv. Legend:** MONETA. HAMBVRGENSIS **Rev:** Crowned imperial eagle, titles of Matthias **Note:** Ref. G#851. Prev. KM#32, 24 Pfennig.

Date	Mintage	VG	F	VF	XF	Unc
1619	—	—	—	—	—	—

Note: Companion issue of Lübeck (city), KM#43

KM# 11 1/16 THALER (2 Schilling)

Silver **Obv:** City arms in circle, date above **Rev:** Crowned imperial eagle, 16 in orb on breast, titles of Rudolph II **Note:** Varieties exist.

Date	Mintage	VG	F	VF	XF	Unc
(1)601 (f)	—	16.00	33.00	65.00	120	—
(1)602 (f)	—	16.00	33.00	65.00	120	—
(1)603 (f)	—	16.00	33.00	65.00	120	—
(1)604 (f)	—	16.00	33.00	65.00	120	—
(1)605 (f)	—	16.00	33.00	65.00	120	—
(1)607 (g)	—	16.00	33.00	65.00	120	—
(1)608 (g)	—	16.00	33.00	65.00	120	—

KM# 29 1/16 THALER (2 Schilling)
Silver **Obv:** Date in legend **Rev:** Imperial eagle with 16 in orb on breast **Note:** Varieties exist.

Date	Mintage	VG	F	VF	XF	Unc
1614 (g)	—	20.00	40.00	80.00	130	—
1615 (g)	—	20.00	40.00	80.00	130	—
1616 (g)	—	20.00	40.00	80.00	130	—
1617 (g)	—	20.00	40.00	80.00	130	—

KM# 28 1/16 THALER (2 Schilling)
Silver **Rev:** Titles of Matthias

Date	Mintage	VG	F	VF	XF	Unc
1614 (g)	—	25.00	45.00	85.00	135	—

KM# 30 1/16 THALER (2 Schilling)
Silver **Rev. Legend:** NON. MIHI. D. SED. NOM. TVO

Date	Mintage	VG	F	VF	XF	Unc
1617	—	33.00	60.00	110	175	—

KM# 21 1/4 THALER (Schau)
Silver **Obv:** City arms in baroque frame, ornate helmet above **Obv. Legend:** DA.PACEM.DOMIN:—IN.DIE:NOSTRIS **Rev:** Nativity scene **Rev. Legend:** IESUS. E: KINT: GEBOREN. V: EIN. IUNCKFRA: AUSERKORN.

Date	Mintage	VG	F	VF	XF	Unc
ND(1606-19)	—	—	—	—	—	—

KM# 22 1/4 THALER (Schau)
Silver **Obv:** City arms in baroque frame, ornate helmet above **Obv. Legend:** DA.PACEM.DOMIN:—IN.DIE:NOSTRIS **Rev:** Nativity scene **Rev. Legend:** PVER. NATVS. EST. NOVIS. E. FILIVS. DATVS. ETS. NOBIS. **Note:** Varieties exist.

Date	Mintage	VG	F	VF	XF	Unc
ND(1606-19)	—	75.00	150	275	500	—

KM# 35 1/4 THALER (Schau)
Silver **Obv:** City arms in baroque frame, ornate helmet **Obv. Legend:** DA.PACEM.DOMIN:—IN.DIE:NOSTRIS **Rev:** Nativity scene **Rev. Legend:** PVER. NATVS. EST. NOBI. E. FILIVS. DATVS. ETS.

Date	Mintage	VG	F	VF	XF	Unc
ND(1620-34)	—	75.00	150	275	500	—

KM# 72 1/4 THALER (Schau)
Silver **Obv:** The Annunciation **Obv. Legend:** AVE MARIA GRATIA. PLENA. DOMINVS TECUM **Rev:** The Nativity **Rev. Legend:** IESUS. E. KINT. GEBORN. V: EIN. IUNCKFRA: AVSERKORN

Date	Mintage	VG	F	VF	XF	Unc
ND(1635-68)	—	60.00	125	245	465	—

KM# 73 1/4 THALER (Schau)
Silver **Obv:** The Annunciation **Obv. Legend:** AVE MARIA GRATIA. PLENA. DOMINVS TECUM **Rev:** The Nativity **Rev. Legend:** PVER NATUS. EST. NOBI E FILIVS. DATVS. EST. NOBIS

Date	Mintage	VG	F	VF	XF	Unc
ND(1635-68)	—	60.00	125	245	465	—

KM# 74 1/4 THALER (Schau)
Silver **Obv:** City arms in shield, ornate helmet above **Obv. Legend:** DA PACEM DOMINE **Rev:** The Nativity **Rev. Legend:** IESUS. E. KINT. GEBORN. V: EIN. IUNCKFRA: AVSERKORN

Date	Mintage	VG	F	VF	XF	Unc
ND(1635-68)	—	75.00	150	275	500	—

KM# 77 1/4 THALER (Schau)
Silver **Obv:** City arms in shield, ornate helmet **Obv. Legend:** DA PACEM DOMINE **Rev:** The Nativity **Rev. Legend:** PVER NATUS. EST. NOBI E FILIVS. DATVS. EST.

Date	Mintage	VG	F	VF	XF	Unc
ND(1635-68)	—	75.00	150	275	500	—

KM# 124 1/4 THALER (Schau)
Silver **Obv:** City arms inside 2 palm branches **Obv. Legend:** MONETA NOVA CIVITATIS HAMBURGEN:. **Rev:** Crowned Imperial Eagle, 4 in orb on breast, titles of Leopold I

Date	Mintage	VG	F	VF	XF	Unc
ND(1687)	—	120	300	450	650	—

KM# 118 1/4 THALER (Schau)
Silver **Obv:** City arms in sprays **Obv. Legend:** * MONETA NOVA CIVITATIS HAMBURGEN: **Rev:** Crowned imperial eagle **Rev. Legend:** LEOPOLDUS • D: G: ROMA: IMP: SEM: AUG •

Date	Mintage	Good	VG	F	VF	XF
ND(1687)	—	55.00	130	275	475	800

KM# 105 1/3 THALER
Silver **Obv:** Arms divide date, value in orb below **Rev:** Crowned imperial eagle

Date	Mintage	VG	F	VF	XF	Unc
ND(1675) HL	—	120	275	400	625	—
1679 HL	—	120	275	400	625	—

KM# 23 1/2 THALER (Schau)
14.4000 g., Silver **Obv:** City arms in baroque frame, ornate helmet **Obv. Legend:** DA.PACEM.DOMIN:—IN.DIE:NOSTRIS **Rev:** Nativity scene **Rev. Legend:** PVER. NATVS. EST. NOVIS. E. FILIVS. DATVS. ETS. **Note:** Klippe; struck on square flan of 1/2 Thaler weight.

Date	Mintage	VG	F	VF	XF	Unc
ND(1606-19)	—	100	200	400	750	—

KM# 78 1/2 THALER (Schau)
Silver **Obv:** Nativity scene **Obv. Legend:** PVER NATVS. EST. NOBI E: FILIVS. DATVS EST. NOBIS. ESA: IX **Rev:** Baptism of Christ **Rev. Legend:** CHRIST. D: HEIL: TAUF. NI: AN. V: SEI: VORLAUF: IM. IORD

Date	Mintage	VG	F	VF	XF	Unc
ND(1635-68)	—	75.00	150	300	600	—

KM# 79 1/2 THALER (Schau)
Silver **Obv:** The Annunciation **Obv. Legend:** AVE MARIA GRATIA. PLENA. DOMINVS **Rev:** The Nativity **Rev. Legend:** PVER NATUS. EST. NOBI E FILIVS. DATVS. EST.

Date	Mintage	VG	F	VF	XF	Unc
ND(1635-68)	—	75.00	150	200	600	—

KM# 106 2/3 THALER
Silver **Obv:** Arms divide date, value below in orb **Rev:** Crowned imperial eagle **Note:** Similar to 1/3 Thaler, KM#105, but value 2/3.

Date	Mintage	VG	F	VF	XF	Unc
ND(1675) HL	—	120	275	500	750	—
ND(1675)	—	120	275	500	750	—
1679 HL	—	120	275	500	750	—

KM# 130 THALER
Silver **Obv:** City arms in baroque frame **Rev:** Crowned imperial eagle **Note:** Dav. #5374.

Date	Mintage	F	VF	XF	Unc	BU
1694 IR	—	190	375	600	1,350	—

KM# 24 THALER (Schau)
Silver **Obv:** City arms in ornamented oval shield, ornate helmet above **Obv. Legend:** DA. PACEM. DOMI. — IN. DIE: NOSTRIS **Rev:** Nativity scene **Rev. Legend:** GLORIA. IN. EXC — ELSIS. DEO

Date	Mintage	VG	F	VF	XF	Unc
ND(1606-19)	—	75.00	150	300	600	—

KM# 36 THALER (Schau)
Silver **Obv:** City arms in rectangular shield with rounded bottom, ornate helmet above **Obv. Legend:** DA. PACEM... **Rev:** Madonna with rays around **Rev. Legend:** SI. DEVS. PRO. NOBIS. — QVIS. CONTRA. NOS

Date	Mintage	VG	F	VF	XF	Unc
ND(1620-34)	—	75.00	150	300	600	—

KM# 82 THALER (Schau)
Silver **Obv:** Nativity scene **Obv. Legend:** PVER NATVS. EST. NOBI E: FILIVS. DATVS EST. NOBIS. **Rev:** Baptism of Christ **Rev. Legend:** CHRIST. D: HEIL: TAUF. NI: AN. V: SEI: VORLAUF: IM.

Date	Mintage	VG	F	VF	XF	Unc
ND(1635-68)	—	65.00	135	275	500	—

KM# 83 THALER (Schau)
Silver **Obv:** The Annunciation **Obv. Legend:** AVE MARIA GRATIA. PLENA. DOMINVS **Rev:** The Nativity **Rev. Legend:** PVER NATUS. EST. NOBI E FILIVS. DATVS. EST.

Date	Mintage	VG	F	VF	XF	Unc
ND(1635-68)	—	65.00	135	275	500	—

KM# 84 THALER (Schau)
Silver **Obv:** Engaged couple, Jehovah in Hebrew and dove above center **Obv. Legend:** QUOS DEUS CONIUNXIT **Rev:** Wedding at Cana **Rev. Legend:** IESUS CHRIST: MACHET

Date	Mintage	VG	F	VF	XF	Unc
ND(1635-68)	—	65.00	135	275	500	—

KM# A25 1-1/4 THALER (Schau)
Silver **Obv:** City arms in ornamented shield, ornate helmet above **Obv. Legend:** DA. PACEM. DOMI. — IN. DIEBVS. NOSTRIS **Rev:** Madonna with sceptre standing on crescent **Rev. Legend:** VERBVM. DOMINI. — MANET. IN ÆTERNVM

Date	Mintage	VG	F	VF	XF	Unc
ND(1606-19)	—	150	250	400	700	—

KM# B25 1-1/2 THALER (Schau)
Silver **Obv:** City arms in ornate shield, ornate helmet above **Obv. Legend:** DA. PACEM. DOMINE'. IN — DIEBVS. NOSTRIS **Rev:** Madonna with sword and sceptre, child with orb **Rev. Legend:** SI. DEVS. PRO. NOBIS. — QVIS. CONTRA. NOS. **Note:** Dav. LS-301.

Date	Mintage	VG	F	VF	XF	Unc
ND(1606-19)	—	225	475	700	1,200	—

KM# C25 1-1/2 THALER (Schau)
Silver **Obv:** City arms in ornamented oval shield, ornate helmet above **Obv. Legend:** DA. PACEM. DOMI. — IN. DIE: NOSTRIS **Rev:** Nativity scene **Rev. Legend:** GLORIA. IN. EXC — ELSIS. DEO

Date	Mintage	VG	F	VF	XF	Unc
ND(1606-19)	—	175	300	450	750	—

KM# 37 1-1/2 THALER (Schau)
Silver, 60 mm. **Obv:** Christ joining a couple in marriage **Obv. Legend:** QUOS DEUS CONIUNXIT — HOMO NON SEPARET **Rev:** Wedding at Cana **Rev. Legend:** IESUS CHRISTUS MACHET WASSER ZU WEIN. IN. CANA. GAL: IOH. II **Note:** Illustration reduced.

Date	Mintage	VG	F	VF	XF	Unc
ND(1620-34)	—	200	375	600	1,000	—

KM# 38 1-1/2 THALER (Schau)
Silver, 60 mm. **Obv:** Marriage scene **Obv. Legend:** WAS GOTT ZUSAMMEN FVGET — DAS SOL KEIN MENSCH SCHEIDEN **Rev:** Similar to KM#37, but variant scene and legend **Rev. Legend:** ...Z. WEIN. IN. CANA. GALI. IOHA. II **Note:** Illustration reduced.

Date	Mintage	VG	F	VF	XF	Unc
ND(1620-34)	—	200	375	600	1,000	—

KM# 39 1-1/2 THALER (Schau)
Silver, 59 mm. **Obv:** Crucifixion scene **Obv. Legend:** CHRISTUS IST UMB UNSER SUNDE WILLEN. GESTORBEN. UND **Rev:** Ascension, Christ with cross and banner **Rev. Legend:** UMB. UNSER. GERECHTIGKEIT. WILLEN. WIDER. AUFFERSTANDE **Note:** Illustration reduced.

Date	Mintage	VG	F	VF	XF	Unc
ND(1620-34)	—	225	400	650	1,150	—

KM# A85 1-1/2 THALER (Schau)
Silver **Obv:** The Nativity **Obv. Legend:** IESUS EIN KINDT GEBORN. V. EINER IUNCKFRAUW: AUSERKORN **Rev:** Baptism of Christ **Rev. Legend:** CHRIST: D. HEILIG: TAUF: NIM. AN. V. SEIM: VORLAUFFER IM. IOR:.

Date	Mintage	VG	F	VF	XF	Unc
ND(1635-68)	—	175	300	450	750	—

KM# B85 1-1/2 THALER (Schau)
Silver **Obv:** Angel with band: HEIL SEI GOTT IN DER HÖH' **Obv. Legend:** IESUS EIN KINDT GEBORN. V. EINER IUNCKFRAUW: AUSERKORN **Rev:** Baptism of Christ **Rev. Legend:** CHRIST: D. HEILIG: TAUF: NIM. AN. V. SEIM: VORLAUFFER IM. IOR:.

Date	Mintage	VG	F	VF	XF	Unc
ND(1635-68)	—	175	300	450	750	—

KM# C85 1-1/2 THALER (Schau)
Silver **Obv:** Engaged couple, Jehovah in Hebrew and dove at top center **Obv. Legend:** QUOS DEIUS CONIUNXIT **Rev:** Wedding at Cana **Rev. Legend:** IESUS CHRISTUS MACHET

Date	Mintage	VG	F	VF	XF	Unc
ND(1635-68)	—	175	300	450	750	—

KM# D85 1-1/2 THALER (Schau)
Silver, 60 mm. **Obv:** Christ performing marriage with a couple **Obv. Legend:** WAS GOT ZUSAMMEN **Rev:** Cana wedding scene, but with couple under canopy, Christ and Mary at left, cellar master at right **Rev. Legend:** IESUS CHRISTUS MACHET **Note:** Illustration reduced.

Date	Mintage	VG	F	VF	XF	Unc
ND(1635-68)	—	150	250	350	650	—

KM# 18 2 THALER
Silver **Note:** Similar to 32 Schilling, KM#17, but date in obverse legend. Dav. #A5358.

Date	Mintage	F	VF	XF	Unc	BU
(1)606	—	550	1,100	2,000	3,250	—
1607	—	550	1,100	2,000	3,250	—

KM# 19 2 THALER
Silver **Note:** Similar to 32 Schilling, KM#17. Dav. #A5359.

Date	Mintage	F	VF	XF	Unc	BU
(1)606/(1)606 Rare	—	—	—	—	—	—

KM# 25 2 THALER
Silver **Note:** Similar to 32 Schilling, KM#20. Dav. #A5360.

Date	Mintage	VG	F	VF	XF	Unc
1610	—	550	1,100	2,000	3,250	—

KM# 66 2 THALER
Silver **Note:** Similar to 32 Schilling, KM#47. Dav. #A5365.

Date	Mintage	VG	F	VF	XF	Unc
1632 Rare	—	—	—	—	—	—
1636 Rare	—	—	—	—	—	—

KM# 116 2 THALER
Silver **Subject:** Peace of Nymwegen **Note:** Similar to 48 Schilling, KM#115. Dav. #5369.

Date	Mintage	VG	F	VF	XF	Unc
1680 HL	—	1,850	3,250	5,500	8,750	—

KM# 120 2 THALER
Silver **Obv:** Crowned imperial eagle, orb on breast, titles of Leopold I **Rev:** City arms, date divided left and right of towes, all in palm wreath **Note:** Dav. #5371.

Date	Mintage	VG	F	VF	XF	Unc
1687 HL	—	1,000	2,000	3,500	5,500	—

KM# 131 2 THALER
Silver **Note:** Similar to 1 Thaler, KM#130. Dav. #5373.

Date	Mintage	VG	F	VF	XF	Unc
1694 IR	—	1,500	2,500	4,250	6,500	—

KM# D25 2 THALER (Schau)
Silver, 56 mm. **Obv:** City arms in oval shield, ornate helmet above, 2 young females as supporters **Obv. Legend:** DA. PACEM. DOMINE. IN. — DIEBVS. NOSTRIS **Rev:** Madonna with sceptre and standing on crescent with child who holds orb **Rev. Legend:** SI. DEVS. PRO. NOBIS. — QVIS. CONTRA. NOS

Date	Mintage	VG	F	VF	XF	Unc
ND(1606-19)	—	350	600	1,000	1,750	—

KM# E25 2 THALER (Schau)
Silver **Obv:** City arms in ornate shield, ornamented helmet above **Obv. Legend:** DA. PACEM **Rev:** Madonna with sceptre and standing on crescent with child who holds orb **Rev. Legend:** SI. DEVS. PRO. NOBIS. — QVIS. CONTRA. NOV **Note:** Dav. LS-306.

Date	Mintage	VG	F	VF	XF	Unc
ND(1606-19)	—	250	450	850	1,500	—

KM# F25 2 THALER (Schau)
Silver, 53 mm. **Obv:** City arms in rectangular shield, ornate helmet above **Obv. Legend:** DA. PACEM. DOMINE. IN. — DIEBVS. NOSTRIS **Rev:** Madonna with sceptre and standing on crescent with child who holds orb **Rev. Legend:** SI. DEVS. PRO. NOBIS. — QVIS. CONTRA. NOV **Note:** Dav. LS-309. Illustration reduced.

Date	Mintage	VG	F	VF	XF	Unc
ND(1606-19)	—	500	900	1,750	3,000	—

KM# G25 2 THALER (Schau)
Silver **Obv:** City arms in ornamented oval shield, ornate helmet above **Obv. Legend:** DA. PACEM. DOMI. — IN. DIEBVS. NOSTRIS **Rev:** Madonna with sceptre standing on crescent **Rev. Legend:** VERBVM. DOMINI. — MANET. IN ÆTERNVM **Note:** Struck from the same dies as KM#A25.

Date	Mintage	VG	F	VF	XF	Unc
ND(1606-19)	—	600	1,000	1,850	3,000	—

KM# H25 2 THALER (Schau)
Silver **Obv:** City arms in oval shield, ornate helmet above, 2 young females as supporters **Obv. Legend:** DA. PACEM. DOMINE. IN. — DIEBVS. NOSTRIS **Rev:** Fortuna on the sea being attacked by Envy **Rev. Legend:** FORTUNÆ COMES IN VIDIA FR

Date	Mintage	VG	F	VF	XF	Unc
ND(1606-19)	—	—	—	—	—	—

KM# I25 2 THALER (Schau)
Silver, 60 mm. **Obv:** City arms in ornamented oval shield, ornate helmet above **Obv. Legend:** DA. PACEM. DOMI. — IN. DIEBVS. NOSTRIS **Rev:** Christ performing marriage of a couple **Rev. Legend:** QUOS. DEVS. CINIVNXIT. HOMO. NON. SEPARET **Note:** Illustration reduced.

Date	Mintage	VG	F	VF	XF	Unc
ND(1606-19)	—	600	1,000	1,850	3,000	—

KM# J25 2 THALER (Schau)
Silver **Obv:** Madonna with sword and sceptre, child with orb **Obv. Legend:** SI. DEVS. PRO. NOBIS. — QVIS. CONTRA. NOS **Rev:** The Resurrection scene **Rev. Legend:** +ICK BIN DE VPERSTANDING VND DAT LEYENT

Date	Mintage	VG	F	VF	XF	Unc
ND(ca.1610-15)	—	250	450	700	1,250	—

KM# K25 2 THALER (Schau)
Silver **Obv:** Nativity scene **Obv. Legend:** PVER. NATVS. EST. NOBIS: ET. FILIVS. DATVS. EST. NOBIS. ESAIA: IX: CA: **Rev:** Scene of 3 wise king's visit to Holy Family **Rev. Legend:** GLORIA. IN. EXCELSIS. DEO. ET. IN. TERRA. PAX. LVCÆ. II. CAPITTEL

Date	Mintage	VG	F	VF	XF	Unc
ND(1606-19)	—	250	450	700	1,250	—

KM# A35 2 THALER (Schau)
Silver **Obv:** Marriage ceremony scene **Obv. Legend:** QUOS DEUS CONIUNXIT HOMO NON SEPARET **Rev:** Wedding at Cana **Rev. Legend:** IESUS CHRISTUS MACHET WASSER ZU GUDEM WEINN. IOHA

Date	Mintage	VG	F	VF	XF	Unc
ND(1619-20)	—	250	450	700	1,250	—

KM# A52 2 THALER (Schau)
Silver, 60 mm. **Obv:** The Annunciation **Obv. Legend:** ZACHARIA: WIRD EIN SOHN GLOBT + MARIA MIT GOTTS. SOHN BEGABT **Rev:** Baptism scene **Rev. Legend:** CHRIST: DE: EHILG: TAUF: NIMPT. AN. V: SEIM. VORLAUFFER. IM. IORDAN **Note:** Illustration reduced.

Date	Mintage	VG	F	VF	XF	Unc
ND(1620-34)	—	250	450	700	1,250	—

KM# B52 2 THALER (Schau)
Silver **Obv:** The Annunciation **Obv. Legend:** ZACHARIA: WIRD EIN SOHN GLOBT + MARIA MIT GOTTS. SOHN BEGABT **Rev:** Armored rider on horseback **Rev. Legend:** IUSTITIA — ET — CONCORDIA

Date	Mintage	VG	F	VF	XF	Unc
ND(ca.1620)	—	250	450	700	1,250	—

KM# C52 2 THALER (Schau)
Silver, 58 mm. **Obv:** Christ joining a couple in marriage **Obv. Legend:** QUOS DEUS CONIUNXIT — HOMO NON SEPARET **Rev:** Wedding at Cana **Rev. Legend:** IESUS CHRISTUS MACHET WASSER ZU WEIN. IN. CANA. GAL: IOH. II

Date	Mintage	VG	F	VF	XF	Unc
ND(1620-34)	—	240	400	650	1,150	—

KM# D52 2 THALER (Schau)
Silver **Obv:** Marriage scene **Obv. Legend:** WAS GOTT ZUSAMMEN FVGET — DAS SOL KEIN MENSCH SCHEIDEN **Rev:** Similar to KM#37, but variant scene and legend **Rev. Legend:** ...Z. WEIN. IN. CANA. GALI. IOHA. II **Note:** Varieties exist.

Date	Mintage	VG	F	VF	XF	Unc
ND(1620-34)	—	180	325	475	900	—

KM# E52 2 THALER (Schau)
Silver, 57 mm. **Obv:** Nativity scene with 3 shepherds **Obv. Legend:** PUER NATUS EST NOBIS **Rev:** Visit of 3 wise Kings **Rev. Legend:** GLORIA. IN. EXCELSIS. DEO **Note:** Illustration reduced.

Date	Mintage	VG	F	VF	XF	Unc
ND(1620-34)	—	275	475	750	1,350	—

KM# F52 2 THALER (Schau)
Silver **Obv:** Flight of the Holy Family to Egypt **Obv. Legend:** CHRISTUS. FLEUCH. IN. EGYPTE. LAND. DAS. IH. HEROD. NICH. MEHR: FAND **Rev:** Ascension, Christ with cross and banner **Rev. Legend:** UMB. UNSER. GERECHTIGKEIT. WILLEN. WIDER. AUFFERSTANDE **Note:** Illustration reduced.

Date	Mintage	VG	F	VF	XF	Unc
ND(1620-34)	—	275	475	750	1,350	—

KM# E85 2 THALER (Schau)
Silver **Obv:** The Nativity **Obv. Legend:** IESUS EIN KINDT GEBORN **Rev:** Baptism of Christ **Rev. Legend:** CHRIST: D. HEILIG: TAUF: NIM **Note:** Illustration reduced.

Date	Mintage	VG	F	VF	XF	Unc
ND(1635-68)	—	250	425	650	1,100	—

KM# F85 2 THALER (Schau)
Silver **Obv:** The Annunciation **Obv. Legend:** AVE MARIA GRATIA. PLENA. DOMINVS **Rev:** The Nativity **Rev. Legend:** PVER NATUS. EST. NOBI E FILIVS. DATVS. EST.

Date	Mintage	VG	F	VF	XF	Unc
ND(1635-68)	—	275	450	750	1,350	—

KM# G85 2 THALER (Schau)
Silver **Obv:** Engaged couple, Jehovah in Hebrew and dove at top center **Obv. Legend:** QUOS DEIUS CONIUNXIT **Rev:** Wedding at Cana **Rev. Legend:** IESUS CHRISTUS MACHET

Date	Mintage	VG	F	VF	XF	Unc
ND(1635-68)	—	275	450	750	1,350	—

KM# H85 2 THALER (Schau)
Obv: Engaged couple, Jehovah in Hebrew and dove at top center **Obv. Legend:** WAS GOTT ZUSAMN FVGT **Rev:** Wedding at Cana **Rev. Legend:** IESUS CHRISTUS MACHET

Date	Mintage	VG	F	VF	XF	Unc
ND(1635-68)	—	275	450	750	1,350	—

KM# L25 2-1/2 THALER (Schau)
Silver **Obv:** City arms in baroque shield, ornate helmet above **Obv. Legend:** DA. PACEM. DOMIN: IN — DIEBVS. NOSTRIS **Rev:** Madonna with sceptre and standing on crescent with child who holds orb **Rev. Legend:** SI. DEVS. PRO. NOBIS. — QVIS. CONTRA. NOV

Date	Mintage	VG	F	VF	XF	Unc
ND(1606-19)	—	275	475	900	1,650	—

KM# M25 3 THALER (Schau)
Silver **Obv:** City arms in baroque shield, ornate helmet above **Obv. Legend:** DA. PACEM. DOMIN: IN — DIEBVS. NOSTRIS **Rev:** Madonna with sceptre and standing on crescent with child who holds orb **Rev. Legend:** SI. DEVS. PRO. NOBIS. — QVIS. CONTRA. NOV **Note:** Struck with same dies as KM#L25.

Date	Mintage	VG	F	VF	XF	Unc
ND(1606-19)	—	300	500	950	1,700	—

KM# A26 3 THALER (Schau)
Silver **Obv:** Madonna with sword and sceptre, child with orb **Obv. Legend:** SI. DEVS. PRO. NOBIS. — QVIS. CONTRA. NOS **Rev:** The Resurrection scene **Rev. Legend:** +ICK BIN DE VPERSTANDING VND DAT LEYENT

Date	Mintage	VG	F	VF	XF	Unc
ND(ca.1610-15)	—	300	500	950	1,700	—

KM# H52 3 THALER (Schau)
Silver, 60 mm. **Obv:** Marriage scene **Obv. Legend:** WAS GOTT ZUSAMMEN FVGET — DAS SOL KEIN MENSCH SCHEIDEN **Rev:** Similar to KM#37, but variant scene and legend **Rev. Legend:** ...Z. WEIN. IN. CANA. GALI. IOHA. II **Note:** Illustration reduced.

Date	Mintage	VG	F	VF	XF	Unc
ND(1620-34)	—	270	450	700	1,100	—

KM# 185 3 THALER (Schau)
Silver **Obv:** Engaged couple, Jehovah in Hebrew and dove at top center **Obv. Legend:** QUOS DEIUS CONIUNXIT **Rev:** Wedding at Cana **Rev. Legend:** IESUS CHRISTUS MACHET **Note:** Illustration reduced.

Date	Mintage	VG	F	VF	XF	Unc
ND(1635-68)	—	240	425	625	950	—

KM# N25 3-1/2 THALER (Schau)
Silver **Obv:** City arms in oval shield, ornate helmet above, 2 young females as supporters **Obv. Legend:** DA. PACEM. DOMINE. IN. — DIEBVS. NOSTRIS **Rev:** Madonna with sceptre standing on crescent with child who holds orb **Rev. Legend:** SI. DEVS. PRO. NOBIS. — QVIS. CONTRA. NOV

Date	Mintage	VG	F	VF	XF	Unc
ND(1606-19)	—	350	550	1,000	1,800	—

TRADE COINAGE

KM# 9 GOLDGULDEN
3.5000 g., 0.9860 Gold 0.1109 oz. AGW **Obv:** St. Peter

Date	Mintage	VG	F	VF	XF	Unc
ND(1606-12) (g)	—	300	600	1,750	3,750	—
1608 (g)	—	300	600	1,750	3,750	—

KM# 31 GOLDGULDEN
3.5000 g., 0.9860 Gold 0.1109 oz. AGW **Rev:** Titles of Matthias

Date	Mintage	VG	F	VF	XF	Unc
1617 (g)	—	425	775	2,300	4,850	—
1619 (g)	—	425	775	2,300	4,850	—

KM# 61 GOLDGULDEN
3.5000 g., 0.9860 Gold 0.1109 oz. AGW **Rev:** Titles of Ferdinand II

Date	Mintage	VG	F	VF	XF	Unc
1628 (i)	—	300	600	1,750	3,750	—

KM# 68 GOLDGULDEN
3.5000 g., 0.9860 Gold 0.1109 oz. AGW **Rev:** Titles of Ferdinand III

Date	Mintage	VG	F	VF	XF	Unc
1637 (j)	—	—	—	—	—	—

KM# 108 GOLDGULDEN
3.5000 g., 0.9860 Gold 0.1109 oz. AGW **Obv:** Helmeted oval arms **Rev:** Crowned imperial eagle, titles of Leopold I

Date	Mintage	VG	F	VF	XF	Unc
1675 HL	—	300	525	1,500	2,800	—

KM# 117 1/4 DUCAT
0.8750 g., 0.9860 Gold 0.0277 oz. AGW

Date	Mintage	VG	F	VF	XF	Unc
1680 HL	—	130	225	500	825	—
ND1692 IR	—	130	225	500	825	—

KM# 140 1/4 DUCAT
0.8750 g., 0.9860 Gold 0.0277 oz. AGW **Obv:** Madonna and child **Rev:** Annunciation scene

Date	Mintage	VG	F	VF	XF	Unc
ND(1700)	—	145	270	600	1,000	—

KM# 107 1/2 DUCAT
1.7500 g., 0.9860 Gold 0.0555 oz. AGW

Date	Mintage	VG	F	VF	XF	Unc
1675 HL	—	150	275	650	1,100	—

KM# 134 1/2 DUCAT
1.7500 g., 0.9860 Gold 0.0555 oz. AGW **Obv:** Crowned imperial eagle, titles of Leopold I

Date	Mintage	VG	F	VF	XF	Unc
ND(1692-1704) IR	—	130	260	575	975	—

KM# 69 DUCAT
3.5000 g., 0.9860 Gold 0.1109 oz. AGW

Date	Mintage	VG	F	VF	XF	Unc
1641 (j)	—	140	230	500	850	—
1642 (j)	—	140	230	500	850	—
1643 (j)	—	140	230	500	850	—
1644 (j)	—	140	230	500	850	—
1645 (j)	—	140	230	500	850	—
1646 (j)	—	140	230	500	850	—
1647 (j)	—	140	230	500	850	—
1649 (j)	—	140	230	500	850	—
1650 (j)	—	140	230	500	850	—
1651 (j)	—	140	230	500	850	—
1652 (j)	—	140	230	500	850	—
1653 (j)	—	140	230	500	850	—
1654 (j)	—	140	230	500	850	—
1655 (j)	—	140	230	500	850	—
1656 (j)	—	140	230	500	850	—
1657 (j)	—	140	230	500	850	—
1658 (j)	—	140	230	500	850	—
1659 (j)	—	140	230	500	850	—
1660 (j)	—	140	230	500	850	—
1661 (j)	—	140	230	500	850	—
1662 (j)	—	140	230	500	850	—
1663 (j)	—	140	230	500	850	—
1664 (j)	—	140	230	500	850	—
1665 (j)	—	140	230	500	850	—
1666 (j)	—	140	230	500	850	—
1667 (j)	—	140	230	500	850	—

KM# 86 DUCAT
3.5000 g., 0.9860 Gold 0.1109 oz. AGW **Rev:** Madonna and child

Date	Mintage	VG	F	VF	XF	Unc
1668 (k)	—	175	280	725	1,250	—
1669 MF (k)	—	175	280	725	1,250	—
1671	—	175	280	725	1,250	—
1674 HL	—	175	280	725	1,250	—
1675 HL	—	175	280	725	1,250	—
1692	—	175	280	725	1,250	—

KM# 121 DUCAT
3.5000 g., 0.9860 Gold 0.1109 oz. AGW **Obv:** Arms in branches **Rev:** Crowned imperial eagle

Date	Mintage	VG	F	VF	XF	Unc
1689 HL	—	240	400	1,000	1,850	—
1692 IR	—	240	400	1,000	1,850	—
1695	—	240	400	1,000	1,850	—
1698	—	240	400	1,000	1,850	—

KM# 132 DUCAT
3.5000 g., 0.9860 Gold 0.1109 oz. AGW **Rev:** Madonna with shield of arms

Date	Mintage	VG	F	VF	XF	Unc
1694 IR	—	175	375	800	1,500	—

KM# 76 2 DUCAT
7.0000 g., 0.9860 Gold 0.2219 oz. AGW **Obv:** Madonna and child in inner circle **Rev:** Madonna and child in inner circle, date in legend

Date	Mintage	VG	F	VF	XF	Unc
1649 MF (j)	—	400	900	2,250	4,250	—
1660 MF (j)	—	400	900	2,250	4,250	—
1666 MF	—	400	900	2,250	4,250	—

KM# 91 2 DUCAT
7.0000 g., 0.9860 Gold 0.2219 oz. AGW **Obv:** Arms with lion supporters **Rev:** Madonna and child, date in legend

Date	Mintage	VG	F	VF	XF	Unc
1669 MF (k)	—	475	875	1,950	3,600	—
1672	—	475	875	1,950	3,600	—
1674 HL	—	475	875	1,950	3,600	—
1679	—	475	875	1,950	3,600	—
1681	—	475	875	1,950	3,600	—
1685	—	475	875	1,950	3,600	—
1690	—	475	875	1,950	3,600	—
1692	—	475	875	1,950	3,600	—
1694	—	475	875	1,950	3,600	—

KM# 109 2 DUCAT
7.0000 g., 0.9860 Gold 0.2219 oz. AGW **Obv:** Crowned imperial eagle, titles of Leopold I **Rev:** City arms between two palm branches

Date	Mintage	VG	F	VF	XF	Unc
ND(1672-92) HL	—	—	—	—	—	—
ND(1692-1705) IR	—	—	—	—	—	—

KM# 122 2 DUCAT
7.0000 g., 0.9860 Gold 0.2219 oz. AGW **Obv:** Crowned imperial eagle, titles of Leopold I **Rev:** Arms in cartouche

Date	Mintage	VG	F	VF	XF	Unc
1689 HL	—	800	1,800	4,000	6,000	—
1692	—	800	1,800	4,000	6,000	—
1696	—	800	1,800	4,000	6,000	—
1698	—	800	1,800	4,000	6,000	—

KM# 49 2-1/2 DUCAT (1/4 Portugalöser)
8.7500 g., 0.9860 Gold 0.2774 oz. AGW **Note:** Similar to 5 Ducat, KM#50.

Date	Mintage	VG	F	VF	XF	Unc
ND(c.1620) Rare	—	—	—	—	—	—

KM# 135 2-1/2 DUCAT (1/4 Portugalöser)

8.7500 g., 0.9860 Gold 0.2774 oz. AGW **Obv:** Crowned imperial eagle, titles of Leopold I **Rev:** Madonna and child

Date	Mintage	VG	F	VF	XF	Unc
ND(1692-1705) IR Rare	—	—	—	—	—	—

KM# O25 5 DUCAT (1/2 Portugalöser)

17.9400 g., Gold **Obv:** City arms in ornamented oval shield, ornate helmet above **Obv. Legend:** DA. PACEM. DOMI. — IN. DIEBVS. NOSTRIS **Rev:** Madonna with sceptre standing on crescent **Rev. Legend:** VERBVM. DOMINI. — MANET. IN ÆTERNVM **Note:** Struck from the same dies as KM#A25.

Date	Mintage	VG	F	VF	XF	Unc
ND(1606-19) Rare	—	—	—	—	—	—

KM# 50 5 DUCAT (1/2 Portugalöser)

17.5000 g., 0.9860 Gold 0.5547 oz. AGW

Date	Mintage	F	VF	XF	Unc	BU
ND(c.1620) Rare	—	—	—	—	—	—

KM# 60 5 DUCAT (1/2 Portugalöser)

17.5000 g., 0.9860 Gold 0.5547 oz. AGW **Rev:** Titles of Ferdinand II **Note:** Struck with 1 Thaler dies.

Date	Mintage	F	VF	XF	Unc	BU
1624 Rare	—	—	—	—	—	—

Note: Stack's International sale, 3/88 XF realized $16,500

KM# 133 5 DUCAT (1/2 Portugalöser)

17.5000 g., 0.9860 Gold 0.5547 oz. AGW **Obv:** Arms in cartouche **Rev:** Crowned imperial eagle, titles of Leopold I

Date	Mintage	F	VF	XF	Unc	BU
1695 IR Rare	—	—	—	—	—	—

KM# P25 10 DUCAT (Portugalöser)

Gold **Obv:** City arms in ornate shield, ornate helmet above **Obv. Legend:** DA. PACEM. DOMINE'. IN — DIEBVS. NOSTRIS **Rev:** Madonna with sword and sceptre, child with orb **Rev. Legend:** SI. DEVS. PRO. NOBIS. — QVIS. CONTRA. NOS **Note:** Struck from the same dies as KM#B25.

Date	Mintage	VG	F	VF	XF	Unc
ND(1606-19) Rare	—	—	—	—	—	—

KM# 51 10 DUCAT (Portugalöser)

35.0000 g., 0.9860 Gold 1.1095 oz. AGW **Rev:** Similar to 5 Ducat, KM#50. **Note:** Illustration reduced.

Date	Mintage	F	VF	XF	Unc	BU
ND(c.1620) Rare	—	—	—	—	—	—

KM# 87 10 DUCAT (Portugalöser)

35.0000 g., 0.9860 Gold 1.1095 oz. AGW **Note:** Similar to KM#51.

Date	Mintage	F	VF	XF	Unc	BU
ND(1668-73) Rare	—	—	—	—	—	—

KM# 138 10 DUCAT (Portugalöser)

35.0000 g., 0.9860 Gold 1.1095 oz. AGW **Subject:** Peace of Ryswick **Obv:** Winged victory standing on prone human figure between palm and pine trees, sailing ships in background **Obv. Legend:** PAX MARE PAX TERRAM PAX VRBES PAX BEATAGROS **Rev:** City view, sailing ships in foreground, Hamburg below, Jehovah in Hebrew in clouds above, legend curves above and below **Rev. Legend:** HÆC VRDS TUTA DEI CLIPEO - PRO TECTA MANEBIT **Note:** (Ref: Gaedechens III: 1681)

Date	Mintage	F	VF	XF	Unc	BU
ND(1697) Rare	—	—	—	—	—	—

REFORM COINAGE

KM# A23 1/2 THALER (Schau)

14.4000 g., Silver, 35 mm. **Obv:** City arms in baroque frame, ornate helmet **Obv. Legend:** DA.PACEM.DOMIN:-- IN.DIE:NOSTRIS **Rev:** Nativity scene **Rev. Legend:** PVER. NATVS. EST. NOVIS. E. FILIVS. DATVS. ETS.

Date	Mintage	F	VF	XF	Unc	BU
ND(1606-19)	—	—	—	—	—	—

HAMELN

Hamlin, Hamelin, Quernhameln City on the Weser river 26 miles southwest of Hannover grew around the abbey of St. Boniface beginning in the 8th century. In 1259 it passed from the abbey of Fulda to the bishopric of Minden, then to the dukes of Brunswick. Became a member of the Hanseatic league and obtained the mint right in the late 15th century and struck coins until 1695. This is the town of the legend of the Pied Piper.

MINTOFFICIALS' INITIALS

Initial	Date	Name
CF or (e)	1615-18	Christof Feustel (Feistel)
DK	1624-25	Unknown
IB or (n)	1671-73	Jonas Bose (Bosen)
(a)	1606-08	Christof Dies (Diess, Dyss)
(b)	1609	Sebastian Schoras
(c)	1611-12	Gert Koler
(d)	1612-15	Jakob Pfahler (Pfaler)
(f)	1619-?	Nicolaus (Claws) Oppermann
(g)	1622-24	Georg Arendes (Arndt, Arndts)
(h)	1626-32	Unknown, perhaps Simon timke
(i)	1633	Unknown
(j)	1635-41	Caspar Hoffmann
(k)	1655-56	Johann Otte (Otto)
(m)	1668-70, 1673	(Peter) Paul Pechstein

Arms

2 mill rinds, often in front of twin-towered church.

CITY

REGULAR COINAGE

KM# 36 PFENNIG

Silver **Note:** Schussel type. Arms in shield divide Q-H, date above.

Date	Mintage	VG	F	VF	XF	Unc
(1)6ZZ	—	27.00	55.00	100	175	—
16Z3	—	27.00	55.00	100	175	—
(1)6Z3	—	27.00	55.00	100	175	—
(1)6Z5	—	27.00	55.00	100	175	—

KM# 40 PFENNIG

Silver **Note:** Shield divides date, QH above.

Date	Mintage	VG	F	VF	XF	Unc
(16)24	—	27.00	55.00	100	175	—

KM# 51 PFENNIG

Copper **Rev:** Date added, 33/STAT/PEN

Date	Mintage	VG	F	VF	XF	Unc
(16)3Z/(16)33	—	13.00	33.00	55.00	90.00	—
1633/(16)33	—	13.00	33.00	55.00	90.00	—

KM# 70 PFENNIG

Silver **Note:** Uniface. Schussel type. Arms divide date.

Date	Mintage	VG	F	VF	XF	Unc
1668	—	—	—	—	—	—
1669	—	—	—	—	—	—
1672	—	—	—	—	—	—

KM# 50 PFENNIG (Stadtpfennig)

Copper **Obv:** Arms, date in legend **Rev:** I/STAT/PEN **Note:** Varieties exist.

Date	Mintage	VG	F	VF	XF	Unc
(16)3Z	—	13.00	33.00	55.00	90.00	—
ND	—	13.00	33.00	55.00	90.00	—
(16)33	—	13.00	33.00	55.00	90.00	—
(1)634	—	13.00	33.00	55.00	90.00	—

KM# 82 2 PFENNIG

Silver **Obv:** Arms divide date **Rev:** II/GUTE/PF **Note:** Gute 2 Pfennig.

Date	Mintage	VG	F	VF	XF	Unc
1672	—	—	—	—	—	—

KM# 16 3 PFENNIG (Dreier)

Silver **Obv:** Arms in shield **Rev:** Imperial orb with 3, date divided above

Date	Mintage	VG	F	VF	XF	Unc
1619	—	—	—	—	—	—
16ZZ	—	—	—	—	—	—
16Z3 (g)	—	—	—	—	—	—

KM# 37 3 PFENNIG (Dreier)

Silver **Obv:** Arms in front of church divide Q-H

Date	Mintage	VG	F	VF	XF	Unc
1622 (g)	—	—	—	—	—	—

KM# 65 3 PFENNIG (Dreier)

Silver **Obv:** Arms in shield **Rev:** Imperial orb with 3 divides date

Date	Mintage	VG	F	VF	XF	Unc
1655 (k)	4,000	—	—	—	—	—
1656 (k)	—	—	—	—	—	—

KM# 71 3 PFENNIG (Dreier)

Silver **Obv:** Arms, date in legend **Rev:** Imperial orb with 3

Date	Mintage	VG	F	VF	XF	Unc
1668 (m)	—	—	—	—	—	—

KM# 83 3 PFENNIG (Dreier)

Silver **Obv:** Arms **Rev:** Imperial orb with 3, date divided above

Date	Mintage	VG	F	VF	XF	Unc
1672 (n)	—	—	—	—	—	—

KM# 90 3 PFENNIG (Dreier)

Silver **Note:** Uniface. Arms, 3 above, date divided below.

Date	Mintage	VG	F	VF	XF	Unc
1695	—	—	—	—	—	—

KM# A90 3 PFENNIG (Dreier)

Silver **Note:** Uniface; Arms, 4 small stars around.

Date	Mintage	VG	F	VF	XF	Unc
ND(ca. late 17th c.)	—	—	—	—	—	—

KM# 54 4 PFENNIG (4 Stadtpfennig; Mattier)
Copper **Obv:** Arms **Rev:** IIII in cartouche divides date, STAT above, PEN below

Date	Mintage	VG	F	VF	XF	Unc
1633	—	16.00	45.00	75.00	120	—
1635 (j)	—	16.00	45.00	75.00	120	—
1636 (j)	—	16.00	45.00	75.00	120	—
1648	—	16.00	45.00	75.00	120	—

KM# 72 4 PFENNIG (4 Stadtpfennig; Mattier)
Silver **Obv:** Arms divide date **Rev:** IIII/GUTE/PF

Date	Mintage	VG	F	VF	XF	Unc
1668 (m)	—	13.00	33.00	45.00	80.00	—
1669 (m)	—	13.00	33.00	45.00	80.00	—
1672 (n)	—	13.00	33.00	45.00	80.00	—
1627 (n) Error; Rare	—	—	—	—	—	—

KM# 91 6 PFENNIG
Silver **Note:** Uniface. 6 above arms, date divided below.

Date	Mintage	VG	F	VF	XF	Unc
1695	—	—	—	—	—	—

KM# 25 FLITTER
Copper **Obv:** Similar to 3 Flitter, KM#27 **Rev:** I/FLIT/TER/date
Note: Kipper Flitter.

Date	Mintage	VG	F	VF	XF	Unc
16Z0	—	13.00	33.00	55.00	100	—

KM# 26 2 FLITTER
Copper **Obv:** Arms in front of church divide date as 1-6/Z-0
Rev: II/FLIT/TRN

Date	Mintage	VG	F	VF	XF	Unc
16Z0	—	13.00	33.00	55.00	120	—
16Z1	—	13.00	33.00	55.00	120	—

KM# 27 3 FLITTER
Copper **Note:** Kipper 3 Flitter.

Date	Mintage	VG	F	VF	XF	Unc
16Z0	—	13.00	33.00	55.00	100	—
16Z1	—	13.00	33.00	55.00	100	—

KM# 34 3 FLITTER
Copper **Rev:** III/FLITT/REN/date

Date	Mintage	VG	F	VF	XF	Unc
16Z1	—	13.00	33.00	55.00	120	—

KM# A28 GOSLAR (1/12 Schilling)
Silver **Obv:** Oval city arms, 4 small rosettes around
Rev: I/GOS/LAR

Date	Mintage	VG	F	VF	XF	Unc
ND(ca.1620)	—	—	—	—	—	—

KM# 28.1 GOSKEN
Copper **Obv:** City arms, IZ below **Rev:** 'I' in center, ANNO, date around

Date	Mintage	VG	F	VF	XF	Unc
16Z0	—	13.00	33.00	55.00	120	—

KM# 28.2 GOSKEN
Copper **Obv:** City gate, arms in entrance, date above
Rev: I/GOS/KEN

Date	Mintage	VG	F	VF	XF	Unc
1620	—	13.00	33.00	55.00	120	—

KM# 29 1-1/2 GOSKEN
Copper **Obv:** Arms, .8. above **Rev:** 1-1/2 in center, ANNO/16Z0 around

Date	Mintage	VG	F	VF	XF	Unc
16Z0	—	25.00	45.00	70.00	125	—

KM# 30 2 GOSKEN
Copper **Obv:** Arms in front of church divide date as 1-6/Z-0
Rev: II center, GOSKEN around

Date	Mintage	VG	F	VF	XF	Unc
16Z0	—	13.00	33.00	55.00	110	—

KM# 31 2 GOSKEN
Copper **Rev:** Date also in legend

Date	Mintage	VG	F	VF	XF	Unc
16Z0	—	13.00	33.00	55.00	110	—
16Z1	—	13.00	33.00	55.00	110	—

KM# 35 2 GOSKEN
Copper **Rev:** Date only in legend

Date	Mintage	VG	F	VF	XF	Unc
16Z1	—	13.00	33.00	55.00	110	—

KM# 33 3 GOSKEN
Copper **Rev:** Date also in legend

Date	Mintage	VG	F	VF	XF	Unc
16Z0	—	25.00	45.00	70.00	120	—

KM# 32 3 GOSKEN
Copper **Obv:** Arms in front of church divide date as 1-6/Z-0
Rev: III in center, GOSKEN around **Note:** Kipper 3 Gosken.

Date	Mintage	VG	F	VF	XF	Unc
16Z0	—	25.00	45.00	70.00	120	—

KM# 38 MARIENGROSCHEN
Silver **Obv:** Arms divide date **Rev:** Madonna and child
Note: Varieties exist.

Date	Mintage	VG	F	VF	XF	Unc
(1)622 (g)	—	27.00	55.00	100	175	—
(1)6Z3 (g)	—	27.00	55.00	100	175	—
1623 (g)	—	27.00	55.00	100	175	—
1624 (g)	—	27.00	55.00	100	175	—
1655 (k)	82,000	27.00	55.00	100	175	—
1668 (m)	—	27.00	55.00	100	175	—
1669 (m)	—	27.00	55.00	100	175	—

KM# 80 4 MARIENGROSCHEN
Silver **Note:** Similar to 6 Mariengroschen, KM#73 but value IIII on reverse.

Date	Mintage	VG	F	VF	XF	Unc
1671 IB	—	—	—	—	—	—

KM# 73 6 MARIENGROSCHEN
Silver **Note:** Varieties exist.

Date	Mintage	VG	F	VF	XF	Unc
1668 (m)	—	27.00	55.00	110	220	—
1669 (m)	—	27.00	55.00	110	220	—
1672 IB	68,000	27.00	55.00	110	220	—

KM# 81 12 MARIENGROSCHEN
Silver **Note:** Similar to 6 Mariengroschen, KM#73 but value XII on reverse.

Date	Mintage	VG	F	VF	XF	Unc
1671 IB	65,000	45.00	110	200	375	—
1672 IB	55,000	45.00	110	200	375	—
1672	—	45.00	110	200	375	—

KM# 5 1/96 THALER
Silver **Obv:** Arms in front of church **Rev:** Imperial orb with 96 divides date in ornamented rhombus

Date	Mintage	VG	F	VF	XF	Unc
1606	—	—	—	—	—	—
1608	—	—	—	—	—	—

KM# 6.2 1/24 THALER (Groschen)
Silver **Rev:** Date divided by cross in outer circle

Date	Mintage	VG	F	VF	XF	Unc
1606	—	20.00	40.00	70.00	130	—
1607	—	20.00	40.00	70.00	130	—
1609	—	20.00	40.00	70.00	130	—

KM# 6.1 1/24 THALER (Groschen)
Silver **Obv:** Arms in front of church **Rev:** Imperial orb with Z4, date divided by cross within inner circle, titles of Rudolf II
Note: Varieties exist.

Date	Mintage	VG	F	VF	XF	Unc
ND (a)	—	20.00	40.00	70.00	125	—
1606 (a)	—	20.00	40.00	70.00	125	—
1607 (a)	—	20.00	40.00	70.00	125	—
1608 (a)	—	20.00	40.00	70.00	125	—
1609 (a)	—	20.00	40.00	70.00	125	—
1609	—	20.00	40.00	70.00	125	—
1609 (b)	—	20.00	40.00	70.00	125	—
1611 (c)	—	20.00	40.00	70.00	125	—

KM# 10 1/24 THALER (Groschen)
Silver **Rev:** Titles of Matthias **Note:** Varieties exist.

Date	Mintage	VG	F	VF	XF	Unc
1612 (c)	—	20.00	40.00	70.00	125	—
1612 (d)	—	20.00	40.00	70.00	125	—
1613 (d)	—	20.00	40.00	70.00	125	—
1614 (d)	—	20.00	40.00	70.00	125	—
1614 (e)	—	20.00	40.00	70.00	125	—
1615/3	—	20.00	40.00	70.00	125	—
1615 (d)	—	20.00	40.00	70.00	125	—
1615 (e)	—	20.00	40.00	70.00	125	—
1616 (e)	60,000	20.00	40.00	70.00	125	—
1617 (e)	—	20.00	40.00	70.00	125	—
1618 (e)	—	20.00	40.00	70.00	125	—

KM# 15 1/24 THALER (Groschen)
Silver **Note:** Klippe.

Date	Mintage	VG	F	VF	XF	Unc
(16)18 (e)	—	—	—	—	—	—

KM# 18 1/24 THALER (Groschen)
Silver **Note:** Klippe.

Date	Mintage	VG	F	VF	XF	Unc
(16)19 (f)	—	—	—	—	—	—

KM# 17 1/24 THALER (Groschen)
Silver **Note:** Kipper 1/24 Thaler. Varieties exist.

Date	Mintage	VG	F	VF	XF	Unc
1619 (f)	—	20.00	40.00	70.00	125	—
(1)619 (f)	—	20.00	40.00	70.00	125	—
(16)19 (f)	—	20.00	40.00	70.00	125	—
(16)Z0 (f)	—	20.00	40.00	70.00	125	—

KM# 19 1/24 THALER (Groschen)
Silver **Note:** Kipper 1/24 Thaler. Varieties exist.

Date	Mintage	VG	F	VF	XF	Unc
(16)19 (f)	—	20.00	40.00	70.00	120	—
(16)20 (f)	—	20.00	40.00	70.00	120	—
(1)620 (f)	—	20.00	40.00	70.00	120	—
ND (f)	—	20.00	40.00	70.00	120	—
1622	—	20.00	40.00	70.00	120	—
(1)6ZZ (g)	—	20.00	40.00	70.00	120	—
1623 (g)	—	20.00	40.00	70.00	120	—

KM# 56 1/24 THALER (Groschen)
Silver **Rev:** Date between church towers

Date	Mintage	VG	F	VF	XF	Unc
1633 (i)	—	—	—	—	—	—

KM# 57 1/24 THALER (Groschen)
Silver **Rev:** Titles of Ferdinand III **Note:** Varieties exist.

Date	Mintage	VG	F	VF	XF	Unc
(16)36 (j)	—	25.00	40.00	80.00	125	—
(16)37 (j)	—	25.00	40.00	80.00	125	—
(16)39 (j)	—	25.00	40.00	80.00	125	—
1641 (j)	21,000	25.00	40.00	80.00	125	—
(1)641 (j)	Inc. above	25.00	40.00	80.00	125	—
1655 (k)	—	25.00	40.00	80.00	125	—

KM# 58 1/24 THALER (Groschen)
Silver **Obv:** Titles of Ferdinand III

Date	Mintage	VG	F	VF	XF	Unc
(1)638 (j)	—	—	—	—	—	—

KM# 7 1/16 THALER (Doppel-Schilling)
Silver **Obv:** Arms in front of church **Rev:** Crowned imperial eagle, 16 in orb on breast, titles of Rudolf II, date divided by crown at top

Date	Mintage	VG	F	VF	XF	Unc
ND	—	200	400	600	1,150	—
1607 (a)	—	200	400	600	1,150	—
1608 (a)	—	200	400	600	1,150	—

KM# 42.1 1/8 THALER (1/2 Reichsort)
Silver **Obv:** I/HALBR./R.ORT/date, titles of Ferdinand II **Rev:** Arms in front of church

Date	Mintage	VG	F	VF	XF	Unc
1624	—	—	—	—	—	—

KM# 42.2 1/8 THALER (1/2 Reichsort)
Silver **Obv:** I/HALBR./R.ORT/date, titles of Ferdinand II **Rev:** Arms in front of church, date divided above value

Date	Mintage	VG	F	VF	XF	Unc
16Z4 (h)	—	—	—	—	—	—

KM# 44 1/8 THALER (1/2 Reichsort)
Silver **Rev:** EIN/HALB./RIKES/ORT, date in legend

Date	Mintage	VG	F	VF	XF	Unc
1625 (h)	—	—	—	—	—	—

KM# 39.1 1/4 THALER (6 Groschen)
Silver **Obv:** Arms in front of Church, date in legend **Rev:** Crowned imperial eagle, 6 on breast, titles of Ferdinand II

Date	Mintage	VG	F	VF	XF	Unc
1623	—	—	—	—	—	—

KM# 39.2 1/4 THALER (6 Groschen)
Silver **Obv:** Arms in front of church, date between towers **Rev:** Crowned imperial eagle, 6 on breast, titles of Ferdinand II

Date	Mintage	VG	F	VF	XF	Unc
16Z3 (g)	—	—	—	—	—	—

KM# 66 1/4 THALER (6 Groschen)
Silver **Obv:** Arms in front of church **Rev:** Crowned imperial eagle, orb without value on breast, titles of Ferdinand III and date in legend

Date	Mintage	VG	F	VF	XF	Unc
1656	—	—	—	—	—	—

KM# 41 1/2 THALER (12 Groschen)
Silver **Obv:** Crowned imperial eagle, 1Z in orb on breast, titles of Ferdinand II **Rev:** Arms in front of church, date between two towers

Date	Mintage	VG	F	VF	XF	Unc
16Z4 (h)	—	—	—	—	—	—
16Z5 (h)	—	—	—	—	—	—
1627 (h)	—	—	—	—	—	—
1629 (h)	—	—	—	—	—	—

KM# 43 1/2 THALER (12 Groschen)
Silver **Rev:** Date in legend

Date	Mintage	VG	F	VF	XF	Unc
(1)625 DK	—	—	—	—	—	—

KM# 52 1/2 THALER (12 Groschen)
Silver **Obv:** Without value in orb on eagle's breast **Rev:** Date divided left and right of church

Date	Mintage	VG	F	VF	XF	Unc
163Z (h)	—	—	—	—	—	—

KM# 55 1/2 THALER (12 Groschen)
Silver **Rev:** Date between church towers

Date	Mintage	VG	F	VF	XF	Unc
1633 (h)	—	—	—	—	—	—

KM# 8 THALER (24 Groschen)
Silver **Obv:** Church with arms in entrance way, date above in inner circle **Obv. Legend:** MONETA.NOVA:CIVITATIS.Q.HAMEL.x **Rev:** Crowned imperial eagle with orb on breast **Rev. Legend:** .RVDOL.II.D.G.ROM.IMP.SE.AVGVST. **Note:** Dav. #5375.

Date	Mintage	VG	F	VF	XF	Unc
1608 (a)	—	1,350	2,250	3,750	6,000	—

KM# 11 THALER (24 Groschen)
Silver **Obv:** Church with arms in entrance way **Obv. Legend:** •MONE•NOVA•CIVI•QVE•HAMELEN• **Rev:** Crowned imperial eagle with orb on breast **Rev. Legend:** MATTH•I•ROMA IMPE• SEMP•AV• **Note:** Dav.#A5377.

Date	Mintage	VG	F	VF	XF	Unc
1614 (d)	—	—	—	—	—	—
1617 GF	1,540	—	—	—	—	—

KM# 12 THALER (24 Groschen)
Silver **Obv:** Church wtih arms in entrance way in inner circle **Obv. Legend:** .MONETA.NOVA.CIVITATIS Q.HAMELE. **Rev:** Crowned imperial eagle with orb on breast, date above **Rev. Legend:** MATH.I.D.G.ROM. IM. SEM. AVGVS. **Note:** Klippe. Dav.#5376. Illustration reduced.

Date	Mintage	VG	F	VF	XF	Unc
1614 (d) Rare	—	—	—	—	—	—

KM# 13 THALER (24 Groschen)
Silver **Obv:** 24 in orb on breast of eagle, titles of Matthias **Rev:** Arms in front of church, date divided by central tower of church **Note:** Klippe. Dav. #5376.

Date	Mintage	VG	F	VF	XF	Unc
1615 (d)	—	—	—	—	—	—
1616 (d)	1,000	—	—	—	—	—

Note: Reported, not confirmed

KM# A13 THALER (24 Groschen)
Silver **Obv:** Church with arms in entrance way, date above in inner circle **Obv. Legend:** MONETA•NOVA•CIVITA•Q• HAMELEN **Rev:** Crowned imperial eagle with orb on breast **Rev. Legend:** MATHI•I•D•G•RO IMP•SEM•AVGVS• **Note:** Dav.#5376.

Date	Mintage	VG	F	VF	XF	Unc
1615	—	—	—	—	—	—

KM# A14 THALER (24 Groschen)
Silver **Obv:** Church with arms in entrance way, date above **Obv. Legend:** •MONETA•NOVA•CIVITATIS•QVERN•HAME LEN• **Rev:** Crowned imperial eagle with orb on breast **Rev. Legend:** MATTH•I•ROMA•IMPE•SEMP•AV• **Note:** Dav.#5376B.

Date	Mintage	VG	F	VF	XF	Unc
1616//1617	—	—	—	—	—	—

KM# 45.3 THALER (24 Groschen)
Silver **Obv:** Church with arms in entrance way **Obv. Legend:** MO•NO••REIP•QUERN•HAMELN•ANNO• **Rev:** Crowned imperial eagle with orb on breast **Rev. Legend:** D•G• FERDI•Z•RO M•IMP•SEM•A• **Note:** Dav.#5377B.

Date	Mintage	VG	F	VF	XF	Unc
(1)1625 D+K	—	1,350	2,250	3,750	6,000	—

KM# 45.1 THALER (24 Groschen)
Silver **Obv:** Church with arms in entrance way **Obv. Legend:** MO•NO•REIP.QUERN HAMELN **Rev:** Crowned imperial eagle with orb on breast **Rev. Legend:** D:G.FERDI.Z.ROM.IMP.S.A.

Date	Mintage	VG	F	VF	XF	Unc
1625 D+K	—	—	—	—	—	—

KM# 45 THALER (24 Groschen)
Silver **Note:** Dav. #5377.

Date	Mintage	VG	F	VF	XF	Unc
1625 DK	—	1,350	2,250	3,750	6,000	—

KM# 45.2 THALER (24 Groschen)
Silver **Obv:** Church with arms in entrance way **Obv. Legend:** MO.NO.REIP.QUERN.HAMELN. **Rev:** Crowned imperial eagle with orb on breast **Rev. Legend:** D:G.FERD.Z.ROM..IMP.SEM.AVG. **Note:** Dav. #5377A.

Date	Mintage	VG	F	VF	XF	Unc
1625 D+K	—	1,350	2,250	3,750	6,000	—

KM# 46.1 THALER (24 Groschen)
Silver **Obv. Legend:** D:G.FERDI.Z.ROM.-IMP*S*AUGU* **Rev:** Date between towers **Rev. Legend:** NOM-*NOUA* REIP...* **Note:** Dav. #5378.

Date	Mintage	VG	F	VF	XF	Unc
(1)625 (h)	—	1,350	2,250	3,750	6,000	—

KM# 46.2 THALER (24 Groschen)
Silver **Obv. Legend:** ...Z.-ROM.IMP.S.A. **Note:** Dav. #5379.

Date	Mintage	VG	F	VF	XF	Unc
1625 (h)	—	1,350	2,250	3,750	6,000	—

KM# 46.3 THALER (24 Groschen)
Silver **Rev:** Three mint mark 1 above church **Rev. Legend:** MONE.NOVA.REIP.QVER.HAMLEN. **Note:** Dav. #5380.

Date	Mintage	VG	F	VF	XF	Unc
(16) (h) Rare	—	—	—	—	—	—

KM# 53.1 THALER (24 Groschen)
Silver **Obv. Legend:** FERDI.Z.DG.ROM... **Note:** Dav. #5382.

Date	Mintage	VG	F	VF	XF	Unc
1632 (h)	—	1,350	2,250	3,750	6,000	—

KM# 53.2 THALER (24 Groschen)
Silver **Obv. Legend:** FERDI.Z.ROM.-... **Note:** Dav. #5383.

Date	Mintage	F	VF	XF	Unc	BU
1632 (h)	—	1,350	2,250	3,750	6,000	—

KM# 60.1 THALER (24 Groschen)
Silver **Obv. Legend:** FERDI:III:D:G:-ROM:... **Rev:** Church in decorative border, arms below **Note:** Dav. #5384.

Date	Mintage	VG	F	VF	XF	Unc
1639 (j)	—	1,350	2,250	3,750	6,000	—

KM# 60.2 THALER (24 Groschen)
Silver **Rev:** Heart above church **Note:** Varieties exist. Dav. #5385.

Date	Mintage	VG	F	VF	XF	Unc
1656 (k) Rare	—	—	—	—	—	—

KM# 76 THALER (24 Groschen)
Silver **Obv:** Crowned imperial eagle, titles of Leopold I **Rev:** Arms in front of church, date between towers **Note:** Dav. #5386.

Date	Mintage	VG	F	VF	XF	Unc
1669 (m) Rare	—	—	—	—	—	—

KM# 9 2 THALER
Silver **Obv:** Arms in front of church **Rev:** Crowned imperial eagle, 16 in orb on breast, titles of Rudolf II, date divided by crown at top

Date	Mintage	VG	F	VF	XF	Unc
1608 (a)	—	—	—	—	—	—

KM# 14 2 THALER
Silver **Obv:** Crowned imperial eagle, date divided by crown, titles of Matthias **Rev:** Arms in front of church, date in legend **Note:** Mule.

Date	Mintage	VG	F	VF	XF	Unc
1616//1617 Rare	—	—	—	—	—	—

KM# 61 2 THALER
Silver **Obv:** Crowned imperial eagle, orb on breast, date in legend below, titles of Ferdinand III

Date	Mintage	VG	F	VF	XF	Unc
1639 (j) Rare	—	—	—	—	—	—

TRADE COINAGE

KM# 59 GOLDGULDEN

3.5000 g., 0.9860 Gold 0.1109 oz. AGW **Obv:** Crowned imperial eagle, titles of Ferdinand III **Rev:** Arms in front of church, date in legend at top

Date	Mintage	VG	F	VF	XF	Unc
1638 (j) Rare	—	—	—	—	—	—

KM# 62 GOLDGULDEN

3.5000 g., 0.9860 Gold 0.1109 oz. AGW **Rev:** Date in legend at bottom

Date	Mintage	VG	F	VF	XF	Unc
(16)39 (j) Rare	—	—	—	—	—	—

KM# 74 GOLDGULDEN

3.5000 g., 0.9860 Gold 0.1109 oz. AGW **Obv:** Arms in front of church **Rev:** Bare-headed soldier standing 3/4 to left with sword and baton, legend **Rev. Legend:** DER.GER - HT.WI.N - V.

Date	Mintage	VG	F	VF	XF	Unc
ND(1668) Rare	—	—	—	—	—	—

KM# 75 GOLDGULDEN

3.5000 g., 0.9860 Gold 0.1109 oz. AGW **Obv:** Crowned imperial eagle, titles of Leopold I **Rev:** City arms in front of church, date above

Date	Mintage	VG	F	VF	XF	Unc
1668 Rare	—	—	—	—	—	—

KM# 85 GOLDGULDEN

3.5000 g., 0.9860 Gold 0.1109 oz. AGW **Rev:** Orb on eagle's breast, date divided by crown

Date	Mintage	VG	F	VF	XF	Unc
1672 Rare	—	—	—	—	—	—

KM# 67 DUCAT

3.5000 g., 0.9860 Gold 0.1109 oz. AGW **Obv:** City arms in front of church **Rev:** Full-length figure of Ferdinand III divides date

Date	Mintage	VG	F	VF	XF	Unc
1656 Rare	—	—	—	—	—	—

KM# 47 4 DUCAT

14.0000 g., 0.9860 Gold 0.4438 oz. AGW **Obv:** Arms in front of church, date between towers **Obv. Legend:** Inner: AMOR-VINZIT-OMNIA; Outer: DES.MENSCHEN.RVM.IST.WIE IN. WEISE.BLOM **Rev:** Bouquet of six flowers, heart pierced by two arrows below, double lily above

Date	Mintage	VG	F	VF	XF	Unc
1625 (h) Rare	—	—	—	—	—	—

KM# 48 10 DUCAT (Portugalöser)

35.0000 g., 0.9860 Gold 1.1095 oz. AGW **Note:** Struck with 1 Thaler dies, KM#46.

Date	Mintage	VG	F	VF	XF	Unc
(1)1625 (h) Rare	—	—	—	—	—	—

PATTERNS

Including off metal strikes

KM#	Date	Mintage	Identification	Mkt Val
Pn2	1672	—	12 Groschen. Gold. KM#81. Crowned imperial eagle, orb on breast, titles of Leopold I, crown divides date at top. Mule.	—

HAMM

A provincial city located in Westphalia, some 20 miles northeast of Dortmund, in the county of Mark. When the ruling house of Mark (see Cleves and Julich-Berg) became extinct in 1609, its territories, including Hamm, went to Brandenburg-Prussia in 1624 after a dispute with Pfalz-Neuburg. Hamm struck a local copper coinage from 1609 to 1749.

ARMS

Fesse of checkerboard

CITY

REGULAR COINAGE

KM# 6 HELLER

Copper **Note:** Uniface. H above arms in ornamented shield.

Date	Mintage	VG	F	VF	XF	Unc
ND(ca.1609)	—	13.00	27.00	45.00	75.00	—

KM# 7 PFENNIG

Copper **Obv:** H above arms in ornamented shield **Rev:** Large I **Note:** Varieties exist.

Date	Mintage	VG	F	VF	XF	Unc
ND(ca. 1609)	—	13.00	27.00	45.00	75.00	—

KM# 8 2 PFENNIG

Copper **Obv:** H above arms in ornamented shield **Rev:** Large II **Note:** Varieties exist.

Date	Mintage	VG	F	VF	XF	Unc
ND(ca. 1609)	—	13.00	27.00	45.00	75.00	—

KM# 46 2 PFENNIG

Copper **Obv:** HAM above arms **Rev:** II above date

Date	Mintage	VG	F	VF	XF	Unc
1637	—	13.00	27.00	45.00	75.00	—

KM# 9 3 PFENNIG

Copper **Obv:** Arms in ornamented shield, H-A-M around in legend **Rev:** Value III in circle

Date	Mintage	VG	F	VF	XF	Unc
ND(ca.1609)	—	12.00	27.00	45.00	75.00	—

KM# 10 3 PFENNIG

Copper **Obv:** H above arms

Date	Mintage	VG	F	VF	XF	Unc
ND(ca.1609)	—	12.00	27.00	45.00	75.00	—

KM# 12 3 PFENNIG

Copper **Obv:** .S.H. above arms

Date	Mintage	VG	F	VF	XF	Unc
ND(ca.1609)	—	12.00	27.00	45.00	75.00	—

KM# 11 3 PFENNIG

Copper **Obv:** H above arms in ornamented shield **Rev:** Large III **Note:** Varieties exist.

Date	Mintage	VG	F	VF	XF	Unc
ND(ca.1609)	—	11.00	20.00	33.00	60.00	—
1618	—	11.00	20.00	33.00	60.00	—

KM# 28 3 PFENNIG

Copper **Obv:** Arms in ornamented shield, STADT.HAM.AN.D., date around **Rev:** Value III in ornamented circle

Date	Mintage	VG	F	VF	XF	Unc
1619	—	12.00	27.00	45.00	75.00	—
1630	—	12.00	27.00	45.00	75.00	—

KM# 41 3 PFENNIG

Copper **Obv:** HAM above arms **Rev:** Value III, date below

Date	Mintage	VG	F	VF	XF	Unc
1635	—	12.00	27.00	45.00	75.00	—

KM# 43 3 PFENNIG

Copper **Obv:** Arms, STADT-date-HAM around **Rev:** Value III in circle

Date	Mintage	VG	F	VF	XF	Unc
1635	—	12.00	27.00	45.00	75.00	—

KM# 42 3 PFENNIG

Copper **Obv:** Arms, STADT. HAM around **Rev:** Value III above date **Note:** Varieties exist.

Date	Mintage	VG	F	VF	XF	Unc
1635	—	12.00	27.00	45.00	75.00	—
1637	—	12.00	27.00	45.00	75.00	—

KM# 50 3 PFENNIG

Copper **Obv:** Arms, STADT. HAMM, date around **Rev. Legend:** III/PFEN

Date	Mintage	VG	F	VF	XF	Unc
1648	—	12.00	27.00	45.00	75.00	—

KM# 55 3 PFENNIG

Copper **Rev:** III only

Date	Mintage	VG	F	VF	XF	Unc
1652	—	11.00	20.00	35.00	60.00	—

KM# 56 3 PFENNIG

Copper **Obv:** H above ornamented arms, H-A-M around in legend **Rev:** III in ornamented square divides date

Date	Mintage	VG	F	VF	XF	Unc
(16)58	—	11.00	27.00	45.00	75.00	—

KM# 57 3 PFENNIG

Copper **Obv:** H above ornamented arms **Rev:** III above date

Date	Mintage	VG	F	VF	XF	Unc
1658	—	11.00	27.00	45.00	75.00	—
1661	—	11.00	27.00	45.00	75.00	—

KM# 58 3 PFENNIG

Copper **Obv:** Arms, HAMM. date around **Rev:** Value III

Date	Mintage	VG	F	VF	XF	Unc
1659	—	10.00	20.00	33.00	55.00	—

KM# 59 3 PFENNIG

Copper **Obv:** Legend S. HAMM. date

Date	Mintage	VG	F	VF	XF	Unc
1659	—	10.00	20.00	33.00	55.00	—

KM# 60 3 PFENNIG

Copper **Obv:** Arms, STADT. HAMM. date around **Rev:** III in palm wreath

Date	Mintage	VG	F	VF	XF	Unc
1669	—	8.00	20.00	33.00	55.00	—
1676	—	8.00	20.00	33.00	55.00	—
1679	—	8.00	20.00	33.00	55.00	—

KM# 65 3 PFENNIG

Copper **Obv:** Arms, STADT. HAMM, date around **Rev:** III PFEN. in palm wreath

Date	Mintage	VG	F	VF	XF	Unc
(16)74	—	7.00	20.00	33.00	55.00	—
1680	—	7.00	20.00	33.00	55.00	—
1682	—	7.00	20.00	33.00	55.00	—
1686	—	7.00	20.00	33.00	55.00	—

KM# 66 3 PFENNIG

Copper **Rev:** III in ornamented circle

Date	Mintage	VG	F	VF	XF	Unc
1676	—	7.00	20.00	33.00	55.00	—

KM# 70 3 PFENNIG

Copper **Obv:** HVS below arms

Date	Mintage	VG	F	VF	XF	Unc
1684	—	7.00	20.00	33.00	55.00	—

KM# 71 3 PFENNIG

Copper **Obv:** Arms **Rev:** Value within wreath

Date	Mintage	VG	F	VF	XF	Unc
1687	—	7.00	20.00	33.00	55.00	—
1699	—	7.00	20.00	33.00	55.00	—
1700	—	7.00	20.00	33.00	55.00	—

KM# 72 3 PFENNIG

Copper **Obv:** Date above arms

Date	Mintage	VG	F	VF	XF	Unc
1687	—	7.00	20.00	33.00	55.00	—
1692	—	7.00	20.00	33.00	55.00	—
1693	—	7.00	20.00	33.00	55.00	—
1696	—	7.00	20.00	33.00	55.00	—

KM# 75 3 PFENNIG

Copper **Obv:** Arms **Rev:** Value within wreath **Note:** Varieties exist.

Date	Mintage	VG	F	VF	XF	Unc
1690	47,000	7.00	20.00	33.00	55.00	—
1699	—	7.00	20.00	33.00	55.00	—

KM# 76 3 PFENNIG

Copper **Obv. Legend:** STADT/date/HAMM

Date	Mintage	VG	F	VF	XF	Unc
1696	—	7.00	20.00	33.00	55.00	—

KM# 14 4 PFENNIG

Copper **Obv:** H-A-M around in legend

Date	Mintage	VG	F	VF	XF	Unc
ND(ca.1609)	—	13.00	30.00	45.00	80.00	—

KM# 13 4 PFENNIG

Copper **Obv:** H above arms in ornamented shield **Rev:** Large IIII **Note:** Varieties exist.

Date	Mintage	VG	F	VF	XF	Unc
ND(ca.1609)	—	13.00	30.00	45.00	80.00	—

KM# 35 4 PFENNIG

Copper **Obv:** Arms, around STADT.HAM.ANNO. date **Rev:** IIII in ornamented oval

Date	Mintage	VG	F	VF	XF	Unc
1620	—	11.00	20.00	33.00	60.00	—

KM# 40 4 PFENNIG

Copper **Obv:** Date **Obv. Legend:** STADT.AHM.AN.D **Note:** Varieties exist.

Date	Mintage	VG	F	VF	XF	Unc
1630	—	11.00	20.00	33.00	60.00	—
1650	—	11.00	20.00	33.00	60.00	—

KM# 47 4 PFENNIG

Copper **Obv:** Arms, around STADT.HAM **Rev:** IIII above date

Date	Mintage	VG	F	VF	XF	Unc
1637	—	11.00	20.00	33.00	60.00	—

KM# 16 6 PFENNIG

Copper **Rev:** Date above VI, H-A-M around legend

Date	Mintage	VG	F	VF	XF	Unc
1609	—	13.00	27.00	45.00	75.00	—

KM# 15 6 PFENNIG

Copper **Obv:** H above arms in ornamented shield **Rev:** Large VI **Note:** Varieties exist.

Date	Mintage	VG	F	VF	XF	Unc
ND(ca.1609)	—	16.00	33.00	60.00	100	—

KM# 26 6 PFENNIG

Copper **Obv:** H-A-M around legend **Rev:** Date below value **Note:** Varieties exist.

Date	Mintage	VG	F	VF	XF	Unc
(1)614	—	27.00	55.00	100	165	—
(1)618	—	13.00	27.00	45.00	70.00	—
1620	—	13.00	27.00	45.00	70.00	—

KM# 36 6 PFENNIG

Copper **Obv:** H above arms, without H-A-M

Date	Mintage	VG	F	VF	XF	Unc
1620	—	16.00	33.00	60.00	100	—

KM# 44 6 PFENNIG

Copper **Rev:** ANNO above value

Date	Mintage	VG	F	VF	XF	Unc
1635	—	13.00	27.00	45.00	75.00	—

KM# 45 6 PFENNIG

Copper **Obv:** HAM above arms **Note:** Varieties exist.

Date	Mintage	VG	F	VF	XF	Unc
1635	—	11.00	20.00	35.00	55.00	—

KM# 5 12 PFENNIG

Copper **Obv:** H above arms

Date	Mintage	VG	F	VF	XF	Unc
(16)05	—	13.00	27.00	45.00	85.00	—

KM# 19 12 PFENNIG

Copper **Rev:** Date below value **Note:** Varieties exist.

Date	Mintage	VG	F	VF	XF	Unc
1609	—	13.00	27.00	45.00	85.00	—
1610	—	13.00	27.00	45.00	85.00	—
1618	—	13.00	27.00	45.00	85.00	—

KM# 17 12 PFENNIG

Copper **Obv:** H above arms in ornamented shield **Rev:** Large XII

Date	Mintage	VG	F	VF	XF	Unc
ND(ca.1609)	—	11.00	20.00	40.00	80.00	—

KM# 18 12 PFENNIG

Copper **Obv:** H-A-M around legend

Date	Mintage	VG	F	VF	XF	Unc
ND(ca.1609)	—	12.00	22.00	45.00	90.00	—

KM# 27 12 PFENNIG
Copper **Obv:** Without H above arms **Note:** Varieties exist.

Date	Mintage	VG	F	VF	XF	Unc
(1)614	—	15.00	30.00	60.00	120	—
1618	—	15.00	30.00	60.00	120	—
1620	—	15.00	30.00	60.00	120	—

HANAU

Located 14 miles east of Frankfurt am Main, Hanau is the site of a Roman frontier settlement. The line of counts can be traced back to the mid-11th century. The county was divided into the lines of Halnau-Lichtenberg and Hanau-Münzenberg in 1451.

HANAU-LICHTENBERG

The younger line of the counts of Hanau. Lands in Alsace, acquired through marriage, the counts taking up residence in Buchsweiler, some 14 miles west of Hagenau. The elder Münzenberg line became extinct in 1642 and all lands passed to Lichtenberg. Raised to the rank of prince in 1696. Became extinct in 1736 and passed to Hesse-Darmstadt in 1785.

RULERS
Johann Reinhard I, 1599-1625
Philipp Wolfgang, 1625-1641
Friedrich Casimir, 1641-1685
Philipp Reinhard, 1685-1712

MINT OFFICIALS' INITIALS

Buchsweiler Mint

Initial	Date	Name
BM, IBM	1663-72	Johann Brettmacher
GHP, HP	1672-73	Georg Hartmann Plappert
IFL	1661-62	Johann Friedrich Lauer
IMG, MG	1659-60	Johann Martin Ganser

Darmstadt Mint

Initial	Date	Name
R	1696-1727	Johann C. Roth, die-cutter

Hanau Mint

Initial	Date	Name
	1603-1607	Peter Arenburch
	1607-1612	Simon Tympe (Timpf)
	1609-1613/14	Gerhard Bodenback, warden
	1613-?	Jakob Thomann
	1613-	Peter Binder, warden
	1614-1616	Melchior Küttner
	1619-1620	Hans Baldwin
IMG, MG	1658-74	Johann Martin Ganser
SM	1674-95	Sebastian Müller

Heidelberg Mint

Initial	Date	Name
IL, JL	1659-1711	Johann Link, die-cutter

Willstett Mint

Initial	Date	Name
	1622-1623	Martin Thomann

Wörth Mint

Initial	Date	Name
(b)=	1596-1601	Jakob Dietrich
V	1601-02	Konrad Vogel

ARMS
Hanau only = 3 chevrons, but often 4-fold arms with central chevron shield.
Hanau-Lichtenberg = 3 chevrons on left, rampant lion on right.
Ochsenstein = 2 horizontal bars

REFERENCE:
S = Reinhard Suchier, **Die Münzen der Grafen von Hanau**, Hanau, 1897.

COUNTSHIP

REGULAR COINAGE

KM# 11 PFENNIG
Silver **Note:** Uniface. Hohl-type. Four-fold arms with central chevron shield, IR above.

Date	Mintage	VG	F	VF	XF	Unc
ND(1605)	75,000	11.00	20.00	40.00	75.00	—

KM# 13 PFENNIG
Silver **Note:** Hohl-type. Three conjoined shields, IR above.

Date	Mintage	VG	F	VF	XF	Unc
ND(1609)	63,000	13.00	27.00	45.00	80.00	—

KM# 77 PFENNIG
Silver **Note:** Hohl-type. Crowned Hanau arms divide H - M, date divided below.

Date	Mintage	VG	F	VF	XF	Unc
1676	—	16.00	27.00	60.00	100	—

KM# 87 PFENNIG
Silver **Note:** Date below divided by SM.

Date	Mintage	VG	F	VF	XF	Unc
1681 SM	—	16.00	33.00	60.00	100	—

KM# 88 PFENNIG
Silver **Note:** Arms divide H-M/S-M.

Date	Mintage	VG	F	VF	XF	Unc
ND(1683-85) SM	—	16.00	33.00	60.00	100	—

KM# 33 2 PFENNIG (1/2 Kreuzer)
Silver **Note:** Hohl-type. Hanau arms divide I - R, date above.

Date	Mintage	VG	F	VF	XF	Unc
1624	—	—	—	—	—	—

KM# 26 4 PFENNIG (Kreuzer)
Silver **Obv:** Crowned arms of Hanau, titles of Ferdinand II **Rev:** Chevron arms, titles of Johann Reinhard I

Date	Mintage	VG	F	VF	XF	Unc
ND(1619-25) Unique	—	—	—	—	—	—

KM# 20 8 PFENNIG (Albus)
Silver **Obv:** Four-fold arms with central chevron shield **Rev:** VIII/PFENNIG/date, DO. I. LIECHT etc. around

Date	Mintage	VG	F	VF	XF	Unc
1610	81,000	33.00	65.00	120	200	—
1611	—	33.00	65.00	120	200	—

KM# 97 ALBUS (8 Pfennig)
Silver **Rev. Inscription:** I/ALBUS/ **Note:** Similar to 6 Albus, KM#99.

Date	Mintage	VG	F	VF	XF	Unc
1693 SM	—	33.00	65.00	120	200	—
1694 SM	—	33.00	65.00	120	200	—
1695 SM	—	33.00	65.00	120	200	—

KM# 32 KREUZER
Silver **Obv:** I/KREI/ZER, titles of Ferdinand II **Rev:** Five-fold arms with central chevron shield, date above **Note:** Varieties exist.

Date	Mintage	VG	F	VF	XF	Unc
1623	—	20.00	40.00	70.00	120	—
1624	—	20.00	40.00	70.00	120	—

KM# 63 KREUZER
Silver **Obv:** Crowned six-fold arms in laurel wreath **Rev:** I/KREVTZ/date/ER in laurel wreath

Date	Mintage	VG	F	VF	XF	Unc
1663 Unique	—	—	—	—	—	—

KM# 68 KREUZER
Silver **Rev:** I/KREV/TZER

Date	Mintage	VG	F	VF	XF	Unc
ND(1667-68)	—	—	—	—	—	—

KM# 69 KREUZER
Silver **Rev:** I/KREVTZ/ER

Date	Mintage	VG	F	VF	XF	Unc
ND(1667-68)	—	—	—	—	—	—

KM# 78 KREUZER
Silver **Obv:** Crowned Hannau-Lichtenberg arms in laurel wreath **Rev:** 16 I 76/KREU/TZER/S.M. in laurel wreath

Date	Mintage	VG	F	VF	XF	Unc
1676 SM	—	—	—	—	—	—

KM# 79 KREUZER
Silver **Rev:** I/KREV/TZER/date/SM **Note:** Varieties exist.

Date	Mintage	VG	F	VF	XF	Unc
1676 SM	—	10.00	20.00	40.00	70.00	—
1677 SM	—	10.00	20.00	40.00	70.00	—
1678 SM	—	10.00	20.00	40.00	70.00	—
1679 SM	487,000	10.00	20.00	40.00	70.00	—
1679 MS Error	Inc. above	10.00	20.00	40.00	70.00	—
1680 SM	—	10.00	20.00	40.00	70.00	—
1681 SM	—	10.00	20.00	40.00	70.00	—
1682 SM	—	10.00	20.00	40.00	70.00	—
1683 SM	—	10.00	20.00	40.00	70.00	—

KM# 85 KREUZER
Silver **Obv:** Crowned heart-shaped three-fold arms without laurel wreath

Date	Mintage	VG	F	VF	XF	Unc
1680 SM	—	13.00	27.00	55.00	90.00	—
1681 SM	—	13.00	27.00	55.00	90.00	—

KM# 102 KREUZER
Silver **Obv:** Crowned oval Hanau-Lichtenberg arms **Rev:** I/KREV/TZER/date

Date	Mintage	VG	F	VF	XF	Unc
1695	—	—	—	—	—	—

KM# 45 2 KREUZER (1/2 Batzen)
Silver **Obv:** II/KREUTZ/ER, titles of Ferdinand II **Rev:** Four-fold arms with central chevron shield, date above

Date	Mintage	VG	F	VF	XF	Unc
1631	—	12.00	25.00	45.00	75.00	—
1632	—	12.00	25.00	45.00	75.00	—

KM# 50 2 KREUZER (1/2 Batzen)
Silver **Obv:** Round seven-fold arms **Rev:** Imperial orb with two in curve-sided rhombus divides date

Date	Mintage	VG	F	VF	XF	Unc
1647	—	—	—	—	—	—

KM# 51 2 KREUZER (1/2 Batzen)
Silver **Obv:** Crowned seven-fold arms **Rev:** Imperial orb with Z (or 2), date divided by cross above, all in wreath **Note:** Varieties exist.

Date	Mintage	VG	F	VF	XF	Unc
1647	—	10.00	20.00	40.00	70.00	—
1647 MG	—	10.00	20.00	40.00	70.00	—
1648 MG	—	10.00	20.00	40.00	70.00	—
1651 MG	—	10.00	20.00	40.00	70.00	—
1653 MG	—	10.00	20.00	40.00	70.00	—
1654 MG	—	10.00	20.00	40.00	70.00	—
1655 MG	—	10.00	20.00	40.00	70.00	—
1656 MG	—	10.00	20.00	40.00	70.00	—
1657 MG	—	10.00	20.00	40.00	70.00	—
1658	—	10.00	20.00	40.00	70.00	—
1666	—	10.00	20.00	40.00	70.00	—
1667	—	10.00	20.00	40.00	70.00	—
1667 MG	—	10.00	20.00	40.00	70.00	—
1668 MG	—	10.00	20.00	40.00	70.00	—
1669 MG	—	10.00	20.00	40.00	70.00	—
1670 MG	—	10.00	20.00	40.00	70.00	—
1671 MG	—	10.00	20.00	40.00	70.00	—
1672 MG	—	10.00	20.00	40.00	70.00	—
1680 SM	—	10.00	20.00	40.00	70.00	—
1681 SM	—	10.00	20.00	40.00	70.00	—
1682 SM	—	10.00	20.00	40.00	70.00	—
1684 SM	—	10.00	20.00	40.00	70.00	—

KM# 60 2 KREUZER (1/2 Batzen)
Silver **Obv:** Crowned seven-fold arms with date below in laurel wreath **Rev:** HANAW (or U) /LICHTEN/BERGI/SCHE/2K in laurel wreath

Date	Mintage	VG	F	VF	XF	Unc
1660 MG	—	—	—	—	—	—

KM# 62 2 KREUZER (1/2 Batzen)
Silver **Obv:** Date above crown

Date	Mintage	VG	F	VF	XF	Unc
1661 IFL	—	11.00	20.00	40.00	75.00	—
1662 IFL	—	11.00	20.00	40.00	75.00	—
1663 IBM	—	11.00	20.00	40.00	75.00	—

KM# 64 2 KREUZER (1/2 Batzen)
Silver **Obv:** Date divided by arms

Date	Mintage	VG	F	VF	XF	Unc
1663 IBM	—	11.00	20.00	40.00	75.00	—
1664/3	—	11.00	20.00	40.00	75.00	—
1664	—	11.00	20.00	40.00	75.00	—
1665	—	11.00	20.00	40.00	75.00	—

KM# 80 2 KREUZER (1/2 Batzen)
Silver **Note:** Similar to KM#51 but date in obverse legend.

Date	Mintage	VG	F	VF	XF	Unc
1678 SM	—	—	—	—	—	—

KM# 90 2 KREUZER (1/2 Batzen)
Silver **Note:** Similar to KM#51 but 2 in orb.

Date	Mintage	VG	F	VF	XF	Unc
1687	—	—	—	—	—	—

KM# 4 3 KREUZER (Groschen)
Silver **Obv:** 4-fold arms with central chevron arms, date above **Rev:** Crowned imperial eagle, 3 in orb on breast, titles of Rudolf II **Note:** Varieties exist.

Date	Mintage	VG	F	VF	XF	Unc
1601	—	12.00	25.00	40.00	70.00	—
1601 V	—	12.00	25.00	40.00	70.00	—
1602	—	12.00	25.00	40.00	70.00	—
1603	—	12.00	25.00	40.00	70.00	—
1604	—	12.00	25.00	40.00	70.00	—
1605	43,000	12.00	25.00	40.00	70.00	—
1606	79,000	12.00	25.00	40.00	70.00	—
1607	93,000	12.00	25.00	40.00	70.00	—
1608	—	12.00	25.00	40.00	70.00	—
1609	—	12.00	25.00	40.00	70.00	—
ND(1610/11)	62,000	12.00	25.00	40.00	70.00	—
1614 Posthumous	—	12.00	25.00	40.00	70.00	—

KM# 5 3 KREUZER (Groschen)
Silver **Note:** Klippe.

Date	Mintage	VG	F	VF	XF	Unc
1600 Rare	—	—	—	—	—	—
1602 Rare	—	—	—	—	—	—

KM# 7 3 KREUZER (Groschen)

Silver **Obv:** Similar to KM#5 but without date **Rev:** Date/ FORTVNAM/VINCE/FERENDO in laurel wreath **Note:** Klippe.

Date	Mintage	VG	F	VF	XF	Unc
1602	—	—	—	—	—	—

KM# 21 3 KREUZER (Groschen)

Silver **Obv:** Titles of Matthias **Note:** Varieties exist.

Date	Mintage	VG	F	VF	XF	Unc
1612	28,000	—	—	—	—	—
ND	12,000	—	—	—	—	—

KM# 34 3 KREUZER (Groschen)

Silver **Obv:** Titles of Ferdinand II

Date	Mintage	VG	F	VF	XF	Unc
1624	—	—	—	—	—	—

KM# 98 2 ALBUS (Batzen)

Silver **Note:** Similar to 6 Albus, KM#99 but value II on reverse.

Date	Mintage	VG	F	VF	XF	Unc
1693 SM	—	30.00	55.00	100	175	—
1694 SM	—	30.00	55.00	100	175	—

KM# 99.1 6 ALBUS (12 Kreuzer)

Silver **Ruler:** Philipp Reinhard **Obv:** Crowned arms **Note:** Varieties exist.

Date	Mintage	VG	F	VF	XF	Unc
1693 SM	—	27.00	45.00	85.00	175	—
1694 SM	—	27.00	45.00	85.00	175	—

KM# 99.2 6 ALBUS (12 Kreuzer)

Silver **Ruler:** Philipp Reinhard **Obv:** Crowned arms
Obv. Legend: PHILIP. REINHARD: G: Z: HANAU
Rev. Legend: NACH • DEM. SCHLUS • DER • STAEND

Date	Mintage	VG	F	VF	XF	Unc
1693	—	—	—	—	—	—

KM# 27 12 KREUZER (Dreibätzner/3 Batzen)

Silver **Obv:** Crowned imperial eagle, 12 in orb on breast, SVB. VMB... **Obv. Legend:** Four-fold arms with central chevron shield, date above **Note:** Varieties exist.

Date	Mintage	VG	F	VF	XF	Unc
1619	—	45.00	100	190	300	—
1620	—	45.00	100	190	300	—
1621	—	45.00	100	190	300	—
ND	—	45.00	100	190	300	—

KM# 35 12 KREUZER (Dreibätzner/3 Batzen)

Silver **Obv:** Shield below date within circle **Rev:** Without 12 in orb, (XII) at top, titles of Ferdinand II

Date	Mintage	VG	F	VF	XF	Unc
1624	—	55.00	110	200	350	—
1625	—	55.00	110	200	350	—

KM# 38 12 KREUZER (Dreibätzner/3 Batzen)

Silver **Obv:** Shield below date within beaded circle, Philipp Wolfgang in legend **Rev:** Double-headed imperial eagle within beaded circle **Note:** Varieties exist.

Date	Mintage	VG	F	VF	XF	Unc
1626	—	60.00	120	220	375	—
1629	—	60.00	120	220	375	—
1630	—	60.00	120	220	375	—
1631	—	60.00	120	220	375	—

KM# 61 12 KREUZER (Dreibätzner/3 Batzen)

Silver **Obv:** Crowned imperial eagle, orb on breast, value (XII) above, titles of Leopold I **Rev:** Crowned six-fold arms, date above crown

Date	Mintage	VG	F	VF	XF	Unc
1660 MG	—	80.00	160	275	450	—
1661/0 IFL	—	80.00	160	275	450	—
1662 IFL	—	80.00	160	275	450	—
ND(1662) IFL	—	80.00	160	275	450	—
ND(1663) FM Error for BM	—	80.00	160	275	450	—

KM# 65 12 KREUZER (Dreibätzner/3 Batzen)

Silver **Obv:** Date divided by crowned arms **Rev:** Double-headed imperial eagle within beaded circle

Date	Mintage	VG	F	VF	XF	Unc
1664	—	80.00	160	275	450	—
1665	—	80.00	160	275	450	—

KM# 70 30 KREUZER (1/3 Thaler)

Silver **Obv:** Bust right **Rev:** Crowned seven-fold arms divide date, value 30 in cartouche at bottom

Date	Mintage	VG	F	VF	XF	Unc
1668 BM	—	—	—	—	—	—
ND(1669)	—	—	—	—	—	—
1672 MG	651	—	—	—	—	—
1673 MG	—	—	—	—	—	—

KM# 75 30 KREUZER (1/3 Thaler)

Silver **Rev:** Date in legend

Date	Mintage	VG	F	VF	XF	Unc
1675 SM Unique	—	—	—	—	—	—

KM# 6 TESTONE (24 Kreuzer)

Silver **Obv:** Four-fold arms with central chevron shield, date above

Date	Mintage	VG	F	VF	XF	Unc
1601	—	80.00	160	220	375	—
1608	—	80.00	160	220	375	—
1609	—	80.00	160	220	375	—
1610	49,000	80.00	160	220	375	—
1611	—	80.00	160	220	375	—
161Z	42,000	80.00	160	220	375	—
1613	16,000	80.00	160	220	375	—
ND(1614-18)	77,000	80.00	160	220	375	—
1621	—	80.00	160	220	375	—
ND(1621)	—	80.00	160	220	375	—

KM# 12 TESTONE (24 Kreuzer)

Silver **Note:** Klippe.

Date	Mintage	VG	F	VF	XF	Unc
1608 Rare	—	—	—	—	—	—

KM# 30 TESTONE (24 Kreuzer)

Silver **Note:** Kipper Testone. Similar to KM#6 but lightweight - 3.6-3.7 grams.

Date	Mintage	VG	F	VF	XF	Unc
ND(1622)	—	45.00	85.00	150	225	—

KM# 8 1/2 THALER

Silver **Note:** Similar to 1 Thaler, KM#9.

Date	Mintage	VG	F	VF	XF	Unc
ND Rare	—	—	—	—	—	—

KM# 71.1 60 KREUZER (2/3 Thaler)

Silver **Rev:** 60 in cartouche below arms

Date	Mintage	VG	F	VF	XF	Unc
1668 BM	—	85.00	150	220	325	—
ND(1668) BM	—	85.00	150	220	325	—

KM# 71.2 60 KREUZER (2/3 Thaler)

Silver **Rev:** Crowned arms divide GH-P at sides

Date	Mintage	VG	F	VF	XF	Unc
ND(1669-72) GHP	—	90.00	150	225	350	—

KM# 71.3 60 KREUZER (2/3 Thaler)

Silver **Rev:** GH-P divided at bottom of crowned arms

Date	Mintage	VG	F	VF	XF	Unc
ND(1669-72) HP	—	100	180	250	375	—

KM# 71.4 60 KREUZER (2/3 Thaler)

Silver

Date	Mintage	VG	F	VF	XF	Unc
1672 MG	18,000	85.00	150	210	300	—
1673 MG	—	85.00	150	210	300	—
1674 MG	—	85.00	150	210	300	—

KM# 71.5 60 KREUZER (2/3 Thaler)

Silver **Note:** Simple and ornate bust varieties exist.

Date	Mintage	VG	F	VF	XF	Unc
1675 SM	—	100	160	240	350	—
1676 SM	—	100	160	240	350	—
1680/76 SM	—	100	160	240	350	—
1680 SM	—	100	160	240	350	—

KM# 95 60 KREUZER (2/3 Thaler)

Silver

Date	Mintage	VG	F	VF	XF	Unc
1691 SM	—	—	—	—	—	—

KM# 96 60 KREUZER (2/3 Thaler)

Silver **Rev:** Oval arms and date divided by crown above **Note:** Varieties exist.

Date	Mintage	VG	F	VF	XF	Unc
1693 SM	—	85.00	150	220	325	—
1693 IL-SM	—	85.00	150	220	325	—
1694 SM	—	85.00	150	220	325	—
1695 SM	—	85.00	150	220	325	—

KM# 9 THALER

Silver **Obv:** Johann Reinhard **Note:** Dav. #6693.

Date	Mintage	VG	F	VF	XF	Unc
ND	2,570	975	2,000	3,600	5,900	—

KM# 15 THALER

Silver **Obv:** Large bust breaking circle at top and bottom **Rev:** Shield dividing date **Note:** Dav. #6694.

Date	Mintage	VG	F	VF	XF	Unc
1609	—	1,100	2,150	3,900	6,500	—

KM# 36 THALER

Silver **Obv:** Smaller full bust within circle **Rev:** Date above shield **Note:** Dav. #6696.

Date	Mintage	VG	F	VF	XF	Unc
1624	—	825	1,700	3,050	4,950	—

KM# 39 THALER

Silver **Obv:** Crowned imperial eagle, orb on breast, titles of Ferdinand II **Rev:** Oval arms in baroque frame, date divided above **Note:** Dav. #6697.

Date	Mintage	VG	F	VF	XF	Unc
1626 Rare	—	—	—	—	—	—

KM# 40 THALER

Silver **Obv:** Bust of Philipp Wolfgang right **Rev:** Four-fold arms with central chevron shield, date divided around **Note:** Dav. #6698.

Date	Mintage	VG	F	VF	XF	Unc
1629 Rare	—	—	—	—	—	—

KM# 52.1 THALER

Silver **Obv:** Crowned imperial eagle, orb on breast, titles of Ferdinand III **Rev:** Crowned ornate seven-fold arms divide date **Note:** Dav. #6699.

Date	Mintage	VG	F	VF	XF	Unc
1647 MG Rare	—	—	—	—	—	—
Note: Dr. Busso Peus Nachfolger Auction 383, 4-05, VF realized approximately $10,695.						
1648 MG Rare	—	—	—	—	—	—
1655 MG Rare	—	—	—	—	—	—

KM# 52.2 THALER

Silver **Obv:** Titles of Leopold I **Rev. Legend:** FRIDERICVS. CASIMIRVS... **Note:** Dav. #6700.

Date	Mintage	VG	F	VF	XF	Unc
1658 MG Rare	—	—	—	—	—	—

KM# 53 THALER

Silver **Obv:** Bust right **Note:** Dav. #A6701.

Date	Mintage	VG	F	VF	XF	Unc
ND MG Rare	—	—	—	—	—	—

KM# 66 THALER

Silver **Obv:** Bust right in circle **Rev:** Helmeted seven-fold arms divide date **Note:** Dav. #6702.

Date	Mintage	VG	F	VF	XF	Unc
1664 BM Rare	—	—	—	—	—	—
Note: Hess-Divo AG Auction 297, 10-03, VF/XF realized approximately $21,250.						
1673 HP Rare	—	—	—	—	—	—

KM# 86 THALER

Silver **Obv:** Large bust without circle **Rev:** Date in legend **Note:** Dav. #6703.

Date	Mintage	VG	F	VF	XF	Unc
1680 SM Rare	—	—	—	—	—	—

KM# 100 THALER

Silver **Obv:** Philipp Reinhard **Rev:** Helmeted seven-fold arms, date in legend **Note:** Dav. #6704.

Date	Mintage	VG	F	VF	XF	Unc
1694 SM	—	1,300	2,850	5,200	9,400	—

KM# 101 THALER

Silver **Rev:** Crowned oval seven-fold arms, date divided at bottom **Note:** Dav. #6705.

Date	Mintage	VG	F	VF	XF	Unc
1694 JL-SM	—	1,150	2,350	4,150	6,800	—

KM# 103.1 THALER

Silver **Obv:** Bust right **Rev:** City view, angel above, crowned and supported oval seven-fold arms below divide date **Note:** Dav. #6706.

Date	Mintage	VG	F	VF	XF	Unc
1695	—	975	2,000	3,600	5,900	—

KM# 103.2 THALER

Silver **Obv:** Bust with different armor, R below **Note:** Dav. #6707.

Date	Mintage	VG	F	VF	XF	Unc
1695 R Rare	—	—	—	—	—	—

KM# 10.1 2 THALER

Silver **Obv:** Bust of Johann Reinhard right **Rev:** Similar to 1 Thaler, KM#9 **Note:** Dav. #6691.

Date	Mintage	VG	F	VF	XF	Unc
ND Rare	—	—	—	—	—	—

KM# 10.2 2 THALER

Silver **Rev. Legend:** IN-LIECH: ET-OCHSE... **Note:** Dav. #6692.

Date	Mintage	VG	F	VF	XF	Unc
ND Rare	—	—	—	—	—	—

KM# 23 2 THALER

Silver **Obv:** Crowned imperial eagle, titles of Matthias and date in legend **Rev:** Helmeted four-fold arms with central chevron shield **Note:** Dav. #6695.

Date	Mintage	VG	F	VF	XF	Unc
1613 Rare	—	—	—	—	—	—

KM# 67 2 THALER

Silver **Obv:** Bust right in circle **Rev:** Helmeted seven-fold arms divide date **Note:** Dav. #6701.

Date	Mintage	VG	F	VF	XF	Unc
1664 BM Rare	—	—	—	—	—	—

KM# 104 2 THALER

Silver **Note:** Similar to 1 Thaler, KM#103.

Date	Mintage	VG	F	VF	XF	Unc
1695 Rare	—	—	—	—	—	—

TRADE COINAGE

KM# 22 GOLDGULDEN

3.5000 g., 0.9860 Gold 0.1109 oz. AGW **Obv:** Bust right **Rev:** Four-fold arms, legend, date **Rev. Legend:** MONE[TA] NO[VA] AUREA BABENHU [SAE] CU [SA] **Mint:** Babenhausen

Date	Mintage	VG	F	VF	XF	Unc
(1)612 Unique	—	—	—	—	—	—

KM# 24 GOLDGULDEN

3.5000 g., 0.9860 Gold 0.1109 oz. AGW **Obv:** Arms in inner circle **Rev:** Crowned imperial eagle in inner circle

Date	Mintage	VG	F	VF	XF	Unc
ND(1612)	—	650	1,250	2,500	5,000	—
1613	252	650	1,250	2,500	5,000	—

KM# 25 GOLDGULDEN
3.5000 g., 0.9860 Gold 0.1109 oz. AGW **Obv:** Date above arms

Date	Mintage	VG	F	VF	XF	Unc
1613	Inc. above	650	1,250	2,500	5,000	—
1614	828	650	1,250	2,500	5,000	—
1615	540	—	—	—	—	—
Note: Reported, not confirmed						
1617	360	650	1,250	2,500	5,000	—
1618	1,350	650	1,250	2,500	5,000	—
1619	1,224	—	—	—	—	—
Note: Reported, not confirmed						

KM# 37 GOLDGULDEN
3.5000 g., 0.9860 Gold 0.1109 oz. AGW **Obv:** Titles of Ferdinand II

Date	Mintage	VG	F	VF	XF	Unc
1624	—	2,000	3,500	6,000	9,000	—

KM# 54 DUCAT
3.5000 g., 0.9860 Gold 0.1109 oz. AGW **Obv:** Ornamental arms **Rev:** Four-line inscription and date in branches, "Jehovah" (in Hebrew) at top

Date	Mintage	VG	F	VF	XF	Unc
1647 Rare	—	—	—	—	—	—
Note: Swiss Bank Auction 25, 9-90 VF realized $13,845						

KM# 55 DUCAT
3.5000 g., 0.9860 Gold 0.1109 oz. AGW **Obv:** Bust of Philipp Casimir right in inner circle **Rev:** Helmeted arms in inner circle

Date	Mintage	VG	F	VF	XF	Unc
ND(1660) Rare	—	—	—	—	—	—

KM# 76 DUCAT
3.5000 g., 0.9860 Gold 0.1109 oz. AGW **Obv:** Bust right **Rev:** Crown above seven-fold arms divides date

Date	Mintage	VG	F	VF	XF	Unc
1675 SM Rare	—	—	—	—	—	—

KM# 89 DUCAT
3.5000 g., 0.9860 Gold 0.1109 oz. AGW **Obv:** Bust of Philipp Reinhard right **Rev:** Crowned ornate seven-fold arms divide S-M

Date	Mintage	VG	F	VF	XF	Unc
ND(1685/6) SM Rare	—	—	—	—	—	—

KM# 31 2 DUCAT
7.0000 g., 0.9860 Gold 0.2219 oz. AGW **Obv:** Bust right **Rev:** Helmeted four-fold arms with central shield, 2 DVCAT in cartouche at bottom, date in legend

Date	Mintage	VG	F	VF	XF	Unc
16ZZ Rare	—	—	—	—	—	—

KM# 91 6 DUCAT
21.0000 g., 0.9860 Gold 0.6657 oz. AGW **Obv:** Bust right **Rev:** Helmeted seven-fold arms, date in legend

Date	Mintage	VG	F	VF	XF	Unc
1688 Rare	—	—	—	—	—	—

KM# 92 10 DUCAT (Portugalöser)
35.0000 g., 0.9860 Gold 1.1095 oz. AGW **Obv:** Bust right **Rev:** Helmeted seven-fold arms, date in legend **Note:** Struck with 1 Thaler dies, but only known in gold.

Date	Mintage	VG	F	VF	XF	Unc
1688 Rare	—	—	—	—	—	—

KM# 105 10 DUCAT (Portugalöser)
35.0000 g., 0.9860 Gold 1.1095 oz. AGW **Obv:** Bust Philipp Reinhard right **Rev:** City view, angel above, crowned and supported seven-fold arms below divide date **Note:** Struck with 1 Thaler dies, KM#103.1.

Date	Mintage	VG	F	VF	XF	Unc
1695 Rare	—	—	—	—	—	—

PATTERNS

Including off metal strikes

KM#	Date	Mintage	Identification	Mkt Val
Pn1	1694 JL-SM	—	Thaler. Gold. KM#101	—

HANAU-MUNZENBERG

Elder line of Hanau founded in division of 1451, but became extinct in 1642 and fell to the line Lichtenberg, line. Hanau-Münzenberg passed to Hesse-Cassel in 1736 upon extinction of Hanau-Lichtenberg.

RULERS
Philipp Ludwig II, 1580-1612
Philipp Moritz, 1612-1638
Katharina Belgia of Nassau-Orange, regent, 1612-1626
Philipp Ludwig III, 1638-1641
Sibylle Christine, regent, 1638-1641
Johann Ernst, 1641-1642

MINT OFFICIALS' INITIALS

Initial	Date	Name
IA, IAL, (a)	1638-39	J(ohann?) Adelmann

ARMS
Hanau only = 3 chevrons, but often 4-fold arms with central chevron shield.
Hanau-Lichtenberg = 3 chevrons on left, 2 horizontal bars of Ochsenstein on right.

REFERENCE:
S = Reinhard Suchier, **Die Münzen der Grafen von Hanau**, Hanau, 1897.

COUNTSHIP

REGULAR COINAGE

KM# 5 PFENNIG
Silver **Note:** Uniface. Hohl type. Shield of Hanau chevron arms in circle of pellets.

Date	Mintage	VG	F	VF	XF	Unc
ND(1603)	663,000	65.00	135	225	—	—

KM# 6 PFENNIG
Silver **Note:** PL above arms.

Date	Mintage	VG	F	VF	XF	Unc
ND(1604)	1,361,000	65.00	135	225	—	—

KM# 9 PFENNIG
Silver **Note:** PL above three shields of arms arranged two above one. Hohl-type.

Date	Mintage	VG	F	VF	XF	Unc
ND(1605)	457,000	45.00	100	190	300	—

KM# 13 PFENNIG
Silver **Note:** Crown above three arms.

Date	Mintage	VG	F	VF	XF	Unc
ND(1606/7)	—	45.00	100	190	300	—

KM# 14 PFENNIG
Silver **Note:** Crown divides P - L, lower shield divides date.

Date	Mintage	VG	F	VF	XF	Unc
1609	—	40.00	80.00	160	275	—

KM# 15 PFENNIG
Silver **Note:** P. L. C. H. E. R. D. I. M., date around three shields.

Date	Mintage	VG	F	VF	XF	Unc
1609	—	40.00	80.00	160	275	—
1610	—	40.00	80.00	160	275	—

KM# 25 PFENNIG
Silver **Note:** Legend P. L. C. I. H., date.

Date	Mintage	VG	F	VF	XF	Unc
1610	—	40.00	80.00	160	275	—

KM# 50 KREUZER
Silver **Rev:** I/KREVT/ZER/date

Date	Mintage	VG	F	VF	XF	Unc
16ZZ	—	—	—	—	—	—

KM# 51 KREUZER
Silver **Rev:** I/KREVTZ/ER/date

Date	Mintage	VG	F	VF	XF	Unc
16ZZ	—	—	—	—	—	—

KM# 49 KREUZER
Silver **Obv:** Crown above three shields, two above one **Rev:** I/KRVTZE/R/date **Note:** Kipper Kreuzer.

Date	Mintage	VG	F	VF	XF	Unc
16ZZ	—	—	—	—	—	—

KM# 60 KREUZER
Silver **Obv:** Crown above three shields, two above one, date in legend **Rev:** Imperial orb with 2 in wreath **Note:** Varieties exist.

Date	Mintage	VG	F	VF	XF	Unc
1638	—	—	—	—	—	—
1638 IAL	—	—	—	—	—	—

KM# 16 ALBUS (2 Kreuzer)
Silver **Obv:** Crown above three shields, two above one **Rev:** 2:CR/VIII/date

Date	Mintage	VG	F	VF	XF	Unc
1609	—	45.00	80.00	140	240	—

KM# 17 ALBUS (2 Kreuzer)
Silver **Rev:** ALB/VIII/ date

Date	Mintage	VG	F	VF	XF	Unc
1609	—	45.00	80.00	140	240	—
1610	—	45.00	80.00	140	240	—

KM# 29 ALBUS (2 Kreuzer)
Silver **Rev:** ALB/NOVVS/date

Date	Mintage	VG	F	VF	XF	Unc
1611	12,000	35.00	60.00	100	180	—

KM# 10 3 KREUZER (Groschen)
Silver **Obv:** Crowned imperial eagle, 3 in orb on breast, titles of Rudolf II **Rev:** Three shields of arms, two above one

Date	Mintage	VG	F	VF	XF	Unc
ND(1605)	898,000	—	—	—	—	—

KM# 11 3 KREUZER (Groschen)
Silver **Obv:** Four-fold arms

Date	Mintage	VG	F	VF	XF	Unc
ND(1605-09)	Inc. above	—	—	—	—	—

KM# 12 3 KREUZER (Groschen)
Silver **Note:** Klippe.

Date	Mintage	VG	F	VF	XF	Unc
ND(1605-09)	—	—	—	—	—	—

KM# 32 3 KREUZER (Groschen)
Silver **Obv:** Crowned shield within circle **Rev:** Value on breast of double-headed imperial eagle within circle **Note:** Varieties exist.

Date	Mintage	VG	F	VF	XF	Unc
161Z	Inc. above	13.00	27.00	45.00	85.00	—
1613	84,000	13.00	27.00	45.00	85.00	—
1614	111,000	13.00	27.00	45.00	85.00	—
1615	—	13.00	27.00	45.00	85.00	—
1618	47,000	13.00	27.00	45.00	85.00	—
1619	53,000	13.00	27.00	45.00	85.00	—

KM# 30 3 KREUZER (Groschen)
Silver **Obv:** Crowned oval four-fold arms, titles of Philipp Ludwig II **Rev:** Titles of Matthias and date in legend

Date	Mintage	VG	F	VF	XF	Unc
1612	—	16.00	33.00	60.00	100	—

KM# 31 3 KREUZER (Groschen)
Silver **Rev:** Crowned oval four-fold arms in baroque frame, MON. TVT. HAN...

Date	Mintage	VG	F	VF	XF	Unc
161Z	68,000	16.00	33.00	60.00	100	—

KM# 38 3 KREUZER (Groschen)
Silver **Obv:** Titles of Ferdinand II

Date	Mintage	VG	F	VF	XF	Unc
(16)19	72,000	13.00	27.00	45.00	85.00	—

KM# 46 3 KREUZER (Groschen)
Silver **Obv:** Arms divide date, titles of Philipp Moritz **Rev:** Double-headed imperial eagle within beaded circle **Note:** Kipper 3 Kreuzer. Varieties exist.

Date	Mintage	VG	F	VF	XF	Unc
16Z1	—	16.00	33.00	60.00	100	—
16ZZ	—	16.00	33.00	60.00	100	—

KM# 26 12 KREUZER (6 Albus)
Silver **Obv:** Crown above 3 shields of arms, 2 above 1 **Rev:** Crowned imperial eagle, 12 in orb on breast, titles of Rudolf II and date in legend

Date	Mintage	VG	F	VF	XF	Unc
1610	8,000	110	225	400	700	—
ND(1610)	Inc. above	110	225	400	700	—

KM# 39 12 KREUZER (6 Albus)
Silver **Obv:** Crowned four-fold arms divide date **Rev:** Crowned imperial eagle, 1Z in orb on breast, titles of Ferdinand II **Note:** Varieties exist.

Date	Mintage	VG	F	VF	XF	Unc
1619	—	110	225	425	725	—
16Z0	—	110	225	425	725	—

KM# 40 24 KREUZER (12 Albus)
Silver **Obv:** Crowned 4-fold arms divide date **Rev:** Crowned imperial eagle, titles of Ferdinand II **Note:** Varieties exist.

Date	Mintage	VG	F	VF	XF	Unc
1619	—	45.00	100	190	350	—
16Z0	—	45.00	100	190	350	—

KM# 36 TESTONE (6 Batzen)
Silver **Obv:** Bust right, two legends around **Rev:** Crowned four-fold arms, date in legend **Note:** Varities exist.

Date	Mintage	VG	F	VF	XF	Unc
1614	12,000	85.00	200	375	650	1,000
1615	3,000	—	—	—	—	—
Note: Reported, not confirmed						
1618/4	16,000	85.00	200	375	650	1,000
1618	Inc. above	85.00	200	375	650	1,000
1619/8/4	34,000	85.00	200	375	650	1,000
16Z0	10,000	—	—	—	—	—
Note: Reported, not confirmed						

KM# 48 TESTONE (6 Batzen)
Silver **Obv:** Bust right **Rev:** Crowned four-fold arms divide date **Note:** Varieties exist.

Date	Mintage	VG	F	VF	XF	Unc
16Z1	—	85.00	200	325	650	—
16ZZ	—	85.00	200	325	650	—

KM# 18 27 ALBUS (Guldenthaler)
Silver **Obv:** Bust right **Rev:** ALBVS/XXVII/Ao. date

Date	Mintage	F	VF	XF	Unc	BU
1609	—	—	—	—	—	—

KM# 27 27 ALBUS (Guldenthaler)
Silver **Rev:** ALB/XX/VII/date

Date	Mintage	F	VF	XF	Unc	BU
1610	646	—	—	—	—	—
ND	—	—	—	—	—	—

KM# 28 27 ALBUS (Guldenthaler)
Silver **Rev:** Crown above three shields of arms, two above one; date between two top shields, lower one divides 27/ALB

Date	Mintage	F	VF	XF	Unc	BU
1610	Inc. above	—	—	—	—	—
1611	525	—	—	—	—	—
Note: Reported, not confirmed						
ND	—	—	—	—	—	—

KM# 47 SCHILLING (1/28 Thaler)
Silver **Obv:** Crown above three shields, two above one; lower shield divides date **Rev:** I/SCHILL **Rev. Legend:** HANAVIS + LANDMVNTZ

Date	Mintage	VG	F	VF	XF	Unc
1621 Rare	—	—	—	—	—	—
1622 Rare	—	—	—	—	—	—

KM# 53 1/4 THALER
Silver **Obv:** Crowned imperial eagle, orb on breast, titles of Ferdinand II and date in legend **Rev:** Crowned arms of Hanau-Munzenberg and Nassau-Orange in ornamented shield, titles of Katharina Belgia

Date	Mintage	VG	F	VF	XF	Unc
16Z3	—	—	—	—	—	—

KM# 54 1/4 THALER
Silver **Rev:** Without ornamentation on shield

Date	Mintage	VG	F	VF	XF	Unc
16Z3	—	—	—	—	—	—

KM# 55 1/2 THALER
Silver **Obv:** Crowned imperial eagle, orb on breast, titles of Ferdinand II and date in legend **Rev:** Crowned arms of Hanau-Munzenberg and Nassau-Orange in ornamented shield, titles of Katharina Belgia

Date	Mintage	VG	F	VF	XF	Unc
16Z3	—	—	—	—	—	—
16Z4	—	—	—	—	—	—

KM# 19 THALER
Silver **Obv:** Bust right **Rev:** Crowned imperial eagle, orb on breast, titles of Rudolf II and date in legend **Note:** Dav. #6681.

Date	Mintage	VG	F	VF	XF	Unc
1609 Rare	—	—	—	—	—	—

KM# 20 THALER
Silver **Obv:** Bust right **Rev:** Crowned four-fold arms with central shield **Note:** Struck on oval flan. Dav. #6682.

Date	Mintage	VG	F	VF	XF	Unc
ND Rare	—	—	—	—	—	—

KM# 33 THALER
Silver **Subject:** Death of Philipp Ludwig II **Obv:** Bust right **Rev:** Seven-line inscription with date **Note:** Dav. #6683.

Date	Mintage	VG	F	VF	XF	Unc
1612 Rare	—	—	—	—	—	—

KM# 52.1 THALER
Silver **Obv:** Crowned ornate shield within circle **Rev:** Crown above double-headed eagle within circle **Note:** Dav. #6686.

Date	Mintage	VG	F	VF	XF	Unc
16ZZ	—	60.00	125	250	500	—
16Z3	—	60.00	125	250	500	—

KM# 52.2 THALER
Silver **Obv:** Crowned ornate shield within circle **Obv. Legend:** MONETA: NOVA:... **Rev:** Crown above double-headed imperial eagle within circle **Note:** Varieties exist. Dav. #6688.

Date	Mintage	VG	F	VF	XF	Unc
1622	—	60.00	125	250	500	—
1623	—	60.00	125	250	500	—
16Z4	—	60.00	125	250	500	—
16Z5	—	60.00	125	250	500	—
16Z6	—	60.00	125	250	500	—
16Z7	—	60.00	125	250	500	—

KM# 56 THALER
Silver **Obv:** Partial date in legend **Rev:** Crowned oval four-fold arms with central shield in baroque frame divide date **Note:** Accession Thaler. Dav. #6689.

Date	Mintage	VG	F	VF	XF	Unc
16Z6/16Z- Rare	—	—	—	—	—	—

KM# 61 THALER
Silver **Obv:** Diamond design divides date within circle **Rev:** Titles of Ferdinand III **Note:** Dav. #6690.

Date	Mintage	VG	F	VF	XF	Unc
1638 IA	—	1,650	2,600	4,550	7,200	—

KM# 21 2 THALER
Silver **Obv:** Bust right **Rev:** Crowned imperial eagle, orb on breast, titles of Rudolf II and date in legend **Note:** Dav. #6680.

Date	Mintage	VG	F	VF	XF	Unc
1609 Rare	—	—	—	—	—	—

KM# 57 2 THALER
Silver **Note:** Similar to 1 thaler, KM#52.1. Dav. #6687.

Date	Mintage	VG	F	VF	XF	Unc
16Z6	—	600	950	1,500	2,150	—

TRADE COINAGE

KM# 7 GOLDGULDEN
3.5000 g., 0.9860 Gold 0.1109 oz. AGW **Obv:** Full-length standing figure of Rudolf II, titles in legend **Rev:** crowned four-fold arms divide date

Date	Mintage	VG	F	VF	XF	Unc
1604	585	—	—	—	—	—
Note: Reported, not confirmed						

KM# 35 GOLDGULDEN
3.5000 g., 0.9860 Gold 0.1109 oz. AGW **Obv:** Crowned imperial eagle, orb on breast, titles of Matthias **Rev:** Crowned arms of Hanau-Munzenberg and Nassau-Orange, titles of Katharina Belgia, date

Date	Mintage	VG	F	VF	XF	Unc
1613	2,194	—	—	—	—	—
Note: Reported, not confirmed						
1614	2,007	—	—	—	—	—
Note: Reported, not confirmed						

KM# 37 GOLDGULDEN
3.5000 g., 0.9860 Gold 0.1109 oz. AGW **Obv:** Date in legend **Rev:** Crown above three shields of arms, two above one

Date	Mintage	VG	F	VF	XF	Unc
1615	756	—	—	—	—	—
1619	1,332	—	—	—	—	—
Note: Reported, not confirmed						

KM# 41 GOLDGULDEN
3.5000 g., 0.9860 Gold 0.1109 oz. AGW **Obv:** Titles of Ferdinand II

Date	Mintage	VG	F	VF	XF	Unc
1619	8,000	—	—	—	—	—
Note: Reported, not confirmed						

KM# 62 DUCAT
3.5000 g., 0.9860 Gold 0.1109 oz. AGW **Obv:** Crowned four-fold arms in rhombus within palm branches **Rev:** Inscription in rhombus, date divided along four sides as 1-6/3-8 **Rev. Inscription:** DV / CATVS / COMITATVS / HANO / M

Date	Mintage	VG	F	VF	XF	Unc
1638 (a) Rare	—	—	—	—	—	—

KM# 63 DUCAT
3.5000 g., 0.9860 Gold 0.1109 oz. AGW **Obv:** Standing full-length figure, crowned oval four-fold arms at left **Rev:** Date, inscription **Rev. Inscription:** /DVCATVS / NOVVS / CVRATE / LAE. HANO / VIENSIS

Date	Mintage	VG	F	VF	XF	Unc
1638 IAL Rare	—	—	—	—	—	—

KM# 64 DUCAT

3.5000 g., 0.9860 Gold 0.1109 oz. AGW **Obv:** Standing full-length figure of soldier at left looking right, crowned four-fold arms at right **Rev:** Inscription in ornamented square, date divided below **Rev. Inscription:** DVCATVS / NOVVS / CVRATE / LAE. HANO / VIENSIS

Date	Mintage	VG	F	VF	XF	Unc
1639 IA Rare	—	—	—	—	—	—

HANNOVER

Located in North Central Germany, Hannover had its beginnings as early as the 12th century. The city obtained the mint right in 1331, but fell under the control of the dukes of Brunswick who later made it their residence. Hannover eventually became the capitol of the Kingdom of the same name. The city coinage lasted until 1674.

MINT OFFICIALS' INITIALS

Initial	Date	Name
(g)= [symbol] or MK	1616	Melchior Kohl
(h)= [symbol] or [symbol]	1616-18	Valentin Block
	1618-19	Andreas Fricke
(i)= [symbol] or TB	1619-20, 22-28	Tönnies Bremer
MB (sometimes in ligature	1628-66	Moritz Bergmann
AS	1666-74	Andreas Schele

ARMS

3-petaled cloverleaf or complex arms consisting of twin-towered city gate, 3-petaled cloverleaf in portal and rampant lion left between towers.

PROVINCIAL CITY

REGULAR COINAGE

KM# 10 PFENNIG

Silver **Note:** Uniface. Arms, date above. Varieties exist

Date	Mintage	VG	F	VF	XF	Unc
1618	—	27.00	60.00	115	200	—
16Z8	54,000	27.00	60.00	115	200	—
1635 MB	—	27.00	60.00	115	200	—
1636 MB	58,000	27.00	60.00	115	200	—
1639 MB	26,000	27.00	60.00	115	200	—
1640 MB	8,000	27.00	60.00	115	200	—
1641 MB	30,000	27.00	60.00	115	200	—
164Z MB	4,000	27.00	60.00	115	200	—
1644 MB	27,000	27.00	60.00	115	200	—
1645 MB	12,000	27.00	60.00	115	200	—
1646 MB	30,000	27.00	60.00	115	200	—
1647 MB	—	27.00	60.00	115	200	—
1648 MB	—	27.00	60.00	115	200	—
1650 MB	11,000	27.00	60.00	115	200	—
1653 MB	—	27.00	60.00	115	200	—
1656 MB	—	27.00	60.00	115	200	—
1657 MB	—	27.00	60.00	115	200	—
1658 MB	21,000	27.00	60.00	115	200	—
1659 MB	14,000	27.00	60.00	115	200	—
1660 MB	—	27.00	60.00	115	200	—
1661 MB	—	27.00	60.00	115	200	—
1663	—	27.00	60.00	115	200	—
1664 MB	—	27.00	60.00	115	200	—
1665 MB	—	27.00	60.00	115	200	—
1666 AS	—	27.00	60.00	115	200	—
1667 AS	—	27.00	60.00	115	200	—
1668 AS	—	27.00	60.00	115	200	—
1670 AS	51,000	27.00	60.00	115	200	—

KM# 50 PFENNIG

Copper **Note:** Uniface. Arms, HANO around.

Date	Mintage	VG	F	VF	XF	Unc
ND(c.1650)	—	—	—	—	—	—

KM# 64 2 PFENNIG

Silver **Obv:** Arms, date above **Rev:** II/GUTE/PEN **Note:** Gute 2 Pfennig.

Date	Mintage	VG	F	VF	XF	Unc
1666 AS	—	—	—	—	—	—

Note: Although the dies exist for this coin, no struck specimens are known

KM# 17 3 PFENNIG (Dreier)

Silver **Obv:** Complete arms **Rev:** Imperial orb with 3 divides date

Date	Mintage	VG	F	VF	XF	Unc
16ZZ	—	27.00	60.00	110	190	—
16ZZ (i)	—	27.00	60.00	110	190	—
16Z3 (i)	—	27.00	60.00	110	190	—

KM# 46 3 PFENNIG (Dreier)

Silver **Obv:** Arms, HANNOVER above **Rev:** Imperial orb with 3 divides date **Note:** Varieties exist.

Date	Mintage	VG	F	VF	XF	Unc
1646 MB	—	16.00	33.00	65.00	135	—
1648 MB	10,000	16.00	33.00	65.00	135	—
1649 MB	20,000	16.00	33.00	65.00	135	—
1650 MB	—	16.00	33.00	65.00	135	—
ND(1650) MB	—	16.00	33.00	65.00	135	—
1651 MB	14,000	16.00	33.00	65.00	135	—
1652 MB	9,000	16.00	33.00	65.00	135	—
1653 MB	—	16.00	33.00	65.00	135	—
1654 MB	8,000	16.00	33.00	65.00	135	—
1655 MB	9,000	16.00	33.00	65.00	135	—
1656 MB	8,000	16.00	33.00	65.00	135	—
1657 MB	3,000	16.00	33.00	65.00	135	—
1658 MB	12,000	16.00	33.00	65.00	135	—
1659 MB	—	16.00	33.00	65.00	135	—
1660 MB	—	16.00	33.00	65.00	135	—
1661 MB	—	16.00	33.00	65.00	135	—
1663 MB	—	16.00	33.00	65.00	135	—
1664 MB	—	16.00	33.00	65.00	135	—

KM# 76 3 PFENNIG (Dreier)

Silver **Obv:** Arms divide date, HANNOVER above **Rev:** Imperial orb with 3

Date	Mintage	VG	F	VF	XF	Unc
1667 AS	—	20.00	40.00	80.00	160	—
1668 AS	—	20.00	40.00	80.00	160	—

KM# 85 3 PFENNIG (Dreier)

Silver **Note:** Similar to KM#46.

Date	Mintage	VG	F	VF	XF	Unc
1670 AS	67,000	20.00	40.00	80.00	160	—
1673 AS	33,000	20.00	40.00	80.00	160	—
1674/3 AS	32,000	20.00	40.00	80.00	160	—

KM# 65 4 PFENNIG

Silver **Obv:** Arms, legend, date **Obv. Legend:** HANNOVER **Rev:** IIII/GUTE (or GVTE)/PEN **Note:** Gute 4 Pfennig.

Date	Mintage	VG	F	VF	XF	Unc
1666 AS	—	—	—	—	—	—
1667 AS	—	—	—	—	—	—

KM# 18 MARIENGROSCHEN

Silver **Obv:** Arms in shield, date in legend **Rev:** Madonna and child **Note:** Kipper Mariengroschen. Varieties exist.

Date	Mintage	VG	F	VF	XF	Unc
16ZZ	—	27.00	55.00	100	200	—
(1)6ZZ	—	27.00	55.00	100	200	—
(1)6ZZ (i)	—	27.00	55.00	100	200	—
16Z3	—	27.00	55.00	100	200	—
16Z3 (i)	—	27.00	55.00	100	200	—
(1)6Z3 (i)	—	27.00	55.00	100	200	—
(1)6Z3	—	27.00	55.00	100	200	—

KM# 19 MARIENGROSCHEN

Silver **Note:** Klippe.

Date	Mintage	VG	F	VF	XF	Unc
(1)6Z3 (i)	—	—	—	—	—	—

KM# 52 MARIENGROSCHEN

Silver **Obv:** Arms in shield, date in legend **Rev:** Madonna and child **Note:** Varieties exist.

Date	Mintage	VG	F	VF	XF	Unc
1652 MB	11,000	27.00	55.00	90.00	180	—
1653 MB	7,000	27.00	55.00	90.00	180	—
1654 MB	3,000	27.00	55.00	90.00	180	—
1655 MB	8,000	27.00	55.00	90.00	180	—
1656 MB	5,000	27.00	55.00	90.00	180	—
1657 MB	10,000	27.00	55.00	90.00	180	—
1658 MB	10,000	27.00	55.00	90.00	180	—
1659 MB	2,000	27.00	55.00	90.00	180	—
1660 MB	—	27.00	55.00	90.00	180	—

KM# 61 MARIENGROSCHEN

Silver **Rev:** Date at top

Date	Mintage	VG	F	VF	XF	Unc
1661 MB	—	—	—	—	—	—

KM# 62 MARIENGROSCHEN

Silver **Rev:** Date above arms **Note:** Varieties exist.

Date	Mintage	VG	F	VF	XF	Unc
1664 MB	—	27.00	55.00	90.00	180	—
1665 MB	—	27.00	55.00	90.00	180	—
1666 MB	—	27.00	55.00	90.00	180	—

KM# 66 MARIENGROSCHEN

Silver **Obv:** Arms in ornamented shield, date above **Rev:** Madonna and child

Date	Mintage	VG	F	VF	XF	Unc
1666 AS	—	20.00	40.00	75.00	150	—
1667 AS	—	20.00	40.00	75.00	150	—
1668 AS	—	20.00	40.00	75.00	150	—
1670 AS	80,000	20.00	40.00	75.00	150	—

KM# 67 MARIENGROSCHEN

Silver **Obv:** Date in legend

Date	Mintage	VG	F	VF	XF	Unc
1666 AS	—	—	—	—	—	—

KM# 77 MARIENGROSCHEN

Silver **Obv:** Arms not in shield

Date	Mintage	VG	F	VF	XF	Unc
1668 AS	—	—	—	—	—	—

KM# 6 1/24 THALER (Groschen)

Silver **Note:** Klippe.

Date	Mintage	VG	F	VF	XF	Unc
1616	—	—	—	—	—	—

KM# 5 1/24 THALER (Groschen)

Silver **Obv:** Imperial orb with Z4, date divided at top in legend by cross, titles of Matthias **Rev:** Arms in ornamented shield **Note:** Varieties exist.

Date	Mintage	VG	F	VF	XF	Unc
1616	—	33.00	65.00	120	240	—
1616 (g)	—	33.00	65.00	120	240	—
1616 MK	—	33.00	65.00	120	240	—
1616 (h)	—	33.00	65.00	120	240	—
1617 (h)	58,000	33.00	65.00	120	240	—
1716 (h) Error	—	33.00	65.00	120	240	—

KM# 7 1/24 THALER (Groschen)

Silver **Rev:** Complex arms **Note:** Varieties exist.

Date	Mintage	VG	F	VF	XF	Unc
1616	—	35.00	60.00	100	200	—
1616 (g)	—	35.00	60.00	100	200	—
1616 MK	—	35.00	60.00	100	200	—
1617	Inc. above	35.00	60.00	100	200	—
1617 (h)	Inc. above	35.00	60.00	100	200	—
1618	—	35.00	60.00	100	200	—
1619 (h)	—	35.00	60.00	100	200	—
16Z0	—	35.00	60.00	100	200	—

KM# 15 1/24 THALER (Groschen)

Silver **Note:** Klippe.

Date	Mintage	VG	F	VF	XF	Unc
16Z0	—	—	—	—	—	—

KM# 16 1/24 THALER (Groschen)

Silver **Obv:** Titles of Ferdinand II **Note:** Kipper 1/24 Thaler. Small flan.

Date	Mintage	VG	F	VF	XF	Unc
(1)6Z0	—	—	—	—	—	—

KM# 20 1/24 THALER (Groschen)

Silver **Obv:** Date divided by cross just above orb, titles of Ferdinand II **Note:** Varieties exist.

Date	Mintage	VG	F	VF	XF	Unc
16Z3 (i)	—	33.00	65.00	120	240	—
1626 (i)	—	33.00	65.00	120	240	—
1632 MB	—	33.00	65.00	120	240	—
1633 MB	3,000	33.00	65.00	120	240	—
1636 MB	—	33.00	65.00	120	240	—

KM# 38 1/24 THALER (Groschen)

Silver **Note:** Varieties exist.

Date	Mintage	VG	F	VF	XF	Unc
1639 MB	6,000	33.00	65.00	120	240	—
1640 MB	13,000	33.00	65.00	120	240	—
1640	Inc. above	33.00	65.00	120	240	—
1641 MB	10,000	33.00	65.00	120	240	—
1642 MB	—	33.00	65.00	120	240	—
1644 MB	9,000	33.00	65.00	120	240	—
1645 MB	4,000	33.00	65.00	120	240	—
1646 MB	11,000	33.00	65.00	120	240	—
1647 MB	2,000	33.00	65.00	120	240	—

KM# 54 1/24 THALER (Groschen)

Silver **Obv:** Date divided by imperial orb with Z4 as 16/M - 58/B and titles of Leopold I

Date	Mintage	VG	F	VF	XF	Unc
1658 MB	1,744	—	—	—	—	—
1659 MB	—	—	—	—	—	—

KM# 71 1/24 THALER (Groschen)

Silver **Obv:** 24 in orb

Date	Mintage	VG	F	VF	XF	Unc
1666 AS	—	—	—	—	—	—

KM# 68 2 MARIENGROSCHEN

Silver **Note:** Varieties exist.

Date	Mintage	VG	F	VF	XF	Unc
1666 AS	—	45.00	85.00	160	300	—
1667 AS	—	45.00	85.00	160	300	—
1668 AS	—	45.00	85.00	160	300	—
1669 AS	—	45.00	85.00	160	300	—

KM# 69 4 MARIENGROSCHEN

Silver **Note:** Varieties exist.

Date	Mintage	VG	F	VF	XF	Unc
1666 AS	—	16.00	33.00	60.00	120	—
1667 AS	—	16.00	33.00	60.00	120	—
1667	—	16.00	33.00	60.00	120	—
1669 AS	—	16.00	33.00	60.00	120	—
1670 AS	—	16.00	33.00	60.00	120	—
1671	—	16.00	33.00	60.00	120	—
1674/0 AS	—	16.00	33.00	60.00	120	—
1674/1 AS	—	16.00	33.00	60.00	120	—

KM# 22 1/2 REICHSORT (1/8 Thaler)

Silver **Obv:** EIM/HALB/REICHS/ORT and titles of Ferdinand II and date **Rev:** Complex arms

Date	Mintage	VG	F	VF	XF	Unc
16Z4 (i)	—	—	—	—	—	—

KM# 26 1/2 REICHSORT (1/8 Thaler)

Silver **Obv:** Date in legend **Note:** Varieties exist.

Date	Mintage	VG	F	VF	XF	Unc
16Z5 (i)	1,334	—	—	—	—	—
16Z8 MB	1,118	—	—	—	—	—
16Z9 MB	2,033	—	—	—	—	—

KM# 70 1/2 REICHSORT (1/8 Thaler)

Silver **Obv:** Lion flanked by towers below date **Rev:** Inscription within circle **Rev. Legend:** LEOPOLD• I • D•G• ROMINUS • SEMP • AUG **Rev. Inscription:** I/HALBER/REICHS/ORT

Date	Mintage	VG	F	VF	XF	Unc
1666 AS	—	55.00	110	200	350	—

KM# 78 6 MARIENGROSCHEN

Silver **Note:** Varieties exist.

Date	Mintage	VG	F	VF	XF	Unc
1668 AS	—	27.00	45.00	90.00	200	—
1668	—	27.00	45.00	90.00	200	—
1669 AS	—	27.00	45.00	90.00	200	—
1671	42,000	27.00	45.00	90.00	200	—
1673 AS	134,000	27.00	45.00	90.00	200	—
1674 AS	58,000	27.00	45.00	90.00	200	—

KM# 88 6 MARIENGROSCHEN

Silver **Obv:** Date in legend

Date	Mintage	VG	F	VF	XF	Unc
1674	—	—	—	—	—	—
1674 AS	—	—	—	—	—	—

KM# 79 12 MARIENGROSCHEN

Silver **Note:** Varieties exist.

Date	Mintage	VG	F	VF	XF	Unc
1669 AS	—	33.00	60.00	110	220	—
1670 AS	—	33.00	60.00	110	220	—
1671	—	33.00	60.00	110	220	—
1672	107,000	33.00	60.00	110	220	—
1674	—	33.00	60.00	110	220	—
1674 AS	—	33.00	60.00	110	220	—

KM# 86 12 MARIENGROSCHEN

Silver **Rev:** XII/MARIEN/GROSCH/date

Date	Mintage	VG	F	VF	XF	Unc
1672 AS	Inc. above	45.00	80.00	140	275	—
1673 AS	12,000	45.00	80.00	140	275	—

KM# 23 1/4 THALER (Reichsort)

Silver **Note:** Similar to 1 Thaler, KM#25.

Date	Mintage	VG	F	VF	XF	Unc
16Z4 (i)	—	—	—	—	—	—
16Z9 MB	988	—	—	—	—	—

KM# 53 1/4 THALER (Reichsort)

Silver **Obv:** Crowned imperial eagle, orb on breast with value 4 (altered from 6), date divided by tail, titles of Ferdinand III **Rev:** Complex arms

Date	Mintage	VG	F	VF	XF	Unc
1654 MB	—	—	—	—	—	—

KM# 72 1/4 THALER (Reichsort)

Silver **Obv:** Titles of Leopold I

Date	Mintage	VG	F	VF	XF	Unc
1666 AS	—	—	—	—	—	—

KM# 24 1/2 THALER

Silver **Note:** Similar to 1 Thaler, KM#25.

Date	Mintage	VG	F	VF	XF	Unc
16Z4 (i)	—	—	—	—	—	—
16Z9 MB	1,966	—	—	—	—	—

KM# 27 1/2 THALER

Silver **Obv:** W/1Z (groschen) in imperial orb

Date	Mintage	VG	F	VF	XF	Unc
16Z5 (i)	—	1,000	2,200	3,300	5,250	—
16Z6 (i)	1,150	1,000	2,200	3,300	5,250	—

KM# 30 1/2 THALER

Silver **Note:** Klippe.

Date	Mintage	VG	F	VF	XF	Unc
16Z9 MB	—	—	—	—	—	—

KM# 73 1/2 THALER

Silver **Obv:** Titles of Leopold I

Date	Mintage	VG	F	VF	XF	Unc
1666 AS	—	—	—	—	—	—

KM# 87 24 MARIENGROSCHEN (2/3 Thaler - Gulden)

Silver **Note:** Similar to 12 Mariengroschen, KM#79, but value XXIIII.

Date	Mintage	VG	F	VF	XF	Unc
1672 AS	—	—	—	—	—	—

KM# 89 24 MARIENGROSCHEN (2/3 Thaler - Gulden)

Silver **Obv:** Lion rampant left above three-petaled cloverleaf **Rev. Inscription:** 24 / MARIEN / GROSCH / date

Date	Mintage	VG	F	VF	XF	Unc
1674 AS	3,608	—	—	—	—	—

KM# 25.1 THALER

Silver **Obv:** Similar to KM#25.2 but larger clover in large door on reverse **Note:** Dav. #5388.

Date	Mintage	VG	F	VF	XF	Unc
16Z4 (i)	—	550	1,000	1,650	—	—

KM# 25.2 THALER

Silver **Note:** Dav. #5390.

Date	Mintage	VG	F	VF	XF	Unc
16Z9 MB	3,344	550	1,000	1,650	3,850	—

KM# 28.1 THALER

Silver **Rev:** Z4 (groschen) in imperial orb **Note:** Dav. #5389.

Date	Mintage	VG	F	VF	XF	Unc
16Z5 (i)	5,748	550	1,000	1,650	—	—

KM# 28.2 THALER

Silver **Rev:** Without 24 in imperial orb **Note:** Dav. #5389A.

Date	Mintage	VG	F	VF	XF	Unc
16Z5 (i)	Inc. above	550	1,000	1,650	—	—

KM# 35 THALER

Silver **Obv:** Shield of complex arms, horned helmet above **Rev:** Crowned imperial eagle, Z4 in orb on breast, date divided by crown at top, titles of Ferdinand II **Note:** Dav. #5392.

Date	Mintage	VG	F	VF	XF	Unc
1630 MB	2,130	550	1,000	1,750	4,000	—

KM# 37 THALER

Silver **Obv:** Lion flanked by towers within beaded circle, without date **Rev:** Z-4 on breast of double-headed imperial eagle within beaded circle **Note:** Dav. #5393.

Date	Mintage	VG	F	VF	XF	Unc
1631 MB	1,780	550	1,000	1,650	3,750	—
1635 MB	—	550	1,000	1,650	3,750	—
1636 MB	—	550	1,000	1,650	3,750	—
1637 MB	311	550	1,000	1,650	3,750	—

KM# 39 THALER

Silver **Rev:** Tail divides date, titles of Ferdinand III **Note:** Dav. #5394.

Date	Mintage	VG	F	VF	XF	Unc
1639 MB Rare	464	—	—	—	—	—

KM# 47 THALER

Silver **Rev:** Date divided at top by crown **Note:** Dav. #5395.

Date	Mintage	VG	F	VF	XF	Unc
1646 MB	128	600	1,100	1,950	—	—

KM# 48 THALER

Silver **Rev:** 24 in orb on breast **Note:** Dav. #5396.

Date	Mintage	VG	F	VF	XF	Unc
1649 MB Unique	—	—	—	—	—	—

KM# 60.1 THALER

Silver **Obv:** Similar to KM#25.2 but without date **Rev:** Titles of Leopold I **Note:** Dav. #5397.

Date	Mintage	VG	F	VF	XF	Unc
1660 MB	—	600	1,100	1,950	—	—

KM# 60.2 THALER

Silver **Rev:** Date not divided **Rev. Legend:** LEOPOLDVS... **Note:** Dav. #5398.

Date	Mintage	VG	F	VF	XF	Unc
1665 Rare	—	—	—	—	—	—

KM# 74 THALER

Silver **Obv:** Lion flanked by towers below date **Rev:** Double-headed imperial eagle **Note:** Dav. #5399.

Date	Mintage	VG	F	VF	XF	Unc
1666 AS	—	550	1,000	1,650	—	—
1670 AS	—	550	1,000	1,650	—	—

KM# 8 2 THALER

Silver **Obv:** Complex arms, date in legend at top **Rev:** Crowned imperial eagle, orb on breast, titles of Matthias **Note:** Dav. #5387.

Date	Mintage	VG	F	VF	XF	Unc
1616 Rare	—	—	—	—	—	—

KM# 36 2 THALER

Silver **Obv:** Shield of complex arms, horned helmet above **Rev:** Crowned imperial eagle, Z4 in orb on breast, date divided by crown at top, titles of Ferdinand II **Note:** Dav. #5391.

Date	Mintage	VG	F	VF	XF	Unc
1630 MB Rare	—	—	—	—	—	—

KM# 9 GOLDGULDEN

3.5000 g., 0.9860 Gold 0.1109 oz. AGW **Obv:** Crowned imperial eagle, orb on breast, titles of Matthias **Rev:** Complex arms, date above **Note:** Fr. #1156.

Date	Mintage	VG	F	VF	XF	Unc
1616	—	1,050	2,250	4,500	7,500	—

KM# 29 GOLDGULDEN

3.5000 g., 0.9860 Gold 0.1109 oz. AGW **Obv:** Titles of Ferdinand II **Note:** Fr. #1156.

Date	Mintage	VG	F	VF	XF	Unc
16Z5 TB	488	850	1,800	3,600	6,000	—
16Z8 TB	2,960	725	1,500	3,000	4,800	—
16Z9 MB	2,061	725	1,500	3,000	4,800	—
1630 MB	627	850	1,800	3,600	6,000	—
1633 MB	323	850	1,800	3,600	6,000	—
1635 MB	527	850	1,800	3,600	6,000	—

KM# 51 GOLDGULDEN

3.5000 g., 0.9860 Gold 0.1109 oz. AGW **Obv:** Titles of Ferdinand III

Date	Mintage	VG	F	VF	XF	Unc
1650 MB	—	950	2,000	3,900	6,600	—

TRADE COINAGE

KM# 45 DUCAT

3.5000 g., 0.9860 Gold 0.1109 oz. AGW **Obv:** Crowned imperial eagle, orb on breast, titles of Matthias **Rev:** Complex arms, date above, legend **Rev. Legend:** DUCAT: NOV... **Note:** Fr. #1157.

Date	Mintage	VG	F	VF	XF	Unc
1640 MB	1,057	1,500	2,750	5,000	8,500	—

KM# A75 DUCAT

3.5000 g., 0.9860 Gold 0.1109 oz. AGW **Obv:** Titles of Leopold I

Date	Mintage	VG	F	VF	XF	Unc
1666	—	1,000	2,000	4,000	7,000	—
1667 AS	—	1,000	2,000	4,000	7,000	—

KM# A54 3 DUCAT

10.5000 g., 0.9860 Gold 0.3328 oz. AGW **Obv:** Crowned imperial eagle, orb on breast with value 4 (altered from 6), date divided by tail, titles of Ferdinand III **Rev:** Complex arms **Note:** Struck with 1/4 Thaler dies, KM#53.

Date	Mintage	VG	F	VF	XF	Unc
1654 MB Rare	—	—	—	—	—	—

KM# 75 3 DUCAT

10.5000 g., 0.9860 Gold 0.3328 oz. AGW **Obv:** Titles of Leopold I **Note:** Fr. #1157. Struck with 1/4 Thaler dies, KM#72.

Date	Mintage	VG	F	VF	XF	Unc
1666 AS Rare	—	—	—	—	—	—

HATZFELD

The origins of this old noble family in Hesse were in the territory around the now ruined castle of Hatzfeld on the Eder River, about 16 miles (26km) north-northwest of Marburg. The earliest known lord of Hatzfeld is Kraft I (1265-1301), whose sons Gottfried I and Kraft II divided their patrimony upon his death. The elder line died out in 1575, but several branches of the younger line continued to thrive into the modern era and undergoing numerous divisions over the next three centuries. The first such division occurred in about 1420, creating the lines of Hatzfeld-Weisweiler and Hatzfeld-Wildenburg. Hatzfeld-Weisweiler was further divided in 1508 into Hatzfeld-Weisweiler-Merten, Hatzfeld-Weisweiler-Werther and Hatzfeld-Weisweiler-Weisweiler. Hatzfeld-Weisweiler-Werther established a cadet line in Schönstein in 1539 and the lord was raised to the rank of count in 1671. A further division of Hatzfeld-Weisweiler-Werther in 1766 created a new branch of Hatzfeld-Weisweiler-Trachenberg, whose count was made a prince in 1803. Meanwhile, the ruler of Hatzfeld-Weisweiler-Weisweiler was raised to a count in 1635 and his son was reconfirmed in the title in 1698. A later count of this line was made a Prussian prince in 1870 and a new line of Hatzfeld-Wildenburg was established from it in 1874.

The original Hatzfeld-Wildenburg line was the only branch of the dynasty which issued coins. Cadet lines were established from it at Heckenbeuhel in 1490 and at Krottendorf in 1569. The latter received part of the countship of Gleichen in 1639, then Trachenberg in 1641, the same year the lord was raised to the rank of count. A further division was effected in 1677 and resulted in the lines of Hatzfeld-Wildenburg-Rosenberg (extinct in 1722) and Hatzfeld-Wildenburg-Krottendorf-Gleichen. The count of Hatzfeld-Wildenburg-Gleichen became a Prussian prince in 1741 and a Prince of the Empire in 1748, but the line died out in 1794 and most of the family's territories were divided between the Archbishopric of Mainz and the Bishopric of Würzburg.

HATZFELD-GLEICHEN

Established from the addition of territories to Hatzfeld-Wildenburg-Krottendorf in 1639 and further divided in 1677 into Hatzfeld-Wildenburg-Rosenberg and Hatzfeld-Wildenburg-Krottendorf.

RULERS

Melchior I, 1630-1658, Count 1641
Hermann, 1658-77
Heinrich, 1677-83 and
Sebastian II, 1677-96
Franz, 1683-1738

REFERENCE:

V = Franz-Eugen Volz, ***Die Münzen und Medaillen des gräflichen Hauses Hatzfeldt.*** in Wolf-Dieter Müller = Jahneke and Franz-Eugen Volz, ***Die Münzen unde Medaillen der gräflicher Häuser Sayn***, Frankfurt am Main, 1975.

COUNTSHIP

REGULAR COINAGE

KM# 5 3 GUTE KREUZER (Groschen)

Silver **Obv:** 3 in small circle of points above GVTE/KREUTZ, year, titles of Franz II **Rev:** Crowned 6-fold arms in ornamented frame **Note:** Struck at Niederstetten. Varieties exist.

Date	Mintage	VG	F	VF	XF	Unc
1684	—	40.00	80.00	140	240	—

KM# 6 3 GUTE KREUZER (Groschen)

Silver **Obv:** 3 in small circle of points above BVTHE/KREVT/ZER, MONETA: HAZFELDIACA

Date	Mintage	VG	F	VF	XF	Unc
ND(ca.1685)	—	40.00	80.00	140	240	—

KM# 7 3 GUTE KREUZER (Groschen)

Silver **Rev:** GVTE/KRVT/ZER

Date	Mintage	VG	F	VF	XF	Unc
ND(ca.1685)	—	40.00	80.00	140	240	—

KM# 1 THALER

Silver **Obv:** Armored bust of Melchior right **Rev:** Seated Madonna and child, Hatzfeld arms below **Mint:** Nurnberg **Note:** Dav. #6709.

Date	Mintage	F	VF	XF	Unc	BU
ND(1666)	—	1,450	2,650	4,500	8,300	—

TRADE COINAGE

KM# 4 DUCAT

Gold **Obv:** Bust of Hermann right, titles of Hermann and Ferdinand III in legend **Rev:** Madonna and child on cloud with shield of Hatzfield arms, PROTECTRIX.NE:DESERAS... **Note:** Fr. #1187.

Date	Mintage	VG	F	VF	XF	Unc
ND(1666) Rare	—	—	—	—	—	—

KM# 3 DUCAT

3.5000 g., 0.9860 Gold 0.1109 oz. AGW **Obv:** Mantled bust to right **Mint:** Nurnberg **Note:** Fr.#1186.

Date	Mintage	VG	F	VF	XF	Unc
ND(1666)	—	1,800	3,400	6,000	9,800	—

HATZFELD-WILDENBURG-KROTTORF

Created from the division of Hatzfeld-Wildenburg in 1569, but reformed in the next generation into Hatzfeld-Gleichen-Trachenberg with the addition of territory.

RULER

Sebastian I, 1569-1630

MINT OFFICIALS

Christian Moller, die-cutter at Nuremberg, ca. 1666
H.N. Kolb, mintmaster at Niederstetten, ca. 1684-1685

ARMS

A house anchor (used to strengthen walls of buildings)

REFERENCE:

V = Franz-Eugen Volz, "Die Münzen und Medaillen des gräflichen Hauses Hatzfeldt," in Wolf-Dieter Müller=Jahneke and Franz-Eugen Volz, ***Die Münzen unde Medaillen der gräflicher Häuser Sayn***, Frankfurt am Main, 1975.

LORDSHIP

REGULAR COINAGE

KM# 3 THALER
Silver **Obv:** Hermann, titles of Hermann and Ferdinand III **Rev:** Madonna seated in clouds with child, arms below

Date	Mintage	F	VF	XF	Unc	BU
ND(1666)	—	1,450	2,650	4,500	8,300	—

KM# 1 THALER
Silver **Obv:** Facing bust of Sebastian I **Rev:** Standing figures of Honor and Virtue, date below **Rev. Legend:** HONOS ET VIRTVS **Note:** Dav. #9249.

Date	Mintage	F	VF	XF	Unc	BU
1597(1666)	—	900	1,850	3,750	6,500	—

Note: Although dated 1597, the above coin was actually struck in Nuremberg in 1666

TRADE COINAGE

KM# 2 DUCAT
3.5000 g., 0.9860 Gold 0.1109 oz. AGW **Obv:** Facing bust of Sebastian I **Rev:** Standing figures of Honor and Virtue, date below **Rev. Legend:** HONOS ET VIRTVS **Note:** Struck at Nürnberg Mint. Fr. #1185.

Date	Mintage	VG	F	VF	XF	Unc
1597(1666)	—	1,500	2,750	4,500	7,000	—

Note: Although dated 1597, the coin was actually struck in Nüremberg in 1666

HEID AND BLEID

The old duel lordships of Heid and Bleid were located north and west of the city of Aachen and were associated with the Bongart family from the early 14th century, vassals of the counts and later dukes of Jülich. Heid was a water castle within the lands of Jülich, whereas Bleid was a place near Maestricht in the Netherlands. The rulers issued several coins during the 16th century. The family split their holdings in the late 17th century and one branch lost its territory during the French Revolution, but descendants of the Bongarts have survived into modern times.

RULER
Wilhelm II von Bongart, 1596-1615

Reference:
M = Julius Menadier, ***Die Aachener Münzen***, Berlin, 1913.

LORDSHIP

REGULAR COINAGE

KM# 1 TESTON (1/4 Thaler)
Silver **Ruler:** Wilhelm II von Bongart **Obv:** Bust left in circle **Obv. Legend:** + GVILI * A * BVNG * DO * HEYD **Rev:** Eagle above 4-fold arms **Rev. Legend:** MO * NO * LIB * BA * I * BLYT

Date	Mintage	VG	F	VF	XF	Unc
ND(1596-1615)	—	—	—	—	—	—

HELFENSTEIN

A line of rulers, eventually counts, with lands near Ulm in Swabia, who traced their origins back to the early 12th century. The family had several divisions of the patrimony, the last occurring in 1548 when the two lines of Helfenstein-Gundelfingen and Helfenstein-Wiesensteig were established. Both became extinct in 1627 and titles passed to Furstenberg and Bavaria, the latter obtaining all of Helfenstein by 1752.

ARMS
Helfenstein – elephant to right
Gundelfingen – long leaf

REFERENCE:
B/E = Christian Binder, Julius Ebner, **Württembergische Münz- und Medaillen-Kunde**, 2 vols., Stuttgart, 1910-12.

HELFENSTEIN-GUNDELFINGEN

RULERS
Froben, 1573-1622
Georg Wilhelm, 1622-1627

COUNTSHIP

TRADE COINAGE

KM# 1 GOLDGULDEN
3.5000 g., 0.9860 Gold 0.1109 oz. AGW **Ruler:** Froben **Obv:** Oval 4-fold arms in baroque frame, date above **Rev:** Crowned imperial eagle, arms of Austria and Burgundy on breast, titles of Rudolf II

Date	Mintage	VG	F	VF	XF	Unc
1611 Rare	—	—	—	—	—	—

HELFENSTEIN-WIESENSTEIG

RULERS
Rudolf V, 1570-1601
Rudolf VI, 1601-1627

COUNTSHIP

REGULAR COINAGE

KM# 1 1/24 THALER (Groschen)
Silver **Ruler:** Rudolf VI **Note:** Counterstamp of elephant and branches, 4-fold arms on Groschen of Magdeburg City KM#240.

Date	Mintage	VG	F	VF	XF	Unc
16ZZ Rare	—	—	—	—	—	—

KM# 2 24 KREUTZER (Dreibätzner)
Silver **Ruler:** Rudolf VI **Obv:** Crowned 4-fold arms, titles of Rudolf VI **Rev:** Crowned imperial eagle, 24 in orb on breast, titles of Ferdinand II **Note:** Kipper 24 Kreutzer. Varieties exist.

Date	Mintage	VG	F	VF	XF	Unc
ND(1621/2)	—	—	—	—	—	—

KM# 3 24 KREUTZER (Dreibätzner)
Silver **Ruler:** Rudolf VI **Obv:** Bust of Rudolf VI right **Rev:** Crowned imperial eagle, 24 in orb on breast, titles of Ferdinand II **Note:** Varieties exist.

Date	Mintage	VG	F	VF	XF	Unc
ND(1621/2)	—	—	—	—	—	—

KM# 4 24 KREUTZER (Dreibätzner)
Silver **Ruler:** Rudolf VI **Obv:** Elephant right in crowned and ornamented oval, titles of Rudolf VI **Rev:** Crowned imperial eagle, value (24) in legend below, titles of Ferdinand II

Date	Mintage	VG	F	VF	XF	Unc
ND(1621/2)	—	—	—	—	—	—

HENNEBERG

The line of counts of Henneberg in southern Thüringia, who traced their ancestors back to the late eighth century became extinct in 1583. The territories went mostly to Saxony with smaller parts to Hesse-Cassel and Brandenburg. Several Saxon duchies issued coins at Ilmenau. In 1660 Henneberg was divided again and redistributed among the duchies of both Albertine Saxony (Electoral Saxony and Saxe-Zeitz) and Ernestine Saxony (Saxe-Gotha and Saxe-Weimar). Each struck coins for its portion.

Joint Sovereignty of Electoral Saxony, Saxe-Gotha, Saxe-Altenburg and Saxe-Weimar

RULERS
Friedrich Wilhelm I of Saxe-Altenburg, 1583-1602, Regent 1591-1601 for Christian II of Electoral Saxony
Johann III of Saxe-Weimar, 1583-1605
Johann Philipp I of Saxe-Altenburg, 1602-39
Friedrich VIII of Saxe-Altenburg, 1602-25
Johann Wilhelm IV of Saxe-Altenburg, 1602-32
Friedrich Wilhelm IV of Saxe-Altenburg, 1603-60
Johann Ernst IV of Saxe-Weimar, 1605-26
Friedrich VII of Saxe-Weimar, 1605-22
Wilhelm IV of Saxe-Weimar, 1605-60
Albrecht II of Saxe-Weimar, 1605-44
Johann Friedrich VI of Saxe-Weimar, 1605-28
Friedrich Wilhelm of Saxe-Weimar, 1605-19
Bernhard of ISaxe-Weimar, 1605-39
Ernst I of Saxe-Gotha (III of Saxe-Weimar), 1605-60
Johann Georg I of Electoral Saxony, 1611-56

MINT MARK
S – Schleusingen Mint

ARMS
Hen standing or walking left
M = Otto Merseburger, **Sammlung Otto Merseburger umfassend Münzen und Medaillen von Sachsen**, Leipzig, 1894.
Sch = Wolfgang Schulten, ***Deutsche Münzen aus der Zeit Karls V.***, Frankfurt am Main, 1976.
S = Hugo Frhr. Von Saurma-Jeltsch, **Die Saurmasche Münzsammlung deutscher, schweizerischer und polnischer Gepräge von etwa dem Beginn der Groschenzeit bis zur Kipperperiode**, Berlin, 1892.
L. Deahna, "Zur hennebergischen Münzkunde," **Frankfurter Münzzeitung** 11 (1911), pp. 194-5, 203-6.

COUNTSHIP

REGULAR COINAGE

KM# 2 3 KREUZER (Groschen)
Silver **Obv:** Date divided at top and bottom **Rev:** Hen in heart-shaped ornamented shield

Date	Mintage	VG	F	VF	XF	Unc
16Z1	—	20.00	45.00	80.00	140	—

KM# 3 3 KREUZER (Groschen)
Silver **Obv:** Date divided near lower shield and 3 in legend at bottom

Date	Mintage	VG	F	VF	XF	Unc
16Z1	—	20.00	45.00	80.00	140	—

KM# 1 3 KREUZER (Groschen)
Silver **Obv:** 3 shields of arms, imperial orb with 3 above, titles of Joahnn Georg I **Rev:** Hen left in ornamental oval **Note:** Kipper 3 Kreuzer.

Date	Mintage	VG	F	VF	XF	Unc
ND(1621)	—	—	—	—	—	—

KM# 7 3 KREUZER (Groschen)
Silver **Obv:** Date in legend, with or without S below orb **Note:** Varieties exist.

Date	Mintage	VG	F	VF	XF	Unc
16ZZ	—	20.00	45.00	80.00	140	—
16ZZ S	—	20.00	45.00	80.00	140	—
1622	—	20.00	45.00	80.00	140	—

KM# 5 24 KREUZER (Doppelschreckenberger)
Silver **Obv:** Date divided by lower shield

Date	Mintage	VG	F	VF	XF	Unc
16Z1	—	27.00	60.00	100	160	—
16Z1 S	—	27.00	60.00	100	160	—
16ZZ S	—	27.00	60.00	100	160	—

KM# 4 24 KREUZER (Doppelschreckenberger)
Silver **Obv:** 3 shields of arms, imperial orb with 24 above, date divided at top and bottom **Rev:** Hen in heart-shaped ornamented shield **Note:** Kipper 24 Kreuzer.

Date	Mintage	VG	F	VF	XF	Unc
16Z1	—	27.00	60.00	100	160	—

KM# 6 24 KREUZER (Doppelschreckenberger)
Silver **Obv:** Date divided by orb at top, with or without S below orb **Note:** Varieties exist.

Date	Mintage	VG	F	VF	XF	Unc
1621 S	—	27.00	60.00	100	160	—
16Z1 S	—	27.00	60.00	100	160	—
16Z1	—	27.00	60.00	100	160	—
16ZZ S	—	27.00	60.00	100	160	—
16ZZ	—	27.00	60.00	100	160	—
1622 S	—	27.00	60.00	100	160	—

KM# 8 24 KREUZER (Doppelschreckenberger)
Silver **Obv:** 24 in orb

Date	Mintage	VG	F	VF	XF	Unc
16ZZ	—	27.00	60.00	100	160	—
16ZZ S	—	27.00	60.00	100	160	—

KM# 9 24 KREUZER (Doppelschreckenberger)
Silver **Rev:** Hen left in oval within baroque frame

Date	Mintage	VG	F	VF	XF	Unc
16ZZ	—	33.00	65.00	120	200	—

KM# 10 24 KREUZER (Doppelschreckenberger)
Silver **Obv:** Value in orb 24

Date	Mintage	VG	F	VF	XF	Unc
1622 S	—	33.00	65.00	120	200	—

KM# 12 1/2 THALER
Silver **Obv:** 3 shields of arms, imperial orb above, date divided at top **Rev:** Hen left in heart-shaped ornamented shield

Date	Mintage	VG	F	VF	XF	Unc
16ZZ S	—	—	—	—	—	—

KM# 13 THALER
Silver **Obv:** 3 shields of arms, imperial orb above, date divided at top **Rev:** Hen left in heart-shaped ornamented shield

Date	Mintage	VG	F	VF	XF	Unc
16ZZ S	—	—	—	—	—	—

KM# 14 THALER
Silver **Obv:** Date divided by lower arms

Date	Mintage	VG	F	VF	XF	Unc
1622 S	—	—	—	—	—	—

KM# 11 40 GROSCHEN (2 Guldentaler)
Silver **Obv:** 3 shield of arms, imperial orb above, date divided at top, 40 in cartouche at bottom **Rev:** Hen left in heart-shaped ornamented shield **Note:** Kipper 40 Groschen.

Date	Mintage	VG	F	VF	XF	Unc
1622	—	2,000	3,250	4,200	6,500	—

KM# 15 3 THALER
Silver **Obv:** 3 shields of arms, imperial orb above, date divided by lower arms **Rev:** Hen left in heart-shaped ornamented shield

Date	Mintage	VG	F	VF	XF	Unc
1622 S Rare	—	—	—	—	—	—

SUCCESSION TO SAXE-GOTHA

Ernestine LIne

RULER
Ernst I, 1660-1675

REGULAR COINAGE

KM# 21 GROSCHEN
Silver **Subject:** Partition of Henneberg and Homage to Ernst **Obv:** Crowned 2-fold arms of Saxony and Henneberg **Rev:** 8-line inscription with date

Date	Mintage	VG	F	VF	XF	Unc
1661	—	15.00	30.00	50.00	90.00	—

KM# 22 1/4 THALER
Silver **Subject:** Partition of Henneberg and Homage to Ernst **Obv:** Crowned 5-fold arms **Rev:** 8-line inscription with Roman numeral date

Date	Mintage	VG	F	VF	XF	Unc
1661	—	—	—	—	—	—

KM# 23 THALER
Silver **Subject:** Partition of Henneberg and Homage to Ernst **Obv:** Crowned 5-fold arms **Rev:** 11-line inscription with Roman numeral date **Note:** Dav. #7446.

Date	Mintage	VG	F	VF	XF	Unc
1661	—	350	750	1,500	2,650	—

SUCCESSION TO SAXE-WEIMAR

RULERS
Wilhelm IV, 1660-62
Johann Ernst II, 1662-83
Wilhelm Ernst, 1683-1728
Johann Ernst, 1683-1707

REGULAR COINAGE

KM# 31 DREIER (3 Pfennig)
Silver **Subject:** Partition of Henneberg and Homage to Wilhelm IV **Obv:** Adjacent ornate arms of Saxony and Henneberg divide date, below Heneb. Hul=/digungs=/muntz **Rev:** 6-line inscription

Date	Mintage	VG	F	VF	XF	Unc
1661	—	16.00	33.00	60.00	100	—

KM# 32 GROSCHEN
Silver **Subject:** Partition of Henneberg and Homage to Wilhelm IV **Obv:** Crowned 5-fold arms **Rev:** 7-line inscription with date

Date	Mintage	VG	F	VF	XF	Unc
1661	—	16.00	33.00	55.00	95.00	—

KM# 33 1/4 THALER
Silver **Subject:** Partition of Henneberg and Homage to Wilhelm IV **Obv:** Bust right **Rev:** Crown above 2 small arms of Saxony and Hennenberg divides date, 5-line inscription below

Date	Mintage	VG	F	VF	XF	Unc
1661	—	—	—	—	—	—

KM# 34 1/2 THALER
Silver **Subject:** Partition of Henneberg and Homage to Wilhelm IV **Obv:** Bust right **Rev:** Crown above 2 small arms of Saxony and Henneberg divides date, 5-line inscription below surrounded by flames and rays

Date	Mintage	VG	F	VF	XF	Unc
1661	—	170	325	550	825	—

KM# 35 THALER
Silver **Subject:** Partition of Henneberg and Homage to Wilhelm IV **Obv:** Bust right **Rev:** Crown above 2 small arms of Saxony and Henneberg divides date, 5-line inscription below surrounded by flames and rays **Note:** Dav. #7548.

Date	Mintage	VG	F	VF	XF	Unc
1661	—	350	750	1,500	2,500	—

HENNEBERG-ILMENAU

SUCCESSION TO SAXE-GOTHA AND WEIMAR

RULERS
Friedrich I of Saxe-Gotha, 1680-91
Friedrich II of Saxe-Gotha, 1691-1732
Wilhelm Ernst of Saxe-Weimar, 1683-1728
Johann Ernst of Saxe-Weimar, 1683-1707

MINT OFFICIALS' INITIALS

Initial	Date	Name
BA	1691-1702	Bastian Altmann at Ilmenau

REGULAR COINAGE

KM# 11 HELLER
Copper

Date	Mintage	VG	F	VF	XF	Unc
1693	—	10.00	27.00	45.00	80.00	—
1694	—	10.00	27.00	45.00	80.00	—

KM# 7 DREIER (3 Pfennig)
Silver **Obv:** Crowned arms, date **Rev:** Hen right

Date	Mintage	VG	F	VF	XF	Unc
1692	—	20.00	40.00	70.00	125	—

KM# 12 DREIER (3 Pfennig)
Silver **Obv:** Hen right **Rev:** Inscription with date

Date	Mintage	VG	F	VF	XF	Unc
1693	—	20.00	40.00	70.00	125	—

KM# 8.1 2 GROSCHEN
Silver **Rev:** Large crown, small arms

Date	Mintage	VG	F	VF	XF	Unc
1692 BA	—	33.00	65.00	120	200	—

KM# 8.2 2 GROSCHEN
Silver **Rev:** Small crown, large arms

Date	Mintage	VG	F	VF	XF	Unc
1692 BA	—	33.00	85.00	160	275	—

KM# 13 1/3 THALER (1/2 Gulden)
Silver **Obv:** Crowned arms, date **Rev:** Hen right, value 1/3 below

Date	Mintage	VG	F	VF	XF	Unc
1693 BA	—	27.00	65.00	115	185	—

KM# 5 2/3 THALER (Gulden)
Silver **Note:** Mining 2/3 Thaler. Similar to KM#10 but larger arms.

Date	Mintage	VG	F	VF	XF	Unc
1691 BA	—	—	—	—	—	—

KM# 9 2/3 THALER (Gulden)
Silver **Obv:** Crown divides date **Note:** Varieties exist.

Date	Mintage	VG	F	VF	XF	Unc
1692 BA	—	40.00	80.00	160	275	—

KM# 10 2/3 THALER (Gulden)
Silver **Obv:** Smaller arms **Note:** Varieties exist.

Date	Mintage	VG	F	VF	XF	Unc
1692 BA	—	40.00	80.00	160	275	—
1693 BA	—	40.00	80.00	160	275	—
1694 BA	—	40.00	80.00	160	275	—

KM# 14 THALER
Silver **Rev:** "JEVOVAH" in Hebrew letters above hen **Note:** Dav. #7481.

Date	Mintage	VG	F	VF	XF	Unc
1693 BA	—	250	600	1,350	2,750	—

KM# 15 THALER
Silver **Rev:** Small hen left in wreath, legend in 3 circles **Note:** Dav. #7482.

Date	Mintage	VG	F	VF	XF	Unc
1693 BA	—	650	1,200	2,100	3,300	—

KM# 16 THALER
Silver **Rev:** Crowned hen walking right **Rev. Legend:** PINGVESCIT DUM ERUIT **Note:** Dav. #7484.

Date	Mintage	VG	F	VF	XF	Unc
1694 BA	—	300	550	900	1,750	—

KM# 25 THALER
Silver **Rev. Legend:** IN RUTILO.. **Note:** Dav. #7485.

Date	Mintage	VG	F	VF	XF	Unc
1695 BA	—	325	575	1,100	2,000	—

KM# 26 THALER

Silver **Rev. Legend:** CRESCIT ET HOC... **Note:** Dav. #7486.

Date	Mintage	VG	F	VF	XF	Unc
1696 BA	—	200	400	750	1,450	—

KM# 28 THALER

Silver **Rev:** Date below hen in ribbon bow **Rev. Legend:** WEIL GOTTES... **Note:** Dav. #7487.

Date	Mintage	VG	F	VF	XF	Unc
1697 BA	—	200	400	750	1,450	—

KM# 30 THALER

Silver **Note:** Dav. #7488.

Date	Mintage	VG	F	VF	XF	Unc
1698 BA	—	250	450	800	1,650	—

KM# 31 THALER

Silver **Note:** Dav. #7489.

Date	Mintage	VG	F	VF	XF	Unc
1699 BA	—	150	300	600	1,150	—

KM# 32 THALER

Silver **Obv:** 2 helmets with plumes and supporters **Rev:** Ribbons instead of palm branches around shields **Note:** Dav. #7490.

Date	Mintage	VG	F	VF	XF	Unc
1699 BA	—	200	400	750	1,450	—

KM# 35 THALER

Silver **Ruler:** Bernard III **Obv:** 2 ornate helmets, figures at right and left **Rev:** Crown above two shields of arms **Note:** Dav. #7491.

Date	Mintage	F	VF	XF	Unc	BU
1700 BA	—	250	450	900	1,850	—

SUCCESSION TO SAXE-MEININGEN

RULER

Bernhard III, 1680-1706

REGULAR COINAGE

KM# 6 HELLER

Copper **Obv:** Crowned Saxon arms **Rev:** Date **Rev. Legend:** I/HELLER/H.MEIN **Note:** Varieties exist.

Date	Mintage	VG	F	VF	XF	Unc
1691	—	7.00	16.00	27.00	45.00	—
1694	—	7.00	16.00	27.00	45.00	—
1696	—	7.00	16.00	27.00	45.00	—
1697	—	7.00	16.00	27.00	45.00	—
1699	—	7.00	16.00	27.00	45.00	—
1700	—	7.00	16.00	27.00	45.00	—

KM# 17 HELLER

Copper **Obv:** Arms between palm branches **Note:** Varieties exist.

Date	Mintage	VG	F	VF	XF	Unc
1694	—	7.00	16.00	27.00	45.00	—
1695	—	7.00	16.00	27.00	45.00	—
1696	—	7.00	16.00	27.00	45.00	—
1699	—	7.00	16.00	27.00	45.00	—

KM# 18 HELLER

Copper **Obv:** Crowned Saxon arms **Rev:** Date **Rev. Legend:** I/HELLER/HEN: MEI

Date	Mintage	VG	F	VF	XF	Unc
1694	—	7.00	16.00	27.00	45.00	—

KM# 19 HELLER

Copper **Rev:** Date **Rev. Legend:** I/HELLER/HEN: MEIN

Date	Mintage	VG	F	VF	XF	Unc
1694	—	7.00	16.00	27.00	45.00	—

KM# 20 HELLER

Copper **Rev:** Date **Rev. Legend:** I/HELLER/HEN: MEIN

Date	Mintage	VG	F	VF	XF	Unc
1694	—	7.00	16.00	27.00	45.00	—

KM# 21 HELLER

Copper **Obv:** Arms between palm branches

Date	Mintage	VG	F	VF	XF	Unc
1694	—	7.00	16.00	27.00	45.00	—

KM# 27 HELLER

Copper **Obv:** Crowned Saxon arms between palm branches **Rev:** Hen right, date below

Date	Mintage	VG	F	VF	XF	Unc
1696	—	6.00	13.00	25.00	40.00	—

KM# 29 HELLER

Copper **Obv:** Without palm branches

Date	Mintage	VG	F	VF	XF	Unc
1697	—	6.00	13.00	25.00	40.00	—
1699	—	6.00	13.00	25.00	40.00	—

KM# 38 HELLER

Copper **Obv:** Crowned hen right on 3 mounds **Rev:** Hen right, date below

Date	Mintage	VG	F	VF	XF	Unc
1700	—	7.00	20.00	33.00	55.00	—

KM# 39 HELLER

Copper **Obv:** Crowned Saxon arms **Rev. Legend:** H/MEIN/HELLER

Date	Mintage	VG	F	VF	XF	Unc
1700	—	7.00	20.00	33.00	45.00	—

KM# 36 HELLER

Copper **Obv:** Crowned hen right on 3 mounds **Rev:** Date **R ev. Legend:** H/MEIN/HELLER **Note:** Varieties exist.

Date	Mintage	VG	F	VF	XF	Unc
1700	—	7.00	20.00	33.00	55.00	—

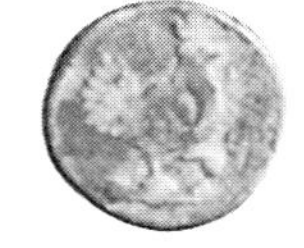

KM# 37 HELLER

Copper **Rev:** Date **Rev. Legend:** MEIN./HELLER **Note:** Varieties exist.

Date	Mintage	VG	F	VF	XF	Unc
1700	—	7.00	20.00	33.00	55.00	—

KM# 24 2 KREUZER (1/2 Batzen)

Silver **Obv:** Crowned arms in palm branches, 2 above **Rev:** Date **Rev. Legend:** NACH/DEM/FRANCKI/SCHEN KREIS/SCHLVS

Date	Mintage	VG	F	VF	XF	Unc
1694	—	—	—	—	—	—

KM# 22 1/36 THALER (8 Pfennig)

Silver **Obv:** 2 oval arms of Saxony and Henneberg in cartouche, crown above **Rev:** Date **Rev. Legend:** 36/EININ.R./THALER

Date	Mintage	VG	F	VF	XF	Unc
1694	—	—	—	—	—	—
1695	—	—	—	—	—	—

KM# 23 1/18 THALER (16 Pfennig)

Silver **Obv:** 2 oval arms of Saxony and Henneberg in cartouche, crown above **Rev:** Date **Rev. Legend:** 1 8/EIN.R./THALER

Date	Mintage	VG	F	VF	XF	Unc
1694	—	—	—	—	—	—

HERFORD

Herford town grew up around the Benedictine abbey of the same name, located about 9 miles northeast of Bielefeld in Westphalia. Herford became a free imperial city in 1631 but had this status removed in 1647. In 1803 it became a possession of Prussia. A series of local coins were struck in Herford from about 1580 until 1670.

PROVINCIAL TOWN

REGULAR COINAGE

KM# 1 PFENNIG

Copper **Obv:** City arms **Obv. Legend:** CIVITAS HERVORIA **Rev:** I in center of legend **Rev. Legend:** ANNO 1636

Date	Mintage	VG	F	VF	XF	Unc
1636	—	55.00	120	175	275	—

KM# 2 PFENNIG

Copper **Obv. Legend:** CIVITAS HERVORD...

Date	Mintage	VG	F	VF	XF	Unc
1636	—	55.00	120	175	275	—

KM# 3 2 PFENNIG
Copper **Obv:** City arms **Obv. Legend:** CIVITAS HERVORIA **Rev:** II in center of legend **Rev. Legend:** ANNO 1636

Date	Mintage	VG	F	VF	XF	Unc
1636	—	40.00	85.00	140	210	—

KM# 4 2 PFENNIG
Copper **Obv. Legend:** CIVITAS HERVORD...

Date	Mintage	VG	F	VF	XF	Unc
1636	—	40.00	85.00	140	220	—

KM# 5 3 PFENNIG
Copper **Obv:** City arms **Obv. Legend:** CIVITAS HERVORIA **Rev:** III in center of legend **Rev. Legend:** ANNO 1636

Date	Mintage	VG	F	VF	XF	Unc
1636	—	20.00	40.00	70.00	115	—

KM# 6 6 PFENNIG
Copper **Obv:** City arms, legend, date **Obv. Legend:** CIVITAS HERVORIA **Rev:** VI in ornamented circle

Date	Mintage	VG	F	VF	XF	Unc
1636	—	20.00	40.00	70.00	115	—

KM# 7 6 PFENNIG
Copper **Obv. Legend:** CIVITAS HERVORD

Date	Mintage	VG	F	VF	XF	Unc
1636	—	20.00	40.00	70.00	115	—

KM# 17 6 PFENNIG
Copper **Obv:** City arms, legend, VI at bottom **Obv. Legend:** STADT HERVORD **Rev:** Crowned scepter divides date in ornamented circle

Date	Mintage	VG	F	VF	XF	Unc
1670	—	16.00	33.00	60.00	110	—

KM# 8 12 PFENNIG
Copper **Obv:** City arms, legend, date **Obv. Legend:** CIVITAS. HERVORDIA **Rev:** XII in ornamented circle

Date	Mintage	VG	F	VF	XF	Unc
1636	—	20.00	40.00	70.00	120	—

KM# 9 12 PFENNIG
Copper **Obv:** ANO before date

Date	Mintage	VG	F	VF	XF	Unc
1636	—	20.00	40.00	70.00	120	—

KM# 18 12 PFENNIG
Copper

Date	Mintage	VG	F	VF	XF	Unc
1670	—	16.00	33.00	60.00	120	—

KM# 10 MARIENGROSCHEN (1/36 Thaler)
Silver **Obv:** City arms, imperial orb with 36 above, legend, date **Obv. Legend:** STAD. HERBORD ANO **Rev:** Madonna and child **Rev. Legend:** MARIEN - GROSCH **Note:** Varieties exist.

Date	Mintage	VG	F	VF	XF	Unc
1638	—	25.00	45.00	80.00	150	—
1640	—	25.00	45.00	80.00	150	—
1646	—	25.00	45.00	80.00	150	—

KM# 15 1/72 THALER (Matthier)
Silver **Obv:** Oval city arms in ornamented circle **Rev. Inscription:** 72 / EHT / HERV / MTIER / date

Date	Mintage	VG	F	VF	XF	Unc
1646	—	400	750	1,200	2,000	—

KM# 11 1/24 THALER (Groschen)
Silver **Obv:** City arms **Rev:** Imperial orb with 24, date above, titles of Ferdinand III **Rev. Legend:** IMPERIALIS. HERVOLDIA.

Date	Mintage	VG	F	VF	XF	Unc
1638	—	—	—	—	—	—

KM# 16 1/24 THALER (Groschen)
Silver **Obv. Legend:** MON. NOVA. REIP. HERVORD.

Date	Mintage	VG	F	VF	XF	Unc
1646	—	—	—	—	—	—

KM# 13 1/2 THALER
Silver **Obv:** City arms divide date **Obv. Legend:** MONETA.NOVA.REIP.HERVORD. **Rev:** Crowned imperial eagle, orb on breast, titles of Ferdinand III

Date	Mintage	VG	F	VF	XF	Unc
1640	—	—	—	—	—	—

KM# 12 THALER
Silver **Obv:** City arms divide date as 1-6/3-8 **Rev:** Crowned imperial eagle, orb on breast, titles of Ferdinand III **Note:** Dav. #5400.

Date	Mintage	VG	F	VF	XF	Unc
1638 Rare	—	—	—	—	—	—
1640 Rare	—	—	—	—	—	—

COUNTERMARKED COINAGE

In 1647, the Elector of Brandenburg, Friedrich Wilhelm (1640-88), took possession of his newly acquired countship of Ravensberg. Herford was located within that territory and the 1636 copper coinage of the town was countermarked to reflect the change in regime. The countermarks used were either a shield of the Herford arms (horizontal bar) or the electoral scepter of Brandenburg. In some cases, both countermarks were used. Another countermark consisting of a horizontal bar in a shield with suspended hunting horn above and sphere below, reportedly representing the Rhenish Imperial Knighthood, was used during this period.

KM# 21 2 PFENNIG
Copper **Note:** Countermark of Herford arms on 2 Pfennig, KM#3 or 4.

CM Date	Host Date	Good	VG	F	VF	XF
ND(1647)	1636	—	—	—	—	—

KM# 24 3 PFENNIG
Copper **Note:** Countermark of Rhemish Imperial Knights on 3 Pfennig, KM#5.

CM Date	Host Date	Good	VG	F	VF	XF
ND(1647-50)	1636	—	—	—	—	—

KM# 28 6 PFENNIG
Copper **Note:** Countermark of Herford and Sceptor arms on 6 Pfennig, KM#6 or 7.

CM Date	Host Date	Good	VG	F	VF	XF
ND(1647)	1636	—	—	—	—	—

KM# 27 6 PFENNIG
Copper **Note:** Countermark of Sceptor arms on 6 Pfennig, KM#6 or 7.

CM Date	Host Date	Good	VG	F	VF	XF
ND(1647)	1636	—	—	—	—	—

KM# 31 12 PFENNIG
Copper **Note:** Countermark of Herford and Sceptor arms on 12 Pfennig, KM#8 or 9.

CM Date	Host Date	Good	VG	F	VF	XF
ND(1647)	1636	—	—	—	—	—

TRADE COINAGE

KM# 14 DUCAT
3.5000 g., 0.9860 Gold 0.1109 oz. AGW **Obv:** 5-line inscription with date in ornamental square **Rev:** Crowned imperial eagle, orb on breast, titles of Ferdinand III

Date	Mintage	F	VF	XF	Unc	BU
1641	—	2,750	3,850	6,100	8,800	—

HERSFELD

Benedictine abbey founded in 769 about 24 miles north-northeast of Fulda. In 1606 the landgraves of Hesse-Cassel replaced the abbots as administrators of Hersfeld. The abbey was secularized and became a part of Hesse-Cassel in 1648.

RULERS
Joachim Ruhl, 1591-1606
Otto of Hesse-Cassel, 1606-1617
Wilhelm II of Hesse-Cassel, 1617-1627
Imperial Occupation, 1627-1631
Wilhelm II of Hesse Cassel, 1631-1637
Hermann III of Hesse-Cassel, 1637-1648

SECULARIZED ABBEY

REGULAR COINAGE

KM# 1 1/2 THALER
14.5800 g., Silver **Ruler:** Wilhelm II of Hesse-Cassel **Obv:** Crowned and mantled 2-fold arms, double-barred cross of Hersfeld left, crowned Hessian lion right **Obv. Legend:** GUILIELMUS D:G:P:A:D:H:A:H: **Rev:** Facing open hand raised from clouds below, all-seeing eye in palm, fore and middle fingers raised vertically, date at end of legend **Rev. Legend:** FIDE. SED. CUI. VIDE. **Note:** Hoffmeister 804.

Date	Mintage	VG	F	VF	XF	Unc
16Z1	—	1,500	2,250	3,500	6,000	—

KM# 2 THALER
Silver **Ruler:** Wilhelm II of Hesse-Cassel **Obv:** Crowned and mantled 2-fold arms with mitre above, double-barred cross of Hersfeld left, crowned Hessian lion right **Obv. Legend:** GUILIELMUS D:G:P:A:D:H:A:H: **Rev:** Facing open hand raised from clouds below, all-seeing eye in palm, fore and middle fingers raised vertically, date at end of legend **Rev. Legend:** FIDE. SED. CUI. VIDE.

Date	Mintage	VG	F	VF	XF	Unc
16Z1 Rare	—	—	—	—	—	—

HESSE-CASSEL

(Hessen-Kassel)

The Hesse principalities were located for the most part north of the Main River, bounded by Westphalia on the west, the Brunswick duchies on the north, the Saxon-Thuringian duchies on the east and Rhine Palatinate and the bishoprics of Mainz and Fulda on the south. The rule of the landgraves of Hesse began in the second half of the 13th century, the dignity of Prince of the Empire being acquired in 1292. In 1567 the patrimony was divided by four surviving sons, only those of Cassel and Darmstadt surviving for more than a generation in Hesse-Cassel the landgrave was raised to the rank of elector in 1803. The electorate formed part of the Kingdom of Westphalia from 1806 to 1813. In 1866 Hesse-Cassel was annexed by Prussia and became the province of Hesse-Nassau.

RULERS
Moritz, 1592-1627
Wilhelm V, 1627-37
Wilhelm VI, 1637-63
Amalie Elisabeth von Hanau, Regent, 1637-50
Wilhelm VII, 1663-70
Hedwig Sophie von Brandenburg, Regent, 1663-77
Karl, 1670-1730

MINT MARKS
C – Cassel
C – Clausthal
(.L.) – Lippoldsberg

MINT OFFICIALS' INITIALS

Initial	Date	Name
	1604-05	Hans Hausmann
	1605-	Christoph Traubell (Draubel)
	1607-08	Baldwin and Jakob von der Rust, mint contractors
	1620	Job Götz, warden at Cassel
	1620	Wilhelm Quensell, mintmaster and warden at Eschwege
	1621	Christoph Wortt (Wordt), mint contractor
	Ca.1621	Zacharias Schwager in Rotenburg
	Ca.1621	Nicholas Kauffunger, mint contractor in Rotenburg
G		Goslar Mint
AG	1637-57	Arnold Gall
GB, IGB	1657-80	Johann Georg Buttner
GK	1637-40	Georg Kruckenberg
IH	1680-81	Johann Heinrich Hoffmann
IVF	1681-97	Johann von Farenberg (Fornenbergk)
LH	1635-38	Lubert Haussmann
TS	1621-34	Terenz Schmidt

ARMS
Hessian lion rampant left

LANDGRAVIATE

REGULAR COINAGE

KM# 15 HELLER
Silver **Ruler:** Moritz **Obv:** Crowned Hessian lion in German shield divides date, M.L.Z.H. above. **Note:** Uniface.

Date	Mintage	VG	F	VF	XF	Unc
1610	—	40.00	120	250	480	—
(1)6ZZ	—	30.00	70.00	150	300	—
ND	—	25.00	50.00	100	200	—

KM# 14 HELLER

Silver **Ruler:** Moritz **Obv:** Arms of Eppstein in Spanish shield **Note:** Uniface.

Date	Mintage	VG	F	VF	XF	Unc
ND(1622)	—	—	—	—	—	—

KM# 28 HELLER

Silver **Ruler:** Moritz **Obv:** Hessian lion in Spanish shield, ML above, Z-H divided left and right **Note:** Schussel-type.

Date	Mintage	VG	F	VF	XF	Unc
ND(1622)	—	20.00	45.00	110	250	—

KM# 59 HELLER

Silver **Ruler:** Moritz **Obv:** Hessian lion in German shield, ML above, Z-H divided left and right, date divided below. **Note:** Schussel-type. Varieties exist.

Date	Mintage	VG	F	VF	XF	Unc
16ZZ	—	25.00	55.00	125	280	—
1623	—	25.00	55.00	125	280	—
(1)6Z3	—	25.00	55.00	125	280	—

KM# 164 HELLER

Silver **Ruler:** Wilhelm V **Obv:** Helmet, W L H above **Note:** Schussel-type. Uniface.

Date	Mintage	VG	F	VF	XF	Unc
ND(1627-37)	—	15.00	35.00	70.00	150	—

KM# 163 HELLER

Silver **Ruler:** Wilhelm V **Obv:** WL / 16H37 / Shamrock **Note:** Uniface.

Date	Mintage	VG	F	VF	XF	Unc
1637	—	30.00	80.00	160	350	—

KM# 206 HELLER

Silver **Ruler:** Wilhelm VI **Obv:** Helmet, date divided to its left and right, WLH above

Date	Mintage	VG	F	VF	XF	Unc
(16)45	—	25.00	60.00	125	250	—
(16)46	—	25.00	60.00	125	250	—

KM# 209 HELLER

Silver **Ruler:** Wilhelm VI **Obv:** Helmet, WLH above, H between horns, date 4-6 flanking

Date	Mintage	VG	F	VF	XF	Unc
(16)46	—	25.00	60.00	125	250	—

KM# 213 HELLER

Silver **Ruler:** Wilhelm VI **Obv:** Helmet, WLZ above, H and 47 between horns

Date	Mintage	VG	F	VF	XF	Unc
(16)47	—	25.00	60.00	125	250	—

KM# A297 HELLER

Silver **Ruler:** Wilhelm VII **Obv:** Crowned W **Note:** Schussel-type. Uniface.

Date	Mintage	VG	F	VF	XF	Unc
ND(1650-1663)	—	25.00	50.00	100	200	—

KM# 238 HELLER

Silver **Ruler:** Wilhelm VI **Obv:** Crowned W divides date as 1-6/5-4. **Note:** Schussel-type.

Date	Mintage	VG	F	VF	XF	Unc
1654 AG	—	30.00	70.00	150	300	—
1656 AG	—	30.00	70.00	150	300	—
1659	—	30.00	70.00	150	300	—
1660	—	30.00	70.00	150	300	—
1661	—	30.00	70.00	150	300	—
1663	—	30.00	70.00	150	300	—

KM# 266 HELLER

Silver **Ruler:** Wilhelm VII **Note:** Similar to KM#238.

Date	Mintage	VG	F	VF	XF	Unc
1665	—	15.00	40.00	90.00	180	—
1667	—	15.00	40.00	90.00	180	—
1668	—	15.00	40.00	90.00	180	—
1670	—	15.00	40.00	90.00	180	—

KM# 297 HELLER

Silver **Ruler:** Karl **Obv:** Crowned script C divides date as 1-6/7-4. **Note:** Schussel-type.

Date	Mintage	VG	F	VF	XF	Unc
1673	—	40.00	90.00	200	400	—
1674	—	40.00	90.00	200	400	—
1676	—	40.00	90.00	200	400	—
1678	—	40.00	90.00	200	400	—
1680	—	40.00	90.00	200	400	—

KM# 316 HELLER

Silver **Ruler:** Karl **Obv:** Crowned CL Monogram divides date as 1-6/8-5. **Note:** Schussel-type.

Date	Mintage	VG	F	VF	XF	Unc
1683	—	40.00	90.00	200	400	—
1685	—	40.00	90.00	200	400	—
1686	—	40.00	90.00	200	400	—
1688	—	40.00	90.00	200	400	—
1690	—	40.00	90.00	200	400	—
1697	—	40.00	90.00	200	400	—

KM# 307 HELLER

Silver **Ruler:** Karl **Obv:** Crowned C, date divided as 16-83 **Note:** Schussel-type. Uniface.

Date	Mintage	VG	F	VF	XF	Unc
1683	—	40.00	90.00	200	400	—

KM# 60 2 HELLER

Silver **Ruler:** Moritz **Obv:** Hessian lion in Spanish shield, ML above, Z-H divided left and right, date divided below. **Note:** Kipper 2 Heller. Uniface. Similar to #59.

Date	Mintage	VG	F	VF	XF	Unc
1623	—	40.00	80.00	160	280	—
(1)6Z3	—	40.00	80.00	160	280	—

KM# 241.1 3 HELLER

Silver **Ruler:** Wilhelm VI **Obv:** Crowned W in palm wreath **Rev:** III, date divided above and to sides

Date	Mintage	VG	F	VF	XF	Unc
1655 AG	—	55.00	110	200	360	—
1656 AG	—	55.00	110	200	360	—
1657 AG	—	55.00	110	200	360	—

KM# 241.2 3 HELLER

Silver **Ruler:** Wilhelm VI **Rev:** III/date

Date	Mintage	VG	F	VF	XF	Unc
1658	—	—	—	—	—	—

Note: Reported, not confirmed

KM# 267 3 HELLER

Silver **Ruler:** Wilhelm VII **Obv:** Crowned W between palm branches **Rev:** Shield with 3, roses besides, date above

Date	Mintage	VG	F	VF	XF	Unc
1665 IGB	—	55.00	110	200	360	—

KM# 280 3 HELLER

Silver **Ruler:** Wilhelm VII **Obv:** Crowned W between palm branches **Rev:** Value 3 in oval baroque frame divides date as 1-6/7-0

Date	Mintage	VG	F	VF	XF	Unc
1668	—	55.00	110	200	360	—
1670	—	55.00	110	200	360	—

KM# 291 3 HELLER

Silver **Ruler:** Karl **Obv:** Crowned script C between palm branches **Rev:** 3 in Rococo shield divides date at 1-6/7-3

Date	Mintage	VG	F	VF	XF	Unc
1673	—	45.00	90.00	185	350	—
1674	—	45.00	90.00	185	350	—
1677	—	45.00	90.00	185	350	—
1681	—	45.00	90.00	185	350	—
1684	—	45.00	90.00	185	350	—
1686	—	45.00	90.00	185	350	—
1694	—	45.00	90.00	185	350	—
1699	—	45.00	90.00	185	350	—

KM# 5 4 HELLER (1/3 Albus)

Silver **Ruler:** Moritz **Obv:** Hessian lion in Spanish shield divides date, MLZH above **Rev:** Landgrave's helmet, 4-H above **Note:** Varieties exist, mainly with the helmet on the reverse.

Date	Mintage	VG	F	VF	XF	Unc
1601	—	8.00	20.00	40.00	80.00	—
160Z	—	8.00	20.00	40.00	80.00	—
1602	—	8.00	20.00	40.00	80.00	—
1603	—	8.00	20.00	40.00	80.00	—
1604	—	8.00	20.00	40.00	80.00	—
(1)604	—	8.00	20.00	40.00	80.00	—
1605	—	8.00	20.00	40.00	80.00	—
1609	—	8.00	20.00	40.00	80.00	—
1610	—	8.00	20.00	40.00	80.00	—
1611	—	8.00	20.00	40.00	80.00	—

KM# 30 4 HELLER (1/3 Albus)

Silver **Ruler:** Moritz **Obv:** Lion in German shield divides date, MLZH above. **Rev:** Helmet, 4-H at sides **Rev. Legend:** LANDT.MUNTZ. **Note:** Kipper 4 Heller.

Date	Mintage	VG	F	VF	XF	Unc
16Z1	—	8.00	25.00	60.00	150	—
16ZZ	—	8.00	25.00	60.00	150	—
(1)6ZZ	—	8.00	25.00	60.00	150	—
16Z3	—	8.00	25.00	60.00	150	—
(1)6Z3	—	8.00	25.00	60.00	150	—

KM# 31 4 HELLER (1/3 Albus)

Silver **Ruler:** Moritz **Obv:** Hessian luion in Spanish shield, date divided 1-6/Z-1 **Rev:** Helmet, 4-H at sides **Rev. Legend:** LANDT * MUNTZ **Note:** Kipper 3 Heller.

Date	Mintage	VG	F	VF	XF	Unc
16Z1	—	20.00	50.00	120	250	—

KM# 32 4 HELLER (1/3 Albus)

Silver **Ruler:** Moritz **Obv:** Hessian lion in German shield, date flanking **Rev:** 4-H divided by helmet **Rev. Legend:** LANDTMUNTZ **Note:** Kipper 4 Heller.

Date	Mintage	VG	F	VF	XF	Unc
16Z1	—	20.00	50.00	120	250	—

KM# 245 4 HELLER (1/3 Albus)

Silver **Ruler:** Wilhelm VI **Obv:** Crowned W in palm wreath **Rev:** IIII, date divided above and at sides, mintmaster initials below **Note:** Varieties exist with value as IIII or II.II.

Date	Mintage	VG	F	VF	XF	Unc
1656 AG	—	8.00	17.00	35.00	60.00	—
1657 AG	—	8.00	17.00	35.00	60.00	—
1657 GB	—	8.00	17.00	35.00	60.00	—
1657 IGB	—	8.00	17.00	35.00	60.00	—
1658 IGB	—	8.00	17.00	35.00	60.00	—

KM# 251 4 HELLER (1/3 Albus)

Silver **Ruler:** Wilhelm VI **Obv:** Crowned ornamented W between palm branches **Rev:** Date/IIII/mintmaster initials

Date	Mintage	VG	F	VF	XF	Unc
1661 IGB	—	20.00	50.00	120	200	—
1663 IGB	—	20.00	50.00	120	200	—

KM# 256 4 HELLER (1/3 Albus)

Silver **Ruler:** Wilhelm VII **Obv:** Hessian lion in crowned Spanish shield between palm branches **Rev:** Date/ IIII/ mintmaster initials

Date	Mintage	VG	F	VF	XF	Unc
1663 IGB	—	27.00	70.00	160	275	—
1665 IGB	—	27.00	70.00	160	275	—
1668 IGB	—	27.00	70.00	160	275	—
1670 IGB	—	27.00	70.00	160	275	—

KM# 290 4 HELLER (1/3 Albus)

Silver **Ruler:** Karl **Obv:** Crowned shield with Hessian lion left, palm branches flank **Rev:** Value, date **Note:** Varieties exist.

Date	Mintage	VG	F	VF	XF	Unc
1671 IGB	—	6.00	16.00	30.00	65.00	—
1673 IGB	—	6.00	16.00	30.00	65.00	—
1674 IGB	—	6.00	16.00	30.00	65.00	—
1675 IGB	—	6.00	16.00	30.00	65.00	—
1676 IGB	—	6.00	16.00	30.00	65.00	—
1677 IGB	—	6.00	16.00	30.00	65.00	—
1678 IGB	—	6.00	16.00	30.00	65.00	—
1679 IGB	—	6.00	16.00	30.00	65.00	—
1680 IGB	—	6.00	16.00	30.00	65.00	—
1681 IH	—	6.00	16.00	30.00	65.00	—
1682 IH	—	6.00	16.00	30.00	65.00	—
1682 IVF	—	6.00	16.00	30.00	65.00	—
1685 IVF	—	6.00	16.00	30.00	65.00	—
1687 IVF	—	6.00	16.00	30.00	65.00	—
1690 IVF	—	6.00	16.00	30.00	65.00	—
1691 IVF	—	6.00	16.00	30.00	65.00	—
1692 IVF	—	6.00	16.00	30.00	65.00	—
1694 IVF	—	6.00	16.00	30.00	65.00	—
1697 IVF	—	6.00	16.00	30.00	65.00	—
1699	—	6.00	16.00	30.00	65.00	—

KM# 215 6 HELLER (1/2 Albus)

Silver **Ruler:** Wilhelm VI **Obv:** Hessian lion **Obv. Legend:** WILHELMVS • HASS • LAND • PRINC • HERSF • **Rev:** Helmet divides date, value 6 between horns

Date	Mintage	VG	F	VF	XF	Unc
1651	—	80.00	140	250	425	—

KM# 242 6 HELLER (1/2 Albus)

Silver **Ruler:** Wilhelm VI **Obv:** Crowned W in wreath, date divided at sides, 1-6 above, 5-6 below **Rev:** Hessian lion, value VI below **Note:** Varieties exist.

Date	Mintage	VG	F	VF	XF	Unc
1655 AG	—	50.00	120	220	400	—
1656 AG	—	40.00	75.00	140	250	—
1657 AG	—	40.00	75.00	140	250	—
1657 IGB	—	40.00	75.00	140	250	—
1658 IGB	—	40.00	75.00	140	250	—

KM# 257 6 HELLER (1/2 Albus)

Silver **Ruler:** Wilhelm VI **Obv:** Crowned and ornamented W date below, between 2 palm branches

Date	Mintage	VG	F	VF	XF	Unc
1663 IGB	—	40.00	75.00	140	280	—

KM# 269 6 HELLER (1/2 Albus)

Silver **Ruler:** Wilhelm VII **Obv:** Crowned W between palm branches, date below in one line

Date	Mintage	VG	F	VF	XF	Unc
1668	—	40.00	75.00	140	250	—

KM# 281 6 HELLER (1/2 Albus)

Silver **Ruler:** Wilhelm VII **Obv:** Crowned W between palm branches, date divided at sides, 1-6 above, 7-0 below

Date	Mintage	VG	F	VF	XF	Unc
1670	—	40.00	75.00	140	250	—

KM# 292 6 HELLER (1/2 Albus)
Silver **Ruler:** Karl **Obv:** Crowned script C, date divided at sides, 1-6 above, 7-3 below, palm branches at sides

Date	Mintage	VG	F	VF	XF	Unc
1673	—	45.00	80.00	150	275	—

KM# 298 6 HELLER (1/2 Albus)
Silver **Ruler:** Karl **Obv:** Crowned script C, date below, palm branches at sides **Rev:** Hessian lion, value VI below
Note: Varieties exist in date numeral placement.

Date	Mintage	VG	F	VF	XF	Unc
1675	—	10.00	22.00	45.00	90.00	—
1679	—	10.00	22.00	45.00	90.00	—
1686	—	10.00	22.00	45.00	90.00	—
1688	—	10.00	22.00	45.00	90.00	—
1695	—	10.00	22.00	45.00	90.00	—

KM# 246 8 HELLER (1/48 Thaler)
Silver **Ruler:** Wilhelm VI **Obv:** VIII in circle, W.L.Z.H. and date in legend **Rev:** Hessian lion, mintmaster's monogram below, all in circle **Note:** Varieties exist.

Date	Mintage	VG	F	VF	XF	Unc
1657 IGB	—	45.00	85.00	160	275	—
1658 IGB	—	45.00	85.00	160	275	—
1659 IGB	—	45.00	85.00	160	275	—

KM# 293 8 HELLER (1/48 Thaler)
Silver **Ruler:** Karl **Obv:** Crowned script C, date divided 1-6 above, 7-3 below, palm branches at sides **Rev:** VIII in heart-shaped cartouche

Date	Mintage	VG	F	VF	XF	Unc
1673	—	33.00	65.00	120	250	—

KM# 49 3 KREUZER
Silver **Subject:** Lordship of Epstein **Obv:** Crowned arms of Eppstein **Rev:** Imperial eagle, 3 in circle on breast, titles of MAVR etc. and of Ferdinand II, date in legend **Note:** Kipper 3 Kreuzer.

Date	Mintage	VG	F	VF	XF	Unc
(1)622 TS	—	—	—	—	—	—
(1)623	—	—	—	—	—	—

Note: Reported, not confirmed

KM# 48 3 KREUZER
Silver **Ruler:** Moritz **Obv:** Crowned Hessian lion to right above C in oval baroque shield, date divided above **Rev:** Imperial orb with 3 **Note:** Kipper 3 Kreuzer.

Date	Mintage	VG	F	VF	XF	Unc
1622 C	—	40.00	90.00	200	400	—

KM# A49 3 KREUZER
Silver **Ruler:** Moritz **Obv:** Crowned arms of Eppstein **Obv. Legend:** CONSILIO ET VIRTUTE... **Rev:** Imperial eagle, 3 in circle on breast **Rev. Legend:** F • E • II • D • G • R • I • S • A •6ZZ

Date	Mintage	VG	F	VF	XF	Unc
(1)6ZZ TS Rare	—	—	—	—	—	—
(1)6ZZ shamrock Rare	—	—	—	—	—	—
(1)622 cross Rare	—	—	—	—	—	—

KM# 50 3 KREUZER
Silver **Ruler:** Moritz **Subject:** Lordship of Plesse **Obv:** Arms of Plesse (pothooks) **Note:** Kipper 3 Kreuzer

Date	Mintage	VG	F	VF	XF	Unc
(1)622 TS	—	—	—	—	—	—
(1)6ZZ shamrock	—	—	—	—	—	—
(1)6ZZ shamrock	—	—	—	—	—	—

KM# 33 12 KREUZER (Schreckenberger)
Silver **Ruler:** Moritz **Obv:** Hessian helmet in circle, horms with three or more branches **Obv. Legend:** MAUR • D • G • LAND • HASS • date **Rev:** Crowned imperial eagle, 12 in circle on breast **Rev. Legend:** FERD • II • D • G • ROM • IMP • SEM • AUGU
Note: Kipper 12 Kreuzer. Prev. KM #33.1.

Date	Mintage	VG	F	VF	XF	Unc
ND	—	40.00	90.00	200	450	—
1621 1 pothook (or rose)	—	25.00	55.00	115	260	—
16Z1 1 pothook	—	25.00	55.00	115	260	—
(1)621 1 pothook	—	25.00	55.00	115	260	—
16Z1 C 3 crossed pothooks	—	25.00	55.00	115	260	—
1621 3 crossed pothooks	—	25.00	55.00	115	260	—
16Z1 3 crossed pothooks	—	20.00	50.00	110	240	—
(1)621 3 crossed pothooks	—	20.00	50.00	110	240	—
(1)6Z1 3 crossed pothooks	—	20.00	50.00	110	240	—
16Z(1) rose	—	30.00	80.00	170	380	—
(1)622 small ring	—	30.00	80.00	170	380	—
(1)622	—	30.00	80.00	170	380	—

KM# 34 12 KREUZER (Schreckenberger)
Silver **Ruler:** Moritz **Obv:** Hessian helmet in circle **Obv. Legend:** MAUR... **Note:** Klippe.

Date	Mintage	VG	F	VF	XF	Unc
(1)6Z1 Rare	—	—	—	—	—	—

Note: Date on obverse

Date	Mintage	VG	F	VF	XF	Unc
1621 Rare	—	—	—	—	—	—

Note: Date on reverse

KM# 36 12 KREUZER (Schreckenberger)
Silver **Ruler:** Moritz **Obv:** Hessian lion in circle without shield **Obv. Legend:** MAUR • D • G • LAND • HASS **Rev:** Crowned imperial eagle, 12 in shield on breast **Rev. Legend:** FERD • II • D • G • ROM • IMP • SEM • AUGU

Date	Mintage	VG	F	VF	XF	Unc
ND rose	—	40.00	90.00	200	450	—
16Z1 rose	—	20.00	50.00	115	275	—
(1)6Z1 rose	—	20.00	50.00	115	275	—
1621 TS	—	28.00	65.00	140	280	—
(1)621 TS	—	20.00	50.00	110	250	—
(1)621 cross	—	28.00	65.00	140	280	—
1621 3 crossed pothooks	—	28.00	65.00	140	280	—
1622 3 crossed pothooks	—	28.00	65.00	140	280	—
(1)622 1 pothook	—	28.00	65.00	140	280	—
(1)622 TS	—	30.00	75.00	160	280	—
(1)622 3 crossed pothooks	—	30.00	75.00	155	350	—
(1)6ZZ 3 crossed pothooks	—	30.00	75.00	155	330	—
16ZZ rose	—	30.00	75.00	155	330	—
1622 rose	—	30.00	75.00	155	330	—
(1)622 rose	—	30.00	75.00	155	330	—
1622 cross	—	30.00	80.00	170	375	—
16ZZ small ring	—	30.00	80.00	170	375	—
1622	—	30.00	75.00	155	330	—
16ZZ	—	30.00	75.00	155	330	—
(1)6ZZ/16ZZ	—	—	—	—	—	—

Note: Reported, not confirmed

KM# 37 12 KREUZER (Schreckenberger)
Silver **Ruler:** Moritz **Obv:** Angel above arms, date in legend, titles of Moritz **Rev:** Imperial eagle, 12 in circle on breast
Note: Varieties exist.

Date	Mintage	VG	F	VF	XF	Unc
16Z1 3 crossed pothooks	—	30.00	80.00	160	350	—
(1)6Z1 3 crossed pothooks	—	35.00	90.00	190	400	—
16ZZ 3 crossed pothooks	—	30.00	80.00	160	350	—
16ZZC 3 crossed pothooks	—	40.00	100	220	450	—
1622 3 crossed pothooks	—	35.00	90.00	190	400	—
(1)622 3 crossed pothooks	—	35.00	90.00	190	400	—

KM# A39 12 KREUZER (Schreckenberger)
Silver **Ruler:** Moritz **Obv:** Hessian lion in crowned shield **Rev:** Imperial eagle, 12 in circle on breast, date

Date	Mintage	VG	F	VF	XF	Unc
(1)6ZZ star	—	45.00	110	250	520	—
(16)ZZ star	—	45.00	110	250	520	—
(16)22 star	—	45.00	110	250	520	—
(16)22 2 stars	—	45.00	110	250	520	—

KM# 39 12 KREUZER (Schreckenberger)
Silver **Ruler:** Moritz **Obv:** Hessian lion in oval or round shield, date **Obv. Legend:** CONSILIO ET VIRTUTE

Date	Mintage	VG	F	VF	XF	Unc
(1)621 3 crossed pothooks	—	40.00	85.00	180	400	—
(1)621/(1)621 3 crossed pothooks	—	45.00	90.00	200	425	—
(1)621	—	40.00	85.00	180	400	—
(1)621/621	—	45.00	90.00	200	425	—

KM# 52 12 KREUZER (Schreckenberger)
Silver **Ruler:** Moritz **Note:** Klippe. Similar to KM#36.1, but date on reverse.

Date	Mintage	VG	F	VF	XF	Unc
(1)6ZZ	—	—	—	—	—	—

Note: Reported, not confirmed

KM# 54 12 KREUZER (Schreckenberger)
Silver **Ruler:** Moritz **Obv:** Hessian lion in double circle, ornaments between the circles, date in legend **Rev:** Crowned imperial eagle, 12 on breast, titles of Ferdinand II

Date	Mintage	VG	F	VF	XF	Unc
(1)621 3 crossed pothooks	—	35.00	80.00	180	400	—
(1)621. V, pothook within and rose	—	25.00	55.00	125	260	—
1621 V, pothook within and rose	—	25.00	55.00	125	260	—
16Z1 V, pothook within	—	25.00	55.00	125	260	—
1621 V, pothook within	—	25.00	55.00	125	260	—
(1)621//16Z1	—	45.00	110	240	520	—
(1)6Z1//16Z1	—	45.00	110	240	520	—
(1)622	—	40.00	90.00	200	440	—
(1)622 TS	—	35.00	80.00	180	400	—
(16)Z2 rose	—	35.00	80.00	180	400	—

Note: Date on reverse

Date	Mintage	VG	F	VF	XF	Unc
(16)22 L	—	40.00	90.00	200	440	—

Note: Date on reverse

KM# 58.1 12 KREUZER (Schreckenberger)
Silver **Ruler:** Moritz **Obv:** Hessian lion in pearl circle
Obv. Legend: ...SPES NON CONFVNDIT

Date	Mintage	VG	F	VF	XF	Unc
1621 O Rare	—	—	—	—	—	—

KM# 58.2 12 KREUZER (Schreckenberger)
Silver **Ruler:** Moritz **Obv:** Crowned arms of Eppstein, flanked by crosses, titles of Maurice in legend, date

Date	Mintage	VG	F	VF	XF	Unc
1621 V, pothook within	—	50.00	100	220	460	—
1622 V, pothook within	—	50.00	100	220	460	—

KM# 56 24 KREUZER (2 Schreckenberger)
Silver **Subject:** Lordship of Eppstein **Obv:** Crowned arms of Eppstein (3 chevrons), date in legend **Obv. Legend:** CONSILIO ET VIRTUTE **Rev:** Crowned imperial eagle, 24 in shield on breast, titles of Ferdinand II **Note:** Kipper 24 Kreuzer.

Date	Mintage	VG	F	VF	XF	Unc
(1)622 Rare	—	—	—	—	—	—
(1)6ZZ Rare	—	—	—	—	—	—

KM# 4 ALBUS (12 Heller)
Silver **Ruler:** Moritz **Obv:** Hessian lion, date below, legend between four arms **Obv. Legend:** MAUR • D • G • LANDGR • HASS **Rev:** Hessian helmet **Rev. Legend:** VALET • I • ALBVM • VEL • 1Z OBVL HASS **Note:** Legend varieties exist.

Date	Mintage	VG	F	VF	XF	Unc
160Z	—	25.00	60.00	150	300	—
1604	—	25.00	70.00	150	280	—
1607	—	25.00	60.00	150	280	—

KM# 8 ALBUS (12 Heller)
Silver **Obv:** Hessian lion in circle, legend divided by 4 small shields **Rev:** Helmet in circle, date above **Rev. Legend:** VALET I ALBVM • VEL • 12 • OBVLOS HASSIACOS

Date	Mintage	VG	F	VF	XF	Unc
(16)05	—	20.00	45.00	110	220	—
(16)06	—	20.00	45.00	110	220	—
(16)07	—	20.00	45.00	110	220	—

KM# 9 ALBUS (12 Heller)
Silver **Obv:** Date divided below lion **Rev:** Date above helmet, between the horns.

Date	Mintage	VG	F	VF	XF	Unc
1607/(16)07	—	30.00	75.00	160	320	—

KM# 10 ALBUS (12 Heller)
Silver, 19-21 mm. **Ruler:** Moritz **Obv:** Date only below lion

Date	Mintage	VG	F	VF	XF	Unc
1607	—	20.00	35.00	65.00	120	—

KM# 16 ALBUS (12 Heller)
Silver **Ruler:** Moritz **Obv:** Without small shields in legend, date divided below lion **Rev. Legend:** ALB • HASSIAC • VALET 1Z • OBVLOS

Date	Mintage	VG	F	VF	XF	Unc
1610	—	35.00	90.00	210	420	—

KM# 21 ALBUS (12 Heller)
Silver **Ruler:** Moritz **Obv:** Date in legend

Date	Mintage	VG	F	VF	XF	Unc
1610	—	30.00	80.00	190	380	—
1611	—	30.00	80.00	190	380	—

KM# 40 ALBUS (12 Heller)
Silver **Ruler:** Moritz **Obv:** Hessian lion in circle **Obv. Legend:** MAUR • D • G • LAND • HAS • **Rev:** Helmet divides date **Rev. Legend:** 1 • ALB • LANDT MUNTZ **Note:** Kipper Albus.

Date	Mintage	VG	F	VF	XF	Unc
16Z1	—	20.00	50.00	130	260	—

KM# 57 ALBUS (12 Heller)
Silver **Ruler:** Moritz **Obv:** Hessian lion, date in legend **Rev:** Helmet **Rev. Legend:** ALB9 • HASSIAC9 • VALET • 1Z • OBUL **Note:** Varieties exist.

Date	Mintage	VG	F	VF	XF	Unc
16ZZ TS	—	20.00	50.00	110	240	—
(1)6ZZ TS	—	20.00	45.00	100	220	—
(1)6Z3 TS	—	20.00	45.00	100	220	—
16Z3 TS	—	20.00	45.00	100	220	—
1624 TS	—	20.00	45.00	100	220	—

KM# 216 ALBUS (12 Heller)
Silver **Ruler:** Wilhelm VI **Obv:** Hessian lion in circle **Obv. Legend:** WILHELMVS HASS: LAND PRINC • HERSF • **Rev:** Helmet, I between, horns, date divided

Date	Mintage	VG	F	VF	XF	Unc
1651 AG	—	25.00	50.00	100	200	—

KM# 224 ALBUS (12 Heller)
Silver **Ruler:** Wilhelm VI **Obv:** Crowned W in palm wreath **Rev:** Crowned Hessian lion, date divided as 16-5Z

Date	Mintage	VG	F	VF	XF	Unc
165Z	—	25.00	45.00	85.00	165	—

KM# 225 ALBUS (12 Heller)
Silver **Ruler:** Wilhelm VI **Obv:** Crowned W in laurel wreath, date divided as 1-6/5-Z **Rev:** Crowned Hessian lion

Date	Mintage	VG	F	VF	XF	Unc
165Z	—	25.00	45.00	85.00	165	—

KM# A225 ALBUS (12 Heller)
Silver **Ruler:** Wilhelm VI **Obv:** Crowned W in palm wreath, date divided 1-6 / 5Z. **Rev:** Crowned Hessian lion

Date	Mintage	VG	F	VF	XF	Unc
165Z	—	25.00	45.00	85.00	165	—

KM# 235 ALBUS (12 Heller)
Silver **Ruler:** Wilhelm VI **Obv:** Crowned W in palm wreath divides date 1-6/5-3 **Rev:** Crowned Hessian lion, mintmaster initials below **Note:** Varieties exist.

Date	Mintage	VG	F	VF	XF	Unc
1653 AG	—	25.00	40.00	80.00	160	—
1654 AG	—	25.00	40.00	80.00	160	—
1655 AG	—	25.00	40.00	80.00	160	—
1656 AG	—	25.00	40.00	80.00	160	—
1657 .o.	—	40.00	70.00	120	220	—
1657 AG	—	25.00	45.00	90.00	170	—
1657	—	40.00	70.00	120	220	—
1657 GB	—	40.00	70.00	120	220	—
1657 IGB	—	40.00	70.00	120	220	—
1658 IGB	—	40.00	70.00	120	220	—
1659 IGB	—	55.00	90.00	155	240	—

KM# 252 ALBUS (12 Heller)
Silver **Ruler:** Wilhelm VI **Obv:** Crowned W with ribbons between palm branches, date in one line **Rev:** Crowned Hessian lion, mint master initials below **Note:** Varieties exist.

Date	Mintage	VG	F	VF	XF	Unc
1661 IGB	—	25.00	45.00	80.00	145	—
166Z IGB	—	25.00	45.00	80.00	145	—
1662 IGB	—	25.00	45.00	80.00	145	—
1663 IGB	—	25.00	45.00	80.00	145	—

KM# A252 ALBUS (12 Heller)
Silver **Ruler:** Wilhelm VI **Obv:** Crowned W between palm branches, date below in one line or as 1-6/6-1

Date	Mintage	VG	F	VF	XF	Unc
1661 IGB	—	40.00	80.00	150	300	—

KM# 268 ALBUS (12 Heller)
Silver **Ruler:** Wilhelm VII **Obv:** Crowned W with ribbons, similar to KM #252 but more ornamented **Rev:** Hessian lion, similar to KM #235

Date	Mintage	VG	F	VF	XF	Unc
1665 IGB	—	30.00	55.00	100	200	—
1667 IGB	—	30.00	55.00	100	200	—
1668 IGB	—	30.00	55.00	100	200	—

KM# A282 ALBUS (12 Heller)
Silver **Ruler:** Wilhelm VII **Obv:** Crowned W without ribbons, within palm branches, date below **Rev:** Hessian lion

Date	Mintage	VG	F	VF	XF	Unc
1668 IGB	—	40.00	80.00	150	300	—

KM# 282 ALBUS (12 Heller)
Silver **Ruler:** Wilhelm VII **Obv:** W within palm branches, date as 1-6/7-0

Date	Mintage	VG	F	VF	XF	Unc
1670 IGB	—	40.00	70.00	120	250	—

KM# 294 ALBUS (12 Heller)
Silver **Ruler:** Karl **Obv:** Crowned double, mirror-image script CL monogram divides date between palm branches **Rev:** Crowned Hessian lion, mintmasters monogram below

Date	Mintage	VG	F	VF	XF	Unc
1673 IGB	—	40.00	80.00	170	340	—

KM# 296 ALBUS (12 Heller)
Silver **Ruler:** Karl **Obv:** Date below C **Note:** Varieties exist especially in design and date placement.

Date	Mintage	VG	F	VF	XF	Unc
1673 IGB	—	12.50	30.00	55.00	90.00	—
1674 IGB	—	12.50	30.00	55.00	90.00	—
1675 IGB	—	12.50	30.00	55.00	90.00	—
1676 IGB	—	12.50	30.00	55.00	90.00	—
1677 IGB	—	12.50	30.00	55.00	90.00	—
1678 IGB	—	12.50	30.00	55.00	90.00	—
1679 IGB	—	12.50	30.00	55.00	90.00	—
1680 IGB	—	12.50	30.00	55.00	90.00	—
1680 IH	—	12.50	30.00	55.00	90.00	—
1681 IH	—	12.50	30.00	55.00	90.00	—
1681 IVF	—	12.50	30.00	55.00	90.00	—
1682 IVF	—	12.50	30.00	55.00	90.00	—
1683 IVF	—	12.50	30.00	55.00	90.00	—
1684 IVF	—	12.50	30.00	55.00	90.00	—
1685 IVF	—	12.50	30.00	55.00	90.00	—
1686 IVF	—	12.50	30.00	55.00	90.00	—
1687 IVF	—	12.50	30.00	55.00	90.00	—
1688 IVF	—	12.50	30.00	55.00	90.00	—
1689 IVF	—	12.50	30.00	55.00	90.00	—
1690 IVF	—	12.50	30.00	55.00	90.00	—

KM# 295 ALBUS (12 Heller)
Silver **Ruler:** Karl **Obv:** Crowned C divides date 1-6 / 7-3, between palm branches

Date	Mintage	VG	F	VF	XF	Unc
1673 IGB	—	25.00	40.00	80.00	140	—
1673 GIB error	—	—	—	—	—	—

KM# 330 ALBUS (12 Heller)
Silver **Ruler:** Karl **Obv:** Crowned CL monogram divides date as 1-6 / 9-1 **Rev:** Lion left without shield **Note:** Variety of crown designs exist.

Date	Mintage	VG	F	VF	XF	Unc
1690	—	—	—	—	—	—
Note: Reported, not confirmed						
1691 IVF	—	20.00	40.00	70.00	120	—
1692 IVF	—	20.00	40.00	70.00	120	—

KM# 331 ALBUS (12 Heller)
Silver **Ruler:** Karl **Obv:** Crowned CL, date flanking as 1-6 / 9-1 **Rev:** Crowned shield with lion **Note:** Many shield and crown varieties exist.

Date	Mintage	VG	F	VF	XF	Unc
1691 IVF	—	20.00	40.00	70.00	120	—
1692 IVF	—	20.00	40.00	70.00	120	—
1693 IVF	—	20.00	40.00	70.00	120	—

KM# 333 ALBUS (12 Heller)
Silver **Ruler:** Karl **Obv:** Bust right **Rev:** Scirpt C, crown above divides date

Date	Mintage	VG	F	VF	XF	Unc
1693 IVF	—	65.00	120	240	400	—

KM# 342 ALBUS (12 Heller)
Silver **Ruler:** Karl **Obv:** Crowned double-script C monogram, L-Z-H between **Rev:** Hessian lion divides date **Note:** Varieties exist in date placement.

Date	Mintage	VG	F	VF	XF	Unc
1694 IVF	—	12.00	25.00	50.00	100	—
1695 IVF	—	12.00	25.00	50.00	100	—
1696 IVF	—	12.00	25.00	50.00	100	—
1697 IVF	—	12.00	25.00	50.00	100	—
1698	—	12.00	25.00	50.00	100	—
1699	—	12.00	25.00	50.00	100	—
1700	—	12.00	25.00	50.00	100	—

KM# A72 2 ALBUS (4 Kreuzer)
Silver **Ruler:** Moritz **Obv:** Hessian lion, date below; all in circle **Obv. Legend:** MAU • D: G • LAND • HASS • C • C • D • Z • E • N • **Rev:** Helmet with two horns **Rev. Legend:** ALB 9 HASS • DVPLIC • VALET 24 • OBUL:

Date	Mintage	VG	F	VF	XF	Unc
16ZZ TS Rare	—	—	—	—	—	—

KM# 72 2 ALBUS (4 Kreuzer)
Silver **Ruler:** Moritz **Obv:** Hessian arms in baroque shield **Obv. Legend:** MAUR: D: G: LAND: HASS: CO: C • D: 2 • E • N • **Rev:** • II •/ ALBUS/ date **Rev. Legend:** VON • REICHS • THALER • SILBER

Date	Mintage	VG	F	VF	XF	Unc
16Z4 TS Rare	—	—	—	—	—	—
16Z5 Rare	—	—	—	—	—	—

KM# 151 2 ALBUS (4 Kreuzer)
Silver **Ruler:** Wilhelm V **Obv:** Hessian lion in circle, date divided around lion **Rev:** Value, Z between horns, helmet **Rev. Legend:** VON REICHS TAHLER SILBER

Date	Mintage	VG	F	VF	XF	Unc
1635	—	—	—	—	—	—

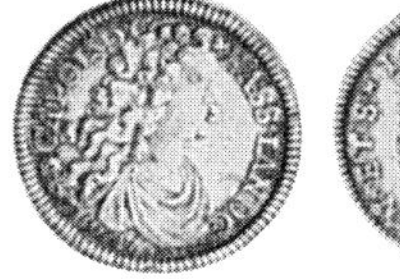

KM# 334 2 ALBUS (4 Kreuzer)
Silver **Ruler:** Karl **Obv:** Bust right **Rev:** 2 crowned script C's between palm branches, date in legend

Date	Mintage	VG	F	VF	XF	Unc
1693 IVF	—	140	250	425	725	—

KM# 305 4 ALBUS (1/8 Thaler)
Silver **Ruler:** Karl **Obv:** Crowned Hessian lion **Rev:** IIII/ ALBUS, date in legend

Date	Mintage	VG	F	VF	XF	Unc
1681 IH	—	55.00	110	180	350	—

KM# 306 4 ALBUS (1/8 Thaler)
Silver **Ruler:** Karl **Obv:** Hessian lion in empty field, without legend **Rev:** IIII/ ALBUS, date **Note:** KM#306 is a possible pattern.

Date	Mintage	VG	F	VF	XF	Unc
1681 IH Rare	—	—	—	—	—	—

KM# 84 1/2 REICHSORT (1/8 Thaler)
Silver **Ruler:** Wilhelm V **Obv:** Hessian helmet, 8-pointed star between horns **Obv. Legend:** WILHELM • D • G... **Rev:** value and date **Rev. Legend:** EIN/ HALBER/ REICHS=/ ORT
Note: Legend varieties.

Date	Mintage	VG	F	VF	XF	Unc
16Z7 TS	—	150	280	580	1,200	—
16Z8 TS	—	120	240	500	950	—

KM# 152 1/2 REICHSORT (1/8 Thaler)
Silver **Ruler:** Wilhelm V **Obv:** Hessian lion in Spanish shield within circle **Obv. Legend:** WIHEL: D: G: LAND: HASS: C • C • Z • E • N **Rev:** Value and date **Rev. Legend:** EINN/ HALBER/ REICHS/ ORTH

Date	Mintage	VG	F	VF	XF	Unc
1635 shamrock Rare	—	—	—	—	—	—

KM# 166.1 1/2 REICHSORT (1/8 Thaler)
Silver **Ruler:** Wilhelm V **Obv:** Tree in storm **Obv. Legend:** VNO VOLENTE HUMILIS LEVABOR **Rev:** Valus and date
Rev. Legend: 1/ HALLBER/ REICHS •/ ORTH•/ 16-37

Date	Mintage	VG	F	VF	XF	Unc
1637 GK crossed pothooks	—	120	300	600	1,150	—

KM# 166.2 1/2 REICHSORT (1/8 Thaler)
Silver **Ruler:** Wilhelm V **Rev. Legend:** EINN/ HALBER/...

Date	Mintage	VG	F	VF	XF	Unc
1637 GK	—	—	—	—	—	—

Note: Reported, not confirmed

KM# 85 1/96 THALER (4 Heller)
Silver **Ruler:** Wilhelm V **Obv:** Ornate helmet divides date, WLZH above **Rev. Legend:** 96/ EIN • R •/ TAHLER/ WERT/ TS

Date	Mintage	VG	F	VF	XF	Unc
(16)Z7 TS	—	—	—	—	—	—
Note: Reported, not confirmed						
(16)Z8 TS	—	65.00	110	185	325	—

KM# 103 1/96 THALER (4 Heller)
Silver **Ruler:** Wilhelm V **Obv:** WLH above ornate helmet
Rev. Legend: 96/ EIN • R •/ TAHLER/ WERT/ TS

Date	Mintage	VG	F	VF	XF	Unc
(16)Z8 TS	—	65.00	110	185	325	—

KM# 104 1/96 THALER (4 Heller)
Silver **Ruler:** Wilhelm V **Obv:** WLZH above helmet
Rev. Legend: 96 • ST • EIN/ R • TAHL/ WERT/ TS

Date	Mintage	VG	F	VF	XF	Unc
(16)Z8 TS	—	65.00	110	185	325	—

KM# 112.1 1/96 THALER (4 Heller)
Silver **Ruler:** Wilhelm V **Obv:** Ornate helmet divides date, WLZH above **Rev. Legend:** 96/ EINN • R/ TAHLER/ WERTH/ TS

Date	Mintage	VG	F	VF	XF	Unc
(16)Z8 TS	—	55.00	90.00	160	300	—
(16)Z9 TS	—	55.00	90.00	160	300	—
(16)29 TS	—	55.00	90.00	160	300	—
(16)30 TS	—	55.00	90.00	160	300	—
(16)31 TS	—	55.00	90.00	160	300	—
(16)33 TS	—	55.00	90.00	160	300	—
(16)35 shamrock	—	55.00	90.00	160	300	—
(16)35 TS	—	55.00	90.00	160	300	—

KM# 112.2 1/96 THALER (4 Heller)
Silver **Ruler:** Wilhelm V **Obv:** Helmet, WLZH above
Rev. Legend: • 96 •/ EINN •R/ TALL •/ WERT **Note:** Varieties exist.

Date	Mintage	VG	F	VF	XF	Unc
ND GK, crossed pothooks	—	55.00	90.00	160	300	—
ND shamrock	—	55.00	90.00	160	300	—
1637 shamrock	—	55.00	90.00	160	300	—

KM# 158 1/96 THALER (4 Heller)
Silver **Ruler:** Wilhelm V **Obv:** Ornate helmet, WLZH above
Rev. Legend: • 96 •/ EINN • R/ THALL/ date

Date	Mintage	VG	F	VF	XF	Unc
1636 shamrock	—	55.00	90.00	160	300	—

KM# 168 1/96 THALER (4 Heller)
Silver **Ruler:** Wilhelm V **Obv:** Helmet, WL above, date between horns **Rev. Legend:** 96/ EINN • R/ THALL/ WERT

Date	Mintage	VG	F	VF	XF	Unc
(16)37 shamrock	—	55.00	90.00	160	300	—

KM# 169 1/96 THALER (4 Heller)
Silver **Ruler:** Wilhelm VI **Obv:** Helmet, WLZ above, H between horns, date divided **Rev. Legend:** 96/ EINN • R/ TAHLL/ WERT

Date	Mintage	VG	F	VF	XF	Unc
(16)37 AG	—	55.00	90.00	160	300	—
(16)40 AG	—	55.00	90.00	160	300	—
ND AG	—	55.00	90.00	160	300	—

KM# 199 1/96 THALER (4 Heller)
Silver **Ruler:** Wilhelm VI **Obv:** Helmet, WLZH above, divides date as 3-9 **Rev. Legend:** 96/ EINN • R/ TAHLL/ VVERT

Date	Mintage	VG	F	VF	XF	Unc
(16)39 GK	—	30.00	75.00	150	300	—

KM# 200 1/96 THALER (4 Heller)
Silver **Ruler:** Wilhelm VI **Obv:** Helmet, date between horns
Rev. Legend: 96/ EINNR •/ TAHLL/ WERT

Date	Mintage	VG	F	VF	XF	Unc
(16)39 GK	—	30.00	75.00	150	300	—

KM# 211 1/96 THALER (4 Heller)
Silver **Ruler:** Wilhelm VI **Obv:** Helmet, WLZ above, H between horns, date divided **Rev. Legend:** 96/ EINN • R/ TAHLL/ WERT

Date	Mintage	VG	F	VF	XF	Unc
(16)40 AG	—	—	—	—	—	—
(16)46 AG	—	—	—	—	—	—

KM# 207 1/96 THALER (4 Heller)
Silver **Ruler:** Wilhelm VI **Obv:** Helmet, WLH above, date divided
Rev. Legend: 96/ S • EIN R/ TAHLER/ WERT

Date	Mintage	VG	F	VF	XF	Unc
(16)45 AG	—	—	—	—	—	—

KM# A212 1/96 THALER (4 Heller)
Silver **Ruler:** Wilhelm VI **Obv:** Helmet, WLZH above, date divided **Rev. Legend:** 96/ EINN • R/ THALL •/ WERT
Note: Varieties exist.

Date	Mintage	VG	F	VF	XF	Unc
(16)49 AG	—	—	—	—	—	—
(16)50 AG	—	—	—	—	—	—

KM# 239 1/96 THALER (4 Heller)
Silver **Ruler:** Wilhelm VI **Obv:** Crowned W divides date as 1-6/5-3 in palm wreath **Rev:** Hessian lion divides 9-6

Date	Mintage	VG	F	VF	XF	Unc
1653 AG	—	60.00	130	250	480	—
1654 AG	—	60.00	130	250	480	—

KM# 212 1/64 THALER (6 Heller)
Silver **Ruler:** Wilhelm VI **Obv:** Hessian lion in shield within circle
Obv. Legend: WILHEL: LANDQ • ZV • HESSEN
Rev. Legend: 64/ ST • EINN/ R • TAHLER/ WERTH

Date	Mintage	VG	F	VF	XF	Unc
1646 AG	—	20.00	50.00	100	180	—
1647 AG	—	20.00	50.00	100	180	—
1649 AG	—	20.00	50.00	100	180	—

KM# 236 1/64 THALER (6 Heller)
Silver **Ruler:** Wilhelm VI **Obv:** Crowned W in palm wreath, date divided above 1-6, below 5-3 **Rev:** Hessian lion divides 6-4

Date	Mintage	VG	F	VF	XF	Unc
1653 AG	—	—	—	—	—	—
1653	—	—	—	—	—	—

KM# 105.1 1/48 THALER (8 Heller)
Silver **Ruler:** Wilhelm V **Obv:** Hessian arms **Obv. Legend:** WIL • LAN • HAS **Rev. Legend:** 48 • ST • EIN THAL WERT

Date	Mintage	VG	F	VF	XF	Unc
16Z8 Rare	—	—	—	—	—	—

KM# 105.2 1/48 THALER (8 Heller)
Silver **Ruler:** Wilhelm V **Obv:** Crowned arms **Obv. Legend:** WILHE: -LAN • HAS **Rev:** Date divided below **Rev. Legend:** 48 ST • EIN • RE TAHLER WERT **Note:** Prev. KM #145. Legend varieties WILHE, WILHL, WILHEL; HA, HAS.

Date	Mintage	VG	F	VF	XF	Unc
1634 3 crossed pothooks, Rare	—	—	—	—	—	—

KM# 106 1/32 THALER (Albus)
Silver **Ruler:** Wilhelm V **Obv:** Helmet, I between horns, title of Wilhelm in legend **Rev:** Value, date **Rev. Legend:** 3Z/ STUCK •/ EIN •• RICHS/ THALER •/ WEHRT **Note:** Nearly 80 varieties exist in obverse legend and reverse value writing combinations.

Date	Mintage	VG	F	VF	XF	Unc
16Z8 TS	—	20.00	40.00	80.00	150	—
16Z9 TS	—	20.00	40.00	80.00	150	—
1630 TS	—	20.00	40.00	80.00	150	—
1631 TS	—	20.00	40.00	80.00	150	—
163Z TS	—	20.00	40.00	80.00	150	—
1633 TS	—	20.00	40.00	80.00	150	—
1634 TS	—	20.00	40.00	80.00	150	—
1635	—	30.00	60.00	120	200	—
1635 o	—	30.00	60.00	120	200	—
1635 shamrock	—	20.00	40.00	80.00	150	—
1636 shamrock	—	20.00	40.00	80.00	150	—
1637 shamrock	—	20.00	40.00	80.00	150	—

KM# 205 1/32 THALER (Albus)
Silver **Ruler:** Wilhelm VI **Note:** Similar to KM#106. Varieties exist.

Date	Mintage	VG	F	VF	XF	Unc
1640 GK	—	18.00	40.00	80.00	170	—
1641 GK Rare	—	—	—	—	—	—
1645 AG	—	18.00	40.00	80.00	170	—
1648 .o.	—	18.00	40.00	80.00	170	—
1650 AG	—	18.00	40.00	80.00	170	—

KM# 17 1/8 THALER (1/2 Ortstaler)
Silver **Ruler:** Moritz **Obv:** Crowned Hessian lion in German shield, helmet above, 4 small arms divide legend **Obv. Legend:** MAURI: -D: GLAN -:HASS: C • - • D • Z • E • N • **Rev:** Crossed flags divide date, branches above, bell and hour glass below, 4 small arms divide legend **Rev. Legend:** CONSILio -et • VIRTU - TE: MO: -NO: IMP

Date	Mintage	VG	F	VF	XF	Unc
1610 Rare	—	—	—	—	—	—

KM# 73 1/8 THALER (1/2 Ortstaler)
Silver **Ruler:** Moritz **Obv:** Crowned Hessian lion in circle, four small shields divide legned **Obv. Legend:** MAU: D: -G • LAND - HASS: C -C • D • Z • E • N **Rev:** Crossed flags divide date, branches above, hourglass below **Rev. Legend:** CONSILIo - ET • VIR: -TUTE • Mo -NO: IM: **Note:** Varieties exist.

Date	Mintage	VG	F	VF	XF	Unc
16Z4 TS	—	100	220	450	900	—
16Z5 TS	—	100	220	450	900	—
16Z6 TS	—	100	220	450	900	—
1627 TS	—	—	—	—	—	—

Note: Reported, not confirmed

KM# 113 1/8 THALER (1/2 Reichsort)
Silver **Ruler:** Wilhelm V **Obv:** Hessian lion, date above, four small shields divide legend **Obv. Legend:** WILHEL • -D • G • LA • -HASS • C • - C • D • Z • N • **Rev:** Tree in storm, four small shields divide legend **Rev. Legend:** DEO • VOL -ENTE • - HUMILIS -LEVABOR

Date	Mintage	VG	F	VF	XF	Unc
16Z9 TS	—	110	250	600	1,200	—

KM# 123 1/8 THALER (1/2 Reichsort)
Silver **Ruler:** Wilhelm V **Obv:** Lion divides date as 1-6/3-0; legend divided by four small sheilds **Obv. Legend:** WILHEL... **Rev:** Tree in storm, four houses beside; four small shield divide legend **Rev. Legend:** DEO VOLENTE HUMILIS LEVABOR
Note: Reverse legend shield position changes.

Date	Mintage	VG	F	VF	XF	Unc
1630	—	110	250	600	1,200	—
1631	—	110	250	600	1,200	—

KM# 124 1/8 THALER (1/2 Reichsort)
Silver **Ruler:** Wilhelm V **Subject:** Death of Moritz **Obv:** 7-line inscription, date **Rev:** Two crossed flags, branches above, hourglass below **Rev. Legend:** MAURITI • MEMENTO MORI • CONSIL • E • VIRTUTE

Date	Mintage	VG	F	VF	XF	Unc
163Z TS	—	100	250	480	900	—

KM# 134.1 1/8 THALER (1/2 Reichsort)
Silver **Ruler:** Wilhelm V **Obv:** Hessian lion without small arms in legend, date between hind claws **Obv. Legend:** WILH: D: G: L: HASS: C: C: D: Z: E: N: TS **Rev:** Tree in storm
Rev. Legend: IEHOVA • VOLENTE • HUMILIS • LEVABOR

Date	Mintage	VG	F	VF	XF	Unc
1633 TS without houses	—	100	220	460	950	—
1633 TS two houses	—	100	220	460	950	—

KM# 134.2 1/8 THALER (1/2 Reichsort)
Silver **Ruler:** Wilhelm V **Obv:** Lion divides date as 1-6/3-3
Obv. Legend: WILHELM • D • G • LAND • HASS • COM • C • D • ZEN **Rev:** Tree in storm **Rev. Legend:** IEHOVA • VOLENTE • HUMILIS • LEVABOR

Date	Mintage	VG	F	VF	XF	Unc
1633 TS//clover two houses	—	120	250	500	950	—
1635 .o.//clover without houses	—	120	250	500	950	—
1637 //clover without houses	—	120	250	500	950	—

KM# 134.3 1/8 THALER (1/2 Reichsort)
Silver **Ruler:** Wilhelm V **Obv:** Date in band below lion

Date	Mintage	VG	F	VF	XF	Unc
1633 TS	—	120	250	500	950	—

KM# 134.4 1/8 THALER (1/2 Reichsort)
Silver **Ruler:** Wilhelm V **Obv:** Lion, date in legend **Obv. Legend:** WILH • D • G • LAND • HAS • AO • 1636 **Rev:** Tree in storm **Rev. Legend:** IEHOVA • VOLENTE • HUMILIS • LEVABOR **Note:** Varieties exist.

Date	Mintage	VG	F	VF	XF	Unc
1636 clover without houses	—	120	250	600	1,200	—

KM# 170 1/8 THALER (1/2 Reichsort)
Silver **Ruler:** Wilhelm V **Obv:** Lion, date divided around lion as 1-6/3-7 or 1-3/6-7 or 16-37, without small shields breaking legend **Rev:** Tree in storm, 4 or 5 houses **Rev. Legend:** VNO • VOLENTE • HUMILIS • LEVABOR **Note:** Varieties exist.

Date	Mintage	VG	F	VF	XF	Unc
1637	—	120	250	550	1,100	—
Note: Date reads vertically						
1637	—	120	250	550	1,100	—
Note: Date reads horizontally						
1637	—	120	250	550	1,100	—
Note: Date split as 16-37						

KM# 171 1/8 THALER (1/2 Reichsort)
Silver **Ruler:** Wilhelm V **Subject:** Death of Wilhelm V **Obv:** 7-line inscription with date **Rev:** Tree in storm, four houses **Rev. Legend:** WILHEL • V • DICT9 • CONSTANS • HASS: LANDGRAVI:

Date	Mintage	VG	F	VF	XF	Unc
1637 GK crossed pothooks	—	85.00	175	350	700	—

KM# 217 1/8 THALER (1/2 Reichsort)
Silver **Ruler:** Wilhelm VI **Subject:** Death of Amalie Elisabth von Hanau, Wife of Wilhelm V, mother of Wilhelm VI **Obv:** 9-line inscription, arabic numeral date **Rev:** Mountain with miner in mine, heart and sun above, clouds and storm beside

Date	Mintage	VG	F	VF	XF	Unc
1651 AG	—	125	250	500	1,000	—

KM# 226 1/8 THALER (1/2 Reichsort)
Silver **Ruler:** Wilhelm VI **Obv:** Complete Hessian arms, date flanking as 1-6/5-2 **Rev:** Sailing ship left **Rev. Legend:** VENTIS • VELA • LEVANTUR • HIS • **Note:** Obverse and reverse legend varieties exist.

Date	Mintage	VG	F	VF	XF	Unc
165Z	—	650	1,300	2,600	5,000	—
1653	—	650	1,300	2,600	5,000	—
1654 AG	—	—	—	—	—	—
1655 AG	—	650	1,300	2,600	5,000	—

KM# 258 1/8 THALER (1/2 Reichsort)
Silver **Ruler:** Wilhelm VI **Subject:** Death of Wilhelm VI **Obv:** Bust half right **Obv. Legend:** WILHELM • VI • D • G • LANDG • HASS • PR • HERSE • CO • CAT • DE • ZI • NI • ET • SCH • **Rev:** 10-line inscription, date in Roman numerals

Date	Mintage	VG	F	VF	XF	Unc
MDCLXIII (1663) IGB	—	150	300	600	1,200	—

KM# 270 1/8 THALER (1/2 Reichsort)
Silver **Ruler:** Wilhelm VII **Obv:** Hessian and Brandenburg arms in crowned divided shield **Obv. Legend:** HEDWIG • SOPHIA • V: G: G: L: Z: H: G: A: C: S: D: M: Z: B: W: V: V: REGENT: **Rev:** Terrestrial globe hanging on a heart, sword cuts rope **Rev. Legend:** DISSOLVER **Note:** Similar to 1 Thaler, KM#273.

Date	Mintage	VG	F	VF	XF	Unc
1669	—	500	1,100	2,200	4,000	—

KM# 283 1/8 THALER (1/2 Reichsort)
Silver **Ruler:** Wilhelm VII **Subject:** Death of Wilhelm VII **Obv:** Helmeted Hessian arms **Obv. Legend:** WILHELM • VII • D • G • LANDG • HASS • PR • HERSE • COM • C • D • Z • N • ET • SHAW * **Rev:** 11-line inscription with Roman numeral date

Date	Mintage	VG	F	VF	XF	Unc
MDCLXX (1670) IGB	—	120	250	500	1,000	—

KM# 317 1/8 THALER (1/2 Reichsort)
Silver **Ruler:** Karl **Obv:** Hession lion **Obv. Legend:** C • L • Z • H • F • Z • H • C • D • Z • N • U • S • **Rev:** Value within legend **Rev. Legend:** HESS LAND MUNTZ

Date	Mintage	VG	F	VF	XF	Unc
1685 IVF	—	30.00	70.00	140	280	—
1689 IVF	—	30.00	70.00	140	280	—

KM# 319 1/8 THALER (1/2 Reichsort)
Silver **Ruler:** Karl **Obv:** Arms, titles of Karl **Rev:** Swan, date in legend **Note:** Similar to 1 Thaler, KM#322. Some sources consider this a medal.

Date	Mintage	VG	F	VF	XF	Unc
1686	—	—	—	—	—	—

KM# 335 1/8 THALER (1/2 Reichsort)
Silver **Ruler:** Karl **Obv:** Bust right **Obv. Legend:** CAROL • DG • HASS • LANDG **Rev:** Four crowned CC monograms forming a cross, date in legend

Date	Mintage	VG	F	VF	XF	Unc
1693 IVF	—	—	650	1,300	2,500	—

KM# 336 1/8 THALER
Silver **Ruler:** Karl **Obv:** Crowned shield **Obv. Legend:** C • L • Z • H • F • Z • H • G • Z • C • D • Z • N • U • S • **Rev:** Value within legend **Rev. Inscription:** VIII/ EINEN/ THALER **Note:** Varieties exist.

Date	Mintage	VG	F	VF	XF	Unc
1693 IVF	—	30.00	70.00	140	280	—
1693 IVF star	—	30.00	70.00	140	280	—

KM# 12 1/4 THALER (Ortstaler)
Silver **Ruler:** Moritz **Obv:** Crowned Hessian lion, date below, four small shields divide legend **Obv. Legend:** MAVRI • S -E • D • G • LA - ND • HASS - C • C • D • Z • E • N **Rev:** Helmet, shamrock between horns **Rev. Legend:** BENEDICTIO DEI E NOVIS • FODI • FRANCOBER

Date	Mintage	VG	F	VF	XF	Unc
1607 Rare	—	—	—	—	—	—

KM# 18 1/4 THALER (Ortstaler)
Silver **Ruler:** Moritz **Obv:** Hessian lion, helmet above; four small shields divide legend **Obv. Legend:** MAURI • -D • G • LAN • -HASS • C • -C • D • Z • ET N • **Rev:** Two crossed flags, branches above, hourglass below **Rev. Legend:** MON • NOV • IMP • CONSILIO ET VIRTVTE

Date	Mintage	VG	F	VF	XF	Unc
1610 Rare	—	—	—	—	—	—

KM# 64 1/4 THALER (Ortstaler)
Silver **Ruler:** Moritz **Obv:** Hessian lion, legend divided by 4 small shields **Rev:** 2 crossed flags divide date, hourglass and bell below, branches above, legend divided by 4 small shields **Rev. Legend:** CONSIL -IO • E • VIR • -TVTEMO • -NO • IMP:

Date	Mintage	VG	F	VF	XF	Unc
1623 TS	—	150	350	700	1,400	—
16Z4 TS	—	150	350	700	1,400	—
16Z5 TS Rare	—	—	—	—	—	—
16Z6 TS	—	150	350	700	1,400	—

KM# 86 1/4 THALER (Ortstaler)
Silver **Ruler:** Wilhelm V **Obv:** Bust of Wilhelm right divides date as 1-6/Z-7, titles of Wilhelm in legend **Rev:** 5-fold arms **Rev. Legend:** UNO

Date	Mintage	VG	F	VF	XF	Unc
1627 Rare	—	—	—	—	—	—

KM# 107 1/4 THALER (Ortstaler)
Silver **Ruler:** Wilhelm V **Obv:** Hessian arms in Spanish shield **Obv. Legend:** WILHELM • D • G • LAND • H • A • H • C • C • D • Z • E • N **Rev:** Tree in storm, date in legend **Rev. Legend:** DEO... **Note:** Varieties exist.

Date	Mintage	VG	F	VF	XF	Unc
(1)6Z8	—	190	380	800	1,600	—
(16)Z8	—	190	380	800	1,600	—
(1)6Z9	—	190	380	800	1,600	—
1630 TS	—	190	380	800	1,600	—
1631 two houses	—	190	380	800	1,600	—

KM# 125 1/4 THALER (Ortstaler)
Silver **Ruler:** Wilhelm V **Subject:** Death of Moritz **Obv:** 7-line inscription **Rev:** Two crossed flags, branches above, hourglass below **Rev. Legend:** MAURITI • MEMENTO MORI CONSI: E: VIRTU

Date	Mintage	VG	F	VF	XF	Unc
163z TS	—	400	1,000	1,800	3,500	—

KM# 138 1/4 THALER (Ortstaler)
Silver **Ruler:** Wilhelm V **Obv:** Oval arms in oval baroque frame, titles of Wilhelm in legend **Obv. Legend:** WILHELM • D • G • LANDGRAV • HASS • COM • C • DIZ • Z • E • N **Rev:** Tree in storm, four houses, date **Rev. Legend:** IEHOVA...

Date	Mintage	VG	F	VF	XF	Unc
(1)633 TS	—	180	380	750	1,600	—

KM# A170 1/4 THALER (Ortstaler)
Silver **Ruler:** Wilhelm V **Obv:** Lion in Spanish shield, 1-6 / 3-5 **Obv. Legend:** WILHELM D G LAND HASS... **Rev:** Tree in storm, houses beside **Rev. Legend:** IEHOVA VOLENTE HUMILIS...

Date	Mintage	VG	F	VF	XF	Unc
1635 clover Rare	—	—	—	—	—	—

KM# 172.1 1/4 THALER (Ortstaler)
Silver **Ruler:** Wilhelm V **Obv:** Hessian lion divides date **Rev:** Tree in storm, 4, 5, or 6 houses **Rev. Legend:** VNO VOLENTE HUMILIS LEVABOR **Note:** Many varieties exist.

Date	Mintage	VG	F	VF	XF	Unc
1637 AG two crossed pothooks	—	200	440	900	1,800	—
1637 GK	—	200	440	900	1,800	—

KM# 172.2 1/4 THALER (Ortstaler)
Silver **Ruler:** Wilhelm V **Obv:** Hessian lion divides date **Rev:** Tree in storm, 3, 4 or 5 houses **Rev. Legend:** IEHOVA VOLENTE HUMILIS LEVABOR

Date	Mintage	VG	F	VF	XF	Unc
(16)37 clover	—	200	440	900	1,800	—

KM# 172.3 1/4 THALER (Ortstaler)
Silver **Ruler:** Wilhelm V **Obv:** Hessian lion, date flanking **Rev:** Tree in storm, 3, 4 or 5 houses **Rev. Legend:** IEHOVA VOLENTE HUMILIS LEVABOR

Date	Mintage	VG	F	VF	XF	Unc
1637	—	200	440	900	1,800	—

KM# 172.4 1/4 THALER (Ortstaler)
Silver **Ruler:** Wilhelm V **Obv:** Hessian lion, date flanking as 3-7 **Rev:** Tree in storm, 3, 4 or 5 houses **Rev. Inscription:** IEHOVA...

Date	Mintage	VG	F	VF	XF	Unc
(16)37 GK	—	200	440	900	1,800	—

KM# 173 1/4 THALER (Ortstaler)
Silver **Ruler:** Wilhelm V **Subject:** Death of Wilhelm V **Obv:** 9-line inscription, Arabic numeral date **Rev:** Tree in storm, 4 houses **Rev. Legend:** VNO VOLENTE HUMILIS LEVABOR

Date	Mintage	VG	F	VF	XF	Unc
1637 GK crossed pothooks	—	140	300	600	1,150	—

Note: Due to engraving style, GK often reads as GR

KM# 196 1/4 THALER (Ortstaler)
Silver **Ruler:** Wilhelm VI **Obv:** Hessian lion, date divided among paws as 1-63-8, star in front denotes Wilhelm VI **Rev:** Tree in storm, 3 houses **Rev. Legend:** IEHOVA VOLENTE HUMILIS LEVABOR

Date	Mintage	VG	F	VF	XF	Unc
1638 LH Rare	—	—	—	—	—	—

KM# 218 1/4 THALER (Ortstaler)
Silver **Ruler:** Wilhelm VI **Subject:** Death of Amalie Elisabeth von Hanau, Wife of Wilhelm V **Obv:** 9-line inscription **Rev:** Mountain with miner in mine, heart and sun above, clouds and storm besides **Rev. Legend:** WIDER MACHT UND LIST MEIN FELS GOTT IST

Date	Mintage	VG	F	VF	XF	Unc
1651 AG	—	160	350	700	1,400	—

KM# 228 1/4 THALER (Ortstaler)
Silver **Ruler:** Wilhelm VI **Obv:** Crowned manifold arms in baroque frame divide date at 1-6/5-Z **Obv. Legend:** WIL: DG: LAND: HASS: PRIN: HERS: CO: CA: DI: ZI: N:& SCH • **Rev:** Sailing ship left **Note:** Varieties exist.

Date	Mintage	VG	F	VF	XF	Unc
165Z	—	600	1,400	2,700	5,200	—
1653	—	—	—	—	—	—
Note: Reported, not confirmed						
1654 AG	—	600	1,400	2,700	5,200	—
1655 AG	—	600	1,400	2,700	5,200	—

Note: Peus Auction 4-03, XF/VF example realized $3775.

KM# 259 1/4 THALER (Ortstaler)
Silver **Ruler:** Wilhelm VI **Subject:** Death of Wilhelm VI **Obv:** Bust half left **Obv. Legend:** WILHELM • VI • G • G • LANDG • HASS • PR • HERSF • CO • CAT • DE • ZI • NI • ET • SCH **Rev:** 10-line inscription, Roman numeral date **Rev. Legend:** PIE -TATA • -FIDE -ET -IVS - TI -TIA -

Date	Mintage	VG	F	VF	XF	Unc
MDCLXIII (1663) IGB	—	250	600	1,200	2,400	—

KM# 271 1/4 THALER (Ortstaler)
Silver **Ruler:** Wilhelm VII **Obv:** Hessian and Brandenburg arms in crowned divided shield **Obv. Legend:** HEDWIG • SOPHIA.... **Rev:** Terrestrial globe hanging on a heart, sword cuts the rope **Rev. Legend:** DISSOLVER **Note:** Similar to 1 Thaler, KM#273.

Date	Mintage	VG	F	VF	XF	Unc
1669	—	600	1,300	2,800	5,200	—

Note: Peus Auction 4-03, XF/VF realized $5100.

KM# 284 1/4 THALER (Ortstaler)
Silver **Ruler:** Wilhelm VII **Subject:** Death of Wilhelm VII **Obv:** 7-fold Hessian arms with 5 helmets **Obv. Legend:** WILHELM • VII • D • G • LANDG • HASS • PR • HERSF • COM • C • D • Z • N • ET • SCHAV * **Rev:** 10-line inscription, Roman numeral date

Date	Mintage	VG	F	VF	XF	Unc
MDCLXX (1670) Rare	—	—	—	—	—	—

KM# 308 1/4 THALER (Ortstaler)
Silver **Ruler:** Karl **Subject:** Death of Hedwig Sophie von Brandenburg, Wife of Wilhelm VI **Obv:** Hessian and Brandenburg arms in divided crowned shield **Obv. Legend:** HEDWIGIS: SOPHIA • HASS: PR • H • NAT • PR • ELECT: BRANDENB: **Rev:** 9-line inscription with date

Date	Mintage	VG	F	VF	XF	Unc
1.6.83	—	650	1,400	2,800	5,500	—

Note: Peus Auction 4-03, VF realized $2830.

KM# 321 1/4 THALER (Ortstaler)
Silver **Ruler:** Karl **Obv:** Crowned arms between palm branches, date below **Rev:** Swan with crown around its neck on pedestal, double C monogram and lion above **Note:** Similar to 1 Thaler, KM#322. Some sources consider this a medal.

Date	Mintage	VG	F	VF	XF	Unc
1686 IVF	—	—	—	—	—	—

KM# 337 1/4 THALER (Ortstaler)
Silver **Ruler:** Karl **Obv:** Bust right **Obv. Legend:** CAROL • DG • - - • HASS • LANDG **Rev:** Double CL monogram in cross angles, crowned

Date	Mintage	VG	F	VF	XF	Unc
1693 IVF	—	—	800	1,450	2,800	—

KM# 22 1/2 THALER
Silver **Ruler:** Moritz **Obv:** Hessian lion in ornamented shield, helmet above, titles of Moritz in legend **Rev:** Crossed flags divide date, branches above, bell and hourglass below **Rev. Legend:** CONSILIO...

Date	Mintage	VG	F	VF	XF	Unc
1611 Rare	—	—	—	—	—	—

KM# 43 1/2 THALER
23.9000 g., Silver **Ruler:** Moritz **Obv:** Helmet above shield with lion, legend between four small shields **Rev:** Crossed lances dividing date at center, legend between four small shields **Note:** Klippe.

Date	Mintage	VG	F	VF	XF	Unc
1621 Unique	—	—	—	—	—	—

KM# 65 1/2 THALER
Silver **Ruler:** Moritz **Obv:** Crowned Hessian lion, 4 small shields divide legend; titles of Maurice **Rev:** Crossed flags divide date, branches above, bell and hourglass below, four small shields divide legend

Date	Mintage	VG	F	VF	XF	Unc
1623 TS	—	300	700	1,400	2,800	—
16Z4 TS	—	270	650	1,250	2,500	—
16Z5 TS	—	270	650	1,250	2,500	—
1626 TS	—	270	650	1,250	2,500	—
1627	—	—	—	—	—	—

Note: Reported, not confirmed

KM# 87 1/2 THALER
Silver **Ruler:** Wilhelm V **Obv:** Facing bust divides date, titles of Wilhelm V in legend **Rev:** Hessian arms in Spanish shield, 3 helmets **Rev. Legend:** UNO • VOLENTE • HUMILIS • LEVABOR •

Date	Mintage	VG	F	VF	XF	Unc
16Z7 TS Rare	—	—	—	—	—	—

KM# 88 1/2 THALER
Silver **Ruler:** Wilhelm V **Obv:** Bust right divides date 1-6/Z-7 or as 16-Z7, titles of Wilhelm V **Obv. Legend:** WILHELM • D • G • LAND • HASS • ADMI • HIR • C • C • D • Z • E • N **Rev:** Hessian arms in German shield, 3 helmets **Rev. Legend:** UNO VOLENTE • HUMILIS • LEVABOR •

Date	Mintage	VG	F	VF	XF	Unc
16Z7 TS Rare	—	—	—	—	—	—
1627	—	—	—	—	—	—

Note: Reported, not confirmed

KM# 108.1 1/2 THALER
Silver **Ruler:** Wilhelm V **Obv:** 5-fold arms in baroque French shield **Obv. Legend:** WILHELM • D • G • LAND • HASS • AD • H • COM • C • D • Z • E • N **Rev:** Tree in storm, without houses, date **Rev. Legend:** DEO • VOLENTE • HUMILIS • LEVABOR •

Date	Mintage	VG	F	VF	XF	Unc
16Z8 TS Rare	—	—	—	—	—	—

KM# 108.2 1/2 THALER
Silver **Ruler:** Wilhelm V **Obv:** Crowned arms in baroque shield **Rev:** Tree in storm, with houses only in 1631 and 1632 **Note:** Reverse background varieties exist.

Date	Mintage	VG	F	VF	XF	Unc
1629 TS	—	400	850	1,750	3,500	—
1630 TS	—	400	850	1,750	3,500	—
1631	—	360	780	1,600	3,000	—
163Z	—	360	780	1,600	3,000	—

KM# 126 1/2 THALER
Silver **Ruler:** Wilhelm V **Subject:** Death of Moritz **Obv:** 9-line inscription, Arabic date **Rev:** Two crossed flags, branches above **Rev. Legend:** MAURITI • MEMENTO MORI • CONSILIO ET VIRTUTE •

Date	Mintage	VG	F	VF	XF	Unc
1632 TS	—	360	780	1,600	3,000	—

KM# 126a 1/2 THALER
Tin **Ruler:** Wilhelm V **Subject:** Death of Moritz **Obv:** 9-line inscription **Rev:** Two crossed flags, branches above **Note:** Off-metal strike of KM#126.

Date	Mintage	VG	F	VF	XF	Unc
1632 TS	—	—	120	260	550	—

KM# 139 1/2 THALER
Silver **Ruler:** Wilhelm V **Obv:** Hessian arms in ornamented oval, crowned, date 1-6-3-3 divided around crown, titles of Wilhelm **Rev:** Tree in storm, 4 houses, date as 633 **Rev. Legend:** IEHOVA...

Date	Mintage	VG	F	VF	XF	Unc
1633//(1)633 clover	—	450	900	1,700	3,400	—

KM# 140 1/2 THALER
Silver **Ruler:** Wilhelm V **Obv:** Bust right divides date **Rev:** Hessian arms in ornamented oval, crowned **Rev. Legend:** FATA • CONSILITS • POTIORA

Date	Mintage	VG	F	VF	XF	Unc
1633	—	—	—	—	—	—

Note: Reported, not confirmed

KM# 146 1/2 THALER
Silver **Ruler:** Wilhelm V **Obv:** Bust right, no legend **Rev:** Ornamented oval arms, no legend **Note:** Some sources consider this a medal.

Date	Mintage	VG	F	VF	XF	Unc
1634	—	—	—	—	—	—

KM# 153 1/2 THALER
Silver **Ruler:** Wilhelm V **Obv:** Crowned Hessian lion divides date as 1-6/3-5 around, titles of Wilhelm in legend **Rev:** Tree in storm **Rev. Legend:** IEHOVA...

Date	Mintage	VG	F	VF	XF	Unc
1635 LH clover	—	220	500	1,000	2,100	—

KM# 175.1 1/2 THALER
Silver **Ruler:** Wilhelm VI **Obv:** Hessian lion, star in front (denotes Wilhelm VI) **Obv. Legend:** WILHEL[M] • D: G: LAND[GRA] • HASS • C[OM] • C • D • Z • E • N • **Rev:** Tree in storm, houses **Rev. Legend:** IEHOVA VOLENTE HUMILIS LEVABOR **Note:** Date placement varies.

Date	Mintage	VG	F	VF	XF	Unc
1637 clover	—	130	260	550	1,200	—
1637 GK crossed pothooks	—	130	260	550	1,200	—
1638 LH	—	130	260	550	1,200	—
1639 GK crossed pothooks	—	130	300	650	1,300	—

KM# 175.2 1/2 THALER
Silver **Ruler:** Wilhelm VI **Obv:** Hessian lion, star. **Rev:** Tree in storm, houses **Rev. Legend:** VNO...

Date	Mintage	VG	F	VF	XF	Unc
1637 GH crossed pothooks	—	130	260	550	1,200	—

KM# 160.1 1/2 THALER

Silver **Ruler:** Wilhelm V **Obv:** Crowned Hessian lion divides date as 16-36 **Rev:** Tree in storm, 4 houses **Rev. Legend:** IEHOVA...

Date	Mintage	VG	F	VF	XF	Unc
1636 2 crosses	—	220	500	1,000	2,100	—
1637 clover	—	220	500	1,000	2,100	—

KM# 160.2 1/2 THALER

Silver **Ruler:** Wilhelm V **Obv:** Crowned Hessian lion **Rev:** Tree in storm, houses **Rev. Legend:** VNO... **Note:** Varieties exist.

Date	Mintage	VG	F	VF	XF	Unc
1637 AG	—	225	500	1,100	2,250	—
1637 LH	—	275	600	1,200	2,450	—
1637 O	—	225	500	1,100	2,250	—

KM# 160.3 1/2 THALER

Silver **Ruler:** Wilhelm V **Obv:** Crowned Hessian lion **Rev:** Tree in storm, houses **Rev. Legend:** VNO...

Date	Mintage	VG	F	VF	XF	Unc
1637 GK two pothooks	—	275	600	1,200	2,450	—

KM# 174 1/2 THALER

Silver **Ruler:** Wilhelm V **Subject:** Death of Wilhelm V **Obv:** 10-line inscription, Arabic date **Obv. Legend:** WILHELM9 • V • DICT9 • CONSTANS • HASS: LANDGR: **Rev:** Tree in storm **Rev. Legend:** VNO VOLENTE HUMILIS LEVABOR

Date	Mintage	VG	F	VF	XF	Unc
1637 GK two pothooks	—	550	1,000	2,000	4,000	—

KM# 219 1/2 THALER

Silver **Ruler:** Wilhelm VI **Subject:** Death of Amalie Elisabeth von Hanau, Wife of Wilhelm V, mother of William VI **Obv:** 9-line inscription with Arabic numeral date **Rev:** Mountain with miner in mine, heart and sun above, clouds and storm besides **Note:** Similar to 1/4 Thaler, KM#218.

Date	Mintage	VG	F	VF	XF	Unc
1651 AG	—	450	900	1,700	3,200	—

KM# 231 1/2 THALER

Silver **Ruler:** Wilhelm VI **Obv:** Crowned Hessian arms in baroque frame divides date, titles of Wilhelm in legend **Rev:** Sailing ship left **Rev. Legend:** VELA VENTIS HIS LEVANTVR **Note:** Varieties exist.

Date	Mintage	VG	F	VF	XF	Unc
1652	—	750	1,500	3,000	5,500	—
1653	—	750	1,500	3,000	5,500	—
1654 AG	—	—	—	—	—	—

Note: Reported, not confirmed

Date	Mintage	VG	F	VF	XF	Unc
1655 AG	—	1,600	1,600	3,200	5,500	—

KM# 261 1/2 THALER

Silver **Ruler:** Wilhelm VI **Subject:** Death of Wilhelm VI **Obv:** Bust right **Obv. Legend:** WILHELM • VI • D • G • LANDG • HASS • PR • HERS • CO • C • D • Z • N • ET • SCHAW **Rev:** 10-line inscription, date in Roman numerals

Date	Mintage	VG	F	VF	XF	Unc
MDCLXIII (1663) IGB	—	250	600	1,300	2,600	—

KM# 272 1/2 THALER

Silver **Ruler:** Wilhelm VII **Obv:** Hessian and brandburg arms in divided crowned shield **Obv. Legend:** HEDWIG • SOPHIA • V: G: G: L: Z: H: G: A: C: S: D: M: Z: B: W: V: V: REGENT: **Rev:** Terrestrial globe hanging on a heart, sword cuts the rope **Rev. Legend:** DISSOLVER **Note:** Similar to 1 Thaler, KM#273.

Date	Mintage	VG	F	VF	XF	Unc
1669	—	500	1,100	2,200	4,000	—

KM# 286 1/2 THALER

Silver **Ruler:** Wilhelm VII **Rev:** Inscription with Arabic numerals date in wreath **Note:** Struck with a 1/4 Thaler die

Date	Mintage	VG	F	VF	XF	Unc
1670	—	—	—	—	—	—

Note: Reported, not confirmed

KM# 285 1/2 THALER

Silver **Ruler:** Wilhelm VII **Subject:** Death of Wilhelm VII **Obv:** Helmeted arms **Obv. Legend:** WILHELM • VII • D • G • LANDG • HASS • PR • HERSF • COM C • D • Z • N • ET SCHAVENB **Rev:** 11-line inscription with Roman numeral date

Date	Mintage	VG	F	VF	XF	Unc
MDCLXX (1670) Rare	—	—	—	—	—	—

KM# 309 1/2 THALER

Silver **Ruler:** Karl **Subject:** Death of Hedwig Sophie von Brandenburg, Wife of Wilhelm VI **Obv:** Hessian and Brandenburg arms in crowned divided shield **Obv. Legend:** HEDWIGIS: SOPHIA • HASS: PR • H • NAT • PR • ELECT: BRANDENB: **Rev:** 9-line inscription with date

Date	Mintage	VG	F	VF	XF	Unc
1683	—	550	1,100	2,000	4,000	—

KM# 318 1/2 THALER

10.7000 g., Silver, 23 mm. **Ruler:** Karl **Obv:** Star **Rev:** Star **Note:** Believed by many now to be a medal

Date	Mintage	VG	F	VF	XF	Unc
1685	—	—	—	—	—	—

KM# 338 1/2 THALER

Silver **Ruler:** Karl **Obv:** Bust right **Obv. Legend:** CAROL • DG • -- HASS: LANDG • **Rev:** Hessian arms in Spanish shield, 5 helmets

Date	Mintage	VG	F	VF	XF	Unc
1693 IVF	—	550	1,100	2,300	4,600	—

KM# 19 THALER

Silver **Ruler:** Moritz **Obv:** Helmeted arms **Rev:** Crossed flags divide date **Note:** Dav.#6711.

Date	Mintage	VG	F	VF	XF	Unc
1610	—	700	1,200	2,400	4,800	—

KM# 20 THALER

Silver **Ruler:** Moritz **Obv:** Hessian lion in oval cartouche, helmet above, legend divided by 4 small shields **Obv. Legend:** MAURIT9 • D: G • LAND: HASS: CO • IN • C • D • Z • E • N • **Rev:** Branches above crossed flags, divided date in the side angles, hourglass and bell below, four small shields divide legend **Rev. Legend:** CONSILIO ET VIRTVTE MON[ETA]: NOV[A]: IMP: **Note:** Dav.#6712.

Date	Mintage	VG	F	VF	XF	Unc
1610	—	—	—	—	—	—

Note: Reported, not confirmed

Date	Mintage	VG	F	VF	XF	Unc
1611	—	700	1,200	2,400	4,800	—

KM# 23 THALER

Silver **Ruler:** Moritz **Obv:** Hessian lion in round shield **Note:** Dav.#6713.

Date	Mintage	VG	F	VF	XF	Unc
1611	—	700	1,200	2,400	5,000	—

KM# 44 THALER

Silver **Ruler:** Moritz **Obv:** Helmeted Hessian lion arms, four small shields divide legend **Note:** Dav.#6716.

Date	Mintage	VG	F	VF	XF	Unc
1621	—	600	1,100	2,200	4,500	—

KM# 45 THALER

Silver **Ruler:** Moritz **Rev:** Date in legend **Note:** Dav.#6717.

Date	Mintage	VG	F	VF	XF	Unc
1621 crossed pothooks	—	600	1,100	2,200	4,500	—

KM# 66 THALER

Silver **Ruler:** Moritz **Obv:** Helmeted Hessian lion arms **Rev:** Crossed lances, hourglass and date below **Note:** Dav.#6718.

Date	Mintage	VG	F	VF	XF	Unc
1623	—	700	1,200	2,400	5,000	—

KM# 69.1 THALER

Silver **Ruler:** Moritz **Obv:** Hessian lion in circle, foru shield break legend **Note:** Dav.#6721.

Date	Mintage	VG	F	VF	XF	Unc
16Z3 TS	—	100	220	460	1,000	—

KM# 69.2 THALER

Silver **Ruler:** Moritz **Obv:** Hessian lion in circle, four shields break legend **Obv. Legend:** MAUR: D: G: LAN: HASS: C: C: D: E: N: **Rev:** Branches above crossed flags **Note:** Dav.#6723. Varieties exist.

Date	Mintage	VG	F	VF	XF	Unc
16Z3 TS	—	100	220	460	1,000	—
16Z3	—	120	250	500	1,200	—
16Z4 TS	—	100	200	430	900	—
16Z5 TS	—	100	200	430	900	—
16Z6 TS	—	100	200	430	900	—
16Z7 TS	—	100	220	460	1,000	—

KM# 67 THALER

Silver **Ruler:** Moritz **Rev:** Crossed flags, hourglass below, date in legend **Note:** Dav.#6719.

Date	Mintage	VG	F	VF	XF	Unc
1623	—	700	1,200	2,400	5,000	—

KM# 68 THALER

Silver **Ruler:** Moritz **Rev:** Crossed lances divide date, branches above **Note:** Dav.#6720.

Date	Mintage	VG	F	VF	XF	Unc
1623	—	700	1,200	2,400	5,000	—

KM# 71 THALER

Silver **Ruler:** Moritz **Obv:** Hessian lion **Obv. Legend:** MAU: G • LAND • HASSIAE C• C • D • E • N • **Rev:** Branches above crossed flags, date divided in the angles **Rev. Legend:** CONSILIO • E • VIRTUTE • M • NO: IMP **Note:** Struck on Thaler flan with 1/2 Thaler dies, date below on reverse Dav.#--.

Date	Mintage	VG	F	VF	XF	Unc
1623 TS	—	—	—	—	—	—

Note: Reported, not confirmed

KM# 76 THALER

Silver **Ruler:** Moritz **Obv:** Hessian lion in circle, four small shield break legend **Rev:** Crossed flags, branches above **Rev. Legend:** CONSILI ET VIRTV MON • NO AURE: IM **Note:** Dav. #6724.

Date	Mintage	VG	F	VF	XF	Unc
16Z6 TS Rare	—	—	—	—	—	—

KM# 98.1 THALER

Silver **Ruler:** Wilhelm V **Obv:** 3 helmets above 5-fold arms in square German shield with round bottom **Obv. Legend:** WILHELM • D • G • LAND... **Rev:** Tree in storm, sun above with Hebrew "JEHOVAH" date in legend **Note:** Dav.#6735.

Date	Mintage	VG	F	VF	XF	Unc
16Z7 TS	—	180	350	750	1,500	—
(1)6Z7 TS	—	170	350	680	1,350	—
16Z8 TS	—	170	350	680	1,350	—

KM# 98.2 THALER

Silver **Ruler:** Wilhelm V **Obv:** 3 helmets above 5-fold Spanish arms in square shield with round bottom **Obv. Legend:** WILHELM • D • G • LAND... **Rev:** Palm tree in storm**Note:** Dav.#6735.

Date	Mintage	VG	F	VF	XF	Unc
16Z8 TS	—	170	330	680	1,350	—
16Z9TS	—	170	330	680	1,350	—

KM# 89 THALER

Silver **Ruler:** Moritz **Obv:** Facing bust, Similar to KM#91 but band around head ANNO.DOMINE.1627. **Rev:** Helmeted arms **Rev. Legend:** UNO VOLENTE HUMILIS LEVABOR MO NO IM **Note:** Dav.#6728.

Date	Mintage	VG	F	VF	XF	Unc
16Z7 TS	—	650	1,200	2,800	6,000	—

KM# 91 THALER

Silver **Ruler:** Wilhelm V **Obv:** Facing bust, *ANNO* *1627* without band around head **Rev:** Helmeted arms IN 5-fold Spanish shield **Note:** Dav.#6729.

Date	Mintage	VG	F	VF	XF	Unc
16Z7 TS	—	600	1,100	2,500	5,500	—

KM# 92 THALER

Silver **Ruler:** Wilhelm V **Obv:** Facing bust of Wilhelm V without date **Rev:** Helmeted arms in 5-fold German shield, date in legend which starts at the bottom **Rev. Legend:** VNO COLENTE HVMILIS LEVABOR **Note:** Dav.#6731. Varieties exist.

Date	Mintage	VG	F	VF	XF	Unc
1627 TS	—	550	1,000	2,400	5,000	—

KM# 93 THALER

Silver **Ruler:** Wilhelm V **Obv:** Facing bust which divides date **Rev:** Helmeted arms, date in legend starting at the bottom **Rev. Legend:** VNO VOLENTE HVMILIS LEVABOR **Note:** Dav.#6732. Date on both sides.

Date	Mintage	VG	F	VF	XF	Unc
16Z7 TS	—	550	1,000	2,400	5,000	—

KM# 95 THALER

Silver **Ruler:** Wilhelm V **Obv:** Facing bust, bust divides date **Rev:** Helmeted arms in 5-fold Spanish shield **Rev. Legend:** UNO VOLENTE HUMILIS LEVABOR MO NO IM **Note:** Dav.#6733. Varieties exist.

Date	Mintage	VG	F	VF	XF	Unc
16Z7 TS	—	500	950	2,200	4,800	—

KM# 96 THALER

Silver **Ruler:** Wilhelm V **Obv:** Bust right **Rev:** Helmeted arms in 5-fold Spanish shield **Rev. Legend:** UNO VOLENTE NUMILIS LEVABOR MO NO IM **Note:** Dav.#6734. Varieties exist, star or rose at end of date.

Date	Mintage	VG	F	VF	XF	Unc
16Z7 TS	—	400	850	200	4,500	—

KM# 115.1 THALER

Silver **Ruler:** Wilhelm V **Obv:** 5-fold arms in crowned oval, crown divides date **Obv. Legend:** WILHELMUS • D: G: LANDTGRAVIVS • HASSIAE • COM: IN: C: D: Z: E: NID **Rev:** Tree in storm, sun above w/Hebrew "JEHOVAH" without houses in the background beside the tree **Rev. Legend:** DEO • VOLETE • HUMILIS • LEVABOR **Note:** Dav.#6737.

Date	Mintage	VG	F	VF	XF	Unc
16Z9 TS	—	110	230	480	950	—
1630 TS	—	110	230	480	950	—

KM# 117 THALER

Silver **Ruler:** Wilhelm V **Obv:** Hessian arms in 5-fold oval, without crown **Obv. Legend:** WILHELMUS • D: G: LANDTGRAV: HASS: CO: C: D: Z: E: N **Rev:** Palm tree in storm **Rev. Legend:** DEO • VILETE • HUMILIS • LEVABOR • ANNO •(date)

Date	Mintage	VG	F	VF	XF	Unc
16Z9 TS	—	110	230	520	1,200	—

KM# 115.2 THALER

Silver **Ruler:** Wilhelm V **Obv. Legend:** LANDTGRAVIUS...C • D • Z • N **Rev:** Tree in storm, town in background **Note:** Dav.#6741.

Date	Mintage	VG	F	VF	XF	Unc
1630 TS	—	150	320	660	1,300	—
1631 TS	—	140	300	630	1,250	—

KM# 120 THALER

Silver **Ruler:** Wilhelm V **Obv:** Bust of Wilhelm V right, date M-D-C-XXX in corners **Rev:** Tree in storm, town in background **Rev. Legend:** DEO VOLENTE HUMILIS LEVABOR **Note:** Klippe. Dav.#6743.

Date	Mintage	VG	F	VF	XF	Unc
MDCXXX (1630)	—	—	2,000	3,500	6,000	—

KM# 115.3 THALER

Silver **Ruler:** Wilhelm V **Obv:** Hessian arms in 5-fold Spanish shield **Obv. Legend:** WILHELM9 • D: G: LANDGRAVI9 **Note:** Dav.#6745.

Date	Mintage	VG	F	VF	XF	Unc
1631 TS	—	140	300	630	1,250	—
1632 TS	—	140	300	630	1,250	—

KM# 115.4 THALER

Silver **Ruler:** Wilhelm V **Obv:** Crown breaks through upper inner circle **Note:** Dav.#6745A.

Date	Mintage	VG	F	VF	XF	Unc
1631	—	85.00	165	300	550	—

KM# 115.6 THALER

Silver **Ruler:** Wilhelm V **Obv:** Hessian arms in 5-fold oval **Obv. Legend:** WILHELM9: D: G: LANDGRAVI9: **Rev:** Palmtree in storm, town in background **Rev. Legend:** IEHOVA **Note:** Dav.#6749.

Date	Mintage	VG	F	VF	XF	Unc
163Z clover//TS	—	150	340	700	1,400	—
1633 clover//TS	—	150	340	700	1,400	—
1634 TS//rose	—	140	300	630	1,250	—
1634 clover//TS	—	—	—	—	—	—
1634 TS//clover	—	140	300	630	1,250	—
1634 clover//rose	—	—	—	—	—	—

KM# 115.5 THALER

Silver **Ruler:** Wilhelm V **Rev. Legend:** V[U]NO.VOLENTE **Note:** Dav.#6746.

Date	Mintage	VG	F	VF	XF	Unc
1632	—	85.00	165	300	550	—

KM# 128 THALER

Silver **Ruler:** Wilhelm V **Subject:** Death of Moritz **Note:** Dav.#6726.

Date	Mintage	VG	F	VF	XF	Unc
1632 TS	—	100	200	375	650	—

KM# 141 THALER

Silver **Ruler:** Wilhelm V **Obv:** Bust right **Obv. Legend:** WILHELM9 • D: G: LANDGRAVI9 HASSIAE • C: C: D: Z: ET: N: **Rev:** Hessian arms in 5-fold oval Spanish shield **Rev. Legend:** FATA CONSILIIS POTIORA **Note:** Dav.#6748.

Date	Mintage	VG	F	VF	XF	Unc
1633 clover	—	900	1,700	2,800	5,400	10,000
1633 crossed pothooks	—	900	1,700	2,800	5,400	10,000
1633 mercury stick	—	900	1,700	2,800	5,400	10,000
1633	—	—	—	—	—	—
Note: Reported, not confirmed						
1634 crossed pothooks	—	900	1,700	2,800	5,400	10,000

KM# 143 THALER

Silver **Ruler:** Wilhelm V **Obv:** Hessian lion left, date scattered in field **Rev:** Tree in storm, town in background **Rev. Legend:** IEHOVA VOLENTE HUMILIS LEVABOR **Note:** Dav.#6752; 6753. Number of houses varies, 4 or 5.

Date	Mintage	VG	F	VF	XF	Unc
1635 LH clover//star	—	150	290	640	1,250	—
1635 LH star//star	—	150	290	640	1,250	—
1636 LH star//star	—	150	290	640	1,250	—
1636 LH star//clover	—	150	290	640	1,250	—

KM# 115.7 THALER

Silver **Ruler:** Wilhelm V **Rev. Legend:** IEHOV **Note:** Dav.#6751.

Date	Mintage	VG	F	VF	XF	Unc
1635	—	85.00	165	300	550	—

KM# 162.1 THALER

Silver **Ruler:** Wilhelm V **Obv:** Hessian lion divides date in inner circle **Rev:** Tree in storm, village in background **Note:** Dav.#6755.

Date	Mintage	VG	F	VF	XF	Unc
1636 LH clover//star	—	150	290	640	1,250	—
1636 LH star//clover	—	150	290	640	1,250	—
1637 LH clover star//star	—	150	290	640	1,250	—

KM# 162.2 THALER

Silver **Ruler:** Wilhelm V **Obv:** Hessian lion left **Rev:** Tree in storm **Note:** Dav.#6757.

Date	Mintage	VG	F	VF	XF	Unc
1637 .o.//star	—	150	290	640	1,250	—

KM# 162.3 THALER

Silver **Ruler:** Wilhelm V **Obv:** Hessian lion left, 16-37 flanking **Rev. Legend:** IEHOVA **Note:** Dav.#6760.

Date	Mintage	VG	F	VF	XF	Unc
1637 G crossed pothooks k	—	150	290	640	1,250	—
1637 GK / crossed pothooks	—	150	290	640	1,250	—

KM# 162.4 THALER

Silver **Ruler:** Wilhelm V **Obv:** 16-37 flanking lion **Rev. Legend:** IEHOVA... **Note:** Dav.#6761.

Date	Mintage	VG	F	VF	XF	Unc
1637 GK crossed pothooks	—	85.00	165	300	550	—

KM# 162.5 THALER
Silver **Ruler:** Wilhelm V **Obv:** Lion running left, date divided by lion above **Note:** Dav.#6762.

Date	Mintage	VG	F	VF	XF	Unc
1637 LH clover	—	85.00	165	300	550	—

KM# 162.6 THALER
Silver **Ruler:** Wilhelm V **Obv:** Hessian lion left, 16-37 flanking **Rev. Legend:** VNO VOLETE HUMILIS LEVABOR **Note:** Dav.#6763; A6764.

Date	Mintage	VG	F	VF	XF	Unc
1637 AG	—	150	290	640	1,250	—
1637 G crossed pothooks K	—	150	290	640	1,250	—

KM# 162.7 THALER
Silver **Ruler:** Wilhelm V **Obv:** Lion's legs divide G-H, mint mark between legs **Note:** Dav.#A6764.

Date	Mintage	VG	F	VF	XF	Unc
1637 GH	—	85.00	165	300	550	—

KM# 176 THALER
Silver **Ruler:** Wilhelm V **Obv:** Date between hind feed **Note:** Dav.#6759. Varieties exist.

Date	Mintage	VG	F	VF	XF	Unc
1637 LH	—	85.00	165	300	550	—

KM# 177 THALER
Silver **Ruler:** Wilhelm V **Subject:** Death of Wilhelm V **Obv:** 10-line inscription with Roman numeral date **Obv. Legend:** WILHELM9 • V • DICT9 • CONSTANS • HASS: LANDGRAVIVS **Rev:** Tree in storm, (4, 5, 6, or 7 houses) **Note:** Dav.#6765.

Date	Mintage	VG	F	VF	XF	Unc
MDCXXXVII (1637) G crossed pothooks K	—	250	500	1,000	2,000	—

KM# 178 THALER
Silver **Ruler:** Wilhelm V **Subject:** Death of Wilhelm V **Obv:** 10-line inscription with arabic numeral date **Obv. Legend:** WILHELM9 • V • DICT9 • CONSTANS • HASS • LANDGRAVIVS **Rev. Legend:** VNO VOLENTE HUMILIS LEBABOR **Note:** Dav.#6766.

Date	Mintage	VG	F	VF	XF	Unc
1637 G crossed pothooks K	—	275	600	1,200	2,400	—

KM# 179.1 THALER
Silver **Ruler:** Wilhelm VI **Obv:** Crowned lion left with star in front, date below **Note:** Dav.#6771.

Date	Mintage	VG	F	VF	XF	Unc
1637 LH	—	150	320	620	1,200	—
1637 GK	—	150	320	620	1,200	—

KM# 179.2 THALER
Silver **Ruler:** Wilhelm VI **Obv:** Crowned lion dividing date, star in front **Rev:** Tree in storm **Note:** Dav.#6775.

Date	Mintage	VG	F	VF	XF	Unc
1637 LH	—	150	320	620	1,200	—
1638 LH	—	150	320	620	1,200	—

KM# 179.3 THALER
Silver **Ruler:** Wilhelm VI **Obv:** Crowned lion left, star in front **Rev:** Tree in storm, no houses **Note:** Dav.#6775A.

Date	Mintage	VG	F	VF	XF	Unc
1637 LH	—	150	320	620	1,200	—
1638 LH	—	150	320	620	1,200	—

KM# 179.4 THALER
Silver **Ruler:** Wilhelm VI **Obv:** Crowned lion dividing date, G (mint mark) K above **Obv. Legend:** WILHELM • D • G • LAND • HASS • C: C • D • Z • ET • N **Rev:** Tree in storm **Note:** Dav.#6778.

Date	Mintage	VG	F	VF	XF	Unc
1639 GK	—	150	320	620	1,200	—

Note: Sometimes the poor die engraving reads GK as GR

KM# 180.1 THALER
Silver **Ruler:** Wilhelm VI **Obv:** Crowned lion left with star in front, date below, L mint mark H behind **Obv. Legend:** ...C: D: Z: E: N: **Rev:** Tree in storm **Note:** Dav.#6770.

Date	Mintage	VG	F	VF	XF	Unc
1637 LH	—	150	320	620	1,200	—

KM# 180.2 THALER
Silver **Ruler:** Wilhelm VI **Obv:** Crowned lion left with star in front, date below **Obv. Legend:** ...C: D: Z: ETN: **Rev:** Tree in storm **Rev. Legend:** VNO VOLENTE HUMILIS LEVABOR **Note:** Dav.#6773.

Date	Mintage	VG	F	VF	XF	Unc
1637 LH	—	150	320	620	1,200	—

KM# 181 THALER
Silver **Ruler:** Wilhelm VI **Obv:** Crowned lion left with star in front, date curved at right behind lion **Note:** Dav.#6772.

Date	Mintage	VG	F	VF	XF	Unc
1637 GK	—	85.00	165	300	550	—

KM# 180.3 THALER
Silver **Ruler:** Wilhelm VI **Obv:** Lion left, star at left **Obv. Legend:** WILHEL • D • G • LANDGRA **Rev:** Tree in storm **Note:** Dav.#6776.

Date	Mintage	VG	F	VF	XF	Unc
1638 LH	—	150	320	620	1,200	—

KM# 180.4 THALER
Silver **Ruler:** Wilhelm VI **Obv:** Crowned lion left with star in front, date curved below, LH above **Rev:** Tree in storm **Note:** Dav.#180.4.

Date	Mintage	VG	F	VF	XF	Unc
1638 LH	—	150	320	620	1,200	—

KM# 220 THALER
Silver **Ruler:** Wilhelm VI **Subject:** Death of Amalie Elisabeth von Hanau, Wife of Wilhelm V **Obv:** 10-line inscription, date in Arabic numerals **Obv. Legend:** AMALIA ELISABETHA • HASSIAE LANDGRAVIA • HANOVIAE COMES: **Rev:** Mountain with miner in mine, hear and sun above, clouds and storm beside **Note:** Similar to 1/4 Thaler, KM#218. Dav.#6768.

Date	Mintage	VG	F	VF	XF	Unc
1651 AG	—	500	1,000	2,100	4,200	—

KM# 232.1 THALER
Silver **Ruler:** Wilhelm VI **Obv:** Crowned 7-fold arms in baroque frame divide date as 1-6/5-Z **Obv. Legend:** WILHELM9: DG • LANDG • HASS: PRINC: HERSF: COM: CATZ • DIETZ • ZIGEN • NID • ET • SCHA • **Rev:** Sailing ship left **Rev. Legend:** HIS VENTIS VELA LEVANTUR **Note:** Dav.#6779.

Date	Mintage	VG	F	VF	XF	Unc
165Z Rare	—	—	—	—	—	—

KM# 232.2 THALER
Silver **Ruler:** Wilhelm VI **Rev. Legend:** VELA VENTIS HIS LEVANTUR **Note:** Dav.#6781.

Date	Mintage	VG	F	VF	XF	Unc
1653 Rare	—	—	—	—	—	—

KM# 232.3 THALER
Silver **Ruler:** Wilhelm VI **Obv. Legend:** CO • CA • DI • ZI • NI • U • SCHAW **Rev:** Sailing ship left **Note:** Dav.#6781A.

Date	Mintage	VG	F	VF	XF	Unc
1653 Rare	—	—	—	—	—	—

KM# 232.4 THALER
Silver **Ruler:** Wilhelm VI **Obv. Legend:** ...& SCH[A] **Rev:** Sailing ship left **Note:** Dav.#6783.

Date	Mintage	VG	F	VF	XF	Unc
1653 Rare	—	—	—	—	—	—
1654 AG Rare	—	—	—	—	—	—
1655 AG	—	—	2,000	4,000	8,000	—

KM# 250 THALER

Silver **Ruler:** Wilhelm VI **Obv:** Bust right **Obv. Legend:** WILHELM • D • G • LANDG • HASS: PR • HERSF • CO • C • D • Z • N • ET • SCHAU **Rev:** Crowned 7-fold arms in French shield within palm branches **Rev. Legend:** FIDE ET IUSTITIA **Note:** Dav.#6784.

Date	Mintage	VG	F	VF	XF	Unc
1660 IGB	—	600	1,200	2,500	5,000	—

KM# 254 THALER

Silver **Ruler:** Wilhelm VI **Obv:** Bust right in wreath **Rev:** Crowned oval arms between palm branches, date in legend **Note:** Dav.#6784A.

Date	Mintage	VG	F	VF	XF	Unc
1661 IGB	—	750	1,500	3,000	7,000	—

KM# 263 THALER

Silver **Ruler:** Wilhelm VI **Obv:** Bust right **Obv. Legend:** WILHELM • D • G • LANDG • HAS • PR • HERSE • CO • C • D • Z • N • ET • SC **Rev:** Crowned 7-fold arms in Franch shield within palm branches **Rev. Legend:** FIDE ET IVSTITIA **Note:** Dav.#6784B.

Date	Mintage	VG	F	VF	XF	Unc
1663 IGB Rare	—	—	—	—	—	—

KM# 264 THALER

Silver **Ruler:** Wilhelm VI **Subject:** Death of Wilhelm VI **Obv:** Bust half-right **Obv. Legend:** WILHELM • VI • D • G • LANDG • HASS • PR • HERSF • COM • CAT • DEC • ZIEG • NID • ET • SCHAWEN • **Rev:** 10-Line inscription with Roman numeral date **Note:** Dav.#6785.

Date	Mintage	VG	F	VF	XF	Unc
MDCLXIII (1663) IGB	—	320	650	1,300	2,500	—

KM# 273 THALER

Silver **Ruler:** Wilhelm VII **Subject:** Hedwig Sophie's death **Obv:** Hessian and Brandenberg arms in crowned divised shield **Rev:** Terrestrial globe hanging on a heart, sword cuts the rope **Note:** Dav.#6786.

Date	Mintage	VG	F	VF	XF	Unc
1669	—	600	1,200	2,700	6,200	—
1671	—	600	1,200	2,700	6,200	—

KM# 274 THALER

Silver **Ruler:** Wilhelm VII **Subject:** Hedwig Sophie's death **Obv:** Hessian and Brandenberg arms in crowned divided shield, date as 1-6/6-9 flanking **Obv. Legend:** HEDWIG • SOPHIA • V: G: G: L: Z: H: G: A: C: S: D: M: Z: B: WIT: V: V: REGENTIN **Rev:** Terrestrial globe hanging on a heart, sword cuts the rope **Rev. Legend:** DISSOLVER **Note:** Dav.#6786A.

Date	Mintage	VG	F	VF	XF	Unc
1669	—	600	1,200	2,700	5,200	—

KM# 287 THALER

Silver **Ruler:** Wilhelm VII **Subject:** Death of Wilhelm VII **Obv:** Hessian arms in shield, 5 helmets above **Obv. Legend:** WILHELM • VII • D • G • LANG • HASS • PR • HERSF • COM • CAT • DEC • ZIEG • NIED ET SCHAV **Rev:** 11-line inscription in wreath with Roman numeral date **Note:** Dav.#6788.

Date	Mintage	VG	F	VF	XF	Unc
MDCLXX (1670) IGB	—	950	1,800	3,500	6,500	—

KM# 288 THALER

Silver **Ruler:** Wilhelm VII **Subject:** Death of Wilhelm VII **Rev:** 6-line inscription **Note:** Dav.#6788A.

Date	Mintage	VG	F	VF	XF	Unc
1670 IGB	—	500	1,000	2,000	3,500	—

KM# 310 THALER

Silver **Ruler:** Karl **Subject:** Death of Hedwig Sophie von Brandenburg, Wife of Wilhelm VI **Obv:** Crowned arms of Hesse and Brandenburg, date 16-49 below **Rev:** 16-line inscription with Roman numeral date **Note:** Dav.#6787.

Date	Mintage	VG	F	VF	XF	Unc
1683	—	500	1,000	2,000	3,500	—

KM# 311 THALER

Silver **Ruler:** Karl **Subject:** Death of Hedwig Sophie **Rev:** 16-line inscription, Roman numeral date **Rev. Legend:** HEDWIGIS SOPHIA NATA PRINC: ELECT: BRANDENBVRGICA **Note:** Dav.#6787A.

Date	Mintage	VG	F	VF	XF	Unc
MDCLXXXIII (1683)	—	500	1,200	2,300	4,500	—

KM# 322 THALER

Silver **Ruler:** Karl **Obv:** Bust right **Rev:** Swan with crown around its neck on pedestal, double-C monogram and lion above **Note:** Dav.#--. Most authorities now consider this a medal.

Date	Mintage	VG	F	VF	XF	Unc
1686 IVF	—	—	—	—	—	—

KM# 325.1 THALER

Silver, 36 mm. **Ruler:** Karl **Obv:** Head right **Obv. Legend:** CAROL: D • G • -HASS: LANDG **Rev:** 7-fold arms in oval, branches flanking **Note:** Dav.#6789.

Date	Mintage	VG	F	VF	XF	Unc
1687 IVF	—	700	1,400	2,800	5,600	—

KM# 325.2 THALER

Silver, 40 mm. **Ruler:** Karl **Obv:** Bust right **Obv. Legend:** CAROLUS... **Rev:** 7-fold arms in oval, plam branches flanking **Note:** Dav.#6790.

Date	Mintage	VG	F	VF	XF	Unc
1692 IVF	—	600	1,200	2,500	5,000	—

KM# 325.3 THALER

Silver **Ruler:** Karl **Obv:** Bust right **Rev:** Crowned oval arms with 16-I-V-F-92 below **Note:** Dav.#6791.

Date	Mintage	VG	F	VF	XF	Unc
1692 IVF	—	600	1,200	2,500	5,000	—

KM# 325.4 THALER

Silver **Ruler:** Karl **Obv:** Larger bust **Rev:** Crowned oval arms **Note:** Dav.#6792.

Date	Mintage	VG	F	VF	XF	Unc
1693 IVF	—	700	1,400	2,800	5,600	—

KM# 340 THALER

Silver **Ruler:** Karl **Obv:** Bust right **Rev:** Helmeted arms divide date **Note:** Dav.#6793.

Date	Mintage	VG	F	VF	XF	Unc
1693	—	450	850	1,600	2,650	—

KM# 46 1-1/2 THALER

Silver **Ruler:** Moritz **Obv:** Hessian lion arms, helmeted, 4 small shields divide legend **Obv. Legend:** MAURIT: D • G • LAND HASS: CO • C • D • Z • E • N: **Rev:** Branches above crossed flags, 4 small shields divide legend **Rev. Legend:** CONSILIO ET • VIRTUTE • MONETA NOV: IMP: **Note:** Klippe. Dav.#6715.

Date	Mintage	VG	F	VF	XF	Unc
16Z1 Rare	—	—	—	—	—	—

Note: Reported, not confirmed

KM# 47 2 THALER

Silver **Ruler:** Moritz **Obv:** Helmeted Hessian lion arms, 4 small sheidls divide legend **Rev:** Branches above crossed flags, 4 small shields divide legend **Note:** Klippe. Dav.#6714.

Date	Mintage	VG	F	VF	XF	Unc
16Z1 3 crossed pothooks Rare	—	—	—	—	—	—

Note: Reported, not confirmed

KM# 80 2 THALER

Silver **Ruler:** Moritz **Obv:** Hessian lion **Obv. Legend:** MAUR: D: G: LAND: HASS: C: C: Z: E: N: **Rev:** Two crossed flags **Rev. Legend:** CONSILIO ET • VIRTUTE • MON NOVA IM **Note:** Similar to 1 Thaler, KM#69, but struck on a thick flan. Dav.#6722.

Date	Mintage	VG	F	VF	XF	Unc
16Z5 TS Rare	—	—	—	—	—	—

Note: Reported, not confirmed

KM# 119 2 THALER

Silver, 54 mm. **Ruler:** Moritz **Obv:** Hessian lions **Obv. Legend:** MAURIT: D: G: LAND: HASSIAE • C: C: D: Z: E: N: **Rev:** Two crossed flags **Rev. Legend:** CONSILI: ET • VIRTU: MONETA • NOVA • IMP: **Note:** Dav.#LS311. Wide 2 Thaler similar to Thaler KM #19, but obverse and reverse the four shields dividing the legends are much bigger and go into the central design area.

Date	Mintage	VG	F	VF	XF	Unc
16Z7 TS	—	—	2,000	3,900	7,800	—

Note: Moller Auction 10, 10-92 VF-XF realized $20,800

KM# 109 2 THALER

Silver **Ruler:** Wilhelm V **Obv:** Hessian arms in 5-fold Spanish shield, three helmets above **Obv. Legend:** WILHELMUS • D • G • LAND... **Rev:** Palm tree in storm, without houses **Rev. Legend:** DEO • VOLENTE • HUMILIS • LEVABOR • ANNO... **Note:** Dav.#LS312.

Date	Mintage	VG	F	VF	XF	Unc
16Z8 TS	—	—	2,000	3,900	7,800	—
16Z9 TS	—	—	2,000	3,900	7,800	—

KM# 121 2 THALER

Silver **Ruler:** Wilhelm V **Obv:** Hessian arms in 5-fold Spanish shield, 3 helmets above **Obv. Legend:** WILHELMUS D • G • LANDGRAVIUS HASSIAE • COMES C • D • Z • ET NIDDA **Rev:** Palm tree in storm, six houses flanking **Rev. Legend:** DEO • VOLENTE HUMILIS LEVABOR **Note:** Dav.#LS315.

Date	Mintage	VG	F	VF	XF	Unc
MDCXXX (1630) TS Rare	—	—	—	—	—	—

Note: Auction Peus #371, 2002 EF realized $7900.

KM# 122 2 THALER

Silver **Ruler:** Wilhelm V **Obv:** Bust of Wilhelm V right, date M-D-C-XXX in corners **Rev:** Tree in storm, town in background **Rev. Legend:** DEO VOLENTE HUMILIS LEVABOR **Note:** Klippe. Dav.#6742.

Date	Mintage	VG	F	VF	XF	Unc
MDCXXX (1630) Rare	—	—	—	—	—	—

KM# 129 2 THALER

Silver **Ruler:** Wilhelm V **Subject:** Death of Moritz **Note:** Similar to 1 Thaler, KM#128. Dav.#6725.

Date	Mintage	VG	F	VF	XF	Unc
1632 TS	—	—	—	—	—	—

Note: Reported, not confirmed

KM# 149 2 THALER

Silver **Ruler:** Wilhelm V **Obv:** Bust left **Note:** Similar to Thaler, KM#142 but struck on a thick flan.

Date	Mintage	VG	F	VF	XF	Unc
1634	—	—	—	—	—	—

KM# 147 2 THALER

Silver **Ruler:** Wilhelm V **Obv:** Hessian arms in 5-fold oval shield, 3 helmets above, Roman numeral date in legend **Obv. Legend:** WILHELMUS9 D: G: LANDGRAVI9 • HASSIAE • COM: C: D: Z: E: N: **Rev:** Palm tree in storm, village in background **Rev. Legend:** IEHOVA • VOLENTE • HUMILIS • LEVABOR • **Note:** Similar to KM#121. Dav.#LS316.

Date	Mintage	VG	F	VF	XF	Unc
MDCXXXIIII (1634) TS Rare	—	—	—	—	—	—

Note: Auction Peus 371, 2002, xf realized $7800. Formerly listed Dav. #6747, KM #148 has been deleted as an error listing.

KM# 148 2 THALER

Silver **Ruler:** Wilhelm V **Obv:** Bust right **Note:** Similar to 1 Thaler, KM#141. Dav.#6747.

Date	Mintage	VG	F	VF	XF	Unc
1634 clover / crossed pothooks Rare	—	—	—	—	—	—

KM# 154 2 THALER

Silver **Ruler:** Wilhelm V **Obv:** crowned Hessian lion to left, legend FATA CONSILIIS POTIORA in inner circle **Obv. Legend:** WILHELM9 D: G: LANDGRAVI9 HASSIAE • COM: C: D: Z: ET • N: ANNO... **Rev:** Tree in storm, 6 houses flanking **Rev. Legend:** IEHOVA VOLENTE HUMILIS LEVABOR **Note:** Dav.#LS318 and LS319 have been combined into one listing.

Date	Mintage	VG	F	VF	XF	Unc
MDCXXXV (1635) L clover H	—	—	—	—	—	—

Note: Auction Peus 383, 2005, VF realized $7500.

KM# 182.1 2 THALER

Silver **Ruler:** Wilhelm V **Obv:** Crowned lion left, dividing date, mintmark below **Obv. Legend:** WILHELM9 • D: G • LANDGRAVI9 • HASSIAE • C: C: D: Z: ET • N: **Rev:** Palm tree in storm, 6 or 8 houses **Rev. Legend:** U[V]NO VOLENTE HUMILIS LEVABOR **Note:** Dav.#6756.

Date	Mintage	VG	F	VF	XF	Unc
1637 .o. Rare	—	—	—	—	—	—
1637 AG Rare	—	—	—	—	—	—

KM# 182.2 2 THALER

Silver **Ruler:** Wilhelm V **Obv:** Lion, date between hind legs **Obv. Legend:** WILHELM9 • D: G: LANDGRAVI9 • HASS: COM: C • D: Z • E • N **Rev. Legend:** IEHOVA VOLENTE HUMILIS LEVABOR **Note:** Dav.#6758.

Date	Mintage	VG	F	VF	XF	Unc
1637 GK crossed pothooks Rare	—	—	—	—	—	—

KM# 183 2 THALER

Silver **Ruler:** Wilhelm V **Subject:** Death of Wilhelm V **Obv:** 10-line inscription, Roman numeral date **Obv. Legend:** WILHELM9 • V • DICT9 • CONSTANS • HASS: LANDGRAVIS **Rev:** Tree in storm, 5 houses **Rev. Legend:** VNO • VOLENTE • HUMILIS • LEVABOR **Note:** Dav.#6764. Legend varieties.

Date	Mintage	VG	F	VF	XF	Unc
1637 G two pothooks K Rare	—	—	—	—	—	—

KM# 184 2 THALER

Silver **Ruler:** Wilhelm VI **Obv:** Lion, date below, star in front **Obv. Legend:** WILHELM9 • D: G: LANDGRAVI9 • HASSIAE • COM: C: D: Z: E: N: **Rev:** Palm tree in storm, 5 houses **Rev. Legend:** IEHOVA VOLENTE HUMILIS LEVABOR **Note:** Similar to 1 Thaler, KM#162. Dav.#6769.

Date	Mintage	VG	F	VF	XF	Unc
1637 L clover H Rare	—	—	—	—	—	—

Note: Auction Moeller 47, 2007, VF+ realized $19,000.

KM# 198 2 THALER

Silver **Ruler:** Wilhelm VI **Obv:** Star in front of lion denoting Wilhelm VI **Note:** Dav.#6774.

Date	Mintage	VG	F	VF	XF	Unc
1638 LH	—	—	—	—	—	—

Note: Reported, not confirmed

KM# 237.1 2 THALER

Silver **Ruler:** Wilhelm VI **Obv:** Crowned manifold arms in baroque frame divide date as 1-6/5-3 **Rev:** Sailing ship left **Note:** Dav.#6780.

Date	Mintage	VG	F	VF	XF	Unc
1653 Rare	—	—	—	—	—	—

KM# 237.2 2 THALER

Silver **Ruler:** Wilhelm VI **Obv. Legend:** ...et SCHA **Note:** Dav.#6782.

Date	Mintage	VG	F	VF	XF	Unc
1655 Rare	—	—	—	—	—	—

KM# 222 2 THALER

Silver **Ruler:** Wilhelm VI **Subject:** Death of Amalie Elisabeth von Hanau, Wife of Wilhelm V **Obv:** Crowned 7-fold arms in baroque frame, date divided as 1-6/5-3 **Obv. Legend:** WILHELM9: DG: LANDG: HASS: PRINC: HERSF: COM: CATz • DIETz • ZIGEN: NID: t SCHA: **Rev:** Sailing ship left **Rev. Legend:** VELA VENTIS HIS LEVANTUR **Note:** Same dies as KM#221. Dav.#6767.

Date	Mintage	VG	F	VF	XF	Unc
1651 AG Rare	—	—	—	—	—	—
1653 Rare	—	—	—	—	—	—

KM# 99 3 THALER

Silver, 54 mm. **Ruler:** Moritz **Note:** Dav.#LS310. Similar to 2 Thaler, KM#119. Struck on a thick flan.

Date	Mintage	VG	F	VF	XF	Unc
16Z7 TS Rare	—	—	—	—	—	—

KM# 118 3 THALER

Silver **Ruler:** Wilhelm V **Obv:** Hessian arms in Spanish shield, 3 helmets above **Obv. Legend:** WILHELMUS • D • G • LAND • HASSIAE • ADMIN • HIRS • COM • C • D • Z • E • N **Rev:** Palm tree in storm, no houses **Rev. Legend:** DEO • VOLENTE • HUMILIS • LEVABOR **Note:** Dav.#LS313. Similar to 2 Thaler, KM#109.

Date	Mintage	VG	F	VF	XF	Unc
16Z9 TS Rare	—	—	—	—	—	—

KM# 155 3 THALER

Silver **Ruler:** Wilhelm V **Obv:** Crowned Hessian lion left, inner legend: FATA CONSILIIS POTIORA **Obv. Legend:** WILHEMUS9 • D:G: LANDGRAVI9 • HASSIAE • COM: C: D: Z: ET • N: **Rev:** Palm tree in storm, 6 houses **Rev. Legend:** IEHOVA VOLENTE HUMILIS LEVABOR **Note:** Similar to 2 Thaler, KM#154. Struck on a thick flan.

Date	Mintage	VG	F	VF	XF	Unc
1635 LH Rare	—	—	—	—	—	—

TRADE COINAGE

KM# 24 GOLDGULDEN

3.5000 g., 0.9860 Gold 0.1109 oz. AGW **Ruler:** Moritz **Obv:** Bust of Maurice right in inner circle **Obv. Legend:** MAURITIUS D: G: LANDGR • HASS • **Rev:** crossed flags and symbols in inner circle **Rev. Legend:** CONSILIO ET VIRTVTE

Date	Mintage	VG	F	VF	XF	Unc
1618	—	—	—	—	—	—

Note: Reported, not confirmed

KM# 77 GOLDGULDEN

3.5000 g., 0.9860 Gold 0.1109 oz. AGW **Ruler:** Moritz **Obv:** Hessian arms in shield **Obv. Legend:** MAUR: D: G: LAND: HASS: C • C • D: Z: E • N **Rev:** Cruciform arms in inner circle, date in legend **Rev. Legend:** MONETA • NOVA • AUREA • HASS:

Date	Mintage	VG	F	VF	XF	Unc
16Z4 TS Rare	—	—	—	—	—	—
16Z6 TS Rare	—	—	—	—	—	—

Note: Peus Auction #379 4-2005 1626 XF realized $18,100.

KM# 100 GOLDGULDEN

3.5000 g., 0.9860 Gold 0.1109 oz. AGW **Ruler:** Wilhelm V **Obv:** Bust of Wilhelm V right in inner circle **Obv. Legend:** WILHELM • D • G• LAND • HASS • A • H • C • C • D • Z • **Rev:** Hessian arms in Spanish shield, date in legend **Rev. Legend:** VNO NOLENTE HUMILIS LEVABOR

Date	Mintage	VG	F	VF	XF	Unc
1627 Rare	—	—	—	—	—	—

KM# 101 GOLDGULDEN

3.5000 g., 0.9860 Gold 0.1109 oz. AGW **Ruler:** Wilhelm V **Obv:** Head right, date as 1-6/2-7 **Obv. Legend:** WILHELM9 • D: G: LAND: HASS: ADM: HIR **Rev:** Hessian arms in Spanish shield

Date	Mintage	VG	F	VF	XF	Unc
1627 Rare	—	—	—	—	—	—

Note: Auction Peus #379, 2004 VF realized $14,500.

KM# 110 GOLDGULDEN

3.5000 g., 0.9860 Gold 0.1109 oz. AGW **Ruler:** Wilhelm V **Obv:** Hessian arms in Spanish shield **Obv. Legend:** WILHELM • D • G • L[AND] • HASS • [A • H •] C • C • D • Z • E • N **Rev:** Tree in storm, no houses **Rev. Legend:** DEO • VOLENTE • HUMILIS • LEVABOR • **Note:** Varieties exist.

Date	Mintage	VG	F	VF	XF	Unc
(16)Z8 TS	—	400	800	1,600	2,800	—
1629 TS	—	400	800	1,600	2,800	—
1630 TS	—	400	800	1,600	2,800	—
1631 TS	—	400	800	1,600	2,800	—
163Z TS	—	400	800	1,600	2,800	—
1633 TS	—	400	800	1,600	2,800	—
1634	—	400	800	1,600	2,800	—

KM# 130 GOLDGULDEN

3.5000 g., 0.9860 Gold 0.1109 oz. AGW **Ruler:** Wilhelm V **Obv:** Hessian arms in Spanish shield **Obv. Legend:** WILHELM • D • G • LAND • HASS • C • C • D • Z • E • N **Rev:** Tree in storm, 2 houses **Note:** Date placement varieties exist.

Date	Mintage	VG	F	VF	XF	Unc
1631	—	400	800	1,600	2,800	—
163Z	—	400	800	1,600	2,800	—

KM# 144 GOLDGULDEN

3.5000 g., 0.9860 Gold 0.1109 oz. AGW **Ruler:** Wilhelm V **Obv:** Hessian arms in Spanish shield, date above **Obv. Legend:** WILHELM • D • G • LAND • HASS • C • C • D • Z • E • N **Rev:** Tree in storm, no houses **Rev. Legend:** IEHOVA • VOLENTE • HUMILIS • LEVABOR

Date	Mintage	VG	F	VF	XF	Unc
1633	—	400	800	1,600	2,800	—
1633 TS	—	400	800	1,600	2,800	—
1634	—	400	800	1,600	2,800	—
1634 TS	—	400	800	1,600	2,800	—

KM# 156 GOLDGULDEN

3.5000 g., 0.9860 Gold 0.1109 oz. AGW **Ruler:** Wilhelm V **Obv:** Hessian lion in Spanish shield, roses flanking **Obv. Legend:** WILHEL[M]: D • G • LAND • HASS • C • C • D • Z • E • N **Rev:** Willow tree in storm, no houses **Rev. Legend:** IEHOVA VOLENTE HUMILIS LEVABOR

Date	Mintage	VG	F	VF	XF	Unc
(1)635 clover	—	550	1,000	2,200	4,400	—
(16)35 clover	—	550	1,000	2,200	4,400	—
(1)63 clover	—	550	1,000	2,200	4,400	—
1636 clover	—	550	1,000	2,200	4,400	—
(1)637	—	550	1,000	2,200	4,400	—
1637 clover	—	550	1,000	2,200	4,400	—

KM# 157 GOLDGULDEN

3.5000 g., 0.9860 Gold 0.1109 oz. AGW **Ruler:** Wilhelm V **Obv:** Hessian lion in Spanish shield, roses flanking, date above **Obv. Legend:** WILHEL[M]: D • G • LAND • HASS • C • C • D • Z • E • N **Rev:** Tree in storm, 2 houses **Rev. Legend:** IEHOVA VOLENTE HUMILIS LEVABOR

Date	Mintage	VG	F	VF	XF	Unc
1637 below lion	—	550	1,000	2,200	4,400	—
1637 behind lion	—	550	1,000	2,200	4,400	—

KM# 185 GOLDGULDEN

3.5000 g., 0.9860 Gold 0.1109 oz. AGW **Ruler:** Wilhelm V **Obv:** Hessian lion in Spanish shield, date as 1-6/3-7 **Obv. Legend:** WILHEL: D: G: LAND: HASS: COM: C: D: Z: E: N: **Rev:** Tree in storm, 4 houses **Rev. Legend:** IEHOVA VOLENTE HUMILIS LEVABOR

Date	Mintage	VG	F	VF	XF	Unc
1637 G two crosshooks K	—	550	1,000	2,200	4,400	—

KM# 186.1 GOLDGULDEN

3.5000 g., 0.9860 Gold 0.1109 oz. AGW **Ruler:** Wilhelm VI **Obv:** Crowned Hessian lion left, star before **Obv. Legend:** WILHE[LM] • D • G • LAND • HASS • C • C • D • Z • E • N **Rev:** Tree in storm, 3 or 4 houses **Rev. Legend:** IEHOVA VOLENTE HUMILIS LEVABOR

Date	Mintage	VG	F	VF	XF	Unc
1637 clover	—	650	1,250	2,500	4,800	—
1637 G crossed pothooks K	—	650	1,250	2,500	4,800	—
1638	—	650	1,250	2,500	4,800	—
1638 LH	—	—	—	—	—	—
1638 GK	—	—	—	—	—	—
1639 GK	—	—	—	—	—	—

KM# 186.2 GOLDGULDEN

3.5000 g., 0.9860 Gold 0.1109 oz. AGW **Ruler:** Wilhelm VI **Obv:** Hessian lion, star in front **Rev:** Tree in storm, 3 houses **Rev. Legend:** VNO VOLENTE HUMILIS LEVABOR

Date	Mintage	VG	F	VF	XF	Unc
1637 GXK	—	650	1,250	2,500	4,800	—

KM# 131 DUCAT

3.5000 g., 0.9860 Gold 0.1109 oz. AGW **Ruler:** Wilhelm V **Subject:** Death of Moritz **Obv:** 7-line inscription, Arabic numeral date **Obv. Legend:** MAURITI9 • HASS: LAND • DEO • ET • IMPERIO • FIDUS • **Rev:** Crossed flags, branches above, bell and hourglass below **Rev. Legend:** MAURITI • MEMENTO MORI • CONSIL • E • VIRTUTE

Date	Mintage	VG	F	VF	XF	Unc
1632 TS Rare	—	—	—	—	—	—

KM# 189 DUCAT

3.5000 g., 0.9860 Gold 0.1109 oz. AGW **Ruler:** Wilhelm V **Subject:** Death of Wilhelm V **Obv:** 10-line inscription, Arabic numeral date **Rev:** Tree in storm, 4, 5, or 6 houses

Date	Mintage	VG	F	VF	XF	Unc
1637	—	300	650	1,250	2,400	—
1637 G crossed pothooks K	—	300	650	1,250	2,400	—
1637 GK	—	—	—	—	—	—

Note: Reported, not confirmed

Date	Mintage	VG	F	VF	XF	Unc
1637 crossed pothooks	—	300	650	1,250	2,400	—
1637 AG	—	300	650	1,250	2,400	—
1637 TS	—	—	—	—	—	—

Note: Reported, not confirmed

KM# 190 DUCAT

3.5000 g., 0.9860 Gold 0.1109 oz. AGW **Ruler:** Wilhelm VI **Subject:** Death of Amalie Elizabeth von Hanau, Wife of Wilhelm V **Obv:** Crowned Hessian diamond arms in laurel wreath **Obv. Legend:** AMELIA ELIZABET • LANDGR • ZU HES voRM • U • REGENTIN **Rev:** Mountain with miner in mine, heart and sun above, clouds and storm flanking **Rev. Legend:** WIEDER MACHT UNDT LIST • MEIN FELS GOTT IST •

Date	Mintage	VG	F	VF	XF	Unc
ND(1651) AG Rare	—	—	—	—	—	—

Note: Only 3 pieces known. Auction Peus 383, 2005, VF realized $11,600.

KM# 233 DUCAT

3.5000 g., 0.9860 Gold 0.1109 oz. AGW **Ruler:** Wilhelm VI **Obv:** Crowned 7-fold Hessian arms in ornamented shield date as 1-6/5-2 **Obv. Legend:** WILHELM9: D • G • LAND: HAS: PRIN: HERSF: C • C • D • Z • N • ET SCHAW **Rev:** Sailing ship **Rev. Legend:** VELA VENTIS HIS LEVANTUR

Date	Mintage	VG	F	VF	XF	Unc
1652	—	650	1,250	2,500	4,800	—
1653	—	—	—	—	—	—

Note: Reported, not confirmed

KM# 255 DUCAT

3.5000 g., 0.9860 Gold 0.1109 oz. AGW **Ruler:** Wilhelm VI **Obv:** Bust of Wilhelm VI right in inner circle **Obv. Legend:** WILHELM • D • G • LAND • HASS • PR • H • C • C • Z • N • ET • SCH **Rev:** Crowned arms, date in legend **Rev. Legend:** FIDE ET IUSTITIA

Date	Mintage	VG	F	VF	XF	Unc
1661 Rare	—	—	—	—	—	—
1663 Rare	—	—	—	—	—	—

Note: Auction UBS 69, 2007, VF relazied $12,250

KM# 265 DUCAT

3.5000 g., 0.9860 Gold 0.1109 oz. AGW **Ruler:** Wilhelm VI **Subject:** Death of Wilhelm VI **Obv:** Facing bust **Rev:** 9-line inscription, Arabic numeral date **Rev. Legend:** PIETATE • FIDE • ET • IUSTITIA

Date	Mintage	VG	F	VF	XF	Unc
1663	—	—	—	—	—	—

Note: Reported, not confirmed

KM# 276 DUCAT

3.5000 g., 0.9860 Gold 0.1109 oz. AGW **Ruler:** Wilhelm VII **Obv:** Bust of Hedwig Sophie right in inner circle **Obv. Legend:** HEDWIG • SOPHIA • V: G: G: L: Z: H: G: A: C: S: D: M: Z: B: W: V: V: REGENTIN **Rev:** Terrestrial globe hanging on a heart, sword cuts the rope **Rev. Legend:** DISSOLVER

Date	Mintage	VG	F	VF	XF	Unc
1669 Rare	—	—	—	—	—	—

Note: Two pieces known. Auction Peus 383, 2005, XF realized $29,000

KM# 289 DUCAT

3.5000 g., 0.9860 Gold 0.1109 oz. AGW **Ruler:** Wilhelm VII **Subject:** Death of Wilhelm VII **Obv:** Helmeted Hessian arms in inner circle **Rev:** 8-line inscription

Date	Mintage	VG	F	VF	XF	Unc
1670 Rare	—	—	—	—	—	—

KM# 299 DUCAT

3.5000 g., 0.9860 Gold 0.1109 oz. AGW **Ruler:** Karl **Obv:** 10-line inscription, Arabic numeral date **Rev:** View of Edder river and surrounding landscape **Rev. Legend:** AN • GOTTES • SEGEN • IST • ALLES • GELEGEN

Date	Mintage	VG	F	VF	XF	Unc
1677 Rare	—	—	—	—	—	—

KM# 323 DUCAT

3.5000 g., 0.9860 Gold 0.1109 oz. AGW **Ruler:** Karl **Obv:** Crowned Hessian arms in oval, date below **Obv. Legend:** CAROLUS • D • G • H • L • PR • H • C • C • D • Z • N • ET • S **Rev:** Swan on pedestal **Rev. Legend:** CANDIDE ET CONSTANTER **Note:** Similar to medal (former 1 Thaler), KM#322.

Date	Mintage	VG	F	VF	XF	Unc
1686 IVF Rare	—	—	—	—	—	—

KM# 341 DUCAT

3.5000 g., 0.9860 Gold 0.1109 oz. AGW **Ruler:** Karl **Obv:** Bust right **Obv. Legend:** CAROL • D • G • HASS • LANDG • **Rev:** Crowned double, mirror-image C monogram, date above

Date	Mintage	VG	F	VF	XF	Unc
1693	—	—	—	—	—	—

Note: Reported, not confirmed

KM# 240 1-1/4 DUCAT

4.3750 g., 0.9860 Gold 0.1387 oz. AGW **Ruler:** Wilhelm VI **Obv:** Crowned 7-fold Hessian arms in ornamented shield **Obv. Legend:** WILHELM9: D G LANDG: HASS PRIN • HERSF • C • C • D • Z • N • T: SCHA **Rev:** Sailing ship **Rev. Legend:** VELA VENTIS HIS LEVANTUR

Date	Mintage	VG	F	VF	XF	Unc
1654 AG Rare	—	—	—	—	—	—

KM# 132 2 DUCAT

7.0000 g., 0.9860 Gold 0.2219 oz. AGW **Ruler:** Wilhelm V **Subject:** Death of Mortiz **Obv:** 7-line inscription Arabic numeral date **Rev:** Crossed flags, branches above, bell and hourglass below **Rev. Legend:** MAURITI MEMENTO MORI • CONSI: E: VIRTU

Date	Mintage	VG	F	VF	XF	Unc
1632 TS Rare	—	—	—	—	—	—

KM# 133 2 DUCAT

7.0000 g., 0.9860 Gold 0.2219 oz. AGW **Ruler:** Wilhelm V **Obv:** Arms divide date in inner circle **Rev:** Willow tree bending in storm in inner circle

Date	Mintage	VG	F	VF	XF	Unc
1632	—	—	—	—	—	—

Note: Reported, not confirmed

KM# 191 2 DUCAT

7.0000 g., 0.9860 Gold 0.2219 oz. AGW **Ruler:** Wilhelm V **Obv:** Crowned Hessian lion in Spanish shield, date as 1-6/3-7 **Obv. Legend:** WILHEL: D: G: LAND: HASS: COM: C: D: Z: E: N: **Rev:** Willow tree bending in storm **Rev. Legend:** IEHOVA VOLENTE HUMILIS LEVABOR

Date	Mintage	VG	F	VF	XF	Unc
1637 GK Rare	—	—	—	—	—	—

KM# 192 2 DUCAT

7.0000 g., 0.9860 Gold 0.2219 oz. AGW **Ruler:** Wilhelm V **Subject:** Death of Wilhelm V **Obv:** 10-line inscription Arabic numeral date **Rev:** Tree in storm, 4 houses **Rev. Legend:** VNO VOLENTE HUMILIS LEVABOR

Date	Mintage	VG	F	VF	XF	Unc
1637 GK crossed pothooks Rare	—	—	—	—	—	—

Note: Some read GK as GR due to poor die engraving

KM# 223 2 DUCAT

7.0000 g., 0.9860 Gold 0.2219 oz. AGW **Ruler:** Wilhelm VI **Subject:** Death of Amalie Elisabeth von Hanau, Wife of Wilhelm V **Obv:** Arms in laurel wreath **Rev:** Mountain with miner in mine, heart and sun above, slouds and storm flanking **Rev. Legend:** WIDER MACHT UND LIST MEIN FELS GOTT IST

Date	Mintage	VG	F	VF	XF	Unc
ND(1651)	—	—	—	—	—	—

Note: Reported, not confirmed

KM# 234 2 DUCAT
7.0000 g., 0.9860 Gold 0.2219 oz. AGW **Ruler:** Wilhelm VI **Obv:** Hessian arms **Rev:** Sailing ship **Note:** Similar to 1 Goldgulden, KM#233.

Date	Mintage	VG	F	VF	XF	Unc
1652 Rare	—	—	—	—	—	—

KM# 312 2 DUCAT
7.0000 g., 0.9860 Gold 0.2219 oz. AGW **Ruler:** Karl **Subject:** Death of Hedwig Sophia, Regend for Wilhelm VII **Obv:** Hessian and Brandenburg arms in divided crowned shield **Obv. Legend:** HEDWIGIS SOPHIA HASS • L • PR • H • HAT • PR • ELECT • BRANDENB • **Rev:** 7-line inscription and date

Date	Mintage	VG	F	VF	XF	Unc
1683	—	—	—	—	—	—

Note: Reported, not confirmed

KM# 313 2 DUCAT
7.0000 g., 0.9860 Gold 0.2219 oz. AGW **Ruler:** Karl **Subject:** Death of Elizabeth Henrietta, Wife of Karl **Obv:** Bust of Elizabeth Henrietta right **Obv. Legend:** HENRIETTA ELISABETA... **Rev:** Crown on pedestal

Date	Mintage	VG	F	VF	XF	Unc
1683 Rare	—	—	—	—	—	—

KM# 243 3 DUCAT
10.5000 g., 0.9860 Gold 0.3328 oz. AGW **Ruler:** Wilhelm VI **Obv:** Crowned manifold arms in baroque frame divide date at 1-6/5-5 **Obv. Legend:** WILHELM9 • DG • LANDG: HASS • PRIN • HERSF • CO: CA • DI • ZI • ET • SCHAW **Rev:** Sailing ship left **Rev. Legend:** VELA VENTIS HIS LEVANTUR

Date	Mintage	VG	F	VF	XF	Unc
1655 AG Rare	—	—	—	—	—	—

Note: Reported, not confirmed

KM# 102 4 DUCAT
14.0000 g., 0.9860 Gold 0.4438 oz. AGW **Ruler:** Moritz **Obv:** Crowned Hessian lion left **Obv. Legend:** MAUR • D • G • LANDG • HASS • C • C • D • Z • E • N **Rev:** Crossed flags, branches above, bell and hourglass below **Rev. Legend:** CONSILIO ET VIRTUTE MON • NOVA IM

Date	Mintage	VG	F	VF	XF	Unc
1627 Rare	—	—	—	—	—	—

KM# 194 4 DUCAT
14.0000 g., 0.9860 Gold 0.4438 oz. AGW **Ruler:** Wilhelm V **Subject:** Death of Wilhelm V **Obv:** 9-line inscription, Arabic numeral date **Obv. Legend:** WILHELM: V • DICT9 • CONSTANS • HASS • LANDGRVIVS **Rev:** Palm tree in storm, 4 houses **Rev. Legend:** VNO VOLENTE HUMILIS LEVABOR

Date	Mintage	VG	F	VF	XF	Unc
1637 GK crossed pothooks Rare	—	—	—	—	—	—

KM# 278 4 DUCAT
14.0000 g., 0.9860 Gold 0.4438 oz. AGW **Ruler:** Wilhelm VII **Subject:** Death of Hedwig Sophie **Obv:** Hessian and Brandenburg arms in divided crowned shield **Obv. Legend:** HEDWIG • SOPHIA • V • G • G... **Rev:** Terrestrial globe hanging on a heat, sword cuts the rope **Rev. Legend:** DISSOLVER **Note:** Similar to 1 Thaler, KM#273.

Date	Mintage	VG	F	VF	XF	Unc
1669 Rare	—	—	—	—	—	—

Note: Reported, not confirmed

KM# 244 5 DUCAT (1/2 Portugalöser)
17.5000 g., 0.9860 Gold 0.5547 oz. AGW **Ruler:** Wilhelm VI **Obv:** Crowned Hessian arms, date as 1-6/5-5 **Rev:** Sailing ship **Rev. Legend:** VELA VENTIS HIS LAVABOR

Date	Mintage	VG	F	VF	XF	Unc
1655	—	—	—	—	—	—

Note: Reported, not confirmed

KM# 111 6 DUCAT
21.0000 g., 0.9860 Gold 0.6657 oz. AGW **Ruler:** Wilhelm V **Obv:** Hessian arms in Spanish shield, 3 helmets above **Rev:** Palm tree in storm, date in legend

Date	Mintage	VG	F	VF	XF	Unc
1628	—	—	—	—	—	—

Note: Reported, not confirmed

KM# 150 6 DUCAT
21.0000 g., 0.9860 Gold 0.6657 oz. AGW **Ruler:** Wilhelm V **Obv:** Bust of Wilhelm V right, date in field **Rev:** Palm tree in storm **Rev. Legend:** IEHOVA...

Date	Mintage	VG	F	VF	XF	Unc
1634	—	—	—	—	—	—

Note: Reported, not confirmed

PATTERNS

Including off metal strikes

KM#	Date	Mintage	Identification	Mkt Val
PnA1	1610	—	4 Heller. Gold. KM#5.	—
Pn2	1610	—	Thaler. Gold. KM#19.	—
Pn3	1628 TS	—	Thaler. Tin. KM#98.	—
Pn4	1634 TS	—	Thaler. Tin. KM#115.	—
Pn5	1638 LH	—	1/2 Thaler. Gold. KM#197.	—
Pn6	1651 AG	—	1/2 Thaler. Gold. KM#219.	—
Pn7	1669	—	Thaler. Gold. KM#274.	—
Pn8	1681	—	3 Heller. Gold. KM#291.	—
Pn9	1686	—	Ducat. Copper. KM#323.	—
Pn10	1686	—	Ducat. Gold. KM#323.	—

HESSE-DARMSTADT

Established by the division of the Landgraviate of Hesse in 1567, Hesse-Darmstadt was the territorially smaller of the two surviving branches of the family. The ruler was raised to the rank of Grand Duke in 1806. In 1815 the Congress of Vienna awarded Hesse-Darmstadt the cities of Mainz and Worms, which were relinquished along with the newly acquired Hesse-Homburg, to the Prussians in 1866. It became part of the German Empire in 1871.

RULERS

Ludwig V, 1596-1626
Georg II, 1626-1661
Ludwig VI, 1661-1678
Ludwig VII, 1678
Ernst Ludwig, 1678-1739

MINT MARKS

N Nidda, 1622

MINT OFFICIALS' INITIALS

Initial	Date	Name
HIS	1619	Johann Schenckh, warden
	1623	Mintmaster
IW	1625-28	Jacob Wiesener (Wiesemann) in Nidda
IS	1654-87	Johann Sartorius
ICF	1681	Johann Carl Falkner
ID	1691-93	Johann Dittmar
IAR, AR	1693-1705	Johann Adam Rephun
GLC	1695-1708	Gabriel Le Clerc, die-cutter and medailleur in Cassel
ICR, R	1696-1707	J.C. Roth, medailleur

LANDGRAVIATE

REGULAR COINAGE

KM# 13 PFENNIG (Heller)
Silver **Ruler:** Ludwig V **Obv:** Cross with M-H / N-F in angles **Note:** Schussel-type.

Date	Mintage	VG	F	VF	XF	Unc
ND(1623-26)	—	27.00	60.00	120	180	—

Note: Minted for coin union of 1623-1626 between Mainz, Hesse-Darmstadt, Nassau and Frankfurt. See Frankfurt, 2 Kreuzer for additional coinage mandated by the union

KM# 14 PFENNIG (Heller)
Silver **Ruler:** Georg II **Obv:** Shield with wheel of Mainz left of Hessian lion. **Note:** Schussel-type.

Date	Mintage	VG	F	VF	XF	Unc
ND(1637-39)	—	45.00	80.00	160	325	—

Note: In 1636 Frankfurt and Nassau finished the cooperation with the union of 1623 because of bad quality of product from the mint at Mainz. Mainz and Hesse-Darmstadt continued with the cooperation until 1639. So it is likely that this Pfennig was minted for the same reason after 1636.

KM# 21.1 PFENNIG (Heller)
Billon **Ruler:** Ludwig V **Obv:** Hessian lion on shield, Z-H flanking, L-L above, date below **Note:** Uniface. Schussle-type. (LLZH = Ludwig Landgrav zu Hessen).

Date	Mintage	VG	F	VF	XF	Unc
1622	—	30.00	60.00	120	180	—
ND	—	—	—	—	—	—

Note: Reported, not confirmed

KM# 21.2 PFENNIG (Heller)
Silver **Ruler:** Georg II **Obv:** Lion in spanish shield **Note:** Schussel-type.

Date	Mintage	VG	F	VF	XF	Unc
ND(1654-61) IS Rare	—	—	—	—	—	—

KM# 45 PFENNIG (Heller)
Silver **Ruler:** Georg II **Obv:** Hessian lion in Spanish shield divides date upwards on left and downwards on right, mintmasters initials above. **Note:** Uniface.

Date	Mintage	VG	F	VF	XF	Unc
1656 IS	—	30.00	65.00	120	240	—
1658 IS Rare	—	—	—	—	—	—
ND(1654-61) IS Rare	—	—	—	—	—	—
1659	—	—	—	—	—	—

Note: Reported, not confirmed

KM# A72 PFENNIG (Heller)
Billon **Ruler:** Ernst Ludwig **Obv:** Hessian lion in crowned shield, H-D above, date in diameter as 1-6 / 8-Z **Note:** Schussel type. Uniface.

Date	Mintage	VG	F	VF	XF	Unc
168Z IS Rare	—	—	—	—	—	—

KM# 72 PFENNIG (Heller)
Silver **Ruler:** Ernst Ludwig **Obv:** Hessian lion in crowned shield divides date and mintmasters initials at 1-6 / 8-5 / I-S. **Note:** Uniface. Schussel-type.

Date	Mintage	VG	F	VF	XF	Unc
1685 IS	—	25.00	60.00	140	280	—
1692	—	25.00	60.00	140	280	—
1693	—	25.00	60.00	140	280	—
1698	—	25.00	60.00	140	280	—

KM# 84 PFENNIG (Heller)
Silver **Ruler:** Ernst Ludwig **Obv:** Hessian lion in shield, H-D above, date below.

Date	Mintage	VG	F	VF	XF	Unc
1692	—	20.00	55.00	125	250	—
1693	—	20.00	55.00	95.00	190	—
1696	—	20.00	55.00	95.00	190	—
1699	—	—	—	—	—	—

KM# 83 PFENNIG (Heller)
Silver **Ruler:** Ernst Ludwig **Rev:** Hessian lion in shield, rose above, date beside as 1-6 / 9-3 **Note:** Uniface.

Date	Mintage	VG	F	VF	XF	Unc
1693	—	45.00	100	175	320	—

KM# 88 PFENNIG (Heller)
Silver **Ruler:** Ernst Ludwig **Obv:** Hessian lion in Spanish shield, date below. **Note:** Schussel-type.

Date	Mintage	VG	F	VF	XF	Unc
1699	—	25.00	55.00	100	190	—

KM# 15 2 PFENNIG (2 Heller)
Silver **Ruler:** Ludwig V **Obv:** Hessian lion divides L-L / Z-H **Rev. Legend:** II/ PFENIG / date

Date	Mintage	VG	F	VF	XF	Unc
1621	—	50.00	110	220	450	—
1622	—	50.00	110	220	450	—

KM# 41.1 ALBUS
Silver **Ruler:** Georg II **Obv:** Hessian lion in laurel wreath **Rev:** Value and date within legend **Rev. Legend:** GEORG LANDGRAF ZV HESS around *I*/ ALBVS

Date	Mintage	VG	F	VF	XF	Unc
1654 IS	—	10.00	25.00	60.00	120	—
1655 IS	—	10.00	25.00	60.00	120	—
1655	—	—	—	—	—	—
1656 IS	—	10.00	25.00	60.00	120	—
1657 IS	—	10.00	25.00	60.00	120	—

KM# 41.2 ALBUS
Silver **Ruler:** Georg II **Obv:** Hessian lion in inner circle, laurel wreath around **Rev:** Value and date within legend **Rev. Legend:** GEORG LANDGRAF ZV HESS around *I*/ ALBVS **Note:** Varieties exist: with or without berries in the laurel wreath, or Small crown on lion within or breaking circle.

Date	Mintage	VG	F	VF	XF	Unc
1656 IS	—	10.00	25.00	60.00	120	—
1657 IS	—	10.00	25.00	60.00	120	—
1658 IS	—	12.00	25.00	60.00	120	—

KM# 71.1 ALBUS
Silver **Ruler:** Ernst Ludwig **Obv:** Hessian lion in shield divides I-S, HESS DARM above, all within laurel wreath **Rev:** I/ ALBVS and date within laurel wreath **Note:** Varieties exist.

Date	Mintage	VG	F	VF	XF	Unc
1680 IS	—	10.00	22.00	55.00	110	—
1681 IS	—	10.00	22.00	55.00	110	—
1682 IS	—	8.00	18.00	45.00	90.00	—
1683 IS	—	8.00	18.00	45.00	90.00	—
1684 IS	—	8.00	18.00	45.00	90.00	—
1687 IS	—	8.00	18.00	45.00	90.00	—

KM# 71.2 ALBUS
Silver **Ruler:** Ernst Ludwig **Obv:** Hessian lion in shield within laurel wreath, rose above **Rev:** *I*/ ALBVS/ date within laurel wreath

Date	Mintage	VG	F	VF	XF	Unc
1686	—	10.00	25.00	55.00	110	—

KM# 71.3 ALBUS
Silver **Ruler:** Ernst Ludwig **Obv:** Hessian lion in shield, HES DAR above, all within laurel wreath **Rev:** *I*/ ALBVS/ date within laurel wreath **Note:** Legend varieties exist.

Date	Mintage	VG	F	VF	XF	Unc
1692 ID	—	10.00	22.00	55.00	110	—
1692	—	10.00	22.00	55.00	110	—
1693 IA-R	—	8.00	18.00	45.00	90.00	—
1694 I.A.R.	—	8.00	18.00	45.00	90.00	—
1695 I.A.R.	—	8.00	18.00	45.00	90.00	—

KM# 71.4 ALBUS
Silver **Ruler:** Ernst Ludwig **Obv:** Hessian lion in shield, H.D. above, all within laurel wreath **Rev:** I/ ALBUS/ date/ mint mark, all within laurel wreath **Note:** Varieties exist with Spanish or French shield.

Date	Mintage	VG	F	VF	XF	Unc
1697 IAR	—	8.00	20.00	50.00	100	—
1699 IAR	—	8.00	20.00	50.00	100	—

KM# 82 2 ALBUS

Silver **Ruler:** Ernst Ludwig **Obv:** Manifold Hessian arms in Spanish shield, HD above, all within laurel wreath **Rev:** II/ ALBUS/ date/ mint mark, all within laurel wreath **Note:** Varieties exit.

Date	Mintage	VG	F	VF	XF	Unc
1692 ID	—	10.00	20.00	50.00	100	—
1693 IAR	—	9.00	18.00	40.00	80.00	—
1694 IAR	—	9.00	18.00	40.00	80.00	—
1695 IAR	—	9.00	18.00	40.00	80.00	—
1697 IAR	—	9.00	18.00	40.00	80.00	—

KM# 19.1 KREUZER

Silver **Ruler:** Ludwig V **Obv:** Hessian lion divides H-LZ, L above, N below

Date	Mintage	VG	F	VF	XF	Unc
1622 N	—	20.00	40.00	75.00	125	—

KM# 19.2 KREUZER

Silver **Ruler:** Ludwig V **Rev. Legend:** KREVT/ ZER

Date	Mintage	VG	F	VF	XF	Unc
1622 N	—	20.00	40.00	75.00	125	—

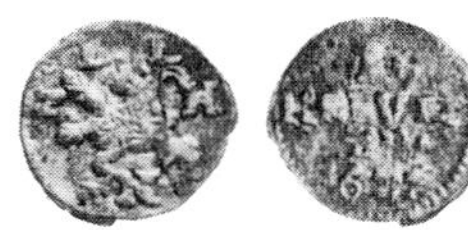

KM# 17.1 KREUZER

Silver **Ruler:** Ludwig V **Obv:** Hessian lion divides L-L / Z-H **Rev. Legend:** *I*/ KREVTZ/ ER/ date **Mint:** Darmstadt

Date	Mintage	VG	F	VF	XF	Unc
16ZZ	—	50.00	110	220	450	—
1622 D	—	50.00	110	220	450	—
1622	—	50.00	110	220	450	—

KM# 17.2 KREUZER

Silver **Ruler:** Ludwig V **Rev. Legend:** I/ KREVT/ ZER **Mint:** Darmstadt

Date	Mintage	VG	F	VF	XF	Unc
1622	—	50.00	110	220	450	—
16ZZ	—	50.00	110	220	450	—

KM# 17.3 KREUZER

Silver **Ruler:** Ludwig V **Rev. Legend:** I/KREV/TZER **Mint:** Darmstadt

Date	Mintage	VG	F	VF	XF	Unc
1622	—	50.00	110	220	450	—
16ZZ	—	50.00	110	220	450	—

KM# 18.1 KREUZER

Silver **Ruler:** Ludwig V **Obv:** Hessian lion divides H-L, L above, N below **Rev. Legend:** .I./ KREVTZ/ ER/ date **Mint:** Nidda **Note:** Varieties exist

Date	Mintage	VG	F	VF	XF	Unc
1622N	—	40.00	85.00	175	350	—
16ZZN	—	40.00	85.00	175	350	—
1622 Rare	—	—	—	—	—	—

KM# 18.2 KREUZER

Silver **Ruler:** Ludwig V **Obv:** Hessian lion divides Z-H, LL above, N below **Rev. Legend:** KREV/ TZER **Mint:** Nidda

Date	Mintage	VG	F	VF	XF	Unc
16ZZN Rare	—	—	—	—	—	—

KM# 18.3 KREUZER

Silver **Ruler:** Ludwig V **Rev. Legend:** KREVTZ/ ER **Mint:** Nidda

Date	Mintage	VG	F	VF	XF	Unc
16ZZN	—	40.00	85.00	175	350	

KM# 70.1 KREUZER

Silver **Ruler:** Ernst Ludwig **Obv:** Hessian lion in French shield between laurel branches, H.D above (1699 has Spanish shield) **Rev:** Value and date between laurel branches **Rev. Legend:** *I*/ KREU/ TZER

Date	Mintage	VG	F	VF	XF	Unc
1680 IS	—	9.00	20.00	45.00	95.00	—
1681 IS	—	9.00	20.00	45.00	95.00	—
1682 IS	—	9.00	20.00	45.00	95.00	—
1683 IS	—	9.00	20.00	45.00	95.00	—
1684	—	—	—	—	—	—
Note: Reported, not confirmed						
1689 IS	—	9.00	20.00	45.00	95.00	—
1699 IAR	—	8.00	18.00	40.00	90.00	—

KM# 73 KREUZER

Silver **Ruler:** Ernst Ludwig **Obv:** Hessian lion (with crown) in Spanish shield, L-E beside, laurel wreath around **Rev:** I/ KREV / TZER/ 1685

Date	Mintage	VG	F	VF	XF	Unc
1685 Rare	—	—	—	—	—	—

Note: Reported, not confirmed

KM# 74 KREUZER

Silver **Ruler:** Ernst Ludwig **Obv:** Hessian lion (uncrowned) in Spanish shield, S-P besides, laurel wreath around **Rev:** I/ KREU/ TZER/ 1686/ LBM

Date	Mintage	VG	F	VF	XF	Unc
1686 LBM	—	20.00	35.00	65.00	120	—

Note: Reported, not confirmed

KM# 8 3 KREUZER (Groschen)

Silver **Ruler:** Ludwig V **Obv:** Hessian arms in Spanish shield, value (3) above **Obv. Legend:** LVDOVICVS • D • G • LANDGRA: HASS* **Rev:** Hssian helmet, date **Rev. Legend:** IN TE DOMINE CONFIDO

Date	Mintage	VG	F	VF	XF	Unc
1619	—	40.00	100	240	500	—

KM# 10 12 KREUZER (Schreckenberger)

Silver **Ruler:** Ludwig V **Obv:** Hessian arms in Spanish sheild, 12 above **Obv. Legend:** LVDOVICVS • D • G • LANDGRA: HASS •*• **Rev:** Helmet, date in legend

Date	Mintage	VG	F	VF	XF	Unc
1619	—	60.00	130	325	600	—

KM# 65.1 60 KREUZER (Gulden)

Silver **Ruler:** Ludwig VI **Obv:** Bust with long hair right **Obv. Legend:** LVDOVIC • VI • D • G • HASSLANDGRAV • PRINC • HERSF * **Rev:** Crowned arms divides mintmaster initials, date above **Rev. Legend:** FVRSTLICHE HESSIS che landmvntz * **Note:** Tall letters.

Date	Mintage	VG	F	VF	XF	Unc
1674 IS	—	60.00	180	450	900	—

KM# 65.2 60 KREUZER (Gulden)

Silver **Ruler:** Ludwig VI **Obv:** Bust with long hair right **Obv. Legend:** LVDOVIC • VI • D • G • HASS • LANDGRAV • PRINC • HERSF * **Rev:** Crowned arms divides I-S, date above **Rev. Legend:** FVRSTLICHE • HESSISC HE LAND MVNTZ* **Note:** Short letters.

Date	Mintage	VG	F	VF	XF	Unc
1674	—	60.00	180	450	900	—
1674 IS	—	—	—	—	—	—

Note: Reported, not confirmed

KM# A5 1/8 THALER

3.6500 g., Silver, 30 mm. **Subject:** Death of Georg I's second wife, Eleonore von Wurttemberg **Obv:** 6-line inscription within square ornamented with foliage, R.N. date above **Obv. Inscription:** F • ELEONORA/ L • Z • H • G • H • Z •/ W • STARB • XII/ IAN • IHRES/ ALTERS • LXVI/ IHAR **Rev:** 2 shields, Hesse and Wurttemberg, rose above, S below, HW at sides **Note:** Many sources now feel this is a medal.

Date	Mintage	VG	F	VF	XF	Unc
MDCXVIII (1618) Rare	—	—	—	—	—	—

KM# 55 1/8 THALER

Silver **Ruler:** Georg II **Obv:** 6-line inscription with Arabic numeral date **Obv. Legend:** DNI DNI GEORGII II L HPH C C DZ H S Y ET B **Rev:** Oak tree with band reading: AETERNI SACRVM **Rev. Legend:** NVM EXEQ PRIN OPT PH PRVD BENEFI

Date	Mintage	VG	F	VF	XF	Unc
1661	—	300	8,700	1,700	3,500	—

Note: The former 55.1 with Roman numeral date does not exist.

KM# 7 1/4 THALER

Silver **Ruler:** Ludwig V **Obv:** 5 shields of arms in cruciform, Hesse in center, Ziegenhain, Katzenelbogen, Diez. **Obv. Legend:** LVDOVICVS • D • G • LANDGRA: HASSIAE **Rev:** Helmet, date in legend **Rev. Legend:** IN • TE • DOMINO • CONFIDO •

Date	Mintage	VG	F	VF	XF	Unc
1618	—	—	1,300	2,800	6,000	—

KM# 12 1/4 THALER

Silver **Ruler:** Ludwig V **Obv:** 5-fold Hessian arms in Spanish shield, ornaments around **Obv. Legend:** LVDOVICVS: D: G: LANDGRA: HASSI * **Rev:** Hessian helmet, date in legend **Rev. Legend:** IN • TE • DOMINO • CONFIDO •

Date	Mintage	VG	F	VF	XF	Unc
1618	—	—	1,200	2,600	5,500	—
1619	—	—	1,200	2,600	5,500	—
16Z1 Rare	—	—	—	—	—	—

KM# 11 1/4 THALER

Silver **Ruler:** Ludwig V **Obv:** 5-fold Hessian arms **Obv. Legend:** LVDOVICVS • D • G • LANDGRA • HASS **Rev:** Hessian helmet, date in legend **Rev. Legend:** IN • DOMINO • CONFIDO • **Note:** Klippe.

Date	Mintage	VG	F	VF	XF	Unc
1619	—	—	—	—	—	—

Note: Reported, not confirmed

KM# 56 1/4 THALER

Silver **Ruler:** Georg II **Subject:** Death of Georg II **Obv:** 8-line inscription with Roman numeral date **Obv. Legend:** DNI • DNI • GEORGII II • LANDHAS • PR • HERSF • COM CDZHS • Y & B around, in center: NASCITUR / XVII • MART MDCV / OBIT • XI • JVNII / MDC • LXI • VIXIT • AN / NOS LVI • MENSES / III • REGNAVIT • / • ANNOS XXXIV / MENX • X • **Rev:** Oak tree, with band reading AETERNITATI SACRVM **Rev. Legend:** NVM EXEQVIAL • PRINCIPS • OPTIMI • PII • PRVDENTIS • BENEF:

Date	Mintage	VG	F	VF	XF	Unc
MDCLXI (1661)	—	—	400	1,000	2,500	6,000

KM# 26 1/2 THALER

Silver **Ruler:** Ludwig V **Obv:** Bust of Ludwig V right **Obv. Legend:** LUDOUIUS: D: G: LANDGR • HASSIÆ • COM • IN • CA • **Rev:** Hessian arms in Spanish shield, date in legend **Rev. Legend:** IN TE * DOMINE * CONFIDO: **Note:** Legend varieties.

Date	Mintage	VG	F	VF	XF	Unc
1625 IW pothook Rare	—	—	—	—	—	—
1626 IW Rare	—	—	—	—	—	—

KM# 31 1/2 THALER

Silver **Ruler:** Georg II **Obv:** Bust of Georg II right **Obv. Legend:** D • G • GEORGIVS • HASSIÆ • LANDGRAVIVS • **Rev:** Hessian arms in ornaments, date in legend **Rev. Legend:** SECVNDVM • VOLVNTATEM • TVAM • DOMINE • **Note:** 1/4 Thaler Octagonal Klippe.

Date	Mintage	VG	F	VF	XF	Unc
1627 Rare	—	—	—	—	—	—

KM# 57 1/2 THALER

Silver **Ruler:** Georg II **Subject:** Death of Georg II **Obv:** 8-line inscription with Roman numeral date **Obv. Legend:** DNI • DNI • GEORGII • II • LAND • HAS • PR: HERSF: COM CDZ • N • S • Y • ET B + around, in center: NASCITUR / XVII • MAR M • DC • V / OBIT • XI • JVNII • / MDCLXI • VVIXIT • AN / NOS • LVI • MENSES / III • REGNAVIT • ANNOS • XXXIV / MENS • X • **Rev:** Oak tree, with band reading AETERNITATI SACRVM **Rev. Legend:** MVM • EXEQVIAL • PRINCIPIS • OPTIMI • PII • PRVDENTIS • BENEF: +

Date	Mintage	VG	F	VF	XF	Unc
MDCLXI (1661) Rare	—	—	—	—	—	—

KM# 80 1/2 THALER

Silver **Ruler:** Ernst Ludwig **Obv:** Bust right **Obv. Legend:** ERNESTVS • LVDOVICVS • I • D • G • HASS • LANDGRAV • PRINC • HERSF * **Rev:** Hessian arms in oval shield with crown, crown above divides date **Rev. Legend:** MONETA • NOVA • ARGENTEA • DARMSTADINA * **Note:** Legend varieties.

Date	Mintage	VG	F	VF	XF	Unc
1691 Rare	—	—	—	—	—	—
1693 IA-R	—	—	—	—	—	—

Note: Reported, not confirmed

KM# 90 1/2 THALER

Silver **Ruler:** Ernst Ludwig **Obv:** Bust right **Obv. Legend:** ERNEST • LUD • I • D • G • HASS • LANDG • PRINC • HERSF * **Rev:** Hessian arms in German shield with 5 helmets **Rev. Legend:** • MONETA • NOVA • ARGENTEA • DARMSTADINA

Date	Mintage	VG	F	VF	XF	Unc
1696 IA-R Rare	—	—	1,500	3,500	7,500	—

Note: Dates of 1697, 1700 and ND formerly listed with this type have been confirmed as not existing or errors in previous catalog appearances

KM# 91 1/2 THALER

Silver **Ruler:** Ernst Ludwig **Obv:** 7-fold Hessian arms in baroque cartouche supported by 2 miners, sun and clouds above, Roman numeral date below **Obv. Legend:** GOTT • BAUE • DAS • HAUS • HESSEN • DARMSTATT **Rev:** Mining scene, man turning windlass in foreground, sun and 3 fires in background **Rev. Legend:** SO • BLICKEN • DIE ERSTLING • DES • SEGENS • HERFUR * **Note:** Mining 1/2 Thaler.

Date	Mintage	VG	F	VF	XF	Unc
MDCXCVI (1696) GLC	—	—	1,400	3,000	6,500	—
MDCXCVI (1696) IAR-R	—	—	—	—	—	—

Note: Reported, not confirmed

Date	Mintage	VG	F	VF	XF	Unc
MDCXCVI (1696)	—	—	—	—	—	—

Note: Reported, but the small mint mark has probably been missed

KM# 22 THALER

Silver **Ruler:** Ludwig V **Obv:** Bust of Ludwig V right **Obv. Legend:** LVDOUICUS • D: G • LANDG: HASSIÆ: CO • I • CA * **Rev:** Hessian manifold arms in German shield with helmet above, ornaments besides, date in legend **Rev. Legend:** INTE: DOMINE: * : CONFIDO: ANNO **Note:** Dav. #6795.

Date	Mintage	VG	F	VF	XF	Unc
1623	—	300	600	1,000	1,600	—
16Z3	—	300	600	1,000	1,600	—

KM# 23.1 THALER

Silver **Ruler:** Ludwig V **Obv:** Bust right, IHS below shoulder **Obv. Legend:** LVDOVICVS: D: G: LANDG: HASSIÆ • COM: I: CA * **Rev:** Hessian manifold arms in German shield, ornaments beside, 3 helmets above **Rev. Legend:** IN TE: DOMINE: CONFIDO: ANN **Note:** Dav. #6796.

Date	Mintage	VG	F	VF	XF	Unc
1623 IHS	—	250	500	1,000	2,000	—
1623 Rare	—	—	—	—	—	—
16Z3 IHS	—	250	500	1,000	2,000	—
16Z3 Rare	—	—	—	—	—	—

KM# 23.2 THALER

Silver **Ruler:** Ludwig V **Obv:** Bust right, I.W. below shoulder **Note:** Dav. #6797.

Date	Mintage	VG	F	VF	XF	Unc
1625 IW	—	250	500	1,000	2,000	—

KM# 23.3 THALER

Silver **Ruler:** Ludwig V **Obv:** Bust right **Obv. Legend:** LVDOVICVS • D: G • LANDGR • HASSIÆ: COM • IN: CA **Rev:** I-W divided by arms **Rev. Legend:** INTE • DOMINE • CONFIDO ANN **Note:** Dav. #6798.

Date	Mintage	VG	F	VF	XF	Unc
1626 IW pothook	—	400	1,000	2,000	4,000	—
(1)626 IW pothook	—	400	1,000	2,000	4,000	—
(1)6Z6 IW pothook	—	400	1,000	2,000	4,000	—

KM# 29 THALER

Silver **Ruler:** Ludwig V **Subject:** Death of Ludwig V **Obv:** 8-line inscription, Roman numeral date **Obv. Legend:** LUDOVICUS • DICTUS • FIDELIS • HASSIÆ • LANDGRAVIUS • around, in center: NATUS • / XXVI • SEPTEMB • / ANNI • M • D • LXXVII • / MORTUUS • XXVII • / JVLII • ANNI M • D • C • XXVI • REGNAVIT • / ANNOS • XXX • MENS • / V • DIES • XIX • **Rev. Legend:** PATRI • PATRIÆ • IMMORTALITATE • DONATO • around, in center: VIVIT •/ POST • FVNERA •/ VIRTUS **Note:** Dav. #6800.

Date	Mintage	VG	F	VF	XF	Unc
MDCXXVI (1626) Rare	—	—	—	—	—	—

KM# 33 THALER

Silver **Ruler:** Georg II **Obv:** Youthful bust of Georg II right divides date **Rev:** 3 helmets above arms **Note:** Dav. #6801.

Date	Mintage	VG	F	VF	XF	Unc
1627 IW	—	—	—	—	—	—

Note: Reported, not confirmed

KM# 36 THALER

Silver, 35 mm. **Ruler:** Georg II **Subject:** 200th Anniversary, Marburg University **Obv:** Bust right **Rev:** 13-line inscription **Note:** Dav. #6802.

Date	Mintage	VG	F	VF	XF	Unc
1627 Rare	—	—	—	—	—	—

Note: This is currently considered a medal.

KM# 34 THALER

Silver **Ruler:** Georg II **Rev:** Date above helmets **Note:** Dav. #--.

Date	Mintage	VG	F	VF	XF	Unc
1627 IW	—	—	—	—	—	—

Note: Now thought to be an incorrect listing

KM# 37 THALER

Silver **Ruler:** Georg II **Subject:** Death of Anna Margarethe von Diepholz, 1st Wife of Philipp zu Butzbach **Obv:** 8-line inscription, Roman numeral date **Obv. Legend:** NATUS / XXIV • SEPTEMB • / ANNI • M • D • LXXVII • / MORTUUS • XXVII • **Rev:** 2 kneeling females, hand from clouds with crown, to one side figures of Satan and Death

Date	Mintage	VG	F	VF	XF	Unc
1629 Rare	—	—	—	—	—	—

Note: Currently thought to be an issue of Hesse-Butzbach, founded by Philip III (Son of Georg II of Hesse-Darmstadt) in 1609, and returned to Hesse-Darmstadt in 1643 at his death.

KM# 48 THALER

Silver **Ruler:** Georg II **Obv:** Mature bust right **Obv. Legend:** :D: G: GEORGIVS • HASSIÆ • LAND • GRAVIVS • COM: IN • C: **Rev:** 5-fold Hessian arms in Spanish sheild, 3 helmets, date in legend **Rev. Legend:** IS SECVNDVM • VOLVNTATEM • TVAM • DOMINE • **Note:** Dav. #6803.

Date	Mintage	VG	F	VF	XF	Unc
1657 IS Rare	—	—	—	—	—	—
1658	—	—	—	—	—	—

Note: Reported, not confirmed

Date	Mintage	VG	F	VF	XF	Unc
1658 IS Rare	—	—	—	—	—	—

KM# 58 THALER

Silver **Ruler:** Georg II **Subject:** Death of Georg II **Obv:** 8-line inscrption, Roman numeral date **Obv. Legend:** DNI • DNI • GEORGII • II • LAND • HAS • PR: HERSF • COM • C • D • Z • N • S • Y • & • B • + around, in center: NASCITVR / XVII • MART MDC / V • ORBIIT • XI • JVNII / MDC • LXI • VIXIT • AN / NOS LVI MENSES / III REGNAVIT • / ANNOS • XXXIV / MENS • X **Rev:** Oak tree, with band reading AETERNITATI SACRVM **Rev. Legend:** NVM • EXEQVIAL: PRINCIPIS • OPTIMI • PII • PRVDENTIS • BENEFICI + **Note:** Dav. #6805.

Date	Mintage	VG	F	VF	XF	Unc
MDCLXI (1661) Rare	—	—	—	—	—	—

KM# 81 THALER

Silver **Ruler:** Ernst Ludwig **Obv:** Bust of Ernst Ludwig right **Obv. Legend:** ERNESTVS • LVDOVICVS • I • D • G • HASS • LANDGRAV • PRINC • HERSF * **Rev:** 7-fold Hessian arms in oval cartouche, crown divides date **Rev. Legend:** MONETA • NOVA • ARGENTEA • DARMSTADINA * **Note:** Dav. #6806.

Date	Mintage	VG	F	VF	XF	Unc
1691 Rare	—	—	—	—	—	—

KM# 87 THALER

Silver **Ruler:** Ernst Ludwig **Obv:** Bust right **Obv. Legend:** ERNEST • LVD • I • D • G • HASS • LANDGR • PR • HERSF * **Rev:** 7-fold Hessian arms in oval cartouche, crown divides date **Rev. Legend:** MONETA • NOVA • ARGENTEA • DARMSTADINA * **Note:** Dav. #6807.

Date	Mintage	VG	F	VF	XF	Unc
1693 IAR	—	—	—	—	—	—

Note: Reported, not confirmed

KM# 93 THALER

Silver **Ruler:** Ernst Ludwig **Obv:** Bust right **Obv. Legend:** ERNEST • LVD • I • D • G • HASS • LANDGRAV • PRINC • HERSF **Rev:** 7-fold Hessian arms in German shield, 5 helmets above, date divided below **Rev. Legend:** MONETA • NOVA • ARGENTEA • DARMSTADINA **Note:** Dav. #6808.

Date	Mintage	VG	F	VF	XF	Unc
1696 ICR-IAR Rare	—	—	—	—	—	—

KM# 94 THALER

Silver **Ruler:** Ernst Ludwig **Obv:** Two miners supporting 7-fold Hessian arms in baroque cartouche, sun and clouds above, Roman numeral date below **Obv. Legend:** GOTT • BAUE • DAS • HAUS • HESSEN • DARMSTATT • **Rev:** Mining scene, man turning windlass in foregorund, suna dn 3 fires in background **Rev. Legend:** SO • BLICKEN • DIE ERSTLING • DES • SEGENS • HERFUR **Note:** Dav. #6810. Mining Thaler.

Date	Mintage	VG	F	VF	XF	Unc
1696	—	1,500	2,800	5,000	8,000	—
1696 IAR	—	1,500	2,800	5,000	8,000	—
1696 GLC Rare	—	—	—	—	—	—
1696 IAR GLC F Rare	—	—	—	—	—	—
1696 IAR R	—	1,500	2,800	5,000	8,000	—

KM# 95.1 THALER

Silver **Ruler:** Ernst Ludwig **Obv:** Bust right in armor, rosette, R below **Obv. Legend:** ERNEST • LVD • I • D • G • HASS • LANDGR • PRINC • HERSF **Rev:** Hessian arms in baroque oval frame supported by 2 lions, crown divides date, Elephant order and IAR below **Rev. Legend:** MONETA • NOVA • ARGENTEA • DARMSTADINA **Note:** Dav. #6809 and Dav. #6811.

Date	Mintage	VG	F	VF	XF	Unc
1696 ICR-IAR	—	—	1,200	2,500	5,000	—
1697 R-IAR	—	—	1,200	2,500	5,000	—

KM# 95.2 THALER

Silver **Ruler:** Ernst Ludwig **Obv:** Bust right in armor **Obv. Legend:** ERNEST • LVD • I • D • G • HASS • LANDGR • PR • HERSF * **Rev:** 7-fold Hessian arms in baroque oval supported by 2 lions, crown divides date, Elephant order and IAR below **Rev. Legend:** MONETA NOVA ARGENTEA DARMSTADINA **Note:** Dav. #6811A.

Date	Mintage	VG	F	VF	XF	Unc
1697 IAR	—	450	900	2,000	4,000	—

KM# 95.3 THALER

Silver **Ruler:** Ernst Ludwig **Obv:** bust right in armor, with rosette, R below **Obv. Legend:** ERNEST • LVD • I • D • G • HASS • LANDGR • PRINC • HERSF **Rev:** Hessian arms in baroque oval supported by 2 lions, crown divides date, Elephant order below **Rev. Legend:** MONETA • NOVA • ARGENTEA • DARMSTADINA **Note:** Dav. #6812. Varieties exist.

Date	Mintage	VG	F	VF	XF	Unc
1700 R-IAR Rare	—	—	—	—	—	—

KM# 24 2 THALER
Silver **Ruler:** Ludwig V **Note:** Similar to 1 Thaler, KM#22. Dav. #6794.

Date	Mintage	VG	F	VF	XF	Unc
16Z3 Rare	—	—	—	—	—	—

KM# 30 2 THALER
Silver **Ruler:** Ludwig V **Subject:** Death of Ludwig V **Obv:** 8-line inscription with Roman numeral date **Obv. Legend:** LUDOVICUS • DICTUS • FIDELIS • HASSIÆ • LANDGRAVIUS • around, in center NATUS • / XXIV • SEPTEMB • / ANNOS • XXX • MENS • / V • DIES • XIX • **Rev. Legend:** PATRI • PATRIÆ • IMMORTALITATE • DONATO around, in center VIVIT •/ POST • FVNERA •/ VIRTUS **Note:** Dav. #6799. Thick planchet, dies of KM#29.

Date	Mintage	VG	F	VF	XF	Unc
MDCXXVI (1626) Rare	—	—	—	—	—	—

TRADE COINAGE

KM# 59 1/2 DUCAT
1.7500 g., 0.9860 Gold 0.0555 oz. AGW **Ruler:** Georg II **Subject:** Death of Georg II **Obv:** 7-line inscription with Arabic numeral date **Rev:** Oak tree at center

Date	Mintage	VG	F	VF	XF	Unc
1661	—	200	650	1,400	2,800	—

KM# 25 DUCAT
3.5000 g., 0.9860 Gold 0.1109 oz. AGW **Ruler:** Ludwig V **Obv:** Crowned arms in inner circle **Rev:** 3 helmets in inner circle, date in legend

Date	Mintage	VG	F	VF	XF	Unc
1621 Rare	—	—	—	—	—	—
1623	—	—	1,200	2,500	5,000	—

KM# 40 DUCAT
3.5000 g., 0.9860 Gold 0.1109 oz. AGW **Ruler:** Georg II **Obv:** Bust of Georg II left with long hair, in inner circle **Rev:** Arms in inner circle, date in legend

Date	Mintage	VG	F	VF	XF	Unc
1651	—	—	—	—	—	—

Note: Reported, not confirmed

KM# 43 DUCAT
3.5000 g., 0.9860 Gold 0.1109 oz. AGW **Ruler:** Georg II **Obv:** Bearded bust

Date	Mintage	VG	F	VF	XF	Unc
1655	—	650	1,500	3,500	7,000	—
1656	—	600	1,400	3,000	6,000	—
1658	—	650	1,500	3,500	7,000	—

KM# 61 DUCAT
3.5000 g., 0.9860 Gold 0.1109 oz. AGW **Ruler:** Georg II **Subject:** Death of Georg II **Obv:** 7-line inscription, with Roman numeral date **Rev:** Oak tree at center

Date	Mintage	VG	F	VF	XF	Unc
MDCLXI (1661)	—	450	1,000	2,500	5,000	—

KM# 68 DUCAT
3.5000 g., 0.9860 Gold 0.1109 oz. AGW **Ruler:** Ludwig VI **Obv:** Bust of Ludwig VI right **Rev:** Crowned arms, date in legend **Rev. Legend:** INTE DOMINE SPERAVI 1675 clover

Date	Mintage	VG	F	VF	XF	Unc
1675 IS	—	450	1,000	2,800	4,600	—

KM# B139 DUCAT
3.5000 g., Gold **Ruler:** Ernst Ludwig **Obv:** Bust right **Rev:** Lion in a square, crowned EL monogram four times around

Date	Mintage	VG	F	VF	XF	Unc
ND(1696-1707)	—	—	—	—	—	—

KM# A139 25 DUCAT
Gold **Ruler:** Ernst Ludwig **Obv:** Bust right, titles of Ernst Ludwig **Rev:** Ornate oval 6-fold arms with central shield, 5 helmets above

Date	Mintage	Good	VG	F	VF	XF
ND(1696-1707) R Rare	—	—	—	—	—	—

PATTERNS

Including off metal strikes

KM#	Date	Mintage	Identification	Mkt Val
PnA1	1626	—	Thaler. Tin. KM#29.	200
Pn1	1657 IS	—	Albus. Gold. KM#41.	—
PnA2	1674 IS	—	60 Kreuzer. Silver. Thaler size planchet, KM#66.	—
Pn2	1696 GLC-R	—	1/2 Thaler. Lead. KM#91.	—

HESSE-HOMBURG

Located in west central Germany, Hesse-Homburg was created from part of Hesse-Darmstadt in 1622. It had six villages along with Homburg (today Bad Homburg) and is mostly known for its famous landgrave, Friedrich II. Commander of the Brandenburg cavalry, Friedrich II (with the silver leg) won the Battle of Fehrbellin in 1675. Hesse-Homburg was mediatized to Hesse-Darmstadt in 1806 and by 1816 had acquired full sovereignty and the lordship of Meisenheim. The Homburg line became extinct in 1866, and along with Hesse-Darmstadt, was annexed by Prussia.

RULERS
Friedrich I, 1622-1638
Margaretha Elisabeth von Leiningen-Westerburg-Schaumburg, regent, 1638-1650
Ludwig Philipp, 1638-1643
Wilhelm Christof, 1643-1669
Friedrich II, 1681-1708

MINT OFFICIALS' INITIALS

Initial	Date	Name
RA	Ca.1692	Johann Reinhard Arnold

LANDGRAVIATE

REGULAR COINAGE

KM# 6 2 ALBUS
Silver **Ruler:** Friedrich II **Obv:** Arms, HH above, in palm branches **Rev:** II/ ALBUS/ date in laurel wreath **Note:** Varieties exist in thickness of arms.

Date	Mintage	VG	F	VF	XF	Unc
1692	—	140	300	600	1,100	—

KM# 7 2/3 THALER (Gulden)
Silver **Ruler:** Friedrich II **Obv:** Bust right **Rev:** Crowned arms, (2/3) below, date in legend

Date	Mintage	VG	F	VF	XF	Unc
1692 RA	—	—	1,000	2,500	6,000	—

Note: Friedrich without Elephant order

Date	Mintage	VG	F	VF	XF	Unc
1692 Restrike	—	—	—	1,500	2,800	—

Note: Friedrich with Elephant order

KM# 8 2/3 THALER (Gulden)
Silver **Ruler:** Friedrich II **Obv:** Crowned arms, 2/3 below, date in legend **Rev:** Large 2/3 in laurel wreath

Date	Mintage	VG	F	VF	XF	Unc
1692 RA	—	—	—	1,000	2,000	—

Note: See note below KM#9

KM# 9 2/3 THALER (Gulden)
Silver **Ruler:** Friedrich II **Obv:** Crowned arms, (2/3) below, date in legend **Rev:** Large 2/3 in laurel wreath

Date	Mintage	VG	F	VF	XF	Unc
ND	—	—	—	1,000	2,000	—

Note: KM#8-9 are restrikes and die-couplings of KM#7 with Hohenlohe-Schillingsfurst 2/3 Thaler, KM#28. Struck in 1860, the original, although rusty, dies were used

TRADE COINAGE

KM# 5 DUCAT
3.5000 g., 0.9860 Gold 0.1109 oz. AGW **Ruler:** Friedrich II **Obv:** Bust of Friedrich right **Rev:** 2 men right and left of mountain, trying to climb

Date	Mintage	VG	F	VF	XF	Unc
1690 Rare	—	—	—	—	—	—

Note: Three known

Date	Mintage	VG	F	VF	XF	Unc
ND Rare	—	—	—	—	—	—

Note: One known

HESSE-MARBURG

When Hesse was divided among four brothers in 1567, one line of landgraves became centered on Marburg, 45 miles southwest of Cassel. Failing to provide any offspring to continue the line after one ruler, Hesse-Marburg reverted to Hesse-Cassel in 1604.

RULER
Ludwig (III) IV, 1567-1604

Initial	Date	Name
(c)= ⚒	1594-ca.1603	Peter Arnsburg (Arnsburgk) in Marburg

LANDGRAVIATE

REGULAR COINAGE

KM# 1 HELLER
Silver **Obv:** Hessian lion in shield divides Z-H, LL above. **Note:** Uniface. Schussel-type.

Date	Mintage	VG	F	VF	XF	Unc
ND	—	40.00	100	200	400	—

KM# 2 HELLER
Silver **Obv:** Hessian lion in shield, LL above **Note:** Schussel-type.

Date	Mintage	VG	F	VF	XF	Unc
ND	—	120	280	550	1,000	—

KM# 3 ALBUS
Silver **Obv:** Three helmets above 5-fold arms **Rev:** Helmet **Rev. Legend:** ALBVS * NOVVS - HASSIAE

Date	Mintage	VG	F	VF	XF	Unc
ND Rare	—	—	—	—	—	—

KM# 10 1/4 THALER
Silver **Subject:** Death of Ludwig IV **Obv:** Three ornate helmets in circle, titles of Ludwig IV **Rev:** 6-line inscription with Roman numeral date

Date	Mintage	VG	F	VF	XF	Unc
MDCIIII (1604) Rare	—	—	—	1,000	2,500	5,000

KM# 11 1/2 THALER
Silver **Obv:** Half-length figure to left, holding helmet, head divides, four small shields divide legend **Rev:** Three helmets

Date	Mintage	VG	F	VF	XF	Unc
1604	—	—	1,000	2,300	4,600	—

KM# 12 1/2 THALER
Silver **Subject:** Death of Ludwig IV **Obv:** Eight-line inscription **Rev:** Three crowned helmets

Date	Mintage	VG	F	VF	XF	Unc
MDCIIII (1604) Rare	—	—	—	—	—	—

KM# 7 THALER
Silver **Note:** Dav. #A6813.

Date	Mintage	VG	F	VF	XF	Unc
1600	—	500	1,000	1,750	2,750	—

KM# 9 THALER
Silver **Obv:** Half-length figure 3/4 left holding helmet and sword **Rev:** Crowned Hessian lion, four small shields divide legend **Note:** Dav. #6814.

Date	Mintage	VG	F	VF	XF	Unc
1603 Rare	—	—	—	—	—	—

Note: One piece known

Date	Mintage	VG	F	VF	XF	Unc
1604 Rare	—	—	—	—	—	—

KM# 14 THALER
Silver **Obv:** Half-length figure 3/4 left, holding helmet and sword **Rev:** Three helmets above oval 5-fold arms **Note:** Dav. #6816.

Date	Mintage	VG	F	VF	XF	Unc
1604	—	—	2,500	5,000	10,000	—

KM# 15 THALER
Silver **Subject:** Death of Ludwig IV **Obv:** 8-line inscription with Roman numeral date **Rev:** Crowned Hessian lion, four small shields divide legend **Note:** Dav. #6817.

Date	Mintage	VG	F	VF	XF	Unc
MDCIIII (1604) Rare	—	—	—	—	—	—

KM# 17 2 THALER
Silver **Obv:** Similar to 1 thaler, KM#9 **Rev:** Crowned Hessian lion, four small shields divide legend **Note:** Dav. #6813.

Date	Mintage	VG	F	VF	XF	Unc
1604 Rare	—	—	—	—	—	—

KM# 16 2 THALER
Silver **Note:** Similar to 1 Thaler, KM#14. Dav. #6815.

Date	Mintage	VG	F	VF	XF	Unc
1604 Rare	—	—	—	—	—	—

HILDESHEIM

A bishopric located in Westphalia, about 18 miles southeast of Hannover, was established in 822. The first mint was installed in the Mundburg Castle c. 977. Hildesheim coins were minted there although the bishopric didn't legally receive the mint right until 1054. There was no episcopal coinage during most of the 16th century, the first being produced only during the reign of Ernst of Bavaria. In 1803 it was secularized and assigned to Prussia. From 1807-1813 it formed part of the Kingdom of Westphalia and in 1813 was given to Hannover.

RULERS

Ernst of Bavaria, 1573-1612
Ferdinand of Bavaria, 1612-50
Maximilian Heinrich of Bavaria, 1650-88
Jobst Edmund von Brabeck, 1688-1702

MINT OFFICIALS' INITIALS

Hildesheim Mint

Initials	Date	Name
GB	1689-90	Georg Binnebohs
GH	Ca.1621-24	?
HB	1674-1711	Heinrich Bonhorst in Clausthal
HS, HIS	1692, 1694-1702	Heinrich Justus Sebastiani
IH	Ca.1611	?, die-cutter
LZ	1678-90	Levin Zernemann, die-cutter in Clausthal and Brunswick
PL	1663-65	Peter Lohr
SC	1660-92, 1693	Simon Conrad

Moritzberg Mint

(Closed 1634)

Initial	Date	Name
CG	1628-33	Caspar Gieseler
(a)= Xᴦ or	1598-1608	Christoph Diess
(b)= (HL)	1608-12	Hans Lachentress
(e)=	1612-18	Andreas Fricke
(f)=	1622-23	Christian Hopfgarten

Peine Mint

1608-1627

Initial	Date	Name
(c)=	1608-09	Paul Lachentress
(d)=	1609-11	Caspar Kohl
(g)=	1620-22	Carl Solter

ARMS

Hildesheim (bishopric): Parted per pale gold and red.
Peine: Wolf leaping left above two corn sheaves.

BISHOPRIC

REGULAR COINAGE

KM# 31 FLITTER

Copper **Obv:** Crowned 4-fold arms of Bavaria-Pfalz, with central shield of Hildesheim **Rev. Inscription:** I / FLIT / TER **Note:** Kipper Flitter.

Date	Mintage	VG	F	VF	XF	Unc
ND(1621/22)	—	13.00	33.00	60.00	100	—

KM# 5 PFENNIG

Silver **Note:** Uniface. Schussel type. 4-fold arms of Bavaria and Hildesheim.

Date	Mintage	VG	F	VF	XF	Unc
ND(ca.1600)	—	33.00	65.00	120	200	—

KM# 45 PFENNIG

Silver **Obv:** Crowned MH monogram divides date as 1-6/6-3.

Date	Mintage	VG	F	VF	XF	Unc
1663	170,000	20.00	33.00	60.00	100	—

KM# 55 PFENNIG

Silver **Obv:** Crowned script JE monogram divides date where present **Note:** Uniface.

Date	Mintage	VG	F	VF	XF	Unc
ND(1688-1702)	—	13.00	27.00	45.00	90.00	—
1691	—	13.00	27.00	45.00	90.00	—
1692	—	13.00	27.00	45.00	90.00	—

KM# 73 PFENNIG

Copper **Obv:** Crowned script JE monogram
Rev. Inscription: I / PFENNIG / SCHEIDE / MUNTZ / date

Date	Mintage	VG	F	VF	XF	Unc
1693	—	9.00	20.00	33.00	60.00	—
1695	—	9.00	20.00	33.00	60.00	—
1696	—	9.00	20.00	33.00	60.00	—
1700	—	9.00	20.00	33.00	60.00	—

KM# 80 2 PFENNIG

Silver **Ruler:** Jobst Edmund von Brabeck **Obv:** Crowned script JE monogram **Rev. Inscription:** II / PFEN / date

Date	Mintage	VG	F	VF	XF	Unc
1696	—	13.00	27.00	55.00	90.00	—

KM# 33 3 PFENNIG (1/96 Thaler)

Silver **Obv:** Crowned 4-fold arms of Bavaria-Pfalz, with central shield of Hildesheim arms **Rev:** Imperial orb with 3 divides date

Date	Mintage	VG	F	VF	XF	Unc
16ZZ (f)	—	—	—	—	—	—

KM# 34 3 PFENNIG (1/96 Thaler)

Silver **Obv:** Arms of Peine in ornate shield

Date	Mintage	VG	F	VF	XF	Unc
16ZZ	—	60.00	115	200	350	—

KM# 46 3 PFENNIG (1/96 Thaler)

Silver **Obv:** Crowned 4-fold arms of Bavaria-Pfalz, with central shield of Hildesheim arms **Note:** Varieties exist.

Date	Mintage	VG	F	VF	XF	Unc
1663	178,000	11.00	25.00	45.00	80.00	—
1664	221,000	8.00	18.00	35.00	55.00	—

KM# 60 3 PFENNIG (1/96 Thaler)

Silver **Obv:** 4-fold arms of Hildesheim and Brabeck, F. B. H. L. M. above

Date	Mintage	VG	F	VF	XF	Unc
1690	—	—	—	—	—	—
1691	—	—	—	—	—	—

KM# 65 4 PFENNIG

Silver **Obv:** Crowned script JE monogram divides date
Rev. Inscription: IIII / PFEN(N) / F. B. H. L. M.

Date	Mintage	VG	F	VF	XF	Unc
1691	—	11.00	20.00	40.00	70.00	—
1692	—	11.00	20.00	40.00	70.00	—

KM# 47 MARIENGROSCHEN

Silver **Obv:** Crowned 4-fold arms of Bavaria-Pfalz, with central shield of Hildesheim arms **Rev:** Madonna and child, date in legend

Date	Mintage	VG	F	VF	XF	Unc
1663	191,000	33.00	55.00	95.00	175	—

KM# 68 MARIENGROSCHEN

Silver **Ruler:** Jobst Edmund von Brabeck **Obv:** Madonna and child **Rev. Inscription:** I / MARIEN / GROS / date

Date	Mintage	VG	F	VF	XF	Unc
1692	—	33.00	55.00	95.00	175	—

KM# 61 6 MARIENGROSCHEN

Silver **Obv:** 4-fold arms of Hildesheim and Brabeck, bishop's cap above, crozier and sword crossed behind in form of St. Andrew's cross **Rev. Inscription:** VI / MARIEN / GROSCH / date

Date	Mintage	VG	F	VF	XF	Unc
1689 GB	—	40.00	85.00	150	225	—
1690	—	40.00	85.00	150	225	—

KM# 74 6 MARIENGROSCHEN

Silver **Obv:** Bust right **Rev. Legend:** NACH DEM...
Rev. Inscription: VI / MARIEN / GROSCH / date

Date	Mintage	VG	F	VF	XF	Unc
1693 HIS	—	40.00	80.00	140	200	—
1694 HIS	—	40.00	80.00	140	200	—

KM# 75 12 MARIENGROSCHEN (1/3 Thaler)

Silver **Obv:** Bust left **Rev. Legend:** NACH DEM...
Rev. Inscription: XII / MARIEN / GROSCH / date

Date	Mintage	VG	F	VF	XF	Unc
1693	—	—	—	—	—	—

KM# 62 24 MARIENGROSCHEN (2/3 Thaler)

Silver **Obv:** Bust right in circle **Rev. Legend:** IN PACE ET AEGUITATE... **Rev. Inscription:** 24 / MARIEN / GROSH / date

Date	Mintage	VG	F	VF	XF	Unc
1690	—	—	—	—	—	—
1691	—	—	—	—	—	—
1692	—	—	—	—	—	—

KM# 69 24 MARIENGROSCHEN (2/3 Thaler)

Silver **Obv:** Crowned oval 4-fold arms of Hildesheim and Brabeck

Date	Mintage	VG	F	VF	XF	Unc
1692	—	—	—	—	—	—

KM# 70 24 MARIENGROSCHEN (2/3 Thaler)

Silver **Rev. Legend:** NACH DEM LEIPZIGE FUES.
Rev. Inscription: XXIIII / MARIEN...

Date	Mintage	VG	F	VF	XF	Unc
1692	—	135	300	450	725	—
1693 HS	—	135	300	450	725	—
1694 HS	—	135	300	450	725	—
1697 HS	—	135	300	450	725	—

KM# 76 24 MARIENGROSCHEN (2/3 Thaler)

Silver **Obv:** Bust right in circle **Rev. Legend:** IN PACE ET AEGUITATE... **Rev. Inscription:** XXIIII / MARIEN / GROSCH, date

Date	Mintage	VG	F	VF	XF	Unc
1693 SC	—	—	—	—	—	—

KM# 77 24 MARIENGROSCHEN (2/3 Thaler)

Silver **Obv:** Crowned oval 4-fold arms of Hildesheim and Brabeck

Date	Mintage	VG	F	VF	XF	Unc
1693 HS	—	—	—	—	—	—
1693 SC	—	—	—	—	—	—

KM# 78 24 MARIENGROSCHEN (2/3 Thaler)

Silver **Obv:** Bust right not in circle **Rev. Legend:** NACH DEM LEIPZIGER FUES

Date	Mintage	VG	F	VF	XF	Unc
1693 HIS	—	375	650	1,075	1,650	—
1694 HIS	—	375	650	1,075	1,650	—
1697 HIS	—	375	650	1,075	1,650	—

KM# 85 24 MARIENGROSCHEN (2/3 Thaler)

Silver **Obv:** Bust left **Rev:** Date in legend **Rev. Inscription:** XXIIII / MARIEN / GROSCH / V:FEINEM SILVER / HIS

Date	Mintage	VG	F	VF	XF	Unc
1698 HIS	—	—	—	—	—	—

KM# 90 24 MARIENGROSCHEN (2/3 Thaler)

Silver **Ruler:** Jobst Edmund von Brabeck **Obv:** Bust right **Rev:** Date in legend **Rev. Inscription:** XXIIII / MARIEN / GROSCH / VIFEINEM SILVER / HIS

Date	Mintage	VG	F	VF	XF	Unc
1700 HIS	—	235	450	925	1,600	—

KM# 6 1/96 THALER (3 Pfennig)

Silver **Obv:** 4-fold arms of Bavaria and Hildesheim **Rev:** Imperial orb with 96

Date	Mintage	VG	F	VF	XF	Unc
ND(ca.1600) (a)	—	40.00	80.00	140	240	—

KM# 7 1/96 THALER (3 Pfennig)

Silver **Rev:** Imperial orb in square

Date	Mintage	VG	F	VF	XF	Unc
ND(ca.1600) (a)	—	40.00	80.00	140	240	—

KM# 12 1/96 THALER (3 Pfennig)

Silver **Obv:** Small shield of Peine arms below arms

Date	Mintage	VG	F	VF	XF	Unc
ND(ca.1609)	—	20.00	33.00	60.00	120	—
ND (d)	—	20.00	33.00	60.00	120	—

KM# 11 1/96 THALER (3 Pfennig)

Silver **Rev:** Imperial orb in rhombus divides date **Note:** Varieties exist.

Date	Mintage	VG	F	VF	XF	Unc
1601 (a)	—	33.00	65.00	115	220	—
160Z (a)	—	33.00	65.00	115	220	—
1604 (a)	—	33.00	65.00	115	220	—
1605 (a)	—	33.00	65.00	115	220	—
ND(ca.1608)	—	27.00	55.00	100	200	—
ND (b)	—	27.00	55.00	100	200	—

KM# 13 1/96 THALER (3 Pfennig)

Silver **Obv:** Small shield of Peine arms below 4-fold arms

Date	Mintage	VG	F	VF	XF	Unc
ND(ca.1609)	—	20.00	33.00	60.00	120	—

KM# 14 1/96 THALER (3 Pfennig)

Silver **Rev:** Imperial orb with 96 in ornamented oval

Date	Mintage	VG	F	VF	XF	Unc
1609	—	20.00	33.00	65.00	135	—

KM# 8 1/24 THALER (Groschen)

Silver **Obv:** Similar to KM#9 **Rev:** Crowned imperial eagle, Z4 in orb on breast, titles of Rudolf II

Date	Mintage	VG	F	VF	XF	Unc
ND (b)	—	—	—	—	—	—

KM# 9 1/24 THALER (Groschen)

Silver **Obv:** Crowned arms **Rev:** Imperial orb with Z4, cross divides date, titles of Rudolf II

Date	Mintage	VG	F	VF	XF	Unc
1601	—	16.00	27.00	55.00	110	—
1601 (a)	—	16.00	27.00	55.00	110	—
1602 (a)	—	16.00	27.00	55.00	110	—
1603 (a)	—	16.00	27.00	55.00	110	—
1604 (a)	—	16.00	27.00	55.00	110	—
1605 (a)	—	16.00	27.00	55.00	110	—
1606 (a)	—	16.00	27.00	55.00	110	—
1607 (a)	—	13.00	27.00	55.00	110	—
1607	—	13.00	27.00	55.00	110	—
1608 (b)	—	13.00	27.00	55.00	110	—
1609 (b)	—	13.00	27.00	55.00	110	—

KM# 15 1/24 THALER (Groschen)

Silver **Obv:** Small shield of Peine arms below arms **Rev:** Date divided by top of cross in legend

Date	Mintage	VG	F	VF	XF	Unc
1609	—	16.00	33.00	65.00	120	—
1609 (c)	—	16.00	33.00	65.00	120	—
1609 (d)	—	16.00	33.00	65.00	120	—

KM# 24 1/24 THALER (Groschen)

Silver **Rev:** Titles of Matthias

Date	Mintage	VG	F	VF	XF	Unc
1613 (e)	—	13.00	27.00	55.00	100	—
1614 (e)	—	13.00	27.00	55.00	100	—
1615 (e)	—	13.00	27.00	55.00	100	—
1616 (e)	—	13.00	27.00	55.00	100	—
1617 (e)	—	13.00	27.00	55.00	100	—
1618 (e)	—	13.00	27.00	55.00	100	—

KM# 25 1/24 THALER (Groschen)

Silver **Rev:** Imperial orb with Z4, date divided in legend at top, titles of Matthias **Note:** Kipper 1/24 Thaler.

Date	Mintage	VG	F	VF	XF	Unc
1619	—	—	—	—	—	—

KM# 26 1/24 THALER (Groschen)

Silver **Note:** Similar to KM#24, but titles of Ferdinand II.

Date	Mintage	VG	F	VF	XF	Unc
1619	—	13.00	25.00	45.00	100	—
1620	—	13.00	25.00	45.00	100	—
1621	—	13.00	25.00	45.00	100	—

KM# 30 1/24 THALER (Groschen)

Silver **Obv:** Ornate shield of Peine arms **Rev:** Imperial orb with Z4, date divided in legend at top, titles of Ferdinand II

Date	Mintage	VG	F	VF	XF	Unc
1620 (g)	—	20.00	33.00	65.00	120	—
1622	—	20.00	33.00	65.00	120	—

KM# 32 1/24 THALER (Groschen)

Silver **Note:** Similar to KM#24 but date divided in obverse legend at top.

Date	Mintage	VG	F	VF	XF	Unc
16Z1	—	13.00	25.00	45.00	100	—
16Z1 GH	—	13.00	25.00	45.00	100	—
16Z3 GH	—	13.00	25.00	45.00	100	—
16Z4 GH	—	13.00	25.00	45.00	100	—

KM# 48 1/24 THALER (Groschen)

Silver **Obv:** Crowned 4-fold arms of Bavaria-Pfalz with central shield of Hildesheim arms **Rev:** Imperial orb with Z4 divides date

Date	Mintage	VG	F	VF	XF	Unc
1663	980	—	—	—	—	—

KM# 66 1/24 THALER (Groschen)

Silver **Obv:** 4-fold arms of Hildesheim and Brabeck **Rev:** Imperial orb with Z4 divides date

Date	Mintage	VG	F	VF	XF	Unc
1691	—	13.00	25.00	45.00	100	—

KM# 10 1/16 THALER (2 Schilling)

Silver **Obv:** Crowned 4-fold arms of Bavaria with central shield of Hildesheim **Rev:** Crowned imperial eagle, 16 in orb on breast, titles of Rudolf II and date divided by crown in legend at top **Note:** Varieties exist.

Date	Mintage	VG	F	VF	XF	Unc
ND (b)	—	27.00	60.00	100	165	—
1602	—	27.00	60.00	100	165	—
1603	—	27.00	60.00	100	165	—
1604	—	27.00	60.00	100	165	—
1605	—	27.00	60.00	100	165	—
1606	—	27.00	60.00	100	165	—
1607	—	27.00	60.00	100	165	—
1608 (b)	—	27.00	60.00	100	165	—
1609 (b)	—	27.00	60.00	100	165	—
(16)09 (b)	—	27.00	60.00	100	165	—
1609 (d)	—	27.00	60.00	100	165	—

KM# 16 1/16 THALER (2 Schilling)

Silver **Rev:** Small shield of Peine arms below 4-fold arms

Date	Mintage	VG	F	VF	XF	Unc
ND(ca.1609)	—	—	—	—	—	—

KM# 57 1/16 THALER (2 Schilling)

Silver **Obv:** Bust right **Rev. Inscription:** XVI / EINEN / REICHS / THAL., date in legend

Date	Mintage	VG	F	VF	XF	Unc
1689	—	13.00	27.00	45.00	100	—
1691	—	13.00	27.00	45.00	100	—
1692	—	13.00	27.00	45.00	100	—

KM# 20 1/12 THALER (2 Groschen)

Silver **Obv:** Similar to 1/24 Thaler, KM#9, but small shield of Peine arms below arms **Rev. Inscription:** NUIE TOPL. / SILBR GROS. / STIFT HILDESH. / date

Date	Mintage	VG	F	VF	XF	Unc
1611	—	27.00	45.00	70.00	115	—

KM# 67 1/12 THALER (2 Groschen)

Silver **Obv:** Crowned 4-fold arms of Hildesheim and Brabeck **Rev. Inscription:** 12 / EINEN / REICHS / THAL / date

Date	Mintage	VG	F	VF	XF	Unc
1691	—	33.00	55.00	85.00	165	—

KM# 71 1/12 THALER (2 Groschen)

Silver **Obv:** Bust right **Rev:** Date in legend **Rev. Inscription:** 12 / EINEN / REICHS / THAL / HIS

Date	Mintage	VG	F	VF	XF	Unc
1692 HIS	—	40.00	70.00	120	200	—
1693 HIS	—	40.00	70.00	120	200	—
1694 HIS	—	40.00	70.00	120	200	—
1696 HIS	—	40.00	70.00	120	200	—
1700 HIS	—	40.00	70.00	120	200	—

KM# 79 1/12 THALER (2 Groschen)

Silver **Rev. Inscription:** 12 / EINEN / REICHS / THAL / date

Date	Mintage	VG	F	VF	XF	Unc
1693	—	40.00	70.00	120	200	—

KM# 82 1/12 THALER (2 Groschen)

Silver **Obv:** Crowned script JE monogram **Rev:** Date in legend **Rev. Inscription:** 12 / EINEN / REICHS / THAL / HIS

Date	Mintage	VG	F	VF	XF	Unc
1697 HIS	—	40.00	70.00	120	200	—
1700 HIS	—	40.00	70.00	120	200	—

KM# 40 1/2 ORT (1/8 Thaler)

Silver **Obv:** Bust right **Rev:** Imperial orb divides G-H above **Rev. Inscription:** EIN / HALB / REICHS / ORTH / date,

Date	Mintage	VG	F	VF	XF	Unc
16Z4 GH	—	—	—	—	—	—

KM# 35 1/4 THALER

Silver **Obv:** Bust right **Rev:** Crowned 4-fold arms of Bavaria-Pfalz with central shield of Hildesheim arms in ornate frame, date divides mintmaster's initials below **Note:** Varieties exist.

Date	Mintage	VG	F	VF	XF	Unc
16Z3 GH	—	—	—	—	—	—
16Z4 GH	—	—	—	—	—	—

KM# 42 1/4 THALER

Silver **Rev:** Date at top of legend **Note:** Varieties exist.

Date	Mintage	VG	F	VF	XF	Unc
16Z5 (f)	—	—	—	—	—	—

KM# 36 1/2 THALER

Silver **Obv:** Bust right **Rev:** Crowned 4-fold arms of Bavaria-Pfalz with central shield of Hildesheim arms in ornate frame, date divides mintmaster's initials below

Date	Mintage	VG	F	VF	XF	Unc
16Z3 GH	—	—	—	—	—	—

KM# 41 1/2 THALER

Silver **Rev:** Date at top of legend

Date	Mintage	VG	F	VF	XF	Unc
16Z3 GH	—	450	850	1,400	—	—
16Z4 (f)	—	450	850	1,400	—	—
1630 CG	—	450	850	1,400	—	—

KM# 49 2/3 THALER (Gulden)

Silver **Obv:** Crowned 4-fold arms of Bavaria-Pfalz with central shield of Hildesheim arms **Rev:** Madonna and child, date in legend

Date	Mintage	VG	F	VF	XF	Unc
1663 PL	88	—	—	—	—	—

KM# 21 THALER

Silver **Obv:** Bust right in circle, date divided by top of head **ev:** Crowned, ornate 4-fold arms of Bavaria-Pfalz with central shield Hildesheim arms, small shield of Peine arms below, IH on edge **Note:** Dav. #5402.

Date	Mintage	VG	F	VF	XF	Unc
1611 IH Rare	—	—	—	—	—	—

KM# 23 THALER

Silver **Obv:** Bust right in circle **Rev:** Crowned 4-fold arms of Bavaria-Pfalz with central shield of Hildesheim arms in ornate frame **Note:** Dav. #5403.

Date	Mintage	VG	F	VF	XF	Unc
ND(ca.1612)	—	3,900	5,900	8,500	—	—

KM# 27 THALER

Silver **Obv:** Similar to KM#37 but date 1 - 6 divided by crown and 1 - 9 divided by arms at sides **Note:** Dav. #5404.

Date	Mintage	VG	F	VF	XF	Unc
1619 Rare	—	—	—	—	—	—

KM# 37.1 THALER

Silver **Note:** Dav. #5405.

Date	Mintage	VG	F	VF	XF	Unc
1623 GH	—	225	450	700	1,200	—

KM# 39 THALER

Silver **Rev:** Similar to KM#37 but date below arms **Note:** Dav. #5405B.

Date	Mintage	VG	F	VF	XF	Unc
1623 GH	—	250	450	700	1,250	—

KM# 38 THALER

Silver **Note:** Klippe. Dav. #5405A.

Date	Mintage	VG	F	VF	XF	Unc
1623 GH Rare	—	—	—	—	—	—

KM# 37.2 THALER

Silver **Obv:** Larger bust **Note:** Varieties exist. Dav. #5406.

Date	Mintage	VG	F	VF	XF	Unc
1623 GH	—	200	400	650	1,150	—
1624 GH	—	200	400	650	1,150	—
1625 GH	—	200	400	650	1,150	—
1630	—	200	400	650	1,150	—
1630 CG	—	200	400	650	1,150	—
1631 CG	—	200	400	650	1,150	—

KM# 50 THALER

Silver **Obv:** Crowned 4-fold arms of Bavaria-Pfalz with central shield of Hildesheim arms **Rev:** Madonna and child, date in legend

Date	Mintage	VG	F	VF	XF	Unc
1663 PL	—	—	—	—	—	—

KM# 56 THALER

Silver **Obv:** Leopold I **Rev:** Ornate helmeted arms of Hildesheim, Madonna and child above, date in legend **Note:** Sede vacante. Dav. #5407.

Date	Mintage	VG	F	VF	XF	Unc
1688 HB/LZ	800	300	500	900	1,600	—

KM# 63 THALER

Silver **Rev:** Helmeted 4-fold arms of Hildesheim and Brabeck in oval supported by two female figures, all dividing date **Note:** Dav. #5408.

Date	Mintage	VG	F	VF	XF	Unc
1690	—	775	1,500	2,650	4,200	—
1690 GB	—	775	1,500	2,650	4,200	—

KM# 72 THALER

Silver **Rev:** Ornately-helmeted 4-fold arms of Hildesheim and Brabeck divide date **Note:** Dav. #5409.

Date	Mintage	VG	F	VF	XF	Unc
1692 SC Rare	—	—	—	—	—	—

KM# 81 THALER

Silver **Obv:** Bust right **Note:** Dav. #5410.

Date	Mintage	VG	F	VF	XF	Unc
1696 HS	—	1,150	2,000	3,300	5,100	—

KM# 83 THALER

Silver **Obv:** Helmeted arms **Rev:** Full-length facing standing figure of St. Anthony **Rev. Legend:** SANCTUS ANTHONIUS... **Note:** Mining Thaler. Dav. #5411.

Date	Mintage	VG	F	VF	XF	Unc
1697 HIS	—	450	950	1,850	3,750	—

KM# 84.1 THALER

Silver **Rev. Legend:** HÆC... **Note:** Mining Thaler. Dav. #5412.

Date	Mintage	VG	F	VF	XF	Unc
1697 HIS	—	350	700	1,250	2,500	—
1698 HIS	—	350	700	1,250	2,500	—
1699 HIS	—	350	700	1,250	2,500	—

KM# 84.2 THALER

Silver **Rev. Legend:** ...SANCTI ANTONII EREMITAE **Note:** Dav. #5413.

Date	Mintage	F	VF	XF	Unc	BU
1698	—	250	550	1,000	2,000	—

KM# 91 THALER

Silver **Obv:** Arms in circle and date in legend **Note:** Mining Thaler. Dav. #5414.

Date	Mintage	VG	F	VF	XF	Unc
1700 HIS Rare	—	—	—	—	—	—

KM# 92 THALER

Silver **Ruler:** Jobst Edmund von Brabeck **Obv:** Ornately-helmeted 4-fold arms **Rev:** St. Anthony in circle **Note:** Mining Thaler. Dav. #5415.

Date	Mintage	VG	F	VF	XF	Unc
1700 HIS Rare	—	—	—	—	—	—

KM# 22 2 THALER

Silver **Note:** Similar to 1 Thaler, KM#21. Dav. #5401.

Date	Mintage	VG	F	VF	XF	Unc
1611 IH Rare	—	—	—	—	—	—

TRADE COINAGE

KM# 64 DUCAT

3.5000 g., 0.9860 Gold 0.1109 oz. AGW **Obv:** Bust of Jobst Edmund right **Rev:** Helmeted arms, date below

Date	Mintage	VG	F	VF	XF	Unc
1690	—	1,000	2,300	5,500	9,000	—
1694 HS	—	1,000	2,300	5,500	9,000	—
1695 HS	—	1,000	2,300	5,500	9,000	—

KM# 51 2 DUCAT

7.0000 g., 0.9860 Gold 0.2219 oz. AGW **Obv:** Crowned oval 4-fold arms of Bavaria-Pfalz in ornate frame, date divided below **Rev:** Madonna seated facing with child

Date	Mintage	VG	F	VF	XF	Unc
1664 Rare	—	—	—	—	—	—

FREE CITY

The town of Hildesheim grew up around the seat of the bishopric and was made a free imperial city in the mid-13th century. The first civic coinage was struck in 1428 and continued more or less continually until the second half of the 18th century. The last silver coins were struck for the city in 1764 and copper coinage was last produced in 1772. Hildesheim came under the control of Prussia in 1803 and like the bishopric, became part of the Kingdom of Westphalia 1807-13. It was awarded to the Kingdom of Hannover in 1813 and reverted to Prussia when the latter absorbed Hannover in 1866.

MINTMASTERS' INITIALS

Initials	Date	Name
(a)=	1573-74, 1589-90,1592-94, 1600-01	Christoph Dyss der Altere
(b)=	1601-03	Henning Hans (Johannis)
(c)=	1603-06	Christoph Diess der Jungere
(d)=	1614-22	Matthais Weber
(e)=	1622-30	Andreas Fricke
	1631-32	Caspar Gieseler
(f)=	1645-48	Caspar Kohl
(g)=	1666-72	Jonas Bose
	1673-74	Peter Paul Peckstein
(h)= I✕B	1674-95	Jonas Bose
HL	1696-1710	Hans Luders

SUPERVISORS

Date	Name
1666-72	Jonas Bose
1696	Joachim Heinrich Bose and Kurd Eberling

MINT WARDENS

Date	Name
1693-96	Hans Luders
1601	Adrian Reimers
1601-19	Jobst Brauns
1615-47	Heinrich Ruden

DIE-CUTTERS

Date	Name
1618-19	Isaac Henniges
1619-28	Lazarus Arens
1630	Isaac Henniges
1637-39	Barthold Kretzer
1666	Henning Benneken
1666-74	Tobias Reuss in Clausthal
1666-68	Paul Franzel
1675-90	Jurgen Lippold Jaster
1691	Heinrich Andreas Fricke

ARMS

Old style are quartered red and gold, new style have upper half of crowned eagle above quarterly.

REGULAR COINAGE

KM# 176 FLITTER (Heller)

Copper **Obv:** Arms in shield with flat top and rounded botttom

Date	Mintage	VG	F	VF	XF	Unc
16Z0	—	9.00	20.00	40.00	75.00	—

KM# 177 FLITTER (Heller)

Copper **Obv:** Oval arms **Rev. Inscription:** I / FLIT / TER / date

Date	Mintage	VG	F	VF	XF	Unc
(1)6Z0	—	9.00	20.00	40.00	75.00	—

KM# 178 FLITTER (Heller)

Copper **Obv:** Ornamented arms

Date	Mintage	VG	F	VF	XF	Unc
(16)Z0	—	9.00	20.00	40.00	75.00	—

KM# 179 FLITTER (Heller)

Copper **Rev. Inscription:** 116 / FLIT / TER / ZO

Date	Mintage	VG	F	VF	XF	Unc
16Z0	—	9.00	20.00	40.00	75.00	—

KM# 180 FLITTER (Heller)

Copper **Obv:** Ornately-shaped arms **Rev. Inscription:** I / FLIT / TER / date

Date	Mintage	VG	F	VF	XF	Unc
(1)6Z0	—	9.00	20.00	40.00	75.00	—

KM# 181 FLITTER (Heller)

Copper **Obv:** Oval arms **Rev. Inscription:** I / FLIT / TER

Date	Mintage	VG	F	VF	XF	Unc
ND(1620/21)	—	9.00	20.00	40.00	75.00	—

KM# 182 FLITTER (Heller)

Copper **Obv:** Ornately-shaped arms

Date	Mintage	VG	F	VF	XF	Unc
ND(1620/21)	—	9.00	20.00	40.00	75.00	—

KM# 175 FLITTER (Heller)

Copper **Obv:** Oval arms, date above **Rev. Inscription:** I / FLIT / TER **Note:** Kipper Flitter.

Date	Mintage	VG	F	VF	XF	Unc
16Z0	—	9.00	20.00	40.00	75.00	—

KM# 135 PFENNIG

Silver **Note:** Uniface. Arms divide date, H above. Varieties exist.

Date	Mintage	VG	F	VF	XF	Unc
16Z8	—	27.00	45.00	80.00	140	—
1628	—	27.00	45.00	80.00	140	—
1630	—	27.00	45.00	80.00	140	—
1631	—	27.00	45.00	80.00	140	—
163Z	—	27.00	45.00	80.00	140	—
1637	—	27.00	45.00	80.00	140	—
1639	—	27.00	45.00	80.00	140	—
1645	—	27.00	45.00	80.00	140	—
1648	—	27.00	45.00	80.00	140	—
1659	—	27.00	45.00	80.00	140	—
1660	—	27.00	45.00	80.00	140	—
1661	—	27.00	45.00	80.00	140	—
1663	—	27.00	45.00	80.00	140	—
1666	—	27.00	45.00	80.00	140	—
1667	—	27.00	45.00	80.00	140	—
1676	—	27.00	45.00	80.00	140	—
1686	—	27.00	45.00	80.00	140	—
1691	—	27.00	45.00	80.00	140	—
1695	—	27.00	45.00	80.00	140	—

KM# 227 2 PFENNIG (Stadt)

Billon **Obv:** Arms in oval shield with pointed bottom, HILDES, date around **Rev. Inscription:** II / STAT / PENN

Date	Mintage	VG	F	VF	XF	Unc
1666	—	13.00	27.00	45.00	80.00	—

KM# 245 2 PFENNIG (Stadt)

Billon **Obv:** 16 HILDES 86 around arms

Date	Mintage	VG	F	VF	XF	Unc
1686	—	13.00	27.00	45.00	80.00	—

KM# 252 2 PFENNIG (Stadt)

Billon **Obv:** City arms **Rev:** Value, date **Note:** Varieties exist.

Date	Mintage	VG	F	VF	XF	Unc
1695	—	10.00	20.00	40.00	80.00	—
1696	—	10.00	20.00	40.00	80.00	—

KM# 183 3 PFENNIG (1/96 Thaler)

Billon **Obv:** Arms in oval **Rev:** Imperial orb with 3 **Note:** Kipper 3 Pfennig.

Date	Mintage	VG	F	VF	XF	Unc
ND(1620/21)	—	20.00	40.00	70.00	120	—

KM# 187 3 PFENNIG (1/96 Thaler)
Billon **Obv:** Oval arms **Rev:** Imperial orb with 3 divides date **Note:** Varieties exist.

Date	Mintage	VG	F	VF	XF	Unc
16ZZ (e)	—	10.00	27.00	45.00	80.00	—
16ZZ	—	10.00	27.00	45.00	80.00	—
1638 (e)	—	10.00	27.00	45.00	80.00	—

KM# 188 3 PFENNIG (1/96 Thaler)
Billon **Obv:** Similar to KM#220 but HILDESHEIM above plain arms **Note:** Varieties exist.

Date	Mintage	VG	F	VF	XF	Unc
16ZZ (e)	—	8.00	20.00	40.00	70.00	—
16Z3	—	8.00	20.00	40.00	70.00	—
1648	—	8.00	20.00	40.00	70.00	—

KM# 221 3 PFENNIG (1/96 Thaler)
Billon **Note:** Klippe.

Date	Mintage	VG	F	VF	XF	Unc
1659 Rare	—	—	—	—	—	—

KM# 220 3 PFENNIG (1/96 Thaler)
Billon **Obv:** HILDES above ornately-shaped arms **Rev:** Imperial orb with value divides date **Note:** Varieties exist.

Date	Mintage	VG	F	VF	XF	Unc
1659	—	7.00	20.00	35.00	66.00	—
1660	—	7.00	20.00	35.00	66.00	—
1661	—	7.00	20.00	35.00	66.00	—
1672	—	7.00	20.00	35.00	66.00	—
1676	—	7.00	20.00	35.00	66.00	—
1679	—	7.00	20.00	35.00	66.00	—
1680	—	7.00	20.00	35.00	66.00	—
1683	—	7.00	20.00	35.00	66.00	—
1685	—	7.00	20.00	35.00	66.00	—
1686	—	7.00	20.00	35.00	66.00	—
1687	—	7.00	20.00	35.00	66.00	—
1690	—	7.00	20.00	35.00	66.00	—
1691	—	7.00	20.00	35.00	66.00	—
1692	—	7.00	20.00	35.00	66.00	—
1694	—	7.00	20.00	35.00	66.00	—
1700	—	7.00	20.00	35.00	66.00	—

KM# 251 4 PFENNIG
Billon **Obv:** Arms within square **Rev:** Value with PF dividing date below **Rev. Inscription:** IIII / STADT / 17PF16 **Note:** Varieties exist.

Date	Mintage	VG	F	VF	XF	Unc
1691	—	10.00	20.00	45.00	90.00	—
1692	—	10.00	20.00	45.00	90.00	—

KM# 226 4 PFENNIG (Matthier)
Billon **Obv:** Arms **Obv. Legend:** MO. NO. CIVIT. HILDES. **Rev. Inscription:** IIII / STAT / PENNI / date **Note:** Stadt 4 Pfennig.

Date	Mintage	VG	F	VF	XF	Unc
1663	—	10.00	20.00	35.00	70.00	—
1666	—	10.00	20.00	35.00	70.00	—

KM# 238 4 PFENNIG (Matthier)
Billon **Rev. Inscription:** IIII / GUTE / 16PF75 **Note:** Gute 4 Pfennig. Varieties exist.

Date	Mintage	VG	F	VF	XF	Unc
ND(ca.1675)	—	10.00	20.00	35.00	70.00	—
1675	—	10.00	20.00	35.00	70.00	—
1676	—	10.00	20.00	35.00	70.00	—
(1)676	—	10.00	20.00	35.00	70.00	—
1679	—	10.00	20.00	35.00	70.00	—
1680	—	10.00	20.00	35.00	70.00	—

KM# 239 4 PFENNIG (Matthier)
Billon **Rev. Inscription:** 1IIII6 /GUTE / 7PF6

Date	Mintage	VG	F	VF	XF	Unc
1676	—	—	—	—	—	—

KM# 190 MARIENGROSCHEN
Silver **Note:** Klippe.

Date	Mintage	VG	F	VF	XF	Unc
(1)6ZZ	—	—	—	—	—	—
(1)6ZZ (e)	—	—	—	—	—	—
(1)6Z3 (e)	—	—	—	—	—	—

KM# 189 MARIENGROSCHEN
1.2200 g., Silver **Obv:** 4-fold arms, date above **Rev:** Madonna and child **Note:** Varieties exist.

Date	Mintage	VG	F	VF	XF	Unc
(1)6ZZ (e)	—	12.00	30.00	55.00	115	—
(1)6ZZ (e)	—	12.00	30.00	55.00	115	—
(1)6Z3 (e)	—	12.00	30.00	55.00	115	—
(1)6Z4	—	12.00	30.00	55.00	115	—
(1)660	—	12.00	30.00	55.00	115	—
1661	—	12.00	30.00	55.00	115	—
(1)663	—	12.00	30.00	55.00	115	—
(1)666	—	12.00	30.00	55.00	115	—
1666	—	12.00	30.00	55.00	115	—
1667	—	12.00	30.00	55.00	115	—
1668	—	12.00	30.00	55.00	115	—
1685	—	12.00	30.00	55.00	115	—
1687	—	12.00	30.00	55.00	115	—

KM# 228 6 MARIENGROSCHEN (1/6 Thaler)
Silver **Obv:** Large arms in oval shield, pointed at bottom **Rev:** Inscription in laurel wreath **Rev. Inscription:** VI / MARIEN / GROSCH / date

Date	Mintage	VG	F	VF	XF	Unc
1666 (g)	—	55.00	100	200	400	—

KM# 229 6 MARIENGROSCHEN (1/6 Thaler)
Silver **Note:** Klippe.

Date	Mintage	VG	F	VF	XF	Unc
1666 (g)	—	—	—	—	—	—

KM# 230 6 MARIENGROSCHEN (1/6 Thaler)
Silver **Note:** Varieties exist.

Date	Mintage	VG	F	VF	XF	Unc
1667	—	27.00	40.00	80.00	160	—
1668	—	27.00	40.00	80.00	160	—
1669	—	27.00	40.00	80.00	160	—
1673	—	27.00	40.00	80.00	160	—
1674	—	27.00	40.00	80.00	160	—
1689	—	27.00	40.00	80.00	160	—
1690	—	27.00	40.00	80.00	160	—
1693	—	27.00	40.00	80.00	160	—
1694	—	27.00	40.00	80.00	160	—
1694 (h)	—	27.00	40.00	80.00	160	—
1696 HL	—	27.00	40.00	80.00	160	—

KM# 236 12 MARIENGROSCHEN (1/3 Thaler)
Silver

Date	Mintage	VG	F	VF	XF	Unc
1674	—	65.00	165	275	475	—
1675	—	65.00	165	275	475	—
1676	—	65.00	165	275	475	—
1677	—	65.00	165	275	475	—
1680	—	65.00	165	275	475	—
1681	—	65.00	165	275	475	—
1693	—	65.00	165	275	475	—
1695 HL	—	65.00	165	275	475	—
1696 HL	—	65.00	165	275	475	—
1697 HL	—	65.00	165	275	475	—
1700 HL	—	65.00	165	275	475	—

KM# 237 24 MARIENGROSCHEN (2/3 Thaler)
Silver **Obv:** Small arms in ovoid shield, pointed at bottom, ornate helmet above, 3/4 length figure of maiden above helmet **Rev:** Value, date below **Rev. Inscription:** 24 / MARIEN / GROSCH **Note:** Varieties exist.

Date	Mintage	VG	F	VF	XF	Unc
1674	—	80.00	160	300	525	—
1680	—	80.00	160	300	525	—
1681	—	80.00	160	300	525	—
1683	—	80.00	160	300	525	—
1684	—	80.00	160	300	525	—
1685	—	80.00	160	300	525	—
1686	—	80.00	160	300	525	—
1687	—	80.00	160	300	525	—
1688	—	80.00	160	300	525	—
1689	—	80.00	160	300	525	—
1690	—	80.00	160	300	525	—
1691	—	80.00	160	300	525	—
1692	—	80.00	160	300	525	—
1693	—	80.00	160	300	525	—
1694	—	80.00	160	300	525	—
1694 (h)	—	80.00	160	300	525	—
1694 HL	—	80.00	160	300	525	—
1695 HL	—	80.00	160	300	525	—
1696 HL	—	80.00	160	300	525	—
1697 HL	—	80.00	160	300	525	—
1698 HL	—	80.00	160	300	525	—
1699 HL	—	80.00	160	300	525	—
1700 HL	—	80.00	160	300	525	—

KM# 143 1/96 THALER (3 Pfennig)
Billon **Obv:** Arms divde date, mintmaster's mark above **Rev:** Imperial orb with 96 in ornamented frame

Date	Mintage	VG	F	VF	XF	Unc
1601 (b)	—	40.00	80.00	130	250	—

KM# 144 1/96 THALER (3 Pfennig)
Billon **Obv:** Arms, mintmaster's mark above **Rev:** Large imperial orb with 96 divides date

Date	Mintage	VG	F	VF	XF	Unc
1601 (b)	—	33.00	65.00	115	220	—
160Z (b)	—	33.00	65.00	115	220	—
160Z	—	33.00	65.00	115	220	—
1603 (b)	—	33.00	65.00	115	220	—
1606	—	33.00	65.00	115	220	—

KM# 153 1/96 THALER (3 Pfennig)
Billon **Obv:** Oval arms **Rev:** Imperial orb with 96, mintmaster's mark above

Date	Mintage	VG	F	VF	XF	Unc
ND(1601-3) (b)	—	20.00	33.00	55.00	110	—
ND(1605-6) (c)	—	20.00	33.00	55.00	110	—

KM# 154 1/96 THALER (3 Pfennig)
Billon **Obv:** Arms, mintmaster's mark above **Rev:** Imperial orb with 96 in oval baroque frame

Date	Mintage	VG	F	VF	XF	Unc
ND(1601-3) (b)	—	20.00	33.00	55.00	110	—

KM# 155 1/96 THALER (3 Pfennig)
Billon **Obv:** Arms in ornate shield, without mintmaster's mark **Rev:** Imperial orb without value in three-lobed triangular frame

Date	Mintage	VG	F	VF	XF	Unc
ND(1601-3)	—	20.00	33.00	55.00	110	—

KM# 156 1/96 THALER (3 Pfennig)
Billon **Rev:** Imperial orb without value in ornamented rhombus

Date	Mintage	VG	F	VF	XF	Unc
ND(1601-3)	—	20.00	33.00	55.00	110	—

KM# 157 1/96 THALER (3 Pfennig)
Billon **Rev:** Large imperial orb without value, but symbol

Date	Mintage	VG	F	VF	XF	Unc
ND(1601-3)	—	20.00	33.00	55.00	110	—

KM# 148 1/96 THALER (3 Pfennig)
Billon **Rev:** Smaller imperial orb with 96 in ornamented rhombus

Date	Mintage	VG	F	VF	XF	Unc
160Z (b)	—	27.00	55.00	85.00	175	—
1603 (b)	—	27.00	55.00	85.00	175	—
1606	—	27.00	55.00	85.00	175	—

KM# 150 1/96 THALER (3 Pfennig)
Billon **Obv:** Arms, mintmaster's mark above **Rev:** Imperial orb with 96 in oval baroque frame, date above

Date	Mintage	VG	F	VF	XF	Unc
160Z (b)	—	27.00	55.00	85.00	175	—
ND (b)	—	27.00	55.00	85.00	175	—

KM# 151 1/96 THALER (3 Pfennig)
Billon **Obv:** Helmet, mintmaster's mark above, divides date **Rev:** Imperial orb with 96 in oval cartouche, date above

Date	Mintage	VG	F	VF	XF	Unc
160Z (b)	—	27.00	55.00	85.00	175	—

KM# 152 1/96 THALER (3 Pfennig)
Billon **Obv:** Mintmaster's mark below helmet **Rev:** Without date

Date	Mintage	VG	F	VF	XF	Unc
160Z (b)	—	27.00	55.00	85.00	175	—

KM# 149 1/96 THALER (3 Pfennig)
Billon **Obv:** Mintmaster's mark left of arms

Date	Mintage	VG	F	VF	XF	Unc
1603 (c)	—	27.00	55.00	85.00	175	—

KM# 160 1/96 THALER (3 Pfennig)
Billon **Obv:** Arms **Rev:** Large imperial orb with 96, mintmaster's mark at upper left

Date	Mintage	VG	F	VF	XF	Unc
ND(1605-6) (c)	—	20.00	33.00	55.00	110	—

KM# 161 1/96 THALER (3 Pfennig)
Billon **Obv:** Oval arms **Rev:** Imperial orb with 96 divides date in ornamented rhombus, mintmaster's mark in one quadrant

Date	Mintage	VG	F	VF	XF	Unc
ND(1605-6) (c)	—	20.00	33.00	55.00	110	—

KM# 137 1/24 THALER (Reichsgroschen)
Silver **Obv:** Imperial orb with 24 or Z4 divides date, titles of Rudolf II **Rev:** Arms

Date	Mintage	VG	F	VF	XF	Unc
1601 (a)	—	20.00	33.00	55.00	85.00	—
1601	—	20.00	33.00	55.00	85.00	—
1601 (b)	—	20.00	33.00	55.00	85.00	—
160Z (b)	—	20.00	33.00	55.00	85.00	—

KM# 139 1/24 THALER (Reichsgroschen)
Silver **Obv:** Imperial orb with Z4 divides date, titles of Rudolf II, partly in Gothic letters **Rev:** Arms, ornate helmet above **Note:** Varieties exist.

Date	Mintage	VG	F	VF	XF	Unc
1603 (c)	—	20.00	33.00	55.00	110	—
1604 (c)	—	20.00	33.00	55.00	110	—
1605 (c)	—	20.00	33.00	55.00	110	—
1605	—	20.00	33.00	55.00	85.00	—
1606	—	20.00	33.00	55.00	85.00	—
1606 (c)	—	20.00	33.00	55.00	85.00	—

KM# 145 1/24 THALER (Reichsgroschen)
Silver **Obv:** Female figure above helmet **Rev:** Roman letters **Note:** Klippe. Varieties exist.

Date	Mintage	VG	F	VF	XF	Unc
1601	—	20.00	33.00	55.00	85.00	—
1601 (b)	—	20.00	33.00	55.00	85.00	—
160Z (b)	—	20.00	33.00	55.00	85.00	—
1603 (b)	—	20.00	33.00	55.00	85.00	—
1605	—	20.00	33.00	55.00	85.00	—
1605 (c)	—	20.00	33.00	55.00	85.00	—

KM# 146 1/24 THALER (Reichsgroschen)
Silver **Note:** Klippe.

Date	Mintage	VG	F	VF	XF	Unc
1601 (b)	—	—	—	—	—	—
160Z (b)	—	—	—	—	—	—
1603 (b)	—	—	—	—	—	—

KM# 162 1/24 THALER (Reichsgroschen)
Silver **Note:** Klippe.

Date	Mintage	VG	F	VF	XF	Unc
1606 (c)	—	—	—	—	—	—

KM# 165 1/24 THALER (Reichsgroschen)
Silver **Obv:** Titles of Matthias **Note:** Varieties exist.

Date	Mintage	VG	F	VF	XF	Unc
(1)614 (d)	—	20.00	33.00	55.00	85.00	—
1614 (d)	—	20.00	33.00	55.00	85.00	—
1615 (d)	—	20.00	33.00	55.00	85.00	—

KM# 166 1/24 THALER (Reichsgroschen)
Silver **Obv:** Date in legend **Note:** Varieties exist.

Date	Mintage	VG	F	VF	XF	Unc
(1)614 (d)	—	20.00	33.00	55.00	85.00	—
(1)614	—	20.00	33.00	55.00	85.00	—
1615 (d)	—	20.00	33.00	55.00	85.00	—
1616 (d)	—	20.00	33.00	55.00	85.00	—
1618	—	20.00	33.00	55.00	85.00	—
1619	—	20.00	33.00	55.00	85.00	—

KM# 167 1/24 THALER (Reichsgroschen)
Silver **Obv:** Arms **Rev:** Titles of Mathias **Note:** Varieties exist.

Date	Mintage	VG	F	VF	XF	Unc
1614 (d)	—	20.00	33.00	55.00	85.00	—
1615 (d)	—	20.00	33.00	55.00	85.00	—
1616 (d)	—	20.00	33.00	55.00	85.00	—

KM# 168 1/24 THALER (Reichsgroschen)
Silver **Obv:** Date in legend **Note:** Varieties exist.

Date	Mintage	VG	F	VF	XF	Unc
(1)614 (d)	—	20.00	33.00	55.00	85.00	—
1614 (d)	—	20.00	33.00	55.00	85.00	—
1615 (d)	—	20.00	33.00	55.00	85.00	—
1616 (d)	—	20.00	33.00	55.00	85.00	—
1617 (d)	—	20.00	33.00	55.00	85.00	—
1618 (d)	—	20.00	33.00	55.00	85.00	—
1619 (d)	—	20.00	33.00	55.00	85.00	—
1619	—	20.00	33.00	55.00	85.00	—

KM# 169 1/24 THALER (Reichsgroschen)
Silver **Note:** Klippe.

Date	Mintage	VG	F	VF	XF	Unc
1616 (d)	—	—	—	—	—	—

KM# 170 1/24 THALER (Reichsgroschen)
Silver **Note:** Klippe.

Date	Mintage	VG	F	VF	XF	Unc
1619 (d)	—	—	—	—	—	—

KM# 185 1/24 THALER (Reichsgroschen)
Silver **Note:** Klippe.

Date	Mintage	VG	F	VF	XF	Unc
(1)6Z0 (d)	—	—	—	—	—	—
(1)6Z1	—	—	—	—	—	—

KM# 184 1/24 THALER (Reichsgroschen)
Silver **Obv:** Titles of Ferdinand II **Note:** Kipper 1/24 Thaler. Varieties exist.

Date	Mintage	VG	F	VF	XF	Unc
(1)6Z0	—	20.00	33.00	55.00	85.00	—
16Z0	—	20.00	33.00	55.00	85.00	—
16Z0 (d)	—	20.00	33.00	55.00	85.00	—
(1)6Z0 (d)	—	20.00	33.00	55.00	85.00	—
ND(1620/21)	—	20.00	33.00	55.00	85.00	—
(1)6Z1	—	20.00	33.00	55.00	85.00	—
(1)6Z1 (d)	—	20.00	33.00	55.00	85.00	—

KM# 192 1/24 THALER (Reichsgroschen)
Silver **Obv:** Arms, ornate helmet and figure of maiden above

Date	Mintage	VG	F	VF	XF	Unc
16ZZ	—	20.00	33.00	55.00	85.00	—
16ZZ (e)	—	20.00	33.00	55.00	85.00	—

KM# 194 1/24 THALER (Reichsgroschen)
Silver **Obv:** Large ornamented arms **Rev:** Imperial orb with 24 or Z4 divides date

Date	Mintage	VG	F	VF	XF	Unc
16ZZ	—	20.00	33.00	55.00	85.00	—

KM# 191 1/24 THALER (Reichsgroschen)
Silver **Obv:** Imperial orb with 24 or Z4 divides date **Rev:** Arms, ornate helmet above **Note:** Varieties exist.

Date	Mintage	VG	F	VF	XF	Unc
1622 (e)	—	20.00	33.00	55.00	85.00	—
16ZZ (e)	—	20.00	33.00	55.00	85.00	—
16ZZ	—	20.00	33.00	55.00	85.00	—
16Z3 (e)	—	20.00	33.00	55.00	85.00	—
16Z3	—	20.00	33.00	55.00	85.00	—

KM# 193 1/24 THALER (Reichsgroschen)
Silver **Obv:** Oval arms **Rev:** Date in legend **Note:** Varieties exist.

Date	Mintage	VG	F	VF	XF	Unc
16ZZ	—	20.00	33.00	55.00	85.00	—
16Z3 (e)	—	20.00	33.00	55.00	85.00	—
16Z4 (e)	—	20.00	33.00	55.00	85.00	—

KM# 216 1/24 THALER (Reichsgroschen)
Silver **Obv:** Arms, ornate helmet and figure of maiden above **Note:** Varieties exist.

Date	Mintage	VG	F	VF	XF	Unc
1645 (f)	—	20.00	33.00	55.00	85.00	—
1646 (f)	—	20.00	33.00	55.00	85.00	—
1647 (f)	—	20.00	33.00	55.00	85.00	—

KM# 215 1/24 THALER (Reichsgroschen)
Silver **Obv:** Imperial orb with Z4 divides date, titles of Ferdinand III **Rev:** Arms

Date	Mintage	VG	F	VF	XF	Unc
1645 (f)	—	20.00	33.00	55.00	85.00	—

KM# 225 1/24 THALER (Reichsgroschen)
Silver **Obv:** Titles of Leopold I

Date	Mintage	VG	F	VF	XF	Unc
1661 (g)	—	—	—	—	—	—

KM# 246 1/24 THALER (Reichsgroschen)
Silver **Obv:** Oval arms with pointed bottom, ornate helmet and figure of maiden above **Obv. Legend:** DA PACEM... **Rev:** Imperial orb with 24 or Z4 divides date **Rev. Legend:** HILDESHEI STADT GELDT **Note:** Varieties exist.

Date	Mintage	VG	F	VF	XF	Unc
1688	—	16.00	27.00	50.00	80.00	—
1689	—	16.00	27.00	50.00	80.00	—
1691	—	16.00	27.00	50.00	80.00	—
1692	—	16.00	27.00	50.00	80.00	—
1693	—	16.00	27.00	50.00	80.00	—
1695	—	16.00	27.00	50.00	80.00	—
1695 HL	—	16.00	27.00	50.00	80.00	—
1696 HL	—	16.00	27.00	50.00	80.00	—
1697 HL	—	16.00	27.00	50.00	80.00	—
1698 HL	—	16.00	27.00	50.00	80.00	—
1699 HL	—	16.00	27.00	50.00	80.00	—
1700 HL	—	16.00	27.00	50.00	80.00	—

KM# 140 1/16 THALER (Doppelschilling)
Silver **Obv:** Crowned imperial eagle, 16 in orb on breast, titles of Rudolf II **Rev:** Arms, date above **Note:** Varieties exist.

Date	Mintage	VG	F	VF	XF	Unc
1601 (b)	—	33.00	80.00	140	200	—
1601 (b)	—	—	—	—	—	—
160Z (c) Rare	—	—	—	—	—	—
1605	—	33.00	80.00	140	200	—
1606	—	33.00	80.00	140	200	—

KM# 147 1/16 THALER (Doppelschilling)
Silver **Obv:** Date divided by arms

Date	Mintage	VG	F	VF	XF	Unc
1601 (b)	—	—	—	—	—	—

KM# 186 1/16 THALER (Doppelschilling)
Silver **Obv:** Crowned imperial eagle, 16 in orb on breast, titles of Ferdinand II **Rev:** Oval arms, ornate helmet and figure of maiden above **Note:** Kipper 1/16 Thaler.

Date	Mintage	VG	F	VF	XF	Unc
16Z0	—	—	—	—	—	—

KM# 196 1/2 REICHSORT (1/8 Thaler)
Silver **Obv:** EIN/HALB/RICHS (or REICHS)/ORT, titles of Ferdinand II and date **Rev:** Oval arms, ornate helmet and figure of maiden above **Note:** Varieties exist.

Date	Mintage	VG	F	VF	XF	Unc
16Z3 (e)	—	—	—	—	—	—
16Z4 (e)	—	—	—	—	—	—
16Z5 (e)	—	—	—	—	—	—
16Z6 (e)	—	—	—	—	—	—
16Z7/6 (e)	—	—	—	—	—	—

KM# 204 1/2 REICHSORT (1/8 Thaler)
Silver **Obv. Inscription:** Date / EIN / HALB / REICHS / ORT

Date	Mintage	VG	F	VF	XF	Unc
16Z4 (E)	—	—	—	—	—	—

KM# 203 1/2 REICHSORT (1/8 Thaler)
Silver **Note:** Klippe.

Date	Mintage	VG	F	VF	XF	Unc
16Z4 (e)	—	—	—	—	—	—

KM# 197 1/4 THALER (Reichsort)
Silver **Obv:** Crowned imperial eagle, orb on breast, titles of Ferdinand II around, date divided in legend at top **Rev:** Ornate arms, ornate helmet and figure of maiden above **Note:** Varieties exist.

Date	Mintage	VG	F	VF	XF	Unc
16Z3 (e)	—	—	—	—	—	—
16Z4 (e)	—	—	—	—	—	—
16Z5 (e)	—	—	—	—	—	—
16Z6 (e)	—	—	—	—	—	—

KM# 159 1/2 THALER
Silver **Obv:** Crowned imperial eagle, orb on breast, titles of Rudolf II **Rev:** Oval arms in baroque frame, figure of maiden above divides date

Date	Mintage	VG	F	VF	XF	Unc
1603 (b)	—	—	—	—	—	—

KM# 198 1/2 THALER
Silver **Obv:** Crowned imperial eagle, orb on breast, titles of Ferdinand II around, date divided in legend at top **Rev:** Ornately-shaped arms, ornate helmet and figure of maiden above

Date	Mintage	VG	F	VF	XF	Unc
16Z3 (e)	—	—	—	—	—	—
16Z4/3 (e)	—	—	—	—	—	—

KM# 206 1/2 THALER
Silver **Obv:** Arms in shield with rounded bottom, flat top

Date	Mintage	VG	F	VF	XF	Unc
16Z4 (e)	—	—	—	—	—	—

KM# 205 1/2 THALER
Silver **Obv:** Oval arms **Note:** Varieties exist.

Date	Mintage	VG	F	VF	XF	Unc
16Z4 (e)	—	—	—	—	—	—
16Z5 (e)	—	—	—	—	—	—
16Z6 (e)	—	—	—	—	—	—
16Z7 (e)	—	—	—	—	—	—
16Z8 (e)	—	—	—	—	—	—

KM# 208 1/2 THALER
Silver **Note:** Klippe.

Date	Mintage	VG	F	VF	XF	Unc
16Z6 (e)	—	—	—	—	—	—

KM# 141 THALER
Silver **Obv:** Crowned imperial eagle, Z4 in orb on breast, date divided by tail below, titles of Rudolf II **Rev:** Arms in ornate shield, ornate helmet and figure of maiden above **Note:** Dav. #5416.

Date	Mintage	VG	F	VF	XF	Unc
160Z (b) Rare	—	—	—	—	—	—

KM# 164 THALER
28.0000 g., Silver **Note:** Similar to 2 Thaler, KM#172. Dav. #LS325.

Date	Mintage	VG	F	VF	XF	Unc
ND(1618)	—	2,500	4,000	6,500	9,500	—

Note: Exists with Hildesheim orb or plain orb

KM# 195.1 THALER
Silver **Obv. Legend:** MONETA * NOVE * - * REIPUB * HILDES **Note:** Similar to KM#195.1. Dav. #5417.

Date	Mintage	VG	F	VF	XF	Unc
16ZZ MW	—	300	600	950	1,400	—

KM# 199 THALER
Silver **Obv:** Date divided in legend at bottom **Note:** Dav. #5418.

Date	Mintage	VG	F	VF	XF	Unc
16Z3 (e)	—	250	500	850	1,250	—

KM# 200 THALER
Silver **Obv:** Date left of crown at top **Note:** Dav. #5418.

Date	Mintage	VG	F	VF	XF	Unc
16Z3 (e)	—	250	500	850	1,250	—
16Z4 (e)	—	250	500	850	1,250	—

KM# 195.2 THALER
Silver **Obv:** Crowned imperial eagle, orb on breast, titles of Ferdinand II around, date divided in legend at top **Rev:** Oval arms in baroque frame, ornate helmet and figure of maiden above **Note:** Dav. #5419.

Date	Mintage	VG	F	VF	XF	Unc
16Z4 (e)	—	250	500	850	1,250	—

KM# 195.3 THALER
Silver **Obv:** Crowned eagle within inner circle **Rev:** Crown above double-headed imperial eagle within beaded circle **Note:** Dav. #5420.

Date	Mintage	VG	F	VF	XF	Unc
16Z4 (e)	—	250	500	850	1,450	—
16Z5 (e)	—	250	500	850	1,450	—
16Z6 (e)	—	250	500	850	1,450	—
16Z7 (e)	—	250	500	850	1,450	—
16Z8 (e)	—	250	500	850	1,450	3,000
1631	—	250	500	850	1,450	—

KM# 250 THALER
Silver **Note:** Similar to KM#72 but titles of Leopold I around, date divided in legend at top. Dav. #5421.

Date	Mintage	VG	F	VF	XF	Unc
1690	—	400	800	1,400	2,250	—

KM# A170 1-1/4 THALER
Silver **Note:** Dav. #LS324. Weight varies: 34.00-36.00 grams. Similar to 2 Thaler, KM#172.

Date	Mintage	VG	F	VF	XF	Unc
ND1618) Rare	—	—	—	—	—	—

KM# 171 1-1/2 THALER
Silver **Note:** Dav. #LS323. Weight varies: 43.00-44.00 grams. Similar to 2 Thaler, KM#172.

Date	Mintage	VG	F	VF	XF	Unc
ND(1618)	—	2,500	4,000	6,500	9,500	—

KM# 172 2 THALER
Silver **Note:** Dav. #LS322. Weight varies: 57.00-58.00 grams.

Date	Mintage	VG	F	VF	XF	Unc
ND(1618)	—	2,500	4,000	6,000	9,000	—

Note: Exists with Hildesheim orb or plain orb

KM# 173 2-1/2 THALER
74.0000 g., Silver **Note:** Dav. #LS321. Similar to 2 Thaler, KM#172.

Date	Mintage	VG	F	VF	XF	Unc
ND(1618) Rare	—	—	—	—	—	—

KM# 174 3 THALER
87.0000 g., Silver **Note:** Dav. #LS320. Similar to 2 Thaler, KM#172.

Date	Mintage	VG	F	VF	XF	Unc
ND(1618) Rare	—	—	—	—	—	—

TRADE COINAGE

KM# 201 1/2 GOLDGULDEN
1.7500 g., 0.9860 Gold 0.0555 oz. AGW **Obv:** Crowned imperial eagle, titles of Ferdinand II and date in legend **Rev:** Arms in baroque frame

Date	Mintage	VG	F	VF	XF	Unc
1623 (e)	—	400	800	1,700	3,300	—

KM# 209 1/2 GOLDGULDEN
1.7500 g., 0.9860 Gold 0.0555 oz. AGW **Obv:** Crowned imperial eagle, orb on breast, titles of Ferdinand II around, date in legend at top **Rev:** Oval arms with pointed bottom, ornate helmet and figure of maiden above

Date	Mintage	VG	F	VF	XF	Unc
1627 (e)	—	400	800	1,700	3,300	—

KM# 158 GOLDGULDEN
3.5000 g., 0.9860 Gold 0.1109 oz. AGW **Obv:** Crowned imperial eagle, orb on breast, titles of Rudolf II **Rev:** Arms, ornate helmet and figure of maiden above divide date

Date	Mintage	VG	F	VF	XF	Unc
1602 (b)	—	500	975	2,300	4,200	—
1603 (b)	—	500	975	2,300	4,200	—
1606/3 (b)	—	500	975	2,300	4,200	—

KM# 202 GOLDGULDEN
3.5000 g., 0.9860 Gold 0.1109 oz. AGW **Obv:** Titles of Ferdinand II, date divided in legend at top

Date	Mintage	VG	F	VF	XF	Unc
1623 (e)	—	400	900	1,700	3,500	—
1627 (e)	—	400	900	1,700	3,500	—
1628 (e)	—	400	900	1,700	3,500	—

KM# 235 GOLDGULDEN
3.5000 g., 0.9860 Gold 0.1109 oz. AGW **Obv:** Titles of Leopold I

Date	Mintage	VG	F	VF	XF	Unc
1672	—	1,300	2,650	5,300	9,000	—

KM# A196 4 GOLDGULDEN
14.4800 g., 0.9860 Gold 0.4590 oz. AGW **Note:** Struck with 1 Thaler dies, KM#195.3.

Date	Mintage	VG	F	VF	XF	Unc
16Z6 (e) Rare	—	—	—	—	—	—

PATTERNS

Including off metal strikes

KM#	Date	Mintage	Identification	Mkt Val
Pn1	16Z4	—	Mariengroschen. Gold.	—
Pn2	16Z6 (e)	—	1/2 Thaler. Gold.	—
Pn4	1700	—	3 Pfennig. Copper.	—

HOHENGEROLDSECK

The line of these lords, who had lands in Baden, began in the late 12th century. Upon the extinction of the dynasty in 1634, the territory passed to Cronberg and finally to Leyen in 1692.

RULER
Jakob, 1569-1634

LORDSHIP

REGULAR COINAGE

KM# 1 12 KREUZER (Schreckenberger)
Silver **Obv:** Crowned imperial eagle, 12 in orb on breast, titles of Ferdinand II **Rev:** Arms **Note:** Kipper 12 Kreuzer.

Date	Mintage	VG	F	VF	XF	Unc
ND(1621/2)	—	—	—	—	—	—

Note: Many forgeries known to exist

HOHENLOHE

A countship located in the vicinity of Uffenheim in Franconia and originally centered on the village and castle of present-day Hohlach. The ruling family derived its name from the place name and has been traced back as far as the 10th century. The counts gradually acquired various territories between Offenheim to Bad Mergentheim and beyond that became the basis for the many branches of the dynasty. The first of these was Weikersheim with its castle overlooking the confluence of the Vorbach with the Tauber River. In 1472, the surviving elder branch of counts was divided into Hohenlohe-Weikersheim and Hohenlohe Neuenstein. The former became extinct in 1545 and its lands reverted to Hohenlohe-Neuenstein, which itself was divided once again into Hohenlohe-Neuenstein-Neuenstein (Protestant) and Hohenlohe-Neuenstein-Waldenburg (Catholic) in 1551. Hohenlohe-Neuenstein-Neuenstein was further divided in 1610 (see) and Hohenlohe-Neuenstein-Waldenburg underwent the same process in 1600 with the establishment of Hohenlohe-Waldenburg-Pfedelbach, Hohenlohe-Waldenburg-Schillingsfürst and Hohenlohe-Waldenburg-Waldenburg. See the sections under each of these branches for the subsequent history of each. The lands of all branches of Hohenlohe were mediatized in 1806, thereafter passing to Bavaria and Württemberg.

JOINT COINAGE

From 1594 to 1622 a joint coinage was issued for all the counts of the various branches of Hohenlohe. See under each branch for names and dates of individual rulers.

MINT MARKS
N = Neuenstein (Kipper period)
S = Schwabach

MINT OFFICIALS' INITIALS

Initial	Date	Name
	1594-?	Paul Diether
	1615-21	Herr Müller

ARMS
Hohenlohe – 2 leopards passant left
Langenburg – crowned lion passant left or right above Lozengy field.

REFERENCE
A = Joseph Albrecht, *Münzgeschichte des Hauses Hohenlohe*, Öhringen, 1865.

COUNTSHIP

From 1594 to 1622 a joint coinage was issued for all the counts of the various branches of Hohenlohe. See under each branch for names and dates of individual rulers.

MINT MARKS
N – Neuenstein (Kipper period)

MINT OFFICIALS' INITIALS

Initial	Date	Name
	1594-?	Paul Diether
I	1615-21	Herr Müller

ARMS
Hohenlohe – 2 leopards passant left
Langenburg – Crowned lion passant left or right above lozengy field

JOINT COINAGE

KM# 9 PFENNIG
Silver **Note:** Uniface. Shields of Hohenlohe and Langenburg arms. Varieties exist.

Date	Mintage	VG	F	VF	XF	Unc
1603	—	27.00	45.00	80.00	140	—
1604	—	27.00	45.00	80.00	140	—
1605	—	27.00	45.00	80.00	140	—
1606	—	27.00	45.00	80.00	140	—
1609	—	27.00	45.00	80.00	140	—
1610	—	27.00	45.00	80.00	140	—
1615	—	27.00	45.00	80.00	140	—
1616	—	27.00	45.00	80.00	140	—

KM# 24 PFENNIG
Silver **Note:** Kipper Pfennig. Langenburg arms with lion striding right, 1 above.

Date	Mintage	VG	F	VF	XF	Unc
ND1621/2)	—	—	—	—	—	—

KM# 25 PFENNIG
Silver **Note:** Lion striding left.

Date	Mintage	VG	F	VF	XF	Unc
ND(1621/2)	—	—	—	—	—	—

KM# 26 2 PFENNIG (1/2 Kreuzer)
Silver **Note:** Uniface. Similar to 1 Pfennig, KM#9 but value 2 above arms.

Date	Mintage	VG	F	VF	XF	Unc
ND1621/2	—	—	—	—	—	—

KM# 8 1/84 THALER (3 Pfennig)
Silver **Obv:** Four-fold arms in ornamented shield **Rev:** Imperial orb with 84 divides date in rhombus **Note:** Varieties exist.

Date	Mintage	VG	F	VF	XF	Unc
1602	—	27.00	55.00	100	170	—
1603	—	27.00	55.00	100	170	—
1604	—	27.00	55.00	100	170	—
1605	—	27.00	55.00	100	170	—
1606	—	27.00	55.00	100	170	—
1609	—	27.00	55.00	100	170	—
1615	—	27.00	55.00	100	170	—

KM# 33 3 KREUZER (Groschen)
Silver **Rev:** Four-fold arms

Date	Mintage	VG	F	VF	XF	Unc
1622	—	33.00	60.00	115	185	—

KM# 34 3 KREUZER (Groschen)
Silver **Obv:** Imperial orb with 3 **Rev:** Hohenlohe arms, date above

Date	Mintage	VG	F	VF	XF	Unc
1622	—	33.00	60.00	115	185	—

KM# 32 3 KREUZER (Groschen)
Silver **Obv:** Crowned imperial eagle, 3 in orb on breast **Rev:** Hohenlohe arms, date in legend **Note:** Kipper 3 Groschen.

Date	Mintage	VG	F	VF	XF	Unc
1622	—	33.00	60.00	115	185	—

KM# 28 12 KREUZER (Schreckenberger)
Silver **Rev:** Four-fold arms divide date

Date	Mintage	VG	F	VF	XF	Unc
1621	—	27.00	70.00	125	200	—

KM# 29 12 KREUZER (Schreckenberger)
Silver **Rev:** Arms, date above

Date	Mintage	VG	F	VF	XF	Unc
1621	—	27.00	65.00	120	200	—

KM# 30 12 KREUZER (Schreckenberger)
Silver **Rev:** Crowned four-fold arms

Date	Mintage	VG	F	VF	XF	Unc
ND(1621)	—	27.00	65.00	120	200	—

KM# 27 12 KREUZER (Schreckenberger)
Silver **Obv:** Crowned imperial eagle, 12 in orb on breast, titles of Ferdinand II **Rev:** Crowned four-fold arms divide date **Note:** Klippe. Kipper 12 Kreuzer.

Date	Mintage	VG	F	VF	XF	Unc
1621	—	27.00	65.00	120	200	—

KM# 31 24 KREUZER (Doppelschreckenberger)
Silver **Obv:** Crowned 4-fold arms divide date **Rev:** Crowned imperial eagle, 24 in orb on breast, titles of Ferdinand II **Note:** Varieties exist.

Date	Mintage	VG	F	VF	XF	Unc
1621	—	33.00	85.00	165	275	—
1621 N	—	33.00	85.00	165	275	—
ND(1621)	—	33.00	85.00	165	275	—

KM# 35 24 KREUZER (Doppelschreckenberger)
Silver **Obv:** Crowned imperial eagle, 24 in orb on breast, MON: NOV:... **Rev:** Crowned four-fold arms, date in legend

Date	Mintage	VG	F	VF	XF	Unc
1622	—	33.00	85.00	165	275	—
1622 N	—	33.00	85.00	165	275	—

KM# 36 24 KREUZER (Doppelschreckenberger)
Silver **Obv:** Crowned four-fold arms divide date **Rev:** Crowned imperial eagle, 24 in circle on breast, titles of Ferdinand II

Date	Mintage	VG	F	VF	XF	Unc
(16)22	—	33.00	85.00	165	275	—

KM# 37 24 KREUZER (Doppelschreckenberger)
Silver **Obv:** Count's crown above 4-fold arms **Rev:** Crowned imperial eagle, 24 in orb on breast **Rev. Legend:** PIETATE...

Date	Mintage	VG	F	VF	XF	Unc
1622	—	33.00	85.00	165	275	—

KM# 10 1/4 THALER
Silver **Note:** Similar to KM#16.

Date	Mintage	VG	F	VF	XF	Unc
1607 Rare	—	—	—	—	—	—
1609 Rare	—	—	—	—	—	—
1610 Rare	—	—	—	—	—	—

KM# 16 1/4 THALER
Silver **Obv:** Titles of Matthias

Date	Mintage	VG	F	VF	XF	Unc
1615 Rare	—	—	—	—	—	—

KM# 12 1/3 THALER (1/2 Gulden)
Silver **Note:** Similar to KM#16.

Date	Mintage	VG	F	VF	XF	Unc
1608 Rare	—	—	—	—	—	—

KM# 11 1/2 THALER
Silver **Note:** Similar to KM#16.

Date	Mintage	VG	F	VF	XF	Unc
1607 Rare	—	—	—	—	—	—
1609 Rare	—	—	—	—	—	—
1610 Rare	—	—	—	—	—	—

KM# 17 1/2 THALER
Silver **Obv:** Titles of Matthias

Date	Mintage	VG	F	VF	XF	Unc
1615 Rare	—	—	—	—	—	—

KM# 5 THALER
Silver **Obv:** 4-fold arms in ornamented shield, date above **Rev:** Crowned imperial eagle, orb on breast, titles of Rudolf II **Note:** Dav# 6818.

Date	Mintage	VG	F	VF	XF	Unc
1601	—	150	275	450	700	—

KM# 6 THALER
Silver **Note:** Varieties exist. Dav. #6819.

Date	Mintage	VG	F	VF	XF	Unc
1603	—	100	200	550	1,450	—
1605	—	100	200	550	1,450	—
1607	—	100	200	550	1,450	—
1608	—	100	200	550	1,450	—
1609	—	100	200	550	1,450	—
1610	—	100	200	550	1,450	—

KM# 18 THALER
Silver **Obv:** Titles of Matthias **Note:** Dav. #6820.

Date	Mintage	VG	F	VF	XF	Unc
1615	—	150	300	750	1,650	—

KM# 19 GOLDGULDEN
3.5000 g., 0.9860 Gold 0.1109 oz. AGW **Obv:** 4-fold arms divide date **Rev:** Crowned imperial eagle, orb on breast, titles of Matthias

Date	Mintage	VG	F	VF	XF	Unc
1615	—	1,500	3,000	6,000	10,500	—

TRADE COINAGE

KM# 7 DUCAT
3.5000 g., 0.9860 Gold 0.1109 oz. AGW **Obv:** 4-fold arms of Hohenlohe and Waldenburg in ornamented frame divide date, MO.NO.COM...begins within small imperial orb **Rev:** Armored and laureate figure of knight with large sword at side, helmet at feet, titles of Rudolf II

Date	Mintage	VG	F	VF	XF	Unc
1608	—	600	1,350	3,000	5,300	—
1610	—	600	1,350	3,000	5,300	—

KM# 13 DUCAT
3.5000 g., 0.9860 Gold 0.1109 oz. AGW **Obv:** 4-fold arms of Hohenlohe and Waldenburg divide date as 1-6/0-8, M: NO; COM:... **Rev:** Crowned imperial eagle, orb on breast, titles of Rudolf II

Date	Mintage	VG	F	VF	XF	Unc
1608	—	1,500	3,000	5,300	8,300	—

KM# 20 DUCAT
3.5000 g., 0.9860 Gold 0.1109 oz. AGW **Obv:** Knight standing 3/4 right, titles of Matthias **Rev:** Four-fold arms in ornamented shield divide date

Date	Mintage	VG	F	VF	XF	Unc
1615	—	—	—	—	—	—

KM# 15 2 DUCAT
7.0000 g., 0.9860 Gold 0.2219 oz. AGW **Obv:** Knight standing 3/4 right, titles of Rudolf II **Rev:** Four-fold arms in ornamented shield divide date

Date	Mintage	VG	F	VF	XF	Unc
1610 Rare	—	—	—	—	—	—

KM# 21 2 DUCAT
7.0000 g., 0.9860 Gold 0.2219 oz. AGW **Obv:** Titles of Matthias

Date	Mintage	VG	F	VF	XF	Unc
1615 Rare	—	—	—	—	—	—

KM# 22 3 DUCAT
10.5000 g., 0.9860 Gold 0.3328 oz. AGW **Obv:** Knight on horseback **Rev:** Ornate helmets, date above **Note:** Similar to 1 Thaler, KM#18.

Date	Mintage	VG	F	VF	XF	Unc
1615 Rare	—	—	—	—	—	—

KM# 23 4 DUCAT
14.0000 g., 0.9860 Gold 0.4438 oz. AGW **Obv:** Knight on horseback **Rev:** Ornate helmets, date above **Note:** Similar to 1 Thaler, KM#18.

Date	Mintage	VG	F	VF	XF	Unc
1615 Rare	—	—	—	—	—	—

HOHENLOHE-LANGENBURG

A branch of Hohenlohe-Neuenstein founded in 1610 and was the Protestant line of the family. It was divided again in 1701, Langenburg being one of the cointinuing entities. The count gained princely rank in 1764, but lost his territory as a result of the mediatization of 1806.

RULERS

Philipp Ernst, 1610-1629
Ludwig Krato, 1629-1632
Joachim Albrecht, 1632-1675
Heinrich Friedrich, 1675-1699
Albrecht Wolfgang, 1699-1715

MINT MARKS

K - Kirchberg
L - Langenburg

MINTMASTERS' INITIALS

Date	Name
1621-23	Egidius Poller at Kirchberg
1621-22	Gerhard Dreyer von Hanau at Langenburg
1622	Jeremias Delssner at Langenburg
1622-23	Jacob de Lannon at Langenburg

PRINCIPALITY

REGULAR COINAGE

KM# 16 1/84 THALER (3 Pfennig)
Silver **Obv:** Adjacent shields of Hohenlohe and Langenburg arms crown above **Rev:** Imperial orb with 84 divides date in rhombus

Date	Mintage	VG	F	VF	XF	Unc
1623	—	—	—	—	—	—

KM# 14 3 KREUZER (Groschen)
Silver

Date	Mintage	VG	F	VF	XF	Unc
16Z3	—	—	—	—	—	—

KM# 15 3 KREUZER (Groschen)
Silver **Obv:** 4-fold arms without crown divide date

Date	Mintage	VG	F	VF	XF	Unc
(16)23	—	—	—	—	—	—

KM# 5 12 KREUZER (Schreckenberger)
Silver **Obv:** Crowned 4-fold arms divide date **Rev:** Crowned imperial eagle, 1Z in orb on breast, titles of Ferdianand II **Note:** Kipper 12 Kreuzer

Date	Mintage	VG	F	VF	XF	Unc
16Z1	—	27.00	55.00	100	165	—

KM# 9 12 KREUZER (Schreckenberger)
Silver **Rev:** Date in legend

Date	Mintage	VG	F	VF	XF	Unc
16ZZ	—	27.00	55.00	100	165	—

KM# 7 24 KREUZER (Doppelschreckenberg)
Silver **Obv:** Bust right **Rev:** Crowned four-fold arms

Date	Mintage	VG	F	VF	XF	Unc
16Z1	—	80.00	160	280	450	—
16ZZ	—	80.00	160	280	450	—

KM# 8 24 KREUZER (Doppelschreckenberg)
Silver **Rev:** Z4 in legend at bottom

Date	Mintage	VG	F	VF	XF	Unc
1621	—	80.00	160	280	450	—

KM# 13 24 KREUZER (Doppelschreckenberg)
Silver **Obv:** Titles of Ferdinand II

Date	Mintage	VG	F	VF	XF	Unc
ND(1621/22)	—	80.00	160	280	450	—

KM# 6 24 KREUZER (Doppelschreckenberg)
Silver **Obv:** Facing bust, 24 in legend **Rev:** Four-fold arms divide date **Note:** Kipper 24 Kreuzer

Date	Mintage	VG	F	VF	XF	Unc
16Z1	—	90.00	170	280	450	—

KM# 12 24 KREUZER (Doppelschreckenberg)
Silver **Obv:** Crowned four-fold arms **Note:** Varieties exist.

Date	Mintage	VG	F	VF	XF	Unc
16ZZ	—	33.00	75.00	125	215	—
16ZZ K	—	33.00	75.00	125	215	—
16ZZ L	—	33.00	75.00	125	215	—

KM# 10 24 KREUZER (Doppelschreckenberg)
Silver **Obv:** Bust right, date below **Rev:** Crowned imperial eagle, Z4 in orb on breast

Date	Mintage	VG	F	VF	XF	Unc
16ZZ K	—	85.00	165	325	550	—

KM# 11 24 KREUZER (Doppelschreckenberg)
Silver **Obv:** Bust right **Rev:** Date in legend

Date	Mintage	VG	F	VF	XF	Unc
16ZZ	—	85.00	165	325	550	—

KM# 17 THALER
Silver **Subject:** 50th Anniversary of Territorial Division **Note:** Dav. #6832.

Date	Mintage	VG	F	VF	XF	Unc
16Z3	—	550	950	1,600	2,400	—

KM# 18 THALER
Silver **Obv:** Oval arms in baroque frame divide date **Note:** Dav. #6833.

Date	Mintage	VG	F	VF	XF	Unc
1623	—	550	950	1,600	2,400	—

HOHENLOHE-NEUENSTEIN-NEUENSTEIN

COUNTSHIP

REGULAR COINAGE

KM# 10 HELLER
Silver **Obv:** Adjacent arms of Hohenlohe and Langenburg in two shields, CGVH above, date below. **Note:** Uniface.

Date	Mintage	VG	F	VF	XF	Unc
(16)23	—	33.00	70.00	120	200	—

KM# 15 1/84 THALER (3 Pfennig - 1 Dreier)
Silver **Obv:** Solitary Hohenlohe arms in crowned rhombus, CG-VH divided near top **Rev:** Imperial orb with 84 divides date in rhombus

Date	Mintage	VG	F	VF	XF	Unc
1623 A	—	40.00	80.00	160	275	—

KM# 21 1/84 THALER (3 Pfennig - 1 Dreier)
Silver **Obv:** Two leopards right in Hohenlohe arms

Date	Mintage	VG	F	VF	XF	Unc
16Z4 IIR	—	40.00	80.00	160	275	—

KM# 11 KREUZER
Silver

Date	Mintage	VG	F	VF	XF	Unc
16Z3	—	40.00	80.00	140	245	—

KM# 12 2 KREUZER (1/2 Batzen)
Silver **Obv:** Imperial orb with 2, titles of Ferdinand II **Rev:** Crowned 3-fold arms, date in legend

Date	Mintage	VG	F	VF	XF	Unc
1623	—	45.00	85.00	165	275	—
1624	—	45.00	85.00	165	275	—

KM# 13 2 KREUZER (1/2 Batzen)
Silver **Obv:** Date divided by orb

Date	Mintage	VG	F	VF	XF	Unc
1623	—	45.00	85.00	165	275	—

KM# 20 2 KREUZER (1/2 Batzen)
Silver **Obv:** Imperial orb with 2 **Rev:** Crowned adjacent arms of Hohenlohe and Langenburg, date above

Date	Mintage	VG	F	VF	XF	Unc
16Z4	—	45.00	85.00	165	275	—

KM# 23 2 KREUZER (1/2 Batzen)
Silver **Obv:** Z in orb on breast

Date	Mintage	VG	F	VF	XF	Unc
1628	—	45.00	85.00	165	275	—

KM# 14 3 KREUZER (Groschen)
Silver **Obv:** Crowned imperial eagle, 3 in shield on breast, titles of Ferdinand II **Rev:** 4-fold arms, date above

Date	Mintage	VG	F	VF	XF	Unc
1623	—	55.00	100	180	300	—
1623 A	—	55.00	100	180	300	—

KM# 30 4 KREUZER (Batzen)
Silver

Date	Mintage	VG	F	VF	XF	Unc
1697 GFN	—	20.00	45.00	85.00	165	—

KM# 5 12 KREUZER (Schreckenberger)
Silver **Obv:** Crowned imperial eagle, 12 in orb on breast, titles of Ferdinand II **Rev:** Crowned 4-fold arms divide date

Date	Mintage	VG	F	VF	XF	Unc
1621	—	—	—	—	—	—

KM# 6 24 KREUZER (Doppelschreckenberger)
Silver **Obv:** Crowned 4-fold arms divide date **Rev:** Crowned imperial eagle, 24 in orb on breast, titles of Ferdinand II **Note:** Kipper 24 Kreuzer.

Date	Mintage	VG	F	VF	XF	Unc
1621	—	45.00	85.00	165	300	—

KM# 7 24 KREUZER (Doppelschreckenberger)
Silver **Obv:** Bust right **Rev:** Crowned 4-fold arms, date above

Date	Mintage	VG	F	VF	XF	Unc
1622	—	—	—	—	—	—

KM# 9 24 KREUZER (Doppelschreckenberger)
Silver **Obv:** Crowned 4-fold arms divide date, titles of Kraft and Philipp Ernst

Date	Mintage	VG	F	VF	XF	Unc
1622	—	—	—	—	—	—

KM# 8 24 KREUZER (Doppelschreckenberger)
Silver **Obv:** Crowned 4-fold arms, date in legend **Rev:** Crowned imperial eagle, 24 in orb on breast **Rev. Legend:** PIETATE... **Mint:** Weickersheim **Note:** Joint issues with Philipp Ernst of Hohenlohe-Neuenstein-Langenburg.

Date	Mintage	VG	F	VF	XF	Unc
1622	—	—	—	—	—	—

KM# 16 THALER
Silver **Obv:** Crowned imperial eagle, titles of Ferdinand II **Rev:** Crowned 4-fold arms divide date **Note:** Dav. #6823.

Date	Mintage	VG	F	VF	XF	Unc
1623	—	1,000	2,000	4,000	6,500	—

KM# 18 THALER
Silver **Note:** Dav. #6824.

Date	Mintage	VG	F	VF	XF	Unc
1623	—	250	450	800	1,500	—
1624	—	300	550	900	1,650	—

KM# 17 THALER
Silver **Note:** Klippe. Dav. #6823A.

Date	Mintage	VG	F	VF	XF	Unc
1623 Rare	—	—	—	—	—	—

KM# 19.1 THALER
Silver Varieties exist. Dav. #6825.

Date	Mintage	VG	F	VF	XF	Unc
1623	—	120	250	500	1,000	—
1624	—	200	350	700	1,200	—
1625	—	200	350	700	1,200	—

KM# 19.2 THALER
Silver **Note:** Dav. #6826.

Date	Mintage	VG	F	VF	XF	Unc
16Z4	—	175	300	600	1,350	2,500

KM# 22 THALER
Silver **Note:** Klippe. Dav. #6825A

Date	Mintage	VG	F	VF	XF	Unc
1625 Rare	—	—	—	—	—	—

KM# 25 THALER
Silver **Obv:** Ornate 4-fold arms with central shield, three helmets above **Rev:** Knight on horseback springing left, globe below divides date **Note:** Dav. #6827.

Date	Mintage	VG	F	VF	XF	Unc
163Z	—	300	550	900	1,650	—

KM# 31 THALER
Silver **Note:** Dav. #6831.

Date	Mintage	VG	F	VF	XF	Unc
1697 GFN	—	120	220	475	1,000	1,650

TRADE COINAGE

KM# 26 DUCAT
3.5000 g., 0.9860 Gold 0.1109 oz. AGW **Obv:** Ornate 4-fold arms with central shield, three helmets above **Rev:** Knight on horseback springing left, globe below divides date

Date	Mintage	VG	F	VF	XF	Unc
1632	—	—	—	—	—	—

KM# 32 DUCAT
3.5000 g., 0.9860 Gold 0.1109 oz. AGW

Date	Mintage	VG	F	VF	XF	Unc
1697 GFN	—	—	600	1,200	2,500	4,000

KM# 33 8 DUCAT
28.0000 g., 0.9860 Gold 0.8876 oz. AGW **Note:** Similar to 1 Thaler, KM#31.

Date	Mintage	VG	F	VF	XF	Unc
1697 GFN Rare	—	—	—	—	—	—

HOHENLOHE-NEUENSTEIN-OEHRINGEN

This principality was located in southern Germany. The Neuenstein-Öhringen line was founded in 1610 and the first prince of the empire from this line was proclaimed in 1764. The line became extinct in 1805 and the lands passed to Ingelfingen.

RULERS
Johann Friedrich I, 1641-1702
Wolfgang Julius von Neuenstein, 1641-1698
Siegfried von Weikersheim, 1645-1684
Johann Ludwig von Künzelsau, 1641-1689

MINT OFFICIALS' INITIALS

Initial	Date	Name
(a) = 2 horseshoes	1668-97	Johann Christoph Holeisen at Augsburg

COUNTSHIP

REGULAR COINAGE

KM# 17 1/8 THALER
Silver **Ruler:** Johann Friedrich I **Mint:** Augsburg **Note:** Similar to 1/4 Thaler, KM#18. Struck from ducat dies, KM# 22.

Date	Mintage	VG	F	VF	XF	Unc
1699 (a)	—	—	—	—	—	—

KM# 18 1/4 THALER
7.2000 g., Silver **Ruler:** Johann Friedrich I **Mint:** Augsburg **Note:** Struck from ducat dies, KM# 22.

Date	Mintage	VG	F	VF	XF	Unc
1699 (a)	—	135	275	525	850	—

KM# 19 1/2 THALER
Silver **Ruler:** Johann Friedrich I **Obv:** Knight on horse leaping left over globe, below which divides date, DEO - DUCE before and after knight, titles of Johann Friedrich I around and value "1/2 Thr. 60 Kr" in margin at bottom **Rev:** Ornately-shaped shield of 4-fold arms with central shield, 3 ornate helmets above, titles continued **Mint:** Augsburg **Note:** Albrecht 131.

Date	Mintage	VG	F	VF	XF	Unc
1699 (a)	—	135	275	525	850	—

KM# 15 THALER
Silver **Ruler:** Johann Friedrich I **Rev:** Age of count is 79 in legend **Mint:** Augsburg **Note:** Dav. #6828.

Date	Mintage	VG	F	VF	XF	Unc
1696 (a)	—	200	350	650	1,200	2,500

KM# 20 THALER

Silver **Ruler:** Johann Friedrich I **Obv:** Knight on horse leaping left over globe, below which divides date, DEO - DUCE before and after knight, titles of Johann Friedrich I around and value "1/2 Thr. 60 kr" in margin at bottom **Rev:** Ornately-shaped shield of 4-fold arms with central shield, 3 ornate helmets above, titles continued **Mint:** Augsburg **Note:** Struck from 1/2 Thaler dies as KM#19. Dav. #6830.

Date	Mintage	VG	F	VF	XF	Unc
1699 (a)	—	175	300	600	1,150	2,500

KM# 21 2 THALER

Silver **Ruler:** Johann Friedrich I **Obv:** Knight on horse leaping left over globe, below which divides date, DEO - DUCE before and after knight, titles of Johann Friedrich I around and value "1/2 Thr. 60 kr" in margin at bottom **Rev:** Ornately-shaped shield of 4-fold arms with central shield, 3 ornate helmets above, titles continued **Mint:** Augsburg **Note:** Struck from 1/2 Thaler dies as KM#19. Dav# 6829.

Date	Mintage	VG	F	VF	XF	Unc
1699 (a) Rare	—	—	—	—	—	—

TRADE COINAGE

KM# 22 DUCAT

3.5000 g., 0.9860 Gold 0.1109 oz. AGW **Ruler:** Johann Friedrich I **Obv:** Equestrian figure of knight riding left above globe dividing date in inner circle **Rev:** Arms topped by 3 helms **Mint:** Augsburg

Date	Mintage	VG	F	VF	XF	Unc
1699 (a)	—	—	—	—	—	—

KM# 23 2 DUCAT

7.0000 g., 0.9860 Gold 0.2219 oz. AGW **Ruler:** Johann Friedrich I **Mint:** Augsburg

Date	Mintage	VG	F	VF	XF	Unc
1699 (a) Rare	—	—	—	—	—	—

KM# 25 7 DUCAT

24.5000 g., 0.9860 Gold 0.7766 oz. AGW **Ruler:** Johann Friedrich I **Obv:** Knight on horse leaping left, globe below divides date **Rev:** Ornate 4-fold arms with central shield, 3 ornate helmets above **Mint:** Augsburg

Date	Mintage	VG	F	VF	XF	Unc
1700 (a) Rare	—	—	—	—	—	—

HOHENLOHE-NEUENSTEIN-WEIKERSHEIM

Established as a branch of Hohenlohe-Neuenstein in the division of 1610, it became extinct in one generation and passed to Hohenlohe-Neuenstein-Neuenstein from which line the younger brothers ruled Weikersheim until 1756.

RULERS

Georg Friedrich, 1610-1645
Siegfried, 1645-1684

MINT MARK

N – Nuremberg

PRINCIPALITY

REGULAR COINAGE

KM# 5.1 THALER

Silver **Obv:** Horseman left, shield below divides date within circle **Obv. Legend:** GEORGE: FRID: COM: -DE: **Rev:** Crowned double eagle with orb on breast **Note:** Dav. #6821.

Date	Mintage	VG	F	VF	XF	Unc
1623	—	300	550	950	1,750	—

KM# 5.2 THALER

Silver **Obv:** Shield below horse divides date and breaks through inner circle **Note:** Dav. #6822.

Date	Mintage	VG	F	VF	XF	Unc
16Z4	—	350	600	1,000	1,850	—

HOHENLOHE-PFEDELBACH

Established as one of three lines of the Waldenburg (Catholic) branch of Hohenlohe in 1600. It became extinct in 1728, passed to Hohenlohe-Bartenstein. A new line was established as Hohenlohe-Bartenstein-Pfedelbach (which see).

RULERS

Ludwig Eberhard, 1600-1650
Friedrich Kraft, 1650-1681
Hiskias, 1681-1685
Ludwig Gottfried, 1685-1728

PRINCIPALITY

REGULAR COINAGE

KM# 5 PFENNIG

Silver **Note:** Uniface. Adjacent shields of Hohenlohe and Langenburg arms, LE above.

Date	Mintage	VG	F	VF	XF	Unc
ND(ca.1610)	—	27.00	55.00	110	170	—

KM# 14 2 KREUZER (1/2 Batzen)

Silver **Obv:** Crowned arms within circle, date above **Rev:** Value within orb

Date	Mintage	VG	F	VF	XF	Unc
1623	—	55.00	110	175	300	—

KM# 10 3 KREUZER (Groschen)

Silver **Obv:** Crowned four-fold arms divide date **Rev:** Crowned imperial eagle, 3 in orb on breast, titles of Ferdinand II

Date	Mintage	VG	F	VF	XF	Unc
(16)21	—	16.00	33.00	60.00	120	—
(16)ZZ	—	16.00	33.00	60.00	120	—

KM# 11 24 KREUZER (Doppelschreckenberger)

Silver **Obv:** 4-fold arms, date divided by crown above **Rev:** Crowned imperial eagle, 24 in orb on breast, titles of Ferdinand II

Date	Mintage	VG	F	VF	XF	Unc
1621	—	33.00	65.00	120	200	—

KM# 12 24 KREUZER (Doppelschreckenberger)

Silver **Rev:** Date divided by arms

Date	Mintage	VG	F	VF	XF	Unc
1622	—	33.00	65.00	120	200	—

KM# 13 THALER

Silver **Note:** Similar to KM#15 but titles of Ludwig Eberhard on reverse. Dav. #6834.

Date	Mintage	VG	F	VF	XF	Unc
1622	—	600	950	1,650	2,800	—

KM# 15 THALER

Silver **Subject:** Joint Coinage with Philipp Heinrich of Hohenlohe-Waldenburg-Waldenburg **Obv:** Titles of both counts **Rev:** Crown above double-headed imperial eagle within circle **Note:** Dav. #6835.

Date	Mintage	VG	F	VF	XF	Unc
1623	—	350	700	1,500	2,500	—

PATTERNS

Including off metal strikes

KM#	Date	Mintage	Identification	Mkt Val
Pn1	1622	—	Thaler. Gold. KM#13	—

HOHENLOHE-WALDENBURG-SCHILLINGSFURST

In 1600 the Pfedelbach, Waldenburg and Schillingsfürst lines of Hohenlohe were established from Waldenburg, the Catholic branch of the family. Waldenburg became extinct in 1679 with all lands passing to Schillingsfurst. The count gained the rank of prince in 1744, but the line only lasted until mediatization in 1806.

RULERS

Georg Friedrich II, 1600-1635
Moritz Friedrich, 1635-1646
Georg Adolf, 1646-1656
Ludwig Gustav, 1656-1697
Philipp Ernst, 1697-1753

MINT MARKS

F - Friedberg

MINTMASTERS' INITIALS

Initial	Date	Name
AD	1689-90	Andreas Dittmar
GFN	1682-1724	Georg Friedrich Nürnberger in Nuremberg
IR	ca.1690	

NOTE: Mints functioned at Bartenstein and Schillingsfürst during the Kipper Period.

PRINCIPALITY

REGULAR COINAGE

KM# 19 1/84 THALER (3 Pfennig)

Silver **Ruler:** Ludwig Gustav **Obv:** Crowned arms of Hohenlohe and Langenburg in ornamented shield **Rev:** Imperial orb with 84 divides date

Date	Mintage	VG	F	VF	XF	Unc
1685	—	33.00	65.00	120	200	—

KM# 20 1/84 THALER (3 Pfennig)

Silver **Ruler:** Ludwig Gustav **Obv:** 3 shields of arms, 2 larger above, 1 smaller below divides date, F in middle, crown above **Rev:** Imperial orb with 84 in ornamented rhombus, alchemical symbols to left and right of orb **Note:** Varieties exist.

Date	Mintage	VG	F	VF	XF	Unc
1685 F	—	20.00	40.00	80.00	165	—
1689 AD	—	20.00	40.00	80.00	165	—
1690 AD	—	20.00	40.00	80.00	165	—
1690 IR	—	20.00	40.00	80.00	165	—
1690	—	20.00	40.00	80.00	165	—
1691	—	20.00	40.00	80.00	165	—

KM# 5 3 KREUZER (Groschen)

Silver **Ruler:** Georg Friedrich II **Obv:** Imperial orb with 3 divides date, titles of Ferdinand II **Rev:** Crowned round 4-fold arms **Note:** Kipper 3 Kreuzer.

Date	Mintage	VG	F	VF	XF	Unc
1622	—	33.00	65.00	120	225	—

KM# 15 3 KREUZER (Groschen)

Silver **Ruler:** Ludwig Gustav

Date	Mintage	VG	F	VF	XF	Unc
1684	—	33.00	65.00	120	225	—
ND	—	33.00	65.00	120	225	—

KM# 21 1/24 THALER (3-3/4 Kreuzer)

Silver **Ruler:** Ludwig Gustav **Obv:** Imperial orb with 24, titles of Ludwig Gustav **Rev:** Crowned oval 4-fold arms

Date	Mintage	VG	F	VF	XF	Unc
ND	—	—	—	—	—	—

KM# 29 4 KREUZER (Batzen)

Silver **Ruler:** Ludwig Gustav

Date	Mintage	VG	F	VF	XF	Unc
1696	—	20.00	40.00	75.00	140	—

KM# 18 6 KREUZER

Silver **Ruler:** Ludwig Gustav **Obv:** Similar to 4 Kreuzer, KM#29 **Rev:** Phoenix in flames, F. VI K. above, date in legend

Date	Mintage	VG	F	VF	XF	Unc
1685	—	40.00	80.00	140	275	—

KM# 25 6 KREUZER

Silver **Ruler:** Ludwig Gustav

Date	Mintage	VG	F	VF	XF	Unc
1691	—	40.00	80.00	140	275	—

KM# 30 1/15 THALER (2 Groschen)

Silver **Ruler:** Ludwig Gustav **Obv:** Crowned 4-fold arms between palm branches **Rev:** Date in legend **Rev. Legend:** +XV/+/EINEN/REICHS/THALR/GFN

Date	Mintage	VG	F	VF	XF	Unc
1696 GFN	—	—	—	—	—	—

KM# 22 1/12 THALER (2 Groschen)

Silver **Ruler:** Ludwig Gustav **Note:** Varieties exist.

Date	Mintage	VG	F	VF	XF	Unc
1685	—	27.00	60.00	100	160	—
1686	—	27.00	60.00	100	160	—
1689	—	27.00	60.00	100	160	—
1690	—	27.00	60.00	100	160	—
1691	—	27.00	60.00	100	160	—
1692	—	27.00	60.00	100	160	—

KM# 26 15 KREUZER

Silver **Ruler:** Ludwig Gustav **Obv:** Bust right **Rev:** Hohenlohe arms, crown above divides date, value XV below

Date	Mintage	VG	F	VF	XF	Unc
1692	—	165	375	550	850	—

KM# 27 15 KREUZER

Silver **Ruler:** Ludwig Gustav **Rev:** Date undivided in legend

Date	Mintage	VG	F	VF	XF	Unc
1692	—	165	375	550	850	—

KM# 10 24 KREUZER (Doppelschreckenberger)

Silver **Ruler:** Georg Friedrich II **Obv:** Bust right, date in legend above, value in legend below **Rev:** 4-fold arms, titles of Georg Friedrich in legend

Date	Mintage	VG	F	VF	XF	Unc
1621	—	—	—	—	2,000	—

KM# 6 24 KREUZER (Doppelschreckenberger)

Silver **Ruler:** Georg Friedrich II **Obv:** Bust right **Rev:** Crowned imperial eagle, 24 on breast **Note:** Kipper 24 Kreuzer.

Date	Mintage	VG	F	VF	XF	Unc
ND(1621/2)	—	—	—	—	—	—

KM# 7 24 KREUZER (Doppelschreckenberger)

Silver **Ruler:** Georg Friedrich II **Obv:** Bust right divides date **Rev:** Crowned 4-fold arms, value (24) in legend

Date	Mintage	VG	F	VF	XF	Unc
1622	—	—	—	—	—	—

KM# 8 24 KREUZER (Doppelschreckenberger)

Silver **Ruler:** Georg Friedrich II **Obv:** Bust right **Rev:** Date in legend

Date	Mintage	VG	F	VF	XF	Unc
16ZZ	—	—	—	—	—	—

KM# 9 24 KREUZER (Doppelschreckenberger)

Silver **Ruler:** Georg Friedrich II **Obv:** Bust right **Rev:** 4-fold arms in ornamented square, value (24) below, date in legend

Date	Mintage	VG	F	VF	XF	Unc
1622	—	—	—	—	—	—

KM# 28 2/3 THALER (Gulden)

Silver **Ruler:** Ludwig Gustav

Date	Mintage	VG	F	VF	XF	Unc
1693	—	—	—	—	—	—

Note: Reportedly struck in Frankfurt about 1861-62

KM# 16 THALER

Silver **Ruler:** Ludwig Gustav **Note:** Dav. #6836.

Date	Mintage	VG	F	VF	XF	Unc
1684 Rare	—	—	—	—	—	—

KM# 31 THALER

Silver **Ruler:** Ludwig Gustav **Note:** Dav. #6837.

Date	Mintage	VG	F	VF	XF	Unc
MDCXCVI (1696 GFN)	—	550	1,000	2,000	3,500	—

KM# 35 THALER

Silver **Ruler:** Philipp Ernst **Obv:** Titles of Philipp Ernst **Note:** Dav. #6838.

Date	Mintage	VG	F	VF	XF	Unc
MDCC (1700 GFN)	—	600	1,100	2,250	3,750	—

TRADE COINAGE

KM# 17 DUCAT

3.5000 g., 0.9860 Gold 0.1109 oz. AGW **Ruler:** Ludwig Gustav

Date	Mintage	VG	F	VF	XF	Unc
1684 Rare	—	—	—	—	—	—

KM# 32 DUCAT

3.5000 g., 0.9860 Gold 0.1109 oz. AGW **Ruler:** Ludwig Gustav **Obv:** Bust left **Obv. Legend:** L. G. S. R. I. C. A-H. E. D. I. L **Rev:** Crowned and mantled arms

Date	Mintage	VG	F	VF	XF	Unc
1696 Rare	—	—	—	—	—	—

KM# 36 8 DUCAT

28.0000 g., 0.9860 Gold 0.8876 oz. AGW **Ruler:** Philipp Ernst **Note:** Struck with 1 Thaler dies, KM#35. Actual weight = 8-1/4 ducat.

Date	Mintage	VG	F	VF	XF	Unc
MDCC (1700 GFN) Rare	—	—	—	—	—	—

HOHENLOHE-WALDENBURG-WALDENBURG

Founded in the division of Waldenburg in 1600 and extinct in 1679. Possessions passed to Hohenlohe-Waldenburg-Schillingsfürst.

RULERS

Philipp Heinrich, 1600-1644
Wolfgang Friedrich, 1644-1658
Philipp Gottfried, 1658-1679

Mints functioned at Waldenburg and Untersteinbach.

COUNTSHIP

REGULAR COINAGE

KM# 1 3 KREUZER (Groschen)

Silver **Obv:** Crowned imperial eagle, 3 in orb on breast, titles of Ferdinand II **Rev:** Four-fold arms **Note:** Kipper 3 Kreuzer. Varieties exist.

Date	Mintage	VG	F	VF	XF	Unc
ND(1621/2)	—	—	—	—	—	—

HOHENZOLLERN-HECHINGEN

Located in southern Germany, the Hechingen line was founded in 1576. The family received the mint right in 1471 and the counts were raised to the rank of prince of the empire in 1623. As a result of the 1848 revolutions the prince abdicated in favor of Prussia in 1849.

RULERS

Eitel Friedrich IV, 1576-1605
Johann Georg, 1605-1623
Eitel Fridrich V, 1623-1662
Philipp Christoph Friedrich, 1662-1671
Friedrich Wilhelm, 1671-1735

ARMS

Hohenzollern: Quartered square, upper left and lower right dark, upper right and lower left light (black and silver).

Hereditary Imperial Chamberlain: Two crossed sceptres.

REFERENCE:

B = **Emil Bahrfeldt,** *Das Münz- und Geldwesen der Fürstenthümer Hohenzollern,* **Berlin, 1900.**

PRINCIPALITY

REGULAR COINAGE

KM# 5 3 KREUZER (Groschen)

Silver **Obv:** Crowned imperial eagle, 3 in orb on breast, titles of Rudolf II **Rev:** Two conjoined shields of Hohenzollern and hereditary chamberlain's arms, date above

Date	Mintage	VG	F	VF	XF	Unc
1606	—	—	—	—	—	—

KM# 13 3 KREUZER (Groschen)

Silver **Obv:** Value (3) in legend below eagle

Date	Mintage	VG	F	VF	XF	Unc
1622	Inc. above	55.00	115	170	225	—

KM# 12 3 KREUZER (Groschen)

Silver **Obv:** Date in legend, titles of Ferdinand II **Rev:** Bust right **Note:** Kipper 3 Kreuzer.

Date	Mintage	VG	F	VF	XF	Unc
1622	691,000	33.00	55.00	115	170	—

KM# 14 3 KREUZER (Groschen)

Silver **Obv:** Bust right, value (3) in legend below **Rev:** Crowned four-fold arms, CAM. HAER..., date in legend **Note:** Varieties exist.

Date	Mintage	VG	F	VF	XF	Unc
1622	Inc. above	—	—	—	—	—

KM# 15 12 KREUZER (Dreibätzner)

Silver **Ruler:** Johann George **Obv:** Bust right **Rev:** Crowned imperial eagle, 12 in orb on breast, titles of Ferdinand II, date divided in legend at top **Note:** Kipper 12 Kreuzer.

Date	Mintage	VG	F	VF	XF	Unc
1622	39,000	—	—	—	—	—

KM# 10 24 KREUZER (1/4 Thaler)

Silver **Obv:** Crowned 4-fold arms **Rev:** Crowned imperial eagle, 24 in orb on breast, titles of Ferdinand II, date divided at top **Note:** Kipper 24 Kreuzer or Sechsbätzner.

Date	Mintage	VG	F	VF	XF	Unc
1621	19,000	—	—	—	—	—

KM# 17 24 KREUZER (1/4 Thaler)

Silver **Note:** Klippe.

Date	Mintage	VG	F	VF	XF	Unc
16ZZ	Inc. above	—	—	—	—	—

KM# 19 24 KREUZER (1/4 Thaler)

Silver **Note:** Klippe.

Date	Mintage	VG	F	VF	XF	Unc
16ZZ	Inc. above	—	—	—	—	—

KM# 16 24 KREUZER (1/4 Thaler)

Silver **Obv:** Bust right **Rev:** Crowned four-fold arms, CAM: HAER..., date in legend **Note:** Varieties exist.

Date	Mintage	VG	F	VF	XF	Unc
16ZZ	223,000	—	—	—	—	—

KM# 18 24 KREUZER (1/4 Thaler)

Silver **Obv:** Value (24) below bust

Date	Mintage	VG	F	VF	XF	Unc
16ZZ	Inc. above	—	—	—	—	—

KM# 11 48 KREUZER (1/2 Thaler)

Silver **Obv:** Crowned 4-fold arms **Rev:** Crowned mperial eagle, 48 in orb on breast, titles of Ferdinand II, date divided in legend at top **Note:** Kipper 48 Kreuzer.

Date	Mintage	VG	F	VF	XF	Unc
1621	31,000	—	—	—	—	—

KM# 20 THALER

Silver **Obv:** St. George on horse right, dragon below **Rev:** Two adjacent helmeted arms of Hohenzollern and hereditary chamberlain **Note:** Dav. #6839.

Date	Mintage	VG	F	VF	XF	Unc
ND(1622) Rare	—	—	—	—	—	—

KM# 21 THALER

Silver **Obv:** Crowned imperial eagle, titles of Ferdinand II, date in legend **Rev:** Bust right **Note:** Dav. #6840.

Date	Mintage	VG	F	VF	XF	Unc
1623 Rare	140	—	—	—	—	—

HOHENZOLLERN-SIGMARINGEN

Located in southern Germany, the Sigmaringen line was founded in 1576. The counts obtained the mint right in 1471 and were raised to the rank of Prince of the Empire in 1623. As a result of the 1848 revolutions the princes abdicated in favor of Prussia in 1849.

RULERS

Karl II, 1576-1606
Johann, 1606-1638
Meinrad I, 1638-1681
Maximilian, 1681-1689
Meinrad II, 1689-1715

ARMS

Hohenzollern: Quartered square, upper left and lower right dark, upper right and lower left light (black and silver).
Sigmaringen – stag left

REFERENCE:

B = Emil Bahrfeldt, *Das Münz- und Geldwesen der Fürstenthümer Hohenzollern,* **Berlin, 1900.**

PRINCIPALITY

REGULAR COINAGE

KM# 5 4 PFENNIG

Copper **Obv:** Hohenzollern arms in baroque frame **Rev:** IIII in wreath **Note:** Kipper 4 Pfennig.

Date	Mintage	VG	F	VF	XF	Unc
ND(1621/22)	—	40.00	85.00	140	200	—

KM# 6 3 KREUZER (Groschen)

Silver **Obv:** Crowned oval Hohenzollern arms in baroque frame **Rev:** Crowned imperial eagle, 3 in orb on breast, titles of Ferdinand II, date in legend

Date	Mintage	VG	F	VF	XF	Unc
1622	428,000	—	—	—	—	—

KM# 7 3 KREUZER (Groschen)

Silver **Rev:** Arms in shield with rounded bottom and flat top

Date	Mintage	VG	F	VF	XF	Unc
1622	Inc. above	—	—	—	—	—

KM# 8 3 KREUZER (Groschen)

Silver **Obv:** Bust of Ferdinand II right, titles around **Rev:** Crowned imperial eagle, shield on breast, value 3 in legend at bottom, date **Rev. Legend:** MON. NOVA. ARG. ZOLL.

Date	Mintage	VG	F	VF	XF	Unc
1622	Inc. above	—	—	—	—	—

KM# 9 24 KREUZER (1/4 Thaler - Sechsbätzner)

Silver **Obv:** Ornately-shaped 4-fold arms with central shield dividing date **Rev:** Crowned imperial eagle, Z4 in orb n breast, titles of Ferdinand II

Date	Mintage	VG	F	VF	XF	Unc
16ZZ	56,000	—	—	—	—	—

KM# 10 24 KREUZER (1/4 Thaler - Sechsbätzner)

Silver **Obv:** 4-fold arms **Rev:** 24 in orb

Date	Mintage	VG	F	VF	XF	Unc
ND(1622)	Inc. above	—	—	—	—	—

KM# 11 THALER

Silver **Ruler:** Johann **Subject:** In the name Johann's younger brother, Ernst Georg (d.1625). **Obv:** Oval 4-fold arms of Hohenzollern and Sigmaringen with central shield in baroque frame, titles of Ernst Georg **Rev:** Crowned imperial eagle, orb on breast, titles of Ferdinand II and date in legend

Date	Mintage	VG	F	VF	XF	Unc
16ZZ Rare	—	—	—	—	—	—

HOHNSTEIN

(Hohenstein)

The counts of Hohnstein, based in the Harz Mountains of central Germany, about 15 miles northeast of Nordhausen, descended from a line dating to the mid-12th century. With the death of Ernst VII in 1593, the dynasty became extinct and the lands were divided among several ecclesiastical and secular principalities. Eventually, most of the territories of Hohnstein went to Brandenburg-Prussia and Brunswick-Wolfenbüttel. Some of these princes struck coinage for Hohnstein.

RULERS

Friedrich Ulrich, Duke of Brunswick-Wolfenbüttel, 1613-1634
Johann VIII, Count of Sayn-Wittgenstein, 1634-1657
Gustav, Count of Sayn-Wittgenstein, 1657-1701

NOTE: For coinage after 1634, see Sayn-Wittgenstein-Hohnstein.

MINT MARKS

EL - Ellrich

MINT OFFICIALS' INITIALS

Initial	Date	Name
(f)= thistle	1620-21	
CO	1613-23	Claus Oppermann at Bayreuth
DF	1684	Daniel Friese at Klettenberg
HCH	1686	Heinrich Christoph Hille at Klettenberg
HM	1675-76	Henning Müller at Ellrich and Klettenberg
HS	1621-24	Henning Schreiber at Lauterberg
IZW	1673-76	Julius Zacharias Wefer at Ellrich
JA, JLA	1684	Johann Leonard Ahrensburg at Klettenberg
JCB	1687-88	Johann Christoph Bar at Klettenberg
PL	1675-76	Peter Lohr at Ellrich and maybe Klettenberg
TLK	1684-90	Thomas Ludolf Koch in Klettenberg

ARMS

Usually 4-fold arms, checkerboard in upper left and lower right, lion passant left above five bars in upper right and lower left, central shield with stag left.
Hohnstein only - checkerboard
Klettenberg only - stag left
Lutterberg only - lion rampant left

COUNTSHIP

REGULAR COINAGE

KM# 12 3 PFENNIG (Dreier)

Copper **Obv:** Klettingberg arms **Rev:** III/PFEN/NING

Date	Mintage	VG	F	VF	XF	Unc
ND(1620/21)	—	60.00	120	200	350	—

KM# 10 3 PFENNIG (Dreier)

Billon Or Silver **Obv:** Vertically divided two-fold arms, date above **Rev:** Imperial orb with 3 **Note:** Kipper 3 Pfennig.

Date	Mintage	VG	F	VF	XF	Unc
16Z0	—	65.00	120	225	375	—

KM# 11 3 PFENNIG (Dreier)

Copper **Obv:** Hohnstein arms, E-L above **Mint:** Ellrich **Note:** Struck at Ellrich Mint.

Date	Mintage	VG	F	VF	XF	Unc
ND(1620/21)	—	60.00	120	200	350	—

KM# 33 3 PFENNIG (Dreier)

Copper **Obv:** Lutterberg arms **Rev:** Imperial orb with 3 divides date

Date	Mintage	VG	F	VF	XF	Unc
16Z1	—	60.00	120	200	350	—

KM# 50 3 PFENNIG (Dreier)

Copper **Obv:** Crowned uncial G divides date **Rev:** Imperial orb with 3

Date	Mintage	VG	F	VF	XF	Unc
167Z	—	45.00	85.00	165	275	—

KM# 51 3 PFENNIG (Dreier)

Copper **Obv:** Ornamented shield, date above

Date	Mintage	VG	F	VF	XF	Unc
167Z	—	45.00	85.00	165	275	—

KM# 34 6 FLITTER (3 Pfennig)

Copper **Obv:** Hohnstein arms, E-L above **Rev:** VI in center, FLITTER, date around **Mint:** Ellrich

Date	Mintage	VG	F	VF	XF	Unc
16Z1	—	80.00	145	250	425	—

KM# 35 6 FLITTER (3 Pfennig)

Copper **Rev:** Imperial orb with VI, cross on orb divides date

Date	Mintage	VG	F	VF	XF	Unc
16Z1	—	85.00	145	250	425	—

KM# 13 8 PFENNIG

Copper **Obv:** Crowned Klettenberg arms **Rev:** VIII in center, PFENNING around **Note:** Kipper 8 Pfennig.

Date	Mintage	VG	F	VF	XF	Unc
ND(1620/21)	—	60.00	115	200	340	—

KM# 5 3 KREUZER (Groschen)

Silver **Obv. Inscription:** IN GOTS GEWALT HAB ICH GESTALT. SO DER HERR GIEBT, DAS MIR GENOGT. **Rev:** Imperial orb with 3, date **Note:** Kipper 3 Kreuzer.

Date	Mintage	VG	F	VF	XF	Unc
1619	—	—	—	—	—	—

KM# 14 3 KREUZER (Groschen)

Silver **Obv:** Crowned Hohnstein arms **Rev:** Crowned imperial eagle, value (3) in legend below, date

Date	Mintage	VG	F	VF	XF	Unc
1620	—	65.00	120	220	375	—

KM# 15 3 KREUZER (Groschen)

Silver **Rev:** 3 in orb on breast

Date	Mintage	VG	F	VF	XF	Unc
1620	—	65.00	120	220	375	—

KM# 32 1/24 THALER (Groschen)

Silver **Obv:** Imperial orb with Z4, titles of Ferdinand II and date **Rev:** Crowned Hohnstien arms, (3) below

Date	Mintage	VG	F	VF	XF	Unc
1620	—	—	—	—	—	—
ND	—	—	—	—	—	—

KM# 6 12 KREUZER (Schreckenberger)

Silver **Obv:** Crowned imperial eagle, 1Z in orb on breast, titles of Matthias **Rev:** Three shields, one above two, SIT NOM...

Date	Mintage	VG	F	VF	XF	Unc
ND(1619)	—	—	—	—	—	—

KM# 17 12 KREUZER (Schreckenberger)

Silver **Obv:** Four-fold arms with central shield **Rev:** Wildman holding tree in right hand, 12 in right field, date **Rev. Legend:** PRO: LEGE: ET: GREGE:

Date	Mintage	VG	F	VF	XF	Unc
1620 (a)	—	33.00	90.00	140	200	—

KM# 18 12 KREUZER (Schreckenberger)

Silver **Rev:** Value (12) below wildman

Date	Mintage	VG	F	VF	XF	Unc
1620	—	33.00	60.00	115	165	—

KM# 19 12 KREUZER (Schreckenberger)

Silver **Rev:** Wildman divides 1-2

Date	Mintage	VG	F	VF	XF	Unc
1620	—	40.00	100	165	225	—

KM# 20 12 KREUZER (Schreckenberger)

Silver **Obv:** Three shields of arms, one above two **Rev:** Wildman holding tree in right hand, 12 in right field

Date	Mintage	VG	F	VF	XF	Unc
1620	—	27.00	60.00	115	170	—
1621	—	27.00	60.00	115	170	—

KM# 22 12 KREUZER (Schreckenberger)

Silver **Obv:** Upper shield of arms divides L-W

Date	Mintage	VG	F	VF	XF	Unc
1620	—	27.00	60.00	115	170	—

KM# 23 12 KREUZER (Schreckenberger)
Silver **Obv:** Three shields of arms, one above two **Rev:** Wildman, 1Z at right, date **Rev. Legend:** PRO LEGE...

Date	Mintage	VG	F	VF	XF	Unc
1620	—	27.00	65.00	125	175	—

KM# 24 12 KREUZER (Schreckenberger)
Silver **Obv:** Crowned Hohnstein arms **Obv. Legend:** PAPS - SN - IL4G - GROS **Rev:** Crowned imperial eagle, 1Z in orb on breast, titles of Ferdinand II

Date	Mintage	VG	F	VF	XF	Unc
ND(1620/21)	—	27.00	80.00	145	190	—

KM# 25 12 KREUZER (Schreckenberger)
Silver **Rev:** Lion left above arms

Date	Mintage	VG	F	VF	XF	Unc
ND(1620/21)	—	27.00	80.00	145	190	—

KM# 26 12 KREUZER (Schreckenberger)
Silver **Obv:** Three shields of arms, one above two, 12 between lower two, date **Obv. Legend:** PRO LEGE... **Rev:** Wildman, tree branch in right hand

Date	Mintage	VG	F	VF	XF	Unc
16Z0	—	27.00	60.00	120	170	—

KM# 27 12 KREUZER (Schreckenberger)
Silver **Obv:** Crowned Hohnstein arms divide date near top **Rev:** Crowned imperial eagle, 12 in orb on breast, SUB: UMBRA

Date	Mintage	VG	F	VF	XF	Unc
1620 CO	—	—	—	—	—	—

KM# 28 12 KREUZER (Schreckenberger)
Silver **Rev:** Without value in orb on eagle's breast

Date	Mintage	VG	F	VF	XF	Unc
1620 CO	—	—	—	—	—	—

KM# 29 12 KREUZER (Schreckenberger)
Silver **Obv:** 5-fold arms with central shield of Klettenberg arms, date in legend **Rev:** 12 in orb on eagle's breast

Date	Mintage	VG	F	VF	XF	Unc
1620	—	33.00	80.00	140	185	—

KM# 39 12 KREUZER (Schreckenberger)
Silver **Obv:** Similar to KM#23 but upper shield divides L-W

Date	Mintage	VG	F	VF	XF	Unc
1620	—	33.00	65.00	120	175	—
1621	—	33.00	65.00	120	175	—

KM# 16 12 KREUZER (Schreckenberger)
Silver **Obv:** Two-fold arms divided horizontally in ornamented shield divides C-O, date divided above **Rev:** Crowned imperial eagle, 12 in orb on breast **Rev. Legend:** SUB: UMBRA: ALARUM: TUAR **Note:** Kipper 12 Kreuzer. Varieties exist.

Date	Mintage	VG	F	VF	XF	Unc
1620 CO	—	—	—	—	—	—

KM# 21 12 KREUZER (Schreckenberger)
Silver **Rev:** Value 1Z below wildman **Note:** Varieties exist.

Date	Mintage	VG	F	VF	XF	Unc
1620	—	27.00	60.00	120	175	—
16Z1	—	27.00	60.00	120	175	—

KM# 36 12 KREUZER (Schreckenberger)
Silver **Obv:** Three shields of arms, value 12 in middle **Rev:** Wildman holding tree in right hand **Note:** Varieties exist.

Date	Mintage	VG	F	VF	XF	Unc
1621	—	27.00	60.00	120	175	—
1621 (a)	—	27.00	60.00	120	175	—

KM# 37 12 KREUZER (Schreckenberger)
Silver **Obv:** 1Z between two lower shields **Note:** Varieties exist.

Date	Mintage	VG	F	VF	XF	Unc
16Z1	—	33.00	65.00	120	180	—

KM# 40 12 KREUZER (Schreckenberger)
Silver **Obv:** Three shields of arms, two above one **Rev:** Wildman, town at left, date **Rev. Legend:** DEO: ET: PATRIAE **Note:** Varieties exist.

Date	Mintage	VG	F	VF	XF	Unc
1621 (a)	—	27.00	80.00	140	185	—

KM# 41.1 12 KREUZER (Schreckenberger)
Silver **Obv:** Crowned three-fold arms **Rev:** Wildman, branch in his right, 12 on left, DEO...

Date	Mintage	VG	F	VF	XF	Unc
1621	—	27.00	80.00	140	185	—

KM# 41.2 12 KREUZER (Schreckenberger)
Silver **Rev:** Similar to reverse legend of KM#38.

Date	Mintage	VG	F	VF	XF	Unc
1621	—	27.00	80.00	140	185	—

KM# 42 12 KREUZER (Schreckenberger)
Silver **Obv:** Crowned imperial eagle, 1Z in orb on breast **Rev:** Wildman, date **Rev. Legend:** PRO LEGE...

Date	Mintage	VG	F	VF	XF	Unc
1621	—	33.00	80.00	140	185	—

KM# 43 12 KREUZER (Schreckenberger)
Silver **Obv:** Crowned imperial eagle, 12 in orb on breast, titles of Ferdinand II **Rev:** Three shields, one above two, 1Z at bottom

Date	Mintage	VG	F	VF	XF	Unc
1621	—	—	—	—	—	—

KM# 38 12 KREUZER (Schreckenberger)
Silver **Rev:** Date **Rev. Legend:** PRO: LEGE:...

Date	Mintage	VG	F	VF	XF	Unc
1621	—	33.00	70.00	125	175	—

KM# 30 24 KREUZER (Doppelschreckenberger)
Silver **Obv:** Crowned imperial eagle, Z4 in orb on breast, titles of Ferdinand II **Rev:** Crowned Hohnstein arms

Date	Mintage	VG	F	VF	XF	Unc
ND(1620/21)	—	45.00	100	185	300	—

KM# 44 24 KREUZER (Doppelschreckenberger)
Silver **Rev:** Date in legend

Date	Mintage	VG	F	VF	XF	Unc
1621	—	45.00	100	185	300	—

KM# 45 24 KREUZER (Doppelschreckenberger)
Silver **Obv:** Crowned arms of two leopards left, value (24) below **Rev:** Wildman, tree branch in right hand, town in right background, date **Rev. Legend:** DEO. ET...

Date	Mintage	VG	F	VF	XF	Unc
1621	—	45.00	100	185	300	—

KM# 46 24 KREUZER (Doppelschreckenberger)
Silver **Rev:** Date **Rev. Legend:** PRO. LEGE...

Date	Mintage	VG	F	VF	XF	Unc
1621	—	45.00	100	185	300	—

KM# 47 24 KREUZER (Doppelschreckenberger)
Silver **Obv:** Crowned Klettenberg arms **Rev:** Z4 on left of wildman

Date	Mintage	VG	F	VF	XF	Unc
1621 CO	—	—	—	—	—	—

KM# 48 24 KREUZER (Doppelschreckenberger)
Silver **Obv:** Crowned imperial eagle, Z4 in orb on breast, titles of Ferdinand II and date in legend **Rev:** Crowned Lutterberg arms

Date	Mintage	VG	F	VF	XF	Unc
1621	—	—	—	—	—	—

KM# 31 6 BATZEN (Sechsbätzner - 24 Kreuzer)
Silver **Obv:** Crowned Hohnstein harms, date divided in legend by crown **Rev:** Crowned imperial eagle, 6 n orb on breast **Rev. Legend:** SUB: ULTRA...

Date	Mintage	VG	F	VF	XF	Unc
1620 CO	—	—	—	—	—	—

INGOLSTADT

A city in Upper Bavaria (Oberbayern) on the Danube at the junction with the Schutter, some 45 miles (75km) north of Munich. When Bavaria was divided in 1375 by the sons of Stephan I, Ingolstadt became the capital of one of the three duchies, but lost that status when the line died out in 1334 and the territory went to the Munich line (see Bavaria). A university was founded in the city in 1472, but was transferred to Landshut in 1800 and then to Munich in 1826. The city was besieged by Gustavus Adolphus in 1632-33 and obsidional coinage was produced to meet the emergency.

REFERENCE

B = Joseph P. Beierlein, **Medaillen und Münzen des Gesammthauses Wittelsbach**, 2 vols., Munich, 1897-1901.

CITY

OBSIDIONAL COINAGE

KM# 1 1/4 GULDEN
4.3500 g., Silver **Ruler:** (no Ruler Information) **Obv:** Crowned Madonna holding child in right arm, palm branch in left, standing on dragon, divides date 16-33 **Obv. Legend:** SANCTA. MARIA. DE. VICTORIA. INGOLSTA **Rev:** View of the city, date 1632 in ribbon and band above **Rev. Legend:** VRBIS. TVTELA. CIVIVM. PATRONA. **Note:** Klippe. Beierlein 806.

Date	Mintage	VG	F	VF	XF	Unc
1633//1632 Rare	—	—	—	—	—	—

ISENBURG

The lands of the counts of Isenburg lay on both sides of the Main River to the east of Frankfurt. The dynasty traces its lineage back to the 10th century and began issuing coins in the mid-13th century. The county underwent many divisions in the Middle Ages, but by the early 17th century only one dominant branch was producing coins. This was Isenburg-Birstein, divided once again into Isenburg-Offenbach-Birstein and Isenburg-Büdingen in 1635. The latter was further divided into four branches in 1673/1687 and two of the substrata became extinct in 1725 and 1780 respectively. Isenburg-Offenbach-Birstein was raised to the rank of prince in 1744 and all other branches had to relinquish their sovereignty to his descendant in 1806. The latter lost his sole leadership in 1813 because he sided with Napoleon and the lands of Isenburg-Offenbach-Birstein were mediatized to Hesse-Darmstadt in 1815. The subdivisions of Isenburg-Büdigen did not issue a regular coinage, but struck the series of the quasi-official snipe hellers during the 19th century.

RULERS

Wolfgang Ernst von Birstein, 1596-1633
Wolfgang Heinrich von Offenbach-Birstein, 1633-1635
Johann Ludwig von Offenbach-Birstein, 1635-1685
Johann Philipp (in Offenbach), 1685-1718

Isenburg-Büdingen

Johann Ernst, 1633-1685
Johann Kasimir, 1685-1693
Ernst Kasimir I, 1693-1749

MINT OFFICIALS' INITIALS

Initial	Date	Name
	1618-1619	Melchior (Michael) Kuttner, in Offenbach
A	CA.1681	
HB, IHB	ca. 1693	
IRA, RA	ca. 1670-1679	

COUNTSHIP

REGULAR COINAGE

KM# 27 KREUZER
Silver **Obv:** Crowned arms **Obv. Legend:** MONETA... **Rev:** I/KREVTZ/ER/date **Rev. Legend:** YSENBVRG. BVDINGEN. **Note:** Kipper Kreuzer.

Date	Mintage	VG	F	VF	XF	Unc
16ZZ	39,000	—	—	—	—	—

KM# 28 KREUZER
Silver **Obv:** I/KREVTZ/ER/date **Obv. Legend:** MONETA... **Rev:** Crowned arms, 5-pointed star on both sides **Rev. Legend:** YSENBVRG. BVDINGEN.

Date	Mintage	VG	F	VF	XF	Unc
16Z3	—	—	—	—	—	—

KM# 35 KREUZER
Silver **Obv:** Crowned arms in laurel wreath **Rev:** I/KREU/TZER/date/A in laurel wreath

Date	Mintage	VG	F	VF	XF	Unc
1681 A	—	135	265	450	800	—

KM# 36 ALBUS
Silver **Obv:** Crowned arms between laurel branches **Rev:** *I*/ALBVS/date/R.A., between laurel branches

Date	Mintage	VG	F	VF	XF	Unc
1681 RA	—	160	275	475	800	—

KM# 5 3 KREUZER (Groschen)
Silver **Obv:** Crowned arms divide date **Rev:** Crowned imperial eagle, 3 in orb on breast, titles of Matthias **Mint:** Budingen **Note:** Struck at Budingen.

Date	Mintage	VG	F	VF	XF	Unc
1618	—	—	—	—	—	—

KM# 22 3 KREUZER (Groschen)
Silver **Rev:** Titles of Ferdinand II and date repeated at end... S. AV. 19.

Date	Mintage	VG	F	VF	XF	Unc
1619	—	—	—	—	—	—

KM# 42 2 ALBUS (Doppelalbus)
Silver **Obv:** Crowned arms between palm branches, titles of Johann Philipp and Wilhelm Moritz **Rev:** *II*/ALBUS/date/H*B **Rev. Legend:** NACH DEM...

Date	Mintage	VG	F	VF	XF	Unc
1693 HB	—	135	225	400	675	—

KM# 6 6 KREUZER
Silver **Obv:** Crowned arms divide date **Rev:** Crowned imperial eagle, 6 in orb on breast, titles of Matthias **Mint:** Budingen **Note:** Varieties exist.

Date	Mintage	VG	F	VF	XF	Unc
1618	—	200	350	600	1,000	—

KM# 40 12 KREUZER
Silver **Obv:** Crowned arms between palm branches, titles of Johann philipp and Wilhelm Moritz **Rev. Legend:** NACH. DEM. SCHLUS... **Rev. Inscription:** XII/KREU/TZER/date/HB

Date	Mintage	VG	F	VF	XF	Unc
1693 HB	—	—	—	—	—	—

KM# 26 4 GROSCHEN
Silver **Obv:** Arms, date in legend **Obv. Legend:** DURA, PATI, VIRTUS **Rev:** Imperial eagle with 4G on breast, titles of Ferdinand II **Note:** Kipper 4 Groschen.

Date	Mintage	VG	F	VF	XF	Unc
1621	—	—	—	—	—	—

KM# 7 1/8 THALER
Silver **Obv:** Crowned arms divide date **Rev:** Imperial eagle, titles of Matthias **Mint:** Budingen **Note:** Struck at Budingen.

Date	Mintage	VG	F	VF	XF	Unc
1618	—	—	—	—	—	—

KM# 18 1/4 THALER
Silver **Obv:** Crowned arms divide date, titles of Wolfgang Ernst **Rev:** Crowned imperial eagle, orb on breast, titles of Matthias **Note:** Varieties exist.

Date	Mintage	VG	F	VF	XF	Unc
1618	—	135	300	425	725	—
1619	—	135	300	425	725	—

KM# 30 60 KREUZER (1 Gulden = 2/3 Thaler)
Silver **Obv:** Ornate arms between two laurel branches, date in legend **Rev:** Crowned imperial eagle, 60 in orb on breast, titles of Leopold I **Note:** Varieties exist.

Date	Mintage	VG	F	VF	XF	Unc
1670 IRA	—	500	825	1,350	2,400	—
1676 IRA	—	500	825	1,350	2,400	—
1678 IRA	—	500	825	1,350	2,400	—
1679 IRA	—	500	825	1,350	2,400	—

KM# 41 60 KREUZER (1 Gulden = 2/3 Thaler)
Silver **Rev:** Crowned arms between palm branches divide date, titles of Johann Philipp and Wilhelm Moritz

Date	Mintage	VG	F	VF	XF	Unc
1693 IHB	—	525	925	1,600	2,700	—

KM# 19 THALER
Silver **Obv:** Ornate baroque arms, double legend, titles of Wolfgang Ernst **Rev:** Crowned imperial eagle, orb on breast, titles of Matthias, date in legend **Note:** Mining Thaler. Dav. #6841.

Date	Mintage	VG	F	VF	XF	Unc
1618 Rare	—	—	—	—	—	—

KM# 25 THALER
Silver **Obv:** Crowned arms, titles of Wolfgang Ernst **Rev:** Titles of Ferdinand II **Note:** Dav. #6842.

Date	Mintage	VG	F	VF	XF	Unc
1620 Rare	—	—	—	—	—	—

KM# 43 2 THALER
Silver **Obv:** Crowned ornate oval arms, titles of Johann Philipp and Wilhelm Moritz, date in legend **Rev:** Crowned imperial eagle, titles of Leopold I **Note:** Dav. #6843.

Date	Mintage	VG	F	VF	XF	Unc
1694 Rare	—	—	—	—	—	—

TRADE COINAGE

KM# 20 DUCAT
3.5000 g., 0.9860 Gold 0.1109 oz. AGW **Obv:** Ornate baroque arms divide date, titles of Wolfgang Ernst in legend **Rev:** Crowned imperial eagle, orb on breast, titles of Matthias **Note:** Varieties exist.

Date	Mintage	VG	F	VF	XF	Unc
1618 Rare	—	—	—	—	—	—

KM# 21 2 DUCAT
7.0000 g., 0.9860 Gold 0.2219 oz. AGW **Obv:** Arms of Isenburg **Rev:** Crowned imperial eagle

Date	Mintage	VG	F	VF	XF	Unc
1619 Rare	—	—	—	—	—	—

ISNY

This south German city, some 17 miles NE of Lindau and the shore of the Bodensee, is first mentioned in the 11th century. It acquired its imperial city status from Emperor Karl IV in 1365 and the mint right in 1507 from Maximilian I. A regular coinage began the following year and continued, on-and-off, until the early 18th century. The city was acquired by Württemberg in 1803 and lost its position as a free city.

ARMS

Eagle with horseshoe in shield on breast. In earlier period, just a horseshoe in shield. Also, sometimes a large, 6-pointed star.

MINT OFFICIALS' INITIALS

Initial	Date	Name
PI	1695-1702	Hans Jakob Hau

REFERENCE

N = Elisabeth Nau, **Die Münzen und Medaillen des oberschwäbischen Städte**, Freiburg im Breisgau, 1964.

REGULAR COINAGE

KM# 5 PFENNIG
Copper **Note:** Uniface. Crowned eagle arms divide date (when present). Varieties exist.

Date	Mintage	VG	F	VF	XF	Unc
ND(ca.1623)	—	16.00	27.00	40.00	70.00	—
1695	—	16.00	27.00	40.00	70.00	—

KM# 10 PFENNIG
Copper **Note:** Eagle without crown above.

Date	Mintage	VG	F	VF	XF	Unc
1695	—	16.00	27.00	40.00	70.00	—
1696	—	16.00	27.00	40.00	70.00	—

KM# 11 PFENNIG
Copper **Note:** Small crowned eagle on arms divide date

Date	Mintage	VG	F	VF	XF	Unc
1698	—	16.00	27.00	40.00	70.00	—

KM# 12 PFENNIG
Copper **Note:** Small crowned eagle divides date.

Date	Mintage	VG	F	VF	XF	Unc
1699	—	16.00	27.00	40.00	70.00	—
1700	—	16.00	27.00	40.00	70.00	—

KM# 6 2 KREUZER (Halbbatzen)
Silver **Obv:** Eagle, legend, date **Obv. Legend:** MON: NO: CIVI: ISSEN: **Rev:** Crowned imperial eagle, value Z in orb on breast, titles of Ferdinand II

Date	Mintage	VG	F	VF	XF	Unc
16Z3	—	—	—	—	—	—

KM# 7 12 KREUZER (Dreibätzner)
Silver **Obv:** Eagle with city arms on breast in ornamented shield divides date, .XII.K. above **Rev:** STAT/MYNZ in round cartouche **Note:** Varieties exist.

Date	Mintage	VG	F	VF	XF	Unc
16Z3	—	—	—	—	—	—

JAGERNDORF

A duchy in Silesia, centered on the town of the same name, which is located on the Oppa (Opava) River, some 14 miles (23km) northwest of Troppau. From earliest recorded times, Jägerndorf had been part of Silesia, but passed to the Duchy of Troppau in 1340. When Troppau was divided by sons of a duke who had died in 1366, Jägerndorf together with Ratibor formed one of the subdivisions. Jägerndorf was occupied by Hungary 1483-93, then by Bohemia through the agency of Johann von Schellenberg in 1493. Johann's son, George, who ruled Jägerndorf on behalf of Bohemia from 1506 to 1523, sold the duchy to Georg the Pious, Margrave of Brandenburg-Ansbach in the latter year. Jägerndorf was briefly in the hands of the Elector of Brandenburg and also for a short period was obtained by the Habsburgs. It shortly thereafter passed to the princes of Liechtenstein who ruled it until the end of World War I in 1918.

RULERS

Georg Friedrich von Brandenburg-Ansbach 1543-1603
Joachim Friedrich von Brandenburg, 1603-1606
Johann Georg von Brandenburg-Ansbach, 1607-1623

MINT OFFICIALS' INITIALS

Initial	Date	Name
Cp	1613-20	Caspar Hennemann
FVC, VCF	1610-12	Franz Carl Uhle
	1610-12	Valentin Janus
	1564-1606	Leonhard Emich, superintendent

DUCHY

REGULAR COINAGE

KM# 30 3 PFENNIG (Drier - Gröschel)
Silver **Obv:** Ornate helmet divides date **Rev:** Crowned Silesian eagle **Note:** Varieties exist.

Date	Mintage	VG	F	VF	XF	Unc
1610	—	27.00	45.00	80.00	125	—
1611	—	27.00	45.00	80.00	125	—
1612	—	27.00	45.00	80.00	125	—

KM# 53 KREUZER
Silver **Obv:** Five shields of arms arranged around central pellet **Rev:** 6-line inscription with date **Note:** Varieties exist.

Date	Mintage	VG	F	VF	XF	Unc
1618	—	—	—	—	—	—
ND	—	—	—	—	—	—

KM# 31 3 KREUZER (Groschen)
Silver **Obv:** Bust right, value (3) below **Rev:** Crowned 4-fold arms with central shield, date in legend **Note:** Varieties exist.

Date	Mintage	VG	F	VF	XF	Unc
(1)610	—	25.00	40.00	70.00	100	—
1611	—	25.00	40.00	70.00	100	—
1612	—	25.00	40.00	70.00	100	—
1613 CP	—	25.00	40.00	70.00	100	—
1614 CP	—	25.00	40.00	70.00	100	—
1615 CP	—	25.00	40.00	70.00	100	—
1616 CP	—	25.00	40.00	70.00	100	—
1617 CP	—	25.00	40.00	70.00	100	—
1618 CP	—	25.00	40.00	70.00	100	—
1619 CP	—	25.00	40.00	70.00	100	—
1620 CP	—	25.00	40.00	70.00	100	—
1621	—	25.00	40.00	70.00	100	—

KM# 39 3 KREUZER (Groschen)
Silver **Note:** Klippe. Varieties exist.

Date	Mintage	VG	F	VF	XF	Unc
1611	—	—	—	—	—	—
1614 CP	—	—	—	—	—	—
1616 CP	—	—	—	—	—	—
1619 CP	—	—	—	—	—	—

KM# 46 3 GROSCHEN
Silver **Obv:** Bust right **Rev:** Two co-joined shields of arms, crowne above, 4-line inscription with date

Date	Mintage	VG	F	VF	XF	Unc
1612	—	—	—	—	—	—

KM# 32 1/4 THALER
Silver **Obv:** Half-length bust right divides date, titles of Johann Georg **Rev:** Crowned 4-fold arms iwth central shield in baroque frame

Date	Mintage	VG	F	VF	XF	Unc
1610 FVC	—	—	—	—	—	—

KM# 6 1/2 THALER

Silver **Obv:** Half-length armored bust right, titles of Georg Friedrich **Rev:** Ornate cross with shield of arms in each angle, shield in center, date in legend at top

Date	Mintage	VG	F	VF	XF	Unc
1602	—	600	1,075	1,650	2,400	—

KM# 13 1/2 THALER

Silver **Obv:** Half-length armored bust right divides date, titles of Joachim Friedrich **Rev:** Ornate 6-fold arms with central shield, titles continued

Date	Mintage	VG	F	VF	XF	Unc
1606	—	800	1,350	2,000	—	—

KM# 14 1/2 THALER

Silver **Obv:** Half-length armored bust right, titles of Johann Georg **Rev:** Oval 12-folds arms, three helmets above

Date	Mintage	VG	F	VF	XF	Unc
ND	—	525	850	1,350	—	—

KM# 33 1/2 THALER

Silver **Obv:** Half-length bust right divides date **Rev:** 12-fold arms, three helmets above

Date	Mintage	VG	F	VF	XF	Unc
1610 FVC	—	525	850	1,350	—	—

KM# 40 1/2 THALER

Silver **Obv:** Half-length armored bust right, date below

Date	Mintage	VG	F	VF	XF	Unc
1611 FVC	—	525	850	1,350	—	—

KM# 62 1/2 THALER (36 Kreuzer)

Silver **Obv:** Half-length bust right **Rev:** Crowned 4-fold arms with central shield, date in legend

Date	Mintage	VG	F	VF	XF	Unc
1621	—	—	—	—	—	—

KM# 7 THALER

Silver **Obv:** Half-length armored bust right turned 1/4 right **Rev:** Ornate crown with shield of arms in each angle, shield in center, date in legend at top

Date	Mintage	VG	F	VF	XF	Unc
1600	—	375	600	975	1,500	—

KM# 8 THALER

Silver **Obv:** Half-figure of Georg Friedrich right **Rev:** Center shield with four shields separated by posts and decorations **Note:** Dav. #6844.

Date	Mintage	VG	F	VF	XF	Unc
1601	—	300	525	900	1,500	—
1602	—	300	525	900	1,500	—

KM# 15 THALER

Silver **Obv:** Half-figure of Joachim Friedrich right dividing 1-606 **Rev:** Helmeted arms **Note:** Dav. #6846.

Date	Mintage	VG	F	VF	XF	Unc
1606 Rare	—	—	—	—	—	—

KM# 16 THALER

Silver **Note:** Similar to KM#17 but oval shield with V-C-F above on reverse. Dav. #6848.

Date	Mintage	VG	F	VF	XF	Unc
ND VCF	—	250	450	950	1,650	—

KM# 17 THALER

Silver **Rev:** Spanish arms **Note:** Dav. #6851.

Date	Mintage	VG	F	VF	XF	Unc
ND	—	265	475	975	1,750	—

KM# 18 THALER

Silver **Obv:** Half-figure right breaks upper legend **Rev:** Helmeted oval arms with F-V-C above **Note:** Dav. #6853.

Date	Mintage	VG	F	VF	XF	Unc
ND FVC	—	250	400	900	1,550	—

KM# 34 THALER

Silver **Obv:** Half-figure right with helmet, date in legend **Rev:** Helmeted arms with F-V-C above **Note:** Dav. #6855.

Date	Mintage	VG	F	VF	XF	Unc
1610 FVC	—	250	450	900	1,550	—

KM# 35 THALER

Silver **Rev:** Smaller shield, initials in helmets **Rev. Legend:** ... CARNO-VIENSIS **Note:** Dav. #6855A.

Date	Mintage	VG	F	VF	XF	Unc
1610	—	265	475	975	1,750	—

KM# 41 THALER

Silver **Obv:** Half-figure half facing, 1611 below **Rev:** Helmeted arms **Rev. Legend:** DVX. CAR.-NOVIEN. X. **Note:** Dav. #6856.

Date	Mintage	VG	F	VF	XF	Unc
1611	—	300	700	1,500	3,000	—

KM# 42 THALER

Silver **Rev. Legend:** DVX. CARN-O. VIENSIS **Note:** Dav. #6856A.

Date	Mintage	VG	F	VF	XF	Unc
1611 FVC	—	300	700	1,500	3,000	—

KM# 47 THALER

Silver **Obv:** Half-figure right, date below **Rev:** Helmeted arms, F-V-C above **Rev. Legend:** DVX. CARNO-VIENSIS X **Note:** Varieties exist. Dav. #6858.

Date	Mintage	VG	F	VF	XF	Unc
1612 FVC	—	300	700	1,500	3,000	—

KM# 10 2 THALER

Silver **Obv:** Half figure right **Note:** Dav. #6844A.

Date	Mintage	VG	F	VF	XF	Unc
1600	—	1,000	1,750	3,000	—	—

KM# 19 2 THALER

Silver **Obv:** Half-figure right dividing 1-606 **Rev:** Helmeted arms **Note:** Dav. #6845.

Date	Mintage	VG	F	VF	XF	Unc
1.606 Rare	—	—	—	—	—	—

Note: Fritz Rudolf Künker Münzenhandlung Auction 131, 10-07, VF realized approximately $9,915.

KM# 20 2 THALER

Silver **Obv:** Half-figure right **Rev:** Helmeted oval arms **Note:** Dav. #6847.

Date	Mintage	VG	F	VF	XF	Unc
ND VCF Rare	—	—	—	—	—	—

Note: Fritz Rudolf Künker Münzenhandlung Auction 113, 6-06, VF realized approximately $10,115.

KM# 21 2 THALER

Silver **Note:** Similar to 1 Thaler, KM#17. Dav. #6850.

Date	Mintage	VG	F	VF	XF	Unc
ND Rare	—	—	—	—	—	—

KM# 22 2 THALER

Silver **Obv:** Half-figure right breaks upper legend **Rev:** Helmeted oval arms with F-V-C above **Note:** Dav. #6852.

Date	Mintage	VG	F	VF	XF	Unc
ND FVC Rare	—	—	—	—	—	—

KM# 36 2 THALER

Silver **Obv:** Half-figure right with helmet, date in legend **Rev:** Helmeted arms with F-V-C above **Note:** Dav. #6854.

Date	Mintage	VG	F	VF	XF	Unc
1610 FVC Rare	—	—	—	—	—	—

Note: Fritz Rudolf Künker Münzenhandlung Auction 135, 01-08, VF realized approximately $9,970

KM# 48 2 THALER
Silver **Obv:** Half-figure right breaking upper legend **Note:** Dav. #6857.

Date	Mintage	VG	F	VF	XF	Unc
1612 FVC Rare	—	—	—	—	—	—

Note: Fritz Rudolf Künker Münzenhandlung Auction 98, 3-05, VF realized approximately $20,685

KM# 12 3 THALER
Silver **Note:** Similar to 1 Thaler, KM#17. Dav. #6849.

Date	Mintage	VG	F	VF	XF	Unc
ND Rare	—	—	—	—	—	—

TRADE COINAGE

KM# 51 1/2 DUCAT
1.7500 g., 0.9860 Gold 0.0555 oz. AGW **Obv:** Crowned arms divide date **Rev:** Six-line inscription

Date	Mintage	VG	F	VF	XF	Unc
1615	—	190	375	750	1,300	—
1617	—	190	375	750	1,300	—
1620	—	190	375	750	1,300	—
1621	—	190	375	750	1,300	—
1622	—	190	375	750	1,300	—

KM# 60 1/2 DUCAT
1.7500 g., 0.9860 Gold 0.0555 oz. AGW **Note:** Klippe.

Date	Mintage	VG	F	VF	XF	Unc
1620	—	—	—	—	—	—

KM# 37 DUCAT
3.5000 g., 0.9860 Gold 0.1109 oz. AGW **Obv:** Johann Georg standing right divides date **Rev:** 12-fold arms, three helmets above

Date	Mintage	VG	F	VF	XF	Unc
1610	—	525	1,150	2,400	4,150	—

KM# 43 DUCAT
3.5000 g., 0.9860 Gold 0.1109 oz. AGW **Rev:** Crowned 12-fold arms, date in legend

Date	Mintage	VG	F	VF	XF	Unc
1611	—	525	1,150	2,400	4,150	—

KM# 49 DUCAT
3.5000 g., 0.9860 Gold 0.1109 oz. AGW **Obv:** Half-length bust of Johann Georg right **Rev:** Crowned 12-fold arms, date in legend

Date	Mintage	VG	F	VF	XF	Unc
1612	—	300	600	1,200	2,250	—
1620	—	300	600	1,200	2,250	—

KM# 50 DUCAT
3.5000 g., 0.9860 Gold 0.1109 oz. AGW **Rev:** Crowned oval arms

Date	Mintage	VG	F	VF	XF	Unc
1614	—	300	600	1,200	2,250	—
1616	—	300	600	1,200	2,250	—
1617	—	300	600	1,200	2,250	—

KM# 61 DUCAT
3.5000 g., 0.9860 Gold 0.1109 oz. AGW **Obv:** Crowned arms divide date **Rev:** Six-line inscription **Note:** Thick planchet.

Date	Mintage	VG	F	VF	XF	Unc
1620	—	375	750	1,800	3,000	—
1621	—	—	—	—	—	—

KM# 52 2 DUCAT
7.0000 g., 0.9860 Gold 0.2219 oz. AGW **Obv:** Crowned arms divide date **Rev:** Six-line inscription **Note:** Thick planchet.

Date	Mintage	VG	F	VF	XF	Unc
1617	—	1,300	2,650	5,300	8,300	—

KM# 54 2 DUCAT
7.0000 g., 0.9860 Gold 0.2219 oz. AGW **Obv:** Johann Georg standing right **Rev:** Crowned oval arms, date in legend

Date	Mintage	VG	F	VF	XF	Unc
1618	—	1,150	2,400	4,500	7,500	—
1620	—	1,150	2,400	4,500	7,500	—
1621	—	1,150	2,400	4,500	7,500	—
ND	—	1,150	2,400	4,500	7,500	—

KM# 55 3 DUCAT
10.5000 g., 0.9860 Gold 0.3328 oz. AGW **Obv:** Johann Georg standing right **Rev:** Crowned oval arms, date in legend

Date	Mintage	VG	F	VF	XF	Unc
ND FVC Rare	—	—	—	—	—	—

KM# A56 3 DUCAT
10.5000 g., 0.9860 Gold 0.3328 oz. AGW **Obv:** Half-length bust Johann Georg right divides date, titles of Johann Georg **Rev:** Crowned 4-fold arms with central shield in baroque frame **Note:** Struck with 1/4 Thaler dies, KM#32.

Date	Mintage	VG	F	VF	XF	Unc
1610 FVC Rare	—	—	—	—	—	—

KM# 23 4 DUCAT
14.0000 g., 0.9860 Gold 0.4438 oz. AGW **Obv:** Half-length armored bust Johann Georg right with titles **Rev:** Oval 12-fold arms, three helmets above **Note:** Struck with 1/2 Thaler dies, KM#14.

Date	Mintage	VG	F	VF	XF	Unc
ND FVC	—	—	—	—	—	—

KM# 38 4 DUCAT
14.0000 g., 0.9860 Gold 0.4438 oz. AGW **Obv:** Half-length armored bust Johann Georg right divides date **Rev:** 12-fold arms, three helmets above **Note:** Struck with 1/2 Thaler dies, KM#33.

Date	Mintage	VG	F	VF	XF	Unc
1610 FVC Rare	—	—	—	—	—	—

KM# 25 5 DUCAT (1/2 Portugalöser)
17.5000 g., 0.9860 Gold 0.5547 oz. AGW **Note:** Struck with 1/2 Thaler dies, KM#14.

Date	Mintage	VG	F	VF	XF	Unc
ND VCF	—	—	—	—	—	—

KM# 44 5 DUCAT (1/2 Portugalöser)
17.5000 g., 0.9860 Gold 0.5547 oz. AGW **Note:** Struck with 1/2 Thaler dies, KM#40.

Date	Mintage	VG	F	VF	XF	Unc
1611 FVC Rare	—	—	—	—	—	—

KM# A45 7 DUCAT
24.5000 g., 0.9860 Gold 0.7766 oz. AGW **Note:** Struck with 1 Thaler dies.

Date	Mintage	VG	F	VF	XF	Unc
1611 Rare	—	—	—	—	—	—

KM# B45 8 DUCAT
28.0000 g., 0.9860 Gold 0.8876 oz. AGW **Note:** Struck with 1 Thaler dies.

Date	Mintage	VG	F	VF	XF	Unc
1611 Rare	—	—	—	—	—	—

KM# 28 10 DUCAT (Portugalöser)
35.0000 g., 0.9860 Gold 1.1095 oz. AGW **Note:** Struck with 1 Thaler dies.

Date	Mintage	VG	F	VF	XF	Unc
ND Rare	—	—	—	—	—	—

KM# 45 10 DUCAT (Portugalöser)
35.0000 g., 0.9860 Gold 1.1095 oz. AGW **Rev. Legend:** DVX. CARN-O. VIENSIS **Note:** Struck with 1 Thaler dies, KM#42.

Date	Mintage	VG	F	VF	XF	Unc
1611 FVC Rare	—	—	—	—	—	—

KM# 26 12 DUCAT
42.0000 g., 0.9860 Gold 1.3314 oz. AGW **Note:** Struck with 2 Thaler dies, KM#22.

Date	Mintage	VG	F	VF	XF	Unc
ND FVC Rare	—	—	—	—	—	—

PATTERNS

Including off metal strikes

KM#	Date	Mintage	Identification	Mkt Val
Pn1	1611	—	Thaler. Lead. KM#41	—
Pn2	1612 FVC	—	Thaler. Lead. KM#47	—

JEVER

A lordship lying on the North Sea coast, Jever's earliest coinage dates from the late 10th and early 11th centuries. For several centuries Jever experienced political disintegration until one powerful lord united the district in the early 15th century. The noble line fell extinct in 1575 and Jever passed by marriage to Oldenburg, then successively to Anhalt-Zerbst in 1667, Russia in 1793, Holland in 1807, Russia again in 1813, and finally to Oldenburg again in 1818.

The coinage struck for Jever under Oldenburg can be distinguished by prominence given to the Jever arms - a lion rampant to the left usually in a central shield imposed over the four-fold arms of Oldenburg and Delmenhorst.

RULERS

Johann XVI von Oldenburg, 1575-1603
Anton Günther von Oldenburg, 1603-1667
Johann Rudolph von Anhalt-Zerbst, 1667 only
Karl Wilhelm von Anhalt-Zerbst, 1667-1718

MINT OFFICIALS' INITIALS

Initial	Date	Name
CDZ, GDZ, Z	1663-71	Georg David Ziegenhorn
CP	1674-91	Christian Pfahler
GW	(ca.1698)	?
IA, IAQ	1666-76	Johann Arendsburg
	1614-22	Nikolaus Wintgens
	1637-49	Gerhard Dreyer
	1649-51	Jürgen Detleffs
	1658-62	Jürgen Hartmann

LORDSHIP

REGULAR COINAGE

KM# 5 SCHWAREN
Billon **Ruler:** Anton Günther **Obv:** Cross, titles of Anton Günther **Rev:** Jever lion, titles

Date	Mintage	VG	F	VF	XF	Unc
ND	7,549	60.00	120	170	—	—

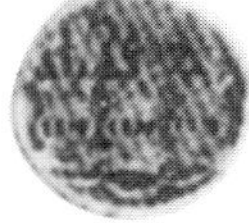

KM# 15 1/4 STUBER (Örtgen)
Billon **Ruler:** Anton Günther **Obv:** Jever lion left **Rev:** 3 ornate helmets

Date	Mintage	VG	F	VF	XF	Unc
ND(c. 1614-22)	—	20.00	40.00	70.00	120	—

KM# 16 1/4 STUBER (Örtgen)
Billon **Ruler:** Anton Günther **Obv:** Cross, titles of Anton Gunther **Rev:** Crowned 4-fold arms with central shield of Jever lion, titles

Date	Mintage	VG	F	VF	XF	Unc
ND	—	70.00	120	200	350	—

KM# 17 1/4 STUBER (Örtgen)
Billon **Ruler:** Anton Günther **Rev:** Jever lion, titles **Note:** Varieties exist.

Date	Mintage	VG	F	VF	XF	Unc
ND	—	20.00	40.00	70.00	125	—

KM# 86 1/4 STUBER (Örtgen)
Billon **Ruler:** Karl Wilhelm **Obv:** Jever lion arms **Obv. Legend:** MON. PRINC. ANH. D. I. &. K. **Rev. Legend:** IN/DOMINO/FIDUCIA/NOST. **Note:** Varieties exist.

Date	Mintage	VG	F	VF	XF	Unc
ND(1667-1718)	—	13.00	27.00	45.00	85.00	—

KM# 85 1/4 STUBER (Örtgen)
Billon **Ruler:** Karl Wilhelm **Obv:** Crowned Jever lion left **Obv. Legend:** MON:NOVA JEVEREN **Rev:** Legend, date **Rev. Legend:** IN/DEO/FACIEM/VIRT **Note:** Varieties exist.

Date	Mintage	VG	F	VF	XF	Unc
1690	—	16.00	30.00	45.00	85.00	—
1699	—	16.00	30.00	45.00	85.00	—

KM# 6 1/2 STUBER
Billon **Ruler:** Anton Günther **Obv:** Crowned 4-fold arms with central shield of Jever lion, titles of Anton Gunther **Rev:** Ornate cross, 1-EV/H-S in 4 angles **Rev. Legend:** IN. M-DOM-SOR-MEA. **Note:** Varieties exist.

Date	Mintage	VG	F	VF	XF	Unc
ND	—	16.00	33.00	55.00	100	—

KM# 7 1/2 STUBER
Billon **Ruler:** Anton Günther **Rev:** I-E/H-S in angles of cross **Rev. Legend:** AUX-IL. M-EA-D. **Note:** Varieties exist.

Date	Mintage	VG	F	VF	XF	Unc
ND	—	16.00	33.00	55.00	100	—

KM# 87 1/2 STUBER
Billon **Ruler:** Karl Wilhelm **Obv:** Ornate burgundian cross **Obv. Legend:** MON-NOV--IEVE-REN **Rev:** Denomination, date

Date	Mintage	VG	F	VF	XF	Unc
1690	—	13.00	27.00	45.00	85.00	—

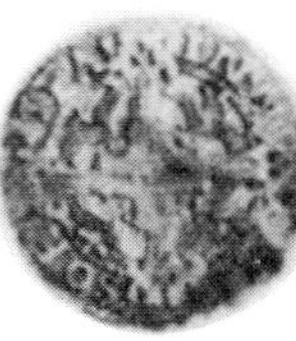

KM# 24 STUBER (10 Witten)
Billon **Ruler:** Anton Günther **Obv:** Crowned 4-fold arms with central shield of Jever lion divides I-S, titles of Anton Gunther **Rev:** Ornate cross **Rev. Legend:** IN. M-DOM-SOR-MEA

Date	Mintage	VG	F	VF	XF	Unc
ND(c. 1618-20)	—	20.00	45.00	80.00	140	—

KM# 56 STUBER (10 Witten)
Billon **Ruler:** Anton Günther **Obv:** Ornate burgundian cross **Obv. Legend:** MON-NOV--IEVE-REN **Rev. Legend:** I/IEVER/STU:VER **Note:** Varieties exist.

Date	Mintage	VG	F	VF	XF	Unc
ND	—	20.00	55.00	80.00	140	—

KM# 57 STUBER (10 Witten)
Billon **Ruler:** Anton Günther **Obv. Legend:** MON-PRIN. ANHA-D. IE. **Note:** Varieties exist.

Date	Mintage	VG	F	VF	XF	Unc
ND	—	20.00	45.00	80.00	140	—

KM# 88 STUBER (10 Witten)
Billon **Ruler:** Karl Wilhelm **Rev:** .I./STUVER./.1690

Date	Mintage	VG	F	VF	XF	Unc
1690	—	16.00	30.00	45.00	95.00	—

KM# 9.1 2 STUBER (Schaf)
Billon **Ruler:** Anton Günther **Obv:** Crowned 4-fold arms with central shield of Jever lion divides II-S, titles of Anton Gunther **Rev:** Ornate cross **Rev. Legend:** IN MANIBVS DOMINI SOR. MEAE*

Date	Mintage	VG	F	VF	XF	Unc
ND	—	27.00	55.00	80.00	140	—

KM# 9.2 2 STUBER (Schaf)
Billon **Ruler:** Anton Günther **Obv:** Value 2-S

Date	Mintage	VG	F	VF	XF	Unc
ND	—	27.00	55.00	80.00	140	—

KM# 9.3 2 STUBER (Schaf)
Billon **Ruler:** Anton Günther **Note:** Klippe.

Date	Mintage	VG	F	VF	XF	Unc
ND	—	—	—	—	—	—

KM# 13 2 STUBER (Schaf)
Billon **Ruler:** Anton Günther **Obv:** Imperial orb inside 2. GROOT. 18 WIT. **Obv. Legend:** Titles of Matthias **Rev:** 4-fold arms with central concave shield of Jever lion, helmet above

Date	Mintage	VG	F	VF	XF	Unc
ND	—	27.00	55.00	80.00	140	—

KM# 18.1 2 STUBER (Schaf)
Billon **Ruler:** Anton Günther **Obv:** Titles of Matthias

Date	Mintage	VG	F	VF	XF	Unc
ND(1614-1619)	—	27.00	55.00	80.00	140	—

KM# 18.2 2 STUBER (Schaf)
Billon **Ruler:** Anton Günther **Obv:** 2 GROOT 18 WIT around small imperial orb within ornamented oval **Obv. Legend:** IN MANIB...

Date	Mintage	VG	F	VF	XF	Unc
ND(1614-1622)	—	27.00	55.00	80.00	140	—

KM# 18.3 2 STUBER (Schaf)
Billon **Ruler:** Anton Günther **Note:** Klippe.

Date	Mintage	VG	F	VF	XF	Unc
ND(1614-1622)	—	—	—	—	—	—

KM# 19 2 STUBER (Schaf)
Billon **Ruler:** Anton Günther **Rev. Legend:** DA. PACEM. DOMINE. IN. DIEBVS. NOSTRIS.

Date	Mintage	VG	F	VF	XF	Unc
ND	—	27.00	55.00	80.00	140	—

KM# 20 2 STUBER (Schaf)
Billon **Ruler:** Anton Günther **Rev. Legend:** AUXILIUM. MEUM.

Date	Mintage	VG	F	VF	XF	Unc
ND	—	27.00	55.00	80.00	140	—

KM# 64 2 STUBER (Schaf)
Billon **Ruler:** Karl Wilhelm **Obv:** Crowned Anhalt arms divide 2-S, titles of Karl Wilhelm **Rev:** Ornate burgundian cross **Rev. Legend:** MONETA NOVA IEVERNSIS

Date	Mintage	VG	F	VF	XF	Unc
ND	—	27.00	55.00	80.00	140	—

KM# 65 2 STUBER (Schaf)
Billon **Ruler:** Karl Wilhelm **Obv:** Crowned 4-fold arms with central shield of Jever lion divides 2-S, titles of Karl Wilhelm **Rev:** Ornate burgundian cross **Rev. Legend:** IN. DOMINO. FIDUCIA. NOSTRA.

Date	Mintage	VG	F	VF	XF	Unc
ND	—	27.00	55.00	80.00	140	—

KM# 10.1 GROTEN (4 Pfennig)
Billon **Ruler:** Anton Günther **Obv:** Crowned 4-fold arms with central shield of Jever lion, titles of Anton Gunther **Rev:** I/OLDEN/BVRGER/GROT/* **Rev. Legend:** AVXILIVM...

Date	Mintage	VG	F	VF	XF	Unc
ND	—	45.00	100	200	350	—

KM# 10.2 GROTEN (4 Pfennig)
Billon **Ruler:** Anton Günther **Rev:** 1/OLDE/GROT/date

Date	Mintage	VG	F	VF	XF	Unc
1658	—	45.00	100	200	350	—
1659	—	45.00	100	200	350	—

KM# 11 GROTEN (4 Pfennig)
Billon **Ruler:** Anton Günther **Obv:** Arms divide I-G

Date	Mintage	VG	F	VF	XF	Unc
ND	—	45.00	100	200	350	—

KM# 12 2 GROTE (Krumster)
Silver **Ruler:** Anton Günther **Obv:** Crowned 4-fold arms with central shield of Jever lion, titles of Anton Gunther **Rev:** Imperial orb **Rev. Legend:** Inner: 2 GROOT 18 WIT; outer: IN. MANIB. DOMI. SORTE, ME.

Date	Mintage	VG	F	VF	XF	Unc
ND	—	70.00	140	225	400	—

KM# 21 2 GROTE (Krumster)
Silver **Ruler:** Anton Günther **Obv. Legend:** Outer: Titles of Matthias **Rev:** Helmeted, ornate 4-fold arms with central shield Jever lion **Note:** Varieties exist.

Date	Mintage	VG	F	VF	XF	Unc
ND(1614-1619)	—	70.00	140	225	400	—

KM# 90 MALL SCHILLING (6 Stüber)
Silver **Ruler:** Karl Wilhelm **Rev:** Crowned imperial eagle, titles of Leopold I, date in legend

Date	Mintage	VG	F	VF	XF	Unc
1698 GW	—	80.00	140	225	300	—

KM# 75 1/192 THALER (Bläffert)
Billon **Ruler:** Karl Wilhelm **Obv:** Jever lion left **Obv. Legend:** CAROL. WILH:. **Rev:** PRIN. ANHALT. 77. around 19Z.

Date	Mintage	VG	F	VF	XF	Unc
(16)77	—	—	—	—	—	—

KM# 30 1/36 THALER (Mariengroschen)
Silver **Ruler:** Anton Günther **Obv:** Crowned ornate 4-fold arms with central shield of Jever lion divides 7-G **Rev:** Imperial eagle with 36 in oval above, titles of Ferdinand III

Date	Mintage	VG	F	VF	XF	Unc
ND(1637-1657)	—	55.00	120	200	325	—

KM# 43 1/36 THALER (Mariengroschen)
Silver **Ruler:** Anton Günther **Obv:** Crowned 4-fold arms with central shield of Jever lion **Rev:** XXXVI./.EIN/RTAL. **Rev. Legend:** AUXILIUM MEUM A DOMINO, date

Date	Mintage	VG	F	VF	XF	Unc
1658	—	55.00	120	200	325	—
1659	—	55.00	120	200	325	—

KM# 44 1/36 THALER (Mariengroschen)
Silver **Ruler:** Anton Günther **Rev. Legend:** AUXILIUM... **Rev. Inscription:** 36 / EIN / R. TAL. / date **Note:** Varieties exist.

Date	Mintage	VG	F	VF	XF	Unc
1659	—	40.00	90.00	160	275	—
1660	—	40.00	90.00	160	275	—
1664	—	40.00	90.00	160	275	—
1665	—	40.00	90.00	160	275	—
1666	—	40.00	90.00	160	275	—

KM# 45 1/36 THALER (Mariengroschen)
Silver **Ruler:** Anton Günther **Obv:** Crowned Jever lion left **Obv. Legend:** MON. PRIN. ANHAL... **Rev. Legend:** IN. DOMINO. FIDVCIA. NOSTRA. **Rev. Inscription:** 36/EIN/RTAL/* **Note:** Varieties exist.

Date	Mintage	VG	F	VF	XF	Unc
ND	—	55.00	120	200	300	—
ND IAQ	—	55.00	120	200	300	—

KM# 58 1/18 THALER (4 Grote)
Silver **Ruler:** Anton Günther **Obv:** Crowned 4-fold arms with central shield of Jever lion, titles of Anton Gunther **Rev. Legend:** AUXILIUM...date **Rev. Inscription:** 18/EIN/R. TAL. /Z **Note:** Varieties exist.

Date	Mintage	VG	F	VF	XF	Unc
1658 (d)	—	115	225	400	675	—
1659 (d)	—	115	225	400	675	—
1660 (d)	—	115	225	400	675	—
1663 Z	—	115	225	400	675	—
1664 Z	—	115	225	400	675	—
1665 Z	—	115	225	400	675	—
1666 Z	—	115	225	400	675	—

KM# 70 1/18 THALER (4 Grote)
Silver **Ruler:** Karl Wilhelm **Obv:** Crowned Jever lion arms **Rev. Legend:** IN DOMINO...date **Rev. Inscription:** 18/EINEN/REICHS/THALER

Date	Mintage	VG	F	VF	XF	Unc
1671	—	—	—	—	—	—

KM# 71 1/18 THALER (4 Grote)
Silver **Ruler:** Karl Wilhelm **Obv:** Anhalt arms **Obv. Legend:** MON. PRINC. ANH... **Rev. Legend:** IN DOMINO **Rev. Inscription:** 18/EINEN/RIAL **Note:** Varieties exist.

Date	Mintage	VG	F	VF	XF	Unc
ND	—	—	—	—	—	—

KM# 50 2 SCHILLING (1/16 Thaler)
Silver **Ruler:** Anton Günther **Obv:** Crowned 4-fold arms with central shield of Jever **Rev:** Titles continued **Rev. Inscription:** II/SCHIL/LNIG/date

Date	Mintage	VG	F	VF	XF	Unc
1654	—	—	—	—	—	—

KM# 73 1/16 THALER (3 Schilling)
Silver **Ruler:** Karl Wilhelm **Obv:** Bust right, titles of Karl Wilhelm **Rev. Legend:** IN. DOMIN:... **Rev. Inscription:** XVI/REICHS/THAL./CP

Date	Mintage	VG	F	VF	XF	Unc
ND(1674-1691)	—	45.00	100	175	300	—

KM# 22 12 GROTE (1/6 Thaler)
Silver **Ruler:** Anton Günther **Obv:** Crowned imperial eagle, orb on breast, titles of Matthias **Rev:** Crowned 4-fold arms with central shield of Jever lion, titles of Anton Gunther

Date	Mintage	VG	F	VF	XF	Unc
ND(1614-1619)	—	—	—	—	—	—

KM# 25 12 GROTE (1/6 Thaler)
Silver **Ruler:** Anton Günther **Obv:** Titles of Ferdinand II **Note:** Klippe.

Date	Mintage	VG	F	VF	XF	Unc
ND(1619-1637)	—	—	—	—	—	—

KM# 41 12 GROTE (1/6 Thaler)
Silver **Ruler:** Anton Günther **Obv:** Bust turned 1/4 to right **Rev:** Crowned 4-fold arms with central shield of Jever lion, XII.GROT below **Rev. Legend:** AVXILIVM and date

Date	Mintage	VG	F	VF	XF	Unc
1658	—	1,350	2,350	—	—	—
1659	—	—	—	—	—	—

KM# 80 1/6 THALER
Silver **Ruler:** Karl Wilhelm **Obv:** Crowned ornate helmet with 3 tall feathers **Rev:** Crowned ornate CWFZA monogram, value (1/6) below, date in legend

Date	Mintage	VG	F	VF	XF	Unc
1689 CP	—	—	—	—	—	—
1690 CP	—	—	—	—	—	—

KM# 23 1/4 THALER
Silver **Ruler:** Anton Günther **Obv:** Crowned 4-fold arms with central shield of Jever lion **Rev:** Crowned imperial eagle, orb on breast, titles of Matthias **Note:** Varieties exist.

Date	Mintage	VG	F	VF	XF	Unc
ND(1614-1619)	—	—	—	—	—	—

KM# 42 24 GROTE (1/3 Thaler)
Silver **Ruler:** Anton Günther **Obv:** Bust turned 1/4 right **Rev:** Crowned 4-fold arms with central shield of Jever lion, XXIIII GROT below **Rev. Legend:** AUXILIUM MEUM A DOMINO, date **Note:** Varieties exist.

Date	Mintage	VG	F	VF	XF	Unc
1658	207,000	225	400	675	1,150	—
1659	Inc. above	225	400	675	1,150	—
1660	Inc. above	225	400	675	1,150	—

KM# 69 1/3 THALER (1/2 Gulden)
Silver **Ruler:** Karl Wilhelm **Obv:** Crowned Jever lion in laurel wreath **Rev:** Mintmaster's initials, date in legend **Rev. Inscription:** III/EINEN/REICHS/THALER/

Date	Mintage	VG	F	VF	XF	Unc
1671 GDZ	—	140	225	350	550	—

KM# 72 1/3 THALER (1/2 Gulden)
Silver **Ruler:** Karl Wilhelm **Obv:** Crowned ornate helmet with 3 tall feathers **Rev:** Date in legend **Rev. Inscription:** III/EINEN/REICHS/THALER **Note:** Varieties exist.

Date	Mintage	VG	F	VF	XF	Unc
1671 CDZ	—	85.00	160	275	475	—
167Z IAG	—	65.00	140	225	400	—
1675 CP	—	75.00	150	240	425	—
1676 IA	—	75.00	150	240	425	—

KM# 26 1/2 THALER
Silver **Ruler:** Anton Günther **Obv:** Crowned 4-fold arms with central shield of Jever lion **Rev:** Crowned imperial eagle, orb on breast, titles of Matthias **Note:** Klippe.

Date	Mintage	VG	F	VF	XF	Unc
ND(1614-1619)	—	—	—	—	—	—

KM# 66 1/2 THALER
Silver **Ruler:** Karl Wilhelm **Subject:** Death of Johann Rudolph **Obv:** Bust right **Rev:** Crowned arms of Anhalt, birth and death dates in legend

Date	Mintage	VG	F	VF	XF	Unc
1667	—	—	—	—	—	—

KM# 35 28 STUBER (Gulden)
Silver **Ruler:** Anton Günther **Obv:** Crowned 4-fold arms with central shield of Jever lion, value (28) below **Obv. Legend:** FLOR • ANT • GV • C(28) • ED • D •LI • E • K - **Rev:** Crowned imperial eagle, 28 in orb on breast **Rev. Legend:** FERD • III • D • G • ROM • IMP • SEMP • AVG • **Note:** Varieties exist. Dav.#713.

Date	Mintage	VG	F	VF	XF	Unc
ND(c. 1640)	—	45.00	85.00	160	275	—

KM# 40 28 STUBER (Gulden)
Silver **Ruler:** Anton Günther **Obv:** Crowned shield within circle **Obv. Legend:** FLOR • AN • GV. C • O (28) E • D • D • I • IE • E • K **Rev:** Value in circle on breast of crowned imperial eagle, 28 in orb on breast within circle **Rev. Legend:** FERD • II • D • G • ROM • IMP • SEMP • AV • **Note:** Varieties exist. Dav. #714.

Date	Mintage	VG	F	VF	XF	Unc
ND(1649-51)	—	33.00	65.00	150	240	—

KM# 59 28 STUBER (Gulden)
Silver **Ruler:** Anton Günther **Obv:** Crowned shield within circle, without value in legend **Obv. Legend:** FLOR • AN • GU • C • O • E • E • DI • IE • E • K • **Rev:** Crowned imperial eagle **Rev. Legend:** • LEOPOLD • D • G • ROM • IMPER • SEMP • AUG * **Note:** Varieties exist. Dav.#715.

Date	Mintage	VG	F	VF	XF	Unc
ND(c. 1660)	—	600	1,125	2,000	3,250	—

KM# 46 48 GROTE (2/3 Thaler)
Silver **Ruler:** Anton Günther **Obv:** Bust turned 1/4 right **Rev:** Crowned 4-fold arms with central shield of Jever lion, 16.48. GROT. 59 above **Rev. Legend:** AUXILIUM MEUM A DOMINO **Note:** Dav.#716.

Date	Mintage	VG	F	VF	XF	Unc
1659	—	500	975	1,800	3,000	—
ND(1660)	—	500	975	1,800	3,000	—

KM# 47 48 GROTE (2/3 Thaler)
Silver **Ruler:** Anton Günther **Rev:** Date in legend **Note:** Varieties exist. Dav.#717.

Date	Mintage	VG	F	VF	XF	Unc
1659	—	500	975	1,800	3,000	—
1660	—	500	975	1,800	3,000	—

KM# 48 48 GROTE (2/3 Thaler)
Silver **Ruler:** Anton Günther **Rev:** Value XXXXVIII GROT. below arms **Note:** Dav.#718.

Date	Mintage	VG	F	VF	XF	Unc
1659 Rare	—	—	—	—	—	—

KM# 89 2/3 THALER (Gulden)
Silver **Ruler:** Karl Wilhelm **Obv:** Crowned ornate helmet with 3 tall feathers **Rev:** Crowned ornate CWFZA monogram, 2/3 below, date in legend **Note:** Dav.#581.

Date	Mintage	VG	F	VF	XF	Unc
1690 CP	—	—	—	—	—	—

KM# 74 40 STUBER (Thaler)
Silver **Ruler:** Karl Wilhelm **Obv:** Knight behind shield **Rev:** Rampant lion left **Note:** Varieties exist.

Date	Mintage	VG	F	VF	XF	Unc
1676	—	400	850	1,650	2,700	—
1677	—	400	850	1,650	2,700	—
1678	—	400	850	1,650	2,700	—

KM# 60 48 GROTE (Thaler weight)

Silver **Ruler:** Anton Günther **Obv. Legend:** Ends with ...IE. ET. KN. **Note:** Approximately 29 grams.

Date	Mintage	VG	F	VF	XF	Unc
1660	—	425	875	1,550	2,600	—

KM# 62 THALER

Silver **Ruler:** Anton Günther **Obv:** Bust left **Obv. Legend:** ANT. GVNT. C. OL. **Rev:** Crowned arms **Note:** Dav. #7114.

Date	Mintage	VG	F	VF	XF	Unc
1664	—	325	650	1,150	1,950	—

KM# A61 48 GROTE (2 Thaler weight)

Silver **Ruler:** Anton Günther **Obv:** Bust turned 1/4 right **Rev:** Crowned 4-fold arms with central shield of Jever lion, 16.48. GROT. 59 above **Rev. Legend:** AUXILIUM MEUM A DOMINO **Note:** Varieties exist. Dav.#7111.

Date	Mintage	VG	F	VF	XF	Unc
1659	—	—	—	—	—	—
ND(1660)	—	—	—	—	—	—

KM# 61 48 GROTE (2 Thaler weight)

Silver **Ruler:** Anton Günther **Obv. Legend:** Ends with ...IE. ET. KN. **Rev:** Date in legend **Note:** Approximately 58 grams. Dav.#7118.

Date	Mintage	VG	F	VF	XF	Unc
1660	—	975	1,750	2,950	—	—

TRADE COINAGE

KM# 63 DUCAT

3.5000 g., 0.9860 Gold 0.1109 oz. AGW **Ruler:** Anton Günther **Obv:** Bust right **Rev:** Crowned 4-fold arms with central shield of Jever lion in palm wreath **Rev. Legend:** AUXILIUM ..., date

Date	Mintage	VG	F	VF	XF	Unc
1664	—	1,450	2,650	4,650	7,000	—

JULICH

The capital of the duchy of Jülich is located on the Roer River 16 miles northeast of Aachen near the border with the Netherlands. The Roman town of Juliacum became the seat of the counts of Jülich by the mid-9th century and that of the dukes beginning in 1356. Three major sieges took place against the city and the first occurred in 1543. In the early 17th century Jülich was besieged twice, in 1610 by Prince Moritz of Nassau-Orange (1618-1625) and in 1621-22 by Count Henry of 's-Heerenberg (d.1638).

CITY

SIEGE COINAGE

1610

Obsidional coinage issued by Baron Johann von Rauschenberg, governor of Julich on behalf of the Hapsburg Archduke Leopold, imperial administrator for the disputed lands of Julich, Cleve, Berg, Mark, and Ravensberg. Most, if not all, of the following items were fashioned or cut from silver or gold dinnerware, some hammered flat and countermarked with identifying stamps and value stamps. There are two types of identifying stamps:

A - in oval, a crowned R (Rauschenberg) above 16L10 (L = Leopold).

B - in oval, V/I. R/1610 (Johann von Rauschenberg).

KM# 1 THALER

Silver **Note:** Weight varies: 1.54-3.50 grams. Uniface, oblong and irregular. Stamp B and I in oblong stamp. Varieties exist.

Date	Mintage	VG	F	VF	XF	Unc
1610	—	1,100	1,800	2,800	4,000	—

KM# 2 THALER

Silver **Note:** On square piece.

Date	Mintage	VG	F	VF	XF	Unc
1610	—	1,100	1,800	2,800	4,000	—

KM# 3 THALER

Silver **Note:** On octagonal piece.

Date	Mintage	VG	F	VF	XF	Unc
1610	—	1,100	1,800	2,800	4,000	—

KM# 4 2 THALER

Silver **Note:** Weight varies: 5.77-6.20 grams. Uniface. Square. Stamp A and II in square stamp.

Date	Mintage	VG	F	VF	XF	Unc
1610	—	800	1,300	2,000	5,600	—

KM# 5 2 THALER

Silver **Note:** Weight varies: 5.98-6.20 grams. Varieties exist.

Date	Mintage	VG	F	VF	XF	Unc
1610	—	1,600	2,600	4,000	5,600	—

KM# 6 2 THALER

Silver **Note:** Weight varies: 2.70-9.30 grams. Small irregular, four sided. Varieties exist.

Date	Mintage	VG	F	VF	XF	Unc
1610	—	1,400	2,300	3,500	5,000	—

KM# 7 3 THALER

Silver **Note:** Weight varies: 7.94-10.00 grams. Uniface, irregular half circle.

Date	Mintage	VG	F	VF	XF	Unc
1610	—	1,300	2,200	3,300	4,800	—

KM# 8 3 THALER

Silver **Note:** Square with rounded corners.

Date	Mintage	VG	F	VF	XF	Unc
1610	—	1,300	2,200	3,300	4,800	—

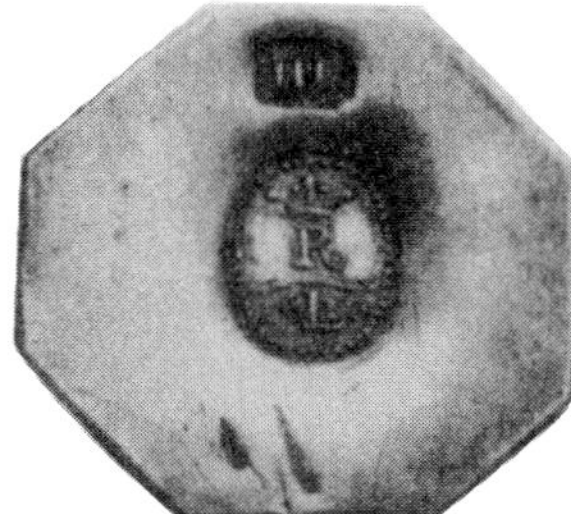

KM# 9 3 THALER

Silver **Note:** Weight varies: 8.60-9.40 grams. Octagonal flan. Varieties exist.

Date	Mintage	VG	F	VF	XF	Unc
1610	—	1,200	2,000	3,100	4,500	—

KM# 10 3 THALER

9.0100 g., Silver **Note:** Square with rounded ends. Stamp B and II in oblong stamp.

Date	Mintage	VG	F	VF	XF	Unc
1610	—	1,450	2,400	3,700	5,300	—

KM# 11 3 THALER

9.0100 g., Silver **Note:** Stamp B and III in rectangular stamp.

Date	Mintage	VG	F	VF	XF	Unc
1610	—	1,400	2,300	3,500	5,100	—

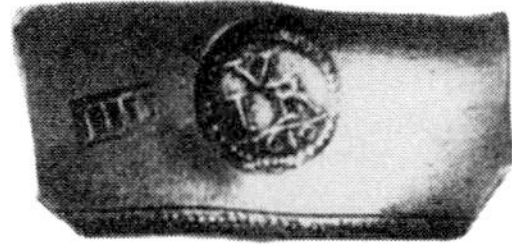

KM# 15 4 THALER

Silver **Note:** Similar to KM#13, but with stamp B.

Date	Mintage	VG	F	VF	XF	Unc
1610	—	1,800	2,900	4,400	6,000	—

KM# 12 4 THALER

Silver **Note:** Weight varies: 11.80-17.42 grams. Uniface irregular octagon. Stamp A and IIII in rectangle.

Date	Mintage	VG	F	VF	XF	Unc
1610	—	1,800	2,900	4,400	6,000	—

KM# 13 4 THALER

Silver **Note:** Weight varies: 11.76-15.78 grams. Irregular rectangle. Stamp A and IIII in oblong stamp. Varieties exist.

Date	Mintage	VG	F	VF	XF	Unc
1610	—	900	1,450	2,200	6,000	—

KM# 14 4 THALER

26.2000 g., Silver **Note:** Unevenly round. Stamp A and IIII in rectangle.

Date	Mintage	VG	F	VF	XF	Unc
1610	—	1,800	2,900	4,400	6,000	—

KM# 16 5 THALER

Silver **Note:** Weight varies: 17.00-18.00 grams. Uniface square with rounded corners. Stamp A and IIIII in rectangle.

Date	Mintage	VG	F	VF	XF	Unc
1610	—	1,900	3,000	4,500	6,500	—

KM# 17 5 THALER

24.7100 g., Silver **Note:** Irregular flan.

Date	Mintage	VG	F	VF	XF	Unc
1610 Rare	—	—	—	—	—	—

Note: Fritz Rudolf Künker Münzenhandlung Auction 122, 3-07, nearly XF realized approximately $14,550

KM# 18 6 THALER

11.8000 g., Silver **Note:** Uniface triangle with rounded angles. Stamp B, V in square at left, I in rectangle at right.

Date	Mintage	VG	F	VF	XF	Unc
1610	—	2,000	3,300	5,000	7,000	—

KM# 19 6 THALER

28.0700 g., Silver **Note:** Piece from bowl rim, square with rounded angles at bottom.

Date	Mintage	VG	F	VF	XF	Unc
1610	—	2,000	3,300	5,000	7,000	—

KM# 20 7 THALER

24.8700 g., Silver, 67 mm. **Note:** Illustration reduced. Uniface triangle with rounded angles. Stamp A in each angle, VII in rectangle at center.

Date	Mintage	VG	F	VF	XF	Unc
1610	—	2,000	3,300	5,000	7,000	—

KM# 21 7 THALER

28.7900 g., Silver **Obv:** Stamp B top left with II in rectangle nearby, stamp A with V in square nearby. **Note:** Illustration reduced. Actual size: 81mm wide. Piece from rim of plate. Varieties exist.

Date	Mintage	VG	F	VF	XF	Unc
1610	—	2,000	3,400	5,300	7,500	—

KM# 22 8 THALER

25.6400 g., Silver **Note:** Uniface square. Stamp A in center, eagle in shield-shaped stamp at left and right, II in square stamp twice each above and below.

Date	Mintage	VG	F	VF	XF	Unc
1610	—	2,000	3,400	5,300	7,500	—

KM# 23 8 THALER

37.5000 g., Silver, 85 mm. **Note:** Illustration reduced. Baroque ornamented handle of tableware. Stamp B, V square at left, III in rectangle at right, stamp A on other side.

Date	Mintage	VG	F	VF	XF	Unc
1610	—	2,000	3,500	5,500	8,000	—

KM# 24 8 THALER

37.5000 g., Silver **Note:** Trapezoid. Stamp B in center, V in square left and III in rectangle at right.

Date	Mintage	VG	F	VF	XF	Unc
1610	—	2,000	3,300	5,000	7,000	—

KM# 25 9 THALER

42.0000 g., Silver **Note:** Rim of baroque ornamented cup in uneven square with rounded corners. Stamp B, V in square at left, IIII in rectangle at right, on other side, arms of Rauschenberg (lion upper right, arrow lower left), winged helmet above, IvR below.

Date	Mintage	VG	F	VF	XF	Unc
1610	—	2,400	4,000	6,000	9,000	—

KM# 26 10 THALER

Silver **Note:** Rim of plate, rounded at one end, inner cut end has rounded corners. Large ornate version of stamp A and VIGILANTE/DEO in two lines below. Other side: Stamp A and X in rectangle. Illustration reduced.

Date	Mintage	VG	F	VF	XF	Unc
1610	—	2,700	7,000	10,000	18,000	—

KM# 27 10 THALER

30.5000 g., Silver **Note:** Uniface irregular square from edge of large bowl. Stamp A and X in square. Varieties exist.

Date	Mintage	VG	F	VF	XF	Unc
1610	—	2,700	4,500	7,000	10,000	—

KM# 28 10 THALER

Silver **Note:** Weight varies: 48.90-53.45 grams. Large piece from rim of plate. Stamp A and X in square.

Date	Mintage	VG	F	VF	XF	Unc
1610 Rare	—	—	—	—	—	—

Note: Fritz Rudolf Künker Münzenhandlung Auction 122, 3-07, nearly XF realized approximately $39,675

KM# 29 10 THALER

Silver **Note:** Similar to KM#27, but stamp B.

Date	Mintage	VG	F	VF	XF	Unc
1610	—	3,000	5,000	7,500	11,000	—

KM# 30 15 THALER

69.8000 g., Silver **Note:** Irregular square with rounded corners. Stamp A and X in rectangle at left, V in square at right, large engraved version of A on other side.

Date	Mintage	VG	F	VF	XF	Unc
1610 Rare	—	—	—	—	—	—

KM# 31 15 THALER

65.1900 g., Silver **Note:** Stamp A in center, X in rectangular at left, a second A at lower right with IIIII in long rectangle at left.

Date	Mintage	VG	F	VF	XF	Unc
1610 Rare	—	—	—	—	—	—

KM# 32 20 THALER

90.8000 g., Silver **Note:** Irregular square with rounded corners. Two A stamps at upper left and right, each with X in square nearby. Smaller Thaler denominations exist.

Date	Mintage	VG	F	VF	XF	Unc
1610 Rare	—	—	—	—	—	—

KM# 33 40 THALER

Gold **Note:** Weight varies: 6.66-6.72 grams. Uniface square with rounded corners. Stamp A in center and at each corner, X in squarish stamp in between along each side. Varieties exist.

Date	Mintage	VG	F	VF	XF	Unc
1610 Rare	—	—	—	—	—	—

SIEGE COINAGE

1621-22

Obsidional coinage issued by Friedrich Pithan, governor of the city. There are 3 main types of stamps:

A - Small shield, F above P monogram divides 16 - Z1/Z - S (2 Stuber).

B - Slightly larger shield, F above P monogram divides 16 - Z1/4 - S (4 Stuber).

C - Large shield with extended corners in upper left and right, F above P monogram divides 16 - Z1/IN - GVL/BE - LE and G below, (beseiged in Julich).

KM# 34 2 STUBER

Silver **Note:** Weight varies: 1.30-1.60 grams. Uniface round. Stamp A. Varieties exist.

Date	Mintage	VG	F	VF	XF	Unc
16Z1	—	550	800	1,050	1,450	—

KM# 35 2 STUBER

Silver **Note:** Weight varies: 0.66-0.81 grams. Triangle with rounded angles. Stamp A. Varieties exist.

Date	Mintage	VG	F	VF	XF	Unc
16Z1	—	550	800	1,050	1,450	—

KM# 36 2 STUBER

Silver **Note:** Weight varies: 0.57-0.71 grams. Octagon. Stamp A.

Date	Mintage	VG	F	VF	XF	Unc
16Z1	—	1,050	1,700	2,700	4,000	—

KM# 37 4 STUBER

Silver **Note:** Weight varies: 0.94-1.62 grams. Uniface irregular round. Stamp B in center. Varieties exist.

Date	Mintage	VG	F	VF	XF	Unc
16Z1	—	1,200	2,000	3,200	4,800	—

KM# 38 4 STUBER

1.2400 g., Silver **Note:** Irregular triangle. Stamp B on one side, GVLICH engraved on other.

Date	Mintage	VG	F	VF	XF	Unc
16Z1	—	1,200	2,000	3,200	4,800	—

KM# 39 4 STUBER

Silver **Note:** Weight varies: 1.92-2.00 grams. Triangular piece from contemporary coin. Stamp B.

Date	Mintage	VG	F	VF	XF	Unc
16Z1	—	2,400	4,000	6,400	9,600	—

KM# 40 8 STUBER

Silver **Note:** Weight varies: 6.05-6.50 grams. Uniface rhombus with rounded corners. Stamp C in center, stamp A in each corner with top inward.

Date	Mintage	VG	F	VF	XF	Unc
16Z1	—	1,350	2,400	4,000	6,000	—

KM# 41 8 STUBER

Silver **Note:** Octagonal flan. Varieties exist.

Date	Mintage	VG	F	VF	XF	Unc
16Z1	—	1,350	2,400	4,000	6,000	—

KM# 42 10 STUBER

7.5800 g., Silver **Note:** Uniface pentagon. Stamp C in center, stamp A five times, tops inward.

Date	Mintage	VG	F	VF	XF	Unc
16Z1	—	1,600	2,700	4,000	6,000	—

KM# 43 12 STUBER

Silver **Note:** Weight varies: 7.17-7.20 grams. Uniface round. Stamp C in center, stamp A six times, tops inward.

Date	Mintage	VG	F	VF	XF	Unc
16Z1	—	1,350	2,400	4,000	6,000	—

KM# 44 12 STUBER

6.3300 g., Silver **Note:** Hexagonal flan.

Date	Mintage	VG	F	VF	XF	Unc
16Z1	—	1,350	2,400	4,000	6,000	—

KM# 45 14 STUBER

Silver **Note:** Weight varies: 4.85-7.70 grams. Uniface seven-sided. Stamp C in center, stamp A seven times at angles, tops inward. Varieties exist.

Date	Mintage	VG	F	VF	XF	Unc
16Z1	—	1,350	2,400	4,000	6,000	—

KM# 46 14 STUBER

Silver **Note:** Round flan.

Date	Mintage	VG	F	VF	XF	Unc
16Z1	—	1,350	2,400	4,000	6,000	—

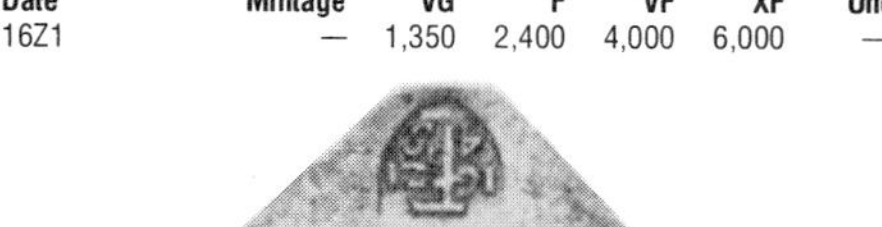

KM# 47 16 STUBER

Silver **Note:** Weight varies: 6.76-6.80 grams. Uniface square with rounded corners. Stamp C in center, stamp B in each of four corners.

Date	Mintage	VG	F	VF	XF	Unc
16Z1	—	1,600	2,700	4,000	6,000	—

KM# 48 16 STUBER

7.0000 g., Silver **Note:** Octagon. Stamp C in cetner, stamp A in each angle, tops inward.

Date	Mintage	VG	F	VF	XF	Unc
16Z1	—	1,850	3,100	4,800	7,000	—

KM# 49 16 STUBER

7.0200 g., Silver **Note:** Round. Stamp C in center, stamp A eight times, tops inward.

Date	Mintage	VG	F	VF	XF	Unc
16Z1	—	1,850	3,100	4,800	7,000	—

KM# 50 20 STUBER

Silver **Note:** Weight varies: 6.99-15.50 grams. Uniface round. Stamp C in center, stamp B five times, tops inward.

Date	Mintage	VG	F	VF	XF	Unc
16Z1	—	1,700	3,000	4,200	6,500	—

KM# 51 20 STUBER

Silver **Note:** Weight varies: 6.60-7.11 grams. Pentagon flan.

Date	Mintage	VG	F	VF	XF	Unc
16Z1	—	1,700	3,000	4,200	6,500	—

KM# 52 24 STUBER

7.6700 g., Silver **Note:** Uniface round. Stamp C in cetner, four A and B stamps alternating, tops inward.

Date	Mintage	VG	F	VF	XF	Unc
16Z1	—	1,350	3,200	4,200	6,500	—

KM# 53 32 STUBER

Silver **Note:** Uniface round. Stamp C in center, stamp B eight times, tops inward.

Date	Mintage	VG	F	VF	XF	Unc
16Z1	—	1,900	3,300	4,800	7,000	—

KM# 54 THALER

Silver **Note:** Weight varies: 27.19-28.08 grams. Uniface. Stmap C on one side of round flan, usually a contemporary thaler or Spanish 8 Reales, hammered flat. Varieties exist.

Date	Mintage	VG	F	VF	XF	Unc
16Z1	—	1,100	3,000	3,600	6,000	—

Note: Note also that many other pieces of this type, on varying size flans with various weights below 10 grams, were probably meant to be passed as thalers, even though no value is stated on coin

JULICH-BERG

The earliest counts of Jülich, located between Aachen and the Rhine (see Jülich, City), are known from the mid-9th century. Successive counts added territories to the nucleus of their domains and obtained the mint right in 1237. Count Wilhelm V (1328-62) attained the rank of Margrave in 1336 and was raised to that of Duke as Wilhelm I in 1356. His son, Wilhelm II, married Maria of Geldern, thus enlarging the duchy greatly. His younger brother married the heiress of Berg (along the east bank of the Rhine) and Ravensberg (in Westphalia). Geldern passed to the Egmont family in 1423 for lack of legitimate heirs in the Jülich line. Jülich itself fell to the younger branch of the family in Berg-Ravensberg in the same year. From this time on, the duchy was known as Jülich-Berg. Wilhelm IV died in 1511 without a male heir and his daughter, Maria, had married Duke Johann III of Cleve the year before. In 1521, the three duchies were united as Jülich-Cleve Berg (see). Following the great controversy after the death of Duke Johann Wilhelm in 1609, Jülich and Berg were occupied jointly by Brandenburg and Pfalz-Neuburg. The latter acquired Jülich-Berg outright in 1624, while Cleve, Mark and Ravensberg went to Brandenburg-Prussia. The dual duchy remained with the Wittelsbachs of the Palatinate until 1801, in which year France occupied it. In the peace settlement at the end of the Napoleonic Wars in 1815, Jülich-Berg was given to Prussia.

RULERS

Disputed, 1609-1624
Wolfgang Wilhelm von Pfalz-Neuburg, 1624-1653
Philipp Wilhelm von Pfalz-Neuburg, 1653-1679
Johann Wilhelm von Pfalz-Neuburg, 1679-1716

MINT MARKS

D - Dusseldorf

MINTOFFICIALS' INITIALS

Initial	Date	Name
IL	1659-1700	Jakob Leer, die-cutter
IL	1689-90	Johann Linck, die-cutter in Heidelberg
ST	1628-35	Simon Timpff
(h) (linden leaf)	1636-65	Simon Huber
(j) (crossed ingot hooks) or IL	1670-81	Johann Longerich in Mülheim
(n) (crossed ingot hooks) or NL	1681-91	Nikolaus Longerich in Mülheim

ARMS

Berg and Pfalz: Lion rampant left.

REFERENCES

N = Alfred Noss, **Die Münzen von Berg und Jülich-Berg I**, Munich, 1929.
Sch = Wolfgang Schulten, **Deutsche Münzen aus der Zeit Karls V.**, Frankfurt am Main, 1976.

DUCHY

REGULAR COINAGE

KM# 11 HELLER

Silver **Note:** Uniface. Rampant lion right.

Date	Mintage	VG	F	VF	XF	Unc
ND(ca.1631)	—	13.00	27.00	55.00	100	—

KM# 79 HELLER

Billon **Note:** Without mintmaster's initials.

Date	Mintage	VG	F	VF	XF	Unc
ND(ca.1685)	—	13.00	27.00	55.00	100	—

KM# 78 HELLER

Billon **Note:** Uniface. Rampant lion left, NL between hind legs.

Date	Mintage	VG	F	VF	XF	Unc
ND(ca.1685)	—	13.00	27.00	55.00	100	—

KM# 5 2 HELLER

Silver **Note:** Uniface. Lion rampant left, legend: 2 HELLER LEICHT.

Date	Mintage	VG	F	VF	XF	Unc
ND(ca.1628)	—	13.00	27.00	45.00	85.00	—

KM# 13 2 HELLER (4 Pfennig)

Silver **Note:** Lion rampant left divides date, value 4 between hind legs.

Date	Mintage	VG	F	VF	XF	Unc
(16)36	—	13.00	27.00	45.00	85.00	—

KM# 50 4 HELLER (Cologne)

Silver **Obv:** Lion rampant right **Obv. Legend:** NVMMVS. IVLIAC. ET. MON **Rev:** Value: IIII in center, legend, date **Rev. Legend:** HELLER. SCHWAR.

Date	Mintage	VG	F	VF	XF	Unc
1662	—	—	—	—	—	—

KM# 25 5 HELLER (Light)

Silver **Obv:** Lion rampant left **Obv. Legend:** MON. IVLIACENSIS **Rev:** Large V in center, dat **Rev. Legend:** HELLER LICHT **Note:** Varieties exist.

Date	Mintage	VG	F	VF	XF	Unc
1640 (h)	—	12.00	24.00	40.00	75.00	—
1641 (h)	—	12.00	24.00	40.00	75.00	—
(1)641 (h)	—	12.00	24.00	40.00	75.00	—
(16)42 (h)	—	12.00	24.00	40.00	75.00	—
1643 (h)	—	12.00	24.00	40.00	75.00	—
(1)643 (h)	—	12.00	24.00	40.00	75.00	—
(16)43 (h)	—	12.00	24.00	40.00	75.00	—
(16)44 (h)	—	12.00	24.00	40.00	75.00	—
ND (h)	—	12.00	24.00	40.00	75.00	—

KM# 39 5 HELLER (Light)

Silver **Note:** Similar to KM#25.

Date	Mintage	VG	F	VF	XF	Unc
(1)655	—	12.00	24.00	40.00	75.00	—

KM# 44 6 HELLER (Light)

Silver **Obv:** Lion rampant left **Obv. Legend:** NVM. IVLIACENSIS. ET **Rev:** Imperial orb with 6, HEL. LE below in legend, MONT - date above

Date	Mintage	VG	F	VF	XF	Unc
(1)659	—	—	—	—	—	—
1659	—	—	—	—	—	—

KM# 6 8 HELLER (1/74 Thaler)

Silver **Obv:** Legend, VIII in center **Obv. Legend:** NVMMVS IVLIACEN **Rev:** Legend, Lxx/VIII in center

Date	Mintage	VG	F	VF	XF	Unc
ND	—	8.00	16.00	33.00	65.00	—

KM# 7 8 HELLER (1/74 Thaler)

Silver **Rev:** Legend, date **Rev. Legend:** CVSVS DVSSELDORP **Note:** Varieties exist.

Date	Mintage	VG	F	VF	XF	Unc
(16)28	—	7.00	16.00	33.00	60.00	—
(1)628	—	7.00	16.00	33.00	60.00	—
(16)29	—	7.00	16.00	33.00	60.00	—
(1)629	—	7.00	16.00	33.00	60.00	—
(1)630	—	7.00	16.00	33.00	60.00	—
(1)631	—	7.00	16.00	33.00	60.00	—
(1)631 ST	—	7.00	16.00	33.00	60.00	—
(1)648 (h)	—	7.00	16.00	33.00	60.00	—
1649	—	7.00	16.00	33.00	60.00	—
(1)649	—	7.00	16.00	33.00	60.00	—
(1)649 (h)	—	7.00	16.00	33.00	60.00	—

KM# 33 8 HELLER (1/74 Thaler)

Silver **Rev:** Rampant lion left in shield **Note:** Varieties exist.

Date	Mintage	VG	F	VF	XF	Unc
(1)649	—	7.00	16.00	33.00	60.00	—
1650	—	7.00	16.00	33.00	60.00	—
(1)650	—	7.00	16.00	33.00	60.00	—
1651	—	7.00	16.00	33.00	60.00	—
(1)651	—	7.00	16.00	33.00	60.00	—
1652	—	7.00	16.00	33.00	60.00	—
(1)652	—	7.00	16.00	33.00	60.00	—
(1)653	—	7.00	16.00	33.00	60.00	—

KM# 54 8 HELLER (1/74 Thaler)

Silver **Obv:** Legend, date **Obv. Legend:** MONE. IVLIA. ET. MONT **Note:** Varieties exist.

Date	Mintage	VG	F	VF	XF	Unc
1663	—	7.00	16.00	33.00	60.00	—
1663	—	7.00	16.00	33.00	60.00	—
(1)664	—	7.00	16.00	33.00	60.00	—
(16)64	—	7.00	16.00	33.00	60.00	—

KM# 51 8 HELLER (1/74 Thaler)

Silver **Obv:** Lion rampant left, date **Obv. Legend:** MONE. IVLIA. ET. MONT. **Rev:** VIII in center **Rev. Legend:** CVSVS. DVSSELDORP.

Date	Mintage	VG	F	VF	XF	Unc
1663	—	8.00	16.00	33.00	65.00	—

KM# 53 8 HELLER (1/74 Thaler)

Silver **Obv:** VIII in ceneter **Obv. Legend:** NVMMVS. IVLIACEN **Rev:** Rampant lion left in shield **Rev. Legend:** CVSVS. DVSSELDORP.

Date	Mintage	VG	F	VF	XF	Unc
1663	—	8.00	16.00	33.00	65.00	—

KM# 52 8 HELLER (1/74 Thaler)

Silver **Obv:** Lion rampant left in shield, date **Obv. Legend:** CVSVS. DVSSELDORP. **Rev:** KM#51 **Note:** Mule.

Date	Mintage	VG	F	VF	XF	Unc
1663	—	8.00	16.00	33.00	65.00	—

KM# 57 8 HELLER (1/74 Thaler)

Silver **Rev:** Date in legend

Date	Mintage	VG	F	VF	XF	Unc
1664	—	7.00	16.00	33.00	60.00	—

KM# 63 8 HELLER (1/74 Thaler)

Silver **Obv:** Titles of Philipp Wilhelm, date **Rev:** VIII in center **Rev. Legend:** MON. IVL. ET. MONT. **Note:** Varieties exist.

Date	Mintage	VG	F	VF	XF	Unc
1676 (j)	—	7.00	16.00	33.00	60.00	—
1676 I(j)L	—	7.00	16.00	33.00	60.00	—
1677 I(j)L	—	7.00	16.00	33.00	60.00	—
1678 I(j)L	—	7.00	16.00	33.00	60.00	—
1679 I(j)L	—	7.00	16.00	33.00	60.00	—

KM# 64 8 HELLER (1/74 Thaler)

Silver **Obv:** Value: VIII in center **Obv. Legend:** MONE. IVLIA. ET. MONT. **Rev:** Arms of Salm (two salmon) in shield **Rev. Legend:** SINGVLA. COLL. IVV. **Note:** Mule.

Date	Mintage	VG	F	VF	XF	Unc
ND	—	—	—	—	—	—

Note: This coin is a mule of reverse type KM#63 and obverse of a fettmannchen of the abbey of Essen date 1671, KM#78

KM# 72 8 HELLER (1/74 Thaler)

Silver **Note:** Similar to KM#63, but titles of Johann Wilhelm II. Varieties exist.

Date	Mintage	VG	F	VF	XF	Unc
1682 N(n)L	—	12.00	24.00	45.00	90.00	—
1683 N(n)L	—	12.00	24.00	45.00	90.00	—

KM# 14 ALBUS

Silver **Obv:** Crowned lion rampant left **Obv. Legend:** NVMMVS. IVLIACEN. **Rev:** Value **Rev. Inscription:** I/ALBg/LEIC/HT **Note:** Light Albus.

Date	Mintage	VG	F	VF	XF	Unc
ND(ca.1636) (h)	—	—	—	—	—	—

KM# 15 ALBUS

Silver **Rev:** Legend, date **Rev. Legend:** CVSVS. DVSSELDOR **Note:** Varieties exist.

Date	Mintage	VG	F	VF	XF	Unc
(1)636	—	16.00	33.00	60.00	120	—
(1)636 (h)	—	16.00	33.00	60.00	120	—
(1)637 (h)	—	16.00	33.00	60.00	120	—

KM# 32 ALBUS

Silver **Obv:** Lion rampant left **Obv. Legend:** MONETA. IVLIACENSIS **Rev:** Value, legend, date **Rev. Legend:** CVSVS. DVSSELDOR **Rev. Inscription:** I/ALBVS/LEICH/T

Date	Mintage	VG	F	VF	XF	Unc
1648 (h)	—	—	—	—	—	—

KM# 37 ALBUS

Silver **Rev. Inscription:** I/ALB/LEIC/HT **Note:** Varieties exist.

Date	Mintage	VG	F	VF	XF	Unc
1654	—	13.00	27.00	55.00	110	—
1655	—	13.00	27.00	55.00	110	—
1658	—	13.00	27.00	55.00	110	—

KM# 62 2 ALBUS (1/2 Bläffert)

Silver **Obv:** Lion rampant left, titles of Philipp Wilhelm **Rev. Legend:** MONET. NOV. IVLIACENSIS **Rev. Inscription:** 2/ALBVS/COLSCH/date **Note:** Varieties exist.

Date	Mintage	VG	F	VF	XF	Unc
1674 (j)	—	8.00	16.00	33.00	65.00	—
1675 (j)	—	8.00	16.00	33.00	65.00	—
1676 (j)	—	8.00	16.00	33.00	65.00	—
1676 I(j)L	—	8.00	16.00	33.00	65.00	—
1677 I(j)L	—	8.00	16.00	33.00	65.00	—
1678 I(j)L	—	8.00	16.00	33.00	65.00	—
1679 I(j)L	—	8.00	16.00	33.00	65.00	—

KM# 68 2 ALBUS (1/2 Bläffert)
Silver **Obv. Legend:** SOLI. DEO. GLORIA. D. S
Rev. Legend: MONETA. NOVA. ARGENTEA.

Date	Mintage	VG	F	VF	XF	Unc
1677	—	—	—	—	—	—

KM# 71 2 ALBUS (1/2 Bläffert)
Silver **Obv:** Titles of Johann Wilhelm II **Note:** Varieties exist.

Date	Mintage	VG	F	VF	XF	Unc
1681 I(j)L	—	8.00	16.00	33.00	65.00	—
1682 N(n)L	—	8.00	16.00	33.00	65.00	—
1683 N(n)L	—	8.00	16.00	33.00	65.00	—
1684 N(n)L	—	8.00	16.00	33.00	65.00	—
1685 N(n)L	—	8.00	16.00	33.00	65.00	—
1688/5 N(n)L	—	8.00	16.00	33.00	65.00	—
1690 N(n)L	—	8.00	16.00	33.00	65.00	—

KM# 16 4 ALBUS (Bläffert)
Silver **Obv:** Crowned 8-fold arms with central shield of Pfalz **Obv. Legend:** IN. DEO... **Rev. Legend:** MONE. NOVA. IVLIACEN. ET. MONT. **Rev. Inscription:** IIII/ALBVS/COLSCH/date **Note:** Varieties exist.

Date	Mintage	VG	F	VF	XF	Unc
(1)636 (h)	—	13.00	27.00	55.00	110	—
1636 (h)	—	13.00	27.00	55.00	110	—
ND(1638) (h)	—	13.00	27.00	55.00	110	—
1639 (h)	—	13.00	27.00	55.00	110	—
(1)641	—	13.00	27.00	55.00	110	—
1643 (h)	—	13.00	27.00	55.00	110	—
1644 (h)	—	13.00	27.00	55.00	110	—
(1)644 (h)	—	13.00	27.00	55.00	110	—
1645 (h)	—	13.00	27.00	55.00	110	—
1646 (h)	—	13.00	27.00	55.00	110	—

KM# 18 4 ALBUS (Bläffert)
Silver **Obv:** Date in legend

Date	Mintage	VG	F	VF	XF	Unc
638 (h)	—	16.00	33.00	60.00	120	—

KM# 19 4 ALBUS (Bläffert)
Silver **Rev. Legend:** NVMMVS. IVLIACEN...

Date	Mintage	VG	F	VF	XF	Unc
639 (h)	—	16.00	33.00	60.00	120	—

KM# 30 4 ALBUS (Bläffert)
Silver **Obv:** Date divided below arms

Date	Mintage	VG	F	VF	XF	Unc
164Z	—	16.00	33.00	60.00	120	—

KM# 31 4 ALBUS (Bläffert)
Silver **Obv:** Date in Roman numerals between MEA and CONSOL

Date	Mintage	VG	F	VF	XF	Unc
(16)42	—	16.00	33.00	60.00	120	—

KM# 77 4 ALBUS (Bläffert)
Silver **Obv:** Titles of Johann Wilhelm II **Rev:** Lion rampant left on line above inscription **Rev. Legend:** MONE. NOV... **Rev. Inscription:** 4.ALB.COL/.date

Date	Mintage	VG	F	VF	XF	Unc
1684 N(n)L	—	—	—	—	—	—

KM# 8 5 ALBUS
Silver **Obv:** Crowned 8-fold arms with central shield of Pfalz divides date **Obv. Legend:** IN. DEO. MEA. CONSOLATIO. **Rev:** Ornate cross with lion left **Rev. Legend:** MON. NOVA. IVLIACENSIS. V. ALB.

Date	Mintage	VG	F	VF	XF	Unc
1629	—	24.00	45.00	90.00	200	—

KM# 10 5 ALBUS
Silver **Note:** Varieties exist.

Date	Mintage	VG	F	VF	XF	Unc
(1)630	—	20.00	40.00	80.00	160	—
(1)631	—	20.00	40.00	80.00	160	—
(1)63Z	—	20.00	40.00	80.00	160	—
(1)633	—	20.00	40.00	80.00	160	—

KM# 26 10 ALBUS (Light)
Silver **Obv:** 8-fold arms with central shield of Pfalz **Obv. Legend:** IN. DEO... **Rev:** Ornamented square tablet with inscription, date divided above and below **Rev. Legend:** MO. NOVA...
Rev. Inscription: X/ALBVS/LICHT

Date	Mintage	VG	F	VF	XF	Unc
1640 (h)	—	100	200	350	—	—

KM# 29 10 ALBUS (Light)
Silver **Rev:** Date in tablet

Date	Mintage	VG	F	VF	XF	Unc
1641 (h)	—	—	—	—	—	—

KM# 60 1/16 THALER (1/2 Schilling)
Silver **Obv:** Crowned 8-fold arms with central shield of Pfalz, titles of Philipp Wilhelm **Rev. Legend:** (j) MON. ARGE. IVLIACENSI **Rev. Inscription:** XVI/I. REICHS/THALER/date **Note:** Varieties exist.

Date	Mintage	VG	F	VF	XF	Unc
1671 (j)	—	80.00	140	225	400	—
1672 (j)	—	80.00	140	225	400	—

KM# 100 1/12 THALER (1/8 Gulden)
Silver **Obv:** Crowned oval 9-fold arms with central shield **Rev. Inscription:** 12/EINEN/REICHS/THAL/date

Date	Mintage	VG	F	VF	XF	Unc
1700 HLO	—	45.00	100	200	350	—

KM# 101 1/12 THALER (1/8 Gulden)
Silver **Obv:** Round arms **Rev:** THALER

Date	Mintage	VG	F	VF	XF	Unc
1700 HLO	—	40.00	80.00	165	300	—

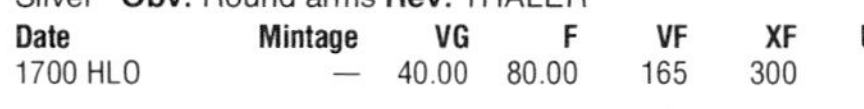

KM# 102 1/12 THALER (1/8 Gulden)
Silver **Obv:** Arms flat on top, rounded at bottom **Note:** Varieties exist.

Date	Mintage	VG	F	VF	XF	Unc
1700 HLO	—	40.00	80.00	165	300	—

KM# 61 1/8 THALER (Schilling)
Silver **Obv:** Crowned 8-fold arms with central shield of Pfalz, titles of Philipp Wilhelm **Rev. Inscription:** VIII/I. REICHS/THALER/date **Note:** Varieties exist.

Date	Mintage	VG	F	VF	XF	Unc
1673 (j)	—	60.00	120	200	375	—
1675 (j)	—	60.00	120	200	375	—

KM# 70 1/8 THALER (Schilling)
Silver **Obv:** Crowned 8-fold arms with central shield of Pfalz divides date, titles of Johann Wilhelm II **Rev:** Rampant lion left holding large oval with 8/I.R **Rev. Legend:** MONET. NOV. IVLIACENS. ET. MONT. **Note:** Permisser Schilling.

Date	Mintage	VG	F	VF	XF	Unc
1680 I(j)L	—	—	—	—	—	—

Note: This coin circulated on par with similar pieces of Liege and Brabant

KM# 35 1/6 THALER (1/4 Gulden)
Silver **Subject:** Death of Wolfgang Wilhelm **Obv:** 11-line inscription with date **Rev:** 5-line inscription with date in chronogram between palm leaves

Date	Mintage	VG	F	VF	XF	Unc
1653	—	200	400	750	—	—

KM# 81 1/6 THALER (1/4 Gulden)
Silver **Obv:** Bust right **Rev:** Crowned 8-fold arms with central shield of Pfalz, value (1/6) below, date

Date	Mintage	VG	F	VF	XF	Unc
1689 N(n)L	—	115	225	350	475	—

KM# 93 1/6 THALER (1/4 Gulden)
Silver **Rev:** 9-fold arms with central shield

Date	Mintage	VG	F	VF	XF	Unc
1691 N(n)L	—	—	—	—	—	—

KM# 94 1/6 THALER (1/4 Gulden)
Silver **Obv:** Large 1/6 in laurel wreath

Date	Mintage	VG	F	VF	XF	Unc
1691 N(n)L	—	—	—	—	—	—

KM# 36 1/4 THALER
Silver **Subject:** Death of Wolfgang Wilhelm **Obv:** 11-line inscription with date **Rev:** 5-line inscription with date in chronogram between palm leaves

Date	Mintage	VG	F	VF	XF	Unc
1653	—	325	600	1,075	1,900	—

KM# 98 1/4 THALER
Silver **Obv:** Bust right, date below **Rev:** Four small crowned shields in cruciform, shield in center, a crowned ornate IW monogram between each shield

Date	Mintage	VG	F	VF	XF	Unc
1696 HHK	—	—	—	—	—	—

KM# 65 2/3 THALER (Gulden)
Silver **Obv:** Bust of Philipp Wilhelm right **Rev:** 8-fold arms with central shield of Pfalz, crown above divides date, value (2/3) below

Date	Mintage	VG	F	VF	XF	Unc
1676 I(j)L	—	—	—	—	—	—

KM# 66 2/3 THALER (Gulden)
Silver **Rev:** Date above crown

Date	Mintage	VG	F	VF	XF	Unc
1676 I(j)L	—	—	—	—	—	—

KM# 82 2/3 THALER (Gulden)
Silver **Obv:** Bust right **Rev:** Date divided by value (2/3) at bottom

Date	Mintage	VG	F	VF	XF	Unc
1689	—	—	—	—	—	—
1689 NL/(n)	—	—	—	—	—	—

KM# 83 2/3 THALER (Gulden)
Silver **Rev:** Crowned 8-fold arms with central shield of Pfalz, value (2/3) below, date in legend **Note:** Varieties exist.

Date	Mintage	VG	F	VF	XF	Unc
1689 (n)NL	—	275	475	1,000	2,000	—
1690 N(n)L	—	275	475	1,000	2,000	—
1690 (n)NL	—	275	475	1,000	2,000	—
1690 NL/(n)	—	275	475	1,000	2,000	—
1690 (n)	—	275	475	1,000	2,000	—
1691 N(n)L	—	275	475	1,000	2,000	—

KM# 90 2/3 THALER (Gulden)
Silver **Obv:** Reverse of KM#83 **Rev:** KM#82 without countermark **Note:** Mule.

Date	Mintage	VG	F	VF	XF	Unc
1690 N(n)L	—	—	—	—	—	—

KM# 95 2/3 THALER (Gulden)
Silver **Rev:** Similar to KM#83, but 9-fold arms in shield

Date	Mintage	VG	F	VF	XF	Unc
1691 N(n)L	—	375	675	1,200	2,000	—

KM# 96 2/3 THALER (Gulden)
Silver

Date	Mintage	VG	F	VF	XF	Unc
1691 IL/N(n)L	—	375	675	1,200	2,000	—
1691 NL/N(n)L	—	375	675	1,200	2,000	—

KM# 103 2/3 THALER (Gulden)
Silver **Rev:** Crowned oval 9-fold arms with central shield

Date	Mintage	VG	F	VF	XF	Unc
1700 HLO	—	800	1,200	1,650	2,400	—

KM# 104 2/3 THALER (Gulden)
Silver **Obv:** Different bust **Rev:** Small oval arms

Date	Mintage	VG	F	VF	XF	Unc
1700 HLO	—	800	1,200	1,650	2,400	—

KM# 105 2/3 THALER (Gulden)
Silver **Rev:** Date divided near bottom by oval arms

Date	Mintage	VG	F	VF	XF	Unc
1700 HLO	—	800	1,200	1,650	2,400	—

KM# 106 2/3 THALER (Gulden)
Silver **Obv:** High collar on neck of bust **Rev:** Larger oval arms

Date	Mintage	VG	F	VF	XF	Unc
1700 HLO	—	800	1,200	1,650	2,400	—

KM# 27 THALER
Silver **Obv:** Bust right, double legend **Rev:** Crowned arms in cartouche **Note:** Dav. #6861.

Date	Mintage	VG	F	VF	XF	Unc
1640 Rare	—	—	—	—	—	—

KM# 40 THALER
Silver **Obv:** Bust right with hair neatly tied back with bow **Rev:** Crowned arms in order chain **Note:** Dav. #6865.

Date	Mintage	VG	F	VF	XF	Unc
1655 Rare	—	—	—	—	—	—

KM# 55 THALER
Silver **Obv:** Bust right with loose flying hair **Note:** Dav. #6867.

Date	Mintage	VG	F	VF	XF	Unc
1663 Rare	—	—	—	—	—	—

KM# 58 THALER
Silver **Obv:** Half-facing bust without inner circle **Note:** Dav. #6868.

Date	Mintage	VG	F	VF	XF	Unc
1667 Rare	—	—	—	—	—	—

KM# 73 THALER
Silver **Note:** Dav. #6870.

Date	Mintage	VG	F	VF	XF	Unc
1682 N(n)L Rare	—	—	—	—	—	—

Note: Fritz Rudolf Künker Münzenhandlung Auction 134, 1-08, nearly XF realized approximately $8,860; Auktionshaus Meister & Sonntag Auction 5, 9-07, XF realized approximately $23,035

KM# 84 THALER
Silver **Obv:** Longer bust showing shoulder **Rev:** Crowned round arms in order collar **Note:** Dav. #6871.

Date	Mintage	VG	F	VF	XF	Unc
1689 IL Rare	—	—	—	—	—	—

KM# 91 THALER
Silver **Subject:** Death of Philipp Wilhelm **Note:** Dav. #6872.

Date	Mintage	VG	F	VF	XF	Unc
1690 NL Rare	—	—	—	—	—	—

KM# 92 THALER
Silver **Obv:** Smaller bust within legend **Obv. Legend:** I. W. D. G. C. P. R. S. R. I. ARCHIT. & EL. **Rev:** Crowned round arms in Order collar **Note:** Dav. #6873.

Date	Mintage	VG	F	VF	XF	Unc
1690 IL Rare	—	—	—	—	—	—

KM# 41 1-1/2 THALER
Silver **Obv:** Bust right **Rev:** Crowned arms divide date **Note:** Dav. #6864.

Date	Mintage	VG	F	VF	XF	Unc
1655 Rare	—	—	—	—	—	—

KM# 12 2 THALER
Silver **Obv:** Bust right within double legend **Rev:** Crowned arms in Order chain **Note:** Dav. #6860.

Date	Mintage	VG	F	VF	XF	Unc
1631 Rare	—	—	—	—	—	—

KM# 42 2 THALER
Silver **Obv:** Bust right with hair neatly tied back with bow **Rev:** Crowned arms in Order chain **Note:** Dav. #6863.

Date	Mintage	VG	F	VF	XF	Unc
1655 Rare	—	—	—	—	—	—

KM# 56 2 THALER
Silver **Obv:** Bust right with loose flying hair **Note:** Dav. #6866.

Date	Mintage	VG	F	VF	XF	Unc
1663 Rare	—	—	—	—	—	—

KM# 74 2 THALER
Silver **Note:** Similar to 1 Thaler, KM#73. Dav. #6869.

Date	Mintage	VG	F	VF	XF	Unc
1682 N(n)L Rare	—	—	—	—	—	—

Note: Auktionshaus H.D. Rauch GmbH Auction 76, 10-05, VF realized approximately $44,510; Westfälische Auktionsgesellschaft Auction 29, 2-05, VF-XF realized approximately $40,840

KM# 43 4 THALER
Silver **Obv:** Bust right with hair neatly tied back with bow **Rev:** Crowned arms in Order chain **Note:** Dav. #6862.

Date	Mintage	VG	F	VF	XF	Unc
1655 Rare	—	—	—	—	—	—

TRADE COINAGE

KM# 17 DUCAT
3.5000 g., 0.9860 Gold 0.1109 oz. AGW **Obv:** Wolfgang Wilhelm **Rev:** Date in legend

Date	Mintage	VG	F	VF	XF	Unc
1636	—	500	1,200	2,400	4,000	—
1643	—	500	1,200	2,400	4,000	—
1650	—	500	1,200	2,400	4,000	—

KM# 38 DUCAT
3.5000 g., 0.9860 Gold 0.1109 oz. AGW **Obv:** Philip Wilhelm **Rev:** Crown divides date

Date	Mintage	VG	F	VF	XF	Unc
1654	—	650	1,500	2,800	4,400	—
1659	—	650	1,500	2,800	4,400	—
1660	—	650	1,500	2,800	4,400	—
1663	—	650	1,500	2,800	4,400	—
1665	—	650	1,500	2,800	4,400	—
1668	—	650	1,500	2,800	4,400	—
1670	—	650	1,500	2,800	4,400	—
1672	—	650	1,500	2,800	4,400	—
1674	—	650	1,500	2,800	4,400	—
1677	—	650	1,500	2,800	4,400	—

KM# 67 DUCAT
3.5000 g., 0.9860 Gold 0.1109 oz. AGW **Obv:** Philip Wilhelm

Date	Mintage	VG	F	VF	XF	Unc
1676	—	375	900	1,800	3,000	—

KM# 75 DUCAT
3.5000 g., 0.9860 Gold 0.1109 oz. AGW **Obv:** Bust of Johan Wilhelm II right **Rev:** Crowned 8-fold arms with central shield of Pfalz, date divided above crown

Date	Mintage	VG	F	VF	XF	Unc
1682 N(n)L	—	750	1,800	3,600	6,000	—
1683 N(n)L	—	750	1,800	3,600	6,000	—

KM# 76 DUCAT
3.5000 g., 0.9860 Gold 0.1109 oz. AGW **Obv:** Larger bust of Johann Wilhelm **Note:** Varieties exist.

Date	Mintage	VG	F	VF	XF	Unc
1683	—	750	1,800	3,600	6,000	—
1686 N(n)L	—	750	1,800	3,600	6,000	—

KM# 97 DUCAT
3.5000 g., 0.9860 Gold 0.1109 oz. AGW **Rev:** Crowned round 9-fold arms with central shield, date in legend

Date	Mintage	VG	F	VF	XF	Unc
1691 IL//NL	—	750	1,800	3,600	6,000	—

KM# 28 2 DUCAT
7.0000 g., 0.9860 Gold 0.2219 oz. AGW **Obv:** Bust of Wolfgang Wilhelm right, titles in legend **Rev:** Bust of second wife, Katharina Charlotte right, titles in legend

Date	Mintage	VG	F	VF	XF	Unc
ND(1640)	—	—	—	—	—	—

KM# 34 2 DUCAT
7.0000 g., 0.9860 Gold 0.2219 oz. AGW **Obv:** Bust of Johann Wilhelm II right **Rev:** Bust of Marie Anne left

Date	Mintage	VG	F	VF	XF	Unc
ND(1679) Rare	—	—	—	—	—	—

KM# A91 10 DUCAT
35.0000 g., 0.9860 Gold 1.1095 oz. AGW **Obv:** Johann Wilhelm longer bust showing shoulder **Rev:** Crowned round arms in Order collar **Note:** Struck with 1 Thaler dies, KM#84.

Date	Mintage	VG	F	VF	XF	Unc
1689 IL Rare	—	—	—	—	—	—

COUNTERMARKED COINAGE

KM# 80 2/3 THALER (Gulden)
Silver **Countermark:** Leaping horse of Brunswick **Obv:** 8-fold arms with central shield of Pfalz, titles of Johann Wilhelm II, date above crown **Rev:** Ship sailing away right, value (2/3) in oval below, oval countermark at right of ship

CM Date	Host Date	Good	VG	F	VF	XF
ND	1688 N(n)L	—	—	—	—	—

PATTERNS

Including off metal strikes

KM#	Date	Mintage	Identification	Mkt Val
Pn2	1700 HLO	—	1/12 Thaler. Copper. KM#101	—

JULICH-CLEVE-BERG

United by marriage in 1510 and formally constituted as a single entity in 1521, the Duchies of Jülick, Cleve and Berg followed a single path during most of the 16th century. Following the death of the last ruler in 1609, the various territories were divided among rival claimants to the inheritance. See Jülich-Berg for a more complete overview of the history.

RULER

Johann Wilhelm I, 1592-1609

MINTMASTERS' PRIVY MARKS

Mark	Date	Name
(h)	1613-15	Heinrich Wintgens in Mülheim
(i)	1602-08	Johann Lambers, die-cutter
(r)	1604-05	Johann Rees in Mülheim
(w)	1611-13	Heinrich Wintgens in Huissen and Emmerich

MINTS

Emmerich in Cleve
Huissen in Cleve
Mülheim in Berg

REFERENCES

N = Alfred Noss, **Die Münzen von Berg und Jülich-Berg I**, Munich, 1929.

Sch = Wolfgang Schulten, **Deutsche Münzen aus der Zeit Karls V.**, Frankfurt am Main, 1976.

S = Hugo Frhr. Von Saurma-Jeltsch, **Die Saurmasche Münzsammlung deutscher, schweizerischer und polnischer Gepräge von etwa dem Beginn der Groschenzeit bis zur Kipperperiode**, Berlin, 1892.

DUCHY

REGULAR COINAGE

KM# 5 1/8 STUBER (Deut)

Copper **Obv:** Crowned arms vertically divided into three parts **Obv. Legend:** MO. POSS. PRIN. CVS. **Rev:** Inscription in wreath **Rev. Inscription:** IN/HVES/SEN **Mint:** Huissen **Note:** Varieties exist.

Date	Mintage	VG	F	VF	XF	Unc
ND	1,286,000	—	—	—	—	—

KM# 6 1/8 STUBER (Deut)

Copper **Rev:** CVSA/HVIS/SIAE in wreath **Note:** Varieties exist.

Date	Mintage	VG	F	VF	XF	Unc
ND	Inc. above	—	—	—	—	—

KM# 10 HELLER

Silver **Note:** Uniface, 5-fold arms, date above.

Date	Mintage	VG	F	VF	XF	Unc
(1)604	206,000	8.00	25.00	30.00	55.00	—

KM# 11 HELLER

Silver **Note:** Mintmaster's symbol above arms instead of date.

Date	Mintage	VG	F	VF	XF	Unc
ND (r)	130,000	8.00	25.00	30.00	55.00	—

KM# 23 1/4 STUBER (Örtchen/Örtgen)

Copper **Obv:** Crowned arms of Julich and Berg divide date **Obv. Legend:** MO-POSSI-PRINC-IVL. ET-MON **Rev:** Crowned 6-fold arms **Rev. Legend:** IVSTITIA. THRONVM. FIRMAT. **Note:** Varieties exist.

Date	Mintage	VG	F	VF	XF	Unc
1609	—	27.00	45.00	100	200	—
1611	45,000	27.00	45.00	100	200	—

KM# 21 8 HELLER (1/74 Thaler)

Silver **Note:** Mule. Two reverses dies of KM#12.

Date	Mintage	VG	F	VF	XF	Unc
(1)604/(1)608	—	—	—	—	—	—

KM# 12 8 HELLER (1/74 Thaler)

Silver **Obv:** VIII in circle **Obv. Legend:** NVMMVS. IVLIACENSI **Rev:** LXX/IIII in circle, legend, date **Rev. Legend:** CVSVS. MOLHEMI **Note:** Varieties exist.

Date	Mintage	VG	F	VF	XF	Unc
(1)604 (r)	23,000	13.00	27.00	45.00	80.00	—
(1)605 (r)	326,000	13.00	27.00	45.00	80.00	—
(1)606 (r)	445,000	13.00	27.00	45.00	80.00	—
(1)607 (r)	228,000	13.00	27.00	45.00	80.00	—
(1)608 (r)	110,000	13.00	27.00	45.00	80.00	—
(1)609 (r)	84,000	13.00	27.00	45.00	80.00	—

KM# 20 8 HELLER (1/74 Thaler)

Silver **Obv:** KM#12 with legend NVMMVS. COLONIEN **Rev:** Obverse of Cologne, KM#11 **Note:** Mule. Varieties exist.

Date	Mintage	VG	F	VF	XF	Unc
(1)605 (r)	—	13.00	27.00	45.00	80.00	—
(1)608 (r)	—	13.00	27.00	45.00	80.00	—
(1)609 (r)	—	13.00	27.00	45.00	80.00	—

KM# 19 8 HELLER (1/74 Thaler)

Silver **Obv:** Date in legend

Date	Mintage	VG	F	VF	XF	Unc
(1)605 (r)	Inc. above	13.00	27.00	45.00	80.00	—

KM# 24 8 HELLER (1/74 Thaler)

Silver **Obv:** KM#12 **Rev:** Reverse of Cologne, KM#11, legend, date **Rev. Legend:** CVSVS. COLONIAE **Note:** Mule.

Date	Mintage	VG	F	VF	XF	Unc
(1)609 (r)	—	—	—	—	—	—

KM# 34 STUBER (21 Heller = 1/56 Thaler)

Silver **Obv:** Crowned 6-fold arms divide I-S **Obv. Legend:** MO:NO:AR:POSS:PRI:21.h. **Rev:** Ornate cross with lily in center, rampant lion left in upper right and lower left angles of cross, 21 in upper left and H in lower right **Rev. Legend:** 56.DVC-:IVLIE-CLI:E-MONT: **Mint:** Huissen **Note:** Varieties exist.

Date	Mintage	VG	F	VF	XF	Unc
ND(1611-13)	404,000	33.00	60.00	110	200	—

KM# 35 STUBER (21 Heller = 1/56 Thaler)

Silver **Rev:** Upper right and lower left angles of cross have a lily and upper left and lower right a rampant lion **Note:** Varieties exist. Illustration reduced.

Date	Mintage	VG	F	VF	XF	Unc
ND(1611-13)	Inc. above	33.00	60.00	110	200	—

KM# 36 STUBER (16 Heller = 1/3 Albus)

Silver **Obv:** Crowned imperial eagle, 16 in orb on breast, titles of Matthias **Rev:** 6-fold arms **Rev. Legend:** MO:POSS:PRIN... **Mint:** Mulheim

Date	Mintage	VG	F	VF	XF	Unc
ND	—	33.00	60.00	110	200	—

KM# 37 STUBER (16 Heller = 1/3 Albus)

Silver **Rev:** Crowned 6-fold arms **Rev. Legend:** MO. NO. AR. POSS. PRI.

Date	Mintage	VG	F	VF	XF	Unc
ND	—	33.00	60.00	110	200	—

KM# 26 SCHILLING

Silver **Obv:** Crowned 6-fold arms, (two each of Julich, Mark, Berg) **Rev:** Crowned imperial eagle, titles of Rudolf **Rev. Legend:** MO.NO.POS...IV.ET.MONT. **Note:** Varieties exist.

Date	Mintage	VG	F	VF	XF	Unc
ND(1609-12)	—	45.00	85.00	160	275	—
ND(1609-12) (w)	—	45.00	85.00	160	275	—

KM# 27 SCHILLING

Silver **Obv:** 6-fold arms of Julich, Cleve, Berg, Mark, Ravensberg, and Mors **Obv. Legend:** IVL. CLE. MONT. **Rev:** Crown above double-headed imperial eagle within rope wreath **Mint:** Emmerich **Note:** Varieties exist.

Date	Mintage	VG	F	VF	XF	Unc
ND(1609-12) (w)	323,000	33.00	65.00	120	200	—

KM# 25 SCHILLING

Silver **Obv:** Ornate 5-fold arms **Obv. Legend:** MONETA. NO. ARGEN. POSS. PRINCIP. **Rev:** Inscription in wreath **Rev. Inscription:** IVSTITIA/THRONVM/FIRMAT. Ao/date **Mint:** Huissen

Date	Mintage	VG	F	VF	XF	Unc
1609	—	200	375	675	1,150	—

KM# 40 SCHILLING

Silver **Obv:** Small crown above arms **Rev:** Crown above double-headed imperial eagle within circle **Mint:** Mulheim

Date	Mintage	VG	F	VF	XF	Unc
ND(1612-13) (h)	54,000	45.00	85.00	160	275	—

KM# 39 SCHILLING

Silver **Obv:** Crowned shield within circle **Rev:** Titles of Matthias **Note:** Varieties exist.

Date	Mintage	VG	F	VF	XF	Unc
ND(1612-13) (w)	Inc. above	33.00	65.00	120	200	—

KM# 41 SCHILLING

Silver **Rev:** Imperial orb on eagle's breast **Note:** Varieties exist.

Date	Mintage	VG	F	VF	XF	Unc
ND(1612-13) (h)	Inc. above	45.00	80.00	160	275	—

KM# 38 STUBER (3 Kreuzer)

Silver **Obv:** (3) in legend at bottom, MO: POS... **Rev. Legend:** Ends: 16.H(eller)

Date	Mintage	VG	F	VF	XF	Unc
ND	—	—	—	—	—	—

KM# 14 THALER

Silver **Note:** Klippe. Dav. #6108A.

Date	Mintage	VG	F	VF	XF	Unc
1604 (j) Rare	Inc. above	—	—	—	—	—

KM# 13 THALER

Silver **Note:** Similar to KM#14, but not a klippe. Varieties exist. Dav. #6108.

Date	Mintage	VG	F	VF	XF	Unc
1604 (j) Rare	3,145	—	—	—	—	—
1605 (r/j) Rare	4,403	—	—	—	—	—

KM# 30 THALER

Silver **Rev:** Crowned arms divide date **Note:** Dav. #6108B.

Date	Mintage	VG	F	VF	XF	Unc
1609 (r/j) Rare	2,580	—	—	—	—	—

KM# 28 THALER

Silver **Subject:** Death of Johann Wilhelm **Obv:** 6-line inscription **Rev:** Arms **Mint:** Huissen **Note:** Dav. #6109.

Date	Mintage	VG	F	VF	XF	Unc
1609 (w) Rare	—	—	—	—	—	—

KM# 16 2 THALER

Silver **Note:** Klippe.

Date	Mintage	VG	F	VF	XF	Unc
1604 (j) Rare	—	—	—	—	—	—

KM# 15 2 THALER

Silver **Note:** Similar to KM#16 but not a klippe. Dav. #6107.

Date	Mintage	VG	F	VF	XF	Unc
1604 (j) Rare	—	—	—	—	—	—

KM# 42 2 THALER

50.8000 g., Silver **Obv:** Crowned shield divides date within circle **Rev:** Crown above double-headed imperial eagle within circle **Mint:** Mulheim **Note:** Klippe. Dav. #6110.

Date	Mintage	VG	F	VF	XF	Unc
1613 (h) Unique	—	—	—	—	—	—

Note: Fritz Rudolf Künker Münzenhandlung Auction 90, 3-03, XF realized approximately $54,175

KM# 17 3 THALER

Silver **Note:** Similar to 2 Thaler, KM#16. Klippe. Dav. #6106.

Date	Mintage	VG	F	VF	XF	Unc
1604 (j) Rare	—	—	—	—	—	—

TRADE COINAGE

KM# 18 GOLDGULDEN

3.5000 g., 0.9860 Gold 0.1109 oz. AGW **Obv:** Four small shields of arms in points of quatrefoil, 6-fold arms, in center date in legend **Rev:** Crowned imperial eagle, orb on breast **Note:** Varieties exist.

Date	Mintage	VG	F	VF	XF	Unc
1604	271	525	1,050	2,200	4,900	—
1605	3,930	450	900	1,900	4,500	—
1608	68	525	1,050	2,200	4,900	—
1609	3,320	450	900	1,900	4,500	—

KM# 43 GOLDGULDEN

3.5000 g., 0.9860 Gold 0.1109 oz. AGW **Obv:** Titles of Matthias **Rev:** Crowned 6-fold arms, legend, date **Mint:** Mulheim

Date	Mintage	VG	F	VF	XF	Unc
1613 (h)	1,220	450	850	1,650	3,500	—

KM# 29 DUCAT

3.5000 g., 0.9860 Gold 0.1109 oz. AGW **Obv:** Full-length figure of emperor (Rudolf II) wearing crown, carrying orb and scepter, striding right, divides date **Obv. Legend:** MO: NO: AVRE-POSS: PRIN. **Rev:** Crowned 6-fold arms, legend, **Rev. Legend:** DVCAT : IVL: CLI ET: MONT.

Date	Mintage	VG	F	VF	XF	Unc
1609 Rare	85	—	—	—	—	—

KAUFBEUREN

As a free city in Bavaria 55 miles southwest of Munich, Kaufbeuren was established c. 842. It was an imperial city from 1286 to 1803 when it passed to Bavaria, and struck a local coinage from about 1540 until 1748.

ARMS

Divided vertically, half of imperial eagle on left, right side divided diagonally from upper left to lower right by band, a 6-pointed star above and below.

REFERENCE

N = Elisabeth Nau, **Die Münzen und Medaillen des oberschwäbischen Städte**, Freiburg im Breisgau, 1964.

FREE CITY

REGULAR COINAGE

KM# 5 PFENNIG

Copper **Obv:** City arms in variety of shield shapes **Note:** Kipper Pfennig. Uniface. Varieties exist.

Date	Mintage	Good	VG	F	VF	XF
ND(1622)	—	24.00	45.00	65.00	120	—

KM# 6 KREUZER

Copper **Obv:** City arms **Rev:** Imperial eagle, 1 in orb on breast **Note:** Kipper Kreuzer; varieties exist.

Date	Mintage	Good	VG	F	VF	XF
ND(1622)	—	16.00	40.00	60.00	110	—

KM# 7 KREUZER

Copper **Obv:** Date above arms **Note:** Varieties exist.

Date	Mintage	Good	VG	F	VF	XF
1622	—	16.00	40.00	60.00	110	—
16zz	—	16.00	40.00	60.00	110	—

KM# 8 KREUZER

Copper **Rev:** Crowned Imperial eagle **Note:** Varieties exist.

Date	Mintage	Good	VG	F	VF	XF
16zz	—	16.00	40.00	60.00	110	—
1622	—	16.00	40.00	60.00	110	—

KEMPTEN

The site of Kempten, 81 miles southwest of Munich, predates the Roman town known as Cambodunum. A monastery was founded there as early as 752 from St. Gall (in present-day Switzerland), but the famous abbey was refounded in 773/4 by Hildegard, wife of Charlemagne. A town grew up around the abbey and was the site of an imperial mint from the early 13th century. In 1289 Kempten became a free imperial city and in 1348 the abbot became a prince of the empire. The city obtained the right to mint coins in 1510 and struck a series from 1511 until 1730. The abbots struck coins in the 12th and 13th centuries, then again from 1572 infrequently until 1748. In 1803 the abbey was secularized and, together with the city, was joined to Bavaria.

RULERS

Johann Adam Renner von Almendingen, 1594-1607
Heinrich VIII von Ulm-Langenrhein, 1607-1616
Johann Eucharius von Wolffurth, 1616-1631
Johann Willibald Schenk von Kastel, 1631-1639
Romanus Bernhard Giel von Gielsperg, 1639-1678
Bernhard Gustav von Baden, 1678
Ruprecht von Bodnau (Bodman), 1678-1728

MINT OFFICIALS' INITIALS

Initial	Date	Name
MW	?	?
(h)= 2 horseshoes		Mintmasters at Augsburg

ARMS

Facing bust of St. Hildegard, usually in shield.

REFERENCE

H = Clemens Maria Haertle, **Die Münzen und Medaillen des Stiftes und der Stadt Kempten, Kempten**, 1993.

ABBEY

REGULAR COINAGE

KM# 5 PFENNIG

Silver **Obv:** Arms in shield divde M - C (Monasterium Campidonensis, above ./I.E.A. (Ioannes Eucharius Abbas) **Note:** Uniface. Varieties exist.

Date	Mintage	VG	F	VF	XF	Unc
ND	—	—	—	—	—	—

KM# 6 PFENNIG

Silver **Note:** Klippe.

Date	Mintage	VG	F	VF	XF	Unc
ND Rare	—	—	—	—	—	—

KM# 7 PFENNIG

Copper **Obv:** Facing bust of St. Hildegard **Rev. Inscription:** CC / XXXX / (blossom)

Date	Mintage	VG	F	VF	XF	Unc
ND	—	—	—	—	—	—

KM# 12 KREUZER

Copper **Obv:** Facing bust of St. Hildegard divides date **Rev:** Crowned Imperial Eagle

Date	Mintage	VG	F	VF	XF	Unc
1623	—	—	—	—	—	—

KM# 11 KREUZER

Silver **Obv:** Facing bust of St. Hildegard, date in legend **Rev:** Eight-armed cross with four short and four long arms, 1 in small oval shield in center, titles of Ferdinand II **Note:** Varieties exist.

Date	Mintage	VG	F	VF	XF	Unc
1623	—	10.00	27.00	55.00	85.00	—
1624	—	10.00	27.00	55.00	85.00	—

KM# 13 KREUZER

Copper **Obv:** Arms divided in two vertically, facing bust of St. Hildegard on left, wolf rampant left above diagonal bands from upper right to lower left in right half **Rev:** Crowned Imperial Eagle, 1 in orb on breast

Date	Mintage	VG	F	VF	XF	Unc
ND(1622-23)	—	33.00	65.00	135	240	—

KM# 14 2 KREUZER (Halbbatzen)

Silver **Obv:** Facing bust of St. Hildegard, date in legend **Rev:** Imperial orb with 2, titles of Ferdinand II **Note:** Varieties exist.

Date	Mintage	VG	F	VF	XF	Unc
1623	—	16.00	33.00	55.00	100	—
1624	—	16.00	33.00	55.00	100	—
1625	—	16.00	33.00	55.00	100	—
1626	—	16.00	33.00	55.00	100	—

KM# 18 2 KREUZER (Halbbatzen)

Silver **Note:** Klippe.

Date	Mintage	VG	F	VF	XF	Unc
1624 Rare	—	—	—	—	—	—

KM# 10 12 KREUZER (Dreibätzner)

Silver **Obv:** Half-length figure of St. Lucius right, arms of Kempten below, titles of Johann Eucharius and date in legend **Rev:** Crowned imperial eagle, 12 in orb on breast, titles of Ferdinand II **Note:** Kipper 12 Kreuzer.

Date	Mintage	VG	F	VF	XF	Unc
(16)22	—	—	—	—	—	—

KM# 15 1/6 THALER

Silver **Obv:** Half-length figure of St. Lucius right, arms of Kempten below, abbot's mitre above **Rev:** Inscription in cartouche **Rev. Inscription:** VI / AVF.EIN / REICHS / TALER / date **Note:** Varieties exist.

Date	Mintage	VG	F	VF	XF	Unc
1623	—	—	—	—	—	—

KM# 17 THALER

Silver **Note:** Klippe.

Date	Mintage	VG	F	VF	XF	Unc
16Z3 Rare	—	—	—	—	—	—

KM# 16 THALER

Silver **Obv:** St. Hildegard holding church model behind arms **Rev:** Crowned imperial eagle **Note:** Varieties exist. Dav. #5422.

Date	Mintage	VG	F	VF	XF	Unc
16Z3	—	900	1,600	2,750	4,000	—

KM# 19 THALER

Silver **Rev:** Smaller coat of arms **Note:** Dav. #5423.

Date	Mintage	VG	F	VF	XF	Unc
16Z5	—	900	1,600	2,750	4,000	—

KM# 32 THALER

Silver **Obv:** Capped arms **Rev:** Crowned bust of saint **Note:** Dav. #5424.

Date	Mintage	VG	F	VF	XF	Unc
1694	—	200	400	700	1,650	3,250

TRADE COINAGE

KM# 25 DUCAT

3.5000 g., 0.9860 Gold 0.1109 oz. AGW **Obv:** Four-fold arms, four helmets above, titles of Johann Willibald, date in legend **Rev:** Crowned Imperial Eagle, titles of Ferdinand II

Date	Mintage	VG	F	VF	XF	Unc
1631 (h) Rare	—	—	—	—	—	—

KM# 30 DUCAT

3.5000 g., 0.9860 Gold 0.1109 oz. AGW **Obv:** Arms topped by four helmets **Rev:** Shield with St. Hildegard topped by helmet and cherub, date at top in legend **Note:** Fr.#1423.

Date	Mintage	VG	F	VF	XF	Unc
1692 (h)	—	625	1,350	3,350	6,300	—
1693 (h)	—	625	1,350	3,350	6,300	—
1695 (h)	—	625	1,350	3,350	6,300	—

KM# 31.1 2 DUCAT

7.0000 g., 0.9860 Gold 0.2219 oz. AGW **Obv:** Arms topped by four helmets **Rev:** Baroque shield with St. Hildegard topped by helmet and cherub, date at top in legend **Note:** Fr. #1422.

Date	Mintage	VG	F	VF	XF	Unc
1693 (h)	—	1,300	2,650	5,300	9,000	—

KM# 31.2 2 DUCAT

7.0000 g., 0.9860 Gold 0.2219 oz. AGW **Rev:** Oval shields with St. Hildegard **Note:** Fr. #1422.

Date	Mintage	VG	F	VF	XF	Unc
1693 (h)	—	1,300	2,650	5,300	9,000	—

FREE CITY

REGULAR COINAGE

KM# 50 PFENNIG

Silver **Obv:** Crowned imperial eagle, K in circle below **Note:** Uniface.

Date	Mintage	VG	F	VF	XF	Unc
ND(ca.1600)	—	13.00	30.00	55.00	85.00	—

KM# 51 PFENNIG

Silver **Rev:** Crowned imperial eagle, K in shield below **Rev. Inscription:** CC/XXXX **Note:** Kipper Pfennig.

Date	Mintage	VG	F	VF	XF	Unc
ND(1622-23)	—	10.00	25.00	45.00	80.00	—

KM# 52 PFENNIG

Silver **Obv:** K in wreath **Note:** Uniface.

Date	Mintage	VG	F	VF	XF	Unc
ND	—	10.00	25.00	45.00	80.00	—

KM# 63 1/2 KREUZER

Silver **Obv:** Three shields with tops towards rim, top shield divides date, K between two at bottom **Note:** Uniface.

Date	Mintage	VG	F	VF	XF	Unc
1623	—	—	—	—	—	—

KM# 53 KREUZER

Copper **Rev:** Crowned imperial eagle, K in shield on breast **Rev. Inscription:** I / KREI / ZER / date **Note:** Kipper Kreuzer. Varieties exist.

Date	Mintage	VG	F	VF	XF	Unc
1622	—	75.00	150	250	—	—

KM# 54 KREUZER

Copper **Rev. Inscription:** I/KREI/TZER/date **Note:** Varieties exist.

Date	Mintage	VG	F	VF	XF	Unc
1622	—	13.00	33.00	45.00	70.00	—

KM# 64 KREUZER

Silver **Obv:** Eagle in shield, shield superimposed on eight-armed cross, legend, date **Obv. Legend:** MON: NO... **Rev:** Crowned imperial eagle, 1 in orb on breast, titles of Ferdinand II **Note:** Varieties exist.

Date	Mintage	VG	F	VF	XF	Unc
1623	—	35.00	70.00	115	200	—

KM# 72 KREUZER

Silver **Rev:** Oval shield **Note:** Varieties exist.

Date	Mintage	VG	F	VF	XF	Unc
1625	—	33.00	65.00	115	200	—

KM# 65 2 KREUZER (Halbbatzen)

Silver **Obv:** Three-fold arms in quatrefoil, titles of Ferdinand II in legend **Rev:** Crowned imperial eagle, 2 in orb on breast, legend, date **Rev. Legend:** MON: NO:... **Note:** Varieties exist.

Date	Mintage	VG	F	VF	XF	Unc
1623	—	13.00	30.00	55.00	85.00	—

KM# 71 2 KREUZER (Halbbatzen)

Silver **Obv:** Three small shields with tops towards rim, titles of Ferdinand II in legend **Note:** Varieties exist.

Date	Mintage	VG	F	VF	XF	Unc
1624	—	10.00	25.00	45.00	80.00	—
1625	—	10.00	25.00	45.00	80.00	—

KM# 66 3 KREUZER (Groschen)

Silver **Obv:** Three small shields with tops towards rim, legend, date **Obv. Legend:** MON: NOVA:... **Rev:** Crowned imperial eagle, 3 in orb on breast, titles of Ferdinand II **Note:** Varieties exist.

Date	Mintage	VG	F	VF	XF	Unc
1623	—	20.00	40.00	85.00	150	—

KM# 57 12 KREUZER (Dreibätzner)

Silver **Rev:** Imperial eagle in cartouche with XII above **Rev. Inscription:** STAT: /MVNTZ/date

Date	Mintage	VG	F	VF	XF	Unc
1622	—	—	—	—	—	—

KM# 58 12 KREUZER (Dreibätzner)

Silver **Obv:** Imperial eagle in shield, XII K above

Date	Mintage	VG	F	VF	XF	Unc
1622	—	—	—	—	—	—

KM# 56 12 KREUZER (Dreibätzner)

Silver **Obv:** STAT/MVNTZ above cross branches, in ornate oval baroque frame **Rev:** Crowned imperial eagle in shield divides date, XII above **Rev. Legend:** MONETA. NOVA... **Note:** Kipper 12 Kreuzer. Varieties exist.

Date	Mintage	VG	F	VF	XF	Unc
1622	—	—	—	—	—	—

KM# 67 12 KREUZER (Dreibätzner)

Silver **Obv:** STAT.MINTZ/date in cartouche **Rev:** Crowned imperial eagle in ornamented shield, XII above **Rev. Legend:** MONETA. NOVA... **Note:** Varieties exist.

Date	Mintage	VG	F	VF	XF	Unc
1623	—	—	—	—	—	—

KM# 55 1/24 THALER (5 Kreuzer)

Silver **Obv. Inscription:** XXIIII / AVF.EIN / REICHS / TALER **Rev:** Crowned imperial eagle, K in shield on breast **Rev. Legend:** MONETA. NOVA... **Note:** Kipper 1/24 Thaler.

Date	Mintage	VG	F	VF	XF	Unc
ND(1622/23)	—	—	—	—	—	—

KM# 59 1/4 THALER

Silver **Obv:** 3 small shields, 2 above 1, date centered above upper 2 shields **Rev:** Half-length laureate figure of emperor 3/4 right, holding orb and scepter, titles of Ferdinand II **Rev. Legend:** MONETA. NOVA...

Date	Mintage	VG	F	VF	XF	Unc
1622	—	225	525	800	1,200	—

KM# 60 1/4 THALER

Silver **Rev:** Crowned imprial eagle in small shield below figure of emperor **Note:** Varieties exist.

Date	Mintage	VG	F	VF	XF	Unc
1622	—	225	525	800	1,200	—

KM# 61 1/2 THALER

Silver **Obv:** Imperial eagle in shield in center, large crown above, small shield at sides and below, date in legend **Rev:** Half-length laureate figure of emporer 3/4 right, holding orb and sceptre, titles of Ferdinand II

Date	Mintage	VG	F	VF	XF	Unc
1622	—	1,350	2,150	3,250	4,500	—

KM# 68 1/2 THALER

Silver

Date	Mintage	VG	F	VF	XF	Unc
1623	—	1,350	2,150	3,250	4,500	—

KM# 73 1/2 THALER

Silver **Note:** Struck from dies of 1 Thaler, KM#69.

Date	Mintage	VG	F	VF	XF	Unc
1623	—	1,150	2,000	3,000	4,200	—

KM# 62 THALER

Silver **Obv:** Half-length figure of emperor facing and holding orb and scepter **Rev:** Crowned arms surrounded by shields and banners **Note:** Dav. #5425.

Date	Mintage	VG	F	VF	XF	Unc
1622	—	1,300	2,250	3,700	5,700	—

KM# 69 THALER
Silver **Obv:** Crowned arms and surrounding shields in cartouches **Rev:** Ruffled bust right **Note:** Dav. #5427.

Date	Mintage	VG	F	VF	XF	Unc
1623	—	650	1,250	2,500	4,000	—

KM# A70 THALER (Regimentstaler)
Silver **Obv:** City view, ribbon band above with CAMPIDONVM in exergue within cartouche, divides date below, small oval shields left and right, imperial eagle to left **Obv. Inscription:** PRÆSIDIVM/ IOVÆ CPNSTANS/ET CERTA/COLVMNA **Rev:** 8 small oval shields of arms of town council members in baroque frames, seven around one in center, 3 angel's heads with wings at top and upper left and right, various other floral ornaments distributed around in field

Date	Mintage	VG	F	VF	XF	Unc
16Z5	—	750	1,450	2,750	4,500	—

KM# 70 2 THALER
Silver **Note:** Similar to 1 Thaler, KM#69. Dav. #5426.

Date	Mintage	VG	F	VF	XF	Unc
1623 Rare	—	—	—	—	—	—

PATTERNS

Including off metal strikes

KM#	Date	Mintage	Identification	Mkt Val
Pn1	1622	—	Thaler. Tin. KM#62.	—
Pn2	1623	—	Thaler. Lead. KM#69.	—

KOLLN

(Cöln)

Originally a separate settlement on the River Spree just southeast of medieval Berlin when first mentioned in 1238, Kölln has been over the centuries absorbed by the great capital city. It was early on the site of a chief mint for the Brandenburg margraves, but also had a short-lived copper coinage during the opening era of the Thirty Years' War.

CITY

REGULAR COINAGE

KM# 1 SCHERF (1/2 Pfennig)
Copper **Ruler:** (no Ruler Information) **Note:** Uniface; Eagle in shield, start to either side of tail, date above.

Date	Mintage	VG	F	VF	XF	Unc
16Z0	—	20.00	45.00	80.00	140	—
16Z1	—	20.00	45.00	80.00	140	—
1621	—	20.00	45.00	80.00	140	—

KM# 2 SCHERF (1/2 Pfennig)
Copper **Ruler:** (no Ruler Information) **Note:** Uniface; Eagle in shield, start to either side of tail, date above; varities exist.

Date	Mintage	VG	F	VF	XF	Unc
1621	—	20.00	45.00	80.00	140	—
16Z1	—	20.00	45.00	80.00	140	—

KROSSEN

(Crossen)

A town situated on the Oder River, about 30 miles southeast of Frankfurt am Oder, founded in 1005. At first the center of a Silesian duchy, Krossen passed to Brandenburg in 1509 by marriage. During much of the 17th century, Krossen was a mint site for the electors of Brandenburg-Prussia, but during the Kipper Period a local coinage was struck.

DUCHY

REGULAR COINAGE

KM# 5 PFENNIG
Bronze **Obv:** Arms with two shields, C below **Note:** Kipper. Uniface.

Date	Mintage	Good	VG	F	VF	XF
ND(1621-22)	—	40.00	70.00	120	180	—

KUSTRIN

(Custrin)

A town on the Oder River, almost due east of Berlin about 50 miles. It came under the control of the Teutonic Order in 1259, later passing to Brandenburg. Local coinage was issued by the town during the Kipper Period.

TOWN

REGULAR COINAGE

KM# 5 PFENNING
Bronze **Obv:** Date divided by orb above shield with two-fold arms **Note:** Kipper Pfennig.

Date	Mintage	VG	F	VF	XF	Unc
1621	—	33.00	55.00	100	160	—
(1)621	—	33.00	55.00	100	160	—
(1)622	—	33.00	55.00	100	160	—
1622	—	33.00	55.00	100	160	—

KYRITZ

This provincial town is located about 50 miles northwest of Berlin. A few small copper coins were issued during the 16th and 17th centuries.

TOWN

REGULAR COINAGE

KM# 5 PFENNIG
Copper **Note:** Uniface. Two adjacent shields of arms, eagle (Brandenburg) on left, double fleur-de-lis on right, "C" below.

Date	Mintage	Good	VG	F	VF	XF
ND(1619-22)	—	40.00	70.00	120	180	—

Note: This issue is distinguished from similar coins of Crossen by lack of a crossbar on the double fleur-de-lis

LAUINGEN

Lauingen, a town on the Danube in Bavaria, about halfway between Ulm and Donauworth, issued a few copper coins during the emergency Kipper Period of the Thirty Years' War.

TOWN

REGULAR COINAGE

KM# 5 1/4 KREUZER (2 Heller)
Copper 0 **Obv:** Monk's head left in wreath **Rev:** Value Z (2) in wreath **Note:** Kipper 1/4 Kreuzer.

Date	Mintage	VG	F	VF	XF	Unc
ND(1620-22)	—	30.00	60.00	115	200	—

KM# 6 1/2 KREUZER (4 Heller)
Copper 0 **Obv:** Crowned monk's head left in wreath **Rev:** Value 4 in wreath **Note:** Kipper 1/2 Kreuzer.

Date	Mintage	VG	F	VF	XF	Unc
ND(1620-22)	—	27.00	55.00	100	165	—

KM# 7 KREUZER (4 Pfennig)
Copper 0 **Note:** Kipper Kreuzer. Similar to 1/2 Kreuzer, KM#6, but ornate script K in wreath on reverse.

Date	Mintage	VG	F	VF	XF	Unc
ND(1620-22)	—	—	—	—	—	—

LEININGEN

The counts, landgraves and princes of Leiningen trace their origin back to early 12th century Alsace. Over the ensuing centuries, through marriage and division, Leiningen became a house of numerous lines with far-flung possessions situated from southwest Germany, throughout the Rhineland, Hesse and Bavaria. Only several of the Leiningen branches struck coins in the 17th and 19th centuries.

LEININGEN-DAGSBURG-FALKENBURG

This line of counts was founded upon the division of Leiningen-Dagsburg-Hartenburg in 1541. The lands of Leiningen-Dagsburg-Falkenburg were located west of Koblenz near the present-day border with Belgium. Its possessions were annexed by France in 1801.

RULERS
Johann Ludwig, 1593-1625
Ludwig of Westerburg, 1597-1622
Emich XII, 1625-1658

MINT OFFICIAL
David Niderlander, warden in Dagsburg, 1620-1621

COUNTSHIP

REGULAR COINAGE

KM# 13 ALBUS (2 Kreuzer)
Silver **Ruler:** Johann Ludwig **Obv:** Crowned oval 4-fold arms with central shield (cross), date in legend **Rev:** Crowned imperial eagle, 2 in orb on breast, titles of Ferdinand **Mint:** Heidesheim **Note:** Varieties exist.

Date	Mintage	VG	F	VF	XF	Unc
1624	—	60.00	110	165	225	—

KM# 5 12 KREUZER (Dreibatzner)
Silver **Obv:** Crowned 4-fold arms w/central shield, (cross) divides date **Rev:** Crowned imperial eagle with 12 in orb on breast, titles of Ferdinand II **Note:** Varieties exist.

Date	Mintage	VG	F	VF	XF	Unc
ND	—	165	275	420	550	—
1620	5,088	200	300	475	650	—

KM# 6 1/4 THALER
Silver **Ruler:** Johann Ludwig **Obv:** Crowned 4-fold arms with central shield (cross) divides date **Rev:** Crowned imperial eagle, titles of Ferdinand II **Mint:** Heidesheim

Date	Mintage	VG	F	VF	XF	Unc
ND	1,044	300	475	625	1,000	—
1620	4,340	325	525	700	1,000	—

KM# 7 THALER
Silver **Obv:** Crowned ornate oval arms divide date **Rev:** Crowned double eagle with orb on breast **Note:** Dav. #6878.

Date	Mintage	VG	F	VF	XF	Unc
1623	—	1,000	1,700	2,900	—	—

KM# 8 THALER
Silver **Rev:** Crowned shield-shaped arms divide date **Note:** Dav. #6879.

Date	Mintage	VG	F	VF	XF	Unc
1623	—	1,050	1,750	3,000	—	—

KM# 9 THALER
Silver **Rev:** Crowned ornate shield-shaped arms, date in legend **Note:** Dav. #6880.

Date	Mintage	VG	F	VF	XF	Unc
1623	—	1,050	1,750	3,000	—	—

KM# 10 THALER
Silver **Obv:** Date divided below crowned double eagle **Rev:** Crowned ornate oval arms **Note:** Dav. #6881.

Date	Mintage	VG	F	VF	XF	Unc
1623	—	1,050	1,750	3,000	—	—

KM# 11 THALER
Silver **Obv:** Crowned ornate oval arms divide slanting date near bottom **Rev:** Crown above double-headed imperial eagle within circle **Note:** Dav. #6882.

Date	Mintage	VG	F	VF	XF	Unc
1623	—	750	1,250	2,250	—	—
1624	—	750	1,250	2,250	—	—

KM# 14 THALER
Silver **Rev:** Date in straight line divided near bottom **Note:** Dav. #6883.

Date	Mintage	VG	F	VF	XF	Unc
1624	—	800	1,350	2,500	—	—

KM# 12 2 THALER
Silver **Obv:** Crowned ornate arms **Rev:** Crowned double eagle **Note:** Dav. #6877.

Date	Mintage	VG	F	VF	XF	Unc
1623 Rare	—	—	—	—	—	—

Note: Giessener Munzhandlung Auction 9 3-76 XF realized $13,420

LEININGEN-LEININGEN

Established by the division of Leiningen-Westerburg in 1547, Leiningen-Leiningen was located some 12 miles southwest of Worms in the Rhineland. When the line fell extinct in 1705, its possessions passed to Leiningen-Schaumburg.

RULERS
Ludwig, 1597-1622
Johann Casimir, 1622-1635
Philipp zu Rikingen, 1635-1668
Ludwig Eberhard, 1668-1688
Philipp Ludwig, 1688-1705

COUNTSHIP

REGULAR COINAGE

KM# 5 PFENNIG
Silver **Obv:** Shield of arms divided into three sections: 1) eagle, 2) two fish, 3) cross **Note:** Uniface.

Date	Mintage	Good	VG	F	VF	XF
ND	444,000	85.00	160	225	300	—

KM# 7 PFENNIG
Silver **Obv:** Small crown above LG **Note:** Varieties exist.

Date	Mintage	Good	VG	F	VF	XF
ND	Inc. above	100	165	250	350	—

KM# 6 PFENNIG
Silver **Ruler:** Ludwig **Obv:** 3 small shields with rounded bottoms towards rims, two above one, LG between top two, Z - L divided by shield on bottom **Mint:** Grünstadt

Date	Mintage	Good	VG	F	VF	XF
ND	Inc. above	85.00	160	225	300	—

KM# 9 8 PFENNIG (2 Kreuzer = 1/2 Batzen)
Silver **Note:** Klippe.

Date	Mintage	Good	VG	F	VF	XF
1610	Inc. above	—	—	—	—	—

KM# 8 8 PFENNIG (2 Kreuzer = 1/2 Batzen)
Silver **Ruler:** Ludwig **Obv:** Crown above three small shields with rounded bottoms toward rim, two above one, LG between top two, Z-L divided by shield on bottom, titles of Ludwig in legend **Rev:** Titles continued from obverse in legend **Rev. Inscription:** VIII/PFENIG/date, **Mint:** Grünstadt **Note:** Varieties exist.

Date	Mintage	Good	VG	F	VF	XF
1610	99,000	45.00	100	160	225	—
1611	32,000	60.00	110	180	275	—

KM# 12 3 KREUZER (Groschen)
Silver **Ruler:** Ludwig **Obv:** Crowned 4-fold arms with central shield (cross), titles fo Ludwig in legend **Rev:** Crowned imperial eagle, 3 in orb on breast, titles of Rudolf II **Mint:** Grünstadt **Note:** Varieties exist.

Date	Mintage	Good	VG	F	VF	XF
1611	36,000	33.00	65.00	135	225	—
ND	Inc. above	33.00	65.00	135	225	—

KM# 13 3 KREUZER (Groschen)
Silver **Ruler:** Ludwig **Obv:** Crowned shield within circle **Rev:** Titles of Matthias **Mint:** Grünstadt **Note:** Varieties exist.

Date	Mintage	Good	VG	F	VF	XF
ND	163,000	33.00	65.00	135	225	—

KM# 20 3 KREUZER (Groschen)
Silver **Obv:** Titles of Ferdinand II **Rev:** Date divided by arms **Note:** Varieties exist.

Date	Mintage	Good	VG	F	VF	XF
1620	—	33.00	65.00	135	225	—
ND	—	33.00	65.00	135	225	—

KM# 21 3 KREUZER (Groschen)
Silver **Ruler:** Ludwig **Obv:** Date in legend **Mint:** Grünstadt **Note:** Varieties exist.

Date	Mintage	Good	VG	F	VF	XF
(16)22	—	33.00	65.00	135	225	—
(1)622	—	33.00	65.00	135	225	—

KM# 22 3 KREUZER (Groschen)
Silver **Note:** Klippe.

Date	Mintage	Good	VG	F	VF	XF
1622	—	—	—	—	—	—

KM# 14 1/4 THALER
Silver **Ruler:** Ludwig **Obv:** Bust of Ludwig right **Rev:** Crowned 4-fold arms with central shield (cross) divides date **Rev. Legend:** DER. RECHT. GLAUBT... **Mint:** Grünstadt **Note:** Varieties exist.

Date	Mintage	VG	F	VF	XF	Unc
ND	6,939	275	600	950	1,500	—
1614	17,000	275	625	1,000	1,600	—

KM# 18 1/2 THALER
Silver **Obv:** Bust right, date below **Rev:** Crowned 4-fold arms iwth central shield **Rev. Legend:** DER. RECHT. GLAUBT...

Date	Mintage	VG	F	VF	XF	Unc
1614	—	—	—	—	—	—

KM# 16 THALER
Silver **Ruler:** Ludwig **Obv:** Bust right in circle **Obv. Legend:** LVD.COM.IN.LEI.ET.RI.DOM.IN.WES.ET.SC.S.R.I.S.L. **Rev:** Crowned ornate 4-fold arms divide date **Rev. Legend:** DER RECHT GLAV: - LAEWIG LEBT **Mint:** Grünstadt **Note:** Dav. #6875.

Date	Mintage	VG	F	VF	XF	Unc
1612 2 known	—	—	—	—	—	—

Note: Gorny & Mosch Giessener Münzhandlung Auction 148, 3-06, good VF realized approximately $21,460.

KM# 17 THALER
Silver **Obv:** Large bust **Rev:** Arms with less ornamentation **Note:** Dav. #6876.

Date	Mintage	VG	F	VF	XF	Unc
1613	1,274	2,000	3,500	5,500	—	—

KM# 10 2 THALER
Silver **Obv:** Bust right, date in front **Rev:** Crowned arms **Note:** Dav. #6874.

Date	Mintage	VG	F	VF	XF	Unc
1610 Rare	—	—	—	—	—	—

KM# 11 2 THALER
Silver **Obv:** Different bust **Rev:** Different shield of arms divides date **Rev. Legend:** GOT. DVT. RETEN. SO DVN. GLAVBEN. **Note:** Klippe.

Date	Mintage	VG	F	VF	XF	Unc
1610 Rare	—	—	—	—	—	—

TRADE COINAGE

KM# 15 GOLDGULDEN
3.5000 g., 0.9860 Gold 0.1109 oz. AGW **Ruler:** Ludwig **Obv:** Bust right in circle, date below. **Obv. Legend:** LV.C.I.L.E.R.D.I.W. S.E.F.S.R.I.S.L(IB). **Rev:** Four-fold arms with central shield, crown above in margin **Rev. Legend:** DER.RECHT.GLAVBT. IA.EWIG.LEB(T). **Mint:** Grünstadt **Note:** Varieties exist.

Date	Mintage	VG	F	VF	XF	Unc
161Z	1,593	425	775	1,650	3,250	—
(1)614	3,488	425	775	1,650	3,250	—
1617	—	425	775	1,650	3,250	—
1618	—	425	775	1,650	3,250	—
1619	—	425	775	1,650	3,250	—
1620	—	425	775	1,650	3,250	—

LEININGEN-SCHAUMBURG-KLEEBERG

This subdivision of Leiningen-Westerburg was established in 1547 and centered in Nassau to the southwest of Limburg. It was further divided in 1695 but none of those branches issued coins.

RULERS

Christof, 1585-1632 and
Philipp Jacob, 1585-1612 and
Reinhart VII, 1585-1655
Georg Wilhelm, 1632-1695

MINT OFFICIALS' INITIALS

Initial	Date	Name
CS	Ca.1663	?
DZ	1670-91	Dietrich Zimmermann at Leiningen
IAB	Ca.1685-89	Johann Adam Bottcher (Bottiger)
	1625-26	Henning Kiessel at Cramberg
	1626-28	Christian Gobel, die-cutter at Cramberg
	1628	Georg Wied at Cramberg

COUNTSHIP

REGULAR COINAGE

KM# 5 PFENNIG

Silver **Obv:** Four-fold arms, LW above. **Mint:** Cramberg **Note:** Kipper Pfennig. Uniface. Varieties exist.

Date	Mintage	Good	VG	F	VF	XF
ND(1621/2)	—	80.00	165	275	450	—

KM# 6 PFENNIG

Silver **Mint:** Cramberg **Note:** Four-fold arms. Varieties exist.

Date	Mintage	Good	VG	F	VF	XF
ND(1621/2)	—	35.00	80.00	135	225	—

KM# 7 PFENNIG

Silver **Note:** LS above arms.

Date	Mintage	Good	VG	F	VF	XF
ND(1621/2)	—	35.00	80.00	135	225	—

KM# 4 PFENNIG

Silver **Ruler:** Reinhart VII **Obv:** Shield of eagle arms, 'L' above, all in circle of pellets **Mint:** Cramberg **Note:** Uniface.

Date	Mintage	VG	F	VF	XF	Unc
ND (1632-55)	—	100	160	225	325	—

KM# 26 8 HELLER

Silver **Ruler:** Georg Wilhelm **Obv:** Cross in shield (Schaumburg), titles of Georg Wilhelm **Rev:** VIII/mintmaster's initials, legend: titles and date **Mint:** Leiningen **Note:** Varieties exist.

Date	Mintage	VG	F	VF	XF	Unc
1676 DZ	—	85.00	165	300	525	—
(1)676	—	85.00	165	300	525	—

KM# 20 KREUZER

Silver **Obv:** Crowned four-fold arms **Rev:** Inscription, mintmaster's initials in wreath **Rev. Inscription:** I/KREVTZ/date/

Date	Mintage	VG	F	VF	XF	Unc
1663 CS	—	—	—	—	—	—

KM# 21 KREUZER

Silver **Rev. Inscription:** I/KREVT/ZER/16CS63

Date	Mintage	VG	F	VF	XF	Unc
1663 CS	—	—	—	—	—	—

KM# 40 KREUZER

Silver **Obv:** Crowned eagle aarms in wreath **Rev:** Inscription in wreath **Rev. Inscription:** I/KREV/TZER/date/mintmaster's initials **Note:** Varieties exist.

Date	Mintage	VG	F	VF	XF	Unc
1685 IAB	—	120	275	425	625	—
1686 IAB	—	120	275	425	625	—

KM# 11 2 KREUZER

Silver **Obv:** Imperial orb with Z, titles of Ferdinand II **Rev:** Ornate cross, small arms in each angle **Note:** Varieties exist.

Date	Mintage	VG	F	VF	XF	Unc
ND(1626)	—	120	275	425	625	—

KM# 9 2 KREUZER

Silver **Obv:** Imperial orb with Z divides date, titles of Reinhart VII **Rev:** Ornate cross, small arms in each angle **Note:** Varieties exist.

Date	Mintage	VG	F	VF	XF	Unc
(16)Z9	—	—	—	—	—	—
ND	—	—	—	—	—	—

KM# 10 2 KREUZER

Silver **Obv:** Titles of Christof **Note:** Varieties exist.

Date	Mintage	VG	F	VF	XF	Unc
ND	—	—	—	—	—	—

KM# 8 3 KREUZER (Groschen)

Silver **Obv:** Crowned imperial eagle, 3 in orb on breast, titles of Ferdinand II and date in legend **Rev:** Four-fold arms, titles of Christof **Note:** Varieties exist.

Date	Mintage	VG	F	VF	XF	Unc
1622	—	—	—	—	—	—
ND	—	—	—	—	—	—

KM# 42 6 KREUZER

Silver **Obv:** Bust right, value (VI) below in legend **Rev:** Eagle in circle, legend, date divided by mintmaster's initials **Rev. Legend:** SOLI DEO GLORIA **Note:** Varieties exist.

Date	Mintage	VG	F	VF	XF	Unc
1689 IAB	—	165	325	525	775	—

KM# 41 15 KREUZER

Silver **Obv:** Bust right **Rev:** Eagle in circle, legend, date **Rev. Legend:** MONETA NOVA ARGENTEA

Date	Mintage	VG	F	VF	XF	Unc
1687	—	60.00	120	225	400	—

KM# 43 15 KREUZER

Silver **Obv:** Value XV below bust in legend **Rev:** Legend, date **Rev. Legend:** SOLI DEO GLORIA **Note:** Varieties exist.

Date	Mintage	VG	F	VF	XF	Unc
1689	—	50.00	115	220	325	—

KM# 45 15 KREUZER

Silver **Rev:** Crowned four-fold arms with central shield (cross) **Note:** Varieties exist.

Date	Mintage	VG	F	VF	XF	Unc
1690	—	40.00	85.00	135	200	—
1691	—	40.00	85.00	135	200	—
1692	—	40.00	85.00	135	200	—

KM# 46 15 KREUZER

Silver **Note:** Similar to KM#45, but value (XV) below arms on reverse.

Date	Mintage	VG	F	VF	XF	Unc
1691	—	65.00	135	250	460	—

KM# 48 15 KREUZER

Silver **Note:** Without indication of value.

Date	Mintage	VG	F	VF	XF	Unc
1692	—	65.00	135	250	460	—

KM# 25 60 KREUZER (Gulden = 2/3 Thaler)

Silver **Ruler:** Georg Wilhelm **Obv:** Bust right, value 60 below **Rev:** Crowned four-fold arms with central shield (cross) in palm branches, date in legend **Mint:** Westerburg **Note:** Varieties exist.

Date	Mintage	VG	F	VF	XF	Unc
1675 DZ	—	600	1,200	2,000	—	—
1676 DZ	—	700	1,500	2,500	—	—
1677 DZ Dav# 608B	—	900	1,800	3,000	—	—

KM# 28 60 KREUZER/16 GUTE GROSCHEN (Gulden = 2/3 Thaler)

Silver **Rev. Inscription:** XVI/GUTE/GROSCH

Date	Mintage	VG	F	VF	XF	Unc
1676	—	—	—	—	—	—

KM# 27 60 KREUZER/16 GUTE GROSCHEN (Gulden = 2/3 Thaler)

Silver **Obv:** Bust right, value below **Rev:** Legend, date **Rev. Legend:** SOLI DEO GLORIA **Rev. Inscription:** 16/GUTE/GROSCH/EN, **Note:** Varieties exist.

Date	Mintage	VG	F	VF	XF	Unc
1676	—	1,000	2,000	3,500	—	—

KM# 15 ALBUS

Silver **Obv:** Crowned four-fold arms with central shield (cross), titles of Georg Wilhelm **Rev:** ALBVS/date in laurel wreath

Date	Mintage	VG	F	VF	XF	Unc
1657	—	—	—	—	—	—

KM# 49 2 ALBUS (4 Kreuzer = Batzen)

Silver **Obv:** Crowned four-fold arms with central shield (cross), L.W above, in laurel wreath **Rev:** II/ALBUS/date, legend **Rev. Legend:** NACH.DEM.SCHLUS.DER.V.STAEND.

Date	Mintage	VG	F	VF	XF	Unc
1693	—	—	—	—	—	—

KM# 29 16 GUTE GROSCHEN (Gulden = 2/3 Thaler)

Silver **Ruler:** Georg Wilhelm **Obv:** Bust right **Rev:** 16/GUTE/GROSCH/EN, legend, date **Rev. Legend:** SOLI DEO GLORIA **Mint:** Westerburg

Date	Mintage	VG	F	VF	XF	Unc
1676	—	1,000	2,000	3,500	—	—

KM# 30 16 GUTE GROSCHEN (Gulden = 2/3 Thaler)

Silver **Obv:** Eagle, legend **Obv. Legend:** MONETA NOVA ARGENTEA

Date	Mintage	VG	F	VF	XF	Unc
1676	—	—	—	—	—	—

KM# 31 24 MARIENGROSCHEN (Gulden = 2/3 Thaler)

Silver **Obv:** Bust right **Rev:** 24/MARIE/GROS, legend, date **Rev. Legend:** SOL DEO GLORIA

Date	Mintage	VG	F	VF	XF	Unc
1676	—	—	—	—	—	—

KM# 36 24 MARIENGROSCHEN (Gulden = 2/3 Thaler)

Silver **Obv. Legend:** XXIIII/MARIE*/GROSCH/date, legend **Rev:** GKIRUA. IN* ECCELSIS*DEO

Date	Mintage	VG	F	VF	XF	Unc
1677	—	—	—	—	—	—

KM# 47 1/12 THALER (2 Groschen)

Silver **Obv:** Crowned oval four-fold arms with central shield (cross) **Rev:** 12/EINEN/REICHS/THALER/1691 in palm wreath **Note:** Varieties exist.

Date	Mintage	VG	F	VF	XF	Unc
1691	—	—	—	—	—	—

KM# 32 1/3 THALER (1/2 Gulden)

Silver **Obv:** Bust right **Rev:** Crowned four-fold arms with central shield (cross) in palm wreath, legend, mintmaster's initials, date **Rev. Legend:** NACH DEM (1/3) LEIBZIGER EVS

Date	Mintage	VG	F	VF	XF	Unc
1676 DZ	—	150	275	500	850	—

KM# 33 1/3 THALER (1/2 Gulden)

Silver **Obv:** Bust right, value (1/3) below **Rev:** Legend, date **Rev. Legend:** SOLI DEO GLORIA

Date	Mintage	VG	F	VF	XF	Unc
1676 DZ	—	200	350	675	1,150	—

KM# 34 2/3 THALER (Gulden)

Silver **Obv:** Bust right, value (2/3) below **Rev:** Crowned four-fold arms with central shield in palm wreath, legend, date **Rev. Legend:** SOLI DEO GLORIA **Note:** Varieties exist.

Date	Mintage	VG	F	VF	XF	Unc
1675	—	375	675	1,250	1,850	—
1676 DZ	—	375	675	1,250	1,850	—

Note: Known struck to weight of 1/2 Thaler, 14.72g.

KM# 35 2/3 THALER (Gulden)

Silver **Obv:** Older bust **Rev:** Larger crown **Note:** Varieties exist.

Date	Mintage	VG	F	VF	XF	Unc
1676 DZ	—	375	675	1,250	1,850	—
1676	—	375	675	1,250	1,850	—

KM# 37 2/3 THALER (Gulden)

Silver **Obv:** Two flowers below bust **Rev:** Value (2/3) at bottom

Date	Mintage	VG	F	VF	XF	Unc
1677	—	400	750	1,350	2,000	—

LINDAU

A town located on the northeast shore of Lake Constance, Lindau dates from the early 9th century. After acquiring the status of free imperial city in 1274, a local coinage was produced for Lindau on and off during the next 5 centuries. During the Kipper Period of the Thirty Years' War, a variety of coins from South German issuing authorities were counterstamped with the linden tree symbol of Lindau. These are not listed here. In 1732 a joint coinage with the towns of Isny, Wangen, and Leutkirch was struck. After the Napoleonic Wars, in 1805, Lindau was made a part of Bavaria.

MINT

Langenargen, of the Swabian imperial circle located in Montfort

MINT OFFICIALS' INITIALS

Initial	Date	Name
	1682-1712	Hans Jakob Kickh
	1685, 1712-19	Johann Albrecht Riedlin von Ulm, die-cutter

IMPERIAL CITY

REGULAR COINAGE

KM# 5 PFENNIG

Copper-Billon **Obv:** 5-leaved linden tree divides date **Note:** Uniface. Varieties exist.

Date	Mintage	Good	VG	F	VF	XF
1661	—	5.00	16.00	30.00	45.00	—
1663	—	5.00	16.00	30.00	45.00	—
1665	—	5.00	16.00	30.00	45.00	—
1675	—	5.00	16.00	30.00	45.00	—
1679	—	5.00	16.00	30.00	45.00	—
1681	—	5.00	16.00	30.00	45.00	—
1682	—	5.00	16.00	30.00	45.00	—
1683	—	5.00	16.00	30.00	45.00	—
1684	—	5.00	16.00	30.00	45.00	—
1686	—	5.00	16.00	30.00	45.00	—
1687	—	5.00	16.00	30.00	45.00	—
1689	—	5.00	16.00	30.00	45.00	—
1691	—	5.00	16.00	30.00	45.00	—
1692	—	5.00	16.00	30.00	45.00	—
1693	—	5.00	16.00	30.00	45.00	—
1694	—	5.00	16.00	30.00	45.00	—
1695	—	5.00	16.00	30.00	45.00	—
1696	—	5.00	16.00	30.00	45.00	—
1697	—	5.00	16.00	30.00	45.00	—
ND	—	5.00	16.00	30.00	45.00	—

LIPPE

The lords of Lippe first established their territory in Westphalia to the west of the Weser River in the early 12th century. The dynasty acquired the rank of count in the early 16th century. In 1613 Lippe was divided into four branches: Lippe-Detmold, Lippe-Sternberg (extinct in 1620 and reverted to Detmold), Lippe-Bracke, and Lippe-Alverdissen. The latter inherited half of the county of Schauenburg (Schaumburg) and founded the line of Schaumburg-Lippe in 1640 (q.v.). Lippe-Brucke became extinct in 1790 and its possessions fell back to the senior branch of Lippe-Detmold, which lasted into the 20th century.

RULERS

Simon VI, 1563-1613
Simon VII, 1613-1627
Hermann Adolf, 1652-1666
Simon Heinrich, 1666-1697

MINT OFFICIALS' INITIALS

Initial	Date	Name
(a)=	1599-1601	Peter Busch von Bielefeld
	1601-04	Alexander Wacherwald, warden
(b)=	1601-02	Caspar Hover
(c)=	1602-06	Henning Hansen
(d)=	1604-06	Ernst Schroder, warden
(e)=	1606-10	Engelbert (Engelhard) Hausmann
	1606-?	Borchard Lachtorp, warden
(f)=	1610-18	Caspar Kholl (Kohl, Khol) in Blomberg

ARMS

5-petaled rose

COUNTSHIP

REGULAR COINAGE

KM# 5 GOSLER (1/2 Pfennig)

Silver **Ruler:** Simon VI **Obv:** Rose in circle **Note:** Uniface.

Date	Mintage	VG	F	VF	XF	Unc
ND(1601)	—	65.00	135	275	400	—

KM# 6 1/96 THALER (Dreier = 3 Pfennig)

Silver **Ruler:** Simon VI **Obv:** Rose **Obv. Legend:** S G V E H Z L **Rev:** Imperial orb with 96 divides date

Date	Mintage	VG	F	VF	XF	Unc
1601	—	100	185	300	475	—
1602 (c)	—	75.00	135	225	350	—
1605(1602)	—	100	185	300	475	—

KM# 9 1/96 THALER (Dreier = 3 Pfennig)

Silver **Ruler:** Simon VI **Obv:** Rose **Obv. Legend:** S. C. E. N. D. D. L. **Rev:** Imperial orb with 96 in rhombus divides date

Date	Mintage	VG	F	VF	XF	Unc
1608	—	85.00	165	275	400	—

KM# 14 1/96 THALER (Dreier = 3 Pfennig)

Silver **Ruler:** Simon VI **Obv:** Rose **Rev:** Imperial orb with 96 divides date

Date	Mintage	VG	F	VF	XF	Unc
1610	—	—	—	—	—	—

KM# 7 MARIENGROSCHEN (1/36 Thaler)

Silver **Ruler:** Simon VI **Obv:** 4-fold arms in ornate shield **Rev:** Madonna and child, date in legend **Note:** Varieties exist.

Date	Mintage	VG	F	VF	XF	Unc
1601 (c)	—	33.00	70.00	120	175	—
1605 (d)	—	33.00	70.00	120	175	—
1605 (e)	—	33.00	70.00	120	175	—
(1)605 (e)	—	33.00	70.00	120	175	—
(1)606 (e)	—	33.00	70.00	120	175	—
1607 (e)	—	33.00	70.00	120	175	—
(1)607 (e)	—	33.00	70.00	120	175	—
1608 (e)	—	33.00	70.00	120	175	—

KM# 8 1/24 THALER (Furstengroschen)

Silver **Ruler:** Simon VI **Obv:** Ornate helmet above 4-fold arms **Rev:** Imperial orb with Z4, date divided upper left and right, titles of Rudolf II **Note:** Varieties exist.

Date	Mintage	VG	F	VF	XF	Unc
1607 (e)	—	27.00	45.00	85.00	140	—
1608 (e)	—	27.00	45.00	85.00	140	—
1609 (f)	—	27.00	45.00	85.00	140	—
1610 (f)	—	27.00	45.00	85.00	140	—
1610 (h)	—	27.00	45.00	85.00	140	—
1611 (h)	—	27.00	45.00	85.00	140	—
161Z (h)	—	27.00	45.00	85.00	140	—

KM# 17 1/24 THALER (Furstengroschen)

Silver **Ruler:** Simon VI **Obv:** Crowned shield **Rev:** Titles of Matthias **Note:** Varieties exist.

Date	Mintage	VG	F	VF	XF	Unc
1613 (h)	—	27.00	45.00	85.00	140	—
1613	—	27.00	45.00	85.00	140	—

KM# 10 THALER

Silver **Ruler:** Simon VI **Note:** Dav. #6884.

Date	Mintage	VG	F	VF	XF	Unc
1601 Rare	—	—	—	—	—	—

KM# 15 THALER

Silver **Ruler:** Simon VI **Obv:** Helmeted arms **Rev:** Crowned imperial eagle with date divided below **Note:** Dav. #6886.

Date	Mintage	VG	F	VF	XF	Unc
1612 (h) Rare	—	—	—	—	—	—

KM# 16 2 THALER

Silver **Ruler:** Simon VI **Obv:** Helmeted arms **Obv. Legend:** RVDOL. II. D. **Rev:** Crowned imperial eagle with date divided below **Note:** Dav. #6885.

Date	Mintage	VG	F	VF	XF	Unc
1612 (h) Rare	—	—	—	—	—	—

LIPPE-DETMOLD

The Counts of Lippe ruled over a small state in northwestern Germany. In 1528/9 they became counts; in 1720 they were raised to the rank of princes, but did not use the title until 1789. Another branch of the family ruled the even smaller Schaumburg-Lippe. Lippe joined North German Confederation in 1866, and became part of the German Empire in 1871. When the insane Prince Alexander succeeded to the throne in 1895, the main branch reached an end, and a ten-year testamentary dispute between the Biesterfeld and the Schaumburg-Lippe lines followed - a Wilhelmine cause celebre. The Biesterfeld line gained the principality in 1905, but abdicated in 1918. In 1947 Lippe was absorbed by the German Land of North Rhine-Westphalia.

RULERS

Simon VI, 1563-1613
Simon VII, 1613-1627
Simon Ludwig, 1627-1636
Simon Philip, 1636-1650
Johann Bernhard, 1650-1652
Hermann Adolf, 1652-1666
Simon Heinrich, 1666-1697
Friedrich Adolf, 1697-1718

MINT OFFICIALS' INITIALS

Initial	Date	Name
B/TB	1678-1716	Thomas (or Tobias) Bernard, die-cutter in Paris
IH/(e)	1671-95	Johann Hoffmann in Detmold
(a)=	1610-18	Caspar Kholl (Kohl, Khol) at Blomberg
(b)=	1619-20	Jacob Pfahler of Marsberg
(c)=	1618	Valentin Riemer
(d)=	1620-21	Ippo Rizema (Ritzema)
	c.1636-55	Michael Kuttner
	1655-58	Johann Kuttneer, superintendant
	1658-60	Christoph Henning Schluter
	1661-69	Hans Georg Moser

PRINCIPALITY

REGULAR COINAGE

KM# 11 1/2 PFENNIG (Groschen)

Copper **Ruler:** Simon VII **Obv:** Rose in circle **Rev:** Value 1/2 in ornate rectangle **Note:** Kipper 1/2 Pfennig. Varieties exist.

Date	Mintage	VG	F	VF	XF	Unc
ND(1619)	100,000	10.00	25.00	45.00	85.00	—

KM# 35 1/2 PFENNIG (Groschen)

0.3200 g., Silver **Ruler:** Simon VII **Obv:** Rose in shield divides date as 2 - 1, crown above. **Note:** Uniface.

Date	Mintage	VG	F	VF	XF	Unc
(16)21	—	9.00	20.00	40.00	80.00	—

KM# 43 1/2 PFENNIG (Groschen)

Copper **Ruler:** Simon VII **Obv:** Rose in ring of 5 small stars alternating with 5 pellets, in circle of pellets **Rev:** Value 1/2 in ornate rectangle, 4 small stars flank upper and lower ornaments, a lily flanks 1/2, in circle of pellets

Date	Mintage	VG	F	VF	XF	Unc
ND(1623)	—	13.00	27.00	55.00	100	—

KM# 50 1/2 PFENNIG (Groschen)

Copper **Ruler:** Simon Philip **Obv:** Linear circle **Rev:** Lily-like ornamentation on sides of rectangle, without outer circle

Date	Mintage	VG	F	VF	XF	Unc
ND(1636-38)	98,000	10.00	20.00	40.00	80.00	—

KM# 60 1/2 PFENNIG (Groschen)

Copper **Ruler:** Simon Philip **Rev:** 1/2 within 4 floral ornaments **Note:** Varieties exist.

Date	Mintage	VG	F	VF	XF	Unc
ND(1644-69)	623,000	10.00	20.00	40.00	80.00	—

KM# 92 1/2 PFENNIG (Groschen)

Billon **Ruler:** Simon Heinrich **Obv:** Rose in center, variety of small stars, rosettes, pellets and/or crosses around **Rev:** 1/2 in center, variety of ornaments around **Note:** Varieties exist.

Date	Mintage	VG	F	VF	XF	Unc
ND(1675-92)	86,000	13.00	27.00	55.00	100	—

KM# 12 PFENNING

Copper **Ruler:** Simon VII **Obv:** Rose in circle **Rev:** Value 1 in ornate rectangle

Date	Mintage	VG	F	VF	XF	Unc
ND(1619)	90,000	27.00	45.00	100	200	—

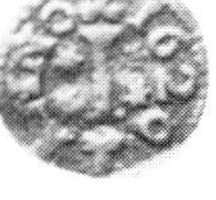

KM# 25 PFENNING

Copper **Ruler:** Simon VII **Obv:** DITMAL around rose **Rev:** ANNO, date around value 1 **Note:** Varieties exist.

Date	Mintage	VG	F	VF	XF	Unc
1620	—	20.00	40.00	80.00	160	—

KM# 44 PFENNING

Copper **Ruler:** Simon VII **Obv:** Rose in ring of 5 small stars alternating with 5 pellets in circle of pellets **Rev:** Value 1 in ornate rectangle, 4 small stars flank upper and lower ornaments, a lily at either side of 1/2, in circle of pellets

Date	Mintage	VG	F	VF	XF	Unc
ND(1623)	—	20.00	40.00	80.00	160	—

KM# 51 PFENNING

Copper **Ruler:** Simon Philip **Obv:** Legend is around rose **Obv. Legend:** LIPP.LANT.MVN(T)Z **Rev:** Value 1 in rectangle, lily-like decorations on sides

Date	Mintage	VG	F	VF	XF	Unc
ND(1636-38)	142,000	16.00	33.00	65.00	135	—

KM# 61 PFENNING

Copper **Ruler:** Simon Philip **Obv:** Rose, 5 large rosettes and 5 small stars around **Rev:** 1 within 4 floral ornaments, flanked by 4 rosettes **Note:** Varieties exist.

Date	Mintage	VG	F	VF	XF	Unc
ND(1644-69)	422,000	16.00	33.00	65.00	135	—

KM# 94 PFENNING

Billon **Ruler:** Simon Heinrich **Obv:** Rose in circle **Rev:** 1 in circle

Date	Mintage	VG	F	VF	XF	Unc
ND(1675-92)	72,000	—	—	—	—	—

KM# 62 1-1/2 PFENNING (1/192 Thaler)

Copper **Ruler:** Simon Philip **Obv:** Leged is around rose **Obv. Legend:** LIPP.LANT.MVNTZ **Rev:** Value 1-1/2 surrounded by circle of small stars and rosettes **Note:** Varieties exist.

Date	Mintage	VG	F	VF	XF	Unc
ND(1644-69)	192,000	7.00	20.00	33.00	55.00	—

KM# 96 1-1/2 PFENNING (1/192 Thaler)

Copper **Ruler:** Simon Heinrich **Obv:** Rose **Rev. Legend:** 1-1/2/LIPP/PFEN/NINGE

Date	Mintage	VG	F	VF	XF	Unc
ND(1675-92)	288,000	7.00	20.00	33.00	55.00	—

KM# 13 2 PFENNING

Copper **Ruler:** Simon VII **Obv:** Rose in circle **Rev:** Value II in ornate rectangle **Note:** Kipper 2 Pfennig.

Date	Mintage	VG	F	VF	XF	Unc
ND(1619)	66,000	9.00	20.00	40.00	70.00	—

KM# 26 2 PFENNING

Copper **Ruler:** Simon VII **Obv:** DITMAL around rose **Rev:** ANNO, date around II **Note:** Varieties exist.

Date	Mintage	VG	F	VF	XF	Unc
1620	—	16.00	33.00	60.00	100	—

KM# 45 2 PFENNING

Copper **Ruler:** Simon VII **Obv:** Rose in ring of 5 small stars alternating with 5 pellets in circle of pellets **Rev:** Value II in ornate rectangle, 4 small stars flank upper and lower ornaments, a lily on sides of 1/2 in circle of pellets **Note:** Varieties exist.

Date	Mintage	VG	F	VF	XF	Unc
ND(1623)	—	16.00	33.00	60.00	100	—

KM# 52 2 PFENNING

Copper **Ruler:** Simon Philip **Obv:** Legend around rose **Obv. Legend:** LIPP.LANT.MVN(T)Z **Rev:** Value II in rectangle, lily-like decorations at sides

Date	Mintage	VG	F	VF	XF	Unc
ND(1636-38)	287,000	13.00	27.00	45.00	100	—

KM# 63 2 PFENNING

Copper **Ruler:** Simon Philip **Obv:** Legend around rose **Obv. Legend:** LIPP.LANT.MVNTZ **Rev:** II within 8 floral ornaments **Note:** Varieties exist.

Date	Mintage	VG	F	VF	XF	Unc
ND(1644-69)	186,000	13.00	27.00	45.00	100	—

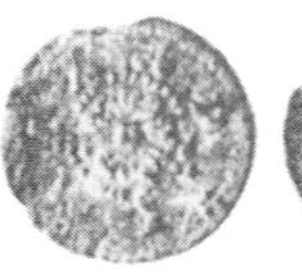 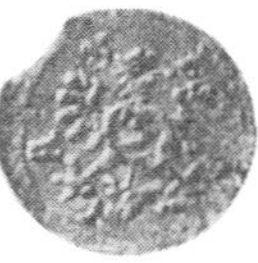

KM# 21 3 PFENNINGE

Silver **Ruler:** Simon VII **Obv:** Rose, around DITMAL **Rev:** Imperial eagle, 3 in orb on breast

Date	Mintage	VG	F	VF	XF	Unc
ND(1619-20)	—	20.00	40.00	65.00	120	—

KM# 14 3 PFENNINGE

Copper **Ruler:** Simon VII **Obv:** Rose in circle **Rev:** Value III in ornate rectangle **Note:** Kipper 3 Pfennig. Varieties exist.

Date	Mintage	VG	F	VF	XF	Unc
ND(1619)	15,000	20.00	40.00	80.00	140	—

KM# 15 3 PFENNINGE

Copper **Ruler:** Simon VII **Obv:** DITMAL around rose **Rev:** ANNO, date around **Note:** Varieties exist.

Date	Mintage	VG	F	VF	XF	Unc
1619	Inc. above	27.00	50.00	100	160	—

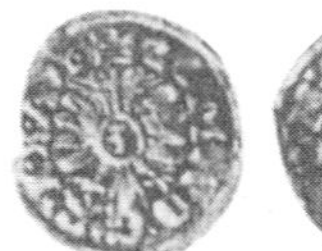

KM# 27 3 PFENNINGE

Silver **Ruler:** Simon VII **Obv:** Rose, titles of Simon VII **Rev:** Crowned imperial eagle, 3 in orb on breast, titles of Matthias (sic) and date

Date	Mintage	VG	F	VF	XF	Unc
1620	—	20.00	40.00	65.00	120	—
16Z0	—	20.00	40.00	65.00	120	—

KM# 41 3 PFENNINGE

Silver **Ruler:** Simon VII **Obv:** 4-fold arms **Rev:** Imperial eagle, 3 in orb on breast, date divided above

Date	Mintage	VG	F	VF	XF	Unc
1622	—	13.00	27.00	55.00	100	—

KM# 46 3 PFENNINGE

Silver **Ruler:** Simon VII **Obv:** Rose in ring of 5 small stars alternating with 5 pellets in circle of pellets **Rev:** Value III in ornate rectangle, 4 small stars flank upper and lower ornaments, a lily on sides of 1/2 in circle of pellets **Note:** Varieties exist.

Date	Mintage	VG	F	VF	XF	Unc
ND(1623)	—	20.00	40.00	65.00	120	—

KM# 53 3 PFENNINGE

Silver **Ruler:** Simon Philip **Obv:** Legend around rose **Obv. Legend:** LIPP.LANT.MVN(T)Z **Rev:** Value III in rectangle, lily-like decorations at sides

Date	Mintage	VG	F	VF	XF	Unc
ND(1636-38)	435,000	9.00	27.00	40.00	80.00	—

KM# 64 3 PFENNINGE

Silver **Ruler:** Simon Philip **Note:** Varieties exist.

Date	Mintage	VG	F	VF	XF	Unc
ND(1644-69)	320,000	9.00	27.00	40.00	80.00	—

KM# 65 6 PFENNIG

Copper **Ruler:** Simon Philip **Obv:** Legend around rose **Obv. Legend:** LIPP.LANT.MVNTZ **Rev:** VI in square, 8 lily-like floral ornaments around **Note:** Varieties exist.

Date	Mintage	VG	F	VF	XF	Unc
ND(1644-69)	167,000	7.00	25.00	35.00	65.00	—

Note: This 6 Pfennig was later countermarked, in 1671, by a small rose with thick petals and again, in 1685, by a double rose

KM# 75 6 PFENNIG

Copper **Ruler:** Simon Heinrich **Countermark:** Small rose with thick petals

Date	Mintage	VG	F	VF	XF	Unc
ND(1671)	—	7.00	25.00	35.00	65.00	—

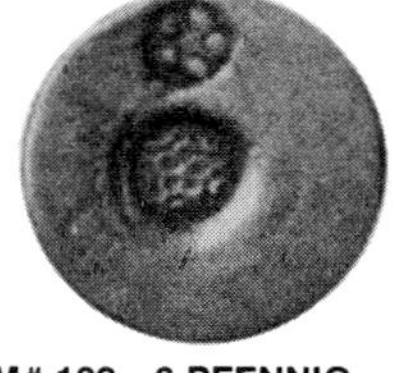 

KM# 102 6 PFENNIG

Copper **Ruler:** Simon Heinrich **Countermark:** Second countermark a double rose

Date	Mintage	VG	F	VF	XF	Unc
ND(1685)	—	9.00	20.00	40.00	80.00	—

KM# 36 3 FLITTER (1-1/2 Pfennig)

Copper **Ruler:** Simon VII **Obv:** Rose in shield **Rev:** III/FLITTERN/date **Note:** Kipper 3 Flitter.

Date	Mintage	VG	F	VF	XF	Unc
(1)6Z1	—	10.00	27.00	40.00	75.00	—

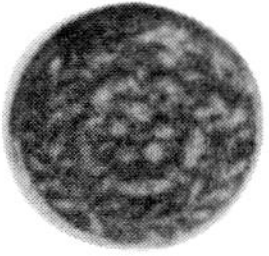 

KM# 77 MATTIER (4 Pfennig)

Silver **Ruler:** Simon Heinrich **Obv:** Rose in laurel wreath **Rev. Legend:** 16I72/MATTIER/GR.LIPP.L./M(UNTZ) **Note:** Varieties exist.

Date	Mintage	VG	F	VF	XF	Unc
1672	35,000	16.00	35.00	70.00	120	—

KM# 78 MATTIER (4 Pfennig)

Silver **Ruler:** Simon Heinrich **Obv:** Rose with alternating rosettes, stars or pellets **Note:** Varieties exist.

Date	Mintage	VG	F	VF	XF	Unc
1672	Inc. above	16.00	35.00	70.00	120	—
1673	32,000	16.00	35.00	70.00	120	—
1683	22,000	16.00	35.00	70.00	120	—

KM# 93 1/12 MARIENGROSCHEN

Copper **Ruler:** Simon Heinrich **Rev:** Value 12

Date	Mintage	VG	F	VF	XF	Unc
ND(1675-92)	Inc. above	33.00	65.00	120	200	—

KM# 95 1/6 MARIENGROSCHEN

Copper **Ruler:** Simon Heinrich **Obv:** Rose **Obv. Legend:** GREFLIGE.LIPP **Rev:** Imperial orb with 6 **Rev. Legend:** LANDT.MUNTZ(E) **Note:** Varieties exist.

Date	Mintage	VG	F	VF	XF	Unc
ND(1675-92)	Inc. above	—	—	—	—	—

KM# 42 MARIENGROSCHEN (1/36 Thaler)

Silver **Ruler:** Simon VII **Obv:** 4-fold arms, titles of Simon VII **Rev:** Madonna and child, date in legend **Note:** Varieties exist.

Date	Mintage	VG	F	VF	XF	Unc
(1)622	42,000	120	200	325	525	—

KM# 76 MARIENGROSCHEN (1/36 Thaler)

Silver **Ruler:** Simon Heinrich **Obv:** Rose in laurel wreath, 36 below **Rev:** I/MARI/GROS, date **Rev. Legend:** GRE.PIPP.LANDT.MUNTZ **Note:** Varieties exist.

Date	Mintage	VG	F	VF	XF	Unc
1671	5,400	33.00	60.00	110	185	—
1672	18,000	33.00	60.00	110	185	—

KM# 79 MARIENGROSCHEN (1/36 Thaler)

Silver **Ruler:** Simon Heinrich **Rev:** I/MARI/GROZ, date **Note:** Varieties exist.

Date	Mintage	VG	F	VF	XF	Unc
1672	30,000	40.00	65.00	120	200	—

KM# 90 MARIENGROSCHEN (1/36 Thaler)

Silver **Ruler:** Simon Heinrich **Rev:** Date **Rev. Legend:** G.LIP.LANT.MUNZ

Date	Mintage	VG	F	VF	XF	Unc
1673	—	60.00	115	200	325	—

KM# 54 2 MARIENGROSCHEN (1/18 Thaler)

Silver **Ruler:** Simon Philip **Obv:** Crowned 4-fold arms, date **Obv. Legend:** DEO.FAVENTE **Rev:** II/MAR/GR **Rev. Legend:** GRAF:LIPP.LANDT.MV(N) **Note:** Varieties exist.

Date	Mintage	VG	F	VF	XF	Unc
1638	25,000	20.00	40.00	80.00	200	—

KM# 70 2 MARIENGROSCHEN (1/18 Thaler)

Silver **Ruler:** Hermann Adolf **Obv:** Crowned HA monogram, date above **Rev:** II/MARI/GR **Note:** Varieties exist.

Date	Mintage	VG	F	VF	XF	Unc
1658	—	55.00	110	200	525	—

KM# 80 2 MARIENGROSCHEN (1/18 Thaler)
Silver **Ruler:** Simon Heinrich **Obv:** Crowned SH monogram **Obv. Legend:** GR.LIPP.SILB.MUNZ **Rev:** 16 II 72/MARI/GR **Rev. Legend:** 18.EINEN.R.THAL.WERT **Note:** Varieties exist.

Date	Mintage	VG	F	VF	XF	Unc
1672	8,550	16.00	33.00	60.00	100	—

KM# 81 2 MARIENGROSCHEN (1/18 Thaler)
Silver **Ruler:** Simon Heinrich **Rev:** Date in legend **Note:** Varieties exist.

Date	Mintage	VG	F	VF	XF	Unc
1672	6,300	16.00	33.00	60.00	100	—

KM# 71 4 MARIENGROSCHEN (1/9 Thaler)
Silver **Ruler:** Hermann Adolf **Obv:** Crowned HA monogram, date above **Obv. Legend:** GR.LIPP.SILBER.MVNTZ **Rev:** IIII/MARI/GR **Rev. Legend:** 9.EINEN.THALER.WEHRT **Note:** Varieties exist.

Date	Mintage	VG	F	VF	XF	Unc
1658	—	80.00	160	325	800	—

KM# 82 4 MARIENGROSCHEN (1/9 Thaler)
Silver **Ruler:** Simon Heinrich **Obv:** Crowned SH monogram, date **Obv. Legend:** G(R).LIPP.SILBER.MVN(T)Z **Note:** Varieties exist.

Date	Mintage	VG	F	VF	XF	Unc
1672 IH/(e)	14,000	20.00	45.00	80.00	120	—

KM# 83 4 MARIENGROSCHEN (1/9 Thaler)
Silver **Ruler:** Simon Heinrich **Rev:** Date in legend **Note:** Varieties exist.

Date	Mintage	VG	F	VF	XF	Unc
1672 IH	12,000	20.00	45.00	80.00	120	—
1672 IH/(e)	Inc. above	20.00	45.00	80.00	120	—

KM# 84 4 MARIENGROSCHEN (1/9 Thaler)
Silver **Ruler:** Simon Heinrich **Rev:** Date **Rev. Inscription:** IIII/MARIEN/GROS **Note:** Varieties exist.

Date	Mintage	VG	F	VF	XF	Unc
1672 IH	59,000	33.00	65.00	120	200	—

KM# A85 6 MARIENGROSCHEN (1/6 Thaler)
Silver **Ruler:** Simon Heinrich **Obv:** Crowned 4-fold arms **Rev. Legend:** G.KIPP.SILBER.MUNTZ.ANNO **Rev. Inscription:** VI / MARIEN / GROS / date

Date	Mintage	VG	F	VF	XF	Unc
1671	—	135	275	525	1,000	—

KM# 85 6 MARIENGROSCHEN (1/6 Thaler)
Silver **Ruler:** Simon Heinrich **Obv:** Crowned 4-fold arms **Rev. Legend:** GR.LIPP.SILBER.MUNTZ **Rev. Inscription:** VI / MARIEN / GROSS / date **Note:** Varieties exist.

Date	Mintage	VG	F	VF	XF	Unc
1672 IH	23,000	115	200	325	600	—

KM# 101 24 MARIENGROSCHEN (2/3 Thale)
Silver **Ruler:** Simon Heinrich **Obv:** Crowned 4-fold arms in baroque frame, value (2/3) below **Rev:** Date **Rev. Inscription:** XXIIII / MARIEN / GROSCH

Date	Mintage	VG	F	VF	XF	Unc
1683 IH	1,815	900	1,600	2,750	4,500	—

KM# 16 12 KREUZER (Driebatzner)
Silver **Ruler:** Simon VII **Obv:** Large, ornate helmet above 4-fold arms **Rev:** Crowned imperial eagle, 12 in orb on breast, titles of Matthias, date **Note:** Varieties exist.

Date	Mintage	VG	F	VF	XF	Unc
1619	8,012	160	300	575	1,000	—

KM# 17 12 KREUZER (Driebatzner)
Silver **Ruler:** Simon VII **Obv:** Titles of Ferdinand II **Note:** Varieties exist.

Date	Mintage	VG	F	VF	XF	Unc
1619	224,000	135	275	460	875	—
16Z0 (b)	—	135	275	460	875	—

KM# 28 12 KREUZER (Driebatzner)
Silver **Ruler:** Simon VII **Rev:** Crowned 4-fold arms

Date	Mintage	VG	F	VF	XF	Unc
16Z0	—	135	275	460	875	—

KM# 29 12 KREUZER (Driebatzner)
Silver **Ruler:** Simon VII **Rev:** Single large rose in shield, large crown above

Date	Mintage	VG	F	VF	XF	Unc
16Z0	—	135	275	460	875	—

KM# 37 12 KREUZER (Driebatzner)
Silver **Ruler:** Simon VII **Obv. Legend:** LANDTMVNZ - ZV - **Rev:** Date in legend **Note:** Varieties exist.

Date	Mintage	VG	F	VF	XF	Unc
1621	—	135	275	460	875	—

KM# 38 12 KREUZER (Driebatzner)
Silver **Ruler:** Simon VII **Obv:** Legend ends GS **Note:** Varieties exist.

Date	Mintage	VG	F	VF	XF	Unc
1621	—	135	275	460	875	—

KM# 97 15 KREUZER (1/6 Thaler)
Silver **Ruler:** Simon Heinrich **Obv:** Crowned imperial eagle, XV in orb on breast, titles of Leopold I **Rev:** Helmeted arms, titles of Simon Heinrich **Note:** Varieties exist.

Date	Mintage	VG	F	VF	XF	Unc
ND(ca. 1675)	4,800	—	—	—	—	—

KM# 5 1/24 THALER (Furstengroschen)
Silver **Ruler:** Simon VII **Obv:** Ornate helmet above 4-fold arms **Rev:** Imperial orb with Z4, cross above divides date, titles of Matthias **Note:** Varieties exist.

Date	Mintage	VG	F	VF	XF	Unc
1614 (a)	—	27.00	55.00	100	165	—
1614 (b)	—	27.00	55.00	100	165	—
1615 (a)	—	27.00	55.00	100	165	—
1615 (b)	—	27.00	55.00	100	165	—
1615	—	27.00	55.00	100	165	—
1616 (a)	—	27.00	55.00	100	165	—
1616 (b)	—	27.00	55.00	100	165	—
1616	—	27.00	55.00	100	165	—
1617 (b)	452,000	27.00	55.00	100	165	—
1618 (b)	—	27.00	55.00	100	165	—
1618 (c)	—	27.00	55.00	100	165	—

KM# 18 1/24 THALER (Furstengroschen)
Silver **Ruler:** Simon VII **Obv:** Helmeted shield within circle **Rev:** Date in legend **Note:** Varieties exist.

Date	Mintage	VG	F	VF	XF	Unc
1619 (b)	165,000	20.00	40.00	70.00	140	—

KM# 19 1/24 THALER (Furstengroschen)
Silver **Ruler:** Simon VII **Rev:** Titles of Ferdinand II **Note:** Varieties exist.

Date	Mintage	VG	F	VF	XF	Unc
1619 (b)	289,000	20.00	40.00	70.00	140	—
1620 (b)	—	20.00	40.00	70.00	140	—
(1)6Z0	—	20.00	40.00	70.00	140	—

KM# 55 1/24 THALER (Furstengroschen)
Silver **Ruler:** Simon Philip **Obv:** Helmeted 4-fold arms **Rev:** Titles of Ferdinand III **Rev. Legend:** MONET:NOV.COMIT.LIPP **Note:** Varieties exist.

Date	Mintage	VG	F	VF	XF	Unc
1638	14,000	60.00	115	225	375	—
1639	Inc. above	65.00	135	275	475	—

KM# 103 1/24 THALER (Furstengroschen)
Silver **Ruler:** Simon Heinrich **Obv:** Helmeted 4-fold arms, titles of Simon Heinrich **Rev:** Imperial orb with 24, cross above divides date **Rev. Legend:** GREFLIGE. LIPP. LANDT. MUNTZ **Note:** Groschen 1/24 Thaler. Varieties exist.

Date	Mintage	VG	F	VF	XF	Unc
1685 IH	432,000	45.00	85.00	160	275	—
1689 IH	502,000	60.00	115	200	325	—

KM# 31 1/21 THALER (1-1/2 Schilling)
Silver **Ruler:** Simon VII **Obv:** Date, 4-fold arms **Obv. Legend:** LANT MVNZ.XII.ZT TH **Rev:** Value in circle on breast of double-headed imperial eagle

Date	Mintage	VG	F	VF	XF	Unc
1620	—	110	200	375	600	—

KM# 30 1/21 THALER (1-1/2 Schilling)
Silver **Ruler:** Simon VII **Obv:** Crowned imperial eagle, 21 in orb on breast **Obv. Legend:** LANT MVNZ 21.ZUM.R.DALER **Rev:** Crowned 4-fold arms, date in legend **Note:** Kipper 1/21 Thaler. Varieties exist.

Date	Mintage	VG	F	VF	XF	Unc
1620 (b)	—	110	200	375	600	—

KM# 32 1/21 THALER (1-1/2 Schilling)
Silver **Ruler:** Simon VII **Obv:** Helmeted arms **Rev:** Value in legend XXI **Note:** Varieties exist.

Date	Mintage	VG	F	VF	XF	Unc
1620	—	100	175	325	525	—
1621	—	100	175	325	525	—

KM# 39 1/21 THALER (1-1/2 Schilling)
Silver **Ruler:** Simon VII **Obv:** Helmeted 4-fold arms, titles of Simon VII, date **Obv. Legend:** LANT MVNZ 21.ZUM.R.DALER

Date	Mintage	VG	F	VF	XF	Unc
1621	—	100	175	325	525	—

KM# 40 1/21 THALER (1-1/2 Schilling)
Silver **Ruler:** Simon VII **Obv:** Helmeted 4-fold arms **Rev:** Without value in orb on eagle's breast

Date	Mintage	VG	F	VF	XF	Unc
1621	—	80.00	165	300	500	—

KM# A72 1/4 THALER
Silver **Ruler:** Hermann Adolf **Obv:** Facing bust, turned slightly right, date in legend **Rev:** Crowned 4-fold arms in ornamented frame **Rev. Legend:** SPES.CONFISA...

Date	Mintage	VG	F	VF	XF	Unc
1658	—	2,500	4,250	7,500	11,000	—

KM# 86 1/3 THALER (1/2 Gulden)
Silver **Ruler:** Simon Heinrich **Rev:** Date in legend **Rev. Inscription:** III / EINEN / REICHS / THAL / I(e)H **Note:** Varieties exist.

Date	Mintage	VG	F	VF	XF	Unc
1672 I(e)H	41,000	55.00	100	190	325	—

KM# 72 1/2 THALER
Silver **Ruler:** Hermann Adolf **Obv:** Facing bust, turned slightly right, date in legend **Rev:** Crowned 4-fold arms in ornamented frame **Rev. Legend:** SPES.CONFISA **Note:** Varieties exist.

Date	Mintage	VG	F	VF	XF	Unc
1658	—	1,650	3,000	6,000	10,000	—

KM# 6 THALER
Silver **Ruler:** Simon VII **Obv:** Crowned imperial eagle with orb on breast, date **Obv. Legend:** MATIAS. I.D.G **Note:** Dav. #6888.

Date	Mintage	VG	F	VF	XF	Unc
1614 (a) Rare	—	—	—	—	—	—

KM# 9 THALER
Silver **Ruler:** Simon VII **Obv:** Helmeted arms within circle **Rev:** Crown above double-headed imperial eagle within circle **Rev. Legend:** MATHI * D * G ** **Note:** Dav. #6890.

Date	Mintage	VG	F	VF	XF	Unc
1617	—	6,500	12,000	20,000	—	—
1618 (d) Rare	—	—	—	—	—	—

KM# 33 THALER
Silver **Ruler:** Simon VII **Rev. Legend:** FERDINAND.II.D.G... **Note:** Dav. #6892.

Date	Mintage	VG	F	VF	XF	Unc
1620 Rare	—	—	—	—	—	—

KM# 47 THALER
Silver **Ruler:** Simon VII **Obv:** Helmeted arms within beaded circle **Rev:** Crown above double-headed eagle within beaded circle **Rev. Legend:** FERDINANDVS: II: D: G: ... **Note:** Dav. #6893.

Date	Mintage	VG	F	VF	XF	Unc
16Z3	3,754	1,200	2,500	4,500	8,000	—

KM# 73 THALER
Silver **Ruler:** Hermann Adolf **Note:** Dav. #6894.

Date	Mintage	VG	F	VF	XF	Unc
1658	—	400	800	1,850	4,500	—

KM# 87 THALER
Silver **Ruler:** Simon Heinrich **Note:** Dav. #6895.

Date	Mintage	VG	F	VF	XF	Unc
1672 IH	610	600	1,200	2,500	4,850	—

KM# 88 THALER
Silver **Ruler:** Simon Heinrich **Rev:** Date above helmeted arms
Note: Dav. #6895A.

Date	Mintage	VG	F	VF	XF	Unc
1672 IH	—	650	1,250	2,650	5,000	—

KM# 89 THALER
Silver **Ruler:** Simon Heinrich **Obv:** Larger head on bust
Note: Dav. #6896.

Date	Mintage	VG	F	VF	XF	Unc
1672 IH	910	650	1,250	2,650	5,000	—

KM# 100 THALER
Silver **Ruler:** Simon Heinrich **Obv:** Bust left **Rev:** Crowned mantled arms **Note:** Dav. #6897.

Date	Mintage	VG	F	VF	XF	Unc
1681	223	1,000	2,000	3,750	6,500	—

KM# 104 THALER
Silver **Ruler:** Simon Heinrich **Obv:** Bust right **Rev:** Crowned and supported arms above palm sprays **Note:** Dav. #6899.

Date	Mintage	VG	F	VF	XF	Unc
1685 IH	194	800	1,600	3,200	5,500	—

KM# 110 THALER
Silver **Ruler:** Simon Heinrich **Rev:** Crowned arms **Note:** Dav. #6900.

Date	Mintage	VG	F	VF	XF	Unc
1692 IH Rare	140	—	—	—	—	—

KM# 7 2 THALER
Silver **Ruler:** Simon VII **Obv:** Helmeted arms
Obv. Legend: I.D.G... **Rev:** Crowned imperial eagle with orb on breast, date below **Note:** Dav. #6887.

Date	Mintage	VG	F	VF	XF	Unc
1614 (a) Rare	—	—	—	—	—	—

KM# 10 2 THALER
Silver **Ruler:** Simon VII **Rev:** Date in legend divided by crown
Rev. Legend: MATHI*... **Note:** Dav. #6889.

Date	Mintage	VG	F	VF	XF	Unc
1617 Rare	—	—	—	—	—	—
1618 (d) Rare	—	—	—	—	—	—

KM# 34 2 THALER
Silver **Ruler:** Simon VII **Rev. Legend:** FERDINAND. II...
Note: Dav. #6891.

Date	Mintage	VG	F	VF	XF	Unc
1620 Rare	—	—	—	—	—	—

KM# 105 2 THALER
Silver **Ruler:** Simon Heinrich **Obv:** Bust right **Rev:** Crowned and supported arms above palm sprays **Note:** Dav. #6898.

Date	Mintage	VG	F	VF	XF	Unc
1685 Rare	—	—	—	—	—	—

TRADE COINAGE

KM# 8 GOLDGULDEN
3.5000 g., 0.9860 Gold 0.1109 oz. AGW **Ruler:** Simon VII
Obv: Ornate helmet above 4-fold arms **Rev:** Crowned imperial eagle, orb on breast, date divided by legs of eagle, titles of Matthias

Date	Mintage	VG	F	VF	XF	Unc
1615 Rare	—	—	—	—	—	—

KM# 20 GOLDGULDEN
3.5000 g., 0.9860 Gold 0.1109 oz. AGW **Ruler:** Simon VII
Obv: Arms topped by helm in inner circle **Rev:** Crowned imperial eagle, date in legend, titles of Matthias

Date	Mintage	VG	F	VF	XF	Unc
1619 Rare	—	—	—	—	—	—

KM# 91 DUCAT
3.5000 g., 0.9860 Gold 0.1109 oz. AGW **Ruler:** Simon Heinrich
Obv: Bust of Simon Heinrich right **Rev:** Arms **Rev. Legend:** CLEMENTE DEO...

Date	Mintage	VG	F	VF	XF	Unc
1673 IH	186	1,200	2,500	4,500	7,500	—
1685	—	1,200	2,500	4,500	7,500	—

KM# 106 DUCAT
3.5000 g., 0.9860 Gold 0.1109 oz. AGW **Ruler:** Simon Heinrich
Obv: Bust right **Rev:** Crowned oval 4-fold arms, supported by 2 lions, palm fronds and date below **Rev. Legend:** NEC TEMERE NEC TIMIDE

Date	Mintage	VG	F	VF	XF	Unc
1685 IH	276	1,200	2,500	4,500	7,500	—

KM# 107 1-1/2 DUCAT
5.2500 g., 0.9860 Gold 0.1664 oz. AGW **Ruler:** Simon Heinrich
Obv: Bust of Simon Heinrich right **Rev:** Crowned arms

Date	Mintage	VG	F	VF	XF	Unc
1685	—	3,000	4,500	7,500	13,000	—
1692 IH	—	3,000	4,500	7,500	13,000	—

KM# 108 3 DUCAT
10.5000 g., 0.9860 Gold 0.3328 oz. AGW **Ruler:** Simon Heinrich
Obv: Bust of Simon Heinrich right **Rev:** Crowned arms

Date	Mintage	VG	F	VF	XF	Unc
1685 Rare	—	—	—	—	—	—
1692 Rare	—	—	—	—	—	—

KM# 109 4 DUCAT
14.0000 g., 0.9860 Gold 0.4438 oz. AGW **Ruler:** Simon Heinrich
Obv: Bust of Simon Heinrich right **Rev:** Crowned arms

Date	Mintage	VG	F	VF	XF	Unc
1685 Rare	—	—	—	—	—	—

KM# A74 5 DUCAT
17.5000 g., 0.9860 Gold 0.5547 oz. AGW **Ruler:** Hermann Adolf

Date	Mintage	VG	F	VF	XF	Unc
1658 Rare	—	—	—	—	—	—

Note: Struck with 1/2 Thaler dies, KM#72

KM# 111 6 DUCAT
21.0000 g., 0.9860 Gold 0.6657 oz. AGW **Ruler:** Simon Heinrich
Note: Struck with 1 Thaler dies, KM#110.

Date	Mintage	VG	F	VF	XF	Unc
1692 IH Rare	—	—	—	—	—	—

PATTERNS

Including off metal strikes

KM#	Date	Mintage	Identification	Mkt Val
Pn2	1672 IH	—	Thaler. Gold. KM#87.	—
Pn3	1673 IH	—	Ducat. Silver. Weight of 1/4 Thaler, KM#91.	—
Pn4	1673 IH	—	Ducat. Silver. Bust right. Crowned ornate arms. Klippe, weight of 1/4 Thaler, KM#91.	—
Pn5	1685 IH	—	Thaler. Gold. KM#104.	—
Pn6	1685 IH	—	Ducat. Silver. Weight of 1/4 Thaler, KM#106.	850

LORRAINE

(Lothringen)

Lorraine was established as a kingdom for Lothaire in the mid-9th century and was a part of the Carolingian Empire. It emerged as a duchy in the early 10th century and eventually became a buffer state between Germany and France. By 955, following several revolts which had their roots in Lorraine, Emperor Otto I (936-73) divided the territory in Lower Lorraine, which later became Brabant, and Upper Lorraine, the region which stretched along the Meuse and Mosel Rivers southwards to Burgundy. It is the latter entity, often associated with Alsace (see), which has come down to modern Europe as Lorraine.

The duchy was often a source of contention between the emperors and the kings of France, especially in the 17th century. France occupied it several times, from 1634-41, 1643-44, 1654-61, and 1673-75, and then again 1690-97. In 1736, duke Franz III married Maria Theresa, daughter of Emperor Karl VI and reigned as Emperor Franz I (1745-65). He exchanged Lorraine with France at the end of 1736 and received the Grand Duchy of Tuscany as compensation in the following year. The former King of Poland, Stanislaw Leszczinski, succeeded Franz III (I) in Lorraine, but the duchy was finally incorporated into France upon his death in 1766. Along with Alsace, Lorraine was acquired by the German Empire after the defeat of France by Prussia in the Franco-Prussian War of 1870-71. The Treaty of Versailles returned Alsace and Lorraine to France in 1919.

RULERS
Renatus II, 1473-1508
Anton, 1508-1544
Franz I, 1544-1545
Nikolaus von Vaudemont, administrator 1545-1552
Karl II, 1545-1608
Heinrich, 1608-1624
Nikolaus, 1624-1625
Franz II, 1625, coins issued in his name 1625-32 by the Badenweiler Mint
Karl III, 1625-34, 1661-73 (died 1675)
Karl IV, 1675-1690
French Occupation, 1690-97
Leopold, (1690) 1697-1729
Franz III, 1729-1736

MINTS
Badenweiler
Florence
Nancy
Romarti (Remiremont)
Stenay

MINT MARKS
G – Unknown mint official at Nancy, late 16th-early 17th c.
A – Paris

ARMS
Lorraine – band from upper left to lower right on which 3 small eagles
Bar – two fish standing on tails, four small crosses around

MONETARY SYSTEM
3 Deniers = 1 Liard
4 Liards = 1 Sol
25 Sols = 1 Livre
6 Livres = 1 Ecu
4 Ecus = 1 Louis D'or

DUCHY

STANDARD COINAGE

KM# 25 OBOL
Copper **Ruler:** Karl III and Nikolaus **Obv:** Crowned double cross
Rev: Ornamental cross **Mint:** Nancy

Date	Mintage	VG	F	VF	XF	Unc
ND(1624-25)	—	20.00	40.00	70.00	120	—

KM# 26 OBOL
Copper **Ruler:** Karl III and Nikolaus **Obv:** Jerusalem cross
Rev: Crowned double cross

Date	Mintage	VG	F	VF	XF	Unc
ND(1624-25)	—	20.00	40.00	70.00	120	—

KM# 27 OBOL

Copper **Ruler:** Karl III **Obv:** Two-part arms **Rev:** Crowned bird

Date	Mintage	VG	F	VF	XF	Unc
ND(1625-34)	—	18.00	35.00	60.00	100	—

KM# 50 OBOL

Copper **Ruler:** French Occupation **Obv:** Sword through crowned double cross **Rev:** Jerusalem cross

Date	Mintage	VG	F	VF	XF	Unc
ND(1634-41)	—	120	200	—	—	—

KM# 10 DENIER

Silver **Ruler:** Heinrich **Obv:** Crowned cross of Lorraine in cartouche **Rev:** Crowned eagle

Date	Mintage	VG	F	VF	XF	Unc
ND(1608-24)	—	16.00	33.00	65.00	130	—

KM# 11 DENIER

Silver **Ruler:** Heinrich **Obv:** Two-sectioned coat of arms **Rev:** Crowned cross of Lorraine between crowned eagles **Mint:** Nancy

Date	Mintage	VG	F	VF	XF	Unc
ND(1608-24)	—	16.00	33.00	65.00	130	—

KM# 12 DENIER

Silver **Ruler:** Heinrich **Obv:** Crowned "H" monogram **Rev:** Arms of Lorraine

Date	Mintage	VG	F	VF	XF	Unc
ND(1608-24)	—	16.00	33.00	65.00	130	—

KM# 28 DENIER

Silver **Ruler:** Karl III and Nikolaus **Obv:** Crowned eagles **Rev:** Crowned arms of Lorraine

Date	Mintage	VG	F	VF	XF	Unc
ND	—	16.00	33.00	65.00	130	—
1625	—	16.00	33.00	65.00	130	—

KM# 40 DENIER

Silver **Ruler:** Karl III **Obv:** Two crowned arms **Rev:** Crowned eagle

Date	Mintage	VG	F	VF	XF	Unc
ND(1626-34)	—	16.00	33.00	65.00	130	—

KM# 41 DENIER

Silver **Ruler:** Karl III **Obv:** Crowned cartouche with arms of Lorraine

Date	Mintage	VG	F	VF	XF	Unc
ND(1626-34)	—	16.00	33.00	65.00	130	—

KM# 51 DENIER

Silver **Ruler:** French Occupation **Obv:** Two-part arms **Rev:** Crowned eagle

Date	Mintage	VG	F	VF	XF	Unc
ND(1634-61)	—	—	—	—	—	—

KM# 52 DENIER

Silver **Ruler:** French Occupation **Obv:** Round arms of Lorraine

Date	Mintage	VG	F	VF	XF	Unc
ND(1634-61)	—	16.00	33.00	65.00	130	—

KM# 70 DENIER

Copper **Ruler:** Leopold Joseph as Leopold I **Obv:** Crowned arms **Rev:** Monogram within four crosses

Date	Mintage	VG	F	VF	XF	Unc
ND(1697-1729)	—	16.00	30.00	60.00	120	—

KM# 71 DENIER

Copper **Ruler:** Leopold Joseph as Leopold I **Rev:** Monogram with cross above and eagles at sides and bottom

Date	Mintage	VG	F	VF	XF	Unc
ND(1697-1729)	—	16.00	30.00	60.00	120	—

KM# 14 2 DENIER

Silver **Ruler:** Heinrich **Obv:** Crowned arms **Rev:** Crowned "H"

Date	Mintage	VG	F	VF	XF	Unc
ND(1608-24)	—	16.00	33.00	65.00	130	—

KM# 15 2 DENIER

Silver **Ruler:** Heinrich **Obv:** Crowned cross of Lorraine **Rev:** Jerusalem cross

Date	Mintage	VG	F	VF	XF	Unc
ND(1608-24)	—	16.00	33.00	65.00	130	—

KM# 13 2 DENIER

Silver **Ruler:** Heinrich **Obv:** Crowned above 2 adjacent arms **Rev:** Crowned eagle **Mint:** Nancy **Note:** Legend varieties exist.

Date	Mintage	VG	F	VF	XF	Unc
ND	—	16.00	33.00	65.00	130	—
1623	—	16.00	33.00	65.00	130	—
1624	—	16.00	33.00	65.00	130	—

KM# 29 2 DENIER

Silver **Ruler:** Karl III and Nikolaus **Obv:** Crowned eagle **Rev:** Crowned two-part arms between crosses of Lorraine

Date	Mintage	VG	F	VF	XF	Unc
1624	—	16.00	33.00	65.00	130	—
1625	—	16.00	33.00	65.00	130	—

KM# 42 2 DENIER

Silver **Ruler:** Karl III **Obv:** Crowned two-part arms **Rev:** Crowned eagle

Date	Mintage	VG	F	VF	XF	Unc
ND(1625-34)	—	9.00	20.00	45.00	100	—

KM# 43 2 DENIER

Silver **Ruler:** Karl III **Obv:** Two crowned arms **Rev:** Crowned cross of Lorraine

Date	Mintage	VG	F	VF	XF	Unc
ND(1625-34)	—	9.00	20.00	45.00	100	—

KM# 53 2 DENIER

Silver **Ruler:** French Occupation **Obv:** Crowned two-part arms **Rev:** Crowned eagle

Date	Mintage	VG	F	VF	XF	Unc
ND(1634-61)	—	—	—	—	—	—

KM# 74 15 DENIERS

Silver **Ruler:** Leopold Joseph as Leopold I **Obv:** Crowned double L monogram, three small eagles in field **Obv. Legend:** LEOP • I • D • G • D • LOT • BA • REX • IER • **Rev:** Cross of Lorraine with eagles in angles

Date	Mintage	VG	F	VF	XF	Unc
ND(1697-1729)	—	20.00	45.00	100	200	—

KM# 76 30 DENIERS

Silver **Ruler:** Leopold Joseph as Leopold I **Obv:** Crowned double L monogram, three small eagles in field **Rev:** Cross of Lorraine with eagles in angles **Note:** Similar to 15 Deniers, KM#74.

Date	Mintage	VG	F	VF	XF	Unc
ND(1697-1729)	—	27.00	45.00	100	210	—

KM# 77 30 DENIERS

Silver **Ruler:** Leopold Joseph as Leopold I **Obv:** Monogram in block letters **Rev:** Cross of Lorraine with eagles in angles **Note:** Similar to 15 Deniers, KM#74.

Date	Mintage	VG	F	VF	XF	Unc
ND(1697-1729)	—	16.00	33.00	65.00	160	—

KM# 82 SOL

Silver **Ruler:** Leopold Joseph as Leopold I **Obv:** Crown above two oval arms **Rev:** Crowned eagle **Mint:** Nancy

Date	Mintage	VG	F	VF	XF	Unc
ND(1697-1729)	—	13.00	27.00	55.00	110	—

KM# 83 SOL

Silver **Ruler:** Leopold Joseph as Leopold I **Obv:** Crowned two-part arms **Rev:** Eagle

Date	Mintage	VG	F	VF	XF	Unc
ND(1697-1729)	—	13.00	27.00	55.00	110	—

KM# 16 1/4 TESTON

Silver **Ruler:** Heinrich **Obv:** Bust right **Rev:** Cross of Lorraine

Date	Mintage	VG	F	VF	XF	Unc
ND(1608-24)	—	80.00	160	275	475	—

KM# 44 1/4 TESTON

Silver **Ruler:** Karl III **Obv:** Bust right **Rev:** Crowned arms **Mint:** Nancy

Date	Mintage	VG	F	VF	XF	Unc
1629	—	80.00	160	275	475	—

KM# 60 1/4 TESTON

Silver **Ruler:** Karl III **Note:** Similar to 1/2 Teston, KM#61.

Date	Mintage	VG	F	VF	XF	Unc
1663	—	75.00	150	240	400	—
1664	—	75.00	150	240	400	—
1665	—	75.00	150	240	400	—
1666	—	75.00	150	240	400	—
1668	—	75.00	150	240	400	—

KM# 61 1/2 TESTON

Silver **Ruler:** Karl III **Obv:** Armored bust **Mint:** Nancy

Date	Mintage	VG	F	VF	XF	Unc
1663	—	80.00	165	280	500	—
1664	—	80.00	165	280	500	—
1665	—	80.00	165	280	500	—
1666	—	80.00	165	280	500	—
1668	—	—	—	—	—	—

KM# 84 1/2 TESTON

Silver **Ruler:** Leopold Joseph as Leopold I **Obv:** Bust right **Rev:** Crowned arms

Date	Mintage	VG	F	VF	XF	Unc
1700	—	35.00	85.00	175	325	—

KM# 17.1 TESTON

9.0000 g., Silver **Ruler:** Heinrich **Obv:** Bust of Heinrich **Obv. Legend:** HENRI. DG. DVX. LOTH. MARCH. DC. BG **Mint:** Nancy

Date	Mintage	VG	F	VF	XF	Unc
ND(1608-24)	—	60.00	120	240	425	—

KM# 17.2 TESTON

9.0000 g., Silver **Ruler:** Heinrich **Obv. Legend:** ends: ...MARC. DC. BG.

Date	Mintage	VG	F	VF	XF	Unc
ND(1608-24)	—	60.00	120	240	425	—

KM# 18 TESTON

9.0000 g., Silver **Ruler:** Heinrich

Date	Mintage	VG	F	VF	XF	Unc
1614	—	60.00	120	240	425	—
1615	—	60.00	120	240	425	—

KM# 30 TESTON

9.0000 g., Silver **Ruler:** Karl III and Nikolaus **Mint:** Nancy

Date	Mintage	VG	F	VF	XF	Unc
1624	—	160	325	675	1,000	—
1625	—	160	325	675	1,000	—
1627	—	160	325	675	1,000	—

KM# 35 TESTON

9.0000 g., Silver **Ruler:** Franz II **Mint:** Badenweiler

Date	Mintage	VG	F	VF	XF	Unc
1626	—	80.00	160	275	475	—
1627	—	80.00	160	275	475	—
1628	—	80.00	160	275	475	—
1629	—	80.00	160	275	475	—
1630	—	80.00	160	275	475	—
1631	—	80.00	160	275	475	—

KM# 45 TESTON

9.0000 g., Silver **Ruler:** Karl III

Date	Mintage	VG	F	VF	XF	Unc
1626	—	110	200	325	650	—
1627	—	110	200	325	650	—
1628	—	110	200	325	650	—
1629	—	110	200	325	650	—
1630	—	110	200	325	650	—
1632	—	110	200	325	650	—

KM# 47 TESTON

9.0000 g., Silver **Ruler:** Karl III **Obv:** Cloaked bust of Christine **Obv. Legend:** CHRIST • LOTH. M. D... **Rev:** Crowned arms **Rev. Legend:** ends: ...FLORENT. CVSA. **Mint:** Florence

Date	Mintage	VG	F	VF	XF	Unc
1630	—	25,000	50,000	80,000	—	—

KM# 55 TESTON

9.0000 g., Silver **Obv:** Bust right **Rev:** Crowned arms

Date	Mintage	VG	F	VF	XF	Unc
1634	—	120	240	400	675	—
1635	—	120	240	400	675	—

KM# 56 TESTON

9.0000 g., Silver **Ruler:** Karl III **Mint:** Romarti

Date	Mintage	VG	F	VF	XF	Unc
1638	—	300	600	950	1,350	—
1639	—	300	600	950	1,350	—

KM# 62 TESTON

9.0000 g., Silver **Mint:** Nancy **Note:** Varieties exist.

Date	Mintage	VG	F	VF	XF	Unc
1663	—	80.00	160	275	475	—
1665	—	80.00	160	275	475	—
1666	—	80.00	160	275	475	—
1667	—	80.00	160	275	475	—
1668	—	80.00	160	275	475	—
1669	—	80.00	160	275	475	—

KM# 90 TESTON

Silver **Ruler:** Leopold Joseph as Leopold I **Obv:** Bust right **Rev:** Crowned plain oval arms **Mint:** Nancy

Date	Mintage	VG	F	VF	XF	Unc
1700	—	100	200	450	875	—

KM# 91 TESTON

Silver **Ruler:** Leopold Joseph as Leopold I **Rev:** Cross of Lorraine on crowned ornate oval arms

Date	Mintage	VG	F	VF	XF	Unc
1700	—	100	200	450	875	—

KM# 92 TESTON

Silver **Ruler:** Leopold Joseph as Leopold I **Obv:** Bust right **Obv. Legend:** LEOP • I • D • G • D • LOT • BA • REX • IE • **Rev:** Crowned oval shield within cartouche **Rev. Legend:** IN • TE • DOMINE • SPERAVI •

Date	Mintage	VG	F	VF	XF	Unc
1700	—	100	200	450	875	—

KM# 5 THALER

Silver **Ruler:** Karl II **Obv:** Bust of Karl II left, date on shoulder **Rev:** Eagle above crowned, mantled and supported arms **Note:** Dav. #6901.

Date	Mintage	VG	F	VF	XF	Unc
1601	—	900	1,800	3,500	6,000	—
1603	—	900	1,800	3,500	6,000	—

KM# 6 THALER

Silver **Ruler:** Karl II **Obv:** Bust breaking circle at bottom, date below **Rev:** Eagle above crowned, helmeted and mantled arms, seven shields around and two monograms in field **Note:** Dav. #6902.

Date	Mintage	VG	F	VF	XF	Unc
1603 Rare	—	—	—	—	—	—

KM# 36 THALER

Silver **Ruler:** Franz II **Obv:** Bust of Franz II right **Rev:** Date above crowned arms **Note:** Dav. #6903.

Date	Mintage	VG	F	VF	XF	Unc
1630 Rare	—	—	—	—	—	—
1632 Rare	—	—	—	—	—	—

KM# 37 THALER

Silver **Ruler:** Franz II **Obv:** Crowned arms divide date at sides **Rev:** Madonna standing in oval of flames **Note:** Dav. #6904.

Date	Mintage	VG	F	VF	XF	Unc
1632 Rare	—	—	—	—	—	—

KM# 63 THALER

Silver **Ruler:** Karl III, 2nd reign **Note:** Thick flan.

Date	Mintage	VG	F	VF	XF	Unc
1665 Rare	—	—	—	—	—	—
1668 Rare	—	—	—	—	—	—

KM# 104 THALER

Silver **Ruler:** Leopold Joseph as Leopold I **Obv:** Bust of Leopold I right **Rev:** Crowned oval arms **Note:** Dav. #6905.

Date	Mintage	VG	F	VF	XF	Unc
1700	—	1,000	2,000	3,750	6,500	—

TRADE COINAGE

KM# 19 1/2 GOLDGULDEN

1.7500 g., 0.9860 Gold 0.0555 oz. AGW **Ruler:** Heinrich **Obv:** Arms **Obv. Legend:** HENRI. D: G. LOTH **Rev:** St. Nicholas standing **Mint:** Nancy **Note:** Fr. #153.

Date	Mintage	VG	F	VF	XF	Unc
ND(1608-24)	—	900	1,800	3,000	4,500	—

KM# 20 GOLDGULDEN

3.5000 g., 0.9860 Gold 0.1109 oz. AGW **Ruler:** Heinrich **Mint:** Nancy **Note:** Fr. #152.

Date	Mintage	VG	F	VF	XF	Unc
ND(1608-24)	—	295	650	1,050	1,550	—

KM# 21.1 GOLDGULDEN

3.5000 g., 0.9860 Gold 0.1109 oz. AGW **Ruler:** Heinrich **Obv:** Bust of Henri **Obv. Legend:** ... MARC. DC. BG. **Note:** Fr. #154.

Date	Mintage	VG	F	VF	XF	Unc
ND(1608-24)	—	575	1,200	2,100	3,000	—

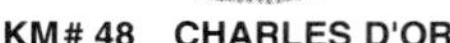

KM# 21.2 GOLDGULDEN
3.5000 g., 0.9860 Gold 0.1109 oz. AGW **Ruler:** Heinrich **Obv. Legend:** ... MARCH. DC. BG. **Note:** Fr. #154.

Date	Mintage	VG	F	VF	XF	Unc
ND(1608-24)	—	575	1,200	2,100	3,000	—

KM# 22 GOLDGULDEN
3.5000 g., 0.9860 Gold 0.1109 oz. AGW **Ruler:** Heinrich **Obv:** Head right **Note:** Fr. #154.

Date	Mintage	VG	F	VF	XF	Unc
1617	—	575	1,200	2,100	3,000	—

KM# 48 CHARLES D'OR
3.3600 g., 0.9520 Gold 0.1028 oz. AGW **Obv:** Bust of Karl III right **Rev:** Cross of crowned C monograms **Mint:** Paris

Date	Mintage	VG	F	VF	XF	Unc
1612A	—	1,900	3,750	6,300	10,500	—

KM# 64 CHARLES D'OR
3.3600 g., 0.9520 Gold 0.1028 oz. AGW **Obv:** Karl III **Mint:** Nancy **Note:** Fr. #157.

Date	Mintage	VG	F	VF	XF	Unc
1661	—	1,200	2,500	5,300	9,000	—
1662	—	1,200	2,500	5,300	9,000	—
1665	—	1,200	2,500	5,300	9,000	—
1668	—	1,200	2,500	5,300	9,000	—
1669	—	1,200	2,250	5,300	9,000	—

KM# 115 LEOPOLD D'OR
6.6900 g., 0.9170 Gold 0.1972 oz. AGW **Ruler:** Leopold Joseph as Leopold I **Obv:** Laureate head right **Obv. Legend:** LEOP • I • D • G • D • LOT • BAR • REX • IE • **Rev:** Crowned L's in cruciform, double crosses at angles **Rev. Legend:** TV • DOMINE • SPES • MEA **Mint:** Nancy **Note:** Fr. #158.

Date	Mintage	VG	F	VF	XF	Unc
1700	—	1,500	3,400	5,600	8,300	—

KM# 57 PISTOLE
6.6500 g., 0.9000 Gold 0.1924 oz. AGW **Obv:** Crowned arms **Obv. Legend:** CAROLVS. D: G... **Rev:** Cross of Jerusalem **Mint:** Romarti **Note:** Fr. #156.

Date	Mintage	VG	F	VF	XF	Unc
1639	—	850	1,750	3,200	5,000	—
ND	—	850	1,750	3,200	5,000	—

KM# A57 2 PISTOLES
13.3000 g., 0.9000 Gold 0.3848 oz. AGW **Ruler:** Karl III **Obv:** Date over large crown above manifold arms with central shield of Lorraine, small cross of Lorraine to either side, titles of Karl III **Obv. Legend:** CAROLUS. D: G... **Rev:** Cross of Jerusalem within octolobe **Rev. Legend:** DA. MIHI. VIRTV. CONTRA. HOSTES. TVOS. **Mint:** Romarti

Date	Mintage	VG	F	VF	XF	Unc
1631	—	1,200	2,600	4,500	6,600	—

LOWENBERG

(Lwowek, Lvuvek)

The city of Löwenberg is located in northwestern Silesia twenty miles southwest of Liegnitz. The Emperor Matthias as king of Bohemia granted the city permission to coin a commemorative thaler on the occasion of a shooting match festival held there in 1615.

MINT OFFICIAL

HR = Hans Rieger der Ältere, die-cutter in Breslau, ca. 1610-1653.

REFERENCES

L/S = Ferdinand Friedensburg and Hans Seger, **Schlesiens Münzen und Medaillen der neueren Zeit**, Breslau, 1901.
J/M = Norbert Jaschke and Fritz P. Maercker, **Schlesische Münzen und Medaillen**, Ihringen, 1985.

PROVINCIAL TOWN

KIPPER COINAGE

KM# 2 HELLER
Silver **Obv:** Lion striding to left **Note:** Uniface. L/S #3599.

Date	Mintage	VG	F	VF	XF	Unc
ND(1621)	—	30.00	70.00	120	—	—

KM# 3 3 HELLER
Copper **Obv:** Lion left in trefoil, date below **Note:** Uniface. J/M #932.

Date	Mintage	VG	F	VF	XF	Unc
1622	—	—	—	—	—	—

REGULAR COINAGE

KM# 5 THALER
Silver **Note:** Dav. #5429.

Date	Mintage	VG	F	VF	XF	Unc
1615 HR	—	200	450	1,000	2,000	—

KM# 6 THALER
Silver **Rev:** Without buds around border **Note:** Dav. #5429A.

Date	Mintage	VG	F	VF	XF	Unc
1615 HR	—	200	450	1,000	2,000	—

KM# 7 THALER
Silver **Rev:** Second line of inscription: DES GROSSEN, small date **Note:** Dav. #5430.

Date	Mintage	VG	F	VF	XF	Unc
1615 HR	—	225	500	1,150	2,250	—

KM# 8 2 THALER
Silver **Note:** Similar to 1 Thaler, KM#5. Dav. #5428.

Date	Mintage	VG	F	VF	XF	Unc
1615 HR Rare	—	—	—	—	—	—

LOWENSTEIN-WERTHEIM

The countship of Löwenstein was established by a division of the county lineage of Calw in northern Württemberg, in 1152. Löwenstein was sold to the Habsburgs in 1281 from which it eventually passed to the Palatinate (Pfalz) in 1441. A new line of counts was established in 1476 from the electoral Palatinate. Wertheim was obtained by marriage in 1600. The division of 1635 resulted in the separation of Löwenstein-Wertheim into 2 branches, Protestant and Catholic.

RULERS

Ludwig II, 1541-1611
Christoph Ludwig, 1611-1618 and
Ludwig III, 1611-1635 and
Wolfgang Ernst, 1611-1636 and
Johann Dietrich, 1611-1644
Friedrich Ludwig, 1618-1635

MINT OFFICIALS

Date	Name
1622 (February)	Heinrich Westermann in Wertheim
1622 (July)	Ernst Knorr the Elder in Wertheim

REFERENCES

K = Ulrich Klein, "Die Münzen der Grafen und Fürsten von Löwenstein-Wertheim," **700 Jahre Stadt Löwenstein**, Löwenstein (Württemberg), 1987.
W = Ferdinand Wibel, **Zur Münzgeschichte der Grafen von Wertheim und des Gesamthauses Löwenstein-Wertheim**, Hamburg, 1880.

COUNTSHIP

REGULAR COINAGE

KM# 14 HELLER
Copper, 25 mm. **Ruler:** Johann Dietrich **Obv:** Bust to right **Obv. Legend:** I. THEO. COM. LE. RO. SVP. CHASP. **Rev:** Crowned shield of 9-fold arms, date at end of legend **Rev. Legend:** IN. CVGNON. CVSVS. **Mint:** Cugnon **Note:** W#177. Prev. Löwenstein-Wertheim-Rochefort KM#12.

Date	Mintage	VG	F	VF	XF	Unc
1623	—	—	—	—	—	—

KM# 1 SCHILLING
Silver **Ruler:** Johann Dietrich **Obv:** Crowned shield of 4-fold arms **Obv. Legend:** MO. NOVA - ARG - ORDINE - CLER. **Rev:** Crowned imperial eagle in circle **Rev. Legend:** NISI TV DOMINE NOBISCVM EPVS. **Note:** Imitation of issue of Schaumburg-Pinneberg KM#75. CLER in obv. legend = Comitis Löwenstein Et Rochefort.

Date	Mintage	VG	F	VF	XF	Unc
ND(1611-35)	—	450	625	850	1,200	—

KM# 26 SCHILLING
Silver **Ruler:** Johann Dietrich **Obv:** Bust to right **Rev:** Date in legend **Mint:** Cugnon **Note:** W#176.

Date	Mintage	VG	F	VF	XF	Unc
1626	—	—	—	—	—	—

KM# 3 3 KREUZER (Groschen)
Silver **Ruler:** Wolfgang Ernst and Johann Dietrich **Obv:** Shield of 4-fold arms divides date **Obv. Legend:** MONETA. NOVA. ARG. ROK. **Rev:** Crowned imperial eagle, 3 in orb on breast **Rev. Legend:** SVB. VMB. ALARVM. TVARVM. **Mint:** Wertheim **Note:** Prev. Löwenstein-Wertheim-Rochefort KM#5.

Date	Mintage	VG	F	VF	XF	Unc
(16)16	—	—	—	—	—	—
1616	—	—	—	—	—	—

KM# 4 3 KREUZER (Groschen)
Silver **Ruler:** Wolfgang Ernst and Johann Dietrich **Obv:** Three small shields of arms, 2 above 1 **Obv. Legend:** MONETA. NOVA. ARG. ROK. **Rev:** Crowned imperial eagle, 3 in orb on breast **Rev. Legend:** SVB. VMB. ALARVM. TVARVM. **Mint:** Wertheim **Note:** Prev. Löwenstein-Wertheim-Rochefort KM#6. Varieties exist.

Date	Mintage	VG	F	VF	XF	Unc
ND(1616)	—	—	—	—	—	—

KM# 5 12 KREUZER (4 Stüber=Dreibätzner)

Silver **Ruler:** Johann Dietrich **Obv:** Bust to right **Obv. Legend:** SIT. NOMEN. DOMINI. BENEDICTVM. **Rev:** Shield of 4-fold arms, date above, where present **Rev. Legend:** MONETA. NOVA. ARGENTIA. CHA. R. **Mint:** Cugnon **Note:** Prev. Löwenstein-Wertheim-Rochefort KM#7. Varieties exist.

Date	Mintage	VG	F	VF	XF	Unc
1617	—	—	—	—	—	—
ND(ca1618)	—	—	—	—	—	—

KM# 9 12 KREUZER (4 Stüber=Dreibätzner)

Silver **Ruler:** Johann Dietrich **Obv:** Bust to right **Obv. Legend:** + SI. DEVS. PRO. NOBIS. QVI. CONT. NOS. **Rev:** Crowned imperial eagle **Rev. Legend:** SVB. VMBRA. ALARVM. TVARVM **Mint:** Wertheim **Note:** Kipper. Prev. Löwenstein-Wertheim-Rochefort KM#11.

Date	Mintage	VG	F	VF	XF	Unc
ND(1621-2)	—	—	—	—	—	—

KM# 10 12 KREUZER (4 Stüber=Dreibätzner)

3.6800 g., Silver **Ruler:** Wolfgang Ernst and Johann Dietrich **Obv:** Crowned shield of 4-fold arms **Obv. Legend:** MONETA - NOVA - ARG * ROK. **Rev:** Crowned imperial eagle **Rev. Legend:** SVB. VMBRA. ALARVM. TUARVM. **Mint:** Rochefort **Note:** Kipper. Prev. Löwenstein-Wertheim-Rochefort KM#10.

Date	Mintage	VG	F	VF	XF	Unc
ND(1622-23)	—	450	625	850	1,200	—

KM# 2 THALER

Silver **Ruler:** Christoph Ludwig **Obv:** Bust to right **Rev:** Helmeted arms **Note:** W#99. Prev. KM#5.

Date	Mintage	VG	F	VF	XF	Unc
ND(1611-18) Rare	—	—	—	—	—	—

KM# 16 THALER

Silver Weight varies: 27.50-28.00g. **Ruler:** Johann Dietrich **Obv:** Armored bust to right in circle, date at top in margin. **Obv. Legend:** IO. THEOD. COM. IN LEWENSTEIN. WERTH. ROCHEF. **Rev:** Shield of 4-fold arms with central shield, 2 ornate helmets flank crest above **Rev. Legend:** ET. MONTAGV. SV. P. IN CHASPIERRE ET CVGNON - ETZ. **Mint:** Cugnon **Note:** Dav. #6909; W#171, 175. Prev. Löwenstein-Wertheim-Rochefort KM#13. Varieties exist.

Date	Mintage	VG	F	VF	XF	Unc
1623	—	500	900	1,650	3,250	—
ND(1624)	—	—	—	—	—	—

KM# 17 THALER

Silver Weight varies: 27.50-28.00g. **Ruler:** Johann Dietrich **Obv:** Armored bust to right in circle, date at top in margin **Obv. Legend:** IO. THEOD. COM. IN LEWENSTEIN. WERGI. ROCHEF. **Rev:** Ornate shield of 4-fold arms with central shield, 2 ornate helmets flank crest above **Rev. Legend:** ET. MONTACV. SV. P. IN CHASFIERRE. **Mint:** Cugnon **Note:** Dav. #6910; W#172. Prev. Löwenstein-Wertheim-Rochefort KM#14.

Date	Mintage	VG	F	VF	XF	Unc
1623	—	500	900	1,650	3,250	—

KM# 18 THALER

Silver Weight varies: 27.50-28.00g., 42-43 mm. **Ruler:** Johann Dietrich **Obv:** Crowned shield of 4-fold arms with central shield in ornamented frame **Obv. Legend:** IO. THEOD. COM. IN. LEWENSTEIN. WERTH. ROCHEF + **Rev:** Crowned imperial eagle, orb on breast, date at end of legend **Rev. Legend:** FERDINAND. II. D.G. ROM. IMP. SEMP. AVGVST. **Mint:** Wertheim **Note:** Dav. #6911; W#169-70. Prev. Löwenstein-Wertheim-Rochefort KM#15.

Date	Mintage	VG	F	VF	XF	Unc
1623	—	400	650	1,250	2,500	—
1624	—	400	650	1,250	2,500	—

KM# 22 THALER

Silver, 42-43 mm. **Ruler:** Johann Dietrich **Obv:** Draped and armored bust to right, date in margin at top **Obv. Legend:** IO. THEOD. COM. IN LEWENSTEIN. WERTH. ROCHEF. **Rev:** Crowned shield of 9-fold arms in ornamented frame **Rev. Legend:** ET. MONTAGV. SV. P. IN CHASPIERRE ET CVGNON - ETZ. **Mint:** Cugnon **Note:** Dav. #6912; W#173. Prev. Löwenstein-Wertheim-Rochefort KM#16.

Date	Mintage	VG	F	VF	XF	Unc
1624 Rare	—	—	—	—	—	—

KM# 24 THALER

Silver Weight varies: 27.50-28.00g., 44 mm. **Ruler:** Johann Dietrich **Obv:** Large armored bust to right in circle, date in margin at top **Obv. Legend:** IO. THEOD. COM IN LEWENSTEIN. WERTH. ROCHEF. **Rev:** Crowned 4-fold arms with central shield, in ornamented frame **Rev. Legend:** ET. MONTAGV. SV. P. IN CHASPIERRE ET CVGNON - ETZ. **Mint:** Cugnon **Note:** Dav. #6913; W#174. Prev. Löwenstein-Wertheim-Rochefort KM#17.

Date	Mintage	VG	F	VF	XF	Unc
1625 Rare	—	—	—	—	—	—

JOINT COINAGE

KM# 20 HELLER

Silver **Ruler:** Christoph Ludwig, Friedrich Ludwig, and Ludwig III **Obv:** Shield of 4-fold arms, date **Note:** Uniface. W#95. Prev. KM#13.

Date	Mintage	VG	F	VF	XF	Unc
1624	—	—	—	—	—	—

KM# 6 2 KREUZER (1/2 Batzen)

Silver **Ruler:** Wolfgang Ernst and Johann Dietrich **Obv:** 2-fold arms divided horizontally, lozenges above, lion walking to right below **Obv. Legend:** ZV: GOTT: MEIN: HOFFNVNG **Rev:** Imperial orb with Z **Rev. Legend:** SOLI: DEO: GLORIA. **Note:** Kipper. K#1b.

Date	Mintage	VG	F	VF	XF	Unc
ND(1619-22)	—	—	—	—	—	—

KM# 7 3 KREUZER (Groschen)

Silver **Ruler:** Wolfgang Ernst and Johann Dietrich **Obv:** Shield of 4-fold arms **Rev:** Crowned imperial eagle, 3 in orb on breast, titles of Ferdinand II **Mint:** Wertheim **Note:** Kipper. W#98.

Date	Mintage	VG	F	VF	XF	Unc
ND(1619-24)	—	—	—	—	—	—

KM# 8 3 KREUZER (Groschen)

Silver **Ruler:** Wolfgang Ernst and Johann Dietrich **Obv:** 2-fold arms divided horizontally **Rev:** Crowned imperial eagle, 3 in orb on breast, titles of Ferdinand II **Mint:** Wertheim **Note:** Kipper. K#1a. Prev. KM#10.

Date	Mintage	VG	F	VF	XF	Unc
1621	—	—	—	—	—	—

KM# 11 24 KREUZER (Sechsbätzner)

Silver **Ruler:** Wolfgang Ernst and Johann Dietrich **Obv:** Crowned rampant lion to right **Rev:** Crowned imperial eagle, 24 in orb on breast, titles of Ferdinand II **Mint:** Wertheim **Note:** Kipper. W#97.

Date	Mintage	VG	F	VF	XF	Unc
ND(ca.1622)	—	—	—	—	—	—

KM# 12 THALER

Silver, 43 mm. **Ruler:** Wolfgang Ernst and Johann Dietrich **Obv:** Two half-length figures facing each other, date in exergue **Obv. Legend:** WOLF. ERN. ET. IOH. THEO. COM. I. LEW. WERTH. R.M. DN. I.S.C.B. H.N. **Rev:** Crowned imperial eagle, orb on breast **Rev. Legend:** FERDINAND. II. D.G. RO. IMP. SEMP. AU. H. B. **Mint:** Wertheim **Note:** Dav. #6906; W#96. Varieties exist.

Date	Mintage	VG	F	VF	XF	Unc
1622 Rare	—	—	—	—	—	—

LOWENSTEIN-WERTHEIM-ROCHEFORT

Rochefort was the Catholic branch of Löwenstein-Wertheim, established in 1635. From 1622 until about 1650, coinage for Löwenstein-Wertheim-Rochefort was struck at the mint of Cugnon in Luxembourg. The ruler was made Prince of the Empire in 1711. All lands in his possession were mediatized in 1806.

RULERS

Wolfgang Ernst, (1611)-1635-1636 and
Johann Dietrich, (1611)-1635-1644
Ferdinand Karl, 1644-1672
Maximilian Karl, 1672-1718

MINT

Cugnon in Luxembourg

MINT OFFICIALS' INITIALS

Initial	Date	Name
(a) = 6-pointed star or PHM	1677-1718	Philipp Heinrich Müller, die-cutter in Augsburg
FS	ca.1691-7	Friedrich Schattauer

REFERENCES

K = Ulrich Klein, "Die Münzen der Grafen und Fürsten von Löwenstein-Wertheim," **700 Jahre Stadt Löwenstein**, Löwenstein (Württemberg), 1987.

W = Ferdinand Wibel, **Zur Münzgeschichte der Grafen von Wertheim und des Gesamthauses Löwenstein-Wertheim**, Hamburg, 1880.

COUNTSHIP
Catholic Branch
REGULAR COINAGE

KM# 28 DENIER (Pfennig)
Copper Weight varies: 0.88-1.32g. **Ruler:** Ferdinand Karl **Obv:** Bust to right in circle **Obv. Legend:** FERDINAN. CHARLE. **Rev:** Four fleurs-de-lis in field **Rev. Legend:** DEN. DE. LA. SOV. DE. CVGN. **Mint:** Cugnon **Note:** W#206.

Date	Mintage	VG	F	VF	XF	Unc
ND(1644-50)	—	—	—	—	—	—

KM# 30 DENIER (Pfennig)
Copper Weight varies: 0.88-1.32g. **Ruler:** Ferdinand Karl **Obv:** Bust to right **Obv. Legend:** FERDINAN.CHARLE **Rev:** Three large rosettes **Rev. Legend:** DEN. DE. LA. SOV. DE. CVGN. **Mint:** Cugnon **Note:** W#202-5. Varieties exist.

Date	Mintage	VG	F	VF	XF	Unc
ND(1644-50)	—	13.00	27.00	55.00	100	—

KM# 29.2 DENIER (Pfennig)
Copper Weight varies: 0.88-1.32g. **Ruler:** Ferdinand Karl **Obv:** Bust to right **Obv. Legend:** F.C.C.D.L.RO.S.S.D.CH.CVG. **Rev:** 3 rosettes in circle **Rev. Legend:** DENIER + DE + CVGNON **Mint:** Cugnon

Date	Mintage	Good	VG	F	VF	XF
ND(1644-50)	—	—	13.00	27.00	55.00	100

KM# 31 DENIER (Pfennig)
Billon **Ruler:** Ferdinand Karl **Obv:** Bust to right **Obv. Legend:** FERDINAN.CHARLE **Rev:** Four fleurs-de-lis in field **Rev. Legend:** DEN.DE.LA.SOV.DE.CVG. **Mint:** Cugnon **Note:** W#187.

Date	Mintage	VG	F	VF	XF	Unc
ND(1644-50)	—	13.00	27.00	55.00	100	—

KM# 32 DENIER (Pfennig)
Billon **Ruler:** Ferdinand Karl **Rev:** Three rosettes **Rev. Legend:** DEN.DE.LA.SOV.DE.CVGN. **Mint:** Cugnon

Date	Mintage	Good	VG	F	VF	XF
ND(1644-50)	—	—	13.00	27.00	55.00	100

KM# 25 DENIER (Pfennig)
Copper Weight varies: 0.88-1.32g. **Ruler:** Ferdinand Karl **Obv:** Bust to right **Obv. Legend:** F.C.C.D.L.R(o).S.S... **Rev:** Two fleurs-de-lis above rosette, date at end of legend **Rev. Legend:** DENIER. DE. CVGNON **Mint:** Cugnon **Note:** W#188-9. Varieties exist.

Date	Mintage	Good	VG	F	VF	XF
1645	—	—	13.00	27.00	55.00	100
1649	—	—	10.00	20.00	40.00	75.00

KM# 26 DENIER (Pfennig)
Copper Weight varies: 0.88-1.32g. **Ruler:** Ferdinand Karl **Obv:** Bust to right **Obv. Legend:** F.C.C.D.L.RO.S.S... **Rev:** Two fleurs-de-lis above rosette, date at end of legend **Rev. Legend:** DENIER. TOVRNOIS. **Mint:** Cugnon **Note:** W#190, 192-4. Varieties exist.

Date	Mintage	Good	VG	F	VF	XF
1645	—	—	13.00	27.00	55.00	100
1649	—	—	13.00	27.00	55.00	100

KM# 27 DENIER (Pfennig)
Copper Weight varies: 0.88-1.32g. **Ruler:** Ferdinand Karl **Obv:** Bust to right **Rev:** Date around field of four rosettes **Rev. Legend:** PRINCE DE CUGNON **Mint:** Cugnon **Note:** W#191.

Date	Mintage	Good	VG	F	VF	XF
1645	—	—	13.00	27.00	55.00	100

KM# 33 DENIER (Pfennig)
Copper Weight varies: 0.88-1.32g. **Ruler:** Ferdinand Karl **Obv:** Bust to right **Obv. Legend:** F.C.C.D.L.RO.S.S... **Rev:** Four fleurs-de-lis in field, date at end of legend **Rev. Legend:** DENIER DE CVGNON **Mint:** Cugnon **Note:** W#195-7, 207. Varieties exist.

Date	Mintage	Good	VG	F	VF	XF
1649	—	—	13.00	27.00	55.00	100
ND(1644-50)	—	—	13.00	27.00	55.00	100

KM# 29.1 DENIER (Pfennig)
Copper Weight varies: 0.88-1.32g. **Ruler:** Ferdinand Karl **Obv:** Bust to right **Obv. Legend:** F.C.C.D.L.RO.S.S.D.CH.CVG. **Rev:** Three large rosettes, date at end of legend **Rev. Legend:** DENIER DE CVGNON **Mint:** Cugnon **Note:** W#198-201. Varieties exist.

Date	Mintage	VG	F	VF	XF	Unc
1649	—	—	—	—	—	—
ND(1644-50)	—	—	—	—	—	—

KM# 20 DOUBLE TOURNOIS (2 Deniers)
Copper Weight varies: 2.40-2.45g. **Ruler:** Johann Dietrich **Obv:** Bust to right in circle. **Obv. Legend:** I.T.H.C.D.LE.RO.S.S.D.CH. CVGN. **Rev:** Four fleurs-de-lis with rosette in center, date at end of legend **Rev. Legend:** DOVBLE.TOVRNOIS. **Mint:** Cugnon **Note:** W#178-86. Varieties exist.

Date	Mintage	VG	F	VF	XF	Unc
1633	—	20.00	33.00	45.00	80.00	—
1634	—	20.00	33.00	45.00	80.00	—
1635	—	30.00	50.00	65.00	120	—
1643	—	30.00	50.00	65.00	120	—

KM# 35 KREUZER
Billon **Ruler:** Maximilian Karl **Obv:** Crowned 3-fold arms **Obv. Legend:** M. C. COM. IN - LOW. WERTH. **Rev:** 4-line inscription with date **Rev. Inscription:** 1/KREU/TZER/(date). **Mint:** Wertheim **Note:** W#213, 215. Varieties exist.

Date	Mintage	Good	VG	F	VF	XF
1697 FS	—	—	13.00	30.00	60.00	115

KM# 37 3 KREUZER (Groschen)
Silver **Ruler:** Maximilian Karl **Rev:** Four-fold arms **Mint:** Wertheim

Date	Mintage	Good	VG	F	VF	XF
1697 FS	—	—	40.00	100	170	250

KM# 36.1 4 KREUZER (Batzen)
Silver, 25 mm. **Ruler:** Maximilian Karl **Obv:** Crowned oval 8-fold arms, date divided by crown in margin **Obv. Legend:** MAX. KARO(L). COM. IN LOW. WERTHEIM. **Rev:** Crowned imperial eagle, 4 in orb on breast **Rev. Legend:** LEOPOLDVS. D.G. ROM. IMP. S. AVG. **Mint:** Wertheim **Note:** W#211, 213. Varieties exist. Prev. KM#36.

Date	Mintage	Good	VG	F	VF	XF
1697 FS	—	—	55.00	90.00	165	250

KM# 36.2 4 KREUZER (Batzen)
Silver, 25 mm. **Ruler:** Maximilian Karl **Obv:** Crowned shield of 8-fold arms, date divided by crown in margin **Obv. Legend:** MAX. KAROL. COM. IN LOW. WERTHEIM.L **Rev:** Shield of 9-fold arms in circle **Rev. Legend:** LEOPOLDVS. D.G. ROM. IMP. S. AVG. **Mint:** Wertheim **Note:** W#212.

Date	Mintage	Good	VG	F	VF	XF
1697 FS	—	—	60.00	100	175	275

KM# 38 THALER
Silver **Ruler:** Maximilian Karl **Obv:** Armored bust to right **Obv. Legend:** MAX • CAROL • COMES IN LOWENSTEIN WERTHEIM • **Rev:** Ornate shield of 8-fold arms divide date near bottom, 3 ornate helmets above **Rev. Legend:** *ROCH • ET MON • S • PR • IN CHAS • D • IN SCHAR • BR • KER • CAS • HERB • ET NEUF **Mint:** Wertheim **Note:** Dav. #6914; W#210.

Date	Mintage	Good	VG	F	VF	XF
1697 PHM//FS	—	—	350	600	1,200	2,150

TRADE COINAGE

KM# 34 DUCAT
3.3900 g., Gold **Ruler:** Maximilian Karl **Obv:** Armored bust turned slightly to right in circle **Obv. Legend:** MAX. CAR. COM. IN LEWENST. WERTH. ROCH. ET MONS. SVPR. **Rev:** Crowned ornately-shaped shield of 8-fold arms, crossed palm fronds divide date below **Rev. Legend:** IN CHASSEP. DOM. IN SCHARH. EREVB. HERB. ET NEVSCH. **Mint:** Cugnon **Note:** FR#1459; W#209.

Date	Mintage	Good	VG	F	VF	XF
1692 Rare	—	—	—	—	—	—

PRINCIPALITY
Catholic Branch
REGULAR COINAGE

KM# 24 DENIER (Pfennig)
1.0900 g., Copper **Obv:** Bust of Ferdinand Charles right **Obv. Legend:** GERDIN. CHARLE **Rev:** Three rosettes, dot in center **Rev. Legend:** DEN. D.L. SOV. D. CVGN. **Mint:** Cugnon

Date	Mintage	VG	F	VF	XF	Unc
ND(1623-24)	—	25.00	50.00	100	165	—

KM# 18 SCHILLING
Silver **Obv:** Bust right, titles in legend **Rev:** Titles, date in legend **Mint:** Cugnon

Date	Mintage	VG	F	VF	XF	Unc
1626	—	—	—	—	—	—

KM# 22 ESCALIN
Silver **Obv:** Rampant lion left with sword and shield **Obv. Legend:** IO.THEOD COM.D.LEW. **Rev:** Crowned eight-fold arms

Date	Mintage	F	VF	XF	Unc	BU
1626	—	—	—	—	—	—

PATTERNS

Including off metal strikes

KM#	Date	Mintage	Identification	Mkt Val
Pn1	1692	—	Ducat. Silver. KM#34.	400

LOWENSTEIN-WERTHEIM-VIRNEBURG

The Protestant branch of the family dates from the division of 1635. There was a further division in 1721 into 3 branches, 2 of which survived more than one generation, only to be mediatized in 1806.

RULERS

Friedrich Ludwig, 1635-1658
Ludwig Ernst, 1658-1681 and
Friedrich Eberhard, 1658-1683
Eucharius Kasimir, 1681-1698
Heinrich Friedrich, 1683-1721

MINT OFFICIALS' INITIALS

Initial	Date	Name
FS	ca.1691-7	Friedrich Schattauer

REFERENCES

K = Ulrich Klein, "Die Münzen der Grafen und Fürsten von Löwenstein-Wertheim," **700 Jahre Stadt Löwenstein**, Löwenstein (Württemberg), 1987.
W = Ferdinand Wibel, **Zur Münzgeschichte der Grafen von Wertheim und des Gesamthauses Löwenstein-Wertheim**, Hamburg, 1880.

COUNTSHIP

Protestant Branch

REGULAR COINAGE

KM# 10 KREUZER
Silver, 15-18 mm. **Ruler:** Eucharius Kasimir Heinrich Friedrich **Obv:** Crowned three-fold arms **Obv. Legend:** E. C. COM. IN. (-) LO(-)W. WERTHEI(M). **Rev:** 4-line inscription with date in wreath **Rev. Inscription:** I/KREU/TZER/(date). **Mint:** Wertheim **Note:** Varieties exist. W#101-2, 110, 112.

Date	Mintage	Good	VG	F	VF	XF
1691	—	—	35.00	70.00	100	160
1697 FS	—	—	35.00	70.00	100	160

KM# 11 KREUZER
Silver **Ruler:** Eucharius Kasimir Heinrich Friedrich **Obv:** Crowned shield of 3-fold arms, no legend **Rev:** 4-line inscription with date **Rev. Inscription:** I/KREU/TZER/(date). **Mint:** Wertheim **Note:** W#103, 113.

Date	Mintage	Good	VG	F	VF	XF
1691	—	—	13.00	27.00	55.00	100
1697	—	—	13.00	27.00	55.00	100

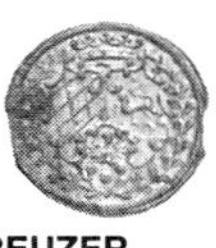

KM# 13 KREUZER
Silver **Ruler:** Eucharius Kasimir Heinrich Friedrich **Obv:** Crowned shield of 3-fold arms in wreath, no legend **Rev:** 4-line inscription with date **Rev. Inscription:** I/KREU/TZER/(date). **Mint:** Wertheim **Note:** W#104.

Date	Mintage	Good	VG	F	VF	XF
1692	—	—	30.00	60.00	85.00	140

KM# 5 3 KREUZER (Groschen)
Silver **Ruler:** Ludwig Ernst and Friedrich Eberhard **Obv:** Shield of 4-fold arms **Rev:** Crowned imperial eagle, 3 in orb on breast, titles of Ferdinand II **Mint:** Wertheim **Note:** W#100.

Date	Mintage	Good	VG	F	VF	XF
ND(1635-37)	—	—	—	—	—	—

KM# 12 4 KREUZER (Batzen)
Silver **Ruler:** Eucharius Kasimir Heinrich Friedrich **Obv:** Crowned shield of 9-fold arms, date in legend **Rev:** Imperial orb with 4 **Mint:** Wertheim **Note:** W#101.

Date	Mintage	Good	VG	F	VF	XF
1691 FS	—	—	—	—	—	—

KM# 14 4 KREUZER (Batzen)
Silver **Ruler:** Eucharius Kasimir Heinrich Friedrich **Obv:** Shield of 9-fold arms, crown above divides date in margin **Obv. Legend:** EUCH. CASIM. COM IN LOW. WERTHEIM. **Rev:** Imperial orb with 4 **Rev. Legend:** ROCHEF. VIRNENBURG. GEILDORF. **Mint:** Wertheim **Note:** W#109.

Date	Mintage	Good	VG	F	VF	XF
1697 FS	—	—	85.00	130	185	270

KM# 15 1/2 THALER
14.6600 g., Silver **Ruler:** Eucharius Kasimir Heinrich Friedrich **Obv:** In half of design, 2 arms holding onto tree branches, band over DUM SCINDITUR FRANGOR, in other half, 2 men working beneath fruit tree, band above ME CONIUNCTIO SERVAT. **Obv. Legend:** EUCH. CASIM. CO. IN LEWENST. WERTH. ROCHEF. VIRNEB. **Rev:** Ornate shield of 9-fold arms divides date near bottom, 4 ornate helmets above **Rev. Legend:** GEILDORF & MONT. S. PR. IN CHASS. D. IN SCHAR. BR. HERB & NEUCH. **Mint:** Wertheim **Note:** W#108.

Date	Mintage	Good	VG	F	VF	XF
1697 FS	—	—	1,750	2,400	3,250	4,500

KM# 16 THALER
Silver Dav. #6908; W#107. **Ruler:** Heinrich Friedrich **Obv:** In half of design, 2 arms holding onto tree branches, band over DUM SCINDITUR FRANGOR, in other half, 2 men working beneath fruit tree, band above ME CONIUNCTIO SERVAT. **Obv. Legend:** EUCH. CASIM. CO. IN LEWENST. WERTH. ROCHEF. VIRNEB. **Rev:** Ornate shield of 9-fold arms divides date near bottom, 4 ornate helmets above **Rev. Legend:** GEILDORF & MONT. S. PR. IN CHASS. D. IN SCHAR. BR. HERB & NEUCH. **Mint:** Wertheim **Note:** Struck at Wertheim. Varieties exist. Dav. #6908.

Date	Mintage	Good	VG	F	VF	XF
1697 FS	—	—	250	600	1,500	2,500

KM# 17 2 THALER
Silver **Ruler:** Eucharius Kasimir Heinrich Friedrich **Obv:** In half of design, 2 arms holding onto tree branches, band over DUM SCINDITUR FRANGOR, in other half, 2 men working beneath fruit tree, band above ME CONIUNCTIO SERVAT. **Obv. Legend:** EUCH. CASIM. CO. IN LEWENST. WERTH. ROCHEF. VIRNEB. **Rev:** Ornate shield of 9-fold arms divides date near bottom, 4 ornate helmets above **Rev. Legend:** GEILDORF & MONT. S. PR. IN CHASS. D. IN SCHAR. BR. HERB & NEUCH. **Mint:** Wertheim **Note:** Dav. #6907; W#105.

Date	Mintage	Good	VG	F	VF	XF
1697 FS Rare	—	—	—	—	—	—

LUBECK

The bishopric was established at Lubeck ca. 1160. The first coins were struck ca. 1190. The bishops became Protestant during the Reformation. Territories were absorbed into Oldenburg during the reign of the last bishop. All the bishops of Lubeck from 1586 until 1802 were dukes of Schleswig-Holstein-Gottorp.

RULERS

Johann Adolf, 1586-1607
Johann Friedrich, 1607-1634
Johann X, 1634-1655
Johann Georg, 1655 (Feb.-Dec.)
Christian Albrecht, 1655-1666
August Friedrich, 1666-1705

MINT OFFICIALS' INITIALS

Initial	Date	Name
AGAH, GAH	Ca.1690	Georg Albrecht Hille?
HR	Ca.1615	Hans Rucke?
HR	1673-1715	Hans Ridder
IG, JG	1603-08	Jonas Georgen in Steinbeck bei Hamburg
MM	1661-66	Michael Moller in gottorp
MP, P	1596-1611	Matthias Puls
PS	Ca.1618	Peter Schrader?

ARMS

Lubeck: A cross.
Schleswig: 2 lions walking left.
Holstein: Nettleleaf.

MONETARY SYSTEM

(1/192 Thaler = 3 Pfennig)

BISHOPRIC

REGULAR COINAGE

KM# 57 DREILING (1/192 Thaler)
Silver **Obv:** Schleswig arms, titles of Christian Albrecht **Rev:** Value 192 between ornaments in center, legend: titles and date

Date	Mintage	VG	F	VF	XF	Unc
166Z MM	—	—	—	—	—	—
1663 MM	—	—	—	—	—	—

KM# 55 SECHSLING (1/96 Thaler)
Silver **Obv:** Holstein arms in center, titles of Christian Albrecht **Rev:** 96 in ornamented shield, titles, date in legend

Date	Mintage	VG	F	VF	XF	Unc
1661 MM	—	—	—	—	—	—

KM# 5 2 SCHILLING
Silver **Obv:** Armored horseman riding right, Z SL below **Rev:** Five lines, V. G. G. / IOH. FRI /. E B. Z. B. V. / L. E. Z. N. H/Z. S. H. **Note:** The 2 and 4 Schilling coins were struck for use in both Bremen and Lubeck.

Date	Mintage	VG	F	VF	XF	Unc
ND	—	—	—	—	—	—

KM# 6 2 SCHILLING
Silver **Obv:** Horseman left **Note:** The 2 and 4 Schilling coins were struck for use in both Bremen and Lubeck.

Date	Mintage	VG	F	VF	XF	Unc
ND	—	—	—	—	—	—

KM# 7 4 SCHILLING
Silver **Obv:** Armored horseman riding right **Rev:** Five lines, V. G. G. / IOH. FRI /. E B. Z. B. V. / L. E. Z. N. H/Z. S. H.
Note: Varieties exist. The 2 and 4 Schilling coins were struck for use in both Bremen and Lubeck.

Date	Mintage	VG	F	VF	XF	Unc
ND	—	—	—	—	—	—

KM# 8 4 SCHILLING
Silver **Obv:** Horseman left **Note:** Varieties exist. The 2 and 4 Schilling coins were struck for use in both Bremen and Lubeck.

Date	Mintage	VG	F	VF	XF	Unc
ND	—	—	—	—	—	—

KM# 26 16 SCHILLING (1/2 Thaler)
Silver **Rev. Legend:** D: S. H. S. E. D.-CO. E. D. M. N. S.
Note: Dav. #5438.

Date	Mintage	VG	F	VF	XF	Unc
1606 MP	—	1,150	2,100	4,000	7,250	—
1607 MP	—	1,150	2,100	4,000	7,250	—
1610 MP	—	1,150	2,100	4,000	7,250	—

KM# 9 4 GROSCHEN (1/6 Thaler)
Silver **Obv:** Bust of Johann Friedrich right **Rev:** Eight-fold arms with central shield of Lubeck cross, 4 GROS. above
Rev. Legend: HERRES. NOR...

Date	Mintage	VG	F	VF	XF	Unc
ND	—	—	—	—	—	—

KM# 10 4 GROSCHEN (1/6 Thaler)
Silver **Rev:** Without indication of value above arms

Date	Mintage	VG	F	VF	XF	Unc
ND	—	—	—	—	—	—

Note: The above 4 Groschen coin circulated in both Bremen and Lubeck

KM# 40 1/36 THALER (Doppelgroten)
Silver **Obv:** Eight-fold arms with cross of Lubeck in center, three helmets above **Rev:** Two crossed keys, date in legend **Note:** This coin was struck for use in both Bremen and Lubeck.

Date	Mintage	VG	F	VF	XF	Unc
1611	—	—	—	—	—	—

KM# 46 1/24 THALER (Groschen)
Silver **Obv:** Imperial orb with Z4 divides date, titles of Matthias **Rev:** Eight-fold arms with central shield of Lubeck cross, titles of Johann Friedrich **Note:** Klippe - 1/24 Thaler.

Date	Mintage	VG	F	VF	XF	Unc
(16)19	—	—	—	—	—	—

KM# 47 1/24 THALER (Groschen)
Silver **Note:** Klippe - 1/24 Thaler.

Date	Mintage	VG	F	VF	XF	Unc
(16)19	—	—	—	—	—	—

KM# 48 1/24 THALER (Groschen)
Silver **Rev:** Date in legend **Note:** Varieties exist.

Date	Mintage	VG	F	VF	XF	Unc
(1)619	—	—	—	—	—	—

KM# 51 1/24 THALER (Groschen)
Silver **Obv:** Imperial orb with Z4, titles of Ferdinand II, date in legend **Rev:** Three-fold arms, bremen and Lubeck above Holstein **Note:** Varieties exist.

Date	Mintage	VG	F	VF	XF	Unc
(1)6Z1	—	—	—	—	—	—
(16)Z1	—	—	—	—	—	—

KM# 13 1/16 THALER
Silver **Rev:** Value 16 in ornamented quatrefoil, legend **Rev. Legend:** MONETA NOVA HOLSATI

Date	Mintage	VG	F	VF	XF	Unc
ND	—	30.00	60.00	110	200	—

KM# 15 1/16 THALER
Silver **Obv:** Imperial orb with 16 divides date, titles of Rudolf II

Date	Mintage	VG	F	VF	XF	Unc
1601	—	30.00	55.00	100	180	—

KM# 12 1/16 THALER
Silver **Obv:** Imperial orb with 16 superimposed on ornamented cross, titles of Rudolf II **Rev:** Six-fold arms with central shield of Lubeck cross, three helmets above **Note:** Varieties exist.

Date	Mintage	VG	F	VF	XF	Unc
ND	—	22.00	45.00	80.00	150	—

KM# 17 1/16 THALER
Silver **Obv:** Titles of Rudolf II, date in legend **Note:** Varieties exist.

Date	Mintage	VG	F	VF	XF	Unc
(1)60Z	—	25.00	45.00	85.00	160	—
1603	—	25.00	45.00	85.00	160	—
(1)604	—	25.00	45.00	85.00	160	—
1604	—	25.00	45.00	85.00	160	—
(1)606	—	25.00	45.00	85.00	160	—
(1)607	—	25.00	45.00	85.00	160	—

KM# 41 1/16 THALER
Silver **Obv:** Crowned imperial eagle, crossed keys in orb on breast, value 1-6 divided by eagle's necks, titles of Rudolf II, date **Rev:** Eight-fold arms with central shield of bremen key and Lubeck cross, three helmets above **Note:** Varieties exist.

Date	Mintage	VG	F	VF	XF	Unc
1611	—	27.00	55.00	100	175	—

KM# 42 1/16 THALER
Silver **Obv:** Eight-fold arms with central shield of Lubeck cross **Rev:** Three helmets, value 16 below legend, date **Rev. Legend:** HER. NOR... **Note:** 1/16 Thaler Doppelschilling. Varieties exist.

Date	Mintage	VG	F	VF	XF	Unc
161Z	—	20.00	45.00	80.00	150	—
1613	—	20.00	45.00	80.00	150	—
1614	—	20.00	45.00	80.00	150	—
1615	—	20.00	45.00	80.00	150	—
1616	—	20.00	45.00	80.00	150	—
(1)617	—	20.00	45.00	80.00	150	—

KM# 44 1/16 THALER
Silver **Obv:** Titles of Matthias **Note:** Varieties exist.

Date	Mintage	VG	F	VF	XF	Unc
1613	—	20.00	45.00	80.00	150	—
1614	—	20.00	45.00	80.00	150	—
(1)615 HR	—	20.00	45.00	80.00	150	—
(1)616	—	20.00	45.00	80.00	150	—
(1)616 HR	—	20.00	45.00	80.00	150	—
(1)617	—	20.00	45.00	80.00	150	—

KM# 45 1/16 THALER
Silver **Rev:** Without value **Note:** 1/16 Thaler Doppelschilling. Varieties exist.

Date	Mintage	VG	F	VF	XF	Unc
(1)617	—	20.00	45.00	80.00	150	—
(1)618	—	20.00	45.00	80.00	150	—
(1)618 PS	—	20.00	45.00	80.00	150	—
(1)619	—	20.00	45.00	80.00	150	—

KM# 50 1/16 THALER
Silver **Obv:** Titles of Ferdinand II

Date	Mintage	VG	F	VF	XF	Unc
(1)6Z0	—	33.00	65.00	120	220	—

KM# 56 1/16 THALER
Silver **Obv:** Bust of Christian Albrecht right **Rev:** Date, value: XVI/1 REIC/HSTHA/ initials **Rev. Legend:** PER. ASPERA. AD. ASTRA **Note:** 1/16 Thaler Duttchen = 3 Schilling. Varieties exist.

Date	Mintage	VG	F	VF	XF	Unc
1661 MM	—	27.00	55.00	100	180	—
166Z MM	—	27.00	55.00	100	180	—
1663 MM	—	27.00	55.00	100	180	—
1664 MM	—	27.00	55.00	100	180	—
1665 MM	—	27.00	55.00	100	180	—

KM# 60 1/16 THALER
Silver **Obv:** Bust of Friedrich right **Rev:** Value and date in legend **Rev. Legend:** DEO SORSQ. SALVSQ. MEA **Note:** Varieties exist.

Date	Mintage	VG	F	VF	XF	Unc
1678	—	33.00	65.00	120	220	—

KM# 25 1/2 THALER
Silver **Obv:** Bust right **Rev:** Three helmets above six-fold arms with central shield of Lubeck cross divide mintmaster's initials and date

Date	Mintage	VG	F	VF	XF	Unc
1606 JG	—	—	—	—	—	—
1607 JG	—	—	—	—	—	—

KM# 34 1/2 THALER
Silver **Rev:** Central shield of Oldenburg arms and year is divided among three helmets

Date	Mintage	VG	F	VF	XF	Unc
1608 MP	—	—	—	—	—	—

KM# 61 2/3 THALER (Gulden)
Silver

Date	Mintage	VG	F	VF	XF	Unc
1678	—	600	1,200	2,200	3,600	—

KM# 62 2/3 THALER (Gulden)
Silver **Rev:** Without value at bottom **Note:** Varieties exist.

Date	Mintage	VG	F	VF	XF	Unc
1678	—	60.00	115	220	375	—
1688	—	60.00	115	220	375	—

KM# 68 2/3 THALER (Gulden)
Silver **Obv:** Smaller bust **Rev:** Smaller arms

Date	Mintage	VG	F	VF	XF	Unc
1689	—	60.00	115	220	375	—
1690 G AH	—	60.00	115	220	375	—
1690 AG/AH	—	60.00	115	220	375	—

KM# 16 THALER
Silver **Obv:** Bust of Johann Adolf left with scepter in right hand **Rev:** Helmeted arms divide date with M P above **Note:** Dav. #5431.

Date	Mintage	VG	F	VF	XF	Unc
(1)601 MP Rare	—	—	—	—	—	—

KM# 18 THALER
Silver **Rev:** Six shields surrounding center 1, MP above **Note:** Dav. #5432.

Date	Mintage	VG	F	VF	XF	Unc
(1)602 MP Rare	—	—	—	—	—	—

KM# 19 THALER
Silver **Obv:** Bust right with scepter **Rev:** Helmeted arms, M-P in helmets, date divided below **Note:** Dav. #5433.

Date	Mintage	VG	F	VF	XF	Unc
1603 MP Rare	—	—	—	—	—	—

KM# 20 THALER
Silver **Subject:** Mutual Oath of Allegiance with King Christian IV of Denmark **Obv:** Bust left with scepter, 30 OCTO below arm **Note:** Dav. #5434.

Date	Mintage	VG	F	VF	XF	Unc
1603 MP Rare	—	—	—	—	—	—

KM# 21 THALER
Silver **Obv:** Without date below arm **Rev:** I-G in helmets **Note:** Dav. #5435.

Date	Mintage	VG	F	VF	XF	Unc
1604 IG Rare	—	—	—	—	—	—

KM# 22 THALER
Silver **Obv:** Similar to KM#26 **Rev:** Helmeted arms wtih M-P above, 60-4 in helmets **Rev. Legend:** DVS. SL. H. S.-E. DI. CO: P. E. D. **Note:** Dav. #5436.

Date	Mintage	VG	F	VF	XF	Unc
(1)604 MP	—	1,000	2,000	3,600	6,000	—

KM# 24 THALER
Silver **Rev:** Helmeted arms with 1-6-0-5 in helmets and M-P **Rev. Legend:** ...HOS.-E. DI. CO: E. D. **Note:** Dav. #5437.

Date	Mintage	VG	F	VF	XF	Unc
1605 MP	—	1,000	2,000	3,600	6,000	—

KM# 23 THALER
Silver **Rev:** Helmeted arms divide date, 60-5 below **Note:** Dav. #A5437.

Date	Mintage	VG	F	VF	XF	Unc
(1)605	—	1,000	2,000	3,600	6,000	—

KM# 28 THALER
Silver **Obv:** Bust right with sceptre **Rev:** Helmeted arms, I-G above, divided date below **Note:** Dav. #A5439.

Date	Mintage	VG	F	VF	XF	Unc
1606 IG Rare	—	—	—	—	—	—

KM# 29 THALER
Silver **Obv:** Bust right **Rev. Legend:** DVX. SL: HO: S:-E... **Note:** Dav. #5439.

Date	Mintage	VG	F	VF	XF	Unc
1606 IG	—	1,000	2,000	3,600	6,000	—
1607 IG	—	1,000	2,000	3,600	6,000	—

KM# 35 THALER
Silver **Subject:** Resignation of Johann Adolf **Obv:** Bust right with sceptre **Rev:** Helmeted arms without Lubeck arms in center **Rev. Legend:** D. S. H. S. E. D... **Note:** Dav. #5440.

Date	Mintage	VG	F	VF	XF	Unc
1608 MP Rare	—	—	—	—	—	—

KM# 36 THALER
Silver **Subject:** Resignation of Johann Adolf **Obv:** Bust right **Rev:** Arms **Rev. Legend:** DVX: SL. HO: S:-E: DI... **Note:** Dav. #5441.

Date	Mintage	VG	F	VF	XF	Unc
1608 IG Rare	—	—	—	—	—	—

KM# 63 THALER

Silver **Obv:** Bust of August Friedrich right **Rev:** Crowned shield in palm branches, H-R at sides, punctuated date in legend **Note:** Dav. #5442.

Date	Mintage	VG	F	VF	XF	Unc
1678 HR Rare	—	—	—	—	—	—
1683 HR Rare	—	—	—	—	—	—

KM# 65 THALER

Silver **Obv:** Fatter bust right **Rev:** Smaller arms **Note:** Dav. #A5443.

Date	Mintage	VG	F	VF	XF	Unc
1683 HR Rare	—	—	—	—	—	—

KM# 66 THALER

Silver **Obv:** Large bust right **Rev:** Helmeted arms, B-M at sides and date divided below **Note:** Dav. #5443.

Date	Mintage	VG	F	VF	XF	Unc
1687 BM Rare	—	—	—	—	—	—

KM# 30 1-1/2 THALER

Silver **Obv:** Three helmets above six-fold arms with central shield of Lubeck cross, date below, titles of Johann Adolf **Rev:** Bust right **Note:** Dav. #LS442.

Date	Mintage	VG	F	VF	XF	Unc
1607 Rare	—	—	—	—	—	—

KM# 31 2 THALER

Silver **Obv:** 1/2-length busts of Johann Adolf and his wife **Rev:** Three helmets above six-fold arms with central shield of Lubeck cross, divides date **Note:** Dav. #LS439.

Date	Mintage	VG	F	VF	XF	Unc
1607 Rare	—	—	—	—	—	—

KM# 32 2 THALER

Silver **Rev:** Duchess offers crown to duke **Note:** Dav. #LS440.

Date	Mintage	VG	F	VF	XF	Unc
1607 P Rare	—	—	—	—	—	—

KM# 33 3 THALER

Silver **Obv:** 1/2-length busts of Johann Adolf and his wife **Rev:** Three helmets above six-fold arms with central shield of Lubeck cross, divides date **Note:** Dav. #LS438.

Date	Mintage	VG	F	VF	XF	Unc
1607 IG Rare	—	—	—	—	—	—

TRADE COINAGE

KM# 43 GOLDGULDEN

Gold **Ruler:** Johann Friedrich **Obv:** Manifold arms, 2-fold central shield of Bremen and Lübeck, 3 helmets above **Obv. Legend:** IO. FR. D.G. A. E. EP. B. ET. L. D. S. H. **Rev:** Full-length standing figure of St. Peter, date nearby **Rev. Legend:** VIVIT POST FVNERA VIRTVS **Note:** Fr. #1504.

Date	Mintage	VG	F	VF	XF	Unc
1612 Rare	—	—	—	—	—	—

MB# A45 GOLDGULDEN

Gold **Ruler:** Johann Friedrich **Obv:** Manifold arms, 2-fold central shield of Bremen and Lübeck, 3 helmets above **Obv. Legend:** I. F. D. G. A. E. EP. B. E. L. D. S. H. **Rev:** Full-length standing figure of St. Peter, date nearby **Rev. Legend:** VIVIT POST FVNERA VIRTVS.

Date	Mintage	VG	F	VF	XF	Unc
1618 Rare	—	—	—	—	—	—

KM# 67 DUCAT

3.5000 g., 0.9860 Gold 0.1109 oz. AGW **Obv:** Armored bust of August Friedrich right in inner circle

Date	Mintage	VG	F	VF	XF	Unc
1688	—	1,800	3,600	6,500	11,000	—
1689	—	1,800	3,600	6,500	11,000	—

KM# 69 DUCAT

3.5000 g., 0.9860 Gold 0.1109 oz. AGW **Obv:** Armored bust of Christian Albrecht right in inner circle **Rev:** Arms in inner circle **Note:** Struck posthumously.

Date	Mintage	VG	F	VF	XF	Unc
1689	—	2,000	4,000	7,000	12,000	—

KM# A17 10 DUCAT

35.0000 g., 0.9860 Gold 1.1095 oz. AGW **Obv:** Bust of Johann Adolf left with scepter in right hand **Rev:** Helmeted arms divide date with MP above **Note:** Struck with 1 Thaler dies, KM#16.

Date	Mintage	VG	F	VF	XF	Unc
(1)601 MP Rare	—	—	—	—	—	—

KM# A33 10 DUCAT

Gold **Ruler:** Johann Friedrich **Obv:** Armored figure to right, 8 small oval shields of arms around **Rev:** Cross in circle, 3 marginal legends **Rev. Legend:** Outer: IOHAN: FRIEDRICH: D:G: ARCH: ET. EP: BRE: ET. LVB.; Middle: HERRES. NORW. DVX. SLES. ET. HOLSACIÆ.; Inner: NOCH. PORTOGALISC: SCHROT: V: KO:. **Note:** Fr. #1505.

Date	Mintage	VG	F	VF	XF	Unc
ND(1607-34) Rare	—	—	—	—	—	—

FREE CITY

Lübeck became a free city of the empire in 1188 and from c. 1190 into the 13th century an imperial mint existed in the town. It was granted the mint right in 1188, 1226 and 1340, but actually began its first civic coinage c.1350. Occupied by the French during the Napoleonic Wars, it was restored as a free city in 1813 and became part of the German Empire in 1871.

MINT OFFICIALS' INITIALS

Initials	Date	Name
(aa)=	1583-1603?	Claes Roethusen
(a)=	1603-14	Statius Wessel II
(bb)=	1617-18	Claus Jaeger
(b)=	1609-44	Heinrich von der Klähren
(c)=	1645-60	Hans Wilms
(d)=	1662-66	Matthias Freude
IF	Ca.1665-67	Dietrich Philipp Zachau
(e)=	1667-72	Lorenz Wagener
(f)=	1673-1715	Hans Ridder

REGULAR COINAGE

KM# A9 1/128 GULDEN (3 Pfennig)

Silver **Obv:** Crowned imperial eagle **Obv. Legend:** CIVITAS IMPERIAL **Rev:** Imperial orb wtih 128 **Rev. Legend:** MONE. NO. LVBEC. **Note:** Varieties exist. Prev. KM#9.

Date	Mintage	VG	F	VF	XF	Unc
(1)603 (a)	—	13.00	27.00	45.00	85.00	—
(1)604 (a)	—	13.00	27.00	45.00	85.00	—

KM# 117 4 PFENNIG

Silver **Obv:** Crowned imperial eagle, city arms on breast, titles of Leopold I **Rev:** Legend, value: III/PFEN/NIG/date **Rev. Legend:** LVB: STAD(T): GE: DT

Date	Mintage	VG	F	VF	XF	Unc
1687	—	—	—	—	—	—

KM# A5 1/64 GULDEN (6 Pfennig)

Silver **Obv:** Crowned imperial eagle **Obv. Legend:** CIVITATIS IMPERIAL **Rev:** Imperial orb with 64, date in legend **Rev. Legend:** MONE NO LVBECK **Note:** Varieties exist. Prev. KM#5.

Date	Mintage	VG	F	VF	XF	Unc
(1)601 (aa)	—	16.00	33.00	60.00	110	—
(1)603 (a)	—	16.00	33.00	60.00	110	—
(1)604 (a)	—	16.00	33.00	60.00	110	—

KM# A56 4 SCHILLING (1/8 Thaler)

Silver **Obv:** Crowned imperial eagle, value 4 in orb on breast, titles of Ferdinand II **Rev:** St. John, city arms below divide date **Rev. Legend:** MONE. NO. LVBECEN. **Note:** Varieties exist. Prev. KM#56.

Date	Mintage	VG	F	VF	XF	Unc
1622 (b)	—	33.00	65.00	120	200	—
1623 (b)	—	33.00	65.00	120	200	—
1629 (b)	—	33.00	65.00	120	200	—
1630 (b)	—	33.00	65.00	120	200	—
1634 (b)	—	33.00	65.00	120	200	—
1635 (b)	—	33.00	65.00	120	200	—
1636 (b)	—	33.00	65.00	120	200	—
1637 (b)	—	33.00	65.00	120	200	—

KM# 71 4 SCHILLING (1/8 Thaler)

Silver **Obv:** Titles of Ferdinand III **Note:** Varieties exist.

Date	Mintage	VG	F	VF	XF	Unc
1639 (b)	—	33.00	65.00	120	200	—
1646 (c)	—	33.00	65.00	120	200	—

KM# A6 8 SCHILLING (1/4 Thaler)

Silver **Obv:** Crowned imperial eagle, value 8 in orb on breast, titles of Rudolf II **Rev:** St. John, city arms below divide date **Note:** Varieties exist. Prev. KM#6.

Date	Mintage	VG	F	VF	XF	Unc
1601 (aa)	—	—	—	—	—	—
(1)603 (a)	—	—	—	—	—	—
(1)606 (a)	—	—	—	—	—	—
(1)609 (a)	—	—	—	—	—	—
1610 (a)	—	—	—	—	—	—
(1)612 (a)	—	—	—	—	—	—

KM# 39 8 SCHILLING (1/4 Thaler)

Silver **Obv:** Titles of Matthias **Rev:** Date divided in legend

Date	Mintage	VG	F	VF	XF	Unc
1617 (bb)	—	—	—	—	—	—

KM# A41 8 SCHILLING (1/4 Thaler)

Silver **Obv:** Titles of Matthias **Rev:** Arms divide date **Note:** Varieties exist. Prev. KM#41.

Date	Mintage	VG	F	VF	XF	Unc
(1)619 (b)	—	—	—	—	—	—
(16)19 (b)	—	—	—	—	—	—

KM# A51 8 SCHILLING (1/4 Thaler)

Silver **Obv:** Titles of Ferdinand II **Note:** Varieties exist. Prev. KM#51.

Date	Mintage	VG	F	VF	XF	Unc
(16)20 (b)	—	—	—	—	—	—
(16)Z0 (b)	—	—	—	—	—	—
(16)21 (b)	—	—	—	—	—	—

KM# A55 8 SCHILLING (1/4 Thaler)

Silver **Rev:** Date divided by shield **Note:** Varieties exist. Prev. KM#55.

Date	Mintage	VG	F	VF	XF	Unc
1621 (b)	—	60.00	125	200	275	—
1622 (b)	—	60.00	125	200	275	—
1623 (b)	—	60.00	125	200	275	—
1625 (b)	—	60.00	125	200	275	—
1626 (b)	—	60.00	125	200	275	—
1627 (b)	—	60.00	125	200	275	—
1628 (b)	—	60.00	125	200	275	—
1629 (b)	—	60.00	125	200	275	—
1631 (b)	—	60.00	125	200	275	—
1632 (b)	—	60.00	125	200	275	—
1633 (b)	—	60.00	125	200	275	—
1634 (b)	—	60.00	125	200	275	—
1635 (b)	—	60.00	125	200	275	—
1637 (b)	—	60.00	125	200	275	—

KM# A67 8 SCHILLING (1/4 Thaler)

Silver **Note:** Varieties exist. Similar to KM#A55, but titles of Ferdinand III. Prev. KM#67.

Date	Mintage	VG	F	VF	XF	Unc
1637 (b)	—	—	—	—	—	—

KM# A78 8 SCHILLING (1/4 Thaler)

Silver **Obv:** Titles of Ferdinand III **Note:** Varieties exist. Prev. KM#78.

Date	Mintage	VG	F	VF	XF	Unc
1645 (c)	—	—	—	—	—	—
1646 (c)	—	—	—	—	—	—

KM# A7 16 SCHILLING (1/2 Thaler)

Silver **Obv:** Imperial orb with 16, date in legend **Rev:** Three-fold arms, Bremen and Lubeck above Holstein **Note:** Varieties exist. Prev. KM#7.

Date	Mintage	VG	F	VF	XF	Unc
1601 (aa)	—	—	—	—	—	—
(1)603 (a)	—	—	—	—	—	—

KM# A26 16 SCHILLING (1/2 Thaler)

Silver **Rev:** Date divided in legend **Note:** Varieties exist. Prev. KM#26.

Date	Mintage	VG	F	VF	XF	Unc
(1)608 (a)	—	100	200	400	—	—
(1)609 (a)	—	100	200	400	—	—
1610 (a)	—	100	200	400	—	—
(1)612 (a)	—	100	200	400	—	—

KM# A42 16 SCHILLING (1/2 Thaler)

Silver **Obv:** Titles of Matthias **Note:** Prev. KM#42.

Date	Mintage	VG	F	VF	XF	Unc
1619 (b)	—	—	—	—	—	—

KM# 52 16 SCHILLING (1/2 Thaler)

Silver **Rev:** Crowned imperial eagle, 16 in orb on breast, titles of Ferdinand II **Note:** Varieties exist.

Date	Mintage	VG	F	VF	XF	Unc
16Z0 (b)	—	275	425	800	1,200	—
1621 (b)	—	275	425	800	1,200	—
1622 (b)	—	275	425	800	1,200	—
1623 (b)	—	275	425	800	1,200	—
1625 (b)	—	275	425	800	1,200	—
1626 (b)	—	275	425	800	1,200	—
1627 (b)	—	275	425	800	1,200	—
1628 (b)	—	275	425	800	1,200	—
1629/8 (b)	—	575	1,200	2,100	3,200	—
1629 (b)	—	275	425	800	1,200	—
1631 (b)	—	275	425	800	1,200	—
1632 (b)	—	275	425	800	1,200	—
1633 (b)	—	275	425	800	1,200	—
1635 (b)	—	275	425	800	1,200	—

KM# A75 16 SCHILLING (1/2 Thaler)

Silver **Obv:** Titles of Ferdinand III **Note:** Prev. KM#75.

Date	Mintage	VG	F	VF	XF	Unc
1640 (b)	—	165	325	600	1,075	—

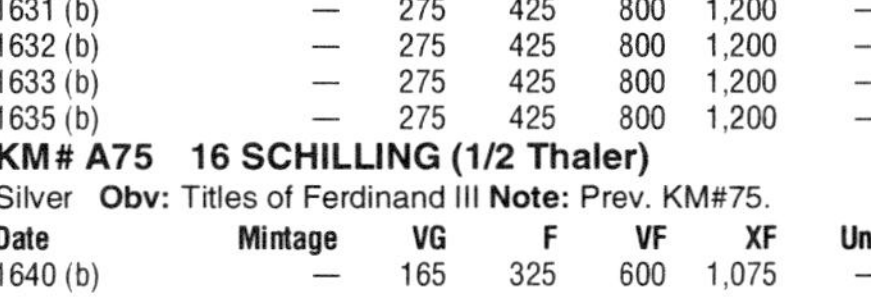

KM# A81 16 SCHILLING (1/2 Thaler)

Silver **Obv:** Standing St. John with paschel lamb facing, arms below, undivided date at top **Obv. Legend:** * MONE NOVA -

LVBECEN **Rev:** Imperial eagle with 16 in orb on breast **Rev. Legend:** FERDINAND: III: D: G: ROM • IMP • SEM: A **Note:** Prev. KM#81.

Date	Mintage	VG	F	VF	XF	Unc
1646 (c)	—	165	325	600	1,075	—

KM# A87 16 SCHILLING (1/2 Thaler)

Silver **Obv:** Date divided by crown in legend **Note:** Prev. KM#87.

Date	Mintage	VG	F	VF	XF	Unc
1654 (c)	—	165	325	600	1,075	—

KM# 97 16 SCHILLING (1/2 Thaler)

Silver **Obv:** Titles of Leopold I, date divided between tail and feet of imperial eagle

Date	Mintage	VG	F	VF	XF	Unc
1662 (d)	—	—	—	—	—	—

KM# 116 16 SCHILLING (1/2 Thaler)

Silver **Obv:** Date divided below eagle's tail **Note:** Varieties exist.

Date	Mintage	VG	F	VF	XF	Unc
1681 (f)	—	—	—	—	—	—
Note: Reported, not confirmed						
1683	—	—	—	—	—	—
Note: Reported, not confirmed						

KM# 106 32 SCHILLING (2/3 Thaler)

18.3200 g., 0.7500 Silver 0.4417 oz. ASW **Obv:** Crowned imperial eagle in wreath, legend **Obv. Legend:** CIVITATIS-IMPERIAL **Rev:** Crowned city arms in wreath divide date, legend **Rev. Legend:** 32. SCHILLING. LVBE. STADT. GELT.

Date	Mintage	VG	F	VF	XF	Unc
1671 (e)	—	80.00	165	325	675	—

KM# 107 32 SCHILLING (2/3 Thaler)

18.3200 g., 0.7500 Silver 0.4417 oz. ASW **Rev:** Date in legend

Date	Mintage	VG	F	VF	XF	Unc
1672 (e)	—	65.00	135	275	525	—

KM# 27 1/192 THALER

Silver **Obv:** Value: 192 in imperial orb **Rev:** Crowned double-headed imperial eagle within circle **Note:** Varieties exist.

Date	Mintage	VG	F	VF	XF	Unc
(160)9 (b)	—	7.00	13.00	33.00	60.00	—
(16)12 (b)	—	7.00	13.00	33.00	60.00	—
(16)20 (b)	—	7.00	13.00	33.00	60.00	—
(16)21 (b)	—	7.00	13.00	33.00	60.00	—
(16)22 (b)	—	7.00	13.00	33.00	60.00	—
(16)24 (b)	—	7.00	13.00	33.00	60.00	—
(16)25 (b)	—	7.00	13.00	33.00	60.00	—
(16)26 (b)	—	7.00	13.00	33.00	60.00	—
(16)27 (b)	—	7.00	13.00	33.00	60.00	—
(16)28 (b)	—	7.00	13.00	33.00	60.00	—
(16)29 (b)	—	7.00	13.00	33.00	60.00	—
(16)92 (b) Error for 1629	—	7.00	13.00	33.00	60.00	—
(16)30 (b)	—	7.00	13.00	33.00	60.00	—
(16)30	—	7.00	13.00	33.00	60.00	—
(16)31 (b)	—	7.00	13.00	33.00	60.00	—
(16)32 (b)	—	7.00	13.00	33.00	60.00	—
(16)33 (b)	—	7.00	13.00	33.00	60.00	—
(1)633 (b)	—	7.00	13.00	33.00	60.00	—
(16)34	—	7.00	13.00	33.00	60.00	—
(16)35 (b)	—	7.00	13.00	33.00	60.00	—
(16)36 (b)	—	7.00	13.00	33.00	60.00	—
(16)37 (b)	—	7.00	13.00	33.00	60.00	—
(16)38 (b)	—	7.00	13.00	33.00	60.00	—
(16)39 (b)	—	7.00	13.00	33.00	60.00	—
(16)41 (b)	—	7.00	13.00	33.00	60.00	—
(16)42 (b)	—	7.00	13.00	33.00	60.00	—
(16)43 (b)	—	7.00	13.00	33.00	60.00	—
(16)44 (b)	—	7.00	13.00	33.00	60.00	—
(16)45 (b)	—	7.00	13.00	33.00	60.00	—
(16)45 (c)	—	7.00	13.00	33.00	60.00	—
(16)46 (c)	—	7.00	13.00	33.00	60.00	—
(16)47 (c)	—	7.00	13.00	33.00	60.00	—
(16)48 (c)	—	7.00	13.00	33.00	60.00	—
(16)49 (c)	—	7.00	13.00	33.00	60.00	—
(16)50 (c)	—	7.00	13.00	33.00	60.00	—
(16)50	—	7.00	13.00	33.00	60.00	—
(16)51 (c)	—	7.00	13.00	33.00	60.00	—
(16)52 (c)	—	7.00	13.00	33.00	60.00	—
(16)54 (c)	—	7.00	13.00	33.00	60.00	—
1655	—	7.00	13.00	33.00	60.00	—
ND (c)	—	7.00	13.00	33.00	60.00	—
(16)65 (d)	—	7.00	13.00	33.00	60.00	—
(16)66 (d)	—	7.00	13.00	33.00	60.00	—
(16)67 (e)	—	7.00	13.00	33.00	60.00	—
(16)71 (e)	—	7.00	13.00	33.00	60.00	—
(16)72 (e)	—	7.00	13.00	33.00	60.00	—
(16)75 (f)	—	7.00	13.00	33.00	60.00	—
ND (f)	—	7.00	13.00	33.00	60.00	—
(16)90	—	7.00	13.00	33.00	60.00	—
(16)92	—	7.00	13.00	33.00	60.00	—
(16)97 (f)	—	7.00	13.00	33.00	60.00	—
(16)98 (f)	—	7.00	13.00	33.00	60.00	—

KM# 88 1/192 THALER

Silver **Rev:** Date in legend **Note:** Varieties exist.

Date	Mintage	VG	F	VF	XF	Unc
(16)55	—	7.00	13.00	33.00	60.00	—
(16)56	—	7.00	13.00	33.00	60.00	—
(16)57	—	7.00	13.00	33.00	60.00	—
(16)58	—	7.00	13.00	33.00	60.00	—
(16)59	—	7.00	13.00	33.00	60.00	—
(16)60 (c)	—	7.00	13.00	33.00	60.00	—
(16)68	—	7.00	13.00	33.00	60.00	—

KM# A50 1/96 THALER

Silver **Rev:** Cross with city arms in center, value: 96 at bottom, date **Rev. Legend:** MONE. NO. LVBEC **Note:** Varieties exist. Prev. KM#50.

Date	Mintage	VG	F	VF	XF	Unc
(1)620 (b)	—	8.00	16.00	33.00	60.00	—
(16)20 (b)	—	8.00	16.00	33.00	60.00	—
(16)21 (b)	—	8.00	16.00	33.00	60.00	—
(16)22 (b)	—	8.00	16.00	33.00	60.00	—
(16)23 (b)	—	8.00	16.00	33.00	60.00	—
(16)24 (b)	—	8.00	16.00	33.00	60.00	—
(16)29 (b)	—	8.00	16.00	33.00	60.00	—
(16)43 (b)	—	8.00	16.00	33.00	60.00	—
(16)44 (b)	—	8.00	16.00	33.00	60.00	—
(16)45 (b)	—	8.00	16.00	33.00	60.00	—
(16)45 (c)	—	8.00	16.00	33.00	60.00	—
(16)46 (c)	—	8.00	16.00	33.00	60.00	—
(16)47 (c)	—	8.00	16.00	33.00	60.00	—
(16)48 (c)	—	8.00	16.00	33.00	60.00	—
(16)49 (c)	—	8.00	16.00	33.00	60.00	—
(16)50 (c)	—	8.00	16.00	33.00	60.00	—
(16)54 (c)	—	8.00	16.00	33.00	60.00	—
(16)59 (c)	—	8.00	16.00	33.00	60.00	—
1661 (d)	—	8.00	16.00	33.00	60.00	—
1662 (d)	—	8.00	16.00	33.00	60.00	—
1664 (d)	—	8.00	16.00	33.00	60.00	—
1665 (d)	—	8.00	16.00	33.00	60.00	—
(16)66 (d)	—	8.00	16.00	33.00	60.00	—
(16)69 (e)	—	8.00	16.00	33.00	60.00	—
1669 (e)	—	8.00	16.00	33.00	60.00	—
1670 (e)	—	8.00	16.00	33.00	60.00	—
(16)75 (f)	—	8.00	16.00	33.00	60.00	—
1675 (f)	—	8.00	16.00	33.00	60.00	—
(16)76 (f)	—	8.00	16.00	33.00	60.00	—
1676 (f)	—	8.00	16.00	33.00	60.00	—

KM# A80 1/96 THALER

Silver **Note:** Klippe 1/96 Thaler. Prev. KM#80.

Date	Mintage	VG	F	VF	XF	Unc
(16)46 (c)	—	—	—	—	—	—

KM# A86 1/96 THALER

Silver **Obv:** Date after legend **Obv. Legend:** CIVITAT IMP **Note:** Prev. KM#86.

Date	Mintage	VG	F	VF	XF	Unc
(16)54 (c)	—	—	—	—	—	—

KM# 53 1/48 THALER (Schilling)

Silver **Obv:** Legend, date, city arms in quatrefoin on cross, value: 48 at bottom **Obv. Legend:** MONE. NOVA-LVBECEN **Rev:** Two crossed keys **Note:** Varieties exist.

Date	Mintage	VG	F	VF	XF	Unc
(1)6Z0 (b)	—	—	—	—	—	—
(1)620 (b)	—	—	—	—	—	—
(16)20 (b)	—	—	—	—	—	—
(1)65Z (c)	—	—	—	—	—	—
(16)5Z (c)	—	—	—	—	—	—
ND (c)	—	—	—	—	—	—
1662 (d)	—	—	—	—	—	—
1667 (e)	—	—	—	—	—	—
1668 (e)	—	—	—	—	—	—
1669 (e)	—	—	—	—	—	—
1670 (e)	—	—	—	—	—	—
1671 (e)	—	—	—	—	—	—

KM# A77 1/24 THALER (2 Schilling)

Silver **Obv:** Legend, imperial eagle with city arms on breast superimposed on cross **Obv. Legend:** CIVI-TATIS-IMPER-ILIS **Rev:** Value: 24/REICHS/DALER/ date **Rev. Legend:** LVBECHS STADT GELDT **Note:** Prev. KM#77.

Date	Mintage	VG	F	VF	XF	Unc
1644 (b)	—	—	—	—	—	—

KM# A79 1/24 THALER (2 Schilling)

Silver **Rev. Legend:** CIVITAT-IMPERIAL **Rev:** Crowned imperial eagle **Note:** Varieties exist. Prev. KM#79.

Date	Mintage	VG	F	VF	XF	Unc
1645 (c)	—	20.00	40.00	80.00	140	—
1646 (c)	—	20.00	40.00	80.00	140	—
1647 (c)	—	20.00	40.00	80.00	140	—
1648 (c)	—	20.00	40.00	80.00	140	—
1649 (c)	—	20.00	40.00	80.00	140	—
1650 (c)	—	20.00	40.00	80.00	140	—
1651 (c)	—	20.00	40.00	80.00	140	—
1652 (c)	—	20.00	40.00	80.00	140	—
1653 (c)	—	20.00	40.00	80.00	140	—
1654 (c)	—	20.00	40.00	80.00	140	—
1655 (c)	—	20.00	40.00	80.00	140	—
1656 (c)	—	20.00	40.00	80.00	140	—
1657 (c)	—	20.00	40.00	80.00	140	—
1658 (c)	—	20.00	40.00	80.00	140	—
1659 (c)	—	20.00	40.00	80.00	140	—
1660 (c)	—	20.00	40.00	80.00	140	—
1665 IF/(d)	—	20.00	40.00	80.00	140	—
1666 IF/(d)	—	20.00	40.00	80.00	140	—
1667 IF	—	20.00	40.00	80.00	140	—
1692 (f)	—	20.00	40.00	80.00	140	—
1693 (f)	—	20.00	40.00	80.00	140	—
1696 (f)	—	20.00	40.00	80.00	140	—
1700 (f)	—	20.00	40.00	80.00	140	—

KM# A43 1/20 THALER (2 Schilling)

Silver **Obv:** St. John above city arms of Lubeck, symbol of mayor Alexander Luneburg (castle tower) in legend between date 16-19 **Obv. Legend:** MONETA-LVBECEN **Rev:** DALER/A. /20. STVC, arms of Lubeck and Hamburg, 24 below **Rev. Legend:** DOMINE. SERVA. NOS

Date	Mintage	VG	F	VF	XF	Unc
1619 (b)	—	—	—	—	—	—

KM# A57 1/16 THALER (3 Schilling)

Silver **Obv:** Crowned imperial eagle, city arms on breast, superimposed on cross **Obv. Legend:** CIVI-TATIS-IMPER-IALIS **Rev:** 16/REICHS/DALER/ date, **Rev. Legend:** LVBECHS. STADT. GELDT. **Note:** Prev. KM#57. Varieties exist.

Date	Mintage	VG	F	VF	XF	Unc
1623 (b)	—	33.00	60.00	110	200	—
1624 (b)	—	33.00	60.00	110	200	—
1629 (b)	—	33.00	60.00	110	200	—
1642 (b)	—	33.00	60.00	110	200	—
1643 (b)	—	33.00	60.00	110	200	—
1644 (b)	—	33.00	60.00	110	200	—
1645 (c)	—	33.00	60.00	110	200	—
1646 (c)	—	33.00	60.00	110	200	—
1647 (c)	—	33.00	60.00	110	200	—
1648 (c)	—	33.00	60.00	110	200	—
1649 (c)	—	33.00	60.00	110	200	—
1651 (c)	—	33.00	60.00	110	200	—
1659 (c)	—	33.00	60.00	110	200	—
1660 (c)	—	33.00	60.00	110	200	—
1662 (d)	—	33.00	60.00	110	200	—
1667 (e)	—	33.00	60.00	110	200	—
1669 (e)	—	33.00	60.00	110	200	—
1670 (d) Error/mule	—	33.00	60.00	110	200	—
1670 (e)	—	33.00	60.00	110	200	—
1671 (e)	—	33.00	60.00	110	200	—
1672 (e)	—	33.00	60.00	110	200	—
1673 (e)	—	33.00	60.00	110	200	—
1683 (f)	—	33.00	60.00	110	200	—

KM# A8 THALER OF 32 SCHILLING

Silver **Obv:** St. John with lamb, city arms below, date above **Rev:** Titles of Rudolph **Note:** Dav. #5444.

Date	Mintage	VG	F	VF	XF	Unc
(1)601 (aa)	—	125	300	700	1,250	—
(1)602 (aa)	—	125	300	700	1,250	—
(1)603 (a)	—	125	300	700	1,250	—
(1)604 (a)	—	125	300	700	1,250	—

KM# A10 THALER OF 32 SCHILLING

Silver **Note:** Similar to 4 Thaler, KM#119. Dav. #LS331. Varieties exist. Prev. KM#10.

Date	Mintage	VG	F	VF	XF	Unc
ND(1603-09) (a) Rare	—	—	—	—	—	—

KM# A23 THALER OF 32 SCHILLING

Silver **Rev:** Date divided by shield below **Note:** Dav. #5445. Prev. KM#23.

Date	Mintage	VG	F	VF	XF	Unc
(1)605 (a)	—	100	250	500	1,250	—
(1)607 (a)	—	100	250	500	1,250	—
(1)608 (a)	—	100	250	500	1,250	—
(1)609 (a)	—	100	250	500	1,250	—

KM# A35 THALER OF 32 SCHILLING

Silver **Rev:** Full date divided by legend **Note:** Dav. #5446. Prev. KM#35. Varieties exist.

Date	Mintage	VG	F	VF	XF	Unc
1610 (a)	—	65.00	125	245	650	—
1611 (a)	—	65.00	125	245	650	—
1612 (a)	—	65.00	125	245	650	—

KM# 38 THALER OF 32 SCHILLING

Silver **Obv:** Titles of Matthias **Note:** Dav. #5447. Varieties exist.

Date	Mintage	VG	F	VF	XF	Unc
1612 (a)	—	65.00	125	245	650	—
1613 (a)	—	65.00	125	245	650	—
1614 (a)	—	65.00	125	245	650	—
1615 (a)	—	65.00	125	245	650	—
1616 (a)	—	65.00	125	245	650	—
1617 (bb)	—	65.00	125	245	650	—
1618 (bb)	—	—	—	—	—	—
Note: Reported, not confirmed						
1619 (b)	—	60.00	120	225	550	—

KM# A44 THALER OF 32 SCHILLING

Silver **Obv:** Symbol of mintmaster Heinrich von der Klahren **Note:** Dav. #LS341. Prev. KM#44.

Date	Mintage	VG	F	VF	XF	Unc
ND(1619-27) (b) Rare	—	—	—	—	—	—

KM# A45 THALER OF 32 SCHILLING

Silver **Obv:** Without halos on eagles **Note:** Dav. #LS341a. Prev. KM#45.

Date	Mintage	VG	F	VF	XF	Unc
ND(1619-27) Rare	—	—	—	—	—	—

KM# 54 THALER OF 32 SCHILLING

Silver **Obv:** Castles flank date **Rev:** Titles of Ferdinand II **Note:** Dav. #5449. Varieties exist.

Date	Mintage	VG	F	VF	XF	Unc
1620 (b)	—	70.00	140	300	1,000	—
1621 (b)	—	70.00	140	300	1,000	—

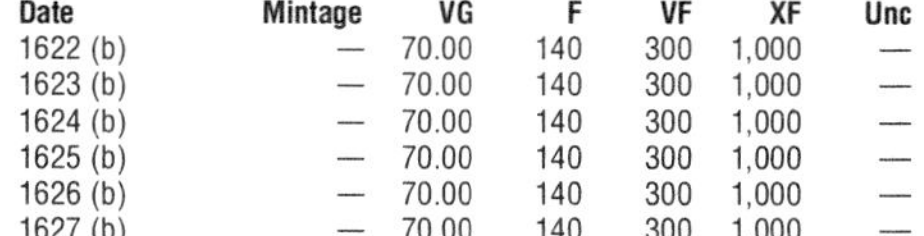

Date	Mintage	VG	F	VF	XF	Unc
1622 (b)	—	70.00	140	300	1,000	—
1623 (b)	—	70.00	140	300	1,000	—
1624 (b)	—	70.00	140	300	1,000	—
1625 (b)	—	70.00	140	300	1,000	—
1626 (b)	—	70.00	140	300	1,000	—
1627 (b)	—	70.00	140	300	1,000	—

KM# A60 THALER OF 32 SCHILLING

Silver **Rev:** Arms of Mayor Lorenz Moller at date **Note:** Dav. #5449B. Prev. KM#60.

Date	Mintage	VG	F	VF	XF	Unc
1627 (b)	—	75.00	150	250	400	—

KM# A61 THALER OF 32 SCHILLING

Silver **Obv:** Arms of Mayors Heinrich Kohler and Lorenz Moller flank arms **Rev:** Crowned double-headed imperial eagle within beaded circle **Note:** Dav. #5449C. Prev. KM#61. Varieties exist.

Date	Mintage	VG	F	VF	XF	Unc
1627 (b)	—	65.00	130	275	750	—
1628 (b)	—	65.00	130	275	750	—
1629 (b)	—	65.00	130	275	750	—
1630 (b)	—	65.00	130	275	750	—
1631 (b)	—	65.00	130	275	750	—
1632 (b)	—	65.00	130	275	750	—
1633 (b)	—	65.00	130	275	750	—
1634 (b)	—	65.00	130	275	750	—
1635 (b)	—	65.00	130	275	750	—

KM# A65 THALER OF 32 SCHILLING

Silver **Obv:** Arms of Mayor Heinrich Kohler (acorns) flank date **Rev:** Crowned double-headed eagle within beaded circle, value in circle on breast **Note:** Dav. #5449D. Prev. KM#65.

Date	Mintage	VG	F	VF	XF	Unc
1634 (b)	—	70.00	140	300	1,000	—
1635 (b)	—	70.00	140	300	1,000	—
1636 (b)	—	70.00	140	300	1,000	—
1637 (b)	—	70.00	140	300	1,000	—
1638 (b)	—	70.00	140	30.00	1,000	—

KM# A69 THALER OF 32 SCHILLING

Silver **Obv:** Date at lower right in legend **Rev:** Titles of Ferdinand III **Note:** Dav. #5450. Prev. KM#69. Varieties exist..

Date	Mintage	VG	F	VF	XF	Unc
1638 (b)	—	175	350	800	1,300	—
1639 (b)	—	175	350	800	1,300	—
1640 (b)	—	175	350	800	1,300	—

KM# A76 THALER OF 32 SCHILLING

Silver **Obv:** Arms of Mayor Heinrich Kohler(acorn) below Saint John, date at upper left **Rev:** Value in circle on breast of double-headed imperial eagle, crown above **Note:** Dav. #5451. Prev. KM#76.

Date	Mintage	VG	F	VF	XF	Unc
1641 (b)	—	150	350	750	1,250	—
1642 (b)	—	150	350	750	1,250	—
1645 (c)	—	150	350	750	1,250	—
1646 (c)	—	150	350	750	1,250	—
1647 (c)	—	150	350	750	1,250	—
1648 (c)	—	150	350	750	1,250	—
1649 (c)	—	150	350	750	1,500	—
1650 (c)	—	150	350	750	1,500	—

KM# 95 THALER OF 32 SCHILLING

Silver **Rev:** Titles of Leopold **Note:** Dav. #5452.

Date	Mintage	VG	F	VF	XF	Unc
1660 (c)	—	425	900	1,600	2,700	—

KM# 96 THALER OF 32 SCHILLING

Silver **Obv:** Saint facing divides beaded circle **Obv. Legend:** MONETA. NOVA.-LUBEC. **Rev:** Value in circle on breast of double-headed imperial eagle, crown above **Rev. Legend:** LEOPOLDUS D: G. ROM: IMP: SEMP: AU: **Note:** Dav. #5453.

Date	Mintage	VG	F	VF	XF	Unc
1661 (c)	—	350	650	1,250	2,250	—

KM# 98 THALER OF 32 SCHILLING

Silver **Obv:** Crowned imperial eagle's tail divides date **Note:** Dav. #5454.

Date	Mintage	VG	F	VF	XF	Unc
1662 (d) Rare	—	—	—	—	—	—

KM# 99 THALER OF 32 SCHILLING

Silver **Obv:** Saint facing above small shields **Rev:** Date in upper left of legend **Rev. Legend:** LEOPOLDUS... **Note:** Dav. #5455. Varieties exist.

Date	Mintage	VG	F	VF	XF	Unc
1662 (d)	—	350	350	1,250	2,250	—
1663 (d)	—	350	650	1,250	2,250	—

KM# 105 THALER OF 32 SCHILLING

Silver **Obv:** Small shields below Saint facing **Obv. Legend:** ...LUBECENSIS **Rev:** Value in circle of breast of double-headed imperial eagle, crown above **Rev. Legend:** LEOPOLD: D. G. RO: **Note:** Dav. #5456.

Date	Mintage	VG	F	VF	XF	Unc
1670 (e)	—	300	650	1,200	2,000	—

KM# 108 THALER OF 32 SCHILLING

Silver **Rev. Inscription:** LEOPOLDUS. D: G: ROMA: I: S: A: **Note:** Dav. #5457.

Date	Mintage	VG	F	VF	XF	Unc
1673 (e)	—	375	875	1,500	2,500	—

KM# 109 THALER OF 32 SCHILLING

Silver **Obv:** Shield below eagle **Note:** Dav. #5458.

Date	Mintage	VG	F	VF	XF	Unc
1676 (f)	—	500	1,000	2,000	5,000	—

KM# 115 THALER OF 32 SCHILLING

Silver **Obv:** Shield below eagle dividing date **Note:** Dav. #5459.

Date	Mintage	VG	F	VF	XF	Unc
1680 (f)	—	400	800	1,500	2,500	—
1683 (f)	—	400	800	1,500	2,500	—

KM# A68 THALER OF 32 SCHILLING

Silver **Note:** Dav. #5449A. Prev. KM#68.

Date	Mintage	VG	F	VF	XF	Unc
1683 (b)	—	75.00	150	350	1,100	—

KM# 120 THALER OF 32 SCHILLING

Silver **Obv:** Smaller lettering **Rev:** Smaller lettering **Note:** Dav. #5460.

Date	Mintage	VG	F	VF	XF	Unc
1690 (f)	—	500	1,000	1,800	3,000	—
1696 (f)	—	500	1,000	1,800	3,000	—

KM# A11 THALER

Silver **Obv. Legend:** Ends: ....OCCASIO **Note:** Dav. #LS331a. Prev. KM#11.

Date	Mintage	VG	F	VF	XF	Unc
ND(1603-09) (a)	—	450	850	1,500	2,500	4,000

KM# A28 THALER

Silver **Obv:** Arms of Mayor Alexander Luneburg (d.1627) in legend **Note:** Dav. #LS336. Prev. KM#28.

Date	Mintage	VG	F	VF	XF	Unc
ND(1603-16) (a) Rare	—	—	—	—	—	—

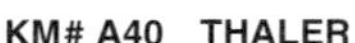

KM# A40 THALER

Silver **Obv:** Symbol of mintmaster Claus Jaeger **Note:** Dav. #LS337. Prev. KM#40.

Date	Mintage	VG	F	VF	XF	Unc
ND(1617-18) (bb) Rare	—	—	—	—	—	—

KM# A12 1-1/2 THALER

Silver **Note:** Similar to 4 Thaler, KM#19. Dav. #LS330. Prev. KM#12.

Date	Mintage	VG	F	VF	XF	Unc
ND(1603-09) (a) Rare	—	—	—	—	—	—

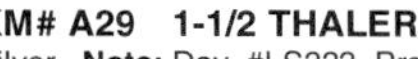

KM# A29 1-1/2 THALER

Silver **Note:** Dav. #LS333. Prev. KM#29.

Date	Mintage	VG	F	VF	XF	Unc
ND(1609-1616) (a) Rare	—	—	—	—	—	—

KM# A30 1-1/2 THALER

Silver **Note:** Similar to 1 thaler, KM#28. Dav. #LS335. Prev. KM#30.

Date	Mintage	VG	F	VF	XF	Unc
ND(1609-16) (a) Rare	—	—	—	—	—	—

KM# A46 1-1/2 THALER

Silver **Note:** Similar to 1 thaler, KM#44. Dav. #LS340. Prev. KM#46.

Date	Mintage	VG	F	VF	XF	Unc
ND(1619-27) (b) Rare	—	—	—	—	—	—

KM# 14 2 THALER

Silver **Obv. Legend:** ACCASIO **Note:** Dav. #LS329a.

Date	Mintage	VG	F	VF	XF	Unc
ND(1603-09) (a) Rare	—	—	—	—	—	—

KM# A15 2 THALER

Silver **Obv:** Redesigned shield **Obv. Legend:** OCCASIO **Note:** Dav. #LS329b. Prev. KM#15.

Date	Mintage	VG	F	VF	XF	Unc
ND(1603-09) (a)	—	1,000	1,650	2,750	4,500	—

KM# A13 2 THALER

Silver **Note:** Similar to 4 Thaler, KM#19. Varieties exist. Dav. #LS329. Prev. KM#13.

Date	Mintage	VG	F	VF	XF	Unc
ND(1603-09) (a) Rare	—	—	—	—	—	—

KM# A24 2 THALER

Silver **Note:** Similar to 1 Thaler, KM#23. Dav. #A5445. Prev. KM#24.

Date	Mintage	VG	F	VF	XF	Unc
(1)605 (a) Rare	—	—	—	—	—	—

KM# A32 2 THALER

Silver **Note:** Similar to 1 Thaler, KM#28 but obverse legend: NVLLA*-PRAE... Dav. #LS334. Prev. KM#32.

Date	Mintage	VG	F	VF	XF	Unc
ND(1609-16) (a)	—	1,000	1,650	2,750	4,500	—

KM# A31 2 THALER

Silver **Note:** Similar to 1-1/2 Thaler, KM#29. Dav. #LS332. Prev. KM#31.

Date	Mintage	VG	F	VF	XF	Unc
ND(1609-16) (a) Rare	—	—	—	—	—	—

KM# 37 2 THALER

Silver **Obv:** Crowned imperial eagle, orb with 32 on breast, titles of Rudolph **Rev:** St. John wtih lamb, city arms below divide date **Note:** Dav. #A5446.

Date	Mintage	VG	F	VF	XF	Unc
1611 (a) Rare	—	—	—	—	—	—

KM# A47 2 THALER

Silver **Note:** Similar to 1 Thaler, KM#44. Dav. #LS339. Prev. KM#47.

Date	Mintage	VG	F	VF	XF	Unc
ND(1619-27) (a) Rare	—	—	—	—	—	—

KM# 58 2 THALER

Silver **Obv:** Titles of Ferdinand II **Note:** Dav. #5448. Varieties exist.

Date	Mintage	VG	F	VF	XF	Unc
1624 (b) Rare	—	—	—	—	—	—
1627 (b) Rare	—	—	—	—	—	—
1628 (b) Rare	—	—	—	—	—	—

KM# A16 2-1/2 THALER

Silver **Note:** Similar to 4 Thaler, KM#19. Dav. #LS328. Prev. KM#16.

Date	Mintage	VG	F	VF	XF	Unc
ND(1603-09) (a) Rare	—	—	—	—	—	—

KM# A18 3 THALER

Silver **Obv:** Revised shield **Obv. Legend:** OCCASio **Note:** Dav. #LS327a. Prev. KM#18.

Date	Mintage	VG	F	VF	XF	Unc
ND(1603-09)	—	1,500	2,400	4,200	6,000	—

KM# B17 3 THALER

Silver **Note:** Similar to 4 Thaler, KM#19. Dav. #LS327. Prev. KM#17.

Date	Mintage	VG	F	VF	XF	Unc
ND(1603-09) (a)	—	1,500	2,400	4,200	6,000	—

KM# A20 4 THALER

Silver **Obv. Legend:** OCCASio **Note:** Dav. #LS326a. Prev. KM#20.

Date	Mintage	VG	F	VF	XF	Unc
ND(1603-09) (a) Rare	—	—	—	—	—	—

KM# A19 4 THALER

Silver **Note:** Varieties exist. Dav. #LS326. Prev. KM#19.

Date	Mintage	VG	F	VF	XF	Unc
ND(1603-09) (a) Rare	—	—	—	—	—	—

KM# A48 4 THALER

Silver **Note:** Similar to 1 Thaler, KM#44. Dav. #LS338. Prev. KM#48.

Date	Mintage	VG	F	VF	XF	Unc
ND(1619-27) (b)	—	2,000	3,500	5,000	8,000	—

KM# 59 4 THALER

Silver **Note:** Similar to 1 Thaler, KM#54. Dav. #A5448.

Date	Mintage	VG	F	VF	XF	Unc
1626 (b) Rare	—	—	—	—	—	—

TRADE COINAGE

KM# A21 GOLDGULDEN

3.5000 g., 0.9860 Gold 0.1109 oz. AGW **Obv:** Orb in shield in inner circle, shield divides date **Rev:** Crowned imperial eagle in inner circle **Note:** Prev. KM#21.

Date	Mintage	VG	F	VF	XF	Unc
(1)603 (a)	—	700	1,500	3,000	5,000	—
(1)603 (aa)	—	700	1,500	3,000	5,000	—
(1)608 (a)	—	700	1,500	3,000	5,000	—
1617 (bb)	—	700	1,500	3,000	5,000	—
1619 (b)	—	700	1,500	3,000	5,000	—
1622 (b)	—	700	1,500	3,000	5,000	—
1623 (b)	—	700	1,500	3,000	5,000	—
1624 (b)	—	700	1,500	3,000	5,000	—
1627 (b)	—	700	1,500	3,000	5,000	—
1629	—	700	1,500	3,000	5,000	—
1637 (b)	—	700	1,500	3,000	5,000	—
1651	—	700	1,500	3,000	5,000	—
1657	—	700	1,500	3,000	5,000	—
1663	—	700	1,500	3,000	5,000	—
1670	—	700	1,500	3,000	5,000	—
1675 (f)	—	700	1,500	3,000	5,000	—

KM# A25 GOLDGULDEN

3.5000 g., 0.9860 Gold 0.1109 oz. AGW **Obv:** Shield of arms in inner circle **Note:** Prev. KM#25.

Date	Mintage	VG	F	VF	XF	Unc
1605	—	425	900	1,800	3,000	—
1611	—	425	900	1,800	3,000	—
1613	—	425	900	1,800	3,000	—
1619	—	425	900	1,800	3,000	—
1625	—	425	900	1,800	3,000	—
1631	—	425	900	1,800	3,000	—
1636	—	425	900	1,800	3,000	—
1637	—	425	900	1,800	3,000	—

KM# A85 1/4 DUCAT

0.8750 g., 0.9860 Gold 0.0277 oz. AGW **Obv:** Orb in shield **Rev:** Crowned imperial eagle **Note:** Prev. KM#85.

Date	Mintage	VG	F	VF	XF	Unc
ND(1650)	—	240	475	900	1,500	—

KM# 110 1/4 DUCAT

0.8750 g., 0.9860 Gold 0.0277 oz. AGW **Obv:** Emperor standing **Rev:** Crowned imperial eagle

Date	Mintage	VG	F	VF	XF	Unc
1679 (f)	—	150	300	475	900	—
1683 (f)	—	150	300	475	900	—
1690 (f)	—	150	300	475	900	—
1692 (f)	—	150	300	475	900	—
1693 (f)	—	150	300	475	900	—
1694 (f)	—	150	300	475	900	—
1697 (f)	—	150	300	475	900	—

KM# 111 1/2 DUCAT

1.7500 g., 0.9860 Gold 0.0555 oz. AGW **Obv:** Emperor standing **Rev:** Crowned imperial eagle

Date	Mintage	VG	F	VF	XF	Unc
1679 (f)	—	180	350	725	1,200	—
1682	—	180	350	725	1,200	—
1683 (f)	—	180	350	725	1,200	—
1688	—	180	350	725	1,200	—
1690 (f)	—	180	350	725	1,200	—
1692 (f)	—	180	350	725	1,200	—
1693 (f)	—	180	350	725	1,200	—
1697 (f)	—	180	350	725	1,200	—
1698	—	180	350	725	1,200	—

KM# A22 DUCAT

3.5000 g., 0.9860 Gold 0.1109 oz. AGW **Obv:** Full-length figure of emperor, date in legend **Rev:** Crowned imperial eagle, city arms on breast **Note:** Varieties exist. Prev. KM#22.

Date	Mintage	VG	F	VF	XF	Unc
(1)603 (a)	—	300	550	1,100	1,800	—
(1)604 (a)	—	300	550	1,100	1,800	—
(1)606 (a)	—	300	550	1,100	1,800	—
(1)607 (a)	—	300	550	1,100	1,800	—
(1)608 (a)	—	300	550	1,100	1,800	—
(1)609 (a)	—	300	550	1,100	1,800	—

KM# A36 DUCAT

3.5000 g., 0.9860 Gold 0.1109 oz. AGW **Obv:** Emperor standing **Rev:** Crowned imperial eagle, date divided **Note:** Varieties exist. Prev. KM#36.

Date	Mintage	VG	F	VF	XF	Unc
1610 (a)	—	240	475	900	1,500	—
161Z (a)	—	240	475	900	1,500	—
1613 (a)	—	240	475	900	1,500	—
1614 (a)	—	240	475	900	1,500	—
1615 (a)	—	240	475	900	1,500	—
1627 (b)	—	240	475	900	1,500	—
1629 (b)	—	240	475	900	1,500	—
1630 (b)	—	240	475	900	1,500	—
1631 (b)	—	240	475	900	1,500	—
1632 (b)	—	—	—	—	—	—
1634 (b)	—	—	—	—	—	—
1636	—	240	475	900	1,500	—
1643 (b)	—	—	—	—	—	—
1645 (c)	—	—	—	—	—	—
1647	—	240	475	900	1,500	—
1648/7 (c)	—	—	—	—	—	—
1649	—	240	475	900	1,500	—
1652	—	240	475	900	1,500	—
1656	—	240	475	900	1,500	—
1657	—	240	475	900	1,500	—
1659	—	240	475	900	1,500	—
1660	—	240	475	900	1,500	—
1663	—	240	475	900	1,500	—
1664	—	240	475	900	1,500	—
1667	—	240	475	900	1,500	—
1672	—	240	475	900	1,500	—
1674	—	240	475	900	1,500	—
1677	—	240	475	900	1,500	—
1683	—	240	475	900	1,500	—
1684	—	240	475	900	1,500	—
1689	—	240	475	900	1,500	—
1690	—	240	475	900	1,500	—
1691	—	240	475	900	1,500	—
1695	—	240	475	900	1,500	—
1697	—	240	475	900	1,500	—
1700	—	240	475	900	1,500	—

KM# 89 2 DUCAT

7.0000 g., 0.9860 Gold 0.2219 oz. AGW **Obv:** Knight with imperial orb and sceptre **Rev:** Crowned double-headed eagle with city arms on breast

Date	Mintage	VG	F	VF	XF	Unc
1656 (c)	—	675	1,200	2,850	4,800	—
1658 (c)	—	675	1,200	2,850	4,800	—
1660 (c)	—	675	1,200	2,850	4,800	—
1666 (d)	—	675	1,200	2,850	4,800	—
1667	—	675	1,200	2,850	4,800	—
1672 (e)	—	675	1,200	2,850	4,800	—
1674 (f)	—	675	1,200	2,850	4,800	—
1675 (f)	—	675	1,200	2,850	4,800	—
1676 (f)	—	675	1,200	2,850	4,800	—
1678 (f)	—	675	1,200	2,850	4,800	—
1681	—	675	1,200	2,850	4,800	—
1682 (f)	—	675	1,200	2,850	4,800	—
1686	—	675	1,200	2,850	4,800	—
1690	—	675	1,200	2,850	4,800	—
1691 (f)	—	675	1,200	2,850	4,800	—
1694	—	675	1,200	2,850	4,800	—
1699	—	675	1,200	2,850	4,800	—

KM# 70 4 DUCAT

14.0000 g., 0.9860 Gold 0.4438 oz. AGW **Note:** Similar to 1 Ducat, KM#36. Thick flan.

Date	Mintage	VG	F	VF	XF	Unc
1638 (b) Rare	—	—	—	—	—	—

KM# A62 5 DUCAT (1/2 Portugaloser)

17.5000 g., 0.9860 Gold 0.5547 oz. AGW **Obv:** Emperor enthroned, 1627 - ANO below **Obv. Legend:** SERVA. NOS. DOMINE. NE. PEREANVS **Rev:** Crowned imperial eagle, city arms on breast, date **Rev. Legend:** EX AVRO. SOLIDO. LIB. IMPER. CIVITAS. LVB. FF **Note:** Prev. KM#62.

Date	Mintage	VG	F	VF	XF	Unc
1628 (b) Rare	—	—	—	—	—	—

KM# A66 5 DUCAT (1/2 Portugaloser)

17.5000 g., 0.9860 Gold 0.5547 oz. AGW **Obv:** City arms in center of large ornate cross, legend, date **Obv. Legend:** EX. AVRO? **Rev:** St. John **Rev. Legend:** SERVA. NOS **Note:** Prev. KM#66.

Date	Mintage	VG	F	VF	XF	Unc
1636 (b) Rare	—	—	—	—	—	—

KM# A109 10 DUCAT

35.0000 g., 0.9860 Gold 1.1095 oz. AGW **Note:** Struck with 1 Thaler dies, KM#108.

Date	Mintage	VG	F	VF	XF	Unc
1673 (e) Rare	—	—	—	—	—	—

PATTERNS

Including off metal strikes

KM#	Date	Mintage	Identification	Mkt Val
Pn1	1665 (d)	—	Sechsling. Gold. KM#50.	—
PnA2	(16)67 (e)	—	Dreiling. Gold. KM#27.	—
PnA3	1669 (e)	—	Sechsling. Gold. KM#50.	—
PnA4	(16)71 (e)	—	Dreiling. Gold. KM#27.	—
Pn6	1681 (f)	—	16 Schilling. Gold. Weight of 2-1/2 Ducat, KM#116.	—
Pn7	1683	—	16 Schilling. Gold. Weight of 2-1/2 Ducat, KM#116.	—
Pn8	1683 (f)	—	1/16 Thaler. Gold. Weight of 2 Ducat, KM#57.	—
Pn9	1687	—	4 Pfennig. Gold. Weight of 1/2 Ducat, KM#117.	—
Pn10	1692 (f)	—	1/24 Thaler. Gold. Weight of 1 Ducat, KM#79.	—
Pn11	(16)98 (f)	—	Dreiling. Gold. KM#27.	—

LUCKAU

Situated about 45 miles (75 km) south-southeast of Berlin, Luckau was the centrally most important town in Lower Lusatia on the way to Dresden. A mint functioned in the town during the 13th and 14th centuries and a mintmaster is mentioned there in the early 15th century. Luckau produced a series of coins for local use during the early period of the Thirty Years' War.

PROVINCIAL TOWN

REGULAR COINAGE

KM# 1 PFENNIG (Kipper)

Copper **Ruler:** (no Ruler Information) **Obv:** Lion leaping left in oval baroque frame, date above **Note:** Uniface.

Date	Mintage	VG	F	VF	XF	Unc
16ZZ Rare	—	—	—	—	—	—

KM# 2 PFENNIG (Kipper)

Copper **Ruler:** (no Ruler Information) **Obv:** Lion leaping left in ornately-shaped shield, date above **Note:** Uniface; varieties exist.

Date	Mintage	VG	F	VF	XF	Unc
16ZZ	—	—	—	—	—	—
1622	—	—	—	—	—	—
16Z2	—	—	—	—	—	—

KM# 3 PFENNIG

Billon **Ruler:** (no Ruler Information) **Obv:** Lion leaping left in ornately-shaped shield, date above **Note:** Uniface; varieties exist.

Date	Mintage	VG	F	VF	XF	Unc
16ZZ Rare	—	—	—	—	—	—

KM# 4 3 KREUZER (Kipper - Groschen)

Silver **Ruler:** (no Ruler Information) **Obv:** Steer walking left **Obv. Legend:** MONETA. NOVA. LUCCANA. **Rev:** Crowned imperial eagle, 3 in orb on breast, titles of Ferdinand II **Note:** Varieties exist.

Date	Mintage	VG	F	VF	XF	Unc
ND(1621/2) Rare	—	—	—	—	—	—

KM# 5 1/24 THALER (Kipper - Groschen)

Silver **Ruler:** (no Ruler Information) **Obv:** Steer walking left, date in margin **Obv. Legend:** MONETA. NOVA. LUCCANA. **Rev:** Crowned imperial eagle, Z4 in orb on breast, titles of Ferdinand II **Note:** Varieties exist.

Date	Mintage	VG	F	VF	XF	Unc
1622 Rare	—	—	—	—	—	—

LUNEBURG

This city 50 miles southeast of Hamburg, chartered in 1247, became a powerful member of The Hanseatic League and received the mint right in 1293. It passed to Hannover in 1705 and to Prussia in 1866. Using a pun on the city name "luna", they showed a half moon on larger coins. Lüneburg had a local coinage, which was produced intermittently from 1293 until 1777.

MINT OFFICIALS' INITIALS

Initials	Date	Name
(a)=	1599-1605	Claus Flegel
(c)= ,AT	1643-49	Andreas Tympfe
(d)= and/or CHS	Ca.1660-	Christoph Hennig Schluter
(e)= HL	1676-89	Hermann Luders
(b)=	1612-45, 49	Jonas Georgens
Knight on horseback rearing left and/or IG (monogram)		
JJJ	1687-1705	Jobst Jacob Janisch in Celle

ARMS

City gate, usually with 3 towers, lion rampant or leopard left in portal. Often depicted with St. John (patron saint) above towers.

CITY

REGULAR COINAGE

KM# 40 FLITTER (1/2 Pfennig)
Silver **Obv:** Lion rampant left **Rev. Inscription:** I/FLIT/TER/date **Note:** Kipper Flitter.

Date	Mintage	VG	F	VF	XF	Unc
(1)6Z0	—	33.00	60.00	100	165	—
(1)6Z1	—	33.00	60.00	100	165	—
ND	—	33.00	60.00	100	165	—

KM# 70 FLITTER (1/2 Pfennig)
Silver **Obv:** Lion rampant left **Rev. Inscription:** 1S/date/LUN

Date	Mintage	Good	VG	F	VF	XF
1641	—	12.00	25.00	40.00	75.00	—

KM# 90 SCHERF (1/2 Pfennig)
Copper **Obv:** Lion rampant left **Rev:** Large S divides date, value 1 above, LVN below **Note:** Varieties exist.

Date	Mintage	VG	F	VF	XF	Unc
1675	—	8.00	16.00	33.00	65.00	—
1683	—	8.00	16.00	33.00	65.00	—
1684	—	8.00	16.00	33.00	65.00	—
1691	—	8.00	16.00	33.00	65.00	—
1694	—	8.00	16.00	33.00	65.00	—

KM# 45 PFENNIG
Copper **Obv:** City arms **Rev. Inscription:** I/PEN/NIG/date

Date	Mintage	VG	F	VF	XF	Unc
16Z1	—	7.00	16.00	33.00	65.00	—
16ZZ	—	7.00	16.00	33.00	65.00	—

KM# 46 PFENNIG
Copper **Obv. Legend:** MONET. CI. LVNEBVRG

Date	Mintage	VG	F	VF	XF	Unc
16Z1	—	7.00	16.00	33.00	65.00	—

KM# 48 PFENNIG
Copper **Rev. Inscription:** I/PEN/NING/date

Date	Mintage	VG	F	VF	XF	Unc
(1)6ZZ	—	7.00	16.00	33.00	65.00	—

KM# 49 PFENNIG
Silver **Obv:** Rampant lion left **Note:** Uniface.

Date	Mintage	VG	F	VF	XF	Unc
ND	—	—	—	—	—	—

KM# 47 3 PFENNIG
Copper **Note:** Kipper 3 Pfennig. Similar to 1 Pfennig, KM#45, but value III.

Date	Mintage	VG	F	VF	XF	Unc
16Z1	—	13.00	27.00	45.00	90.00	—

KM# 50 3 PFENNIG
Copper **Obv. Legend:** ...LUNEBURG

Date	Mintage	VG	F	VF	XF	Unc
(1)6ZZ	—	13.00	27.00	45.00	90.00	—

KM# 44 SECHSLING (6 Pfennig)
Silver **Obv:** City arms **Obv. Legend:** MONET. CI. LUNEBURG **Rev. Legend:** STADT GELT. ANO **Rev. Inscription:** I/SECS/LING, date

Date	Mintage	VG	F	VF	XF	Unc
(1)6Z1	—	40.00	65.00	120	200	—

KM# 51 1/64 THALER (1/2 Schilling)
Silver **Obv:** Imperial orb with 64, titles of Ferdinand II and date in legend **Rev:** City arms **Rev. Legend:** MO NO CP. LUNEBURG

Date	Mintage	VG	F	VF	XF	Unc
16ZZ IG	—	33.00	60.00	115	185	—

KM# 62 1/64 THALER (1/2 Schilling)
Silver **Rev. Legend:** MO: NO: CIV: LUNEBURGENSIS

Date	Mintage	VG	F	VF	XF	Unc
1627 (b)	—	33.00	60.00	115	185	—

KM# 71 1/64 THALER (1/2 Schilling)
Silver **Rev:** Legend, date **Rev. Legend:** STADT: GELDT **Note:** Varieties exist.

Date	Mintage	VG	F	VF	XF	Unc
1643	—	27.00	55.00	95.00	165	—
1647	—	27.00	55.00	95.00	165	—

KM# 56 1/32 THALER (Schilling)
Silver **Obv:** City arms, date in legend **Rev:** Ornamented quatrefoil with 32 in center **Rev. Legend:** DA. PAC...

Date	Mintage	VG	F	VF	XF	Unc
(1)6Z3 (b)	—	—	—	—	—	—

KM# 58 1/32 THALER (Schilling)
Silver **Rev:** Date in legend **Note:** Varieties exist.

Date	Mintage	VG	F	VF	XF	Unc
16Z6 IG	—	20.00	33.00	65.00	115	—
1627 (b)	—	20.00	33.00	65.00	115	—
1629 (b)	—	20.00	33.00	65.00	115	—

KM# 73 1/32 THALER (Schilling)
Silver **Note:** Similar to KM#58. Varieties exist.

Date	Mintage	VG	F	VF	XF	Unc
1647	—	20.00	33.00	65.00	115	—
1648	—	20.00	33.00	65.00	115	—

KM# 10 1/16 THALER (2 Schilling)
Silver **Obv:** St. John above city arms **Obv. Legend:** MO: NO. C. - LVNEBVR **Rev:** Crowned imperial eagle, 16 in orb on breast, titles of Rudolf II and date in legend

Date	Mintage	VG	F	VF	XF	Unc
(1)601 (A)	—	—	—	—	—	—

KM# 32 1/16 THALER (2 Schilling)
Silver **Obv:** Titles of Matthias **Note:** Varieties exist.

Date	Mintage	VG	F	VF	XF	Unc
1614 (b)	—	45.00	80.00	120	180	—
1615 (b)	—	45.00	80.00	120	180	—
1616 (b)	—	45.00	80.00	120	180	—

KM# 41 1/16 THALER (2 Schilling)
Silver **Obv:** City arms divide date **Obv. Legend:** MO. NO. CI. LVNAEBVRGE. **Rev:** St. John, value (16) below **Rev. Legend:** DA. PAC. D: I.-DIEB. NOS. **Note:** Kipper 1/16 Thaler.

Date	Mintage	VG	F	VF	XF	Unc
1620 (b)	—	—	—	—	—	—

KM# 52 1/16 THALER (2 Schilling)
Silver **Obv:** City arms in shield imposed on cross, which divides legend **Obv. Legend:** MONE-LUNE-BURG-date **Rev:** St. John, value 16 between feet **Rev. Legend:** DA. PA... **Note:** Varieties exist.

Date	Mintage	VG	F	VF	XF	Unc
(1)6ZZ (b)	—	55.00	85.00	140	200	—
(1)6Z4 (b)	—	55.00	85.00	140	200	—

KM# 59 1/16 THALER (2 Schilling)
Silver **Obv:** Date above arms **Note:** Varieties exist.

Date	Mintage	VG	F	VF	XF	Unc
16Z6 (b)	—	27.00	55.00	90.00	150	—
1627 (b)	—	27.00	55.00	90.00	150	—
16Z8 (b)	—	27.00	55.00	90.00	150	—
16Z9 (b)	—	27.00	55.00	90.00	150	—
1632 (b)	—	27.00	55.00	90.00	150	—
1633 (b)	—	27.00	55.00	90.00	150	—
1637 (b)	—	27.00	55.00	90.00	150	—
1643 (c)	—	27.00	55.00	90.00	150	—
1644	—	27.00	55.00	90.00	150	—
1646 AT	—	27.00	55.00	90.00	150	—
1647 (c)	—	27.00	55.00	90.00	150	—
1647 AT	—	27.00	55.00	90.00	150	—

KM# 85 1/16 THALER (2 Schilling)
Silver **Obv:** Date divided by mintmaster's initials or symbol in legend

Date	Mintage	VG	F	VF	XF	Unc
1660 (d)	—	27.00	55.00	90.00	150	—
1677 (e)	—	27.00	55.00	90.00	150	—

KM# 57 1/4 THALER
Silver **Obv:** Crowned imperial eagle, orb on breast, titles of Ferdinand II and date **Rev:** City arms, date in legend

Date	Mintage	VG	F	VF	XF	Unc
(1)6Z5/1625 (b)	—	100	185	325	550	—

KM# A53 8 SCHILLING
Silver **Obv:** City arms, date in margin **Obv. Legend:** MON • NOV • CIV • LUNEBERGEN • **Rev:** Crowned imperial eagle, 8 in orb on breast **Rev. Legend:** FERDINANDUS • II • DG • RO • I • S • A •

Date	Mintage	VG	F	VF	XF	Unc
16ZZ (b)	—	—	—	—	—	—

KM# 63 8 SCHILLING
Silver **Rev:** 8 in orb on imperial eagle's breast and date **Note:** Varieties exist.

Date	Mintage	VG	F	VF	XF	Unc
(1)6ZZ (b)	—	—	—	—	—	—
1629 (b)	—	120	225	400	650	—
1632 (b)	—	120	225	400	650	—

KM# 86 8 SCHILLING
Silver **Obv:** Titles of Leopold I

Date	Mintage	VG	F	VF	XF	Unc
1660 CHS (d)	—	—	—	—	—	—

KM# 53 16 SCHILLING (1/2 Thaler)
Silver **Obv:** Towered building facade within beaded circle **Rev:** Value in circle on breast of double-headed imperial eagle within beaded circle **Note:** Varieties exist.

Date	Mintage	VG	F	VF	XF	Unc
16ZZ (b)	—	275	500	675	1,125	—
16Z9 (b)	—	275	500	675	1,125	—
1632 (b)	—	275	500	675	1,125	—

KM# 11 THALER OF 32 SCHILLING
Silver **Obv:** Gate and towers **Obv. Legend:** MONETA. NOVA: CIVI: LVNEBVGENS **Rev:** Crowned imperial eagle with orb and 32 on breast **Rev. Legend:** RVDOLP: II. G. RO. I. SE. AVG. P. F. D. **Note:** Dav. #5461.

Date	Mintage	VG	F	VF	XF	Unc
1601 Rare	—	—	—	—	—	—

KM# 12 THALER OF 32 SCHILLING
Silver **Obv. Legend:** ...IM. SEM. AUGU. P. F. D. **Rev. Legend:** ...CIUITATTS. LUNEBURGENSIS **Note:** Dav. #5462.

Date	Mintage	VG	F	VF	XF	Unc
1602 Rare	—	—	—	—	—	—

KM# 14 THALER OF 32 SCHILLING
Silver **Obv:** Tilted small shield below towered building facade, within beaded circle **Rev:** Value in circle on breast of double-headed imperial eagle, crown above **Note:** Dav. #5464.

Date	Mintage	VG	F	VF	XF	Unc
1609	—	240	475	900	1,500	—
1610	—	240	475	900	1,500	—
1611	—	240	475	900	1,500	—
1612	—	240	475	900	1,500	—

KM# 20 THALER OF 32 SCHILLING
Silver **Obv:** KM#12 **Rev:** KM#31 **Note:** Mule. Dav. #A5465.

Date	Mintage	VG	F	VF	XF	Unc
1610 Rare	—	—	—	—	—	—

KM# 21 THALER OF 32 SCHILLING
Silver **Note:** Similar to 2 Thaler, KM#22. Dav. #LS342A.

Date	Mintage	VG	F	VF	XF	Unc
ND(1611-12) Rare	—	—	—	—	—	—

KM# 25 THALER OF 32 SCHILLING
Silver **Note:** Similar to 2 Thaler, KM#30 but with fuller cape. Dav. #LS346.

Date	Mintage	VG	F	VF	XF	Unc
ND(1612) Rare	—	—	—	—	—	—

KM# 26 THALER OF 32 SCHILLING
Silver **Obv:** Similar to 2 Thaler, KM#29 **Note:** Dav. #LS348.

Date	Mintage	VG	F	VF	XF	Unc
ND(1612) Rare	—	—	—	—	—	—

KM# 24 THALER OF 32 SCHILLING
Silver **Note:** Similar to 2 Thaler, KM#15. Dav. #LS-B342.

Date	Mintage	VG	F	VF	XF	Unc
ND(1612) Rare	—	—	—	—	—	—

KM# 31 THALER OF 32 SCHILLING
Silver **Obv:** Titles of Matthias **Rev:** Date divided 16-27 by towers **Note:** Dav. #5465.

Date	Mintage	VG	F	VF	XF	Unc
1613	—	350	850	1,750	3,000	—
1615	—	350	850	1,750	3,000	—
1617 (b)	—	350	850	1,750	3,000	—
1619	—	350	850	1,750	3,000	—

KM# 33 THALER OF 32 SCHILLING
Silver **Obv:** Date divided 1-6-1-7 by towers **Rev:** Crowned double-headed imperial eagle **Note:** Dav. #5465A.

Date	Mintage	VG	F	VF	XF	Unc
1617	—	400	900	1,850	3,200	—

KM# 34 THALER OF 32 SCHILLING
Silver **Note:** Similar to 2 Thaler, KM#30. Dav. #LS344A.

Date	Mintage	VG	F	VF	XF	Unc
ND(1617) Rare	—	900	1,650	3,250	5,500	—

KM# 54 THALER OF 32 SCHILLING
Silver **Obv:** Without date in legend **Note:** Dav. #5468.

Date	Mintage	VG	F	VF	XF	Unc
ND(1619-37) (b)	—	450	1,000	2,000	3,500	—

KM# 55 THALER OF 32 SCHILLING
Silver **Rev:** Titles of Ferdinand II **Note:** Dav. #5466.

Date	Mintage	VG	F	VF	XF	Unc
1622 (b)	—	125	250	550	1,150	—
1623	—	125	250	550	1,150	—
1624 (b)	—	125	250	550	1,150	—
1625	—	125	250	550	1,150	—
1626 (b)	—	125	250	500	1,150	—

KM# 60 THALER OF 32 SCHILLING
Silver **Obv:** Towered building facade within circle **Rev:** Value in circle of breast of double-headed imperial eagle, crown above, date in legend **Note:** Dav. #5467.

Date	Mintage	VG	F	VF	XF	Unc
1626 (b)	—	125	250	550	1,150	—
1627	—	125	250	550	1,150	—
1628	—	125	250	550	1,150	—
1629	—	125	250	550	1,150	—
1630	—	125	250	550	1,150	—
1632	—	125	250	550	1,150	—
1636	—	125	250	500	1,150	—

KM# 87 THALER OF 32 SCHILLING
Silver **Obv:** Large towers **Rev:** Titles of Leopold I **Note:** Dav. #5469.

Date	Mintage	VG	F	VF	XF	Unc
1660 CHS Rare	—	—	—	—	—	—

KM# 27 1-1/2 THALER
Silver **Note:** Similar to 2 Thaler, KM#30 but with fuller cape. Dav. #LS-A346.

Date	Mintage	VG	F	VF	XF	Unc
ND(1612) Rare	—	—	—	—	—	—

KM# 35 1-1/2 THALER
Silver **Note:** Similar to 2 Thaler, KM#30. Dav. #LS344.

Date	Mintage	VG	F	VF	XF	Unc
ND(1617) Rare	—	—	—	—	—	—

KM# 13 2 THALER
Silver **Obv:** Gate and towers **Rev:** Crowned imperial eagle with orb and 32, titles of Rudolph **Note:** Dav. #5463.

Date	Mintage	VG	F	VF	XF	Unc
1606	—	900	1,500	2,500	3,750	—

KM# 15 2 THALER
Silver **Rev:** T between feet **Note:** Dav. #LS-A342.

Date	Mintage	VG	F	VF	XF	Unc
ND(1609)	—	1,500	2,500	4,000	6,000	—

KM# 22 2 THALER
Silver **Obv:** Crowned helmeted arms **Rev:** Standing figure facing, profile right within cresent at left **Note:** Dav. #LS342.

Date	Mintage	VG	F	VF	XF	Unc
ND(1611-12)	—	850	1,500	3,000	5,000	—

KM# 23 2 THALER
Silver **Obv:** Crowned helmeted arms **Obv. Legend:** QVISCONTRA NOS... **Rev:** Standing figure facing, profile right within cresent at left **Note:** Dav. #LS342a.

Date	Mintage	VG	F	VF	XF	Unc
ND(1611-12)	—	750	1,350	2,850	4,800	—

KM# 30 2 THALER
Silver **Rev:** Lion between shield between feet **Note:** Dav. #LS343.

Date	Mintage	VG	F	VF	XF	Unc
ND(1612)	—	1,500	2,500	4,000	6,000	—

KM# 29 2 THALER
Silver **Obv:** Inner legend **Obv. Legend:** QUIS - CONTRA NOS **Note:** Dav. #LS347.

Date	Mintage	VG	F	VF	XF	Unc
ND(1612) Rare	—	—	—	—	—	—

KM# 28 2 THALER
Silver **Note:** Similar to KM#30 but with fuller cape. Dav. #LS345.

Date	Mintage	VG	F	VF	XF	Unc
ND(1612) Rare	—	—	—	—	—	—

TRADE COINAGE

MB# 99 GOLDGULDEN
Gold **Obv:** Rampant lion to left **Rev:** Imperial eagle **Rev. Legend:** RVDOLPH... **Note:** Fr. #1519.

Date	Mintage	VG	F	VF	XF	Unc
ND(1576-1612)	—	900	1,800	3,250	5,500	—

KM# 5 GOLDGULDEN
3.5000 g., 0.9860 Gold 0.1109 oz. AGW **Obv:** St. John standing, rampant lion in shield at feet, legend in style of Venetian ducat **Obv. Legend:** MONETA-LVNEBVR **Rev:** Crescent moon with profile face right **Rev. Legend:** VISITAVIT:-N-ORIE. EX. ALTO

Date	Mintage	VG	F	VF	XF	Unc
ND(1585-1612)	—	750	1,500	2,750	4,500	—

KM# 6 GOLDGULDEN
3.5000 g., 0.9860 Gold 0.1109 oz. AGW **Obv:** Imperial eagle in inner circle **Rev:** St. John standing in inner circle

Date	Mintage	VG	F	VF	XF	Unc
1601	1,233	450	900	1,800	3,000	—
1602	343	450	900	1,800	3,000	—
1603	—	450	900	1,800	3,000	—
1604	—	450	900	1,800	3,000	—
1606	155	450	900	1,800	3,000	—
1607	—	450	900	1,800	3,000	—
1609	733	450	900	1,800	3,000	—
1610	784	450	900	1,800	3,000	—
1612	900	450	900	1,800	3,000	—
1613	220	450	900	1,800	3,000	—
1614	396	450	900	1,800	3,000	—
1615	432	450	900	1,800	3,000	—
1616	288	450	900	1,800	3,000	—
1617 (b)	828	450	900	1,800	3,000	—
1623	—	450	900	1,800	3,000	—
1629	—	450	900	1,800	3,000	—
1635	—	450	900	1,800	3,000	—

KM# 39 GOLDGULDEN
3.5000 g., 0.9860 Gold 0.1109 oz. AGW **Obv:** St. John standing

Date	Mintage	VG	F	VF	XF	Unc
ND(1613-37)	—	575	1,200	2,250	3,750	—

KM# 61 GOLDGULDEN

3.5000 g., 0.9860 Gold 0.1109 oz. AGW **Obv:** Bust of St. John in inner circle **Rev:** Orb in trilobe

Date	Mintage	VG	F	VF	XF	Unc
1626	—	500	975	2,050	3,400	—
1629	—	500	975	2,050	3,400	—

MB# 101 2 GOLDGULDEN

Gold **Obv:** City arms in circle **Rev:** Imperial eagle in circle **Rev. Legend:** RVDOLPHVS... **Note:** Fr. #1518.

Date	Mintage	VG	F	VF	XF	Unc
ND(1576-1612) Rare	—	—	—	—	—	—

KM# 4 2 GOLDGULDEN

7.0000 g., 0.9860 Gold 0.2219 oz. AGW **Obv:** St. John standing in oval, arms at bottom **Rev:** Crescent moon with face right in inner circle

Date	Mintage	VG	F	VF	XF	Unc
ND(1585-1612)	—	1,500	2,750	4,750	7,500	—

KM# 42 2-1/2 GOLDGULDEN

8.7500 g., 0.9860 Gold 0.2774 oz. AGW **Obv:** St. John standing in inner circle **Rev:** Arms superimposed on cross in inner circle

Date	Mintage	VG	F	VF	XF	Unc
ND(ca.1620) Rare	—	—	—	—	—	—

KM# 43 3 GOLDGULDEN

10.5000 g., 0.9860 Gold 0.3328 oz. AGW **Obv:** St. John standing in inner circle **Rev:** Arms superimposed on cross in inner circle

Date	Mintage	VG	F	VF	XF	Unc
ND(ca.1612) Rare	—	—	—	—	—	—

KM# 72 DUCAT

3.5000 g., 0.9860 Gold 0.1109 oz. AGW **Obv:** St. John standing in oval, arms at bottom **Rev:** Crescent moon with face right in inner circle

Date	Mintage	VG	F	VF	XF	Unc
1645	—	675	1,350	2,700	4,500	—
1647	—	675	1,350	2,700	4,500	—

MB# 88 5 DUCAT

Gold **Obv:** City arms (gate) in circle **Rev:** Large Maltese cross in circle **Note:** Fr. #1517.

Date	Mintage	VG	F	VF	XF	Unc
ND(1576-1612)	—	—	—	—	—	—

KM# A31 6 DUCAT

21.0000 g., 0.9860 Gold 0.6657 oz. AGW **Rev:** St. John standing facing at center, crescent moon with face right in inner circle **Note:** Struck with 2 Thaler dies, KM#29. Actual weight 19.90 grams.

Date	Mintage	VG	F	VF	XF	Unc
ND(1612) Rare	—	—	—	—	—	—

KM# 98 6 DUCAT

21.0000 g., 0.9860 Gold 0.6657 oz. AGW **Obv:** St. John standing holding lamb beside two palm trees, harbor scene in background **Rev:** Face in crescent, huntsman above, fisherman below

Date	Mintage	VG	F	VF	XF	Unc
ND(1650) Rare	—	—	—	—	—	—

KM# 99 10 DUCAT

35.0000 g., 0.9860 Gold 1.1095 oz. AGW **Note:** Similar to 6 Ducat, KM#98.

Date	Mintage	VG	F	VF	XF	Unc
ND(1650) Rare	—	—	—	—	—	—

MAGDEBURG

The small 9th century settlement on the Elbe River, about 85 miles (140 km) west-southwest of Berlin, grew into an important religious and trading center. A convent was established in Magdeburg by Otto the Great (962-73) in 937, while he was still King of the Germans and not yet Emperor. Otto followed this pious act by placing an imperial mint in the town in 942 and facilitated the establishment of an archbishopric there in 968. It was not long before the archbishops were striking coins, in the name of the emperor at first, then in their own names beginning in the late 11th-early 12th century. Archiepiscopal coinage was struck more or less continuously from the late 14th century until 1679. Long under the influence of Brandenburg-Prussia, the Archbishopric of Magdeburg passed, along with the city, into the possession of that powerful state in 1680.

RULERS

Ernst, Herzog von Sachsen, 1476-1513
Albrecht IV, Markgraf von Brandenburg, Administrator, 1513-1545
Johann Albrecht, Markgraf von Brandenburg, 1545-1551
Friedrich IV, Markgraf von Brandenburg, 1551-1552
Sigmund, Markgraf von Brandenburg, 1552-1566
Joachim Friedrich, Markgraf von Brandenburg, 1566-1598
Regents of the Chapter, 1598-1607
Christian Wilhelm von Brandenburg, 1608-1631
Leopold Wilhelm of Austria, 1631-1638
Regents of the Chapter, 1635-1638
August von Sachsen-Weissenfels, 1638-1680

MINT OFFICIALS' INITIALS

Initial	Date	Name
(a)= and/or GM	1595-1613	Georg Meinhard in Halle
(b)=	1613-17	Jonas Wedemeyer in Halle
IH/H	1614	Isaak Henniges, die-cutter
	1617-?	Heinrich Mayer
W	Ca.1619-22	
FD	1622	Franz Thimo
H	Ca.1622	
	1622	Anton Koburger the Elder
AK	1623-25	Anton Koburger the Younger
MK	1638	
ML	1638	
(c)= and/or PS	1638-41	Peter Schrader
ABK	1668	Anton Bernhard Koburger
HHF	1668-77	Hans Heinrich Friese in Halle
(d)=	1675-85	Johann Georg Breyer (Breuer), die-cutter and mintmaster in Brunswick City
SM	Ca.1677	
AF	Ca.1679	

ARMS

Archbishopric and cathedral chapter - 2-fold arms, divided horizontally in half, usually upper, foliated or floral ornament or otherwise shaded to denote red, lower half blank to denote silver, sometimes with patron Saint Moritz.

References

S = Friedrich Freiherrn von Schrötter, ***Beschreibung der Neuzeitlichen Münzen des Erzstifts und der Stadt Magdeburg 1400-1682***. Magdeburg, 1909.

B = Emil Bahrfeldt, Magdeburger Münzen. Nachträge und Berichtigungen zu Friedrich Freiherrn v. Schrötters Buche über die neuzeitlichen Münzen von Magdeburg, ***Berliner Münzblätter*** 43 (1922), pp. 290-91, 345-46, 390-93, 410ff.

Saur = Hugo Frhr. Von Saurma-Jeltsch, ***Die Saurmasche Münzsammlung deutscher, schweizerischer und polnischer Gepräge von etwa dem Beginn der Groschenzeit bis zur Kipperperiode***. Berlin, 1892.

Sch = Wolfgang Schulten, ***Deutsche Münzen aus der Zeit Karls V***. Frankfurt am Main, 1974.

ARCHBISHOPRIC

REGULAR COINAGE

KM# 70 PFENNIG

Silver **Note:** Uniface. Schussel type: Four-fold arms iwth central shield of Madgeburg, date above.

Date	Mintage	VG	F	VF	XF	Unc
(16)ZZ	—	7.00	13.00	27.00	60.00	—

KM# 75 PFENNIG

Silver **Obv:** Arms divide mintmaster's initials **Note:** Varieties exist.

Date	Mintage	VG	F	VF	XF	Unc
(16)Z3	—	7.00	13.00	27.00	60.00	—
(16)Z4	—	7.00	13.00	27.00	60.00	—

KM# 76 PFENNIG

Silver **Obv:** Adjacent arms of Brandenburg and Zollern, date above **Rev:** Imperial orb in shield divides mintmaster's initials

Date	Mintage	VG	F	VF	XF	Unc
(16)Z3	—	7.00	13.00	27.00	60.00	—

KM# 25 3 PFENNIG (Dreier)

Silver **Obv:** Helmeted eagle arms of Brandenburg, date divided at top **Rev:** Imperial orb with 3 in ornamented oval frame

Date	Mintage	VG	F	VF	XF	Unc
1613	—	20.00	40.00	70.00	120	—
1615	—	—	—	—	—	—

KM# 41 3 PFENNIG (Dreier)

Silver **Obv:** Three shields of arms, Brandenburg, Zollern, and Magdeburg **Rev:** Imperial orb with 3

Date	Mintage	VG	F	VF	XF	Unc
1615	—	20.00	40.00	65.00	120	—

KM# 49 3 PFENNIG (Dreier)

Silver **Obv:** Four-fold arms with central shield of Magdeburg in cartouche **Rev:** Imperial orb with 3 divides date near top

Date	Mintage	VG	F	VF	XF	Unc
1617	—	20.00	40.00	65.00	120	—

KM# 50 3 PFENNIG (Dreier)

Silver **Obv:** Adjacent shields of Brandenburg and Zollern

Date	Mintage	VG	F	VF	XF	Unc
1617 (b)	—	25.00	45.00	80.00	140	—

KM# 67 3 PFENNIG (Dreier)
Silver **Obv:** Four-fold arms with central shield of Magdeburg, small annulet at either side and above **Rev:** Imperial orb with 3 divides date **Note:** Kipper 3 Pfennig. Varieties exist.

Date	Mintage	VG	F	VF	XF	Unc
16Z1	—	20.00	40.00	70.00	120	—

KM# 72 3 PFENNIG (Dreier)
Silver **Obv:** Five-line inscription with date, Brandenburg eagle in oval shield divides lower three lines **Obv. Inscription:** CHRIS/WIL: D: G: /P: A:-M: C/H.-D: P:/ date **Rev:** Imperial orb with 3 divides mintmaster's initials in ornamented rhombus **Note:** Varieties exist.

Date	Mintage	VG	F	VF	XF	Unc
(16)ZZ FD	—	33.00	60.00	100	170	—
(16)ZZ FD-H	—	33.00	60.00	100	170	—

KM# 71 3 PFENNIG (Dreier)
Silver **Obv:** Four-fold arms with central shield of Magdeburg, date above **Rev:** Imperial orb with 3 in ornamented rhombus

Date	Mintage	VG	F	VF	XF	Unc
16ZZ	—	20.00	40.00	65.00	120	—
16ZZ FD	—	20.00	40.00	65.00	120	—

KM# 77 3 PFENNIG (Dreier)
Silver **Obv:** Adjacent arms of Brandenburg and Magdeburg, date above **Rev:** Imperial orb with 3 divides mintmaster's initials **Note:** Varieties exist.

Date	Mintage	VG	F	VF	XF	Unc
16Z3 AK	—	33.00	60.00	100	170	—
16Z4 AK	—	33.00	60.00	100	170	—

KM# 53 4 GROSCHEN (3 Kreuzer - Schreckenberger)
Silver **Obv:** Crowned imperial eagle with orb on breast **Rev:** Four-fold arms with central shield of Magdeburg superimposed on ornamented cross **Note:** Kipper 4 Groschen. Varieties exist.

Date	Mintage	VG	F	VF	XF	Unc
ND(1619-22)	—	40.00	80.00	125	220	—

KM# 54 4 GROSCHEN (3 Kreuzer - Schreckenberger)
Silver **Obv:** Crowned ornate shield **Rev:** Value 4 in imperial orb **Note:** Varieties exist.

Date	Mintage	VG	F	VF	XF	Unc
ND(1619-22)	—	40.00	80.00	125	220	—

KM# 55 4 GROSCHEN (3 Kreuzer - Schreckenberger)
Silver **Obv:** Smaller cross **Note:** Varieties exist.

Date	Mintage	VG	F	VF	XF	Unc
ND(1619-22) W	—	40.00	80.00	125	220	—

KM# 7 1/24 THALER (Groschen)
Silver **Obv:** Imperial orb with Z4 divides date, titles of Rudolf II **Rev:** St. Moritz standing full-length holding flag and chapter arms in shield **Note:** Cathedral Chapter issue. Varieties exist.

Date	Mintage	VG	F	VF	XF	Unc
1607 (a)	—	33.00	55.00	85.00	165	—

KM# 26 1/24 THALER (Groschen)
Silver **Obv:** Helmeted Magdeburg arms **Rev:** Small imperial orb with Z4 divides date, beow adjacent arms of Brandenburg and Zollern

Date	Mintage	VG	F	VF	XF	Unc
1613 (b)	—	13.00	27.00	45.00	85.00	—

KM# 27 1/24 THALER (Groschen)
Silver **Ruler:** Christian Wilhelm von Brandenburg **Obv:** Oval Magdeburg arms, ornate helmet above **Obv. Legend:** CRIS. WIL. D.G. PA. A. G. P. G MB **Rev:** Imperial orb with 'Z4' divides date **Rev. Legend:** MATI. D.G. RO. IM. SEM. AV **Note:** Varieties exist.

Date	Mintage	VG	F	VF	XF	Unc
1613 (b)	—	13.00	27.00	45.00	85.00	—
1614 (b)	—	13.00	27.00	45.00	85.00	—
1614	—	13.00	27.00	45.00	85.00	—

KM# 34 1/24 THALER (Groschen)
Silver **Ruler:** Christian Wilhelm von Brandenburg **Obv:** Magdeburg arms above two adjacent arms, Brandenburg and Zollern **Note:** Varieties exist.

Date	Mintage	VG	F	VF	XF	Unc
1614 (b)	—	13.00	27.00	45.00	85.00	—

KM# 37 1/24 THALER (Groschen)
Silver **Obv:** Shields with pointed bottoms and scalloped tops **Note:** Varieties exist.

Date	Mintage	VG	F	VF	XF	Unc
1614 (b)	—	13.00	27.00	45.00	85.00	—
1615 (b)	—	13.00	27.00	45.00	85.00	—

KM# 33 1/24 THALER (Groschen)
Silver **Obv:** Four-fold arms with central shield of Magdeburg

Date	Mintage	VG	F	VF	XF	Unc
1614	—	13.00	27.00	45.00	85.00	—

KM# 36 1/24 THALER (Groschen)
Silver **Obv:** Arms in oval shields

Date	Mintage	VG	F	VF	XF	Unc
1614 (b)	—	13.00	27.00	45.00	85.00	—

KM# 35 1/24 THALER (Groschen)
Silver **Note:** Klippe

Date	Mintage	VG	F	VF	XF	Unc
1614 (b)	—	—	—	—	—	—

KM# 42 1/24 THALER (Groschen)
Silver **Rev. Legend:** MARCH. BR. D. PRVS. **Note:** Varieties exist.

Date	Mintage	VG	F	VF	XF	Unc
1615 (b)	—	16.00	30.00	55.00	90.00	—

KM# 43 1/24 THALER (Groschen)
Silver **Ruler:** Christian Wilhelm von Brandenburg **Obv:** Four-fold arms in various shapes, with central shield of Magdeburg **Note:** Varieties exist.

Date	Mintage	VG	F	VF	XF	Unc
1615 (b)	—	16.00	30.00	55.00	95.00	—
1616 (b)	—	16.00	30.00	55.00	95.00	—
1617 (b)	—	16.00	30.00	55.00	95.00	—

KM# 44 1/24 THALER (Groschen)
Silver **Obv:** Titles of Matthias **Note:** Varieties exist.

Date	Mintage	VG	F	VF	XF	Unc
1615 (b)	—	16.00	30.00	55.00	95.00	—

KM# 51 1/24 THALER (Groschen)
Silver **Rev. Legend:** COAD. HALB. M. B. D. P. **Note:** Varieties exist.

Date	Mintage	VG	F	VF	XF	Unc
1617 (b)	—	16.00	30.00	55.00	95.00	—

KM# 52 1/24 THALER (Groschen)
Silver **Obv:** 16-fold arms with central shield of Magdeburg arms **Rev:** Imperial orb with Z4 divides date, titles of Christian Wilhelm **Rev. Legend:** PRO: LE-GE. ET.-GREGE **Note:** Klippe. Reverse of this coin struck with same dies as goldgulden, KM#47.

Date	Mintage	VG	F	VF	XF	Unc
1617 (b)	—	—	—	—	—	—

KM# 58 1/24 THALER (Groschen)
Silver **Ruler:** Christian Wilhelm von Brandenburg **Obv:** Four-fold arms with central shield of Magdeburg, titles of Christian Wilhelm **Rev:** Imperial orb with Z4, date divided above **Note:** Kipper Coinage. Varieties exist.

Date	Mintage	VG	F	VF	XF	Unc
1619	—	16.00	30.00	55.00	95.00	—
16Z0	—	16.00	30.00	55.00	95.00	—
(16)Z0	—	16.00	30.00	55.00	95.00	—
16Z1	—	16.00	30.00	55.00	95.00	—
(16)Z1	—	16.00	30.00	55.00	95.00	—
(16)1Z Error	—	16.00	30.00	55.00	95.00	—

KM# 65 1/24 THALER (Groschen)
Silver **Note:** Klippe.

Date	Mintage	VG	F	VF	XF	Unc
(16)Z0	—	—	—	—	—	—

KM# 73 1/24 THALER (Groschen)
Silver **Rev:** Arms divide mintmaster's initials

Date	Mintage	VG	F	VF	XF	Unc
16ZZ FD	—	16.00	30.00	55.00	95.00	—

KM# 74 1/24 THALER (Groschen)
Silver **Rev:** Date above arms

Date	Mintage	VG	F	VF	XF	Unc
16ZZ	—	16.00	30.00	55.00	95.00	—

KM# 78 1/24 THALER (Groschen)
Silver **Obv:** Imperial orb with Z4 divides mintmaster's initials, date divided at top **Rev:** Three oval shields of arms, Magdeburg above Brandenburg and Zollern

Date	Mintage	VG	F	VF	XF	Unc
16Z3 AK	—	20.00	33.00	60.00	120	—
16Z4 AK	—	20.00	33.00	60.00	120	—

KM# 145 1/24 THALER (Groschen)
Silver **Ruler:** August von Sachsen-Weissenfels **Obv:** Oval 2-fold arms of Magdeburg and Saxony in baroque frame **Obv. Legend:** AUGUSTUS. DEI. GRAT. P. A. **Rev:** Imperial orb with '24' divides mintmaster's initials, date at end of legend **Rev. Legend:** A - M. DUX. SAX.-I. C. E. M. **Note:** Varieties exist.

Date	Mintage	VG	F	VF	XF	Unc
1668 ABK	—	13.00	27.00	45.00	85.00	—
1669 HHF	—	13.00	27.00	45.00	85.00	—
1670 HHF	—	13.00	27.00	45.00	85.00	—

KM# 38 1/16 THALER (Doppelschilling)
Silver **Obv:** Crowned imperial eagle, 16 in orb on breast, crown at top divides date, titles in legend **Rev:** Four-fold arms with central shield of Magdeburg superimposed on ornate cross **Rev. Legend:** MO. N. NO-CRISTI.-WIL. AR-EP. MAG. **Note:** Klippe.

Date	Mintage	VG	F	VF	XF	Unc
1614	—	—	—	—	—	—

KM# 45 1/16 THALER (Doppelschilling)
Silver **Note:** Similar to KM#38 but round.

Date	Mintage	VG	F	VF	XF	Unc
1615	—	—	—	—	—	—

KM# 59 1/16 THALER (Doppelschilling)
Silver **Note:** Kipper 1/16 Thaler. Varieties exist.

Date	Mintage	VG	F	VF	XF	Unc
1619	—	—	—	—	—	—

KM# 66 1/16 THALER (Doppelschilling)
Silver **Obv. Legend:** CRI-SIA-WIL-HEL **Rev:** Intertwined DS (Doppelschilling), titles in legend with date

Date	Mintage	VG	F	VF	XF	Unc
(16)Z0	—	—	—	—	—	—

KM# 15 1/14 THALER (Doppelgroschen)
Silver **Obv:** Facing bust turned slightly right **Rev:** Small imperial orb with 14 divides date above NEWE. TOP/PEL. SILBER/ GROSCHEN/G(a)M

Date	Mintage	VG	F	VF	XF	Unc
1610 G(a)M	—	—	—	—	—	—

KM# 18 1/14 THALER (Doppelgroschen)
Silver **Obv:** Bust right **Obv. Inscription:** NE-WE/TOPPEL. SIL/BER.GROS:/G(a)M **Rev:** Small imperial orb with 14 divides date and first line of inscription **Note:** Varieties exist.

Date	Mintage	VG	F	VF	XF	Unc
161Z G(a)M	—	—	—	—	—	—

KM# 56 1/12 THALER
Silver **Obv:** Value 1Z in imperial orb **Note:** Varieties exist.

Date	Mintage	VG	F	VF	XF	Unc
ND(1619/22)	—	33.00	65.00	115	180	—

KM# 57 1/12 THALER
Silver **Obv:** Smaller cross **Note:** Varieties exist.

Date	Mintage	VG	F	VF	XF	Unc
ND(1619/22)	—	33.00	65.00	115	180	—

KM# 91 1/12 THALER
Silver **Obv:** Half-length bust right **Rev. Inscription:** EIN / HALBER / REICHS / ORT / date

Date	Mintage	VG	F	VF	XF	Unc
16Z4 AK	—	—	—	—	—	—

KM# 146 1/6 THALER
Silver **Ruler:** August von Sachsen-Weissenfels **Obv:** Half-length bust right, value (1/6) below **Rev:** Crowned four-fold arms with central shield of Magdeburg divides date and mintmaster's initials

Date	Mintage	VG	F	VF	XF	Unc
1668 ABK	—	45.00	80.00	125	220	—

KM# 147 1/6 THALER
Silver **Rev:** Date in legend **Note:** Varieties exist.

Date	Mintage	VG	F	VF	XF	Unc
1668 HHF	—	45.00	80.00	125	220	—
1669 HHF	—	45.00	80.00	125	220	—

KM# 165 1/6 THALER
Silver **Rev:** Value (1/6) at bottom **Note:** Varieties exist.

Date	Mintage	VG	F	VF	XF	Unc
1670 HHF	—	33.00	60.00	110	165	—

KM# 166 1/6 THALER

Silver **Rev:** Large bust **Note:** Varieties exist.

Date	Mintage	VG	F	VF	XF	Unc
1670 HHF	—	33.00	60.00	110	165	—

KM# 79 1/4 THALER

Silver **Obv:** 3/4-length bust right **Obv. Inscription:** PRO.LEGE.-ET.GREGE **Rev:** Small helmeted arms of Magdeburg in center, oval arms of Brandenburg above and Zollern below divided inscription, margin of 14 small oval arms **Note:** Varieties exist.

Date	Mintage	VG	F	VF	XF	Unc
ND (b)	—	—	—	—	—	—
(16)Z3 AK	—	—	—	—	—	—

KM# 81 1/4 THALER

Silver **Obv:** Half-length bust right

Date	Mintage	VG	F	VF	XF	Unc
(16)Z3 AK	—	—	—	—	—	—

KM# 92 1/4 THALER

Silver **Rev:** 15-fold arms with central shields of Magdeburg and Brandenburg above that of Zollern, date in legend

Date	Mintage	VG	F	VF	XF	Unc
(16)Z4 AK	—	—	—	—	—	—

KM# 80 1/4 THALER

Silver **Note:** Klippe.

Date	Mintage	VG	F	VF	XF	Unc
ND (b)	—	—	—	—	—	—

KM# 105 1/4 THALER

Silver **Obv:** Helmeted arms of Magdeburg divide date and mintmaster's initials **Rev:** Full-length figure of St. Moritz holding Magdeburg banner in right hand, shield with imperial eagle in left hand **Note:** Cathedral Chapter issue.

Date	Mintage	VG	F	VF	XF	Unc
1638 MK	—	135	275	375	500	—

KM# 106 1/4 THALER

Silver **Obv:** Date divided above

Date	Mintage	VG	F	VF	XF	Unc
1638 PS (c)	—	135	275	375	500	—

KM# 130 1/4 THALER

Silver **Obv:** Facing bust of August **Rev:** Four-fold arms with central shield of Magdeburg, bishop's mitre above, date divided in legend at top

Date	Mintage	VG	F	VF	XF	Unc
1640 PS	—	—	—	—	—	—

KM# 148 1/3 THALER (1/2 Gulden)

Silver **Ruler:** August von Sachsen-Weissenfels **Obv:** Value (1/3) below bust **Rev:** 4-fold arms with central shield of Magdeburg divide date and mintmaster's initials **Note:** Varieties exist.

Date	Mintage	VG	F	VF	XF	Unc
1668 ABK	—	—	—	—	—	—

KM# 149 1/3 THALER (1/2 Gulden)

Silver **Rev:** Date in legend **Note:** Varieties exist.

Date	Mintage	VG	F	VF	XF	Unc
1668 HHF	—	35.00	65.00	115	190	—
1669 HHF	—	35.00	65.00	115	190	—

KM# 152 1/3 THALER (1/2 Gulden)

Silver **Rev:** Date divided by crown

Date	Mintage	VG	F	VF	XF	Unc
1669 HHF	—	35.00	65.00	115	190	—

KM# 153 1/3 THALER (1/2 Gulden)

Silver **Obv:** Larger bust without circle

Date	Mintage	VG	F	VF	XF	Unc
1669 HHF	—	35.00	65.00	115	190	—
1670 HHF	—	35.00	65.00	115	190	—

KM# 167 1/3 THALER (1/2 Gulden)

Silver **Rev:** Value (1/3) at bottom

Date	Mintage	VG	F	VF	XF	Unc
1670 HHF	—	45.00	80.00	140	225	—

KM# 168 1/3 THALER (1/2 Gulden)

Silver **Obv:** Larger head **Note:** Varieties exist.

Date	Mintage	VG	F	VF	XF	Unc
1670 HHH	—	40.00	80.00	125	220	—
1671 HHH	—	40.00	80.00	125	220	—
1672 HHH	—	40.00	80.00	125	220	—
1674 HHH	—	40.00	80.00	125	220	—
1675 HHH	—	40.00	80.00	125	220	—

KM# 19 1/2 THALER

Silver **Obv:** Half-length bust right, imperial orb at lower right **Rev:** Three helmets above 13-fold arms with central shield of Magdeburg

Date	Mintage	VG	F	VF	XF	Unc
(1)61Z GM	—	—	—	—	—	—

KM# 85 1/2 THALER (20 Groschen)

Silver **Obv:** 3/4-length bust right **Obv. Inscription:** PRO. LEG.--ET. GREGE **Rev:** Small helmeted arms of Magdeburg in center, oval arms above, Zollern below divided inscription, margin of 14 small oval arms

Date	Mintage	VG	F	VF	XF	Unc
ND	—	—	—	—	—	—

KM# 68 1/2 THALER (20 Groschen)

Silver **Obv:** Oval four-fold arms with central shield of Brandenburg in cartouche **Rev:** Angel above heart-shaped shield of Magdeburg, date above, 20 G. in cartouche in margin at bottom **Note:** Kipper 1/2 Thaler. Varieties exist.

Date	Mintage	VG	F	VF	XF	Unc
16Z1	—	—	—	—	—	—

KM# 82 1/2 THALER (20 Groschen)

Silver **Note:** Varieties exist.

Date	Mintage	VG	F	VF	XF	Unc
ND	—	135	325	450	625	—
(16)Z3	—	135	325	450	625	—
(16)Z4 AK	—	135	325	450	625	—
16Z4 AK	—	135	325	450	625	—

KM# 86 1/2 THALER (20 Groschen)

Silver **Obv:** Half-length bust right **Rev:** 15-fold arms with central shield of Magdeburg

Date	Mintage	VG	F	VF	XF	Unc
(16)Z3 AK	—	—	—	—	—	—

KM# 93 1/2 THALER (20 Groschen)

Silver **Rev:** 16-fold arms with central shields of Magdeburg and Brandenburg above that of Zollern, date in legend **Note:** Varieties exist.

Date	Mintage	VG	F	VF	XF	Unc
16Z4 AK	—	275	525	1,000	1,700	—
(16)Z4 AK	—	275	525	1,000	1,700	—
(16)Z5 AK	—	275	525	1,000	1,700	—

KM# 83 1/2 THALER (20 Groschen)

Silver **Obv:** Half-length bust right **Rev:** 16-fold arms with central shield of Magdeburg

Date	Mintage	VG	F	VF	XF	Unc
ND	—	—	—	—	—	—

KM# 84 1/2 THALER (20 Groschen)

Silver **Obv. Legend:** CRIST. D. G. P. ADM...WILHJ

Date	Mintage	VG	F	VF	XF	Unc
ND	—	—	—	—	—	—

KM# 107 1/2 THALER (20 Groschen)

Silver **Obv:** Helmeted arms of Magdeburg divide date and mintmaster's initials **Rev:** Full-length figure of St. Moritz holding Magdeburg banner in right hand, shield with imperial eagle in left hand

Date	Mintage	VG	F	VF	XF	Unc
1638 (c)	—	165	225	600	875	—

KM# 108 1/2 THALER (20 Groschen)

Silver **Obv:** Date divided above arms **Note:** Varieties exist.

Date	Mintage	VG	F	VF	XF	Unc
1638 PS (c)	—	260	400	625	925	—

KM# 131 1/2 THALER (20 Groschen)

Silver **Obv:** Facing bust of August **Rev:** 4-fold arms with central shield of Magdeburg, bishop's mitre above, date divided in legend at top **Note:** Varieties exist.

Date	Mintage	VG	F	VF	XF	Unc
1640 PS Rare	—	—	—	—	—	—

KM# 155 2/3 THALER (Gulden)

Silver **Note:** Varieties exist.

Date	Mintage	VG	F	VF	XF	Unc
1669 HHF	—	80.00	125	200	300	—

KM# 156 2/3 THALER (Gulden)

Silver **Obv:** Without circle around bust **Note:** Varieties exist.

Date	Mintage	VG	F	VF	XF	Unc
1669 HHF	—	80.00	125	200	300	—
1670 HHF	—	80.00	125	200	300	—

KM# 169 2/3 THALER (Gulden)

Silver **Obv:** Larger bust **Note:** Varieties exist.

Date	Mintage	VG	F	VF	XF	Unc
1670 HHF	—	45.00	80.00	140	225	—
1671 HHF	—	45.00	80.00	140	225	—
1672 HHF	—	45.00	80.00	140	225	—
1673 HHF	—	45.00	80.00	140	225	—
1674 HHF	—	45.00	80.00	140	225	—

KM# 171 2/3 THALER (Gulden)

Silver **Ruler:** August von Sachsen-Weissenfels **Rev:** Arms divide 2/3-T, date divided below arms **Note:** Varieties exist.

Date	Mintage	VG	F	VF	XF	Unc
1674	—	45.00	80.00	140	225	—
1675	—	45.00	80.00	140	225	—

KM# 173 2/3 THALER (Gulden)

Silver **Rev:** Swan swimming right, value 2/3 in oval below, legend, date **Rev. Legend:** SILENDO. ET. SPERANDO. **Note:** Varieties exist.

Date	Mintage	VG	F	VF	XF	Unc
1675 (d)	—	45.00	80.00	140	225	—
ND (d)	—	45.00	80.00	140	225	—

KM# 172 2/3 THALER (Gulden)

Silver **Rev:** 21-fold arms divide three stars - 2/3

Date	Mintage	VG	F	VF	XF	Unc
1675 (d)	—	45.00	80.00	140	225	—

KM# 174 2/3 THALER (Gulden)

Silver **Obv:** Bust right wtih lion's head on shoulder **Rev:** Date divided by arms

Date	Mintage	VG	F	VF	XF	Unc
1675 HHF	—	45.00	80.00	140	225	—

KM# 175.1 2/3 THALER (Gulden)

Silver **Ruler:** August von Sachsen-Weissenfels **Rev:** Shield with indented sides

Date	Mintage	VG	F	VF	XF	Unc
1675 HHF	—	45.00	80.00	140	225	—

KM# 175.2 2/3 THALER (Gulden)

Silver **Ruler:** August von Sachsen-Weissenfels **Obv:** Date below bust

Date	Mintage	VG	F	VF	XF	Unc
1675 HHF	—	45.00	80.00	140	225	—
1676 HHF	—	45.00	80.00	140	225	—

KM# 176 2/3 THALER (Gulden)

Silver **Rev:** Mintmaster's initials divided by value below arm **Note:** Varieties exist.

Date	Mintage	VG	F	VF	XF	Unc
1676 HHF	—	45.00	80.00	140	225	—

KM# 179 2/3 THALER (Gulden)

Silver **Obv:** Bust right with lion's head on shoulder, mintmaster's initials below **Note:** Varieties exist.

Date	Mintage	VG	F	VF	XF	Unc
1679 AF	—	55.00	100	200	300	—

KM# 5 THALER

Silver **Obv:** Helmeted arms with divided date above and G-M below **Rev:** Saint standing with standard and shield **Note:** Cathedral Chapter issue. Varieties exist. Dav.#5471.

Date	Mintage	VG	F	VF	XF	Unc
1602 GM	1,000	110	240	450	725	—
1603 GM	1,525	110	240	450	725	—
1604 GM	3,432	110	240	450	725	—
1605 GM	6,371	110	240	450	725	—
1606 GM	7,080	110	240	450	725	—
1607 GM	4,401	110	240	450	725	—

KM# 8 THALER

Silver **Ruler:** Christian Wilhelm von Brandenburg **Obv:** Bust of Christian Wilhelm right **Obv. Legend:** CHRIST: WILH: D: G: P: ARCHIEP: MAGD: P: G: M: B: **Rev:** Helmeted arms with divided date above, G-M below **Note:** Dav.#5473.

Date	Mintage	VG	F	VF	XF	Unc
1608 GM	—	600	1,200	2,250	3,500	—
1609 GM	—	600	1,200	2,250	3,500	—

KM# 9 THALER

Silver **Ruler:** Christian Wilhelm von Brandenburg **Obv:** Narrower bust **Obv. Legend:** CHRISTI:... **Note:** Dav.#5474. Varieties exist.

Date	Mintage	VG	F	VF	XF	Unc
1608 GM	—	200	550	850	2,200	—
1609 GM	—	200	550	850	2,200	—
1610 GM	—	200	550	850	2,200	—
1611 GM	—	200	550	850	2,200	—
1612 GM	—	200	550	850	2,200	—

KM# 16 THALER

Silver **Rev:** G-M in legend **Note:** Dav.#5474A.

Date	Mintage	VG	F	VF	XF	Unc
1611 GM	—	250	400	900	2,250	—

KM# 17 THALER

Silver **Obv. Legend:** CHRISTI: VILH:... **Rev:** G16-11M below arms **Note:** Dav.#5474B.

Date	Mintage	VG	F	VF	XF	Unc
1611 GM	—	250	400	900	2,250	—

KM# 20 THALER

Silver **Rev:** Legend starting on the right **Note:** Dav.#5474C.

Date	Mintage	VG	F	VF	XF	Unc
1612 GM	—	250	400	900	2,250	—

KM# 21 THALER

Silver **Rev:** G-M divided by arms **Note:** Dav.#5474D.

Date	Mintage	VG	F	VF	XF	Unc
1612 GM	—	250	400	900	2,250	—

KM# 22 THALER

Silver **Obv. Legend:** ...ARCHIEP: IAGD:... **Note:** Dav.#5474E.

Date	Mintage	VG	F	VF	XF	Unc
1612 GM	—	250	400	900	2,250	—

KM# 23 THALER

Silver **Obv:** Longer bust right **Rev:** Date divided in legend at top **Note:** Dav.#5475.

Date	Mintage	VG	F	VF	XF	Unc
1612 GM	—	250	400	900	2,250	—

KM# 24 THALER

Silver **Obv. Legend:** CHRISTIAN... **Note:** Dav.#5475A.

Date	Mintage	VG	F	VF	XF	Unc
1612 GM	—	250	400	900	2,250	—

KM# 28 THALER

Silver **Obv:** Different bust with wing collar **Rev:** Date divided by helmets above arms **Note:** Dav.#5476.

Date	Mintage	VG	F	VF	XF	Unc
1613 GM	—	250	400	900	2,250	—

KM# 29 THALER

Silver **Obv:** Half-bust facing **Obv. Legend:** CHRIS. WILH D. G. -P. ADM. MAG. D. PR. **Note:** Dav.#5477.

Date	Mintage	VG	F	VF	XF	Unc
1613 GM Rare	—	—	—	—	—	—

KM# 31 THALER

Silver **Rev:** Fourteen shields surround legend which surrounds Bishop's shield with small shields above and below **Rev. Legend:** PRO: LEGE.-ET. GREGE **Note:** Dav.#5479.

Date	Mintage	VG	F	VF	XF	Unc
ND	—	300	500	1,000	2,500	—

KM# 32 THALER

Silver **Ruler:** Christian Wilhelm von Brandenburg **Obv:** Large facing figure **Rev:** Different frames and shapes of center shield **Note:** Dav.#5480.

Date	Mintage	VG	F	VF	XF	Unc
ND IH-(b)	—	300	500	1,000	2,500	—

KM# 30 THALER

Silver **Obv:** Small half-bust right **Obv. Legend:** CHRIST. WILH. AR. EP. MAGDEB. MAR. BRAND. D. PRVS. **Note:** Dav.#5478.

Date	Mintage	VG	F	VF	XF	Unc
1613 IH/(b) Rare	—	—	—	—	—	—
1613 (b) Rare	—	—	—	—	—	—

KM# 39 THALER

Silver **Obv:** Date above figure **Obv. Legend:** CRISTI. WILH. D: G. AR... **Rev:** St. Mortitz standing with standard and shield, Cathedral at left **Note:** Dav.#5482.

Date	Mintage	VG	F	VF	XF	Unc
1614 IH-(b) Rare	—	—	—	—	—	—

KM# 69 THALER

Silver **Obv:** Oval four-fold arms with central shield of Brandenburg in cartouche **Rev:** Angel above heart-shaped shield of Magdeburg, date above

Date	Mintage	VG	F	VF	XF	Unc
16Z1	—	—	—	—	—	—
1621	—	—	—	—	—	—

KM# 87 THALER

Silver **Ruler:** Christian Wilhelm von Brandenburg **Obv:** Bust right, date below **Rev:** Similar to Dav. #5480 but center arms helmeted with staffs **Note:** Dav. #5483.

Date	Mintage	VG	F	VF	XF	Unc
1623 AK	—	300	500	1,000	2,500	—

KM# 88 THALER

Silver **Obv:** Without date below bust **Note:** Dav. #5484.

Date	Mintage	VG	F	VF	XF	Unc
ND	—	250	500	900	2,000	—

KM# 89 THALER

Silver **Obv. Legend:** CHRIS. WILH. D: G: P. ADM. MAG. MARCH. BR. DVX. P: COAD. HALB: **Note:** Dav. #5485.

Date	Mintage	VG	F	VF	XF	Unc
ND	—	250	500	900	2,000	—

KM# 90 THALER

Silver **Obv. Legend:** CRIS. WILH... **Note:** Dav. #5485A.

Date	Mintage	VG	F	VF	XF	Unc
ND	—	250	500	900	2,000	—

KM# 94 THALER

Silver **Obv:** Legend, date **Obv. Legend:** CRIS. WIL: D: G: P: AD: M: COA: HAL: MAR: BR: DVX: PRV **Note:** Dav. #5486.

Date	Mintage	VG	F	VF	XF	Unc
1624 AK	—	150	300	600	1,200	—

KM# 95 THALER

Silver **Obv. Legend:** CHRIS: WILH: D: G: POST: AD: MAG: E: HALB: M: B: D: P **Note:** Dav. #5487.

Date	Mintage	VG	F	VF	XF	Unc
(16)24 AK	—	100	200	500	1,000	—

KM# 97 THALER

Silver **Ruler:** Christian Wilhelm von Brandenburg **Obv. Legend:** CHRIS*WILH*... **Rev:** Shield separating A-K, date in legend **Note:** Dav. #5490.

Date	Mintage	VG	F	VF	XF	Unc
(16)24 AK	—	100	200	500	1,000	—
(16)25 AK	—	100	200	500	1,000	—

KM# 96 THALER

Silver **Rev:** Shield separating Z-4 and A-K **Note:** Dav. #5488. Varieties exist.

Date	Mintage	VG	F	VF	XF	Unc
(16)Z4 AK	—	—	—	—	—	—
1624 AK	—	125	250	600	1,200	—

KM# 98 THALER

Silver **Ruler:** Christian Wilhelm von Brandenburg **Obv. Legend:** CRIS: WIL: D: G: POSTVL:... **Note:** Dav. #5491.

Date	Mintage	VG	F	VF	XF	Unc
(16)25 AK	—	125	250	600	1,200	—

KM# 99 THALER

Silver **Obv. Legend:** CRIS. WILH. D: G. P... **Note:** Dav. #5492. Varieties exist.

Date	Mintage	VG	F	VF	XF	Unc
ND	—	125	250	600	1,200	—

KM# 100 THALER

Silver **Note:** Similar to KM#99 but without helmet above arms.

Date	Mintage	VG	F	VF	XF	Unc
ND	—	—	—	—	—	—

KM# 109 THALER

Silver **Note:** Cathedral Chapter issue. Similar to KM#110 but PS-X below arms. Dav. #5495.

Date	Mintage	VG	F	VF	XF	Unc
1638 PS(c)	—	125	250	600	1,200	—

KM# 110 THALER

Silver **Obv:** M-K divided above helmeted arms **Note:** Dav. #5495A.

Date	Mintage	VG	F	VF	XF	Unc
1638 MK	—	125	250	600	1,200	—

KM# 111 THALER

Silver **Obv:** M-K divided below helmeted arms **Note:** Dav. #5495B.

Date	Mintage	VG	F	VF	XF	Unc
1638 MK	—	125	250	600	1,200	—

KM# 112 THALER

Silver **Obv:** PS-X divided below helmeted arms **Note:** Dav. #5495C.

Date	Mintage	VG	F	VF	XF	Unc
1638 PS(c)	—	125	250	600	1,200	—

KM# 113 THALER

Silver **Obv:** PS dividing date below helmeted arms **Note:** Dav. #5495D.

Date	Mintage	VG	F	VF	XF	Unc
1638 PS	—	125	250	600	1,200	—

KM# 114 THALER

Silver **Obv:** PSX dividing date below helmeted arms **Note:** Dav. #5495E.

Date	Mintage	VG	F	VF	XF	Unc
1638 PS(c)	—	125	250	600	1,200	—

KM# 115 THALER

Silver **Obv:** PS left of arms, date divided by arms **Note:** Dav. #5496.

Date	Mintage	VG	F	VF	XF	Unc
1638 PS(c)	—	150	300	700	1,400	—

KM# 116 THALER

Silver **Obv:** PS-X and 16-38 below arms **Note:** Dav. #5496A.

Date	Mintage	VG	F	VF	XF	Unc
1638 PS(c)	—	150	300	700	1,400	—

KM# 117 THALER

Silver **Obv:** P S X below arms **Note:** Dav. #5496B.

Date	Mintage	VG	F	VF	XF	Unc
1638 PS(c)	—	150	300	700	1,400	—

KM# 118 THALER
Silver **Obv:** P S X right and 16-38 below arms **Note:** Dav. #5496C. Varieties exist.

Date	Mintage	VG	F	VF	XF	Unc
1638 PS(c)	—	150	300	700	1,400	—

KM# 119 THALER
Silver **Obv:** 11-line inscription **Note:** Dav. #5497. Varieties exist.

Date	Mintage	VG	F	VF	XF	Unc
1638 PS(c)	—	300	500	1,000	2,500	—

KM# 120 THALER
Silver **Rev:** City view at left **Note:** Dav. #5498. Varieties exist.

Date	Mintage	VG	F	VF	XF	Unc
1638 PS(c)S/ML	—	250	500	900	2,000	—

KM# 132 THALER
Silver **Obv:** Facing bust **Obv. Legend:** AUGUSTUS. D: G. POSTULATUS. ARCHIEPISCOPUS. MAGDEBURGEN **Rev:** Helmeted arms, PS-X at sides, date divided at top **Rev. Legend:** PRIMAS. GERMA: DUX-SAX. IUL. CL. E. MONT. **Note:** Dav. #5502.

Date	Mintage	VG	F	VF	XF	Unc
1640 PS(c)	—	350	600	1,200	2,750	—

KM# 133 THALER
Silver **Ruler:** August von Sachsen-Weissenfels **Obv. Legend:** ...POSTUL: ARCHIEP:... **Note:** Dav. #5502A.

Date	Mintage	VG	F	VF	XF	Unc
1640 PS(c)	—	350	600	1,200	2,750	—

KM# 136 THALER
Silver **Rev:** Arms divide PS-X **Rev. Legend:** ...DU-X. SAX... **Note:** Dav. #5503.

Date	Mintage	VG	F	VF	XF	Unc
1641 PS(c)	—	350	600	1,200	2,750	—

KM# 137 THALER
Silver **Obv. Legend:** ...POSTULATUS. ARCHIEPISCOPUS... **Note:** Dav. #5503A.

Date	Mintage	VG	F	VF	XF	Unc
1641 PS(c)	—	350	600	1,200	2,750	—

KM# 138 THALER
Silver **Obv. Legend:** ...MAGDEBURGE **Note:** Dav. #5503B.

Date	Mintage	VG	F	VF	XF	Unc
1641 PS(c)	—	350	600	1,200	2,750	—

KM# 157 THALER
Silver **Obv:** Facing bust with longer, curlier hair **Obv. Legend:** ...POST:ADMI:ARCHI=EP:MADGEB. **Rev:** Date in legend **Note:** Dav. #5504.

Date	Mintage	VG	F	VF	XF	Unc
1669 HHF	—	350	600	1,200	2,750	—

KM# 158 THALER
Silver **Obv:** Bust right **Obv. Legend:** ARCHI-EP **Note:** Dav. #5505.

Date	Mintage	VG	F	VF	XF	Unc
1669 HHF	—	400	650	1,350	3,000	—

KM# 159 THALER
Silver **Rev. Legend:** ...I.C.E.M. **Note:** Dav. #5505A.

Date	Mintage	VG	F	VF	XF	Unc
1669 HHF	—	400	650	1,350	3,000	—

KM# 177 THALER
Silver **Obv:** Larger bust right **Obv. Legend:** D. G. AUGUSTUS... **Note:** Dav. #5506.

Date	Mintage	VG	F	VF	XF	Unc
1677 HHF-SM	—	400	650	1,350	3,000	—

KM# 178 THALER
Silver **Obv:** Different harnessed bust **Note:** Dav. #5507.

Date	Mintage	VG	F	VF	XF	Unc
1677 HHF-SM	—	400	650	1,350	3,000	—

KM# 6 2 THALER
Silver **Note:** Cathedral Chapter issue. Similar to 1 Thaler, KM#5. Dav. #5470.

Date	Mintage	VG	F	VF	XF	Unc
1603 GM Rare	—	—	—	—	—	—
1606 GM Rare	—	—	—	—	—	—

KM# 10 2 THALER
Silver **Obv:** Bust right **Rev:** Helmeted arms with divided date above and G M below **Note:** Archepiscopal issue. Dav. #5472.

Date	Mintage	VG	F	VF	XF	Unc
1609 GM Rare	—	—	—	—	—	—

KM# 40 2 THALER
Silver **Obv:** Half-figure facing with head right, date above **Rev:** St. Moritz standing with standard and shield, Cathedral at left **Note:** Dav. #5481.

Date	Mintage	VG	F	VF	XF	Unc
1614 (b)-IH Rare	—	—	—	—	—	—

KM# 101 2 THALER
Silver **Note:** Similar to 1 Thaler, KM#97. Dav. #5489.

Date	Mintage	VG	F	VF	XF	Unc
1625 AK Rare	—	—	—	—	—	—

KM# 124 2 THALER
Silver **Obv:** Eleven-line inscription **Rev:** Saint standing with banner, sword, and shield **Note:** Dav. #A5497.

Date	Mintage	VG	F	VF	XF	Unc
1638 PS(c) Rare	—	—	—	—	—	—

KM# 122 2 THALER
Silver **Note:** Similar to 1 Thaler, KM#110 but date divided 16-38-PXS. Dav. #5494B.

Date	Mintage	VG	F	VF	XF	Unc
1638 PS(c) Rare	—	—	—	—	—	—

KM# 123 2 THALER
Silver **Subject:** Enthronement of August von Sachsen-Weissenfels **Note:** Similar to 1 Thaler, KM#115. Dav. #A5496.

Date	Mintage	VG	F	VF	XF	Unc
1638 PS(c) Rare	—	—	—	—	—	—

KM# 121 2 THALER
Silver **Note:** Cathedral Chapter issue. Similar to 1 Thaler, KM#110 but with date divided 16-P X S-38. Dav. #5494A.

Date	Mintage	VG	F	VF	XF	Unc
1638 PS(c) Rare	—	—	—	—	—	—

KM# 134 2 THALER
Silver **Obv:** Facing bust **Rev:** Helmeted arms **Note:** Dav. #5501.

Date	Mintage	VG	F	VF	XF	Unc
1640 PS(c) Rare	—	—	—	—	—	—

TRADE COINAGE

KM# 46 1/2 GOLDGULDEN
1.7500 g., 0.9860 Gold 0.0555 oz. AGW **Obv:** Bust of Christian Wilhelm right in inner circle **Rev:** Arms in inner circle

Date	Mintage	VG	F	VF	XF	Unc
ND(1613)	—	375	900	2,200	4,200	—

KM# 61 GOLDGULDEN
3.5000 g., 0.9860 Gold 0.1109 oz. AGW **Note:** Hexagonal klippe.

Date	Mintage	VG	F	VF	XF	Unc
ND(1613) (b) Rare	—	—	—	—	—	—

KM# 47 GOLDGULDEN
3.5000 g., 0.9860 Gold 0.1109 oz. AGW **Obv:** Bust of Christian Wilhelm right in inner circle **Rev:** Arms in inner circle

Date	Mintage	VG	F	VF	XF	Unc
ND(1613) (b)	—	—	—	—	—	—
1615	—	400	975	2,300	4,550	—
(16)23	—	400	975	2,300	4,550	—
ND	282	400	975	2,300	4,550	—

KM# 48 2 GOLDGULDEN
7.0000 g., 0.9860 Gold 0.2219 oz. AGW **Obv:** Bust of Christian Wilhelm right in inner circle **Rev:** Three vertical shields in circle of fourteen shields

Date	Mintage	VG	F	VF	XF	Unc
ND (b) Rare	—	—	—	—	—	—

KM# 125 DUCAT
3.5000 g., 0.9860 Gold 0.1109 oz. AGW **Obv:** Oval arms topped by helmet dividing date, in inner circle **Rev:** St. Maurice standing with banner, sword, and shield in inner circle **Note:** Cathedral Chapter issue.

Date	Mintage	VG	F	VF	XF	Unc
1638 PS(c)	—	300	650	1,300	2,300	—

KM# 126 DUCAT
3.5000 g., 0.9860 Gold 0.1109 oz. AGW **Subject:** Enthronement of Archbishop August **Obv:** Nine-line inscription with date **Rev:** St. Moritz

Date	Mintage	VG	F	VF	XF	Unc
1638	—	325	725	1,450	2,750	—

KM# 135 DUCAT
3.5000 g., 0.9860 Gold 0.1109 oz. AGW **Ruler:** August von Sachsen-Weissenfels **Obv:** August

Date	Mintage	VG	F	VF	XF	Unc
1640 PS	—	400	850	1,800	3,350	—
1641 PS	—	400	850	1,800	3,350	—

CITY

The city of Magdeburg encompassed the seat of the archbishopric. The town received the mint right in 1479 but had already been striking local coinage in the previous century. Magdeburg was besieged in 1550-1551 and again in 1629, during the Thirty Years' War, leading to interesting obsidional coinages. In 1631 the imperial forces under Tilly burned Magdeburg to the ground causing the deaths of 30,000 inhabitants, an act which shocked all of Europe. The city was rebuilt in 1638 and was absorbed by Brandenburg in 1680. The last city coinage is dated 1682. Magdeburg became a mint for Brandenburg-Prussia (q.v.) beginning in 1683. The city was taken by the French in 1806 and reverted to Prussia in 1814.

MINT OFFICIALS' INITIALS

Initial	Date	Name
(a)= [symbol] or [symbol]	1571-1606	Konrad Hundt
HS	1614-26	Henning Schreiber in Halberstadt
(b)= [symbol] or [symbol] and/or HM	1616-18	Heinrich Meyer
PS	1622-39	Peter Schrader
IL	1664-75	Johann Liebmann, warden in Berlin
HPK	1661-63	Hans Philipp Koburger
EFS	1669-70	Ernst Friedrich Schneider
CP	1672-78, 82-83	Christoph Pflug
IE	1673, 78-80	Johann Elers

ARMS

City gate, usually with two towers, maiden holding wreath above gate; sometimes just maiden with wreath.

REGULAR COINAGE

KM# 205 PFENNIG
Silver **Note:** Uniface. Hohl type. City arms. Varieties exist.

Date	Mintage	VG	F	VF	XF	Unc
ND(1592-1612)	—	7.00	13.00	27.00	60.00	—

KM# 230 PFENNIG
Copper **Note:** Kipper Pfennig. Uniface. City arms, date below. Varieties exist.

Date	Mintage	VG	F	VF	XF	Unc
16Z1	—	5.00	11.00	20.00	40.00	—

KM# 265 PFENNIG
Silver **Note:** Uniface. City arms, date divided above.

Date	Mintage	VG	F	VF	XF	Unc
1630	—	7.00	13.00	25.00	45.00	—

KM# 266 PFENNIG
Silver **Note:** City arms divide date.

Date	Mintage	VG	F	VF	XF	Unc
(16)30	—	7.00	13.00	25.00	45.00	—

KM# 318 PFENNIG
Silver **Obv:** City arms **Rev. Inscription:** 1/PFENG/date/mintmaster's initials

Date	Mintage	VG	F	VF	XF	Unc
1675 CP	—	—	—	—	—	—

KM# 212 3 PFENNIG (Dreier)
Silver **Obv:** City arms **Rev:** Imperial orb with 3 divides date **Note:** Varieties exist.

Date	Mintage	VG	F	VF	XF	Unc
1617 (b)	—	16.00	33.00	55.00	95.00	—

KM# 236 3 PFENNIG (Dreier)
Silver **Obv:** City arms in oval baroque frame **Rev:** Imperial orb with 3 divides date within ornamented rhombus **Note:** Varieties exist.

Date	Mintage	VG	F	VF	XF	Unc
16ZZ	—	16.00	30.00	45.00	80.00	—

KM# 239 3 PFENNIG (Dreier)
Silver **Obv:** Without M below arms **Note:** Varieties exist.

Date	Mintage	VG	F	VF	XF	Unc
16ZZ	—	13.00	27.00	45.00	80.00	—
16Z3	—	13.00	27.00	45.00	80.00	—
16Z3 PS	—	13.00	27.00	45.00	80.00	—
1670	—	13.00	27.00	45.00	80.00	—
1670 EFS	—	13.00	27.00	45.00	80.00	—
1673 CP	—	13.00	27.00	45.00	80.00	—
1674 CP	—	13.00	27.00	45.00	80.00	—
1675 CP	—	13.00	27.00	45.00	80.00	—
1676 CP	—	13.00	27.00	45.00	80.00	—
1677	—	13.00	27.00	45.00	80.00	—
1679 IE	—	13.00	27.00	45.00	80.00	—
1680 IE	—	13.00	27.00	45.00	80.00	—

KM# 237 3 PFENNIG (Dreier)
Silver **Rev:** Larger orb without rhombus divides date

Date	Mintage	VG	F	VF	XF	Unc
16ZZ	—	16.00	30.00	45.00	80.00	—

KM# 238 3 PFENNIG (Dreier)
Silver **Obv:** City arms, M below, all in circle **Rev:** Imperial orb with 3 divides date

Date	Mintage	VG	F	VF	XF	Unc
16ZZ	—	16.00	30.00	45.00	80.00	—

KM# 206 1/24 THALER (Groschen)
Silver **Obv:** City arms **Obv. Legend:** MO. NO. CI. MAGDEBVR. **Rev:** Imperial orb with Z4 divides date, titles of Rudolf II **Note:** Varieties exist. Weight varies: 2.2-2.4 grams.

Date	Mintage	VG	F	VF	XF	Unc
1601 (a)	—	16.00	35.00	60.00	120	—
1606 (a)	—	16.00	35.00	60.00	120	—

KM# 210 1/24 THALER (Groschen)
Silver **Obv:** Crowned city arms, titles of Matthias, date divided in legend at top **Note:** Weight varies: 2.2-2.4 grams.

Date	Mintage	VG	F	VF	XF	Unc
1616 (b)	—	13.00	27.00	55.00	95.00	—

KM# 211 1/24 THALER (Groschen)
Silver **Obv:** Without crown above arms **Note:** Varieites exist. Weight varies: 2.2-2.4 grams.

Date	Mintage	VG	F	VF	XF	Unc
1616 (b)	—	13.00	27.00	55.00	95.00	—
1617 (b)	—	13.00	27.00	55.00	95.00	—
1617	—	13.00	27.00	55.00	95.00	—
1618	—	13.00	27.00	55.00	95.00	—

KM# 225 1/24 THALER (Groschen)
Silver **Note:** Kipper 1/24 Thaler. Struck on smaller flan. Weight varies: 0.45-1.24 grams.

Date	Mintage	VG	F	VF	XF	Unc
1619	—	25.00	35.00	55.00	95.00	—

KM# 226 1/24 THALER (Groschen)
4.8100 g., Silver **Note:** Klippe.

Date	Mintage	VG	F	VF	XF	Unc
1619	—	33.00	60.00	100	180	—

KM# 233 1/24 THALER (Groschen)
Silver **Obv:** Titles of Ferdinand II **Note:** Varieties exist.

Date	Mintage	VG	F	VF	XF	Unc
16Z1	—	25.00	40.00	55.00	95.00	—

KM# 234 1/24 THALER (Groschen)
Silver **Obv:** Date above arms **Note:** Varieties exist.

Date	Mintage	VG	F	VF	XF	Unc
16Z1	—	25.00	40.00	55.00	95.00	—

KM# 240 1/24 THALER (Groschen)
Silver **Obv:** Date divided by cross on orb **Note:** Varieties exist. Weight varies: 1.90-2.30 grams.

Date	Mintage	VG	F	VF	XF	Unc
16ZZ	—	20.00	33.00	45.00	100	—

KM# 253 1/24 THALER (Groschen)
Silver **Obv:** City arms **Rev:** Date divided in legend at top **Note:** Varieties exist.

Date	Mintage	VG	F	VF	XF	Unc
16Z3 PS	—	20.00	33.00	45.00	100	—
16Z4 PS	—	20.00	33.00	45.00	100	—
16Z6 PS	—	20.00	33.00	45.00	100	—
1630 PS	—	20.00	33.00	45.00	100	—
1631 PS	—	20.00	33.00	45.00	100	—

KM# 254 1/24 THALER (Groschen)
Silver **Obv:** Date divided above arms **Note:** Varieties exist.

Date	Mintage	VG	F	VF	XF	Unc
16Z3 PS	—	20.00	33.00	45.00	100	—

KM# 261 1/24 THALER (Groschen)
Billon **Obv:** City arms **Rev:** Rose in circle, date **Rev. Legend:** NECESSI(TAS): CARET. LEGE **Note:** Weight varies: 0.75-1.20 grams.

Date	Mintage	VG	F	VF	XF	Unc
16Z9	—	20.00	33.00	45.00	100	—

Note: These siege coins are often found with a rose countermark

KM# 280 1/24 THALER (Groschen)
Silver **Obv:** City arms **Rev:** Imperial orb with 24, titles of Leopold I and date in legend **Rev. Legend:** MO. NO...

Date	Mintage	VG	F	VF	XF	Unc
1661 HPK	—	20.00	33.00	45.00	100	—

KM# 286 1/24 THALER (Groschen)
Silver **Obv:** City arms **Obv. Legend:** MAG DE BURGER **Rev. Legend:** STAD-GELD **Rev. Inscription:** 23 / 1 R: / THALER / date

Date	Mintage	VG	F	VF	XF	Unc
1668 IL	—	20.00	33.00	45.00	100	—

KM# 287 1/24 THALER (Groschen)
Silver **Obv:** City arms **Rev. Inscription:** 24/EINEN/REICHS/THALER/date

Date	Mintage	VG	F	VF	XF	Unc
1669	—	20.00	33.00	45.00	100	—

KM# 288 1/24 THALER (Groschen)
Silver **Rev:** Border of flowers and arches

Date	Mintage	VG	F	VF	XF	Unc
1669	—	15.00	33.00	45.00	100	—

KM# 289 1/24 THALER (Groschen)
Silver **Rev:** Imperial orb wtih 24 divides date, border of flowers and arches **Note:** Varieties exist.

Date	Mintage	VG	F	VF	XF	Unc
1669	—	20.00	33.00	45.00	100	—
1670 EFS	—	20.00	33.00	45.00	100	—

KM# 296 1/24 THALER (Groschen)
Silver **Rev:** Imperial orb with 24 divides date in circle, border of laurel leaves **Note:** Varieties exist.

Date	Mintage	VG	F	VF	XF	Unc
1670 EFS	—	20.00	33.00	45.00	100	—

KM# 298 1/24 THALER (Groschen)
Silver **Rev:** Imperial orb with 24 divides mintmaster's initials left and date right **Rev. Legend:** VERB. DOM. MANET. IN. AETERN. **Note:** Varieties exist.

Date	Mintage	VG	F	VF	XF	Unc
1670 EFS	—	20.00	33.00	45.00	100	—

KM# 299 1/24 THALER (Groschen)
Silver **Rev:** Date and mintmaster's initials divided by orb **Note:** Varieties exist.

Date	Mintage	VG	F	VF	XF	Unc
1670 EFS	—	20.00	33.00	45.00	100	—
1672 CP	—	20.00	33.00	45.00	100	—
1673 CP	—	20.00	33.00	45.00	100	—
1674 CP	—	20.00	33.00	45.00	100	—
1675 CP	—	20.00	33.00	45.00	100	—
1676 CP	—	20.00	33.00	45.00	100	—
1679 IE	—	20.00	33.00	45.00	100	—
1680 IE	—	20.00	33.00	45.00	100	—

KM# 295 1/24 THALER (Groschen)
Silver **Rev:** Orb divides mintmaster's initials left and date right

Date	Mintage	VG	F	VF	XF	Unc
1670 EFS	—	20.00	33.00	45.00	100	—

KM# 297 1/24 THALER (Groschen)
Silver **Rev:** Date and mintmaster's initials divided ".E.F. 16-70. S." in circle around orb

Date	Mintage	VG	F	VF	XF	Unc
1670 EFS	—	20.00	33.00	45.00	100	—

KM# 323 1/24 THALER (Groschen)
Silver **Obv:** City arms in oval baroque frame

Date	Mintage	VG	F	VF	XF	Unc
1677 CP	—	20.00	33.00	45.00	100	—

KM# 334 1/24 THALER (Groschen)
Silver **Obv:** City arms, MO. NO... in half circle above **Rev. Legend:** VERB. DOM... **Rev. Inscription:** 24/EINEN/REICHS/THAL/date

Date	Mintage	VG	F	VF	XF	Unc
1682 CP	—	20.00	33.00	45.00	100	—

KM# 235 1/16 THALER (Doppelschilling)
Silver **Obv:** Intertwined DS, date above **Obv. Legend:** MO. NO... **Rev:** Crowned imperial eagle, blank orb on breast, titles of Ferdinand II **Note:** Kipper 1/16 Thaler.

Date	Mintage	VG	F	VF	XF	Unc
16Z1	—	—	—	—	—	—

KM# 256 1/2 ORT (1/8 Thaler)
Silver **Obv:** City arms **Obv. Legend:** MO. NO. CI... **Rev:** Date divided by small orb at top, titles of Ferdinand II **Rev. Inscription:** EIN / HALB / REICHS / ORT **Note:** Varieties exist.

Date	Mintage	VG	F	VF	XF	Unc
16Z4 PS	—	—	—	—	—	—

KM# 302 1/6 THALER
Silver **Obv:** City arms **Rev:** Inscription between laurel and palm branches, date divided by orb at top **Rev. Legend:** VERBUM. DOMINI... **Rev. Inscription:** VI / EINEN / REICHS / THALER / mintmaster's initials

Date	Mintage	VG	F	VF	XF	Unc
1672 CP	—	—	—	—	—	—

KM# 231 12 KREUZER (4 Groschen - Schreckenberger)
Silver **Obv:** City arms, date above **Rev:** Crowned imperial eagle, 1Z in orb on breast, titles of Ferdinand II **Note:** Kipper 12 Kreuzer. Varieties exist.

Date	Mintage	VG	F	VF	XF	Unc
16Z1	—	40.00	65.00	100	160	—

KM# 232 4 GROSCHEN (12 Kreuzer - Schreckenberger)
Silver **Obv:** City arms, date above **Rev:** Crowned imperial eagle, 4 in orb on breast, titles of Ferdinand II **Note:** Kipper 4 Groschen. Varieties exist.

Date	Mintage	VG	F	VF	XF	Unc
16Z1	—	55.00	85.00	165	275	—

KM# 331 4 GROSCHEN (12 Kreuzer - Schreckenberger)
Silver **Obv:** City arms **Rev. Legend:** VERBUM DOMINI... **Rev. Inscription:** IIII / GUTE / GROSCHEN / date / mintmaster's initials **Note:** Gute 4 Groschen.

Date	Mintage	VG	F	VF	XF	Unc
1682 CP	—	—	—	—	—	—

KM# 249 6 GROSCHEN (Ort - 1/4 Thaler)
Silver **Obv:** Helmeted city arms in shield **Rev:** Crowned imperial eagle, 6 in orb on breast, titles of Ferdinand II, date divided at top **Rev. Legend:** MO. NO. CIVI...

Date	Mintage	VG	F	VF	XF	Unc
16Z3 PS	—	115	220	375	625	—

KM# 250 6 GROSCHEN (Ort - 1/4 Thaler)
Silver **Obv:** City arms **Rev:** Value in circle on breast of double-headed imperial eagle, crown above **Note:** Varieties exist.

Date	Mintage	VG	F	VF	XF	Unc
16Z3 PS	—	85.00	165	300	575	—
16Z4 PS	—	85.00	165	300	575	—

KM# 259 6 GROSCHEN (Ort - 1/4 Thaler)
Silver **Obv:** City arms **Rev. Legend:** NECESSITAS. LEGEM. NON. HABET. **Rev. Inscription:** VI / GROSCHEN / MAGDEBVR: / STATGELT / date

Date	Mintage	VG	F	VF	XF	Unc
16Z9	—	100	200	350	600	—

Note: The above are often found with a rose countermark

KM# 300 1/3 THALER (1/2 Gulden)
Silver **Note:** Varieties exist.

Date	Mintage	VG	F	VF	XF	Unc
1670 EFS	—	80.00	140	200	350	—
1671	—	80.00	140	200	350	—
1672 CP	—	80.00	140	200	350	—
1673 CP	—	80.00	140	200	350	—
1674 CP	—	80.00	140	200	350	—

KM# 314 1/3 THALER (1/2 Gulden)
Silver **Obv:** Value 1/3 in oval baroque frame within oak and palm branches, date at top **Rev:** City arms

Date	Mintage	VG	F	VF	XF	Unc
1674 CP	—	85.00	160	230	375	—

KM# 319 1/3 THALER (1/2 Gulden)
Silver **Obv:** City view from river, "Jehovah" in rayed oval above **Rev:** Helmeted four-fold arms, date in legend

Date	Mintage	VG	F	VF	XF	Unc
1675 CP	—	—	—	—	—	—

KM# 332 8 GUTE GROSCHEN
Silver **Obv:** City arms **Rev. Legend:** VERBUM DOMINI... **Rev. Inscription:** VIII / GUTE / GROSCHEN / date, mintmaster's initials

Date	Mintage	VG	F	VF	XF	Unc
1682 CP	—	—	—	—	—	—

KM# 213 12 GROSCHEN (1/2 Thaler)
Silver **Obv:** City arms, date above **Rev:** Crowned imperial eagle, 1Z in orb on breast, titles of Matthias

Date	Mintage	VG	F	VF	XF	Unc
1617 HM	—	—	—	—	—	—

KM# 251 12 GROSCHEN (1/2 Thaler)
Silver **Obv:** Helmeted city arms in shield **Rev:** Date divided by crown at top, titles of Ferdinand II

Date	Mintage	VG	F	VF	XF	Unc
16Z3 PS	—	275	450	800	1,350	—

KM# 252 12 GROSCHEN (1/2 Thaler)
Silver **Obv:** Plain city arms **Rev:** Value in circle on breast of double-headed imperial eagle, crown above **Note:** Varieties exist.

Date	Mintage	VG	F	VF	XF	Unc
16Z3 PS	—	225	400	675	1,200	—
16Z4 PS	—	225	400	675	1,200	—
16Z5 PS	—	225	400	675	1,200	—
16Z7 PS	—	225	400	675	1,200	—
1630 PS	—	225	400	675	1,200	—

KM# 260 12 GROSCHEN (1/2 Thaler)
Silver **Obv:** City arms **Rev. Legend:** NECESSITAS.LEGEM. NON.HABET. **Rev. Inscription:** XII / GROSCHEN / MAGDEBVR: / STATGELT / date **Note:** Varieties exist.

Date	Mintage	VG	F	VF	XF	Unc
16Z9	—	135	275	450	850	—

KM# 214 1/2 THALER (12 Groschen)
Silver **Subject:** Centennial of the Protestant Reformation **Note:** Similar to 1 Thaler, KM#215.

Date	Mintage	VG	F	VF	XF	Unc
1617	—	135	225	400	525	—

KM# 273 1/2 THALER (12 Groschen)
Silver **Obv:** City arms, date in legend **Rev:** Crowned imperial eagle, bust of emperor in oval on breast, titles of Ferdinand III

Date	Mintage	VG	F	VF	XF	Unc
1639	—	—	—	—	—	—

KM# 324 1/2 THALER (12 Groschen)
Silver **Obv:** City view from river, "Jehovah" in rayed oval above **Rev:** Helmeted four-fold arms, date in legend

Date	Mintage	VG	F	VF	XF	Unc
1678 IE	—	—	—	—	—	—

KM# 301 16 GUTE GROSCHEN
Silver **Obv:** City arms in oval baroque frame **Rev:** Inscription in laurel and palm wreath **Rev. Inscription:** XVI / GUTE / GROSCHEN / date

Date	Mintage	VG	F	VF	XF	Unc
1672 CP	—	400	675	1,150	1,600	—
1673 CP	—	400	675	1,150	1,600	—

KM# 306 16 GUTE GROSCHEN
Silver **Rev:** GROSCH:... **Note:** Varieties exist.

Date	Mintage	VG	F	VF	XF	Unc
1673 CP	—	400	675	1,150	1,600	—
1674 CP	—	400	675	1,150	1,600	—

KM# 313 16 GUTE GROSCHEN
Silver **Obv:** Round arms in floral ring **Obv. Legend:** MONETA. NOVA...

Date	Mintage	VG	F	VF	XF	Unc
1674 CP	—	400	675	1,150	1,600	—

KM# 333 16 GUTE GROSCHEN
Silver **Obv:** City arms **Rev:** XVI/GUTE/GROSCHEN/date/mintmaster's initials **Rev. Legend:** VERBUM DOMINI... **Note:** Varieties exist.

Date	Mintage	VG	F	VF	XF	Unc
1682 CP	—	135	275	450	800	—

KM# 303 2/3 THALER (Gulden)
Silver **Obv:** Helmeted four-fold arms **Obv. Legend:** MONETA. NOVA... **Rev:** Inscription divided by 2/3, all in laurel and palm wreath **Rev. Inscription:** VERBUM / DOMINI / MANET.IN. / AETERNUM / date **Note:** Varieties exist.

Date	Mintage	VG	F	VF	XF	Unc
1672 CP	—	—	—	—	—	—

KM# 304 2/3 THALER (Gulden)
Silver **Obv:** City arms in oval baroque frame **Note:** Varieties exist.

Date	Mintage	VG	F	VF	XF	Unc
1672 CP	—	—	—	—	—	—

KM# 305 2/3 THALER (Gulden)
Silver **Obv:** City arms **Rev:** Inscription divided by 2/3, in laurel and palm wreath **Rev. Inscription:** VERBUM / DOMINI / MANET.IN. / AETERNUM / date

Date	Mintage	VG	F	VF	XF	Unc
1672 CP	—	—	—	—	—	—

KM# 316 2/3 THALER (Gulden)
Silver **Obv:** City arms in oval baroque frame **Rev:** Inscription divided by 2/3, in laurel and palm wreath **Rev. Inscription:** VERBUM / DOMINI / MANET.IN. / AETERNUM / date

Date	Mintage	VG	F	VF	XF	Unc
1674 CP	—	65.00	125	200	350	—

KM# 317.1 2/3 THALER (Gulden)
Silver **Obv:** City arms in circle, date divided by rosette at top **Obv. Legend:** MONETA. NOV: CIV. MAGDEBURG **Rev:** 4-line inscription, value '2/3' in oval below, border of laurel and palm branches **Rev. Inscription:** VERB. / DOMINI / MANET. IN / ÆTERN **Note:** Varieties exist.

Date	Mintage	VG	F	VF	XF	Unc
1674 CP	—	45.00	85.00	140	275	—

KM# 317.2 2/3 THALER (Gulden)
Silver, 34 mm. **Obv:** City arms with lower part in half circle, date divided by rosette above. **Obv. Legend:** MONETA. NOV. CIV. MAGDEBURG **Rev:** 4-line inscription, value '2/3' in oval below, laurel and palm branches in margin **Rev. Inscription:** VERV / DOMINI / MAET. IN /ÆTERN

Date	Mintage	VG	F	VF	XF	Unc
1674 cp	—	45.00	85.00	140	275	—

KM# 315 2/3 THALER (Gulden)
Silver **Note:** Varieties exist.

Date	Mintage	VG	F	VF	XF	Unc
1674 CP	—	65.00	125	200	325	—
1675 CP	—	65.00	125	200	325	—

KM# 320 2/3 THALER (Gulden)
Silver **Note:** Varieties exist.

Date	Mintage	VG	F	VF	XF	Unc
1675 CP	—	45.00	85.00	140	275	—

KM# 321 2/3 THALER (Gulden)
Silver **Obv:** Date complete in obverse legend **Note:** Varieties exist.

Date	Mintage	VG	F	VF	XF	Unc
1675 CP	—	55.00	100	160	300	—
1676 CP	—	55.00	100	160	300	—

KM# 325 2/3 THALER (Gulden)
Silver **Obv:** City arms, date divided at top **Rev:** Similar to KM#320

Date	Mintage	VG	F	VF	XF	Unc
1678 CP	—	55.00	100	160	300	—

KM# 208 THALER (24 Groschen)
Silver **Obv:** Young lady above city gate **Rev:** Crowned imperial ealge with 24 in orb on breast, date above **Note:** Dav. #5508.

Date	Mintage	VG	F	VF	XF	Unc
1603 (a) Rare	—	—	—	—	—	—

KM# 216 THALER (24 Groschen)
Silver **Note:** Dav. #5509A. Klippe.

Date	Mintage	VG	F	VF	XF	Unc
1617 HM Rare	—	—	—	—	—	—

KM# 217 THALER (24 Groschen)
Silver **Obv:** Young lady above city gate, date above **Obv. Legend:** MATTHIAS: II: D: G: ROM: IMP: SEM: AV: **Rev:** Crowned imperial eagle, H-M below **Rev. Legend:** MONETA: NO: CI: MAGDEBVRGK **Note:** Dav. #5510.

Date	Mintage	VG	F	VF	XF	Unc
1617 HM	—	300	700	1,500	3,000	—

KM# 218 THALER (24 Groschen)
Silver **Obv. Legend:** MATTHI-II-D-G-RO-IMP-SEM-A **Rev. Legend:** MO NO. AVR. CI. MAGDEBVR **Note:** Dav. #5511.

Date	Mintage	VG	F	VF	XF	Unc
1617	—	300	700	1,500	3,000	—

KM# 215 THALER (24 Groschen)
Silver **Subject:** 100th Anniversary of the Reformation **Obv:** Crowned imperial eagle with arms on breast **Rev:** Half busts of Huss and Luther within double legend **Note:** Dav. #5509. Varieties exist.

Date	Mintage	VG	F	VF	XF	Unc
1617	—	350	600	1,250	2,750	—
1617 HM	—	—	—	—	—	—

KM# 221 THALER (24 Groschen)
Silver **Obv. Legend:** MATHI. D. G. ROM. -IMP. SEMP. AVGVS. **Rev:** Legend, date **Rev. Legend:** MON * NOVA * CIVITAT * MAGDEBVRCK **Note:** Dav. #5512.

Date	Mintage	VG	F	VF	XF	Unc
1618	—	300	700	1,500	3,000	—

KM# 222 THALER (24 Groschen)
28.5300 g., Silver **Subject:** Founding of the City **Obv:** Emperor Otto I (936-73) on horseback to right, date in exergue **Rev:** Crowned imperial eagle, 4-fold arms on breast **Note:** Dav. #5514.

Date	Mintage	VG	F	VF	XF	Unc
1618 Rare	—	—	—	—	—	—

KM# 241 THALER (24 Groschen)
Silver **Obv:** Emperor riding galloping horse right, date divided below **Rev:** Wagon pulled left towards city by two doves and two swans with standing Venus and the Three Graces, four-line inscription in tablet below divides date

Date	Mintage	VG	F	VF	XF	Unc
16ZZ HS	—	850	1,500	2,250	5,000	—

KM# 242 THALER (24 Groschen)
Silver **Obv:** Emperor Otto I and Empress Edith enthroned, imperial eagle in shield centered above, four-line inscription with foundation date 938 below **Rev:** City view, arms above in band MAGDA-BVRG, divide Roman numeral date, three-line inscription in cartouche below

Date	Mintage	VG	F	VF	XF	Unc
16ZZ PS	—	—	—	—	—	—

KM# 255 THALER (24 Groschen)
Silver **Obv:** Large city arms, towers break circle at upper left and right **Rev:** Crowned imperial eagle, 'Z4' in orb on breast, date divided by crown at top, mintmaster's initials divided to left and right of eagle's claws **Rev. Legend:** FERDINAND II - D:G: RO: IM. S.A **Note:** Dav. #5516. Varieties exist.

Date	Mintage	VG	F	VF	XF	Unc
16Z3 PS	—	125	250	750	1,650	—
16Z4 PS	—	125	250	750	1,650	—
16Z5 PS	—	125	250	750	1,650	—
16Z6 PS	—	125	250	750	1,650	—
16Z7 PS	—	125	250	750	1,650	—
16Z8 PS	—	125	250	750	1,650	—
16Z9 PS	—	125	250	750	1,650	—
1630 PS	—	125	250	750	1,650	—

KM# A255 THALER (24 Groschen)
Silver, 41.5 mm. **Rev:** Mintmaster's initials divided by eagles' necks to left and right.

Date	Mintage	VG	F	VF	XF	Unc
1630 PS	—	125	250	750	1,650	—

KM# 267 THALER (24 Groschen)
Silver **Subject:** Rebuilding the City **Obv:** Maiden above helmeted arms **Rev:** Crowned imperial eagle with Emperor's bust, legend in straight lines around **Note:** Dav. #5518.

Date	Mintage	VG	F	VF	XF	Unc
1638 PS	—	300	600	1,250	2,000	—

KM# 268 THALER (24 Groschen)
Silver **Subject:** Reconstruction of the City, 1638-1642 **Obv:** Maiden facing, flanked by towers **Rev:** Oval shield on breast of double-headed imperial eagle **Note:** Dav. #5520.

Date	Mintage	VG	F	VF	XF	Unc
1638 PS	—	250	550	1,000	1,900	—

KM# 282 THALER (24 Groschen)
Silver **Rev:** Helmeted arms with girl above dividing date **Note:** Dav. #5521.

Date	Mintage	VG	F	VF	XF	Unc
1661 HPK	—	1,650	3,000	5,000	8,100	—

KM# 283 THALER (24 Groschen)
Silver **Rev:** Girl above city gate dividing date **Note:** Dav. #5523.

Date	Mintage	VG	F	VF	XF	Unc
1661 HPK	—	1,650	3,000	5,000	8,100	—

KM# 285 THALER (24 Groschen)
Silver **Rev. Legend:** MONETA: ARGENTEA: CIVITATIS. MAGDEBVRG **Note:** Dav. #5524.

Date	Mintage	VG	F	VF	XF	Unc
1662 HPK	—	1,650	3,000	5,000	8,100	—

KM# 307 THALER (24 Groschen)
Silver **Obv:** "Jehovah" in Hebrew above city view **Note:** Dav. #5526.

Date	Mintage	VG	F	VF	XF	Unc
1673 CP	—	1,000	2,150	3,650	5,000	—

KM# 308 THALER (24 Groschen)
Silver **Obv. Legend:** MON. NO. CIV. MAGDEB. **Note:** Dav. #5527.

Date	Mintage	VG	F	VF	XF	Unc
1673 CP	—	700	1,500	2,500	4,000	—

KM# 326 THALER (24 Groschen)
Silver **Rev:** Girl breaks legend at top and divides date **Note:** Dav. #5528.

Date	Mintage	VG	F	VF	XF	Unc
1678 IE	—	1,000	1,800	3,000	5,000	—
1680 IE	—	1,000	1,800	3,000	5,000	—

KM# 330 THALER (24 Groschen)
Silver **Rev:** Inner circle ends with legend **Note:** Dav. #5529.

Date	Mintage	VG	F	VF	XF	Unc
1680 IE	—	1,100	1,900	3,200	5,000	—

KM# 335 THALER (24 Groschen)
Silver **Subject:** Deliverance from the Plague **Obv:** City view, sun shining from clouds, inscription in band above **Rev:** Two maidens in landscape, Eye of God with rays in clouds above, inscription in band above, three-line inscription with date below

Date	Mintage	VG	F	VF	XF	Unc
168Z CP Rare	—	—	—	—	—	—

KM# 309 1-1/4 THALER
Silver **Note:** Dav. #A5525.

Date	Mintage	VG	F	VF	XF	Unc
1673 CP Rare	—	—	—	—	—	—

KM# 243 1-1/2 THALER
Silver **Subject:** Founding of the City by Emperor Otto I the Great **Obv:** Emperor riding galloping horse right, date divided below **Rev:** Wagon pulled left towards city by two doves and two swans with standing Venus and the Three Graces, four-line inscription in tablet below divides date

Date	Mintage	VG	F	VF	XF	Unc
16ZZ HS Rare	—	—	—	—	—	—

KM# 310 1-1/2 THALER
Silver **Note:** Similar to 1-1/4 Thaler, KM#309. Dav. #B5525.

Date	Mintage	VG	F	VF	XF	Unc
1673 CP Rare	—	—	—	—	—	—

KM# 227 2 THALER
Silver **Subject:** Founding of the City **Obv:** Emperor Otto on horseback right **Rev:** Crowned double eagle with shield on breast **Note:** Dav. #5513.

Date	Mintage	VG	F	VF	XF	Unc
1618 Rare	—	—	—	—	—	—

KM# 245 2 THALER
Silver **Note:** Hexagonal klippe.

Date	Mintage	VG	F	VF	XF	Unc
16ZZ HS Rare	—	—	—	—	—	—

KM# 244 2 THALER
Silver **Obv:** Emperor riding galloping horse right, date divided below **Rev:** Wagon pulled left by two doves and two swans with standing Venus and the Three Graces, four-line inscription in tablet below divides date

Date	Mintage	VG	F	VF	XF	Unc
16ZZ HS Rare	—	—	—	—	—	—

KM# 257 2 THALER
Silver **Note:** Similar to 1 Thaler, KM#255. Dav. #5515.

Date	Mintage	VG	F	VF	XF	Unc
1624 PS Rare	—	—	—	—	—	—
1625 PS Rare	—	—	—	—	—	—

KM# 269 2 THALER
Silver **Subject:** Rebuilding of the City **Obv:** Crowned double eagle with Emperor's bust, legend in straight lines around **Rev:** Maiden above helmeted arms **Note:** Dav. #5517.

Date	Mintage	VG	F	VF	XF	Unc
1638 PS Rare	—	—	—	—	—	—

KM# 270 2 THALER
Silver **Subject:** Reconstruction of the City, 1638-1642 **Note:** Dav. #5519. Similar to 1 Thaler, KM#268.

Date	Mintage	VG	F	VF	XF	Unc
1638 PS Rare	—	—	—	—	—	—

KM# 284 2 THALER
Silver **Rev:** Girl above city gate dividing date **Note:** Dav. #5522.

Date	Mintage	VG	F	VF	XF	Unc
1661 HPK Rare	—	—	—	—	—	—

KM# 311 2 THALER
Silver **Note:** Dav. #5525. Similar to 1-1/4 Thaler, KM#309.

Date	Mintage	VG	F	VF	XF	Unc
1673 CP Rare	—	—	—	—	—	—

Note: Giessener Munzhandlung Auction 6 11-73 VF realized approximately $6,300

KM# 246 3 THALER
Silver **Subject:** Founding of the City by Emperor Otto I the Great **Obv:** Emperor riding galloping horse right, date divided below **Rev:** Wagon pulled left towards city by two doves and two swans with standing Venus and the Three Graces, four-line inscription in tablet divides date

Date	Mintage	VG	F	VF	XF	Unc
16ZZ HS Rare	—	—	—	—	—	—

TRADE COINAGE

KM# 207 GOLDGULDEN
3.5000 g., 0.9860 Gold 0.1109 oz. AGW **Obv:** Crowned imperial eagle in inner circle, titles of Rudolf II **Rev:** Young women above two-towered city gate in inner circle

Date	Mintage	VG	F	VF	XF	Unc
1605 (a)	—	300	550	1,200	2,150	—
1606 (a)	—	300	550	1,200	2,150	—

KM# 219 GOLDGULDEN
3.5000 g., 0.9860 Gold 0.1109 oz. AGW **Obv:** Titles of Matthias

Date	Mintage	VG	F	VF	XF	Unc
1617 (b)	—	525	1,150	2,400	4,500	—

KM# 220 GOLDGULDEN
3.5000 g., 0.9860 Gold 0.1109 oz. AGW **Obv:** Crowned imperial eagle in inner circle, titles of Matthias **Rev:** Arms topped by helmet in inner circle

Date	Mintage	VG	F	VF	XF	Unc
ND	—	400	850	1,800	3,350	—

KM# 247 GOLDGULDEN
3.5000 g., 0.9860 Gold 0.1109 oz. AGW **Obv:** Titles of Ferdinand II

Date	Mintage	VG	F	VF	XF	Unc
1622 PS	—	220	450	725	1,750	—
1624 PS	—	275	600	1,250	2,550	—

KM# 258 GOLDGULDEN
3.5000 g., 0.9860 Gold 0.1109 oz. AGW **Rev:** Titles of Ferdinand II **Note:** Varieties exist.

Date	Mintage	VG	F	VF	XF	Unc
1626 PS	—	220	450	725	1,750	—
1627 PS	—	220	450	725	1,750	—
1628 PS	—	220	450	725	1,750	—
1629 PS	—	220	450	725	1,750	—
1630 PS	—	220	450	725	1,750	—

KM# 271 DUCAT
3.5000 g., 0.9860 Gold 0.1109 oz. AGW **Subject:** Rebuilding of the City **Obv:** Crowned imperial eagle in inner circle **Rev:** Value and date in tablet

Date	Mintage	VG	F	VF	XF	Unc
1638 PS	—	260	575	1,100	2,300	—
1641 PS	—	260	575	1,100	2,300	—
1642 PS	—	260	575	1,100	2,300	—

KM# 312 DUCAT
3.5000 g., 0.9860 Gold 0.1109 oz. AGW **Rev:** Arms topped by helmet in inner circle

Date	Mintage	VG	F	VF	XF	Unc
1673 CP	—	450	1,050	2,250	4,500	—

KM# 274 2 DUCAT
7.0000 g., 0.9860 Gold 0.2219 oz. AGW **Obv:** Crowned imperial eagle in inner circle **Rev:** Young woman above two-towered city gate

Date	Mintage	VG	F	VF	XF	Unc
1639 Rare	—	—	—	—	—	—

KM# 322 2 DUCAT
7.0000 g., 0.9860 Gold 0.2219 oz. AGW **Obv:** View of Magdeburg **Rev:** Arms topped by helmet in inner circle

Date	Mintage	VG	F	VF	XF	Unc
1675 CP Rare	—	—	—	—	—	—

KM# A323 4 DUCAT
14.0000 g., 0.9860 Gold 0.4438 oz. AGW **Obv:** View of Magdeburg **Rev:** Arms topped by helmet

Date	Mintage	VG	F	VF	XF	Unc
1675 CP Rare	—	—	—	—	—	—

KM# A223 5 DUCAT (1/2 Portugaloser)

Gold **Obv:** City arms in arc beginning at right **Obv. Legend:** MONETA. NOVA. AVREA. CIVITA. MAGDEBV. **Obv. Inscription:** NACH-PORTV-SCHROT **Rev:** Large ornate cross **Rev. Legend:** CRVX. XPI SALVS. NOSTRA. & REDEMPTIO. E. **Note:** FR#1534.

Date	Mintage	VG	F	VF	XF	Unc
ND(1573-1606) (a)	—	—	—	—	—	—

KM# 272 5 DUCAT (1/2 Portugaloser)

17.5000 g., 0.9860 Gold 0.5547 oz. AGW **Subject:** Rebuilding of the City **Obv:** Crowned imperial eagle with Emperor's bust, legend in straight lines around **Rev:** Maiden above helmeted arms

Date	Mintage	VG	F	VF	XF	Unc
1638 PS Rare	—	—	—	—	—	—

KM# 223 10 DUCAT (Portugaloser)

35.0000 g., 0.9860 Gold 1.1095 oz. AGW **Obv:** City arms, NACH-PORTV-SCHROT in arc beginning at right **Obv. Legend:** MONETA. NOVE. AVREA. CIVITA. MAGDEBV. **Rev:** Large ornate cross **Rev. Legend:** CRVX. XPI. SALVS. NOSTRA. & REDEMPTIO. E. **Note:** Fr.#1533.

Date	Mintage	VG	F	VF	XF	Unc
ND(1573-1606) (a) Rare	—	—	—	—	—	—

KM# 224 10 DUCAT (Portugaloser)

35.0000 g., 0.9860 Gold 1.1095 oz. AGW **Obv:** Crowned imperial eagle with shield on breast **Rev:** Emperor Otto on horseback right **Note:** Varieties exist.

Date	Mintage	VG	F	VF	XF	Unc
1618 (b)	—	—	—	14,500	20,000	—

KM# 248 10 DUCAT (Portugaloser)

35.0000 g., 0.9860 Gold 1.1095 oz. AGW **Subject:** Founding of the City by Emperor Otto I the Great **Obv:** Emperor riding galloping horse right, date divided below **Rev:** Wagon pulled left towards city by two doves and two swans with standing Venus and the Three Graces, four-line inscription in tablet below divides date

Date	Mintage	VG	F	VF	XF	Unc
16ZZ HS	—	—	—	12,000	17,500	—

PATTERNS

Including off metal strikes

KM#	Date	Mintage	Identification	Mkt Val
Pn1	ND(1623)	—	1/4 Thaler. Copper. Klippe.	—

TRIAL STRIKES

KM#	Date	Mintage	Identification	Mkt Val
TS1	1617	—	1/30 Thaler. Silver. Klippe. Imperial orb wtih 30, cross divides date.	—

MAINZ

Mainz, located on the Rhine 25 miles west of Frankfurt, became an archbishopric in 747. It was a residence and mint of Charlemagne, and the Imperial Mint established then functioned into the 11th century. The archbishops were recognized as presidents of the electoral college and arch-chancellors of the Empire by the Golden Bull of 1356. In 1797, Mainz was ceded to France and in 1801 the French annexed all of the territories on the left bank of the Rhine. The remaining lands were secularized in 1803 and portions were divided between Hesse-Darmstadt, Nassau and Prussia.

Mainz became a Free City of the Empire in 1118 but lost the title in 1163 through an unsuccessful revolt against ecclesiastical authority. The city obtained the mint right in 1420 but rarely availed itself of the privilege. It was occupied by Sweden from 1631 to 1635 during the 30 Years' War. Siege coins were struck in 1793 when the French garrison was besieged by the Prussians.

RULERS

Wolfgang von Dalberg, 1582-1601
Johann Adam von Bicken, 1601-1604
Johann Schweickhard von Kronberg, 1604-1626
Georg Friedrich von Greiffenklau zu Wollrath, 1626-1629
Anselm Casimir Wamboldt von Umstaedt, 1629-1647
Swedish, 1631-1635
Johann Philipp, Graf von Schönborn, 1647-1673
Lothar Friedrich, Freiherr von Metternich-Burscheid, 1673-1675
Damian Hartard, Freiherr von der Leyen, 1675-1678
Karl Heinrich von Metternich-Winneburg, Jan.-Sept. 1679
Anselm Franz, Freiherr von Ingelheim, 1679-1695
Lothar Franz, Graf von Schönborn, 1695-1729

MINT OFFICIALS' INITIALS

Initial	Date	Name
AD	1690	Andreas Dittmar in Erfurt
	1690-92	In Mainz
AE	1618-36	Kaspar Ayrer in Frankfurt am Main
AK	Ca.1693	
AL	1678-83	Adam Longerich in Coblenz
	1683-84	In Mainz
BR	Ca.1641	
BS	1629-33	Benedict Stephani
CB	1692-96	Conrad Bethmann in Aschaffenburg
DA	1627-29, 33-36	Daniel Ayrer in Mainz
Et	1643-44	Ernst Textor
ET	1644-51	Etherius Hettinger
F, MF	1652-83	Matthias Fischer
GB	1692	Johann Gerhard Bender in Mainz
GFN	1682-1724	Georg Friedrich Nurnberger in Nürnberg
GFS	1689	Georg Friedrich Staude in Erfurt
HC	Ca.1641	
ICD	1673-76	Johann Christoph Durr in Erfurt
ICS	1690-91	Johann Christoph Staude in Erfurt
IGL	1691-92	Johann (Hans) Georg Langbehn (Langbein) in Aschaffenburg
IH	1675-76	Johann Horcher, mint treasurer in Erfurt
IS	Ca.1602	
KD	Ca.1676	
LS	1611-30	Lorenz Schilling, die-cutter in Frankfurt am Main
MG	1642	Johann Martin Ganser in Hanau
PE	Ca.1642	
VBW	1684-88, 1702-14	Ulrich Burkhard Willerding
	1586-1607	Andreas Wachsmuth the Elder
	1609-19	Hennig Kissels in Aschaffenburg
	1621-23	Andreas Wachsmuth the Younger
	1622-?	Johann Wolf Palm, warden
	Ca.1628	Philipp Schad (Scheid), warden
	1629-?	Michael Kapp (Capp), warden
	1636-40	Adolf Koch, warden
	1636-42	Philipp Schad, warden 2nd time
	1640-42	Hans Georg Dumwald von Geinhausen, warden
	1690-?	Johann Jacob Birkenholz, warden
	1691-?	Johann Georg Bickel, die-cutter

ARMS

A wheel with six spokes

ARCHBISHOPRIC

REGULAR COINAGE

KM# 54 8 HELLER

Silver **Note:** Uniface. G/ARS/8.

Date	Mintage	VG	F	VF	XF	Unc
ND	—	33.00	65.00	135	200	—

KM# 5 PFENNIG

Silver **Note:** Uniface. Schussel type. 4-fold arms of Mainz and Bicken, IA above. Varieties exist.

Date	Mintage	VG	F	VF	XF	Unc
ND(1601-04)	—	8.00	13.00	27.00	55.00	—

KM# 30 PFENNIG

Silver **Note:** Uniface. Hohl type. Arms of Mianz (wheel), ML (Mainzer Landmunze) above.

Date	Mintage	VG	F	VF	XF	Unc
ND(1622)	—	8.00	13.00	27.00	55.00	—

KM# 39 PFENNIG

Silver **Note:** Crowned 4-fold arms of Mainz and Umstadt.

Date	Mintage	VG	F	VF	XF	Unc
ND(1629-47)	—	8.00	13.00	27.00	55.00	—

KM# 91 PFENNIG

Silver **Note:** 2-fold arms divided vertically, Mainz on left, Unstadt right, mintmaster's initials above.

Date	Mintage	VG	F	VF	XF	Unc
ND(1643-46) ET	—	8.00	13.00	27.00	55.00	—

KM# 97 PFENNIG

Silver **Note:** 2-fold arms of Mainz and Schonborn divided vertically, 6-petalled rose above.

Date	Mintage	VG	F	VF	XF	Unc
ND(1647-73)	—	8.00	13.00	27.00	55.00	—

KM# 99 PFENNIG

Silver **Note:** MF above arms.

Date	Mintage	VG	F	VF	XF	Unc
ND(1647-73?)	—	8.00	13.00	27.00	55.00	—

KM# 98 PFENNIG

Silver **Note:** Schussel type. W. W. above arms.

Date	Mintage	VG	F	VF	XF	Unc
ND(1647-73?)	—	8.00	13.00	27.00	55.00	—

KM# 132 PFENNIG

Silver **Note:** Arms of Mainz and Leyen divided vertically.

Date	Mintage	VG	F	VF	XF	Unc
ND(1675-78)	—	8.00	13.00	27.00	45.00	—

KM# 156 PFENNIG

Silver **Obv:** Crowned arms of Mainz, date divided near top **Rev:** Imperial orb with 1 in cartouche

Date	Mintage	VG	F	VF	XF	Unc
1677	—	8.00	13.00	27.00	45.00	—

KM# 175 PFENNIG

Silver **Note:** Uniface. Arms of Mainz and Ingelheim divided vertically, mintmaster's initials above. Varieties exist.

Date	Mintage	VG	F	VF	XF	Unc
ND(ca.1680/1) MF	—	8.00	13.00	27.00	45.00	—
ND(ca.1692/6) CB	—	8.00	13.00	27.00	45.00	—

KM# 157 2 PFENNIG

Silver **Obv:** Three shields of arms around cetner, lower one divides date **Rev:** II/PFEN

Date	Mintage	VG	F	VF	XF	Unc
1677	—	—	—	—	—	—

KM# 133 3 PFENNIG

Silver **Obv:** Three separate arms of Mainz, Leyen, and Worms, crown above central shield, two crossed palm branches below **Rev:** Imperial orb with 3 in cartouche divides date **Note:** Varieties exist.

Date	Mintage	VG	F	VF	XF	Unc
1675 ICD	—	11.00	20.00	33.00	60.00	—
1676 ICD	—	12.00	20.00	35.00	65.00	—

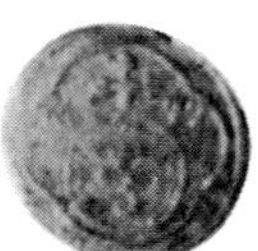

KM# 144 3 PFENNIG

Silver **Obv:** Three arms of Mainz, Leyen, and Worms in triangular cartouche, crown above, D. H. E. M. at top **Rev:** Imperial orb with 3 divides date **Note:** Varieties exist.

Date	Mintage	VG	F	VF	XF	Unc
1676 IH	—	11.00	16.00	35.00	65.00	—
1676 ICD	—	11.00	16.00	35.00	65.00	—
1677 ICD	—	11.00	16.00	35.00	65.00	—
1677	—	11.00	16.00	35.00	65.00	—

KM# 176 3 PFENNIG

Silver **Obv:** 4-fold arms of Mainz and Ingelheim in palm leaves, AF-EM above **Rev:** Imperial orb with 3 divides date in laurel wreath **Note:** Varieties exist.

Date	Mintage	VG	F	VF	XF	Unc
1680	—	11.00	16.00	35.00	65.00	—
1681	—	11.00	16.00	35.00	65.00	—
1682	—	11.00	16.00	35.00	65.00	—
1685	—	11.00	16.00	35.00	65.00	—
1686	—	11.00	16.00	35.00	65.00	—
1688	—	11.00	16.00	35.00	65.00	—
1689	—	11.00	16.00	35.00	65.00	—
1690 ICS	—	11.00	16.00	35.00	65.00	—

KM# 146 6 PFENNIG (Sechser)

Silver **Obv:** Date in legend **Rev:** Orb divides mintmaster's initials

Date	Mintage	VG	F	VF	XF	Unc
1676 ICD	—	27.00	45.00	80.00	125	—

KM# 145 6 PFENNIG (Sechser)

Silver **Obv:** Crowned 3-fold arms **Rev:** Imperial orb with 6, date in legend **Note:** Struck at Erfurt.

Date	Mintage	VG	F	VF	XF	Unc
1676	—	33.00	55.00	85.00	145	—

KM# 147 6 PFENNIG (Sechser)

Silver **Obv:** Crowned 3-fold arms of Mainz, Leyen, and Worms, date in legend **Rev:** Imperial orb with 6 divides mintmaster's initials, within palm branches **Note:** Varieties exist.

Date	Mintage	VG	F	VF	XF	Unc
1676 KD	—	25.00	40.00	65.00	120	—
1676 ICD	—	25.00	40.00	65.00	120	—

KM# 158 6 PFENNIG (Sechser)

Silver **Rev:** Facing bust of St. Martin, value 6 in round frame below

Date	Mintage	VG	F	VF	XF	Unc
1677	—	27.00	40.00	75.00	120	—

KM# 115 KREUZER

Silver **Obv:** 2-fold arms divided vertically, Mainz (wheel) on left and Schonborn on right, in laurel wreath **Rev:** Value: I/KREVTZ/date/initials, in laurel wreath

Date	Mintage	VG	F	VF	XF	Unc
1661 MF	—	13.00	27.00	45.00	80.00	—

KM# 203 KREUZER

Silver **Obv:** 4-fold arms of Mainz and Ingelheim in laurel wreath **Rev:** Value: I/KREU/TZER/date/initials, in laurel wreath **Note:** Varieties exist.

Date	Mintage	VG	F	VF	XF	Unc
1691 AD	—	11.00	20.00	40.00	70.00	—
1693 CB	—	11.00	20.00	40.00	70.00	—

KM# 81 2 KREUZER (1 Albus)

Silver **Obv:** 4-fold arms of Mainz and Umstadt in laurel wreath **Rev:** Imperial orb with 2, date above, legend, mintmaster's initials **Rev. Legend:** MAINTZER. ALBVS.

Date	Mintage	VG	F	VF	XF	Unc
1641 BS	—	40.00	80.00	140	200	—

KM# 215 3 KREUZER (Groschen)

Silver **Subject:** Death of Anselm Franz **Obv:** Crowned oval ornate 4-fold arms of Mainz and Ingelheim **Rev:** 6-line inscription with dates, small imperial orb with 3 at bottom

Date	Mintage	VG	F	VF	XF	Unc
1695	—	55.00	110	200	350	—

KM# 204 12 KREUZER

Silver **Obv:** Crowned 4-fold arms of Mainz and Ingelheim in palm branches **Rev:** XII/KREU/TZER/date/mintmaster's initials **Rev. Legend:** CHURFURSTL... **Note:** Varieties exist.

Date	Mintage	VG	F	VF	XF	Unc
1691 IGL	—	33.00	65.00	100	200	—

Date	Mintage	VG	F	VF	XF	Unc
1692 IGL	—	33.00	65.00	100	200	—
1692 CB	—	33.00	65.00	100	200	—

KM# 208 12 KREUZER

Silver **Rev. Legend:** NACH. DE. SCHLUS...

Date	Mintage	VG	F	VF	XF	Unc
1693 CB	—	27.00	55.00	85.00	185	—
1694 CB	—	27.00	55.00	85.00	185	—

KM# 177 15 KREUZER (1/4 Gulden)

Silver **Obv:** Bust right **Obv. Legend:** Crowned 4-fold arms of Mainz and Ingelheim, palm branches at each side, value (15) in legend below, date in legend at top

Date	Mintage	VG	F	VF	XF	Unc
1680 MF	—	—	—	—	—	—

KM# 195 15 KREUZER (1/4 Gulden)

Silver **Obv:** Value XV below shoulder of bust **Rev:** Date divided in legend by mintmaster's initials **Note:** Varieties exist.

Date	Mintage	VG	F	VF	XF	Unc
1689 GFS	—	27.00	55.00	80.00	140	—
1690 ICS	—	27.00	55.00	80.00	140	—
1691 ICS	—	27.00	55.00	80.00	140	—

KM# 200 15 KREUZER (1/4 Gulden)

Silver **Rev:** Value XV at bottom **Note:** Varieties exist.

Date	Mintage	VG	F	VF	XF	Unc
1690 AD	—	45.00	90.00	200	325	—

KM# 120 30 KREUZER (1/3 Thaler)

Silver **Obv:** Bust right **Rev:** 6-fold arms with central shield of Schonborn, value 30 in legend at bottom, date in legend **Note:** Varieties exist.

Date	Mintage	VG	F	VF	XF	Unc
1671 MF	—	65.00	120	250	400	—
1672 MF	—	65.00	120	250	400	—

KM# 135 30 KREUZER (1/3 Thaler)

Silver **Rev:** Crowned 4-fold arms of Mainz and Worms with central shield of Leyen, palm branches at either side, value (30) below, date in legend **Note:** Varieties exist.

Date	Mintage	VG	F	VF	XF	Unc
1675 MF	—	60.00	115	220	380	—
1676 MF	—	60.00	115	220	380	—

KM# 134 30 KREUZER (1/3 Thaler)

Silver **Rev:** Crowned 6-fold arms with central shield of Metternich, value 30 and date in legend

Date	Mintage	VG	F	VF	XF	Unc
1675 MF	—	120	225	420	725	—

KM# 148 30 KREUZER (1/3 Thaler)

Silver **Rev:** Very small arms, date divided in legend at top

Date	Mintage	VG	F	VF	XF	Unc
1676	—	—	—	—	—	—

KM# 162 30 KREUZER (1/3 Thaler)

Silver **Rev:** 4-fold arms of Mainz and Worms, with inner shield of 4-fold arms of Winneburg and Beilstein, with central shield of Metternich, in laurel wreath, crown above

Date	Mintage	VG	F	VF	XF	Unc
1679 MF	—	—	—	—	—	—

KM# 178 30 KREUZER (1/3 Thaler)

Silver **Rev:** Crowned 4-fold arms of Mainz and Ingelheim, palm branch at each side, value 30 in legend below, legend, date **Rev. Legend:** DEXTERA DOMINI - EXALTAVIT ME

Date	Mintage	VG	F	VF	XF	Unc
1680 MF	—	—	—	—	—	—

KM# 121 60 KREUZER (2/3 Thaler)

Silver **Obv:** Date in legend **Rev:** Value 60 at bottom **Note:** Varieties exist.

Date	Mintage	VG	F	VF	XF	Unc
1671 MF	—	65.00	120	200	325	—
1672 MF	—	65.00	120	200	325	—

KM# 123 60 KREUZER (2/3 Thaler)

Silver **Rev:** Crowned 6-fold arms with central shield of Metternich, value (60) in legend at bottom, date in legend **Note:** Varieties exist.

Date	Mintage	VG	F	VF	XF	Unc
1673 MF	—	65.00	120	200	325	—
1674 MF	—	65.00	120	200	325	—
1675 MF	—	65.00	120	200	325	—

KM# 136 60 KREUZER (2/3 Thaler)

Silver **Rev:** Crowned 4-fold arms of Mainz and Worms with central shield of Leyen divide date and mintmaster's initials, ERFFURT in small band below, value in legend at bottom **Note:** Varieties exist.

Date	Mintage	VG	F	VF	XF	Unc
1675 ICD	—	65.00	120	220	400	—

KM# 141 60 KREUZER (2/3 Thaler)

Silver **Obv:** Different bust **Note:** Varieties exist.

Date	Mintage	VG	F	VF	XF	Unc
1675 MF	—	90.00	180	325	500	—
1676 MF	—	90.00	180	325	500	—

KM# 137 60 KREUZER (2/3 Thaler)

Silver **Rev:** Without ERFFURT, palm branches at sides of arms, date in legend

Date	Mintage	VG	F	VF	XF	Unc
1675 MF	—	600	1,000	2,000	2,700	—

KM# 138 60 KREUZER (2/3 Thaler)

Silver **Rev:** Large crown above arms, without palm branches, arms divide date and mintmaster's initials

Date	Mintage	VG	F	VF	XF	Unc
1675 ICD	—	600	1,000	2,000	2,700	—

KM# 139 60 KREUZER (2/3 Thaler)

Silver **Rev:** Palm branches crossed below arms

Date	Mintage	VG	F	VF	XF	Unc
1675 ICD	—	600	1,000	2,000	2,700	—

KM# 140 60 KREUZER (2/3 Thaler)

Silver **Rev:** Squarish arms with date divided in legend at top

Date	Mintage	VG	F	VF	XF	Unc
1675 ICD	—	100	200	400	1,000	—

KM# 163 60 KREUZER (2/3 Thaler)

Silver **Obv:** Bust right **Rev:** 4-fold arms of Mainz and Worms, inner shield of 4-fold arms of Winneburg and Beilstein, central shield of Metternich, in laurel wreath, crown above value 60 in legend below

Date	Mintage	VG	F	VF	XF	Unc
1679 MF	—	140	275	675	1,150	—

KM# 179 60 KREUZER (2/3 Thaler)

Silver **Rev:** Youthful bust and value 60. **Note:** Similar to KM#201.

Date	Mintage	VG	F	VF	XF	Unc
1680 MF	—	60.00	115	200	325	—

KM# 201 60 KREUZER (2/3 Thaler)

Silver **Obv:** Older bust **Note:** Varieties exist.

Date	Mintage	VG	F	VF	XF	Unc
1690 AD	—	80.00	165	275	425	—
1693 CB	—	80.00	165	275	425	—
1695 CB	—	80.00	165	275	425	—

KM# 32 ALBUS (2 Kreuzer)

Silver **Obv:** Ornamented shield of Mainz arms in circle with laurel wreath around, M*L (Mainzer Landmunze) in legend at top **Rev:** I/ALBVS in laurel wreath **Note:** Kipper Albus.

Date	Mintage	VG	F	VF	XF	Unc
ND(1622)	—	—	—	—	—	—

KM# 93 ALBUS (2 Kreuzer)

4.2200 g., Silver **Note:** Klippe.

Date	Mintage	VG	F	VF	XF	Unc
1644 ET Rare	—	—	—	—	—	—

KM# 92 ALBUS (2 Kreuzer)

Silver **Obv:** 4-fold arms of Mainz and Ulmstadt in laurel wreath **Rev:** I/ALBVS/date/mintmaster's initials in laurel wreath **Note:** Varieties exist.

Date	Mintage	VG	F	VF	XF	Unc
1644 ET	—	13.00	27.00	55.00	85.00	—
1645 ET	—	13.00	27.00	55.00	85.00	—
1646 ET	—	13.00	27.00	55.00	85.00	—

KM# 100 ALBUS (2 Kreuzer)

Silver **Note:** Varieties exist.

Date	Mintage	VG	F	VF	XF	Unc
1648 ET	—	8.00	16.00	33.00	55.00	—
1650 ET	—	8.00	16.00	33.00	55.00	—
1651 ET	—	8.00	16.00	33.00	55.00	—
1652 MF	—	8.00	16.00	33.00	55.00	—
1653 MF	—	8.00	16.00	33.00	55.00	—
1654 MF	—	8.00	16.00	33.00	55.00	—
1655 MF	—	8.00	16.00	33.00	55.00	—
1656 MF	—	8.00	16.00	33.00	55.00	—
1657 MF	—	8.00	16.00	33.00	55.00	—
1658 MF	—	8.00	16.00	33.00	55.00	—

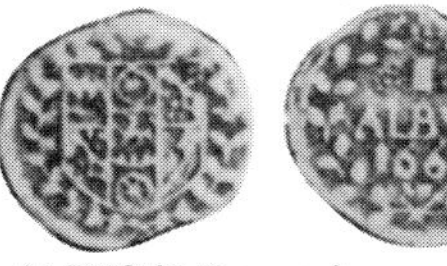

KM# 117 ALBUS (2 Kreuzer)

Silver **Obv:** 6-fold arms with central shiedl of Schonborn **Note:** Varieties exist.

Date	Mintage	VG	F	VF	XF	Unc
1664 MF	—	8.00	16.00	33.00	55.00	—
1666 MF	—	8.00	16.00	33.00	55.00	—
1667 MF	—	8.00	16.00	33.00	55.00	—
1668 MF	—	8.00	16.00	33.00	55.00	—
1669 MF	—	8.00	16.00	33.00	55.00	—
1670 MF	—	8.00	16.00	33.00	55.00	—
1671 MF	—	8.00	16.00	33.00	55.00	—

KM# 129 ALBUS (2 Kreuzer)

Silver **Obv:** Central shield of Metternich arms

Date	Mintage	VG	F	VF	XF	Unc
1674 MF	—	13.00	27.00	55.00	85.00	—

KM# 159 ALBUS (2 Kreuzer)

Silver **Obv:** 4-fold arms of Mainz and Worms with central shield of Leyen, in laurel wreath

Date	Mintage	VG	F	VF	XF	Unc
1678 MF	—	13.00	27.00	55.00	85.00	—

KM# 164 ALBUS (2 Kreuzer)

Silver **Obv:** Three small arms of Mainz, Worms, and Metternich above 4-fold arms of Winneburg and Beilstein, with central shield of Metternich, crown above, crossed palm branches below **Rev:** Value: I/ALBVS/date/initials in laurel wreath

Date	Mintage	VG	F	VF	XF	Unc
1679 MF	—	16.00	33.00	65.00	120	—

KM# 165 ALBUS (2 Kreuzer)

Silver **Obv:** Without palm branches

Date	Mintage	VG	F	VF	XF	Unc
1679 MF	—	16.00	33.00	65.00	120	—

KM# 166 ALBUS (2 Kreuzer)

Silver **Obv:** 4-fold arms of Mainz and Worms, with inner shield of 4-fold arms of Winneburg and Beilstein, with central shield of Metternich, in laurel wreath

Date	Mintage	VG	F	VF	XF	Unc
1679 MF	—	16.00	33.00	65.00	115	—

KM# 167 ALBUS (2 Kreuzer)

4.2200 g., Silver **Obv:** 4-fold arms of Mainz and Ingelheim in laurel wreath **Rev:** Value: I/ALBVS/date/initials, in laurel wreath **Note:** Varieties exist.

Date	Mintage	VG	F	VF	XF	Unc
1679 MF	—	13.00	27.00	55.00	85.00	—
1680 MF	—	13.00	27.00	55.00	85.00	—
1681 MF	—	13.00	27.00	55.00	85.00	—
1692 CB	—	13.00	27.00	55.00	85.00	—
1692 GB	—	13.00	27.00	55.00	85.00	—

KM# 216 ALBUS (2 Kreuzer)

4.2200 g., Silver **Rev. Legend:** NACHDEMSCHL. D. V. STAND.

Date	Mintage	VG	F	VF	XF	Unc
1695 CB	—	13.00	27.00	55.00	85.00	—

KM# 184 2 ALBUS (4 Kreuzer)

Silver **Obv:** 4-fold arms of Mainz and Ingelheim in laurel wreath **Rev:** Value: II/ALBVS/date/initials, in laurel wreath **Note:** Varieties exist.

Date	Mintage	VG	F	VF	XF	Unc
1681 MF	—	20.00	40.00	80.00	140	—
1690 AD	—	20.00	40.00	80.00	140	—
1691 AD	—	20.00	40.00	80.00	140	—
1693 CB	—	20.00	40.00	80.00	140	—

KM# 202 2 ALBUS (4 Kreuzer)

Silver **Mint:** Erfurt

Date	Mintage	VG	F	VF	XF	Unc
1690 ICS	—	20.00	40.00	80.00	140	—

KM# 209 2 ALBUS (4 Kreuzer)

Silver **Rev. Legend:** NACH. DEM. SCHLUS. DER. V. STAND.

Date	Mintage	VG	F	VF	XF	Unc
1693 CB	—	16.00	33.00	65.00	115	—
1694 CB	—	16.00	33.00	65.00	115	—
1695 CB	—	16.00	33.00	65.00	115	—

KM# 124 GROSCHEN (3 Kreuzer)

Silver **Subject:** Death of Johann Philipp and Accession of Lothar Friedrich **Obv:** Crowned 6-fold arms with central shield of Schonborn in palm branches **Rev:** Crowned 6-fold arms with central shield of Metternich in palm branches, date in legend

Date	Mintage	VG	F	VF	XF	Unc
1673	—	40.00	80.00	165	325	—

KM# 142 GROSCHEN (3 Kreuzer)

Silver **Subject:** Death of Lothar Friedrich **Obv:** Crowned 6-fold arms with central shield of Metternich, palm branches at sides **Rev:** 12-line inscription with dates

Date	Mintage	VG	F	VF	XF	Unc
1675	—	40.00	80.00	165	325	—

KM# 160 GROSCHEN (3 Kreuzer)

Silver **Subject:** Death of Damian Hartard **Obv:** Crowned 4-fold arms with central shield of Leyen in palm branches **Rev:** 9-line inscription with date

Date	Mintage	VG	F	VF	XF	Unc
1678	—	40.00	80.00	165	325	—

KM# 168 GROSCHEN (3 Kreuzer)

Silver **Subject:** Death of Karl Heinrich **Obv:** Crowned 4-fold arms with central shield of Metternich **Rev:** 10-line inscription with dates

Date	Mintage	VG	F	VF	XF	Unc
1679	—	40.00	80.00	165	325	—

KM# 217 GROSCHEN (3 Kreuzer)

Silver **Subject:** Death of Anselm Franz and Accessin of Lothar Franz **Obv:** Crowned 6-fold arms with central shield of Schonborn, date in legend **Rev:** Crowned 4-fold arms of Mainz and Ingelheim, titles of Anselm Franz

Date	Mintage	VG	F	VF	XF	Unc
1695	—	80.00	140	165	325	—

KM# 149 4 GROSCHEN

Silver **Obv:** Bust right **Rev:** 3-fold arms of Mainz, Worms and Leyen divide date, crown above **Rev. Legend:** C. F. M. SILBER M above, IIII. GUT. GROSCH below

Date	Mintage	VG	F	VF	XF	Unc
1676	—	45.00	100	200	325	—

KM# 150 4 GROSCHEN

Silver **Rev. Legend:** C. F. M. L. M. V. FEIN. SIL, IIII. GUT. GROSCH. **Note:** Varieties exist.

Date	Mintage	VG	F	VF	XF	Unc
1676	—	45.00	100	200	325	—

KM# 186 SOL

Silver **Subject:** French Occupation **Obv:** Crowned ornamented oval, within four intertwined cursive L's (for Louis XIV) **Rev:** Value 1 in center

Date	Mintage	VG	F	VF	XF	Unc
ND(1689)	—	60.00	120	200	325	—

KM# 187 SOL

Silver **Rev:** 1/SOL/date

Date	Mintage	VG	F	VF	XF	Unc
1689	—	45.00	100	165	300	—

KM# 188 2 SOLS

Silver **Subject:** French Occupation **Obv:** Crowned ornamented oval, within four intertwined L's (for Louis XIV), value (3) in legend below **Obv. Legend:** MONE. NOV-ARGENTEA **Rev. Legend:** GLOR. IN. EXCELS. DEO. **Rev. Inscription:** II / SOLS / date

Date	Mintage	VG	F	VF	XF	Unc
1689	—	85.00	165	275	425	—

KM# 189 1/24 THALER (Groschen)

Silver **Obv:** Crowned 4-fold arms of Mainz and Ingelheim in baroque frame **Rev:** Imperial orb with value: 24 divides date near top **Rev. Legend:** CHURFURST... **Mint:** Erfurt

Date	Mintage	VG	F	VF	XF	Unc
1689 GFS	—	45.00	100	165	225	—

KM# 210 1/24 THALER (Groschen)

Silver **Obv:** Ornate round arms **Rev:** Legend, date **Rev. Legend:** NACH DEM LEIPZIGER FUSS

Date	Mintage	VG	F	VF	XF	Unc
1693 ICS	—	45.00	100	165	225	—

KM# 125 1/12 THALER (Doppelgroschen)

Silver **Subject:** Death of Johann Philipp and Accession of Lothar Friedrich **Obv:** Crowned 6-fold arms of Mainz, Worms, and Wurzburg with central shield of Schonborn, palm branches at sides **Rev:** Crowned 6-fold arms of Mainz with central shield of Metternich, palm branches at sides, date in legend

Date	Mintage	VG	F	VF	XF	Unc
1673	—	80.00	160	275	400	—

KM# 143 1/12 THALER (Doppelgroschen)

Silver **Subject:** Death of Lothar Friedrich **Obv:** Crowned 6-fold arms with central shield of Metternich, palm branches at sides **Rev:** 12-line inscription/date

Date	Mintage	VG	F	VF	XF	Unc
1675	—	80.00	140	225	—	—

KM# 190 1/12 THALER (Doppelgroschen)

Silver **Rev. Inscription:** 12 / EINEN / REICHS / THALER / date **Mint:** Erfurt **Note:** Varieties exist.

Date	Mintage	VG	F	VF	XF	Unc
1689 GFS	—	20.00	35.00	60.00	100	—
1690 ICS	—	20.00	35.00	60.00	100	—
1691 AD	—	33.00	70.00	120	165	—
1692 AD	—	20.00	35.00	60.00	100	—
1692 CB	—	20.00	35.00	60.00	100	—

KM# 205 1/12 THALER (Doppelgroschen)

Silver **Rev:** Value: 12/EINEN/THALER/date

Date	Mintage	VG	F	VF	XF	Unc
1691 ICS	—	—	—	—	—	—

KM# 161 1/8 THALER

Silver **Subject:** Death of Damian Hartard **Obv:** Crowned 4-fold arms of Mainz and Worms between palm branches **Rev:** 9-line inscription with dates

Date	Mintage	VG	F	VF	XF	Unc
1678	—	100	200	325	—	—

KM# 169 1/8 THALER

Silver **Subject:** Death of Karl Heinrich **Obv:** Crowned 4-fold arms of Mainz and Worms with 4-fold central shield of Metternich arms with central shield of Mainz alone, palm branches at sides **Rev:** 10-line inscription with dates

Date	Mintage	VG	F	VF	XF	Unc
1679	—	65.00	135	200	325	—

KM# 191 1/6 THALER

Silver **Subject:** French Occupation **Obv:** Crowned ornamented oval, within four intertwined cursive L's (for Louis XIV) **Obv. Legend:** MONETA. NOVA. ARGENTEA **Rev:** Large 1/6 in center, GLORIA..., date in legend

Date	Mintage	VG	F	VF	XF	Unc
1689	—	90.00	190	375	725	—

KM# 6 1/4 THALER

Silver **Obv:** Oval 4-fold arms of Mainz and Bicken, mitre above **Rev:** St. Martin riding left on horse, kneeling beggar underneath, wheel of Mainz in cartouche below, date in legend

Date	Mintage	VG	F	VF	XF	Unc
160Z	—	65.00	135	200	325	—

KM# 15 1/4 THALER

Silver **Subject:** Laying of Cornerstone for New Archepiscopal Residence at Aschaffenburg **Obv:** Ornate 4-fold arms of Mainz and Kronberg, three helmets above **Rev:** View of castle, Roman numeral date in legend **Note:** Varieties exist.

Date	Mintage	VG	F	VF	XF	Unc
1614 LS	—	675	1,000	1,350	1,650	—

KM# 63 1/4 THALER

Silver **Obv:** Bust of Anselm Casimir right **Rev:** Helmeted 4-fold arms of Mainz and Umstadt

Date	Mintage	VG	F	VF	XF	Unc
ND	—	375	650	1,000	1,350	—

KM# 61 1/4 THALER

Silver **Obv:** Bust right **Rev:** 4-fold arms of Mainz and Umstadt, three helmets above, date in legend

Date	Mintage	VG	F	VF	XF	Unc
1636	—	375	650	1,000	1,350	—

KM# 62 1/4 THALER

Silver **Obv:** Smaller bust and value 1/4 below

Date	Mintage	VG	F	VF	XF	Unc
1636	—	375	650	1,000	1,350	—

KM# 127 1/3 THALER (30 Kreuzer)

Silver **Obv:** Bust right, date in legend **Rev:** Triangle with streaming rays above Metternich arms (three mussel shells) **Rev. Legend:** IN TRIBVS PACITVM EST MEO. ECCL. 25

Date	Mintage	VG	F	VF	XF	Unc
1673	—	—	—	—	—	—

KM# 126 1/3 THALER (30 Kreuzer)

Silver **Obv:** Bust right **Rev:** Crowned 6-fold arms with central shield of Metternich, date in legend **Note:** Varieties exist.

Date	Mintage	VG	F	VF	XF	Unc
1673 MF	—	110	200	375	675	—

KM# 192 1/3 THALER (30 Kreuzer)

Silver **Subject:** French Occupation **Obv:** Crowned ornamented oval, within four intertwined cursive L's (for Louis XIV) **Obv. Legend:** MONETA. NOVA. ARGENTEA. **Rev:** Large 1/3 in center, GLORIA..., date in legend

Date	Mintage	VG	F	VF	XF	Unc
1689	—	275	450	700	1,125	—

KM# 11 1/2 THALER

Silver **Obv:** Oval 4-fold arms of Mainz and Bicken, three helmets above **Rev:** St. Martin riding horse left, beggar below ar right, round arms of Mainz in ornamented frame in margin at lower left, date in legend at top

Date	Mintage	VG	F	VF	XF	Unc
1603	—	800	1,350	2,000	2,600	—

KM# 16 1/2 THALER

Silver **Subject:** Laying the Cornerstone of the New Archepiscopal Residence at Aschaffenburg **Obv:** Ornate 4-fold arms of Mainz and Kronberg, three helmets above **Rev:** View of castle, Roman numeral date in legend

Date	Mintage	VG	F	VF	XF	Unc
1614 LS	—	800	1,350	2,000	2,600	—

KM# 17 1/2 THALER

Silver **Note:** Klippe.

Date	Mintage	VG	F	VF	XF	Unc
1614 LS	—	700	1,500	2,400	3,250	—

KM# 50 1/2 THALER

Silver **Obv:** Bust turned 1/4 to right **Rev:** Ornate 4-fold arms of Mainz and Umstadt, three helmets above, date in legend

Date	Mintage	VG	F	VF	XF	Unc
1630 LS/AD	—	2,000	3,500	4,500	—	—

KM# 69 1/2 THALER

Silver **Obv:** Bust right

Date	Mintage	VG	F	VF	XF	Unc
1637 BS	—	2,000	3,500	4,500	—	—

KM# 80 1/2 THALER

Silver **Obv:** Crowned 4-fold arms of Mainz and Umstadt **Rev:** Date/MONETA NOVA/ARGENTEA/MOGVNITINA, legend in laurel wreath **Rev. Legend:** S: ROM: IMP **Note:** Varieties exist.

Date	Mintage	VG	F	VF	XF	Unc
1640	—	525	850	1,350	2,000	—
1641	—	525	850	1,350	2,000	—
1642	—	525	850	1,350	2,000	—

KM# 82 1/2 THALER

Silver **Subject:** Meeting of Imperial Diet in Regensburg **Obv:** Wreath in outer margin enclosing crowned arms of the seven electors in cartouches, above the standing imperial eagle, inscription in center within laurel wreath REICHS/TAG/ZV REGEN/SPVRG/date **Rev:** Laureate bust of emperor right, shield of Regensburg arms below, angel's head under crown above, titles of Ferdinand III **Note:** Show 1/2 Thaler.

Date	Mintage	VG	F	VF	XF	Unc
1641 HC/BR	—	1,250	2,000	3,250	—	—

KM# 84 1/2 THALER

Silver **Obv:** 4-fold arms of Mainz and Umstadt in baroque frame, half eagle and flowers on each side **Rev:** Inscription in laurel wreath, titles of Anselm Casimir **Rev. Inscription:** Date / MONETA: NOVA / ARGENTEA / MOGVN / TINAE **Note:** Varieties exist.

Date	Mintage	VG	F	VF	XF	Unc
1642 MG	—	525	800	1,350	2,000	—
1645 MG	—	525	800	1,350	2,000	—

KM# 193 2/3 THALER (60 Kreuzer)

Silver **Subject:** French Occupation **Obv:** Crowned ornamented oval, four intertwined cursive L's (for Louis XIV) **Obv. Legend:** MONETA NOVA ARGENTEA **Rev:** Large 2/3 in center, GLORIA..., date in legend

Date	Mintage	VG	F	VF	XF	Unc
1689	—	1,600	2,600	4,000	—	—

KM# 194 2/3 THALER (60 Kreuzer)

Silver **Obv:** Smaller oval with crown dividing date, without legend

Date	Mintage	VG	F	VF	XF	Unc
1689	—	1,600	2,600	4,000	—	—

KM# 4 THALER

Silver **Note:** Dav. #9468.

Date	Mintage	VG	F	VF	XF	Unc
1601	—	1,500	2,500	3,500	—	—

KM# 7 THALER

Silver **Obv:** Capped and helmeted arms **Rev:** St. Martin facing on horseback, beggar under horse **Note:** Dav. #5531. Varieties exist.

Date	Mintage	VG	F	VF	XF	Unc
1602	—	450	850	1,750	3,500	—

KM# 8 THALER

Silver **Rev:** Beggar at rear of horse **Note:** Dav. #5533. Varieties exist.

Date	Mintage	VG	F	VF	XF	Unc
1602	—	450	850	1,750	3,500	—
1603	—	450	850	1,750	3,500	—

KM# 19 THALER

Silver, 46 mm. **Note:** Dav. #5536A.

Date	Mintage	VG	F	VF	XF	Unc
1614	—	1,050	1,900	3,000	6,000	—

KM# 20 THALER

Silver **Note:** Klippe. Dav. #5536B.

Date	Mintage	VG	F	VF	XF	Unc
1614 LS	—	2,250	3,750	6,000	—	—

KM# 18 THALER

Silver **Subject:** Laying of Cornerstone for New Archepiscopal Residence at Aschaffenburg **Obv:** Crowned and helmeted shield **Rev:** Aschaffenburg Castle **Note:** Thick Thaler. Dav. #5536.

Date	Mintage	VG	F	VF	XF	Unc
1614 LS	—	1,050	1,900	3,000	6,000	—

KM# 22 THALER

Silver **Note:** Similar to KM#23 but sterner portrait of Johann on obverse and ANNO added in reverse legend. Dav. #5537.

Date	Mintage	VG	F	VF	XF	Unc
1618	—	1,050	1,900	3,000	5,300	—

KM# 23 THALER

Silver **Note:** Dav. #5539.

Date	Mintage	VG	F	VF	XF	Unc
1619	—	1,050	2,050	3,750	6,000	—

KM# 35 THALER

Silver **Obv:** Bust of Georg Friedrich right, LS on arm **Rev:** Helmeted arms **Note:** Dav. #5541.

Date	Mintage	VG	F	VF	XF	Unc
1627 AE	—	500	1,100	2,500	4,000	—

KM# 34 THALER

Silver **Note:** Similar to KM#35 but smaller bust with date and LS on arm and smaller shield on reverse. Dav. #5540.

Date	Mintage	VG	F	VF	XF	Unc
1627 AE	—	500	1,100	2,500	3,600	—

KM# 40 THALER

Silver **Obv:** Closer bust with date and LS on arm **Rev:** Helmeted arms with AD left, mint mark right **Note:** Dav. #5543.

Date	Mintage	VG	F	VF	XF	Unc
1629 LS/DA	—	500	1,100	2,500	4,000	—
ND AD Rare	—	—	—	—	—	—

KM# 51 THALER

Silver **Obv:** Facing bust of Anselm **Rev:** Helmeted arms **Note:** Dav. #5544.

Date	Mintage	VG	F	VF	XF	Unc
1629 LS/DA	—	1,300	2,500	4,500	7,500	—

KM# 53 THALER

Silver **Obv:** Bust of Anselm right **Note:** Dav. #5546.

Date	Mintage	VG	F	VF	XF	Unc
1630 BS	—	350	700	1,300	2,200	—

KM# 52 THALER

Silver **Note:** Octagonal klippe. Dav. #5545.

Date	Mintage	VG	F	VF	XF	Unc
1630 BS	—	3,000	5,300	7,500	—	—

KM# 64 THALER

Silver **Obv:** Different cloak on bust **Obv. Legend:** ANSELMI. **Rev. Legend:** MONET-A: NOVA: ARGENTEA: MOG-V-NTINA. **Note:** Dav. #5547.

Date	Mintage	VG	F	VF	XF	Unc
1636	—	265	500	900	1,300	—

KM# 65 THALER

Silver **Obv. Legend:** ANSELMUS... **Note:** Dav. #5548.

Date	Mintage	VG	F	VF	XF	Unc
1636	—	190	375	675	1,150	—
1637 BS	—	190	375	675	1,150	—

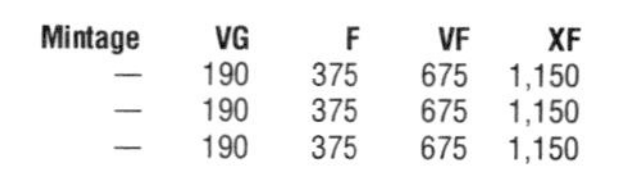

Date	Mintage	VG	F	VF	XF	Unc
1641 BS	—	190	375	675	1,150	—
ND BS	—	190	375	675	1,150	—
ND	—	190	375	675	1,150	—

KM# 70 THALER

Silver **Rev:** Date below shield **Note:** Dav. #5549.

Date	Mintage	VG	F	VF	XF	Unc
1637 BS	—	250	500	1,000	2,750	—
1638 BS	—	250	500	1,000	2,750	—
1639 BS	—	250	500	1,000	2,750	—

KM# 72 THALER

Silver **Obv:** Similar to 3 Thaler, KM#73 **Rev:** Similar to KM#65 **Note:** Dav. #5551.

Date	Mintage	VG	F	VF	XF	Unc
1639 BS	—	250	500	1,000	2,750	—

KM# 83 THALER

Silver **Subject:** Meeting of Imperial Diet in Regensburg **Obv:** Laureate bust of emperor right, shield of Regensburg arms below, angel's head under crown above, titles of Ferdinand III **Rev:** Wreath in outer margin enclosing crowned arms of the seven electors in cartouches, above the standing imperial eagle, inscription in center within laurel wreath **Rev. Inscription:** REICHS / TAG / ZV REGEN / SPVRG / date **Note:** Show Thaler.

Date	Mintage	VG	F	VF	XF	Unc
1641 HC/BR	—	—	—	—	—	—

KM# 85 THALER

Silver **Obv:** Facing bust of Anselm **Rev:** Helmeted arms with mitre divide date **Note:** Dav. #5552. Varieties exist.

Date	Mintage	VG	F	VF	XF	Unc
1642 MG	—	500	1,000	2,000	3,500	—

KM# 86 THALER

Silver **Obv:** Without MOG on legend **Note:** Dav. #5553. Varieties exist.

Date	Mintage	VG	F	VF	XF	Unc
1642 MG	—	500	1,000	2,000	3,500	—

KM# 94 THALER

Silver **Obv:** Bust right **Rev:** Helmeted arms, date above **Note:** Dav. #5554.

Date	Mintage	VG	F	VF	XF	Unc
1644	—	300	600	1,300	2,500	—

KM# 109 THALER

Silver **Obv:** Facing bust of Johann Philipp left **Rev:** Capped and helmeted arms **Note:** Dav. #5556.

Date	Mintage	VG	F	VF	XF	Unc
ND ET	—	1,200	1,900	3,000	4,000	—

KM# 110 THALER

Silver **Obv:** Bust of Johann Philipp right **Note:** Dav. #5558.

Date	Mintage	VG	F	VF	XF	Unc
1658 MF	—	375	750	1,450	2,400	—

KM# 130 THALER

Silver **Note:** Similar to 2 Thaler, KM#131. Dav. #5560.

Date	Mintage	VG	F	VF	XF	Unc
1674 MF	—	3,000	5,300	7,500	—	—

KM# 151 THALER

Silver **Obv:** Bust of Damian Hartard right **Rev:** Helmeted arms **Note:** Dav. #5562.

Date	Mintage	VG	F	VF	XF	Unc
1676 MF	—	800	1,600	3,250	6,000	—

KM# 152 THALER

Silver **Obv. Legend:** ... D. G. S. S. M. A. E. **Rev. Legend:** S. R. I. P. G. AR. CAN. PR. EL. EP. WORM. **Note:** Dav. #5563.

Date	Mintage	VG	F	VF	XF	Unc
1676	—	700	1,300	2,400	4,000	—

KM# 153 THALER

Silver **Obv. Legend:** ... HARTARDT. D. G. S. S. MOG. ARCH. E. **Note:** Dav. #5564.

Date	Mintage	VG	F	VF	XF	Unc
1676 ICD	—	700	1,300	2,400	4,000	—

KM# 170 THALER

Silver **Obv:** Bust of Karl Heinrich right **Rev:** Helmeted arms **Note:** Dav. #5566.

Date	Mintage	VG	F	VF	XF	Unc
1679 MF	—	2,500	3,900	5,600	8,400	—

KM# 180 THALER

Silver **Subject:** Peace of Nymegen **Obv:** Bust of Anselm Franz right **Rev:** Hand holding scale weighing sword and olive branch **Note:** Dav. #5567.

Date	Mintage	VG	F	VF	XF	Unc
ND	—	500	1,000	2,250	3,750	—

KM# 181 THALER

Silver **Rev:** Helmeted arms **Note:** Dav. #5569. Varieties exist.

Date	Mintage	VG	F	VF	XF	Unc
1680 MF	—	250	600	1,250	2,750	—
1682 MF	—	250	600	1,250	2,750	—
1682 AL	—	250	600	1,250	2,750	—
1682 VBW	—	250	600	1,250	2,750	—

KM# 206 THALER

Silver **Rev:** Different shaped arms **Note:** Dav. #5570.

Date	Mintage	VG	F	VF	XF	Unc
1691 AD	—	450	900	1,500	3,000	—
1691 CB	—	675	1,200	2,250	4,000	—

KM# 211 THALER
Silver **Rev:** Without inner circle **Note:** Dav. #5571. Varieties exist.

Date	Mintage	VG	F	VF	XF	Unc
1692 CB	—	450	900	1,500	3,000	—
1693 CB	—	450	900	1,500	3,000	—

KM# 212 THALER
Silver **Obv:** Bust right **Rev:** Helmeted round 4-fold arms of Mainz and Ingelheim, date in legend

Date	Mintage	VG	F	VF	XF	Unc
1693 AK	—	1,900	3,400	5,300	—	—

KM# 214 THALER
Silver **Obv:** Different bust **Rev:** Smaller, altered arms **Note:** Dav. #5572.

Date	Mintage	VG	F	VF	XF	Unc
1694 CB	—	450	750	1,750	3,500	—
1695 CB	—	450	750	1,750	3,500	—

KM# 219 THALER
Silver **Obv:** Bust of Lothar Franz right **Rev:** Capped round arms with crozier and sword, cross above cap, date divided below **Note:** Dav. #5574.

Date	Mintage	VG	F	VF	XF	Unc
1696	—	450	750	1,500	3,000	—

KM# 10 2 THALER
Silver **Obv:** Capped and helmeted arms **Rev:** St. Martin on horseback facing out, beggar at rear of horse **Note:** Dav. #5532.

Date	Mintage	VG	F	VF	XF	Unc
1602	—	1,800	3,000	5,300	7,500	—

KM# 9 2 THALER
Silver **Note:** Similar to 1 Thaler, KM#7. Dav. #5530. Varieties exist.

Date	Mintage	VG	F	VF	XF	Unc
1602	—	1,800	3,000	5,300	7,500	—

KM# 29 2 THALER
Silver **Subject:** Laying of the Cornerstone for the New Archepiscopal Residence at Schaffenburg **Note:** Similar to 1 Thaler, KM#18. Thick flan.

Date	Mintage	VG	F	VF	XF	Unc
1614 LS	—	3,000	5,300	7,500	—	—

KM# 24 2 THALER
Silver **Note:** Similar to 1 Thaler, KM#23. Dav. #5538.

Date	Mintage	VG	F	VF	XF	Unc
1619	—	3,000	5,300	7,500	—	—

KM# 41 2 THALER
Silver **Obv:** Bust of Georg Friedrich right **Rev:** Helmeted arms **Note:** Dav. #5542.

Date	Mintage	VG	F	VF	XF	Unc
1629 LS/AD Rare	—	—	—	—	—	—

KM# 95 2 THALER
Silver **Obv:** Bust of Anselm right **Rev:** Helmeted arms **Note:** Dav. #A5554.

Date	Mintage	VG	F	VF	XF	Unc
1644	—	3,000	5,300	7,500	—	—

KM# 111 2 THALER
Silver **Obv:** Facing bust of Johann Philipp left **Rev:** Capped and helmeted arms **Note:** Dav. #5555.

Date	Mintage	VG	F	VF	XF	Unc
ND ET	—	3,000	5,300	7,500	—	—

KM# 112 2 THALER
Silver **Note:** Similar to 1 Thaler, KM#110. Dav. #5557.

Date	Mintage	VG	F	VF	XF	Unc
1658 MF	—	3,500	6,300	9,500	14,000	—

KM# 131 2 THALER
Silver **Obv:** Bust of Lothar Friedrich **Note:** Dav. #5559.

Date	Mintage	VG	F	VF	XF	Unc
1674 MF	—	2,800	4,200	6,300	8,400	—

KM# 154 2 THALER
Silver **Note:** Dav. #5561.

Date	Mintage	VG	F	VF	XF	Unc
1676 MF	—	1,500	3,000	4,500	7,500	—

KM# 171 2 THALER
Silver **Note:** Similar to 1 Thaler, KM#170. Dav. #5565.

Date	Mintage	VG	F	VF	XF	Unc
1679 MF	—	3,750	6,400	9,000	—	—

KM# 182 2 THALER
Silver **Obv:** Bust of Anselm Franz right **Note:** Dav. #5568. Varieties exist.

Date	Mintage	VG	F	VF	XF	Unc
1680 MF	—	2,500	4,200	7,000	11,000	—
1685 VBW	—	2,500	4,200	7,000	11,000	—

KM# 207 2 THALER
Silver **Note:** Similar to 1 Thaler, KM#181 but different arms. Varieties exist.

Date	Mintage	VG	F	VF	XF	Unc
1691 AD	—	3,000	5,300	7,500	—	—
1691 CB	—	3,000	5,300	7,500	—	—

KM# 213 2 THALER
Silver **Note:** Similar to 1 Thaler, KM#211.

Date	Mintage	VG	F	VF	XF	Unc
1693 AK	—	4,900	7,900	11,500	—	—

KM# 218 2 THALER
Silver **Note:** Similar to 1 Thaler, KM#218.

Date	Mintage	VG	F	VF	XF	Unc
1695 AK	—	4,900	7,900	11,500	—	—

KM# 73 3 THALER
Silver **Obv:** Bust of Anselm Casimir right **Rev:** Helmeted arms in wreath **Note:** Dav. #5550.

Date	Mintage	VG	F	VF	XF	Unc
1639	—	7,000	12,500	17,500	—	—

TRADE COINAGE

KM# 33 GOLDGULDEN
3.5000 g., 0.9860 Gold 0.1109 oz. AGW **Obv:** Arms in inner circle **Rev:** Four batons cruciform with shields of arms in angles in inner circle

Date	Mintage	VG	F	VF	XF	Unc
16Z6	40,000	400	900	1,600	2,500	—
16Z7 AE	Inc. above	400	900	1,600	2,500	—
1627 DA	—	—	—	—	—	—

KM# 36 GOLDGULDEN
3.5000 g., 0.9860 Gold 0.1109 oz. AGW **Rev:** St. Martin and beggar in inner circle

Date	Mintage	VG	F	VF	XF	Unc
16Z8	—	1,200	2,400	3,750	5,300	—

KM# 37 DUCAT
3.5000 g., 0.9860 Gold 0.1109 oz. AGW

Date	Mintage	VG	F	VF	XF	Unc
16Z8	—	180	350	725	1,200	—
16Z9	—	180	350	725	1,200	—

KM# 38 DUCAT
3.5000 g., 0.9860 Gold 0.1109 oz. AGW **Note:** Klippe.

Date	Mintage	VG	F	VF	XF	Unc
1628	—	700	1,400	2,700	6,000	—

KM# 42 DUCAT
3.5000 g., 0.9860 Gold 0.1109 oz. AGW **Obv:** Facing bust of Anselm Casimir in inner circle **Rev:** Arms in inner circle

Date	Mintage	VG	F	VF	XF	Unc
1629	—	600	1,300	2,500	5,500	—

KM# 60 DUCAT
3.5000 g., 0.9860 Gold 0.1109 oz. AGW **Obv:** Anselm Casimir **Rev:** Crowned arms in inner circle

Date	Mintage	VG	F	VF	XF	Unc
1633 BS	—	240	475	850	1,800	—
1638 BS	—	240	475	850	1,800	—
1644	—	240	475	850	1,800	—
ND BS	—	240	475	850	1,800	—

KM# 66 DUCAT
3.5000 g., 0.9860 Gold 0.1109 oz. AGW **Obv:** Bust of Anselm Casimir right **Rev:** Arms in inner circle

Date	Mintage	VG	F	VF	XF	Unc
1636	—	265	525	1,050	2,250	—
1638	—	265	525	1,050	2,250	—

KM# 67 DUCAT
3.5000 g., 0.9860 Gold 0.1109 oz. AGW **Obv:** Arms divide date in inner circle **Rev:** Value in tablet

Date	Mintage	VG	F	VF	XF	Unc
1636	—	180	350	725	1,200	—
1641 BS	—	180	350	725	1,200	—

KM# 87 DUCAT
3.5000 g., 0.9860 Gold 0.1109 oz. AGW

Date	Mintage	VG	F	VF	XF	Unc
1642 MG	—	240	475	875	1,600	—
1646	—	240	475	875	1,600	—

KM# 96 DUCAT
3.5000 g., 0.9860 Gold 0.1109 oz. AGW **Obv:** Crowned arms in wreath

Date	Mintage	VG	F	VF	XF	Unc
1645	—	180	350	650	1,200	—
1646 ET	—	180	350	650	1,200	—

KM# 101 DUCAT
3.5000 g., 0.9860 Gold 0.1109 oz. AGW **Obv:** Bust of Johann Philip facing

Date	Mintage	VG	F	VF	XF	Unc
1648 ET	—	300	600	1,000	2,000	—
1649 ET	—	300	600	1,000	2,000	—
1650	—	300	600	1,000	2,000	—

KM# 105 DUCAT
3.5000 g., 0.9860 Gold 0.1109 oz. AGW **Obv:** Bust of Johann Philip left

Date	Mintage	VG	F	VF	XF	Unc
1650 ET	—	190	375	625	1,250	—
1651	—	190	375	625	1,250	—
1651/0	—	190	375	625	1,250	—

KM# 106 DUCAT
3.5000 g., 0.9860 Gold 0.1109 oz. AGW **Obv:** Large bust of Johann Philip left

Date	Mintage	VG	F	VF	XF	Unc
1652 MF	—	190	375	625	1,250	—
1653 MF	—	190	375	625	1,250	—

KM# 107 DUCAT
3.5000 g., 0.9860 Gold 0.1109 oz. AGW **Obv:** Small bust of Johann Philip left

Date	Mintage	VG	F	VF	XF	Unc
1652 MF	—	190	375	625	1,250	—
1653 MF	—	190	375	625	1,250	—
1654 MF	—	190	375	625	1,250	—
1655 MF	—	190	375	625	1,250	—
1657 MF	—	190	375	625	1,250	—
1658 MF	—	325	625	1,500	2,500	—
1659 MF	—	325	625	1,500	2,500	—
1660 MF	—	190	375	625	1,250	—
1661 MF	—	190	375	625	1,250	—

KM# 108 DUCAT
3.5000 g., 0.9860 Gold 0.1109 oz. AGW **Obv. Legend:** (I) OANN...

Date	Mintage	VG	F	VF	XF	Unc
1655 MF	—	190	375	625	1,250	—

KM# 116 DUCAT
3.5000 g., 0.9860 Gold 0.1109 oz. AGW **Obv:** Large bust of Johann Philip left

Date	Mintage	VG	F	VF	XF	Unc
1663 MF	—	220	450	825	1,500	—
1664 MF	—	220	450	825	1,500	—

KM# 118 DUCAT
3.5000 g., 0.9860 Gold 0.1109 oz. AGW **Obv:** Small bust of Johann Philip right

Date	Mintage	VG	F	VF	XF	Unc
1667	—	190	350	625	1,050	—
1668 MF	—	190	350	625	1,050	—
1670	—	190	350	625	1,050	—

KM# 122 DUCAT
3.5000 g., 0.9860 Gold 0.1109 oz. AGW **Obv:** Large bust of Johann Philip right

Date	Mintage	VG	F	VF	XF	Unc
1671 MF	—	190	350	625	1,000	—

KM# 128 DUCAT
3.5000 g., 0.9860 Gold 0.1109 oz. AGW **Obv:** Bust of Lothar Friedrich right in inner circle

Date	Mintage	VG	F	VF	XF	Unc
1673 MF	—	1,050	2,150	4,550	7,800	—

KM# 155 DUCAT
3.5000 g., 0.9860 Gold 0.1109 oz. AGW **Obv:** Bust of Damian Hartard right in inner circle

Date	Mintage	VG	F	VF	XF	Unc
1676 MF	—	600	1,400	3,300	6,000	—

KM# 172 DUCAT
3.5000 g., 0.9860 Gold 0.1109 oz. AGW **Obv:** Bust of Karl Heinrich right **Rev:** Crowned 4-fold arms with central shield of Metternich in palm branches, date in legend

Date	Mintage	VG	F	VF	XF	Unc
1679 MF	—	—	—	—	—	—

KM# 185 DUCAT
3.5000 g., 0.9860 Gold 0.1109 oz. AGW **Obv:** Bust of Anselm Franz right in inner circle

Date	Mintage	VG	F	VF	XF	Unc
1684 AL	—	325	625	1,500	2,500	—

KM# 220 DUCAT
3.5000 g., 0.9860 Gold 0.1109 oz. AGW **Subject:** Treaty of Ryswick

Date	Mintage	VG	F	VF	XF	Unc
ND(1696) GFN	—	425	750	1,050	1,650	—

KM# 221 DUCAT
3.5000 g., 0.9860 Gold 0.1109 oz. AGW **Subject:** Treaty of Ryswick **Rev:** Altar wtih burning weapons on top

Date	Mintage	VG	F	VF	XF	Unc
1696	—	270	475	800	1,300	—

KM# 222 DUCAT
3.5000 g., 0.9860 Gold 0.1109 oz. AGW **Subject:** Treaty of Ryswick **Rev:** Minerva standing

Date	Mintage	VG	F	VF	XF	Unc
1696	—	250	500	1,000	1,750	—

KM# 43 2 DUCAT
7.0000 g., 0.9860 Gold 0.2219 oz. AGW **Obv:** Facing bust of Anselm Casimir in inner circle **Rev:** Arms in inner circle **Note:** Struck with 1 Ducat dies.

Date	Mintage	VG	F	VF	XF	Unc
1629	—	850	1,900	4,900	8,500	—

KM# 68 2 DUCAT
7.0000 g., 0.9860 Gold 0.2219 oz. AGW **Obv:** Bust of Anselm Casimir right **Rev:** Arms in inner circle **Note:** Struck with 1 Ducat dies.

Date	Mintage	VG	F	VF	XF	Unc
1636	—	750	1,500	3,300	6,000	—

KM# 71 2 DUCAT
7.0000 g., 0.9860 Gold 0.2219 oz. AGW **Obv:** Small crowned arms

Date	Mintage	VG	F	VF	XF	Unc
ND	—	275	450	825	1,650	—
1638 BS	—	275	450	825	1,650	—

KM# 74 2 DUCAT
7.0000 g., 0.9860 Gold 0.2219 oz. AGW **Obv:** Large crowned arms

Date	Mintage	VG	F	VF	XF	Unc
1639 BS	—	275	450	825	1,650	—

KM# 88 2 DUCAT
7.0000 g., 0.9860 Gold 0.2219 oz. AGW **Obv:** Facing bust of Anselm Casimir in inner circle **Rev:** Crowned arms in inner circle

Date	Mintage	VG	F	VF	XF	Unc
1642	—	700	1,400	2,400	4,500	—

KM# 89 2 DUCAT
7.0000 g., 0.9860 Gold 0.2219 oz. AGW **Obv:** Bust of Anselm Casimir right in inner circle

Date	Mintage	VG	F	VF	XF	Unc
1642 MG	—	425	850	1,450	2,700	—
1644 ET	—	425	850	1,450	2,700	—
1646 ET	—	425	850	1,450	2,700	—
1647 ET	—	425	850	1,450	2,700	—

KM# 90 2 DUCAT
7.0000 g., 0.9860 Gold 0.2219 oz. AGW **Obv:** Bust of Anselm Casimir right in inner circle **Rev:** Arms topped by three helmets in inner circle

Date	Mintage	VG	F	VF	XF	Unc
1642 MG	—	600	1,200	2,700	4,050	—

KM# 183 2 DUCAT
7.0000 g., 0.9860 Gold 0.2219 oz. AGW **Subject:** Anselm Franz

Date	Mintage	VG	F	VF	XF	Unc
1680 MF	—	550	1,450	3,950	5,500	—

KM# 223 2 DUCAT
7.0000 g., 0.9860 Gold 0.2219 oz. AGW **Subject:** Treaty of Ryswick **Obv:** Crowned and mantled arms **Rev:** Concordia seated left with wreath and cornucopia

Date	Mintage	VG	F	VF	XF	Unc
ND(1696)	—	475	950	1,800	3,000	—

KM# 224 2 DUCAT
7.0000 g., 0.9860 Gold 0.2219 oz. AGW **Subject:** Treaty of Ryswick **Rev:** Altar with burning weapons on top

Date	Mintage	VG	F	VF	XF	Unc
1696	—	400	800	1,500	2,500	—

KM# 225 2 DUCAT
7.0000 g., 0.9860 Gold 0.2219 oz. AGW **Subject:** Treaty of Ryswick **Rev:** Minerva standing

Date	Mintage	VG	F	VF	XF	Unc
1696	—	400	800	1,500	2,500	—

KM# 21 3 DUCAT
10.5000 g., 0.9860 Gold 0.3328 oz. AGW **Subject:** Laying the Cornerstone for the New Archepiscopal Residence at Aschaffenburg **Note:** Similar to 1 Thaler, KM#18.

Date	Mintage	VG	F	VF	XF	Unc
1614 LS	—	6,600	10,000	14,500	—	—

KM# A132 5 DUCAT (1/2 Portugaloser)
17.5000 g., 0.9860 Gold 0.5547 oz. AGW **Note:** Struck with 1 Thaler dies, KM#130.

Date	Mintage	VG	F	VF	XF	Unc
1674 MF Rare	—	—	—	—	—	—

KM# A156 5 DUCAT (1/2 Portugaloser)
17.5000 g., 0.9860 Gold 0.5547 oz. AGW **Obv:** Hartard bust right within inner circle **Obv. Legend:** DAMIAN HARTARD: DG: ARCHIEPVS: MOGVNTINVS: **Rev. Legend:** S • R • I • P • GERM • ARCHICAN & PRIN: EL: EPS: WOR: **Note:** Struck with 1 Thaler dies, KM#154. Fr. #1659a.

Date	Mintage	VG	F	VF	XF	Unc
1676 MF Rare	—	—	—	—	—	—

KM# A184 5 DUCAT (1/2 Portugaloser)
17.5000 g., 0.9860 Gold 0.5547 oz. AGW

Date	Mintage	VG	F	VF	XF	Unc
1680 MF	—	—	—	12,500	16,500	—
1682 MF	—	—	—	12,500	16,500	—

KM# B156 7 DUCAT
24.5000 g., 0.9860 Gold 0.7766 oz. AGW **Note:** Struck with 1 Thaler dies, KM#151.

Date	Mintage	VG	F	VF	XF	Unc
1676 MF Rare	—	—	—	—	—	—

KM# B184 10 DUCAT (Portugaloser)
35.0000 g., 0.9860 Gold 1.1095 oz. AGW **Note:** Struck with 1 Thaler dies, KM#181.

Date	Mintage	VG	F	VF	XF	Unc
1680 MF	—	—	—	14,000	18,500	—
1682 MF	—	—	—	14,000	18,500	—
1684 AL	—	—	—	14,000	18,500	—

TRADE COINAGE

Swedish Issues - 1631-1635

KM# 500 DUCAT
3.5000 g., 0.9860 Gold 0.1109 oz. AGW **Obv:** Gustav II Adolf facing

Date	Mintage	VG	F	VF	XF	Unc
1631 Rare	—	—	—	—	—	—

KM# 502 DUCAT
3.5000 g., 0.9860 Gold 0.1109 oz. AGW **Obv:** Bust right

Date	Mintage	VG	F	VF	XF	Unc
1632 HA	—	260	525	1,150	2,300	—
1632 HE	—	260	525	1,150	2,300	—

KM# 503 DUCAT
3.5000 g., 0.9860 Gold 0.1109 oz. AGW **Obv. Inscription:** IN PVGNIS...

Date	Mintage	VG	F	VF	XF	Unc
1632	—	1,100	1,800	2,750	—	—

KM# 504 DUCAT
3.5000 g., 0.9860 Gold 0.1109 oz. AGW **Obv:** Bust right **Rev. Inscription:** IN PVGNIS...

Date	Mintage	VG	F	VF	XF	Unc
1632	—	300	600	1,200	2,400	—

KM# 505 DUCAT
3.5000 g., 0.9860 Gold 0.1109 oz. AGW **Rev. Inscription:** HEROS MAGNANIMBS...

Date	Mintage	VG	F	VF	XF	Unc
1632	—	1,500	2,500	3,850	—	—

KM# 506 DUCAT

3.5000 g., 0.9860 Gold 0.1109 oz. AGW **Obv:** Ruler standing **Rev. Inscription:** IN PVGNIS/FVERATLEO, REX...

Date	Mintage	VG	F	VF	XF	Unc
1632	—	1,500	2,500	3,850	—	—

KM# 507 DUCAT

3.5000 g., 0.9860 Gold 0.1109 oz. AGW **Rev:** Crowned shield

Date	Mintage	VG	F	VF	XF	Unc
1632	—	1,500	2,500	3,850	—	—

KM# 508 DUCAT

3.5000 g., 0.9860 Gold 0.1109 oz. AGW **Rev. Legend:** DVCATVS NOVVU

Date	Mintage	VG	F	VF	XF	Unc
1632	—	1,500	2,500	3,850	—	—

KM# 511 DUCAT

3.5000 g., 0.9860 Gold 0.1109 oz. AGW **Obv:** Facing bust of Kristina **Rev:** Crowned shield

Date	Mintage	VG	F	VF	XF	Unc
ND(1635) Rare	—	—	—	—	—	—

KM# 501 2 DUCAT

7.0000 g., 0.9860 Gold 0.2219 oz. AGW **Obv:** Gustav II Adolf **Rev:** Arms in inner circle

Date	Mintage	VG	F	VF	XF	Unc
1631	—	3,000	5,400	8,400	—	—

KM# 509 2 DUCAT

7.0000 g., 0.9860 Gold 0.2219 oz. AGW **Obv:** Gustav II Adolf profile **Rev:** Value and date on tablet

Date	Mintage	VG	F	VF	XF	Unc
1632	—	3,000	5,400	8,400	—	—

KM# 510 2 DUCAT

7.0000 g., 0.9860 Gold 0.2219 oz. AGW **Obv:** Gustav II Adolf standing

Date	Mintage	VG	F	VF	XF	Unc
1632	—	4,200	6,600	10,000	—	—

KM# 512 2 DUCAT

7.0000 g., 0.9860 Gold 0.2219 oz. AGW **Obv:** Facing bust of Kristina **Rev:** Crowned shield

Date	Mintage	VG	F	VF	XF	Unc
ND(1635) Rare	—	—	—	—	—	—

UNION OF MAINZ AND HESSE-DARMSTADT

JOINT COINAGE

KM# 1 HELLER

Silver **Obv:** Hesse lion and Mainz wheel in shield, L above **Note:** Uniface.

Date	Mintage	VG	F	VF	XF	Unc
ND(1623-26)	—	20.00	45.00	110	220	—

KM# 684.1 2 KREUZER (Albus)

Silver **Obv:** Imperial orb with Z in laurel wreath **Obv. Legend:** MEINTZ. VNC. HES. DARM. **Rev:** Adjacent oval arms of Mainz and Hesse, M-H above, date below, in laurel wreath **Note:** Varieties exist.

Date	Mintage	VG	F	VF	XF	Unc
16Z9	—	13.00	33.00	65.00	150	—
1630	—	13.00	33.00	65.00	150	—

KM# 684.2 2 KREUZER (Albus)

Silver **Obv:** Similar to KM#684.1, adjacent oval arms of Mainz and Hesse, M-H above, date below, no laurel wreath **Rev. Legend:** MEINTZ.VND.HAS.DARMST.BS (Bundes Scheidemünze)

Date	Mintage	VG	F	VF	XF	Unc
163Z	—	16.00	35.00	70.00	150	—
1635	—	16.00	35.00	70.00	150	—
1637	—	16.00	35.00	70.00	150	—
1638	—	16.00	35.00	70.00	150	—
1639	—	16.00	35.00	70.00	150	—

KM# 684.3 2 KREUZER (Albus)

Silver **Obv:** Similar to KM#684.1, adjacent oval arms of Mainz and Hesse, M-H above, date below, no laurel wreath **Rev. Legend:** MEINTZ.VND.HAS.DARMST.BS (Bundes Scheidemünze)

Date	Mintage	VG	F	VF	XF	Unc
1637	—	13.00	33.00	65.00	150	—
1638	—	13.00	33.00	65.00	150	—
1639	—	13.00	33.00	65.00	150	—

UNION OF HESSE-DARMSTADT, MAINZ, NASSAU-SAARBRUCKE

Mainz joined a union with Hesse-Darmstadt, Nassau-Saarbrucken and Frankfurt to strike some minor coins during the Thirty Years' War. Official coinage was to be minted at Frankfurt. Unofficial issues struck by Mainz foiled the union, ending the four-state corroboration in 1636. A two-state union for Hesse-Darmstadt and Mainz continued to mint amended Halbbatzen in Mainz from 1637-1639.

JOINT COINAGE

KM# 652 PFENNIG

Silver **Obv:** Cross with M-H/N-F in angles **Note:** Uniface. Schussel type.

Date	Mintage	VG	F	VF	XF	Unc
ND(1623-30)	—	16.00	40.00	90.00	200	—

KM# 653.1 2 KREUZER (Albus)

Silver **Obv:** Imperial orb with Z divides date **Obv. Legend:** MEINTZ. HAS. NAS. FRANC **Rev:** Ornate cross, arms of each of four members of monetary union in angles

Date	Mintage	VG	F	VF	XF	Unc
16Z5	—	13.00	30.00	55.00	100	—
16Z8 Æ	—	13.00	30.00	55.00	100	—
16Z8 HE	—	13.00	30.00	55.00	100	—
1629 Æ	—	13.00	30.00	55.00	100	—
16Z9 HE	—	13.00	30.00	55.00	100	—
16Z9 HS	—	13.00	30.00	55.00	100	—
(16)Z9	—	13.00	30.00	55.00	100	—
1630 Æ	—	13.00	30.00	55.00	100	—
163Z	—	13.00	30.00	55.00	100	—
1635	—	13.00	30.00	55.00	100	—
1635 HE	—	13.00	30.00	55.00	100	—
1636	—	13.00	30.00	55.00	100	—
1636 BS	—	13.00	30.00	55.00	100	—
ND	—	13.00	30.00	55.00	100	—

KM# 653.2 2 KREUZER (Albus)

Silver **Obv:** Imperial orb with Z divides date **Obv. Legend:** MEINTZ.HAS.NAS.FRANC. **Rev:** Ornate cross, arms of each of 4 members of the monetary union in angles

Date	Mintage	VG	F	VF	XF	Unc
16Z9	—	—	—	—	—	—

FRENCH OCCUPATION

REGULAR COINAGE

KM# 550 UNKNOWN DENOMINATION

12.6000 g., Silver **Note:** Klippe. Crowned arms of Mainz in ornate baroque shield, griffin rampant at right, legend: KURF MAINZ - NOTH MVN, date in cartouche above.

Date	Mintage	VG	F	VF	XF	Unc
1688 Rare	—	—	—	—	—	—

KM# 551 UNKNOWN DENOMINATION

Pewter, 34 mm. **Note:** Octagonal klippe. Date struck separately below round impression of arms.

Date	Mintage	VG	F	VF	XF	Unc
1688	—	—	—	—	—	—

PATTERNS

Including off metal strikes

KM#	Date	Mintage	Identification	Mkt Val
Pn1	1629 BS	—	Thaler. Pewter. KM#51.	—
Pn2	ND(1647) VBW	—	Pfennig. Gold. VBW above arms. KM#98.	—
Pn3	1652 MF	—	Albus. Gold. KM#100.	—
Pn4	1658 MF	—	Albus. Gold. KM#100.	—
Pn5	1674 MF	—	Albus. Gold. KM#129.	—
Pn6	16Z7 Æ	—	2 Kreuzer. Gold. KM#653.1.	—
Pn7	1636	—	2 Kreuzer. Gold. KM#653.1.	—
Pn8	1679 MF	—	Albus. Gold. KM#164.	—
Pn9	1680	—	3 Pfennig. Gold. KM#176.	—
	1680	—	3 Pfennig. Gold. KM#176.	—
Pn10	1682 MF	—	Thaler. Gold. KM#181.	18,500
Pn11	1684 AL	—	Thaler. Gold. KM#181.	18,500
Pn12	1690 AD	—	2 Albus. Gold. KM#184.	—
Pn13	1695 AK	—	2 Thaler. Pewter. KM#218.	—

MANSFELD

A small, silver mining state, located between Anhalt and Thuringia. Bracteats were struck c. 1200. The ruling family of Mansfeld was much divided during the 15th and 16th centuries and they were prolific coin issuers during this period. The county of Mansfeld was annexed to Electoral Saxony in 1780 and then passed to Prussia in 1815.

RULERS

Vorderort Line

BORNSTEDT

Bruno II, 1546-1615
Wolfgang III, 1615-1638
Bruno III, 1615-1644
Joachim Friedrich, 1615-1623
Philip V, 1615-1657
Karl Adam, 1638-1662
Georg Albrecht, 1657-1696
Maximilian Philip, 1657-1664
Franz Maximilian, 1644-1692
Heinrich Franz, 1644-1715

EISLEBEN

Jobst II, 1579-1619
Ernst IV, 1579-1609
Hoyer Christof, 1579-1587
Johann Georg II, 1619-1647

FRIEDEBURG

Peter Ernst I, 1532-1604

ARNSTEIN

Wilhelm I, 1601-1615

ARTERN

Johann Georg IV, 1585-1615
Volrat VI, 1585-1627

Hinterort Line

Ernst VI, 1567-1609
Friedrich Christof, 1579-1631
David, 1592-1628
Ernst Ludwig, 1631-1632
Christian Friedrich, 1632-1666

MINT MARKS

A, AR - Artern
B - Blumrode
F - Friedeburg
K - Katharinenrieth
L, LS - Leimbach
M -- Mansfeld
MF - Thal Mansfeld
NA - New-Asseburg
OWS - Oberwiederstedt bei Hettstedt
V - Voigtstedt
W - Welbsleben

MINT OFFICIALS' INITIALS

Initial	Date	Name
ABK	1667-80	Anton Bernhard Koburger in Eisleben
AK	1615-32	Anton Koburger (the Elder) in Eisleben
CW	1688-1739	Christian Wermuth, die-cutter in Gotha
DM		Daniel Mebes in Gerbstadt
GB		Unknown
GM	1595-1615	Georg Meinhart in Eisleben
HB		Hardenberg in Wiederstadt
HB		Hans Bergkmann in Artern
HI	1619-23	Hans (Johann/Heinrich)Jacob in Saalfeld
HPK	1632-65	Hans (Johann) Philipp Koburger in Eisleben
HS		Hans Simons
IS	1621-?	Johann Sommer in Artern
PH		Philipp von Hausen in Arnstein castle Johann/Jacob Elias

ARMS

Mansfeld (lordship) – two rows of three lozenges (diamond shapes)

Old Mansfeld (until about 1550) – 4-fold with Querfurt in upper left and lower right, Mansfeld in upper right and lower left

New Mansfeld (from about 1550 onwards) – 4-fold of old Mansfeld in upper left and lower right, Arnstein in upper right, Heldrungen in lower left

Querfurt – six horizontal bars, every other one shaded

Arnstein – eagle

Heldrungen – rampant lion striding upwards to left on checkered diagonal bar

REFERENCE

T = Otto Tornau, ***Münzwesen und Münzen der Grafschaft Mansfeld***, Prague, 1937.

JOINT COINAGE

I – Günther IV, Ernst II, Hoyer VI, Gebhard VII, Albrecht VII
II – Ernst II, Hoyer VI, Gebhard VII, Albrecht VII
III – Hoyer VI, Gebhard VII, Albrecht VII, Philipp II
IV – Hoyer VI, Gebhard VII, Albrecht VII, Johann Georg I

COUNTSHIP

ANONYMOUS COINAGE

1619-1625

KM# 6 3 FLITTER (1-1/2 Pfennig)

Copper **Obv:** Rampant lion left (Heldrungen) divides date in ornamented shield **Rev:** III/FLIT/TER

Date	Mintage	VG	F	VF	XF	Unc
(16)Z1	—	—	—	—	—	—

KM# 7 3 FLITTER (1-1/2 Pfennig)

Copper **Obv:** Oval Querfurt arms (four horizontal bars), value III above

Date	Mintage	VG	F	VF	XF	Unc
ND(1621/22)	—	—	—	—	—	—

KM# 19 PFENNIG

Silver **Obv:** 4-fold arms divide mintmaster's initials, date above **Note:** Uniface, Schussel type. Varieties exist.

Date	Mintage	VG	F	VF	XF	Unc
(16)24 HI	—	13.00	27.00	55.00	95.00	—
(16)25 AK	—	13.00	27.00	55.00	95.00	—
1625 AK	—	13.00	27.00	55.00	95.00	—

KM# 5 3 PFENNIG (Dreier)

Silver **Obv:** 4-fold arms divide date, mintmaster's initials above **Rev:** Small imperial orb with 3 in ornamented rhombus

Date	Mintage	VG	F	VF	XF	Unc
(16)19	—	—	—	—	—	—

KM# 9 3 PFENNIG (Dreier)

Copper **Obv:** 4-fold arms, date above **Rev:** Rampant lion left in shield (Heldrungen), value 3 above

Date	Mintage	VG	F	VF	XF	Unc
16Z1	—	12.00	25.00	40.00	50.00	—

KM# 10 3 PFENNIG (Dreier)

Copper **Obv:** Rampant lion left in shield **Rev:** Imperial orb with 3 divides date

Date	Mintage	VG	F	VF	XF	Unc
(16)Z1	—	12.00	24.00	40.00	70.00	—

KM# 11 3 PFENNIG (Dreier)

Copper **Obv:** Rampant lion left in circle **Rev:** Ornamented heart-shaped shield with 3

Date	Mintage	VG	F	VF	XF	Unc
ND(1621/22)	—	12.00	24.00	40.00	70.00	—

KM# 12 3 PFENNIG (Dreier)

Copper **Obv:** Value III above lion

Date	Mintage	VG	F	VF	XF	Unc
ND(1621/22)	—	12.00	24.00	40.00	70.00	—

KM# 8 3 PFENNIG (Dreier)

Copper **Obv:** 3-fold arms **Rev:** Imperial orb with 3 **Note:** Kipper 3 Pfennig.

Date	Mintage	VG	F	VF	XF	Unc
ND(1621/22)	—	12.00	24.00	40.00	70.00	—

KM# 13 3 PFENNIG (Dreier)

Silver **Obv:** 4-fold arms, crown above divides mintmaster's initials **Rev:** Imperial orb with 3, cross divides date **Note:** Varieties exist.

Date	Mintage	VG	F	VF	XF	Unc
16ZZ HI	—	8.00	16.00	33.00	60.00	—
16Z3 HI	—	8.00	16.00	33.00	60.00	—

KM# 14 3 PFENNIG (Dreier)

Silver **Obv:** Mintmaster's initials divided by arms **Note:** Varieties exist.

Date	Mintage	VG	F	VF	XF	Unc
16ZZ HI	—	8.00	16.00	33.00	60.00	—
16Z3 HI	—	8.00	16.00	33.00	60.00	—

KM# 15 3 PFENNIG (Dreier)

Silver **Obv:** 4-fold arms, crown above divides mintmaster's initials **Rev:** Orb divides date within ornamented rhombus

Date	Mintage	VG	F	VF	XF	Unc
16ZZ HI	—	13.00	27.00	45.00	80.00	—

KM# 16 3 PFENNIG (Dreier)

Silver **Obv:** 3-fold arms, crown above divides mintmaster's initials **Rev:** Imperial orb with 3, cross divides date

Date	Mintage	VG	F	VF	XF	Unc
16ZZ HI	—	13.00	27.00	45.00	80.00	—

KM# 17 3 PFENNIG (Dreier)

Silver **Obv:** Mintmaster's initials divided by arms

Date	Mintage	VG	F	VF	XF	Unc
16ZZ HI	—	13.00	27.00	45.00	80.00	—

KM# 18 3 PFENNIG (Dreier)

Silver **Obv:** Without crown above arms

Date	Mintage	VG	F	VF	XF	Unc
16ZZ HI	—	13.00	27.00	45.00	80.00	—

MANSFELD-ARTERN

Founded in the division of 1530/32, Artern became extinct in 1631 and its lands and titles reverted to Bornstedt.

RULERS

Johann Georg IV, 1585-1615
Philipp Ernst, 1585-1631

JOINT COINAGE

I - Volrat VI, Jobst II, and Wolfgang III
II - Volrat VI, Jobst II, Wolfgang III and Bruno III
III - Volrat VI and Jobst II
IIIa - Volrat VI, Wolfgang III and Albrecht Wolff
IIIb - Volrat VI, Philipp Ernst and Albrecht Wolff
IV - Volrat VI, Wolfang III and Johann Georg II
V - Philipp Ernst, Wolfgang III and Johann Georg II

COUNTSHIP

JOINT COINAGE

KM# 60 FLITTER (1/2 Pfennig)

Copper **Ruler:** Volrat VI, Philipp Ernst, Albrecht Wolff **Obv:** Rampant lion left (Heldrungen) in ornamented shield **Rev:** Querfurt arms (four horizontal bars) in shield **Note:** Kipper Flitter. Struck at Thal Mansfeld Mint.

Date	Mintage	VG	F	VF	XF	Unc
ND(1621/22)	—	—	—	—	—	—

KM# 65 3 FLITTER (1-1/2 Pfennig)

Copper **Ruler:** Volrat VI, Philipp Ernst, Albrecht Wolff **Mint:** Katharinenrieth

Date	Mintage	VG	F	VF	XF	Unc
(16)Z1	—	—	—	—	—	—

KM# 61 3 FLITTER (1-1/2 Pfennig)

Copper **Ruler:** Volrat VI, Philipp Ernst, Albrecht Wolff **Obv:** Rampant lion left (Heldrungen) in ornate shield **Rev:** Querfurt arms (four horizontal bars) below **Rev. Inscription:** III / FLITT / ER **Mint:** Thal Mansfeld **Note:** Kipper 3 Flitter. Varieties exist.

Date	Mintage	VG	F	VF	XF	Unc
ND(1621/22)	—	—	—	—	—	—

KM# 62 3 FLITTER (1-1/2 Pfennig)

Copper **Ruler:** Volrat VI, Philipp Ernst, Albrecht Wolff **Rev:** Date divided by arms **Note:** Varieties exist.

Date	Mintage	VG	F	VF	XF	Unc
1621	—	—	—	—	—	—

KM# 63 3 FLITTER (1-1/2 Pfennig)

Copper **Ruler:** Volrat VI, Philipp Ernst, Albrecht Wolff **Rev:** III above Querfurt arms **Note:** Varieties exist.

Date	Mintage	VG	F	VF	XF	Unc
ND(1621/22)	—	—	—	—	—	—

KM# 64 3 FLITTER (1-1/2 Pfennig)

Copper **Ruler:** Volrat VI, Philipp Ernst, Albrecht Wolff **Obv:** Two-fold arms divided vertically in ornate shield **Rev:** III in circle, date **Rev. Legend:** FLITTER **Note:** Varieties exist.

Date	Mintage	VG	F	VF	XF	Unc
16Z1	—	—	—	—	—	—

KM# 31 3 PFENNIG (Dreier)

Copper **Ruler:** Volrat VI, Philipp Ernst, Albrecht Wolff **Obv:** Four-fold arms, small heart above **Rev:** Imperial orb with 3 divides date **Mint:** Thal Mansfeld

Date	Mintage	VG	F	VF	XF	Unc
1618	—	20.00	40.00	75.00	120	—
161Z Error for 16Z1	—	20.00	40.00	75.00	120	—

KM# 66 3 PFENNIG (Dreier)

Copper **Ruler:** Volrat VI, Philipp Ernst, Albrecht Wolff **Obv:** Arnstein egle in circle **Rev:** Imperial orb with 3

Date	Mintage	VG	F	VF	XF	Unc
ND(1621/22)	—	27.00	45.00	80.00	165	—
ND(1621/22) MF	—	27.00	45.00	80.00	165	—

KM# 67 3 PFENNIG (Dreier)

Copper **Ruler:** Volrat VI, Philipp Ernst, Albrecht Wolff **Obv:** Two-fold arms divided vertically in ornate shield **Rev:** Imperial orb with 3 divides date, in rhombus

Date	Mintage	VG	F	VF	XF	Unc
16Z1	—	16.00	33.00	60.00	100	—

KM# 69 3 PFENNIG (Dreier)

Copper **Ruler:** Volrat VI, Philipp Ernst, Albrecht Wolff **Obv:** Date divided by arms

Date	Mintage	VG	F	VF	XF	Unc
(16)21/16Z1 K	—	—	—	—	—	—

KM# 70 3 PFENNIG (Dreier)

Copper **Ruler:** Volrat VI, Philipp Ernst, Albrecht Wolff **Obv:** Four-fold arms divide date, A above **Rev:** Imperial orb with 3 divides A-R **Note:** Struck at Artern Mint. Varieties exist.

Date	Mintage	VG	F	VF	XF	Unc
(16)1Z A/AR Error for Z1	—	—	—	—	—	—

KM# 68 3 PFENNIG (Dreier)

Copper **Ruler:** Volrat VI, Philipp Ernst, Albrecht Wolff **Obv:** Four-fold arms, K above **Rev:** Imperial orb with 3 divides date **Note:** Struck at Katharinenrieth Mint.

Date	Mintage	VG	F	VF	XF	Unc
(16)Z1 K	—	—	—	—	—	—
16Z1 K	—	—	—	—	—	—
1621 K	—	—	—	—	—	—

KM# 114 GROSCHEN

Silver **Ruler:** Volrat VI, Philipp Ernst, Albrecht Wolff **Subject:** Death of Volrat VI **Obv:** Crowned four-fold arms **Rev:** Seven-line inscription with dates **Note:** Varieties exist.

Date	Mintage	VG	F	VF	XF	Unc
16Z7	—	—	—	—	—	—

KM# 73 12 KREUZER (Schreckenberger)

Silver **Ruler:** Volrat VI, Philipp Ernst, Albrecht Wolff **Obv:** Three small shields of arms, above two, upper one divides date **Rev:** St. George slaying dragon at right

Date	Mintage	VG	F	VF	XF	Unc
16Z1	—	65.00	135	225	325	—

KM# 74 12 KREUZER (Schreckenberger)

Silver **Ruler:** Volrat VI, Philipp Ernst, Albrecht Wolff **Obv:** Single arms at bottom divides date

Date	Mintage	VG	F	VF	XF	Unc
(16)Z1	—	65.00	135	225	325	—

KM# 76 12 KREUZER (Schreckenberger)

Silver **Ruler:** Volrat VI, Philipp Ernst, Albrecht Wolff **Rev:** Helmet with eight small banners from top, date in legend

Date	Mintage	VG	F	VF	XF	Unc
1621	—	85.00	140	275	400	—

KM# 78 12 KREUZER (Schreckenberger)

Silver **Ruler:** Volrat VI, Philipp Ernst, Albrecht Wolff **Obv:** Three small shields of arms, one above two, upper one divides date

Date	Mintage	VG	F	VF	XF	Unc
1621	—	65.00	135	225	325	—

KM# 71 12 KREUZER (Schreckenberger)

Silver **Ruler:** Volrat VI, Philipp Ernst, Albrecht Wolff **Obv:** Four-fold arms **Rev:** Crowned imperial eagle, 1Z in orb on breast **Note:** Kipper 12 Kreuzer.

Date	Mintage	VG	F	VF	XF	Unc
ND(1621/22)	—	65.00	135	225	325	—

KM# 79 12 KREUZER (Schreckenberger)

Silver **Ruler:** Volrat VI, Philipp Ernst, Albrecht Wolff **Obv:** Two adjacent ornate shields of arms, date above **Note:** Struck at Hettstedt Mint.

Date	Mintage	VG	F	VF	XF	Unc
16Z1 HS	—	115	195	275	350	—

KM# 75 12 KREUZER (Schreckenberger)

Silver **Ruler:** Volrat VI, Philipp Ernst, Albrecht Wolff **Obv:** Three small shields of arms, one above two, upper one divides date **Rev:** Crowned imperial eagle, 1Z in orb on breast, titles of Ferdinand II **Note:** Varieties exist.

Date	Mintage	VG	F	VF	XF	Unc
16Z1	—	65.00	135	225	350	—

KM# 77 12 KREUZER (Schreckenberger)

Silver **Ruler:** Volrat VI, Philipp Ernst, Albrecht Wolff **Obv:** Two adjacent ornate shields of arms, date above **Rev:** Crowned imperial eagle 1Z in orb on breast, titles of Ferdinand II **Note:** Varieties exist.

Date	Mintage	VG	F	VF	XF	Unc
16Z1	—	85.00	160	275	400	—

KM# 81 24 KREUZER (Doppelschreckenburger)

Silver **Ruler:** Volrat VI, Philipp Ernst, Albrecht Wolff **Rev:** Crowned imperial eagle, Z4 in orb on breast

Date	Mintage	VG	F	VF	XF	Unc
ND(1621/22)	—	—	—	—	—	—

KM# 82 24 KREUZER (Doppelschreckenburger)

Silver **Ruler:** Volrat VI, Philipp Ernst, Albrecht Wolff **Obv:** Ornamented four-fold arms **Rev:** Crowned imperial eagle, Z4 in orb on breast, titles of Ferdinand II

Date	Mintage	VG	F	VF	XF	Unc
ND(1621/22)	—	—	—	—	—	—

KM# 80 24 KREUZER (Doppelschreckenburger)

Silver **Ruler:** Volrat VI, Philipp Ernst, Albrecht Wolff **Obv:** Angel above heart-shaped two-fold arms **Rev:** Two adjacent ornate shields of arms, value Z4 above **Note:** Kipper 24 Kreuzer.

Date	Mintage	VG	F	VF	XF	Unc
ND(1621/22)	—	—	—	—	—	—

KM# 83 30 KREUZER

Silver **Ruler:** Volrat VI, Philipp Ernst, Albrecht Wolff **Obv:** Angel above three-fold arms **Rev:** Crowned imperial eagle, 30 in orb on breast **Note:** Kipper 30 Kreuzer.

Date	Mintage	VG	F	VF	XF	Unc
ND(1621/22)	—	—	—	—	—	—

KM# 88 1/24 THALER

Silver **Ruler:** Volrat VI, Wolfgang III, Johann Georg II **Rev:** Date and mintmaster's initials divided by orb

Date	Mintage	VG	F	VF	XF	Unc
16ZZ HI	—	27.00	55.00	85.00	140	—

KM# 87 1/24 THALER

Silver **Ruler:** Volrat VI, Wolfgang III, Johann Georg II **Obv:** Two helmets above four-fold arms **Rev:** Imperial orb with 24 divides mintmaster's initials, cross above divides date **Note:** Varieties exist.

Date	Mintage	VG	F	VF	XF	Unc
16ZZ HI	—	27.00	55.00	85.00	140	—
16Z3 HI	—	27.00	55.00	85.00	140	—
(16)Z3 HI	—	27.00	55.00	85.00	140	—
16Z4 HI	—	27.00	55.00	85.00	140	—

KM# 89 1/24 THALER

Silver **Ruler:** Philipp Ernst, Wolfgang III, Johann Georg II **Obv:** Four-fold arms divide mintmaster's initials, date above **Rev:** Imperial orb with Z4 **Note:** Varieties exist.

Date	Mintage	VG	F	VF	XF	Unc
16ZZ AK	—	20.00	45.00	80.00	125	—
16Z3 AK	—	20.00	45.00	80.00	125	—
16Z4 AK	—	20.00	45.00	80.00	125	—
16Z4 HI	—	20.00	45.00	80.00	125	—
1624 HI	—	20.00	45.00	80.00	125	—
16Z5 AK	—	20.00	45.00	80.00	125	—
1625 AK	—	20.00	45.00	80.00	125	—
1626 AK	—	20.00	45.00	80.00	125	—
16Z7 AK	—	20.00	45.00	80.00	125	—
16Z8 AK	—	20.00	45.00	80.00	125	—

KM# 103 1/24 THALER
Silver **Ruler:** Volrat VI, Wolfgang III, Johann Georg II **Obv:** Two helmets above oval arms **Rev:** Imperial orb with 24 divides mintmaster's initials, cross above divides date

Date	Mintage	VG	F	VF	XF	Unc
16Z4	—	27.00	55.00	85.00	145	—

KM# 104 1/24 THALER
Silver **Ruler:** Philipp Ernst, Wolfgang III, Johann Georg II

Date	Mintage	VG	F	VF	XF	Unc
16Z4 HI	—	27.00	55.00	85.00	145	—

KM# 105 1/24 THALER
Silver **Ruler:** Volrat VI, Wolfgang III, Johann Georg II **Obv:** Four-fold arms divide mintmaster's initials, date above

Date	Mintage	VG	F	VF	XF	Unc
1624 HI	—	27.00	55.00	85.00	145	—

KM# 115 1/24 THALER
Silver **Ruler:** Volrat VI, Wolfgang III, Johann Georg II **Rev:** Imperial orb with 24 or Z4, date divided in legend at top

Date	Mintage	VG	F	VF	XF	Unc
16Z7 AK	—	27.00	55.00	85.00	145	—

KM# 120 1/24 THALER
Silver **Ruler:** Volrat VI, Wolfgang III, Johann Georg II **Rev:** Date divided at top in legend

Date	Mintage	VG	F	VF	XF	Unc
1629 AK	—	33.00	60.00	100	165	—

KM# 119 1/24 THALER
Silver **Ruler:** Volrat VI, Wolfgang III, Johann Georg II **Rev:** Imperial orb with 24 or Z4 **Note:** Varieties exist.

Date	Mintage	VG	F	VF	XF	Unc
1629 AK	—	33.00	60.00	100	165	—

KM# 121 1/24 THALER
Silver **Ruler:** Volrat VI, Wolfgang III, Johann Georg II **Rev:** Date divided by orb **Note:** Varieties exist.

Date	Mintage	VG	F	VF	XF	Unc
16Z9/1630 AK	—	33.00	60.00	100	165	—
1629/1630 AK	—	33.00	60.00	100	165	—

KM# 122 1/24 THALER
Silver **Ruler:** Volrat VI, Wolfgang III, Johann Georg II **Note:** Name of an unknown Wilhelm Georg replaces that of Wolfgang III; probably a die-cutter's error.

Date	Mintage	VG	F	VF	XF	Unc
1629/1630 AK	—	—	—	—	—	—

KM# 130 1/24 THALER
Silver **Ruler:** Volrat VI, Wolfgang III, Johann Georg II **Rev:** Date divided by orb **Note:** Varieties exist.

Date	Mintage	VG	F	VF	XF	Unc
1630 AK	—	33.00	60.00	100	165	—

KM# 131 1/24 THALER
Silver **Ruler:** Volrat VI, Wolfgang III, Johann Georg II **Obv:** Mintmaster's initials above arms

Date	Mintage	VG	F	VF	XF	Unc
1630 AK	—	33.00	60.00	100	165	—

KM# 10 1/21 THALER
Silver **Ruler:** Volrat VI, Jobst II, Wolfgang III **Obv:** Two helmets above four-fold arms **Rev:** Imperial orb with Z1 divides mintmaster's initials, cross above divides date **Note:** Varieties exist.

Date	Mintage	VG	F	VF	XF	Unc
1616 AK	—	—	—	—	—	—

KM# 19 1/21 THALER
Silver **Ruler:** Volrat VI, Jobst II, Wolfgang III, Bruno III

Date	Mintage	VG	F	VF	XF	Unc
1617 AK	—	—	—	—	—	—
Note: Reported, not confirmed						
1618 AK	—	—	—	—	—	—
Note: Reported, not confirmed						

KM# 5 1/4 THALER
Silver **Ruler:** Volrat VI, Jobst II, Wolfgang III, Bruno III **Subject:** Death of Johann Georg IV **Obv:** Four-fold arms divide mintmaster's initials, two helmets above divide date **Rev:** Seven-line inscription with dates, legend divided by orb and three small shields **Rev. Legend:** TRAV-IST-MIS-LISH

Date	Mintage	VG	F	VF	XF	Unc
1615 GM	—	—	—	—	—	—

KM# 11 1/4 THALER
Silver **Ruler:** Volrat VI, Jobst II, Wolfgang III **Obv:** Four-fold arms, date and mintmaster's initials between and around two helmets above **Rev:** St. George slaying dragon at right **Note:** Varieties exist.

Date	Mintage	VG	F	VF	XF	Unc
1616 AK	—	80.00	140	220	325	—

KM# 20 1/4 THALER
Silver **Ruler:** Volrat VI, Jobst II, Wolfgang III, Bruno III **Obv:** Date and mintmaster's initials divided

Date	Mintage	VG	F	VF	XF	Unc
1617 AK	—	80.00	140	220	325	—

KM# 35 1/4 THALER
Silver **Ruler:** Volrat VI, Jobst II, Wolfgang III, Bruno III **Obv:** Mintmaster's initials between helmets

Date	Mintage	VG	F	VF	XF	Unc
1619 AK	—	80.00	140	220	325	—

KM# 36 1/4 THALER
Silver **Ruler:** Volrat VI, Jobst II **Obv:** St. George slaying dragon at right **Rev:** Ornate four-fold arms, two helmets above divide date and mintmaster' initials

Date	Mintage	VG	F	VF	XF	Unc
1619 HI	—	40.00	75.00	140	275	—

KM# 50 1/4 THALER
Silver **Ruler:** Volrat VI, Wolfgang III, Johann Georg II **Obv:** St. George slaying dragon, titles of Philipp Ernst **Rev:** Four-fold arms, two helmets above divided by date and mintmaster's initials **Note:** Spruch 1/4 Thaler. Varieties exist.

Date	Mintage	VG	F	VF	XF	Unc
16Z0 HI	—	27.00	55.00	120	275	—
16Z3 HI	—	27.00	55.00	120	275	—

KM# 90 1/4 THALER
Silver **Ruler:** Volrat VI, Wolfgang III, Johann Georg II **Obv:** Date left of St. George **Rev:** Mintmaster's initials divided by arms

Date	Mintage	VG	F	VF	XF	Unc
16ZZ HI	—	40.00	75.00	140	275	—

KM# 94 1/4 THALER
Silver **Ruler:** Volrat VI, Wolfgang III, Johann Georg II **Rev:** Date in legend, mintmaster's initials divided by arms

Date	Mintage	VG	F	VF	XF	Unc
1623 HI	—	40.00	75.00	140	275	—

KM# 95 1/4 THALER
Silver **Ruler:** Volrat VI, Wolfgang III, Johann Georg II **Rev:** Date divided at top

Date	Mintage	VG	F	VF	XF	Unc
1623 HI	—	40.00	75.00	140	275	—

KM# 96 1/4 THALER
Silver **Ruler:** Volrat VI, Wolfgang III, Johann Georg II **Rev:** Date between two helmets

Date	Mintage	VG	F	VF	XF	Unc
16Z3 HI	—	40.00	75.00	140	275	—

KM# 97 1/4 THALER
Silver **Ruler:** Volrat VI, Wolfgang III, Johann Georg II **Rev:** Date in legend at top, mintmaster's initials divided by arms

Date	Mintage	VG	F	VF	XF	Unc
1623 HI	—	—	—	—	—	—

KM# 107 1/4 THALER
Silver **Ruler:** Volrat VI, Wolfgang III, Johann Georg II **Rev:** Date between helmets

Date	Mintage	VG	F	VF	XF	Unc
1624 HI	—	33.00	70.00	140	275	—

KM# 106 1/4 THALER
Silver **Ruler:** Volrat VI, Wolfgang III, Johann Georg II **Rev:** Date divided by arms **Note:** Varieties exist.

Date	Mintage	VG	F	VF	XF	Unc
16Z4 AK	—	33.00	70.00	140	275	—
16Z6 AK	—	33.00	70.00	140	275	—

KM# 108 1/4 THALER
Silver **Ruler:** Volrat VI, Wolfgang III, Johann Georg II **Rev:** Date divided by arms **Note:** Varieties exist.

Date	Mintage	VG	F	VF	XF	Unc
1624 HI	—	33.00	70.00	140	275	—

KM# 116 1/4 THALER
Silver **Ruler:** Volrat VI, Wolfgang III, Johann Georg II **Subject:** Death of Volrat VI **Obv:** St. George slaying dragon at right **Rev:** Seven-line inscription with dates, imperial orb above

Date	Mintage	VG	F	VF	XF	Unc
16Z7	—	—	—	—	—	—
Note: Reported, not confirmed						

KM# 123 1/4 THALER
Silver **Ruler:** Philipp Ernst, Wolfgang III, Johann Georg II **Rev:** Mintmaster's initials between helmets

Date	Mintage	VG	F	VF	XF	Unc
16Z9 AK	—	33.00	70.00	140	275	—
1630 AK	—	—	—	—	—	—
Note: Reported, not confirmed						

KM# 6 1/2 THALER
Silver **Ruler:** Philipp Ernst, Wolfgang III, Johann Georg II **Subject:** Death of Johann Georg IV **Obv:** Four-fold arms divide mintmaster's initials, two helmets above divide date **Rev:** Seven-line inscription with dates, legend divided by orb and three small shields **Rev. Legend:** TRAV-UST-MIS-LICH **Note:** Varieties exist.

Date	Mintage	VG	F	VF	XF	Unc
1615 GM	—	—	—	—	—	—

KM# 7 1/2 THALER
Silver **Ruler:** Philipp Ernst, Wolfgang III, Johann Georg II **Obv:** Date in legend **Note:** Varieties exist.

Date	Mintage	VG	F	VF	XF	Unc
1615 GM	—	—	—	—	—	—

KM# 12 1/2 THALER
Silver **Ruler:** Volrat VI, Jobst II, Wolfgang III **Obv:** Four-fold arms, date and mintmaster's initials between and around two helmets above **Rev:** St. George slaying dragon at right **Note:** Varieties exist.

Date	Mintage	VG	F	VF	XF	Unc
1616 AK	—	165	325	450	800	—
1617 AK	—	165	325	450	800	—

KM# 22 1/2 THALER
Silver **Ruler:** Volrat VI, Wolfgang III, Johann Georg II **Note:** Spruch 1/2 Thaler. Broad flan. Similar to 1 Thaler, KM#18. Varieties exist.

Date	Mintage	VG	F	VF	XF	Unc
1617 AK	—	—	—	—	—	—
1618 AK	—	—	—	—	—	—
1619 AK	—	—	—	—	—	—

KM# 21 1/2 THALER
Silver **Ruler:** Volrat VI, Jobst II, Wolfgang III, Bruno III **Obv:** Date and mintmaster's initials divided by arms

Date	Mintage	VG	F	VF	XF	Unc
1617 AK	—	165	325	450	800	—

KM# 33 1/2 THALER
Silver **Ruler:** Volrat VI, Jobst II, Wolfgang III, Bruno III **Obv:** Date between helmets

Date	Mintage	VG	F	VF	XF	Unc
(16)18 AK	—	165	325	450	800	—

KM# 32 1/2 THALER
Silver **Ruler:** Volrat VI, Jobst II, Wolfgang III, Bruno III **Obv:** Mintmaster's initials between helmets **Note:** Varieties exist.

Date	Mintage	VG	F	VF	XF	Unc
1618 AK	—	165	325	450	800	—
1619 AK	—	165	325	450	800	—

KM# 37 1/2 THALER
Silver **Ruler:** Volrat VI, Jobst II **Obv:** St. George slaying dragon at right **Rev:** Ornate four-fold arms, two helmets above divide date and mintmaster's initials

Date	Mintage	VG	F	VF	XF	Unc
1619 HI	—	—	—	—	—	—

KM# 38 1/2 THALER
Silver **Rev:** Date divided by arms **Note:** Varieties exist.

Date	Mintage	VG	F	VF	XF	Unc
1619 AK	—	—	—	—	—	—
16Z3 HI	—	—	—	—	—	—
16Z4 HI	—	—	—	—	—	—

KM# 51 1/2 THALER
Silver **Ruler:** Volrat VI, Wolfgang III, Johann Georg II **Rev:** Date and mintmaster's initials between helmets

Date	Mintage	VG	F	VF	XF	Unc
16Z0 HI	—	—	—	—	—	—

KM# 52 1/2 THALER
Silver **Ruler:** Volrat VI, Wolfgang III, Johann Georg II **Note:** Similar to 1 Thaler, KM#29. Varieties exist.

Date	Mintage	VG	F	VF	XF	Unc
16Z0 HI	—	—	—	—	—	—
16Z4 HI	—	—	—	—	—	—

KM# 91 1/2 THALER
Silver **Ruler:** Volrat VI, Wolfgang III, Johann Georg II **Rev:** Date divided by arms **Note:** Varieties exist.

Date	Mintage	VG	F	VF	XF	Unc
16ZZ HI	—	45.00	85.00	140	275	—
16Z3 HI	—	45.00	85.00	140	275	—
16Z4 HI	—	45.00	85.00	140	275	—
16Z4 AK	—	45.00	85.00	140	275	—

Date	Mintage	VG	F	VF	XF	Unc
16Z5 AK	—	45.00	85.00	140	275	—
16Z6 AK	—	45.00	85.00	140	275	—

KM# 92 1/2 THALER

Silver **Ruler:** Philipp Ernst, Wolfgang III, Johann Georg II **Obv:** Date left of St. George **Rev:** Mintmaster's initials divided by arms **Note:** Varieties exist.

Date	Mintage	VG	F	VF	XF	Unc
16ZZ HI	—	55.00	100	165	275	—

KM# 99 1/2 THALER

Silver **Ruler:** Volrat VI, Wolfgang III, Johann Georg II **Note:** Broad flan.

Date	Mintage	VG	F	VF	XF	Unc
16Z3 HI	—	55.00	100	165	275	—

KM# 98 1/2 THALER

Silver **Ruler:** Philipp Ernst, Wolfgang III, Johann Georg II **Obv:** Date at top in legend

Date	Mintage	VG	F	VF	XF	Unc
16Z3 HI	—	55.00	100	165	275	—

KM# 101 1/2 THALER

Silver **Ruler:** Volrat VI, Wolfgang III, Johann Georg II **Rev:** Date divided in legend at top

Date	Mintage	VG	F	VF	XF	Unc
16Z3 H: I	—	55.00	100	165	275	—

KM# 100 1/2 THALER

Silver **Ruler:** Volrat VI, Wolfgang III, Johann Georg II **Rev:** Date in legend at top, mintmaster's initials divided by arms **Note:** Varieties exist.

Date	Mintage	VG	F	VF	XF	Unc
16Z3 HI	—	55.00	100	165	275	—
16Z4 HI	—	55.00	100	165	275	—
16Z5 HI	—	55.00	100	165	275	—

KM# 109 1/2 THALER

Silver **Ruler:** Volrat VI, Wolfgang III, Johann Georg II **Rev:** Date divided by arms

Date	Mintage	VG	F	VF	XF	Unc
16Z4 HI	—	55.00	100	165	275	—

KM# 110 1/2 THALER

Silver **Ruler:** Volrat VI, Wolfgang III, Johann Georg II **Rev:** Date between two helmets

Date	Mintage	VG	F	VF	XF	Unc
16Z4 HI	—	55.00	100	165	275	—

KM# 117 1/2 THALER

Silver **Ruler:** Volrat VI, Wolfgang III, Johann Georg II **Subject:** Death of Volrat VI **Obv:** St. George slaying dragon at right **Rev:** Seven-line inscription with dates, imperial orb above

Date	Mintage	VG	F	VF	XF	Unc
16Z7	—	—	—	—	—	—

KM# 124 1/2 THALER

Silver **Ruler:** Volrat VI, Wolfgang III, Johann Georg II **Rev:** Mintmaster's initials between helmets

Date	Mintage	VG	F	VF	XF	Unc
16Z9 AK	—	—	—	—	—	—

KM# 132 1/2 THALER

Silver **Rev:** Mintmaster's initials also divided by arms

Date	Mintage	VG	F	VF	XF	Unc
1630 AK	—	—	—	—	—	—

KM# 133 1/2 THALER

Silver **Ruler:** Volrat VI, Wolfgang III, Johann Georg II **Rev:** Date between helmets

Date	Mintage	VG	F	VF	XF	Unc
1630 AK	—	—	—	—	—	—

KM# 8 THALER

Silver **Ruler:** Volrat VI, Wolfgang III, Johann Georg II **Subject:** Death of Johann Georg IV **Obv:** Helmeted arms divide date above, G-M below **Rev:** Seven-line inscription **Note:** Varieties exist. Dav. #6949.

Date	Mintage	VG	F	VF	XF	Unc
1615 GM Rare	—	1,250	2,500	4,500	7,500	—

KM# 13 THALER

Silver **Ruler:** Volrat VI, Jobst II, Wolfgang III **Obv. Legend:** BOLRA. IOBST. E. WOLFG. P. **Note:** Varieties exist. Dav. #6950.

Date	Mintage	VG	F	VF	XF	Unc
1616 AK	—	75.00	190	265	400	—
1617 AK	—	75.00	190	265	400	—

KM# 16 THALER

Silver **Ruler:** Volrat VI, Jobst II, Wolfgang III **Obv:** Date divided by shield **Note:** Varieties exist. Dav. #6952.

Date	Mintage	VG	F	VF	XF	Unc
1616 AK	—	75.00	190	265	400	—
1617 AK	—	75.00	190	265	400	—

KM# 15 THALER

Silver **Ruler:** Volrat VI, Jobst II, Wolfgang III **Obv:** A-K divided in helmets **Note:** Dav. #6951A.

Date	Mintage	VG	F	VF	XF	Unc
1616 AK	—	—	—	—	—	—

KM# 17 THALER

Silver **Ruler:** Volrat VI, Jobst II, Wolfgang III, Bruno III **Obv:** Date divided in helmets, A-K below **Obv. Legend:** VOLRAT. IOBST. WOLF. E. BRV. **Note:** Varieties exist.

Date	Mintage	VG	F	VF	XF	Unc
1616 AK	—	75.00	190	265	400	—
1617 AK	—	75.00	190	265	400	—
1618 AK	—	75.00	190	265	400	—
1619 AK	—	75.00	190	265	400	—

KM# 14 THALER

Silver **Ruler:** Volrat VI, Jobst II, Wolfgang III **Obv:** Solid or divided date in helmets **Note:** Varieties exist. Dav. #6991.

Date	Mintage	VG	F	VF	XF	Unc
1616 AK	—	75.00	190	265	400	—
1617 AK	—	75.00	190	265	400	—

KM# 23 THALER

Silver **Ruler:** Volrat VI, Jobst II, Wolfgang III, Bruno III **Obv:** Clover and A-K between helmets, date divided by shield below **Note:** Varieties exist.

Date	Mintage	VG	F	VF	XF	Unc
1617 AK	—	75.00	190	265	400	—
1618 AK	—	75.00	190	265	400	—
1619 AK	—	75.00	190	265	400	—

KM# 27 THALER

Silver **Ruler:** Volrat VI, Jobst II, Wolfgang III, Bruno III **Rev:** Helmeted arms divide date and initials below **Note:** Varieties exist. Dav. #6967.

Date	Mintage	VG	F	VF	XF	Unc
1617 AK	—	75.00	190	265	400	—
1618 AK	—	75.00	190	265	400	—
1619 AK	—	115	225	375	600	—
16Z1 HI	—	75.00	190	265	400	—
16ZZ HI	—	—	—	—	—	—
1624 HI	—	75.00	190	265	400	—
1625 HI	—	75.00	190	265	400	—
1626 HI	—	75.00	190	265	400	—
1627 HI	—	75.00	190	265	400	—

KM# 24 THALER

Silver **Ruler:** Volrat VI, Jobst II, Wolfgang III, Bruno III **Obv:** A-K below **Note:** Dav. #6955A.

Date	Mintage	VG	F	VF	XF	Unc
1617 AK	—	75.00	190	265	400	—
1618 AK	—	75.00	190	265	400	—
1619 AK	—	75.00	190	265	400	—

KM# 25 THALER

Silver **Ruler:** Volrat VI, Jobst II, Wolfgang III, Bruno III **Obv:** A-K above date **Note:** Dav. #6955B.

Date	Mintage	VG	F	VF	XF	Unc
1617 AK	—	75.00	190	265	400	—
1618 AK	—	75.00	190	265	400	—
1619 AK	—	75.00	190	265	400	—

KM# 26 THALER

Silver **Ruler:** Volrat VI, Jobst II, Wolfgang III, Bruno III **Obv:** Without A-K **Note:** Dav. #6955C.

Date	Mintage	VG	F	VF	XF	Unc
1617	—	75.00	190	265	400	—
1618	—	75.00	190	265	400	—
1619	—	75.00	190	265	400	—

KM# 39 THALER

Silver **Ruler:** Volrat VI, Jobst II **Obv:** Helmeted arms, X/H. I/date between helmets **Obv. Legend:** VOLRATH. ET. IOBST. PATR. COM. ET. COM. **Note:** Varieties exist. Dav. #6956.

Date	Mintage	VG	F	VF	XF	Unc
1619 HI	—	75.00	190	265	400	—
1620 HI	—	75.00	190	265	400	—

KM# 40 THALER

Silver **Ruler:** Volrat VI, Jobst II **Obv:** St. George and dragon **Obv. Legend:** VOLRATH ET. JOBST. PATRVELES **Rev:** Wreaths horizontal **Note:** Varieties exist. Dav. #6957.

Date	Mintage	VG	F	VF	XF	Unc
1619 HI	—	75.00	190	265	400	—

KM# 41 THALER

Silver **Ruler:** Volrat VI, Jobst II **Rev:** Wreaths vertical **Note:** Varieties exist. Dav. #6957A.

Date	Mintage	VG	F	VF	XF	Unc
1619 HI	—	75.00	190	265	400	—

KM# 42 THALER

Silver **Ruler:** Volrat VI, Jobst II **Rev:** X/HI/date between helmets **Note:** Varieties exist. Dav. #6969.

Date	Mintage	VG	F	VF	XF	Unc
1619 HI	—	75.00	190	265	400	—
1620 HI	—	75.00	190	265	400	—
1621 HI	—	75.00	190	265	400	—
1622 HI	—	75.00	190	265	400	—

KM# 54 THALER

Silver **Ruler:** Volrat VI, Wolfgang III, Johann Georg II **Obv. Legend:** VOLRAT. WOLF: IOH: GEOR: PATR: CO: E: DO: **Note:** Varieties exist. Dav. #6960.

Date	Mintage	VG	F	VF	XF	Unc
1620 HI	—	75.00	190	265	400	—
1621 HI	—	75.00	190	265	400	—
1622 HI	—	75.00	190	265	400	—

KM# 55 THALER

Silver **Ruler:** Volrat VI, Wolfgang III, Johann Georg II **Obv. Legend:** VOLR: WOLF: IOH: GEOR: PATR. **Rev:** Spanish or German shields **Note:** Varieties exist. Dav. #6962.

Date	Mintage	VG	F	VF	XF	Unc
16Z0 HI	—	75.00	190	265	400	—
16Z1 HI	—	75.00	190	265	400	—
16ZZ HI	—	75.00	190	265	400	—
16Z3 HI	—	75.00	190	265	400	—
16Z4 HI	—	75.00	190	265	400	—
16Z4 AK	—	75.00	190	265	400	—
16Z5 AK	—	75.00	190	265	400	—
16Z6 AK	—	75.00	190	265	400	—
16Z7 AK	—	75.00	190	265	400	—

KM# 53 THALER

Silver **Ruler:** Volrat VI, Jobst II **Rev:** X/O/H-I between helmets, date divided below **Note:** Dav. #6958.

Date	Mintage	VG	F	VF	XF	Unc
1620 HI	—	75.00	190	265	400	—

KM# 85 THALER

Silver **Ruler:** Volrat VI, Wolfgang III, Johann Georg II **Rev:** H-I divided by shield **Note:** Dav. #6963A.

Date	Mintage	VG	F	VF	XF	Unc
1621 HI	—	75.00	190	265	400	—
1622 HI	—	75.00	190	265	400	—
1623 HI	—	75.00	190	265	400	—

KM# 84 THALER

Silver **Ruler:** Volrat VI, Wolfgang III, Johann Georg II **Note:** Similar to KM#85 but HI between helmets. Dav. #6963.

Date	Mintage	VG	F	VF	XF	Unc
1621 HI	—	75.00	190	265	400	—
1622 HI	—	75.00	190	265	400	—
1623 HI	—	75.00	190	265	400	—

KM# 102 THALER

Silver **Ruler:** Volrat VI, Wolfgang III, Johann Georg II **Obv. Legend:** VOLRAT. WOLFGANG. E. IOHAN. GEORG. PATRVELIS. **Note:** Dav. #6964.

Date	Mintage	VG	F	VF	XF	Unc
1623 HI	—	75.00	190	265	400	—
1624 HI	—	75.00	190	265	400	—

KM# 118 THALER

Silver **Ruler:** Volrat VI, Wolfgang III, Johann Georg II **Subject:** Death of Volrat VI **Obv:** St. George and dragon **Rev:** Seven-line inscription **Note:** Dav. #6965.

Date	Mintage	VG	F	VF	XF	Unc
1627	—	115	225	350	525	—

KM# 125 THALER

Silver **Ruler:** Volrat VI, Wolfgang III, Johann Georg II **Obv. Legend:** PHILIP: ERN: SEN: WOL: ET: IO-HA. GEOR. PA: **Rev:** Helmeted arms divide date and A-K **Note:** Dav. #6970. Varieties exist.

Date	Mintage	VG	F	VF	XF	Unc
1629	—	75.00	190	265	400	—
1630	—	75.00	190	265	400	—

KM# 126 THALER

Silver **Ruler:** Volrat VI, Wolfgang III, Johann Georg II **Rev:** A-K between helmets **Note:** Dav. #6970A. Varieties exist.

Date	Mintage	VG	F	VF	XF	Unc
1629	—	75.00	190	265	400	—

KM# 9 2 THALER

Silver **Ruler:** Volrat VI, Wolfgang III, Johann Georg II **Subject:** Death of Johann Georg IV **Obv:** Helmeted arms divide date above, G-M below **Rev:** Seven-line inscription **Note:** Dav. #6948. Varieties exist.

Date	Mintage	VG	F	VF	XF	Unc
1615 GM Rare	—	—	—	—	—	—

KM# 28 2 THALER

Silver **Ruler:** Volrat VI, Jobst II, Wolfgang III, Bruno III **Note:** Spruch 2 Thaler. Similar to 1 Thaler, KM#27. Varieties exist. Dav. #6966.

Date	Mintage	VG	F	VF	XF	Unc
1617 AK	—	600	1,150	1,900	3,000	—
1618 AK	—	600	1,150	1,900	3,000	—
1619 AK	—	600	1,150	1,900	3,000	—
1621 HI	—	600	1,150	1,900	3,000	—
16Z5 AK	—	600	1,150	1,900	3,000	—

KM# 34 2 THALER

Silver **Ruler:** Volrat VI, Jobst II, Wolfgang III, Bruno III **Obv:** Helmeted arms with divided date and A-K between helmets **Obv. Legend:** VOLRAT. IOBST. WOLF. E. BRV. **Note:** Dav. #6954.

Date	Mintage	VG	F	VF	XF	Unc
1618 AK	—	600	1,050	1,800	3,000	—

KM# 56 2 THALER

Silver **Ruler:** Volrat VI, Wolfgang III, Johann Georg II **Note:** Similar to 1 Thaler, KM#54. Dav. #6959.

Date	Mintage	VG	F	VF	XF	Unc
1620 HI	—	600	1,050	1,800	3,000	—

KM# 86 2 THALER

Silver **Ruler:** Volrat VI, Wolfgang III, Johann Georg II **Note:** Similar to 1 Thaler, KM#42. Dav. #6968.

Date	Mintage	VG	F	VF	XF	Unc
16Z1 HI	—	600	1,150	1,900	3,000	—

KM# 112 2 THALER

Silver **Ruler:** Volrat VI, Wolfgang III, Johann Georg II **Note:** Similar to 1 Thaler, KM#55. Varieties exist. Dav. #6961.

Date	Mintage	VG	F	VF	XF	Unc
1626	—	600	1,050	1,800	3,000	—

TRADE COINAGE

KM# 57 1/2 GOLDGULDEN

1.7500 g., 0.9860 Gold 0.0555 oz. AGW **Ruler:** Volrat VI, Wolfgang III, Johann Georg II **Obv:** St. George and dragon in inner circle **Rev:** Three shields as trilobe, date divided at bottom

Date	Mintage	VG	F	VF	XF	Unc
1620	—	375	575	1,300	2,500	—

KM# 18 GOLDGULDEN

3.5000 g., 0.9860 Gold 0.1109 oz. AGW **Ruler:** Volrat VI, Jobst II, Wolfgang III, Bruno III **Obv. Legend:** VOLRATH • IOBST • E • WOLFGANG...

Date	Mintage	VG	F	VF	XF	Unc
1616	—	270	425	850	1,750	—
1617	—	270	425	850	1,750	—

KM# 29 GOLDGULDEN

3.5000 g., 0.9860 Gold 0.1109 oz. AGW **Ruler:** Volrat VI, Wolfgang III, Johann Georg II **Obv. Legend:** VOLRAT • IOBST • WOLFGANG • E • BRUNO...

Date	Mintage	VG	F	VF	XF	Unc
1617	—	270	425	850	1,750	—
1618	—	270	425	850	1,750	—

KM# 43 GOLDGULDEN

3.5000 g., 0.9860 Gold 0.1109 oz. AGW **Ruler:** Volrat VI, Jobst II **Obv. Legend:** VOLRAT • ET • JOBST ...

Date	Mintage	VG	F	VF	XF	Unc
1619	—	270	425	850	1,750	—

KM# 58 GOLDGULDEN

3.5000 g., 0.9860 Gold 0.1109 oz. AGW **Ruler:** Volrat VI, Wolfgang III, Johann Georg II **Obv. Legend:** VOLRAT • ET • IOBST...

Date	Mintage	VG	F	VF	XF	Unc
16Z0 HI	—	240	350	775	1,600	—
16Z1 HI	—	240	350	775	1,600	—
16Z6 AK	—	240	350	775	1,600	—

KM# 134 GOLDGULDEN

3.5000 g., 0.9860 Gold 0.1109 oz. AGW **Ruler:** Volrat VI, Wolfgang III, Johann Georg II **Rev:** Three shields as trilobe, date divided at bottom

Date	Mintage	VG	F	VF	XF	Unc
1630	—	300	550	1,150	2,150	—

KM# 93 2 GOLDGULDEN

7.0000 g., 0.9860 Gold 0.2219 oz. AGW **Ruler:** Volrat VI, Wolfgang III, Johann Georg II **Obv:** St. George slaying dragon at right, date at left **Rev:** Ornate four-fold arms, two helmets above, Mintmaster's initials divided by arms

Date	Mintage	VG	F	VF	XF	Unc
16ZZ HI Rare	—	—	—	—	—	—

KM# 113 2 GOLDGULDEN

7.0000 g., 0.9860 Gold 0.2219 oz. AGW **Ruler:** Volrat VI, Wolfgang III, Johann Georg II **Rev:** Date divided by arms

Date	Mintage	VG	F	VF	XF	Unc
16Z6 AK Rare	—	—	—	—	—	—

KM# 127 2 GOLDGULDEN

7.0000 g., 0.9860 Gold 0.2219 oz. AGW **Ruler:** Philipp Ernst, Wolfgang III, Johann Georg II **Rev:** Two helmets above divided by date and mintmaster's initials **Note:** Varieties exist.

Date	Mintage	VG	F	VF	XF	Unc
16Z9 AK Rare	—	—	—	—	—	—

KM# 59 2 DUCAT

7.0000 g., 0.9860 Gold 0.2219 oz. AGW **Obv:** St. George slaying dragon, titles of Philipp Ernst **Rev:** Four-fold arms, two helmets above divided by date and mintmaster's initials

Date	Mintage	VG	F	VF	XF	Unc
16Z0 HI Rare	—	—	—	—	—	—

KM# 111 2 DUCAT

7.0000 g., 0.9860 Gold 0.2219 oz. AGW **Rev:** Date between helmets

Date	Mintage	VG	F	VF	XF	Unc
16Z4 HI Rare	—	—	—	—	—	—

KM# 30 3 DUCAT

10.5000 g., 0.9860 Gold 0.3328 oz. AGW **Ruler:** Volrat VI, Jobst II, Wolfgang III, Bruno III **Obv:** Four-fold arms, date and mintmaster's initials between two helmets above **Rev:** St. George slaying dragon at right

Date	Mintage	VG	F	VF	XF	Unc
1617 AK Rare	—	—	—	—	—	—
1619 AK Rare	—	—	—	—	—	—

KM# 135 4 DUCAT

14.0000 g., 0.9860 Gold 0.4438 oz. AGW **Ruler:** Philipp Ernst, Wolfgang III, Johann Georg II **Note:** Struck with 1 Thaler dies, KM#27.

Date	Mintage	VG	F	VF	XF	Unc
1630 AK Rare	—	—	—	—	—	—

KM# 136 4 DUCAT

14.0000 g., 0.9860 Gold 0.4438 oz. AGW **Ruler:** Philipp Ernst, Wolfgang III, Johann Georg II **Note:** Struck with 1 Thaler dies, KM#42.

Date	Mintage	VG	F	VF	XF	Unc
1630 AK Rare	—	—	—	—	—	—

MANSFELD-BORNSTEDT

Founded upon the division of Mansfeld in 1530/32. Raised to the rank of Prince of the Empire in 1709. The line became extinct in 1780 and its titles fell to Colloredo.

RULERS

Bruno II, 1546-1615
Wolfgang III, 1615-1638
Karl Adam, 1638-1662
Franz Maximilian, 1644-1692
Heinrich Franz, 1644-1715
Georg Albrecht, 1657-1696
Maximilian Philipp, 1657-1664
Karl Franz, 1692-1717

JOINT COINAGE

V - Wolfgang III, Bruno III, Joachim Friedrich and Philipp V

REFERENCE

T = Otto Tornau, **Münzwesen und Münzen der Grafschaft Mansfeld**, Prague, 1937.

COUNTSHIP

STANDARD COINAGE

KM# 55 2 PFENNIG

Copper **Ruler:** Bruno II, Wilhelm I, Johann Georg IV, Volrat VI and Jobst II **Obv:** 3-fold arms, .I.I. above **Mint:** Schraplau **Note:** Kipper 2 Pfennig. Uniface.

Date	Mintage	VG	F	VF	XF	Unc
ND(1621/22)	—	—	—	—	—	—

KM# 31 3 PFENNIG (Dreier)

Silver **Ruler:** Bruno II, Wilhelm I, Johann Georg IV, Volrat VI and Jobst II **Obv:** Ornate 4-fold arms with mintmaster's initials above **Rev:** Imperial orb with 3 divides date, within ornamented rhombus **Note:** Varieties exist.

Date	Mintage	VG	F	VF	XF	Unc
161Z GM	—	—	—	—	—	—
1613 GM	—	—	—	—	—	—

KM# 56 3 PFENNIG (Dreier)

Copper **Obv:** Round 4-fold arms **Rev:** Imperial orb with 3 divides date **Note:** Kipper 3 Pfennig. Varieties exist.

Date	Mintage	Good	VG	F	VF	XF
(16)Z1	—	11.00	20.00	35.00	70.00	—

KM# 57 3 PFENNIG (Dreier)

Copper **Ruler:** Bruno II, Wilhelm I, Johann Georg IV, Volrat VI and Jobst II **Obv:** Rampant lion to left (Heldrungen), OWS below **Rev:** Imperial orb with 3 **Mint:** Oberwiederstedt bei Hettstedt

Date	Mintage	Good	VG	F	VF	XF
ND(1621/22) OWS	—	20.00	33.00	60.00	100	—

KM# 58 3 PFENNIG (Dreier)

Copper **Ruler:** Bruno II, Wilhelm I, Johann Georg IV, Volrat VI and Jobst II **Obv:** 4-fold arms, W above **Rev:** Imperial orb with 3 divides date **Mint:** Welbsleben

Date	Mintage	Good	VG	F	VF	XF
(16)Z1 W	—	20.00	33.00	60.00	100	—

KM# 59 3 PFENNIG (Dreier)

Copper **Ruler:** Wolfgang III and David **Obv:** 3-fold arms in ornate shield **Rev:** Imperial orb with 3 **Mint:** Schraplau **Note:** Varieties exist.

Date	Mintage	Good	VG	F	VF	XF
ND(1621/22)	—	20.00	33.00	60.00	100	—

KM# 60 3 PFENNIG (Dreier)

Copper **Ruler:** Wolfgang III and David **Note:** Uniface. 3-fold arms in ornate shield.

Date	Mintage	Good	VG	F	VF	XF
ND(1621/22)	—	20.00	33.00	60.00	100	—

KM# 61 3 PFENNIG (Dreier)

Copper **Ruler:** Wolfgang III and David **Obv:** 4-fold arms, date above **Rev:** Rampant lion to left (Heldrungen) in circle, 3 below **Note:** Varieties exist.

Date	Mintage	Good	VG	F	VF	XF
16Z1	—	11.00	20.00	35.00	65.00	—

KM# 62 3 PFENNIG (Dreier)

Copper **Ruler:** Wolfgang III and David **Rev:** Lion in squarish shield, value 3 above

Date	Mintage	Good	VG	F	VF	XF
16Z1	—	11.00	20.00	33.00	65.00	—

KM# 63 3 PFENNIG (Dreier)

Copper **Ruler:** Wolfgang III and David **Rev:** Ornately-shaped shield

Date	Mintage	Good	VG	F	VF	XF
16Z1	—	11.00	20.00	35.00	65.00	—

KM# 64 3 PFENNIG (Dreier)

Copper **Ruler:** Wolfgang III and David **Rev:** Value: I.I.I. above lion arms

Date	Mintage	Good	VG	F	VF	XF
16Z1	—	11.00	20.00	33.00	65.00	—

KM# 65 3 PFENNIG (Dreier)

Copper **Ruler:** Wolfgang III and Joachim Friedrich **Obv:** Shield of Arnstein eagle divides date, F above **Rev:** Imperial orb with 3 **Note:** Struck at Friedeburg.

Date	Mintage	Good	VG	F	VF	XF
(16)Z1	—	20.00	33.00	60.00	100	—

KM# 40 GROSCHEN

Silver **Ruler:** Bruno II, Wilhelm I, Volrat VI and Jobst II **Subject:** Death of Bruno II **Obv:** 4-fold arms divide mintmaster's initials **Rev:** 8-line inscription with dates **Note:** Varieties exist.

Date	Mintage	VG	F	VF	XF	Unc
1615 GM	—	—	—	—	—	—

KM# 32 3-1/2 GROSCHEN

Silver **Ruler:** Bruno II, Wilhelm I, Johann Georg IV, Volrat VI and Jobst II **Obv:** 4-fold arms divide 3 1/Z - gl, two helmets above, date in legend

Date	Mintage	VG	F	VF	XF	Unc
161Z	—	—	—	—	—	—

KM# 66 12 KREUZER (Schreckenburger)

Silver **Ruler:** Wolfgang III, Bruno III and Joachim Friedrich **Obv:** Crowned imperial eagle, 1Z in orb on breast, titles of Ferdinand II **Rev:** Crowned 4-fold arms divide date, angel above **Note:** Kipper 12 Kreuzer.

Date	Mintage	VG	F	VF	XF	Unc
(16)21	—	—	—	—	—	—

KM# 67 12 KREUZER (Schreckenburger)

Silver **Ruler:** Wolfgang III, Bruno III, Joachim Friedrich and Philipp V **Obv:** Crowned 4-fold arms **Rev:** St. George slaying dragon at right, date divided by imperial orb in legend at top

Date	Mintage	VG	F	VF	XF	Unc
16Z1	—	—	—	—	—	—

KM# 68 12 KREUZER (Schreckenburger)

Silver **Ruler:** Wolfgang III, Bruno III, Joachim Friedrich and Philipp V **Obv:** Value (1Z) at bottom

Date	Mintage	VG	F	VF	XF	Unc
16Z1	—	—	—	—	—	—

KM# 69 12 KREUZER (Schreckenburger)

Silver **Ruler:** Wolfgang III, Bruno III, Joachim Friedrich and Philipp V **Obv:** 3 small shields of arms around central point, titles of Wolfgang III **Rev:** Three small shields of arms around central point, titles of Wolfgang III **Rev. Legend:** FATA. VIAM. INVENIENT

Date	Mintage	VG	F	VF	XF	Unc
1621	—	—	—	—	—	—

KM# 70 12 KREUZER (Schreckenburger)

Silver **Ruler:** Wolfgang III, Bruno III, Joachim Friedrich and Philipp V **Rev:** St. George slaying dragon at right

Date	Mintage	VG	F	VF	XF	Unc
1621	—	—	—	—	—	—

KM# 71 12 KREUZER (Schreckenburger)

Silver **Ruler:** Wolfgang III, Bruno III, Joachim Friedrich and Philipp V **Obv:** 4-fold arms **Rev:** Crowned imperial eagle, 1Z in orb on breast, legend, date **Rev. Legend:** FATA. VIAM. INVENIENT

Date	Mintage	VG	F	VF	XF	Unc
16Z1	—	—	—	—	—	—
1621	—	—	—	—	—	—

KM# 72 12 KREUZER (Schreckenburger)

Silver **Ruler:** Wolfgang III and Joachim Friedrich **Obv:** Crowned 4-fold arms divide date, angel above **Rev:** Crowned imperial eagle, 1Z in orb on breast

Date	Mintage	VG	F	VF	XF	Unc
16Z1	—	—	—	—	—	—

KM# 73 12 KREUZER (Schreckenburger)

Silver **Ruler:** Wolfgang III and Joachim Friedrich **Obv:** 4-fold arms surmounted on cross with lilies at ends, titles of Joachim Friedrich

Date	Mintage	VG	F	VF	XF	Unc
ND(1621/22)	—	—	—	—	—	—

KM# 75 24 KREUZER (Doppelschreckenberger)

Silver **Ruler:** Wolfgang III **Obv:** Ornate 4-fold arms of Mansfeld, angel's head and wings above **Obv. Legend:** WOL: COM: E: E: I. MANS. ND: I. H. **Rev:** Three small ornate shields of arms, 1 above 2, upper shield divides 2 - 4, date at end of legend **Rev. Legend:** RATA. VIAM. INVENIENT. **Mint:** Schraplau **Note:** Kipper 24 Kreuzer.

Date	Mintage	Good	VG	F	VF	XF
16Z1 Rare	—	—	—	—	—	—

KM# 95 1/2 ORT (1/8 Thaler)

Silver **Ruler:** Wolfgang III and Joachim Friedrich **Obv:** Two helmets above 4-fold arms, titles of Karl Adam **Rev. Inscription:** EIN. / HALB. / REICHS. / ORT. / date

Date	Mintage	VG	F	VF	XF	Unc
1655	—	—	—	—	—	—

KM# 20 1/28 THALER

Silver **Ruler:** Bruno II, Wilhelm I, Johann Georg IV, Volrat VI and Jobst II **Obv:** Two hlemets above 4-fold arms **Rev:** Imperial orb with Z8 divides date **Note:** Varieties exist.

Date	Mintage	VG	F	VF	XF	Unc
1610	—	—	—	—	—	—
1610 GM	—	—	—	—	—	—
1611 GM	—	—	—	—	—	—

KM# 22 1/28 THALER

Silver **Ruler:** Bruno II, Wilhelm I, Johann Georg IV, Volrat VI and Jobst II **Rev:** Date in legend **Note:** Varieties exist.

Date	Mintage	VG	F	VF	XF	Unc
1611 GM	—	—	—	—	—	—

KM# 23 1/28 THALER

Silver **Ruler:** Bruno II, Wilhelm I, Johann Georg IV, Volrat VI and Jobst II **Note:** Mule. Reverse of issue of Friedrich Christoph of Eigentliche-Hinterort.

Date	Mintage	VG	F	VF	XF	Unc
1611 GM	—	—	—	—	—	—

KM# 77 1/24 THALER

Silver **Ruler:** Wolfgang III, Bruno III, Joachim Friedrich and Philipp V **Obv:** Crowned 4-fold arms **Rev:** Imperial orb with 24, date divided in legend at top **Note:** Kipper 1/24 Thaler. Prev. KM #74.

Date	Mintage	VG	F	VF	XF	Unc
16Z1	—	—	—	—	—	—

KM# 102 1/24 THALER

Silver **Ruler:** Wolfgang III, Bruno III, Joachim Friedrich and Philipp V **Obv:** Ornamented oval 4-folds arms, titles of Karl Adam **Rev:** Imperial orb with 24 divides date

Date	Mintage	VG	F	VF	XF	Unc
1657 HPK	—	—	—	—	—	—

KM# 116 1/24 THALER

Silver **Ruler:** Franz Mazimilian and Heinrich Franz **Obv:** Date divided by cross on top of orb

Date	Mintage	VG	F	VF	XF	Unc
1668 ABK	—	—	—	—	—	—

KM# 115 1/24 THALER

Silver **Ruler:** Franz Mazimilian and Heinrich Franz **Obv:** Imperial orb with 24 divides date and mintmaster's initials **Rev:** Crowned 4-fold arms **Note:** Varieties exist.

Date	Mintage	VG	F	VF	XF	Unc
1668 ABK	—	—	—	—	—	—
1670 ABK	—	—	—	—	—	—
1673 ABK	—	—	—	—	—	—

KM# 117 1/24 THALER

Silver **Ruler:** Franz Mazimilian and Heinrich Franz **Rev:** Without crown above arms **Note:** Varieties exist.

Date	Mintage	VG	F	VF	XF	Unc
1668 ABK	—	—	—	—	—	—

KM# 27 1/21 THALER

Silver **Ruler:** Franz Mazimilian and Heinrich Franz **Rev:** Without value shown in orb

Date	Mintage	VG	F	VF	XF	Unc
1611 GM	—	16.00	33.00	55.00	100	—

KM# 24 1/21 THALER
Silver **Ruler:** Franz Mazimilian and Heinrich Franz
Note: Varieties exist.

Date	Mintage	VG	F	VF	XF	Unc
1611 GM	—	16.00	33.00	55.00	100	—
161Z GM	—	16.00	33.00	55.00	100	—
161Z	—	16.00	33.00	55.00	100	—
1613 GM	—	16.00	33.00	55.00	100	—
1614 GM	—	16.00	33.00	55.00	100	—
1615 GM	—	16.00	33.00	55.00	100	—

KM# 26 1/21 THALER
Silver **Ruler:** Franz Mazimilian and Heinrich Franz **Rev:** Date divided by orb **Note:** Varieties exist.

Date	Mintage	VG	F	VF	XF	Unc
1611	—	16.00	33.00	55.00	100	—
1611 GM	—	16.00	33.00	55.00	100	—
161Z GM	—	16.00	33.00	55.00	100	—

KM# 33 1/21 THALER
Silver **Ruler:** Bruno II, Wilhelm I, Volrat VI and Jobst II
Obv: Ornamented 4-fold arms **Rev:** Imperial orb with Z1 divides mintmaster's initials, date in legend

Date	Mintage	VG	F	VF	XF	Unc
161Z GM	—	16.00	33.00	55.00	100	—

KM# 25 1/21 THALER
Silver **Ruler:** Franz Mazimilian and Heinrich Franz **Note:** Klippe.

Date	Mintage	VG	F	VF	XF	Unc
1613 GM	—	—	—	—	—	—

KM# 28 1/8 THALER
Silver **Ruler:** Bruno II, Wilhelm I, Johann Georg IV, Volrat VI and Jobst II **Obv:** 4-fold arms divide date and mintmaster's initials, angel above **Rev:** St. George slaying dragon

Date	Mintage	VG	F	VF	XF	Unc
1611 GM	—	—	—	—	—	—

KM# 29 1/8 THALER
Silver **Note:** Varieties exist.

Date	Mintage	VG	F	VF	XF	Unc
1611 GM	—	—	—	—	—	—
161Z GM	—	—	—	—	—	—

KM# 41 1/8 THALER
Silver **Ruler:** Bruno II, Wilhelm I, Johann Georg IV, Volrat VI and Jobst II **Subject:** Death of Bruno II **Obv:** 4-fold arms, mintmaster's initials above **Rev:** 8-line inscription with dates

Date	Mintage	VG	F	VF	XF	Unc
1615 GM	—	—	—	—	—	—

KM# 5 1/4 THALER
Silver **Ruler:** Bruno II, Wilhelm I (V) and Johann Georg IV
Obv: Two helmets divided by date above 4-fold arms
Rev: St. George slaying dragon, imperial orb above horse's head
Note: Varieties exist.

Date	Mintage	VG	F	VF	XF	Unc
(1)604 GM	—	65.00	120	200	325	—
1605 GM	—	65.00	120	200	325	—
1606 GM	—	65.00	120	200	325	—

KM# 13 1/4 THALER
Silver **Ruler:** Bruno II, Wilhelm I, Johann Georg IV and Volrat VI **Note:** Varieties exist.

Date	Mintage	VG	F	VF	XF	Unc
1607 GM	—	65.00	120	200	325	—
1608 GM	—	65.00	120	200	325	—
1609 GM	—	65.00	120	200	325	—
1610 GM	—	65.00	120	200	325	—
161Z GM	—	65.00	120	200	325	—
1613 GM	—	65.00	120	200	325	—
1614 GM	—	65.00	120	200	325	—
1615 GM	—	65.00	120	200	325	—
ND GM	—	65.00	120	200	325	—

KM# 42 1/4 THALER
Silver **Ruler:** Bruno II, Wilhelm I, Johann Georg IV and Volrat VI **Subject:** Death of Bruno II **Obv:** St. George slaying dragon at left, sword raised above head **Rev:** 8-line inscription with dates **Note:** Varieties exist.

Date	Mintage	VG	F	VF	XF	Unc
1615 GM	—	135	225	400	675	—

KM# 83 1/4 THALER
Silver **Ruler:** Wolfgang III and Johann Georg II **Obv:** St. George slaying dragon, imperial orb above horse's head **Rev:** Two helmets above 4-fold arms divide date **Note:** Varieties exist.

Date	Mintage	VG	F	VF	XF	Unc
1635 HPK	—	115	165	275	400	—

KM# 96 1/4 THALER
Silver **Ruler:** Wolfgang III and Johann Georg II **Obv:** Two helmets above 4-fold arms, date divided by arms, titiles of Karl Adam
Rev: St. George slaying dragon, imperial orb above horse's head

Date	Mintage	VG	F	VF	XF	Unc
1655 HPK	—	115	165	275	400	—
1660 HPK	—	—	—	—	—	—

Note: Reported, not confirmed

KM# 105 1/4 THALER
Silver **Ruler:** Wolfgang III and Johann Georg II **Rev:** Obverse of issue of Christoph Friedrich of Eigentliche-Hinterort **Note:** Mule.

Date	Mintage	VG	F	VF	XF	Unc
1660 HPK	—	—	—	—	—	—

KM# 108 1/4 THALER
Silver **Ruler:** Franz Mazimilian and Heinrich Franz **Obv:** St. George slaying dragon below **Rev:** 4-fold arms, two helmets above divided by date, mintmaster's initials outside helmets

Date	Mintage	VG	F	VF	XF	Unc
1667 ABK	—	135	200	325	500	—

KM# 119 1/3 THALER (1/2 Gulden)
Silver **Ruler:** Franz Mazimilian and Heinrich Franz **Rev:** Palm branches at sides of arms, mintmaster's initials below

Date	Mintage	VG	F	VF	XF	Unc
1669 ABK	—	55.00	80.00	220	300	—

KM# 120 1/3 THALER (1/2 Gulden)
Silver **Ruler:** Franz Mazimilian and Heinrich Franz
Rev: Without palm branches

Date	Mintage	VG	F	VF	XF	Unc
1669 ABK	—	55.00	80.00	220	300	—

KM# 118 1/3 THALER (1/2 Gulden)
Silver **Obv:** St. George slaying dragon. value 1/3 in oval at bottom **Rev:** 4-fold arms divide mintmaster's initials, crown above divides date **Note:** Varieties exist.

Date	Mintage	VG	F	VF	XF	Unc
1669 ABK	—	33.00	55.00	90.00	160	—
1670 ABK	—	33.00	55.00	90.00	160	—

KM# 125 1/3 THALER (1/2 Gulden)
Silver **Ruler:** Franz Mazimilian and Heinrich Franz **Rev:** Arms divide date and mintmaster's initials **Note:** Varieties exist.

Date	Mintage	VG	F	VF	XF	Unc
1670 ABK	—	27.00	45.00	90.00	165	—
1671 ABK	—	27.00	45.00	90.00	165	—
1672 ABK	—	27.00	45.00	90.00	165	—
1673 ABK	—	27.00	45.00	90.00	165	—

KM# 127 1/3 THALER (1/2 Gulden)
Silver **Ruler:** Franz Mazimilian and Heinrich Franz **Rev:** 4-fold oval arms divide mintmaster's initials, crown above divides date

Date	Mintage	VG	F	VF	XF	Unc
1673 ABK	—	—	—	—	—	—

KM# 6 1/2 THALER
Silver **Ruler:** Bruno II, Wilhelm I (V) and Johann Georg IV
Note: Varieties exist.

Date	Mintage	VG	F	VF	XF	Unc
(1)604 GM	—	65.00	135	225	400	—
1605 GM	—	65.00	135	225	400	—
1606 GM	—	65.00	135	225	400	—

KM# 10 1/2 THALER
Silver **Ruler:** Bruno II, Wilhelm I, Johann Georg IV and Volrat VI

Date	Mintage	VG	F	VF	XF	Unc
1606 GM	—	60.00	100	165	275	—
1607 GM	—	60.00	100	165	275	—
1608 GM	—	60.00	100	165	275	—
1609 GM	—	60.00	100	165	275	—
1610 GM	—	60.00	100	165	275	—
1611 GM	—	60.00	100	165	275	—
161Z GM	—	60.00	100	165	275	—
1613 GM	—	60.00	100	165	275	—
1614 GM	—	60.00	100	165	275	—
1615 GM	—	60.00	100	165	275	—
ND GM	—	60.00	100	165	275	—

KM# 14 1/2 THALER
Silver **Ruler:** Bruno II, Wilhelm I, Johann Georg IV and Volrat VI **Note:** Broad flan.

Date	Mintage	VG	F	VF	XF	Unc
1608 GM	—	—	—	—	—	—

KM# 34 1/2 THALER
Silver **Ruler:** Bruno II, Wilhelm I, Johann Georg IV, Volrat VI and Jobst II **Obv:** Date in legend **Note:** Varieties exist.

Date	Mintage	VG	F	VF	XF	Unc
161Z GM	—	—	—	—	—	—

KM# 43 1/2 THALER
Silver **Ruler:** Bruno II, Wilhelm I, Johann Georg IV, Volrat VI and Jobst II **Subject:** Death of Bruno II **Obv:** St. George slaying dragon at left, sword raised above head **Rev:** 8-line inscription with dates **Note:** Varieties exist.

Date	Mintage	VG	F	VF	XF	Unc
1615 GM	—	—	—	—	—	—

KM# 84 1/2 THALER
Silver **Ruler:** Wolfgang III and Johann Georg II **Obv:** St. George slaying dragon, imperial orb above horse's head **Rev:** Two helmets above 4-fold arms divide date **Note:** Varieties exist.

Date	Mintage	VG	F	VF	XF	Unc
1635 HPK	—	115	220	375	600	—
1638 HPK	—	115	220	375	600	—

KM# 97 1/2 THALER

Silver **Ruler:** Wolfgang III and Johann Georg II **Obv:** Two helmets above 4-fold arms, date divided by arms, titles of Karl Adam **Rev:** St. George slaying dragon, imperial orb above horse's head **Note:** Varieties exist.

Date	Mintage	VG	F	VF	XF	Unc
1655 HPK	—	60.00	120	190	300	—
1657 HPK	—	60.00	120	190	300	—
1658 HPK	—	60.00	120	190	300	—
1659 HPK	—	60.00	120	190	300	—
1660 HPK	—	60.00	120	190	300	—

KM# 109 1/2 THALER

Silver **Ruler:** Wolfgang III and Johann Georg II **Obv:** St. George slaying dragon below **Rev:** 4-fold arms divide date, two helmets above, mintmaster's initials outside helmets **Note:** Varieties exist.

Date	Mintage	VG	F	VF	XF	Unc
1667 HPK	—	65.00	135	200	325	—

KM# 107 2/3 THALER (Gulden)

Silver **Ruler:** Franz Mazimilian and Heinrich Franz **Obv:** St. George slaying dragon, value: 2/3 in oval at bottom **Rev:** 4-fold arms divide mintmaster's initials crown above divides date **Note:** Varieties exist.

Date	Mintage	VG	F	VF	XF	Unc
1665 ABK	—	55.00	85.00	190	200	—
1675 ABK	—	55.00	85.00	190	200	—
1676 ABK	—	55.00	85.00	190	200	—

KM# 128 2/3 THALER (Gulden)

Silver **Ruler:** Franz Mazimilian and Heinrich Franz **Rev:** Two helmets above arms instead of crowne, date outside left helmet **Note:** Varieties exist.

Date	Mintage	VG	F	VF	XF	Unc
1675 ABK	—	40.00	65.00	115	180	—

KM# 129 2/3 THALER (Gulden)

Silver **Ruler:** Franz Mazimilian and Heinrich Franz **Rev:** Date divided by helmets **Note:** Varieties exist.

Date	Mintage	VG	F	VF	XF	Unc
1675 ABK	—	45.00	80.00	130	190	—

KM# 130 2/3 THALER (Gulden)

Silver **Ruler:** Franz Mazimilian and Heinrich Franz **Rev:** Date and mintmaster's initials divided by arms **Note:** Varieties exist.

Date	Mintage	VG	F	VF	XF	Unc
1675 ABK	—	45.00	80.00	125	190	—
1676 ABK	—	45.00	80.00	125	190	—

KM# 131 2/3 THALER (Gulden)

Silver **Ruler:** Franz Mazimilian and Heinrich Franz **Obv:** Date divided in legend near top **Note:** Varieties exist.

Date	Mintage	VG	F	VF	XF	Unc
1676 ABK	—	45.00	80.00	125	190	—
ND ABK	—	45.00	80.00	125	190	—

KM# 7 THALER

Silver **Ruler:** Bruno II, Wilhelm I (V) and Johann Georg IV **Obv:** Helmeted arms, G-M and date above **Obv. Legend:** BRVNO. SENIOR. WILH: H: GE: P: **Rev:** St. George and dragon, orb at upper right **Rev. Legend:** COM: E: DOMI: I: MAN-SFE: NO: D: I: H: **Note:** Dav. #6916.

Date	Mintage	VG	F	VF	XF	Unc
1604 GM	—	75.00	190	265	400	—
1605 GM	—	75.00	190	265	400	—
1606 GM	—	75.00	190	265	400	—
1607 GM	—	75.00	190	265	400	—

KM# 8 THALER

Silver **Ruler:** Bruno II, Wilhelm I (V) and Johann Georg IV **Obv:** St. George and dragon **Obv. Legend:** COMI: E: DOMI: IN: MANSFE: NOB: DO: I. h: **Rev:** St. George and dragon, legend similar to KM#7 but with single dots **Note:** Mule. Dav. #6917.

Date	Mintage	VG	F	VF	XF	Unc
ND(1604)	—	75.00	190	265	400	—

KM# 9 THALER

Silver **Ruler:** Bruno II, Wilhelm I, Johann Georg IV and Volrat VI **Obv. Legend:** BRVNO. SENI: WILH: HA: GE: VOLR: P. **Note:** Dav. #6919.

Date	Mintage	VG	F	VF	XF	Unc
1605	—	75.00	190	265	400	—
1607	—	75.00	190	265	400	—
1608	—	75.00	190	265	400	—
(1)609	—	75.00	190	265	400	—
1609	—	75.00	190	265	400	—
1610	—	75.00	190	265	400	—
1611	—	75.00	190	265	400	—
1612	—	75.00	190	265	400	—
1613 GM	—	75.00	190	265	400	—
1614 GM	—	75.00	190	265	400	—
1615 GM	—	75.00	190	265	400	—

KM# 36 THALER

Silver **Ruler:** Bruno II, Wilhelm I, Johann Georg IV and Volrat VI **Obv. Legend:** BRVNO. S: WILH. HANS. GEOR. VOLRAT. P. **Note:** Dav. #6921.

Date	Mintage	VG	F	VF	XF	Unc
1612 GM	—	75.00	190	265	400	—
1613 GM	—	75.00	190	265	400	—
1614 GM	—	75.00	190	265	400	—
1615 GM	—	75.00	190	265	400	—
ND	—	75.00	190	265	400	—

KM# 37 THALER

Silver **Ruler:** Bruno II, Wilhelm I, Johann Georg IV, Volrat VI and Jobst II **Obv. Legend:** BRVNO: S: WILH. HANS: G. VOL: IOB: P: **Note:** Dav. #6922.

Date	Mintage	VG	F	VF	XF	Unc
1612 GM	—	—	—	—	—	—

KM# 44 THALER

Silver **Ruler:** Bruno II, Wilhelm I, Johann Georg IV, Volrat VI and Jobst II **Subject:** Death of Bruno **Obv:** Large GM, hooves within circle **Note:** Dav. #6923.

Date	Mintage	VG	F	VF	XF	Unc
1615 GM	—	120	215	350	550	—

KM# 45 THALER

Silver **Ruler:** Bruno II, Wilhelm I, Johann Georg IV, Volrat VI and Jobst II **Obv:** Small GM, hooves break circle **Note:** Dav. #6923A.

Date	Mintage	VG	F	VF	XF	Unc
1615 GM	—	130	230	375	600	—

KM# 35 THALER

Silver **Ruler:** Bruno II, Wilhelm I, Johann Georg IV and Volrat VI **Note:** Klippe. Cross-reference number Dav. #6919D.

Date	Mintage	VG	F	VF	XF	Unc
1615 Rare	—	—	—	—	—	—

KM# 48 THALER

Silver **Ruler:** Wolfgang III, Bruno III, Joachim Friedrich and Philipp V **Obv. Legend:** WOLFGAN: BRVNO: IOACHIM: FRIDERIC. ET. PHILIP: F. **Rev:** Date and HI between helmets **Note:** Dav. #6924.

Date	Mintage	VG	F	VF	XF	Unc
1619	—	90.00	180	350	550	—

KM# 49 THALER

Silver **Ruler:** Wolfgang III, Bruno III, Joachim Friedrich and Philipp V **Rev:** H-I divided by helmets **Note:** Dav. #6924A.

Date	Mintage	VG	F	VF	XF	Unc
1619	—	90.00	180	350	550	—

KM# 50 THALER

Silver **Ruler:** Wolfgang III and Bruno III **Obv. Legend:** WOLFGAN: ET. BRVNO: FRAT: COM: ET: DOMI: **Note:** Dav. #6925.

Date	Mintage	VG	F	VF	XF	Unc
1619 XHI	—	90.00	180	350	550	—
1620 XHI	—	90.00	180	350	550	—
1622 XHI	—	90.00	180	350	550	—

KM# 80 THALER

Silver **Ruler:** Wolfgang III and Johann Georg II **Obv. Legend:** WOLFG: ET. IOHA: GEOR: PAT: COMI: ET. **Note:** Dav. #6927.

Date	Mintage	VG	F	VF	XF	Unc
1631 HPK	—	75.00	190	265	400	—
1632 HPK	—	75.00	190	265	400	—
1635 HPK	—	75.00	190	265	400	—
1637 HPK	—	75.00	190	265	400	—
1638 HPK	—	75.00	190	265	400	—
ND HPK	—	75.00	190	265	400	—

KM# 81 THALER

Silver **Ruler:** Wolfgang III and Johann Georg II **Obv. Legend:** ...IOHAN. GEORG... **Rev:** Double-helmeted arms **Note:** Dav. #6928.

Date	Mintage	VG	F	VF	XF	Unc
ND HPK	—	75.00	190	265	400	—

KM# 98 THALER

Silver **Ruler:** Wolfgang III and Johann Georg II **Obv:** Helmeted arms, date divided below **Rev:** St. George and the dragon **Note:** Dav. #6930.

Date	Mintage	VG	F	VF	XF	Unc
1655 HPK	—	75.00	190	265	400	—
1656 HPK	—	75.00	190	265	400	—
1657 HPK	—	75.00	190	265	400	—
1658 HPK	—	75.00	190	265	400	—
1659 HPK	—	75.00	190	265	400	—
1660 HPK	—	75.00	190	265	400	—

KM# 110 THALER

Silver **Ruler:** Franz Mazimilian and Heinrich Franz **Obv:** Large winged dragon **Obv. Legend:** FRANZ MAX. HEINR. FRANZ. COMIT. I. MANSFELT. **Note:** Dav. #6931.

Date	Mintage	VG	F	VF	XF	Unc
1667 ABK	—	80.00	200	290	450	—

KM# 111 THALER

Silver **Ruler:** Franz Mazimilian and Heinrich Franz **Obv:** Small winged dragon **Note:** Dav. #6931A.

Date	Mintage	VG	F	VF	XF	Unc
1667 ABK	—	80.00	200	290	450	—

KM# 15 2 THALER

Silver **Ruler:** Bruno II, Wilhelm I, Johann Georg IV and Volrat VI **Note:** Similar to 1 Thaler, KM#9. Dav. #6918.

Date	Mintage	VG	F	VF	XF	Unc
1609 GM	—	600	1,050	1,800	3,000	—
1615 GM	—	600	1,050	1,800	3,000	—

KM# 38 2 THALER

Silver **Ruler:** Bruno II, Wilhelm I, Johann Georg IV and Volrat VI **Obv. Legend:** BRVNO. S. WILH. HANS. GEOR. VOLRAT. P. **Note:** Dav. #6920.

Date	Mintage	VG	F	VF	XF	Unc
1612 GM	—	600	1,050	1,800	3,000	—

KM# 85 2 THALER

Silver **Ruler:** Wolfgang III and Johann Georg II **Obv:** St. George right and dragon **Obv. Legend:** WOLFG: ET. IOHA: GEOR: PAT: COMI: ET. **Note:** Dav. #6926.

Date	Mintage	VG	F	VF	XF	Unc
1635 HPK	—	600	1,050	1,800	3,000	—

KM# 99 2 THALER

Silver **Ruler:** Wolfgang III and Johann Georg II **Note:** Similar to 1 Thaler, KM#98. Dav. #6929.

Date	Mintage	VG	F	VF	XF	Unc
1655 HPK	—	600	1,150	1,900	3,000	—
1656 HPK	—	600	1,150	1,900	3,000	—
1657 HPK	—	600	1,150	1,900	3,000	—

KM# 11 3 THALER

Silver **Ruler:** Bruno II, Wilhelm I (V) and Johann Georg IV **Obv:** Helmeted arms **Obv. Legend:** BRVNO. SENIOR. WILH: H: GE: P: **Rev:** St. George and dragon **Note:** Dav. #6915.

Date	Mintage	VG	F	VF	XF	Unc
1606 GM Rare	—	—	—	—	—	—

TRADE COINAGE

KM# 12 GOLDGULDEN

3.5000 g., 0.9860 Gold 0.1109 oz. AGW **Ruler:** Bruno II, Wilhelm I (V) and Johann Georg IV

Date	Mintage	VG	F	VF	XF	Unc
1606	—	250	500	1,000	2,000	—

KM# 30 GOLDGULDEN

3.5000 g., 0.9860 Gold 0.1109 oz. AGW **Ruler:** Bruno II, Wilhelm I (V) and Johann Georg IV **Rev:** Three shields as trilobe, date divided at bottom

Date	Mintage	VG	F	VF	XF	Unc
1611	—	280	500	975	2,050	—

KM# 39 GOLDGULDEN

3.5000 g., 0.9860 Gold 0.1109 oz. AGW **Ruler:** Bruno II, Wilhelm I, Johann Georg IV, Volrat VI and Jobst II **Obv:** Three shields of arms in trefoil form, bottom arms divide date **Rev:** St. George slaying dragon **Note:** Varieties exist.

Date	Mintage	VG	F	VF	XF	Unc
1614	—	—	—	—	—	—

KM# 47 GOLDGULDEN

3.5000 g., 0.9860 Gold 0.1109 oz. AGW **Ruler:** Bruno II, Wilhelm I, Johann Georg IV, Volrat VI and Jobst II **Subject:** Death of Bruno II **Obv:** 4-fold arms divide mintmaster's initials **Rev:** 8-line inscription with dates **Note:** Varieties exist.

Date	Mintage	VG	F	VF	XF	Unc
1615 GM	—	—	—	—	—	—

KM# 46 GOLDGULDEN

3.5000 g., 0.9860 Gold 0.1109 oz. AGW **Ruler:** Bruno II, Wilhelm I, Johann Georg IV, Volrat VI and Jobst II

Date	Mintage	VG	F	VF	XF	Unc
1615	—	280	500	975	2,050	—
ND	—	280	500	975	2,050	—

KM# 126 1/4 DUCAT

0.8750 g., 0.9860 Gold 0.0277 oz. AGW **Ruler:** Franz Mazimilian and Heinrich Franz **Obv:** St. George and dragon **Rev:** Arms, value and date

Date	Mintage	VG	F	VF	XF	Unc
1670	—	145	220	375	650	—
1671	—	145	220	375	650	—

KM# 82 DUCAT

3.5000 g., 0.9860 Gold 0.1109 oz. AGW **Ruler:** Wolfgang III and Johann Georg II **Rev:** Value and date on tablet

Date	Mintage	VG	F	VF	XF	Unc
1631	—	270	550	1,200	2,250	—
1632	—	270	550	1,200	2,250	—
1635	—	270	550	1,200	2,250	—
1638	—	270	550	1,200	2,250	—

KM# 101 DUCAT

3.5000 g., 0.9860 Gold 0.1109 oz. AGW **Ruler:** Wolfgang III and Johann Georg II

Date	Mintage	VG	F	VF	XF	Unc
1656	—	270	550	1,200	2,250	—

KM# 112 DUCAT

3.5000 g., 0.9860 Gold 0.1109 oz. AGW **Ruler:** Franz Mazimilian and Heinrich Franz **Obv:** St. George slaying dragon **Obv. Legend:** FRANZ MAX

Date	Mintage	VG	F	VF	XF	Unc
1667	—	145	255	425	725	—

KM# 135 DUCAT

3.5000 g., 0.9860 Gold 0.1109 oz. AGW **Ruler:** Franz Mazimilian and Heinrich Franz **Obv:** St. George horseback right slaying dragon **Obv. Legend:** FRANZ • MAX • HEINR • FRANZ • COMIT • IN MANSFELT **Rev:** Ornate crowned arms in order chain **Rev. Legend:** • NOB • DOM • INHELD • UNGENSEB • E • SER • **Note:** Fr#1573.

Date	Mintage	VG	F	VF	XF	Unc
1687	—	190	375	750	1,250	—

KM# 86 2 DUCAT

7.0000 g., 0.9860 Gold 0.2219 oz. AGW **Ruler:** Wolfgang III and Johann Georg II **Obv:** St. George slaying dragon, imperial orb above horse's head **Rev:** Two helmets above 4-fold arms, date divided by arms **Note:** Varieties exist.

Date	Mintage	VG	F	VF	XF	Unc
1635 HPK	—	650	1,150	2,150	3,750	—

KM# 100 2 DUCAT
7.0000 g., 0.9860 Gold 0.2219 oz. AGW **Ruler:** Wolfgang III and Johann Georg II **Obv:** Two helmets above 4-fold arms, date divided by arms, titles of Karl Adam **Rev:** St. George slaying dragon, imperial orb above horse's head

Date	Mintage	VG	F	VF	XF	Unc
1655 HPK	—	825	1,400	2,750	4,400	—

KM# 113 2 DUCAT
7.0000 g., 0.9860 Gold 0.2219 oz. AGW **Ruler:** Franz Mazimilian and Heinrich Franz **Obv:** St. George slaying dragon **Obv. Legend:** FRANZ MAX...

Date	Mintage	VG	F	VF	XF	Unc
1667	—	725	1,200	2,400	4,200	—

KM# 21 3 DUCAT
10.5000 g., 0.9860 Gold 0.3328 oz. AGW **Ruler:** Bruno II, Wilhelm I, Johann Georg IV and Volrat VI **Note:** Similar to 1/2 Thaler, KM#6.

Date	Mintage	VG	F	VF	XF	Unc
1610 GM Rare	387	—	—	—	—	—
1615 GM Rare	—	—	—	—	—	—

KM# 106 3 DUCAT
10.5000 g., 0.9860 Gold 0.3328 oz. AGW **Ruler:** Karl Adam **Obv:** Two helmets above 4-fold arms, date divided by arms, titles of Karl Adam **Rev:** St. George slaying dragon, imperial orb above horse's head

Date	Mintage	VG	F	VF	XF	Unc
1660 HPK	—	1,050	2,050	3,850	6,600	—

KM# 114 3 DUCAT
10.5000 g., 0.9860 Gold 0.3328 oz. AGW **Ruler:** Franz Mazimilian and Heinrich Franz **Obv:** St. George slaying dragon **Obv. Legend:** FRANZ MAX • HEINR • FRANZ...

Date	Mintage	VG	F	VF	XF	Unc
1667 AB-K	—	900	1,600	3,300	5,400	—

KM# 87 5 DUCAT (1/2 Portugaloser)
17.5000 g., 0.9860 Gold 0.5547 oz. AGW **Ruler:** Wolfgang III and Johann Georg II **Obv:** St. George slaying dragon, imperial orb above horse's head **Rev:** Two helmets above 4-fold arms divide date **Note:** Varieties exist.

Date	Mintage	VG	F	VF	XF	Unc
1635 HPK	—	2,000	3,000	5,000	8,500	—
1637 HPK	—	2,000	3,000	5,000	8,500	—

KM# 88 10 DUCAT (Portugaloser)
35.0000 g., 0.9860 Gold 1.1095 oz. AGW **Ruler:** Wolfgang III and Johann Georg II **Note:** Similar to 1 Thaler, KM#80. Varieties exist.

Date	Mintage	VG	F	VF	XF	Unc
1635 HPK Rare	—	—	—	—	—	—
1637 HPK Rare	—	—	—	—	—	—

MANSFELD-EIGENTLICHE-HINTERORT

Founded in 1486 when the Hinterort line of Mansfeld was divided into this and the Schraplau branches. Upon the extinction of Eigentliche-Hinterort in 1666, the lands and titles reverted to Mansfeld-Vorderort-Bornstedt.

RULERS
David, 1592-1628
Friedrich Christoph, 1609-1631
Ernst Ludwig, 1631-1632
Christian Friedrich, 1632-1666

JOINT COINAGE
I - Ernst VI and Friedrich Christoph
II - Ernst VI, Friedrich Christoph and David
III - Friedrich Christoph and David

COUNTSHIP

JOINT COINAGE

KM# 87 3 FLITTER (1-1/2 Pfennig)
Copper **Rev:** Value: FLITTER

Date	Mintage	VG	F	VF	XF	Unc
16Z1 M	—	—	—	—	—	—

KM# 86 3 FLITTER (1-1/2 Pfennig)
Copper **Obv:** Four-fold arms, M above **Rev:** III in center, FLITTER, date around **Mint:** Mansfeld **Note:** Kipper 3 Flitter. Struck at Mansfeld Mint.

Date	Mintage	VG	F	VF	XF	Unc
16Z1 M	—	—	—	—	—	—

KM# 88 PFENNIG
Copper **Note:** Uniface. Four-fold arms divide mintmaster's initials, date above.

Date	Mintage	VG	F	VF	XF	Unc
16Z1 DM	—	—	—	—	—	—

KM# 142 PFENNIG
Silver **Note:** Anonymous Kipper. Uniface. Schussel type. Oval four-fold arms, date above divides mintmaster's initials.

Date	Mintage	VG	F	VF	XF	Unc
16Z3 AK	—	—	—	—	—	—

KM# 35 3 PFENNIG (Dreier)
Silver **Obv:** Helmeted four-fold arms **Rev:** Small imperial orb with 3 divides date, in ornamented rhombus

Date	Mintage	VG	F	VF	XF	Unc
1611	—	33.00	60.00	100	165	—

KM# 55 3 PFENNIG (Dreier)
Silver **Obv:** Four-fold arms, mintmaster's initials above **Rev:** Imperial orb with 3 divides date

Date	Mintage	VG	F	VF	XF	Unc
161Z GM	—	33.00	60.00	100	165	—

KM# 56 3 PFENNIG (Dreier)
Silver **Rev:** Value in orb III

Date	Mintage	VG	F	VF	XF	Unc
161Z GM	—	33.00	60.00	100	165	—

KM# 90 3 PFENNIG (Dreier)
Copper **Obv:** Rampant lion (Heldrungen) left, value III above **Rev:** Large "B" between annulets and stars **Mint:** Blumrode **Note:** Struck at Blumrode Mint.

Date	Mintage	Good	VG	F	VF	XF
ND(1621/22) B	—	16.00	33.00	65.00	110	—

KM# 92 3 PFENNIG (Dreier)
Copper **Obv:** Four-fold arms with M above **Rev:** Imperial orb with 3 in double rhombus **Mint:** Mansfeld **Note:** Struck at Mansfeld Mint.

Date	Mintage	Good	VG	F	VF	XF
ND(1621/22) M	—	16.00	33.00	65.00	110	—

KM# 95 3 PFENNIG (Dreier)
Copper **Obv:** Four-fold arms in heart-shaped shield, III above **Rev:** Heart-shaped shield with 3 **Note:** Struck at unknown mint.

Date	Mintage	Good	VG	F	VF	XF
ND(1621/22)	—	16.00	33.00	65.00	110	—

KM# 97 3 PFENNIG (Dreier)
Copper **Rev:** Arms in oval shield **Note:** Varieties exist.

Date	Mintage	Good	VG	F	VF	XF
ND(1621/22)	—	16.00	33.00	65.00	110	—

KM# 91 3 PFENNIG (Dreier)
Copper **Obv:** Large "B" between floral ornaments **Rev:** Value 3 in ornamented heart-shaped shield

Date	Mintage	Good	VG	F	VF	XF
ND(1621/22) B	—	16.00	33.00	65.00	110	—

KM# 93 3 PFENNIG (Dreier)
Copper **Obv:** Oval four-fold arms, M above **Rev:** Imperial orb with 3 divides date

Date	Mintage	Good	VG	F	VF	XF
(16)21 M	—	16.00	33.00	65.00	110	—

KM# 94 3 PFENNIG (Dreier)
Copper **Obv:** Arms in squarish shield

Date	Mintage	Good	VG	F	VF	XF
(16)Z1 M	—	16.00	33.00	65.00	110	—

KM# 96 3 PFENNIG (Dreier)
Copper **Obv:** Without value **Rev. Legend:** *3 PFENNIG...

Date	Mintage	Good	VG	F	VF	XF
ND(1621/22)	—	16.00	33.00	65.00	110	—

KM# 98 3 PFENNIG (Dreier)
Copper **Obv:** Date above four-fold arms **Rev:** Imperial orb with 3

Date	Mintage	Good	VG	F	VF	XF
16Z1	—	20.00	40.00	80.00	130	—

KM# 99 3 PFENNIG (Dreier)
Copper **Obv:** Ornamented four-fold arms **Rev:** Imperial orb with 3, date divided above

Date	Mintage	Good	VG	F	VF	XF
16Z1	—	20.00	40.00	80.00	130	—

KM# 100 3 PFENNIG (Dreier)
Copper **Obv:** Oval arms

Date	Mintage	Good	VG	F	VF	XF
(16)Z1	—	20.00	40.00	80.00	130	—
(16)22	—	20.00	40.00	80.00	130	—

KM# 101 3 PFENNIG (Dreier)
Copper **Obv:** Four-fold arms, date above **Rev:** Ornamented oval frame with 3, date above

Date	Mintage	Good	VG	F	VF	XF
16Z1/16Z1	—	20.00	40.00	80.00	130	—

KM# 102 3 PFENNIG (Dreier)
Copper **Obv:** Heart-shaped four-fold arms **Rev:** 3 in large ornamented frame divides date

Date	Mintage	Good	VG	F	VF	XF
(16)21	—	20.00	40.00	80.00	130	—

KM# 89 3 PFENNIG (Dreier)
Silver **Obv:** Crowned four-fold arms divide date and mintmaster's initials **Rev:** Imperial orb with 3 in rhombus **Note:** Anonymous Kipper. Varieties exist.

Date	Mintage	VG	F	VF	XF	Unc
16Z1 AK	—	16.00	33.00	65.00	110	—
16ZZ AK	—	16.00	33.00	65.00	110	—

KM# 122 3 PFENNIG (Dreier)
Silver **Rev:** Without rhombus **Note:** Varieties exist.

Date	Mintage	VG	F	VF	XF	Unc
16ZZ AK	—	27.00	55.00	90.00	165	—

KM# 123 3 PFENNIG (Dreier)
Silver **Obv:** Crowned four-fold arms divide mintmaster's initials **Rev:** Imperial orb with 3 divides date **Note:** Varieties exist.

Date	Mintage	VG	F	VF	XF	Unc
16ZZ AK	—	27.00	55.00	90.00	165	—
16Z3 AK	—	27.00	55.00	90.00	165	—

KM# 124 3 PFENNIG (Dreier)
Copper **Obv:** St. George slaying dragon at right **Rev:** Imperial orb with 3 divides date

Date	Mintage	Good	VG	F	VF	XF
(16)ZZ	—	—	—	—	—	—

KM# 120 3 PFENNIG (Dreier)
Silver **Obv:** Crown above four-fold arms divide date **Rev:** Imperial orb with 3 in rhombus

Date	Mintage	VG	F	VF	XF	Unc
16ZZ	—	27.00	55.00	90.00	165	—

KM# 121 3 PFENNIG (Dreier)
Silver **Obv:** Four-fold arms, crown above divides mintmaster's initials **Rev:** Imperial orb with 3 divides date, within rhombus

Date	Mintage	VG	F	VF	XF	Unc
16ZZ AK	—	27.00	55.00	90.00	165	—

KM# 104 6 PFENNIG
Copper **Obv:** Date above arms

Date	Mintage	VG	F	VF	XF	Unc
16Z1	—	16.00	27.00	45.00	85.00	—

KM# 105 6 PFENNIG
Copper **Obv:** Imperial orb with 6

Date	Mintage	VG	F	VF	XF	Unc
16Z1	—	16.00	27.00	45.00	85.00	—

KM# 103 6 PFENNIG
Copper **Obv:** Ornate four-fold arms, eight-pointed star above **Rev:** VI/PFENNIG above imperial orb **Note:** Kipper 6 Pfennig.

Date	Mintage	VG	F	VF	XF	Unc
ND(1621/22)	—	9.00	20.00	33.00	60.00	—

KM# 168 GROSCHEN (1/28 Thaler)
Silver **Subject:** Death of David **Obv:** Crown divides date above ornaented oval four-fold arms **Rev:** Eight-line inscription with dates **Note:** Varieties exist.

Date	Mintage	VG	F	VF	XF	Unc
(16)Z8	—	—	—	—	—	—

KM# 186 GROSCHEN (1/28 Thaler)
Silver **Subject:** Death of Friedrich Christoph **Obv:** Five-line inscription with dates, titles of Friedrich Christoph **Rev:** Crowned oval four-fold arms **Rev. Legend:** GEDVLDT IN . VNSHVLDT. **Note:** Varieties exist.

Date	Mintage	VG	F	VF	XF	Unc
(16)31	—	135	225	375	—	—

KM# 190 GROSCHEN (1/28 Thaler)
Silver **Subject:** Death of Ernest Ludwig **Obv:** Crowned oval four-fold arms **Rev:** Seven-line inscription with date **Note:** Varieties exist.

Date	Mintage	VG	F	VF	XF	Unc
(1)632	—	—	—	—	—	—

KM# 107 12 KREUZER (Schreckenburger)
Silver **Rev:** Angel above four-fold arms

Date	Mintage	VG	F	VF	XF	Unc
ND(1621/22)	—	65.00	120	200	300	—

KM# 108 12 KREUZER (Schreckenburger)
Silver **Rev:** Ornamented oval arms

Date	Mintage	VG	F	VF	XF	Unc
ND(1621/22)	—	65.00	120	200	300	—

KM# 109 12 KREUZER (Schreckenburger)
Silver **Obv:** Crowned imperial eagle, 1Z in orb on breast, titles of Ferdinand II **Rev:** Crowned four-fold arms, titles of Friedrich Christoph

Date	Mintage	VG	F	VF	XF	Unc
ND(1621/22)	—	65.00	120	200	300	—

KM# 110 12 KREUZER (Schreckenburger)
Silver **Obv:** Arms divide mintmaster's initials **Rev:** Date **Rev. Legend:** IUST. NVN.-VS

Date	Mintage	VG	F	VF	XF	Unc
16Z1 GB	—	65.00	120	200	300	—
161Z GB	—	65.00	120	200	300	—

Note: Error with retrograde B

KM# 112 12 KREUZER (Schreckenburger)
Silver **Rev:** Titles of David in legend

Date	Mintage	VG	F	VF	XF	Unc
ND(1621/22)	—	—	—	—	—	—

KM# 111 12 KREUZER (Schreckenburger)
Silver **Obv:** Crowned imperial eagle, 1Z in orb on breast, titles of Ferdinand II **Rev:** Crowned four-fold arms, titles of Friedrich Christoph **Mint:** Hedersleben **Note:** Struck at Hedersleben Mint.

Date	Mintage	VG	F	VF	XF	Unc
1621	—	65.00	120	200	300	—

KM# 113 12 KREUZER (Schreckenburger)
Silver **Rev:** Date added **Mint:** Schraplau **Note:** Struck at Schraplau Mint.

Date	Mintage	VG	F	VF	XF	Unc
16Z1	—	85.00	155	225	350	—

KM# 106 12 KREUZER (Schreckenburger)
Silver **Obv:** St. George slaying dragon at left **Rev:** Crowned four-fold arms **Note:** Varieties exist.

Date	Mintage	VG	F	VF	XF	Unc
ND(1621/22)	—	65.00	120	200	300	—

KM# 16 1/28 THALER

Silver **Obv:** Imperial orb with Z8, date in legend at top **Rev:** BEI GOT/IST RAHT/VND THAT above four-fold arms dividing mintmaster's initials **Note:** Spruch 1/28 Thaler.

Date	Mintage	VG	F	VF	XF	Unc
1606 GM	—	—	—	—	—	—

KM# 17 1/28 THALER

Silver **Rev:** BEI/GOTT IST/RAHT VND/TH-AT

Date	Mintage	VG	F	VF	XF	Unc
ND GM	—	—	—	—	—	—

KM# 30 1/28 THALER

Silver **Obv:** Date divided by cross on orb **Rev:** Date divided by arms

Date	Mintage	VG	F	VF	XF	Unc
1610/1610 GM	—	—	—	—	—	—

KM# 31 1/28 THALER

Silver **Rev:** Date divided by arms

Date	Mintage	VG	F	VF	XF	Unc
1610	—	—	—	—	—	—

KM# 32 1/28 THALER

Silver **Obv:** Imperial orb with Z8 divides mintmaster's initials, titles of Friedrich Christoph and date in legend **Rev:** Helmeted four-fold arms **Note:** Varieties exist.

Date	Mintage	VG	F	VF	XF	Unc
1610 GM	—	—	—	—	—	—

KM# 39 1/28 THALER

Silver **Rev:** Date divided by orb, mintmaster's initials in legend at top **Note:** Varieties exist.

Date	Mintage	VG	F	VF	XF	Unc
1611 GM	—	—	—	—	—	—

KM# 36 1/28 THALER

Silver **Obv:** Imperial orb with 28, Date divided by cross on orb **Rev:** BEI/GOTT IST/RAHT VND/TH-AT above four-fold arms dividing mintmaster's initials

Date	Mintage	VG	F	VF	XF	Unc
1611 GM	—	—	—	—	—	—

KM# 37 1/28 THALER

Silver **Obv:** Mintmaster's initials divided by cross

Date	Mintage	VG	F	VF	XF	Unc
1611 GM	—	—	—	—	—	—

KM# 38 1/28 THALER

Silver **Obv:** Titles of Friedrich Christoph **Rev:** Imperial orb with Z8 divides mintmaster's initials, date in legend

Date	Mintage	VG	F	VF	XF	Unc
1611 GM	—	—	—	—	—	—

KM# 40 1/28 THALER

Silver **Rev:** Mintmaster's initials divided by arms

Date	Mintage	VG	F	VF	XF	Unc
1611 GM	—	—	—	—	—	—

KM# 84 1/24 THALER

Silver **Obv:** Crowned four-fold arms divide mintmaster's initials, titles of Freidrich Christoph **Rev:** Imperial orb with 24 divides date **Note:** Varieties exist. Kipper 1/24 Thaler.

Date	Mintage	VG	F	VF	XF	Unc
16Z0 AK	—	20.00	45.00	80.00	120	—
16Z8 AK	—	20.00	45.00	80.00	120	—
16Z9 AK	—	20.00	45.00	80.00	120	—
1630 AK	—	20.00	45.00	80.00	120	—
1631 AK	—	20.00	45.00	80.00	120	—

KM# 115 1/24 THALER

Silver **Obv:** Lion rampant left (Heldrungen) **Rev:** Imperial orb with 24, titles of Ferdinand II and date in legend **Note:** Varieties exist.

Date	Mintage	VG	F	VF	XF	Unc
(16)Z1	—	27.00	55.00	90.00	160	—
ND(1621/22)	—	27.00	55.00	90.00	160	—

KM# 117 1/24 THALER

Silver **Rev:** Date divided at top in legend **Note:** Varieties exist.

Date	Mintage	VG	F	VF	XF	Unc
(16)Z1	—	13.00	27.00	55.00	95.00	—

KM# 118 1/24 THALER

Silver **Obv:** Crowned four-fold arms divide mintmaster's initials **Rev:** Imperial orb with Z4, cross above divides date **Note:** Varieties exist.

Date	Mintage	VG	F	VF	XF	Unc
16Z1 AK	—	11.00	22.00	45.00	80.00	—
16Z4 AK	—	11.00	22.00	45.00	80.00	—
16Z5 AK	—	11.00	22.00	45.00	80.00	—
16Z6 AK	—	11.00	22.00	45.00	80.00	—

KM# 114 1/24 THALER

Silver **Obv:** Imperial orb with 24, titles of David in legend **Rev:** Lion rampant left (Heldrungen) **Rev. Legend:** FATA. VIAM. INVENIE.

Date	Mintage	VG	F	VF	XF	Unc
ND(1621/22)	—	27.00	55.00	90.00	160	—

KM# 116 1/24 THALER

Silver **Obv:** Crowned four-fold arms **Rev:** Imperial orb with Z4

Date	Mintage	VG	F	VF	XF	Unc
ND(1621/22)	—	13.00	27.00	55.00	95.00	—

KM# 125 1/24 THALER

Silver **Obv:** Imperial orb with 24, cross divides mintmaster's initials, date divided at top **Rev:** Helmet with six small pennants above four-fold arms

Date	Mintage	VG	F	VF	XF	Unc
16ZZ AK	—	13.00	27.00	55.00	95.00	—

KM# 127 1/24 THALER

Silver **Rev:** Change in legend from D. I. MANSF... **Rev. Legend:** MANSF...

Date	Mintage	VG	F	VF	XF	Unc
16ZZ AK	—	13.00	27.00	55.00	95.00	—

KM# 128 1/24 THALER

Silver **Rev:** Mintmaster's initials divided by arms

Date	Mintage	VG	F	VF	XF	Unc
16ZZ AK	—	13.00	27.00	55.00	95.00	—

KM# 126 1/24 THALER

Silver **Obv:** Imperial orb with 24 or Z4 divides mintmaster's initials, date divided in legend at top **Rev:** Helmeted four-fold arms **Note:** Varieties exist.

Date	Mintage	VG	F	VF	XF	Unc
16ZZ AK	—	13.00	27.00	55.00	95.00	—

KM# 147 1/24 THALER

Silver **Rev:** Mintmaster's initials divided by orb

Date	Mintage	VG	F	VF	XF	Unc
16Z4 AK	—	13.00	27.00	55.00	95.00	—

KM# 161 1/24 THALER

Silver **Obv:** Imperial orb with date divided at top **Rev:** Crowned four-fold arms divide mintmaster's initials, titles of Friedrich Christoph **Note:** Varieties exist.

Date	Mintage	VG	F	VF	XF	Unc
16Z7 AK	—	11.00	22.00	45.00	80.00	—
16Z8 AK	—	11.00	22.00	45.00	80.00	—
16Z9 AK	—	11.00	22.00	45.00	80.00	—
1630 AK	—	11.00	22.00	45.00	80.00	—

KM# 162 1/24 THALER

Silver **Obv:** Four-fold arms, crown above divides mintmaster's initials **Rev:** Imperial orb with 24 or Z4, date divided in legend at top **Note:** Varieties exist.

Date	Mintage	VG	F	VF	XF	Unc
16Z7 AK	—	11.00	22.00	45.00	80.00	—
16Z8 AK	—	11.00	22.00	45.00	80.00	—

KM# 173 1/24 THALER

Silver **Rev:** Imperial orb with 24 divides date

Date	Mintage	VG	F	VF	XF	Unc
16Z9 AK	—	13.00	27.00	55.00	95.00	—

KM# 174 1/24 THALER

Silver **Obv:** Crowned round arms, mintmaster's initials divided by crown above arms

Date	Mintage	VG	F	VF	XF	Unc
16Z9 AK	—	13.00	27.00	55.00	95.00	—

KM# 185 1/24 THALER

Silver **Rev:** Orb divides both date and mintmaster's initials

Date	Mintage	VG	F	VF	XF	Unc
1630/Z4 AK	—	13.00	27.00	55.00	95.00	—

Note: Reverse die of KM#147 with date altered from 16Z4 to 1630

KM# 208 1/24 THALER

Silver **Obv:** Crowned four-fold arms divide mintmaster's initials, date divided in legend at top **Rev:** Imperial orb with 24, date divided in legend at top **Note:** Varieties exist.

Date	Mintage	VG	F	VF	XF	Unc
(16)45/1646 HPK	—	13.00	27.00	55.00	95.00	—
(16)45/1647 HPK	—	13.00	27.00	55.00	95.00	—

KM# 209 1/24 THALER

Silver **Note:** Date only on reverse. Varieties exist.

Date	Mintage	VG	F	VF	XF	Unc
1646 HPK	—	13.00	27.00	55.00	95.00	—
1647 HPK	—	13.00	27.00	55.00	95.00	—

KM# 41 1/21 THALER

Silver **Obv:** Imperial orb with Z1, mintmaster's initials divided by cross on orb **Rev:** BEI/GOTT IST/RAHT VND/TH-AT

Date	Mintage	VG	F	VF	XF	Unc
1611 GM	—	13.00	27.00	55.00	95.00	—
161Z GM	—	13.00	27.00	55.00	95.00	—

KM# 43 1/21 THALER

Silver **Obv:** Mintmaster's initials divided by cross on orb **Rev:** Mintmaster's initials divided by arms

Date	Mintage	VG	F	VF	XF	Unc
1611 GM	—	13.00	27.00	55.00	95.00	—
1613 GM	—	13.00	27.00	55.00	95.00	—

KM# 42 1/21 THALER

Silver **Obv:** Mintmaster's initials divided in legend at top, date divided by orb **Note:** Varieties exist.

Date	Mintage	VG	F	VF	XF	Unc
1611 GM	—	13.00	27.00	55.00	95.00	—
161Z	—	13.00	27.00	55.00	95.00	—
1613 GM	—	13.00	27.00	55.00	95.00	—
1615 GM	—	13.00	27.00	55.00	95.00	—

KM# 44 1/21 THALER

Silver **Obv:** Imperial orb with Z1 divides date and mintmaster's initials **Rev:** Helmeted four-fold arms **Note:** Varieties exist.

Date	Mintage	VG	F	VF	XF	Unc
1611 GM	—	13.00	27.00	55.00	95.00	—

KM# 45 1/21 THALER

Silver **Obv:** Date divided in legend at top **Note:** Varieties exist.

Date	Mintage	VG	F	VF	XF	Unc
1611 GM	—	13.00	27.00	55.00	95.00	—
161Z GM	—	13.00	27.00	55.00	95.00	—

KM# 58 1/21 THALER

Silver **Obv:** Mintmaster's initials divided at top of legend **Note:** Varieties exist.

Date	Mintage	VG	F	VF	XF	Unc
161Z GM	—	13.00	27.00	55.00	95.00	—
1615 GM	—	13.00	27.00	55.00	95.00	—

KM# 57 1/21 THALER

Silver **Obv:** Reverse of Mansfeld-Vorderort-Borstedt KM#24

Date	Mintage	VG	F	VF	XF	Unc
161Z GM	—	13.00	27.00	55.00	90.00	—

KM# 61 1/21 THALER

Silver **Obv:** Mintmaster's initials divided by arms

Date	Mintage	VG	F	VF	XF	Unc
1616 AK	—	13.00	27.00	55.00	90.00	—

KM# 46 1/8 THALER

Silver **Obv:** St. George slaying dragon at left **Rev:** BEI GOT/IST RATH/VND THAT above four-fold arms which divide date and mintmaster's initials **Note:** Spruch 1/8 Thaler.

Date	Mintage	VG	F	VF	XF	Unc
1611 GM	—	—	—	—	—	—

KM# 47 1/4 THALER

Silver **Obv:** St. George slaying dragon at left **Rev:** BEI GOT/IST RATH/VND THAT above four-fold arms which divide date and mintmaster's initials **Note:** Spruch 1/4 Thaler. Varieties exist.

Date	Mintage	VG	F	VF	XF	Unc
1611 GM	—	60.00	120	225	400	—
1613 GM	—	60.00	120	225	400	—
1614 GM	—	60.00	120	225	400	—
1615 GM	—	60.00	120	225	400	—

KM# 48 1/4 THALER

Silver **Obv:** Four-fold arms divide mintmaster's initials, helmet above divides date, titles of Friedrich Christoph **Rev:** St. George slaying dragon at left **Note:** Varieties exist.

Date	Mintage	VG	F	VF	XF	Unc
1611 GM	—	60.00	120	225	400	—
161Z GM	—	60.00	120	225	400	—

KM# 62 1/4 THALER

Silver **Obv:** St. George slaying dragon at left **Rev:** Ornamented four-fold arms divide mintmaster's initials, crown above divides date **Rev. Legend:** BEY. GOTT. IST. RATH. VND. THAT **Note:** Varieties exist.

Date	Mintage	VG	F	VF	XF	Unc
1616 AK	—	60.00	120	225	400	—
1618 AK	—	60.00	120	225	400	—

KM# 65 1/4 THALER

Silver **Rev:** Date divided by arms and mintmaster's initials divided by crown

Date	Mintage	VG	F	VF	XF	Unc
1617 AK	—	60.00	120	225	400	—

KM# 66 1/4 THALER

Silver **Rev:** Date and mintmaster's initials divided

Date	Mintage	VG	F	VF	XF	Unc
1617 AK	—	60.00	120	225	400	—

KM# 72 1/4 THALER

Silver **Obv:** St. George slaying dragon at left, titles of Friedrich Christoph **Rev:** Four-fold arms divide mintmaster's initials near top, helmet above divides date **Rev. Legend:** PATIENTA - VINCIT - OMNIA **Note:** Spruch 1/4 Thaler.

Date	Mintage	VG	F	VF	XF	Unc
1619 HI	—	60.00	120	225	400	—

KM# 80 1/4 THALER
Silver **Rev. Legend:** EST. DEVS. AYXUKUI. CIBSUKUI. QVE. POTIS. **Note:** Similar to KM#66 but reverse legend differs.

Date	Mintage	VG	F	VF	XF	Unc
16Z0 HI	—	60.00	120	225	400	—

KM# 129 1/4 THALER
Silver **Obv:** St. George slaying dragon at left, titles of Friedrich Christoph **Rev:** Helmeted four-fold arms divide date and mintmaster's initials **Note:** Varieties exist.

Date	Mintage	VG	F	VF	XF	Unc
16ZZ AK	—	60.00	120	225	400	—
16ZZ	—	60.00	120	225	400	—
16Z3 AK	—	60.00	120	225	400	—
16Z4 AK	—	60.00	120	225	400	—

KM# 163 1/4 THALER
Silver **Subject:** Death of David **Obv:** Six-line inscription with dates **Rev:** Crowned four-fold arms divide date and mintmaster's initials

Date	Mintage	VG	F	VF	XF	Unc
Z8 AK	—	—	—	—	—	—

KM# 164 1/4 THALER
Silver **Obv:** Seven-line inscription

Date	Mintage	VG	F	VF	XF	Unc
(16)Z8 AK	—	—	—	—	—	—

KM# 165 1/4 THALER
Silver **Obv:** Eight-line inscription

Date	Mintage	VG	F	VF	XF	Unc
(16)Z8 AK	—	—	—	—	—	—

KM# 175 1/4 THALER
Silver **Obv:** St. George slaying dragon at left, titles of Friedrich Christoph **Rev:** Helmeted four-fold arms with date divided by helmet above arms **Note:** Varieties exist.

Date	Mintage	VG	F	VF	XF	Unc
16Z9	—	60.00	120	225	400	—
ND AK	—	60.00	120	225	400	—

KM# 187 1/4 THALER
Silver **Subject:** Death of Friedrich Christoph **Obv:** St. George slaying dragon at left **Rev:** Eight-line inscription with dates **Note:** Varieties exist.

Date	Mintage	VG	F	VF	XF	Unc
1631	—	—	—	—	—	—

KM# 191 1/4 THALER
Silver **Subject:** Death of Ernst Ludwig **Obv:** St. George slaying dragon at left **Rev:** Seven-line inscription with dates **Note:** Varieties exist.

Date	Mintage	VG	F	VF	XF	Unc
(1)63Z	—	—	—	—	—	—

KM# 200 1/4 THALER
Silver **Note:** Similar to 1/2 Thaler, KM#201. Varieties exist.

Date	Mintage	VG	F	VF	XF	Unc
1641 HPK	—	27.00	55.00	120	200	—
1642 HPK	—	27.00	55.00	120	200	—
1649 HPK	—	27.00	55.00	120	200	—
1649	—	27.00	55.00	120	200	—
1653 HPK	—	27.00	55.00	120	200	—
1661 HPK	—	27.00	55.00	120	200	—

KM# 227 1/4 THALER
Silver **Rev:** Mintmaster's initials and date divided by helmet **Note:** Varieties exist.

Date	Mintage	VG	F	VF	XF	Unc
1663 HPK	—	85.00	165	275	525	—

KM# 228 1/4 THALER
Silver **Rev:** Date divided by arms **Note:** Varieties exist.

Date	Mintage	VG	F	VF	XF	Unc
1663 HPK	—	—	—	—	—	—
1665 HPK	—	—	—	—	—	—

KM# 15 1/2 THALER
Silver **Note:** Spruch 1/2 Thaler. Similar to 1 Thaler, KM#7.

Date	Mintage	VG	F	VF	XF	Unc
1605 GM	—	—	—	—	—	—

KM# 23 1/2 THALER
Silver **Note:** Similar to 1 Thaler, KM#18. Varieties exist.

Date	Mintage	VG	F	VF	XF	Unc
1609 GM	—	55.00	95.00	140	225	—
1611 GM	—	55.00	95.00	140	225	—

KM# 49 1/2 THALER
Silver **Obv:** St. George slaying dragon at left **Rev:** BEI GOT/IST RATH/VND THAT above four-fold arms which divide date and mintmaster's initials **Note:** Varieties exist.

Date	Mintage	VG	F	VF	XF	Unc
1611 GM	—	80.00	165	300	500	—
1613 GM	—	80.00	165	300	500	—
1614 GM	—	80.00	165	300	500	—
1615 GM	—	80.00	165	300	500	—

KM# 50 1/2 THALER
Silver **Obv:** Four-fold divide mintmaster's initials, helmet above divides date, titles of Friedrich Christoph **Rev:** St. George slaying dragon at left **Note:** Varieties exist.

Date	Mintage	VG	F	VF	XF	Unc
1611 GM	—	80.00	165	300	500	—
161Z GM	—	80.00	165	300	500	—
1613 GM	—	80.00	165	300	500	—
1617 AK	—	80.00	165	300	500	—

KM# 63 1/2 THALER
Silver **Obv:** St. George slaying dragon at left **Rev:** Ornamented four-fold arms divide mintmaster's initials, crown above divides date **Rev. Legend:** BEY. GOTT. IST. RATH. VND. THAT **Note:** Spruch 1/2 Thaler.

Date	Mintage	VG	F	VF	XF	Unc
1616 AK	—	—	—	—	—	—

KM# 67 1/2 THALER
Silver **Note:** Broad flan. Similar to 1 Thaler, KM#64.

Date	Mintage	VG	F	VF	XF	Unc
1617 AK	—	—	—	—	—	—

KM# 68 1/2 THALER
Silver **Note:** Normal flan. Similar to 1 Thaler, KM#64. Varieties exist.

Date	Mintage	VG	F	VF	XF	Unc
1617 AK	—	175	235	290	350	—
1618 AK	—	175	235	290	350	—

KM# 73 1/2 THALER
Silver **Obv:** St. George slaying dragon at left, titles of Friedrich Christoph **Rev:** Four-fold arms divide mintmaster's initials near top, helmet above divides date **Rev. Legend:** PATIENTA - VINCIT - OMNIA **Note:** Varieties exist.

Date	Mintage	VG	F	VF	XF	Unc
1619 HI	—	—	—	—	—	—

KM# 82 1/2 THALER
Silver **Note:** Similar to 1 Thaler, KM#75 but mintmaster's initials above date. Varieties exist.

Date	Mintage	VG	F	VF	XF	Unc
16Z0 HI	—	135	220	275	350	—
16Z1 AK	—	135	220	275	350	—
1624 AK	—	135	220	275	350	—

KM# 81 1/2 THALER
Silver **Rev:** Ornamented four-fold arms divide mintmaster's initials, crown above divides date **Rev. Legend:** EST DEVS. AUXILIO. CONSILIO. QVE. POTIS.

Date	Mintage	VG	F	VF	XF	Unc
16Z0 HI	—	—	—	—	—	—

KM# 130 1/2 THALER
Silver **Obv:** St. George slaying dragon at left, titles of Friedrich Christoph **Rev:** Helmeted four-fold arms divide date and mintmaster's initials **Note:** Varieties exist.

Date	Mintage	VG	F	VF	XF	Unc
16ZZ AK	—	45.00	85.00	140	220	—
16Z3 AK	—	45.00	85.00	140	220	—
16Z4 AK	—	45.00	85.00	140	220	—
16Z9 AK	—	45.00	85.00	140	220	—

KM# 131 1/2 THALER
Silver **Rev:** Date divided by helmet above arms **Note:** Varieties exist.

Date	Mintage	VG	F	VF	XF	Unc
(16)ZZ AK	—	60.00	120	200	340	—
16Z9 AK	—	60.00	120	200	340	—

KM# 151 1/2 THALER
Silver **Obv:** St. George slaying dragon at left **Rev:** Helmeted four-fold arms divide date and mintmaster's initials near bottom

Date	Mintage	VG	F	VF	XF	Unc
16Z6 AK	—	100	200	350	550	—

KM# 152 1/2 THALER
Silver **Rev:** Mansfeld-Artern, KM#91

Date	Mintage	VG	F	VF	XF	Unc
16Z6 AK	—	100	200	350	550	—

KM# 166 1/2 THALER
Silver **Subject:** Death of David **Obv:** Seven-line inscription **Rev:** Crowned four-fold arms divid date and mintmaster's initials. **Note:** Varieties exist.

Date	Mintage	VG	F	VF	XF	Unc
16Z8 AK	—	—	—	—	—	—

KM# 188 1/2 THALER
Silver **Subject:** Death of Friedrich Christoph **Obv:** Eight-line inscription with dates **Rev:** St. George slaying dragon at left **Rev. Legend:** GEDVLDT. IN. VNSCHVLDT. TREW IST WILPRET. **Note:** Varieties exist.

Date	Mintage	VG	F	VF	XF	Unc
1631	—	—	450	750	1,150	—

KM# 192 1/2 THALER
Silver **Subject:** Death of Ernst Ludwig **Obv:** St. George slaying dragon at left **Rev:** Seven-line inscription with dates

Date	Mintage	VG	F	VF	XF	Unc
1632	—	—	—	—	—	—

KM# 201 1/2 THALER
Silver **Note:** Varieties exist.

Date	Mintage	VG	F	VF	XF	Unc
1642 HPK	—	60.00	120	190	250	—
1646	—	60.00	120	190	250	—
1649 HPK	—	60.00	120	190	250	—
1649	—	60.00	120	190	250	—
1651 HPK	—	60.00	120	190	250	—
1653 HPK	—	60.00	120	190	250	—

KM# 220 1/2 THALER
Silver **Rev:** Mintmaster's initials also divided by helmet **Note:** Varieties exist.

Date	Mintage	VG	F	VF	XF	Unc
1651 HPK	—	—	—	—	—	—

KM# 225 1/2 THALER
Silver **Obv:** Date in legend

Date	Mintage	VG	F	VF	XF	Unc
1661 HPK	—	55.00	100	165	275	—

KM# 229 1/2 THALER
Silver **Rev:** Date divided by legend **Note:** Varieties exist.

Date	Mintage	VG	F	VF	XF	Unc
1663 HPK	—	45.00	85.00	110	120	—
1664 HPK	—	45.00	85.00	110	120	—
1665 HPK	—	45.00	85.00	110	120	—

KM# 24 2/3 THALER (Gulden)
Silver **Note:** Spruch 2/3 Thaler. Broad flan. Similar to 1 Thaler, KM#18.

Date	Mintage	VG	F	VF	XF	Unc
1609 GM	—	—	—	—	—	—

KM# 148 2/3 THALER (Gulden)
Silver **Note:** Similar to 1 Thaler, KM#145.

Date	Mintage	VG	F	VF	XF	Unc
1624 AK	—	—	—	—	—	—

KM# 5 THALER
Silver **Obv:** Crowned imperial eagle above crowned arms divide date and G-M, titles of Rudolf II **Rev. Legend:** ERNESTVS. FRI: CHRIST: E. DAVID. CO. MANSF: **Note:** Dav. #6996.

Date	Mintage	VG	F	VF	XF	Unc
1602 GM	—	75.00	190	265	400	—
1603 GM	—	75.00	190	265	400	—

KM# 9 THALER
Silver **Rev. Legend:** ERNESTVS. E: FRID: CHRIST: CO: E: DO: I: MANSFEL **Note:** Dav. #6998.

Date	Mintage	VG	F	VF	XF	Unc
1603 GM	—	75.00	190	265	400	—

KM# 7 THALER

Silver **Obv:** Helmeted arms with helmets dividing G-M **Rev:** St. George left and dragon **Note:** Dav. #6974.

Date	Mintage	VG	F	VF	XF	Unc
1603 GM	—	75.00	190	265	400	—
1605 GM	—	75.00	190	265	400	—

KM# 8 THALER

Silver **Obv:** Arms divide G-M **Note:** Varieties exist. Dav. #6974A.

Date	Mintage	VG	F	VF	XF	Unc
1603 GM	—	75.00	190	265	400	—
1605 GM	—	75.00	190	265	400	—
1615 GM Error for 1605	—	75.00	190	265	400	—

KM# 13 THALER

Silver **Obv:** Helmeted arms with divided date above and G-M below **Rev. Legend:** ...D: I: MAN **Note:** Varieties exist. Dav. #7000.

Date	Mintage	VG	F	VF	XF	Unc
1604 GM	—	75.00	190	265	400	—
1605 GM	—	75.00	190	265	400	—
1606 GM	—	75.00	190	265	400	—
1607 GM	—	75.00	190	265	400	—
1608 GM	—	75.00	190	265	400	—
1609 GM	—	75.00	190	265	400	—
1611 GM	—	75.00	190	265	400	—

KM# 18 THALER

Silver **Obv:** St. George left and dragon **Rev:** Shield dividing date and G-M, three-line inscription above **Note:** Dav. #6977.

Date	Mintage	VG	F	VF	XF	Unc
1606	—	75.00	190	265	400	—
1607	—	75.00	190	265	400	—
1608	—	75.00	190	265	400	—
1609	—	75.00	190	265	400	—
1610	—	75.00	190	265	400	—
1611	—	75.00	190	265	400	—
1612	—	75.00	190	265	400	—
1613	—	75.00	190	265	400	—
1614	—	75.00	190	265	400	—
1615	—	75.00	190	265	400	—

KM# 33 THALER

Silver **Obv:** Helmeted arms, divided date above and initials below **Rev:** St. George and dragon **Note:** Dav. #7002.

Date	Mintage	VG	F	VF	XF	Unc
1610 GM	—	75.00	190	265	400	—
1611 GM	—	75.00	190	265	400	—
1612 GM	—	75.00	190	265	400	—
1613 GM	—	75.00	190	265	400	—
1614 GM	—	75.00	190	265	400	—
1615 GM	—	75.00	190	265	400	—
1616 AK	—	75.00	190	265	400	—
1617 AK	—	75.00	190	265	400	—
1618 AK	—	75.00	190	265	400	—
1619 AK	—	75.00	190	265	400	—
1621 AK	—	75.00	190	265	400	—

KM# 52 THALER

Silver **Obv:** G-M above arms, date below **Note:** Dav. #7003.

Date	Mintage	VG	F	VF	XF	Unc
1611 GM	—	75.00	190	265	400	—

KM# 53 THALER

Silver **Obv:** Without initials above arms **Note:** Dav. #7003A.

Date	Mintage	VG	F	VF	XF	Unc
1611	—	75.00	190	265	400	—

KM# 51 THALER

Silver **Rev:** Four-line inscription above shield **Note:** Dav. #6977A.

Date	Mintage	VG	F	VF	XF	Unc
1611 GM	—	75.00	190	265	400	—
1614 GM	—	75.00	190	265	400	—
1615 GM	—	75.00	190	265	400	—

KM# 64 THALER

Silver **Rev:** Crowned shield divide date and A-K **Note:** Dav. #6979.

Date	Mintage	VG	F	VF	XF	Unc
1616	—	75.00	190	265	400	—
1618	—	75.00	190	265	400	—
1620	—	75.00	190	265	400	—

KM# 69 THALER

Silver **Rev:** A-K above date **Note:** Dav. #6979A.

Date	Mintage	VG	F	VF	XF	Unc
1617	—	75.00	190	265	400	—
1618	—	75.00	190	265	400	—
1619	—	75.00	190	265	400	—

KM# 74 THALER

Silver **Rev:** A-K above crown **Note:** Dav. #6979B.

Date	Mintage	VG	F	VF	XF	Unc
1619	—	75.00	190	265	400	—

KM# 75 THALER

Silver **Note:** Dav. #6980.

Date	Mintage	VG	F	VF	XF	Unc
1619 H-I	—	75.00	190	265	400	—
1620 H-I	—	75.00	190	265	400	—

KM# 76 THALER

Silver **Obv:** St. George and dragon **Rev:** Helmeted arms, date divided above, A-K divided at center **Note:** Dav. #7005.

Date	Mintage	VG	F	VF	XF	Unc
1619 AK	—	75.00	190	265	400	—
1620 AK	—	75.00	190	265	400	—

KM# 83 THALER

Silver **Rev:** H-I above date **Note:** Dav. #6980A.

Date	Mintage	VG	F	VF	XF	Unc
1620	—	75.00	190	265	400	—

KM# 119 THALER

Silver **Obv:** St. George and dragon smaller **Rev:** Crowned arms dividing date and H-I **Note:** Dav. #6981.

Date	Mintage	VG	F	VF	XF	Unc
1621	—	75.00	190	265	400	—

KM# 132 THALER

Silver **Obv. Legend:** DAVID: C. E. DO: I. MANSF. NO: DO: I. HEL SE. E. SC. **Rev:** Spanish shield divides A-K **Rev. Legend:** BEI: GOTT: IST: RAHT. VNND THATT **Note:** Dav. #6982.

Date	Mintage	VG	F	VF	XF	Unc
1622	—	75.00	190	265	400	—

KM# 133 THALER

Silver **Rev:** A-K above date **Note:** Dav. #6982A.

Date	Mintage	VG	F	VF	XF	Unc
1622	—	75.00	190	265	400	—

KM# 134 THALER

Silver **Rev:** Heart-shaped shield, A-K above date **Note:** Dav. #6982B.

Date	Mintage	VG	F	VF	XF	Unc
1622	—	75.00	190	265	400	—

KM# 135 THALER

Silver **Rev:** Date above A-K **Note:** Dav. #7006.

Date	Mintage	VG	F	VF	XF	Unc
1622	—	75.00	190	265	400	—
1623	—	75.00	190	265	400	—
1624	—	75.00	190	265	400	—
1625	—	75.00	190	265	400	—

KM# 136 THALER

Silver **Obv:** Small rider within circle above dragon on back **Note:** Dav. #7006A.

Date	Mintage	VG	F	VF	XF	Unc
1622 AK	—	75.00	190	265	400	—

KM# 137 THALER

Silver **Rev:** A-K above date **Note:** Dav. #7006B.

Date	Mintage	VG	F	VF	XF	Unc
1622	—	75.00	190	265	400	—
1623	—	75.00	190	265	400	—
1624	—	75.00	190	265	400	—
1625	—	75.00	190	265	400	—

KM# 138 THALER

Silver **Rev. Legend:** MANSF. NOBILES. DOM... **Note:** Dav. #7007.

Date	Mintage	VG	F	VF	XF	Unc
1622 AK	—	75.00	190	265	400	—

KM# 139 THALER

Silver **Obv:** St. George left and dragon **Obv. Legend:** FRIDERI: CHRIS: ET. DAVID. CO: E: D: IN **Rev:** Helmeted arms dividing date and A-K below **Note:** Dav. #7013. Varieties exist for legend and shield.

Date	Mintage	VG	F	VF	XF	Unc
1622	—	75.00	190	265	400	—
1623	—	75.00	190	265	400	—
1624	—	75.00	190	265	400	—
1625	—	75.00	190	265	400	—
1626	—	75.00	190	265	400	—

KM# 143 THALER

Silver **Obv. Legend:** DAVID: C. E. DO: I. MANSF. NO: DO: I. HEL. SE. E. SC. **Rev. Legend:** IN. MANSF. NOBI. DOM. IN. HEL. SEB. ET. SC. **Note:** Mule. Dav. #6986.

Date	Mintage	VG	F	VF	XF	Unc
1623 AK	—	75.00	190	265	400	—

KM# 144 THALER

Silver **Obv. Legend:** ...DOM. I. MANS. N: D. I. H: S: E. S: **Rev. Legend:** BEI. GOTT. IST. RAHT. VNND. THADT **Note:** Mule. Dav. #6987.

Date	Mintage	VG	F	VF	XF	Unc
1623 AK	—	75.00	190	265	400	—

KM# 146 THALER

Silver **Rev. Legend:** IN. MANSF. NOBI. DOM... **Note:** Dav. #7008.

Date	Mintage	VG	F	VF	XF	Unc
1623 AK	—	75.00	190	265	400	—

KM# 145 THALER

Silver **Note:** Dav. #6989.

Date	Mintage	VG	F	VF	XF	Unc
1623 A-K	—	75.00	190	265	400	—
1624 A-K	—	75.00	190	265	400	—
1625 A-K	—	75.00	190	265	400	—
1626 A-K	—	75.00	190	265	400	—
1627 A-K	—	75.00	190	265	400	—
1628 A-K	—	75.00	190	265	400	—

KM# 156 THALER

Silver **Obv:** Date below St. George **Rev:** Date above crowned arms in legend **Note:** Dav. #6990.

Date	Mintage	VG	F	VF	XF	Unc
1624	—	75.00	190	265	400	—
1626//624 AK	—	75.00	190	265	400	—

KM# 150 THALER

Silver **Rev:** Date divided above arms **Note:** Dav. #7014.

Date	Mintage	VG	F	VF	XF	Unc
1625 AK	—	75.00	190	265	400	—
1626 AK	—	75.00	190	265	400	—

KM# 153 THALER

Silver **Obv. Legend:** DAVID: CO: ET. DO: IN. MANSF. N. :D: I. H. S. E. **Rev. Legend:** MANST. NO. DO. IN. HEL. SEB. ET. SC. **Note:** Mule. Dav. #6983.

Date	Mintage	VG	F	VF	XF	Unc
1626//1622 AK	—	75.00	190	265	400	—

KM# 154 THALER

Silver **Rev. Legend:** COM. ET. DOM. IN. MANSF. NO. DOM. IN. HEL: **Note:** Mule. Dav. #6984.

Date	Mintage	VG	F	VF	XF	Unc
1626//1622 AK	—	75.00	190	265	400	—

KM# 155 THALER

Silver **Rev:** Double helmets and complex arms **Note:** Mule. Dav. #6985.

Date	Mintage	VG	F	VF	XF	Unc
1626//1622 AK	—	75.00	190	265	400	—

KM# 157 THALER

Silver **Rev:** Elaborate shield **Note:** Dav. #6990A.

Date	Mintage	VG	F	VF	XF	Unc
1626//1626 AK	—	75.00	190	265	400	—

KM# 158 THALER

Silver **Obv:** Similar to KM#156 **Rev:** Similar to KM#145 **Note:** Dav. #6991.

Date	Mintage	VG	F	VF	XF	Unc
1626//1625 AK	—	75.00	190	265	400	—

KM# 159 THALER

Silver **Rev:** Crowned arms divide date and A-K **Note:** Dav. #6993.

Date	Mintage	VG	F	VF	XF	Unc
1626 AK	—	75.00	190	265	400	—

KM# 167 THALER

Silver **Subject:** Death of David **Obv:** Seven-line inscription **Rev:** Crowned arms **Note:** Dav. #6994.

Date	Mintage	VG	F	VF	XF	Unc
1628 AK	—	130	265	400	625	—

KM# 176 THALER

Silver **Obv. Legend:** FRIDERI: CHRI:... **Rev. Legend:** MANSF: NOBI. DOM. IN. HEL... **Note:** Dav. #7010.

Date	Mintage	VG	F	VF	XF	Unc
1629 AK	—	75.00	190	265	400	—
1630 AK	—	75.00	190	265	400	—

KM# 177 THALER

Silver **Rev:** Initials divided by helmets, date below **Note:** Cross-reference number Dav. #7011.

Date	Mintage	VG	F	VF	XF	Unc
1629 AK	—	75.00	190	265	400	—

KM# 189 THALER
Silver **Subject:** Death of Friedrich Christoph **Note:** Dav. #7012.

Date	Mintage	VG	F	VF	XF	Unc
1631	—	130	265	400	625	—

KM# 193 THALER
Silver **Subject:** Death of Ernst Ludwig **Obv:** St. George and dragon **Rev:** Seven-line inscription **Note:** Dav. #7016.

Date	Mintage	VG	F	VF	XF	Unc
1632 Rare	—	—	—	—	—	—

KM# 202 THALER
Silver **Rev:** Helmeted arms dividing date above and HP-K below **Note:** Dav. #7019.

Date	Mintage	VG	F	VF	XF	Unc
1642 HPK	—	75.00	190	265	400	—
1643 HPK	—	75.00	190	265	400	—
1644 HPK	—	75.00	190	265	400	—
1645 HPK	—	75.00	190	265	400	—
1646 HPK	—	75.00	190	265	400	—
1647 HPK	—	75.00	190	265	400	—
1648 HPK	—	75.00	190	265	400	—
1649 HPK	—	75.00	190	265	400	—
1651 HPK	—	75.00	190	265	400	—
1652 HPK	—	75.00	190	265	400	—
1653 HPK	—	75.00	190	265	400	—
1663 HPK	—	75.00	190	265	400	—
1665 HPK	—	75.00	190	265	400	—

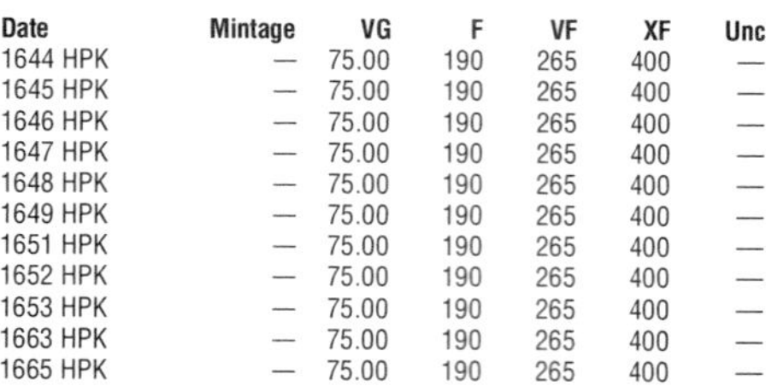

KM# 211 THALER
Silver **Rev:** Without initials **Note:** Dav. #7019A.

Date	Mintage	VG	F	VF	XF	Unc
1648	—	75.00	190	265	400	—
1649	—	75.00	190	265	400	—
1651	—	75.00	190	265	400	—

KM# 221 THALER
Silver **Rev:** HP-K above date **Note:** Dav. #7019B.

Date	Mintage	VG	F	VF	XF	Unc
1651	—	75.00	190	265	400	—

KM# 222 THALER
Silver **Note:** Dav. #7021.

Date	Mintage	VG	F	VF	XF	Unc
1653 HPK	—	75.00	190	265	400	—
1661 HPK	—	75.00	190	265	400	—
1662 HPK	—	75.00	190	265	400	—
1663 HPK	—	75.00	190	265	400	—
1664 HPK	—	75.00	190	265	400	—
1665 HPK	—	75.00	190	265	400	—
ND HP-K	—	75.00	190	265	400	—

KM# 6 2 THALER
Silver **Obv:** Crowned double eagle above crowned arms **Rev:** St. George left and dragon **Note:** Dav. #6995.

Date	Mintage	VG	F	VF	XF	Unc
1602 GM	—	600	1,050	1,800	3,000	—

KM# 11 2 THALER
Silver **Rev. Legend:** ERNESTVS. E: FRID: CHRIST: CO: E: DO: I: MANSFEL **Note:** Dav. #6997.

Date	Mintage	VG	F	VF	XF	Unc
1603 GM	—	600	1,050	1,800	3,000	—

KM# 10 2 THALER
Silver **Obv:** Helmeted arms with helmets dividing G-M **Rev:** St. George left and dragon **Note:** Dav. #6973.

Date	Mintage	VG	F	VF	XF	Unc
1603 GM	—	600	1,050	1,800	3,000	—

KM# 14 2 THALER
Silver **Obv:** Helmeted arms with divided date above and G-M below **Rev:** St. George and dragon **Rev. Legend:** NOBILES. DOMINI... **Note:** Dav. #6999.

Date	Mintage	VG	F	VF	XF	Unc
1604 GM	—	600	1,050	1,800	3,000	—
1606 GM	—	600	1,050	1,800	3,000	—

KM# 20 2 THALER
Silver **Note:** Similar to 1 Thaler, KM#18. Dav. #6976.

Date	Mintage	VG	F	VF	XF	Unc
1607 GM	—	600	1,050	1,800	3,000	—
1610 GM	—	600	1,050	1,800	3,000	—
1611 GM	—	600	1,050	1,800	3,000	—
1615 GM	—	600	1,050	1,800	3,000	—

KM# 25 2 THALER
Silver **Rev. Legend:** NOBILIS. DOMINVS... **Note:** Dav. #6999A.

Date	Mintage	VG	F	VF	XF	Unc
1609 GM	—	600	1,050	1,800	3,000	—

KM# 34 2 THALER
Silver **Note:** Similar to 1 Thaler, KM#33. Dav. #7001.

Date	Mintage	VG	F	VF	XF	Unc
1610 GM	—	600	1,050	1,800	3,000	—
1612 GM	—	600	1,050	1,800	3,000	—

KM# 70 2 THALER
Silver **Rev:** Crowned shield divides date and A-K **Note:** Dav. #6978.

Date	Mintage	VG	F	VF	XF	Unc
1617 AK	—	600	1,050	1,800	3,000	—

KM# 85 2 THALER
Silver **Obv:** St. George and dragon **Rev:** Helmeted arms with date divided above and H-I divided at center **Note:** Dav. #7004.

Date	Mintage	VG	F	VF	XF	Unc
1620 HI	—	600	1,050	1,800	3,000	—

KM# 149 2 THALER
Silver **Note:** Similar to 1 Thaler, KM#145. Dav. #6988.

Date	Mintage	VG	F	VF	XF	Unc
1624 AK	—	600	1,050	1,800	3,000	—

KM# 178 2 THALER
Silver **Obv:** St. George and dragon **Rev:** Helmeted arms divide date and mintmaster's initials **Note:** Dav. #3250.

Date	Mintage	VG	F	VF	XF	Unc
16Z9 AK	—	—	—	—	—	—

KM# 194 2 THALER
Silver **Subject:** Death of Ernst Ludwig **Obv:** St. George and dragon **Rev:** Seven-line inscription **Note:** Dav. #7015.

Date	Mintage	VG	F	VF	XF	Unc
1632 Rare	—	—	—	—	—	—

KM# 206 2 THALER
Silver **Note:** Similar to 1 Thaler, KM#202. Dav. #7018.

Date	Mintage	VG	F	VF	XF	Unc
1644 HPK	—	600	1,050	1,800	3,000	—
1646 HPK	—	600	1,050	1,800	3,000	—
1651 HPK	—	600	1,050	1,800	3,000	—
1665 HPK	—	600	1,050	1,800	3,000	—

KM# 223 2 THALER
Silver **Note:** Similar to 1 Thaler, KM#222. Dav. #7020.

Date	Mintage	VG	F	VF	XF	Unc
1653 HPK	—	600	1,050	1,800	3,000	—
1662 HPK	—	600	1,050	1,800	3,000	—

KM# 26 3 THALER
Silver **Note:** Similar to 1 Thaler, KM#18. Dav. #6975.

Date	Mintage	VG	F	VF	XF	Unc
1609 GM Rare	—	—	—	—	—	—

KM# 160 4 THALER
Silver **Obv:** St. George and dragon **Rev:** Crowned arms **Note:** Dav. #6992.

Date	Mintage	VG	F	VF	XF	Unc
1626 AK Rare	—	—	—	—	—	—

KM# 210 4 THALER
Silver **Note:** Similar to 1 Thaler, KM#202. Dav. #7017.

Date	Mintage	VG	F	VF	XF	Unc
1646 Rare	—	—	—	—	—	—

TRADE COINAGE

KM# 19 GOLDGULDEN
3.5000 g., 0.9860 Gold 0.1109 oz. AGW **Obv:** St. George slaying dragon **Rev:** Two-line inscription above arms

Date	Mintage	VG	F	VF	XF	Unc
1606	—	325	650	1,300	2,200	—
1607 GM	—	—	—	—	—	—
1608 GM	—	—	—	—	—	—
1609 GM	—	—	—	—	—	—
1610 GM	—	—	—	—	—	—
1611 GM	—	—	—	—	—	—
1612 GM	—	—	—	—	—	—
1613 GM	—	—	—	—	—	—
1614 GM	—	—	—	—	—	—
1618	—	325	650	1,300	2,200	—

KM# 21 GOLDGULDEN
3.5000 g., 0.9860 Gold 0.1109 oz. AGW **Rev:** Arms topped by helmet in inner circle

Date	Mintage	VG	F	VF	XF	Unc
1607	—	325	650	1,300	2,200	—

KM# 140 GOLDGULDEN
3.5000 g., 0.9860 Gold 0.1109 oz. AGW **Rev:** Arms topped by helmet in inner circle

Date	Mintage	VG	F	VF	XF	Unc
1622	—	425	850	1,650	2,850	—

KM# 59 2 GOLDGULDEN
7.0000 g., 0.9860 Gold 0.2219 oz. AGW **Obv:** St. George slaying dragon at left **Rev:** Inscription above four-fold arms which divide date and mintmaster's initials **Rev. Inscription:** BEI GOT/IST RATH/VND THAT **Note:** Varieties exist.

Date	Mintage	VG	F	VF	XF	Unc
1614 GM	—	—	—	—	—	—
1615 GM	—	—	—	—	—	—

KM# 77 DUCAT
3.5000 g., 0.9860 Gold 0.1109 oz. AGW **Obv:** St. George and dragon in inner circle **Rev:** Crowned arms in inner circle

Date	Mintage	VG	F	VF	XF	Unc
1619	—	400	750	1,500	2,700	—

KM# 141 DUCAT
3.5000 g., 0.9860 Gold 0.1109 oz. AGW **Obv:** St. George slaying dragon at left **Rev:** Arms topped by helmet in inner circle

Date	Mintage	VG	F	VF	XF	Unc
1622	—	275	550	1,100	2,200	—

KM# 207 DUCAT
3.5000 g., 0.9860 Gold 0.1109 oz. AGW

Date	Mintage	VG	F	VF	XF	Unc
1644	—	220	425	1,000	1,800	—
1647	—	220	425	1,000	1,800	—
1652	—	220	425	1,000	1,800	—

KM# 169 1-3/4 DUCAT
6.1250 g., 0.9860 Gold 0.1942 oz. AGW **Subject:** Death of David **Obv:** Seven-line inscription with dates **Rev:** Crowned four-fold arms divide date and mintmaster's initials

Date	Mintage	VG	F	VF	XF	Unc
(16)Z8 AK Rare	—	—	—	—	—	—

KM# 54 2 DUCAT
7.0000 g., 0.9860 Gold 0.2219 oz. AGW **Obv:** St. George slaying dragon left **Rev:** Inscription above four-fold arms which divide date and mintmaster's initials **Rev. Inscription:** BEI GOT/IST RATH/VND THAT

Date	Mintage	VG	F	VF	XF	Unc
1611 Rare	—	—	—	—	—	—

KM# 170 2 DUCAT
7.0000 g., 0.9860 Gold 0.2219 oz. AGW **Subject:** Death of David **Obv:** Six-line inscription with dates **Rev:** Crowned four-fold arms divide date and mintmaster's initials

Date	Mintage	VG	F	VF	XF	Unc
(16)Z8 AK Rare	—	—	—	—	—	—

KM# 171 2 DUCAT
7.0000 g., 0.9860 Gold 0.2219 oz. AGW **Obv:** Eight-line inscription with dates

Date	Mintage	VG	F	VF	XF	Unc
(16)Z8 AK Rare	—	—	—	—	—	—

KM# 195 2 DUCAT
7.0000 g., 0.9860 Gold 0.2219 oz. AGW **Subject:** Death of Ernst Ludwig **Obv:** St. George slaying dragon at left **Rev:** Seven-line inscription with dates

Date	Mintage	VG	F	VF	XF	Unc
(1)63Z Rare	—	—	—	—	—	—

KM# 203 2 DUCAT
7.0000 g., 0.9860 Gold 0.2219 oz. AGW **Rev:** Four-fold arms divide mintmaster's initials, helmet above divides date
Note: Varieties exist.

Date	Mintage	VG	F	VF	XF	Unc
1642 HPK	—	—	—	—	—	—
1649 HPK	—	—	—	—	—	—

KM# 172 2-3/4 DUCAT
9.6200 g., 0.9860 Gold 0.3049 oz. AGW **Subject:** Death of David **Obv:** Seven-line inscription with dates **Rev:** Crowned four-fold arms divide date and mintmaster's initials **Note:** Varieties exist.

Date	Mintage	VG	F	VF	XF	Unc
16Z8 AK Rare	—	—	—	—	—	—

KM# 60 3 DUCAT
10.5000 g., 0.9860 Gold 0.3328 oz. AGW **Obv:** St. George slaying dragon at left **Rev:** Inscription above four-fold arms which divide date and mintmaster's initials **Rev. Inscription:** BEI GOT/IST RATH/VND THAT **Note:** Spruch 3 Ducat.

Date	Mintage	VG	F	VF	XF	Unc
1614 GM	—	1,650	3,100	5,500	8,800	—
1615 GM Rare	—	—	—	—	—	—

KM# 212 3 DUCAT
10.5000 g., 0.9860 Gold 0.3328 oz. AGW **Rev:** Helmeted four-fold arms divide date and mintmaster's initials

Date	Mintage	VG	F	VF	XF	Unc
1649 HPK Rare	—	—	—	—	—	—
1649 Rare	—	—	—	—	—	—

KM# 204 4 DUCAT
14.0000 g., 0.9860 Gold 0.4438 oz. AGW **Obv:** St. George slaying dragon to left **Rev:** Date divided by helmet, four-fold arms divide mintmaster's initials

Date	Mintage	VG	F	VF	XF	Unc
1642 HPK Rare	—	—	—	—	—	—

KM# 213 4 DUCAT
14.0000 g., 0.9860 Gold 0.4438 oz. AGW **Rev:** Helmeted four-fold arms divide date and mintmaster's initials

Date	Mintage	VG	F	VF	XF	Unc
1649 HPK Rare	—	—	—	—	—	—

KM# 22 5 DUCAT (1/2 Portugaloser)
14.0000 g., 0.9860 Gold 0.4438 oz. AGW **Note:** Spruch 5 Ducat. Similar to 1 Thaler, KM#18.

Date	Mintage	VG	F	VF	XF	Unc
1608 GM Rare	—	—	—	—	—	—
1609 GM Rare	—	—	—	—	—	—

KM# 71 5 DUCAT (1/2 Portugaloser)
14.0000 g., 0.9860 Gold 0.4438 oz. AGW **Note:** Similar to 1 Thaler, KM#64.

Date	Mintage	VG	F	VF	XF	Unc
1617 AK Rare	—	—	—	—	—	—

KM# 226 5 DUCAT (1/2 Portugaloser)
14.0000 g., 0.9860 Gold 0.4438 oz. AGW **Note:** Similar to 1 Thaler, KM#222.

Date	Mintage	VG	F	VF	XF	Unc
1661 HPK Rare	—	—	—	—	—	—

KM# 12 10 DUCAT (Portugaloser)
35.0000 g., 0.9860 Gold 1.1095 oz. AGW **Obv:** St. George slaying dragon left **Obv. Legend:** ERNESTVS. FRI: CHRIST: E. DAVID. CO. MANSF: **Rev:** Crowned double eagle above crowned arms divide date and G-M

Date	Mintage	VG	F	VF	XF	Unc
1603 GM Rare	—	—	—	—	—	—

KM# 205 10 DUCAT (Portugaloser)
35.0000 g., 0.9860 Gold 1.1095 oz. AGW **Obv:** St. George slaying dragon at left **Rev:** Seven flags above arms divide date **Note:** Struck with 1 Thaler dies, KM#202.

Date	Mintage	VG	F	VF	XF	Unc
1642 HPK Rare	—	—	—	—	—	—

MANSFELD-EISLEBEN

This line resulted from the division of 1530/32. Upon the extinction of Eisleben in 1710, all lands and titles reverted to the Bornstedt line.

RULERS
Jobst II, 1596-1619
Johann Georg II, 1619-1647
Hoyer Christof II, 1647-1663
Johann Georg III, 1663-1710

COUNTSHIP

REGULAR COINAGE

KM# 21 3 FLITTER (1-1/2 Pfennig)
Copper **Obv:** Four-fold arms, L above **Rev:** III in center, FLITTER, date in legend **Mint:** Leimbach **Note:** Kipper 3 Flitter.

Date	Mintage	VG	F	VF	XF	Unc
16Z1 L	—	—	—	—	—	—

KM# 22 3 PFENNIG
Copper **Obv:** St. George right slaying dragon **Rev:** Imperial orb with 3 divides L-S **Mint:** Leimbach **Note:** Kipper 3 Pfennig.

Date	Mintage	VG	F	VF	XF	Unc
ND(1621/22) LS	—	27.00	55.00	100	200	—

KM# 24 3 PFENNIG
Copper **Obv:** Four-fold arms **Rev:** Imperial orb with 3 divides L-S **Note:** Varieties exist.

Date	Mintage	VG	F	VF	XF	Unc
ND(1621/22) LS	—	27.00	55.00	100	200	—

KM# 25 3 PFENNIG
Copper **Obv:** L above arms **Rev:** Date divided by orb
Note: Varieties exist.

Date	Mintage	VG	F	VF	XF	Unc
16Z1 L/LS	—	27.00	55.00	100	200	—
(16)Z1 L/LS	—	27.00	55.00	100	200	—

KM# 23 3 PFENNIG
Copper **Obv:** St. George right slaying dragon divides date
Rev: L-S divided above imperial orb with 3

Date	Mintage	VG	F	VF	XF	Unc
(16)Z1 LS	—	27.00	55.00	100	200	—
(16)ZZ LS	—	27.00	55.00	100	200	—

KM# 30 3 PFENNIG

Copper **Obv:** Date above arms

Date	Mintage	VG	F	VF	XF	Unc
(16)ZZ LS	—	27.00	55.00	100	200	—

KM# 32 3 PFENNIG

Copper **Obv:** Four-fold arms divide date, L above **Rev:** Imperial orb with 3 divides L-S

Date	Mintage	VG	F	VF	XF	Unc
(16)ZZ L/LS	—	27.00	55.00	100	200	—

KM# 31 3 PFENNIG

Copper **Rev:** Orb divides date and mint initials **Note:** Varieties exist.

Date	Mintage	VG	F	VF	XF	Unc
(16)ZZ LS	—	27.00	55.00	100	200	—

KM# 45 3 PFENNIG (Dreier)

Silver **Obv:** Ornamented oval four-fold arms divide date **Rev:** Small imperial orb with 3 divides mintmaster's initials in ornamented rhombus

Date	Mintage	VG	F	VF	XF	Unc
1634 HPK	—	16.00	33.00	65.00	135	—

KM# 75 3 PFENNIG (Dreier)

Silver **Obv:** Crowned four-fold arms, mintmaster's initials above **Rev:** Imperial orb with 3, date above

Date	Mintage	VG	F	VF	XF	Unc
1671 ABK	—	—	—	—	—	—

KM# 76 6 PFENNIG (Sechser)

Silver **Obv:** Imperial orb with 6 divides mintmaster's initials **Rev:** Crowned four-fold arms divide date **Note:** Varieties exist.

Date	Mintage	VG	F	VF	XF	Unc
1671 ABK	—	—	—	—	—	—

KM# 20 12 KREUZER (Schreckenburger)

Silver **Obv:** Crowned imperial eagle, 12 in orb on breast, titles of Ferdinand II **Rev:** Four-fold arms divide date, angel above **Note:** Kipper 12 Kreuzer.

Date	Mintage	VG	F	VF	XF	Unc
(16)20	—	40.00	70.00	120	200	—

KM# 26 12 KREUZER (Schreckenburger)

Silver **Obv:** Ornamented 4-fold arms, date in legend **Rev:** Crowned imperial eagle, 12 in orb on breast, (NA) at bottom in legend **Mint:** Neu-Asseburg **Note:** Varieties exist.

Date	Mintage	VG	F	VF	XF	Unc
16Z1 NA	—	40.00	70.00	120	200	—

KM# 27 12 KREUZER (Schreckenburger)

Silver **Obv:** 2 ornate helmets above oval with L, date in legend **Rev:** Crowned imperial eagle, 1Z in orb on breast, titles of Johann Georg II **Mint:** Leimbach

Date	Mintage	VG	F	VF	XF	Unc
16Z1 L	—	40.00	70.00	120	200	—

KM# 28 1/24 THALER (Groschen)

Silver **Obv:** St. George right slaying dragon **Rev:** Four-fold arms, value Z4 below, date in legend

Date	Mintage	VG	F	VF	XF	Unc
1621	—	—	—	—	—	—

KM# 29 1/24 THALER (Groschen)

Silver **Obv:** Crowned four-fold arms **Rev:** Imperial orb with 24

Date	Mintage	VG	F	VF	XF	Unc
ND(1621/22)	—	16.00	33.00	60.00	110	—

KM# 39 1/24 THALER (Groschen)

Silver **Obv:** Four-fold arms divide mintmaster's initials, date above **Rev:** Imperial orb with 24 **Note:** Varieties exist.

Date	Mintage	VG	F	VF	XF	Unc
1630	—	20.00	40.00	80.00	125	—
163Z AK	—	20.00	40.00	80.00	125	—
1633 HPK	—	20.00	40.00	80.00	125	—
1634 HPK	—	20.00	40.00	80.00	125	—
1635 HPK	—	20.00	40.00	80.00	125	—
1636 HPK	—	20.00	40.00	80.00	125	—
1644 HPK	—	20.00	40.00	80.00	125	—

KM# 40 1/24 THALER (Groschen)

Silver **Obv:** Mintmaster's initials above arms **Rev:** Date divided at top **Note:** Varieties exist.

Date	Mintage	VG	F	VF	XF	Unc
1623 HPK Error for 1632	—	—	—	—	—	—
163Z HPK	—	20.00	40.00	80.00	125	—
1636 HPK	—	20.00	40.00	80.00	125	—
1637 HPK	—	20.00	40.00	80.00	125	—
1638 HPK	—	20.00	40.00	80.00	125	—
1639 HPK	—	20.00	40.00	80.00	125	—
1640 HPK	—	20.00	40.00	80.00	125	—
1640	—	20.00	40.00	80.00	125	—
1641 HPK	—	20.00	40.00	80.00	125	—
1642 HPK	—	20.00	40.00	80.00	125	—
ND HPK	—	20.00	40.00	80.00	125	—

KM# 44 1/24 THALER (Groschen)

Silver **Rev:** Date divided by imperial orb **Note:** Varieties exist.

Date	Mintage	VG	F	VF	XF	Unc
1636 HPK	—	20.00	40.00	80.00	125	—
1637 HPK	—	20.00	40.00	80.00	125	—
1640 HPK	—	20.00	40.00	80.00	125	—
1645 HPK	—	20.00	40.00	80.00	125	—

KM# 50 1/24 THALER (Groschen)

Silver **Obv:** Mintmaster's initials divided by arms **Note:** Varieties exist.

Date	Mintage	VG	F	VF	XF	Unc
1641 HPK	—	20.00	40.00	80.00	125	—
1645 HPK	—	20.00	40.00	80.00	125	—
1646 HPK	—	20.00	40.00	80.00	125	—
1647 HPK	—	20.00	40.00	80.00	125	—

KM# 51 1/24 THALER (Groschen)

Silver **Subject:** Death of Johann Georg II **Obv:** Eight-line inscription with dates **Rev:** Imperial orb with 24 **Rev. Legend:** DENNOCH **Note:** Varieties exist.

Date	Mintage	VG	F	VF	XF	Unc
1647	—	—	—	—	—	—

KM# 55 1/24 THALER (Groschen)

Silver **Obv:** Four-fold arms divide mintmaster's initials **Rev:** Imperial orb with 24 divides date **Note:** Varieties exist.

Date	Mintage	VG	F	VF	XF	Unc
1648 HPK	—	16.00	33.00	60.00	100	—
1652 HPK	—	16.00	33.00	60.00	100	—
1657 HPK	—	16.00	33.00	60.00	100	—
ND HPK	—	16.00	33.00	60.00	100	—

KM# 65 1/24 THALER (Groschen)

Silver **Obv:** Imperial orb with 24 divides date and mintmaster's initials **Rev:** Crowned four-fold arms **Note:** Varieties exist.

Date	Mintage	VG	F	VF	XF	Unc
1668 ABK	—	16.00	33.00	60.00	100	—
1669 ABK	—	16.00	33.00	60.00	100	—
1670 ABK	—	16.00	33.00	60.00	100	—

KM# 66 1/6 THALER

Silver **Note:** Similar to 1/3 Thaler, KM#67 but value (1/6) below St. George. Varieties exist.

Date	Mintage	VG	F	VF	XF	Unc
1668 ABK	—	45.00	85.00	165	325	—
1669 ABK	—	45.00	85.00	165	325	—

KM# 68 1/6 THALER

Silver **Rev:** Mintmaster's initials below arms

Date	Mintage	VG	F	VF	XF	Unc
1669 ABK	—	45.00	85.00	165	325	—

KM# 11 1/4 THALER

Silver **Note:** Klippe.

Date	Mintage	VG	F	VF	XF	Unc
1619 HI	—	—	—	—	—	—

KM# 10 1/4 THALER

Silver **Subject:** Death of Jobst II **Obv:** Crowned four-fold arms divide date and mintmaster's initials **Rev:** Eight-line inscription with dates **Note:** Varieties exist.

Date	Mintage	VG	F	VF	XF	Unc
1619 HI	—	—	—	—	—	—

KM# 41 1/4 THALER

Silver **Obv:** St. George right slaying dragon **Rev:** Ornate four-fold arms divide date, mintmaster's initials between two helmets above **Note:** Varieties exist.

Date	Mintage	VG	F	VF	XF	Unc
1632 HPK	—	—	—	—	—	—
1634 HPK	—	—	—	—	—	—

KM# 52 1/4 THALER

Silver **Subject:** Death of Johann Georg II **Obv:** Eight-line inscription with dates **Rev:** St. George right slaying dragon **Note:** Varieties exist.

Date	Mintage	VG	F	VF	XF	Unc
1647	—	—	—	—	—	—

KM# 60 1/4 THALER

Silver **Obv:** St. George right slaying dragon **Rev:** Ornate four-fold arms, date and mintmaster's initials in legend **Note:** Spruch 1/4 Thaler.

Date	Mintage	VG	F	VF	XF	Unc
1667 ABK	—	80.00	140	225	375	—

KM# 67 1/3 THALER (1/2 Gulden)

Silver **Note:** Varieties exist.

Date	Mintage	VG	F	VF	XF	Unc
1668 ABK	—	45.00	80.00	140	225	—
1669 ABK	—	45.00	80.00	140	225	—
1670 ABK	—	45.00	80.00	140	225	—
1671 ABK	—	45.00	80.00	140	225	—
1672 ABK	—	45.00	80.00	140	225	—
1673 ABK	—	45.00	80.00	140	225	—

KM# 69 1/3 THALER (1/2 Gulden)

Silver **Rev:** Mintmaster's initials divided below arms

Date	Mintage	VG	F	VF	XF	Unc
1669 ABK	—	45.00	80.00	140	225	—

KM# 12 1/2 THALER

Silver **Subject:** Death of Jobst II **Obv:** St. George left slaying dragon **Rev:** Eight-line inscription with dates

Date	Mintage	VG	F	VF	XF	Unc
1619 HI	—	85.00	140	200	300	—

KM# 13 1/2 THALER

Silver **Obv:** Crowned four-fold arms divide date and mintmaster's initials

Date	Mintage	VG	F	VF	XF	Unc
1619 HI	—	85.00	140	200	300	—

KM# 42 1/2 THALER

Silver **Obv:** St. George right slaying dragon **Rev:** Ornate four-fold arms with date between helmets, mintmaster's initials divided by arms **Note:** Varieties exist.

Date	Mintage	VG	F	VF	XF	Unc
1634 HPK	—	—	—	—	—	—

KM# 53 1/2 THALER

Silver **Subject:** Death of Johann George II **Obv:** Eight-line inscription with dates **Rev:** St. George right slaying dragon **Note:** Varieties exist.

Date	Mintage	VG	F	VF	XF	Unc
1647	—	—	—	—	—	—

KM# 5 THALER

Silver **Obv:** St. George slaying the dragon **Rev:** Helmeted arms **Note:** Dav. #6932.

Date	Mintage	VG	F	VF	XF	Unc
1603 GM	—	75.00	190	265	400	—
1604 GM	—	75.00	190	265	400	—
1605 GM	—	75.00	190	265	400	—
1606 GM	—	75.00	190	265	400	—
1607 GM	—	75.00	190	265	400	—
1608 GM	—	75.00	190	265	400	—
1609 GM	—	75.00	190	265	400	—
1610 GM	—	75.00	190	265	400	—
1611 GM	—	75.00	190	265	400	—

KM# 6 THALER

Silver **Rev. Legend:** COM: E: DOMI: IN: MANSFE: NOB: **Note:** Dav. #6933.

Date	Mintage	VG	F	VF	XF	Unc
1608 GM	—	90.00	220	300	450	—

KM# 14 THALER
Silver **Subject:** Death of Jobst II **Obv:** St. George left with dragon **Rev:** Eight-line inscription **Note:** Dav. #6935.

Date	Mintage	VG	F	VF	XF	Unc
1619 HI	—	120	250	500	1,250	—

KM# 15 THALER
Silver **Note:** Klippe. Dav. #6935A.

Date	Mintage	VG	F	VF	XF	Unc
1619 HI Rare	—	—	—	—	—	—

KM# 34 THALER
Silver **Ruler:** Johann Georg II **Obv:** St. George right with dragon **Rev:** Helmeted arms with date and A-K between helmets **Note:** Dav. #6936.

Date	Mintage	VG	F	VF	XF	Unc
16Z9 AK	—	85.00	205	290	425	—

KM# 43 THALER
Silver **Obv. Legend:** HP-K below arms **Rev. Legend:** MANSF: NO. DOM: IN. HELDRVNG: SE: ET. SC: **Note:** Dav. #6937.

Date	Mintage	VG	F	VF	XF	Unc
1634 HPK	—	85.00	205	290	425	—

KM# 54 THALER
Silver **Subject:** Death of Johann George II **Note:** Dav. #6938.

Date	Mintage	VG	F	VF	XF	Unc
1647	—	120	250	550	1,250	—

KM# 61 THALER
Silver **Obv:** St. George and dragon right **Obv. Legend:** IOAN. GEOR. COMES. I. MANSF. NOB. DYNASTA... **Rev:** Helmeted arms, legend, date, ABK **Rev. Legend:** FORTITER. ET CONSTANTER. **Note:** Dav. #6940.

Date	Mintage	VG	F	VF	XF	Unc
1667 ABK	—	85.00	205	290	425	—

KM# 62 THALER
Silver **Rev:** AB-K by helmets, date divided below **Note:** Dav. #6941.

Date	Mintage	VG	F	VF	XF	Unc
1667 ABK	—	85.00	205	290	425	—

KM# 63 THALER
Silver **Rev. Legend:** NOB: DOM: IN: HELDRUNGEN. SEB. E. SR: **Note:** Dav. #6942.

Date	Mintage	VG	F	VF	XF	Unc
1667 abk	—	85.00	205	290	425	—

KM# 70 THALER
Silver **Obv. Legend:** ...GEORG... **Rev:** Date between helnets, AB-K below arms **Note:** Dav. #6944.

Date	Mintage	VG	F	VF	XF	Unc
1669 ABK	—	75.00	190	265	400	—
1671 ABK	—	75.00	190	265	400	—

KM# 35 2 THALER
Silver **Note:** Similar to 1 Thaler KM#14. Dav. #6934.

Date	Mintage	VG	F	VF	XF	Unc
1619 HI Rare	—	—	—	—	—	—

KM# 64 2 THALER
Silver **Obv:** St. George right and dragon **Obv. Legend:** IOAN. GEOR. COMES. I MANSF. NOB. DYNASTA... **Rev:** Helmeted arms, legend, date, ABK **Rev. Legend:** FORTITER. ET. CONSTANTER. **Note:** Dav. #6939.

Date	Mintage	VG	F	VF	XF	Unc
1667 ABK	—	600	1,050	1,800	3,000	—

KM# 77 2 THALER
Silver **Obv. Legend:** ...GEORG... **Rev:** Date between helmets, AB-K below arms **Note:** Dav. #6943.

Date	Mintage	VG	F	VF	XF	Unc
1671 ABK	—	600	1,050	1,800	3,000	—

TRADE COINAGE

KM# 46 GOLDGULDEN
3.5000 g., 0.9860 Gold 0.1109 oz. AGW

Date	Mintage	VG	F	VF	XF	Unc
1632	—	240	425	850	1,750	—
1635	—	240	425	850	1,750	—
1636	—	240	425	850	1,750	—
1637	—	240	425	850	1,750	—

MANSFELD-FRIEDEBURG

Founded in the division of 1530/32 and became extinct in 1604. Titles passed to Bornstedt.

RULERS
Peter Ernst I, 1532-1604
Peter Ernst IV, 1580-1626
Gebhard VIII von Arnstein, 1586-1601

JOINT COINAGE
I - Peter Ernst I, Bruno II, Gebhard VIII and Johann Georg IV
II - Peter Ernst I, Bruno II, Wilhelm I and Johann Georg IV

REFERENCE
T = Otto Tornau, **Münzwesen und Münzen der Grafschaft Mansfeld**, Prague, 1937.

COUNTSHIP

JOINT COINAGE

KM# 10 1/4 THALER
Silver **Obv:** 4-fold arms, two helmets above divided by date and mintmaster's initials **Rev:** St. George right slaying dragon **Note:** Varieties exist.

Date	Mintage	VG	F	VF	XF	Unc
160Z GM	—	80.00	140	220	325	—
(1)603 GM	—	80.00	140	220	325	—

KM# 12 1/2 THALER
Silver **Note:** Broad flan. Similar to 1 thaler, KM#9. Varieties exist.

Date	Mintage	VG	F	VF	XF	Unc
160Z GM	—	65.00	120	220	325	—

KM# 11 1/2 THALER
Silver **Obv:** 4-fold arms, two helmets above divided by date and mintmaster's initials **Rev:** St. George right slaying dragon **Note:** Varieties exist.

Date	Mintage	VG	F	VF	XF	Unc
160Z GM	—	65.00	120	220	325	—
(1)603 GM	—	65.00	120	220	325	—
(1)604 GM	—	65.00	120	220	325	—
1604 GM	—	65.00	120	220	325	—

KM# 7 THALER
Silver **Obv:** Helmeted arms **Obv. Legend:** PETER. ERN: BRVNO: GE: HA: GE: P: **Rev:** St. George right with dragon **Note:** Dav. #6945.

Date	Mintage	VG	F	VF	XF	Unc
1601 GM	—	95.00	230	325	475	—

KM# 9 THALER
Silver **Obv. Legend:** PETER. ERN: BRVNO: WILH: HA: GE: P: **Note:** Dav. #6947.

Date	Mintage	VG	F	VF	XF	Unc
1601 GM	—	75.00	190	265	425	900
160Z GM	—	75.00	190	265	425	900
1603 GM	—	75.00	190	265	425	900
1604 GM	—	75.00	190	265	425	900

KM# 13 4 THALER
Silver **Note:** Similar to 1 Thaler, KM#9. Dav. #6946.

Date	Mintage	VG	F	VF	XF	Unc
160Z GM Rare	—	—	—	—	—	—

TRADE COINAGE

KM# 14 GOLDGULDEN
3.5000 g., 0.9860 Gold 0.1109 oz. AGW **Obv:** Three shields as trilobe, date divided at bottom **Rev:** St. George and dragon in inner circle

Date	Mintage	VG	F	VF	XF	Unc
1603	—	240	475	950	1,800	—

MANSFELD-SCHRAPLAU

This branch was founded on the division of 1486. It became extinct in 1602 and its lands passed to Eigentliche-Hinterort.

RULER
Heinrich II, 1591-1602

REFERENCE
T = Otto Tornau, **Münzwesen und Münzen der Grafschaft Mansfeld**, Prague, 1937.

COUNTSHIP

REGULAR COINAGE

KM# 8 1/4 THALER
Silver **Obv:** Helmeted four-fold arms divide date **Rev:** St. George left slaying dragon

Date	Mintage	VG	F	VF	XF	Unc
160Z GM	—	—	—	—	—	—

Note: Reported, not confirmed

KM# 5 1/2 THALER
Silver **Obv:** Helmeted four-fold arms divide date **Rev:** St. George left slaying dragon **Note:** Broad flan. Spruch 1/2 Thaler.

Date	Mintage	VG	F	VF	XF	Unc
1601 GM	—	60.00	130	200	325	—

KM# 9 1/2 THALER
Silver **Note:** Normal flan.

Date	Mintage	VG	F	VF	XF	Unc
160Z GM	—	60.00	130	200	325	—

KM# 6 THALER
Silver **Obv:** Helmeted arms **Rev:** St. George and dragon **Note:** Dav. #6972.

Date	Mintage	VG	F	VF	XF	Unc
1601 GM	—	125	325	450	650	—
1602 GM	—	125	325	450	650	—

KM# 7 2 THALER
Silver **Obv:** Helmeted arms **Rev:** St. George and dragon **Note:** Dav. #6971.

Date	Mintage	VG	F	VF	XF	Unc
1601 GM	—	1,000	1,750	3,000	5,000	—

MARK

The county of Mark was established in the early 13th century in Westphalia, with the capital located in the town of Hamm. Through marriages during the 14th century, Mark inherited the counties of Berg and Cleves. By the late 15th century, those three counties were united with those of Jülich and Ravensberg and all five figured in the succession controversy stemming from the extinction of the ruling line in 1609. Mark, along with Cleves and Ravensberg, went to Brandenburg (Prussia) in 1624. Several decades later, the electors of Brandenburg struck a special local coinage for Mark.

RULERS
Johann Wilhelm, 1592-1609
Georg Wilhelm, 1619-1640
Friedrich Wilhelm, 1640-1688

ARMS
Horizontal bar of checkerboard design

COUNTSHIP

REGULAR COINAGE

KM# 9 6 PFENNIG (1/104 Thaler)
Billon **Obv:** Crowned 4-fold arms of Mark and Cleves **Obv. Legend:** MONET MARCANA **Rev. Inscription:** VI / PFEN / NING / date **Mint:** Lunen **Note:** Varieties exist.

Date	Mintage	VG	F	VF	XF	Unc
1660	15,000	65.00	135	225	500	—
1663	—	65.00	135	225	500	—

KM# 6 SCHILLING (1/52 Thaler)
Silver **Obv:** Crowned 4-fold arms of Mark nad Cleves, titiles of Friedrich Wilhelm **Obv. Legend:** MONET MARCANA **Rev:** Inscription, legend, date **Rev. Legend:** MON NOV CIV LUNENSIS **Rev. Inscription:** I / SCHIL / LING / MM (Moneta Marcena), **Note:** Varieties exist.

Date	Mintage	VG	F	VF	XF	Unc
1659	7,600	40.00	80.00	140	300	—

KM# 7 SCHILLING (1/52 Thaler)
Silver **Rev:** Inscription, legend, date **Rev. Legend:** MON NOV MARCANA **Rev. Inscription:** 1 / SCHIL / LING / 52, **Mint:** Lunen **Note:** Varieties exist.

Date	Mintage	VG	F	VF	XF	Unc
1659	Inc. above	27.00	55.00	95.00	200	—
1660	44,000	27.00	55.00	95.00	200	—

KM# 8 2 SCHILLING (1/16 Thaler)
Silver **Obv:** Bust right, value (16) above, titles of Friedrich Wilhelm **Rev:** Brandenburg eagle, scepter arms on breast, arms of Cleves and Mark on wings, legend, date **Rev. Legend:** MONETA NOVA MARCANA **Mint:** Lunen **Note:** Varieties exist.

Date	Mintage	VG	F	VF	XF	Unc
1659	4,700	200	400	650	1,500	—
1660	10,000	135	265	475	1,000	—

KM# 3 20 SCHILLING
Silver **Obv:** Crowned 9-fold arms in baroque frame **Obv. Legend:** IN DEO SPES ET SALUS MEA **Rev:** Crowned imperial eagle, orb on breast **Rev. Legend:** NVMMVS ARG CO MAR VIG SOLID **Mint:** Huissen **Note:** Prev. Brandenburg-Prussia KM #5.

Date	Mintage	VG	F	VF	XF	Unc
ND(ca.1620's)	—	2,000	4,000	6,500	—	—

KM# 5 THALER
Silver **Ruler:** Friedrich Wilhelm **Obv:** 3/4 facing bust **Rev:** Eagle with three shields on breast and wings, crown above divided date **Mint:** Lunen **Note:** Dav. #6189. Prev. Brandenburg-Prussia KM #291.

Date	Mintage	VG	F	VF	XF	Unc
1657 Rare	—	—	—	—	—	—

KM# 10 THALER
Silver **Ruler:** Friedrich Wilhelm **Obv:** Bust right in circle **Rev:** Eagle with three arms on breast and wings, date divided by legend **Mint:** Lunen **Note:** Dav. #6190. Prev. Brandenburg-Prussia KM #316.

Date	Mintage	VG	F	VF	XF	Unc
1660 MM Rare	—	—	—	—	—	—

TRADE COINAGE

KM# 8A DUCAT
3.5000 g., 0.9860 Gold 0.1109 oz. AGW **Ruler:** Friedrich Wilhelm **Obv:** Facing bust of Friedrich Wilhelm in inner circle **Rev:** Capped four-fold arms **Mint:** Lunen **Note:** Prev. Brandenburg-Prussia KM #306.

Date	Mintage	VG	F	VF	XF	Unc
1659 MM	—	1,300	3,350	5,800	9,000	—

KM# 11 DUCAT
3.5000 g., 0.9860 Gold 0.1109 oz. AGW **Ruler:** Friedrich Wilhelm **Obv:** Bust of Friedrich Wilhelm right in inner circle **Rev:** Capped arms divide date in inner circle **Mint:** Lunen **Note:** Prev. Brandenburg-Prussia KM #317.

Date	Mintage	VG	F	VF	XF	Unc
1660	—	600	1,550	2,750	4,200	—
1662	—	600	1,550	2,750	4,200	—

KM# 12 DUCAT
3.5000 g., 0.9860 Gold 0.1109 oz. AGW **Ruler:** Friedrich Wilhelm **Obv:** Facing bust of Friedrich Wilhelm in inner circle **Rev:** Capped arms in inner circle, date in legend **Mint:** Lunen **Note:** Prev. Brandenburg-Prussia KM #334.

Date	Mintage	VG	F	VF	XF	Unc
1664	—	600	1,000	2,500	3,600	—

MARSBERG

A town in Westphalia, which is located on the Diemel River west of Warburg. Its origins are obscure, but Marsberg had a mint in the 13th century. During the first half of the 17th century, Marsberg had a local coinage, some issues being struck in the name of the archbishop/elector of Cologne. The town was included in the Kingdom of Westphalia from 1807 to 1813 and passed to Prussia in 1815.

RULERS
Ernst von Bayern, 1583-1612
Ferdinand von Bayern, 1612-1650

MINT OFFICIALS' INITIALS

Initial	Date	Name
VFH	1630	Urban Felgenhauer
(a)= [mark]	1601-18	Jacob Pfahler

TOWN

REGULAR COINAGE

KM# 21 PFENNIG
0.8000 g., Copper **Obv:** I in circle **Obv. Legend:** FERDINAN ELECT **Rev:** A and upright key in center, small shield above with cross of Cologne divides date **Rev. Legend:** MARSPERG

Date	Mintage	VG	F	VF	XF	Unc
1638	—	20.00	45.00	90.00	150	—

KM# 22 PFENNIG
0.8000 g., Copper **Rev:** Date undivided in legend

Date	Mintage	VG	F	VF	XF	Unc
1638	—	20.00	45.00	90.00	150	—

KM# 23 PFENNIG
0.2400 g., Silver **Obv:** Upright key, two-towered city gate behind **Rev:** Large A, four rosettes around

Date	Mintage	VG	F	VF	XF	Unc
ND	—	—	—	—	—	—

KM# 7 3 PFENNIG (Dreier)
Silver **Obv:** City gate with two towers, A and upright key in entrance, Cologne cross above **Rev:** Imperial orb with 3 divides date, all within trefoil **Note:** Varieties exist. Weight varies: 0.7-0.8 grams.

Date	Mintage	VG	F	VF	XF	Unc
1606 (a)	—	—	—	—	—	—

KM# 11 3 PFENNIG (Dreier)
Silver **Obv:** Three shields of amrs, one above two, date divided by one above **Rev:** Without date **Note:** Varieties exist.

Date	Mintage	VG	F	VF	XF	Unc
1609 (a)	—	—	—	—	—	—

KM# 15 3 PFENNIG (Dreier)
Silver **Rev:** Date divided by orb

Date	Mintage	VG	F	VF	XF	Unc
1614	—	—	—	—	—	—

KM# 20 SCHILLING (1/28 Thaler)
2.5200 g., Silver **Obv:** Large A and upright key in front of two-towered city gate, date scattered about design, mintmaster's monogram **Obv. Legend:** MONETA NOV CI MONT MARTIS **Rev:** Crowned imperial eagle, Z8 in orb on breast, titles of Ferdinand II

Date	Mintage	VG	F	VF	XF	Unc
1630 VFH	—	—	—	—	—	—

KM# 12 1/28 THALER (Groschen)
1.4000 g., Silver **Obv:** Three shields of arms, one above two **Rev:** Imperial orb with Z8, titles of Rudolf II, date divided by cross at top

Date	Mintage	VG	F	VF	XF	Unc
1609 (a)	—	225	375	600	—	—

KM# 5 1/24 THALER (Groschen)
Silver **Obv:** Three shields of arms, one above two **Rev:** Imperial orb with Z4, titles of Rudolf II, date divided by cross at top **Note:** Varieties exist. Weight varies: 1.5-1.7 grams.

Date	Mintage	VG	F	VF	XF	Unc
1601 (a)	—	33.00	60.00	120	170	—
1606 (a)	—	33.00	60.00	120	170	—
1606	—	33.00	60.00	120	170	—
1607	—	33.00	60.00	120	170	—
1608 (a)	—	33.00	60.00	120	170	—
1609 (a)	—	33.00	60.00	120	170	—
1610 (a)	—	33.00	60.00	120	170	—
1611 (a)	—	33.00	60.00	120	170	—

KM# 6 1/24 THALER (Groschen)
Silver **Obv:** A and upright key in two-towered city gate, small shield above with cross of Cologne **Rev:** Date divided by upper part of orb **Note:** Varieties exist.

Date	Mintage	VG	F	VF	XF	Unc
1605	—	35.00	100	180	275	—
1606	—	35.00	100	180	275	—
1607	—	35.00	100	180	275	—

KM# 8 1/24 THALER (Groschen)
Silver **Rev:** Value in orb 24, date divided by cross at top

Date	Mintage	VG	F	VF	XF	Unc
1606	—	55.00	100	180	275	—

KM# 9 1/24 THALER (Groschen)
Silver **Rev:** Date undivided in legend

Date	Mintage	VG	F	VF	XF	Unc
1608 (a)	—	55.00	100	180	275	—

KM# 10 1/24 THALER (Groschen)
Silver **Rev:** Value erroneously 4Z in orb

Date	Mintage	VG	F	VF	XF	Unc
1608 (a)	—	55.00	100	180	275	—

KM# 16 1/24 THALER (Groschen)
Silver **Obv:** Shield with A and upright key superimposed on cross **Rev:** 4Z in orb, titles of Matthias **Note:** Varieties exist.

Date	Mintage	VG	F	VF	XF	Unc
1614	—	60.00	120	200	300	—
1615	—	60.00	120	200	300	—

KM# 17 1/24 THALER (Groschen)
Silver **Obv:** A and upright key in two-towered city gate, small shield above, date divided by cross at top **Rev:** Titles of Matthias **Note:** Varieties exist.

Date	Mintage	VG	F	VF	XF	Unc
1616	—	60.00	120	210	320	—
1617	—	60.00	115	200	300	—

MECKLENBURG-GUSTROW

The shortest in duration of the Mecklenburg divisions was founded in 1610 by Johann Albrecht II, son of Johann VII of Mechlenburg-Schwerin. His son, Gustav Adolf was the last of the line when he died in 1695. Mecklenburg-Strelitz was the claimant thereafter.

RULERS

Ulrich III, regent, 1555-1603
Karl I, 1603-1610
Johann Albrecht II, 1611-1636
Gustav Adolph, 1636-1695

MINT OFFICIALS' PRIVY MARKS

Boizenburg Mint

Mark	Date	Name
(a)=	1608-09	Simon Ludermann
(b)=	1615-18	Joachim Konecke
(c)=crowned heart	1618	Samuel Nebeltau

Gadebusch Mint

Mark	Date	Name
(d)=acorn	1605-08	Nicolaus Isebein

Gluckstadt Mint

Mark	Date	Name
HH	1692-93	Christoph Woldtrecht

Groien Mint

Mark	Date	Name
	1615-18	Lorentz Leiser
(e)=crowned heart	1618	Samuel Nebeltau
(f) front half of unicorn left	1621-22	Nicolaus Netzebrandt
(g)= hand to right	1622-24	Heinrich Hantschen
(h)=	1632-35	Hans Puls

Gustrow Mint

Mark	Date	Name
	1668	Daniel Syvertz
(l)= lion left	1670-73	Hans Memmies der Altere
(ii)= lion left and/or IM	1673-83	Johann (Hans) Memmies der Jüngere

Marienehe Mint

Mark	Date	Name
(j)=acorn	1601-05	Nicolaus Isebein

Rostock Mint

Mark	Date	Name
(k)= lion left and/or IM	1686-95	Johann (Hans) Memmies der Jüngere

Schwaan Mint

Mark	Date	Name
HIH or HH	1692-93	Heinrich Johann Hille

Wismar Mint

Mark	Date	Name
	1666, 1668	Henning Stor

DUCHY

REGULAR COINAGE

KM# 35 PFENNIG

Copper **Obv:** Facing steer's head, titles of Johann Albrecht II **Rev. Inscription:** 1/PFEN/NING/date **Mint:** Groien

Date	Mintage	Good	VG	F	VF	XF
16Z1	—	9.00	22.00	33.00	65.00	—

KM# 36 2 PFENNIG

Copper **Rev:** Similar to 3 Pfennig, KM#37 but value II on reverse. **Mint:** Groien **Note:** Varieties exist.

Date	Mintage	Good	VG	F	VF	XF
1621	—	11.00	27.00	45.00	80.00	—
16Z1	—	11.00	27.00	45.00	80.00	—

KM# 37 3 PFENNIG

Copper **Rev:** Value III **Mint:** Groien

Date	Mintage	Good	VG	F	VF	XF
16Z1	—	11.00	27.00	45.00	80.00	—
16ZZ	—	11.00	27.00	45.00	80.00	—

KM# 94 3 PFENNIG

Copper **Obv:** GA monogram in laurel wreath **Rev:** III/date **Rev. Legend:** LANDWITT **Mint:** Gustrow **Note:** Varieties exist.

Date	Mintage	Good	VG	F	VF	XF
1674	—	8.00	13.00	25.00	45.00	—
1675	—	8.00	13.00	25.00	45.00	—
1676	—	8.00	13.00	25.00	45.00	—
1677	—	8.00	13.00	25.00	45.00	—
1678	—	8.00	13.00	25.00	45.00	—
1679	—	8.00	13.00	25.00	45.00	—
ND	—	8.00	13.00	25.00	45.00	—

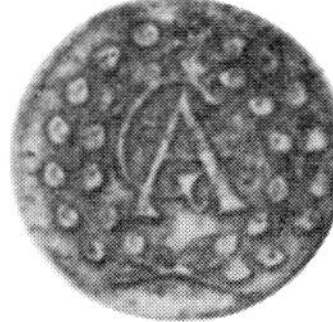

KM# 109 3 PFENNIG

Copper **Mint:** Rostock **Note:** Varieties exist.

Date	Mintage	Good	VG	F	VF	XF
1688	29,000	5.00	13.00	24.00	45.00	—
1690	27,000	5.00	13.00	24.00	45.00	—
1692	211,000	5.00	13.00	24.00	45.00	—
1692 (k)	149,000	5.00	13.00	24.00	45.00	—

KM# 45 SECHSLING (6 Pfennig)

Silver **Obv:** Similar to 3 Pfennig, KM#37 **Rev:** Inscription divided by mint symbol **Rev. Inscription:** I / SOSLI / MECHE / LNVB / date

Date	Mintage	VG	F	VF	XF	Unc
16ZZ (g)	—	13.00	35.00	55.00	100	—
16Z4 (g)	—	13.00	35.00	55.00	100	—

KM# 46 SECHSLING (6 Pfennig)

Silver **Rev:** 1/SOSLI/NG MEC/HELN/date divided by mint symbol

Date	Mintage	VG	F	VF	XF	Unc
16ZZ (g)	—	13.00	35.00	55.00	100	—

KM# 120 SECHSLING (6 Pfennig)

Billon **Obv:** Crowned GA monogram, legend, and date **Obv. Legend:** ANNO **Rev:** Imperial orb with 6 **Mint:** Rostock

Date	Mintage	VG	F	VF	XF	Unc
1692	124,000	11.00	22.00	40.00	80.00	—

KM# 38 SCHILLING

Silver **Obv:** Similar to 3 Pfennig, KM#37 **Rev. Inscription:** 1 SCHIL / LING / date **Mint:** Groien **Note:** Varieties exist.

Date	Mintage	VG	F	VF	XF	Unc
1621	—	16.00	40.00	70.00	120	—
16Z1	—	16.00	40.00	70.00	120	—

KM# 47 SCHILLING

Silver **Obv:** Five-fold arms, titles of Johann Albrecht **Rev:** Inscription, date divided by mint symbol. **Rev. Inscription:** I/SCHIL/LING ME/CHELN/BVRG/(date). **Note:** Varieties exist.

Date	Mintage	VG	F	VF	XF	Unc
16ZZ (g)	—	13.00	33.00	60.00	100	—
16Z3/Z (g)	—	13.00	33.00	60.00	100	—
16Z3 (g)	—	13.00	33.00	60.00	100	—
16Z4/3 (g)	—	13.00	33.00	60.00	100	—
16Z4 (g)	—	13.00	33.00	60.00	100	—

KM# 5 2 SCHILLING (Doppelschilling)

Silver **Obv:** Ornate four-fold arms with central shield, legend, mintmaster's symbol **Obv. Legend:** Z - CH - M **Rev:** Intertwined DS in shield, imperial orb above, date. below

Date	Mintage	VG	F	VF	XF	Unc
(1)603 (j)	17,000	40.00	85.00	140	225	—
(1)604 (j)	24,000	40.00	85.00	140	225	—

KM# 6 2 SCHILLING (Doppelschilling)

Silver **Rev:** Date around shield **Note:** Varieties exist.

Date	Mintage	VG	F	VF	XF	Unc
1604 (j)	Inc. above	27.00	65.00	120	200	—
1605 (j)	3,109	27.00	65.00	120	200	—
1606 (d)	8,280	27.00	65.00	120	200	—
1607 (d)	5,909	27.00	65.00	120	200	—
1608 (d)	9,348	27.00	65.00	120	200	—
1608 (a)	13,000	27.00	65.00	120	200	—
1609 (a)	58,000	27.00	65.00	120	200	—

KM# 20 2 SCHILLING (Doppelschilling)

Silver **Obv:** Similar to KM#5 but date in place of four letters in legend **Note:** Varieties exist.

Date	Mintage	VG	F	VF	XF	Unc
1614	—	24.00	45.00	80.00	125	—
1615 (b)	131,000	24.00	45.00	80.00	125	—
1615	139,000	24.00	45.00	80.00	125	—
1616 (b)	—	24.00	45.00	80.00	125	—
1616	120,000	24.00	45.00	80.00	125	—
1617 (b)	218,000	24.00	45.00	80.00	125	—
1617	273,000	24.00	45.00	80.00	125	—
1618	—	24.00	45.00	80.00	125	—
ND (b)	—	24.00	45.00	80.00	125	—

KM# 27 2 SCHILLING (Doppelschilling)

Silver **Rev:** Date in legend **Note:** Varieties exist.

Date	Mintage	VG	F	VF	XF	Unc
1617	—	24.00	45.00	80.00	125	—
1618	—	24.00	45.00	80.00	125	—
ND	—	24.00	45.00	80.00	125	—

KM# 29 2 SCHILLING (Doppelschilling)

Silver **Obv:** KM#13 **Rev:** KM#15 **Note:** Mule.

Date	Mintage	VG	F	VF	XF	Unc
1617/1618	—	—	—	—	—	—

KM# 28 2 SCHILLING (Doppelschilling)

Silver **Rev:** Date only in legend **Note:** Varieties exist.

Date	Mintage	VG	F	VF	XF	Unc
1618	—	24.00	45.00	80.00	125	—
1618 (c)	—	24.00	45.00	80.00	125	—

KM# 22 4 SCHILLING

Silver **Obv:** Crowned four-fold arms with central shield divide date, titles of Johann Albrecht II **Rev:** Crowned imperial eagle, titles of Matthias **Note:** Kipper 4 Schilling. Varieties exist.

Date	Mintage	VG	F	VF	XF	Unc
1616 (b)	26,000	35.00	60.00	120	200	—
ND (b)	—	35.00	60.00	120	200	—
ND	—	35.00	60.00	120	200	—

KM# 23 4 SCHILLING

Silver **Rev:** Imperial orb on eagle's breast **Note:** Varieties exist.

Date	Mintage	VG	F	VF	XF	Unc
1616 (b)	—	35.00	60.00	120	200	—
ND	—	35.00	60.00	120	200	—

KM# 24 4 SCHILLING

Silver **Rev:** Value 4 in imperial orb **Note:** Varieties exist.

Date	Mintage	VG	F	VF	XF	Unc
1616 (b)	—	35.00	60.00	120	200	—
ND	—	35.00	60.00	120	200	—

KM# 39 1/2 ORT (1/8 Thaler)

Silver **Obv:** Four-fold arms with central shield, three helmets above **Rev:** HALB/REICHS/ORTH/date **Note:** Varieties exist.

Date	Mintage	VG	F	VF	XF	Unc
16Z1 (f)	—	90.00	165	235	—	—
16Z1	—	90.00	165	235	—	—

KM# 40 1/2 ORT (1/8 Thaler)

Silver **Obv:** Bust right **Note:** Varieties exist.

Date	Mintage	VG	F	VF	XF	Unc
16Z1 (f)	—	120	200	325	—	—

KM# 50 1/2 ORT (1/8 Thaler)

Silver **Obv:** Date divided by bust **Note:** Varieties exist.

Date	Mintage	VG	F	VF	XF	Unc
(1)6ZZ/16ZZ (f)	—	120	200	325	—	—

KM# 51 1/2 ORT (1/8 Thaler)

Silver **Obv:** Bust facing, slightly to right **Rev:** Four-fold arms with central shield, date in legend **Note:** Varieties exist.

Date	Mintage	VG	F	VF	XF	Unc
16ZZ (g)	—	80.00	140	200	300	—

KM# 72 1/2 ORT (1/8 Thaler)

Silver **Note:** Similar to 1/4 Thaler, KM#52. Varieties exist.

Date	Mintage	VG	F	VF	XF	Unc
1634 (h)	—	—	—	—	—	—

KM# 100 GULDEN (1/2 Thaler)

Silver **Obv:** Crowned 7-fold arms **Rev. Inscription:** EIN / GVLDEN / MECKLEN / BVRGS / date **Mint:** Gustrow **Note:** Varieties exist. Dav. #671.

Date	Mintage	VG	F	VF	XF	Unc
1679	—	225	400	675	1,125	—
1680	—	225	400	675	1,125	—

KM# 111 24 MARIENGROSCHEN (Gulden = 2/3 Thaler)

Silver **Obv:** Bust right **Rev:** Inscription, legend, date **Rev. Legend:** MONETA NOVA ARGENTEA **Rev. Inscription:** XXIIII / MARIEN / GROSS **Mint:** Glückstadt **Note:** Dav. #676.

Date	Mintage	VG	F	VF	XF	Unc
1689	—	85.00	180	275	450	—

Note: Struck in 1692

KM# 48 1/96 THALER (Sechsling = 6 Pfennig)

Silver **Obv:** Similar to 3 Pfennig, KM#37 **Rev:** Imperial orb with 96, mint mark, date **Rev. Legend:** HERTZ MECH

Date	Mintage	VG	F	VF	XF	Unc
16ZZ (g)	—	—	—	—	—	—

KM# 90 1/96 THALER (Sechsling = 6 Pfennig)

Billon **Obv:** GA monogram in laurel wreath **Rev:** Value 96 in shield, date in legend **Note:** Varieties exist.

Date	Mintage	VG	F	VF	XF	Unc
1671 (i)	—	20.00	33.00	60.00	120	—
1675 (ii)	—	20.00	33.00	60.00	120	—
1676 (ii)	—	20.00	33.00	60.00	120	—
1677 (ii)	—	20.00	33.00	60.00	120	—
1679 (ii)	—	20.00	33.00	60.00	120	—
1688 (k)	206,000	20.00	33.00	60.00	120	—
1689 (k)	96,000	20.00	33.00	60.00	120	—
1689	—	20.00	33.00	60.00	120	—
1692 (k)	—	—	—	—	—	—
ND	—	20.00	33.00	60.00	120	—

Note: Mintage icluded in KM#120.

KM# 49 1/48 THALER (Schilling)

Silver **Obv:** Five-fold arms, titles of Johann Albrecht **Rev:** Imperial orb with 48 divides date

Date	Mintage	VG	F	VF	XF	Unc
16ZZ (f)	—	—	—	—	—	—

KM# 80 1/48 THALER (Schilling)

Silver **Obv:** 7-fold arms **Rev:** Inscription, date in legend **Rev. Inscription:** 48 / EINEN / REICH / DALE **Mint:** Wismar **Note:** Varieties exist.

Date	Mintage	VG	F	VF	XF	Unc
1666	14,000	—	—	—	—	—

KM# 91 1/48 THALER (Schilling)

Silver **Rev:** 48/REICHS/DALER/date **Note:** Varieties exist.

Date	Mintage	VG	F	VF	XF	Unc
1671 (i)	—	16.00	30.00	55.00	100	—
1675 (ii)	—	16.00	30.00	55.00	100	—
1676 (ii)	—	16.00	30.00	55.00	100	—
1677 (ii)	—	16.00	30.00	55.00	100	—
1679 (ii)	—	16.00	30.00	55.00	100	—
1680 (ii)	—	16.00	30.00	55.00	100	—
1694 (k)	—	16.00	30.00	55.00	100	—

KM# 112 1/48 THALER (Schilling)

Silver **Obv:** Crowned GA monogram, legend, date **Obv. Legend:** ANNO **Rev:** Value 48 in wreath **Note:** Varieties exist.

Date	Mintage	VG	F	VF	XF	Unc
1689	—	16.00	30.00	55.00	100	—
1691	—	16.00	30.00	55.00	100	—
1692	504,000	13.00	27.00	45.00	90.00	—

KM# 113 1/24 THALER (Doppelschilling)

Silver **Obv:** Crowned GA monogram, legend, date **Obv. Legend:** Imperial orb with 24 divides mintmaster's initials **Note:** Varieties exist.

Date	Mintage	VG	F	VF	XF	Unc
1689 IM	1,440,000	—	—	—	—	—
1692 HIH	36,000	—	—	—	—	—
1692	—	—	—	—	—	—

KM# 121 1/24 THALER (Doppelschilling)

Silver **Obv:** Crowned 7-fold arms **Rev:** 24/EINEN/REICHS/THAL, date in legend **Note:** Varieties exist.

Date	Mintage	VG	F	VF	XF	Unc
1692 HIH	Inc. above	—	—	—	—	—

KM# 122 1/24 THALER (Doppelschilling)

Silver **Rev:** Imperial orb with 24 divides mintmaster's initials, date in legend

Date	Mintage	VG	F	VF	XF	Unc
1692	—	—	—	—	—	—

KM# 92 1/16 THALER (Dutchen)

Silver **Obv:** Seven-fold arms **Rev:** 16/REICHS/DALER/date **Note:** Varieties exist.

Date	Mintage	VG	F	VF	XF	Unc
1671 (i)	—	33.00	65.00	130	250	—
1672 (i)	—	33.00	65.00	130	250	—
1673 (i)	—	40.00	80.00	160	275	—

KM# 95 1/16 THALER (Dutchen)

Silver **Obv:** Bust right **Rev:** XVI/REICHS/THALER/mintmaster's initials, date in legend **Note:** Varieties exist.

Date	Mintage	VG	F	VF	XF	Unc
1677 (k) IM	—	—	—	—	—	—
1678 (k)	—	—	—	—	—	—

KM# 99 1/16 THALER (Dutchen)

Silver **Rev:** XVI/REICH/THAL **Mint:** Gustrow **Note:** Varieties exist.

Date	Mintage	VG	F	VF	XF	Unc
1678	—	—	—	—	—	—

KM# 124 1/12 THALER

Silver **Obv:** Crowned ornate GA monogram

Date	Mintage	VG	F	VF	XF	Unc
1692	—	—	—	—	—	—

KM# 125 1/12 THALER

Silver **Obv:** Crowned seven-fold arms divide date **Rev:** 12/ EINEN/REICHS/THAL/mintmaster's initials

Date	Mintage	VG	F	VF	XF	Unc
1692 HIH	Inc. above	—	—	—	—	—

KM# 123 1/12 THALER

Silver **Obv:** Crowned seven-fold arms **Rev:** 12/EINEN/ REICHS/THAL/date **Mint:** Glückstadt **Note:** Varieties exist.

Date	Mintage	VG	F	VF	XF	Unc
1692 HIH	—	—	—	—	—	—
1692	36,000	—	—	—	—	—

KM# 114 1/6 THALER

Silver **Obv:** Bust right **Rev:** VI/EINEN/REICHS/THAL/date **Rev. Legend:** MONETA... **Mint:** Glückstadt

Date	Mintage	VG	F	VF	XF	Unc
1689	—	85.00	165	275	450	—

Note: Struck in 1692

KM# 126 1/6 THALER

Silver **Rev. Legend:** NACH DEM...

Date	Mintage	VG	F	VF	XF	Unc
1692 HIH	—	—	—	—	—	—

KM# 127 1/6 THALER

Silver **Obv:** Crowned seven-fold arms divide mintmaster's initials

Date	Mintage	VG	F	VF	XF	Unc
1692 HIH	—	—	—	—	—	—

KM# 41 1/4 THALER (Ort)

Silver **Obv:** Bust right divides date **Rev:** Four-fold arms with central shield, three helmets above **Note:** Varieties exist.

Date	Mintage	VG	F	VF	XF	Unc
16Z1 (f)	—	200	375	550	900	—
16ZZ (f)	—	200	375	550	900	—

KM# 52 1/4 THALER (Ort)

Silver **Note:** Varieties exist.

Date	Mintage	VG	F	VF	XF	Unc
16ZZ (g)	—	225	400	675	1,150	—

KM# 7 1/2 THALER

Silver **Obv:** Half-length armored bust right holding scepter, head divides date, titles of Karl **Rev:** Five-fold arms supported by steer and griffin, three helmets above

Date	Mintage	VG	F	VF	XF	Unc
1607 (d)	—	—	—	—	—	—

KM# 10 1/2 THALER

Silver **Obv:** Half-length armored bust right holding imperial orb **Rev:** Five-fold arms, three helmets above

Date	Mintage	VG	F	VF	XF	Unc
1608 (a)	—	—	—	—	—	—

KM# 15 1/2 THALER

Silver **Obv:** Date in legend above duke's head

Date	Mintage	VG	F	VF	XF	Unc
1609 (a)	—	—	—	—	—	—

KM# 42 1/2 THALER

Silver **Obv:** Four-fold arms with central shield, three helmets above **Note:** Varieties exist.

Date	Mintage	VG	F	VF	XF	Unc
16Z1 (f)	—	275	550	950	1,550	—
16Z1	—	275	550	950	1,550	—
16ZZ (f)	—	275	550	950	1,550	—
16ZZ (g)	—	275	550	950	1,550	—

KM# 53 1/2 THALER

Silver **Note:** Similar to 1/4 Thaler, KM#52. Varieties exist.

Date	Mintage	VG	F	VF	XF	Unc
16ZZ (g)	—	400	725	1,200	2,000	—
16Z3 (g)	—	400	725	1,200	2,000	—
(1)634 (h)	—	400	725	1,200	2,000	—

KM# 60 1/2 THALER

Silver **Obv:** Small bust right **Note:** Similar to 1/4 Thaler, KM#52.

Date	Mintage	VG	F	VF	XF	Unc
16Z4 (g)	—	—	—	—	—	—

KM# 108 2/3 THALER (Gulden)

Silver **Obv:** Bust right, date below **Rev:** Crowned seven-fold arms divide mintmaster's initials, value (2/3) in oval at bottom

Date	Mintage	VG	F	VF	XF	Unc
1687 IM	—	—	—	—	—	—

KM# 110 2/3 THALER (Gulden)

Silver **Mint:** Rostock **Note:** Varieties exist. Dav. #672.

Date	Mintage	VG	F	VF	XF	Unc
1688	—	100	200	300	525	—

KM# 115 2/3 THALER (Gulden)

Silver **Mint:** Glückstadt **Note:** Dav. #675.

Date	Mintage	VG	F	VF	XF	Unc
1689	—	85.00	170	275	425	—

Note: Struck in 1692

KM# 8 THALER

Silver **Obv:** Bust right dividing date **Obv. Legend:** CAROLUS. DEI. GRACIA. DUX. MEGAPOLENSI. **Rev:** Helmeted arms **Rev. Legend:** PRIN. VA. COM. -SU. ROS. - - TOC. E. STAR. D. **Note:** Dav. #7044.

Date	Mintage	VG	F	VF	XF	Unc
1607 (d)	—	1,000	2,000	3,500	—	—

KM# 9 THALER

Silver **Obv:** Bust half facing right **Obv. Legend:** ...MEGAPOLENS **Note:** Dav. #7045.

Date	Mintage	VG	F	VF	XF	Unc
1607 (d) Rare	—	—	—	—	—	—

KM# 11 THALER

Silver **Obv:** Bust half facing right with scepter dividing date **Obv. Legend:** ...MEGAPOLENSI **Rev:** Helmeted and supported arms **Note:** Dav. #7047.

Date	Mintage	VG	F	VF	XF	Unc
1608 (d)	—	1,800	3,500	6,000	—	—

KM# 12 THALER

Silver **Obv:** Bust right with orb in hand **Note:** Dav. #7050.

Date	Mintage	VG	F	VF	XF	Unc
1608 (a)	—	1,800	2,250	4,500	7,500	—
1609	—	1,800	2,250	4,500	7,500	—

KM# 16 THALER

Silver **Obv:** Without orb **Note:** Dav. #7050A.

Date	Mintage	VG	F	VF	XF	Unc
1609 (a)	—	1,800	2,250	4,500	7,500	—

KM# 21 THALER

Silver **Obv:** Bust right **Obv. Legend:** IOHANNES. ALBERTVS. D: G: DVX. MEGAPOLE **Rev:** Helmeted arms, date **Rev. Legend:** NON. EST. MORTALE. QVOD. OPTO. AN: DO: **Note:** Dav. #7051.

Date	Mintage	VG	F	VF	XF	Unc
1615	—	1,200	2,500	4,000	—	—

KM# 25 THALER

Silver **Subject:** Death of Margaret Elisabeth, Wife of Johann Albrecht **Obv:** Helmeted arms **Rev:** Eight-line inscription **Note:** Dav. #7052.

Date	Mintage	VG	F	VF	XF	Unc
1616 Rare	—	—	—	—	—	—

KM# 30 THALER

Silver **Obv:** Bust right **Obv. Legend:** IOANNES. ALBERTVS. D: G: COAD. EPISC. RATZEBURG **Rev:** Helmeted arms dividing date **Rev. Legend:** DVX. MEGAPOLENSIS. NON. EST MORTALE. QUOD: OPTO. X. **Note:** Dav. #7053.

Date	Mintage	VG	F	VF	XF	Unc
1618 (b)	—	1,200	2,500	4,000	—	—

KM# 43 THALER

Silver **Obv:** Bust right dividing date **Obv. Legend:** HANS. ALBRECHT: V: G: G: HER: ZV. MECHLEN: **Rev:** Helmeted arms, unicorn **Rev. Legend:** FVRST. ZV. WEN: GRA: ZV: SWE: D: L: R: V: S: HER **Note:** Dav. #7054.

Date	Mintage	VG	F	VF	XF	Unc
16Z1 (f)	—	875	1,750	3,500	—	—

KM# 44 THALER

Silver **Rev:** Without unicorn in legend **Note:** Dav. #7054A.

Date	Mintage	VG	F	VF	XF	Unc
16Z1	—	875	1,750	3,500	—	—

KM# 54 THALER

Silver **Obv. Legend:** ...MECHLN **Rev:** Unicorn in legend **Rev. Legend:** ...GRA...ZV... **Note:** Dav. #7055.

Date	Mintage	VG	F	VF	XF	Unc
16ZZ (f)	—	450	950	1,850	—	—

KM# 55 THALER

Silver **Obv:** Thinner bust **Rev:** Unicorn in legend **Rev. Legend:** FVRST. ZVWEN: GRA...Z:... **Note:** Dav. #7055A.

Date	Mintage	VG	F	VF	XF	Unc
16ZZ (f)	—	450	950	1,850	—	—

KM# 56 THALER

Silver **Obv:** Facing bust **Rev:** Helmeted arms, hand, date **Rev. Legend:** NON. EST. MORTALE. QVOD: OPTO: **Note:** Dav. #7057.

Date	Mintage	VG	F	VF	XF	Unc
16ZZ (g)	—	750	1,500	2,500	—	—
16Z3	—	750	1,500	2,500	—	—

KM# 57 THALER

Silver **Obv:** Bust right, scalloped lace collar **Rev:** Helmeted arms **Note:** Dav. #7058.

Date	Mintage	VG	F	VF	XF	Unc
16ZZ (g)	—	350	800	1,800	—	—
16Z3 (g)	—	350	800	1,800	—	—

KM# 59 THALER

Silver **Rev. Legend:** QVOD: hand OPTO: **Note:** Dav. #7058A.

Date	Mintage	VG	F	VF	XF	Unc
16Z3	—	350	800	1,800	—	—

KM# 61 THALER

Silver **Obv:** Full lace collar without dots, shoulder circles, dashes **Note:** Dav. #7058B.

Date	Mintage	VG	F	VF	XF	Unc
16Z4 (g)	—	325	650	1,350	2,250	—

KM# 62 THALER

Silver **Obv:** Full lace collar with dots, shoulder circles, dots **Note:** Dav. #7058C.

Date	Mintage	VG	F	VF	XF	Unc
16Z4 (g)	—	325	650	1,350	2,250	—

KM# 65 THALER

Silver **Obv:** Facing bust **Obv. Legend:** V. G. G. HANS. ALBRECHT. HERT. Z. MECHELN. **Rev. Legend:** MONETA. NOVA. MEGELENB. **Note:** Dav. #7059.

Date	Mintage	VG	F	VF	XF	Unc
1633	—	1,350	2,750	4,500	—	—

KM# 66 THALER

Silver **Obv. Legend:** NON EST MORTALE-QUOD OPTO **Note:** Dav. #7060.

Date	Mintage	VG	F	VF	XF	Unc
1633 (h)	—	850	1,250	3,500	5,500	—
1634 (h)	—	850	1,250	3,500	5,500	—
1635 (h)	—	850	1,250	3,500	5,500	—

KM# 67 THALER

Silver **Obv:** Small bust, dots lower breast plate **Note:** Dav. #7060A.

Date	Mintage	VG	F	VF	XF	Unc
1633 (h)	—	850	1,750	3,500	5,500	—

KM# 73 THALER

Silver **Obv:** Large bust, stars lower breast plate **Rev. Legend:** NON EST MORTAL:-QUAD OPTO **Note:** Varieties exist. Dav. #7060B.

Date	Mintage	VG	F	VF	XF	Unc
1634 (h)	—	850	1,750	3,500	5,500	—

KM# 82 THALER

Silver **Obv:** Bust right, date below **Obv. Legend:** DEI GRATIA. GUSTAV. ADOLPHUS. DUX. MECKLENBURG **Rev:** Helmeted and supported arms **Rev. Legend:** QVID. RETRIBUAM. DOMINO **Note:** Dav. #7062.

Date	Mintage	VG	F	VF	XF	Unc
1668 Rare	—	—	—	—	—	—

KM# 96 THALER

Silver **Obv:** Without inner circle **Obv. Legend:** D. G. GVST. ADOLP: DVX. MECKLENB: **Rev:** Helmeted arms in palm sprays in inner circle **Note:** Dav. #7064.

Date	Mintage	VG	F	VF	XF	Unc
1677 Rare	—	—	—	—	—	—

KM# 97 THALER

Silver **Obv. Legend:** ...ADOLP.- DVX... **Note:** Dav. #7065.

Date	Mintage	VG	F	VF	XF	Unc
1677 Rare	—	—	—	—	—	—

Note: Fritz Rudolf Künker Münzenhandlung Auction 92, 6-04, VF realized approximately $8,225

KM# 106 THALER

Silver **Rev:** Helmeted arms supported by a buffalo and griffin **Note:** Dav. #7068.

Date	Mintage	VG	F	VF	XF	Unc
1680 Rare	—	—	—	—	—	—

KM# 116 THALER

Silver **Note:** Dav. #7069.

Date	Mintage	VG	F	VF	XF	Unc
1689 Rare	—	—	—	—	—	—

KM# 128 THALER

Silver **Obv. Legend:** D. G. GUSTAVUS ADOLPHUS DUX... **Rev:** Helmeted, hatted and supported arms **Note:** Dav. #7070.

Date	Mintage	VG	F	VF	XF	Unc
1692 IM Rare	—	—	—	—	—	—

KM# 129 THALER

Silver **Obv:** Without IM below **Rev:** HI-H below arms **Note:** Dav. #7071.

Date	Mintage	VG	F	VF	XF	Unc
1693 HIH Rare	—	—	—	—	—	—

KM# 130 THALER

Silver **Subject:** Death of Gustav Adolf **Note:** Dav. #7072.

Date	Mintage	VG	F	VF	XF	Unc
1696 Rare	—	—	—	—	—	—

KM# 13 1-1/2 THALER

Silver **Note:** Similar to 1 Thaler, KM#12. Dav. #7049.

Date	Mintage	VG	F	VF	XF	Unc
1608 (d) Rare	—	—	—	—	—	—

KM# 14 2 THALER

Silver **Obv:** Bust right with scepter dividing date **Rev:** Helmeted and supported arms **Note:** Dav. #7046.

Date	Mintage	VG	F	VF	XF	Unc
1608 (d) Rare	—	—	—	—	—	—

KM# 17 2 THALER

Silver **Note:** Similar to 1 Thaler, KM#12. Cross-reference number Dav. #7048.

Date	Mintage	VG	F	VF	XF	Unc
1609 (a) Rare	—	—	—	—	—	—

KM# 26 2 THALER

Silver **Note:** Similar to 1 Thaler, KM#25. Dav. #7052A.

Date	Mintage	VG	F	VF	XF	Unc
1616	—	—	—	—	—	—

KM# 31 2 THALER

Silver **Note:** Similar to 1 Thaler, KM#30. Dav. #7053A.

Date	Mintage	VG	F	VF	XF	Unc
1618 (b)	—	—	—	—	—	—

KM# 58 2 THALER

Silver **Note:** Similar to 1 Thaler, KM#56. Dav. #7056.

Date	Mintage	VG	F	VF	XF	Unc
16ZZ (f) Rare	—	—	—	—	—	—

KM# 83 2 THALER

Silver **Obv:** Bust of Gustav Adolf right, date below **Rev:** Helmeted and supported arms **Note:** Dav. #7061.

Date	Mintage	VG	F	VF	XF	Unc
1668 Rare	—	—	—	—	—	—

KM# 98 2 THALER

Silver **Obv:** Bust right without inner circle **Rev:** Hatted arms in palm sparys **Note:** Dav. #7063.

Date	Mintage	VG	F	VF	XF	Unc
1677 Rare	—	—	—	—	—	—

KM# 107 2 THALER

Silver **Obv:** Bust right dividing date without inner circle **Rev:** Helmeted and supported arms **Note:** Dav. #7066.

Date	Mintage	VG	F	VF	XF	Unc
1680 Rare	—	—	—	—	—	—

TRADE COINAGE

KM# 68 DUCAT

3.5000 g., 0.9860 Gold 0.1109 oz. AGW **Obv:** Johann Albrecht

Date	Mintage	VG	F	VF	XF	Unc
1633 (h)	—	575	1,200	2,800	5,600	—

KM# 69 DUCAT

3.5000 g., 0.9860 Gold 0.1109 oz. AGW **Note:** Similar to 1/2 Ort, KM#72.

Date	Mintage	VG	F	VF	XF	Unc
1633 (h)	—	—	—	—	—	—

KM# 81 DUCAT

3.5000 g., 0.9860 Gold 0.1109 oz. AGW **Obv:** Bust of Gustav Adolph right in inner circle **Rev:** Arms in inner circle, date in legend **Mint:** Wismar

Date	Mintage	VG	F	VF	XF	Unc
1666 (h)	1,000	525	1,150	2,650	4,050	—
1668	—	525	1,150	2,650	4,050	—

KM# 93 DUCAT

3.5000 g., 0.9860 Gold 0.1109 oz. AGW **Mint:** Gustrow

Date	Mintage	VG	F	VF	XF	Unc
1671	—	500	1,050	2,650	4,050	—
1672	—	500	1,050	2,650	4,050	—
1674	—	500	1,050	2,650	4,050	—
1680 IM	—	500	1,050	2,650	4,050	—
1686	—	500	1,050	2,650	4,050	—
1687	—	500	1,050	2,650	4,050	—
1688 PP	—	500	1,050	2,650	4,050	—
1689 PP	—	500	1,050	2,650	4,050	—

KM# 70 2 DUCAT

7.0000 g., 0.9860 Gold 0.2219 oz. AGW **Obv:** Johann Albrecht standing in inner circle **Rev:** Arms in inner circle

Date	Mintage	VG	F	VF	XF	Unc
1633	—	1,550	3,650	5,900	9,800	—

KM# 71 3 DUCAT

10.5000 g., 0.9860 Gold 0.3328 oz. AGW **Obv:** Johann Albrecht standing in inner circle **Rev:** Arms in inner circle

Date	Mintage	VG	F	VF	XF	Unc
1633 Rare	—	—	—	—	—	—

PATTERNS

Including off metal strikes

KM#	Date	Mintage	Identification	Mkt Val
Pn1	1689	—	1/6 Thaler. Copper. KM#114	—

MECKLENBURG-SCHWERIN

The duchy of Mecklenburg was located along the Baltic coast between Holstein and Pomerania. Schwerin was annexed to Mecklenburg in 1357. During the Thirty Years' War, the dukes of Mecklenburg sided with the Protestant forces against the emperor. Albrecht von Wallenstein, the imperialist general, ousted the Mecklenburg dukes from their territories in 1628. They were restored to their lands in 1632. In 1658 the Mecklenburg dynasty was divided into two lines. No coinage was produced for Mecklenburg-Schwerin from 1708 until 1750. The 1815 Congress of Vienna elevated the duchy to the status of grand duchy and it became a part of the German Empire in 1871 until 1918 when the last grand duke abdicated.

RULERS

Adolf Friedrich I, 1592-1628, 1632-1658
Christian Ludwig I, 1658-1692
Friedrich Wilhelm, 1692-1713

MINT MARKS

A - Berlin
B - Hannover

MINT OFFICIALS' INITIALS & PRIVY MARKS

DOMITZ MINT

Initial or Mark	Date	Name
(a)= [mark]	1669-73	Henning Kemper
WE	1675-79	Werner Eberhardt

GADEBUSCH MINT

Initial or Mark	Date	Name
(b)= [mark]	1611-19	Simon Ludemann
(c)= mermaid or CE	1621-24	Christian Emerich

RATZEBURG MINT

Initial or Mark	Date	Name
(d)= [mark] and AH	1678(Jan.–May)	Andreas Hille
(e)= [mark] and/or PBH	1678-79	Peter Brasshaver
DB monogram	1679-81	Dietrich Bauer
(f)= [mark]	1682-85	Michael Wagner
(g) none	1686-89	Gabriel Christian Rodatz

SCHWERIN MINT

Initial or Mark	Date	Name
(h)= [mark]	1651-52	Berthold Krause
	1658-63	Peter Lohe
ZDK	1695-1708	Zacharias Daniel Kelpe

WISMAR MINT

Initial or Mark	Date	Name
(l)= [mark] or ID	1625, 1632-47	Johann Dase

GRAND DUCHY

REGULAR COINAGE

KM# 40 PFENNIG

Copper **Ruler:** Adolf Friedrich I **Obv:** Facing steer head; titles of Adolph Friedrich **Rev:** Date **Rev. Inscription:** I / PFEN / NING **Mint:** Gadebusch **Note:** Varieties exist.

Date	Mintage	Good	VG	F	VF	XF
16Z1	—	11.00	27.00	45.00	80.00	—
1621	—	11.00	27.00	45.00	80.00	—
(1)622	—	11.00	27.00	45.00	80.00	—

KM# 41 2 PFENNIG (Zweier)

Copper **Ruler:** Adolf Friedrich I **Obv:** Facing steer head, titles of Adolph Friedrich **Rev. Inscription:** Z / PFEN / NING / date **Mint:** Gadebusch **Note:** Varieties exist.

Date	Mintage	Good	VG	F	VF	XF
1621	—	11.00	27.00	45.00	80.00	—

KM# 42 2 PFENNIG (Zweier)

Copper **Ruler:** Adolf Friedrich I **Rev. Inscription:** II / PFEN / NING / date **Note:** Varieties exist.

Date	Mintage	Good	VG	F	VF	XF
1621	—	11.00	27.00	45.00	80.00	—

KM# 43 3 PFENNIG (Dreier)

Copper **Ruler:** Adolf Friedrich I **Obv:** Facing steer head, titles of Adolph Friedrich **Mint:** Gadebusch **Note:** Varieties exist.

Date	Mintage	Good	VG	F	VF	XF
1621	—	9.00	16.00	27.00	45.00	—
1622	—	9.00	16.00	27.00	45.00	—

KM# 95 3 PFENNIG (Dreiling)

Silver **Ruler:** Christian Ludwig I **Obv:** Crowned CL monogram **Rev:** Imperial orb with 3 divides date **Mint:** Domitz **Note:** Varieties exist.

Date	Mintage	VG	F	VF	XF	Unc
1676	—	11.00	22.00	40.00	90.00	—
1677	—	11.00	22.00	40.00	90.00	—

KM# 85 SECHSLING (6 Pfennig)

Silver **Ruler:** Christian Ludwig I **Obv:** Facing steer head, titles of Christian Ludwig **Rev:** Date **Rev. Inscription:** I / SOSLING / MECHLE / NBVRG **Mint:** Schwerin **Note:** Varieties exist.

Date	Mintage	VG	F	VF	XF	Unc
1661	—	—	—	—	—	—

KM# 96 SECHSLING (6 Pfennig)

Silver **Ruler:** Christian Ludwig I **Obv:** Crowned CL monogram, **Obv. Legend:** LANDMVNZ **Rev:** Date **Rev. Inscription:** I/SECHS/LING **Mint:** Domitz

Date	Mintage	VG	F	VF	XF	Unc
1676	—	—	—	—	—	—

KM# 44 SCHILLING

Silver **Ruler:** Adolf Friedrich I **Obv:** Facing steer head, titles of Adolph Friedrich **Rev:** Value and date **Rev. Inscription:** 1 / SCHIL / LING

Date	Mintage	VG	F	VF	XF	Unc
1621 (c)	—	—	—	—	—	—

KM# 86 SCHILLING

Silver **Ruler:** Christian Ludwig I **Obv:** Crowned 7-fold arms **Rev:** Value and date **Rev. Inscription:** 1 / SCHILLI / NG MECH / LENBVRG **Mint:** Schwerin **Note:** Varieties exist.

Date	Mintage	VG	F	VF	XF	Unc
1661	—	—	—	—	—	—

KM# 97 SCHILLING

Silver **Ruler:** Christian Ludwig I **Obv:** Crowned CL monogram, date **Obv. Legend:** LANDMVNTZ **Rev:** Value and mintmasters symbol **Rev. Inscription:** I / SCHIL / LING ME / CKELN / BVRG **Note:** Varieties exist.

Date	Mintage	VG	F	VF	XF	Unc
1670 (a)	—	20.00	40.00	80.00	140	—
1671 (a)	—	20.00	40.00	80.00	140	—
1672 (a)	—	20.00	40.00	80.00	140	—

KM# 10 2 SCHILLING (Doppelschilling)

Silver **Ruler:** Adolf Friedrich I **Obv:** 4-fold arms with central shield, titles of Adolph Friedrich **Rev:** Large intertwined DS divides date

Date	Mintage	VG	F	VF	XF	Unc
1611 (b)	—	27.00	65.00	135	200	—

KM# 21 2 SCHILLING (Doppelschilling)

Silver **Ruler:** Adolf Friedrich I **Note:** Klippe 2 Schilling.

Date	Mintage	VG	F	VF	XF	Unc
1613 (b)	—	—	—	—	—	—

KM# 19 2 SCHILLING (Doppelschilling)

Silver **Ruler:** Adolf Friedrich I **Rev:** DS in shield **Note:** Varieties exist.

Date	Mintage	VG	F	VF	XF	Unc
1613 (b)	—	33.00	65.00	135	200	—
(16)15 (b)	—	33.00	65.00	135	200	—

KM# 20 2 SCHILLING (Doppelschilling)

Silver **Ruler:** Adolf Friedrich I **Rev:** Date in legend **Note:** Varieties exist.

Date	Mintage	VG	F	VF	XF	Unc
1613 (b)	—	27.00	55.00	115	165	—
(1)613 (b)	—	27.00	55.00	115	165	—
1614 (b)	—	27.00	55.00	115	165	—
(1)614 (b)	—	27.00	55.00	115	165	—
(16)14 (b)	—	27.00	55.00	115	165	—
(16)15 (b)	—	27.00	55.00	115	165	—

KM# 22 2 SCHILLING (Doppelschilling)

Silver **Ruler:** Adolf Friedrich I **Note:** Similar to KM#20 but part of date divided by shield, rest below shield. Varieties exist.

Date	Mintage	VG	F	VF	XF	Unc
1614 (b)	—	27.00	55.00	115	165	—
1615 (b)	—	27.00	55.00	115	165	—
(16)15 (b)	—	27.00	55.00	115	165	—
1616 (b)	—	27.00	55.00	115	165	—

KM# 33 2 SCHILLING (Doppelschilling)

Silver **Ruler:** Adolf Friedrich I **Rev:** DS not in shield **Note:** Varieties exist.

Date	Mintage	VG	F	VF	XF	Unc
1616 (b)	—	24.00	45.00	90.00	160	—
(16)16 (b)	—	24.00	45.00	90.00	160	—
(1)6(1)7 (b)	—	24.00	45.00	90.00	160	—
1617 (b)	—	24.00	45.00	90.00	160	—
ND(1618) (b)	—	24.00	45.00	90.00	160	—

KM# 130 2 SCHILLING (Doppelschilling)

Silver **Ruler:** Friedrich Wilhelm **Obv:** Crowned 7-fold arms **Rev:** Date, mintmaster's initials **Rev. Inscription:** II / SCHIL / LING **Note:** Varieties exist.

Date	Mintage	VG	F	VF	XF	Unc
1696 ZDK	—	16.00	33.00	60.00	120	—
1699 ZDK	10,000	16.00	33.00	60.00	120	—

KM# 135 4 GUTE GROSCHEN (1/6 Thaler)

Silver **Ruler:** Friedrich Wilhelm **Obv:** Bust right **Rev:** Legend is 4 crowned ornate FW monograms in cruciform around date in circle in center, VIER GVTE GROS CEN **Mint:** Schwerin

Date	Mintage	VG	F	VF	XF	Unc
1698	—	—	—	—	—	—

KM# 136 16 GUTE GROSCHEN (2/3 Thaler)

Silver **Ruler:** Friedrich Wilhelm **Obv:** Bust right **Rev:** Date **Rev. Inscription:** XVI / GVTE / GROSCH / EN **Mint:** Schwerin

Date	Mintage	VG	F	VF	XF	Unc
1698	60	—	—	—	—	—

KM# 75 1/192 THALER (Dreiling)

Silver **Ruler:** Adolf Friedrich I **Obv:** Date in legend **Mint:** Wismar **Note:** Varieties exist.

Date	Mintage	VG	F	VF	XF	Unc
(16)43	—	13.00	30.00	60.00	120	—
(16)45	—	13.00	30.00	60.00	120	—

KM# 87 1/192 THALER (Dreiling)

Silver **Ruler:** Christian Ludwig I **Obv:** Titles of Christian Ludwig **Rev:** Imperial orb divides date **Mint:** Schwerin

Date	Mintage	VG	F	VF	XF	Unc
1661	—	—	—	—	—	—

KM# 5 1/192 THALER (Dreiling)

Silver **Ruler:** Friedrich Wilhelm **Obv:** Facing steer head, titles of Adolph Friedrich **Rev:** Imperial orb with 192 **Mint:** Gadebusch

Date	Mintage	VG	F	VF	XF	Unc
ND	—	—	—	—	—	—

KM# 47 1/96 THALER (Sechsling)

Silver **Ruler:** Adolf Friedrich I **Obv:** Facing steer head, titles of Adolph Friedrich, date in legend **Rev:** Imperial orb with 96 **Note:** Varieties exist.

Date	Mintage	VG	F	VF	XF	Unc
(1)622 CE	—	13.00	27.00	55.00	115	—
(16)22 CE	—	13.00	27.00	55.00	115	—
(16)23 CE	—	13.00	27.00	55.00	115	—

KM# 48 1/96 THALER (Sechsling)

Silver **Ruler:** Adolf Friedrich I **Obv:** Date divided by steer's head **Note:** Varieties exist.

Date	Mintage	VG	F	VF	XF	Unc
(1)622 CE	—	13.00	27.00	55.00	115	—
(16)22 CE	—	13.00	27.00	55.00	115	—
(16)22	—	13.00	27.00	55.00	115	—
(16)23 CE	—	13.00	27.00	55.00	115	—
(16)23	—	13.00	27.00	55.00	115	—

KM# 137 1/96 THALER (Sechsling)

Silver **Ruler:** Friedrich Wilhelm **Obv:** Date in legend **Rev:** Value: 96 on imperial orb **Mint:** Schwerin **Note:** Varieties exist.

Date	Mintage	VG	F	VF	XF	Unc
1698	125,000	13.00	24.00	45.00	100	—
1699	115,000	13.00	24.00	45.00	100	—

KM# 11 1/64 THALER

Silver **Ruler:** Adolf Friedrich I **Obv:** Facing steer head in shield, titles of Adolph Friedrich **Rev:** Imperial orb with 64, date in legend

Date	Mintage	VG	F	VF	XF	Unc
161Z (b)	—	—	—	—	—	—
1613 (b)	—	—	—	—	—	—

KM# 12 1/64 THALER

Silver **Ruler:** Adolf Friedrich I **Rev:** Date divided by imperial orb

Date	Mintage	VG	F	VF	XF	Unc
161Z (b)	—	—	—	—	—	—

KM# 49 1/48 THALER (Schilling)

Silver **Ruler:** Adolf Friedrich I **Obv:** Facing steer head in shield, titles of Adolph Friedrich **Rev:** Imperial orb with 48 **Note:** Varieties exist.

Date	Mintage	VG	F	VF	XF	Unc
1622 CE	—	—	—	—	—	—
(16)22 CE	—	—	—	—	—	—

KM# 115 1/48 THALER (Schilling)

Silver **Ruler:** Christian Ludwig I **Obv:** Crowned CL monogram **Rev:** Date **Rev. Inscription:** 48 / EINEN / REICHS / THALER **Mint:** Ratzeburg

Date	Mintage	VG	F	VF	XF	Unc
1678	—	—	—	—	—	—

KM# 138 1/48 THALER (Schilling)

Silver **Ruler:** Friedrich Wilhelm **Obv:** Crowned ornate FW monogram **Rev:** Crowned 2-fold arms divided vertically, date **Rev. Legend:** MONETA (48) NOVA **Mint:** Schwerin

Date	Mintage	VG	F	VF	XF	Unc
1698	—	—	—	—	—	—

KM# 60 1/24 THALER (Groschen)

Silver **Ruler:** Adolf Friedrich I **Obv:** 4-fold arms with central shield, titles of Adolph Friedrich **Rev:** Date, small imperial orb at top **Rev. Inscription:** 24 / REICHS / DALER **Note:** Varieties exist.

Date	Mintage	VG	F	VF	XF	Unc
1632 (i)	—	40.00	75.00	160	245	—
1633 (i)	—	40.00	75.00	160	245	—
1646 (i)	—	40.00	75.00	160	245	—
1647 (i)	—	40.00	75.00	160	245	—
1650 (i)	—	40.00	75.00	160	245	—
1651 (h)	—	40.00	75.00	160	245	—
1652 (h)	—	40.00	75.00	160	245	—

KM# 80 1/24 THALER (Doppelschilling)

Silver **Ruler:** Christian Ludwig I **Obv:** Bust right **Mint:** Schwerin **Note:** Varieites exist.

Date	Mintage	VG	F	VF	XF	Unc
1659	—	—	—	—	—	—

KM# 88 1/24 THALER (Doppelschilling)

Silver **Ruler:** Christian Ludwig I **Obv:** 7-fold arms

Date	Mintage	VG	F	VF	XF	Unc
1661	—	—	—	—	—	—

KM# 98 1/24 THALER (Doppelschilling)

Silver **Ruler:** Christian Ludwig I **Obv:** Crowned CL monogram within Order chain **Note:** Varieties exist.

Date	Mintage	VG	F	VF	XF	Unc
1670 (a)	—	33.00	60.00	120	190	—
1671 (a)	—	33.00	60.00	120	190	—
1672 (a)	—	33.00	60.00	120	190	—
1673 (a)	—	33.00	60.00	120	190	—

KM# 123 1/24 THALER (Doppelschilling)

Silver **Ruler:** Christian Ludwig I **Obv:** Bust right

Date	Mintage	VG	F	VF	XF	Unc
1682	—	—	—	—	—	—

Note: Reported, not confirmed

KM# 131 1/24 THALER (Doppelschilling)

Silver **Ruler:** Friedrich Wilhelm **Obv:** Crowned 7-fold arms **Rev:** Date, mintmasters initials **Rev. Inscription:** 24 / EINEN / REICHS / THALER **Note:** Varieties exist.

Date	Mintage	VG	F	VF	XF	Unc
1696 ZDK	203,000	—	—	—	—	—

KM# 53 1/16 THALER (Dutchen)

Silver **Ruler:** Adolf Friedrich I **Obv:** 4-fold arms with central shield, titles of Adolph Friedrich **Rev:** Date, small imperial orb above **Rev. Inscription:** 16 / REICHS / DALER **Note:** Varieties exist.

Date	Mintage	VG	F	VF	XF	Unc
1632 (i)	—	45.00	80.00	165	275	—
1633 (i)	—	45.00	80.00	165	275	—
1646 (i)	—	45.00	80.00	165	275	—

KM# 110 1/16 THALER (Dutchen)

Silver **Ruler:** Christian Ludwig I **Obv:** Bust right **Rev:** Mintmasters initials, date in legend **Rev. Inscription:** XVI / REICHS / DALER **Note:** Varieties exist.

Date	Mintage	VG	F	VF	XF	Unc
1676 WE	—	40.00	75.00	150	225	—
1677 WE	—	40.00	75.00	150	225	—

KM# 111 1/16 THALER (Dutchen)

Silver **Ruler:** Christian Ludwig I **Rev:** Mintmasters initials **Rev. Inscription:** XVI / REICHS / THAL(E)R **Note:** Varieties exist.

Date	Mintage	VG	F	VF	XF	Unc
1676	—	40.00	75.00	150	225	—
1678 PBH	—	40.00	75.00	150	225	—
1678 (f)	—	40.00	75.00	150	225	—

Note: 1678 with star mint mark struck ca.1682-1685

KM# 46 1/8 THALER (1/2 Reichsort)
Silver **Ruler:** Adolf Friedrich I **Rev:** Date **Rev. Inscription:** HALB / REICH / S ORTH **Note:** Klippe 1/8 Thaler.

Date	Mintage	VG	F	VF	XF	Unc
1621 (c)	—	—	—	—	—	—

KM# 45 1/8 THALER (1/2 Reichsort)
Silver **Ruler:** Adolf Friedrich I **Obv:** 1/2-length bust right, titles of Adolph Friedrich **Rev:** Date **Rev. Inscription:** HALB / REICHS / ORTH **Note:** Varieties exist.

Date	Mintage	VG	F	VF	XF	Unc
1621 (c)	—	60.00	120	200	325	—
1622 CE	—	60.00	120	200	325	—

KM# 50 1/8 THALER (1/2 Reichsort)
Silver **Ruler:** Adolf Friedrich I **Rev:** 4-fold arms with central shield, 3 helmets above, date divided above

Date	Mintage	VG	F	VF	XF	Unc
(1)622 CE	—	—	—	—	—	—

KM# 56 1/8 THALER (1/2 Reichsort)
Silver **Ruler:** Adolf Friedrich I **Note:** Similar to KM#46, but not Klippe.

Date	Mintage	VG	F	VF	XF	Unc
1625	—	—	—	—	—	—

Note: Reported, not confirmed

KM# 54 1/4 THALER (Reichsort)
Silver **Ruler:** Adolf Friedrich I **Obv:** 1/2 length bust right, titles of Adolph Friedrich **Rev:** 4-fold arms with central shield dividing date, 3 helmets above

Date	Mintage	VG	F	VF	XF	Unc
(1)623 CE	—	—	—	—	—	—

KM# 62 1/4 THALER (Reichsort)
Silver **Ruler:** Adolf Friedrich I **Subject:** Death of Anna Marie, Wife of Adolph Friedrich I **Obv:** 10-line inscription with date **Rev:** 4-line inscription

Date	Mintage	VG	F	VF	XF	Unc
1634	—	—	—	—	—	—

KM# 103 1/3 THALER (1/2 Gulden)
Silver **Ruler:** Christian Ludwig I **Obv:** Crowned CL monogram, 1/3 in oval below **Rev:** Crowned 7-fold arms, in order chain, date in legend

Date	Mintage	VG	F	VF	XF	Unc
1671 (a)	—	—	—	—	—	—

KM# 116 1/3 THALER (1/2 Gulden)
Silver **Ruler:** Christian Ludwig I **Obv:** Bust right, 1/3 in oval below **Rev:** Crowned 7-fold arms, supporters at sides, Order chain at bottom, date in legend **Note:** Varieties exist.

Date	Mintage	VG	F	VF	XF	Unc
1678 WE	—	—	—	—	—	—

KM# 31 1/2 THALER
Silver **Ruler:** Adolf Friedrich I **Obv:** 1/2 length bust right, titles of Adolph Friedrich **Rev:** 4-fold arms with central shield supported, 3 helmets above, date in upper left legend **Note:** Varieties exist.

Date	Mintage	VG	F	VF	XF	Unc
1615 (b)	—	—	—	—	—	—
1618 (b)	—	—	—	—	—	—
(1)622	—	—	—	—	—	—
(1)623 CE	—	—	—	—	—	—

KM# 63 1/2 THALER
Silver **Ruler:** Adolf Friedrich I **Subject:** Death of Anna Maria, Wife of Adolph Friedrich I **Obv:** 11-line inscription with date **Rev:** 6-line inscription

Date	Mintage	VG	F	VF	XF	Unc
1634	—	—	—	—	—	—

KM# 90 1/2 THALER
Silver **Ruler:** Christian Ludwig I **Obv:** Bust right **Rev:** Crowned and mantled 7-fold arms, Order chain around, date divided at bottom of crown **Mint:** Domitz

Date	Mintage	VG	F	VF	XF	Unc
1669	—	—	—	—	—	—

KM# 89 2/3 THALER (Gulden)
Silver **Ruler:** Christian Ludwig I **Obv:** Crowned CL monogram, 2/3 in oval below **Rev:** Crowned and mantled 7-fold arms, Order chain around, date divided at bottom of crown **Note:** Dav. #665. Varieties exist.

Date	Mintage	VG	F	VF	XF	Unc
1670 (a)	—	650	1,250	2,500	4,000	—
1671 (a)	—	650	1,250	2,500	4,000	—

KM# 104 2/3 THALER (Gulden)
Silver **Ruler:** Christian Ludwig I **Obv:** Without mantle, angels hold up crown **Note:** Dav. #666. Varieties exist.

Date	Mintage	VG	F	VF	XF	Unc
1671 (a)	—	500	1,000	2,000	3,500	—
1672 (a)	—	500	1,000	2,000	3,500	—
1673 (a)	—	500	1,000	2,000	3,500	—

KM# A106 2/3 THALER (Gulden)
Silver **Ruler:** Christian Ludwig I **Obv:** Bust of Christian right with value in oval below **Rev:** Angels support crowned arms, Order chain below **Note:** Dav. #667-669. Varieties exist.

Date	Mintage	VG	F	VF	XF	Unc
1675 WE	—	40.00	85.00	160	425	—
1676 WE	—	40.00	85.00	160	425	—
1677 WE	—	40.00	85.00	160	425	—
1678 (d)	—	40.00	85.00	160	425	—
1678 (f) Star	—	40.00	85.00	160	425	—
1688 (g)	—	40.00	85.00	160	425	—

KM# 106 2/3 THALER (Gulden)
Silver **Ruler:** Christian Ludwig I **Obv:** Armored bust **Rev:** Different crown, small order chain under shield

Date	Mintage	VG	F	VF	XF	Unc
1676 (d)	—	40.00	85.00	150	325	—
1678 (d) AH	—	40.00	85.00	150	325	—
1678 (e) PBH	—	40.00	85.00	150	325	—
1680 DB	—	40.00	85.00	150	325	—

KM# 13 THALER
Silver **Ruler:** Adolf Friedrich I **Obv:** Bust of Adolf right **Rev:** Fortuna **Note:** Dav. #7023.

Date	Mintage	VG	F	VF	XF	Unc
1612 (b)	—	350	750	1,650	3,250	—

KM# 14 THALER
Silver **Ruler:** Adolf Friedrich I **Obv:** Longer bust right **Rev:** Helmeted arms **Note:** Dav. #7025.

Date	Mintage	VG	F	VF	XF	Unc
1612 (b)	—	350	700	1,200	2,000	—

KM# 23 THALER
Silver **Ruler:** Adolf Friedrich I **Rev:** Helmeted and supported arms, divided date **Note:** Dav. #7026.

Date	Mintage	VG	F	VF	XF	Unc
1613 (b)	—	200	600	1,200	3,250	—
1614 (b)	—	200	600	1,200	3,250	—
1615 (b)	—	215	450	875	1,650	—
1616 (b)	—	215	450	875	1,650	—
1617 (b)	—	225	450	1,000	2,250	—
1618 (b)	—	225	450	1,000	2,250	—

KM# 24 THALER
Silver **Ruler:** Adolf Friedrich I **Rev:** Date not divided in legend **Note:** Dav. #7026A.

Date	Mintage	VG	F	VF	XF	Unc
1613 (b)	—	250	600	1,200	3,000	—
1614 (b)	—	250	600	1,200	3,000	—
1615 (b)	—	250	600	1,200	3,000	—
1616 (b)	—	250	600	1,200	3,000	—
1617 (b)	—	250	600	1,200	3,000	—
1618 (b)	—	225	500	1,150	2,750	—

KM# 25 THALER
Silver **Ruler:** Adolf Friedrich I **Note:** Similar to 2 Thaler, KM#27. Dav. #LS359.

Date	Mintage	VG	F	VF	XF	Unc
1613 (b) Rare	—	—	—	—	—	—

KM# 51 THALER
Silver **Ruler:** Adolf Friedrich I **Obv:** Bust right **Obv. Legend:** ADOLPH.FRIDR.V G.G. HERTZ. Z. MECKLENBVR **Rev:** Helmeted arms, date **Rev. Legend:** F. Z. -W. -G. Z. S. D. L. R. V.S. HER **Note:** Dav. #7027.

Date	Mintage	VG	F	VF	XF	Unc
1622 CE	—	225	500	1,150	2,750	—

KM# 52 THALER
Silver **Ruler:** Adolf Friedrich I **Obv:** Bust right **Obv. Legend:** ...HERT. Z. **Rev:** Date dividied **Rev. Legend:** ...G. Z. S. D. L. R. -V. S. HER. H **Note:** Dav. #7028.

Date	Mintage	VG	F	VF	XF	Unc
1622 CE Rare	—	—	—	—	—	—

KM# 55 THALER
Silver **Ruler:** Adolf Friedrich I **Obv:** Different bust right **Rev:** Helmeted and supported arms **Note:** Dav. #7029.

Date	Mintage	VG	F	VF	XF	Unc
1623 CE	—	225	500	1,150	2,750	—
1623 CE	—	225	500	1,150	2,750	—

KM# 61 THALER

Silver **Ruler:** Adolf Friedrich I **Obv:** Facing bust **Rev:** Helmeted arms **Note:** Dav. #7030.

Date	Mintage	VG	F	VF	XF	Unc
1633 (i)	—	500	975	1,800	3,050	—
1634 (i)	—	525	1,050	1,950	3,250	—

KM# 64 THALER

Silver **Ruler:** Adolf Friedrich I **Subject:** Death of Anna Maria, Wife of Adolf Friedrich **Obv:** 12-line inscription **Rev:** Sun **Rev. Inscription:** VIVIT.POST / FUNERA / VIRTUS **Note:** Dav. #7031.

Date	Mintage	VG	F	VF	XF	Unc
1634 Rare	—	—	—	—	—	—

Note: Fritz Rudolf Künker Münzenhandlung Auction 92, 6-04, XF realized approximately $10,880

KM# 66 THALER

Silver **Ruler:** Adolf Friedrich I **Obv:** Facing bust **Rev:** Helmeted arms **Note:** Dav. #7033.

Date	Mintage	VG	F	VF	XF	Unc
1637 (i)	—	300	600	1,100	2,000	—
1639 (i)	—	300	600	1,100	2,000	—
1642 (i)	—	300	600	1,100	2,000	—
1647 (i)	—	300	600	1,100	2,000	—

KM# 91 THALER

Silver **Ruler:** Christian Ludwig I **Obv:** Head of Christian Ludwig right **Rev:** Similar to KM#99 **Note:** Dav. #7034.

Date	Mintage	VG	F	VF	XF	Unc
1669 (a)	—	600	1,150	1,900	3,000	—
1670 (a)	—	600	1,150	1,900	3,000	—

KM# 99 THALER

Silver **Ruler:** Christian Ludwig I **Obv:** Bust right **Note:** Dav. #7036.

Date	Mintage	VG	F	VF	XF	Unc
1670	—	1,500	3,000	5,000	7,500	—

KM# 100 THALER

Silver **Ruler:** Christian Ludwig I **Obv:** Smaller bust right **Obv. Legend:** CHRISTIAN: LVDOVI: D: G: DVX MEGAPOLITAN **Note:** Dav. #7037.

Date	Mintage	VG	F	VF	XF	Unc
1670	—	1,500	3,000	6,500	11,000	—

KM# 105 THALER

Silver **Ruler:** Christian Ludwig I **Rev:** Crowned arms **Rev. Legend:** NON EST MORT-ALE... **Note:** Dav. #7038.

Date	Mintage	VG	F	VF	XF	Unc
1671	—	750	1,500	3,000	6,500	—

KM# 107 THALER

Silver **Ruler:** Christian Ludwig I **Subject:** Death of Duke Johann Georg of Mirow **Note:** Dav. #LS363.

Date	Mintage	VG	F	VF	XF	Unc
1675	—	1,200	2,500	4,500	7,500	—

KM# 112 THALER

Silver **Ruler:** Christian Ludwig I **Obv. Legend:** ...LUDOV: D: G: DUX... **Rev. Legend:** NON EST MOR-TALE.. **Note:** Dav. #7041.

Date	Mintage	VG	F	VF	XF	Unc
1677 WE Rare	—	—	—	—	—	—

KM# 120 THALER

Silver **Ruler:** Christian Ludwig I **Obv:** Different bust right **Obv. Legend:** CHRIST. LVD. D. G... **Rev:** Crowned arms in Order band, date below **Note:** Dav. #7043.

Date	Mintage	VG	F	VF	XF	Unc
1681 Rare	—	—	—	—	—	—

KM# 15 1-1/2 THALER

Silver **Ruler:** Adolf Friedrich I **Note:** Similar to 3 Thaler, KM#18. Dav. #LS353.

Date	Mintage	VG	F	VF	XF	Unc
1612 (b) Rare	—	—	—	—	—	—

KM# 26 1-1/2 THALER

Silver **Ruler:** Adolf Friedrich I **Note:** Similar to 2 Thaler, KM#27. Dav. #LS358.

Date	Mintage	VG	F	VF	XF	Unc
1613 (b) Rare	—	—	—	—	—	—

KM# 108 1-1/2 THALER

Silver **Ruler:** Christian Ludwig I **Subject:** Death of Duke Johann Georg of Mirow **Note:** Similar to 1 Thaler, KM#107. Dav. #LS362.

Date	Mintage	VG	F	VF	XF	Unc
1675 Rare	—	—	—	—	—	—

KM# 113 1-1/2 THALER

Silver **Ruler:** Christian Ludwig I **Note:** Similar to Thaler, KM#114. Dav. #7040.

Date	Mintage	VG	F	VF	XF	Unc
1677 WE Rare	—	—	—	—	—	—

KM# 16 2 THALER

Silver **Ruler:** Adolf Friedrich I **Obv:** Bust right **Rev:** Fortuna standing with sail, tree and cavalry riding right in background **Note:** Dav. #7022.

Date	Mintage	VG	F	VF	XF	Unc
1612 (b) Rare	—	—	—	—	—	—

Note: Fritz Rudolf Künker Münzenhandlung Auction 96, 9-04, VF-XF realized approximately $9,225

KM# 17 2 THALER

Silver **Ruler:** Adolf Friedrich I **Rev:** Helmeted arms, date divided at left in legend **Note:** Dav. #7024.

Date	Mintage	VG	F	VF	XF	Unc
1612 (b)	—	2,050	3,400	6,000	—	—

KM# 27 2 THALER

Silver **Ruler:** Adolf Friedrich I **Note:** Dav. #LS357.

Date	Mintage	VG	F	VF	XF	Unc
1613 (b)	—	1,700	2,800	4,700	7,700	—

KM# 34 2 THALER

Silver **Ruler:** Adolf Friedrich I **Subject:** Death of Margaret Elizabeth, Wife of Johann Albrecht **Obv:** Helmeted arms **Rev:** 10-line inscription **Note:** Dav. #LS360.

Date	Mintage	VG	F	VF	XF	Unc
1616 Rare	—	—	—	—	—	—

KM# 67 2 THALER

Silver **Ruler:** Adolf Friedrich I **Note:** Similar to 1 Thaler, KM#66. Dav. #7032.

Date	Mintage	VG	F	VF	XF	Unc
1639 (i) Rare	—	—	—	—	—	—

KM# 101 2 THALER

Silver **Ruler:** Christian Ludwig I **Note:** Similar to 1 Thaler, KM#99.

Date	Mintage	VG	F	VF	XF	Unc
1670 Rare	—	—	—	—	—	—

KM# 109 2 THALER

Silver **Ruler:** Christian Ludwig I **Subject:** Death of Duke Johann Georg of Nirow **Note:** Similar to 1 Thaler, KM#107. Dav. #LS361.

Date	Mintage	VG	F	VF	XF	Unc
1675 Rare	—	—	—	—	—	—

KM# 114 2 THALER

Silver **Ruler:** Christian Ludwig I **Obv:** Bust of Christian Ludwig right in inner circle **Rev:** Crowned and mantled arms in bands, date and initials above **Note:** Dav. #7040.

Date	Mintage	F	VF	XF	Unc	BU
1677 WE Rare	—	—	—	—	—	—

KM# 121 2 THALER
Silver **Ruler:** Christian Ludwig I **Obv:** Different bust right without inner circle **Rev:** Crowned arms in order band, date below
Note: Dav. #7042.

Date	Mintage	F	VF	XF	Unc	BU
1681 Rare	—	—	—	—	—	—

KM# 18 3 THALER
Silver **Ruler:** Adolf Friedrich I **Obv:** Bust of Adolf Friedrich right **Rev:** Fortuna with sail, tree and cavalry riding right in background **Note:** Dav. #LS351.

Date	Mintage	VG	F	VF	XF	Unc
1612 (b) Rare	—	—	—	—	—	—

KM# 28 3 THALER
Silver **Ruler:** Adolf Friedrich I **Note:** Similar to 2 Thaler, KM#27. Dav. #LS356.

Date	Mintage	VG	F	VF	XF	Unc
1613 (b) Rare	—	—	—	—	—	—

KM# 29 4 THALER
Silver **Ruler:** Adolf Friedrich I **Note:** Similar to 2 Thaler, KM#27. Dav. #LS355.

Date	Mintage	VG	F	VF	XF	Unc
1613 (b) Rare	—	—	—	—	—	—

KM# 30 5 THALER
Silver **Ruler:** Adolf Friedrich I **Note:** Similar to 2 Thaler, KM#27. Dav. #LS354.

Date	Mintage	VG	F	VF	XF	Unc
1613 Rare	—	—	—	—	—	—

TRADE COINAGE

KM# 32 GOLDGULDEN
3.5000 g., 0.9860 Gold 0.1109 oz. AGW **Ruler:** Adolf Friedrich I **Obv:** Bust of Adolf Friedrich right in inner circle **Rev:** Helmeted arms in inner circle

Date	Mintage	VG	F	VF	XF	Unc
1615 (b)	—	900	1,800	3,750	6,000	—
1616 (b)	—	900	1,800	3,750	6,000	—
ND (b)	—	—	—	—	—	—

KM# 57 GOLDGULDEN
3.5000 g., 0.9860 Gold 0.1109 oz. AGW **Ruler:** Adolf Friedrich I **Obv:** Different bust of Adolf Friedrich right in inner circle

Date	Mintage	VG	F	VF	XF	Unc
1625 ID	—	575	1,150	2,350	3,900	—

KM# 65 GOLDGULDEN
3.5000 g., 0.9860 Gold 0.1109 oz. AGW **Ruler:** Adolf Friedrich I **Obv:** Facing bust, slightly right **Rev:** 4-fold arms with central shield, date in legend

Date	Mintage	VG	F	VF	XF	Unc
1634 (i)	—	700	1,500	3,000	5,000	—

KM# A19 3 GOLDGULDEN
10.5000 g., 0.9860 Gold 0.3328 oz. AGW **Ruler:** Adolf Friedrich I **Note:** Struck with 1 Thaler dies, KM#13.

Date	Mintage	VG	F	VF	XF	Unc
1612 (b) Rare	—	—	—	—	—	—

KM# A68 4 GOLDGULDEN
14.0000 g., 0.9860 Gold 0.4438 oz. AGW **Ruler:** Adolf Friedrich I

Date	Mintage	VG	F	VF	XF	Unc
1637 (i) Rare	—	—	—	—	—	—

Note: Struck with 1 Thaler dies, KM#66

KM# B19 5 GOLDGULDEN
17.5000 g., 0.9860 Gold 0.5547 oz. AGW **Ruler:** Adolf Friedrich I **Note:** Struck with 1 Thaler dies, KM#13.

Date	Mintage	VG	F	VF	XF	Unc
1612 (b) Rare	—	—	—	—	—	—

KM# C19 6 GOLDGULDEN
21.0000 g., 0.9860 Gold 0.6657 oz. AGW **Ruler:** Adolf Friedrich I **Note:** Struck with 1 Thaler dies, KM#13.

Date	Mintage	VG	F	VF	XF	Unc
1612 (b) Rare	—	—	—	—	—	—

KM# A40 6 GOLDGULDEN
21.0000 g., 0.9860 Gold 0.6657 oz. AGW **Ruler:** Adolf Friedrich I **Note:** Struck with 1 Thaler dies, KM#66.

Date	Mintage	VG	F	VF	XF	Unc
1639 (i) Rare	—	—	—	—	—	—
1642 (i) Rare	—	—	—	—	—	—

KM# B68 8 GOLDGULDEN
28.0000 g., 0.9860 Gold 0.8876 oz. AGW **Ruler:** Adolf Friedrich I **Note:** Struck with 1 Thaler dies, KM#66.

Date	Mintage	VG	F	VF	XF	Unc
1637 (i) Rare	—	—	—	—	—	—

KM# D19 10 GOLDGULDEN
35.0000 g., 0.9860 Gold 1.1095 oz. AGW **Ruler:** Adolf Friedrich I **Note:** Struck with 1 Thaler dies, KM#13.

Date	Mintage	VG	F	VF	XF	Unc
1612 (b) Rare	—	—	—	—	—	—

KM# 68 DUCAT
3.5000 g., 0.9860 Gold 0.1109 oz. AGW **Ruler:** Adolf Friedrich I **Obv:** Bust of Adolf Friedrich in inner circle **Rev:** Arms topped with 3 helmets in inner circle, date in legend **Mint:** Wismar

Date	Mintage	VG	F	VF	XF	Unc
1639 (i)	—	625	1,350	2,800	5,300	—

KM# 102 DUCAT
3.5000 g., 0.9860 Gold 0.1109 oz. AGW **Ruler:** Christian Ludwig I **Obv:** Bust of Christian Ludwig right in inner circle **Rev:** Arms in inner circle

Date	Mintage	VG	F	VF	XF	Unc
1670	—	750	1,500	3,750	6,000	—
1671	—	750	1,500	3,750	6,000	—
1681	—	750	1,500	3,750	6,000	—

KM# 132 DUCAT
3.5000 g., 0.9860 Gold 0.1109 oz. AGW
Ruler: Friedrich Wilhelm **Obv:** Crowned FW monogram

Date	Mintage	VG	F	VF	XF	Unc
1696	850	825	1,750	4,150	6,800	—

KM# 134 DUCAT
3.5000 g., 0.9860 Gold 0.1109 oz. AGW
Ruler: Friedrich Wilhelm **Rev:** Crowned FW monogram

Date	Mintage	VG	F	VF	XF	Unc
1696	Inc. above	825	1,750	4,150	6,800	—

KM# 133 DUCAT
3.5000 g., 0.9860 Gold 0.1109 oz. AGW
Ruler: Friedrich Wilhelm **Obv:** Bust of Friedrich Wilhelm right
Rev. Legend: NON EST MORTALE...

Date	Mintage	VG	F	VF	XF	Unc
1696	Inc. above	825	1,750	4,150	6,800	—

KM# 69 2 DUCAT
7.0000 g., 0.9860 Gold 0.2219 oz. AGW **Ruler:** Adolf Friedrich I **Note:** Klippe 2 Ducat. Similar to 1 Ducat, KM#68.

Date	Mintage	VG	F	VF	XF	Unc
1639 (i) Rare	—	—	—	—	—	—

KM# 122 2 DUCAT
7.0000 g., 0.9860 Gold 0.2219 oz. AGW
Ruler: Christian Ludwig I **Obv:** Christian Ludwig

Date	Mintage	VG	F	VF	XF	Unc
1681 Rare	—	—	—	—	—	—

KM# A45 10 DUCAT
35.0000 g., 0.9860 Gold 1.1095 oz. AGW
Ruler: Adolf Friedrich I **Note:** Struck with 1 Thaler dies, KM#66.

Date	Mintage	VG	F	VF	XF	Unc
1647 (i) Rare	—	—	—	—	—	—

Note: Struck with 1 Thaler dies, KM#66

PIEFORTS

KM#	Date	Mintage	Identification	Mkt Val
P1	1678 (e) PBH	—	2/3 Thaler. Silver. 36.5000 g. Dav.#668, KM#106.	—
P2	1680 DB	—	2/3 Thaler. Silver. Dav.#668, KM#106.	—

MECKLENBURG-STRELITZ

The duchy of Mecklenburg was located along the Baltic Coast between Holstein and Pomerania. The Strelitz line was founded in 1658 when the Mecklenburg line was divided into two lines. The 1815 Congress of Vienna elevated the duchy to the status of grand duchy. It became a part of the German Empire in 1871 until 1918 when the last grand duke died.

RULER
Adolf Friedrich II, 1692-1708

GRAND DUCHY

REGULAR COINAGE

KM# 4 THALER
Silver **Obv:** Bust of Adolph Friedrich II right dividing date **Rev:** Helmeted, crowned and supported arms **Note:** Dav. #7073.

Date	Mintage	VG	F	VF	XF	Unc
1694 Rare	—	—	—	—	—	—

MEMMINGEN

This former free imperial city is located in southern Bavaria, about 35 miles southwest of Augsburg. It is the site of an early church foundation of the mid-8th century, but the town itself is mentioned only from the first part of the 11th century. In 1286, free city status and mint rights were granted.

The town struck bracteates into the 14th century. A local town coinage was also issued in the 17th and early 18th centuries. The city was annexed to Bavaria in 1802.

MINTMASTERS
Johannes Vogel, 1622-1623 and 1635-1636

ARMS
Normally 2-fold, divided vertically, half of imperial eagle on left, cross on right.

FREE CITY

REGULAR COINAGE

KM# 10 2 KREUZER (1/2 Batzen)
Silver **Obv:** City arms, legend and date **Obv. Legend:** MEMINGEN **Rev:** 2 in baroque frame **Rev. Legend:** STATT MU(V)NZ **Note:** Varieties exist.

Date	Mintage	Good	VG	F	VF	XF
1635	—	—	30.00	60.00	150	350
1636	—	—	30.00	60.00	150	350

KM# 6 3 KREUZER (Groschen)
Silver **Obv:** City arms in oval baroque frame divide date **Rev:** Inscription in oval baroque frame **Rev. Inscription:** ST: /MEM: /.3. **Note:** Varieties exist.

Date	Mintage	Good	VG	F	VF	XF
1623	—	—	40.00	80.00	185	400

KM# 5 12 KREUZER (Dreibatzner)
Silver **Obv:** City arms in oval baroque frame divide date, XII above **Rev:** Inscription in oval baroque frame **Rev. Inscription:** STAT / MEMIN / GEN **Note:** Varieties exist.

Date	Mintage	Good	VG	F	VF	XF
16ZZ	—	—	27.00	55.00	120	300
1622	—	—	27.00	55.00	120	300
1623	—	—	27.00	55.00	120	300

METZ

The capital of Lorraine (Lothringen), Metz is located 36 miles (60 km) west of Saarbrücken and 80 mi. (132 km) west-northwest of Strasburg in present-day France. It has existed as a place prior to the Roman conquest of Gaul and was named by the Romans Divodurum. It was the site of a bishopric at least from the 4th century which grew in importance in the High Middle Ages. Metz functioned as the location of an imperial mint from the 9th through early 12th centuries and the first coins of the bishops were struck in the mid-10th century. The city was attacked and occupied Metz during 1552 and 1553, at which time the coinage of the bishops began to assume the French model upon forfeiting their rights to the conquerors. The Peace of Westphalia ending the Thirty Years' War in 1648 gave formal recognition to the seizure of the city and the last local coinage was issued around 1660.

RULERS
Karl II, Herzog von Lothringen-Guise, 1578-1607
Annas von Peruffe d'Escars von Givry, 1608-1612
Heinrich III, Marquis von Verneuil, 1612-1652 (d.1682)
Under Guardianship of the Cathedral Chapter, 1612-1621

ARMS
Cross

BISHOPRIC

REGULAR COINAGE

KM# 7 DENIER

Silver **Ruler:** Heinrich III **Obv:** Crown on cross, mitre **Obv. Legend:** VIC. HENRI. D. G. EPVS. METENSIS. **Rev:** Crowned H **Rev. Legend:** MONETA. NOVA. VICENSIS.

Date	Mintage	VG	F	VF	XF	Unc
ND(1612-52)	—	55.00	115	225	400	—

KM# 10 2 DENIER

Silver **Ruler:** Heinrich III **Obv:** Similar to 1 Denier, KM#7 **Rev:** Crowned "Alerion"

Date	Mintage	VG	F	VF	XF	Unc
ND(1612-52)	—	60.00	120	240	440	—

KM# 4 1/4 ECU

Silver **Ruler:** Karl II **Obv:** Bust of bishop **Obv. Legend:** CAROL. D. CARD. LOTH. EP. ARGENT. ET. NET **Rev. Legend:** ALSAS. LANGRA.

Date	Mintage	VG	F	VF	XF	Unc
ND(1578-1607)	—	—	—	—	—	—

CITY

The pre-Roman settlement of Metz was the seat of a bishopric from the 4th century (see) and became a free imperial city in the 13th century. The city was accorded the right to mint its own coins in 1383, which production came to an end after the conclusion of the Peace of Westphalia, the treaty ending the Thirty Years' War in 1648-50. The city and surrounding territory then formally passed to France. The last city coinage was struck in 1650.

CITY ARMS

Shield divided vertically into two sections, right half usually shaded

REFERENCES

Sch = Wolfgang Schulten, **Deutsche Münzen aus der Zeit Karls V.**, Frankfurt am Main, 1976.

S = Hugo Frhr. Von Saurma-Jeltsch, **Die Saurmasche Münzsammlung deutscher, schweizerischer und polnischer Gepräge von etwa dem Beginn der Groschenzeit bis zur Kipperperiode**, Berlin, 1892.

REGULAR COINAGE

KM# 1 6 GROSCHEN (1/2 Franc)

Silver **Obv:** Oval city arms in baroque frame, value "VI.G." in exergue **Obv. Legend:** MONETA. CIVITA. METENSIS. **Rev:** Bust of St. Stephen left, date in exergue **Rev. Legend:** S • STEPHAN • PROTHOM **Note:** Varieties exist.

Date	Mintage	VG	F	VF	XF	Unc
1611	—	40.00	80.00	140	200	—
1612	—	40.00	80.00	140	200	—
1613	—	40.00	80.00	140	200	—
1614	—	40.00	80.00	140	200	—
1616	—	40.00	80.00	140	200	—
1617	—	40.00	80.00	140	200	—
16Z3	—	40.00	80.00	140	200	—
1641	—	40.00	80.00	140	200	400

KM# 2 12 GROSCHEN (Franc)

Silver **Obv:** Oval city arms in baroque frame, value "XII.G." in exergue **Obv. Legend:** MONETA. NOVA. METENSIS **Rev:** Bust of St. Stephen left, date in exergue **Note:** Varieties exist.

Date	Mintage	VG	F	VF	XF	Unc
1611	—	45.00	100	165	275	—
1613	—	45.00	100	165	275	—
1614	—	45.00	100	165	275	—
1616	—	45.00	100	165	275	—
1617	—	45.00	100	165	275	—
1657	—	45.00	100	165	275	—

KM# 6 1/4 THALER (Teston)

Silver

Date	Mintage	VG	F	VF	XF	Unc
1628	—	27.00	55.00	100	160	—

KM# 20 1/4 THALER (Teston)

Silver **Obv:** Ornate arms **Obv. Legend:** MONETA CIVITA METENSIS **Rev:** Bust of St. Stephan left, value 1/4 below **Rev. Legend:** ❊ S. STEPANVS PROTOMARTYR

Date	Mintage	VG	F	VF	XF	Unc
1640	—	525	1,200	3,300	—	—

KM# 12 1/2 THALER

Silver **Obv:** Arms in scalloped frame **Obv. Legend:** MONETA CIVITA METENSIS **Rev:** Bust of St. Stephan left, value 1/2 below **Rev. Legend:** S.STEPHANVS PROTOMARTIR

Date	Mintage	VG	F	VF	XF	Unc
1638	—	—	1,125	3,000	5,250	—

DAV# 5580 THALER

Silver **Obv:** St. Stefan standing in oval **Rev:** Double eagle with arms on breast, date in legend

Date	Mintage	VG	F	VF	XF	Unc
1628	—	105	210	350	600	—
1629	—	105	210	350	600	—
1630	—	105	210	350	600	—
1631	—	105	210	350	600	—
1632	—	105	210	350	600	—
1633	—	115	225	400	675	—
1634	—	105	210	350	600	—

KM# 8 THALER

Silver **Obv:** Imperial eagle, city arms on breast, date **Obv. Legend:** MONETA. NOVA. METENSIS **Rev:** Full-length standing figure of St. Stephan holding palm branch in elongated oval **Note:** Varieties exist.

Date	Mintage	VG	F	VF	XF	Unc
1628	—	105	210	350	600	—
1629	—	105	210	350	600	—
1630	—	105	210	350	600	—
1631	—	105	210	350	600	—
1632	—	105	210	350	600	—
1633	—	105	210	350	600	—
1634	—	105	210	350	600	—

KM# 15 THALER

Silver **Obv:** City arms with scalloped sides in ornamented frame, date **Obv. Legend:** MONETA CIVITAMETENSIS **Rev:** Bust of St. Stephan left in circle **Rev. Legend:** S. STEPHANVS PROTOMARTIR. **Note:** Varieties exist.

Date	Mintage	VG	F	VF	XF	Unc
1638	—	90.00	180	300	525	—
1639	—	90.00	180	300	525	—
1640	—	90.00	180	300	525	—
1641	—	90.00	180	300	525	—
1643	—	90.00	180	300	525	—
1645	—	90.00	180	300	525	—

KM# 13 THALER

Silver **Obv:** City arms in hexalobe, date **Obv. Legend:** MONETA CIVITATISMETEN **Rev:** Full-length standing figure of St. Stephan holding palm branch in elongated oval

Date	Mintage	VG	F	VF	XF	Unc
1638	—	105	210	350	600	—

KM# 14 THALER

Silver **Obv:** Oval city arms in baroque frame, date **Obv. Legend:** MONETA CIVITATIS METEN **Rev:** Full-length standing figure of St. Stephan holding palm branch in elongated oval **Rev. Legend:** S • STE[JAMVS • • PROTHOMART

Date	Mintage	VG	F	VF	XF	Unc
1638	—	205	400	675	1,300	—

KM# 16 THALER

Silver **Obv:** City arms with scalloped sides in ornamented frame, date **Obv. Legend:** MONETA CIVITA METENSIS **Rev:** Bust of St. Stephan left in circle **Rev. Legend:** S. STEPHANVS PROTHOMART

Date	Mintage	VG	F	VF	XF	Unc
1638	—	90.00	180	300	525	—

DAV# 5581 THALER

Silver **Obv:** Shield in scalloped frame

Date	Mintage	VG	F	VF	XF	Unc
1638	—	90.00	180	300	525	—

DAV# 5582 THALER

Silver **Obv:** Oval arms in more decorative shield

Date	Mintage	VG	F	VF	XF	Unc
1638	—	210	400	675	1,150	—

DAV# 5583 THALER

Silver **Rev. Legend:** S. STEPHANVS PROTOMARTIR

Date	Mintage	VG	F	VF	XF	Unc
1638	—	90.00	195	400	550	—
1639	—	90.00	195	400	550	—
1640	—	90.00	195	400	550	—
1641	—	90.00	195	400	550	—
1643	—	90.00	195	400	550	—
1645	—	90.00	195	400	550	—

DAV# 5583A THALER

Silver **Rev. Legend:** S. STEPHANVS. PROTHOMART.

Date	Mintage	VG	F	VF	XF	Unc
1638	—	90.00	195	400	550	—

DAV# 5583B THALER

Silver **Rev. Legend:** S • STEPHANVS • PROTO • MARTIR •

Date	Mintage	VG	F	VF	XF	Unc
1646	—	90.00	195	400	550	—
1647	—	90.00	195	400	550	—
1650	—	90.00	195	400	550	—

KM# 22 THALER

Silver **Obv:** City arms with scalloped sides in ornamented frame, date **Obv. Legend:** MONETA CIVITA METENSIS **Rev:** Bust of St. Stephan left in circle **Rev. Legend:** S STEPHANVS • PROTO • MARTIR **Note:** Varieties exist.

Date	Mintage	VG	F	VF	XF	Unc
1646	—	90.00	180	300	525	—
1647	—	90.00	180	300	525	—
1650	—	90.00	180	300	525	—

KM# A10 2 THALER

Silver **Obv:** Imperial eagle, city arms on breast, date **Obv. Legend:** MONETA. NOVA. METENSIS **Rev:** Full-length standing figure of St. Stephan in elongated oval

Date	Mintage	VG	F	VF	XF	Unc
1630 Rare	—	—	—	—	—	—

DAV# A5580 2 THALER

Silver **Note:** Similar to 1 Thaler, Dav. #5580.

Date	Mintage	VG	F	VF	XF	Unc
1630 Rare	—	—	—	—	—	—

TRADE COINAGE

KM# A4 GOLDGULDEN

3.5000 g., 0.9860 Gold 0.1109 oz. AGW **Obv:** City arms in hexalobe **Obv. Legend:** FLORENVS. CIVITAT. METENS. **Rev:** Full-length figure of St. Stephan standing, holding stone and palm branch, divides date, all in elongated oval **Note:** Varieties exist.

Date	Mintage	VG	F	VF	XF	Unc
1620	—	175	300	500	900	—
1623	—	175	300	500	900	—
1624	—	175	300	500	900	—
1631	—	175	300	500	900	—
ND	—	175	300	500	900	—

KM# 18 GOLDGULDEN

3.5000 g., 0.9860 Gold 0.1109 oz. AGW **Obv:** City arms in hexalobe **Obv. Legend:** FLORENVS. CIVITAT. METENS. **Rev:** Bust of St. Stephan to left

Date	Mintage	VG	F	VF	XF	Unc
1639	—	350	650	1,350	2,000	—

FR# 164 GOLDGULDEN (Florin)

3.5000 g., 0.9860 Gold 0.1109 oz. AGW **Obv:** City arms in hexalobe **Obv. Legend:** FLORENVS CIVITATIS METENSID **Rev:** Full-length figure of St. Stefan standing holding stone and palm branch, all in elongated oval **Rev. Legend:** S. STEPHANUS - OROTHOMAR.

Date	Mintage	VG	F	VF	XF	Unc
1620	—	300	600	900	1,500	—
1623	—	300	600	900	1,500	—
1624	—	300	600	900	1,500	—
1631	—	300	600	900	1,500	—

FR# 165 GOLDGULDEN (Florin)

3.5000 g., 0.9860 Gold 0.1109 oz. AGW **Rev:** Bust of St. Stefan left

Date	Mintage	VG	F	VF	XF	Unc
1639	—	425	850	1,650	2,500	—
1645	—	425	850	1,650	2,500	—
ND	—	425	850	1,650	2,500	—

MINDEN

The town of Minden in Westphalia, some 60 miles east of Osnabruck, was made the seat of a bishopric by Charlemagne in 803. The bishop gained the mint right in 997 and obtained the right to maintain a mint at Eisleben in 1045. Only a small variety of coin types were struck during the first half of the 17th century, most notably the city seige issues of 1634. For the coinage of Bishop Christian, see listings for him under Brunswick-Luneburg-Celle. As part of the Peace of Westphalia ending the Thirty Years' War in 1648, Minden was secularized and handed over to Brandenburg-Prussia. The latter established a mint for the territory in Minden with coins first struck in 1652. From 1807 until 1814, Minden was part of the Kingdom of Westphalia and was returned to Prussia thereafter.

RULERS

Christian von Braunschweig-Luneburg, 1599-1633
Franz Wilhelm von Wartenberg, 1633-1648

ARMS

2 crossed keys

REFERENCE

S = Ewald Stange, **Geld- und Münzgeschichte des Bistums Minden**, Berlin, 1915.

BISHOPRIC

TRADE COINAGE

KM# 13 DUCAT

3.5000 g., 0.9860 Gold 0.1109 oz. AGW **Ruler:** Franz Wilhelm von Wartenberg **Obv:** Christ handing key to St. Peter, titles of Franz Wilhelm **Rev:** 4-fold arms with central shield of Wartenberg, crossed sword and crozier behind, titles continued around

Date	Mintage	VG	F	VF	XF	Unc
ND(ca.1643) Rare	500	—	—	—	—	—

TOWN

STANDARD COINAGE

KM# 1 3 PFENNIG (Dreier)

Copper **Ruler:** Christian von Braunschweig-Luneburg **Obv:** Lion in field of hearts in inner circle **Obv. Legend:** CHRIST. D. G. EP. MINDEN **Rev:** Large 'III' over 'GP' **Rev. Legend:** DVX. BRVNS. ET. LVNEBVR

Date	Mintage	VG	F	VF	XF	Unc
ND(1599-1633)	—	13.00	27.00	55.00	100	—

KM# 5 3 PFENNIG (Dreier)

Silver **Obv:** Crossed keys divide 1 - 6, 34 below **Rev. Inscription:** III / PENNI

Date	Mintage	VG	F	VF	XF	Unc
1634	—	—	—	—	—	—

SIEGE COINAGE

KM# 6 MATTHIER (1/2 Mariengroschen = 4 Pfennig)

Silver **Obv:** MIN/OBSES, crossed keys below divide date **Rev. Inscription:** Value: EIN/MATTI/ER

Date	Mintage	VG	F	VF	XF	Unc
1634	6,156	175	400	850	1,375	—

KM# 7 MARIENGROSCHEN

Silver **Obv:** Inscription, crossed keys below divide date **Obv. Inscription:** MIN / OBSES **Rev. Inscription:** I / GROS

Date	Mintage	VG	F	VF	XF	Unc
1634	24,000	100	200	350	—	—

KM# 8 2 MARIENGROSCHEN

Silver **Obv:** Crossed keys, legend, date **Obv. Legend:** MINDA OBSESSA Ao **Rev. Legend:** DVRVM TELVM NECESSITAS **Rev. Inscription:** II / GROS

Date	Mintage	VG	F	VF	XF	Unc
1634	4,549	275	450	800	—	—

KM# 9 4 MARIENGROSCHEN (1/2 Kopstucke)

Silver **Obv:** Crossed keys, legend, date **Obv. Legend:** MINDA OBSESSA Ao **Rev. Legend:** DVRVM TELVM NECESSITAS **Rev. Inscription:** IIII / GROS

Date	Mintage	VG	F	VF	XF	Unc
1634	70,000	—	—	—	—	—

KM# 10 4 MARIENGROSCHEN (1/2 Kopstucke)
Copper **Obv:** Two stamps: Crossed keys and IIIIG.
Note: Uniface, square, approximately 13.4 grams.

Date	Mintage	VG	F	VF	XF	Unc
ND(1634)	—	200	400	600	950	—

KM# 10a 4 MARIENGROSCHEN (1/2 Kopstucke)
7.6000 g., Tin

Date	Mintage	VG	F	VF	XF	Unc
ND(1634)	—	—	—	—	—	—

KM# 12 8 MARIENGROSCHEN (Kopstucke)
Copper **Obv:** Crossed keys, legend, date **Obv. Legend:** MINDA OBSESSA Ao **Rev. Legend:** DVRVM TELVM NECESSITAS **Rev. Inscription:** VIII/GROS

Date	Mintage	VG	F	VF	XF	Unc
1634	2,099	—	—	—	—	—

KM# 11 8 MARIENGROSCHEN (Kopstucke)
Silver **Obv:** Inscription in circle **Obv. Inscription:** MINDA / OBSESSA / date **Rev:** Inscription in circle, countermarked with two crossed keys **Rev. Inscription:** 8 / GROS / CHEN **Shape:** Square **Note:** Approximately 3.6 grams.

Date	Mintage	VG	F	VF	XF	Unc
1634	—	90.00	170	225	375	—

MITTWEIDA

The town of Mittweida in Saxony is located 11 miles (18km) north of Chemnitz. During the Kipper Period of the Thirty Years' War, a local coinage was struck there.

REFERENCE
M = Otto Merseburger, **Sammlung Otto Merseburger umfassend Münzen und Medaillen von Sachsen**, Leipzig, 1894.

PROVINCIAL TOWN

KIPPER COINAGE

KM# 1 3 PFENNIG (Dreier)
Lead **Ruler:** (no Ruler Information) **Obv:** Town arms (two lions), MZ (Mittweidischer Zeichen) above **Rev:** Value '3' and date **Note:** M-2650.

Date	Mintage	VG	F	VF	XF	Unc
16Z1 Rare	—	—	—	—	—	—

MOMPELGART

(Mömpelgard, Mümpelgard, Montbéliard)

The Countship of Mömpelgart was located southwest of the rhine, between the county of Burgundy and the Landgraviate of Upper Alsace. Its capital was the town of the same name situated near the confluence of the Allaine and Lisaine Rivers, 36 miles (60 kilometers) northeast of Besançon. When the last count of the old line died without a male heir, the territory and titles passed by way of his daughter Henriette through her marriage in 1408 to Count Eberhard IV of Württemberg (ruled 1417-19). Eberhard's son, Ludwig I (1419-50), inherited Mömpelgart outright when his mother died in 1444. The Countship was ruled from this point by either the Counts (dukes from 1495) of Württemberg themselves or their brothers and cousins until a separate line was established in 1608. When that line became extinct in 1723, the titles and lands reverted to Württemberg. France annexed Mömpelgart in 1796 and all association with Württemberg ended.

RULERS
Friedrich I, 1558-1608
Under guardianship of his uncle, Ludwig III (Duke 1568-93)
Ludwig Friedrich, 1608-1631
Leopold Friedrich, 1631-1662
Georg II, 1662-1699
French Occupation, 1684-1697
Leopold Eberhard, 1699-1723

MINT MARKS
M – Mömpelgart Mint
R – Reichenweier (Riquewihr Mint

MINT OFFICIALS' INITIALS

Initial	Date	Name
	1579-1616	Franz Briot
	1613-19	Franz Guichart
	1622	André Hubner
	1623-24	Jacob Kolb
	1624-25	3 brothers Wittenauer
S	1692	Johann Friedrich Schattauer, die-cutter and mintmaster in Brenz

ARMS
Mömpelgart – 2 fish standing on tails
Württemberg – 3 stag horns
Flag with eagle (Hereditary flag-bearer of the Empire)
Teck – field of lozenges (diamond shapes)
Urach – hunting horn

REFERENCE
B&E = Christian Binder and Julius Ebner, **Württembergische Münz- und Medaillen-Kunde**, 2 vols., Stuttgart, 1910-12.

COUNTSHIP

REGULAR COINAGE

KM# 4 KREUZER
Silver **Ruler:** Ludwig Friedrich **Obv:** Mömpelgart arms, titles of Ludwig Friedrich **Rev:** 'LF' monogram, 4 fleur-de-lis in cruciform, date **Rev. Legend:** M—N—M—

Date	Mintage	VG	F	VF	XF	Unc
(1)622	—	33.00	60.00	120	240	—

KM# 5 KREUZER
Silver **Ruler:** Ludwig Friedrich **Obv:** Mömpelgart arms, 'I' left and right, titles of Ludwig Friedrich **Rev:** 'LF' monogram, 4 fleur-de-lis in cruciform, 'I' left and right, date

Date	Mintage	VG	F	VF	XF	Unc
1622	—	33.00	60.00	120	240	—

KM# 7 2 KREUZER (1/2 Batzen = Halbbatzen)
0.8800 g., Silver **Ruler:** Ludwig Friedrich **Obv:** Württemberg arms, titles of Ludwig Friedrich **Rev:** Mömpelgart arms, date **Rev. Legend:** MON: NOVA: MONT:

Date	Mintage	VG	F	VF	XF	Unc
1622	—	55.00	100	200	375	—

Note: Known also struck on thick flan of 2.82 grams

KM# 8 2 KREUZER (1/2 Batzen = Halbbatzen)
0.8800 g., Silver **Ruler:** Ludwig Friedrich **Obv:** 3 small shields of arms, 2 above 1, which divides date below, value '2' at top, titles of Ludwig Friedrich **Rev:** Flag with eagle, 'M' below, titles continued

Date	Mintage	VG	F	VF	XF	Unc
1624 M	22,000	60.00	120	220	400	—

KM# 9 3 KREUZER (Groschen)
Silver **Ruler:** Ludwig Friedrich **Obv:** Württemberg arms, '3' above, titles of Ludwig Friedrich **Rev:** Mömpelgart arms, '3' above, date **Rev. Legend:** MON:NOVA:MOMP: **Note:** Weight varies 1.03-1.24 grams.

Date	Mintage	VG	F	VF	XF	Unc
16Z3	143,000	40.00	80.00	160	320	—
16Z4	124,000	40.00	80.00	160	320	—

KM# 9a 3 KREUZER (Groschen)
3.8000 g., Silver **Ruler:** Ludwig Friedrich **Obv:** Württemberg arms, '3' above, titles of Ludwig **Rev:** Mömpelgart arms, '3' above, date **Rev. Legend:** MON:NOVA:MOMP: **Note:** Klippe.

Date	Mintage	VG	F	VF	XF	Unc
16Z4	—	—	—	—	—	—

KM# 15 12 KREUZER (Dreibätzner)
Silver **Ruler:** Ludwig Friedrich **Obv:** Bust right, value '12' below, titles of Ludwig Friedrich **Rev:** Crowned 4-fold arms divide date **Rev. Legend:** SECVNDM.VOLVNTATEM.DEI.

Date	Mintage	VG	F	VF	XF	Unc
1622	—	165	325	525	850	—

KM# 16 12 KREUZER (Dreibätzner)
Silver **Ruler:** Ludwig Friedrich **Obv:** 3 small shields of arms, 2 above 1, value '12' above, titles of Ludwig Friedrich **Rev:** Shield with eagle flag, date **Rev. Legend:** COMES.MOMPELGART

Date	Mintage	VG	F	VF	XF	Unc
1623	—	165	325	525	850	—

KM# 17 12 KREUZER (Dreibätzner)
Silver **Ruler:** Ludwig Friedrich **Obv:** 3 small shields of arms, 2 above 1, value '12' above, titles of Ludwig Friedrich **Rev:** Shield with eagle flag, date **Rev. Legend:** MONTPELIGAR or MONTBELIGAR

Date	Mintage	VG	F	VF	XF	Unc
1624	—	165	325	525	850	—

KM# 18 2 SCHILLING
Silver **Ruler:** Ludwig Friedrich **Obv:** 3 small shields of arms, 2 above 1, value '2' above, titles of Ludwig Friedrich **Rev:** Shield with eagle flag, date **Rev. Legend:** MONTPELIGAR or MONTBELIGAR

Date	Mintage	VG	F	VF	XF	Unc
1624	31,000	27.00	55.00	95.00	170	—
1625	41,000	27.00	55.00	95.00	170	—

KM# 19 1/4 THALER
Silver **Ruler:** Ludwig Friedrich **Obv:** Bust right in circle, titles of Ludwig Friedrich **Rev:** Crowned 4-fold arms divide II—II (=1/4 Taler), date **Rev. Legend:** SECVNDVM.VOLVNTATEM.DEI

Date	Mintage	VG	F	VF	XF	Unc
1622	—	—	—	—	—	—

KM# 20 1/2 THALER (Shooting)
Silver **Ruler:** Ludwig Friedrich **Obv:** Large 'LF' monogram in circle, wreath border **Rev:** Crossbow vertical divides date in circle, wreath border

Date	Mintage	VG	F	VF	XF	Unc
1612	—	—	—	—	—	—

Note: The '2' in the date is retrograde

KM# 21 2/3 THALER (Gulden)
Silver **Ruler:** Georg II **Obv:** Bust right, titles of Georg II **Rev:** Crowned oval 4-fold arms within palm branches, date **Rev. Legend:** CONCORDIA.RES.PARVÆ.CRESCVNT

Date	Mintage	VG	F	VF	XF	Unc
1692 S	—	—	—	—	—	—

KM# 22 THALER (Shooting)
Silver **Ruler:** Ludwig Friedrich **Obv:** Large 'LF' monogram in circle, wreath border **Rev:** Crowned 4-fold arms in rhombus divide date, all within circle, wreath border

Date	Mintage	VG	F	VF	XF	Unc
1614 Rare	—	—	—	—	—	—

KM# 23 THALER (Shooting)
Silver **Ruler:** Ludwig Friedrich **Obv:** Ruffed collared bust in circle, titles of Ludwig Friedrich **Rev:** Crowned ornate 4-fold arms, date **Rev. Legend:** SECVNDVM.VOLVNTATEM.DEI **Note:** Dav. 7075, Varieties Exist.

Date	Mintage	VG	F	VF	XF	Unc
1622	11,000	2,250	4,750	7,750	—	—

Note: Fritz Rudolf Künker Münzenhandlung Auction 134, 1-08, VF realized approximately $7,680; Hess-Divo AG Auction 304, 5-06, VF realized approximately $15,640; Fritz Rudolf Künker Münzenhandlung Auction 98, 3-05, VF realized approximately $5,070

Date	Mintage	VG	F	VF	XF	Unc
16Z3 Rare	—	—	—	—	—	—

KM# 24 2 THALER
Silver **Ruler:** Ludwig Friedrich **Obv:** Bust in circle, titles of Ludwig Friedrich **Rev:** Crowned ornate 4-fold arms, date
Rev. Legend: SECVNDVM.VOLVNTATEM.DEI

Date	Mintage	VG	F	VF	XF	Unc
1624 Rare	—	—	—	—	—	—

KM# 25 1/4 DUCAT
Gold **Ruler:** Ludwig Friedrich **Obv:** Mömpelgart arms, titles of Ludwig **Rev:** 'LF' monogram, 4 fleur-de-lis in cruciform, date **Rev. Legend:** M—N—M— **Note:** Struck from the same dies as Kreuzer KM#4.

Date	Mintage	VG	F	VF	XF	Unc
(1)622	—	1,200	2,400	3,600	5,400	—

KM# 26 1/2 DUCAT
Gold **Ruler:** Ludwig Friedrich **Obv:** Württemberg arms, titles of Ludwig Friedrich **Rev:** Mömpelgart arms, date **Rev. Legend:** MON:NOVA:MONT: **Note:** Struck from the same dies as 2 Kreuzer, KM#7.

Date	Mintage	VG	F	VF	XF	Unc
1622	—	1,500	2,700	4,200	6,000	—

MONTFORT

Montfort struck their first coins, bracteates, in the 13th century. The first Count of Montfort ruled ca. 1200.

After many divisions and consolidations, Montfort was sold to Austria in 1780.

RULERS
Hugo and Johann VII, 1619-1625
Hugo, 1619-1662
Johann VIII, 1662-1686
Anton II, regent, 1686-1693
Anton III, the Younger, 1693-1734

MINTMASTER'S INITIALS
FIG - Franz Josef Gully

COUNTSHIP

STANDARD COINAGE

KM# 13 4 HELLER (2 Pfennig)
Copper, 17 mm. **Obv:** Monogram HGZM in pearl circle, IIII at top, date at bottom **Rev:** Montfort arms between flowers

Date	Mintage	VG	F	VF	XF	Unc
1622	—	200	325	675	1,075	—

KM# 22 PFENNIG
Copper **Obv:** Flag in cartouche divides date, "H" above
Note: Uniface.

Date	Mintage	VG	F	VF	XF	Unc
1624	—	200	325	675	1,075	—

KM# 22a PFENNIG
Silver **Obv:** Flag in cartouche divides date, "H" above **Note:** Uniface.

Date	Mintage	VG	F	VF	XF	Unc
1624	—	—	—	—	—	—

KM# 30 PFENNIG
Copper, 22 mm. **Obv:** Flag in cartouche divides date, "H" above
Note: Uniface

Date	Mintage	VG	F	VF	XF	Unc
(16)27	—	200	325	675	1,075	—

KM# 32 PFENNIG
Copper, 12 mm. **Obv:** Montfort arms divide date, "H" above
Note: Uniface.

Date	Mintage	VG	F	VF	XF	Unc
(16)29	—	200	325	675	1,075	—

KM# 35 PFENNIG
Copper, 11 mm. **Obv:** Flag on plain shield **Note:** Uniface.

Date	Mintage	VG	F	VF	XF	Unc
ND(1662-86)	—	135	275	525	1,000	—

KM# 48 PFENNIG
Copper, 13 mm. **Obv:** Crowned arms in elongated shield divides date **Note:** Uniface.

Date	Mintage	VG	F	VF	XF	Unc
1676	—	165	300	600	1,000	—

KM# 14 1/2 KREUZER
Copper, 16 mm. **Obv:** Arms with "H" between flowers above, "K" below divides date **Note:** Uniface.

Date	Mintage	VG	F	VF	XF	Unc
1622	—	200	325	675	1,075	—

KM# 17 KREUZER
0.6600 g., Silver, 16 mm. **Obv:** Crowned double eagle, "K" in orb on breast **Rev:** Montfort arms divide date

Date	Mintage	VG	F	VF	XF	Unc
1623	—	165	325	600	1,000	—

KM# 25 KREUZER
Silver **Obv:** Double eagle, "1" in orb on breast
Obv. Legend: FER II... **Rev:** Montfort arms on double cross

Date	Mintage	VG	F	VF	XF	Unc
1625	—	165	325	600	1,000	—

KM# 28 KREUZER
Silver **Obv. Legend:** FERD II...

Date	Mintage	VG	F	VF	XF	Unc
1626	—	165	325	600	1,000	—

KM# 36 KREUZER
Silver **Obv:** Crowned double eagle, "I" on breast **Rev:** Montfort arms in cartouche

Date	Mintage	VG	F	VF	XF	Unc
ND(1662-86)	—	165	275	525	850	—

KM# 70 KREUZER
Silver **Obv:** Crowned double eagle with "I" on breast dividing date **Rev:** Crowned arms **Rev. Legend:** ...MON.

Date	Mintage	VG	F	VF	XF	Unc
1680	—	135	275	525	850	—

KM# 71 KREUZER
Silver **Rev. Legend:** ...MONTF.

Date	Mintage	VG	F	VF	XF	Unc
1680	—	135	275	525	850	—

KM# 90 KREUZER
Silver, 15 mm. **Obv:** Armored bust right **Rev:** Crowned arms between palm fronds

Date	Mintage	VG	F	VF	XF	Unc
1696	—	80.00	160	300	525	—

KM# 91 KREUZER
Silver **Obv:** Crowned shield **Obv. Legend:** ... MON.
Rev: Crowned double eagle, "I" in orb on breast

Date	Mintage	VG	F	VF	XF	Unc
(16)96	—	60.00	120	225	400	—
(16)96	—	60.00	120	225	400	—

KM# 92 KREUZER
Silver **Rev. Legend:** ...MONTF.

Date	Mintage	VG	F	VF	XF	Unc
1696 IK	—	80.00	160	300	525	—

KM# 93 KREUZER
Silver **Rev. Legend:** ...MON:F.

Date	Mintage	VG	F	VF	XF	Unc
1696	—	80.00	160	300	525	—

KM# 18 2 KREUZER
1.2500 g., Silver, 18 mm. **Obv:** Orb with denomination
Obv. Legend: FERD.II... **Rev:** Church flag in ornamented shield

Date	Mintage	VG	F	VF	XF	Unc
ND	—	27.00	55.00	100	220	—

KM# 19 2 KREUZER
Silver, 19 mm. **Rev:** Montfort arms in ornamentation and legend

Date	Mintage	VG	F	VF	XF	Unc
1623	—	33.00	60.00	115	225	—
1624	—	33.00	60.00	115	225	—

KM# 27 2 KREUZER
Silver **Note:** Double dot legend dividers; (16)26 date also exists with a Lindau countermark.

Date	Mintage	VG	F	VF	XF	Unc
1625	—	27.00	45.00	90.00	210	—
1626	—	27.00	45.00	90.00	210	—
(16)26	—	27.00	45.00	90.00	210	—
(16)27	—	27.00	45.00	90.00	210	—
(16)28	—	27.00	45.00	90.00	210	—
1629	—	27.00	45.00	90.00	210	—
(16)29	—	27.00	45.00	90.00	210	—
(16)29(29) Error date	—	27.00	45.00	90.00	210	—

KM# 26 2 KREUZER
Silver **Note:** Single dot legend dividers.

Date	Mintage	VG	F	VF	XF	Unc
1625	—	33.00	60.00	115	225	—

KM# 83 4 KREUZER
4.0000 g., Silver, 23 mm. **Obv:** Manteled arms with helmet and flag **Obv. Legend:** ...COMES.IN... **Rev:** Crowned imperial eagle, 4 in orb on breast **Rev. Legend:** ...COMES.IN...

Date	Mintage	VG	F	VF	XF	Unc
1694	—	27.00	55.00	110	225	—
(16)94	—	27.00	55.00	110	225	—

KM# 85 4 KREUZER
4.0000 g., Silver **Ruler:** Anton III, the Younger
Obv. Legend: "COM:" **Note:** Many varieties exist.

Date	Mintage	VG	F	VF	XF	Unc
(16)94	—	27.00	55.00	110	225	—
1695	—	27.00	55.00	110	225	—
1697	—	27.00	55.00	110	225	—

KM# 84 4 KREUZER
Silver **Ruler:** Anton III, the Younger **Obv:** Manteled arms with helmet and mitre above **Obv. Legend:** ANTONIVS. COMES.IN. MONTFOR. **Rev:** Crowned imperial eagle, 4 in orb on breast **Rev. Legend:** LEOPOLDVS. D.G. ROM. IMP. S. AVG.

Date	Mintage	VG	F	VF	XF	Unc
1694	—	27.00	55.00	110	225	—

KM# 8 12 KREUZER
Silver

Date	Mintage	VG	F	VF	XF	Unc
1621	—	1,000	1,650	—	—	—

KM# 9 12 KREUZER
2.0000 g., Silver, 26 mm. **Obv:** Armored bust left with sword on right shoulder and sceptre in left hand **Rev:** Crowned imperial eagle, 12 in orb on breast **Note:** Kipper.

Date	Mintage	VG	F	VF	XF	Unc
ND	—	850	1,600	—	—	—

KM# 11 12 KREUZER
Silver **Obv:** Montfort shield in field next to bust

Date	Mintage	VG	F	VF	XF	Unc
ND	—	850	1,600	—	—	—

KM# 40 15 KREUZER

Silver, 31 mm. **Obv:** Crowned Montfort arms between palm branches **Rev:** Crowned imperial eagle above XV
Rev. Legend: IN. MONTFORT.

Date	Mintage	VG	F	VF	XF	Unc
1674	—	200	375	675	—	—

KM# 41 15 KREUZER

Silver **Obv:** Crowned Montfort arms between palm branches **Obv. Legend:** MONTFOR. **Rev:** Crowned imperial eagle above XV

Date	Mintage	VG	F	VF	XF	Unc
1674	—	200	375	675	—	—

KM# 42 15 KREUZER

Silver, 31 mm. **Obv:** Crowned Montfort arms between palm branches **Obv. Legend:** I.MONTFORT: **Rev:** Crowned imperial eagle above XV

Date	Mintage	VG	F	VF	XF	Unc
1674	—	200	375	675	—	—

KM# 43 15 KREUZER

5.6500 g., Silver, 29 mm. **Obv:** Armored bust right **Obv. Legend:** IOANN... **Rev:** Crowned arms between 2 branches

Date	Mintage	VG	F	VF	XF	Unc
1675	—	135	275	450	—	—

KM# 44 15 KREUZER

5.6500 g., Silver, 29 mm. **Obv:** Armored bust right **Obv. Legend:** IOANNES... **Rev:** Crowned arms between 2 branches

Date	Mintage	VG	F	VF	XF	Unc
1675	—	135	275	450	—	—

KM# 49 15 KREUZER

Silver **Obv:** Armored bust right, dots at beginning and end of legend **Rev:** Crowned arms between 2 branches

Date	Mintage	VG	F	VF	XF	Unc
1676	—	45.00	85.00	165	375	—

KM# 50 15 KREUZER

Silver **Obv:** Armored bust right, without dots at beginning and end of legend **Rev:** Crowned arms between 2 branches

Date	Mintage	VG	F	VF	XF	Unc
1676	—	45.00	85.00	165	375	—

KM# 51 15 KREUZER

Silver **Obv:** Armored bust right, tight curls

Date	Mintage	VG	F	VF	XF	Unc
1676	—	45.00	85.00	165	375	—

KM# 52 15 KREUZER

Silver **Obv:** Armored bust right, continuous legend below **Rev:** Crowned arms between 2 branches

Date	Mintage	VG	F	VF	XF	Unc
1678	—	40.00	80.00	160	320	—

KM# 53 15 KREUZER

Silver **Obv:** Armored bust right, divides legend at bottom **Rev:** Crowned arms between 2 branches

Date	Mintage	VG	F	VF	XF	Unc
1678	—	40.00	80.00	160	320	—

KM# 54 15 KREUZER

Silver **Obv:** Armored bust right, divides legend **Obv. Legend:** ...COM + - + MES... **Rev:** Crowned arms between 2 branches

Date	Mintage	VG	F	VF	XF	Unc
1678	—	40.00	80.00	160	320	—

KM# 58 15 KREUZER

Silver **Obv:** Armored bust right, continuous legend **Rev:** Crowned arms between 2 branches

Date	Mintage	VG	F	VF	XF	Unc
1679	—	40.00	80.00	160	320	—

KM# 59 15 KREUZER

Silver **Obv:** Armored bust right, divides legend **Obv. Legend:** "COMES * - * DE" **Rev:** Crowned arms between 2 branches

Date	Mintage	VG	F	VF	XF	Unc
1679	—	40.00	80.00	160	320	—

KM# 82 15 KREUZER

Silver, 30 mm. **Obv:** Armored bust right **Rev:** Crowned arms between 2 branches

Date	Mintage	VG	F	VF	XF	Unc
1692	—	33.00	65.00	135	325	—

KM# 55 30 KREUZER (1/2 Gulden)

Silver **Obv:** Armored bust **Rev:** Crowned arms between branches

Date	Mintage	VG	F	VF	XF	Unc
1678	—	200	375	725	1,350	—

KM# 60 30 KREUZER (1/2 Gulden)

Silver **Obv:** Armored bust **Rev:** Heart-shaped shield

Date	Mintage	VG	F	VF	XF	Unc
1679	—	200	375	725	1,350	—

KM# 75 30 KREUZER (1/2 Gulden)

Silver, 33 mm. **Obv:** Armored bust **Rev:** Crowned arms between branches

Date	Mintage	VG	F	VF	XF	Unc
1690	—	200	325	600	1,075	—
1690 FIG	—	200	325	600	1,075	—
1691/10 FIG	—	—	—	—	—	—

KM# 79 30 KREUZER (1/2 Gulden)

Silver **Obv:** Armored bust right **Rev:** Crowned arms between branches

Date	Mintage	VG	F	VF	XF	Unc
1691 FIG	—	200	325	600	1,075	—

KM# 56 60 KREUZER (Gulden)

18.5000 g., Silver, 37 mm. **Obv:** Bust right **Rev:** Crowned arms between branches

Date	Mintage	VG	F	VF	XF	Unc
1678	—	115	225	425	725	—

KM# 57 60 KREUZER (Gulden)

Silver **Obv:** Bust right **Rev:** Crowned arms between branches, heart-shaped shield

Date	Mintage	VG	F	VF	XF	Unc
1678	—	135	275	525	850	—

KM# 61 60 KREUZER (Gulden)

Silver **Obv:** Bust right **Rev:** Crowned arms between branches **Note:** This coin also exists with Franconian Circle and Salzburg countermarks.

Date	Mintage	VG	F	VF	XF	Unc
1679	—	115	225	425	725	—

KM# 62 60 KREUZER (Gulden)

Silver **Obv:** Bust right **Rev:** Crowned arms between branches, legend in rope borders

Date	Mintage	VG	F	VF	XF	Unc
1679	—	115	225	425	725	—

KM# 63 60 KREUZER (Gulden)

Silver **Obv:** Bust right, legend divided at bottom **Rev:** Crowned arms between branches

Date	Mintage	VG	F	VF	XF	Unc
1679	—	100	200	375	650	—

KM# 64 60 KREUZER (Gulden)

Silver **Obv:** Portrait with modified nose **Rev:** Crowned arms between branches

Date	Mintage	VG	F	VF	XF	Unc
1679	—	135	275	450	800	—

KM# 76 60 KREUZER (Gulden)

16.2500 g., Silver, 38 mm. **Obv:** Portrait with loose curls **Rev:** Crowned arms between 2 branches **Note:** This coin also exists with Franconian Circle countermark.

Date	Mintage	VG	F	VF	XF	Unc
1690 FIG	—	100	200	375	650	—

KM# 77 60 KREUZER (Gulden)

Silver **Obv:** Portrait with tight curls **Rev:** Crowned arms between 2 branches **Note:** This coin also exists with Franconian Circle countermark.

Date	Mintage	VG	F	VF	XF	Unc
1690 FIG	—	100	200	375	650	—

KM# 78 60 KREUZER (Gulden)

Silver **Obv:** Portrait with tight scale-like curls **Rev:** Large crown **Note:** This coin also exists with Franconian Circle countermark.

Date	Mintage	VG	F	VF	XF	Unc
1690	—	100	200	375	650	—

KM# 80 60 KREUZER (Gulden)

Silver **Obv. Legend:** ...ADMINI.

Date	Mintage	VG	F	VF	XF	Unc
1691 FIG	—	100	200	375	650	—

KM# 81 60 KREUZER (Gulden)

Silver **Obv. Legend:** ...ADMINIST.

Date	Mintage	VG	F	VF	XF	Unc
1691/0 FIG	—	100	200	375	650	—
1691 FIG	—	100	200	375	650	—
1691	—	100	200	375	650	—
1691 E	—	100	200	375	650	—

KM# 24 1/4 THALER

Silver **Ruler:** Hugo and Johann VII **Obv:** Shield of Montfort arms. **Rev:** Bust of Ferdinand II.

Date	Mintage	VG	F	VF	XF	Unc
1624	—	450	850	1,600	2,650	—

KM# 86 1/4 THALER

Silver **Ruler:** Anton III, the Younger **Obv:** Bust right **Rev:** Manteled arms with helmet and flag

Date	Mintage	VG	F	VF	XF	Unc
1694	—	450	850	1,600	2,650	—

KM# A87 1/2 THALER

Silver **Ruler:** Anton III, the Younger **Obv:** Armored bust right

Date	Mintage	VG	F	VF	XF	Unc
1694	—	400	800	1,350	2,400	—

KM# 87 1/2 THALER

14.6500 g., Silver, 36 mm. **Ruler:** Anton III, the Younger **Obv:** Draped armored bust right **Rev:** Arms

Date	Mintage	VG	F	VF	XF	Unc
1695	—	400	800	1,350	2,400	—

Note: Contemporary counterfeit of 1695 coin is struck from smaller oval shaped dies in lower grade silver

KM# 45 2/3 THALER (Gulden)

18.3000 g., Silver **Obv:** Portrait with loose curls **Note:** This coin also exists with Franconian Circle countermark.

Date	Mintage	VG	F	VF	XF	Unc
1675	—	135	300	575	925	—

KM# 46 2/3 THALER (Gulden)
Silver **Obv:** Portrait with tight curls

Date	Mintage	VG	F	VF	XF	Unc
1675	—	160	325	600	1,075	—

KM# 47 2/3 THALER (Gulden)
Silver **Rev:** Arms ornamented with 2 griffin heads

Date	Mintage	VG	F	VF	XF	Unc
1675	—	200	375	675	1,125	—

KM# 65 2/3 THALER (Gulden)
Silver **Obv:** Armored bust **Rev:** Montfort arms, denomination "2/3"

Date	Mintage	VG	F	VF	XF	Unc
1679	—	200	375	675	1,125	—

KM# 5 THALER
Silver **Obv:** Helmeted arms within beaded circle **Rev:** Double-headed imperial eagle, value in orb on breast **Note:** Dav.#7077.

Date	Mintage	VG	F	VF	XF	Unc
16Z0	—	175	350	650	1,100	—

KM# 6 THALER
Silver **Obv:** Arabesque begins legend **Rev:** Arabesque before date **Note:** Dav.#7077A.

Date	Mintage	VG	F	VF	XF	Unc
16Z0	—	250	500	850	1,350	—

KM# 7 THALER
Silver **Obv:** Arms with pointed shield **Rev:** Double-headed imperial eagle, value in orb on breast **Note:** Dav.#7078.

Date	Mintage	VG	F	VF	XF	Unc
16Z0	—	175	350	650	1,100	—

KM# 12 THALER
Silver **Obv:** Arms with rounded shield **Rev:** Double-headed imperial eagle, value in orb on breast **Note:** Dav.#7079.

Date	Mintage	VG	F	VF	XF	Unc
16Z1	—	200	400	750	1,250	—

KM# 15 THALER
Silver **Obv:** 1/2 Length bust right, small shield below **Rev:** Double-headed imperial eagle within beaded circle, crown above **Rev. Legend:** FERDINAN:II:... **Note:** Dav.#7080.

Date	Mintage	VG	F	VF	XF	Unc
16ZZ	—	500	900	1,500	—	—

KM# 16 THALER
Silver **Rev. Legend:** FERDINANDVS II...

Date	Mintage	VG	F	VF	XF	Unc
16ZZ	—	600	1,000	1,700	—	—

KM# 20 THALER
Silver **Obv:** Bust 1/4 right divides date, small shield below **Rev:** Double-headed imperial eagle within beaded circle, crown above **Note:** Single dot legend dividers; Dav.#7081.

Date	Mintage	VG	F	VF	XF	Unc
1623	—	500	900	1,500	—	—

KM# 21 THALER
Silver **Ruler:** Hugo and Johann VII **Obv:** Bust right divides date, small shield below **Obv. Legend:** MONETA NOVA HVGONIS... **Rev:** Double-headed imperial eagle within circle, crown above **Note:** Double-dot legend dividers; Dav.#7082.

Date	Mintage	VG	F	VF	XF	Unc
16Z3	—	400	750	1,250	—	—

KM# 31 THALER
Silver **Obv:** St. John of Montfort standing with shield at left, date below, double legend **Rev:** Crowned double eagle with orb on breast **Note:** Dav.#7084.

Date	Mintage	VG	F	VF	XF	Unc
1627 Rare	—	—	—	—	—	—

KM# 33 THALER
Silver **Obv:** Bust of Johann VIII with arms **Rev:** Crowned double eagle **Note:** Dav.#7085; previous KM#32.

Date	Mintage	VG	F	VF	XF	Unc
ND Rare	—	—	—	—	—	—

KM# 72 THALER
Silver **Obv:** Helmeted, mitred and draped arms with banner behind **Note:** Dav.#7086.

Date	Mintage	VG	F	VF	XF	Unc
1680	—	400	800	1,600	2,750	—

KM# 88 THALER
29.3000 g., Silver, 40 mm. **Obv:** Rounded shield, helmeted, mantled arms within beaded cirrcle **Obv. Legend:** ANTONIVS... **Rev:** Double-headed imperial eagle , value in orb on breast within beaded circle, crown above **Rev. Legend:** LEOPOLDVS... **Note:** Dav.#7087.

Date	Mintage	VG	F	VF	XF	Unc
1694	—	275	550	1,150	2,250	—
1695/4	—	275	550	1,150	2,250	—
1695	—	275	550	1,150	2,250	—
1696 IK	—	275	550	1,150	2,250	—

KM# 89 THALER
Silver **Obv:** Bust of Anton right **Rev:** Helmeted, mitred and draped arms with banner behind **Note:** Dav.#7088.

Date	Mintage	VG	F	VF	XF	Unc
1694	—	500	900	1,750	3,250	—

KM# 29 2 THALER
Silver **Obv:** Helmeted, mitred and draped arms **Rev:** Crowned double eagle **Note:** Dav.#7083.

Date	Mintage	VG	F	VF	XF	Unc
1626 Rare	—	—	—	—	—	—

PATTERNS

Including off metal strikes

KM#	Date	Mintage	Identification	Mkt Val
Pn1	1627	—	Thaler. Gold. KM#31	—

KM# 6 BATZEN (4 Kreuzer)
Silver **Obv:** Shield of city arms superimposed on long cross, MONETA, etc. **Rev:** Imperial Eagle, 1 in orb on breast, date below, EX VNO, etc.

Date	Mintage	VG	F	VF	XF	Unc
1623	—	400	725	1,250	2,000	—

KM# 7 DREIBATZNER (12 Kreuzer)
Silver **Obv:** Shield of city arms superimposed on long cross, MONETA, etc. **Obv. Legend:** MON—OVAMI—NA. **Rev:** Crowned Imperial Eagle with 12 in orb on breast, EX VNO, etc.

Date	Mintage	VG	F	VF	XF	Unc
1623	—	—	—	—	—	—

KM# 8 DREIBATZNER (12 Kreuzer)
Silver **Obv:** Ornate city arms, date **Obv. Legend:** MONETA*NOVA*MILHVSINIA* **Rev:** Crowned Imperial Eagle with value '12' below eagle, EX VNO, etc.

Date	Mintage	VG	F	VF	XF	Unc
1623	—	—	—	—	—	—

KM# 9.1 THALER
Silver **Obv:** Rappant Lion left holding city arms, MONETA, etc. **Rev:** Crowned imperial eagle **Rev. Legend:** EX VNO OMNIS NOSTRA SALVS **Note:** Dav. #5586.

Date	Mintage	VG	F	VF	XF	Unc
1623 Rare	—	—	—	—	—	—

KM# 10.1 THALER
Silver **Obv:** Rappant Lion left holding city arms, MONETA, etc. **Rev:** Crowned imperial eagle **Rev. Legend:** EX VNO OMNIS NOSTRA SAL **Note:** Dav. #5587.

Date	Mintage	VG	F	VF	XF	Unc
1623	—	1,000	1,750	3,000	5,000	—

KM# 11 THALER
Silver **Obv:** Ornate city arms, date in margin above, MONETA, etc. **Rev:** Crowned imperial eagle **Rev. Legend:** EX VNO OMNIS NOSTRA SALVS **Note:** Dav. #5588.

Date	Mintage	VG	F	VF	XF	Unc
1623	—	400	750	1,250	2,500	—

KM# 9.2 THALER
Silver **Obv:** Rappant Lion left holding city arms, MONETA, etc. **Rev:** Crowned Imperial Eagle **Rev. Legend:** EX VNO OMNIS NOSTRA SALVS **Note:** Klippe. Dav. #5586A.

Date	Mintage	VG	F	VF	XF	Unc
1623 Rare	—	—	—	—	—	—

KM# 10.2 THALER
Silver **Obv:** Rappant Lion left holding city arms, MONETA, etc. **Rev:** Crowned Imperial Eagle **Rev. Legend:** EX VNO OMNIS NOSTRA SAL **Note:** Klippe. Dav. #5587A.

Date	Mintage	VG	F	VF	XF	Unc
1623 Rare	—	—	—	—	—	—

MUHLHAUSEN ALSACE

(Mulhouse)

Not to be confused with the Mühlhausen in Thüringen, this town is located in southern Alsace, 58 miles (96 km) south of Strassburg. Mühlhausen was made a free imperial city during the 14th century. The town did not exercise its right to strike coins until the early phase of the Thirty Years' War. At the conclusion of hostilities in 1648, Mühlhausen joined the Swiss Confederation, but was annexed to France in 1798.

ARM

A millwheel, sometimes just half a millwheel and half an eagle.

FREE CITY

REGULAR COINAGE

KM# 1 RAPPEN (Pfennig)
Silver **Obv:** Half eagle and half a mill-wheel in circle within circle of pellets **Note:** Uniface. Hohl-type.

Date	Mintage	VG	F	VF	XF	Unc
ND(ca.1623)	—	55.00	115	225	375	—

KM# 2 RAPPEN (Pfennig)
Silver **Obv:** Half eagle and half a mill-wheel in circle within shield **Note:** Uniface. Hohl-type.

Date	Mintage	VG	F	VF	XF	Unc
(ca.1623)	—	55.00	115	225	375	—

KM# 3.1 1/2 KREUZER
Silver **Obv:** Arms as Rappen, KM#1, date **Obv. Legend:** MO.NO.MILHVSINA **Rev:** Ornate cross **Rev. Legend:** EX.VNO.OMN:NOST.SAL(VS).

Date	Mintage	VG	F	VF	XF	Unc
1622	—	65.00	125	240	400	—
1623	—	65.00	125	240	400	—

KM# 3.2 1/2 KREUZER
Silver **Obv:** Arms as Rappen, date **Obv. Legend:** MO. NO. MILHVSINA **Rev:** Ornate cross **Rev. Legend:** EX. VNO. OMN: NOST. SAL(VS). **Note:** Klippe.

Date	Mintage	VG	F	VF	XF	Unc
1623	—	—	—	—	—	—

KM# 4 KREUZER
Silver **Obv:** City arms, date divided at top **Obv. Legend:** MO.NO:MILHVSINA **Rev:** Ornate cross **Rev. Legend:** EX.VNO.OMN:NOST.SAL(VS).

Date	Mintage	VG	F	VF	XF	Unc
1623	—	200	375	600	925	—

KM# 5 KREUZER
Silver **Obv:** City arms **Obv. Legend:** MO.NO:MILHVSINA **Rev:** Ornate cross **Rev. Legend:** EX.VNO.OMN:NOST.SAL(VS).

Date	Mintage	VG	F	VF	XF	Unc
1623	—	200	375	600	925	—

MUHLHAUSEN THURINGEN

(in Thuringia)

The city of Mühlhausen is located 20 miles (34km) north-northwest of Gotha and is one of the oldest towns in Thuringia (Thüringen). Walls and fortifications were built during the reign of Emperor Heinrich I (918-36), who gave Mühlhausen a number of special privileges. An imperial mint was located there in the 12th and 13th centuries. After obtaining the right to mint its own coinage, Mühlhausen issued a long series dated from 1496-1767. Mühlhausen came under Prussian rule in 1802, then was dominated by Westphalia from 1807. It was returned to Prussia in 1815, by the terms of the peace which ended the Napoleonic Wars.

MINT OFFICIALS' INITIALS

Initial	Date	Name
	1616	Lubert Hausmann of Cassel
	1618-20	Andreas Weber
	1618-19	Zacharias Wolf, warden
	1621	Jacob Wossner of Munden
	1621-22	Heinrich Schwellenburg
	1626-72	Henning Schluter of Zellerfeld
	1665	Hieronymus Hollenbach, die-cutter
IZW and/or X	1676	Julius Zacharias Wefer (Weber)
	1676	Henning Christoph Meyer, warden

NOTE: Coinage of 1665 minted in Zellerfeld, Brunswick.

ARMS

Archaic type: Upper half of eagle above mill-rind.

Newer type: Eagle with two mill-rinds on wings.

NOTE: there are some variations on the above types found on some coins.

FREE CITY

REGULAR COINAGE

KM# 15 PFENNINGE
Copper **Obv:** Muhlhausen eagle, date divided by tail **Note:** Uniface. Kipper Pfennige.

Date	Mintage	VG	F	VF	XF	Unc
(16)Z1	—	30.00	65.00	110	165	—

KM# 16 3 PFENNINGE (Dreier)
Copper **Obv:** Muhlhausen eagle, head divides 3 - , tail divides date **Note:** Kipper 3 Pfenninge. Uniface. Varieties exist.

Date	Mintage	VG	F	VF	XF	Unc
(16)21	—	30.00	65.00	110	165	—
(16)22	19,000	30.00	65.00	110	165	—

KM# 5 1/24 THALER (Groschen)
Silver **Obv:** Muhlhausen eagle **Obv. Legend:** MON. NO. IM. CI. MULHUS **Rev:** Imperial orb with Z4, titles of Matthias, date divided at top

Date	Mintage	VG	F	VF	XF	Unc
1619	—	—	—	—	—	—

KM# 26 2/3 THALER (Gulden)
Silver **Obv:** Helmeted shield **Rev. Legend:** CIVIT... **Note:** Dav. #688.

Date	Mintage	VG	F	VF	XF	Unc
1676 IZW	—	450	925	1,500	—	—

KM# 6 THALER
Silver **Obv:** Shield with crowned eagle arms, 2 mill-rinds on wings, ornate helmet above **Obv. Legend:** MON:NOV:CIV:—IMP:MULHUS. **Rev:** Crowned imperial eagle, orb on breast, titles of Matthias, date divided by crown at top **Note:** Dav. #5584.

Date	Mintage	VG	F	VF	XF	Unc
1619 Rare	—	—	—	—	—	—

Note: Fritz Rudolf Künker Münzenhandlung Auction 113, 6-06, VF realized approximately $10,115

KM# 25 THALER

Silver **Obv:** Crowned imperial eagle, orb with Z4, titles of Leopold **Note:** Dav. #5585.

Date	Mintage	VG	F	VF	XF	Unc
1665	500	500	1,250	2,750	5,000	—

SIEGE COINAGE

KM# 7 DUCAT

3.5000 g., 0.9860 Gold 0.1109 oz. AGW **Obv:** Legend, Muhlhausen eagle **Obv. Legend:** MON: NOV: CIVI - IMP : MULHUS **Rev:** Crowned imperial eagle, orb on breast, date divided at top, titles of Matthias

Date	Mintage	VG	F	VF	XF	Unc
1619 Rare	—	—	—	—	—	—

MUNSTER

St. Ludger founded the bishopric near the end of the 8th or the beginning of the 9th century in Westphalia. The town of Münster, which means "monastery," grew up around the ecclesiastical establishment (which see). The earliest anonymous coins of the bishopric date from the late 11th century and a long series of issues in the name of the bishops followed over the centuries. In 1802, Münster was secularized and divided among several principalities. Those were soon mediatized and part of the territory went to Hannover. Münster belonged to the Duchy of Berg from 1806 until 1810, then to France until 1814, when it was acquired by Prussia.

During the 16th and 17th centuries treasury tokens, mostly counterstamped with the arms or initials of the current treasurer were issued. These were replaced in the middle of the 17th century by Cathedral coins, showing St. Paul with a sword. They last appeared at the end of the 18th century.

RULERS

Ernst, Herzog von Bayern, 1585-1612
Ferdinand, Herzog von Bayern, 1612-1650
Christof Bernhard von Galen, 1650-1678
Ferdinand von Fürstenberg, 1678-1683
Maximilian Heinrich von Bayern, 1683-1688
Friedrich Christian von Plettenberg, 1688-1706

MINT OFFICIALS' INITIALS & PRIVY MARKS

Initials or Privy Mark	Date	Name
EK	1638-56	Englebert Kettler
GS	Ca.1683-88	Gottfried Storp
HLO, HO	1696-1700, 1704, 1706	Heinrich Lorenz Odendahl
IL	1664-80	Johann Longerich
IO/JO	1692-96	Johann Odendahl
(a) – bird	1638-1656	Engelbert Kettler
(b) – flower		?
(c) - rosette		?

ARMS

Horizontal bar, usually shaded by cross-hatching

BISHOPRIC

REGULAR COINAGE

KM# 36 3 PFENNIG (1/112 Thaler)

Silver **Obv:** Crowned 4-fold arms with central shield of Munster, titles of Ferdinand, (112) in legend at bottom **Rev:** Titles in legend **Rev. Inscription:** III / PFEN / date **Note:** Varieties exist.

Date	Mintage	VG	F	VF	XF	Unc
1641 EK	—	20.00	40.00	65.00	120	—
1645 EK	—	20.00	40.00	65.00	120	—
1646 EK	—	20.00	40.00	65.00	120	—

KM# 40 3 PFENNIG (1/112 Thaler)

Silver **Obv:** Crowned 4-fold arms, titles of Ferdinand, (112) in legend at bottom **Rev:** Bust of St. Paul, date also in legend **Rev. Inscription:** III / PFEN / date

Date	Mintage	VG	F	VF	XF	Unc
1643 EK	—	20.00	40.00	65.00	120	—

KM# 44 3 PFENNIG (1/112 Thaler)

Silver **Rev:** Inscription, titles in legend **Rev. Inscription:** III / PFEN / date

Date	Mintage	VG	F	VF	XF	Unc
1647	—	20.00	40.00	65.00	120	—
1648	—	20.00	40.00	65.00	120	—

KM# 58 3 PFENNIG (1/112 Thaler)

Silver **Obv:** 4-fold arms with central shield of Galen (3 wolf traps), titles of Christoph Bernhard, (112) in legend at bottom **Rev:** Inscription, titles in legend **Rev. Inscription:** III / PFEN / date **Note:** Varieties exist.

Date	Mintage	VG	F	VF	XF	Unc
1652	—	20.00	40.00	65.00	120	—
1653	—	20.00	40.00	65.00	120	—
1655	—	20.00	40.00	65.00	120	—

KM# 37 4 PFENNIG (1/84 Thaler)

Silver **Obv:** Crowned 4-fold arms, titles of Ferdinand, (80) in legend at bottom **Rev:** Inscription, titles in legend **Rev. Inscription:** IIII / PFEN / date

Date	Mintage	VG	F	VF	XF	Unc
1641 EK	—	—	—	—	—	—

KM# 41 4 PFENNIG (1/84 Thaler)

Silver **Rev:** Value: 4

Date	Mintage	VG	F	VF	XF	Unc
1643 EK	—	—	—	—	—	—

KM# 25 6 PFENNIG (1/56 Thaler)

Silver **Obv:** Crowned 4-fold arms in rhombus-form, titles of Ferdinand in legend, (56) in legend at bottom **Rev:** Inscription, titles in legend **Rev. Inscription:** VI / PFEN / date **Note:** Varieties exist.

Date	Mintage	VG	F	VF	XF	Unc
1639 EK	—	20.00	40.00	65.00	120	—
1641 EK	—	20.00	40.00	65.00	120	—
1642 EK	—	20.00	40.00	65.00	120	—
1643 EK	—	20.00	40.00	65.00	120	—
1645 EK	—	20.00	40.00	65.00	120	—
1646 EK	—	20.00	40.00	65.00	120	—
1648 EK	—	20.00	40.00	65.00	120	—

KM# 59 6 PFENNIG (1/56 Thaler)

Silver **Obv:** 4-fold arms with central shield of Galen (3 wolf traps), titles of Christoph Bernhard, (56) in legend at bottom **Rev:** VI/PFEN(N), date **Note:** Varieties exist.

Date	Mintage	VG	F	VF	XF	Unc
1652	—	20.00	40.00	65.00	120	—
1654	—	20.00	40.00	65.00	120	—
1655	—	20.00	40.00	65.00	120	—

KM# 117 6 PFENNIG (1/56 Thaler)

Silver **Obv:** Crowned 6-fold arms with central shield of Plettenberg (line down center of shield), titles of Friedrich Christian in legend **Rev:** Inscription, legend, (56) at bottom **Rev. Legend:** EPISCOPVS. MONASTERIENS **Rev. Inscription:** VI / PFEN / date **Note:** Varieties exist.

Date	Mintage	VG	F	VF	XF	Unc
1695 JO	—	13.00	27.00	45.00	90.00	—
1696 HO	—	13.00	27.00	45.00	90.00	—

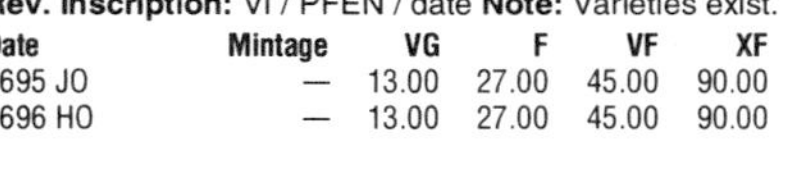

KM# 30 SCHILLING (1/28 Thaler)

Silver **Obv:** Crowned 4-fold arms iwth central shield of Munster, titles of Ferdinand, (28) in legend at bottom **Rev:** 1/2-length bust of St. Paul, below 1.SCHIL/date **Note:** Varieties exist.

Date	Mintage	VG	F	VF	XF	Unc
1640 (a)	—	25.00	45.00	80.00	140	—
1641 (a)	—	25.00	45.00	80.00	140	—
1647 (a)	—	25.00	45.00	80.00	140	—

KM# 31 SCHILLING (1/28 Thaler)

Silver **Ruler:** Ferdinand von Bayern **Rev:** Date in legend **Note:** Varieties exist.

Date	Mintage	VG	F	VF	XF	Unc
1640 EK	—	25.00	45.00	80.00	140	—
1642 EK	—	25.00	45.00	80.00	140	—
1643 EK	—	25.00	45.00	80.00	140	—
1645 EK	—	25.00	45.00	80.00	140	—
1646 EK	—	25.00	45.00	80.00	140	—
1647 EK	—	25.00	45.00	80.00	140	—
1648 EK	—	25.00	45.00	80.00	140	—

KM# 55 SCHILLING (1/28 Thaler)

Silver **Obv:** Cathedral arms with 1/2-length bust of St. Paul divides date **Rev:** Crowned imperial eagle, orb on breast, titles of Ferdinand III, (28) in legend at bottom **Note:** Sede vacante issue.

Date	Mintage	VG	F	VF	XF	Unc
1650	—	60.00	115	200	325	—

KM# 60 SCHILLING (1/28 Thaler)

Silver **Obv:** Crowned 4-fold arms with central shield of Galen arms, titles of Christoph Bernhard, (28) in legend at bottom **Rev:** Similar to KM#30 **Note:** Varieties exist.

Date	Mintage	VG	F	VF	XF	Unc
1652 EK	—	20.00	40.00	70.00	120	—
1653 EK	—	20.00	40.00	70.00	120	—
1654 EK	—	20.00	40.00	70.00	120	—

KM# 66 SCHILLING (1/28 Thaler)

Silver **Rev:** Date divided by head of St. Paul

Date	Mintage	VG	F	VF	XF	Unc
1655 EK	—	20.00	40.00	70.00	120	—

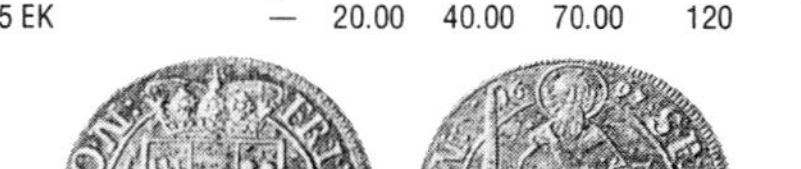

KM# 118 SCHILLING (1/28 Thaler)

Silver **Obv:** Crowned 6-fold arms with central shield of Plettenberg, titles of Friedrich Christian, (28) in legend at bottom

Date	Mintage	VG	F	VF	XF	Unc
1695 JO	—	16.00	33.00	45.00	80.00	—
1696 HO	—	16.00	33.00	45.00	80.00	—
1697 HO	—	16.00	33.00	45.00	80.00	—

KM# 32 2 SCHILLING (1/14 Thaler)

Silver **Obv:** Crowned 4-fold arms with central shield of Munster, titles of Ferdinand, (14) in legend at bottom **Rev:** Full-length figure of St. Paul with sword, date in legend

Date	Mintage	VG	F	VF	XF	Unc
1640 (a)	—	33.00	65.00	120	225	—

KM# 38 2 SCHILLING (1/14 Thaler)

Silver **Ruler:** Ferdinand von Bayern **Rev:** Date divided by figure of saint **Note:** Varieties exist.

Date	Mintage	VG	F	VF	XF	Unc
1640 (a)	—	33.00	65.00	120	225	—
1641 (a)	—	33.00	65.00	120	225	—
1643 (a)	—	33.00	65.00	120	225	—
1645 (a)	—	33.00	65.00	120	225	—
1646 (a)	—	33.00	65.00	120	225	—

Date	Mintage	VG	F	VF	XF	Unc
1647 (a)	—	33.00	65.00	120	225	—
1648	—	33.00	65.00	120	225	—

KM# 46 2 SCHILLING (1/14 Thaler)

Silver **Rev:** Date divided at top

Date	Mintage	VG	F	VF	XF	Unc
1648	—	33.00	65.00	120	225	—

KM# 61 2 SCHILLING (1/14 Thaler)

Silver **Obv:** Central shield of Galen arms, titles of Christoph Bernhard **Note:** Varieties exist.

Date	Mintage	VG	F	VF	XF	Unc
1652 (a)	—	33.00	65.00	120	225	—
1654 (a)	—	33.00	65.00	120	225	—
1655 (a)	—	33.00	65.00	120	225	—
1678 IL	—	33.00	65.00	120	225	—

KM# 120 2 SCHILLING (1/14 Thaler)

Silver **Obv:** Crowned 6-fold arms with central shield of Plettenberg, titles of Friedrich Christian

Date	Mintage	VG	F	VF	XF	Unc
1696 HLO	—	—	—	—	—	—

KM# 100 12 MARIENGROSCHEN (1/2 Gulden)

Silver **Rev. Inscription:** XII / MARIEN / GROS / date. **Note:** Similar to 24 Mariengroschen, KM#101. Varieties exist.

Date	Mintage	VG	F	VF	XF	Unc
1692 JO	—	27.00	55.00	115	225	—
1693 JO	—	27.00	55.00	115	225	—
1694 JO	—	27.00	55.00	115	225	—

KM# 102 24 MARIENGROSCHEN (Gulden)

Silver **Rev:** ...GROSCH

Date	Mintage	VG	F	VF	XF	Unc
1692 IO	—	45.00	85.00	165	325	—

KM# 101 24 MARIENGROSCHEN (Gulden)

Silver **Obv:** Crowned oval 6-fold arms with central shield of Plettenberg, titles of Friedrich Christian **Rev:** Inscription, titles in legend **Rev. Inscription:** XXIIII / MARIEN / GROS / date **Note:** Varieties exist.

Date	Mintage	VG	F	VF	XF	Unc
1692 JO	—	45.00	85.00	165	325	—
1693 JO	—	45.00	85.00	165	325	—
1694 JO	—	45.00	85.00	165	325	—

KM# 111 24 MARIENGROSCHEN (Gulden)

Silver **Rev:** ...GROSCH **Note:** Varieties exist.

Date	Mintage	VG	F	VF	XF	Unc
1694 JO	—	33.00	65.00	135	275	—
1695 JO	—	33.00	65.00	135	275	—

KM# 110 24 MARIENGROSCHEN (Gulden)

Silver **Obv:** Shield of arms squared at top, round at bottom (Spanish type)

Date	Mintage	VG	F	VF	XF	Unc
1694 JO	—	33.00	65.00	135	275	—

KM# 85 1/4 GULDEN (4 Schilling)

Silver **Obv:** Crowned 8-fold arms with central shield of Galen arms, titles of Christoph Bernhard, date **Rev:** Inscription, 6/EIN R. TR. below in laurel wreath **Rev. Inscription:** 1/4 / REICHS / GVLDEN / IIII SCHIL / VIII PFENN / MVNST / date

Date	Mintage	VG	F	VF	XF	Unc
1678 IL	—	—	—	—	—	—

KM# 86 1/4 GULDEN (4 Schilling)

Silver **Obv:** Crowned 8-fold arms with central shield of Galen arms, titles of Christoph Bernhard, date **Rev:** Inscription, 3/EIN R. TR. below in laurel wreath **Rev. Inscription:** 1/2 / REICHS / GVLDEN / VIIII SCHIL / IIII PFENNI

Date	Mintage	VG	F	VF	XF	Unc
1678 IL	—	—	—	—	—	—

KM# 87 GULDEN (18 Schilling)

Silver **Obv:** Crowned 8-fold arms with central shield of Galen arms, titles of Christoph Bernhard, date **Rev:** Inscription, 1-1/2/EIN-RTLR below **Rev. Inscription:** I / REICHS / GVLDEN / XVIII SCHIL / VIII PFENNI / MVNST / date

Date	Mintage	VG	F	VF	XF	Unc
1678	—	—	—	—	—	—

KM# 103 1/48 THALER (Halbgroschen)

Silver **Obv:** Crowned FC monogram **Rev:** Inscription, legend, date **Rev. Legend:** F.M.L. MVNTZ **Rev. Inscription:** 48 / I / REICHS / TH **Note:** Varieties exist.

Date	Mintage	VG	F	VF	XF	Unc
1692 JO	—	13.00	27.00	45.00	75.00	—

KM# 88 1/24 THALER (Groschen)

Silver **Obv:** Crowned 8-fold arms with central shield of Galen arms, titles of Christoph Bernhard **Rev:** Inscription, date in legend **Rev. Inscription:** 24 / I / REICHS / THAL., FVRST?, **Note:** Varieties exist.

Date	Mintage	VG	F	VF	XF	Unc
1678 IL	—	20.00	40.00	80.00	140	—

KM# 104 1/24 THALER (Groschen)

Silver **Obv:** Crowned oval 6-fold arms with central shield of Plettenberg, titles of Friedrich Christian **Rev:** FVRST..., date in legend **Rev. Inscription:** 24/I/REICHS/THAL. **Note:** Varieties exist.

Date	Mintage	VG	F	VF	XF	Unc
1692 IO	—	16.00	33.00	65.00	120	—
1693 IO	—	16.00	33.00	65.00	120	—

KM# 89 1/16 THALER

Silver **Obv:** Crowned 8-fold arms with central shield of Galen arms divide date **Rev:** 1/2-length bust of St. Paul with sword and book, below XVI/R. tr.

Date	Mintage	VG	F	VF	XF	Unc
1678 IL	—	33.00	65.00	115	200	—

KM# 105 1/12 THALER (Doppelgroschen)

Silver **Obv:** Crowned 6-fold arms with central shield of Plettenberg arms, titles of Friedrich Christian **Rev:** Legend, date, value **Rev. Legend:** FVRSTL? **Rev. Inscription:** 12 / EINEN / REICHS / THAL **Note:** Varieties exist.

Date	Mintage	VG	F	VF	XF	Unc
1692 IO	—	27.00	55.00	95.00	165	—
1692 JO	—	27.00	55.00	95.00	165	—
1693 IO	—	27.00	55.00	95.00	165	—
1693 JO	—	27.00	55.00	95.00	165	—
1695 IO	—	27.00	55.00	95.00	165	—
1695 JO	—	27.00	55.00	95.00	165	—
1696 JO	—	27.00	55.00	95.00	165	—

KM# 90 1/8 THALER (Blamuser)

Silver **Obv:** Crowned 8-fold arms with central shield of Galen arms divides date **Rev:** 1/2-length bust of St. Paul with sword and book, VIII/R. tr. below **Note:** Varieties exist.

Date	Mintage	VG	F	VF	XF	Unc
1678 IL	—	65.00	120	200	325	—

KM# 5 1/4 THALER

Silver **Obv:** Crowned 4-fold arms with central shield of Munster, titles of Ferdinand **Rev:** Full-length figure of St. Paul divides date **Note:** Varieties exist.

Date	Mintage	VG	F	VF	XF	Unc
1633	—	—	—	—	—	—
1637	—	—	—	—	—	—

KM# 6 1/2 THALER

Silver **Obv:** Crowned 4-fold arms with central shiedl of Munster, titles of Ferdinand **Rev:** Full-length figure of St. Paul divides date

Date	Mintage	VG	F	VF	XF	Unc
1633	—	—	—	—	—	—
1635 (b)	—	—	—	—	—	—

KM# 56 1/2 THALER

Silver **Obv:** Cathedral arms with 1/2-length bust of St. Paul divides date **Rev:** Full-length figure of Ferdinand III with sword and orb

Date	Mintage	VG	F	VF	XF	Unc
1650	—	—	—	—	—	—

KM# 106 2/3 THALER (Gulden)

Silver **Obv:** 1/2-length bust of St. Paul with sword and book, value 2/3 below **Rev:** Crowned 6-fold arms with central shield of Plettenberg divide date, titles of Friedrich Christian

Date	Mintage	VG	F	VF	XF	Unc
1692 IO	—	—	—	—	—	—

KM# 7 THALER

Silver **Obv:** Mitered arms, legend **Obv. Legend:** FERDINANDVS... **Rev:** St. Paul standing dividing date, mint mark between feet **Note:** Dav. #5589.

Date	Mintage	VG	F	VF	XF	Unc
1633 (c) Rare	—	—	—	—	—	—

KM# 8 THALER

Silver **Obv:** Crowned arms **Rev:** St. Paul **Note:** Dav. #5591.

Date	Mintage	VG	F	VF	XF	Unc
1633	—	190	375	675	1,050	—
1633 (b)	—	190	375	675	1,050	—

Date	Mintage	VG	F	VF	XF	Unc
1634 (b)	—	190	375	675	1,050	—
1635 (b)	—	190	375	675	1,050	—
1635	—	190	375	675	1,050	—
1635 (a)	—	190	375	675	1,050	—
1636 (a)	—	190	375	675	1,050	—
1637 (a)	—	190	375	675	1,050	—
1638 (a)	—	190	375	675	1,050	—
1639 (a)	—	190	375	675	1,050	—
1640 (a)	—	190	375	675	1,050	—
1643 (a)	—	190	375	675	1,050	—
1645 (a)	—	190	375	675	1,050	—
1646 (a)	—	190	375	675	1,050	—

KM# 11 THALER

Silver **Note:** Klippe. Dav. #5591A.

Date	Mintage	VG	F	VF	XF	Unc
1634 (b) Rare	—	—	—	—	—	—

KM# 12 THALER

Silver **Rev:** St. Paul above city view, date below **Note:** Dav. #5593.

Date	Mintage	VG	F	VF	XF	Unc
1638 EK	—	1,650	3,000	5,000	8,800	—
1647 EK	—	—	—	—	—	—

KM# 13 THALER

Silver **Obv:** St. Paul in cloud above city view, date below **Rev:** Adoration of the Magi **Note:** Dav. #5595.

Date	Mintage	VG	F	VF	XF	Unc
1638 EK	—	—	—	—	—	—
1647 EK	—	750	1,500	3,000	5,000	—

KM# 14 THALER

Silver **Obv:** Adoration of the Magi **Rev:** Circumcision of Jesus **Note:** Dav. #5596.

Date	Mintage	VG	F	VF	XF	Unc
ND(1647) EK	—	120	225	500	1,250	—

KM# 47 THALER

Silver **Subject:** Peace of Westphalia **Obv:** 1/2-length figure of St. Paul with sword and book, titles of Emperor Ferdinand III and Bishop Ferdinand I **Obv. Inscription:** BONVM CERTAMEN / CERTABE. FIDEM / SERVAVI **Rev:** Two arms from clouds at left and right, shaking hands and clasping caduceus and olive branches, 5-line inscription with date **Note:** Broad flan.

Date	Mintage	VG	F	VF	XF	Unc
1648	—	—	—	—	—	—

KM# 57 THALER

Silver **Note:** Sede vacante. Dav. #5597.

Date	Mintage	VG	F	VF	XF	Unc
1650 EK	—	350	1,000	2,000	5,000	—
1651 EK	—	—	—	—	—	—

KM# 62 THALER

Silver **Rev:** St. Paul **Note:** Dav. #5599.

Date	Mintage	VG	F	VF	XF	Unc
1652 (a)	—	200	450	1,000	2,000	—
1653 (a)	—	250	550	1,150	2,250	—
1654 (a)	—	250	550	1,150	2,250	—

KM# 67 THALER

Silver **Obv:** Helmeted arms **Rev:** St. Paul standing, date divided above in legend **Note:** Dav. #5600.

Date	Mintage	VG	F	VF	XF	Unc
1659	—	500	1,000	2,250	4,500	—

KM# 68 THALER

Silver **Rev:** Crucifix dividing date, inner legend **Note:** Dav. #5601.

Date	Mintage	VG	F	VF	XF	Unc
1659	—	300	650	1,400	2,800	—

KM# 76 THALER

Silver **Rev:** Oval arms **Note:** Dav. #5603A.

Date	Mintage	VG	F	VF	XF	Unc
1661	—	200	400	850	1,500	—

KM# 77 THALER

Silver **Obv:** Different city view **Rev:** Elaborate frame for arms **Note:** Size varies: 39-40mm. Dav. #5604.

Date	Mintage	VG	F	VF	XF	Unc
1661	—	250	500	100	2,000	4,200

KM# 75 THALER

Silver **Rev:** Bust of St. Paul above city view **Note:** Broad flan. Varieties exist. Dav. #5603.

Date	Mintage	VG	F	VF	XF	Unc
MDCLXI (1661)	—	100	200	500	950	—

KM# 91 THALER

Silver **Subject:** Death of the Bishop **Rev:** 11-line inscription **Note:** Broad flan. Dav. #5605.

Date	Mintage	VG	F	VF	XF	Unc
MDCLXXVIII (1678)	—	275	550	1,100	2,200	—

KM# 95 THALER

Silver **Obv:** Leopold **Note:** Sede vacante. Dav. #5607.

Date	Mintage	VG	F	VF	XF	Unc
1683 GS	—	500	1,000	2,150	3,500	—

KM# 97 THALER

Silver **Obv:** Different bust of Leopold right **Rev:** Saint with sword and book dividing date **Note:** Varieites exist. Sede vacante. Dav. #5608.

Date	Mintage	VG	F	VF	XF	Unc
1688 GS	—	350	700	1,500	3,250	6,000

KM# 107 THALER

Silver **Obv:** Bust of Friedrich Christian right **Rev:** Crowned oval arms dividing I-O, date in legend above **Note:** Dav. #5609.

Date	Mintage	F	VF	XF	Unc	BU
1693 IO	—	1,500	3,000	5,000	—	—

KM# 108 THALER

Silver **Rev:** Helmeted arms, I-O at sides, date in legend **Note:** Dav. #5610.

Date	Mintage	F	VF	XF	Unc	BU
1693 JO	—	1,500	3,000	5,000	—	—
1695 JO	—	1,500	3,000	5,000	—	—

KM# 112 THALER

Silver **Rev:** Helmeted square arms, J-O at sides **Note:** Dav. #5611.

Date	Mintage	F	VF	XF	Unc	BU
1694 JO	—	1,500	3,000	5,000	—	—

KM# 113 THALER

Silver **Rev:** Crowned arms in palm branches, J-O at sides **Note:** Dav. #5612.

Date	Mintage	F	VF	XF	Unc	BU
1694 JO	—	1,500	3,000	5,000	—	—

KM# 114 THALER

Silver **Rev:** Date divided at top **Note:** Dav. #5613.

Date	Mintage	F	VF	XF	Unc	BU
1694	—	1,500	3,000	5,000	—	—

KM# 121 THALER

Silver **Obv. Legend:** FRIDERICVS. CHRISTIANVS... **Rev:** Crowned oval arms in palm branches, date above, J-O at sides **Note:** Dav. #5614.

Date	Mintage	F	VF	XF	Unc	BU
1696 JO	—	1,200	2,000	3,500	5,500	—

KM# 122 THALER

Silver **Obv. Legend:** FRIDER: CHRISTI:... **Note:** Dav. #5615.

Date	Mintage	F	VF	XF	Unc	BU
1696	—	700	1,500	3,000	5,000	—
1696 HLO	—	700	1,500	3,000	5,000	—

KM# 123 THALER

Silver **Note:** Dav. #5616.

Date	Mintage	F	VF	XF	Unc	BU
1697 HLO	—	700	1,500	3,000	5,000	—
1698 HLO	—	700	1,500	3,000	5,000	—

KM# 124 THALER

Silver **Rev:** Date below arms diviided by mintmaster's initials

Date	Mintage	F	VF	XF	Unc	BU
1699 IO	—	700	1,500	3,000	5,000	—

KM# 49 1-1/4 THALER (Shau)

35.8800 g., Silver, 51 mm. **Ruler:** Ferdinand von Bayern **Subject:** Peace of Westphalia **Obv:** Two angels above city view **Obv. Legend:** HINC ? TOTI ? PAX ? INSONAT ? ORBI **Obv. Inscription:** MONASTERIVM / WESTPHA / 1648 **Rev:** Clasped hands in front of two crossed cornucopiae, date in chronogram **Rev. Legend:** C?SARIS ET. REGVM. IVNXIT. PAX. AVREA. DEXTER. AS. 24. 8bris. **Note:** Prev. X#M11.

Date	Mintage	F	VF	XF	Unc	BU
1648 EK	—	—	850	1,200	—	—

KM# 15 1-1/4 THALER

Silver **Obv:** Crowned arms **Rev:** St. Paul above city view **Note:** Klippe. Dav. #A5592.

Date	Mintage	VG	F	VF	XF	Unc
1638 EK Rare	—	—	—	—	—	—
1647 EK Rare	—	—	—	—	—	—

KM# 48 1-1/4 THALER

Silver **Ruler:** Ferdinand von Bayern **Subject:** Peace of Westphalia **Obv:** 1/2-length figure of St. Paul with sword and book, titles of Emperor Ferdinand III and Bishop Ferdinand I **Obv. Inscription:** BONVM CERTAMEN / CERTAVI. FIDEN / SERVAVI **Rev:** Two arms from clouds at left and right, clasped hands and holding caduceus and olive branches, 5-line inscription with date

Date	Mintage	VG	F	VF	XF	Unc
1648 Rare	—	—	—	—	—	—

KM# 17 1-1/2 THALER

Silver **Note:** Klippe. Similar to 1 Thaler, KM#12.

Date	Mintage	VG	F	VF	XF	Unc
1638 EK Rare	—	—	—	—	—	—

KM# 16 1-1/2 THALER

Silver **Note:** Klippe. Similar to 1 Thaler, KM#13. Dav. #A5594.

Date	Mintage	VG	F	VF	XF	Unc
1638 EK Rare	—	—	—	—	—	—

KM# 9 2 THALER

Silver **Note:** Similar to 1 Thaler, KM#12. Dav. #5590.

Date	Mintage	VG	F	VF	XF	Unc
1633 Rare	—	—	—	—	—	—
1633 (b) Rare	—	—	—	—	—	—
1634 (b) Rare	—	—	—	—	—	—
1636 (a) Rare	—	—	—	—	—	—
1637 (a) Rare	—	—	—	—	—	—
1639 (a) Rare	—	—	—	—	—	—

KM# 20 2 THALER

Silver **Note:** Similar to 1 Thaler, KM#13. Dav. #5594.

Date	Mintage	VG	F	VF	XF	Unc
1638 EK Rare	—	—	—	—	—	—
1647 EK	—	—	—	—	—	—

Note: Reported, not confirmed

KM# 18 2 THALER

Silver **Obv:** Crowned arms **Rev:** St. Paul above city view **Note:** Dav. #B5592.

Date	Mintage	VG	F	VF	XF	Unc
1638 EK Rare	—	—	—	—	—	—
1647 EK Rare	—	—	—	—	—	—

KM# 19 2 THALER

Silver **Note:** Klippe. Dav. #C5592.

Date	Mintage	VG	F	VF	XF	Unc
1638 EK Rare	—	—	—	—	—	—
1647 EK Rare	—	—	—	—	—	—

KM# 63 2 THALER

Silver **Note:** Similar to 1 Thaler, KM#62. Dav. #5598.

Date	Mintage	VG	F	VF	XF	Unc
1652 (a) Rare	—	—	—	—	—	—
1653 Rare	—	—	—	—	—	—
1654 Rare	—	—	—	—	—	—

KM# 69 2 THALER

Silver **Note:** Similar to 1 Thaler, KM#68. Dav. #A5601.

Date	Mintage	VG	F	VF	XF	Unc
1659 Rare	—	—	—	—	—	—

KM# 79 2 THALER

Silver **Rev:** Oval arms

Date	Mintage	VG	F	VF	XF	Unc
1661	—	550	950	1,750	2,800	—

KM# 78 2 THALER

Silver **Note:** Broad flan. Dav. #5602.

Date	Mintage	VG	F	VF	XF	Unc
MDCLXI (1661)	—	750	1,500	3,000	5,000	—

KM# 96 2 THALER

Silver **Note:** Sede vacante. Similar to 1 Thaler, KM#95. Dav. #5606.

Date	Mintage	VG	F	VF	XF	Unc
1683 GS Rare	—	—	—	—	—	—

KM# 115 2 THALER

Silver **Obv:** Bust right **Rev:** Crowned arms in palm branches **Note:** Dav. #A5612.

Date	Mintage	VG	F	VF	XF	Unc
1694 JO Rare	—	—	—	—	—	—

KM# A22 2-1/2 THALER

72.8600 g., Silver **Ruler:** Ferdinand von Bayern **Obv:** Crowned arms **Rev:** St. Paul above city view **Note:** Klippe. Same as Dav. 5592.

Date	Mintage	VG	F	VF	XF	Unc
1638 EK Rare	—	—	—	—	—	—

Note: Fritz Rudolf Künker Münzenhandlung Auction 140, 6-08, VF realized approximately $28,685; Fritz Rudolf Künker Münzenhandlung Auction 84, 6-03, VF realized approximately $14,615

KM# 21 3 THALER

Silver **Obv:** Crowned arms **Rev:** St. Paul above city view **Note:** Dav. #D5592.

Date	Mintage	VG	F	VF	XF	Unc
1638 EK Rare	—	—	—	—	—	—

KM# 22 3 THALER

Silver **Note:** Klippe. Dav. #5592.

Date	Mintage	VG	F	VF	XF	Unc
1638 EK Rare	—	—	—	—	—	—

KM# 116 3 THALER

Silver **Note:** Dav. #LS364. Illustration reduced.

Date	Mintage	VG	F	VF	XF	Unc
1694 JO Rare	—	—	—	—	—	—

Note: Spink Taisei Zurich Milas sale 4-92 XF realized $12,230

TRADE COINAGE

KM# 10 DUCAT

3.5000 g., 0.9860 Gold 0.1109 oz. AGW **Obv:** Crowned arms **Rev:** St. Paul standing

Date	Mintage	VG	F	VF	XF	Unc
1633	—	900	1,800	3,400	6,000	—
1634	—	900	1,800	3,400	6,000	—
1635	—	900	1,800	3,400	6,000	—
1636	—	900	1,800	3,400	6,000	—
1637	—	900	1,800	3,400	6,000	—

KM# 23 DUCAT

3.5000 g., 0.9860 Gold 0.1109 oz. AGW

Date	Mintage	VG	F	VF	XF	Unc
1638	—	650	1,150	2,800	4,250	—
1640	—	650	1,150	2,800	4,250	—
1641	—	650	1,150	2,800	4,250	—

KM# 24 DUCAT

3.5000 g., 0.9860 Gold 0.1109 oz. AGW **Obv:** Crowned oval 4-fold arms with central shield of Munster **Rev:** 5-line inscription with date divided in first line, in wreath

Date	Mintage	VG	F	VF	XF	Unc
1638	—	700	1,250	3,000	4,550	—
1639	—	700	1,250	3,000	4,550	—

KM# 26 DUCAT

3.5000 g., 0.9860 Gold 0.1109 oz. AGW **Note:** Klippe.

Date	Mintage	VG	F	VF	XF	Unc
1639 Rare	—	—	—	—	—	—

KM# 33 DUCAT

3.5000 g., 0.9860 Gold 0.1109 oz. AGW **Rev:** Date in last of four lines

Date	Mintage	VG	F	VF	XF	Unc
1640	—	650	1,150	2,800	4,250	—
1641	—	650	1,150	2,800	4,250	—
1647	—	650	1,150	2,800	4,250	—

KM# 64 DUCAT

3.5000 g., 0.9860 Gold 0.1109 oz. AGW **Obv:** Crowned arms **Rev:** Value in branches

Date	Mintage	VG	F	VF	XF	Unc
1652	—	825	1,750	3,400	6,000	—
1665	—	825	1,750	3,400	6,000	—

KM# 65 DUCAT

3.5000 g., 0.9860 Gold 0.1109 oz. AGW **Note:** Klippe.

Date	Mintage	VG	F	VF	XF	Unc
1652 Rare	—	—	—	—	—	—

KM# 43 DUCAT

3.5000 g., 0.9860 Gold 0.1109 oz. AGW **Obv:** Madonna and child **Rev:** Crowned arms

Date	Mintage	VG	F	VF	XF	Unc
ND(1661-78)	—	2,400	4,800	7,800	12,000	—

KM# 92 DUCAT

3.5000 g., 0.9860 Gold 0.1109 oz. AGW **Subject:** Death of Christoph Bernhard

Date	Mintage	VG	F	VF	XF	Unc
1678	—	825	1,750	3,300	6,000	—

KM# 109 DUCAT

3.5000 g., 0.9860 Gold 0.1109 oz. AGW **Obv:** Bust of Friedrich Christian right **Rev:** Crowned oval arms, date in legend

Date	Mintage	VG	F	VF	XF	Unc
1693 IO	—	1,700	3,450	5,600	10,000	—

KM# 119 DUCAT

3.5000 g., 0.9860 Gold 0.1109 oz. AGW **Obv:** Bust of Friedrich Christian right **Rev:** Crowned arms

Date	Mintage	VG	F	VF	XF	Unc
1695 JO	—	1,250	2,700	4,700	8,100	—

KM# 34 2 DUCAT

7.0000 g., 0.9860 Gold 0.2219 oz. AGW **Obv:** Crowned arms **Rev:** 3-line inscription and date in branches **Note:** Klippe.

Date	Mintage	VG	F	VF	XF	Unc
1640 Rare	—	—	—	—	—	—

KM# 45 2 DUCAT

7.0000 g., 0.9860 Gold 0.2219 oz. AGW **Obv:** Crowned oval 4-fold arms with central shield of Munster **Rev:** 4-line inscription with date in last line, in wreath **Note:** Klippe.

Date	Mintage	VG	F	VF	XF	Unc
1647 Rare	—	—	—	—	—	—

KM# 35 2 DUCAT

7.0000 g., 0.9860 Gold 0.2219 oz. AGW **Obv:** Madonna and child **Rev:** Crowned arms

Date	Mintage	VG	F	VF	XF	Unc
ND(1661-78)	—	2,650	5,400	8,400	14,500	—

KM# 39 3 DUCAT

10.5000 g., 0.9860 Gold 0.3328 oz. AGW **Obv:** Crowned oval 4-fold arms with central shield of Munster **Rev:** 4-line inscription with date in last line, in wreath

Date	Mintage	VG	F	VF	XF	Unc
1641 Rare	—	—	—	—	—	—

KM# 80 3 DUCAT

10.5000 g., 0.9860 Gold 0.3328 oz. AGW **Note:** Similar to 1 Thaler, KM#75.

Date	Mintage	VG	F	VF	XF	Unc
1661 Rare	—	—	—	—	—	—

KM# 81 3 DUCAT

10.5000 g., 0.9860 Gold 0.3328 oz. AGW, 34.5 mm. **Obv:** Ornate helmeted 9-fold arms **Obv. Legend:** CHRIST: BERN: D. G: EPIS. PRINCEPS • MONA **Rev:** 1/2-length figure of Charlemagne right holding orb and sceptre **Rev. Legend:** CAROLVS • MAGNVS • FVNDATOR

Date	Mintage	VG	F	VF	XF	Unc
ND(1661-78)	—	2,500	4,500	7,500	10,000	—

KM# 70 4 DUCAT

14.0000 g., 0.9860 Gold 0.4438 oz. AGW **Note:** Similar to 1 Thaler, KM#68.

Date	Mintage	VG	F	VF	XF	Unc
1659 Rare	—	—	—	—	—	—

KM# 82 6 DUCAT

21.0000 g., 0.9860 Gold 0.6657 oz. AGW **Obv:** Helmeted arms **Rev:** Bust of St. Paul, city view of Munster below

Date	Mintage	VG	F	VF	XF	Unc
1661	—	1,000	2,000	4,500	7,000	—

KM# 93 6 DUCAT

21.0000 g., 0.9860 Gold 0.6657 oz. AGW **Subject:** Death of Christian Bernhard **Rev:** 11-line inscription **Note:** Similar to 1 Thaler, KM#91.

Date	Mintage	VG	F	VF	XF	Unc
MDCLXXVIII (1678)	—	2,000	4,000	7,000	12,000	—

CITY

The history of the city is one of continuous struggle with the bishops for recognition of its autonomy. It was an important member of the Hanseatic League in the 13th and 14th centuries. Figured as the center of the Anabaptist revolt of 1534-35. Bishop took city as his seat in 1660 and deprived it of free status, yet local coinage was struck from the mid-16th to mid-18th century.

MINT OFFICIALS' INITIALS

Initial	Date	Name
	Ca.1600	Paul Potthof
IP	1601-04	Johann Potthof der Altere
	1604-35	Hermann Potthof
	1635-ca.1644	Johann Potthof der Jüngere
	1645-77	Johann Scharlaken
	1678-79	Engelbert Johann Scharlaken
	1680-1719	Johann Tomhulse
	1740-58	Johann Joseph Rensinck
	Ca.1750	Johann Heinrich Hase, die-cutter

NOTE: Numbers on some 3 Schilling and 12 Pfennig coins ranging from 1 to 11 are die-numbers.

REGULAR COINAGE

KM# 330 HELLER

Copper **Obv:** Small, plain city arms with point in center **Obv. Legend:** STADT. MVNSTER **Rev:** Value, I/H in ornamented circle

Date	Mintage	Good	VG	F	VF	XF
ND(1700-1740)	—	4.00	8.00	22.00	40.00	—

KM# 300 PFENNIG

Copper **Obv:** Ornate city arms, legend beginning and ending with rosette **Obv. Legend:** STADT. M-VNSTER **Rev:** Value I in ornamented rhombus

Date	Mintage	Good	VG	F	VF	XF
ND(ca.1600-35)	—	8.00	13.00	27.00	45.00	—

KM# 315 PFENNIG

Copper **Obv:** Narrow shield of arms, legend continuous, stops are +'s

Date	Mintage	Good	VG	F	VF	XF
ND(ca.1650)	—	8.00	13.00	27.00	45.00	—

KM# 320 PFENNIG

Copper **Obv:** Stops are 6-pointed stars

Date	Mintage	Good	VG	F	VF	XF
ND(ca.1700)	—	8.00	13.00	27.00	45.00	—

KM# 331 PFENNIG

Copper **Obv:** Shield shaped more ornately, with bottom ending in sharp point **Rev:** Value smaller

Date	Mintage	Good	VG	F	VF	XF
ND(ca.1700)	—	8.00	13.00	27.00	45.00	—

KM# 301 2 PFENNING
Copper **Obv:** Lion rampant left holding shield of Munster arms **Obv. Legend:** STAD-T. MV-NSTER **Rev:** Value II in ornamented square **Note:** Struck 1603 to 1697 in varieties.

Date	Mintage	Good	VG	F	VF	XF
ND(1603-97)	—	11.00	16.00	33.00	60.00	—

KM# 302 3 PFENNING
Copper **Obv:** City arms in ornate frame, legend, date **Obv. Legend:** STADT. MVNSTER. ANo. **Rev:** III in circle, ornamented border **Note:** Struck in varieties during 17th century.

Date	Mintage	Good	VG	F	VF	XF
1602	—	8.00	13.00	27.00	45.00	—

KM# 327 3 PFENNING
Copper **Rev:** Small module

Date	Mintage	Good	VG	F	VF	XF
1662	—	—	—	—	—	—

KM# 303 4 PFENNIG
Copper **Obv:** Small city arms in ornate frame, legend, date **Obv. Legend:** STADT. MVNSTER. ANo **Rev:** Value IIII in ornate rectangle

Date	Mintage	Good	VG	F	VF	XF
1602	—	13.00	27.00	45.00	75.00	—

Note: Struck until end of 17th century

KM# 304 4 PFENNIG
Copper **Note:** Similar to 2 Pfennig, KM#301, but value IIII.

Date	Mintage	Good	VG	F	VF	XF
ND	—	8.00	13.00	27.00	45.00	—

Note: Struck 1689 to 1694 in varieties

KM# 305 6 PFENNIG
Copper **Obv:** City arms in ornate frame, legend, date **Obv. Legend:** STADT. MV-NSTER. A-No **Rev:** Value VI in ornamented rectangle

Date	Mintage	Good	VG	F	VF	XF
1602	—	20.00	55.00	80.00	120	—

Note: Varieties exist. Struck until about 1637. Some pieces are known countermarked 1660 (during siege).

KM# 306 12 PFENNIG
Copper **Obv:** City arms in ornate frame, legend, jewel countermark **Obv. Legend:** STADT. MVNSTER **Rev:** Value XII with date divided among ciphers, all in ornately framed rectangle, a number from 1 to 11 at top

Date	Mintage	Good	VG	F	VF	XF
1602	—	30.00	65.00	100	145	—

Note: Struck until about 1635

KM# 307 3 SCHILLING
Copper **Obv:** City arms in ornate frame, lion supporters on each side, STADT above, MVNSTER below near bottom, a small countermark - a jewel. **Rev:** Value III in central rectangle, date divided between three I's of value, in ornamented frame, small M in oval above, small S in oval below **Rev. Legend:** 1 (OR OTHER NUMBER UP TO 10)-QVI DAT-PAVPERI-NON IND-IGEBIT **Note:** Struck until about 1639.

Date	Mintage	Good	VG	F	VF	XF
1602 IP	—	30.00	65.00	100	145	—

KM# 310 3 SCHILLING
Copper **Obv:** Additional countermark, small city arms with date 1639 in center, near top

Date	Mintage	Good	VG	F	VF	XF
1639	—	—	—	—	—	—

COUNTERMARKED SIEGE COINAGE

1660

KM# A321 6 PFENNIG
Copper **Countermark:** 1660 **Note:** Countermark on KM#305.

Date	Mintage	Good	VG	F	VF	XF
ND	—	—	—	—	—	—

SIEGE COINAGE

KM# 321 1/2 THALER
Silver **Obv. Legend:** MONAST: WESTPH: OBSESSVM **Note:** Uniface. Klippe. City arms in baroque frame, date divided by jewel at top

Date	Mintage	Good	VG	F	VF	XF
1660	—	115	225	500	750	—

KM# 322 1/2 THALER
Silver **Obv:** City arms in baroque frame, large jewel above **Rev. Inscription:** MONAST: / OBSES= / SVM / date **Note:** Klippe.

Date	Mintage	VG	F	VF	XF	Unc
1660	—	—	—	—	—	—

KM# 323 THALER
Silver **Obv:** Legend, date **Obv. Legend:** MONAST: WESTPH: OBSESSVM **Note:** Uniface.

Date	Mintage	VG	F	VF	XF	Unc
1660	—	135	275	600	875	—

KM# 324 2 DUCAT
7.0000 g., 0.9860 Gold 0.2219 oz. AGW **Note:** Klippe. Struck with 1/2 Thaler dies, KM#321.

Date	Mintage	VG	F	VF	XF	Unc
1660 Rare	—	—	—	—	—	—

KM# 325 3 DUCAT
10.5000 g., 0.9860 Gold 0.3328 oz. AGW **Note:** Klippe. Struck with 1/2 Thaler dies, KM#321.

Date	Mintage	VG	F	VF	XF	Unc
1660 Rare	—	—	—	—	—	—

KM# 326 5 DUCAT
17.5000 g., 0.9860 Gold 0.5547 oz. AGW **Note:** Klippe. Struck with 1 Thaler dies, KM#19.

Date	Mintage	VG	F	VF	XF	Unc
1660 Rare	—	—	—	—	—	—

CATHEDRAL CHAPTER

RULER
EVB = Engelbert von Brabeck, leader of Cathedral Chapter.

Initial	Date	Name
K	Ca. 1608	Kettler?
R	Ca. 1633	

NOTE: Coinage until after 1633 consisted of bursary tokens issued by Cathedral Chapter members of local nobility.

REGULAR COINAGE

KM# 405 HELLER
Copper **Obv:** Legend, St. Paul seated on chair **Obv. Legend:** SANCTVS. PAVLVS. APOST. **Rev:** Legend, date, small I above H **Rev. Legend:** BVRSA DOMINORVM

Date	Mintage	Good	VG	F	VF	XF
1608 with countermark	—	16.00	33.00	65.00	120	—

Note: The 1608 with countermark issues are found with countermark of Galen arms (3 wolftraps) at bottom of reverse

Date	Mintage	Good	VG	F	VF	XF
1608	—	16.00	33.00	65.00	120	—

KM# 406 HELLER
Copper **Obv:** Legend, facing bust of St. Paul **Obv. Legend:** SANCTVS. PAVLVS. APOST. **Rev:** Legend, date, value: I **Rev. Legend:** BVRSA DOMINORVM

Date	Mintage	Good	VG	F	VF	XF
1608 with countermark	—	—	27.00	55.00	100	—

Note: The 1608 with countermark issues are found with countermark of Galen arms (3 wolftraps) at bottom of reverse

Date	Mintage	Good	VG	F	VF	XF
1608	—	13.00	27.00	55.00	100	—

KM# 410 HELLER
Copper **Obv:** Inscription in circle **Obv. Inscription:** ELE / I **Note:** Uniface.

Date	Mintage	Good	VG	F	VF	XF
ND	—	40.00	80.00	160	320	—

Note: Struck during the first half of the 17th century

KM# 415 HELLER
Copper **Obv:** 1/2-length figure of St. Paul holding sword and book divides S-P **Obv. Legend:** MO. CATH. ECCL. MONAS. **Rev:** Wreath of palm leaves, legend: date in center as 16/61 **Note:** Varieties exist.

Date	Mintage	Good	VG	F	VF	XF
1661	—	8.00	16.00	33.00	55.00	—
1669	—	8.00	16.00	33.00	55.00	—

KM# 416 PFENNIG
Copper **Obv:** Full-length facing figure of St. Paul divides S-P near bottom. **Obv. Legend:** M:CATHED:ECCL:MONASTA **Rev:** Large 'I' divides date in wreath

Date	Mintage	Good	VG	F	VF	XF
1661	—	8.00	16.00	33.00	55.00	—
1699	—	8.00	16.00	33.00	55.00	—

KM# 407 2 PFENNING
Copper **Obv:** Legend, St. Paul seated **Obv. Legend:** SANCTVS. PAVLVS. APOST **Rev:** Legend, date, value: II **Rev. Legend:** BVRSA DOMINORVM

Date	Mintage	Good	VG	F	VF	XF
1608 with countermark	—	—	20.00	40.00	65.00	—

Note: The 1608 with countermark issues are found with countermark of Galen arms (3 wolftraps) at bottom of reverse

Date	Mintage	Good	VG	F	VF	XF
1608	—	11.00	20.00	40.00	65.00	—

KM# 411 2 PFENNING
Copper **Note:** Uniface. ELE/II in circle.

Date	Mintage	Good	VG	F	VF	XF
ND	—	60.00	115	225	375	—

Note: Struck during the first half of the 17th century

KM# 417 2 PFENNING
Copper **Obv:** 3/4-length figure of St. Paul with sword and book, S.P. below **Obv. Legend:** MO.CATH.ECCL.MONAS **Rev:** Value, II in center divides date, wreath of palm leaves **Note:** Varieties exist.

Date	Mintage	VG	F	VF	XF	Unc
1661	—	9.00	20.00	40.00	75.00	—
1669	—	9.00	20.00	40.00	75.00	—

KM# 400 3 PFENNING
Copper **Note:** Varieties exist.

Date	Mintage	Good	VG	F	VF	XF
1603	—	9.00	16.00	35.00	65.00	—
1608 with countermark	—	9.00	16.00	35.00	65.00	—

Note: The 1608 with countermark issues are found with countermark of Galen arms (3 wolftraps) at bottom of reverse

Date	Mintage	Good	VG	F	VF	XF
1608	—	9.00	16.00	35.00	65.00	—

KM# 412 3 PFENNING
Copper **Obv:** Inscription in circle **Obv. Inscription:** ELE / III **Note:** Uniface.

Date	Mintage	Good	VG	F	VF	XF
ND	—	65.00	135	275	425	—

Note: Struck during the first half of the 17th century

KM# 418 3 PFENNING
Copper **Note:** Varieties exist.

Date	Mintage	Good	VG	F	VF	XF
1661	—	8.00	13.00	33.00	55.00	—
1669	—	8.00	13.00	33.00	55.00	—
1692	—	8.00	13.00	33.00	55.00	—
1696	—	8.00	13.00	33.00	55.00	—
1699	—	8.00	13.00	33.00	55.00	—

KM# 401 4 PFENNING
Copper **Note:** Similar to 3 Pfenning KM#400. Varieties exist.

Date	Mintage	Good	VG	F	VF	XF
1603	—	13.00	27.00	45.00	90.00	—
1608 with countermark	—	13.00	27.00	45.00	90.00	—

Note: The 1608 with countermark issues are found with countermark of Galen arms (3 wolftraps) at bottom of reverse

Date	Mintage	Good	VG	F	VF	XF
1608	—	13.00	27.00	45.00	90.00	—

KM# 413 4 PFENNING
Copper **Obv:** Inscription in circle **Obv. Inscription:** ELE / IIII **Note:** Uniface. Varieties exist.

Date	Mintage	Good	VG	F	VF	XF
ND	—	85.00	165	325	525	—

Note: Struck during the first half of the 17th century

KM# 419 4 PFENNING
Copper **Rev:** Baroque frame around IIII/date instead of wreath **Note:** Varieties exist.

Date	Mintage	Good	VG	F	VF	XF
1661	—	9.00	16.00	35.00	55.00	—
1662	—	9.00	16.00	35.00	55.00	—
1696	—	9.00	16.00	35.00	55.00	—
1699	—	9.00	16.00	35.00	55.00	—

KM# 402 6 PFENNIG
Copper **Note:** Varieties exist.

Date	Mintage	Good	VG	F	VF	XF
1603	—	11.00	20.00	40.00	80.00	—
1608	—	11.00	20.00	40.00	80.00	—

Note: Some 1608 issues have countermark of Galen arms (3 wolftraps) at bottom of reverse

Date	Mintage	Good	VG	F	VF	XF
1633	—	11.00	20.00	40.00	80.00	—

KM# 403 12 PFENNIG
Copper **Note:** Similar to 6 Pfennig, KM#402, but value on reverse XII. Varieties exist.

Date	Mintage	Good	VG	F	VF	XF
1603	—	27.00	55.00	85.00	165	—
1608 with countermark	—	27.00	55.00	85.00	165	—

Note: The 1608 with countermark issues are found with countermark of Galen arms (3 wolftraps) at bottom of reverse

Date	Mintage	Good	VG	F	VF	XF
1608	—	27.00	55.00	85.00	165	—
1633	—	27.00	55.00	85.00	165	—

KM# 404 3 SCHILLING
Copper **Obv:** St. Paul on horse galloping left **Obv. Legend:** SAVLE. SAVLE QUID. ME. PERSEQVE. **Rev:** Inscription, date above, countermark below in shield form with EVB/von Brabeck arms, all in ornamented circle **Rev. Inscription:** ++ S ++ I ++ I ++ I ++, **Note:** Varieties exist.

Date	Mintage	Good	VG	F	VF	XF
1603	—	13.00	27.00	55.00	85.00	—
1608 with countermark	—	13.00	27.00	55.00	85.00	—

Note: The 1608 with countermark issues are found with countermark of Galen arms (3 wolftraps) at bottom of reverse

Date	Mintage	Good	VG	F	VF	XF
1608	—	13.00	27.00	55.00	85.00	—
1633	—	20.00	40.00	75.00	125	—

MUNSTERBERG

The duchy of Münsterberg was located in Silesia south of the city of Breslau. It was united with the duchy of Öls from 1495 until 1569, when Karl II sold Münsterberg to Bohemia from which it eventually was acquired by Austria in 1647. The line of dukes continued to rule in Öls, however. Austria granted the duchy to Count Johann Weikhard of Auersperg in 1653 and made him duke of Münsterberg the next year. Auersperg sold Münsterberg to russia in 1793.

MUNSTERBERG-OELS

The duchies of Munsterberg and Oels were located in Silesia, south and north of Breslau respectively. Munsterberg passed to Bohemia in 1462 and was created a separate duchy. Oels was acquired in 1495 and the two became a single entity under a long dynastic succession. The last duke died in 1647 and Munsterberg passed to Austria, while Oels was acquired through marriage by Wurttemberg (see Wurttemberg-Oels). In 1653, the count of Auersperg received Munsterberg and was made duke there in 1654 (see Munsterberg).

RULERS
Karl II, 1587-1617
Heinrich Wenzel, 1617-1639
Karl Friedrich, 1617-1647

MINT OFFICIALS' INITIALS

Initial	Date	Name
(a)= * * * or * * *	1611-12	Christoph Hedwiger in Oels
(b)=	1612-14	Basilius von Sonn in Oels
(c)= HT monogram	1614-16	Hans Tuchmann in Oels
BH	1619-21	Burkhart Hase in Oels
HT	1620-22	Hans Tuchmann, mintmaster and warden in Oels
BZ	1622-23	Balthasar Zwirner, mint-lessee

ARMS
Horizontal bar across upper half of shield.

DUCHY

REGULAR COINAGE

KM# 67 3 HELLER
Silver **Obv:** Three small shields of arms in trefoil form, III above two upper shields, lower shield divides date and mintmaster's initials **Note:** Uniface.

Date	Mintage	VG	F	VF	XF	Unc
1622 BZ	—	13.00	27.00	55.00	100	—
1623 BZ	—	13.00	27.00	55.00	100	—

KM# 68 3 HELLER
Silver **Obv:** Crowned Munsterberg arms divide date, III. H below **Note:** Uniface.

Date	Mintage	VG	F	VF	XF	Unc
1622	—	13.00	27.00	55.00	100	—
1622 BZ	—	13.00	27.00	55.00	100	—
1623 BZ	—	13.00	27.00	55.00	100	—

KM# 72 6 HELLER
Silver **Obv:** Two adjacent shields of arms, crown above, date divided at sides, VI below **Rev:** Silesian eagle

Date	Mintage	VG	F	VF	XF	Unc
1623	—	20.00	40.00	75.00	140	—

KM# 9 3 PFENNIG (Dreier)
Silver **Obv:** Silesian eagle, Munsterberg arms on breast, date divided lower left and right **Rev:** Four small shields of arms in cruciform

Date	Mintage	VG	F	VF	XF	Unc
1612	—	—	—	—	—	—

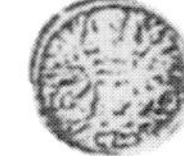

KM# 61 1/4 KREUZER (Pfennig)
Silver **Obv:** Silesian eagle, Munsterberg arms on breast **Note:** Uniface.

Date	Mintage	VG	F	VF	XF	Unc
ND(ca.1621) Rare	—	—	—	—	—	—

KM# 5 3 KREUZER (Groschen)
Silver **Obv:** Bust right, 3 in oval below, titles of Karl II **Rev:** Four-fold arms with central shield of Munsterberg, small imperial orb above, date in legend **Note:** Varieties exist.

Date	Mintage	VG	F	VF	XF	Unc
(1)611 (a)	—	16.00	33.00	60.00	110	—
(1)61Z (a)	—	16.00	33.00	60.00	110	—
(1)61Z (b)	—	16.00	33.00	60.00	110	—
(1)613 (b)	—	16.00	33.00	60.00	110	—
(1)614 (b)	—	16.00	33.00	60.00	110	—
(1)614 (c)	—	16.00	33.00	60.00	110	—
(1)615 (c)	—	16.00	33.00	60.00	110	—
(1)616 (c)	—	16.00	33.00	60.00	110	—

KM# 39 3 KREUZER (Groschen)
Silver **Obv:** Four-fold arms with central shield of Munsterberg, small imperial orb above **Rev:** Silesian eagle, 3 in oval below, date in legend **Note:** Kipper 3 Kreuzer. Varieties exist.

Date	Mintage	VG	F	VF	XF	Unc
(1)619 BH	—	16.00	33.00	60.00	110	—
(1)619	—	16.00	33.00	60.00	110	—
(1)620 BH	—	16.00	33.00	60.00	110	—
(1)620 HT	—	16.00	33.00	60.00	110	—
(1)621 BH	—	16.00	33.00	60.00	110	—
(1)621 HT	—	16.00	33.00	60.00	110	—
(1)622 HT	—	16.00	33.00	60.00	110	—

KM# 70 3 KREUZER (Groschen)
Silver **Obv:** Right shield with two curving bands

Date	Mintage	VG	F	VF	XF	Unc
1622 BZ	—	20.00	40.00	80.00	140	—

KM# 69 3 KREUZER (Groschen)
Silver **Obv:** Two adjacent shields of arms, Silesian eagle on left, checkerboard on right, crown above, 3 below **Rev:** Silesian eagle, date in legend **Note:** Varieties exist.

Date	Mintage	VG	F	VF	XF	Unc
16ZZ BZ	—	20.00	40.00	75.00	125	—
16Z3 BZ	—	20.00	40.00	75.00	125	—

KM# 62 24 KREUZER (Doppelschreckenberger)
Silver **Note:** Kipper 24 Kreuzer. Similar to 48 Kreuzer KM#64, but 24 below eagle. Varieties exist.

Date	Mintage	VG	F	VF	XF	Unc
1621 BH	—	60.00	100	140	200	—
1621 HT	—	60.00	100	140	200	—
1621	—	60.00	100	140	200	—

KM# 63 24 KREUZER (Doppelschreckenberger)
Silver **Obv:** Busts of two ducal brothers facing each other, date below **Rev:** Crowned ornate four-fold arms with central shield of Munsterberg, 24 below **Note:** Varieties exist.

Date	Mintage	VG	F	VF	XF	Unc
1621 HT	—	45.00	85.00	125	200	—
1622 HT	—	45.00	85.00	125	200	—
1622	—	45.00	85.00	125	200	—
1622 BZ	—	45.00	85.00	125	200	—
1623 BZ	—	45.00	85.00	125	200	—
1623	—	45.00	85.00	125	200	—

KM# 71 24 KREUZER (Doppelschreckenberger)
Silver **Rev:** Date in legend

Date	Mintage	VG	F	VF	XF	Unc
1622 HT	—	—	—	—	—	—

KM# 65 48 KREUZER (4 Schreckenberger)
Silver **Rev:** Without indication of value

Date	Mintage	VG	F	VF	XF	Unc
1621	—	—	—	—	—	—

KM# 64 48 KREUZER (4 Schreckenberger)
Silver **Note:** Kipper 48 Kreuzer. Varieties exist.

Date	Mintage	VG	F	VF	XF	Unc
1621 BH	—	85.00	160	220	300	—
1621 HT	—	85.00	160	220	300	—
1621	—	85.00	160	220	300	—

KM# 33 1/8 THALER
Silver **Subject:** Death of Karl II

Date	Mintage	VG	F	VF	XF	Unc
MDCXVII (1617)	—	100	165	325	500	—

KM# 18 1/4 THALER
Silver **Obv:** Bust right, small imperial orb in legend at top **Rev:** Crowned four-fold arms with central shield of Munsterberg, date in legend

Date	Mintage	VG	F	VF	XF	Unc
(1)613 (b)	—	85.00	160	325	500	—
(1)614 (b)	—	85.00	160	325	500	—

KM# 10 1/2 THALER
Silver **Obv:** Titles of Karl II, small imperial orb in legend at top

Date	Mintage	VG	F	VF	XF	Unc
161Z (a)	—	200	325	600	1,075	—

KM# 19 1/2 THALER
Silver **Rev:** Four-fold arms with central shield of Munsterberg, three small helmets above, date in legend

Date	Mintage	VG	F	VF	XF	Unc
(1)613 (b)	—	275	525	850	1,350	—

KM# 26 1/2 THALER
Silver **Obv:** Larger bust **Rev:** Four-fold arms shaped differently

Date	Mintage	VG	F	VF	XF	Unc
(1)614 (b)	—	—	—	—	—	—

KM# 34 1/2 THALER
Silver **Subject:** Death of Karl II

Date	Mintage	VG	F	VF	XF	Unc
MDCXVII (1617)	—	135	275	475	750	—

KM# 40 1/2 THALER
Silver **Obv:** Busts of two ducal brothers facing each other **Rev:** Four-fold arms with central shield of Munsterberg, three small helmets above, date in legend **Note:** Varieties exist.

Date	Mintage	VG	F	VF	XF	Unc
(1)619 BH	—	85.00	160	325	525	—
(1)620 BH	—	85.00	160	325	525	—
(1)621 BH	—	85.00	160	325	525	—

KM# A55 1/2 THALER
Silver **Ruler:** Heinrich Wenzel **Obv:** Half-length figures of two brothers facing each other, date in exergue, small imperial orb at top in margin **Obv. Legend:** D.G. HEINRI• WENC• ET• CAROL • FRID (E) • FRAT• **Rev:** 4-fold arms with central shield of Münsterberg, 5 ornate helmets above **Rev. Legend:** DVC • SIL • MONS - •E•T• OLS • CO • GLA • **Mint:** Oels

Date	Mintage	F	VF	XF	Unc	BU
1620 BH	—	—	—	—	—	—
1621 BH	—	—	—	—	—	—

KM# 55 1/2 THALER
Silver **Obv:** Half-length bust right, five small shields in legend **Rev:** Half-length bust left, date divided above, five small shields in legend

Date	Mintage	VG	F	VF	XF	Unc
1620 BH	—	—	—	—	—	—

KM# 6 THALER
Silver **Obv:** Bust right **Rev:** Helmeted arms **Note:** Dav. #7089.

Date	Mintage	VG	F	VF	XF	Unc
1611	—	600	1,200	2,500	4,500	8,500
161Z (a)	—	250	500	1,000	2,000	—

KM# 20 THALER
Silver **Obv:** Different bust **Note:** Dav. #7091.

Date	Mintage	VG	F	VF	XF	Unc
1613 (b)	—	750	1,500	3,000	5,000	9,500
1616 (c)	—	750	1,500	3,000	5,000	9,500

KM# 27 THALER

Silver **Obv:** Different bust **Note:** Dav. #7092.

Date	Mintage	VG	F	VF	XF	Unc
1614 (b)	—	750	1,500	3,000	5,000	—
1615 (c)	—	750	1,500	3,000	5,000	—

KM# 35 THALER

Silver **Subject:** Death of Karl II **Obv:** Bust right, arms below **Rev:** Inscription **Note:** Dav. #7093.

Date	Mintage	VG	F	VF	XF	Unc
1617	—	450	950	2,000	4,000	6,500

KM# 41 THALER

Silver **Obv:** Facing busts with ornament below **Rev:** Helmeted arms **Note:** Dav. #7094.

Date	Mintage	VG	F	VF	XF	Unc
1619 BH	—	650	1,350	2,750	4,500	—

KM# 42 THALER

Silver **Obv:** Bust right with shields in legend and 2 below **Rev:** Bust left dividing date with shields in legend **Note:** Dav. #7096.

Date	Mintage	VG	F	VF	XF	Unc
1619 BH	—	450	950	2,000	4,000	—
1620 BH	—	450	950	2,000	4,000	—

KM# 43 THALER

Silver **Obv:** Facing busts with date below **Rev:** Helmeted arms **Note:** Varieties exist. Dav. #7097.

Date	Mintage	VG	F	VF	XF	Unc
1619 BH	—	—	—	—	—	—
1620 BH	—	300	700	1,500	2,500	—

KM# 56 2 THALER

Silver **Note:** Similar to 1 Thaler, KM#42. Dav. #7095.

Date	Mintage	VG	F	VF	XF	Unc
1620 BH Rare	—	—	—	—	—	—

KM# 21 3 THALER

Silver **Note:** Similar to 1 Thaler, KM#6. Dav. #7090.

Date	Mintage	VG	F	VF	XF	Unc
161Z (a) Rare	—	—	—	—	—	—

TRADE COINAGE

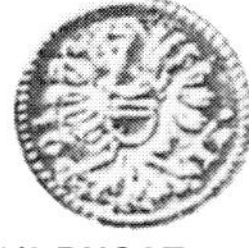

KM# 11 1/2 DUCAT

1.7500 g., 0.9860 Gold 0.0555 oz. AGW **Obv:** Displayed eagle with shield on breast **Rev:** Cruciform arms

Date	Mintage	VG	F	VF	XF	Unc
1612	—	240	350	725	1,300	—

KM# 32 1/2 DUCAT

1.7500 g., 0.9860 Gold 0.0555 oz. AGW **Rev:** Crowned arms

Date	Mintage	VG	F	VF	XF	Unc
1616 (c)	—	240	400	775	1,400	—

KM# 7 DUCAT

3.5000 g., 0.9860 Gold 0.1109 oz. AGW **Obv:** Bust of Karl II right in inner circle **Rev:** Crowned arms **Note:** Varieties exist.

Date	Mintage	VG	F	VF	XF	Unc
1611	—	270	550	1,100	2,000	—
1612	—	270	550	1,100	2,000	—
1613	—	270	550	1,100	2,000	—
1614	—	270	550	1,100	2,000	—
1615 (c)	—	270	550	1,100	2,000	—
1616 (c)	—	270	550	1,100	2,000	—

KM# 22 DUCAT

3.5000 g., 0.9860 Gold 0.1109 oz. AGW **Obv:** Bust of Karl II breaks through top of circle

Date	Mintage	VG	F	VF	XF	Unc
1613	—	270	550	1,100	2,000	—

KM# 44 DUCAT

3.5000 g., 0.9860 Gold 0.1109 oz. AGW **Obv:** Bust of Heinrich Wenzel right in inner circle **Rev:** Bust of Karl Friedrich left in inner circle **Note:** Varieties exist.

Date	Mintage	VG	F	VF	XF	Unc
1619 BH	—	375	750	1,500	3,000	—
1620 BH	—	375	750	1,500	3,000	—
1621 BH	—	375	750	1,500	3,000	—

KM# 45 DUCAT

3.5000 g., 0.9860 Gold 0.1109 oz. AGW **Obv:** Busts break inner circle at top **Rev:** Busts break inner circle at top

Date	Mintage	VG	F	VF	XF	Unc
1619	—	375	750	1,500	3,000	—

KM# 12 2 DUCAT

7.0000 g., 0.9860 Gold 0.2219 oz. AGW **Obv:** Bust of Karl II to right in inner circle **Rev:** Crowned arms

Date	Mintage	VG	F	VF	XF	Unc
1612 (a)	—	600	1,200	2,700	4,500	—

KM# 28 2 DUCAT

7.0000 g., 0.9860 Gold 0.2219 oz. AGW **Rev:** Arms topped by three helmets in inner circle, date in legend

Date	Mintage	VG	F	VF	XF	Unc
1614	—	450	950	2,000	3,250	—
1615 (c)	—	450	950	2,000	3,250	—

KM# 36 2 DUCAT

7.0000 g., 0.9860 Gold 0.2219 oz. AGW **Subject:** Death of Karl II **Rev:** Five-line inscription

Date	Mintage	VG	F	VF	XF	Unc
1617	—	825	1,750	3,750	4,500	—

KM# 66 2 DUCAT

7.0000 g., 0.9860 Gold 0.2219 oz. AGW **Obv:** Bust of Heinrich Wenzel right in inner circle, five shields in border **Rev:** Bust of Karl Friedrich left in inner circle, five shields on border

Date	Mintage	VG	F	VF	XF	Unc
1621 BH	—	450	900	2,100	3,000	—

KM# 13 3 DUCAT

10.5000 g., 0.9860 Gold 0.3328 oz. AGW **Obv:** Bust of Karl II right in inner circle **Rev:** Five shields in inner circle

Date	Mintage	VG	F	VF	XF	Unc
161Z (a)	—	600	1,200	2,700	5,400	—

KM# 23 3 DUCAT

10.5000 g., 0.9860 Gold 0.3328 oz. AGW **Rev:** Arms below three helmets in inner circle, date in legend

Date	Mintage	VG	F	VF	XF	Unc
1613 (b)	—	550	1,150	2,600	4,200	—
1614	—	550	1,150	2,600	4,200	—

KM# 46.1 3 DUCAT

10.5000 g., 0.9860 Gold 0.3328 oz. AGW **Obv:** Heinrich Wenzel and Karl Friedrich **Note:** Varieties exist.

Date	Mintage	VG	F	VF	XF	Unc
1619 BH	—	550	1,150	2,600	4,200	—
1621 BH	—	550	1,150	2,600	4,200	—

KM# 57 3 DUCAT

10.5000 g., 0.9860 Gold 0.3328 oz. AGW **Obv:** Bust of Heinrich Wenzel right in inner circle, five shields in border **Rev:** Bust of Karl Friedrich left divides date in inner circle, five shields in border

Date	Mintage	VG	F	VF	XF	Unc
1620 BH	—	725	1,400	3,050	5,500	—
1621 BH	—	725	1,400	3,050	5,500	—

KM# 46.2 3 DUCAT

10.5000 g., 0.9860 Gold 0.3328 oz. AGW **Obv:** Heinrich Wenzel and Karl Friedrich **Rev:** Oval arms below three helmets **Note:** Varieties exist.

Date	Mintage	VG	F	VF	XF	Unc
1621 HT	—	450	950	2,200	3,500	—
1622 HT	—	450	950	2,200	3,500	—

KM# 14 4 DUCAT

14.0000 g., 0.9860 Gold 0.4438 oz. AGW **Obv:** Armored bust of Karl II right **Rev:** Four large shields surround small shield in center

Date	Mintage	VG	F	VF	XF	Unc
161Z (a)	—	1,000	2,000	4,000	6,500	—

KM# 24 4 DUCAT

14.0000 g., 0.9860 Gold 0.4438 oz. AGW **Rev:** Arms below three helmets in inner circle, date in legend

Date	Mintage	VG	F	VF	XF	Unc
1613 (b)	—	1,000	2,000	4,000	6,500	—
1615 (c)	—	1,000	2,000	4,000	6,500	—

KM# 47.1 4 DUCAT

14.0000 g., 0.9860 Gold 0.4438 oz. AGW **Obv:** Heinrich Wenzel and Karl Friedrich **Rev:** Square topped arms below three helmets

Date	Mintage	VG	F	VF	XF	Unc
1619 BH	—	775	1,600	3,600	6,500	—
1621 BH	—	775	1,600	3,600	6,500	—

KM# 58 4 DUCAT

14.0000 g., 0.9860 Gold 0.4438 oz. AGW **Obv:** Heinrich Wenzel right **Rev:** Karl Friedrich left

Date	Mintage	VG	F	VF	XF	Unc
1620 BH	—	775	1,600	3,600	6,100	—

KM# 47.3 4 DUCAT

Gold **Ruler:** Heinrich Wenzel **Obv:** Half-length figures of two brothers facing each other, date in exergue, small imperial orb at top in margin **Obv. Legend:** D.G. HEINRI • WENC • ET • CAROL • FRID • FRAT • **Rev:** 4-fold arms with central shield of Münsterberg, 5 ornate helmets above **Rev. Legend:** DVG • SIL • MONS • - •ET • OLS • CO • GLA • **Mint:** Oels **Note:** Struck from 1/2 Thaler dies, KM#55a.

Date	Mintage	VG	F	VF	XF	Unc
1620 BH	—	—	—	—	—	—
1621 BH Rare	—	—	—	—	—	—

Note: UBS Gold & Numismatics Auction 69, 1-07, VF-XF realized approximately $8,875

KM# 47.2 4 DUCAT

14.0000 g., 0.9860 Gold 0.4438 oz. AGW **Obv:** Heinrich Wenzel and Karl Friedrich **Rev:** Oval arms below three helmets

Date	Mintage	VG	F	VF	XF	Unc
1621 HT	—	—	—	—	—	—
1622 HT Rare	—	—	—	—	—	—

Note: Fritz Rudolf Künker Münzenhandlung Auction 135, 1-08, XF realized approximately $16,985

KM# 8 5 DUCAT

17.5000 g., 0.9860 Gold 0.5547 oz. AGW **Note:** Similar to 1 Thaler, KM#6.

Date	Mintage	VG	F	VF	XF	Unc
(1)611	—	1,100	2,200	4,500	7,500	—
(1)61Z (a)	—	1,100	2,200	4,500	7,500	—

KM# 15 5 DUCAT

17.5000 g., 0.9860 Gold 0.5547 oz. AGW **Note:** Similar to 1 Thaler, KM#20. Varieties exist.

Date	Mintage	VG	F	VF	XF	Unc
(1)61Z (a)	—	1,100	2,200	4,500	7,500	—
(1)613 (b)	—	1,100	2,200	4,500	7,500	—
(1)616 (c)	—	1,100	2,200	4,500	7,500	—

KM# 29 5 DUCAT

17.5000 g., 0.9860 Gold 0.5547 oz. AGW **Note:** Similar to 1 Thaler, KM#27, but different bust. Varieties exist.

Date	Mintage	VG	F	VF	XF	Unc
(1)615	—	1,100	2,200	4,500	7,500	—

KM# 59 5 DUCAT

17.5000 g., 0.9860 Gold 0.5547 oz. AGW **Note:** Similar to 1 Thaler, KM#43. Varieties exist.

Date	Mintage	VG	F	VF	XF	Unc
(1)6Z0 BH	—	1,200	2,500	4,750	8,500	—
(1)6Z1 BH	—	1,200	2,500	4,750	8,500	—

KM# A9 6 DUCAT

21.0000 g., 0.9860 Gold 0.6657 oz. AGW **Ruler:** Karl II **Obv:** Bust of Karl II right **Rev:** Helmeted ornate arms **Note:** Fr.#3241.

Date	Mintage	VG	F	VF	XF	Unc
1611	—	1,100	2,150	5,400	9,600	—

KM# 31 6 DUCAT

21.0000 g., 0.9860 Gold 0.6657 oz. AGW **Rev:** Date in legend

Date	Mintage	VG	F	VF	XF	Unc
(1)615 (c)	—	1,700	3,300	6,000	9,600	—
(1)616 (c)	—	1,700	3,300	6,000	9,600	—

KM# 30 6 DUCAT

21.0000 g., 0.9860 Gold 0.6657 oz. AGW **Note:** Similar to 1 Thaler, KM#27, but date below different bust on obverse.

Date	Mintage	VG	F	VF	XF	Unc
(1)615 (c)	—	1,700	3,300	6,000	9,600	—
(1)616 (c)	—	1,700	3,300	6,000	9,600	—

KM# 37 6 DUCAT

21.0000 g., 0.9860 Gold 0.6657 oz. AGW **Subject:** Death of Karl II **Note:** Similar to 1/2 Thaler, KM#34.

Date	Mintage	VG	F	VF	XF	Unc
1617 Rare	—	—	—	—	—	—

KM# 48 6 DUCAT

21.0000 g., 0.9860 Gold 0.6657 oz. AGW

Date	Mintage	VG	F	VF	XF	Unc
1619 BH Rare	—	—	—	—	—	—

KM# A60 6 DUCAT

21.0000 g., 0.9860 Gold 0.6657 oz. AGW **Ruler:** Heinrich Wenzel **Obv:** Facing 1/2 length figures of Heinrich Wenzel and Karl Friedrich **Rev:** Helmeted ornate arms **Note:** Fr.#3256.

Date	Mintage	VG	F	VF	XF	Unc
16Z0 Rare	—	—	—	—	—	—

KM# 60 8 DUCAT

28.0000 g., 0.9860 Gold 0.8876 oz. AGW **Note:** Similar to 1 Thaler, KM#43.

Date	Mintage	VG	F	VF	XF	Unc
1620 BH Rare	—	—	—	—	—	—

KM# 16 9 DUCAT

31.5000 g., 0.9860 Gold 0.9985 oz. AGW **Note:** Similar to 1 Thaler, KM#6.

Date	Mintage	VG	F	VF	XF	Unc
(1)61Z (a)	—	—	—	10,000	16,500	—

KM# 17 10 DUCAT

35.0000 g., 0.9860 Gold 1.1095 oz. AGW **Note:** Similar to 1 Thaler, KM#6.

Date	Mintage	VG	F	VF	XF	Unc
(1)61Z (a) Rare	—	—	—	—	—	—

KM# 25 10 DUCAT

35.0000 g., 0.9860 Gold 1.1095 oz. AGW **Note:** Similar to 1 Thaler, KM#20.

Date	Mintage	VG	F	VF	XF	Unc
(1)613 (b) Rare	—	—	—	—	—	—

KM# A38 10 DUCAT
35.0000 g., 0.9860 Gold 1.1095 oz. AGW **Note:** Similar to 1 Thaler, KM#20.

Date	Mintage	VG	F	VF	XF	Unc
(1)616 (c) Rare	—	—	—	—	—	—

KM# 38 10 DUCAT
35.0000 g., 0.9860 Gold 1.1095 oz. AGW **Subject:** Death of Karl II **Note:** Similar to 1 Thaler, KM#35.

Date	Mintage	VG	F	VF	XF	Unc
1617 Rare	—	—	—	—	—	—

KM# A39 12-1/2 DUCAT
43.7500 g., 0.9860 Gold 1.3868 oz. AGW **Subject:** Death of Karl II **Obv:** Bust of Karl II right, arms below **Rev:** 8 line inscription **Note:** Struck with 1 Thaler dies, KM#35.

Date	Mintage	VG	F	VF	XF	Unc
1617 Rare	—	—	—	—	—	—

MURBACH & LUDERS

Murbach and Lüders were neighboring abbeys in Upper Alsace founded in the 8th century. Almost from their inception they had a common ruling abbot. A local 12th and 13th century coinage preceded the official granting in 1544 of the right to mint coins. Their territories were absorbed into France in 1680, and secularization followed in 1764.

ABBOTS
Andreas, Erzherzog von Österreich, 1587-1600
Leopold V, Erzherzog von Österreich, 1601-1625, abdicated
Johann Wilhelm, Erzherzog von Österreich, (1625) 1632-1662
Colomban von Andlau, 1663-1665
Franz Egon, Fürst von Fürstenberg-Heiligenberg, 1665-1682

MINTS
Ensisheim
Gebweiler (French Guebwiller)

ARMS
Murbach – hand raised vertically with first two fingers extended in sign of Episcopal benediction
Lüders – dog rampant left

ABBEY

REGULAR COINAGE

KM# 1 PFENNING
Billon **Obv:** Arms of Furstenberg with those of Murbach and Luders **Note:** Uniface.

Date	Mintage	VG	F	VF	XF	Unc
ND(1665-82)	—	20.00	45.00	80.00	160	—

KM# 5 1/2 BATZEN
Billon **Obv:** 4-fold arms **Obv. Legend:** COLVMBAN. E. AP... **Rev:** Faving bust of St. Leodegar, date at end of legend

Date	Mintage	VG	F	VF	XF	Unc
1664	—	20.00	40.00	65.00	135	—

KM# 30 2 BATZEN
Billon **Obv:** Adjacent shield of 2 abbeys, date above, value 2 in circle below **Obv. Legend:** MONETA • NOVA • MVR • ETLVDR **Rev:** Full length figure of St. Leodegar facing

Date	Mintage	VG	F	VF	XF	Unc
1624//1624	—	33.00	65.00	135	300	—

KM# 50 10 BATZEN
Silver **Obv:** Francis Egon **Rev:** Shield with four arms

Date	Mintage	VG	F	VF	XF	Unc
1666	—	40.00	80.00	150	300	—

KM# 23 1/4 THALER
7.4900 g., Silver **Obv:** Bust of Leopold right in inner circle **Rev:** Crowned arms

Date	Mintage	VG	F	VF	XF	Unc
ND	—	55.00	100	165	325	—

KM# 12 THALER
Silver **Obv:** St. Leodegarius with shield **Obv. Legend:** LEODEGARIVS... **Rev:** Crowned imperial eagle **Rev. Legend:** FERDINANDVS ? II ? D:G:? **Note:** Dav. #5617.

Date	Mintage	VG	F	VF	XF	Unc
ND(ca. 1630)	—	250	450	875	1,600	—

KM# 13 THALER
Silver **Obv. Legend:** LEODEGARIvS **Note:** Dav. #5617A.

Date	Mintage	VG	F	VF	XF	Unc
ND(ca. 1630)	—	250	450	875	1,600	—

KM# 14 THALER
Silver **Obv:** St. Leodegarius with shield **Obv. Legend:** LEODEGARIVs... **Rev:** Crowned double-headed imperial eagle **Note:** Dav. #5617B.

Date	Mintage	VG	F	VF	XF	Unc
ND(ca 1630)	—	250	450	875	1,600	—

KM# 15 THALER
Silver **Obv:** Seated St. Lodegarius with right arm raised, small shield between feet **Rev:** Crowned double-headed imperial eagle **Note:** Dav. #5618. Varieties exist.

Date	Mintage	VG	F	VF	XF	Unc
ND(ca 1626)	—	400	800	1,500	2,500	—

KM# 28 THALER
Silver **Obv:** Bust of Leopold right, date below **Rev:** Crowned imperial shield, arms of the abbeys at left and right **Note:** Dav. #5620.

Date	Mintage	VG	F	VF	XF	Unc
1625	—	700	1,350	2,500	4,000	—

KM# 35 THALER
Silver **Obv:** Date in front of bust **Note:** Dav. #5620A.

Date	Mintage	VG	F	VF	XF	Unc
1625	—	700	1,350	2,500	4,000	—

NASSAU

The Countship of Nassau had its origins in the area of the Lahn of the central Rhineland, with territory on both sides of that river. The first count who attained the title with recognition from the emperor was Walram in 1158. His grandsons, Walram I (1255-88) and Otto I (1255-90), divided their patrimony. Walram claimed the left bank of the lahn and made Weisbaden his principal seat, whereas Otto took the right bank and ruled from Siegen. Thus, the division of 1255 established the two main lines over the ensuing centuries.

Several times, various branches of the family issued joint coinage, notably in the late 17th and again in the early 19th centuries. Eventually, through extinction of the various lines and the elevation of one ruler to the throne of the Netherlands, all Nassau was reunited under the house of Nassau-Weilburg.

ARMS
Nassau – lion rampant left on field of billets (small vertical rectangles)
Holzappel – griffin rampant left holding apple

REFERENCE
I = Julius Isenbeck, **Das nassauische Münzwesen**, Wiesbaden, 1879.

DUCHY

Joint Rulers

RULERS
Johann Franz of Siegen
Heinrich of Dillenburg
Wilhelm Moritz of Siegen
Heinrich Casimir of Dietz
Franz Alexander of Hademar

STANDARD COINAGE

DAV# 7098 THALER
Silver **Obv:** Five princes standing facing, date below **Rev:** Crowned, supported arms

Date	Mintage	VG	F	VF	XF	Unc
1681	—	750	1,500	3,000	5,000	—

NASSAU-DILLENBURG

One of the divisions of the Ottonian line of the house of Nassau which was founded in 1290 by Heinrich I, son of Otto I (1255-1290). Through the years this branch developed strong ties with the Netherlands. The last duke of Nassau-Dillenburg, Christian, died in 1739 and the lands passed to Nassau-Dietz.

RULER
Heinrich, 1662-1701

Duchy

STANDARD COINAGE

DAV# 7099 THALER
Silver **Obv:** Bust right **Rev:** Crowned, supported arms

Date	Mintage	VG	F	VF	XF	Unc
1683 Rare	—	—	—	—	—	—

TRADE COINAGE

Separate coinage of Nassau-Weilburg

FR# 1785 DUCAT
3.5000 g., 0.9860 Gold 0.1109 oz. AGW **Obv:** Bust of Heinrich right **Rev:** Shield of arms

Date	Mintage	VG	F	VF	XF	Unc
1688	—	5,000	9,000	14,500	22,500	—

NASSAU-WEILBURG

Duchy

STANDARD COINAGE

DAV# 7100 THALER
Silver **Obv:** Bust of Johann Ernst right **Rev:** Helmeted arms, ANNO-date below

Date	Mintage	VG	F	VF	XF	Unc
1691 Rare	—	—	—	—	—	—

NEURUPPIN

A provincial town located 35 miles (60km) northwest of Berlin, Neuruppin became a mint site for the margraves of Brandenburg in the early 16th century. A local coinage was produced during the first part of the Thirty Years' War.

PROVINCIAL TOWN

REGULAR COINAGE

KM# 1 PFENNIG
Copper **Obv:** Brandenburg eagle in circle, head divides N ? R. **Note:** Uniface. Kipper Pfennig.

Date	Mintage	VG	F	VF	XF	Unc
ND(1621-22)	—	12.00	22.00	35.00	70.00	—

KM# 2 PFENNIG
Copper **Obv:** Brandenburg eagle in circle divides date, head divides N ? R **Note:** Uniface. Kipper Pfennig. Varieties exist.

Date	Mintage	VG	F	VF	XF	Unc
(16)Z1	—	13.00	24.00	40.00	85.00	—
(16)21	—	13.00	24.00	40.00	85.00	—
(16)ZZ	—	13.00	24.00	40.00	85.00	—

NORDHAUSEN

Located north of Thuringia (Thüringen) and 25 miles (40km) northeast of Mühlhausen in Thuringia, the town of Nordhausen is found mentioned in records from as early as 874. It was the site of an imperial mint in the 12th and 13th centuries and was designated a free imperial city in 1253. Coinage was struck locally from about this time until nearly the end of the 17th century, but issues were not continuous throughout this period. Nordhausen was annexed at first to Prussia in 1803 and this was made a permanent arrangement in 1813.

MINT OFFICIALS' INITIALS

Initial	Date	Name
HG	1618-24	Hans Gruber
CM	1624	Conrad Marquard
IK	1660	Johann König
AD	1685-86	Andreas Detmar

ARMS
Eagle, head left, sometimes crowned

FREE IMPERIAL CITY

REGULAR COINAGE

KM# 3 3 PFENNIG
Silver **Obv:** Eagle, head left in circle **Rev:** Imperial orb in ornamented rhombus

Date	Mintage	VG	F	VF	XF	Unc
ND(ca.1610)	—	11.00	20.00	40.00	75.00	—

KM# 5 3 PFENNIG
Silver **Obv:** City arms in ornamented oval **Rev:** Imperial orb in ornamented rhombus

Date	Mintage	VG	F	VF	XF	Unc
ND(ca.1615)	—	13.00	27.00	50.00	85.00	—

KM# 6 3 PFENNIG
Silver **Obv:** City arms in ornamented oval **Rev:** Imperial orb with 3 divides date

Date	Mintage	VG	F	VF	XF	Unc
1615	—	13.00	27.00	50.00	85.00	—

KM# 22 3 PFENNIG
Copper **Obv:** City arms **Rev:** Imperial orb with 3 divides date **Note:** Kipper 3 Pfennig.

Date	Mintage	VG	F	VF	XF	Unc
1622	—	11.00	16.00	40.00	—	—

KM# 25 12 KREUZER (Schreckenberger)
Silver **Obv:** Crowned city arms in ornate frame **Obv. Legend:** MO. NO. CI. IM. NORTHAVSN **Rev:** Crowned imperial eagle, 12 in orb on breast **Rev. Legend:** FERD. II. ROM. IMP. SEMP. A

Date	Mintage	VG	F	VF	XF	Unc
ND(ca.1622)	—	45.00	85.00	155	250	—

KM# 23 12 KREUZER (Schreckenberger)
Silver **Obv:** Ornate helmet above small city arms, MO. NO. C - IM. NORT **Rev:** Crowned imperial eagle, 12 in orb on breast, titles of Ferdinand II and date **Note:** Kipper 12 Kreuzer.

Date	Mintage	VG	F	VF	XF	Unc
16ZZ	—	40.00	75.00	125	220	—

KM# 24 12 KREUZER (Schreckenberger)
Silver **Note:** Similar to KM#5 but MO. OCI - IM. NORT on obverse and 12 in orb and no date on reverse.

Date	Mintage	VG	F	VF	XF	Unc
ND(ca.1622)	—	45.00	85.00	155	250	—

KM# 37 16 GUTE GROSCHEN (2/3 Thaler = Gulden)
Silver **Obv:** Similar to 24 Mariengroschen, KM#8 **Rev:** 16/GUTE/ GROSCHN/date, MONETA NOVA ARGENTEA **Note:** Dav. #708.

Date	Mintage	VG	F	VF	XF	Unc
1685	—	400	750	1,250	—	—

KM# 35 24 MARIENGROSCHEN (2/3 Thaler)
Silver **Obv:** Ornate helmet above pointed-bottom oval city arms, CIVITATIS - NORTHUSAE **Rev:** 4-line inscription in circle **Rev. Legend:** MONETA : NOVA : ARGENTEA **Rev. Inscription:** XXIIII / MARIEN / GROSCH: / date **Note:** Dav. #706.

Date	Mintage	VG	F	VF	XF	Unc
1685	—	200	400	850	1,750	—
1686	—	200	400	850	1,750	—

KM# 36 24 MARIENGROSCHEN (2/3 Thaler)
Silver **Obv:** Squarish arms with rounded top and bottom **Rev. Inscription:** XXIII / MARIEN / GROSC / HEN / date **Note:** Dav. #707.

Date	Mintage	VG	F	VF	XF	Unc
1685 AD	—	400	800	1,600	2,750	—

KM# 7 1/24 THALER (Groschen)
Silver **Obv:** Ornate helmet over small city arms, MO. NO. CI. NORTHA. **Rev:** Imperial orb with Z4, date divided at top, titles of Matthias

Date	Mintage	VG	F	VF	XF	Unc
1616	—	45.00	85.00	175	300	—

KM# 8 1/24 THALER (Groschen)
Silver **Obv:** Oval city arms, MON. IMPE.NORTHAVS **Rev:** Similar to KM#10 **Note:** Varieties exist. Dav.#5621.

Date	Mintage	VG	F	VF	XF	Unc
1616	—	33.00	65.00	120	225	—
1617	—	33.00	65.00	120	225	—
1618	—	33.00	65.00	120	225	—

KM# 16 1/24 THALER (Groschen)
Silver **Obv:** Small oval city arms, MO : NO :... **Rev:** Imperial orb with 4 **Note:** Kipper 1/24 Thaler.

Date	Mintage	VG	F	VF	XF	Unc
1620	—	80.00	160	275	—	—

KM# 40 2/3 THALER (Gulden)
Silver **Obv:** Ornate helmet divides date above city arms, MO : N. LIB? **Rev:** Column, sun left, personification of wind right, 2.3 in oval below **Rev. Legend:** INCLINATA RURSUS - IN DEO ERIGAR ? **Note:** Dav. #704.

Date	Mintage	VG	F	VF	XF	Unc
1685 AD	—	325	675	1,200	2,100	—

KM# 41 2/3 THALER (Gulden)
Silver **Obv. Legend:** MO : NO : LII :? **Rev. Legend:** RURSU... **Note:** Dav. #705.

Date	Mintage	VG	F	VF	XF	Unc
1685 AD	—	375	725	1,350	2,400	—

KM# 11 THALER
Silver **Obv:** Crowned imperial eagle with orb **Obv. Legend:** MATTHI. I. D: G. ROMA... **Rev:** Helmeted arms, date above **Rev. Legend:** MO. NO.

Date	Mintage	VG	F	VF	XF	Unc
1616 Rare	—	—	—	—	—	—

KM# 18.1 THALER
Silver **Obv. Legend:** FERDI. II... **Rev. Legend:** MON: MOV: CIV.-IMP: NORTHUS. **Note:** Dav.#5623.

Date	Mintage	VG	F	VF	XF	Unc
1620	—	1,000	2,000	4,150	7,100	—

KM# 19 THALER
Silver **Obv:** Crowned imperial eagle, date divided above **Rev:** Crowned eagle separating H-G above **Note:** Dav.#5626.

Date	Mintage	VG	F	VF	XF	Unc
1620 HG	—	1,000	2,000	4,000	6,900	—
1623 HG	—	1,000	2,000	4,000	6,900	—

KM# 18.2 THALER
Silver **Obv. Legend:** * MON • NOV • CIV* * IMP • NORTHUS **Rev:** Crowned imperial eagle **Note:** Dav.#5626A

Date	Mintage	VG	F	VF	XF	Unc
1620 HG	—	1,000	2,000	4,150	7,100	—

KM# 27 THALER
Silver **Rev:** Helmeted arms in fancy decoration **Rev. Legend:** MO: NOV: CIV:-IMP: NORTHV: **Note:** Dav.#5627.

Date	Mintage	VG	F	VF	XF	Unc
1623	—	1,000	2,000	4,000	6,900	—

KM# 30 THALER
Silver **Obv:** C-M above eagle, date not divided in legend **Rev:** Without initials in arms **Rev. Legend:** MON. NO. CIV.-IM. **Note:** Dav.#5629.

Date	Mintage	VG	F	VF	XF	Unc
1624 CM	—	875	1,750	3,150	5,600	—

KM# 29 THALER
Silver **Rev:** H-G in arms **Rev. Legend:** MON. MO. CIVI... **Note:** Varieties exist. Dav.#5628.

Date	Mintage	VG	F	VF	XF	Unc
1624 HG	—	1,000	2,000	4,000	6,900	—

KM# 32 THALER
Silver **Obv. Legend:** LEOPOLDVS. D. G... **Rev:** Date divided above helmeted arms **Note:** Dav.#5631.

Date	Mintage	VG	F	VF	XF	Unc
1660 IK	—	1,000	2,000	4,150	7,100	—

KM# 20 2 THALER
Silver **Obv:** Crowned imperial eagle, date divided above **Rev:** Helmeted arms with fancy decoration **Note:** Dav.#5622.

Date	Mintage	VG	F	VF	XF	Unc
1620 Rare	—	—	—	—	—	—

KM# 28 2 THALER
Silver **Obv:** Crowned eagle dividing H-G above **Note:** Dav.#5625.

Date	Mintage	VG	F	VF	XF	Unc
1623 HG Rare	—	—	—	—	—	—

KM# 33 2 THALER
Silver **Note:** Dav.#5630.

Date	Mintage	VG	F	VF	XF	Unc
1660 IK Rare	—	—	—	—	—	—

TRADE COINAGE

FR# 1791 4 GOLDGULDEN
14.0000 g., 0.9860 Gold 0.4438 oz. AGW **Obv:** Arms **Rev:** Imperial eagle

Date	Mintage	VG	F	VF	XF	Unc
1619 Rare	—	—	—	—	—	—

FR# 1792 DUCAT
3.5000 g., 0.9860 Gold 0.1109 oz. AGW **Obv:** Theodosis seated facing **Rev:** Shield of arms in inner circle

Date	Mintage	VG	F	VF	XF	Unc
1619 Rare	—	—	—	—	—	—

KM# 14 4 DUCAT
Gold **Obv:** City arms **Rev:** Crowned imperial eagle, titles of Ferdinand II **Note:** Fr.#1791.

Date	Mintage	VG	F	VF	XF	Unc
1619 Rare	—	—	—	—	—	—

NORTHEIM

(Nordheim)

The city of Northeim, lying 15 miles north of Gottingen in Brunswick-Luneburg, is known from records dating to the early 11th century. Never gaining status as a Free City of the Empire, Northeim was under the control of the dukes of Brunswick-Luneburg who allowed a local coinage to be struck from the 16th century until 1676.

MINT OFFICIALS' INITIALS

Initial	Date	Name
(a)= [symbol]	1609-14	Jakob Pfahler
	1614-16	Dietrich Schmidt, warden
	1617	Andreas Einbeck, warden
(b)= [symbol] or [symbol] or [symbol]	1615-18	Valentin Block
	1618-21	Heinrich von Eck
	Ca. 1619-20	Henning Westermann
	Ca. 1620-21	Wilhelm Nordmeier, warden
	1621	Philipp Kahle
	1622	Levin Brockmann
	1622-23	Hans von Eck
PL or (pl) [symbol]	1662-70	Peter Lohr
WN	1655-59	Wilhelm Nordmeier
(c)= [symbol] and/or [symbol]	1671-76	Johann Heinrich Hoffman

CITY

REGULAR COINAGE

KM# 12 FLITTER (1/2 Pfennig)
Copper **Obv:** N flanked by 3-petalled leaf, 8-pointed star above and below **Rev. Inscription:** *1* / FLIT / TER **Note:** Kipper Flitter.

Date	Mintage	Good	VG	F	VF	XF
ND(1621/22)	—	11.00	27.00	45.00	75.00	—

KM# 13 PFENNIG
Copper **Obv:** N flanked by various ornaments, star above and below **Rev. Inscription:** I / PFEN / NING **Note:** Kipper Pfennig. Varieties exist.

Date	Mintage	Good	VG	F	VF	XF
ND(1621/22)	—	11.00	27.00	45.00	75.00	—

KM# 19 PFENNIG
Silver **Obv:** Crowned gothic N superimposed on cross **Note:** Uniface. Schussel type. Varieties exist.

Date	Mintage	VG	F	VF	XF	Unc
ND(ca.1623)	—	20.00	40.00	70.00	125	—

KM# 25 PFENNIG
Copper **Obv:** Crowned gothic N divides date **Rev. Inscription:** I / STAT / PEN **Note:** Stadt Pfennig. Varieties exist.

Date	Mintage	Good	VG	F	VF	XF
1655	—	12.00	24.00	45.00	85.00	—
1656	—	12.00	24.00	45.00	85.00	—
1657	—	12.00	24.00	45.00	85.00	—

KM# 36 PFENNIG
Silver **Obv:** Crowned gothic N divides date **Note:** Uniface. Schussel type. Varieties exist.

Date	Mintage	VG	F	VF	XF	Unc
1664	—	16.00	33.00	60.00	120	—
1667	—	16.00	33.00	60.00	120	—
1669	—	16.00	33.00	60.00	120	—
1673 (c)	—	16.00	33.00	60.00	120	—
1674 (c)	—	16.00	33.00	60.00	120	—
1675 (c)	—	16.00	33.00	60.00	120	—
1676 (c)	—	16.00	33.00	60.00	120	—

KM# 15 3 PFENNIG

Copper **Obv:** Crowned gothic N divides date **Rev:** III in circle, around PFENN. NIGE

Date	Mintage	Good	VG	F	VF	XF
16Z1	—	9.00	20.00	40.00	70.00	—

KM# 14 3 PFENNIG

Copper **Obv:** Crowned gothic N between two rosettes **Rev:** III in circle, legend, date **Rev. Legend:** PFENN. NIG **Note:** Kipper Pfennig.

Date	Mintage	Good	VG	F	VF	XF
16Z1	—	9.00	20.00	40.00	70.00	—

KM# 17 3 PFENNIG (Dreier)

Silver **Obv:** Gothic N superimposed on cross **Rev:** Imperial orb with 3, cross on orb divides date

Date	Mintage	VG	F	VF	XF	Unc
16ZZ	—	33.00	60.00	120	200	—

KM# 20 3 PFENNIG (Dreier)

Silver **Obv:** Gothic N superimposed on cross

Date	Mintage	VG	F	VF	XF	Unc
16Z3	—	33.00	60.00	120	200	—

KM# 26 3 PFENNIG (Dreier)

Copper **Obv:** Mintmasters' initials divided at bottom

Date	Mintage	Good	VG	F	VF	XF
1655 WN	—	6.00	16.00	33.00	60.00	—

KM# 27 3 PFENNIG (Dreier)

Copper **Obv:** Crowned gothic N superimposed on cross, date divided in legend **Rev:** III/STAT/PEN/NI

Date	Mintage	Good	VG	F	VF	XF
1655	—	9.00	20.00	40.00	70.00	—

KM# 35 3 PFENNIG (Dreier)

Silver **Obv:** Crowned gothic N divides date **Rev:** Imperial orb with 3 **Note:** Varieties exist.

Date	Mintage	VG	F	VF	XF	Unc
166Z	—	20.00	40.00	70.00	120	—
1664	—	20.00	40.00	70.00	120	—
1665	—	20.00	40.00	70.00	120	—
1666	—	20.00	40.00	70.00	120	—
1669	—	20.00	40.00	70.00	120	—
1670 (c)	—	20.00	40.00	70.00	120	—
1671 (c)	—	20.00	40.00	70.00	120	—
1672 (c)	—	20.00	40.00	70.00	120	—
1673 (c)	—	20.00	40.00	70.00	120	—
1674 (c)	—	20.00	40.00	70.00	120	—
1675 (c)	—	20.00	40.00	70.00	120	—
1676 (c)	—	20.00	40.00	70.00	120	—

KM# 16 4 PFENNIG

Copper **Obv:** Crowned gothic N between two rosettes **Rev:** IIII in circle, around PFENNINGE, date **Note:** Kipper Pfennig. Varieties exist.

Date	Mintage	Good	VG	F	VF	XF
16Z1	—	13.00	27.00	55.00	100	—

KM# 40 4 PFENNIG

Silver **Obv:** Crowned gothic N divides date **Rev:** IIII/GUTE/PF **Note:** Gute 4 Pfennig. Varieties exist.

Date	Mintage	VG	F	VF	XF	Unc
1670 (pl)	—	27.00	45.00	75.00	125	—
1670 (c)	—	27.00	45.00	75.00	125	—
1671 (c)	—	27.00	45.00	75.00	125	—
1672 (c)	—	27.00	45.00	75.00	125	—
1673 (c)	—	27.00	45.00	75.00	125	—

KM# 21 MARIENGROSCHEN

Silver **Obv:** Crowned ornate gothic N superimposed on cross, legend, date **Obv. Legend:** MO. NO. NORTHE. **Rev:** Madonna and child in circle **Rev. Legend:** MARIA. M-AT. DOM.

Date	Mintage	VG	F	VF	XF	Unc
16Z3	—	27.00	45.00	85.00	165	—

KM# 28 MARIENGROSCHEN

Silver **Obv:** Crowned gothic N, legend, date **Obv. Legend:** MO. NO. NORTHE **Rev:** Madonna and child **Rev. Legend:** MAR. MATER. DO. **Note:** Varieties exist.

Date	Mintage	VG	F	VF	XF	Unc
1655 WN	—	20.00	33.00	60.00	120	—
166Z	—	20.00	33.00	60.00	120	—
1664	—	20.00	33.00	60.00	120	—
1665	—	20.00	33.00	60.00	120	—
1666	—	20.00	33.00	60.00	120	—
1669	—	20.00	33.00	60.00	120	—
1670	—	20.00	33.00	60.00	120	—
1671	—	20.00	33.00	60.00	120	—

KM# 41 4 MARIENGROSCHEN (1/9 Thaler)

Silver **Obv:** Similar to 6 Mariengroschen KM#38 but legend variation, date **Obv. Legend:** STAD. NORTHEIM. **Rev. Legend:** VON FEINEM SILBER **Rev. Inscription:** IIII / MARIEN / GROS **Note:** Varieties exist.

Date	Mintage	VG	F	VF	XF	Unc
1671 (c)	—	—	—	—	—	—

KM# 38 6 MARIENGROSCHEN (1/6 Thaler)

Silver **Obv. Legend:** NORTHEIMISCH STADTGELD **Rev:** Legend, date **Rev. Legend:** ANNO DOMINI **Note:** Varieties exist.

Date	Mintage	VG	F	VF	XF	Unc
1669 PL	—	40.00	80.00	140	240	—
1669 (pl)	—	40.00	80.00	140	240	—
1670 (pl)	—	40.00	80.00	140	240	—
1671 (c)	—	40.00	80.00	140	240	—
1672 (c)	—	40.00	80.00	140	240	—

KM# 44 24 MARIENGROSCHEN (2/3 Thaler)

Silver **Obv:** Similar to 6 Mariengroschen KM#38 but legend variation, date **Obv. Legend:** ANNO CHRISTI **Rev. Legend:** MON: NOVA CIVIT: NORTHEIMENSIS **Rev. Inscription:** XXIIII / MARIEN / GROSCH / mintmaster's initials **Note:** Varieties exist.

Date	Mintage	VG	F	VF	XF	Unc
1674 (c)	—	—	—	—	—	—

KM# 5 1/24 THALER (Groschen)

Silver **Obv:** Imperial orb with Z4, date divided by cross on orb, titles of Matthias **Rev:** Crowned gothic N superimposed on long-armed cross **Rev. Legend:** MON: CIVIT: NORTHEIM

Date	Mintage	VG	F	VF	XF	Unc
1614 (a)	—	27.00	55.00	100	165	—

KM# 6 1/24 THALER (Groschen)

Silver **Rev:** Without cross in background **Rev. Legend:** MO. NO: CIVI. NORTHEIM **Note:** Varieties exist.

Date	Mintage	VG	F	VF	XF	Unc
1615 (b)	—	24.00	45.00	80.00	140	—
1616	—	24.00	45.00	80.00	140	—

KM# 7 1/24 THALER (Groschen)

Silver **Obv:** Date divided in legend at top **Note:** Varieties exist.

Date	Mintage	VG	F	VF	XF	Unc
1616	—	24.00	45.00	80.00	140	—
1616 (b)	—	24.00	45.00	80.00	140	—
1618	—	24.00	45.00	80.00	140	—
1619	—	24.00	45.00	80.00	140	—
(1)6Z0	—	24.00	45.00	80.00	140	—
16Z0	—	24.00	45.00	80.00	140	—

KM# 11 1/24 THALER (Groschen)

Silver **Note:** Klippe.

Date	Mintage	VG	F	VF	XF	Unc
16Z0	—	—	—	—	—	—

KM# 10 1/24 THALER (Groschen)

Silver **Obv:** Titles of Ferdinand II

Date	Mintage	VG	F	VF	XF	Unc
16Z0	—	27.00	55.00	90.00	160	—

KM# 18 1/24 THALER (Groschen)

Silver **Obv:** Imperial orb with Z4, cross on orb divides date, titles of Ferdinand II **Rev:** Crowned gothic N with cross in background **Rev. Legend:** MONE. NOVA. NORTHEIM.

Date	Mintage	VG	F	VF	XF	Unc
16ZZ	—	27.00	55.00	100	160	—

KM# 39 1/24 THALER (Groschen)

Silver **Rev:** Date left of crown

Date	Mintage	VG	F	VF	XF	Unc
1670	—	27.00	55.00	100	160	—

KM# 42 1/24 THALER (Groschen)

Silver **Obv:** Imperial orb with Z4, titles of Leopold I **Rev:** Date **Rev. Legend:** MO. NO. NORTHEI

Date	Mintage	VG	F	VF	XF	Unc
1671 (c)	—	27.00	55.00	100	175	—

KM# 37 THALER

Silver **Obv:** Lion dividing P-L city arms of 5-towered gateway **Rev:** Crowned imperial eagle with arms on breast, date below, titles of Leopold **Note:** Dav. #5632.

Date	Mintage	VG	F	VF	XF	Unc
1665 PL Rare	—	—	—	—	—	—

KM# 43 THALER

Silver **Obv:** Arms and 24 on breast of eagle **Rev:** Details added into arms **Rev. Legend:** MON: NOVA. CICIT:... **Note:** Dav. #5633.

Date	Mintage	VG	F	VF	XF	Unc
1671 (c) Rare	—	—	—	—	—	—

NURNBERG

(Nuremberg)

The Franconian town of Nürnberg, located some 120 miles (200 kilometers) north-northwest of Munich, is known from documents at least as early as 1050. It was already mentioned as the site of an imperial mint in 1062 and its early massive fortifications probably date from this period. The first identifiable coins struck in the imperial mint are from the reign of Emperor Konrad III von Hohenstaufen (1138-52). In 1219, Emperor Friedrich II (1215-50) granted free status to Nürnberg and the mint continued to strike imperial coinage from that date. In 1422, the city received the right to strike its own coins and the first issues in silver appeared two years later. The first gold coins of Nürnberg date from about 1429. From then onwards, an almost unbroken succession of coinage was produced by the Nürnberg mint. On 15 September 1806, Nürnberg formally became part of Bavaria, although the last city coins were struck in 1807.

MINT OFFICIALS' INITIALS

Initial or Mark	Date	Name
DSD	End of 17th century	Daniel Sigmund Dockler, die-cutter
H/GH	1679-1712	George Hautsch (1745), die-cutter
I.L.OE., OEXELEIN		Johann Leonhard Oexelein
K.R.		George Knoll and Riedner
(a)= 3 wheat ears	1616-18, 20-ca.31	Hans Putzere
(b)=Star	1619-39	Hans Christoph Lauer
(c)=Cross	1622-57	Georg Nurnberger (elder)
(d)=Star	1639-45	Hans David Lauer
(e)=Cross	1655-77	Georg Nurnberger (younger)
(f)= Cross and/or GFN	1677-1716	Georg Friedrich Nurnberger

CITY ARMS

Divided vertically, eagle (or half eagle) on left, six diagonal bars downward to right on right side.

Paschal Lamb

The paschal lamb, Lamb of God or Agnes Dei was used in the gold Ducat series. It appears standing on a globe holding a banner with the word "PAX" (peace).

REFERENCES

K = Hans-Jörg Kellner, **Die Münzen der Freien Reichsstadt Nürnberg**, Grünwald bei München, 1957.

Sch = Wolfgang Schulten, **Deutsche Münzen aus der Zeit Karls V.**, Frankfurt am Main, 1976.

S = Hugo Frhr. Von Saurma-Jeltsch, **Die Saurmasche Münzsammlung deutscher, schweizerischer und polnischer Gepräge von etwa dem Beginn der Groschenzeit bis zur Kipperperiode**, Berlin, 1892.

FREE IMPERIAL CITY

REGULAR COINAGE

KM# 54 3 HELLER

Copper **Obv:** Nurnberg arms divide date, 3 H above **Note:** Uniface. Kipper 3 Heller.

Date	Mintage	VG	F	VF	XF	Unc
1622	—	—	—	—	—	—

KM# 5 PFENNIG

Billon **Obv:** Two adjacent shields of arms, date above, N below **Note:** Varieties exist. Known struck on thick flan using two dies of 1598, so not uniface. Kellner 267.

Date	Mintage	VG	F	VF	XF	Unc
1601	—	8.00	16.00	24.00	45.00	—
1602	—	8.00	16.00	24.00	45.00	—
1603	—	8.00	16.00	24.00	45.00	—
1604	—	8.00	16.00	24.00	45.00	—
1605	—	8.00	16.00	24.00	45.00	—
1606	—	8.00	16.00	24.00	45.00	—
1607	—	8.00	16.00	24.00	45.00	—
1609	—	8.00	16.00	24.00	45.00	—
1610	—	8.00	16.00	24.00	45.00	—
1611	—	8.00	16.00	24.00	45.00	—
1612	—	8.00	16.00	24.00	45.00	—
1613	—	8.00	16.00	24.00	45.00	—

KM# 9 PFENNIG

Billon **Note:** Klippe. Uniface.

Date	Mintage	VG	F	VF	XF	Unc
1602	—	—	—	—	—	—
1604	—	—	—	—	—	—

KM# 21 PFENNIG

Billon **Obv:** Two adjacent oval arms, date above, N below **Note:** Uniface. Varieties exist.

Date	Mintage	VG	F	VF	XF	Unc
1614	—	8.00	16.00	24.00	45.00	—
1615	—	8.00	16.00	24.00	45.00	—
1616	—	8.00	16.00	24.00	45.00	—
1617	—	8.00	16.00	24.00	45.00	—
1618	—	8.00	16.00	24.00	45.00	—
1619	—	8.00	16.00	24.00	45.00	—
1620	—	8.00	16.00	24.00	45.00	—

KM# 35 PFENNIG

Billon **Obv:** Nurnberg arms divide date, value I above **Note:** Kipper Pfennig.

Date	Mintage	VG	F	VF	XF	Unc
1620	—	11.00	20.00	33.00	60.00	—
1621	—	13.00	27.00	40.00	65.00	—

KM# 45 PFENNIG

Silver **Obv:** Nurnberg arms divide date, N above **Note:** Uniface.

Date	Mintage	VG	F	VF	XF	Unc
1621	—	—	—	—	—	—

KM# 55 PFENNIG

Copper **Obv:** City arms in rhomboid shaped shield **Note:** Uniface. Kellner 272.

Date	Mintage	VG	F	VF	XF	Unc
ND(1622)	—	11.00	20.00	33.00	55.00	—

KM# 35a PFENNIG

Copper

Date	Mintage	VG	F	VF	XF	Unc
1622	—	11.00	20.00	33.00	60.00	—

KM# 64 PFENNIG

Billon **Note:** Uniface. Varieties exist.

Date	Mintage	VG	F	VF	XF	Unc
1623	—	8.00	16.00	24.00	45.00	—
1624	—	8.00	16.00	24.00	45.00	—

Date	Mintage	VG	F	VF	XF	Unc
1625	—	8.00	16.00	24.00	45.00	—
1627	—	8.00	16.00	24.00	45.00	—
1628	—	8.00	16.00	24.00	45.00	—
1629	—	8.00	16.00	24.00	45.00	—
1630	—	8.00	16.00	24.00	45.00	—
1631	—	8.00	16.00	24.00	45.00	—
1632	—	8.00	16.00	24.00	45.00	—
1633	—	8.00	16.00	24.00	45.00	—
1634	—	8.00	16.00	24.00	45.00	—
1635	—	8.00	16.00	24.00	45.00	—
1636	—	8.00	16.00	24.00	45.00	—
1637	—	8.00	16.00	24.00	45.00	—
1638	—	8.00	16.00	24.00	45.00	—
1639	—	8.00	16.00	24.00	45.00	—
1640	—	8.00	16.00	24.00	45.00	—
1641	—	8.00	16.00	24.00	45.00	—
1642	—	8.00	16.00	24.00	45.00	—
1643	—	8.00	16.00	24.00	45.00	—
1644	—	8.00	16.00	24.00	45.00	—
1646	—	8.00	16.00	24.00	45.00	—
1647	—	8.00	16.00	24.00	45.00	—
1649	—	8.00	16.00	24.00	45.00	—
1650	—	8.00	16.00	24.00	45.00	—
1652	—	8.00	16.00	24.00	45.00	—
1654	—	8.00	16.00	24.00	45.00	—
1655	—	8.00	16.00	24.00	45.00	—
1656	—	8.00	16.00	24.00	45.00	—
1657	—	8.00	16.00	24.00	45.00	—
1658	—	8.00	16.00	24.00	45.00	—
1659	—	8.00	16.00	24.00	45.00	—
1660	—	8.00	16.00	24.00	45.00	—
1661	—	8.00	16.00	24.00	45.00	—
1662	—	8.00	16.00	24.00	45.00	—
1663	—	8.00	16.00	24.00	45.00	—
1664	—	8.00	16.00	24.00	45.00	—
1665	—	8.00	16.00	24.00	45.00	—
1666	—	8.00	16.00	24.00	45.00	—
1667	—	8.00	16.00	24.00	45.00	—
1668	—	8.00	16.00	24.00	45.00	—
1669	—	8.00	16.00	24.00	45.00	—
1670	—	8.00	16.00	24.00	45.00	—
1671	—	8.00	16.00	24.00	45.00	—
1672	—	8.00	16.00	24.00	45.00	—
1673	—	8.00	16.00	24.00	45.00	—
1674	—	8.00	16.00	24.00	45.00	—

KM# 86 PFENNIG

Billon **Obv:** Two adjacent oval arms, surmounted by angel's head, date above, N below **Note:** Varieties exist.

Date	Mintage	VG	F	VF	XF	Unc
1628	—	9.00	20.00	33.00	55.00	—
1629	—	9.00	20.00	33.00	55.00	—
1630	—	9.00	20.00	33.00	55.00	—
1631	—	9.00	20.00	33.00	55.00	—

KM# 193 PFENNIG

Billon **Obv:** Nurnberg arms divide date, S.I. above, + to lower right **Note:** Uniface. Varieties exist.

Date	Mintage	VG	F	VF	XF	Unc
1675 (e)	—	7.00	13.00	24.00	45.00	—
1676 (e)	—	7.00	13.00	24.00	45.00	—
1677 (e)	—	7.00	13.00	24.00	45.00	—
1678 (f)	—	7.00	13.00	24.00	45.00	—
1679 (f)	—	7.00	13.00	24.00	45.00	—
1680 (f)	—	7.00	13.00	24.00	45.00	—
1681 (f)	—	7.00	13.00	24.00	45.00	—
1682 (f)	—	7.00	13.00	24.00	45.00	—
1683 (f)	—	7.00	13.00	24.00	45.00	—
1684 (f)	—	7.00	13.00	24.00	45.00	—
1685 (f)	—	7.00	13.00	24.00	45.00	—
1686 (f)	—	7.00	13.00	24.00	45.00	—
1687 (f)	—	7.00	13.00	24.00	45.00	—
1688 (f)	—	7.00	13.00	24.00	45.00	—
1689 (f)	—	7.00	13.00	24.00	45.00	—
1690 (f)	—	7.00	13.00	24.00	45.00	—
1692 (f)	—	7.00	13.00	24.00	45.00	—
1693 (f)	—	7.00	13.00	24.00	45.00	—
1695 (f)	—	7.00	13.00	24.00	45.00	—
1696 (f)	—	7.00	13.00	24.00	45.00	—
1698 (f)	—	7.00	13.00	24.00	45.00	—
1699 (f)	—	7.00	13.00	24.00	45.00	—
1700 (f)	—	7.00	13.00	24.00	45.00	—

KM# 174 1-1/2 PFENNIG

Silver **Obv:** Nurnberg arms divide date, value 1 1/2 (pfg) above **Rev:** N, 1 1/2 (pfg) below

Date	Mintage	VG	F	VF	XF	Unc
1659 (e)	—	—	—	—	—	—

KM# 36 2 PFENNIG (Zweier)

Silver **Obv:** Nurnberg arms divide date, value II above **Note:** Uniface.

Date	Mintage	VG	F	VF	XF	Unc
1620	—	11.00	20.00	33.00	55.00	—

 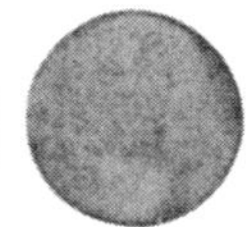

KM# 36a 2 PFENNIG (Zweier)

Copper **Obv:** Nurnberg arms divide date, value II above **Note:** Uniface

Date	Mintage	VG	F	VF	XF	Unc
1621	—	8.00	16.00	27.00	55.00	—
1622	—	8.00	16.00	27.00	55.00	—

KM# 65 2 PFENNIG (Zweier)

Silver **Obv:** Two adjacent shields or arms, II divides date above, N below **Note:** Varieties exist.

Date	Mintage	VG	F	VF	XF	Unc
1623	—	8.00	16.00	27.00	45.00	—
1624	—	8.00	16.00	27.00	45.00	—
1628	—	8.00	16.00	27.00	45.00	—
1630	—	8.00	16.00	27.00	45.00	—
1631	—	8.00	16.00	27.00	45.00	—
1633	—	8.00	16.00	27.00	45.00	—

KM# 28 3 PFENNIG (Dreier)

Silver **Subject:** Enlargement of the City Hall **Obv:** Similar to KM#22 **Rev:** Four-line inscription

Date	Mintage	VG	F	VF	XF	Unc
1616	—	16.00	33.00	55.00	110	—

 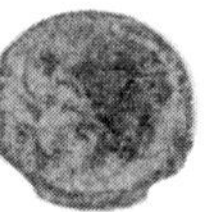

KM# 56 3 PFENNIG (Dreier)

Copper **Obv:** Shield of arms, date at sides, 3 and a pfennigmark above **Note:** Uniface.

Date	Mintage	VG	F	VF	XF	Unc
1622	—	—	—	—	—	—

KM# 66 3 PFENNIG (Dreier)

Silver **Obv:** Two adjacent shields of arms, date above, N below **Rev:** Imperial orb with 3 in baroque frame

Date	Mintage	VG	F	VF	XF	Unc
1623	—	11.00	20.00	33.00	55.00	—
1624	—	11.00	20.00	33.00	55.00	—
1625	—	11.00	20.00	33.00	55.00	—

KM# 107 3 PFENNIG (Dreier)

Silver **Obv:** Nurnberg arms in baroque frame, date divided near top

Date	Mintage	VG	F	VF	XF	Unc
1631	—	13.00	27.00	40.00	70.00	—

KM# 108 3 PFENNIG (Dreier)

Silver **Obv:** Nurnberg arms in ornamented rhombus **Rev:** Imperial orb with 3 divides date, all in ornamented rhombus

Date	Mintage	VG	F	VF	XF	Unc
1631	—	11.00	20.00	33.00	55.00	—
1632	—	11.00	20.00	33.00	55.00	—
1659	—	11.00	20.00	33.00	55.00	—
1662	—	—	—	—	—	—

KM# 6 3 PFENNIG (1/84 Gulden)

Silver **Obv:** Ornamented oval shield of city arms divide date **Rev:** Imperial orb with 84 in ornamented rhombus **Note:** Varieties exist. Kellner 250.

Date	Mintage	VG	F	VF	XF	Unc
1601	—	11.00	20.00	33.00	55.00	—
1602	—	11.00	20.00	33.00	55.00	—
1603	—	11.00	20.00	33.00	55.00	—
1604	—	11.00	20.00	33.00	55.00	—
1605	—	11.00	20.00	33.00	55.00	—
1606	—	11.00	20.00	33.00	55.00	—
1607	—	11.00	20.00	33.00	55.00	—
1608	—	11.00	20.00	33.00	55.00	—
1609	—	11.00	20.00	33.00	55.00	—
1610	—	11.00	20.00	33.00	55.00	—
1611	—	11.00	20.00	33.00	55.00	—
1612	—	11.00	20.00	33.00	55.00	—
1613	—	11.00	20.00	33.00	55.00	—

KM# 22 3 PFENNIG (1/84 Gulden)

Silver **Obv:** Nurnburg arms in baroque frame, date above **Rev:** Imperial orb with 84 in laurel wreath

Date	Mintage	VG	F	VF	XF	Unc
1614	—	11.00	20.00	33.00	55.00	—
1615	—	11.00	20.00	33.00	55.00	—
1616	—	11.00	20.00	33.00	55.00	—

KM# 29 3 PFENNIG (1/84 Gulden)

Silver **Obv:** Oval arms

Date	Mintage	VG	F	VF	XF	Unc
1617	—	11.00	20.00	33.00	55.00	—
1618	—	11.00	20.00	33.00	55.00	—
1619	—	11.00	20.00	33.00	55.00	—
1620	—	11.00	20.00	33.00	55.00	—

KM# 46 1/84 GULDEN (3 Pfennig)

Copper **Obv:** Heart-shaped Nurnberg arms in baroque frame, date divided at top **Rev:** 84 in wreath **Note:** Varieties exist.

Date	Mintage	VG	F	VF	XF	Unc
1621 (a)	—	11.00	20.00	33.00	55.00	—
1622 (a)	—	11.00	20.00	33.00	55.00	—
1622 (b)	—	11.00	20.00	33.00	55.00	—
1622 (c)	—	11.00	20.00	33.00	55.00	—

KM# 40 1/2 KREUZER (2 Pfennig)

Silver **Obv:** Nurnberg arms divide date, 1/2 K above **Note:** Uniface.

Date	Mintage	VG	F	VF	XF	Unc
1620	—	11.00	20.00	33.00	55.00	—

KM# 37 KREUZER (4 Pfennig)

Copper **Obv:** Nurnberg arms, N above **Rev:** I/KREUTZ/ER/date **Note:** Kipper Kreuzer. Varieties exist.

Date	Mintage	VG	F	VF	XF	Unc
1620	—	11.00	20.00	33.00	55.00	—
1621	—	11.00	20.00	33.00	55.00	—
1622	—	11.00	20.00	33.00	55.00	—

KM# 68 KREUZER (4 Pfennig)

Silver **Obv:** Double cross (x on ++) **Rev:** Two adjacent arms, date above, I below

Date	Mintage	VG	F	VF	XF	Unc
1623 (c)	—	11.00	20.00	33.00	55.00	—
1624 (a)	—	11.00	20.00	33.00	55.00	—
1630 (a)	—	11.00	20.00	33.00	55.00	—

KM# 67 KREUZER (4 Pfennig)

Silver **Obv:** Imperial eagle, orb on breast with I **Rev:** Two adjacent shields of arms, date above, N below **Note:** Varieties exist.

Date	Mintage	VG	F	VF	XF	Unc
1623	—	13.00	27.00	40.00	70.00	—

KM# 90 KREUZER (4 Pfennig)

Silver **Obv:** Double cross **Rev:** Nurnberg arms in ornamented shield divide date

Date	Mintage	VG	F	VF	XF	Unc
1629 (b)	—	11.00	24.00	40.00	65.00	—

KM# 100 KREUZER (4 Pfennig)

Silver **Obv:** Two coats of arms below date with N at bottom **Rev:** Double cross. Legend begins with star **Note:** Similar to KM#51 but legend begins with star. Varieties exist.

Date	Mintage	VG	F	VF	XF	Unc
1630 (b)	—	11.00	20.00	33.00	55.00	—
1631 (b)	—	11.00	20.00	33.00	55.00	—
1632 (b)	—	11.00	20.00	33.00	55.00	—
1633 (b)	—	11.00	20.00	33.00	55.00	—
1634 (b)	—	11.00	20.00	33.00	55.00	—
1635 (b)	—	11.00	20.00	33.00	55.00	—
1636 (b)	—	11.00	20.00	33.00	55.00	—
1637 (b)	—	11.00	20.00	33.00	55.00	—
1638 (b)	—	11.00	20.00	33.00	55.00	—
1639 (b)	—	11.00	20.00	33.00	55.00	—
1640 (b)	—	11.00	20.00	33.00	55.00	—
1641 (b)	—	11.00	20.00	33.00	55.00	—

KM# 109 KREUZER (4 Pfennig)

Silver **Obv:** Double cross **Rev:** Two adjacent shields of arms with date above

Date	Mintage	VG	F	VF	XF	Unc
1631 (a)	—	11.00	20.00	33.00	55.00	—
1631 (b)	—	11.00	20.00	33.00	55.00	—

KM# 151 KREUZER (4 Pfennig)

Silver **Note:** Legend begins with cross. Varieties exist.

Date	Mintage	VG	F	VF	XF	Unc
1639 (c)	—	11.00	20.00	33.00	55.00	—
1641 (c)	—	11.00	20.00	33.00	55.00	—
1642 (c)	—	11.00	20.00	33.00	55.00	—
1643 (c)	—	11.00	20.00	33.00	55.00	—
1645 (c)	—	11.00	20.00	33.00	55.00	—
1646 (c)	—	11.00	20.00	33.00	55.00	—
1647 (c)	—	11.00	20.00	33.00	55.00	—
1654 (c)	—	11.00	20.00	33.00	55.00	—
1656 (c)	—	11.00	20.00	33.00	55.00	—
1659 (e)	—	11.00	20.00	33.00	55.00	—
1661 (e)	—	11.00	20.00	33.00	55.00	—
1662 (3)	—	11.00	20.00	33.00	55.00	—
1664 (e)	—	11.00	20.00	33.00	55.00	—
1667 (e)	—	11.00	20.00	33.00	55.00	—

Date	Mintage	VG	F	VF	XF	Unc
1670 (e)	—	11.00	20.00	33.00	55.00	—
1673 (e)	—	11.00	20.00	33.00	55.00	—

KM# 194 KREUZER (4 Pfennig)
Silver **Obv:** Double cross, mint mark (++) divides date at top **Rev:** Oval Nurnberg arms in baroque frame **Note:** Varieties exist.

Date	Mintage	VG	F	VF	XF	Unc
1676 (e)	—	11.00	20.00	33.00	55.00	—
1678 (f)	—	11.00	20.00	33.00	55.00	—
1679 (f)	—	11.00	20.00	33.00	55.00	—
1680 (f)	—	11.00	20.00	33.00	55.00	—
1681 (f)	—	11.00	20.00	33.00	55.00	—

KM# 215 KREUZER (4 Pfennig)
Silver **Obv:** Double cross, date in margin, mint mark (++) at top **Rev:** Two adjacent arms, angel's head above, N below **Note:** Varieties exist.

Date	Mintage	VG	F	VF	XF	Unc
1691 (f)	—	9.00	20.00	33.00	60.00	—
1692 (f)	—	9.00	20.00	33.00	60.00	—
1693 (f)	—	9.00	20.00	33.00	60.00	—
1694 (f)	—	9.00	20.00	33.00	60.00	—
1700 (f)	—	9.00	20.00	33.00	60.00	—

KM# 38 2 KREUZER (1/2 Batzen)
Silver **Obv:** Ornately-shaped Nurnberg arms **Rev. Inscription:** II / KREUTZ / ER / date

Date	Mintage	VG	F	VF	XF	Unc
1620	—	13.00	22.00	33.00	65.00	—
1620 (a)	—	13.00	22.00	33.00	65.00	—

KM# 57 2 KREUZER (1/2 Batzen)
Silver **Obv:** Nurnberg arms, N above **Note:** Kipper Kreuzer. Varieties exist.

Date	Mintage	VG	F	VF	XF	Unc
1620	—	13.00	27.00	40.00	70.00	—
1621	—	13.00	27.00	40.00	70.00	—
1622	—	13.00	27.00	40.00	70.00	—

KM# 157 2 KREUZER (1/2 Batzen)
Silver **Obv:** Eagle, head right **Rev:** Nurnberg arms, 2.K. above

Date	Mintage	VG	F	VF	XF	Unc
ND(1643) (c)	—	11.00	20.00	33.00	65.00	—

KM# 184 2 KREUZER (1/2 Batzen)
Silver **Obv:** Nurnberg arms divide date, 2 above **Rev:** Crowned imperial eagle, Nurnberg arms on breast, titles of Leopold I

Date	Mintage	VG	F	VF	XF	Unc
1665 (e)	—	13.00	24.00	40.00	70.00	—

KM# 200 2 KREUZER (1/2 Batzen)
Silver **Rev:** II K. above arms

Date	Mintage	VG	F	VF	XF	Unc
1680 (f)	—	16.00	27.00	45.00	80.00	—

KM# 221 2 KREUZER (1/2 Batzen)
Silver **Rev:** 2 on eagle's breast

Date	Mintage	VG	F	VF	XF	Unc
1694 (f)	—	13.00	24.00	40.00	70.00	—
1695 (f)	—	13.00	24.00	40.00	70.00	—

KM# 222 4 KREUZER (Batzen)
Silver **Obv:** Oval Nurnberg arms in baroque frame, date divided below **Rev:** Crowned imperial eagle, 4 in oval on breast, titles of Leopold I

Date	Mintage	VG	F	VF	XF	Unc
1694 (F)	—	16.00	33.00	65.00	120	—

KM# 58 5 KREUZER
Silver **Obv:** Nürnberg arms divide date, V.K. above **Rev:** Crowned imperial eagle, Nurnberg arms on breast, titles of Leopold I **Note:** Kipper 5 Kreuzer. Varieties exist.

Date	Mintage	VG	F	VF	XF	Unc
1622 (a)	—	20.00	33.00	60.00	120	—
1622 (b)	—	20.00	33.00	60.00	120	—
1622 (c)	—	20.00	33.00	60.00	120	—

KM# 39 6 KREUZER
Silver **Obv:** Nurnberg arms in baroque frame **Rev. Inscription:** VI / KREUTZ / ER / date

Date	Mintage	VG	F	VF	XF	Unc
1620	—	16.00	33.00	55.00	120	—

KM# 201 6 KREUZER
Silver **Obv:** Shield of city arms divides date, value K/VI in two lines above **Obv. Legend:** + MON: NOV: ARGENT: REIP: NORIMBERG **Rev:** Crowned imperial eagle with small shield of Nürnberg arms on breast **Rev. Legend:** LEOPOLDVS: D: G: ROM: IMPER: S: A. **Note:** Varieties exist.

Date	Mintage	VG	F	VF	XF	Unc
1680 (f)	—	15.00	30.00	50.00	90.00	—

KM# 59 10 KREUZER (1/12 Thaler)
Silver **Obv:** Nurnberg arms divide date, value X.K above **Rev:** Crowned imperial eagle, Nurnberg arms on breast, titles of Ferdinand II **Note:** Kipper 10 Kreuzer. Varieties exist.

Date	Mintage	VG	F	VF	XF	Unc
1622 (a)	—	20.00	33.00	60.00	120	—
1622 (b)	—	20.00	33.00	60.00	120	—
1622 (c)	—	20.00	33.00	60.00	120	—

KM# 60 15 KREUZER (1/8 Thaler)
Silver **Note:** Kipper 15 Kreuzer. Varieties exist.

Date	Mintage	VG	F	VF	XF	Unc
1622 (a)	—	11.00	20.00	40.00	80.00	—
1622 (b)	—	11.00	20.00	40.00	80.00	—
1622 (c)	—	11.00	20.00	40.00	80.00	—

KM# 61 20 KREUZER
Silver **Obv:** Nurnberg arms divide date, value K. / XX above **Rev:** Crowned imperial eagle, Nurnberg arms on breast, titles of Ferdinand II **Note:** Kipper 20 Kreuzer. Varieties exist.

Date	Mintage	VG	F	VF	XF	Unc
1622 (a)	—	20.00	40.00	85.00	155	—
1622 (c)	—	20.00	40.00	85.00	155	—

KM# 7 30 KREUZER (1/2 Reichsgulden)
Silver **Obv:** Two shields of arms **Obv. Inscription:** RE SPVB / NVRENBERG / F•F **Rev:** Crowned imperial eagle, 30 in orb on breast **Note:** Varieties exist. Kellner 142.

Date	Mintage	VG	F	VF	XF	Unc
MDCI (1601)	—	55.00	115	200	325	—
MDCII (1602)	—	55.00	115	200	325	—
MDCIII (1603)	—	55.00	115	200	325	—
MDCIV (1604)	—	55.00	115	200	325	—
MDCV (1606)	—	55.00	115	200	325	—
MDCVI (1607)	—	55.00	115	200	325	—
MDCVII (1608)	—	55.00	115	200	325	—
MDCVIII (1609)	—	55.00	115	200	325	—
MDCIX (1610)	—	55.00	115	200	325	—
MDCX (1611)	—	55.00	115	200	325	—
MDCXI (1612)	—	55.00	115	200	325	—

KM# 18 30 KREUZER (1/2 Reichsgulden)
Silver **Obv:** 2 shields of arms, angel heads above, date below. **Rev:** Crowned imperial eagle, 30 in orb on breast, titles of Matthias **Note:** Varieties exist.

Date	Mintage	VG	F	VF	XF	Unc
1613	—	55.00	115	200	325	—
1614	—	55.00	115	200	325	—
1615	—	55.00	115	200	325	—
1616	—	55.00	115	200	325	—
1617	—	55.00	115	200	325	—
1618	—	55.00	115	200	325	—
1619	—	55.00	115	200	325	—

KM# 41 30 KREUZER (1/2 Reichsgulden)
Silver **Obv:** Titles of Ferdinand II **Note:** Varieties exist.

Date	Mintage	VG	F	VF	XF	Unc
1620	—	55.00	115	200	325	—
1621	—	55.00	115	200	325	—
1622 (b)	—	55.00	115	200	325	—

Date	Mintage	VG	F	VF	XF	Unc
1623 (b)	—	55.00	115	200	325	—
1624 (b)	—	55.00	115	200	325	—
1625 (b)	—	55.00	115	200	325	—
1626 (b)	—	55.00	115	200	325	—
1627 (b)	—	55.00	115	200	325	—
1628 (b)	—	55.00	115	200	325	—
1629 (b)	—	55.00	115	200	325	—
1630 (b)	—	55.00	115	200	325	—
1631 (b)	—	55.00	115	200	325	—
1632 (b)	—	55.00	115	200	325	—
1633 (b)	—	55.00	115	200	325	—
1635 (b)	—	55.00	115	200	325	—
1636 (b)	—	55.00	115	200	325	—
1637 (b)	—	55.00	115	200	325	—

KM# 62 30 KREUZER (1/4 Thaler)
Silver **Obv:** Nurnberg arms divide date, value K. /XXX above **Rev:** Crowned imperial eagle, Nurnberg arms on breast, titles of Leopold I **Note:** Kipper 30 Kreuzer. Varieties exist.

Date	Mintage	VG	F	VF	XF	Unc
1622 (a)	—	—	—	—	—	—
1622 (b)	—	—	—	—	—	—
1622 (c)	—	—	—	—	—	—

KM# 75 30 KREUZER (1/2 Gulden)
Silver **Obv:** Winged Genius, shield of arms at both sides of legs, date below **Rev:** Crowned double-headed imperial eagle, orb on breast **Note:** Varieties exist.

Date	Mintage	VG	F	VF	XF	Unc
1625 (c)	—	65.00	165	275	450	—
1626 (c)	—	65.00	165	275	450	—
1627 (c)	—	65.00	165	275	450	—
1628 (c)	—	65.00	165	275	450	—
1629 (c)	—	65.00	165	275	450	—
1631 (c)	—	65.00	165	275	450	—

KM# 101 30 KREUZER (1/2 Gulden)
Silver **Rev:** St. Sebald holding model of church, two small arms at both sides of legs, Roman numeral date at bottom **Note:** Varieties exist.

Date	Mintage	VG	F	VF	XF	Unc
1630 (c)	—	50.00	115	200	325	—
1631 (c)	—	50.00	115	200	325	—
1632 (c)	—	50.00	115	200	325	—
1633 (c)	—	50.00	115	200	325	—
1634 (c)	—	50.00	115	200	325	—
1635 (c)	—	50.00	115	200	325	—
1636 (c)	—	50.00	115	200	325	—
1637 (c)	—	50.00	115	200	325	—

KM# 140 30 KREUZER (1/2 Gulden)
Silver **Obv:** Two shields of arms, angel heads above, date below **Rev:** Crowned imperial eagle, 30 in orb on breast, titles of Ferdinand II **Note:** Varieties exist.

Date	Mintage	VG	F	VF	XF	Unc
1638 (b)	—	50.00	115	200	325	—
1639 (b)	—	50.00	115	200	325	—
1640 (d)	—	50.00	115	200	325	—
1642 (d)	—	50.00	115	200	325	—

KM# 141 30 KREUZER (1/2 Gulden)
Silver **Obv:** St. Sebald holding model of Church, two small arms at both sides of legs, Roman numeral date at bottom **Note:** Varieties exist.

Date	Mintage	VG	F	VF	XF	Unc
1638 (c)	—	50.00	115	200	325	—
1639 (c)	—	50.00	115	200	325	—
1640 (c)	—	50.00	115	200	325	—
1641 (c)	—	50.00	115	200	325	—
1642 (c)	—	50.00	115	200	325	—
1643 (c)	—	50.00	115	200	325	—
1645 (c)	—	50.00	115	200	325	—
1646 (c)	—	50.00	115	200	325	—

KM# 165 30 KREUZER (1/2 Gulden)
Silver **Obv:** Figure of St. Sebald divides date at middle **Note:** Varieties exist.

Date	Mintage	VG	F	VF	XF	Unc
1650 (c)	—	50.00	115	200	325	—
1657 (c)	—	50.00	115	200	325	—
1658 (e)	—	50.00	115	200	325	—

KM# 8 60 KREUZER
Silver **Obv:** Two shields of arms **Obv. Inscription:** RESPVB / NVRENBERG / F•F **Rev:** Crowned imperial eagle, 60 in orb on

eagle's breast **Rev. Legend:** +RVDOLPH: II: ROM:-IMP: AVG: P: F: DEC: **Note:** Reichsgulden 60 Kreuzer. Varieties exist. Dav. #89; Kellner 127.

Date	Mintage	VG	F	VF	XF	Unc
MDCI (1601)	—	120	165	275	425	—
MDCII (1602)	—	120	165	275	425	—
MDCIII (1603)	—	120	165	275	425	—
MDCIV (1604)	—	120	165	275	425	—
MDCV (1605)	—	120	165	275	425	—
MDCVI (1606)	—	120	165	275	425	—
MDCVII (1607)	—	120	165	275	425	—
MDCVIII (1608)	—	120	165	275	425	—
MDCIX (1609)	—	120	165	275	425	—
MDCX (1610)	—	120	165	275	425	—
MDCXI (1611)	—	120	165	275	425	—
MDCXII (1612)	—	120	165	275	425	—

KM# 19 60 KREUZER

Silver **Obv:** 2 Adjacent angels with rounded shields on chest, inscription above, date below **Rev:** Crowned double-headed imperial eagle, value in orb on breast **Note:** Titles of Matthias. Varieties exist. Dav. #90.

Date	Mintage	VG	F	VF	XF	Unc
1613	—	120	165	260	400	—
1614	—	120	165	260	400	—
1615	—	120	165	260	400	—
1616	—	120	165	260	400	—
1617	—	120	165	260	400	—
1618	—	120	165	260	400	—
1619	—	120	165	260	400	—

KM# 42 60 KREUZER

Silver **Note:** Similar to 30 Kreuzer, KM#41 but 60 in orb on eagle's breast, titles of Ferdinand II. Varieties exist. Dav. #91.

Date	Mintage	VG	F	VF	XF	Unc
1620	—	120	165	260	400	—
1621	—	120	165	260	400	—
1622 (b)	—	120	165	260	400	—
1623 (b)	—	120	165	260	400	—
1624 (b)	—	120	165	260	400	—
1625 (b)	—	120	165	260	400	—
1626 (b)	—	120	165	260	400	—
1627 (b)	—	120	165	260	400	—
1628 (b)	—	120	165	260	400	—
1629 (b)	—	120	165	260	400	—
1631 (b)	—	120	165	260	400	—
1632 (b)	—	120	165	260	400	—
1633 (b)	—	120	165	260	400	—
1634 (b)	—	120	165	260	400	—
1635 (b)	—	120	165	260	400	—

KM# 63 60 KREUZER (1/2 Thaler)

Silver **Obv:** Value: K./LX above **Rev:** Crowned double-headed imperial eagle, small shield on breast **Note:** Kipper 60 Kreuzer.

Date	Mintage	VG	F	VF	XF	Unc
1622 (b)	—	120	200	275	475	—
1622 (c)	—	120	200	275	475	—

KM# 74 60 KREUZER (1/2 Thaler)

Silver **Obv:** Two oval arms in baroque frame, angel's head above, date in legend **Rev:** Crowned double-headed imperial eagle, 60 in orb on eagle breast **Note:** Reichsgulden 60 Kreuzer. Dav. #92.

Date	Mintage	VG	F	VF	XF	Unc
1624 (a)	—	100	165	250	400	—

KM# 76 60 KREUZER (1/2 Thaler)

Silver **Rev:** Winged Genius, shield of arms at both sides of legs, date below **Note:** Varieties exist. Dav. #93.

Date	Mintage	VG	F	VF	XF	Unc
1625 (c)	—	120	200	300	525	—
1626 (c)	—	120	200	300	525	—
1627 (c)	—	120	200	300	525	—
1628 (c)	—	120	200	300	525	—
1629 (c)	—	120	200	300	525	—

KM# 102 60 KREUZER (1/2 Thaler)

Silver **Obv:** St. Sebald holding model of church, 2 small arms at both sides of legs, Roman numeral date at bottom **Rev:** Crowned imperial eagle, 60 in orb on breast **Note:** Varieties exist.

Date	Mintage	VG	F	VF	XF	Unc
1630 (c)	—	100	180	270	450	—
1631 (c)	—	100	180	270	450	—
1632 (c)	—	100	180	270	450	—
1633 (c)	—	100	180	270	450	—
1634 (c)	—	100	180	270	450	—
1635 (c)	—	100	180	270	450	—
1636 (c)	—	100	180	270	450	—
1637 (c)	—	100	180	270	450	—

KM# 102.1 60 KREUZER (1/2 Thaler)

Silver **Obv. Legend:** FERDINAND: II: D: G: ROM. IMP SEM... **Rev:** St. Sebald holding model of church, two small arms at both sides of legs, Roman numeral date at bottom **Note:** Dav. #94.

Date	Mintage	VG	F	VF	XF	Unc
1630 (c)	—	100	180	270	450	—
1631 (c)	—	100	180	270	450	—
1632 (c)	—	100	180	270	450	—
1633 (c)	—	100	180	270	450	—
1634 (c)	—	100	180	270	450	—

KM# 102.2 60 KREUZER (1/2 Thaler)

Silver **Obv. Legend:** FERDINAND: II: DG: ROM. SE: AU:... **Note:** Varieties exist. Dav. #95.

Date	Mintage	VG	F	VF	XF	Unc
1635 (c)	—	100	180	270	450	—
1636 (c)	—	100	180	270	450	—
1637 (c)	—	100	180	270	450	—

KM# 142 60 KREUZER (1/2 Thaler)

Silver **Obv:** Titles of Ferdinand III **Rev:** Angel head above two shields, date between **Note:** Varieties exist. Dav. #96.

Date	Mintage	VG	F	VF	XF	Unc
1638 (b)	—	100	190	275	475	—
1639 (d)	—	100	190	275	475	—
1640 (b)	—	100	190	275	475	—

KM# 143 60 KREUZER (1/2 Thaler)

Silver **Rev:** Roman numeral date below saint **Note:** Varieties exist. Dav. #97.

Date	Mintage	VG	F	VF	XF	Unc
1638 (c)	—	100	180	270	450	—
1639 (c)	—	100	180	270	450	—
1640 (c)	—	100	180	270	450	—
1641 (c)	—	100	180	270	450	—
1642 (c)	—	100	180	270	450	—
1643 (c)	—	100	180	270	450	—
1645 (c)	—	100	180	270	450	—
1646 (c)	—	100	180	270	450	—

KM# 166 60 KREUZER (1/2 Thaler)

Silver **Rev:** St. Sebald divides date **Note:** Varieties exist. Dav. #98.

Date	Mintage	VG	F	VF	XF	Unc
1650 (c)	—	100	180	270	450	—
1657 (c)	—	100	180	270	450	—
1658 (e)	—	100	180	270	450	—

KM# 180 60 KREUZER (1/2 Thaler)

Silver **Obv:** Titles of Leopold I **Note:** Varieties exist. Dav. #99.

Date	Mintage	VG	F	VF	XF	Unc
1660 (e)	—	110	200	275	475	—

KM# A29 1/21 THALER (Reichsgroschen)

Silver **Subject:** Centennial of the Reformation **Obv:** Basket held by robed hand from right, inverted over lit candle **Obv. Legend:** ECCLESIA NORI - CA IUBILANS. **Rev:** 4-line inscription containing date in chronogram in ornamented square tablet, angel's head and wings above **Note:** Saurma 1149.

Date	Mintage	VG	F	VF	XF	Unc
MDLLVVVII(1617)	—	—	—	—	—	—

KM# 69 1/9 THALER

Silver **Obv:** 3 small oval shields of arms, 1 above 2 divides date **Rev:** Crowned imperial eagle, 9 in shield on breast, titles of Ferdinand II

Date	Mintage	VG	F	VF	XF	Unc
1623 (b)	—	20.00	45.00	85.00	165	—
1624 (b)	—	20.00	45.00	85.00	165	—

KM# 144 1/9 THALER

Silver **Obv:** Titles of Ferdinand III

Date	Mintage	VG	F	VF	XF	Unc
1638 (b)	—	27.00	55.00	90.00	175	—
1644 (d)	—	27.00	55.00	90.00	175	—

KM# 47 1/8 THALER

Silver **Note:** Without indication of value.

Date	Mintage	VG	F	VF	XF	Unc
1621 (b)	—	27.00	55.00	90.00	175	—
1623 (b)	—	27.00	55.00	90.00	175	—

KM# 77 1/8 THALER

Silver **Rev:** 1/8 in oval on eagle's breast **Note:** Varieties exist.

Date	Mintage	VG	F	VF	XF	Unc
1625 (b)	—	24.00	45.00	80.00	165	—
1626 (b)	—	24.00	45.00	80.00	165	—
1628 (b)	—	24.00	45.00	80.00	165	—
1629 (b)	—	24.00	45.00	80.00	165	—
1630 (b)	—	24.00	45.00	80.00	165	—
1631 (b)	—	24.00	45.00	80.00	165	—
1632 (b)	—	24.00	45.00	80.00	165	—
1634 (b)	—	24.00	45.00	80.00	165	—

KM# 132 1/8 THALER

Silver **Rev:** Oval Nurnberg arms in baroque frame divide date **Note:** Varieties exist.

Date	Mintage	VG	F	VF	XF	Unc
1635 (b)	—	20.00	40.00	80.00	165	—
1636 (b)	—	20.00	40.00	80.00	165	—
1637 (b)	—	20.00	40.00	80.00	165	—

KM# 145 1/8 THALER

Silver

Date	Mintage	VG	F	VF	XF	Unc
1638 (b)	—	20.00	40.00	80.00	165	—
1640 (d)	—	20.00	40.00	80.00	165	—
1641 (d)	—	20.00	40.00	80.00	165	—

KM# 217 1/8 THALER

Silver **Obv:** Laureate bust of Leopold I to right **Rev:** Eagle holding two shields of arms in talons, date between shields, 1/8 in cartouche at bottom

Date	Mintage	VG	F	VF	XF	Unc
1693 GFN	—	27.00	55.00	115	200	—

KM# 70 1/6 THALER

Silver **Obv:** 6 in shield on eagle's breast

Date	Mintage	VG	F	VF	XF	Unc
1623 (b)	—	27.00	55.00	100	200	—
1624 (b)	—	27.00	55.00	100	200	—

KM# 146 1/6 THALER

Silver **Obv:** Titles of Ferdinand III **Note:** Varieties exist.

Date	Mintage	VG	F	VF	XF	Unc
1638 (b)	—	27.00	55.00	100	200	—
1639 (b)	—	27.00	55.00	100	200	—
1641 (d)	—	27.00	55.00	100	200	—
1642 (d)	—	27.00	55.00	100	200	—
1643 (d)	—	27.00	55.00	100	200	—

KM# 48 1/4 THALER

Silver **Note:** Similar to 1/8 Thaler, KM#47. Varieties exist.

Date	Mintage	VG	F	VF	XF	Unc
1621	—	45.00	85.00	140	225	—
1622	—	45.00	85.00	140	225	—
1623 (a)	—	45.00	85.00	140	225	—
1623 (b)	—	45.00	85.00	140	225	—
1624 (a)	—	45.00	85.00	140	225	—
1624 (b)	—	45.00	85.00	140	225	—
1624 (c)	—	45.00	85.00	140	225	—
1625 (a)	—	45.00	85.00	140	225	—

KM# 80 1/4 THALER

Silver **Note:** Similar to 1/8 Thaler, KM#47, but value 1/4 in oval on eagle's breast. Varieties exist.

Date	Mintage	VG	F	VF	XF	Unc
1626 (a)	—	45.00	85.00	140	225	—
1627 (a)	—	45.00	85.00	140	225	—
1628 (a)	—	45.00	85.00	140	225	—
1629 (a)	—	45.00	85.00	140	225	—
1631 (a)	—	45.00	85.00	140	225	—
1632 (a)	—	45.00	85.00	140	225	—
1633 (a)	—	45.00	85.00	140	225	—
1634 (a)	—	45.00	85.00	140	225	—
1635 (a)	—	45.00	85.00	140	225	—
1636 (a)	—	45.00	85.00	140	225	—
1637 (a)	—	45.00	85.00	140	225	—

KM# 147 1/4 THALER

Silver **Obv:** Titles of Ferdinand III

Date	Mintage	F	VF	XF	Unc
1638 (a)	—	45.00	85.00	150	275	—
1640 (a)	—	45.00	85.00	150	275	—
1645 (a)	—	45.00	85.00	150	275	—

KM# 218 1/4 THALER

Silver

Date	Mintage	VG	F	VF	XF	Unc
1693 GFN	—	45.00	90.00	200	400	—

KM# 148 1/3 THALER (1/2 Gulden)

Silver **Obv:** Large oval Nurnberg arms in baroque frame, date divided below, 1/3 in cartouche at bottom **Rev:** Crowned imperial eagle, Nurnberg arms on breast, titles of Ferdinand III **Note:** Varieties exist.

Date	Mintage	VG	F	VF	XF	Unc
1638 (c)	—	45.00	85.00	150	275	—
1639 (c)	—	45.00	85.00	150	275	—
1640 (c)	—	45.00	85.00	150	275	—
1641 (c)	—	45.00	85.00	150	275	—
1642 (c)	—	45.00	85.00	150	275	—
1645 (c)	—	45.00	85.00	150	275	—
1646 (c)	—	45.00	85.00	150	275	—
1657 (c)	—	45.00	85.00	150	275	—
1658 (e)	—	45.00	85.00	150	275	—

KM# 23 1/2 THALER

Silver **Obv:** Three small oval arms in baroque frames, one above two, date below **Rev:** Crowned imperial eagle, titles of Matthias **Note:** Varieties exist.

Date	Mintage	VG	F	VF	XF	Unc
1614	—	45.00	100	165	325	—
1615	—	45.00	100	165	325	—
1616	—	45.00	100	165	325	—

KM# 30 1/2 THALER

Silver **Subject:** Centennial of the Reformation **Obv:** Basket held by robed hand from right, inverted over lit candle, cherub's head and wings in each corner **Obv. Legend:** ECCLESIA NORI - CA IUBILANS. **Rev:** 4-line inscription containing date in chronogram in ornamented square tablet, angel's head and wings above, floral ornaments in each corner **Rev. Inscription:** MARTINVS / LVTHERVS / THEOLOGIE / D:. **Note:** Klippe.

Date	Mintage	VG	F	VF	XF	Unc
MDLLVVVII (1617) Rare	—	—	—	—	—	—

KM# 49 1/2 THALER

Silver **Obv:** Titles of Ferdinand II **Rev:** Upper arms (eagle) divide date **Note:** Varieties exist.

Date	Mintage	VG	F	VF	XF	Unc
1621 (a)	—	45.00	100	165	325	—
1623 (a)	—	45.00	100	165	325	—
1624 (a)	—	45.00	100	165	325	—

KM# 50 1/2 THALER

Silver **Rev:** Upper arms are imperial eagle **Note:** Varieties exist.

Date	Mintage	VG	F	VF	XF	Unc
1621 (b)	—	45.00	100	165	325	—
1623 (b)	—	45.00	100	165	325	—
1624 (b)	—	45.00	100	165	325	—
1625 (b)	—	45.00	100	165	325	—
1625 (c)	—	45.00	100	165	325	—

KM# 78 1/2 THALER

Silver **Obv:** Similar to 1/8 Thaler, KM#47, but 1/2 in oval on eagle's breast **Note:** Varieties exist.

Date	Mintage	VG	F	VF	XF	Unc
1625 (b)	—	45.00	100	165	325	—
1626 (b)	—	45.00	100	165	325	—
1628 (b)	—	45.00	100	165	325	—

KM# 103 1/2 THALER

Silver **Obv:** Similar to KM#129 but inscription in chronogram **Obv. Inscription:** PAX BONA NVNC REDEAT MARS PEREATQVE FEROX, date **Rev:** Crowned imperial eagle, sword and scepter in claws, imperial bust in shield on breast

Date	Mintage	VG	F	VF	XF	Unc
ND(1630) (b)	—	55.00	120	200	400	—

KM# 110 1/2 THALER

Silver **Obv:** Date in chronogram **Obv. Inscription:** VIVIDA PAX CHRISTI SERVERT NOS TEMPORE TRISTI

Date	Mintage	VG	F	VF	XF	Unc
ND(1631) (b)	—	55.00	120	200	400	—

KM# 129 1/2 THALER

Silver **Obv:** 3 Shields above city view, date in chronogram **Obv. Inscription:** SVBVENIAT FINIS IVDICIVMVE PIIS **Rev:** Crowned double-headed imperial eagle, without sword, scepter or imperial bust

Date	Mintage	VG	F	VF	XF	Unc
ND(1633) (b)	—	55.00	120	200	400	—

KM# 182 1/2 THALER

Silver **Obv:** City view with "Jehovah" in Hebrew above, Roman numeral date in cartouche below **Rev:** Three ornate shields of amrs, one above two **Note:** Varieties exist.

Date	Mintage	VG	F	VF	XF	Unc
1661 (e)	—	55.00	120	200	400	—
1662 (e)	—	55.00	120	200	400	—
1680 (f)	—	55.00	120	200	400	—

KM# 219 1/2 THALER

Silver **Obv:** Three oval shields of arms in baroque frame, one above two, date in margin at upper left **Rev:** Crowned imperial eagle, Nurnberg arms on breast, titles of Leopold I around

Date	Mintage	VG	F	VF	XF	Unc
1693 GFN	—	45.00	110	200	400	—

KM# 149 2/3 THALER (Gulden)

Silver **Obv:** Large oval Nurnberg arms in baroque frame, value and date divided near top of arms **Rev:** Crowned imperial eagle, Nurnberg arms on breast, titles of Ferdinand III **Note:** Varieties exist.

Date	Mintage	VG	F	VF	XF	Unc
1638 (c)	—	85.00	140	225	400	—
1639 (c)	—	85.00	140	225	400	—
1640 (c)	—	85.00	140	225	400	—
1641 (c)	—	85.00	140	225	400	—
1642 (c)	—	85.00	140	225	400	—
1645 (c)	—	85.00	140	225	400	—
1646 (c)	—	85.00	140	225	400	—
1657 (c)	—	85.00	140	225	400	—
1658 (e)	—	85.00	140	225	400	—

KM# 24 THALER

Silver **Obv:** Three shields with date below **Obv. Legend:** MATTHIAS... **Rev:** Crowned double eagle **Note:** Dav. #5634.

Date	Mintage	VG	F	VF	XF	Unc
1614	—	300	650	1,250	2,150	—
1615	—	300	650	1,250	2,150	—
1616	—	300	650	1,250	2,150	—
1617	—	200	500	1,000	1,750	—
1618	—	250	600	1,200	2,000	—
1619	—	250	600	1,200	2,000	—

KM# 51 THALER

Silver **Obv:** Three shields with date above **Rev. Legend:** FERDINANDVS. II: **Note:** Dav. #5635.

Date	Mintage	VG	F	VF	XF	Unc
1621 (a) Rare	—	—	—	—	—	—

Note: Hess-Divo AG Auction 301, 5-05, nice XF realized approximately $20,725

KM# 52 THALER

Silver **Obv:** Upper shield with imperial eagle **Rev:** Crowned double-headed imperial eagle, without sword, scepter or imperial bust **Rev. Legend:** FERDINANDI. II... **Note:** Dav. #5636.

Date	Mintage	VG	F	VF	XF	Unc
1621 (b)	—	50.00	100	175	375	700
1622 (b)	—	50.00	100	175	375	—
1622 (c)	—	50.00	100	175	375	—
1623 (b)	—	50.00	100	175	375	650
1623 (c)	—	50.00	100	175	375	650
1624 (b)	—	50.00	100	175	375	650
1624 (c)	—	50.00	100	175	375	—
1625 (b)	—	50.00	100	175	375	—
1625 (c)	—	50.00	100	175	375	—
1626 (b)	—	50.00	100	175	375	—
1626 (c)	—	50.00	100	175	375	—
1627 (b)	—	50.00	100	175	375	650
1627 (c)	—	50.00	100	175	375	650
1628 (b)	—	50.00	100	175	375	—

KM# 71 THALER

Silver **Obv:** 3 Ornate rounded shields, upper shield is imperial eagle, divided date above **Rev:** Crowned double-headed imperial eagle, without sword, scepter and imperial breast **Rev. Legend:** FERDINANDVS. II:... **Note:** Dav. #5637.

Date	Mintage	VG	F	VF	XF	Unc
1623 (a)	—	50.00	100	185	400	675
1624 (a)	—	50.00	100	185	400	675
1624 (c)	—	50.00	100	185	400	—
1625 (a)	—	50.00	100	185	400	—
1628 (a)	—	50.00	100	185	400	—

KM# 81 THALER

Silver **Rev. Legend:** ...NVRENBERGENSIS. **Note:** Dav. #5639.

Date	Mintage	VG	F	VF	XF	Unc
1626	—	1,750	3,500	6,000	—	—

KM# 83 THALER

Silver **Obv:** Equestrian figure **Rev:** Winged cherub, date in roman numerals **Rev. Legend:** ...NVRENBERGENSIS. **Note:** Dav. #5640.

Date	Mintage	VG	F	VF	XF	Unc
1627	—	800	1,500	2,500	3,750	—
1628 Rare	—	—	—	—	—	—

Note: Fritz Rudolf Künker Münzenhandlung Auction 134, 1-08, XF realized approximately $12,550; Hess-Divo AG Auction 301, 5-05, XF realized approximately $20,725

Date	Mintage	VG	F	VF	XF	Unc
1630 Rare	—	—	—	—	—	—

KM# 87 THALER

Silver **Obv:** 3 shields supported by 2 mermaids **Rev:** Crowned imperial eagle with shield on breast **Note:** Dav. #5641.

Date	Mintage	VG	F	VF	XF	Unc
16Z8 (a)	—	700	1,350	2,750	4,750	—

KM# 88 THALER

Silver **Obv:** Cherub surrounded by three shields, date in exergue **Rev:** Crowned imperial eagle with arms on breast **Note:** Dav. #5642.

Date	Mintage	VG	F	VF	XF	Unc
1628 (c)	—	65.00	125	275	550	—

KM# 89 THALER

Silver **Rev:** Three shields above city view, date in chronogram in exergue **Rev. Inscription:** CANDIDIA PAX REDEAT / PAX REGNET IN OR. / BE. ET. IN VRBE. / **Note:** Dav. #5643.

Date	Mintage	VG	F	VF	XF	Unc
ND(1628) (b) Rare	—	—	—	—	—	—

Note: Fritz Rudolf Künker Münzenhandlung Auction 134, 1-08, VF realized approximately $10,705; Hess-Divo AG Auction 301, 5-05, VF+ realized approximately $17,410

KM# 91 THALER

Silver **Obv:** Date in chronogram in exergue: VENI AVT SVBVENITV/IS O CHRISTE RED/EMPTOR **Rev:** Bust on breast of crowned double-headed eagle, larger crown above **Note:** Dav. #5644.

Date	Mintage	VG	F	VF	XF	Unc
ND(1629) (B)	—	85.00	175	350	650	—

KM# 92 THALER

Silver **Obv:** Arms in cartouche **Rev:** Crowned imperial eagle with arms on breast **Note:** Dav. #5645.

Date	Mintage	VG	F	VF	XF	Unc
1629 (c)	—	275	550	950	1,650	—

KM# 93 THALER

Silver **Obv:** Arms in frame with face above and below **Rev:** Crowned imperial eagle with shield on breast **Note:** Dav. #5646.

Date	Mintage	VG	F	VF	XF	Unc
1629 (a)	—	400	900	2,000	5,750	—
1630 (a)	—	400	900	2,000	5,750	—
1631 (a)	—	400	900	2,000	5,750	—

KM# 94 THALER

Silver **Obv:** Three shields dividing date above **Rev:** Crowned imperial eagle **Note:** Dav. #5647.

Date	Mintage	VG	F	VF	XF	Unc
1629 (b)	—	60.00	120	250	500	—
1630 (b)	—	60.00	120	250	500	—
1631 (b)	—	60.00	120	250	500	—
1632 (b)	—	60.00	120	250	500	—
1633 (b)	—	60.00	120	250	500	—
1634 (b)	—	60.00	120	250	500	—
1635 (b)	—	60.00	120	250	500	—
1636 (b)	—	60.00	120	250	500	—
1637 (b)	—	60.00	120	250	500	—

KM# 104 THALER

Silver **Obv:** Cherub in center of 3 shields, date in exergue, legend, breast **Obv. Legend:** MONETA. NOVA. ARGENTEA... **Rev:** Crowned imperial eagle with arms on breast **Note:** Dav. #5648.

Date	Mintage	VG	F	VF	XF	Unc
1630 (c)	—	75.00	150	300	500	1,175

KM# 105 THALER

Silver **Obv:** Three shields above city view, legend in exergue **Obv. Legend:** NVRINBERGA DIV CHRISTI SIT TVTA SVB VMBRA **Rev:** Crowned imperial eagle with bust on breast **Note:** Dav. #5649.

Date	Mintage	VG	F	VF	XF	Unc
1630 (b)	—	150	300	700	1,750	—

KM# 111 THALER

Silver **Rev:** Inscription in exergue, date in chronogram **Rev. Inscription:** VIVIDA PAX CHRISTI SERVETNOS TEMPORE TRISTI **Note:** Dav. #5650.

Date	Mintage	VG	F	VF	XF	Unc
ND(1631) (b)	—	175	350	800	1,550	—

KM# 119 THALER

Silver **Obv:** Cherub surrounded by three shields, date in exergue **Rev:** Crowned imperial eagle with arms on breast, titles of Ferdinand II **Note:** Dav. #5651.

Date	Mintage	VG	F	VF	XF	Unc
1632 (c)	—	75.00	150	325	750	—
1634 (c)	—	85.00	165	350	800	—
ND (c)	—	75.00	150	325	750	—

KM# 118 THALER

Silver **Obv:** Bust of Gustav II Adolphus right **Rev:** Crowned arms **Note:** Swedish issue. Dav. #4550.

Date	Mintage	VG	F	VF	XF	Unc
1632 (b)	—	175	325	700	1,650	4,500

KM# 130 THALER

Silver **Obv:** Shields above city view, date in chronogram in exergue **Obv. Inscription:** PAX ADSIT BELLVM FVGIAT PESTISQVE SEVERA **Rev:** Crowned double-headed imperial eagle without sword and scepter **Note:** Dav. #5652.

Date	Mintage	VG	F	VF	XF	Unc
ND(1633) (b)	—	175	375	750	1,250	—

KM# 133 THALER

Silver **Obv:** Arms in frame **Rev:** Cherub flying above city view, date in chronogram **Note:** Dav. #5653.

Date	Mintage	VG	F	VF	XF	Unc
ND(1635) (b)	—	700	1,500	3,000	5,000	15,000

KM# 134 THALER

Silver **Obv:** Cherub surrounded by three shields with date above **Rev:** Crowned double-headed imperial eagle with shield on breast **Note:** Dav. #5654.

Date	Mintage	VG	F	VF	XF	Unc
1635 (c)	—	100	200	475	750	—
1636 (c)	—	100	200	475	750	—
1637 (c)	—	100	200	475	750	—

KM# 138 THALER

Silver **Rev. Legend:** FERDINAND: II:... **Note:** Dav. #5655.

Date	Mintage	VG	F	VF	XF	Unc
1637 (c)	—	100	200	475	750	—
1638 (c)	—	100	200	475	750	—

KM# 139 THALER

Silver **Obv:** Three shields in cartouche with date in frame below **Rev:** Crowned imperial eagle **Note:** Dav. #5656.

Date	Mintage	VG	F	VF	XF	Unc
1637 (b)	—	150	275	550	900	—
1638 (b)	—	150	275	550	900	—
1639 (b)	—	150	275	550	900	—
1641 (d)	—	150	275	550	900	—

KM# 150 THALER

Silver **Obv:** Arms in frame **Rev:** Crowned imperial eagle with shield **Note:** Dav. #5657.

Date	Mintage	VG	F	VF	XF	Unc
1638 (c)	—	250	500	900	1,500	—

KM# 156 THALER

Silver **Obv:** Angel between two shields, Roman numeral date below **Rev:** Crowned imperial eagle with arms on breast **Note:** Dav. #5658.

Date	Mintage	VG	F	VF	XF	Unc
1642 (c)	—	300	650	1,750	3,500	8,500
1645 (c)	—	300	650	1,750	3,500	8,500
1646 (c)	—	300	650	1,750	3,500	8,500
1648 (c)	—	300	650	1,750	3,500	8,500
1649 (c)	—	300	650	1,750	3,500	8,500
1657 (c)	—	300	650	1,750	3,500	8,500

KM# 172 THALER

Silver **Obv:** 3 Shields **Rev:** "Jehovah" above city view, Roman numeral date in ornate frame below **Note:** Dav. #5659.

Date	Mintage	VG	F	VF	XF	Unc
1658 (c)	—	225	450	950	2,000	5,750
1661 (c)	—	225	450	950	2,000	5,750
1662 (c)	—	225	450	950	2,000	5,750
1663 (c)	—	225	450	950	2,000	5,750
1677 (c)	—	225	450	950	2,000	5,750

KM# 202 THALER
Silver **Obv:** 3 Shields **Rev:** Different city view and ornate frame **Note:** Dav. #5661.

Date	Mintage	VG	F	VF	XF	Unc
MDCLXXX (1680) (f)	—	150	300	500	800	1,250

KM# 203 THALER
Silver **Rev:** Crowned eagle above City Hall, seated figure of Nuremburg in foreground **Note:** Dav. #5663.

Date	Mintage	VG	F	VF	XF	Unc
ND(1688) PHM-F	—	—	—	2,000	4,000	6,750

KM# 204 THALER
Silver **Obv:** Different city view **Rev:** D. S. D. below figure, without cross **Note:** Dav. #5664.

Date	Mintage	VG	F	VF	XF	Unc
ND(1688) DSD	—	—	—	2,500	5,000	8,000

KM# 220 THALER
Silver **Obv:** Bust of Leopold right **Rev:** Eagle above two shields, date between, GFN below **Note:** Dav. #5665.

Date	Mintage	VG	F	VF	XF	Unc
1693 GFN	—	120	250	550	1,000	2,000

KM# 223 THALER
Silver **Obv:** Three shields with decorations, GFN below **Rev:** "Jehovah" above city view, Roman numeral date in ornate frame below **Note:** Dav. #5666.

Date	Mintage	VG	F	VF	XF	Unc
1694 GFN	—	120	250	550	900	1,850

KM# 224 THALER
Silver **Rev:** Crowned imperial eagle wtih arms on breast **Note:** Dav. #5667.

Date	Mintage	VG	F	VF	XF	Unc
1694 GFN	—	850	1,750	3,500	7,500	12,500

KM# 228 THALER
Silver **Obv:** Eye of God above city view, Roman numeral date in cartouche below **Rev:** Angel with two shields of arm **Note:** Dav. #5668.

Date	Mintage	VG	F	VF	XF	Unc
1696 GFN	—	75.00	150	375	900	1,750

KM# 230 THALER
Silver **Subject:** Peace of Ryswick **Obv:** "Jehovah" above city view, inscription and date below **Rev:** Peace standing above two genii holding shields of arms **Note:** Dav. #5669.

Date	Mintage	VG	F	VF	XF	Unc
1698 GFN	—	150	375	800	1,500	2,500

KM# 82 2 THALER
Silver **Obv:** 3 shields dividing date above **Rev:** Crowned imperial eagle, titles of Ferdinand II **Note:** Dav. #5638.

Date	Mintage	VG	F	VF	XF	Unc
1626 Rare	—	—	—	—	—	—

Note: Hess-Divo AG Auction 301, 5-05, VF-XF realized approximately $26,525

KM# 84 2 THALER
Silver **Obv:** Equestrian figure of Ferdinand II right **Rev:** Winged cherub with two shields of arms, date in exergue **Note:** Dav. #A5640.

Date	Mintage	VG	F	VF	XF	Unc
MDCXXVII (1627)	—	1,000	1,800	2,750	5,000	—
MDCXXVIII (1628)	—	1,000	1,800	2,750	5,000	—
MDCXXX (1630)	—	1,000	1,800	2,750	5,000	—

KM# 205 2 THALER
Silver **Note:** Similar to 1 Thaler, KM#203. Dav. #5662.

Date	Mintage	VG	F	VF	XF	Unc
ND(1688) PHM (F) Rare	—	—	—	—	—	—

KM# 206 3 THALER
Silver **Note:** Similar to 1 Thaler, KM#202. Dav. #5660.

Date	Mintage	VG	F	VF	XF	Unc
1680 (f) Rare	—	—	—	—	—	—

TRADE COINAGE

KM# 10 GOLDGULDEN
3.5000 g., 0.9860 Gold 0.1109 oz. AGW **Obv:** Eagle with N on breast **Obv. Legend:** + NVREMBERG + MONE + REIPVB **Rev:** St. Lawerence **Rev. Legend:** SANCTVS - LAVRENTIVS

Date	Mintage	VG	F	VF	XF	Unc
1611	—	220	450	650	1,050	—
1612	—	220	450	650	1,050	—
1613	—	220	450	650	1,050	—

KM# 15 GOLDGULDEN
3.5000 g., 0.9860 Gold 0.1109 oz. AGW **Obv:** Matthias and Anna **Rev:** Three shields of arms

Date	Mintage	VG	F	VF	XF	Unc
1612	—	650	1,500	2,500	3,500	—

KM# 25.1 GOLDGULDEN
3.5000 g., 0.9860 Gold 0.1109 oz. AGW **Obv:** Oval arms in ornate frame **Rev:** St. Lawrence standing holding gridiron facing right

Date	Mintage	VG	F	VF	XF	Unc
1614	—	300	500	700	1,250	—
1615	—	300	500	700	1,250	—

KM# 25.2 GOLDGULDEN
3.5000 g., 0.9860 Gold 0.1109 oz. AGW **Rev:** St. Lawrence standing holding gridiron facing left

Date	Mintage	VG	F	VF	XF	Unc
1617	—	300	500	750	1,450	—

KM# 31 GOLDGULDEN
3.5000 g., 0.9860 Gold 0.1109 oz. AGW **Obv:** Angel above arms **Rev:** St. Lawrence standing holding gridiron

Date	Mintage	VG	F	VF	XF	Unc
1618	—	325	550	800	1,600	—

KM# 32 GOLDGULDEN
3.5000 g., 0.9860 Gold 0.1109 oz. AGW **Obv:** Oval arms

Date	Mintage	VG	F	VF	XF	Unc
1619	—	325	550	750	1,350	—

KM# 43 GOLDGULDEN
3.5000 g., 0.9860 Gold 0.1109 oz. AGW **Obv:** Oval arms **Rev:** St. Lawrence standing

Date	Mintage	VG	F	VF	XF	Unc
1620	—	220	450	650	1,050	—
1621	—	220	450	650	1,050	—
1622	—	220	450	650	1,050	—

KM# 44 GOLDGULDEN
3.5000 g., 0.9860 Gold 0.1109 oz. AGW **Obv:** Eagle with N on shield **Note:** Varieties exist.

Date	Mintage	VG	F	VF	XF	Unc
1620	—	300	500	700	1,250	—
1621	—	300	500	700	1,250	—
1623	—	300	500	700	1,250	—

KM# 73 GOLDGULDEN
3.5000 g., 0.9860 Gold 0.1109 oz. AGW **Obv:** Displayed eagle with N on breast **Rev:** St. Sebaldus **Note:** Varieties exist.

Date	Mintage	VG	F	VF	XF	Unc
1623	—	1,200	2,400	4,500	7,700	—
1624	—	1,200	2,400	4,500	7,700	—
1625	—	1,200	2,400	4,500	7,700	—
1626	—	1,200	2,400	4,500	7,700	—
1633	—	1,200	2,400	4,500	7,700	—
1634	—	1,200	2,400	4,500	7,700	—
1636	—	1,200	2,400	4,500	7,700	—
1637	—	1,200	2,400	4,500	7,700	—
1642	—	1,200	2,400	4,500	7,700	—
1643	—	1,200	2,400	4,500	7,700	—
1646	—	1,200	2,400	4,500	7,700	—
1686	—	1,200	2,400	4,500	7,700	—

KM# 72 GOLDGULDEN
3.5000 g., 0.9860 Gold 0.1109 oz. AGW **Obv:** Eagle with N on shield **Note:** Varieties exist.

Date	Mintage	VG	F	VF	XF	Unc
1623	—	300	600	900	1,450	—
1626	—	300	600	900	1,450	—
1629	—	300	600	900	1,450	—
1632	—	300	600	900	1,450	—
1634	—	300	600	900	1,450	—
1635	—	300	600	900	1,450	—
1636	—	300	600	900	1,450	—
1639	—	300	600	900	1,450	—
1640	—	300	600	900	1,450	—
1686	—	300	600	900	1,450	—

KM# 95 GOLDGULDEN
3.5000 g., 0.9860 Gold 0.1109 oz. AGW **Obv:** Oval arms in cartouche in inner circle

Date	Mintage	VG	F	VF	XF	Unc
1629	—	1,200	2,400	4,500	7,700	—
1630	—	1,200	2,400	4,500	7,700	—

KM# 16 2 GOLDGULDEN

7.0000 g., 0.9860 Gold 0.2219 oz. AGW **Obv:** Jugate busts of Matthias and Anna right **Rev:** Three shields in inner circle, date at bottom

Date	Mintage	VG	F	VF	XF	Unc
1612 Rare	—	—	—	—	—	—

KM# 26 2 GOLDGULDEN

7.0000 g., 0.9860 Gold 0.2219 oz. AGW **Obv:** Oval arms in cartuoche in inner circle **Rev:** St. Lawrence standing holding gridiron and book

Date	Mintage	VG	F	VF	XF	Unc
1614 Rare	—	—	—	—	—	—

KM# 27 2 GOLDGULDEN

7.0000 g., 0.9860 Gold 0.2219 oz. AGW **Obv:** Imperial eagle **Note:** Varieties exist.

Date	Mintage	VG	F	VF	XF	Unc
1615 Rare	—	—	—	—	—	—
1617 Rare	—	—	—	—	—	—
1618 Rare	—	—	—	—	—	—
1619 Rare	—	—	—	—	—	—

KM# 53 2 GOLDGULDEN

7.0000 g., 0.9860 Gold 0.2219 oz. AGW **Obv:** Titles of Ferdinand II

Date	Mintage	VG	F	VF	XF	Unc
1621	—	—	—	—	—	—

KM# 17 3 GOLDGULDEN

10.5000 g., 0.9860 Gold 0.3328 oz. AGW **Obv:** Displayed eagle wtih N on breast in inner circle **Rev:** St. Lawrence standing holding gridiron and book

Date	Mintage	VG	F	VF	XF	Unc
1612 Rare	—	—	—	—	—	—

KM# 20 3 GOLDGULDEN

10.5000 g., 0.9860 Gold 0.3328 oz. AGW **Obv:** Imperial eagle

Date	Mintage	VG	F	VF	XF	Unc
1613 Rare	—	—	—	—	—	—

KM# 79 6 GOLDGULDEN

21.0000 g., 0.9860 Gold 0.6657 oz. AGW **Obv:** Imperial eagle

Date	Mintage	VG	F	VF	XF	Unc
1625 (c) Rare	—	—	—	—	—	—

KM# 245 1/32 DUCAT

0.1094 g., 0.9860 Gold 0.0035 oz. AGW **Obv:** Shield of arms **Rev:** Paschal lamb

Date	Mintage	VG	F	VF	XF	Unc
ND(1700)	—	50.00	100	200	325	—

KM# 246 1/16 DUCAT

0.2188 g., 0.9860 Gold 0.0069 oz. AGW **Obv:** Crowned arms in branches **Rev:** Paschal lamb

Date	Mintage	VG	F	VF	XF	Unc
ND(1700)	—	100	135	190	300	—

KM# 247 1/16 DUCAT

0.2188 g., 0.9860 Gold 0.0069 oz. AGW **Note:** Klippe.

Date	Mintage	VG	F	VF	XF	Unc
ND(1700)	—	65.00	95.00	130	210	—

KM# 248 1/8 DUCAT

0.4375 g., 0.9860 Gold 0.0139 oz. AGW **Obv:** Crowned arms in branches **Rev:** Paschal lamb

Date	Mintage	VG	F	VF	XF	Unc
ND(1700) GFN	—	95.00	125	190	250	—

KM# 249 1/8 DUCAT

0.4375 g., 0.9860 Gold 0.0139 oz. AGW **Note:** Klippe.

Date	Mintage	VG	F	VF	XF	Unc
ND(1700) GFN	—	95.00	125	190	250	—

KM# 250 1/4 DUCAT

0.8750 g., 0.9860 Gold 0.0277 oz. AGW **Obv:** Crowned arms in branches **Rev:** Paschal lamb

Date	Mintage	VG	F	VF	XF	Unc
1700 GFN	—	130	175	235	325	—

KM# 251 1/4 DUCAT

0.8750 g., 0.9860 Gold 0.0277 oz. AGW **Note:** Klippe.

Date	Mintage	VG	F	VF	XF	Unc
1700	—	130	175	235	325	—

KM# 252 1/4 DUCAT

0.8750 g., 0.9860 Gold 0.0277 oz. AGW

Date	Mintage	VG	F	VF	XF	Unc
ND(1700) GFN	—	80.00	110	150	210	—

KM# 253 1/4 DUCAT

0.8750 g., 0.9860 Gold 0.0277 oz. AGW **Obv:** Crowned arms in branches **Rev:** Paschal lamb **Note:** Klippe.

Date	Mintage	VG	F	VF	XF	Unc
ND(1700)	—	80.00	110	150	210	—

KM# 216 1/2 DUCAT

1.7500 g., 0.9860 Gold 0.0555 oz. AGW **Obv:** Three shields of arms **Rev:** Paschal lamb, date in exergue

Date	Mintage	VG	F	VF	XF	Unc
1692	—	225	450	725	975	—

KM# 254 1/2 DUCAT

1.7500 g., 0.9860 Gold 0.0555 oz. AGW **Obv:** Three shields of arms **Rev:** Paschal lamb, date in legend

Date	Mintage	VG	F	VF	XF	Unc
1700 GFN	—	175	265	350	525	—
1700 CGL	—	175	265	350	525	—
Note: Restruck 1746-55)						
1700 IMF	—	175	265	350	525	—
Note: Restruck 1755-64						

KM# 255 1/2 DUCAT

1.7500 g., 0.9860 Gold 0.0555 oz. AGW

Date	Mintage	VG	F	VF	XF	Unc
1700	—	175	265	350	525	—

KM# 256 1/2 DUCAT

1.7500 g., 0.9860 Gold 0.0555 oz. AGW **Note:** Klippe.

Date	Mintage	VG	F	VF	XF	Unc
1700	—	175	265	400	575	—

KM# 112 DUCAT

3.5000 g., 0.9860 Gold 0.1109 oz. AGW **Obv:** Bust of Gustav II Adolphus facing **Rev:** Crowned arms **Note:** Swedish issue.

Date	Mintage	VG	F	VF	XF	Unc
1631	—	500	1,000	2,000	3,200	—

KM# 120 DUCAT

3.5000 g., 0.9860 Gold 0.1109 oz. AGW **Obv:** Bust of Gustav II Adolphus facing **Rev:** Crowned arms **Note:** Swedish issue.

Date	Mintage	VG	F	VF	XF	Unc
1632 (b)	—	250	500	800	1,500	—

KM# 121 DUCAT

3.5000 g., 0.9860 Gold 0.1109 oz. AGW **Obv:** Gustav II Adolphus standing **Rev:** Crowned arms **Note:** Swedish issue.

Date	Mintage	VG	F	VF	XF	Unc
1632	—	350	700	1,350	2,250	—

KM# 122 DUCAT

3.5000 g., 0.9860 Gold 0.1109 oz. AGW **Obv:** Bust of Gustav II Adolphus right **Rev:** 7-line inscription in wreath **Note:** Swedish issue.

Date	Mintage	VG	F	VF	XF	Unc
1632	—	500	1,000	2,000	3,200	—

KM# 123 DUCAT

3.5000 g., 0.9860 Gold 0.1109 oz. AGW **Obv:** Arms **Rev:** Paschal lamb holding palm frond atop globe **Note:** City coinage resumed.

Date	Mintage	VG	F	VF	XF	Unc
1632	—	165	275	425	725	—

KM# 131 DUCAT

3.5000 g., 0.9860 Gold 0.1109 oz. AGW **Obv:** Ornate arms **Rev:** Cross from cloud above lying lamb

Date	Mintage	VG	F	VF	XF	Unc
1633	—	250	400	650	1,000	—

KM# 135 DUCAT

3.5000 g., 0.9860 Gold 0.1109 oz. AGW **Obv:** Displayed eagle **Rev:** Two shields of arms hanging from knotted ribbon, date in chronogram

Date	Mintage	VG	F	VF	XF	Unc
ND(1635)	—	600	1,400	2,400	3,300	—

KM# 136 DUCAT

3.5000 g., 0.9860 Gold 0.1109 oz. AGW **Obv:** Ornate arms **Rev:** 4-line inscription in ornate square frame

Date	Mintage	VG	F	VF	XF	Unc
1635 (b)	—	200	350	525	950	—
1636 (b)	—	200	350	525	950	—
1637 (b)	—	200	350	525	950	—
1638 (b)	—	200	350	525	950	—
1639 (b)	—	200	350	525	950	—
1640 (d)	—	200	350	525	950	—
1641 (d)	—	200	350	525	950	—
1642 (d)	—	200	350	525	950	—
1643 (d)	—	200	350	525	950	—
1644 (d)	—	200	350	525	950	—
1645 (d)	—	200	350	525	950	—

KM# 137 DUCAT

3.5000 g., 0.9860 Gold 0.1109 oz. AGW **Subject:** Peace ducat **Obv:** Displayed eagle **Rev:** Genius standing with two shields, date in chronogram **Note:** Varieties exist

Date	Mintage	VG	F	VF	XF	Unc
ND(1635) (c)	—	250	500	750	1,200	—
ND(1637) (c)	—	200	350	525	950	—
ND(1640) (c)	—	250	425	650	950	—
ND(1648) (c)	—	200	350	525	950	—
ND(1686) (f)	—	200	350	525	950	—

KM# 155 DUCAT

3.5000 g., 0.9860 Gold 0.1109 oz. AGW **Obv:** Eagle with head to left **Rev:** Two adjacent arms, angel's head above, date in chronogram

Date	Mintage	VG	F	VF	XF	Unc
1640 (c)	—	250	500	750	1,450	—

KM# 158 DUCAT

3.5000 g., 0.9860 Gold 0.1109 oz. AGW **Obv:** Displayed eagle **Rev:** Winged figure staning with two shields

Date	Mintage	VG	F	VF	XF	Unc
1646 (c)	—	450	600	1,100	1,750	—
1647 (c)	—	450	600	1,100	1,750	—

KM# 159 DUCAT

3.5000 g., 0.9860 Gold 0.1109 oz. AGW **Obv:** Three shields of arms **Rev:** Paschal lamb

Date	Mintage	VG	F	VF	XF	Unc
1649 (c)	—	350	500	800	1,500	—

KM# 167 DUCAT

3.5000 g., 0.9860 Gold 0.1109 oz. AGW **Obv:** 6-line inscription, arms divide date at bottom **Rev:** Hand reaching down from heaven with laurel wreath above globe

Date	Mintage	VG	F	VF	XF	Unc
1650 (c)	—	600	900	1,600	2,250	—

KM# 168 DUCAT

3.5000 g., 0.9860 Gold 0.1109 oz. AGW **Subject:** Treaty of Westphalia **Obv:** Hand holds laurel wreath above displayed eagle **Rev:** 6-line inscription, above arms divide Roman numeral date at bottom

Date	Mintage	VG	F	VF	XF	Unc
ND(1650) (c)	—	600	900	1,750	2,650	—

KM# 173 DUCAT

3.5000 g., 0.9860 Gold 0.1109 oz. AGW **Obv:** Laureate bust of Leopold I right **Rev:** Three shields above date

Date	Mintage	VG	F	VF	XF	Unc
1658	—	1,700	3,300	6,000	10,000	—

KM# 181 DUCAT

3.5000 g., 0.9860 Gold 0.1109 oz. AGW **Obv:** Shield of arms **Rev:** 4-line inscription and date in tablet

Date	Mintage	VG	F	VF	XF	Unc
1660	—	675	1,350	2,850	4,050	—

KM# 257 DUCAT

3.5000 g., 0.9860 Gold 0.1109 oz. AGW **Obv:** Three shields of arms **Rev:** Paschal lamb, date in chronogram

Date	Mintage	VG	F	VF	XF	Unc
MDCC (1700) GFN	—	265	425	575	800	—
MDCC (1700)	—	265	425	575	800	—

KM# 258 DUCAT

3.5000 g., 0.9860 Gold 0.1109 oz. AGW **Obv:** 3 shields of arms **Rev:** Paschal lamb, date in chronogram **Note:** Klippe.

Date	Mintage	VG	F	VF	XF	Unc
MDCC (1700) GFN	—	225	350	525	750	—
MDCC (1700) CGL	—	225	350	525	750	—
Note: Restruck 1746-55						
MDCC (1700) IMF	—	225	350	525	750	—
Note: Restruck 1755-64						

KM# 113 2 DUCAT

7.0000 g., 0.9860 Gold 0.2219 oz. AGW **Note:** Swedish occupation. Similar to 1 Ducat, KM#112.

Date	Mintage	VG	F	VF	XF	Unc
1631	—	850	1,750	3,500	6,000	—

KM# 124 2 DUCAT

7.0000 g., 0.9860 Gold 0.2219 oz. AGW **Note:** Similar to 1 Ducat, KM#120.

Date	Mintage	VG	F	VF	XF	Unc
1632	—	750	1,500	3,000	5,500	—

KM# 125 2 DUCAT

7.0000 g., 0.9860 Gold 0.2219 oz. AGW **Subject:** Death of Gustav II Adolfus

Date	Mintage	VG	F	VF	XF	Unc
1632	—	850	1,750	3,500	6,000	—

KM# 126 2 DUCAT

7.0000 g., 0.9860 Gold 0.2219 oz. AGW **Obv:** Shield of arms **Rev:** Paschal lamb holding palm fron on globe

Date	Mintage	VG	F	VF	XF	Unc
1632	—	450	900	1,700	2,400	—

KM# 160 2 DUCAT

7.0000 g., 0.9860 Gold 0.2219 oz. AGW **Obv:** Three shields of arms **Rev:** Paschal lamb

Date	Mintage	VG	F	VF	XF	Unc
1649 (c)	—	450	900	1,750	2,500	—

KM# 169 2 DUCAT

7.0000 g., 0.9860 Gold 0.2219 oz. AGW **Obv:** 7-line inscription inside outer legend, arms above **Rev:** Hand reaching down from heaven with laurel wreath for hands reaching from globe, all in inner circle

Date	Mintage	VG	F	VF	XF	Unc
1650 (c)	—	600	1,200	2,400	3,550	—

KM# 259 2 DUCAT

7.0000 g., 0.9860 Gold 0.2219 oz. AGW **Obv:** Three shields of arms **Rev:** Paschal lamb, date in chronogram

Date	Mintage	VG	F	VF	XF	Unc
MDCC (1700) GFN	—	325	575	825	1,250	—

KM# 260 2 DUCAT

7.0000 g., 0.9860 Gold 0.2219 oz. AGW **Obv:** Three shields of arms **Rev:** Paschal lamb, date in chronogram **Note:** Klippe.

Date	Mintage	VG	F	VF	XF	Unc
MDCC (1700) GFN	—	1,000	2,000	3,700	6,500	—

KM# A105 3 DUCAT

10.5000 g., 0.9860 Gold 0.3328 oz. AGW **Obv:** 3 shields of arms above city view, inscription in exergue, date in chronogram **Obv. Inscription:** PAX BONA... **Rev:** Crowned imperial eagle with bust on breast **Note:** Struck with 1/2 Thaler dies, KM#103.

Date	Mintage	VG	F	VF	XF	Unc
ND(1630) (b) Rare	—	—	—	—	—	—

KM# 161 3 DUCAT

10.5000 g., 0.9860 Gold 0.3328 oz. AGW **Obv:** 5-line inscription over shield of arms **Rev:** Paschal lamb, date in chronogram **Note:** Klippe.

Date	Mintage	VG	F	VF	XF	Unc
1648 Rare	—	—	—	—	—	—

KM# 170 3 DUCAT

10.5000 g., 0.9860 Gold 0.3328 oz. AGW **Obv:** 7-line inscription inside outer legend, arms above **Rev:** Hand reaching down from heaven with laurel wreath for hands reaching from globe, all in inner circle **Shape:** Square **Note:** Klippe.

Date	Mintage	VG	F	VF	XF	Unc
1650 (c)	—	2,300	4,500	8,000	13,000	—

KM# 261 3 DUCAT

10.5000 g., 0.9860 Gold 0.3328 oz. AGW **Obv:** Three shields with dove flying above **Rev:** Lamb holding banner on globe in inner circle **Note:** Klippe. Date in chronogram.

Date	Mintage	VG	F	VF	XF	Unc
ND(1700)	—	1,600	3,200	6,200	8,500	—

KM# 114 4 DUCAT

14.0000 g., 0.9860 Gold 0.4438 oz. AGW **Obv:** 3 shields of arms above city view, inscription in exergue, date in chronogram **Obv. Inscription:** VIVIDIA PAX..., **Rev:** Crowned imperial eagle with bust on breast **Note:** Struck with 1/2 Thaler dies, KM#110.

Date	Mintage	VG	F	VF	XF	Unc
ND(1631) (b) Rare	—	—	—	—	—	—

KM# A131 4 DUCAT

14.0000 g., 0.9860 Gold 0.4438 oz. AGW **Obv:** 3 shields of arms above city view, inscription in exergue, date in chronogram **Obv. Inscription:** SVBVENIAT FINIS... **Rev:** Crowned imperial eagle, titles of Ferdinand II **Note:** Struck with 1/2 Thaler dies, KM#129.

Date	Mintage	VG	F	VF	XF	Unc
ND(1633) (b) Rare	—	—	—	—	—	—

KM# 171 4 DUCAT

14.0000 g., 0.9860 Gold 0.4438 oz. AGW **Obv:** 7-line inscription inside outer legend, arms above **Rev:** Hand reaching down from heaven with laurel wreath for hands reaching from globe, all in inner circle

Date	Mintage	VG	F	VF	XF	Unc
1650 (c) Rare	—	—	—	—	—	—

KM# 183 4 DUCAT

14.0000 g., 0.9860 Gold 0.4438 oz. AGW **Obv:** City view with "Jehovah" in Hebrew above, Roman numeral date in cartouche below **Rev:** Three ornate shields of arms, one above two **Note:** Struck with 1/2 Thaler dies, KM#182.

Date	Mintage	VG	F	VF	XF	Unc
1662 (e) Rare	—	—	—	—	—	—

KM# 190 4 DUCAT

14.0000 g., 0.9860 Gold 0.4438 oz. AGW **Obv:** Laureate bust of Leopold I right **Rev:** Cherub left holding two shields of arms

Date	Mintage	VG	F	VF	XF	Unc
ND(1670) Rare	—	—	—	—	—	—

KM# A203 4 DUCAT

14.0000 g., 0.9860 Gold 0.4438 oz. AGW **Obv:** Three shields of arms **Rev:** City view with "Jehovah" in Hebrew above, Roman numeral date in cartouche below **Note:** Struck with 1/2 Thaler dies, KM#182.

Date	Mintage	VG	F	VF	XF	Unc
1680 Rare	—	—	—	—	—	—

KM# 231 4 DUCAT

14.0000 g., 0.9860 Gold 0.4438 oz. AGW **Subject:** Peace of Ryswick **Obv:** City view with "Jehovah" in Hebrew above, inscription and date below **Rev:** Peace standing above two cherubs holding shields of amrs

Date	Mintage	VG	F	VF	XF	Unc
1698 GFN Rare	—	—	—	—	—	—

KM# 127 5 DUCAT

17.5000 g., 0.9860 Gold 0.5547 oz. AGW **Obv:** Bust of Gustav II Adolphus right **Rev:** Crowned arms **Note:** Swedish issue.

Date	Mintage	VG	F	VF	XF	Unc
1632 (b) Rare	—	—	—	—	—	—

KM# 191 5 DUCAT

17.5000 g., 0.9860 Gold 0.5547 oz. AGW **Obv:** Bust of Leopold right **Rev:** Cherub walking left iwth two shields of arms **Note:** City coingag resumed.

Date	Mintage	VG	F	VF	XF	Unc
ND(1670) Rare	—	—	—	—	—	—

KM# 195 5 DUCAT

17.5000 g., 0.9860 Gold 0.5547 oz. AGW **Obv:** Cherub walking left iwth two shields of arms **Rev:** City view with "Jehovah" in Hebrew above, date in exergue

Date	Mintage	VG	F	VF	XF	Unc
1677 (c) Rare	—	—	—	—	—	—

KM# 225 5 DUCAT

17.5000 g., 0.9860 Gold 0.5547 oz. AGW **Obv:** Three shields with decorations, angel head above **Rev:** City view with "Jehovah" in Hebrew above date below

Date	Mintage	VG	F	VF	XF	Unc
MDCXCIV (1694) Rare	—	—	—	—	—	—

KM# 229 5 DUCAT

17.5000 g., 0.9860 Gold 0.5547 oz. AGW **Obv:** Eye of God above city view, Roman numeral date in exergue below **Rev:** Angel with two shields of arms **Note:** Struck with 1 Thaler dies, KM#228.

Date	Mintage	VG	F	VF	XF	Unc
MDCXCVI (1696) GFN Rare	—	—	—	—	—	—

KM# 232 5 DUCAT

17.5000 g., 0.9860 Gold 0.5547 oz. AGW **Obv:** City view with "Jehovah" in Hebrew above, inscription and date below **Rev:** Peace standing above two genii holding shields of arms **Note:** Struck with 1 Thaler dies, KM#230.

Date	Mintage	VG	F	VF	XF	Unc
1698 GFN	—	—	—	5,500	8,500	—

KM# 115 6 DUCAT

21.0000 g., 0.9860 Gold 0.6657 oz. AGW **Note:** Swedish issue. Similar to 4 Ducat, KM#114.

Date	Mintage	VG	F	VF	XF	Unc
1631 (b) Rare	—	—	—	—	—	—

KM# 128 6 DUCAT

21.0000 g., 0.9860 Gold 0.6657 oz. AGW **Note:** City coinage resumed. Similar to 5 Ducat, KM#127.

Date	Mintage	VG	F	VF	XF	Unc
1632 Rare	—	—	—	—	—	—

KM# 192 6 DUCAT

21.0000 g., 0.9860 Gold 0.6657 oz. AGW **Obv:** Laureate bust of Leopold I right **Rev:** Cherub left holding two shields of arms

Date	Mintage	VG	F	VF	XF	Unc
ND(1670) Rare	—	—	—	—	—	—

KM# 234 6 DUCAT
21.0000 g., 0.9860 Gold 0.6657 oz. AGW **Obv:** City view with "Jehovah" in Hebrew above, inscription and date below **Rev:** Peace standing above two genii holding shields of arms **Note:** Similar to 5 Ducat, KM#232.

Date	Mintage	VG	F	VF	XF	Unc
1698 GFN	—	—	—	6,000	9,500	—

KM# 235 6 DUCAT
21.0000 g., 0.9860 Gold 0.6657 oz. AGW **Note:** Klippe.

Date	Mintage	VG	F	VF	XF	Unc
1698 GFN Rare	—	—	—	—	—	—

KM# 116 8 DUCAT
28.0000 g., 0.9860 Gold 0.8876 oz. AGW **Note:** Swedish issue. Similar to 4 Ducat, KM#114.

Date	Mintage	VG	F	VF	XF	Unc
1631 (b) Rare	—	—	—	—	—	—

KM# 226 8 DUCAT
28.0000 g., 0.9860 Gold 0.8876 oz. AGW **Obv:** Crowned imperial eagle with arms on breast **Rev:** City view with "Jehovah" in Hebrew above, date below **Note:** City coinage resumed.

Date	Mintage	VG	F	VF	XF	Unc
1694 GFN Rare	—	—	—	—	—	—

KM# 240 8 DUCAT
28.0000 g., 0.9860 Gold 0.8876 oz. AGW **Note:** Klippe. Similar to 5 ducat, KM#232.

Date	Mintage	VG	F	VF	XF	Unc
1698 GFN Rare	—	—	—	—	—	—

KM# 241 9 DUCAT
31.5000 g., 0.9860 Gold 0.9985 oz. AGW **Note:** Similar to 5 ducat, KM#232.

Date	Mintage	VG	F	VF	XF	Unc
1698 GFN Rare	—	—	—	—	—	—

KM# 85 10 DUCAT
35.0000 g., 0.9860 Gold 1.1095 oz. AGW **Obv:** Equestrian figure of Ferdinand II right **Rev:** Cherub standingholding two shields of arms, Roman numeral date in exergue **Note:** Struck with 2 Thaler dies, KM#84.

Date	Mintage	VG	F	VF	XF	Unc
ND(1627) Rare	—	—	—	—	—	—
ND(1630) Rare	—	—	—	—	—	—

KM# 117 10 DUCAT
35.0000 g., 0.9860 Gold 1.1095 oz. AGW **Note:** Swedish issue. Similar to 4 Ducat, KM#114.

Date	Mintage	VG	F	VF	XF	Unc
1631 (b) Rare	—	—	—	—	—	—

KM# 189 10 DUCAT
35.0000 g., 0.9860 Gold 1.1095 oz. AGW **Obv:** Laureate bust of Leopold I right **Rev:** Cherub holding two shields of arms **Note:** City coinage resumed.

Date	Mintage	VG	F	VF	XF	Unc
ND(1670) Rare	—	—	—	—	—	—

KM# 208 10 DUCAT
35.0000 g., 0.9860 Gold 1.1095 oz. AGW **Obv:** Eye of God above city view, 4-line inscrition in exergue **Rev:** Crowned eagle above City Hall, seated figure of Nurnberg in foreground **Note:** Struck with 1 Thaler dies, KM#203.

Date	Mintage	VG	F	VF	XF	Unc
ND(1688) PHM/(f) Rare	—	—	—	—	—	—

KM# 227 10 DUCAT
35.0000 g., 0.9860 Gold 1.1095 oz. AGW **Note:** Similar to 8 Ducat, KM#226.

Date	Mintage	VG	F	VF	XF	Unc
1694 GFN Rare	—	—	—	—	—	—

KM# 209 12 DUCAT
42.0000 g., 0.9860 Gold 1.3314 oz. AGW **Note:** Similar to 10 Ducat, KM#208. Struck with 1 Thaler dies, KM#203.

Date	Mintage	VG	F	VF	XF	Unc
ND(1688) PHM/(f) Rare	—	—	—	—	—	—

KM# 210 14 DUCAT
49.0000 g., 0.9860 Gold 1.5533 oz. AGW **Note:** Similar to 10 Ducat, KM#208. Struck with 1 Thaler dies, KM#203.

Date	Mintage	VG	F	VF	XF	Unc
ND(1688) PHM/(f) Rare	—	—	—	—	—	—

PATTERNS

Including off metal strikes

KM#	Date	Mintage	Identification	Mkt Val
Pn1	1610	—	Pfennig. Gold. Two-side strike	—
Pn2	1612	—	Goldgulden. Silver. KM#15	500
Pn3	ND(1617)	—	Goldgulden. Silver. KM#30; date in chronogram.	125
Pn8	1650	—	3 Ducat. Silver. KM#70. Klippe.	350
Pn10	ND(1700) GFN	—	2 Ducat. Silver. KM#259. Date in chronogram.	250

OLDENBURG

The county of Oldenburg was situated on the North Seacoast, to the east of the principality of East Friesland. It was originally part of the old duchy of Saxony and the first recorded lord ruled from the beginning of the 11th century. The first count was named in 1091and had already acquired the county of Delmenhorst prior to that time. The first identifiable Oldenburg coinage was struck in the first half of the 13thcentury. Oldenburg was divided into Oldenburg and Delmenhorst in 1270, but the two lines were reunited by marriage five generations later. Through another marriage to the heiress of the duchy of Schleswig and county of Holstein, the royal house of Denmark descended through the Oldenburg line beginning in 1448, while a junior branch continued as counts of Oldenburg. The lordship of Jever was added to the county's domains in 1575. In 1667, the last count died without a direct heir and Oldenburg reverted to Denmark until 1773. In the following year, Oldenburg was given to the bishop of Lübeck, of the Holstein-Gottorp line, and raised to the status of a duchy. Oldenburg was occupied several times during the Napoleonic Wars and became a grand duchy in 1829. In 1817, Oldenburg acquired the principality of Birkenfeld from Prussia and struck coins in denominations used there. World War I spelled the end of temporal power for the grand duke in 1918, but the title has continued up to the present time. Grand Duke Anton Gunther was born in 1923.

RULERS
Anton Gunther, 1603-1667
Friedrich III of Denmark, 1667-1670
Christian V of Denmark, 1670-1699
Friedrich IV of Denmark, 1699-1730

MINT OFFICIALS' INITIALS

Initial	Date	Name
(a)= .:. or ⚜ or ✹	1614-22	Nicolaus Wintgens
	1616-44	Anton Paris, warden
Z	1622-37	
(b)= ☽ or ✱	1637-49	Gerhard Dreyer
(c)= HE	1649-51	Jurgen Detleffs
	1653-	Konrad Delbruck
(d)= ⚘ or ⚔ or ✕	1658-67	Jurgen Hartmann in Munden
	1660-62	Hermann Vogelsang, warden and die-cutter
Z	1663-71	Georg David Ziegenhorn, mintmaster
IGP	Ca. 1665	Unknown die-cutter
CW	1680-1702	Christopher Woltereck in Gluckstadt

ARMS
Oldenburg: Two bars on field.
Delmenhorst: Cross with pointed bottom bar.
Jever: Lion rampant to left.
NOTE: Coins struck for lordship of Jever are listed under the latter.

COUNTSHIP

REGULAR COINAGE

KM# 5 SCHWAREN (3 Light Pfennig)
Silver **Ruler:** Friedrich V of Denmark **Obv:** Delmenhorst arms in circle, titles of Anton Gunther **Rev. Inscription:** I / OLD.B / VR.SW / ARN

Date	Mintage	VG	F	VF	XF	Unc
ND	—	—	—	—	—	—

KM# 21 GROTEN (1/144 Thaler)
Silver **Ruler:** Anton Gunther **Obv:** Crown above 3 small arms, Oldenburg and Jever above Delmenhorst, titles of Anton Gunther **Rev:** Titles continued **Rev. Inscription:** O / OLDEN / BORG / GROT **Note:** Varieties exist.

Date	Mintage	VG	F	VF	XF	Unc
ND(1614-22)	—	20.00	40.00	75.00	150	—

KM# 22 GROTEN (1/144 Thaler)
Silver **Ruler:** Anton Gunther **Rev. Inscription:** I / OLDEN / BVRG / GROT **Note:** Varieties exist.

Date	Mintage	VG	F	VF	XF	Unc
ND(1614-22)	—	20.00	40.00	75.00	150	—

KM# 31 GROTEN (1/144 Thaler)
Silver **Ruler:** Anton Gunther **Obv:** 3 Shields **Obv. Legend:** EN.OLDEN.BVRG.GROT **Rev:** Crowned imperial eagle, orb on breast, titles of Ferdinand II **Note:** Varieties exist.

Date	Mintage	VG	F	VF	XF	Unc
ND(1619-22)	—	16.00	33.00	60.00	120	—

KM# 32 GROTEN (1/144 Thaler)
Silver **Ruler:** Anton Gunther **Obv:** Arms of Oldenburg and Delmenhorst above Jever arms **Rev. Legend:** EIN or EEN OLDEN... **Note:** Varieties exist.

Date	Mintage	VG	F	VF	XF	Unc
ND(1619-22)	—	20.00	35.00	70.00	140	—
ND(1619-22) (a)	—	20.00	35.00	70.00	140	—

KM# 75 GROTEN (1/144 Thaler)
Silver **Ruler:** Anton Gunther **Obv:** Jever arms divide date, legend **Obv. Legend:** I GROT.OLD.BOR.LANT.G **Rev:** Titles of Ferdinand III **Note:** Varieties exist.

Date	Mintage	VG	F	VF	XF	Unc
1651	—	20.00	35.00	70.00	140	—
(16)51	—	20.00	35.00	70.00	140	—

KM# 77 2 GROTE (1/36 Thaler)
Silver **Ruler:** Anton Gunther **Obv:** Crown at top, 2 small arms above 1 **Rev:** Date **Rev. Inscription:** XXXVI / EIN / R.TALAVXILIVM...

Date	Mintage	VG	F	VF	XF	Unc
1658	—	70.00	140	250	400	—
1659 (d)	—	70.00	140	250	400	—

KM# 20 1/2 SCHILLING (Flindrich)
Silver **Ruler:** Anton Gunther **Obv:** Crowned 4-fold arms, titles of Anton Gunther **Rev:** Crowned imperial eagle, orb on breast, titles of Matthias **Note:** Varieties exist.

Date	Mintage	VG	F	VF	XF	Unc
ND(1612-19)	—	60.00	120	200	375	—

KM# 23 1/2 SCHILLING (Flindrich)
Silver **Ruler:** Anton Gunther **Obv:** Ornate floriated cross, Jever lion in center **Obv. Legend:** SORS. MEA... **Rev:** Arms in six-foil

Date	Mintage	VG	F	VF	XF	Unc
ND(1614-1622)	—	60.00	120	200	375	—

KM# A32 1/2 SCHILLING (Flindrich)
Silver **Ruler:** Anton Gunther **Obv:** Titles of Ferdinand II **Note:** Prev. KM#32.

Date	Mintage	VG	F	VF	XF	Unc
ND(1619-37)	—	—	—	—	—	—

KM# 60 1/2 SCHILLING (Flindrich)
Silver **Ruler:** Anton Gunther **Obv:** Titles of Ferdinand III **Rev:** Ornaments around arms **Note:** Varieties exist.

Date	Mintage	VG	F	VF	XF	Unc
ND(1637-57)	—	—	—	—	—	—

KM# 28 SCHILLING (6 Stuber)
Silver **Ruler:** Anton Gunther **Note:** Klippe Schilling.

Date	Mintage	VG	F	VF	XF	Unc
ND(1614-19)	—	—	—	—	—	—

KM# 24 SCHILLING (6 Stuber)
Silver **Ruler:** Anton Gunther **Obv:** Crowned imperial eagle **Obv. Legend:** IN.MANIBVS... **Rev:** Crowned 4-fold arms, titles of Anton Gunther **Note:** Varieties exist.

Date	Mintage	VG	F	VF	XF	Unc
ND(1614)	—	20.00	40.00	75.00	140	—

KM# 25 SCHILLING (6 Stuber)
Silver **Ruler:** Anton Gunther **Obv:** Crowned shield **Rev:** Imperial orb on eagle's breast **Note:** Varieties exist.

Date	Mintage	VG	F	VF	XF	Unc
ND(1614)	—	20.00	40.00	75.00	140	—

KM# 26 SCHILLING (6 Stuber)
Silver **Ruler:** Anton Gunther **Obv:** Crowned shield **Rev:** Titles of Matthias **Note:** Varieties exist.

Date	Mintage	VG	F	VF	XF	Unc
ND(1614-19)	—	20.00	40.00	75.00	140	—

KM# 27 SCHILLING (6 Stuber)
Silver **Ruler:** Anton Gunther **Obv:** Crowned shield **Rev:** Imperial orb on eagle's breast **Note:** Varieties exist.

Date	Mintage	VG	F	VF	XF	Unc
ND(1614-19)	—	20.00	40.00	75.00	140	—

KM# 33 SCHILLING (6 Stuber)
Silver **Ruler:** Anton Gunther **Obv:** Crowned shield **Rev:** Titles of Ferdinand II **Note:** Varieties exist.

Date	Mintage	VG	F	VF	XF	Unc
ND(1619-37)	—	33.00	65.00	120	265	—

KM# 100 SCHILLING (6 Stuber)
Silver **Ruler:** Anton Gunther **Obv:** Titles of Ferdinand III **Note:** Varieties exist.

Date	Mintage	VG	F	VF	XF	Unc
ND(1637-57)	—	—	—	—	—	—

KM# 76 SCHILLING (6 Stuber)
Silver **Ruler:** Anton Gunther **Obv:** Crowned shield **Rev:** Titles of Leopold I

Date	Mintage	VG	F	VF	XF	Unc
ND(1657-67)	—	65.00	135	275	475	—

KM# 80 SCHILLING (6 Stuber)
Silver **Ruler:** Anton Gunther **Obv:** Crowned AG monogram, titles of Anton Gunther **Rev:** 2-fold arms, Jever above Delmenhorst **Rev. Legend:** IN.MA.DOMI.SORS.MEA

Date	Mintage	VG	F	VF	XF	Unc
ND	—	—	—	—	—	—

KM# 81 SCHILLING (6 Stuber)
Silver **Ruler:** Anton Gunther **Obv:** VG monogram in error

Date	Mintage	VG	F	VF	XF	Unc
ND	—	—	—	—	—	—

KM# 55 15 SCHAF (Gulden)
Silver **Ruler:** Anton Gunther **Obv:** Crowned 4-fold arms, titles of Anton Gunther **Rev:** Crowned imperial eagle, 15 in orb on breast **Rev. Legend:** IN.MANIBVS **Note:** Varieties exist.

Date	Mintage	VG	F	VF	XF	Unc
ND(1620)	—	275	525	1,000	1,500	—

KM# 56 15 SCHAF (30 Stuber)
Silver **Ruler:** Anton Gunther **Obv:** 30 in orb on eagle's breast

Date	Mintage	VG	F	VF	XF	Unc
ND	—	—	—	—	—	—

KM# 35 1/4 MARK (8 Grote)
Silver **Ruler:** Anton Gunther **Note:** Klippe 1/4 Mark.

Date	Mintage	VG	F	VF	XF	Unc
ND	—	—	—	—	—	—

KM# 34 1/4 MARK (8 Grote)
Silver **Ruler:** Anton Gunther **Obv:** Crown above 3 small shields of arms, 2 above 1, titles of Anton Gunther **Rev. Inscription:** 1/4 / OLDENB / MARCK.ZU / 8. GROT. OD / IEV. 6 / STV **Note:** Varieties exist.

Date	Mintage	VG	F	VF	XF	Unc
ND (a)	—	60.00	120	225	425	—

KM# 36 1/4 MARK (8 Grote)
Silver **Ruler:** Anton Gunther **Rev:** Legend is 5 lines **Rev. Legend:** /IEV. 5 3/4 **Note:** Varieties exist.

Date	Mintage	VG	F	VF	XF	Unc
ND (a)	—	100	200	375	600	—

KM# 37 1/2 MARK (16 Grote)
Silver **Ruler:** Anton Gunther **Rev. Inscription:** 1/2 / OLDENBV / MARCK. ZU / XVI. GROT / OD. IEVER / 11 1/2. STV **Note:** Varieties exist.

Date	Mintage	VG	F	VF	XF	Unc
ND (a)	—	165	375	675	1,200	—

KM# 38 1/2 MARK (16 Grote)
Silver **Ruler:** Anton Gunther **Rev. Inscription:** 1/2 / OLDEN / BVRGER / MARCK.ZU / XVI / GROOT **Note:** Varieties exist.

Date	Mintage	VG	F	VF	XF	Unc
ND	—	200	400	625	1,350	—

KM# 41 MARK (32 Grote)
Silver **Ruler:** Anton Gunther **Obv:** Legend is continuation, in error, of titles

Date	Mintage	VG	F	VF	XF	Unc
ND (a)	—	—	—	—	—	—

KM# 40 MARK (32 Grote)
Silver **Ruler:** Anton Gunther **Rev. Inscription:** OLDENB / MARCK / ZU / XXXII / GROOT. OD / IEV. 23 / STV **Note:** Similar to 1/4 Mark, KM#34. Varieties exist.

Date	Mintage	VG	F	VF	XF	Unc
ND (a)	—	425	900	1,500	2,400	—

KM# 39 MARK (32 Grote)
Silver **Ruler:** Anton Gunther **Obv:** Crown above 3 small shields, 2 above 1 **Rev:** Crowned imperial eagle, imperial orb on breast, titles of Ferdinand II **Rev. Legend:** OLDENB. MARCK. ZU. 32. GROT. OD. IEV. 23 STV

Date	Mintage	VG	F	VF	XF	Unc
ND(1619-22) (a)	—	—	—	—	—	—

KM# 45 MARK (32 Grote)
Silver **Ruler:** Anton Gunther **Rev. Inscription:** I / OLDEN / BVRGER / MARCK. ZV / XXXII / GROOT **Note:** Varieties exist.

Date	Mintage	VG	F	VF	XF	Unc
ND (a)	—	525	1,075	1,800	2,700	—

KM# 44 MARK (32 Grote)
Silver **Ruler:** Anton Gunther **Obv:** Crown above 3 small shields of arms, 2 above 1, titles of Anton Gunther **Rev. Inscription:** ...IEV.24 / STV **Note:** Varieties exist.

Date	Mintage	VG	F	VF	XF	Unc
ND (a)	—	—	—	—	—	—

KM# 43 MARK (32 Grote)
Silver **Ruler:** Anton Gunther **Note:** Klippe Mark.

Date	Mintage	VG	F	VF	XF	Unc
ND(1619-22) (a)	—	—	—	—	—	—

KM# 42 MARK (32 Grote)
Silver **Ruler:** Anton Gunther **Rev:** Crowned imperial eagle, imperial orb on breast, titles of Ferdinand II **Rev. Legend:** OLDENB • MARCK • ZU • 32 GROT • OD • IEV • 24 ST **Note:** Varieties exist.

Date	Mintage	VG	F	VF	XF	Unc
ND(1619-22) (a)	—	—	—	—	—	—

KM# 90 1/8 THALER
Silver **Ruler:** Anton Gunther **Subject:** Death of Anton Gunther **Obv:** 9-line inscription with dates **Rev:** Crowned 4-fold arms **Rev. Legend:** AUXILIUM MEUM A DOMINO **Note:** Varieties exist.

Date	Mintage	VG	F	VF	XF	Unc
1667	—	85.00	165	300	500	—

KM# 46 1/4 THALER
Silver **Ruler:** Anton Gunther **Obv:** Bust of Anton Gunther right, titles in legend **Rev:** 4-fold arms, 3 helmets above, titles continued in legend

Date	Mintage	VG	F	VF	XF	Unc
ND(1619) (a)	—	—	—	—	—	—

KM# 47 1/4 THALER
Silver **Ruler:** Anton Gunther **Obv:** Crowned imperial eagle, imperial orb on breast, titles of Ferdinand II **Rev:** Crowned 4-fold arms, titles of Anton Gunther **Note:** Varieties exist.

Date	Mintage	VG	F	VF	XF	Unc
ND(1619-22)	—	—	—	—	—	—

KM# 91 1/4 THALER
Silver **Ruler:** Anton Gunther **Subject:** Death of Anton Gunther **Obv:** 9-line inscription with date **Rev:** Crowned 4-fold arms **Rev. Legend:** AUXILIUM MEUM A DOMINO

Date	Mintage	VG	F	VF	XF	Unc
1667	—	—	—	—	—	—

KM# 29 1/2 THALER
Silver **Ruler:** Anton Gunther **Obv:** Crowned imperial eagle, imperial orb on breast, titles of Matthias **Rev:** 4-fold arms, 2 helmets above, titles of Anton Gunther

Date	Mintage	VG	F	VF	XF	Unc
ND(1614-19) (a)	—	—	—	—	—	—

KM# 48 1/2 THALER
Silver **Ruler:** Anton Gunther **Obv:** Bust of Anton Gunther, right, titles in legend **Rev:** 4-fold arms, 3 helmets above, titles continued in legend **Note:** Klippe 1/2 Thaler.

Date	Mintage	VG	F	VF	XF	Unc
ND(1619) (a)	—	—	—	—	—	—

KM# 62 1/2 THALER
Silver **Ruler:** Anton Gunther **Subject:** Death of Anton Gunther's Sister **Obv:** Helmeted arms **Obv. Legend:** ANNA \ SOPHIA.. **Rev:** 8-line inscription **Note:** Varieties exist.

Date	Mintage	VG	F	VF	XF	Unc
1639 (b)	—	—	—	—	—	—

KM# 61 1/2 THALER
Silver **Ruler:** Anton Gunther **Subject:** Death of Anton Gunther's Sister **Obv:** 7-line inscription **Rev:** 8-line inscription with Roman numeral dates

Date	Mintage	VG	F	VF	XF	Unc
1639	—	—	—	—	—	—

KM# 92 1/2 THALER
Silver **Ruler:** Anton Gunther **Subject:** Death of Anton Gunther **Obv:** Crowned 4-fold arms **Rev:** 9-line inscription with dates **Rev. Legend:** AUXILIUM MEUM A DOMINO

Date	Mintage	VG	F	VF	XF	Unc
1667	—	125	265	500	850	—

KM# 97 2/3 THALER (Gulden)
17.3230 g., 0.7500 Silver 0.4177 oz. ASW **Ruler:** Christian V of Denmark **Obv:** Large Shield with open crown on top supported by two wildmen **Obv. Legend:** COMITAT : OLDENB : ET DELM : * **Rev:** Large 2/3 in center, date in legend **Rev. Legend:** MONETA NOVA ARGENTEA . 1690.C*W. or .C.W.* **Mint:** Glückstadt

Date	Mintage	VG	F	VF	XF	Unc
1690 CW	—	4,000	6,000	10,000	20,000	—

KM# 98 2/3 THALER (Gulden)
Silver **Ruler:** Christian V of Denmark **Obv:** Wildmen supporting crowned shield **Rev:** Large 2/3 within legend

Date	Mintage	VG	F	VF	XF	Unc
1690	—	4,000	6,000	8,500	—	—

Note: Some of these gulden are known with the countermark of the Franconian Circle, valued at 60 Kreuzer

KM# 63 3/4 THALER
21.2000 g., Silver **Ruler:** Anton Gunther **Subject:** Death of Anton Gunther's Sister **Obv:** Helmeted arms
Obv. Legend: ANNA.SOPHIA.. **Rev:** 8-line inscription

Date	Mintage	VG	F	VF	XF	Unc
1639 (b)	—	—	—	—	—	—

Note: Thalers Dav. #7113, Dav. #7113A and Dav. #7114 formerly listed in Oldenburg are now located in Jever

KM# 6 THALER
Silver **Ruler:** Anton Gunther **Obv. Legend:** ... RO + IMPER • SEMP + AVGV • **Note:** Dav. #7102.

Date	Mintage	VG	F	VF	XF	Unc
ND (a) Rare	—	—	—	—	—	—

KM# 7 THALER
Silver **Ruler:** Anton Gunther **Obv. Legend:** ROM + IMPERA + SEMP + AVG **Note:** Klippe Thaler. Dav. #7103.

Date	Mintage	VG	F	VF	XF	Unc
ND (a)	—	3,000	5,000	7,500	—	—

KM# 8 THALER
Silver **Ruler:** Anton Gunther **Obv:** Helmeted 4-fold shield **Rev:** Crowned double-headed imperial eagle **Rev. Legend:** ROM • IMPERAT • SEMP • AVGV **Note:** Dav. #7104.

Date	Mintage	VG	F	VF	XF	Unc
ND (a)	—	2,700	4,500	7,000	—	—

KM# 9 THALER
Silver **Ruler:** Anton Gunther **Obv. Legend:** COMES: IN: OLDENB **Rev. Legend:** ET • DELMENH • DOM... **Note:** Dav. #7107.

Date	Mintage	VG	F	VF	XF	Unc
ND (a)	—	1,100	1,900	3,300	—	—

KM# 10 THALER
Silver **Ruler:** Anton Gunther **Obv. Legend:** COM•OLDENBVRG? **Rev. Legend:** ET • DEL • DO • IN? **Note:** Dav. #7107A.

Date	Mintage	VG	F	VF	XF	Unc
ND (a)	—	1,100	1,900	3,300	—	—

KM# 11 THALER
Silver **Ruler:** Anton Gunther **Note:** Klippe Thaler. Dav. #7107B.

Date	Mintage	VG	F	VF	XF	Unc
ND (a)	—	2,400	4,000	7,000	—	—

KM# 12 THALER
Silver **Ruler:** Anton Gunther **Obv:** Helmeted arms
Rev: Crowned imperial eagle with orb on breast, titles of Ferdinand II **Note:** Dav, #7109.

Date	Mintage	VG	F	VF	XF	Unc
ND (a)	—	850	1,750	3,500	5,750	—

KM# 64 THALER
Silver **Ruler:** Anton Gunther **Subject:** Death of Anton Gunther's Sister **Obv:** Helmeted arms **Obv. Legend:** ANNA • SOPHIA... **Rev:** 8-line inscription **Note:** Dav. #7110.

Date	Mintage	VG	F	VF	XF	Unc
1639 (b)	—	1,150	2,250	4,500	7,500	—

KM# 84 THALER
Silver **Ruler:** Anton Gunther **Subject:** 82nd Birthday of Count Anton Gunther **Obv:** Bust right, AETAT: 82 at left, REGIMI at right **Rev:** Helmeted arms separating IG-P, date in legend **Note:** Dav. #7115.

Date	Mintage	VG	F	VF	XF	Unc
1665 IGP	—	850	1,750	3,500	7,000	—

KM# 86 THALER
Silver **Ruler:** Anton Gunther **Subject:** 83rd Birthday of Count Anton Gunther **Obv:** Bust right, within inner circle - AETATIS. 83 at left, REGIMINIS. 63 at right **Rev:** Helmeted arms, date in legend **Note:** Dav. #7116.

Date	Mintage	VG	F	VF	XF	Unc
1666	—	750	1,550	3,200	5,500	—

KM# 93 THALER
Silver **Ruler:** Anton Gunther **Subject:** Death of Count Anton Gunther **Obv:** Crowned arms **Rev:** 9-line inscription **Note:** Dav. #7118.

Date	Mintage	VG	F	VF	XF	Unc
1667	—	1,350	2,750	5,000	8,500	—

KM# 65 1-1/4 THALER
35.0000 g., Silver **Ruler:** Anton Gunther **Note:** Klippe 1-1/4 Thaler; Similar to 1 Thaler, KM#9. Dav. #--.

Date	Mintage	VG	F	VF	XF	Unc
ND (a) Rare	—	—	—	—	—	—

KM# 66 1-1/2 THALER
Silver **Ruler:** Anton Gunther **Obv:** Bust of Anton Gunther right **Rev:** Helmeted arms **Note:** Klippe. Dav. #7106.

Date	Mintage	VG	F	VF	XF	Unc
ND (a) Rare	—	—	—	—	—	—

Note: Fritz Rudolf Künker Münzenhandlung Auction 69, 10-01, XF realized approximately $13,895

KM# 13 2 THALER
58.0000 g., Silver **Ruler:** Anton Gunther **Note:** Octagonal Klippe 2 Thaler; Similar to 1 Thaler, KM#9. Dav. #--.

Date	Mintage	VG	F	VF	XF	Unc
ND (a) Rare	—	—	—	—	—	—

Note: Thalers Dav. #7111 and Dav. #7112 formerly listed in Oldenberg are now located under Jever

KM# 14 2 THALER
58.0000 g., Silver **Ruler:** Anton Gunther **Rev. Legend:** RO ++ IMPER • SEMP ++ AVGV • **Note:** Klippe. Similar to 1 Thaler, KM#8. Dav. #7101.

Date	Mintage	VG	F	VF	XF	Unc
ND (a) Rare	—	—	—	—	—	—

Note: Dr. Busso Peus Nachfolger Auction 373, 10-02, XF realized approximately $24,760

KM# 15 2 THALER

58.0000 g., Silver **Ruler:** Anton Gunther **Note:** Similar to KM#16 but reverse legend ends ...RN. Dav. #7105.

Date	Mintage	VG	F	VF	XF	Unc
ND (a) Rare	—	—	—	—	—	—

KM# 16 2 THALER

58.0000 g., Silver **Ruler:** Anton Gunther **Rev. Legend:** ...KNIP **Note:** Dav. #7105A. Illustration reduced.

Date	Mintage	VG	F	VF	XF	Unc
ND (a) Rare	—	—	—	—	—	—

KM# 17 2 THALER

58.0000 g., Silver **Ruler:** Anton Gunther **Obv:** Helmeted arms **Rev:** Crowned imperial eagle with orb on breast **Note:** Dav. #7108.

Date	Mintage	VG	F	VF	XF	Unc
ND Rare	—	—	—	—	—	—

KM# 94 2 THALER

58.0000 g., Silver **Ruler:** Anton Gunther **Subject:** Death of Anton Gunther **Obv:** Crowned arms **Rev:** 9-line inscription **Note:** Dav. #7117.

Date	Mintage	VG	F	VF	XF	Unc
1667 Rare	—	—	—	—	—	—

TRADE COINAGE

KM# 82 3 DUCAT

10.5000 g., 0.9860 Gold 0.3328 oz. AGW **Ruler:** Anton Gunther **Obv:** Bust of Anton Gunther facing 1/3 right **Rev:** Crowned arms

Date	Mintage	VG	F	VF	XF	Unc
1660	—	4,000	6,500	11,500	17,500	—

KM# 95 4 DUCAT

14.0000 g., 0.9860 Gold 0.4438 oz. AGW **Ruler:** Anton Gunther **Subject:** Death of Anton Gunther **Obv:** 9-line inscription with dates **Rev:** Crowned 4-fold arms **Rev. Legend:** AUXILIUM MEUM A DOMINO

Date	Mintage	VG	F	VF	XF	Unc
1667 Rare	—	—	—	—	—	—

Note: Struck with 1/2 Thaler dies, KM#92

KM# 87 5 DUCAT

17.5000 g., 0.9860 Gold 0.5547 oz. AGW **Ruler:** Anton Gunther **Subject:** 83rd Birthday of Anton Gunther **Obv:** Bust right **Rev:** Helmeted arms **Note:** Struck with 1 Thaler dies, KM#86.

Date	Mintage	VG	F	VF	XF	Unc
1666 Rare	—	—	—	—	—	—

KM# 85 10 DUCAT

35.0000 g., 0.9860 Gold 1.1095 oz. AGW **Ruler:** Anton Gunther **Subject:** 82nd Birthday of Anton Gunther **Obv:** Bust right **Rev:** Helmeted arms **Note:** Struck with 1 Thaler dies, KM#84.

Date	Mintage	VG	F	VF	XF	Unc
1665 IGP Rare	—	—	—	—	—	—

KM# 88 10 DUCAT

35.0000 g., 0.9860 Gold 1.1095 oz. AGW **Ruler:** Anton Gunther **Subject:** 83rd Birthday of Anton Gunther **Note:** Similar to 5 Ducat, KM#87. Struck with 1 Thaler dies, KM#86.

Date	Mintage	VG	F	VF	XF	Unc
1666 Rare	—	—	—	—	—	—

KM# 89 10 DUCAT

35.0000 g., 0.9860 Gold 1.1095 oz. AGW **Ruler:** Anton Gunther **Obv:** Bust left

Date	Mintage	VG	F	VF	XF	Unc
1666 Rare	—	—	—	—	—	—

KM# 96 10 DUCAT

35.0000 g., 0.9860 Gold 1.1095 oz. AGW **Ruler:** Anton Gunther **Subject:** Death of Anton Gunther **Note:** Similar to 4 Ducat, KM#95. Struck with 1 Thaler dies, KM#93

Date	Mintage	VG	F	VF	XF	Unc
1667 Reported, not confirmed	—	—	—	—	—	—

Note: Struck with 1 Thaler dies, KM#93

OSNABRUCK

A bishopric was established in the town, 30 miles (50 km) northeast of Munster, in 804. The town grew into a small, fortified city around the cathedral and the bishopric expanded its territory north and east of the county of Tecklenburg. The bishops enjoyed the right of coinage from 889 and extended it to their mint in Wiedenbruck (q.v.) in 952. The cathedral chapter issued its own coins in the 17th and 18th centuries. After joining the Hanseatic League independently of the bishops, the city itself minted coins from the mid-16th century until 1805. Both the bishopric and city became part of the kingdom of Hannover in 1803.

BISHOPRIC

RULERS

Konrad IV, Graf von Rietberg, 1482-1508
Erich II, Herzog von Braunschweig-Grubenhagen, 1508-1532
Franz, Graf von Waldeck, 1532-1553
Johann IV, Graf von Hoya, 1553-1574
Heinrich II, Herzog von Sachsen-Lauenburg, 1574-1585
Wilhelm von Schenking, 1585
Bernhard, Graf von Waldeck, 1585-1591
Philip Sigismund of Brunswick, 1591-1623
Eitel Friedrich of Hohenzollern, 1623-1625
Franz Wilhelm, Graf von Wartenberg, 1625-1634
Gustav Gustavson, Graf von Wasaborg, 1634-1648
Franz Wilhelm, Graf von Wartenberg, 1648-1661
Ernst August of Brunswick, 1662-1698
Sede Vacante, 1698
Karl von Lothringen, 1698-1715

ARMS

Wheel w/6 spokes (usually) and also on city+
Braunschweig (Brunswick): 2 leopards
Hoya: 2 bear paws
Minden: 2 crossed keys
Münster: Broad horizontal bar
Paderborn: Cross
Rietburg: Eagle
Waldeck: 8-pointed star
Wartenberg: Crowned lion rampant left

MINT OFFICIALS' INITIALS

Initial	Date	Name
EK	1605-06	Elias Kempfzer, mintmaster in Annaberg, Saxony for cathedral chapter
IL	Ca. 1633	Johann Loidtmann
EK	1637	Engelbert Kettler
	1641-?	Johann and Heinrich Pothoff
	1655-71	Hermann von der Hardt at Melle
HS	1625-72	Henning Schlüter in Zellerfeld
AS	1666-74	Andreas Scheele in Hannover City

REGULAR COINAGE

KM# 62 1-1/2 PFENNIG (1/8 Schilling)

Silver **Ruler:** Franz Wilhelm **Obv:** Osnabrück arms in hexalobe **Rev:** In 3 lines, 16I57 / / F.O.P. **Mint:** Melle

Date	Mintage	VG	F	VF	XF	Unc
1657	39,000	30.00	65.00	100	160	—

KM# 64 1-1/2 PFENNIG (1/8 Schilling)

Silver **Ruler:** Franz Wilhelm **Obv:** Osnabrück arms in simple circle **Mint:** Melle **Note:** Similar to KM#62.

Date	Mintage	VG	F	VF	XF	Unc
1657	Inc. above	30.00	65.00	100	160	—

KM# 66 2 PFENNIG (1/6 Schilling)

Silver **Ruler:** Franz Wilhelm **Obv:** Osnabrück arms **Rev:** Large Roman numeral II divides date / F.O.P. **Mint:** Melle

Date	Mintage	VG	F	VF	XF	Unc
1657	27,000	25.00	55.00	95.00	—	—

KM# 67 2 PFENNIG (1/6 Schilling)

Silver **Ruler:** Franz Wilhelm **Obv:** Similar to KM#66 **Rev. Inscription:** II / 1657 / F.O.P. **Mint:** Melle

Date	Mintage	VG	F	VF	XF	Unc
1657	Inc. above	25.00	55.00	95.00	—	—

KM# 68 3 PFENNIG (1/4 Schilling)

Silver **Ruler:** Franz Wilhelm **Obv:** Similar to 2 Pfennig, KM#66 **Rev. Inscription:** 1657 / III / F.O.P. **Mint:** Melle **Note:** Varieties exist.

Date	Mintage	VG	F	VF	XF	Unc
1657	19,000	40.00	80.00	140	200	—

KM# 70 4 PFENNIG (1/3 Schilling)

Silver **Ruler:** Franz Wilhelm **Obv:** Similar to 2 Pfennig, KM#66 **Rev:** 1657 / IIII / F.O.P. **Mint:** Melle **Note:** Varieties exist.

Date	Mintage	VG	F	VF	XF	Unc
1657	13,000	30.00	60.00	120	175	—

KM# 72 5 PFENNIG (1/50 Thaler)

Silver **Ruler:** Franz Wilhelm **Obv:** Similar to 2 Pfennig, KM#66 **Rev. Inscription:** 1657 / V / F.O.P. **Mint:** Melle

Date	Mintage	VG	F	VF	XF	Unc
1657	5,900	30.00	60.00	120	—	—

KM# 74 6 PFENNIG (1/2 Schilling)

Silver **Ruler:** Franz Wilhelm **Obv:** Similar to 2 Pfennig, KM#66 **Rev. Inscription:** 1657/ VI / F.O.P. **Mint:** Melle **Note:** Varieties exist.

Date	Mintage	VG	F	VF	XF	Unc
1657	9,780	30.00	60.00	120	—	—

KM# 111 6 PFENNIG (1/2 Schilling)

Silver **Ruler:** Ernst August I **Obv:** Crowned EA monogram in palm branches **Rev:** Date in 5-line inscription **Rev. Inscription:** / VI / PFENN / OSNAB / (4Z) **Mint:** Melle **Note:** Varieties exist

Date	Mintage	VG	F	VF	XF	Unc
1664	—	33.00	70.00	125	180	—
1665	—	33.00	70.00	125	180	—
1666	—	33.00	70.00	125	180	—

KM# 24 SCHILLING (12 Pfennig)

Copper **Ruler:** Franz Wilhelm **Obv:** Crown above FWE monogram **Rev:** Value .X.I.I., Osnabrück arms above divide date

Date	Mintage	Good	VG	F	VF	XF
1633 IL	—	45.00	85.00	120	165	—

KM# 50 SCHILLING (1/21 Thaler)

Silver **Ruler:** Gustav Gustavson **Obv:** 3 shields of arms, 2 above 1, lower arms divide value 2 - 1 **Rev:** 3 shields of arms, 2 above 1

Date	Mintage	VG	F	VF	XF	Unc
ND(1642-49)	—	40.00	75.00	135	—	—

KM# 99 SCHILLING (1/21 Thaler)

Silver **Ruler:** Ernst August I **Obv:** Crowned EA monogram, date above, value (Z1) at bottom **Rev:** Crowned 12-fold arms **Mint:** Melle

Date	Mintage	VG	F	VF	XF	Unc
1663	—	40.00	75.00	135	—	—

KM# 25 SCHILLING

Silver **Ruler:** Franz Wilhelm **Obv:** W above Osnabrück arms **Note:** Uniface. Klippe. Siege issue.

Date	Mintage	VG	F	VF	XF	Unc
ND(1633)	—	—	—	—	—	—

KM# 27 2 SCHILLING

Silver **Ruler:** Franz Wilhelm **Obv:** Wheel arms of Osnabrück **Note:** Uniface. Klippe. Siege issue.

Date	Mintage	VG	F	VF	XF	Unc
ND(1633)	—	—	—	—	—	—

KM# 29 3 SCHILLING

Copper **Ruler:** Franz Wilhelm **Obv:** Crown above FWE monogram **Rev:** I.I.I.S, Osnabrück arms divide date above

Date	Mintage	Good	VG	F	VF	XF
1633 IL	—	40.00	80.00	120	175	—

KM# 84 GROSCHEN (1/24 Thaler)

Silver **Ruler:** Ernst August I **Obv:** Crowned EA monogram **Rev:** Crowned Osnabrück arms, date divided above **Mint:** Zellerfeld

Date	Mintage	VG	F	VF	XF	Unc
1662 HS	—	40.00	75.00	135	—	—

KM# 100 GROSCHEN (1/24 Thaler)

Silver **Ruler:** Ernst August I **Rev:** Value Z4 at bottom **Mint:** Melle **Note:** Similar to KM#84. Varieties exist.

Date	Mintage	VG	F	VF	XF	Unc
1663	—	40.00	85.00	140	185	—
1664	—	40.00	85.00	140	185	—

KM# 101 GROSCHEN (1/24 Thaler)

Silver **Ruler:** Ernst August I **Rev:** Value Z - 4 divided by arms **Mint:** Melle **Note:** Similar to 1 Groschen, KM#100.

Date	Mintage	VG	F	VF	XF	Unc
1663	—	40.00	75.00	135	—	—

KM# 102 GROSCHEN (1/24 Thaler)

Silver **Ruler:** Ernst August I **Obv:** Die of Mariengroschen, KM240 **Rev:** Die of KM#100 **Mint:** Melle **Note:** Mule.

Date	Mintage	VG	F	VF	XF	Unc
1663	—	40.00	75.00	135	—	—

KM# 53 FURSTENGROSCHEN (1/28 Thaler)

Silver **Ruler:** Franz Wilhelm **Obv:** Crowned Wartenberg arms divide date, titles of Franz Wilhelm around **Rev:** 1/2-length figure of St. Peter holding key and book, value 28 below **Mint:** Melle **Note:** Varieties exist.

Date	Mintage	VG	F	VF	XF	Unc
1656	—	50.00	110	165	—	—

KM# 80 FURSTENGROSCHEN (1/28 Thaler)

Silver **Ruler:** Franz Wilhelm **Obv:** Cardinal's hat above 4-fold arms with central shield of Wartenberg **Rev:** Similar to KM#53, but with date in margin **Mint:** Melle

Date	Mintage	VG	F	VF	XF	Unc
1661	—	50.00	110	165	—	—

KM# 55 2 FURSTENGROSCHEN (1/14 Thaler)

Silver **Ruler:** Franz Wilhelm **Obv:** Crowned Wartenberg arms, titles of Franz Wilhelm around, value 14 below **Rev:** St. Peter standing, holding key and book, divides date **Mint:** Melle **Note:** Varieties exist

Date	Mintage	VG	F	VF	XF	Unc
1656	—	45.00	100	150	—	—
1657	—	45.00	100	150	—	—

KM# 76 2 FURSTENGROSCHEN (1/14 Thaler)

Silver **Ruler:** Franz Wilhelm **Obv:** Arms divide date **Mint:** Melle **Note:** Similar to KM#55. Varieties exist

Date	Mintage	VG	F	VF	XF	Unc
1657	—	45.00	100	150	—	—

KM# 122 2 FURSTENGROSCHEN (1/14 Thaler)

Silver **Ruler:** Ernst August I **Obv:** Crowned EA monogram, value

(14) at bottom **Rev:** Crowned 12-fold arms, date in margin **Mint:** Melle **Note:** Varieties exist

Date	Mintage	VG	F	VF	XF	Unc
1667	—	55.00	125	175	275	—
1668	—	55.00	125	175	275	—

KM# 105 MATIER

Silver **Ruler:** Ernst August I **Obv:** Crowned EA monogram **Rev:** 3-line inscription, last line is date **Rev. Inscription:** EIN / MATIER / **Mint:** Melle

Date	Mintage	VG	F	VF	XF	Unc
1663	—	40.00	85.00	140	200	—

KM# 107 MARIENGROSCHEN (1/36 Thaler)

Silver **Ruler:** Ernst August I **Obv:** Crowned EA monogram, date above **Rev:** Madonna and child, rays around, legend in margin **Rev. Legend:** MARIEN - GROSCHE **Mint:** Melle

Date	Mintage	VG	F	VF	XF	Unc
1663	—	40.00	75.00	135	—	—

KM# 57 2 MARIENGROSCHEN (1/18 Thaler)

Silver **Ruler:** Franz Wilhelm **Obv:** Crowned FWE monogram, titles of Franz Wilhelm around **Rev:** Legend around inscription, date **Rev. Legend:** II / MARI / GRO **Rev. Inscription:** MONE NO ARGENT **Mint:** Melle

Date	Mintage	VG	F	VF	XF	Unc
1656	7,416	70.00	150	225	—	—

KM# 115 2 MARIENGROSCHEN (1/18 Thaler)

Silver **Ruler:** Ernst August I **Obv:** Crowned EA monogram **Rev:** Legend around inscription, date **Rev. Legend:** II / MARIE / GROS / **Rev. Inscription:** 18 AUF EIN REICHS THALER **Mint:** Melle **Note:** Varieties exist

Date	Mintage	VG	F	VF	XF	Unc
1665	—	40.00	75.00	125	—	—
1666	—	40.00	75.00	125	—	—
1667	—	40.00	75.00	125	—	—
1668	—	40.00	75.00	125	—	—

KM# 125.1 2 MARIENGROSCHEN (1/18 Thaler)

Silver **Ruler:** Ernst August I **Obv:** Braunschweig helmet with horse crest **Rev:** Legend with date around inscription **Rev. Legend:** II / MARI / GR / **Rev. Inscription:** VON FEINEM SILBER **Mint:** Melle

Date	Mintage	VG	F	VF	XF	Unc
1669	—	60.00	120	200	—	—

KM# 125.2 2 MARIENGROSCHEN (1/18 Thaler)

Silver **Ruler:** Ernst August I **Rev:** Legend, date **Rev. Legend:** II / MARIE / GROS **Mint:** Melle **Note:** Similar to 125.1.

Date	Mintage	VG	F	VF	XF	Unc
1669	—	60.00	120	200	—	—

KM# 59 4 MARIENGROSCHEN (1/2 Kopfstuck)

Silver **Ruler:** Franz Wilhelm **Obv:** Crowned Wartenberg arms divide date, titles of Franz Wilhelm around **Rev:** Legend around inscription **Rev. Legend:** IIII / MARIE / GRO(S) **Rev. Inscription:** MONETA NOVA... **Mint:** Melle **Note:** Varieties exist.

Date	Mintage	VG	F	VF	XF	Unc
1656	26,000	50.00	110	170	—	—
1657	—	50.00	110	170	—	—

KM# 127 4 MARIENGROSCHEN (1/2 Kopfstuck)

Silver **Ruler:** Ernst August I **Obv:** Braunschweig helmet with horse crest **Rev:** Legend around inscription, date **Rev. Legend:** IIII / MARIE / GROS **Rev. Inscription:** VON FEINEM SILBER **Mint:** Melle **Note:** Varieties exist.

Date	Mintage	VG	F	VF	XF	Unc
1669	—	65.00	145	200	275	—

KM# 129 6 MARIENGROSCHEN (1/6 Thaler)

Silver **Ruler:** Ernst August I **Rev. Legend:** VI / MARIE / GROS **Note:** Similar to 4 Mariengroschen, KM#127.

Date	Mintage	VG	F	VF	XF	Unc
1669	—	75.00	160	250	—	—

KM# 130 12 MARIENGROSCHEN (1/3 Thaler)

Silver **Ruler:** Ernst August I **Rev. Legend:** XII / MARIEN / GROS **Mint:** Hannover **Note:** Similar to 4 Mariengroschen, KM#127. Varieties exist.

Date	Mintage	VG	F	VF	XF	Unc
1669	—	70.00	150	225	350	—
1669 AS	—	70.00	150	225	350	—
1670	—	70.00	150	225	350	—
1670 AS	—	70.00	150	225	350	—

KM# 131 12 MARIENGROSCHEN (1/3 Thaler)

Silver **Ruler:** Ernst August I **Obv:** Helmet enclosed in circle **Mint:** Hannover **Note:** Similar to KM#130. Varieties exist.

Date	Mintage	VG	F	VF	XF	Unc
1669	—	70.00	150	225	350	—
1670	—	70.00	150	225	350	—

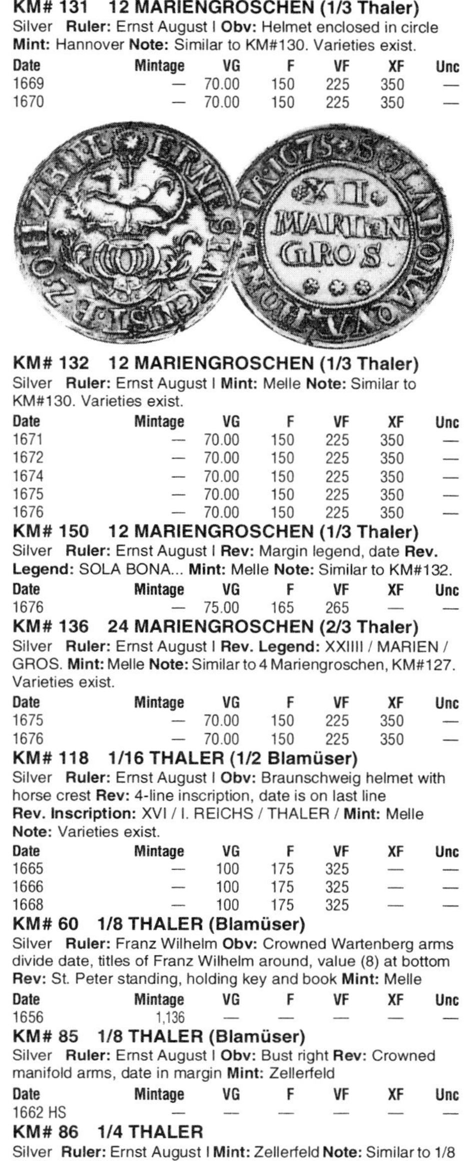

KM# 132 12 MARIENGROSCHEN (1/3 Thaler)

Silver **Ruler:** Ernst August I **Mint:** Melle **Note:** Similar to KM#130. Varieties exist.

Date	Mintage	VG	F	VF	XF	Unc
1671	—	70.00	150	225	350	—
1672	—	70.00	150	225	350	—
1674	—	70.00	150	225	350	—
1675	—	70.00	150	225	350	—
1676	—	70.00	150	225	350	—

KM# 150 12 MARIENGROSCHEN (1/3 Thaler)

Silver **Ruler:** Ernst August I **Rev:** Margin legend, date **Rev. Legend:** SOLA BONA... **Mint:** Melle **Note:** Similar to KM#132.

Date	Mintage	VG	F	VF	XF	Unc
1676	—	75.00	165	265	—	—

KM# 136 24 MARIENGROSCHEN (2/3 Thaler)

Silver **Ruler:** Ernst August I **Rev. Legend:** XXIIII / MARIEN / GROS. **Mint:** Melle **Note:** Similar to 4 Mariengroschen, KM#127. Varieties exist.

Date	Mintage	VG	F	VF	XF	Unc
1675	—	70.00	150	225	350	—
1676	—	70.00	150	225	350	—

KM# 118 1/16 THALER (1/2 Blamüser)

Silver **Ruler:** Ernst August I **Obv:** Braunschweig helmet with horse crest **Rev:** 4-line inscription, date is on last line **Rev. Inscription:** XVI / I. REICHS / THALER / **Mint:** Melle **Note:** Varieties exist.

Date	Mintage	VG	F	VF	XF	Unc
1665	—	100	175	325	—	—
1666	—	100	175	325	—	—
1668	—	100	175	325	—	—

KM# 60 1/8 THALER (Blamüser)

Silver **Ruler:** Franz Wilhelm **Obv:** Crowned Wartenberg arms divide date, titles of Franz Wilhelm around, value (8) at bottom **Rev:** St. Peter standing, holding key and book **Mint:** Melle

Date	Mintage	VG	F	VF	XF	Unc
1656	1,136	—	—	—	—	—

KM# 85 1/8 THALER (Blamüser)

Silver **Ruler:** Ernst August I **Obv:** Bust right **Rev:** Crowned manifold arms, date in margin **Mint:** Zellerfeld

Date	Mintage	VG	F	VF	XF	Unc
1662 HS	—	—	—	—	—	—

KM# 86 1/4 THALER

Silver **Ruler:** Ernst August I **Mint:** Zellerfeld **Note:** Similar to 1/8 Thaler, KM#85.

Date	Mintage	VG	F	VF	XF	Unc
1662 HS	—	—	—	—	—	—

KM# 30 1/2 THALER

Silver **Ruler:** Franz Wilhelm **Obv:** St. Peter standing behind 4-fold arms, holding key and book, divides date **Note:** Uniface Klippe. Siege issue.

Date	Mintage	VG	F	VF	XF	Unc
1633	—	—	—	—	—	—

KM# 88 1/2 THALER

Silver **Ruler:** Ernst August I **Mint:** Zellerfeld **Note:** Similar to 1/8 Thaler, KM#85.

Date	Mintage	VG	F	VF	XF	Unc
1662 HS	—	—	—	—	—	—

KM# 22 THALER

Silver **Ruler:** Franz Wilhelm **Obv:** Franz Wilhelm **Rev:** Date above shield **Note:** Dav. #5670.

Date	Mintage	VG	F	VF	XF	Unc
1631	—	2,000	4,000	7,500	—	—

KM# 33 THALER

Silver **Ruler:** Franz Wilhelm **Note:** Klippe. Similar to 1/2 Thaler, KM#30. Siege issue.

Date	Mintage	VG	F	VF	XF	Unc
1633	—	—	—	—	—	—

KM# 46 THALER

Silver **Obv:** Bust of Franz Wilhelm right to bottom of coin **Rev:** Oval arms divide date above, E-K below **Note:** Dav. #5672.

Date	Mintage	VG	F	VF	XF	Unc
1637 EK Rare	—	—	—	—	—	—
ND(ca.1637) EK	—	1,250	2,500	5,000	—	—

KM# 78 THALER

Silver **Ruler:** Franz Wilhelm **Rev:** Different arms, 4-fold arms with central shield of Wartenberg, date divided near top **Mint:** Melle **Note:** Similar to KM#46. Dav. #5672.

Date	Mintage	VG	F	VF	XF	Unc
1657 Rare	—	—	—	—	—	—

KM# 82 THALER

Silver **Ruler:** Franz Wilhelm **Obv:** Bust right of elderly Franz Wilhelm as cardinal, titles as such, date in margin **Rev:** Cardinal's hat above 4-fold arms with central shield of Wartenberg

Date	Mintage	VG	F	VF	XF	Unc
1661 Rare	—	—	—	—	—	—

KM# 90 THALER
Silver **Ruler:** Ernst August I **Obv:** Ernst August **Rev:** Helmeted arms, date in legend **Note:** Dav. #5673. The Thaler dated 1663 was struck at the Melle mint.

Date	Mintage	VG	F	VF	XF	Unc
1662	—	750	1,500	3,000	6,000	—
1663	—	900	1,850	3,750	—	—

KM# 154 THALER
Silver **Ruler:** Sede Vacante **Obv:** Standing saint with small shield in front **Rev:** Church with short crosses, stars and long trail banner above **Note:** Dav. #5674.

Date	Mintage	VG	F	VF	XF	Unc
1698	—	300	600	1,200	2,000	—

KM# A154 THALER
Silver **Ruler:** Sede Vacante **Obv:** Standing saint with small shield in front **Rev:** Church with tall crosses, stars and short trail banner above **Mint:** Hannover **Note:** Dav. #5674A.

Date	Mintage	VG	F	VF	XF	Unc
1698	1,381	325	675	1,350	2,250	—

KM# A230 1-1/2 THALER
Silver **Note:** Klippe. Similar to 1 Thaler, KM#46 but struck on a square flan.

Date	Mintage	VG	F	VF	XF	Unc
ND(ca.1637) EK Rare	—	—	—	—	—	—

KM# B230 2 THALER
Silver **Note:** Similar to 1 Thaler, KM#46. Dav. #B5671.

Date	Mintage	VG	F	VF	XF	Unc
ND Rare	—	—	—	—	—	—

KM# C230 2 THALER
Silver **Note:** Klippe. Dav. #C5671.

Date	Mintage	VG	F	VF	XF	Unc
ND Rare	—	—	—	—	—	—

KM# 230 3 THALER
Silver **Note:** Similar to 1 Thaler, KM#46. Dav. #5671.

Date	Mintage	VG	F	VF	XF	Unc
ND Rare	—	—	—	—	—	—

KM# 93 3 THALER
Silver **Ruler:** Ernst August I **Obv:** 5 helmets above 12-fold arms **Rev:** Crossed sword and crozier above city view, value 3 stamped at bottom **Mint:** Zellerfeld **Note:** Dav. #229.

Date	Mintage	VG	F	VF	XF	Unc
ND(1662) HS	—	—	—	—	—	—

KM# 94 4 THALER
Silver **Ruler:** Ernst August I **Rev:** Value 4 stamped at bottom **Mint:** Zellerfeld **Note:** Dav. #228. Similar to 3 Thalers, KM#93.

Date	Mintage	VG	F	VF	XF	Unc
ND(1662) HS	—	—	—	—	—	—

KM# 95 4 THALER
Silver **Ruler:** Ernst August I **Obv:** Similar to KM#94 **Rev:** Arm from clouds holds wheel of Osnabrück by ribbon, city view in background, value 4 stamped at bottom **Mint:** Zellerfeld **Note:** Dav. #230.

Date	Mintage	VG	F	VF	XF	Unc
ND(1662) HS	—	—	—	—	—	—

KM# 97 5 THALER
Silver, 80 mm. **Ruler:** Ernst August I **Rev:** Value 5 stamped at bottom **Mint:** Zellerfeld **Note:** Dav. #227. Similar to 3 Thalers, KM#93. Illustration reduced.

Date	Mintage	VG	F	VF	XF	Unc
ND(1662) HS	—	—	—	—	—	—

TRADE COINAGE

KM# 48 DUCAT
3.5000 g., 0.9860 Gold 0.1109 oz. AGW **Obv:** St. Peter standing **Rev:** Arms in ornamental shield in inner circle **Note:** Fr#1938.

Date	Mintage	VG	F	VF	XF	Unc
1637 EK	—	900	1,800	3,750	6,800	—

KM# 52 DUCAT
3.5000 g., 0.9860 Gold 0.1109 oz. AGW **Obv:** Three shields in inner circle **Rev:** Three different shields in inner circle **Note:** Fr. #1939.

Date	Mintage	VG	F	VF	XF	Unc
ND(1642)	—	500	1,150	2,250	4,150	—

KM# 120 DUCAT
3.5000 g., 0.9860 Gold 0.1109 oz. AGW **Obv:** Bust of Ernst August in inner circle **Rev:** Crowned arms in inner circle **Mint:** Melle **Note:** Fr. #1940.

Date	Mintage	VG	F	VF	XF	Unc
1666	—	675	1,500	3,000	5,300	—

KM# 109 15 DUCAT
51.0900 g., 0.9860 Gold 1.6195 oz. AGW **Mint:** Melle **Note:** Struck with 1 Thaler dies, KM#90. Prev. KM#2.

Date	Mintage	VG	F	VF	XF	Unc
1663 Unique, 1 known	—	—	—	—	—	—

CATHEDRAL CHAPTER

MINT
Eversburg

REGULAR COINAGE

KM# 10 PFENNIG
Copper **Obv:** St. Peter on throne holding key and book, arms of Osnabrück below in front around legend **Obv. Legend:** DOM CAPITEL OSNABRVK **Rev:** Value I divides date in circle **Mint:** Eversburg

Date	Mintage	Good	VG	F	VF	XF
1606	—	15.00	30.00	65.00	—	—

KM# 13 2 PFENNIG
Copper **Obv:** Different legend in margin than KM#10 **Obv. Legend:** DOM CAPITEL - ZV - OSNABRVK **Rev:** Value with date as 1I6016 **Mint:** Eversburg

Date	Mintage	Good	VG	F	VF	XF
1606 EK	—	15.00	30.00	65.00	—	—

KM# 15 3 PFENNIG
Copper **Rev:** Value with date in ornamented rectangle, 1I6I0I6 **Mint:** Eversburg **Note:** Similar to 2 Pfennig, KM#13.

Date	Mintage	Good	VG	F	VF	XF
1606 EK	—	15.00	30.00	65.00	—	—

KM# 3 6 PFENNIG
Copper **Rev:** Value on reverse VI and date at top in margin **Mint:** Eversburg **Note:** Similar to 1 Pfennig, KM#10.

Date	Mintage	Good	VG	F	VF	XF
1605	—	20.00	40.00	85.00	—	—

KM# 17 6 PFENNIG
Copper **Rev:** Value and date in ornamented rectangle on reverse, 1V6016 **Mint:** Eversburg **Note:** Similar to KM#3.

Date	Mintage	Good	VG	F	VF	XF
1606 EK	—	20.00	40.00	85.00	—	—

KM# 6 9 PFENNIG
Copper **Rev:** Value on reverse I and stylized X **Mint:** Eversburg **Note:** Similar to 6 Pfennig, KM#3.

Date	Mintage	Good	VG	F	VF	XF
1605	—	25.00	50.00	100	120	—

KM# 19 9 PFENNIG
Copper **Rev:** Value and date 1V6I0I16I **Mint:** Eversburg **Note:** Similar to 6 Pfennig, KM#17.

Date	Mintage	Good	VG	F	VF	XF
1606 EK	—	30.00	60.00	100	145	—

KM# 8 12 PFENNIG (Schilling)
Copper **Rev:** Value on reverse, stylized XII **Mint:** Eversburg **Note:** Similar to 6 Pfennig, KM#3.

Date	Mintage	Good	VG	F	VF	XF
1605	—	40.00	70.00	120	—	—

KM# 20 12 PFENNIG (Schilling)
Copper **Rev:** Value and date 1X6016I **Mint:** Eversburg **Note:** Similar to 6 Pfennig, KM#17.

Date	Mintage	Good	VG	F	VF	XF
1606 EK	—	35.00	65.00	110	150	—

SWEDISH OCCUPATION

REGULAR COINAGE

KM# 35 THALER
Silver **Obv:** Bust of Gustavus Adolphus left **Rev:** Crown above inscription **Rev. Inscription:** IOHAN • 10/ EIN • GVTER • HIRT/ LESSET • SEIN • LE:/ BEN • FVR • DIE •/ SCHAAFFE •/ OSNABRVGK/ +1663+ **Note:** Dav. #4551.

Date	Mintage	VG	F	VF	XF	Unc
1633 Rare	—	—	—	—	—	—

KM# 36 THALER
Silver **Rev. Inscription:** ...HRT/ LESST • SEIN • LE/ BEN • F • DI • SCH/ AFFE/ 16 0SNABR 33 **Note:** Similar to KM#37. Dav. #4553.

Date	Mintage	VG	F	VF	XF	Unc
1633	—	175	375	800	1,350	—

KM# 37 THALER

Silver **Rev:** Date divided below inscription **Rev. Inscription:** ...SCHAFFE/ OSNABRVG **Note:** Dav. #4554.

Date	Mintage	VG	F	VF	XF	Unc
1633	—	100	200	500	850	—

KM# 38 THALER

Silver **Rev:** Date above inscription in legend **Rev. Inscription:** ...SCHAFFE/ OSNABRV **Note:** Dav. #4555.

Date	Mintage	VG	F	VF	XF	Unc
1633	—	150	350	750	1,250	—

KM# 39 THALER

Silver **Rev. Inscription:** ...LESSET • SEIN/ LEBEN • F • DIE •/... **Note:** Dav. #4556.

Date	Mintage	VG	F	VF	XF	Unc
1633	—	200	425	850	1,400	—

KM# 42 2 THALER

Silver **Rev. Inscription:** ...HRT/ LESST • SEIN • LE/ BEN • F • DI • SCH/ AFFE/ 16 OSNABR 33. **Note:** Similar to 1 Thaler, KM#37. Dav. #4552.

Date	Mintage	VG	F	VF	XF	Unc
1633 Unique	—	—	—	—	—	—

TRADE COINAGE

FR# 1943 DUCAT

3.5000 g., 0.9860 Gold 0.1109 oz. AGW **Obv:** Laureate bust of Gustav II Adolphus left **Rev:** Crown above 5-line legend

Date	Mintage	VG	F	VF	XF	Unc
1633	—	325	650	1,300	2,200	—

KM# 44 10 DUCAT

35.0000 g., 0.9860 Gold 1.1095 oz. AGW **Obv:** Laureate bust of Gustav II Adolphus left **Rev:** Crown above 5-line inscription with OSNABRVC in bracket and date below **Note:** Struck with 1 Thaler dies, KM#37. Prev. KM#1.

Date	Mintage	VG	F	VF	XF	Unc
1633 Rare	—	—	—	—	—	—

CITY

The city of Osnabrück is located northeast of Münster. Although the city owed its original growth to the bishopric it achieved considerable independence from the bishops and joined the Hanseatic League. It had its own local coinage from the early 16th century until 1805. It was absorbed by Hannover in 1803.

Initial	Date	Name
CD	1586-1633	Cordt Dellebrügk
HB	1667-82	Hermann Brauwe
	1691-98	Johann Brockmann
IM	1690-98	Jürgen Meyer, die-cutter

REGULAR COINAGE

MB# 100 PFENNIG

Copper **Obv:** Osnabrück arms in ornamented shield, around inscription, date **Obv. Inscription:** STADT OSNABRVGK **Rev:** Value I in ornamented frame **Note:** Varieties exist.

Date	Mintage	VG	F	VF	XF	Unc
1622	—	8.00	16.00	33.00	60.00	—

KM# 139.1 PFENNIG

Copper **Note:** Similar to MB#100. Varieties exist.

Date	Mintage	VG	F	VF	XF	Unc
1676 HB	8,280	8.00	16.00	33.00	60.00	—
1691	17,000	8.00	16.00	33.00	60.00	—
1698	91,000	8.00	16.00	33.00	60.00	—

KM# 139.2 PFENNIG

Copper **Note:** Similar to MB#100. Klippe.

Date	Mintage	VG	F	VF	XF	Unc
1698	—	—	—	—	—	—

MB# 103 1-1/2 PFENNIG

Copper **Rev:** Value I over I--I **Note:** Similar to 1 Pfennig, MB#100.

Date	Mintage	VG	F	VF	XF	Unc
1622	3,192	20.00	33.00	60.00	120	—

KM# 141 1-1/2 PFENNIG

Copper **Note:** Similar to MB#103.

Date	Mintage	VG	F	VF	XF	Unc
1676	55,000	20.00	33.00	60.00	120	—

MB# 107 3 PFENNIG

Copper **Rev:** Value III **Note:** Similar to 1 Pfennig, MB#100. Varieties exist.

Date	Mintage	VG	F	VF	XF	Unc
1622 CD	4,200	8.00	16.00	27.00	55.00	—

KM# 144 3 PFENNIG

Copper **Note:** Similar to MB#107. Varieties exist. Those with CD mintmaster's initials were struck with old reverse dies.

Date	Mintage	VG	F	VF	XF	Unc
1676	Inc. above	8.00	16.00	27.00	55.00	—
1676 CD	125,000	8.00	16.00	27.00	55.00	—
1676 HB	Inc. above	8.00	16.00	27.00	55.00	—

MB# 110 4 PFENNIG

Copper **Rev:** Value IIII **Note:** Similar to 1 Pfennig, MB#100. Varieties exist.

Date	Mintage	VG	F	VF	XF	Unc
1625	—	8.00	16.00	27.00	45.00	—

KM# 146 4 PFENNIG

Copper **Note:** Similar to MB#110. Varieties exist. The issue with '69' is an error for 1690.

Date	Mintage	VG	F	VF	XF	Unc
1676 HB	47,000	8.00	16.00	27.00	45.00	—
(1)69(0) IM	—	8.00	16.00	27.00	45.00	—
1690 IM	94,000	8.00	16.00	27.00	45.00	—

MB# 91 5 PFENNIG (Stüber)

Copper **Obv:** Osnabrück arms in ornamented shield, around inscription, date **Rev:** Value V within wreath **Note:** Varieties exist.

Date	Mintage	VG	F	VF	XF	Unc
(16)25	—	9.00	16.00	30.00	60.00	—
(16)26	—	9.00	16.00	30.00	60.00	—
1650	—	9.00	16.00	30.00	60.00	—
1660	—	9.00	16.00	30.00	60.00	—
1695	—	9.00	16.00	30.00	60.00	—

MB# 92 6 PFENNIG

Copper **Rev:** Value VI in ornamented frame within wreath **Note:** Similar to 5 Pfennig, MB#91. Varieties exist.

Date	Mintage	VG	F	VF	XF	Unc
(16)25 CD	72,000	11.00	25.00	40.00	60.00	—

MB# 96 8 PFENNIG

Copper **Rev:** Value VIII **Note:** Similar to 7 Pfennig, MB#94. Varieties exist.

Date	Mintage	VG	F	VF	XF	Unc
1625 CD	—	11.00	20.00	33.00	60.00	—

MB# 97 9 PFENNIG

Copper **Obv:** Round shield of city arms in ornamented frame, date at end of legend **Obv. Legend:** STADT. OSNABRVGK. Ao **Rev:** Value VIIII in ornamented frame on reverse and no wreath **Note:** Varieties exist.

Date	Mintage	VG	F	VF	XF	Unc
1625 CD	181,000	12.00	27.00	45.00	80.00	—

MB# 112 12 PFENNIG (Schilling)

Copper **Rev:** Value XII in ornamented circle **Note:** Similar to 1 Pfennig, MB#100. Varieties exist.

Date	Mintage	VG	F	VF	XF	Unc
1615 CD	—	13.00	27.00	45.00	75.00	—
1623 CD	—	13.00	27.00	45.00	75.00	—
1633 CD	—	13.00	27.00	45.00	75.00	—

OTTINGEN

The counts of Öttingen, with lands in Swabia north of Nördlingen, trace their descent in a long line back to the early 10th century. The counts obtained the right to coin money in 1393. During the Reformation, Öttingen was divided into the Protestant Öttingen-Öttingen and the Catholic Öttingen-Wallerstein lines of counts. Öttingen-Öttingen gained the rank of prince in 1674, but became extinct in 1731 and was divided between Öttingen-Wallerstein-Spielberg and Öttingen-Wallerstein-Wallerstein. In 1602 Öttingen-Wallerstein was split into 3 lines: Öttingen-Wallerstein-Spielberg (prince in 1734, mediatized in the early 19th century), Öttingen-Wallerstein-Wallerstein (prince in 1774, mediatized in the early 19th century) and Öttingen-Wallerstein-Katzenstein, which became extinct in 1798. Only 3 lines actually struck coins during the 16th to 19th centuries.

OTTINGEN-OTTINGEN

This line of Öttingen counts was founded as the Protestant branch in 1557 during the Reformation. The count was granted the rank of prince in 1674. When it became extinct in 1731, its holdings were divided between Öttingen-Wallerstein-Spielberg and Öttingen-Wallerstein-Wallerstein.

RULERS

Gottfried, 1569-1622
Ludwig Eberhard, 1622-1634
Joachim Ernst, 1634-1659

Kraft Ludwig, 1659-1660
Albrecht Ernst I, 1660-1683
Albrecht Ernst II, 1683-1731

MINT OFFICIALS' INITIALS

Initial	Date	Name
CM, ICM	1670-95	Johann Christoph Müller, die-cutter in Stuttgart
GS, S		

COUNTSHIP

REGULAR COINAGE

KM# 26 PFENNIG

Silver **Ruler:** Ludwig Eberhard **Obv:** Two conjoined shields of arms, LEG above, O below **Note:** Uniface.

Date	Mintage	VG	F	VF	XF	Unc
ND(ca.1625)	—	13.00	27.00	55.00	90.00	—

KM# 5 3 PFENNIG (Dreier)

Silver **Ruler:** Gottfried **Obv:** Arms of Ottingen, date above, titles of Gottfried **Rev:** Imperial eagle, 3 in orb on breast, titles of Ferdinand II

Date	Mintage	VG	F	VF	XF	Unc
1622 Rare	—	—	—	—	—	—

KM# 10 KREUZER

Silver **Ruler:** Ludwig Eberhard **Obv:** Arms divide Z-O, arms with LEG above **Rev:** Imperial orb with value I divdes date **Note:** Varieties exist.

Date	Mintage	VG	F	VF	XF	Unc
1623	—	27.00	60.00	120	185	—
1624	—	27.00	60.00	120	185	—
1625	—	27.00	60.00	120	185	—

KM# 27 KREUZER

Silver **Ruler:** Ludwig Eberhard **Obv:** Oval arms, LEGZO above **Rev:** Value I between two stars, KREYZ/ER* in two line below **Note:** Varieties exist.

Date	Mintage	VG	F	VF	XF	Unc
ND(ca.1625)	—	27.00	55.00	90.00	145	—

KM# 6 2 KREUZER (1/2 Batzen)

Silver **Ruler:** Gottfried **Obv:** Öttingen arms in ornamented shield, titles of Gottfried **Rev:** Imperial eagle with Z in orb on breast, titles of Ferdinand II

Date	Mintage	VG	F	VF	XF	Unc
ND(ca.1622/3)	—	—	—	—	—	—

KM# 11 2 KREUZER (1/2 Batzen)

Silver **Ruler:** Ludwig Eberhard **Obv:** Oval arms divide date, titles of Ludwig Eberhard **Rev:** Imperial orb with value 2, titles of Ferdinand II **Note:** Varieties exist.

Date	Mintage	VG	F	VF	XF	Unc
(16)23	—	65.00	135	225	375	—

KM# 12 2 KREUZER (1/2 Batzen)

Silver **Ruler:** Ludwig Eberhard **Obv:** Large X within ornate shield **Rev:** Date divided by cross on orb **Note:** Varieties exist.

Date	Mintage	VG	F	VF	XF	Unc
(16)23	—	20.00	40.00	80.00	140	—
(16)24	—	20.00	40.00	80.00	140	—
(16)25	—	20.00	40.00	80.00	140	—
(16)26	—	20.00	40.00	80.00	140	—

KM# 22 2 KREUZER (1/2 Batzen)

Silver **Ruler:** Ludwig Eberhard **Note:** Klippe. Similar to KM#12 but struck on square flan.

Date	Mintage	VG	F	VF	XF	Unc
(16)24 Rare	—	—	—	—	—	—

KM# 15 3 KREUZER (1 Groschen)

Silver **Ruler:** Ludwig Eberhard **Rev:** Full date above arms

Date	Mintage	VG	F	VF	XF	Unc
1623	—	27.00	60.00	120	175	—

KM# 13 3 KREUZER (1 Groschen)

Silver **Ruler:** Ludwig Eberhard **Obv:** Oval arms in ornamental frame, titles of Ludwig Eberhard **Rev:** Imperial orb with 3 divides date, titles of Ferdinand II **Note:** Varieties exist.

Date	Mintage	VG	F	VF	XF	Unc
(16)23	—	27.00	60.00	120	175	—

KM# 14 3 KREUZER (1 Groschen)

Silver **Ruler:** Ludwig Eberhard **Rev:** Date divided by arms **Note:** Varieties exist.

Date	Mintage	VG	F	VF	XF	Unc
(16)23	—	27.00	60.00	120	175	—

KM# 35 3 KREUZER (1 Groschen)

Silver **Ruler:** Albrecht Ernst I **Obv:** Bust right **Rev:** Crowned arms between two laurel branches, legend, date **Rev. Legend:** DOMINVS PR (3) VIDEBIT

Date	Mintage	VG	F	VF	XF	Unc
1673	—	100	200	375	600	—

KM# 28 4 KREUZER (1 Batzen)

Silver **Ruler:** Ludwig Eberhard **Obv:** Ornate Ottingen arms; value ? 1 ? 1 ? 1 ? 1 ? above **Rev:** Crowned imperial eagle, date divided by crown at top, titles of Ferdinand II

Date	Mintage	VG	F	VF	XF	Unc
(16)25	—	135	225	400	675	—

KM# 36 12 KREUZER (Zwolfer)

Silver **Ruler:** Albrecht Ernst I **Obv:** Crowned arms between two laurel branches **Obv. Legend:** +ALBERTVS ERNESTVS COMES OTTINGENSIS **Rev:** Hound's head left, value (XII) in margin at bottom, date at end of legend **Rev. Legend:** DOMINVS PRO - VIDEBIT

Date	Mintage	VG	F	VF	XF	Unc
1673	—	60.00	120	200	325	—

KM# 7 24 KREUZER (6 Batzen)

Silver **Ruler:** Gottfried **Obv:** Arms surmounted by dog's head left which divides date, titles of Gottfried **Rev:** Crowned imperial eagle, 24 in orb on breast, titles of Ferdinand II

Date	Mintage	VG	F	VF	XF	Unc
1622 Rare	—	—	—	—	—	—

KM# 8 24 KREUZER (6 Batzen)

Silver **Ruler:** Gottfried **Rev:** Dog's head right

Date	Mintage	VG	F	VF	XF	Unc
1622 Rare	—	—	—	—	—	—

KM# 9 24 KREUZER (6 Batzen)

Silver **Ruler:** Gottfried **Rev:** Two conjoined shield of arms, dog's head, date above, titles of Gottfried **Note:** Varieties exist.

Date	Mintage	VG	F	VF	XF	Unc
1622	—	375	625	1,075	1,650	—

KM# 16 30 KREUZER (1/2 Guldenthaler)

Silver **Ruler:** Gottfried **Obv:** Arms of Ottingen, crowned angel's head above, titles of Gottfried **Rev:** Crowned imperial eagle, 30 in shield on breast, titles of Ferdinand II

Date	Mintage	VG	F	VF	XF	Unc
ND(ca.1620) Rare	—	—	—	—	—	—

KM# 17 30 KREUZER (1/2 Gulden)

Silver **Ruler:** Ludwig Eberhard **Obv:** Titles of Ludwig Eberhard

Date	Mintage	VG	F	VF	XF	Unc
1623 Rare	—	—	—	—	—	—

KM# 19 60 KREUZER (Gulden)

Silver **Ruler:** Ludwig Eberhard **Obv:** Ottingen arms divide date, titles of Ludwig Eberhard

Date	Mintage	VG	F	VF	XF	Unc
1623 Rare	—	—	—	—	—	—

KM# 37 60 KREUZER (Gulden)

Silver **Ruler:** Albrecht Ernst I **Obv:** Bust right within circle **Obv. Legend:** ALBERTVS ERNESTVS COMES OTTINGENSIS **Rev:** Crowned arms between two laurel branches, value (60) below in margin, date at end of legend **Rev. Legend:** DOMINVS: PRO - VIDEBIT

Date	Mintage	VG	F	VF	XF	Unc
1673	—	625	1,075	1,650	2,350	—

KM# 39 60 KREUZER (Gulden)

Silver **Ruler:** Albrecht Ernst I **Obv:** Bust to right **Obv. Legend:** ALBERTVS • ERNESTVS • COMES • OTTINGENSIS **Rev:** Crowned oval arms in baroque frame, value (60) divides date below **Rev. Legend:** DOMINVS - PROVIDEBIT **Note:** Varieties exist.

Date	Mintage	VG	F	VF	XF	Unc
1674	—	225	525	850	1,150	—
1674 S	—	225	525	850	1,150	—

KM# 29 1/9 THALER

Silver **Ruler:** Ludwig Eberhard **Obv:** Arms, date above **Rev:** Crowned imperial eagle, value 1/9 on breast, titles of Ferdinand II

Date	Mintage	VG	F	VF	XF	Unc
1629 Rare	—	—	—	—	—	—

KM# 23 1/6 THALER

Silver **Ruler:** Ludwig Eberhard **Obv:** Öttingen arms with angel's head above, date divided **Rev:** Crowned imperial eagle, 1/6 in cirlce on breast, titles of Ferdinand II

Date	Mintage	VG	F	VF	XF	Unc
1624 Rare	—	—	—	—	—	—

KM# 24 1/4 THALER

Silver **Ruler:** Ludwig Eberhard **Obv:** Shield of arms with ornate helmet above, dog's head crest divides date **Rev:** Crowned imperial eagle, value 1/4 in orb on breast, titles of Ferdinand II

Date	Mintage	VG	F	VF	XF	Unc
1624 Rare	—	—	—	—	—	—

KM# 41 1/3 THALER (1/2 Gulden)

Silver **Ruler:** Albrecht Ernst I **Obv:** Bust right **Obv. Legend:** ALBERTVS • ERNESTVS • COMES • OTTINGENSIS **Rev:** Crowned arms between two laurel branches, value (1/3) at bottom divides date **Rev. Legend:** DOMINVS • PROVIDEBIT

Date	Mintage	VG	F	VF	XF	Unc
1674	—	—	—	—	—	—

KM# 42 1/3 THALER (1/2 Gulden)

Silver **Ruler:** Albrecht Ernst I **Obv:** Bust to right **Obv. Legend:** ALBERTVS• ERNESTVS • COMES • OTTINGENSIS **Rev:** Crowned oval arms in baroque frame, value (1/3) divides date below **Rev. Legend:** DOMINVS • PROVIDEBIT

Date	Mintage	VG	F	VF	XF	Unc
1674 CM	—	—	—	—	—	—

KM# 43 2/3 THALER (Gulden)

Silver **Ruler:** Albrecht Ernst I **Obv:** Bust to right **Obv. Legend:** ALBERTVS • ERNESTVS • COMES • OTTINGENSIS **Rev:** Crowned arms in laurel wreath, date divided by value (2/3) below **Rev. Legend:** DOMINVS • PROVIDEBIT **Note:** Varieties exist.

Date	Mintage	VG	F	VF	XF	Unc
1674	—	165	300	450	850	—

KM# 44 2/3 THALER (Gulden)

Silver **Ruler:** Albrecht Ernst I **Obv:** Bust to right **Obv. Legend:** ALBERTVS•ERNESTVS•COMES•OTTINGENSIS **Rev:** Value 2/3 punched over 60 **Rev. Legend:** DOMINVS • PROVIDEBIT

Date	Mintage	VG	F	VF	XF	Unc
1674 ICM	—	—	—	—	—	—

KM# 20 THALER
Silver **Ruler:** Ludwig Eberhard **Obv:** Shield of arms with ornate helmet above, dog's head crest divides date **Obv. Legend:** * LUDWIG * EBERHARD * COMES * OTING * **Rev:** Crowned imperial eagle **Rev. Legend:** FERDINANDVS • II • ROM • IMP • SE(M)(P) • AVG(VS) **Note:** Dav. #7136.

Date	Mintage	VG	F	VF	XF	Unc
1623	—	85.00	175	350	600	—
1624	—	85.00	175	350	600	—
1625	—	85.00	175	350	600	—

KM# 21 THALER
Silver **Ruler:** Ludwig Eberhard **Obv:** Shield of arms with ornate helmet above, dog's head crest divides date **Obv. Legend:** * LVDWIG * EBERHART * COMES * OTING * **Rev:** Crowned imperial eagle **Rev. Legend:** FERDINANDVS • II • ROM • IMP • SE(M)(P) • AVG(VS) **Note:** Dav. #7136A.

Date	Mintage	VG	F	VF	XF	Unc
1623	—	85.00	175	350	600	—

KM# 25 THALER
Silver **Ruler:** Ludwig Eberhard **Obv:** St. Michael with sword and shield standing on dragon, L • E • G • Z • Ö at left, date at right **Obv. Legend:** DA PACEM DOMINE IN DIEBVS NOSTRIS **Rev:** Crowned imperial eagle **Rev. Legend:** FERDINANDVS • II • ROM • IMP • SEM • AVGVS **Note:** Dav. #7137.

Date	Mintage	VG	F	VF	XF	Unc
1624	—	1,000	1,850	3,500	6,000	—
1625	—	1,000	1,850	3,500	6,000	—

PRINCIPALITY

REGULAR COINAGE

KM# 65 PFENNIG
Silver **Ruler:** Albrecht Ernst II **Obv:** Crown above script monogram AE, date around crown

Date	Mintage	VG	F	VF	XF	Unc
1690	—	—	—	—	—	—

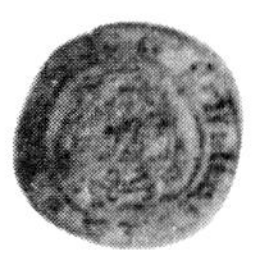

KM# 60 KREUZER
Silver **Ruler:** Albrecht Ernst I **Obv:** Crowned oval shield of arms in baroque frame **Rev:** Cross in circle, date in legend **Rev. Legend:** FVRST: OTTING: KREVTZER

Date	Mintage	VG	F	VF	XF	Unc
1680	—	40.00	75.00	125	200	—

KM# 61 2 KREUZER (1/2 Batzen)
Silver **Ruler:** Albrecht Ernst I **Obv:** Crowned arms **Rev:** Imperial orb with value 2 divides date **Note:** Varieties exist.

Date	Mintage	VG	F	VF	XF	Unc
1680	—	45.00	80.00	140	220	—

KM# 58 3 KREUZER (1 Groschen)
Silver **Ruler:** Albrecht Ernst I **Obv:** Bust to right **Obv. Legend:** ALBERT, ERNEST, D:G. PRINC. OTTING **Rev:** Crowned oval shield of arms in baroque frame, value (3) divides date below **Rev. Legend:** DOMINVS - PROVIDEBIT

Date	Mintage	VG	F	VF	XF	Unc
1675	—	45.00	100	165	300	—

KM# 48 4 KREUZER (1 Batzen)
Silver **Ruler:** Albrecht Ernst I **Obv:** Bust right in circle **Obv. Legend:** ALBERT, ERNEST, D:G. PRINCEPS OTTING **Rev:** Crowned oval arms in baroque frame, value (6) divides date below **Rev. Legend:** DOMINVS - PROVIDEB **Note:** Varieties exist.

Date	Mintage	VG	F	VF	XF	Unc
1675	—	25.00	45.00	100	165	—
1676	—	25.00	45.00	100	165	—
1677	—	25.00	45.00	100	165	—
1678	—	25.00	45.00	100	165	—

KM# 38 30 KREUZER (1/2 Gulden)
Silver **Ruler:** Albrecht Ernst I **Obv:** Bust right **Obv. Legend:** ALBERT, ERNEST, D.G. PRINCEPS. OTTING. **Rev:** Crowned oval arms in baroque frame, value (30) divides date below **Rev. Legend:** PROVIDEBIT - DOMINUS

Date	Mintage	VG	F	VF	XF	Unc
1674	—	55.00	120	200	300	—
1675	—	55.00	120	200	300	—

KM# 18 60 KREUZER (Gulden)
Silver **Ruler:** Gottfried **Obv:** Ottingen arms divide date, titles of Gottfried **Rev:** Crowned imperial eagle, 60 in orb on breast, titles of Ferdinand II **Note:** Dav. #102.

Date	Mintage	VG	F	VF	XF	Unc
1623 Rare; posthumous	—	—	—	—	—	—

KM# 40 60 KREUZER (Gulden)
Silver **Ruler:** Albrecht Ernst I **Obv:** Bust to right **Obv. Legend:** ALBERT, ERNEST, PRINCEPS. OTTING. **Rev:** Crowned oval arms in baroque frame, value (60) divides date below **Rev. Legend:** DOMINUS - PROVIDEBIT **Note:** Varieties exist.

Date	Mintage	VG	F	VF	XF	Unc
1674	—	60.00	120	185	275	—
1674 S	—	60.00	120	185	275	—
1674 GS	—	60.00	120	185	275	—
1675	—	60.00	120	185	275	—
1676	—	60.00	120	185	275	—
1677	—	60.00	120	185	275	—
1678	—	60.00	120	185	275	—

KM# A39 60 KREUZER (Gulden)
19.4600 g., Silver **Ruler:** Albrecht Ernst I **Obv:** Bust right **Obv. Legend:** ALBERTVS ERNSTVS COMES OTTINGENSIS **Rev:** Crowned squarish arms in sprays, legend above **Rev. Legend:** DOMINVS PROVIDEBIT

Date	Mintage	Good	VG	F	VF	XF
1674	—	27.00	60.00	120	200	—

KM# 49 60 KREUZER (Gulden)
Silver **Ruler:** Albrecht Ernst I **Obv:** Crowned AEO monogram divides date, value (60) in margin at bottom **Obv. Legend:** DOMINVS. PROVIDEBIT **Rev:** Hound walking left in circle **Rev. Legend:** VIGILANTIA ET FIDELITATE **Note:** Varieties exist. L-321-3; Dav. #737.

Date	Mintage	VG	F	VF	XF	Unc
1675	—	225	375	600	800	—

KM# 70 1/4 THALER
Silver **Ruler:** Albrecht Ernst II **Subject:** Death of Eberhardine Sophie, Wife of Christian Eberhard, Prince of Ostfriesland **Obv:** Vintner cutting heavily-laden vine **Rev:** Seven-line inscription with date, death's head below

Date	Mintage	VG	F	VF	XF	Unc
1700 Rare	—	—	—	—	—	—

KM# 50 THALER
Silver **Ruler:** Albrecht Ernst I **Subject:** Albert Ernst I raised to rank of Prince **Obv:** Bust right in circle, legend contains date in chronogram **Obv. Legend:** ALBERTVS • ERNESTVS • FAVENTE • DEI • GRATIA • PRIMVS • ÖTTING: PRINCEPS A **Rev:** Crowned oval shield of arms in baroque frame, legend contains date in chronogram **Rev. Legend:** NVMEN • UNICA • IN TERRIS • SALVS • PROVIDEBIT **Note:** Dav. #7138.

Date	Mintage	VG	F	VF	XF	Unc
1675	—	1,300	2,400	4,000	6,000	—

KM# 52 THALER
Silver **Ruler:** Albrecht Ernst I **Obv:** Bust right **Obv. Legend:** ALBERT • ERNEST • D: G: PRINCEPS • OTTINGEN **Rev:** Crowned shield of arms divides date **Rev. Legend:** FVRSTLICH: OTTING: REICHSTHALER **Note:** Dav. #7139.

Date	Mintage	VG	F	VF	XF	Unc
1677	—	1,400	2,500	4,200	6,500	—

KM# 62 THALER
Silver **Ruler:** Albrecht Ernst I **Obv:** Bust to right in circle **Obv. Legend:** ALBERT 9 ERNEST 9 D: G: PRINCEPTS • OTTINGEN **Rev:** Crowned shield of oval arms in baroque frame, date divided at top **Rev. Legend:** FVRSTLICH: OTTING: REICHSTAHALER **Note:** Dav. #7140.

Date	Mintage	VG	F	VF	XF	Unc
1680	—	1,300	2,400	4,000	6,000	—

TRADE COINAGE

KM# 45 1/4 DUCAT
0.8750 g., 0.9860 Gold 0.0277 oz. AGW **Ruler:** Albrecht Ernst I **Subject:** Attaining the Rank of Prince **Obv:** Crowned oval arms **Rev:** Allegorical figure standing by altar, arm from clouds with crown

Date	Mintage	VG	F	VF	XF	Unc
ND(1674) Rare	—	—	—	—	—	—

KM# 46 1/4 DUCAT
0.8750 g., 0.9860 Gold 0.0277 oz. AGW **Ruler:** Albrecht Ernst I **Obv:** AE monogram **Rev:** Shield of arms **Note:** Fr. #1955.

Date	Mintage	VG	F	VF	XF	Unc
ND PGN	—	425	900	1,800	3,000	—

KM# 47 1/2 DUCAT
1.7500 g., 0.9860 Gold 0.0555 oz. AGW **Ruler:** Albrecht Ernst I **Obv:** AE monogram **Rev:** Crowned and mantled arms **Note:** Klippe. Fr. #1954.

Date	Mintage	VG	F	VF	XF	Unc
ND	—	725	1,500	3,000	4,800	—

KM# 51 DUCAT
3.5000 g., 0.9860 Gold 0.1109 oz. AGW **Ruler:** Albrecht Ernst I **Obv:** Bust to right **Rev:** Shield of arms **Note:** Fr. #1952.

Date	Mintage	VG	F	VF	XF	Unc
1675	—	1,600	3,300	6,000	9,600	—

KM# 53 DUCAT
3.5000 g., 0.9860 Gold 0.1109 oz. AGW **Ruler:** Albrecht Ernst I **Obv:** Bust to right **Rev:** Five-line inscription with date above arms **Note:** Fr. #1953.

Date	Mintage	VG	F	VF	XF	Unc
1677	—	3,750	5,300	9,000	14,500	—

KM# 55 DUCAT
3.5000 g., 0.9860 Gold 0.1109 oz. AGW **Ruler:** Albrecht Ernst I **Subject:** Peace of Nimwegen **Obv:** Cannon firing right, clouds above **Rev:** Nine-line inscription with date in chronogram

Date	Mintage	VG	F	VF	XF	Unc
1679 Rare	—	—	—	—	—	—

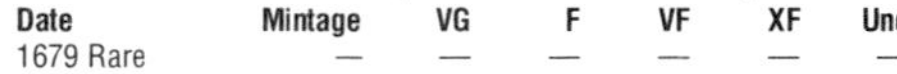

KM# 56 DUCAT
3.5000 g., 0.9860 Gold 0.1109 oz. AGW **Ruler:** Albrecht Ernst II **Obv:** Armored bust to right **Rev:** Crowned and mantled arms **Note:** Fr. #1956.

Date	Mintage	VG	F	VF	XF	Unc
ND	—	1,900	3,750	6,800	10,500	—

KM# 54 2 DUCAT
7.0000 g., 0.9860 Gold 0.2219 oz. AGW **Ruler:** Albrecht Ernst I **Obv:** Bust to right **Rev:** Shield of arms **Note:** Fr. #1951.

Date	Mintage	VG	F	VF	XF	Unc
1677 Rare	—	—	—	—	—	—

KM# 57 2 DUCAT
7.0000 g., 0.9860 Gold 0.2219 oz. AGW **Ruler:** Albrecht Ernst I **Subject:** Peace of Nimwegen **Obv:** Allegorical figure **Rev:** Ten-line inscription with Roman numeral date

Date	Mintage	VG	F	VF	XF	Unc
1679 Rare	—	—	—	—	—	—

PATTERNS

Including off metal strikes

KM#	Date	Mintage	Identification	Mkt Val
Pn1	ND	—	Ducat. Silver. KM#56	—

OTTINGEN-WALLERSTEIN-WALLERSTEIN

Founded upon the 1602 division of Öttingen-Wallerstein, this line of counts became princes in 1774. Their territories were mediatized in the early 19th century.

RULERS
Ernst II, 1602-1670
Wilhelm IV, 1670-1692 and
Philipp, 1670-1680
Wolfgang IV, 1692-1708 and
Ignaz, 1692-1723

MINT OFFICIALS' INITIALS

Initial	Date	Name
(h)= 2 horseshoes	1668-97	Johann Christoph Holeisen in Augsburg

COUNTSHIP

REGULAR COINAGE

KM# 5 2 KREUZER (1/2 Batzen)
Silver **Obv:** Arms in ornamented frame **Rev:** Imperial orb with value 2, date in legend **Mint:** Augsburg **Note:** Struck at Augsburg Mint.

Date	Mintage	VG	F	VF	XF	Unc
1694 (h)	—	100	200	400	600	—

KM# 6 4 KREUZER (1 Batzen)
Silver **Obv:** Crowned arms **Rev:** Crowned imperial eagle, 4 in heart-shaped shield on breast, date in legend **Mint:** Augsburg

Date	Mintage	VG	F	VF	XF	Unc
1694 (h)	—	125	250	450	700	—

KM# 7 THALER
Silver **Obv:** Crowned imperial eagle, LI in heart-shaped shield on breast, date in legend above, 90 in frame below **Rev:** Crowned and supported arms **Mint:** Augsburg **Note:** Dav. #7141.

Date	Mintage	F	VF	XF	Unc	BU
1694	—	1,200	2,000	3,200	4,500	—

KM# 8 THALER
Silver **Obv:** Hand from heaven watering flowers **Rev:** Helmeted arms **Mint:** Augsburg **Note:** Dav. #7142.

Date	Mintage	F	VF	XF	Unc	BU
1694	—	450	850	1,650	2,750	—

KM# 9 THALER
Silver **Obv:** Helmeted arms **Rev:** Crowned imperial eagle with LI in heart on breast **Mint:** Augsburg **Note:** Dav. #7143.

Date	Mintage	F	VF	XF	Unc	BU
1694	—	950	1,600	2,500	3,500	—

PADERBORN

One of the principal cities of Westphalia and the seat of a bishopric from its founding by Charlemagne in 795, Paderborn is situated 23 miles (38 kilometers) south-southeast of Bielefeld and about 50 miles (80 kilometers) southeast of Münster. The bishop received the right to strike coins in 1028 and was raised to the rank of Prince of the Empire in about 1100. By the late 12th to early 13th century, the bishops were employing nine different mints in their territories. In 1802, the bishopric was secularized and its domains, as well as the city of Paderborn, were annexed to Prussia. The former bishopric was part of the Kingdom of Westphalia from 1807 to 1813, after which it was returned to Prussia. In addition to the episcopal coinage, the cathedral chapter issued a series of coins in the early 17th century and during the several interregnal years.

The town, and later city, of Paderborn grew up around the cathedral and became a member of the Hanseatic League, but failed to obtain the mint right. Eventually, the townspeople converted to Protestantism and found themselves in opposition to the Catholic bishop. The bishop prevailed and had a series of coins struck for the city in 1605. Paderborn also issued a local coinage during the early period of the Thirty Years' War.

RULERS
Theodor von Fürstenberg, 1585-1618
Ferdinand I, Herzog von Bayern, 1618-50
Theodor Adolf von der Recke, 1650-1661
Ferdinand II von Fürstenberg, 1661-1683
Hermann Werner, Wolff-Metternich zu Gracht,1683-1704

MINT OFFICIALS' INITIALS

Initial	Date	Name
(a)=	1611-	Jacob Pfaler
(b)=	ca. 1616-17	Unknown
(c)=	1652-54, 75-76	Jost Dietrich Koch
(d)= or IDK		
PL	1655-58	Peter Löhr

BISHOPRIC

REGULAR COINAGE

C# A4 PFENNIG
Copper **Obv:** Oval shield in cartouche **Rev:** Denomination in ornamented oval

Date	Mintage	VG	F	VF	XF	Unc
1693	—	8.00	20.00	33.00	65.00	—

DAV# 5675 THALER
Silver **Obv:** Crowned imperial eagle divides date **Rev:** Arms, titles of Theodor

Date	Mintage	VG	F	VF	XF	Unc
1611 Rare	—	—	—	—	—	—

DAV# 5677 THALER
Silver **Obv:** Facing bust of Theodorich **Rev:** Helmeted arms with date divided below

Date	Mintage	VG	F	VF	XF	Unc
1612 Rare	—	—	—	—	—	—

DAV# 5680 THALER
Silver **Obv:** Crowned imperial eagle, orb on breast, date divided 1-6-1-8 **Rev:** Helmeted arms

Date	Mintage	VG	F	VF	XF	Unc
1618 Rare	—	—	—	—	—	—

DAV# 5681 THALER
Silver **Obv:** Crowned imperial eagle with orb **Rev:** Helmeted arms, date in legend

Date	Mintage	VG	F	VF	XF	Unc
1618 Rare	—	—	—	—	—	—

DAV# 5680a THALER
Silver **Note:** Klippe.

Date	Mintage	VG	F	VF	XF	Unc
1618 Rare	—	—	—	—	—	—

DAV# 5684 THALER
Silver **Obv:** Bust right **Obv. Legend:** ...ELE. ADM. HIL. EPI. PADERB. **Rev:** Crowned arms, date in legend

Date	Mintage	VG	F	VF	XF	Unc
1620 Rare	—	—	—	—	—	—

DAV# 5685 THALER
Silver **Obv. Legend:** ...EPI. PAD. ET. ADM. HILD.

Date	Mintage	VG	F	VF	XF	Unc
1620 Rare	—	—	—	—	—	—

DAV# 5686 THALER
Silver **Obv:** Crowned arms, date in legend **Rev:** St. Liborius standing facing divides S-L

Date	Mintage	VG	F	VF	XF	Unc
1620 Rare	—	—	—	—	—	—

DAV# 5688 THALER
Silver **Rev:** St. Liborius standing divides SANCTVS-LIBORIVS

Date	Mintage	VG	F	VF	XF	Unc
1620 Rare	—	—	—	—	—	—

DAV# 5689 THALER
Silver **Obv:** Crowned arms **Rev:** St. Liborius standing divides SANCTVS-LIBORIVS

Date	Mintage	VG	F	VF	XF	Unc
1620 Rare	—	—	—	—	—	—

DAV# 5690 THALER
Silver **Obv:** Bust of Theodor Adolf right **Rev:** Mitred and helmeted arms

Date	Mintage	VG	F	VF	XF	Unc
1654 Rare	—	—	—	—	—	—

DAV# 5692 THALER
Silver **Obv:** Facing bust of Theodor Adolf **Obv. Legend:** Ends: PIRMON **Rev:** Arms divide P-L, legend, date **Rev. Legend:** FORTITER * RECTE * PIE * AO •

Date	Mintage	VG	F	VF	XF	Unc
1656	—	750	1,500	3,250	5,500	—

DAV# 5693 THALER
Silver **Obv. Legend:** Ends: PYRMO **Rev:** Legend without *, ANO:1.6.57.

Date	Mintage	VG	F	VF	XF	Unc
1657	—	900	1,850	4,000	6,500	—

DAV# 5694 THALER
Silver **Obv:** Similar to Dav. #5692 **Rev:** Mitred and helmeted arms divide date at bottom

Date	Mintage	VG	F	VF	XF	Unc
1659	—	1,000	2,000	4,250	7,000	—

DAV# 5696 THALER
Silver **Rev:** Standing saint holding church, stag at left

Date	Mintage	VG	F	VF	XF	Unc
1663	—	350	750	1,650	2,750	—

DAV# 5698 THALER
Silver

Date	Mintage	VG	F	VF	XF	Unc
MDCLXIIII (1663) Rare	—	—	—	—	—	—

DAV# 5699 THALER
Silver **Obv:** Helmeted arms with center shield **Rev:** 9-line inscription

Date	Mintage	VG	F	VF	XF	Unc
MDCLXVIII (1668)	—	400	900	1,850	3,500	—

DAV# 5700 THALER
Silver **Obv:** Larger 4-part arms without centre shield **Obv. Legend:** ...S • R • I • PRINC • COM • PYRM •

Date	Mintage	VG	F	VF	XF	Unc
MDCLXVIII (1668)	—	400	900	1,850	3,500	—

DAV# 5699A THALER
Silver **Note:** Klippe.

Date	Mintage	VG	F	VF	XF	Unc
1668 Rare	—	—	—	—	—	—

DAV# 5701 THALER
Silver **Obv:** Facing bust of Ferdinand **Rev:** Helmeted arms, date in legend

Date	Mintage	VG	F	VF	XF	Unc
1671 Rare	—	—	—	—	—	—

DAV# 5702 THALER
Silver **Rev:** Helmeted arms divide date at bottom

Date	Mintage	VG	F	VF	XF	Unc
1671 Rare	—	—	—	—	—	—

DAV# 5704 THALER
Silver

Date	Mintage	VG	F	VF	XF	Unc
1676	—	1,000	1,750	3,000	5,000	—

DAV# 5707 THALER
Silver **Subject:** Herman Werner

Date	Mintage	VG	F	VF	XF	Unc
1683 Rare	—	—	—	—	—	—

DAV# 5706 THALER
Silver **Obv:** Saint **Rev:** Charlemagne **Note:** Sede vacante.

Date	Mintage	VG	F	VF	XF	Unc
1683	—	300	700	1,500	2,750	—

DAV# 5709 THALER
Silver **Rev:** Helmeted arms divide date

Date	Mintage	VG	F	VF	XF	Unc
1684	—	750	1,250	2,500	4,500	—

DAV# 5710 THALER
Silver **Obv:** St. Anthony of Padua holding Christ child, Mary at right

Date	Mintage	VG	F	VF	XF	Unc
1685	—	235	475	875	1,500	—
1687	—	235	475	875	1,500	—
1693	—	270	550	1,000	1,700	—

DAV# 5712 THALER

Silver

Date	Mintage	VG	F	VF	XF	Unc
1693	—	650	1,200	1,650	3,000	—

DAV# 5713 THALER

Silver **Obv:** Bust with ornamented cape **Rev:** Large arms

Date	Mintage	VG	F	VF	XF	Unc
1694	—	400	800	1,500	2,500	—

DAV# 5713A THALER

Silver **Obv:** Short collar **Rev:** Punctuated date

Date	Mintage	VG	F	VF	XF	Unc
1694	—	450	900	1,750	3,500	—

DAV# 5676 2 THALER

Silver **Obv:** Facing bust of Theodor **Rev:** Helmeted arms, date divided below

Date	Mintage	VG	F	VF	XF	Unc
1612 Rare	—	—	—	—	—	—

DAV# 5678 2 THALER

Silver **Obv:** Helmeted arms **Obv. Legend:** TH-EODO • A • FVRSTENB • D • G • EC • C • PAD • EPIS **Rev:** Crowned imperial eagle **Rev. Legend:** MA • TIAS • I • D • G • ROMA • IMP • E • SEM • AV •

Date	Mintage	VG	F	VF	XF	Unc
1615 Rare	—	—	—	—	—	—

DAV# 5679 2 THALER

Silver **Obv. Legend:** THEODO • A • FVRSTENBERG • D • G • EPIS... **Rev. Legend:** RO: IMPER: SEMPER • AVGVST •

Date	Mintage	VG	F	VF	XF	Unc
1618 Rare	—	—	—	—	—	—

DAV# 5682 2 THALER

Silver **Subject:** Death of Theodor **Obv:** Helmeted arms **Rev:** 7-line inscription

Date	Mintage	VG	F	VF	XF	Unc
MDCXIIX (1618) Rare	—	—	—	—	—	—

DAV# 5683 2 THALER

Silver **Obv:** Bust of Ferdinand right **Rev:** Crowned arms

Date	Mintage	VG	F	VF	XF	Unc
1620 Rare	—	—	—	—	—	—

DAV# A5687 2 THALER

Silver **Obv:** Standing saint dividing SANCTVS-LIBORIVS **Rev:** Crowned arms

Date	Mintage	VG	F	VF	XF	Unc
1620 Rare	—	—	—	—	—	—

DAV# A5689 2 THALER

Silver **Obv:** Crowned arms **Rev:** Standing saint dividing SANCTVS-LIBORIVS **Note:** Dav. #5689.

Date	Mintage	VG	F	VF	XF	Unc
1621 Rare	—	—	—	—	—	—

DAV# 5691 2 THALER

Silver **Note:** Similar to 1 Thaler, Dav. #5692.

Date	Mintage	VG	F	VF	XF	Unc
1656 PL	—	1,000	2,000	3,500	6,000	—

DAV# 5695 2 THALER

Silver **Note:** Similar to 1 Thaler, Dav. #5696.

Date	Mintage	VG	F	VF	XF	Unc
1663	—	900	1,650	3,250	5,500	—

DAV# 5697 2 THALER

Silver **Note:** Similar to 1 Thaler, Dav. #5698.

Date	Mintage	VG	F	VF	XF	Unc
MDCLXIII (1663) Rare	—	—	—	—	—	—

DAV# A5701 2 THALER

Silver **Obv:** Facing bust of Ferdinand **Rev:** Helmeted arms, date in legend

Date	Mintage	VG	F	VF	XF	Unc
1671 Rare	—	—	—	—	—	—

DAV# 5703 2 THALER

Silver

Date	Mintage	VG	F	VF	XF	Unc
1676 IDK	—	1,200	2,250	4,000	7,000	—

DAV# 5705 2 THALER

Silver **Note:** Similar to 1 Thaler, Dav. #5706.

Date	Mintage	VG	F	VF	XF	Unc
1683	—	900	1,650	3,250	5,500	—

DAV# 5708 2 THALER

Silver **Note:** Similar to 1 Thaler, Dav. #5709.

Date	Mintage	VG	F	VF	XF	Unc
1684 Rare	—	—	—	—	—	—

DAV# 5711 2 THALER

Silver **Note:** Similar to 1 Thaler, Dav. #5712.

Date	Mintage	VG	F	VF	XF	Unc
1693 Rare	—	—	—	—	—	—

DAV# 5714 2 THALER

Silver

Date	Mintage	VG	F	VF	XF	Unc
1698 Rare	—	—	—	—	—	—

DAV# 5687 3 THALER

Silver **Obv:** St. Liborius standing facing between SANCTVS-LIBORIVS **Rev:** Arms, date in legend

Date	Mintage	VG	F	VF	XF	Unc
1620 Rare	—	—	—	—	—	—

TRADE COINAGE

FR# 1958 DUCAT

3.5000 g., 0.9860 Gold 0.1109 oz. AGW **Obv:** Bust of Theodor Adolph in inner circle **Rev:** Arms in inner circle

Date	Mintage	VG	F	VF	XF	Unc
1651	—	1,350	2,800	5,600	9,800	—
1653	—	1,350	2,800	5,600	9,800	—

FR# 1960 DUCAT

3.5000 g., 0.9860 Gold 0.1109 oz. AGW **Obv:** Bust of Ferdinand II right in inner circle

Date	Mintage	VG	F	VF	XF	Unc
1674	—	1,050	2,050	4,150	7,500	—

FR# 1961 DUCAT

3.5000 g., 0.9860 Gold 0.1109 oz. AGW **Obv:** Bust of Herman Werner right in inner circle

Date	Mintage	VG	F	VF	XF	Unc
1684	—	850	1,750	3,500	6,000	—
1693	—	850	1,750	3,500	6,000	—

FR# 1959 6 DUCAT

21.0000 g., 0.9860 Gold 0.6657 oz. AGW **Obv:** Bust of Ferdinand II right **Rev:** Helmeted arms **Note:** Struck with 1 Thaler dies, Dav. #5704.

Date	Mintage	VG	F	VF	XF	Unc
1676 Rare	—	—	—	—	—	—

FR# 1960a 6 DUCAT

21.0000 g., 0.9860 Gold 0.6657 oz. AGW **Obv:** Bust of Herman Werner right **Rev:** Helmeted arms **Note:** Struck with 1 Thaler dies, Dav. #5709.

Date	Mintage	VG	F	VF	XF	Unc
1684 Rare	—	—	—	—	—	—

PASSAU

The Bishopric, in Bavaria, near the Austrian border, was established in 738. The bishops obtained the mint right prior to 999 but they originally struck coins jointly at the imperial mint in Passau. Ecclesiastical coinage began in the 12th century. In 1803, Passau was secularized and divided between Bavaria and Salzburg. In 1805 Bavaria absorbed the Salzburg portion.

RULERS

Leopold, Erzherzog von Österreich, 1598-1625
Leopold Wilhelm, Erzherzog von Österreich, 1625-1662
Karl Josef, Erzherzog von Österreich, 1662-1664
Wenzeslaus, Graf von Thun, 1664-1673
Sebastian, Graf von Pötting, 1673-1689
Johann Philipp, Graf von Lamberg, 1689-1712

ARMS

Springing or rampant wolf, usually 1 and w/arms of bishop's own family.

MINT OFFICIALS' INITIALS

Initial	Date	Name
	1622-32	Martin Schall in Gebweiler
	Ca. 1680	Friedrich Schattauer
(a)= Pinecone between 2 horseshoes	1668-97	Johann Christoph Holeisen in Augsburg
M*F or MF	1674-1700	Michael Federer, mintmaster and die-cutter in Regensburg
PHM or (b)= star	1677-1718	Philipp Heinrich Müller, die-cutter in Augsburg
SEIZ	Ca. 1688-1706	V. Seiz, die-cutter in Passau and Salzburg

BISHOPRIC

REGULAR COINAGE

KM# 1 KREUZER

Silver **Obv:** Bust right, titles of Sebastian **Rev:** 5-fold arms, date above

Date	Mintage	VG	F	VF	XF	Unc
1674	—	—	—	—	—	—

KM# 2 2 KREUZER

Silver **Obv:** Bust right, value '2' below, titles of Sebastian **Rev:** 5-fold arms, date above

Date	Mintage	VG	F	VF	XF	Unc
1674	—	—	—	—	—	—

KM# 3 2 KREUZER

Silver **Obv:** Passau arms divide date, value 2 below, titles of Johann Philipp **Rev:** Crowned 4-fold arms with central shield, titles continued

Date	Mintage	VG	F	VF	XF	Unc
1694	—	90.00	160	325	525	—
1699	—	90.00	160	325	525	—

KM# 5 3 KREUZER (Groschen)

21.0000 g., 0.9860 Gold 0.6657 oz. AGW **Obv:** 4-fold arms, titles of Sebastian **Rev:** St. Stephen standing behind Passau arms divides date, (3) below

Date	Mintage	VG	F	VF	XF	Unc
1682	—	—	—	—	—	—

KM# 7 6 KREUZER

Silver **Obv:** Bust right, (VI) below, titles of Sebastian **Rev:** Ornate 5-fold arms, date in margin at top

Date	Mintage	VG	F	VF	XF	Unc
1674	—	—	—	—	—	—

MB# 23 12 KREUZER

Silver **Obv:** Bust right, 12 in cartouche below, titles of Leopold **Rev:** 4-fold arms, 12 in cartouche below

Date	Mintage	VG	F	VF	XF	Unc
ND(1598-1625)	—	—	—	—	—	—

KM# 8 15 KREUZER (1/4 Gulden)

Silver **Obv:** Ornate 4-fold arms, titles of Sebastian **Rev:** St. Stephen standing behind Passau arms divides date, value (15) below

Date	Mintage	VG	F	VF	XF	Unc
1682	—	—	—	—	—	—

KM# 9 30 KREUZER (1/2 Reichsguildiner)

Silver **Obv:** Ornate 4-fold arms divides 'Kr', titles of Sebastian **Rev:** St. Stephen standing behind Passau arms divides date, value (30) below

Date	Mintage	VG	F	VF	XF	Unc
1682	—	550	1,000	1,800	3,000	—

KM# 11 60 KREUZER (Reichsguildiner)

Silver **Obv:** Bust right, date below, titles of Leopold **Rev:** Crowned 3-fold arms, titles continue

Date	Mintage	VG	F	VF	XF	Unc
1621	—	300	600	1,150	1,850	—

KM# 12 60 KREUZER (Reichsguildiner)

Silver **Obv:** Bust right, titles of Leopold **Rev:** Crowned 3-fold arms, titles continue

Date	Mintage	VG	F	VF	XF	Unc
ND(1623-25)	—	275	525	1,000	1,650	—

KM# 10 60 KREUZER (Reichsguildiner)

Silver **Obv:** Ornate 4-fold arms, value (60) below, titles of Sebastian **Rev:** St. Stephen standing behind Passau arms divides date

Date	Mintage	VG	F	VF	XF	Unc
1682	—	—	—	—	—	—

KM# 14 1/2 THALER

Silver **Obv:** Ornate 4-fold arms, titles of Sebastian **Rev:** St. Stephen standing behind Passau arms divides date

Date	Mintage	VG	F	VF	XF	Unc
1680	—	—	—	—	—	—
1682	—	—	—	—	—	—

KM# 15 1/2 THALER

Silver **Obv:** Crowned ornate 4-fold arms with central shield, titles of Johann Philipp **Rev:** St. Stephen standing divides date, oval Passau arms below

Date	Mintage	VG	F	VF	XF	Unc
1694	—	100	200	350	650	—

DAV# 5715 THALER

Silver **Ruler:** Sebastian **Obv:** Crowned arms **Rev:** Saint standing with small shield in front dividing date

Date	Mintage	VG	F	VF	XF	Unc
1680 Rare	—	—	—	—	—	—

DAV# 5716 THALER

Silver **Ruler:** Johann Philipp **Obv:** Ornate crowned arms **Rev:** Saint with arms wider open

Date	Mintage	VG	F	VF	XF	Unc
1694 MF	—	275	550	1,000	1,800	—

DAV# 5717 THALER

Silver **Ruler:** Johann Philipp

Date	Mintage	VG	F	VF	XF	Unc
1696 PHM/(a)	—	300	600	1,350	2,250	—
1697 PHM/MF	—	270	550	1,200	2,200	—

TRADE COINAGE

FR# 2067 1/6 DUCAT

0.5833 g., 0.9860 Gold 0.0185 oz. AGW **Ruler:** Sebastian **Obv:** Bust of Sebastian right **Rev:** Arms topped by cross, crown and mitre

Date	Mintage	VG	F	VF	XF	Unc
1674	—	300	750	1,450	2,800	—

FR# 2066 1/4 DUCAT

0.8750 g., 0.9860 Gold 0.0277 oz. AGW **Ruler:** Sebastian **Obv:** Bust of Sebastian right **Rev:** Arms topped by cross, crown and mitre

Date	Mintage	VG	F	VF	XF	Unc
1674	—	375	825	1,800	3,000	—

FR# A2069 DUCAT

3.5000 g., 0.9860 Gold 0.1109 oz. AGW **Ruler:** Johann Philipp **Obv:** Bust of Johann Philip right **Rev:** Crowned round arms divide date

Date	Mintage	VG	F	VF	XF	Unc
1698 (b)/(a)	—	600	1,200	2,400	4,150	—

FR# 2068 2 DUCAT

7.0000 g., 0.9860 Gold 0.2219 oz. AGW **Ruler:** Johann Philipp **Obv:** Bust of Johann Philip right **Rev:** Crowned oval arms, date below

Date	Mintage	VG	F	VF	XF	Unc
1698 (b)/(a)	—	1,500	3,000	6,000	9,800	—

KM# 18 5 DUCAT

Gold **Obv:** Crowned ornate 4-fold arms with central shield, titles of Johann Philipp **Rev:** St. Stephen standing divides date, oval Passau arms below **Note:** Struck from the same dies as 1/2 Thaler KM#15.

Date	Mintage	VG	F	VF	XF	Unc
1694 Rare	—	—	—	—	—	—

KM# 100 5 DUCAT

17.5000 g., 0.9860 Gold 0.5547 oz. AGW **Ruler:** Johann Philipp **Obv:** Crowned ornate 4-fold arms with central shield, titles of Johann Philipp **Rev:** St. Stephen standing divides date, oval Passau arms below **Note:** Struck with 1/2 Thaler dies.

Date	Mintage	VG	F	VF	XF	Unc
1694 Rare	—	—	—	—	—	—

KM# 105 10 DUCAT

35.0000 g., 0.9860 Gold 1.1095 oz. AGW **Ruler:** Johann Philipp **Obv:** Bust of Johann Philipp right, "10" stamped incuse into field at chest line **Rev:** Crowned arms divide date **Note:** Struck with 1 Thaler dies, Dav. #5717.

Date	Mintage	VG	F	VF	XF	Unc
1697 PHM/MF Rare	—	—	—	—	—	—

PFALZ

(Rhenish Palatinate, Rheinpfalz)

The Counts Palatine originally administered and exercised judicial functions over the imperial household of the Holy Roman Emperor, based at the center of Charlemagne's empire, Aachen. They gradually acquired territories in the middle Rhine. From1214 onwards the position was hereditary in the Wittelsbach family, who also controlled Bavaria. For a time the electoral dignity alternated between the Bavarian and Palatinate branches of the Wittelsbach family, until the Golden Bull in1356 settled it upon the Palatinate branch.

When the Protestant nobles in Prague elected Friedrich V, who was also a Protestant, as King of Bohemia in 1618, it precipitated a conflict which became known as the Thirty Years' War. Bohemia had been ruled by the Catholic Habsburg Emperors from Vienna since 1527 and Ferdinand II, was incensed at being rebuffed for the crown. Friedrich V lost his battles with Ferdinand II's armies and had to flee to the Hague and to the protection of his father-in-law, King James I of England. He would forever after be known as "The Winter King" in ridicule of his short reign. As punishment, the electoral dignity was taken from the Pfalz branch of the Wittelsbachs and given to the rival branch, the Catholic Duke of Bavaria. As one of the general conditions set forth in the Peace of Westphalia in 1648-50, an eighth electorship was created for Pfalz and thus the dignity was restored to the family.

The conversion of the electors to Roman Catholicism led to the expulsion of Huguenots and other Protestants from their territories, many of whom made their way to America, founding New Paltz, New York. In the course of the later seventeenth and eighteenth centuries, the various branches of the Palatinate were left without any legitimate heirs, so that Karl The odor was able to combine the thrones of Jülich-Berg, the Palatinate, and Bavaria after the War of the Bavarian Succession.

Karl Theodor was a great Maecenas, whose orchestra at Mannheim was one of the greatest in Europe. He was a patron of Mozart, who wrote *Idomeneo* for the opera house in Munich, and of the chemist Benjamin Thompson, later Count Rumford, who fled Massachusetts when the American Revolution broke out and sought refuge in Bavaria.

The Palatinate was administered as part of Bavaria from1777, and did not mint any separate coins after 1802. The territories which composed the Palatinate were scattered over central Germany, and now form part of the West German states of Bavaria, Baden, Hesse, and Rheinland-Pfalz. The chief industry is bulk chemicals, from the great BASF factory at Ludwigshafen.

In 1753 Bavaria and Austria concluded a monetary convention, reducing the fineness of the thaler to the point that 20 gulden could be coined from a Mark of fine silver. The most important result was that henceforth the gulden, rather than being worth 2/3 of a thaler, was henceforth worth half a thaler. This Convention standard was soon afterwards adopted by most of the states of southwest Germany, including the Palatinate.

The Electors Palatine and the Saxon Elector acted as Vicars of the Empire after the death of a Holy Roman Emperor and before a new one was elected; the Elector Palatine in the areas of Franconian and Suevic law, the Saxon Elector in the areas where Saxon law applied. Both principalities issued coins commemorating the vicariates. Thus the Elector, Palatine Karl Theodor Actedas, Vicar of the Empire in 1790, after the death of Josef II, and again in 1792, after the early death of Leopold II, and issued coins in those two years. These coins are analogous to the "Sede Vacante" coins of ecclesiastical principalities.

PFALZ-ELECTORAL PFALZ

(Rhenish Pfalz, Rheinpfalz, Churpfalz, Kurpfalz)
Line of Succession in the Electoral Dignity

Once the electorship was vested in the Palatine line of the Wittelsbachs, it passed by right of succession through the senior male line until the death of Friedrich II in 1556. His nephew Otto Heinrich then received the dignity, but this failed at his death three years later. The branch of the family with the highest seniority aft this time was that of Pfalz-Simmern and it was to it that the electoral office passed. The electorship was lost, as stated above, in 1623 as a result of Friedrich V's actions and not restored until the end of the Thirty Years' War in 1648 as part of the peace settlement. The royal coinage of Friedrich V for Bohemia is listed under that entity. From 1622 until 1648, the Upper Palatinate and part of the Rhenish Palatinate were administered by Bavaria, which struck coins for use in those territories. See Bavaria for listings of those issues. The Simmern line died out in 1685 and the office of elector fell to Pfalz-Neuburg, the rulers of which were also dukes of Jülich-Berg. The coinage issued of these Pfalz-Neuburg rulers are often confused one with the other and it is sometimes difficult to separate issues for Electoral Pfalz from those of Jülich-Berg, particularly because some issues for one principality were produced or at least the dies were made in the mint of the other territory. The fate of extinction befell the Pfalz-Neuburg line in 1742 and all its lands and titles passed to Pfalz-Sulzbach for one generation. The Elector also became duke and elector in Bavaria when the Wittelsbach line in that principality became extinct and the two branches of the family were finally united after a breach of centuries. Once again the electoral dignity passed to another branch of the Palatine family, this time to Pfalz-Birkenfeld in 1799. With the abolition of the Holy Roman Empire by Napoleon in 1806, the electoral college was no longer needed and passed quietly away.

RULERS

Friedrich IV von Simmern, 1583-1610
Johann Kasimir von Lautern, Regent 1583-92
Friedrich V, "The Winter King", 1610-23, died 1632
Johann II von Zweibrücken, Regent 1610-14
Bavarian Rule, 1622-48
Karl Ludwig von Simmern, 1648-80
Karl von Simmern, 1680-85
Philipp Wilhelm von Neuburg, 1685-90
Johann Wilhelm von Neuburg, 1690-1716

MINT OFFICIALS' INITIALS

HEIDELBERG MINT

Initials	Date	Name
	1620	Johan Ludwig Eichesstein, mintmaster
GP	1650-63	Georg Pfründt, die-cutter in Nürnberg
(a)	1656-59	Johan Kasimir Herman, mintmaster
	1659-76	Johann Kaspar Herman, mintmaster
	1657-?	Michael Koch, warden
ISS	1658-59	Unknown die-cutter
	1659-76	Sebastian Müller, warden
IL, L	1659-1711	Johann Linck, die-cutter and mintmaster
GB	1684-92	Johann Gerhard Bender, mintmaster
IMW, MW	1694-1709	Johann Michael Wunsch, mintmaster

MANNHEIM MINT

Initials	Date	Name
	1607-10	Johann Ludwig Eichelstein, mintmaster

ARMS

Pfalz – rampant lion to left or right
Bavaria or old Wittelsbach – field of lozenges (diamond shapes)
Electorate – blank shield, sometimes shaded with closely spaced horizontal lines or ..arabesques
..- also, an imperial orb

MONETARY SYSTEMS

8 Pfenning = 2 Kreuzer = 1 Albus
16 Pfenning = 4 Kreuzer = 2 Albus = 1 Batzen

ELECTORATE

REGULAR COINAGE

KM# 62 HELLER

Copper **Ruler:** Friedrich V **Obv:** Crowned Bohemian lion right holding orb **Mint:** Amberg **Note:** Kipper. Uniface.

Date	Mintage	VG	F	VF	XF	Unc
ND(1621-22)	—	15.00	30.00	65.00	—	—

KM# 3 PFENNIG

Billon **Ruler:** Friedrich IV **Obv:** Round 4-fold arms, HEIDELBERG, date around **Mint:** Heidelberg **Note:** Uniface. Prev. Pfalz-Simmern KM#6.

Date	Mintage	VG	F	VF	XF	Unc
1608	—	16.00	33.00	60.00	120	—
1609	—	16.00	33.00	60.00	120	—

KM# 28 PFENNIG

Silver **Ruler:** Johann II **Obv:** Shield of 4-fold arms of Pfalz and

Bavaria, IAP above (=Johann Admin. Palat.) **Note:** Uniface hohl-type.

Date	Mintage	VG	F	VF	XF	Unc
ND(1610-15)	—	15.00	30.00	65.00	—	—

KM# 58 PFENNIG

Silver **Ruler:** Friedrich V **Obv:** Shield of 3-fold arms with scalloped sides of Pfalz, Electorate and Bavaria divides date, "IC" in ligature above **Mint:** Heidelberg **Note:** Uniface.

Date	Mintage	VG	F	VF	XF	Unc
ND(1615-20)	—	15.00	30.00	65.00	—	—

KM# 64 PFENNIG

Copper **Ruler:** Friedrich V **Obv:** Crowned Bohemian lion to right holding orb **Mint:** Heidelberg **Note:** Kipper, uniface.

Date	Mintage	VG	F	VF	XF	Unc
ND(1621-22)	—	15.00	30.00	65.00	—	—

KM# 77 PFENNIG

Copper **Ruler:** Karl Ludwig **Obv:** Round 3-fold arms in baroque frame, C*L above **Mint:** Heidelberg **Note:** Uniface. Prev. Pfalz-Simmern KM#9.

Date	Mintage	VG	F	VF	XF	Unc
ND(1648-80)	—	25.00	45.00	85.00	150	—

KM# 101 2 PFENNIG

Silver **Ruler:** Karl Ludwig **Note:** Prev. Pfalz-Simmern KM#107.

Date	Mintage	VG	F	VF	XF	Unc
1662	—	20.00	40.00	75.00	150	—
ND	—	20.00	40.00	75.00	150	—

KM# 5 4 PFENNIG (1/2 Albus)

Silver **Ruler:** Friedrich IV **Obv:** Pfalz lion right in circle holding orb **Obv. Legend:** MO. NO. IIII. NVM. MANHEIM **Rev:** Shield of Wittelsbach arms, date above in circle **Rev. Legend:** C(H)VRF. PFALTS. LANDMVNTZ **Mint:** Mannheim **Note:** Varieties exist. Prev. Pfalz-Simmern KM#10.

Date	Mintage	VG	F	VF	XF	Unc
1608	—	33.00	65.00	120	220	—
1609	—	33.00	65.00	120	220	—

KM# 24 4 PFENNIG (1/2 Albus)

Silver **Ruler:** Friedrich IV **Obv:** Bust right in circle, titles of Friedrich IV **Rev:** 4-fold arms, legend, date **Rev. Legend:** MO. NO. IIII. NVM. MAHEM **Mint:** Mannheim

Date	Mintage	VG	F	VF	XF	Unc
1610	—	20.00	40.00	80.00	—	—

KM# 7 ALBUS

Silver **Ruler:** Friedrich IV **Obv:** Bust right in circle **Obv. Legend:** NOV. ALBVS MANHEIMII CVSVS **Rev:** 3 small shields of arms, 2 above, 1 below which divides date, electoral hat above **Rev. Legend:** CH. FVRST. PFALTZ. LANDMVNZ. **Mint:** Mannheim **Note:** Prev. Pfalz-Simmern KM#13.

Date	Mintage	VG	F	VF	XF	Unc
1608	—	65.00	135	225	400	—

KM# 27 ALBUS

Silver **Ruler:** Friedrich IV **Obv:** Bust right in circle, titles of Friedrich IV **Rev:** 4-fold arms, date **Rev. Legend:** NOV. ALBVS. MANHE. CV. **Mint:** Mannheim

Date	Mintage	VG	F	VF	XF	Unc
(1)610	—	65.00	135	225	400	—

KM# 120 ALBUS

Silver **Ruler:** Karl von Simmern **Obv:** Large script 'C', date divided between crown and 'C' **Rev:** Crowned Pfalz lion left within palm and laurel branches **Mint:** Heidelberg

Date	Mintage	VG	F	VF	XF	Unc
1682	—	50.00	100	200	350	—

KM# 128 ALBUS

Silver **Ruler:** Philipp Wilhelm **Obv:** Bust right with titles of Elector Philipp Wilhelm **Rev:** 3 shields - lion, orb and lozenge, electoral hat above **Note:** Prev. Pfalz-Neuburg KM#40.

Date	Mintage	VG	F	VF	XF	Unc
1685	—	50.00	100	200	350	—

KM# 126 ALBUS

Silver **Ruler:** Philipp Wilhelm **Obv:** Bust right with titles of Elector Philipp Wilhelm **Rev:** 3 shields - lion, orb, and lozenge, electoral hat above **Mint:** Heidelberg **Note:** Prev. Pfalz-Neuburg KM#40.

Date	Mintage	VG	F	VF	XF	Unc
1685	—	50.00	100	200	350	—

KM# 132 ALBUS

Silver **Ruler:** Philipp Wilhelm **Obv:** Crowned Pfalz lion left in circle, titles of Philipp Wilhelm **Rev:** Crowned 8-fold arms with central shield, titles continued ending ALB9 date **Mint:** Heidelberg

Date	Mintage	VG	F	VF	XF	Unc
1688 GB	—	50.00	100	200	350	—

KM# 140 ALBUS

Silver **Ruler:** Johann Wilhelm **Obv:** Crowned Pfalz lion left in circle, titles of Johann Wilhelm **Rev:** Mintmaster's initials, titles cont. and date **Rev. Inscription:** *I* / ALBVS / **Mint:** Heidelberg

Date	Mintage	VG	F	VF	XF	Unc
1691 GB	—	50.00	100	200	350	—

KM# 26 ALBUS (8 Pfennig)

Silver **Ruler:** Friedrich IV **Obv:** Bust right in circle, titles of Friedrich IV **Rev:** 4-fold arms, legend, date **Rev. Legend:** NOV. ALBVS. MA(N)HEMII. C(V) **Mint:** Mannheim **Note:** Prev. Pfalz-Simmern KM#12.

Date	Mintage	VG	F	VF	XF	Unc
1610	—	30.00	50.00	90.00	—	—

KM# 114 ALBUS (8 Pfennig)

Silver **Ruler:** Karl von Simmern **Obv:** Large script 'C', crown above divides date **Obv. Legend:** SVSTENTANTE DEO. **Rev:** Crowned Pfalz lion left within palm and laurel branches **Mint:** Heidelberg

Date	Mintage	VG	F	VF	XF	Unc
1681	—	20.00	30.00	70.00	—	—

KM# 144 2 ALBUS

1.7500 g., Billon **Ruler:** Johann Wilhelm **Obv:** Crowned lion rampant left in laurel wreath divides C - P **Rev:** Inscription in laurel wreath **Rev. Inscription:** II / ALBUS / (date) **Note:** Prev. Pfalz-Neuburg KM#51. Varieties exist. Some are counterfeits.

Date	Mintage	VG	F	VF	XF	Unc
1700 IMW	—	27.00	40.00	85.00	180	—

KM# 9 3-1/4 ALBUS (1/8 Gulden)

Silver **Ruler:** Friedrich IV **Obv:** Bust right in circle, behind III.ALB, in front .II. ... (= 2 Pfennig or 1/4 Albus) **Obv. Legend:** MONE. ARGENT. MANHEMII. CVSA. **Rev:** 3 small shields of arms, 2 above 1 below which divides date, electoral hat above **Rev. Legend:** CHVRF. FVRST. PFALTZ. LANDMVNZ. **Mint:** Mannheim **Note:** Varieties exist.

Date	Mintage	VG	F	VF	XF	Unc
1608	—	—	—	—	—	—

KM# 29 3-1/4 ALBUS (1/8 Gulden)

Ruler: Friedrich IV **Obv:** Bust right in circle, titles of Friedrich IV **Rev:** 4-fold arms divide III - 2... **Mint:** Mannheim

Date	Mintage	VG	F	VF	XF	Unc
1610	—	—	—	—	—	—

KM# 146 6 ALBUS

Silver **Ruler:** Johann Wilhelm **Obv:** Crowned oval 9-fold arms, titles of Johann Wilhelm **Rev:** Value inscription, date, mintmaster's initials **Rev. Legend:** NACH DEM SCHLUS DER V. STÆND. **Rev. Inscription:** ★ VI ★ / ALBUS/ **Note:** Prev. Pfalz-Neuburg KM#52. Varieties exist.

Date	Mintage	VG	F	VF	XF	Unc
1700 IMW	—	45.00	90.00	200	325	—

KM# 12 6-1/2 ALBUS

Silver **Ruler:** Friedrich IV **Obv:** Bust right in circle **Obv. Legend:** MON. NO. ARG. VI ... ALB. MANHEMII. CVSA (or variant) **Rev:** 3 small shields of arms, 2 above 1 below which divides date, electoral hat above **Rev. Legend:** CHVRFVRST. PFALTZ. LANDMVNZ. **Mint:** Mannheim **Note:** Klippe.

Date	Mintage	VG	F	VF	XF	Unc
1608	—	—	—	—	—	—

KM# 11 6-1/2 ALBUS

Silver **Ruler:** Friedrich IV **Obv:** Bust right in circle **Obv. Legend:** MON. NO. ARG. VI ... ALB. MANHEMII. CVSA (or variant) **Rev:** 3 small shields of arms, 2 above 1 below which divides date, electoral hat above **Rev. Legend:** CHVRFVRST. PFALTZ. LANDMVNZ. **Mint:** Mannheim **Note:** Prev. Pfalz-Simmern KM#14. Varieties exist.

Date	Mintage	VG	F	VF	XF	Unc
1608	—	80.00	165	275	475	—

KM# 30 6-1/2 ALBUS

Silver **Ruler:** Friedrich IV **Obv:** Bust right in circle, titles of Friedrich IV **Rev:** 4-fold arms divide VI - ... **Mint:** Mannheim

Date	Mintage	VG	F	VF	XF	Unc
1610	—	—	—	—	—	—

KM# 14 13 ALBUS (1/2 Gulden)

Silver **Ruler:** Friedrich IV **Obv:** Bust right in circle, XIII - ALB. behind and in front of bust **Rev:** 3 small shields of arms divide date at bottom, electoral hat above **Mint:** Mannheim **Note:** Prev. Pfalz-Simmern KM#15.

Date	Mintage	VG	F	VF	XF	Unc
1608	—	200	425	850	1,550	—

KM# 16 26 ALBUS (Gulden)

Silver **Ruler:** Friedrich IV **Obv:** Bust right divides XXVI at left and ALB at right in inner circle **Rev:** Date divided by lion on top of helmet **Mint:** Mannheim **Note:** Dav.#744. Prev. Pfalz-Simmern KM#16.

Date	Mintage	VG	F	VF	XF	Unc
1608	—	275	525	1,000	1,650	—

KM# 65 KREUZER

Billon **Ruler:** Friedrich V **Obv:** Crowned Bohemian lion to left **Rev:** Shield of Wittelsbach arms divides date, '4' above **Mint:** Heidelberg **Note:** Kipper.

Date	Mintage	VG	F	VF	XF	Unc
1621	—	30.00	60.00	120	—	—
1622	—	30.00	60.00	120	—	—

KM# 82 KREUZER

Silver **Ruler:** Karl Ludwig **Obv:** Pfalz lion left in circle, titles of Karl Ludwig **Rev:** Blank oval shield of arms in baroque frame, legend, date **Mint:** Heidelberg **Note:** Prev. Pfalz-Simmern KM#95.

Date	Mintage	VG	F	VF	XF	Unc
1657	—	20.00	40.00	90.00	—	—
1658	—	20.00	40.00	90.00	—	—
1663	—	20.00	40.00	90.00	—	—

KM# 83 KREUZER

Silver **Ruler:** Karl Ludwig **Obv:** Ornate helmet over 3 small shields of arms **Rev:** Inscription in laurel wreath **Rev. Inscription:** I / date / KREVZ / ER **Note:** Prev. Pfalz-Simmern KM#1.

Date	Mintage	VG	F	VF	XF	Unc
1661	—	—	—	—	—	—

KM# 134 KREUZER

Silver **Ruler:** Philipp Wilhelm **Obv:** Crowned Pfalz lion left in circle, titles of Philipp Wilhelm, date in legend **Rev:** Mintmasters' initials in circle, titles cont. **Rev. Inscription:** I / KREV / TZER / **Mint:** Heidelberg **Note:** Prev. Pfalz-Neuburg KM#41.

Date	Mintage	VG	F	VF	XF	Unc
1688 GB	—	—	—	—	—	—

KM# 148 KREUZER

Silver **Ruler:** Johann Wilhelm **Obv:** Pfalz lion left in laurel wreath **Rev:** 3-line inscription, date in laurel wreath **Rev. Inscription:** I / KREU / ZER / **Mint:** Heidelberg **Note:** Prev. Pfalz-Neuburg KM#50.

Date	Mintage	VG	F	VF	XF	Unc
1700	—	45.00	85.00	160	275	—

KM# 79 2 KREUZER

Billon **Ruler:** Karl Ludwig **Obv:** Crowned rampant lion left in circle, titles of Karl Ludwig **Rev:** Oval blank shield in baroque frame with 2 small points in center, legend, date **Rev. Legend:** S • R • I • EL • & VIC • B • D • DN • PVIDEBIT **Mint:** Heidelberg **Note:** Prev. Pfalz-Simmern KM#91. Vicariat issue.

Date	Mintage	VG	F	VF	XF	Unc
1657 (a)	163,000	33.00	65.00	135	225	—
1658 (a)	—	33.00	65.00	135	225	—

KM# 80 2 KREUZER

Billon **Ruler:** Karl Ludwig **Obv:** Crowned rampant lion left in circle, titles of Karl Ludwig **Rev:** Large '2' in ornamented oval, legend, date **Rev. Legend:** DOMINVS PROVIDEBIT **Mint:** Heidelberg **Note:** Prev. Pfalz-Simmern KM#90.

Date	Mintage	VG	F	VF	XF	Unc
1657 (a)	Inc. above	33.00	65.00	135	225	—

KM# 104 2 KREUZER

Silver **Ruler:** Karl Ludwig **Obv:** Crowned rampant lion left in circle, titles of Karl Ludwig **Obv. Legend:** CAROL • LUD • D • G • DOM ... **Rev:** Oval blank shield in baroque frame **Rev. Legend:** S • R • I • EL • & B • D • DN • PVIDEBIT **Mint:** Heidelberg **Note:** Prev. Pfalz-Simmern KM#108. Varieties exist.

Date	Mintage	VG	F	VF	XF	Unc
1662 (a)	—	35.00	70.00	150	250	—
1663 (a)	—	35.00	70.00	150	250	—
1664 (a)	—	35.00	70.00	150	250	—
1665 (a)	—	35.00	70.00	150	250	—
1667 (a)	—	35.00	70.00	150	250	—
1668 (a)	—	35.00	70.00	150	250	—
1669 (a)	—	35.00	70.00	150	250	—
1670 (a)	—	35.00	70.00	150	250	—
1673 (a)	—	35.00	70.00	150	250	—

KM# 75 4 KREUZER

Copper **Ruler:** Friedrich V **Obv:** Rampant Bohemian lion left **Rev:** Bavarian lozenges divide date, value above **Note:** Prev. Pfalz-Simmern KM#55. Kipper.

Date	Mintage	VG	F	VF	XF	Unc
1622	—	40.00	85.00	160	275	—

KM# 67 12 KREUZER
Billon **Ruler:** Friedrich V **Obv:** Rampant Bohemian lion left **Rev:** 3 shields - lion, orb, and Bavarian lozenge **Mint:** Heidelberg **Note:** Klippe. Pfalz-Simmern KM#44.

Date	Mintage	VG	F	VF	XF	Unc
1621	—	45.00	100	200	320	—

KM# 66 12 KREUZER
Billon **Ruler:** Friedrich V **Obv:** Rampant Bohemian lion left **Rev:** 3 shields - lion, orb, and Bavarian lozenge **Mint:** Heidelberg **Note:** Prev. Pfalz-Simmern KM#43. Kipper.

Date	Mintage	VG	F	VF	XF	Unc
1621	—	45.00	100	200	320	—
1622	—	45.00	100	200	320	—
ND	—	45.00	100	200	320	—

KM# 87 15 KREUZER (1/4 Gulden)
Silver **Ruler:** Karl Ludwig **Obv:** Bust right in circle, titles of Karl Ludwig **Rev:** 3 small shields of arms, 2 above 1, lower shield divides date, electoral hat above all, value (15) at bottom **Rev. Legend:** DOMINVS - PROVIDEBIT **Mint:** Heidelberg **Note:** Prev. Pfalz-Simmern KM#96.

Date	Mintage	VG	F	VF	XF	Unc
1658 (a)	—	55.00	110	200	325	—
1660 (a)	—	55.00	110	200	325	—
1661 (a)	—	55.00	110	200	325	—

KM# 98 15 KREUZER (1/4 Gulden)
Silver **Ruler:** Karl Ludwig **Obv:** Bust right in circle, titles of Karl Ludwig **Rev:** 3 small shields of arms, date divided above middle shield **Rev. Legend:** CHUR FURST LICHER - PFALTZ LANDMUNTZ **Mint:** Heidelberg **Note:** Varieties exist.

Date	Mintage	VG	F	VF	XF	Unc
1661 (a)	—	55.00	110	200	325	—
1662 GP/(a)	—	55.00	110	200	325	—
1666 (a)	—	55.00	110	200	325	—
1668	—	55.00	110	200	325	—
1672	—	55.00	110	200	325	—

KM# 68 24 KREUZER (Sechsbätzner)
Silver **Ruler:** Friedrich V **Obv:** Crowned Bohemian lion rampant left in circle, titles of Friedrich V as king of Bohemia **Rev:** Crown above 3 ornate sields of arms, 2 aove 1 below which divides date, titles cont. **Mint:** Heidelberg **Note:** Kipper.

Date	Mintage	VG	F	VF	XF	Unc
1621	—	—	—	—	—	—
ND	—	—	—	—	—	—

KM# 69 24 KREUZER (Sechsbätzner)
Silver **Ruler:** Friedrich V **Obv:** Crowned Bohemian lion rampant left in circle, titles of Friedrich V as king of Bohemia **Rev:** Crown above 3 ornate shields of arms, 2 above 1 below which divides date, titles cont., legend error REHNI instead of RHENI **Mint:** Heidelberg **Note:** Kipper.

Date	Mintage	VG	F	VF	XF	Unc
ND(1621)	—	—	—	—	—	—

KM# 89 30 KREUZER (1/2 Gulden)
Silver **Ruler:** Karl Ludwig **Obv:** Bust right in circle, titles of Karl Ludwig **Rev:** 3 small shields of arms, 2 above 1, lower shield divides date, electoral hat above all, value (30) at bottom **Mint:** Heidelberg **Note:** Prev. Pfalz-Simmern KM#97.

Date	Mintage	VG	F	VF	XF	Unc
1658 (a)	—	80.00	160	275	475	—
1660 (a)	—	80.00	160	275	475	—
1661 (a)	—	80.00	160	275	475	—

KM# 100 30 KREUZER (1/2 Gulden)
Silver **Ruler:** Karl Ludwig **Obv:** Bust right in circle, titles of Karl Ludwig **Rev:** 3 small shields of arms, middle shield divides date, value (30) at bottom **Mint:** Heidelberg **Note:** Prev. Pfalz-Simmern KM#97.

Date	Mintage	VG	F	VF	XF	Unc
1661 (a)	—	80.00	160	275	475	—
1664 (a)	—	80.00	160	275	475	—
1665 (a)	—	80.00	160	275	475	—
1666 (a)	—	80.00	160	275	475	—
1668	—	80.00	160	275	475	—
1672	—	80.00	160	275	475	—
1673	—	80.00	160	275	475	—

KM# 91 60 KREUZER (Guldenthaler)
Silver **Ruler:** Karl Ludwig **Obv:** Bust right in circle, titles of Karl Ludwig **Rev:** 3 small shields of arms, ornate helmet above arms, lion crest on top divides date, value (60) at bottom **Mint:** Heidelberg **Note:** Prev. Pfalz-Simmern KM#98.

Date	Mintage	VG	F	VF	XF	Unc
1658 ISS	—	100	200	375	600	—
1659 ISS	—	100	200	375	600	—
1660	—	100	200	375	600	—

KM# 95 60 KREUZER (Guldenthaler)
Silver **Ruler:** Karl Ludwig **Obv:** Bust right in circle, titles of Karl Ludwig **Rev:** 3 small shields of arms, lower shield divides date at bottom **Mint:** Heidelberg **Note:** Prev. Pfalz-Simmern KM#98.

Date	Mintage	VG	F	VF	XF	Unc
1660 (a)	—	100	200	375	600	—
1661 (a)	—	100	200	375	600	—

KM# 96 60 KREUZER (Guldenthaler)
Silver **Ruler:** Karl Ludwig **Obv:** Bust right in circle, titles of Karl Ludwig **Rev:** 3 small shields of arms, 2 above 1, lower shield divides date, electoral hat above all **Rev. Legend:** CHUR FURSTLICHER - PFALZ LANDMUNTZ (or V's for U's) **Mint:** Heidelberg **Note:** Prev. Pfalz-Simmern KM#105. Varieties exist.

Date	Mintage	VG	F	VF	XF	Unc
1660 (a)	—	80.00	185	350	600	—
1661 CP/(a)	—	80.00	185	350	600	—
1662 P/(a)	—	80.00	185	350	600	—
1664	—	80.00	185	350	600	—
1665	—	80.00	185	350	600	—
1666	—	80.00	185	350	600	—
1667 (a)	—	80.00	185	350	600	—
1668 (a)	—	80.00	185	350	600	—
1670 (a)	—	80.00	185	350	600	—
1672	—	80.00	185	350	600	—
1673 (a)	—	80.00	185	350	600	—
1676 (a)	—	80.00	185	350	600	—

KM# 18 GULDEN
Silver **Ruler:** Friedrich III **Obv:** Bust right divides value in circle **Rev:** 3 shields of arms **Mint:** Mannheim

Date	Mintage	VG	F	VF	XF	Unc
1608	—	—	—	—	—	—

KM# 32 1/4 THALER
Silver **Ruler:** Friedrich IV **Obv:** Bust with sword over right shoulder, orb in left hand **Rev:** Crowned arms divide large date **Note:** Klippe. Prev. Pfalz-Simmern KM#26.

Date	Mintage	VG	F	VF	XF	Unc
1610	—	—	—	—	—	—

KM# 31 1/4 THALER
Silver **Ruler:** Friedrich IV **Obv:** Bust with sword over right shoulder, left hand holds orb right in inner circle **Rev:** Crowned arms divide large date **Note:** Prev. Pfalz-Simmern KM#25.

Date	Mintage	VG	F	VF	XF	Unc
1610	—	—	—	—	—	—

KM# 46 1/4 THALER
Silver **Ruler:** Johann II **Obv:** Bust right in circle, outer legend titles of Johann II **Obv. Legend:** Inner leg. VICARIUS DUX B. CO. V. & SPAN. **Rev:** Crowned imperial eagle, 3-fold arms of Pfalz, Electorate and Bavaria on breast, date at end of legend **Rev. Legend:** VERBUM DOMINI MANET IN ÆTERNUM **Mint:** Heidelberg **Note:** Vicariat issue.

Date	Mintage	VG	F	VF	XF	Unc
161Z	—	—	—	—	—	—

KM# 33 1/2 THALER
Silver **Ruler:** Johann II **Obv:** Bust right in circle, titles of Johann II **Rev:** 3 small shields of arms, 2 above 1, electoral hat above, all in circle, date at end of legend **Rev. Legend:** VERBUM • DOMINI • MANET • IN • ÆTERNVM **Mint:** Heidelberg

Date	Mintage	VG	F	VF	XF	Unc
1610	—	—	—	—	—	—

KM# 48 1/2 THALER
Silver **Ruler:** Johann II **Obv:** Bust right in circle, outer legend, titles of Johann II **Obv. Legend:** Inner leg: VICARIUS DUX B. CO. V. & SPAN **Rev:** Crowned imperial eagle, 3-fold arms of Pfalz, Electorate and Bavaria on breast, date at end of legend **Rev. Legend:** VERBUM DOMINI MANET IN ÆTERN **Mint:** Heidelberg **Note:** Vicariat issue.

Date	Mintage	VG	F	VF	XF	Unc
161Z	—	—	—	—	—	—

KM# 20 THALER
Silver **Ruler:** Friedrich IV **Obv:** Bust with sword and orb right **Rev:** Crowned arms divide date **Mint:** Mannheim **Note:** Dav. #7144. Prev. Pfalz-Simmern KM#17.

Date	Mintage	VG	F	VF	XF	Unc
1608	—	850	1,650	3,750	6,500	—

KM# 37 THALER
Silver **Ruler:** Friedrich IV **Obv:** 1/2-length bust right, sword on right shoulder, orb in left hand in inner circle **Rev:** Crowned arms divide larger date **Mint:** Mannheim **Note:** Dav. #7146. Prev. Pfalz-Simmern KM#28.

Date	Mintage	VG	F	VF	XF	Unc
1610	—	850	1,650	3,750	6,500	—

KM# 35 THALER
Silver **Ruler:** Johann II **Obv:** Bust right **Obv. Legend:** IOHAN. D. G. CO. PAL. RH ... **Rev:** 3 shields crowned, date in legend **Note:** Dav. #7180. Prev. Pfalz-Zweibrücken KM#5.

Date	Mintage	VG	F	VF	XF	Unc
1610 Rare	—	—	—	—	—	—

KM# 36 THALER
Silver **Ruler:** Johann II **Obv:** Bust right **Obv. Legend:** IOHAN. D. G. C. PA. RH ... **Rev:** 3 shields crowned, date in legend **Mint:** Heidelberg **Note:** Dav. #7181. Prev. Pfalz-Zweibrücken KM#6.

Date	Mintage	VG	F	VF	XF	Unc
1610 Rare	—	—	—	—	—	—

KM# 41 THALER
Silver **Ruler:** Johann II **Obv:** Bust right **Rev:** 3 shields capped, date below **Mint:** Heidelberg **Note:** Dav. #7182. Prev. Pfalz-Zweibrücken KM#7.

Date	Mintage	VG	F	VF	XF	Unc
1611 Rare	—	—	—	—	—	—

KM# 42 THALER
Silver **Ruler:** Johann II **Obv:** Bust right **Obv. Legend:** IOHAN. D. G. CO. PAL. RH ... **Rev:** 3 shields crowned, scrollwork around date **Mint:** Heidelberg **Note:** Dav. #7182A. Prev. Pfalz-Zweibrücken KM#8.

Date	Mintage	VG	F	VF	XF	Unc
1611 Rare	—	—	—	—	—	—

KM# 43 THALER
Silver **Ruler:** Johann II **Obv:** Bust right **Obv. Legend:** IOHAN. D. G. CO. PAL. RH ... **Rev:** 3 shields crowned, date punctuated 1.6. - .11. **Mint:** Heidelberg **Note:** Dav. #7182B. Prev. Pfalz-Zweibrücken KM#9.

Date	Mintage	VG	F	VF	XF	Unc
1611 Rare	—	—	—	—	—	—

KM# 44 THALER
Silver **Ruler:** Johann II **Obv:** Bust right **Obv. Legend:** IOHAN. D. G. CO. PAL. RH ... **Rev:** 3 shields crowned, date in legend divided by shield **Mint:** Heidelberg **Note:** Dav. #7183. Prev. Pfalz-Zweibrücken KM#10.

Date	Mintage	VG	F	VF	XF	Unc
1611 Rare	—	—	—	—	—	—

KM# 50 THALER

Silver **Ruler:** Johann II **Obv:** Bust right, titles of Johann II **Obv. Legend:** IOHAN • D • G • CO • V • & S • ... **Rev:** Crowned double-headed eagle **Mint:** Heidelberg **Note:** Dav. #7184. Prev. Pfalz-Zweibrücken KM#12. Vicariat issue.

Date	Mintage	VG	F	VF	XF	Unc
161Z	—	950	1,850	4,000	6,500	—

KM# 51 THALER

Silver **Ruler:** Johann II **Obv:** Bust right in inner circle **Obv. Legend:** ... CO. V. & SPANH. **Rev:** Crowned double-headed eagle **Mint:** Heidelberg **Note:** Dav. #7184A. Prev. Pfalz-Zweibrücken KM#13. Vicariat issue.

Date	Mintage	VG	F	VF	XF	Unc
161Z	—	950	1,850	4,000	6,500	—

KM# 57 THALER

Silver **Ruler:** Friedrich V **Obv:** King standing between shields **Rev:** 5-fold arms **Rev. Legend:** ... LVSA. 1620. **Mint:** Mannheim **Note:** Dav. #7147. Prev. Pfalz-Simmern KM#40.

Date	Mintage	VG	F	VF	XF	Unc
1620 Rare	—	—	—	—	—	—

KM# 59 THALER

Silver **Ruler:** Friedrich V **Obv:** King standing between shields **Rev:** 5-fold arms **Rev. Legend:** ... + LUX. *1620. **Mint:** Mannheim **Note:** Dav. #7147A. Prev. Pfalz-Simmern KM#41.

Date	Mintage	VG	F	VF	XF	Unc
1620 Rare	—	—	—	—	—	—

KM# 60 THALER

Silver **Ruler:** Friedrich V **Obv:** King standing between shields **Rev:** 5-fold arms **Rev. Legend:** ... LVSA.A 1620 **Mint:** Mannheim **Note:** Dav. #7147B. Prev. Pfalz-Simmern KM#42.

Date	Mintage	VG	F	VF	XF	Unc
1620 Rare	—	—	—	—	—	—

KM# 70 THALER

Silver **Ruler:** Friedrich V **Obv:** Crowned Bohemian lion **Rev:** Crown above 3 shields divide date **Mint:** Mannheim **Note:** Dav. #7148. Prev. Pfalz-Simmern KM#46.

Date	Mintage	VG	F	VF	XF	Unc
1621	—	1,250	2,500	4,750	7,500	—

KM# 71 THALER

Silver **Ruler:** Friedrich V **Obv:** Crowned Bohemian lion left **Rev:** Crown above 3 shields, date divided by bottom shield **Mint:** Mannheim **Note:** Dav. #7149. Prev. Pfalz-Simmern KM#47.

Date	Mintage	VG	F	VF	XF	Unc
1621	—	1,000	2,000	4,000	6,500	—

KM# 72 THALER

Silver **Ruler:** Friedrich V **Obv:** Crowned Bohemian lion left, legend has reversed D **Rev:** 3 longer and thinner shields, bottom shield divides date **Mint:** Mannheim **Note:** Dav. #7150. Prev. Pfalz-Simmern KM#48. Varieties exist.

Date	Mintage	VG	F	VF	XF	Unc
1621	—	1,200	2,250	4,250	7,000	—

KM# 84 THALER

Silver **Ruler:** Karl Ludwig **Obv:** 9-line inscription, date **Rev:** Lion above 3 helmeted shields **Mint:** Heidelberg **Note:** Dav. #7151. Prev. Pfalz-Simmern KM#92. Vicariat issue.

Date	Mintage	VG	F	VF	XF	Unc
1657 (a)	—	300	600	1,250	2,250	—

KM# 85 THALER

Silver **Ruler:** Karl Ludwig **Obv:** Bust right in inner circle **Obv. Legend:** CAR. LVD. D. G. C. PR. **Rev:** 3 shields of arms, legend, date **Rev. Legend:** DOMINVS PROVIDEBIT. **Mint:** Heidelberg **Note:** Dav. #7152. Prev. Pfalz-Simmern KM#93.

Date	Mintage	VG	F	VF	XF	Unc
1657	—	500	1,000	2,000	3,500	—

KM# 93 THALER

Silver **Ruler:** Karl Ludwig **Obv:** Bust of Karl Ludwig right **Rev:** 3 shields of arms in inner circle, legend, date **Mint:** Heidelberg **Note:** Dav. #7153. Prev. Pfalz-Simmern KM#99.

Date	Mintage	VG	F	VF	XF	Unc
1659	—	235	450	950	1,850	—
166Z	—	235	450	950	1,850	—
1667	—	235	450	950	1,850	—
1669	—	235	450	950	1,850	—
1670	—	235	450	950	1,850	—

KM# 103 THALER

Silver **Ruler:** Christian August **Obv:** Bust right without inner circle **Rev:** Crowned arms in Order of the Garter Band, date above **Mint:** Heidelberg **Note:** Dav. #7154. Prev. Pfalz-Simmern KM#106.

Date	Mintage	VG	F	VF	XF	Unc
1661	—	500	1,000	2,000	3,500	—

KM# 106 THALER

Silver **Ruler:** Karl Ludwig **Obv:** Facing busts, legend around **Rev:** 5-line inscription, date on 5th line, mint officials' below **Note:** Dav. #7155. Prev. Pfalz-Simmern KM#M1.

Date	Mintage	VG	F	VF	XF	Unc
1671 IL	—	1,000	2,000	3,500	6,000	—

KM# 117 THALER

Silver **Ruler:** Karl von Simmern **Obv:** Bust right, dots at shoulder **Rev:** Helmeted and supported arms within Garter Order band, date below **Mint:** Heidelberg **Note:** Dav. #7156. Prev. Pfalz-Simmern KM#115.

Date	Mintage	VG	F	VF	XF	Unc
1681 IL	—	350	700	1,500	3,750	—

KM# 118 THALER

Silver **Ruler:** Karl von Simmern **Obv:** Bust right with smaller head, shorter hair, lion's face at shoulder **Mint:** Heidelberg **Note:** Dav. #7156A. Prev. Pfalz-Simmern KM#116.

Date	Mintage	VG	F	VF	XF	Unc
1681	—	300	600	1,250	3,500	—

KM# 138 THALER

Silver **Ruler:** Philipp Wilhelm **Obv:** Bust of Philipp Wilhelm right **Obv. Legend:** P. W. C. P. R. ... **Rev:** Crowned arms, date at end of legend **Rev. Legend:** M. D. C. V. S. M. R. & M. D. I. R. **Note:** Dav. #7176. Prev. Pfalz-Neuburg KM#42.

Date	Mintage	VG	F	VF	XF	Unc
1688 Rare	—	—	—	—	—	—

KM# 142 THALER

Silver **Ruler:** Johann Wilhelm **Obv:** Bust of Johann Wilhelm right, legend begins at 8 o'clock **Obv. Legend:** I. W. D. G. C. ... **Rev. Legend:** B. I. C. & M. D ... **Note:** Dav. #7177. Prev. Pfalz-Neuburg KM#46.

Date	Mintage	VG	F	VF	XF	Unc
1694 Rare	—	—	—	—	—	—

Note: Dr. Busso Peus Nachfolger Auction 381, 11-04, XF/Unc realized approximately $35,555

KM# 150 THALER

Silver **Ruler:** Christian August **Obv:** Bust of Christian August right, legend begins at 8 o'clock **Obv. Legend:** I. W. D. G. C. P. R. & ARCHIT & . L. L. **Rev. Legend:** B. I. C. ... M. D. C. V. S. ... **Note:** Dav. #7179. Prev. Pfalz-Neuburg KM#53.

Date	Mintage	VG	F	VF	XF	Unc
1700 IL	—	700	1,400	2,580	4,750	—

KM# 76 1-1/2 THALER

Silver **Ruler:** Bavarian Rule **Obv:** Bust of Maximilian I right **Obv. Legend:** MAXIMILIANVS D:G: COM: PAL: RHENI ... TRI: BAVARIA • DVX • **Rev:** Supported arms **Rev. Legend:** SACRI ROM • IMP • ARCHIDAR ... E • PRINCEPS • ELECTOR **Mint:** Heidelberg **Note:** Dav. #6095. Prev. Pfalz-Simmern KM#77.

Date	Mintage	VG	F	VF	XF	Unc
1627 Rare	—	—	—	—	—	—

KM# 39 2 THALER

Silver **Ruler:** Friedrich IV **Obv:** 1/2-length bust right, sword on right shoulder, orb in left hand **Rev:** 3-fold arms divide date **Mint:** Mannheim **Note:** Dav. #7145. Prev. Pfalz-Simmern KM#29.

Date	Mintage	VG	F	VF	XF	Unc
1610 Rare	—	—	—	—	—	—

KM# 130 2 THALER

Silver **Ruler:** Philipp Wilhelm **Obv:** 3 gothic canopies, St. Peter enthroned under central canopy, Counts Ruprecht I and II kneeling in left and right canopies **Obv. Legend:** VNIVERSITATIS. HEIDELBERG FESTVM. SECVLARE. III **Rev:** 13-line inscription with Roman Numeral date

Date	Mintage	VG	F	VF	XF	Unc
MDCXXCVI (1686) IL Rare	—	—	—	—	—	—

KM# 152 2 THALER

Silver **Ruler:** Johann Wilhelm **Obv:** Bust of Johann Wilhelm right **Rev:** Shield of arms **Note:** Dav. #7178. Prev. Pfalz-Neuburg KM#54.

Date	Mintage	VG	F	VF	XF	Unc
1700 Rare	—	—	—	—	—	—

TRADE COINAGE

KM# 73 GOLDGULDEN

3.5000 g., 0.9860 Gold 0.1109 oz. AGW **Ruler:** Friedrich V **Obv:** Lion **Rev:** Palatine arms in 3 shields **Mint:** Heidelberg **Note:** Fr. #1998. Prev. Pfalz-Simmern KM#52.

Date	Mintage	VG	F	VF	XF	Unc
1621	—	750	1,600	3,400	6,100	—

KM# 74 GOLDGULDEN

3.5000 g., 0.9860 Gold 0.1109 oz. AGW **Ruler:** Friedrich IV **Obv:** Rampant lion in inner circle **Mint:** Heidelberg **Note:** Fr. #1999. Prev. Pfalz-Simmern KM#53.

Date	Mintage	VG	F	VF	XF	Unc
1621	—	475	1,300	2,700	4,750	—

KM# 22 2-3/4 GOLDGULDEN

3.5000 g., 0.9860 Gold 0.1109 oz. AGW **Ruler:** Friedrich IV **Obv:** 1/2-figure of Friedrich IV w/sword and orb right **Rev:** Crown above 3 shields of arms, date divided below **Mint:** Mannheim **Note:** Fr. #1994. Prev. Pfalz-Simmern KM#18.

Date	Mintage	VG	F	VF	XF	Unc
1608	—	550	1,200	3,000	4,800	—

KM# 34 10 GOLDGULDEN (Portugalöser)

Gold, 40 mm. **Ruler:** Johann II **Obv:** Bust to right in circle **Obv. Legend:** IOHAN. D.G. CO. PAL. RH. TV. ET. ADMI. EL. PAL. D. BA. C. V. E. S. **Rev:** Three small shields of arms, 2 over 1, crown above, date at end of legend **Rev. Legend:** VERBVM. DOMINI. MANET. IN AETERNVM. A. **Note:** Struck from Thaler dies, KM#35.

Date	Mintage	Good	VG	F	VF	XF
1610 Rare	—	—	—	—	—	—

KM# 110 1/4 DUCAT

0.8750 g., Gold **Ruler:** Karl Ludwig **Obv:** Bust of Karl Ludwig right in inner circle **Rev:** Helmet above 3 shields of arms in inner circle, date in legend **Note:** Fr. #2004. Prev. Pfalz-Simmern KM#111.

Date	Mintage	VG	F	VF	XF	Unc
1674	—	500	1,000	2,200	4,250	—

KM# 108 1/2 DUCAT

1.7500 g., 0.9860 Gold 0.0555 oz. AGW **Ruler:** Karl Ludwig **Obv:** Bust of Karl Ludwig right **Rev:** 3 shields of arms **Note:** Fr. #2003. Prev. Pfalz-Simmern KM#110.

Date	Mintage	VG	F	VF	XF	Unc
1673	—	600	1,350	3,300	5,300	—

KM# 112 1/2 DUCAT

1.7500 g., 0.9860 Gold 0.0555 oz. AGW **Ruler:** Karl Ludwig **Obv:** Bust of Karl Ludwig right in inner circle **Rev:** Date in legend at right **Note:** Fr. #2002. Prev. Pfalz-Simmern KM#112. Rhine Gold.

Date	Mintage	VG	F	VF	XF	Unc
1674	—	500	1,200	2,550	4,750	—

KM# 54 DUCAT

Gold **Ruler:** Friedrich V **Obv:** Full-length facing armored figure holding orb, helmet at feet, titles of Friedrich V **Rev:** 3 small shields of arms, 2 above 1, electoral hat above, all in circle, date at end of legend **Rev. Legend:** MONETA. NOVA. AVREA. ANNO. **Mint:** Heidelberg

Date	Mintage	VG	F	VF	XF	Unc
1612 Rare	—	—	—	—	—	—

KM# 49 DUCAT

3.5000 g., 0.9860 Gold 0.1109 oz. AGW **Ruler:** Friedrich V **Obv:** Equestrian figure of Friedrich V right in inner circle **Rev:** Crown above 3 shields of arms in inner circle, date in legend **Note:** Fr. #1997. Prev. Pfalz-Simmern KM#31.

Date	Mintage	VG	F	VF	XF	Unc
1612	—	550	1,200	2,950	4,750	—

KM# 86 DUCAT

3.5000 g., 0.9860 Gold 0.1109 oz. AGW **Ruler:** Karl Ludwig **Obv:** Bust of Karl Ludwig right in inner circle **Rev:** Crown above 3 shields **Note:** Fr. #2000. Vicariat issue. Prev. Pfalz-Simmern KM#94.

Date	Mintage	VG	F	VF	XF	Unc
1657	—	900	1,800	4,200	7,200	—

KM# 94 DUCAT

3.5000 g., 0.9860 Gold 0.1109 oz. AGW **Ruler:** Karl Ludwig **Obv:** Bust of Karl Ludwig right **Rev:** Crowned 3 shields in inner circle **Note:** Fr. #2001. Prev. Pfalz-Simmern KM#100.

Date	Mintage	VG	F	VF	XF	Unc
1659	—	475	1,100	2,650	4,200	—
1662	—	475	1,100	2,650	4,200	—
1673	—	475	1,100	2,650	4,200	—

KM# 122 DUCAT

3.5000 g., 0.9860 Gold 0.1109 oz. AGW **Ruler:** Karl von Simmern **Obv:** Bust of Karl right in inner circle **Note:** Fr. #2005. Prev. Pfalz-Simmern KM#117.

Date	Mintage	VG	F	VF	XF	Unc
1682	—	650	1,350	3,000	6,000	—
1683	—	650	1,350	3,000	6,000	—

KM# 124 DUCAT

3.5000 g., 0.9860 Gold 0.1109 oz. AGW **Ruler:** Philipp Wilhelm **Obv:** Bust of Johann Wilhelm right **Rev:** Crowned arms **Note:** Prev. Pfalz-Sulzbach KM#6.

Date	Mintage	VG	F	VF	XF	Unc
1683	—	300	700	1,600	2,800	—
1686	—	300	700	1,600	2,800	—

KM# 53 2 DUCAT

7.0000 g., 0.9860 Gold 0.2219 oz. AGW **Ruler:** Friedrich V **Obv:** Equestrian figure of Friedrich V right in inner circle **Rev:** Crown above 3 shields of arms in inner circle, date in legend **Note:** Fr. #1996. Prev. Pfalz-Simmern KM#32.

Date	Mintage	VG	F	VF	XF	Unc
1612 Rare	—	—	—	—	—	—

KM# 56 2 DUCAT

Gold **Ruler:** Johann II **Obv:** Bust right in circle, date at end of inner legend, outer legend - titles of Johann II **Obv. Legend:** VICARIVS DVXB. CO. V. & SPAN **Rev:** Crowned imperial eagle, legend divided by crown at top and 3 small shields of arms at left, right and bottom **Rev. Legend:** VERB. - DOMI. - MANI. - ?TER. **Mint:** Heidelberg **Note:** Vicariat issue.

Date	Mintage	VG	F	VF	XF	Unc
161Z Rare	—	—	—	—	—	—

KM# 55 4 DUCAT

14.0000 g., 0.9860 Gold 0.4438 oz. AGW **Ruler:** Friedrich V **Obv:** Equestrian figure of Friedrich V right **Rev:** Crown above 3 shields in inner circle **Note:** Fr. #1995. Prev. Pfalz-Simmern KM#33.

Date	Mintage	VG	F	VF	XF	Unc
1612 Rare	—	—	—	—	—	—

PFALZ-NEUBURG

Pfalz-Neuburg takes its name designation from the town Neuburg on the Danube, 11 miles (18 kilometers) west of Ingolstadt, in the Upper Palatinate (Oberpfalz). It was acquired by Electoral Pfalz from Bavaria-Landshut when the ducal line of that principality became extinct in 1504. Two nephews of the elector ruled in Pfalz-Neuburg jointly, then the survivor continued until he succeeded to the electorate in 1556. In the following year, Wolfgang, the count Palatine (Pfalzgraf) of Pfalz-Zweibrücken purchased Neuburg and Sulzbach. The new line of Pfalz-Neuburg was founded by the eldest son of Wolfgang in the division of 1569. Pfalz-Neuburg acquired Pfalz-Sulzbach in 1604, then divided into Pfalz-Neuburg and Pfalz-Sulzbach in 1614. In 1685, the male line of descent in the Electoral Line from Pfalz-Simmern failed and the electoral dignity passed to Pfalz-Neuburg. See Electoral Pfalz for coinage after 1685.

RULERS

Philipp Ludwig, 1569-1614
Wolfgang-Wilhelm, 1614-1653
Philipp Wilhelm, 1653-1685, died 1690

MINT OFFICIALS' INITIALS

Other than Neuburg itself, mints were opened in four locations during the Kipper Period of the Thirty Years' War. Gundelfingen is a town on the River Brenz close to where it joins the Danube, next to the larger town of Lauingen and about halfway between Ulm and Donauwörth. Höchstädt is a town on the Danube about 12 miles (21km) southwest of Donauwörth. Stockau is a very small village on the River Paar 14 miles (23km) east-southeast of Neuburg and Kallmünz is a village at the junction of the Naab and Vils Rivers, 11 miles (19km) northwest of Regensburg.

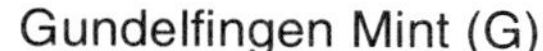

Gundelfingen Mint (G)

Initial	Date	Name
	July, 1621	Abraham Jud
(a)=	1621-22	Heinrich Brandes
(b)=	Jan. 1622	Johann Rentsch
	Aug. 1622-	Friedrich Gebhardt
	1622	Joachim Friedrich Krauss, warden

Höchstädt Mint (H)

Initial	Date	Name
	Jan. 1622-	Johann Rentsch

Kallmünz Mint (K or C)

Initial	Date	Name
(e)= or	1622	Heinrich Brandes
CE	1623-25	Karl Ernst
	1623	Jonas Federer
(f)=	1626-27	Friedrich held
	Ca. 1629	Christof Resel, die-cutter
(g)= or	1625-32	Jörg (Georg) Thomas Paul
ITP/GTP		Jörg (Georg) Thomas paul
(h)= face in half moon to left	1625	Christof Geissler

Stockau Mint (S)

Initial	Date	Name
	Sept. 1621	Abraham Jud
(c)=	1622	Schottmüller
(d)=	Jan. 1622	Johann Rentsch

REFERENCE

N = Alfred Noss, *Die pfälzischen Münzen des Hauses Wittelsbach*, **v. 4**, *Pfalz-Veldenz, Pfalz-Neuburg, Pfalz-Sulzbach*, **Munich, 1938.**

PALATINE COUNTSHIP

REGULAR COINAGE

KM# 53 PFENNIG

Silver **Ruler:** Wolfgang-Wilhelm **Obv:** Large 'N' with date above in circle **Rev:** Oval Wittelsbach arms divide mintmaster's initials, 'C' above, all in circle **Mint:** Kallmunz **Note:** Ref. N#341.

Date	Mintage	VG	F	VF	XF	Unc
1624 CE	—	10.00	20.00	40.00	—	—

KM# 62 PFENNIG

Silver **Ruler:** Wolfgang-Wilhelm **Obv:** Large double 'W' **Rev:** Small Spanish shield of Wittelsbach arms in circle **Mint:** Kallmunz **Note:** Ref. N#406-07. Varieties exist.

Date	Mintage	VG	F	VF	XF	Unc
ND(1625-30)	—	10.00	20.00	40.00	—	—

KM# 66 PFENNIG

Silver **Ruler:** Wolfgang-Wilhelm **Obv:** Large double 'W', C.P.R. (Comes Palatinus Rheni) above, date below, all in circle **Rev:** Small spanish shield of Wittelsbach arms in circle **Mint:** Kallmunz **Note:** Ref. N#365.

Date	Mintage	VG	F	VF	XF	Unc
1626	—	10.00	20.00	40.00	—	—

KM# 30 1/2 SCHILLING (1/16 Thaler)

Silver **Ruler:** Wolfgang-Wilhelm **Obv:** Crowned oval 8-fold arms with central shield, all within Order of Golden Fleece **Obv. Legend:** IN DEO MEA - CONSOLATIO **Rev:** 7-line inscription **Rev. Inscription:** HALBER / BAIRISCH. SC. / HILLING. NACH / ALTEM. VALOR / .XVI. FVR. EIN / REICHSDALER / (date) **Mint:** Gundelfingen **Note:** Bavarian standard. Ref. N#279.

Date	Mintage	VG	F	VF	XF	Unc
1622 (a)	—	—	—	—	—	—

KM# 31 1/2 SCHILLING (1/16 Thaler)

Silver **Ruler:** Wolfgang-Wilhelm **Obv:** Crowned oval 8-fold arms with central shield, al within Order of Golden Fleece **Obv. Legend:** IN DEO MEA - CONSOLATIO **Rev:** 7-line inscription, date at end **Rev. Inscription:** HALBER / BAIRISCH. SC. / HILLING. NACH / ALTEM. VALER / .XVI. FVR. EIN / REISCHSDALER **Mint:** Gundelfingen **Note:** Ref. N#280.

Date	Mintage	VG	F	VF	XF	Unc
1622 (a)	—	—	—	—	—	—

KM# 3 1/2 KREUZER

Billon **Ruler:** Wolfgang-Wilhelm **Obv:** Similar to KM#2 but w/oval 8-fold arms with central shield within Order of Golden Fleece **Mint:** Kallmunz **Note:** Kipper. Ref. N#299.

Date	Mintage	Good	VG	F	VF	XF
ND(1621-22)	—	8.00	15.00	30.00	65.00	—

KM# 2 1/2 KREUZER

Billon **Ruler:** Wolfgang-Wilhelm **Obv:** 3 small adjacent shields of arms with electoral hat above divide date, titles of Wolfgang Wilhelm **Rev:** Inscription in wreath **Rev. Inscription:** 120 / 1/2 K **Mint:** Kallmunz **Note:** Kipper. Ref. N#297-98.

Date	Mintage	VG	F	VF	XF	Unc
1621	—	18.00	32.00	70.00	—	—
1622	—	18.00	32.00	70.00	—	—

KM# 8 1/2 KREUZER

Silver **Ruler:** Wolfgang-Wilhelm **Obv:** 3 small shields of arms, 2 above 1, electoral hat above **Obv. Legend:** W ★ W ★ - ★ CP ★ R ★ (Wolfgang Wilhelm Comes Palatinus Rheni) **Mint:** Kallmunz **Note:** Ref. N#320-21. Varieties exist. Uniface.

Date	Mintage	VG	F	VF	XF	Unc
ND(1622-23)	—	20.00	40.00	85.00	—	—

KM# 38 1/2 KREUZER

Silver **Ruler:** Wolfgang-Wilhelm **Obv:** Hatted 3-fold arms in Spanish shield **Obv. Legend:** W. W. C. P. R. **Rev:** Imperial orb with 1/2 divides date **Mint:** Kallmunz **Note:** Ref. N#330-31. Varieties exist.

Date	Mintage	VG	F	VF	XF	Unc
1623	—	20.00	40.00	85.00	—	—

KM# 55 1/2 KREUZER

Silver **Ruler:** Wolfgang-Wilhelm **Obv:** 3 small shields of arms, 2 above 1, electoral hat divides date **Mint:** Kallmunz **Note:** Uniface. Ref. N#340, 350, 361-64, 383, 404. Varieties exist.

Date	Mintage	VG	F	VF	XF	Unc
1624	—	15.00	30.00	50.00	90.00	—
1625	—	15.00	30.00	50.00	90.00	—
1626	—	15.00	30.00	50.00	90.00	—
1628	—	15.00	30.00	50.00	90.00	—
1632	—	15.00	30.00	50.00	90.00	—

KM# 75 1/2 KREUZER

Silver **Ruler:** Wolfgang-Wilhelm **Obv:** Oval 3-fold arms, electoral hat above divides date, legend around **Obv. Legend:** W. W. C. P. R. **Mint:** Kallmunz **Note:** Ref. N#384. Uniface.

Date	Mintage	VG	F	VF	XF	Unc
1628	—	20.00	40.00	85.00	—	—

KM# 10 KREUZER

Billon **Ruler:** Wolfgang-Wilhelm **Obv:** 8-fold arms with central shield, electoral hat above divides date, titles of Wolfgang Wilhelm **Rev:** 60/K in wreath **Mint:** Kallmunz **Note:** Ref. N#296. Kipper.

Date	Mintage	VG	F	VF	XF	Unc
1622	—	8.00	15.00	30.00	65.00	—

KM# 68 KREUZER

Silver **Ruler:** Wolfgang-Wilhelm **Obv:** Double-cross in circle, value 'I' in small central shield, date divided at top, titles of Wolfgang Wilhelm **Rev:** Hatted 8-fold arms with central shield, titles continued **Mint:** Kallmunz **Note:** Ref. N#359-60, 376. Varieties exist.

Date	Mintage	VG	F	VF	XF	Unc
1626	—	15.00	25.00	45.00	—	—
1627	—	15.00	25.00	45.00	—	—

KM# 77 KREUZER

Silver **Ruler:** Wolfgang-Wilhelm **Obv:** Cross with lily ends in circle, value 'I' in small central shield, date divided at top, titles of Woldgang Wilhelm **Mint:** Kallmunz **Note:** Ref. N#382.

Date	Mintage	VG	F	VF	XF	Unc
1628 (g)	—	15.00	25.00	45.00	—	—

KM# 41 KREUZER

Billon **Ruler:** Philipp Wilhelm **Obv:** Crowned lion rampant left in circle **Obv. Legend:** P. W. C. P. R. S... **Rev:** 1 KREUTZER **Rev. Legend:** B. I. C. M. D. C...

Date	Mintage	VG	F	VF	XF	Unc
1688 gb	—	18.00	32.00	65.00	125	—

KM# 11 KREUZER (4 Pfennig)

Copper **Ruler:** Wolfgang-Wilhelm **Obv:** Hatted 8-fold arms with central shield divide date, titles of Wolfgang Wilhelm **Rev:** II + II in circle **Mint:** Kallmunz **Note:** Ref. N#300.

Date	Mintage	VG	F	VF	XF	Unc
1622	1,053,000	12.00	25.00	45.00	80.00	—

KM# 12 KREUZER (4 Pfennig)

Copper **Ruler:** Wolfgang-Wilhelm **Obv:** Hatted oval arms with central shield dividing date, titles of Wolfgang Wilhelm **Rev:** II + II in circle **Mint:** Kallmunz **Note:** Ref. N#301-07. Varieties exist.

Date	Mintage	VG	F	VF	XF	Unc
ND(1622-23)	—	9.00	20.00	35.00	60.00	—

KM# 40 2 KREUZER (1/2 Batzen)

1.0800 g., Silver, 19 mm. **Ruler:** Wolfgang-Wilhelm **Obv:** Hatted 8-fold arms with central shield, titles of Wolfgang Wilhelm **Rev:** Imperial orb with 2 or Z divides date **Rev. Legend:** MON. NOVA. PAL(A)NEOBVRG (or variant) **Mint:** Kallmunz **Note:** Ref. N#326-29, 334-39, 343-49, 353-58, 368-75, 377-81, 387-89, 393-95, 399-403, 405. Varieties exist.

Date	Mintage	VG	F	VF	XF	Unc
1623	—	10.00	18.00	30.00	50.00	—
1623 (a)	—	10.00	18.00	30.00	50.00	—
1624	—	10.00	18.00	30.00	50.00	—
1625	—	10.00	18.00	30.00	50.00	—
1625 (g)	—	10.00	18.00	30.00	50.00	—
1625 (h)	—	10.00	18.00	30.00	50.00	—
1626 (c)	—	10.00	18.00	30.00	50.00	—
1626 (g)	—	10.00	18.00	30.00	50.00	—
1627 (g)	—	10.00	18.00	30.00	50.00	—
1628	—	10.00	18.00	30.00	50.00	—
1628 (g)	—	10.00	18.00	30.00	50.00	—
1629 (g)	—	10.00	18.00	30.00	50.00	—
1630 (g)	—	10.00	18.00	30.00	50.00	—
1631 (g)	—	10.00	18.00	30.00	50.00	—
1632 (g)	—	10.00	18.00	30.00	50.00	—
163Z (g)	—	10.00	18.00	30.00	50.00	—
1634 (g)	—	10.00	18.00	30.00	50.00	—

KM# 42 3 KREUZER (Groschen)

Silver **Ruler:** Wolfgang-Wilhelm **Obv:** Crowned rampant Pfalz lion to left in circle, titles of Wolfgang Wilhelm **Rev:** Imperial orb with 3 divides date, titles continued **Note:** Ref. N#325.

Date	Mintage	VG	F	VF	XF	Unc
1623 (b)	—	—	—	—	—	—

KM# 5 24 KREUZER (Sechsbätzner)

Silver **Ruler:** Wolfgang-Wilhelm **Obv:** Crowned lion rampant left holding ornamented oval with 24 **Obv. Legend:** MONETA. NOVA ... **Rev:** Ornate 8-fold arms with central shield, Order of Golden Fleece around, electoral hat above **Rev. Legend:** IN DEO MEA - CONSOLATIO **Mint:** Gundelfingen **Note:** Ref. N#263. Kipper.

Date	Mintage	VG	F	VF	XF	Unc
ND(1621) (a)	—	200	325	500	725	—

KM# 6 24 KREUZER (Sechsbätzner)

Silver **Ruler:** Wolfgang-Wilhelm **Obv:** Crowned lion rampant left holding ornamented oval, date below with value **Obv. Legend:** MONETA. NOVA ... **Rev:** Ornate 8-fold arms with central shield, Order of Golden Fleece around, electoral hat above **Rev. Legend:** IN DEO MEA - CONSOLATIO **Mint:** Gundelfingen **Note:** Ref. N#264-65, 278. Kipper.

Date	Mintage	VG	F	VF	XF	Unc
1621 (a)	—	150	275	450	700	—
1622 (g)	—	150	275	450	700	—
1622 G	—	150	275	450	700	—

KM# 14 24 KREUZER (Sechsbätzner)

Silver **Ruler:** Wolfgang-Wilhelm **Obv:** Crowned lion rampant left with mint mark 'G' below, ornamented oval with 24 **Obv. Legend:** MONETA. NOVA ... **Rev:** Ornate 8-fold arms with central shield, Order of Golden Fleece around, electoral hat above **Rev. Legend:** IN DEO MEA - CONSOLATIO. **Mint:** Gundelfingen **Note:** Ref. N#266-67, 271-72. Kipper.

Date	Mintage	VG	F	VF	XF	Unc
1622 G	—	150	275	450	700	—
ND G	—	150	275	450	700	—

KM# 15 24 KREUZER (Sechsbätzner)

Silver **Ruler:** Wolfgang-Wilhelm **Obv:** Crowned lion rampant left holding ornamented oval with 24, date at end of legend **Obv. Legend:** MONETA. NOVA **Rev:** Ornate 8-fold arms with central shield, Order of Golden Fleece around, electoral hat above **Rev. Legend:** IN DEO MEA - CONSOLATIO **Mint:** Gundelfingen **Note:** Ref. N#268. Kipper.

Date	Mintage	VG	F	VF	XF	Unc
1622 (b)	—	150	275	450	700	—

KM# 16 24 KREUZER (Sechsbätzner)

Silver **Ruler:** Wolfgang-Wilhelm **Obv:** Crowned lion rampant left holding ornamented oval with 24, mint mark 'G' below lion, date at end of legend **Obv. Legend:** MONETA. NOVA ... **Rev:** Ornate 8-fold arms with central shield, Order of Golden Fleece around, electoral hat above **Rev. Legend:** IN DEO MEA - CONSOLATIO **Mint:** Gundelfingen **Note:** Ref. N#269-70.

Date	Mintage	VG	F	VF	XF	Unc
1622	—	150	275	450	700	—

KM# 17 24 KREUZER (Sechsbätzner)

Silver **Ruler:** Wolfgang-Wilhelm **Obv:** Crowned lion rampant left holding ornamented oval with 24, mint mark 'G' below lion, date by hind leg of lion **Obv. Legend:** MONETA. NOVA ... **Rev:** Ornate 8-fold arms with central shield, Order of Golden Fleece around, electoral hat abaove **Rev. Legend:** IN DEO MEA - CONSOLATIO **Mint:** Gundelfingen **Note:** Kipper. Ref. N#276-77.

Date	Mintage	VG	F	VF	XF	Unc
1622 G	—	150	275	450	700	—

KM# 18 24 KREUZER (Sechsbätzner)

Silver **Ruler:** Wolfgang-Wilhelm **Obv:** Crowned lion rampant left holding ornamented oval with 24 **Obv. Legend:** MONETA. NOVA ... **Rev:** Oval arms, Order of Golden Fleece around, electoral hat above **Rev. Legend:** IN DEO MEA - CONSOLATIO **Mint:** Stockau **Note:** Kipper. Ref. N#284.

Date	Mintage	VG	F	VF	XF	Unc
ND(1622) (c)	—	150	275	450	700	—

KM# 19 24 KREUZER (Sechsbätzner)

Silver **Ruler:** Wolfgang-Wilhelm **Obv:** Crowned lion rampant left holding ornamented oval with 24, 'S' below lion **Obv. Legend:** MONETA. NOVA ... **Rev:** Oval arms, Order of Golden Fleece around, electoral hat above **Rev. Legend:** IN DEO MEA - CONSOLATIO **Mint:** Stockau **Note:** Kipper. Ref. N#285, 287-88. Varieties exist.

Date	Mintage	VG	F	VF	XF	Unc
ND(1622) S	—	150	275	450	700	—
ND(1622) S (d)	—	150	275	450	700	—

KM# 20 24 KREUZER (Sechsbätzner)

Silver **Ruler:** Wolfgang-Wilhelm **Obv:** Crowned lion rampant left holding ornamented oval with 24, mint mark 'S' below lion **Obv. Legend:** MONETA. NOVA ... **Rev:** Oval arms, Order of Golden Fleece around, electoral hat above, date at end of legend **Rev. Legend:** IN DEO MEA - CONSOLATIO **Mint:** Stockau **Note:** Kipper. Ref. N#286.

Date	Mintage	VG	F	VF	XF	Unc
1622 S (d)	—	150	275	450	700	—

KM# 21 24 KREUZER (Sechsbätzner)

Silver **Ruler:** Wolfgang-Wilhelm **Obv:** Crowned lion rampant left holding ornamented oval with 24 **Obv. Legend:** MONETA. NOVA ... **Rev:** Ornate 8-fold arms with central shield, Order of Golden Fleece around, electoral hat above, date at end of legend **Rev. Legend:** IN DEO MEA - CONSOLATIO **Mint:** Hochstadt **Note:** Ref. N#289. Kipper.

Date	Mintage	VG	F	VF	XF	Unc
1622 H	—	150	275	450	700	—

KM# 22 24 KREUZER (Sechsbätzner)

Silver **Ruler:** Wolfgang-Wilhelm **Obv:** Crowned lion rampant left holding ornamented oval with 24, mint mark 'H' engraved over 'G' **Obv. Legend:** MONETA. NOVA ... **Rev:** Ornate 8-fold arms with central shield, Order of Golden Fleece around **Rev. Legend:** IN DEO MEA - CONSOLATIO **Mint:** Hochstadt **Note:** Ref. N#290. Kipper.

Date	Mintage	VG	F	VF	XF	Unc
ND(1622) H	—	150	275	450	700	—

KM# 23 24 KREUZER (Sechsbätzner)

Silver **Ruler:** Wolfgang-Wilhelm **Obv:** Crowned lion rampant left holding ornamental oval with 24, 'K' below lion **Obv. Legend:** MONETA. NOVA ... **Rev:** Ornately shaped arms, Order of Golden Fleece around, electoral hat above **Rev. Legend:** IN DEO MEA - CONSOLATIO **Mint:** Kallmunz **Note:** Ref. N#291-94. Kipper. Varieties exist.

Date	Mintage	VG	F	VF	XF	Unc
1622 K (e)	—	150	275	450	700	—
1622 K	—	150	275	450	700	—

KM# 95 30 KREUZER (1/2 Gulden)

Silver **Ruler:** Philipp Wilhelm **Obv:** Armored bust right, titles of Philip Wilhelm ending with date at top **Rev:** Crowned 8-fold arms with central shield, all in Order of Golden Fleece, value (30) below **Rev. Legend:** MONETA. NOVA ... **Mint:** Kallmunz **Note:** Ref. N#415.

Date	Mintage	VG	F	VF	XF	Unc
1674	—	225	450	625	850	—

KM# 25 48 KREUZER

Silver **Ruler:** Wolfgang-Wilhelm **Obv:** Crowned facing lion, seated and holding oval with '48' in paw, head divides date **Obv. Legend:** MONETA. NOVA ... **Rev:** Oval 8-fold arms with central shield, Order of Golden Fleece around, electoral hat above **Rev. Legend:** IN DEO MEA - CONSOLATIO **Mint:** Gundelfingen **Note:** Ref. N#273. Kipper. Varieties exist.

Date	Mintage	VG	F	VF	XF	Unc
1622 (a)	—	—	—	—	—	—

KM# 26 48 KREUZER

Silver **Ruler:** Wolfgang-Wilhelm **Obv:** Crowned facing lion, seated and holding oval with 48 in paw, date at end of legend **Obv. Legend:** MONETA. NOVA ? **Rev:** Oval 8 fold arms with central shield, Order of Golden Fleece around, electoral hat above **Rev. Legend:** IN DEO MEA - CONSOLATIO **Mint:** Gundelfingen **Note:** Ref. N#274. Varieties exist.

Date	Mintage	VG	F	VF	XF	Unc
1622	—	—	—	—	—	—

KM# 27 48 KREUZER

Silver **Ruler:** Wolfgang-Wilhelm **Obv:** Crowned, seated lion 1/2-right holding oval with 48 in paw, mint mark G below, head divides date **Obv. Legend:** MONETA. NOVA ... **Rev:** Oval 8-fold arms with central shield, Order of Golden Fleece around, electoral hat above **Rev. Legend:** IN DEO MEA - CONSOLATIO **Mint:** Gundelfingen **Note:** Ref. N#275.

Date	Mintage	VG	F	VF	XF	Unc
1622 G	—	—	—	—	—	—

KM# 28 48 KREUZER

Silver **Ruler:** Wolfgang-Wilhelm **Obv:** Crowned seated lion 1/2-right holding oval with 48 in paw, 'S' mint mark, no date **Obv. Legend:** MONETA. NOVA ... **Rev:** Oval 8-fold arms with central shield, Order of Golden Fleece around, electoral hat above **Rev. Legend:** IN DEO MEA - CONSOLATIO **Mint:** Stockau **Note:** Ref. N#281-83. Varieties exist.

Date	Mintage	VG	F	VF	XF	Unc
ND(1622) S	—	—	—	—	—	—
ND(1622) S (c)	—	—	—	—	—	—

KM# 97 60 KREUZER (1 Gulden)

Silver **Ruler:** Philipp Wilhelm **Obv:** Armored bust right divides date, titles of Philipp Wilhelm **Rev:** Crowned 8-fold arms with central shield, all within Order of Golden Fleece, value (60) below **Rev. Legend:** MONETA. NOVA ... **Mint:** Stockau **Note:** Dav. #757. Varieties exist.

Date	Mintage	VG	F	VF	XF	Unc
1674	—	125	250	475	700	—

KM# 98 60 KREUZER (1 Gulden)

Silver **Ruler:** Philipp Wilhelm **Obv:** Armored bust right, titles of Philipp Wilhelm ending with date above or divided by crown **Rev:** Crowned 8-fold arms with central shield, all in Order of Golden Fleece, value (60) below arms **Rev. Legend:** MONETA. NOVA ... **Mint:** Stockau **Note:** Dav. #758. Varieties exist.

Date	Mintage	VG	F	VF	XF	Unc
1674	—	100	200	325	525	—
1675	—	100	200	325	525	—

KM# 83 1/6 THALER

Silver **Ruler:** Wolfgang-Wilhelm **Obv:** Bust right in circle, value 1/6 in oval below, titles of Wolfgang Wilhelm **Rev:** Ornate 8-fold arms with central shield within Order of Golden Fleece divide mintmaster's initials, titles continued, date in legend **Mint:** Neuburg **Note:** Ref. N#392.

Date	Mintage	VG	F	VF	XF	Unc
1631 GTP	—	—	—	—	—	—

KM# 88 1/4 THALER

Silver **Ruler:** Wolfgang-Wilhelm **Obv:** Bust right in circle, titles of Wolfgang Wilhelm **Rev:** Ornate 8-fold arms with central shield within Order of Golden Fleece divide mintmaster's initials, titles continued **Mint:** Neuburg **Note:** Ref. N#319.

Date	Mintage	VG	F	VF	XF	Unc
ND(1632-35) (b)	—	—	—	—	—	—

KM# 44 1/2 THALER

Silver **Ruler:** Wolfgang-Wilhelm **Obv:** Collared bust right, outer legend with titles of Wolfgang Wilhelm **Obv. Legend:** IN DEO MEA - CONSOLATIO **Rev:** 8-fold arms with central shield, all within Order of Golden Fleece, crown above divides date, titles continued **Mint:** Neuburg **Note:** Ref. N#313, 318.

Date	Mintage	VG	F	VF	XF	Unc
1623	—	800	1,150	1,600	2,100	—
ND	—	800	1,150	1,600	2,100	—

KM# 57 1/2 THALER

Silver **Ruler:** Wolfgang-Wilhelm **Obv:** Collared bust right, value '1/2' at top, outer legend titles of Wolfgang Wilhelm **Rev:** 8-fold arms with central shield, all within Order of Golden Fleece, crown above, titles continued with date at end **Mint:** Neuburg **Note:** Ref. N#333.

Date	Mintage	VG	F	VF	XF	Unc
1624	—	500	850	1,200	1,500	—

KM# 90 1/2 THALER

Silver **Ruler:** Wolfgang-Wilhelm **Obv:** Armored bust right, titles of Wolfgang Wilhelm **Obv. Legend:** IN DEO MEA - CONSOLATIO **Rev:** 8-fold arms with central shield, all within Order of Golden Fleece, crown above, titles continued, date at end of legend **Mint:** Neuburg **Note:** Ref. N#397.

Date	Mintage	VG	F	VF	XF	Unc
1632 (g)	—	—	—	—	—	—

KM# 33 THALER

Silver **Ruler:** Wolfgang-Wilhelm **Obv:** Ruffled bust right, inside legend **Obv. Legend:** IN. DEO. MEO. CONSOLATIO. **Rev:** Crowned arms divide date **Note:** Dav. #7158. Prev. KM#5.

Date	Mintage	VG	F	VF	XF	Unc
1622	—	270	550	1,000	1,600	—

KM# 35 THALER

Silver **Ruler:** Wolfgang-Wilhelm **Note:** Klippe. Dav. #7158A. Prev. KM#6.

Date	Mintage	VG	F	VF	XF	Unc
1622 Rare	—	—	—	—	—	—

KM# 36 THALER

Silver **Ruler:** Wolfgang-Wilhelm **Obv:** Inside legend **Obv. Legend:** IN. DEO. MEA. CONSLATIO **Note:** Dav. #7159. Prev. KM#7.

Date	Mintage	VG	F	VF	XF	Unc
1622	—	270	550	1,000	1,600	—

KM# 46 THALER

Silver **Ruler:** Wolfgang-Wilhelm **Obv:** Large collar, fuller beard **Rev:** Crowned arms divide date above **Note:** Dav. #7160.

Date	Mintage	VG	F	VF	XF	Unc
1623	—	205	400	800	1,350	—

KM# 47 THALER

Silver **Ruler:** Wolfgang-Wilhelm **Obv. Legend:** WOLF. GVIL. CO. PAL. RH. DVX... **Note:** Dav. #7161. Prev. KM#10.

Date	Mintage	VG	F	VF	XF	Unc
1623	—	205	400	800	1,350	—

KM# 48 THALER

Silver **Ruler:** Wolfgang-Wilhelm **Obv. Legend:** ...CLI. ET. MONT. **Note:** Dav. #7162. Prev. KM#11.

Date	Mintage	VG	F	VF	XF	Unc
1623	—	205	400	800	1,350	—

KM# 49 THALER

Silver **Ruler:** Wolfgang-Wilhelm **Obv:** Larger head **Obv. Legend:** ... MO: **Note:** Dav. #7162A. Prev. KM#12.

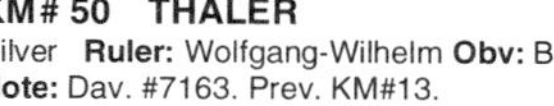

Date	Mintage	VG	F	VF	XF	Unc
1623	—	205	400	800	1,350	—

KM# 50 THALER

Silver **Ruler:** Wolfgang-Wilhelm **Obv:** Bust right divides date **Note:** Dav. #7163. Prev. KM#13.

Date	Mintage	VG	F	VF	XF	Unc
1623	—	205	400	800	1,350	—

KM# 51 THALER

Silver **Ruler:** Wolfgang-Wilhelm **Obv:** Ruffled bust divides inner legend **Rev:** Crowned arms **Note:** Dav. #7164. Prev. KM#14.

Date	Mintage	VG	F	VF	XF	Unc
ND (b)	—	205	400	800	1,350	—

KM# 59 THALER

Silver **Ruler:** Wolfgang-Wilhelm **Obv:** Ruffled bust right, ornamented shoulder, inner legend **Rev:** Crowned arms in Order chain **Note:** Dav. #7166. Prev. KM#15.

Date	Mintage	VG	F	VF	XF	Unc
1624 CE	—	205	400	800	1,350	—

KM# 64 THALER

Silver **Ruler:** Wolfgang-Wilhelm **Obv:** Plain inner field **Rev:** Crowned ornate arms, date in legend **Note:** Dav. #7167. Prev. KM#17.

Date	Mintage	VG	F	VF	XF	Unc
1625 (h)	—	205	400	800	1,350	—
1626 ITP	—	205	400	800	1,350	—

KM# 70 THALER

Silver **Ruler:** Wolfgang-Wilhelm **Obv:** Bust right in inner circle, titles of Wolfgang-Wilhelm **Rev:** Crowned shield of arms **Note:** Dav. #7168. Prev. KM#18.

Date	Mintage	VG	F	VF	XF	Unc
1626 GTP	—	350	675	1,200	2,050	—

KM# 72 THALER

Silver **Ruler:** Wolfgang-Wilhelm **Rev:** Capped arms in Order chain divide GT-P **Note:** Dav. #7170. Prev. KM#19.

Date	Mintage	VG	F	VF	XF	Unc
1627 GTP Rare	—	—	—	—	—	—

KM# 79 THALER

Silver **Ruler:** Wolfgang-Wilhelm **Obv:** Taller bust **Note:** Dav. #7172. Prev. KM#21.

Date	Mintage	VG	F	VF	XF	Unc
16Z9 GTP	—	350	675	1,200	2,050	—

KM# 81 THALER

Silver **Ruler:** Wolfgang-Wilhelm **Rev:** City view with angels above, NEOBVRG below **Note:** Varieties exist. Dav. #7173. Prev. KM#22. Tiny letters between pillars of bridge G-T-P-M-M-I-C-O-L-M = Georg Thomas Paur Münz Meister in Colmünz and on the bridge itself in tiny letters CHRISTOF RESEL, the name of the die-cutter.

Date	Mintage	VG	F	VF	XF	Unc
16Z9 GTP Rare	—	—	—	—	—	—

KM# 85 THALER

Silver **Ruler:** Wolfgang-Wilhelm **Obv:** Small bust **Obv. Legend:** ...ET: MON. **Rev:** Crowned arms, date in legend **Note:** Dav. #7174. Prev. KM#30.

Date	Mintage	VG	F	VF	XF	Unc
1631 GTP Rare	—	—	—	—	—	—

KM# 86 THALER

Silver **Ruler:** Wolfgang-Wilhelm **Obv. Legend:** ...ET: MO. **Note:** Dav. #7174A. Prev. KM#31.

Date	Mintage	VG	F	VF	XF	Unc
1631 GTP Rare	—	—	—	—	—	—

KM# 92 THALER

Silver **Ruler:** Wolfgang-Wilhelm **Obv. Legend:** ...MONE. **Rev:** Oval arms supported by angels **Note:** Dav. #7175. Prev. KM#32.

Date	Mintage	VG	F	VF	XF	Unc
1632 (g)	—	270	550	1,000	1,600	—

KM# 93 THALER

Silver **Ruler:** Wolfgang-Wilhelm **Obv. Legend:** ...MONT. **Note:** Dav. #7175A. Prev. KM#33.

Date	Mintage	VG	F	VF	XF	Unc
1632 (g)	—	270	550	1,000	1,600	—

KM# 34 2 THALER

Silver **Ruler:** Wolfgang-Wilhelm **Obv:** Ruffled bust right, inner legend **Obv. Legend:** IN. DEO. MEO. CONSOLATIO. **Rev:** Crowned arms divide date **Note:** Similar to 1 Thaler, KM#33. Dav. #7157. Prev. KM#8.

Date	Mintage	VG	F	VF	XF	Unc
1622 Rare	—	—	—	—	—	—

KM# 60 2 THALER

Silver **Ruler:** Wolfgang-Wilhelm **Obv:** Ruffled bust right in inner circle, titles of Wolfgang **Obv. Legend:** WOLFG • WIL • D • G • C • PA • RHE • D • BA • CL • EM • T * **Rev:** Crowned shield of arms, date at end of legend **Rev. Legend:** CO. VEL. SP. MAR • RA - MOR • D • RA • **Note:** Klippe. Similar to 1 Thaler, KM#59. Dav. #7165.

Date	Mintage	VG	F	VF	XF	Unc
1624 CE Rare	—	—	—	—	—	—

KM# 73 2 THALER

Silver **Ruler:** Wolfgang-Wilhelm **Note:** Dav. #7169. Prev. KM#20. Similar to 1 Thaler, KM#72.

Date	Mintage	VG	F	VF	XF	Unc
1627 GTP Rare	—	—	—	—	—	—

KM# 80 2 THALER

Silver **Ruler:** Wolfgang-Wilhelm **Obv:** Smaller bust right **Rev:** Crowned arms **Note:** Dav. #7171. Prev. KM#23.

Date	Mintage	VG	F	VF	XF	Unc
16Z9 GTP Rare	—	—	—	—	—	—

PFALZ-SIMMERN

One of the four branches of the Pfalz stemming from the division of 1410, Pfalz-Simmern was itself divided into the Simmern and Zweibrücken lines after one generation in 1459. When the electoral line in the Rhenish Pfalz (Rheinpfalz) came to an end a century later, the electoral dignity passed to the eldest of three brothers in Pfalz-Simmern, while the younger two ruled successively in Simmern. After the last brother died, Pfalz-Simmern was ruled by the electoral line until 1610, at which time the younger brother of the Elector was given the countship there. This final line in Simmern only lasted two generations and reverted to the Elector once again in 1674. However, the Electoral line itself became extinct in 1685 and the Electorate with all its titles passed to Pfalz-Neuburg.

RULERS

Friedrich IV, 1598-1610
Ludwig Philipp, 1610-55
Ludwig Heinrich Moritz, 1655-74

MINT OFFICIALS' INITIALS

Initial	Date	Name
IGP	1661-62	Johann Georg Pfründt in Stromberg

ARMS

Sponheim (associated with Simmern line) – checkerboard
Wittelsbach family – field of lozenges (diamond shapes)

REFERENCES

S = Hugo Frhr. Von Saurma-Jeltsch, ***Die Saurmasche Münzsammlung deutscher, schweizerischer und polnischer Gepräge von etwa dem Beginn der Groschenzeit bis zur Kipperperiode***, Berlin, 1892.

Sch = Wolfgang Schulten, ***Deutsche Münzen aus dere Zeit Karls V.***, Frankfurt am Main, 1974.

PALATINE COUNTSHIP

REGULAR COINAGE

KM# 3 KREUZER

Silver **Ruler:** Ludwig Heinrich Moritz **Obv:** Ornate helmet over 3 small shields of arms **Rev:** Inscription in laurel wreath **Rev. Inscription:** I/ date/ KREVZ/ ER **Mint:** Stromberg

Date	Mintage	VG	F	VF	XF	Unc
1661	—	—	—	—	—	—

KM# 15 ALBUS (2 Kreuzer)

Silver **Ruler:** Ludwig Heinrich Moritz **Obv:** Ornate helmet above 3 small shields of arms **Rev:** 3-line inscription, date on last line in laurel wreath **Rev. Inscription:** 1/ALBVS/ **Mint:** Stromberg **Note:** Varieties exist.

Date	Mintage	VG	F	VF	XF	Unc
1663	—	45.00	90.00	165	275	—
1667	—	33.00	70.00	150	250	—

KM# 5 15 KREUZER (1/4 Gulden)

Silver **Ruler:** Ludwig Heinrich Moritz **Obv:** Bust right in circle **Rev:** Ornate helmet over 3 small shields of arms, value (15) at bottom, date **Rev. Legend:** MONETA NOVA **Mint:** Stromberg

Date	Mintage	VG	F	VF	XF	Unc
1661	—	—	—	—	—	—

KM# 7 60 KREUZER (1 Gulden)

Silver **Ruler:** Ludwig Heinrich Moritz **Obv:** Bust right in circle **Rev:** Ornate helmet above 3 small shields of arms, value (60) at bottom, date **Rev. Legend:** MONETA NOVA **Mint:** Stromberg **Note:** Dav. #754.

Date	Mintage	VG	F	VF	XF	Unc
1661	—	—	—	—	—	—

KM# 8 60 KREUZER (1 Gulden)

Silver **Ruler:** Ludwig Heinrich Moritz **Obv:** Bust right in circle **Rev:** Ornate helmet above 3 small shields of arms divides date, value (60) at bottom **Rev. Legend:** MONETA NOVA... **Mint:** Stromberg

Date	Mintage	VG	F	VF	XF	Unc
1661	—	—	—	—	—	—

KM# 9 60 KREUZER (1 Gulden)

Silver **Ruler:** Ludwig Heinrich Moritz **Obv:** Bust right in circle **Rev:** Ornate helmet above 3 small shields of arms divides date, value (60) at bottom **Rev. Legend:** FVRSTLICHE: PFALTZ — SIMEREN: LANDMVNTZ

Date	Mintage	VG	F	VF	XF	Unc
1661 IGP	—	1,750	3,000	5,000	—	—

KM# 11 60 KREUZER (1 Gulden)

Silver **Ruler:** Ludwig Heinrich Moritz **Obv:** Bust right in circle

Rev: Ornate helmet above 3 small shields of arms divides date, value (60) at bottom **Rev. Legend:** FVRSTLICHE: PFALTZ — SIMERN. LANDMVNTZ **Mint:** Stromberg **Note:** Dav. #756. Varieties exist

Date	Mintage	VG	F	VF	XF	Unc
1661 IGP	—	550	900	1,600	2,700	—

TRADE COINAGE

KM# 13 DUCAT
Gold **Ruler:** Ludwig Heinrich Moritz **Obv:** Bust right in circle **Rev:** Ornate helmet over 3 small shields of arms in circle, Roman numeral date **Rev. Legend:** DUCATUS NOVUS SIMERIENSIS **Mint:** Stromberg

Date	Mintage	VG	F	VF	XF	Unc
MDCLXII (1662) Rare	—	—	—	—	—	—

PFALZ-SULZBACH

Originally one of the four lines established in 1569, the first ruler died childless in 1604 and Sulzbach went to the eldest brother in Pfalz-Neuburg. The latter's younger son began a new line in 1614 upon the division of Pfalz-Neuburg. Early in the 18th century, the electoral dignity had passed to Pfalz-Neuburg, but that line also became extinct and all titles, including the electorate, reverted to Pfalz-Sulzbach in 1742 (see Electoral Pfalz for listings after this date).

RULERS
Otto Heinrich, 1569-1604
August, 1614-32
Christian August, 1632-1708

MINT MARKS
All coins struck in Nürnberg mint, but there are no distinguishing marks or symbols.

REFERENCE
N = Alfred Noss, ***Die pfälzischen Münzen des Hauses Wittelsbach***, v. 4, ***Pfalz-Veldenz, Pfalz-Neuburg, Pfalz-Sulzbach***, Munich, 1938.

PALATINE COUNTSHIP

STANDARD COINAGE

KM# 1 THALER
Silver **Ruler:** Christian August **Obv:** Hatted bust right **Rev:** Crowned oval 8-fold arms with central shield of Pfalz in baroque frame, Roman numeral date at end of legend at bottom **Rev. Legend:** SI VIS VINCE - RE PERDE **Mint:** Nurnberg

Date	Mintage	VG	F	VF	XF	Unc
MDCLXV (1665) Rare	—	—	—	—	—	—

TRADE COINAGE

KM# 3 1/4 DUCAT
Gold **Ruler:** Christian August **Obv:** Crowned oval 8-fold arms with central shield in baroque frame **Rev:** Christ rising from grave, mourner to either side **Rev. Legend:** VERBVM CRVCIS VIRTVS DEI **Mint:** Nurnberg **Note:** Fr. #2053.

Date	Mintage	VG	F	VF	XF	Unc
ND(ca1682)	—	600	1,150	2,000	3,500	—

KM# 4 DUCAT
Gold **Ruler:** Christian August **Obv:** Armored bust right **Rev:** Crowned oval 8-fold arms with central shield in baroque frame divide date near bottom **Rev. Legend:** SI VIS VINCE - RE PERDE **Mint:** Nurnberg **Note:** Fr. #2052.

Date	Mintage	VG	F	VF	XF	Unc
1682	—	1,400	2,750	4,950	8,300	—

KM# 2 6 DUCAT
Gold **Ruler:** Christian August **Obv:** Hatted bust right **Rev:** Crowned oval 8-fold arms with central shield of Pfalz in baroque frame, Roman numeral date at bottom **Rev. Legend:** SI VIS VINCE - RE PERDE **Mint:** Nurnberg **Note:** Struck with Thaler dies, KM#1.

Date	Mintage	VG	F	VF	XF	Unc
MDCLXV (1665) Rare	—	—	—	—	—	—

PATTERNS

Including off metal strikes

KM#	Date	Mintage	Identification	Mkt Val
Pn1	1682	—	Ducat. Silver. KM#4.	150

PFALZ-VELDENZ

This line of Counts Palatine controlled territory centered on Veldenz, overlooking the Mosel River, 20 miles (33km) northeast of Trier. Their principal residence was the castle at Lauterecken on the Glan, some 16 miles (27km) north-northwest of Kaiserslautern. Pfalz-Veldenz was established in 1514 when Pfalz-Zweibrücken-Veldenz was divided into Pfalz-Zweibrücken and Pfalz-Veldenz. However, the younger of the two brothers did not receive full recognition of his rights until 1543. The line of Pfalz-Veldenz fell extinct in 1694, the lands and titles having then been divided by Pfalz-Birkenfeld-Zweibrücken and Pfalz-Sulzbach.

RULERS
Georg Gustav, 1592-1634
Johann August, 1592-1611, in Lützelstein 1598-1611
Ludwig Philipp, 1592-1601
Georg Johann (Hans) II, 1592-1634, in Lützelstein 1611-54
Leopold Ludwig, 1634-94

MINT OFFICIALS' INITIALS

Initial	Date	Name
(f)= ✿	1600-02	Georg Gustav Preyell in Rockenhausen
(g)= ✿/✶/✶	1603-?	Jakob Dietrich in Rockenhausen
(h)= ⚒ or ⸸ plus HI	1608-09	Hans Jakob in Veldenz
	1608-09	Hans Stumpff in Veldenz
	1619	Johann Jakob Eiselstein in Rothau
	1619	Gümbel G. Wolkenhauer in Rothau
BM	1671-75	Johann Brettmacher in Weinburg

ARMS
Crowned rampant lion left

REFERENCE
N = Alfred Noss, ***Die pfälzischen Münzen des Hauses Wittelsbach***, v. 4, ***Pfalz-Veldenz, Pfalz-Neuburg, Pfalz-Sulzbach***, Munich, 1938.

PALATINE COUNTSHIP

REGULAR COINAGE

KM# 32 HELLER
0.2350 g., Silver, 12 mm. **Ruler:** Leopold Ludwig **Obv:** Crowned 4-fold arms of Pfalz and Bavaria with central shield of Veldenz divide date, H below **Mint:** Weinburg **Note:** Uniface schüssel-type. N#258.

Date	Mintage	Good	VG	F	VF	XF
1673	—	25.00	50.00	90.00	—	—

MB# 75 PFENNIG
Silver Weight varies: 0.185-0.31g., 12.5-13.5 mm. **Ruler:** Johann August **Obv:** Shield of 4-fold arms of Pfalz and Bavaria, IAP (=Johann August Pfalzgraf) above **Mint:** Weinburg **Note:** Coinage for Lützelstein; uniface schüssel-type. N#239-41. Varieties exist.

Date	Mintage	Good	VG	F	VF	XF
ND(1598-1611)	—	20.00	40.00	85.00	165	—

KM# 4 PFENNIG
Silver Weight varies: 0.185-0.21g., 13 mm. **Ruler:** Georg Gustav **Obv:** 2-fold arms divided diagonally, Pfalz lion in upper left, Bavarian lozenges in lower right, GGP above (=Georg Gustav Pfalzgraf) **Mint:** Rockenhausen **Note:** Uniface schüssel-type. N#174.

Date	Mintage	Good	VG	F	VF	XF
ND(ca1603-5)	—	20.00	40.00	85.00	165	—

KM# 34 PFENNIG
0.2500 g., Silver, 19 mm. **Ruler:** Leopold Ludwig **Obv:** Crowned 4-fold arms of Pfalz and Bavaria with central shield of Veldenz divide date **Mint:** Weinburg **Note:** Uniface schüssel-type. N#257.

Date	Mintage	Good	VG	F	VF	XF
1673	—	40.00	75.00	135	—	—

KM# 22 KREUZER
Silver Weight varies: 0.49-0.58g., 17-17.5 mm. **Ruler:** Leopold Ludwig **Obv:** Crowned 4-fold arms of Pfalz and Bavaria with central shield of Veldenz divide date **Rev:** Imperial orb with 1K, legend around, all within laurel wreath **Rev. Legend:** PFALTZ. VELDENTZ. **Mint:** Weinburg **Note:** Varieties exist. N#245, 262.

Date	Mintage	Good	VG	F	VF	XF
1669	—	30.00	60.00	125	200	325
1674 BM	—	30.00	60.00	125	200	325

KM# 24 2 KREUZER (1/2 Batzen)
Silver, 20 mm. **Ruler:** Leopold Ludwig **Obv:** Crowned 4-fold arms of Pfalz and Bavaria with central shield of Veldenz, date divided to left, above and right of crown, all in laurel wreath **Rev:** Imperial orb with 2K in circle **Rev. Legend:** PFALTZ. VELDENTZISCHE. **Mint:** Weinburg **Note:** N#244.

Date	Mintage	Good	VG	F	VF	XF
1669	—	25.00	45.00	90.00	—	—

KM# 46 2 KREUZER (1/2 Batzen)
1.2200 g., Silver, 20 mm. **Ruler:** Leopold Ludwig **Obv:** Crowned 4-fold arms of Pfalz and Bavaria with central shield of Veldenz divide date, all within laurel wreath **Rev:** Imperial orb with 2K in circle **Rev. Legend:** PFALTZ. VELDENTZISCHE. **Mint:** Weinburg **Note:** N#261.

Date	Mintage	Good	VG	F	VF	XF
1674 BM	—	25.00	45.00	90.00	—	—

KM# 2 3 KREUZER (Groschen)
Silver Weight varies: 1.38-1.90g., 20.5-22.5 mm. **Ruler:** Georg Gustav **Obv:** 4-fold arms in spanish shield with central shield of Veldenz, date above **Obv. Legend:** GE(OR). GV(S)(T). D.G. C(O). R(A). R(H). D(V). B(A). C(O). V(E). (E.S.). **Rev:** Crowned imperial eagle, 3 in orb on breast **Rev. Legend:** RVDOL. (Z.) (II.) (RO.) IM(-)P. (SE.) AVG. (P.F. DEC.) **Mint:** Rockenhausen **Note:** Varieties exist. N#165-7, 169-70.

Date	Mintage	Good	VG	F	VF	XF
160Z (f)	—	30.00	65.00	100	140	200
1603 (g)	—	30.00	65.00	100	140	200
ND(ca1603) (g)	—	30.00	50.00	90.00	125	175

KM# 7 3 KREUZER (Groschen)
Silver Weight varies: 1.49-1.58g., 22-23 mm. **Ruler:** Georg Gustav **Obv:** Ornately-shaped shield of 4-fold arms of Pfalz and Bavaria with central shield of Veldenz **Obv. Legend:** GE. GVS. D.G. C(O). P(A). R(H). D. B(A). C. V. (E.) (S.). **Rev:** Crowned imperial eagle, 3 in orb on breast **Rev. Legend:** RVDOL. (Z.)(II.) (RO.) IMP. (-) (SE.) AVG. (P. F. DEC). **Mint:** Rockenhausen **Note:** Varieties exist. N#171-3.

Date	Mintage	Good	VG	F	VF	XF
ND(ca1603) (g)	—	35.00	75.00	125	—	—

KM# 6 3 KREUZER (Groschen)
6.8500 g., Silver, 24x25 mm. **Ruler:** Georg Gustav **Obv:** Spanish shield with 4-fold arms of Pfalz and Bavaria with central shield of Veldenz **Obv. Legend:** GE. GV. D.G. CO. PA. RH. DV. BA. CO. V. **Rev:** Crowned imperial eagle, 3 in orb on breast. **Rev. Legend:** RVDOL. II. RO. IMP. AVG. P. F. DEC. **Mint:** Rockenhausen **Note:** Klippe. N#168.

Date	Mintage	Good	VG	F	VF	XF
ND(ca1603) (g)	—	35.00	75.00	125	—	—

KM# 9 3 KREUZER (Groschen)
Silver Weight varies: 1.25-1.80g., 21-22 mm. **Ruler:** Georg Gustav **Obv:** Spanish shield of 4-fold arms of Pfalz and Bavaria with central shield of Veldenz, date above **Obv. Legend:** GE. GVS. D.G. CO. PA. (RH.) D. B. C. V. (E.) ET. S. **Rev:** Crowned imperial eagle, 3 in orb on breast **Rev. Legend:** RVDOL. Z. IMP. AVG. P. F. DEC. **Mint:** Veldenz **Note:** Varieties exist. N#175-7, 180.5.

Date	Mintage	Good	VG	F	VF	XF
(1)608 (h)	—	15.00	30.00	60.00	85.00	125
(1)609 (h)	—	15.00	30.00	60.00	85.00	125

KM# 10 3 KREUZER (Groschen)
Silver Weight varies: 1.59-1.70g., 20.5-22 mm. **Ruler:** Georg Gustav **Obv:** Ornately-shaped shield of 4-fold arms of Pfalz and Bavaria with central shield of Veldenz divide date **Obv. Legend:** GE GVS. D.G(.) CO. PA. RH. D(V). B(A). C. V(.)E. ET. S. **Rev:** Crowned imperial eagle, 3 in orb on breast **Rev. Legend:** RVDOL. Z. IMP. AVG. P. F. DEC **Mint:** Veldenz **Note:** Varieties exist. N#178-80.

Date	Mintage	Good	VG	F	VF	XF
(1)608 (h)	—	15.00	30.00	60.00	85.00	125
(1)609 (h)	—	15.00	30.00	60.00	85.00	125

KM# 12 3 KREUZER (Groschen)
Silver Weight varies: 1.32-1.505g., 22 mm. **Ruler:** Georg Gustav **Obv:** Ornately-shaped shield of 4-fold arms of Pfalz and Bavaria with central shield of Veldenz **Obv. Legend:** GE. GVS(T). D.G. C(O). P. R. D. B. C(O). V. E. S. **Rev:** Crowned imperial eagle, 3 in orb on breast **Rev. Legend:** MATT(H)(IAS). II. RO(M). IMP(ER). S(E). A(VG). **Mint:** Rothau **Note:** Varieties exist. N#224-5.

Date	Mintage	Good	VG	F	VF	XF
ND(ca1619)	—	25.00	40.00	75.00	120	—

KM# 13 3 KREUZER (Groschen)
Silver Weight varies: 1.13-1.93g., 20-22 mm. **Ruler:** Georg Gustav **Obv:** Spanish shield of 4-fold arms of Pfalz and Bavaria with central shield of Veldenz **Obv. Legend:** GE. GVST. D.G. C(O). P. R. D. B. (C)(O). V. E. S. **Rev:** Crowned imperial eagle, 3 in orb on breast **Rev. Legend:** MATT(H)(I)(AS). I(I). RO(M). IM(P)(E)(R). S. A. **Mint:** Rothau **Note:** Varieties exist. N#226-37.

Date	Mintage	Good	VG	F	VF	XF
ND(ca1619)	—	—	—	—	—	—

KM# 15 12 KREUZER (Dreibätzner)
Silver Weight varies: 5.11-5.19g., 27.5 mm. **Ruler:** Georg Gustav **Obv:** Crowned ornately-shaped shield of 4-fold arms of Pfalz and Bavaria with central shield of Veldenz **Obv. Legend:** GEORG GVST. D. G. C. P. R. D. B. C. V. E. S. **Rev:** Imperial eagle with orb on breast, (XII) at top in margin **Rev. Legend:** FERDINAND. II. ROM. IM. P. S. AV. **Mint:** Rothau **Note:** N#238.

Date	Mintage	Good	VG	F	VF	XF
ND(1619-34)	—	120	225	400	650	1,000

KM# 36 12 KREUZER (Dreibätzner)
Silver Weight varies: 4.59-5.16g., 26-28.5 mm. **Ruler:** Leopold Ludwig **Obv:** Crowned shield of 4-fold arms of Pfalz and Bavaria with central shield of Veldenz divides date **Obv. Legend:** LEOP. LVD. D.G. C. P. R. D. B. ET. COM. VELDENTIÆ. **Rev:** Crowned imperial eagle in circle, orb on breast, (XII) in margin at top **Rev. Legend:** LEOPOLDVS. I. ROM. IMP. SEMP AVG. **Mint:** Weinburg **Note:** N#256, 260.

Date	Mintage	Good	VG	F	VF	XF
1673 BM	—	45.00	75.00	125	—	—
1674/3 BM	—	45.00	75.00	125	—	—

KM# 17 12 KREUZER (Schreckenberger)
Silver Weight varies: 2.45-3.02g., 25-26 mm. **Ruler:** Georg Gustav **Obv:** Bust to right in circle **Obv. Legend:** GEORG. GVST. D.G. C(O). P(A). R(H). D. G. C(O). V. E. S. **Rev:** Ornamented Spanish shield of 4-fold arms of Pfalz and Bavaria with central shield of Veldenz, value (12) above, date at end of legend **Rev. Legend:** SOLI. DEO. GLORIA. **Mint:** Rothau **Note:** Kipper Coinage. Varieties exist. N#220-3.

Date	Mintage	Good	VG	F	VF	XF
1621	—	35.00	70.00	125	275	500
1622	—	35.00	70.00	125	275	500

KM# 20 24 KREUZER (Sechsbätzner)
Silver Weight varies: 8.28-8.92g., 31x30, 32x32 mm. **Ruler:** Georg Gustav **Obv:** Armored bust to right in circle **Obv. Legend:** GEORG. GVST. D.G. CO. PA. RH. D. G. C. V. E. S. **Rev:** Crowned shield of 4-fold arms of Pfalz and Bavaria with central shield of Veldenz **Rev. Legend:** SOLI. DEO. GLORIA. **Mint:** Rothau **Note:** Kipper coinage, Klippe. N#181, 206.

Date	Mintage	Good	VG	F	VF	XF
ND(1621-22)	—	40.00	90.00	200	350	—

KM# 19 24 KREUZER (Sechsbätzner)
Silver Weight varies: 6.98-9.17g., 28-31 mm. **Ruler:** Georg Gustav **Obv:** Armored bust to right in circle **Obv. Legend:** GEORG. GVST. D.G. C(O)(M). R(A). R(H). D. B. C(O). V. E. S. **Rev:** Crowned shield of 4-fold arms of Pfalz and Bavaria with central shield of Veldenz **Rev. Legend:** SOLI. DEO. GLORIA. **Mint:** Rothau **Note:** Kipper coinage, varieties exist. N#181-219.

Date	Mintage	Good	VG	F	VF	XF
ND(1621-22)	—	49.00	90.00	200	350	—

KM# 26 30 KREUZER (1/2 Gulden)
Silver Weight varies: 9.57-9.88g., 32 mm. **Ruler:** Leopold Ludwig **Obv:** Armored bust to right in circle **Obv. Legend:** LEOPOLD. LVD. D.G. C. P. R. D. B. ET. COM. VELDENTIÆ. **Rev:** Two ornate helmets divide date above shield of 4-fold arms of Pfalz and Bavaria with central shield of Veldenz, (30) below in margin **Rev. Legend:** VERBVM DOMINI MA - NET IN ÆTERNVM. **Mint:** Weinburg **Note:** Varieties exist. N#243, 254.

Date	Mintage	Good	VG	F	VF	XF
1669	—	—	—	—	—	—
1673 BM	—	—	—	—	—	—

KM# 38 45 KREUZER (3/4 Gulden)
14.5200 g., Silver, 34 mm. **Ruler:** Leopold Ludwig **Obv:** Armored bust to right in circle **Obv. Legend:** LEOPOLD. LVDOVIC. D.G. C. P. R. D. B. ET. COM. VELDENTIÆ. **Rev:** Shield of 4-fold arms of Pfalz and Bavaria with central shield of Veldenz, 2 ornate helmets above divide date, (45) in margin at bottom **Rev. Legend:** VERBVM. DOMINI. - MANET. IN. ÆTERNVM. **Mint:** Weinburg **Note:** N#253.

Date	Mintage	Good	VG	F	VF	XF
1673 BM	—	—	—	—	—	—

KM# 28 60 KREUZER (Gulden)
Silver Weight varies: 18.78-19.29g., 36 mm. **Ruler:** Leopold Ludwig **Obv:** Armored bust to right in circle **Obv. Legend:** LEOPOLD. LVDOVIC. D.G. COM. PAL. RH. D. BAV. ET. COM. VELDENT. **Rev:** Shield of 4-fold arms of Pfalz and Bavaria with central shield of Veldenz, date divided among crests of 2 ornate helmets above, (60) in margin at bottom **Rev. Legend:** + VERBVM. DOMINI - MANET. IN. ÆTERNVM. **Mint:** Weinburg **Note:** Varieties exist. Dav. #759; N#242, 246.

Date	Mintage	Good	VG	F	VF	XF
1669	—	—	—	—	—	—
1670/69	—	—	—	—	—	—

KM# 30 60 KREUZER (Gulden)
19.8200 g., Silver, 35.5 mm. **Ruler:** Leopold Ludwig **Obv:** Large armored bust to right in circle **Obv. Legend:** LEOPOLD. LVDOVIC. D.G. C. P. R. D. B. ET. COM. VELDENTIÆ. **Rev:** Shield of 4-fold arms of Pfalz and Bavaria with central shield of Veldenz, date divided among crests of 2 ornate helmets above, (60) in margin at bottom **Rev. Legend:** VERBVM. DOMINI - MANET. IN. ÆTERNVM. **Mint:** Weinburg **Note:** Dav. #760; N#248.

Date	Mintage	Good	VG	F	VF	XF
1672	—	300	600	1,000	1,500	2,250

KM# 40 60 KREUZER (Gulden)
Silver Weight varies: 18.63-19.45g., 32-37 mm. **Ruler:** Leopold Ludwig **Obv:** Armored bust to right in circle **Obv. Legend:** LEOPOLD. LVD(OV)(W)IC. D.G. C. P. R. D. B. ET. COM. VELDENTIÆ. **Rev:** Shield of 4-fold arms of Pfalz and Bavaria with central shield of Veldenz, date divided by crests of 2 ornate helmets above, (60) in margin at bottom **Rev. Legend:** VERBVM. DOMINI. (-) MA (-) NET. IN ÆTERNVM. **Mint:** Weinburg **Note:** Varieties exist. Dav. #760; N#251-2, 259.

Date	Mintage	Good	VG	F	VF	XF
1673 BM	—	275	500	875	1,200	1,750
1674 BM	—	275	500	875	1,200	1,750

KM# 42 1/4 THALER
7.2300 g., Silver, 31 mm. **Ruler:** Leopold Ludwig **Obv:** Armored bust to right in circle **Obv. Legend:** LEOPOLD. LVD. D.G. C. P. R. D. B. ET. COM. VELDENTIÆ. **Rev:** Shield of 4-fold arms of Pfalz and Bavaria with central shield of Veldenz, date divided by crests of 2 ornate helmets above, (1/4) in margin at bottom **Rev. Legend:** VERBVM. DOMINI MA - NET. IN. ÆTERNVM. **Mint:** Weinburg **Note:** N#255.

Date	Mintage	Good	VG	F	VF	XF
1673 BM	—	300	600	900	1,350	2,000

KM# 39 1/2 THALER
11.8700 g., Silver, 32 mm. **Ruler:** Leopold Ludwig
Obv: Armored bust to right in circle **Obv. Legend:** LEOPOLD. LVD. D.G. C. P. R. D. B. ET. COM. VELDENTIÆ. **Rev:** Ornate shield of 4-fold arms of Pfalz and Bavaria with central shield of Veldenz, crest on ornate helmet above divides date
Rev. Legend: VERBVM. DOMINI MA - NET. IN. ÆTERNVM. **Mint:** Weinburg **Note:** Struck from 1/4 Thaler dies, KM#42.

Date	Mintage	Good	VG	F	VF	XF
1673 BM	—	—	1,650	3,000	4,250	6,000

KM# 43 3/4 THALER
14.5300 g., Silver, 33 mm. **Ruler:** Leopold Ludwig
Obv: Armored bust to right in circle **Obv. Legend:** LEOPOLD. LVD. D.G. C. P. R. D. B. ET. COM. VELDENTIÆ. **Rev:** Ornate shield of 4-fold arms of Pfalz and Bavaria with central shield of Veldenz, crest on ornate helmet above divides date
Rev. Legend: VERBVM. DOMINI MA - NET. IN. ÆTERNVM. **Mint:** Weinburg **Note:** Struck from 1/4 Thaler dies, KM#42.

Date	Mintage	Good	VG	F	VF	XF
1673 BM	—	—	—	—	—	—

KM# 29 THALER
Silver **Ruler:** Leopold Ludwig **Obv:** Armored and draped bust to right **Obv. Legend:** LEOPOLD. LVDOVIC. D.G. C. P. R. D. B. &. COM. VELDENTIÆ. **Rev:** Ornately-shaped shield of 4-fold arms of Bavaria and Pfalz with central shield of Veldenz, two ornate helmets above divide date **Rev. Legend:** VERBVM. DOMINI. MANET. IN ÆTERNVM. **Mint:** Weinburg **Note:** Dav. #7191; N#247, 250.

Date	Mintage	VG	F	VF	XF	Unc
1671	—	1,000	1,850	3,250	5,500	12,500
1673 MB	—	1,000	1,850	3,250	5,500	12,500

TRADE COINAGE

KM# 44 DUCAT
3.5000 g., 0.9860 Gold 0.1109 oz. AGW, 21 mm.
Ruler: Leopold Ludwig **Obv:** Armored bust to right, date at end of legend **Obv. Legend:** LEOPOLD. LVD. D.G. C. P. R. D. B. ET. COM. VELDENTIÆ. **Rev:** Shield of 4-fold arms of Bavaria and Pfalz, central shield of Veldenz, 2 helmets above
Rev. Legend: VERBVM DOMINI MANET IN ÆTERNVM. **Mint:** Weinburg **Note:** FR#2055; N#249.

Date	Mintage	VG	F	VF	XF	Unc
1673 Rare	—	—	—	—	—	—

PATTERNS

(Including off metal strikes)

KM#	Date	Mintage	Identification	Mkt Val
Pn1	1621	—	12 Kreuzer. Lead. 26x27 mm. Klippe of KM#17.	400

PFALZ-ZWEIBRUCKEN

This branch of Rhinegraves was established upon the division of Pfalz-Simmern in 1459 and was known first as Pfalz-Zweibrücken-Veldenz until 1514, when a separate line at Veldenz was founded. In 1557, Neuburg and Sulzbach were acquired by purchase from Electoral Pfalz. Four brothers divided their inheritance in 1569 and founded new lines at Neuburg, Sulzbach, Birkenfeld and the continued line of Zweibrücken. The male succession failed several times, once in 1661 when the title passed to a cousin of the Pfalz-Landsberg line, then again in 1731. After more than three years of imperial sequestration, Zweibrücken was acquired by Pfalz-Birkenfeld in 1734, which was known henceforth as Pfalz-Birkenfeld-Zweibrücken. The capital of the principality, Zweibrücken, meaning "Two Bridges", is located not far from the border with France, 17 miles (28km) east of Saarbrücken. The mint town of Meisenheim is on the River Glan, 20 miles (33km) east of Zweibrücken.

RULERS

Ludwig I, 1459-1489
Alexander, 1489-1514
Ludwig II, 1514-1532
Wolfgang, 1532-1569
Johann I der Ältere, 1569-1604
Johann II der Jüngere, 1604-35,
  Administrator and Regent in Electoral Pfalz, 1610-15
Friedrich, 1635-61
Friedrich Ludwig von Pfalz-Landsberg, 1661-81
  French Occupation, 1677-93
Adolf Johann, 1681-89
Karl XI (King of Sweden), 1681-97
Karl XII (King of Sweden), 1697-1718
Gustav Samuel Leopold von Pfalz-Kleeburg, 1718-1731

MINT OFFICIALS' INITIALS

Initial	Date	Name
(a)=	Ca.1590-1605	Jakob Taglang
	Ca.1592-1604	H. Cunzelmann, die-cutter in Zweibrücken and Meisenheim
	Ca.1600	Balthasar Mey (Meyel)
	1600-07	Johann Ludwig Eichelstein
(b)=	1611-21	Johann Jakob (or Philipp) Mey (May)
(c)=	1611-21	Johann Jakob (or Philipp) Mey (May)
	Ca. 1613	Christoph Peyel, warden
HT/IHT (often in legature)	1621-23	Johann Heinrich Taglang in Meisenheim
	1621-26	In Zweibrücken
(d)=	1623-24	Hans Tuchmann (Christmann Tucher) in Zweibrücken and Meisenheim
(e)=	1624	Paul Dietherr der Jüngere
M	1624-25	Philibert Ludwig Messerschmid

ARMS

Zweibrücken – lion rampant left
Wittelsbach – field of lozenges (Diamond shapes)
Wittelsbach (old) – eagle, head to left

PALATINE COUNTSHIP

REGULAR COINAGE

MB# 59 HELLER
Silver **Ruler:** Johann I **Obv:** Shield of 4-fold arms of Pfalz and Bavaria **Note:** Uniface schüssel-type

Date	Mintage	VG	F	VF	XF	Unc
ND(1569-1604)	—	—	—	—	—	—

MB# 62 PFENNIG
Silver **Ruler:** Johann I **Obv:** Three small adjacent shields of arms, 2 over 1, IP above (=Johann Pfalzgraf) **Note:** Uniface sch?ssel-type. S#2019.

Date	Mintage	VG	F	VF	XF	Unc
ND(1569-1604)	—	8.00	16.00	35.00	80.00	—

MB# 63 PFENNIG
Silver **Ruler:** Johann I **Obv:** Shield of 3-fold arms, IP above (=Johann Pfalzgraf) **Note:** Uniface schüssel-type. S#2020.

Date	Mintage	VG	F	VF	XF	Unc
ND(1569-1604)	—	11.00	20.00	45.00	110	—

KM# 4 PFENNIG
Silver **Ruler:** Johann II **Obv:** Shield of Wittelsbach arms divides Z - B, with P above (=Pfalz-Zwei-Brücken) **Note:** Uniface schüssel-type.

Date	Mintage	VG	F	VF	XF	Unc
ND(1604-35)	—	8.00	15.00	35.00	70.00	—

KM# 37 PFENNIG
Ruler: Johann II **Obv:** Shield of Wittelsbach arms divides date, P above **Note:** Uniface hohl-type.

Date	Mintage	VG	F	VF	XF	Unc
(16)22	—	8.00	15.00	35.00	70.00	—

KM# 5 8 PFENNIG
, 17 mm. **Ruler:** Johann II **Obv:** 3-line inscription with value **Obv. Inscription:** M/ VIII/ PF (symbol) **Mint:** Meisenheim **Note:** Uniface. Attribution to Johann II is uncertain.

Date	Mintage	VG	F	VF	XF	Unc
ND(1604-35)	—	8.00	15.00	35.00	70.00	—

KM# 6 2 KREUZER (1/2 Batzen)
0.8600 g., Silver **Ruler:** Johann II **Obv:** Zweibrücken lion rampant to left in circle **Obv. Legend:** IO DG C P R D B IV CL ET MO. **Rev:** 3-line inscription of value **Rev. Legend:** MONETA NOVA BIPONT. **Rev. Inscription:** II/ KREVTZ/ ER

Date	Mintage	VG	F	VF	XF	Unc
ND(1604-35)	—	20.00	40.00	75.00	125	—

KM# 49 2 KREUZER (1/2 Batzen)
Silver **Ruler:** Johann II **Obv:** Three small shields of arms, 2 above 1, in circle **Obv. Legend:** IOHAN. D.G. CO. PA. RH. DV. BA. C. V. E. S. **Rev:** Imperial orb with Z divides date, large M at top **Rev. Legend:** FERDI. II. RO. IMP. AVG. P. F. DEC. **Mint:** Meisenheim

Date	Mintage	VG	F	VF	XF	Unc
16Z4 M	—	20.00	40.00	80.00	150	—
16Z5 M	—	20.00	40.00	80.00	150	—

KM# 2 3 KREUZER (Groschen)
Silver **Ruler:** Johann I **Obv:** 3-fold arms in spanish shield, date above **Obv. Legend:** IOHA. D.G. CO. PA. RH. DV. BA. C. V. E. **Rev:** Crowned imperial eagle, 3 in orb on breast
Rev. Legend: RVDOL. Z. IMP. AVG. P. F. DE. **Mint:** Zweibrücken **Note:** Varieties exist. S#2013-17.

Date	Mintage	VG	F	VF	XF	Unc
1601	—	16.00	33.00	60.00	120	—
1602	—	16.00	33.00	60.00	120	—
1603	—	16.00	33.00	60.00	120	—
1604	—	16.00	33.00	60.00	120	—

KM# 8 3 KREUZER (Groschen)
Silver **Ruler:** Johann II **Obv:** Three small shields of arms, 2 over 1, date above, all in circle **Obv. Legend:** IOH. D.G. CO. PA. RH. DV. BA. C. V. E. S. **Rev:** Crowned imperial eagle, 3 in orb on breast **Rev. Legend:** RVDOL. Z. RO. IMP. AVG. P. F. DE. **Mint:** Zweibrücken **Note:** Varieties exist. S#2025-29.

Date	Mintage	VG	F	VF	XF	Unc
1604	—	6.00	9.00	15.00	30.00	—
1605	—	6.00	9.00	15.00	30.00	—
1606	—	6.00	9.00	15.00	30.00	—
1607	—	6.00	9.00	15.00	30.00	—
1608	—	6.00	9.00	15.00	30.00	—
ND(ca1610-11)	—	6.00	9.00	15.00	30.00	—

KM# 15 3 KREUZER (Groschen)
1.6400 g., Silver, 21.5 mm. **Ruler:** Johann II **Obv:** 3-fold arms in spanish shield **Obv. Legend:** IOH. D.G. CO. PA. RH. DV. BA. C. V. E. S. **Rev:** Crowned imperial eagle, 3 in orb on breast **Rev. Legend:** RVDOL. Z. RO. IMP. AVG. P. F. DE. **Mint:** Zweibrücken **Note:** S#2030.

Date	Mintage	VG	F	VF	XF	Unc
ND(1611-12) (b)	—	25.00	50.00	90.00	165	—

KM# 16 3 KREUZER (Groschen)
Silver **Ruler:** Johann II **Obv:** 3-fold arms in spanish shield **Obv. Legend:** IOH. D.G. CO. PA. RH. DV. BA. C. V. E. S. **Rev:** Crowned imperial eagle, 3 in orb on breast **Rev. Legend:** MATHI. I. RO. IMP. AVG. P. F. **Mint:** Zweibrücken **Note:** S#2031.

Date	Mintage	VG	F	VF	XF	Unc
ND(1612-19) (b)	—	25.00	50.00	90.00	165	—

KM# 33 12 KREUZER (Schreckenberger)

Silver, 27 mm. **Ruler:** Johann II **Obv:** Bust to right in circle **Obv. Legend:** IOHAN. D.G. CO. PA. RHE. DV. BA. CO. VE. ET. S(P). **Rev:** Shield of 4-fold arms of Pfalz and Bavaria with central shield of Zweibrücken divides date, (1Z) above **Rev. Legend:** + VERBVM. DOMINI. MANET. IN ÆTERN(V). **Mint:** Zweibrücken **Note:** Kipper coinage. Varieties exist.

Date	Mintage	VG	F	VF	XF	Unc
16Z0 (b)	—	125	235	325	425	700
16Z1 (b)	—	125	235	325	425	700
16ZZ (c)	—	125	235	325	425	700

KM# 39 12 KREUZER (Schreckenberger)

Silver **Ruler:** Johann II **Obv:** Bust to right in circle **Obv. Legend:** IOHAN. D.G. CO. PA. RHE. DV. BA. CO. VE. ET. S. **Rev:** Shield of 4-fold arms of Pfalz and Bavaria with central shield of Zweibrücken, date at end of legend **Rev. Legend:** VERBVM. DOMINI. MANET. IN AETE. **Note:** Kipper coinage.

Date	Mintage	VG	F	VF	XF	Unc
16ZZ	—	—	—	—	—	—

KM# 57 12 KREUZER (Dreibätzner)

Silver **Ruler:** Johann II **Obv:** Bust to right in circle **Rev:** Shield of 4-fold arms of Pfalz and Bavaria with central shield of Zweibrücken divides date, (1Z) above

Date	Mintage	VG	F	VF	XF	Unc
1627	—	—	—	—	—	—

KM# 35 24 KREUZER (Doppelschreckenberger)

Silver Weight varies: 4.69-5.68g., 29 mm. **Ruler:** Johann II **Obv:** Bust to right in circle **Obv. Legend:** IOHAN. D.G. CO. PA. RHE. DV. BA. CO. VE(L). ET. SP(O). **Rev:** Shield of 4-fold arms of Pfalz and Bavaria with central shield of Zweibrücken, date at end of legend **Rev. Legend:** + VERBVM. DOMINI. MANET. IN ÆTE(R)(N). **Mint:** Zweibrücken **Note:** Kipper coinage. Varieties exist.

Date	Mintage	VG	F	VF	XF	Unc
16Z0	—	80.00	135	200	350	—
16Z1	—	80.00	135	200	350	—
16ZZ	—	80.00	135	200	350	—
ND(1621-22)	—	80.00	135	200	350	—

KM# 53 24 KREUZER (Sechsbätzner)

Silver, 31-32 mm. **Ruler:** Johann II **Obv:** Bust to right in circle **Obv. Legend:** IOHAN. D.G. CO. PA. RH. DV. BA. IVL. CLI. ET. MONT. **Rev:** Shield of manifold arms, date above, (XXIIII) in margin at top **Rev. Legend:** CO. VE. SP. MA. ET. RA. DO. IN. RAVEN. **Mint:** Zweibrücken

Date	Mintage	VG	F	VF	XF	Unc
1626 HT	—	—	—	—	—	—

KM# 41 1/8 THALER

Silver, 30-31 mm. **Ruler:** Johann II **Obv:** Ornate shield of manifold arms in circle **Obv. Legend:** IOHANNES DEI GRATIA COMES PALATINVS RHENI BAVARIÆ. **Rev:** Seated lion facing, holding tablet on which is 8.FVR/I.R.T., all in circle, date at end of legend **Rev. Legend:** IVLIÆ. CL. ET BER. DVX CO. VEL. SPO. MAR. ET RA. DO. IN RAV.

Date	Mintage	VG	F	VF	XF	Unc
1623	—	—	—	—	—	—

KM# 42 1/8 THALER

Silver **Ruler:** Johann II **Obv:** Bust to right in circle **Rev:** Shield of manifold arms, value 1/8 below

Date	Mintage	VG	F	VF	XF	Unc
1623	—	—	—	—	—	—

KM# 18 1/4 THALER

Silver Weight varies: 8.31-8.73g. **Ruler:** Johann II **Obv:** Armored bust to right in circle **Obv. Legend:** IOHAN. D. G. CO(M). PA. RH(E). (-) T (- E). AD. E. P. D. B. C. V. E. S. **Rev:** Shield with 4-fold arms of Pfalz and Bavaria with central shield of Zweibrücken lion, date above **Rev. Legend:** VERBVM. DOM(M)IN(I). MANET. IN. ÆTERN. **Mint:** Heidelberg **Note:** S#2023-24. Varieties exist.

Date	Mintage	VG	F	VF	XF	Unc
1611	—	150	225	350	500	—
161Z	—	150	225	350	500	—
ND(1611)	—	80.00	125	200	325	—

KM# 19 1/4 THALER

Silver **Ruler:** Johann II **Obv:** Armored bust to right in circle **Obv. Legend:** IOHAN. D.G. CO. PA. RHE. DV. BA. CO. VE. ET. SP. **Rev:** Shield of 4-fold arms of Pfalz and Bavaria with central shield of Zweibrücken lion **Rev. Legend:** VERBVM. DOMINI. MANET. IN. ÆTERN. **Mint:** Zweibrücken

Date	Mintage	VG	F	VF	XF	Unc
ND(1616-21) (b)	—	150	300	425	600	—
ND(1616-21) (c)	—	150	300	425	600	—

KM# 47 THALER

Silver, 41-42 mm. **Ruler:** Johann II **Obv:** Bust to right in circle **Obv. Legend:** IOHAN. D.G. CO. PA(L). RHE. DVX. BA. IVL. CLI. ET. MON. **Rev:** Manifold arms, 5 ornate helmets above, date at end of margin **Rev. Legend:** CO. VE. SP. MA. ET. - RA. DO. IN. RAV(E). **Mint:** Meisenheim **Note:** Dav. #7189. Prev. KM#23.

Date	Mintage	Good	VG	F	VF	XF
16Z3	—	—	210	425	775	1,250
16Z4 (e)	—	—	210	425	775	1,250

KM# 44 THALER

Silver, 41 mm. **Ruler:** Johann II **Obv:** Bust to right in circle **Obv. Legend:** IOHAN. D.G. COM. PA. RHE. DVX. PA. IVL. CLI. ET. MONT. **Rev:** Manifold arms, 5 ornate helmets above, date at end of legend **Rev. Legend:** CO. VE. SPO. MAR. ET. RAV. - DO. IN. RAVENST. **Note:** Dav. #7186. Prev. KM#20.

Date	Mintage	VG	F	VF	XF	Unc
16Z3	—	210	425	775	1,250	—

KM# 45 THALER

Silver, 40 mm. **Ruler:** Johann II **Obv:** Bust to right in circle, N's reversed in legend **Obv. Legend:** IOHAN. D.G. CO. PAL. RHE. DVX. BA. IVL. CLI. ET. MON. **Rev:** Manifold arms, 5 ornate helmets above, date at end of legend **Rev. Legend:** CO. VEL. SPOL. MAR. ET RAV. - DO. IN. RAVENS(T). **Note:** Dav. #7187. Prev. KM#21.

Date	Mintage	VG	F	VF	XF	Unc
16Z3	—	115	230	450	750	—
16Z4	—	115	230	450	750	—

KM# 46 THALER

Silver, 43 mm. **Ruler:** Johann II **Obv:** Bust to right in circle, N's reversed in legend **Obv. Legend:** IOHAN. D.G. CO. PAL. RHE.

DVX. BA. IVL. CLI. ET. MON. **Rev:** Manifold arms, 5 ornate helmets above, date at end of legend **Rev. Legend:** CO.-VE. SP. MA. ET. R. - DO. IN. RAVEN. **Note:** Dav. #7188. Prev. KM#22.

Date	Mintage	VG	F	VF	XF	Unc
16Z3 (d)	—	145	290	525	875	—
16Z4 (d)	—	145	290	525	875	—

KM# 55 THALER

Silver, 42-43 mm. **Ruler:** Johann II **Obv:** Facing armored bust, turned slightly to right, in circle **Obv. Legend:** IOHAN. D.G. COM. PALA. RHE. DVX. BA. IVL. CLI. ET. MONT. **Rev:** Shield of manifold arms, 5 ornate helmets above, date at end of legend near top **Rev. Legend:** CO. - VE. SPO. MAR. ET. R. - AV. DO. IN. RAV. **Mint:** Zweibrücken **Note:** Dav. #7190. Prev. KM#24.

Date	Mintage	VG	F	VF	XF	Unc
16Z6 HT	—	975	1,900	3,300	5,300	—

TRADE COINAGE

MB# 66 GOLDGULDEN

Gold **Ruler:** Johann I **Obv:** Spanish shield with 4-fold arms of Pfalz and Bavaria in circle **Obv. Legend:** IOHA. D. G. CO. PA. RHE. DV. BA. C. V. E. S. **Rev:** Crowned imperial eagle, orb on breast **Rev. Legend:** MONE. NOVA. AVREA. BIPONT. **Mint:** Zweibrücken

Date	Mintage	Good	VG	F	VF	XF
AH(1569-1604)	—	—	—	—	—	—

KM# 25 GOLDGULDEN

Gold **Ruler:** Johann II **Obv:** 4-fold arms of Pfalz and Bavaria, date above, titles as administrator of Electoral Pfalz **Obv. Legend:** IOH. D.G. C. PA. RHE. T. E. AD. E. P. D. B. C. V. E. S. **Rev:** Crowned imperial eagle, orb on breast **Rev. Legend:** MONE. NOVA. AVREA. BIPONT. **Mint:** Zweibrücken **Note:** FR#2059. Prev. KM#11.

Date	Mintage	VG	F	VF	XF	Unc
1611 (b)	—	500	950	1,750	3,000	—

KM# 27 GOLDGULDEN

3.1000 g., Gold **Ruler:** Johann II **Obv:** 4-fold arms of Pfalz and Bavaria, date above, titles as Administrator of Electoral Pfalz **Obv. Legend:** IOH. D.G. C. PA. RHE. T. E. AD. E. P. D. B. C. V. E. S. **Rev:** Crowned imperial eagle, orb on breast **Rev. Legend:** MONE. NOVA. AVREA. BIPONT. **Mint:** Zweibrücken **Note:** FR#2059.

Date	Mintage	VG	F	VF	XF	Unc
161Z (b)	—	1,500	2,100	3,250	4,000	—

KM# 29 GOLDGULDEN

3.2200 g., Gold **Ruler:** Johann II **Obv:** 4-fold arms of Pfalz and Bavaria in circle **Obv. Legend:** IOHA. D.G. CO. PA. RH. DV. BA. C. V. E. S. **Rev:** Crowned imperial eagle, orb on breast **Rev. Legend:** MONE. NOVA. AVREA. BIPONT. **Mint:** Zweibrücken **Note:** FR#2059.

Date	Mintage	VG	F	VF	XF	Unc
ND(1615-16) (c)	—	1,250	2,200	3,000	5,000	—

KM# 31 GOLDGULDEN

3.1600 g., Gold **Ruler:** Johann II **Obv:** Shield of manifold arms, date above **Obv. Legend:** IOH. D.G. C. P. R. D. B. I. C. ET. M. C. V. SP. M. ET. R. D. I(N). R(A). **Rev:** Crowned imperial eagle, orb on breast **Rev. Legend:** MONET. NOVA. AVREA. BIPONT. **Mint:** Zweibrücken **Note:** FR#2059. Prev. KM#11.

Date	Mintage	VG	F	VF	XF	Unc
1616 (b)	—	250	550	1,200	2,000	—
1617 (b)	—	250	550	1,200	2,000	—
1618 (b)	—	250	550	1,200	2,000	—
1619 (b)	—	250	550	1,200	2,000	—
1621 (b)	—	250	550	1,200	2,000	—

KM# 51 GOLDGULDEN

Gold, 22 mm. **Ruler:** Johann II **Obv:** Large shield of manifold arms, date above, M in margin at top **Obv. Legend:** IOH. D.G. C. P. R. D. B. I. C. ET. M. C. V. SP. M. ET. R. D. I. R. **Rev:** Crowned imperial eagle, orb on breast **Rev. Legend:** MONET. NOVA. AVREA. BIPONT. **Mint:** Meisenheim

Date	Mintage	Good	VG	F	VF	XF
16Z4 M	—	—	—	—	—	—
16Z5 M	—	—	—	—	—	—

POMERANIA

(Pommern)

The territory that became Pomerania, stretching along the Baltic coast from the Oder to the Vistula Rivers, was populated by Slavic peoples at least as early as the 5th century. A local ruler named Svantibor took the title of Duke of Pomerania in the late 11th century, thus announcing his claim of independence from Poland. Upon Svantibor's death in 1107, the duchy was divided by his four sons into Inner and Outer Pomerania. In 1181, Pomerania was admitted a constituent state of the Holy Roman Empire. Over the next several centuries, Pomerania underwent several divisions, although that centered on Wolgast emerged as the dominant branch by the early 15th century. Other family members ruled at Barth, Rügenwalde and most importantly, in Stettin, the eventural capital of united Pomerania. Several brothers of the dukes, as well as some dukes themselves, ruled as bishops of Cammin (see) some 20 miles (33km) north-northeast of Stettin.

The line at Wolgast became extinct in 1625 and its territories and titles passed to the Stettin branch, thus united all of Pomerania. The line at Stettin was established in 1569 and lost political power in 1637. The nephew of Bogislaw XIV, Ernst Bogislaw von Croy, was Bishop of Cammin from 1637 until 1650. Upon his death in 1684, the ducal line of almost 700 years came to an end.

Pomerania suffered severely during the Thirty Years' War and when the last duke succeeded to the bishopric of Cammin in 1637, as mentioned above, Sweden annexed the duchy. As part of the terms of the Treaty of Westphalia ending the war, Sweden was forced to pass the eastern part of Pomerania, called Hinter-Pommern, to Brandenburg-Prussia. Sweden did retain Stettin as the capital of its province of West Pomerania and struck a long series of coins specifically for that territory. Swedish control over its portion of Pomerania was continually challenged by the margraves of Brandenburg-Prussia, which succeeded in gaining part of the province in 1679, then all of West Pomerania to the River Peene in 1720. The remaining enclaves of Stralsund, Wolgast and Rügen were awarded to Prussia in 1815.

RULERS

Stettin Line

Barnim XII, 1600-1603, in Rügenwalde 1560-1603
Bogislaw XIII, 1603-1606, in Barth 1569-1606
Philip II, 1606-1618
Georg III, in Rügenwalde 1606-1617
Franz, 1618-1620
Bogislaw XIV, 1620-1637, in Rügenwalde 1617-1620

Wolgast Line

Bogislaw X the Great, 1474-1523
Georg I, 1523-1531
Philipp I, 1531-1560
Ernst Ludwig, 1560-1592
Philipp III Julius, 1592-1625

Swedish Occupation

Christian of Sweden, 1632-1654
Karl X of Sweden, 1654-1660
Karl XI of Sweden, 1660-1697
Karl XII of Sweden, 1697-1718
Adolf Fredrik of Sweden, 1751-1771
Gustav III, King of Sweden, 1771-1792
Gustav IV Adolf of Sweden, 1792-1809

MINT OFFICIALS' INITIALS

Stettin

Initial	Date	Name
BA	1681-85	Bastian Altmann
CS	1680-81	Christoph Sucro
DHM	1685-88	David Heinrich Matthaus
DS	1610-1620	Daniel Sailer of Augsburg, die-cutter
DS	1672-76	Daniel Syvertz
GT (sometimes in ligature, and/or (z) =	Ca. 1618-1637, 1654	Gottfried Tabbert, die-cutter
HIH, (b)=battle axe	1666-71	Heinrich Johann Hille
HS (sometimes S superimposed on H)	1612-19	Johann (Hans) Schampan
ICA	1695-98	Julius Christian Arensburg
ILA, (c)= crossed battle axes	1688-95	Johann Leonhard Arensburg
IM	1705-10	Johann Memmies
VB	1633-63	Ulrich Butkau

Franzburg

Initial	Date	Name
CR	1608-?	Caspar Rotermund, mint contractor
	1608-?	Joachim Köneke (König)
	1615-?	Michael Martens
HP and/or (d) = acorn	1621-1625	Hans Puls, mint contractor
	1621-1625	Jürgen Stange, warden

Köslin

Initial	Date	Name
CW	ca. 1631	Christian Wilke

ARMS

Pomerania – griffin, usually rampant to left
Barth – rampant griffin to right with two large feathers
Gützkow – St. Andrew's cross with rose in each angle
Rügen – upper half of rampant crowned lion to left over a double set of stairs
Stettin – rampant crowned griffin to right
Wolgast – upper half of rampant griffin to left over checkerboard

REFERENCES

H = Johannes Hildisch, **Die Münzen der pommerschen Herzöge**, Cologne/Vienna: Böhlau Verlag, 1980.
S = Hugo Frhr. Von Saurma-Jeltsch, **Die Saurmasche Münzsammlung deutscher, schweizerischer und polnischer Gepräge von etwa dem Beginn der Groschenzeit bis zur Kipperperiode**, Berlin, 1892.
Sch = Wolfgang Schulten, **Deutsche Münzen aus der Zeit Karls V.**, Frankfurt am Main, 1976.

POMERANIA-STETTIN

RULERS

Barnim XII, 1600-1603, in Rügenwalde 1560-1603
Bogislaw XIII, 1603-1606, in Barth 1569-1606
Philip II, 1606-1618
Georg III, in Rügenwalde 1606-1617
Franz, 1618-1620
Bogislaus XIV, 1620-1637, in Rügenwalde 1617-1620

DUCHY

REGULAR COINAGE

KM# 11 3 PFENNIG (Dreier)

0.7400 g., Silver, 16-17 mm. **Ruler:** Philipp II **Obv:** Ornate helmet over small shield of arms, PHD - SPO above **Rev:** Ornate helmet over small shield of arms, date divided near top **Mint:** Stettin **Note:** Varieties exist. H#67-9, 70.

Date	Mintage	Good	VG	F	VF	XF
161Z	—	10.00	15.00	30.00	60.00	—
1613	—	10.00	15.00	30.00	60.00	—
1614	—	10.00	15.00	30.00	60.00	—
1615	—	10.00	15.00	30.00	60.00	—

KM# 97 3 PFENNIG (Dreier)
0.6300 g., Silver, 15-16 mm. **Ruler:** Bogislaw XIV
Obv: Crowned griffin left holding sword, around B.H. - Z.S.P. **Rev:** Ornate helmet over arms, date divided near top **Mint:** Stettin **Note:** H#138.

Date	Mintage	Good	VG	F	VF	XF
16ZZ	—	10.00	15.00	30.00	60.00	—
(1)6ZZ	—	10.00	15.00	30.00	60.00	—

KM# 94 1/2 GROSCHEN POMMERSCH
0.6000 g., Silver, 14 mm. **Ruler:** Bogislaw XIV **Obv:** Blank shield superimposed on cross in circle **Obv. Legend:** BVGSL. DVX. S. POM. **Rev:** 3-line inscription, date at end of legend **Rev. Legend:** SOLI. PATRIÆ. **Rev. Inscription:** HALB/GROS/POM. **Mint:** Stettin **Note:** H#151.

Date	Mintage	Good	VG	F	VF	XF
16ZZ	—	—	—	—	—	—

KM# 98 WITTEN (4 Pfennig)
0.9500 g., Silver, 16 mm. **Ruler:** Bogislaw XIV **Obv:** Griffin to left in circle with sword **Obv. Legend:** BVGSL. D.G. D. ST. POM. **Rev:** Short cross in circle, date in angles **Rev. Legend:** DEVS. ADIVTOR. MEVS. **Mint:** Stettin **Note:** H#150.

Date	Mintage	Good	VG	F	VF	XF
16ZZ	—	—	—	—	—	—

KM# 61 2 SCHILLING (Doppelschilling)
Silver Weight varies: 1.62-1.90g., 22-23 mm. **Ruler:** Franz **Obv:** Crowned griffin to left in circle holding sword **Obv. Legend:** FRANCIS(C). I. D.G. DVX. S. P(O)(M). **Rev:** Intertwined DS in circle, date at end of legend **Rev. Legend:** ADSIT. AB. ALTO. **Mint:** Stettin **Note:** H#122-4. Prev. Pomerania KM#63.

Date	Mintage	Good	VG	F	VF	XF
1618	—	6.00	10.00	18.00	30.00	55.00
1619	—	6.00	10.00	18.00	30.00	55.00
16Z0	—	6.00	10.00	18.00	30.00	55.00

KM# 84 2 SCHILLING (Doppelschilling)
Silver, 21-21.5 mm. **Ruler:** Bogislaw XIV **Obv:** Crowned griffin to left in circle holding sword **Obv. Legend:** BVGSLAVS. (D.G.) DVX. S. P(OM). **Rev:** Intertwined DS in circle **Rev. Legend:** DEVS. ADIVTOR. MEVS. **Mint:** Stettin **Note:** H#140-1.

Date	Mintage	Good	VG	F	VF	XF
ND(1620-25)	—	15.00	25.00	40.00	75.00	—

KM# 85 2 SCHILLING (Doppelschilling)
Silver, 23 mm. **Ruler:** Bogislaw XIV **Obv:** Crowned griffin to left in circle **Obv. Legend:** BVGSLAVS. DVX. S. POM. **Rev:** Intertwined DS in circle divides date **Rev. Legend:** DEVS. ADIVTOR. MEVS. **Mint:** Stettin **Note:** H#142-3. Prev. Pomerania KM#63.

Date	Mintage	Good	VG	F	VF	XF
(16)Z0	—	15.00	25.00	40.00	75.00	—
(16)Z1	—	15.00	25.00	40.00	75.00	—

KM# 83 2 SCHILLING (Doppelschilling)
1.3100 g., Silver, 22 mm. **Ruler:** Bogislaw XIV **Obv:** Crowned griffin to left in circle **Obv. Legend:** BVGSLAVS. D. G. DVX. S. P. **Rev:** Intertwined DS in circle **Rev. Legend:** DEVS. ADIVTOR. MEVS. **Mint:** Stettin **Note:** H#139.

Date	Mintage	Good	VG	F	VF	XF
ND(1620-25) (z)	—	15.00	25.00	40.00	75.00	—
ND(1620-25)	—	15.00	25.00	40.00	75.00	—

KM# 95 2 SCHILLING (Doppelschilling)
1.2600 g., Silver, 21-22 mm. **Ruler:** Bogislaw XIV **Obv:** Crowned griffin to left in circle holding sword **Obv. Legend:** BVGSLAVS. (D.G.) DVX. (X.) S. P(O)(M). **Rev:** Intertwined DS in circle divides date **Rev. Legend:** DEVS. ADIVTOR. MEVS. **Mint:** Stettin **Note:** H#144-9, 366-7. Varieties exist. Prev. Pomerania KM#63.

Date	Mintage	Good	VG	F	VF	XF
(16)Z1 (z)	—	10.00	18.00	30.00	45.00	80.00
(16)ZZ (z)	—	10.00	18.00	30.00	45.00	80.00
(16)Z3	—	10.00	18.00	30.00	45.00	80.00
(16)Z4	—	10.00	18.00	30.00	45.00	80.00
(16)Z5	—	10.00	18.00	30.00	45.00	80.00
(16)Z8 (z)	—	10.00	18.00	30.00	45.00	80.00
(16)Z9 (z)	—	10.00	18.00	30.00	45.00	80.00

KM# 12 1/24 THALER (Reichsgroschen)
1.4800 g., Silver, 20-21 mm. **Ruler:** Philipp II **Obv:** Crowned griffin to left with sword and book in circle **Obv. Legend:** PHILIPPVS. II. DVX. STE(O). (P)(B)O. **Rev:** Imperial orb with Z4 divides date **Rev. Legend:** CHRI(S)TO. ET. REIPV(B)(R)LI. **Mint:** Stettin **Note:** H#60-66. Varieties exist.

Date	Mintage	Good	VG	F	VF	XF
161Z	—	15.00	30.00	50.00	75.00	115
1613	—	15.00	30.00	50.00	75.00	115
1614	—	15.00	30.00	50.00	75.00	115
1615	—	15.00	30.00	50.00	75.00	115
1616	—	15.00	30.00	50.00	75.00	115
1617	—	15.00	30.00	50.00	75.00	115
1618	—	15.00	30.00	50.00	75.00	115

KM# 62 1/24 THALER (Reichsgroschen)
1.4400 g., Silver, 20 mm. **Ruler:** Franz **Obv:** Crowned griffin to left in circle holding sword **Obv. Legend:** FRANCIS. I. D.G. DVX. S. P. **Rev:** Imperial orb with Z4 **Rev. Legend:** ADSIT. AB. ALTO + **Mint:** Stettin **Note:** H#119.

Date	Mintage	Good	VG	F	VF	XF
ND(1618-20)	—	—	—	—	—	—

KM# 63 1/24 THALER (Reichsgroschen)
1.4400 g., Silver, 19 mm. **Ruler:** Franz **Obv:** Crowned griffin to left in circle holding sword **Obv. Legend:** FRANCIS(C). (I.) D.G. DVX. S. P(O)(M). **Rev:** Imperial or with Z4, date at end of legend **Rev. Legend:** ADSIT. AB. ALTO. **Mint:** Stettin **Note:** H#120-21. Varieties exist. Prev. Pomerania KM#64.

Date	Mintage	Good	VG	F	VF	XF
1618	—	8.00	15.00	30.00	60.00	120
1619	—	8.00	15.00	30.00	60.00	120
(16)19	—	8.00	15.00	30.00	60.00	120

KM# 64 1/24 THALER (Dreipölker)
Silver Weight varies: 0.92-1.40g., 20 mm. **Ruler:** Bogislaw XIV **Obv:** Shield of 4-fold arms, (3) in oval at bottom **Obv. Legend:** BVGSLAV(S). - DVX. S. POM. **Rev:** Imperial orb with Z4 divides date **Rev. Legend:** DEVS. ADIVTOR. MEV(S). **Mint:** Stettin **Note:** Coinage for Rügenwalde. H#283-5. Varieties exist.

Date	Mintage	Good	VG	F	VF	XF
(16)18	—	10.00	18.00	35.00	70.00	140
(16)19	—	10.00	18.00	35.00	70.00	140
(16)Z0	—	10.00	18.00	35.00	70.00	140
(16)0Z error for 1620, value error 4Z in orb	—	10.00	18.00	35.00	70.00	140

KM# 96 1/24 THALER (Dreipölker)
0.8800 g., Silver, 19-20 mm. **Ruler:** Bogislaw XIV **Obv:** Shield of 4-fold arms, value (3) at bottom **Obv. Legend:** BVGSLAV. - DVX. S. POM. **Rev:** Imperial orb with Z4 OR 24 divides date **Rev. Legend:** DEVS. ADIVTOR. MEV(S). **Mint:** Stettin **Note:** H#135-7. Varieties exist.

Date	Mintage	Good	VG	F	VF	XF
(16)Z1	—	10.00	18.00	35.00	70.00	140
(16)ZZ	—	10.00	18.00	35.00	70.00	140
(16)Z3	—	10.00	18.00	35.00	70.00	140
(16)23	—	10.00	18.00	35.00	70.00	140

KM# 100 1/16 THALER (Düttchen)
2.8900 g., Silver, 27-28 mm. **Ruler:** Bogislaw XIV **Obv:** Griffin to left in shield superimposed on long cross **Obv. Legend:** BOGIS. - LAVS. - XIV D.G - DVX. S. P. **Rev:** 4-line inscription with date **Rev. Legend:** REICHS. SC(H)ROT. VND KORN. **Rev. Inscription:** 16. ST./REICHS/TALER/(date) **Mint:** Stettin **Note:** H#362-5. Varieties exist.

Date	Mintage	Good	VG	F	VF	XF
16Z8	—	25.00	45.00	80.00	135	200
16Z9	—	25.00	45.00	80.00	135	200
1630	—	25.00	45.00	80.00	135	200
1631	—	25.00	45.00	80.00	135	200

KM# 99 1/16 THALER (Düttchen)
2.8900 g., Silver, 26-27 mm. **Ruler:** Bogislaw XIV
Obv: Crowned griffin to left in circle holding sword and book **Obv. Legend:** MONETA. NOVA. BOGISLAI. XIV. D.S. PO. **Rev:** 5-line inscription with date **Rev. Legend:** PRIN. RVG. COM. GVT. TERR. LEOB. E. BV. D(N). **Rev. Inscription:** 16/STVK./EIN. R./TALER/(date). **Mint:** Stettin **Note:** H#361.

Date	Mintage	Good	VG	F	VF	XF
16Z8	—	30.00	50.00	90.00	150	—
1628	—	30.00	50.00	90.00	150	—

KM# 31 1/8 THALER (1/2 Reichsort)
3.5800 g., Silver, 25 mm. **Ruler:** Philipp II **Subject:** Death of Anna von Schleswig-Holstein, Widow of Bogislaw XIII **Obv:** Skull above crossed scepter and scythe in circle **Obv. Legend:** OPTIMA PHILOSOPHIA. **Rev:** 5-line inscription with date, floral ornaments at top and bottom **Rev. Inscription:** MEMORIÆ/ FVNEBRI: DN/ ANNÆ DV:/ POM: MAT:/ CARIS. (date). **Mint:** Stettin **Note:** H#91.

Date	Mintage	Good	VG	F	VF	XF
1616	—	—	—	—	—	—

KM# 38 1/8 THALER (1/2 Reichsort)
3.6100 g., Silver, 26 mm. **Ruler:** Philipp II **Subject:** Death of Georg III **Obv:** Wind blowing from clouds at upper right on rose bush below **Obv. Legend:** FLORIS. RAPIT. AVRA. DECOREM. **Rev:** 5-line inscription with Roman numeral date, floral ornaments at top and bottom **Rev. Inscription:** LVCTVS/ PVBLICI/ MEMORIA/ XXVI MAI/ AO DCXVII. **Mint:** Stettin **Note:** H#97.

Date	Mintage	Good	VG	F	VF	XF
DCXVII(1617)	—	—	—	—	—	—

KM# 66 1/8 THALER (1/2 Reichsort)
3.5000 g., Silver, 26-27 mm. **Ruler:** Franz **Subject:** Death of Philipp II **Obv:** Rose bush in circle **Obv. Legend:** VT. ROSA RODIMVR OMNES. **Rev:** 5-line inscription with date in wreath **Rev. Inscription:** (date)/ CHRISTO/ ET/ REIPVBLI/ CAE. **Mint:** Stettin **Note:** H#111.

Date	Mintage	Good	VG	F	VF	XF
1618	—	—	—	—	—	—

KM# 87 1/8 THALER (1/2 Reichsort)
3.5000 g., Silver, 26-27 mm. **Ruler:** Bogislaw XIV **Subject:** Death of Franz **Obv:** Skull over crossed scepter and scythe, all in wreath **Rev:** 6-line inscription **Rev. Inscription:** PACIFI/ CVM RAPV/ IT VERVM/ NON DEFI/ CIT: AL/ TER. **Mint:** Stettin **Note:** H#134.

Date	Mintage	Good	VG	F	VF	XF
ND(1620)	—	—	—	—	—	—

KM# 140 1/8 THALER (1/2 Reichsort)
3.4400 g., Silver, 26 mm. **Ruler:** Bogislaw XIV **Obv:** Bust to right in circle, date at end of legend **Obv. Legend:** BOGISLAVS. XIV. D.G. DVX. S. P. **Rev:** 4-line inscription in circle, date at end of legend **Rev. Legend:** DEVS. ADIVTOR. MEVS. (AŌ). **Mint:** Stettin **Note:** H#360.

Date	Mintage	Good	VG	F	VF	XF
1636//1636	—	—	—	—	—	—

KM# 142 1/8 THALER (1/2 Reichsort)
3.5500 g., Silver, 26-27 mm. **Ruler:** Bogislaw XIV **Subject:** Entombment of Bogislaw XIV **Obv:** Tree stump with two young limbs in leaf, view of Stettin behind, sun shining down from upper left divides DEO - DIRIGENTE **Rev:** 11-line inscription with dates in wreath **Rev. Inscription:** NVMMVS/ EXEQVIALIS/ OPTIMI PRINCI/ PIS. BOGISLAI/ DVCIS. STET. POME/ EIVS NOMINIS. XIV./ ET. VLTIMI/ NATI. 31 MART 1580/ DEN. X. MAR 1637/ SEP. 25 MAY/ 1654. **Mint:** Stettin **Note:** H#387.

Date	Mintage	Good	VG	F	VF	XF
1654	600	—	—	—	—	—

KM# 2 1/4 THALER (Reichsort)
7.0600 g., Silver, 30 mm. **Ruler:** Philipp II **Obv:** Bust to right in circle **Obv. Legend:** PHILIPPVS. II. D.G. DVX. STET. POM. **Rev:** Skull above crossed scepter and scythe **Rev. Legend:** MEDIT. MORT. OPTIMA. PHILOSOPHIA. **Mint:** Stettin **Note:** H#59.

Date	Mintage	Good	VG	F	VF	XF
ND(1606-18)	—	—	—	—	—	—

KM# 32 1/4 THALER (Reichsort)
7.1500 g., Silver, 30 mm. **Ruler:** Philipp II **Subject:** Death of Anna von Schleswig-Holstein, Widow of Bogislaw XIII **Obv:** Skull above crossed scepter and scythe **Obv. Legend:** MEDIT. MORT. OPTIMA. PHILOSOPHIA. **Rev:** 7-line inscription with Roman numeral date **Rev. Inscription:** MEMORIÆ/ FVNEBRI. DÑ/ ANNÆ. DVCIS/ POM. MATRIS/ CARISS. ANNO/ MDCXVI. VIII/ APRILIS. **Mint:** Stettin **Note:** H#90.

Date	Mintage	Good	VG	F	VF	XF
MDCXVI(1616)	—	—	—	—	—	—

KM# 39 1/4 THALER (Reichsort)
7.1700 g., Silver, 30 mm. **Ruler:** Philipp II **Subject:** Death of Georg III **Obv:** Sun shining on rose bush **Obv. Legend:** REDIENS. SOL. SVSCITAT. HERBAS. **Rev:** 6-line inscription with Roman numeral date **Rev. Inscription:** MEMORI? / GEORGI D PO. / MERAN A FRAT. / PHILIP. II SACRA / TVM. XXVI. MAI / AO. DCXVII. **Mint:** Stettin **Note:** H#96.

Date	Mintage	Good	VG	F	VF	XF
DCXVII(1617)	—	—	—	—	—	—

KM# 67 1/4 THALER (Reichsort)
7.0100 g., Silver, 29.5 mm. **Ruler:** Franz **Subject:** Death of Philipp II **Obv:** Bust to right in ornamented circle **Obv. Legend:** PHILIPPVS. II. D.G. DVX. POM. **Rev:** 7-line inscription with Roman numeral date **Rev. Inscription:** PATRI/PATRIÆ. PIO/PACIFICO MODE/RATO. LITERA/TO. C. LAC. R.P./AŌ MDCXIIX/XIX MART. **Mint:** Stettin **Note:** H#110.

Date	Mintage	Good	VG	F	VF	XF
MDCXIIX (1618) DS	—	—	—	—	—	—

KM# 88 1/4 THALER (Reichsort)
7.2400 g., Silver, 30-31 mm. **Ruler:** Bogislaw XIV **Subject:** Death of Franz **Obv:** Skull over crossed scepter and scythe, all in wreath **Rev:** 6-line inscription **Rev. Legend:** FRANCISCVS. I. DG. DVX. STETIN. P. **Rev. Inscription:** PACIFI/CVM. RAPV/IT. VERVM/NON. DEFI/CIT: AL/TER. **Mint:** Stettin **Note:** H#133.

Date	Mintage	Good	VG	F	VF	XF
ND(1620) GT	—	—	—	—	—	—

KM# 101 1/4 THALER (Reichsort)
7.1500 g., Silver, 28 mm. **Ruler:** Bogislaw XIV **Obv:** Half-length figure to right divides date in circle **Obv. Legend:** BOGIS. XIV. D.G. DVX. STET. POM. CAS. ET. VAN. **Rev:** Large shield of 9-fold arms in ornate frame within circle **Rev. Legend:** PRIN. RUG. COM. GUTZ. TER. LEOB. ET. BU. DN. **Mint:** Stettin **Note:** H#357.

Date	Mintage	Good	VG	F	VF	XF
16Z8	—	—	—	—	—	—

KM# 102 1/4 THALER (Reichsort)
7.1500 g., Silver, 32 mm. **Ruler:** Bogislaw XIV **Obv:** Bust to right in circle **Obv. Legend:** BOGISLAVS. XIV. D.G. DVX. ST. PO. C. E. V. **Rev:** Ornamented spanish shield of 9-fold arms, date above, in circle **Rev. Legend:** PRIN. RVG. CO. GVT. TER. LEOB. E. BV. DO. **Mint:** Stettin **Note:** H#358.

Date	Mintage	Good	VG	F	VF	XF
16Z8	—	—	—	—	—	—

KM# 135 1/4 THALER (Reichsort)
7.1500 g., Silver, 31 mm. **Ruler:** Bogislaw XIV **Obv:** Small bust to right in circle **Obv. Legend:** BOGISLAVS. XIV. D.G. DVX. STE. POM. **Rev:** 10-fold arms in baroque frame, ducal cap above, date at end of legend **Rev. Legend:** DEVS. ADIVTOR. MEVS. **Mint:** Stettin **Note:** H#359.

Date	Mintage	Good	VG	F	VF	XF
1635	—	—	—	—	—	—

KM# 143 1/4 THALER (Reichsort)
7.1400 g., Silver Weight varies: 7.12-7.14g., 30 mm. **Ruler:** Bogislaw XIV **Subject:** Entombment of Bogislaw XIV **Obv:** Tree stump with two young limbs in leaf, view of Stettin behind, sun shining down from upper left, DEO DIRIGENTE to right of sun **Rev:** 11-line inscription with date within wreath **Rev. Inscription:** NVMMVS.EXEQVIALIS/ OPTIMI. PRINCI/ PIS. BOGISLAI / DVCIS. STET. POME / EIVS. NOMINIS. XIV / ET VLTIMI / NATI. 31 MART 1580 / DEN. 10. MAR. 1637 / SEP. 25 MAY / 1654. **Mint:** Stettin **Note:** H#386.

Date	Mintage	Good	VG	F	VF	XF
1654	100	300	500	750	1,000	1,500

KM# 3 1/2 THALER
14.0000 g., Silver, 33-34 mm. **Ruler:** Philipp II **Obv:** Bust to right in circle **Obv. Legend:** PHILIPPVS. II. D.G. DVX. POMERANORVM. **Rev:** Crowned griffin to left holding sword in circle, 10 oval shields of arms around, legend in small letters between tops of shields **Rev. Legend:** CR - IS - TO - ET - RE - IP - VB - LI - C - Æ. **Mint:** Stettin **Note:** H#58. Varieties exist.

Date	Mintage	Good	VG	F	VF	XF
ND(1606-18) DS	—	—	—	—	—	—
ND(1606-18)	—	—	—	—	—	—

KM# 40 1/2 THALER
14.6000 g., Silver, 35 mm. **Ruler:** Philipp II **Subject:** Centennial of the Reformation **Obv:** Armored bust wearing ruffed collar to right in circle **Obv. Legend:** PHILIPPVS. II. D.G. DVX. POMERANORVM. **Rev:** Small sailboat, man at tiller, being blown to right by wind from clouds at upper left, legend ends with Roman numeral date **Rev. Legend:** SAPIENTIA NON VIOLENTIA. ANNO. MDCXVII. **Mint:** Stettin **Note:** H#84.

Date	Mintage	Good	VG	F	VF	XF
MDCXVII(1617)	—	—	—	—	—	—

KM# 41 1/2 THALER
14.6000 g., Silver, 35 mm. **Ruler:** Philipp II **Subject:** Centennial of the Reformation **Obv:** Armored bust to right in circle **Obv. Legend:** PHILIPPVS. II. DVX. POMERANORVM. **Rev:** Small sailboat, man at tiller, being blown to right by wind from clouds at upper left, Roman numeral date at end of legend **Rev. Legend:** SAPIENTIA NON VIOLENTIA. ANNO. MDCXVII. **Mint:** Stettin **Note:** H#85.

Date	Mintage	Good	VG	F	VF	XF
MDCXVII(1617)	—	—	—	—	—	—

KM# 42 1/2 THALER
13.8500 g., Silver, 35 mm. **Ruler:** Philipp II **Subject:** Death of Georg III **Obv:** Wildman standing to left of table holding ornately-shaped shield of Pomeranian arms, hourglass, flower and skull on table, the front of which is a square tablet with birth and death dates in Roman numerals **Obv. Inscription:** NATVS / XXX. IAN / M.DLXXXII / OBIIT / XXVII MART / MDCXVII. **Rev:** 9-line inscription with Roman numeral date **Rev. Inscription:** PHILIPPVS/II DVX STETTIN/ET POMERANIÆ. GEORGI III / FRATR DESIDERAT / MEMORIÆ / CVM LACRYM FF / XXVI MAII / MDCXVII. **Mint:** Stettin **Note:** H#95.

Date	Mintage	Good	VG	F	VF	XF
MDCXVII(1617)	—	—	—	—	—	—

KM# 43 1/2 THALER
14.3800 g., Silver, 35 mm. **Ruler:** Philipp II **Subject:** Centennial of the Reformation **Obv:** Samson wrestling with lion, date at end of legend **Obv. Legend:** OBTVRAVIT OS LEONIS. **Rev:** 7-line inscription with Roman numeral date **Rev. Inscription:** IN MEMO/RIAM. IVBILÆI/EVANGELICI/ANNO. M.D.XVII/ CELERATI. PHI/LIPPVS. II. DVX/POM. F.F. **Mint:** Stettin **Note:** H#104.

Date	Mintage	Good	VG	F	VF	XF
1617//MDXVII(1517)	—	—	—	—	—	—

KM# 44 1/2 THALER
14.3800 g., Silver, 35 mm. **Ruler:** Philipp II **Subject:** Centennial of the Reformation **Obv:** Samson wrestling with lion on grass, date at end of legend **Obv. Legend:** OBTVRAVIT OS LEONIS. **Rev:** 7-line inscription with Roman numeral date **Rev. Inscription:** IN MEMO/RIAM. IVBILÆI/EVANGELICI/ANNO. M.D.C.XVII/CELEBRATI. PHI/LIPPVS. II. DVX/POM. F.F. **Mint:** Stettin **Note:** H#105.

Date	Mintage	Good	VG	F	VF	XF
1517//MDCXVII(1617)	—	—	—	—	—	—

KM# 68 1/2 THALER
14.1900 g., Silver, 35 mm. **Ruler:** Franz **Subject:** Death of Philipp II **Obv:** Armored bust wearing ruffed collar to right in ornamented circle **Obv. Legend:** PHILIPPVS. II. D.G. DVX. POMERANORVM. **Rev:** 10-line inscription with dates **Rev. Inscription:** NVMMVS/MEMOR. FVNEBRI/PHILIPPI. II/DVCIS. STET. POMER/QVI. NATVS. Z8. IVL. AÕ.1573, DEBAT, 3, FEB, AÕ. 1618/CONSECRATVS/A. FRANC. I. SEDINET/POMER. DVCE. FRAT/ET. SVCCESS. **Mint:** Stettin **Note:** H#109.

Date	Mintage	Good	VG	F	VF	XF
1618	—	—	—	—	—	—

KM# 69 1/2 THALER
14.2100 g., Silver, 35 mm. **Ruler:** Franz **Obv:** Armored bust to right in circle **Obv. Legend:** D.G. FRANCISCVS. I. DVX. SEDINI. POMERAN. CASSVB. ET. VAN. **Rev:** Ornate shield of 9-fold arms supported by 2 wildmen, 3 ornate helmets above **Rev. Legend:** PRINC. RVGIÆ. COM GVTZK. TERR. LEOPOL. ET. BVTOV. DNS. **Mint:** Stettin **Note:** H#117.

Date	Mintage	Good	VG	F	VF	XF
ND(1618-20)	—	—	—	—	—	—

KM# 71 1/2 THALER
14.3300 g., Silver, 35 mm. **Ruler:** Franz **Subject:** Death of Anna Maria von Brandenburg, Widow of Barnim XII **Obv:** Crowned griffin to left holding sword and ornate shield, 10 small shields of arms on wings, standing on ornate tablet which is blank, no legend **Rev:** 10-line inscription with Roman numeral dates **Rev. Inscription:** MEMORIÆ. FVNEB/ANNÆ MARIÆ/IOH. GEORG. EL. BR. FILIÆ/BARNI. XI. DVC. POM. VIDVÆ/NATÆ. M.D.LXVII/DENA. M.DCXIIX/SEP. 17. XB. STET. Ã. EOD/FRANCISCVS. I. DVX. STET. POM/F. F. **Mint:** Stettin **Note:** H#127.

Date	Mintage	Good	VG	F	VF	XF
MDCXIIX(1618)	—	—	—	—	—	—

KM# 70 1/2 THALER
14.2100 g., Silver, 35 mm. **Ruler:** Franz **Obv:** Armored bust to right in circle **Obv. Legend:** D.G. FRANCISCVS. I. DVX. SEDINI. POMERAN. CASSVB. ET. VAN. **Rev:** Ornate shield of 9-fold arms supported by 2 wildmen, 3 ornate helmets above **Rev. Legend:** PRINC. RVGIÆ. COM. GVTZK. TERR. LEOPOL. ET. BVTOV. DN. **Mint:** Stettin **Note:** H#118.

Date	Mintage	Good	VG	F	VF	XF
ND(1618-20) GT	—	—	—	—	—	—

KM# 89 1/2 THALER
13.7500 g., Silver, 35 mm. **Ruler:** Bogislaw XIV **Subject:** Death of Franz **Obv:** Armored bust to right in circle **Obv. Legend:** D.G. FRANCISCVS. I. DVX. SEDINI. POMERAN. CASSVB. ET. VAN. **Rev:** 10-line inscription with dates **Rev. Inscription:** NVMMVS/NOVISSIMO. HONORI/FRANCISCI. I/DVCIS. STET. POM. QVI/NATVS. XXIV. MART. AÕ. 1577/MORTVVS. XXVII. NOVE/ANNO. 1620. DICATVS/A. BOGISLAO. SIV/FRATRE. ET. SVC/CESSORE. **Mint:** Stettin **Note:** H#132.

Date	Mintage	Good	VG	F	VF	XF
1620 GT	—	—	—	—	—	—

KM# 103 1/2 THALER
13.9400 g., Silver, 36 mm. **Ruler:** Bogislaw XIV **Obv:** Half-length armored figure to right divides date in circle **Obv. Legend:** BOGISLAVS. XIV. D.G. DVX. STE. POM. CASS. ET. VAN. **Rev:** Shield of 9-fold arms in ornate frame within circle **Rev. Legend:** PRINCEPS. RVG. COM. GVTZK. TERR. LEOB. ET. BVT. DN. **Mint:** Stettin **Note:** H#353.

Date	Mintage	Good	VG	F	VF	XF
16Z8	—	—	—	—	—	—

KM# 104 1/2 THALER
13.9400 g., Silver, 36-37 mm. **Ruler:** Bogislaw XIV **Obv:** Large armored half-length figure to right divides date and breaks circle at top **Obv. Legend:** BOGISLAVS. XIV. D.G. DVX. STET. POM. CAS. E. VA. **Rev:** Shield of 9-fold arms in ornate frame within circle **Rev. Legend:** PRINCEPS. RVG. COM. GVTZK. TERR. LEOB. ET. BVT. DN. **Mint:** Stettin **Note:** H#354.

Date	Mintage	Good	VG	F	VF	XF
16Z8	—	—	—	—	—	—

KM# 105 1/2 THALER
13.9400 g., Silver, 33 mm. **Ruler:** Bogislaw XIV **Obv:** Half-length armored figure to right divides date in circle **Obv. Legend:** BOGIS. XIV. D.G. DVX. STET. POM. CASSVB. ET. VANDA. **Rev:** Shield of 9-fold arms in ornate frame within circle **Rev. Legend:** PRINCEPS. RVG. COM. GVTZ. TER. LEOB. ET. BVT. DN. **Mint:** Stettin **Note:** H#355.

Date	Mintage	Good	VG	F	VF	XF
16Z8	—	—	—	—	—	—

KM# 106 1/2 THALER
13.9400 g., Silver, 38 mm. **Ruler:** Bogislaw XIV **Obv:** Bust to right in circle **Obv. Legend:** BOGISLAVS. XIV. D.G. DVX. STE. POM. CAS. E. V. **Rev:** Squarish shield of 9-fold arms, 3 ornate helmets above, date divided at top in margin **Rev. Legend:** PRINC. RVG. COM. GVT. TER. LEOB. E. BV. D. **Mint:** Stettin **Note:** H#356. Varieties exist.

Date	Mintage	Good	VG	F	VF	XF
16Z8	—	—	—	—	—	—
16Z8 error XVI for XIV	—	—	—	—	—	—

KM# 144 1/2 THALER
14.2900 g., Silver, 42 mm. **Ruler:** Bogislaw XIV **Subject:** Entombment of Bogislaw XIV **Obv:** Bust to right in wreath **Obv. Legend:** BOGISLAVS. XIV. D.G. DVX. STET. POM. C. &. V. P. RV. E. C. C. G. T. L. E. B. D. **Rev:** 12-line inscription with dates in wreath **Rev. Inscription:** NVMMVS / EXEQVALIS. / OPTIMI PRINCIPIS / *BOGISLAI* / DVCIS STET. POM EIVS / NOMINIS. 14. ET VLTIMI / NATI. 31. MART. 1580 / DENATI. 10. MART. 1637 / CONDITI. 25. MAI. 1654 / REG. C. R. S. ET. F. W / M. &. E. B. D. P / P.P. **Mint:** Stettin **Note:** H#382.

Date	Mintage	Good	VG	F	VF	XF
1654	200	—	—	—	—	—

KM# 145 1/2 THALER
14.2900 g., Silver, 34 mm. **Ruler:** Bogislaw XIV **Subject:** Entombment of Bogislaw XIV **Obv:** Bust to right in wreath, double legend with dates **Obv. Legend:** IN MEMORIAM VLTIMI EX GRYPHICA STIRPE DVCIS POMERAN BOGISLAI. 14. // NATI. 31. MART. 1580. DENATI. 10. MART. 1637. HVMATI. 25. MAI. 1654. **Rev:** Tree stump with two young limbs in leaf, crowned griffin standing on top, skull below, crowned oval arms of Sweden and Brandenburg at lower left and right, sun shining down from above, all in wreath **Rev. Legend:** GRYPS TRIBUS ECCE CORONIS ET SCEPTRO CEDIT. **Mint:** Stettin **Note:** H#383.

Date	Mintage	Good	VG	F	VF	XF
1654	Inc. above	400	700	1,000	1,600	2,250

KM# 146 1/2 THALER
14.2900 g., Silver, 32 mm. **Ruler:** Bogislaw XIV **Subject:** Entombment of Bogislaw XIV **Obv:** Tree stump with two young limbs in leaf, view of Stettin behind, sun shiniing down from upper left, DEO DIRIGENTE to right of sun **Rev:** 11-line inscription with dates in wreath **Rev. Inscription:** NVMMVS / EXEQVIALIS / OPTIMI PRINCI / PIS BOGISLAI / DVCIS. STET. POME / EIVS. NOMINIS. XIV / ET. VLTIMI / NATI. 31. MART. 1580 / DEN. X. MAR. 1637 / SEP. 25. MAY / 1654. **Mint:** Stettin **Note:** H#384.

Date	Mintage	Good	VG	F	VF	XF
1654	Inc. above	—	—	—	—	—

KM# 147 1/2 THALER
14.2900 g., Silver, 28 mm. **Ruler:** Bogislaw XIV **Obv:** Tree stump with two young limbs in leaf, view of Stettin behind, sun shining down from upper left divides DEO - DIRIGENTE. **Rev:** 11-line inscription with dates in wreath **Rev. Inscription:** NVMMVS/EXEQVIALIS/OPTIMI PRINCI/PIS. BOGISLAI/DVCIS. STET. POMER/EIVS. NOMINIS. SIV/ET. VLTIMI/NATI. 31. MART. 1580/DEN. 10. MAR. 1637/SEP. 25. MAY/1654. **Mint:** Stettin **Note:** H#385. Struck on thick flan from 1/8 Thaler dies.

Date	Mintage	Good	VG	F	VF	XF
1654	Inc. above	—	—	—	—	—

KM# 4 THALER
Silver, 40.5-42 mm. **Ruler:** Philipp II **Obv:** Bust to right in ornamented circle **Obv. Legend:** PHILIPPVS. II. D.G. DVX. POMERANORVM **Rev:** Crowned griffin to left holding sword in circle, 10 oval shields of arms around, legend in small letters between tops of shields **Rev. Legend:** CR - IS - TO - ET - RE - IP - VB - LI - C - Æ. **Mint:** Stettin **Note:** Dav. #7215; H#50. Prev. Pomerania KM#40.

Date	Mintage	VG	F	VF	XF	Unc
ND(1606-18) DS	—	700	1,400	2,500	4,250	—
ND(1606-18)	—	700	1,400	2,500	4,250	—

KM# 5 THALER
28.7100 g., Silver, 41-42 mm. **Ruler:** Philipp II **Obv:** Bust to right in circle **Obv. Legend:** PHILIPPVS. II. DVX. POMERANORVM. **Rev:** Crowned griffin left holding sword in circle, 10 oval shields of arms around, legend in small letters between tops of shields **Rev. Legend:** CR - IS - TO - ET - RE - IP - VB - LI - C - Æ. **Mint:** Stettin **Note:** Dav. #7211; H#51. Prev. Pomerania KM#38.

Date	Mintage	Good	VG	F	VF	XF
ND(1606-18)	—	—	750	1,500	2,750	4,650

KM# 6 THALER
28.7000 g., Silver, 40-41 mm. **Ruler:** Philipp II **Obv:** Bust to right in ornamented circle **Obv. Legend:** PHILIPPVS. II. D.G. DVX.

POMERANORVM. **Rev:** Crowned griffin left holding sword and book, 10 small shields of arms on wings, 2-line inscription in ornate tablet below **Rev. Inscription:** CHRISTO. ET. REIP/ VBLICÆ. **Mint:** Stettin **Note:** Dav. #7213; H#52. Prev. Pomerania KM#39.

Date	Mintage	VG	F	VF	XF	Unc
ND(1606-18)	—	750	1,500	2,750	4,650	—

KM# 13 THALER

28.7000 g., Silver, 42-43 mm. **Ruler:** Philipp II **Obv:** Bust to right in circle, legend divided by 5 small shields of arms in margin **Obv. Legend:** V. G. G. - PHI. - LIPS - H. Z. S. - POM. **Rev:** Crowned griffin left holding sword and book, legend divided by 5 small shields of arms in margin, date at end of legend **Rev. Legend:** CHRI - STO. ET - REIP - ANNO - (date) **Mint:** Stettin **Note:** Dav. #7205; H#53, 55. Prev. Pomerania KM#23.

Date	Mintage	VG	F	VF	XF	Unc
1613	—	1,400	2,500	4,150	6,900	—
1614	—	1,400	2,500	4,150	6,900	—

KM# 18 THALER

28.7000 g., Silver, 42 mm. **Ruler:** Philipp II **Obv:** Bust to right in circle **Obv. Legend:** PHILIPPVS. II. DVX. POMERANORVM. **Rev:** Shield of 9-fold arms supported by 2 helmeted wildmen, ornate helmet above, date at end of legend **Rev. Legend:** CHRISTO. ET. REIPVBLICÆ. **Mint:** Stettin **Note:** Dav. #7208; H#54, 54. Prev. Pomerania KM#27.

Date	Mintage	VG	F	VF	XF	Unc
1614	—	1,150	2,150	3,750	6,300	—
1616	—	1,150	2,150	3,750	6,300	—

KM# 19 THALER

Silver **Ruler:** Philipp II **Obv:** Bust to right in circle, legend divided by 5 small shields of arms **Obv. Legend:** V. G. G. - PHI. - LIPS - H. A. S. - POM. **Rev:** Crowned griffin to left holding sword and book, legend divided by 5 small shields of arms, date at end of legend **Rev. Legend:** CHRI - STO. ET - REIP - ANNO - (date) **Mint:** Stettin **Note:** Klippe. Dav. #7205A; H#KL55. Prev. Pomerania KM#26.

Date	Mintage	VG	F	VF	XF	Unc
1614 Rare	—	—	—	—	—	—

KM# 25 THALER

Silver, 43 mm. **Ruler:** Philipp II **Obv:** Bust to right in circle, legend divided by 5 small shields of arms **Obv. Legend:** V. G. G. - PHI. - LIPS - H. Z. S. - POM. **Rev:** 11-line inscription with date **Rev. Inscription:** (date) / A. DEO / OMNIA. OR / NAMENTA / REIPVBLICAE. ET / FVNDAMEN / TVM. EIVS / EST. NON / GAVDE / REVA / NIS **Mint:** Stettin **Note:** Dav. #7209; H#56. Prev. Pomerania KM#35.

Date	Mintage	VG	F	VF	XF	Unc
1615 Rare	—	—	—	—	—	—

KM# 33 THALER

27.2600 g., Silver, 42 mm. **Ruler:** Philipp II **Subject:** Death of Anna von Schleswig-Holstein, Widow of Bogislaw XIII **Obv:** Bust to right in circle **Obv. Legend:** PHILIPPVS. II. DVX. POMERANORVM. **Rev:** 9-line inscription with Roman numeral dates **Rev. Inscription:** ANNA FILIA/ IOHAN. DVCIS/ HOLS. VIDVA. BOGIS/ LAI. SEN. DVCIS POM./ MATER CARISS. NATA/ MDLXXVII. VII. OCT/ DENATA. MDCXVI/ XXX IAN. SEPVL/ VIII. APRI. **Mint:** Stettin **Note:** Dav. #7218; H#89. Prev. Pomerania KM#41.

Date	Mintage	VG	F	VF	XF	Unc
MDCXVI(1616)	—	700	1,400	2,500	4,250	—

KM# 45 THALER

28.6000 g., Silver, 41 mm. **Ruler:** Philipp II **Subject:** Centennial of the Reformation **Obv:** Bust to right in ornamented circle **Obv. Legend:** PHILIPPVS. II. D.G. DVX. POMERANORVM. **Rev:** Small sailboat, man at tiller, being blown to right by wind from clouds at upper left. Roman numeral date at end of legend **Rev. Legend:** SAPIENTIA NON VIOLENTIA. ANNO. MDCXVII. **Mint:** Stettin **Note:** Dav. #7226; H#82. Prev. Pomerania KM#50.2.

Date	Mintage	VG	F	VF	XF	Unc
MDCXVII(1617)	—	800	1,500	2,500	4,200	—

KM# 46 THALER

27.2500 g., Silver, 42 mm. **Ruler:** Philipp II **Subject:** Centennial of the Reformation **Obv:** Bust to right in circle **Obv. Legend:** PHILIPPVS. II. DVX. POMERANORVM. **Rev:** Small sailboat, man at tiller, being blown to right by wind from clouds at upper left, Roman numeral date at end of legend **Rev. Legend:** SAPIENTIA NON VIOLENTIA. ANNO. MDCXVII. **Mint:** Stettin **Note:** Dav. #7224; H#83. Prev. Pomerania KM#50.1.

Date	Mintage	VG	F	VF	XF	Unc
MDCXVII(1617)	—	800	1,500	2,500	4,200	—

KM# 47 THALER

28.6100 g., Silver, 43 mm. **Ruler:** Philipp II **Subject:** Death of Georg III **Obv:** Wildman standing to left of table holding ornately-shaped shield of Pomeranian arms, hourglass, flower and skull on table, the front of which is a square tablet with birth and death dates in Roman numerals **Obv. Inscription:** NATVS/ XXX. IAN/ M.DLXXXII/ OBIIT/ XXVII MART/ MDCXVII. **Rev:** 9-line inscription with Roman numeral date **Rev. Inscription:** PHILIPPVS/ II DVX STETTIN/ ET POMERANIÆ. GEORGI III/ FRATR DESIDERAT/ MEMORIÆ/ CVM LACRYM FF/ XXVI MAII/ MDCXVII. **Mint:** Stettin **Note:** Dav. #7221; H#94. Prev. Pomerania KM#49.

Date	Mintage	VG	F	VF	XF	Unc
MDCXVII(1617)	—	1,650	3,000	5,000	8,100	—

KM# 48 THALER

28.4400 g., Silver, 37 mm. **Ruler:** Philipp II **Subject:** Centennial of the Reformation **Obv:** Samson wrestling with lion on grass, date at end of legend **Obv. Legend:** OBTVRAVIT OS LEONIS. **Rev:** 7-line inscription with Roman numeral date **Rev. Inscription:** IN MEMO/ RIAM. IVBILÆI/ EVANGELICI/ ANNO. M.D.C.XVII/ CELEBRATI. PHI/ LIPPVS. II. DVX/ POM. F.F. **Mint:** Stettin **Note:** Dav. #7229; H#103. Prev. Pomerania KM#51.

Date	Mintage	VG	F	VF	XF	Unc
1517//MDCXVII (1617) Rare	—	—	—	—	—	—

KM# 49 THALER

28.4400 g., Silver, 37 mm. **Ruler:** Philipp II **Subject:** Centennial of the Reformation **Obv:** Samson wrestling with lion, date at end of legend **Obv. Legend:** OBTVRAVIT OS LEONIS. **Rev:** 7-line inscription with Roman numeral date **Rev. Inscription:** IN MEMO/ RIAM. IVBILÆI/ EVANGELICI/ ANNO. M.D.XVII/ CELERATI. PHI/ LIPPVS. II. DVX/ POM. F.F. **Mint:** Stettin **Note:** H#102.

Date	Mintage	VG	F	VF	XF	Unc
1617//MDXVII (1517) Rare	—	—	—	—	—	—

KM# 72 THALER

28.7400 g., Silver, 43-44 mm. **Ruler:** Franz **Subject:** Death of Philipp II **Obv:** Armored bust wearing ruffed collar to right in ornamented circle **Obv. Legend:** PHILIPPVS. II. D.G. DVX. POMERANORVM. **Rev:** 10-line inscription with dates **Rev. Inscription:** NVMMVS/ MEMOR. FVNEBRI/ PHILIPPI. II/ DVCIS. STET. POMER/ QVI. NATVS. Z8. IVL. AÕ.1573, DEBAT, 3, FEB, AÕ. 1618/ CONSECRATVS/ A. FRANC. I. SEDINET/ POMER. DVCE. FRAT/ ET. SVCCESS. **Mint:** Stettin **Note:** Dav. #7232; H#108. Prev. Pomerania KM#65.

Date	Mintage	VG	F	VF	XF	Unc
1618	—	750	1,500	2,750	4,500	—

KM# 73 THALER

28.7000 g., Silver, 42-43 mm. **Ruler:** Franz **Obv:** Armored bust to right in circle **Obv. Legend:** D.G. FRANCISCVS. I. DVX. SEDINI. POMERAN. CASSVB. ET. VAN. **Rev:** Ornate shield of 9-fold arms supported by 2 wildmen, 3 ornate helmets above **Rev. Legend:** PRINC. RVGIÆ. COM GVTZK. TERR. LEOPOL. ET. BVTOV. DNS. **Mint:** Stettin **Note:** Dav. #7233; H#116. Prev. Pomerania KM#66.

Date	Mintage	VG	F	VF	XF	Unc
ND(1618-20)	—	1,400	2,500	4,150	6,900	—

KM# 74 THALER

28.7000 g., Silver, 42-43 mm. **Ruler:** Franz **Obv:** Armored bust to right in circle **Obv. Legend:** D.G. FRANCISCVS. I. DVX. SEDINI. POMERAN. CASSVB. ET. VAN. **Rev:** Ornate shield of 9-fold arms supported by 2 wildmen, 3 ornate helmets above **Rev. Legend:** PRINC. RVGIÆ. COM. GVTZK. TERR. LEOPOL. ET. BVTOV. DN. **Mint:** Stettin **Note:** Dav. #7233A; H#115.

Date	Mintage	VG	F	VF	XF	Unc
ND(1618-20) GT	—	1,400	2,500	4,150	6,900	—

KM# 75 THALER

28.5900 g., Silver, 42-43 mm. **Ruler:** Franz **Subject:** Death of Anna Maria von Brandenburg, Widow of Barnim XII **Obv:** Crowned griffin to left holding sword and ornate shield, 10 small shields of arms on wings, standing on ornate tablet which is blank, no legend **Rev:** 10-line inscription with Roman numeral dates **Rev. Inscription:** MEMORIÆ. FVNEB/ ANNÆ MARIÆ/ IOH. GEORG. EL. BR. FILIÆ/ BARNI. XI. DVC. POM. VIDVÆ/ NATÆ. M.D.LXVII/ DENA. M.DCXIIX/ SEP. 17. XB. STET. Ã. EOD/ FRANCISCVS. I. DVX. STET. POM/ F. F. **Mint:** Stettin **Note:** Dav. #7236; H#126. Prev. Pomerania KM#67.

Date	Mintage	VG	F	VF	XF	Unc
MDCXIIX(1618)	—	1,150	2,150	3,750	6,300	—

KM# 90 THALER

29.0500 g., Silver, 43 mm. **Ruler:** Bogislaw XIV **Subject:** Death of Franz **Obv:** Armored bust to right in circle **Obv. Legend:** D.G. FRANCISCVS. I. DVX. SEDINI. POMERAN. CASSVB. ET. VAN. **Rev:** 10-line inscription with dates **Rev. Inscription:** NVMMVS/ NOVISSIMO. HONORI/ FRANCISCI. I/ DVCIS. STET. POM. QVI/ NATVS. XXIV. MART. AÕ. 1577/ MORTVVS. XXVII. NOVE/ ANNO. 1620. DICATVS/ A. BOGISLAO. SIV/ FRATRE. ET. SVC/ CESSORE. **Mint:** Stettin **Note:** Dav. #7239; H#131. Prev. Pomerania KM#82.

Date	Mintage	VG	F	VF	XF	Unc
1620 GT	—	700	1,400	2,500	4,250	—

KM# 115 THALER

Silver **Ruler:** Bogislaw XIV **Obv:** Half-length figure to right, wearing highly ornamented armor, divides date **Obv. Legend:** BOGISLAVS. XIV. D.G. DVX. STET. POM. CAS. ET. VAN.

Rev: Ornate shield of 9-fold arms with ornate helmet above, supported by 2 wildmen wearing helmets **Rev. Legend:** PRINCEPS. RVG. CO. GVTZK. TERR. LEOB. E. B. D(N). **Mint:** Stettin **Note:** Dav. #7254; H#343-4. Prev. Pomerania KM#110. 1628 not in Hildisch and may not exist.

Date	Mintage	Good	VG	F	VF	XF
1628 Reported, not confirmed	—	—	—	—	—	—
1629/8	—	—	550	1,100	2,000	3,300
1630	—	—	550	1,100	2,000	3,300

KM# 110 THALER

28.5500 g., Silver, 42-43 mm. **Ruler:** Bogislaw XIV **Obv:** Bust to right in circle **Obv. Legend:** BOGISLAVS. XIV. D.G. DVX. STET. POM. CASSVB. ET. VAN. **Rev:** Shield of 9-fold arms, ornate helmet above, supported by 2 wildmen wearing helmets, date divided at top **Rev. Legend:** PRINC. RVG. COM GVTZK. TERR. LEOB. E. BVT. DO. **Mint:** Stettin **Note:** Dav. #7248. Prev. Pomerania KM#105.

Date	Mintage	Good	VG	F	VF	XF
16Z8	—	—	175	350	600	1,000

KM# 107 THALER

28.5500 g., Silver, 43 mm. **Ruler:** Bogislaw XIV **Obv:** Bust to right divides date in circle **Obv. Legend:** BOGISLAVS. XIV. D.G. DVX. STET. POM. CASSVB. ET. VAN. **Rev:** Griffin to right holding sword in ornate shield, ducal cap above divides date **Rev. Legend:** PRINC. RVG. COM. GVTZK. TERR. LEOBVRG. ET. BVTOV. DN. **Mint:** Stettin **Note:** Dav. #7244. Prev. Pomerania KM#102.

Date	Mintage	VG	F	VF	XF	Unc
16Z8//16Z8 (z)	—	625	1,300	2,400	4,000	—

KM# 108 THALER

28.5500 g., Silver, 43 mm. **Ruler:** Bogislaw XIV **Obv:** Bust to right divides date in circle **Obv. Legend:** BOGISLAVS. XIV. D.G. DVX. STET. POM. CASSVB. ET. VAN. **Rev:** Griffin to right holding sword in ornate shield, ducal cap above divides date **Rev. Legend:** PRINC. RVG. COM. GVTZK. TERR. LEOBVRG. ET. BVTO. DN. **Mint:** Stettin **Note:** Dav. #7244A. Prev. Pomerania KM#103.

Date	Mintage	VG	F	VF	XF	Unc
16Z8//16Z8 (z)	—	625	1,300	2,400	4,000	—

KM# 109 THALER

28.5500 g., Silver, 43 mm. **Ruler:** Bogislaw XIV **Obv:** Bust to right in circle **Obv. Legend:** BOGISLAVS. XIV. D.G. DVX. STET. POM. CASSVB. ET. VAN. **Rev:** Griffin to right holding sword in ornate shield, ducal cap above divides date **Rev. Legend:** PRINC. RVG. COM. GVTZK. TERR. LEOBVRG. ET. BVTOV. DN. **Mint:** Stettin **Note:** Dav. #7246. Prev. Pomerania KM#104. Varieties exist.

Date	Mintage	VG	F	VF	XF	Unc
16Z8 (z)	—	525	1,050	1,800	3,000	—

KM# 111 THALER

28.5500 g., Silver, 41 mm. **Ruler:** Bogislaw XIV **Obv:** Half-length armored figure to right divides date **Obv. Legend:** BOGISLAVS. XIV. D.G. DVX. STET. POM. CASSVB. ET. VAN. **Rev:** Shield of 9-fold arms with ornate helmet above, supported by 2 wildmen wearing helmets **Rev. Legend:** PRINC. RVGIÆ. COM. GVTZK. TERR. LEOPOL. ET. BVTOV. DN. **Mint:** Stettin **Note:** Dav. #7249. Prev. Pomerania KM#106. Varieties exist.

Date	Mintage	VG	F	VF	XF	Unc
16Z8 GT(z)	—	700	1,400	2,500	4,150	—

KM# 112 THALER

28.5500 g., Silver, 46 mm. **Ruler:** Bogislaw XIV **Obv:** Half-length armored figure to right divides date **Obv. Legend:** BOGISLAVS. XIV. D.G. DVX. STET. POM. CASS. ET. VAN. **Rev:** Ornate shield of 9-fold arms with ornate helmet above, supported by 2 wildmen wearing helmets **Rev. Legend:** PRINCEPS. RVG. COM. GVTZK. TERR. LEOB. ET. BVT. DN. **Mint:** Stettin **Note:** Dav. #7251. Prev. Pomerania KM#107.

Date	Mintage	VG	F	VF	XF	Unc
1628 Rare	—	—	—	—	—	—

KM# 113 THALER

28.5500 g., Silver, 42 mm. **Ruler:** Bogislaw XIV **Obv:** Small and thin half-length armored figure to right divides date **Obv. Legend:** BOGISLAVS. XIV. D.G. DVX. STET. POM. CAS. ET. VAN. **Rev:** Ornate shield of 9-fold arms with ornate helmet above, supported by 2 wildmen wearing helmets **Rev. Legend:** PRINCEPS. RVG. COM. GVTZK. TERR. LEOB. E. B. D. **Mint:** Stettin **Note:** Dav. #7252. Prev. Pomerania KM#108.

Date	Mintage	VG	F	VF	XF	Unc
16Z8	—	700	1,400	2,500	4,150	—

KM# 114 THALER

28.5500 g., Silver **Ruler:** Bogislaw XIV **Obv:** Half-length armored figure to right divides date **Obv. Legend:** BOGISLAVS. XIV. D.G. DVX. STETIN. POM. CAS. ET. VAN. **Rev:** Ornate shield of 9-fold arms with ornate helmet above, supported by 2 wildmen wearing helmets **Rev. Legend:** PRINC. RVG. COM. GVTZK. TERR. LEOBVRG. ET. BVTOV. DN. **Mint:** Stettin **Note:** Dav. #7253; H#337. Prev. Pomerania KM#109.

Date	Mintage	VG	F	VF	XF	Unc
16Z8	—	700	1,400	2,500	4,150	—

KM# 121 THALER

Silver **Ruler:** Bogislaw XIV **Obv:** Half-length armored figure to right divides date **Obv. Legend:** BOGISLAVS. XIV. D.G. DVX. STET. POM. CAS. ET. VAN. **Rev:** Ornate shield of 9-fold arms with ornate helmet above, supported by 2 wildmen wearing helmets **Rev. Legend:** PRIN. RVG. COM. GVTZK. TERR. LEOB. ET. B. DN. **Mint:** Stettin **Note:** Dav. #7255. Prev. Pomerania KM#128.1.

Date	Mintage	VG	F	VF	XF	Unc
1630	—	700	1,400	2,500	4,150	—

KM# 122 THALER

Silver **Ruler:** Bogislaw XIV **Obv:** Half-length armored figure to right divides date **Obv. Legend:** BOGISLAVS. XIV. D.G. DVX. STET. POM. CAS. ET. VAN. **Rev:** Ornate shield of 9-fold arms with ornate helmet above, supported by 2 wildmen wearing helmets **Rev. Legend:** PRINCEPS. RVG. COM. GVTZK. TERR. LEOB. ET. B. DN. **Mint:** Stettin **Note:** Dav. #7255A. Prev. Pomerania KM#128.2.

Date	Mintage	VG	F	VF	XF	Unc
1630	—	700	1,400	2,500	4,150	—

KM# 123 THALER

Silver **Ruler:** Bogislaw XIV **Obv:** Half-length armored figure to right divides date **Obv. Legend:** BOGISLAVS. XIV. D.G. DVX. STET. POM. CAS. ET. VAN. **Rev:** Ornate shield of 9-fold arms with ornate helmet above, supported by 2 wildmen wearing helmets **Rev. Legend:** PRIN. RVG. COM. GVTZK. TERR. LEOB. E. T. B. D. **Mint:** Stettin **Note:** Dav. #7255B. Prev. Pomerania KM#128.3.

Date	Mintage	VG	F	VF	XF	Unc
1630	—	700	1,400	2,500	4,150	—

KM# 124 THALER

Silver **Ruler:** Bogislaw XIV **Obv:** Half-length armored figure to right divides date **Obv. Legend:** BOGISLAVS. XIV. D.G. SVX. STET. POM. CAS. ET. VAN. **Rev:** Ornate shield of 9-fold arms with ornate helmet above, supported by 2 wildmen wearing helmets **Rev. Legend:** PRIN. RVG. COM. GVTZK. TERR. LEOB. E. G. DN. **Mint:** Stettin **Note:** Dav. #7255C. Prev. Pomerania KM#128.4.

Date	Mintage	VG	F	VF	XF	Unc
1630	—	700	1,400	2,500	4,150	—

KM# 126 THALER

Silver, 43-45 mm. **Ruler:** Bogislaw XIV **Obv:** Large half-length armored figure to right **Obv. Legend:** BOGISLAVS. XIV. D.G. DVX. STE. PO. CAS. ET. V. **Rev:** Ornate shield of 9-fold arms with ornate helmet above, supported by 2 wildmen wearing helmets, date divide near top by crest of helmet, where present **Rev. Legend:** PRIN. RVG. COM. GVTZK. TERR. LEOB. ET. B. D(N). **Mint:** Köslin **Note:** Dav. #7256; H#346. Prev. Pomerania KM#146.

Date	Mintage	VG	F	VF	XF	Unc
1631 CW	—	875	1,500	2,750	4,650	—
ND(1631)	—	625	1,250	2,250	3,750	—

KM# 127 THALER

Silver **Ruler:** Bogislaw XIV **Obv:** Half-length armored figure to right divides date **Obv. Legend:** BOGISLAVS. XIV. D.G. DVX. STET. POM. CAS. ET. VAN. **Rev:** Ornate shield of 9-fold arms with ornate helmet above, supported by 2 wildmen wearing helmets **Rev. Legend:** PRIN. RVG. COM. GVTZK. TERR. LEOB. ET. B. DN. **Mint:** Stettin **Note:** Dav. #7257; H#347. Prev. Pomerania KM#147.

Date	Mintage	Good	VG	F	VF	XF
1631	—	—	250	500	900	1,500

KM# 128 THALER

Silver **Ruler:** Bogislaw XIV **Obv:** Large armored bust to right divides date **Obv. Legend:** BOGISLAVS. XIV. D. G. DVX. STE. PO. CAS. ET. VAND. **Rev:** Ornate shield of 9-fold arms with ornate helmet above, supported by 2 wildmen wearing helmets, date divided by crest of helmet near top **Rev. Legend:** PRIN. RVG. COM. GVTZK. TERR. LEOB. ET. BVT. - DN. **Mint:** Stettin **Note:** Dav. #7258. Prev. Pomerania KM#153.1.

Date	Mintage	VG	F	VF	XF	Unc
163Z/163Z Rare	—	—	—	—	—	—

KM# 129 THALER

Silver **Ruler:** Bogislaw XIV **Obv:** Large armored bust to right divides date **Obv. Legend:** BOGISLAVS. XIV. D.G. DVX. STE. PO. CAS. ET. VAND. **Rev:** Ornate shield of 9-fold arms with ornate helmet above, supported by 2 wildmen wearing helmets, date divided by crest of helmet near top **Rev. Legend:** PRIN. RVG. COM. GVTZK. TERR. LEOB. ET. B. DN. **Mint:** Stettin **Note:** Dav. #7258A; H#348. Prev. Pomerania KM#153.2.

Date	Mintage	VG	F	VF	XF	Unc
163Z//163Z Rare	—	—	—	—	—	—

KM# 130 THALER

Silver **Ruler:** Bogislaw XIV **Obv:** Large armored bust to right breaks circle at top **Obv. Legend:** BOGISLAVS. XIV. D.G. DVX. STE. PO. CAS. E. VAN. **Rev:** Ornate shield of 9-fold arms with ornate helmet above, supported by 2 wildmen wearing helmets, date divided by crest of helmet near top **Rev. Legend:** PRIN. RVG. COM. GVTZK. TERR. LEOB. ET. BVT. DN. **Mint:** Stettin **Note:** Dav. #7259; H#349. Prev. Pomerania KM#157.1.

Date	Mintage	VG	F	VF	XF	Unc
1633	—	450	900	1,650	2,700	—

KM# 131 THALER

Silver **Ruler:** Bogislaw XIV **Obv:** Large armored bust to right breaks circle at top **Obv. Legend:** BOGISLAVS. XIV. D.G. DVX. STE. PO. CAS. E. V. **Rev:** Ornate shield of 9-fold arms with ornate helmet above, supported by 2 wildmen wearing helmets, date divided by crest of helmet near top **Rev. Legend:** PRIN. RVG. COM GVTZK. TERR. LEOB. ET. B. DN. **Mint:** Stettin **Note:** Dav. #7259A; H#349. Prev. Pomerania KM#157.2.

Date	Mintage	VG	F	VF	XF	Unc
1633	—	450	900	1,650	2,700	—

KM# 134 THALER

Silver **Ruler:** Bogislaw XIV **Obv:** Large armored bust to right breaks circle at top **Obv. Legend:** BOGISLAVS. XIV. D.G. DVX. STE. P. CAS. E(T). VAN. **Rev:** Ornate shield of 9-fold arms with ornate helmet above, supported by 2 wildmen wearing helmets, date divided by crest of helmet near top **Rev. Legend:** PRIN. RVG. CO. GVTZK. TERR. LEOB. ET. BVT. DN. **Mint:** Stettin **Note:** Dav. #7260; H#350. Prev. Pomerania KM#170.

Date	Mintage	VG	F	VF	XF	Unc
1634 Rare	—	—	—	—	—	—
1635 Rare	—	—	—	—	—	—

KM# 136 THALER

Silver **Ruler:** Bogislaw XIV **Obv:** Large armored bust to right breaks circle at top **Obv. Legend:** BOGISLAVS. XIV. D.G. DVX. STE. P. CAS. E(T). VAN. **Rev:** Ornate shield of 9-fold arms with ornate helmet above, supported by 2 wildmen wearing helmets, date divided by crest of helmet near top **Rev. Legend:** PRIN. RVG. CO. GVTZK. TERR. LEOB. ET. B. D. **Mint:** Stettin **Note:** H#351.

Date	Mintage	VG	F	VF	XF	Unc
1635 Rare	—	—	—	—	—	—

KM# 137 THALER

27.1700 g., Silver, 43 mm. **Ruler:** Bogislaw XIV **Obv:** Duke on horseback galloping to right, small oval Pomeranian arms below **Obv. Legend:** BOGISLAVS. XIV - DG. - DVX. S. P. **Rev:** Ornate shield of 10-fold arms with ornate helmet above, supported by 2 wildmen wearing helmets, date above left wildman **Rev. Legend:** CASSVB. ET. VAND. PRINC. RVB. EP. CAM. COM. GVTZK. TER. LEOB. ET. BV. DO. **Mint:** Stettin **Note:** H#370.

Date	Mintage	VG	F	VF	XF	Unc
1635 GT Rare	—	—	—	—	—	—

KM# 141 THALER

Silver **Ruler:** Bogislaw XIV **Obv:** Large armored bust to right breaks circle at top. **Obv. Legend:** BOGISLAVS. XIV. D.G. DVX. STE. P. CAS. ET. VA. **Rev:** Ornate shield of 9-fold arms with ornate helmet above, supported by 2 wildmen wearing helmets, date divided by crest of helmet **Rev. Legend:** PRIN. RVG. COM. GVTZK. TERR. LEOB. E. B. D. **Mint:** Stettin **Note:** Dav. #7261; H#352. Prev. Pomerania KM#178.

Date	Mintage	VG	F	VF	XF	Unc
1636 Rare	—	—	—	—	—	—

KM# 148 THALER

28.8000 g., Silver, 44 mm. **Ruler:** Bogislaw XIV **Subject:** Entombment of Bogislaw XIV **Obv:** Duke on horseback galloping to right, small oval Pomeranian arms below **Obv. Legend:** BOGISLAVS. XIV - DG. - DVX. S. P. **Rev:** Skull within wreath, triple circular legends around **Rev. Legend:** IN MEMORIAM ULTIMI EX GRYPHICA STIRPE DUCIS POMER/ BOGISLAI. XIV. NATI. XXXI. MART. 1580. DENATI. X/ MART. 1637. HVMATI. 25. MAI. 1654. **Mint:** Stettin **Note:** H#378.

Date	Mintage	VG	F	VF	XF	Unc
1654 GT Rare	120	—	—	—	—	—

KM# 149 THALER

28.8000 g., Silver **Ruler:** Bogislaw XIV **Subject:** Entombment of Bogislaw XIV **Obv:** Armored bust to right in wreath **Obv. Legend:** BOGISLAVS. XIV. D.G. DVX. ST. POM. C. &. VAND. P. RV. EP. C. CO. G. T. L. &. B. D. **Rev:** 15-line inscription with dates **Rev. Inscription:** NOVISSIMIS / HONORIBVS / BOGISLAI. DVC. STET / POMER. EIVS. NOMINIS / 14. ET. VLTIMI / NATI. 31. MART. 1637 / HVMATI. 25. MAI. 1654 / CHRISTINA. D. G. SVECOR / GOTHOR. VANDAL. REGI / ET/FRIDERICVS. WILH. / D. G. MARC. &. EL. B/ DVCE. POM / F. F. **Mint:** Stettin **Note:** Dav. #LS372B; H#379. Prev. Pomerania KM#211.

Date	Mintage	VG	F	VF	XF	Unc
1654	Inc. above	—	—	3,150	5,000	—

KM# 150 THALER

28.8000 g., Silver, 45 mm. **Ruler:** Bogislaw XIV **Subject:** Entombment of Bogislaw XIV **Obv:** Large crowned griffin to left standing on tree trunk lying on ground, 10 small shields of arms on wings, small tree to right, skull to lower left, several young branches growing up from it with arms of Sweden and Brandenburg attached, sun shining dow **Rev:** 11-line inscription with date in wreath, triple marginal legend in Gothic letters **Rev. Inscription:** NVMMVS / EXEQVIALIS / OPTIMI.PRINCI / PIS.BOGISLAI / DVCIS.STET.POM / EIVS.NOMINIS.14 / ET.VLTIMI / NATI.31.MAR.1580 / DEN.X.MAR.1637 / SEP.25.MAI / 1654. **Mint:** Stettin **Note:** H#380.

Date	Mintage	VG	F	VF	XF	Unc
1654 GT Rare	Inc. above	—	—	—	—	—

KM# 151 THALER

28.8000 g., Silver, 33 mm. **Ruler:** Bogislaw XIV **Subject:** Entombment of Bogislaw XIV **Obv:** Tree stump with two young limbs in leaf, view of Stettin behind, sun shining down from upper left, DEO DIRIGENTE to right of sun **Rev:** 11-line inscription with dates in wreath **Rev. Inscription:** NVMMVS/ EXEQVIALIS/ OPTIMI PRINCI/ PIS BOGISLAI/ DVCIS. STET. POME/ EIVS. NOMINIS. XIV/ ET. VLTIMI/ NATI. 31. MART. 1580/ DEN. X. MAR. 1637/ SEP. 25. MAY/ 1654. **Mint:** Stettin **Note:** H#381. Struck from 1/2 Thaler dies, KM#146.

Date	Mintage	Good	VG	F	VF	XF
1654 Rare	Inc. above	—	—	—	—	—

KM# 14 1-1/2 THALER

42.8200 g., Silver, 42 mm. **Ruler:** Philipp II **Obv:** Bust to right in circle, legend divided by 5 small shields of arms in margin **Obv. Legend:** V. G. G. - PHI. - LIPS - H. Z. S. - POM. **Rev:** Crowned griffin left holding sword and book, legend divided by 5 small shields of arms in margin, date at end of legend **Rev. Legend:** CHRI - STO. ET - REIP - ANNO - (date) **Mint:** Stettin **Note:** Dav. #7204; H#49. Prev. Pomerania KM#24.

Date	Mintage	VG	F	VF	XF	Unc
1613 Rare	—	—	—	—	—	—

KM# 15 1-1/2 THALER

Silver **Ruler:** Bogislaw XIV **Obv:** Bust to right in circle, legend divided by 5 small shields of arms in margin **Obv. Legend:** V. G. G. - PHI. - LIPS - H. Z. S. - POM. **Rev:** Crowned griffin left holding sword and book, legend divided by 5 small shields of arms in margin, date at end of legend **Rev. Legend:** CHRI - STO. ET - REIP - ANNO - (date) **Mint:** Stettin **Note:** Klippe. Dav. #7204A; H#KL49.

Date	Mintage	VG	F	VF	XF	Unc
1613 Rare	—	—	—	—	—	—

KM# 7 2 THALER

57.2600 g., Silver, 41 mm. **Ruler:** Philipp II **Obv:** Bust to right in ornamented circle **Obv. Legend:** PHILIPPVS. II. D.G. DVX. POMERANORVM. **Rev:** Crowned griffin left holding sword in circle, 10 oval shields of arms around, legend in small letters between tops of shields **Rev. Legend:** CR - IS - TO - ET - RE - IP - VB - LI - C - Æ. **Mint:** Stettin **Note:** Dav. #7214; H#41. Prev. Pomerania KM#44.

Date	Mintage	VG	F	VF	XF	Unc
ND(1606-18) Rare	—	—	—	—	—	—

KM# 8 2 THALER

57.2600 g., Silver, 41 mm. **Ruler:** Philipp II **Obv:** Bust to right in circle **Obv. Legend:** PHILIPPVS. II. DVX. POMERANORVM. **Rev:** Crowned griffin left holding sword in circle, 10 oval shields of arms around, legend in small letters between tops of shields **Rev. Legend:** CR - IS - TO - ET - RE - IP - VB - LI - C - Æ. **Mint:** Stettin **Note:** Dav. #7210; H#42. Prev. Pomerania KM#42.

Date	Mintage	VG	F	VF	XF	Unc
ND(1606-18) Rare	—	—	—	—	—	—

KM# 9 2 THALER

57.2500 g., Silver, 40-41 mm. **Ruler:** Philipp II **Obv:** Bust to right in ornamented circle **Obv. Legend:** PHILIPPVS. II. D.G. DVX. POMERANORVM. **Rev:** Crowned griffin left holding sword and book, 10 small shields of arms on wings, 2-line inscription in ornate tablet below **Rev. Inscription:** CHRISTO. ET. REIP / VBLICÆ. **Mint:** Stettin **Note:** Dav. #7212; H#43. Prev. Pomerania KM#43.

Date	Mintage	VG	F	VF	XF	Unc
ND(1606-18) Rare	—	—	—	—	—	—

KM# 16 2 THALER

Silver **Ruler:** Philipp II **Obv:** Bust to right in circle, legend divided by 5 small shields of arms in margin **Obv. Legend:** V. G. G. - PHI. - LIPS - H. Z. S. - POM. **Rev:** Crowned griffin left holding sword and book, legend divided by 5 small shields of arms in margin, date at end of legend **Rev. Legend:** CHRI - STO. ET - REIP - ANNO - (date) **Mint:** Stettin **Note:** Dav. #7203; H#44, 46. Prev. Pomerania KM#25.

Date	Mintage	VG	F	VF	XF	Unc
1613 Rare	—	—	—	—	—	—
1614 Rare	—	—	—	—	—	—

KM# 20 2 THALER

Silver **Ruler:** Philipp II **Obv:** Bust to right in circle **Obv. Legend:** PHILIPPVS. II. DVX. POMERANORVM. **Rev:** Shield of 9-fold arms supported by 2 helmeted wildmen, ornate helmet above, date at end of legend **Rev. Legend:** CHRISTO. ET. REIPVBLICÆ. **Mint:** Stettin **Note:** Dav. #7207; H#45, 48. Prev. Pomerania KM#28.

Date	Mintage	VG	F	VF	XF	Unc
1614	—	5,600	8,800	12,500	—	—
1616	—	5,600	8,800	12,500	—	—

KM# 26 2 THALER

Silver, 43 mm. **Ruler:** Philipp II **Obv:** Bust to right in circle, legend divided by 5 small shields of arms **Obv. Legend:** V. G. G. - PHI. - LIPS - H. Z. S. - POM. **Rev:** 11-line inscription with date **Rev. Inscription:** (date)/ A. DEO/ OMNIA. OR/ NAMENTA/ REIPVBLICAE. ET/ FVNDAMEN/ TVM. EIVS/ EST. NON/ GAVDE/ REVA/ NIS **Mint:** Stettin **Note:** Dav. #A7209; H#47.

Date	Mintage	VG	F	VF	XF	Unc
1615 Rare	—	—	—	—	—	—

KM# 34 2 THALER

57.3300 g., Silver, 43 mm. **Ruler:** Philipp II **Subject:** Death of Anna vn Schleswig-Holstein, Widow of Bogislaw XIII **Obv:** Bust to right in circle **Obv. Legend:** PHILIPPVS. II. DVX. POMERANORVM. **Rev:** 9-line inscription with Roman numeral dates **Rev. Inscription:** ANNA FILIA/ IOHAN. DVCIS/ HOLS. VIDVA. BOGIS/ LAI. SEN. DVCIS POM./ MATER CARISS. NATA/ MDLXXVII. VII. OCT/ DENATA. MDCXVI/ XXX IAN. SEPVL/ VIII. APRI. **Mint:** Stettin **Note:** Dav. #7217; H#88. Prev. Pomerania KM#45.

Date	Mintage	VG	F	VF	XF	Unc
MDCXVI(1616)	—	3,750	6,300	8,800	12,500	—

KM# 52 2 THALER

57.4200 g., Silver, 43 mm. **Ruler:** Philipp II **Subject:** Death of Georg III **Obv:** Wildman standing to left of table holding ornately-shaped shield of Pomeranian arms, hourglass, flower and skull on table, the front of which is a square tablet with birth and death dates in Roman numerals **Obv. Inscription:** NATVS/ XXX. IAN/ M.DLXXXII/ OBIIT/ XXVII MART/ MDCXVII. **Rev:** 9-line inscription with Roman numeral date **Rev. Inscription:** PHILIPPVS/ II DVX STETTIN/ ET POMERANIÆ. GEORGI III/ FRATR DESIDERAT/ MEMORIÆ/ CVM LACRYM FF/ XXVI MAII/ MDCXVII. **Mint:** Stettin **Note:** Dav. #7220; H#93. Prev. Pomerania KM#52.

Date	Mintage	VG	F	VF	XF	Unc
MDCXVII(1617) Rare	—	—	—	—	—	—

KM# 53 2 THALER

57.7300 g., Silver, 58-59 mm. **Ruler:** Philipp II **Subject:** Centennial of the Reformation **Obv:** Luther kneeling in church pew and holding book **Obv. Legend:** PERIERAT. ET. INVENTVS EST. 1517. **Rev:** Priest placing book on chest inscribed ANNO IVBEL/ 1617. **Rev. Legend:** INVENI QVEM DILIGIT ANIMA MEA **Mint:** Stettin **Note:** Dav. #7228; H#101. Prev. Pomerania KM#55.

Date	Mintage	VG	F	VF	XF	Unc
1617 Rare	—	—	—	—	—	—

KM# 50 2 THALER

58.8000 g., Silver, 41 mm. **Ruler:** Philipp II **Subject:** Centennial of the Reformation **Obv:** Bust to right in ornamented circle **Obv. Legend:** PHILIPPVS. II. D.G. DVX. POMERANORVM. **Rev:** Small sailboat, man at tiller, being blown to right by wind from clouds at upper left. Roman numeral date at end of legend **Rev. Legend:** SAPIENTIA NON VIOLENTIA. ANNO. MDCXVII. **Mint:** Stettin **Note:** Dav. #7225; H#80. Prev. Pomerania KM#54.

Date	Mintage	VG	F	VF	XF	Unc
MDCXVII(1617)	—	3,150	5,600	8,800	12,500	—

KM# 51 2 THALER

58.8000 g., Silver, 42 mm. **Ruler:** Philipp II **Subject:** Centennial of the Reformation **Obv:** Bust to right in circle **Obv. Legend:** PHILIPPVS. II. DVX. POMERANORVM. **Rev:** Small sailboat, man at tiller, being blown to right by wind from clouds at upper left, Roman numeral date at end of legend **Rev. Legend:** SAPIENTIA NON VIOLENTIA. ANNO. MDCXVII. **Mint:** Stettin **Note:** Dav. #7223; H#81. Prev. Pomerania KM#53.

Date	Mintage	VG	F	VF	XF	Unc
MDCXVII(1617)	—	3,150	5,600	8,800	12,500	—

KM# 76 2 THALER

58.2000 g., Silver, 43-44 mm. **Ruler:** Franz **Subject:** Death of Philipp II **Obv:** Armored bust wearing ruffed collar to right in ornamented circle **Obv. Legend:** PHILIPPVS. II. D.G. DVX. POMERANORVM. **Rev:** 10-line inscription with dates **Rev. Inscription:** NVMMVS/ MEMOR. FVNEBRI/ PHILIPPI. II/ DVCIS. STET. POMER/ QVI. NATVS. Z8. IVL. AÕ.1573, DEBAT, 3, FEB, AÕ. 1618/ CONSECRATVS/ A. FRANC. I. SEDINET/ POMER. DVCE. FRAT/ ET. SVCCESS. **Mint:** Stettin **Note:** Dav. #7231; H#107. Prev. Pomerania KM#68.

Date	Mintage	VG	F	VF	XF	Unc
1618	—	3,150	5,600	8,800	12,500	—

KM# 77 2 THALER

Silver, 42-43 mm. **Ruler:** Franz **Subject:** Death of Anna Maria von Brandenburg, Widow of Barnim XII **Obv:** Crowned griffin to left holding sword and ornate shield, 10 small shields of arms on wings, standing on ornate tablet which is blank, no legend **Rev:** 10-line inscription with Roman numeral dates **Rev. Inscription:** MEMORIÆ. FVNEB/ ANNÆ MARIÆ/ IOH. GEORG. EL. BR. FILIÆ/ BARNI. XI. DVC. POM. VIDVÆ/ NATÆ. M.D.LXVII/ DENA. M.DCXIIX/ SEP. 17. XB. STET. Ã. EOD/ FRANCISCVS. I. DVX. STET. POM/ F. F. **Mint:** Stettin **Note:** Dav. #7235. Prev. Pomerania KM#69. Unlisted in Hildisch, existence questionable.

Date	Mintage	VG	F	VF	XF	Unc
MDCXIIX(1618) Rare	—	—	—	—	—	—

KM# 91 2 THALER
Silver, 43 mm. **Ruler:** Bogislaw XIV **Subject:** Death of Franz **Obv:** Armored bust to right in circle **Obv. Legend:** D.G. FRANCISCVS. I. DVX. SEDINI. POMERAN. CASSVB. ET. VAN. **Rev:** 10-line inscription with dates **Rev. Inscription:** NVMMVS/ NOVISSIMO. HONORI/ FRANCISCI. I/ DVCIS. STET. POM. QVI/ NATVS. XXIV. MART. AÕ. 1577/ MORTVVS. XXVII. NOVE/ ANNO. 1620. DICATVS/ A. BOGISLAO. SIV/ FRATRE. ET. SVC/ CESSORE. **Mint:** Stettin **Note:** Dav. #A7239; H#130.

Date	Mintage	VG	F	VF	XF	Unc
1620 GT Rare	—	—	—	—	—	—

KM# 116 2 THALER
55.4800 g., Silver, 43 mm. **Ruler:** Bogislaw XIV **Obv:** Bust to right in circle **Obv. Legend:** BOGISLAVS. XIV. D.G. DVX. STET. POM. CASSVB. ET. VAN. **Rev:** Griffin to right holding sword in ornate shield, ducal cap above divides date **Rev. Legend:** PRINC. RVG. COM. GVTZK. TERR. LEOBVRG. ET. BVTOV. DN. **Mint:** Stettin **Note:** Dav. #7245; H#334. Prev. Pomerania KM#117.

Date	Mintage	VG	F	VF	XF	Unc
16Z8 (z) Rare	—	—	—	—	—	—

KM# 117 2 THALER
55.4800 g., Silver, 42-43 mm. **Ruler:** Bogislaw XIV **Obv:** Bust to right in circle **Obv. Legend:** BOGISLAVS. XIV. D.G. DVX. STET. POM. CASSVB. ET. VAN. **Rev:** Shield of 9-fold arms, ornate helmet above, supported by 2 wildmen wearing helmets, date divided at top **Rev. Legend:** PRINC. RVG. COM GVTZK. TERR. LEOB. E. BVT. DO. **Mint:** Stettin **Note:** Dav. #7247. Prev. Pomerania KM#118.

Date	Mintage	VG	F	VF	XF	Unc
16Z8 Rare	—	—	—	—	—	—

KM# 118 2 THALER
55.4800 g., Silver, 46 mm. **Ruler:** Bogislaw XIV **Obv:** Half-length armored figure to right divides date **Obv. Legend:** BOGISLAVS. XIV. D.G. DVX. STET. POM. CASS. ET. VAN. **Rev:** Ornate shield of 9-fold arms with ornate helmet above, supported by 2 wildmen wearing helmets **Rev. Legend:** PRINCEPS. RVG. COM. GVTZK. TERR. LEOB. ET. BVT. DN. **Mint:** Stettin **Note:** Dav. #7250. Prev. Pomerania KM#119.

Date	Mintage	VG	F	VF	XF	Unc
1628 Rare	—	—	—	—	—	—

KM# 138 2 THALER
57.0000 g., Silver, 43 mm. **Ruler:** Bogislaw XIV **Obv:** Duke on horseback galloping to right, small oval Pomeranian arms below **Obv. Legend:** BOGISLAVS. XIV - DG. - DVX. S. P. **Rev:** Ornate shield of 10-fold arms with ornate helmet above, supported by 2 wildmen wearing helmets, date above left wildman **Rev. Legend:** CASSVB. ET. VAND. PRINC. RVB. EP. CAM. COM. GVTZK. TER. LEOB. ET. BV. DO. **Mint:** Stettin **Note:** H#369.

Date	Mintage	VG	F	VF	XF	Unc
1635 GT	—	—	—	—	—	—

KM# 152 2 THALER
51.0100 g., Silver **Ruler:** Bogislaw XIV **Subject:** Entombment of Bogislaw XIV **Obv:** Armored bust to right in wreath **Obv. Legend:** BOGISLAVS. XIV. D.G. DVX. ST. POM. C. &. VAND. P. RV. EP. C. CO. G. T. L. &. B. D. **Rev:** 15-line inscription with dates **Rev. Inscription:** NOVISSIMIS / HONORIBVS / BOGISLAI. DVC. STET / POMER. EIVS. NOMINIS / 14. ET. VLTIMI / NATI. 31. MART. 1637 / HVMATI. 25. MAI. 1654 / CHRISTINA. D. G. SVECOR / GOTHOR. VANDAL. REGI / ET / FRIDERICVS. WILH. / D. G. MARC. &. EL. B / DVCE. POM / F. F. **Mint:** Stettin **Note:** Dav. #LS372A; H#377. Prev. Pomerania KM#212.

Date	Mintage	VG	F	VF	XF	Unc
1654	50	—	—	5,600	9,400	—

KM# 17 3 THALER
84.5100 g., Silver, 44 mm. **Ruler:** Philipp II **Obv:** Bust to right in circle, legend divided by 5 small shields of arms in margin **Obv. Legend:** V. G. G. - PHI. - LIPS - H. Z. S. - POM. **Rev:** Crowned griffin left holding sword and book, legend divided by 5 small shields of arms in margin, date at end of legend **Rev. Legend:** CHRI - STO. ET - REIP - ANNO - (date) **Mint:** Stettin **Note:** Dav. #A7203; H#38, 40.

Date	Mintage	VG	F	VF	XF	Unc
1613 Rare	—	—	—	—	—	—
1614 Rare	—	—	—	—	—	—

KM# 21 3 THALER
Silver **Ruler:** Philipp II **Obv:** Bust to right in circle **Obv. Legend:** PHILIPPVS. II. DVX. POMERANORVM. **Rev:** Shield of 9-fold arms supported by 2 helmeted wildmen, ornate helmet above, date at end of legend **Rev. Legend:** CHRISTO. ET. REIPVBLICÆ. **Mint:** Stettin **Note:** Dav. #7206; ;H#39. Prev. Pomerania KM#29.

Date	Mintage	VG	F	VF	XF	Unc
1614 Rare	—	—	—	—	—	—

KM# 54 3 THALER
Silver, 42 mm. **Ruler:** Philipp II **Subject:** Centennial of the Reformation **Obv:** Bust to right in circle **Obv. Legend:** PHILIPPVS. II. DVX. POMERANORVM. **Rev:** Small sailboat, man at tiller, being blown to right by wind from clouds at upper left, Roman numeral date at end of legend **Rev. Legend:** SAPIENTIA NON VIOLENTIA. ANNO. MDCXVII. **Mint:** Stettin **Note:** Dav. #7222; H#79. Prev. Pomerania KM#57.

Date	Mintage	VG	F	VF	XF	Unc
MDCXVII(1617) Rare	—	—	—	—	—	—

KM# 55 3 THALER
86.1600 g., Silver, 44 mm. **Ruler:** Philipp II **Subject:** Death of Georg III **Obv:** Wildman standing to left of table holding ornately-shaped shield of Pomeranian arms, hourglass, flower and skull on table, the front of which is a square tablet with birth and death dates in Roman numerals **Obv. Inscription:** NATVS/ XXX. IAN/ M.DLXXXII/ OBIIT/ XXVII MART/ MDCXVII. **Rev:** 9-line inscription with Roman numeral date **Rev. Inscription:** PHILIPPVS/ II DVX STETTIN/ ET POMERANIÆ. GEORGI III/ FRATR DESIDERAT/ MEMORIÆ/ CVM LACRYM FF/ XXVI MAII/ MDCXVII. **Mint:** Stettin **Note:** Dav. #7219; H#92. Prev. Pomerania KM#56.

Date	Mintage	VG	F	VF	XF	Unc
MDCXVII(1617) Rare	—	—	—	—	—	—

KM# 56 3 THALER
Silver, 49 mm. **Ruler:** Philipp II **Subject:** Centennial of the Reformation **Obv:** Luther kneeling in church pew and hlding book **Obv. Legend:** PERIERAT. ET. INVENTVS EST. 1517. **Rev:** Priest placing book on chest inscribed ANNO IVBEL/ 1617. **Rev. Legend:** INVENI QVEM DILIGET ANIMA MEA. **Mint:** Stettin **Note:** Dav. #7227; H#100. Prev. Pomerania KM#58.

Date	Mintage	VG	F	VF	XF	Unc
1617 Rare	—	—	—	—	—	—

KM# 78 3 THALER
86.5500 g., Silver, 43 mm. **Ruler:** Franz **Subject:** Death of Anna Maria von Brandenburg, Widow of Barnim XII **Obv:** Crowned griffin to left holding sword and ornate shield, 10 small shields of arms on wings, standing on ornate tablet which is blank, no legend **Rev:** 10-line inscription with Roman numeral dates **Rev. Inscription:** MEMORIÆ. FVNEB/ ANNÆ MARIÆ/ IOH. GEORG. EL. BR. FILIÆ/ BARNI. XI. DVC. POM. VIDVÆ/ NATÆ. M.D.LXVII/ DENA. M.DCXIIX/ SEP. 17. XB. STET. Ã. EOD/ FRANCISCVS. I. DVX. STET. POM/ F. F. **Mint:** Stettin **Note:** Dav. #7234; H#125. Prev. Pomerania KM#70.

Date	Mintage	VG	F	VF	XF	Unc
MDCXIIX(1618) Rare	—	—	—	—	—	—

KM# 92 3 THALER
88.4700 g., Silver, 43 mm. **Ruler:** Bogislaw XIV **Subject:** Death of Franz **Obv:** Armored bust to right in circle **Obv. Legend:** D.G. FRANCISCVS. I. DVX. SEDINI. POMERAN. CASSVB. ET. VAN. **Rev:** 10-line inscription with dates **Rev. Inscription:** NVMMVS/ NOVISSIMO. HONORI/ FRANCISCI. I/ DVCIS. STET. POM. QVI/ NATVS. XXIV. MART. AÕ. 1577/ MORTVVS. XXVII. NOVE/ ANNO. 1620. DICATVS/ A. BOGISLAO. SIV/ FRATRE. ET. SVC/ CESSORE. **Mint:** Stettin **Note:** Dav. #7238; H#129. Prev. Pomerania KM#87.

Date	Mintage	VG	F	VF	XF	Unc
1620 GT Rare	—	—	—	—	—	—

KM# 153 3 THALER
86.9300 g., Silver, 50 mm. **Ruler:** Bogislaw XIV **Subject:** Entombment of Bogislaw XIV **Obv:** Armored bust to right in wreath **Obv. Legend:** BOGISLAVS. XIV. D.G. DVX. ST. POM. C. &. VAND. P. RVG. EP. CAM. COM. GVTZ. TER. LEOB. &. BVTO. DNS. **Rev:** 17-line inscription with Roman numeral dates **Rev. Inscription:** INFERIÆ / OPTIMI. PRINCIP / BOGISLAI / DVCIS. STETINI. POMERA / EIVS. NOMINIS. XIV. ET. VLTIMI / NATI. XXXI. MART. MDLXXX / DENATI. X. MART. MDCXXXVII / CONDITI. XXV. MAI. MDCLIV / ADORNATÆ / A / CHRISTINA. D.G. SVECORVM. GO / THORVM. VANDALORQ. REGI(N)/ ET / FRIDERICO. WIL **Mint:** Stettin **Note:** Dav. #LS371; H#376. Prev. Pomerania KM#213.

Date	Mintage	VG	F	VF	XF	Unc
MDCLIV(1654) GT	36	—	—	11,500	19,000	—

KM# 22 4 THALER
Silver **Ruler:** Philipp II **Obv:** Bust to right in circle **Obv. Legend:** PHILIPPVS. II. DVX. POMERANORVM. **Rev:** Shield of 9-fold arms supported by 2 helmeted wildmen, ornate helmet above, date at end of legend **Rev. Legend:** CHRISTO. ET. REIPVBLICÆ. **Mint:** Stettin **Note:** Dav. #A7206; H#37.

Date	Mintage	VG	F	VF	XF	Unc
1614 Rare	—	—	—	—	—	—

KM# 35 4 THALER
Silver **Ruler:** Philipp II **Subject:** Death of Anna von Schleswig-Holstein, Widow of Bogislaw XIII **Obv:** Bust to right in circle **Obv. Legend:** PHILIPPVS. II. DVX. POMERANORVM. **Rev:** 9-line inscription with Roman numeral dates **Rev. Inscription:** ANNA FILIA / IOHAN. DVCIS / HOLS. VIDVA. BOGIS / LAI. SEN. DVCIS POM. / MATER CARISS. NATA / MDLXXVII. VII. OCT / DENATA. MDCXVI / XXX IAN. SEPVL / VIII. APRI. **Mint:** Stettin **Note:** Dav. #7216; H#87. Prev. Pomerania KM#46.

Date	Mintage	VG	F	VF	XF	Unc
MDCXVI(1616)	—	7,500	11,500	16,500	22,500	—

KM# 79 4 THALER
114.6500 g., Silver, 43-44 mm. **Ruler:** Franz **Subject:** Death of Philipp II **Obv:** Armored bust wearing ruffed collar to right in ornamented circle **Obv. Legend:** PHILIPPVS. II. D.G. DVX. POMERANORVM. **Rev:** 10-line inscription with dates **Rev. Inscription:** NVMMVS / MEMOR. FVNEBRI / PHILIPPI. II / DVCIS. STET. POMER / QVI. NATVS. Z8. IVL. AÕ.1573, DEBAT, 3, FEB, AÕ. 1618 / CONSECRATVS / A. FRANC. I. SEDINET / POMER. DVCE. FRAT / ET. SVCCESS. **Mint:** Stettin **Note:** Dav. #7230; H#106. Prev. Pomerania KM#71.

Date	Mintage	VG	F	VF	XF	Unc
1618 Rare	—	—	—	—	—	—

KM# 93 4 THALER
115.2800 g., Silver, 43 mm. **Ruler:** Bogislaw XIV **Subject:** Death of Franz **Obv:** Armored bust to right in circle **Obv. Legend:** D.G. FRANCISCVS. I. DVX. SEDINI. POMERAN. CASSVB. ET. VAN. **Rev:** 10-line inscription with dates **Rev. Inscription:** NVMMVS / NOVISSIMO. HONORI / FRANCISCI. I / DVCIS. STET. POM. QVI / NATVS. XXIV. MART. AÕ. 1577 / MORTVVS. XXVII. NOVE / ANNO. 1620. DICATVS / A. BOGISLAO. SIV / FRATRE. ET. SVC / CESSORE. **Mint:** Stettin **Note:** Dav. #7237; H#128. Prev. Pomerania KM#88.

Date	Mintage	VG	F	VF	XF	Unc
1620 GT Rare	—	—	—	—	—	—

KM# 154 4 THALER
114.8800 g., Silver, 68 mm. **Ruler:** Bogislaw XIV **Subject:** Entombment of Bogislaw XIV **Obv:** Bust to right in wreath **Obv. Legend:** BOGISLAVS. XIV. D.G. DVX. STET. POM. CAS. &. VAND. PR. RV(G). EP. CAM. CO(M). GVTZ. TER. LE(OB). &. BV(TO). DNS. **Rev:** 17-line inscription with Roman numeral dates **Rev. Inscription:** INFERIÆ / OPTIMI. PRINCIP(IS) / BOGISLAI / DVCIS. STETINI. POMERA(N) / EIVS. NOMINIS. XIV.(&) (ET). VLTI(M)(I) / NATI. XXXI. MART. MDLXXX / DENATI. X. MART. MDCXXXVII / CONDITI. XXV. MAI. MDCLIV / ADORNATÆ / A / CHRISTINA. D.G. SVECORVM. GO / THORVM. VANDALORQ. REGI(N)(A) / **Mint:** Stettin **Note:** Dav. #LS370; H#374. Prev. Pomerania KM#214. Varieties exist.

Date	Mintage	VG	F	VF	XF	Unc
MDCLIV(1654) GT Rare	36	—	—	—	—	—

KM# 155 4 THALER
115.0000 g., Silver, 50 mm. **Ruler:** Bogislaw XIV **Subject:** Entombment of Bogislaw XIV **Obv:** Bust to right in wreath **Obv. Legend:** BOGISLAVS. XIV. D.G. DVX. ST. POM. C. &. VAND. P. RV. EP. C. CO. G. T. L. &. B. **Rev:** 15-line inscription with dates **Rev. Inscription:** NOVISSIMIS / HONORIBVS / BOGISLAI. DVC. STET / POMER. EIVS. NOMINIS / 14. ET. VLTIMI / NATI. 31. MART. 1580 / DENATI. 10. MART. 1637 / HVMATI. 25. MAI. 1654 / CHRISTINA. D.G. SVECORV / GOTHOR. VANDAL. REGIN / ET / FRIDERICVS. WILHEL / D.G. MARC. &. EL. BRA / DVCES. POMER / F **Mint:** Stettin **Note:** H#375.

Date	Mintage	VG	F	VF	XF	Unc
1654 Rare	Inc. above	—	—	—	—	—

TRADE COINAGE

KM# A13 GOLDGULDEN
3.1800 g., Gold, 22 mm. **Ruler:** Philipp II **Obv:** Bust to right in circle **Obv. Legend:** PHILIPPVS. II. DVX. STET. POM. **Rev:** Shield of 9-fold arms in circle, date at end of legend **Rev. Legend:** CHRISTO. ET. REIPVBLI. (date). **Mint:** Stettin **Note:** FR#2080; H#30, 31. Prev. Pomerania KM#16.

Date	Mintage	VG	F	VF	XF	Unc
161Z	—	400	1,000	2,400	4,000	—
1613	—	400	1,000	2,400	4,000	—

KM# 23 GOLDGULDEN
Gold Weight varies: 3.16-3.21g., 21.5 mm. **Ruler:** Philipp II **Obv:** Bust to right in circle **Obv. Legend:** PHILIPPVS. II. DVX. STET. POM. **Rev:** Sword vertical superimposed on quill pointed to left, all in circle **Rev. Legend:** ALLES. ZU. SEINER. ZEIT. (date). **Mint:** Stettin **Note:** FR#2083; H#73, 74. Prev. Pomerania KM#30.

Date	Mintage	VG	F	VF	XF	Unc
1614	—	1,800	3,000	4,250	5,200	—
1615	—	1,800	3,000	4,250	5,200	—

KM# 28 GOLDGULDEN
3.2000 g., Gold, 22 mm. **Ruler:** Philipp II **Obv:** Bust to right in circle **Obv. Legend:** PHILIPPVS. II. DVX. STETIN. POMER. **Rev:** Stag standing to left towards cascading falls, date at end of legend **Rev. Legend:** IN. TE. SITIT. ANIMA. MEA. (date). **Mint:** Stettin **Note:** FR#2087; H#32, 33. Prev. Pomerania KM#36.

Date	Mintage	VG	F	VF	XF	Unc
1615	—	300	750	1,800	3,000	—
1616	—	300	750	1,800	3,000	—

KM# 27 GOLDGULDEN
3.2000 g., Gold, 21.5 mm. **Ruler:** Philipp II **Obv:** Bust to right in circle **Obv. Legend:** PHILIPPVS. II. DVX. STET. POM. **Rev:** Sword vertical superimposed on quill pointed to right, all in circle **Rev. Legend:** ALLES. ZU. SEINER. ZEIT. (date). **Mint:** Stettin **Note:** H#75.

Date	Mintage	VG	F	VF	XF	Unc
1615	—	750	1,450	2,750	4,500	—

KM# 36 GOLDGULDEN
3.2000 g., Gold, 22 mm. **Ruler:** Philipp II **Obv:** Bust to right in circle **Obv. Legend:** PHILIPPVS. II. DVX. STETI(N). POM(ER). **Rev:** 4-line inscription with date in palm and laurel wreath **Rev. Inscription:** SOLI / DEO GLO / RIA / (date) **Mint:** Stettin **Note:** FR#2091; H#34-6. Prev. Pomerania KM#47. Varieties exist.

Date	Mintage	VG	F	VF	XF	Unc
1616	—	500	1,250	3,000	5,000	—
1617	—	500	1,250	3,000	5,000	—
1618	—	500	1,250	3,000	5,000	—

KM# 57 GOLDGULDEN
3.2000 g., Gold, 22 mm. **Ruler:** Philipp II **Obv:** Bust to right in circle **Obv. Legend:** PHILIPPVS. II. DVX. STETIN. POMER. **Rev:** Snail gliding over twig to left in cirle, date at end of legend **Rev. Legend:** LENTE. SED. ATTENTE. (date). **Mint:** Stettin **Note:** FR#2089; H#76-8. Prev. Pomerania KM#61. Varieties exist.

Date	Mintage	VG	F	VF	XF	Unc
1617	—	700	1,750	4,200	7,000	—
1618	—	700	1,750	4,200	7,000	—

KM# 58 GOLDGULDEN
3.1700 g., Gold, 21 mm. **Ruler:** Philipp II **Subject:** Enlargement of Stettin Palace **Obv:** Bust to right in circle **Obv. Legend:** PHILIPPVS. II. DVX. STETIN. POMER. **Rev:** 5-line inscription with date **Rev. Inscription:** MEMOR / AMPLIFIC / ARCIS / STETINEN / (date). **Mint:** Stettin **Note:** FR#2094; H#86.

Date	Mintage	VG	F	VF	XF	Unc
1617	—	850	1,750	3,500	6,000	—

KM# 59 GOLDGULDEN
3.1700 g., Gold, 22 mm. **Ruler:** Philipp II **Subject:** Centennial of the Reformation **Obv:** The Good Shepherd holding lamb before lion in circle **Obv. Legend:** DE ORE. LEONIS - 1517. **Rev:** 5-line inscription with date **Rev. Inscription:** NVMMVS / SÆCVLARIS / PHILIPPI. II / DVCIS. POM / (date) **Mint:** Stettin **Note:** FR#2093; H#98. Prev. Pomerania KM#60.

Date	Mintage	VG	F	VF	XF	Unc
1617	—	400	1,000	2,400	4,000	—

KM# 60 GOLDGULDEN
3.1700 g., Gold, 22 mm. **Ruler:** Philipp II **Subject:** Centennial of the Reformation **Obv:** Bust to right in circle **Obv. Legend:** PHILIPPVS. II. DVX. STETIN. POMER. **Rev:** 5-line inscription with date **Rev. Inscription:** NVMMVS / SÆCVLARIS / PHILIPPI. II / DVCIS. POM / (date) **Mint:** Stettin **Note:** FR#2092; H#99. Prev. Pomerania KM#59.

Date	Mintage	VG	F	VF	XF	Unc
1617	—	400	1,000	2,400	4,000	—

KM# 80 GOLDGULDEN
3.1800 g., Gold, 22 mm. **Ruler:** Franz **Obv:** Bust to right in circle **Obv. Legend:** FRANCIS. I. D.G. DVX. S. POM. **Rev:** Crowned griffin to left in circle holding sword, date at end of legend **Rev. Legend:** ADSIT. AB. ALTO. (date). **Mint:** Stettin **Note:** FR#2095; H#114. Prev. Pomerania KM#72.

Date	Mintage	VG	F	VF	XF	Unc
1618	—	600	1,500	3,600	6,000	—

KM# 119 GOLDGULDEN
3.1400 g., Gold, 21 mm. **Ruler:** Bogislaw XIV **Obv:** Half-length figure to right in circle **Obv. Legend:** BOGISLAVS. XIV. D.G. DVX. STE(T). P(O). **Rev:** Crowned griffin to left holding sword and book in circle, date at end of legend **Rev. Legend:** HIC. REGIT. ILLE. TVETVR. (date). **Mint:** Stettin **Note:** FR#2099; H#288. Prev. Pomerania KM#133.

Date	Mintage	VG	F	VF	XF	Unc
16Z9	—	500	1,250	3,000	5,000	—

KM# 24 2 GOLDGULDEN
6.9400 g., Gold, 22 mm. **Ruler:** Philipp II **Obv:** Bust to right in circle **Obv. Legend:** PHILIPPVS. II. DVX. STETIN. POMER. **Rev:** King David facing left, playing harp to flock of sheep, date at end of legend **Rev. Legend:** EGO. TVLI. TE. DE. GREGE. (date). **Mint:** Stettin **Note:** FR#2082; H#71. Prev. Pomerania KM#31.

Date	Mintage	VG	F	VF	XF	Unc
1614 Rare	—	—	—	—	—	—

KM# 29 2 GOLDGULDEN
6.3700 g., Gold, 21 mm. **Ruler:** Philipp II **Obv:** Bust to right in circle **Obv. Legend:** PHILIPPVS. II. DVX. STETIN. POMER. **Rev:** Stag standing to left towards cascading fals, date at end of legend **Rev. Legend:** IN. TE. SITIT. ANIMA. MEA. (date). **Mint:** Stettin **Note:** FR#2086; H#27. Prev. Pomerania KM#37.

Date	Mintage	VG	F	VF	XF	Unc
1615 Rare	—	—	—	—	—	—

KM# 30 2 GOLDGULDEN
6.4000 g., Gold, 22 mm. **Ruler:** Philipp II **Obv:** Bust to right in circle **Obv. Legend:** PHILIPPVS. II. DVX. STETI. POM. **Rev:** Candlestick with burning taper in circle, date at end of legend **Rev. Legend:** OFFICIO. MIHI. OFFICIO. (date). **Mint:** Stettin **Note:** FR#2084; H#72.

Date	Mintage	VG	F	VF	XF	Unc
1615 Rare	—	—	—	—	—	—

KM# 37 2 GOLDGULDEN
6.3300 g., Gold, 22 mm. **Ruler:** Philipp II **Obv:** Armored bust to right in circle **Obv. Legend:** PHILIPPVS. II. DVX. STETIN. POMER. **Rev:** 4-line inscription with date in palm and laurel wreath **Rev. Inscription:** SOLI/DEO GLOR/RIA/(date). **Mint:** Stettin **Note:** FR#2090; H#28, 29. Prev. Pomerania KM#48.

Date	Mintage	VG	F	VF	XF	Unc
1616 Rare	—	—	—	—	—	—

Note: Leu Numismatik AG Auction 85, 10-02, VF realized approximately $8,320

Date	Mintage	VG	F	VF	XF	Unc
1617 Rare	—	—	—	—	—	—

KM# 156 1/2 DUCAT
1.7300 g., Gold, 18 mm. **Ruler:** Bogislaw XIV **Subject:** Entombment of Bogislaw XIV **Obv:** 8-line inscription with date **Obv. Inscription:** NVMMVS / EXEQVIALIS / BOGISLAI / DVCIS. STETI / POMERANOR / EIVS. NOMIN / 14.ET.VLT / 1654. **Rev:** Skull in wreath, curved legend above **Rev. Legend:** SPERO VITAM **Mint:** Stettin **Note:** FR#2103; H#373.

Date	Mintage	VG	F	VF	XF	Unc
1654 Rare	50	—	—	—	—	—

KM# 120 DUCAT
3.4300 g., Gold, 23 mm. **Ruler:** Bogislaw XIV **Obv:** Full-length standing figure, head turned to right, divides date **Obv. Legend:** BOGISLAVS. XIV. (-) D.G. - D (-) VX. STETIN. P(OMM). **Rev:** Shield of 9-fold arms in ornamented frame **Rev. Legend:** PRIN. RVG. COM. GVTZ. TERR. LEOB. E. B(V). D. **Mint:** Stettin **Note:** H#292-3. Prev. Pomerania KM#134. Varieties exist.

Date	Mintage	VG	F	VF	XF	Unc
16Z9	—	400	800	1,600	2,800	—
1631	—	400	800	1,600	2,800	—

KM# 125 DUCAT
3.4300 g., Gold, 23 mm. **Ruler:** Bogislaw XIV **Obv:** Full-length standing figure, head turned to right **Obv. Legend:** BOGISL. XIV - D.G. D. ST. PO. **Rev:** Shield of 9-fold arms, 3 ornate helmets above **Rev. Legend:** MO: NO: - AVREA. **Mint:** Stettin **Note:** FR#2101; H#289.

Date	Mintage	VG	F	VF	XF	Unc
ND(ca1630-5)	—	450	900	1,850	3,250	—

KM# 132 DUCAT
3.4400 g., Gold, 24 mm. **Ruler:** Bogislaw XIV **Obv:** Full-length standing figure, head turned to right, divides date **Obv. Legend:** BOGISL. XIV - D.G. D(VX). S(T). P(O). (C. ET. V. P. R.) **Rev:** Shield of 9-fold arms, 3 ornate helmets above **Rev. Legend:** MO: NO: - AVREA. **Mint:** Stettin **Note:** FR#2101; H#295. Prev. Pomerania KM#169.

Date	Mintage	VG	F	VF	XF	Unc
1633	—	450	900	1,850	3,250	—

KM# 133 DUCAT
3.4300 g., Gold, 23 mm. **Ruler:** Bogislaw XIV **Obv:** Full-length standing figure, head turned to right, divides date **Obv. Legend:** BOGISLAVS. XIV. - D. - G. DVX. STE. P. C. E. **Rev:** Oval shield of 9-fold arms **Rev. Legend:** P. R. CO. G. TER. LEOB. ET. BVT. DOM. **Mint:** Stettin **Note:** H#296.

Date	Mintage	VG	F	VF	XF	Unc
1633	—	450	900	1,850	3,250	—

KM# 157 DUCAT
3.4500 g., Gold, 24 mm. **Ruler:** Bogislaw XIV **Obv:** 11-line inscription with dates **Obv. Inscription:** NVMMVS / EXEQVIALIS / OPTIMI.PRINCI / PIS. BOGISLAI / DVCIS. STET. POM / EIVS. NOMINIS. 14 / ET. ELTIMI / NATI. 31. MAR. 1580 / DEN. 10. MAR. 1637 / SEP. 25. MAY / 1654. **Rev:** Skull, curved legend above, all in wreath **Rev. Legend:** SPERO VITAM **Mint:** Stettin **Note:** FR#2102; H#372.

Date	Mintage	VG	F	VF	XF	Unc
1654	25	—	—	—	—	—

KM# 10 6 DUCAT
Gold, 42 mm. **Ruler:** Philipp II **Obv:** Bust to right in ornamented circle **Obv. Legend:** PHILIPPVS. II. D.G. DVX. POMERANORVM. **Rev:** Crowned griffin to left holding sword in circle, 10 oval shields of arms around, legend in small letters between tops of shields **Rev. Legend:** CR - IS - TO - ET - RE - IP - VB - LI - C - Æ. **Mint:** Stettin **Note:** H#26. Struck from Thaler dies, KM#4.

Date	Mintage	VG	F	VF	XF	Unc
ND(1606-18) DS Rare	—	—	—	—	—	—

KM# 81 6 DUCAT
20.4800 g., Gold, 42 mm. **Ruler:** Franz **Obv:** Armored bust to right in circle **Obv. Legend:** D.G. FRANCISCVS. I. DVX. SEDINI. POMERAN. CASSVB. ET. VANDAL. **Rev:** Shield of 9-fold arms, ornate helmet above, supported by 2 wildmen wearing helmets **Rev. Legend:** PRINC. RVGIÆ. COM. GVTZK. TERR. LEOPOL. ET. BVTOV. DNS. **Mint:** Stettin **Note:** H#113.

Date	Mintage	VG	F	VF	XF	Unc
ND(1618-20) DS Rare	—	—	—	—	—	—

KM# 82 10 DUCAT (Portugalöser)
34.7900 g., Gold, 42 mm. **Ruler:** Franz **Obv:** Armored bust to right wearing ruffed collar, in circle **Obv. Legend:** D.G. FRANCISCVS. I. DVX. SEDINI. POMERAN. CASSVB. ET. VANDAL. **Rev:** Shield of 9-fold arms with ornate helmet above, supported by 2 wildmen wearing helmets **Rev. Legend:** PRINC. RVGIÆ. COM. GVTZK. TERR. LEOPOL. ET. BVTOV. DNS. **Mint:** Stettin **Note:** FR#2096; H#112.

Date	Mintage	VG	F	VF	XF	Unc
ND(1618-20) DS Rare	—	—	—	—	—	—

KM# 139 10 DUCAT (Portugalöser)
34.5700 g., Gold, 43 mm. **Ruler:** Bogislaw XIV **Obv:** Duke on horseback galloping to right, small oval Pomeranian arms below **Obv. Legend:** BOGISLAVS. XIV - DG. - DVX. S. P. **Rev:** Ornate shield of 10-fold arms with ornate helmet above, supported by 2 wildmen wearing helmets, date above left wildman **Rev. Legend:** CASSVB. ET. VAND. PRINC. RVB. EP. CAM. COM. GVTZK. TER. LEOB. ET. BV. DO. **Mint:** Stettin **Note:** H#368.

Date	Mintage	VG	F	VF	XF	Unc
1635 GT Rare	—	—	—	—	—	—

KM# 158 10 DUCAT (Portugalöser)
34.5000 g., Gold, 43 mm. **Ruler:** Bogislaw XIV **Subject:** Entombment of Bogislaw XIV **Obv:** Duke on horseback galloping to right, small oval Pomeranian arms below **Obv. Legend:** BOGISLAVS. XIV - DG. - DVX. S. P. **Rev:** Skull in wreath, triple marginal legends with dates **Rev. Legend:** IN MEMORIAM ULTIMI EX GRYPHICA STIRPE DUCIS POMER//BOGISLAI. XIV. NATI. XXXI. MART. 1580. DENATI. X//MART. 1637. HVMATI. 25. MAI. 1654. **Mint:** Stettin **Note:** H#371.

Date	Mintage	VG	F	VF	XF	Unc
1654 GT Rare	10	—	—	—	—	—

PATTERNS

Including off metal strikes

KM#	Date	Mintage	Identification	Mkt Val
Pn1	1615	—	Thaler. Bronze. 43 mm. KM# 25. Prev. Pomerania KM#35.	—

POMERANIA-WOLGAST

RULERS
Philip III Julius, 1592-1625

DUCHY

REGULAR COINAGE

KM# 1 PFENNIG
1.0000 g., Copper, 18 mm. **Ruler:** Philipp III Julius **Obv:** 4-line inscription with date **Obv. Inscription:** PHIL/ IVLIVS/ H.Z.S.P./ (date) **Rev:** Crowned griffin to left **Note:** H#229.

Date	Mintage	Good	VG	F	VF	XF
1609	—	65.00	125	185	275	750

KM# 28 3 PFENNIG (Pommersch)

1.2900 g., Copper, 18 mm. **Ruler:** Philipp III Julius **Obv:** Griffin to left in circle **Obv. Legend:** PHILIPPVS. IVL. H.Z.S.P. **Rev:** 5-line inscription with date **Rev. Inscription:** III/ PFEN/ NING/ POM/ (date). **Note:** H#228.

Date	Mintage	Good	VG	F	VF	XF
16ZZ	—	15.00	25.00	45.00	80.00	—

KM# 18 WITTEN (4 Pfennig)

0.5500 g., Silver, 14-15 mm. **Ruler:** Philipp III Julius **Obv:** Griffin to left in circle **Obv. Legend:** PHILIPPVS. IVLIVS. **Rev:** Short cross in circle, date divided in angles **Rev. Legend:** D.G. SVX. STET. POM. **Note:** H#220.

Date	Mintage	Good	VG	F	VF	XF
1619	—	30.00	65.00	125	200	—

KM# 29 6 PFENNIG (Pommersch)

2.0400 g., Copper, 22 mm. **Ruler:** Philipp III Julius **Obv:** Griffin to left in circle **Obv. Legend:** PHILIPPVS. IVL. H.Z.S.P. **Rev:** 5-line inscription with date **Rev. Inscription:** VI/ PFEN/ NING/ POM(E)/ (date). **Note:** H#227.

Date	Mintage	Good	VG	F	VF	XF
16ZZ	—	18.00	30.00	50.00	85.00	150

KM# 13.1 6 PFENNIG (1/64 Thaler)

1.4900 g., Silver, 20 mm. **Ruler:** Philipp III Julius **Obv:** Griffin to left in circle **Obv. Legend:** PHILIPPVS. IULIUS. **Rev:** Imperial orb with 64 in circle, date at end of legend **Rev. Legend:** HERT. Z. STE. POM. **Note:** H#215, 216.

Date	Mintage	Good	VG	F	VF	XF
(1)610	—	12.00	25.00	45.00	90.00	—
1615	—	12.00	25.00	45.00	90.00	—

KM# 13.2 6 PFENNIG (1/64 Thaler)

0.6400 g., Silver, 18 mm. **Ruler:** Philipp III Julius **Obv:** Griffin to left in circle **Obv. Legend:** PHILIPPVS. IVLIVS. **Rev:** Imperial orb with 64 divides date **Rev. Legend:** D.G. DVX. STE(T). P(O)(M). **Note:** H#217-19. Kipper coinage. Varieties exist.

Date	Mintage	Good	VG	F	VF	XF
1619	—	12.00	25.00	45.00	90.00	—
16Z0	—	12.00	25.00	45.00	90.00	—
16Z1	—	12.00	25.00	45.00	90.00	—

MB# 11 SCHILLING (12 Pfennig)

1.0500 g., Silver, 19 mm. **Ruler:** Ernst Ludwig **Obv:** Shield of Wolgast arms, small imperial orb above **Obv. Legend:** ERNEST. LVDO. D.G. DVX. S. PO. **Rev:** Crowned griffin to left in circle, date at end of legend **Rev. Legend:** SPES. MEA. CHRISTV(S). **Note:** H#154-55. Varieties exist.

Date	Mintage	Good	VG	F	VF	XF
1590	—	—	—	—	—	—
159Z	—	—	—	—	—	—
1592	—	—	—	—	—	—

KM# 25 SCHILLING (Pommersch)

0.6500 g., Silver, 16-17 mm. **Ruler:** Philipp III Julius **Obv:** Griffin to left in circle **Obv. Legend:** PHILIPPVS. IVL. H.Z.S.P. **Rev:** 5-line inscription with date **Rev. Inscription:** I/ SCHIL/ LING/ POM(E)/ (date). **Mint:** Franzburg **Note:** H#222-6. Varieties exist.

Date	Mintage	Good	VG	F	VF	XF
16Z1 (d)	—	12.00	20.00	40.00	75.00	—
16ZZ (d)	—	12.00	20.00	40.00	75.00	—
16Z3 (d)	—	12.00	20.00	40.00	75.00	—
16Z4 (d)	—	12.00	20.00	40.00	75.00	—
16Z5 (d)	—	12.00	20.00	40.00	75.00	—

KM# 19 SCHILLING (12 Pfennig Lübisch)

0.9700 g., Silver, 19 mm. **Ruler:** Philipp III Julius **Obv:** Griffin to left in circle **Obv. Legend:** PHILIPPVS. IVLIVS. D.G. **Rev:** Shield of Rügen arms, 1Z P.L. above, date at end of legend **Rev. Legend:** DVX. STET. POM. **Note:** H#213-14.

Date	Mintage	Good	VG	F	VF	XF
16Z0	—	12.00	20.00	40.00	75.00	—
16Z1	—	12.00	20.00	40.00	75.00	—

KM# 5 2 SCHILLING (Doppelschilling)

Silver Weight varies: 1.39-2.53g., 22-26 mm. **Ruler:** Philipp III Julius **Obv:** Shield of 4-fold arms divides date to left, top and right **Obv. Legend:** PHILIPPUS. IU(L)(I)(U)(S). H. Z. S. (P.) **Rev:** Intertwined DS in ornamented shield **Rev. Legend:** RECTE. FACI. NE. METUAS. **Mint:** Franzburg **Note:** H#199-212. Varieties exist, V's instead of U's on some examples.

Date	Mintage	Good	VG	F	VF	XF
1609	—	18.00	30.00	50.00	85.00	135
1610	—	18.00	30.00	50.00	85.00	135
1611	—	18.00	30.00	50.00	85.00	135
161Z	—	18.00	30.00	50.00	85.00	135
1613	—	18.00	30.00	50.00	85.00	135
1614	—	18.00	30.00	50.00	85.00	135
1615	—	18.00	30.00	50.00	85.00	135
1616	—	18.00	30.00	50.00	85.00	135
1617	—	18.00	30.00	50.00	85.00	135
1618	—	18.00	30.00	50.00	85.00	135
1619	—	18.00	30.00	50.00	85.00	135
16Z0	—	18.00	30.00	50.00	85.00	135
16Z1	—	18.00	30.00	50.00	85.00	135

KM# 2 2 SCHILLING (Doppelschilling)

2.5300 g., Silver, 26 mm. **Ruler:** Philipp III Julius **Obv:** Shield of 9-fold arms in circle **Obv. Legend:** P. I. H. Z. S. P. NEMINEM. METUA. **Rev:** Intertwined DS in ornamented shield **Rev. Legend:** RECTE. FACI. NEM. TIMEAS. **Note:** H#193.

Date	Mintage	Good	VG	F	VF	XF
ND(1609-13)	—	—	—	—	—	—

KM# 3 2 SCHILLING (Doppelschilling)

2.5300 g., Silver, 26 mm. **Ruler:** Philipp III Julius **Obv:** Shield of 9-fold arms in circle **Obv. Legend:** P. I/ H. Z. S. P. - NEMINEM. METUAS. **Rev:** Intertwined DS in ornamented shield, date at end of legend **Rev. Legend:** RE (-) CTE. (-) FACIE (-) NDO. **Note:** H#195-6. Varieties exist.

Date	Mintage	Good	VG	F	VF	XF
1609	—	—	—	—	—	—

KM# 4.1 2 SCHILLING (Doppelschilling)

2.5300 g., Silver, 26 mm. **Ruler:** Philipp III Julius **Obv:** Shield of 9-fold arms in circle **Obv. Legend:** P. I. H. Z. S. P. - NEMINEM. MET(U)(V)S. **Rev:** Intertwined DS in ornamented shield which divides date to left, top and right **Rev. Legend:** RECTE. FACIE. NE(MI). MET(U)(V)A(S). **Note:** H#197. Varieties exist.

Date	Mintage	Good	VG	F	VF	XF
1609	—	18.00	30.00	65.00	100	165

KM# 4.2 2 SCHILLING (Doppelschilling)

2.5300 g., Silver, 26 mm. **Ruler:** Philipp III Julius **Obv:** Shield of 9-fold arms in circle **Obv. Legend:** PHILIPPUS. IULIUS. H. Z. S. P. (A.) **Rev:** Intertwined DS in ornamented shield which divides date to left, top and right **Rev. Legend:** RECTE. FAC(I)(E). NE. METUA(S). **Mint:** Franzburg **Note:** H#198.

Date	Mintage	Good	VG	F	VF	XF
1609 CR	—	20.00	35.00	70.00	110	185

KM# 16 2 SCHILLING (Doppelschilling)

2.2300 g., Silver, 23 mm. **Ruler:** Philipp III Julius **Obv:** Shield of 4-fold arms in circle **Obv. Legend:** PHILIPPUS. IUL. H. Z. S. P. **Rev:** Intertwined DS in ornamented shield **R ev. Legend:** RECTE. FA. NE. METVAS. **Note:** H#194.

Date	Mintage	Good	VG	F	VF	XF
ND(1614-17)	—	—	—	—	—	—

KM# 30 2 SCHILLING (Pommersch)

1.0600 g., Silver, 20 mm. **Ruler:** Philipp III Julius **Obv:** Griffin to left in circle **Obv. Legend:** PHILIPPVS. IVL. H. Z. S. P. **Rev:** 5-line inscription with date **Rev. Inscription:** II/ SCHILL/ ING. POM/ MERSCH/ (date). **Mint:** Franzburg **Note:** H#221. Varieties exist.

Date	Mintage	Good	VG	F	VF	XF
16ZZ (d)	—	80.00	150	215	275	385

KM# 17 4 SCHILLING

3.6400 g., Silver, 30 mm. **Ruler:** Philipp III Julius **Obv:** Crowned shield of 4-fold arms divides date in circle **Obv. Legend:** PHILIPPVS. IULIUS. V. G. G. HZ. STET. P. **Rev:** Crowned imperial eagle **Rev. Legend:** MATTHIAS. I. D. G. R. I S. AUGUSTU. **Note:** H#187.

Date	Mintage	Good	VG	F	VF	XF
1616	—	—	—	—	—	—

KM# 7 1/24 THALER (Reichsgroschen)

1.6500 g., Silver, 20-21 mm. **Ruler:** Philipp III Julius **Obv:** Shield of 4-fold arms in circle **Obv. Legend:** PHILIP(US). IULI(US). H. Z. S. P(O). **Rev:** Imperial orb with Z4, first half of date divided at top, second half by orb **Rev. Legend:** SI. DEUS. P. N. Q. C(O). NO(S). **Mint:** Franzburg **Note:** H#181-6. Varieties exist.

Date	Mintage	Good	VG	F	VF	XF
1609 CR	—	12.00	25.00	40.00	60.00	90.00
1610	—	12.00	25.00	40.00	60.00	90.00
1611	—	12.00	25.00	40.00	60.00	90.00
161Z	—	12.00	25.00	40.00	60.00	90.00
1613	—	12.00	25.00	40.00	60.00	90.00
1616	—	12.00	25.00	40.00	60.00	90.00

KM# 6 1/24 THALER (Reichsgroschen)

1.6500 g., Silver, 23 mm. **Ruler:** Philipp III Julius **Obv:** Shield of 4-fold arms in circle **Obv. Legend:** PHILIP. IULIUS. D. S(T). P(O). **Rev:** Imperial orb with Z4 divides date **Rev. Legend:** SI. DEUS. P. N. Q. C(O). NOS. **Mint:** Franzburg **Note:** H#180.

Date	Mintage	Good	VG	F	VF	XF
(1)609 CR	—	—	—	—	—	—
1609	—	—	—	—	—	—

KM# 31 1/16 THALER (Düttchen)

3.0900 g., Silver, 27-28 mm. **Ruler:** Philipp III Julius **Obv:** Griffin to left in shield superimposed on long cross **Obv. Legend:** PHILI - PPVS. - IVLIVS. - H.Z.S.P. **Rev:** 7-line inscription with date **Rev. Inscription:** NACH/ ALTEN. SC/ HROT. VND/ KORN. XVI. ST/ VCKE. EINEN/ REICHS. TA/ LER. (date) **Mint:** Franzburg **Note:** H#188.

Date	Mintage	Good	VG	F	VF	XF
16ZZ (d)	—	—	—	—	—	—

KM# 37 1/16 THALER (Düttchen)

3.0900 g., Silver, 27-28 mm. **Ruler:** Philipp III Julius **Obv:** Griffin to left in shield superimposed on long cross **Obv. Legend:** PHILI - PPVS. - IVLIVS. - H.Z.S.P. **Rev:** 4-line inscription with date **Rev. Legend:** REICHS. SCHROT. V(ND) KORN. **Rev. Inscription:** 16. ST/ REICHS/ TALER/ (date). **Mint:** Franzburg **Note:** H#189-90.

Date	Mintage	Good	VG	F	VF	XF
16Z3 (d)	—	30.00	55.00	100	165	285
16Z4 (d)	—	120	225	325	475	650

KM# 38 1/16 THALER (Düttchen)

3.0900 g., Silver, 27-28 mm. **Ruler:** Philipp III Julius **Obv:** Griffin to left in shield, head breaks shield at top, superimposed on long cross **Obv. Legend:** PHILIP - PVS. IV - LIVS. H. - Z.S.P. **Rev:** 4-line inscription with date **Rev. Legend:** REICHS. SCHROT. VND KORN. **Rev. Inscription:** 16. ST/ REICHS/ TALER/ (date). **Mint:** Franzburg **Note:** H#191-2. Varieties exist, U's substituted for V's.

Date	Mintage	Good	VG	F	VF	XF
16Z4 (d)	—	18.00	30.00	55.00	85.00	130
16Z5 (d)	—	18.00	30.00	55.00	85.00	130

MB# 9 1/8 THALER (1/2 Reichsort)

3.4600 g., Silver, 25 mm. **Ruler:** Ernst Ludwig **Obv:** Facing bust turned slightly to right breaks circle at top **Obv. Legend:** ERENEST. LVDOV. D.G. DVX. STETI. POME. **Rev:** Ornamented shield of 9-fold arms, date divided at bottom by mintmaster's symbol **Rev. Legend:** AVXILIVM. MEVM. A. DOMINO. **Mint:** Stettin **Note:** H#153.

Date	Mintage	Good	VG	F	VF	XF
1585 (f)	—	—	—	—	—	—

KM# 32 1/8 THALER (1/2 Reichsort)

3.3100 g., Silver, 24-25 mm. **Ruler:** Philipp III Julius **Obv:** Crowned griffin to left in circle **Obv. Legend:** V. G. G. PHILIPPVS. IVL. H. A. Z. P. **Rev:** 4-line inscription with date **Rev. Legend:** FATA. F. FERAM. P. PATI. PALMAM. **Rev. Inscription:** HALB/ REICHS/ ORTH/ (date). **Note:** H#179.

Date	Mintage	Good	VG	F	VF	XF
16ZZ	—	—	—	—	—	—

KM# 39 1/8 THALER (1/2 Reichsort)

3.6400 g., Silver, 28 mm. **Ruler:** Philipp III Julius **Subject:** Death of Philipp III Julius **Obv:** Bust to right divides date **Obv. Legend:** PHILIPP. IVL. D.G. DVX. STE. POM. **Rev:** Sun shining on flowering plant **Rev. Legend:** ADHVC. MEA. MESSIS. IN. HERBA. **Mint:** Franzburg **Note:** H#234.

Date	Mintage	Good	VG	F	VF	XF
(1)6Z5 (d)	—	—	—	—	—	—

KM# 33 1/4 THALER (Reichsort)

7.0700 g., Silver, 31 mm. **Ruler:** Philipp III Julius **Obv:** Crowned griffin to left in double circle **Obv. Legend:** V. G. G. PHILIPPVS. IVLIVS. H. Z. S. P. **Rev:** 4-line inscription with date **Rev. Legend:** FATA. FER. FE. PART. PATIE. PALMAM. **Rev. Inscription:** REI/CHES.ORTH/ (date). **Mint:** Franzburg **Note:** H#178.

Date	Mintage	Good	VG	F	VF	XF
16ZZ (d)	—	—	—	—	—	—

KM# 40 1/4 THALER (Reichsort)

7.0300 g., Silver, 34 mm. **Ruler:** Philipp III Julius **Subject:** Death of Philipp III Julius **Obv:** Bust to right in circle **Obv. Legend:** PHILIPPVS. IVLIVS. D.G. DVX. S. P. C. E. V. **Rev:** Sun shining on flowering plant, date at end of legend **Rev. Legend:** ADHVC. MEA. MESSIS. IN. HERBA. **Mint:** Franzburg **Note:** H#233.

Date	Mintage	Good	VG	F	VF	XF
16Z5 (d)	—	—	—	—	—	—

KM# 34 1/2 THALER

14.1600 g., Silver, 35 mm. **Ruler:** Philipp III Julius **Obv:** Bust with double high ruffed collar to right in circle **Obv. Legend:** PHILIPPVS. IVLIVS. D.G. DVX. STE. POME. **Rev:** Shield of 9-fold arms, ornate helmet above, supported by 2 wildmen wearing helmets, date divided by crest of helmet at upper left **Rev. Legend:** FATA. F. FE. PARI. P. PALM. **Mint:** Franzburg **Note:** H#176.

Date	Mintage	Good	VG	F	VF	XF
16ZZ (d)	—	—	—	—	—	—
(16)ZZ (d)	—	—	—	—	—	—

KM# 35 1/2 THALER

14.1600 g., Silver, 36 mm. **Ruler:** Philipp III Julius **Obv:** Large armored bust to right breaks circle at top **Obv. Legend:** V. G. G. PHILIPPVS. IVLIVS. H. Z. S. PO. **Rev:** Shield of 9-fold arms, ornate helmet above, supported by 2 wildmen wearing helmets, date divided by crests of middle and right helmets **Rev. Legend:** FATA. F. FE. PARI. P. PALM. **Mint:** Franzburg **Note:** H#177.

Date	Mintage	Good	VG	F	VF	XF
16ZZ HP	—	—	—	—	—	—

KM# 41 1/2 THALER

14.4200 g., Silver, 38-39 mm. **Ruler:** Philipp III Julius **Subject:** Death of Philipp III Julius **Obv:** Armored bust to right in circle **Obv. Legend:** PHILIPPVS. IVLIVS. D.G. DVX. STE. POM. CAS. E. VAN. **Rev:** 10-line inscription with dates **Rev. Inscription:** NVMVS. EX/TREMÆ. MEMOR/PHILIPP. IVLII. DV/S.P. NATI. AN. 1584/Z7. DEC. DENATI. 17Z5.6. FEB. A. PATRUELE/ET. SVCCESSORE/BOGISLAO. 14. DV/STE. POM. CON/SECRATVS. **Mint:** Franzburg **Note:** H#232.

Date	Mintage	Good	VG	F	VF	XF
16Z5 (d)	—	—	—	—	—	—

KM# 8 THALER

28.4100 g., Silver, 41 mm. **Ruler:** Philipp III Julius **Obv:** High-collared bust to right in circle **Obv. Legend:** PHILIPPUS. IULIUS. D.G. DUX. STETIN. POMER. **Rev:** Shield of 9-fold arms, ornate helmet above, supported by 2 wildmen wearing helmets **Rev. Legend:** FATA. FEREN. FE. PARI. PATIEN. PALMAM. **Note:** Dav. #7201; H#168. Prev. Pomerania KM#95.

Date	Mintage	VG	F	VF	XF	Unc
ND(1609-10) Rare	—	—	—	—	—	—

KM# 9 THALER

28.4100 g., Silver, 40 mm. **Ruler:** Philipp III Julius **Obv:** Bust to right in circle divides date **Obv. Legend:** PHILIPPUS. IULIUS. D.G. D. STETIN. POM **Rev:** Shield of 9-fold arms, ornate helmet above, supported by 2 wildmen wearing helmets **Rev. Legend:**

FATA. FEREN. FE. PARI. PATIEN. PALMAM. **Mint:** Franzburg **Note:** Dav. #7192; H#169. Prev. Pomerania KM#11.1.

Date	Mintage	VG	F	VF	XF	Unc
(1)609 CR	—	500	1,050	1,900	3,200	—

KM# 10 THALER

28.4100 g., Silver, 40 mm. **Ruler:** Philipp III Julius **Obv:** Bust to right in circle divides date **Obv. Legend:** PHILIPPUS. IULIUS. D.G. D. STETIN. POM. **Rev:** Shield of 9-fold arms, ornate helmet above, supported by 2 wildmen wearing helmets **Rev. Legend:** FATA. FEREN. FE. PARI. PATIEN. PALMAm. **Mint:** Franzburg **Note:** Dav. #7192A. Prev. Pomerania KM#11.2. Second 'M' in PALMAM is small.

Date	Mintage	VG	F	VF	XF	Unc
(1)609 CR	—	500	1,050	1,900	3,200	—

KM# 14 THALER

Silver, 41-42 mm. **Ruler:** Philipp III Julius **Obv:** Armored bust to right in circle divides date **Obv. Legend:** PHILIPPUS. IULIUS. D.G. D. STETIN. POME. **Rev:** Shield of 9-fold arms, ornate helmet above, supported by 2 wildmen wearing helmets **Rev. Legend:** FATA. FEREN. FE. PARI. PATIEN. PALMAM. **Note:** Dav. #7194; H#170-1. Prev. Pomerania 21.

Date	Mintage	VG	F	VF	XF	Unc
1610	—	500	1,050	1,900	3,200	—
1611	—	500	1,050	1,900	3,200	—
ND(1610-11)	—	500	1,050	1,900	3,200	—

KM# 20 THALER

28.4000 g., Silver, 41-42 mm. **Ruler:** Philipp III Julius **Obv:** Bust to right in circle divides date **Obv. Legend:** PHILIPPUS. IULIUS. D.G. D. STET. POMER. **Rev:** Shield of 9-fold arms, ornate helmet above, supported by 2 wildmen wearing helmets **Rev. Legend:** FATA. FEREN. FE. PARI. PATIEN. PALMAM. **Note:** Dav. #7197; H#172. Prev. Pomerania KM#83.

Date	Mintage	VG	F	VF	XF	Unc
16Z0	—	300	575	1,150	2,250	—
1620	—	300	575	1,150	2,250	—

KM# 21 THALER

28.4000 g., Silver, 43 mm. **Ruler:** Philipp III Julius **Obv:** Armored bust to right in circle **Obv. Legend:** PHILIPPUS. IULIUS. D.G. DUX. STETIN. POMER. **Rev:** Shield of 9-fold arms, ornate helmet above, supported by 2 wildmen wearing helmets, date divided in margin at top **Rev. Legend:** FATA. FEREN. FE. PARI. PATIENT. PALMAM. **Note:** Dav. #7198; H#172-3. Prev. Pomerania KM#84.

Date	Mintage	VG	F	VF	XF	Unc
16Z0 Rare	—	—	—	—	—	—

KM# 26 THALER

28.4000 g., Silver, 40 mm. **Ruler:** Philipp III Julius **Obv:** Bust to right in circle wearing double ruffed collar **Obv. Legend:** PHILIPPUS. IULIUS. D.G. DUX. STETIN. POMER. **Rev:** Shield of 9-fold arms, ornate helmet above, supported by 2 wildmen wearing helmets, date divided in margin at top **Rev. Legend:** FATA. FEREN. FE. PARI. PATIEN. PALMAM. **Note:** Dav. #7200; H#174. Prev. Pomerania KM#89.

Date	Mintage	VG	F	VF	XF	Unc
16Z1	—	300	650	1,300	2,500	—
ND(1621)	—	300	650	1,300	2,500	—

KM# 36 THALER

28.4000 g., Silver, 41 mm. **Ruler:** Philipp III Julius **Obv:** Bust to right in circle divides date **Obv. Legend:** PHILIPPVS. IVLIVS. D.G. DVX. STETTIN. POMER. **Rev:** Shield of 9-fold arms, ornate helmet above, supported by 2 wildmen wearing helmets **Rev. Legend:** FATA. FEREN. FE. PARI. PATIENT. PALMAM. **Mint:** Franzburg **Note:** Dav. #7201; H#175. Prev. Pomerania KM#95.

Date	Mintage	VG	F	VF	XF	Unc
16ZZ (d) Rare	—	—	—	—	—	—

KM# 42 THALER

28.6500 g., Silver, 49 mm. **Ruler:** Philipp III Julius **Subject:** Death of Philipp III Julius **Obv:** Draped bust to right in circle **Obv. Legend:** PHILIPPVS. IVLIUS. D.G. DVX. STET. POM. CASSV. ET. VAN. **Rev:** 10-line inscription with dates **Rev. Inscription:** NVMVS. EX/ TREMÆ. MEMOR/ PHILIPPI. IVLII. DV/ S. POM. NATI. A. 1584/ Z7. DEC. DENATI. A. 16Z5/ 6. FEB. A. PATRUELE/ ET. SVCCESSORE/ BOGISLAO. 14. DVC/ STE. POM. CON/ SECRATVS. **Mint:** Franzburg **Note:** jDav. #7207; H#231. Prev. Pomerania KM#101.

Date	Mintage	VG	F	VF	XF	Unc
16Z5 (d)	—	900	1,700	3,000	5,000	—

KM# 22 1-1/2 THALER

40.6600 g., Silver, 41 mm. **Ruler:** Philipp III Julius **Obv:** Bust to right in circle divides date **Obv. Legend:** PHILIPPUS. IULIUS. D.G. D. STET. POMER. **Rev:** Shield of 9-fold arms, ornate helmet above, supported by 2 wildmen wearing helmets **Rev. Legend:** FATA. FEREN. FE. PARI. PATIEN. PALMAM. **Note:** Dav. #7196; H#167. Prev. Pomerania KM#85.

Date	Mintage	VG	F	VF	XF	Unc
16Z0	—	3,000	5,000	7,000	11,000	—

KM# 11 2 THALER

Silver, 40 mm. **Ruler:** Philipp III Julius **Obv:** Bust to right in circle divides date **Obv. Legend:** PHILIPPUS. IULIUS. D.G. D. STETIN. POM. **Rev:** Shield of 9-fold arms, ornate helmet above, supported by 2 wildmen wearing helmets **Rev. Legend:** FATA. FEREN. FE. PARI. PATIEN. PALMAM. **Mint:** Franzburg **Note:** Dav. #A7192.

Date	Mintage	VG	F	VF	XF	Unc
(1)609 CR Rare	—	—	—	—	—	—

KM# 15 2 THALER

57.5800 g., Silver, 42 mm. **Ruler:** Philipp III Julius **Obv:** Bust to rght in circle divides date **Obv. Legend:** PHILIPPUS. IULIUS. D.G. D. STETIN. POME. **Rev:** Shield of 9-fold arms, ornate helmet above, supported by 2 wildmen wearing helmets **Rev. Legend:** FATA. FEREN. FE. PARI. PATIEN. PALMAM. **Note:** Dav. #7193; H#164. Prev. Pomerania KM#22.

Date	Mintage	VG	F	VF	XF	Unc
1610 Rare	—	—	—	—	—	—

KM# 23 2 THALER

57.6000 g., Silver, 43-44 mm. **Ruler:** Philipp III Julius **Obv:** Bust to right in circle divides date **Obv. Legend:** PHILIPPUS. IULIUS. D.G. D. STET. POMER. **Rev:** Shield of 9-fold arms, ornate helmet above, supported by 2 wildmen wearing helmets **Rev. Legend:** FATA. FEREN. FE. PARI. PATIEN(T). PALMAM. **Note:** Dav. #7195; H#165. Prev. Pomerania KM#86.

Date	Mintage	VG	F	VF	XF	Unc
16Z0 Rare	—	—	—	—	—	—
1620 Rare	—	—	—	—	—	—

KM# 24 2 THALER

Silver, 42x44 mm. **Ruler:** Philipp III Julius **Obv:** Bust to right in circle divides date **Obv. Legend:** PHILIPPUS. IULIUS. D.G. D. STET. POMER. **Rev:** Shield of 9-fold arms, ornate helmet above, supported by 2 wildmen wearing helmets **Rev. Legend:** FATA. FEREN. FE. PARI. PATIENT. PALMAM. **Note:** Klippe. Dav. #7195A; H#KL165.

Date	Mintage	VG	F	VF	XF	Unc
16Z0 Rare	—	—	—	—	—	—

KM# 27 2 THALER

57.6000 g., Silver, 40-41 mm. **Ruler:** Philipp III Julius **Obv:** Bust wearing high ruffed collar to right in circle **Obv. Legend:** PHILIPPUS. IULIUS. D.G. DUX. STETIN. POMER. **Rev:** Shield of 9-fold arms, ornate helmet above, supported by 2 wildmen wearing helmets, date divided in margin at top **Rev. Legend:** FATA. FEREN. FE. PARI. PATIEN. PALMAM. **Note:** Dav. #7199; H#166. Prev. Pomerania KM#90.

Date	Mintage	VG	F	VF	XF	Unc
16Z1 Rare	—	—	—	—	—	—

KM# 43 2 THALER
56.8000 g., Silver, 52 mm. **Ruler:** Philipp III Julius **Obv:** Draped bust to right in circle **Obv. Legend:** PHILIPPVS. IVLIVS. D.G. DVX. STET. POM. CASSV. ET. VAN. **Rev:** 10-line inscription with dates **Rev. Inscription:** NVMVS. EX / TREMÆ. MEMOR / PHILIPPI. IVLII. DV / S. POM. NATI. A. 1584 / Z7. DEC. DENATI. A. 16Z5 / 6. FEB. A. PATRUELE / ET. SVCCESSORE / BOGISLAO. 14. DVC / STE. POM. CON / SECRATVS. **Mint:** Franzburg **Note:** Dav. #A7202 and LS368; H#230. Prev. Pomerania KM#102.

Date	Mintage	VG	F	VF	XF	Unc
16Z5 (d)	—	2,000	4,000	6,500	10,000	—

TRADE COINAGE

KM# 12 GOLDGULDEN
3.0600 g., Gold, 23 mm. **Ruler:** Philipp III Julius **Obv:** Bust to right in circle divides date **Obv. Legend:** PHILIPPUS. IULIUS. D.G. D.S. P(O). **Rev:** Shield of 9-fold arms in circle **Rev. Legend:** DESPERAND(U)(V)M. DEO. D(U)(VCE). NIL. **Mint:** Franzburg **Note:** FR#2079; H#162-3. Prev. Pomerania KM#12. Varieties exist.

Date	Mintage	VG	F	VF	XF	Unc
(1)609	—	350	850	2,050	3,400	—
(1)609 CR	—	350	850	2,050	3,400	—
(1)611 CR	—	350	850	2,050	3,400	—

SWEDISH OCCUPATION

RULERS
Christina of Sweden, 1637-1654
Karl X of Sweden, 1654-1660
Karl XI of Sweden, 1660-1697
Karl XII of Sweden, 1697-1718

REGULAR COINAGE

KM# 207 WITTEN (1/192 Thaler)
Silver **Obv:** Crowned griffin left in inner circle **Obv. Legend:** KRISTINA... **Rev:** Value and date in inner circle

Date	Mintage	VG	F	VF	XF	Unc
1650	—	33.00	65.00	135	275	—
1651	—	33.00	65.00	135	275	—
1654	—	33.00	65.00	135	275	—

KM# 216 WITTEN (1/192 Thaler)
Silver **Obv:** Griffin holding sword **Obv. Legend:** CAROLUS. GUSTAVUS...

Date	Mintage	VG	F	VF	XF	Unc
1655	—	40.00	80.00	160	320	—
1656	—	40.00	80.00	160	320	—
1657	—	65.00	135	275	525	—

KM# 238 WITTEN (1/192 Thaler)
Silver **Obv:** Crowned griffin **Obv. Legend:** CAROLUS XI... **Rev:** Value: WITT, date in inner circle

Date	Mintage	VG	F	VF	XF	Unc
1666	—	33.00	65.00	135	275	—

KM# 240 WITTEN (1/192 Thaler)
Silver **Rev:** Value: WIT

Date	Mintage	VG	F	VF	XF	Unc
1668 Rare	—	—	—	—	—	—
1670 Rare	—	—	—	—	—	—

KM# 296 WITTEN (1/192 Thaler)
Silver **Rev:** Value: WITTEN

Date	Mintage	VG	F	VF	XF	Unc
1684 Rare	—	—	—	—	—	—

KM# 297 WITTEN (1/192 Thaler)
Silver **Obv:** BA below griffin **Rev:** Value in three lines

Date	Mintage	VG	F	VF	XF	Unc
1684 BA	—	40.00	80.00	160	320	—

KM# 298 WITTEN (1/192 Thaler)
Silver **Rev:** WITTEN

Date	Mintage	VG	F	VF	XF	Unc
1684 BA Rare	—	—	—	—	—	—
1685 BA	—	33.00	65.00	160	320	—
1686 BA Rare	—	—	—	—	—	—

KM# 306 WITTEN (1/192 Thaler)
Silver **Obv:** Initials below griffin

Date	Mintage	VG	F	VF	XF	Unc
1686 DHM	—	33.00	65.00	160	320	—

KM# 315 WITTEN (1/192 Thaler)
Silver **Rev:** Value/initials/date

Date	Mintage	VG	F	VF	XF	Unc
1687 DHM	—	33.00	65.00	160	320	—

KM# 321 WITTEN (1/192 Thaler)
Silver **Rev:** Value/date/initials

Date	Mintage	VG	F	VF	XF	Unc
1688 DHM	—	33.00	65.00	160	320	—

KM# 336 WITTEN (1/192 Thaler)
Silver **Rev:** Value/date/initials

Date	Mintage	VG	F	VF	XF	Unc
1690 ILA	—	33.00	65.00	140	275	—

KM# 258 1/192 THALER (Witten)
Silver **Obv:** Crowned griffin left **Rev:** Value in orb, date in legend

Date	Mintage	VG	F	VF	XF	Unc
1673	—	45.00	100	200	400	—
1674	—	45.00	100	200	400	—

KM# 259 1/96 THALER (Sechsling)
Silver

Date	Mintage	VG	F	VF	XF	Unc
1673	—	45.00	100	200	400	—
1674 Rare	—	—	—	—	—	—

KM# 299 1/96 THALER (Sechsling)
Silver **Obv:** Initials below griffin **Rev:** Value, date below

Date	Mintage	VG	F	VF	XF	Unc
1684 BA	—	33.00	65.00	135	275	—
1685 BA Rare	—	—	—	—	—	—
1685 DHM Rare	—	—	—	—	—	—
1687 DHM	—	33.00	65.00	135	275	—

KM# 316 1/96 THALER (Sechsling)
Silver **Rev:** Value, date, initials

Date	Mintage	VG	F	VF	XF	Unc
1687 DHM	—	33.00	65.00	135	275	—
1688 DHM	—	33.00	65.00	135	275	—

KM# 324 1/96 THALER (Sechsling)
Silver **Obv:** Crowned C, date divided by crown **Rev:** Orb dividing initials

Date	Mintage	VG	F	VF	XF	Unc
1689 ILA	—	33.00	65.00	135	275	—
1690 ILA	—	33.00	65.00	135	275	—
1691 ILA	—	33.00	65.00	135	275	—
1692 ILA Rare	—	—	—	—	—	—

KM# 251.1 1/48 THALER (Schilling)
Silver **Obv:** Crowned griffin, initials below in inner circle **Rev:** Value in inner circle, date in legend

Date	Mintage	VG	F	VF	XF	Unc
1661 VB Rare	—	—	—	—	—	—
1670 HIH Rare	—	—	—	—	—	—
1671 HIH Rare	—	—	—	—	—	—
1672 DS	—	13.00	27.00	55.00	110	—
1672 DS	—	13.00	27.00	55.00	110	—
1673 DS	—	13.00	27.00	55.00	110	—
1674 DS Rare	—	—	—	—	—	—
1675 DS Rare	—	—	—	—	—	—
1676 DS Rare	—	—	—	—	—	—
1680 CS Rare	—	—	—	—	—	—
1681 CS	—	20.00	40.00	80.00	160	—
1681 BA	—	20.00	40.00	80.00	160	—
1682 BA Rare	—	—	—	—	—	—
1683 BA Rare	—	—	—	—	—	—
1684 BA	—	13.00	27.00	55.00	110	—
1685 BA Rare	—	—	—	—	—	—
1685 BA Rare	—	—	—	—	—	—
1686 DHM Rare	—	—	—	—	—	—
1689 DHM	—	27.00	55.00	110	220	—
1690 ILA	—	20.00	33.00	65.00	135	—
1691 ILA	—	20.00	33.00	65.00	135	—
1692 ILA	—	20.00	33.00	65.00	135	—
1693 ILA	—	27.00	55.00	110	220	—
1694 ILA Rare	—	—	—	—	—	—

KM# 251.2 1/48 THALER (Schilling)
Silver **Rev:** Initials in legend

Date	Mintage	VG	F	VF	XF	Unc
1681 CS	—	13.00	27.00	55.00	110	—

KM# 251.3 1/48 THALER (Schilling)
Silver **Obv:** Initials in legend

Date	Mintage	VG	F	VF	XF	Unc
1687 DHM Rare	—	—	—	—	—	—

KM# 317 1/48 THALER (Schilling)
Silver **Rev:** Value and initials in inner circle

Date	Mintage	VG	F	VF	XF	Unc
1687 DHM	—	20.00	33.00	65.00	135	—
1688 DHM Rare	—	—	—	—	—	—

KM# 224 DOPPEL-SCHILLING (1/16 Thaler)
Silver **Obv:** Griffin holding sword in inner circle **Obv. Legend:** CAROL GVST... **Rev:** DS in inner circle, date in legend

Date	Mintage	VG	F	VF	XF	Unc
1656	—	20.00	40.00	70.00	140	—
1657	—	20.00	40.00	70.00	140	—
1658	—	20.00	40.00	70.00	140	—
1659	—	20.00	40.00	70.00	140	—
1660	—	20.00	40.00	70.00	140	—

KM# 241 DOPPEL-SCHILLING (1/16 Thaler)
Silver **Obv. Legend:** CAROL XI...

Date	Mintage	VG	F	VF	XF	Unc
1662	—	20.00	40.00	70.00	140	—
1666	—	40.00	80.00	160	320	—
1666 HIH (b)	—	27.00	55.00	110	220	—
1667 (b)	—	20.00	40.00	70.00	140	—
1668	—	20.00	40.00	70.00	140	—
1668 (b)	—	20.00	40.00	70.00	140	—
1669	—	20.00	40.00	70.00	140	—
1669 (b)	—	20.00	40.00	70.00	140	—
1670	—	20.00	40.00	70.00	140	—

KM# 273 DOPPEL-SCHILLING (1/16 Thaler)
Silver **Rev:** Legend begins at bottom

Date	Mintage	VG	F	VF	XF	Unc
1670	—	27.00	55.00	110	220	—

KM# 232 1/24 THALER (Groschen)
Silver **Obv:** Shield in inner circle **Rev:** Orb divides date and initials in inner circle

Date	Mintage	VG	F	VF	XF	Unc
1661 VB	—	135	275	400	675	—
1662 VB	—	165	325	675	1,000	—

KM# 247.1 1/24 THALER (Groschen)
Silver **Obv:** Griffin with sword left **Rev:** Value and initials in inner circle, date in legend

Date	Mintage	VG	F	VF	XF	Unc
1670 HIH	—	27.00	55.00	90.00	200	—
1671 HIH	—	20.00	40.00	80.00	160	—
1687 DHM	—	17.00	33.00	65.00	135	—
1688 DHM	—	20.00	40.00	80.00	160	—

KM# 247.2 1/24 THALER (Groschen)
Silver **Rev:** Without initials

Date	Mintage	VG	F	VF	XF	Unc
1671	—	27.00	55.00	110	220	—

KM# 249.1 1/24 THALER (Groschen)
Silver **Rev:** Initials in legend at top

Date	Mintage	VG	F	VF	XF	Unc
1671 HIH	—	10.00	20.00	40.00	80.00	—
1675 DS	—	20.00	40.00	80.00	160	—
1676 DS	—	27.00	55.00	110	220	—
1680 CS Rare	—	—	—	—	—	—
1681 CS	—	10.00	20.00	40.00	80.00	—

KM# 249.2 1/24 THALER (Groschen)
Silver **Rev:** Initials divide date in legend

Date	Mintage	VG	F	VF	XF	Unc
1671 HIH	—	13.00	27.00	55.00	110	—

KM# 252 1/24 THALER (Groschen)
Silver **Rev:** Initials below griffin in inner circle

Date	Mintage	VG	F	VF	XF	Unc
1672 DS	—	10.00	20.00	40.00	80.00	—
1681 CS	—	13.00	27.00	55.00	110	—
1681 BA	—	13.00	27.00	55.00	110	—
1682 BA	—	27.00	55.00	110	220	—
1683 BA Rare	—	—	—	—	—	—
1684 BA	—	27.00	55.00	110	220	—

KM# 253 1/24 THALER (Groschen)
Silver **Obv. Legend:** CAROLUS...DS...

Date	Mintage	VG	F	VF	XF	Unc
1672 DS	—	13.00	27.00	55.00	110	—

KM# 254 1/24 THALER (Groschen)
Silver **Obv. Legend:** CAROLUS XI...DS...

Date	Mintage	VG	F	VF	XF	Unc
1672 DS	—	13.00	27.00	55.00	110	—

KM# 282 1/24 THALER (Groschen)
Silver **Obv:** Initials below griffin **Rev:** Mintmaster's initials in legend

Date	Mintage	VG	F	VF	XF	Unc
1681 CS	—	27.00	55.00	110	220	—
1687 DHM Rare	—	—	—	—	—	—

KM# 281 1/24 THALER (Groschen)
Silver, 22 mm. **Ruler:** Karl XI of Sweden **Obv:** Rampant griffin to left in circle **Obv. Legend:** CAROLUS XI. D.G. REX. SUECIÆ. **Rev:** 4-line inscription, date at end of legend **Rev. Legend:** IN IEHOUA SORS MEA. **Rev. Inscription:** 24 / EINEN / REICHS / DALER **Mint:** Stettin **Note:** Mule: obverse of KM#254 and reverse of KM#282.

Date	Mintage	VG	F	VF	XF	Unc
1681 DS//CS	—	20.00	40.00	80.00	160	—

KM# 302.1 1/24 THALER (Groschen)
Silver **Obv:** Right leg of griffin divides initials

Date	Mintage	VG	F	VF	XF	Unc
1685 BA	—	20.00	40.00	80.00	160	—

KM# 302.2 1/24 THALER (Groschen)
Silver **Obv:** Initials between hind legs of griffin

Date	Mintage	VG	F	VF	XF	Unc
1685 DHM	—	27.00	55.00	110	220	—
1687 DHM	—	13.00	27.00	55.00	110	—
1688 DHM	—	13.00	27.00	55.00	110	—

KM# 302.3 1/24 THALER (Groschen)
Silver **Obv:** Initials below hind legs of griffin

Date	Mintage	VG	F	VF	XF	Unc
1686 DHM	—	13.00	27.00	55.00	110	—

KM# 312 1/24 THALER (Groschen)
Silver **Obv:** Initials in oval below griffin

Date	Mintage	VG	F	VF	XF	Unc
1686 DHM	—	13.00	27.00	55.00	110	—

KM# 325 1/24 THALER (Groschen)
Silver **Obv:** Crowned shield **Rev:** Value and initials in inner circle, date in legend

Date	Mintage	VG	F	VF	XF	Unc
1689 ILA	—	40.00	80.00	160	320	—
1690 ILA	—	27.00	55.00	110	220	—
1692 ILA Rare	—	—	—	—	—	—

KM# 283.1 1/12 THALER (2 Groschen)
Silver **Obv:** Crowned griffin in inner circle **Rev:** Value and initials in inner circle, date in legend

Date	Mintage	VG	F	VF	XF	Unc
1681 CS	—	20.00	40.00	80.00	160	—
1681 3 stars Rare	—	—	—	—	—	—
1681 BA	—	33.00	65.00	135	275	—
1682 BA	—	40.00	80.00	160	320	—
1688 DHM	—	33.00	65.00	135	275	—

KM# 283.2 1/12 THALER (2 Groschen)
Silver **Obv:** Crowned griffin in small circle **Rev:** Value, date, and initials in inner circle, date in legend

Date	Mintage	VG	F	VF	XF	Unc
1688 DHM Rare	—	—	—	—	—	—

KM# 323 1/12 THALER (2 Groschen)
Silver **Obv:** Crowned straight-sided shield **Rev:** Value and initials in inner circle, date in legend

Date	Mintage	VG	F	VF	XF	Unc
1689 ILA	—	20.00	40.00	80.00	160	—
1690 ILA	—	16.00	33.00	65.00	135	—
1691 ILA	—	16.00	33.00	65.00	135	—
1692 ILA	—	27.00	55.00	110	220	—
1693 ILA	—	16.00	33.00	65.00	135	—

KM# 337 1/12 THALER (2 Groschen)
Silver **Obv:** Griffin left in coat of arms

Date	Mintage	VG	F	VF	XF	Unc
1690 ILA	—	33.00	65.00	135	275	—
1691 ILA	—	27.00	55.00	110	220	—

KM# 343 1/12 THALER (2 Groschen)
Silver **Obv:** Crowned, curved shield divides initials

Date	Mintage	VG	F	VF	XF	Unc
1693 ILA	—	24.00	45.00	90.00	190	—
1664 ILA Error for 1694	—	135	200	400	800	—
1694 ILA	—	40.00	80.00	160	320	—
1695 ILA	—	40.00	80.00	160	320	—
1695 ICA	—	33.00	65.00	135	275	—
1696 ICA	—	45.00	100	200	400	—
1697 ICA	—	45.00	100	200	400	—

KM# 345 1/12 THALER (2 Groschen)
Silver

Date	Mintage	VG	F	VF	XF	Unc
1694 ILA	—	40.00	80.00	160	320	—

KM# 208 1/8 THALER (1/2 Reichsort)
Silver **Obv:** Christina right in inner circle **Rev:** Value, date below in inner circle

Date	Mintage	VG	F	VF	XF	Unc
1653 Rare	—	—	—	—	—	—

KM# 210 1/8 THALER (1/2 Reichsort)
Silver **Rev:** Value in inner circle, date in legend **Note:** Varieties of reverse exist.

Date	Mintage	VG	F	VF	XF	Unc
1654 Rare	—	—	—	—	—	—

KM# 326.1 1/6 THALER (4 Groschen)
Silver **Obv:** Bust right with chest armor **Rev:** Crowned, supported arms, value below divides date

Date	Mintage	VG	F	VF	XF	Unc
1689 ILA	—	65.00	135	275	525	—

KM# 327 1/6 THALER (4 Groschen)
Silver **Obv:** Bust right with chest armor **Rev:** Value in four lines in inner circle

Date	Mintage	VG	F	VF	XF	Unc
1689 ILA-KMK Unique	—	—	—	—	—	—

KM# 326.2 1/6 THALER (4 Groschen)
Silver **Obv:** Bust right with chest armor and shoulder armor **Rev:** Crowned, supported arms, value below divides date

Date	Mintage	VG	F	VF	XF	Unc
1693 ILA	—	135	275	525	1,075	—

KM# 233 1/4 THALER (Reichsort)
Silver **Obv:** Laureate bust right **Rev:** Shield divides initials in inner circle, date in legend

Date	Mintage	VG	F	VF	XF	Unc
1661 VB Rare	—	—	—	—	—	—

KM# 234 1/4 THALER (Reichsort)
Silver **Obv:** Bust right

Date	Mintage	VG	F	VF	XF	Unc
1661 VB Rare	—	—	—	—	—	—

KM# 221 REICHSORT (1/4 Thaler)
Silver **Obv:** Charles X right in inner circle **Rev:** Arms, date in legend

Date	Mintage	VG	F	VF	XF	Unc
1658 VB Rare	—	—	—	—	—	—

KM# 261 1/3 THALER (1/2 Gulden)
Silver **Obv:** Draped laureate bust with hair locks on chest and back **Rev:** Crowned, supported shield, value and initials below, date in legend

Date	Mintage	VG	F	VF	XF	Unc
1672 DS Rare	—	—	—	—	—	—
1673 DS	—	40.00	80.00	160	320	—

KM# 255 1/3 THALER (1/2 Gulden)
Silver **Obv:** Draped laureate bust with short wig and shoulder flaps

Date	Mintage	VG	F	VF	XF	Unc
1672 DS Rare	—	—	—	—	—	—
1673 DS	—	65.00	135	275	525	—

KM# 256 1/3 THALER (1/2 Gulden)
Silver **Obv:** Long wig

Date	Mintage	VG	F	VF	XF	Unc
1672 DS Rare	—	—	—	—	—	—
1673 DS	—	55.00	110	220	425	—

KM# 260 1/3 THALER (1/2 Gulden)
Silver **Obv:** Long wig, initials below bust

Date	Mintage	VG	F	VF	XF	Unc
1673 DS	—	33.00	65.00	135	275	—
1674 DS	—	33.00	65.00	135	275	—

KM# 262 1/3 THALER (1/2 Gulden)
Silver **Obv:** Draped bust with hair locks on back, initials below

Date	Mintage	VG	F	VF	XF	Unc
1674 DS	—	33.00	65.00	135	275	650
1681 CS Rare	—	—	—	—	—	—

KM# 263 1/3 THALER (1/2 Gulden)
Silver **Obv:** Laureate draped bust with hair locks and shoulder armor, initials below

Date	Mintage	VG	F	VF	XF	Unc
1674 DS	—	33.00	65.00	135	275	—
1675 DS	—	33.00	65.00	135	275	—

KM# 268 1/3 THALER (1/2 Gulden)
Silver **Obv:** Laureate draped bust with chest and shoulder armor

Date	Mintage	VG	F	VF	XF	Unc
1674 DS	—	65.00	135	275	525	—

KM# 284 1/3 THALER (1/2 Gulden)
Silver **Obv:** Draped bust **Rev:** Crowned, supported shield divides initials

Date	Mintage	VG	F	VF	XF	Unc
1681 CS Rare	—	—	—	—	—	—

KM# 285 1/3 THALER (1/2 Gulden)
Silver **Obv:** Draped bust with ornamented chest and shoulder armor, initials below

Date	Mintage	VG	F	VF	XF	Unc
1681 CA Rare	—	—	—	—	—	—
1682 BA Rare	—	—	—	—	—	—
1684 BA Rare	—	—	—	—	—	—
1685 DHM Rare	—	—	—	—	—	—
1686 DHM Rare	—	—	—	—	—	—

KM# 294 1/3 THALER (1/2 Gulden)
Silver **Obv:** Draped bust with ornamented chest armor

Date	Mintage	VG	F	VF	XF	Unc
1683 BA Rare	—	—	—	—	—	—

KM# 304 1/3 THALER (1/2 Gulden)
Silver **Obv:** Draped bust with plain chest armor

Date	Mintage	VG	F	VF	XF	Unc
1685 DHM Rare	—	—	—	—	—	—

KM# 328 1/3 THALER (1/2 Gulden)
Silver **Obv:** Draped bust with riveted chest armor, divided legend

Date	Mintage	VG	F	VF	XF	Unc
1689 ILA Rare	—	—	—	—	—	—
1689 ILA - crossed flags Rare	—	—	—	—	—	—
1690 ILA	—	80.00	160	320	650	—
1690 ILA - crossed flags	—	80.00	160	320	650	—

KM# 347 1/3 THALER (1/2 Gulden)
Silver **Obv:** Draped bust with ornamented chest and shoulder armor, divided legend **Rev:** Indented, crowned arms

Date	Mintage	VG	F	VF	XF	Unc
1696 ICA Rare	—	—	—	—	—	—

KM# 187 1/2 THALER
Silver **Obv:** Half-length portrait of Christina **Rev:** Christ holding orb above shield dividing date

Date	Mintage	VG	F	VF	XF	Unc
1640 Rare	—	—	—	—	—	—

KM# 189 1/2 THALER
Silver **Obv:** Half-length portrait in ornamental circle

Date	Mintage	VG	F	VF	XF	Unc
1641 Rare	—	—	—	—	—	—

KM# 192 1/2 THALER
Silver **Obv:** Bust left

Date	Mintage	VG	F	VF	XF	Unc
1642 Rare	—	—	—	—	—	—
1646 Rare	—	—	—	—	—	—

KM# 231 1/2 THALER
Silver **Obv:** Laureate bust right **Rev:** Shield divides initials in inner circle, date in legend

Date	Mintage	VG	F	VF	XF	Unc
1661 Unique	—	—	—	—	—	—

KM# 264 2/3 THALER (Gulden)
Silver **Obv:** Draped laureate bust with shoulder flaps right, initials below **Rev:** Crowned, supported arms, value below, date in legend

Date	Mintage	VG	F	VF	XF	Unc
1673 DS	—	100	200	400	800	—

KM# 286 2/3 THALER (Gulden)
Silver **Obv:** Draped laureate bust with shoulder armor

Date	Mintage	VG	F	VF	XF	Unc
1681 CS	—	80.00	160	320	650	—

KM# 287 2/3 THALER (Gulden)
Silver **Obv:** Draped bust

Date	Mintage	VG	F	VF	XF	Unc
1681 CS	—	80.00	160	320	650	—

KM# 288 2/3 THALER (Gulden)
Silver **Rev:** Arms divide initials

Date	Mintage	VG	F	VF	XF	Unc
1681 CS-CS	—	100	200	400	800	—

KM# 289 2/3 THALER (Gulden)
Silver

Date	Mintage	VG	F	VF	XF	Unc
1681 Rare	—	—	—	—	—	—
1681 CS	—	80.00	160	320	650	—
1684/3 BA	—	85.00	165	330	675	—
1684 BA	—	80.00	160	320	650	—

KM# 290 2/3 THALER (Gulden)
Silver

Date	Mintage	VG	F	VF	XF	Unc
1681 BA	—	65.00	135	275	525	—

KM# 291 2/3 THALER (Gulden)
Silver **Obv:** Riveted armor

Date	Mintage	VG	F	VF	XF	Unc
1681 BA	—	60.00	120	240	480	—
1683 BA	—	65.00	135	275	525	—
1685 BA	—	110	220	425	850	—
1686 DHM	—	100	200	400	800	—
1688 DHM	—	120	240	450	975	—

KM# 292 2/3 THALER (Gulden)
Silver **Obv:** Ornamented bust armor

Date	Mintage	VG	F	VF	XF	Unc
1681 BA	—	65.00	135	275	525	—
1682 BA Rare	—	—	—	—	—	—
1683 BA	—	65.00	135	275	525	—
1685 BA	—	110	220	425	850	—

KM# 295 2/3 THALER (Gulden)
Silver

Date	Mintage	VG	F	VF	XF	Unc
1683 BA	—	80.00	160	320	650	—
1684/3 BA	—	65.00	135	275	525	—
1684 BA	—	65.00	135	275	525	—
1685 DHM Rare	—	—	—	—	—	—

KM# 307.1 2/3 THALER (Gulden)
Silver

Date	Mintage	VG	F	VF	XF	Unc
1686 DHM	—	100	200	400	800	—
1687 DHM	—	80.00	160	320	650	900
1688 DHM Rare	—	—	—	—	—	—
1689	—	100	200	400	800	—
1689 ILA	—	55.00	110	220	440	750
1689 ILA/(c)	—	65.00	135	275	525	800
1690 ILA	—	65.00	135	275	525	800
1660 ILA Rare; error for 1690	—	—	—	—	—	—
1690 ILA/(c)	—	55.00	110	220	440	750
1691 ILA	—	70.00	150	300	600	850
1692 ILA	—	65.00	135	275	525	800

KM# 308.1 2/3 THALER (Gulden)
Silver **Obv:** Draped bust with chest armor and shoulder rosette, full legend

Date	Mintage	VG	F	VF	XF	Unc
1686 DHM	—	100	200	400	800	—

KM# 308.2 2/3 THALER (Gulden)
Silver **Obv:** Divided legend

Date	Mintage	VG	F	VF	XF	Unc
1686 DHM	—	100	200	400	800	—

KM# 319 2/3 THALER (Gulden)
Silver **Obv:** Draped bust with plain chest armor, divided legend

Date	Mintage	VG	F	VF	XF	Unc
1687 DHM	—	80.00	160	320	640	—
1688 DHM	—	100	200	400	800	—

KM# 307.2 2/3 THALER (Gulden)
Silver **Obv:** Without G++V

Date	Mintage	VG	F	VF	XF	Unc
1690 ILA/(c)	—	65.00	135	275	525	—

KM# 341 2/3 THALER (Gulden)
Silver

Date	Mintage	VG	F	VF	XF	Unc
1692 ILA	—	65.00	135	275	525	—
1693 ILA	—	70.00	150	300	600	—
1694 ILA Rare	—	—	—	—	—	—
1695 ILA	—	70.00	150	300	600	—
1695 ICA	—	70.00	150	300	600	—
1695 ICA/(C)	—	70.00	150	300	600	—
1696 ICA beside truncation	—	—	—	—	—	—
1696 ICA below truncation	—	—	—	—	—	—
1697 ICA on truncation	—	65.00	135	275	525	—
1697 ICA beside truncation	—	60.00	120	240	480	—

KM# 188.1 THALER
Silver **Obv:** Half-length portrait in ornamented circle, large crown at left **Rev:** Christ above supported arms **Note:** Dav. #4571.

Date	Mintage	VG	F	VF	XF	Unc
1640	—	500	1,000	1,900	3,150	—
1641	—	500	1,000	1,900	3,150	—

KM# 188.2 THALER

Silver **Obv:** Small crown at left **Note:** Dav. #4571A.

Date	Mintage	VG	F	VF	XF	Unc
1641	—	500	1,000	1,900	3,150	—

KM# 193.2 THALER

Silver **Obv:** Bust with curly hair **Note:** Dav. #4573.

Date	Mintage	VG	F	VF	XF	Unc
164Z	—	375	750	1,400	2,400	—
1644	—	1,450	2,750	4,500	—	—
1647	—	500	1,000	1,900	3,150	—
1654 Rare	—	—	—	—	—	—

KM# 190 THALER

Silver **Obv:** Bust left in ornamented circle **Rev:** Helmeted, supported arms **Note:** Dav. #4575.

Date	Mintage	VG	F	VF	XF	Unc
1642 Rare	—	—	—	—	—	—

KM# 193.1 THALER

Silver **Obv:** Bust with wavy hair in plain circle **Note:** Dav. #A4573.

Date	Mintage	VG	F	VF	XF	Unc
1642	—	450	900	1,650	2,850	—

KM# 217.1 THALER

Silver **Obv:** Karl X **Rev:** Helmeted, supported arms **Note:** Varieties of portraits exist. Dav. #4577.

Date	Mintage	VG	F	VF	XF	Unc
1655	—	500	975	1,800	3,000	—

KM# 217.2 THALER

Silver **Obv:** Larger bust **Note:** Portrait varieties exist. Dav. #4577A.

Date	Mintage	VG	F	VF	XF	Unc
1657 VB	—	525	1,050	2,000	3,300	—

KM# 265.1 THALER

Silver **Obv:** Laureate bust with hair locks on shoulder and back **Rev:** Crowned, supported straight sided arms, DS below **Note:** Dav. #4578.

Date	Mintage	VG	F	VF	XF	Unc
1673 DS Rare	—	—	—	—	—	—

KM# 265.2 THALER

Silver **Obv:** DS below bust **Note:** Dav. #4578A.

Date	Mintage	VG	F	VF	XF	Unc
1673 DS Rare	—	—	—	—	—	—

KM# 266 THALER

Silver **Obv:** Hair locks on back **Note:** Dav. #4579.

Date	Mintage	VG	F	VF	XF	Unc
1674 DS	—	2,500	4,150	6,800	11,500	—

KM# 271 THALER

Silver **Obv:** Hair locks on bust and back **Rev:** Round shield **Note:** Dav. #4580.

Date	Mintage	VG	F	VF	XF	Unc
1675 DS	—	1,650	2,750	4,500	7,500	—

KM# 310 THALER

Silver **Obv:** Bust with rosette **Rev:** Shield with indented sides **Note:** Dav. #4581.

Date	Mintage	VG	F	VF	XF	Unc
1686 DHM Rare	—	—	—	—	—	—
1687 DHM Rare	—	—	—	—	—	—

KM# 329 THALER

Silver **Obv:** Bust with chest armor **Rev:** Plumes above crowned round arms divide date **Note:** Dav. #4582.

Date	Mintage	VG	F	VF	XF	Unc
1689 ILA-(c) Rare	—	—	—	—	—	—
1690 Rare	—	—	—	—	—	—

KM# 196.2 2 THALER

Silver **Obv:** Bust in plain circle **Note:** Dav. #4572.

Date	Mintage	VG	F	VF	XF	Unc
1642 Rare	—	—	—	—	—	—
1647 Rare	—	—	—	—	—	—

KM# 196.1 2 THALER

Silver **Obv:** Bust of Christina left in ornamented circle **Rev:** Helmeted, supported arms, date in legend **Note:** Dav. #4574.

Date	Mintage	VG	F	VF	XF	Unc
1642 Rare	—	—	—	—	—	—

KM# 218 2 THALER

57.3000 g., Silver **Obv:** Bust of Karl X right in inner circle **Rev:** Plume of helmet on crowned arms divide date **Note:** Dav. #4576.

Date	Mintage	VG	F	VF	XF	Unc
1655 Rare	—	—	—	—	—	—
1657 VB Rare	—	—	—	—	—	—

TRADE COINAGE

KM# 191 DUCAT

3.5000 g., 0.9860 Gold 0.1109 oz. AGW **Obv:** Facing half-figure of Christina in ornate inner circle **Rev:** Christ holding orb above shield of arms in inner circle

Date	Mintage	VG	F	VF	XF	Unc
1641	—	300	675	1,500	2,700	—

KM# 198 DUCAT

3.5000 g., 0.9860 Gold 0.1109 oz. AGW **Obv:** Without ornamentation on inner circle **Rev:** Shield of arms, date in legend

Date	Mintage	VG	F	VF	XF	Unc
1642	—	350	750	1,800	3,000	—

KM# 199.1 DUCAT

3.5000 g., 0.9860 Gold 0.1109 oz. AGW **Obv:** Christina

Date	Mintage	VG	F	VF	XF	Unc
1642	—	250	575	1,250	2,250	—
1653	—	250	575	1,250	2,250	—

KM# 199.2 DUCAT

3.5000 g., 0.9860 Gold 0.1109 oz. AGW **Rev:** Arms in inner circle

Date	Mintage	VG	F	VF	XF	Unc
1646	—	250	575	1,250	2,250	—
1653	—	250	575	1,250	2,250	—
1654	—	250	575	1,250	2,250	—

KM# 215.1 DUCAT

3.5000 g., 0.9860 Gold 0.1109 oz. AGW **Obv:** Karl X standing holding scepter and orb **Rev:** Shield of arms, date in legend

Date	Mintage	VG	F	VF	XF	Unc
1654	—	1,200	2,550	5,100	9,400	—
1656 VB	—	1,200	2,550	5,100	9,400	—
1658 VB	—	1,200	2,550	5,100	9,400	—

KM# 215.2 DUCAT

3.5000 g., 0.9860 Gold 0.1109 oz. AGW **Rev:** Arms in inner circle

Date	Mintage	VG	F	VF	XF	Unc
1659 VB	—	1,200	2,550	5,100	9,400	—

KM# 235 DUCAT

3.5000 g., 0.9860 Gold 0.1109 oz. AGW **Obv:** Laureate bust of Karl XI right in inner circle **Rev:** Crowned shield of arms, date in legend

Date	Mintage	VG	F	VF	XF	Unc
1662	—	725	1,600	3,600	7,200	—

KM# 239.1 DUCAT

3.5000 g., 0.9860 Gold 0.1109 oz. AGW **Obv:** Laureate bust of Karl XI in narrow armor left **Rev:** Shield of arms, date in legend

Date	Mintage	VG	F	VF	XF	Unc
1666 HIH/(b)	—	650	1,450	3,400	6,800	—

KM# 239.2 DUCAT

3.5000 g., 0.9860 Gold 0.1109 oz. AGW **Obv:** Bust in wide armor **Note:** Varieties exist.

Date	Mintage	VG	F	VF	XF	Unc
1666 HIH/(b) Rare	—	—	—	—	—	—

KM# 257.1 DUCAT

3.5000 g., 0.9860 Gold 0.1109 oz. AGW **Obv:** Large laureate bust of Karl XI right **Rev:** Arms topped by helmet with wildmen supporters

Date	Mintage	VG	F	VF	XF	Unc
1672 DS Rare	—	—	—	—	—	—

KM# 257.2 DUCAT

3.5000 g., 0.9860 Gold 0.1109 oz. AGW **Obv:** Small bust

Date	Mintage	VG	F	VF	XF	Unc
1673 DS	—	1,100	2,500	5,500	9,500	—
1674 DS	—	1,100	2,500	5,500	9,500	—

KM# 257.3 DUCAT

3.5000 g., 0.9860 Gold 0.1109 oz. AGW **Rev:** Round shield

Date	Mintage	VG	F	VF	XF	Unc
1675 DS	—	1,100	2,500	5,500	9,500	—

KM# 257.4 DUCAT

3.5000 g., 0.9860 Gold 0.1109 oz. AGW **Obv:** Older bust

Date	Mintage	VG	F	VF	XF	Unc
1682 BA	—	1,100	2,500	5,500	9,500	—

KM# 300.1 DUCAT

3.5000 g., 0.9860 Gold 0.1109 oz. AGW **Obv:** Bust right with ornamented chest armor

Date	Mintage	VG	F	VF	XF	Unc
1684 BA	—	1,100	2,500	5,500	9,500	—

KM# 300.2 DUCAT

3.5000 g., 0.9860 Gold 0.1109 oz. AGW **Obv:** Bust right with plain chest armor

Date	Mintage	VG	F	VF	XF	Unc
1685 BA	—	1,100	2,500	5,500	9,500	—

KM# 313.1 DUCAT

3.5000 g., 0.9860 Gold 0.1109 oz. AGW **Rev:** Full legend

Date	Mintage	VG	F	VF	XF	Unc
1686 DHM Rare	—	—	—	—	—	—

KM# 313.2 DUCAT

3.5000 g., 0.9860 Gold 0.1109 oz. AGW **Rev:** Divided legend

Date	Mintage	VG	F	VF	XF	Unc
1686 DHM Rare	—	—	—	—	—	—

KM# 330 DUCAT

3.5000 g., 0.9860 Gold 0.1109 oz. AGW **Obv:** Bust right with shoulder armor

Date	Mintage	VG	F	VF	XF	Unc
1689 ILA/(c)	—	1,100	2,500	5,500	9,500	—
1690 ILA/(c)	—	1,100	2,500	5,500	9,500	—

KM# 340.1 DUCAT

3.5000 g., 0.9860 Gold 0.1109 oz. AGW **Obv:** Legend divided **Rev:** ILA added

Date	Mintage	VG	F	VF	XF	Unc
1691 ILA/(c)	—	1,100	2,500	5,500	9,500	—
1693 ILA	—	1,100	2,500	5,500	9,500	—
1694 ILA	—	1,100	2,500	5,500	9,500	—

KM# 340.2 DUCAT

3.5000 g., 0.9860 Gold 0.1109 oz. AGW **Obv:** ICA added **Note:** Varieties exist.

Date	Mintage	VG	F	VF	XF	Unc
1695 ICA Rare	—	—	—	—	—	—
1696 ICA	—	1,100	2,500	5,500	9,500	—
1697 ICA	—	1,100	2,500	5,500	9,500	—

KM# 220 1-1/2 DUCAT

5.2500 g., 0.9860 Gold 0.1664 oz. AGW **Obv:** Armored bust of Karl XI **Rev:** Wheat sheaf holding crown, orb and crossed sword and scepter in inner circle

Date	Mintage	VG	F	VF	XF	Unc
ND ILA Unique	—	—	—	—	—	—

KM# 222 2 DUCAT

7.0000 g., 0.9860 Gold 0.2219 oz. AGW **Subject:** Karl X

Date	Mintage	VG	F	VF	XF	Unc
1658	—	700	1,400	3,250	6,300	—

KM# 236.1 2 DUCAT

7.0000 g., 0.9860 Gold 0.2219 oz. AGW **Subject:** Karl XI

Date	Mintage	VG	F	VF	XF	Unc
1661	—	625	1,400	3,900	7,700	—

KM# 236.2 2 DUCAT

7.0000 g., 0.9860 Gold 0.2219 oz. AGW **Obv:** Plain head of Karl XI

Date	Mintage	VG	F	VF	XF	Unc
1661	—	900	1,900	4,500	9,000	—

KM# 301 2 DUCAT

7.0000 g., 0.9860 Gold 0.2219 oz. AGW **Obv:** Armored bust of Karl XI

Date	Mintage	VG	F	VF	XF	Unc
1684 BA	—	825	1,650	3,900	7,500	—

KM# 320 2 DUCAT

7.0000 g., 0.9860 Gold 0.2219 oz. AGW **Obv:** Bust with draped shoulder

Date	Mintage	VG	F	VF	XF	Unc
1687 DHM	—	825	1,650	3,900	7,500	—

KM# 339 2 DUCAT

7.0000 g., 0.9860 Gold 0.2219 oz. AGW **Obv:** Divided legend **Note:** Varieties exist.

Date	Mintage	VG	F	VF	XF	Unc
1690 ILA	—	825	1,650	3,900	7,500	—
1695 ILA	—	825	1,650	3,900	7,500	—

KM# 342 2 DUCAT

7.0000 g., 0.9860 Gold 0.2219 oz. AGW **Obv:** Armored bust of Karl XI **Rev:** Wheat sheaf holding crown, orb, crossed sword, and scepter in inner circle **Note:** Varieties exist.

Date	Mintage	VG	F	VF	XF	Unc
1692 ILA	—	800	1,600	3,500	6,400	—
1693 ILA	—	800	1,600	3,500	6,400	—
1694 ILA	—	800	1,600	3,500	6,400	—
1696 ICA	—	500	1,000	2,200	4,000	—
1697 ICA	—	600	1,200	3,000	5,000	—
ND ILA	—	800	1,600	3,500	6,400	—

KM# 209 2-1/2 DUCAT

8.7500 g., 0.9860 Gold 0.2774 oz. AGW **Obv:** Laureate bust of Christina right in inner circle **Rev:** Shield of arms, date in legend

Date	Mintage	VG	F	VF	XF	Unc
1653 Rare	—	—	—	—	—	—

KM# 270 3 DUCAT

10.5000 g., 0.9860 Gold 0.3328 oz. AGW **Obv:** Laureate bust of Karl XI right **Rev:** Crowned arms with wildmen supporters, date in legend

Date	Mintage	VG	F	VF	XF	Unc
1674 Unique	—	—	—	—	—	—

PRENZLAU

(Prenzlow)

The town of Prenzlau is in Pomerania, about 28 miles (47km) southwest of Stettin, and appears as a mint for the dukes of Pomerania from the second half of the 12th century. By the mid-13th century, Prenzlau came under the control of the margraves of Brandenburg and was soon producing coins for those rulers. The town had its own coinage in the latter 15th century and again during the Kipper Period of the Thirty Years' War.

PROVINCIAL TOWN

REGULAR COINAGE

KM# 1 PFENNIG (Kipper)

Copper **Obv:** Brandenburg eagle, feathered helmet above, all in a circle **Rev:** I/PFEN/ date **Note:** Varieties exist.

Date	Mintage	VG	F	VF	XF	Unc
16Z1	—	16.00	27.00	55.00	90.00	—
16ZZ	—	16.00	27.00	55.00	90.00	—
1622	—	16.00	27.00	55.00	90.00	—

KM# 2 PFENNIG

Silver **Note:** Uniface; Brandenburg eagle, feathered helmet above divides date, all in a circle.

Date	Mintage	VG	F	VF	XF	Unc
1622	—	—	—	—	—	—

QUEDLINBURG

The small provincial town of Quedlinburg, 8 miles (13km) south-southeast of Halberstadt and slightly north of the Harz Mountains, was founded in 922. The town itself had its own coinage during the middle of the 17th century, but most of the local coinage was produced in and for the abbey. Near the village in 966, Emperor Otto I the Great (962-73) founded an abbey primarily for princesses of his imperial Saxon family. Otto I's grandson, Otto III (983-1002), established an imperial mint in the town and gave the abbesses the right to strike their own coinage at about the same time. Many of the abbesses were members of the House of Saxony or from noble families closely associated with it. When the Electorate and Duchy of Saxony itself became officially Protestant during the Reformation, Quedlinburg followed the same path in 1539. The coinage of the abbesses came to an end in 1697 when Elector Friedrich August I of Saxony (1694-1733) sold his rights over Quedlinburg to Brandenburg-Prussia in order to become King of Poland. A brief and scarce issue of a few types occurred in 1759, but otherwise the abbesses had only their 40-square mile (65-square km) territory to administer. Even this was secularized and annexed by Prussia in 1803.

RULERS

Anna III von Stolberg-Wernigerode, 1584-1601
Maria von Sachsen-Weimar, 1601-10
Dorothea von Sachsen, 1610-1617
Dorothea Sophia von Sachsen-Altenburg, 1618-1645
Anna Sophia I von Pfalz-Birkenfeld, 1645-1680
Anna Sophia II von Hessen-Darmstadt, 1681-1683
Anna Dorothea von Sachsen-Weimar, 1684-1704

MINT OFFICIALS' INITIALS

Initials	Date	Name
TE	1615-17	Tobias Eitze, mintmaster
HL	1617-19	Heinrich Löhr, mintmaster
	June-Aug 1619	Heinrich Meyer, mintmaster
	Oct-Dec 1619	Heinrich Oppermann, mintmaster
HL	1620-24, 1633-37	Hans Lauch, mintmaster
	Aug-Nov 1621	Johann Lampe, mintmaster
	1623-25	Georg Koch, mintmaster
AH	1674-76	August Hackeberg, mint director
	1674-80	Heinrich Römer, mint director
GF	1675-77	Georg Fromholtz, warden
	Ca.1675	Martin Müller, die-cutter
HAR	1676-?	Heinricyh Albert Reinecke, mintmaster
	Ca.1685	Johann Arensburger, mintmaster
	Ca.1690?	Philipp Ernst, mintmaster
HCH	1689-1729	Heinrich Christoph Hille, mintmaster in Braunschweig
HIC	1676-?	Henning Jürgen Cammer (Kemmer), warden

ARMS

Two crossed fish, but also sometimes an eagle or a three-towered city gate, or a combination of these.

Electoral and Ducal Saxony arms often appear on coins of abbesses from that family.

REFERENCE

D = Adalbert Düning, ***Übersich über die Münzgeschichte des kaiserlichen freien weltlichen Stifts Quedlinburg***, Quedlinburg, 1886.

ABBEY

REGULAR COINAGE

KM# 23 PFENNIG (Kipper)

Copper **Ruler:** Dorothea Sophia **Obv:** Heart-shaped 2-fold arms of ducal Saxony and Quedlingburg **Rev:** Large 'Q', date below **Note:** Reference D-33.

Date	Mintage	VG	F	VF	XF	Unc
1620	—	16.00	33.00	60.00	100	—
1621	—	16.00	33.00	60.00	100	—
1622	—	16.00	33.00	60.00	100	—

KM# 24 PFENNIG (Kipper)

Copper **Ruler:** Dorothea Sophia **Note:** Uniface; Heart-shaped 2-fold arms of ducal Saxony and Quedlingburg.

Date	Mintage	VG	F	VF	XF	Unc
ND(1620-22)	—	16.00	33.00	60.00	100	—

KM# 25 PFENNIG (Straubpfennig)
Copper **Ruler:** Dorothea Sophia **Obv:** 2-fold arms of ducal Saxony and Quedlinburg **Rev. Legend:** I/ STRAV/ PHEN

Date	Mintage	VG	F	VF	XF	Unc
ND(ca.1620)	—	20.00	40.00	70.00	120	—

KM# 42 PFENNIG (Straubpfennig)
Silver **Ruler:** Dorothea Sophia **Obv:** Heart-shaped 2-fold arms of Ducal and Electoral Saxony divide mintmaster's initials, date divided below. **Note:** Uniface. Reference D-32.

Date	Mintage	VG	F	VF	XF	Unc
(16)34 HL	—	—	—	—	—	—

KM# 67 PFENNIG (Straubpfennig)
Silver **Ruler:** Anna Sophie I **Obv:** 2-fold arms of Quedlingburg and Pfalz, rampant lion left, divide date. **Note:** Uniface.

Date	Mintage	VG	F	VF	XF	Unc
(16)77	—	—	—	—	—	—

KM# 28 3 PFENNIG (Dreier)
Copper **Ruler:** Dorothea Sophia **Obv:** Crowned 2-fold arms of ducal Saxony and Quedlingburg in baroque frame **Rev:** Imperial orb with '3' divides date

Date	Mintage	VG	F	VF	XF	Unc
(16)Z1	—	16.00	33.00	60.00	100	—

KM# 34 3 PFENNIG (Dreier)
Copper **Ruler:** Dorothea Sophia **Obv:** Crowned 2-fold arms of ducal Saxony and Quedlingburg in baroque frame **Rev:** Complete date over Imperial orb

Date	Mintage	VG	F	VF	XF	Unc
1622	—	20.00	40.00	70.00	120	—

KM# 29 3 PFENNIG (Dreier)
Silver **Ruler:** Dorothea Sophia **Obv:** Ornate 2-fold arms of ducal and electoral Saxony **Rev:** Imperial orb with '3' divides date in baroque frame **Note:** Reference D-31.

Date	Mintage	VG	F	VF	XF	Unc
1621 HL	—	12.00	25.00	40.00	75.00	—
1622 HL	—	12.00	25.00	40.00	75.00	—

KM# 59 3 PFENNIG (Dreier)
Silver **Ruler:** Anna Sophie I **Obv:** Crowned heart-shaped 2-fold arms of Quedlinburg and Pfalz, rampant lion left, within palm branches **Rev:** Imperial orb with '3' divides date **Note:** Reference D-38.

Date	Mintage	VG	F	VF	XF	Unc
1676	—	—	—	—	—	—
1677	—	—	—	—	—	—

KM# 30 4 GROSCHEN (Schreckenberger)
Silver **Ruler:** Dorothea Sophia **Obv:** Heart-shaped 2-fold arms of ducal Saxony and Quedlinburg in ornate frame, date at top **Obv. Legend:** MO. NO. D-G. DORT. SOPHI **Rev:** Crowned Imperial Eagle, '4' in circle on breast **Rev. Legend:** DVCISS. SAX. ABBAT. QVEDLB **Note:** Varieties exist. Reference D-28.

Date	Mintage	VG	F	VF	XF	Unc
16Z1	—	30.00	50.00	100	—	—

KM# 31 4 GROSCHEN (Schreckenberger)
Silver **Ruler:** Dorothea Sophia **Obv:** Heart-shaped 2-fold arms of ducal Saxony and Quedlinburg in ornate frame, date at top **Obv. Legend:** MO. NO. D-G. DORT. SOPHI **Rev:** Crowned Imperial Eagle, '4' in circle on breast **Rev. Legend:** DVCISS. SAX. ABBAT. QVEDLB **Note:** Klippe. Reference D-28

Date	Mintage	VG	F	VF	XF	Unc
16Z1	—	30.00	50.00	100	—	—

KM# 32 12 KREUZER (Schreckenberger)
Silver **Ruler:** Dorothea Sophia **Obv:** Heart-shaped 2-fold arms of ducal Saxony and Quedlingburg, date above **Obv. Legend:** MO. NO. D-G. DORO. SO **Rev:** Crowned Imperial Eagle, '12' in circle on breast **Rev. Legend:** DUCIS. SA. ABBA. QUE **Note:** Varieties exist. Reference D-29.

Date	Mintage	VG	F	VF	XF	Unc
1621	—	25.00	45.00	95.00	—	—

KM# 3 1/24 THALER (Groschen)
Silver **Ruler:** Dorothea **Obv:** 2-fold arms of Ducal and Electoral Saxony in circle **Obv. Legend:** MO. NO. D.G. DOROTHEÆ **Rev:** Imperial orb with Z4, date divided by cross at top **Rev. Legend:** DVC. SAX. AB. QVEDL **Note:** Varieties exist. Reference D-25.

Date	Mintage	VG	F	VF	XF	Unc
1612	—	15.00	30.00	60.00	100	—
1614	—	15.00	30.00	60.00	100	—
1615 TE	—	15.00	30.00	60.00	100	—
1616 TE	—	15.00	30.00	60.00	100	—
1616	—	15.00	30.00	60.00	100	—
1617	—	15.00	30.00	60.00	100	—
1617/5 TE	—	15.00	30.00	60.00	100	—
1617 TE	—	15.00	30.00	60.00	100	—
1617 HL	—	15.00	30.00	60.00	100	—

KM# 18 1/24 THALER (Groschen)
Silver **Ruler:** Dorothea Sophia **Obv:** 2-fold arms of Ducal and Electoral Saxony in circle. **Obv. Legend:** MO. NO. D.G. DOROTHEÆ **Rev:** Imperial orb with Z4, date divided by cross at top **Rev. Legend:** DVC. SAX. AB. QVEDL **Note:** Varieties exist. Reference D-30.

Date	Mintage	VG	F	VF	XF	Unc
1618 HL	—	15.00	30.00	60.00	100	—
1619 HL	—	15.00	30.00	60.00	100	—
1620 HL	—	15.00	30.00	60.00	100	—
1621 HL	—	15.00	30.00	60.00	100	—
1622 HL	—	15.00	30.00	60.00	100	—
ND HL	—	15.00	30.00	60.00	100	—

KM# 22 1/24 THALER (Groschen)
Silver **Ruler:** Dorothea Sophia **Obv:** 2-fold arms of ducal and electoral Saxony in circle, titles of Dorothea Sophia **Obv. Legend:** MO. NO. D.G. DOROTHEÆ **Rev:** Imperial orb with Z4, date divided by cross at top **Rev. Legend:** DVC. SAX. AB. QVEDL **Note:** Klippe. Reference D-30.

Date	Mintage	VG	F	VF	XF	Unc
1620 HL	—	—	—	—	—	—
1622 HL	—	—	—	—	—	—

KM# 45 1/24 THALER (Groschen)
Silver **Ruler:** Anna Sophie I **Obv:** Crowned 6-fold arms with central shield of Quedlinburg divides mintmaster's initials. **Rev:** Imperial orb with 24 divides date **Rev. Legend:** MONETA . NOVA... **Note:** Reference D-37.

Date	Mintage	VG	F	VF	XF	Unc
1675 GF	—	—	—	—	—	—
1676 GF	—	—	—	—	—	—

KM# 35 1/4 THALER
Silver, 30 mm. **Ruler:** Dorothea Sophia **Obv:** Manifold arms with central shield of Quedlinburg **Obv. Legend:** MO: NO: D:G: DOR: SOPH: DV: SA: A **Rev:** Crowned imperial eagle, orb on breast, date divided above **Rev. Legend:** FERDI: II. D:G: ROM: IMP: SEM: AVG

Date	Mintage	VG	F	VF	XF	Unc
16Z4	—	165	375	525	1,000	—

KM# 46 1/3 THALER (1/2 Gulden)
Silver **Ruler:** Anna Sophie I **Obv:** Crowned 6-fold arms with central shield of Quedlinburg divide date, value 1/3 in oval **Obv. Legend:** MONETA . NOVA... **Rev:** Crowned ornate script monogram **Rev. Legend:** BESCHAW. DAS. ZIEL. SAGE. NICHT. VIEL

Date	Mintage	VG	F	VF	XF	Unc
1675 GF	—	—	—	—	—	—

KM# 47 1/3 THALER (1/2 Gulden)
Silver **Ruler:** Anna Sophie I **Obv:** Bust left, titles of Anna Sophia I **Rev:** 6-fold arms with central shield of Quedlinburg, 3 helmets above, divide date

Date	Mintage	VG	F	VF	XF	Unc
1675 GF	—	—	—	—	—	—

KM# 36 1/2 THALER
Silver **Ruler:** Dorothea Sophia **Note:** Similar to KM#37.2; Dav. #5721.

Date	Mintage	VG	F	VF	XF	Unc
1623 HL	—	—	—	—	—	—

KM# 48 1/2 THALER
Silver **Ruler:** Anna Sophie I **Obv:** Bust left in sprays **Rev:** Helmeted arms, date divided among helmets. **Note:** Similar to KM#55; Dav. #5726.

Date	Mintage	VG	F	VF	XF	Unc
1675 GF	—	—	—	—	—	—

KM# 49 1/2 THALER
Silver **Ruler:** Anna Sophie I **Subject:** 30th Anniversary of the Investiture of Anna Sophia I **Obv:** Bust left **Rev:** 9-line inscription **Note:** Similar to KM#55; Dav. #5727.

Date	Mintage	VG	F	VF	XF	Unc
1675	—	—	—	—	—	—

KM# 51 2/3 THALER (Gulden)
Silver **Ruler:** Anna Sophie I **Obv:** Bust left. **Obv. Legend:** ANNA SOPHIA: P:B:R:H:I:B:A:Z:Q:G:Z:V:V:S. **Rev:** 3 helmets above manifold arms, oval with value '2/3' below, date at end of legend. **Rev. Legend:** MONETA. NOVA. ARG. - DIOEC. QVEDLINB. **Note:** Dav. #773.

Date	Mintage	VG	F	VF	XF	Unc
1675 GF	—	—	—	—	—	—

KM# 54 2/3 THALER (Gulden)
Silver **Ruler:** Anna Sophie I **Obv:** Crowned ornate script monogram, crossed palm fronds below. **Obv. Inscription:** BESCHAW. DAS. ZIEL. SAGE. NICHT. VIEL. **Rev:** Crowned 6-fold arms with central shield of Quedlinburg, value '2/3' in oval below, date at end of legend. **Rev. Legend:** MONETA NOVA ARG: - DIOEC. QVEDLINB. **Note:** Dav. #776.

Date	Mintage	VG	F	VF	XF	Unc
1675 GF	—	—	—	—	—	—

KM# 52 2/3 THALER (Gulden)
Silver **Ruler:** Anna Sophie I **Obv:** Bust right, titles of Anna Sophia I **Note:** Dav. 774.

Date	Mintage	VG	F	VF	XF	Unc
1675 GF	—	300	700	1,200	—	—
1676 GF	—	300	700	1,200	—	—

KM# 61 2/3 THALER (Gulden)
Silver **Ruler:** Anna Sophie I **Obv:** Bust left, titles of Anna Sophia I **Rev:** Date divided by arms **Note:** Reference Dav. 775B.

Date	Mintage	VG	F	VF	XF	Unc
1676 HAR	—	135	225	300	475	—
1677 HAR	—	135	225	300	475	—

KM# 53 2/3 THALER (Gulden)
Silver **Ruler:** Anna Sophie I **Obv:** Bust left, titles of Anna Sophia I **Rev:** Crowned arms and date divided **Note:** Varieties exist. Reference Dav. 775A.

Date	Mintage	VG	F	VF	XF	Unc
1676 AH	—	135	225	300	475	—
1676 HAR	—	135	225	300	475	—
1676	—	135	225	300	475	—
1677 HAR	—	135	225	300	475	—

KM# 62 2/3 THALER (Gulden)
Silver **Ruler:** Anna Sophie I **Obv:** Crowned ornate script monogram, crossed palm fronds below. **Obv. Legend:** BESCHAW. DAS ZIEL. SAGE NICHT VIEL. **Rev:** Crowned 6-fold arms with central shield of Quedlinburg divide date and

mintmaster's initials, value '2/3' in oval below. **Rev. Legend:** MONETA. NOVA. ARG. - DIOEC. QVEDLINB. **Note:** Dav. #777.

Date	Mintage	VG	F	VF	XF	Unc
1676 GF	—	85.00	140	220	375	—
1676 HIC	—	85.00	140	220	375	—

KM# 63 2/3 THALER (Gulden)

Silver **Ruler:** Anna Sophie I **Obv:** Bust right, titles of Anna Sophia I, date divided by arms **Rev:** Crowned ornate script monogram, date above **Rev. Legend:** BESCHAW. DAS. ZIEL. SAGE. NICHT. VIEL **Note:** Dav. #777A.

Date	Mintage	VG	F	VF	XF	Unc
1676 GF	—	—	—	—	—	—

KM# 64 2/3 THALER (Gulden)

Silver **Ruler:** Anna Sophie I **Obv:** Bust right, titles of Anna Sophia I, date divided by arms **Rev:** Crowned ornate script monogram, date above **Rev. Legend:** BESCHAW. DAS. ZIEL. SAGE. NICHT. VIEL **Note:** Mule; 2 different dates.

Date	Mintage	VG	F	VF	XF	Unc
1676//1677 GF	—	—	—	—	—	—

KM# 5 THALER

Silver **Ruler:** Dorothea **Obv:** Crowned imperial eagle with orb on breast, date above in legend **Rev:** Helmeted arms **Note:** Dav. #5718.

Date	Mintage	VG	F	VF	XF	Unc
1615 TE	—	500	900	1,600	2,000	—
1617/5 TE Rare	—	—	—	—	—	—
Note: UBS Gold & Numismatics Auction 57, 9-03, XF realized approximately $12,345						
1617 HL Rare	—	—	—	—	—	—

KM# 9 THALER

Silver **Ruler:** Dorothea **Subject:** Centennial of the Reformation **Obv:** 3 ornate helmets above manifold arms, date divided at top. **Obv. Legend:** DOROTHE: D:G. ABBATIS. -QVEDELB. DVCIS: SAXO. **Rev:** Full-length standing figure of Emperor Heinrich I (918-36) holding sword and orb, town view in background. **Rev. Legend:** HEINR AVG. D.G ROM IM SAX - DVX. ABB: QVEDLB: FVND. **Note:** Dav. #LS374; 28.50 grams - 29.37 grams.

Date	Mintage	VG	F	VF	XF	Unc
1617 HL	—	700	1,200	2,000	3,200	—
1617 HL/IH	—	700	1,200	2,000	3,200	—

KM# 26 THALER

Silver **Ruler:** Dorothea Sophia **Obv. Legend:** MATHI. D. G. ROM-IMP... **Rev. Legend:** MO. NO D. G. DOROT-SOP... **Note:** Dav.#5719.

Date	Mintage	VG	F	VF	XF	Unc
1618 HL	—	450	900	1,500	—	—

KM# 37.1 THALER

Silver **Ruler:** Dorothea Sophia **Note:** Similar to Dav. #5721 but reverse legend:...QVED

Date	Mintage	VG	F	VF	XF	Unc
1623	—	500	1,000	1,750	—	—

KM# 37.2 THALER

Silver **Ruler:** Dorothea Sophia **Rev. Legend:** Ends: ...QVE **Note:** Dav. #5721.

Date	Mintage	VG	F	VF	XF	Unc
1623 HL	—	400	750	1,350	—	—

KM# 37.3 THALER

Silver **Ruler:** Dorothea Sophia **Obv:** 3 ornate helmets above manifold arms which divide mintmaster's initials. **Obv. Legend:** MO. NO. D.G. DOROT. SOPH. DV. SAX. A. QVED. **Rev:** Crowned imperial eagle, orb on breast, date divided at top. **Rev. Legend:** FERDI. II. D.G. ROM. IMP: SEMP: AVGV. **Note:** Similar to Dav. #5721.

Date	Mintage	VG	F	VF	XF	Unc
1623 HL	—	450	750	1,350	—	—

KM# 39 THALER

Silver **Ruler:** Dorothea Sophia **Rev:** Legend ends:...AVGVS **Note:** Dav. #5722. Weight varies: 28.50-29.37 grams.

Date	Mintage	VG	F	VF	XF	Unc
1624	—	400	800	1,400	—	—
16Z9	—	400	800	1,400	—	—

KM# 40 THALER

Silver **Ruler:** Dorothea Sophia **Obv:** Similar to Dav. #5724 but legend: MON. NOV... **Rev:** Crowned arms, date below **Rev. Legend:** DVC. SAX. ABBAT... **Note:** Dav. #5723.

Date	Mintage	VG	F	VF	XF	Unc
1633 HL	—	600	1,050	1,750	—	—

KM# 44 THALER

Silver **Ruler:** Dorothea Sophia **Obv. Legend:** MONET. NOV... **Rev. Legend:** DVCIS. SAXON... **Note:** Dav. #5724.

Date	Mintage	VG	F	VF	XF	Unc
1634 HL	—	300	600	1,000	1,650	—

KM# 55 THALER

Silver **Ruler:** Anna Sophie I **Obv:** Bust left in sprays **Rev:** Helmeted arms with helmets dividing date **Note:** Dav. #5726.

Date	Mintage	VG	F	VF	XF	Unc
1675 GF Rare	—	—	—	—	—	—

KM# 56 THALER

Silver **Ruler:** Anna Sophie I **Subject:** 30th Anniversary of Investiture of Anna Sophia **Obv:** Bust left **Rev:** Nine-line inscription **Note:** Dav. #1675.

Date	Mintage	VG	F	VF	XF	Unc
1675 Rare	—	—	—	—	—	—

KM# 69 THALER

Silver **Ruler:** Anna Sophie I **Obv:** Large crown above shield with Thuringian lion rampant left holding crossed Quedlinburg fish, date divided at left and right. **Obv. Legend:** ANNA. SOPHIA. P: B: R: H: I: B: A: Z: Q: G: Z: V: V: S. **Rev:** Three medallions, 2 above 1, each with tree, town view and legend, floral sprays around. **Note:** Dav. #5728.

Date	Mintage	VG	F	VF	XF	Unc
1677	—	950	1,750	3,250	5,500	—

KM# 11 1-1/2 THALER

Silver **Ruler:** Dorothea **Subject:** Centennial of the Reformation **Note:** Similar to 2 Thaler, Dav. #LS373.

Date	Mintage	VG	F	VF	XF	Unc
1617 HL	—	1,450	2,400	3,900	6,600	—

KM# 12 2 THALER

57.4000 g., Silver **Ruler:** Dorothea **Subject:** Centennial of the Reformation **Obv:** 3 ornate helmets above manifold arms, date divided at top. **Obv. Legend:** DOROTHE. D:G. ABBATIS - QVEDELB. DVCIS: SAXO. **Rev:** Full-length standing figure of Emperor Heinrich I (918-36) holding sword and orb, town view in background. **Rev. Legend:** HEINR: AVG. D:G. RO. IM: SAX - DVX. ABB: QVEDLB: FVND-AT. **Note:** Dav. #LS373.

Date	Mintage	VG	F	VF	XF	Unc
1617 HL/IH	—	2,200	3,600	5,500	8,300	—

KM# 57 2 THALER

57.4000 g., Silver **Ruler:** Anna Sophie I **Obv:** Bust left in sprays **Rev:** Helmeted arms with helmet dividing date, G-F below **Note:** Dav. #5725.

Date	Mintage	VG	F	VF	XF	Unc
1675 GF Rare	—	—	—	—	—	—

TRADE COINAGE

KM# 8 DUCAT

Gold **Ruler:** Dorothea **Obv:** Full-length facing figure of St. Servatius divides legend **Obv. Legend:** S — S DOROT. D.G. DVC. — SAX. AB. QVED **Rev:** Manifold arms with central shield of Quedlingburg, date divided at top **Rev. Legend:** V.D.M. — I. Æ **Note:** Klippe. Reference D-24.

Date	Mintage	VG	F	VF	XF	Unc
1616	—	—	—	—	—	—

KM# 7 DUCAT

Gold **Ruler:** Dorothea **Obv:** Full-length facing figure of St. Servatius divides legend **Obv. Legend:** S — S DOROT. D.G. DVC. — SAX. AB. QVED **Rev:** Manifold arms with central shield of Quedlingburg, date divided at top **Rev. Legend:** V.D.M. — I. Æ **Note:** Reference D-24.

Date	Mintage	VG	F	VF	XF	Unc
1616	—	—	—	—	—	—

KM# 20 DUCAT

3.5000 g., 0.9860 Gold 0.1109 oz. AGW **Ruler:** Dorothea Sophia **Obv:** Crowned arms of Quedlinburg in inner circle, titles of Dorothea Sophia **Rev:** Crowned arms of Saxony in inner circle **Note:** Fr. #2445.

Date	Mintage	VG	F	VF	XF	Unc
ND	—	725	1,500	2,600	4,550	—

KM# 14 8 DUCAT

26.6400 g., 0.9860 Gold 0.8445 oz. AGW **Ruler:** Dorothea **Subject:** Centennial of the Reformation **Obv:** Helmeted arms, titles of Dorothea **Rev:** Heinrich I standing with sword and orb, city in background **Note:** Struck with 2 Thaler dies, Dav. #LS373.

Date	Mintage	VG	F	VF	XF	Unc
1617 HL Rare	—	—	—	—	—	—

KM# 17 10 DUCAT

35.0000 g., 0.9860 Gold 1.1095 oz. AGW **Ruler:** Dorothea **Subject:** Centennial of the Reformation **Note:** Fr. #2443, similar to 8 Ducat, Fr. #2444. Struck with 2 Thaler dies, KM #12.

Date	Mintage	VG	F	VF	XF	Unc
1617 HL Rare	—	—	—	—	—	—

KM# 16 10 DUCAT

Gold **Ruler:** Dorothea **Subject:** Centennial of the Reformation **Note:** Fr. #2443. Struck from the same dies as KM#9.

Date	Mintage	VG	F	VF	XF	Unc
1617 HL Rare	—	—	—	—	—	—

TOWN

REGULAR COINAGE

KM# 70 3 PFENNIG (Dreier)

Copper **Obv:** 'Q' in circle divides date **Rev:** Value 'III' in circle

Date	Mintage	VG	F	VF	XF	Unc
(16)62 Rare	—	—	—	—	—	—

RANTZAU

(Ranzau)

The small county of Rantzau was situated in Holstein and its seat was the castle of Breitenburg, located just a few miles south of Itzehoe and ten miles (17km) north-northeast from Glückstadt on the Elbe River. The ruling family of Rantzau is mentioned in sources as early as 1362, which refer back to a certain Schalko Rantzau who was Burggraf of Leisnig in Saxony in 1283. Meanwhile, the rule of Count Adolf II of Holstein (1128-64) saw the beginnings of a Saxon colonization of his territories. It seems that some members of the Rantzau family relocated to that region during the following century or two. Johann Rantzau (1492-1565) built the castle of Breitenburg, the foundation stone of which bears the date 1501. His great-grandson, Christian, was granted the title of count and the mint right by Emperor Ferdinand III in 1650. The line of counts became extinct in 1734, but other branches of the family continued in widely separate territories – Leisnig, Bohemia, Mecklenburg, Prussia, Hannover, Württemberg, Oldenburg, Denmark and the Netherlands. Breitenburg passed in marriage to Kastell-Rüdenhausen and eventually back to the Rantzau-Ahrensburg branch of the family.

RULERS

Gerhard, 1598-1627
Christian, 1627-1663
Detlef, 1663-1697
Christian Detlef, 1697-1721
Wilhelm Adolf, 1721-1734

Initial	Date	Name
(a)= [symbol]	1635-68	Matthias Freude der Ältere in Hamburg

ARMS

Usually 4-fold arms (quartered) with a central shield, Rantzau in quarters 1 and 4, divided vertically with right side shaded; quarters 2 and 3, for Burggrafs of Leisnig, are divided by diagonal bar with six lozenges (Diamonds) on each side of bar; central shield has rampant lion left for lordship of Penik in Bohemia.

REFERENCE

M = Adolph Meyer, ***Die Münzen und Medaillen der Herren von Rantzau***, Vienna, 1882.

COUNTSHIP

REGULAR COINAGE

KM# 4 2/3 THALER (Gulden)

Silver **Ruler:** Detlef **Obv:** Bust right, value '2/3' in oval at bottom. **Obv. Legend:** DETHLEF. S. R. I. C. I. R(ANZOVV). ET(&) L. D. I. B. **Rev:** Large crown above 4-fold arms in baroque frame with central shield of Penik lion, date divided in margin at bottom. **Rev. Legend:** RECTE. FACIENDO. NEMINEM. TIMEAS. **Note:** Dav. #778, Meyer 9-14.

Date	Mintage	VG	F	VF	XF	Unc
1689	—	675	1,000	1,350	2,000	—

KM# 2 THALER

Silver **Ruler:** Christian I **Obv:** Bust right in circle. **Obv. Legend:** CHRISTIAN: COM: IN: RANTZOU. DOM: IN. BREITENB:. **Rev:** 4-fold arms with central shield of Penik lion, mintmaster's symbol at beginning and date at end of legend. **Rev. Legend:** DEO DVCE COMITE FORTVNA. **Note:** Dav. #7290, Meyer 7, 8.

Date	Mintage	VG	F	VF	XF	Unc
1656 (a)	—	2,400	3,900	6,600	11,000	—
1657 (a)	—	2,100	3,600	6,000	10,000	—

TRADE COINAGE

KM# 1 DUCAT

3.5000 g., 0.9860 Gold 0.1109 oz. AGW **Ruler:** Christian I **Obv:** Bust right in circle. **Obv. Legend:** CHRISTIAN. COM. IN RANTZ. DOM. IN BREITENB. **Rev:** 4-fold arms with central shield of Penik lion divide date near bottom, 3 ornate helmets above. **Rev. Legend:** DEO DVCE COMITE FORTVNA. **Note:** Fr. #2449, Meyer 1, 2, 4, 5.

Date	Mintage	VG	F	VF	XF	Unc
1655 (a)	—	1,500	3,000	5,300	9,000	—
1656 (a)	—	1,500	3,000	5,300	9,000	—
1658 (a)	—	1,500	3,000	5,300	9,000	—

KM# 5 DUCAT

3.5000 g., 0.9860 Gold 0.1109 oz. AGW **Ruler:** Detlef **Obv:** Bust right. **Obv. Legend:** DETHLEF. S. R. I. C. R. ET L. D. I. B. **Rev:** 4-fold arms with central shield of Penik lion, 3 ornate helmets above divide date. **Rev. Legend:** RECTE. FACIENDO. NEMINEM. TIMEAS. **Note:** Fr. #2450, Meyer 6.

Date	Mintage	VG	F	VF	XF	Unc
1689	—	2,650	4,500	7,500	12,000	—

KM# 3 2 DUCAT

7.0000 g., 0.9860 Gold 0.2219 oz. AGW **Ruler:** Christian I **Obv:** Bust right in circle, titles of Christian I. **Rev:** 4-fold arms with central shield of Penik lion divide date near bottom, 3 ornate helmets above. **Rev. Legend:** DEO DVCE COMITE FORTVNA. **Note:** Fr. #2448, Meyer 3.

Date	Mintage	VG	F	VF	XF	Unc
1656 (a) Rare	—	—	—	—	—	—

RATZEBURG

Located in northern Germany, 12 miles (20 km) south-southeast of Lubeck, Ratzeburg became the seat of a bishopric about the middle of the 12th century. The first bishop was installed in 1158, but it was not until after the conversion of the see to Protestantism in 1566 that coins were struck there. At the conclusion of the Thirty Years' War in 1648, the bishopric was erected into a secular entity and annexed to Mecklenburg-Schwerin. Thus, the bishopric followed the fate of the medieval countship of Ratzeburg, which had been absorbed by Mecklenburg in 1216. Special coins were struck for the principality of Ratzeburg in the 1670s.

RULERS

Karl, Herzog von Mecklenburg, 1592-1610
August, Herzog von Braunschweig-Luneburg-Celle, 1610-1636
Gustaf Adolf, Herzog von Mecklenburg--Gustrow, 1636-1648 (d. 1695)
Christian I Ludwig, Herzog von Mecklenburg-Schwerin, 1658-1692

MINT OFFICIALS' INITIALS

Mark or Initial	Date	Name
(a)	Ca.1617	Unknown
(b) or	Ca.1617	Unknown
(c)	Ca.1617-18	Unknown
(d)	Ca.1619-20	Unknown
(e)	Ca.1623	Unknown, Berthold Krause?
	1650-60	Wismar and Mecklenburg-Schwerin
HS	1622-40	Henning Schreiber in Clausthal
	1626-72	Henning Schluter in Goslar
	1626-72	Henning Schluter in Zellerfeld
(f)	1671-73	Henning Kemper

ARMS

Crenelated city gate, usually with bishop's miter above.

BISHOPRIC

REGULAR COINAGE

DAV# 5730 THALER

Silver **Rev:** Rearing horse, city scene below

Date	Mintage	VG	F	VF	XF	Unc
1617 (b)	—	250	450	750	1,250	—

DAV# 5729 THALER

Silver **Obv:** Helmeted arms **Rev:** Horseman right, date divided below by horse's front feet **Note:** Varieties exist.

Date	Mintage	VG	F	VF	XF	Unc
1617 (b)	—	250	450	750	1,250	—
1620 (b)	—	250	450	750	1,250	—

DAV# 5731 THALER

Silver **Rev:** 16-BK-23 between horse's legs **Note:** Varieties exist.

Date	Mintage	VG	F	VF	XF	Unc
1623 (e)	—	275	500	825	1,400	—

DAV# 5732 THALER

Silver **Rev:** Helmeted arms **Note:** Varieties exist.

Date	Mintage	VG	F	VF	XF	Unc
1634	—	110	220	375	650	—
1635	—	110	220	375	650	—
1636	—	110	220	375	650	—

DAV# 5733 THALER

Silver **Obv:** Facing bust **Rev:** Date in legend

Date	Mintage	VG	F	VF	XF	Unc
1634 Rare	—	—	—	—	—	—

Note: Fritz Rudolf Künker Münzenhandlung Auction 95, 9-04, VF-XF realized approximately $9840

DAV# 5734 THALER

Silver **Rev:** Legend, date **Rev. Legend:** PATRIIS-UIRTUTIBUS-H/S

Date	Mintage	VG	F	VF	XF	Unc
1634 Rare	—	—	—	—	—	—

DAV# 5735 THALER

Silver **Obv. Legend:** ...EP: RATZB:... **Rev:** Legend, date **Rev. Legend:** VIRTUTIBUS-ANNO. DO:

Date	Mintage	VG	F	VF	XF	Unc
1634 Rare	—	—	—	—	—	—

Note: Fritz Rudolf Künker Münzenhandlung Auction 86, 9-03, XF realized approximately $9180

DAV# 5736 THALER

Silver **Obv:** Helmeted arms **Rev:** Wildman

Date	Mintage	VG	F	VF	XF	Unc
1636	—	115	205	350	575	—

DAV# 5736A THALER

Silver **Obv:** Legend broken by shield at bottom

Date	Mintage	VG	F	VF	XF	Unc
1636	—	75.00	135	225	450	—

DAV# 5737 THALER

Silver **Note:** Similar to Dav. #5736A but legend ...-RACE. DUX...

Date	Mintage	VG	F	VF	XF	Unc
1636	—	85.00	145	235	525	—

DAV# 5737A THALER

Silver **Obv. Legend:** -RATC. DUX...

Date	Mintage	VG	F	VF	XF	Unc
1636	—	85.00	145	235	525	—

DAV# 5738 THALER

Silver **Subject:** Death of August **Note:** Varieties exist.

Date	Mintage	VG	F	VF	XF	Unc
1636	—	175	350	750	1,500	—

DAV# A5738 2 THALER

Silver **Subject:** Death of August **Note:** Similar to 1 Thaler, Dav. #5738.

Date	Mintage	VG	F	VF	XF	Unc
1636 Rare	—	—	—	—	—	—

TRADE COINAGE

FR# 2451 GOLDGULDEN

3.5000 g., 0.9860 Gold 0.1109 oz. AGW **Obv:** Equestrian figure of August right in inner circle **Rev:** Large arms in inner circle, date in legend

Date	Mintage	VG	F	VF	XF	Unc
1618 (c) Rare	—	—	—	—	—	—

FR# 2452 DUCAT

3.5000 g., 0.9860 Gold 0.1109 oz. AGW **Obv:** August standing facing **Rev:** Crowned arms

Date	Mintage	VG	F	VF	XF	Unc
ND HS	—	500	1,100	2,000	3,500	—

RAVENSBERG

A countship in Westphalia surrounded by the bishoprics of Minden on the northeast, Osnabruck on the northwest, Munster on the west, the lordships of Rheda and Rechenberg and the countship of Rietberg on the southwest, and the countship of Lippe on the southeast. The dynasty of rulers emerged in the late 11th century. The countship of Berg was obtained through marriage in the early 14th century, then Ravensberg itself passed in marriage to the duchy of Julich later in the same century. In the first part of the 16th century, these territories were joined to the duchy of Cleveland the county of Mark by marriage. The coinage of each of these principalities has been listed elsewhere. When the last ruler of Julich-Cleve-Berg-Mark-Ravensberg died without heir in 1609, it set off the greatest controversy of the age and was one of the disputes leading to the general conflagration known as the Thirty Years' War (1618-1648).Brandenburg-Prussia and Pfalz-Neuburg laid claim to Ravensberg and the two struck a joint coinage for the countship from 1609 until 1614. Brandenburg controlled the countship from 1614 to 1623, striking coins for the territory it regarded as its own. However, from 1623 to 1647, while Brandenburg was occupied with the war against the Empire farther to the east, Pfalz-Neuburg maintained a presence in Ravensberg. Beginning in 1647, Brandenburg obtained permanent control of Ravensberg and struck a separate coinage for the countship until 1667. The chief mint of Ravensberg was Bielefeld.

RULERS

Johann Wilhelm, Herzog von Jülich-Kleve-Berg 1592-1609
Johann Sigismund of Brandenburg-Prussia, 1614-1619
Georg Wilhelm of Brandenburg-Prussia, 1619-1623
Wolfgang Wilhelm, 1623-1647
Friedrich Wilhelm of Brandenburg-Prussia, 1647-1688

MINT OFFICIALS' INITIALS

Bielefeld

Initial	Date	Name
(a)= or	1591-1616	Peter Busch
	?-1614	Ernst Schroder, warden
	1615-22	Anton Hoyer at Emmerich (Cleve)
	1615-38	Henning Brauns, warden
	1616-19, 27-29	Georg Kuhne
	1620-27	Julius Billerbeck
(b)=	1629-54	Jobst Koch
	1654-66	Johann Koch
	1655-56	Jobst Dietrich Koch

ARMS

3 chevrons (Ravensberg), usually in combination with the arms of the other four principalities, Ravensberg is in the lower right-hand division lion rampant left (Pfalz) scepter vertical (Brandenburg), usually with electoral cap above.

REFERENCE

S = Ewald Stange, **Geld- und Münzgeschichte der Grafschaft Ravensberg**, Münster, 1951.

COUNTSHIP

REGULAR COINAGE

KM# 20 PFENNIG

Copper **Obv:** Ravensberg arms in ornamented shield **Obv. Legend:** NVMVS RAVENSBERG **Rev:** Value: I in ornamented square, date above

Date	Mintage	VG	F	VF	XF	Unc
1620	—	24.00	45.00	75.00	120	—

KM# 21 PFENNIG

Copper **Obv. Legend:** NVM - RAV **Rev:** Value: Large I divides date in ornamented circle

Date	Mintage	VG	F	VF	XF	Unc
1620	—	24.00	45.00	75.00	120	—

KM# 22 2 PFENNIG

Copper **Obv:** Ravensberg arms in ornamented shield **Obv. Legend:** NVMMVS **Rev:** Value: II in ornamented square, date above

Date	Mintage	VG	F	VF	XF	Unc
1620	—	24.00	45.00	75.00	120	—

KM# 26 2 PFENNIG

Copper **Obv. Legend:** NVMVS RAVENSPVRG **Rev:** Value: II divides date

Date	Mintage	VG	F	VF	XF	Unc
16Z1	—	24.00	45.00	75.00	120	—

KM# 23 3 PFENNIG

Copper **Obv:** Ravensberg arms in ornamented shield **Obv. Legend:** NVMMVS RAVENSPVRG **Rev:** Value: III divides date in ornamented circle

Date	Mintage	VG	F	VF	XF	Unc
1620	—	27.00	55.00	100	165	—

KM# 27 3 PFENNIG

Copper **Rev:** Date divided among III

Date	Mintage	VG	F	VF	XF	Unc
16Z1	—	33.00	60.00	120	200	—

KM# 57 3 PFENNIG

Copper **Obv:** Capped scepter divides date **Obv. Legend:** RAVENSB. LANT. MVN. **Rev:** Ornamented square with III **Note:** Varieties exist.

Date	Mintage	VG	F	VF	XF	Unc
1655	—	20.00	40.00	70.00	120	—

KM# 58 3 PFENNIG

Copper **Obv:** Without date **Obv. Legend:** RAVENSB. LANDT. MVNTZ

Date	Mintage	VG	F	VF	XF	Unc
ND	—	16.00	33.00	45.00	75.00	—

KM# 24 6 PFENNIG

Copper **Obv:** Ravensberg arms in ornamented shield **Rev:** Value: VI with date above in ornamented circle **Note:** Varieties exist.

Date	Mintage	VG	F	VF	XF	Unc
1620	—	18.00	35.00	55.00	90.00	—
16Z1	—	18.00	35.00	55.00	90.00	—

KM# 59 6 PFENNIG

Copper

Date	Mintage	VG	F	VF	XF	Unc
1655	—	18.00	35.00	55.00	90.00	—

KM# 25 12 PFENNIG (1 Schilling)

Copper **Note:** Varieties exist.

Date	Mintage	VG	F	VF	XF	Unc
1620	—	16.00	33.00	60.00	90.00	—
16Z1	—	16.00	33.00	60.00	90.00	—

KM# 60 12 PFENNIG (1 Schilling)

Copper **Note:** Varieties exist.

Date	Mintage	VG	F	VF	XF	Unc
1655	—	24.00	45.00	75.00	125	—
1663	—	24.00	45.00	75.00	125	—

KM# 29 KORTLING (6 Heller-3 Pfennig-1/4 Mariengroschen)

Copper **Obv:** Five-fold arms **Obv. Legend:** MO. NO. D. C. E. M. C. R. A. **Rev:** Date, imperial orb with 6 **Rev. Legend:** IN. DEO. SPES. MEA **Note:** Lightweight Kortling. Varieties exist.

Date	Mintage	VG	F	VF	XF	Unc
1629 (b)	6,000	27.00	55.00	85.00	140	—
1630 (b)	26,000	27.00	55.00	85.00	140	—
163Z (b)	—	27.00	55.00	85.00	140	—
1634	1,280	27.00	55.00	85.00	140	—
1643 (b)	—	27.00	55.00	85.00	140	—
ND	—	27.00	55.00	85.00	140	—

KM# 30 KORTLING (6 Heller-3 Pfennig-1/4 Mariengroschen)

Copper **Obv:** Six-fold arms with that of Brandenburg in lower center **Obv. Legend:** MO. NO. EL. BRAND... **Rev:** Imperial orb with 6, around legend **Rev. Legend:** S. P. D. CO. M. RA. D. IN. R. (or variant) **Note:** Varieties exist.

Date	Mintage	VG	F	VF	XF	Unc
ND (b)	28,000	27.00	55.00	85.00	140	—
ND	Inc. above	27.00	55.00	85.00	140	—

KM# 35 MATTIER (1/2 Mariengroschen)

Silver **Obv:** Value: EIN/MATTH/IER. RAV/ENSPV/date **Rev:** Madonna and child **Rev. Legend:** MARIA. MA. DOMINI.

Date	Mintage	VG	F	VF	XF	Unc
1630 (b)	—	—	—	—	—	—

KM# 47 MATTIER (1/2 Mariengroschen)

Silver **Obv:** Value: EIN/MATIER/RAVEN/SPVRG/date

Date	Mintage	VG	F	VF	XF	Unc
164Z	—	—	—	—	—	—

KM# 55 MATTIER (1/2 Mariengroschen)

Silver **Obv:** Capped scepter divides date **Obv. Legend:** MO. NO. EL. BRAN... **Rev:** Value: EIN/MATIER/RAVENS/BURG **Note:** Varieties exist.

Date	Mintage	VG	F	VF	XF	Unc
1651	—	45.00	80.00	120	170	—
1652	—	45.00	80.00	120	170	—
1653	—	45.00	80.00	120	170	—
1660	—	45.00	80.00	120	170	—
1661	—	45.00	80.00	120	170	—
1664	—	45.00	80.00	120	170	—
1665	—	45.00	80.00	120	170	—

KM# 31 MARIENGROSCHEN (1/36 Thaler)

Silver **Obv:** Five-fold arms **Obv. Legend:** MO. NO. D. I. CLI. E. MO. C. RAV. **Rev:** Date, Madonna and child **Rev. Legend:** MARIA. MA. DOMIN **Note:** Varieties exist.

Date	Mintage	VG	F	VF	XF	Unc
1629 (b)	—	27.00	55.00	90.00	175	—
1630 (b)	13,000	27.00	55.00	90.00	175	—
1631 (b)	2,376	27.00	55.00	90.00	175	—
163Z (b)	3,564	27.00	55.00	90.00	175	—
1633 (b)	—	27.00	55.00	90.00	175	—
1634 (b)	7,000	27.00	55.00	90.00	175	—
ND (b)	11,000	27.00	55.00	90.00	175	—
ND	Inc. above	27.00	55.00	90.00	175	—

KM# 51 MARIENGROSCHEN (1/36 Thaler)

Silver **Obv:** Date in legend **Rev:** Date, Madonna and child **Rev. Legend:** MARIEN - GROSCHE **Note:** Varieties exist.

Date	Mintage	VG	F	VF	XF	Unc
1648	—	27.00	55.00	95.00	175	—
1653 (b)	—	27.00	55.00	95.00	175	—
1660 (b)	—	27.00	55.00	95.00	175	—
1661	—	27.00	55.00	95.00	175	—
1662	—	27.00	55.00	95.00	175	—
1663	—	27.00	55.00	95.00	175	—
1664	—	27.00	55.00	95.00	175	—

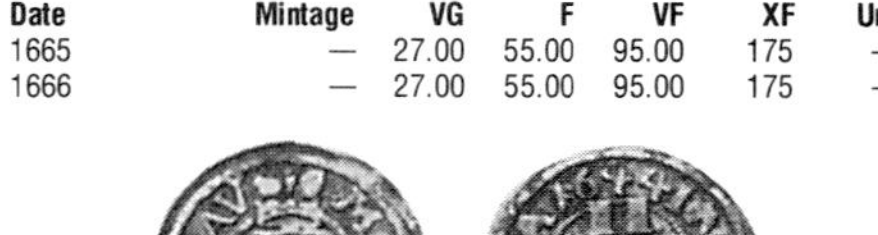

Date	Mintage	VG	F	VF	XF	Unc
1665	—	27.00	55.00	95.00	175	—
1666	—	27.00	55.00	95.00	175	—

KM# 48 2 MARIENGROSCHEN

Silver **Obv:** Crowned five-fold arms **Obv. Legend:** MO. NO... **Rev:** Date, value: II/MAR/GR. **Rev. Legend:** IN. DEO. SPE. MEA **Note:** Varieties exist.

Date	Mintage	VG	F	VF	XF	Unc
1644	—	20.00	40.00	75.00	125	—
1646	—	20.00	40.00	75.00	125	—

KM# 49 2 MARIENGROSCHEN

Silver **Rev:** Value: II/MAR/GRO/date **Rev. Legend:** S. P. D. CO. M. RA. D. IN. R. **Note:** Varieties exist.

Date	Mintage	VG	F	VF	XF	Unc
1647	—	20.00	40.00	75.00	125	—
1647 (b)	—	20.00	40.00	75.00	125	—
1649 (b)	—	20.00	40.00	75.00	125	—
1653	—	20.00	40.00	75.00	125	—
1664	—	20.00	40.00	75.00	125	—
1665	—	20.00	40.00	75.00	125	—
1666	—	20.00	40.00	75.00	125	—
1667	—	20.00	40.00	75.00	125	—
ND	—	20.00	40.00	75.00	125	—

KM# 56 2 MARIENGROSCHEN

Silver **Rev:** Date in legend

Date	Mintage	VG	F	VF	XF	Unc
1653	—	20.00	40.00	75.00	125	—

KM# 5 1/24 THALER (Reichsgroschen)

Silver **Ruler:** Johann Wilhelm, Herzog von Jülich-Kleve-Berg **Obv:** Five-fold arms, three helmets above, small shield of Ravensberg at bottom **Obv. Legend:** DEVS. REF(V)-(V)GIVM. ME(V)(M) **Rev:** Imperial orb with Z4, cross above divides date **Rev. Legend:** MO. NO. DVC. IVL. CL(I). ET. MO(N). **Mint:** Bielefeld **Note:** Varieties exist.

Date	Mintage	VG	F	VF	XF	Unc
1601 (a)	30,916	16.00	30.00	45.00	120	—
160Z (a)	26,992	16.00	30.00	45.00	120	—
1603 (a)	30,688	16.00	30.00	45.00	120	—
1604 (a)	6,160	16.00	30.00	45.00	120	—
1605 (a)	21,616	16.00	30.00	45.00	120	—
1606 (a)	20,584	16.00	30.00	45.00	120	—
1607 (a)	8,516	16.00	30.00	45.00	120	—
1608 (a)	11,200	16.00	30.00	45.00	120	—
1609 (a)	7,840	16.00	30.00	45.00	120	—

KM# 15 1/24 THALER (Reichsgroschen)

Silver **Rev:** Date divided in legend at top **Note:** Varieties exist.

Date	Mintage	VG	F	VF	XF	Unc
1618	—	—	—	—	—	—

KM# A16 1/24 THALER (Reichsgroschen)

Silver, 19 mm. **Obv:** 5-fold arms, 3 helmets above **Obv. Legend:** DEVS. REFVGIVM. ME. **Rev:** Imperial orb with Z4 **Rev. Legend:** MONOIVLCLI ET M. **Mint:** Bielefeld **Note:** Klipper coinage.

Date	Mintage	F	VF	XF	Unc	BU
ND(1620-3)	—	—	—	—	—	—

KM# 28 1/24 THALER (Reichsgroschen)

Silver **Ruler:** Georg Wilhelm of Brandenburg-Prussia **Obv:** 5-fold arms, 3 helmets above **Obv. Legend:** DEVS. REFVG. ME. **Rev:** Imperial orb with Z4 **Rev. Legend:** MO NO IVL CLI ET M. **Note:** Kipper coinage.

Date	Mintage	F	VF	XF	Unc	BU
ND(1622-23)	—	—	—	—	—	—

KM# 32 1/24 THALER (Reichsgroschen)

Silver **Obv:** Imperial orb with Z4, cross divides date, titles of Ferdinand II **Rev:** Crowned 8-fold arms with central shield of Pfalz, titles of Wolfgang Wilhelm **Note:** Gute 1/24 Thaler. Varieties exist.

Date	Mintage	VG	F	VF	XF	Unc
16Z9 (b)	—	16.00	33.00	50.00	115	—
1630 (b)	6,000	16.00	33.00	50.00	115	—
1631 (b)	5,000	16.00	33.00	50.00	115	—
1632 (b)	8,000	16.00	33.00	50.00	115	—
1635 (b)	—	16.00	33.00	50.00	115	—
1635	—	16.00	33.00	50.00	115	—
1636	23,000	16.00	33.00	50.00	115	—
1637	11,000	16.00	33.00	50.00	115	—
1638 (b)	—	16.00	33.00	50.00	115	—
ND	—	16.00	33.00	50.00	115	—

KM# 39 1/24 THALER (Reichsgroschen)

Silver **Obv:** Crowned arms within circle **Rev:** Titles of Ferdinand III

Date	Mintage	VG	F	VF	XF	Unc
1639 (b)	—	40.00	80.00	140	225	—

KM# 8 1/4 THALER (Reichsort-Ortstaler-Orter)

Silver **Obv:** Half-length bust of Johann Wilhelm right, holding mace **Rev:** Five-fold arms, three helmets above, small shield of Ravensberg arms at bottom, date divided in legend at upper left and top

Date	Mintage	VG	F	VF	XF	Unc
(1)608 (a)	—	—	—	—	—	—

KM# 6 THALER

Silver **Obv:** Johann Wilhelm **Rev:** Helmeted arms **Note:** Dav. #7293.

Date	Mintage	VG	F	VF	XF	Unc
1603 (a)	22,000	1,100	2,000	3,500	6,000	—
1604 (a)	26,000	1,100	2,000	3,500	6,000	—
1608 (a)	10,000	1,100	2,000	3,500	6,000	—
1609 (a)	4,000	1,100	2,000	3,500	6,000	—

KM# 9 THALER

Silver **Note:** Dav. #7293A.

Date	Mintage	VG	F	VF	XF	Unc
1608 (a) Rare	—	—	—	—	—	—

KM# 36 THALER

Silver **Obv. Legend:** WOLFG. WIL...; inner legend: IN DEO-MEA CONSOLA **Note:** Similar to KM#Pn1. Dav. #7294.

Date	Mintage	VG	F	VF	XF	Unc
1630 (b) Rare	352	—	—	—	—	—
1632 (b) Rare	480	—	—	—	—	—

Note: Fritz Rudolf Künker Münzenhandlung Auction 93, 6-04 nearly XF realized approximately $14,510

Date	Mintage	VG	F	VF	XF	Unc
1633 (b) Rare	200	—	—	—	—	—

KM# 38 THALER

Silver **Obv:** New bust right **Obv. Legend:** Inner: IN DEO MEA-CONSOLA **Rev:** Decoration around shield changed **Note:** Varieties in punctuation exist. Dav. #7295.

Date	Mintage	VG	F	VF	XF	Unc
1638 (b) Rare	—	—	—	—	—	—
1640 (b) Rare	—	—	—	—	—	—

Note: Fritz Rudolf Künker Münzenhandlung Auction 93, 6-04, VF realized approximately $7,860

KM# 45 THALER

Silver **Obv:** New bust right, without inner circle between legends **Rev:** Crowned arms without inner circle **Note:** Dav. #7296.

Date	Mintage	VG	F	VF	XF	Unc
1641 (b)	—	1,500	3,000	5,000	—	—

KM# 46 THALER

Silver **Obv:** New bust right **Rev:** Less shield decoration **Note:** Dav. #7297.

Date	Mintage	VG	F	VF	XF	Unc
1641 (b) Rare	—	—	—	—	—	—
1642 (b) Rare	—	—	—	—	—	—

KM# 10 1-1/2 THALER

Silver **Note:** Similar to 1 Thaler, KM#6 but Klippe. Dav. #7292.

Date	Mintage	VG	F	VF	XF	Unc
1608 (b) Rare	—	—	—	—	—	—

KM# 7 2 THALER

Silver **Note:** Similar to 1 Thaler, KM#6 but Klippe. Dav. #7291. Illustration reduced.

Date	Mintage	VG	F	VF	XF	Unc
1604 (a) Rare	—	—	—	—	—	—
1608 (a) Rare	—	—	—	—	—	—

TRADE COINAGE

KM# 37 GOLDGULDEN

3.5000 g., 0.9860 Gold 0.1109 oz. AGW **Obv:** Bust right, date below **Rev:** Without order chain

Date	Mintage	VG	F	VF	XF	Unc
1631 Rare	324	—	—	—	—	—

KM# 40 DUCAT

3.5000 g., 0.9860 Gold 0.1109 oz. AGW **Obv:** Crowned eight-fold arms with central shield of Pfalz, chain of Order around **Rev:** DVCATVS/NOVVS. RAVENS/BVR; date in ornamented square

Date	Mintage	VG	F	VF	XF	Unc
1639 Rare	—	—	—	—	—	—

KM# 50 DUCAT

3.5000 g., 0.9860 Gold 0.1109 oz. AGW **Obv:** Five-fold arms with central shield of Brandenburg scepter, large electoral hat above, titles of Friedrich Wilhelm **Rev:** DUCATUS/NOVUS. COM/RAVENS/BERG date **Note:** Varieties exist.

Date	Mintage	VG	F	VF	XF	Unc
1647 Rare	—	—	—	—	—	—
1648 Rare	—	—	—	—	—	—

KM# 52 DUCAT
3.5000 g., 0.9860 Gold 0.1109 oz. AGW **Obv:** Bust right, titles of Friedrich Wilhelm **Rev:** 5-fold arms with central Brandenburg scepter divide date and elector's titles continued

Date	Mintage	VG	F	VF	XF	Unc
1648 Rare	—	—	—	—	—	—

PATTERNS

Including off metal strikes

KM#	Date	Mintage	Identification	Mkt Val
Pn1	1632	—	Thaler. Pewter. Dav. #7294.	100

RAVENSBURG

(Ravenspurg)

Not to be confused with Ravensberg in Westphalia, Ravensburg is located some 13 miles (22 kilometers) north of Lake Constance in lower Swabia. The earliest structures of the city fortifications date from about 750. The city takes its name from the old German personal name Ravan, that is Rabe in modern German, meaning raven or crow, but who this actually refers to is lost to history. By the middle of the 11th century, Ravensburg was a growing town and received the right to hold markets early in the 12th century. Although Ravensburg is mentioned as the site of an imperial mint in the 12th century, then as a mint for the bishops of Constance early in the next century, it did not receive the mint right for municipal coinage until the 14th century. The first city coinages known date from the later 1300s. Ravensburg had been elevated to the rank of an imperial city in 1276. From the inception of its coinage until the early 18th century, Ravensburg produced intermittent issue of coins. The city also had a short-lived joint coinage with Ulm and Überlingen in the early 16th century (see the latter for these). During the Napoleonic Wars, Ravensburg was annexed by Bavaria in 1803 and transferred to Württemberg in 1810.

MINT OFFICIALS' INITIALS

Bielefeld

Initial	Date	Name
DS	1620-1625	Daniel Sailer, die-cutter in Augsburg
	1622	Konrad Beck
	1693	Daniel Sommer

ARMS

City gate with two crenelated towers.

FREE CITY

REGULAR COINAGE

KM# 15 PFENNIG (1/4 Kreuzer)
Copper **Obv:** Uniface: city arms, '4' above.

Date	Mintage	VG	F	VF	XF	Unc
ND (ca1693)	—	13.00	33.00	55.00	100	—

KM# 28 KREUZER (4 Pfennig)
Silver **Obv:** City arms in baroque frame **Rev:** Crowned imperial eagle, 'K' in oval on breast

Date	Mintage	VG	F	VF	XF	Unc
1700	—	30.00	65.00	125	220	—

REGENSBURG

(Ratisbon)

Regensburg is located in Bavaria. Coinage was first struck jointly with the dukes of Bavaria beginning in the 10th century then later on its own. It was secularized in 1810 and ceded to Bavaria.

MINTMASTERS' INITIALS

Initial	Date	Name
HF	1653-73	Hieronymus Federer
MF	1673-1700	Michael Federer
Cinquefoil	1635-37	Christoph Leinmuth
Wing	1639-53	Hans Siegmund Federer
3 ears of grain	1637-38	Hans Putzer
Hat	1623-34	Balthasar Ziegler
Fleur-de-lis	1639-40	Unknown
	1598-ca. 1619	Haubold Lehner

WARDENS

Date	Name
1586-1604	Georg Fraisslich
1637-?	Hans Putzer
1660-85	Friedrich Hungar
1688-?	Johann Gottlieb Stotz
1700-18	Johann Georg Kramer

DIE-CUTTERS and ENGRAVERS

Date	Name
1626	Christoph Pessle
1633	Georg Thomas Paur
1660	Ulrich Gravenauer
1663-89	Georg Sigmundt Renz
1690	Tobias Pannesperger
1691-1706	Johann Adam Seitz

BISHOPRIC

The town of Regensburg, located on the Danube River in Bavaria about 35 miles (57km) northeast of Ingolstadt, became the seat of a bishopric in 470. The first coins of the bishops were joint issues with the dukes of Bavaria from the mid-10th century. In the 11th century, independent episcopal coinage made its appearance. Most of the bishops were members of the local Bavarian nobility. Karl Theodor von Dalberg, the last one with territorial control transferred those lands to Bavaria in 1810, having been raised to the rank of archbishop in 1805. He was given Frankfurt am Main in exchange by Napoleon, who made him a grand duke as well. When Napoleon lost his empire, the bishop was left with only his ecclesiastic title as archbishop of Regensburg.

RULERS

Wolfgang II von Hausen, 1600-1613
Albrecht IV von Törring, 1613-1649
Franz Wilhelm von Wartenberg, 1649-1661
Johann Georg von Herberstein, 1661-1663
Adam Lorenz von Törring, 1663-1666
Guidobald von Thun-Hohnstein, 1666-1668
Albrecht Sigmund, Herzog von Bayern, 1668-1685
Josef Clemens, Herzog von Bayern, 1685-1716

ARMS

Bishopric – diagonal band from upper left to lower right
Bergstall – 2-fold, 2 weapons hurlers, forepart of camel
Pappenheim – 6 monks' hoods, 3 above 2 above 1, also – 2 crossed swoards for hereditary office of Marshall of the Empire
Sinzenhof – 6 pie-slice shaped segments, points meeting in center, every other one shaded

REFERENCE

E/K = Hubert Emmerig and Otto Kozinowski, **Die Münzen und Medaillen der Regensburger Bishöfe und des Domkapitels seit dem 16. Jahrhundert**, Stuttgart, 1998.

REGULAR COINAGE

KM# 25 THALER
Silver **Obv:** 5-line inscription **Obv. Inscription:** ALBERTVS / .G.D. / EPISCOBVS / RATISBON / ENSIS. **Rev:** Date in inner circle at center of star **Note:** Dav. #5739.

Date	Mintage	VG	F	VF	XF	Unc
1621	—	1,000	2,000	4,000	7,000	—

KM# 144 THALER
Silver **Note:** Similar to KM#145 but with date divided 1-6-5-7 above arms, rosette below arms. Dav. #5740.

Date	Mintage	VG	F	VF	XF	Unc
1657	—	2,500	5,000	8,000	—	—
ND	—	2,500	5,000	8,000	—	—

KM# 145 THALER
Silver **Obv:** Franz Wilhelm **Rev:** Without date above and rosette below arms **Note:** Dav. #5740A.

Date	Mintage	VG	F	VF	XF	Unc
ND	—	2,750	5,500	8,500	—	—

KM# 168 THALER
Silver **Obv:** Capped bust **Rev:** Bishop's cap above oval arms **Note:** Dav. #5741.

Date	Mintage	VG	F	VF	XF	Unc
1661	—	1,500	2,900	5,000	8,100	—

FREE CITY

The site of Regensburg was settled before the arrival of the Romans, who called the place Ratisbona. After the establishment of a bishopric there in the 5th century, the town was also the chief residence of the early dukes of Bavaria. From the 10th century through the early 13th century, Regensburg contained a mint which produced coins for the dukes and bishops. Regensburg was elevated to a free imperial city in 1180 and obtained the mint right in 1230. A long series of issues dating from 1508 and continuing into the early 19th century ensued.

Regensburg was the site of the Imperial Diet (Reichstag) or Parliament, which met continuously in the Reichssaal of the city hall from 1663 until 1806, when Napoleon dissolved the Holy Roman Empire. The opening of each year's session, attended by the emperor in person, all the secular princes and ecclesiastic rulers of the empire, was a source of great pride and prestige for the city. However, Regensburg lost its independence and was handed over to the bishop in 1803. It came into the possession of Bavaria, along with the bishopric, in 1810.

REGULAR COINAGE

KM# 34 HELLER
Copper **Obv:** Regensburg arms in square **Rev:** .1.

Date	Mintage	VG	F	VF	XF	Unc
ND(1622-23)	—	33.00	80.00	125	175	—

KM# 33 HELLER
Copper **Obv:** Regensburg arms in square **Rev:** "R" in circle of pellets **Note:** Kipper Heller.

Date	Mintage	VG	F	VF	XF	Unc
ND(1622-23)	—	20.00	45.00	80.00	125	—

KM# 192 HELLER
Copper **Note:** Diamond-shaped with rounded corners, Regensburg arms divide date, R above, H below.

Date	Mintage	VG	F	VF	XF	Unc
1677	—	7.00	16.00	27.00	55.00	—
1679	159,000	7.00	16.00	27.00	55.00	—
1681	190,000	7.00	16.00	27.00	55.00	—
1682	374,000	7.00	16.00	27.00	55.00	—
1684	296,000	7.00	16.00	27.00	55.00	—
1686	147,000	7.00	16.00	27.00	55.00	—
1687	210,000	7.00	16.00	27.00	55.00	—
1689	289,000	7.00	16.00	27.00	55.00	—
1691	178,000	7.00	16.00	27.00	55.00	—
1692	314,000	7.00	16.00	27.00	55.00	—
1693	336,000	7.00	16.00	27.00	55.00	—
1694	445,000	7.00	16.00	27.00	55.00	—
1695	226,000	7.00	16.00	27.00	55.00	—
1696	605,000	7.00	16.00	27.00	55.00	—
1697	—	7.00	16.00	27.00	55.00	—
1698	411,000	7.00	16.00	27.00	55.00	—
1699	371,000	7.00	16.00	27.00	55.00	—
1700	380,000	7.00	16.00	27.00	55.00	—

KM# 10 PFENNING (1/84 Gulden)
Silver **Obv:** Regensburg arms in ornamented shield **Rev:** Imperial orb with 84 in baroque frame divides date **Note:** Varieties exist.

Date	Mintage	VG	F	VF	XF	Unc
1611	—	33.00	80.00	125	175	—
1613	—	33.00	80.00	125	175	—
ND	—	27.00	60.00	100	160	—

KM# 26 PFENNING (1/84 Gulden)

Billon **Note:** Kipper Pfenning. Uniface. Regensburg arms, "R" above, date below.

Date	Mintage	VG	F	VF	XF	Unc
16Z1	—	27.00	60.00	100	160	—

KM# 26a PFENNING (1/84 Gulden)

Copper **Note:** Uniface.

Date	Mintage	VG	F	VF	XF	Unc
16ZZ	—	20.00	45.00	80.00	125	—

KM# 37 PFENNING (1/84 Gulden)

Silver **Note:** Uniface. Regensburg arms in ornamented shield, date above.

Date	Mintage	VG	F	VF	XF	Unc
1623	—	9.00	16.00	33.00	60.00	—

KM# 42 PFENNING (1/84 Gulden)

Silver **Note:** Regensburg arms in plain shield, date above.

Date	Mintage	VG	F	VF	XF	Unc
1624	—	9.00	16.00	33.00	60.00	—
1625	—	9.00	16.00	33.00	60.00	—
1626	—	9.00	16.00	33.00	60.00	—

KM# 53 PFENNING (1/84 Gulden)

Silver **Note:** Regensburg arms in baroque cartouche-like shield, date above.

Date	Mintage	VG	F	VF	XF	Unc
1627	—	9.00	16.00	33.00	60.00	—
1628	—	9.00	16.00	33.00	60.00	—
1629	—	9.00	16.00	33.00	60.00	—

KM# 60 PFENNING (1/84 Gulden)

Silver **Note:** Date divided at top by ornament.

Date	Mintage	VG	F	VF	XF	Unc
1629	—	9.00	16.00	33.00	60.00	—
1631	—	9.00	16.00	33.00	60.00	—

KM# 92 PFENNING (1/84 Gulden)

Silver **Note:** Regensburg arms in oval baroque frame, date divided above by ornament. Varieties exist.

Date	Mintage	VG	F	VF	XF	Unc
1639	—	9.00	16.00	33.00	60.00	—
1640	—	9.00	16.00	33.00	60.00	—
1641	—	12.00	20.00	40.00	75.00	—
1642	—	12.00	20.00	40.00	75.00	—
1644	—	12.00	20.00	40.00	75.00	—
1647	—	9.00	16.00	33.00	60.00	—

KM# 125 PFENNING (1/84 Gulden)

Silver **Note:** Regensburg arms in heart-shaped shield, date divided above.

Date	Mintage	VG	F	VF	XF	Unc
1651	—	9.00	16.00	33.00	60.00	—
1652	—	9.00	16.00	33.00	60.00	—

KM# 132 PFENNING (1/84 Gulden)

Silver **Note:** Mintmaster's initials below shield

Date	Mintage	VG	F	VF	XF	Unc
1653 HF	—	9.00	16.00	33.00	60.00	—
1656 HF	—	9.00	16.00	33.00	60.00	—

KM# 169 PFENNING (1/84 Gulden)

Silver **Note:** Regensburg arms in rhombus, date divided to upper left and right.

Date	Mintage	VG	F	VF	XF	Unc
1660	—	12.00	20.00	40.00	75.00	—
1661	—	9.00	16.00	33.00	60.00	—

KM# 175 PFENNING (1/84 Gulden)

Silver **Note:** Regensburg arms in heart-shaped shield, date above. Varieties exist.

Date	Mintage	VG	F	VF	XF	Unc
1665	—	8.00	13.00	27.00	55.00	—
1668	—	8.00	13.00	27.00	55.00	—
1673	—	8.00	13.00	27.00	55.00	—
1674	—	8.00	13.00	27.00	55.00	—
1677	—	8.00	13.00	27.00	55.00	—
1680	60,000	8.00	13.00	27.00	55.00	—
1684	—	8.00	13.00	27.00	55.00	—
1685	—	8.00	13.00	27.00	55.00	—
1687	57,000	8.00	13.00	27.00	55.00	—
1691	36,000	8.00	13.00	27.00	55.00	—

KM# 200 PFENNING (1/84 Gulden)

Silver **Note:** Regensburg arms in oval baroque frame, date above.

Date	Mintage	VG	F	VF	XF	Unc
1693	78,000	12.00	20.00	40.00	75.00	—

KM# 201 PFENNING (1/84 Gulden)

Silver **Note:** Regensburg arms in wreath-like frame, date above.

Date	Mintage	VG	F	VF	XF	Unc
1693	Inc. above	9.00	16.00	33.00	60.00	—

KM# 204 PFENNING (1/84 Gulden)

Silver **Note:** Regensburg arms in frame of two joined ovals, date above.

Date	Mintage	VG	F	VF	XF	Unc
1696	—	9.00	16.00	33.00	60.00	—

KM# 100 1/2 KREUZER (2 Pfennig)

Silver **Note:** Uniface. Regensburg arms in heart-shaped frame, value: 1/2 in oval above divides date. Varieties exist.

Date	Mintage	VG	F	VF	XF	Unc
1640	—	11.00	20.00	33.00	60.00	—
1641	—	9.00	16.00	27.00	55.00	—
1644	—	9.00	16.00	27.00	55.00	—
1645	—	9.00	16.00	27.00	55.00	—
1646	—	9.00	16.00	27.00	55.00	—
1647	—	11.00	20.00	33.00	60.00	—
1651	—	11.00	20.00	33.00	60.00	—
1652	—	11.00	20.00	33.00	60.00	—
1653	—	11.00	20.00	33.00	60.00	—

KM# 112 1/2 KREUZER (2 Pfennig)

Silver **Note:** Imperial eagle, Regensburg arms in shield on breast, all in rhombus, value: 1/2 in circle at top, date divided at upper left and right.

Date	Mintage	VG	F	VF	XF	Unc
1647	—	13.00	27.00	45.00	75.00	—

KM# 133 1/2 KREUZER (2 Pfennig)

Silver **Note:** Regensburg arms in cartouche, value: 1/2 in circle above divides date.

Date	Mintage	VG	F	VF	XF	Unc
1653	—	11.00	20.00	33.00	60.00	—

KM# 156 1/2 KREUZER (2 Pfennig)

Silver **Note:** Similar to KM#133, but mintmaster's initials at bottom.

Date	Mintage	VG	F	VF	XF	Unc
1659 HF	—	9.00	16.00	27.00	55.00	—
1666 HF	—	9.00	16.00	27.00	55.00	—

KM# 190 1/2 KREUZER (2 Pfennig)

Silver **Note:** Similar to KM#100, but heart-shaped more defined, bottom closed. Varieties exist.

Date	Mintage	VG	F	VF	XF	Unc
1674	—	11.00	20.00	33.00	60.00	—
1680	—	11.00	20.00	33.00	60.00	—
1690	—	11.00	20.00	33.00	60.00	—

KM# 205 1/2 KREUZER (2 Pfennig)

Silver **Obv:** Regensburg arms in cartouche, value: 1/2 in ornament above divides date **Note:** Uniface

Date	Mintage	VG	F	VF	XF	Unc
1696	—	8.00	16.00	33.00	60.00	—

Note: 1/2 Kreuzer dated 1696 reported struck in 1696, 1701 and 1734; Mintage reported only in latter year at 6,048 pieces

KM# 206 1/2 KREUZER (2 Pfennig)

Silver **Note:** Regensburg arms with value: 1/2 above in baroque frame, initial below.

Date	Mintage	VG	F	VF	XF	Unc
ND B	—	16.00	27.00	55.00	90.00	—

KM# 28 KREUZER

Billon **Rev:** Double cross (x on ++), value I in shield in center

Date	Mintage	VG	F	VF	XF	Unc
1621	—	13.00	30.00	60.00	100	—
1622	—	13.00	30.00	60.00	100	—

KM# 27 KREUZER

Billon **Obv:** Regensburg arms in ornamented shield, date above **Rev:** Imperial orb in ornamented shield **Note:** Kipper Kreuzer.

Date	Mintage	VG	F	VF	XF	Unc
1621	—	27.00	80.00	120	185	—

KM# 36 KREUZER

Billon **Obv:** Regensburg arms in ornate shield **Rev:** R in shield superimposed on cross

Date	Mintage	VG	F	VF	XF	Unc
ND(1622-23)	—	16.00	33.00	65.00	115	—

KM# 38 KREUZER

Billon **Obv:** Regensburg arms in ornamented shield, date above **Rev:** Imperial eagle, shield on breast with I **Note:** Varieties exist.

Date	Mintage	VG	F	VF	XF	Unc
1623	—	11.00	20.00	33.00	60.00	—
1624	—	11.00	20.00	33.00	60.00	—
1625	—	11.00	20.00	33.00	60.00	—
1626	—	11.00	20.00	33.00	60.00	—

KM# 54 KREUZER

Billon **Obv:** Crowned imperial eagle, value: I in shield on breast **Rev:** Regensburg arms in rounded shield, date divided by ornament at top **Note:** Varieties exist.

Date	Mintage	VG	F	VF	XF	Unc
1627	—	12.00	25.00	45.00	80.00	—
1628	—	11.00	20.00	33.00	60.00	—
1631	—	11.00	20.00	33.00	60.00	—
1637 (b)	—	12.00	25.00	45.00	80.00	—

KM# 93 KREUZER

Billon **Obv:** Regensburg arms in oval baroque frame, date divided by ornament above **Rev:** Double-headed imperial eagle, orb on breast **Note:** Varieties exist.

Date	Mintage	VG	F	VF	XF	Unc
1639	—	11.00	20.00	33.00	60.00	—
1640	—	11.00	20.00	33.00	60.00	—
1641	—	11.00	20.00	33.00	60.00	—
1642	—	11.00	20.00	33.00	60.00	—
1643	—	11.00	20.00	33.00	60.00	—
1644	—	11.00	20.00	33.00	60.00	—
1645	—	11.00	20.00	33.00	60.00	—
1646	—	11.00	20.00	33.00	60.00	—
1647	—	11.00	20.00	33.00	60.00	—
1648	—	11.00	20.00	33.00	60.00	—
1649	—	11.00	20.00	33.00	60.00	—
1650	—	11.00	20.00	33.00	60.00	—
1651	—	11.00	20.00	33.00	60.00	—
1652	—	11.00	20.00	33.00	60.00	—
1653	—	11.00	20.00	33.00	60.00	—
1655 HF	—	11.00	20.00	33.00	60.00	—

KM# 116 KREUZER

Billon **Obv:** Crowned imperial eagle, value: I in orb on breast, titles of Ferdinand III **Rev:** Legend, date **Rev. Legend:** MONE... **Note:** Varieties exist.

Date	Mintage	VG	F	VF	XF	Unc
1648	—	9.00	16.00	27.00	55.00	—
1649	—	11.00	20.00	33.00	60.00	—

KM# 126 KREUZER

Billon **Obv:** Crowned imperial eagle, arms of austria on breast **Rev:** Regensburg arms in baroque frame, divide date, value: I above

Date	Mintage	VG	F	VF	XF	Unc
1651	—	11.00	20.00	33.00	60.00	—

KM# 176 KREUZER

Billon **Obv:** Heart-shaped cartouche encloses arms, date above **Rev:** Crowned imperial eagle, value: I in shield on breast **Note:** Varieties exist.

Date	Mintage	VG	F	VF	XF	Unc
1665 HF	—	9.00	20.00	40.00	80.00	—
1680 HF	—	9.00	20.00	40.00	80.00	—
1691 HF	—	9.00	20.00	40.00	80.00	—
1693 HF	6,600	9.00	20.00	40.00	80.00	—
1696 HF	—	9.00	20.00	40.00	80.00	—

KM# 40 2 KREUZER (Halbbatzen)

Silver **Note:** Klippe.

Date	Mintage	VG	F	VF	XF	Unc
1623	—	110	165	240	350	—

KM# 39 2 KREUZER (Halbbatzen)

Silver **Obv:** Regensburg arms in plain shield, date above **Obv. Legend:** MONE... **Rev:** Crowned imperial eagle, Z in shield on breast **Rev. Legend:** DA. PACEM... **Note:** Varieties exist.

Date	Mintage	VG	F	VF	XF	Unc
1623	—	9.00	20.00	40.00	80.00	—
1624	—	9.00	20.00	40.00	80.00	—
1625	—	9.00	20.00	40.00	80.00	—

KM# 46 2 KREUZER (Halbbatzen)

Silver **Obv:** Arms in cartouche, date in legend **Rev:** Crowned double-headed imperial eagle **Note:** Varieties exist.

Date	Mintage	VG	F	VF	XF	Unc
1626	—	13.00	30.00	55.00	90.00	—
1627	—	13.00	30.00	55.00	90.00	—
1628	—	9.00	20.00	40.00	80.00	—
1629	—	9.00	20.00	40.00	80.00	—
1630	—	9.00	20.00	40.00	80.00	—
1631	—	9.00	20.00	40.00	80.00	—

KM# 45 2 KREUZER (Halbbatzen)

Silver **Obv:** Value: 2 in shield **Rev:** Ornamented shield

Date	Mintage	VG	F	VF	XF	Unc
1626	—	13.00	30.00	55.00	90.00	—

KM# 72 2 KREUZER (Halbbatzen)

Silver **Obv:** Z in circle on eagle's breast

Date	Mintage	VG	F	VF	XF	Unc
1631	—	12.00	24.00	45.00	85.00	—

KM# 73 2 KREUZER (Halbbatzen)

Silver **Obv:** Z in imperial orb on breast **Note:** Varieties exist.

Date	Mintage	VG	F	VF	XF	Unc
1632	—	12.00	24.00	45.00	85.00	—
1633	—	12.00	24.00	45.00	85.00	—
1634	—	12.00	24.00	45.00	85.00	—

KM# 80 2 KREUZER (Halbbatzen)

Silver **Obv:** Mintmaster's symbol in heart-shaped cartouche at bottom **Rev:** Crowned double-headed eagle, value in orb on breast

Date	Mintage	VG	F	VF	XF	Unc
1634 (a)	—	13.00	30.00	55.00	90.00	—

Note: Struck in 1635-37

KM# 81 2 KREUZER (Halbbatzen)

Silver **Rev:** Mintmaster's symbol at top

Date	Mintage	VG	F	VF	XF	Unc
1634 (b)	—	16.00	33.00	60.00	110	—

Note: Struck in 1637-38

KM# 82 2 KREUZER (Halbbatzen)

Silver **Rev:** Mintmaster's symbol at bottom

Date	Mintage	VG	F	VF	XF	Unc
1634 (c)	—	15.00	33.00	55.00	100	—

Note: Struck in 1639-40

KM# 165 2 KREUZER (Halbbatzen)

Silver **Obv:** Regensburg arms in oval baroque frame, date in legend **Rev:** Crowned imperial eagle, value: 2 in circle on breast **Rev. Legend:** SERVA. NOBIS...

Date	Mintage	VG	F	VF	XF	Unc
1660	—	20.00	45.00	80.00	125	—

KM# 171 2 KREUZER (Halbbatzen)

Silver **Obv:** Value: 2 on breast, imperial orb

Date	Mintage	VG	F	VF	XF	Unc
1663	—	20.00	40.00	75.00	120	—

KM# 184 2 KREUZER (Halbbatzen)

Silver **Rev:** Heart-shaped arms **Note:** Varieties exist.

Date	Mintage	VG	F	VF	XF	Unc
1668 HF	—	16.00	33.00	65.00	115	—
1680 MF	—	16.00	33.00	65.00	115	—
1694 MF	31,000	16.00	33.00	65.00	115	—

KM# 17 10 KREUZER (1/6 Guldenthaler)

Silver **Obv:** City arms in ornate frame divide date **Obv. Legend:** MONETA. REIPVBLICÆ. RATISBONENSIS. **Rev:** Crowned imperial eagle, orb with '10' on breast **Rev. Legend:** MATHIÆ. ROM. IMP. AVG. P. F. DECRETO.

Date	Mintage	VG	F	VF	XF	Unc
(16)19	—	125	220	320	500	—

KM# 11 30 KREUZER (1/2 Guldenthaler)

Silver **Obv:** Regensburg arms in shield **Rev:** Crowned imperial eagle, 30 in orb on breast, titles of Matthias

Date	Mintage	VG	F	VF	XF	Unc
1613	—	500	825	1,200	1,800	—
ND	—	275	550	950	1,350	—

KM# 29 30 KREUZER (1/2 Guldenthaler)

Silver **Obv:** Titles of Ferdinand II

Date	Mintage	VG	F	VF	XF	Unc
(16)Z1	—	500	825	1,200	1,800	—

KM# 70 30 KREUZER (1/2 Guldenthaler)

Silver **Obv:** Oval Regensburg arms in baroque frame, angel above, date in legend **Rev:** Crowned double-headed imperial eagle, value in orb on breast

Date	Mintage	VG	F	VF	XF	Unc
1630	—	2,200	2,800	4,000	5,750	—

KM# 47 1/9 THALER

Silver **Obv:** Crowned imperial eagle, arms of Austria on breast, titles of Ferdinand II **Rev:** Regensburg arms, angel above, value: 1/9 in oval below, date in legend

Date	Mintage	VG	F	VF	XF	Unc
1626	—	200	375	600	825	—

KM# 61 1/9 THALER

Silver **Obv:** Crowned imperial eagle in circle, value: 1/9 in circle on breast, titles of Ferdinand II and date in legend **Rev:** Regensburg arms in oval shield with point at bottom, angel above

Date	Mintage	VG	F	VF	XF	Unc
16Z9	—	220	400	625	875	—

KM# 86 1/9 THALER

Silver **Obv:** Crowned imperial eagle, value: 1/9 in oval at bottom, titles of Ferdinand III **Rev:** Oval Regensburg arms in baroque frame, angel's head above, date in legend **Note:** Varieties exist.

Date	Mintage	VG	F	VF	XF	Unc
1638	—	175	340	550	800	—
1641	—	180	375	600	825	—
1645	—	210	400	625	850	—
1646	—	180	375	600	825	—
1647	—	180	375	600	825	—

KM# 117 1/9 THALER

Silver **Obv:** Large crowned imperial eagle **Rev:** Without angel at top

Date	Mintage	VG	F	VF	XF	Unc
1648 (c)	—	180	375	600	825	—

KM# 139 1/9 THALER

Silver **Obv:** Regensburg arms in oval baroque frame, date in margin **Rev:** Crowned imperial eagle, value: 1/9 inorb on breast, titles of Ferdinand III **Note:** Varieties exist.

Date	Mintage	VG	F	VF	XF	Unc
1654 HF	—	180	375	600	825	—
1655 HF	—	180	375	600	825	—
1656 HF	—	180	375	600	825	—
1657 HF	—	180	375	600	825	—

KM# 146 1/9 THALER

Silver **Obv:** Titles of Leopold I **Note:** Varieties exist.

Date	Mintage	VG	F	VF	XF	Unc
1657	—	—	—	—	—	—

Note: Coin dated 1657, if it exists, would be a mule of obverse die for KM#139 and reverse die for KM#146; Reported, not confirmed

Date	Mintage	VG	F	VF	XF	Unc
1659 HF	—	185	375	600	825	—
1661 HF	—	185	375	600	825	—
1662 HF	—	185	375	600	825	—
1663 HF	—	185	375	600	825	—
1664 HF	—	185	375	600	825	—
1665 HF	—	185	375	600	825	—
1667 HF	—	185	375	600	825	—

KM# 48 1/6 THALER (1/4 Gulden)

Silver **Obv:** Crowned imperial eagle, arms of Austria on breast, titles of Ferdinand II **Rev:** Regensburg arms, angel above, value: 1/6 in oval below, date in legend

Date	Mintage	VG	F	VF	XF	Unc
1626	—	425	675	975	1,500	—
1627	—	425	675	975	1,500	—

KM# 55 1/6 THALER (1/4 Gulden)

Silver **Obv:** Crowned imperial eagle in circle, Austria arms on breast, value: 1/6 in oval below, titles of Ferdinand II **Rev:** Ornately-shaped Regensburg arms, angel above, date in legend

Date	Mintage	VG	F	VF	XF	Unc
1627	—	425	675	975	1,500	—
1628	—	325	575	800	1,250	—

KM# 87 1/6 THALER (1/4 Gulden)

Silver **Obv:** Value: 1/6 below eagle **Note:** Varieties exist.

Date	Mintage	VG	F	VF	XF	Unc
1638 (b)	—	325	575	800	1,250	—
1641 (c)	—	325	575	800	1,250	—

KM# 107 1/6 THALER (1/4 Gulden)

Silver **Obv:** Value: 1/6 in orb on eagle's breast **Note:** Varieties exist.

Date	Mintage	VG	F	VF	XF	Unc
1644 (c)	—	325	575	800	1,250	—
1645 (c)	—	325	575	800	1,250	—
1646 (c)	—	325	575	800	1,250	—
1647 (c)	—	325	575	800	1,250	—
1651 (c)	—	325	575	800	1,250	—

KM# 128 1/6 THALER (1/4 Gulden)

Silver **Obv:** Without angel's head above arms **Rev:** Crowned double-headed imperial eagle, value in orb on breast

Date	Mintage	VG	F	VF	XF	Unc
1652 (c)	—	500	800	1,150	1,650	—

KM# 134 1/6 THALER (1/4 Gulden)

Silver **Obv:** Without inner circle **Rev:** Without inner circle

Date	Mintage	VG	F	VF	XF	Unc
1653	—	325	575	800	1,250	—
1657 HF	—	260	450	700	1,175	—

KM# 140 1/6 THALER (1/4 Gulden)

Silver **Obv:** Enclosed in circle

Date	Mintage	VG	F	VF	XF	Unc
1654 HF	—	325	575	800	1,250	—
1656 HF	—	325	575	800	1,250	—

KM# 157 1/6 THALER (1/4 Gulden)

Silver **Obv:** Titles of Leopold I **Note:** Varieties exist.

Date	Mintage	VG	F	VF	XF	Unc
1659 HF	—	260	450	775	1,175	—
1662 HF	—	260	450	775	1,175	—
1663 HF	—	260	450	775	1,175	—
1664 HF	—	500	800	1,150	1,650	—

KM# 179 1/6 THALER (1/4 Gulden)

Silver **Rev:** Heart-shaped arms

Date	Mintage	VG	F	VF	XF	Unc
1667 HF	—	325	550	800	1,250	—
1680 MF	—	325	550	800	1,250	—

Note: 1680-dated coins struck from altered 1667 dies

KM# 49 1/4 THALER

Silver **Obv:** Crowned imperial eagle, arms of Austria on breast, titles of Ferdinand II **Rev:** Regensburg arms, angel above, value: 1/4 in oval below, date in legend

Date	Mintage	VG	F	VF	XF	Unc
1626	—	500	800	1,200	1,800	—

KM# 50 1/4 THALER

Silver **Obv:** Value: 1/4 on bottom, oval **Rev:** Ornately-shaped arms **Note:** Varieties exist.

Date	Mintage	VG	F	VF	XF	Unc
1626	—	425	675	1,000	1,400	—
1627	—	425	675	1,000	1,400	—
1628	—	425	675	1,000	1,400	—

KM# 88 1/4 THALER

Silver **Note:** Similar to 1/9 Thaler, KM#86, but value: 1/4 on obverse. Varieties exist.

Date	Mintage	VG	F	VF	XF	Unc
1638 (b)	—	500	800	1,200	1,800	—
1641 (c)	—	425	675	1,000	1,400	—
1642 (c)	—	425	675	1,000	1,400	—
1645 (c)	—	450	800	1,150	1,650	—
1646 (c)	—	450	800	1,150	1,650	—

KM# 108 1/4 THALER

Silver **Obv:** Ornate arms **Rev:** Crowned double-headed eagle, value in orb on breast

Date	Mintage	VG	F	VF	XF	Unc
1644 (c)	—	425	675	1,600	1,400	—
1646 (c)	—	450	800	1,150	1,650	—
1647 (c)	—	450	800	1,150	1,650	—

KM# 113 1/4 THALER
Silver **Obv:** Modified oval shield **Rev:** Heart-shaped shield with value on eagle's breast

Date	Mintage	VG	F	VF	XF	Unc
1647 (c)	—	500	800	1,200	1,800	—

KM# 129 1/4 THALER
Silver **Obv:** Ornate arms **Rev:** Crowned double-headed eagle, value in orb on breast **Note:** Varieties exist.

Date	Mintage	VG	F	VF	XF	Unc
1652 (c)	—	425	675	1,000	1,450	—
1654	—	425	675	1,000	1,450	—
1655	—	425	675	1,000	1,450	—

KM# 142 1/4 THALER
Silver **Obv:** Without inner circle **Rev:** Without inner circle

Date	Mintage	VG	F	VF	XF	Unc
1656 HF	—	425	675	1,000	1,450	—

KM# 147 1/4 THALER
Silver **Obv:** Ornate oval arms, date in legend **Rev:** Crowned double-headed imperial eagle, value in orb on breast

Date	Mintage	VG	F	VF	XF	Unc
1657 HF	—	425	675	1,000	1,450	—

KM# 158 1/4 THALER
Silver **Obv:** Value: 1/4 in orb, titles of Leopold I **Note:** Varieties exist.

Date	Mintage	VG	F	VF	XF	Unc
1660 HF	—	425	675	1,000	1,450	—
1661 HF	—	425	675	1,000	1,450	—
1662 HF	—	425	675	1,000	1,450	—
1663 HF	—	425	675	1,000	1,450	—
1664 HF	—	425	675	1,000	1,450	—

KM# 177 1/4 THALER
Silver **Obv:** Heart-shaped arms **Rev:** Heart-shaped shield on eagle's breast **Note:** Varieties exist.

Date	Mintage	VG	F	VF	XF	Unc
1665 HF	—	450	800	1,150	1,650	—
1666 HF	—	425	675	1,000	1,450	—
1667 HF	—	425	675	1,000	1,450	—
1672 HF	—	425	675	1,000	1,450	—
1680 HF	—	450	800	1,150	1,650	—

Note: 1680 dated coins struck from altered 1672 dies

KM# 202 1/4 THALER
Silver **Note:** Modified and more ornate oval shield of arms, date divided at top

Date	Mintage	VG	F	VF	XF	Unc
1694 MF	—	500	800	1,200	1,800	—

KM# 110 1/3 THALER (1/2 Gulden)
Silver **Note:** Similar to 1/4 Thaler, KM#113, but value: 1/3 in shield on breast.

Date	Mintage	VG	F	VF	XF	Unc
1646 (c)	—	725	1,200	1,600	2,000	—

KM# 130 1/3 THALER (1/2 Gulden)
Silver **Note:** Similar to 1/6 Thaler, KM#128, but value: 1/3 in orb.

Date	Mintage	VG	F	VF	XF	Unc
1652 (c)	—	725	1,200	1,600	2,000	—

KM# 141 1/3 THALER (1/2 Gulden)
Silver **Obv:** Ornate arms **Rev:** Crowned double-headed imperial eagle, value in orb on breast **Note:** Varieties exist.

Date	Mintage	VG	F	VF	XF	Unc
1654 HF	—	725	1,200	1,600	2,000	—
1655 HF	—	725	1,200	1,600	2,000	—
1656 HF	—	525	1,000	1,500	2,000	—
1657 HF	—	525	1,000	1,500	2,000	—

KM# 159 1/3 THALER (1/2 Gulden)
Silver **Obv:** Titles of Leopold I **Note:** Varieties exist.

Date	Mintage	VG	F	VF	XF	Unc
1659 HF	—	525	1,000	1,500	2,000	—
1663 HF	—	525	1,000	1,500	2,000	—
1664 HF	—	525	1,000	1,500	2,000	—
1666 HF	—	525	1,000	1,500	2,000	—

KM# 180 1/3 THALER (1/2 Gulden)
Silver **Note:** Similar to 1/4 Thaler, KM#177, but value: 1/3 in shield.

Date	Mintage	VG	F	VF	XF	Unc
1667 HF	—	450	900	1,450	1,850	—
1672 HF	—	525	1,000	1,500	2,000	—
1680 HF	—	525	1,000	1,500	2,000	—

Note: 1680 dated coins struck from altered 1672 dies

KM# 43 1/2 THALER
Silver **Obv:** Cherub above shield **Rev:** Double-headed imperial eagle, shield on breast **Note:** Similar to 1/4 Thaler, KM#50, but without indication of value.

Date	Mintage	VG	F	VF	XF	Unc
1625	—	425	675	1,000	1,450	—
1627	—	425	675	1,000	1,450	—

KM# 62 1/2 THALER
Silver **Rev:** Oval Regensburg arms in baroque frame

Date	Mintage	VG	F	VF	XF	Unc
1629	—	425	675	1,000	1,450	—

KM# 63 1/2 THALER
Silver **Obv:** Oval arms pointed at bottom **Rev:** Crowned double-headed imperial eagle, shield on breast

Date	Mintage	VG	F	VF	XF	Unc
1629	—	425	675	1,000	1,450	—

KM# 89 1/2 THALER
Silver **Obv:** Ornate arms **Rev:** Crowned double-headed imperial eagle, shield on breast, without indication of value

Date	Mintage	VG	F	VF	XF	Unc
1638 (b)	—	500	800	1,200	1,900	—
1639	—	500	1,000	1,375	2,000	—

KM# 101 1/2 THALER
Silver **Obv:** Ornate arms **Rev:** Crown above double-headed imperial eagle, shield on breast **Note:** Varieties exist.

Date	Mintage	VG	F	VF	XF	Unc
1640 (c)	—	550	1,000	1,375	2,000	—
1643 (c)	—	500	800	1,200	1,800	—

KM# 105 1/2 THALER
Silver **Obv:** Bust right, titles of Ferdinand III **Rev:** Date divided at top **Note:** Varieties exist.

Date	Mintage	VG	F	VF	XF	Unc
1644 (c)	—	500	800	1,200	1,800	—
1645 (c)	—	500	800	1,200	1,800	—
1646 (c)	—	425	675	1,000	1,450	—

KM# 114 1/2 THALER
Silver **Obv:** Ornate arms **Rev:** Value in shield on eagle's breast **Note:** Varieties exist.

Date	Mintage	VG	F	VF	XF	Unc
1647 (c)	—	525	850	1,250	2,000	—
1653 (c)	—	600	1,000	1,450	2,100	—
1654 HF	—	600	1,000	1,450	2,100	—

KM# 143 1/2 THALER
Silver **Obv:** Ornate arms **Rev:** Value in orb on breast

Date	Mintage	VG	F	VF	XF	Unc
1656 HF	—	500	800	1,200	1,800	—
1657 HF	—	500	800	1,200	1,800	—

KM# 148 1/2 THALER
Silver **Obv:** Arms of Austria on eagle's breast, without indication of value

Date	Mintage	VG	F	VF	XF	Unc
1657	—	—	—	—	—	—

Note: Reported, not confirmed

KM# 152 1/2 THALER
Silver **Obv:** Large ornate oval arms **Rev:** SVB VMBRA ALARUM TVARUM instead of emperor's titles

Date	Mintage	VG	F	VF	XF	Unc
1658 HF	—	1,600	2,100	2,800	3,500	—

KM# 166 1/2 THALER
Silver **Obv:** Ornate arms **Rev:** Value in orb on breast
Note: Varieties exist.

Date	Mintage	VG	F	VF	XF	Unc
1660 HF	—	500	800	1,200	1,800	—
1661 HF	—	500	800	1,200	1,800	—
1662 HF	—	475	800	1,150	1,700	—
1663 HF	—	475	800	1,150	1,700	—
1664 HF	—	475	800	1,150	1,700	—

KM# 178 1/2 THALER
Silver **Obv:** Heart-shaped ornate arms, cherub face and wings above **Rev:** Value in orb on breast **Note:** Varieties exist.

Date	Mintage	VG	F	VF	XF	Unc
1665 HF	—	475	800	1,150	1,650	—
1666/5 HF	—	475	800	1,150	1,650	—
1667 HF	—	475	800	1,150	1,650	—
1672 HF	—	475	800	1,150	1,650	—
1680 MF	—	500	800	1,200	1,800	—

Note: Struck from altered 1672 dies

Date	Mintage	VG	F	VF	XF	Unc
1691 MF	—	500	900	1,350	2,000	—
1694 MF	1,245	475	800	1,150	1,650	—

Note: Struck from altered 1672 dies

KM# 207 1/2 THALER
Silver **Obv:** Ornate modified oval Regensburg arms, date divided at top **Rev:** Crowned imperial eagle, Austrian arms in heart-shaped shield on breast, titles of Leopold I

Date	Mintage	VG	F	VF	XF	Unc
1696 MF	—	450	800	1,150	1,650	—

KM# 111 2/3 THALER (Gulden)
Silver **Obv:** Ornate arms **Rev:** Crowned double-headed eagle, heart shaped shield with value on breast **Note:** Similar to 1/4 Thaler, KM#113, but value: 2/3 in shield on eagle's breast. Dav. #783, 784.

Date	Mintage	VG	F	VF	XF	Unc
1646 (c)	—	1,250	1,900	2,400	3,100	—
1655 HF	—	1,250	1,900	2,400	3,100	—

KM# 149 2/3 THALER (Gulden)
Silver **Note:** Similar to 1/3 Thaler, KM#141, but value: 2/3 in heart-shaped shield on eagle's breast. Dav. #785.

Date	Mintage	VG	F	VF	XF	Unc
1657 HF	—	1,150	1,650	2,200	3,000	—

KM# 170 2/3 THALER (Gulden)
Silver **Obv:** Ornate arms **Rev:** Crowned double-headed imperial eagle with value in orb on breast **Note:** Similar to 1/3 Thaler, KM#141, but value: 2/3 in orb, titles of Leopold I. Dav. #786, 787.

Date	Mintage	VG	F	VF	XF	Unc
1662 HF	—	1,150	1,650	2,200	3,000	—
1663 HF	—	1,150	1,650	2,200	3,000	—
1664 HF	—	1,150	1,650	2,200	3,000	—
1666 HF	—	1,150	1,650	2,200	3,000	—
1667 HF	—	1,150	1,650	2,200	3,000	—
1672 HF	—	1,150	1,650	2,200	3,000	—
1680 HF	—	1,150	1,650	2,200	3,000	—

Note: 1680 dated coins struck from altered 1672 die

KM# 12 GULDENTHALER OF 60 KREUZER
Silver **Obv:** Value: 60 in orb on breast of crowned imperial eagle **Obv. Legend:** MATHIAE * ROM: IMP: AVG: P*F: DECRETO* **Rev:** Arms dividing date **Rev. Legend:** MONETA * REIPVLICAE * RATISPONENSIS * **Note:** Dav. #115.

Date	Mintage	VG	F	VF	XF	Unc
1613	—	900	1,700	2,950	4,900	—

KM# 13 GULDENTHALER OF 60 KREUZER
Silver **Obv:** Simplified eagle **Rev:** Revised arms **Note:** Dav. #115.

Date	Mintage	VG	F	VF	XF	Unc
ND	—	850	1,550	2,600	4,550	—

KM# 14 GULDENTHALER OF 60 KREUZER
Silver **Rev:** Ornate arms **Note:** Dav. #115.

Date	Mintage	VG	F	VF	XF	Unc
ND	—	650	1,200	2,000	3,500	—

KM# 15 GULDENTHALER OF 60 KREUZER
Silver **Rev:** Dots divide legend, simplified arms **Note:** Dav. #115.

Date	Mintage	VG	F	VF	XF	Unc
ND	—	850	1,550	2,600	4,550	—

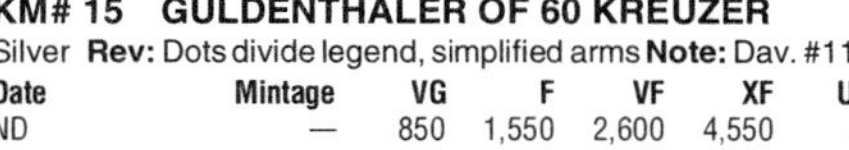

KM# 18 GULDENTHALER OF 60 KREUZER
Silver **Obv:** City arms divide date encircled by wreath, senators arms with initials around **Rev:** Crowned double-headed imperial eagle, value in orb on breast **Rev. Legend:** MONETA * REIPVBLICAE * RATISPONENSIS * **Note:** Dav. #118.

Date	Mintage	VG	F	VF	XF	Unc
1619	—	1,050	1,950	3,250	5,200	—

KM# 30 GULDENTHALER OF 60 KREUZER
Silver **Obv. Legend:** • MATHIAE • ROM • IMP • AVG:P*F DECRETO* • **Rev:** Arms divide date

Date	Mintage	VG	F	VF	XF	Unc
1621	—	—	—	—	—	—

Note: Reported, not confirmed

KM# 31 GULDENTHALER OF 60 KREUZER
Silver **Obv:** Flower breaks legend at top, arms on shield in inner circle **Rev:** Double-headed eagle, crown above, value in orb on breast, legend around **Rev. Legend:** FERDINANDI • II • ROM • IMP • S:AVG • P • F DECRETO **Note:** Dav. #119.

Date	Mintage	VG	F	VF	XF	Unc
16Z1	—	525	900	1,550	2,600	—

KM# 32 GULDENTHALER OF 60 KREUZER
Silver **Obv:** *'s begin and end legend, revised border on arms **Rev:** Crowned double-headed imperial eagle, value in orb on breast **Note:** Dav. #119.

Date	Mintage	VG	F	VF	XF	Unc
1621	—	525	900	1,550	2,600	—

KM# 71 GULDENTHALER OF 60 KREUZER
Silver **Obv:** Legend, angel above arms **Obv. Legend:** •MONE: REIPVB: -RATISPON: 1640 **Rev:** Crowned double-headed imperial eagle, value in orb on breast **Rev. Legend:** FERDINANDVS • II • ROM: IMP: ABG: P • F • DECRETO **Note:** Dav. #120.

Date	Mintage	VG	F	VF	XF	Unc
1630	—	650	1,150	1,950	3,250	—

KM# 41 THALER
Silver **Obv:** Ornate shield divides date **Rev:** Crowned double-headed imperial eagle, shield on breast, different punctuation **Note:** Dav. #5744.

Date	Mintage	VG	F	VF	XF	Unc
1623	—	275	575	1,150	2,000	—

KM# 44 THALER
Silver **Obv:** Angel holding shield before him **Obv. Legend:** MONETA* REIPVLICAE... **Rev. Legend:** ...AVGVSTVS. **Note:** Dav. #5745.

Date	Mintage	VG	F	VF	XF	Unc
1625	—	275	575	1,150	2,000	—

KM# 51 THALER
Silver **Obv. Legend:** ...D. R. ROM. IMP. SEM... **Rev. Legend:** MONETA. REIPVB... **Note:** Dav. #5746.

Date	Mintage	VG	F	VF	XF	Unc
1626	—	275	575	1,150	2,000	—
1628	—	275	575	1,150	2,000	—

KM# 52 THALER
Silver **Obv:** Angel above ornate shield **Obv. Legend:** MONE... **Rev:** Crown above double-headed imperial eagle, shield on breast, legend, titles of Ferdinand **Note:** Dav. #5747.

Date	Mintage	VG	F	VF	XF	Unc
1626	—	175	350	650	1,250	2,500
1627	—	175	350	650	1,250	2,500

KM# 64 THALER
Silver **Obv:** Date below eagle **Rev:** Similar to Dav. #5749 **Note:** Dav. #5748.

Date	Mintage	VG	F	VF	XF	Unc
1629	—	600	1,150	2,250	3,750	—

KM# 74 THALER
Silver **Obv:** Angel above ornate egg-shaped shield **Rev:** Crown above double-headed imperial eagle, shield on breast **Note:** Dav. #5749.

Date	Mintage	VG	F	VF	XF	Unc
1632	—	600	1,150	2,250	4,250	—

Note: Fritz Rudolf Künker Münzenhandlung Auction 113, 6-06, nearly Unc. realized approximately $14,540

KM# 77 THALER
Silver **Subject:** Conquest of Regensburg by Duke Bernhard of Saxony **Note:** Dav. #5750.

Date	Mintage	VG	F	VF	XF	Unc
1633	—	500	1,000	2,000	5,500	—

KM# 78 THALER
Silver **Obv:** Similar to KM#77, but inscription within wreath **Rev:** City view in inner circle **Note:** Dav. #5751.

Date	Mintage	VG	F	VF	XF	Unc
1633 Rare	—	—	—	—	—	—

KM# 83 THALER
Silver **Obv:** Similar to KM#74 **Rev:** City view in inner circle **Note:** Dav. #5752.

Date	Mintage	VG	F	VF	XF	Unc
1634 Rare	—	—	—	—	—	—

KM# 90 THALER
Silver **Obv:** Arms in round frame **Rev:** Crowned imperial eagle without sword or scepter, Austrian arms on chest **Note:** Dav. #5754.

Date	Mintage	VG	F	VF	XF	Unc
1638 (b)	—	400	800	1,650	2,750	—

KM# 94 THALER
Silver **Rev:** Similar to KM#74 **Note:** Dav. #5755.

Date	Mintage	VG	F	VF	XF	Unc
1639	—	650	1,150	2,150	5,750	—

KM# 102 THALER
Silver **Obv:** Angel head, two eagle heads above arms **Rev:** Crown above imperial eagle, orb between necks, shield on breast **Note:** Dav. #5758.

Date	Mintage	VG	F	VF	XF	Unc
1641 (c)	—	250	500	1,000	1,850	—
1642 (c)	—	250	500	1,000	1,850	—

KM# 106 THALER
Silver **Obv:** Crowned imperial eagle with Emperor's bust on breast **Rev:** Angel above arms in frame **Note:** Dav. #5760.

Date	Mintage	VG	F	VF	XF	Unc
1643 (c)	—	350	750	1,500	2,500	—
1644 (c)	—	350	750	1,500	2,500	—

KM# 109 THALER
Silver **Obv. Legend:** ...ROMA: IMP:... **Note:** Dav. #5761.

Date	Mintage	VG	F	VF	XF	Unc
1645 (c)	—	300	650	1,350	2,250	4,000
1646 (c)	—	300	650	1,350	2,250	—
1647 (c)	—	300	650	1,350	2,500	—

KM# 115 THALER

Silver **Rev:** Oval shield without angel **Note:** Dav. #5762.

Date	Mintage	VG	F	VF	XF	Unc
1647 (c)	—	650	1,150	2,150	5,750	—

KM# 118 THALER

Silver **Obv:** Angel above arms **Rev:** Crowned imperial eagle with oval arms on breast **Note:** Dav. #5763.

Date	Mintage	VG	F	VF	XF	Unc
1649 (c)	—	150	375	850	1,750	3,750

KM# 131 THALER

Silver **Obv:** Crowned imperial eagle with emperor's head on breast **Rev:** Angel head above arms in round frame **Note:** Dav. #5764.

Date	Mintage	VG	F	VF	XF	Unc
1652 (c)	—	650	1,250	2,500	6,000	—
1653 (c)	—	650	1,250	2,500	6,000	—
1654 HF	—	—	—	—	—	—

KM# 151 THALER

Silver **Obv:** Angel head above arms in inner circle **Rev:** Crowned imperial eagle with nothing on breast **Note:** Dav. #5766.

Date	Mintage	VG	F	VF	XF	Unc
1656 HF	—	400	800	1,650	2,750	—
1657 HF	—	400	800	1,650	2,750	—

KM# 153 THALER

Silver **Obv:** Arms in frame, HF below **Rev:** Crowned double-headed imperial eagle **Note:** Dav. #5767.

Date	Mintage	VG	F	VF	XF	Unc
1658 HF	—	700	1,350	2,750	4,500	—

KM# 167 THALER

Silver **Obv:** Arms in frame, without inner circle, HF below **Rev:** Crowned imperial eagle with Austrian arms in heart shield **Note:** Dav. #5769.

Date	Mintage	VG	F	VF	XF	Unc
1660 HF	—	400	800	1,650	2,850	—
1661 HF	—	400	800	1,650	2,850	—
1662 HF	—	400	800	1,650	2,850	—
1663 HF	—	400	800	1,650	2,850	—

KM# 172 THALER

Silver **Obv:** Ornate oval shield **Rev:** Crowned imperial eagle with arms on breast **Note:** Dav. #5770.

Date	Mintage	VG	F	VF	XF	Unc
1664 HF	—	400	800	1,650	3,250	—
1665 HF	—	400	800	1,650	3,250	—
1666 HF	—	400	800	1,650	3,250	—
1667 HF	—	600	1,200	2,500	4,250	—
1672 HF	—	600	1,200	2,500	4,250	—

KM# 191 THALER

Silver **Obv:** Crowned imperial eagle without shield on breast **Note:** Dav. #5771.

Date	Mintage	VG	F	VF	XF	Unc
1676 MF Rare	—	—	—	—	—	—

KM# 195 THALER

Silver **Obv:** Eagle with heart-shaped Austrian arms on breast **Rev:** Arms in frame, MF below **Note:** Dav. #5772.

Date	Mintage	VG	F	VF	XF	Unc
1680/72 MF	—	700	1,350	2,750	4,500	—
1680 MF	—	700	1,350	2,750	4,500	—
1681 MF	—	425	850	1,750	3,500	5,500
1691 MF	—	450	900	1,850	3,750	—
1694 MF	6,821	450	900	1,850	3,750	—

KM# 203 THALER

Silver **Rev:** Angel above arms in frame **Note:** Dav. #5773.

Date	Mintage	F	VF	XF	Unc	BU
1694 MF	Inc. above	200	375	700	1,850	—
1696 MF	307	275	575	1,150	2,250	—

KM# 19 1-1/2 GULDENTHALER

Silver **Note:** Similar to 1 Guldenthaler, KM#18.

Date	Mintage	VG	F	VF	XF	Unc
1619	—	4,000	5,300	6,300	8,300	—

KM# 5 1-1/2 THALER

Silver **Obv:** Angel holding imprial and city shields **Rev:** 7-line inscription **Note:** Klippe. Dav. #A5742.

Date	Mintage	VG	F	VF	XF	Unc
1608 Rare	—	—	—	—	—	—

KM# 20 2 GULDENTHALER

Silver **Note:** Similar to 1 Guldenthaler, KM#18.

Date	Mintage	VG	F	VF	XF	Unc
1619 Rare	—	—	—	—	—	—

KM# 6 2 THALER

Silver **Obv:** Angle holding imperial and city shields **Rev:** 7-line inscription **Note:** Klippe. Dav. #5742.

Date	Mintage	VG	F	VF	XF	Unc
1608 Rare	—	—	—	—	—	—

TRADE COINAGE

MB# 65 GOLDGULDEN

3.5000 g., 0.9860 Gold 0.1109 oz. AGW **Subject:** Election of Rudolf II as King of Rome **Obv:** 5-line inscription in circle **Obv. Legend:** + RVDOLPHVS. II. D.G. ROM. REX. EL

Obv. Inscription: XXVII/OCT. COR/.I. NOV/M.D.LXXV/RATISBO **Rev:** Table with 6 orbs, another orb above **Rev. Legend:** + CONSENTIENTIBVS. VOTIS

Date	Mintage	VG	F	VF	XF	Unc
MDLXXV (1575)	—	1,200	2,250	3,500	—	—

KM# 16 GOLDGULDEN

3.5000 g., 0.9860 Gold 0.1109 oz. AGW **Obv:** Crossed key arms topped by date in inner circle **Rev:** Crowned imperial eagle, titles of Leopold I

Date	Mintage	VG	F	VF	XF	Unc
1617	—	1,450	2,800	5,000	8,500	14,500
Note: UBS Regensburg Auction 60, 9-04, nearly FDC realized $14,170						
1618	—	1,450	2,800	5,000	8,500	14,500

KM# 209 1/3 DUCAT

1.1666 g., 0.9860 Gold 0.0370 oz. AGW

Date	Mintage	VG	F	VF	XF	Unc
1696	—	350	650	1,200	2,100	—

KM# 135 1/2 DUCAT

1.1666 g., 0.9860 Gold 0.0370 oz. AGW **Obv:** Crowned legend **Obv. Legend:** FERDINAND IV... **Rev:** Legend on ribbon **Rev. Legend:** PRO DEO ET...

Date	Mintage	VG	F	VF	XF	Unc
1653	—	150	300	650	1,150	—

KM# 56 DUCAT

3.5000 g., 0.9860 Gold 0.1109 oz. AGW **Obv:** Trinity Church **Rev:** Inscription

Date	Mintage	VG	F	VF	XF	Unc
1627	—	600	1,200	2,250	3,750	—

KM# 75 DUCAT

3.5000 g., 0.9860 Gold 0.1109 oz. AGW **Obv:** Crowned imperial eagle with arms on breast in inner circle, titles of Ferdinand II **Rev:** Crossed keys in cartouche in inner circle, date divided at top

Date	Mintage	VG	F	VF	XF	Unc
1632	—	1,000	2,000	4,000	6,500	—

KM# 79 DUCAT

3.5000 g., 0.9860 Gold 0.1109 oz. AGW **Subject:** Triumphal Entry into City of Bernhard of Saxe-Weimar on Nov. 4, 1633 **Rev:** 6-line inscription

Date	Mintage	VG	F	VF	XF	Unc
1633	—	1,250	2,500	4,500	8,000	—

KM# 84 DUCAT

3.5000 g., 0.9860 Gold 0.1109 oz. AGW **Rev:** City of Regensburg

Date	Mintage	VG	F	VF	XF	Unc
1634	—	1,000	2,000	4,000	6,500	—

KM# 85 DUCAT

3.5000 g., 0.9860 Gold 0.1109 oz. AGW **Subject:** Coronation of Ferdinand III

Date	Mintage	VG	F	VF	XF	Unc
1636	—	1,250	2,500	4,500	—	—

KM# 91 DUCAT

3.5000 g., 0.9860 Gold 0.1109 oz. AGW **Obv:** Crossed keys in cartouche in inner circle, cherub head at top, date in legend **Rev:** Crowned imperial eagle **Note:** Varieties exist.

Date	Mintage	VG	F	VF	XF	Unc
1638 (b)	—	400	850	1,750	3,500	6,000
1639 (b)	—	400	850	1,750	3,500	6,000
1640 (c)	—	400	850	1,750	3,500	6,000
1641 (c)	—	400	850	1,750	3,500	6,000
1642 (c)	—	400	850	1,750	3,500	6,000
1643 (c)	—	400	850	1,750	3,500	6,000
1644 (c)	—	400	850	1,750	3,500	6,000
1645	—	425	900	1,800	4,000	6,750
1646 (c)	—	400	850	1,750	3,500	6,000
1647 (c)	—	400	850	1,750	3,500	6,000
1651	—	450	950	1,850	4,500	8,000
1652	—	400	850	1,750	3,500	6,000
1656 HF	—	400	850	1,750	3,500	6,000
1657 HF	—	450	950	1,850	4,000	6,750

KM# 103 DUCAT

3.5000 g., 0.9860 Gold 0.1109 oz. AGW **Subject:** 200th Anniversary of the Reformation in Regensburg **Obv:** 5-line inscription, arms divide date at top **Rev:** Light and hands

Date	Mintage	VG	F	VF	XF	Unc
1641	—	850	1,650	3,000	5,000	—

KM# 104 DUCAT

3.5000 g., 0.9860 Gold 0.1109 oz. AGW **Obv:** 5-line inscription, arms divide date at top **Rev:** Candle above Bible on stand, banner at top

Date	Mintage	VG	F	VF	XF	Unc
1642	—	175	350	725	1,350	2,200

KM# 119 DUCAT

3.5000 g., 0.9860 Gold 0.1109 oz. AGW

Date	Mintage	VG	F	VF	XF	Unc
1649 (c)	—	500	1,050	2,050	3,800	6,300

KM# 127 DUCAT

3.5000 g., 0.9860 Gold 0.1109 oz. AGW **Obv:** Crowned imperial eagle **Rev:** 3-line inscription on mantle, divided date below

Date	Mintage	VG	F	VF	XF	Unc
1651	—	1,200	2,400	4,800	7,800	—

KM# 136 DUCAT

3.5000 g., 0.9860 Gold 0.1109 oz. AGW **Obv:** Crowned legend **Obv. Legend:** FERDINAND IV... **Rev:** Legend on ribbon **Rev. Legend:** PRO DEO ET...

Date	Mintage	VG	F	VF	XF	Unc
1653	—	220	425	800	1,600	—

KM# 137 DUCAT

3.5000 g., 0.9860 Gold 0.1109 oz. AGW **Obv:** Wreath **Rev:** Crowned imperial eagle

Date	Mintage	VG	F	VF	XF	Unc
1653	—	550	1,150	2,000	3,500	—

KM# 154 DUCAT

3.5000 g., 0.9860 Gold 0.1109 oz. AGW **Note:** Similar to KM#160.

Date	Mintage	VG	F	VF	XF	Unc
1658 HF	—	1,200	2,400	4,800	7,800	—

KM# 160 DUCAT

3.5000 g., 0.9860 Gold 0.1109 oz. AGW **Obv:** Crossed keys in cartouche, date in legend, titles of Leopold I **Rev:** Crowned imperial eagle with shield on breast **Note:** Varieties exist.

Date	Mintage	VG	F	VF	XF	Unc
1659 HF	—	750	1,550	3,150	5,000	—
1660 HF	—	750	1,550	3,150	5,000	—
1661 HF	—	750	1,550	3,150	5,000	—
1662 HF	—	750	1,550	3,150	5,000	—
1663 HF	—	750	1,550	3,150	5,000	—
1664 HF	—	750	1,550	3,150	5,000	—
1665 HF	—	750	1,550	3,150	5,000	—
1666 HF	—	750	1,550	3,150	5,000	—
1668 HF	—	750	1,550	3,150	5,000	—
1672 HF	—	750	1,550	3,150	5,000	—
1680 HF	334	750	1,550	3,150	5,000	—
1696 MF	7	—	—	—	—	—

KM# A38 2 DUCAT

7.0000 g., 0.9860 Gold 0.2219 oz. AGW **Subject:** Coronation of Ferdinand III as King of Rome **Obv. Inscription:** FERDINAND: III/HVG: ET BÖH: REX/CORON: IN REG/ROMANOR:/XXX. DECB:/MDCXXXVI **Rev:** Cross surmounted on scales, crossed sword and scepter behind **Rev. Legend:** FIRMAMENTA. — REGNORVM **Note:** FR#2464.

Date	Mintage	VG	F	VF	XF	Unc
MDCXXXVI (1636)	—	650	1,150	2,000	3,500	—

KM# 57 2 DUCAT

7.0000 g., 0.9860 Gold 0.2219 oz. AGW **Obv:** Trinity Church **Rev:** Inscription **Note:** Struck with 1 Ducat dies, KM#56.

Date	Mintage	VG	F	VF	XF	Unc
1627	—	1,350	2,700	4,950	8,100	—

KM# 76 2 DUCAT

7.0000 g., 0.9860 Gold 0.2219 oz. AGW **Obv:** Arms in cartouche, date divided at top **Rev:** Crowned imperial eagle with shield on breast in inner circle **Note:** Struck with 1 Ducat dies, KM#75.

Date	Mintage	VG	F	VF	XF	Unc
1632	—	1,900	3,750	6,000	10,500	—

KM# A39 2 DUCAT

7.0000 g., 0.9860 Gold 0.2219 oz. AGW **Subject:** Centennial of Reformation in Regensburg **Obv:** City arms in cartouche divide date above 5-line inscription **Obv. Inscription:** NVN LEICHT DIS / LICHT VNS 100 IAHR / DASSELB NOCH FORT / VS GOTT BEWAHR / S.P.Q.R. **Rev:** Hands and arms extending from clouds at left and right, holding candle over table on the top of which is S. BIBLIA, and on facing side, CONFES/AVGVST/ANA, inscription in ribbon above V.D.M.I.Æ. **Rev. Legend:** DEN. XV. — OCTOB: **Note:** FR#2467.

Date	Mintage	VG	F	VF	XF	Unc
1642	—	—	—	1,800	3,000	4,500

KM# A53 2 DUCAT

7.0000 g., 0.9860 Gold 0.2219 oz. AGW **Subject:** Coronation of Ferdinand IV as King of Rome **Obv:** Imperial crown and palm fronds to left and right above 6-line inscription **Obv. Inscription:** FERDINAND: IV / HVNG: ET: BOH REX / CORON IN REGEM / ROMANORVM / XVIII. IVNV / MDCLIII. **Rev:** Scepter standing vertically, top reaching into clouds with Eye of God above, palm fronds to lower left and right, ribbon behind with inscription **Rev. Legend:** PRO DEO — ET POPVLO. **Note:** FR#2471a.

Date	Mintage	VG	F	VF	XF	Unc
MDCLIII (1653)	—	—	—	1,350	2,500	4,500

KM# 150 2 DUCAT

7.0000 g., 0.9860 Gold 0.2219 oz. AGW **Obv:** Crossed keys in ornate border **Rev:** Crowned imperial eagle, titles of Leopold I

Date	Mintage	VG	F	VF	XF	Unc
ND(1657-1705) HF	—	1,350	2,750	5,000	8,500	12,000

Note: UBS Regensburg Auction 60, 9-04, XF-nearly FDC realized $10,970

KM# 58 3 DUCAT

10.5000 g., 0.9860 Gold 0.3328 oz. AGW **Obv:** Trinity Church **Rev:** Inscription

Date	Mintage	VG	F	VF	XF	Unc
1627	—	1,500	3,000	5,500	9,000	—

KM# 155 3 DUCAT

10.5000 g., 0.9860 Gold 0.3328 oz. AGW **Obv:** Crowned imperial eagle with heart-shaped arms on breast, titles of Leopold I **Rev:** Arms in cartouche

Date	Mintage	VG	F	VF	XF	Unc
ND(1658-1705) Rare	—	—	—	—	—	—

KM# 173 4 DUCAT

14.0000 g., 0.9860 Gold 0.4438 oz. AGW **Obv:** Ornate arms **Rev:** Crowned imperial eagle, heart shaped shield on breast, titles of Leopold I

Date	Mintage	VG	F	VF	XF	Unc
1664 HF Rare	—	—	—	—	—	—

Note: UBS Regensburg Auction 60, 9-04, FDC realized $21,940

KM# 138 5 DUCAT

17.5000 g., 0.9860 Gold 0.5547 oz. AGW **Obv:** Crowned 5-line inscription: FERDINAND IV... **Rev:** Legend on ribbon **Rev. Legend:** PRO DEO ET...

Date	Mintage	VG	F	VF	XF	Unc
1653	—	2,000	3,500	6,000	10,000	—

KM# 174 5 DUCAT

17.5000 g., 0.9860 Gold 0.5547 oz. AGW **Obv:** Arms **Rev:** Crowned imperial eagle, titles of Leopold I

Date	Mintage	VG	F	VF	XF	Unc
1664 HF Rare	—	—	—	—	—	—

Note: UBS Regensburg Auction 60, 9-04, XF realized $14,625

KM# 181 6 DUCAT

21.0000 g., 0.9860 Gold 0.6657 oz. AGW **Obv:** Arms divide date in cartouche **Rev:** Crowned double-headed imperial eagle, heart shaped shield on breast, titles of Leopold I

Date	Mintage	VG	F	VF	XF	Unc
1667 HF Rare	—	—	—	—	—	—
ND IMF/HF Rare	—	—	—	—	—	—

Note: UBS Regensburg Auction 60, 9-04, XF realized $21,940 (1667 HF)

KM# 182 8 DUCAT

28.0000 g., 0.9860 Gold 0.8876 oz. AGW **Obv:** Crowned imperial eagle with crowned hear-shaped arms on breast **Rev:** Crossed keys divide date in cartouche

Date	Mintage	VG	F	VF	XF	Unc
1667 HF Rare	—	—	—	—	—	—

KM# 59 10 DUCAT

35.0000 g., 0.9860 Gold 1.1095 oz. AGW **Obv:** Crowned imperial eagle **Rev:** Ornate arms

Date	Mintage	VG	F	VF	XF	Unc
1627 Rare	—	—	—	—	—	—

KM# 183 10 DUCAT

35.0000 g., 0.9860 Gold 1.1095 oz. AGW **Obv:** Ornate arms **Rev:** Crowned imperial eagle, heart shaped shield on breast, titles of Leopold

Date	Mintage	VG	F	VF	XF	Unc
1667 HF Rare	—	—	—	—	—	—
ND IMF/HF Rare	—	—	—	—	—	—

Note: UBS Regensburg Auction 60, 9-04, nearly FDC realized $29,250 (1667 HF)

Note: UBS Regensburg Auction 60, 9-04, XF realized $43,875 (ND IMF/HF)

PATTERNS

Including off metal strikes

KM#	Date	Mintage	Identification	Mkt Val
Pn1	1619	—	Guldenthaler Of 60 Kreuzer. Gold. 36.6000 g. Klippe. KM#18.	—
Pn2	1640	—	Kreuzer. Gold. KM#93.	1,550
Pn3	1653	—	1/2 Kreuzer. Gold. 1/4 Ducat weight. KM#133.	—
Pn4	1680	—	1/2 Kreuzer. Gold. 1/6 Ducat weight. KM#190.	—
Pn5	1680	—	Kreuzer. Gold. KM#176.	1,850
Pn6	1687	—	Pfennig. Gold. 1/8 Ducat weight. KM#175.	—
Pn7	1691	—	Pfennig. Gold. 1/8 Ducat weight. KM#175.	—
Pn8	1693	—	Heller. Gold. KM#192.	1,850
Pn9	1693	—	Pfennig. Gold. 1/10 Ducat weight. KM#200.	1,250
Pn10	1693	—	Pfennig. Gold. 1/8 Ducat weight. KM#201.	—
Pn11	1696	—	Pfennig. Gold. 1/8 Ducat weight. KM#204.	1,250
Pn12	1696	—	Pfennig. Gold. 1/5 Ducat weight. KM#204.	1,650
Pn13	1696	—	Kreuzer. Gold. KM#176.	1,850
Pn14	1699	—	Heller. Gold. KM#192.	1,850

REGENSTEIN

The counts of Regenstein trace their line of descent from the younger branch of the counts of Blankenburg from the early 13th century. The seat of power for the early counts was the castle of Regenstein, 12 miles (20km) southwest of the city of Halberstadt. When the counts of Blankenburg became extinct about 1370, those lands and titles passed to Regenstein. The last count of the line died in 1599 and the twin counties were divided by Brunswick and the bishopric of Halberstadt. There followed a succession of rulers until Brunswick and Brandenburg, which had received Halberstadt as part of the settlement stemming from the Peace of Westphalia, divided the two counties between them. Brandenburg (q.v.) subsequently struck coins in and for Regenstein.

RULERS

Johann Ernst to Brunswick and Halberstadt, 1599-1629
Johann von Merode, 1629-1631
To Brunswick, 1631-1643
Wilhelm Leopold von Tättenbach, 1643-1661
Johann Erasmus von Tättenbach, 1661-1671

NOTE: The copper 3 Pfennig of Brunswick-Wolfenbüttel (q.v.) dated 1621, KM#237, with crowned R, was issued for Regenstein.

COUNTSHIP

REGULAR COINAGE

KM# 1 1/2 THALER

Silver **Obv:** Bust right, titles of Johann Erasmus around **Rev:** Crowned 9-fold arms with small helmeted shield of arms to either side, date **Rev. Legend:** SOLI. DEO. GLORIA

Date	Mintage	VG	F	VF	XF	Unc
1663 Rare	—	—	—	—	—	—

DAV# 7299 THALER

Silver **Note:** Similar to 2 Thaler, Dav. #7298.

Date	Mintage	VG	F	VF	XF	Unc
1663 Rare	—	—	—	—	—	—

DAV# 7298 2 THALER

Silver **Obv:** Bust of Johann Erasmus right **Rev:** Helmeted arms

Date	Mintage	VG	F	VF	XF	Unc
1663 Rare	—	—	—	—	—	—

REUSS

The Reuss family, whose lands were located in Thuringia, was founded c. 1035. By the end of the 12th century, the custom of naming all males in the ruling house Heinrich had been established. The Elder Line modified this strange practice in the late 17th century to numbering all males from 1 to 100, then beginning over again. The Younger Line, meanwhile, decided to start the numbering of Heinrichs with the first male born in each century. Greiz was founded in 1303. Upper and Lower Greiz lines were founded in 1535 and the territories were divided until 1768. In 1778 the ruler was made a prince of the Holy Roman Empire. The principality endured until 1918.

MINT MARKS

A - Berlin
B – Hannover

MINT OFFICIALS' INITIALS

Initial	Date	Name
ES	1622	Ernst Schultes in Gera
	1623	In Lobenstein
HO	1621-?	Heinrich Oppermann in Moschlitz
IAB	1678-79	Johann Adam Bottcher in Schleiz
ICF	1681	Johann Carl Falkner in Darmstadt
	1692-93	In Eisenach
ILH	1698-1716	Johann Lorenz Holland in Dresden
IS	1624-35	Johann Schneider, known as Weissmantel in Erfurt
MR	1632-73	Martin Reinmann in Saalfeld
SD	1669-75, 78-80	Simon Dannes in Schleiz
TL	1621	Tobias Lippold, mint lessee in Gera
WA	1604-24 (d. 1634)	Wolf Albrech in Saalfeld

LORDSHIP

JOINT COINAGE

of Younger Line

KM# 5 1/24 THALER (Groschen)

Silver **Obv:** Crowned heart-shaped 4-fold arms in baroque frame **Rev:** Imperial orb with 24 divides date, legend **Rev. Legend:** OBER SAXSISCHEN KREISSES GROSCH

Date	Mintage	VG	F	VF	XF	Unc
1655	—	100	155	210	275	—

KM# 6 1/4 THALER
Silver **Rev. Legend:** VIVIT POST FVNERA VIRTVS **Note:** Similar to 1 Thaler, KM#7.

Date	Mintage	VG	F	VF	XF	Unc
1655 MR	—	85.00	125	200	325	—

KM# 7 THALER
Silver **Note:** Dav. #7313

Date	Mintage	VG	F	VF	XF	Unc
MDCLV (1655) MR	—	235	475	875	1,500	—

REUSS-BURGK

The Elder Line in Untergreiz divided their lands in about1582 and Reuss-Burgk was thus founded. When this branch died out after 3 generations, Burgk reverted to Untergreiz.

RULERS
Heinrich II, 1582-1608
Heinrich II, 1608-1639
Heinrich III, 1639-1640

COUNTSHIP

REGULAR COINAGE

KM# 5 12 KREUZER (3 Batzen)
Silver **Obv:** Crowned imperial eagle, 12 in orb on breast, date divided near bottom, titles of Ferdinand II **Rev:** Crowned arms in ornamented shield divided vertically, lion left and crane right **Rev. Legend:** MO. NO...

Date	Mintage	VG	F	VF	XF	Unc
1621 HO	—	110	200	—	—	—

KM# 6 24 KREUZER (6 Batzen)
Silver **Obv:** Crowned imperial eagle, 24 in orb on breast, titles of Ferdinand II **Rev:** Crowned oval four-fold arms in baroque frame divide date near bottom, titles of Heinrich II

Date	Mintage	VG	F	VF	XF	Unc
1621 HO	—	135	225	—	—	—

KM# 7 24 KREUZER (6 Batzen)
Silver **Rev:** Date divided near bottom

Date	Mintage	VG	F	VF	XF	Unc
1621	—	135	225	—	—	—

KM# 8 24 KREUZER (6 Batzen)
Silver **Obv:** Without titles of Heinrich II **Obv. Legend:** MON. NOV. ARGENT. RVTHENICA BVR. **Note:** Varieties exist.

Date	Mintage	VG	F	VF	XF	Unc
1621	—	135	225	—	—	—
1622	—	135	225	—	—	—

KM# 9 24 KREUZER (6 Batzen)
Silver **Obv:** Crowned imperial eagle, 24 in orb on breast, titles of Ferdinand II **Rev:** Lion rampant left in ornamented oval shield, titles of Heinrich II

Date	Mintage	VG	F	VF	XF	Unc
ND	—	135	225	—	—	—

KM# 15 GROSCHEN
Silver **Subject:** Death of Heinrich II **Obv:** Crowned four-fold arms in ornamented heart-shaped shield, titles of Heinrich II **Obv. Legend:** Six-line inscription with date **Rev:** AN. GottES...

Date	Mintage	VG	F	VF	XF	Unc
1639	—	27.00	55.00	100	165	—

KM# 16 1/4 THALER
Silver **Subject:** Death of Heinrich II **Note:** Similar to 1 Groschen KM#15, but seven-line inscription on reverse.

Date	Mintage	VG	F	VF	XF	Unc
1639 Rare	—	—	—	—	—	—

KM# 17 1/2 THALER
Silver **Subject:** Death of Heinrich II **Obv:** Half-length figure of armored Heinrich right, titles in legend **Rev:** Seven-line inscription with date **Rev. Legend:** AN GOTTES...

Date	Mintage	VG	F	VF	XF	Unc
1639 Rare	—	—	—	—	—	—

KM# 10 THALER
Silver **Obv:** Helmeted arms **Rev:** Crowned imperial eagle with orb between necks **Note:** Dav. #7302.

Date	Mintage	VG	F	VF	XF	Unc
1624 WA	—	400	800	1,500	2,400	—

KM# 19 THALER
Silver **Rev:** Roman numeral date **Rev. Legend:** ...GREITZ. DECEM... **Note:** Dav. #7303A.

Date	Mintage	VG	F	VF	XF	Unc
1639 Rare	—	—	—	—	—	—

KM# 20 THALER
Silver **Subject:** Death of Heinrich II **Rev:** Seven-line inscription, legend divided by arms **Note:** Dav. #7304.

Date	Mintage	VG	F	VF	XF	Unc
1639 Rare	—	—	—	—	—	—

KM# 18 THALER
Silver **Subject:** Death of Heinrich II **Obv:** Half figure right **Rev:** Crowned shield **Note:** Varieties exist. Dav. #7303.

Date	Mintage	VG	F	VF	XF	Unc
1639 Rare	—	—	—	—	—	—

REUSS-DOLAU

Originally an offshoot of Reuss-Burgk from 1616, it reverted to the main Burgk line in 1636 and was transferred to Reuss-Obergreiz in 1640.

RULERS
Heinrich IV, 1616-1636
Heinrich XVI von Obergreiz, 1681-1698

COUNTSHIP

REGULAR COINAGE

KM# 5 24 KREUZER (6 Batzen)
Silver **Obv:** Crowned imperial eagle, 24 in orb on breast, titles of Ferdinand II **Rev:** Four-fold arms in ornamented frame **Rev. Legend:** MON. NOV. ARGENT. RVTHENICA. DOL. **Note:** Kipper 24 Kreuzer. Varieties exist.

Date	Mintage	VG	F	VF	XF	Unc
ND	—	—	—	—	—	—

KM# 6 1/24 THALER (1 Groschen)
Silver **Obv:** Value: 24 on imperial orb, titles of Ferdinand II **Rev:** Arms of Reuss lion left **Rev. Legend:** MO. NO. AR. RVTHE. D"O. **Note:** Kipper 1/24 Thaler.

Date	Mintage	VG	F	VF	XF	Unc
ND	—	80.00	150	—	—	—

REUSS-GERA

This lordship was founded in 1206 and became extinct in 1550, passing to Greiz. The Younger Line established a new branch in Gera in the same year. In 1635, Gera was divided into the lines of Gera, Lobenstein, Saalburgand Schleiz. Gera fell extinct again in 1802 and the title passed to Schleiz.

RULERS
Heinrich II Posthumous, 1572-1635
Heinrich II the Younger, 1635-1670
Heinrich IV, 1670-1686
Heinrich XVIII, 1686-1735

PRINCIPALITY

REGULAR COINAGE

KM# 24 3 PFENNIG (Dreier)
Silver **Subject:** Lordship of Lobenstein **Obv:** Imperial orb with 3 **Rev:** Helmet with dog head divides date, LOB above

Date	Mintage	VG	F	VF	XF	Unc
1622 ES	—	27.00	55.00	100	180	—

KM# 41 3 PFENNIG (Dreier)
Silver **Rev. Legend:** LOBENST... **Note:** Varieties exist.

Date	Mintage	VG	F	VF	XF	Unc
16Z3 ES	—	27.00	55.00	100	180	—

KM# 42 3 PFENNIG (Dreier)
Silver **Rev:** Imperial orb in baroque frame

Date	Mintage	VG	F	VF	XF	Unc
16Z3 MR	—	27.00	55.00	100	180	—

KM# 43 3 PFENNIG (Dreier)
Silver **Obv:** Legend around orb **Obv. Legend:** MONETA-RVTHENICA

Date	Mintage	VG	F	VF	XF	Unc
1623	—	—	—	—	—	—

Note: Reported, not confirmed

KM# 44 6 PFENNIG (Sechser)
Silver **Subject:** Lordship of Lobenstein **Obv:** VI in orb **Rev:** Helmet with dog head divides date

Date	Mintage	VG	F	VF	XF	Unc
1623 ES	—	—	—	—	—	—

Note: Reported, not confirmed

KM# 14 3 KREUZER (Groschen)
Silver **Subject:** Lordship of Lobenstein **Obv:** Crowned imperial eagle, 3 in orb on breast, titles of Ferdinand II **Rev:** Lion left in baroque frame **Rev. Legend:** MO. NO. AR. RVTHE. L. **Note:** Kipper 3 Kreuzer.

Date	Mintage	VG	F	VF	XF	Unc
ND	—	65.00	120	180	250	—

KM# 12 12 KREUZER (3 Batzen)
Silver **Subject:** Lordship of Lobenstein **Obv:** Date in legend at top **Rev:** Shield of lion arms, dog head above **Rev. Legend:** HERRSCAFT. LOBENSTEIN **Note:** Varieties exist.

Date	Mintage	VG	F	VF	XF	Unc
16Z0	—	—	—	—	—	—

KM# 16 12 KREUZER (3 Batzen)
Silver **Rev:** Legend, date **Rev. Legend:** MO: NO: ARG: RVTHENICA **Note:** Varieties exist.

Date	Mintage	VG	F	VF	XF	Unc
16Z1	—	80.00	135	220	325	—
1621	—	80.00	135	220	325	—

KM# 15 12 KREUZER (3 Batzen)
Silver **Obv:** Crowned imperial eagle, 12 in orb on breast, titles of Ferdinand II **Rev:** Oval lion arms, dog head above divides date

Date	Mintage	VG	F	VF	XF	Unc
1621	—	80.00	125	200	300	—

KM# 13 24 KREUZER (6 Batzen)
Silver **Subject:** Lordship of Lobenstein **Obv:** 24 in orb **Rev:** Shield of lion arms, dog head above **Rev. Legend:** HERRSCHAFT

Date	Mintage	VG	F	VF	XF	Unc
1620	—	—	—	—	—	—

KM# 22 24 KREUZER (6 Batzen)
Silver **Rev:** Arms divide date **Rev. Legend:** MO: NO: ARG: RVTHENICA. DOM. 4

Date	Mintage	VG	F	VF	XF	Unc
1621	—	—	—	—	—	—

KM# 23 24 KREUZER (6 Batzen)
Silver **Rev:** Date in legend

Date	Mintage	VG	F	VF	XF	Unc
1621	—	—	—	—	—	—

KM# 17 24 KREUZER (6 Batzen)
Silver **Obv:** Crowned imperial eagle, 24 in orb on breast, titles of Ferdinand II **Rev:** Ornamented four-fold arms, date and mint mark in legend **Note:** Kipper 24 Kreuzer. Varieties exist.

Date	Mintage	VG	F	VF	XF	Unc
(16)21 G	—	80.00	135	220	325	—
(1)621 G	—	80.00	135	220	325	—
1622 G	—	80.00	135	220	325	—

KM# 18 24 KREUZER (6 Batzen)
Silver **Note:** Klippe.

Date	Mintage	VG	F	VF	XF	Unc
(16)21 G	—	—	—	—	—	—

KM# 19 24 KREUZER (6 Batzen)
Silver **Obv:** Date divided by arms **Obv. Legend:** Ends: GE or GER **Rev:** Double-headed imperial eagle, value in orb on breast **Note:** Varieties exist.

Date	Mintage	VG	F	VF	XF	Unc
1621 TL	—	55.00	115	165	275	—
ND TL	—	55.00	115	165	275	—

KM# 21 24 KREUZER (6 Batzen)
Silver **Rev:** Oval lion arms, dog head left above divides date **Note:** Varieties exist.

Date	Mintage	VG	F	VF	XF	Unc
1621	—	65.00	120	200	300	—
ND	—	65.00	120	200	300	—

KM# 20 24 KREUZER (6 Batzen)
Silver **Rev:** Oval lion arms, plume of helmet above divides date

Date	Mintage	VG	F	VF	XF	Unc
1621	—	65.00	120	200	300	—

KM# 25 24 KREUZER (6 Batzen)
Silver **Rev:** Date divided by dog head **Rev. Legend:** Ends: RVTHENICA*L. **Note:** Varieties exist.

Date	Mintage	VG	F	VF	XF	Unc
16ZZ	—	65.00	120	200	300	—
1622	—	65.00	120	200	300	—

KM# 26 24 KREUZER (6 Batzen)
Silver **Note:** Klippe. Mintmaster's initials in two of the corners

Date	Mintage	VG	F	VF	XF	Unc
1622 IS	—	—	—	—	—	—

KM# 27 1/24 THALER (Groschen)
Silver **Subject:** Lordship of Lobenstein **Obv:** Helmet with dog head right **Obv. Legend:** ...RVTHEN:L. **Rev:** Imperial orb with 24 divides date, titles of Ferdinand II **Note:** .55-.65 grams. Kipper 1/24 Thaler.

Date	Mintage	VG	F	VF	XF	Unc
16ZZ	—	65.00	120	200	300	—

KM# 28 1/24 THALER (12 Pfennig)
1.2500 g., Silver **Obv:** Lion arms with dog head left **Obv. Legend:** NACH. DEM. AL: SCH: V: KOR: **Rev:** Imperial orb with 1Z divides date

Date	Mintage	VG	F	VF	XF	Unc
16ZZ	—	45.00	100	140	200	—

KM# 29 1/24 THALER (12 Pfennig)
1.2500 g., Silver **Rev:** Imperial orb with 24 divides date, titles of Ferdinand II **Note:** Varieties exist.

Date	Mintage	VG	F	VF	XF	Unc
16ZZ ES	—	55.00	110	160	240	—
16Z3 ES	—	55.00	110	160	240	—
16Z3 MR	—	55.00	110	160	240	—

KM# 55 1/24 THALER (12 Pfennig)
1.2500 g., Silver **Subject:** Death of Heinrich II **Obv:** Four-fold arms, titles of Heinrich II **Rev:** Six-line inscription I. B. A. G/NAT9IO. IV/NII. Ao 1572/OBIIIt. 3. DECEMB. Ao/1635 **Rev. Legend:** PIETAS-AD-OMNIA-VTILIS

Date	Mintage	VG	F	VF	XF	Unc
1635	2,410	—	—	—	—	—

KM# 30 1/4 THALER
Silver **Subject:** Lordship of Lobenstein **Obv:** Two helmets with dog head and crane, date above **Rev:** Phoenix rising from flames on short column, imperial orb above, hands from clouds on either side with palm branch and sword

Date	Mintage	VG	F	VF	XF	Unc
16ZZ	—	—	—	—	—	—

KM# 47 1/4 THALER
Silver **Obv:** Crowned imperial eagle, orb on breast, titles of Ferdinand II **Rev:** Two helmets facing forward with dog head and crane, date below

Date	Mintage	VG	F	VF	XF	Unc
16Z4 WA	—	—	—	—	—	—

KM# 56 1/4 THALER
Silver **Subject:** Death of Heinrich II Posthumous **Obv:** Four-fold arms, two helmets with dog head and crane above **Rev:** Six-line inscription I. B. A. G. /NAT910. IV/NII. Ao 1572/OBIIt. 3. DE/CEMB. Ao/1635

Date	Mintage	VG	F	VF	XF	Unc
1635	140	950	1,650	2,700	4,500	—

KM# 31 1/2 THALER (30 Groschen)
20.5400 g., Silver **Obv:** Oval four-fold arms surmounted by two ornate helmets **Rev:** Phoenix rising from flames on short column, orb above, from clouds at left a hand with palm branch, at right with sword, date in legend, value (30) at bottom

Date	Mintage	VG	F	VF	XF	Unc
1622	—	—	—	—	—	—

KM# 33 1/2 THALER (30 Groschen)
20.5400 g., Silver **Obv:** Squarish four-fold arms, two helmets above with dog head and crane **Rev:** Similar to KM#31 but without indication of value

Date	Mintage	VG	F	VF	XF	Unc
1622 ES	—	—	—	—	—	—

KM# 32 1/2 THALER (30 Groschen)
20.5400 g., Silver **Subject:** Lordship of Lobenstein **Obv:** Crowned imperial eagle, 1Z in orb on breast, titles of Ferdinand II and date in legend **Rev:** Oval four-fold arms, two helmets above with dog head and crane **Note:** Varieties exist.

Date	Mintage	VG	F	VF	XF	Unc
16ZZ ES	—	—	—	—	—	—

KM# 45 1/2 THALER (30 Groschen)
20.5400 g., Silver **Obv:** Similar to KM#32 **Rev:** Heart-shaped four-fold arms, two helmets above

Date	Mintage	VG	F	VF	XF	Unc
1623	—	—	—	—	—	—

KM# 48 1/2 THALER (30 Groschen)
20.5400 g., Silver **Obv:** Ornamented four-fold arms, two helmets with dog head and crane above **Rev:** Crowned double-headed imperial eagle, orb on breast, titles of Ferdinand II, date in legend

Date	Mintage	VG	F	VF	XF	Unc
16Z4 WA	—	—	—	—	—	—

KM# 57 1/2 THALER (30 Groschen)
20.5400 g., Silver **Subject:** Death of Heinrich II Posthumous **Obv:** Gothic letters in field around head; Ich Bau - auff Gott **Rev:** Eight-line inscription **Note:** Varieties exist.

Date	Mintage	VG	F	VF	XF	Unc
1635	274	450	675	1,000	1,350	—

KM# 10 THALER
Silver **Note:** Varieties exist. Dav. #7308.

Date	Mintage	VG	F	VF	XF	Unc
1620	4,730	500	1,000	1,900	3,150	—

KM# 34 THALER (Groschen)
Silver **Obv:** Oval four-fold arms surmounted by two ornate helmets **Rev:** Phoenix rising from flames on short column, orb above, from clouds at left a hand with palm branch, at right with sword, date in legend, value (60) at bottom **Note:** Varieties exist.

Date	Mintage	VG	F	VF	XF	Unc
1622	—	—	—	—	—	—

KM# 35 THALER (Groschen)
Silver **Note:** Klippe. Varieties exist.

Date	Mintage	VG	F	VF	XF	Unc
1622 Rare	—	—	—	—	—	—

KM# 36 THALER (Groschen)
Silver **Subject:** Lordship of Lobenstein **Note:** Varieties exist. Dav. #7309

Date	Mintage	VG	F	VF	XF	Unc
1622 ES	—	375	700	1,250	2,400	—

KM# 37 THALER (Groschen)

Silver **Rev. Legend:** ...HVNG: ET: BOH: REX:... **Note:** Varieties exist. Dav. #7310

Date	Mintage	VG	F	VF	XF	Unc
1622 ES	—	600	1,200	2,500	4,000	—

KM# 38 THALER (Groschen)

Silver **Obv:** Ornate oval shield **Rev:** Crown above double-headed imperial eagle, value in orb on breast **Rev. Legend:** Error: BON instead of BOH in legend **Note:** Dav. #7310A.

Date	Mintage	VG	F	VF	XF	Unc
1622	—	650	1,250	2,600	4,250	—

KM# 46 THALER (Groschen)

Silver **Obv:** Ornate oval shield **Obv. Legend:** ...SEN: RVH: DN: **Rev:** Crown above double-headed imperial eagle, value in orb on breast **Note:** Dav. #7311.

Date	Mintage	VG	F	VF	XF	Unc
16Z3 MR	—	325	625	1,050	2,250	—

KM# 58 THALER (Groschen)

Silver **Subject:** Death of Heinrich II **Rev:** Eight-line inscription **Note:** Dav. #7312.

Date	Mintage	VG	F	VF	XF	Unc
MDCXXXV (1635)	257	300	600	1,250	2,200	—

KM# 59 THALER (Groschen)

Silver **Rev:** Ten-line inscription **Note:** Dav. #7312A.

Date	Mintage	VG	F	VF	XF	Unc
MDCXXXV (1635)	Inc. above	350	700	1,450	2,500	—

KM# 11 2 THALER

Silver **Note:** Similar to 1 Thaler, KM#10. Dav. #7307.

Date	Mintage	VG	F	VF	XF	Unc
1620 Rare	—	—	—	—	—	—

TRADE COINAGE

KM# 5 GOLDGULDEN

3.5000 g., 0.9860 Gold 0.1109 oz. AGW **Obv:** Two helmets with dog head and crane, titles of Heinrich II **Rev:** Four-fold arms, date above

Date	Mintage	VG	F	VF	XF	Unc
1619 WA	—	1,000	2,000	3,500	6,000	—

KM# 39 GOLDGULDEN

3.5000 g., 0.9860 Gold 0.1109 oz. AGW **Subject:** Lordship of Lobenstein **Obv:** Ornamented four-fold arms, small imperial orb above divides date **Rev:** Two helmets surmounted by dog head and crane, titles of Heinrich II

Date	Mintage	VG	F	VF	XF	Unc
1622	—	1,000	2,000	3,500	6,000	—

KM# 60 GOLDGULDEN

3.5000 g., 0.9860 Gold 0.1109 oz. AGW **Subject:** Death of Heinrich II **Note:** Similar to 1/2 Thaler, KM#57.

Date	Mintage	VG	F	VF	XF	Unc
1635	—	—	—	—	—	—

Note: Reported, not confirmed

KM# 40 3 DUCAT

10.5000 g., 0.9860 Gold 0.3328 oz. AGW **Subject:** Lordship of Lobenstein **Obv:** Squarish four-fold arms, two helmets above with dog head and crane **Rev:** Eight-line inscription, date

Date	Mintage	VG	F	VF	XF	Unc
1622 ES Rare	—	—	—	—	—	—

REUSS-GREIZ

RULERS

Heinrich IV von Reuss-Obergreiz and
Heinrich V von Reuss-Untergreiz

COUNTSHIP

JOINT COINAGE

1604-29

KM# 5 12 KREUZER (3 Batzen)

Silver **Obv:** Crowned imperial eagle, 12 in orb on breast, titles of Ferdinand II **Rev:** Helmeted oval lion arms, plume of helmet divides date **Note:** Kipper 12 Kreuzer. Varieties exist.

Date	Mintage	VG	F	VF	XF	Unc
1621	—	80.00	140	220	325	—

KM# 6 24 KREUZER (6 Batzen)

Silver **Obv:** Crowned imperial eagle, 24 in orb on breast, titles of Ferdinand II **Rev:** Oval lion arms, helmet and dog head above divide date **Note:** Kipper 24 Kreuzer.

Date	Mintage	VG	F	VF	XF	Unc
1621	—	65.00	120	200	300	—

KM# 8 24 KREUZER (6 Batzen)

Silver **Note:** Klippe. Varieties exist.

Date	Mintage	VG	F	VF	XF	Unc
1621	—	—	—	—	—	—
(16)21	—	—	—	—	—	—
ND	—	—	—	—	—	—

KM# 7 24 KREUZER (6 Batzen)

Silver **Rev:** Crowned four-fold arms, date in legend **Note:** Varieties exist.

Date	Mintage	VG	F	VF	XF	Unc
1621	—	55.00	115	195	275	—
ND	—	55.00	115	195	275	—

KM# 9 THALER

Silver **Obv:** Ornate helmeted arms **Rev:** Crown above double-headed imperial eagle, orb on breast **Note:** Varieties exist. Dav. #7305.

Date	Mintage	VG	F	VF	XF	Unc
1624 WA	—	550	1,150	2,200	3,500	—

JOINT COINAGE

1619

KM# 15 1/2 THALER

14.3600 g., Silver **Obv:** Ornate four-fold arms **Rev:** Phoenix rising from flames on top of short column, imperial orb above from clouds; hand with palm branch on left, sword on right; date in legend

Date	Mintage	VG	F	VF	XF	Unc
1619 WA	—	—	—	—	—	—

KM# 16.1 THALER

Silver **Obv:** Helmeted arms **Obv. Legend:** Ends:...G: C: G: S: ET. L:* **Rev:** Phoenix in flames under orb on pedestal, hand with palm frond at left, sword at right **Note:** Dav. #7301.

Date	Mintage	VG	F	VF	XF	Unc
1619 WA	—	375	750	1,500	2,500	—

KM# 16.2 THALER

Silver **Rev:** Different clouds **Note:** Dav. #7301A.

Date	Mintage	VG	F	VF	XF	Unc
1619 WA	—	375	750	1,500	2,500	—

KM# 16.3 THALER

Silver **Obv. Legend:** Ends:...G: C: G: S: ET.LO. **Note:** Dav. #7301B.

Date	Mintage	VG	F	VF	XF	Unc
1619 WA	—	375	750	1,500	2,500	—

KM# 17 2 THALER

Silver **Note:** Similar to 1 Thaler, KM#16. Dav. #7300.

Date	Mintage	VG	F	VF	XF	Unc
1619 WA Rare	—	—	—	—	—	—

REUSS-OBERGREIZ

The other branch of the division of 1635, Obergreiz went through a number of consolidations and further divisions. Upon the extinction of the Ruess-Untergreiz line in 1768, the latter passed to Reuss-Obergreiz and this line continued on into the 20th century, obtaining the rank of count back in 1673 and that of prince in 1778.

RULERS
Heinrich I, 1580-1607
Heinrich II, 1607-1616
Heinrich IV, 1616-1629
Heinrich I, 1629-1681
Heinrich VI, 1681-1697
Heinrich I, 1697-1714

LORDSHIP

REGULAR COINAGE

KM# 5 HELLER
Copper **Ruler:** Heinrich I **Obv:** 3-line inscription with date **Obv. Inscription:** R/HELLER/(date) **Note:** Uniface. Varieties exist.

Date	Mintage	Good	VG	F	VF	XF
1660	—	5.00	13.00	27.00	60.00	—
1661	—	5.00	13.00	27.00	60.00	—
1667	—	5.00	13.00	27.00	60.00	—
1668	—	5.00	13.00	27.00	60.00	—

KM# 6 HELLER
Copper **Ruler:** Heinrich I **Obv:** Crowned lion **Rev:** Date **Rev. Legend:** R/HELLER **Note:** Varieties exist.

Date	Mintage	Good	VG	F	VF	XF
1660	—	7.00	13.00	22.00	45.00	—
1661	—	7.00	13.00	22.00	45.00	—

KM# 7 HELLER
Copper **Ruler:** Heinrich I **Obv:** Helmet with hound's head crest **Rev:** Date **Rev. Legend:** REISI/HELER

Date	Mintage	Good	VG	F	VF	XF
1661	—	—	—	—	—	—

COUNTSHIP

REGULAR COINAGE

KM# 10 HELLER
Copper **Ruler:** Heinrich I **Obv:** Crowned lion rampant left in shield **Rev:** Date **Rev. Legend:** R/HELLER

Date	Mintage	Good	VG	F	VF	XF
1676	—	—	—	—	—	—

KM# 11 HELLER
Copper **Ruler:** Heinrich I **Obv:** Crowned rampant lion left **Note:** Varieties exist.

Date	Mintage	Good	VG	F	VF	XF
1676	—	4.00	11.00	24.00	40.00	—
1677	—	4.00	11.00	24.00	40.00	—
1678	—	4.00	11.00	24.00	40.00	—

KM# 9 HELLER
Copper **Ruler:** Heinrich I **Obv:** 3-line inscription with date **Obv. Inscription:** R/HELLER/(date) **Note:** Uniface. Varieties exist.

Date	Mintage	Good	VG	F	VF	XF
1676	—	4.00	10.00	20.00	45.00	—
1677	—	4.00	10.00	20.00	45.00	—
1678	—	4.00	10.00	20.00	45.00	—
1681	—	4.00	10.00	20.00	45.00	—

KM# 12 HELLER
Copper **Ruler:** Heinrich I **Obv:** Lion right **Rev:** Date **Rev. Legend:** R/HE.ER

Date	Mintage	Good	VG	F	VF	XF
1677	—	—	—	—	—	—

KM# 13 HELLER
Copper **Ruler:** Heinrich I **Obv:** Crowned lion rampant left **Rev:** Reusisch:/Obergratzi=/sche Heller/date

Date	Mintage	Good	VG	F	VF	XF
1678	—	4.00	11.00	24.00	40.00	—

KM# 14 HELLER
Copper **Ruler:** Heinrich I **Obv:** Helmet with dog head right above **Rev:** Crowned lion rampant left, date spaced around

Date	Mintage	Good	VG	F	VF	XF
ND	—	—	—	—	—	—

KM# 15 HELLER
Copper **Ruler:** Heinrich I **Obv:** Dog head left **Rev:** Similar to KM#5 **Note:** Varieties exist.

Date	Mintage	Good	VG	F	VF	XF
1678	—	4.00	11.00	24.00	40.00	—

KM# 20 HELLER
Copper **Ruler:** Heinrich I **Obv:** Helmet with dog head right above **Rev:** Dog head turned right divides date **Note:** Varieties exist.

Date	Mintage	Good	VG	F	VF	XF
1679	—	4.00	11.00	24.00	40.00	—
1680	—	4.00	11.00	24.00	40.00	—

KM# 22 HELLER
Copper **Ruler:** Heinrich I **Rev. Legend:** REUSISCH/ OBERGRAITZI:/SCHE HELLER **Note:** Varieties exist.

Date	Mintage	Good	VG	F	VF	XF
1679	—	4.00	11.00	24.00	40.00	—
1680	—	4.00	11.00	24.00	40.00	—
1681	—	4.00	11.00	24.00	40.00	—

KM# 21 HELLER
Copper **Ruler:** Heinrich I **Obv:** Dog head right divides date **Rev. Legend:** GR/REUss/heller/O G

Date	Mintage	Good	VG	F	VF	XF
1679	—	5.00	13.00	27.00	45.00	—

KM# 28 HELLER
Copper **Ruler:** Heinrich VI **Obv:** Helmet with hound's head crest **Rev. Inscription:** REIS I/HELER/(date)

Date	Mintage	Good	VG	F	VF	XF
1681	—	—	—	—	—	—

KM# 31 HELLER
Copper **Ruler:** Heinrich VI **Note:** Crowned lion rampant left, space around. Uniface. Varieties exist.

Date	Mintage	Good	VG	F	VF	XF
1686	—	5.00	13.00	27.00	60.00	—
ND	—	5.00	13.00	27.00	60.00	—

KM# 35 HELLER
Copper **Ruler:** Heinrich VI **Note:** Dog head left.

Date	Mintage	Good	VG	F	VF	XF
ND	—	—	—	—	—	—

KM# 34 HELLER
Copper **Ruler:** Heinrich VI **Note:** Helmet with dog head right above.

Date	Mintage	Good	VG	F	VF	XF
ND	—	4.00	11.00	24.00	40.00	—

KM# 33 HELLER
Copper **Ruler:** Heinrich VI **Note:** Lion right.

Date	Mintage	Good	VG	F	VF	XF
ND	—	—	—	—	—	—

KM# 32 HELLER
Copper **Ruler:** Heinrich VI **Note:** Lion without crown.

Date	Mintage	Good	VG	F	VF	XF
1686	—	—	—	—	—	—

KM# 29 HELLER
Copper **Ruler:** Heinrich VI **Obv:** 3-line inscription with date **Obv. Inscription:** R/HELLER/(date) **Note:** Uniface. Varieties exist.

Date	Mintage	Good	VG	F	VF	XF
1686	—	4.00	10.00	20.00	45.00	—
1691	—	4.00	10.00	20.00	45.00	—

KM# 40 HELLER
Copper **Ruler:** Heinrich VI **Note:** R/HL-LR/date.

Date	Mintage	Good	VG	F	VF	XF
1691	—	4.00	11.00	24.00	40.00	—

KM# 16 PFENNIG
Silver **Ruler:** Heinrich I **Obv:** Crane left **Obv. Legend:** GR. PFENIGE **Note:** Varieties exist.

Date	Mintage	VG	F	VF	XF	Unc
1678	—	9.00	20.00	33.00	60.00	—
1679	—	9.00	20.00	33.00	60.00	—
1680	—	9.00	20.00	33.00	60.00	—

KM# 30 PFENNIG
Silver **Ruler:** Heinrich I **Obv:** Lion rampant left **Obv. Legend:** GR. PFENNIGE **Rev:** Imperial orb with symbol divides date

Date	Mintage	VG	F	VF	XF	Unc
1680	—	16.00	33.00	55.00	85.00	—

KM# 17 3 PFENNIG
Silver **Ruler:** Heinrich I **Obv. Legend:** GR/DREYER **Rev:** Value: 3 on imperial orb divides date as 1 - 6/7 - 8

Date	Mintage	VG	F	VF	XF	Unc
1678	—	9.00	20.00	40.00	80.00	—

KM# 18 1/84 THALER (3 Pfennig)
Silver **Ruler:** Heinrich I **Obv:** Value: 84 on imperial orb divides date, titles of Heinrich I **Rev:** 3 small shields of arms, 2 above 1 **Note:** Varieties exist.

Date	Mintage	VG	F	VF	XF	Unc
1678	—	27.00	40.00	65.00	120	—
1680	—	27.00	40.00	65.00	120	—

KM# 19 1/24 THALER (Groschen)
Silver **Ruler:** Heinrich I **Obv:** Crowned 4-fold arms **Obv. Legend:** AN GOTTES SEGEN... **Rev:** Value: 24 on imperial orb divides date **Rev. Legend:** GR. G. W. REUSISCHE. GROSCHEN **Note:** Varieties exist.

Date	Mintage	VG	F	VF	XF	Unc
1678	—	13.00	30.00	55.00	100	—
1679/78	—	20.00	40.00	70.00	125	—

Date	Mintage	VG	F	VF	XF	Unc
1679	—	13.00	30.00	55.00	100	—
1680	—	13.00	30.00	55.00	100	—

KM# 23 1/6 THALER (1/4 Gulden)
Silver **Ruler:** Heinrich I **Obv:** Value 1/6 in oval below arms **Rev:** Cross in center with IHS; date **Rev. Legend:** IN HOC VICTORIA CERTA; OMNIA - CUM - DEO **Note:** Varieties exist.

Date	Mintage	VG	F	VF	XF	Unc
1679	—	40.00	80.00	140	225	—

KM# 24 1/6 THALER (1/4 Gulden)
Silver **Ruler:** Heinrich I **Obv:** Date, bust right **Obv. Legend:** OMNIA CUM DEO **Note:** Varieties exist.

Date	Mintage	VG	F	VF	XF	Unc
1679	—	65.00	135	225	375	—

KM# 25 1/3 THALER (1/2 Gulden)
Silver **Ruler:** Heinrich I **Obv:** Titles of Heinrich I

Date	Mintage	VG	F	VF	XF	Unc
1679	—	40.00	110	160	325	—

KM# 26 1/3 THALER (1/2 Gulden)
Silver **Ruler:** Heinrich I **Note:** Similar to 1/6 Thaler, KM#24, but value: 1/3.

Date	Mintage	VG	F	VF	XF	Unc
1679	—	—	—	—	—	—

KM# 27 2/3 THALER (1 Gulden)
Silver **Ruler:** Heinrich I

Date	Mintage	VG	F	VF	XF	Unc
1679	—	200	375	550	1,000	—

KM# 41 THALER

Silver **Ruler:** Heinrich I **Subject:** Internment of Heinrich VI (died 1697, buried 1698) **Note:** Dav. #7306.

Date	Mintage	VG	F	VF	XF	Unc
1698 ILH	—	—	450	900	1,650	2,900

TRADE COINAGE

KM# 42 5 DUCAT

17.5000 g., 0.9860 Gold 0.5547 oz. AGW **Ruler:** Heinrich I **Subject:** Internment of Heinrich VI **Obv:** Bust right **Rev:** 11-line inscription, date

Date	Mintage	VG	F	VF	XF	Unc
1698 ILH Rare	—	—	—	—	—	—

Note: Struck with 1 Thaler dies, KM#41

REUSS-ROTHENTHAL

The smallest of the Reuss branches, only Heinrich V of lower Greiz issued coins for this division.

RULER

Heinrich V, 1668-1698

COUNTSHIP

TRADE COINAGE

KM# 5 DUCAT

3.5000 g., 0.9860 Gold 0.1109 oz. AGW **Obv:** Bust of Heinrich right in inner circle **Rev:** Arms in inner circle

Date	Mintage	VG	F	VF	XF	Unc
1679 ICF Rare	—	—	—	—	—	—

REUSS-SCHLEIZ

Originally part of the holdings of Reuss-Gera, Schleiz was ruled separately on and off during the first half of the 16th century. When the Gera line died out in 1550, Schleiz passed to Obergreiz. Schleiz was reintegrated into a new line of Gera and a separate countship at Schleiz was founded in 1635, only to last one generation. At its extinction in 1666, Schleiz passed to Reuss-Saalburg which thereafter took the name of Reuss-Schleiz.

RULERS

Heinrich II, 1580-1616
Heinrich II Posthumous, 1616-1635
Heinrich IX, 1635-1666
Heinrich I, 1666-1692
Heinrich XI, 1692-1726

PRINCIPALITY

REGULAR COINAGE

KM# 30 PFENNIG

Silver **Obv:** Dog head above helmet **Rev:** Imperial orb with 1 dividing date and initials

Date	Mintage	VG	F	VF	XF	Unc
1680 SD	—	20.00	40.00	80.00	240	—

KM# 31 PFENNIG

Silver **Rev:** Imperial orb with 1 dividing R-S and date **Mint:** Friedenstein bei Gotha **Note:** Struck at Friedenstein bei Gotha.

Date	Mintage	VG	F	VF	XF	Unc
1683	—	16.00	35.00	65.00	200	—

KM# 32 2 PFENNIG

Silver **Obv:** Dog head above helmet **Rev:** Imperial orb dividing R-S and date **Mint:** Friedenstein bei Gotha **Note:** Struck at Friedenstein bei Gotha.

Date	Mintage	VG	F	VF	XF	Unc
1683	—	24.00	45.00	80.00	240	—

KM# 10 3 PFENNIG

Silver **Obv:** Dog head above helmet **Obv. Legend:** SCHLAIZER DREIER **Rev:** Value: 84 on imperial orb dividing initials, date above

Date	Mintage	VG	F	VF	XF	Unc
1669 SD	—	13.00	25.00	40.00	135	—

KM# 23 3 PFENNIG

Silver **Obv. Legend:** SCHLAITZ: DREYER **Rev:** Orb divides date and initials **Note:** Varieties exist.

Date	Mintage	VG	F	VF	XF	Unc
1679 SD	—	11.00	20.00	33.00	100	—

KM# 16 2 SILBER GROSCHEN (1/12 Thaler)

Silver **Subject:** Death of Heinrich I's Wife, Maximilane von Hardegg **Mint:** Friedenstein bei Gotha **Note:** Similar to 2/3 Thaler KM#19, but obverse with value "2 gl" in oval.

Date	Mintage	VG	F	VF	XF	Unc
1678	—	35.00	65.00	110	325	—

KM# 24 1/24 THALER (Groschen)

Silver **Obv:** Crowned four-fold arms in palm wreath **Rev:** Value: 24/EINEN/REICHS/THALER/date **Mint:** Friedenstein bei Gotha **Note:** Varieties exist.

Date	Mintage	VG	F	VF	XF	Unc
1679 SD	—	13.00	27.00	55.00	140	—

KM# 17 1/4 THALER

Silver **Subject:** Death of Heinrich I's Wife, Maximilane von Hardegg **Mint:** Friedenstein bei Gotha **Note:** Similar to 2/3 Thaler KM#19, but obverse with value "2 gl" in oval on obverse replaced by skull.

Date	Mintage	VG	F	VF	XF	Unc
1678	—	100	200	300	525	—

KM# 18 1/3 THALER (1/2 Gulden)

Silver **Obv:** Bust right **Rev:** Crowned round four-fold arms, value: 1/3 in oval below divides date **Mint:** Friedenstein bei Gotha **Note:** Varieties exist.

Date	Mintage	VG	F	VF	XF	Unc
1678 SD	—	—	—	—	—	—
1679 SD	—	—	—	—	—	—

KM# 15 2/3 THALER (Gulden)

Silver **Obv:** Bust right **Rev:** Crowned arms in round shield, value: 2/3 divides date below **Mint:** Friedenstein bei Gotha

Date	Mintage	VG	F	VF	XF	Unc
1670 SD	—	—	—	—	—	—

KM# 19 2/3 THALER (Gulden)

Silver **Subject:** Death of Heinrich I's Wife, Maximilane von Hardegg **Obv:** Value: 2/3 in oval below frame **Note:** Varieties exist.

Date	Mintage	VG	F	VF	XF	Unc
1678 SD	—	225	300	375	775	—

KM# 20 2/3 THALER (Gulden)

Silver **Note:** Varieties exist.

Date	Mintage	VG	F	VF	XF	Unc
1678 SD	—	135	200	275	525	—
1679 SD	—	135	200	275	525	—

KM# 21 2/3 THALER (Gulden)

Silver **Rev:** Arm extending from clouds holding scale, value: 2/3 below, date in legend **Note:** Varieties exist.

Date	Mintage	VG	F	VF	XF	Unc
1678 SD	—	275	400	550	1,150	—

KM# 25 2/3 THALER (Gulden)

Silver **Obv:** Bust 3/4 right **Rev:** Small oval four-fold arms in crossed oak branches, value: 2/3 in oval divides date **Note:** Varieties exist.

Date	Mintage	VG	F	VF	XF	Unc
1679 SD	—	—	—	—	—	—

KM# 26 THALER

Silver **Note:** Dav. #7314.

Date	Mintage	VG	F	VF	XF	Unc
1679 IAB	—	525	900	1,800	3,750	—

KM# 27 THALER

Silver **Note:** Dav. #7316.

Date	Mintage	VG	F	VF	XF	Unc
1679 IAB	—	600	1,000	2,050	4,250	—

KM# 28 2 THALER

Silver **Note:** Similar to 1 Thaler, KM#27. Dav. #7315.

Date	Mintage	VG	F	VF	XF	Unc
1679 IAB Rare	—	—	—	—	—	—

TRADE COINAGE

KM# 5 GOLDGULDEN

3.5000 g., 0.9860 Gold 0.1109 oz. AGW **Obv:** Arms in inner circle **Rev:** Two helmets vis-a-vis

Date	Mintage	VG	F	VF	XF	Unc
1619	—	—	450	900	1,900	2,800
1622	—	—	450	900	1,900	2,800

PATTERNS

Including off metal strikes

KM#	Date	Mintage	Identification	Mkt Val
Pn1	1678	—	Goldgulden. Silver.	—

REUSS-UNTERGREIZ

Founded in 1535, inherited Burgk in 1550. After several acquisitions and subsequent divisions, the line died out in 1768 and all holdings passed to Reuss-Obergreiz.

RULERS

Heinrich V, 1572-1604
Heinrich III, 1604-1609
Heinrich IV, 1609-1616
Heinrich V, 1609-(1625)-1667
Heinrich II, 1668-1697
Heinrich IV, 1668-1675
Heinrich V, 1668-1698
Heinrich XIII, 1675-1733

PRINCIPALITY

REGULAR COINAGE

KM# 5 3 PFENNIG (1/84 Thaler)

Silver **Obv:** Helmet with dog head divides date **Obv. Legend:** OBER SAX: KREISSES **Rev:** Value: 3 on imperial orb divides initials

Date	Mintage	VG	F	VF	XF	Unc
1657 MR	—	27.00	55.00	110	225	—

KM# 6 3 PFENNIG (1/84 Thaler)

Silver **Obv:** Two ornamented helmets with dog head and crane divide date **Rev:** Value: 3 on imperial orb in ornamental frame

Date	Mintage	VG	F	VF	XF	Unc
1659	—	27.00	55.00	110	225	—

KM# 16 6 PFENNIG

Silver **Obv:** Helmet with dog head left divides G-R **Rev:** Value: 6 on imperial orb divides date **Note:** Sechser 6 Pfennig. Varieties exist.

Date	Mintage	VG	F	VF	XF	Unc
1690	—	20.00	40.00	80.00	160	—
1691	—	20.00	40.00	80.00	160	—

KM# 15 1/48 THALER

Silver **Obv:** Helmet with dog head left divides GR-DR **Rev:** Value: 84 on imperial orb divides date, all in rhombus

Date	Mintage	VG	F	VF	XF	Unc
1690	—	24.00	45.00	95.00	165	—
1691	—	24.00	45.00	95.00	165	—

KM# 10 2/3 THALER (Gulden)

Silver **Obv:** Bust right, titles of Heinrich II **Rev:** Crowned four-fold arms with central shield, date 16 above crown, rest divided by arms, value: 2/3 in oval below **Note:** Varieties exist.

Date	Mintage	VG	F	VF	XF	Unc
1678	—	325	600	1,075	1,650	—
1683	—	325	600	1,075	1,650	—

RHEINE

(Reine)

Located on the River Ems in Westphalia about 25 miles (42km) west of Osnabrück and 24 miles (39km) northwest of Münster, the town of Rheine received municipal rights from the bishop of the latter city in 1327. The town leaders petitioned Ernst of Bavaria, Administrator of Münster in the late 16th century for permission to issue minor coinage. The request was granted several years later and coins were produced from about 1602 until 1609.

TOWN ARMS

Shield with horizontal band across middle in which are three stars in line.

REFERENCES

D = Wilhelm Döll, **Die Kupfermünzen und Kupfermarken der Stadt Rheine**, Rheine, 1980.
W = Joseph Weingärtner, **Beschreibung der Kupfermünzen Westfalens nebst historischen Nachrichten**, 2 vols., Paderborn, 1872-81.

PROVINCIAL TOWN

REGULAR COINAGE

KM# 1 HELLER

Copper **Obv:** Shield of town arms **Obv. Legend:** STADT — REINE **Rev:** 'I' inset with upper half of H, within 2 ornamented circles **Note:** Size varies 14.5-16 mm; weight varies .6-1.1 grams.

Date	Mintage	Good	VG	F	VF	XF
ND(1602)	—	16.00	33.00	55.00	85.00	—

KM# 2 PFENNIG

Copper **Obv:** Shield of town arms **Obv. Legend:** STADT — REINE **Rev:** 'I' in ornamented rhombus with arches in sides, all within a circle **Note:** Size varies 14.5-18.5 mm; weight varies .77-1.52 grams.

Date	Mintage	Good	VG	F	VF	XF
ND(1602)	—	16.00	33.00	55.00	90.00	—

KM# 3 2 PFENNIG

Copper **Obv:** Lion striding to left, holding shield of town arms in forepaws **Obv. Legend:** STAD — T. R — EINE **Rev:** 'II' in ornamented square **Note:** Size varies 16-17.5 mm; weight varies .96-1.6 grams; obverse legend varies.

Date	Mintage	Good	VG	F	VF	XF
ND(1602) Rare	—	—	—	—	—	—

KM# 4 3 PFENNIG

Copper **Obv:** Shield of town arms, date **Obv. Legend:** STADT . R — EINE **Rev:** 'III' with arabesques around **Note:** Size varies 19.5-21 mm; weight varies 1.07-2.7; varieties exist.

Date	Mintage	Good	VG	F	VF	XF
160Z	—	16.00	27.00	55.00	90.00	—
1602	—	16.00	27.00	55.00	90.00	—
1609	—	16.00	27.00	55.00	90.00	—

KM# 5 4 PFENNIG

Copper **Obv:** Shield of town arms, date **Obv. Legend:** STADT . R — EINE **Rev:** 'IIII' with arabesques around **Note:** Size varies 20-21 mm; weight varies 1.06-3.035 grams.

Date	Mintage	Good	VG	F	VF	XF
160Z	—	16.00	27.00	55.00	90.00	—
1602	—	16.00	27.00	55.00	90.00	—
1609	—	16.00	27.00	55.00	90.00	—

KM# 6 6 PFENNIG

Copper **Obv:** Shield of town arms, date **Obv. Legend:** STADT— REINE **Rev:** "VI' in circle, ornamented border of either 20 or 24 small crescents **Note:** Size varies 21-23 mm; weight varies 1.4-3.2 grams; varieties exist.

Date	Mintage	Good	VG	F	VF	XF
160Z	—	24.00	45.00	80.00	125	—
1602	—	24.00	45.00	80.00	125	—

KM# 7 8 PFENNIG

Copper **Obv:** Ornamented shield of town arms, date **Obv. Legend:** STADT. REINE **Rev:** 'VIII' with arabesques around **Note:** Size varies 21.5-23.5 mm; weight varies 1.51-2.07 grams; varieties exist.

Date	Mintage	Good	VG	F	VF	XF
160Z	—	30.00	60.00	115	160	—
1602	—	30.00	60.00	115	160	—

KM# 8 12 PFENNIG

Copper **Obv:** Ornamented shield of town arms, date **Obv. Legend:** STADT . REINE **Rev:** Gothic '12' in circle, outer margin of striations **Note:** Size varies 29-32 mm; weight varies 2.595-8.15 grams; varieties exist.

Date	Mintage	Good	VG	F	VF	XF
160Z	—	45.00	75.00	115	180	—

RIETBERG

The counts of Rietberg held lands along the River Ems in Westphalia. Rietberg castle and town are located on the river about 15 miles (25 km) west-northwest of Paderborn. The line of Rietberg counts was established by Heinrich II (1185-1207), the younger brother of Count Gottfried II of Arnsberg (1185-1235). The line in Rietberg had the misfortune to become extinct in the male line more than once. When Konrad IV died in 1439, he was succeeded by his grandson through his daughter. In the mid-16th century, Johann II left only two daughters. Irmgard married first Erich von Hoya, second Simon von Lippe, who ruled Rietberg briefly after his wife died in 1583. Meanwhile, Walburg had married Enno III von Ostfriesland and their daughter Sabina Katharina eventually married her uncle, Johann III von Ostfriesland. Johann III ruled Rietberg and their son was the first of a new line of counts there. When that line became extinct as well in 1690, Rietberg passed in marriage to the counts of Kaunitz. The countship was raised to a principality in 1764 and was mediatized in 1807, passing to Westphalia thereafter.

RULERS

Johann I, 1481-1516
Otto III, 1516-1535
Otto IV, 1535-1551
Johann II der Tolle, 1535-1557 (d. 1564)
Interregnum, 1557-1564
Irmgard, 1564-1583
Walburg, 1564-1586
Enno III von Ostfriesland, 1586-1600
Sabina Katharina, 1600-1618 and
Johann III von Ostfriesland, 1600-1625
Ernst Christof I, 1625-1640
Johann IV, 1640-1660
Friedrich Wilhelm, 1660-1677
Franz Adolf Wilhelm, 1677-1685
Ferdinand Maximilian, 1685-1687
Franz Adolf Wilhelm, again 1687-1690
Maria Ernestine Franziska, 1690-1758
Maximilian Ulrich von Kaunitz, 1699-1746
Wenzel Anton, 1746-1794, Prince 1764
Ernst Christof II, 1794-1797
Dominikus Anon, 1797-1807 (d. 1812)

REFERENCE

B = W. Buse, "Münzgeschichte der Grafschaft Rietberg,, ***Zeitschrift für Numismatik*** 29 (1912), pp. 254-362, pls. 6-9.
Sch = Wolfgang Schulten, ***Deutsche Münzen aus der Zeit Karls. V.*** Frankfurt am Main, 1974.

COUNTSHIP

REGULAR COINAGE

KM# 60 4 PFENNIG

Copper **Obv:** Eagle **Rev:** Denomination: II•II and date

Date	Mintage	VG	F	VF	XF	Unc
1654	—	325	525	—	—	—

KM# 61 6 PFENNIG

Copper **Obv:** Eagle **Rev:** Denomination VI and date

Date	Mintage	VG	F	VF	XF	Unc
1654	—	400	675	—	—	—

KM# 17 SCHILLING

Silver **Obv:** Crowned arms on St. Andrew's cross **Rev:** Imperial eagle, titles of Matthias

Date	Mintage	VG	F	VF	XF	Unc
1617	—	45.00	100	200	400	—

KM# 18 SCHILLING

Silver **Rev:** Without St. Andrew's cross under arms **Note:** Several legend varieties exist.

Date	Mintage	VG	F	VF	XF	Unc
1617	—	40.00	80.00	160	350	—
1618	—	40.00	80.00	160	350	—
1619	—	40.00	80.00	160	350	—

KM# 22 SCHILLING

Silver **Obv:** Crowned arms **Rev:** Crowned imperial eagle, titles of Ferdinand II

Date	Mintage	VG	F	VF	XF	Unc
1619	—	45.00	100	200	400	—

KM# 21 SCHILLING
11.0000 g., Silver **Obv:** Crowned arms **Rev:** Double-headed imperial eagle, orb on breast **Note:** Klippe.

Date	Mintage	VG	F	VF	XF	Unc
ND(1619)	—	—	—	—	—	—

KM# 23 SCHRECKENBERGER
Silver **Ruler:** Johann III von Ostfriesland **Obv:** Arms **Rev:** Crowned imperial eagle, titles of Matthias

Date	Mintage	VG	F	VF	XF	Unc
1618	—	80.00	160	300	600	—
1619	—	80.00	160	300	600	—

KM# 24 SCHRECKENBERGER
Silver **Ruler:** Johann III von Ostfriesland **Obv:** Arms **Rev:** Crowned imperial eagle, titles of Ferdinand II **Note:** Kipper Coinage

Date	Mintage	VG	F	VF	XF	Unc
1619	—	75.00	125	245	500	—

KM# 25 SCHRECKENBERGER
10.8000 g., Silver **Obv:** Arms **Rev:** Crowned imperial eagle, titles of Ferdinand II **Note:** Klippe.

Date	Mintage	VG	F	VF	XF	Unc
1619	—	—	—	—	—	—

KM# 62 2 MARIENGROSCHEN
1.1150 g., Silver **Obv:** Arms **Rev:** Denomination

Date	Mintage	VG	F	VF	XF	Unc
1654	—	525	850	—	—	—

KM# 14 1/24 THALER (Groschen)
1.3000 g., Silver **Ruler:** Sabina Katharina **Obv:** Arms of Rietberg and Ostfriesland **Rev:** Imperial orb, titles of Matthias

Date	Mintage	VG	F	VF	XF	Unc
1615	—	13.00	27.00	55.00	115	—
1616	—	13.00	27.00	55.00	115	—
1616 (a)	—	13.00	27.00	55.00	115	—
1617	—	13.00	27.00	55.00	115	—
1617 (a)	—	13.00	27.00	55.00	115	—
1618	—	13.00	27.00	55.00	115	—
1618 (a)	—	13.00	27.00	55.00	115	—

KM# 15 1/24 THALER (Groschen)
Silver **Obv:** 2 Shields, legend around **Rev:** Imperial orb, value within **Note:** Klippe.

Date	Mintage	VG	F	VF	XF	Unc
1616	—	—	—	—	—	—

KM# 19 1/24 THALER (Groschen)
Silver **Ruler:** Johann III von Ostfriesland **Obv:** 2 Shields, legend around **Rev:** Imperial orb, value within **Note:** Smaller, cruder strike with legend varieties. Many varieties exist.

Date	Mintage	VG	F	VF	XF	Unc
1617 (a)	—	13.00	27.00	55.00	115	—
1618 (a)	—	13.00	27.00	55.00	115	—
1619 (a)	—	13.00	27.00	55.00	115	—

KM# 26 1/24 THALER (Groschen)
Silver **Ruler:** Johann III von Ostfriesland **Obv:** 2 Shields, legend around **Rev:** Titles of Ferdinand II **Note:** Kipper Coinage

Date	Mintage	VG	F	VF	XF	Unc
1619	—	20.00	40.00	80.00	160	—
16Z0	—	20.00	40.00	80.00	160	—

KM# 35 1/21 THALER (Fürstengroschen)
Silver **Ruler:** Johann III von Ostfriesland **Obv:** Round 2-fold arms of Rietburg and Ostfriesland. **Obv. Legend:** LANTMVNTZ. XXI. ZV R. DALER. **Rev:** Imperial eagle, '1Z' in circle on breast. **Rev. Legend:** FERD. II. D.G. ROM. IM. SEM. AVG. **Note:** Kipper 1/21 Thaler. Many varieties exist.

Date	Mintage	VG	F	VF	XF	Unc
ND	—	33.00	55.00	85.00	150	—

KM# 36 1/21 THALER (Fürstengroschen)
Silver **Obv:** Error, 1Z in orb

Date	Mintage	VG	F	VF	XF	Unc
ND	—	33.00	55.00	85.00	150	—

KM# 37 1/21 THALER (Fürstengroschen)
Silver **Ruler:** Johann III von Ostfriesland **Obv:** Round 2-fold arms of Rietburg and Ostfriesland **Obv. Legend:** IOH. COM. ET DO. FR. OR. ET. RIT. **Rev:** Crowned imperial eagle, 'Z1' in circle on breast. **Rev. Legend:** RITP. MVNTZ. XXI. ZV R. DALER. **Note:** Kipper coinage. Many varieties exist.

Date	Mintage	VG	F	VF	XF	Unc
ND	—	27.00	45.00	80.00	150	—

KM# 38 1/21 THALER (Fürstengroschen)
Silver **Obv:** Helmeted arms **Rev:** Crowned imperial eagle, 1Z in orb on eagle's chest, titles of Ferdinand II **Note:** Varieties exist.

Date	Mintage	VG	F	VF	XF	Unc
ND	—	40.00	65.00	110	180	—

KM# 27 1/4 THALER
Silver **Obv:** Crowned imperial eagle, titles of Matthias **Rev:** Arms **Note:** Legend varieties exist.

Date	Mintage	VG	F	VF	XF	Unc
1619	—	—	—	—	—	—

KM# 28 1/4 THALER
Silver **Obv:** Crowned imperial eagle, titles of Ferdinand II **Rev:** Arms **Note:** Legend varieties exist.

Date	Mintage	VG	F	VF	XF	Unc
1619	—	—	—	—	—	—

KM# 81 1/3 THALER (Half Gulden)
9.1000 g., Silver **Obv:** Crowned arms **Rev:** Denomination and horse countermark

Date	Mintage	VG	F	VF	XF	Unc
1688 Rare	—	—	—	—	—	—

KM# 63 1/2 THALER
13.2000 g., Silver **Obv:** 3 Helmeted shields **Rev:** Crowned imperial eagle above date, titles of Ferdinand III

Date	Mintage	VG	F	VF	XF	Unc
1654 Rare	—	—	—	—	—	—

KM# 64 2/3 THALER (Gulden)
Silver **Obv:** Crowned imperial eagle, titles of Ferdinand III, denomination divides date **Rev:** Helmeted arms

Date	Mintage	VG	F	VF	XF	Unc
1654 Rare	—	—	—	—	—	—

KM# 82 2/3 THALER (Gulden)
Silver **Obv:** Crowned arms **Rev:** Denomination and horse countermark **Note:** 18.1-18.7 grams.

Date	Mintage	VG	F	VF	XF	Unc
1688 PNC Rare	—	—	—	—	—	—
1688 PN	—	—	—	—	—	—

KM# 90 2/3 THALER (Gulden)
Silver **Obv:** Regent's portrait **Rev:** Crowned arms

Date	Mintage	VG	F	VF	XF	Unc
1693 PN Rare	—	—	—	—	—	—

KM# 16 THALER
Silver **Obv:** Crowned imperial eagle with orb on breast, date divided below **Obv. Legend:** MATTIAS. I. D. G. ROMAN… **Rev:** Helmeted arms **Rev. Legend:** IOAN. COM. E-DO… **Note:** Dav. #7317.

Date	Mintage	VG	F	VF	XF	Unc
1616 Rare	—	—	—	—	—	—

KM# 20 THALER
Silver **Obv:** Date divided by helmets 1-6-1-8 **Obv. Legend:** …ET: DO:…ET: RIT. **Rev:** Crown above double-headed imperial eagle, orb on breast **Rev. Legend:** MATHI. I. D. G. RA. ROMAN… **Note:** Dav. #7318.

Date	Mintage	VG	F	VF	XF	Unc
1618 Rare	—	—	—	—	—	—

KM# 41 THALER
Silver **Ruler:** Johann III von Ostfriesland **Obv:** Arms **Rev:** Crown above double-headed imperial eagle, orb on breast **Note:** Dav. #7320.

Date	Mintage	VG	F	VF	XF	Unc
1621 Rare	—	—	—	—	—	—

KM# 43 THALER
Silver **Ruler:** Johann III von Ostfriesland **Obv:** Arms **Rev:** Crown above double-headed imperial eagle, orb on breast **Rev. Legend:** FERDI*I. I. D: G*EL*ROM*IMP... **Note:** Dav. #7321.

Date	Mintage	VG	F	VF	XF	Unc
1621 Rare	—	—	—	—	—	—
ND(1625) Rare	—	—	—	—	—	—
1625 Rare	—	—	—	—	—	—

KM# 42 THALER
Silver **Obv:** Arms, legend around **Rev:** Crown above double-headed imperial eagle, orb on breast **Note:** Klippe. Dav. #7320A. Illustration reduced.

Date	Mintage	VG	F	VF	XF	Unc
1621 Rare	—	—	—	—	—	—

KM# 50 THALER
Silver **Obv:** Arms **Rev:** Crown above double-headed imperial eagle, orb on breast **Rev. Legend:** FER*II*D: G*EL*RO*IM... **Note:** Dav. #7323.

Date	Mintage	VG	F	VF	XF	Unc
ND Rare	—	—	—	—	—	—

KM# 51 THALER
Silver **Obv. Legend:** IOAN. CO. E. D. -FR… **Note:** Dav. #7324.

Date	Mintage	VG	F	VF	XF	Unc
ND Rare	—	—	—	—	—	—

KM# 52 THALER
Silver **Ruler:** Johann IV **Obv:** Helmeted arms **Obv. Legend:** IOAN: COM: ET: DO: FRI: OR… **Rev:** Crown above double-headed imperial eagle, orb on breast **Rev. Legend:** FERDINAND: I. I. I. D. GRA… **Note:** Dav. #7325.

Date	Mintage	VG	F	VF	XF	Unc
ND Rare	—	—	—	—	—	—

Note: Dr. Busso Peus Nachfolger Auction 389, 11-06, VF realized approximately $26,830

KM# 53 THALER
Silver **Ruler:** Johann IV **Obv. Legend:** FERDINAND: I. I. I. I... **Note:** Dav. #7325A.

Date	Mintage	VG	F	VF	XF	Unc
ND Rare	—	—	—	—	—	—

KM# 71.2 THALER
Silver Plated Copper **Ruler:** Johann IV **Obv. Legend:** ...EOED RIDTHE. **Note:** Dav. #7326A.

Date	Mintage	VG	F	VF	XF	Unc
1660	—	75.00	150	300	—	—

Note: This coin is a contemporary copy of the then current Netherlands Lowenthaler type struck in Rietberg by Johann IV

KM# 71.3 THALER
Silver Plated Copper **Ruler:** Johann IV **Obv. Legend:** ...EOED RIDTH. **Note:** Dav. #7326B.

Date	Mintage	VG	F	VF	XF	Unc
1660	—	100	200	350	—	—

KM# 72.1 THALER
Silver Plated Copper **Rev. Legend:** ...MOVETFVR **Note:** Dav. #7326C.

Date	Mintage	VG	F	VF	XF	Unc
1660	—	100	200	350	—	—

KM# 71.1 THALER
Silver Plated Copper **Ruler:** Johann IV **Obv:** Knight behind arms **Obv. Legend:** ...EOFD RIDTHF. **Rev:** Lion, date **Note:** 20.00-25.00 grams. Dav. #7326.

Date	Mintage	VG	F	VF	XF	Unc
1660	—	75.00	150	300	—	—

Note: This coin is a contemporary copy of the then current Netherlands Lowenthaler type struck in Rietberg by Johann IV

KM# 72.2 THALER
Silver Plated Copper **Rev. Legend:** ...MOVETVIR
Note: Additional varieties exist. Some with reversed D's. Dav. #7326D.

Date	Mintage	VG	F	VF	XF	Unc
1660	—	100	200	350	—	—

KM# 40 2 THALER
Silver **Rev. Legend:** FER*II*... **Note:** Dav. #7322.

Date	Mintage	VG	F	VF	XF	Unc
ND Rare	—	—	—	—	—	—

KM# 39 2 THALER
Silver **Note:** Similar to 1 Thaler, KM#41. Dav. #7319.

Date	Mintage	VG	F	VF	XF	Unc
1621 Rare	—	—	—	—	—	—

CITY COINAGE

KM# 140 PFENNIG
Copper **Obv:** Eagle, legend around **Rev:** Denomination, date to right

Date	Mintage	VG	F	VF	XF	Unc
1617	—	200	400	800	—	—
1626	—	200	400	800	—	—
1639	—	200	400	800	—	—

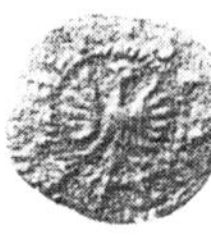

KM# 148 PFENNIG
Copper **Ruler:** Johann IV

Date	Mintage	VG	F	VF	XF	Unc
1651	—	200	400	800	—	—

KM# 142 3 PFENNIG
Copper **Obv:** Eagle facing left in beaded circle, legend around **Rev:** Tall numerals of denomination in beaded circle

Date	Mintage	VG	F	VF	XF	Unc
1617	—	135	275	525	—	—
1639	—	135	275	525	—	—

KM# 150 3 PFENNIG
Copper **Obv:** Eagle facing right in corded circle, legend around **Rev:** Denomination in corded circle

Date	Mintage	VG	F	VF	XF	Unc
1651	—	160	300	600	—	—

KM# 146 4 PFENNIG
Copper **Obv:** Eagle, legend around **Rev:** Denomination

Date	Mintage	VG	F	VF	XF	Unc
1626	—	225	450	925	—	—

KM# 152 4 PFENNIG
Copper

Date	Mintage	VG	F	VF	XF	Unc
1651	—	225	450	925	—	—
1654	—	225	450	925	—	—

TRADE COINAGE

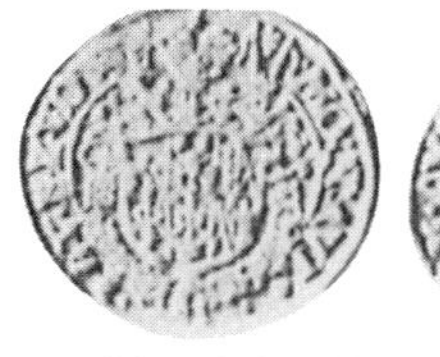

KM# 5 GOLDGULDEN
3.5000 g., 0.9860 Gold 0.1109 oz. AGW **Obv:** Crowned arms **Rev:** Crowned imperial eagle, titles of Matthias

Date	Mintage	VG	F	VF	XF	Unc
ND(1601-25) Rare	—	—	—	—	—	—

KM# 6 1-1/2 GOLDGULDEN
5.2500 g., 0.9860 Gold 0.1664 oz. AGW **Obv:** Crowned arms **Rev:** Double crowned eagle, titles of Matthias

Date	Mintage	VG	F	VF	XF	Unc
ND(1601-25) Rare	—	—	—	—	—	—

ROSTOCK

The town of Rostock is first mentioned in 1030 and was the seat of a lordship of the same name in the 13th century. It is located just a few miles inland from where the Warnow River enters the Baltic Sea and was an important trading center from earliest times. Although Rostock was usually under some control by the Mecklenburg dukes, it functioned somewhat as a free city, gaining a municipal charter as early as 1218. The city obtained control of its own coinage in 1323 and received the mint right unconditionally in 1361. From 1381, Rostock was a member of the Wendischen Münzverein (Wendish Monetary Union) and joined the Hanseatic League not long afterwards. The city coinage was struck from the 14th century until 1864.

MINTMASTERS' MARKS

Mark	Date	Name
(g)=	1594-1606	Sebastian Schoras
(h)=	1605/6-1609	Joachim Konike (Köneke)
(i)= or or	1609-14	Marcus Hoyer
(j)=	1614-15	Hans Klein
(k)=	1615-16 or 18	Hironymus Sulzberger
	1620-23	Georg Stange
	1621-22/3	Hans Klein, 2nd time
HD (sometimesin ligature)	1623-29	Hans Dethloff
(l)=	1629-35	Mathias Freude
(m)=	1635-56	Samuel Timpfe
(n)=	1659-60	Andreas Timpfe
(o)=	1661-70	Johann Freude
(p)= or PE	1670-72	Paul Eggers
(q)= or or AH	1672-79	Arnold Hille
IM	1679-1711	Johann Memmies

ARMS

Griffin, usually rampant to left. Also, shield divided by horizontal band above griffin walking left, below arabesques or sometimes an arrow.

CITY

REGULAR COINAGE

KM# 27 PFENNIG

Copper **Obv:** Griffin **Obv. Legend:** CIVIT ROSTOCK **Rev:** Denomination and date **Edge:** Plain

Date	Mintage	F	VF	XF	Unc	BU
1621	—	20.00	30.00	55.00	—	—
1622	—	20.00	30.00	55.00	—	—
1638	—	20.00	30.00	55.00	—	—
1647	—	20.00	30.00	55.00	—	—
1654	—	20.00	30.00	55.00	—	—

KM# 95 PFENNIG

Copper **Obv:** Griffin to left in circle **Obv. Legend:** ROSTOCKER **Rev:** Value and date **Rev. Inscription:** I/(date) **Note:** Prev. C#A1.

Date	Mintage	VG	F	VF	XF	Unc
1666	—	11.00	20.00	50.00	120	—
1682	—	11.00	20.00	50.00	120	—
1689	—	11.00	20.00	50.00	120	—
1699	—	11.00	20.00	50.00	120	—

KM# 28 2 PFENNIG

Copper **Obv:** Griffin **Obv. Legend:** CIVIT ROSTOCK **Rev:** Denomination and date **Edge:** Plain

Date	Mintage	F	VF	XF	Unc	BU
1621	—	20.00	33.00	60.00	—	—

KM# 22 3 PFENNIG

Copper **Obv:** Griffin **Obv. Legend:** CIVIT ROSTOCK **Rev:** Denomination and date **Edge:** Plain

Date	Mintage	F	VF	XF	Unc	BU
1621	—	16.00	27.00	45.00	—	—
1622	—	16.00	27.00	45.00	—	—
1638	—	16.00	27.00	45.00	—	—
1647	—	16.00	27.00	45.00	—	—
1654	—	16.00	27.00	45.00	—	—

KM# 85 3 PFENNIG

Copper **Obv:** Griffin left in circle **Obv. Legend:** CIVITA. — ROSTOC(H)(I). **Rev:** Value and date **Rev. Inscription:** III/(date)

Date	Mintage	VG	F	VF	XF	Unc
1660 (n)	—	8.00	16.00	27.00	45.00	—
1666 (o)	—	8.00	16.00	27.00	45.00	—
1672 PE	—	8.00	16.00	27.00	45.00	—
1673 (q)	—	8.00	16.00	27.00	45.00	—
1686 IM	—	8.00	16.00	27.00	45.00	—
1687 IM	—	8.00	16.00	27.00	45.00	—
1692 IM	—	8.00	16.00	27.00	45.00	—
1695 IM	—	8.00	16.00	27.00	45.00	—
1697 IM	—	8.00	16.00	27.00	45.00	—
1699 IM	—	8.00	16.00	27.00	45.00	—

KM# 3 THALER

Silver **Obv:** Griffin **Rev:** Crowned double-headed imperial eagle, orb on breast **Note:** Dav. #5778; Varieties exist.

Date	Mintage	VG	F	VF	XF	Unc
(1)605	—	500	1,000	2,000	3,500	—
(1)607	—	500	1,000	2,000	3,500	—
(1)609	—	500	1,000	2,000	3,500	—
(1)610	—	400	900	1,850	3,250	—
(1)611	—	500	1,000	2,000	3,500	—

KM# 10 THALER

Silver **Obv:** Partial date above eagle **Rev:** Full date in legend **Note:** Dav. #5780.

Date	Mintage	VG	F	VF	XF	Unc
1607//1607	—	650	1,250	2,750	5,000	—
1609//1609	—	650	1,250	2,750	5,000	—

KM# 9 THALER

Silver **Rev:** Full dates in legend **Note:** Dav. #5780; Varieties exist.

Date	Mintage	VG	F	VF	XF	Unc
1607	—	500	1,000	2,000	3,500	—
1608	—	550	1,100	2,250	4,250	—
1609	—	550	1,100	2,250	4,250	—
1611	—	600	1,200	2,500	4,500	—
1612	—	600	1,200	2,500	4,500	—

KM# 15 THALER

Silver **Subject:** Baptism of Prince Hans Christoph, eldest son of Duke Johann Albrecht II **Obv:** Ornate shield **Rev:** Crown above double-headed imperial eagle, orb on breast **Note:** Dav. #5782.

Date	Mintage	VG	F	VF	XF	Unc
1612	—	1,500	3,000	5,500	10,000	—

Note: Fritz Rudolf Künker Münzenhandlung Auction 141, 6-08, XF+ realized approximately $13,940

KM# 16 THALER

Silver **Rev:** Date **Rev. Legend:** MONETA: NOVA: ROSTOCHIENSIS **Note:** Dav. #5783.

Date	Mintage	VG	F	VF	XF	Unc
1612 Rare	—	—	—	—	—	—

KM# 17 THALER

Silver **Obv:** Griffin **Rev:** Crown above double-headed imperial eagle, orb on breast **Rev. Legend:** MATTIAS. I. D. G. RO... **Note:** Dav. #5784; Varieties exist.

Date	Mintage	VG	F	VF	XF	Unc
1612	—	350	750	1,600	3,250	—
1613	—	350	750	1,600	3,250	—
1618	—	600	1,250	3,000	5,000	—
ND	—	350	750	1,600	5,250	—

KM# 20 THALER

Silver **Obv:** Griffin **Rev:** Crown above double-headed imperial eagle, orb on breast **Rev. Legend:** MATTH. D: G: ROM:-IMP. **Note:** Dav. #5785.

Date	Mintage	VG	F	VF	XF	Unc
1613	—	450	850	1,750	3,500	—
ND	—	450	850	1,750	3,500	—

KM# 23 THALER

Silver **Subject:** Baptism of Prince Carl Heinrich, second son of Duke Johann Albrecht II **Note:** Dav. #LS381.

Date	Mintage	VG	F	VF	XF	Unc
1616	—	1,650	2,900	4,800	7,900	—

KM# 36 THALER

Silver **Obv:** Griffin with claws **Rev:** Crowned imperial eagle **Rev. Legend:** FERDINAN: II: D: G: R:... **Note:** Dav. #5786.

Date	Mintage	VG	F	VF	XF	Unc
1623	—	625	1,250	2,250	4,150	—
1624 HD	—	625	1,250	2,250	4,150	—
1625 HD	—	625	1,250	2,250	4,150	—
1626 HD	—	625	1,250	2,250	4,150	—

KM# 40 THALER

Silver **Subject:** Baptism of Prince Christian, oldest son of Duke Adolph Friedrich I **Note:** Dav. #LS385.

Date	Mintage	VG	F	VF	XF	Unc
1624 HD	—	650	1,200	2,000	3,500	—

KM# 45 THALER

Silver **Obv:** Crowned imperial eagle **Obv. Legend:** FERDINANDVS II... **Rev:** Griffin **Rev. Legend:** MONE. NOVA... **Note:** Dav. #5787.

Date	Mintage	VG	F	VF	XF	Unc
1626 HD	—	625	1,250	2,250	4,150	—
1627 HD	—	625	1,250	2,250	4,150	—

KM# 46 THALER

Silver **Obv:** Griffin **Obv. Legend:** HD*MONETA... **Rev:** Crown above double-headed imperial eagle, orb on breast **Note:** Dav. #5788.

Date	Mintage	VG	F	VF	XF	Unc
1627 HD	—	900	1,850	3,750	6,250	—

KM# 47 THALER

Silver **Obv. Legend:** ...D: G: RO: I: S: A:... **Rev:** Griffin with hooves **Rev. Legend:** ...ROSTOCHIENSIS. **Note:** Dav. #5789.

Date	Mintage	VG	F	VF	XF	Unc
1627 HD	—	300	650	1,350	2,250	—
1628 HD	—	300	650	1,350	2,250	—
1629 HD	—	300	650	1,350	2,250	—
1631	—	350	700	1,450	2,500	—
1632	—	350	700	1,450	2,500	—
1633	—	350	700	1,450	2,500	—

KM# 50 THALER

Silver **Rev. Legend:** ROS. THOCHI. ENSIS. **Note:** Dav. #5789A.

Date	Mintage	VG	F	VF	XF	Unc
1629 HD	—	300	650	1,350	2,250	—

KM# 51 THALER

Silver **Obv:** Crowned imperial eagles with halos, date divided by crown **Obv. Legend:** FERDIN. II. D. G. RO:... **Note:** Dav. #5791.

Date	Mintage	VG	F	VF	XF	Unc
1630	—	400	750	1,500	2,750	—
1631	—	400	750	1,500	2,750	—
1632	—	400	750	1,500	2,750	—
1633	—	400	750	1,500	2,750	—

KM# 54 THALER

Silver **Obv:** Griffin **Rev:** Crown above double-headed imperial eagle, value in orb on breast **Rev. Legend:** ...D: G: ROMIO: I: S: A:... **Note:** Dav. #5789B.

Date	Mintage	VG	F	VF	XF	Unc
1631	—	300	650	1,350	2,250	—

KM# 59 THALER

Silver **Obv. Legend:** ...ROSTOCK. IENSIS: **Note:** Dav. #5791A.

Date	Mintage	VG	F	VF	XF	Unc
1633	—	400	750	1,500	2,750	—

KM# 60 THALER

Silver **Obv:** Eagles without halos **Note:** Dav. #5791B.

Date	Mintage	VG	F	VF	XF	Unc
1633	—	400	750	1,500	2,750	—

KM# 61 THALER

Silver **Obv. Legend:** FERDINAND: II...IMP: SEMP: **Rev. Legend:** ...ROSTOCK: IENSIS:X. **Note:** Dav. #5792.

Date	Mintage	VG	F	VF	XF	Unc
ND Rare	—	—	—	—	—	—

KM# 62 THALER

Silver **Rev. Legend:** ...ROS. THOCHI: EN. SIS. **Note:** Dav. #5792A.

Date	Mintage	VG	F	VF	XF	Unc
ND Rare	—	—	—	—	—	—

KM# 63 THALER

Silver **Obv:** Crowned imperial eagle without halos **Rev. Legend:** ...NOVA. CIVIT:... **Note:** Dav. #5793.

Date	Mintage	VG	F	VF	XF	Unc
1633	—	300	650	1,350	2,250	—
1634	—	300	650	1,350	2,250	—

KM# 64 THALER

Silver **Obv. Legend:** FERDINANDUS. II. ROMA: IMP:... **Note:** Dav. #5794.

Date	Mintage	VG	F	VF	XF	Unc
1633	—	275	600	1,250	2,000	—
1634	—	275	600	1,250	2,000	—
1635	—	275	600	1,250	2,000	—
1636	—	275	600	1,250	2,000	—
1637	—	275	600	1,250	2,000	—

KM# 58 THALER

Silver **Obv:** Eagle with halos

Date	Mintage	VG	F	VF	XF	Unc
1633	—	275	600	1,250	2,000	—

KM# 75 THALER

Silver **Obv:** Griffin **Rev:** Crown above double-headed imperial eagle, value in orb on breast **Rev. Legend:** FERDINANDUS. III... **Note:** Dav. #5795.

Date	Mintage	VG	F	VF	XF	Unc
1637	—	275	600	1,250	2,000	—
1639	—	275	600	1,250	2,000	—

KM# 79 THALER

Silver **Obv. Legend:** MON. NOVA:... **Note:** Dav. #5796.

Date	Mintage	VG	F	VF	XF	Unc
1640	—	275	600	1,250	2,000	—

KM# 80 THALER

Silver **Obv:** Griffin, date in legend **Obv. Legend:** ...CIVITA... **Rev:** Crowned imperial eagle dividing date below **Rev. Legend:** ...ROMANO... **Note:** Dav. #5797.

Date	Mintage	VG	F	VF	XF	Unc
1642//1642	—	450	900	1,850	3,250	—
1643//1642	—	600	1,200	2,250	—	—
1646//1642	—	600	1,200	2,250	—	—

KM# 89 THALER

Silver **Obv. Legend:** LEOPOLDUS. D: G: ROMA: IMP: SE: AUG: **Rev:** Mint mark before griffin **Note:** Dav. #5798.

Date	Mintage	VG	F	VF	XF	Unc
1661	—	450	1,000	2,000	3,500	—
1664	—	450	1,000	2,000	3,500	—

KM# 93 THALER

Silver **Obv:** Date **Obv. Legend:** ...ROM: I: M: S: A: **Note:** Dav. #5799.

Date	Mintage	VG	F	VF	XF	Unc
1663	—	275	525	950	1,750	—

KM# 4 1-1/2 THALER

Silver **Obv:** Helmeted arms **Rev:** Crown above double-headed imperial eagle, orb on breast **Note:** Dav. #LS378.

Date	Mintage	VG	F	VF	XF	Unc
1605 Rare	—	—	—	—	—	—

KM# 41 1-1/2 THALER

Silver **Subject:** Baptism of Prince Adolph Friedrich **Note:** Dav. #LS383.

Date	Mintage	VG	F	VF	XF	Unc
1624 HD	—	1,600	3,000	5,000	8,000	—

KM# 5 2 THALER

Silver **Note:** Similar to 1-1/2 Thaler. Dav. #LS377.

Date	Mintage	VG	F	VF	XF	Unc
1605 Rare	—	—	—	—	—	—

KM# 11 2 THALER

Silver **Note:** Previous Dav.#5779.

Date	Mintage	VG	F	VF	XF	Unc
1609 Rare	—	—	—	—	—	—

KM# 13 2 THALER

Silver **Obv:** Helmeted arms **Rev:** Crowned imperial eagle, orb on breast **Note:** Dav. #LS380.

Date	Mintage	VG	F	VF	XF	Unc
1611 Rare	—	—	—	—	—	—

KM# 24 2 THALER

Silver **Subject:** Baptism of Prince Carl Heinrich, second son of Duke Johann Albrecht II **Note:** Dav. #LS381.

Date	Mintage	VG	F	VF	XF	Unc
1616	—	2,300	4,000	7,000	11,000	—

KM# 42 2 THALER

Silver **Subject:** Baptism of Prince Adolph Friedrich **Note:** Dav. #LS382.

Date	Mintage	VG	F	VF	XF	Unc
1624 HD	—	1,900	3,300	5,500	9,000	—

KM# 43 2 THALER

Silver **Subject:** Baptism of Prince Christian, oldest son of Duke Adolph Friedrich **Note:** Dav. #LS384.

Date	Mintage	VG	F	VF	XF	Unc
1624 HD	—	1,600	3,000	5,000	8,000	—

KM# 48 2 THALER

Silver **Obv:** Griffin with claws, date above in legend **Rev:** Crowned imperial eagle **Rev. Legend:** FERDINANDUS II... **Note:** Dav. #A5787.

Date	Mintage	VG	F	VF	XF	Unc
1627 HD Rare	—	—	—	—	—	—

KM# 52 2 THALER

Silver **Note:** Dav. #5790.

Date	Mintage	VG	F	VF	XF	Unc
1630 Rare	—	—	—	—	—	—

KM# 6 3 THALER

Silver **Note:** Dav. #LS376.

Date	Mintage	VG	F	VF	XF	Unc
1605 Rare	—	—	—	—	—	—

KM# 14 3 THALER

Silver **Note:** Dav. #LS379.

Date	Mintage	VG	F	VF	XF	Unc
1611 Rare	—	—	—	—	—	—

KM# 7 4 THALER

Silver **Note:** Dav. #LS375.

Date	Mintage	VG	F	VF	XF	Unc
1605 Rare	—	—	—	—	—	—

TRADE COINAGE

KM# 8 GOLDGULDEN

3.5000 g., 0.9860 Gold 0.1109 oz. AGW **Obv:** Griffin in inner circle **Rev:** Crowned imperial eagle in inner circle, titles of Rudolf II **Note:** Fr. #2583.

Date	Mintage	VG	F	VF	XF	Unc
1606	—	500	925	1,800	3,050	—
1608	—	500	925	1,800	3,050	—
1609	—	500	925	1,800	3,050	—
1610	—	500	925	1,800	3,050	—
1611	—	500	925	1,800	3,050	—
ND	—	500	925	1,800	3,050	—

KM# 21 GOLDGULDEN

3.5000 g., 0.9860 Gold 0.1109 oz. AGW **Obv:** Griffin in inner circle, date in legend **Rev:** Crowned imperial eagle in inner circle, titles of Matthias **Note:** Fr. #2584.

Date	Mintage	VG	F	VF	XF	Unc
1613	—	600	1,200	2,400	4,200	—
1614	—	600	1,200	2,400	4,200	—
1615	—	600	1,200	2,400	4,200	—
1616	—	600	1,200	2,400	4,200	—
1617	—	600	1,200	2,400	4,200	—

KM# 44 GOLDGULDEN

3.5000 g., 0.9860 Gold 0.1109 oz. AGW **Rev:** Crowned imperial eagle in inner circle, titles of Ferdinand II **Note:** Fr. #2586.

Date	Mintage	VG	F	VF	XF	Unc
1625	—	575	1,150	2,200	3,750	—
1626	—	575	1,150	2,200	3,750	—
1627	—	575	1,150	2,200	3,750	—
1629 HD	—	575	1,150	2,200	3,750	—
1630	—	575	1,150	2,200	3,750	—
1631	—	575	1,150	2,200	3,750	—

KM# 37 2 GOLDGULDEN

7.0000 g., 0.9860 Gold 0.2219 oz. AGW **Obv:** Griffin in inner circle, date in legend **Rev:** Crowned imperial eagle in inner circle, titles of Ferdinand II **Note:** Fr. #2585.

Date	Mintage	VG	F	VF	XF	Unc
1623	—	1,100	2,100	4,200	6,600	—

KM# 109 1/4 DUCAT

0.8750 g., 0.9860 Gold 0.0277 oz. AGW **Obv:** Griffin, titles of Leopold I **Rev:** Value and date **Note:** FR#2594.

Date	Mintage	VG	F	VF	XF	Unc
1696	—	190	400	875	1,550	—

KM# 106 1/2 DUCAT

1.7500 g., 0.9860 Gold 0.0555 oz. AGW **Obv:** Griffin, date in legend **Rev:** Crowned imperial eagle, titles of Leopold I **Note:** Fr. #2592.

Date	Mintage	VG	F	VF	XF	Unc
1695	—	250	500	1,050	2,200	—

KM# 57 DUCAT

3.5000 g., 0.9860 Gold 0.1109 oz. AGW **Obv:** Arms in inner circle, date in legend **Rev:** Crowned imperial eagle, titles of Ferdinand II **Note:** Fr. #2587.

Date	Mintage	VG	F	VF	XF	Unc
1632	—	220	500	1,000	1,750	—
1633	—	220	500	1,000	1,750	—
1634	—	220	500	1,000	1,750	—
1636	—	220	500	1,000	1,750	—

KM# 73 DUCAT

3.5000 g., 0.9860 Gold 0.1109 oz. AGW **Obv:** Ornate arms within beaded circle **Rev:** Titles of Ferdinand III **Note:** Fr. #2589.

Date	Mintage	VG	F	VF	XF	Unc
1636	—	210	475	900	1,600	—
1639	—	210	475	900	1,600	—
1646	—	210	475	900	1,600	—
1655	—	210	475	900	1,600	—

KM# 90 DUCAT

3.5000 g., 0.9860 Gold 0.1109 oz. AGW **Obv:** Arms in inner circle, date in legend **Rev:** Crowned imperial eagle in inner circle, titles of Leopold I **Note:** Fr. #2591. Varieties exist.

Date	Mintage	VG	F	VF	XF	Unc
1661	—	325	625	1,250	2,250	—
1664	—	325	625	1,250	2,250	—
1665	—	325	625	1,250	2,250	—
1672	—	325	625	1,250	2,250	—
1677 AH	—	325	625	1,250	2,250	—
1682 IM	—	325	625	1,250	2,250	—
1694 IM	—	325	625	1,250	2,250	—

KM# 78 2 DUCAT

7.0000 g., 0.9860 Gold 0.2219 oz. AGW **Obv:** Oval arms divides date within square disign with inscription **Rev:** Crowned imperial eagle, titles of Ferdinand III **Note:** Fr. #2588.

Date	Mintage	VG	F	VF	XF	Unc
1639	—	600	1,200	2,500	4,000	—

KM# 81 2 DUCAT

7.0000 g., 0.9860 Gold 0.2219 oz. AGW **Obv:** Arms in inner circle, date in legend **Rev:** Crowned imperial eagle, titles of Leopold I **Note:** Fr. #2590.

Date	Mintage	VG	F	VF	XF	Unc
1661	—	1,100	2,100	4,200	6,600	—
1695 IM	—	1,100	2,100	4,200	6,600	—

ROTHENBURG

A city located in Bavaria on the Tauber River southeast of Wurzburg. Population: 11,882. Exports include soap and textiles.

Nobles of Rothenburg, whose castle lay in the Harz Mountains, were the cadet line of the counts of Beichlingen. Founded by Friedrich IV (1252-1313) the city became an imperial city in 1274 and reached the height of its prosperity at the end of the 14th century.

CITY

TRADE COINAGE

KM# 4 DUCAT

3.5000 g., 0.9860 Gold 0.1109 oz. AGW **Subject:** 100th Anniversary of Reformation **Obv:** Castle and legend **Rev:** Inscription

Date	Mintage	VG	F	VF	XF	Unc
1617	—	1,250	2,500	4,500	7,000	—

PATTERNS

Including off metal strikes

KM#	Date	Mintage	Identification	Mkt Val
Pn1	1617	—	Ducat. Silver. KM#4.	450

ROTTWEIL

The city of Rottweil is located on the upper Neckar River, northwest of the Swabian Alps and about 32 miles (53km) south-southwest of Tübingen. The place was first mentioned in records as early as 771 and became an established market town from about 1140. During the third quarter of the 12th century, bracteates with the eagle arms of the town were struck in Rottweil. Subsequent issues appeared in the 13th century prior to its elevation to the status of a Free City of the Empire in 1268. The earliest seal with the eagle city arms is known from 1280. The first mint right was granted by the Count of Zähringen in 1218, but the imperial concession was made in 1285. A new mint privilege was granted by Emperor Maximilian I in 1512, although some coins had been struck in and for the city prior to that date. Only a few issues were struck during the 16th century and a few more were issued by the city in the early period of the Thirty Years' War. Records show that the last coins minted in Rottweil were Kreuzers in the year 1701, but none are known to exist. The city lost its free status during the Napoleonic Wars and in 1803, Rottweil was absorbed by Württemberg.

Initial	Date	Name
IM	1623-24	Johann Martin
	1623-24	Thomas Linckh von Zug, warden

ARMS

Eagle with wings spread

REFERENCES

N = Elisabeth Nau, **Die Münzen und Medaillen des oberschwäbischen Städte**, Freiburg im Breisgau, 1964.

Sch = Wolfgang Schulten, **Deutsche Münzen aus der Zeit Karls V.**, Frankfurt am Main, 1976.

FREE CITY

REGULAR COINAGE

KM# 4 3 KREUZER (Groschen)

Silver **Obv:** City arms in circle **Obv. Legend:** MONE. ROTWILENSIS., (date) **Rev:** Crowned imperial eagle, value 3 in circle on breast **Rev. Legend:** FERDINA(N)D. II. I(M). S. AV. **Note:** Kipper. 17-18.5mm. .70-1.59g.

Date	Mintage	VG	F	VF	XF	Unc
16ZZ	—	33.00	45.00	85.00	150	—

KM# 2 3 KREUZER (Groschen)

Silver **Obv:** Latin cross divides date **Obv. Legend:** SALVE. CRVX. SANCTA. **Rev:** Eagle, 3 in circle on breast, legend around **Rev. Legend:** MO. NO. ROTWILENSIS **Note:** Kipper; varieties exist.

Date	Mintage	VG	F	VF	XF	Unc
16ZZ	—	33.00	65.00	115	180	—

KM# 3 3 KREUZER (Groschen)

Silver **Obv:** City arms within circle, date in legend **Obv. Legend:** MONE. NO. ROTWILENSI **Rev:** Crowned imperial eagle, 3 in circle on breast **Rev. Legend:** FERDINAND. II IM. S. AV. **Note:** Varieties of design and legend exist.

Date	Mintage	VG	F	VF	XF	Unc
16ZZ	—	40.00	80.00	165	325	—

KM# 5 6 KREUZER

Silver **Obv:** Latin cross divides date, legend around **Obv. Legend:** SALVE. CRVX. SANCTA **Rev:** Imperial eagle within beaded circle **Rev. Legend:** MONETA. NOVA. ROTWILENSIS.6. **Note:** Kipper; varieties exist.

Date	Mintage	VG	F	VF	XF	Unc
16ZZ	—	70.00	150	—	—	—

KM# 1 12 KREUZER (Dreibätzner)

Silver **Obv:** Eagle with 12 in circle on breast, legend around **Obv. Legend:** MONETA. NOVA. ROTWILENSIS **Rev:** Latin cross divides date, legend around **Rev. Legend:** SALVE. CRVX. SANCTA **Note:** Kipper; varieties exist; weight varies 2.09 - 3.19 grams.

Date	Mintage	VG	F	VF	XF	Unc
16Z1	—	50.00	100	—	—	—
16ZZ	—	50.00	100	—	—	—

KM# 6 12 KREUZER (Dreibätzner)

Silver **Obv:** Eagle with cross in shield on breast, legend and date around **Obv. Legend:** MONE. NO. ROTWILENSIS **Rev:** Crowned imperial eagle, 12 in circle on breast, titles of Ferdinand II around **Note:** Kipper; varieties exist; weight varies 2.09 - 3.19 grams.

Date	Mintage	VG	F	VF	XF	Unc
16ZZ	—	50.00	100	—	—	—

KM# 7 24 KREUZER (Sechsbätzner = Dicken)

Silver **Obv:** Latin cross divides date within circle **Obv. Legend:** SALVE. CRVX. SANCTA **Rev:** Imperial eagle within beaded circle **Rev. Legend:** MONETA. NOVA. ROTWILENSIS **Note:** Kipper; varieties exist; weight varies 4.29 - 4.97 grams.

Date	Mintage	VG	F	VF	XF	Unc
16ZZ	—	60.00	120	—	—	—

KM# 8 THALER

29.9000 g., Silver, 30 mm. **Obv:** Eagle, head to left, legend around **Obv. Legend:** MONETA. NOVA. ROTWILENSIS **Rev:** Latin cross divides date, legend around **Rev. Legend:** SALVE. CRVX. SANCTA **Note:** Klippe; struck on square flan with same dies as KM#6.

Date	Mintage	VG	F	VF	XF	Unc
16ZZ Rare	—	—	—	—	—	—

KM# 9 THALER

Silver **Obv:** Displayed eagle in circle, date at end of legend **Obv. Legend:** MONETA: NOVA: ROTWILENSIS **Rev:** Crowned imperial eagle **Rev. Legend:** FERDINANDVS: II: ROM: IMP: SEMPE: AVG. **Note:** Dav. #5803.

Date	Mintage	VG	F	VF	XF	Unc
1623 IM Rare	—	—	—	—	—	—

Note: Fritz Rudolf Künker Münzenhandlung Auction 69, 10-01, nearly XF realized approximately $10,655

KM# 10 THALER

Silver **Obv:** Displayed eagle in circle, date at end of legend **Obv. Legend:** MONETA. NOVA. ROTVVILENSIS. **Rev:** Crowned imperial eagle within circle **Rev. Legend:** FERDINANDVS. II. ROM. IMP. SEMPER. AVGVSTVS. **Note:** Dav. #5804.

Date	Mintage	VG	F	VF	XF	Unc
1623 Rare	—	—	—	—	—	—

Note: Auktionshaus Meister & Sonntag Auction 5, 9-07, XF realized approximately $15,355; Fritz Rudolf Künker Münzenhandlung Auction 113, 6-06, VF-XF realized approximately $8,220

KM# 11 1-1/4 THALER

Silver **Obv:** Displayed eagle in circle, date at end of legend **Obv. Legend:** MONETA. NOVA. ROTWILENSIS. **Rev:** Crowned imperial eagle **Rev. Legend:** FERDINANDVS. II. ROM. IMP. SEMPE. AV. **Note:** Dav. #5803A. Klippe.

Date	Mintage	VG	F	VF	XF	Unc
1623 IM Rare	—	—	—	—	—	—

Note: Auktionshaus Meister & Sonntag Auction 5, 9-07, XF realized approximately $55,835

SALM

The earliest rulers of this county, with widely scattered territories in the border region of present-day Germany, France and Belgium, descended from the counts of Luxembourg in the second half of the 11th century. The patrimony was divided between two succeeding sons about 1130-35. Lower Salm was located in the Ardenne region of France and became extinct in 1416 with the death of Heinrich VI. It passed by marriage to the lord of Reifferscheidt who in turn established the line of Salm-Reifferscheidt in 1455. The other division of old Salm was Upper Salm and was located in the Vosges to the southwest of Strassburg. This line underwent several divisions, one of which died out and passed to Lorrainein 1503. Another branch subdivided and half passed to as on who left the area and established himself as progenitor of the Salm-Neuburg line in Austria. The remaining half of Salm went to the older son and was inherited through marriage upon his death in 1475 by a ruler styled Wild and Rhinegrave. This latter individual was well-established in lands which stretched along the Rhine between Trier and Mainz. Thus, the early modern lines of Salm and its subdivisions in Germany came into being. The old castle of Salm, seat of the earliest counts is located southwest of Strassburg, but the dynastic name was transferred to the Rhineland counts, who became from that point on, the Wild- and Rhinegraves of Salm. Two main lines were founded in 1499.

ARMS

Salm - 2 fish (salmon) standing on tails
Rhinegraves - lion with double tail
Wildgraves - crowned lion
Kyrburg - 3 lions, 2 above 1

SALM-DHAUN

(Salm-Daun)

The seat of this branch was at Dhaun (Daun), about 37 miles (62 km) east of Trier, near Kirn an der Nahe. It was further divided in 1561 into three lines: Salm-Neuweiler, Salm-Dhaun and Salm-Grumbach. Salm-Dhaun has a final division in 1697 into Salm-Dhaun and Salm-Püttlingen. The last count died and Püttlingen passed by marriage to Lowenstein-Wertheim-Rochefort in 1750.

RULERS

Adolf Heinrich, 1561-1606
Wolfgang Friedrich, 1606-1638
under guardianship of his mother
Juliane, 1606-1617
Johann Ludwig, 1638-1673
Johann Philipp, 1673-1693
Karl, 1693-1733

MINT OFFICIALS' INITIALS

Meddersheim Mint

Symbol	Date	Name
	ca. 1605	Andreas Wachsmuth
	ca. 1605	Georg Müller
	ca. 1612	Wilhelm Schreiner, warden
	ca. 1613	Henning Kissel
H	ca. 1615-18	Peter Hex
	ca. 1619-?	Christian Ulmen

COUNTSHIP

REGULAR COINAGE

KM# 1 PFENNIG

Silver **Obv:** Coat of arms in circle of dots **Note:** Uniface. Schussel type.

Date	Mintage	VG	F	VF	XF	Unc
ND(1561-1606)	—	9.00	20.00	40.00	65.00	—

DAV# 7330 THALER

Silver **Obv:** Crowned imperial eagle, orb on breast, date **Obv. Legend:** RVDOLP*II*IMP*AVG*P* **Rev:** Helmeted arms **Rev. Legend:** AD. HE. CO:SI.-E.

Date	Mintage	VG	F	VF	XF	Unc
1601 Rare	—	—	—	—	—	—

DAV# 7329 2 THALER

Silver **Obv:** Crowned imperial eagle, orb on breast, date **Obv. Legend:** RVDOLP*II*IMP AVG*P* **Rev:** Helmeted arms **Rev. Legend:** AD. HE. CO:SI.-E.

Date	Mintage	VG	F	VF	XF	Unc
1601 Rare	—	—	—	—	—	—

DAV# 7331 2 THALER

Silver **Obv. Legend:** RVDOLF. II. ROM... **Rev. Legend:** AD. HEIN. SYLVES. RHENIQ...

Date	Mintage	VG	F	VF	XF	Unc
1601 Rare	—	—	—	—	—	—

DAV# 7332 2 THALER

Silver **Obv. Legend:** *RVDOLP*II*ROM*... **Rev. Legend:** AD: HEIN: SYL-VES: RHENIQ...

Date	Mintage	VG	F	VF	XF	Unc
1602 Rare	—	—	—	—	—	—

DAV# 7332A 2 THALER

Silver **Obv. Legend:** RVDOLF...

Date	Mintage	VG	F	VF	XF	Unc
1602 Rare	—	—	—	—	—	—

DAV# 7333 2 THALER

Silver **Obv:** Legend, date **Obv. Legend:** RVDOLP*II*IMP*AVG*P*F*DECRE **Rev:** Helmeted oval arms

Date	Mintage	VG	F	VF	XF	Unc
1604 Rare	2,567	—	—	—	—	—

DAV# 7334 2 THALER

Silver **Obv. Legend:** RVDOLF: ROM: IMP: AVGVSTVS... **Rev:** Helmeted arms **Rev. Legend:** REINGRAFSCHA-FT...

Date	Mintage	VG	F	VF	XF	Unc
ND(1606-12) Rare	—	—	—	—	—	—

TRADE COINAGE

FR# 2602 GOLDGULDEN

3.5000 g., 0.9860 Gold 0.1109 oz. AGW **Obv:** Crowned imperial eagle in inner circle, titles of Matthias **Rev:** Arms in inner circle

Date	Mintage	VG	F	VF	XF	Unc
(1)617 Rare	360	—	—	—	—	—

FR# 2603 GOLDGULDEN

3.5000 g., 0.9860 Gold 0.1109 oz. AGW

Date	Mintage	VG	F	VF	XF	Unc
1619 Rare	—	—	—	—	—	—

SALM-KYRBURG

Founded in 1499, this branch took its name from Kyrburg Castle, the ruins of which are located three miles (5 km) west-southwest of Dhaun. A further subdivision was made in 1607, resulting in the lines of Salm-Kyrburg,Salm-Morchingen and Salm-Tronecken, the latter lasting only one generation. The main line became extinct in 1681 and fell to Salm-Morchingen, which in turn ended in the male line in 1688. All Salm-Kyrburg lands and titles then reverted to Salm-Salm. After several subdivisions of that senior branch, a new line of Salm-Kyrburg was established from Salm-Neuweiler-Lenze in 1738. The count was raised to the rank of Prince of the Empire in 1742. All territories of the family were mediatized in 1806, but the Salm-Kyrburg line has survived down to modern times.

RULERS

Otto I, 1548-1607
Johann Kasimer, 1607-1651
with Johann IX von Salm-Morchingen, 1607-1623
and Otto II von Salm-Tronecken, 1607-1637
then Johann Philipp von Salm-Morchingen,
1623-1638 and Otto Ludwig von Salm-Morchingen, 1623-1634
George Friedrich, 1651-1681

MINT OFFICIALS' INITIALS

Initials or Mark	Date	Name
(c)	1602-09	
(d)	1623-30	
(e)	1631-35	Johann Philipp Mey in Diemeringen
(g)		Darmstadt Mint

COUNTSHIP

REGULAR COINAGE

DAV# 7328 THALER

Silver **Ruler:** Otto I **Obv:** Helmeted arms Crowned imperial eagle with orb on breast, date divided below **Obv. Legend:** OT-TO. CO: SILV.-E:... **Rev:** Crowned imperial eagle with orb on breast, date divided below **Rev. Legend:** RVDOL. II. ROM...

Date	Mintage	VG	F	VF	XF	Unc
1604 (c) Rare	—	—	—	—	—	—

DAV# 7327 2 THALER

Silver **Ruler:** Otto I **Obv:** Helmeted arms Crowned imperial eagle with orb on breast, date divided below **Obv. Legend:** OT-TO. CO: SILV-E... **Rev:** Crowned imperial eagle with orb on breast, date divided below **Rev. Legend:** RVDOL. II. ROM...OT-TO. CO: SILV-E...

Date	Mintage	VG	F	VF	XF	Unc
1602 (c) Rare	—	—	—	—	—	—
1604 (c) Rare	—	—	—	—	—	—

TRADE COINAGE

FR# 2605 GOLDGULDEN

3.5000 g., 0.9860 Gold 0.1109 oz. AGW **Ruler:** Johann Kasimer **Obv:** Lion with shield of arms in inner circle **Rev:** Crowned imperial eagle in inner circle

Date	Mintage	VG	F	VF	XF	Unc
ND(1623-30) (d) Rare	—	—	—	—	—	—

SAXE-ALTENBURG

(Sachsen-Alt-Altenburg)

This early division of Saxe-Old-Weimar was effectively created in 1573 when the two sons of Johann Wilhelm agreed on joint rule of their territories while founding lines which eventually became separately administered entities. For the joint coinage up to 1602, see Saxe-Old-Weimar. In 1672, the Saxe-Old-Altenburg line became extinct and most of the territory and titles were inherited by Saxe-New-Gotha (see). In 1826, the Duke of Saxe-Hildburghausen received Altenburg in exchange for Hildburghausen and established the line of Saxe-(New)-Altenburg (which see).

RULERS

Friedrich Wilhelm I, 1573-1602
Johann Philipp I, 1602-1639
Friedrich VIII, 1602-1625
Johann Wilhelm IV, 1602-1632
Friedrich Wilhelm II, 1639-1669
Friedrich Wilhelm III, 1669-1672

Note: Joint coinages were issued by the four brothers 1603-1625, three brothers 1626-1632, and two brothers 1633-1639.

MINT OFFICIALS

A large number of mints operated for Saxe-Altenburg during the Kipper Period of the Thirty Years' War. Therefore, the mints are arranged here in alphabetical order and the persons employed in each of those mints are listed with as precise dates of tenure as possible.

Allstedt Mint

Initial	Date	Name
	July-Winter 1621	Anton von Wingen (Wenigen)
	Feb-July 1622	Johannes Schmill (Schmell)
	July 1622-March 1623	Matthias Winterstein
(d) = crescent	March-June 1623	Wilhelm Quendel (Cuendel)

Altenburg ('A' in circle or 'AB')

	March-May 1621	Gerhard Han (Haen)
	Sept 1621	Nikolaus Wode (Wohde, Woidte)
	late 1621-April 1622	David Ursinus
AS	ca.1621	Unknown die-cutter
DW	1621-1625, mintmaster from Feb 1623	David Wölke (Wölcke)
	1623	David Haussmann, warden

Bürgel Mint ('BV')

acorn	Dec 1620-June 1621	Georg Oppermann
	July 1621-?	Curt Marquart
	1622	Wolf Zschezsching

Camburg Mint ('CB')

	July 1621	Hans Jakob
	Late 1521-Feb. 1622	Unknown
EFS/ES	1636-72	Ernst Friedrich Schneider in Coburg
Arm holding sickle		

Dornburg Mint ('DB')

Rose	1621	Hans Dechandt

Eisenberg Mint ('EB')

(i)	Feb-June 1621	Arnold Tilly
Z	July 1621-Feb 1622	Hermann Zindel

Gotha Mint

IB	Sept-Dec 1650	Johann Braun in Gotha

Gräfenthal Mint ('GT', 'G' or G)

July 1621	Wolf Albrecht
Sept 1621	Heinrich Abel Ziegenmeyer
Sept 1621	Heinrich Koch
Oct 1621	Benedict Scheuner
March 1622	Georg Gross

Jüdewein Mint

Feb 1622	Martin Eckhard
March 1622	David Wölke (Wölcke)
March 1622	Vincenz Will

Kahla Mint ('C')

March 1621	Christian Oppermann
August 1621	Georg Richter

Lehesten Mint

1621	Martin Eckhardt
March 1622	Hans Fiedler

Lucka Mint ('L' in circle)

August 1621	Wolf Dietrich
Late 1621	Christian Oppermann
1622	Wolf Zschezsching

Meuselwitz or Münsa Mint ('M' or 'MZ' in circle or 'MM')

Nobitz Mint ('N' in circle)

Pölzig Mint ('P' or 'PZ')

Roda Mint ('R' in circle or 'RO')

Spring 1621	Nikolaus Sindt
August 1621	Daniel Busso
Autumn 1621 – Feb 1622	Otto Hoffmann

Rossla Mint

Sept 1621	Wolf Zschezsching
1622	Nikolaus Wode (Wohde, Woidte)

Saalfeld Mint ('S')

WA (sometimes in ligature)	1604-19, 22-30	Wolf Albrecht
HI or H	1619-22	Hans Jacob
	1621-22	Hans Heinrich Jacob
Heart with 2 flowers	Aug 1622-23	Gottfried Ehrlich, warden
MR (with or without)	1630-73	Martin Reimann

Schmölln Mint

June 1621 – Feb 1622	Basche (Paschallis) Hachenberg

Windischleuba Mint ('WL,' sometimes in ligature)

DUCHY

REGULAR COINAGE

C# A5 3 PFENNIG

Copper **Obv:** Coat of arms divides A-B **Rev:** III in orb divides date

Date	Mintage	VG	F	VF	XF	Unc
1622	—	13.00	27.00	55.00	100	—
1623	—	13.00	27.00	55.00	100	—

DAV# 7361 THALER

Silver **Subject:** 4 Brothers **Obv:** Facing busts **Rev:** Two facing busts, date above

Date	Mintage	VG	F	VF	XF	Unc
1605	—	50.00	100	175	350	—
1606	—	50.00	100	175	350	—
1607	—	50.00	100	175	350	—
1608	—	50.00	100	175	350	—
1609	—	50.00	100	175	350	—
1610	—	50.00	100	175	350	—
1611	—	50.00	100	175	350	—
1612	—	50.00	100	175	350	—

DAV# 7363 THALER

Silver **Obv:** Four facing busts **Rev:** Arms with date above within legend **Rev. Legend:** DISCORDIA...within 17 shields in circle within legend: LANDG:THV:MAR:MIS:

Date	Mintage	VG	F	VF	XF	Unc
1612	—	60.00	110	185	400	—
1613	—	60.00	110	185	400	—

DAV# 7365 THALER

Silver **Rev:** Helmeted arms dividing date

Date	Mintage	VG	F	VF	XF	Unc
1613	—	50.00	100	175	350	—
1614	—	50.00	100	175	350	—
1615	—	50.00	100	175	350	—
1616	—	50.00	100	175	350	—
1617	—	50.00	100	175	350	—
1618	—	50.00	100	175	350	—

DAV# 7367 THALER

Silver **Obv:** 1/2 figure right dividing date above, two shields below **Rev:** Three busts right, two shields below

Date	Mintage	VG	F	VF	XF	Unc
1618 WA	—	50.00	100	175	350	—
1619 WA	—	50.00	100	175	350	—
16Z0 WA	—	50.00	100	175	350	—
16Z1 HXI	—	50.00	100	175	350	—
16ZZ HXI	—	50.00	100	175	350	—
16Z2 WA	—	50.00	100	175	350	—
16Z3 WA	—	50.00	100	175	350	—

DAV# 7367A THALER

Silver **Note:** Klippe.

Date	Mintage	VG	F	VF	XF	Unc
1621 Rare	—	—	—	—	—	—

DAV# 7369 THALER

Silver **Rev:** Three half figures right, two shields below

Date	Mintage	VG	F	VF	XF	Unc
16Z3 WA	—	50.00	100	175	350	—
16Z4 WA	—	50.00	100	175	350	—
16Z5 WA	—	50.00	100	175	350	—

DAV# 7371 THALER

Silver **Rev:** Middle figure holds baton

Date	Mintage	VG	F	VF	XF	Unc
1623	—	50.00	100	175	350	—
1624	—	50.00	100	175	350	—
1625	—	50.00	100	175	350	—

DAV# 7382 THALER

Silver **Obv:** Facing bust **Rev:** Helmeted arms divide ANNO and date

Date	Mintage	VG	F	VF	XF	Unc
1623	—	325	575	1,000	2,000	—

DAV# 7371A THALER

Silver **Obv:** WA added below shields

Date	Mintage	VG	F	VF	XF	Unc
1625	—	50.00	100	175	350	—

DAV# 7373 THALER

Silver **Subject:** Death of Friedrich VIII **Obv:** Figure right, date divided above **Rev:** 9-line inscription

Date	Mintage	VG	F	VF	XF	Unc
1625	—	325	575	1,000	2,000	—

DAV# 7374 THALER

Silver **Subject:** Death of Friedrich VIII **Rev:** 8-line inscription

Date	Mintage	VG	F	VF	XF	Unc
1625	—	325	575	1,000	2,000	—

DAV# 7376 THALER

Silver **Subject:** 3 Brothers **Obv:** Bust right, date divided above, shield below **Rev:** Two facing busts dividing M-R, two shields below

Date	Mintage	VG	F	VF	XF	Unc
16Z6 WA	—	55.00	110	185	375	—
16Z7 WA	—	55.00	110	185	375	—
16Z8 WA	—	55.00	110	185	375	—
16Z9 WA	—	55.00	110	185	375	—
1630 WA	—	55.00	110	185	375	—
1631 WA	—	55.00	110	185	375	—
1631 MR	—	55.00	110	185	375	—
1632 WA	—	55.00	110	185	375	—
1632 MR	—	55.00	110	185	375	—

DAV# 7376A THALER

Silver **Rev:** Without initials in field behind busts

Date	Mintage	VG	F	VF	XF	Unc
16Z6	—	55.00	110	185	375	—
1631	—	55.00	110	185	375	—

DAV# 7376B THALER

Silver **Rev:** Without hands showing

Date	Mintage	VG	F	VF	XF	Unc
1626	—	55.00	110	185	375	—
1628	—	55.00	110	185	375	—
1629	—	55.00	110	185	375	—

DAV# 7377 THALER

Silver **Subject:** Two Sons of Friedrich Wilhelm **Obv:** Bust right **Rev:** Bust left divides date

Date	Mintage	VG	F	VF	XF	Unc
1634	—	115	210	350	550	—

DAV# 7378 THALER

Silver **Obv:** Bust right without bow behind head **Rev:** Bust left divides date above

Date	Mintage	VG	F	VF	XF	Unc
1637	—	115	210	350	550	—

DAV# 7379 THALER

Silver **Obv:** Bust left **Rev:** Date divided lower down

Date	Mintage	VG	F	VF	XF	Unc
1637	—	115	220	350	550	—

DAV# 7380 THALER

Silver **Obv:** Half-figure right **Rev:** Half-figure right divides date

Date	Mintage	VG	F	VF	XF	Unc
1637	—	115	220	350	550	—

DAV# 7381 THALER

Silver **Rev:** Half-figure left with MR in front

Date	Mintage	VG	F	VF	XF	Unc
1637	—	115	220	350	550	—
1638	—	115	220	350	550	—

DAV# 7383 THALER

Silver **Subject:** Death of Johann Philipp **Obv:** Bust right with angels above **Rev:** 14-line inscription in diamond

Date	Mintage	VG	F	VF	XF	Unc
1639	—	450	775	1,300	2,000	—

DAV# 7383A THALER

Silver **Rev:** 13-line inscription

Date	Mintage	VG	F	VF	XF	Unc
1639	—	450	775	1,300	2,000	—

DAV# 7385 THALER

Silver **Obv:** Bust of Friedrich Wilhelm right with helmet in front **Rev:** Helmeted arms divide EF-S

Date	Mintage	VG	F	VF	XF	Unc
ND Rare	—	—	—	—	—	—

DAV# 7387 THALER

Silver **Obv:** Bust right divides date **Rev. Legend:** ...ET. RA. D. I. RA.

Date	Mintage	VG	F	VF	XF	Unc
1640 Rare	—	—	—	—	—	—

DAV# 7387A THALER

Silver **Rev. Legend:** ...ET. RAV. D. I. RAV.

Date	Mintage	VG	F	VF	XF	Unc
1640 Rare	—	—	—	—	—	—

DAV# 7388 THALER

Silver **Obv:** Helmet in front of bust facing right **Rev:** Helmeted arms dividing date and EF-S

Date	Mintage	VG	F	VF	XF	Unc
1640	—	1,000	2,000	3,250	—	—

DAV# 7389 THALER

Silver **Rev:** Helmeted arms divide EF-S above and date below **Rev. Legend:** LAN. THV. MAR. MIS. COMARERDIR.

Date	Mintage	VG	F	VF	XF	Unc
1640	—	1,000	2,000	3,250	—	—

DAV# 7393 THALER

Silver **Obv:** Half-figure right with helmet **Rev. Legend:** LANDG: THVR: MAR: MIS: COM: MAR:

Date	Mintage	VG	F	VF	XF	Unc
1641	—	350	750	1,500	2,500	—

DAV# 7401 THALER

Silver **Rev:** Larger shield and decoration **Rev. Legend:** DOM. I: IN. R.

Date	Mintage	VG	F	VF	XF	Unc
1641	—	350	750	1,500	2,500	—
1642	—	350	750	1,500	2,500	—
1643	—	350	750	1,500	2,500	—
1644	—	350	750	1,500	2,500	—
1645	—	350	750	1,500	2,500	—

DAV# 7395 THALER

Silver **Rev. Legend:** GRAF. THVR: MAR:...

Date	Mintage	VG	F	VF	XF	Unc
1642	—	325	700	1,450	2,500	—

DAV# 7398 THALER

Silver **Obv:** Similar to Dav. #7399 but new figure **Rev:** Similar to Dav. #7399 but legend ends:...RAV: D: I. R.

Date	Mintage	VG	F	VF	XF	Unc
1642	—	300	650	1,350	2,850	—

DAV# 7397 THALER

Silver **Rev. Legend:** ...MARCK. GRAF. MIS. **Note:** Similar to Dav. #7395 but M-R divided by shield.

Date	Mintage	VG	F	VF	XF	Unc
1642	—	275	600	1,250	2,250	—
1643	—	275	600	1,250	2,250	—
1644	—	275	600	1,250	2,250	—

DAV# 7399 THALER

Silver **Rev:** Legend, date **Rev. Legend:** ...DOM: I: RAV:

Date	Mintage	VG	F	VF	XF	Unc
1643	—	300	650	1,350	2,250	—

DAV# 7402 THALER

Silver **Obv:** Bust right **Rev:** Center shield divides M-R, surrounded by 18 shields within legend

Date	Mintage	VG	F	VF	XF	Unc
1649	—	250	500	1,000	1,850	—
1650	—	250	500	1,000	1,850	—
1651	—	250	500	1,000	1,850	—

DAV# 7384 THALER

Silver **Subject:** Death of Elisabeth, Wife of Johann Philipp **Obv:** Crowned, heart-shaped arms **Rev:** 12-line inscription

Date	Mintage	VG	F	VF	XF	Unc
1650	—	400	800	1,650	2,750	—

DAV# 7406 THALER

Silver **Subject:** Death of Magdalena Sybilla, Second Wife of Friedrich Wilhelm II

Date	Mintage	VG	F	VF	XF	Unc
1668	—	350	750	1,500	2,500	—

DAV# 7404 THALER

Silver **Note:** Similar to 2 Thaler, Dav. #7403.

Date	Mintage	VG	F	VF	XF	Unc
1669	—	350	750	1,500	2,500	—

DAV# 7407 THALER

Silver **Obv:** Bust of Friedrich Wilhelm III right **Rev:** Round arms in center, circle of 18 shields around

Date	Mintage	VG	F	VF	XF	Unc
1672	—	650	1,250	2,500	4,250	—

DAV# 7409 THALER

Silver **Subject:** Death of Friedrich Wilhelm III **Obv:** Bust right **Rev:** 12-line inscription

Date	Mintage	VG	F	VF	XF	Unc
MDCLXXII (1672)	—	300	600	1,200	2,000	—

DAV# 7367B 1-1/4 THALER

Silver **Note:** Similar to 1 Thaler, Dav. #7367 but Klippe.

Date	Mintage	VG	F	VF	XF	Unc
1621 Rare	—	—	—	—	—	—

DAV# 7360 2 THALER

Silver **Note:** Similar to 1 Thaler, Dav. #7361.

Date	Mintage	VG	F	VF	XF	Unc
1606	—	675	1,200	1,900	3,000	—

DAV# 7364 2 THALER
Silver **Note:** Similar to 1 Thaler, Dav. #7365.

Date	Mintage	VG	F	VF	XF	Unc
1613	—	675	1,200	1,900	3,000	—
1616	—	675	1,200	1,900	3,000	—

DAV# 7362 2 THALER
Silver **Obv:** Four facing busts **Rev:** Arms with date above dividing A-H at sides in circle of 17 shields

Date	Mintage	VG	F	VF	XF	Unc
1613	—	675	1,200	1,900	3,000	—

DAV# 7366 2 THALER
Silver **Note:** Similar to 1 Thaler, Dav. #7367.

Date	Mintage	VG	F	VF	XF	Unc
1619	—	675	1,200	1,900	3,000	—
1623	—	675	1,200	1,900	3,000	—

DAV# 7368 2 THALER
Silver **Note:** Similar to 1 Thaler, Dav. #7370 but central figure without baton.

Date	Mintage	VG	F	VF	XF	Unc
1623	—	675	1,200	1,900	3,000	—

DAV# 7372 2 THALER
Silver **Note:** Similar to 1 Thaler, Dav. #7373.

Date	Mintage	VG	F	VF	XF	Unc
1625 Rare	—	—	—	—	—	—

DAV# 7370 2 THALER
Silver **Rev:** Central figure with baton

Date	Mintage	VG	F	VF	XF	Unc
1625	—	800	1,400	2,200	3,500	—

DAV# 7375 2 THALER
Silver **Subject:** 3 Brothers **Note:** Similar to 1 Thaler, Dav. #7376.

Date	Mintage	VG	F	VF	XF	Unc
1626 Rare	—	—	—	—	—	—

DAV# 7386 2 THALER
Silver **Obv:** Bust of Friedrich Wilhelm II right dividing date **Rev:** Helmeted arms divide EF-S

Date	Mintage	VG	F	VF	XF	Unc
1640 Rare	—	—	—	—	—	—

DAV# 7391 2 THALER
Silver **Obv:** Half-figure with baton down right **Rev:** Helmeted arms divide EF-S **Rev. Legend:** ...DOM. I. R.

Date	Mintage	VG	F	VF	XF	Unc
1641	—	975	1,750	2,900	4,400	—

DAV# 7392 2 THALER
Silver **Rev:** Helmeted arms divide E-G at sides and date below

Date	Mintage	VG	F	VF	XF	Unc
1641	—	975	1,750	2,900	4,400	—

DAV# 7396 2 THALER
Silver **Rev:** Smaller shield within circle divides M-R, date in legend

Date	Mintage	VG	F	VF	XF	Unc
1643	—	—	—	—	—	—
1644 Rare	—	—	—	—	—	—

DAV# 7400 2 THALER
Silver **Obv:** New figure with helmet **Rev:** Larger shield and decoration **Rev. Legend:** ...DOMI: IN. R.

Date	Mintage	VG	F	VF	XF	Unc
1644 Rare	—	—	—	—	—	—

DAV# 7405 2 THALER
Silver **Subject:** Death of Magdalena Sybilla, Second Wife of Friedrich Wilhelm II **Note:** Similar to 1 Thaler, Dav. #7406.

Date	Mintage	VG	F	VF	XF	Unc
1668	—	1,050	1,900	3,250	4,950	—

DAV# 7403 2 THALER
Silver **Subject:** Death of Friedrich Wilhelm II **Obv:** Facing bust **Rev:** 7-line inscription

Date	Mintage	VG	F	VF	XF	Unc
1669	—	1,500	2,650	4,400	6,600	—

DAV# A7407 2 THALER
Silver

Date	Mintage	VG	F	VF	XF	Unc
1672	—	1,500	2,650	4,400	6,600	—

DAV# 7408 2 THALER
Silver **Subject:** Death of Friedrich Wilhelm III **Obv:** Bust right **Rev:** 12-line inscription

Date	Mintage	VG	F	VF	XF	Unc
1672	7	1,300	2,250	3,750	5,600	—

DAV# 7390 3 THALER
Silver **Obv:** Figure right with helmet **Rev:** Helmeted arms dividing EF-S

Date	Mintage	VG	F	VF	XF	Unc
1641 Rare	—	—	—	—	—	—

TRADE COINAGE

FR# 2904 GOLDGULDEN
3.5000 g., 0.9860 Gold 0.1109 oz. AGW **Obv:** Four brothers - two facing two - in inner circle **Rev:** Arms with date above in inner circle

Date	Mintage	VG	F	VF	XF	Unc
1614	—	375	750	1,350	2,500	—
1619	—	375	750	1,350	2,500	—
1622	—	375	750	1,350	2,500	—

FR# 2906 DUCAT
3.5000 g., 0.9860 Gold 0.1109 oz. AGW **Obv:** Bust of Johann Philip right in inner circle **Rev:** Bust of Friedrich Wilhelm left in inner circle

Date	Mintage	VG	F	VF	XF	Unc
1638	—	325	725	1,300	2,200	—

FR# 2907 DUCAT
3.5000 g., 0.9860 Gold 0.1109 oz. AGW **Subject:** Death of Johann Philipp **Obv:** Bust of Johann Philipp right, two angels with wreath above head, three shields below **Rev:** 9-line inscription in rhombus

Date	Mintage	VG	F	VF	XF	Unc
1639	—	600	1,200	2,400	4,200	—

FR# 2908 DUCAT
3.5000 g., 0.9860 Gold 0.1109 oz. AGW **Obv:** Bust of Friedrich Wilhelm right divides date **Rev:** Elaborate arms with six helmets

Date	Mintage	VG	F	VF	XF	Unc
1640	—	425	900	1,800	3,000	—

KM# 150 DUCAT
3.5000 g., 0.9860 Gold 0.1109 oz. AGW **Obv:** Older bust of Friedrich Wilhelm II right divides date **Rev:** Manifold arms

Date	Mintage	VG	F	VF	XF	Unc
1654	—	725	1,450	2,650	4,200	—

FR# 2910 DUCAT
3.5000 g., 0.9860 Gold 0.1109 oz. AGW **Subject:** Death of Magdalena Sybilla, second wife of Friedrich Wilhelm II **Obv:** Crowned MS monogram in inner circle **Rev:** 8-line inscription

Date	Mintage	VG	F	VF	XF	Unc
1668	—	550	1,100	2,100	3,600	—

FR# 2912 DUCAT
3.5000 g., 0.9860 Gold 0.1109 oz. AGW **Subject:** Death of Friedrich Wilhelm II **Obv:** Facing bust of Friedrich Wilhelm in inner circle **Rev:** 8-line inscription

Date	Mintage	VG	F	VF	XF	Unc
MDCLXIX (1669)	—	600	1,200	2,400	4,200	—

FR# 2905 2 DUCAT
7.0000 g., 0.9860 Gold 0.2219 oz. AGW **Obv:** John Philip

Date	Mintage	VG	F	VF	XF	Unc
1637	—	900	1,800	3,300	5,400	—

KM# 200 10 DUCAT
3.5000 g., 0.9860 Gold 0.1109 oz. AGW **Subject:** Death of Friedrich Wilhelm III **Obv:** 7-line inscription in inner circle **Rev:** 3-line inscription in laurel wreath

Date	Mintage	VG	F	VF	XF	Unc
1672 Rare	—	—	—	—	—	—

SAXE-BARBY

(Sachsen-Barby)

When the line of counts of Barby (q.v.) became extinct in 1659, the lands of that county fell to Electoral Saxony. In 1680, a separate line of Saxe-Barby was established by a son of the duke of Saxe-Weissenfels. It was short-lived, however, and reverted to Saxe-Weissenfels in 1739. The latter also became extinct in 1746 and Barby was integrated from that time into the kingdom of Saxony.

RULER
Heinrich, 1680-1728

DUCHY

REGULAR COINAGE

KM# 1 2/3 THALER (Gulden)
Silver **Ruler:** Heinrich **Obv:** Bust of Heinrich right **Rev:** Crowned 4-fold arms of Saxony with central shield of Barby, divide date, value 2/3 in oval below **Note:** Dav.#834.

Date	Mintage	VG	F	VF	XF	Unc
1687 Rare	—	—	—	—	—	—

Note: Fritz Rudolf Künker Münzenhandlung Auction 80, 3-03, VF realized approximately $13,265

SAXE-COBURG

Coburg, a town and county in southern Thüringia – now belonging to Bavaria - came to the Wettins thru a marriage in the fourteenth century. In the division of the Saxon territories in 1485 it went to the Ernestine branch. It was apparently first a separate duchy under Johann Ernst I (1542-1553), then passed into the Old Gotha, Old Altenburg, and finally New Gotha line. In 1680 it was created a separate duchy for Albrecht III, second son of Ernst the Pious. At his death in 1699 there was vehement contention among his surviving brothers, but eventually it was assigned to his youngest brother Johann Ernst VIII of Saalfeld.

RULER
Albrecht III, 1680-1699

MINT OFFICIALS' INITIALS

Initial	Date	Name
SM	1674-95	Sebastian Muller in Hanau
RA	1676-1690?	Johann Reinhart Arnold, warden in Hanau
GFS	1677-80	Georg Friedrich Staude in Gotha
(a) ⚒ and/or PFC	1686-1714	Paul Friedrich Crumm, warden and mintmaster in Coburg
HEA	1686-1705	Heinrich Ernst Angerstein in Coburg

DUCHY

REGULAR COINAGE

KM# 5 HELLER
Copper

Date	Mintage	VG	F	VF	XF	Unc
1680	—	7.00	13.00	27.00	55.00	—
1681	—	7.00	13.00	27.00	55.00	—

DAV# 7410 THALER
Silver **Subject:** Receiving the Order of the Elephant **Obv:** Bust right **Rev:** Arm from clouds with crown above eagle on rose bush

Date	Mintage	VG	F	VF	XF	Unc
ND(1684) HEA (a)	—	350	650	1,100	1,650	—

DAV# 7411 THALER
Silver **Obv:** Bust right **Rev:** Crowned and mantled arms

Date	Mintage	VG	F	VF	XF	Unc
1687 PFC	—	800	1,500	2,400	3,700	—

DAV# 7412 THALER
Silver **Obv:** Without inner circles **Rev:** Without inner circles **Edge:** Date

Date	Mintage	VG	F	VF	XF	Unc
1694 HEA (a)	—	800	1,500	2,400	3,700	—

TRADE COINAGE

KM# 30 DUCAT
3.5000 g., 0.9860 Gold 0.1109 oz. AGW **Obv:** Bust Albrecht III right **Rev:** Four-fold arms with central shield of Saxony, crown above divides date **Mint:** Coburg

Date	Mintage	VG	F	VF	XF	Unc
1687 PFC Rare	—	—	—	—	—	—

SAXE-EISENACH

(Sachsen-Eisenach)

One of the Ernestine Saxon duchies in Thuringia (Thüringen), Saxe-Eisenach was first ruled separately by one of eight brothers beginning in 1640. It reverted back to Saxe-Middle-Weimar in 1644, but a new line was established by the second son of Duke Wilhelm IV as Saxe-(New)-Weimar in 1622. This second line became extinct very shortly thereafter and Eisenach passed to Wilhelm IV's third son in 1671. Sayn-Altenkirchen (q.v.) was added to the duke's possessions through marriage in 1686. Again, the line passed out of existence and Eisenach was returned to Saxe-Weimar in 1741. See Saxe-Weimar-Eisenach for subsequent coinages.

RULERS
Albrecht II, 1640-1644
Adolph Wilhelm, 1662-1668
Johann Georg I, 1671-1686
Johann Georg II, 1686-1698
Johann Wilhelm, 1698-1729

MINT OFFICIALS' INITIALS

Initial	Date	Name
CW	1688-1739	Christian Wermuth, die-cutter in Gotha
HCM/HGM w/or w/o two crossed ingot hooks	1689-90	Heinrich Christian Müller
HD	1693-?	Hubertus Dönnigke
ICF	1692-93	Johann Carl Falkner
	1692-?	Johann Matthias Obermüller
IEK	1689-90	Johann Esaias Krauel (Grauel)
IGW	1683-90	Johann Gottfried Wichmannshausen in Gotha
SC	1700-01	Simon Conradi

DUCHY

REGULAR COINAGE

KM# 32 HELLER
Copper **Ruler:** Johann Wilhelm **Obv:** Crowned Saxony arms between palm branches **Rev:** 1/HELLER/ F.E.L., date

Date	Mintage	VG	F	VF	XF	Unc
1700	—	8.00	16.00	33.00	60.00	—

KM# 33 2 PFENNIG (Leuchte)
Silver **Ruler:** Johann Wilhelm **Obv:** 3 small oval shields of arms, crown above **Rev:** 2/LEUCHTE/PFENN/F.E.L.M., date

Date	Mintage	VG	F	VF	XF	Unc
1700	—	12.00	27.00	55.00	95.00	—

KM# 34 3 PFENNIG (Dreier)
Silver **Ruler:** Johann Wilhelm **Obv:** Crowned script 'IW' monogram divides date **Rev:** Imperial orb with 3 **Rev. Legend:** NACH DEM LEIPZIGER FUS

Date	Mintage	VG	F	VF	XF	Unc
1700	—	20.00	40.00	80.00	145	—

KM# 15 GROSCHEN
Silver **Ruler:** Johann Georg I **Subject:** Death of Johann Georg I's Son, Friedrich August **Obv:** Bust left **Rev:** 6-line inscription, Roman numeral dates in legend

Date	Mintage	VG	F	VF	XF	Unc
MDCLXXXIV (1684)	—	—	—	—	—	—

KM# 35 GROSCHEN
Silver **Ruler:** Johann Wilhelm **Obv:** Bust right **Rev:** 4 small crowned shields of arms in cruciform divide date, 1/GROS in center circle **Rev. Legend:** NACH - LEIPZ - FUS

Date	Mintage	VG	F	VF	XF	Unc
1700 SC	—	16.00	33.00	65.00	115	—

KM# 36 GROSCHEN
Silver **Ruler:** Johann Wilhelm **Obv:** Bust left **Rev:** 4 small crowned shields of arms in cruciform divide date, 1/GROS in center circle **Rev. Legend:** NACH - DEM - LEIPZ - FUS

Date	Mintage	VG	F	VF	XF	Unc
1700 SC	—	16.00	33.00	65.00	115	—

KM# 26 1/12 THALER (Doppelgroschen)
Silver **Ruler:** Johann Georg II **Obv:** Arms of Saxony **Rev:** 12/EINEN, date

Date	Mintage	VG	F	VF	XF	Unc
1692	—	—	—	—	—	—
1693	—	—	—	—	—	—

KM# 27 1/6 THALER (1/4 Gulden)
Silver **Ruler:** Johann Georg II **Obv:** Bust right **Rev:** Crowned arms in center of 4 crowned IG monograms within palm branches forming quatrefoil, value 1/6 in oval below divided date

Date	Mintage	VG	F	VF	XF	Unc
1693 ICF	—	—	—	—	—	—
1694 HD	—	—	—	—	—	—

KM# 3 1/4 THALER
Silver **Ruler:** Albrecht II **Subject:** Death and Interment of Albrecht II **Obv:** Jehovah's name in rayed sun above palm sprays with W.H.Z.S. A.H.Z.S.E.H.Z.S. **Rev:** 8-line inscription

Date	Mintage	VG	F	VF	XF	Unc
1644-45	—	—	—	—	—	—

KM# 37 1/3 THALER (1/2 Gulden)
Silver **Ruler:** Johann Wilhelm **Obv:** Bust right **Rev:** 4 small crowned IW monograms with palm branches in cruciform, Saxony arms in center, value 1/3 in oval below divides date

Date	Mintage	VG	F	VF	XF	Unc
1700 SC	—	—	—	—	—	—

KM# 16 1/2 THALER
Silver **Ruler:** Johann Georg I **Subject:** Death of Johann Georg I's Son, Friedrich August **Obv:** Bust left **Rev:** 7-line inscription in palm wreath

Date	Mintage	VG	F	VF	XF	Unc
1684 IGW	—	—	—	—	—	—

KM# 13 2/3 THALER (Gulden)
Silver **Ruler:** Johann Georg I **Obv:** Crowned manifold arms with date **Rev:** 2/3 in wreath **Rev. Legend:** DOMINVS PROVIDEBIT **Note:** Dav. #839.

Date	Mintage	VG	F	VF	XF	Unc
1682	—	—	—	—	—	—

KM# 14 2/3 THALER (Gulden)
Silver **Ruler:** Johann Georg I **Obv:** Crowned manifold arms, titles of Johann Georg I **Rev:** Large 2/3 in circle **Rev. Legend:** DOMINVS PROVIDEBIT **Note:** Dav. #840.

Date	Mintage	VG	F	VF	XF	Unc
ND(ca.1682)	—	—	—	—	—	—

KM# 19 2/3 THALER (Gulden)
Silver **Ruler:** Johann Georg II **Obv:** Bust right **Rev:** Crowned and ornamented manifold arms, 2/3 in oval cartouche divides date below

Date	Mintage	VG	F	VF	XF	Unc
1689 IEK	—	—	—	—	—	—

KM# 20 2/3 THALER (Gulden)
Silver **Ruler:** Johann Georg II **Obv:** Bust right **Rev:** Crowned manifold arms in palm branches divide date, value 2/3 in oval below

Date	Mintage	VG	F	VF	XF	Unc
1690 HCM	—	—	—	—	—	—
1690 HGM	—	—	—	—	—	—

KM# 21 2/3 THALER (Gulden)
Silver **Ruler:** Johann Georg II **Obv:** Bust right within circle **Rev:** Crowned manifold arms in palm branches divide date, value 2/3 in oval below, all in circle

Date	Mintage	VG	F	VF	XF	Unc
1690 HGM	—	—	—	—	—	—

KM# 22 2/3 THALER (Gulden)
Silver **Ruler:** Johann Georg II **Obv:** Bust right **Rev:** Crowned manifold arms in palm branches, value 2/3 in oval below divides date

Date	Mintage	VG	F	VF	XF	Unc
1690 HCM	—	80.00	150	220	300	—

KM# 23 2/3 THALER (Gulden)
Silver **Ruler:** Johann Georg II **Obv:** Crowned ornate, intertwined JGS monogram, value 2/3 in center, date divided to upper left and right **Rev:** Sailing ship to right, FORTUNA & ZEPHYRO

Date	Mintage	VG	F	VF	XF	Unc
1690	—	—	—	—	—	—

KM# 25 2/3 THALER (Gulden)
Silver **Ruler:** Johann Georg II **Obv:** Bust right **Rev:** Crowned manifold arms in palm branches, date divided by value in oval at bottom **Note:** Dav. #844.

Date	Mintage	VG	F	VF	XF	Unc
1691	—	80.00	150	220	300	—

KM# 38 2/3 THALER (Gulden)
Silver **Ruler:** Johann Wilhelm **Obv:** Bust right **Rev:** 4 small crowned IW monograms within palm branches in cruciform, Saxony arms in center, value 2/3 in oval below divided date

Date	Mintage	VG	F	VF	XF	Unc
1700 SC	—	—	—	—	—	—

KM# 28 2/3 THALER
Silver **Ruler:** Johann Georg II **Obv:** Bust right **Rev:** Crowned arms in center of 4 crowned IG monograms within palm branches forming quatrefoil, value 2/3 in oval below divided date **Note:** Dav. #845.

Date	Mintage	VG	F	VF	XF	Unc
1693 ICF	—	—	—	—	—	—

KM# 4 THALER
Silver **Ruler:** Albrecht II **Subject:** Death and Interment of Albrecht II. **Obv:** Jehovah's name in rayed sun above palm sprays. **Obv. Legend:** W.H.Z.S., A.H.Z.S.E.H.Z.S. **Rev:** 8-line inscription. **Note:** Dav# 7414.

Date	Mintage	Good	VG	F	VF	XF
1645	—	450	900	1,850	3,850	6,200

KM# 5 THALER
Silver **Ruler:** Albrecht II **Subject:** Death and Interment of Albrecht II. **Obv:** Jehovah's name in rayed sun above bust of Albrecht, inner initials. **Obv. Legend:** A.H.Z.-S.I.C.V.B. **Note:** Dav# 7415.

Date	Mintage	Good	VG	F	VF	XF
1645	—	450	850	1,750	3,750	6,000

KM# 11 THALER

Silver **Ruler:** Adolph Wilhelm **Subject:** Death of Adolph Wilhelm **Obv:** Facing bust of Adolph Wilhelm **Rev:** 21-line inscription **Note:** Dav# 7416

Date	Mintage	VG	F	VF	XF	Unc
1668 Rare	—	—	—	—	—	—

KM# 17 THALER

Silver **Ruler:** Johann Georg I **Subject:** Death of Friedrich August, son of Johann Georg I **Obv:** Bust left **Rev:** Seven-line inscription **Note:** Dav# 7417.

Date	Mintage	VG	F	VF	XF	Unc
1684 IGW	—	900	1,850	3,850	6,200	—

KM# 18 THALER

Silver **Ruler:** Johann Georg I **Subject:** Death of Johann Georg I **Obv:** Bust right **Rev:** 24-line inscription **Note:** Dav# 7418.

Date	Mintage	VG	F	VF	XF	Unc
1686 Rare	—	—	—	—	—	—

KM# 30 THALER

Silver **Ruler:** Johann Georg II **Subject:** Death of Johann Georg II **Obv:** Bust right **Rev:** 23-line inscription **Note:** Dav# 7419.

Date	Mintage	VG	F	VF	XF	Unc
1698 Rare	—	—	—	—	—	—

KM# 6 1-1/4 THALER

Silver **Ruler:** Albrecht II **Subject:** Death and Interment of Albrecht II **Obv:** Jehovah's name in rayed sun above palm sprays w/initials. **Obv. Legend:** W.H.Z.S., A.H.Z.S., E.H.Z.S. **Rev:** 8-line inscription. **Note:** Dav# 7413.

Date	Mintage	VG	F	VF	XF	Unc
1645 Rare	—	—	—	—	—	—

KM# 7 1-1/4 THALER

Silver **Ruler:** Albrecht II **Subject:** Death and Interment of Albrecht II **Note:** Klippe. Dav#7413A.

Date	Mintage	VG	F	VF	XF	Unc
1645 Rare	—	—	—	—	—	—

TRADE COINAGE

KM# 8 DUCAT

3.5000 g., 0.9860 Gold 0.1109 oz. AGW **Ruler:** Albrecht II **Subject:** Death and Interment of Albrecht II **Obv:** Jehovah's name in rayed sun above bust, inner initials: A.H.Z.-S.I.C.V.B.

Date	Mintage	VG	F	VF	XF	Unc
1644-45	—	—	—	—	—	—

KM# 9 DUCAT

3.5000 g., 0.9860 Gold 0.1109 oz. AGW **Ruler:** Albrecht II **Subject:** Death and Interment of Albrecht II **Obv:** Jehovah's name in rayed sun above palm sprays with W.H.Z.S. A.H.Z.S.E.H.Z.S. **Rev:** 8-line inscription

Date	Mintage	VG	F	VF	XF	Unc
1644-45	—	—	—	—	—	—

KM# 39 DUCAT

3.5000 g., 0.9860 Gold 0.1109 oz. AGW **Ruler:** Johann Wilhelm **Obv:** Bust of Johann Wilhelm right **Rev:** Monograms in script letters

Date	Mintage	VG	F	VF	XF	Unc
1700 CW	—	1,500	3,000	5,300	8,300	—

FR# 2916 DUCAT

3.5000 g., 0.9860 Gold 0.1109 oz. AGW **Ruler:** Johann Wilhelm **Obv:** Bust of Johann Wilhelm 3/4 right **Rev:** Crowned and helmeted arms

Date	Mintage	VG	F	VF	XF	Unc
1700 CW	—	1,500	3,000	5,300	8,300	—

KM# 40 DUCAT

3.5000 g., 0.9860 Gold 0.1109 oz. AGW **Ruler:** Johann Wilhelm **Obv:** Bust of Johann Wilhelm right **Rev:** 4 crowned cruciform JW monograms with small oval arms of ducal Saxony in center **Note:** Fr# 2916.

Date	Mintage	VG	F	VF	XF	Unc
1700 CW	—	1,500	3,000	5,300	8,300	—

SAXE-EISENBERG

Short-lived branch of the Ernestine Saxon house which was created for Christian, fifth son of Ernst the Pious of Saxe-Gotha. The line became extinct with the death of Christian in 1707 and passed to Saxe-Hildburghausen.

RULER

Christian, 1680-1707

MINT OFFICIALS' INITIALS

Initials	Date	Name
HM	1681-1683	Christian Henning Müller, mintmaster in Gotha
IA	1692-1706	Julius Angerstein, die-cutter and mintmaster

DUCHY

REGULAR COINAGE

KM# 17 8 PFENNIG

Silver **Ruler:** Christian **Obv:** Facing bust **Obv. Legend:** CHRISTIAN. D.G. DUX. SAX: I. CL. &. MON. **Rev:** Crowned 4-fold arms of Saxony in baroque frame, value (8) in oval at bottom, date at end of legend **Rev. Legend:** VON FEINEM — SILBER

Date	Mintage	VG	F	VF	XF	Unc
1683	—	65.00	110	140	200	—

KM# 38 1/24 THALER (16 Pfennig)

Silver **Ruler:** Christian **Obv:** Armored bust to right **Obv. Legend:** D:G. CHRISTIAN; S. I. C. M. A. &. W. D: **Rev:** Imperial orb with 24 divides date and mintmaster's initials **Rev. Legend:** NACH REICHS SCHROTT U. KORN

Date	Mintage	VG	F	VF	XF	Unc
1698	—	—	—	—	—	—

KM# 39 1/24 THALER (16 Pfennig)

Silver **Ruler:** Christian **Obv:** Helmeted oval arms of ducal Saxony **Obv. Legend:** D:G. CHRISTIANUS SAX. I. C. M. A. &. W. DUX **Rev:** Imperial orb with 24 divides date and mintmaster's initials **Rev. Legend:** NACH REICHS SCHROTT UND KORN

Date	Mintage	VG	F	VF	XF	Unc
1698 IA	—	40.00	80.00	165	250	—

KM# 2 1/4 THALER

Silver **Ruler:** Christian **Subject:** Death of Christian's Wife, Christiane von Sachsen-Merseburg **Obv:** 8-line inscription with dates **Rev:** Cherub on scroll with flower and incense urn

Date	Mintage	VG	F	VF	XF	Unc
1679	—	—	—	—	—	—

KM# 3 1/2 THALER

Silver **Ruler:** Christian **Subject:** Death of Christian's Wife, Christiane von Sachsen-Merseburg **Obv:** 9-line inscription with dates **Obv. Legend:** +NUMM. EXEQ: CHRISTIANÆ. D:G. DUC S. I. C. &. MON. PIÆ. MEM **Obv. Inscription:** QUÆ/NATA. MARTISB./d. 1. IUN. A. 1659./DESPONSATA/IBID. d. 13 FEBRU. 1677./DENATA/d. 13. MART. ET. MOR/HUMATA. d. 29./APR. 1679 **Rev:** Child sitting on skull playing flute, vase with flowers at lower left, smoking urn at lower right, arms from clouds hold ribbon with inscription above **Rev. Inscription:** OMNIA VANITAS

Date	Mintage	VG	F	VF	XF	Unc
1679	—	—	—	—	—	—

KM# 26 1/2 THALER

Silver **Ruler:** Christian **Obv:** Armored bust to right **Obv. Legend:** D:G. CHRISTIAN'. SAX. I. C. M. A. &. W. DUX: **Rev:** Small crowned arms of ducal Saxony in center between palm fronds, four small crowned shields of arms around in cruciform wtih palm fronds, 4 crowned double-C monograms with palm fronds in angles, date divided at top **Rev. Legend:** DE — O — PAT — RIÆ — PROX — IMO — SAC — RUM.

Date	Mintage	VG	F	VF	XF	Unc
1692	—	1,200	1,600	2,500	3,300	—

KM# 31 1/2 THALER

Silver **Ruler:** Christian **Obv:** Bust to right **Rev:** Helmeted oval manifold arms of Saxony, date divided to either side of helmets in margin

Date	Mintage	VG	F	VF	XF	Unc
1697 IA	—	—	—	—	—	—

KM# 10 2/3 THALER (Gulden)

Silver **Ruler:** Christian **Obv:** Bust right in circle **Obv. Legend:** CHRISTIANUS. D.G. DUX. SAX. IUL. CLIV. ET. MONT **Rev:** Heart on altar, arms from clouds above hold shield and palm branch, inscription curved in band at top, value 2/3 in oval at bottom, date at end of legend **Rev. Legend:** NACH DEM OBER-SACH — CREYS SCHLUS **Rev. Inscription:** DEO PROTECTORI MEO **Note:** Dav# 850.

Date	Mintage	VG	F	VF	XF	Unc
1682 HM	—	225	400	650	925	—

KM# 23 2/3 THALER (Gulden)

Silver **Ruler:** Christian **Obv:** Bust right in circle **Obv. Legend:** CHRISTIANUS. D.G. DUX. SAX. IUL. CLIV. ET. MONT **Rev:** Table with hat, sword and palm branch, oval 4-fold arms in baroque frame divide date below in front, 2/3 in oval at bottom **Rev. Legend:** IN UTROQUE DEO. — MON. NOV. ARG. AD. LEGEM IMP. **Note:** Dav# 851.

Date	Mintage	VG	F	VF	XF	Unc
1686	—	1,600	2,000	2,650	4,000	—

Note: Only 2 reportedly known

KM# 27 2/3 THALER (Gulden)

Silver **Ruler:** Christian **Obv:** Bust right **Obv. Legend:** D.G. CHRISTIAN9 SAX. I. C. M. A. &. W. DVX **Rev:** Crowned oval arms between palm branches, value 2/3 below, date at end of legend **Rev. Legend:** NACH DEM LEIPZIGER FUS **Note:** Dav# 852.

Date	Mintage	VG	F	VF	XF	Unc
1692	—	—	—	—	—	—

KM# 4 THALER

Silver **Ruler:** Christian **Subject:** Death of Christian's Wife, Christiane von Sachsen-Merseburg **Obv:** Twelve-line inscription **Obv. Legend:** + D.G. CHRISTIANÆ. D. SAX. I. C. &. M. L. TH. M. MIS. &. VT: LUS. PR. HEN. C. M. &. R. DN. INI RAV. **Obv. Inscription:** HOC/MONUMENTUM/AMORIS POSITUM./QUÆ NATA./MARTISB. 1. IUN. A. 1659./DESPONSATA/IBID. d. 13 FEBRU. 1677./DENATA POSTPACTUM/FILIOLÆ d. 13. MARTIJ./ET. HUMATA./MARTISB. d. 29. APR./1679 **Rev:** Child sitting on skull playing flute, vase with flowers at lower left, smoking urn at lower right, arms from clouds hold ribbon with inscription above **Rev. Inscription:** OMNIA VANITAS **Note:** Dav# 7421.

Date	Mintage	VG	F	VF	XF	Unc
1679	—	250	500	950	1,750	2,800

KM# 12 THALER

Silver **Ruler:** Christian **Obv:** Young bust **Rev:** Helmeted arms divide date at top and H-M at bottom **Note:** Dav# 7422.

Date	Mintage	VG	F	VF	XF	Unc
1682 HM	—	750	1,500	2,750	4,800	—

DAV# 7422A THALER

Silver **Obv:** Armored bust right **Obv. Legend:** CHRISTIANUS•D•G•DUX•SAX•IUL•CLIV•ET•MONTIUM **Rev:** Royal insignia, arms in palm branches below **Rev. Legend:** NOV•ARGENT

Date	Mintage	VG	F	VF	XF	Unc
1686	—	750	1,500	2,750	4,800	—

KM# 29 THALER
Silver **Ruler:** Christian **Obv:** Older bust **Rev:** Arms surrounded by crowned shields and crowned intertwined C's, date above **Note:** Dav# 7423.

Date	Mintage	VG	F	VF	XF	Unc
1692	—	750	1,500	2,750	4,800	—

KM# 32 THALER
Silver **Ruler:** Christian **Obv:** Bust right without inner circle **Rev:** Helmeted arms, date divided at top, I-A below **Note:** Dav# 7424.

Date	Mintage	VG	F	VF	XF	Unc
1697 IA	—	700	1,400	2,500	4,650	—
1699 IA	—	700	1,400	2,500	4,650	—

KM# 5 2 THALER
Silver **Ruler:** Christian **Subject:** Death of Christiane, Wife of Christian **Note:** Dav# 7420. Similar to Thaler, KM# 4.

Date	Mintage	VG	F	VF	XF	Unc
1679 Rare	—	—	—	—	—	—

TRADE COINAGE

KM# 22 GOLDGULDEN
3.5000 g., 0.9860 Gold 0.1109 oz. AGW **Ruler:** Christian **Obv:** Crowned arms **Rev:** Standing palm tree **Note:** Fr# 2926.

Date	Mintage	VG	F	VF	XF	Unc
1684	—	1,050	2,050	3,750	6,300	—

KM# 19 1/4 DUCAT
0.8750 g., 0.9860 Gold 0.0277 oz. AGW **Ruler:** Christian **Obv:** Facing armored bust **Obv. Legend:** + CHRISTIAN: D.G. DUX. SAX: I. C. ET. MONT. **Rev:** Crowned 4-fold arms of Saxony in baroque frame, 1/4 in oval at bottom, date at end of legend **Rev. Legend:** DEO PROTEC — TORI MEO **Note:** Fr# 2921.

Date	Mintage	VG	F	VF	XF	Unc
1683	—	240	425	725	1,200	—
ND	—	240	425	725	1,200	—

KM# 20 1/2 DUCAT
1.7500 g., 0.9860 Gold 0.0555 oz. AGW **Ruler:** Christian **Obv:** Bust of Christian right **Rev:** Crowned arms in branches, value below **Note:** Fr# 2920.

Date	Mintage	VG	F	VF	XF	Unc
1683	—	375	675	1,350	2,250	—

KM# 34 1/2 DUCAT
1.7500 g., 0.9860 Gold 0.0555 oz. AGW **Ruler:** Christian **Rev:** Crowned and mantled arms **Note:** Fr# 2925.

Date	Mintage	VG	F	VF	XF	Unc
ND	—	425	725	1,450	2,400	—

KM# 14 DUCAT
3.5000 g., 0.9860 Gold 0.1109 oz. AGW **Ruler:** Christian **Obv:** Facing armored bust **Obv. Legend:** CHRISTIANUS. D.G. DUX. SAX. IUL. CLIV. ET. MONT. **Rev:** Heart on altar, crossed arms and hands from clouds above holding symbols, date in margin at top **Rev. Legend:** DEO — PROTECTORI — MEO. **Note:** Fr# 2918.

Date	Mintage	VG	F	VF	XF	Unc
1682	—	1,050	1,750	3,750	6,100	—

KM# 25 DUCAT
3.5000 g., 0.9860 Gold 0.1109 oz. AGW **Ruler:** Christian **Rev:** Table holding palm and sword **Note:** Fr# 2922.

Date	Mintage	VG	F	VF	XF	Unc
1686	—	900	1,750	3,250	5,500	—

KM# 35 DUCAT
3.5000 g., 0.9860 Gold 0.1109 oz. AGW **Ruler:** Christian **Obv:** Bust of Christian right **Rev:** Crowned and mantled arms, date divided at top **Note:** Fr# 2924.

Date	Mintage	VG	F	VF	XF	Unc
1697	—	1,000	2,000	3,600	6,000	—

KM# 15 2 DUCAT
7.0000 g., 0.9860 Gold 0.2219 oz. AGW **Ruler:** Christian **Obv:** Christian **Note:** Fr# 2919.

Date	Mintage	VG	F	VF	XF	Unc
ND(1682) Rare	—	—	—	—	—	—

KM# 36 2 DUCAT
7.0000 g., 0.9860 Gold 0.2219 oz. AGW **Ruler:** Christian **Rev:** Crowned and mantled arms, date divided at top **Note:** Fr# 2923. Struck on thick planchet from Ducat dies, KM# 35.

Date	Mintage	VG	F	VF	XF	Unc
1697 Rare	—	—	—	—	—	—

KM# 7 4 DUCAT
14.0000 g., 0.9860 Gold 0.4438 oz. AGW **Ruler:** Christian **Subject:** Death of Christian's Wife, Christiane von Sachsen-Merseburg **Obv:** 9-line inscription with dates **Obv. Legend:** +NUMM. EXEQ: CHRISTIANÆ. D:G. DUC S. I. C. &. MON. PIÆ. MEM **Obv. Inscription:** QUÆ/NATA. MARTISB./d. 1. IUN. A. 1659./DESPONSATA/IBID. d. 13 FEBRU. 1677./DENATA/d. 13. MART. ET. MOR/HUMATA. d. 29./APR. 1679 **Rev:** Child sitting on skull playing flute, vase with flowers lower left, smoking urn lower right, arms from clouds hold ribbon with inscription above **Rev. Inscription:** OMNIA VANITAS **Note:** Struck from 1/2 Thaler dies, KM# 3.

Date	Mintage	VG	F	VF	XF	Unc
1679 Rare	—	—	—	—	—	—

KM# 8 10 DUCAT
35.0000 g., 0.9860 Gold 1.1095 oz. AGW **Ruler:** Christian **Subject:** Death of Christian's Wife, Christiane von Sachsen-Merseburg **Obv:** 12-line inscription with dates **Obv. Legend:** + D.G. CHRISTIANÆ. D. SAX. I. C. &. M. L. TH. M. MIS. &. VT: LUS. PR. HEN. C. M. &. R. DN. INI RAV. **Obv. Inscription:** HOC/ MONUMENTUM/AMORIS POSITUM./QUÆ NATA./ MARTISB. 1. IUN. A. 1659./DESPONSATA/IBID. d. 13 FEBRU. 1677./DENATA POSTPACTUM/FILIOLÆ d. 13. MARTIJ./ET. HUMATA./MARTISB. d. 29. APR./1679 **Rev:** Child sitting on skull playing flute, with flowers at lower left, smoking urn at lower right, arms from clouds hold ribbon with inscription above **Rev. Inscription:** OMNIA VANITAS **Note:** Struck from Thaler dies, KM# 4.

Date	Mintage	VG	F	VF	XF	Unc
1679 Rare	—	—	—	—	—	—

PATTERNS

Including off metal strikes

KM#	Date	Mintage	Identification	Mkt Val
Pn1	1682	—	Ducat. Silver. KM# 14.	—

SAXE-OLD GOTHA

(Sachsen-Alt-Gotha)

In the aftermath of the religious struggles of the first half of the 16th century, Ernestine Saxony was ruled jointly, divided, and ruled jointly again in relentless succession. The sons of Johann Friedrich I effected a division of the domains in 1565. When the older brother was imprisoned two years later, Gotha reverted to Saxe-Old Weimar. Gotha was ceded in 1572 by Weimar to the Coburg branch of the family, but reverted to the former again in 1638. Upon its extinction in the latter year, Gotha fell to Weimar a third time, from which a new Gotha line was established in 1640.

RULERS

Johann Wilhelm, 1565-1567
And Johann Ernst II von Eisenach, 1572-1638

MINT OFFICIALS' INITIALS

Initial	Date	Name
WA	1604-12	Wolf Albrecht der Jüngere in Coburg
	1612-20, 23-32	Wolf Albrecht der Jüngere in Saalfeld
(c)=	1578-1603	Gregor Bechstedt (Bechstädt) in Saalfeld
(d)=	1603-04	Barther Bechstedt in Saalfeld
(e)= ☿ or WF	1620-April 1621	Wolfgang Frömell in Coburg (Ehrenburg)
	April-Dec. 1621	In Hildburghausen
	Early 1622	In Gotha
	1622-23	In Coburg
	1622	Tobias Rentsch in Neustadt an der Heide
(f)= ♀	1622	Johann Stopffel in Gotha
	1622	Hans Brauer (Brawer) in Hildburghausen
(g)= or	1620-21	Johann Ziessler in Eisenach
(h)=	1621-22	Hans Schmidt in Körner (Amt Volkenroda)
(i)= or MR	1633-39	Martin Reimann in Saalfeld
(j)= arm with sickle or EF/EFS	1636-72	Ernst Friedrich Schneider in Coburg
E		Ehrenburg mint in Coburg

DUCHY

REGULAR COINAGE

DAV# 7426 THALER
Silver **Obv:** Facing busts **Rev:** Date above center shield dividing C-O in circle of thirteen shields

Date	Mintage	VG	F	VF	XF	Unc
1601 (c)	—	70.00	160	280	450	—
160Z (c)	—	70.00	160	280	450	—
1603 (c)	—	70.00	160	280	450	—
1604 (d)	—	70.00	160	280	450	—
1604 WA	—	70.00	160	280	450	—
1605 WA	—	70.00	160	280	450	—
1606 WA	—	70.00	160	280	450	—
1607 WA	—	70.00	160	280	450	—
1608 WA	—	70.00	160	280	450	—
1609 WA	—	70.00	160	280	450	—
1610 WA	—	70.00	160	280	450	—
1611 WA	—	70.00	160	280	450	—
1612 WA	—	70.00	160	280	450	—

DAV# 7427 THALER
Silver **Rev:** Sixteen shields around knight on horseback, date below horse

Date	Mintage	VG	F	VF	XF	Unc
1612 WA	—	250	500	850	—	—

DAV# 7429 THALER

Silver **Rev:** Knight on horse dividing date

Date	Mintage	VG	F	VF	XF	Unc
1612 WA	—	75.00	170	300	750	—
1613 WA	—	75.00	170	300	750	—
1614 WA	—	75.00	170	300	750	—
1615 WA	—	75.00	170	300	750	—
1616 WA	—	75.00	170	300	750	—
1617 WA	—	75.00	170	300	750	—
1618 WA	—	75.00	170	300	750	—
1619 WA	—	75.00	170	300	750	—

DAV# 7431 THALER

Silver **Obv:** Bust right divides date; Ligate WA appears either below or after VERZEHRT at right **Rev:** Bust left with arm at left and right

Date	Mintage	VG	F	VF	XF	Unc
1623 WA	—	80.00	160	295	675	—
1624 WA	—	80.00	160	295	675	—
1625 WA	—	80.00	160	295	675	—
1626 WA	—	80.00	160	295	675	—
1627 WA	—	80.00	160	295	675	—
1628 WA	—	80.00	160	295	675	—
1629 WA	—	80.00	160	295	675	—

DAV# 7432 THALER

Silver **Obv:** Larger and thicker bust, without date **Rev:** Shorter and thicker bust, date in field behind bust

Date	Mintage	VG	F	VF	XF	Unc
1633 MR(i)	—	300	600	1,200	2,000	—

DAV# 7433 THALER

Silver **Subject:** Death of Johann Casimir **Obv:** Bust right **Rev:** Six-line inscription

Date	Mintage	VG	F	VF	XF	Unc
1633 MR	—	375	750	1,500	2,500	—

DAV# 7434 THALER

Silver **Obv:** Bust of Johann Ernst **Rev:** Sixteen shields around knight on horseback, dividing date

Date	Mintage	VG	F	VF	XF	Unc
1633 MR-(i)	—	485	850	1,750	2,800	—
1635 MR-(i)	—	485	850	1,750	2,800	—

DAV# A7435 THALER

Silver **Rev:** Helmeted shield divides date within inner circle **Rev. Legend:** DO: IN RAVE:

Date	Mintage	VG	F	VF	XF	Unc
1633 MR	—	450	875	1,500	2,500	—

DAV# 7435 THALER

Silver **Obv:** Facing half figure **Rev:** Helmeted shield reaches edge of coin, date divided at bottom

Date	Mintage	VG	F	VF	XF	Unc
1635 EFS-(j)	—	375	750	1,450	2,400	—

DAV# 7435A THALER

Silver **Rev:** Arms don't break border at bottom

Date	Mintage	VG	F	VF	XF	Unc
1636 EFS-(j)	—	375	750	1,450	2,400	—

DAV# 7436 THALER

Silver **Obv:** Bust right

Date	Mintage	VG	F	VF	XF	Unc
1636 EFS-(j)	—	375	750	1,450	2,400	—

DAV# 7437 THALER

Silver **Obv:** Smaller bust right **Rev:** Helmeted shield within inner circle divides date **Rev. Legend:** DO: IN RAVE:

Date	Mintage	VG	F	VF	XF	Unc
1636 EFS-(j)	—	375	750	1,450	2,400	—
1637 EFS-(j)	—	375	750	1,450	2,400	—
ND	—	375	750	1,450	2,400	—

DAV# 7438 THALER

Silver **Obv:** Bust right, date in legend **Rev:** Helmeted shield divides EF-S **Rev. Legend:** ...RAVENS

Date	Mintage	VG	F	VF	XF	Unc
1637 EFS-(j)	—	375	750	1,450	2,400	—
1638 EFS-(j)	—	375	750	1,450	2,400	—

DAV# 7439 THALER
Silver **Rev:** Helmeted arms divide legend at top, date and E-F below

Date	Mintage	VG	F	VF	XF	Unc
1637 EF-(j)	—	300	600	1,200	2,000	—
1638 EF-(j)	—	300	600	1,200	2,000	—

DAV# 7440 THALER
Silver **Subject:** Death of Johann Ernst **Rev:** Six-line inscription, nineteen shields around border

Date	Mintage	VG	F	VF	XF	Unc
1638 EFS-(j)	—	375	645	1,275	2,150	—

DAV# 7425 2 THALER
Silver **Note:** Similar to 1 Thaler, Dav. #7426.

Date	Mintage	VG	F	VF	XF	Unc
1603 (c)	—	825	1,500	2,700	—	—
1604 WA	—	825	1,500	2,700	—	—
1610 WA	—	825	1,500	2,700	—	—
1611 WA	—	825	1,500	2,700	—	—

DAV# 7428 2 THALER
Silver **Note:** Similar to 1 Thaler, Dav. #7429.

Date	Mintage	VG	F	VF	XF	Unc
1613 WA	—	825	1,500	2,700	—	—
1614 WA	—	825	1,500	2,700	—	—
1615 WA	—	825	1,500	2,700	—	—

DAV# 7430 2 THALER
Silver **Note:** Similar to 1 Thaler, Dav. #7431.

Date	Mintage	VG	F	VF	XF	Unc
1624 WA	—	525	975	1,800	3,000	—
1625 WA	—	525	975	1,800	3,000	—

DAV# LS411 2 THALER
Silver, 61 mm. **Obv:** Duke on horseback right, grass below **Rev:** Helmeted arms divide date, W-A divided below **Note:** Illustration reduced.

Date	Mintage	VG	F	VF	XF	Unc
1624 WA	—	1,200	2,100	3,400	—	—

DAV# LS413 2 THALER
58.0000 g., Silver **Obv:** Castle below duke on horseback **Note:** Illustration reduced.

Date	Mintage	VG	F	VF	XF	Unc
1624 WA	—	900	1,500	2,700	—	—
1625 WA	—	900	1,500	2,700	—	—
1626 WA	—	900	1,500	2,700	—	—

DAV# LS415 2 THALER
58.0000 g., Silver **Rev:** Without inner circle

Date	Mintage	VG	F	VF	XF	Unc
1625 WA	—	800	1,400	2,250	—	—
1626 WA	—	800	1,400	2,250	—	—

DAV# LS416 2 THALER
58.0000 g., Silver **Obv:** Duke on horseback looking back, without inner circle

Date	Mintage	VG	F	VF	XF	Unc
1626 WA Rare	—	—	—	—	—	—

DAV# A7433 2 THALER
58.0000 g., Silver **Obv:** Bust right in medallion, eighteen shields around **Rev:** Duke on horseback right

Date	Mintage	VG	F	VF	XF	Unc
1627 Rare	—	—	—	—	—	—

DAV# LS417 2 THALER
58.0000 g., Silver **Obv:** Duke on horseback right, tree clump below **Rev:** Helmeted arms divide date and W-A below **Note:** Illustration reduced.

Date	Mintage	VG	F	VF	XF	Unc
1627 WA	—	825	1,450	2,650	4,300	—
1629 WA	—	825	1,450	2,650	4,300	—

DAV# LS418 2 THALER

57.8000 g., Silver **Obv:** Duke looks back, castle and date below horse **Rev:** W-A divided by helmeted arms

Date	Mintage	VG	F	VF	XF	Unc
1629 WA	—	1,100	1,900	3,050	4,350	—

DAV# LS419 2 THALER

58.0000 g., Silver **Obv:** Duke on horseback looks right, without castle below

Date	Mintage	VG	F	VF	XF	Unc
1629 WA	—	1,200	2,100	3,300	4,900	—

DAV# LS420 2 THALER

58.0000 g., Silver **Obv:** Flowers below duke on horseback, date in exergue **Rev:** Helmeted arms divide M-R

Date	Mintage	VG	F	VF	XF	Unc
1633 MR-(i) Rare	—	—	—	—	—	—

DAV# 7435B 2 THALER

58.0000 g., Silver **Obv:** 1 Thaler, Dav. #7435 **Rev:** Similar to 1 Thaler, Dav. #7437

Date	Mintage	VG	F	VF	XF	Unc
1636 EFS-(j) Rare	—	—	—	—	—	—

DAV# LS410 3 THALER

86.5000 g., Silver **Note:** Similar to 2 Thaler, Dav. #LS411.

Date	Mintage	VG	F	VF	XF	Unc
1624 WA Rare	—	—	—	—	—	—

DAV# LS412 3 THALER

87.0000 g., Silver **Note:** Similar to 2 Thaler, Dav. #LS413.

Date	Mintage	VG	F	VF	XF	Unc
1624 WA Rare	—	—	—	—	—	—
1625 WA Rare	—	—	—	—	—	—

DAV# LS414 3 THALER

87.0000 g., Silver **Note:** Similar to 2 Thaler, Dav. #LS415.

Date	Mintage	VG	F	VF	XF	Unc
1626 WA Rare	—	—	—	—	—	—

DAV# LS-A416 3 THALER

87.0000 g., Silver **Note:** Similar to 2 Thaler, Dav. #LS416.

Date	Mintage	VG	F	VF	XF	Unc
1626 WA Rare	—	—	—	—	—	—

DAV# LS419A 3 THALER

87.2000 g., Silver **Note:** Similar to 2 Thaler, Dav. #LS419.

Date	Mintage	VG	F	VF	XF	Unc
1629 WA Rare	—	—	—	—	—	—

DAV# LS420A 3 THALER

87.2000 g., Silver **Obv:** Dav. #LS419 **Rev:** Dav. #LS420

Date	Mintage	VG	F	VF	XF	Unc
1633/1629 MR-(i)	—	—	—	—	—	—

TRADE COINAGE

FR# 2944 DUCAT

3.5000 g., 0.9860 Gold 0.1109 oz. AGW **Obv:** Johann Ernst facing **Rev:** Helmeted arms **Rev. Legend:** LANT. M. M. C?

Date	Mintage	VG	F	VF	XF	Unc
1635 (j)	—	250	500	1,150	2,050	—
1636 (j)	—	250	500	1,150	2,050	—
1637 (j)	—	250	500	1,150	2,050	—

FR# 2945 DUCAT

3.5000 g., 0.9860 Gold 0.1109 oz. AGW **Rev. Legend:** GOTT BESS?

Date	Mintage	VG	F	VF	XF	Unc
1637 (j)	—	250	500	1,150	2,050	—
1638 EF	—	250	500	1,150	2,050	—

FR# 2946 DUCAT

3.5000 g., 0.9860 Gold 0.1109 oz. AGW **Subject:** Death of Johann Ernst II **Rev:** Six-line inscription in inner circle

Date	Mintage	VG	F	VF	XF	Unc
1638 (j)	—	375	875	1,900	3,150	—

FR# 2942 2 DUCAT

7.0000 g., 0.9860 Gold 0.2219 oz. AGW **Subject:** Death of Johann Casimir **Obv:** Bust of Johann Casimir right holding helmet and sceptor, in inner circle **Rev:** Six-line inscription in inner circle

Date	Mintage	VG	F	VF	XF	Unc
1633 (i)	—	1,150	2,200	4,050	6,900	—

SAXE-NEW GOTHA

Short-lived branch of the Ernestine Saxon house which was created for Ernst III, 6th son of Johann III of Saxe-Middle-Weimar. When Ernst died in 1675 his seven sons ruled jointly until 1680 and then divided their holdings into seven branches.

RULERS

Ernst I (III) the Pious, 1640-1675
Joint Rule of Seven Brothers, 1675-1680
- Friedrich I of Altenburg
- Albrecht III of Middle-Coburg
- Bernhard III of Meiningen
- Heinrich III of Römhild
- Christian of Eisenberg
- Ernst IV of Hildburghausen
- Johan Ernst VIII of Saalfeld

DUCHY

REGULAR COINAGE

DAV# 7442 THALER

Silver **Subject:** Peace of Westphalia **Obv:** Saxon arms divide date **Rev:** Five-line inscription, Hebrew letters in sun above **Note:** Struck in 1672-75.

Date	Mintage	VG	F	VF	XF	Unc
1650	—	200	400	700	1,200	—

DAV# 7444 THALER

Silver **Subject:** Peace of Westphalia **Obv:** Saxon arms divide date **Rev:** Four-line inscription, Hebrew letters in sun above **Note:** Struck in 1672-75.

Date	Mintage	VG	F	VF	XF	Unc
1650	—	200	400	700	1,200	—

DAV# 7445 THALER

Silver **Subject:** Death of Johann Ernst, Son of Ernst **Obv:** JESVS, four-line inscription within heart **Rev:** Crowned shield within double legend

Date	Mintage	VG	F	VF	XF	Unc
MDCLVII (1657)	—	375	700	1,150	2,000	—

DAV# 7447 THALER

Silver **Subject:** The Catechism **Obv:** Three lines around sun, nine beams radiating from the sun with qualities of God **Rev:** Ten-line inscription

Date	Mintage	VG	F	VF	XF	Unc
1668	258	200	400	700	1,200	—
1671	—	200	400	700	1,200	—

DAV# 7448 THALER

Silver **Obv:** JESUS in sun above crown, inverted heart with eight-line inscription **Rev:** Ten-line inscription

Date	Mintage	VG	F	VF	XF	Unc
1668	204	235	475	825	1,400	—
1671	1,300	235	475	825	1,400	—

DAV# 7449 THALER

Silver **Subject:** Marriage of Friedrich and Magdalena Sybilla **Obv:** "JEHOVAH" with rays descending on wedding couple **Rev:** Twelve-line inscription

Date	Mintage	VG	F	VF	XF	Unc
1669	747	220	400	650	1,150	—

DAV# 7450 THALER

Silver **Subject:** Baptism of Princess Anna Sophia, Oldest Daughter of Prince Friedrich **Obv:** Baptismal scene with twelve-line inscription in field **Rev:** Ten-line inscription

Date	Mintage	VG	F	VF	XF	Unc
1670	—	270	500	800	1,400	—

DAV# 7451 THALER

Silver **Subject:** Marriage of Bernhard and Maria Hedwig **Obv:** "JEHOVAH" with rays descending on wedding couple **Rev:** Twelve-line inscription

Date	Mintage	VG	F	VF	XF	Unc
1671	700	220	400	650	1,150	—

DAV# 7453 THALER

Silver **Subject:** Baptism of Daughter of Prince Friedrich **Obv:** Baptism scene with eleven-line inscription in field **Rev:** Ten-line inscription

Date	Mintage	VG	F	VF	XF	Unc
1671	—	200	400	850	1,500	—

DAV# A7454 THALER

Silver **Subject:** The "Happiness" Thaler **Obv:** Eleven-line inscription **Rev:** Ten-line inscription

Date	Mintage	VG	F	VF	XF	Unc
1672	405	190	375	700	1,150	—

DAV# B7454 THALER

Silver **Subject:** The "Happiness" Thaler **Obv:** Considerable modifications **Rev:** Considerable modifications **Note:** Mintage included with Dav. #A7454.

Date	Mintage	VG	F	VF	XF	Unc
1672	—	300	600	1,200	2,000	—

DAV# 7455 THALER

Silver **Subject:** Death of Ernst **Obv:** Bust right **Rev:** Nine-line inscription within ring of eighteen shields

Date	Mintage	VG	F	VF	XF	Unc
1675	—	175	300	500	850	—

DAV# 7458 THALER

Silver **Subject:** Death of Ernst **Obv:** Different bust **Rev:** Larger crowned arms at top in circle of eighteen shields

Date	Mintage	VG	F	VF	XF	Unc
1675	—	225	400	750	1,650	3,000

DAV# 7457 1-1/2 THALER

Silver **Subject:** Death of Ernst **Note:** Similar to 1 Thaler, Dav. #7458.

Date	Mintage	VG	F	VF	XF	Unc
1675 Rare	—	—	—	—	—	—

DAV# 7441 2 THALER

Silver **Subject:** Peace of Westphalia **Note:** Similar to 1 Thaler, Dav. #7442.

Date	Mintage	VG	F	VF	XF	Unc
1650 Rare	—	—	—	—	—	—

Note: Struck in 1672-75

DAV# 7443 2 THALER

Silver **Subject:** Peace of Westphalia **Note:** Similar to 1 Thaler, Dav. #7444.

Date	Mintage	VG	F	VF	XF	Unc
1650 Rare	—	—	—	—	—	—

Note: Struck in 1672-75; Fritz Rudolf Künker Münzenhandlung Auction 98, 3-05, VF realized approximately $12,680

DAV# 7454 2 THALER

Silver **Subject:** Death of Ernst **Note:** Similar to 1 Thaler, Dav. #7455.

Date	Mintage	VG	F	VF	XF	Unc
1675	—	500	950	1,650	2,800	—

DAV# 7456 2 THALER

Silver **Subject:** Death of Ernst **Note:** Similar to 1 Thaler, Dav. #7458.

Date	Mintage	VG	F	VF	XF	Unc
1675 Rare	—	—	—	—	—	—

DAV# 7452 3 THALER

Silver **Subject:** Baptism of Daughter of Prince Friedrich **Note:** Similar to 1 Thaler, Dav. #7453.

Date	Mintage	VG	F	VF	XF	Unc
1671 ABK Rare	—	—	—	—	—	—

TRADE COINAGE

FR# 2953 1/4 DUCAT

0.8750 g., 0.9860 Gold 0.0277 oz. AGW **Obv:** Oval Saxon arms **Rev:** Four-line inscription

Date	Mintage	VG	F	VF	XF	Unc
1675	—	140	220	450	775	—

FR# 2949 1/2 DUCAT

1.7500 g., 0.9860 Gold 0.0555 oz. AGW **Subject:** Peace of Westphalia **Obv:** Five-line inscription in Gothic letters **Rev:** Five-line inscription in Gothic letters, date above

Date	Mintage	VG	F	VF	XF	Unc
1650	—	150	300	650	1,000	—

Note: Struck in 1672-73

FR# 2952 1/2 DUCAT

1.7500 g., 0.9860 Gold 0.0555 oz. AGW **Obv:** Oval Saxon arms **Rev:** Five-line inscription

Date	Mintage	VG	F	VF	XF	Unc
1673	—	150	350	700	1,200	—

FR# 2948 DUCAT

3.5000 g., 0.9860 Gold 0.1109 oz. AGW **Subject:** Peace of Westphalia **Obv:** Five-line inscription **Rev:** Five-line inscription, date above

Date	Mintage	VG	F	VF	XF	Unc
1650	1,278	325	575	1,200	2,200	—

FR# 2955 DUCAT

3.5000 g., 0.9860 Gold 0.1109 oz. AGW **Subject:** Death of Ernst the Pious **Obv:** Bust of Ernst the Pious right **Rev:** Nine-line inscription with date below

Date	Mintage	VG	F	VF	XF	Unc
1675 IB	143	475	950	1,800	3,000	—

FR# 2947 2 DUCAT

7.0000 g., 0.9860 Gold 0.2219 oz. AGW **Subject:** Peace of Westphalia **Obv:** Five-line inscription **Rev:** Five-line inscription, date above

Date	Mintage	VG	F	VF	XF	Unc
1650	—	825	1,600	3,050	4,950	—

FR# 2959a 2 DUCAT

7.0000 g., 0.9860 Gold 0.2219 oz. AGW **Subject:** Consecration of Castle of Friedrichswerth

Date	Mintage	VG	F	VF	XF	Unc
1689 Rare	—	—	—	—	—	—

KM# 30 8 DUCAT

28.0000 g., 0.9860 Gold 0.8876 oz. AGW **Subject:** Baptism of Princess Anna Sophia **Obv:** Baptismal scene, counterstamp small "8K" **Rev:** Ten-line inscription **Note:** Struck with 1 Thaler dies, Dav. #7450.

Date	Mintage	VG	F	VF	XF	Unc
1670 Rare	—	—	—	—	—	—

SAXE-GOTHA-ALTENBURG

(Sachsen-Gotha-Altenburg)

When the seven sons of Ernst the Pious of Saxe-New-Gotha divided the lands of their father in 1680, the eldest established the line of Saxe-Gotha-Altenburg. The line became extinct in 1825 and the following year witnessed the division of the territory which resulted in a general reorganization of the Thuringian duchies. Altenburg itself was inherited by the duke of Saxe-Hildburghausen, who transferred Hildburghausen to Saxe-Meiningen and became the founder of a new line of Saxe-Altenburg. Saxe-Meiningen also received Saalfeld from Saxe-Coburg, which in turn had acquired Gotha as part of the proceedings. The line of Saxe-Coburg-Gotha was established as a result. See under each of the foregoing regarding developments after the realignment of 1826. For a short period of time, from 1688 to 1692, the duke leased the abbey of Walkenried from Brunswick-Wolfenbüttel and struck a series of coins for that district.

RULERS

Friedrich I, 1680-1691
Friedrich II, 1691-1732
Jointly with brother Johann Wilhelm, 1691-1707

MINT OFFICIALS' INITIALS

Initials	Date	Name
GFS	1677-80	Georg Friedrich Staude, mintmaster in Gotha
HM	1681-83	Henning Müller, mintmaster in Gotha
CF or F	1681-88	Christian Fischer, warden in Gotha
	1688-90	mintmaster
IGS	1681-87	Johann Georg Sorberger, die-cutter in Gotha
IGW	1683-90	Johann Gottfried Wichmannshausen, mintmaster in Gotha
ICB	1688-89	Johann Christoph Bähr, mintmaster in Walkenried
	1690-93	warden in Gotha
	1693-96	mintmaster
CW or W	1688-1739	Christian Wermuth, die-cutter in Gotha
IT	1690-1723	Johann Thun, mintmaster in Gotha

DUCHY

REGULAR COINAGE

DAV# 7459 THALER

Silver **Subject:** Assuming the Regency After the Inheritance of Saalfeld from the Old Altenburg Line **Obv:** Crowned shield, date above **Rev:** Man in center of landscape

Date	Mintage	VG	F	VF	XF	Unc
1673 MR	—	525	1,050	1,950	3,250	—

DAV# 7460 THALER

Silver **Subject:** Building of the Castle in Friedrichswerth **Obv:** Bust right **Rev:** Castle, date below

Date	Mintage	VG	F	VF	XF	Unc
1680	—	475	950	1,700	2,950	—

DAV# 7461 THALER

Silver **Obv:** Bust right, titles of Friedrich I **Rev:** Crowned and supported arms, date below **Rev. Legend:** CONSILIO. — ET. ARMIS

Date	Mintage	VG	F	VF	XF	Unc
1680 Rare	—	—	—	—	—	—
1681 Rare	—	—	—	—	—	—

DAV# 7463 THALER

Silver **Subject:** Death of Magdalena Sybilla, First Wife of Friedrich **Obv:** Bust of Magdalena left, date in Roman numerals **Rev:** 8-line inscription on pedestal between palm sprays

Date	Mintage	VG	F	VF	XF	Unc
MDCLXXXI (1681)	—	350	700	1,300	2,200	—

DAV# 7464 THALER

Silver **Rev:** Scales on pillow, date in legend

Date	Mintage	VG	F	VF	XF	Unc
1683 IGW	—	225	450	825	1,450	—

DAV# 7465 THALER

Silver **Obv:** Bust right in circle, legend unbroken at top **Rev:** Helmeted arms dividing date and IG-W

Date	Mintage	VG	F	VF	XF	Unc
1685 Rare	—	—	—	—	—	—

DAV# 7465A THALER

Silver **Note:** Similar to Dav. #7465.

Date	Mintage	VG	F	VF	XF	Unc
1687	—	—	—	—	—	—

DAV# 7473 THALER

Silver **Ruler:** Friedrich I **Obv:** Seven busts facing left and right **Rev:** Date divided at top

Date	Mintage	F	VF	XF	Unc	BU
1688 IGW	—	425	850	1,750	4,250	—
1690 IT	—	425	850	1,750	4,250	—

DAV# 7466 THALER

Silver **Obv:** Bust right breaks legend at top and bottom, without inner circle **Rev:** Helmeted arms within circle at top, date in legend at bottom divided by arms

Date	Mintage	VG	F	VF	XF	Unc
1688 IGW Rare	—	—	—	—	—	—

DAV# 7468 THALER

Silver **Obv:** 6 medallions with busts either left or right around center medallion of bust turned 3/4 to left, D-S-I-&-M in margin **Rev:** 6-helmeted manifold arms divide mintmaster's initials in middle, date near bottom **Rev. Legend:** LANDG: TH: MARCH: M: PRINC: DIC: HENN:

Date	Mintage	VG	F	VF	XF	Unc
1688 IGW	—	—	265	525	1,050	1,900

DAV# 7468A THALER

Silver **Obv:** Similar to Dav. #7468 **Rev:** Similar to Dav. #7470

Date	Mintage	VG	F	VF	XF	Unc
1688	—	—	265	525	1,050	1,900

DAV# 7470 THALER

Silver **Obv:** 6 medallions with busts either left or right around center medallion of bust right **Obv. Legend:** DUCES-SAXON-IVL.-CLIV.-ET-MONT:

Date	Mintage	VG	F	VF	XF	Unc
1688 IGW	—	—	175	350	700	1,400
1690 IT	—	—	175	350	700	1,400
1691 IT	—	—	175	350	700	1,400

DAV# 7471 THALER

Silver **Obv:** 6 medallions with busts either left or right around center medallion of bust right **Rev:** Helmeted arms in inner circle, date in legend below

Date	Mintage	VG	F	VF	XF	Unc
1688 IGW	—	—	210	425	850	1,500

DAV# 7474 THALER

Silver **Subject:** Inauguration of the Castle **Rev:** Castle, date below

Date	Mintage	F	VF	XF	Unc	BU
1689 W	—	450	850	1,650	3,750	—

DAV# LS421B THALER

Silver **Note:** Similar to 1-1/2 Thaler, Dav. #LS421A.

Date	Mintage	VG	F	VF	XF	Unc
ND	—	—	650	1,200	2,500	—

DAV# LS422A THALER

Silver **Note:** Similar to 1-1/2 Thaler, Dav. #LS422.

Date	Mintage	VG	F	VF	XF	Unc
ND	—	—	650	1,200	2,500	—

DAV# 7475 THALER

Silver **Ruler:** Friedrich I **Subject:** Death of Friedrich **Rev:** 9-line inscription, arms above with 19 shields around

Date	Mintage	VG	F	VF	XF	Unc
1691 IT	—	—	650	1,200	2,500	4,000

DAV# 7476 THALER

Silver, 46 mm.

Date	Mintage	VG	F	VF	XF	Unc
1691 IT Rare	—	—	—	—	—	—

DAV# 7477 THALER

Silver **Subject:** Allegiance of Gotha **Obv:** Two busts left and two busts right **Rev:** Helmeted round arms, date below

Date	Mintage	VG	F	VF	XF	Unc
1692 IT	—	—	600	1,200	2,000	—

DAV# 7478 THALER

Silver **Obv:** Bust of Friedrich II right **Rev:** Arms at center, five shields and 32/GR in palm sprays with F's between

Date	Mintage	VG	F	VF	XF	Unc
1692	—	—	1,300	2,100	3,300	—

DAV# 7478A THALER

Silver **Obv:** Similar to Dav. #7478 **Rev:** Quartered round arms

Date	Mintage	VG	F	VF	XF	Unc
1692	—	—	1,350	2,250	3,500	—

DAV# 7479 THALER

Silver **Rev:** Helmeted arms divide date and I-T

Date	Mintage	VG	F	VF	XF	Unc
1694 IT	—	—	750	1,350	2,250	—

DAV# 7480 THALER

Silver **Obv:** Crowned wreath with 7-line inscription, shields in corners **Rev:** 19-line inscription

Date	Mintage	F	VF	XF	Unc	BU
1699 CW Rare	—	—	—	—	—	—

DAV# LS421A 1-1/2 THALER

32.5000 g., Silver

Date	Mintage	VG	F	VF	XF	Unc
ND(1683-88) IGW	—	—	—	2,500	4,500	—

DAV# LS422 1-1/2 THALER

Silver **Note:** Similar to 2 Thaler, Dav. #LS-A422.

Date	Mintage	VG	F	VF	XF	Unc
ND(1683-88) IGW	—	—	—	3,000	5,000	—

DAV# A7464 2 THALER

Silver **Note:** Similar to 1 Thaler, Dav. #7464.

Date	Mintage	VG	F	VF	XF	Unc
1683	—	—	—	—	—	—

DAV# LS421 2 THALER

43.3000 g., Silver **Note:** Similar to 1-1/2 Thaler, Dav. #LS421A.

Date	Mintage	VG	F	VF	XF	Unc
ND(1683-88) IGW	—	—	—	3,500	5,500	—

DAV# 7467 2 THALER

Silver **Obv:** Seven medallions with busts **Obv. Legend:** D-S-I-C-&-M **Rev:** Helmeted arms, IG-W divided at center, date divided below

Date	Mintage	VG	F	VF	XF	Unc
1688 IGW Rare	—	—	—	—	—	—

DAV# 7469 2 THALER

Silver **Note:** Similar to 1 Thaler, Dav. #7470.

Date	Mintage	VG	F	VF	XF	Unc
1688 IGW Rare	—	—	—	—	—	—
1691 IT Rare	—	—	—	—	—	—

DAV# A7471 2 THALER

Silver **Note:** Similar to 1 Thaler, Dav. #7471.

Date	Mintage	VG	F	VF	XF	Unc
1688 Rare	—	—	—	—	—	—

DAV# 7472 2 THALER

Silver **Note:** Similar to 1 Thaler, Dav. #7473.

Date	Mintage	VG	F	VF	XF	Unc
1688 IGW Rare	—	—	—	—	—	—

DAV# LS423 2 THALER

Silver **Subject:** Admission into the Pegnitzschafer Order **Obv:** Rural scene **Rev:** 4 lines in scroll, value punched near bottom **Note:** Varieties with and without 2 stamped at lower reverse.

Date	Mintage	VG	F	VF	XF	Unc
ND	—	—	—	5,000	8,500	—

DAV# LS-A421 4 THALER

Silver **Note:** Similar to 1-1/2 Thaler, Dav. #LS421A.

Date	Mintage	VG	F	VF	XF	Unc
ND(1683-88) IGW Rare	—	—	—	—	—	—

TRADE COINAGE

FR# 2959 GOLDGULDEN

3.5000 g., 0.9860 Gold 0.1109 oz. AGW **Obv:** Crowned 4-fold arms in inner circle **Rev:** Figure of Fortune on globe

Date	Mintage	VG	F	VF	XF	Unc
1684 IGW	—	625	1,350	2,450	4,200	—

FR# 2966 1/4 DUCAT

0.8750 g., 0.9860 Gold 0.0277 oz. AGW **Obv:** Bust of Friedrich I right **Rev:** Crowned oval arms

Date	Mintage	VG	F	VF	XF	Unc
1682 HIM	—	120	300	550	950	—
1684 IGW	—	120	300	550	950	—

FR# 2961 1/2 DUCAT

1.7500 g., 0.9860 Gold 0.0555 oz. AGW **Obv:** Bust of Friedrich I right **Rev:** Cruciform arms with F in angles

Date	Mintage	VG	F	VF	XF	Unc
1689	—	300	600	1,300	2,250	—
1690	—	300	600	1,300	2,250	—

FR# 2963 1/2 DUCAT

1.7500 g., 0.9860 Gold 0.0555 oz. AGW **Rev:** Ship at sea

Date	Mintage	VG	F	VF	XF	Unc
1690	—	375	750	1,500	2,500	—

FR# 2957 DUCAT

3.5000 g., 0.9860 Gold 0.1109 oz. AGW **Ruler:** Friedrich I **Obv:** Bust to right **Rev:** Crowned oval manifold arms in baroque frame, date in legend at upper left

Date	Mintage	VG	F	VF	XF	Unc
1681 HM	—	450	925	1,800	3,300	—
1683 IGW	—	450	925	1,800	3,300	—

FR# 2958 DUCAT

3.5000 g., 0.9860 Gold 0.1109 oz. AGW **Subject:** Death of Magdalena Sybilla, Wife of Friedrich I **Obv:** Laureate head of Magdalena Sybilla left **Rev:** 6-line inscription

Date	Mintage	VG	F	VF	XF	Unc
1681	—	600	1,200	2,400	4,200	—

FR# 2960 DUCAT

3.5000 g., 0.9860 Gold 0.1109 oz. AGW **Obv:** Bust of Friedrich I right **Rev:** Cruciform arms with F in angles

Date	Mintage	VG	F	VF	XF	Unc
1689 F	—	425	850	1,800	3,300	—

FR# 2962 DUCAT

3.5000 g., 0.9860 Gold 0.1109 oz. AGW **Rev:** Ship at sea

Date	Mintage	VG	F	VF	XF	Unc
1690	—	575	1,250	2,400	4,250	—

FR# 2965 DUCAT

3.5000 g., 0.9860 Gold 0.1109 oz. AGW **Subject:** Friedrich I Awarded Danish Order of Danneborg **Obv:** Head of Friedrich I right **Rev:** Star of Danneborg flanked by cruciform arms with F in angles

Date	Mintage	VG	F	VF	XF	Unc
1690 F	—	450	925	1,800	3,300	—

FR# 2967 DUCAT

3.5000 g., 0.9860 Gold 0.1109 oz. AGW **Subject:** Death of Friedrich I **Obv:** Armored bust of Friedrich I right **Rev:** 8-line inscription in palm branches

Date	Mintage	VG	F	VF	XF	Unc
1691 IT	—	350	775	1,700	3,300	—

FR# 2970 DUCAT

3.5000 g., 0.9860 Gold 0.1109 oz. AGW **Ruler:** Friedrich II and Johann Wilhelm **Obv:** Bust with high coiffure facing right **Rev:** Crowned oval manifold arms in baroque frame **Rev. Legend:** LANDGR. TH. etc.

Date	Mintage	VG	F	VF	XF	Unc
1692	—	325	725	1,550	3,050	—
1694	—	325	725	1,550	3,050	—
1698	—	325	725	1,550	3,050	—
1699	—	325	725	1,550	3,050	—

FR# 2967a 2 DUCAT

7.0000 g., 0.9860 Gold 0.2219 oz. AGW **Obv:** Bust of Friedrich I right, Roman numeral date **Rev:** Busts of Friedrich II and Johann Wilhelm right

Date	Mintage	VG	F	VF	XF	Unc
ND(1690)	—	850	1,600	3,300	5,400	—

SAXE-JENA

(Sachsen-Jena)

As a branch of the Ernestine line of Saxony, the duchy of Saxe-Jena was established upon the division of Saxe-Weimar-Eisenach in 1662. The Saxe-Jena branch only lasted for two generations, becoming extinct in 1690, and its lands reverted to Saxe-Eisenach.

RULERS

Bernhard II, 1662-1678
Johann Wilhelm, 1678-1690

MINT OFFICIALS' INITIALS

Initial	Date	Name
ABC/ABK	1667-80	Anton Bernhard Koburger in Eisleben
HIW	d. 1690	Hans Jacob Wolrab, die-cutter in Nuremberg

DUCHY

REGULAR COINAGE

KM# 17 3 PFENNIG (Dreier)

Silver **Subject:** Internment of Bernhard II **Obv:** Crowned oval arms of Saxony in baroque frame **Rev:** Six-line inscription with dates

Date	Mintage	VG	F	VF	XF	Unc
1678	—	—	—	—	—	—

KM# 25 3 PFENNIG (Dreier)

Silver **Subject:** Death of Marie, Wife of Bernhard II **Obv:** Crowned M, ribbons trailing down each side **Rev:** Seven-line inscription with dates

Date	Mintage	VG	F	VF	XF	Unc
1682	—	20.00	40.00	65.00	115	—

KM# 35 3 PFENNIG (Dreier)
Silver **Subject:** Interment of Johann Wilhelm III **Obv:** Intertwined JW monogram, crown above, cross below **Rev:** Six-line inscription with date

Date	Mintage	VG	F	VF	XF	Unc
1691	—	—	—	—	—	—

KM# 18 GROSCHEN (1/24 Thaler)
Silver **Subject:** Interment of Bernhard II **Obv:** Crowned oval arms of Saxony in baroque frame **Rev:** Seven-line inscription with dates

Date	Mintage	VG	F	VF	XF	Unc
1678	—	—	—	—	—	—

KM# 26 GROSCHEN (1/24 Thaler)
Silver **Subject:** Death of Marie, Wife of Bernhard II **Obv:** Crowned M, ribbons trailing down each side **Rev:** Seven-line inscription with dates

Date	Mintage	VG	F	VF	XF	Unc
1682	—	33.00	65.00	120	200	—

KM# 30 GROSCHEN (1/24 Thaler)
Silver **Subject:** Acceptance of the Chancellorship of Jena University for Johann Wilhelm III **Obv:** Six-line inscription with date **Rev:** Six-line inscription with titles

Date	Mintage	VG	F	VF	XF	Unc
1688	—	27.00	55.00	110	200	—

KM# 36 GROSCHEN (1/24 Thaler)
Silver **Subject:** Interment of Johann Wilhelm III **Obv:** Crowned arms of Saxony, inscriptions above and below in arcs **Rev:** Nine-line inscription, Roman numeral dates, titles in legend

Date	Mintage	VG	F	VF	XF	Unc
ND(1691)	—	24.00	45.00	80.00	140	—

KM# 5 1/8 THALER
Silver **Subject:** Completion of Jena Palace **Obv:** Bust right **Rev:** View of palace, date above, legend around

Date	Mintage	VG	F	VF	XF	Unc
1661	—	—	—	—	—	—

KM# 6 1/4 THALER
Silver **Subject:** Completion of Jena Palace **Obv:** Bust right **Rev:** View of palace, date above, legend around

Date	Mintage	VG	F	VF	XF	Unc
1661	—	—	—	—	—	—

KM# 19 1/4 THALER
Silver **Subject:** Interment of Bernhard II **Obv:** Wigged bust right **Rev:** Nine-line inscription, Roman numeral dates, crown above

Date	Mintage	VG	F	VF	XF	Unc
ND(1678)	—	—	—	—	—	—

KM# 27 1/4 THALER
Silver **Subject:** Death of Marie, Wife of Bernhard II **Obv:** Bust turned 1/4 right, titles and date in legend **Rev:** Rectangular altar, seven-line inscription on side

Date	Mintage	VG	F	VF	XF	Unc
1682	—	90.00	160	275	425	—

KM# 31 1/4 THALER
Silver **Subject:** Acceptance of the Chancellorship of Jena University for Johann Wilhelm III **Obv:** Winged cadeuceus surmounted with crowned arms of Saxony, view of Jena in background, rays streaming from sun above, legend at sides **Obv. Legend:** TUETUR - ET ORNAT **Rev:** Nine-line inscription with date

Date	Mintage	VG	F	VF	XF	Unc
1688	—	100	200	400	750	—

KM# 37 1/4 THALER
Silver **Subject:** Interment of Johann Wilhelm III **Obv:** Epitaph on tablet in five lines **Obv. Legend:** NON PERITVRA NECE **Rev:** Five-line inscription, Roman numeral dates within two palm branches

Date	Mintage	VG	F	VF	XF	Unc
ND(1691)	—	160	275	450	800	—

KM# 10 1/3 THALER (1/2 Gulden)
Silver **Obv:** Bust right **Rev:** Crowned oval manifold arms, branches at sides, value 1/3 in oval below, date in legend **Note:** Varieties exist.

Date	Mintage	VG	F	VF	XF	Unc
1673 ABK	—	225	400	675	1,075	—
1673 ABC	—	225	400	675	1,075	—
1674 ABC	—	225	400	675	1,075	—

KM# 20 1/2 THALER
Silver **Subject:** Interment of Bernhard II **Obv:** Wigged bust right **Rev:** Ten-line inscription, Roman numeral dates, crown above

Date	Mintage	VG	F	VF	XF	Unc
ND(1678)	—	—	—	—	—	—

KM# 28 1/2 THALER
Silver **Subject:** Death of Marie, Wife of Bernhard II **Obv:** Bust turned 1/4 right, titles and date in legend **Rev:** Rectangular seven-line inscription on side

Date	Mintage	VG	F	VF	XF	Unc
1682	—	—	—	—	—	—

KM# 32 1/2 THALER
Silver **Subject:** Acceptance of the Chancellorship of Jena University for Johann Wilhelm III **Obv:** Winged cadeuceus surmounted with crowned arms of Saxony, view of Jena in background, rays streaming from sun above, legend at sides **Obv. Legend:** TUETUR - ET ORNAT **Rev:** Nine-line inscription with date

Date	Mintage	VG	F	VF	XF	Unc
1688 HIW	—	45.00	90.00	165	300	—

KM# 38 1/2 THALER
Silver **Subject:** Interment of Johann Wilhelm III **Obv:** Facing wigged bust, turned slightly right **Rev:** Epitaph on tablet in nine lines, Roman numeral date, crown above **Note:** Varieties exist.

Date	Mintage	VG	F	VF	XF	Unc
ND(1691)	—	—	—	—	—	—

KM# 11 2/3 THALER (Gulden)
Silver **Obv:** Bust right in circle **Rev:** Crowned arms of Saxony between two branches, date at top, value 2/3 at bottom **Note:** Varieties exist.

Date	Mintage	VG	F	VF	XF	Unc
1673 ABC	—	225	375	600	925	—
1674 ABC	—	225	375	600	925	—

KM# 16 2/3 THALER (Gulden)
Silver **Obv:** Bust not in circle **Note:** Varieties exist.

Date	Mintage	VG	F	VF	XF	Unc
1674 ABC	—	225	375	600	925	—

KM# 12 THALER
Silver **Obv:** Bust right **Rev:** Crowned arms divide date and AB-C **Note:** Dav. #7492.

Date	Mintage	VG	F	VF	XF	Unc
1673	—	700	1,400	2,500	4,000	—

KM# 13 THALER
Silver **Rev:** Date above crowned arms **Note:** Dav. #7493.

Date	Mintage	VG	F	VF	XF	Unc
1673 ABK	—	700	1,400	2,500	4,000	—

KM# 14 THALER
Silver **Rev:** Smaller letters, BANCO THALER added in inner row **Note:** Dav. #7494.

Date	Mintage	VG	F	VF	XF	Unc
1673 Rare	—	—	—	—	—	—

KM# 21 THALER
Silver **Subject:** Interment of Bernhard II **Obv:** Bust right **Rev:** Eleven-line inscription **Note:** Dav. #7495.

Date	Mintage	VG	F	VF	XF	Unc
1678 Rare	—	—	—	—	—	—

KM# 29 THALER
Silver **Subject:** Death of Marie, Wife of Bernhard II **Rev:** Seven-line inscription on tablet with rope border **Note:** Dav. #7496.

Date	Mintage	VG	F	VF	XF	Unc
1682	—	550	1,100	2,000	3,500	—

KM# 33 THALER
Silver **Subject:** Acceptance of the Chancellorship of Jena University for Johann Wilhelm III **Obv:** Winged cadeuceus surmounted with crowned arms of Saxony, view of Jena in background, rays streaming from sun above, legend at sides **Obv. Legend:** TUETUR - ET ORNAT **Rev:** Nine-line inscription with date **Note:** Varieties exist.

Date	Mintage	VG	F	VF	XF	Unc
1688	—	750	1,500	3,000	5,000	—

KM# 39 THALER
Silver **Subject:** Death of Johann Wilhelm **Obv:** Bust right **Rev:** Crowned entablature with ten-line inscription **Note:** Dav. #7497.

Date	Mintage	VG	F	VF	XF	Unc
1691	—	500	1,000	1,800	3,000	—

KM# 15 1-1/2 THALER
Silver **Subject:** 35th Birthday of Bernhard II **Obv:** Two-masted ship sailing right towards rocks, two-line inscription in curved band above **Rev:** Ten-line inscription, Roman numeral date

Date	Mintage	VG	F	VF	XF	Unc
ND(1673) ABK Rare	—	—	—	—	—	—

TRADE COINAGE

KM# A16 5 DUCAT
17.5000 g., 0.9860 Gold 0.5547 oz. AGW **Obv:** Bust of Bernhard II right **Rev:** Crowned arms in sprays **Note:** Struck with 1 Thaler dies, KM#14.

Date	Mintage	VG	F	VF	XF	Unc
1673 ABK Unique	—	—	—	—	—	—

KM# B16 10 DUCAT
35.0000 g., 0.9860 Gold 1.1095 oz. AGW **Subject:** 35th Birthday of Bernhard II **Obv:** Two-masted sailing ship right, two-line inscription in curved band above **Rev:** Ten-line inscription, Roman numeral date **Note:** Struck with 1-1/2 Thaler dies, KM#15.

Date	Mintage	VG	F	VF	XF	Unc
ND(1673) ABK	—	—	—	—	—	—

PATTERNS

Including off metal strikes

KM#	Date	Mintage	Identification	Mkt Val
Pn1	1661	—	1/8 Thaler. Tin. KM#5	—
Pn2	1661	—	1/8 Thaler. Gold. KM#5	—

SAXE-LAUENBURG

(Sachsen-Lauenburg)

One of older branches of the Saxon house, founded in 1260 by Johann I, the line became extinct in 1689 with the death of Julius Franz.. Lauenburg passed to Brunswick-Luneburg, then to Hanover, then Prussia, Denmark and finally, back to Prussia in 1864.

RULERS
Magnus II, 1581-1603
Moritz, 1581-1612
Franz II, 1581-1619
August II, 1619-1656
Julius Heinrich, 1656-1665
Franz Erdmann, 1665-1666
Julius Franz, 1666-1689

MINT OFFICIALS' INITIALS and MARKS

Initial or Mark	Date	Name
IG (monogram)	1609-19	Jonas Georgens
(a)	Clenched fist holding ingot hook	Christoph Feustel

(b) [mark]	1620-24	Barthold Bartels
(c) [mark]	1645-46	Simon Timpe
IS	1656	Johann Schultze
(d) [mark]	1657-62	Matthias Freude
(e) [mark] or HI	1670-71	Henning Jiders
IW	1672-73	Johann Wagner
(f) [mark]	1673	Georg Nurnberger dere Jungere
(g) 3 small stars	1678-89	Lorenz Wagner

DUCHY

REGULAR COINAGE

KM# 6 THALER

Silver **Obv:** Duke on horseback left **Rev:** Helmeted arms **Note:** Dav. #7336.

Date	Mintage	Good	VG	F	VF	XF
(1)609 IG	—	300	600	1,150	1,800	—

KM# 7 THALER

Silver **Obv:** Bust with ruffled collar right **Obv. Legend:** FRANC: II: D: G: DUX: SAXO:... **Rev:** Date in legend **Note:** Dav. #7337.

Date	Mintage	Good	VG	F	VF	XF
(1)609 IG	—	300	600	1,150	1,800	—

KM# 30 THALER

Silver **Obv. Legend:** FRANCIS:...SAX **Rev:** Arms with straight sides **Note:** Dav. #7338.

Date	Mintage	Good	VG	F	VF	XF
(1)611 IG	—	220	450	825	1,300	—

KM# 31 THALER

Silver **Obv. Legend:** ...SAXO: ANGA:... **Rev:** Helmeted arms break legend and divide date at bottom **Note:** Dav. #7339.

Date	Mintage	Good	VG	F	VF	XF
1611	—	250	500	950	1,500	—

KM# 32 THALER

Silver **Obv:** Bust right with lion head on shoulder **Obv. Legend:** FRANC: II:... **Note:** Dav. #7340.

Date	Mintage	Good	VG	F	VF	XF
1611	—	250	500	950	1,500	—

KM# 39 THALER

Silver **Obv:** Head right **Obv. Legend:** FRANCIS: II. D: G:...WEST **Rev:** Helmeted arms with date divided by helmets **Note:** Dav. #7342.

Date	Mintage	Good	VG	F	VF	XF
1613 IG	—	300	600	1,150	1,800	—
1617 IG	—	350	700	1,300	2,100	—
1619 IG	—	350	700	1,300	2,100	—

KM# 35 THALER

Silver **Obv:** Duke on horseback right **Rev:** Helmeted arms **Note:** Dav. #7341.

Date	Mintage	Good	VG	F	VF	XF
ND IG Rare	—	—	—	—	—	—

KM# 50 THALER

Silver **Obv:** Head right **Rev:** Ten-line inscription **Note:** Dav. #7343.

Date	Mintage	Good	VG	F	VF	XF
1619 IG Rare	—	—	—	—	—	—

KM# 51 THALER

29.0000 g., Silver **Subject:** Death of Franz II **Obv:** Bust with scepter right, helmet in front **Rev:** Ten-line inscription, three lines in exergue **Note:** Dav. #LS433.

Date	Mintage	VG	F	VF	XF	Unc
1619 IG	—	850	1,450	2,400	4,200	—

KM# 62 THALER

29.0000 g., Silver **Obv:** Bust of August II **Rev:** Helmeted arms **Note:** Dav. #7344.

Date	Mintage	Good	VG	F	VF	XF
1620 (b)	—	190	375	675	1,200	—
1621 (b)	—	190	375	675	1,200	—
1622 (b)	—	190	375	675	1,200	—
1624 (b)	—	155	325	575	1,000	—

KM# 87 THALER

29.0000 g., Silver **Rev:** Eight-line inscription **Note:** Dav. #7345.

Date	Mintage	Good	VG	F	VF	XF
1624 (b)	—	350	750	1,500	2,500	—

KM# 89 THALER

29.0000 g., Silver **Obv:** Facing bust divides date **Rev:** Helmeted arms **Note:** Dav. #7347.

Date	Mintage	Good	VG	F	VF	XF
1645 (c)	—	425	825	1,500	2,650	—

KM# 92 THALER

29.0000 g., Silver **Subject:** Death of Johann Adolph, Son of August II **Obv:** Helmeted arms **Rev:** Six-line inscription **Note:** Dav. #7348.

Date	Mintage	Good	VG	F	VF	XF
1646 (c) Rare	—	—	—	—	—	—

KM# 95 THALER

29.0000 g., Silver **Obv:** 3/4-length figure right, helmet in front **Rev:** Helmeted arms **Note:** Dav. #LS437.

Date	Mintage	VG	F	VF	XF	Unc
ND (b) Rare	—	950	1,850	3,750	—	—

KM# 100 THALER

29.0000 g., Silver **Subject:** Death of August II **Obv:** Helmeted arms **Rev:** Nine-line inscription **Note:** Dav. #7351.

Date	Mintage	VG	F	VF	XF	Unc
1656 (d) Rare	—	—	—	—	—	—

KM# 107 THALER

29.0000 g., Silver **Subject:** Death of Julius Heinrich **Obv:** Bust right **Rev:** Church

Date	Mintage	VG	F	VF	XF	Unc
1665 Rare	—	—	—	—	—	—

KM# 109 THALER
29.0000 g., Silver **Rev:** Eagle above, crown in sprays at center **Note:** Dav. #7353.

Date	Mintage	VG	F	VF	XF	Unc
1670	—	900	1,800	3,300	5,500	—

KM# 115 THALER
29.0000 g., Silver **Obv:** Bust right **Rev:** Capped arms divide date **Note:** Dav. #7354.

Date	Mintage	VG	F	VF	XF	Unc
1673 (f) Rare	—	—	—	—	—	—

KM# 116 THALER
29.0000 g., Silver **Rev:** Helmeted arms **Note:** Dav. #7355.

Date	Mintage	VG	F	VF	XF	Unc
1673 (f) Rare	—	—	—	—	—	—

KM# 124 THALER
29.0000 g., Silver **Rev:** Crowned arms **Note:** Dav. #7356.

Date	Mintage	VG	F	VF	XF	Unc
1678 Rare	—	—	—	—	—	—

KM# 126 THALER
29.0000 g., Silver **Obv:** Large bust right **Note:** Dav. #7358.

Date	Mintage	VG	F	VF	XF	Unc
1679	—	900	1,800	3,300	5,500	—

KM# 128 THALER
29.0000 g., Silver **Note:** Dav. #7359.

Date	Mintage	VG	F	VF	XF	Unc
1680	—	575	1,150	2,050	3,450	—

KM# 130 THALER
Silver, 40 mm. **Note:** Smaller flan. Dav. #7359A.

Date	Mintage	VG	F	VF	XF	Unc
1683	—	575	1,150	2,050	3,450	—

KM# 94 THALER (32 Schilling)
29.0000 g., Silver **Obv:** Bust right **Rev:** Crowned double eagle with 32 in orb on breast **Note:** Dav. #7349.

Date	Mintage	Good	VG	F	VF	XF
ND (b)	—	350	625	1,100	1,750	—

KM# 20 1-1/4 THALER
25.0000 g., Silver **Rev:** Helmeted arms, date in legend **Note:** Dav. #LS430.

Date	Mintage	VG	F	VF	XF	Unc
1610	—	950	1,550	2,500	4,400	—

KM# 21 1-1/4 THALER
25.0000 g., Silver **Obv:** Bust right, helmet in front **Rev:** Helmeted arms **Note:** Dav. #LS431B.

Date	Mintage	VG	F	VF	XF	Unc
ND Rare	—	—	—	—	—	—

KM# 96 1-1/4 THALER
25.0000 g., Silver **Note:** Dav. #LS436. Similar to 1 Thaler, KM#95.

Date	Mintage	VG	F	VF	XF	Unc
ND Rare	—	—	—	—	—	—

KM# 8 1-1/2 THALER
Silver **Obv:** Circle within triangle, within double circles **Rev:** Triangle within double circles **Note:** Dav. #LS427A.

Date	Mintage	VG	F	VF	XF	Unc
ND	—	1,500	2,700	4,500	—	—

KM# 22 1-1/2 THALER
Silver **Note:** Dav. #LS429. Similar to 1-1/4 Thaler, KM#20.

Date	Mintage	VG	F	VF	XF	Unc
1610	—	1,600	2,700	4,500	7,500	—

KM# 23 1-1/2 THALER
Silver **Note:** Dav. #LS431A. Similar to 1-1/4 Thaler, KM#21.

Date	Mintage	VG	F	VF	XF	Unc
ND Rare	—	—	—	—	—	—

KM# 97 1-1/2 THALER
Silver **Note:** Dav. #LS435. Similar to 1 Thaler, KM#95.

Date	Mintage	VG	F	VF	XF	Unc
ND Rare	—	—	—	—	—	—

KM# 9 2 THALER
Silver **Note:** Dav. #7336. Similar to 1 Thaler, KM#6.

Date	Mintage	VG	F	VF	XF	Unc
1609 Rare	—	—	—	—	—	—

KM# 10 2 THALER
57.0000 g., Silver **Note:** Dav. #LS427. Similar to 1-1/2 Thaler, KM#8.

Date	Mintage	VG	F	VF	XF	Unc
ND	—	1,550	2,750	5,000	8,500	—

KM# 24 2 THALER
57.0000 g., Silver **Note:** Dav. #LS428. Similar to 1-1/4 Thaler, KM#20.

Date	Mintage	VG	F	VF	XF	Unc
1610	—	1,250	2,050	3,450	5,600	—

KM# 25 2 THALER
57.0000 g., Silver **Note:** Dav. #LS431. Similar to 1-1/4 Thaler, KM#21.

Date	Mintage	VG	F	VF	XF	Unc
ND Rare	—	—	—	—	—	—

KM# 52 2 THALER
57.0000 g., Silver **Note:** Dav. #LS433. Similar to 1 Thaler, KM#51.

Date	Mintage	VG	F	VF	XF	Unc
1619	—	1,450	2,400	3,500	7,200	—

KM# 90 2 THALER
57.0000 g., Silver **Rev:** Helmeted arms **Note:** Dav. #7346.

Date	Mintage	VG	F	VF	XF	Unc
1645 (c) Rare	—	—	—	—	—	—

Note: Fritz Rudolf Künker Münzenhandlung Auction 80, 3-03, XF realized approximately $61,355

KM# 101 2 THALER
57.0000 g., Silver **Subject:** Death of August II **Obv:** Helmeted arms **Rev:** Nine-line inscription **Note:** Dav. #7350.

Date	Mintage	VG	F	VF	XF	Unc
1656 (d) Rare	—	—	—	—	—	—

KM# 11 3 THALER
86.0000 g., Silver **Note:** Dav. #LS426. Similar to 1-1/2 Thaler, KM#8.

Date	Mintage	VG	F	VF	XF	Unc
ND Rare	—	—	—	—	—	—

KM# 98 3 THALER
86.0000 g., Silver **Note:** Dav. #LS434. Similar to 1 Thaler, KM#98.

Date	Mintage	VG	F	VF	XF	Unc
ND Rare	—	—	—	—	—	—

KM# 12 4 THALER
Silver **Note:** Dav. #LS425. Similar to 1-1/2 Thaler, KM#8.

Date	Mintage	VG	F	VF	XF	Unc
ND Rare	—	—	—	—	—	—

KM# 13 5 THALER
143.0000 g., Silver **Note:** Dav. #LS424. Similar to 1-1/2 Thaler, KM#8.

Date	Mintage	VG	F	VF	XF	Unc
ND Rare	—	—	—	—	—	—

TRADE COINAGE

KM# 33 GOLDGULDEN
3.5000 g., 0.9860 Gold 0.1109 oz. AGW **Obv:** Bust of Franz II right in inner circle **Rev:** Helmeted arms in inner circle **Note:** Fr. #2982.

Date	Mintage	VG	F	VF	XF	Unc
1611 IG	—	725	1,400	2,750	5,250	—

KM# 26 8 GOLDGULDEN
28.0000 g., 0.9860 Gold 0.8876 oz. AGW **Obv:** Equestrian figure of Julius Heinrich right **Rev:** Helmeted arms in inner circle **Note:** Fr. #2983.

Date	Mintage	VG	F	VF	XF	Unc
ND IG Rare	—	—	—	—	—	—

KM# 102 DUCAT
3.5000 g., 0.9860 Gold 0.1109 oz. AGW **Obv:** Bust of Julius Heinrich right in inner circle **Rev:** Helmeted arms in inner circle **Note:** Fr. #2985.

Date	Mintage	VG	F	VF	XF	Unc
1657 (d)	—	1,050	2,050	3,750	6,300	—
1662 (d)	—	1,050	2,050	3,750	6,300	—

KM# 104 DUCAT
3.5000 g., 0.9860 Gold 0.1109 oz. AGW **Rev:** Madonna and child in inner circle **Note:** Fr. #2986.

Date	Mintage	VG	F	VF	XF	Unc
1659 (d)	—	1,050	2,050	3,750	6,300	—

KM# 108 DUCAT
3.5000 g., 0.9860 Gold 0.1109 oz. AGW **Obv:** Bust of Julius Franz right **Rev:** Cap and sprays in large trefoil **Note:** Fr. #2988.

Date	Mintage	VG	F	VF	XF	Unc
1670	—	775	1,600	3,150	5,250	—
1673	—	775	1,600	3,150	5,250	—
ND	—	775	1,600	3,150	5,250	—

KM# 106 2 DUCAT
7.0000 g., 0.9860 Gold 0.2219 oz. AGW **Obv:** Bust of Julius Heinrich right in inner circle **Rev:** Helmeted arms in inner circle **Note:** Fr. #2984.

Date	Mintage	VG	F	VF	XF	Unc
1662 (d) Rare	—	—	—	—	—	—

KM# 117 2 DUCAT
7.0000 g., 0.9860 Gold 0.2219 oz. AGW **Obv:** Bust of Julius Franz right **Rev:** Cap and sprays in large trefoil **Note:** Fr. #2987.

Date	Mintage	VG	F	VF	XF	Unc
1673	—	1,800	3,400	5,700	9,000	—
1678	—	1,800	3,400	5,700	9,000	—
1680	—	1,800	3,400	5,700	9,000	—
1681	—	1,800	3,400	5,700	9,000	—
1683	—	1,800	3,400	5,700	9,000	—
ND	—	1,800	3,400	5,700	9,000	—

SAXE-MEININGEN

(Sachsen-Meiningen)

The duchy of Saxe-Meiningen was located in Thuringia, sandwiched between Saxe-Weimar-Eisenach on the west and north and the enclave of Schmalkalden belonging to Hesse-Cassel on the east. It was founded upon the division of the Ernestine line in Saxe-Gotha in 1680. In 1735, due to an exchange of some territory, the duchy became known as Saxe-Coburg-Meiningen. In 1826, Saxe-Coburg-Gotha assigned Saalfeld to Saxe-Meiningen. The duchy came under the strong influence of Prussia from 1866, when Bernhard II was forced to abdicate because of his support of Austria. The monarchy ended with the defeat of Germany in 1918.

RULERS
Bernhard, 1680-1706

MINT OFFICIALS' INITIALS

Initial	Date	Name
CW, W	1688-1739	Christian Wermuth, die-cutter in Gotha
GFA	1673-76	Georg Friedrich Staude in Weimar
	1677-80	In Gotha
	1687	In Meiningen
	1687	In Erfurt
HeA	1686-1705	Heinrich Ernst Angerstein in Coburg and
	1687-1714	Ernst Friedrich Angerstein in Coburg
IGS	1689-90	Johann Georg Sorberger in Meiningen
IT	1690-1723	Johann thun in Gotha
PFC	1685-1714	Paul Friedrich Crum in Coburg
VOIGT		J. C. Voigt, die-cutter and medailleur

NOTE: Between 1691 and 1703, Saxe-Meiningen struck coins in various denominations for its part of Henneberg-Ilmenau.

DUCHY

REGULAR COINAGE

KM# 32.1 HELLER

Copper **Ruler:** Bernhard **Obv:** Crowned arms **Rev:** Value, date **Rev. Legend:** MEIN/HELLER

Date	Mintage	VG	F	VF	XF	Unc
1699	—	5.00	12.00	25.00	40.00	—

KM# 32.2 HELLER

Copper **Ruler:** Bernhard **Rev:** Value, date **Rev. Legend:** M/HELLER

Date	Mintage	VG	F	VF	XF	Unc
1699	—	5.00	12.00	25.00	40.00	—

KM# 5 GROSCHEN

Silver **Ruler:** Bernhard **Subject:** Death of Bernhard's First Wife, Marie Hedwig of Hesse-Darmstadt **Obv:** Intertwined M and H, ducal crown above, titles of Marie Hedwig in legend **Rev:** 7-line inscription with dates

Date	Mintage	VG	F	VF	XF	Unc
1680	—	60.00	115	200	325	—

KM# 26 GROSCHEN

Silver **Ruler:** Bernhard **Obv:** Armored bust of Bernhard right in inner circle **Rev:** View of Meiningen castle

Date	Mintage	VG	F	VF	XF	Unc
1692	—	27.00	45.00	75.00	125	—

KM# 27 GROSCHEN

Silver **Ruler:** Bernhard **Subject:** Homage of Gotha **Obv:** 2 conjoined busts right, titles in legend **Rev:** 2 joined hands ending in lozenges, MVTVA FIDE above, 4-line inscription with Roman numeral date below

Date	Mintage	VG	F	VF	XF	Unc
1692 IT Rare	—	—	—	—	—	—

KM# 19 1/12 THALER (Doppelgroschen)

Silver **Ruler:** Bernhard **Obv:** Crowned oval 4-fold arms in baroque frame **Rev:** Value, date and initials **Rev. Legend:** 12/EINEN/REICHS/THALER

Date	Mintage	VG	F	VF	XF	Unc
1689 IGS	—	27.00	55.00	100	165	—
1690 IGS	—	27.00	55.00	100	165	—

KM# 6 1/4 THALER

Silver **Ruler:** Bernhard **Subject:** Death of Bernhard's First Wife, Marie Hedwig of Hesse-Darmstadt **Obv:** Intertwined M and H, ducal crown above, legend titles of Marie Hedwig **Rev:** 8-line inscription with dates

Date	Mintage	VG	F	VF	XF	Unc
1680 Rare	—	—	—	—	—	—

KM# 9 1/3 THALER (1/2 Gulden)

Silver **Ruler:** Bernhard **Obv:** Bust right **Rev:** Crowned 4-fold arms in palm branches, value 1/3 below, date in legend

Date	Mintage	VG	F	VF	XF	Unc
1687 GFS	—	—	—	—	—	—

KM# 10 1/3 THALER (1/2 Gulden)

Silver **Ruler:** Bernhard **Obv:** Date divided at bottom by bust

Date	Mintage	VG	F	VF	XF	Unc
1687	—	—	—	—	—	—

KM# 7 1/2 THALER

Silver **Ruler:** Bernhard **Subject:** Death of Bernhard's First Wife, Marie Hedwig of Hesse-Darmstadt

Date	Mintage	VG	F	VF	XF	Unc
1680 Rare	—	—	—	—	—	—

KM# 11 2/3 THALER (Gulden)

Silver **Ruler:** Bernhard **Obv:** Bust right **Rev:** Crowned 4-fold arms in palm branches, value 2/3 below, date in legend

Date	Mintage	VG	F	VF	XF	Unc
1687 GFS	—	45.00	90.00	165	300	—

KM# 14 2/3 THALER (Gulden)

Silver **Ruler:** Bernhard **Obv:** Bust right **Rev:** Helmeted ornate 18-fold arms, value 2/3 below, date in legend

Date	Mintage	VG	F	VF	XF	Unc
1687 Rare	—	—	—	—	—	—

KM# 15 2/3 THALER (Gulden)

Silver **Ruler:** Bernhard **Obv:** Crowned intertwined BHZS monogram, value 2/3 below, date in legend **Rev:** Crowned 4-fold arms in palm branches

Date	Mintage	VG	F	VF	XF	Unc
1687	—	225	375	600	1,000	—

KM# 16 2/3 THALER (Gulden)

Silver **Ruler:** Bernhard **Rev:** Figure seated on stone holding a ring high

Date	Mintage	VG	F	VF	XF	Unc
1687	—	200	325	525	850	—

KM# 12 2/3 THALER (Gulden)

Silver **Ruler:** Bernhard **Obv:** Date divided by bust at bottom and reads facing outwards **Note:** Varieties exist.

Date	Mintage	VG	F	VF	XF	Unc
1687 GFS	—	45.00	90.00	165	300	—
1689 IGS	—	45.00	90.00	165	300	—

KM# 13 2/3 THALER (Gulden)

Silver **Ruler:** Bernhard **Obv:** Date reads inwards **Note:** Varieties exist.

Date	Mintage	VG	F	VF	XF	Unc
1687 GFS	—	45.00	90.00	165	300	—
1689/7 IGS	—	45.00	90.00	165	300	—
1689 IGS	—	45.00	90.00	165	300	—
1689	—	45.00	90.00	165	300	—

KM# 25 2/3 THALER (Gulden)

Silver **Ruler:** Bernhard

Date	Mintage	VG	F	VF	XF	Unc
1691 IGS	—	45.00	90.00	165	300	—

KM# 8 THALER

Silver **Ruler:** Bernhard **Subject:** Death of Bernhard's First Wife, Maria Hedwig of Hesse-Darmstadt **Rev:** Crowned arms above 8-line inscription, 11 arms around **Note:** Dav. #7498.

Date	Mintage	VG	F	VF	XF	Unc
1680	—	850	1,750	3,500	5,750	8,500

KM# 24 THALER

Silver **Ruler:** Bernhard **Subject:** Dedication of the Chapel at Elisabethenburg Palace **Rev:** "Jehovah" in sun above castle **Note:** Dav. #7500.

Date	Mintage	VG	F	VF	XF	Unc
1692	—	400	800	1,650	2,750	—

KM# 28 THALER

Silver **Ruler:** Bernhard **Subject:** Homage of Gotha **Obv:** 2 conjoined busts right **Rev:** Large helmeted ornate 18-fold arms w/round shield, without value shown **Note:** Dav. #--.

Date	Mintage	VG	F	VF	XF	Unc
1692 Rare	—	—	—	—	—	—

KM# 32 THALER

Silver **Ruler:** Bernhard **Rev:** Helmeted arms **Note:** Dav. #7501.

Date	Mintage	VG	F	VF	XF	Unc
1694 Rare	—	—	—	—	—	—

TRADE COINAGE

KM# 18 DUCAT

3.5000 g., 0.9860 Gold 0.1109 oz. AGW **Ruler:** Bernhard **Obv:** Armored bust of Bernhard right in inner circle **Rev:** Arms in inner circle

Date	Mintage	VG	F	VF	XF	Unc
1687	—	725	1,450	2,650	4,200	—
1688	—	725	1,450	2,650	4,200	—

KM# 29 DUCAT

3.5000 g., 0.9860 Gold 0.1109 oz. AGW **Ruler:** Bernhard **Subject:** Homage of Gotha **Obv:** 2 conjoined busts right, titles in legend **Rev:** 2 joined hands ending in lozenges, MVTVA FIDE above, 4-line inscription with Roman numeral date below

Date	Mintage	VG	F	VF	XF	Unc
1692 IT	—	420	850	1,650	2,750	—

KM# 30 DUCAT

3.5000 g., 0.9860 Gold 0.1109 oz. AGW **Ruler:** Bernhard **Rev:** View of Meiningen castle

Date	Mintage	VG	F	VF	XF	Unc
1692	—	600	1,200	2,400	3,850	—

KM# 31 2 DUCAT

7.0000 g., 0.9860 Gold 0.2219 oz. AGW **Ruler:** Bernhard **Obv:** Armored bust of Bernhard right in inner circle **Rev:** View of Meiningen castle

Date	Mintage	VG	F	VF	XF	Unc
1692	—	1,200	2,400	4,800	7,800	—

KM# A25 10 DUCAT

35.0000 g., 0.9860 Gold 1.1095 oz. AGW **Ruler:** Bernhard **Subject:** Dedication of the Chapel at Elizabethenburg Palace **Obv:** Bust of Bernhard right **Rev:** Jehovah in Hebrew above castle **Note:** Struck with 1 Thaler dies, KM#24.

Date	Mintage	VG	F	VF	XF	Unc
1692 Rare	—	—	—	—	—	—

SAXE-ROMHILD

Short-lived branch of the Ernestine Saxon house which was created for Heinrich III, 4th son of Ernst the Pious of Saxe-Gotha. The line became extinct in 1710 at Heinrich's death and properties were divided by Gotha, Meiningen and Saalfeld.

RULER

Heinrich III, 1680-1710

DUCHY

REGULAR COINAGE

DAV# 7502 THALER

Silver **Rev:** Helmeted oval arms

Date	Mintage	VG	F	VF	XF	Unc
1692 ML	—	750	1,500	2,700	4,500	—

TRADE COINAGE

FR# 2997 DUCAT

3.5000 g., 0.9860 Gold 0.1109 oz. AGW **Obv:** Bust of Heinrich III right in inner circle **Rev:** Crowned arms in inner circle

Date	Mintage	VG	F	VF	XF	Unc
1698	—	550	1,200	2,150	3,500	—

SAXE-SAALFELD

As a branch of the Ernestine Saxon house, Saxe-Saalfeld was purchased from Meissen-Thuringia in 1389. It was created as a duchy for Johann Ernst VIII, 7th son of Ernst the Pious of Saxe-Gotha. Coburg was added to the holdings in 1735 and thereafter the dukes took the name of Saxe-Coburg-Saalfeld. Later coinage is listed there.

RULER

Johann Ernst VIII, 1680-1729

DUCHY

REGULAR COINAGE

DAV# 7505 THALER

Silver **Rev:** Helmeted arms

Date	Mintage	VG	F	VF	XF	Unc
1687	—	350	700	1,250	2,100	—

DAV# 7508 THALER

Silver **Subject:** Marriage of Johann Ernst VIII and Charlotte Johanna **Obv:** Accolated busts right **Rev:** Arms in sprays, date below

Date	Mintage	VG	F	VF	XF	Unc
1690	—	675	1,350	2,500	4,150	—

DAV# 7509 THALER

Silver **Obv:** Bust right **Rev:** Helmeted arms, date divided below

Date	Mintage	VG	F	VF	XF	Unc
1690 Rare	—	—	—	—	—	—
1691 Rare	—	—	—	—	—	—

DAV# 7510 THALER

Silver **Obv:** Bust right, helmet in front **Rev:** City view

Date	Mintage	VG	F	VF	XF	Unc
1692 Rare	—	—	—	—	—	—

DAV# 7511 THALER

Silver **Obv:** Bust right, helmet in front **Rev:** Helmeted oval arms

Date	Mintage	VG	F	VF	XF	Unc
1694	—	450	850	1,500	2,500	—

DAV# 7513 THALER

Silver **Obv:** Similar to Dav. #7511 **Rev:** Hand from clouds with wreath above city view

Date	Mintage	VG	F	VF	XF	Unc
1697 Rare	—	—	—	—	—	—
1698 Rare	—	—	—	—	—	—

DAV# 7514 THALER

Silver **Obv:** Similar to Dav. #7511 **Rev:** Helmeted arms divide date below

Date	Mintage	VG	F	VF	XF	Unc
1698 Rare	—	—	—	—	—	—

DAV# 7504 1-1/2 THALER

Silver **Note:** Similar to 2 Thaler, Dav. #7503.

Date	Mintage	VG	F	VF	XF	Unc
1687	—	1,050	2,100	3,750	6,300	—

DAV# 7507 1-1/2 THALER

Silver **Subject:** Marriage of Johann Ernst and Charlotte Johanna **Note:** Similar to 1 Thaler, Dav. #7508.

Date	Mintage	VG	F	VF	XF	Unc
1690 Rare	—	—	—	—	—	—

DAV# 7512 1-1/2 THALER

Silver **Obv:** Bust right **Rev:** Hand from clouds with wreath above city view, Roman numeral date below

Date	Mintage	VG	F	VF	XF	Unc
1697 Rare	—	—	—	—	—	—

DAV# 7503 2 THALER

Silver **Rev:** Helmeted arms

Date	Mintage	VG	F	VF	XF	Unc
1687	—	1,150	2,200	3,950	6,600	—

DAV# 7506 2 THALER

Silver **Subject:** Marriage of Johann Ernst and Charlotte Johanna **Note:** Similar to 1 Thaler, Dav. #7508.

Date	Mintage	VG	F	VF	XF	Unc
1690 Rare	—	—	—	—	—	—

TRADE COINAGE

FR# 3000 DUCAT
3.5000 g., 0.9860 Gold 0.1109 oz. AGW **Ruler:** Johann Ernst VIII **Obv:** Young armored bust right in inner circle **Rev:** Elaborate arms topped by 6 helmets, date divided below

Date	Mintage	VG	F	VF	XF	Unc
1698	—	350	700	1,450	2,500	—

FR# 2999 2 DUCAT
7.0000 g., 0.9860 Gold 0.2219 oz. AGW **Obv:** Bust of Johann Ernst VIII right **Rev:** Oval manifold arms, six helmets above, date divided at bottom

Date	Mintage	VG	F	VF	XF	Unc
1698 Rare	—	—	—	—	—	—

FR# 2998 6 DUCAT
21.0000 g., 0.9860 Gold 0.6657 oz. AGW **Obv:** Bust of Johann Ernst VIII right **Rev:** Crowned arms **Note:** Struck with 1 Thaler dies, Dav. #7514.

Date	Mintage	VG	F	VF	XF	Unc
1698 Rare	—	—	—	—	—	—

SAXE-WEIMAR

(Sachsen-Neu-Weimar)

Founded from Saxe-Middle-Weimar in 1640, the division ended the joint rule of the duchy begun by all eight sons of Johann III. In 1662, the four sons of Wilhelm IV divided their inheritance into the lines of Saxe-(New)-Weimar, Saxe-Eisenach, Saxe-Marksuhl and Saxe-Jena. When the line in Eisenach became extinct in 1741, that territory and titles reverted to Weimar, which became known from that time on as Saxe-Weimar-Eisenach

RULERS
Wilhelm IV, 1640-1662
Johann Ernst II (V), 1662-1683
Wilhelm Ernst, 1683-1728

MINT OFFICIALS' INITIALS

Initial	Date	Name
(a) arm with sickle or EF or EFS	1636-72	Ernst Friedrich Schneider in Coburg
ID	Ca. 1660	Unknown
GFS	1673-77	George Friedrich Staude in Weimar
	1677-80	In Gotha
BA	1687-90	Bastian Altmann in Weimar

DUCHY

STANDARD COINAGE

DAV# 7541 THALER
Silver **Subject:** Peace in Weimar **Obv:** Two hands holding wreath above coat of arms, sword at left, olive branch at right **Rev:** Three clasped hands above a sword, date in chronogram

Date	Mintage	VG	F	VF	XF	Unc
1650	—	675	1,350	2,750	4,500	—

DAV# 7542 THALER
Silver **Subject:** Rebuilding the Weimar Castle **Obv:** Rebuilt castle **Rev:** Burning castle

Date	Mintage	VG	F	VF	XF	Unc
1652	—	700	1,450	2,850	5,000	8,000

DAV# 7543 THALER
Silver **Obv. Legend:** ... SAXON. IVL. CLIV. &MONT. **Rev:** Legend starts at lower left **Rev. Legend:** AULA...

Date	Mintage	VG	F	VF	XF	Unc
1653	—	800	1,600	3,000	6,000	—

DAV# 7544 THALER
Silver **Subject:** Death of Wilhelmina Eleonora, Daughter of Wilhelm IV **Obv:** IESUSEI both ways in a cross, biographical data in field **Obv. Legend:** Crowned wreath with W E inside, WILHELMINA-ELEONORA at sides

Date	Mintage	VG	F	VF	XF	Unc
1653 Rare	—	—	—	—	—	—

DAV# 7545 THALER
Silver **Subject:** Duke Bernhard Assuming the Rectorship of Jena University **Obv:** Two crowned hearts with bust of Johann Friedrich and two shields at center **Rev:** Two busts in center of Johann Friedrich and Johann Wilhelm

Date	Mintage	VG	F	VF	XF	Unc
1654	—	625	1,250	2,500	4,250	—

DAV# 7537 THALER
Silver **Subject:** Entombment of Bernhard in Weimar **Rev:** Nine-line inscription

Date	Mintage	VG	F	VF	XF	Unc
1655	—	550	1,100	2,250	4,000	—

DAV# 7546 THALER
Silver **Subject:** Death of Friedrich, Son of Wilhelm IV **Obv:** FRIDERICVS both ways on a cross, biographical data in field **Rev:** Sun behind clouds, biographical data below

Date	Mintage	VG	F	VF	XF	Unc
1656	—	600	1,200	2,500	4,250	—

DAV# 7547 THALER
Silver **Subject:** New Castle Wilhelmsburg **Rev:** Palace, five-line inscription below

Date	Mintage	VG	F	VF	XF	Unc
1658	—	525	675	1,350	2,250	—

DAV# 7549 THALER
Silver **Obv:** Bust right **Rev:** Wilhelmsburg Castle at Weimar

Date	Mintage	VG	F	VF	XF	Unc
1662 Rare	—	—	—	—	—	—

DAV# 7550 THALER
Silver **Subject:** Death of Wilhelm IV **Obv:** Obelisk with ribbons **Rev:** Two arms from clouds tying four arrows together below a crown **Note:** Varieties exist.

Date	Mintage	VG	F	VF	XF	Unc
1662	—	150	300	650	1,250	—

DAV# 7552 THALER
Silver **Obv:** Bust of Johann Ernst **Rev:** Female figure seated by column with staff, palace behind

Date	Mintage	VG	F	VF	XF	Unc
ND(1663) Rare	—	—	—	—	—	—

DAV# 7551 THALER
Silver **Subject:** Death of Eleonora Dorothea, Widow of Wilhelm IV **Obv:** Eight-line inscription **Rev:** Hands from clouds holding crown above heart inscribed JESUS

Date	Mintage	VG	F	VF	XF	Unc
1665	—	175	350	750	1,500	—

DAV# 7554 THALER
Silver **Subject:** Death of Christiane Elisabeth, Wife of Johann Ernst **Obv:** "JEHOVAH" in Hebrew above in sun with clouds, moon, and earth below **Rev:** Twelve-line inscription

Date	Mintage	VG	F	VF	XF	Unc
1679	—	650	1,250	2,500	—	—

DAV# 7555 THALER
Silver **Subject:** Death of Johann Ernst **Obv:** Bust right in laurel branches **Rev:** Eight-line inscription below crowned arms on tomb, Roman numeral date

Date	Mintage	VG	F	VF	XF	Unc
ND(1683) Rare	—	—	—	—	—	—

Note: Westfälische Auktionsgesellschaft Auction 40, 2-07, nearly XF realized approximately $8,920

DAV# 7537A 1-1/4 THALER
Silver **Subject:** Entombment of Bernhard in Weimar
Note: Similar to 1 Thaler, Dav. #7537.

Date	Mintage	VG	F	VF	XF	Unc
1655 Rare	—	—	—	—	—	—

DAV# 7537B 3 THALER
Silver **Subject:** Entombment of Bernhard in Weimar
Note: Similar to 1 Thaler, Dav. #7537.

Date	Mintage	VG	F	VF	XF	Unc
1655 Rare	—	—	—	—	—	—

TRADE COINAGE

FR# 3019 1/4 DUCAT
0.8750 g., 0.9860 Gold 0.0277 oz. AGW **Obv:** Crowned arms **Rev:** "Jehovah" in Hebrew and legend

Date	Mintage	VG	F	VF	XF	Unc
1651	—	120	240	475	775	—

FR# 3024 1/4 DUCAT
0.8750 g., 0.9860 Gold 0.0277 oz. AGW **Obv:** Saxon arms in branches **Rev:** "Jehovah" at top, four-line inscription, date at bottom

Date	Mintage	VG	F	VF	XF	Unc
1658	—	125	250	500	825	—

FR# 3029 1/4 DUCAT
0.8750 g., 0.9860 Gold 0.0277 oz. AGW **Obv:** Bust of Wilhelm right **Rev:** Crowned Saxon arms, divided date below

Date	Mintage	VG	F	VF	XF	Unc
1662	—	150	280	575	950	—

FR# 3018 1/2 DUCAT
1.7500 g., 0.9860 Gold 0.0555 oz. AGW **Obv:** Crowned arms **Rev:** "Jehovah" and legend

Date	Mintage	VG	F	VF	XF	Unc
1651	—	170	350	700	1,150	—
1652	—	170	350	700	1,150	—

FR# 3023 1/2 DUCAT
1.7500 g., 0.9860 Gold 0.0555 oz. AGW **Obv:** Saxon arms in branches in inner circle **Rev:** "Jehovah" at top, four-line inscription, date at bottom

Date	Mintage	VG	F	VF	XF	Unc
1651	—	170	350	700	1,150	—
1656	—	170	350	700	1,150	—

FR# 3021 1/2 DUCAT
1.7500 g., 0.9860 Gold 0.0555 oz. AGW **Obv:** Wilhelm

Date	Mintage	VG	F	VF	XF	Unc
1654	—	145	270	575	950	—

FR# 3017 DUCAT
3.5000 g., 0.9860 Gold 0.1109 oz. AGW **Obv:** Crowned arms **Rev:** "Jehovah" and legend

Date	Mintage	VG	F	VF	XF	Unc
1651	—	325	625	1,250	2,100	—

FR# 3022 DUCAT
3.5000 g., 0.9860 Gold 0.1109 oz. AGW **Rev:** "Jehovah" at top

Date	Mintage	VG	F	VF	XF	Unc
1651	—	325	625	1,250	2,100	—

FR# 3026 DUCAT
3.5000 g., 0.9860 Gold 0.1109 oz. AGW **Obv:** Arms of Henneberg-Ilmenau **Rev:** Five-line inscription

Date	Mintage	VG	F	VF	XF	Unc
1661	—	500	1,000	1,900	3,150	—

FR# 3028 DUCAT
3.5000 g., 0.9860 Gold 0.1109 oz. AGW **Obv:** Bust of Wilhelm right in inner circle **Rev:** Jena Castle

Date	Mintage	VG	F	VF	XF	Unc
1661	—	500	1,000	1,900	3,150	—

FR# 3024b 2 DUCAT
Gold **Ruler:** Wilhelm IV **Obv:** Bust in circle turned slightly to left, date at top in margin **Obv. Legend:** D.G. WILHELM. DVX. SAX. IVL. CLIV. & MONT. **Rev:** 7-line inscription with date in chronogram **Rev. Inscription:** SIC BENE/WILHELMVS/FECIT FACIET/QVE BENE VLTRA./VT RATA VERIF DVO/EST ELLOGIO/GENITRIX **Note:** Fr. #3024b.

Date	Mintage	VG	F	VF	XF	Unc
1658 Unique	—	—	—	—	—	—

FR# 3027 2 DUCAT
Gold **Ruler:** Wilhelm IV **Obv:** Armored bust to right, legend in Gothic script **Rev:** Crown above 2 small ornate shields of arms divides date, 5-line inscription below **Note:** Fr. #3027.

Date	Mintage	VG	F	VF	XF	Unc
1661 Rare	—	—	—	—	—	—

FR# 3024d 3 DUCAT
Gold **Ruler:** Wilhelm IV **Obv:** Armored bust turned slightly to right, date at top in margin **Obv. Legend:** D.G. WILHELM, DVX SAX. IVL. CLIV. ET MONT. **Rev:** View of courtyard of palace, Wilhelms=Burg in Gothic letters in ribbon above, 5-line inscription with chronogram below **Rev. Inscription:** SIC bene WILheLMVs feCIt/faCIetaVe VLtra/Vt rata VerIfLVo/est eLLogio/genItrIX **Note:** Fr. 3024d.

Date	Mintage	VG	F	VF	XF	Unc
1658 Rare	—	—	—	—	—	—

SAXE-WEIMAR, MIDDLE

(Sachsen-Mittel Weimar)

Upon the death of Johann III of Saxe-Old-Weimar in 1605, his eight sons ruled the duchy together. Both Eisenach and Gotha were acquired from Saxe-Old Gotha when Johann Ernst II died in 1638. By 1640, three brothers alone remained and they divided the territory into Saxe-(New)-Weimar, Saxe-Eisenach and Saxe-(Middle) Gotha.

RULERS
Joint Rule, 1605-1640
Johann Ernst IV, 1605-1626
Friedrich VII, 1605-1622
Wilhelm IV, 1605-1640
Albrecht II, 1605-1640
Johann Friedrich VI, 1605-1628
Ernst III the Pious, 1605-1640
Friedrich Wilhelm, 1605-1619
Bernhard the Great, 1605-1639, Duke of Franconia 1633-1634

MINT OFFICIALS' INITIALS

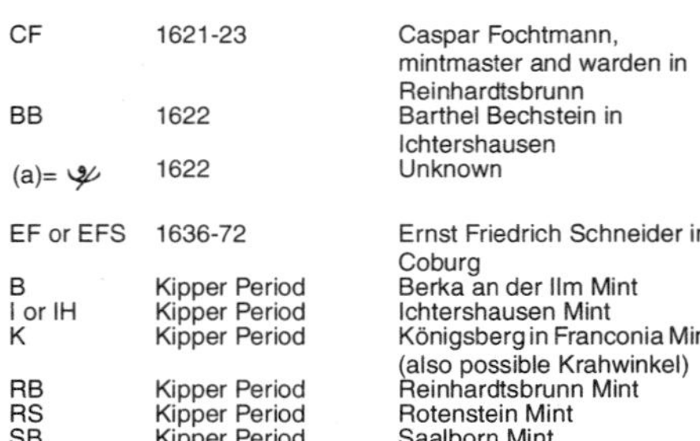

Initial	Date	Name
WA	1604-12	Wolf Albrecht der Jüngere in Coburg
	1612-20, 23-32	In Saalfeld
CVL	1616-20	Cyriacus von Lehr in Weimar
	1622	In Hornstein
GA	1620-24	Georg Andreae (known as Gabriel Andresse) in Weimar
CF	1621-23	Caspar Fochtmann, mintmaster and warden in Reinhardtsbrunn
BB	1622	Barthel Bechstein in Ichtershausen
(a)=	1622	Unknown
EF or EFS	1636-72	Ernst Friedrich Schneider in Coburg
B	Kipper Period	Berka an der Ilm Mint
I or IH	Kipper Period	Ichtershausen Mint
K	Kipper Period	Königsberg in Franconia Mint (also possible Krahwinkel)
RB	Kipper Period	Reinhardtsbrunn Mint
RS	Kipper Period	Rotenstein Mint
SB	Kipper Period	Saalborn Mint

DUCHY

STANDARD COINAGE

DAV# 7523 THALER
Silver **Obv:** 4 half-figures facing, inscription below **Obv. Inscription:** MON: NOV: ARG: ... **Rev:** 4 half-figures facing, 2-line inscription below, date below **Rev. Inscription:** LINEASE VINA / RIENSIS. **Note:** "8 Brothers" design.

Date	Mintage	VG	F	VF	XF	Unc
1607 WA	—	70.00	125	200	375	—
1608 WA	—	70.00	125	200	375	—
1609 WA	—	70.00	125	200	375	—
1610 WA	—	70.00	125	200	375	—
1611 WA	—	70.00	125	200	375	—
1612 WA	—	70.00	125	200	375	—

DAV# 7525 THALER
Silver **Obv:** DISCORDIAE/FOMES INNRIA below figures **Rev:** 8 FRAT. DVC: SAXON: /IVL: CLI: MOT: above figures

Date	Mintage	VG	F	VF	XF	Unc
1612 WA	—	70.00	125	220	375	—
1613 WA	—	70.00	125	220	375	—

DAV# 7527 THALER
Silver **Obv:** 4 half-figures facing, scrollwork below

Date	Mintage	VG	F	VF	XF	Unc
1612 WA	—	70.00	125	200	375	—
1613 WA	—	70.00	125	200	375	—
1614 WA	—	70.00	125	200	375	—
1615 WA	—	70.00	125	200	375	—
1616 WA	—	70.00	125	200	375	—

DAV# 7529 THALER

Silver **Obv:** Figure right with 7 busts around **Rev:** Helmeted arms divide date

Date	Mintage	VG	F	VF	XF	Unc
1616 WA	—	75.00	135	275	550	—
1617 WA	—	75.00	135	275	550	—
1618 WA	—	75.00	135	275	550	—
1619 WA	—	75.00	135	275	550	—

DAV# 7521 THALER

Silver **Subject:** Death of Dorothea Marie, Widow of Johann III **Obv:** Crowned heart-shaped arms **Rev:** 12-line inscription with date

Date	Mintage	VG	F	VF	XF	Unc
1617 WA	—	350	700	1,250	2,000	—

DAV# 7531 THALER

28.9400 g., Silver **Obv:** Figure of Pallas standing with spear and shield, spear divides date **Rev:** Helmeted spears **Note:** "6 Brothers" design.

Date	Mintage	VG	F	VF	XF	Unc
1622 GA	—	85.00	175	350	750	—
1623 GA	—	85.00	175	350	750	—

DAV# 7530 THALER

Silver **Subject:** Death of Frederick VII **Rev:** Arms above 7-line inscription

Date	Mintage	VG	F	VF	XF	Unc
1622 (a)	—	125	250	450	1,000	—

DAV# 7532 THALER

Silver **Obv:** Wreath in field, helmet on Pallas divides date **Rev:** Helmeted arms divide letters at bottom

Date	Mintage	VG	F	VF	XF	Unc
1623 GA	—	75.00	150	300	650	—

DAV# 7532A THALER

Silver **Obv:** Rough wreath, helmet divides date

Date	Mintage	VG	F	VF	XF	Unc
1623 CF	—	75.00	150	300	650	—

DAV# 7533 THALER

Silver **Subject:** Death of Johann Ernst IV **Obv:** Bust right **Rev:** 10-line inscription

Date	Mintage	VG	F	VF	XF	Unc
1626 WA Rare	—	—	—	—	—	—

DAV# 4557 THALER

Silver **Obv:** Bust of Gustavus Adolphus right **Rev:** Crowned oval 4-fold arms with central shield in ornate frame, date in margin **Note:** Swedish issue.

Date	Mintage	VG	F	VF	XF	Unc
1631 GA Rare	—	—	—	—	—	—

DAV# 7540 THALER

Silver **Subject:** Death of Johann Wilhelm, Son of Wilhelm IV **Obv:** 9-line inscription **Rev:** 2 arms bound together holding a wreath with initials of the duke, duchess and dead son

Date	Mintage	VG	F	VF	XF	Unc
1639 Rare	—	—	—	—	—	—

DAV# 7536 THALER

Silver **Obv:** Bust right **Rev:** 2 busts **Note:** "3 Brothers" design.

Date	Mintage	VG	F	VF	XF	Unc
1639 EF Rare	—	—	—	—	—	—

DAV# 7553 1-1/2 THALER

Silver **Obv:** Bust **Rev:** Arms

Date	Mintage	VG	F	VF	XF	Unc
1679 Rare	—	—	—	—	—	—

DAV# 7522 2 THALER

Silver **Note:** "8 Brothers" design. Similar to 1 Thaler, Dav. #7523.

Date	Mintage	VG	F	VF	XF	Unc
1607 WA	—	500	950	1,600	2,700	—
1608 WA	—	500	950	1,600	2,700	—
1609 WA	—	500	950	1,600	2,700	—

DAV# 7526 2 THALER

Silver **Ruler:** Duke of Franconia **Note:** Similar to 1 Thaler, Dav. #7527.

Date	Mintage	VG	F	VF	XF	Unc
1613 WA	—	500	950	1,600	2,700	—
1614 WA	—	500	950	1,600	2,700	—

DAV# 7524 2 THALER

Silver **Obv:** 4 half figures facing, DISCORDIAE/... below **Rev:** 4 half figures facing, 8 FRAT. DVC:... above

Date	Mintage	VG	F	VF	XF	Unc
1613 WA	—	500	950	1,600	2,700	—
1614 WA	—	500	950	1,600	2,700	—

DAV# 7528 2 THALER

Silver **Note:** Similar to 1 Thaler, Dav. #7529.

Date	Mintage	VG	F	VF	XF	Unc
1617 WA	—	625	1,150	1,900	3,250	—
1619 WA	—	625	1,150	1,900	3,250	—

TRADE COINAGE

FR# 3014 GOLDGULDEN

3.5000 g., 0.9860 Gold 0.1109 oz. AGW **Obv:** Johann Ernst and 3 brothers **Rev:** 4 additional brothers

Date	Mintage	VG	F	VF	XF	Unc
1613 WA	—	150	295	575	1,000	—
1615 WA	—	150	295	575	1,000	—
1617 WA	—	150	295	575	1,000	—
1619 WA	—	150	295	575	1,000	—

FR# 3015 GOLDGULDEN

3.5000 g., 0.9860 Gold 0.1109 oz. AGW **Obv:** Crowned Saxon arms in branches, date divided at top **Rev:** Arms in inner circle

Date	Mintage	VG	F	VF	XF	Unc
1623 GA	—	475	1,000	2,000	3,300	—

FR# 3020 2 DUCAT

7.0000 g., 0.9860 Gold 0.2219 oz. AGW **Obv:** Bust of Wilhelm **Rev:** 4-line inscription on banner before military trophies, date at top

Date	Mintage	VG	F	VF	XF	Unc
1654	—	750	1,500	2,800	5,000	—

SAXE-WEIMAR, OLD

(Sachsen-Alt Weimar)

After the loss of the electoral dignity by Johann Friedrich I in 1547 (see Saxony-Ernestine Line) and his death in 1554, his sons ruled jointly in Wittenberg and Thuringia (Thüringen) until 1565. Weimar and Altenburg were separated and ruled by Johann Friedrich's second son, who also appropriated Gotha in 1567. In 1573, the lines of Saxe-Old-Altenburg and Saxe-Middle-Weimar were founded, but the two sons ruled together and issued a series of joint coinages.

RULERS

Friedrich Wilhelm I of Altenburg, 1573-1602
and Johann III of Weimar, 1573-1605

MINT OFFICIALS

Mark	Date	Name
(c)= [symbol]	1578-1603	Gregor Bechstedt (Bechstädt) in Saalfeld
(e)= flower or WA (ligature)	1604-12	Wolf Albrecht der Jüngere in Coburg
	161612-20, 1623-32	Wolf Albrecht der Jüngere in Saalfeld

DUCHY

STANDARD COINAGE

KM# 17 PFENNIG

Copper **Ruler:** Johann III **Subject:** Death of Johann III **Obv:** Ornate 9-fold arms with central shield of Saxony **Rev:** Arabesque, date **Rev. Legend:** OMNIA/CONANDO/DOCILISSO/LERTIA. VI=/NCIT

Date	Mintage	VG	F	VF	XF	Unc
1605	—	—	—	—	—	—

KM# 18 SCHRECKENBERGER (1/8 Thaler)

Silver **Ruler:** Johann III **Subject:** Death of Johann III **Obv:** 1/2-length figure of angel behind S arms, titles of Johann III **Rev:** 8-line inscription with dates **Rev. Legend:** DOMINE DIRIGE. ME. IN. VERBO. TVO

Date	Mintage	VG	F	VF	XF	Unc
1605 WA	—	45.00	85.00	150	275	—

KM# 9 1/4 THALER

Silver **Ruler:** Johann III **Subject:** Death of Friedrich Wilhelm I **Obv:** Saxony arms in ornate frame, titles of Friedrich Wilhelm I **Rev:** 8-line inscription with dates in circle **Rev. Legend:** DOMINE CONSERVA...

Date	Mintage	VG	F	VF	XF	Unc
160Z	—	—	—	—	—	—

KM# 19 1/4 THALER

Silver **Ruler:** Johann III **Subject:** Death of Johann III **Obv:** Bust right in circle **Rev:** 8-line inscription with dates
Rev. Legend: DOMINE DIRIGE. ME. IN. VERBO. TVO

Date	Mintage	VG	F	VF	XF	Unc
1605 WA	—	175	350	600	1,000	—

KM# 10 1/2 THALER

Silver **Ruler:** Johann III **Subject:** Death of Friedrich Wilhelm I **Obv:** Saxony arms in ornate frame, titles of Friedrich I
Rev: 8-line inscription with dates in circle **Rev. Legend:** DOMINE CONSERVA...

Date	Mintage	VG	F	VF	XF	Unc
160Z WA	—	125	225	375	675	—

KM# 20 1/2 THALER

Silver **Ruler:** Johann III **Obv:** Bust of Johann III **Rev:** Helmeted arms

Date	Mintage	VG	F	VF	XF	Unc
1605 WA	—	400	750	1,250	—	—

KM# 21 1/2 THALER

Silver **Ruler:** Johann III **Subject:** Death of Johann III **Obv:** Bust right in circle **Rev:** 8-line inscription with dates
Rev. Legend: DOMINE DIRIGE. ME. IN. VERBO. TVO

Date	Mintage	VG	F	VF	XF	Unc
1605 WA	—	150	275	450	—	—

KM# 3 THALER

Silver **Ruler:** Johann III **Obv:** Two 1/2-length figures of dukes facing each other, small imperial orb above, titles around **Rev:** Saxony arms in ornate shield with date above in circle, 12 small shields around, legend in outer margin **Rev. Legend:** LANTG. THVRI. ET. MARCHIO

Date	Mintage	VG	F	VF	XF	Unc
1597 (c)	—	70.00	135	200	375	—
1598 (c)	—	70.00	135	200	375	—
1599 (c)	—	70.00	135	200	375	—
1600 (c)	—	70.00	135	200	375	—
1601 (c)	—	70.00	135	200	375	—

KM# 5 THALER

Silver **Ruler:** Johann III **Obv:** Two 1/2-length figures of dukes facing each other, small imperial orb above, titles around
Rev: Saxony arms in ornate shield with date above in circle, 12 small shields around, legend in outer margin **Rev. Legend:** LANTG. THURI. ET. MARCHIO **Note:** Dav. #7515.

Date	Mintage	VG	F	VF	XF	Unc
1601 (c)	—	80.00	175	325	700	—

KM# 6 THALER

Silver **Ruler:** Johann III **Obv:** Two 1/2-length figures of dukes facing each other, small imperial orb above, titles around **Rev:** 3 helmets above 11-fold arms, bottom of shield divides date **Note:** Dav. #7517.

Date	Mintage	VG	F	VF	XF	Unc
1601 (c)	—	80.00	150	275	650	—
160Z (c)	—	80.00	150	275	650	—

KM# 11 THALER

Silver **Ruler:** Johann III **Subject:** Death of Friedrich Wilhelm **Obv:** 1/2-length armored bust right, titles of Friedrich Wilhelm **Rev:** 7-line inscription with dates **Rev. Legend:** DOMINE CONSERVA **Note:** Previous Dav.#7518.

Date	Mintage	VG	F	VF	XF	Unc
160Z (c)	—	200	400	700	1,150	—
160Z WA	—	200	400	700	1,150	—
160Z	—	200	400	700	1,150	—

KM# 14 THALER

Silver **Ruler:** Johann III **Obv:** Bust of Johann III **Obv. Legend:** ...SAXONIAE.LANDT:THUR **Rev:** Helmeted arms **Note:** Dav. #7519.

Date	Mintage	VG	F	VF	XF	Unc
(1)604 WA	—	155	325	575	950	—
1604	—	155	325	575	950	—
1605 WA	—	155	325	575	950	—

KM# 15 THALER

Silver **Ruler:** Johann III **Obv:** Armored bust of Johann III right **Obv. Legend:** ...SAXONIAE. LANDT:THUR **Rev:** Helmeted arms **Note:** Dav. #7519A.

Date	Mintage	VG	F	VF	XF	Unc
1604	—	155	325	575	950	—

KM# 22 THALER

Silver **Ruler:** Johann III **Subject:** Death of Johann III **Rev:** Eight-line inscription in inner circle **Note:** Dav. #7520.

Date	Mintage	VG	F	VF	XF	Unc
1605	—	150	280	500	850	—

KM# 7 2 THALER

Silver **Ruler:** Johann III **Obv:** Two 1/2-length figures of dukes with batons in hand, facing each other, small imperial orb above, titles around **Rev:** 3 helmets above 11-fold arms, bottom of shield divides date

Date	Mintage	VG	F	VF	XF	Unc
1601 (c) Rare	—	—	—	—	—	—

KM# 12 2 THALER

Silver **Ruler:** Johann III **Obv:** Two 1/2-length figures of dukes facing each other, small imperial orb above, titles around **Rev:** 3 helmets above 11-fold arms, bottom of shield divides date **Note:** Dav. #7516.

Date	Mintage	VG	F	VF	XF	Unc
160Z (c) Rare	—	—	—	—	—	—

SAXE-WEISSENFELS

Branch of the Albertine Saxon house, which was created in 1656 for August, 2nd son of the Elector of Saxony, Johann Georg I. The line became extinct with the death of Johann Adolf II in 1746 and the territories reverted to Electoral Saxony.

RULERS

August, 1656-1680
Johann Adolf I, 1680-1697
Johann Georg, 1697-1712

MINT OFFICIALS' INITIALS

Initials	Date	Name
IHF or HHF	1669-1670	Johann (Hans) Heinrich Friese, mintmaster in Halle
SQ	1686	Samuel Querfurt, mintmaster in Weissenfels

REFERENCE

M = Otto Merseburger, **Sammlung Otto Merseburger umfassend Münzen und Medaillen von Sachsen**, Leipzig, 1894.

DUCHY

STANDARD COINAGE

KM# 5 GROSCHEN (1/24 Thaler)

Silver, 23 mm. **Ruler:** August **Subject:** Death of August's First Wife, Anna Maria von Mecklenburg-Schwerin **Obv:** Crowned AM monogram in palm branches **Obv. Legend:** DEVM QVI HABET OMNIA HABET. **Rev:** 7-line inscription with dates **Rev. Inscription:** NATA./SVER. 1. IVL. 1627./DENAT./HAL. 10. DEC. 1669/ÆTAT./XLII. M.5. D./10. **Mint:** Halle **Note:** M#2319.

Date	Mintage	VG	F	VF	XF	Unc
1669 HHF	—	30.00	60.00	100	185	—

KM# 17 GROSCHEN (1/24 Thaler)

Silver **Ruler:** Johann Adolf I **Subject:** Death of Johann Adolf I's Wife, Johanna Magdalena von Sachsen-Altenburg **Obv:** Crowned script JM monogram **Rev:** 8-line inscription with dates **Rev. Inscription:** NAT./ALTENB:14/IAN: Ao. 1656./DEN: LEUCOPE=/TRÆ. 22. IAN: Ao. 1686. ÆTAT/XXX. D. IX./S.Q. **Mint:** Weissenfels **Note:** M#2327.

Date	Mintage	VG	F	VF	XF	Unc
1686 SQ	—	35.00	70.00	120	200	—

KM# 7 1/4 THALER

7.2500 g., Silver **Ruler:** August **Subject:** Death of August's First Wife, Anna Maria von Mecklenburg-Schwerin **Obv:** Crowned AM monogram in palm branches **Obv. Legend:** DEVM. QVI. HABET. OMNIA. HABET. **Rev:** 7-line inscription with dates **Rev. Inscription:** NATA/SVER. 1. IVL. 1627./DENAT./HAL. 11. DEC. 1669/ÆTAT./XLII. M. 5. D./10. **Mint:** Halle **Note:** M#2318.

Date	Mintage	VG	F	VF	XF	Unc
1669 HHF	—	40.00	80.00	150	250	—

KM# 18 1/4 THALER

Silver **Ruler:** Johann Adolf I **Subject:** Death of Johann Adolf I's Wife, Johanna Magdalena von Sachsen-Altenburg **Obv:** Crowned script JM monogram **Obv. Legend:** + PROVIDENTIA. DOMINI. SUFFICIENTIA MIHI. **Rev:** 8-line inscription with dates **Mint:** Weissenfels

Date	Mintage	VG	F	VF	XF	Unc
1686 SQ	—	175	350	600	1,000	—

KM# 8 1/2 THALER

14.5800 g., Silver **Ruler:** August **Subject:** Death of August's First Wife, Anna Maria von Mecklenburg-Schwerin **Obv:** Jacob wrestling with the archangel **Obv. Legend:** DEVM. QVI. HABET. OMNIA. HABET. **Rev:** 11-line inscription with dates **Rev. Legend:** + D.G. ANNA MARIA. DUX. SAX. IUL. CLIV. ET. MONT. **Rev. Inscription:** NAT./E. DOM. MEG./SVER. 1. IUL. 1627./NUPTA/IBID. 23. NOV. 1647./DENATA/HAL. 11. DEC. 1669/VIXIT/ANNOS. XLII./MENS. 5. D. 10./IH.F. **Mint:** Halle **Note:** M#2317.

Date	Mintage	VG	F	VF	XF	Unc
1669 IHF	—	75.00	150	275	450	—

KM# 19 1/2 THALER

Silver **Ruler:** Johann Adolf I **Subject:** Death of Johann Adolf I's Wife, Johanna Magdalena von Sachsen-Altenburg **Obv:** Figure of Jesus as the Good Shepherd, carrying staff, with lamb over shoulders **Obv. Legend:** + PROVIDENTIA. DOMINI. SUFFICIENTIA. MIHI. **Rev:** 8-line inscription with dates **Rev. Legend:** + D.G. IOHANNA. MAGDALENA. D. S. I. C. & M. **Rev. Inscription:** NATA/ALTENBURGI/14. IAN: Ao. 1656./DENAT: LEUCOPE=/TRÆ. 22. IAN: Ao./1686, ÆTAT:/XXX. D. IX./S.Q. **Mint:** Weissenfels **Note:** M#2326.

Date	Mintage	VG	F	VF	XF	Unc
1686 SQ	—	75.00	150	275	450	—

KM# 3 THALER

Silver **Ruler:** August **Subject:** Laying Foundation Stone of New Palace Church **Obv:** IESUS above altar, hands in prayer and Bible with inscriptions **Obv. Legend:** SANCTA TRINITAS MEA HEREDITAS. **Rev:** 12-line inscription with date **Mint:** Halle **Note:** Dav. #7658

Date	Mintage	VG	F	VF	XF	Unc
1663	—	150	300	525	1,200	2,000

KM# 9 THALER

29.2000 g., Silver **Ruler:** August **Subject:** Death of August's First Wife, Anna Maria von Mecklenburg-Schwerin **Obv:** Jacob wrestling with the archangel **Obv. Legend:** DEVM. QVI. HABET. OMNIA. HABET. **Rev:** 11-line inscription with dates **Rev. Legend:** + D.G. ANNA MARIA. DUX. SAX. IUL. CLIV. ET. MONT. **Rev. Inscription:** NAT./E. DOM. MEG./SVER. 1. IUL 1627./NUPTA/IBID 23. NOV. 1647./DENATA/HAL 11. DEC. 1669/VIXIT/ANNOS. XLIIL/MENS. 5. D./IH. 10. F. **Mint:** Halle **Note:** Dav. #7659.

Date	Mintage	VG	F	VF	XF	Unc
1669 IHF	—	200	400	950	1,850	3,250

KM# 10 THALER

Silver **Ruler:** August **Subject:** Death of August's First Wife, Anna Maria von Mecklenburg-Schwerin **Obv:** Jacob wrestling with the archangel **Obv. Legend:** DEUM. QVI. HABET. OMNIA. HABET. **Rev:** 11-line inscription with dates **Rev. Legend:** + D.G. ANNA MARIA. DUX. SAX. IUL. CLIV. ET. MONT. **Rev. Inscription:** NAT./E. DOM. MEG./SVER. 1. IUL 1627./NUPTA/IBID 23. NOV. 1647./DENATA/HAL 11. DEC. 1669/VIXIT/ANNOS. XLIIL/MENS. 5. D. 10/HHF. **Mint:** Halle **Note:** DAV. #7659A.

Date	Mintage	VG	F	VF	XF	Unc
1669 HHF	—	250	450	1,000	2,000	—

KM# 13 THALER

Silver **Ruler:** Johann Adolf I **Subject:** Birth of Prince Adolf **Obv:** Crowned JA's in palm sprays, shields in corners **Obv. Legend:** AUF DER NEUEN AUGUSTUS BURG ZU WEISSENFELS **Rev:** Sun above child in cradle, Roman numeral date divided in corners **Rev. Legend:** BUCHSEN SCHIESSEN BEY DER PRINZLICHEN EINSEGNUNG **Note:** Klippe. Dav. #7662.

Date	Mintage	VG	F	VF	XF	Unc
MDCLXXXV(1685)	—	500	1,000	2,000	3,500	—

KM# 20 THALER

Silver **Ruler:** Johann Adolf I **Subject:** Death of Johann Adolf I's Wife, Johanna Magdalena von Sachsen-Altenburg **Obv:** Figure of Jesus as the Good Shepherd, holding staff, with lamb on shoulders **Obv. Legend:** + PROVIDENTIA DOMINI SUFFICIENTIA MIHI **Rev:** 8-line inscription with dates **Rev. Legend:** + D.G. IOHANNA. MAGDALENA. D.S.I.C. &. M. **Rev. Inscription:** NATA/ALTENBURGI./14. IAN: Ao. 1656./DENAT. LEUCOPE=/TR. E. 22. IANUAR:/Ao. 1686. ÆTATE:/Ao. XXX. DIE./S. IX. Q. **Mint:** Weissenfels **Note:** Dav. #7663.

Date	Mintage	VG	F	VF	XF	Unc
1686 SQ	—	200	450	950	1,750	—

KM# 25 THALER (Shooting)

Silver **Ruler:** Johann Georg **Obv:** Cross in center of 8-rayed star, ribbon with Order of the Elephant around **Rev:** Large crown above two adjacent oval shields, ducal Saxony in left, JG monogram in right, Roman numeral date divided in corners **Rev. Legend:** + SCHIESEN BEY DEM CARNEVAL AUF DER NEUEN AUGUSTUSBURG Z. WE. **Note:** Klippe. Dav. #7664.

Date	Mintage	VG	F	VF	XF	Unc
MDCIC(1699)	—	1,650	2,750	—	—	—

Note: Baldwin's Auctions Ltd Auction 49, 9-06, ex-mounted, tooled, otherwise VF realized approximately $2,565

KM# 28 THALER (Shooting)

Silver **Ruler:** Johann Georg **Obv:** Cross in 8-pointed star, ribbon of Order of the Elephant around **Rev:** Crown over two adjacent oval shields, ducal Saxony in left, JG monogram in right, Roman numeral date divided in corners **Rev. Legend:** + SCHIESEN BEY SR. HOCHF. DURCHL. GEBURTSTAG. AUF. DER NEUEN AUGUSTUSB. Z. WEISENF. **Note:** Klippe. Dav. #7665.

Date	Mintage	VG	F	VF	XF	Unc
MDCC(1700)	—	1,050	1,800	3,600	6,000	—

KM# 14 1-1/2 THALER

Silver **Ruler:** Johann Adolf I **Subject:** Birth of Prince Adolf **Obv:** Crowned JA's in palm sprays, shields in corners **Obv. Legend:** AUF DER NEUEN AUGUSTUS BURG ZU WEISSENFELS **Rev:** Sun above child in cradle, Roman numeral date divided in corners **Rev. Legend:** RINGEL RENNEN BEY DER PRINZLICHEN EINSEGNUNG **Note:** Klippe. Dav. #7661.

Date	Mintage	VG	F	VF	XF	Unc
MDCLXXXV(1685) Rare	—	—	—	—	—	—

KM# 15 2 THALER

Silver **Ruler:** Johann Adolf I **Subject:** Birth of Prince Adolf **Obv:** Crowned JA's in palm sprays, shields in corners **Obv. Legend:** AUF DER NEUEN AUGUSTUS BURG ZU WEISSENFELS **Rev:** Sun above child in cradle, Roman numeral date divided in corners **Rev. Legend:** RINGEL RENNEN BEY DER PRINZLICHEN EINSEGNUNG **Note:** Klippe. Dav. #7660.

Date	Mintage	VG	F	VF	XF	Unc
MDCLXXXV(1685) Rare	—	—	—	—	—	—

TRADE COINAGE

KM# 11 DUCAT

Gold **Ruler:** August **Subject:** Death of August's First Wife, Anna Maria von Mecklenburg-Schwerin **Obv:** Crowned AM monogram in palm branches **Obv. Legend:** DEVM. QVI. HABET. OMNIA. HABET. **Rev:** 7-line inscription with dates **Rev. Inscription:** NATA./SVER. 1. IVL. 1627./DENAT./HAL. 11. DEC. 1669/ÆTAT./XLII. M. 5. D./10. **Mint:** Halle **Note:** Struck from Groschen dies, KM #5; FR#1561.

Date	Mintage	VG	F	VF	XF	Unc
1669 HHF	—	525	1,050	2,050	3,450	—

KM# 21 DUCAT

3.5000 g., 0.9860 Gold 0.1109 oz. AGW **Ruler:** Johann Adolf I **Subject:** Death of Johanna Magdalena, Wife of Johann Adolf **Obv:** Capped JA monogram **Rev:** 8-line inscription **Mint:** Weissenfels **Note:** FR#3044.

Date	Mintage	VG	F	VF	XF	Unc
1686 SQ	—	525	1,050	2,050	3,450	—

KM# 23 DUCAT

3.5000 g., 0.9860 Gold 0.1109 oz. AGW **Ruler:** Johann Georg **Subject:** Denmark's Order of the Elephant Conferred upon Johann Georg **Obv:** Full-length figure of duke to right with hand on altar **Rev:** Round Saxony arms in baroque frame, date divided below, surrounded by Order of the Elephant, crown above **Note:** FR#3045.

Date	Mintage	VG	F	VF	XF	Unc
1698	—	650	1,300	2,600	4,500	—

KM# 24 2 DUCAT
Gold **Ruler:** Johann Georg **Subject:** Marriage of Johann Georg and Friderike Elisabeth von Sachsen-Eisenach **Obv:** Two hearts on altar, arms of Saxony infront, rays streaming down from clouds above **Obv. Legend:** COELESTIBVS - IGNIBVS ARDENT **Rev:** 10-line inscription with date

Date	Mintage	VG	F	VF	XF	Unc
1698 Rare	—	—	—	—	—	—

KM# 26 2 DUCAT
Gold **Ruler:** Johann Georg **Subject:** Homage of Langensalza **Obv:** Flaming altar, legend curved above in Gothic letters, 2-line Gothic inscription in exergue **Obv. Legend:** Ein ewiger - Saltz = Bund. **Rev:** 9-line inscription in Gothic letters with date

Date	Mintage	VG	F	VF	XF	Unc
1699 CW Rare	—	—	—	—	—	—

SAXE-ZEITZ-NAUMBURG

Saxe-Zeitz was created at the same time as Saxe-Weissenfels for the fourth son of the elector Johann Georg I., Moritz, was administrator also of the bishopric of Naumburg-Zeitz and a part of Henneberg. At the death of his son Moritz-Wilhelm, a Catholic, in 1718, this line became extinct and reverted to the electoral line.

RULER
Moritz, 1656-1681

DUCHY

STANDARD COINAGE

DAV# 7666 THALER
28.9900 g., Silver **Ruler:** Moritz **Obv:** Bust of Moritz facing **Rev:** Mauritzburg Castle

Date	Mintage	VG	F	VF	XF	Unc
1667	—	650	1,250	2,500	4,000	—

DAV# 7666A 2 THALER
52.1000 g., Silver **Ruler:** Moritz **Note:** Similar to 1 Thaler, Dav. #7666.

Date	Mintage	VG	F	VF	XF	Unc
1667	—	1,900	3,200	4,800	7,200	—

SAXONY

Saxony, located in southeast Germany was founded in 850. The first coinage was struck c. 990. It was divided into two lines in 1464. The electoral right was obtained by the elder line in 1547. During the time of the Reformation, Saxony was one of the more powerful states in central Europe. It became a kingdom in 1806. At the Congress of Vienna in 1815, they were forced to cede half its territories to Prussia.

RULERS
Friedrich Wilhelm von Saxe-Altenburg, Regent, 1591-1601
Christian II, Johann Georg I and August, jointly 1591-1611
Johann Georg I and August, jointly 1611-1615
Johann Georg I, alone 1615-1656
Johann Georg II, 1656-1680
Johann Georg III, 1680-1691
Johann Georg IV, 1691-1694
Friedrich August I, 1694-1733

MINT MARKS
L - Leipzig

MINT OFFICIALS' INITIALS

Annaberg Mint

Initial	Date	Name
Acorn on twig	1621-23	Michael Rothe

Bautzen Mint

CR	1640-78	Constantin Rothe in Dresden for Bautzen
HI	1666-67	Hennig Idlers

Bitterfeld Mint

Acorn w/o twig	1621	Barthel Eckardt

Chemnitz Mint

K in shield	1621-22	Christoph Sundtheim
CF, 2 fish	1678-86	Christoph Fischer
CM	1635	Cornelius Meide
CR, acorn	1640-78	Constantin Rothe
HB ligate	1556-1604	Hans Biener
HvR ligate, swan	1605-24	Heinrich von Rehnen
HI	1624-35	Hans Jacob
IK, 2 crossed arrows	1688-98	Johann Koch
ILH	1698-1716	Johann Lorenz Holland
SD	1635-40	Sebald Dierleber

Eckartsberga Mint

	1621	Christian Gerlach
EB	1621-22	Bernhard Hillard

Ehrenfriedersdorf Mint

Finger ring w/tapered stone	1622	Unknown

Eilenburg Mint

E in shield	1621	Unknown

Gommern Mint

6-pointed star	1621-22	Paul Lieber Paus

Grossenhain Mint

MB and/or 3-pointed rosette	1621-22	Marcus Brun

Grunthal Mint

	1621-23	August Rothe

Langensalza Mint

3 towers	1621	Andreas Becker

Leipzig Mint

EPH, fish	1693-1714	Ernst Peter Hecht
SL, as monogram in shield or w/hunting horn between 2 stag's antlers	1621-22	Stadt Leipzig Reichard Jager

Liebenwerda Mint

LW	1621	Jobst Wenighausen

Lutzen Mint

WQ and/or 4 L's in shape of cross	1621	Wilhelm Quendal

Merseburg Mint

MB and/or rooster	1621-22	Georg Sommerling

Naumburg Mint

N w/ or w/o heart	June 1621	Georg Oppermann
	Summer 1621	Curt Marquardt
	September 1621	Sebastian Hartel
	October 1621	Friedrich Ulm

Neustadt an der Orla Mint

N and/or HT monogram	1621-22	Hans Treuttner
	1621-22	Christoph Krafft

Pirna Mint

GS monogram w/pear on twig	1621-22	Georg Stange

Sangerhausen Mint

S	1621	Heinrich Ulm

Schkeuditz Mint

HVS monogram	1621	Heinrich Ulm

Taucha Mint

T in shield	1621	Matthias von Neuss and David Wolke

Tennstedt Mint

Tree	1621	Unknown

Weida Mint

W (sometimes in shield)	1621-22	Christoph Sundtheim

Zwickau Mint

Anchor and/or 3 swans	1621-22	Adam Prellhoff, Jacob Cern, die-cutter

Arms of Electoral Saxony

2-fold arms divided vertically, 2 crossed swords on left, opened crown curving diagonally from upper left to lower right on right side.

DUCHY AND ELECTORATE

REGULAR COINAGE

KM# 5 PFENNIG
Silver **Obv:** Sasxony arms, initials above **Rev:** Imperial orb in baroque shield divides date **Note:** Varieties exist.

Date	Mintage	VG	F	VF	XF	Unc
1601 HB	—	7.00	13.00	25.00	45.00	—
1602 HB	—	7.00	13.00	25.00	45.00	—
1603 HB	—	7.00	13.00	25.00	45.00	—
1604 HB	—	7.00	13.00	25.00	45.00	—
1605 HB	—	7.00	13.00	25.00	45.00	—
1606 HvR	—	7.00	13.00	25.00	45.00	—
1607 HvR	—	7.00	13.00	25.00	45.00	—
1609 HvR	—	7.00	13.00	25.00	45.00	—
1609 HB	—	7.00	13.00	25.00	45.00	—

Note: Varieties exist

KM# 65 PFENNIG
Silver **Note:** Similar to KM#5.

Date	Mintage	VG	F	VF	XF	Unc
1613 HvR	—	7.00	13.00	25.00	45.00	—
1615 HvR	—	7.00	13.00	25.00	45.00	—

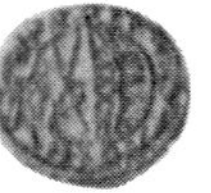

KM# 130 PFENNIG
Silver **Obv:** Oval arms in baroque frame, initials below **Rev:** Imperial orb within shield **Note:** Varieties exist.

Date	Mintage	VG	F	VF	XF	Unc
1620 HvR	—	7.00	13.00	25.00	45.00	—
1621 HvR	—	7.00	13.00	25.00	45.00	—
1622 HvR	—	7.00	13.00	25.00	45.00	—
1623 HvR	—	7.00	13.00	25.00	45.00	—
1624 HvR	—	7.00	13.00	25.00	45.00	—
1625 HI	—	7.00	13.00	25.00	45.00	—
1626 HI	—	7.00	13.00	25.00	45.00	—
1627 HI	—	7.00	13.00	25.00	45.00	—
1628 HI	—	7.00	13.00	25.00	45.00	—
1629 HI	—	7.00	13.00	25.00	45.00	—
1630 HI	—	7.00	13.00	25.00	45.00	—
1631 HI	—	7.00	13.00	25.00	45.00	—
1632 HI	—	7.00	13.00	25.00	45.00	—
1636 SD	—	7.00	13.00	25.00	45.00	—

Date	Mintage	VG	F	VF	XF	Unc
1637 SD	—	7.00	13.00	25.00	45.00	—
1638 SD	—	7.00	13.00	25.00	45.00	—
1639 SD	—	7.00	13.00	25.00	45.00	—
1640 CR	—	7.00	13.00	25.00	45.00	—
1640 SD	—	7.00	13.00	25.00	45.00	—
1641 CR	—	7.00	13.00	25.00	45.00	—
1642 CR	—	7.00	13.00	25.00	45.00	—
1643 CR	—	7.00	13.00	25.00	45.00	—
1644 CR	—	7.00	13.00	25.00	45.00	—
1645 CR	—	7.00	13.00	25.00	45.00	—
1646 CR	—	7.00	13.00	25.00	45.00	—
1647 CR	—	7.00	13.00	25.00	45.00	—
1648 CR	—	7.00	13.00	25.00	45.00	—
1649 CR	—	7.00	13.00	25.00	45.00	—
1650 CR	—	7.00	13.00	25.00	45.00	—
1651 CR	—	7.00	13.00	25.00	45.00	—
1652 CR	—	7.00	13.00	25.00	45.00	—
1653 CR	—	7.00	13.00	25.00	45.00	—
1654 CR	—	7.00	13.00	25.00	45.00	—
1654 CR	—	7.00	13.00	25.00	45.00	—

Note: Varieties exist

KM# 139 PFENNIG

Copper **Note:** Struck at Leipzig. Heart-shaped Saxony arms in ornamented frame, date divided above, S - L divided below.

Date	Mintage	VG	F	VF	XF	Unc
16Z1 SL	—	5.00	11.00	20.00	40.00	—

KM# 138 PFENNIG

Copper **Note:** Date divided above arms. Varieties exist.

Date	Mintage	VG	F	VF	XF	Unc
16Z1	—	5.00	11.00	20.00	40.00	—
16ZZ	—	5.00	11.00	20.00	40.00	—
16Z3	—	5.00	11.00	20.00	40.00	—

KM# 137 PFENNIG

Copper **Note:** Kipper Pfenning. Uniface. Struck at Grunthal. Oval Saxony arms in baroque frame, date above. Varieties exist.

Date	Mintage	VG	F	VF	XF	Unc
16Z1	—	5.00	11.00	20.00	40.00	—
1621	—	5.00	11.00	20.00	40.00	—
1622	—	5.00	11.00	20.00	40.00	—

KM# 140 PFENNIG

Copper **Note:** Oval arms.

Date	Mintage	VG	F	VF	XF	Unc
16Z1 SL	—	5.00	11.00	20.00	40.00	—

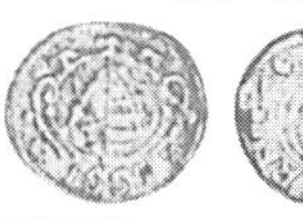

KM# 455 PFENNIG

Copper **Obv:** Round Saxony arms in baroque frame divide initials, date below **Rev:** Imperial orb **Rev. Legend:** OBER. SAX. KREISSES. **Note:** Varieties exist.

Date	Mintage	VG	F	VF	XF	Unc
1657 CR	—	7.00	13.00	25.00	45.00	—
1658 CR	—	7.00	13.00	25.00	45.00	—
1659 CR	—	7.00	13.00	25.00	45.00	—
1660 CR	—	7.00	13.00	25.00	45.00	—
1661 CR	—	7.00	13.00	25.00	45.00	—
1662 CR	—	7.00	13.00	25.00	45.00	—
1663 CR	—	7.00	13.00	25.00	45.00	—
1664 CR	—	7.00	13.00	25.00	45.00	—
1665 CR	—	7.00	13.00	25.00	45.00	—
1667 CR	—	7.00	13.00	25.00	45.00	—

Note: Varieties exist

Date	Mintage	VG	F	VF	XF	Unc
1667 CR	—	7.00	13.00	25.00	45.00	—

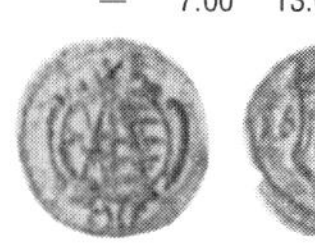

KM# 519 PFENNIG

Billon **Obv:** Oval Saxony arms in ornamented frame, initials below **Rev:** Imperial orb in shield divides date **Note:** Varieties exist.

Date	Mintage	VG	F	VF	XF	Unc
1667 CR	—	7.00	13.00	25.00	45.00	—
1668 CR	—	7.00	13.00	25.00	45.00	—
1669 CR	—	7.00	13.00	25.00	45.00	—
1670 CR	—	7.00	13.00	25.00	45.00	—
1671 CR	—	7.00	13.00	25.00	45.00	—
1672 CR	—	7.00	13.00	25.00	45.00	—
1673 CR	—	7.00	13.00	25.00	45.00	—
1674 CR	—	7.00	13.00	25.00	45.00	—
1675 CR	—	7.00	13.00	25.00	45.00	—
1676 CR	—	7.00	13.00	25.00	45.00	—
1677 CR	—	7.00	13.00	25.00	45.00	—
1679 CF	—	7.00	13.00	25.00	45.00	—

Note: Varieties exist

Date	Mintage	VG	F	VF	XF	Unc
1679 CF	—	7.00	13.00	25.00	45.00	—

KM# 573 PFENNIG

Billon **Obv:** Crowned Saxony arms between 2 palm branches, initials divided below **Note:** Varieties exist.

Date	Mintage	VG	F	VF	XF	Unc
1681 CF	—	7.00	13.00	25.00	45.00	—
1682 CF	—	7.00	13.00	25.00	45.00	—
1683 CF	—	7.00	13.00	25.00	45.00	—
1684 CF	—	7.00	13.00	25.00	45.00	—
1685 CF	—	7.00	13.00	25.00	45.00	—
1686 CF	—	7.00	13.00	25.00	45.00	—
1687	—	7.00	13.00	25.00	45.00	—
1689 IK	—	7.00	13.00	25.00	45.00	—
1691 IK	—	7.00	13.00	25.00	45.00	—

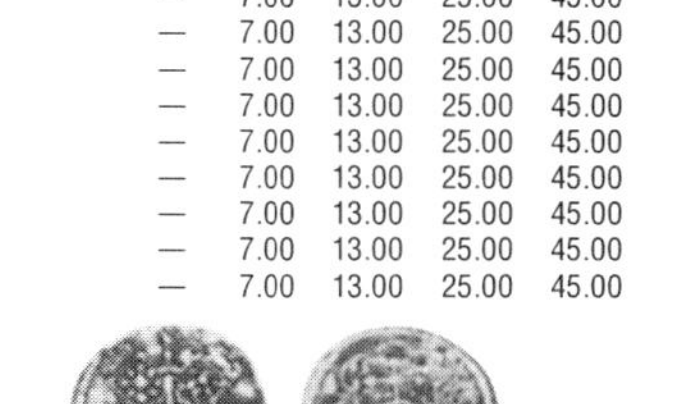
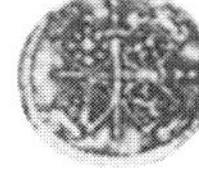

KM# 623 PFENNIG

Billon **Obv:** 4 small crowned shields of arms, 1 in each angle of 2 crossed swords **Rev:** Initials divided at bottom

Date	Mintage	VG	F	VF	XF	Unc
1692 IK	—	7.00	13.00	25.00	45.00	—

KM# 636 PFENNIG

Billon **Obv:** 2 adjacent oval arms in baroque frame, crown above **Note:** Varieties exist.

Date	Mintage	VG	F	VF	XF	Unc
1693 IK	—	7.00	13.00	25.00	45.00	—
1694 EPH	—	7.00	13.00	25.00	45.00	—
1694 IK	—	7.00	13.00	25.00	45.00	—

KM# 663 PFENNIG

Billon **Rev:** Initials at bottom **Note:** Varieties exist.

Date	Mintage	VG	F	VF	XF	Unc
1695 EPH	—	7.00	13.00	25.00	45.00	—
1695 IK	—	7.00	13.00	25.00	45.00	—
1695 EPH	—	7.00	13.00	25.00	45.00	—
1696 IK	—	7.00	13.00	25.00	45.00	—
1697 IK	—	7.00	13.00	25.00	45.00	—
1698 IK	—	7.00	13.00	25.00	45.00	—

KM# 674 PFENNIG

Billon **Obv:** Initials at bottom

Date	Mintage	VG	F	VF	XF	Unc
1696 EPH	—	7.00	13.00	25.00	45.00	—
1697 EPH	—	7.00	13.00	25.00	45.00	—

KM# 702 PFENNIG

Billon, 13.1 mm. **Ruler:** Friedrich August I **Obv:** Crowned 4-fold arms with central shield within palm branches **Rev:** Imperial orb in cartouche divides date

Date	Mintage	VG	F	VF	XF	Unc
1698 ILH	—	7.00	13.00	24.00	45.00	—
1698 LIH	—	7.00	13.00	24.00	45.00	—
1699 ILH	—	7.00	13.00	24.00	45.00	—
1700 ILH	—	7.00	13.00	24.00	45.00	—

KM# 720 PFENNIG

Billon **Obv:** Crowned 4-fold arms with central shild between palm branches **Rev:** Imperial orb in cartouche, date above

Date	Mintage	VG	F	VF	XF	Unc
1700 ILH	—	8.00	16.00	33.00	60.00	—

KM# 6 3 PFENNIGE

Silver **Obv:** 3 small ornate shields of arms, 1 above 2, divide date, mintmasters initials monogram below **Rev:** Imperial orb in baroque frame **Note:** Varieties exist.

Date	Mintage	VG	F	VF	XF	Unc
(16)01 HB	—	13.00	30.00	55.00	100	—
(16)02 HB	—	13.00	30.00	55.00	100	—
(16)03 HB	—	13.00	30.00	55.00	100	—
(16)04 HB	—	13.00	30.00	55.00	100	—
(16)04 HvR	—	13.00	30.00	55.00	100	—
(16)05 HB	—	13.00	30.00	55.00	100	—
(16)06 HvR	—	13.00	30.00	55.00	100	—
(16)07 HvR	—	13.00	30.00	55.00	100	—
(16)08 HvR	—	13.00	30.00	55.00	100	—
(16)09 HvR	—	13.00	30.00	55.00	100	—

Note: Varieties exist

KM# 48 3 PFENNIGE

Silver **Rev:** Orb in ornamented rhombus **Note:** Varieties exist.

Date	Mintage	VG	F	VF	XF	Unc
1612 HvR	—	16.00	33.00	60.00	110	—
1613 HvR	—	16.00	33.00	60.00	110	—
1614 HvR	—	16.00	33.00	60.00	110	—
1615 HvR	—	16.00	33.00	60.00	110	—

KM# 131 3 PFENNIGE

Silver **Rev:** Imperial orb in baroque frame **Note:** Kipper 3 Pfenning. Struck at Dresden.

Date	Mintage	VG	F	VF	XF	Unc
1620 (swan)	—	13.00	30.00	55.00	95.00	—

KM# 152 3 PFENNIGE

Silver **Note:** Ornately-shaped arms, without value III.

Date	Mintage	VG	F	VF	XF	Unc
1621	—	9.00	25.00	40.00	80.00	—

KM# 141 3 PFENNIGE

Silver **Obv:** 3 small shields of arms, 1 above 2 **Rev:** Imperial orb with 3 divides date **Note:** Struck at Grossenhain.

Date	Mintage	VG	F	VF	XF	Unc
1621	—	13.00	30.00	55.00	95.00	—

KM# 142 3 PFENNIGE

Silver **Obv:** Ornate 2-fold arms, angel's head above, symbol in margin at top **Rev:** Value: 3 on imperial orb, date divided in legend at top **Note:** Struck at Merseburg.

Date	Mintage	VG	F	VF	XF	Unc
1621 (rooster	—	13.00	30.00	55.00	95.00	—

KM# 150 3 PFENNIGE

Silver **Note:** Uniface. Heart-shaped two-fold arms in baroque frame, value: III above divides date.

Date	Mintage	VG	F	VF	XF	Unc
1621	—	9.00	25.00	40.00	80.00	—

KM# 144 3 PFENNIGE

Silver **Obv:** 2 adjacent leaf-shaped shields of arms, 5-petaled rosettes above, 3 below **Rev:** Value: 3 on imperial orb divdes date, all in rhombus

Date	Mintage	VG	F	VF	XF	Unc
(16)21	—	9.00	25.00	40.00	80.00	—

KM# 145 3 PFENNIGE

Silver **Obv:** Ornate 2-fold arms, 6-petaled rosette divides date above **Rev:** Value: 3 on imperial orb, 6-petaled rosette at left and right, date divided by cross above

Date	Mintage	VG	F	VF	XF	Unc
(16)21/(16)21	—	9.00	25.00	40.00	80.00	—

KM# 146 3 PFENNIGE

Silver **Obv:** Without date **Rev:** With date

Date	Mintage	VG	F	VF	XF	Unc
(16)21	—	9.00	25.00	40.00	80.00	—

KM# 147 3 PFENNIGE

Silver **Obv:** Ornate 2-fold arms between two 6-petaled rosettes, value: III above divides date

Date	Mintage	VG	F	VF	XF	Unc
1621	—	9.00	25.00	40.00	80.00	—

KM# 148 3 PFENNIGE

Silver **Rev:** Date replaces rosettes

Date	Mintage	VG	F	VF	XF	Unc
16Z1	—	9.00	25.00	40.00	80.00	—

KM# 149 3 PFENNIGE

Silver **Obv:** Without date

Date	Mintage	VG	F	VF	XF	Unc
(16)Z1	—	9.00	25.00	40.00	80.00	—

KM# 344 3 PFENNIGE

Silver **Obv:** Ornate 2-fold arms **Rev:** Value: 3 on imperial orb divides date

Date	Mintage	VG	F	VF	XF	Unc
1622	—	9.00	25.00	40.00	80.00	—

KM# 345 3 PFENNIGE

Silver **Obv:** 2 ornamented adjoining shields of arms **Rev:** Imperial orb in baroque frame divides date

Date	Mintage	VG	F	VF	XF	Unc
(16)22	—	9.00	25.00	40.00	80.00	—

KM# 143 3 PFENNIGE

Silver **Obv:** 3 ornate shields of arms, 1 above 2, divide date **Rev:** 2 crossed swords above 3 in baroque frame

Date	Mintage	VG	F	VF	XF	Unc
1622	—	13.00	30.00	55.00	95.00	—

KM# 385 3 PFENNIGE

Silver **Obv:** 3 small ornate shields of arms, 1 above 2, divide date, initials monogram below **Rev:** Imperial orb in baroque frame **Note:** Varieties exist.

Date	Mintage	VG	F	VF	XF	Unc
1623 HvR	—	9.00	25.00	35.00	65.00	—
1624 HvR	—	9.00	25.00	35.00	65.00	—
1625 HvR	—	9.00	25.00	35.00	65.00	—
1626 HI	—	9.00	25.00	35.00	65.00	—
1627 HI	—	9.00	25.00	35.00	65.00	—
1628 HI	—	9.00	25.00	35.00	65.00	—
1629 HI	—	9.00	25.00	35.00	65.00	—
1630 HI	—	9.00	25.00	35.00	65.00	—
1631 HI	—	9.00	25.00	35.00	65.00	—
1632 HI	—	9.00	25.00	35.00	65.00	—

Date	Mintage	VG	F	VF	XF	Unc
1634 HI	—	9.00	25.00	35.00	65.00	—
1635 HI	—	9.00	25.00	35.00	65.00	—
1636 SD	—	9.00	25.00	35.00	65.00	—
1637 SD	—	9.00	25.00	35.00	65.00	—
1638 SD	—	9.00	25.00	35.00	65.00	—
1639 SD	—	9.00	25.00	35.00	65.00	—
1641 CR	—	9.00	25.00	35.00	65.00	—
1642 CR	—	9.00	25.00	35.00	65.00	—
1643 CR	—	9.00	25.00	35.00	65.00	—
1645 CR	—	9.00	25.00	35.00	65.00	—
1647 CR	—	9.00	25.00	35.00	65.00	—
1648 CR	—	9.00	25.00	35.00	65.00	—
1649 CR	—	9.00	25.00	35.00	65.00	—
1651 CR	—	9.00	25.00	35.00	65.00	—
1652 CR	—	9.00	25.00	35.00	65.00	—
1654 CR	—	9.00	25.00	35.00	65.00	—

KM# 445 3 PFENNIGE

Silver **Obv:** Ornate oval 2-fold arms divide initials, date below **Rev:** Imperial orb with 3 **Rev. Legend:** OBER. SAX. KREISSES **Note:** Varieties exist.

Date	Mintage	VG	F	VF	XF	Unc
1656 CR	—	9.00	25.00	40.00	80.00	—
1659 CR	—	9.00	25.00	40.00	80.00	—
1660 CR	—	9.00	25.00	40.00	80.00	—
1661 CR	—	9.00	25.00	40.00	80.00	—
1662 CR	—	9.00	25.00	40.00	80.00	—
1663 CR	—	9.00	25.00	40.00	80.00	—
1664 CR	—	9.00	25.00	40.00	80.00	—
1665 CR	—	9.00	25.00	40.00	80.00	—

KM# 508 3 PFENNIGE

Silver **Obv:** Angular shield of arms

Date	Mintage	VG	F	VF	XF	Unc
1665 CR	—	9.00	25.00	40.00	80.00	—

KM# 523 3 PFENNIGE

Silver **Obv:** Oval 2-fold arms in baroque frame, date divided by acorn at bottom **Rev:** Imperial orb in baroque frame divides initials **Note:** Varieties exist.

Date	Mintage	VG	F	VF	XF	Unc
1669 CR	—	9.00	25.00	40.00	80.00	—
1679 CF	—	9.00	25.00	40.00	80.00	—

KM# 574 3 PFENNIGE

Silver **Obv:** Crowned 2-fold arms between palm branches, date divided by 2 small fish below

Date	Mintage	VG	F	VF	XF	Unc
1681 CF	—	11.00	27.00	45.00	90.00	—
1682 CF	—	11.00	27.00	45.00	90.00	—

KM# 605 3 PFENNIGE

Silver **Obv:** 2 adjacent oval arms in baroque frames, crown above divides initials **Rev:** Imperial orb with 3 in baroque frame divides date, crossed arrows below

Date	Mintage	VG	F	VF	XF	Unc
1690 IK	—	9.00	25.00	35.00	65.00	—
1691 IK	—	9.00	25.00	35.00	65.00	—

KM# 624 3 PFENNIGE

Silver **Obv:** 4 small crowned shields of arms, 1 in each angle of 2 crossed swords

Date	Mintage	VG	F	VF	XF	Unc
1692 IK	—	9.00	25.00	40.00	80.00	—

KM# 637 3 PFENNIGE

Silver **Obv:** Initials in between arms, near bottom

Date	Mintage	VG	F	VF	XF	Unc
1693 IK	—	9.00	25.00	40.00	70.00	—
1694 IK	—	9.00	25.00	40.00	70.00	—

KM# 665 3 PFENNIGE

Silver **Obv:** Crowned oval 2-fold arms between palm branches **Rev:** Imperial orb with 3 in baroque frame divides date, initials below

Date	Mintage	VG	F	VF	XF	Unc
1695 EPH	—	13.00	30.00	55.00	100	—
1696 EPH	—	13.00	30.00	55.00	100	—

KM# 664 3 PFENNIGE

Silver **Note:** Similar to KM#637.

Date	Mintage	VG	F	VF	XF	Unc
1695 IK	—	9.00	25.00	40.00	70.00	—
1696 IK	—	9.00	25.00	40.00	70.00	—
1697 IK	—	9.00	25.00	40.00	70.00	—

KM# 711 3 PFENNIGE

Silver, 18 mm. **Ruler:** Friedrich August I **Obv:** Crowned round 4-fold arms with central shield of 2-fold arms between 2 palm branches, initials below **Rev:** Value: 3 on imperial orb in baroque frame, date at top

Date	Mintage	VG	F	VF	XF	Unc
1699 ILH	—	11.00	27.00	45.00	90.00	—
1700 ILH	—	11.00	27.00	45.00	90.00	—

KM# 509 6 PFENNIGE (Sechser)

Silver **Obv:** Crowned 2-fold arms in ornamented frame, date below **Rev:** Imperial orb with 6 divides initials **Rev. Legend:** OBER SAX KREISS

Date	Mintage	VG	F	VF	XF	Unc
1665 CR	—	33.00	60.00	100	160	—

KM# 154 3 KREUZER

Silver **Obv:** 2-fold arms in baroque frame **Rev:** Crowned imperial eagle, orb on breast with 3, date above **Note:** Kipper 3 Kreuzer. Struck at Bitterfeld.

Date	Mintage	VG	F	VF	XF	Unc
(16)21 (acorn)	—	25.00	45.00	90.00	150	—
ND1621 (acorn)	—	—	—	—	—	—
ND (acorn)	—	25.00	45.00	90.00	150	—
ND (acorn)	—	25.00	45.00	90.00	150	—

Note: Varieties exist

KM# 155 3 KREUZER

Silver **Obv:** Heart-shaped arms

Date	Mintage	VG	F	VF	XF	Unc
ND (acorn)	—	33.00	60.00	120	200	—

KM# 159 3 KREUZER

Silver **Obv:** 2-fold arms in baroque frame divide date **Rev:** Crowned imperial eagle, orb on breast with 3

Date	Mintage	VG	F	VF	XF	Unc
(16)21 (rosette)	—	33.00	60.00	120	200	—
ND (rosette)	—	33.00	60.00	120	200	—

KM# 163 3 KREUZER

Silver **Rev:** Date divided by crown at top

Date	Mintage	VG	F	VF	XF	Unc
1621 SL	—	33.00	60.00	120	200	—

KM# 165 3 KREUZER

Silver **Obv:** Round 2-fold arms in baroque frame, angel's head above **Rev:** Crowned imperial eagle, 3 in orb on breast, date divided above crown

Date	Mintage	VG	F	VF	XF	Unc
(16)Z1	—	27.00	55.00	110	180	—
(16)21	—	27.00	55.00	110	180	—

KM# 166 3 KREUZER

Silver **Obv:** Round 2-fold arms in plain circle, angel's head above **Rev:** Crowned imperial eagle, 3 on breast, date in legend

Date	Mintage	VG	F	VF	XF	Unc
(16)Z1	—	27.00	55.00	110	180	—

KM# 168 3 KREUZER

Silver **Obv:** Date divided at top **Rev:** Crowned imperial eagle, 3 in orb on breast

Date	Mintage	VG	F	VF	XF	Unc
16)Z1/(16)Z1	—	27.00	55.00	110	180	—

KM# 169 3 KREUZER

Silver **Obv:** Oval 2-fold arms in baroque frame **Rev:** Crowned imperial eagle, 3 in orb on breast, date divided by crown

Date	Mintage	VG	F	VF	XF	Unc
16Z1	—	27.00	55.00	110	180	—

KM# 160 3 KREUZER

5.0400 g., Silver **Note:** Kipper 3 Kreuzer.

Date	Mintage	VG	F	VF	XF	Unc
(16)21 (rosette)	—	40.00	65.00	135	225	—

KM# 167 3 KREUZER

Silver **Note:** Klippe.

Date	Mintage	VG	F	VF	XF	Unc
(16)Z1	—	33.00	60.00	120	200	—

KM# 156 3 KREUZER

Silver **Obv:** 2-fold arms in baroque frame **Rev:** Crowned imperial eagle, orb on breast with 3, date divided above **Note:** Struck at Eckartsberga.

Date	Mintage	VG	F	VF	XF	Unc
16Z1 EB	—	33.00	60.00	120	200	—

KM# 157 3 KREUZER

Silver **Note:** Struck at Gommern. Similar to KM#156. Varieties exist.

Date	Mintage	VG	F	VF	XF	Unc
16Z1 (star)	—	33.00	60.00	120	200	—
1621 (star)	—	33.00	60.00	120	200	—
ND (star)	—	33.00	60.00	120	200	—

KM# 158 3 KREUZER

Silver **Obv:** 2-fold arms in baroque frame, date above **Rev:** Crowned imperial eagle, orb on breast with 3, HAIN above **Note:** Struck at Grossenhain.

Date	Mintage	VG	F	VF	XF	Unc
1621 (rosette)	—	33.00	60.00	120	200	—

KM# 162 3 KREUZER

Silver **Obv:** Round 2-fold arms **Rev:** Crowned imperial eagle, 3 in orb on breast, date in legend **Note:** Struck at Leipzig.

Date	Mintage	VG	F	VF	XF	Unc
16Z1 SL	—	33.00	60.00	120	200	—
1621 SL	—	33.00	60.00	120	200	—

KM# 164 3 KREUZER

Silver **Obv:** Oval 2-fold arms in baroque frame, angel's head above **Rev:** Crowned imperial eagle, 3 in orb on breast, date in legend **Note:** Struck at Merseburg.

Date	Mintage	VG	F	VF	XF	Unc
1621 (rooster)	—	33.00	60.00	120	200	—

KM# 512 3 KREUZER

Silver **Note:** Coinage for Oberlausitz. Struck at Bautzen. Similar to 15 Kreuzer, KM#514 but 3 in oval at bottom.

Date	Mintage	VG	F	VF	XF	Unc
1666 HI	—	65.00	135	250	400	—

KM# 513 6 KREUZER

Silver **Note:** Coinage for Oberlausitz. Struck at Bautzen. Similar to 15 Kreuzer, KM#514 but VI in oval at bottom.

Date	Mintage	VG	F	VF	XF	Unc
1666 HI	—	—	—	—	—	—
1666 HI	—	—	—	—	—	—

KM# 182 12 KREUZER

Silver **Rev:** Without value indicated

Date	Mintage	VG	F	VF	XF	Unc
1621 SVH	—	40.00	80.00	160	275	—

KM# 183 12 KREUZER

Silver **Obv:** Oval arms

Date	Mintage	VG	F	VF	XF	Unc
1621 SVH	—	40.00	80.00	160	275	—

KM# 185 12 KREUZER

Silver **Ruler:** Johann Georg I **Obv:** Heart-shaped arms **Rev:** T in shield at top

Date	Mintage	VG	F	VF	XF	Unc
1621 T	—	45.00	85.00	175	300	—

KM# 187 12 KREUZER

Silver **Rev:** Value (12) in legend at bottom

Date	Mintage	VG	F	VF	XF	Unc
1621 (tree)	—	45.00	85.00	175	300	—

KM# 190 12 KREUZER

Silver **Rev:** 12 in orb on breast

Date	Mintage	VG	F	VF	XF	Unc
16Z1 NN	—	33.00	65.00	135	250	—

KM# 191 12 KREUZER

Silver **Obv:** Heart-shaped arms

Date	Mintage	VG	F	VF	XF	Unc
16Z1	—	40.00	80.00	160	275	—

KM# 192 12 KREUZER

Silver **Obv:** Oval arms

Date	Mintage	VG	F	VF	XF	Unc
16Z1	—	33.00	65.00	135	250	—

KM# 176 12 KREUZER

Silver **Note:** Klippe.

Date	Mintage	VG	F	VF	XF	Unc
1621 (rooster)	—	—	—	—	—	—

KM# 181 12 KREUZER

Silver **Note:** Klippe.

Date	Mintage	VG	F	VF	XF	Unc
1621 SVH	—	—	—	—	—	—

KM# 170 12 KREUZER

Silver **Obv:** Oval 2-fold arms, angel above **Rev:** Crowned imperial eagle, orb on breast, with 1Z, date in legend **Note:** Struck at Bitterfeld. Varieties exist.

Date	Mintage	VG	F	VF	XF	Unc
16Z1 (acorn)	—	40.00	80.00	160	275	—

KM# 171 12 KREUZER

Silver **Obv:** Ornamented heart-shaped arms **Rev:** Value (12) at bottom **Note:** Struck at Grossenhain.

Date	Mintage	VG	F	VF	XF	Unc
1621 (rosette)	—	45.00	85.00	175	300	—

KM# 174 12 KREUZER
Silver **Rev:** Value 12 at bottom **Note:** Struck at Langensalza.

Date	Mintage	VG	F	VF	XF	Unc
1621 (3 towers)	—	45.00	85.00	175	300	—

KM# 175 12 KREUZER
Silver **Obv:** Arms nearly flat on top, rounded on bottom, value (1Z) below **Note:** Struck at Merseburg.

Date	Mintage	VG	F	VF	XF	Unc
1621 (rooster)	—	40.00	80.00	160	275	—

KM# 179 12 KREUZER
Silver **Obv:** Date above angel **Note:** Struck at Pirna.

Date	Mintage	VG	F	VF	XF	Unc
1621 GS	—	40.00	80.00	160	275	—

KM# 180 12 KREUZER
Silver **Rev:** 2 angels behind upper arms, date above, 12 in legend at bottom **Note:** Struck at Schkeuditz. Varieties exist.

Date	Mintage	VG	F	VF	XF	Unc
1621 SVH	—	40.00	80.00	160	275	—
ND SVH	—	40.00	80.00	160	275	—

KM# 184 12 KREUZER
Silver **Rev:** T in small shield in legend at top divides date, where present **Note:** Struck at Taucha. Varieties exist.

Date	Mintage	VG	F	VF	XF	Unc
1621 T	—	45.00	85.00	175	300	—
ND T	—	45.00	85.00	175	300	—

KM# 186 12 KREUZER
Silver **Rev:** Tree between 2 lower arms **Note:** Struck at Tennstedt.

Date	Mintage	VG	F	VF	XF	Unc
1621 (tree)	—	45.00	85.00	175	200	—

KM# 172 12 KREUZER
Silver **Obv:** Oval arms **Rev:** With value **Note:** Varieties exist.

Date	Mintage	VG	F	VF	XF	Unc
1621 (rosette)	—	40.00	80.00	160	275	—
ND (rosette)	—	40.00	80.00	160	275	—

KM# 177 12 KREUZER
Silver **Obv:** Crowned ornamented 2-fold arms **Rev:** 3 small shields of arms, 1 above 2, upper shield divides date

Date	Mintage	VG	F	VF	XF	Unc
1622 MB	—	40.00	80.00	160	275	—
1622 (rooster)	—	40.00	80.00	160	275	—

KM# 193 15 KREUZER (1/6 Thaler)
Silver **Note:** Kipper 15 Kreuzer. Struck at Chemnitz. Similar to 20 Groschen, KM#187 but 15 in small orb at top on reverse.

Date	Mintage	VG	F	VF	XF	Unc
1621 K	—	—	—	—	—	—

KM# 514 15 KREUZER (1/6 Thaler)
Silver **Note:** Coinage for Oberlausitz. Struck at Bautzen.

Date	Mintage	VG	F	VF	XF	Unc
1666 HI	—	90.00	190	325	525	—
1667 HI	—	90.00	190	325	525	—

KM# 524 15 KREUZER (1/6 Thaler)
Silver **Note:** Coinage for Meissen. Struck at Leipzig. Similar to 60 Kreuzer, KM#526, but 15 in legend at bottom on reverse.

Date	Mintage	VG	F	VF	XF	Unc
1669	—	80.00	240	300	500	—

KM# 204 24 KREUZER (8 Groschen)
Silver **Rev:** Date in legend

Date	Mintage	VG	F	VF	XF	Unc
(16)21 SVH	—	45.00	90.00	200	300	—

KM# 194 24 KREUZER (8 Groschen)
Silver **Obv:** Oval 2-fold arms, angel above. **Rev:** Crowned imperial eagle, orb on breast **Note:** Kipper 24 Kreuzer. Struck at Bitterfeld.

Date	Mintage	VG	F	VF	XF	Unc
16Z1 (acorn)	—	55.00	110	220	325	—

KM# 196 24 KREUZER (8 Groschen)
Silver **Obv:** Ornamented heart-shaped arms, angel above **Rev:** 2 angels behind upper arms, date above, 24 in legend **Note:** Struck at Grossenhain.

Date	Mintage	VG	F	VF	XF	Unc
1621 (rooster)	—	60.00	120	225	375	—
1621 MB	—	60.00	120	225	375	—

KM# 197 24 KREUZER (8 Groschen)
Silver **Obv:** Oval 2-fold arms, angel above **Rev:** 3 small shields of arms, 1 above 2, upper shield divides date, value (24) at bottom **Note:** Struck at Langensalza.

Date	Mintage	VG	F	VF	XF	Unc
1621 (3 towers)	—	60.00	120	225	375	—

KM# 201 24 KREUZER (8 Groschen)
Silver **Obv:** Ornamented heart-shaped 2-fold arms, angel above **Rev:** Date above arms, value Z4 in small orb at top in legend **Note:** Struck at Naumburg. Varieties exist.

Date	Mintage	VG	F	VF	XF	Unc
16Z1 ND	—	45.00	90.00	200	300	—
1621 ND	—	45.00	90.00	200	300	—
ND ND	—	45.00	90.00	200	300	—

KM# 202 24 KREUZER (8 Groschen)
Silver **Obv:** Value (24) in legend at bottom **Note:** Struck at Sangerhausen.

Date	Mintage	VG	F	VF	XF	Unc
1621	—	45.00	90.00	200	300	—
1621 S	—	45.00	90.00	200	300	—

KM# 203 24 KREUZER (8 Groschen)
Silver **Obv:** Heart-shaped arms, angel above **Rev:** 2 angels behind upper arms, date above **Note:** Struck at Schkeuditz. Varieties exist.

Date	Mintage	VG	F	VF	XF	Unc
1621 SVH	—	45.00	90.00	200	300	—
(16)21 SVH	—	45.00	90.00	200	300	—
ND SVH	—	45.00	90.00	200	300	—

KM# 206 24 KREUZER (8 Groschen)
Silver **Obv:** Oval 2-fold arms, angel above **Rev:** Date divided at top **Note:** Struck at Taucha. Varieties exist.

Date	Mintage	VG	F	VF	XF	Unc
1621 T	—	65.00	120	250	400	—

KM# 207 24 KREUZER (8 Groschen)
Silver **Obv:** Heart-shaped arms, angel above **Rev:** 3 small shields of arms, 1 above 2, upper shield divides date, tree between lower shields **Note:** Struck at Tennstedt.

Date	Mintage	VG	F	VF	XF	Unc
1621 (tree)	—	65.00	120	250	400	—

KM# 208 24 KREUZER (8 Groschen)
Silver **Obv:** Arms almost oval **Rev:** 2 angels behind upper arms, date above **Note:** Struck at Weida.

Date	Mintage	VG	F	VF	XF	Unc
16Z1 W	—	45.00	90.00	200	300	—
ND W	—	45.00	90.00	200	300	—

KM# 205 24 KREUZER (8 Groschen)
Silver **Obv:** Value (24) at bottom **Rev:** Without angels **Note:** Varieties exist.

Date	Mintage	VG	F	VF	XF	Unc
1621 SVH	—	45.00	90.00	200	300	—
1622 SVH	—	45.00	90.00	200	300	—

KM# 198 24 KREUZER (8 Groschen)
Silver **Obv:** Heart-shaped arms

Date	Mintage	VG	F	VF	XF	Unc
1621 (3 towers)	—	60.00	120	225	375	—

KM# 200 24 KREUZER (8 Groschen)
Silver **Obv:** Crowned ornamented 2-fold arms, value (24) below

Date	Mintage	VG	F	VF	XF	Unc
1622 (rooster)	—	55.00	110	210	325	—
ND (rooster)	—	55.00	110	210	325	—

KM# 199 24 KREUZER (8 Groschen)
Silver **Obv:** Arms nearly flat on top, rounded on bottom, and (Z4) below **Note:** Struck at Merseburg.

Date	Mintage	VG	F	VF	XF	Unc
1622 (rooster)	—	55.00	110	210	325	—

KM# 211 30 KREUZER (1/3 Thaler)
Silver **Obv:** Oval arms, angel above. **Rev:** Crowned imperial eagle with 30 in orb on breast, date in legend **Note:** Kipper 30 Kreuzer. Struck at Eilenburg.

Date	Mintage	VG	F	VF	XF	Unc
1621 E	—	40.00	80.00	160	275	—

KM# 212 30 KREUZER (1/3 Thaler)
Silver **Rev:** Value 30 in small orb at top **Note:** Struck at Grossenhain.

Date	Mintage	VG	F	VF	XF	Unc
1621 (rosette)	—	40.00	80.00	160	275	—

KM# 213 30 KREUZER (1/3 Thaler)
Silver **Obv:** Ornamented heart-shaped 2-fold arms, angel above, value 30 in orb **Rev:** 3 small shields of arms, 1 above 2, angels at sides of upper shield, date divided by lower 2 shields **Note:** Struck at Naumburg.

Date	Mintage	VG	F	VF	XF	Unc
1621 N	—	45.00	90.00	180	300	—

KM# 214 30 KREUZER (1/3 Thaler)
Silver **Obv:** Ornamented heart-shaped arms **Rev:** 2 arms above 1, lower arms divides date **Note:** Struck at Pirna.

Date	Mintage	VG	F	VF	XF	Unc
1621 GS	—	45.00	90.00	180	300	—

KM# 215 30 KREUZER (1/3 Thaler)
Silver **Obv:** Oval 2-fold arms, angel above, value 30 in legend **Rev:** 3 small shields of arms, 1 above 2, upper shield divides date **Note:** Struck at Sangerhausen.

Date	Mintage	VG	F	VF	XF	Unc
1621 S	—	40.00	80.00	160	275	—

KM# 216 30 KREUZER (1/3 Thaler)
Silver **Obv:** Heart-shaped arms **Rev:** 2 arms above 1, lower arms divide date **Note:** Struck at Schkeuditz.

Date	Mintage	VG	F	VF	XF	Unc
1621 SH-S	—	55.00	110	200	325	—

KM# 217 30 KREUZER (1/3 Thaler)
Silver **Obv:** Oval 2-fold arms, angel above **Rev:** Crowned imperial eagle, orb with 30 on breast, date in legend **Note:** Struck at Taucha.

Date	Mintage	VG	F	VF	XF	Unc
1621 T	—	45.00	90.00	180	300	—

KM# 218 30 KREUZER (1/3 Thaler)
Silver **Obv:** Heart-shaped arms, angel above **Rev:** 3 small shields of arms, 1 above 2, upper shield divides date, 30 in legend at top **Note:** Struck at Tennstedt.

Date	Mintage	VG	F	VF	XF	Unc
1621 (tree)	—	55.00	110	200	325	—

KM# 525 30 KREUZER (1/3 Thaler)
Silver **Note:** Coinage for Meissen. Struck at Leipzig.

Date	Mintage	VG	F	VF	XF	Unc
1669	—	60.00	120	220	375	—

KM# 221 60 KREUZER (2/3 Thaler)
Silver **Obv:** Heart-shaped 2-fold arms, angel above (60) at bottom **Rev:** 3 small shields of arms, 1 above 2, date divided by upper arms, T in shield at bottom **Note:** Kipper 60 Kreuzer. Struck at Taucha.

Date	Mintage	VG	F	VF	XF	Unc
1621 T	—	—	—	—	—	—

KM# 526 60 KREUZER (2/3 Thaler)
Silver **Note:** Coinage for Meissen. Struck at Leipzig.

Date	Mintage	VG	F	VF	XF	Unc
1669	—	100	200	375	600	—
1670	—	100	200	375	600	—

KM# 222 120 KREUZER
Silver **Obv:** Heart-shaped 2-fold arms, angel above, (120) at bottom **Rev:** 3 small shields of arms, 1 above 2, 2 angels flank upper arms, date above **Note:** Kipper 120 Kreuzer. Struck at Taucha.

Date	Mintage	VG	F	VF	XF	Unc
ND T	—	—	—	—	—	—
1621 T	—	—	—	—	—	—
ND T T	—	—	—	—	—	—

KM# 224 SCHRECKENBERGER (12 Kreuzer)
Silver **Obv:** Heart-shaped arms **Rev:** 2 angels behind upper arms, date above **Mint:** Dresden

Date	Mintage	VG	F	VF	XF	Unc
1620 (swan)	—	100	200	375	600	—
1621 (swan)	—	100	200	375	600	—

KM# 225 SCHRECKENBERGER (12 Kreuzer)
Silver **Obv:** Arms almost oval

Date	Mintage	VG	F	VF	XF	Unc
1620 (swan)	—	85.00	180	325	525	—
1621 (swan)	—	85.00	180	325	525	—

KM# 226 SCHRECKENBERGER (12 Kreuzer)
Silver **Obv:** Round arms

Date	Mintage	VG	F	VF	XF	Unc
1621 (swan)	—	85.00	180	325	525	—
1622 (swan)	—	85.00	180	325	525	—

KM# 223 SCHRECKENBERGER (12 Kreuzer)
Silver **Obv:** Oval 2-fold arms, angel above **Rev:** 3 small shields of arms, 1 above 2, upper shield divides date **Note:** Struck at Bitterfeld. Varieties exist.

Date	Mintage	VG	F	VF	XF	Unc
1621 (acorn)	—	85.00	180	325	525	—
ND (acorn)	—	85.00	180	325	525	—

KM# 227 SCHRECKENBERGER (12 Kreuzer)
Silver **Obv:** Arms almost oval **Note:** Struck at Eilenburg.

Date	Mintage	VG	F	VF	XF	Unc
1621 E	—	—	—	—	—	—
1621 E	—	—	—	—	—	—

KM# 228 SCHRECKENBERGER (12 Kreuzer)
Silver **Note:** Struck at Gommern.

Date	Mintage	VG	F	VF	XF	Unc
16Z1 (star)	—	—	—	—	—	—

KM# 235 2 SCHRECKENBERGER (24 Kreuzer)
Silver **Obv:** Ornamented heart-shaped 2-fold arms, angel above **Rev:** 3 small arms, 1 above 2, angels left and right of upper shield, date above arms

Date	Mintage	VG	F	VF	XF	Unc
16Z1 W	—	30.00	60.00	120	200	—

KM# 236 2 SCHRECKENBERGER (24 Kreuzer)
Silver **Obv:** Heart-shaped arms, angel above **Rev:** 3 small shields of arms, 1 above 2, upper shield divides date

Date	Mintage	VG	F	VF	XF	Unc
16Z1 W	—	30.00	60.00	120	200	—

KM# 238 2 SCHRECKENBERGER (24 Kreuzer)
Silver **Obv:** Heart-shaped arms **Rev:** 2 angels behind upper arms, date in legend

Date	Mintage	VG	F	VF	XF	Unc
16Z1	—	27.00	45.00	100	180	—

KM# 240 2 SCHRECKENBERGER (24 Kreuzer)
Silver **Rev:** 3 small shields of arms, 1 above 2, upper shield divides date

Date	Mintage	VG	F	VF	XF	Unc
1621	—	27.00	45.00	100	200	—

KM# 229 2 SCHRECKENBERGER (24 Kreuzer)
Silver **Obv:** Ornamented heart-shaped 2-fold arms, angel above **Rev:** 3 small arms, 1 above 2, angels left and right of upper shield, date divided by lower 2 shields **Note:** Kipper 2 Schreckenberger. Struck at Chemnitz.

Date	Mintage	VG	F	VF	XF	Unc
1621 K	—	30.00	60.00	120	200	—

KM# 230 2 SCHRECKENBERGER (24 Kreuzer)
Silver **Obv:** Oval 2-fold arms, angel above **Rev:** Crowned imperial eagle, orb on breast, date in legend **Note:** Struck at Eilenburg.

Date	Mintage	VG	F	VF	XF	Unc
1621 E	—	30.00	60.00	120	200	—

KM# 231 2 SCHRECKENBERGER (24 Kreuzer)
Silver **Obv:** Arms almost oval **Rev:** 2 angels behind upper arms, date above. **Note:** Struck at Gommern.

Date	Mintage	VG	F	VF	XF	Unc
16Z1 (star)	—	30.00	60.00	120	200	—
(16)Z1 (star)	—	30.00	60.00	120	200	—

KM# 232 2 SCHRECKENBERGER (24 Kreuzer)
Silver **Obv:** Heart-shaped arms **Note:** Struck at Leipzig.

Date	Mintage	VG	F	VF	XF	Unc
16Z1 (4L)	—	30.00	60.00	120	200	—
(16)Z1 (4L)	—	30.00	60.00	120	200	—

KM# 233 2 SCHRECKENBERGER (24 Kreuzer)
Silver **Obv:** Arms almost oval **Note:** Struck at Pirna.

Date	Mintage	VG	F	VF	XF	Unc
1621 GS	—	30.00	60.00	120	200	—

KM# 234 2 SCHRECKENBERGER (24 Kreuzer)
Silver **Obv:** Heart-shaped arms **Rev:** 3 small shields of arms, 1 above 2, upper shield divides date **Note:** Struck at Sangerhausen.

Date	Mintage	VG	F	VF	XF	Unc
1621 S	—	30.00	60.00	120	200	—

KM# 237 2 SCHRECKENBERGER (24 Kreuzer)
Silver **Obv:** Oval 2-fold arms, angel above **Note:** Struck at Zwickau.

Date	Mintage	VG	F	VF	XF	Unc
1621 (anchor/3 swans)	—	30.00	60.00	120	200	—

KM# 239 2 SCHRECKENBERGER (24 Kreuzer)
Silver **Rev:** 2 angels behind upper arms, date above **Note:** Varieties exist.

Date	Mintage	VG	F	VF	XF	Unc
16Z1 (bear above shield)	—	27.00	45.00	100	190	—
1621	—	27.00	45.00	100	190	—
ND	—	27.00	45.00	100	190	—

KM# 446 GROSCHEN (1/24 Thaler)
Silver **Subject:** Death of Johann Georg I **Obv:** Bust right holding sword over right shoulder **Rev:** 8-line inscription with Roman numeral dates

Date	Mintage	VG	F	VF	XF	Unc
MDCLVI (1656)	—	20.00	33.00	65.00	120	—

KM# 478 GROSCHEN (1/24 Thaler)
Silver **Subject:** Death of Johann Georg II's Mother, Magdalene Sibylle **Obv:** 7-line inscription **Rev:** 6-line inscription with Roman numeral dates

Date	Mintage	VG	F	VF	XF	Unc
1659 (acorn)	—	33.00	65.00	120	200	—

KM# 592 GROSCHEN (1/24 Thaler)
Silver **Subject:** Death of Johann Georg III's Mother, Magdalene Sibylle **Obv:** MANET in wreath, SOLA. SPES. MEA in band at top **Rev:** 7-line inscription with dates

Date	Mintage	VG	F	VF	XF	Unc
1687	—	—	—	—	—	—

KM# 608 GROSCHEN (1/24 Thaler)
Silver **Subject:** Death of Johann Georg III **Obv:** Arms from clouds holding partly furled flag **Obv. Legend:** IEHOVA VEXILLIVM MEVM **Rev:** 7-line inscription with Roman numeral dates, 1 in small circle at bottom

Date	Mintage	VG	F	VF	XF	Unc
MDCXCI (1691) IK	—	27.00	55.00	90.00	160	—

KM# 643 GROSCHEN (1/24 Thaler)
Silver **Subject:** Death of Johann Georg IV **Obv:** Pyramid with crowned shields of arms on 2 sides **Rev:** 6-line inscription with Roman numeral dates, 1 in small circle below

Date	Mintage	VG	F	VF	XF	Unc
MDCXCIV (1694) IK	—	27.00	55.00	90.00	160	—

KM# 242 2 GROSCHEN (1/12 Thaler)
Silver **Obv:** Ornate 2-fold arms **Rev:** 3 shields of arms, small imperial orb above, date divided at top **Note:** Kipper 2 Groschen. Struck at Dresden.

Date	Mintage	VG	F	VF	XF	Unc
1621 (swan) Rare	—	—	—	—	—	—

KM# 609 2 GROSCHEN (1/12 Thaler)
Silver **Subject:** Death of Johann Georg III **Rev:** Value 2 in oval

Date	Mintage	VG	F	VF	XF	Unc
MDCXCI (1691) IK	—	27.00	55.00	100	165	—

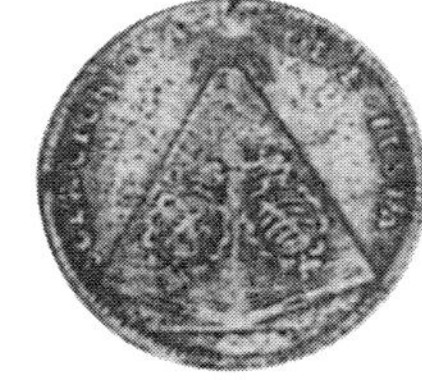

KM# 644 2 GROSCHEN (1/12 Thaler)
Silver **Subject:** Death of Johann Georg IV

Date	Mintage	VG	F	VF	XF	Unc
MDCXCIV (1694) IK	—	27.00	55.00	100	165	—
1694 IK	—	27.00	55.00	100	165	—

KM# 244 4 GROSCHEN
Silver **Obv:** Oval 2-fold arms, angel above **Rev:** Crowned imperial eagle, orb with 4 on breast, date in legend **Note:** Struck at Liebenwerda. Varieties exist.

Date	Mintage	VG	F	VF	XF	Unc
(16)Z1 LW	—	—	—	—	—	—

KM# 246 4 GROSCHEN
Silver **Rev:** 3 small shields of arms, 1 above 2, upper shield divides date **Note:** Struck at Lutzen. Varieties exist.

Date	Mintage	VG	F	VF	XF	Unc
1621 (4L) WQ	—	27.00	55.00	110	220	—
ND (4L)	—	27.00	55.00	110	220	—
1621 (4L)	—	27.00	55.00	110	220	—

KM# 248 4 GROSCHEN
Silver **Obv:** Date above angel **Rev:** Crowned imperial eagle, 4 in orb on eagle's breast **Note:** Struck at Pirna. Varieties exist.

Date	Mintage	VG	F	VF	XF	Unc
1621 GS	—	33.00	60.00	120	225	—

KM# 251 4 GROSCHEN
Silver **Rev:** Mint symbol in legend at top

Date	Mintage	VG	F	VF	XF	Unc
1621	—	20.00	40.00	85.00	180	—

KM# 245 4 GROSCHEN
Silver **Obv:** Heart-shaped arms **Note:** Varieties exist.

Date	Mintage	VG	F	VF	XF	Unc
(16)Z1 LW	—	—	—	—	—	—

KM# 250 4 GROSCHEN
Silver

Date	Mintage	VG	F	VF	XF	Unc
1622 (rosette)	—	20.00	40.00	85.00	190	—

KM# 243 4 GROSCHEN
Silver **Obv:** Crowned ornamented 2-fold arms, value 4 gr. below **Rev:** 3 small shields of arms, 1 above 2, upper shield divides date **Note:** Struck at Leipzig.

Date	Mintage	VG	F	VF	XF	Unc
1622 SL	—	33.00	60.00	120	225	—

KM# 249 4 GROSCHEN
Silver **Note:** Struck at Zwickau. Similar to 8 Groschen, KM#359, but value 4 gr at bottom on reverse.

Date	Mintage	VG	F	VF	XF	Unc
1622 (anchor & 3 swans)	—	33.00	60.00	120	225	—

KM# 252 5 GROSCHEN
Silver **Note:** Kipper 5 Groschen. Struck at Dresden. Similar to 20 Groschen, KM#253, but value (5) bottom reverse.

Date	Mintage	VG	F	VF	XF	Unc
1622 (swan)	—	—	—	—	—	—

KM# 349 8 GROSCHEN (1/3 Thaler)
Silver **Note:** Kipper 8 Groschen. Struck at Annaberg. Similar to 20 Groschen, KM#253, but value (8gr) at bottom of obverse.

Date	Mintage	VG	F	VF	XF	Unc
1622 (acorn)	—	27.00	45.00	90.00	180	—

KM# 347 8 GROSCHEN (1/3 Thaler)
Silver **Note:** Klippe.

Date	Mintage	VG	F	VF	XF	Unc
1622 SL	—	—	—	—	—	—

KM# 353 8 GROSCHEN (1/3 Thaler)
Silver **Obv:** Crowned ornamented 2-fold arms, value 8 gr below **Note:** Struck at Chemnitz. Varieties exist.

Date	Mintage	VG	F	VF	XF	Unc
16ZZ K	—	27.00	45.00	100	190	—
1622 K	—	27.00	45.00	100	190	—

KM# 354 8 GROSCHEN (1/3 Thaler)
Silver **Obv:** Crowned 2-fold arms in baroque frame **Rev:** Value at bottom **Note:** Struck at Ehrenfriedersdorf. Varieties exist.

Date	Mintage	VG	F	VF	XF	Unc
1622 (ring)	—	30.00	60.00	120	200	—

KM# 346 8 GROSCHEN (1/3 Thaler)
Silver **Obv:** Crowned ornamented 2-fold arms, value 8 gr below **Rev:** 3 small shields of arms, 1 above 2, upper shield divides date **Note:** Struck at Leipzig. Varieties exist.

Date	Mintage	VG	F	VF	XF	Unc
16ZZ SL	—	33.00	65.00	135	240	—
1622 SL	—	33.00	65.00	135	240	—

KM# 355 8 GROSCHEN (1/3 Thaler)
Silver **Note:** Struck at Neustadt. Similar to KM#359, but value at bottom on obverse.

Date	Mintage	VG	F	VF	XF	Unc
1622 N - HT	—	27.00	45.00	100	190	—

KM# 358 8 GROSCHEN (1/3 Thaler)
Silver **Note:** Struck at Pirna. Similar to KM#359.

Date	Mintage	VG	F	VF	XF	Unc
1622 GS	—	30.00	60.00	120	200	—

KM# 359 8 GROSCHEN (1/3 Thaler)
Silver **Note:** Struck at Weida. Varieties exist.

Date	Mintage	VG	F	VF	XF	Unc
16ZZ W	—	27.00	45.00	100	190	—

KM# 360 8 GROSCHEN (1/3 Thaler)
Silver **Note:** Struck at Zwickau.

Date	Mintage	VG	F	VF	XF	Unc
1622 (anchor/3 swan)	—	27.00	45.00	100	190	—

KM# 357 8 GROSCHEN (1/3 Thaler)
Silver **Obv:** Large, ornately-shaped arms. **Note:** Varieties exist.

Date	Mintage	VG	F	VF	XF	Unc
16ZZ N	—	30.00	60.00	120	200	—

KM# 348 8 GROSCHEN (1/3 Thaler)
Silver **Obv:** Value 8 at top

Date	Mintage	VG	F	VF	XF	Unc
1622 SL	—	33.00	65.00	135	240	—

KM# 350 8 GROSCHEN (1/3 Thaler)
Silver **Rev:** Value at bottom

Date	Mintage	VG	F	VF	XF	Unc
1622 (acorn)	—	27.00	45.00	90.00	180	—

KM# 351 8 GROSCHEN (1/3 Thaler)
Silver **Rev:** Similar to KM#359

Date	Mintage	VG	F	VF	XF	Unc
1622 (acorn)	—	27.00	45.00	90.00	180	—

KM# 352 8 GROSCHEN (1/3 Thaler)
Silver **Obv:** Crowned 2-fold arms in baroque frame, value at bottom in legend

Date	Mintage	VG	F	VF	XF	Unc
1622 (acorn)	—	27.00	45.00	90.00	180	—
1623 (acorn)	—	27.00	45.00	90.00	180	—

KM# 356 8 GROSCHEN (1/3 Thaler)
Silver **Rev:** Value at bottom

Date	Mintage	VG	F	VF	XF	Unc
16ZZ N	—	27.00	45.00	100	190	—

KM# 361 8 GROSCHEN (1/3 Thaler)
Silver

Date	Mintage	VG	F	VF	XF	Unc
16ZZ (rosette)	—	20.00	35.00	75.00	140	—
1622 (rosette)	—	20.00	35.00	75.00	140	—
16ZZ (rosette/star)	—	20.00	35.00	75.00	140	—
1622 (:8:)	—	20.00	35.00	75.00	140	—

KM# 527 8 GROSCHEN (1/3 Thaler)
Silver **Note:** Coinage for Meissen. Struck at Leipzig. Similar to 60 Kreuzer, KM#526, but date divided by crown above arms, value (8gr) on reverse.

Date	Mintage	VG	F	VF	XF	Unc
1669	—	135	275	425	725	—

KM# A362 10 GROSCHEN
Silver **Note:** Kipper 10 Groschen. Struck at Annaberg. Similar to 20 Groschen, KM#253, but value (10gr) on obverse. Prev. KM#362.

Date	Mintage	VG	F	VF	XF	Unc
1622 (acorn)	—	45.00	80.00	160	275	—

KM# A364 10 GROSCHEN
Silver **Obv:** Round arms **Note:** Similar to 8 Groschen, KM#359, but value: 10gr. Prev. KM#364.

Date	Mintage	VG	F	VF	XF	Unc
1622 (swan)	—	40.00	65.00	135	275	—
1623 (swan)	—	40.00	65.00	135	275	—

KM# A363 10 GROSCHEN
Silver **Obv:** Round arms **Note:** Struck at Dresden. Prev. KM#363.

Date	Mintage	VG	F	VF	XF	Unc
16ZZ (swan)	—	40.00	65.00	135	275	—
1622 (swan)	—	40.00	65.00	135	275	—
1623 (swan)	—	40.00	65.00	135	275	—

KM# 256 20 GROSCHEN
Silver **Obv:** Heart-shaped 2-fold arms **Note:** Struck at Dresden.

Date	Mintage	VG	F	VF	XF	Unc
1620 (swan)	—	55.00	110	220	375	—

KM# 257 20 GROSCHEN
Silver **Obv:** Arms nearly flat on top, curved on bottom **Note:** Varieties exist.

Date	Mintage	VG	F	VF	XF	Unc
1620 (swan)	—	33.00	65.00	135	225	—
1621 (swan)	—	33.00	65.00	135	225	—
16Z1 (swan)	—	33.00	65.00	135	225	—
1622 (swan)	—	33.00	65.00	135	225	—

KM# 258 20 GROSCHEN
Silver **Obv:** Without indication of value. Hybrid strike

Date	Mintage	VG	F	VF	XF	Unc
1621 (swan)	—	33.00	65.00	135	225	—

KM# 261 20 GROSCHEN
Silver **Rev:** 3 small arms, 1 above 2, angels at left and right of upper shield, date above

Date	Mintage	VG	F	VF	XF	Unc
1621 (rooster)	—	45.00	80.00	160	275	—

KM# 253 20 GROSCHEN
Silver **Obv:** Heart-shaped 2-fold arms in baroque frame, angel below, value: 20gr in legend at bottom **Rev:** 3 small arms, 1 above 2, angels at left and right of upper shield, date above **Note:** Kipper 20 Groschen. Struck at Annaberg.

Date	Mintage	VG	F	VF	XF	Unc
1621 (acorn)	—	45.00	80.00	160	275	—

KM# 265 20 GROSCHEN
Silver **Note:** Klippe.

Date	Mintage	VG	F	VF	XF	Unc
1621 (anchor & 3 swans)	—	—	—	—	—	—

KM# 260 20 GROSCHEN
Silver **Obv:** Arms nearly flat on top, curved on bottom divide date **Note:** Struck at Merseburg.

Date	Mintage	VG	F	VF	XF	Unc
1621 (rooster)	—	45.00	80.00	160	275	—

KM# 262 20 GROSCHEN
Silver **Obv:** Arms nearly flat on top, curved on bottom **Note:** Struck at Naumburg.

Date	Mintage	VG	F	VF	XF	Unc
1621 N	—	55.00	110	220	375	—

KM# 263 20 GROSCHEN
Silver **Note:** Struck at Pirna.

Date	Mintage	VG	F	VF	XF	Unc
1621 GS	—	55.00	110	220	375	—

KM# 264 20 GROSCHEN
Silver **Obv:** Value in legend at top **Note:** Struck at Zwickau.

Date	Mintage	VG	F	VF	XF	Unc
1621 (anchor & 3 swans)	—	33.00	65.00	135	225	—
1622 (anchor & 3 swans)	—	33.00	65.00	135	225	—

KM# 254 20 GROSCHEN
Silver **Obv:** Arms nearly flat on top , curved on bottom **Note:** Varieties exist.

Date	Mintage	VG	F	VF	XF	Unc
1621 (acorn)	—	45.00	80.00	160	275	—
1622 (acorn)	—	45.00	80.00	160	275	—

KM# 255 20 GROSCHEN
Silver **Note:** Struck at Chemnitz.

Date	Mintage	VG	F	VF	XF	Unc
1622 K	—	55.00	110	220	375	—

KM# 259 20 GROSCHEN
Silver **Note:** Struck at Leipzig. Similar to KM#253, but oval arms on obverse.

Date	Mintage	VG	F	VF	XF	Unc
1622 SL	—	55.00	110	220	375	—

KM# 266 30 GROSCHEN
Silver **Obv:** Arms nearly flat on top, curved on bottom, angel above, value (30 gr) in legend at bottom **Rev:** Similar to 20 Groschen, KM#253 **Note:** Kipper 30 Groschen. Struck at Annaberg. Varieties exist.

Date	Mintage	VG	F	VF	XF	Unc
1621 (acorn)	—	40.00	85.00	160	275	—
1622 (acorn)	—	40.00	85.00	160	275	—
1623 (acorn)	—	40.00	85.00	160	275	—

KM# 273 30 GROSCHEN
Silver **Note:** Klippe.

Date	Mintage	VG	F	VF	XF	Unc
1621 N	—	—	—	—	—	—

KM# 272 30 GROSCHEN
Silver **Note:** Struck at Naumburg.

Date	Mintage	VG	F	VF	XF	Unc
1621 N	—	40.00	85.00	160	275	—

KM# 277 30 GROSCHEN
Silver **Rev:** T in small shield **Note:** Struck at Taucha.

Date	Mintage	VG	F	VF	XF	Unc
1621 T	—	60.00	120	220	375	—

KM# 274 30 GROSCHEN
Silver **Rev:** N in small shield at top **Note:** Varieties exist.

Date	Mintage	VG	F	VF	XF	Unc
16Z1 N	—	40.00	85.00	160	275	—
16ZZ N	—	40.00	85.00	160	275	—

KM# 278 30 GROSCHEN
Silver **Rev:** W at top **Note:** Struck at Weida. Varieties exist.

Date	Mintage	VG	F	VF	XF	Unc
1622 W	—	60.00	120	220	375	—

KM# 279 30 GROSCHEN
Silver **Note:** Struck at Zwickau.

Date	Mintage	VG	F	VF	XF	Unc
1622 (anchor & 3 swans)	—	45.00	85.00	160	275	—

KM# 276 30 GROSCHEN
Silver **Obv:** Arms nearly flat on top, curved on bottom **Note:** Struck at Pirna. Varieties exist.

Date	Mintage	VG	F	VF	XF	Unc
1622 GS	—	60.00	120	220	375	—
Note: Varieties exist						
1622 GS	—	60.00	120	220	375	—

KM# 270 30 GROSCHEN
Silver **Obv:** Arms nearly flat on top, curved on bottom

Date	Mintage	VG	F	VF	XF	Unc
1622 SL	—	55.00	90.00	180	300	—

KM# 275 30 GROSCHEN
Silver **Obv:** Arms almost round

Date	Mintage	VG	F	VF	XF	Unc
16ZZ N	—	40.00	85.00	160	275	—

KM# 280 30 GROSCHEN
Silver **Note:** Klippe.

Date	Mintage	VG	F	VF	XF	Unc
1622 (anchor & 3 swans)	—	65.00	120	200	325	—

KM# 267 30 GROSCHEN
Silver **Rev:** K in shield at top **Note:** Struck at Chemnitz.

Date	Mintage	VG	F	VF	XF	Unc
1622 K	—	60.00	120	220	375	—

KM# 268 30 GROSCHEN
Silver **Note:** Struck at Dresden. Similar to 20 Groschen, KM#253 but (30 gr) in legend at bottom on obverse. Varieties exist.

Date	Mintage	VG	F	VF	XF	Unc
1622 (swan)	—	40.00	85.00	160	275	—
1623 (swan)	—	40.00	85.00	160	275	—

KM# 269 30 GROSCHEN
Silver **Obv:** Oval arms **Note:** Struck at Leipzig.

Date	Mintage	VG	F	VF	XF	Unc
1622 SL	—	55.00	90.00	180	300	—

KM# 271 30 GROSCHEN
Silver **Note:** Struck at Merseburg.

Date	Mintage	VG	F	VF	XF	Unc
1622 (rooster)	—	60.00	120	220	375	—

KM# 284 40 GROSCHEN
Silver **Note:** Varieties exist.

Date	Mintage	VG	F	VF	XF	Unc
1620 (swan)	—	55.00	110	200	375	—
1621 (swan)	—	55.00	110	200	375	—
16Z1 (swan)	—	55.00	110	200	375	—
1622 (swan)	—	55.00	110	200	375	—

KM# 281 40 GROSCHEN

Silver **Rev:** Shield divides 2 half-length men in inner circle, legend around **Mint:** Annaberg **Note:** Similar to KM#284. Varieties exist.

Date	Mintage	VG	F	VF	XF	Unc
1621 (acorn)	—	65.00	135	275	475	—
1622 (acorn)	—	65.00	135	275	475	—

KM# 286 40 GROSCHEN

Silver **Obv:** Date divided by arms **Note:** Struck at Merseburg.

Date	Mintage	VG	F	VF	XF	Unc
1621 (rooster)	—	80.00	160	300	500	—

KM# 289 40 GROSCHEN

Silver **Note:** Struck at Naumburg. Similar to KM#284.

Date	Mintage	VG	F	VF	XF	Unc
1621 N	—	65.00	135	275	450	—

KM# 291 40 GROSCHEN

Silver **Note:** Struck at Pirna. Similar to KM#284. Varieties exist.

Date	Mintage	VG	F	VF	XF	Unc
1621 GS	—	55.00	110	200	375	—
1622 GS	—	55.00	110	200	375	—

KM# 292 40 GROSCHEN

Silver **Rev:** Date divided by T in shield at top **Note:** Struck at Taucha. Varieties exist.

Date	Mintage	VG	F	VF	XF	Unc
1621 T	—	80.00	160	300	500	—
ND T	—	80.00	160	300	500	—

KM# 295 40 GROSCHEN

Silver **Note:** Struck at Weida. Similar to KM#284, but W in shield at top on reverse. Varieties exist.

Date	Mintage	VG	F	VF	XF	Unc
16ZZ W	—	55.00	110	200	375	—
16Z1 W	—	55.00	110	200	375	—
16ZZ W	—	55.00	110	200	375	—

Note: Varieties exist

KM# 287 40 GROSCHEN

Silver **Obv:** Date above arms

Date	Mintage	VG	F	VF	XF	Unc
1621 (rooster)	—	80.00	160	300	500	—

KM# 290 40 GROSCHEN

Silver **Obv:** Large oval 2-fold arms in baroque frame, value (40) in legend at bottom. **Rev:** N in small shield at top

Date	Mintage	VG	F	VF	XF	Unc
16Z1 N	—	65.00	135	275	475	—

KM# 293 40 GROSCHEN

Silver **Obv:** Oval arms **Rev:** Date below T in shield at top

Date	Mintage	VG	F	VF	XF	Unc
1621 T	—	80.00	160	300	500	—

KM# 296 40 GROSCHEN

Silver **Obv:** Crowned nearly oval 2-fold arms in baroque frame, value 40 gr in legend at top **Rev:** 3 shields of arms, 1 above 2, upper arms divide date

Date	Mintage	VG	F	VF	XF	Unc
1621 (anchor & 3 swans)	—	45.00	80.00	140	250	—

KM# 298 40 GROSCHEN

Silver **Obv:** Date divided by arms

Date	Mintage	VG	F	VF	XF	Unc
1621 (anchor & 3 swans)	—	33.00	60.00	120	220	—

KM# 299 40 GROSCHEN

Silver **Obv:** Value (40 gr) in legend at bottom

Date	Mintage	VG	F	VF	XF	Unc
1621 (anchor & 3 swans)	—	33.00	60.00	120	220	—

KM# 288 40 GROSCHEN

Silver **Obv:** Similar to KM#286 **Rev:** Similar to KM#287 **Note:** Hybrid Strike.

Date	Mintage	VG	F	VF	XF	Unc
1621/1621 (rooster)	—	80.00	160	300	500	—
1622/1622 (rooster)	—	80.00	160	300	500	—

KM# 300 40 GROSCHEN

Silver **Rev:** Similar to KM#297 **Note:** Hybrid Strike.

Date	Mintage	VG	F	VF	XF	Unc
1621/1621 (anchor & 3 swans)	—	33.00	60.00	120	220	—

KM# 297 40 GROSCHEN

Silver **Note:** Similar to KM#284, but value in legend at top of obverse.

Date	Mintage	VG	F	VF	XF	Unc
1621 (anchor & 3 swans)	—	45.00	80.00	145	280	—
1622 (anchor & 3 swans)	—	45.00	80.00	145	280	—

KM# 301 40 GROSCHEN

Silver **Note:** Similar to KM#284.

Date	Mintage	VG	F	VF	XF	Unc
1622 (anchor & 3 swans)	—	33.00	60.00	120	220	—

KM# 282 40 GROSCHEN

Silver **Note:** Struck at Chemnitz. Similar to KM#216, but K in shield at top of reverse.

Date	Mintage	VG	F	VF	XF	Unc
1622 K	—	55.00	165	300	500	—

KM# 285 40 GROSCHEN

Silver **Obv:** Oval arms **Note:** Struck at Leipzig.

Date	Mintage	VG	F	VF	XF	Unc
1622 SL	—	85.00	165	300	500	—

KM# 371 60 GROSCHEN

Silver **Note:** Klippe.

Date	Mintage	VG	F	VF	XF	Unc
16Z1 N	—	—	—	—	—	—

KM# 375 60 GROSCHEN

Silver **Obv:** Heart-shaped arms **Rev:** T in shield bottom **Note:** Struck at Taucha.

Date	Mintage	VG	F	VF	XF	Unc
1621 T	—	325	525	1,000	1,650	—

KM# 376 60 GROSCHEN

Silver **Rev:** W at top **Note:** Struck at Weida. Varieties exist.

Date	Mintage	VG	F	VF	XF	Unc
16ZZ W	—	60.00	120	220	375	—
16ZZ W	—	60.00	120	220	375	—

Note: Varieties exist

KM# 369 60 GROSCHEN

Silver **Note:** Struck at Naumburg.

Date	Mintage	VG	F	VF	XF	Unc
1621 N	—	45.00	85.00	165	275	—

KM# 370 60 GROSCHEN

Silver **Rev:** N in small shield at top **Note:** Struck at Neustadt.

Date	Mintage	VG	F	VF	XF	Unc
16Z1 N	—	45.00	85.00	165	275	—
16ZZ N	—	45.00	85.00	165	275	—
16ZZ N - HT	—	45.00	85.00	165	275	—

KM# 373 60 GROSCHEN

Silver **Obv:** Arms nearly flat on top, curved at bottom **Note:** Struck at Pirna. Varieties exist.

Date	Mintage	VG	F	VF	XF	Unc
1622 GS	—	45.00	85.00	165	275	—

KM# 377 60 GROSCHEN

Silver **Obv:** Arms nearly flat on top, curved at bottom, value in legend at top **Note:** Struck at Zwickau.

Date	Mintage	VG	F	VF	XF	Unc
1622 (anchor & 3 swans)	—	55.00	100	200	325	—

KM# 366 60 GROSCHEN

Silver **Obv:** Arms nearly flat on top, curved on bottom, value (60 gr) **Note:** Varieties exist.

Date	Mintage	VG	F	VF	XF	Unc
16ZZ SL	—	45.00	85.00	165	275	—
1622 SL	—	45.00	85.00	165	275	—

KM# 380 60 GROSCHEN

Silver **Note:** Varieties exist.

Date	Mintage	VG	F	VF	XF	Unc
1622 (flying bird)	—	40.00	80.00	160	275	—
1622 (trefoil)	—	40.00	80.00	160	275	—

KM# 374 60 GROSCHEN

Silver **Note:** Klippe.

Date	Mintage	VG	F	VF	XF	Unc
1622 GS	—	—	—	—	—	—

KM# 379 60 GROSCHEN

Silver **Note:** Klippe.

Date	Mintage	VG	F	VF	XF	Unc
1622 (anchor & 3 swans)	—	—	—	—	—	—

KM# 362 60 GROSCHEN

Silver **Obv:** Arms nearly flat on top, curved at bottom, value (60 gr) in legend at bottom **Rev:** 3 shields of arms, 1 above 2, upper arms divide date **Note:** Struck at Annaberg. Varieties exist.

Date	Mintage	VG	F	VF	XF	Unc
1622 (acorn)	—	45.00	85.00	165	275	—
1623 (acorn)	—	45.00	85.00	165	275	—

KM# 363 60 GROSCHEN

Silver **Rev:** K in shield at top **Note:** Struck at Chemnitz.

Date	Mintage	VG	F	VF	XF	Unc
1622 K	—	60.00	120	220	375	—

KM# 364 60 GROSCHEN

Silver **Rev:** Without initial in shield at top **Note:** Struck at Dresden. Varieties exist.

Date	Mintage	VG	F	VF	XF	Unc
1622 (swan)	—	45.00	85.00	165	275	—
1623 (swan)	—	45.00	85.00	165	275	—

KM# 365 60 GROSCHEN

Silver **Note:** Struck at Leipzig. Similar to 20 Groschen, KM#253, but value (60 gr) on obverse.

Date	Mintage	VG	F	VF	XF	Unc
1622 SL	—	45.00	85.00	165	275	—

KM# 367 60 GROSCHEN

Silver **Obv:** Arms nearly flat on top, curved at bottom, (60 gr) in legend at bottom **Rev:** 3 shields of arms, 1 above 2, upper arms divide date **Note:** Struck at Merseburg.

Date	Mintage	VG	F	VF	XF	Unc
1622 MB(rooster)	—	45.00	85.00	165	275	—
1622 (rooster)	—	45.00	85.00	165	275	—

KM# 372 60 GROSCHEN

Silver **Obv:** Heart-shaped arms

Date	Mintage	VG	F	VF	XF	Unc
16ZZ N	—	—	—	—	—	—

KM# 378 60 GROSCHEN

Silver **Obv:** Value in legend at bottom

Date	Mintage	VG	F	VF	XF	Unc
1622 (anchor & 3 swans)	—	45.00	85.00	165	275	—

KM# 368 60 GROSCHEN

Silver **Note:** Klippe.

Date	Mintage	VG	F	VF	XF	Unc
1622 MB/(rooster)	—	—	—	—	—	—

KM# 625 1/48 THALER (1/2 Groschen)

Silver **Obv:** Mintmasters initials at bottom **Rev:** Value: 48/EINEN/THAL/date, titles of Johann Georg IV

Date	Mintage	VG	F	VF	XF	Unc
1692 IK	—	8.00	16.00	33.00	60.00	—

KM# 666 1/48 THALER (1/2 Groschen)

Silver **Obv:** Crowned 2-fold arms between palm branches, initials divided near bottom **Note:** Varieties exist.

Date	Mintage	VG	F	VF	XF	Unc
1695 EPH	—	8.00	16.00	33.00	60.00	—
1695 IK	—	8.00	16.00	33.00	60.00	—
1696 EPH	—	8.00	16.00	33.00	60.00	—
1696 IK	—	8.00	16.00	33.00	60.00	—

KM# 703 1/48 THALER (1/2 Groschen)

Silver **Ruler:** Friedrich August I **Obv:** Small branch at sides of arms **Rev:** Crossed palm fronds

Date	Mintage	VG	F	VF	XF	Unc
1698 ILH	—	8.00	16.00	33.00	60.00	—

KM# 712 1/48 THALER (1/2 Groschen)
Silver **Ruler:** Johann Georg IV **Obv:** Crowned round 4-fold arms with crowned central shield of 2-fold arms, between 2 crossed palm branches, initials below **Rev:** Value and date in palm wreath

Date	Mintage	VG	F	VF	XF	Unc
1699 ILH	—	8.00	16.00	33.00	60.00	—
1700 ILH	—	8.00	16.00	33.00	60.00	—

KM# 7 1/24 THALER (Groschen)
Silver **Obv:** 2 ornate adjacent shields of arms, small imperial orb divides date above, titles of 3 brothers **Rev:** Ornate helmet above arms of crossed swords, titles continued

Date	Mintage	VG	F	VF	XF	Unc
1601 HB	—	45.00	85.00	160	275	—

KM# 11 1/24 THALER (Groschen)
Silver **Obv:** Ornate helmet above arms of crossed swords, titles of Christian II **Rev:** 2 ornate adjacent shields of arms, small imperial orb divides date above, titles continued **Note:** Varieties exist.

Date	Mintage	VG	F	VF	XF	Unc
1601 HB	—	33.00	65.00	120	225	—
1602 HB	—	33.00	65.00	120	225	—
1603 HB	—	33.00	65.00	120	225	—
1604 HB	—	33.00	65.00	120	225	—
1605 HB	—	33.00	65.00	120	225	—
1605 HvR	—	33.00	65.00	120	225	—
1606 HvR	—	33.00	65.00	120	225	—
1607 HvR	—	33.00	65.00	120	225	—
1608 HvR	—	33.00	65.00	120	225	—
1610 HvR	—	33.00	65.00	120	225	—
1611 HvR	—	33.00	65.00	120	225	—

KM# 37 1/24 THALER (Groschen)
Silver **Obv:** 2 small adjacent shields of arms, small orb above divides date, titles of Johann Georg I **Rev:** 3 small shields of arms, 1 above 2, titles of August

Date	Mintage	VG	F	VF	XF	Unc
1611 (swan)	—	40.00	75.00	140	250	—
1612 (swan)	—	40.00	75.00	140	250	—

KM# 49 1/24 THALER (Groschen)
Silver **Obv:** 2-fold arms in baroque frame divide date, small orb above, titles of Johann Georg I **Rev:** 4-fold arms, vicariat titles **Note:** Vicariat Issue

Date	Mintage	VG	F	VF	XF	Unc
1612 (swan)	—	—	—	—	—	—

KM# 66 1/24 THALER (Groschen)
Silver **Obv:** Ornamented 2-fold arms divide date, small orb above, titles of Johann Georg I **Rev:** Ornamented 4-fold arms, titles of August

Date	Mintage	VG	F	VF	XF	Unc
1613 (swan)	—	40.00	70.00	140	250	—
1614 (swan)	—	40.00	70.00	140	250	—

KM# 70 1/24 THALER (Groschen)
Silver **Obv:** Oval 2-fold arms in baroque frame, titles of Johann Georg I **Rev:** 3 small ornately-shaped shields of arms, 2 above 1, small orb divides date at top, titles of August

Date	Mintage	VG	F	VF	XF	Unc
1614 (swan)	—	33.00	65.00	120	225	—
1615 (swan)	—	33.00	65.00	120	225	—

KM# 71 1/24 THALER (Groschen)
Silver **Obv:** Titles of Johann Georg I **Note:** Kipper 1/24 Thaler. All Kipper groschen are of a small module, usually under 20 mm in diameter. Varieties exist.

Date	Mintage	VG	F	VF	XF	Unc
1614 (swan)	—	33.00	65.00	120	225	—
1616 (swan)	—	33.00	65.00	120	225	—
1619 (swan)	—	33.00	65.00	120	225	—
1620 (swan)	—	33.00	65.00	120	225	—
1621 (swan)	—	33.00	65.00	120	225	—
1622 (swan)	—	33.00	65.00	120	225	—
1623 (swan)	—	33.00	65.00	120	225	—
1624 (swan)	—	33.00	65.00	120	225	—
1624 HI	—	33.00	65.00	120	225	—
1625 HI	—	33.00	65.00	120	225	—
1626 HI	—	33.00	65.00	120	225	—
1627 HI	—	33.00	65.00	120	225	—
1628 HI	—	33.00	65.00	120	225	—
1629 HI	—	33.00	65.00	120	225	—
1630 HI	—	33.00	65.00	120	225	—
1631 HI	—	33.00	65.00	120	225	—
1632 HI	—	33.00	65.00	120	225	—
1633 HI	—	33.00	65.00	120	225	—
1634 HI	—	33.00	65.00	120	225	—
1635 CM	—	33.00	65.00	120	225	—
1635 HI	—	33.00	65.00	120	225	—
1636 SD	—	33.00	65.00	120	225	—
1637 SD	—	33.00	65.00	120	225	—
1638 SD	—	33.00	65.00	120	225	—
1639 SD	—	33.00	65.00	120	225	—
1640 CR	—	33.00	65.00	120	225	—
1640 SD	—	33.00	65.00	120	225	—
1641 CR	—	33.00	65.00	120	225	—
1642 CR	—	33.00	65.00	120	225	—
1643 CR	—	33.00	65.00	120	225	—
1644 CR	—	33.00	65.00	120	225	—
1645 CR	—	33.00	65.00	120	225	—
1646 CR	—	33.00	65.00	120	225	—
1648 CR	—	33.00	65.00	120	225	—
1649 CR	—	33.00	65.00	120	225	—
1650 CR	—	33.00	65.00	120	225	—
1651 CR	—	33.00	65.00	120	225	—
1652 CR	—	33.00	65.00	120	225	—
1653 CR	—	33.00	65.00	120	225	—
1655 CR	—	33.00	65.00	120	225	—

KM# 307 1/24 THALER (Groschen)
Silver **Obv:** Oval 2-fold arms in baroque frame, angel's head and wings above **Rev:** 3 small, ornately-shaped shields of arms, 2 above 1, imperial orb with 24 at top divides date **Note:** Struck at Dresden. Varieties exist.

Date	Mintage	VG	F	VF	XF	Unc
1620 (swan)	—	27.00	55.00	100	200	—
16Z1 (swan)	—	27.00	55.00	100	200	—
1621 (swan)	—	27.00	55.00	100	200	—

KM# 309 1/24 THALER (Groschen)
Silver **Obv:** Plain 2-fold arms between E - B **Note:** Struck at Eckartsberga.

Date	Mintage	VG	F	VF	XF	Unc
16Z1 EB	—	27.00	60.00	120	220	—

KM# 302 1/24 THALER (Groschen)
Silver **Obv:** 2-fold arms in baroque frame, angel's head and wings above **Rev:** Imperial orb with 24 divides date **Note:** Struck at Annaberg. Varieties exist.

Date	Mintage	VG	F	VF	XF	Unc
16Z1 (acorn)	—	27.00	60.00	120	220	—

KM# 303 1/24 THALER (Groschen)
Silver **Obv:** 2-fold arms **Rev:** Imperial orb with Z4, date divided in legend at top **Note:** Struck at Bitterfeld.

Date	Mintage	VG	F	VF	XF	Unc
16Z1 (acorn)	—	27.00	60.00	120	220	—

KM# 313 1/24 THALER (Groschen)
Silver **Rev:** Date divided in legend at top **Note:** Struck at Leipzig. Varieties exist.

Date	Mintage	VG	F	VF	XF	Unc
16Z1 SL	—	27.00	55.00	100	200	—
1622 SL	—	27.00	55.00	100	200	—
Note: Varieties exist						
1622 SL	—	27.00	55.00	100	200	—

KM# 308 1/24 THALER (Groschen)
Silver **Rev:** Value: 24 on imperial orb divides date **Note:** Varieties exist.

Date	Mintage	VG	F	VF	XF	Unc
16Z1 (swan)	—	27.00	55.00	100	200	—
16ZZ (swan)	—	27.00	55.00	100	200	—
16Z3 (swan)	—	27.00	55.00	100	200	—

KM# 333 1/24 THALER (Groschen)
Silver **Rev:** 24 in orb **Rev. Legend:** SA. RO... **Note:** Varieties exist.

Date	Mintage	VG	F	VF	XF	Unc
1621 (flying bird)	—	13.00	27.00	60.00	120	—
(16)21 (flying bird)	—	13.00	27.00	60.00	120	—
(16)22 (cross)	—	13.00	27.00	60.00	120	—
1622 (5-petaled rosette)	—	13.00	27.00	60.00	120	—
ND (crown)	—	13.00	27.00	60.00	120	—

KM# 334 1/24 THALER (Groschen)
Silver **Rev. Legend:** SA. ROMANI... **Note:** Varieties exist.

Date	Mintage	VG	F	VF	XF	Unc
16Z1 (5-petaled rosette)	—	13.00	27.00	60.00	120	—
ND (4-petaled rosette)	—	13.00	27.00	60.00	120	—

KM# 336 1/24 THALER (Groschen)
Silver **Obv:** 3 small shields of arms, 1 above 2 **Rev:** Imperial orb with 24 **Rev. Legend:** SA. R..., date divided at top **Note:** Varieties exist.

Date	Mintage	VG	F	VF	XF	Unc
1621 (cross)	—	13.00	27.00	60.00	120	—
ND (cross)	—	13.00	27.00	60.00	120	—
1621	—	13.00	27.00	60.00	120	—
ND	—	13.00	27.00	60.00	120	—

KM# 327 1/24 THALER (Groschen)
Silver **Note:** Klippe.

Date	Mintage	VG	F	VF	XF	Unc
1621 (3 swans)	—	33.00	65.00	120	225	—

KM# 328 1/24 THALER (Groschen)
Silver **Rev:** Imperial orb with 24, date divided at top

Date	Mintage	VG	F	VF	XF	Unc
1621 (3 swans)	—	27.00	60.00	120	220	—
1622 (3 swans)	—	27.00	60.00	120	220	—

KM# 338 1/24 THALER (Groschen)
Silver **Rev:** Round arms, date at top **Rev. Legend:** ARCHIM. E. ELECT.

Date	Mintage	VG	F	VF	XF	Unc
16Z1 (trefoil)	—	13.00	27.00	60.00	120	—

KM# 314 1/24 THALER (Groschen)
Silver **Obv:** 3 small ornately-shaped shields, 2 above 1

Date	Mintage	VG	F	VF	XF	Unc
1621 SL	—	27.00	55.00	100	200	—

KM# 326 1/24 THALER (Groschen)
Silver **Obv:** Ornate 2-fold arms **Rev:** 3 small shields of arms, 1 above 2, divide date **Note:** Struck at Zwickau.

Date	Mintage	VG	F	VF	XF	Unc
1621 (3 swans)	—	27.00	60.00	120	220	—

KM# 332 1/24 THALER (Groschen)
Silver **Rev:** Round arms and date at top **Note:** Varieties exist.

Date	Mintage	VG	F	VF	XF	Unc
1621 (lily)	—	13.00	27.00	60.00	120	—
1621 (double-lily)	—	13.00	27.00	60.00	120	—
ND	—	13.00	27.00	60.00	120	—

KM# 315 1/24 THALER (Groschen)
Silver **Rev:** Date undivided at end of legend

Date	Mintage	VG	F	VF	XF	Unc
1622 SL	—	27.00	55.00	100	200	—

KM# 317 1/24 THALER (Groschen)
Silver **Obv:** Without angel's head and wings **Rev:** 24 in orb

Date	Mintage	VG	F	VF	XF	Unc
1622 (rooster)	—	27.00	55.00	100	200	—
1622 (rooster)/MD	—	27.00	55.00	100	200	—

KM# 325 1/24 THALER (Groschen)
Silver **Rev:** Z4 in orb

Date	Mintage	VG	F	VF	XF	Unc
1622 W	—	27.00	60.00	120	220	—

KM# 330 1/24 THALER (Groschen)
Silver **Rev:** Date undivided at end of legend

Date	Mintage	VG	F	VF	XF	Unc
1622 (3 swans)	—	27.00	60.00	120	220	—

KM# 329 1/24 THALER (Groschen)
Silver **Note:** Klippe.

Date	Mintage	VG	F	VF	XF	Unc
1622 (3 swans)	—	33.00	65.00	120	225	—

KM# 322 1/24 THALER (Groschen)
Silver **Rev:** Date divided in legend at top **Note:** Varieties exist.

Date	Mintage	VG	F	VF	XF	Unc
16ZZ N	—	27.00	60.00	120	220	—

KM# 331 1/24 THALER (Groschen)
Silver **Obv:** Heart-shaped 2-fold arms, mint symbol at top **Rev:** Imperial orb with Z4, titles of Ferdinand II, date at top, when present **Note:** Varieties exist.

Date	Mintage	VG	F	VF	XF	Unc
16ZZ (lily)	—	13.00	27.00	60.00	120	—
1622 (trefoil)	—	13.00	27.00	60.00	120	—

KM# 306 1/24 THALER (Groschen)
Silver **Rev:** Date divided by orb **Rev. Legend:** SA ROM I M... **Note:** Varieties exist.

Date	Mintage	VG	F	VF	XF	Unc
16ZZ	—	27.00	55.00	100	200	—

KM# 316 1/24 THALER (Groschen)
Silver **Obv:** 2-fold arms in baroque frame, angel's head and wings above **Rev:** Imperial orb with Z4, date divided in legend at top **Note:** Struck at Merseburg.

Date	Mintage	VG	F	VF	XF	Unc
1622 (rooster)	—	27.00	55.00	100	200	—

KM# 323 1/24 THALER (Groschen)

Silver **Obv:** Ornate 2-fold arms **Rev:** Imperial orb with 24, date divided at top **Note:** Struck at Pirna. Varieties exist.

Date	Mintage	VG	F	VF	XF	Unc
1622 GS	—	27.00	60.00	120	220	—

KM# 324 1/24 THALER (Groschen)

Silver **Obv:** W in legend at top **Note:** Struck at Weida.

Date	Mintage	VG	F	VF	XF	Unc
1622 W	—	27.00	60.00	120	220	—

KM# 310 1/24 THALER (Groschen)

Silver **Obv:** 2-fold arms **Note:** Struck at Ehrenfriedersdorf. Varieties exist.

Date	Mintage	VG	F	VF	XF	Unc
16ZZ (finger ring)	—	27.00	60.00	120	220	—
ND (finger ring)	—	27.00	60.00	120	220	—

KM# 471 1/24 THALER (Groschen)

Silver **Obv:** Oval 2-fold arms in baroque frame, titles of Johann Georg II **Rev:** Imperial orb with 24 divides date and initials **Rev. Legend:** OBER SAXSISCH KREISSES GROSCH **Note:** Varieties exist.

Date	Mintage	VG	F	VF	XF	Unc
1658 CR	—	11.00	20.00	40.00	80.00	—
1659 CR	—	11.00	20.00	40.00	80.00	—
1660 CR	—	11.00	20.00	40.00	80.00	—
1661 CR	—	11.00	20.00	40.00	80.00	—
1662 CR	—	11.00	20.00	40.00	80.00	—
1663 CR	—	11.00	20.00	40.00	80.00	—
1664 CR	—	11.00	20.00	40.00	80.00	—
1665 CR	—	11.00	20.00	40.00	80.00	—
1666 CR	—	11.00	20.00	40.00	80.00	—
1667 CR	—	11.00	20.00	40.00	80.00	—
1668 CR	—	11.00	20.00	40.00	80.00	—

KM# 520 1/24 THALER (Groschen)

Silver **Rev. Legend:** SAC. ROM... **Note:** Varieties exist.

Date	Mintage	VG	F	VF	XF	Unc
1667 CR	—	11.00	20.00	40.00	80.00	—
1668 CR	—	11.00	20.00	40.00	80.00	—
1669 CR	—	11.00	20.00	40.00	80.00	—
1670 CR	—	11.00	20.00	40.00	80.00	—
1671 CR	—	11.00	20.00	40.00	80.00	—
1672 CR	—	11.00	20.00	40.00	80.00	—
1673 CR	—	11.00	20.00	40.00	80.00	—
1674 CR	—	11.00	20.00	40.00	80.00	—
1677 CR	—	11.00	20.00	40.00	80.00	—
1678 CF	—	11.00	20.00	40.00	80.00	—
1678 CR	—	11.00	20.00	40.00	80.00	—
1679 CF	—	11.00	20.00	40.00	80.00	—
1680 CF	—	11.00	20.00	40.00	80.00	—
Note: Varieties exist						
1680 CF	—	11.00	20.00	40.00	80.00	—

KM# 570 1/24 THALER (Groschen)

Silver **Obv:** Crowned 2-fold arms between 2 palm branches **Note:** Varieties exist.

Date	Mintage	VG	F	VF	XF	Unc
1680 CF	—	11.00	20.00	40.00	80.00	—
1681 CF	—	11.00	20.00	40.00	80.00	—
1682 CF	—	11.00	20.00	40.00	80.00	—
1683 CF	—	11.00	20.00	40.00	80.00	—
1684 CF	—	11.00	20.00	40.00	80.00	—
1685 CF	—	11.00	20.00	40.00	80.00	—
1686 CF	—	11.00	20.00	40.00	80.00	—
1687	—	11.00	20.00	40.00	80.00	—
1688	—	11.00	20.00	40.00	80.00	—
1688 IK	—	11.00	20.00	40.00	80.00	—
1689 IK	—	11.00	20.00	40.00	80.00	—
1690 IK	—	11.00	20.00	40.00	80.00	—
1691 IK	—	11.00	20.00	40.00	80.00	—

KM# 610 1/24 THALER (Groschen)

Silver **Obv:** Titles of Johann Georg IV **Rev:** 24/EINEN/THAL/ date, SAC. ROM...

Date	Mintage	VG	F	VF	XF	Unc
1691 IK	—	11.00	20.00	40.00	80.00	—
1692 IK	—	11.00	20.00	40.00	80.00	—
1693 IK	—	11.00	20.00	40.00	80.00	—
1694 IK	—	11.00	20.00	40.00	80.00	—
Note: Varieties exist						
1694 IK	—	11.00	20.00	40.00	80.00	—

KM# A645 1/24 THALER (Groschen)

Silver **Obv:** 2 ornamented heraldic shields

Date	Mintage	VG	F	VF	XF	Unc
1693 IK	—	11.00	20.00	40.00	80.00	—

KM# 645 1/24 THALER (Groschen)

Silver **Obv:** Crowned round 2-fold arms in crossed palm branches, mintmaster's initials below **Note:** Varieties exist.

Date	Mintage	VG	F	VF	XF	Unc
1694 IK	—	11.00	20.00	40.00	80.00	—
1695 EPH	—	11.00	20.00	40.00	80.00	—
1695 IK	—	11.00	20.00	40.00	80.00	—
1696 EPH	—	11.00	20.00	40.00	80.00	—
1696 IK	—	11.00	20.00	40.00	80.00	—
1696 EPH	—	11.00	20.00	40.00	80.00	—
1697 EPH	—	11.00	20.00	40.00	80.00	—
1697 IK	—	11.00	20.00	40.00	80.00	—
1698 EPH	—	11.00	20.00	40.00	80.00	—
1699 EPH	—	11.00	20.00	40.00	80.00	—

KM# 682 1/24 THALER (Groschen)

Silver **Ruler:** Johann Georg IV **Obv:** Crowned round 4-fold arms with crowned central shield of 2-fold arms **Rev:** Value: 24/EINEN/THAl/date in palm wreath

Date	Mintage	VG	F	VF	XF	Unc
1697 IK	—	11.00	20.00	40.00	80.00	—
1697 ILH	—	11.00	20.00	40.00	80.00	—
1698 ILH	—	11.00	20.00	40.00	80.00	—
1699 ILH	—	11.00	20.00	40.00	80.00	—
1700 ILH	—	11.00	20.00	40.00	80.00	—

KM# 515 1/15 THALER

Silver **Obv:** 2 ornately-shaped shields of arms above small city arms of Bautzen, divide date **Rev. Legend:** MONETA NOVA..., value: XV/EIN/REICHS/THAL/initials

Date	Mintage	VG	F	VF	XF	Unc
1666 HI	—	—	—	—	—	—

KM# 606 1/12 THALER (Doppelgroschen)

Silver

Date	Mintage	VG	F	VF	XF	Unc
1690 IK	—	—	—	—	—	—
1691 IK	—	—	—	—	—	—

KM# 611 1/12 THALER (Doppelgroschen)

Silver **Note:** Varieties exist.

Date	Mintage	VG	F	VF	XF	Unc
1691 IK	—	13.00	27.00	40.00	85.00	—
1692 IK	—	13.00	27.00	40.00	85.00	—
1693 IK	—	13.00	27.00	40.00	85.00	—

KM# 638 1/12 THALER (Doppelgroschen)

Silver **Obv:** 2 adjacent oval arms in baroque frames, crown above, initials below, where present **Rev:** Value: 12/EINEN/THAL/date **Note:** Varieties exist.

Date	Mintage	VG	F	VF	XF	Unc
1693	—	13.00	27.00	40.00	85.00	—
1693 IK	—	13.00	27.00	40.00	85.00	—
1693 EPH	—	13.00	27.00	40.00	85.00	—
1694 IK	—	13.00	27.00	40.00	85.00	—
1694 EPH	—	13.00	27.00	40.00	85.00	—

KM# 646 1/12 THALER (Doppelgroschen)

Silver **Obv:** Crowned oval 2-fold arms framed by crossed palm branches, initials below **Note:** Varieties exist.

Date	Mintage	VG	F	VF	XF	Unc
1694 EPH	—	13.00	27.00	40.00	85.00	—
1695 EPH	—	13.00	27.00	40.00	85.00	—
1695 IK	—	13.00	27.00	40.00	85.00	—
1696 EPH	—	13.00	27.00	40.00	85.00	—
1696 IK	—	13.00	27.00	40.00	85.00	—
1697 EPH	—	13.00	27.00	40.00	85.00	—
1698 EPH	—	13.00	27.00	40.00	85.00	—

KM# A683 1/12 THALER (Doppelgroschen)

Silver

Date	Mintage	VG	F	VF	XF	Unc
1697 EPH	—	13.00	27.00	40.00	85.00	—
1698 EPH	—	13.00	27.00	40.00	85.00	—
1699 ILH	—	13.00	27.00	40.00	85.00	—

KM# 12 1/8 THALER

Silver **Obv:** Bust of Christian II right, small imperial orb above, shield of crossed swords below **Rev:** Busts of Johann Georg I and August facing each other, small shield of open crown arms above, date in legend

Date	Mintage	VG	F	VF	XF	Unc
1601	—	—	—	—	—	—

KM# 35 1/8 THALER

Silver **Obv:** Oval Electoral Saxony arms in baroque frame, titles of three brothers **Rev:** Oval ducal Saxony arms in baroque frame, titles continued and date in legend

Date	Mintage	VG	F	VF	XF	Unc
1610 (swan)	—	—	—	—	—	—
1611 (swan)	—	—	—	—	—	—

KM# 50 1/8 THALER

Silver **Obv:** Titles of Johann Georg I and August only

Date	Mintage	VG	F	VF	XF	Unc
1612 (swan)	—	—	—	—	—	—

KM# 51 1/8 THALER

Silver **Obv:** 1/2-length crowned bust of Johann Georg I right holding sword over right shoulder **Rev:** Ornate 4-fold arms with central shield of electoral Saxony, date divided above

Date	Mintage	VG	F	VF	XF	Unc
1612 (swan)	—	65.00	135	275	475	—

KM# 93 1/8 THALER

Silver **Subject:** Reformation Centennial **Obv:** 1/2-length figure holding sword over right shoulder divides IOH - GEOR, 4-fold arms with central shield below, date divided at bottom **Rev:** 1/2-length figure holding sword over right shoulder divides FRID - III, 2-fold arms of Saxony below, 15 - 17 at bottom

Date	Mintage	VG	F	VF	XF	Unc
1617	—	33.00	65.00	135	250	—

KM# 115 1/8 THALER

Silver **Obv:** Equestrian figure of Johann Georg I right with sword over right shoulder divides date, oval 2-fold arms below **Rev:** 12-line inscription **Note:** Vicariat Issue.

Date	Mintage	VG	F	VF	XF	Unc
1619	—	55.00	110	220	375	—

KM# 386 1/8 THALER

Silver **Obv:** Bust right, sword over shoulder **Rev:** 2-fold arms, date

Date	Mintage	VG	F	VF	XF	Unc
1623 (swan)	—	—	—	—	—	—
1624 (swan)	—	—	—	—	—	—

KM# 387 1/8 THALER

Silver **Rev:** 3-fold arms **Note:** Varieties exist.

Date	Mintage	VG	F	VF	XF	Unc
1624 HI	—	20.00	40.00	80.00	145	—
1625 HI	—	20.00	40.00	80.00	145	—
1627 HI	—	20.00	40.00	80.00	145	—
1628 HI	—	20.00	40.00	80.00	145	—
1629 HI	—	20.00	40.00	80.00	145	—
1630 HI	—	20.00	40.00	80.00	145	—
1635 HI	—	20.00	40.00	80.00	145	—
1635 SD	—	20.00	40.00	80.00	145	—
1636 SD	—	20.00	40.00	80.00	145	—
1637 SD	—	20.00	40.00	80.00	145	—
1638 SD	—	20.00	40.00	80.00	145	—
1639 SD	—	20.00	40.00	80.00	145	—
1640 CR	—	20.00	40.00	80.00	145	—
1641 CR	—	20.00	40.00	80.00	145	—
1642 CR	—	20.00	40.00	80.00	145	—
1643 CR	—	20.00	40.00	80.00	145	—
1644 CR	—	20.00	40.00	80.00	145	—
1645 CR	—	20.00	40.00	80.00	145	—
1646 CR	—	20.00	40.00	80.00	145	—
1647 CR	—	20.00	40.00	80.00	145	—
1648 CR	—	20.00	40.00	80.00	145	—
1649 CR	—	20.00	40.00	80.00	145	—
1650 CR	—	20.00	40.00	80.00	145	—
1651 CR	—	20.00	40.00	80.00	145	—
1652 CR	—	20.00	40.00	80.00	145	—
1653 CR	—	20.00	40.00	80.00	145	—
1654 CR	—	20.00	40.00	80.00	145	—
1655 CR	—	20.00	40.00	80.00	145	—
1656 CR	—	20.00	40.00	80.00	145	—

KM# 405 1/8 THALER

Silver **Subject:** Centennial of Augsburg Confession **Obv:** 1/2-length figure of Johann Georg I, sword over right shoulder, divides IOH - GEO, oval 4-fold arms with central shield below, full date divided by head **Rev:** 1/2-length figure of Duke Johann, sword over right shoulder, divides IOH - NES, 4 small shields of arms around, full date (1530) divided by head

Date	Mintage	VG	F	VF	XF	Unc
1630	—	45.00	85.00	160	275	—

KM# 447 1/8 THALER

Silver **Subject:** Death of Johann Georg I **Obv:** Bust facing slightly right, sword over shoulder **Rev:** 8-line inscription with Roman numeral date

Date	Mintage	VG	F	VF	XF	Unc
MDCLVI (1656)	—	60.00	120	200	375	—

KM# 456 1/8 THALER

Silver **Obv:** Duke on horseback, with sword over shoulder, oval 2-fold arms below, date in legend **Rev:** 10-line inscription **Note:** Vacariat Issue.

Date	Mintage	VG	F	VF	XF	Unc
1657	—	45.00	85.00	160	275	—

KM# 472 1/8 THALER

Silver **Obv:** Bust right with sword over right shoulder **Rev:** 3-fold arms, mintmasters initials below **Note:** Varieties exist.

Date	Mintage	VG	F	VF	XF	Unc
1658 CR	—	27.00	55.00	110	180	—
1659 CR	—	27.00	55.00	110	180	—
1660 CR	—	27.00	55.00	110	180	—
1661 CR	—	27.00	55.00	110	180	—
1662 CR	—	27.00	55.00	110	180	—
1663 CR	—	27.00	55.00	110	180	—
1664 CR	—	27.00	55.00	110	180	—
1665 CR	—	27.00	55.00	110	180	—
1666 CR	—	27.00	55.00	110	180	—
1667 CR	—	27.00	55.00	110	180	—
1668 CR	—	27.00	55.00	110	180	—
1673 CR	—	27.00	55.00	110	180	—
1674 CR	—	27.00	55.00	110	180	—
1675 CR	—	27.00	55.00	110	180	—
1676 CR	—	27.00	55.00	110	180	—
1678 CR	—	27.00	55.00	110	180	—
1680 CR	—	27.00	55.00	110	180	—

KM# 575 1/8 THALER

Silver **Obv:** 1/2-length figure right with sword over shoulder **Rev:** 3-fold arms, date in legend **Note:** Varieties exist.

Date	Mintage	VG	F	VF	XF	Unc
1681 CF	—	—	—	—	—	—
1688 IK	—	—	—	—	—	—

KM# 593 1/8 THALER

Silver **Subject:** Death of Johann Georg III's Mother, Magdalene Sibylle **Note:** Similar to 1 Groschen, KM#592.

Date	Mintage	VG	F	VF	XF	Unc
1687	—	—	—	—	—	—

KM# 647 1/8 THALER

Silver **Obv:** Large bust right **Rev:** Crowned oval 2-fold arms between palm branches divides mintmasters initials, date in legend **Note:** Varieties exist.

Date	Mintage	VG	F	VF	XF	Unc
1694 IK	—	27.00	45.00	90.00	170	—
1695 IK	—	27.00	45.00	90.00	170	—
1696 IK	—	27.00	45.00	90.00	170	—
1697 IK	—	27.00	45.00	90.00	170	—

KM# 721 1/8 THALER

Silver **Ruler:** Johann Georg IV **Obv:** Large bust right **Rev:** Crowned flat top 2-fold arms between palm branches divides initials, date in legend **Note:** Varieties exist.

Date	Mintage	VG	F	VF	XF	Unc
1700 ILH	—	20.00	40.00	80.00	140	—

KM# 516 1/6 THALER (1/4 Gulden)

Silver **Note:** Coinage for Oberlausitz. Struck at Bautzen. Varieties exist.

Date	Mintage	VG	F	VF	XF	Unc
1666 HI	—	40.00	85.00	160	275	—
1667 HI	—	40.00	85.00	160	275	—
1668 CR	—	40.00	85.00	160	275	—

KM# 521 1/6 THALER (1/4 Gulden)

Silver **Obv:** Bust right **Rev:** Crowned 4-fold arms with central shield of electoral Saxony divide initials, 1/6 in oval below, date at top in legend

Date	Mintage	VG	F	VF	XF	Unc
1668 CR	—	40.00	85.00	160	275	—
1669 CR	—	40.00	85.00	160	275	—
1672 CR	—	40.00	85.00	160	275	—
1673 CR	—	40.00	85.00	160	275	—
1674 CR	—	40.00	85.00	160	275	—

KM# 558 1/6 THALER (1/4 Gulden)

Silver **Obv:** Small bust right **Rev:** Crowned oval 2-fold arms between 2 palm branches, value 1/6 in oval below, date in legend at top

Date	Mintage	VG	F	VF	XF	Unc
1678 CF	—	35.00	75.00	150	240	—
1679 CF	—	35.00	75.00	150	240	—
1680 CF	—	35.00	75.00	150	240	—

KM# 576 1/6 THALER (1/4 Gulden)

Silver **Obv:** Bust right **Rev:** Crowned 2-fold arms between 2 palm branches, value 1/6 in oval below, date in legend at top **Note:** Varieties exist.

Date	Mintage	VG	F	VF	XF	Unc
1681 CF	—	35.00	70.00	150	240	—
1682 CF	—	35.00	70.00	150	240	—
1683 CF	—	35.00	70.00	150	240	—
1684 CF	—	35.00	70.00	150	240	—
1685 CF	—	35.00	70.00	150	240	—
1686 CF	—	35.00	70.00	150	240	—
1687	—	35.00	70.00	150	240	—
1688	—	35.00	70.00	150	240	—
1688 IK	—	35.00	70.00	150	240	—
1689 IK	—	35.00	70.00	150	240	—
1690 IK	—	35.00	70.00	150	240	—
1691 IK	—	35.00	70.00	150	240	—

KM# 612 1/6 THALER (1/4 Gulden)

Silver **Subject:** Death of Johann Georg III **Note:** Similar to 1 Groschen, KM#608, but value: 1/6 in oval at bottom of reverse.

Date	Mintage	VG	F	VF	XF	Unc
MDCXCI (1691) IK	—	55.00	110	200	300	—
1691 IK	—	55.00	110	200	300	—

KM# 626 1/6 THALER (1/4 Gulden)

Silver **Rev:** Similar to obverse of 1 Pfening, KM#623, but date divided at top and value: 1/6 divided in upper and lower angles of crossed swords

Date	Mintage	VG	F	VF	XF	Unc
1692 IK	—	—	—	—	—	—
1693 IK	—	—	—	—	—	—

KM# 648 1/6 THALER (1/4 Gulden)

Silver **Subject:** Death of Johann Georg IV **Note:** Similar to 1 Groschen, KM#643, but reverse has 9-line inscription and value: 1/6 in oval at bottom

Date	Mintage	VG	F	VF	XF	Unc
MDCXCIV (1694) IK	—	—	—	—	—	—

KM# 667 1/6 THALER (1/4 Gulden)

Silver **Rev:** Crowned oval 2-fold arms between 2 palm branches, date divided above, value: 1/6 in oval below **Note:** Varieties exist.

Date	Mintage	VG	F	VF	XF	Unc
1695 IK	—	35.00	70.00	150	240	—
1696 IK	—	35.00	70.00	150	240	—
1696 EPH	—	35.00	70.00	150	240	—

KM# 704 1/6 THALER (1/4 Gulden)

Silver **Rev:** 2 adjacent shields of arms **Note:** Varieties exist.

Date	Mintage	VG	F	VF	XF	Unc
1698 ILH	—	35.00	70.00	150	240	—
1698 EPH	—	35.00	70.00	150	240	—
1699 ILH	—	35.00	70.00	150	240	—
1699 EPH EPH	—	35.00	70.00	150	240	—
1699 EPH	—	35.00	70.00	150	240	—
1700 ILH	—	35.00	70.00	150	240	—

KM# 722 1/6 THALER (1/4 Gulden)

Silver **Ruler:** Friedrich August I **Rev:** 2 adjacent shields between palm branches, with 4-fold arms, with central shield of electoral Saxony, large crown above, value: 1/6 in oval below, date in legend

Date	Mintage	VG	F	VF	XF	Unc
1700 ILH	—	35.00	70.00	150	240	—

KM# 8 1/4 THALER

Silver **Obv:** 3 facing 1/2-length figures, date divided above, small imperial orb at top **Rev:** Ornate 2-fold arms in baroque frame

Date	Mintage	VG	F	VF	XF	Unc
1600 HB	—	45.00	100	200	400	—
1601 HB	—	45.00	100	200	400	—

KM# 13 1/4 THALER

Silver **Obv:** Half-length bust, with sword over right shoulder divides date, small crossed swords arms below **Rev:** 2 busts facing each other, small open-crown arms below **Note:** Varieties exist.

Date	Mintage	VG	F	VF	XF	Unc
1601 HB	—	40.00	85.00	180	375	—
1602 HB	—	40.00	85.00	180	375	—
1603 HB	—	40.00	85.00	180	375	—
1604 HB	—	40.00	85.00	180	375	—
1605 HB	—	40.00	85.00	180	375	—
1605 HvR	—	40.00	85.00	180	375	—
1606 HvR	—	40.00	85.00	180	375	—
1607 HvR	—	40.00	85.00	180	375	—
1608 HvR	—	40.00	85.00	180	375	—
1609 HvR	—	40.00	85.00	180	375	—
1610 HvR	—	40.00	85.00	180	375	—
1611 HvR	—	40.00	85.00	180	375	—

KM# 40 1/4 THALER

Silver **Obv:** 1/2-length bust of Johann Georg I right with sword over right shoulder divides date, crossed swords arms below **Rev:** 1/2-length bust of August right, 4 small shields of arms in legend **Note:** Varieties exist.

Date	Mintage	VG	F	VF	XF	Unc
1611 (swan)	—	65.00	135	275	500	—
1612 (swan)	—	65.00	135	275	500	—
1613 (swan)	—	65.00	135	275	500	—
1614 (swan)	—	65.00	135	275	500	—
1615 (swan)	—	65.00	135	275	500	—
1616 (swan)	—	65.00	135	275	500	—

KM# 38 1/4 THALER

Silver **Subject:** Death of Christian II **Obv:** 9-line inscription with Roman numeral date **Rev:** 6-line inscription

Date	Mintage	VG	F	VF	XF	Unc
1611	—	55.00	110	220	425	—

KM# 39 1/4 THALER

Silver **Subject:** Accession of Johann Georg I **Obv:** Full-length figure of Johann Georg I with sword and scepter **Rev:** Bear and ape by tree

Date	Mintage	VG	F	VF	XF	Unc
ND	—	—	—	—	—	—

KM# 52 1/4 THALER

Silver **Obv:** 1/2-length crowned bust of Johann Georg I right holding sword over right shoulder **Rev:** Ornate 4-fold arms with central shield of electoral Saxony, date divided above **Note:** Vicariat Issue.

Date	Mintage	VG	F	VF	XF	Unc
1612 (swan)	—	100	200	400	750	—

KM# 77 1/4 THALER

Silver **Subject:** Death of August II **Obv:** Bust right with baton and helmet **Rev:** 4-line inscription

Date	Mintage	VG	F	VF	XF	Unc
1615	—	65.00	135	275	500	—

KM# 78 1/4 THALER

Silver **Obv:** Bust right, sword over shoulder **Rev:** Round 2-fold arms

Date	Mintage	VG	F	VF	XF	Unc
1615 (swan)	—	—	—	—	—	—
1616 (swan)	—	—	—	—	—	—

KM# 88 1/4 THALER

Silver **Rev:** Squarish arms **Note:** Varieties exist.

Date	Mintage	VG	F	VF	XF	Unc
1616 (swan)	—	55.00	110	220	450	—
1617 (swan)	—	55.00	110	220	450	—
1618 (swan)	—	55.00	110	220	450	—
1619 (swan)	—	55.00	110	220	450	—
1620 (swan)	—	55.00	110	220	450	—
1621 (swan)	—	55.00	110	220	450	—
1622 (swan)	—	55.00	110	220	450	—
1623 (swan)	—	55.00	110	220	450	—
1624 (swan)	—	55.00	110	220	450	—

KM# 96 1/4 THALER

Silver **Note:** Similar to 1/8 Thaler, KM#93.

Date	Mintage	VG	F	VF	XF	Unc
1617	—	100	180	325	575	—

KM# 94 1/4 THALER

Silver **Subject:** Reformation Centennial **Obv:** Standing figure before seated king **Obv. Legend:** VT SALOMON..., date **Rev:** Mailed hands holding up severed arms

Date	Mintage	VG	F	VF	XF	Unc
1617	—	80.00	140	275	500	—

KM# 95 1/4 THALER

Silver **Obv:** Johann Georg I standing before his mother **Obv. Legend:** HONOR... **Rev:** Hands between 2 cornucopia, date in legend

Date	Mintage	VG	F	VF	XF	Unc
1617	—	100	180	325	575	—

KM# 116 1/4 THALER

Silver **Obv:** Duke on horseback divides date. **Note:** Vicariat Issue.

Date	Mintage	VG	F	VF	XF	Unc
1619	—	65.00	120	250	475	—

KM# 117 1/4 THALER

Silver **Note:** Thick flan.

Date	Mintage	VG	F	VF	XF	Unc
1619	—	—	—	—	—	—

KM# 388 1/4 THALER

Silver **Rev:** 4-fold arms with central shield on reverse **Note:** Similar to KM#407.

Date	Mintage	VG	F	VF	XF	Unc
1623	—	55.00	110	220	425	—
1624 HI	—	55.00	110	220	425	—
1625 HI	—	55.00	110	220	425	—
1627 HI	—	55.00	110	220	425	—

KM# 407 1/4 THALER

Silver **Obv:** Bust right with sword on shoulder **Rev:** 3-fold arms, date at top **Note:** Varieties exist.

Date	Mintage	VG	F	VF	XF	Unc
1628 HI	—	55.00	110	220	425	—
1630 HI	—	55.00	110	220	425	—
1631 HI	—	55.00	110	220	425	—
1632 HI	—	55.00	110	220	425	—
1634 HI	—	55.00	110	220	425	—
1635 CM	—	55.00	110	220	425	—
1635 HI	—	55.00	110	220	425	—
1635 SD	—	55.00	110	220	425	—
1636 SD	—	55.00	110	220	425	—
1637 SD	—	55.00	110	220	425	—
1638 SD	—	55.00	110	220	425	—
1639 SD	—	55.00	110	220	425	—
1640 SD	—	55.00	110	220	425	—
1640 CR	—	55.00	110	220	425	—
1641 CR	—	55.00	110	220	425	—
1642 CR	—	55.00	110	220	425	—
1643 CR	—	55.00	110	220	425	—
1644 CR	—	55.00	110	220	425	—
1645 CR	—	55.00	110	220	425	—
1646 CR	—	55.00	110	220	425	—
1647 CR	—	55.00	110	220	425	—
1648 CR	—	55.00	110	220	425	—
1649 CR	—	55.00	110	220	425	—
1650 CR	—	55.00	110	220	425	—
1651 CR	—	55.00	110	220	425	—
1652 CR	—	55.00	110	220	425	—
1653 CR	—	55.00	110	220	425	—
1654 CR	—	55.00	110	220	425	—
1655 CR	—	55.00	110	220	425	—
1656 CR	—	55.00	110	220	425	—

KM# 406 1/4 THALER

Silver **Subject:** Augsburg Confession Centennial

Date	Mintage	VG	F	VF	XF	Unc
1630	—	65.00	120	250	450	—

KM# 448 1/4 THALER
Silver **Subject:** Death of Johann Georg I

Date	Mintage	VG	F	VF	XF	Unc
MDCLVI (1656)	—	85.00	165	300	575	—

KM# 449 1/4 THALER
Silver **Obv:** Titles of Johann Georg II

Date	Mintage	VG	F	VF	XF	Unc
1656 CR	—	55.00	110	220	425	—
1658 CR	—	55.00	110	220	425	—
1659 CR	—	55.00	110	220	425	—
1660 CR	—	55.00	110	220	425	—
1661 CR	—	55.00	110	220	425	—
1662 CR	—	55.00	110	220	425	—
1663 CR	—	55.00	110	220	425	—
1664 CR	—	55.00	110	220	425	—
1665 CR	—	55.00	110	220	425	—
1666 CR	—	55.00	110	220	425	—
1667 CR	—	55.00	110	220	425	—
1668 CR	—	55.00	110	220	425	—
1675 CR	—	55.00	110	220	425	—
1677 CR	—	55.00	110	220	425	—
1679 CF	—	55.00	110	220	425	—
1680 CF	—	55.00	110	220	425	—

Note: Varieties exist

KM# 457 1/4 THALER
Silver **Obv:** Duke on horseback right with sword over shoulder, oval 2-fold arms below, date in legend **Rev:** 10-line inscription **Note:** Vicariat Issue.

Date	Mintage	VG	F	VF	XF	Unc
1657	—	60.00	120	240	475	—

KM# 535 1/4 THALER
Silver **Subject:** Wechsel Succession **Obv:** Bust of Johann Georg II right **Rev:** Crowned oval 2-fold arms in baroque frame, WECHSEL THALER below, date in legend

Date	Mintage	VG	F	VF	XF	Unc
1670 CR	—	—	—	—	—	—

KM# 577 1/4 THALER
Silver **Note:** Similar to KM#407, but titles of Johann Georg III. Varieties exist.

Date	Mintage	VG	F	VF	XF	Unc
1681 CF	—	60.00	120	240	450	—
1683 CF	—	60.00	120	240	450	—
1687	—	60.00	120	240	450	—
1688 IK	—	60.00	120	240	450	—
1690 IK	—	60.00	120	240	450	—
1691 IK	—	60.00	120	240	450	—

KM# 594 1/4 THALER
Silver **Subject:** Death of Johann Georg III's Mother, Magdalene Sibylle **Note:** Similar to 1 Groschen, KM#592.

Date	Mintage	VG	F	VF	XF	Unc
1687	—	—	—	—	—	—

KM# 639 1/4 THALER
Silver **Note:** Similar to KM#407, but titles of Johann Georg IV on obverse and electoral hat above arms on reverse.

Date	Mintage	VG	F	VF	XF	Unc
1693 IK	—	60.00	120	240	450	—
1694 EPH	—	60.00	120	240	450	—

Note: Varieties exist

Date	Mintage	VG	F	VF	XF	Unc
1694 IK	—	60.00	120	240	450	—

KM# 650 1/4 THALER
Silver **Note:** Similar to KM#639, but titles of Friedrich August I.

Date	Mintage	VG	F	VF	XF	Unc
1694 IK	—	60.00	120	240	450	—
1695 IK	—	60.00	120	240	450	—
1696 IK	—	60.00	120	240	450	—
1697 IK	—	60.00	120	240	450	—

Note: Varieties exist

KM# 649 1/4 THALER
Silver **Subject:** Homage of Dresden to Friedrich August I **Obv:** 4 crowned double-F monograms in cruciform, A in each angle, crossed-swords arms in center **Rev:** Hand in center holding up 2 fingers, curved inscription below, all in wreath, outer marginal inscription with Roman numeral date

Date	Mintage	VG	F	VF	XF	Unc
1694	—	—	—	—	—	—

KM# 676 1/4 THALER
Silver **Obv:** Crowned bust right **Rev:** Crowned 4-fold arms of Poland and Lithuania with central shield of Saxony arms divide 1-8, date in margin

Date	Mintage	VG	F	VF	XF	Unc
1698	—	—	—	—	—	—

Note: Struck for circulation in Poland

KM# 705 1/4 THALER
Silver **Ruler:** Friedrich August I **Obv:** Large bust right **Rev:** Round arms between palm branches dividing initials

Date	Mintage	VG	F	VF	XF	Unc
1698 ILH	—	45.00	110	220	425	—
1699 ILH	—	45.00	110	220	425	—
1700 ILH	—	45.00	110	220	425	—

KM# 517 1/3 THALER (1/2 Gulden)
Silver **Note:** Coinage for Oberlaustiz. Struck at Bautzen.

Date	Mintage	VG	F	VF	XF	Unc
1666 HI	—	60.00	120	200	400	—
1667 HI	—	60.00	120	200	400	—
1668 CR	—	60.00	120	200	400	—

Note: Varieties exist

KM# 522 1/3 THALER (1/2 Gulden)
Silver **Note:** Similar to 1/8 Thaler, KM#472, but value: 1/3 at bottom on reverse.

Date	Mintage	VG	F	VF	XF	Unc
1668 CR	—	45.00	90.00	180	350	—
1669 CR	—	45.00	90.00	180	350	—
1670 CR	—	45.00	90.00	180	350	—

Note: Varieties exist

KM# 547 1/3 THALER (1/2 Gulden)
Silver **Obv:** Bust right **Rev:** Crowned 4-fold arms with central shield of crossed swords divide mintmasters initials, value: 1/3 in oval below

Date	Mintage	VG	F	VF	XF	Unc
1672 CR	—	33.00	65.00	135	275	—
1673 CR	—	33.00	65.00	135	275	—
1674 CR	—	33.00	65.00	135	275	—
1675 CR	—	33.00	65.00	135	275	—

Note: Varieties exist

KM# 548 1/3 THALER (1/2 Gulden)
Silver **Obv:** Bust right **Rev:** Crowned oval 2-fold arms in palm branches, date in legend at top, value: 1/3 in oval below

Date	Mintage	VG	F	VF	XF	Unc
1675 CR	—	40.00	80.00	160	325	—
1676 CR	—	40.00	80.00	160	325	—
1677 CR	—	40.00	80.00	160	325	—
1678 CR	—	40.00	80.00	160	325	—
1678 CF	—	40.00	80.00	160	325	—
1679 CF	—	40.00	80.00	160	325	—
1680 CF	—	40.00	80.00	160	325	—

Note: Varieties exist

KM# 578 1/3 THALER (1/2 Gulden)
Silver **Rev:** Squarish arms

Date	Mintage	VG	F	VF	XF	Unc
1681 CF	—	40.00	80.00	160	325	—
1682 CF	—	40.00	80.00	160	325	—
1683 CF	—	40.00	80.00	160	325	—
1684 CF	—	40.00	80.00	160	325	—
1685 CF	—	40.00	80.00	160	325	—
1686 CF	—	40.00	80.00	160	325	—
1687	—	40.00	80.00	160	325	—
1688 IK	—	40.00	80.00	160	325	—
1689 IK	—	40.00	80.00	160	325	—
1690 IK	—	40.00	80.00	160	325	—
1691 IK	—	40.00	80.00	160	325	—

Note: Varieties exist

KM# 613 1/3 THALER (1/2 Gulden)
Silver **Subject:** Death of Johann Georg III

Date	Mintage	VG	F	VF	XF	Unc
MDCXCI (1691) IK	—	45.00	90.00	190	350	—

KM# 627 1/3 THALER (1/2 Gulden)
Silver **Obv:** Bust right **Rev:** Similar to obverse of 1 Pfennig, KM#623, but date divided at top and value: 1/3 divided in upper and lower angles of crossed swords

Date	Mintage	VG	F	VF	XF	Unc
1692 IK	—	45.00	85.00	160	300	—
1693 IK	—	55.00	100	200	350	—

KM# 640 1/3 THALER (1/2 Gulden)
Silver **Obv:** Bust right **Rev:** 2 adjacent oval arms in baroque frame, crown above divides date, value: 1/3 in oval below divides initials

Date	Mintage	VG	F	VF	XF	Unc
1693 IK	—	85.00	160	300	500	—
1694 EPH	—	85.00	160	300	500	—

Note: Varieties exist

Date	Mintage	VG	F	VF	XF	Unc
1694 IK	—	85.00	160	300	500	—

KM# 651 1/3 THALER (1/2 Gulden)
Silver **Subject:** Death of Johann Georg IV

Date	Mintage	VG	F	VF	XF	Unc
MDCXCIV (1694) IK	—	45.00	90.00	180	350	—

KM# 652 1/3 THALER (1/2 Gulden)

Silver **Obv:** Bust right **Rev:** Crowned oval 2-fold arms between 2 palm branches, date divided above, value 1/3 in oval below

Date	Mintage	VG	F	VF	XF	Unc
1694 IK	—	—	—	—	—	—
1695 EPH	—	40.00	80.00	160	300	—
1695 IK	—	40.00	80.00	160	300	—
1696 EPH	—	40.00	80.00	160	300	—
1696 IK	—	40.00	80.00	160	300	—
1697 EPH	—	40.00	80.00	160	300	—
Note: Varieties exist						
1697 IK	—	40.00	80.00	160	300	—

KM# 706 1/3 THALER (1/2 Gulden)

Silver **Rev:** 2 adjacent shields of arms

Date	Mintage	VG	F	VF	XF	Unc
1698 EPH	—	35.00	70.00	150	250	—
1698 ILH	—	40.00	80.00	160	300	—
1699 EPH	—	35.00	70.00	150	250	—
1699 ILH	—	40.00	80.00	160	300	—
1700 ILH	—	35.00	70.00	150	250	—
Note: Varieties exist						

KM# 723 1/3 THALER (1/2 Gulden)

Silver **Ruler:** Friedrich August I **Obv:** Armored bust right **Rev:** Crown above two shields **Note:** Similar to 1/6 Thaler, KM#722, but value: 1/3 on reverse.

Date	Mintage	VG	F	VF	XF	Unc
1700 ILH	—	35.00	70.00	150	250	—

KM# 10 1/2 THALER

Silver **Rev:** 2-fold arms in ornamented heart-shaped shield

Date	Mintage	VG	F	VF	XF	Unc
1600 HB	—	80.00	160	325	500	—

KM# 14 1/2 THALER

Silver **Note:** Varieties exist.

Date	Mintage	VG	F	VF	XF	Unc
1601 HB	—	65.00	120	240	475	—
1602 HB	—	65.00	120	240	475	—
1603 HB	—	65.00	120	240	475	—
1604 HB	—	65.00	120	240	475	—
1605 HvR	—	65.00	120	240	475	—
1606 HvR	—	65.00	120	240	475	—
1607 HvR	—	65.00	120	240	475	—
1608 HvR	—	65.00	120	240	475	—
1609 HvR	—	65.00	120	240	475	—
1610 HvR	—	65.00	120	240	475	—
1611 HvR	—	65.00	120	240	475	—

KM# 22 1/2 THALER

Silver **Note:** Thick flan.

Date	Mintage	VG	F	VF	XF	Unc
1602 HB	—	135	275	525	800	—
1610 HvR	—	135	275	525	800	—

KM# 42 1/2 THALER

Silver **Subject:** Accession of Johann Georg I **Obv:** Full-length figure of Johann Georg I with sword and scepter **Rev:** Bear and ape by tree

Date	Mintage	VG	F	VF	XF	Unc
1611	—	—	—	—	—	—

KM# 41 1/2 THALER

Silver **Subject:** Death of Christian II **Note:** Similar to 1/4 Thaler, KM#38.

Date	Mintage	VG	F	VF	XF	Unc
MDCXI (1611)	—	100	200	375	575	—

KM# 53 1/2 THALER

Silver

Date	Mintage	VG	F	VF	XF	Unc
1612 (swan)	—	45.00	90.00	200	375	—
1613 (swan)	—	45.00	90.00	200	375	—
1614 (swan)	—	45.00	90.00	200	375	—
1615 (swan)	—	45.00	90.00	200	375	—

KM# 54 1/2 THALER

Silver **Note:** Vicariat Issue.

Date	Mintage	VG	F	VF	XF	Unc
1612 (swan)	—	80.00	165	325	525	—

KM# 79 1/2 THALER

Silver **Note:** Similar to KM#53, but thick flan.

Date	Mintage	VG	F	VF	XF	Unc
1615 (swan)	—	—	—	—	—	—

KM# 80 1/2 THALER

Silver **Subject:** Death of August II **Obv:** Bust right with baton and helmet **Rev:** 4-line inscription

Date	Mintage	VG	F	VF	XF	Unc
1615	—	—	—	—	—	—

KM# 81 1/2 THALER

Silver **Obv:** Bust right with sword and helmet, band over left shoulder **Rev:** Helmeted arms divide date at top

Date	Mintage	VG	F	VF	XF	Unc
1615 (swan)	—	60.00	120	220	425	—
1616 (swan)	—	60.00	120	220	425	—

KM# 97 1/2 THALER

Silver **Subject:** Reformation Centennial

Date	Mintage	VG	F	VF	XF	Unc
1617	—	200	400	700	1,150	—

KM# 99 1/2 THALER

Silver

Date	Mintage	VG	F	VF	XF	Unc
1617	—	100	200	350	525	—

KM# 100 1/2 THALER

Silver

Date	Mintage	VG	F	VF	XF	Unc
1617	—	100	200	350	525	—

KM# 102 1/2 THALER

Silver **Note:** Similar to 1 Thaler, KM#90. Varieties exist.

Date	Mintage	VG	F	VF	XF	Unc
1617 (swan)	—	60.00	120	220	425	—
1618 (swan)	—	60.00	120	220	425	—
1619 (swan)	—	60.00	120	220	425	—
1620 (swan)	—	60.00	120	220	425	—
1621 (swan)	—	60.00	120	220	425	—
1623 (swan)	—	60.00	120	220	425	—
1624 (swan)	—	60.00	120	220	425	—

KM# 98 1/2 THALER

Silver **Note:** Thick flan.

Date	Mintage	VG	F	VF	XF	Unc
1617	—	—	—	—	—	—

KM# 101 1/2 THALER
Silver **Note:** Thick flan.

Date	Mintage	VG	F	VF	XF	Unc
1617	—	—	—	—	—	—

KM# 118 1/2 THALER
Silver **Note:** Vicariat Issue. Similar to 1/4 Thaler, KM#116.

Date	Mintage	VG	F	VF	XF	Unc
1619	—	85.00	165	325	500	—

KM# 381 1/2 THALER
Silver **Note:** Similar to 1 Thaler, KM#90, but 4-fold arms with central shield of crossed swords in ornamented frame.

Date	Mintage	VG	F	VF	XF	Unc
1622 (swan)	—	60.00	120	220	425	—
1623 (swan)	—	60.00	120	220	425	—
16Z6 HI	—	60.00	120	220	425	—

KM# 389 1/2 THALER
Silver **Note:** Similar to 1 Thaler, KM#132. Varieties exist.

Date	Mintage	VG	F	VF	XF	Unc
1624 HI	—	55.00	110	220	400	—
1625 HI	—	55.00	110	220	400	—
1626 HI	—	55.00	110	220	400	—
1627 HI	—	55.00	110	220	400	—
1628 HI	—	55.00	110	220	400	—
1629 HI	—	55.00	110	220	400	—

KM# 408 1/2 THALER
Silver **Subject:** Augsburg Confession Centennial

Date	Mintage	VG	F	VF	XF	Unc
1630	—	65.00	120	240	425	—

KM# 409 1/2 THALER
Silver **Note:** Thick flan.

Date	Mintage	VG	F	VF	XF	Unc
1630	—	—	—	—	—	—

KM# 410 1/2 THALER
Silver **Rev:** Without helmets above 4-fold arms, central shield of crossed swords **Note:** Varieties exist.

Date	Mintage	VG	F	VF	XF	Unc
1630 HI	—	55.00	110	220	400	—
1631 HI	—	55.00	110	220	400	—
1632 HI	—	55.00	110	220	400	—
1633 HI	—	55.00	110	220	400	—
1634 HI	—	55.00	110	220	400	—
1635 CM	—	55.00	110	220	400	—
1635 HI	—	55.00	110	220	400	—
1635 SD	—	55.00	110	220	400	—
1636 SD	—	55.00	110	220	400	—
1637 SD	—	55.00	110	220	400	—
1638 SD	—	55.00	110	220	400	—
1639 SD	—	55.00	110	220	400	—
1640 CR	—	55.00	110	220	400	—
1641 CR	—	55.00	110	220	400	—
1642 CR	—	55.00	110	220	400	—
1644 CR	—	55.00	110	220	400	—
1645 CR	—	55.00	110	220	400	—
1646 CR	—	55.00	110	220	400	—
1647 CR	—	55.00	110	220	400	—
1648 CR	—	55.00	110	220	400	—
1649 CR	—	55.00	110	220	400	—
1650 CR	—	55.00	110	220	400	—
1651 CR	—	55.00	110	220	400	—
1652 CR	—	55.00	110	220	400	—
1653 CR	—	55.00	110	220	400	—
1654 CR	—	55.00	110	220	400	—
1655 CR	—	55.00	110	220	400	—
1656 CR	—	55.00	110	220	400	—

KM# 450 1/2 THALER
Silver **Subject:** Death of Johann Georg I

Date	Mintage	VG	F	VF	XF	Unc
MDCLVI (1656)	—	60.00	120	250	425	—

KM# 459 1/2 THALER
Silver **Note:** Thick flan.

Date	Mintage	VG	F	VF	XF	Unc
1657	—	—	—	—	—	—

KM# 458 1/2 THALER
Silver **Note:** Vicariat Issue. Similar to 1/8 Thaler, KM#456.

Date	Mintage	VG	F	VF	XF	Unc
1657	—	60.00	120	250	425	—
1658	—	60.00	120	250	425	—

KM# 473 1/2 THALER
Silver

Date	Mintage	VG	F	VF	XF	Unc
1658 CR	—	60.00	120	250	425	—
1659 CR	—	60.00	120	250	425	—
1660 CR	—	60.00	120	250	425	—
1661 CR	—	60.00	120	250	425	—
1662 CR	—	60.00	120	250	425	—
1663 CR	—	60.00	120	250	425	—
1665 CR	—	60.00	120	250	425	—

KM# 479 1/2 THALER
Silver **Subject:** Death of Johann Georg II's Mother, Magdalene Sibylle

Date	Mintage	VG	F	VF	XF	Unc
1659 Rare	—	—	—	—	—	—

KM# 495 1/2 THALER
Silver **Note:** Thick flan.

Date	Mintage	VG	F	VF	XF	Unc
1661 CR	—	165	325	600	1,000	—
1666 CR	—	165	325	600	1,000	—

KM# 510 1/2 THALER
Silver **Note:** Similar to KM#473, but elector in armor on obverse. Varieties exist.

Date	Mintage	VG	F	VF	XF	Unc
1665 CR	—	60.00	120	250	425	—
1666 CR	—	60.00	120	250	425	—
1667 CR	—	60.00	120	250	425	—
1671 CR	—	60.00	120	250	425	—
1672 CR	—	60.00	120	250	425	—
1673 CR	—	60.00	120	250	425	—
1679 CR	—	60.00	120	250	425	—

KM# 518 1/2 THALER
Silver **Obv:** Johann Georg II galloping on horseback right, small oval 2-fold arms below **Rev:** 9-line inscription with date **Note:** Show 1/2 Thaler. Struck at Bautzen.

Date	Mintage	VG	F	VF	XF	Unc
1666	—	—	—	—	—	—

KM# 536 1/2 THALER
Silver **Subject:** Wechsel Succession **Note:** Similar to 1 Thaler, KM#538.

Date	Mintage	VG	F	VF	XF	Unc
1670 CR	—	135	275	475	800	—

KM# 579 1/2 THALER
Silver **Note:** Similar to KM#473, but titles of Johann George III.

Date	Mintage	VG	F	VF	XF	Unc
1681 CF	—	55.00	90.00	165	325	—
1683 CF	—	55.00	90.00	165	325	—
1684 CF	—	55.00	90.00	165	325	—
1686 CF	—	55.00	90.00	165	325	—
1687	—	55.00	90.00	165	325	—
1688 IK	—	55.00	90.00	165	325	—
1689 IK	—	55.00	90.00	165	325	—
1690 IK	—	55.00	90.00	165	325	—
1691 IK	—	55.00	90.00	165	325	—

Note: Varieties exist

KM# 595 1/2 THALER
Silver **Subject:** Death of Johann Georg III's Mother, Magdalene Sibylla **Note:** Similar to 1 Groschen, KM#592.

Date	Mintage	VG	F	VF	XF	Unc
1687	—	—	—	—	—	—

KM# 614 1/2 THALER
Silver **Note:** Similar to 1 Thaler, KM#618.

Date	Mintage	VG	F	VF	XF	Unc
1691 IK	—	—	—	—	—	—
1692 IK	—	—	—	—	—	—
1693 IK	—	—	—	—	—	—
1694 IK	—	—	—	—	—	—

Note: Varieties exist

KM# 653 1/2 THALER
Silver **Note:** Similar to 1/4 Thaler, KM#407, but 4-fold arms with central shield of crossed swords.

Date	Mintage	VG	F	VF	XF	Unc
1694 EPH	—	—	—	—	—	—

KM# 668 1/2 THALER
Silver **Note:** Similar to 1 Thaler, KM#669.

Date	Mintage	VG	F	VF	XF	Unc
1695 IK	—	—	—	—	—	—
Note: IK						
1696 IK	—	—	—	—	—	—
Note: IK						

KM# 724 1/2 THALER
Silver **Ruler:** Friedrich August I **Obv:** Laureate bust right **Obv. Legend:** DG.FRID.AUG.REX.POL — DUX SAX. I.C.M.A & W. **Rev:** Crowned, round 4-fold arms with crowned central shield of 2-fold arms, between 2 palm branches crossed at bottom, date at top **Rev. Legend:** SAC. ROMANI. IMP. ARCHIMARS. ET. ELECT. **Note:** Varieties exist.

Date	Mintage	VG	F	VF	XF	Unc
1698 ILH	—	90.00	200	375	600	—
1700 ILH	—	90.00	200	375	600	—

KM# 549 2/3 THALER (Gulden)
Silver **Note:** Varieties exist.

Date	Mintage	VG	F	VF	XF	Unc
1675 CR	—	55.00	90.00	165	325	—
1676 CR	—	55.00	90.00	165	325	—
1677 CR	—	55.00	90.00	165	325	—
1678 CR	—	55.00	90.00	165	325	—

KM# 559 2/3 THALER (Gulden)
Silver **Obv:** Smaller bust **Note:** Varieties exist.

Date	Mintage	VG	F	VF	XF	Unc
1678 CF	—	55.00	90.00	165	325	—
1679 CF	—	55.00	90.00	165	325	—
1680 CF	—	55.00	90.00	165	325	—

KM# 571 2/3 THALER (Gulden)
Silver **Note:** Varieties exist. Dav. #810.

Date	Mintage	VG	F	VF	XF	Unc
1680 CF	—	55.00	90.00	165	325	—
1681 CF	—	55.00	90.00	165	325	—
1682 CF	—	55.00	90.00	165	325	—
1683 CF	—	55.00	90.00	165	325	—
1684 CF	—	55.00	90.00	165	325	—
1685 CF	—	55.00	90.00	165	325	—
1686 CF	—	55.00	90.00	165	325	—
1687	—	55.00	90.00	165	325	—
1688	—	55.00	90.00	165	325	—
1688 IK	—	55.00	90.00	165	325	—
1689	—	55.00	90.00	165	325	—
1689 IK	—	55.00	90.00	165	325	—
1690 IK	—	55.00	90.00	165	325	—
1691 IK	—	55.00	90.00	165	325	—

KM# 596 2/3 THALER (Gulden)
Silver **Subject:** Death of Johann Georg III's Mother, Magdalene Sibylle

Date	Mintage	VG	F	VF	XF	Unc
1687	—	—	—	—	—	—

KM# 615 2/3 THALER (Gulden)
Silver **Subject:** Death of Johann Georg III

Date	Mintage	VG	F	VF	XF	Unc
MDCXCI (1691) IK	—	45.00	100	220	400	—

KM# 628 2/3 THALER (Gulden)
Silver

Date	Mintage	VG	F	VF	XF	Unc
1692 IK	—	35.00	65.00	135	225	—
1693 IK	—	35.00	65.00	135	225	—

KM# 641 2/3 THALER (Gulden)
Silver

Date	Mintage	VG	F	VF	XF	Unc
1693	—	—	—	—	—	—
1693 IK	—	35.00	65.00	135	225	—
1693 SD	—	40.00	70.00	140	275	—
1693 EPH	—	—	—	—	—	—
1694 IK	—	35.00	65.00	135	225	—
1694 EPH	—	40.00	70.00	140	275	—

KM# 654 2/3 THALER (Gulden)
Silver **Subject:** Death of Johann Georg IV

Date	Mintage	VG	F	VF	XF	Unc
MDCXCIV (1694) IK	—	60.00	120	250	425	—

KM# 655 2/3 THALER (Gulden)
Silver **Note:** Varieties exist.

Date	Mintage	VG	F	VF	XF	Unc
1694 IK	—	35.00	65.00	135	240	—
1694 EPH	—	40.00	70.00	140	275	—
1695 IK	—	35.00	65.00	135	240	—
1695 EPH	—	40.00	70.00	140	275	—
1696 IK	—	35.00	65.00	135	240	—
1696 EPH	—	40.00	70.00	140	275	—
1697 IK	—	35.00	65.00	135	240	—
1697 EPH	—	40.00	70.00	140	275	—

KM# 685 2/3 THALER (Gulden)
Silver **Ruler:** Friedrich August I **Obv:** Armored, laureate bust right **Obv. Legend:** DG • FRID • AUGUST • REX POLONIARUM

Rev: Crown above two shields, value below **Rev. Legend:** DUX • SAX • I • C • M • A • & • W • S • R • I • ... **Note:** Similar to 1 Thaler, KM#707, but value: 2/3 on reverse. Dav.#819.

Date	Mintage	VG	F	VF	XF	Unc
1697 EPH	—	35.00	65.00	135	240	—
1697 IK	—	35.00	65.00	135	240	—
1698 EPH	—	35.00	65.00	135	240	—
1698 ILH	—	35.00	65.00	135	240	—
1699 EPH	—	35.00	65.00	135	240	—
1699 ILH	—	35.00	65.00	135	240	—
1700 EPH	—	35.00	65.00	135	240	—
1700 ILH	—	35.00	65.00	135	240	—

KM# 15 THALER

Silver **Obv:** 3 half figures facing with date divided above **Rev:** Helmeted arms **Note:** Dav. #7557.

Date	Mintage	VG	F	VF	XF	Unc
1600	—	90.00	170	225	350	—
1601 HB	—	90.00	170	225	350	—

KM# 16 THALER

28.7700 g., Silver **Obv:** Bust right with sword and helmet, date divided above **Rev:** 2 facing busts in a circle of 14 shields **Note:** Dav. #7561.

Date	Mintage	VG	F	VF	XF	Unc
1601 HB	—	90.00	170	225	350	—
160Z HB	—	90.00	170	225	350	—
1603 HB	—	90.00	170	225	350	—
1604 HB	—	90.00	170	225	350	—
1605 HB	—	90.00	170	225	350	—

KM# 24 THALER

Silver **Obv:** Bust right with sword and helmet divide date **Rev:** Busts facing one another **Note:** Dav. #7566.

Date	Mintage	VG	F	VF	XF	Unc
1604 HR	—	90.00	170	225	350	—
1605 HR	—	90.00	170	225	350	—
1606 HR	—	90.00	170	225	350	—
1607 HR	—	90.00	170	225	350	—
1608 HR	—	90.00	170	225	350	—
1609 HR	—	90.00	170	225	350	—
1610 HR	—	90.00	170	225	350	—
1611 HR	—	90.00	170	225	350	—

KM# 43 THALER

Silver **Subject:** Death of Christian II **Obv:** Bust right, 2 rows of legends around **Rev:** 6-line inscription **Note:** Dav. #7569.

Date	Mintage	VG	F	VF	XF	Unc
1611	—	195	375	675	1,150	—

KM# 44 THALER

Silver **Obv:** Bust right with sword and helmet dividing date **Rev:** Circle of 18 shields around bust right **Note:** Dav. #7573.

Date	Mintage	VG	F	VF	XF	Unc
1611 swan	—	90.00	170	225	350	—
1612 swan	—	90.00	170	225	350	—
1613 swan	—	90.00	170	225	350	—
1614 swan	—	90.00	170	225	350	—
1615 swan	—	90.00	170	225	350	—
1616 swan	—	90.00	170	225	350	—

KM# 125 THALER

Silver **Subject:** Accession After the Settlement of the Ducal Succession in Julich **Obv:** Standing figure with sword **Rev:** Bear and ape by tree **Note:** Dav. #7575.

Date	Mintage	VG	F	VF	XF	Unc
1611 Rare	—	—	—	—	—	—

Note: Fritz Rudolf Künker Münzenhandlung Auction 119, 2-07, XF realized approximately $13,025

KM# 55 THALER

Silver **Subject:** Death of Emperor Rudolf **Obv:** Capped bust with sword **Rev:** Shield dividing date **Note:** Dav. #7579.

Date	Mintage	VG	F	VF	XF	Unc
1612 swan	—	125	250	700	1,500	—

KM# 56 THALER

Silver **Rev:** Arms dividing date at top **Note:** Dav. #7580.

Date	Mintage	VG	F	VF	XF	Unc
1612 swan	—	150	300	900	1,650	—

KM# 72 THALER

Silver **Subject:** Baptism of August, Son of Johann Georg **Obv:** 1/2 figure right with baton and helmet **Rev:** Crowned crossed swords in branches **Note:** Klippe. Dav. #7583.

Date	Mintage	VG	F	VF	XF	Unc
1614	—	300	550	900	1,500	—

KM# 82 THALER

Silver **Subject:** Baptism of Christian, Son of Johann Georg **Obv:** 1/2 figure in different armor right with baton and helmet **Note:** Klippe. Dav. #7587.

Date	Mintage	VG	F	VF	XF	Unc
1615	—	215	400	650	1,850	—

KM# 83 THALER

Silver **Subject:** Death of August, Administrator of Naumburg **Obv:** Bust right with baton and helmet **Rev:** 4-line inscription **Note:** Dav. #7588.

Date	Mintage	VG	F	VF	XF	Unc
1615	—	210	400	750	2,000	—

KM# 89 THALER

Silver **Obv:** Bust right with sword and helmet, band over left shoulder **Rev:** Helmeted arms divide date at top **Note:** Dav. #7589.

Date	Mintage	VG	F	VF	XF	Unc
1616 swan	—	165	325	425	625	—

KM# 90 THALER

Silver **Obv:** Bust right with sword and helmet, band over right shoulder **Note:** Dav. #7591.

Date	Mintage	VG	F	VF	XF	Unc
1616 swan	—	130	250	325	500	1,150
1617 swan	—	130	250	325	500	1,150
1618 swan	—	130	250	325	500	1,150
1619 swan	—	130	250	325	500	1,150
1620 swan	—	130	250	325	500	1,150

KM# 103 THALER

Silver **Subject:** Centennial of the Reformation **Obv:** Capped bust right with sword dividing IOH-GEORG **Rev:** Capped bust right dividing FRID-III **Note:** Dav. #7595.

Date	Mintage	VG	F	VF	XF	Unc
1617	—	195	375	675	1,150	—

KM# 119 THALER

Silver **Subject:** Death of Emperor Matthias **Obv:** Elector on horseback right dividing date **Rev:** 12-line inscription **Note:** Dav. #7597.

Date	Mintage	VG	F	VF	XF	Unc
1619	—	130	250	450	750	—

KM# 132 THALER

Silver **Rev:** Helmeted arms **Note:** Dav. #7601.

Date	Mintage	VG	F	VF	XF	Unc
1620 HvR swan	—	65.00	170	325	475	—
1621 HvR swan	—	65.00	170	325	475	—
1622 HvR swan	—	65.00	170	325	475	—
1623 HvR swan	—	65.00	170	325	475	—
1624 HI	—	65.00	170	325	475	—
1625 HI	—	65.00	170	325	475	—
1626 HI	—	65.00	170	325	475	—
1627 HI	—	65.00	170	325	475	—
1628 HI	—	65.00	170	325	475	—
1629 HI	—	65.00	170	325	475	—
1630 HI	—	65.00	170	325	475	—
1631 HI	—	65.00	170	325	475	—
1632 HI	—	65.00	170	325	475	—
1633 HI	—	65.00	170	325	475	—
1634 HI	—	65.00	170	325	475	—
1635 CM	—	65.00	170	325	475	—
1635 HI	—	65.00	170	325	475	—
1635 SD	—	65.00	170	325	475	—
1636 SD	—	65.00	170	325	475	—
1637 SD	—	65.00	170	325	475	—
1638 SD	—	65.00	170	325	475	—

KM# 339 THALER

Silver **Note:** Kipper Thaler. Struck at Merseburg. Similar to 20 Groschen, KM#253, but oval arms and without indication of value.

Date	Mintage	VG	F	VF	XF	Unc
1621 (rooster)	—	—	—	—	—	—

KM# 340 THALER

Silver **Note:** Similar to 20 Groschen, KM#253, but arms nearly flat on top, curved on bottom without indication of value.

Date	Mintage	VG	F	VF	XF	Unc
1622 (rooster)	—	—	—	—	—	—
1622 MB/(rooster)	—	—	—	—	—	—

KM# 394 THALER

Silver **Note:** Similar to 2 Thaler, KM#392. Dav. #LS390.

Date	Mintage	VG	F	VF	XF	Unc
1628 Rare	—	—	—	—	—	—

KM# 411 THALER

Silver **Subject:** Centennial of Augsburg Confession **Obv:** Capped bust holding sword with two hands right **Obv. Legend:** ...EXHIBITAE... **Note:** Dav. #7605.

Date	Mintage	VG	F	VF	XF	Unc
1630	—	100	190	300	650	—

KM# 412 THALER

Silver **Subject:** Centennial of Augsburg Confession **Obv:** Capped bust holding sword with one hand **Note:** Dav. #7605A.

Date	Mintage	VG	F	VF	XF	Unc
1630	—	130	250	400	850	—

KM# 413 THALER

Silver **Subject:** Centennial of Augsburg Confession **Obv:** 25 Juny-1630 below in legend **Obv. Legend:** ...EXHIBIT... **Rev:** 25 Juny-1530 divided below in legend **Note:** Dav. #7606.

Date	Mintage	VG	F	VF	XF	Unc
1630	—	130	250	400	650	—

KM# 414 THALER

Silver **Subject:** Marriage of Maria Elisabeth, Daughter of Johann Georg, to Friedrich III **Obv:** Clasped and chained hands **Note:** Dav. #7609.

Date	Mintage	VG	F	VF	XF	Unc
1630	—	270	500	800	1,300	—

KM# 425 THALER

Silver **Rev:** 8 helmets above shield dividing date **Note:** Dav. #7612.

Date	Mintage	VG	F	VF	XF	Unc
1638 SD	—	80.00	155	250	375	—
1639 SD	—	80.00	155	250	375	—
1640 CR	—	80.00	155	250	375	—
1640 SD	—	80.00	155	250	375	—
1641 CR	—	80.00	155	250	375	—
1642 CR	—	80.00	155	250	375	—
1643 CR	—	80.00	155	250	375	—
1644 CR	—	80.00	155	250	375	—

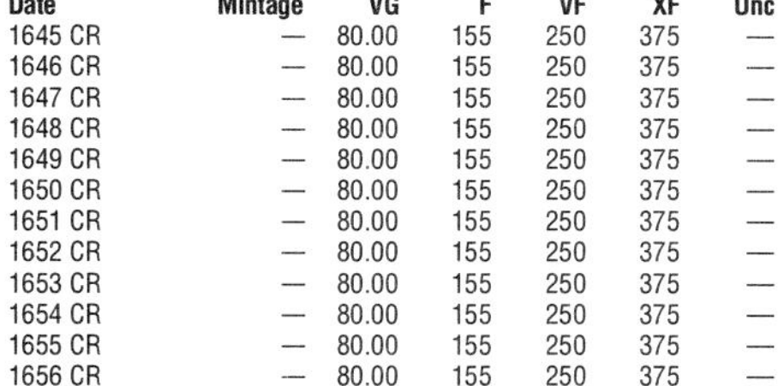

Date	Mintage	VG	F	VF	XF	Unc
1645 CR	—	80.00	155	250	375	—
1646 CR	—	80.00	155	250	375	—
1647 CR	—	80.00	155	250	375	—
1648 CR	—	80.00	155	250	375	—
1649 CR	—	80.00	155	250	375	—
1650 CR	—	80.00	155	250	375	—
1651 CR	—	80.00	155	250	375	—
1652 CR	—	80.00	155	250	375	—
1653 CR	—	80.00	155	250	375	—
1654 CR	—	80.00	155	250	375	—
1655 CR	—	80.00	155	250	375	—
1656 CR	—	80.00	155	250	375	—

KM# 451 THALER

Silver **Subject:** Death of Johann Georg I **Obv:** Facing bust within 2 outer legends **Rev:** 10-line inscription **Note:** Dav. #7614.

Date	Mintage	VG	F	VF	XF	Unc
1656	—	130	250	450	750	—

KM# 481 THALER

Silver **Subject:** Death of Emperor Ferdinand III **Obv. Legend:** DEO ET - PATRIAE begins at 2 o'clock **Note:** Dav. #7630.

Date	Mintage	VG	F	VF	XF	Unc
1657 acorn	—	85.00	175	375	750	—
1658 acorn	—	85.00	175	375	750	—

KM# 480 THALER

Silver **Subject:** Death of the Emperor Ferdinand III **Obv. Legend:** DEO ET-PATRIAE **Note:** Similar to Dav. #7630 but obverse legend begins at 9 o'clock. Dav. #7628.

Date	Mintage	VG	F	VF	XF	Unc
1657 acorn	—	90.00	180	400	785	—

KM# 474 THALER

Silver **Obv:** Bust with sword right, cap in front **Rev:** Helmeted arms, date divided by helmets **Note:** Dav. #7617.

Date	Mintage	VG	F	VF	XF	Unc
1658 CR	—	130	250	425	625	—
1659 CR	—	130	250	425	625	—
1660 CR	—	130	250	425	625	—
1661 CR	—	130	250	425	625	—
1662 CR	—	130	250	425	625	—
1663 CR	—	130	250	425	625	—
1664 CR	—	130	250	425	625	—
1665 CR	—	130	250	425	625	—
1666 CR	—	130	250	425	625	—
1667 CR	—	130	250	425	625	—
1678 CR	—	130	250	425	625	—
1679 CR	—	130	250	425	625	—
1680 CR	—	130	250	425	625	—

KM# 476 THALER

Silver **Obv:** Bust in armor, helmet in front **Note:** Dav. #7617.

Date	Mintage	VG	F	VF	XF	Unc
1658 CR	—	130	250	425	625	—
1659 CR	—	130	250	425	625	—
1660 CR	—	130	250	425	625	—
1664 CR	—	130	250	425	625	—
1665 CR	—	130	250	425	625	—
1666 CR	—	130	250	425	625	—
1667 CR	—	130	250	425	625	—
1668 CR	—	130	250	425	625	—

KM# 482 THALER

Silver **Subject:** Death of Magdalena Sibylla, Wife of Johann Georg I **Obv:** 10-line inscription **Rev:** 11-line inscription **Note:** Dav. #7615.

Date	Mintage	VG	F	VF	XF	Unc
1659	—	140	270	500	800	—

KM# 475 THALER

Silver **Note:** Thick flan. Dav. #7617A. Struck with 1/4 Thaler dies, KM#449.

Date	Mintage	VG	F	VF	XF	Unc
1660 CR	—	130	250	425	625	—
1661 CR	—	130	250	425	625	—
1662 CR	—	130	250	425	625	—
1666 CR	—	130	250	425	625	—

KM# 500 THALER

Silver **Subject:** Marriage of Erdmuthe Sophie, Daughter of Johann Georg, to Christian Ernst **Obv:** Arms with wreath from clouds above pillars and monument **Rev:** 9-line inscription, arms in four corners **Note:** Klippe. Dav. #7631. Illustration reduced.

Date	Mintage	VG	F	VF	XF	Unc
1662	—	200	400	900	1,850	—

KM# 502 THALER

Silver **Subject:** Confessional Issue **Note:** Similar to 2 Thaler, KM#504.

Date	Mintage	VG	F	VF	XF	Unc
1663	—	—	—	—	—	—

KM# 528 THALER

Silver **Subject:** Birth of Johann Georg IV, Grandson of Johann Georg II **Obv:** IG4 monogram **Rev:** Young Hercules in a cradle grasping a snake, date in corners **Note:** Klippe. Dav. #7632. Illustration reduced.

Date	Mintage	VG	F	VF	XF	Unc
1669	—	—	500	1,150	2,000	—

KM# 538 THALER

Silver **Obv:** Different bust right **Rev:** WECHSEL., THALER below arms **Note:** Dav. #7625.

Date	Mintage	VG	F	VF	XF	Unc
1670 CR	—	125	250	475	750	—
1671 CR	—	125	250	475	750	—

KM# 537 THALER

Silver **Obv:** Bust right **Rev:** Capped arms in frame **Note:** Dav. #7621.

Date	Mintage	VG	F	VF	XF	Unc
1670 CR	—	130	250	425	625	—
1671 CR	—	130	250	425	625	—

KM# 544 THALER

Silver **Obv:** Larger bust **Rev:** Oval shield and different frame **Note:** Dav. #7624.

Date	Mintage	VG	F	VF	XF	Unc
1671 CR	—	115	225	295	450	—

KM# 565 THALER
22.4800 g., Silver **Subject:** Election to the Order of the Garter **Obv:** St. George slaying the dragon **Rev:** 9-line inscription in laurel wreath **Note:** Dav. #7633.

Date	Mintage	VG	F	VF	XF	Unc
MDCLXXI (1671)	—	130	250	450	1,000	2,000
MDCLXXVIII (1678)	—	130	250	450	1,000	2,000

KM# 550 THALER
Silver **Obv:** Heavier bust **Rev:** Differently shaped shield **Note:** Dav. #7626.

Date	Mintage	VG	F	VF	XF	Unc
1675 CR	—	120	250	425	625	—
1676 CR	—	120	250	425	625	—
1677 CR	—	120	250	425	625	—
1678 CR	—	120	250	425	625	—

KM# 560 THALER
Silver **Obv:** Thinner bust with long hair **Rev:** Differently shaped shield dividing C-F **Note:** Dav. #7627.

Date	Mintage	VG	F	VF	XF	Unc
1678 CF	—	175	375	750	1,250	—
1679 CF	—	175	375	750	1,250	—
1680 CF	—	175	375	750	1,250	—

KM# 561 THALER
Silver **Subject:** Shooting Match at Dresden **Obv:** Bust right, arms in corners **Rev:** 7-line inscription in wreath, arms in corners **Note:** Klippe. Dav. #7635.

Date	Mintage	VG	F	VF	XF	Unc
1678	—	225	425	675	1,150	—

KM# 562 THALER
21.8800 g., Silver **Subject:** Shooting Match at Dresden **Obv:** Capped arms in Order band with motto, arms in corners **Rev:** Hercules standing with club date in Roman numerals **Note:** Klippe. Dav. #7636.

Date	Mintage	VG	F	VF	XF	Unc
MDC-LXXVIII (1678)	—	165	300	525	2,500	—

KM# 564 THALER
Silver **Subject:** Peace of Nijmegen **Obv:** 6-line inscription in wreath, arms in corners **Rev:** Hand from cloud with wreath above Hercules on a cloud **Note:** Klippe. Dav.#7637.

Date	Mintage	VG	F	VF	XF	Unc
1679	—	205	375	600	1,000	—

KM# 572 THALER
Silver **Subject:** Death of Johann Georg II **Obv:** Fama above capped shields, Saturn below **Rev:** 16-line inscription **Note:** Dav.#7638.

Date	Mintage	VG	F	VF	XF	Unc
1680	—	200	400	850	1,500	—

KM# 580 THALER

Silver **Obv:** Bust right with helmet in front **Rev:** Helmeted arms separating initials, date divided at top **Note:** Dav. #7640.

Date	Mintage	VG	F	VF	XF	Unc
1681 CF	—	115	225	425	675	1,550
1682 CF	—	115	225	425	675	1,550
1683 CF	—	115	225	425	675	1,550
1684 CF	—	115	225	425	675	1,550
1685 CF	—	115	225	425	675	1,550
1686 CF	—	115	225	425	675	1,550
1687	—	115	225	425	675	1,550
1688	—	115	225	425	675	1,550
1688 IK	—	115	225	425	675	1,550
1689 IK	—	115	225	425	675	1,550

KM# 599 THALER

Silver **Subject:** Relief of Turkish Siege of Vienna **Obv:** Helmeted and armored bust of Johann Georg III right **Rev:** Elector's hat above field marshall's staff, dividing city view below, crossed swords between arms of Saxony, turban at right below arms **Designer:** Johann Höhn

Date	Mintage	VG	F	VF	XF	Unc
ND(1683) Rare	—	—	—	—	—	—

Note: Baldwin's Auctions Ltd Auction 41, 5-05, good VF realized approximately $6,090

KM# 597 THALER

Silver **Subject:** Death of Johann Georg II's Wife, Magdalena Sibylla of Brandenburg-Bayreuth **Obv:** 9-line inscription **Obv. Inscription:** +/ D • G •/ MAGDALENA/ SIBYLLA • ELECTRIX •/ SAXONIÆ • E • PROSAP •/ MARCH • BRANDENB •/ NAT • 1612 • DENAT • 1687/ DIE • 20 MART •/ + **Rev:** Large crown above 4-banded rainbow beneath which a 2-line inscription, all in laurel wreath **Rev. Inscription:** SOLA •/ SPES• MEA • **Note:** Dav# 7641.

Date	Mintage	VG	F	VF	XF	Unc
1687	—	325	675	1,500	2,500	—

KM# 607 THALER

Silver **Rev:** Helmeted arms **Note:** Dav. #7642.

Date	Mintage	VG	F	VF	XF	Unc
1690 IK	—	150	300	650	1,200	—
1691 IK	—	150	300	650	1,200	—

KM# 616 THALER

Silver **Subject:** Death of Johann Georg III **Obv:** Arm from clouds holding flag **Rev:** 11-line inscription **Note:** Dav. #7643.

Date	Mintage	VG	F	VF	XF	Unc
1691 IK	—	100	225	600	1,000	—

KM# 617 THALER

Silver **Subject:** Death of Johann Georg III **Obv:** Bust right in center, 3 legends around **Rev:** 15-line inscription **Note:** Dav. #7645.

Date	Mintage	VG	F	VF	XF	Unc
1691 IK	—	175	375	850	1,650	—

KM# 618 THALER

Silver **Obv:** Bust right, helmet in front **Rev:** Helmeted arms separating initials, date divided at top **Note:** Dav. #7647.

Date	Mintage	VG	F	VF	XF	Unc
1691 IK	—	250	450	1,000	2,000	3,750
1692 IK	—	250	450	1,000	2,000	3,750
1693 IK	—	250	450	1,000	2,000	3,750
1694 IK	—	250	450	1,000	2,000	3,750

KM# 642 THALER

Silver **Subject:** Johann Georg IV Receiving the Order of the Garter **Obv:** JG4 monogram in Garter band, arms in corners **Rev:** Capped wreath with crossed swords, arms in corners **Note:** Klippe. Dav. #7649.

Date	Mintage	VG	F	VF	XF	Unc
1693	—	100	200	400	800	1,650

KM# 656 THALER

Silver **Rev:** Capped arms dividing initials, date in legend **Note:** Dav. #7648.

Date	Mintage	VG	F	VF	XF	Unc
1694 EP-H	—	600	1,200	2,000	3,500	—

KM# 657 THALER

Silver **Subject:** Death of Johann Georg IV **Obv:** Pyramid with arms on 2 sides, churches in background **Rev:** Pyramid with 14-line inscription, tents and guns in background, flags and cannons in foreground **Note:** Dav. #7650.

Date	Mintage	VG	F	VF	XF	Unc
1694 IK	—	140	270	500	800	—

KM# 658 THALER

Silver **Subject:** Death of Johann Georg IV **Obv:** Bust right, 3 legends around **Rev:** 16-line inscription **Note:** Dav. #7651.

Date	Mintage	VG	F	VF	XF	Unc
1694 IK	—	150	300	650	1,250	2,250

KM# 669 THALER

Silver **Obv:** Bust right, sword and helmet in front **Rev:** Helmeted arms divide initials, date divided above **Note:** Dav. #7652.

Date	Mintage	VG	F	VF	XF	Unc
1695 IK	—	300	700	1,500	2,500	—
1696 IK	—	300	700	1,500	2,500	—
1697 IK	—	300	700	1,500	2,500	—
1698 IK	—	300	700	1,500	2,500	—

KM# 675 THALER

Silver **Subject:** Birth of Friedrich August II **Obv:** Knight holding large shield, door in background **Rev:** FAS in cloud above city view of Dresden **Note:** Dav. #7653.

Date	Mintage	VG	F	VF	XF	Unc
1696 IK	—	350	750	1,550	2,550	5,750

KM# 686 THALER

Silver **Obv:** Crowned FAC monogram in sprays, date divided above **Rev:** Hand with wreath from cloud above Hercules on a cloud **Note:** Klippe. Dav. #7654.

Date	Mintage	VG	F	VF	XF	Unc
1697	—	175	350	750	1,850	—

KM# 707 THALER

Silver **Ruler:** Friedrich August I **Rev:** 2 shields crowned between palm branches **Note:** Dav. #7656.

Date	Mintage	F	VF	XF	Unc	BU
1698 IK	—	350	750	1,500	3,750	—
1698 ILH	—	350	750	1,500	3,750	—
1699 ILH	—	350	750	1,500	3,750	—
1700 ILH	—	350	750	1,500	3,750	—

KM# 713 THALER

Silver **Ruler:** Friedrich August I **Obv:** Crowned A in sprays, date divided above **Rev:** Hand with wreath from cloud above Hercules on a cloud **Rev. Legend:** VIRTUTE PARATA **Shape:** 4-Sided **Note:** Klippe. Dav. #7657 and Dav. #2648. Illustration reduced.

Date	Mintage	F	VF	XF	Unc	BU
1699	—	400	900	2,000	3,200	—

KM# 395 1-1/2 THALER

Silver **Note:** Similar to 2 Thaler, KM#392. Dav. #LS389. Illustration reduced.

Date	Mintage	VG	F	VF	XF	Unc
16Z8	—	850	1,650	2,750	—	—

KM# 503 1-1/2 THALER

Silver **Note:** Similar to 2 Thaler, KM#504. Dav. #LS405.

Date	Mintage	VG	F	VF	XF	Unc
1663	—	750	1,250	1,950	3,250	—

KM# 17 2 THALER

Silver **Obv:** 3 half figures facing, date divided above **Rev:** Helmeted arms **Note:** Dav. #7556.

Date	Mintage	VG	F	VF	XF	Unc
1601 HB	—	525	825	1,350	2,250	—

KM# 18 2 THALER

Silver **Note:** Similar to 1 Thaler, KM#16. Dav. #7560.

Date	Mintage	VG	F	VF	XF	Unc
1601 HB	—	350	600	1,000	1,900	—
160Z HB	—	350	600	1,000	1,900	—
1603 HB	—	350	600	1,000	1,900	—
1604 HB	—	350	600	1,000	1,900	—
1605 HB	—	350	600	1,000	1,900	—

KM# 26 2 THALER

Silver **Note:** Similar to 1 Thaler, KM#24. Dav. #7565.

Date	Mintage	VG	F	VF	XF	Unc
1605 HvR	—	350	600	1,000	1,900	—
1606 HvR	—	350	600	1,000	1,900	—
1607 HvR	—	350	600	1,000	1,900	—
1608 HvR	—	350	600	1,000	1,900	—
1609 HvR	—	350	600	1,000	1,900	—
1610 HvR	—	350	600	1,000	1,900	—
1611 HvR	—	350	600	1,000	1,900	—

KM# 45 2 THALER

Silver **Subject:** Death of Christian II **Note:** Similar to 1 Thaler, KM#43. Dav. #7568.

Date	Mintage	VG	F	VF	XF	Unc
1611	—	650	1,250	2,000	3,750	—

KM# 46 2 THALER

Silver **Note:** Similar to 1 Thaler, KM#44. Dav. #7572.

Date	Mintage	VG	F	VF	XF	Unc
1611	—	550	950	1,450	2,500	—
1612	—	550	950	1,450	2,500	—
1613	—	550	950	1,450	2,500	—
1614	—	550	950	1,450	2,500	—
1615	—	550	950	1,450	2,500	—

KM# 124 2 THALER

Silver **Subject:** Accession After the Settlement of the Ducal Succession in Julich **Obv:** Standing figure with sword **Rev:** Bear and ape by tree **Note:** Dav. #7574.

Date	Mintage	VG	F	VF	XF	Unc
1611 Rare	—	—	—	—	—	—

KM# 57 2 THALER

Silver **Ruler:** Johann Georg I and August **Subject:** Death of Emperor Rudolph **Note:** Similar to 1 Thaler, KM#55. Dav. #7578.

Date	Mintage	VG	F	VF	XF	Unc
1612 swan	—	750	1,500	2,500	—	—

KM# 73 2 THALER

Silver **Subject:** Baptism of August, Son of Johann Georg I **Note:** Klippe. Similar to KM#74, but sword pointing to last A in AMONA. Dav. #7582.

Date	Mintage	VG	F	VF	XF	Unc
1614	—	650	1,200	2,400	4,250	—

KM# 74 2 THALER

Silver **Subject:** Baptism of August, Son of Johann Georg I **Rev:** Sword pointing to S in SVIS **Note:** Klippe. Dav. #7582A.

Date	Mintage	VG	F	VF	XF	Unc
1614	—	600	1,200	2,450	4,250	—

KM# 84 2 THALER

Silver **Subject:** Baptism of Christian, Son of Johann Georg I **Obv:** Different armor **Note:** Klippe. Dav. #7586.

Date	Mintage	VG	F	VF	XF	Unc
1615	—	650	1,250	2,500	4,500	—

KM# 91 2 THALER

Silver **Ruler:** Johann Georg I **Note:** Similar to 1 Thaler KM#90. Dav. #7590A.

Date	Mintage	VG	F	VF	XF	Unc
1616 swan	—	450	850	1,750	3,000	—
1617 swan	—	450	850	1,750	3,000	—
1618 swan	—	450	850	1,750	3,000	—
1619 swan	—	450	850	1,750	3,000	—

KM# 104 2 THALER

Silver **Subject:** Centennial of the Reformation **Obv:** Capped bust dividing IOH-GEOR **Rev:** Capped bust dividing FRID-III **Note:** Dav. #7594.

Date	Mintage	VG	F	VF	XF	Unc
1617	—	800	1,600	3,250	5,500	—

KM# 120 2 THALER

Silver **Subject:** Death of Emperor Matthias **Note:** Similar to 1 Thaler, KM#119. Dav. #7596.

Date	Mintage	VG	F	VF	XF	Unc
1619	—	850	1,650	3,400	5,750	—

KM# 133 2 THALER

Silver **Ruler:** Johann Georg I **Note:** Similar to 1 Thaler, KM#132. Dav. #7600.

Date	Mintage	VG	F	VF	XF	Unc
1620 HR	—	240	475	900	2,250	—
1621 HR	—	240	475	900	2,250	—
1623 HR	—	240	475	900	2,250	—
1625 HS	—	240	475	900	2,250	—
1626 HS	—	240	475	900	2,250	—
1627 HS	—	240	475	900	2,250	—
1628 HS	—	240	475	900	2,250	—
1629 HS	—	240	475	900	2,250	—
1631	—	240	475	900	2,250	—
1632 HS	—	240	475	900	2,250	—
1633 HS	—	240	475	900	2,250	—
1634 HS	—	240	475	900	2,250	—
1635 CM	—	240	475	900	2,250	—
1635 HS	—	240	475	900	2,250	—
1635 SD	—	240	475	900	2,250	—
1636 SD	—	240	475	900	2,250	—
1637 SD	—	240	475	900	2,250	—
1638 SD	—	240	475	900	2,250	—

KM# 341 2 THALER

Silver **Note:** Kipper 2 Thaler. Similar to 20 Groschen, KM#253 but without indication of value, and date at bottom of obverse.

Date	Mintage	VG	F	VF	XF	Unc
1621 (rooster)	—	—	—	—	—	—

KM# 342 2 THALER

Silver **Note:** Also dated above angels on reverse.

Date	Mintage	VG	F	VF	XF	Unc
1621/1621 (rooster)	—	—	—	—	—	—

KM# 343 2 THALER

Silver **Note:** Date only above angels on reverse.

Date	Mintage	VG	F	VF	XF	Unc
1622 (rooster)	—	—	—	—	—	—
1622 MB/(rooster)	—	—	—	—	—	—

KM# 392 2 THALER

Silver **Obv:** Duke on horseback, Dresden and Elbe River bridge below **Rev:** Helmeted arms divide date **Note:** Illustration reduced. Dav. #LS388.

Date	Mintage	VG	F	VF	XF	Unc
1626 HI	—	1,000	2,000	3,500	—	—
1627 HI	—	1,000	2,000	3,500	—	—
1628 HI	—	1,000	2,000	3,500	—	—

KM# 391 2 THALER

Silver **Obv:** Bust in cloak with sword right **Rev:** Capped arms divide date at top **Note:** Dav. #7602.

Date	Mintage	VG	F	VF	XF	Unc
1626 HI	—	600	1,200	2,250	3,750	—
1627 HI	—	600	1,200	2,250	3,750	—
1628 HI	—	600	1,200	2,250	3,750	—

KM# 415 2 THALER

Silver **Subject:** Centennial of Augsburg Confession **Obv:** Johann Georg with sword in 2 hands **Note:** Dav. #7604.

Date	Mintage	VG	F	VF	XF	Unc
1630	—	500	1,000	2,000	3,500	—

KM# 416 2 THALER

Silver **Subject:** Centennial of Augsburg Confession **Note:** Similar to 1 Thaler, KM#412. Dav. #7604A.

Date	Mintage	VG	F	VF	XF	Unc
1630	—	500	1,000	2,000	3,500	—

KM# 417 2 THALER

Silver **Subject:** Marriage of Maria Elisabeth, Daughter of Johann Georg, and Friedrich III **Rev:** Clasped and chained hands **Note:** Dav. #7608.

Date	Mintage	VG	F	VF	XF	Unc
1630	—	450	850	1,750	3,000	—

KM# 430 2 THALER

Silver **Note:** Similar to 1 Thaler, KM#425. Dav. #7611.

Date	Mintage	VG	F	VF	XF	Unc
1645 CR	—	375	750	1,500	2,500	—
1646 CR	—	375	750	1,500	2,500	—
1654 CR	—	375	750	1,500	2,500	—
1655 CR	—	3,753	750	1,500	2,500	—

KM# 435 2 THALER

58.0000 g., Silver **Subject:** Peace of Westphalia **Note:** Similar to 3 Thaler, KM#436. Dav. #LS395.

Date	Mintage	VG	F	VF	XF	Unc
1650 CR	—	1,500	2,450	3,750	5,500	—

KM# 443 2 THALER

Silver **Obv:** 1/2 figure facing with sword **Rev:** 8 helmets above shield **Note:** Dav. #7613.

Date	Mintage	VG	F	VF	XF	Unc
1652 CR	—	900	1,850	3,500	6,000	—
1653 CR	—	900	1,850	3,500	6,000	—

KM# 460 2 THALER

Silver, 51 mm. **Subject:** Death of Emperor Ferdinand III **Obv:** Duke on horseback, arms below **Rev:** 12-line inscription **Note:** Dav. #LS398.

Date	Mintage	VG	F	VF	XF	Unc
1657 acorn	—	1,000	2,000	3,500	5,000	—
1658 acorn	—	1,000	2,000	3,500	5,000	—

KM# 496 2 THALER

Silver, 64 mm. **Ruler:** Johann Georg II **Subject:** Chapel at Moritzburg **Note:** Illustration reduced. Dav. #LS401.

Date	Mintage	VG	F	VF	XF	Unc
1661 acorn	—	500	900	1,750	2,750	—

KM# 499 2 THALER

Silver **Obv:** Bust with sword right, cap in front **Rev:** Helmeted arms **Note:** Dav. #7616.

Date	Mintage	VG	F	VF	XF	Unc
1662 CR	—	550	950	1,850	3,000	—
1677 CR	—	550	950	1,850	3,000	—

KM# 504 2 THALER

58.0000 g., Silver **Subject:** For the Confession **Note:** Illustration reduced. Dav. #LS404.

Date	Mintage	VG	F	VF	XF	Unc
1663 CR	—	1,050	1,750	2,700	3,950	—

KM# 511 2 THALER

Silver **Note:** Similar to 1 Thaler, KM#476. Dav. #7618.

Date	Mintage	VG	F	VF	XF	Unc
1665 CR	—	1,050	2,000	3,300	5,300	—

KM# 539 2 THALER

Silver **Note:** Similar to 1 Thaler, KM#537. Dav. #7620.

Date	Mintage	VG	F	VF	XF	Unc
1670 CR	—	1,050	2,000	3,300	5,300	—

KM# 545 2 THALER

58.0000 g., Silver **Rev:** Capped oval shield in frame **Note:** Dav. #7623.

Date	Mintage	VG	F	VF	XF	Unc
1671 CR	—	1,050	2,000	3,300	5,300	—

KM# 598 2 THALER

Silver **Note:** Similar to 1 Thaler, KM#580. Dav. #7639.

Date	Mintage	VG	F	VF	XF	Unc
1687	—	1,150	2,050	3,400	5,600	—

KM# 619 2 THALER

Silver **Note:** Similar to 1 Thaler, KM#617. Dav. #7644.

Date	Mintage	VG	F	VF	XF	Unc
1691 IK	—	900	1,800	3,000	5,000	—

KM# 629 2 THALER

Silver **Note:** Similar to 1 Thaler, KM#618. Dav. #7646.

Date	Mintage	VG	F	VF	XF	Unc
1692 IK Rare	—	—	—	—	—	—

KM# 708 2 THALER

Silver **Rev:** 2 shields crowned between palm branches, date divided at top **Note:** Dav. #7655.

Date	Mintage	VG	F	VF	XF	Unc
1698 ILH Rare	—	—	—	—	—	—
1699 ILH Rare	—	—	—	—	—	—

KM# 554 2-1/2 THALER

Silver **Subject:** Dedication of Spire at Dresden Palace **Obv:** View of palace with spire in center **Rev:** 15-line inscription with Roman numeral date **Note:** Show 2-1/2 Thaler.

Date	Mintage	VG	F	VF	XF	Unc
1676 Rare	—	—	—	—	—	—

KM# 25 3 THALER

Silver **Note:** Similar to 1 Thaler, KM#16. Dav. #7559.

Date	Mintage	VG	F	VF	XF	Unc
1604 HB	—	1,250	2,250	3,700	5,700	—

KM# 27 3 THALER

Silver **Note:** Similar to 1 Thaler, KM#24. Dav. #7564.

Date	Mintage	VG	F	VF	XF	Unc
1606 HvR	—	1,250	2,250	3,700	5,700	—
1610 HvR	—	1,250	2,250	3,700	5,700	—

KM# 47 3 THALER

Silver **Note:** Similar to 1 Thaler, KM#43. Dav. #7567.

Date	Mintage	VG	F	VF	XF	Unc
1611 Rare	—	—	—	—	—	—

KM# 67 3 THALER

Silver **Note:** Similar to 1 Thaler, KM#44. Dav. #7571.

Date	Mintage	VG	F	VF	XF	Unc
1613	—	1,250	2,250	3,700	5,700	—
1614	—	1,250	2,250	3,700	5,700	—

KM# 75 3 THALER

Silver **Subject:** Baptism of August, Son of Johann Georg **Note:** Klippe. Similar to 1 Thaler, KM#72. Dav. #7581.

Date	Mintage	VG	F	VF	XF	Unc
1614 Rare	—	—	—	—	—	—

KM# 85 3 THALER

Silver **Subject:** Baptism of Christian, Son of Johann Georg **Note:** Klippe. Similar to 1 Thaler, KM#82. Dav. #7585.

Date	Mintage	VG	F	VF	XF	Unc
1615 Rare	—	—	—	—	—	—

KM# 105 3 THALER

Silver **Subject:** Centennial of the Reformation **Note:** Similar to 1 Thaler, KM#103. Dav. #7593.

Date	Mintage	VG	F	VF	XF	Unc
1617	—	1,250	2,250	3,700	5,700	—

KM# 393 3 THALER

87.0000 g., Silver **Note:** Similar to 2 Thaler, KM#392. Dav. #LS387.

Date	Mintage	VG	F	VF	XF	Unc
1626 HI	—	1,500	2,650	4,000	5,600	—
1627 HI	—	1,500	2,650	4,000	5,600	—
1628 HI	—	1,500	2,650	4,000	5,600	—

KM# 396 3 THALER

87.0000 g., Silver **Note:** Similar to 1 Thaler, KM#132. Dav. #7599.

Date	Mintage	VG	F	VF	XF	Unc
1628 HS	—	1,250	2,250	3,700	5,700	—
1629 HS	—	1,250	2,250	3,700	5,700	—

KM# 418 3 THALER

87.0000 g., Silver **Subject:** Centennial of the Augsburg Confession **Note:** Similar to 1 Thaler, KM#411. Dav. #7603.

Date	Mintage	VG	F	VF	XF	Unc
1630 Rare	—	—	—	—	—	—

KM# 419 3 THALER

87.0000 g., Silver **Subject:** Marriage of Maria Elisabeth, Daughter of Johann Georg to Friedrich III **Note:** Klippe. Similar to 1 Thaler, KM#415. Dav. #7607.

Date	Mintage	VG	F	VF	XF	Unc
1630 Rare	—	—	—	—	—	—

KM# 436 3 THALER

Silver **Subject:** Peace of Westphalia **Note:** Illustration reduced. Dav. #LS394.

Date	Mintage	VG	F	VF	XF	Unc
1650 CR	—	1,150	2,250	4,500	7,500	—

KM# 452 3 THALER

Silver **Note:** Similar to 1 Thaler, KM#425. Dav. #7610.

Date	Mintage	VG	F	VF	XF	Unc
1656 CR	—	1,250	2,250	3,700	5,700	—

KM# 461 3 THALER

88.0000 g., Silver **Note:** Similar to 2 Thaler, KM#460. Dav. #LS397. Illustration reduced.

Date	Mintage	VG	F	VF	XF	Unc
1657 acorn	—	1,500	3,000	6,000	9,750	—

KM# 497 3 THALER
87.0000 g., Silver **Subject:** Chapel at Moritzburg **Note:** Similar to 2 Thaler, KM#496. Dav. #LS400. Illustration reduced.

Date	Mintage	VG	F	VF	XF	Unc
1661 acorn	—	1,800	3,000	4,600	6,500	—

KM# 505 3 THALER
Silver **Subject:** For the Confession **Note:** Similar to 2 Thaler, KM#504. Dav. #LS403. Illustration reduced.

Date	Mintage	VG	F	VF	XF	Unc
1663 CR	—	2,350	3,950	6,100	8,800	—

KM# 555 3 THALER
Silver **Subject:** Shooting Festival at Dresden, Magdalena Sybil as Queen **Note:** Klippe. Illustration reduced. Dav. #LS409.

Date	Mintage	VG	F	VF	XF	Unc
1676 Rare	—	—	—	—	—	—

KM# 23 4 THALER
Silver **Note:** Similar to 1 Thaler, KM#16. Dav. #7558.

Date	Mintage	VG	F	VF	XF	Unc
1603 HB Rare	—	—	—	—	—	—
1604 HB Rare	—	—	—	—	—	—

KM# 28 4 THALER
Silver **Note:** Similar to 1 Thaler, KM#24. Dav. #7563.

Date	Mintage	VG	F	VF	XF	Unc
1606 HvR	—	2,250	3,950	6,200	—	—
1608 HvR	—	2,250	3,950	6,200	—	—
1609 HvR	—	2,250	3,950	6,200	—	—
1610 HvR	—	2,250	3,950	6,200	—	—
1611 HvR	—	2,250	3,950	6,200	—	—

KM# 68 4 THALER
Silver **Subject:** Death of Emperor Rudolph **Note:** Similar to 1 Thaler, KM#55. Dav. #7577.

Date	Mintage	VG	F	VF	XF	Unc
1612 (swan)	—	2,700	4,500	7,300	—	—

KM# 69 4 THALER
Silver **Note:** Similar to 1 Thaler, KM#44. Dav. #7570.

Date	Mintage	VG	F	VF	XF	Unc
1613	—	2,050	3,600	6,200	10,000	—
1614	—	2,050	3,600	6,200	10,000	—
1615	—	2,050	3,600	6,200	10,000	—

KM# 86 4 THALER
Silver **Subject:** Baptism of Christian, Son of Johann Georg **Note:** Klippe. Similar to 1 Thaler, KM#82. Dav. #7584.

Date	Mintage	VG	F	VF	XF	Unc
1615 Rare	—	—	—	—	—	—

KM# 106 4 THALER
Silver **Subject:** Centennial of the Reformation **Note:** Dav. #7592.

Date	Mintage	VG	F	VF	XF	Unc
1617 Rare	—	—	—	—	—	—

KM# 114 4 THALER
Silver **Note:** Similar to 1 Thaler, KM#90. Dav. #7590.

Date	Mintage	VG	F	VF	XF	Unc
1618 (swan) Rare	—	—	—	—	—	—

KM# 397 4 THALER
Silver **Note:** Similar to 1 Thaler, KM#132. Dav. #7598.

Date	Mintage	VG	F	VF	XF	Unc
1628 HS Rare	—	—	—	—	—	—

KM# 398 4 THALER
Silver **Note:** Similar to 1 Thaler, KM#392. Dav. #LS386. Illustration reduced.

Date	Mintage	VG	F	VF	XF	Unc
1628 HI	—	2,700	4,500	7,100	10,000	—

KM# 437 4 THALER
Silver **Subject:** Peace of Westphalia **Note:** Similar to 3 Thaler, KM#436. Dav. #LS393.

Date	Mintage	VG	F	VF	XF	Unc
1650 CR Rare	—	—	—	—	—	—

KM# 462 4 THALER
Silver, 67 mm. **Obv:** Duke mounted with sword right **Obv. Legend:** PATRIAE DEO ET **Rev:** 12-line inscription **Note:** Dav. #LS396. Illustration reduced.

Date	Mintage	VG	F	VF	XF	Unc
1657 (acorn) Rare	—	—	—	—	—	—

KM# 498 4 THALER
87.0000 g., Silver **Subject:** Chapel at Moritzburg **Note:** Similar to 2 Thaler, KM#496. Dav. #LS399.

Date	Mintage	VG	F	VF	XF	Unc
1661 (acorn) Rare	—	—	—	—	—	—

KM# 506 4 THALER
87.0000 g., Silver **Subject:** For the Confession **Note:** Similar to 2 Thaler, KM#504. Dav. #LS402.

Date	Mintage	VG	F	VF	XF	Unc
1663 CR Rare	—	—	—	—	—	—

KM# 546 4 THALER
87.0000 g., Silver **Note:** Similar to 1 Thaler, KM#544. Dav. #7622.

Date	Mintage	VG	F	VF	XF	Unc
1671 CR Rare	—	—	—	—	—	—

KM# 556 4 THALER
87.0000 g., Silver **Subject:** Shooting Festival at Dresden **Note:** Klippe. Similar to 3 Thaler, KM#555. Dav. #LS408.

Date	Mintage	VG	F	VF	XF	Unc
1676 Rare	—	—	—	—	—	—

KM# 563 4 THALER
87.0000 g., Silver **Subject:** Shooting Match at Dresden **Note:** Klippe. Similar to 1 Thaler, KM#561. Dav. #7634.

Date	Mintage	VG	F	VF	XF	Unc
1678 Rare	—	—	—	—	—	—

KM# 30 5 THALER
Silver **Note:** Similar to 1 Thaler, KM#24. Dav. #7562.

Date	Mintage	VG	F	VF	XF	Unc
1609 HvR Rare	—	—	—	—	—	—

KM# 58 5 THALER
Silver **Subject:** Death of Emperor Rudolph **Note:** Similar to 1 Thaler, KM#55. Dav. #7576.

Date	Mintage	VG	F	VF	XF	Unc
1612 swan Rare	—	—	—	—	—	—

KM# 438 5 THALER
Silver **Subject:** Peace of Westphalia **Note:** Similar to 3 Thaler, KM#436. Dav. #LS392.

Date	Mintage	VG	F	VF	XF	Unc
1650 CR Rare	—	—	—	—	—	—

KM# 439 6 THALER
Silver **Subject:** Peace of Westphalia **Note:** Similar to 3 Thaler, KM#436. Dav. #LS391.

Date	Mintage	VG	F	VF	XF	Unc
1650 CR Rare	—	—	—	—	—	—

KM# 557 6 THALER
Silver **Note:** Klippe. Similar to 3 Thaler, KM#555. Dav. #LS407

Date	Mintage	VG	F	VF	XF	Unc
1676 Rare	—	—	—	—	—	—

KM# 399 9 THALER
Silver **Note:** Similar to 2Thaler, KM#392. Dav. #LS-A386

Date	Mintage	VG	F	VF	XF	Unc
1628 HI Rare	—	—	—	—	—	—

TRADE COINAGE

KM# 87 GOLDGULDEN
3.5000 g., 0.9860 Gold 0.1109 oz. AGW **Obv:** 1/2 figure of Johann Georg I right with sword and helmet in inner circle **Rev:** Arms in inner circle, date divided at top in legend **Mint:** Dresden

Date	Mintage	VG	F	VF	XF	Unc
1615 HR ligate	—	300	700	1,500	2,800	—
1616 HR ligate	—	300	700	1,500	2,800	—
1618 (swan)	—	300	700	1,500	2,800	—
1619 (swan)	—	300	700	1,500	2,800	—
1620 (swan)	—	300	700	1,500	2,800	—
1625 HI	—	300	700	1,500	2,800	—
1632 HI	—	300	700	1,500	2,800	—
1641 CR	—	300	700	1,500	2,800	—

KM# 540 GOLDGULDEN
3.5000 g., 0.9860 Gold 0.1109 oz. AGW **Obv:** Bust right **Rev:** Crowned 3-fold arms divide date **Rev. Legend:** MONETA ARGENTEA MISNICA **Mint:** Leipzig **Note:** Coinage for Meissen.

Date	Mintage	VG	F	VF	XF	Unc
1670	—	600	1,200	2,400	4,200	—

KM# 134 2 GOLDGULDEN
7.0000 g., 0.9860 Gold 0.2219 oz. AGW **Obv:** 1/2 figure of Johann Georg I right with sword and helmet in inner circle **Rev:** Arms in inner circle, date divided at top in legend

Date	Mintage	VG	F	VF	XF	Unc
1620 (swan)	—	775	1,600	3,300	5,400	—
1651 CR	—	775	1,600	3,300	5,400	—

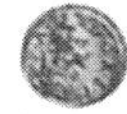

KM# A678 1/12 DUCAT
0.2900 g., 0.9860 Gold 0.0092 oz. AGW **Obv:** Bust of Friedrich August I right **Rev:** Arm holding sword

Date	Mintage	VG	F	VF	XF	Unc
ND(1694-1733)	—	—	—	—	—	—

KM# 59 1/8 DUCAT
0.4375 g., 0.9860 Gold 0.0139 oz. AGW **Obv:** Bare-headed bust right **Rev:** Oval 4-fold arms with central shield of crossed swords in baroque frame, date below **Note:** Vicariat Issue.

Date	Mintage	VG	F	VF	XF	Unc
1612	—	—	—	—	—	—

KM# 60 1/4 DUCAT
0.8750 g., 0.9860 Gold 0.0277 oz. AGW **Obv:** Bare-headed bust right **Rev:** Oval 4-fold arms with central shield of crossed swords in baroque frame, date below **Note:** Vicariat Issue.

Date	Mintage	VG	F	VF	XF	Unc
1612	—	—	—	—	—	—

KM# 441 1/4 DUCAT
0.8750 g., 0.9860 Gold 0.0277 oz. AGW **Obv:** 1/2 figure of Johann Georg I right with sword and helmet in inner circle **Rev:** Arms in inner circle, date divided at top in legend **Mint:** Dresden

Date	Mintage	VG	F	VF	XF	Unc
1651 CR	—	175	350	600	1,000	—

KM# 541 1/4 DUCAT
0.8750 g., 0.9860 Gold 0.0277 oz. AGW **Obv:** Bust right **Rev:** Crowned 3-fold arms divide date **Rev. Legend:** MONETA ARGENTEA MISNICA **Mint:** Leipzig **Note:** Coinage for Meissen.

Date	Mintage	VG	F	VF	XF	Unc
1670	—	—	—	—	—	—

KM# 678 1/4 DUCAT
0.8750 g., 0.9860 Gold 0.0277 oz. AGW **Obv:** Bust of Friedrich August I right

Date	Mintage	VG	F	VF	XF	Unc
1696 IK	—	100	205	425	825	—

KM# 687 1/4 DUCAT
0.8750 g., 0.9860 Gold 0.0277 oz. AGW **Obv:** Equestrian figure of Friedrich August I right **Rev:** Crowned and mantled arms, date divided at top **Mint:** Leipzig

Date	Mintage	VG	F	VF	XF	Unc
1697	—	100	205	425	825	—

KM# 725 1/4 DUCAT
0.8750 g., 0.9860 Gold 0.0277 oz. AGW **Ruler:** Friedrich August I **Obv:** Bust right **Rev:** Crowned arms **Mint:** Dresden

Date	Mintage	VG	F	VF	XF	Unc
1700 ILH	—	95.00	180	325	600	—

KM# 61 1/2 DUCAT
1.7500 g., 0.9860 Gold 0.0555 oz. AGW **Obv:** Bare-headed bust right **Rev:** Oval 4-fold arms with central shield of crossed swords in baroque frame, date below **Note:** Vicariat Issue.

Date	Mintage	VG	F	VF	XF	Unc
1612	—	—	—	—	—	—

KM# 442 1/2 DUCAT
1.7500 g., 0.9860 Gold 0.0555 oz. AGW **Obv:** John George I standing in inner circle **Rev:** Arms in cartouche in inner circle, date divided at top **Mint:** Dresden

Date	Mintage	VG	F	VF	XF	Unc
1651 CR	—	200	450	1,000	1,800	—
1652 CR	—	200	450	1,000	1,800	—
1653 CR	—	200	450	1,000	1,800	—
1655 CR	—	200	450	1,000	1,800	—

KM# 483 1/2 DUCAT
1.7500 g., 0.9860 Gold 0.0555 oz. AGW **Obv:** Robed 1/2 figure of Johann Georg II holding sword and elector's hat in inner circle **Rev:** Arms in cartouche in inner circle, date divided at top

Date	Mintage	VG	F	VF	XF	Unc
1659 acorn	—	150	350	850	1,500	—
1660 acorn	—	150	350	850	1,500	—
1662 acorn	—	150	350	850	1,500	—
1664 acorn	—	150	350	850	1,500	—
1665 acorn	—	150	350	850	1,500	—
1666 acorn	—	150	350	850	1,500	—

KM# 587 1/2 DUCAT
1.7500 g., 0.9860 Gold 0.0555 oz. AGW **Obv:** Robed 1/2 figure of Johann Georg III holding sword and elector's hat in inner circle **Rev:** Crowned arms in palm branches, date at top

Date	Mintage	VG	F	VF	XF	Unc
1683 CF	—	145	300	725	1,200	—
1684 CF	—	145	300	725	1,200	—
1686 CF	—	145	300	725	1,200	—
1688	—	145	300	725	1,200	—
1690 IK	—	145	300	725	1,200	—
1691 IK	—	145	300	725	1,200	—

KM# 630 1/2 DUCAT
1.7500 g., 0.9860 Gold 0.0555 oz. AGW **Obv:** Robed 1/2 figure of Johann Georg IV holding sword and elector's hat in inner circle **Rev:** Crowned arms in cartouche, date at top

Date	Mintage	VG	F	VF	XF	Unc
1692 IK	—	170	375	875	1,550	—
1693 IK	—	170	375	875	1,550	—
1694 IK	—	170	375	875	1,550	—

KM# 679 1/2 DUCAT
1.7500 g., 0.9860 Gold 0.0555 oz. AGW **Obv:** Bust of Friedrich August I right in inner circle **Rev:** Lion holding upraised sword and shield of arms, date at top

Date	Mintage	VG	F	VF	XF	Unc
1696 IK	—	125	250	625	1,200	—

KM# 688 1/2 DUCAT
1.7500 g., 0.9860 Gold 0.0555 oz. AGW **Obv:** Equestrian figure of Friedrich August I right in inner circle **Rev:** Crowned and mantled arms, date divided at top **Mint:** Leipzig

Date	Mintage	VG	F	VF	XF	Unc
1697 EPH	—	125	250	625	1,200	—

KM# 689 1/2 DUCAT
1.7500 g., 0.9860 Gold 0.0555 oz. AGW **Subject:** Coronation of Friedrich August I as August II of Poland **Obv:** Bust of Friedrich August I right, titles as king of Poland **Rev:** Crown **Rev. Legend:** A DEO

Date	Mintage	VG	F	VF	XF	Unc
ND	—	110	220	550	1,050	—

KM# 690 1/2 DUCAT
1.7500 g., 0.9860 Gold 0.0555 oz. AGW **Rev. Legend:** HANC DEVS IPSE DEDIT

Date	Mintage	VG	F	VF	XF	Unc
ND	—	110	220	550	1,050	—

KM# 714 1/2 DUCAT
1.7500 g., 0.9860 Gold 0.0555 oz. AGW **Ruler:** Friedrich August I **Obv:** Bust right **Rev:** Date in legend **Mint:** Dresden

Date	Mintage	VG	F	VF	XF	Unc
1699 ILH	—	100	220	525	925	—

KM# 542 3/4 DUCAT
2.6250 g., 0.9860 Gold 0.0832 oz. AGW **Obv:** Bust right **Rev:** crowned 3-fold arms divide date **Rev. Legend:** MONETA ARGENTEA MISNICA **Mint:** Leipzig **Note:** Coinage for Meissen.

Date	Mintage	VG	F	VF	XF	Unc
1670	—	—	—	—	—	—

KM# 19 DUCAT
3.5000 g., 0.9860 Gold 0.1109 oz. AGW **Note:** Similar to 1 Thaler, KM#15.

Date	Mintage	VG	F	VF	XF	Unc
1601 Rare	—	—	—	—	—	—

KM# 62 DUCAT
3.5000 g., 0.9860 Gold 0.1109 oz. AGW **Obv:** Bare-headed bust right **Rev:** Oval 4-fold arms with central shield of crossed swords in baroque frame, date below **Note:** Vicariat Issue.

Date	Mintage	VG	F	VF	XF	Unc
1612	—	—	—	—	—	—

KM# 126 DUCAT

3.5000 g., 0.9860 Gold 0.1109 oz. AGW **Mint:** Dresden
Note: This coin was restruck periodically until 1812.

Date	Mintage	VG	F	VF	XF	Unc
1616	—	—	—	—	—	—

KM# 107 DUCAT

3.5000 g., 0.9860 Gold 0.1109 oz. AGW **Subject:** Reformation Centennial **Note:** Similar to 1/2 Thaler, KM#97.

Date	Mintage	VG	F	VF	XF	Unc
1617	—	350	750	1,500	2,500	—

KM# 108 DUCAT

3.5000 g., 0.9860 Gold 0.1109 oz. AGW **Note:** Similar to 1/2 Thaler, KM#99.

Date	Mintage	VG	F	VF	XF	Unc
1617	—	425	900	1,800	3,000	—

KM# 109 DUCAT

3.5000 g., 0.9860 Gold 0.1109 oz. AGW **Subject:** Centennial of the Reformation **Obv:** Johann Georg I **Rev:** Friedrich III

Date	Mintage	VG	F	VF	XF	Unc
1617	—	150	300	650	1,200	—

KM# 121 DUCAT

3.5000 g., 0.9860 Gold 0.1109 oz. AGW **Obv:** Johann Georg I
Note: Vicariat Issue.

Date	Mintage	VG	F	VF	XF	Unc
1619	—	300	550	1,100	2,000	—

KM# 135 DUCAT

3.5000 g., 0.9860 Gold 0.1109 oz. AGW **Subject:** Military Campaign in Oberlausitz **Obv:** Oval 4-fold arms with central shield of crossed swords in baroque frame, date divided date
Rev: Arms and armor in center **Rev. Legend:** ZVM GLVCKLICHEN ANFANG VND GVTEM ENDE

Date	Mintage	VG	F	VF	XF	Unc
1620	—	—	—	—	—	—

KM# 382 DUCAT

3.5000 g., 0.9860 Gold 0.1109 oz. AGW **Subject:** Baptism of Prince Heinrich **Obv:** Crowned shield of arms **Rev:** St. George slaying the dragon

Date	Mintage	VG	F	VF	XF	Unc
1622	—	375	700	1,400	2,600	—

KM# 383 DUCAT

3.5000 g., 0.9860 Gold 0.1109 oz. AGW **Obv:** Johann Georg I
Mint: Dresden

Date	Mintage	VG	F	VF	XF	Unc
1622 (swan)	—	240	425	900	1,600	—

KM# 390 DUCAT

3.5000 g., 0.9860 Gold 0.1109 oz. AGW

Date	Mintage	VG	F	VF	XF	Unc
1625 HI	—	190	325	625	1,000	—
1627 HI	—	190	325	625	1,000	—
1628 HI	—	190	325	625	1,000	—
1629 HI	—	190	325	625	1,000	—
1632 HI	—	190	325	625	1,000	—
1633 HI	—	190	325	625	1,000	—
1634 HI	—	190	325	625	1,000	—
1635 CM	—	325	500	1,000	1,550	—
1635 SD	—	190	325	625	1,000	—
1636 SD	—	190	325	625	1,000	—
1637 SD	—	190	325	625	1,000	—
1638 SD	—	190	325	625	1,000	—
1639 SD	—	190	325	625	1,000	—
1640 SD	—	190	325	625	1,000	—
1640 CR	—	220	350	700	1,150	—
1641 CR	—	220	350	700	1,150	—
1642 CR	—	220	350	700	1,150	—
1643 CR	—	220	350	700	1,150	—
1644 CR	—	220	350	700	1,150	—
1645 CR	—	220	350	700	1,150	—
1646 CR	—	220	350	700	1,150	—
1648 CR	—	220	350	700	1,150	—
1649 CR	—	220	350	700	1,150	—
1650 CR	—	220	350	700	1,150	—
1652 CR	—	220	350	700	1,150	—
1653 CR	—	220	350	700	1,150	—
1655 CR	—	220	350	700	1,150	—

KM# 420 DUCAT

3.5000 g., 0.9860 Gold 0.1109 oz. AGW **Subject:** Centennial of the Augsburg Confession **Obv:** Bust of Johann Georg I right
Rev: Bust of Johann right

Date	Mintage	VG	F	VF	XF	Unc
1630	—	200	350	700	1,250	—

KM# 424 DUCAT

3.5000 g., 0.9860 Gold 0.1109 oz. AGW **Subject:** Peace of Prague

Date	Mintage	VG	F	VF	XF	Unc
1635	—	225	450	850	1,500	—

KM# 444 DUCAT

3.5000 g., 0.9860 Gold 0.1109 oz. AGW **Subject:** Birth of Johann Georg I's Granddaughter, Erdmuthe Sophie **Obv:** Three small flames in wreath, inscription around **Rev:** Plant with 3 blossoms, date in legend

Date	Mintage	VG	F	VF	XF	Unc
1654	—	275	500	925	1,650	—

KM# 463 DUCAT

3.5000 g., 0.9860 Gold 0.1109 oz. AGW **Obv:** Equestrian figure of Johann Georg II right **Rev:** 6-line inscription **Note:** Vicariat Issue.

Date	Mintage	VG	F	VF	XF	Unc
1657	—	300	600	1,200	2,200	—

KM# 484 DUCAT

3.5000 g., 0.9860 Gold 0.1109 oz. AGW **Subject:** Death of Johann Georg II's Mother, Magdalene Sibylle **Obv:** 7-line inscription **Rev:** 6-line inscription with Roman numeral date

Date	Mintage	VG	F	VF	XF	Unc
1659 (acorn)	—	—	—	—	—	—

KM# 485 DUCAT

3.5000 g., 0.9860 Gold 0.1109 oz. AGW **Obv:** Johann Georg II

Date	Mintage	VG	F	VF	XF	Unc
1659 CR	—	375	775	1,600	2,800	—
1660 CR	—	375	775	1,600	2,800	—
1662 CR	—	375	775	1,600	2,800	—
1664 CR	—	375	775	1,600	2,800	—
1665 CR	—	375	775	1,600	2,800	—
1672 CR	—	425	850	1,750	3,100	—

KM# 529 DUCAT

3.5000 g., 0.9860 Gold 0.1109 oz. AGW **Obv:** Equestrian figure of Johann Georg II above arms in inner circle **Rev:** Sword and quill behind shield on ornamental column, date at sides

Date	Mintage	VG	F	VF	XF	Unc
1669	—	525	1,050	2,200	3,750	—

KM# 543 DUCAT

3.5000 g., 0.9860 Gold 0.1109 oz. AGW **Obv:** Bust right
Rev: Crowned 3-fold arms divide date **Rev. Legend:** MONETA ARGENTEA MISNICA **Mint:** Leipzig **Note:** Coinage for Meissen.

Date	Mintage	VG	F	VF	XF	Unc
1670	—	—	—	—	—	—

KM# 581 DUCAT

3.5000 g., 0.9860 Gold 0.1109 oz. AGW **Obv:** Robed 1/2 figure of Johann Georg III right with sword and elector's cap in inner circle **Rev:** Crowned arms in palm branches, date at top

Date	Mintage	VG	F	VF	XF	Unc
1681 CF	—	325	650	1,400	2,400	—
1683 CF	—	325	650	1,400	2,400	—
1684 CF	—	325	650	1,400	2,400	—
1686 CF	—	325	650	1,400	2,400	—
1687	—	325	650	1,400	2,400	—
1690 IK	—	325	650	1,400	2,400	—
1691 IK	—	325	650	1,400	2,400	—

KM# 591 DUCAT

3.5000 g., 0.9860 Gold 0.1109 oz. AGW **Obv:** Bust of Johann Georg III right in inner circle **Rev:** Crossed swords with shields of arms in angles

Date	Mintage	VG	F	VF	XF	Unc
1686	—	350	700	1,450	2,500	—

KM# 620 DUCAT

3.5000 g., 0.9860 Gold 0.1109 oz. AGW **Subject:** Death of Johann Georg III **Obv:** 6-line inscription **Rev:** Banner held by arm from clouds

Date	Mintage	VG	F	VF	XF	Unc
1691	—	350	700	1,450	2,500	—

KM# 621 DUCAT

3.5000 g., 0.9860 Gold 0.1109 oz. AGW **Obv:** Bust of Johann Georg IV holding sword to right in inner circle **Rev:** Crowned arms, date at top

Date	Mintage	VG	F	VF	XF	Unc
1691 IK	—	825	1,750	3,000	5,300	—
1692 IK	—	825	1,750	3,000	5,300	—
1693 IK	—	825	1,750	3,000	5,300	—
1694 IK	—	825	1,750	3,000	5,300	—

KM# 659 DUCAT

3.5000 g., 0.9860 Gold 0.1109 oz. AGW **Mint:** Leipzig

Date	Mintage	VG	F	VF	XF	Unc
1694 EPH	—	300	600	1,250	2,200	—

KM# 660 DUCAT

3.5000 g., 0.9860 Gold 0.1109 oz. AGW **Obv:** Bust of Friedrich August I with sword to right in inner circle **Rev:** Crowned arms, date at top **Mint:** Dresden

Date	Mintage	VG	F	VF	XF	Unc
1694 IK	—	350	700	1,450	2,500	—

KM# 670 DUCAT

3.5000 g., 0.9860 Gold 0.1109 oz. AGW **Subject:** Hungarian Campaign **Obv:** Friedrich August I

Date	Mintage	VG	F	VF	XF	Unc
1695	—	225	475	1,000	1,850	—
ND	—	225	475	1,000	1,850	—

KM# 671 DUCAT

3.5000 g., 0.9860 Gold 0.1109 oz. AGW **Obv:** Robed 1/2 figure of Friedrich August I to right with sword and elector's hat in inner circle **Rev:** Lion holding upraised sword and shield of arms, date at top

Date	Mintage	VG	F	VF	XF	Unc
1695 IK	—	350	700	1,450	2,500	—
1696 IK	—	350	700	1,450	2,500	—
1697 IK	—	350	700	1,450	2,500	—

KM# 691 DUCAT

3.5000 g., 0.9860 Gold 0.1109 oz. AGW **Obv:** Equestrian figure of Friedrich August I right **Rev:** Draped arms **Mint:** Leipzig

Date	Mintage	VG	F	VF	XF	Unc
1697 EPH	—	260	525	975	1,750	—

KM# 692 DUCAT

3.5000 g., 0.9860 Gold 0.1109 oz. AGW **Note:** Struck with 1/2 Ducat dies, KM #688.

Date	Mintage	VG	F	VF	XF	Unc
1697	—	260	525	975	1,750	—

KM# 693 DUCAT

3.5000 g., 0.9860 Gold 0.1109 oz. AGW **Note:** Struck with 1/4 Ducat dies.

Date	Mintage	VG	F	VF	XF	Unc
1697 EPH	—	300	625	1,250	2,100	—

KM# 694 DUCAT

3.5000 g., 0.9860 Gold 0.1109 oz. AGW **Subject:** Coronation of Friedrich August I as August II of Poland **Mint:** Dresden

Date	Mintage	VG	F	VF	XF	Unc
1697	—	180	350	725	1,200	—

KM# 695 DUCAT

3.5000 g., 0.9860 Gold 0.1109 oz. AGW

Date	Mintage	VG	F	VF	XF	Unc
1697 IK	—	180	350	725	1,200	—

KM# 696 DUCAT

3.5000 g., 0.9860 Gold 0.1109 oz. AGW **Subject:** Coronation of Friedrich August I as August II of Poland **Obv:** Bust of Friedrich August I right **Rev:** Large crown at center

Date	Mintage	VG	F	VF	XF	Unc
1697	—	180	350	725	1,200	—

KM# 697 DUCAT

3.5000 g., 0.9860 Gold 0.1109 oz. AGW **Subject:** Coronation of Friedrich August I as King of Poland in 1697 **Obv:** Friedrich August I mounted on horse right **Note:** Struck with 1/2 Ducat dies.

Date	Mintage	VG	F	VF	XF	Unc
ND	—	250	500	1,000	1,800	—

KM# 709 DUCAT

3.5000 g., 0.9860 Gold 0.1109 oz. AGW **Ruler:** Friedrich August I **Obv:** Draped bust right **Obv. Legend:** D • G • FRID: AUG: REX POL DUX SAX:.. **Rev:** Crowned arms within branches

Date	Mintage	VG	F	VF	XF	Unc
1698 ILH	—	240	450	1,200	2,050	—
1699 ILH	—	240	450	1,200	2,050	—
1700 ILH	—	240	450	1,200	2,050	—

KM# 582 1-1/2 DUCAT

5.2500 g., 0.9860 Gold 0.1664 oz. AGW **Obv:** Armored bust of Johann Georg III right **Rev:** Crowned arms in palm branches, date divided at top

Date	Mintage	VG	F	VF	XF	Unc
1681 CF	—	350	775	1,700	3,000	—
1683 CF	—	350	775	1,700	3,000	—
1684 CF	—	350	775	1,700	3,000	—
1688	—	350	775	1,700	3,000	—
1690 IK	—	350	775	1,700	3,000	—

KM# 631 1-1/2 DUCAT

5.2500 g., 0.9860 Gold 0.1664 oz. AGW **Obv:** Bust of Johann Georg IV right **Rev:** Crossed swords with shields of arms in angles

Date	Mintage	VG	F	VF	XF	Unc
1692 IK	—	350	775	1,700	3,000	—
1693 IK	—	350	775	1,700	3,000	—
1694 IK	—	350	775	1,700	3,000	—

KM# 698 1-1/2 DUCAT

5.2500 g., 0.9860 Gold 0.1664 oz. AGW **Obv:** Equestrian figure of Friedrich August I right **Rev:** Draped arms

Date	Mintage	VG	F	VF	XF	Unc
1697 EPH	—	275	550	1,200	2,200	—

KM# 20 2 DUCAT

7.0000 g., 0.9860 Gold 0.2219 oz. AGW **Note:** Similar to 1 Thaler, KM#15.

Date	Mintage	VG	F	VF	XF	Unc
1601 HB Rare	—	—	—	—	—	—

KM# 63 2 DUCAT

7.0000 g., 0.9860 Gold 0.2219 oz. AGW **Obv:** Bare-headed bust right **Rev:** Oval 4-fold arms with central shield of crossed swords in baroque frame, date below **Note:** Vicariat Issue.

Date	Mintage	VG	F	VF	XF	Unc
1612	—	—	—	—	—	—

KM# 127 2 DUCAT

7.0000 g., 0.9860 Gold 0.2219 oz. AGW **Note:** Similar to 1 Ducat, KM#126.

Date	Mintage	VG	F	VF	XF	Unc
1616	—	850	1,750	3,500	6,000	—

KM# 92 2 DUCAT

7.0000 g., 0.9860 Gold 0.2219 oz. AGW **Obv:** 1/2 figure of Johann Georg I right with sword and helm in inner circle **Mint:** Dresden

Date	Mintage	VG	F	VF	XF	Unc
1616 (swan)	—	750	1,500	3,000	5,300	—
1625 HI	—	750	1,500	3,000	5,300	—

KM# 110 2 DUCAT

7.0000 g., 0.9860 Gold 0.2219 oz. AGW **Subject:** Reformation Centennial **Note:** Similar to 1/2 Thaler, KM#97.

Date	Mintage	VG	F	VF	XF	Unc
1617	—	400	800	1,650	2,750	—

KM# 111 2 DUCAT

7.0000 g., 0.9860 Gold 0.2219 oz. AGW **Note:** Similar to 1/2 Thaler, KM#99.

Date	Mintage	VG	F	VF	XF	Unc
1617 Rare	—	—	—	—	—	—

KM# 112 2 DUCAT

7.0000 g., 0.9860 Gold 0.2219 oz. AGW **Subject:** Centennial of the Reformation **Obv:** Johann Georg I **Rev:** Friedrich III

Date	Mintage	VG	F	VF	XF	Unc
1617	—	450	750	1,350	2,400	—

KM# 122 2 DUCAT

7.0000 g., 0.9860 Gold 0.2219 oz. AGW **Obv:** Equestrian figure of Johann Georg I above arms right **Rev:** 6-line inscription **Note:** Vicariat Issue.

Date	Mintage	VG	F	VF	XF	Unc
1619	—	450	900	2,100	3,750	—

KM# 136 2 DUCAT

7.0000 g., 0.9860 Gold 0.2219 oz. AGW **Obv:** Johann Georg I

Date	Mintage	VG	F	VF	XF	Unc
1620 (swan)	—	625	1,250	2,500	4,400	—

KM# 384 2 DUCAT

7.0000 g., 0.9860 Gold 0.2219 oz. AGW **Subject:** Baptism of Prince Heinrich **Obv:** Crowned shield of arms **Rev:** St. George slaying the dragon

Date	Mintage	VG	F	VF	XF	Unc
1622 Rare	—	—	—	—	—	—

KM# 400 2 DUCAT

7.0000 g., 0.9860 Gold 0.2219 oz. AGW

Date	Mintage	VG	F	VF	XF	Unc
1628 HI	—	375	750	1,800	3,000	—
1629 HI	—	375	750	1,800	3,000	—
1632 HI	—	375	750	1,800	3,000	—
1635 CM	—	450	900	2,100	3,750	—
1636 SD	—	425	675	1,650	2,650	—
1637 SD	—	425	675	1,650	2,650	—
1638 SD	—	425	675	1,650	2,650	—
1639 SD	—	425	675	1,650	2,650	—
1640 CR	—	425	675	1,650	2,650	—
1641 CR	—	425	675	1,650	2,650	—
1642 CR	—	425	675	1,650	2,650	—
1643 CR	—	425	675	1,650	2,650	—
1644 CR	—	425	675	1,650	2,650	—
1645 CR	—	425	675	1,650	2,650	—
1646 CR	—	425	675	1,650	2,650	—
1652 CR	—	425	675	1,650	2,650	—
1654 CR	—	425	675	1,650	2,650	—

KM# 421 2 DUCAT

7.0000 g., 0.9860 Gold 0.2219 oz. AGW **Subject:** Centennial of the Augsburg Confession **Obv:** Bust of Johann Georg I right **Rev:** Bust of Johann right

Date	Mintage	VG	F	VF	XF	Unc
1630	—	325	650	1,300	2,200	—

KM# 464 2 DUCAT

7.0000 g., 0.9860 Gold 0.2219 oz. AGW **Obv:** Johann Georg II **Note:** Vicariat Issue.

Date	Mintage	VG	F	VF	XF	Unc
1657	—	400	800	1,500	2,500	—

KM# 486 2 DUCAT

7.0000 g., 0.9860 Gold 0.2219 oz. AGW **Obv:** Robed 1/2 figure of Johann Georg II with sword and elector's cap in inner circle **Rev:** Arms in cartouche, date at top

Date	Mintage	VG	F	VF	XF	Unc
1659 CR	—	700	1,400	3,100	4,900	—
1660 CR	—	700	1,400	3,100	4,900	—
1662 CR	—	700	1,400	3,100	4,900	—

KM# 507 2 DUCAT
7.0000 g., 0.9860 Gold 0.2219 oz. AGW **Note:** Confessional Issue. Similar to 2 Thaler, KM#504.

Date	Mintage	VG	F	VF	XF	Unc
1663	—	—	—	—	—	—

KM# 551 2 DUCAT
7.0000 g., 0.9860 Gold 0.2219 oz. AGW **Obv:** Armored bust of Johann Georg II right **Rev:** Crowned arms in palm branches, date at top

Date	Mintage	VG	F	VF	XF	Unc
1675 CR	—	550	1,200	2,600	4,200	—
1676 CR	—	550	1,200	2,600	4,200	—

KM# 583 2 DUCAT
7.0000 g., 0.9860 Gold 0.2219 oz. AGW **Obv:** Armored bust of Johann Georg III right **Rev:** Crowned arms in palm branches, date divided at top

Date	Mintage	VG	F	VF	XF	Unc
1681 CF	—	550	1,200	2,600	4,200	—
1683 CF	—	550	1,200	2,600	4,200	—
1684 CF	—	550	1,200	2,600	4,200	—
1686 CF	—	550	1,200	2,600	4,200	—
1688	—	550	1,200	2,600	4,200	—
1689 IK	—	550	1,200	2,600	4,200	—
1691 IK	—	550	1,200	2,600	4,200	—

KM# 590 2 DUCAT
7.0000 g., 0.9860 Gold 0.2219 oz. AGW **Obv:** 1/2 length figure of Johann Georg III with sword and elector's cap in inner circle **Rev:** Crowned arms in inner circle

Date	Mintage	VG	F	VF	XF	Unc
1685 F	—	675	1,350	3,000	4,800	—

KM# 622 2 DUCAT
7.0000 g., 0.9860 Gold 0.2219 oz. AGW **Obv:** Bust of Johann Georg III with sword and helmet **Rev:** Crowned arms

Date	Mintage	VG	F	VF	XF	Unc
1691 IK	—	550	1,200	2,600	4,200	—

KM# 632 2 DUCAT
7.0000 g., 0.9860 Gold 0.2219 oz. AGW **Obv:** Bust of Johann Georg IV right **Rev:** Crossed swords with shields of arms in angles

Date	Mintage	VG	F	VF	XF	Unc
1692 IK	—	550	1,200	2,600	4,200	—
1693 IK	—	550	1,200	2,600	4,200	—
1694 IK	—	550	1,200	2,600	4,200	—

KM# 661 2 DUCAT
7.0000 g., 0.9860 Gold 0.2219 oz. AGW **Mint:** Leipzig

Date	Mintage	VG	F	VF	XF	Unc
1694 EPH	—	475	1,000	2,200	3,600	—

KM# 672 2 DUCAT
7.0000 g., 0.9860 Gold 0.2219 oz. AGW **Obv:** Bust of Friedrich August I with sword in inner circle **Rev:** Crowned arms in inner circle **Mint:** Dresden

Date	Mintage	VG	F	VF	XF	Unc
1695 IK	—	675	1,350	3,000	4,800	—

KM# 673 2 DUCAT
7.0000 g., 0.9860 Gold 0.2219 oz. AGW **Subject:** Hungarian Campaign **Obv:** Equestrian figure of Friedrich August I right **Rev:** Draped arms

Date	Mintage	VG	F	VF	XF	Unc
1695	—	325	625	1,400	2,500	—

KM# 680 2 DUCAT
7.0000 g., 0.9860 Gold 0.2219 oz. AGW **Obv:** Friedrich August I standing right beside desk **Rev:** 2 shields of arms topped by elector's cap

Date	Mintage	VG	F	VF	XF	Unc
1696	—	525	1,050	2,200	3,950	—

KM# 681 2 DUCAT
7.0000 g., 0.9860 Gold 0.2219 oz. AGW **Obv:** Friedrich August I standing **Rev:** Altar

Date	Mintage	VG	F	VF	XF	Unc
1696	—	375	675	1,500	3,000	—

KM# 699 2 DUCAT
7.0000 g., 0.9860 Gold 0.2219 oz. AGW **Subject:** Coronation of Friedrich August I as August II of Poland **Obv:** Friedrich August I

Date	Mintage	VG	F	VF	XF	Unc
1697	—	250	500	1,150	2,200	—

KM# 700 2 DUCAT
7.0000 g., 0.9860 Gold 0.2219 oz. AGW **Subject:** Coronation of Friedrich August I as August II of Poland **Obv:** Bust of Friedrich August I right **Obv. Legend:** FRID. AUG... **Rev:** Large crown at center

Date	Mintage	VG	F	VF	XF	Unc
1697	—	350	750	1,650	3,250	—

KM# 701 2 DUCAT
7.0000 g., 0.9860 Gold 0.2219 oz. AGW
Obv. Legend: FRIDERICUS AUGUST...

Date	Mintage	VG	F	VF	XF	Unc
1697	—	240	475	950	1,800	—

KM# 710.1 2 DUCAT
7.0000 g., 0.9860 Gold 0.2219 oz. AGW **Ruler:** Friedrich August I **Obv:** Armored, laureate bust right **Obv. Legend:** D G FRID AUG REX POL - DUX ... **Rev:** Date above crown **Note:** Some dates struck from 1/2 Thaler dies, KM# 724.

Date	Mintage	VG	F	VF	XF	Unc
1698 ILH	—	450	1,050	2,250	4,150	—
1700 ILH	—	450	1,050	2,250	4,150	—

KM# 739 2 DUCAT
7.0000 g., 0.9860 Gold 0.2219 oz. AGW **Ruler:** Friedrich August I **Obv:** Bust right **Rev:** Crowned round 4-fold arms with central shield of 2-fold arms, flanked by 2 palm branches crossed at bottom, date at top **Note:** Struck from 1/8 Thaler dies, KM# 721.

Date	Mintage	VG	F	VF	XF	Unc
1700 ILH	—	—	—	—	—	—

KM# A422 3 DUCAT
10.5000 g., 0.9860 Gold 0.3328 oz. AGW **Subject:** Centennial of the Augsburg Confession **Obv:** Bust of Johann Georg right **Rev:** Bust of Johann right

Date	Mintage	VG	F	VF	XF	Unc
1630	—	700	1,350	2,500	4,000	—

KM# 465 3 DUCAT
10.5000 g., 0.9860 Gold 0.3328 oz. AGW **Note:** Similar to 1 Ducat, KM#463.

Date	Mintage	VG	F	VF	XF	Unc
1657 (acorn)	—	—	—	—	—	—
1658 (acorn)	—	—	—	—	—	—

KM# 552 3 DUCAT
10.5000 g., 0.9860 Gold 0.3328 oz. AGW **Obv:** Armored bust of Johann Georg II right **Rev:** Crowned arms in palm branches, date at top

Date	Mintage	VG	F	VF	XF	Unc
1675 CR	—	775	1,600	3,400	6,000	—
1679 CF	—	775	1,600	3,400	6,000	—

KM# 584 3 DUCAT
10.5000 g., 0.9860 Gold 0.3328 oz. AGW

Date	Mintage	VG	F	VF	XF	Unc
1681 CF	—	750	1,500	3,700	6,000	—
1683 CF	—	750	1,500	3,700	6,000	—
1684 CF	—	750	1,500	3,700	6,000	—
1686 CF	—	750	1,500	3,700	6,000	—
1688 IK	—	750	1,500	3,700	6,000	—
1689 IK	—	750	1,500	3,700	6,000	—
1690 IK	—	750	1,500	3,700	6,000	—
1691 IK	—	750	1,500	3,700	6,000	—

KM# 633 3 DUCAT
10.5000 g., 0.9860 Gold 0.3328 oz. AGW **Obv:** Johann Georg IV

Date	Mintage	VG	F	VF	XF	Unc
1692 IK	—	850	1,800	3,600	6,000	—

KM# 726 3 DUCAT
10.5000 g., 0.9860 Gold 0.3328 oz. AGW **Obv:** Bust right **Rev:** Crowned round 4-fold arms with central shield of 2-fold arms between 2 palm branches crossed at bottom, date at top **Note:** Struck with 1/2 Thaler dies, KM#724.

Date	Mintage	VG	F	VF	XF	Unc
1700 ILH	—	—	—	—	—	—

KM# 21 4 DUCAT
14.0000 g., 0.9860 Gold 0.4438 oz. AGW **Obv:** 3 half-figures facing with date divided above **Rev:** Helmeted arms

Date	Mintage	VG	F	VF	XF	Unc
1601 HB Rare	—	—	—	—	—	—

KM# A123 4 DUCAT

13.8600 g., Gold **Obv:** Equestrian figure of Johann Georg I right **Obv. Legend:** PROLEGE-ET GREGE **Rev:** 12-line inscription **Note:** Vicariat issue. Fr#2673.

Date	Mintage	VG	F	VF	XF	Unc
1619	—	—	—	—	16,000	—

KM# A421 4 DUCAT

14.0000 g., 0.9860 Gold 0.4438 oz. AGW **Subject:** Centennial of the Augsburg Confession **Obv:** Bust of Johann Georg I right **Rev:** Bust of Johann right

Date	Mintage	VG	F	VF	XF	Unc
1630	—	800	1,650	3,000	5,000	—

KM# 466 4 DUCAT

14.0000 g., 0.9860 Gold 0.4438 oz. AGW **Note:** Vicariat Issue. Similar to 1 Ducat, KM#463.

Date	Mintage	VG	F	VF	XF	Unc
1657 (acorn)	—	—	—	—	—	—
1658 (acorn)	—	—	—	—	—	—

KM# 553 4 DUCAT

14.0000 g., 0.9860 Gold 0.4438 oz. AGW **Obv:** Armored bust of Johann Georg II right **Rev:** Crowned arms in palm branches, date at top

Date	Mintage	VG	F	VF	XF	Unc
1675 CR	—	—	—	—	—	—

KM# 585.1 4 DUCAT

14.0000 g., 0.9860 Gold 0.4438 oz. AGW **Obv:** Johann Georg II **Mint:** Dresden

Date	Mintage	VG	F	VF	XF	Unc
1681 CF	—	1,150	2,200	5,000	8,800	—
1683 CF	—	950	1,900	4,400	7,500	—
1684 CF	—	950	1,900	4,400	7,500	—
1685 CF	—	1,150	2,200	5,000	8,800	—
1688	—	950	1,900	4,400	7,500	—

KM# 585.2 4 DUCAT

14.0000 g., 0.9860 Gold 0.4438 oz. AGW **Obv:** Draped armored bust of Johann Georg II

Date	Mintage	VG	F	VF	XF	Unc
1690 IK	—	750	1,700	3,750	6,300	—
1691 IK	—	875	1,900	4,400	6,900	—

KM# 634 4 DUCAT

14.0000 g., 0.9860 Gold 0.4438 oz. AGW **Note:** Similar to 3 Ducat, KM#633.

Date	Mintage	VG	F	VF	XF	Unc
1692 IK	—	1,150	2,200	4,700	8,100	—

KM# 662 4 DUCAT

14.0000 g., 0.9860 Gold 0.4438 oz. AGW **Obv:** Bust of Johann Georg IV holding sword right in inner circle **Rev:** Crowned arms, date at top

Date	Mintage	VG	F	VF	XF	Unc
1694 Rare	—	—	—	—	—	—

KM# 64 5 DUCAT (1/2 Portugalöser)

17.5000 g., 0.9860 Gold 0.5547 oz. AGW **Obv:** Bare-headed bust right **Rev:** Oval 4-fold arms with central shield of crossed swords in baroque frame, date below **Note:** Vicariat Issue.

Date	Mintage	VG	F	VF	XF	Unc
1612 Rare	—	—	—	—	—	—

KM# 76 5 DUCAT (1/2 Portugalöser)

17.5000 g., 0.9860 Gold 0.5547 oz. AGW **Obv:** 1/2 length figure of Johann Georg with sword and helmet in inner circle **Rev:** Cross within circle of 19 shields of arms **Mint:** Dresden

Date	Mintage	VG	F	VF	XF	Unc
1614 Rare	—	—	—	—	—	—

KM# 123 5 DUCAT (1/2 Portugalöser)

17.5000 g., 0.9860 Gold 0.5547 oz. AGW **Obv:** Equestrian figure of Johann Georg I right **Rev:** 12-line inscription **Note:** Vicariat Issue.

Date	Mintage	VG	F	VF	XF	Unc
1619 Rare	—	—	—	—	—	—

KM# 422 5 DUCAT (1/2 Portugalöser)

17.5000 g., 0.9860 Gold 0.5547 oz. AGW **Subject:** Centennial of the Augsburg Confession **Obv:** Johann Georg I **Rev:** Johann

Date	Mintage	VG	F	VF	XF	Unc
1630	—	775	1,600	3,300	5,400	—

KM# 453 5 DUCAT (1/2 Portugalöser)

17.5000 g., 0.9860 Gold 0.5547 oz. AGW **Subject:** Death of Johann Georg I **Note:** Similar to 1 Thaler, KM#451. Struck from same dies.

Date	Mintage	VG	F	VF	XF	Unc
1656 Rare	—	—	—	—	—	—

KM# 467 5 DUCAT (1/2 Portugalöser)

17.5000 g., 0.9860 Gold 0.5547 oz. AGW **Note:** Vicariat Issue. Similar to 1 Ducat, KM#463.

Date	Mintage	VG	F	VF	XF	Unc
1657 (acorn)	—	—	—	—	—	—
1658 (acorn)	—	—	—	—	—	—

KM# 586 5 DUCAT (1/2 Portugalöser)

17.5000 g., 0.9860 Gold 0.5547 oz. AGW **Note:** Similar to 3 Ducat, KM#584.

Date	Mintage	VG	F	VF	XF	Unc
1681 CF Rare	—	—	—	—	—	—
1688 Rare	—	—	—	—	—	—

KM# 635 5 DUCAT (1/2 Portugalöser)

17.5000 g., 0.9860 Gold 0.5547 oz. AGW **Note:** Similar to 3 Ducat, KM#633.

Date	Mintage	VG	F	VF	XF	Unc
1692 IK Rare	—	—	—	—	—	—

KM# 727 5 DUCAT (1/2 Portugalöser)

17.5000 g., 0.9860 Gold 0.5547 oz. AGW **Note:** Similar to 3 Ducat, KM#726. Struck with 1 Thaler dies, KM#707.

Date	Mintage	VG	F	VF	XF	Unc
1700 OLH	—	—	—	—	—	—

KM# 113 6 DUCAT

21.0000 g., 0.9860 Gold 0.6657 oz. AGW **Subject:** Anniversary of the Reformation **Obv:** Johann Georg **Rev:** Frederick III

Date	Mintage	VG	F	VF	XF	Unc
1617 Rare	—	—	—	—	—	—

KM# A423 6 DUCAT

21.0000 g., 0.9860 Gold 0.6657 oz. AGW **Note:** Similar to 10 Ducat, KM#423.

Date	Mintage	VG	F	VF	XF	Unc
1630	—	1,500	2,750	5,000	8,000	—

KM# 468 6 DUCAT

21.0000 g., 0.9860 Gold 0.6657 oz. AGW **Note:** Vicariat Issue. Similar to 1 Ducat, KM#463.

Date	Mintage	VG	F	VF	XF	Unc
1657 (acorn) Rare	—	—	—	—	—	—

KM# 588 6 DUCAT

21.0000 g., 0.9860 Gold 0.6657 oz. AGW **Obv:** Half-length bust right **Rev:** Helmeted 8-fold arms

Date	Mintage	VG	F	VF	XF	Unc
1684 Rare	—	—	—	—	—	—
1685 Rare	—	—	—	—	—	—
1690 Rare	—	—	—	—	—	—

KM# 589 6 DUCAT

21.0000 g., 0.9860 Gold 0.6657 oz. AGW **Note:** Similar to 3 Ducat, KM#584.

Date	Mintage	VG	F	VF	XF	Unc
1685 CF Rare	—	—	—	—	—	—

KM# B423 7 DUCAT

24.5000 g., 0.9860 Gold 0.7766 oz. AGW **Note:** Similar to 10 Ducat, KM#423.

Date	Mintage	VG	F	VF	XF	Unc
1630	—	1,650	3,250	6,000	9,000	—

KM# A418 8 DUCAT

28.0000 g., 0.9860 Gold 0.8876 oz. AGW **Obv:** 1/2-length bust with sword **Rev:** Arms

Date	Mintage	VG	F	VF	XF	Unc
1628 Rare	—	—	—	—	—	—

KM# C423 8 DUCAT

28.0000 g., 0.9860 Gold 0.8876 oz. AGW **Subject:** Centennial of the Augsburg Confession **Obv:** Bust of Johann Georg right **Rev:** Bust of Johann right

Date	Mintage	VG	F	VF	XF	Unc
1630	—	2,000	3,500	6,500	9,500	—

KM# 469 8 DUCAT

28.0000 g., 0.9860 Gold 0.8876 oz. AGW **Note:** Vicariat Issue. Similar to 1 Ducat, KM#463.

Date	Mintage	VG	F	VF	XF	Unc
1657 (acorn) Rare	—	—	—	—	—	—

KM# D423 9 DUCAT

31.5000 g., 0.9860 Gold 0.9985 oz. AGW **Note:** Similar to 10 Ducat, KM#423.

Date	Mintage	VG	F	VF	XF	Unc
1630	—	2,500	4,000	7,500	16,500	—

KM# 29 10 DUCAT (Portugalöser)

35.0000 g., 0.9860 Gold 1.1095 oz. AGW **Obv:** Bust of Friedrich August I right **Rev:** Helmeted arms **Note:** Struck with 1 Thaler dies, KM#707.

Date	Mintage	VG	F	VF	XF	Unc
1606 Rare	—	—	—	—	—	—

KM# B123 10 DUCAT (Portugalöser)

35.0000 g., 0.9860 Gold 1.1095 oz. AGW **Obv:** Equestrian figure of Johann Georg I right **Rev:** 12-line inscription **Note:** Vicariat Issue. Struck with 1 Thaler dies, KM#119. Prev. KM#A123.

Date	Mintage	VG	F	VF	XF	Unc
1619 Rare	—	—	—	—	—	—

KM# B418 10 DUCAT (Portugalöser)

35.0000 g., 0.9860 Gold 1.1095 oz. AGW **Obv:** 1/2-length bust with sword **Rev:** Arms

Date	Mintage	VG	F	VF	XF	Unc
1628 Rare	—	—	—	—	—	—

KM# 423 10 DUCAT (Portugalöser)

35.0000 g., 0.9860 Gold 1.1095 oz. AGW **Subject:** Centennial of the Augsburg Confession **Obv:** Bust of Johann Georg right **Rev:** Bust of Johann right

Date	Mintage	VG	F	VF	XF	Unc
1630	—	—	—	9,500	13,500	—

KM# 470 10 DUCAT (Portugalöser)

35.0000 g., 0.9860 Gold 1.1095 oz. AGW **Note:** Vicariat Issue. Similar to 1 Ducat, KM#463. Struck with 1 Thaler dies, KM#481.

Date	Mintage	VG	F	VF	XF	Unc
1657 (acorn) Rare	—	—	—	—	—	—

KM# 487 10 DUCAT (Portugalöser)

35.0000 g., 0.9860 Gold 1.1095 oz. AGW **Subject:** Death of Johann Georg II's Mother, Magdalene Sibylle **Note:** Similar to 1 Ducat, KM#484. Struck with 1 Thaler dies, KM#482.

Date	Mintage	VG	F	VF	XF	Unc
1659 (acorn) Rare	—	—	—	—	—	—

KM# 501 10 DUCAT (Portugalöser)

35.0000 g., 0.9860 Gold 1.1095 oz. AGW **Subject:** Marriage of Erdmuthe Sophie to Christian Ernst **Note:** Struck with 1 Thaler dies, KM#500.

Date	Mintage	VG	F	VF	XF	Unc
1662 Rare	—	—	—	—	—	—

KM# 530 10 DUCAT (Portugalöser)

35.0000 g., 0.9860 Gold 1.1095 oz. AGW **Subject:** Birth of Johann Georg IV **Note:** Struck with 1 Thaler dies, KM#528.

Date	Mintage	VG	F	VF	XF	Unc
1669 Rare	—	—	—	—	—	—

KM# A424 12 DUCAT

42.0000 g., 0.9860 Gold 1.3314 oz. AGW **Note:** Similar to 10 Ducat, KM#423.

Date	Mintage	VG	F	VF	XF	Unc
1630 Rare	—	—	—	—	—	—

KM# A419 16 DUCAT

57.0000 g., 0.9860 Gold 1.8069 oz. AGW **Obv:** Equestrian figure on horse in front of Dresden city view **Rev:** 6-fold helmeted arms

Date	Mintage	VG	F	VF	XF	Unc
1627 Rare	—	—	—	—	—	—

KM# 36 20 DUCAT (Doppel Portugalöser)

70.0000 g., 0.9860 Gold 2.2190 oz. AGW **Note:** Similar to 1 Thaler, KM#24. Struck with 2 Thaler dies, KM#26.

Date	Mintage	VG	F	VF	XF	Unc
1610 Rare	—	—	—	—	—	—

KM# B419 20 DUCAT (Doppel Portugalöser)

70.0000 g., 0.9860 Gold 2.2190 oz. AGW **Obv:** Equestrian figure on horse in front of Dresden city view **Rev:** 6-fold helmeted arms

Date	Mintage	VG	F	VF	XF	Unc
1628 Rare	—	—	—	—	—	—

KM# 454 20 DUCAT (Doppel Portugalöser)

70.0000 g., 0.9860 Gold 2.2190 oz. AGW **Subject:** Death of Johann Georg I **Note:** Struck with 1 Thaler dies, KM#451.

Date	Mintage	VG	F	VF	XF	Unc
1656 Rare	—	—	—	—	—	—

KM# 477 20 DUCAT (Doppel Portugalöser)

70.0000 g., 0.9860 Gold 2.2190 oz. AGW **Note:** Vicariat Issue. Struck with 2 Thaler dies, KM#489.

Date	Mintage	VG	F	VF	XF	Unc
1658 (acorn) Rare	—	—	—	—	—	—

KM# 488 20 DUCAT (Doppel Portugalöser)

70.0000 g., 0.9860 Gold 2.2190 oz. AGW **Subject:** Death of Johann Georg II's Mother, Magdalene Sibylle **Note:** Struck with 1 Thaler dies, KM#482.

Date	Mintage	VG	F	VF	XF	Unc
1659 (acorn) Rare	—	—	—	—	—	—

KM# C419 25 DUCAT

87.5000 g., 0.9860 Gold 2.7737 oz. AGW **Obv:** Equestrian figure on horse in front of Dresden city view **Rev:** 6-fold helmeted arms

Date	Mintage	VG	F	VF	XF	Unc
1628 Rare	—	—	—	—	—	—

PATTERNS

Including off metal strikes

KM#	Date	Mintage	Identification	Mkt Val
Pn1	1630	—	10 Ducat. Silver. 34.7000 g. KM423.	—
PnA2	1694	—	Pfennig. Gold. KM636.	—
Pn2	1700 ILH	—	2 Ducat. Silver. KM710.	—

SAYN-ALTENKIRCHEN

The counts of Sayn of the Rhineland are first mentioned in the 12th century. They issued a sporadic coinage from the 13th century and acquired possessions in various parts of western Germany. Divided in 1605 into the branches of Sayn-Sayn, Sayn-Wittgenstein and Sayn-Berleburg. Sayn-Altenkirchen was an off-shoot of Sayn-Sayn. With the extinction of the line of Eisenach dukes in 1741, it was acquired by Brandenburg-Ansbach until 1791, went to Prussia until 1803, and finally to Nassau in 1803.

RULERS

Johanetta, 1648-1686 (1701)
Johann Wilhelm of Saxe-Eisenach, 1686-1729

COUNTSHIP

STANDARD COINAGE

KM# 3 ALBUS

Silver **Obv:** Crowned arms in branches in inner circle, long legend **Rev:** Value and date in inner circle **Rev. Legend:** NACH DEM SCHLVS DER V STAND **Mint:** Friedewald

Date	Mintage	VG	F	VF	XF	Unc
1693	—	—	—	—	—	—

KM# 4 ALBUS

Silver **Obv:** Shorter legend **Obv. Legend:** I. W. H. Z. S. G. Z. S. **Rev. Legend:** NACH DEM FRANCKF. SCHLVS.

Date	Mintage	VG	F	VF	XF	Unc
1693	—	—	—	—	—	—

KM# 6 2 ALBUS

Silver **Obv:** Crowned arms in branches in inner circle **Rev:** Value and date in inner circle **Mint:** Friedewald

Date	Mintage	VG	F	VF	XF	Unc
1693	—	—	—	—	—	—

KM# 8 15 KREUZER

Silver **Obv:** Armored bust of Johann Wilhelm left in inner circle **Rev:** Crowned arms of Saxony and Sayn in branches in inner circle, value below, date at top **Mint:** Friedewald

Date	Mintage	VG	F	VF	XF	Unc
1693	—	175	350	675	1,125	—

KM# 9 15 KREUZER
Silver **Rev:** Date at upper left

Date	Mintage	VG	F	VF	XF	Unc
1693	—	175	350	675	1,125	—

KM# 11 1/6 THALER
Silver **Ruler:** Johann Wilhelm of Saxe-Eisenbach
Obv: Armored bust of Johann Wilhelm left **Rev:** 1/6 with date in angles in inner circle **Mint:** Friedewald

Date	Mintage	VG	F	VF	XF	Unc
1692	—	—	—	—	—	—

KM# 13 2/3 THALER
Silver **Ruler:** Johann Wilhelm of Saxe-Eisenbach
Obv: Armored bust of Johann Wilhelm to left in inner circle
Rev: Crowned arms of Saxony and Sayn in branches in inner circle, value below, date at top **Mint:** Friedewald

Date	Mintage	VG	F	VF	XF	Unc
1693	—	—	—	—	—	—

SAYN-BERLEBURG

RULERS
Georg V, 1605-1631
Georg Wilhelm, 1643-1684

COUNTSHIP

STANDARD COINAGE

KM# 5 PFENNIG
Billon **Obv:** Three boars' heads **Note:** Uniface.

Date	Mintage	VG	F	VF	XF	Unc
ND	—	27.00	40.00	75.00	140	—

KM# 6 PFENNIG
Billon **Obv:** Two-fold arms, three boars' heads and pale below H

Date	Mintage	VG	F	VF	XF	Unc
ND	—	27.00	40.00	75.00	140	—

KM# 7 PFENNIG
Billon **Obv:** Two-fold arms, four points and lion rampant below H

Date	Mintage	VG	F	VF	XF	Unc
ND	—	27.00	40.00	75.00	140	—

KM# 8 PFENNIG
Billon **Obv:** Two-fold arms, pale and lion rampant below H

Date	Mintage	VG	F	VF	XF	Unc
ND	—	27.00	40.00	75.00	140	—

KM# 9 PFENNIG
Billon **Obv:** Two-fold arms, pale and lion rampant below arrow

Date	Mintage	VG	F	VF	XF	Unc
ND	—	27.00	40.00	75.00	140	—

KM# 10 PFENNIG
Billon **Obv:** Crowned G W monogram

Date	Mintage	VG	F	VF	XF	Unc
ND	—	27.00	40.00	75.00	140	—

KM# 40 4 GUTE PFENNIG
Billon **Obv:** Crowned G divides date **Rev:** Value **Mint:** Berleburg

Date	Mintage	VG	F	VF	XF	Unc
1660	—	—	—	—	—	—

KM# 21 3 KREUZER (1/8 Thaler)
Base Silver **Obv:** Multiple arms at center

Date	Mintage	VG	F	VF	XF	Unc
1622 Rare	—	—	—	—	—	—

KM# 20 3 KREUZER (1/8 Thaler)
Base Silver **Obv:** 2-towered gate in inner circle **Rev:** Crowned imperial eagle with value on breast **Mint:** Berleburg **Note:** Kipper 3 Kreuzer.

Date	Mintage	VG	F	VF	XF	Unc
1622 Rare	—	—	—	—	—	—

KM# 11 12 KREUZER (1/2 Thaler)
Base Silver **Obv:** Lion rampant in inner circle **Rev:** Crowned imperial eagle with value on breast **Mint:** Berleburg **Note:** Kipper 12 Kreuzer.

Date	Mintage	VG	F	VF	XF	Unc
ND Rare	—	—	—	—	—	—

KM# 22 24 KREUZER (1 Thaler)
Base Silver **Obv:** Bust of Georg right in inner circle, date in legend **Rev:** Crowned imperial eagle with value on breast in inner circle **Mint:** Berleburg **Note:** Kipper 24 Kreuzer.

Date	Mintage	VG	F	VF	XF	Unc
1622 Rare	—	—	—	—	—	—

KM# 45 30 KREUZER (1/2 Gulden)
Silver **Obv:** Large bust of Georg Wilhelm right, value below
Rev: Crowned arms, date in legend **Mint:** Berleburg

Date	Mintage	VG	F	VF	XF	Unc
1675	—	325	675	1,200	2,000	—

KM# 46 30 KREUZER (1/2 Gulden)
Silver **Obv:** Small bust of Georg Wilhelm right, value below

Date	Mintage	VG	F	VF	XF	Unc
1675 IB	—	250	500	900	1,500	—

KM# 55 30 KREUZER (1/2 Gulden)
Silver **Obv:** Crowned arms in branches, date in legend

Date	Mintage	VG	F	VF	XF	Unc
1676	—	325	675	1,200	2,000	—

KM# 47 60 KREUZER (2/3 Thaler)
Silver **Obv:** Georg Wilhelm

Date	Mintage	VG	F	VF	XF	Unc
1675 IB	—	165	300	600	1,000	—

KM# 48 60 KREUZER (2/3 Thaler)
Silver **Obv:** Dot before GEORG

Date	Mintage	VG	F	VF	XF	Unc
1675 IB	—	165	300	600	1,000	—

KM# 49 60 KREUZER (2/3 Thaler)
Silver **Obv:** Three dots before GEORG

Date	Mintage	VG	F	VF	XF	Unc
1675 IB	—	165	300	600	1,000	—

KM# 50 60 KREUZER (2/3 Thaler)
Silver **Rev:** Without dots before date

Date	Mintage	VG	F	VF	XF	Unc
1675 IB	—	165	300	600	1,000	—

KM# 51 60 KREUZER (2/3 Thaler)
Silver **Rev:** Dots before and after GRUIS

Date	Mintage	VG	F	VF	XF	Unc
1675	—	165	300	600	1,000	—

KM# 52 60 KREUZER (2/3 Thaler)
Silver **Obv:** Two dots below 60

Date	Mintage	VG	F	VF	XF	Unc
1675 IB	—	165	300	600	1,000	—

KM# 53 60 KREUZER (2/3 Thaler)
Silver **Rev:** Rosettes in legend

Date	Mintage	VG	F	VF	XF	Unc
1675 IB	—	165	300	600	1,000	—

KM# 54 60 KREUZER (2/3 Thaler)
Silver **Rev:** Straight-sided shield

Date	Mintage	VG	F	VF	XF	Unc
1675 IB	—	165	300	600	1,000	—

KM# 56 60 KREUZER (2/3 Thaler)
Silver **Obv:** Bust of Georg Wilhelm right **Rev:** Crowned arms, date in legend

Date	Mintage	VG	F	VF	XF	Unc
1676 IB	—	120	240	400	725	—

KM# 57 60 KREUZER (2/3 Thaler)
Silver **Rev:** Crown breaks inner circle, arms in branches, date in legend

Date	Mintage	VG	F	VF	XF	Unc
1676	—	120	240	400	725	—

KM# 58 60 KREUZER (2/3 Thaler)
Silver **Rev:** Crowned arms in branches in inner circle, date in legend

Date	Mintage	VG	F	VF	XF	Unc
1676	—	120	240	400	725	—

KM# 59 60 KREUZER (2/3 Thaler)
Silver **Obv:** Older bust of Georg Wilhelm right **Rev:** Crowned arms in branches without inner circle, date in legend

Date	Mintage	VG	F	VF	XF	Unc
1676 IVB	—	120	240	400	725	—

KM# 60 60 KREUZER (2/3 Thaler)
Silver **Obv:** Different bust of Georg Wilhelm right in inner circle **Rev:** Round arms in cartouche in inner circle

Date	Mintage	VG	F	VF	XF	Unc
1676	—	120	240	400	725	—

KM# 61 24 MARIENGROSCHEN
Silver **Rev:** Value and date in inner circle

Date	Mintage	VG	F	VF	XF	Unc
1676	—	400	750	1,250	2,100	—

KM# 23 1/2 REICHSTHALER
Silver **Obv:** Arms in circle **Rev:** Crowned imperial eagle in inner circle, date in legend **Mint:** Berleburg

Date	Mintage	VG	F	VF	XF	Unc
1625	—	—	—	—	—	—

KM# 62 2/3 THALER
Silver **Obv:** Bust of Gustav of Sayn-Wittgenstein-Hohenstein right in inner circle **Rev:** Crowned arms in inner circle, value below, date in legend

Date	Mintage	VG	F	VF	XF	Unc
1676	—	450	800	1,350	2,400	—

DAV# 7667 REICHSTHALER
Silver **Obv:** Helmeted arms in inner circle **Rev:** Crowned imperial eagle with orb on breast in inner circle **Mint:** Berleburg

Date	Mintage	VG	F	VF	XF	Unc
1624	—	4,500	7,500	12,000	—	—
1625	—	4,500	7,500	12,000	—	—

DAV# 7667B REICHSTHALER
Silver **Obv:** Arms in quatrefoil in inner circle

Date	Mintage	VG	F	VF	XF	Unc
1624	—	4,500	7,500	12,000	—	—
(1)625	—	4,500	7,500	12,000	—	—

DAV# 7668 REICHSTHALER
Silver **Obv:** Bust of Georg right in inner circle, date in legend

Date	Mintage	VG	F	VF	XF	Unc
1625 Rare	—	—	—	—	—	—

DAV# 7669 REICHSTHALER
Silver **Obv:** Bust of Georg Wilhelm right in inner circle
Rev: Helmeted arms in inner circle, date in legend

Date	Mintage	VG	F	VF	XF	Unc
1678 IVB Rare	—	—	—	—	—	—

TRADE COINAGE

FR# 3051 GOLDGULDEN
3.5000 g., 0.9860 Gold 0.1109 oz. AGW **Obv:** Shield of arms in inner circle **Rev:** Crowned imperial eagle in inner circle, titles of Ferdinand II

Date	Mintage	VG	F	VF	XF	Unc
ND	—	1,300	2,600	5,200	8,500	—

KM# 80 GOLDGULDEN
3.5000 g., 0.9860 Gold 0.1109 oz. AGW **Rev:** Helmeted arms in inner circle

Date	Mintage	VG	F	VF	XF	Unc
1624	—	—	—	—	—	—

FR# 3053 GOLDGULDEN
3.5000 g., 0.9860 Gold 0.1109 oz. AGW **Obv:** Orb in trilobe in inner circle

Date	Mintage	VG	F	VF	XF	Unc
ND	—	1,050	2,250	4,150	6,800	—

FR# 3054 GOLDGULDEN
3.5000 g., 0.9860 Gold 0.1109 oz. AGW **Obv:** Three shields of arms in inner circle **Rev:** Crowned imperial eagle in inner circle, titles of Ferdinand II

Date	Mintage	VG	F	VF	XF	Unc
ND	—	750	1,500	3,000	5,300	—

FR# 3056 GOLDGULDEN
3.5000 g., 0.9860 Gold 0.1109 oz. AGW **Rev:** Three shields of arms with tops toward each other in inner circle

Date	Mintage	VG	F	VF	XF	Unc
ND	—	650	1,500	3,200	5,600	—

FR# 3057 GOLDGULDEN
3.5000 g., 0.9860 Gold 0.1109 oz. AGW **Rev:** Two shields of arms joined in inner circle

Date	Mintage	VG	F	VF	XF	Unc
ND	—	650	1,500	3,200	5,600	—

FR# 3052 GOLDGULDEN
3.5000 g., 0.9860 Gold 0.1109 oz. AGW **Obv:** Orb in ornamental trilobe in inner circle **Rev:** Two shields of arms in ornamental inner circle

Date	Mintage	VG	F	VF	XF	Unc
ND	—	875	2,000	4,400	7,200	—

SAYN-HACKENBERG-ALTENKIRCHEN

RULERS
Wilhelm III, 1606-1623
Ernst, 1623-1641

COUNTSHIP

STANDARD COINAGE

KM# 5 PFENNIG
Billon **Ruler:** Wilhelm III **Obv:** Arms in beaded circle **Note:** Uniface.

Date	Mintage	VG	F	VF	XF	Unc
ND(ca. 1609)	—	33.00	45.00	85.00	160	—

KM# 16 1/16 REICHSTHALER
Silver **Subject:** Death of Luise Juliane **Obv:** 6-line inscription **Rev:** 6-line inscription

Date	Mintage	VG	F	VF	XF	Unc
1670	300	110	200	325	600	—

KM# 17 1/16 REICHSTHALER
Silver **Obv:** Laureate bust of Leopold I in inner circle **Rev:** Arms divide date and value in inner circle **Mint:** Dortmund

Date	Mintage	VG	F	VF	XF	Unc
1670	12,000	—	—	—	—	—
1671	Inc. above	—	—	—	—	—

KM# 18 1/4 REICHSTHALER
Silver **Subject:** Death of Luise Juliane **Obv:** 8-line inscription **Rev:** Praying countess in boat in stormy sea in inner circle

Date	Mintage	VG	F	VF	XF	Unc
1670	200	325	525	850	1,350	—

KM# 10 1/2 REICHSTHALER
Silver **Subject:** Death of Luise Juliane **Obv:** 8-line inscription **Rev:** Praying countess in boat in stormy sea in inner circle **Note:** Prev. Sayn-Hackenberg-Altenkirchen KM#19.

Date	Mintage	VG	F	VF	XF	Unc
1670	100	450	850	1,350	2,100	—

SAYN-WITTGENSTEIN-HOHNSTEIN

County in 1261 in western Germany, northeast of Coblenz. Count Salentin married the heiress of Wittgenstein c. 1359 to establish the line. Count Gustav (1657-1701) was a prolific issuer of coins, not all of them genuinely his to issue. This caused some concern among his neighbors. The last member of the line was made a prince in 1804 and died in 1837.

RULERS
Johann VIII, 1634-1657
Gustav, 1657-1701

COUNTSHIP

STANDARD COINAGE

KM# 80 KREUZER
Billon **Obv:** Sayn arms in palm branches **Rev:** Value and date in palm branches **Mint:** Berleburg

Date	Mintage	VG	F	VF	XF	Unc
1682 ICF	—	60.00	115	200	325	—
1683 IVB	—	60.00	115	200	325	—
1683 IUB	—	60.00	115	200	325	—
1684 IVB	—	60.00	115	200	325	—
1684 IUB	—	60.00	115	200	325	—

KM# 81 KREUZER
Billon **Mint:** Wittgenstein

Date	Mintage	VG	F	VF	XF	Unc
1685 HM	—	60.00	115	200	325	—
1685 CHM	—	60.00	115	200	325	—
1685 IVB	—	60.00	115	200	325	—
1686 ICF	—	60.00	115	200	325	—

KM# 20 3 KREUZER
Billon **Obv:** Crowned G divides date **Rev:** Orb with 3 near bottom **Mint:** Ellrich

Date	Mintage	VG	F	VF	XF	Unc
1672	—	45.00	85.00	160	275	—

KM# 21 3 KREUZER
Billon **Obv:** Arms with date above

Date	Mintage	VG	F	VF	XF	Unc
1672	—	45.00	85.00	160	275	—

KM# 5 ALBUS
Billon **Obv:** Arms with W above **Rev:** Value and date in wreath

Date	Mintage	VG	F	VF	XF	Unc
1657 Large date	—	100	200	325	—	—
1657 Small date	—	100	200	325	—	—

KM# 82 ALBUS
Billon **Obv:** Sayn arms in palm branches **Rev:** Value and date in palm branches

Date	Mintage	VG	F	VF	XF	Unc
1681 ICF	—	65.00	135	225	400	—

KM# 105 2 ALBUS
Billon **Obv:** Arms in palm branches **Rev:** Value and date in palm branches

Date	Mintage	VG	F	VF	XF	Unc
1692	—	85.00	160	300	425	—

KM# 83 8 HELLER
Billon **Obv:** Arms of Sayn **Rev:** Value in inner circle, date in legend

Date	Mintage	VG	F	VF	XF	Unc
1681 JCF	—	16.00	30.00	55.00	100	—
1682 ICF	—	16.00	30.00	55.00	100	—
1682 IC	—	16.00	30.00	55.00	100	—
ND ICF	—	16.00	30.00	55.00	100	—

KM# 6 MARIENGROSCHEN
Billon **Obv:** Lion in inner circle, date in legend **Rev:** Radiant figure of Madonna holding child in inner circle **Note:** Legend varieties.

Date	Mintage	VG	F	VF	XF	Unc
1653	—	45.00	80.00	135	225	—
1655	—	45.00	80.00	135	225	—
1656	—	45.00	80.00	135	225	—
1657	—	45.00	80.00	135	225	—

KM# 22 MARIENGROSCHEN
Billon **Obv:** Crowned G divides date **Rev:** Without inner circle

Date	Mintage	VG	F	VF	XF	Unc
1672	—	33.00	60.00	100	165	—
1673	—	33.00	60.00	100	165	—

KM# 23 MARIENGROSCHEN
Billon **Obv:** Crowned arms divide date in inner circle

Date	Mintage	VG	F	VF	XF	Unc
1672	—	40.00	65.00	120	200	—

KM# 7 2 MARIENGROSCHEN
Billon **Obv:** Crowned arms divide date in inner circle **Rev:** Value in inner circle **Note:** Punctuation varieties.

Date	Mintage	VG	F	VF	XF	Unc
1654	—	16.00	40.00	80.00	140	—
1655	—	16.00	40.00	80.00	140	—
1656	—	16.00	40.00	80.00	140	—

KM# 8 4 MARIENGROSCHEN
Silver **Obv:** Crowned arms divide date in inner circle **Rev:** Value in inner circle **Note:** Ornamentation varieties.

Date	Mintage	VG	F	VF	XF	Unc
1655	—	33.00	65.00	135	275	—
1656	—	33.00	65.00	135	275	—
1657	—	33.00	65.00	135	275	—

KM# 84 6 MARIENGROSCHEN
Silver **Obv:** Armored bust of Gustav right **Rev:** Value and date in inner circle

Date	Mintage	VG	F	VF	XF	Unc
1688	—	45.00	85.00	165	325	—
1689	—	45.00	85.00	165	325	—

KM# 24 12 MARIENGROSCHEN
Silver **Obv:** Klettenberg arms in inner circle **Rev:** Value XII in inner circle, MARIA/GROS, date in legend **Mint:** Ellrich

Date	Mintage	VG	F	VF	XF	Unc
167Z	—	200	375	600	—	—

KM# 25 12 MARIENGROSCHEN
Silver **Rev:** XII/MARIEN/GROSCH

Date	Mintage	VG	F	VF	XF	Unc
1672	—	200	375	600	—	—
1673 IZW	—	200	375	600	—	—

KM# 26 12 MARIENGROSCHEN
Silver **Obv:** Bust of Gustav right **Rev:** Value in inner circle, date in legend

Date	Mintage	VG	F	VF	XF	Unc
1673	—	225	425	725	—	—
1673 IZW	—	225	425	725	—	—
1674 IZW	—	225	425	725	—	—

KM# 27 16 GUTE GROSCHEN (2/3 Thaler)
Silver **Obv:** Walking stag in inner circle **Rev:** Value divides date in inner circle

Date	Mintage	VG	F	VF	XF	Unc
1675	—	250	500	950	1,550	—

KM# 28 16 GUTE GROSCHEN (2/3 Thaler)
Silver **Obv:** Crowned arms in palm branches in inner circle, fraction below **Rev:** Value and date in inner circle

Date	Mintage	VG	F	VF	XF	Unc
1675	—	200	400	725	1,250	—

KM# 29 16 GUTE GROSCHEN (2/3 Thaler)
Silver **Obv:** Value and date in inner circle, titles of Gustav **Rev:** Crowned arms in inner circle

Date	Mintage	VG	F	VF	XF	Unc
1675	—	200	400	725	1,250	—

KM# 30 16 GUTE GROSCHEN (2/3 Thaler)
Silver **Obv:** Helmeted arms in inner circle **Rev:** Value in inner circle, Roman numeral date in legend

Date	Mintage	VG	F	VF	XF	Unc
1676	—	115	200	325	525	—

KM# 31 16 GUTE GROSCHEN (2/3 Thaler)
Silver

Date	Mintage	VG	F	VF	XF	Unc
1676	—	160	325	525	1,075	—

KM# 32 16 GUTE GROSCHEN (2/3 Thaler)
Silver **Obv:** Value and Roman numeral date in inner circle **Rev:** Walking stag in inner circle

Date	Mintage	VG	F	VF	XF	Unc
1676	—	180	375	600	1,150	—

KM# 33 16 GUTE GROSCHEN (2/3 Thaler)
Silver **Obv:** Running stag in inner circle **Rev:** Value and date in inner circle

Date	Mintage	VG	F	VF	XF	Unc
1677	—	185	375	625	1,200	—

KM# 34 16 GUTE GROSCHEN (2/3 Thaler)
Silver **Obv:** Bust of Gustav right

Date	Mintage	VG	F	VF	XF	Unc
1677	—	200	400	750	1,250	—

KM# 35 24 MARIENGROSCHEN (2/3 Thaler)
Silver **Obv:** Klettenberg arms (stag) in inner circle **Rev:** XXIIII value in inner circle, date in legend **Rev. Legend:** PIE ET CAUTE

Date	Mintage	VG	F	VF	XF	Unc
1673 IZW	—	90.00	180	375	750	—
1675	—	90.00	180	375	750	—

KM# 36 24 MARIENGROSCHEN (2/3 Thaler)
Silver **Obv:** Bust of Gustav

Date	Mintage	VG	F	VF	XF	Unc
1673 IZW	—	200	400	750	—	—
1674 IZW	—	200	400	750	—	—

KM# 37 24 MARIENGROSCHEN (2/3 Thaler)
Silver **Rev:** Small letters in value

Date	Mintage	VG	F	VF	XF	Unc
1674	—	40.00	100	165	300	—

KM# 38 24 MARIENGROSCHEN (2/3 Thaler)
Silver **Obv:** Stag in inner circle **Rev:** Value in inner circle, date in legend

Date	Mintage	VG	F	VF	XF	Unc
1675	—	65.00	135	225	375	—

KM# 39 24 MARIENGROSCHEN (2/3 Thaler)
Silver **Obv:** Large bust of Gustav right in inner circle **Rev:** Value and date in inner circle **Rev. Legend:** VERBIUM DOMINI MANET IN AETERNUM

Date	Mintage	VG	F	VF	XF	Unc
1675	—	200	400	675	1,200	—

KM# 40 24 MARIENGROSCHEN (2/3 Thaler)
Silver **Obv:** Helmeted arms in inner circle **Rev:** Value in inner circle, date in legend **Rev. Legend:** TANDEM FORTUNA OBSTETRICE

Date	Mintage	VG	F	VF	XF	Unc
1676	—	185	375	600	1,150	—
1677	—	185	375	600	1,150	—

KM# 41 24 MARIENGROSCHEN (2/3 Thaler)
Silver **Obv:** Gustav **Rev. Legend:** AD PALMAM PRAESSA LAETIUS RESURGO

Date	Mintage	VG	F	VF	XF	Unc
1676	—	45.00	100	165	300	—

KM# 42 24 MARIENGROSCHEN (2/3 Thaler)
Silver **Obv:** Older bust osf Gustav right in inner circle **Rev:** Value in inner circle, date in legend **Rev. Legend:** PIE ET CAUTE

Date	Mintage	VG	F	VF	XF	Unc
1677	—	65.00	135	225	375	—

KM# 85 24 MARIENGROSCHEN (2/3 Thaler)
Silver **Rev. Legend:** MONETA NOVA ARGENTEA

Date	Mintage	VG	F	VF	XF	Unc
1689	—	—	—	—	—	—

KM# 106 24 MARIENGROSCHEN (2/3 Thaler)
Silver **Obv:** Helmeted arms in inner circle **Rev:** Running stag in inner circle

Date	Mintage	VG	F	VF	XF	Unc
1690	—	—	—	—	—	—

KM# 107 24 MARIENGROSCHEN (2/3 Thaler)
Silver **Obv:** Bust of Gustav right in inner circle **Rev:** Value in inner circle **Rev. Legend:** TANDEM FORTUNA OBSTETRICE

Date	Mintage	VG	F	VF	XF	Unc
ND(1690)	—	200	400	675	1,200	—

KM# 104 24 MARIENGROSCHEN (2/3 Thaler)
Silver **Obv:** Smaller bust of Gustav right in inner circle **Rev:** Value in inner circle, date in Roman numerals in legend

Date	Mintage	VG	F	VF	XF	Unc
1691	—	225	450	800	1,350	—

KM# 44 1/24 THALER
Silver **Rev:** Legend, date **Rev. Legend:** PIE. ET. CAUTE

Date	Mintage	VG	F	VF	XF	Unc
1672	—	65.00	135	225	375	—

KM# 43 1/24 THALER
Silver **Obv:** Klettenberg arms (stag) in inner circle **Rev:** Orb in inner circle with 24 near bottom, titles of Gustav in legend **Note:** Struck at Ellrich Mint.

Date	Mintage	VG	F	VF	XF	Unc
ND(1672)	—	80.00	160	275	425	—

KM# A45 1/24 THALER
Silver **Obv:** Hohnstein arms divide mintmaster's initials **Rev:** Imperial orb with 24 divides date as 1-6/8-4 **Note:** Struck at Klettenberg Mint.

Date	Mintage	VG	F	VF	XF	Unc
1684 DF	—	65.00	135	250	400	—

KM# 86 1/16 THALER
Silver **Obv:** Crowned G monogram in palm branches **Rev:** Value in inner circle, date in legend

Date	Mintage	VG	F	VF	XF	Unc
1683	—	—	—	—	—	—

KM# 87 1/16 THALER
Silver **Obv:** Gustav

Date	Mintage	VG	F	VF	XF	Unc
1683	—	165	325	600	1,075	—

KM# 90 1/12 THALER (Doppelgroschen)
Silver **Obv:** Crowned arms divide date in inner circle **Rev:** Value in inner circle

Date	Mintage	VG	F	VF	XF	Unc
1684	—	85.00	165	275	450	—

KM# 88 1/12 THALER (Doppelgroschen)
Silver **Obv:** Crowned six-fold arms with central shield divide date as 1-6/8-4 **Rev:** 12/EINEN/REICHS/THAL/ER **Note:** Struck at Klettenberg Mint.

Date	Mintage	VG	F	VF	XF	Unc
1684 DF	—	85.00	165	275	450	—

KM# 89 1/12 THALER (Doppelgroschen)
Silver **Obv:** Crowned arms **Rev:** Value in inner circle, date in legend

Date	Mintage	VG	F	VF	XF	Unc
1689	—	115	200	325	—	—

KM# 91 1/6 THALER
Silver **Obv:** Gustav **Rev:** Value in inner circle, date in legend

Date	Mintage	VG	F	VF	XF	Unc
1688	—	325	600	1,000	1,650	—

KM# 92 1/6 THALER
Silver **Rev:** Value and date in inner circle

Date	Mintage	VG	F	VF	XF	Unc
1688	—	325	600	1,000	1,650	—

KM# 93 1/6 THALER
Silver **Obv:** Older bust of Gustav right **Rev:** Value in inner circle, date in legend

Date	Mintage	VG	F	VF	XF	Unc
1689	—	350	625	1,075	1,700	—

KM# 94 1/6 THALER
Silver **Rev:** Value and date in inner circle

Date	Mintage	VG	F	VF	XF	Unc
1689	—	350	625	1,075	1,700	—

KM# 95 1/6 THALER
Silver **Obv:** Bust of Gustav right breaks legend at top

Date	Mintage	VG	F	VF	XF	Unc
1689	—	350	625	1,075	1,700	—

KM# 45 1/4 THALER
Silver **Obv:** Bust of Gustav right in inner circle **Rev:** Ship at sea with setting sun in background

Date	Mintage	VG	F	VF	XF	Unc
ND Unique	—	—	—	—	—	—

Note: Struck from dies of unknown double ducat and with silver from the Netherlands East Indies

KM# 46 1/3 THALER

Silver **Obv:** Bust of Gustav right **Rev:** Crowned six-fold arms, fraction below, date in legend **Rev. Legend:** UT PRESSA PALM

Date	Mintage	VG	F	VF	XF	Unc
1674 IZW	—	100	200	375	600	—
1676 PL	—	100	200	375	600	—

KM# 47 1/3 THALER

Silver **Rev:** Legend, date **Rev. Legend:** PIE ET CAUTE-ANNO

Date	Mintage	VG	F	VF	XF	Unc
1674 ZIW	—	100	200	375	600	—

KM# 48 1/3 THALER

Silver **Rev:** Crowned arms divide P-L, fraction below, date in legend **Rev. Legend:** UT PRESSA PALM

Date	Mintage	VG	F	VF	XF	Unc
1676 PL	—	100	200	375	600	—

KM# 49 1/3 THALER

Silver **Obv:** Different bust of Gustav right
Rev. Legend: TANDEM FORTUNA-OBSTETRILE

Date	Mintage	VG	F	VF	XF	Unc
1676 PL	—	85.00	180	325	575	—
1676	—	85.00	180	325	575	—
1677	—	85.00	180	325	575	—

KM# 50.1 2/3 THALER (60 Kreuzer)

Silver **Obv:** Bust of Gustav right **Rev:** Crowned arms, fraction below, date in legend **Rev. Legend:** PIE ET CAUTE

Date	Mintage	VG	F	VF	XF	Unc
1673	—	80.00	160	325	675	—

KM# 50.2 2/3 THALER (60 Kreuzer)

Silver **Rev:** Legend, date **Rev. Legend:** PIE ET CAUTE.ANNO

Date	Mintage	VG	F	VF	XF	Unc
1674 IZW	—	65.00	135	275	525	—

KM# 51 2/3 THALER (60 Kreuzer)

Silver **Rev. Legend:** UT PRESSA PALM

Date	Mintage	VG	F	VF	XF	Unc
1674 IZW	—	65.00	135	275	525	—
1675 IZW	—	65.00	135	275	525	—
1676 PL	—	65.00	135	275	525	—

KM# 52 2/3 THALER (60 Kreuzer)

Silver **Obv:** Larger head and broader hair arrangement, with flower at shoulder

Date	Mintage	VG	F	VF	XF	Unc
1674 IZW	—	85.00	165	300	600	—

KM# 53 2/3 THALER (60 Kreuzer)

Silver **Obv:** Different bust of Gustav right **Rev:** Crowned arms divide P-L, fraction below, date in legend

Date	Mintage	VG	F	VF	XF	Unc
1675 PL	—	65.00	135	275	525	—

KM# 55 2/3 THALER (60 Kreuzer)

Silver **Obv:** Crowned GGZSVH monogram in branches, value below **Rev:** Helmeted arms **Rev. Legend:** AD INSTAR GRUIS

Date	Mintage	VG	F	VF	XF	Unc
1675 WI	—	—	—	—	—	—

KM# 56 2/3 THALER (60 Kreuzer)

Silver **Obv:** Large bust of Gustav right, value below **Rev:** Crowned arms, date in legend

Date	Mintage	VG	F	VF	XF	Unc
1675 IB	—	65.00	135	275	525	—

KM# 57 2/3 THALER (60 Kreuzer)

Silver **Obv:** Smaller bust of Gustav

Date	Mintage	VG	F	VF	XF	Unc
1675 IB	—	65.00	135	275	525	—
1676 IB	—	65.00	135	275	525	—

KM# 59 2/3 THALER (60 Kreuzer)

Silver **Obv:** Different crowned GGZSVH monogram with date below in inner circle **Rev:** Large 2/3 in inner circle

Date	Mintage	VG	F	VF	XF	Unc
1675	—	—	—	—	—	—

KM# 60 2/3 THALER (60 Kreuzer)

Silver **Obv:** Bust of Gustav right **Rev:** Crowned arms divide date, value below

Date	Mintage	VG	F	VF	XF	Unc
1675	—	80.00	160	300	525	—

KM# 61 2/3 THALER (60 Kreuzer)

Silver **Obv:** Older bust of Gustav right in inner circle, value below **Rev:** Crowned arms in inner circle, date above crown

Date	Mintage	VG	F	VF	XF	Unc
1676	—	110	200	325	575	—

KM# 62 2/3 THALER (60 Kreuzer)

Silver **Obv:** Gustav

Date	Mintage	VG	F	VF	XF	Unc
1676	—	65.00	135	225	375	—

KM# 63 2/3 THALER (60 Kreuzer)

Silver **Obv:** Fine style bust of Gustav right in inner circle

Date	Mintage	VG	F	VF	XF	Unc
1676	—	90.00	160	300	525	—

KM# 64 2/3 THALER (60 Kreuzer)

Silver **Obv:** Gustav **Rev:** Crowned arms divide date in inner circle, value below

Date	Mintage	VG	F	VF	XF	Unc
1676	—	65.00	135	225	375	—
1678	—	65.00	135	225	375	—

KM# 66 2/3 THALER (60 Kreuzer)

Silver **Obv:** Older bust of Gustav right

Date	Mintage	VG	F	VF	XF	Unc
1676	—	100	180	300	525	—

KM# 67 2/3 THALER (60 Kreuzer)

Silver **Obv:** Tall bust of Gustav

Date	Mintage	VG	F	VF	XF	Unc
1676	—	65.00	135	225	375	—

KM# 78 2/3 THALER (60 Kreuzer)

Silver **Obv:** Tall mature bust of Gustav right in inner circle **Rev:** Wide crown above arms

Date	Mintage	VG	F	VF	XF	Unc
1676	—	80.00	150	250	400	—

KM# 69 2/3 THALER (60 Kreuzer)

Silver **Obv:** Youthful bust of Gustav right with plume below **Rev:** Helmeted arms with value below, date in legend

Date	Mintage	VG	F	VF	XF	Unc
1676	—	—	—	—	—	—

KM# 79 2/3 THALER (60 Kreuzer)
Silver **Obv:** Without inner circle **Rev:** Wide arms, date in legend

Date	Mintage	VG	F	VF	XF	Unc
1676	—	80.00	150	250	400	—

KM# 65 2/3 THALER (60 Kreuzer)
Silver **Obv:** Squarish bust of Gustav **Note:** Varieties exist with wide or narrow arms for both dates.

Date	Mintage	VG	F	VF	XF	Unc
1676	—	60.00	120	200	350	—
1678	—	60.00	120	200	350	—

KM# 68 2/3 THALER (60 Kreuzer)
Silver **Obv:** Stocky bust of Gustav right in inner circle **Note:** Varieties exist.

Date	Mintage	VG	F	VF	XF	Unc
1676	—	45.00	100	165	300	—

KM# 70 2/3 THALER (60 Kreuzer)
Silver **Obv:** Short mature bust of Gustav right in inner circle **Rev:** Crowned arms divide date in inner circle, value below **Note:** Varieties exist.

Date	Mintage	VG	F	VF	XF	Unc
1676	—	45.00	100	165	300	—
1677	—	45.00	100	165	300	—

KM# 58 2/3 THALER (60 Kreuzer)
Silver **Obv:** Crowned GGZSVH monogram with date and value below in branches

Date	Mintage	VG	F	VF	XF	Unc
1676	—	—	—	—	—	—

KM# 54 2/3 THALER (60 Kreuzer)
Silver **Rev:** Large crowned six-fold arms with central shield divides date, 2/3 in oval at bottom **Rev. Legend:** AD • PALMUM • PRESSA • LAETIUE • SURGIT •

Date	Mintage	VG	F	VF	XF	Unc
1676 PL	—	65.00	135	275	525	—

KM# A55 2/3 THALER (60 Kreuzer)
Silver **Rev:** Crowned six-fold arms with central shield,value 2/3 in oval below, legend, date **Rev. Legend:** TANDEM FORTUNA-OBSTETRICE

Date	Mintage	VG	F	VF	XF	Unc
1676 PL	—	80.00	160	325	675	—

KM# 77 2/3 THALER (60 Kreuzer)
Silver **Rev:** Flower at each side of arms

Date	Mintage	VG	F	VF	XF	Unc
1677	—	65.00	135	225	375	—

KM# 71 2/3 THALER (60 Kreuzer)
Silver **Obv:** Without inner circle **Rev:** Without inner circle

Date	Mintage	VG	F	VF	XF	Unc
1677	—	65.00	135	225	375	—

KM# 72 2/3 THALER (60 Kreuzer)
Silver **Obv:** Small bust of Gustav right **Rev:** Crowned arms divide date in inner circle, value below

Date	Mintage	VG	F	VF	XF	Unc
1678	—	65.00	135	225	375	—

KM# 73 2/3 THALER (60 Kreuzer)
Silver **Obv:** Smiling bust of Gustav right in inner circle

Date	Mintage	VG	F	VF	XF	Unc
1678	—	80.00	160	275	425	—

KM# 96 2/3 THALER (60 Kreuzer)
Silver **Obv:** Armored bust of Gustav **Rev:** Crowned arms in inner circle, value below

Date	Mintage	VG	F	VF	XF	Unc
1683	—	275	525	850	1,350	—
1684	—	300	600	1,000	1,600	—
1686	—	300	600	1,000	1,600	—
1687	—	300	600	1,000	1,600	—

KM# 97 2/3 THALER (60 Kreuzer)
Silver **Obv:** Older armored bust of Gustav right **Rev:** Large 2/3 in inner circle, date in legend

Date	Mintage	VG	F	VF	XF	Unc
1688	—	—	—	—	—	—
1689	—	—	—	—	—	—

KM# 98 2/3 THALER (60 Kreuzer)
Silver **Obv:** Bust of Gustav right in inner circle, value below **Rev:** Crowned arms in straight-sided shield in inner circle, date above crown

Date	Mintage	VG	F	VF	XF	Unc
1689	—	—	—	—	—	—

KM# 108 2/3 THALER (60 Kreuzer)
Silver **Obv:** Bust of Gustav right in inner circle **Rev:** Crowned arms divide date in inner circle, value below

Date	Mintage	VG	F	VF	XF	Unc
1690	—	80.00	160	275	425	—

KM# 109 2/3 THALER (60 Kreuzer)
Silver **Rev:** Helmeted arms in inner circle, date in legend

Date	Mintage	VG	F	VF	XF	Unc
1690	—	135	275	450	800	—

KM# 110 2/3 THALER (60 Kreuzer)
Silver **Rev:** Value at bottom

Date	Mintage	VG	F	VF	XF	Unc
1691	—	135	275	450	800	—

DAV# 7670 THALER
Silver **Obv:** Armored bust of Johann VIII right in inner circle

Date	Mintage	VG	F	VF	XF	Unc
1654	—	1,350	2,250	4,500	7,500	—
1656	—	1,350	2,250	4,500	7,500	—

DAV# A7671 THALER
Silver **Obv:** Armored bust of Johann VIII facing in ornamented circle **Rev:** Helmeted arms in inner circle, date below **Mint:** Minden

Date	Mintage	VG	F	VF	XF	Unc
1654 Rare	—	—	—	—	—	—

DAV# 7671 THALER
Silver **Obv:** Ludwig Christian **Mint:** Wittgenstein

Date	Mintage	VG	F	VF	XF	Unc
1667	—	1,000	2,000	4,000	7,000	—

DAV# 7672 THALER
Silver **Obv:** Armored bust of Gustav right in inner circle **Rev:** Helmeted arms in inner circle, date in legend **Mint:** Schwarzenau

Date	Mintage	VG	F	VF	XF	Unc
1682 ICF Rare	—	—	—	—	—	—

TRADE COINAGE

FR# 3058 DUCAT
3.5000 g., 0.9860 Gold 0.1109 oz. AGW **Obv:** Bust of Johann right in inner circle **Rev:** Arms topped by four helmets divides date

Date	Mintage	VG	F	VF	XF	Unc
1654 Rare	—	—	—	—	—	—

KM# 112 DUCAT
Silver **Obv:** Armored bust of Gustav right in inner circle **Rev:** Helmeted arms with date above in inner circle **Mint:** Berleburg **Note:** Ducat struck in silver only.

Date	Mintage	VG	F	VF	XF	Unc
1681	—	—	—	—	—	—

FR# 3059 2 DUCAT
7.0000 g., 0.9860 Gold 0.2219 oz. AGW **Obv:** Bust of Gustav right in inner circle **Rev:** Goat on rocks with castle in foreground, date divided at sides

Date	Mintage	VG	F	VF	XF	Unc
1687 Rare	—	—	—	—	—	—

SCHAUMBURG-LIPPE

The tiny countship of Schaumburg-Lippe, with an area of only 131 square miles (218 square kilometers) in northwest Germany, was surrounded by the larger states of Brunswick-Lüneburg-Calenberg, an enclave of Hesse-Cassel, and the bishopric of Minden (part of Brandenburg-Prussia from 1648). It was founded in 1640 when Schaumburg-Gehmen was divided between Hesse-Cassel and Lippe-Alverdissen. The two became known as Schaumburg-Hessen and Schaumburg-Lippe. Philipp II, the youngest son of Count Simon VI of Lippe came into the possession of Alverdissen and Lipperode upon his father's death in 1613. In 1640, he also inherited half of Schaumburg-Bückeburg, becoming the first Count of Schaumburg-Lippe. A separate line of Schaumburg-Alverdissen was established in 1681 and, upon the extinction of the elder line in 1777, the lands and titles devolved onto Alverdissen, becoming the ruling line in the countship. In 1807, the count was raised to the rank of prince and Schaumburg-Lippe was incorporated into the Rhine Confederation. It became a part of the German Confederation in 1815 and joined the North German Confederation in 1866. The principality became a member state in the German Empire in 1871. The last sovereign prince resigned as a result of World War I.

See Schaumburg-Hessen for coinage which also circulated in Schaumburg-Lippe.

RULERS
Philipp I, 1644-1681
Friedrich Christian, 1681-1728

MINT OFFICIALS

Initial or mark	Date	Name
PL	1659-60	Peter Löhr, mintmaster Bückeburg
IHH	1676-77	Johann Hinrich Hoffmann, mintmaster Bückeburg

REFERENCE
W = Paul Weinmeister, ***"Die Münzen und Medaillen von Schaumburg-Lippe,"*** Blätter für Münzfreunde 42 (1907), col. 3615ff.

COUNTSHIP

REGULAR COINAGE

KM# 1 6 PFENNIG
Copper **Ruler:** Philipp I **Obv:** Arms in circle, wreath border with value VI at bottom **Rev:** Crowned Hessian lion to left **Mint:** Rinteln **Note:** W-1.

Date	Mintage	Good	VG	F	VF	XF
ND(1648) Rare	—	—	—	—	—	—

DAV# 7673 THALER
Silver **Ruler:** Philipp I **Obv:** Facing bust **Rev:** Helmeted arms divide date at top

Date	Mintage	VG	F	VF	XF	Unc
1660	200	2,000	3,500	5,500	9,000	—

SCHAUMBURG-PINNEBERG

(Schauenburg-Pinneberg)

County in northwest Germany. First count in 1030. In 1106 it became part of Holstein, which remained for over 2 centuries. Many churchmen came from this house. Raised to the rank of prince in 1620. Senior line died out in 1622 and title reverted to Holstein-Schauenburg-Gehmen branch, which had been established in 1581. Gehmen itself became extinct in 1640 and Holstein-Schauenburg was divided among various states. Pinneberg was given to Denmark, Buckeburg was split between Hesse-Cassel and Lippe-Alverdissen and renamed Schaumburg-Hessen and Schaumburg-Lippe respectively. Gehmen went to Limburg-Styrum.

RULERS
Adolf XIII, 1576-1601
Ernst III, 1601-1622
Jobst Hermann, 1622-1635
Otto VI, 1635-1640

MINT OFFICIALS' INITIALS

Rineteln Mint

Initial	Date	Name
(a)=	1603-04	Henning Hanses
(b)=	1618-20	Julius Bilderbeck

Oldendorf Mint

Initial	Date	Name
(c)=	1604-05	Henning Hanses
(d)=	1609-11	Kaspar Kohl
(e)=	1611-17	Christoph Feistell
(f)=	1617-18	Julius Bilderbeck
(g), (h)=	1620-21	Kaspar Kohl
(i), (j)=	1621-22	Justus Arnoldi
(k)=	1622-23	Ernst Beissner
(l)=	1623-24	Kaspar Gieseler
(m)=	1624-25	Christoph Feistell
(n)=	1635-40	Kaspar Kohl

Altona Mint

Initial	Date	Name
(o)=	1592-1600	Klaus Isenbehn

Mark	Date	Name
(p)=	1599-1605	Daniel Kostede
(q), (r), (s)=	1605-18	Henning Hanses
(t), (u)=	1618-20	Christoph Feistell
	1621	Henning Hanses
(v)=	1621-24	Thomas Eisenbein
(w)=	1624-40	Christoph Feistell

ARMS

Nettleleaf, often as central shield in 4-fold arms.

REFERENCES

W = Paul Weinmeister, ***"Münzgeschichte der Grafschaft Holstein-Schauenburg,"*** Zeitschrift für Numismatik 26 (1908), pp. 348-481 and 27 (1909), pp. 278-83.

S = Hugo Frhr. Von Saurma-Jeltsch, **Die Saurmasche Münzsammlung deutscher, schweizerischer und polnischer Gepräge von etwa dem Beginn der Groschenzeit bis zur Kipperperiode**, Berlin, 1892.

COUNTY

STANDARD COINAGE

KM# 85 PFENNIG (1/12 Groschen)

Copper **Obv:** Arms, 1Z above **Rev:** I in square

Date	Mintage	Good	VG	F	VF	XF
ND(ca.1620)	—	20.00	40.00	85.00	140	—

KM# 86 1-1/2 PFENNIG (1/8 Groschen)

Copper **Obv:** Arms divide date, 8 above **Rev:** Ornamented square with 1-1/2

Date	Mintage	Good	VG	F	VF	XF
16Z0	—	40.00	85.00	140	185	—
ND	—	40.00	85.00	140	185	—

KM# 87 3 PFENNIG

Copper **Obv:** Arms, 3 above **Rev:** III in ornamented square

Date	Mintage	Good	VG	F	VF	XF
ND(ca.1620)	—	45.00	100	160	275	—

KM# 123 3 PFENNIG

Silver **Obv:** Imperial orb with 3 divides date **Rev:** Four-fold arms, with central shield, titles of Jobst Hermann around

Date	Mintage	VG	F	VF	XF	Unc
16ZZ	—	60.00	120	250	—	—

KM# 88 4 PFENNIG

Copper **Obv:** Arms with 4 above divide date **Rev:** IIII in ornamented square

Date	Mintage	Good	VG	F	VF	XF
(16)Z0	—	45.00	115	160	250	—
ND	—	45.00	115	160	250	—

KM# 89 4 PFENNIG

Copper **Rev:** IV in ornamented square

Date	Mintage	Good	VG	F	VF	XF
(16)Z0	—	45.00	115	160	250	—

KM# 90 6 PFENNIG

Copper **Obv:** Arms, 6 above **Rev:** VI in ornamented square

Date	Mintage	Good	VG	F	VF	XF
ND(ca.1620)	—	65.00	135	200	325	—

KM# 91 12 PFENNIG (Furstengroschen)

Silver Or Billon **Obv:** Crowned imperial eagle, orb on breast **Obv. Legend:** F. LANDT. MVN. ZV. IZ. **Rev:** Four-fold arms with central shield, titles of Ernst III **Note:** Varieties exist.

Date	Mintage	VG	F	VF	XF	Unc
ND (after 1620)	—	40.00	80.00	140	225	—

KM# 92 12 PFENNIG (Furstengroschen)

Silver Or Billon **Obv. Legend:** LANDT. MVNZE. ZC. 1Z. PN. **Rev:** Large crown above four-fold arms with central shield, cross behind arms **Note:** Varieties exist.

Date	Mintage	VG	F	VF	XF	Unc
ND (after 1620)	—	40.00	80.00	135	225	—

KM# 93 12 PFENNIG (Furstengroschen)

Silver Or Billon **Obv. Legend:** FVR. SCHAV. LAN. MVN ... **Note:** Varieties exist.

Date	Mintage	VG	F	VF	XF	Unc
ND (after 1620)	—	40.00	80.00	140	225	—

KM# 94 12 PFENNIG (Furstengroschen)

Silver Or Billon **Rev:** Three separate shields of arms, one above two

Date	Mintage	VG	F	VF	XF	Unc
ND (after 1620)	—	40.00	80.00	135	225	—

KM# 95 12 PFENNIG (Furstengroschen)

Silver Or Billon **Rev:** Large ornate helmet, titles of Ernst III

Date	Mintage	VG	F	VF	XF	Unc
ND (after 1620)	—	40.00	80.00	135	225	—

KM# 96 12 PFENNIG (Furstengroschen)

Silver Or Billon **Obv. Legend:** LANT.MVNZE.ZV.1Z.

Date	Mintage	VG	F	VF	XF	Unc
ND (after 1620)	—	40.00	80.00	135	225	—

KM# 97 3 KREUZER (1 Groschen)

Silver **Obv:** Crowned 4-fold arms with central shield, titles of Ernst III **Rev:** Crowned imperial eagle, 3 in circle on breast, titles of Ferdinand II

Date	Mintage	VG	F	VF	XF	Unc
ND(1620)	—	40.00	80.00	135	225	—

KM# A134 2 MARIENGROSCHEN

Silver **Obv:** II/ MARI/ GRO **Obv. Legend:** LANDT. MVNZ. V. FEIN. SILB. **Rev:** Crowned nettle leaf divides date as 1-6/Z-4 **Note:** Prev. KM#134.

Date	Mintage	VG	F	VF	XF	Unc
1624	—	45.00	85.00	140	250	—
1626	—	45.00	85.00	140	250	—

KM# 135 4 MARIENGROSCHEN

Silver **Obv. Legend:** LANDT. MVNZ. V. FEIN. SILB. **Obv. Inscription:** IIII/ MARI/ GRO **Rev:** Crowned nettle leaf divides date as 1-6/Z-4

Date	Mintage	VG	F	VF	XF	Unc
1624	—	65.00	110	200	325	—

KM# 115 4 GROSCHEN

Silver **Note:** Klippe.

Date	Mintage	VG	F	VF	XF	Unc
(16)Z1	—	—	—	—	—	—

KM# 114 4 GROSCHEN

Silver **Obv:** Crowned 4-fold arms with central shield, cross behind **Rev:** 4G in orb on eagle's breast, titles of Ferdinand II and date in legend **Note:** Varieties exist.

Date	Mintage	VG	F	VF	XF	Unc
(1)6Z1	—	80.00	160	325	—	—
(16)Z1	—	80.00	160	325	—	—
ND	—	80.00	160	325	—	—

KM# 125 8 GROSCHEN

Silver **Obv:** 8 in orb on crowned imperial eagle's breast **Rev:** Four-fold arms with central shield, three helmets above

Date	Mintage	VG	F	VF	XF	Unc
ND(ca.1622)	—	100	200	400	—	—

KM# 98 16 GROSCHEN

Silver **Obv:** 4-fold arms with central shield, 3 helmets above **Rev:** Crowned imperial eagle, 16 in orb on breast **Note:** Countermarked examples known.

Date	Mintage	VG	F	VF	XF	Unc
(1)620	—	65.00	135	275	—	—
ND	—	55.00	120	240	—	—

KM# 55 28 GROSCHEN

Silver **Obv:** Z8 in orb on breast, date divided below **Rev:** Four-fold arms with central shield, three helmets above **Note:** Varieties exist.

Date	Mintage	VG	F	VF	XF	Unc
1610 (q)	—	165	300	500	750	—
1611 (q)	—	165	300	500	750	—
1613 (q)	—	165	300	500	750	—
ND	—	165	300	500	750	—

KM# 63 28 GROSCHEN

Silver **Obv:** Date in legend

Date	Mintage	VG	F	VF	XF	Unc
1611 (q)	—	165	300	500	750	—

KM# 76 SCHRECKENBERGER (12 Kreuzer)

Silver **Note:** Klippe.

Date	Mintage	VG	F	VF	XF	Unc
ND(1616-19)	—	—	—	—	—	—

KM# 75 SCHRECKENBERGER (12 Kreuzer)

Silver **Obv:** Titles of Matthias **Rev:** Titles of Ernst III **Note:** Varieties exist.

Date	Mintage	VG	F	VF	XF	Unc
ND(1616-19)	—	27.00	60.00	120	165	—
ND(1616-19) (e)	—	27.00	60.00	120	165	—
ND(1616-19) (t)	—	27.00	60.00	120	165	—

KM# 6 1/24 THALER (Groschen)

Silver **Ruler:** Adolf XIII **Rev:** Three helmets above arms

Date	Mintage	VG	F	VF	XF	Unc
(1)600 (p)	—	16.00	27.00	45.00	75.00	—
(1)601 (p)	—	16.00	27.00	45.00	75.00	—

KM# 8 1/24 THALER (Groschen)

Silver **Obv:** Three helmets above arms **Rev:** Imperial w/Z4 within **Note:** Varieties exist.

Date	Mintage	VG	F	VF	XF	Unc
(1)601 (p)	—	16.00	27.00	45.00	75.00	—
(1)60Z (p)	—	16.00	27.00	45.00	75.00	—
(1)603 (p)	—	16.00	27.00	45.00	75.00	—
1603 (a)	—	16.00	27.00	45.00	75.00	—
(1)604 (p)	—	16.00	27.00	45.00	75.00	—
(1)604 (a)	—	16.00	27.00	45.00	75.00	—
1604 (a)	—	16.00	27.00	45.00	75.00	—
(1)605 (a)	—	16.00	27.00	45.00	75.00	—
(1)606 (c)	—	16.00	27.00	45.00	75.00	—
1606 (q)	—	16.00	27.00	45.00	75.00	—
(1)607 (p)	—	16.00	27.00	45.00	75.00	—
(1)607 (q)	—	16.00	27.00	45.00	75.00	—
(1)608 (q)	—	16.00	27.00	45.00	75.00	—
(1)609 (q)	—	16.00	27.00	45.00	75.00	—

KM# 7 1/24 THALER (Groschen)

Silver **Rev:** Without helmets above arms, titles of Ernst III **Note:** Varieties exist.

Date	Mintage	VG	F	VF	XF	Unc
(1)601 (p)	—	16.00	27.00	45.00	75.00	—
(1)60Z (p)	—	16.00	27.00	45.00	75.00	—
(1)603 (p)	—	16.00	27.00	45.00	75.00	—
(1)604 (p)	—	16.00	27.00	45.00	75.00	—
1604 (p)	—	16.00	27.00	45.00	75.00	—
(1)1604 (c)	—	16.00	27.00	45.00	75.00	—

KM# 64 1/24 THALER (Groschen)

Silver **Obv:** Three helmets above arms **Rev:** Z4 in orb, titles of Matthias, date in legend **Note:** Varieties exist.

Date	Mintage	VG	F	VF	XF	Unc
(1)611	—	20.00	33.00	55.00	80.00	—
1612	—	20.00	33.00	55.00	80.00	—
1614	—	20.00	33.00	55.00	80.00	—
1615 (e)	—	20.00	33.00	55.00	80.00	—
1616	—	20.00	33.00	55.00	80.00	—
(1)618 (t)	—	20.00	33.00	55.00	80.00	—

KM# 99 1/24 THALER (Groschen)

Silver **Obv:** Similar to KM#7, but titles of Ferdinand II **Note:** Kipper 1/24 Thaler. Varieties exist.

Date	Mintage	VG	F	VF	XF	Unc
(1)6Z0	—	16.00	27.00	45.00	75.00	—
Z0(16)	—	16.00	27.00	45.00	75.00	—
ND	—	16.00	27.00	45.00	75.00	—

KM# 124 1/24 THALER (Groschen)
Silver **Rev:** Titles of Jobst Hermann **Note:** Varieties exist.

Date	Mintage	VG	F	VF	XF	Unc
16ZZ	—	27.00	60.00	100	160	—
16ZZ (k)	—	27.00	60.00	100	160	—
16Z3 (k)	—	27.00	60.00	100	160	—
16Z4 (l)	—	27.00	60.00	100	160	—
16Z5 (m)	—	27.00	60.00	100	160	—
16Z6 (m)	—	27.00	60.00	100	160	—
16Z6	—	27.00	60.00	100	160	—
16Z7 (m)	—	27.00	60.00	100	160	—
1630 (m)	—	27.00	60.00	100	160	—
1631 (m)	—	27.00	60.00	100	160	—
163Z (m)	—	27.00	60.00	100	160	—
1633 (m)	—	27.00	60.00	100	160	—
1635 (m)	—	27.00	60.00	100	160	—

KM# 150 1/24 THALER (Groschen)
Silver **Obv:** Titles of Ferdinand III **Rev:** Titles of Otto VI **Note:** Varieties exist.

Date	Mintage	VG	F	VF	XF	Unc
1638 (n)	—	27.00	60.00	100	160	—
(16)38 (n)	—	27.00	60.00	100	160	—
(16)39 (n)	—	27.00	60.00	100	160	—

KM# 73 1/24 THALER (Adlergroschen)
Silver **Obv:** Without 24 in orb **Note:** Varieties exist.

Date	Mintage	VG	F	VF	XF	Unc
1614	—	16.00	27.00	45.00	75.00	—
1614 (e)	—	16.00	27.00	45.00	75.00	—
1615 (e)	—	16.00	27.00	45.00	75.00	—
1616 (e)	—	16.00	27.00	45.00	75.00	—
1616	—	16.00	27.00	45.00	75.00	—
1617	—	16.00	27.00	45.00	75.00	—
1617 (e)	—	16.00	27.00	45.00	75.00	—
1618	—	16.00	27.00	45.00	75.00	—
1618 (e)	—	16.00	27.00	45.00	75.00	—
(1)618 (e)	—	16.00	27.00	45.00	75.00	—
1619	—	16.00	27.00	45.00	75.00	—
1619 (e)	—	16.00	27.00	45.00	75.00	—
(!)619 (e)	—	16.00	27.00	45.00	75.00	—
(16)19 (e)	—	16.00	27.00	45.00	75.00	—
16Z0	—	16.00	27.00	45.00	75.00	—
16Z0 (e)	—	16.00	27.00	45.00	75.00	—

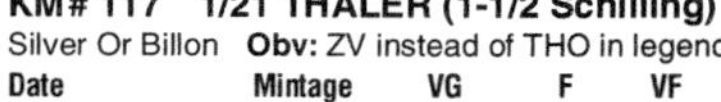

KM# 117 1/21 THALER (1-1/2 Schilling)
Silver Or Billon **Obv:** ZV instead of THO in legend

Date	Mintage	VG	F	VF	XF	Unc
ND(1621)	—	65.00	135	225	325	—

Note: This issue was struck for the Westphalian part of the county

KM# 116 1/21 THALER (1-1/2 Schilling)
Silver Or Billon **Obv:** Crowned imperial eagle, Z1 in orb on breast **Obv. Legend:** XXI THO EINEM. THALER **Note:** Kipper 1/21 Thaler.

Date	Mintage	VG	F	VF	XF	Unc
ND(1621)	—	65.00	135	225	325	—

Note: This issue was struck for the Westphalian part of the county

KM# 66 1/18-1/2 THALER
Silver **Note:** Klippe.

Date	Mintage	VG	F	VF	XF	Unc
(1)611 (q)	—	115	225	400	675	—

KM# 65 1/18-1/2 THALER
Silver **Note:** Similar to 1/16 thaler, KM#18 but 18-1/2 in orb on eagle's breast. Varieties exist.

Date	Mintage	VG	F	VF	XF	Unc
(1)611 (q)	—	27.00	55.00	100	160	—
(1)612 (q)	—	27.00	55.00	100	160	—
(1)613 (q)	—	27.00	55.00	100	160	—

KM# 72 1/18-1/2 THALER
Silver **Obv:** Titles of Matthias **Note:** Varieties exist.

Date	Mintage	VG	F	VF	XF	Unc
(1)613 (q)	—	33.00	60.00	120	190	—
(1)614 (q)	—	33.00	60.00	120	190	—
(1)615 (q)	—	33.00	60.00	120	190	—
(1)616 (q)	—	33.00	60.00	120	190	—

KM# 47 1/16 THALER (2 Schilling)
Silver **Obv:** Titles of Rudolf II **Note:** Varieties exist.

Date	Mintage	VG	F	VF	XF	Unc
(1)608 (q)	—	20.00	45.00	85.00	140	—
(1)609 (q)	—	20.00	45.00	85.00	140	—
(1)611	—	20.00	45.00	85.00	140	—

KM# 77 1/16 THALER (2 Schilling)
Silver **Obv:** Titles of Matthias **Note:** Varieties exist.

Date	Mintage	VG	F	VF	XF	Unc
(1)616 (f)	—	27.00	55.00	100	160	—
(1)617 (f)	—	27.00	55.00	100	160	—
(1)617 (q)	—	27.00	55.00	100	160	—
(1)618 (t)	—	27.00	55.00	100	160	—
(1)619 (t)	—	27.00	55.00	100	160	—
(1)6Z0 (t)	—	27.00	55.00	100	160	—

KM# 100 1/16 THALER (2 Schilling)
Silver **Obv:** Titles of Ferdinand II **Note:** Kipper 1/16 Thaler.

Date	Mintage	VG	F	VF	XF	Unc
(1)6Z0	—	27.00	55.00	100	160	—
(1)6Z0 (b)	—	27.00	55.00	100	160	—
(1)6Z1 (i)	—	27.00	55.00	100	160	—

KM# 101 1/16 THALER (2 Schilling)
Silver **Note:** Klippe.

Date	Mintage	VG	F	VF	XF	Unc
(1)6Z0	—	115	225	400	675	—

KM# 118 1/16 THALER (2 Schilling)
Silver **Obv:** 16 below eagle **Rev:** Date divided by arms

Date	Mintage	VG	F	VF	XF	Unc
16Z1 (p)/16Z1 (h)	—	30.00	60.00	110	165	—

KM# 119 1/16 THALER (2 Schilling)
Silver **Rev:** Date left of arms

Date	Mintage	VG	F	VF	XF	Unc
(16)Z1/16Z1	—	30.00	60.00	110	165	—

KM# 120 1/16 THALER (2 Schilling)
Silver **Obv:** Without date or value

Date	Mintage	VG	F	VF	XF	Unc
(16)Z1	—	30.00	60.00	110	165	—

KM# 121 1/16 THALER (2 Schilling)
Silver **Obv:** Date, similar to 2 Thaler, KM#328 but without value

Date	Mintage	VG	F	VF	XF	Unc
16Z1 (h)	—	30.00	60.00	110	165	—

KM# 122 1/16 THALER (2 Schilling)
Silver **Obv:** 16 below eagle

Date	Mintage	VG	F	VF	XF	Unc
16Z1 (h)	—	27.00	55.00	100	160	—
ND (h)	—	27.00	55.00	100	160	—

KM# 136 1/16 THALER (2 Schilling)
Silver **Rev:** Titles of Jobst Hermann

Date	Mintage	VG	F	VF	XF	Unc
1624	—	33.00	65.00	120	225	—

KM# 48 1/4 THALER
Silver **Obv:** Crowned imperial eagle, orb on breast, titles of Rudolf II and date in legend **Rev:** Four-fold arms with central shield, three helmets above

Date	Mintage	VG	F	VF	XF	Unc
(1)608	—	450	1,000	1,650	2,650	—

KM# 57 1/4 THALER
Silver **Rev:** Date divided by arms

Date	Mintage	VG	F	VF	XF	Unc
(1)610	—	450	1,000	1,650	2,650	—
ND	—	450	1,000	1,650	2,650	—

KM# 126 1/4 THALER
Silver **Obv:** Titles of Ferdinand II **Rev:** Arms break legend at bottom

Date	Mintage	VG	F	VF	XF	Unc
(1)6ZZ	—	450	1,000	1,650	2,650	—

KM# 58 1/2 THALER
Silver **Obv:** Crowned imperial eagle, orb on breast, titles of Rudolf II **Rev:** Four-fold arms with central shield, three helmets above, date divided among helmets

Date	Mintage	VG	F	VF	XF	Unc
1610 (q)	—	850	1,600	2,500	3,300	—
1613 (q)	—	850	1,600	2,500	3,300	—

KM# 69 1/2 THALER
Silver **Rev:** Date divided by arms

Date	Mintage	VG	F	VF	XF	Unc
(1)61Z	—	850	1,600	2,500	3,300	—

KM# 102 1/2 THALER
Silver **Obv:** Bust right **Rev:** Four-fold arms with central shield, three helmets above, date divided among helmets

Date	Mintage	VG	F	VF	XF	Unc
(16)Z0	—	—	—	—	—	—
ND	—	—	—	—	—	—

KM# 103 1/2 THALER
Silver **Obv:** Four-fold arms with central shield, three helmets above titles of Ernst III **Rev:** Count on horseback galloping right

Date	Mintage	VG	F	VF	XF	Unc
ND Rare	—	—	—	—	—	—

KM# 104 1/2 THALER
Silver **Obv:** Presentation of the Miracle in the Wedding at Cana, the turning of water into wine

Date	Mintage	VG	F	VF	XF	Unc
ND Rare	—	—	—	—	—	—

KM# 105 1/2 THALER
Silver **Obv:** Scene from Cana - the seven-headed dragon of Babylon with one head severed

Date	Mintage	VG	F	VF	XF	Unc
ND Rare	—	—	—	—	—	—

KM# 128 1/2 THALER
Silver

Date	Mintage	VG	F	VF	XF	Unc
(1)6ZZ	—	850	1,600	2,500	3,300	—
1618 Error for 1628	—	850	1,600	2,500	3,300	—
ND	—	850	1,600	2,500	3,300	—

KM# 127 1/2 THALER
Silver **Subject:** Death of Ernst III **Note:** Similar to 1 Thaler, KM#130.

Date	Mintage	VG	F	VF	XF	Unc
1622 (MDCXXII) Rare	—	—	—	—	—	—

KM# 137 1/2 THALER
Silver **Obv:** Date divided below eagle

Date	Mintage	VG	F	VF	XF	Unc
16Z4	—	850	1,600	2,500	3,300	—

KM# 17 THALER
Silver **Obv:** Crowned double-headed eagle with orb on breast **Obv. Legend:** RVDOLP. II. ROM. IMP. SEMP. AVGVST. **Rev:** Helmeted arms divide date **Rev. Legend:** ERNESTUS. HOL. SC. E. ST. CO. DOM. GEMMAE. **Note:** Dav. #3723.

Date	Mintage	VG	F	VF	XF	Unc
1602	—	125	250	450	725	—

KM# 18 THALER
Silver **Rev. Legend:** S. E. S: CO: D: GEMM. **Note:** Dav. #3724.

Date	Mintage	VG	F	VF	XF	Unc
1602	—	125	250	450	725	—

KM# 19 THALER
Silver **Obv. Legend:** RUDOL II. D: G. RO. IM. SEM... **Rev. Legend:** ...SC. E. ST. CO. D: GEMMAE. **Note:** Dav. #3725.

Date	Mintage	VG	F	VF	XF	Unc
1602	—	125	250	450	725	—

KM# 20 THALER
Silver **Obv:** Eagle divides date at bottom **Obv. Legend:** ...ROMA. IMPER. SEMPER AVGVS. **Rev. Legend:** D. G. HOL. SC. E. ST. CO. D: G. **Note:** Dav. #3726.

Date	Mintage	VG	F	VF	XF	Unc
1603	—	125	250	450	725	—

KM# 21 THALER
Silver **Obv. Legend:** RUDOL. II. ROMA. IMP. SEMPER AUGUS. **Note:** Dav. #3726A.

Date	Mintage	VG	F	VF	XF	Unc
1603	—	125	250	450	725	—

KM# 22 THALER
Silver **Note:** Similar to 2 Thaler, KM#25. Dav. #LS465.

Date	Mintage	VG	F	VF	XF	Unc
1603 Rare	—	—	—	—	—	—

KM# 28 THALER
Silver **Obv. Legend:** D. G. ROMA. IMPER. SEMPER. AVGVS. **Note:** Dav. #3727.

Date	Mintage	VG	F	VF	XF	Unc
1604	—	125	250	450	725	—

KM# 29 THALER
Silver **Note:** Similar to 1-1/2 Thaler, KM#32. Dav. #LS467.

Date	Mintage	VG	F	VF	XF	Unc
1606 Rare	—	—	—	450	725	—

KM# 30 THALER
Silver **Note:** Dav. #LS474.

Date	Mintage	VG	F	VF	XF	Unc
ND	—	1,900	3,000	4,750	6,800	—

KM# 31 THALER
Silver **Note:** Similar to 5 Thaler, KM#13. Dav. #LS483.

Date	Mintage	VG	F	VF	XF	Unc
ND Rare	—	—	—	—	—	—

KM# 46 THALER
Silver **Obv:** Helmeted arms divide date **Obv. Legend:** ERNESTUS. HOL... **Rev. Legend:** ...ROM: IMP: SEMP: AUGUSTUS. **Note:** Dav. #3728.

Date	Mintage	VG	F	VF	XF	Unc
1607	—	125	250	450	725	—

KM# 49 THALER
Silver **Obv:** Helmeted arms **Rev:** Double-headed imperial eagle, orb on breast **Rev. Legend:** RVDOL. II. D: G. RO: IM: SEM... **Note:** Dav. #3729.

Date	Mintage	VG	F	VF	XF	Unc
1608	—	—	—	—	—	—
ND	—	125	250	450	725	—

KM# 50 THALER
Silver **Obv. Legend:** ROMA.IMPER:SEMPER:AVG. **Rev:** Helmeted arms with date divided in helmets **Rev. Legend:** ...D. G. HOL. SE. S: CO. D: GE. **Note:** Dav. #3730.

Date	Mintage	VG	F	VF	XF	Unc
1608	—	125	250	450	725	—
1609	—	125	250	450	725	—
1611	—	125	250	450	725	—
1613	—	125	250	450	725	—

KM# 51 THALER
Silver **Obv. Legend:** RO: IM: SEM: AVGVST. P. F. D. **Note:** Dav. #3730A.

Date	Mintage	VG	F	VF	XF	Unc
1608	—	125	250	450	725	—

KM# 59 THALER
Silver **Obv. Legend:** ...ROMAN. IMPER. SEMPER. AUGV. **Rev:** Helmeted oval arms, date below **Rev. Legend:** ...H. S. E. C. O. D. G. **Note:** Dav. #3731.

Date	Mintage	VG	F	VF	XF	Unc
1610	—	125	250	450	725	—

KM# 62 THALER
Silver **Obv:** Helmeted arms, date in legend **Note:** Dav. #3733.

Date	Mintage	VG	F	VF	XF	Unc
1610	—	125	250	450	725	—
1611	—	125	250	450	725	—

KM# 60 THALER
Silver **Obv:** 28 on breast of eagle **Obv. Legend:** ...ROMA. IMPER. SEMPRE. AUG. **Note:** Dav. #3731A.

Date	Mintage	VG	F	VF	XF	Unc
1610	—	125	250	450	725	—

KM# 61 THALER
Silver **Obv:** Helmeted arms with date divided in helmets **Note:** Dav. #3732.

Date	Mintage	VG	F	VF	XF	Unc
1610	—	125	250	450	725	—

KM# 68 THALER
Silver **Obv:** Bust of Ernest right **Rev:** Helmeted arms with date in helmets **Note:** Dav. #3737.

Date	Mintage	VG	F	VF	XF	Unc
1611	—	250	400	725	1,200	—
1614	—	250	400	725	1,200	—
1615	—	250	400	725	1,200	—
1616	—	250	400	725	1,200	—
1618	—	250	400	725	1,200	—
ND	—	250	400	725	1,200	—

KM# 67 THALER
Silver **Rev:** Eagle with 28 in orb on breast **Note:** Dav. #3734.

Date	Mintage	VG	F	VF	XF	Unc
1611	—	125	250	450	725	—

KM# 70 THALER
Silver **Rev:** Date divided in helmets above arms **Note:** Dav. #3735.

Date	Mintage	VG	F	VF	XF	Unc
1612	—	125	250	450	725	—

KM# 71 THALER
Silver **Obv. Legend:** ERNESTUS. D. G. - H. S. E. S. CO. D. G. **Note:** Dav. #3736.

Date	Mintage	VG	F	VF	XF	Unc
ND	—	125	250	450	725	—

KM# 74 THALER
Silver **Rev:** Helmeted arms, date below **Note:** Dav. #3738.

Date	Mintage	VG	F	VF	XF	Unc
1615	—	250	400	725	1,200	—
1616	—	250	400	725	1,200	—
1617	—	250	400	725	1,200	—
1618	—	250	400	725	1,200	—
1619	—	250	400	725	1,200	—

KM# 79 THALER
Silver **Note:** Klippe. Dav. #3738A.

Date	Mintage	VG	F	VF	XF	Unc
1617	—	—	—	—	—	—
1618	—	—	—	—	—	—

KM# 106 THALER
Silver **Rev:** Helmeted arms, date in cartouche below **Rev. Legend:** COM. -GE: 620 **Note:** Dav. #3739.

Date	Mintage	VG	F	VF	XF	Unc
1620	—	250	400	725	1,200	—

KM# 107 THALER
Silver **Obv:** KM#106 **Rev:** KM#74 **Note:** Mule. Dav. #3740.

Date	Mintage	VG	F	VF	XF	Unc
(1620)/1619	—	250	400	725	1,200	—

KM# 108 THALER
Silver **Obv:** Bust right **Obv. Legend:** ERNESTUS: D. G. PRINC: ET. COMES: HOLS: SCHAW. **Rev:** Helmeted arms **Rev. Legend:** COMES: STERNB: DOMINVS: GE, 6Z0 **Note:** Dav. #3741.

Date	Mintage	VG	F	VF	XF	Unc
1620	—	250	400	725	1,200	—

KM# 109 THALER
Silver **Rev. Legend:** COM: STERNB: DOM: GEHM, 6ZO **Note:** Dav. #3741A.

Date	Mintage	VG	F	VF	XF	Unc
1620	—	250	400	725	1,200	—

KM# 110 THALER
Silver **Obv. Legend:** ...COMES: HOLS: SCHAW. **Rev:** Helmeted arms with 16-2-0 in helmets **Rev. Legend:** ...DOMIN: GEHM **Note:** Dav. #3742.

Date	Mintage	VG	F	VF	XF	Unc
1620	—	250	400	725	1,200	—

KM# 111 THALER
Silver **Rev:** Only 2-0 in helmets **Note:** Dav. #3742A.

Date	Mintage	VG	F	VF	XF	Unc
(16)20	—	250	400	725	1,200	—

KM# 112 THALER
Silver **Obv:** Helmeted arms **Obv. Legend:** ERNESTVS. D: G: C: HO: S: E: ST: D: I: G: **Rev:** Horseman **Note:** Dav. #3743.

Date	Mintage	VG	F	VF	XF	Unc
ND	—	250	400	725	1,200	—

KM# 113 THALER
Silver **Obv. Legend:** ...DG: HOL: SCA: E: STE: C: D: G: **Note:** Dav. #3744.

Date	Mintage	VG	F	VF	XF	Unc
ND	—	250	400	725	1,200	—

KM# 129 THALER
Silver **Subject:** Death of Ernest **Obv:** Arms in frame **Obv. Legend:** ERNEST: D: G: S: R: I. PRINC. CO: HOLS: SCHAUMB: STER: D: G: **Rev:** Nine-line inscription **Note:** Dav. #3745.

Date	Mintage	VG	F	VF	XF	Unc
1622	—	400	650	1,050	1,800	—

KM# 134 THALER
Silver **Obv:** Helmeted arms **Obv. Legend:** IUST. HER. D.G. CO. H. S. E. S. D. G. ET. B. **Rev:** Crown above double-headed imperial eagle, orb on breast **Rev. Legend:** FERDINAND U: D. G. R. IM. S. AU. **Note:** Dav. #3749.

Date	Mintage	VG	F	VF	XF	Unc
16ZZ	—	125	250	450	725	—
(1)6ZZ	—	125	250	450	725	—
16Z3	—	125	250	450	725	—
ND	—	125	250	450	725	—

KM# 130 THALER
Silver **Subject:** Death of Ernest **Obv. Legend:** ...COM: HOLSAT. SCHAVMB. STERNB. DN: GEH. **Note:** Dav. #3746.

Date	Mintage	VG	F	VF	XF	Unc
1622	—	400	650	1,050	1,800	—

KM# 131 THALER
Silver **Obv:** Crowned double-headed eagle with orb on breast **Obv. Legend:** FERDINANDUS. II. D: G: ROMA: IM: S: A:, 6ZZ **Rev:** Helmeted arms **Rev. Legend:** IOBST. HERMAIN: - D: G: CO: H: E: S: D: G: **Note:** Dav. #3747.

Date	Mintage	VG	F	VF	XF	Unc
(1)6ZZ	—	125	250	450	725	—

KM# 132 THALER
Silver **Obv:** Helmeted arms **Obv. Legend:** IUSTUS. HARM. D. G. C. H. S. S. D. G. **Rev:** Crown above double-headed imperial eagle, orb on breast **Rev. Legend:** ...ROM. IM. S. A., 16ZZ **Note:** Dav. #3748.

Date	Mintage	VG	F	VF	XF	Unc
16ZZ	—	125	250	450	725	—

KM# 133 THALER
Silver **Obv:** With date 6ZZ **Note:** Dav. #3748A.

Date	Mintage	VG	F	VF	XF	Unc
(1)6ZZ	—	125	250	450	725	—

KM# 139 THALER
Silver **Obv:** Helmeted arms **Rev:** Double-headed imperial eagle, orb on breast, date below eagle **Note:** Dav. #3751.

Date	Mintage	VG	F	VF	XF	Unc
16Z4	—	125	250	450	725	—

KM# 138 THALER
Silver **Obv. Legend:** FERDINANDUS II. D. G. RO... **Rev. Legend:** OVST. HERM. D. G. C... **Note:** Dav. #3750.

Date	Mintage	VG	F	VF	XF	Unc
1624	—	125	250	450	725	—

KM# 140 THALER
Silver **Obv. Legend:** ...IM. S. AU, 1628 **Rev. Legend:** IUS. HER. D. G. CO. HOL.S . ET. S. D. G. ET. B. **Note:** Dav. #3752.

Date	Mintage	VG	F	VF	XF	Unc
1628	—	125	250	425	725	—
ND	—	125	250	425	725	—

KM# 141 THALER
Silver **Obv. Legend:** IM. S. AV, 16Z8 **Note:** Dav. #3752A.

Date	Mintage	VG	F	VF	XF	Unc
1628	—	125	250	450	725	—

KM# 142 THALER
Silver **Obv:** Helmeted arms **Rev:** Eagle with 3Z on orb on breast **Note:** Dav. #3752B.

Date	Mintage	VG	F	VF	XF	Unc
1628	—	125	250	450	725	—

KM# 143 THALER
Silver **Obv:** Helmeted arms **Rev:** Double-headed imperial eagle, orb on breast, divided date below eagle **Note:** Dav. #3753.

Date	Mintage	VG	F	VF	XF	Unc
1628	—	125	250	425	725	—

KM# 23 1-1/2 THALER
Silver **Note:** Dav. #LS463.

Date	Mintage	VG	F	VF	XF	Unc
1603 Rare	—	—	—	—	—	—

KM# 32 1-1/2 THALER
Silver **Obv:** Helmeted arms **Rev:** Horseman **Note:** Dav. #LS466.

Date	Mintage	VG	F	VF	XF	Unc
1606 Rare	—	—	—	—	—	—

KM# 33 1-1/2 THALER

43.0500 g., Silver **Obv:** Helmeted arms within circle **Note:** Dav. #LS473.

Date	Mintage	VG	F	VF	XF	Unc
ND	—	1,200	2,050	3,400	5,300	—

KM# 34 1-1/2 THALER

43.0000 g., Silver **Note:** Dav. #LS476.

Date	Mintage	VG	F	VF	XF	Unc
ND Rare	—	—	—	—	—	—

KM# 35 1-1/2 THALER

43.0000 g., Silver **Note:** Similar to 5 Thaler, KM#13. Dav. #LS482.

Date	Mintage	VG	F	VF	XF	Unc
ND	—	2,250	3,750	6,000	9,000	—

KM# 9 2 THALER

58.0000 g., Silver **Obv:** Helmeted arms **Rev:** Horseman **Note:** Dav. #LS458.

Date	Mintage	VG	F	VF	XF	Unc
1601 Rare	—	—	—	—	—	—

KM# 11 2 THALER

58.0000 g., Silver **Obv. Legend:** ERNST: D: G: CH... **Note:** Dav. #LS460.

Date	Mintage	VG	F	VF	XF	Unc
(1)601	—	3,000	5,300	8,300	11,500	—
(1)602	—	3,000	5,300	8,300	11,500	—

KM# 10 2 THALER

58.0000 g., Silver **Obv. Legend:** ADOLP. D: G. COM. HOL. SCH... **Note:** Dav. #LS549.

Date	Mintage	VG	F	VF	XF	Unc
ND Rare	—	—	—	—	—	—

KM# 24 2 THALER

58.0000 g., Silver **Note:** Similar to 3 Thaler, KM#26. Dav. #LS462.

Date	Mintage	VG	F	VF	XF	Unc
(1)603	—	2,250	3,750	6,000	9,000	—

KM# 25 2 THALER

58.0000 g., Silver **Obv:** Helmeted arms **Rev:** Horseman **Note:** Dav. #LS464.

Date	Mintage	VG	F	VF	XF	Unc
(1)603 Rare	—	—	—	—	—	—

KM# 36 2 THALER

58.0000 g., Silver **Rev:** Without decoration below horse, only ground **Note:** Dav. #LS468.

Date	Mintage	VG	F	VF	XF	Unc
(1)606 Rare	—	—	—	—	—	—

KM# 37 2 THALER

58.0000 g., Silver **Note:** Similar to 3 Thaler, KM#42. Dav. #LS470.

Date	Mintage	VG	F	VF	XF	Unc
(1)606 Rare	—	—	—	—	—	—

KM# 38 2 THALER

58.0000 g., Silver **Note:** Dav. #LS472. Illustration reduced.

Date	Mintage	VG	F	VF	XF	Unc
ND	—	1,350	2,250	3,750	6,000	—

KM# 39 2 THALER
58.0000 g., Silver **Obv:** Helmeted arms **Rev:** Horseman **Note:** Dav. #LS475. Illustration reduced.

Date	Mintage	VG	F	VF	XF	Unc
ND	—	2,250	3,750	6,000	9,000	—

KM# 40 2 THALER
58.0000 g., Silver **Obv:** Helmeted oval arms within circle **Rev:** Horseman within circle **Note:** Dav. #LS479. Illustration reduced.

Date	Mintage	VG	F	VF	XF	Unc
ND	—	3,000	5,300	8,300	11,500	—

KM# 41 2 THALER
58.0000 g., Silver **Obv. Legend:** ERNEST: D: G: PRINC: E:... **Note:** Similar to 5 Thaler, KM#13. Dav. #LS481.

Date	Mintage	VG	F	VF	XF	Unc
ND Rare	—	—	—	—	—	—

KM# 12 2-1/2 THALER
Silver **Note:** Similar to 2 Thaler, KM#40. Dav. #LS478.

Date	Mintage	VG	F	VF	XF	Unc
ND Rare	—	—	—	—	—	—

KM# 26 3 THALER
87.0000 g., Silver **Obv:** Helmeted arms **Rev:** Horseman **Note:** Dav. #LS461.

Date	Mintage	VG	F	VF	XF	Unc
(1)603 Rare	—	—	—	—	—	—
ND	—	—	—	—	—	—

KM# 42 3 THALER
87.0000 g., Silver **Rev:** Horseman with ground below **Note:** Dav. #LS469.

Date	Mintage	VG	F	VF	XF	Unc
(1)606 Rare	—	—	—	—	—	—

KM# 43 3 THALER
87.0000 g., Silver **Note:** Similar to 1-1/2 Thaler, KM#33. Dav. #LS471.

Date	Mintage	VG	F	VF	XF	Unc
ND	—	2,250	3,750	5,600	8,300	—

KM# 44 3 THALER
87.0000 g., Silver **Note:** Similar to 2 Thaler, KM#40. Dav. #LS477.

Date	Mintage	VG	F	VF	XF	Unc
ND Rare	—	—	—	—	—	—

KM# 45 3 THALER
87.0000 g., Silver **Obv:** Helmeted arms **Obv. Legend:** IVSTVS... **Rev:** Horseman **Note:** Dav. #LS485.

Date	Mintage	VG	F	VF	XF	Unc
ND Rare	—	—	—	—	—	—

KM# 13 5 THALER
146.0000 g., Silver **Obv:** Helmeted arms **Rev:** Horseman **Note:** Dav. #LS480.

Date	Mintage	VG	F	VF	XF	Unc
ND Rare	—	—	—	—	—	—

TRADE COINAGE

KM# 27 GOLDGULDEN
3.5000 g., 0.9860 Gold 0.1109 oz. AGW **Obv:** Helmeted arms in inner circle **Rev:** Crowned imperial eagle in inner circle, titles of Rudolf II, date in legend

Date	Mintage	VG	F	VF	XF	Unc
1603 (a)	—	550	1,200	2,550	5,200	—
1604 (a)	—	550	1,200	2,550	5,200	—
1608 (q)	—	550	1,200	2,550	5,200	—
1610 (q)	—	550	1,200	2,550	5,200	—
1612 (q)	—	550	1,200	2,550	5,200	—
1612	—	550	1,200	2,550	5,200	—

KM# 78 GOLDGULDEN
3.5000 g., 0.9860 Gold 0.1109 oz. AGW **Rev:** Titles of Matthias

Date	Mintage	VG	F	VF	XF	Unc
1616	—	650	1,450	2,800	5,600	—

KM# 14 5 DUCAT (1/2 Portugalloser)
17.5000 g., 0.9860 Gold 0.5547 oz. AGW **Note:** Similar to 10 Ducat, KM#15.

Date	Mintage	VG	F	VF	XF	Unc
ND Rare	—	—	—	—	—	—

KM# 15 10 DUCAT (1 Portugalloser)
35.0000 g., 0.9860 Gold 1.1095 oz. AGW **Obv:** Helmeted arms **Rev:** Equestrian figure of Ernst III right **Note:** Also reported in 51 millimeter diameter.

Date	Mintage	VG	F	VF	XF	Unc
ND Rare	—	—	—	—	—	—

KM# 16 20 DUCAT (2 Portugalloser)

70.0000 g., 0.9860 Gold 2.2190 oz. AGW **Obv:** Scene from Cana - the seven-headed dragon of Babylon with one head severed **Note:** Similar to 10 Ducat, KM#15

Date	Mintage	VG	F	VF	XF	Unc
ND Unique	—	—	—	—	—	—

KM# A17 20 DUCAT (2 Portugalloser)

70.0000 g., 0.9860 Gold 2.2190 oz. AGW **Note:** Similar to 10 Ducat, KM#15

Date	Mintage	VG	F	VF	XF	Unc
ND Rare	—	—	—	—	—	—

SCHLESWIG-HOLSTEIN

Christian I, son of Count Dietrich of Oldenburg (1423-40), was elected King of Denmark in 1448. By virtue of his marriage to Hedwig, the last surviving heir of the countship of Holstein-Rendsburg (see Holstein), Christian I became Duke of Schleswig and Count of Holstein in 1459. His status over Holstein was raised to that of duke in 1474 and from that year onwards, the dual duchies of Schleswig-Holstein were ruled by the Danish royal house. In 1533, a separate line for one of Friedrich I's sons was established in Gottorp. Similarly, a son of Christian III was given Sonderburg as his domain in 1559. The Danish kings continued to have coins struck for their remaining portions of Schleswig-Holstein during the next several centuries. Upon the dissolution of the Holy Roman Empire by Napoleon in 1806, Holstein was made a part of Denmark. However, Holstein, without Schleswig, joined the German Confederation following the final defeat of Napoleon in 1815. After Denmark tried to annex Schleswig and Holstein in 1846, she fought a war with Prussia for three years over control of the duchies, but it was inconclusive. In 1863, Denmark declared that Schleswig was part of that country although it had a German majority in the population. A second war was fought between Denmark against Prussia and Austria and Schleswig-Holstein was occupied by the victorious Prussians. The administration of Holstein was given to Austria, while that of Schleswig was obtained by Prussia in 1865. However, Austria was forced to give up Holstein after losing a war with Prussia in 1866. Schleswig-Holstein were controlled by Prussia and became part of the German Empire in 1871. Following World War I, a plebiscite was held in Schleswig and the northern part, with its majority Danish population, was ceded to Denmark in 1920.

RULERS

Danish Royal Line

Christian IV, 1588-1648
Frederik III, 1648-1670
Christian V, 1670-1699

MINT OFFICIALS INITIALS & MARKS

Initial or Mark	Date	Name
(c) = [mark] or [mark] or MP (sometimes in ligature)	1596-ca.1609	Matz Puls, mint contractor Schleswig
(f) = Bird standing left	1598-1601	Christian Vogell, mintmaster Steinbeck
	1601-15	Jacob Stein, warden Steinbeck bei Hamburg
(g) = Knight on horseback left or IG (ligature)	1606-08	Jonas Georgens (or Jürgensen), mintmaster Steinbeck
(h) = [mark]	1612-17	Simon Timpf der Ältere, mintmaster Burg auf Fehmarn
(t) = [mark] or [mark]	1617-20	Samuel Timpf, mintmaster Burg auf Fehmarn
	1620-22	In Steinbeck
or ST (ligature)	1627?	In Schleswig
(i) = [mark]	1618-25	Thomas Timpf, mintmaster Burg auf Fehmarn
HP	1622	Heinrich Puls, mintmaster Schleswig
(j) = [mark] or [mark]	Ca.1628-36	Peter Timpf, mintmaster Schleswig
Blum Fe	1631-60	Johann Blum, medailleur in Bremen
ST (ligature)	1640-43	Simon Timpf der Jüngere, mintmaster Glückstadt
HG	1641-44	Hans Gläser, mintmaster Scshleswig
(k) = M[mark]M	1644-59; 1661-66	Michael Möller, mintmaster Schleswig
D, SD (sometimes in ligature)	Ca. 1650-54	Sebastian Dadler (Dattler), die-cutter
IS	1657-60	Jacob Schwiegelt, mintmaster Glückstadt
IR	Ca.1664-1720	Johann Retecke, die-cutter in Hamburg
Breuer or B, BR, GB, JGB,	Ca. 1666-95	Johann Georg Breuer, die-cutter
(l) = [mark] or CP	1668-72	Christian Pfahler, mintmaster Schleswig
MF	1668-73	Mathias Freude der Jüngere mintmaster Hamburg
AH	1674-78	Andreas Hille, mintmaster Schleswig
CMB, CIMB, CMMB	1674-82	Claus Jakob Mecklenburg, mintmaster Schleswig
HL	1674-92	Hermann Lüders, mintmaster Hamburg
CR	1677-83	Caspar Riddr, mintmasster Plön
IH	1677-93	Johann Höhn der Jüngere, die-cutter in Danzig
HCH	Ca.1684-1729	Heinrich Christian Hille, mintmaster & Medailleur
HHL (ligature)	1689-95	Hans Heinrich Lüders, mintmaster Tönning
SC	1690-93	Simon Conrad?, mintmaster Steuerwald
C X W	1692-96	Christopher Woltereck, 1692-96
	1695-1701	Jacob Musaphia, mintmaster Tönning
	Ca.1695-1702	Johann Heinrich Storkau, warden Tönning

ARMS

Holstein – nettle leaf
Oldenburg – 2, 3, or 4 horizontal bars, usually shaded
Schleswig – 2 lions passant to left, one above the other

NOTE

The term Lübsch refers to coins struck on the standard of Lübeck.

REFERENCES

L = Christian Lange, ***Chr. Lange's Sammiun Schleswig-Holsteinischer Münzen und Medaillen***. 2 vols., Berlin, 1908-12

Sch = Wolfgang Schulten, ***Deutsche Münzen aus der Zeit Karls V***. Frankfurt am Main, 1974.

DUCHY

REGULAR COINAGE

KM# 1 6 PFENNIG

Silver **Ruler:** Christian IV **Obv:** Crown above large 'C' which encloses '4', divides date **Rev. Inscription:** I / SOES / LINCK / LVBS **Note:** Varieties exist.

Date	Mintage	VG	F	VF	XF	Unc
16Z3	—	80.00	160	300	475	—
(16)Z4	—	80.00	160	300	475	—
(16)Z5	—	80.00	160	300	475	—

KM# 4 6 PFENNIG

Silver **Ruler:** Christian IV **Obv:** Crowned 'C' enclosing '4' within circle, titles of Christian IV **Rev:** Inscription in circle, titles continued, date **Rev. Inscription:** I / SECH / SLIN

Date	Mintage	VG	F	VF	XF	Unc
164Z ST	—	55.00	90.00	190	325	—

KM# 5 6 PFENNIG

Silver **Ruler:** Frederik III **Obv:** Crowned 'F' with superimposed '3' in circle, titles of Friedrich III **Rev:** Mintmaster's initials, titles continued, date **Rev. Inscription:** I / SECH / SLI(N) **Note:** Varieties exist.

Date	Mintage	VG	F	VF	XF	Unc
1658 IS	—	45.00	85.00	165	300	—
1659 IS	—	45.00	85.00	165	300	—
1660 IS	—	45.00	85.00	165	300	—

KM# 2 2 SCHILLING (Doppelschilling)

Silver **Ruler:** Christian IV **Obv:** King on horseback to right, 2 SL or Z SL below **Rev:** Titles of Christian IV in 6 lines

Date	Mintage	VG	F	VF	XF	Unc
ND(ca.1640)	—	13.00	27.00	60.00	120	—

KM# 3 4 SCHILLING (Lübsch)

Silver **Ruler:** Christian IV **Obv:** King on horseback to right, 4 SL below **Rev:** Titles of Christian IV in 6 lines

Date	Mintage	VG	F	VF	XF	Unc
ND(ca.1640)	—	—	—	—	—	—

KM# 7 KRONE

Silver **Ruler:** Frederik III **Obv:** Crowned F3 monogram **Rev:** Crowned Danish arms divide date **Note:** Dav. #3674; Prev. Holstein KM#5.

Date	Mintage	VG	F	VF	XF	Unc
1659	—	65.00	120	200	375	—
1660	—	65.00	120	200	375	—

KM# 8 KRONE

Silver **Ruler:** Frederik III **Rev:** Date in legend at upper left **Note:** Dav. #3675; Prev. Holstein KM#6.

Date	Mintage	VG	F	VF	XF	Unc
1659	—	65.00	120	200	375	—
1660	—	65.00	120	200	375	—

KM# 15 KRONE

Silver **Ruler:** Christian V **Obv:** Crowned C5 monogram **Rev:** Crowned Danish arms in frame **Note:** Dav. #3678. Prev. Holstein KM#15.

Date	Mintage	VG	F	VF	XF	Unc
1671	—	65.00	120	200	275	—
1672	—	65.00	120	200	275	—
1673	—	65.00	120	200	275	—
1674	—	65.00	120	200	275	—
1675	—	65.00	120	200	275	—
1676	—	65.00	120	200	275	—
1677	—	65.00	120	200	275	—
1678	—	65.00	120	200	275	—
1679	—	65.00	120	200	275	—
1680	—	65.00	120	200	275	—
1681	—	65.00	120	200	275	—
1682	—	65.00	120	200	275	—

KM# 25 KRONE

Silver **Ruler:** Christian V **Obv:** Crowned 'C5' monogram in palm branches **Rev:** Crowned Danish arms **Note:** Dav. #3679. Prev. Holstein KM#25.

Date	Mintage	VG	F	VF	XF	Unc
1692 CW	—	80.00	140	225	400	—
1693 CW	—	80.00	140	225	400	—
1694 CW	—	80.00	140	225	400	—

KM# 26 KRONE

Silver **Ruler:** Christian V **Rev:** Date below arms **Note:** Dav. #3679A. Prev. Holstein KM#26.

Date	Mintage	VG	F	VF	XF	Unc
1693	—	80.00	140	225	400	—

KM# 27 KRONE

Silver **Ruler:** Christian V **Obv:** Similar to KM#25 but laurel around monogram **Rev:** Smaller frame around arms **Note:** Dav. #3680. Prev. Holstein KM#27.

Date	Mintage	VG	F	VF	XF	Unc
1694 CW	—	80.00	140	225	400	—
1695 CW	—	80.00	140	225	400	—
1696 CW	—	80.00	140	225	400	—

KM# 10 THALER

Silver **Ruler:** Frederik III **Obv. Legend:** FRIDERICUS: 3: D: G: DAN: NOR: VA: GOT: REX. **Rev:** I. XW and punctuated date below Fortuna **Note:** Specie Thaler. Dav. #3673. Prev. Holstein KM#10.

Date	Mintage	VG	F	VF	XF	Unc
1664 Rare	—	—	—	—	—	—
1666 Rare	—	—	—	—	—	—

KM# 11 THALER

Silver **Ruler:** Christian V **Obv:** King standing with scepter and globe **Rev:** Crowned C5 monograms **Note:** Dav. #3676. Prev. Holstein KM#11.

Date	Mintage	VG	F	VF	XF	Unc
ND(ca.1670) Rare	—	—	—	—	—	—

KM# 20 THALER

Silver **Ruler:** Christian V **Obv:** Bust of Christian V right **Rev:** Three crowned C5 monograms **Note:** Dav. #3677. Prev. Holstein KM#20.

Date	Mintage	VG	F	VF	XF	Unc
1683 Rare	—	—	—	—	—	—

PATTERNS

Inlcuding off metal strikes

KM#	Date	Mintage	Identification	Mkt Val
Pn1	1659 IS	—	Thaler. Silver. Dav. #3671. Specie Thaler.	—
Pn2	1659 IS	—	Thaler. Silver. Dav. #3672. Specie Thaler.	—
Pn3	1659 IS	—	Thaler. Silver. Pn2. Pn1. Specie Thaler.	—
Pn4	1788	—	10 Schilling. Gold.	—
Pn6	1799	—	20 Schilling. Copper. C#7.	200

SCHLESWIG-HOLSTEIN-GLUCKSBURG

Established upon the division of Schleswig-Holstein-Sonderburg in 1622, the duchy of Schleswig-Holstein-Glücksburg existed for about one and a half centuries. When the line became extinct in 1779, the lands and titles passed to Denmark.

RULERS
Philipp, 1622-1663
Christian, 1663-1698
Philipp Ernst, 1698-1729

DUCHY

STANDARD COINAGE

KM# 5 THALER
Silver **Obv:** Philip right **Rev:** Helmeted arms, date in legend **Note:** Dav. #3718.

Date	Mintage	VG	F	VF	XF	Unc
1632 Rare	—	—	—	—	—	—
ND Rare	—	—	—	—	—	—

Note: UBS Gold & Numismatics Auction 53, 1-2002, VF realized approximately $6,295.

TRIAL STRIKES

KM#	Date	Mintage	Identification	Mkt Val
TS1	ND	—	Thaler. Lead. Uniface, Christian.	—

SCHLESWIG-HOLSTEIN-GOTTORP

The line of Gottorp was established in 1533 as a territorial domain for the youngest son of Friedrich I, King of Denmark and Duke of Schleswig-Holstein. Many members of this line and a cadet line founded in 1702 became bishops of Lübeck (see). Duke Karl Peter Ulrich, whose father, Karl Friedrich, had married Anna of Russia, became Czar Peter III in 1762, but was killed shortly after his accession to the throne. His son, Paul, traded Gottorp to Denmark for Oldenburg in 1773 (see Oldenburg) and ruled Russia as Czar Paul I (1798-1901).

RULERS
Friedrich III, 1616-1659
Christian Albrecht, 1659-1694
Land occupied by Danes, 1675-79 and 1683-89
Friedrich IV, 1694-1702

DUCHY

REGULAR COINAGE

KM# 89 PFENNIG
Silver **Note:** Uniface. Hohl type. Arms, date above.

Date	Mintage	VG	F	VF	XF	Unc
16Z4	—	27.00	60.00	110	170	—
16Z5	—	27.00	60.00	110	170	—

KM# A96 PFENNIG
Silver **Note:** Hohl type. Arms, 16 above, Z-6 on left and right. Varieties exist.

Date	Mintage	VG	F	VF	XF	Unc
16Z6	—	27.00	60.00	110	170	—
16Z7	—	27.00	60.00	110	170	—
(16)Z7	—	27.00	60.00	110	170	—
ND	—	27.00	60.00	110	170	—

KM# A105 PFENNIG
Silver **Note:** 3-8 on left and right of arms.

Date	Mintage	VG	F	VF	XF	Unc
(16)38	—	—	—	—	—	—

KM# A110 PFENNIG
Silver **Note:** Date entirely above arms.

Date	Mintage	VG	F	VF	XF	Unc
1640	—	—	—	—	—	—

KM# 50 1/192 THALER (Dreiling)
Silver **Obv:** Two lions walking left **Rev:** 192 in sunburst

Date	Mintage	VG	F	VF	XF	Unc
1661	—	27.00	55.00	95.00	150	—
1662	—	27.00	55.00	95.00	150	—
1663	—	27.00	55.00	95.00	150	—
1668	—	27.00	55.00	95.00	150	—
1670	—	27.00	55.00	95.00	150	—
1671	—	27.00	55.00	95.00	150	—
1675	—	27.00	55.00	95.00	150	—

KM# 51 1/96 THALER (Sechsling)
Silver **Obv:** Three arrows and nine rays with ball ends around shield **Rev:** 96 in sunburst

Date	Mintage	VG	F	VF	XF	Unc
1661	—	16.00	33.00	60.00	120	—
1662	—	16.00	33.00	60.00	120	—
1663	—	16.00	33.00	60.00	120	—

KM# 55 1/96 THALER (Sechsling)
Silver **Obv:** Three arrows and 11 thick wedges around shield **Rev:** 96 in center

Date	Mintage	VG	F	VF	XF	Unc
1668	—	16.00	33.00	60.00	120	—
1670	—	16.00	33.00	60.00	120	—
1671	—	16.00	33.00	60.00	120	—
1672	—	16.00	33.00	60.00	120	—
1675	—	16.00	33.00	60.00	120	—
1676	—	16.00	33.00	60.00	120	—

KM# 52 1/16 THALER
Silver **Obv:** Tall bust right breaks inner circle at top **Rev:** Value within legend **Note:** Reichs 1/16 Thaler.

Date	Mintage	VG	F	VF	XF	Unc
1661	—	27.00	55.00	85.00	140	—
1662	—	27.00	55.00	85.00	140	—
1663	—	27.00	55.00	85.00	140	—
1664	—	27.00	55.00	85.00	140	—
1665	—	27.00	55.00	85.00	140	—

KM# 56 1/16 THALER
Silver **Obv:** Tall bust right breaks inner circle at bottom

Date	Mintage	VG	F	VF	XF	Unc
1668	—	27.00	55.00	85.00	140	—
1669	—	27.00	55.00	85.00	140	—

KM# 57 1/16 THALER
Silver **Obv:** Short bust right within inner circle

Date	Mintage	VG	F	VF	XF	Unc
1669	—	33.00	55.00	85.00	140	—
1670	—	33.00	55.00	85.00	140	—
1671	—	33.00	55.00	85.00	140	—
1675	—	33.00	55.00	85.00	140	—

KM# 68 1/16 THALER
Silver **Obv:** Short bust right without inner circle

Date	Mintage	VG	F	VF	XF	Unc
1675	—	27.00	55.00	85.00	140	—

KM# 69 1/4 THALER
Silver **Obv:** Bust right **Rev:** Shield of six parts

Date	Mintage	VG	F	VF	XF	Unc
1675	—	325	600	1,000	2,000	—
1676	—	325	600	1,000	2,000	—

KM# 61 1/2 THALER
Silver **Obv:** Armored and draped bust right **Rev:** Crowned shield between palm branches

Date	Mintage	VG	F	VF	XF	Unc
1673	—	600	1,250	2,200	4,000	—

KM# 60 2/3 THALER
Silver **Obv:** Crowned CA monogram **Rev:** Crowned shield, value below

Date	Mintage	VG	F	VF	XF	Unc
1672	—	—	—	—	—	—

KM# 70 2/3 THALER

Silver **Rev:** Crowned shield, mintmaster's initials below

Date	Mintage	VG	F	VF	XF	Unc
1676	—	1,000	1,650	3,000	4,700	—

KM# 71 2/3 THALER

Silver **Obv:** Armored and draped bust right **Rev:** Crowned shield between palm branches

Date	Mintage	VG	F	VF	XF	Unc
1676	—	—	—	—	—	—

KM# 79 2/3 THALER

Silver **Rev:** Crowned shield divides date

Date	Mintage	VG	F	VF	XF	Unc
1683	—	1,000	1,650	3,000	4,700	—
1688	—	1,000	1,650	3,000	4,700	—

KM# 80 2/3 THALER

Silver **Obv:** Value in oval below armored and draped bust right **Rev:** Crowned shield

Date	Mintage	VG	F	VF	XF	Unc
1689	—	1,000	1,650	3,000	4,700	—

KM# 5 THALER

Silver **Obv:** Bust right **Obv. Legend:** IOHAN: ADOLPH: D: G: HERES * NORWEGI. **Rev:** Helmeted arms in cartouche design, date divided in helmets **Rev. Legend:** DVX. SLE. HO. S. - E: DI. CO: O: E. DE. **Note:** Dav. #3682.

Date	Mintage	VG	F	VF	XF	Unc
1608 Rare	—	—	—	—	—	—
1609 Rare	—	—	—	—	—	—

KM# 6 THALER

Silver **Obv:** Bust with scepter **Obv. Legend:** ...ADOLF...NORV.DVX.SL **Rev:** Helmeted arms in shield design **Rev. Legend:** D S H S E DI - C O E D M N S **Note:** Dav. #3683.

Date	Mintage	VG	F	VF	XF	Unc
1608 Rare	—	—	—	—	—	—

KM# 7 THALER

Silver **Obv:** Bust right **Obv. Legend:** ...ADOLF...NORWEGI **Rev. Legend:** D. S. H. S. E. DI. - C. O. E. D. M. N. S. **Note:** Dav. #3684.

Date	Mintage	VG	F	VF	XF	Unc
1609 Rare	—	—	—	—	—	—

KM# 8 THALER

Silver **Obv:** Older bust with beard **Obv. Legend:** IOH. ADOL. D. G. HAER... **Rev:** Helmeted arms wider at bottom, date **Rev. Legend:** E DITM. COM. OLDENB. & DELMENHOR **Note:** Dav. #3687.

Date	Mintage	VG	F	VF	XF	Unc
1609 Rare	—	—	—	—	—	—

KM# 13 THALER

28.7100 g., Silver **Rev:** Date divided at bottom by arms **Note:** Dav. #3689.

Date	Mintage	VG	F	VF	XF	Unc
1611	—	190	325	575	950	—
1612	—	190	325	575	950	—

KM# 12 THALER

Silver **Obv. Legend:** IOHAN*ADOLPH*D*G*HERES... **Rev. Legend:** SLEIS • HOL • ST. - DIT • CO • O. E. DE. **Note:** Some coins have an orb above the duke's head in the legend. Dav. #3688.

Date	Mintage	VG	F	VF	XF	Unc
1611	—	190	325	575	950	—
1612	—	190	325	575	950	—
1615	—	190	325	575	950	—

KM# 14 THALER

Silver **Rev. Legend:** ...E: DI: CO: O: E. DE. **Note:** Dav. #3690.

Date	Mintage	VG	F	VF	XF	Unc
1611	—	250	600	1,250	2,500	—

KM# 15 THALER

Silver **Obv:** Bust with ruff **Obv. Legend:** ...NORWEGIAE: DVX **Rev:** Date divided in helmets **Note:** Dav. #3691.

Date	Mintage	VG	F	VF	XF	Unc
1613 Rare	—	—	—	—	—	—

KM# 16 THALER

Silver **Obv:** Bust right **Rev. Legend:** ...DIT. CO: O: E: DEL. **Note:** Dav. #3692.

Date	Mintage	VG	F	VF	XF	Unc
1614	—	225	450	900	1,900	—

KM# 17 THALER

Silver **Rev:** Date divided below arms **Rev. Legend:** D: C: O: E: CE: **Note:** Dav. #3693.

Date	Mintage	VG	F	VF	XF	Unc
1617	—	225	450	900	1,900	—

KM# 18 THALER

Silver **Obv:** Bust of Frederik right **Obv. Legend:** FRIDERICUS • D: G: HAERES • NORWEGIAE **Rev:** Helmeted arms, date divided in helmets **Rev. Legend:** DVX • SLES: HOL • - ST: DIT: C: OE: DE: **Note:** Dav. #3695.

Date	Mintage	VG	F	VF	XF	Unc
1618	—	275	575	1,150	2,000	—
1620	—	275	575	1,150	2,000	—

KM# 25 THALER

Silver **Obv. Legend:** ...G: DUX. SLES: ET. HOLSA: **Rev. Legend:** VIRTUTIS GLOR - RIA MERCES 6Z1 **Note:** Dav. #3696.

Date	Mintage	VG	F	VF	XF	Unc
1621	—	275	575	1,150	2,000	—

KM# 26 THALER

Silver **Obv. Legend:** FRIDERICH • D: G: HERES • NORWE: DVX **Rev:** Date in helmets above arms **Rev. Legend:** SLEIS. HOL... **Note:** Dav. #3697.

Date	Mintage	VG	F	VF	XF	Unc
1622	—	265	450	800	1,300	—

KM# 27 THALER

Silver **Obv:** Bust in wide lace collar **Obv. Legend:** FRIDERICUS • D: G • DVS... **Rev:** Helmeted arms with date in helmets **Rev. Legend:** VIRTUT: GLO - RIA. MER. **Note:** Dav. #3698.

Date	Mintage	VG	F	VF	XF	Unc
1622 ST	—	225	375	675	1,150	—
1623 ST	—	225	375	675	1,150	—
1624 ST	—	225	375	675	1,150	—
1625 ST	—	225	375	675	1,150	—
1626 ST	—	225	375	675	1,150	—

KM# 28 THALER

Silver **Rev:** Date in legend **Note:** Dav. #3698A.

Date	Mintage	VG	F	VF	XF	Unc
1622	—	225	375	675	1,150	—

KM# 29 THALER

Silver **Rev:** Date by lower arms **Note:** Dav. #3698B.

Date	Mintage	VG	F	VF	XF	Unc
1622	—	225	375	675	1,150	—

KM# 30 THALER

Silver **Obv:** Bust right with pointy beard, thin lace collar **Rev:** Differently shaped shield **Note:** Dav. #3699.

Date	Mintage	VG	F	VF	XF	Unc
1626	—	225	375	675	1,150	—
1627	—	225	375	675	1,150	—
1628	—	225	375	675	1,150	—

KM# 35 THALER

Silver **Obv:** Bust right **Obv. Legend:** ...HERES * NORWEGIAE. DUX. **Rev:** Date in legend **Rev. Legend:** SLES: E: HOL - SATIAE **Note:** Dav. #3700.

Date	Mintage	VG	F	VF	XF	Unc
1634	—	350	750	1,250	—	—
1636	—	350	750	1,250	—	—
1637	—	350	750	1,250	—	—

KM# 40 THALER

Silver **Obv. Legend:** ... H: N: DUX: SLES: ET: HOLSA **Rev:** Legend, date **Rev. Legend:** VIRTUT: GLORIA: MERC: **Note:** Dav. #3701.

Date	Mintage	VG	F	VF	XF	Unc
1647 Rare	—	—	—	—	—	—

KM# 45 THALER

Silver **Subject:** Death of Frederik III **Obv:** Old bust right **Rev:** Nine-line inscription, with DECMR. and MXM. **Note:** Dav. #3702.

Date	Mintage	VG	F	VF	XF	Unc
1659	—	700	1,200	2,000	3,300	—

KM# 46 THALER

Silver **Rev. Legend:** Nine-line inscription with: DECEMB **Note:** Dav. #3702A.

Date	Mintage	VG	F	VF	XF	Unc
1659	—	700	1,200	2,000	3,300	—

KM# 47 THALER

Silver **Rev. Legend:** Nine-line inscription with: MXM. **Note:** Dav. #3702B.

Date	Mintage	VG	F	VF	XF	Unc
1659	—	700	1,200	2,000	3,300	—

KM# 62 THALER

Silver **Obv:** Bust right of Christian **Rev:** M-F above arms, date in legend **Note:** Dav. #3703.

Date	Mintage	VG	F	VF	XF	Unc
1673 MF	—	1,250	2,500	4,050	6,900	—
1674 MF	—	1,250	2,500	4,050	6,900	—

KM# 63 THALER

Silver **Obv:** Bust right of Christian, different drapery **Note:** Dav. #3704.

Date	Mintage	VG	F	VF	XF	Unc
1674 AH	—	1,250	2,500	4,050	6,900	—

KM# 64 THALER

Silver **Obv:** Bust right of Christian, legend is unbroken and starts at top **Note:** Dav. #3705.

Date	Mintage	VG	F	VF	XF	Unc
1674	—	1,250	2,500	4,050	6,900	—

KM# 77 THALER

Silver **Rev:** Helmeted arms with rounded bottom, date above, CI - MB below **Note:** Dav. #3706.

Date	Mintage	VG	F	VF	XF	Unc
1681 Rare	—	—	—	—	—	—

KM# 78 THALER

Silver **Rev:** Helmeted arms with flat bottom divide date at bottom **Note:** Dav. #3707.

Date	Mintage	VG	F	VF	XF	Unc
1682 Rare	—	—	—	—	—	—

KM# 85 THALER

Silver **Rev:** S.C. 1693 in cartouche below arms **Note:** Dav. #3708.

Date	Mintage	VG	F	VF	XF	Unc
1693 Rare	—	—	—	—	—	—

KM# 86 THALER

Silver **Obv:** Bust of Frederik IV right **Rev:** Crowned arms with six shields around, flag behind **Note:** Dav. #3710.

Date	Mintage	VG	F	VF	XF	Unc
1697 Rare	—	—	—	—	—	—

KM# 88 THALER

Silver **Rev:** Crowned arms with six shields around in decoration **Note:** Dav. #3711.

Date	Mintage	VG	F	VF	XF	Unc
1698 Rare	—	—	—	—	—	—

KM# 95 THALER

Silver **Rev:** Crowned arms in palm branches **Note:** Dav. #3712.

Date	Mintage	VG	F	VF	XF	Unc
1700 Rare	—	—	—	—	—	—

KM# 9 2 THALER
Silver **Obv:** Bust of Johann Adolf right **Rev:** Helmeted arms with H-P above and date divided in helmets **Note:** Dav. #3681.

Date	Mintage	VG	F	VF	XF	Unc
1609 Rare	—	—	—	—	—	—

KM# 10 2 THALER
Silver **Obv:** Older bust right **Rev:** Helmeted arms, date in legend **Note:** Dav. #3686.

Date	Mintage	VG	F	VF	XF	Unc
1609 Rare	—	—	—	—	—	—

KM# 19 2 THALER
Silver **Obv:** Bust of Frederik right **Rev:** Helmeted arms iwth date divided by helmets **Note:** Dav. #3694.

Date	Mintage	VG	F	VF	XF	Unc
1618 Rare	—	—	—	—	—	—

KM# 65 2 THALER
Silver **Obv:** Bust of Christian right **Rev:** Crowned oval arms in wreath **Note:** Dav. #A3705.

Date	Mintage	VG	F	VF	XF	Unc
1674 Rare	—	—	—	—	—	—

KM# 87 2 THALER
Silver **Obv:** Bust of Frederik IV right **Rev:** Crowned arms with six shields around, flags behing **Note:** Dav. #3709.

Date	Mintage	VG	F	VF	XF	Unc
1697 Rare	—	—	—	—	—	—

KM# 11 3 THALER
Silver **Obv:** Bust of Johann Adolf right **Rev:** Helmeted arms, date in legend **Note:** Dav. #3685.

Date	Mintage	VG	F	VF	XF	Unc
1609 Rare	—	—	—	—	—	—

KM# 75 MARK
Silver **Obv:** Wreath around shield design **Rev:** Value within legend

Date	Mintage	VG	F	VF	XF	Unc
1681	—	—	—	—	—	—

KM# 76 2 MARK
Silver **Obv:** Crowned monogram, value below **Rev:** Crowned shield between palm branches

Date	Mintage	VG	F	VF	XF	Unc
1681 CIMB	—	175	350	650	—	—

TRADE COINAGE

KM# 24 GOLDGULDEN
3.5000 g., 0.9860 Gold 0.1109 oz. AGW **Obv:** Bust of Friedrich III right in inner circle **Rev:** Arms topped by three helmets, date in legend

Date	Mintage	VG	F	VF	XF	Unc
1619	—	1,500	3,000	6,000	9,800	—

KM# 34 GOLDGULDEN
3.5000 g., 0.9860 Gold 0.1109 oz. AGW **Obv:** Friedrich III standing right in inner circle

Date	Mintage	VG	F	VF	XF	Unc
1627	—	975	2,050	3,750	6,000	—

KM# 53 GOLDGULDEN
3.5000 g., 0.9860 Gold 0.1109 oz. AGW **Obv:** Bust of Christian Albrecht right in inner circle **Rev:** Orb at center

Date	Mintage	VG	F	VF	XF	Unc
1664	—	1,300	2,700	4,950	8,300	—

KM# 4 DUCAT
3.5000 g., 0.9860 Gold 0.1109 oz. AGW **Obv:** Johann Adolf standing right in inner circle **Rev:** Crowned arms in inner circle

Date	Mintage	VG	F	VF	XF	Unc
1601 Rare	—	—	—	—	—	—

KM# 39 DUCAT
3.5000 g., 0.9860 Gold 0.1109 oz. AGW **Obv:** Bust of Friedrich III right in inner circle **Rev:** Arms topped by three helmets in inner circle

Date	Mintage	VG	F	VF	XF	Unc
1642	—	750	1,550	2,900	4,950	—

KM# 54 DUCAT
3.5000 g., 0.9860 Gold 0.1109 oz. AGW **Subject:** Christian Albrecht **Rev:** Crowned oval arms

Date	Mintage	VG	F	VF	XF	Unc
1664	—	1,800	3,700	6,500	11,000	—

KM# 66 DUCAT
3.5000 g., 0.9860 Gold 0.1109 oz. AGW **Obv:** Smaller bust, without inner circle

Date	Mintage	VG	F	VF	XF	Unc
1674 AH	—	1,800	3,700	6,500	11,000	—

KM# 81 DUCAT
3.5000 g., 0.9860 Gold 0.1109 oz. AGW **Rev:** Crowned shield, date below

Date	Mintage	VG	F	VF	XF	Unc
1689 Rare	—	—	—	—	—	—

KM# 82 DUCAT
3.5000 g., 0.9860 Gold 0.1109 oz. AGW **Rev:** Crowned mountain, date in cartouche at bottom

Date	Mintage	VG	F	VF	XF	Unc
1689	—	825	1,650	3,300	5,800	—

KM# A89 DUCAT
3.5000 g., 0.9860 Gold 0.1109 oz. AGW **Obv:** Crowned shield with lions **Rev:** View of Holm fortress with guidance from above, date at top

Date	Mintage	VG	F	VF	XF	Unc
1698	—	1,050	2,150	4,000	6,400	—

KM# 90 DUCAT
3.5000 g., 0.9860 Gold 0.1109 oz. AGW **Obv:** Bust of Friedrich IV right

Date	Mintage	VG	F	VF	XF	Unc
1698	—	750	1,500	3,000	5,300	—

KM# 91 DUCAT
3.5000 g., 0.9860 Gold 0.1109 oz. AGW **Rev:** Crowned shield with lions at center

Date	Mintage	VG	F	VF	XF	Unc
1698	—	750	1,500	3,000	5,300	—
1700	—	750	1,500	3,000	5,300	—

KM# 92 DUCAT
3.5000 g., 0.9860 Gold 0.1109 oz. AGW **Rev:** Shield with lions surrounded by six shields of arms

Date	Mintage	VG	F	VF	XF	Unc
1698	—	975	2,050	3,750	6,000	—

KM# 67 5 DUCAT
17.5000 g., 0.9860 Gold 0.5547 oz. AGW

Date	Mintage	VG	F	VF	XF	Unc
1674 Rare	—	—	—	—	—	—

SCHLESWIG-HOLSTEIN-NORBURG

Established upon the division of Schleswig-Holstein-Sonderburg in 1622. The first line became extinct after two generations and passed to Schleswig-Holstein-Plön, from which a second line was begun in 1679. When the Plön branch of the family died out in 1706, Norburg acquired the lands and titles. Schleswig-Holstein-Norburg passed to Denmark in 1761.

RULER
August, 1676-1699

DUCHY

REGULAR COINAGE

KM# 5 THALER
Silver **Subject:** Conclusion of Oldensburg Succession Dispute **Obv:** Helmeted shield, date flanking in straight line, 16 - 76 **Note:** Dav. #3722.

Date	Mintage	VG	F	VF	XF	Unc
1676 CP	—	600	1,200	2,000	3,250	—

KM# 6 THALER

Silver **Subject:** Conclusion of Oldensburg Succession Dispute **Obv:** Helmeted shield, date below on a curve **Note:** Dav. #3722A.

Date	Mintage	VG	F	VF	XF	Unc
1676 GP	—	600	1,200	2,000	3,250	—

TRADE COINAGE

KM# 7 3 DUCAT

10.5000 g., 0.9860 Gold 0.3328 oz. AGW **Subject:** Conclusion of Oldenburg's Succession Dispute **Obv:** 5-fold arms with central shield, 3 ornate helmets above, date divided near bottom, titles of August **Rev:** Eagle flying above view of mining scene, carrying a scale in his claws, sun shining with rays from above **Rev. Legend:** DIVINA BENEDICTIONE ET CÆSAREA IUSTITIA

Date	Mintage	VG	F	VF	XF	Unc
1676 CP Rare	—	—	—	—	—	—

KM# 8 4 DUCAT

14.0000 g., 0.9860 Gold 0.4438 oz. AGW **Subject:** Conclusion of Oldenburg's Succession Dispute **Obv:** 5-fold arms with central shield, 3 ornate helmets above, date divided near bottom, titles of August **Rev:** Eagle in flight holding scales above mining scene,sun shining with rays from above **Rev. Legend:** DIVINA BENEDICTIONE ET CÆSAREA IUSTITIA

Date	Mintage	VG	F	VF	XF	Unc
1676 CP Rare	—	—	—	—	—	—

SCHLESWIG-HOLSTEIN-PLOEN

One of the branches of Schleswig-Holstein founded upon the division of Schleswig-Holstein-Sonderburg in 1622. It fell extinct in 1706 and all lands and titles reverted to Schleswig-Holstein-Norburg.

RULERS

Joachim Ernst, 1622-1671
Johann Adolf, 1671-1704

COUNTY

REGULAR COINAGE

KM# 10 2 MARK (Lübsch)

Silver **Ruler:** Johann Adolf **Obv:** Crowned 5-fold arms with central shield divide date, titles of Johann Adolf **Rev. Legend:** Palm tree divides mintmaster's initials, large stone resting in branches

Date	Mintage	VG	F	VF	XF	Unc
1677 CR	—	60.00	120	225	400	—

KM# 11 1/16 THALER

Silver **Ruler:** Johann Adolf **Obv:** Draped bust right **Rev:** Value, date within legend

Date	Mintage	VG	F	VF	XF	Unc
1677 CR	—	55.00	115	220	350	—

KM# 13 1/12 THALER

Silver **Ruler:** Johann Adolf **Obv:** Crowned shield **Rev:** Value within legend

Date	Mintage	VG	F	VF	XF	Unc
1690	—	45.00	90.00	165	300	—

KM# 14 2/3 THALER

Silver **Ruler:** Johann Adolf **Obv:** Draped, armored bust right, value in oval below **Rev:** Crowned shield between palm branches

Date	Mintage	VG	F	VF	XF	Unc
1690	—	60.00	115	200	325	—

KM# 15 2/3 THALER

Silver **Ruler:** Johann Adolf **Rev:** Crowned shield

Date	Mintage	VG	F	VF	XF	Unc
1690	—	60.00	115	200	325	—

KM# 16 2/3 THALER

Silver **Ruler:** Johann Adolf **Obv:** Large armored bust right **Rev:** Crowned shield in circle, value below

Date	Mintage	VG	F	VF	XF	Unc
1690	—	35.00	85.00	165	300	—

KM# 17 2/3 THALER

Silver **Ruler:** Johann Adolf **Rev:** Fraction within legend

Date	Mintage	VG	F	VF	XF	Unc
1690	—	45.00	85.00	165	300	—

KM# 5 THALER

Silver **Ruler:** Joachim Ernst **Obv:** Bust of Joachim Ernst right **Rev:** Helmeted arms, date in legend **Note:** Dav.#3719.

Date	Mintage	VG	F	VF	XF	Unc
1625 MA Rare	—	—	—	—	—	—

KM# 6 THALER

Silver **Ruler:** Joachim Ernst **Obv:** Helmeted arms **Rev:** Crowned, double-headed eagle, orb with 32 on breast **Note:** Dav. #3720.

Date	Mintage	VG	F	VF	XF	Unc
1625 MA Rare	—	—	—	—	—	—

KM# 18 THALER

Silver **Ruler:** Johann Adolf **Obv:** Bust of Johann Adolf right, date below **Rev:** Helmeted arms

Date	Mintage	VG	F	VF	XF	Unc
1690 Rare	—	—	—	—	—	—

TRADE COINAGE

KM# 12 DUCAT

3.5000 g., 0.9860 Gold 0.1109 oz. AGW **Ruler:** Johann Adolf **Obv:** Arms in inner circle **Rev:** Crowned JA monogram

Date	Mintage	VG	F	VF	XF	Unc
1677 CR	—	1,250	2,250	4,500	7,000	—

KM# 19 DUCAT

3.5000 g., 0.9860 Gold 0.1109 oz. AGW **Ruler:** Johann Adolf **Obv:** Bust of Johann Adolf right in inner circle **Rev:** Arms in inner circle

Date	Mintage	VG	F	VF	XF	Unc
1690	—	1,650	3,000	5,500	9,000	—

PATTERNS

(Including off metal strikes)

KM#	Date	Mintage	Identification	Mkt Val
Pn2	1677	—	Ducat. Copper. KM#12; 10-sided klippe.	—
Pn1	1690	—	Thaler. Tin. KM#18.	—

SCHLESWIG-HOLSTEIN-SONDERBURG

Sonderburg was split away from Schleswig-Holstein in 1559 and created as a separate duchy for a younger son of King Christian III of Denmark. Divisions of Schleswig-Holstein-Sonderburg occurred in 1622 and again in 1627. The first division resulted in the branches of Glücksburg, Norburg and Plön, all of which were acquired by Denmark in the second half of the 18th century.

RULERS

Johann der Jüngere, 1559-1622
Alexander, 1622-1627

MINT OFFICIALS' INITIALS

Initial	Date	Name
PH	1608-	P. Hanssen in Sonderburg
(r)= R	1618-1620	Tobias Reinhardt in Reinfeld
	1620	Christoph Mittelbach in Reinfeld
(s)= [symbol]	1625-27	Johann Lilienthal in Sonderburg and Reinfeld

DUCHY

REGULAR COINAGE

KM# 4 2 SCHILLING (Lübsch)

Silver **Ruler:** Johann the Younger **Obv:** Rider on horse leaping to left, value: Z SL below **Rev:** Titles of Johann in 6-line inscription

Date	Mintage	VG	F	VF	XF	Unc
ND(1618-22)	—	16.00	40.00	65.00	120	—

KM# 11 2 SCHILLING (Lübsch)

Silver **Ruler:** Johann the Younger **Obv:** Nettle leaf of Holstein divides value: 2 - L or Z - L, date above **Rev:** Titles of Johann in 6-line inscription **Note:** Varieties exist.

Date	Mintage	VG	F	VF	XF	Unc
16Z0	—	16.00	40.00	65.00	120	—
16Z1	—	16.00	40.00	65.00	120	—
16Z3 Posthumous	—	16.00	40.00	65.00	120	—
16Z5 Posthumous	—	16.00	40.00	65.00	120	—

KM# 5 2 SCHILLING (Doppelschilling)
Silver **Ruler:** Johann the Younger **Obv:** 5-fold arms with central shield, titles of Johann in legend **Rev:** Large intertwined 'DS' in circle, small imperial orb above, titles continued in legend, date **Note:** Varieties exist.

Date	Mintage	VG	F	VF	XF	Unc
(16)18	—	60.00	110	180	250	—
(16)18 (r)	—	60.00	110	180	250	—
(16)19 (r)	—	60.00	110	180	250	—

KM# 13 4 SCHILLING (Lübsch)
Silver **Ruler:** Johann the Younger **Obv:** Rider on horse leaping to left, value: 4 SL below **Rev:** Titles of Johann in 6-line inscription

Date	Mintage	VG	F	VF	XF	Unc
ND(1618-22)	—	65.00	135	300	400	—

KM# 12 4 SCHILLING (Lübsch)
Silver **Ruler:** Johann the Younger **Obv:** Rider on horse leaping to left, value: 4 SL below **Rev:** Titles of Johann in 7-line inscription, date in last line

Date	Mintage	VG	F	VF	XF	Unc
16ZZ	—	85.00	165	300	475	—

KM# 14 1/96 THALER (Sechsling)
Silver **Ruler:** Johann the Younger **Obv:** Quatrefoil superimposed on floriated cross, titles of Johann **Rev:** Imperial orb with 96, date **Rev. Legend:** SLES. E. HOLS

Date	Mintage	VG	F	VF	XF	Unc
(1)622	—	—	—	—	—	—

KM# 8 1/64 THALER (Sechsling)
Silver **Ruler:** Johann the Younger **Obv:** Shield of lion rampant left (Norway) superimposed on cross, titles of Johann in legend **Rev:** Imperial orb with 64, titles and date in legend

Date	Mintage	VG	F	VF	XF	Unc
(1)619 (r)	—	65.00	120	225	400	—

KM# 3 1/16 THALER
Silver **Ruler:** Johann the Younger **Obv:** 16 within orb **Rev:** Helmeted shield **Note:** Prev. KM#5.

Date	Mintage	VG	F	VF	XF	Unc
1604	—	120	225	425	850	—

KM# 6 1/16 THALER
Silver **Obv:** Group of shields **Rev:** 16 within orb **Note:** Prev. KM#10.

Date	Mintage	VG	F	VF	XF	Unc
1618 (r)	—	135	275	475	925	—
1619 (r)	—	135	275	475	925	—

KM# 9 1/16 THALER
Silver **Obv:** Helmeted shield **Rev:** Eagle with 16 on breast **Note:** Prev. KM#11.

Date	Mintage	VG	F	VF	XF	Unc
1619 (r)	—	135	275	475	925	—
1620 (r)	—	135	275	475	925	—

KM# 25 1/16 THALER
Silver **Subject:** Alexander

Date	Mintage	VG	F	VF	XF	Unc
(1)6Z5 (s)	—	180	300	550	—	—

KM# 7 1/4 THALER
Silver **Obv:** Bust right **Rev:** Helmeted shield **Note:** Prev. KM#15.

Date	Mintage	VG	F	VF	XF	Unc
ND(1618-22) (r)	—	—	—	—	—	—

KM# 16 1/4 THALER
Silver **Subject:** Death of Johann

Date	Mintage	VG	F	VF	XF	Unc
1622	—	650	1,075	2,000	3,200	—

KM# 27 1/4 THALER
Silver **Subject:** Death of Alexander

Date	Mintage	VG	F	VF	XF	Unc
1627	—	—	—	—	—	—

KM# 17 1/2 THALER
Silver **Subject:** Death of Johann

Date	Mintage	VG	F	VF	XF	Unc
1622	—	1,000	1,800	3,000	5,000	—

KM# 18 THALER
Silver **Obv:** Bust of Johann right **Rev:** Helmeted arms **Note:** Dav. #3714.

Date	Mintage	VG	F	VF	XF	Unc
(1)622	—	1,500	3,000	5,000	—	—

KM# 19 THALER
Silver **Rev:** Narrower shield **Note:** Dav. #3714A.

Date	Mintage	VG	F	VF	XF	Unc
(1)622	—	1,500	3,000	5,000	—	—

KM# 20 THALER
Silver **Obv:** Bow knot on duke's shoulder **Note:** Dav. #3714B.

Date	Mintage	VG	F	VF	XF	Unc
(1)622 (r)	—	1,500	3,000	5,000	—	—

KM# 21 THALER
Silver **Subject:** Death of Johann **Note:** Similar to 2 Thaler, KM#23. Dav. #3715.

Date	Mintage	VG	F	VF	XF	Unc
1622	—	1,500	2,500	4,000	6,000	—

KM# 26 THALER
Silver **Obv:** Bust of Alexander right **Rev:** Helmeted arms **Note:** Dav. #3716.

Date	Mintage	VG	F	VF	XF	Unc
(1)626 (s)	—	1,350	2,750	4,500	—	—

KM# 28 THALER
Silver **Subject:** Death of Alexander **Obv:** 8-line inscription inside inner circle **Rev:** Helmeted arms, date (1)626 **Note:** Dav. #3717.

Date	Mintage	VG	F	VF	XF	Unc
1627 (s)	—	1,000	2,000	3,250	—	—

KM# 22 2 THALER
Silver **Obv:** Bust of Johann right **Rev:** Helmeted arms **Note:** Dav. #3713.

Date	Mintage	VG	F	VF	XF	Unc
1622 Rare	—	—	—	—	—	—

KM# 23 2 THALER
Silver **Subject:** Death of Johann **Note:** Dav. #A3715.

Date	Mintage	VG	F	VF	XF	Unc
1622	—	2,000	3,000	5,000	8,000	—

TRADE COINAGE

KM# 10 GOLDGULDEN
3.5000 g., 0.9860 Gold 0.1109 oz. AGW **Obv:** Bust of Johann right in inner circle **Rev:** Orb in inner circle **Note:** Prev. Fr.12.

Date	Mintage	VG	F	VF	XF	Unc
1619 (r)	—	1,400	2,800	4,900	8,400	—

FR# 24 GOLDGULDEN
3.5000 g., 0.9860 Gold 0.1109 oz. AGW **Obv:** Crowned shields in inner circle

Date	Mintage	VG	F	VF	XF	Unc
1624	—	1,050	2,100	3,850	6,300	—

SCHWARZBURG

The countship of Schwarzburg had its beginnings in central Thuringia (Thüringen) and the ruling family eventually held numerous small territories from northern to central Thuringia. The earliest rulers known with any historical certainty were counts of Käfernburg in the 12th century. The line was divided into Käfernburg and Schwarzburg in the early 13th century, but when that of Käfernburg became extinct in 1385, most of its territories reverted to Schwarzburg. Several divisions of the countship took place during the next several centuries and at the beginning of the 16th century, there existed the branches of Schwarzburg-Arnstadt, Schwarzburg-Blankenburg and Schwarzburg-Leutenberg. The rulers of the various lines usually struck a joint coinage during the 16th century, but some of the counts issued coins in their own right as well. In 1526, the lines of Schwarzburg-Frankenhausen and Schwarzburg-Sondershausen were established from Schwarzburg-Blankenburg. Frankenhausen only lasted for one generation, but Schwarzburg-Sondershausen was further divided into Schwarzburg-Arnstadt, Schwarzburg-Rudolstadt and Schwarzburg-Sondershausen in 1552 (see separate listings for each of these). The Arnstadt line also failed after a single generation, but was reestablished as a branch of Schwarzburg-Sondershausen in 1642.

RULERS

Joint Coinage VI

Albrecht VII von Rudolstadt, 1586-1605
Günther XLII von Sondershausen, 1586-1643
Anton Heinrich von Sondershausen, 1586-1638
Johann Günther II von Sondershausen, 1586-1631
Christian Günther I von Sondershausen, 1586-1642

Joint Coinage VII

Karl Günther von Rudolstadt, 1605-1630Ludwig Günther von Rudolstadt, 1605-1646Albrecht Günther von Rudolstadt, 1605-1634Günther XLII von Sondershausen, 1586-1643Anton Heinrich von Sondershausen, 1586-1638Johann Günther II von Sondershausen, 1586-1631Christian Günther I von Sondershausen, 1586-1642

MINT OFFICIALS

Initial or mark	Date	Name
(b) = Gr	1597-1606	Florian Gruber, mintmaster in Erfurt
	Ca.1597-1606	Hans Weber, warden in Erfurt
HG	1606-09	Hieronymus Gronberger, mintmaster in Erfurt
WA	Ca.1611-13	Wolf Albrecht, mintmaster in Saalfeld

ARMS

Schwarzburg – (1) early arms, a crowned lion, often to right, (2) the symbols of a two-tined fork and a comb are often found as part of the arms, usually at the bottom of the main body of the arms, (3) the imperial eagle with arms on breast were adopted by all branches of the family who became princes of the empire in the late 17th and early 18th centuries

Arnstadt – eagle
Hohnstein – checkerboard
Klettenberg – striding deer
Lutterberg – crowned striding lion above four horizontal bars
Sondershausen – deer antlers

REFERENCES

F = Ernst Fischer, **Die Münzen des Hauses Schwarzburg**, Heidelberg, 1904.

R = Ernst Helmuth von Betha, **Schwarzburger Münzen und Medaillen: Sammlung des Schlossmuseums in Rudolstadt**, Halle (Saale), 1903.

COUNTSHIP

STANDARD COINAGE

KM# 3 THALER

Silver **Ruler:** Joint Coinage VI Albrecht VII, Günther XLII, Anton Heinrich, Johann Günther II and Christian Günther I **Obv:** Helmeted and supported arms, divided date above **Obv. Legend:** ALB. GVN. AN. HE. HA. GV. CH... **Rev:** Crowned double eagle wtih orb and cross **Rev. Legend:** RUDOLPH... **Mint:** Erfurt **Note:** Dav. #7674.

Date	Mintage	VG	F	VF	XF	Unc
1601 (b)	—	240	450	725	1,200	—
1602 (b)	—	240	450	725	1,200	—
1603 (b)	—	240	450	725	1,200	—
1604 (b)	—	240	450	725	1,200	—
1605 (b)	—	240	450	725	1,200	—

KM# 12 THALER

Silver **Ruler:** Joint Coinage VII **Obv:** Helmeted and supported arms **Obv. Legend:** GVNT: AN. HEIN: CAR... **Rev:** St. Martin and beggar, orb above divides date **Mint:** Erfurt **Note:** Dav. #7675.

Date	Mintage	VG	F	VF	XF	Unc
1605 (b)	—	215	400	650	1,100	—

KM# 15 THALER

Silver **Ruler:** Joint Coinage VII **Obv:** Helmeted and supported arms divide date **Rev:** St. Martin and beggar, orb above divides date **Mint:** Erfurt **Note:** Dav. #7676.

Date	Mintage	VG	F	VF	XF	Unc
1606//1606 (b)	—	240	450	725	1,200	—

KM# 16 THALER

Silver **Ruler:** Joint Coinage VII **Rev:** St. Martin and seated beggar **Mint:** Erfurt **Note:** Dav. #7677.

Date	Mintage	VG	F	VF	XF	Unc
1606 (b)	—	215	400	650	1,100	—
1607 HG	—	215	400	650	1,100	—
1608 HG	—	215	400	650	1,100	—
1609 HG	—	215	400	650	1,100	—

KM# 17 THALER

Silver **Ruler:** Joint Coinage VII **Rev:** Beggar reclining **Mint:** Erfurt **Note:** Dav. #7677A.

Date	Mintage	VG	F	VF	XF	Unc
1606 HG	—	215	400	650	1,100	—
1608 HG	—	215	400	650	1,100	—

KM# 18 THALER

Silver **Ruler:** Joint Coinage VII **Obv:** Helmeted arms with date in helmets **Rev:** Similar to KM #17 **Mint:** Erfurt **Note:** Dav. #7678.

Date	Mintage	VG	F	VF	XF	Unc
1606 (b)	—	240	450	725	1,200	—

KM# 21 THALER

Silver **Ruler:** Joint Coinage VII **Rev:** Beggar seated right **Mint:** Erfurt **Note:** Dav. #7677B.

Date	Mintage	VG	F	VF	XF	Unc
1608 HG	—	240	450	725	1,200	—

KM# 23 THALER

Silver **Ruler:** Joint Coinage VII **Rev:** Date appears: AN. 16-09 **Mint:** Erfurt **Note:** Dav. #7677C.

Date	Mintage	VG	F	VF	XF	Unc
1609 HG	—	240	450	725	1,200	—

KM# 25 THALER

Silver **Ruler:** Joint Coinage VII **Obv:** Date above helmets **Mint:** Saalfeld **Note:** Dav. #7679.

Date	Mintage	VG	F	VF	XF	Unc
1613 WA	—	300	550	900	1,500	—

KM# 61 THALER

Silver **Ruler:** Joint Coinage VII **Obv:** Helmeted arms divide date at helmets **Obv. Legend:** GVNT. ANT. HEIN. HAN-S... **Rev:** St. Martin and beggar above legend **Rev. Legend:** HH ++ O ++ **Note:** Dav. #7680.

Date	Mintage	VG	F	VF	XF	Unc
1623 HHO	—	240	450	725	1,200	—

KM# 62 THALER

Silver **Ruler:** Joint Coinage VII **Rev. Legend:** LIN ++ ARN ++ ER ++ SONND **Note:** Dav. #7680B.

Date	Mintage	VG	F	VF	XF	Unc
1623 HHO	—	240	450	725	1,200	—

KM# 63 THALER

Silver **Ruler:** Joint Coinage VII **Obv. Legend:** HEIN. HANS-GVNT... **Note:** Dav. #7680C.

Date	Mintage	VG	F	VF	XF	Unc
1623 HHO	—	240	450	725	1,200	—

KM# 65 THALER

Silver **Ruler:** Joint Coinage VII **Subject:** Death of Johann Günther II **Obv:** Facing bust **Rev:** 11-line inscription **Note:** Dav. #7681.

Date	Mintage	VG	F	VF	XF	Unc
1632	—	425	775	1,300	2,150	—

KM# 68 THALER

Silver **Subject:** Death of Anton Heinrich **Obv:** Helmeted arms **Rev:** 7-line inscription **Note:** Dav. #7682.

Date	Mintage	VG	F	VF	XF	Unc
1638 IBM	—	300	500	850	1,450	—

KM# 72 THALER

Silver **Subject:** Death of Anna, Sister of the 4 Counts **Obv:** 10-line inscription **Rev:** 8-line inscription **Note:** Dav. #7683.

Date	Mintage	VG	F	VF	XF	Unc
1640 Rare	—	—	—	—	—	—

KM# 77 THALER

Silver **Subject:** Memorial Thaler for Christian Günther I **Obv:** Helmeted arms, DVRVM PATIETIA MOLLIT below **Rev:** 9-line inscription **Note:** Dav. #7684.

Date	Mintage	VG	F	VF	XF	Unc
1643 Rare	—	—	—	—	—	—

KM# 78 THALER

Silver **Subject:** Death of Günther XLII **Obv:** Helmeted and supported arms, PIETATE ET. IUSTITIA below **Rev:** 10-line inscription **Note:** Dav. #7685.

Date	Mintage	VG	F	VF	XF	Unc
1643 Rare	—	—	—	—	—	—

SCHWARZBURG-ARNSTADT

The seat of this branch of Schwarzburg is located about 10 miles (16 kilometers) south of Erfurt. The town, castle and surrounding territory were acquired by the counts of Schwarzburg in the early 14th century and a line was soon established separate from Schwarzburg-Blankenburg. The latter fell extinct in the mid-14th century and passed to Arnstadt. Generations later, the lines of Schwarzburg-Sondershausen and Schwarzburg-Rudolstadt were founded and Arnstadt was absorbed by the former, only to reemerge as a separate line in 1642. The last count of Schwarzburg-Arnstadt was raised to the rank of prince in 1709, but died without heirs in 1716.

RULERS

Christian Günther I zu Sondershausen, 1586-1642
Christian Günther II, 1642-1666
Johann Günther IV, 1666-1669
Anton Günther II, 1669-1716, Prince 1709

MINT OFFICIALS

Initial or mark	Date	Name
HM+	1675-81	Henning Müller, mintmaster in Sondershausen
(a)= [crossed hammers mark]	1676-78	Henning Müller, mintmaster in Keula
HCH	1685-89	Heinrich Christoph Hille, mintmaster in Arnstadt

Arms: See under Schwarzburg

REFERENCES:

F = Ernst Fischer, *Die Münzen des Hauses Schwarzburg*, **Heidelberg, 1904.**

R = Ernst Helmuth von Bethe, *Schwarzburger Münzen und Medaillen: Sammlung des Schlossmuseums in Rudolstadt,* **Halle (Saale), 1903.**

COUNTSHIP

REGULAR COINAGE

KM# 4 THALER

Silver **Ruler:** Christian Günther II **Subject:** Death of Christian Günther II **Obv:** Helmeted and supported arms **Rev:** Five-line inscription within wreath **Note:** Prev. Dav#7686.

Date	Mintage	VG	F	VF	XF	Unc
1666	—	350	625	1,150	2,000	—

KM# 6 THALER

Silver **Ruler:** Johann Günther IV **Subject:** Death of Johann Günther IV **Obv:** Helmeted and supported arms **Rev:** Nine-line inscription within wreath **Note:** Prev. Dav#7687.

Date	Mintage	VG	F	VF	XF	Unc
1669	—	900	1,500	2,500	4,350	—

TRADE COINAGE

KM# 29 DUCAT

3.5000 g., 0.9860 Gold 0.1109 oz. AGW, 21.5 mm. **Ruler:** Anton Günther II **Obv:** Armored bust to left **Obv. Legend:** ANTHON. GUNTHER. E. IV. COM. IMP:. **Rev:** Manifold arms supported by wildman and woman, 3 ornate helmets above, date at end of legend **Rev. Legend:** COM. DE. SCHVVARTZB: — ET HONSTEIN. (date). **Note:** Fr#3108.

Date	Mintage	VG	F	VF	XF	Unc
1680 HM	—	700	1,500	3,000	5,000	—

SCHWARZBURG-RUDOLSTADT

Established upon the division of Schwarzburg-Sondershausen in 1552, the younger main branch of Schwarzburg, centered on the castle and town of Rudolstadt, 17 miles (29 kilometers) south of Weimar, flourished until the end of World War I. The count was raised to the rank of prince in 1711. The three sons of Albrecht VII, the first Count of Schwarzburg-Rudolstadt, ruled and issued coinage jointly, followed by a long succession of sole rulers descended from the middle son, Ludwig Günther I.

RULERS

Albrecht VII, 1552-1605
Joint Rule:
Karl Günther zu Kranichfeld, 1605-1630
Ludwig Günther I zu Rudolstadt, 1605-1646
Albrecht Günther zu Stadtilm, 1605-1634
Albrecht Anton, 1646-1710

MINTMARKS AND MINT OFFICIALS' INITIALS

Initials	Date	Name
R	1621-1623	Rudolstadt mint
BB	1621, 1622-1625	Barthel Bechstett (or Bechstein), mintmaster in Rudolstadt
	1621	Christoph Carpe, mintmaster in Rudolstadt
F	1621-1622	Friedeburg mint
Z	1621-1623	Heinrich Abel Ziegenmeier, mintmaster in Friedeburg
K, KS	1621-1622	Königsee mint
	1620-1621	Heinrich Meyer von Halle, mintmaster in Königsee
S	1621-1623	Peter Schrader von Magdeburg, mintmaster in Königsee
L	1621-1622	Leutenberg mint
P	1621-1623	Johann Pabst, mintmaster in Leutenberg
	1621-1622	Wolf Albrecht, mintmaster in Leutenberg
	1622	Barthel Bechstett (or Bechstein), mintmaster in Kranichfeld
	1622	Caspar Urleben, mintmaster in Kranichfeld

Arms: See under Schwarzburg

REFERENCES:

F = Ernst Fischer, ***Die Münzen des Hauses Schwarzburg***, **Heidelberg, 1904.**

R = Ernst Helmuth von Bethe, ***Schwarzburger Münzen und Medaillen: Sammlung des Schlossmuseums in Rudolstadt***, Halle (Saale), 1903.

COUNTSHIP

REGULAR COINAGE

KM# 81 THALER

Silver **Ruler:** Ludwig Günther I and Albrecht Günther Jointly **Subject:** Death of Karl Günther **Rev:** 8-line inscription **Note:** Dav #7694.

Date	Mintage	VG	F	VF	XF	Unc
1630	—	700	1,300	2,400	4,000	—

KM# 85 THALER

Silver **Ruler:** Ludwig Günther I **Subject:** Death of Albrecht Günther **Rev:** 8-line inscription **Note:** Dav #7698.

Date	Mintage	VG	F	VF	XF	Unc
1634 Rare	—	—	—	—	—	—

KM# 88 THALER

Silver **Ruler:** Ludwig Günther I **Subject:** Death of Ludwig Günther I **Rev:** Crowned arms **Note:** Dav #7696.

Date	Mintage	VG	F	VF	XF	Unc
1646	—	525	975	1,750	3,150	—

KM# 89 THALER

Silver **Ruler:** Ludwig Günther I **Obv:** Order of Johann cross on right breast **Note:** Dav #7696A.

Date	Mintage	VG	F	VF	XF	Unc
1646	—	525	975	1,750	3,150	—

KM# 91 THALER

Silver **Ruler:** Albrecht Anton **Subject:** Death of Anna Sophia, Wife of Karl Günther **Obv:** Crowned arms of Anhalt and Schwarzburg **Rev:** 11-line inscription **Note:** Dav #7695.

Date	Mintage	VG	F	VF	XF	Unc
1652	—	800	1,500	2,700	4,500	—

KM# 95 THALER
Silver **Ruler:** Albrecht Anton **Subject:** Death of Emilie, Wife of Ludwig Günther **Obv:** 2 crowned shields **Rev:** Cross with hearts at top and base **Note:** Dav #7697.

Date	Mintage	VG	F	VF	XF	Unc
1670	—	1,000	1,800	3,300	5,500	—

SCHWARZBURG-SONDERSHAUSEN

As the elder main line of Schwarzburg established in 1552, the counts of Schwarzburg-Sondershausen controlled their scattered territories from the castle of Sondershausen in northern Thuringia (Thüringen), 10 miles (16 kilometers) southeast of Nordhausen. Count Christian Wilhelm I was raised to the rank of prince in 1697 and the line descended from him until it finally became extinct in 1909. All titles and territories then passed to Schwarzburg-Rudolstadt.

RULERS

Joint Coinage (1619-23):
Günther XLII, 1586-1643
Anton Heinrich, 1586-1638,
Johann Günther II, 1586-1631
Christian Günther I, 1586-1642
Anton Günther I, 1642-1666
Ludwig Günther II zu Ebeleben, 1642-1681
Christian Wilhelm I, 1666-1721, Prince 1697
Jointly with Anton Günther II zu Arnstadt, 1677-1679

MINTMARKS AND MINT OFFICIALS' INITIALS

Initial	Date	Name
A, AR	1621-22	Arnstadt mint
WF	1621	Wolfgang Fröhmel, mintmaster in Arnstadt
G, GR	1621-22	Greussen mint
CO	1620-22	Claus Oppermann, mintmaster in Greussen
HHO	1622-23	Hans Heinrich Otte, mintmaster in Greussen;
	1622-23	In Hohnstein
(b)= [symbol] or HE	1620-22	Hans von Eck, mintmaster in Clingen
	1621-22	Volkmar Happe, mintmaster in Keula
LW	1621-22	Lipold Wefer, mintmaster in Lohra or Kelbra(?)
SH	1621-22	Sondershausen mint
	1624	Johann Schulthess, mintmaster in Sondershausen
IBM	1631-50	Joachim Blum (Monetarius), die-cutter in Bremen
HM	1675-82	Henning Müller, mintmaster in Sondershausen
(a)= [symbol]	1676-79	Henning Müller, mintmaster in Arnstadt and Keula
IH	ca1683-84	Johann Hercher, mintmaster in Sondershausen
IT	1684-89 or 1690	Johann Thun, mintmaster in Sondershausen
W	ca1677, 1686-88	Christian Wermuth, die-cutter in Sondershausen

ARMS: See under Schwarzburg

REFERENCES:

F = Ernst Fischer, *Die Münzen des Hauses Schwarzburg,* **Heidelberg, 1904.**

R = Ernst Helmuth von Bethe, *Schwarzburger Münzen und Medaillen: Sammlung des Schlossmuseums in Rudolstadt,* **Halle (Saale), 1903.**

COUNTSHIP

REGULAR COINAGE

KM# 82 THALER
Silver **Ruler:** Anton Günther I **Subject:** Death of Anton Günther I **Obv:** Helmeted and supported arms **Rev:** 8-line inscription in wreath **Note:** Dav #7688.

Date	Mintage	VG	F	VF	XF	Unc
1666	—	700	1,250	2,050	3,450	—

KM# 102 THALER
Silver **Ruler:** Christian Wilhelm I jointly with Anton Günther II **Obv:** Horse in landscape **Rev:** Ornate shield of manifold arms divide mintmaster's initials, 3 ornate helmets above **Note:** Dav #7689. Prev. KM #M1.

Date	Mintage	VG	F	VF	XF	Unc
1677 HM	—	525	975	1,800	3,000	—

KM# 103 THALER
Silver **Ruler:** Christian Wilhelm I jointly with Anton Günther II **Obv:** Horse in different landscape **Note:** Dav #7690. Prev. KM#M2.

Date	Mintage	VG	F	VF	XF	Unc
1677 HM/W	—	625	1,100	2,100	3,500	—

KM# 104 2 THALER
51.0800 g., Silver **Ruler:** Christian Wilhelm I jointly with Anton Günther II **Note:** Dav #7690A. Prev. KM #M3.

Date	Mintage	VG	F	VF	XF	Unc
1677 HM/W	—	1,700	2,800	4,550	7,000	—

PRINCIPALITY

REGULAR COINAGE

KM# 112 THALER
Silver **Ruler:** Christian Wilhelm I **Subject:** Death of Ludwig Günther II **Note:** Similar to 2 Thaler, KM# 113. Prev. Dav #LS486A.

Date	Mintage	VG	F	VF	XF	Unc
1681 HM	—	1,400	2,400	4,000	6,500	—

KM# 124 THALER
Silver **Ruler:** Christian Wilhelm I **Obv:** Bust of Christian Wilhelm right **Rev:** Helmeted and supported arms, I-T below **Note:** Dav #7691.

Date	Mintage	VG	F	VF	XF	Unc
1687 IT Rare	—	—	—	—	—	—

KM# 113 2 THALER
Silver **Ruler:** Christian Wilhelm I jointly with Anton Günther II **Subject:** Death of Ludwig Günther II **Obv:** 13-line inscription **Rev:** Helmeted and supported arms **Note:** Prev. Dav #LS486.

Date	Mintage	VG	F	VF	XF	Unc
1681 HM	—	2,000	3,500	5,700	9,500	—

TRADE COINAGE

KM# 121 1/4 DUCAT
0.8750 g., 0.9860 Gold 0.0277 oz. AGW **Ruler:** Christian Wilhelm I jointly with Anton Günther II **Obv:** Bust of Christian Wilhelm right **Rev:** Shield of arms **Note:** Prev. Fr#3106.

Date	Mintage	VG	F	VF	XF	Unc
1684 IT	—	220	450	875	1,650	—
1686 IT	—	220	450	875	1,650	—

KM# 107 DUCAT
3.5000 g., 0.9860 Gold 0.1109 oz. AGW **Ruler:** Christian Wilhelm I jointly with Anton Günther II **Obv:** Bust of Christian Wilhelm right **Rev:** Crowned arms with wild man and wild woman supporters **Note:** Prev. Fr#3107.

Date	Mintage	VG	F	VF	XF	Unc
1679 HM	—	625	1,250	2,500	4,400	—
1684	—	625	1,250	2,500	4,400	—
1689 IT	—	625	1,250	2,500	4,400	—

SCHWARZENBERG

The princes of Schwarzenberg based their land holdings in Franconia after Erkinger I of Stefansberg bought the lordship of Schwarzenberg sometime between 1405 and 1411. He became a member of the Imperial Diet in 1429 and upon his death in 1437, his two sons founded the lines of Schwarzenberg-Stefansberg and Schwarzenberg-Hohenlandsberg. The younger line, which was raised to the rank of count in 1566, became extinct in 1646. Its lands and titles reverted to Stefansberg, which attained the countship in 1599. In 1670, the count of Schwarzenberg was made a prince and, a generation later, the territories of Sulz and Kettgau were added to the family holdings through marriage, followed by Krumau in 1719. Having acquired Gimborn earlier, the prince sold that county to Wallmoden in 1783. Klettgau was sold to Baden in 1813, but not before the principality in Franconia was mediatized to Bavaria when the Holy Roman Empire came to an end in 1806. Members of the family retained their titles and held extensive lands in Bavaria, Austria and Bohemia/Czechoslovakia well into the 20th century. Several princes von Schwarzenberg distinguished themselves in both civil and military service to Austria.

RULERS

Schwarzenberg-Hohenlandsberg
Georg Ludwig, 1596-1646
Schwarzenberg-Stefansberg
Adam, 1599-1641
Johann Adolf, 1641-1683, prince 1670
Ferdinand Wilhelm Eusebius, 1683-1703

MINT OFFICIALS' INITIALS

Cologne Mint

Initials	Date	Name
PN	1680-98	Peter Newers
	ca. 1697	Martin Brunner, diecutter

Kremnitz Mint

MIM	ca. 1696	Martin Josef Mayerl, warden
	ca. 1696 (1650-1736)	Johann Michael Hofmann, die-cutter

Nuremberg Mint

(n)		Nuremberg mint (either struck or dies from there)
VM	1569-1603 (died 1603)	Valentin Maler, die-cutter
GFN	1677-1716	Georg Friedrich Nürnberg, mintmaster
	ca. 1696	Martin Brunner, die-cutter

Vienna Mint

(a)	1648-ca. 1682	Johann (Hans) Konrad Richthausen, mintmaster
	ca. 1682-? (1650-1736)	Johann Michael Hofmann, die-cutter
(b) or MM	1679-99	Matthias Mittermayer von Waffenberg, mintmaster

PRINCIPALITY

REGULAR COINAGE

KM# 5 THALER
Silver **Ruler:** Johann Adolf **Obv:** Bust of Johann Adolf right **Rev:** Crowned arms **Mint:** Vienna **Note:** Dav# 7699.

Date	Mintage	VG	F	VF	XF	Unc
1682 (a)	—	325	600	1,100	1,800	—

KM# 12 THALER
Silver **Ruler:** Ferdinand Wilhelm Eusebius **Obv:** Ferdinand Wilhelm Eusebius **Rev:** Crowned arms in Order chain **Mint:** Nuremberg **Note:** Dav# 7700.

Date	Mintage	VG	F	VF	XF	Unc
1696 GF-N	—	205	375	700	1,150	—

KM# 16 THALER
Silver **Ruler:** Ferdinand Wilhelm Eusebius **Obv:** Accolated busts of Ferdinand and Maria Anna **Rev:** Two crowned and mantled shield, date above, legend begins at top **Rev. Legend:** PRINCEPS. A... **Mint:** Vienna **Note:** Dav# 7701.

Date	Mintage	VG	F	VF	XF	Unc
1696 MM	—	100	255	425	600	—

KM# 17 THALER
Silver **Ruler:** Ferdinand Wilhelm Eusebius **Rev:** Legend begins at bottom **Rev. Legend:** D: G: PRINC. A... **Mint:** Kremnitz **Note:** Dav# 7702.

Date	Mintage	VG	F	VF	XF	Unc
1696 MIM	—	85.00	210	350	500	—

KM# 18 THALER
Silver **Ruler:** Ferdinand Wilhelm Eusebius **Obv:** Bust of Ferdinand right **Rev:** Crowned arms **Mint:** Cologne **Note:** Dav# 7703.

Date	Mintage	VG	F	VF	XF	Unc
1697 P-N	—	350	650	1,150	1,950	—

TRADE COINAGE

KM# 7 DUCAT
3.5000 g., 0.9860 Gold 0.1109 oz. AGW **Ruler:** Johann Adolf **Obv:** Bust of Johann Adolf right **Rev:** Capped arms in Order collar **Mint:** Vienna **Note:** Prev. Fr# 92.

Date	Mintage	VG	F	VF	XF	Unc
1682 (a)	—	600	1,450	3,000	4,500	—

KM# 10 DUCAT
3.5000 g., 0.9860 Gold 0.1109 oz. AGW **Ruler:** Ferdinand Wilhelm Eusebius **Obv:** Bust of Ferdinand Wilhelm Eusebius right **Rev:** Capped arms in Order collar **Mint:** Vienna **Note:** Fr# 94.

Date	Mintage	VG	F	VF	XF	Unc
1693 (b)	—	425	850	1,700	3,000	—
1695 (b)	—	425	850	1,700	3,000	—

KM# 14 10 DUCAT
35.0000 g., 0.9860 Gold 1.1095 oz. AGW **Ruler:** Ferdinand Wilhelm Eusebius **Obv:** Draped and armored bust to right **Obv. Legend:** FERDINAND. D.G. PR. — A SCHWARTZENBERG. **Rev:** Crowned shield of 4-fold arms in chain of order divides date **Rev. Legend:** DOM. IN HOHEN LANDSBERG. GIMB. MUR. WIT. ET FRAUENBERG. **Mint:** Nuremberg **Note:** Struck with Thaler dies, KM# 12 (Dav #7700). Prev. KM# 60.

Date	Mintage	VG	F	VF	XF	Unc
1696 GFN Rare	—	—	—	—	—	—

SCHWEINFURT

Schweinfurt was a Free City located in Lower Franconia some 27 miles northeast of Würzburg. It was first mentioned in 790, became a Free City in the 13th century. Immediately after becoming free, Schweinfurt was the site of a short-lived royal bracteat mint.

The only Schweinfurt local coinage appeared in 1622, though a 1717 series of Reformation commemoratives may have passed as coins.

In 1803 the town was annexed to Bavaria.

MINT OFFICIAL
FEW = Friedrich Ernst Wermuth, mintmaster in Hildburghausen, 1716-1718

FREE CITY

REGULAR COINAGE

KM# 1 1/84 GULDEN
1.2300 g., Copper **Obv:** City arms divide date, "S-S-M" (Schweinfurt Stadt Münz) at left, top and right **Rev:** Denomination "84" in wreath **Note:** Size varies 17.4 - 17.8mm.

Date	Mintage	Good	VG	F	VF	XF
1622	—	—	25.00	45.00	75.00	100

KM# 2 KREUZER
Copper **Obv:** City arms **Rev:** "I/KREUZ/ER" and date

Date	Mintage	Good	VG	F	VF	XF
1622	—	—	45.00	75.00	120	170

SILESIA

The territory of Silesia was historically located between Bohemia and Poland, but was Germanic in character from an early period. The first ruling dynasty, that of the Piasts, was descended from the Polish royal line and soon had divided Silesia into a number of smaller entities. Silesia proper became a part of the Holy Roman Empire in the 14th century and came under the influence of Bohemia, which began striking coins for that territory. After the mid-14th century, Breslau (see) became the capital and the principal mint of the duchy. In 1526, Silesia, along with Bohemia, came into the possession of the Habsburg imperial family. The Austrian-style coinage of Silesia was struck from that time until 1740, with few gaps, most notably during the Thirty Years' War, when the estates struck a series of emergency coinage. All during the period of Habsburg domination, the various semi-independent small duchies, in all their branches, continued to strike their own coins. The bishops of Breslau and a number of towns and cities also issued coinages in their own names (see under Breslau and the town names).

In the 1740's, Prussia conquered the greater portion of Silesia and established a mint in Breslau which struck coins within the Prussian system from 1743 until 1797 (see under Prussia). Silesia remained a province of Prussia throughout the 18th and 19th centuries, only to be divided and partly awarded to Poland after World War I. Following the Second World War, the rest of Silesia was united with Poland and remains as part of that country up to the present day.

RULERS

Habsburg Dynasty

Rudolf II, 1576-1612
Matthias, 1612-1619
Ferdinand II, 1619-1637
Ferdinand III, 1637-1657
Leopold I, 1657-1705

MINT MARKS

A - Berlin
B - Breslau
W - Wratislawia (i.e. Breslau)

MINT OFFICIALS' INITIALS

BRESLAU MINT

(Wroclaw, Vratislav)
(in Silesia)

Coat of arms sometimes at top center of crowned shield. Other times just Austrian arms on imperial eagle's breast. Legend usually ends: DVX S, SI or SIL.

MINT OFFICIALS' INITIALS

Initials	Dates	Names
BZ	1623-24	B. Zwirner
FBDL	1664	Franz Baron de Lisola
FBL	1664-65	Franz Baron de Lisola
GFH, G	1678-79, 1709	George Franz Hoffmann, die-cutter
HR	1624-35	Hans Riedel, warden
HT	1623-24	H. Tuchmann
HZ	1632-35	Hans Ziesler
IE	Ca.1683	Jan Engelhart
IZ	1630-34	Johann Ziesler
IZHZ	1631-34	Hans Ziesler
MI	1637-46	Michael Jan, warden
MMW	1692-1702	M.M.v. Wackerl
SHS, SH	1664-91	Salomon Hammerschmidt, warden

MINT OFFICIALS' PRIVY MARKS

Privy Mark	Description	Dates	Names
AT	Stylized AT	1625-26	Andreas Tschorr
(b) -	Metal hook	1627, 1635-36	Johann Ziesler
(bh) - HZ	H battle axe Z	1635-37	Hans Ziesler
(cb) -	Crossed halberd	1627-33, 1636	Johan Ziesler
(2ch)	2 crossed halberds		
(3ch)	3 crossed halberds		
(cbh)	HZ, crossed halberd	1636	Hans Ziesler
(f) -	Flags	1628-34	Johann Ziesler
(fa) - H-Z	HZ above flags	1633-36	Hans Ziesler
(fb) - H Z	Flags between H and Z	1636	Hans Ziesler
(fl) -	GH, double fleur de lis in circle	1648-64	Georg Hubner, warden
(g) - GR	Goose in circle	1637-67	Georg Reichart
(h)	HR monogram		
(ha)	Halberd		
(hp)	HP monogram		
(ht)	HT monogram		
(p)	PH monogram		

BRIEG MINT

(Breh, Brzeg)
(in Silesia)

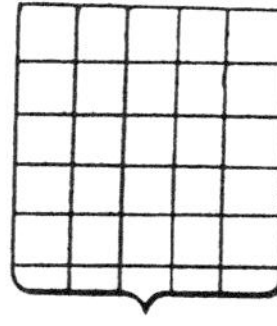

Coat of arms in legend.

MINT MARKS

Initials	Dates	Name
MB	1693-1702	
MBL	1665	

MINT OFFICIALS' INITIALS

Initials	Dates	Name
CB	1677-1713	Christoph Brettschneider

GLOGAU MINT

(Glogow, Hlohov)
(in Silesia)

Large coat of arms, like Vienna, on imperial eagle's breast. Legend usually ends MO.

MINT MARK

G - Glogau, 1623

MINT OFFICIALS' INITIALS

Initials	Dates	Names
BZ	1623	B. Zwirner
HR, ligate HR	-	Hans Riedel
IH, IIH	1623	J. J. Huser
II	1625	J. Jamnitzer

MINT OFFICIALS' PRIVY MARKS

Privy Mark	Description	Dates	Names
(m) -	4 above M	-	Matthaus Jachtmann
(p) - Z	ZP monogram	-	Zacharius Petzold

NEISSE MINT

(Nysa, Nisa)
(in Silesia)

Large coat of arms, like Vienna, on imperial eagle's breast. Legend usually ends MO.CO.T.

MINT OFFICIALS' INITIALS

Initials	Dates	Names
BZ	1623-24	Balthasar Zwirner
DVB	1624-25	D. V. Bren

MINT OFFICIALS' PRIVY MARKS

Privy Mark	Description	Dates	Names
(dt)	Double trefoil		-
(f)	Varieties of fleur de lis	1622-25	-
(s)	Star & star in crescents	1622-24	-

OELS MINT

(Olesnica, Olesnice)
(in Silesia)

Revolutionary types of Friedrich von der Pfalz

MINT OFFICIALS' PRIVY MARKS

Privy mark	Description	Date	Name
HT -	Ligate HT	1621	Hans Tuchmann

OPPELN MINT

(Opole, Opoli)
(in Silesia)

Large coat of arms, like Vienna, on imperial eagle's breast or coat of arms, like Breslau, on minor types without eagle. Legend usually ends CO.T or CO.TY.

MINT MARKS

(f) - - double fleur de lis

MINT OFFICIALS' INITIALS

Initials	Dates	Names
FIK	1673-85	Franz Ignaz Kirschenhofer, Warden
FN	1699-1705	Franz Nowak, warden
SF	1625	Salomon Franzel, warden

MINT OFFICIALS' PRIVY MARKS

Privy Marks	Description	Dates	Names
MMW	MMW	1685-99	Martin Max. v. Wackerl, warden

RATIBOR MINT

(Raciborz)
(in Silesia)

Large coat of arms, like Vienna on imperial eagle's breast. Legend ends TY.

MINT OFFICIALS' INITIALS

Initials	Dates	Names
DR, R	1624-25	D. Raschke
SD	1624-25	S. Dyringer

SAGAN MINT

(Zagan, Zahan)
(in Silesia)

Large coat of arms, like Vienna on imperial eagle's breast. Legend ends CO.TY.

MINT OFFICIALS' INITIALS

Initials	Dates	Names
GE	-	Gottfried Ehrlich, warden
HDM	1625	-

MINT OFFICIALS' PRIVY MARKS

Privy Marks	Description	Dates	Names
VM VM	VM	1625	
HZ, IZ	3 crossed metal hooks	1628-29	Jan Ziesler
(f) -	Metal hook	1629-31	Jan Henryk Jacob
(h)	Halberd		

SCHWEIDNITZ MINT

MINT OFFICIALS' INITIALS

Initial	Date	Name
	1525-28	Paul Monau and Konrad Saurman
AE, AHE	1743-51	Adam Heinrich von Ehrenberg
D	1735-67	Ignaz Donner, die-cutter and medailleur

ARMS:

Eagle with crescent on breast, sometimes with small cross on crescent.

REFERENCES

Ferdinand Friedensburg and Hans Seger, ***Schlesiens Münzen und Medaillen der Neueren Zeit***, Breslau, 1901 (reprint Frankfurt/Main)

Norbert Jaschke and Fritz P. Maercker, ***Schlesische Münzen und Medaillen***, Ihringen, 1985.

Viktor Miller zu Aichholz, A. Loehr, E. Holzmaair, ***Österreichische Münzprägungen 1519-1938,*** 2 vols., 2nd edn., Chicago, 1981

Hugo Frhr. Von Saurma-Jeltsch, ***Die Saurmasche Münzsammlung deutscher, schweizerischer und polnischer Gepräge von etwa dem Beginn der Groschenzeit bis zur Kipperperiode***, Berlin, 1892

Hugo Frhr. Von Saurma-Jeltsch, ***Schlesische Münzen und Medaillen***, Breslau, 1883.

Wolfgang Schulten, ***Deutsche Münzen aus der Zeit Karls V.***, Frankfurt am Main, 1974

DUCHY

STANDARD COINAGE

MB# 62 HELLER

Silver **Ruler:** Rudolf II **Obv:** Crowned 'M' divides date **Mint:** Breslau **Note:** Uniface. S/Sch#82-83, 90-99.

Date	Mintage	VG	F	VF	XF	Unc
160Z	—	7.00	15.00	25.00	50.00	—
1603	—	7.00	15.00	25.00	50.00	—
1604	—	7.00	15.00	25.00	50.00	—

KM# 1 HELLER

Silver **Ruler:** Rudolf II **Obv:** Crowned 'R' divides mint marks, date below **Mint:** Breslau **Note:** Uniface. S/Sch.# 101-102, 104-106. Varieties exist.

Date	Mintage	VG	F	VF	XF	Unc
1605 RB	—	7.00	15.00	25.00	50.00	—
1606	—	7.00	15.00	25.00	50.00	—
1608	—	7.00	15.00	25.00	50.00	—
1609	—	7.00	15.00	25.00	50.00	—
1610	—	7.00	15.00	25.00	50.00	—

KM# 2 HELLER

Silver **Ruler:** Matthias **Obv:** Crowned 'M' divides B-B or R-B, date below **Mint:** Breslau **Note:** Uniface. S/Sch#107-109.

Date	Mintage	VG	F	VF	XF	Unc
1613	—	8.00	16.00	20.00	60.00	—
1614	—	8.00	16.00	20.00	60.00	—
1617	—	8.00	16.00	20.00	60.00	—

KM# 3 HELLER

Silver **Ruler:** Ferdinand II **Obv:** Crowned FII divides R - B, date below **Mint:** Breslau **Note:** Uniface. S/Sch#114.

Date	Mintage	VG	F	VF	XF	Unc
1619	—	10.00	20.00	40.00	80.00	—

KM# 377 HELLER

Billon **Ruler:** Ferdinand III **Obv:** Crowned Gothic Y in center circle **Rev:** Crowned eagle in inner circle, date in legend **Mint:** Teschen **Note:** Prev. Austria KM#970 (1690). Varieties exist.

Date	Mintage	VG	F	VF	XF	Unc
1650	—	6.00	12.00	20.00	40.00	—
1651	—	6.00	12.00	20.00	40.00	—
1652	—	6.00	12.00	20.00	40.00	—
1653	—	6.00	12.00	20.00	40.00	—
1654	—	6.00	12.00	20.00	40.00	—
1655	—	6.00	12.00	20.00	40.00	—

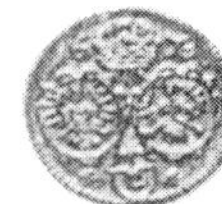

KM# 510 4 HELLER (Vierer)

Billon **Ruler:** Leopold I **Obv:** Crown divides date above two shields of arms, value below **Mint:** Oppeln **Note:** Prev. Austria #1277 (KM#1276). Varieties exist.

Date	Mintage	VG	F	VF	XF	Unc
1674	—	8.00	16.00	35.00	70.00	—
1675	—	8.00	16.00	35.00	70.00	—
1676	—	8.00	16.00	35.00	70.00	—
1677 FIK	—	8.00	16.00	35.00	70.00	—
1678	—	8.00	16.00	35.00	70.00	—
1679	—	8.00	16.00	35.00	70.00	—
1681	—	8.00	16.00	35.00	70.00	—
1684	—	8.00	16.00	35.00	70.00	—
1686	—	8.00	16.00	35.00	70.00	—
1689	—	8.00	16.00	35.00	70.00	—
1691	—	8.00	16.00	35.00	70.00	—

KM# 534 4 HELLER (Vierer)

Billon **Ruler:** Leopold I **Obv:** Date divided at bottom **Mint:** Oppeln **Note:** Prev. Austria KM#1300 (KM#1278).

Date	Mintage	VG	F	VF	XF	Unc
1678	—	15.00	30.00	60.00	—	—

KM# 540 4 HELLER (Vierer)

Billon **Ruler:** Leopold I **Mint:** Oppeln **Note:** Prev. Austria KM#1301 (KM#1277). Klippe of Austria KM#1277.

Date	Mintage	VG	F	VF	XF	Unc
1679	—	15.00	30.00	60.00	—	—

KM# 648 4 HELLER (Vierer)

Billon **Ruler:** Leopold I **Obv:** Orb with value **Mint:** Oppeln **Note:** Prev. Austria KM#1396 (KM#1275).

Date	Mintage	VG	F	VF	XF	Unc
1699	—	15.00	30.00	60.00	—	—

KM# 72 PFENNIG

Billon **Ruler:** Ferdinand II **Obv:** Straight-sided shield divides date in diamond, F above shield, HR below **Mint:** Breslau **Note:** Uniface. Prev. Austria KM#465 (KM#10).

Date	Mintage	VG	F	VF	XF	Unc
1624 W-(h)	—	12.50	25.00	45.00	65.00	—
1624 HR-W	—	12.50	25.00	45.00	65.00	—
1624 (h)	—	12.50	25.00	45.00	65.00	—
1624 W	—	12.50	25.00	45.00	65.00	—
1625 (h)	—	12.50	25.00	45.00	65.00	—

KM# 162 PFENNIG

Billon **Ruler:** Ferdinand II **Obv:** Shield with concave sides **Mint:** Breslau **Note:** Uniface. Prev. Austria KM#561 (KM#11).

Date	Mintage	VG	F	VF	XF	Unc
1625 (h)	—	12.50	25.00	40.00	65.00	—

KM# 54 2 PFENNIG

Billon **Ruler:** Ferdinand II **Obv:** Crown with arabesque below, above two shields, crown divides date **Mint:** Neisse **Note:** Uniface. Varieties exist. Prev. Austria KM#436 (KM#1195).

Date	Mintage	VG	F	VF	XF	Unc
1623 (dt)	—	20.00	40.00	85.00	150	—
1624 (dt)	—	20.00	40.00	85.00	150	—
1625 (dt)	—	20.00	40.00	85.00	150	—

KM# 75 2 PFENNIG

Billon **Ruler:** Ferdinand II **Obv:** Crown above two shields, in trilobe, crown divides date **Mint:** Breslau **Note:** Uniface. Varieties exist. Prev. Austria KM#468 (KM#12).

Date	Mintage	VG	F	VF	XF	Unc
1624 HR	—	15.00	30.00	55.00	80.00	—

KM# 78 2 PFENNIG

Billon **Ruler:** Ferdinand II **Obv:** Date above crown **Mint:** Breslau **Note:** Prev. Austria KM#469 (KM#13).

Date	Mintage	VG	F	VF	XF	Unc
1624 W	—	15.00	30.00	55.00	80.00	—

KM# 81 2 PFENNIG

Billon **Ruler:** Ferdinand II **Rev:** "IIH" **Mint:** Neisse **Note:** Prev. Austria KM#470 (KM#1196).

Date	Mintage	VG	F	VF	XF	Unc
1624 (dt)	—	20.00	40.00	85.00	150	—

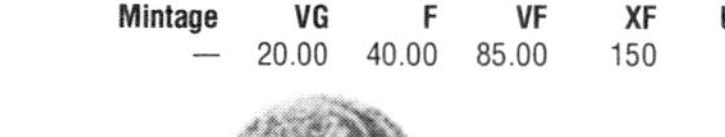

KM# 165 2 PFENNIG

Billon **Ruler:** Ferdinand II **Obv:** Crown above two shields tilted inward **Mint:** Breslau **Note:** Prev. Austria KM#562 (KM#14).

Date	Mintage	VG	F	VF	XF	Unc
1625 HR	—	12.50	27.50	20.00	75.00	—

KM# 168 2 PFENNIG

Billon **Ruler:** Ferdinand II **Obv:** Arabesque below crown, shields tilted slightly **Mint:** Breslau **Note:** Prev. Austria KM#563 (KM#15).

Date	Mintage	VG	F	VF	XF	Unc
1625 HR	—	12.50	27.50	50.00	75.00	—
1627 W (h)	—	12.50	27.50	50.00	75.00	—
1628 IIH	—	12.50	27.50	50.00	75.00	—
1643 MI	—	12.50	27.50	50.00	75.00	—

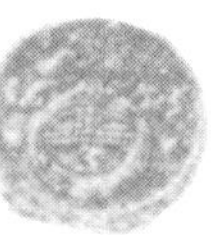
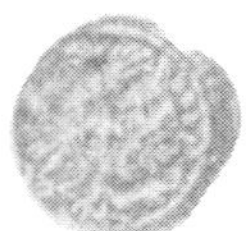

KM# 93 3 PFENNIG

Billon **Ruler:** Ferdinand II **Obv:** Orb with value within, date divided by orb **Rev:** Imperial eagle **Mint:** Glogau **Note:** Prev. Austria KM#472 (KM#325). Varieties exist with and without dots in and around orb.

Date	Mintage	VG	F	VF	XF	Unc
1624	—	7.00	12.00	22.00	45.00	—
1625 II	—	7.00	12.00	22.00	45.00	—
1625 DR	—	7.00	12.00	22.00	45.00	—

KM# 84.1 3 PFENNIG

Billon **Ruler:** Ferdinand II **Obv:** Orb with value within divides date **Rev:** Imperial eagle with arms on breast **Mint:** Breslau **Note:** Prev. Austria KM#471.1 (KM#16.1).

Date	Mintage	VG	F	VF	XF	Unc
1624	—	15.00	32.50	60.00	90.00	—

KM# 84.2 3 PFENNIG

Billon **Ruler:** Ferdinand II **Mint:** Breslau **Note:** Prev. Austria KM#471.2 (KM#16.2). Privy mark on obverse and reverse.

Date	Mintage	VG	F	VF	XF	Unc
1624 (h)	—	15.00	32.50	60.00	90.00	—

KM# 84.3 3 PFENNIG

Billon **Ruler:** Ferdinand II **Mint:** Breslau **Note:** Prev. Austria KM#471.3 (KM#16.3). Privy mark on obverse.

Date	Mintage	VG	F	VF	XF	Unc
1624 (h)	—	15.00	32.50	60.00	90.00	—
1625 (h)	—	15.00	32.50	60.00	90.00	—

KM# 96 3 PFENNIG

Billon **Ruler:** Ferdinand II **Obv:** Orb with value wihtin divides date **Rev:** Imperial eagle **Mint:** Neisse **Note:** Prev. Austria KM#473 (KM#1197).

Date	Mintage	VG	F	VF	XF	Unc
1624 (dt)	—	15.00	30.00	85.00	150	—
1624 IIH	—	15.00	30.00	85.00	150	—

Note: Dots may appear in top quarter of orb or in field

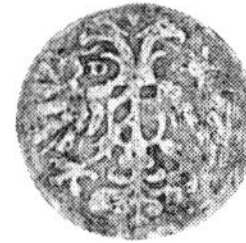

KM# 183 3 PFENNIG

Billon **Ruler:** Ferdinand II **Obv:** Orb with value within divides date in diamond **Mint:** Neisse **Note:** Prev. Austria KM#567 (KM#1198). Varieties exist.

Date	Mintage	VG	F	VF	XF	Unc
1625 DVB	—	15.00	30.00	85.00	150	—

KM# 186 3 PFENNIG

Billon **Ruler:** Ferdinand II **Obv:** Orb with value within, date divided by orb **Rev:** Crowned imperial eagle **Mint:** Oppeln **Note:** Prev. Austria KM#568 (KM#1265). Varieties exist.

Date	Mintage	VG	F	VF	XF	Unc
1625 SF Rare	—	—	—	—	—	—

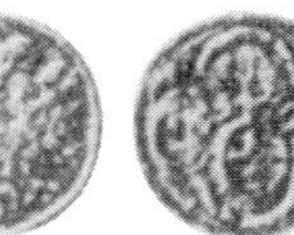

KM# 189 3 PFENNIG

Billon **Ruler:** Ferdinand II **Obv:** Orb with value within divides date in quatrefoil **Mint:** Oppeln **Note:** Prev. Austria KM#569 (KM#1266). Varieties exist.

Date	Mintage	VG	F	VF	XF	Unc
1625 SF Rare	—	—	—	—	—	—

KM# 192 3 PFENNIG

Billon, 16.5 mm. **Ruler:** Ferdinand II **Obv:** Imperial eagle **Rev:** Orb with value within, arched date divided by orb **Mint:** Sagan **Note:** Prev. Austria KM#570 (KM#1580).

Date	Mintage	VG	F	VF	XF	Unc
1625 (h) Rare	—	—	—	—	—	—

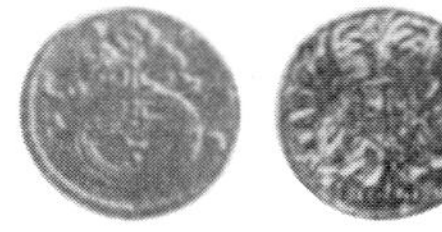

KM# 195 3 PFENNIG

Billon **Ruler:** Ferdinand II **Obv:** Straight date divided by orb **Mint:** Sagan **Note:** Prev. Austria KM#571 (KM#1581).

Date	Mintage	VG	F	VF	XF	Unc
1625 (h) Rare	—	—	—	—	—	—

KM# 198 3 PFENNIG

Billon **Ruler:** Ferdinand II **Obv:** Orb with value within, arched date divided by orb, all in diamond **Mint:** Sagan **Note:** Prev. Austria KM#572 (KM#1582).

Date	Mintage	VG	F	VF	XF	Unc
1625 VM Rare	—	—	—	—	—	—

KM# 84.4 3 PFENNIG

Billon **Ruler:** Ferdinand II **Rev:** Two dots and two crosses **Mint:** Breslau **Note:** Prev. Austria KM#471.4 (KM#16.4).

Date	Mintage	VG	F	VF	XF	Unc
1625 AT	—	15.00	32.50	60.00	90.00	—

KM# 84.5 3 PFENNIG

Billon **Ruler:** Ferdinand II **Rev:** Four dots **Mint:** Breslau **Note:** Prev. Austria KM#471.5 (KM#16.5).

Date	Mintage	VG	F	VF	XF	Unc
1625 AT	—	15.00	32.50	60.00	90.00	—

KM# 84.6 3 PFENNIG

Billon **Ruler:** Ferdinand II **Rev:** Four crosses **Mint:** Breslau **Note:** Prev. Austria KM#471.6 (KM#16.6).

Date	Mintage	VG	F	VF	XF	Unc
1625 AT	—	15.00	32.50	60.00	90.00	—

KM# 84.7 3 PFENNIG

Billon **Ruler:** Ferdinand II **Rev:** Four rosettes **Mint:** Breslau **Note:** Prev. Austria KM#471.7 (16.7).

Date	Mintage	VG	F	VF	XF	Unc
1625 AT	—	15.00	32.50	60.00	90.00	—

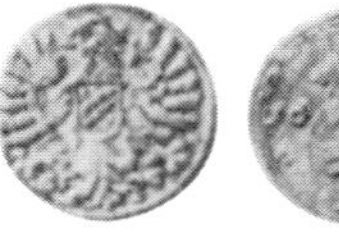

KM# 372 3 PFENNIG

Billon **Ruler:** Ferdinand III **Obv:** Displayed eale with arms on breast **Rev:** Orb with value within; date divided at sides **Mint:** Teschen **Note:** Prev. Austria KM#965 (KM#1691). Varieites exist.

Date	Mintage	VG	F	VF	XF	Unc
1649	—	5.00	10.00	20.00	40.00	—
1650	—	5.00	10.00	20.00	40.00	—

KM# 378 3 PFENNIG

Billon **Ruler:** Ferdinand III **Obv:** Orb divides date in diamond; ornamentation in outer fields **Mint:** Teschen **Note:** Prev. Austria KM#971 (KM#1692).

Date	Mintage	VG	F	VF	XF	Unc
1650	—	5.00	10.00	20.00	40.00	—
1651	—	5.00	10.00	20.00	40.00	—
1652	—	5.00	10.00	20.00	40.00	—
1653	—	5.00	10.00	20.00	40.00	—
1654	—	5.00	10.00	20.00	40.00	—
1655	—	5.00	10.00	200	40.00	—

KM# 438 3 PFENNIG

Billon **Ruler:** Leopold I **Obv:** Orb with value within divides date, ornamentation at sides **Mint:** Oppeln **Note:** Prev. Austria KM#1279, (1184). Varieties exist.

Date	Mintage	VG	F	VF	XF	Unc
1661	—	9.00	20.00	40.00	80.00	—
1663	—	9.00	20.00	40.00	80.00	—
1668	—	9.00	20.00	40.00	80.00	—
1669	—	9.00	20.00	40.00	80.00	—
1670	—	9.00	20.00	40.00	80.00	—
1671	—	9.00	20.00	40.00	80.00	—
1672	—	9.00	20.00	40.00	80.00	—
1673	—	9.00	20.00	40.00	80.00	—
1674	—	9.00	20.00	40.00	80.00	—
1679	—	9.00	20.00	40.00	80.00	—

Date	Mintage	VG	F	VF	XF	Unc
1680	—	9.00	20.00	40.00	80.00	—
1681	—	9.00	20.00	40.00	80.00	—
1682	—	9.00	20.00	40.00	80.00	—
1683	—	9.00	20.00	40.00	80.00	—
1684	—	9.00	20.00	40.00	80.00	—
1686	—	9.00	20.00	40.00	80.00	—
1687	—	9.00	20.00	40.00	80.00	—
1688	—	9.00	20.00	40.00	80.00	—
1689	—	9.00	20.00	40.00	80.00	—
1690	—	9.00	20.00	40.00	80.00	—
1691	—	9.00	20.00	40.00	80.00	—
1692	—	9.00	20.00	40.00	80.00	—
1693	—	9.00	20.00	40.00	80.00	—
1694	—	9.00	20.00	40.00	80.00	—
1695	—	9.00	20.00	40.00	80.00	—
1696	—	9.00	20.00	40.00	80.00	—
1697	—	9.00	20.00	40.00	80.00	—

KM# 594 3 PFENNIG

Silver **Ruler:** Leopold I **Obv:** Imperial eagle with arms on breast **Rev:** Value within orb dividing date **Mint:** Brieg **Note:** Prev. Austria KM#170 (KM#1365). Varieties exist.

Date	Mintage	VG	F	VF	XF	Unc
1693MB	—	8.00	16.00	35.00	75.00	—
1694MB	—	8.00	16.00	35.00	75.00	—
1695MB	—	8.00	16.00	35.00	75.00	—
1696MB	—	8.00	16.00	35.00	75.00	—
1697MB	—	8.00	16.00	35.00	75.00	—

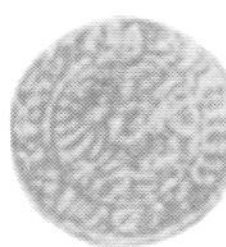

KM# 99 KREUZER

Silver **Ruler:** Ferdinand II **Obv:** Laureate bust right in inner circle **Rev:** Crowned imperial eagle with value on breast in inner circle, date in legend **Mint:** Breslau **Note:** Prev. Austira KM#477 (KM#19).

Date	Mintage	VG	F	VF	XF	Unc
1624 W	—	10.00	20.00	35.00	60.00	—
1625 W	—	10.00	20.00	35.00	60.00	—

KM# 102 KREUZER

Silver **Ruler:** Ferdinand II **Rev:** Privy mark added **Mint:** Breslau **Note:** Prev. Austria KM#478 (KM#20). Varieties exist.

Date	Mintage	VG	F	VF	XF	Unc
1624 W-HR	—	10.00	20.00	35.00	60.00	—
1625 W-(h)	—	10.00	20.00	35.00	60.00	—
1625 W-HR	—	10.00	20.00	35.00	60.00	—
1626 W-(h)	—	10.00	20.00	35.00	60.00	—
1627 W-(h)	—	10.00	20.00	35.00	60.00	—
1627 W(ha)-(h)	—	10.00	20.00	35.00	60.00	—
1632 W-HZ	—	10.00	20.00	35.00	60.00	—
1632 W-(3ch)	—	10.00	20.00	35.00	60.00	—
1633 W-(3ch)	—	10.00	20.00	35.00	60.00	—
1633 HZ-(3ch)	—	10.00	20.00	35.00	60.00	—
1633 W-HZ	—	10.00	20.00	35.00	60.00	—
1633 HZ-HZ	—	10.00	20.00	35.00	60.00	—
1635 (ha)	—	10.00	20.00	35.00	60.00	—
1636 (ha)	—	10.00	20.00	35.00	60.00	—

KM# 111 KREUZER

Silver **Ruler:** Ferdinand II **Obv:** Laureate bust right in inner circle **Rev:** Crowned imperial eagle with value on breast in inner circle; dates in legend **Mint:** Ratibor **Note:** Prev. Austria KM#485 (KM#1565).

Date	Mintage	VG	F	VF	XF	Unc
1624 SD Rare	—	—	—	—	—	—
1625 SD Rare	—	—	—	—	—	—

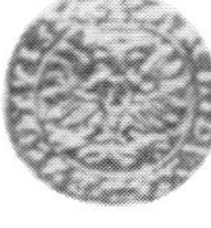

KM# 105 KREUZER

Silver **Ruler:** Ferdinand II **Obv:** Laureate bust right in inner circle **Rev:** Crowned imperial eagle with value on breast in inner circle, date in legend **Mint:** Neisse **Note:** Prev. Austria KM#482 (KM#1199).

Date	Mintage	VG	F	VF	XF	Unc
1624 BZ	—	15.00	30.00	65.00	125	—
1624 BZ/dt)	—	15.00	30.00	65.00	125	—
1624 (dt) BZ	—	15.00	30.00	65.00	125	—
1624 IIH	—	15.00	30.00	65.00	125	—
1624 DVB/(dt)	—	15.00	30.00	65.00	125	—
1624 DVB	—	15.00	30.00	65.00	125	—

KM# 108 KREUZER

Silver **Ruler:** Ferdinand II **Rev:** Coat of arms below eagle **Mint:** Neisse **Note:** Prev. Austria KM#483 (KM#1200).

Date	Mintage	VG	F	VF	XF	Unc
1624 BZ	—	15.00	30.00	65.00	125	—
1624 BZ/(dt)	—	15.00	30.00	65.00	125	—

KM# 207 KREUZER

Silver **Ruler:** Ferdinand II **Rev:** Shield of arms on cross in inner circle, date in legend **Mint:** Oppeln **Note:** Prev. Austria KM#579 (KM#1268).

Date	Mintage	VG	F	VF	XF	Unc
1625 SF Rare	—	—	—	—	—	—

KM# 210 KREUZER

Silver **Ruler:** Ferdinand II **Obv:** Shield of arms on cross in inner circle; date in legend **Mint:** Ratibor **Note:** Prev. Austria KM#580 (KM#1566). Varieties exist.

Date	Mintage	VG	F	VF	XF	Unc
1625 SD Rare	—	—	—	—	—	—

KM# 201 KREUZER

Silver **Ruler:** Ferdinand II **Rev:** Value on imperial eagle shield on double cross **Mint:** Neisse **Note:** Prev. Austria KM#576 (KM#1201).

Date	Mintage	VG	F	VF	XF	Unc
1625 DVB	—	12.00	25.00	45.00	90.00	—
1625 DVB/(dt)	—	12.00	25.00	45.00	90.00	—

KM# 204 KREUZER

Silver **Ruler:** Ferdinand II **Obv:** Laureate bust right in inner circle **Rev:** Crowned imperial eagle with value on breast, date in legend **Mint:** Oppeln **Note:** Prev. Austria KM#578 (KM#1267). Varieties exist.

Date	Mintage	VG	F	VF	XF	Unc
1625 (dt) Rare	—	—	—	—	—	—
1625 SF Rare	—	—	—	—	—	—

KM# 333 KREUZER

Silver **Ruler:** Ferdinand III **Mint:** Breslau **Note:** Prev. Austria KM#828 (KM#60). Varieties exist.

Date	Mintage	VG	F	VF	XF	Unc
1637	—	10.00	20.00	35.00	70.00	—
1638	—	10.00	20.00	35.00	70.00	—
1639	—	10.00	20.00	35.00	70.00	—
1640	—	10.00	20.00	35.00	70.00	—
1641	—	10.00	20.00	35.00	70.00	—
1642	—	10.00	20.00	35.00	70.00	—
1643	—	10.00	20.00	35.00	70.00	—
1644	—	10.00	20.00	35.00	70.00	—
1649	—	10.00	20.00	35.00	70.00	—
1651	—	10.00	20.00	35.00	70.00	—
1652	—	10.00	20.00	35.00	70.00	—
1653	—	10.00	20.00	35.00	70.00	—
1654	—	10.00	20.00	35.00	70.00	—

KM# 363 KREUZER

Silver **Ruler:** Ferdinand III **Obv:** Laureate bust in inner circle, value below **Rev:** Crowned arms in inner circle, date in legend **Mint:** Teschen **Note:** Prev. Austria KM#919 (KM#1693). Varieties exist.

Date	Mintage	VG	F	VF	XF	Unc
1644	—	8.00	16.00	35.00	60.00	—
1645	—	8.00	16.00	35.00	60.00	—
1646	—	8.00	16.00	35.00	60.00	—
1647	—	8.00	16.00	35.00	60.00	—
1648	—	8.00	16.00	35.00	60.00	—
1649	—	8.00	16.00	35.00	60.00	—

KM# 405 KREUZER

Silver **Ruler:** Leopold I **Obv:** Laureate bust right in inner circle **Rev:** Crowned imperial eagle with value on breast, date in legend **Mint:** Breslau **Note:** Prev. Austria KM#1132 (KM#75). Varieties exist.

Date	Mintage	VG	F	VF	XF	Unc
1659 G-H	—	8.00	16.00	35.00	85.00	—
1660 G-H	—	8.00	16.00	35.00	85.00	—
1661 G-H	—	8.00	16.00	35.00	85.00	—
1665 S-H	—	8.00	16.00	35.00	85.00	—

KM# 498 KREUZER

Silver **Ruler:** Leopold I **Rev:** Crown divides date **Mint:** Breslau **Note:** Prev. Austria KM#1267 (KM#76). Varieties exist.

Date	Mintage	VG	F	VF	XF	Unc
1670	—	7.00	15.00	30.00	60.00	—
1671	—	7.00	15.00	30.00	60.00	—
1672	—	7.00	15.00	30.00	60.00	—
1698	—	7.00	15.00	30.00	60.00	—
1699	—	7.00	15.00	30.00	60.00	—

KM# 606 KREUZER

Silver **Ruler:** Leopold I **Obv:** Laureate bust right in inner circle **Rev:** Crowned imperial eagle with value on breast, crown divides date **Mint:** Brieg **Note:** Prev. Austria KM#171 (1373). Varieties exist.

Date	Mintage	VG	F	VF	XF	Unc
1694 CB	—	8.00	16.00	35.00	75.00	—
1696 CB	—	8.00	16.00	35.00	75.00	—
1697 CB	—	8.00	16.00	35.00	75.00	—
1698 CB	—	8.00	16.00	35.00	75.00	—
1699 CB	—	8.00	16.00	35.00	75.00	—
1700 CB	—	8.00	16.00	35.00	75.00	—

KM# 612 KREUZER

Silver **Ruler:** Leopold I **Obv:** Bust right in inner circle **Obv. Legend:** LEOPOLDVS • D • G • R • I • S • ... **Rev:** Crowned imperial eagle with value on breast in inner circle, crown divides date **Mint:** Oppeln **Note:** Prev. Austria KM#1280 (1382). Varieties exist.

Date	Mintage	VG	F	VF	XF	Unc
1695	—	11.00	22.00	45.00	90.00	—
1697	—	11.00	22.00	45.00	90.00	—
1698	—	11.00	22.00	45.00	90.00	—
1698 FN	—	11.00	22.00	45.00	90.00	—
1699 FN	—	11.00	22.00	45.00	90.00	—
1700 FN	—	11.00	22.00	45.00	90.00	—

KM# 639 KREUZER

Silver **Ruler:** Leopold I **Obv:** Without inner circle **Mint:** Brieg **Note:** Prev. Austria KM#1394 (KM#172).

Date	Mintage	VG	F	VF	XF	Unc
1697 CB	—	—	—	—	—	—

KM# 36 3 KREUZER

Silver **Ruler:** Ferdinand II **Mint:** Breslau **Note:** Prev. Austria KM#385 (KM#21).

Date	Mintage	VG	F	VF	XF	Unc
1622	—	15.00	30.00	45.00	75.00	—
1623	—	15.00	30.00	45.00	75.00	—

KM# 39 3 KREUZER

Silver **Ruler:** Ferdinand II **Obv:** Orb **Rev:** Value below Silesian eagle **Mint:** Breslau **Note:** Prev. Austria KM#386 (KM#22).

Date	Mintage	VG	F	VF	XF	Unc
1622	—	15.00	30.00	45.00	75.00	—

KM# 42 3 KREUZER

Silver **Ruler:** Ferdinand II **Mint:** Neisse **Note:** 3 Kipper Kreuzer. Similar to KM#495. Prev. Austria KM#392 (KM#1202).

Date	Mintage	VG	F	VF	XF	Unc
1622	—	12.00	25.00	45.00	90.00	—

KM# 114 3 KREUZER

Silver **Ruler:** Ferdinand II **Obv:** Laureate bust right in inner circle **Rev:** Crowned imperial eagle in inner circle, date in legend, value at bottom **Mint:** Breslau **Note:** Prev. Austria KM#491 (KM#23). Varieties exist.

Date	Mintage	VG	F	VF	XF	Unc
1624	—	12.00	25.00	40.00	75.00	—
1624 HR	—	12.00	25.00	40.00	75.00	—
1624 BZ	—	12.00	25.00	40.00	75.00	—
1624 W	—	12.00	25.00	40.00	75.00	—
1624 BZ-HT	—	12.00	25.00	40.00	75.00	—
1624 BZ-HR	—	12.00	25.00	40.00	75.00	—
1625	—	12.00	25.00	40.00	75.00	—
1625 AT	—	12.00	25.00	40.00	75.00	—
1625 W	—	12.00	25.00	40.00	75.00	—
1625 HR	—	12.00	25.00	40.00	75.00	—
1626 HR	—	12.00	25.00	40.00	75.00	—
1627 HR	—	12.00	25.00	40.00	75.00	—
1627 (ch)-HR	—	12.00	25.00	40.00	75.00	—
1627 (h)-HR	—	12.00	25.00	40.00	75.00	—
1628 (ch)-(h)	—	12.00	25.00	40.00	75.00	—
1629 (ch)-(h)	—	12.00	25.00	40.00	75.00	—
1630 (2ch)-HR	—	12.00	25.00	40.00	75.00	—
1630 (3ch)-HR	—	12.00	25.00	40.00	75.00	—
1631 (3ch)-HR	—	12.00	25.00	40.00	75.00	—
1632 (3ch)-HR	—	12.00	25.00	40.00	75.00	—
1632 (3ch)-HZ	—	12.00	25.00	40.00	75.00	—
1633 (3ch)-HZ	—	12.00	25.00	40.00	75.00	—
1634 (3ch)-HZ	—	12.00	25.00	40.00	75.00	—
1635 HZ	—	12.00	25.00	40.00	75.00	—
1635 H(ha)-Z	—	12.00	25.00	40.00	75.00	—
1636 H(3ch)-Z	—	12.00	25.00	40.00	75.00	—
1636 H(ha)-Z	—	12.00	25.00	40.00	75.00	—
1637 H(ha)-Z	—	12.00	25.00	40.00	75.00	—
ND HR	—	12.00	25.00	40.00	75.00	—

KM# 117 3 KREUZER

Silver **Ruler:** Ferdinand II **Obv:** Without privy mark or denomination **Rev:** Without privy mark or denomination **Mint:** Breslau **Note:** Prev. Austria KM#492 (KM#25).

Date	Mintage	VG	F	VF	XF	Unc
1624	—	—	—	—	—	—

KM# 120 3 KREUZER

Silver **Ruler:** Ferdinand II **Mint:** Neisse **Note:** Prev. Austria KM#495 (KM#1203). Varieties exist.

Date	Mintage	VG	F	VF	XF	Unc
1624 BZ	—	12.00	25.00	45.00	90.00	—
1624 IIH	—	12.00	25.00	45.00	90.00	—
1624 DVB/(dt)	—	12.00	25.00	45.00	90.00	—
1624 DVB	—	12.00	25.00	45.00	90.00	—
1625 DVB/(dt)	—	12.00	25.00	45.00	90.00	—
1625 DVB	—	12.00	25.00	45.00	90.00	—

KM# 213 3 KREUZER

Silver **Ruler:** Ferdinand II **Obv:** Value below bust **Mint:** Breslau **Note:** Prev. Austria KM#581 (KM#27). Varieties exist.

Date	Mintage	VG	F	VF	XF	Unc
1625 HR	—	12.00	25.00	40.00	70.00	—
1626 HR	—	12.00	25.00	40.00	70.00	—
1627 HR	—	12.00	25.00	40.00	70.00	—
1629	—	12.00	25.00	40.00	70.00	—
1630	—	12.00	25.00	4.00	70.00	—
1631	—	12.00	25.00	40.00	70.00	—
1632	—	12.00	25.00	40.00	70.00	—
1633	—	12.00	25.00	40.00	70.00	—
1634	—	12.00	25.00	40.00	70.00	—
1635	—	12.00	25.00	40.00	70.00	—
1636	—	12.00	25.00	40.00	70.00	—
1637	—	12.00	25.00	40.00	70.00	—

KM# 216 3 KREUZER

Silver **Ruler:** Ferdinand II **Obv:** Laureate bust right in inner circle, value below **Rev:** Crowned imperial eagle in inner circle, date in legend **Mint:** Oppeln **Note:** Prev. Austria KM#585 (KM#1269). Varieties exist.

Date	Mintage	VG	F	VF	XF	Unc
1625 SF Rare	—	—	—	—	—	—

KM# 222 3 KREUZER

Silver **Ruler:** Ferdinand II **Obv:** Laureate bust right in inner circle **Rev:** Crowned imperial eagle in inner circle, value below, date in legend **Mint:** Ratibor **Note:** Prev. Austria KM#587 (KM#1567). Varieties exist.

Date	Mintage	VG	F	VF	XF	Unc
1625 SD Rare	—	—	—	—	—	—

KM# 225 3 KREUZER

Silver **Ruler:** Ferdinand II **Obv:** Laureate bust right in inner circle **Rev:** Crowned imperial eagle in inner circle; value below, date in legend **Mint:** Sagan **Note:** Prev. Austria KM#588 (KM#1583). Varieties exist.

Date	Mintage	VG	F	VF	XF	Unc
1625 (h) Rare	—	—	—	—	—	—
1625 HDM Rare	—	—	—	—	—	—

KM# 219 3 KREUZER

Silver **Ruler:** Ferdinand II **Rev:** Three shields, one above two - points together, ornamentation between in inner circle, date in legend **Mint:** Oppeln **Note:** Prev. Austria KM#586 (KM#1270). Varieties exist.

Date	Mintage	VG	F	VF	XF	Unc
1625 (dt)-SF Rare	—	—	—	—	—	—
1625 SF Rare	—	—	—	—	—	—

KM# 282 3 KREUZER

Silver **Ruler:** Ferdinand II **Obv:** Date below bust in inner circle **Mint:** Breslau **Note:** Prev. Austria KM#691 (KM#28).

Date	Mintage	VG	F	VF	XF	Unc
1628 (ch)-HR	—	—	—	—	—	—

KM# 288 3 KREUZER

Silver **Ruler:** Ferdinand II **Mint:** Breslau **Note:** Prev. Austria KM#708 (KM#24). Klippe.

Date	Mintage	VG	F	VF	XF	Unc
1629 (ch)-HR	—	—	—	—	—	—

KM# 297 3 KREUZER

Silver **Ruler:** Ferdinand II **Obv:** Bust with plain collar **Mint:** Breslau **Note:** Prev. Austria KM#742 (KM#26). Varieties exist.

Date	Mintage	VG	F	VF	XF	Unc
1630 (p)	—	—	—	—	—	—

KM# 336 3 KREUZER

Silver **Ruler:** Ferdinand III **Obv:** Ferdinand III **Rev:** Date in legend **Mint:** Breslau **Note:** Prev. Austria KM#831 (KM#61). Varieties exist.

Date	Mintage	VG	F	VF	XF	Unc
1637	—	12.00	20.00	38.00	75.00	—
1638	—	12.00	20.00	38.00	75.00	—
1639	—	12.00	20.00	38.00	75.00	—
1640	—	12.00	20.00	38.00	75.00	—
1641	—	12.00	20.00	38.00	75.00	—
1642	—	12.00	20.00	38.00	75.00	—
1643	—	12.00	20.00	38.00	75.00	—
1644	—	12.00	20.00	38.00	75.00	—
1645	—	12.00	20.00	38.00	75.00	—
1646	—	12.00	20.00	38.00	75.00	—
1647	—	12.00	20.00	38.00	75.00	—
1648	—	12.00	20.00	38.00	75.00	—
1649	—	12.00	20.00	38.00	75.00	—
1650	—	12.00	20.00	38.00	75.00	—
1651	—	12.00	20.00	38.00	75.00	—
1652	—	12.00	20.00	38.00	75.00	—
1653	—	12.00	20.00	38.00	75.00	—
1654	—	12.00	20.00	38.00	75.00	—
1655	—	12.00	20.00	38.00	75.00	—
1656	—	12.00	20.00	38.00	75.00	—
1657 GH	—	12.00	20.00	38.00	75.00	—

KM# 354 3 KREUZER

Silver **Ruler:** Ferdinand III **Obv:** Laureate bust right in inner circle, value below **Rev:** Crowned arms in inner circle, date in legend **Mint:** Teschen **Note:** Prev. Austria KM#907 (KM#1694).

Date	Mintage	VG	F	VF	XF	Unc
1642 DR	—	10.00	20.00	38.00	75.00	—
1644 HL	—	10.00	20.00	38.00	75.00	—
1646 HL	—	10.00	20.00	38.00	75.00	—
1647 H	—	10.00	20.00	38.00	75.00	—
1647 DR	—	10.00	20.00	38.00	75.00	—
1648 HL	—	10.00	20.00	38.00	75.00	—
1648 LB	—	10.00	20.00	38.00	75.00	—
1649 HL	—	10.00	20.00	38.00	75.00	—
1649 LB	—	10.00	20.00	38.00	75.00	—

KM# 357 3 KREUZER

Silver **Ruler:** Ferdinand III **Rev:** Eagle **Mint:** Teschen **Note:** Prev. Austria KM#917 (KM#1695).

Date	Mintage	VG	F	VF	XF	Unc
1643 HL	—	10.00	20.00	38.00	75.00	—
1649 GG	—	10.00	20.00	38.00	75.00	—
1652 GG	—	10.00	20.00	38.00	75.00	—

KM# 369 3 KREUZER

Silver **Ruler:** Ferdinand III **Obv:** Crowned bust of Wladislaus IV right in inner circle **Rev:** Crowned arms, date right of arms **Note:** Prev. Poland-Silesia KM#5.

Date	Mintage	VG	F	VF	XF	Unc
1647 Rare	—	—	—	—	—	—

KM# 390 3 KREUZER

Silver **Ruler:** Leopold I **Obv:** Laureate of John Casimir right in inner circle, value below **Rev:** Displayed eagle in inner circle, date in legend **Note:** Prev. Poland-Silesia KM#10.

Date	Mintage	VG	F	VF	XF	Unc
1657 Rare	—	—	—	—	—	—

KM# 402 3 KREUZER

Silver **Ruler:** Leopold I **Rev:** Without AT **Note:** Prev. Poland-Silesia KM#11.

Date	Mintage	VG	F	VF	XF	Unc
1658 Rare	—	—	—	—	—	—

KM# 399 3 KREUZER

Silver **Ruler:** Ferdinand III **Mint:** Breslau **Note:** Prev. Austria KM#1113 (KM#62). Posthumous issue.

Date	Mintage	VG	F	VF	XF	Unc
1658 GH	—	—	—	—	—	—

KM# 408 3 KREUZER

Silver **Ruler:** Leopold I **Obv:** Crowned bust holding septer and orb right in inner circle, value below **Rev:** Crowned imperial eagle in inner circle, date in legend **Mint:** Breslau **Note:** Prev. Austria KM#1138 (KM#77).

Date	Mintage	VG	F	VF	XF	Unc
1659 G-H	—	—	—	—	—	—

KM# 411.1 3 KREUZER

Silver **Ruler:** Leopold I **Obv:** Laureate bust right in inner circle, value below **Mint:** Breslau **Note:** Prev. Austria KM#1139.1 (KM#78.1). Varieties exist.

Date	Mintage	VG	F	VF	XF	Unc
1659 G-H	—	7.00	15.00	30.00	60.00	—
1660 G-H	—	7.00	15.00	30.00	60.00	—
1661 G-H	—	7.00	15.00	30.00	60.00	—
1662 G-H	—	7.00	15.00	30.00	60.00	—
1663 G-H	—	7.00	15.00	30.00	60.00	—
1664 G-H	—	7.00	15.00	30.00	60.00	—
1665 S-H	—	7.00	15.00	30.00	60.00	—

KM# 426 3 KREUZER

Silver **Ruler:** Leopold I **Rev:** Crowned displayed eagle in inner circle, date in legend **Note:** Prev. Poland-Silesia KM#15.

Date	Mintage	VG	F	VF	XF	Unc
1660 TT Rare	—	—	—	—	—	—
1661 Rare	—	—	—	—	—	—
1661 TT Rare	—	—	—	—	—	—

KM# 411.2 3 KREUZER

Silver **Ruler:** Leopold I **Obv:** Value inverted **Mint:** Breslau **Note:** Prev. Austria KM#1139.2 (KM#78.2).

Date	Mintage	VG	F	VF	XF	Unc
1664	—	8.00	16.00	35.00	70.00	—

KM# 471 3 KREUZER

Silver **Ruler:** Leopold I **Obv:** Bust right **Obv. Legend:** LEOPOLDUS • D • G •R • I •... **Rev:** Crowned double, eagle, crown divides date **Mint:** Breslau **Note:** Varieties exist. Prev. Austria KM#79 (KM#1230).

Date	Mintage	VG	F	VF	XF	Unc
1665 FBL	—	9.00	20.00	40.00	80.00	—
1665 SHS	—	9.00	20.00	40.00	80.00	—
1666 SHS	—	9.00	20.00	40.00	80.00	—
1667 SHS	—	9.00	20.00	40.00	80.00	—
1668 SHS	—	9.00	20.00	40.00	80.00	—
1669 SHS	—	9.00	20.00	40.00	80.00	—
1670 SHS	—	9.00	20.00	40.00	80.00	—
1672	—	9.00	20.00	40.00	80.00	—
1693	—	9.00	20.00	40.00	80.00	—
1695	—	9.00	20.00	40.00	80.00	—
1696	—	9.00	20.00	40.00	80.00	—
1697	—	9.00	20.00	40.00	80.00	—
1698	—	9.00	20.00	40.00	80.00	—

KM# 504 3 KREUZER

Silver **Ruler:** Leopold I **Obv:** Laureate bust right in inner circle, value below **Rev:** Crowned imperial eagle in inner circle, crown divides date **Mint:** Oppeln **Note:** Prev. Austria KM#1281 (KM#1273). Varieties exist.

Date	Mintage	VG	F	VF	XF	Unc
1672	—	7.00	15.00	30.00	60.00	—
1673	—	7.00	15.00	30.00	60.00	—
1673 FIK	—	7.00	15.00	30.00	60.00	—
1674 FIK	—	7.00	15.00	30.00	60.00	—
1675 FIK	—	7.00	15.00	30.00	60.00	—
1699 F-N	—	7.00	15.00	30.00	60.00	—
1699 FN	—	7.00	15.00	30.00	60.00	—
1700 FN	—	7.00	15.00	30.00	60.00	—

KM# 516 3 KREUZER

Silver **Ruler:** Leopold I **Obv:** Laureate bust right in inner circle, value below **Rev:** Crowned imperial eagle in inner circle, crown divides date **Mint:** Brieg **Note:** Prev. Austria KM#173 (KM#1287). Varieties exist.

Date	Mintage	VG	F	VF	XF	Unc
1676 CB	—	9.00	20.00	40.00	85.00	—
1695 CB	—	9.00	20.00	40.00	85.00	—
1696 CB	—	9.00	20.00	40.00	85.00	—
1697 CB	—	9.00	20.00	40.00	85.00	—
1698 CB	—	9.00	20.00	40.00	85.00	—
1699 CB	—	9.00	20.00	40.00	85.00	—
1700 CB	—	9.00	20.00	40.00	85.00	—

KM# 381 3 KREUZER

Silver **Ruler:** Ferdinand III **Obv:** Crowned bust facing in inner circle **Rev:** Crowned eagle in inner circle, date in legend **Mint:** Teschen **Note:** Prev. Austria KM#981 (KM#1696).

Date	Mintage	VG	F	VF	XF	Unc
1683	—	10.00	20.00	40.00	80.00	—

KM# 474 6 KREUZER

Silver **Ruler:** Leopold I **Obv:** Laureate bust right in inner circle, value in Roman numerals below **Rev:** Crowned imperial eagle in inner circle, date in legend **Mint:** Breslau **Note:** Prev. Austria KM#1232 (KM#81).

Date	Mintage	VG	F	VF	XF	Unc
1665 S-H	—	8.00	18.00	35.00	70.00	—
1666 S-H	—	8.00	18.00	35.00	70.00	—
1666 SHS	—	8.00	18.00	35.00	70.00	—

KM# 507 6 KREUZER

Silver **Ruler:** Leopold I **Rev:** Crown divides date **Mint:** Breslau **Note:** Prev. Austria KM#1274 (KM#82). Varieties exist.

Date	Mintage	VG	F	VF	XF	Unc
1672 SHS	—	8.00	18.00	35.00	65.00	—
1673 SHS	—	8.00	18.00	35.00	65.00	—
1674 SHS	—	8.00	18.00	35.00	65.00	—
1675 SHS	—	8.00	18.00	35.00	65.00	—
1676 SHS	—	8.00	18.00	35.00	65.00	—
1677 SHS	—	8.00	18.00	35.00	65.00	—
1678 SHS	—	8.00	18.00	35.00	65.00	—
1679 SHS	—	8.00	18.00	35.00	65.00	—
1680 SHS	—	8.00	18.00	35.00	65.00	—
1681 SHS	—	8.00	18.00	35.00	65.00	—
1682 SHS	—	8.00	18.00	35.00	65.00	—
1683 SHS	—	8.00	18.00	35.00	65.00	—
1684 SHS	—	8.00	18.00	35.00	65.00	—
1685 SHS	—	8.00	18.00	35.00	65.00	—
1686 SHS	—	8.00	18.00	35.00	65.00	—
1687 SHS	—	8.00	18.00	35.00	65.00	—
1688 SHS	—	8.00	18.00	35.00	65.00	—
1689 SHS	—	8.00	18.00	35.00	65.00	—
1690 SHS	—	8.00	18.00	35.00	65.00	—
1691 SHS	—	8.00	18.00	35.00	65.00	—
1692	—	8.00	18.00	35.00	65.00	—
1693	—	8.00	18.00	35.00	65.00	—

KM# 517 6 KREUZER

Silver **Ruler:** Leopold I **Mint:** Oppeln **Note:** Prev. Austria KM#1278 (KM#1282). Varieties exist.

Date	Mintage	VG	F	VF	XF	Unc
1675 FIK	—	15.00	40.00	75.00	135	—
1676 FIK	—	15.00	40.00	75.00	135	—
1677 FIK	—	15.00	40.00	75.00	135	—
1678 FIK	—	15.00	40.00	75.00	135	—
1679 FIK	—	15.00	40.00	75.00	135	—
1681 FIK	—	15.00	40.00	75.00	135	—
1682 FIK	—	15.00	40.00	75.00	135	—
1683 FIK	—	15.00	40.00	75.00	135	—
1685	—	15.00	40.00	75.00	135	—
1686	—	15.00	40.00	75.00	135	—
1688	—	15.00	40.00	75.00	135	—
1689	—	15.00	40.00	75.00	135	—
1690	—	15.00	40.00	75.00	135	—

KM# 522 6 KREUZER

Silver **Ruler:** Leopold I **Obv:** Laureate bust right in inner circle, value below **Rev:** Crowned imperial eagle in inner circle, crown divides date **Mint:** Brieg **Note:** Prev. Austria KM#1297 (KM#174). Varieties exist.

Date	Mintage	VG	F	VF	XF	Unc
1677 CB	—	20.00	40.00	75.00	150	—

KM# 57 15 KREUZER

Silver **Ruler:** Ferdinand II **Mint:** Glogau **Note:** Prev. Austria KM#439 (KM#326). Varieties exist.

Date	Mintage	VG	F	VF	XF	Unc
1623 IH	—	9.00	20.00	35.00	60.00	—
1623 G/BZ	—	9.00	20.00	35.00	60.00	—

KM# 414 15 KREUZER

Silver **Ruler:** Leopold I **Obv:** Laureate bust right in inner circle, value below **Rev:** Crowned imperial ealge in inner circle, date in legend **Mint:** Breslau **Note:** Prev. Austria KM#1143 (KM#83). Varieties exist.

Date	Mintage	VG	F	VF	XF	Unc
1659 G-H	—	10.00	20.00	40.00	85.00	—
1660 G-H	—	10.00	20.00	40.00	85.00	—
1661 G-H	—	10.00	20.00	40.00	85.00	—
1662 G-H	—	10.00	20.00	40.00	85.00	—
1663 G-H	—	10.00	20.00	40.00	85.00	—
1664 G-H	—	10.00	20.00	40.00	85.00	—
1664 S-HS	—	10.00	20.00	40.00	85.00	—

KM# 462 15 KREUZER

Silver **Ruler:** Leopold I **Obv:** Crown divides date **Mint:** Breslau **Note:** Prev. Austria KM#1218 (KM#84). Varieties exist.

Date	Mintage	VG	F	VF	XF	Unc
1664 FBDL	—	10.00	20.00	40.00	85.00	—
1664 FBL	—	10.00	20.00	40.00	85.00	—

Date	Mintage	VG	F	VF	XF	Unc
1664 SH	—	10.00	20.00	40.00	85.00	—
1665 FBL	—	10.00	20.00	40.00	85.00	—
1665 SH	—	10.00	20.00	40.00	85.00	—
1674 SHS	—	10.00	20.00	40.00	85.00	—
1675 SHS	—	10.00	20.00	40.00	85.00	—
1676 SHS	—	10.00	20.00	40.00	85.00	—
1692	—	10.00	20.00	40.00	85.00	—
1693	—	10.00	20.00	40.00	85.00	—
1694	—	10.00	20.00	40.00	85.00	—
1695	—	10.00	20.00	40.00	85.00	—
1696	—	10.00	20.00	40.00	85.00	—

KM# 465 15 KREUZER

Silver **Ruler:** Leopold I **Obv:** Laureate bust of John Casimir right in inner circle, value below **Rev:** Crowned displayed eagle in inner circle, date in legend **Note:** Prev. Poland-Silesia KM#16.

Date	Mintage	VG	F	VF	XF	Unc
1664 AT Rare	—	—	—	—	—	—

KM# 525 15 KREUZER

Silver **Ruler:** Leopold I **Obv:** Laureate bust right in inner circle, value below **Rev:** Crowned imperial eagle in inner circle, crown divides date **Mint:** Brieg **Note:** Prev. Austria KM#1298 (KM#175). Varieties exist.

Date	Mintage	VG	F	VF	XF	Unc
1677 CB	—	25.00	50.00	110	250	—
1693 CB	—	25.00	50.00	110	250	—
1694 CB	—	25.00	50.00	110	250	—

KM# 393 18 KREUZER

Silver **Ruler:** Leopold I **Obv:** Crowned arms divide value in inner circle **Mint:** Breslau **Note:** Prev. Austria KM#1001 (KM#85).

Date	Mintage	VG	F	VF	XF	Unc
1657 G-H	—	—	—	—	—	—

KM# 9 24 KREUZER

Silver **Ruler:** Friedrich von der Pfalz **Mint:** Oels **Note:** Prev. KM#304 (KM#1225).

Date	Mintage	VG	F	VF	XF	Unc
1621 HT monogram Rare	—	—	—	—	—	—

KM# 48 24 KREUZER

Silver **Ruler:** Ferdinand II **Mint:** Neisse **Note:** Prev. Austria KM#398. 24 Kipper Kreuzer. Varieties exist.

Date	Mintage	VG	F	VF	XF	Unc
1622	—	20.00	40.00	85.00	150	—
1623 BZ	—	20.00	40.00	85.00	150	—
1623 (dt)	—	20.00	40.00	85.00	150	—
1624 BZ	—	20.00	40.00	85.00	150	—

KM# 60 24 KREUZER

Silver **Ruler:** Ferdinand II **Mint:** Breslau **Note:** Prev. Austria KM#440 (KM#30). 24 Kipper Kreuzer.

Date	Mintage	VG	F	VF	XF	Unc
1623 BZ	—	14.00	30.00	50.00	90.00	—
1623 HT	—	14.00	30.00	50.00	90.00	—
1623 BZ-HT	—	14.00	30.00	50.00	90.00	—

KM# 63 24 KREUZER

Silver **Ruler:** Ferdinand II **Mint:** Glogau **Note:** Prev. Austria KM#441 (KM#327). 24 Kipper Kreuzer.

Date	Mintage	VG	F	VF	XF	Unc
1623 G/BZ	—	9.00	22.00	38.00	65.00	—
1623 IH	—	9.00	22.00	38.00	65.00	—
1623 IIH	—	9.00	22.00	38.00	65.00	—

KM# 12 30 KREUZER

Silver **Ruler:** Ferdinand II **Obv:** Four-line denomination in rectangle **Rev:** Silesian eagle **Mint:** Breslau **Note:** Prev. Austria KM#308 (KM#31).

Date	Mintage	VG	F	VF	XF	Unc
1621 HR	—	—	—	—	—	—

KM# 15 48 KREUZER

Silver **Ruler:** Friedrich von der Pfalz **Mint:** Oels **Note:** Prev. Austria KM#258 (KM#1226). Similar to 24 Kreuzer KM#239.

Date	Mintage	VG	F	VF	XF	Unc
1621 Ht monogram Rare	—	—	—	—	—	—

KM# 51 150 KREUZER

Silver **Ruler:** Ferdinand II **Mint:** Neisse **Note:** Prev. Austria KM#421 (KM#1205). Varieties exist.

Date	Mintage	VG	F	VF	XF	Unc
1622 (dt) Rare	—	—	—	—	—	—
1623 (dt) Rare	—	—	—	—	—	—

KM# 123 1/4 THALER

Silver **Ruler:** Ferdinand II **Obv:** Laureate bust right in inner circle **Rev:** Crowned imperial eagle in inner circle, date in legend **Mint:** Neisse **Note:** Prev. Austria KM#505 (KM#1206).

Date	Mintage	VG	F	VF	XF	Unc
1624 BZ Rare	—	—	—	—	—	—

KM# 348 1/4 THALER

Silver **Ruler:** Ferdinand III **Obv:** Crowned bust right in inner circle **Rev:** Crowned imperial eagle in inner circle, date in legend **Mint:** Breslau **Note:** Prev. Austria KM#894 (KM#63). Varieties exist.

Date	Mintage	VG	F	VF	XF	Unc
1641	—	15.00	25.00	60.00	100	—
1642	—	15.00	25.00	60.00	100	—
1643	—	15.00	25.00	60.00	100	—
1644	—	15.00	25.00	60.00	100	—
1645	—	15.00	25.00	60.00	100	—
1646	—	15.00	25.00	60.00	100	—
1648	—	15.00	25.00	60.00	100	—
1649	—	15.00	25.00	60.00	100	—
1650	—	15.00	25.00	60.00	100	—
1651	—	15.00	25.00	60.00	100	—
1653	—	15.00	25.00	60.00	100	—
1654	—	15.00	25.00	60.00	100	—
1655	—	15.00	25.00	60.00	100	—
1657	—	15.00	25.00	60.00	100	—

KM# 429 1/4 THALER

Silver **Ruler:** Leopold I **Obv:** Laureate bust right in inner circle **Rev:** Crowned imperial eagle in inner circle, crown divides date **Mint:** Breslau **Note:** Prev. Austria KM#1171 (KM#86). Varieties exist.

Date	Mintage	VG	F	VF	XF	Unc
1660 G-H	—	20.00	40.00	60.00	100	—
1662 G-H	—	20.00	40.00	60.00	100	—
1664 G-H	—	20.00	40.00	60.00	100	—
1666 S-HS	—	20.00	40.00	60.00	100	—
1695	—	20.00	40.00	60.00	100	—

KM# 432 1/4 THALER

Silver **Ruler:** Leopold I **Obv:** Crowned bust holding septer **Rev:** Heart-shaped arns on double eagle **Mint:** Breslau **Note:** Prev. Austria KM#1172 (KM#87).

Date	Mintage	VG	F	VF	XF	Unc
1660 GH	—	25.00	50.00	100	150	—

KM# 126 1/2 THALER

Silver **Ruler:** Ferdinand II **Obv:** Laureate bust right in inner circle **Rev:** Crowned imperial eagle in inner circle, date in legend **Mint:** Neisse **Note:** Prev. Austria KM#512 (KM#1207).

Date	Mintage	VG	F	VF	XF	Unc
1624 (dt) - BZ Rare	—	—	—	—	—	—

KM# 228 1/2 THALER

Silver **Ruler:** Ferdinand II **Obv:** Bust right **Rev:** Heraldic double eagle **Mint:** Oppeln **Note:** Prev. Austria KM#593 (KM#1271).

Date	Mintage	VG	F	VF	XF	Unc
1625 SF Rare	—	—	—	—	—	—

KM# 231 1/2 THALER

Silver **Ruler:** Ferdinand II **Obv:** Laureate bust right in inner circle **Rev:** Crowned imperial eagle in inner circle, date in legend **Mint:** Ratibor **Note:** Prev. Austria KM#594 (KM#1568).

Date	Mintage	VG	F	VF	XF	Unc
1625 DR-SD Rare	—	—	—	—	—	—

KM# 285 1/2 THALER

Silver **Ruler:** Ferdinand II **Mint:** Breslau **Note:** Prev. Austria KM#697(KM#32). Varieties exist.

Date	Mintage	VG	F	VF	XF	Unc
1628 W-(3ch)	—	125	250	400	650	—
1631 W/HR-(3ch)IZ	—	125	250	400	650	—
1632 W-(3ch)/IZ	—	125	250	400	650	—

KM# 318 1/2 THALER

Silver **Ruler:** Ferdinand II **Mint:** Breslau **Note:** Prev. Austria KM#781 (KM#33). Varieties exist.

Date	Mintage	VG	F	VF	XF	Unc
1632 W/HR-(3ch)/IZ	—	125	250	400	650	—

KM# 340 1/2 THALER

Silver **Ruler:** Ferdinand III **Obv:** Bust right in inner circle **Rev:** Inner circle added **Mint:** Breslau **Note:** Prev. Austria KM#853 (KM#64). Varieties exist.

Date	Mintage	VG	F	VF	XF	Unc
1638	—	25.00	50.00	100	200	—
1639	—	25.00	50.00	100	200	—
1641	—	25.00	50.00	100	200	—
1642	—	25.00	50.00	100	200	—
1643	—	25.00	50.00	100	200	—
1644	—	25.00	50.00	100	200	—
1645	—	25.00	50.00	100	200	—
1646	—	25.00	50.00	100	200	—
1648	—	25.00	50.00	100	200	—
1651	—	25.00	50.00	100	200	—
1653	—	25.00	50.00	100	200	—
1654	—	25.00	50.00	100	200	—
1655	—	25.00	50.00	100	200	—
1657	—	25.00	50.00	100	200	—

KM# 366 1/2 THALER

Silver **Ruler:** Ferdinand III **Mint:** Breslau **Note:** Prev. Austria KM#928 (KM#65).

Date	Mintage	VG	F	VF	XF	Unc
1646	—	25.00	50.00	125	300	—
1650	—	25.00	50.00	125	300	—

KM# 417 1/2 THALER

Silver **Ruler:** Leopold I **Mint:** Breslau **Note:** Prev. Austria KM#1146 (KM#88).

Date	Mintage	VG	F	VF	XF	Unc
1659 G-H	—	300	500	800	1,200	—
1660 G-H	—	300	500	800	1,200	—
1662 G-H	—	300	500	800	1,200	—
1663 G-H	—	300	500	800	1,200	—
1664 G-H	—	300	500	800	1,200	—

KM# 477 1/2 THALER

Silver **Ruler:** Leopold I **Obv:** Laureate bust **Rev:** Crowned imperial eagle in inner circle, crown divides date **Mint:** Breslau **Note:** Varieties exist. Prev. Austria KM#89 (KM#1236).

Date	Mintage	VG	F	VF	XF	Unc
1665 SH	—	135	275	425	650	—
1670 SHS	—	135	275	425	650	—
1672 SHS	—	135	275	425	650	—
1677 SHS	—	135	275	425	650	—
1679 SHS	—	135	275	425	650	—
1689 SHS	—	135	275	425	650	—
1695	—	135	275	425	650	—
1696	—	135	275	425	650	—

KM# 579 1/2 THALER

Silver **Ruler:** Leopold I **Obv:** Laureate bust right in inner circle **Rev:** Crowned imperial eagle in inner circle, crown divides date **Mint:** Oppeln **Note:** Prev. Austria KM#1347 (KM#1283). Varieties exist.

Date	Mintage	VG	F	VF	XF	Unc
1690 Rare	—	—	—	—	—	—
1700 FN Rare	—	—	—	—	—	—

KM# 615 1/2 THALER

Silver **Ruler:** Leopold I **Obv:** Laureate bust right in inner circle **Rev:** Crowned imperial eagle in inner circle, crown divides date **Mint:** Brieg **Note:** Prev. Austria KM#176 (KM#1384).

Date	Mintage	VG	F	VF	XF	Unc
1695 CB	—	200	400	675	1,000	—

KM# 18 3/4 THALER

Silver **Ruler:** Ferdinand II **Obv:** Silesian eagle within legend; M, HR, and SP monograms in corners **Mint:** Glogau **Note:** Prev. Austria KM#332 (KM#328). Uniface. Klippe.

Date	Mintage	VG	F	VF	XF	Unc
1621 Rare	—	—	—	—	—	—

KM# 129.1 THALER

Silver **Ruler:** Ferdinand II **Obv:** Bust right **Obv. Legend:** FERDINANDVS. II. D: G. R. IM. S. A. G. H. B. REX. DV. X. S. **Rev:** Crowned double eagle **Rev. Legend:** NEC NON ARCHID (W) AV. DVX. BV. M. M. C. T. **Mint:** Breslau **Note:** Prev. Austria KM#516.1 (KM#34.1, Dav.#3151).

Date	Mintage	VG	F	VF	XF	Unc
ND W/(3ch)	—	400	700	1,200	1,800	—
ND W/(2ch)	—	400	700	1,200	1,800	—
ND W	—	400	700	1,200	1,800	—

KM# 144 THALER

Silver **Ruler:** Ferdinand II **Mint:** Neisse **Note:** Prev. Austria KM#524 (Dav.#3164, KM#1209). Varieties exist.

Date	Mintage	VG	F	VF	XF	Unc
1624 BZ	—	1,150	2,250	4,500	7,500	—
1624 (dt)-BZ	—	1,150	2,250	4,500	7,500	—
1624 BZ-BZ	—	1,150	2,250	4,500	7,500	—

Date	Mintage	VG	F	VF	XF	Unc
1624 BZ	—	1,150	2,250	4,500	7,500	—
Note: Strike mark on reverse						
1624 (dt)	—	1,150	2,250	4,500	7,500	—

KM# 129.2 THALER

Silver **Ruler:** Ferdinand II **Obv. Legend:** D: G. RO. IM. S. AV. GER. HV. BOH. REX. **Rev. Legend:** ARCHIDVX. AVSTRI. DVX. BVRG. SILESIAE **Mint:** Breslau **Note:** Prev. Austria KM#516.2 (KM#34.2, Dav.#3152).

Date	Mintage	VG	F	VF	XF	Unc
1624 BZ/HR	—	400	700	1,200	1,800	—

KM# 129.3 THALER

Silver **Ruler:** Ferdinand II **Rev. Legend:** ARCHIDVX. AVS. DVX. BVR. MAR. MO. CO. TYR. **Mint:** Breslau **Note:** Prev. Austria KM#516.3 (Dav.#3153, KM#34.3).

Date	Mintage	VG	F	VF	XF	Unc
1624 BZ	—	400	700	1,000	1,800	—

KM# 129.4 THALER

Silver **Ruler:** Ferdinand II **Rev. Legend:** ARCHIDVX. AVS. DVX. BVR. MAR. MO. CO. TYR. **Mint:** Breslau **Note:** Prev. Austria KM#516.4 (Dav.#3154, KM#34.4)

Date	Mintage	VG	F	VF	XF	Unc
1624 BZ/BZ	—	2,500	4,750	7,750	—	—

KM# 141 THALER

Silver **Ruler:** Ferdinand II **Obv:** Laureate half-figure right holding orb and scepter in inner circle **Rev:** Crowned imperial eagle with round arms on breast in inner circle, date in legend **Mint:** Neisse **Note:** Prev. Austria KM#523 (Dav.#3165, KM#1208).

Date	Mintage	VG	F	VF	XF	Unc
1624 (dt) Rare	—	—	—	—	—	—

KM# 234 THALER

Silver **Ruler:** Ferdinand II **Obv:** Ferdinand II right in ornamented inner circle **Mint:** Breslau **Note:** Prev. Austria KM#595 (KM#36, Dav.#A.3155). Thick planchet.

Date	Mintage	VG	F	VF	XF	Unc
1625 HR Rare	—	—	—	—	—	—

KM# 237 THALER

Silver **Ruler:** Ferdinand II **Obv:** Ferdinand II in plain inner circle, date below legend **Obv. Legend:** ...D: G. R. I. S. A. G. H. B. REX. DV. S **Rev:** Crowned arms in Order chain **Rev. Legend:** NEC NON ARCHIDVX - A. DVX. BVR. M. M. C. TY - R. **Mint:** Breslau **Note:** Prev. Austria KM#596 (KM#37, Dav.#3155).

Date	Mintage	VG	F	VF	XF	Unc
1625 Rare	—	—	—	—	—	—

KM# 240 THALER

Silver **Ruler:** Ferdinand II **Mint:** Oppeln **Note:** Prev. Austria KM#597 (KM#1272, Dav.#3166).

Date	Mintage	VG	F	VF	XF	Unc
1625 SF Rare	—	—	—	—	—	—

KM# 246 THALER

Silver **Ruler:** Ferdinand II **Obv:** Facing bust with scepter and orb **Rev:** Soldiers and city view **Mint:** Breslau **Note:** Prev. Austria KM#627 (KM#38).

Date	Mintage	VG	F	VF	XF	Unc
1626 HR Rare	—	—	—	—	—	—

KM# 129.5 THALER

Silver **Ruler:** Ferdinand II **Obv:** Date below legend **Obv. Legend:** D: G. R. IMP. S .A. GER. H: B: REX. DVX. SIL **Rev. Legend:** NEC NON ARCHIN (W) AV. DV. BV. MA. MO. C. T. **Mint:** Breslau **Note:** Prev. Austria KM#516.5 (KM#34.5, Dav.#3156).

Date	Mintage	VG	F	VF	XF	Unc
1627 W/(2ch)	—	400	700	1,200	1,800	—

KM# 129.6 THALER

Silver **Ruler:** Ferdinand II **Rev. Legend:** ... ARCHIDVX (W) AVS. DVX. BVR. M. M. C. T. **Mint:** Breslau **Note:** Prev. Austria KM#516.6 (KM#34.6, Dav.#3156A).

Date	Mintage	VG	F	VF	XF	Unc
1627 W/(2ch) Rare	—	—	—	—	—	—

KM# 276 THALER

Silver **Ruler:** Ferdinand II **Mint:** Breslau **Note:** Prev. Austria KM#674 (KM#35). Klippe. Similar to KM#129.5.

Date	Mintage	VG	F	VF	XF	Unc
1627 W/(2ch) Rare	—	—	—	—	—	—

KM# 129.7 THALER

Silver **Ruler:** Ferdinand II **Obv. Legend:** ... IM. S. A. G. H. B. REX. DV. X. S. **Rev:** Eagle divides date at bottom **Mint:** Breslau **Note:** Prev. Austria KM#516.7 (KM#34.7, Dav.#3157).

Date	Mintage	VG	F	VF	XF	Unc
1629 W/(2ch)	—	260	450	775	1,150	—

KM# 300 THALER

Silver **Ruler:** Ferdinand II **Obv. Legend:** ... D. G. ROM. IMP. S. A. G. H. B. REX. **Rev:** Date divided below eagle **Rev. Legend:** AR: AV: D. BV: MA: MO (W) DVX SILESIAE & PH **Mint:** Breslau **Note:** Prev. Austria KM#745 (KM#34.8, Dav.#3158).

Date	Mintage	VG	F	VF	XF	Unc
1630 W/(p)	—	400	700	1,200	1,800	—

KM# 315 THALER

Silver **Ruler:** Ferdinand II **Obv. Legend:** ... D. G. R. IM. S. A. G. H. B. REX. DVX. SI **Rev. Legend:** NEC NON ARCHIDVX. (W) AVS. DVX. BVR. M. M. C. T. **Mint:** Breslau **Note:** Prev. Austria KM#767 (KM#34.9, Dav.#3159).

Date	Mintage	VG	F	VF	XF	Unc
1631 W/IZ(3ch)	—	400	700	1,200	1,800	—
1631 IZ/(3ch)	—	400	700	1,200	1,800	—

KM# 129.10 THALER

Silver **Ruler:** Ferdinand II **Obv. Legend:** ...DVX. S. **Rev:** Date in legend **Rev. Legend:** ARCHIDVX, AVST. DVX. (W)BVFRG. SILE ze **Mint:** Breslau **Note:** Prev. Austria KM#516.10 (KM#34.10, Dav.#3160).

Date	Mintage	VG	F	VF	XF	Unc
1632 W/IZ/(3ch)	—	400	700	1,200	1,800	—

KM# 129.11 THALER

Silver **Ruler:** Ferdinand II **Rev:** Date after legend **Rev. Legend:** ....AVSTRI. DVX. BVR(G) SILESI. ze **Mint:** Breslau **Note:** Prev. Austria KM#516.11 (KM#34.11, Dav.#3161).

Date	Mintage	VG	F	VF	XF	Unc
1632 IZ/(3ch)	—	350	875	1,350	2,250	—

KM# 129.12 THALER

Silver **Ruler:** Ferdinand II **Obv. Legend:** D: G(W)R. I. CS. A. G. HVNG. BO. REX **Rev:** Date after legend **Rev. Legend:** ...AVSTRIDVX. BVRG. SILESI. ze **Mint:** Breslau **Note:** Prev. Austria KM#516.12 (KM#34.12, Dav.#3162).

Date	Mintage	VG	F	VF	XF	Unc
1632 IZ/(3ch) Rare	—	—	—	—	—	—

KM# 345.1 THALER

Silver **Ruler:** Ferdinand III **Obv:** Crowned bust right in inner circle **Rev:** Crowned imperial eagle in inner circle, date in legend **Mint:** Breslau **Note:** Prev. Austria KM#875.1 (KM#66.1, Dav.#3219). Legend varieties exist.

Date	Mintage	VG	F	VF	XF	Unc
1639 M-I	—	275	550	1,250	2,250	—
1641 M-I	—	275	550	1,250	2,250	—
1642 M-I	—	275	550	1,250	2,250	—
1643 M-I	—	275	550	1,250	2,250	—

Date	Mintage	VG	F	VF	XF	Unc
1645 M-I	—	275	550	1,250	2,250	—
1646 M-I	—	275	550	1,250	2,250	—
1648 M-I	—	275	550	1,250	2,250	—
1650 G-I	—	275	550	1,250	2,250	—
1651 G-I	—	275	550	1,250	2,250	—
1653 G-I	—	275	550	1,250	2,250	—
1654 G-I	—	275	550	1,250	2,250	—
1655	—	275	550	1,250	2,250	—

KM# 375 THALER

Silver **Ruler:** Ferdinand III **Obv:** Laureate bust right with wide lace collar in inner circle **Mint:** Breslau **Note:** Prev. Austria KM#966 (KM#67, Dav.#3220).

Date	Mintage	VG	F	VF	XF	Unc
1649 G-H	—	1,650	3,250	5,500	—	—

KM# 384 THALER

Silver **Ruler:** Ferdinand III **Obv:** Narrow laureate bust right in inner circle **Mint:** Breslau **Note:** Prev. Austria KM#991 (KM#68, Dav.#3221).

Date	Mintage	VG	F	VF	XF	Unc
1655 G-H Rare	—	—	—	—	—	—
1656 G-H Rare	—	—	—	—	—	—

KM# 345.2 THALER

Silver **Ruler:** Ferdinand III **Rev:** Modified arms **Mint:** Breslau **Note:** Prev. Austria KM#875.2 (KM#66.2, Dav.#3222).

Date	Mintage	VG	F	VF	XF	Unc
1656	—	275	550	1,250	2,250	—
1657 G-H	—	275	550	1,250	2,250	—

KM# 420 THALER

Silver **Ruler:** Leopold I **Mint:** Breslau **Note:** Prev. Austria KM#1155 (KM#90, Dav.#3285).

Date	Mintage	VG	F	VF	XF	Unc
1659 G-H Rare	—	—	—	—	—	—
1660 G-H Rare	—	—	—	—	—	—

KM# 435.1 THALER

Silver **Ruler:** Leopold I **Obv:** Young laureate bust right **Obv. Legend:** ...BOHEN.ZC.REX. **Rev:** Eagle with arms in Order collar on breast, date **Rev. Legend:** BURGUND.COMES.TYR **Mint:** Breslau **Note:** Prev. Austria KM#1174.1 (KM#92.1, Dav#3286).

Date	Mintage	VG	F	VF	XF	Unc
1660 GH Rare	—	—	—	—	—	—

KM# 447 THALER

Silver **Ruler:** Leopold I **Rev:** Sword and scepter in eagle claws **Mint:** Breslau **Note:** Prev. Austria KM#1199 (KM#91, Dav.#3287).

Date	Mintage	VG	F	VF	XF	Unc
1662 GH Rare	—	—	—	—	—	—
1663 GH Rare	—	—	—	—	—	—

KM# 435.2 THALER

Silver **Ruler:** Leopold I **Obv. Legend:** ...BO.H.ETC.REX **Rev:** Date after legend **Rev. Legend:** ...BURG.COM TYROL **Mint:** Breslau **Note:** Prev. Austria KM#1174.2 (KM#92.2, Dav.#A3288).

Date	Mintage	VG	F	VF	XF	Unc
1663 GH Rare	—	—	—	—	—	—

KM# 480.1 THALER

Silver **Ruler:** Leopold I **Mint:** Breslau **Note:** Prev. Austria KM#1221.1 (KM#93.1, Dav.#3288).

Date	Mintage	VG	F	VF	XF	Unc
1664 GH Rare	—	—	—	—	—	—
1665 SH	—	1,750	3,250	5,500	—	—

KM# 480.2 THALER

Silver **Ruler:** Leopold I **Mint:** Breslau **Note:** Prev. Austria KM#1221.2 (KM#93.2, Dav.#3288A).

Date	Mintage	VG	F	VF	XF	Unc
1665 Rare	—	—	—	—	—	—

KM# 483.1 THALER

Silver **Ruler:** Leopold I **Obv:** Laureate bust **Obv. Legend:** LEOPOLDVS. D: G. EL. RO. LSE. AVG. GER. HV. BO: REX. **Rev. Legend:** ARCHI. DVX. AVST. SHS DVX. BURG. ET. SIL... **Mint:** Breslau **Note:** Prev. Austria KM#1244.1 (KM#94.1, Dav.#3289).

Date	Mintage	VG	F	VF	XF	Unc
1666 shs	—	1,000	2,000	4,000	6,500	—

KM# 483.2 THALER

Silver **Ruler:** Leopold I **Obv:** Lion's head on shoulder **Mint:** Breslau **Note:** Prev. Austria KM#1244.2 (KM#94.2, Dav.#3290).

Date	Mintage	VG	F	VF	XF	Unc
1668 SHS	—	1,000	2,000	4,000	6,500	—
1669 SHS	—	1,000	2,000	4,000	6,500	—

KM# 483.3 THALER

Silver **Ruler:** Leopold I **Obv. Legend:** ...R. LSE. AVG. GE... **Rev. Legend:** ...ET. SILE: **Mint:** Breslau **Note:** Prev. Austria KM#1244.3 9KM#94.3, Dav.#3291).

Date	Mintage	VG	F	VF	XF	Unc
1670 SHS	—	750	1,500	3,000	5,000	—
1672 SHS	—	750	1,500	3,000	5,000	—
1673 SHS	—	750	1,500	3,000	5,000	—
1674 SHS	—	750	1,500	3,000	5,000	—

KM# 483.4 THALER

Silver **Ruler:** Leopold I **Obv. Legend:** ...ROM IMP: SE: AV: GE: HV: BO: REX. **Rev. Legend:** ARCHIDVX... **Mint:** Breslau **Note:** Prev. Austria KM#1244.4 (KM#94.4, Dav.#3292).

Date	Mintage	VG	F	VF	XF	Unc
1677 SHS	—	750	1,500	3,000	5,000	—

KM# 483.5 THALER

Silver **Ruler:** Leopold I **Obv:** Bust with GFH on shoulder **Obv. Legend:** ...DG: EL... GER... **Rev. Legend:** ...BVR. ET. SILESIAE. **Mint:** Breslau **Note:** Prev. Austria KM#1244.5 (KM#94.5, Dav.#3293).

Date	Mintage	VG	F	VF	XF	Unc
1678 SHS	—	750	1,500	3,000	5,000	—
1679 SHS	—	750	1,500	3,000	5,000	—

KM# 483.7 THALER

Silver **Ruler:** Leopold I **Obv. Legend:** ...HV. & BO. REX. **Mint:** Breslau **Note:** Prev. Austria KM#1244.7 (KM#94.7, Dav.#3295).

Date	Mintage	VG	F	VF	XF	Unc
1683 SHS	—	950	1,750	3,500	6,000	—
1684 SHS	—	950	1,750	3,500	6,000	—

KM# 483.6 THALER

Silver **Ruler:** Leopold I **Obv. Legend:** ...DG. ROM. IMP. SE. AVE. GER. HV. BO **Rev. Legend:** ...SILES **Mint:** Breslau **Note:** Prev. Austria KM#1244.6 (KM#94.6, Dav.#3294).

Date	Mintage	VG	F	VF	XF	Unc
1683 SHS	—	650	1,250	2,500	4,750	—

KM# 483.8 THALER

Silver **Ruler:** Leopold I **Obv:** Bust right with lion's head on arm **Obv. Legend:** ...SEM: AVG:. **Rev. Legend:** ... AVSTRI: SHSDVX. BVRG: ET. SILE. **Mint:** Breslau **Note:** Prev. Austria KM#1224.8 (KM#9438, Dav.#3296).

Date	Mintage	VG	F	VF	XF	Unc
1685 SHS	—	800	1,600	3,250	5,500	—
1686 SHS	—	800	1,600	3,250	5,500	—
1687 SHS	—	800	1,600	3,250	5,500	—
1688 SHS	—	800	1,600	3,250	5,500	—

KM# 483.9 THALER

Silver **Ruler:** Leopold I **Obv:** Armored bust **Mint:** Breslau **Note:** Prev. Austria KM#1224.9 (KM#94.9, Dav.#3296A).

Date	Mintage	VG	F	VF	XF	Unc
1686 SHS	—	800	1,600	3,250	5,500	—

KM# 483.10 THALER

Silver **Ruler:** Leopold I **Obv. Legend:** ...D: G: ROM... **Mint:** Breslau **Note:** Prev. Austria KM#1224.10 (KM#94.10, Dav.#3297).

Date	Mintage	VG	F	VF	XF	Unc
1689 SHS	—	375	750	1,500	2,500	—
1690 SHS	—	375	750	1,500	2,500	—

KM# 483.11 THALER

Silver **Ruler:** Leopold I **Obv. Legend:** ...DG. ROM...HVN & BOH. REX **Rev. Legend:** AVSTRIAE MMW DVX. BVRG & SILESIAE. **Mint:** Breslau **Note:** Prev. Austria KM#1224.11 (KM#94.11, Dav.#3298).

Date	Mintage	VG	F	VF	XF	Unc
1691 SHS	—	375	750	1,500	2,500	—
1692	—	375	750	1,500	2,500	—
1693	—	375	750	1,500	2,500	—

KM# 483.12 THALER

Silver **Ruler:** Leopold I **Obv:** Bust divides legend **Obv. Legend:** ...AV. GE. H. B. REX. **Rev. Legend:** ...AVST. MMW...& SILE. **Mint:** Breslau **Note:** Prev. Austria KM#1224.12 (KM#94.12, Dav.#3299).

Date	Mintage	VG	F	VF	XF	Unc
1694	—	450	900	1,850	3,250	—

KM# 483.13 THALER

Silver **Ruler:** Leopold I **Obv:** Thin bust **Obv. Legend:** ...D: G:... AVG: GERM: HU: & BO: REX. **Rev. Legend:** AVSTRIAE... SILESIAE. **Mint:** Breslau **Note:** Prev. Austria KM#1224.13 (KM#94.13, Dav.#3300).

Date	Mintage	VG	F	VF	XF	Unc
1695	—	400	800	1,650	2,750	—
1696	—	400	800	1,650	2,750	—

KM# 621.1 THALER

Silver **Ruler:** Leopold I **Obv:** Laureate bust right separates inner circle **Rev:** Crowned imperial eagle in inner circle, crown divides date **Mint:** Brieg **Note:** Prev. Austria KM#1386.1 (KM#177.1, Dav.#3304).

Date	Mintage	VG	F	VF	XF	Unc
1695 CB	—	325	700	1,350	2,250	—

KM# 621.2 THALER

Silver **Ruler:** Leopold I **Obv:** Laureate bust right in inner circle **Obv. Legend:** LEOPOLDUS. DG: ROM: IMPERATOR ... **Mint:** Brieg **Note:** Prev. KM#1386.2 (KM#177.2, Dav.#3305)

Date	Mintage	VG	F	VF	XF	Unc
1696 CB	—	325	700	1,350	2,250	—
1697 CB	—	325	700	1,350	2,250	—

KM# 483.14 THALER

Silver **Ruler:** Leopold I **Obv:** Armored bust right without inner circle **Obv. Legend:** LEOPOLDUS. DG: ROM: IMP: SE: AV: GE:... **Rev. Legend:** Ends: SILESI **Mint:** Breslau **Note:** Prev. Austria KM#1224.14 (KM#94.14, Dav.#3301).

Date	Mintage	VG	F	VF	XF	Unc
1697	—	450	900	1,850	3,250	—
1698	—	450	900	1,850	3,250	—

KM# 651.1 THALER

Silver **Ruler:** Leopold I **Obv:** Laureate armored bust right **Obv. Legend:** LEOPOLDUS • D • G • ROM: IMP: SEM: AVG: GER: HU: BO: REX • **Rev:** Crowned imperial eagle with arms on breast **Rev. Legend:** ARCHIDUX • AVSTRIAE DUX • BVRG •... **Mint:** Oppeln **Note:** Dav. #3303. Prev. Austria KM#1284.1 (KM#1398.1).

Date	Mintage	VG	F	VF	XF	Unc
1699 Rare	—	—	—	—	—	—
1700 FN	—	375	750	1,500	2,500	—

KM# 21 1-1/2 THALER

Silver **Ruler:** Ferdinand II **Obv:** Silesian eagle within legend ; M. HR, and SP monograms in corners **Mint:** Glogau **Note:** Prev. Austria KM#351 (KM#329). Klippe. Uniface.

Date	Mintage	VG	F	VF	XF	Unc
1621 Rare	—	—	—	—	—	—

KM# 249 1-1/2 THALER

Silver **Ruler:** Ferdinand II **Obv:** Laureate bust half right holding orb and scepter **Rev:** City view of Breslau with horseman and companion in foreground in inner circle **Mint:** Breslau **Note:** Prev. Austria KM#635 (KM#39).

Date	Mintage	VG	F	VF	XF	Unc
1626 (h) Rare	—	—	—	—	—	—

KM# 4.1 2 THALER

Silver **Ruler:** Ferdinand II **Obv:** Laureate bust right in inner circle **Obv. Legend:** FERNINANDVS. II. D: G. R. IM. S. A. G. H. B. REX. DV. X. S **Rev:** Crowned imperial eagle with date divided below in inner circle **Rev. Legend:** NEC NON ARCHIS (W) AV. DVX. BV. M. M. C. T. **Mint:** Breslau **Note:** Prev. Austria KM#269.1 (KM#40.1, Dav.#3150).

Date	Mintage	VG	F	VF	XF	Unc
ND W/(2ch) Rare	—	—	—	—	—	—

KM# 6 2 THALER

Silver **Ruler:** Ferdinand II **Mint:** Breslau **Note:** Prev. Austria KM#270 (KM#41). Klippe.

Date	Mintage	VG	F	VF	XF	Unc
ND Rare	—	—	—	—	—	—

KM# 147 2 THALER

Silver **Ruler:** Ferdinand II **Obv:** Laureate bust right in inner circle **Rev:** Crowned imperial eagle in inner circle, date in legend **Mint:** Neisse **Note:** Prev. Austria KM#543 (KM#1210, Dav.#A3163).

Date	Mintage	VG	F	VF	XF	Unc
1624 BZ Rare	—	—	—	—	—	—

KM# 252 2 THALER

Silver **Ruler:** Ferdinand II **Obv:** Laureate bust half right holding orb and scepter in inner circle **Rev:** City view of Breslau with horseman and companion in foreground in inner circle **Mint:** Breslau **Note:** Prev. Austria KM#638 (KM#42).

Date	Mintage	VG	F	VF	XF	Unc
1626 (h) Rare	—	—	—	—	—	—

KM# 40.2 2 THALER

Silver **Ruler:** Ferdinand II **Obv:** Date below bust **Obv. Legend:** ...IMP. S. A. GER. H: B. RX. DVX. SIL **Rev. Legend:** DV. BV. MA. MO. C. T. **Mint:** Breslau **Note:** Prev. Austria KM#269.2 (KM#40.2, Dav.#A3156).

Date	Mintage	VG	F	VF	XF	Unc
1627 W/(2ch) Rare	—	—	—	—	—	—

KM# 40.3 2 THALER

Silver **Ruler:** Ferdinand II **Obv. Legend:** IM. S. A. G. H. B. REX. DV. X. S. **Rev:** Date divied by eagle **Rev. Legend:** ARCHIDVX (W) AVX. DVX. BVR. M. M. C. T. **Mint:** Breslau **Note:** Prev. Austria KM#269.3 (KM#40.3, Dav.#A3157).

Date	Mintage	VG	F	VF	XF	Unc
1629 W/(2ch) Rare	—	—	—	—	—	—

KM# 40.4 2 THALER

Silver **Ruler:** Ferdinand II **Obv. Legend:** ...D. G. ROM. IMP. S. A. G. H. B. REX. **Rev:** Date below legend **Rev. Legend:** AR: AV: D. BV: MA: MO (W) DVX SILESIAE & PH **Mint:** Breslau **Note:** Prev. Austria KM#269.4 (KM#40.4, Dav.#A3158). Varieties exist.

Date	Mintage	VG	F	VF	XF	Unc
1630 W/(hp) Rare	—	—	—	—	—	—

KM# 360.1 2 THALER

Silver **Ruler:** Ferdinand III **Obv:** Crowned bust right in inner circle **Rev:** Crowned imperial eagle in inner circle, date in legend **Mint:** Breslau **Note:** Prev. Austria KM#918.1 (KM#69.1, Dav.#3218). Legend varieties exist.

Date	Mintage	VG	F	VF	XF	Unc
1643 M-I Rare	—	—	—	—	—	—
1646 M-I Rare	—	—	—	—	—	—
1650 G-H Rare	—	—	—	—	—	—

KM# 396 2 THALER

Silver **Ruler:** Ferdinand III **Rev:** Modified arms **Mint:** Breslau **Note:** Prev. Austria KM#1006 (KM#69.2, Dav.#A3222).

Date	Mintage	VG	F	VF	XF	Unc
1657 G-H Rare	—	—	—	—	—	—

KM# 450 2 THALER

Silver **Ruler:** Leopold I **Obv:** Young laureate bust right in inner circle **Rev:** Crowned imperial eagle in inner circle, date in legend **Mint:** Breslau **Note:** Prev. Austria KM#1201 (KM#95, Dav.#A3287).

Date	Mintage	VG	F	VF	XF	Unc
1662 GH Rare	—	—	—	—	—	—

KM# 24 3 THALER

12.2800 g., Silver **Ruler:** Ferdinand II **Mint:** Glogau **Note:** Prev. Austria KM#358 (KM#330). Struck with 3/4 Thaler dies KM#332. Uniface. Klippe.

Date	Mintage	VG	F	VF	XF	Unc
1621 Rare	—	—	—	—	—	—

KM# 150 3 THALER
86.0300 g., Silver **Ruler:** Ferdinand II **Obv:** Laureate bust right in inner circle **Rev:** Crowned imperial eagle in inner circle, date in legend **Mint:** Neisse **Note:** Prev. Austria KM#548 (KM#1211, Dav.#3163).

Date	Mintage	VG	F	VF	XF	Unc
1624 BZ/(dt) Rare	—	—	—	—	—	—

KM# 153 3 THALER
86.0300 g., Silver **Ruler:** Ferdinand II **Mint:** Neisse **Note:** Prev. Austria KM#549 (KM#1212, Dav.#3163A). Octagonal klippe.

Date	Mintage	VG	F	VF	XF	Unc
1624 BZ Rare	—	—	—	—	—	—

KM# 255 3 THALER
Silver **Ruler:** Ferdinand II **Obv:** Laureate bust half right holding orb and scepter in inner circle **Rev:** City view of Breslau with horseman and companion in foreground in inner circle **Mint:** Breslau **Note:** Prev. Austria KM#646 (KM#43).

Date	Mintage	VG	F	VF	XF	Unc
1626 (h) Rare	—	—	—	—	—	—

KM# 258 4 THALER
115.2000 g., Silver **Ruler:** Ferdinand II **Obv:** Laureate bust half right holding orb and scepter in inner circle **Rev:** City view of Breslau with horseman and companion in foreground in inner circle **Mint:** Breslau **Note:** Prev. Austria KM#655 (KM#44).

Date	Mintage	VG	F	VF	XF	Unc
1626 (h) Rare	—	—	—	—	—	—

KM# 27 6 THALER
24.3200 g., Silver **Ruler:** Ferdinand II **Obv:** Silesian eagle within legend; M, HR, and SP monograms in corners **Mint:** Glogau **Note:** Prev. Austria KM#360 (KM#331). Uniface. Klippe.

Date	Mintage	VG	F	VF	XF	Unc
1621 Rare	—	—	—	—	—	—

KM# 33 25 THALER
Silver **Ruler:** Ferdinand II **Obv:** Five-line denomination in rectangle **Rev:** Silesian eagle **Mint:** Breslau **Note:** Prev. Austria KM#45.

Date	Mintage	VG	F	VF	XF	Unc
1621 HR Rare	—	—	—	—	—	—

TRADE COINAGE

KM# 543 1/12 DUCAT
0.2917 g., 0.9860 Gold 0.0092 oz. AGW **Ruler:** Leopold I **Obv:** Laureate bust of Leopold right in inner circle, value at shoulder **Rev:** Crowned imperial eagle in inner circle **Mint:** Breslau **Note:** Prev. Austria KM#1310 (KM#96).

Date	Mintage	VG	F	VF	XF	Unc
1681	—	70.00	145	215	400	—
1682	—	70.00	145	215	400	—
1683	—	70.00	145	215	400	—
1687	—	70.00	145	215	400	—
1688	—	70.00	145	215	400	—
1690	—	70.00	145	215	400	—
ND	—	70.00	145	215	400	—

KM# 585 1/12 DUCAT
0.2917 g., 0.9860 Gold 0.0092 oz. AGW **Ruler:** Leopold I **Obv:** Tall laureate bust right, value at shoulder **Mint:** Breslau **Note:** Prev. Austria KM#1357 (KM#97).

Date	Mintage	VG	F	VF	XF	Unc
1692	—	70.00	145	230	425	—
1693	—	70.00	145	230	425	—
1694	—	70.00	145	230	425	—
1695	—	70.00	145	230	425	—
1696	—	70.00	145	230	425	—
1698	—	70.00	145	230	425	—

KM# 654 1/12 DUCAT
0.2917 g., 0.9860 Gold 0.0092 oz. AGW **Ruler:** Leopold I **Obv:** Laureate head right, value at shoulder **Rev:** Crowned imperial eagle in inner circle **Mint:** Oppeln **Note:** Prev. Austria KM#1399 (KM#1285).

Date	Mintage	VG	F	VF	XF	Unc
1699	—	120	210	425	900	—

KM# 564 1/8 DUCAT
0.4375 g., 0.0139 Gold 0.0002 oz. AGW **Ruler:** Leopold I **Obv:** Crown divides date above two shields, value below **Mint:** Breslau **Note:** Prev. Austria KM#1339 (KM#98). Uniface.

Date	Mintage	VG	F	VF	XF	Unc
1686	—	110	215	400	900	—
1690	—	110	215	400	900	—
1694	—	110	215	400	900	—
1698	—	110	215	400	900	—

KM# 573 1/8 DUCAT
0.4375 g., 0.9860 Gold 0.0139 oz. AGW **Ruler:** Leopold I **Rev:** Crowned imperial eagle **Mint:** Breslau **Note:** Prev. Austria KM#1345 (KM#99).

Date	Mintage	VG	F	VF	XF	Unc
1688 SHS	—	110	215	400	900	—
1690 SHS	—	110	215	400	900	—
1693	—	110	215	400	900	—
1695	—	110	215	400	900	—
1696	—	110	215	400	900	—
1697	—	110	215	400	900	—

KM# 657 1/8 DUCAT
0.5834 g., 0.9860 Gold 0.0185 oz. AGW **Ruler:** Leopold I **Obv:** Laureate head right, value at shoulder **Rev:** Crowned imperial eagle in inner circle **Mint:** Oppeln **Note:** Prev. Austria KM#1400 (KM#1286).

Date	Mintage	VG	F	VF	XF	Unc
1699	—	180	325	475	950	—

KM# 492 1/6 DUCAT
0.5834 g., 0.9860 Gold 0.0185 oz. AGW **Ruler:** Leopold I **Mint:** Breslau **Note:** Prev. Austria KM#1259 (KM#100).

Date	Mintage	VG	F	VF	XF	Unc
1669 SHS	—	60.00	110	205	425	—
1670 SHS	—	60.00	110	205	425	—
1671 SHS	—	60.00	110	205	425	—
1673 SHS	—	60.00	110	205	425	—
1674 SHS	—	60.00	110	205	425	—
1675 SHS	—	60.00	110	205	425	—
1676 SHS	—	60.00	110	205	425	—
1677 SHS	—	60.00	110	205	425	—
1679 SHS	—	60.00	110	205	425	—
1681 SHS	—	60.00	110	205	425	—
1682 SHS	—	60.00	110	205	425	—

KM# 567 1/6 DUCAT
0.5834 g., 0.9860 Gold 0.0185 oz. AGW **Ruler:** Leopold I **Obv:** Lauerate bust right, value at shoulder **Rev:** Crowned imperial eagle **Mint:** Breslau **Note:** Prev. Austria KM#1342 (KM#101).

Date	Mintage	VG	F	VF	XF	Unc
1687 SHS	—	60.00	110	205	425	—
1688 SHS	—	60.00	110	205	425	—
1690 SHS	—	60.00	110	205	425	—
1691 SHS	—	60.00	110	205	425	—
1693	—	60.00	110	205	425	—
1694	—	60.00	110	205	425	—
1695	—	60.00	110	205	425	—
1696	—	60.00	110	205	425	—
1698	—	60.00	110	205	425	—

KM# 495 1/4 DUCAT
0.8750 g., 0.9860 Gold 0.0277 oz. AGW **Ruler:** Leopold I **Obv:** Laureate bust right in inner circle **Rev:** Crowned imperial eagle in inner circle **Mint:** Breslau **Note:** Prev. Austria KM#1260 (KM#102).

Date	Mintage	VG	F	VF	XF	Unc
1669 SHS	—	95.00	240	425	900	—
1671 SHS	—	95.00	240	425	900	—
1675 SHS	—	95.00	240	425	900	—
1676 SHS	—	95.00	240	425	900	—
1678 SHS	—	95.00	240	425	900	—
1679 SHS	—	95.00	240	425	900	—
1680 SHS	—	95.00	240	425	900	—
1681 SHS	—	95.00	240	425	900	—
1682 SHS	—	95.00	240	425	900	—
1683 SHS	—	95.00	240	425	900	—
1684 SHS	—	95.00	240	425	900	—

KM# 570 1/4 DUCAT
1.7500 g., 0.9860 Gold 0.0555 oz. AGW **Ruler:** Leopold I **Obv:** Standing figure right between two shields **Rev:** Heraldic imperial eagle **Mint:** Breslau **Note:** Prev. Austria KM#1343 (KM#103).

Date	Mintage	VG	F	VF	XF	Unc
1687 SHS	—	95.00	240	425	900	—
1688 SHS	—	95.00	240	425	900	—
1689 SHS	—	95.00	240	425	900	—
1690 SHS	—	95.00	240	425	900	—
1691 SHS	—	95.00	240	425	900	—

KM# 597 1/4 DUCAT
0.8750 g., 0.9860 Gold 0.0277 oz. AGW **Ruler:** Leopold I **Obv:** Laureate bust right in inner circle, value at shoulder **Rev:** Crowned imperial eagle without inner circle **Mint:** Breslau **Note:** Prev. Austria KM#104 (KM#1369).

Date	Mintage	VG	F	VF	XF	Unc
1693	—	95.00	240	425	900	—
1694	—	95.00	240	425	900	—
1696	—	95.00	240	425	900	—
1698	—	95.00	240	425	900	—

KM# 660 1/4 DUCAT
0.8750 g., 0.9860 Gold 0.0277 oz. AGW **Ruler:** Leopold I **Obv:** Laureate bust right in inner circle, value at shoulder **Rev:** Crowned imperial eagle **Mint:** Oppeln **Note:** Prev. Austria KM#1401 (KM#1287).

Date	Mintage	VG	F	VF	XF	Unc
1699	—	240	425	725	1,450	—

KM# 441 1/3 DUCAT
1.7500 g., 0.9860 Gold 0.0555 oz. AGW **Ruler:** Leopold I **Obv:** Crowned bust right in inner circle **Rev:** Oval arms on crowned imperial eagle in inner circle **Mint:** Breslau **Note:** Prev. Austria KM#1188 (KM#106).

Date	Mintage	VG	F	VF	XF	Unc
1661 GH	—	180	325	550	1,100	—
1663 GH	—	180	325	550	1,100	—

KM# 468 1/3 DUCAT
1.7500 g., 0.9860 Gold 0.0555 oz. AGW **Ruler:** Leopold I **Mint:** Breslau **Note:** Prev. Austria KM#1222 (KM#107).

Date	Mintage	VG	F	VF	XF	Unc
1664 GH	—	180	325	550	1,100	—

KM# 486 1/3 DUCAT
1.7500 g., 0.9860 Gold 0.0555 oz. AGW **Ruler:** Leopold I **Obv:** Laureatebust right in inner circle **Rev:** Shield of arms on crowned imperial eagle in inner circle **Mint:** Breslau **Note:** Prev. Austria KM#1249 (KM#108).

Date	Mintage	VG	F	VF	XF	Unc
1667 SHS	—	150	270	500	1,000	—
1668 SHS	—	150	270	500	1,000	—
1669 SHS	—	150	270	500	1,000	—
1670 SHS	—	150	270	500	1,000	—
1671 SHS	—	150	270	500	1,000	—
1674 SHS	—	150	270	500	1,000	—
1675 SHS	—	150	270	500	1,000	—
1676 SHS	—	150	270	500	1,000	—
1677 SHS	—	150	270	500	1,000	—
1678 SHS	—	150	270	500	1,000	—
1679 SHS	—	150	270	500	1,000	—
1680 SHS	—	150	270	500	1,000	—
1681 SHS	—	150	270	500	1,000	—
1682 SHS	—	150	270	500	1,000	—
1683 SHS	—	150	270	500	1,000	—
1684 SHS	—	150	270	500	1,000	—
1686 SHS	—	150	270	500	1,000	—
1687 SHS	—	150	270	500	1,000	—
1688 SHS	—	150	270	500	1,000	—
1689 SHS	—	150	270	500	1,000	—
1690 SHS	—	150	270	500	1,000	—
1691 SHS	—	150	270	500	1,000	—

KM# 546 1/3 DUCAT
1.1667 g., 0.9860 Gold 0.0370 oz. AGW **Ruler:** Leopold I **Obv:** Laureate bust right in inner circle, value at shoulder **Rev:** Crowned imperial eagle in inner circle **Mint:** Breslau **Note:** Prev. Austria KM#1311 (KM#105).

Date	Mintage	VG	F	VF	XF	Unc
1681 SHS	—	120	270	475	1,000	—
1683 SHS	—	120	270	475	1,000	—
1688 SHS	—	120	270	475	1,000	—
1690 SHS	—	120	270	475	1,000	—

KM# 600 1/3 DUCAT
1.1667 g., 0.9860 Gold 0.0370 oz. AGW **Ruler:** Leopold I **Mint:** Breslau **Note:** Prev. Austria KM#1370 (KM#A106).

Date	Mintage	VG	F	VF	XF	Unc
1693	—	120	270	475	1,000	—
1694	—	120	270	475	1,000	—
1696	—	120	270	475	1,000	—
1698	—	120	270	475	1,000	—

KM# 603 1/3 DUCAT
1.7500 g., 0.9860 Gold 0.0555 oz. AGW **Ruler:** Leopold I **Mint:** Breslau **Note:** Prev. Austria KM#1371 (KM#A109).

Date	Mintage	VG	F	VF	XF	Unc
1693	—	150	270	500	1,000	—
1694	—	150	270	500	1,000	—
1696	—	150	270	500	1,000	—
1698	—	150	270	500	1,000	—

KM# 330 1/2 DUCAT
Gold **Ruler:** Ferdinand II **Obv:** Standing figure right between two shields **Rev:** Heraldic imperial eagle **Mint:** Breslau **Note:** Prev. Austria KM#818 (KM#46).

Date	Mintage	VG	F	VF	XF	Unc
1636 HZ/(2ch)	—	—	—	—	—	—
Note: Reported, not confirmed						
1636 HZ above (2ch)	—	190	300	725	1,900	—

MB# 66 DUCAT
3.5000 g., 0.9860 Gold 0.1109 oz. AGW **Ruler:** Rudolf II **Obv:** Full-length crowned and armored figure, head and torso turned to right, holding scepter over right shoulder **Obv. Legend:** RVDOL. II. D.G. RO. IM. - S - AVG. G. H. B. REX. **Rev:** Crowned imperial eagle, large shield of 4-fold arms with central shield of Silesia superimposed on breast, date at end of legend **Rev. Legend:** ARCHIDVX. AVST. DVX. BVR. ET. SILESIAE **Mint:** Breslau **Note:** Fr. #79.

Date	Mintage	VG	F	VF	XF	Unc
ND(ca. 1583)	—	300	600	1,200	2,000	—

KM# 66 DUCAT
3.5000 g., 0.9860 Gold 0.1109 oz. AGW **Ruler:** Ferdinand II **Obv:** Laureate bust **Rev:** Silesian eagle **Mint:** Breslau **Note:** Prev. Austria KM#458 (KM#47).

Date	Mintage	VG	F	VF	XF	Unc
1623	—	625	1,250	2,300	3,750	—

KM# 69 DUCAT

3.5000 g., 0.9860 Gold 0.1109 oz. AGW **Ruler:** Ferdinand II **Obv:** Ferdinand II standing right divides date in inner circle **Rev:** Crowned imperial eagle in inner circle **Mint:** Breslau **Note:** Prev. Austria KM#459 (KM#48).

Date	Mintage	VG	F	VF	XF	Unc
1623 (ht)	—	175	280	625	1,900	—
1625 W-(h)	—	175	280	625	1,900	—

KM# 261 DUCAT

3.5000 g., 0.9860 Gold 0.1109 oz. AGW **Ruler:** Ferdinand II **Obv:** Crowned shield of arms added at each side of standing figure **Rev:** Date in legend **Mint:** Breslau **Note:** Prev. Austria KM#656(KM#49).

Date	Mintage	VG	F	VF	XF	Unc
1626 W-(h)	—	175	280	625	1,900	—
1629 W-(h)	—	175	280	625	1,900	—
1630 W-(hp)	—	175	280	625	1,900	—
1633 W(3ch)IZ	—	175	280	625	1,900	—
1633 W-HZ above (3ch)	—	175	280	625	1,900	—

KM# 306 DUCAT

3.5000 g., 0.9860 Gold 0.1109 oz. AGW **Ruler:** Ferdinand II **Obv:** Bust right **Mint:** Breslau **Note:** Prev. Austria KM#755 (KM#50).

Date	Mintage	VG	F	VF	XF	Unc
1630 W/(3ch)/IZ	—	—	—	—	—	—

KM# 309 DUCAT

3.5000 g., 0.9860 Gold 0.1109 oz. AGW **Ruler:** Ferdinand II **Obv:** Crowned bust in inner circle **Mint:** Breslau **Note:** Prev. Austria KM#756 (KM#51).

Date	Mintage	VG	F	VF	XF	Unc
1630 W/(3ch)/IZ	—	—	—	—	—	—
1631 W(3ch)IZ	—	250	400	875	2,050	—
1632 W(3ch)IZ	—	250	400	875	2,050	—
1635 HZ-(2ch)	—	250	400	875	2,050	—
1636 HZ-(2ch)	—	250	400	875	2,050	—

KM# 339 DUCAT

3.5000 g., 0.9860 Gold 0.1109 oz. AGW **Ruler:** Ferdinand III **Obv:** Crowned bust right in inner circle **Rev:** Crowned imperial eagle in inner circle, date in legend **Mint:** Breslau **Note:** Prev. Austria KM#842 (KM#70).

Date	Mintage	VG	F	VF	XF	Unc
1637	—	190	400	750	1,900	—
1638	—	190	400	750	1,900	—
1639	—	190	400	750	1,900	—
1640	—	190	400	750	1,900	—
1641	—	190	400	750	1,900	—
1642	—	190	400	750	1,900	—
1643	—	190	400	750	1,900	—
1644	—	190	400	750	1,900	—
1645	—	190	400	750	1,900	—
1646	—	190	400	750	1,900	—
1647	—	190	400	750	1,900	—
1648	—	190	400	750	1,900	—
1649	—	190	400	750	1,900	—
1650	—	190	400	750	1,900	—
1651	—	190	400	750	1,900	—
1652	—	190	400	750	1,900	—
1653	—	190	400	750	1,900	—
1654	—	190	400	750	1,900	—
1655	—	190	400	750	1,900	—
1656	—	190	400	750	1,900	—
1657	—	190	400	750	1,900	—

KM# 423 DUCAT

3.5000 g., 0.9860 Gold 0.1109 oz. AGW **Ruler:** Leopold I **Obv:** Crowned bust right in inner circle **Rev:** Crowned imperial eagle in inner circle, date in legend **Mint:** Breslau **Note:** Prev. Austria KM#1157 (KM#109).

Date	Mintage	VG	F	VF	XF	Unc
1659 GH	—	220	475	950	2,000	—
1660 GH	—	220	475	950	2,000	—
1661 GH	—	220	475	950	2,000	—
1663 GH	—	220	475	950	2,000	—
1664 GH	—	220	475	950	2,000	—
1665 GH	—	220	475	950	2,000	—

KM# 497 DUCAT

3.5000 g., 0.9860 Gold 0.1109 oz. AGW **Ruler:** Leopold I **Obv:** Laureate bust right in inner circle **Rev:** Crowned imperial eagle in inner circle, crown divides date **Mint:** Breslau **Note:** Prev. Austria KM#1262 (KM#110).

Date	Mintage	VG	F	VF	XF	Unc
1669 SHS	—	155	400	850	1,550	—
1673 SHS	—	155	400	850	1,550	—
1674 SHS	—	155	400	850	1,550	—
1675 SHS	—	155	400	850	1,550	—
1676 SHS	—	155	400	850	1,550	—
1677 SHS	—	155	400	850	1,550	—
1678 SHS	—	155	400	850	1,550	—
1680 SHS	—	155	400	850	1,550	—
1681 SHS	—	155	400	850	1,550	—
1682 SHS	—	155	400	850	1,550	—
1684 SHS	—	155	400	850	1,550	—
1685 SHS	—	155	400	850	1,550	—
1688 SHS	—	155	400	850	1,550	—
1689 SHS	—	155	400	850	1,550	—
1690 SHS	—	155	400	850	1,550	—
1691 SHS	—	155	400	850	1,550	—

KM# 531 DUCAT

3.5000 g., 0.9860 Gold 0.1109 oz. AGW **Ruler:** Leopold I **Obv:** Laureate bust right in inner circle **Rev:** Crowned imperial eagle in inner circle, crown divides date **Mint:** Brieg **Note:** Prev. Austria KM#1299 (KM#178).

Date	Mintage	VG	F	VF	XF	Unc
1677 CB	—	200	400	875	2,000	—

KM# 588 DUCAT

3.5000 g., 0.9860 Gold 0.1109 oz. AGW **Ruler:** Leopold I **Obv:** Fuller laureate bust right in inner circle **Rev:** Crowned imperial eagle, crown divides date **Mint:** Breslau **Note:** Prev. Austria KM#111 (KM#1358).

Date	Mintage	VG	F	VF	XF	Unc
1692	—	155	400	850	1,550	—
1693	—	155	400	850	1,550	—
1694	—	155	400	850	1,550	—
1696	—	155	400	850	1,550	—
1697	—	155	400	850	1,550	—
1698	—	155	400	850	1,550	—

KM# 636 DUCAT

3.5000 g., 0.9860 Gold 0.1109 oz. AGW **Ruler:** Leopold I **Obv:** Smaller bust right in inner circle **Rev:** Crowned imperial eagle in inner circle, date in legend **Mint:** Brieg **Note:** Prev. Austria KM#179 (KM#1393).

Date	Mintage	VG	F	VF	XF	Unc
1696 CB	—	155	400	850	1,750	—
1697 CB	—	155	400	850	1,750	—

KM# 666 DUCAT

3.5000 g., 0.9860 Gold 0.1109 oz. AGW **Ruler:** Leopold I **Obv:** Laureate armored bust right in inner circle **Rev:** Crowned arms in Order collar in inner circle **Mint:** Oppeln **Note:** Prev. Austria KM#1409 (KM#1288)

Date	Mintage	VG	F	VF	XF	Unc
1700 FN	—	450	1,300	2,750	5,200	—

KM# 351 2 DUCAT

7.0000 g., 0.9860 Gold 0.2219 oz. AGW **Ruler:** Ferdinand III **Obv:** Crowned bust right in inner circle **Rev:** Crowned imperial eagle **Mint:** Breslau **Note:** Prev. Austria KM#898 (KM#71). Legend varieties exist.

Date	Mintage	VG	F	VF	XF	Unc
1641	—	350	850	2,200	5,200	—
1642	—	350	850	2,200	5,200	—
1643	—	350	850	2,200	5,200	—
1645	—	350	850	2,200	5,200	—

KM# 444 2 DUCAT

7.0000 g., 0.9860 Gold 0.2219 oz. AGW **Ruler:** Leopold I **Obv:** Crowned bust right in inner circle **Rev:** Crowned imperial eagle in inner circle, date in legend **Mint:** Breslau **Note:** Prev. Austria KM#112 (KM#1189).

Date	Mintage	VG	F	VF	XF	Unc
1661	—	400	850	2,450	6,000	—
1665 SH	—	400	850	2,450	6,000	—
1669 SHS	—	400	850	2,450	6,000	—
1671 SHS	—	400	850	2,450	6,000	—
1672 SHS	—	400	850	2,450	6,000	—
1673 SHS	—	400	850	2,450	6,000	—
1679 SHS	—	400	850	2,450	6,000	—
1684 SHS	—	400	850	2,450	6,000	—
1687 SHS	—	400	850	2,450	6,000	—
1692	—	400	850	2,450	6,000	—

KM# 663 2 DUCAT

7.0000 g., 0.9860 Gold 0.2219 oz. AGW **Ruler:** Leopold I **Obv:** Laureate bust right in inner circle **Rev:** Crowned eagle with wreath around head in inner circle **Mint:** Oppeln **Note:** Prev. Austria KM#1402 (KM#1289).

Date	Mintage	VG	F	VF	XF	Unc
1699 FN	—	550	1,100	3,150	9,400	—

KM# 456 3 DUCAT

10.5000 g., 0.9860 Gold 0.3328 oz. AGW **Ruler:** Leopold I **Obv:** Crowned bust right in inner circle **Rev:** Crowned imperial eagle in inner circle, date in legend **Mint:** Breslau **Note:** Prev. Austria KM#1213 (KM#113).

Date	Mintage	VG	F	VF	XF	Unc
1663 GH	—	725	1,600	6,100	10,500	—
1665/3 SH	—	725	1,600	6,100	10,500	—
1667 SHS	—	725	1,600	6,100	10,500	—

KM# 513 3 DUCAT

10.5000 g., 0.9860 Gold 0.3328 oz. AGW **Ruler:** Leopold I **Obv:** Laureate bust right in inner circle **Rev:** Crowned imperial eagle in inner circle, crown divides date **Mint:** Breslau **Note:** Prev. Austria KM#1285 (KM#114).

Date	Mintage	VG	F	VF	XF	Unc
1675 SHS	—	525	1,050	3,600	7,200	—
1684 SHS	—	525	1,050	3,600	7,200	—
1689 SHS	—	525	1,050	3,600	7,200	—

KM# 624 3 DUCAT

10.5000 g., 0.9860 Gold 0.3328 oz. AGW **Ruler:** Leopold I **Mint:** Breslau **Note:** Prev. Austria KM#1390 (KM#A115).

Date	Mintage	VG	F	VF	XF	Unc
1695 MMW	—	525	1,050	3,600	7,200	—
1696 MMW	—	525	1,050	3,600	7,200	—

KM# 669 3 DUCAT

10.5000 g., 0.9860 Gold 0.3328 oz. AGW **Ruler:** Leopold I **Obv:** Laureate bust right in inner circle **Rev:** Crowned imperial eagle in inner circle **Mint:** Oppeln **Note:** Prev. Austria KM#1290 (KM#1411).

Date	Mintage	VG	F	VF	XF	Unc
1700 FN	—	650	1,300	4,400	9,400	—

KM# 519 4 DUCAT

14.0000 g., 0.9860 Gold 0.4438 oz. AGW **Ruler:** Leopold I **Obv:** Laureate bust right in inner circle **Rev:** Crowned imperial eagle in inner circle **Mint:** Breslau **Note:** Prev. Austria KM#1291 (KM#115).

Date	Mintage	VG	F	VF	XF	Unc
1676 SHS	—	1,100	2,200	650	11,000	—

KM# 591 4 DUCAT

14.0000 g., 0.9860 Gold 0.4438 oz. AGW **Ruler:** Leopold I **Mint:** Breslau **Note:** Prev. Austria KM#1359 (KM#A116).

Date	Mintage	VG	F	VF	XF	Unc
1692 MMW	—	1,100	2,200	6,600	11,000	—
1695 MMW	—	1,100	2,200	6,600	11,000	—

KM# 627 4 DUCAT

14.0000 g., 0.9860 Gold 0.4438 oz. AGW **Ruler:** Leopold I **Obv:** Older bust **Mint:** Breslau **Note:** Prev. Austria KM#1391 (KM#116).

Date	Mintage	VG	F	VF	XF	Unc
1695	—	1,400	3,850	8,300	12,500	—

MB# 78 5 DUCAT

17.5000 g., 0.9860 Gold 0.5547 oz. AGW **Ruler:** Rudolf II **Obv:** Crowned and armored 1/2-length figure to right, holding sceptre over right shoulder and imperial orb in left hand **Obv. Legend:** RVDOLPHVS. II. D.G. RO. IM. S. A. GE. GV. BO. REX. **Rev:** Crowned imperial eagle in circle, large 4-fold arms with central shield of Silesia superimposed on breast, date at end of legend **Rev. Legend:** ARCHIDVX. AV. DVX - BV. ET. SILESIAE. **Mint:** Breslau **Note:** Struck with Thaler dies, MB#72. Fr. #74.

Date	Mintage	VG	F	VF	XF	Unc
1587 (db) Rare	—	—	—	—	—	—

KM# 264 5 DUCAT
17.5000 g., 0.9860 Gold 0.5547 oz. AGW **Ruler:** Ferdinand II **Obv:** Laureate bust right in inner circle **Rev:** Crowned imperial eagle in inner circle **Mint:** Breslau **Note:** Prev. Austria KM#658 (KM#53).

Date	Mintage	VG	F	VF	XF	Unc
1626 HR	—	650	1,600	3,300	7,200	—
1627 HR	—	650	1,600	3,300	7,200	—
1628	—	650	1,600	3,300	7,200	—
1629	—	650	1,600	3,300	7,200	—

KM# 342 5 DUCAT
17.5000 g., 0.9860 Gold 0.5547 oz. AGW **Ruler:** Ferdinand III **Obv:** Laureate bust right in inner circle **Rev:** Crowned imperial eagle **Mint:** Breslau **Note:** Prev. Austria KM#862 (KM#72).

Date	Mintage	VG	F	VF	XF	Unc
1638	—	650	1,200	3,050	6,600	—
1643	—	650	1,200	3,050	6,600	—

KM# 555 5 DUCAT
17.5000 g., 0.9860 Gold 0.5547 oz. AGW **Ruler:** Leopold I **Obv:** Laureate bust right in inner circle **Rev:** Crowned imperial eagle in inner circle **Mint:** Breslau **Note:** Prev. Austria KM#1328 (KM#117).

Date	Mintage	VG	F	VF	XF	Unc
1684 SHS	—	650	1,650	4,700	8,800	—
1690 SHS	—	650	1,650	4,700	8,800	—

KM# 630 5 DUCAT
17.5000 g., 0.9860 Gold 0.5547 oz. AGW **Ruler:** Leopold I **Obv:** Laureate bust right in inner circle **Rev:** Crowned imperial eagle in inner circle **Mint:** Brieg **Note:** Prev. Austria KM#1392 (KM#180).

Date	Mintage	VG	F	VF	XF	Unc
1695 CB	—	825	1,800	4,700	8,800	—

KM# 645 5 DUCAT
17.5000 g., 0.9860 Gold 0.5547 oz. AGW **Ruler:** Leopold I **Mint:** Breslau **Note:** Prev. Austria KM#1395 (KM#A118).

Date	Mintage	VG	F	VF	XF	Unc
1698	—	650	1,650	4,700	8,800	—

KM# 156 6 DUCAT
21.0000 g., 0.9860 Gold 0.6657 oz. AGW **Ruler:** Ferdinand II **Obv:** Bust right **Rev:** Heraldic imperial eagle **Mint:** Breslau **Note:** Prev. Austria KM#554 (KM#54).

Date	Mintage	VG	F	VF	XF	Unc
1624 BZ/HR Rare	—	—	—	—	—	—

KM# 159 10 DUCAT
35.0000 g., 0.9860 Gold 1.1095 oz. AGW **Ruler:** Ferdinand II **Mint:** Neisse **Note:** Prev. Austria KM#555 (KM#1214). Struck with 1 Thaler dies of KM#599.

Date	Mintage	VG	F	VF	XF	Unc
1624 (dt) - BZ Rare	—	—	—	—	—	—

KM# 243 10 DUCAT
35.0000 g., 0.9860 Gold 1.1095 oz. AGW **Ruler:** Ferdinand II **Obv:** Bust right **Rev:** Heraldic imperial eagle **Mint:** Oppeln **Note:** Prev. Austria KM#621 (KM#1273).

Date	Mintage	VG	F	VF	XF	Unc
1625 SF Rare	—	—	—	—	—	—

KM# 267 10 DUCAT
35.0000 g., 0.9860 Gold 1.1095 oz. AGW **Ruler:** Ferdinand II **Obv:** Frontal portrait with scepter and orb **Rev:** Soldiers with city view in background **Mint:** Breslau **Note:** Prev. Austria KM#663 (KM#55).

Date	Mintage	VG	F	VF	XF	Unc
1626 (h) Rare	—	—	—	—	—	—

PATTERNS

Including off metal strikes

KM#	Date	Mintage	Identification	Mkt Val
PnBR1	ND(1649)	—	Kreuzer. Gold.	—
PnBR2	ND(1652)	—	Kreuzer. Gold.	—
PnBR3	ND(1653)	—	Kreuzer. Gold.	—
PnOP2	ND(1680)	—	3 Pfennig. Gold.	—
PnOP3	ND(1686)	—	3 Pfennig. Gold.	—
PnOP4	ND(1687)	—	3 Pfennig. Gold.	—
PnOP5	ND(1688)	—	3 Pfennig. Gold.	—
PnOP6	ND(1689)	—	3 Pfennig. Gold.	—
PnOP7	ND(1690)	—	3 Pfennig. Gold.	—
PnOP8	ND(1693)	—	3 Pfennig. Gold.	—
PnOP9	ND(1694)	—	3 Pfennig. Gold.	—
PnOP10	ND(1695)	—	4 Heller. Gold.	—
PnOP11	ND(1696)	—	3 Pfennig. Gold.	—
PnOP12	ND(1699)	—	4 Heller. Gold.	—
PnOP13	ND(1699)	—	3 Pfennig. Gold.	—

SILESIA-LIEGNITZ-BRIEG

One of the major divisions of Silesia and notably having two administrative centers, Silesia-Liegnitz-Brieg went through periods when its two parts were ruled separately by various family members. Liegnitz is northwest of the traditional Silesian capital of Breslau and separated from it by the territory of Neumarkt. Brieg is southwest of Breslau, with the district of Ohlau separating the two entities.

The seemingly numerous divisions of Silesia-Liegnitz-Brieg in reality were not an alienation of the various components of the duchy, but rather a division of the administration by members of the ruling family. Therefore, all parts of Silesia-Liegnitz-Brieg were under a single ruler during some years, whereas the districts of Liegnitz, Brieg, Ohlau, Lüben, Wohlau and Goldberg-Haynau had their own individual dukes during other periods. The rulers sometimes issued joint coinages under this system.

When the last duke died childless in 1675, Silesia-Liegnitz-Brieg passed to the control of the Habsburg emperors as Kings of Bohemia. The duchy finally was acquired by Prussia through force of arms in the 1740's, along with most of the rest of Silesia.

RULERS

Friedrich IV, Liegnitz with
Anna von Württemberg, Haynau, 1594-1616
Joachim Friedrich, in Brieg, 1586-1602
in Liegnitz, 1596-1602
Anna Maria von Anhalt-Dessau, Ohlau, 1602-1605
Georg Rudolph, Liegnitz & Goldberg, 1602-1653
Johann Christian, in Brieg, 1602-1639
Georg III, in Brieg, 1639-1664
Ludwig IV, in Liegnitz, 1653-1663
Anna Sophie von Mecklenburg, Parchwitz, 1663-1667
Christian, in Liegnitz, 1663-1672
in Brieg, 1664-1672
in Ohlau, 1639-1672
Louise von Anhalt, in Ohlau, 1672-1680, regent for
Georg Wilhelm, in Liegnitz-Brieg, 1672-1675

MINT OFFICIALS' INITIALS or MARKS

Brieg Mint

Initial or Mark	Date	Name
BH (sometimes in ligature)	1616-22	Burkhard Hase, also Kreuzburg
	1621-?	Joachim Stein, mint contractor
	? – 1623	Caspar Wecker, mintmaster
	1623	Blasius Pförtner, mintmaster
EW	1657-73	Elilas Weiss, warden & mintmaster
CB, CBS	1668-1713	Christoph Brettschneider, warden and Mintmaster
SK	1674-75	Samuel Koller, goldsmith and medailleur

Breslau Mint

Initial or Mark	Date	Name
HR	1614-35	Hans Rieger, warden and die-cutter, also in Ohlau and Reichenstein
(fs)= [mark] or FS	1625	Friedrich Schönau, die-cutter
GH	1645-65	Georg Hübner, imperial warden
DVF, VOGT	1659-63	D. Vogt, medailleur
GFH	1666-1706	Georg Franz Hoffmann, die-cutter

Haynau Mint

Initial or Mark	Date	Name
(mt)= [mark] or MT	1620-23	Markus Täubner

Liegnitz Mint

Initial or Mark	Date	Name
(c) = [mark] or CC	1612-21	Christoph Cantor
GH	1612-23	Georg Heinecke (Heinke)
(mt) = [mark] or MT	1620-21	Markus Täubner

Liegnitz and Brieg Mints

Initial or Mark	Date	Name
(d)= [mark]	1607-10	Christoph Tuchmann
(e)= [mark]	1602-05, 1621-22	Unknown
AK	1621	Unknown
IB	1638-70	Johann Bensheim, die-cutter
VT	1651-52	Unknown warden
(pf)= [mark] or [mark] or [mark]	1652-65	Christian Pfahler
ER	Ca. 1673-74	Unknown die-cutter

Wohlau Mint

Initial or Mark	Date	Name
IK	1621-23	Johann Knoblauch

ARMS

Silesia – eagle with crescent on breast
Brieg – checkerboard
Liegnitz-Brieg – 4-fold, quartered with arms of Silesia and Brieg

REFERENCES

B = Walter Baum, ***Zur Geschichte der Liegnitzer Münze***, **Lorch**, Württemberg, 1981.

F/S = Ferdinand Friedensburg and Hans Seger, ***Schlesiens Münzen und Medaillen der neueren Zeit***, Breslau, 1901 (reprint Frankfurt/Main, 1976).

J/M = Norbert Jaschke and Fritz P. Maercker, ***Schlesische Münzen und Medaillen***, Ihringen, 1985.

S = Hugo Frhr. Von Saurma-Jeltsch, ***Die Saurmasche Münzsammlung deutscher, schweizerischer und polnischer Gepräge von etwa dem Beginn der Groschenzeit bis zur Kipperperiode***, Berlin, 1892.

S/Sch = Hugo Frhr. Von Saurma-Jeltsch, ***Schlesische Münzen und Medaillen***, Breslau, 1883.

Sch = Wolfgang Schulten, ***Deutsche Münzen aus der Zeit Karls V***,. Frankfurt am Main, 1974.

DUCHY

REGULAR COINAGE

KM# 511 3 PFENNIG (DREIER)
Silver **Ruler:** Christian zu Ohlau **Obv:** Silesian eagle divides mintmaster's initials **Rev:** 2 ornately shaped adjacent shields of arms, crown above, date below where present **Note:** Ref: F/S#1955-57.

Date	Mintage	VG	F	VF	XF	Unc
1673	—	12.00	25.00	50.00	100	—
1673 CB	—	12.00	25.00	50.00	100	—
ND ER	—	12.00	25.00	50.00	100	—

KM# 368 KREUZER
Silver, 16.6 mm. **Ruler:** Georg III, Ludwig IV and Christian **Obv:** 3 facing 1/2-length figures, small imperial orb above **Obv. Legend:** D.G. GEORG • LUD • ET • CHRI • FRAT • **Rev:** Silesian eagle in circle, (I) below, date at end of legend **Rev. Legend:** DUCES • SI • LIG • - ET • BREG • **Mint:** Kreuzburg **Note:** Ref: F/S#1712, 1722-23.

Date	Mintage	VG	F	VF	XF	Unc
1651	—	10.00	20.00	40.00	90.00	—
165Z	—	10.00	20.00	40.00	90.00	—
165Z GH	—	10.00	20.00	40.00	90.00	—

KM# 426 3 KREUZER (1/24 Thaler)
Silver **Ruler:** Ludwig IV **Obv:** Mantled bust right, value '3' in oval below **Obv. Legend:** D.G. LUDOV (IC) • DUX • - SIL • L • B • & GOLDB. **Rev:** Silesian eagle in circle, date at end of legend **Rev. Legend:** MONETA. NOVA - ARGENT. **Note:** Ref. F/S#1870, 1872-73, 79-80, 1884-86. Varieties exist.

Date	Mintage	VG	F	VF	XF	Unc
1659 (pf)	—	12.00	25.00	45.00	85.00	—
1660 (pf)	—	12.00	25.00	45.00	85.00	—
1660 (pf) - EW	—	12.00	25.00	45.00	85.00	—

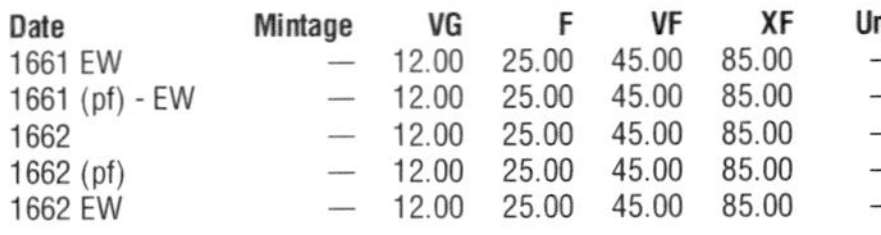

Date	Mintage	VG	F	VF	XF	Unc
1661 EW	—	12.00	25.00	45.00	85.00	—
1661 (pf) - EW	—	12.00	25.00	45.00	85.00	—
1662	—	12.00	25.00	45.00	85.00	—
1662 (pf)	—	12.00	25.00	45.00	85.00	—
1662 EW	—	12.00	25.00	45.00	85.00	—

KM# 425 3 KREUZER (1/24 Thaler)
Silver, 22 mm. **Ruler:** Georg III **Obv:** Mantled bust right, value '3' in oval below **Obv. Legend:** D.G. GEORGI • DVX • - SIL • L(IGN) • & BREG • **Rev:** Silesian eagle in circle, date at end of legend **Rev. Legend:** MONETA • NOVA - ARGENT • **Note:** Ref: F/S#1834, 1843, 1850-51, 1854-55. Varieties exist.

Date	Mintage	VG	F	VF	XF	Unc
1659 (pf)	—	12.00	25.00	45.00	85.00	—
1660 (pf) - EW	—	12.00	25.00	45.00	85.00	—
1661 (pf)	—	12.00	25.00	45.00	85.00	—
1661 (pf) - EW	—	12.00	25.00	45.00	85.00	—
1662 (pf)	—	12.00	25.00	45.00	85.00	—
1662 EW	—	12.00	25.00	45.00	85.00	—

KM# 150 3 KREUZER
Silver **Ruler:** Johann Christian and Georg Rudolph **Obv:** Silesian eagle **Obv. Legend:** IO. CHR. ET. GEO. RVD. DVC. SIL. L. B. **Rev:** 2 adjacent shields of arms, Silesian eagle left, Brieg right, large crown above, 3 in oval below, date at end of legend **Rev. Legend:** MO. NOV. ARG. REICHST. **Mint:** Reichenstein **Note:** Varieties exist. Ref: F/S#1493, 1496, 1500-01, 1503, 1514-15, 1518, 1537, 1545-46, 1556, J/M#114.

Date	Mintage	VG	F	VF	XF	Unc
1614 (c)	—	20.00	27.00	40.00	75.00	—
1615 (c)	—	20.00	27.00	40.00	75.00	—
1616	—	20.00	27.00	40.00	75.00	—
1616 (c)	—	20.00	27.00	40.00	75.00	—
1616 BH	—	20.00	27.00	40.00	75.00	—
1617 BH	—	20.00	27.00	40.00	75.00	—
1617 HR	—	20.00	27.00	40.00	75.00	—
1618 HR	—	20.00	27.00	40.00	75.00	—
168 HR (error)	—	20.00	27.00	40.00	75.00	—
1619 HR	—	20.00	27.00	40.00	75.00	—
16Z0 HR	—	20.00	27.00	40.00	75.00	—
16Z1 HR	—	20.00	27.00	40.00	75.00	—

KM# 370 3 KREUZER
Silver **Ruler:** Georg III, Ludwig IV and Christian **Obv:** 3 facing 1/2-length figures, value 3 in oval below **Obv. Legend:** D.G. GEORG. LUDW - ET. CHRISTIAN. **Rev:** Silesian eagle in circle, date at end of legend **Rev. Legend:** FRAT. DUC. SIL. - LIG. BREG. **Note:** Ref: F/S#1711, 1720-21.

Date	Mintage	VG	F	VF	XF	Unc
1651 (pf) - VT	—	12.00	25.00	50.00	90.00	—
1652	—	12.00	25.00	50.00	90.00	—
1652 GH	—	12.00	25.00	50.00	90.00	—

KM# 500 3 KREUZER
Silver **Ruler:** Christian zu Ohlau **Obv:** Mantled bust right, value '3' in oval below **Obv. Legend:** CHRISTIANVS ? - ? D?G ? DVX ? SIL **Rev:** Silesian eagle, crown above divides date in margin **Rev. Legend:** LIGNIC ? BREGENS ? & ? WOLAV. **Note:** Ref. F/S#1928, 1931, 1936.

Date	Mintage	VG	F	VF	XF	Unc
1668 CB	—	8.00	13.00	27.00	45.00	95.00
1669 CB	—	8.00	13.00	27.00	45.00	95.00
1670 CB	—	8.00	13.00	27.00	45.00	95.00

KM# 516 6 KREUZER
Silver **Ruler:** Louise **Obv:** Silesian eagle, crown above, (VI) below **Obv. Legend:** MONETA NOV. AR - GENT. DUC. SIL(E) **Rev:** 2 adjacent oval arms in baroque frame, crown above, date at top in margin **Rev. Legend:** LIGN(ICENS). BREG(ENS). (ET) (&). WOLA(V) (U) IE (NSIS). **Note:** Ref. F/S#1950-51. Varieties exist.

Date	Mintage	VG	F	VF	XF	Unc
1673	—	—	—	—	—	—
1673 CB	—	9.00	15.00	25.00	45.00	—

KM# 521 6 KREUZER
Silver **Ruler:** Georg Wilhelm **Obv:** Armored and mantled bust right **Obv. Legend:** GEORG. WILHELM. D.G. DVX. SIL. **Rev:** Silesian eagle, crown above divides date in margin, (VI) below **Rev. Legend:** LIGNIC. BREGE - NS. & WOLAVI. **Note:** Ref. F/S#1960.

Date	Mintage	VG	F	VF	XF	Unc
1674 CB	—	30.00	42.00	60.00	85.00	—

KM# 430 15 KREUZER (1/6 Thaler)
, 28 mm. **Ruler:** Georg III **Obv:** Armored bust to right, value (XV) below **Obv. Legend:** D.G. GEORGIUS. DUX. - SIL. LIGN. ET. BREG. **Rev:** Silesian eagle in circle, date at end of legend **Rev. Legend:** MONETA. NOVA. - ARGENTEA. **Note:** Ref. F/S#1833, 1842, 1848-49, 1852-53, 1856, 1860. Varieties exist.

Date	Mintage	VG	F	VF	XF	Unc
1659 (pf)	—	30.00	60.00	100	200	—
1660 (pf) - EW	—	30.00	60.00	100	200	—
1661 (pf) - EW	—	30.00	60.00	100	200	—
1661 EW	—	30.00	60.00	100	200	—
1662 (pf)	—	30.00	60.00	100	200	—
1662 EW	—	30.00	60.00	100	200	—
1663 (pf)	—	30.00	60.00	100	200	—
1664 (pf)	—	30.00	60.00	100	200	—

KM# 397 1/8 THALER
Silver **Ruler:** Johann Christian and Georg Rudolph **Obv:** Facing bust, turned slightly to right **Obv. Legend:** D.G. GEORG. RUDOLPH. DUX. SIL. LIG. BREG & GOLDBE. **Rev:** 6-line inscription with dates **Rev. Legend:** S. CÆS. MAI. VICAR. REG. SUPR. PRÆF. PER. UTRAM & SIL. **Rev. Inscription:** NATUS / 22. IANUARII / ANNO 1595 / OBIIT 14 / IANUARII / 1653 **Note:** Ref. F/S#1702.

Date	Mintage	VG	F	VF	XF	Unc
1653	—	150	250	350	500	—

KM# 506 1/2 THALER
Silver **Ruler:** Georg Wilhelm **Subject:** Death of Christian **Obv:** Armored and mantled bust to right **Obv. Legend:** CONSTANTER. ET. SINCERE. **Rev:** 6-line inscription with Roman numeral dates, arabesques above and below **Rev. Legend:** CHRISTIANVS. D.B. DVX. SIL. LIG. BREG. ET. WOL. **Rev. Inscription:** NAT. OLAV. / A.C. MDCXIIX. / XIX. APRIL / DENAT. LIGNICI. / A.C. MDCLXXII / XXIX. FEBR. **Note:** Ref. F/S#1947.

Date	Mintage	VG	F	VF	XF	Unc
1672	—	—	—	—	—	—

KM# 532 1/2 THALER
Silver **Subject:** Death of Georg Wilhelm **Obv:** Mantled bust to right **Obv. Legend:** GEORG. WILHELM. D.G. DVX. SILESIÆ. **Rev:** 10-line inscription with dates **Rev. Inscription:** PIASTEÆ / REG. FAM. ULTIM. / VIRTUTE. PRIMUS. / ANIMAM. / DIE. 20. SEPTEMB. 1660. / ACCEPTAM / DEO. ITA. IUBENTI. / D. 21. NOVEMB. 1675 / ILLACHRYM. SILES. / REDDIDIT. **Note:** Ref. F/S#1974.

Date	Mintage	VG	F	VF	XF	Unc
1675 SK	—	65.00	100	150	225	—

KM# 14 THALER
Silver **Ruler:** Joachim Friedrich zu Liegnitz **Obv:** Armored bust with high collar to right **Obv. Legend:** IOACH. FRID. HERZ. I. SCHL. Z. L. V. B. T. Z. M. **Rev:** Bust right of Anna Marie von Anhalt wearing ruffed collar and small cap, date at top **Rev. Legend:** A. MARIA. G. F. Z. AN. HERZ. I. SCHL. Z. L. V. B. **Note:** Dav. #7705. Ref. F/S#1384.

Date	Mintage	VG	F	VF	XF	Unc
160Z Rare	—	—	—	—	—	—

KM# 15 THALER
Silver **Subject:** Death of Joachim Friedrich **Obv:** Armored and collared bust to right **Obv. Legend:** ✠ MEMOR. IOACH. FRID. DVCIS. SILES. LEGN. BREGENSIS **Rev:** 10-line inscription with Roman numeral dates **Rev. Inscription:** ✠ / DEO. OPT. / MAX. IN. ÆTERN. / VIVENS. SVM. PATR. / LVCIV. PLACIDE. OBI / IT. AN. M.D.C II. M. MA / RT. XX. V. HORA. P. MER / VI. CVM. VIRISSET / AN. LI. MEN. S.V / DIES. XXVI. **Note:** Ref. F/S#1388. Struck on thick flan from 1/2 Thaler dies, KM#10.

Date	Mintage	VG	F	VF	XF	Unc
MDCII (1602) Rare	—	—	—	—	—	—

KM# 42 THALER
Silver **Ruler:** Johann Christian and Georg Rudolph **Subject:** Death of Anna Maria von Anhalt, Widow of Joachim Friedrich **Obv:** Crowned 4-fold arms **Obv. Legend:** IO. CHR. ET. GE. RVD. FR. DVC. SL. LIG. ET. BREG. **Rev:** Crowned shield of 8-fold arms within central shield of Anhalt, double marginal legends with Roman numeral date **Rev. Legend:** Outer leg: MEM. IL. MAT. ANNÆ. MAR. PR. ANHAL. DVCI. SIL. LEG. BREG. QVÆ. Inner leg: PIA. OBIIT. M. NOV. DIE. XIV. M.D.C.V.F.F. **Note:** Dav. #7706. Ref. F/S#1395. Struck on thick flan from 1/2 Thaler dies, KM#40.

Date	Mintage	VG	F	VF	XF	Unc
MDCV (1605) Rare	—	—	—	—	—	—

KM# 53 THALER

Silver **Ruler:** Johann Christian and Georg Rudolph **Obv:** Two 1/2-length figures facing each other behind flat surface with arabesques in exergue **Obv. Legend:** D.G. IOHAN. CHRIST. ET. GEOR(G). RVD. FRA **Rev:** 4-fold arms, 3 ornate helmets above, date at end of legend **Rev. Legend:** DVC. SIL. LIG. - ET. BREG. **Note:** Dav. #7708. Ref. F/S#1410, 1416, 1420, 1424, 1438, 1456.

Date	Mintage	VG	F	VF	XF	Unc
(1)606	—	150	375	800	1,650	—
(1)607	—	150	375	800	1,650	—
(1)607 (d)	—	150	375	800	1,650	—
(1)608 (d)	—	150	375	800	1,650	—
(1)609 (d)	—	150	375	800	1,650	—
(1)610 (d)	—	150	375	800	1,650	—

KM# 63 THALER

Silver **Ruler:** Johann Christian and Georg Rudolph **Obv:** Two 1/2-length figures facing each other **Obv. Legend:** D.G. IOAN. CHRIST. ET. GEORG. RVD. FRA. **Rev:** Ornately shaped shield of 4-fold arms, 3 helmets above, date at end of legend **Rev. Legend:** DVC. SIL. LIG. - ET. BREG. **Note:** Dav. #7710. Ref. F/S#1425, 1436.

Date	Mintage	VG	F	VF	XF	Unc
(1)608 (d)	—	200	400	925	1,850	—
(1)609 (d)	—	200	400	925	1,850	—

KM# 64 THALER

Silver **Ruler:** Johann Christian and Georg Rudolph **Obv:** Two 1/2-length figures facing each other **Obv. Legend:** D.G. IOAN. CHRIST. ET. GEORG. RVD. FRA. **Rev:** Shield of 4-fold arms with flat top, 3 helmets above, date at end of legend **Rev. Legend:** DVC. SIL. LIG. - ET. BREG. **Note:** Dav. #7710A.

Date	Mintage	VG	F	VF	XF	Unc
(1)608 (d)	—	200	400	925	1,850	—

KM# 74 THALER

Silver **Ruler:** Johann Christian and Georg Rudolph **Obv:** Two 1/2-length figures facing each other, ornamented fillet below **Obv. Legend:** D.G. IOAN. CHRIST. ET. GEORG. RVD. FRA. **Rev:** Shield of 4-fold arms with flat top, 3 helmets above, date at end of legend **Rev. Legend:** DVC. DIL. LIG. - ET. BREG. **Note:** Dav. #7710B. Ref. F/S#1437.

Date	Mintage	VG	F	VF	XF	Unc
(1)609 (d)	—	225	450	1,000	2,000	—

KM# 76 THALER

Silver **Ruler:** Johann Christian and Georg Rudolph **Obv:** Two 1/2-length figures facing each other, wearing different armor, nothing below **Obv. Legend:** D.G. IOHAN. CHRIST. ET. GEORG. RVD. FRA. **Rev:** Oval shield of 4-fold arms, 3 helmets above, date at end of legend **Rev. Legend:** DVC. SIL. LIG. - ET. BREG. **Note:** Dav. #7713.

Date	Mintage	VG	F	VF	XF	Unc
(1)609 (d)	—	200	400	925	1,850	—
(1)610 (d)	—	200	400	925	1,850	—

KM# 75 THALER

Silver **Ruler:** Johann Christian and Georg Rudolph **Obv:** Two 1/2-length figures facing each other over horizontal line below **Obv. Legend:** D.G. IOHAN. CHRIST. ET. GEORG. RVD. FRA. **Rev:** Flat shield with rounded bottom of 4-fold arms, 3 helmets above, date at end of legend **Rev. Legend:** DVC. SIL. LIG. - ET. BREG. **Note:** Dav. #7712.

Date	Mintage	VG	F	VF	XF	Unc
(1)609 (d)	—	250	500	1,150	2,250	—

KM# 95 THALER

Silver **Ruler:** Johann Christian and Georg Rudolph **Obv:** Two 1/2-length figures facing each other **Obv. Legend:** D.G. IOAN. CHRIST. ET. GEORG. RVD. FRA. **Rev:** Oval shield of 4-fold arms, 3 helmets above, date at end of legend **Rev. Legend:** DVC. SIL. LIG. - ET. BREG. **Note:** Dav. #7713A.

Date	Mintage	VG	F	VF	XF	Unc
(1)610 (d)	—	200	400	925	1,850	—

KM# 128 THALER

Silver **Ruler:** Johann Christian and Georg Rudolph **Obv:** Draped bust to right, legend begins at bottom, divided by 2 small shields of arms at left and right, small imperial orb in circle at bottom **Obv. Legend:** D.G. IO - HANN. CHRISTI. - AN. ET. **Rev:** Draped bust to left divides date, legend begins at upper left, 2 small shields of arms at left and right **Rev. Legend:** GEOR. RVD. FRA. D. - SIL. LIG. ET. BREG. **Note:** Dav. #7715. Ref. F/S#1472.

Date	Mintage	VG	F	VF	XF	Unc
1611	—	300	600	1,250	2,500	—

KM# 129 THALER

Silver **Ruler:** Johann Christian and Georg Rudolph **Obv:** Draped bust to right, legend begins at bottom, divided by 2 small shields of arms at left and right, small imperial orb in circle at bottom **Obv. Legend:** D.G. IO - HANN. CHRISTI. - AN. ET. **Rev:** Draped bust to left divides date, legend begins at upper left, 2 small shields of arms at left and right **Rev. Legend:** GEOR. RVD. FRA. D. - SIL. LIG. ET. BREG. **Note:** Klippe. Dav. #7715A. Ref. F/S#1473.

Date	Mintage	VG	F	VF	XF	Unc
1611	—	675	1,350	2,250	—	—

KM# 155 THALER

Silver **Ruler:** Johann Christian and Georg Rudolph **Obv:** Bust right, legend begins at upper left, divided by 2 small shields of arms at left and right **Obv. Legend:** D.G. IO. CHR. ET. G - EO. RVD. DVX. SI. L. B. **Rev:** Bust left, legend ends with date, 2 small shields of arms at left and right **Rev. Legend:** MON. NOV. ARGE. - REICHST. **Mint:** Reichenstein **Note:** Klippe. Dav. #7716A. Ref. F/S#1492, 1495, 1498. Varieties exist.

Date	Mintage	VG	F	VF	XF	Unc
1614 Rare	—	—	—	—	—	—
1615 Rare	—	—	—	—	—	—
1616 Rare	—	—	—	—	—	—

KM# 154 THALER

Silver **Ruler:** Johann Christian and Georg Rudolph **Obv:** Bust right, legend begins at upper left, divided by 2 small shields of arms at left and right **Obv. Legend:** D.G. IO. CHR. ET. G - EO. RVD. DVX. SI. L. B. **Rev:** Bust left, legend ends with date, 2 small shields of arms at left and right **Rev. Legend:** MON. NOV. ARGE. - REICHST. **Mint:** Reichenstein **Note:** Dav. #7716. Ref. F/S#1511. Varieties exist.

Date	Mintage	VG	F	VF	XF	Unc
1614 Rare	—	—	—	—	—	—
1615 Rare	—	—	—	—	—	—
1616 Rare	—	—	—	—	—	—
1617 Rare	—	—	—	—	—	—

KM# 169 THALER

Silver **Ruler:** Johann Christian and Georg Rudolph **Obv:** 2 armored 1/2-length figures facing each other, horizontal line with ornamentation below **Obv. Legend:** D.G. IOHAN. CHRIS(T). ET. GEORG. RVDO. FRAT(R). **Rev:** Shield with flat top and rounded bottom of 4-fold arms, 3 ornate helmets above, date at end of legend **Rev. Legend:** DVC. SIL. LIGNIC. ET. BREGE. **Mint:** Reichenstein **Note:** Dav. #7718. Ref. F/S#1512, 1531, 1542. Varieties exist.

Date	Mintage	VG	F	VF	XF	Unc
1617 HR	—	500	1,000	2,500	4,250	—
1618 HR	—	500	1,000	2,500	4,250	—
1619 HR	—	500	1,000	2,500	4,250	—
1620 HR	—	750	1,500	3,000	6,250	—
1621 HR	—	750	1,500	3,000	6,250	—
1621	—	750	1,500	3,000	6,250	—

KM# 184 THALER

Silver **Ruler:** Johann Christian and Georg Rudolph **Obv:** 2 armored 1/2-length figures facing each other, horizontal line with ornamentation below **Obv. Legend:** D.G. IOHAN. CHRIS(T). ET. GEORG. RVDO. FRAT(R). **Rev:** Shield with flat top and rounded bottom of 4-fold arms, 3 ornate helmets above, date at end of legend **Rev. Legend:** DVC. SIL. LIGNIC. ET. BREGE. **Mint:** Reichenstein **Note:** Klippe. Dav. #7718B. Ref. F/S#1517, 1532.

Date	Mintage	VG	F	VF	XF	Unc
1618 HR	—	1,850	3,500	6,000	—	—
1619 HR	—	1,850	3,500	6,000	—	—
1621	—	1,850	3,500	6,000	—	—

KM# 193 THALER

Silver **Ruler:** Johann Christian and Georg Rudolph **Obv:** 2 armored 1/2-length figures facing each other **Obv. Legend:** D.G. IOHAN. CHRIS(T). ET. GEORG. RVDO. FRAT(R). **Rev:** Shield with flat top and rounded bottom of 4-fold arms, 3 ornate helmets above, date at end of legend **Rev. Legend:** DVC. SIL. LIGNIC. ET. BREGE. **Mint:** Reichenstein **Note:** Dav. #7718A. Ref. F/S#1517, 1532.

Date	Mintage	VG	F	VF	XF	Unc
1619	—	500	1,000	2,150	4,250	—

KM# 266 THALER

Silver **Ruler:** Johann Christian **Obv:** Armored bust to right **Obv. Legend:** D.G. IOHAN. CHRISTIAN. DVX. SIL. **Rev:** 4-fold arms, 3 helmets above, date at top in margin **Rev. Legend:** LIGN. ET. BREG. SVP. CAPVT. SIL. **Mint:** Ohlau **Note:** Dav. #7719. Ref. F/S#1562.

Date	Mintage	VG	F	VF	XF	Unc
16Z1 HR Rare	—	—	—	—	—	—

KM# 270 THALER

Silver **Ruler:** Georg Rudolf **Obv:** Armored bust right, small imperial orb at top **Obv. Legend:** D.G. GEORG. RVDOLPHVS. DVC. SILESIÆ. **Rev:** 4-fold arms, 3 helmets above, date at end of legend **Rev. Legend:** LIGNICEN. ET. - BREGEN **Mint:** Liegnitz **Note:** Dav. #7724. Ref. F/S#1688, 1692.

Date	Mintage	VG	F	VF	XF	Unc
16Z1 (e)	—	—	—	—	—	—
16ZZ (e)	—	1,850	3,500	6,000	—	—

KM# 267 THALER

Silver **Ruler:** Johann Christian **Obv:** Armored bust to right divides date, small imperial orb at top in margin **Obv. Legend:** D. G. IOHANES • CHRISTIANVS • DVX **Rev:** 4-fold arms, 3 helmets above **Rev. Legend:** SIL. LIGNI. - ET. BREGE. **Mint:** Ohlau **Note:** Dav. #7720. Ref. F/S#1563.

Date	Mintage	VG	F	VF	XF	Unc
1621 HR Rare	—	—	—	—	—	—

Note: Fritz Rudolf Künker Münzenhandlung Auction 135, 1-08, near XF realized approximately $7,750

KM# 268 THALER

Silver **Ruler:** Johann Christian **Obv:** Armored bust to right divides date, small imperial orb at top in margin **Obv. Legend:** D.G. IOHANES. CHRISTIANVS. DVX. **Rev:** 4-fold arms, 3 helmets above **Rev. Legend:** SIL. LIGNI. - ET. BREGE. **Mint:** Ohlau **Note:** Klippe. Dav. #7720A. Ref. F/S#1564.

Date	Mintage	VG	F	VF	XF	Unc
1621 HR Rare	—	—	—	—	—	—

KM# 269 THALER
Silver **Ruler:** Georg Rudolf **Obv:** Armored bust right, small imperial orb at top **Obv. Legend:** D.G. GEORG. RVDOLPHVS. DVC. SILES. **Rev:** 4-fold arms, 3 helmets above, date at end of legend **Rev. Legend:** LIGNIC • ET • BREG • **Mint:** Haynau **Note:** Dav. #7723.

Date	Mintage	VG	F	VF	XF	Unc
16Z1 MT Rare	—	—	—	—	—	—

KM# 345 THALER
Silver **Ruler:** Johann Christian **Obv:** Armored and mantled bust to right, small imperial orb at top in margin **Obv. Legend:** D: G. IOHAN. CHRISTIAN. DVX. SILES. LIGNI. ET. BREG. **Rev:** 4-fold arms, 3 helmets above, date at end of legend **Rev. Legend:** MONETA • NOVA • CRVCIBVRGENSIS. **Mint:** Kreuzburg **Note:** Dav. #7721. Ref. F/S#1598.

Date	Mintage	VG	F	VF	XF	Unc
1622 (fs) Rare	—	—	—	—	—	—

Note: Fritz Rudolf Künker Münzenhandlung Auction 135, 1-08, XF realized approximately $38,395

KM# 346 THALER
Silver **Ruler:** Georg Rudolf **Obv:** 1/2-length armored figure to right, legend begins with small imperial orb **Obv. Legend:** D.G. GEORGIVS. RVDOLPHVS. DVX. SILESIÆ. **Rev:** 4-fold arms, 3 helmets above, date divided at top **Rev. Legend:** LIGNICENSIS. ET. - BREGENSIS. **Mint:** Liegnitz **Note:** Dav. #7725. Ref. F/S#1690.

Date	Mintage	VG	F	VF	XF	Unc
16ZZ (e) Rare	—	—	—	—	—	—

KM# 347 THALER
Silver **Ruler:** Georg Rudolf **Obv:** 1/2-length armored figure to right, legend begins with small imperial orb **Obv. Legend:** D.G. GEORGIVS. RVDOLPHVS. DVX. SILESIÆ. **Rev:** City view of Liegnitz with battlements in foreground, date at end of legend **Rev. Legend:** SI. DEVS. PRO. NOBIS. QVIS. CONTRA. NOS. **Mint:** Liegnitz **Note:** Dav. #7726. Ref. F/S#1691.

Date	Mintage	VG	F	VF	XF	Unc
16ZZ (e) Rare	—	—	—	—	—	—

KM# 376 THALER
Silver **Ruler:** Georg III, Ludwig IV and Christian **Obv:** Three facing 1/2-length figures, horizontal line below with arabesques in exergue, small imperial orb at top **Obv. Legend:** D.G. GEORG. LUDOVIC. ET. CHRISTIAN. FRATRES. **Rev:** 3 helmets above ornate 4-fold arms, date at end of legend **Rev. Legend:** DUCES. SILESIÆ. LIGN. - ET. BREGENES. **Note:** Dav. #7727. Ref. F/S#1707-08, 1716.

Date	Mintage	VG	F	VF	XF	Unc
1651 (pf)	—	300	600	1,150	2,250	—
1651 (pf)-VT	—	750	1,500	3,000	6,250	—
165Z (pf)-VT	—	750	1,500	3,000	6,250	—

KM# 388 THALER
Silver **Ruler:** Georg III, Ludwig IV and Christian **Obv:** 3 facing 1/2-length figures, horizontal line below with arabesques in exergue, small imperial orb at top **Obv. Legend:** D.G. GEORG. LUDOVIC. ET. CHRISTIAN. FRATRES. **Rev:** 3 helmets above ornate 4-fold arms, date at end of legend **Rev. Legend:** DUCES. SILESI?. LIGN. - ET. BREGENES. **Note:** Ref. F/S#1718. Struck on thick flan from 1/2 Thaler dies, KM#374.

Date	Mintage	VG	F	VF	XF	Unc
165Z (pf)-VT	—	—	—	—	—	—

KM# 407.1 THALER
Silver **Ruler:** Georg III, Ludwig IV and Christian **Obv:** 3 facing 3/4-length figures, horizontal line below with arabesques in exergue, small imperial orb at top **Obv. Legend:** D.G. GEORGIVS. LUDOVICVS. ET. CHRISTIANVS. FRATR. **Rev:** 3 helmets above ornate 4-fold arms, date at end of legend **Rev. Legend:** DVCES. SILESI. LIGNI. BR - EGENES. ET. WOLAV. **Note:** Dav. #7729. Ref. F/S#1749. Varieties exist.

Date	Mintage	VG	F	VF	XF	Unc
1656 (pf)	—	350	950	2,250	4,500	—

KM# 407.2 THALER
Silver **Ruler:** Georg III, Ludwig IV and Christian **Obv:** 3 facing 1/2 length figures, horizontal line below, batons at waist **Obv. Legend:** D.G. GEORGIVS. LUDOVICVS. ET. CHRISTIANVS. FRATR. **Rev:** 3 helmets above ornate 4-fold arms, date at end of legend. **Rev. Legend:** DVCES. SILESI. LIGNI. BR - EGENES. ET. WOLAV. **Note:** Dav. #7729A. Ref. F/S#1749. Varieties exist.

Date	Mintage	VG	F	VF	XF	Unc
1656 (pf)	—	500	1,200	3,000	6,250	—

KM# 414.1 THALER
Silver **Ruler:** Georg III, Ludwig IV and Christian **Obv:** 3 facing armored 1/2-length figures, small imperial orb at top, arabesques in exergue **Obv. Legend:** D.G. GEORGIUS. LUDOVICVS. & CHRISTIANVS. FRATRES. **Rev:** 3 helmets above oval 4-fold arms, date at end of legend, EW below **Rev. Legend:** DVCES. SILESIÆ. LIGNIC. BRE - GENS. ET. WOLAVIENSES. **Note:** Dav. #7731. Ref. F/S#1759, 1768-69, 1778. Varieties exist.

Date	Mintage	VG	F	VF	XF	Unc
1657 (pf)-EW	—	450	1,100	2,750	5,750	—
1658 (pf)-EW	—	450	1,100	2,750	5,750	—
1659 (pf)-EW	—	450	1,100	2,750	5,750	—

KM# 414.2 THALER
Silver **Ruler:** Georg III, Ludwig IV and Christian **Obv:** 3 facing 1/2-length figures, horizontal line below with arabesques in exergue, small imperial orb at top **Obv. Legend:** D.G. GEORGIVS. LUDOVICVS. & CHRISTIANVS. FRATRES. **Rev:** 3 helmets above oval 4-fold arms, date at end of legend, no EW below **Rev. Legend:** DVCES. SILESIÆ. LIGNIC. BRE - GENS. ET. WOLAVIENSES **Note:** Dav. #7731. Ref. F/S#1759, 1768-69, 1778. Varieties exist.

Date	Mintage	VG	F	VF	XF	Unc
1657 (pf)	—	450	1,100	2,750	5,750	—
1658 (pf)	—	450	1,100	2,750	5,750	—

KM# 413 THALER
Silver **Ruler:** Georg III, Ludwig IV and Christian **Obv:** 3 facing armored 1/2-length figures, small imperial orb at top, arabesques in exergue **Obv. Legend:** D.G. GEORGIUS. LUDOVICUS. & CHRISTIANUS. FRATRES. **Rev:** 3 helmets above ornate 4-fold arms, date at end of legend **Rev. Legend:** DUCES. SILESI?. LIGNIC - ENSES. ET. BREGENSES. **Note:** Ref. F/S#1757-58.

Date	Mintage	VG	F	VF	XF	Unc
1657 (pf)	—	500	1,200	3,000	6,250	—
1657 (pf)-EW	—	500	1,200	3,000	6,250	—

KM# 444 THALER
Silver **Ruler:** Christian zu Ohlau **Obv:** Mantled bust to right, crown in margin at top **Obv. Legend:** D.G. CHRISTIANUS. DUX. SILESIÆ. LIGNIC. BREG. ET. WOL. **Rev:** Round 4-fold arms in baroque frame, 3 ornate helmets above, date at end of legend **Rev. Legend:** SUFFICIT MIHI GRA - TIA TUA DOMINE A. **Note:** Dav. #7739. Ref. F/S#1894, 1904.

Date	Mintage	VG	F	VF	XF	Unc
1660 (pf)-EW	—	400	1,000	2,500	5,000	—
1661 (pf)-EW	—	400	1,000	2,500	5,000	—

KM# 445 THALER
Silver **Ruler:** Christian zu Liegnitz **Obv:** Mantled bust to right, crown in margin at top **Obv. Legend:** D.G. CHRISTIANUS. DUX. SILESIÆ. LIGNIC. BREG. ET. WOL. **Rev:** Round 4-fold arms in baroque frame, 3 ornate helmets above, date at end of legend **Rev. Legend:** CONSILIUM IEHOVÆ STABIT. AN. **Note:** Dav. #7740. Ref. F/S#1897, 1903.

Date	Mintage	VG	F	VF	XF	Unc
1660 (pf)-EW	—	400	1,000	2,500	5,000	—
1661 EW	—	400	1,000	2,500	5,000	—

KM# 442 THALER
Silver **Ruler:** Georg III, Ludwig IV and Christian **Obv:** 3 facing 1/2-length figures, horizontal line below with arabesques in exergue, small imperial orb at top **Obv. Legend:** D.G. GEORGIVS. LUDOVICVS. & CHRISTIANVS. FRATRES. **Rev:** 3 helmets above oval 4-fold arms, date at end of legend **Rev. Legend:** SUFFICIT MIHI GRA - TIA TUA DOMINE A. **Note:** Dav. #7732. Ref. F/S#1786.

Date	Mintage	VG	F	VF	XF	Unc
1660 (pf)-EW	—	450	1,100	2,750	5,750	—

KM# 443 THALER
Silver **Ruler:** Georg III **Obv:** Mantled bust right, crown in margin at top **Obv. Legend:** D.G. GEORGIUS. DUX. SILESIÆ. LIGNIC. ET. BREGEN. **Rev:** Round 4-fold arms in baroque frame, 3 ornate helmets above, date at end of legend **Rev. Legend:** SORS MEA A-DOMINO AN. **Note:** Dav. #7735. Ref. F/S#1840-41.

Date	Mintage	VG	F	VF	XF	Unc
1660 (pf)-EW	—	400	1,000	2,250	5,000	—
1660	—	400	1,000	2,250	5,000	—

KM# 452 THALER
Silver **Ruler:** Georg III, Ludwig IV and Christian **Obv:** 3 facing 1/2 length figures, horizontal line below with arabesques in exergue, small imperial orb at top **Obv. Legend:** D.G. GEORGIVS. LUDOVICVS. & CHRISTIANVS. FRATRES. **Rev:** 3 helmets above oval 4-fold arms, date at end of legend **Rev. Legend:** CONSILIUM IEHOVÆ STABIT. AN. **Note:** Dav. #7733. Ref. F/S#1789.

Date	Mintage	VG	F	VF	XF	Unc
1661 EW	—	450	1,150	2,750	5,750	—

KM# 453 THALER
Silver **Ruler:** Georg III **Obv:** Mantled bust right, crown in margin at top **Obv. Legend:** D.G. GEORGIUS. DUX. SILESIÆ. LIGNIC. ET. BREGEN. **Rev:** 3 helmets above oval 4-fold arms, date at end of legend **Rev. Legend:** CONSILIUM IEHOVÆ STABIT. AN. **Note:** Dav. #7736. Ref. F/S#1847.

Date	Mintage	VG	F	VF	XF	Unc
1661 EW	—	450	1,150	2,750	5,500	—

KM# 454 THALER
Silver **Ruler:** Ludwig IV **Obv:** Crown above bust right of LudwigMantled bust right, crown in margin at top **Obv. Legend:** D.G. LUDOVICUS. DUX. SILESIÆ. LIGNIC. BREG. ET. GOLDBER. **Rev:** Round 4-fold arms in baroque frame, 3 ornate helmets above, date at end of legend **Rev. Legend:** CONSILIUM IEHOVÆ STABIT. AN. **Note:** Dav. #7738. Ref. F/S#1876.

Date	Mintage	VG	F	VF	XF	Unc
1661 EW	—	500	1,200	3,000	6,250	—

KM# 490 THALER

Silver **Ruler:** Christian zu Liegnitz **Obv:** Armored and mantled bust to right **Obv. Legend:** CHRISTIANVS. D.G. DVX. SILESIÆ. LIGNICE(NSIS). **Rev:** Silesian eagle, crown above divides date in margin, mintmaster's initials in oval at bottom **Rev. Legend:** BREGENSIS. E(T). - WOLAVIENSIS. **Note:** Dav. #7741. Ref. F/S#1924, 1940-41, 1946. Varieties exist.

Date	Mintage	VG	F	VF	XF	Unc
1666 GFH/CBS	—	450	800	1,350	2,250	—
1671 GFH/CBS	—	450	800	1,350	2,250	—
1671 CBS	—	400	725	1,250	2,050	—
1672 CBS	—	400	725	1,250	2,050	—

KM# 534 THALER

Silver **Ruler:** Georg Wilhelm **Obv:** Armored bust to right **Obv. Legend:** + GEORGIVS. WILHELM. D.G. DVX. SILESIAE **Rev:** Silesian eagle, date divided by head, large crown above **Rev. Legend:** LIGNICENSIS. BREGENSIS. ET. WOLAVIENSIS. **Note:** Dav. #7742. Ref. F/S#1967.

Date	Mintage	VG	F	VF	XF	Unc
1675 CB	—	550	1,250	3,000	6,000	11,500

DAV# LS488 1-1/4 THALER

Silver **Subject:** Death of Georg Wilhelm **Rev:** Sixteen-line inscription **Note:** Weight varies: 33.00-34.00 grams.

Date	Mintage	VG	F	VF	XF	Unc
1675	—	1,250	2,500	5,000	8,500	13,500

KM# 538 1-1/2 THALER

Silver **Ruler:** Georg Wilhelm **Subject:** Death of Georg Wilhelm **Obv:** Armored and mantled bust turned 3/4 right **Obv. Legend:** +GEORG+ WILHELM+ D.G+ DVX+ SILESIAE+ LIGN+ BREG+ & WOLAVIENS+ **Rev:** 16-line inscription with Roman numeral dates **Rev. Inscription:** PIASTI • / ET NARCIIÆ POLONIÆ/ ULTIMUS. NEPOS. PRIN(ceps)/ XV. VIX. ANNOS. NAT. SEDTA(men)/ DIE. XXI. NOVEMB. A. MDCLXXV./SIBI. REGIÆ FAMILIÆ./NOVEMQ' SECULORUM. SENIO./ FATALEM. FIGIT. TERMINUM./ AMBIGENTE. SILESIA/ NUM. PIASTI. NATA. LIB, (PL), **Note:** Dav.#LS487 (F/S-1973). Illustration reduced.

Date	Mintage	VG	F	VF	XF	Unc
MDCLXXV (1675) SK	—	1,500	3,000	6,000	9,500	15,500

KM# 17 2 THALER

Silver **Ruler:** Joachim Friedrich zu Liegnitz **Obv:** Armored bust with high collar to right **Obv. Legend:** IOACH. FRID. HERZ. I. SCHL. Z. L. V. B. T. Z. M. **Rev:** Bust right of Anna Marie von Anhalt wearing ruffed collar and small cap, date at top **Rev. Legend:** A. MARIA. G. F. Z. AN. HERZ. I. SCHL. Z. L. V. B. **Note:** Dav. #7704. Ref. F/S-1415.

Date	Mintage	VG	F	VF	XF	Unc
160Z Rare	—	—	—	—	—	—

KM# 59 2 THALER

Silver **Ruler:** Johann Christian and Georg Rudolph **Obv:** Two 1/2-length figures facing each other behind flat surface with arabesques in exergue **Obv. Legend:** D. G. IOHAN. CHRIST. ET. GEOR(G). RVD. FRA. **Rev:** 4-fold arms, 3 ornate helmets above, date at end of legend **Rev. Legend:** DVC. SIL. LIG. - ET. BREG. **Note:** Dav. #7707. Ref. F/S-1415.

Date	Mintage	VG	F	VF	XF	Unc
(1)607 Rare	—	—	—	—	—	—
(1)607 (d) Rare	—	—	—	—	—	—

KM# 78 2 THALER

Silver **Ruler:** Johann Christian and Georg Rudolph **Obv:** Two 1/2-length figures facing **Obv. Legend:** D. G. IOHAN. CHRIST. ET. GEOR(G). RVD. FRA. **Rev:** 4-fold arms, 3 ornate helmets above, date at end of legend **Rev. Legend:** DVC. SIL. LIG. - ET. BREG. **Note:** Dav. #7709.

Date	Mintage	VG	F	VF	XF	Unc
(1)609 (d) Rare	—	—	—	—	—	—

KM# 79 2 THALER

Silver **Ruler:** Johann Christian and Georg Rudolph **Obv:** Two 1/2-length figures facing behind flat surface with ornamented fillet below **Obv. Legend:** D. G. IOHAN. CHRIST. ET. GEOR(G). RVD. FRA. **Rev:** 4-fold arms, 3 ornate helmets above, date at end of legend **Rev. Legend:** DVC. SIL. LIG. - ET. BREG. **Note:** Dav. #7709A. Ref. F/S-1434.

Date	Mintage	VG	F	VF	XF	Unc
(1)609 (d) Rare	—	—	—	—	—	—

KM# 80 2 THALER

Silver **Ruler:** Johann Christian and Georg Rudolph **Obv:** Two 1/2-length figures facing each other behind flat surface with ornamented fillet below **Obv. Legend:** D. G. IOHAN. CHRIST. ET. GEOR(G). RVD. FRA. **Rev:** 4-fold arms, 3 ornate helmets above, date at end of legend **Rev. Legend:** DVC. SIL. LIG. - ET. BREG. **Note:** Klippe. Dav. #7709B. Ref. F/S-1435.

Date	Mintage	VG	F	VF	XF	Unc
(1)609 (d) Rare	—	—	—	—	—	—

KM# 81 2 THALER

Silver **Ruler:** Johann Christian and Georg Rudolph **Obv:** Two 1/2-length figures facing each other over horizontal line below **Obv. Legend:** D. G. IOHAN. CHRIST. ET. GEORG. RVD. FRA. **Rev:** Flat shield with rounded bottom of 4-fold arms, 3 helmets above, date at end of legend **Rev. Legend:** DVC. SIL. LIG. - ET. BREG. **Note:** Dav. #7711.

Date	Mintage	VG	F	VF	XF	Unc
(1)609 Rare	—	—	—	—	—	—

KM# 131 2 THALER

Silver **Ruler:** Johann Christian and Georg Rudolph **Obv:** Draped bust to right, legend begins at bottom, divided by 2 small shields of arms at left and right, small imperial orb in circle at bottom **Obv. Legend:** D. G. IO - HANN. CHRISTI. - AN. ET. **Rev:** Draped bust to left divides date, legend begins at upper left, 2 small shields of arms at left and right **Rev. Legend:** GEOR. RVD. FRA. D. - SIL. LIG. ET. BREG. **Note:** Dav. #7714. Ref. F/S-1470.

Date	Mintage	VG	F	VF	XF	Unc
1611 Rare	—	—	—	—	—	—

KM# 132 2 THALER

Silver **Ruler:** Johann Christian and Georg Rudolph **Obv:** Draped bust to right, legend begins at bottom, divided by 2 small shields of arms at left and right, small imperial orb in circle at bottom **Obv. Legend:** D. G. IO - HANN. CHRISTI. - AN. ET. **Rev:** Draped bust to left divides date, legend begins at upper left, 2 small shields of arms at left and right **Rev. Legend:** GEOR. RVD. FRA. D. - SIL. LIG. ET. BREG. **Note:** Klippe. Dav. #7714A. Ref. F/S-1471.

Date	Mintage	VG	F	VF	XF	Unc
1611 Rare	—	—	—	—	—	—

KM# 195 2 THALER

Silver **Ruler:** Johann Christian and Georg Rudolph **Obv:** 2 armored 1/2-length figures facing each other, horizontal line with ornamentation below **Obv. Legend:** D. G. IOHAN. CHRIS(T). ET. GEORG. RVDO. FRAT(R). **Rev:** Shield with flat top and rounded bottom of 4-fold arms, 3 ornate helmets above, date at end of legend **Rev. Legend:** DVC. SIL. LIGNIC. ET. BREGE. **Note:** Klippe. Dav. #7717. Ref. F/S-1530.

Date	Mintage	VG	F	VF	XF	Unc
1619 HR Rare	—	—	—	—	—	—
1621 Rare	—	—	—	—	—	—

KM# 272 2 THALER

Silver **Ruler:** Johann Christian and Georg Rudolph **Obv:** 2 armored 1/2-length figures facing each other, horizontal line with ornamentation below **Obv. Legend:** D. G. IOHAN. CHRIS(T). ET. GEORG. RVDO. FRAT(R). **Rev:** Shield with flat top and rounded bottom of 4-fold arms, 3 ornate helmets above, date at end of legend **Rev. Legend:** DVC. SIL. LIGNIC. ET. BREGE. **Note:** Klippe. Dav. #7717A. Ref. F/S-1548.

Date	Mintage	VG	F	VF	XF	Unc
1621 Rare	—	—	—	—	—	—

KM# 273 2 THALER

Silver **Ruler:** Georg Rudolf **Obv:** Armored bust right, small imperial orb at top **Obv. Legend:** D. G. GEORG. RVDOLPHVS. DVX. SILESI. **Rev:** 4-fold arms, 3 helmets above, date at end of legend **Rev. Legend:** LIGNIC. ET. BEG. HERNS. **Note:** Dav. #7722. Ref. F/S-1680.

Date	Mintage	VG	F	VF	XF	Unc
1621 IK Rare	—	—	—	—	—	—

KM# 349 2 THALER

Silver **Ruler:** Georg Rudolf **Obv:** 1/2-length armored figure to right, legend begins with small imperial orb **Obv. Legend:** D. G. GEORGIVS. RVDOLPHVS. DVX. SILESIÆ. **Rev:** 4-fold arms, 3 helmets above, date divided at top **Rev. Legend:** LIGNICENSIS. ET. - BREGENSIS. **Mint:** Liegnitz **Note:** Dav. #A7725. Ref. J/M-123.

Date	Mintage	VG	F	VF	XF	Unc
16ZZ (e) Rare	—	—	—	—	—	—

KM# 409 2 THALER
Silver **Ruler:** Georg III, Ludwig IV and Christian **Obv:** 3 facing 3/4-lentth figures, horizontal line abelow with arabesques in exergue, small imperial orb at top **Obv. Legend:** D. G. GEORGIVS. LUDOVICVS. ET. CHRISTIANVS. FRATR. **Rev:** 3 helmets above ornate 4-fold arms, date at end of legend **Rev. Legend:** DVCES. SILESI. LIGNI. BR - EGENES. ET. WOLAV. **Note:** Dav. #7728. Ref. F/S-1748.

Date	Mintage	VG	F	VF	XF	Unc
1656 (pf) Rare	—	—	—	—	—	—

KM# 416 2 THALER
Silver **Ruler:** Georg III, Ludwig IV and Christian **Obv:** 3 facing armored 1/2-length figures, small imperial orb at top, arabesques in exergue **Obv. Legend:** D. G. GEORGIUS. LUDOVICUS. & CHRISTIANUS. FRATRES. **Rev:** 3 helmets above ornate 4-fold arms, date at end of legend **Rev. Legend:** DUCES. SILESIÆ. LIGNIC - ENSES. ET. BREGENSES. **Note:** Ref. F/S #1756.

Date	Mintage	VG	F	VF	XF	Unc
1657 (pf)	—	—	—	—	—	—

KM# 418 2 THALER
Silver **Ruler:** Georg III, Ludwig IV and Christian **Obv:** 3 facing 1/2-length figures, horizontal line below with arabesques in exergue, small imperial orb at top **Obv. Legend:** D. G. GEORGIVS. LUDOVICVS. & CHRISTIANVS. FRATRES. **Rev:** 3 helmets above oval 4-fold arms, date at end of legend **Rev. Legend:** DVCES. SILESIÆ. LIGNIC. BRE - GENS. ET. WOLAVIENSES. **Note:** Dav. #7730. Ref. F/S-1777, J/M-132.

Date	Mintage	VG	F	VF	XF	Unc
1658 (pf) Rare	—	—	—	—	—	—
1659 (pf)-EW Rare	—	—	—	—	—	—

KM# 447 2 THALER
Silver **Ruler:** Georg III **Obv:** Mantled bust to right, crown in margin at top **Obv. Legend:** D. G. GEORGIUS. DUX. SILESIÆ. LIGNIC. ET. BREGEN. **Rev:** Round 4-fold arms in baroque frame, 3 ornate helmets above, date at end of legend **Rev. Legend:** SORS MEA A - DOMINO AN. **Note:** Dav. #7734. Ref. F/S-1839.

Date	Mintage	VG	F	VF	XF	Unc
1660 (pf)-EW Rare	—	—	—	—	—	—

KM# 456 2 THALER
Silver **Ruler:** Ludwig IV **Obv:** Mantled bust right, crown in margin at top **Obv. Legend:** D. G. LUDOVICUS. DUX. SILESIÆ. LIGNIC. BREG. ET. GOLDBER. **Rev:** Round 4-fold arms in baroque frame, 3 ornate helmets above, date at end of legend **Rev. Legend:** CONSILIUM IEHOVÆ STABIT. AN. **Note:** Dav. #7737. Ref. F/S-1875.

Date	Mintage	VG	F	VF	XF	Unc
1661 EW Rare	—	—	—	—	—	—

TRADE COINAGE

KM# 97 1/4 DUCAT
0.8750 g., 0.9860 Gold 0.0277 oz. AGW **Ruler:** Johann Christian and Georg Rudolph **Obv:** Crowned ornate 4-fold arms divide date **Rev:** 6-line inscription **Rev. Inscription:** MO. / AVR. D.G. IO. / CHR. ET. GE. / RVD. FR. D. SL. / LIG. ET. BRE / GEN. **Mint:** Liegnitz

Date	Mintage	VG	F	VF	XF	Unc
1610	—	—	—	—	—	—

KM# 197 1/4 DUCAT
0.8750 g., 0.9860 Gold 0.0277 oz. AGW **Obv:** 2 adjacent oval arms of Silesian eagle and Brieg in baroque frames, crown above **Rev:** 4-line inscription with date **Rev. Inscription:** MONE / TA. NOVA. / AVREA. / 1619. **Note:** Fr. #3174.

Date	Mintage	VG	F	VF	XF	Unc
1619	—	150	300	500	900	—

KM# 198 1/4 DUCAT
0.8750 g., 0.9860 Gold 0.0277 oz. AGW **Obv:** 2 adjacent oval arms of Silesian eagle and Brieg in baroque frames, crown above **Rev:** 4-line inscription with date **Rev. Inscription:** MONE / TA. NOVA. / AVREA. / 1619. **Note:** Fr. #3175. Klippe.

Date	Mintage	VG	F	VF	XF	Unc
1619	—	200	450	800	1,250	—

KM# 213 1/4 DUCAT
0.8750 g., 0.9860 Gold 0.0277 oz. AGW **Ruler:** Johann Christian and Georg Rudolph **Obv:** 2 busts facing each other, legend begins with small imperial orb **Obv. Legend:** D.G. IOH. CHRI. ET. GEORG. RVD. FRA. **Rev:** 4-fold arms, 3 ornate helmets above, date divided at top **Rev. Legend:** MO. AV. DVC. SI. LI. ET. BRE. **Mint:** Liegnitz

Date	Mintage	VG	F	VF	XF	Unc
16Z0	—	—	—	—	—	—

KM# 523 1/4 DUCAT
0.8750 g., 0.9860 Gold 0.0277 oz. AGW **Ruler:** Louise **Obv:** Facing bust of Louise slightly right, mother of Georg Wilhelm, in inner circle **Obv. Legend:** + LOVISE. D.G. DVC. SIL. LIG. BREG. E. WOLAV. **Rev:** 2 adjacent oval arms in baroque frame, crown above date below **Rev. Legend:** NAT. PD. ANH. CO. ASC. DO. SER. ET. RER. TV. ET. GV. **Note:** Fr. #3214.

Date	Mintage	VG	F	VF	XF	Unc
1674	—	250	500	950	1,650	—

KM# 540 1/4 DUCAT
0.8750 g., 0.9860 Gold 0.0277 oz. AGW **Ruler:** Georg Wilhelm **Obv:** Armored bust of Georg Wilhelm right in inner circle **Obv. Legend:** GEORG. WILHELM. D.G. DVX. SIL. **Rev:** Crowned Silesian eagle in inner circle, crown divides date in margin at top **Rev. Legend:** LIGNIC. BREGENS. ET. WOLAVIEN. **Note:** Fr. #3217.

Date	Mintage	VG	F	VF	XF	Unc
167 CB (error)	—	—	—	—	—	—
1675 CB	—	150	300	500	850	—

KM# 99 1/2 DUCAT
1.7500 g., 0.9860 Gold 0.0555 oz. AGW **Ruler:** Johann Christian and Georg Rudolph **Obv:** Crowned ornate 4-fold arms divide date **Rev:** 6-line inscription **Rev. Inscription:** MO. / AVR. D.G. IO. / CHR. ET. GE. / RVD. FR. D. SL. / LIG. ET. BRE / GEN. **Note:** Fr. #3168.

Date	Mintage	VG	F	VF	XF	Unc
1610	—	175	350	700	1,150	—

KM# 100 1/2 DUCAT
1.7500 g., 0.9860 Gold 0.0555 oz. AGW **Ruler:** Johann Christian and Georg Rudolph **Obv:** Crowned ornate 4-fold arms divide date **Rev:** 5-line inscription **Rev. Inscription:** MO. / AVR. D.G. IO. / CHR. ET. GE. / RVD. FR. D. SL. / LIG. ET. BREGEN. **Note:** Fr. #3169.

Date	Mintage	VG	F	VF	XF	Unc
1610	—	175	350	700	1,150	—

KM# 200 1/2 DUCAT
1.7500 g., 0.9860 Gold 0.0555 oz. AGW **Ruler:** Johann Christian and Georg Rudolph **Obv:** Facing busts of Johann Christian and Georg Rudolf in inner circle, 2 adjacent oval arms in baroque frame in exergue **Rev:** 7-line inscription with date **Rev. Inscription:** MO. / AVR. D.G. IO. / CHR. ET. GEO. / RVD. FRA. D / SIL. LIGNI. / ET. BREG. / 1619. **Note:** Fr. #3172.

Date	Mintage	VG	F	VF	XF	Unc
1619	—	175	350	700	1,150	—

KM# 201 1/2 DUCAT
1.7500 g., 0.9860 Gold 0.0555 oz. AGW **Ruler:** Johann Christian and Georg Rudolph **Obv:** 1/2-length busts of Johann Christian and Georg Rudolf facing in inner circle, 2 adjacent oval arms in baroque frame in exergue **Rev:** 7-line inscription with date **Rev. Inscription:** MO. / AVR. D.G. IO. / CHR. ET. GEO. / RVD. FRA. D / SIL. LIGNI. / ET. BREG. / 1619. **Note:** Fr. #3173. Klippe.

Date	Mintage	VG	F	VF	XF	Unc
1619	—	280	625	1,200	2,050	—

KM# 19 1/2 DUCAT
1.7500 g., 0.9860 Gold 0.0555 oz. AGW **Ruler:** Johann Christian and Georg Rudolph **Obv:** Facing 1/2-length busts of Johann Christian and Georg Rudolf facing each other in inner circle, legend begins with small imperial orb **Obv. Legend:** D.G. IOH. CHRI ET. GEOR. RVD. FRA. **Rev:** Crowned ornate 4-fold arms in inner circle **Rev. Legend:** MO. AV. D. - S. L. BR. **Note:** Fr. #3146.

Date	Mintage	VG	F	VF	XF	Unc
ND(1602-21)	—	210	425	700	1,250	—

KM# 215 1/2 DUCAT
1.7500 g., 0.9860 Gold 0.0555 oz. AGW **Ruler:** Johann Christian and Georg Rudolph **Obv:** Busts of Johann Christian and Georg Rudolph facing, legend begins with small imperial orb **Obv. Legend:** D.G. IOH. CHRI. ET. GEORG. RVD. FRA. **Rev:** 4-fold arms, 3 ornate helmets above, date divided at top **Rev. Legend:** MO. AV. DVC. SI. LI. ET. BRE. **Note:** Fr. #3155.

Date	Mintage	VG	F	VF	XF	Unc
1620	—	210	425	700	1,250	—

KM# 216 1/2 DUCAT
1.7500 g., 0.9860 Gold 0.0555 oz. AGW **Ruler:** Johann Christian and Georg Rudolph **Obv:** Busts of Johann Christian and Georg Rudolph facing, legend begins with small imperial orb **Obv. Legend:** D.G. IOH. CHRI. ET. GEORG. RVD. FRA. **Rev:** 4-fold arms, 3 ornate helmets abaove, date divided at top **Rev. Legend:** MO. AV. DVC. SI. LI. ET. BRE. **Note:** Klippe.

Date	Mintage	VG	F	VF	XF	Unc
16Z0	—	—	—	—	—	—

KM# 378 1/2 DUCAT
1.7500 g., 0.9860 Gold 0.0555 oz. AGW **Ruler:** Georg III, Ludwig IV and Christian **Obv:** Facing 1/2-length figures of Georg, Ludwig, and Christian in inner circle, horizontal line below with arabesques in exergue, small imperial orb at top **Obv. Legend:** D:G • GEORG • LUDOVIC • ET • CHRISTIAN • FRATRES • **Rev:** Ornate 4-fold arms topped by three helmets in inner circle, date at end of legend **Rev. Legend:** DUCES • SILESIÆ • LIGN • - ET • BREGENES • **Note:** Fr. #3201.

Date	Mintage	VG	F	VF	XF	Unc
1651	—	190	375	675	1,300	—
1652	—	190	375	675	1,300	—
1656	—	190	375	675	1,300	—

KM# 400 1/2 DUCAT
1.7500 g., 0.9860 Gold 0.0555 oz. AGW **Ruler:** Georg III, Ludwig IV and Christian **Obv:** 3 armored 1/2-length figures of Georg, Ludwig and Christian in inner circle, small imperial orb at top, arabesques in exergue **Obv. Legend:** D:G • GEORGIUS • LUDOVICUS • & CHRISTIANUS • FRATRES • **Rev:** 3 helmets above ornate 4-fold arms, date at end of legend **Rev. Legend:** DUCES • SILESIÆ • LIGNIC - ENSES • ET • BREGENSES. **Note:** Fr. #3201.

Date	Mintage	VG	F	VF	XF	Unc
1653/2/1	—	150	300	600	1,050	—
1653/Z	—	150	300	600	1,050	—
1654/Z	—	150	300	600	1,050	—
1656	—	150	300	600	1,050	—

KM# 542 1/2 DUCAT
1.7500 g., 0.9860 Gold 0.0555 oz. AGW **Ruler:** Georg Wilhelm **Obv:** Armored bust of Georg Wilhelm facing right in inner circle **Obv. Legend:** GEORG. WILHELM. D.G. DVX. SI. **Rev:** Crowned Silesian eagle in inner circle, crown above divides date in margin at top **Rev. Legend:** LIGNIC. BREGENS. ET. WOLAVI. **Mint:** Brieg **Note:** Fr. #3219.

Date	Mintage	VG	F	VF	XF	Unc
1675 CB	—	280	550	1,050	1,900	—

KM# 1 DUCAT
3.5000 g., 0.9860 Gold 0.1109 oz. AGW **Ruler:** Joachim Friedrich zu Liegnitz **Obv:** Collared bust of Joachim Friedrich right in inner circle **Obv. Legend:** (flower) MO. NO. AVR. IOACHIMI. FRIDERICI. **Rev:** Crowned 4-fold arms in inner circle, date at end of legend **Rev. Legend:** DVCIS. LEGNICEN. ET BREGEN. **Note:** Fr. #3139.

Date	Mintage	VG	F	VF	XF	Unc
1600	—	250	500	1,000	1,850	—
1601	—	250	500	1,000	1,850	—

KM# 32 DUCAT
3.5000 g., 0.9860 Gold 0.1109 oz. AGW **Ruler:** Johann Christian and Georg Rudolph **Obv:** Facing busts of Johann Christian and Georg Rudolf in inner circle, horizontal line below, date in exergue **Obv. Legend:** MON. NOVA. AVR. IOAN. CHRIS. GEORG. RV. **Rev:** Crowned 4-fold arms **Rev. Legend:** DVCVM. LIGNI. ET. BREGEN. FRA. **Note:** Fr. #3142.

Date	Mintage	VG	F	VF	XF	Unc
1604	—	300	600	1,200	2,200	—

KM# 33 DUCAT
3.5000 g., 0.9860 Gold 0.1109 oz. AGW **Ruler:** Johann Christian and Georg Rudolph **Obv:** Large facing busts of Johann Christian & Georg Rudolph **Obv. Legend:** MO. NO. AVR. IOA. CHR. ET. GEOR. RV. FR. **Rev:** Crowned ornate 4-fold arms divide date **Rev. Legend:** DVC. SIL. LIGNICEN. ET. BREG. **Note:** Fr. #3142.

Date	Mintage	VG	F	VF	XF	Unc
1604	—	300	600	1,200	2,200	—

KM# 44 DUCAT
3.5000 g., 0.9860 Gold 0.1109 oz. AGW **Ruler:** Johann Christian and Georg Rudolph **Obv:** Large facing busts of Johann Christian and Georg Rudolph **Obv. Legend:** MO. NO. AVR. IOAN. CHR. ET. GEOR. RVD. FRA. **Rev:** Crowned ornate 4-fold arms, date at end of legend **Rev. Legend:** DVC. SIL. LEG. ET. BREG. **Note:** Fr. #3142.

Date	Mintage	VG	F	VF	XF	Unc
1605	—	300	600	1,200	2,200	—
1606	—	300	600	1,200	2,200	—

KM# 55 DUCAT
3.5000 g., 0.9860 Gold 0.1109 oz. AGW **Ruler:** Johann Christian and Georg Rudolph **Obv:** Small facing busts of John Christian and Georg Rudolf **Obv. Legend:** MO • AVR • IOAN • CHR • ET • GEOR • RVD • FR(A) • **Rev:** Crowned 4-fold arms, date at end of legend **Rev. Legend:** DVC • SIL • LIG • - ET • BREG • **Note:** Fr. #3145.

Date	Mintage	VG	F	VF	XF	Unc
1606	—	300	600	1,200	2,200	—
1607	—	300	600	1,200	2,200	—
1608	—	300	600	1,200	2,200	—
1609	—	300	600	1,200	2,200	—
1609 (d)	—	300	600	1,200	2,200	—

KM# 102 DUCAT
3.5000 g., 0.9860 Gold 0.1109 oz. AGW **Ruler:** Johann Christian and Georg Rudolph **Obv:** Armored bust of Johann Christian right in inner circle, legend divided by 2 small shields of arms **Obv. Legend:** MO. AVREA. D.G. - IOHAN. CHR. ET. **Rev:** Armored bust of Georg Rudolf left divides date in inner circle, legend divided by 2 small shields of arms **Rev. Legend:** GEOR. RVD. FR. D. - SL. LIG. ET. BRE. **Note:** Fr. #3166.

Date	Mintage	VG	F	VF	XF	Unc
1610 (d)	—	220	450	925	1,600	—
1611	—	220	450	925	1,600	—

KM# 103 DUCAT
3.5000 g., 0.9860 Gold 0.1109 oz. AGW **Ruler:** Johann Christian and Georg Rudolph **Obv:** Crowned, ornate 4-fold arms divide date **Rev:** 6-line inscription **Rev. Inscription:** MO. / AVR. D.G. IO. / CHR. ET. GE. / RVD. FR. D. SL. / LIG. ET. BRE / GEN.

Note: Thick planchet. Fr. #3167. Struck on thick flan with 1/2 Ducat dies, KM#99.

Date	Mintage	VG	F	VF	XF	Unc
1610	—	375	750	1,500	2,500	—

KM# 146 DUCAT

3.5000 g., 0.9860 Gold 0.1109 oz. AGW **Ruler:** Johann Christian and Georg Rudolph **Obv:** Armored 1/2-length busts of Johann Christian and Georg Rudolf facing each other **Obv. Legend:** MO • AVR • IOAN • CHR • ET • GEOR • RVD • FRA • **Rev:** 2 adjacent shields of arms, Silesian eagle left, Brieg right, large crown above, date below **Rev. Legend:** DVC • SIL • LIGNI • ET • BREGEN • **Note:** Fr. #3170.

Date	Mintage	VG	F	VF	XF	Unc
161Z	—	260	525	1,100	2,000	—

KM# 156 DUCAT

3.5000 g., 0.9860 Gold 0.1109 oz. AGW **Ruler:** Johann Christian and Georg Rudolph **Obv:** Armored bust of Johann Christian right, legend divided by 2 small shields of arms **Obv. Legend:** D.G. IO. - CH. ET. GE. RV. DV - SIL. L. B. **Rev:** Armored bust of Georg Rudolph left, legend divided by 2 small shields of arms which ends with date **Rev. Legend:** MO. NOV. - AVR. REICHST. - (date). **Mint:** Reichenstein **Note:** Fr. #3178.

Date	Mintage	VG	F	VF	XF	Unc
1614	—	350	725	1,450	2,400	—

KM# 205 DUCAT

3.5000 g., 0.9860 Gold 0.1109 oz. AGW **Ruler:** Johann Christian and Georg Rudolph **Obv:** 1/2-length figures of Johann Christian and Georg Rudolph facing each other, 2 adjacent oval arms in baroque frame in exergue **Rev:** 7-line inscription with date **Rev. Inscription:** MO. / AVR. D.G. IO. / CHR. ET. GEO. / RVD. FRA. D/ SIL. LIGNI. / ET. BREG. / 1619. **Mint:** Reichenstein **Note:** Fr. #3171. Struck on thick flan with 1/2 Ducat dies, KM#200.

Date	Mintage	VG	F	VF	XF	Unc
1619	—	325	625	1,250	2,300	—

KM# 203 DUCAT

3.5000 g., 0.9860 Gold 0.1109 oz. AGW **Ruler:** Johann Christian and Georg Rudolph **Obv:** Large armored bust of Johann Christian right, legend divided by 2 small shields of arms **Obv. Legend:** D.G. I - OH. CHR. ET. GEO. - RV. FR. **Rev:** Large armored bust of Georg Rudolph left, legend divided by 2 small shields of arms which ends with date **Rev. Legend:** MO. AV. - DVX. SI. LI. ET. BR - EG. **Mint:** Reichenstein **Note:** Fr. #3166.

Date	Mintage	VG	F	VF	XF	Unc
1619	—	250	500	1,050	1,800	—

KM# 204 DUCAT

3.5000 g., 0.9860 Gold 0.1109 oz. AGW **Ruler:** Johann Christian and Georg Rudolph **Obv:** Small armored bust of Johann Christian right, legend divided by 2 small shields of arms **Obv. Legend:** D.G. I - OH. CHR. ET. GEO. - RV. FR. **Rev:** Small armored bust of Georg Rudolph left, legend divided by 2 small shields of arms which ends with date **Rev. Legend:** MO. AV. - DVX. SI. LI. ET. BR - EG. **Mint:** Reichenstein **Note:** Fr. #3166.

Date	Mintage	VG	F	VF	XF	Unc
1619	—	190	375	750	1,250	—

KM# 218 DUCAT

3.5000 g., 0.9860 Gold 0.1109 oz. AGW **Ruler:** Johann Christian and Georg Rudolph **Obv:** Busts of Johann Christian and Georg Rudolph facing each other, legend begins with small imperial orb **Obv. Legend:** D.G. IOHA. CHRI. ET. GEORG. RVD. FRAT. **Rev:** 4-fold arms, 3 ornate helmets above, date divided at top **Rev. Legend:** MO. AVR. DVC. SIL. LE. ET. BRE. **Mint:** Reichenstein **Note:** Fr. #3154.

Date	Mintage	VG	F	VF	XF	Unc
16Z0	—	220	450	925	1,700	—

KM# 275 DUCAT

3.5000 g., 0.9860 Gold 0.1109 oz. AGW **Ruler:** Georg Rudolf **Obv:** High-collared bust of Georg Rudolf right in inner circle **Obv. Legend:** D.G. GEOR. RVD. DVC. SI. LI. ET. BR. **Rev:** 3 helmets above 4-fold arms, date at end of legend **Rev. Legend:** MONETA. AVREA. **Mint:** Haynau **Note:** Fr. #3194.

Date	Mintage	VG	F	VF	XF	Unc
16Z1 MT	—	240	475	1,000	1,850	—

KM# 276 DUCAT

3.5000 g., 0.9860 Gold 0.1109 oz. AGW **Ruler:** Georg Rudolf **Obv:** High-collared bust of Georg Rudolph right **Obv. Legend:** D.G. GEOR. RVD. DVC. SI. LI. ET. BR. **Rev:** 3 helmets above 4-fold arms, date at end of legend **Rev. Legend:** MONETA. AVREA. **Note:** Fr. #3194.

Date	Mintage	VG	F	VF	XF	Unc
16Z1	—	325	650	1,300	2,200	—

KM# 277 DUCAT

3.5000 g., 0.9860 Gold 0.1109 oz. AGW **Ruler:** Georg Rudolf **Obv:** Armored bust of Georg Rudolph right **Obv. Legend:** D.G. GEOR. RVD. DVC. SI. LI. ET. BR. **Rev:** 3 helmets above 4-fold arms, date at end of legend **Rev. Legend:** MONETA. AVREA. **Note:** Fr. #3194.

Date	Mintage	VG	F	VF	XF	Unc
16Z1	—	325	650	1,300	2,200	—

KM# 351 DUCAT

3.5000 g., 0.9860 Gold 0.1109 oz. AGW **Ruler:** Georg Rudolf **Obv:** Armored bust of Georg Rudolph right, small imperial orb at top **Obv. Legend:** D.G. GEORG. RVDO. DVX. SIL. LI. & BRE. **Rev:** Crowned ornamented 4-fold arms, date at end of legend **Rev. Legend:** MONETA. AVREA. ANNO.

Date	Mintage	VG	F	VF	XF	Unc
1622	—	325	650	1,300	2,200	—

KM# 380 DUCAT

3.5000 g., 0.9860 Gold 0.1109 oz. AGW **Ruler:** Georg III, Ludwig IV and Christian **Obv:** 1/2-length busts of Georg III, Ludwig IV & Christian facing, horizontal line below with arabesques in exergue, small imperial orb at top **Obv. Legend:** D.G. GEORG. LUDOVIC. ET. CHRISTIAN. FRATRES. **Rev:** 3 helmets above ornate 4-fold arms, date at end of legend **Rev. Legend:** DUCES. SILESIÆ. LIGN. - ET. BREGENES. **Note:** Fr. #3200. Struck at either Liegnitz or Brieg mint.

Date	Mintage	VG	F	VF	XF	Unc
1651 VT	—	165	325	650	875	—
165Z VT	—	165	325	650	875	—
165Z/1 VT	—	165	325	650	875	—

KM# 401 DUCAT

3.5000 g., 0.9860 Gold 0.1109 oz. AGW **Ruler:** Georg III, Ludwig IV and Christian **Obv:** Armored 1/2-length busts of Georg, Ludwig, and Christian facing, small imperial orb at top, arabesques in exergue **Obv. Legend:** D.G. GEORGIUS. LUDOVICUS. & CHRISTIANUS. FRATRES. **Rev:** 3 helmets above ornate 4-fold arms, date at end of legend **Rev. Legend:** DUCES. SILESIÆ. LIGNIC - ENSES. ET. BREGENSES. **Note:** Fr. #3200. Struck at Liegnitz or Brieg mint. Varieties exist.

Date	Mintage	VG	F	VF	XF	Unc
1653 (pf)	—	165	325	650	1,000	—
1654	—	165	325	650	1,000	—
1655	—	165	325	650	1,000	—
1656 (pf)	—	—	—	—	—	—
1657 (pf)	—	—	—	—	—	—
1657 (pf) - EW	—	165	325	650	1,000	—
1658 (pf)	—	—	—	—	—	—
1658 (pf) - EW	—	165	325	650	1,000	—
1659 (pf) - EW	—	165	325	650	1,000	—
1660 (pf)	—	—	—	—	—	—
1660 (pf) - EW	—	165	325	650	1,000	—
1661	—	165	325	650	1,000	—
1662 EW	—	165	325	650	1,000	—

KM# 449 DUCAT

3.5000 g., 0.9860 Gold 0.1109 oz. AGW **Ruler:** Georg III **Obv:** Mantled bust of Georg III right in inner circle, crown in margin at top **Obv. Legend:** D.G. GEORGIUS. DUX. SILESIÆ. LIGNIC. ET. BREGEN. **Rev:** Round 4-fold arms in baroque frame, 3 ornate helmets above, date at end of legend **Rev. Legend:** SORS MEA A - DOMINO AN. **Note:** Fr. #3202. Struck at either Liegnitz or Brieg mints.

Date	Mintage	VG	F	VF	XF	Unc
1660 (pf) - EW	—	325	625	1,250	2,300	—

KM# 450 DUCAT

3.5000 g., 0.9860 Gold 0.1109 oz. AGW **Ruler:** Christian zu Ohlau **Obv:** Mantled bust of Christian right in inner circle, crown above in margin **Obv. Legend:** D.G. CHRISTIANUS. DUX. SIL. L. BREG. & W. **Rev:** 3 helmets above ornate 4-fold arms, date at end of legend **Rev. Legend:** DUCES. SILESIÆ. LIGNIC - ENSES. ET. BREGENSES. **Note:** Fr. #3207. Struck at Liegnitz or Brieg mints.

Date	Mintage	VG	F	VF	XF	Unc
1660 (pf) - EW	—	325	625	1,250	2,300	—

KM# 462 DUCAT

3.5000 g., 0.9860 Gold 0.1109 oz. AGW **Ruler:** Christian zu Ohlau **Obv:** Mantled bust of Christian right, crown above in margin **Obv. Legend:** D.G. CHRISTIANUS. DUX. SIL. L. BREG. & W. **Rev:** Round 4-fold arms in baroque frame, 3 ornate helmets above, date at end of legend **Rev. Legend:** CONSILIUM IEHOVÆ STABIT. AN. **Mint:** Brieg **Note:** Fr. #3208.

Date	Mintage	VG	F	VF	XF	Unc
1661 EW	—	280	575	1,150	1,900	—

KM# 461 DUCAT

3.5000 g., 0.9860 Gold 0.1109 oz. AGW **Ruler:** Christian zu Ohlau **Obv:** Armored and mantled bust of Christian right, crown above in margin **Obv. Legend:** D.G. CHRISTIANUS. DUX. SIL. L. BREG. & WOL. **Rev:** Round 4-fold arms in baroque frame, 3 ornate helmets above, date at end of legend **Rev. Legend:** SUFFICIT MIHI GRA - TIA TUA DOMINE A. **Note:** Fr. #3208. Struck at either Liegnitz or Brieg mints.

Date	Mintage	VG	F	VF	XF	Unc
1661 (pf) - EW	—	325	625	1,250	2,300	—

KM# 460 DUCAT

3.5000 g., 0.9860 Gold 0.1109 oz. AGW **Ruler:** Ludwig IV **Obv:** Mantled bust of Ludwig right in inner circle, crown in margin at top **Obv. Legend:** D.G. LUDOVICUS. DUX. SIL. LIGNIC. B. & GOLD. **Rev:** Round 4-fold arms in baroque frame, 3 ornate helmets above, date at end of legend **Rev. Legend:** CONSILIUM IEHOVÆ STABIT. AN. **Mint:** Brieg **Note:** Fr. #3205.

Date	Mintage	VG	F	VF	XF	Unc
1661 EW	—	325	625	1,250	2,300	—

KM# 458 DUCAT

3.5000 g., 0.9860 Gold 0.1109 oz. AGW **Ruler:** Georg III, Ludwig IV and Christian **Obv:** Armored 1/2-length figures of Georg III, Ludwig IV & Christian facing, small imperial orb at top, arabesques in exergue **Obv. Legend:** D.G. GEORGIUS. LUDOVICUS. & CHRISTIANUS. FRATRES. **Rev:** 3 helmets above ornate 4-fold arms, date at end of legend. **Rev. Legend:** SUFFICIT MIHI GRA - TIA TUA DOMINE A. **Note:** Fr. #3200.

Date	Mintage	VG	F	VF	XF	Unc
1661 (pf) - EW	—	180	350	725	950	—

KM# 459 DUCAT

3.5000 g., 0.9860 Gold 0.1109 oz. AGW **Ruler:** Georg III, Ludwig IV and Christian **Obv:** Armored 1/2-length figures of Georg III, Ludwig IV & Christian facing, small imperial orb at top, arabesques in exergue **Obv. Legend:** D.G. GEORGIUS. LUDOVICUS. & CHRISTIANUS. FRATRES. **Rev:** 3 helmets above ornate 4-fold arms, date at end of legend **Rev. Legend:** CONSILIUM IEHOVÆ STABIT. AN. **Mint:** Brieg **Note:** Fr. #3200.

Date	Mintage	VG	F	VF	XF	Unc
1661 EW	—	180	350	725	950	—

KM# 466 DUCAT

3.5000 g., 0.9860 Gold 0.1109 oz. AGW **Ruler:** Ludwig IV **Obv:** Mantled bust of Ludwig IV right, crown in margin at top **Obv. Legend:** D.G. LUDOVICUS. DUX. SIL. LIGNIC. B. & GOLD. **Rev:** 3 helmets above ornate 4-fold arms, date at end of legend **Rev. Legend:** DUCES. SILESIÆ. LIGNIC - ENSES. ET. BREGENSES. **Mint:** Brieg **Note:** Fr. #3206.

Date	Mintage	VG	F	VF	XF	Unc
1662 EW	—	250	500	1,000	1,850	—

KM# 477 DUCAT

3.5000 g., 0.9860 Gold 0.1109 oz. AGW **Ruler:** Georg III **Obv:** Bust of Georg III right, crown above in margin **Obv. Legend:** D.G. GEORGIUS. DUX. SIL. LIGN. & BREG. **Rev:** Round 4-fold arms, 3 helmets above, date at end of legend **Rev. Legend:** MONETA. AVRE. NOVA. REICHSTENIENSI. **Mint:** Reichenstein **Note:** Fr. #3203.

Date	Mintage	VG	F	VF	XF	Unc
1664	—	525	1,050	2,050	3,400	—

KM# 492 DUCAT

3.5000 g., 0.9860 Gold 0.1109 oz. AGW **Ruler:** Christian zu Liegnitz **Obv:** Armored and mantled bust of Christian right in inner circle **Obv. Legend:** CHRISTIANVS. D.G. DVX. SILESIÆ. LIGNICE. **Rev:** Crowned Silesian eagle in inner circle, crown above divides date in margin, mintmaster's initials in oval at bottom **Rev. Legend:** BREGENSIS. ET. - WOLAVIENSIS. **Mint:** Brieg **Note:** Fr. #3213.

Date	Mintage	VG	F	VF	XF	Unc
1666 CBS	—	325	625	1,300	2,300	—
1670 CB	—	325	625	1,300	2,300	—
1672 CB	—	325	625	1,300	2,300	—
1672 CBS	—	325	625	1,300	2,300	—

KM# 525 DUCAT

3.5000 g., 0.9860 Gold 0.1109 oz. AGW **Ruler:** Georg Wilhelm **Obv:** Armored bust of Georg Wilhelm right **Obv. Legend:** GEORG. WILHELM. D.G. DVX. SIL. **Rev:** Silesian eagle, crown above divides date in margin at top **Rev. Legend:** LIGNIC. BREG. & WOLAVIEN. **Mint:** Brieg **Note:** Fr. #3216.

Date	Mintage	VG	F	VF	XF	Unc
1674	—	350	700	1,450	2,550	—
1675 CB	—	350	700	1,450	2,550	—

KM# 544 DUCAT

3.5000 g., 0.9860 Gold 0.1109 oz. AGW **Ruler:** Georg Wilhelm **Obv:** Armored, facing bust of Georg Wilhelm right in inner circle **Obv. Legend:** GEORG. WILHELM. D.G. DVX. SI. **Rev:** Silesian eagle, crown above divides date in margin at top **Rev. Legend:** LIGNIC. BREGENS. ET. WOLAVI. **Mint:** Brieg **Note:** Struck on thick flan with 1/2 Ducat dies, KM#542. Fr. #3218.

Date	Mintage	VG	F	VF	XF	Unc
1675	—	425	875	1,800	3,200	—

KM# 21 2 DUCAT

7.0000 g., 0.9860 Gold 0.2219 oz. AGW **Subject:** Death of Joachim Friedrich **Obv:** Armored and collared bust of Joachim Friedrich right in inner circle **Obv. Legend:** ✠ MEMOR. IOACH. FRID. DVCIS. SILES. LEGN. BREGENSIS. **Rev:** 8-line inscription with R.N. date, circular marginal inscription **Rev. Legend:** ✠ DEO. OPT. MAX. IN. ÆTERN. VIVENS. SVM. PATR. **Rev. Inscription:** OBIIT. AN / NO. M.D. C II. / M. MART. XXV. / HORA. P. MER. VI / CVM. / VIXISSMI. / AN. LI. MENS. V / DIES. XXVI. / ✠. **Note:** Fr. #3141. Struck with 1/2 Thaler dies, KM#12.

Date	Mintage	VG	F	VF	XF	Unc
MDCII (1602)	—	650	1,300	2,800	4,900	—

KM# 66 2 DUCAT
7.0000 g., 0.9860 Gold 0.2219 oz. AGW **Ruler:** Johann Christian and Georg Rudolph **Obv:** Small busts of Johann Christian & Georg Rudolph slightly facing each other **Obv. Legend:** MO. AVR. IOAN. CHR. ET. GEOR. RVD. FR(A). **Rev:** Crowned 4-fold arms, date at end of legend **Rev. Legend:** DVC. SIL. LIG. - ET. BREG. **Note:** Klippe. Fr. #3143.

Date	Mintage	VG	F	VF	XF	Unc
1608	—	825	1,600	3,050	4,950	—

KM# 83 2 DUCAT
7.0000 g., 0.9860 Gold 0.2219 oz. AGW **Ruler:** Johann Christian and Georg Rudolph **Obv:** Small facing busts of Johann Christian and Georg Rudolf in inner circle **Obv. Legend:** MO. AVR. IOAN. CHR. ET. GEOR. RVD. FR(A). **Rev:** Crowned oval shield of 4-fold arms, date at end of legend **Rev. Legend:** DVC. SIL. LIG. - ET. BREG. **Note:** Fr. #3144.

Date	Mintage	VG	F	VF	XF	Unc
1609	—	550	1,100	2,350	4,150	—

KM# 84 2 DUCAT
7.0000 g., 0.9860 Gold 0.2219 oz. AGW **Ruler:** Johann Christian and Georg Rudolph **Obv:** Armored bust of Johann Christian right, legend begins at lower left, divided by 2 small shields of arms **Obv. Legend:** D.G. IO - HANN. CHRISTI - AN. ET. **Rev:** Armored bust of Georg Rudolf left divides date, legend begins at upper left, divided by 2 small shields of arms **Rev. Legend:** GEOR. RVD. FR. D. - SL. LIG. ET. BREG. **Note:** Fr. #3164. Struck at either Liegnitz or Brieg mints.

Date	Mintage	VG	F	VF	XF	Unc
1609 (d)	—	475	950	2,000	3,400	—
1609	—	475	950	2,000	3,400	—
1610 (d)	—	475	950	2,000	3,400	—

KM# 105 2 DUCAT
7.0000 g., 0.9860 Gold 0.2219 oz. AGW **Ruler:** Johann Christian and Georg Rudolph **Obv:** Armored bust of Johann Christian right, legend begins at lower left, divided by 2 small shields of arms **Obv. Legend:** D.G. IO - HANN. CHRISTI - AN. ET. **Rev:** Armored bust of Georg Rudolph left divides date, legend begins at upper left, divided by 2 small shields of arms. **Rev. Legend:** GEOR. RVD. FR. D. - SL. LIG. ET. BREG. **Note:** Klippe. Struck at either Liegnitz or Brieg mints. Fr. #3165.

Date	Mintage	VG	F	VF	XF	Unc
1610 (d)	—	625	1,250	2,500	4,200	—
1611	—	625	1,250	2,500	4,200	—

KM# 157 2 DUCAT
7.0000 g., 0.9860 Gold 0.2219 oz. AGW **Ruler:** Johann Christian and Georg Rudolph **Obv:** Armored bust of Johann Christian right, legend divided by 2 small shields of arms **Obv. Legend:** D.G. IO. - CH. ET. GE. RV. DV - SIL. L. B. **Rev:** Armored bust of Georg Rudolph left, legend divided by 2 small shields of arms which ends with date **Rev. Legend:** MO. NOV. - AVR. REICHST. - (date). **Mint:** Reichenstein **Note:** Fr. #3177.

Date	Mintage	VG	F	VF	XF	Unc
1614	—	1,450	2,800	5,300	9,000	—

KM# 353 2 DUCAT
7.0000 g., 0.9860 Gold 0.2219 oz. AGW **Ruler:** Georg Rudolf **Obv:** Armored bust of Georg Rudolf right in inner circle, small imperial orb at top **Obv. Legend:** D.G. GEO. RVD. DVX. SIL. LIG. & BRE. **Rev:** Crowned ornamented 4-fold arms in inner circle, date at end of legend **Rev. Legend:** MONETA. AVREA. ANNO. **Note:** Fr. #3190.

Date	Mintage	VG	F	VF	XF	Unc
16ZZ	—	675	1,350	2,700	4,400	—

KM# 382 2 DUCAT
7.0000 g., 0.9860 Gold 0.2219 oz. AGW **Ruler:** Georg III, Ludwig IV and Christian **Obv:** 1/2-length figures of Georg III, Ludwig IV & Christian facing, horizontal line below with arabesques in exergue, small imperial orb at top **Obv. Legend:** D.G. GEORG. LUDOVIC. ET. CHRISTIAN. FRATRES. **Rev:** 3 helmets above ornate 4-fold arms, date at end of legend **Rev. Legend:** DUCES. SILESIÆ. LIGN. - ET. BREGENES. **Note:** Fr. #3199.

Date	Mintage	VG	F	VF	XF	Unc
1651 (pf)	—	450	875	1,800	3,050	—

KM# 402 2 DUCAT
7.0000 g., 0.9860 Gold 0.2219 oz. AGW **Subject:** Death of Georg Rudolf **Obv:** Facing bust of Georg Rudolf right in inner circle **Obv. Legend:** D.G. GEORG. RUDOLPH. DUX. SIL. LIG. BREG & GOLDBE. **Rev:** 6-line inscription with date in inner circle **Rev. Legend:** S. CÆS. MAI. VICAR. REG. SUPR. PRÆF. PER. UTRAM & SIL. **Rev. Inscription:** NATUS / 22. IANUARII / ANNO 1595 / OBIIT 14 / IANUARII / 1653. **Note:** Fr. #3195.

Date	Mintage	VG	F	VF	XF	Unc
1653	—	950	2,000	3,600	6,000	—

KM# 403 2 DUCAT
7.0000 g., 0.9860 Gold 0.2219 oz. AGW **Ruler:** Georg III, Ludwig IV and Christian **Obv:** Armored facing 1/2-length busts of Georg, Ludwig, and Christian, small imperial orb at top, arabesques in exergue **Obv. Legend:** D.G. GEORGIUS. LUDOVICUS. & CHRISTIANUS. FRATRES. **Rev:** 3 helmets above ornate 4-fold arms, date at end of legend **Rev. Legend:** DUCES. SILESIÆE. LIGNIC - ENSES. ET. BREGENSES. **Note:** Struck at either Liegnitz or Brieg mints. Varieties exist. Fr. #3199.

Date	Mintage	VG	F	VF	XF	Unc
1653 (pf)	—	425	850	1,800	3,000	—
1657 (pf) - EW	—	425	850	1,800	3,000	—
1658 (pf)	—	425	850	1,800	3,000	—
1659 (pf) - EW	—	425	850	1,800	3,000	—

KM# 480 2 DUCAT
7.0000 g., 0.9860 Gold 0.2219 oz. AGW **Subject:** Death of Georg III **Obv:** Facing long-haired bust of Georg III in inner circle **Obv. Legend:** GEORGIUS. III. DUX. SILES. LIGN. BREG. SUPR. CAP. SIL. **Rev:** 6-line inscription and date in inner circle **Rev. Legend:** DEO. PATRIÆ ET CÆSARI. **Rev. Inscription:** NATUS / A. 1611. D. 4. SEP. / DENATUS / A. 1664. D. 14. IUL. / ÆTAT. 5Z. MENS. / X. DIE. X. **Note:** Fr. #3204. Struck with 1/4 Thaler dies, KM#476.

Date	Mintage	VG	F	VF	XF	Unc
1664	—	950	2,000	3,600	6,000	—

KM# 494 2 DUCAT
7.0000 g., 0.9860 Gold 0.2219 oz. AGW **Ruler:** Christian zu Liegnitz **Obv:** Armored and mantled bust of Christian right in inner circle **Obv. Legend:** CHRISTIANVS. D.G. DVX. SILESIÆ. LIGNICE. **Rev:** Crowned Silesian eagle in inner circle, crown above divides date in margin, mintmaster's initials in oval at bottom **Rev. Legend:** BREGENSIS. ET. - WOLAVIENSIS. **Mint:** Brieg **Note:** Fr. #3212.

Date	Mintage	VG	F	VF	XF	Unc
1666 CBS	—	750	1,500	3,000	5,300	—
1670 CBS	—	750	1,500	3,000	5,300	—
1672 CBS	—	750	1,500	3,000	5,300	—

KM# 546 2 DUCAT
7.0000 g., 0.9860 Gold 0.2219 oz. AGW **Ruler:** Georg Wilhelm **Obv:** Armored bust of Georg Wilhelm right in inner circle **Obv. Legend:** + GEORGIVS. WILHELM. D.G. DVX. SILESIAE. **Rev:** Silesian eagle, date divided by crown in margin at top **Rev. Legend:** LIGNICENSIS. BREGENSIS. ET. WOLAVIENSIS. **Mint:** Brieg **Note:** Fr. #3215.

Date	Mintage	VG	F	VF	XF	Unc
1675 CBS	—	750	1,500	3,250	5,600	—

KM# 547 2 DUCAT
7.0000 g., 0.9860 Gold 0.2219 oz. AGW **Subject:** Death of Georg Wilhelm **Obv:** Armored and mantled bust of Georg Wilhelm right **Obv. Legend:** GEORG. WILH. D.G. DVX. SILE. LIGN. BREG. & WOL. **Rev:** 10-line inscription with R.N. dates in inner circle **Rev. Inscription:** PIASTEÆ / REG. FAM. ULTIM / VIRTUTI. INT. PRI. MOS / ANIMAM. / D. XXIX. SEPT. MDCLX / ACCEPTAM / DEO. ITA. IUBENTI / DXXI. NOV. MDCLXXV / ILLACHRYM. SILES / REDDIDIT. **Note:** Fr. #3221. Struck with 1/4 Thaler dies, KM#529.

Date	Mintage	VG	F	VF	XF	Unc
MDCLXXV (1675)	—	725	1,450	3,100	5,400	—

KM# 47 3 DUCAT
10.5000 g., 0.9860 Gold 0.3328 oz. AGW **Ruler:** Johann Christian and Georg Rudolph **Subject:** Death of Joachim Friedrich's Widow, Anna Maria von Anhalt **Obv:** Crowned 4-fold arms **Obv. Legend:** IO. CHR. ET. GE. RVD. FR. DVC. SL. LIG. ET. BREG. **Rev:** Crowned shield of 8-fold arms with central shield of Anhalt, double marginal legends with R.N. date **Rev. Legend:** Outer: MEM. IL. MAT. ANNÆ. MAR. PR. ANHAL. DVCI. SIL. LEG. BREG. QVÆ. Inner: PIA. OBIIT. M. NOV. DIE. XIV. M.D.C.V. F.F. **Note:** Klippe.

Date	Mintage	VG	F	VF	XF	Unc
MDCV (1605) Rare	—	—	—	—	—	—

KM# 46 3 DUCAT
10.5000 g., 0.9860 Gold 0.3328 oz. AGW **Ruler:** Johann Christian and Georg Rudolph **Subject:** Death of Joachim Friedrich's Widow, Anna Maria von Anhalt **Obv:** Crowned 4-fold arms **Obv. Legend:** IO. CHR. ET. GE. RVD. FR. DVC. SL. LIG. ET. BREG **Rev:** Crowned shield of 8-fold arms with central shield of Anhalt, double marginal legends with R.N. dates **Rev. Legend:** Outer: MEM. IL. MAT. ANNÆ. MAR. PR. ANHAL. DVCI. SIL. LEG. BREG. QVÆ. Inner: PIA. OBIIT. M. NOV. DIE. XIV. M.D.C. V. F.F. **Note:** Struck with 1/2 Thaler dies, KM#40.

Date	Mintage	VG	F	VF	XF	Unc
MDCV (1605) Rare	—	—	—	—	—	—

KM# 108 3 DUCAT
10.5000 g., 0.9860 Gold 0.3328 oz. AGW **Ruler:** Johann Christian and Georg Rudolph **Obv:** 1/2-length figures of Johann Christian and Georg Rudolf facing each other behind flat surface with arabesques in exergue **Obv. Legend:** D:G • IOHAN • CHRIST • ET • GEORG • RVD • FRA • **Rev:** 4-fold arms, 3 ornate helmets above, date at end of legend **Rev. Legend:** DVC • SIL • LIG • - ET • BREG • **Note:** Fr. #3153. Struck with 1/2 Thaler dies, KM#93. Struck at either Liegnitz or Brieg mints.

Date	Mintage	VG	F	VF	XF	Unc
(1)610 (d)	—	675	1,350	2,700	4,400	—
1613	—	675	1,350	2,700	4,400	—

KM# 107 3 DUCAT
10.5000 g., 0.9860 Gold 0.3328 oz. AGW **Ruler:** Johann Christian and Georg Rudolph **Obv:** Armored bust of Johann Christian right, legend divided by 2 small shields of arms **Obv. Legend:** MO. AVREA. D.G. - IOHAN. CHR. ET. **Rev:** Armored bust of Georg Rudolph left divides date, legend divided by 2 small shields of arms **Rev. Legend:** GEOR. RVD. FR. D. - SL. LIG. ET. BRE. **Note:** Klippe. Fr. #3163. Struck at either Liegnitz or Brieg mints.

Date	Mintage	VG	F	VF	XF	Unc
1610 (d)	—	1,000	2,050	3,750	6,300	—

KM# 134 3 DUCAT
10.5000 g., 0.9860 Gold 0.3328 oz. AGW **Ruler:** Johann Christian and Georg Rudolph **Obv:** Draped bust of Christian right in inner circle, legend begins at bottom, divided by 2 small crowned shields of arms at left and right **Obv. Legend:** D:G • IO - HANN • CHRISTI • - AN • ET • **Rev:** Draped bust of Georg Rudolf to left divides date in inner circle, legend begins at upper left, 2 small crowned shields of arms at left and right **Rev. Legend:** GEOR • RVD • FR • D • - SI • LIG • ET • BREG • **Note:** Fr. #3162. Struck with 1/2 Thaler dies, KM#125.

Date	Mintage	VG	F	VF	XF	Unc
1611	—	700	1,400	2,800	4,550	—

KM# A135 3 DUCAT
10.5000 g., 0.9860 Gold 0.3328 oz. AGW **Ruler:** Johann Christian and Georg Rudolph **Obv:** 1/2-length armored figures of Johann Christian & Georg Rudolph facing each other **Obv. Legend:** MO. AVR. IOAN. CHR. ET. GEOR. RVD. FRA. **Rev:** Ornate 4-fold arms, 3 helmets above, date at end of legend **Rev. Legend:** DVC. SIL. LIGN. ET. BREG. **Mint:** Liegnitz **Note:** Fr. #3153.

Date	Mintage	VG	F	VF	XF	Unc
1613 CC	—	600	1,200	2,500	4,150	—

KM# 171 3 DUCAT
10.5000 g., 0.9860 Gold 0.3328 oz. AGW **Ruler:** Johann Christian and Georg Rudolph **Obv:** Bust of Johann Christian right, legend begins at upper left, divided by 2 small crowned shields of arms at left and right **Obv. Legend:** D.G. IOHA. CHRI. ET. - GEORG. RVD. FRA. **Rev:** Bust of Georg Rudolph left, legend ends with date, 2 small crowned shields of arms at left and right **Rev. Legend:** DVX. SIL. LIGNI. ET. - BREGEN. **Mint:** Breslau **Note:** Fr. #3162. Struck with 1/2 Thaler dies, KM#190.

Date	Mintage	VG	F	VF	XF	Unc
1617 HR	—	625	1,250	2,500	4,050	—

KM# 207 3 DUCAT

10.5000 g., 0.9860 Gold 0.3328 oz. AGW **Ruler:** Johann Christian and Georg Rudolph **Obv:** Bust of Johann Christian right, legend begins at upper left, divided by 2 small crowned shields of arms at left and right **Obv. Legend:** D.G. IOH. CHR - ET. GEO. RVD. FR. **Rev:** Bust of Georg Rudolph left, legend ends with date, 2 small crowned shields of arms at left and right **Rev. Legend:** DVX. SIL. LI. - ET. BRE. **Mint:** Breslau **Note:** Fr. #3162. Struck with 1/4 Thaler dies, KM#167.

Date	Mintage	VG	F	VF	XF	Unc
1619 HR	—	625	1,250	2,500	4,050	—

KM# 279 3 DUCAT

10.5000 g., 0.9860 Gold 0.3328 oz. AGW **Ruler:** Georg Rudolf **Obv:** Bust of Johann Christian right, legend begins at upper left, divided by 2 small shields of arms at left and right **Obv. Legend:** D.G. IOH. CHR - ET. GEO. RVD. FR. **Rev:** Bust Georg Rudolph left, legend ends with date, 2 small shields of arms at left and right **Rev. Legend:** DVX. SIL. LI. - ET. BRE. **Mint:** Liegnitz **Note:** Struck with 24 Kreuzer dies, KM#248.

Date	Mintage	VG	F	VF	XF	Unc
16Z1 MT Rare	—	—	—	—	—	—

KM# 355 3 DUCAT

10.5000 g., 0.9860 Gold 0.3328 oz. AGW **Ruler:** Johann Christian **Obv:** Armored bust of Johann Christian right in inner circle, date at lower right within the circle around bust, small imperial orb at top **Obv. Legend:** D.G. IOHANNES. CHRISTIANUS. DUX. **Rev:** Oval 4-fold arms topped by three helmets in inner circle **Rev. Legend:** SIL. LIGN. - ET. BREG. **Mint:** Ohlau **Note:** Fr. #3186.

Date	Mintage	VG	F	VF	XF	Unc
16ZZ HR Rare	—	—	—	—	—	—

KM# 356 3 DUCAT

10.5000 g., 0.9860 Gold 0.3328 oz. AGW **Ruler:** Johann Christian **Mint:** Ohlau **Note:** Klippe. Fr. #3187.

Date	Mintage	VG	F	VF	XF	Unc
16ZZ HR Rare	—	—	—	—	—	—

KM# 357 3 DUCAT

10.5000 g., 0.9860 Gold 0.3328 oz. AGW **Ruler:** Georg Rudolf **Obv:** Armored bust of Georg Rudolf right in inner circle, small imperial orb at top **Obv. Legend:** D.G. GEO. RVD. DVX. SIL. LIG. & BRE. **Rev:** Crowned ornamented 4-fold arms in inner circle, date at end of legend **Rev. Legend:** MONETA. AVREA. ANNO. **Note:** Fr. #3189.

Date	Mintage	VG	F	VF	XF	Unc
16ZZ	—	1,750	3,150	5,200	8,300	—

KM# 384 3 DUCAT

10.5000 g., 0.9860 Gold 0.3328 oz. AGW **Ruler:** Georg III, Ludwig IV and Christian **Obv:** Facing 1/2-figures of Georg, Ludwig, and Christian in inner circle, horizontal line below with arabesques in exergue, small imperial orb at top **Obv. Legend:** D.G. GEORG LUDOVIC. ET. CHRISTIAN. FRATRES. **Rev:** Ornate 4-fold arms topped by three helmets in inner circle, date at end of legend **Rev. Legend:** DUCES. SILESIÆ. LIGN. - ET. BREGENES. **Note:** Fr. #3198. Struck at Liegnitz or Brieg mints.

Date	Mintage	VG	F	VF	XF	Unc
1651 (pf) - VT	—	625	1,250	2,500	4,050	—

KM# 420 3 DUCAT

10.5000 g., 0.9860 Gold 0.3328 oz. AGW **Ruler:** Georg III, Ludwig IV and Christian **Obv:** Armored 1/2-length figures of Georg, Ludwig & Christian facing **Obv. Legend:** D.G. GEORGIUS. LUDOVICUS. & CHRISTIANUS. FRATRES. **Rev:** 3 helmets above ornate 4-fold arms, date at end of legend **Rev. Legend:** DUCES. SILESIÆ. LIGNIC - ENSES. ET. BREGENSES. **Note:** Fr. #3198. Struck at Liegnitz or Brieg mints.

Date	Mintage	VG	F	VF	XF	Unc
1658 (pf)	—	625	1,250	2,500	4,050	—
1660 (pf) - EW	—	625	1,250	2,500	4,050	—

KM# 464 3 DUCAT

10.5000 g., 0.9860 Gold 0.3328 oz. AGW **Ruler:** Georg III, Ludwig IV and Christian **Obv:** Armored 1/2-length figures of Georg, Ludwig & Christian facing, small imperial orb at top, arabesques in exergue **Obv. Legend:** D.G. GEORGIUS. LUDOVICUS. & CHRISTIANUS. FRATRES. **Rev:** 3 helmets above ornate 4-fold arms, date at end of legend **Rev. Legend:** SUFFICIT MIHI GRA - TIA TUA DOMINE A **Note:** Struck at either Liegnitz or Brieg mints.

Date	Mintage	VG	F	VF	XF	Unc
1661 (pf) - EW	—	—	—	—	—	—

KM# 496 3 DUCAT

10.5000 g., 0.9860 Gold 0.3328 oz. AGW **Ruler:** Christian zu Ohlau **Obv:** Armored and mantled bust of Georg Wilhelm right in inner circle **Obv. Legend:** CHRISTIANVS • D:G • DVX • SILESIÆ • LIGNICE • **Rev:** Crowned Silesian eagle in inner circle, crown divides date in margin, mintmaster's initials in oval at bottom **Rev. Legend:** BREGENSIS • ET • - WOLAVIENSIS • **Mint:** Brieg **Note:** Fr. #3211.

Date	Mintage	VG	F	VF	XF	Unc
1666 CBS	—	1,800	3,300	5,400	8,400	—

KM# 49 4 DUCAT

14.0000 g., 0.9860 Gold 0.4438 oz. AGW **Ruler:** Johann Christian and Georg Rudolph **Obv:** Small 1/2-length figures of Johann Christian and Georg Rudolf facing each other behind flat surface with arabesques in exergue **Obv. Legend:** D:G • IOHAN • CHRIST • ET • GEOR(G) • RVD • FRA • **Rev:** 4-fold arms topped by three helmets, date at end of legend **Rev. Legend:** DVC • SIL • LIG • - ET • BREG • **Note:** Fr. #3152. Struck with Thaler dies, KM#53. Struck at either Liegnitz or Brieg mints.

Date	Mintage	VG	F	VF	XF	Unc
(1)605	—	1,000	2,050	3,750	6,300	—
(1)607	—	1,000	2,050	3,750	6,300	—
(1)607 (d)	—	1,000	2,050	3,750	6,300	—
(1)609	—	1,000	2,050	3,750	6,300	—
(1)610	—	1,000	2,050	3,750	6,300	—

KM# 110 4 DUCAT

14.0000 g., 0.9860 Gold 0.4438 oz. AGW **Ruler:** Johann Christian and Georg Rudolph **Obv:** 1/2-length figures of Johann Christian & Georg Rudolph facing each other behind flat surface with arabesques in exergue **Obv. Legend:** D:G • IOHAN • CHRIST • ET • GEORG • RVD • FRA • **Rev:** 4-fold arms, 3 ornate helmets above, date at end of legend **Rev. Legend:** DVC • SIL • LIG • - ET • BREG • **Note:** Fr. #3152. Struck with 1/2 Thaler dies, KM#93. Struck at either Liegnitz or Brieg mints.

Date	Mintage	VG	F	VF	XF	Unc
(1)610 (d)	—	1,000	2,050	3,750	6,300	—

KM# 111 4 DUCAT

14.0000 g., 0.9860 Gold 0.4438 oz. AGW **Ruler:** Johann Christian and Georg Rudolph **Obv:** Armored bust of Johann Christian right, legend divided by 2 small shields of arms **Obv. Legend:** MO. AVREA. D.G. - IOHAN. CHR. ET. **Rev:** Armored bust of Georg Rudolph left divides date, legend divided by 2 small shields of arms **Rev. Legend:** GEOR. RVD. FR. D. - SL. LIG. ET. BRE. **Note:** Klippe. Struck at either Liegnitz or Brieg mints on thick, square flan with Ducat dies, KM#102. Fr. #3161.

Date	Mintage	VG	F	VF	XF	Unc
1610 (d)	—	1,500	3,000	6,000	9,800	—
1611	—	1,500	3,000	6,000	9,800	—

KM# 136 4 DUCAT

14.0000 g., 0.9860 Gold 0.4438 oz. AGW **Ruler:** Johann Christian and Georg Rudolph **Obv:** Draped bust of Johann Christian right, legend begins at bottom divided by 2 small shields of arms at left and right **Obv. Legend:** D:G • IO - HANN • CHRISTI • - AN • ET • **Rev:** Draped bust of Georg Rudolf left divides date, legend begins at upper left, 2 small shields of arms at left and right **Rev. Legend:** GEOR • RVD • FR • D • - SI • LIG • ET • BREG • **Note:** Fr. #3160. Struck with 1/2 Thaler dies, KM#134.

Date	Mintage	VG	F	VF	XF	Unc
1611	—	1,000	2,050	3,750	6,300	—

KM# 159 4 DUCAT

14.0000 g., 0.9860 Gold 0.4438 oz. AGW **Ruler:** Johann Christian and Georg Rudolph **Obv:** Armored bust of Johann Christian right, legend divided by 2 small shields of arms **Obv. Legend:** D.G. IO. - CH. ET. GE. RV. DV - SIL. L. B. **Rev:** Armored bust of Georg Rudolph left, legend divided by 2 small shields of arms which ends with date **Rev. Legend:** MO. NOV. - AVR. REICHST. - (date). **Mint:** Reichenstein **Note:** Fr. #3176.

Date	Mintage	VG	F	VF	XF	Unc
1614 Rare	—	—	—	—	—	—

KM# 173 4 DUCAT

14.0000 g., 0.9860 Gold 0.4438 oz. AGW **Ruler:** Johann Christian and Georg Rudolph **Obv:** Draped bust of Johann Christian right, legend begins at bottom, divided by 2 small shields of arms at left and right **Obv. Legend:** D.G. IO - HANN. CHRISTI. - AN. ET. **Rev:** Draped bust of Georg Rudolph left divides date, legend begins at upper left, 2 small shields of arms at left and right **Rev. Legend:** GEOR. RVD. FR. D. - SI. LIG. ET. BREG. **Mint:** Breslau

Date	Mintage	VG	F	VF	XF	Unc
1617 HR Rare	—	—	—	—	—	—

KM# 359 4 DUCAT

14.0000 g., 0.9860 Gold 0.4438 oz. AGW **Ruler:** Johann Christian **Obv:** Armored bust of Johann Christian right, date at lower right within the circle around bust, small imperial orb at top **Obv. Legend:** D.G. IOHANNES. CHRISTIANUS. DUX. **Rev:** Oval 4-fold arms topped by three helmets in inner circle **Rev. Legend:** SIL. LIGN. - ET. BREG. **Mint:** Ohlau **Note:** Fr. #3185.

Date	Mintage	VG	F	VF	XF	Unc
16ZZ HR Rare	—	—	—	—	—	—

KM# 390 4 DUCAT

14.0000 g., 0.9860 Gold 0.4438 oz. AGW **Ruler:** Georg III, Ludwig IV and Christian **Obv:** Facing 1/2-length figures of Georg, Ludwig, and Christian in inner circle, horizontal line below with arabesques in exergue, small imperial orb at top **Obv. Legend:** D.G. GEORG. LUDOVIC. ET. CHRISTIAN. FRATRES. **Rev:** 3 helmets above ornate 4-fold arms, date at end of legend **Rev. Legend:** DUCES. SILESIÆ. LIGN. - ET. BREGENES. **Note:** Fr. #3197. Struck with 1/2 Thaler dies, KM#374. Struck at either Liegnitz or Brieg mints.

Date	Mintage	VG	F	VF	XF	Unc
165Z (pf) - VT	—	1,000	2,050	3,750	6,300	—

KM# 422 4 DUCAT

14.0000 g., 0.9860 Gold 0.4438 oz. AGW **Ruler:** Georg III, Ludwig IV and Christian **Obv:** Facing, armored 1/2-length figures of Georg, Ludwig & Christian, small imperial orb at top, arabesques in exergue **Obv. Legend:** D.G. GEORGIUS. LUDOVICUS. & CHRISTIANUS. FRATRES. **Rev:** 3 helmets above ornate 4-fold arms, date at end of legend **Rev. Legend:** DUCES. SILESIÆ. LIGNIC - ENSES. ET. BREGENSES. **Note:** Fr. #3197. Struck at either Liegnitz or Brieg mints. Struck with 1/4 Thaler dies, KM#399.

Date	Mintage	VG	F	VF	XF	Unc
1658 (pf)	—	1,000	2,050	3,750	6,300	—
1659 (pf) - EW	—	1,000	2,050	3,750	6,300	—

KM# 23 5 DUCAT

17.5000 g., 0.9860 Gold 0.5547 oz. AGW **Subject:** Death of Joachim Friedrich **Obv:** Armored and collared bust of Joachim Friedrich right in inner circle **Obv. Legend:** ✠ MEMOR. IOACH. FRID. DVCIS. SILES. LEGN. BREGENSIS. **Rev:** 8-line inscription with R.N. date, circular marginal inscription **Rev. Legend:** ✠ DEO. OPT. MAX. IN. ÆTERN. VIVENS. SVM. PATR. **Rev. Designer:** OBIIT. AN / NO. M.D. C II. / M. MART. XXV. / HORA. P. MER. VI / CVM. / VIXISSMI. / AN. LI. MENS. V / DIES. XXVI. / ✠. **Note:** Fr. #3140. Struck from 1/2 Thaler dies, KM#12.

Date	Mintage	VG	F	VF	XF	Unc
MDCII (1602) Rare	—	—	—	—	—	—

KM# 67 5 DUCAT

17.5000 g., 0.9860 Gold 0.5547 oz. AGW **Ruler:** Johann Christian and Georg Rudolph **Obv:** Small busts of Johann Christian and Georg Rudolf facing each other, date below **Obv. Legend:** D.G. IOHAN. CHRIST. ET. GEOR. RVD. FRA. **Rev:** 4-fold arms, 3 ornate helmets above **Rev. Legend:** DVC. SIL. LIG. - ET. BREGEN. **Note:** Fr. #3151. Struck with 1/2 Thaler dies, KM#57. Struck at either Liegnitz or Brieg mints.

Date	Mintage	VG	F	VF	XF	Unc
(1)608 (d)	—	1,250	2,500	5,000	8,100	—

KM# 86 5 DUCAT

17.5000 g., 0.9860 Gold 0.5547 oz. AGW **Ruler:** Johann Christian and Georg Rudolph **Obv:** 1/2-length figures of Johann Christian & Georg Rudolph facing each other **Obv. Legend:** D:G • IOAN • CHRIST • ET • GEORG • RVD • FRA • **Rev:** 4-fold arms, 3 ornate helmets above, date at end of legend **Rev. Legend:** DVC • SIL • LIG • - ET • BREG • **Note:** Fr. #3151. Struck with 1/2 Thaler dies, KM#72.

Date	Mintage	VG	F	VF	XF	Unc
(1)609 (d)	—	1,200	2,300	4,400	7,500	—

KM# 113 5 DUCAT

17.5000 g., 0.9860 Gold 0.5547 oz. AGW **Ruler:** Johann Christian and Georg Rudolph **Obv:** 1/2-length figures of Johann Christian & Georg Rudolph facing each other behind flat surface with arabesques in exergue **Obv. Legend:** D.G. IOHAN. CHRIST. ET.

GEOR(G). RVD. FRA. **Rev:** 4-fold arms, 3 ornate helmets above, date at end of legend **Rev. Legend:** DVC. SIL. LIG. - ET. BREG. **Note:** Fr. #3151. Struck with Thaler dies, KM#53.

Date	Mintage	VG	F	VF	XF	Unc
(1)610 (d)	—	1,200	2,300	4,400	7,500	—

KM# 138 5 DUCAT

17.5000 g., 0.9860 Gold 0.5547 oz. AGW **Ruler:** Johann Christian and Georg Rudolph **Obv:** Draped bust of Johann Christian right in inner circle, legend begins at bottom, divided by 2 small shields of arms at left and right **Obv. Legend:** D.G. IO - HANN. CHRISTI. - AN. ET. **Rev:** Draped bust of Georg Rudolf left divides date in inner circle, legend begins at upper left, 2 small shields of arms at left and right **Rev. Legend:** GEOR. RVD. FR. D. - SI. LIG. ET. BREG. **Note:** Fr. #3159. Struck with 1/2 Thaler dies, KM#134.

Date	Mintage	VG	F	VF	XF	Unc
1611	—	1,250	2,500	5,000	8,100	—

KM# 161 5 DUCAT

17.5000 g., 0.9860 Gold 0.5547 oz. AGW **Ruler:** Johann Christian and Georg Rudolph **Obv:** Bust of Johann Christian right, legend begins at upper left, divided by 2 small shields of arms at left and right **Obv. Legend:** D.G. IO. CHR. ET. G - EO. RVD. DVX. SI. L. B. **Rev:** Bust of Georg Rudolph left, legend ends with date, 2 small shields of arms at left and right **Rev. Legend:** MON. NOV. ARGE. - REICHST. **Mint:** Reichenstein **Note:** Fr. #3182. Struck with Thaler dies, KM#154.

Date	Mintage	VG	F	VF	XF	Unc
1615 Rare	—	—	—	—	—	—
1616 Rare	—	—	—	—	—	—

KM# 175 5 DUCAT

17.5000 g., 0.9860 Gold 0.5547 oz. AGW **Ruler:** Johann Christian and Georg Rudolph **Obv:** Bust of Johann Christian right, legend begins at upper left, divided by 2 small shields of arms at left and right **Obv. Legend:** D.G. IOHA. CHRI. ET. - GEORG. RVD. FRA. **Rev:** Bust of Georg Rudolph left, legend ends with date, 2 small shields of arms at left and right **Rev. Legend:** DVX. SIL. LIGNI. ET. - BREGEN. **Mint:** Reichenstein **Note:** Fr. #3159. Struck with 1/2 Thaler dies, KM#190.

Date	Mintage	VG	F	VF	XF	Unc
1617 HR	—	1,200	2,500	4,500	7,500	—

KM# 209 5 DUCAT

17.5000 g., 0.9860 Gold 0.5547 oz. AGW **Ruler:** Johann Christian and Georg Rudolph **Obv:** Armored, 1/2-length figures of Johann Christian and Georg Rudolph facing each other, horizontal line with ornamentation below **Obv. Legend:** D.G. IOHAN. CHRIS(T). ET. GEORG. RVDO. FRAT(R). **Rev:** Shield with flat top and rounded bottom of 4-fold arms, 3 ornate helmets above, date at end of legend **Rev. Legend:** DVC. SIL. LIGNIC. ET. BREGE. **Mint:** Reichenstein **Note:** Fr. #3151. Struck with Thaler dies, KM#169.

Date	Mintage	VG	F	VF	XF	Unc
1619 HR	—	1,350	2,650	4,900	8,300	—

KM# 281 5 DUCAT

17.5000 g., 0.9860 Gold 0.5547 oz. AGW **Ruler:** Georg Rudolf **Obv:** Armored bust of Georg Rudolph right, small imperial orb at top in margin **Obv. Legend:** D.G. GEOR. RVD. DVX. SIL. LIG. BRI. ET. GO. **Rev:** Crowned Spanish shield of 4-fold arms in baroque frame, date at end of legend **Rev. Legend:** MONETA. NOVA. AVREA. **Note:** Fr. #3188.

Date	Mintage	VG	F	VF	XF	Unc
1621 Rare	—	—	—	—	—	—

KM# 362 5 DUCAT

17.5000 g., 0.9860 Gold 0.5547 oz. AGW **Ruler:** Johann Christian **Obv:** Armored and mantled bust of Johann Christian right, small imperial orb at top in margin **Obv. Legend:** D.G. IOHAN. CHRIST. DVX. SIL. LIG. ET. B. **Rev:** 4-fold arms, 3 helmets above, date at end of legend **Rev. Legend:** MONETA. NOVA. CRVCIBVRGENSIS. **Mint:** Kreuzburg **Note:** Fr. #3184.

Date	Mintage	VG	F	VF	XF	Unc
1622 FS Rare	—	—	—	—	—	—

KM# 361 5 DUCAT

17.5000 g., 0.9860 Gold 0.5547 oz. AGW **Ruler:** Johann Christian **Obv:** Bust of Johann Christian right in inner circle, small imperial orb at top in margin **Obv. Legend:** D.G. IOHAN. CHRIST. DVX. SIL. LIG. ET. B. **Rev:** 4-fold arms topped by three helmets in inner circle, date at end of legend **Rev. Legend:** MONETA. NOVA. CRVCIBVRGENSIS. **Mint:** Kreuzburg **Note:** Fr. #3184. Struck with 1/2 Thaler dies, KM#343.

Date	Mintage	VG	F	VF	XF	Unc
1622 FS Rare	—	—	—	—	—	—

KM# 411 5 DUCAT

17.5000 g., 0.9860 Gold 0.5547 oz. AGW **Ruler:** Georg III, Ludwig IV and Christian **Obv:** Armored 1/2-length figures of Georg, Ludwig, and Christian facing, small imperial orb at top, arabesques in exergue **Obv. Legend:** D.G. GEORGIUS. LUDOVICUS. & CHRISTIANUS. FRATRES. **Rev:** 3 helmets above ornate 4-fold arms, date at end of legend **Rev. Legend:** DUCES. SILESIÆ. LIGNIC - ENSES. ET. BREGENSES. **Note:** Fr. #3196. Struck with 1/2 Thaler dies, KM#305 at either Liegnitz or Brieg mints. Varieties exist.

Date	Mintage	VG	F	VF	XF	Unc
1656 (pf)	—	850	1,800	4,200	6,600	—
1658 (pf)	—	725	1,500	3,600	6,000	—
1659 (pf) - EW	—	725	1,500	3,600	6,000	—

KM# 508 5 DUCAT

17.5000 g., 0.9860 Gold 0.5547 oz. AGW **Ruler:** Christian zu Brieg **Obv:** Armored and mantled bust of Christian right in inner circle **Obv. Legend:** CHRISTIANVS. D.G. DVX. SILESIÆ. LIGNICE. **Rev:** Crowned Silesian eagle in inner circle, crown divides date in margin, mintmaster's initials in oval at bottom **Rev. Legend:** BREGENSIS. ET. - WOLAVIENSIS. **Mint:** Brieg **Note:** Fr. #3210.

Date	Mintage	VG	F	VF	XF	Unc
1672 CBS Rare	—	—	—	—	—	—

FR# 3220 5 DUCAT

17.5000 g., 0.9860 Gold 0.5547 oz. AGW **Subject:** Death of Georg Wilhelm **Note:** Similar to 2 Ducat, Fr. #3221.

Date	Mintage	VG	F	VF	XF	Unc
1675 Rare	—	—	—	—	—	—

FR# A3150 6 DUCAT

21.0000 g., 0.9860 Gold 0.6657 oz. AGW **Obv:** Small busts of Johann Christian and Georg Rudolf **Note:** Struck with 1/2 Thaler dies.

Date	Mintage	VG	F	VF	XF	Unc
1605 Rare	—	—	—	—	—	—

KM# 61 6 DUCAT

21.0000 g., 0.9860 Gold 0.6657 oz. AGW **Ruler:** Johann Christian and Georg Rudolph **Obv:** 1/2-length figures of Johann Christian & Georg Rudolph facing each other behind flat surface with arabesques in exergue **Obv. Legend:** D.G. IOHAN. CHRIST. ET. GEOR. RVD. FRA. **Rev:** 4-fold arms, 3 ornate helmets above, date at end of legend **Rev. Legend:** DVC. SIL. LIG. - ET. BREGEN. **Note:** Fr. #3150. Struck with Thaler dies, KM#53.

Date	Mintage	VG	F	VF	XF	Unc
(1)607 Rare	—	—	—	—	—	—

KM# 115 6 DUCAT

21.0000 g., 0.9860 Gold 0.6657 oz. AGW **Ruler:** Johann Christian and Georg Rudolph **Obv:** 1/2-length figures of Johann Christian & Georg Rudolph facing each other behind flat surface with arabesques in exergue **Obv. Legend:** D.G. IOHAN. CHRIST. ET. GEOR(G). RVD. FRA. **Rev:** 4-fold arms, 3 ornate helmets above, date at end of legend **Rev. Legend:** DVC. SIL. LIG. - ET. BREG. **Note:** Fr. #3150. Struck at either Liegnitz or Brieg mints.

Date	Mintage	VG	F	VF	XF	Unc
(1)610 (d) Rare	—	—	—	—	—	—

KM# 140 6 DUCAT

21.0000 g., 0.9860 Gold 0.6657 oz. AGW **Ruler:** Johann Christian and Georg Rudolph **Obv:** Draped bust of Johann Christian right in inner circle, legend begins at bottom, divided by 2 small shields of arms at left and right, small imperial orb in circle at bottom **Obv. Legend:** D.G. IO - HANN. CHRISTI. - AN. ET. **Rev:** Draped bust of Georg Rudolf left divides date in inner circle, legend begins at upper left, 2 small shields of arms at left and right **Rev. Legend:** GEOR. RVD. FRA. D. - SIL. LIG. ET. BREG. **Note:** Fr. #3158. Struck with Thaler dies, KM#128.

Date	Mintage	VG	F	VF	XF	Unc
1611 Rare	—	—	—	—	—	—

KM# 163 6 DUCAT

21.0000 g., 0.9860 Gold 0.6657 oz. AGW **Ruler:** Johann Christian and Georg Rudolph **Obv:** Bust of Johann Christian right, legend begins at upper left, divided by 2 small shields of arms at left and right **Obv. Legend:** D.G. IO. CHR. ET. G - EO. RVD. DVX. SI. L. B. **Rev:** Bust of Georg Rudolph left, legend ends with date, 2 small shields of arms at left and right **Rev. Legend:** MON. NOV. ARGE. - REICHST. **Mint:** Reichenstein **Note:** Fr. #3181. Struck with Thaler dies, KM#154. Specimen dated 1616 sold at auction in 1983 as XF for SFr 30,500.

Date	Mintage	VG	F	VF	XF	Unc
1615 Rare	—	—	—	—	—	—
1616 Rare	—	—	—	—	—	—

KM# 177 6 DUCAT

21.0000 g., 0.9860 Gold 0.6657 oz. AGW **Ruler:** Johann Christian and Georg Rudolph **Obv:** Armored 1/2-length figures of Johann Christian and Georg Rudolf facing each other, horizontal line with ornamentation below **Obv. Legend:** D.G. IOHA(N). CHRIS(T). ET. GEOR(G). RVDO. FRAT(R). **Rev:** Shield with flat top and rounded bottom of 4-fold arms, 3 ornate helmets above, date at end of legend **Rev. Legend:** DVC. SIL. LIGNIC. ET. BREGE. **Mint:** Reichenstein **Note:** Fr. #3150. Struck with Thaler dies, KM#169.

Date	Mintage	VG	F	VF	XF	Unc
1616 Rare	—	—	—	—	—	—
1617 HR Rare	—	—	—	—	—	—
1619 HR Rare	—	—	—	—	—	—
1621 Rare	—	—	—	—	—	—

KM# 283 6 DUCAT

21.0000 g., 0.9860 Gold 0.6657 oz. AGW **Ruler:** Georg Rudolf **Obv:** Armored bust of Georg Rudolph right in inner circle, small imperial orb at top **Obv. Legend:** D.G. GEORG. RVDOLPHVS. DVC. SILES. **Rev:** 4-fold arms topped by three helmets in inner circle, date at end of legend **Rev. Legend:** LIGNIC. ET. BREG. **Mint:** Haynau **Note:** Fr. #3193. Struck with Thaler dies, KM#269.

Date	Mintage	VG	F	VF	XF	Unc
16Z1 MT Rare	—	—	—	—	—	—

KM# 117 7 DUCAT

24.5000 g., 0.9860 Gold 0.7766 oz. AGW **Ruler:** Johann Christian and Georg Rudolph **Obv:** 1/2-length figures of Johann Christian and Georg Rudolf facing each other behind flat surface with arabesques in exergue **Obv. Legend:** D.G. IOHAN. CHRIST. ET. GEOR(G). RVD. FRA. **Rev:** 4-fold arms, 3 ornate helmets above, date at end of legend **Rev. Legend:** DVC. SIL. LIG. - ET. BREG. **Note:** Fr. #3149. Struck with Thaler dies, KM#53 at either Liegnitz or Brieg mints.

Date	Mintage	VG	F	VF	XF	Unc
(1)610 (d) Rare	—	—	—	—	—	—

KM# 285 7 DUCAT

24.5000 g., 0.9860 Gold 0.7766 oz. AGW **Ruler:** Johann Christian **Obv:** Armored bust of Johann Christian right **Obv. Legend:** D.G. IOHAN. CHRISTIAN. DVX. SIL. **Rev:** 4-fold arms, 3 helmets above, date at top in margin **Rev. Legend:** LIGN. ET. BREG. SVP. CAPVT. SIL. **Mint:** Ohlau **Note:** Fr. #3183. Struck with Thaler dies, KM#266.

Date	Mintage	VG	F	VF	XF	Unc
16Z1 HR Rare	—	—	—	—	—	—

KM# 286 7 DUCAT

24.5000 g., 0.9860 Gold 0.7766 oz. AGW **Ruler:** Georg Rudolf **Obv:** Armored bust of Georg Rudolph right, small imperial orb at top **Obv. Legend:** D.G. GEORG. RVDOLPHVS. DVC. SILES. **Rev:** 4-fold arms, 3 helmets above, date at end of legend **Rev. Legend:** LIGNIC. ET. BREG. **Mint:** Haynau **Note:** Fr. #3192. Struck with Thaler dies, KM#269.

Date	Mintage	VG	F	VF	XF	Unc
16Z1 MT Rare	—	—	—	—	—	—

KM# 179 8 DUCAT

28.0000 g., 0.9860 Gold 0.8876 oz. AGW **Ruler:** Johann Christian and Georg Rudolph **Obv:** Large bust of Johann Christian right, legend begins at upper left, divided by 2 small shields of arms at left and right **Obv. Legend:** D.G. IO. CHR. ET. G - EO. RVD. DVX. SI. L. B. **Rev:** Large bust of Georg Rudolph left, legend ends with date, 2 small shields of arms at left and right **Rev. Legend:** MON. NOV. ARGE. - REICHST. **Mint:** Reichenstein **Note:** Fr. #3180. Struck with Thaler dies, KM#154.

Date	Mintage	VG	F	VF	XF	Unc
1617 Rare	—	—	—	—	—	—

KM# 288 8 DUCAT

28.0000 g., 0.9860 Gold 0.8876 oz. AGW **Ruler:** Georg Rudolf **Obv:** Armored bust of Georg Rudolph right, small imperial orb at top **Obv. Legend:** D.G. GEORG. RVDOLPHVS. DVC. SILES. **Rev:** 4-fold arms, 3 helmets above, date at end of legend **Rev. Legend:** LIGNIC. ET. BREG. **Mint:** Haynau **Note:** Fr. #3191. Struck with Thaler dies, KM#269.

Date	Mintage	VG	F	VF	XF	Unc
16Z1 MT Rare	—	—	—	—	—	—

KM# 51 10 DUCAT

35.0000 g., 0.9860 Gold 1.1095 oz. AGW **Ruler:** Johann Christian and Georg Rudolph **Subject:** Death of Joachim Friedrich's Widow, Anna Maria von Anhalt **Obv:** Facing bust wearing small hat **Rev:** Crowned shield of 8-fold arms within central shield of Anhalt, double marginal legends with R.N. date. **Rev. Legend:** Outer: MEM. IL. MAT. ANNÆ. MAR. PR. ANHAL. DVCI. SIL. LEG. BREG. QVÆ.; Inner: PIA. ORIIT. M. NOV. DIE. XIV. M.D.C.V. F.F.

Date	Mintage	VG	F	VF	XF	Unc
MDCV (1605) Rare	—	—	—	—	—	—

KM# 89 10 DUCAT

35.0000 g., 0.9860 Gold 1.1095 oz. AGW **Ruler:** Johann Christian and Georg Rudolph **Obv:** Small busts of Johann Christian and Georg Rudolf facing each other **Obv. Legend:** D.G. IOAN. CHRIST. ET. GEORG. RVD. FRA. **Rev:** Ornately shaped shield of 4-fold arms, 3 helmets above, date at end of legend **Rev. Legend:** DVC. SIL. LIG. - ET. BREG. **Note:** Fr. #3148. Struck with Thaler dies, KM#269 at either Liegnitz or Brieg mints.

Date	Mintage	VG	F	VF	XF	Unc
(1)609 (d) Rare	—	—	—	—	—	—

KM# 88 10 DUCAT

35.0000 g., 0.9860 Gold 1.1095 oz. AGW **Ruler:** Johann Christian and Georg Rudolph **Obv:** 3/4-length armored figure to right divides date, small imperial orb at top, 2 small shields of arms below **Obv. Legend:** D.G. IOHANN - CHRISTIAN. ET. **Rev:** 3/4-length armored figure to left, 2 small shields of arms below **Rev. Legend:** (Large cross) GEORG. RVD. FRAT - DVC. SIL. LIG. ET. BRE. **Note:** Fr. #3156.

Date	Mintage	VG	F	VF	XF	Unc
1609 Rare	—	—	—	—	—	—

KM# 119 10 DUCAT

35.0000 g., 0.9860 Gold 1.1095 oz. AGW **Ruler:** Johann Christian and Georg Rudolph **Obv:** Small 1/2-length figures facing each other behind flat surface with arabesques in exergue **Obv. Legend:** D.G. IOHAN. CHRIST. ET. GEOR(G). RVD. FRA. **Rev:** 4-fold arms, 3 ornate helmets above, date at end of legend **Rev. Legend:** DVC. SIL. LIG. - ET. BREG. **Note:** Fr. #3148. Struck with Thaler dies, KM#53 at either Liegnitz or Brieg mints.

Date	Mintage	VG	F	VF	XF	Unc
(1)610 (d) Rare	—	—	—	—	—	—

KM# 142 10 DUCAT

35.0000 g., 0.9860 Gold 1.1095 oz. AGW **Ruler:** Johann Christian and Georg Rudolph **Obv:** Draped bust of Johann Christian right, legend begins at bottom, divided by 2 small shields of arms at left and right, small imperial orb in circle at bottom **Obv. Legend:** D.G. IO - HANN. CHRISTI. - AN. ET. **Rev:** Draped bust of Georg Rudolph left divides date, legend begins at upper left, 2 small shields of arms at left and right **Rev. Legend:** GEOR. RVD. FRA. D. - SIL. LIG. ET. BREG. **Note:** Fr. #3157. Struck with Thaler dies, KM#128.

Date	Mintage	VG	F	VF	XF	Unc
1611 Rare	—	—	—	—	—	—

KM# 181 10 DUCAT

35.0000 g., 0.9860 Gold 1.1095 oz. AGW **Ruler:** Johann Christian and Georg Rudolph **Obv:** Large bust of Johann Christian right, legend begins at upper left, divided by 2 small shields of arms at left and right **Obv. Legend:** D.G. IO. CHR. ET. G - EO. RVD. DVX. SI. L. B. **Rev:** Large bust of Georg Rudolph left, legend ends with date, 2 small shields of arms at left and right **Rev. Legend:** MON. NOV. ARGE. - REICHST. **Mint:** Reichenstein **Note:** Fr. #3179. Struck with Thaler dies, KM#154.

Date	Mintage	VG	F	VF	XF	Unc
1617 Rare	—	—	—	—	—	—

KM# 182 10 DUCAT

35.0000 g., 0.9860 Gold 1.1095 oz. AGW **Ruler:** Johann Christian and Georg Rudolph **Obv:** Armored 1/2-length figures of Johann Christian and Georg Rudolph facing each other, horizontal line with ornamentation below **Obv. Legend:** D.G. IOHAN. CHRIS(T). ET. GEORG. RVDO. FRAT(R). **Rev:** Shield with flat top and rounded bottom of 4-fold arms, 3 ornate helmets above, date at end of legend **Rev. Legend:** DVC. SIL. LIGNIC. ET. BREGE. **Mint:** Reichenstein **Note:** Fr. #3148. Struck with Thaler dies, KM#169.

Date	Mintage	VG	F	VF	XF	Unc
1617 HR Rare	—	—	—	—	—	—
1619 HR Rare	—	—	—	—	—	—

KM# 290 10 DUCAT

35.0000 g., 0.9860 Gold 1.1095 oz. AGW **Ruler:** Georg Rudolf **Obv:** Armored bust of Georg Rudolph right, small imperial orb at top **Obv. Legend:** D.G. GEORG. RVDOLPHVS. DVC. SILES. **Rev:** 4-fold arms, 3 helmets above, date at end of legend **Rev. Legend:** LIGNIC. ET. BREG. **Mint:** Haynau **Note:** Struck with Thaler dies, KM#269.

Date	Mintage	VG	F	VF	XF	Unc
16Z1 MT Rare	—	—	—	—	—	—

KM# 498 10 DUCAT

35.0000 g., 0.9860 Gold 1.1095 oz. AGW **Ruler:** Christian zu Brieg **Obv:** Armored and mantled bust of Christian right **Obv. Legend:** CHRISTIANVS. D.G. DVX. SILESIÆ. LIGNICE(NSIS). **Rev:** Silesian eagle, crown above divides date in margin, mintmaster's initials in oval at bottom **Rev. Legend:** BREGENSIS. E(T). - WOLAVIENSIS. **Note:** Fr. #3209. Struck with Thaler dies, KM#490 at Brieg or Breslau mints.

Date	Mintage	VG	F	VF	XF	Unc
1666 GFH/CBS Rare	—	—	—	—	—	—

KM# 440 12 DUCAT

42.0000 g., 0.9860 Gold 1.3314 oz. AGW **Ruler:** Georg III, Ludwig IV and Christian **Obv:** 1/2-length figures of Georg, Ludwig & Christian facing, horizontal line below with arabesques in exergue, small imperial orb at top **Obv. Legend:** D.G. GEORGIVS. LVDOVICVS. & CHRISTIANVS. FRATRES. **Rev:** 3 helmets above oval 4-fold arms, date at end of legend **Rev. Legend:** DVCES. SILESIÆ. LIGNIC. BRE - GENS. ET. WOLAVIENSES. **Note:** Struck with Thaler dies, KM#414 at either Liegnitz or Brieg mints.

Date	Mintage	VG	F	VF	XF	Unc
1659 (pf) - EW Rare	—	—	—	—	—	—

FR# 3147 20 DUCAT

70.0000 g., 0.9860 Gold 2.2190 oz. AGW **Obv:** Small busts of Johann Christian and Georg Rudolf

Date	Mintage	VG	F	VF	XF	Unc
1617 Rare	—	—	—	—	—	—

CITY

REGULAR COINAGE

KM# 5 2 HELLER

Copper **Note:** Uniface. Two crossed keys divide G- H, L above, II below.

Date	Mintage	VG	F	VF	XF	Unc
ND GH	—	6.00	12.00	20.00	40.00	—

KM# 6 3 HELLER

Copper **Note:** Uniface. Bohemian lion striding left towards two crossed keys at left, L above, G III H below.

Date	Mintage	VG	F	VF	XF	Unc
ND GH	—	6.00	12.00	20.00	40.00	—

KM# 7 3 HELLER

Copper **Note:** Trefoil with L in top lobe dividing G - H, crossed keys lower left, Bohemian lion lower right, III below.

Date	Mintage	VG	F	VF	XF	Unc
ND GH	—	6.00	12.00	20.00	40.00	—
ND	—	6.00	12.00	20.00	40.00	—

KM# 8 3 HELLER

Copper **Note:** Trefoil with L in top lobe dividing date, lion lower left, crossed keys lower right, III below.

Date	Mintage	VG	F	VF	XF	Unc
16ZZ GH	—	6.00	12.00	20.00	40.00	—

KM# 9 3 HELLER

Copper **Note:** Uniface. Crossed keys below L divide G - H.

Date	Mintage	VG	F	VF	XF	Unc
16ZZ GH	—	6.00	12.00	20.00	40.00	—

SOEST

Soest is a town in Westphalia, 27 miles (46 km) east of Dortmund. It was important in trade and as an imperial mint from at least the 11th-12th centuries. After Westphalia, for the most part, came under the control of the archbishops of Cologne and Soest grew in its role as a member of the Hanseatic League, the two came into increasing conflict. By the mid-15th century, Soest sought protection from the duke of Cleves. The town produced its own coinage in the late 15th century and then from the second half of the 16th until the mid-18th centuries. Prussia annexed Soest in 1813.

ARMS

A key, usually with ornate tabs, standing vertically.

MINT OFFICIALS

Date	Name
1601-12	Heinrich Holtkamp, die-cutter
1616-354	Gottfried Nase, die-cutter
1637	Jorgen in dem Brande, die-cutter
1654	Hermann Schoneberg, die-cutter
1662-83	Johann Schotte, die-cutter
1680, 1703	Goswin Schönberg, die-cutter
Ca, 1700	Georg Harnold

CITY

REGULAR COINAGE

KM# 5 2 SHILLINGS

Silver **Obv:** City key in oval cartouche **Rev:** Value II in branches

Date	Mintage	VG	F	VF	XF	Unc
1620	—	9.00	20.00	40.00	90.00	—

SOLMS

The earliest count of Solms whose name has come down to us was Marquard I (1129-1141). Although the original center of power may have been any one of three places, the most likely location is Burg-Solms, also known by the old name of Hohensolms. Burgsolms is located on the Lahr River about 5 miles (8 km) west of Wetzlar and 7 miles (11 km) northeast of Weilburg in the Sauerland, north of Frankfurt am Main. This region became the center of mining and smelting in medieval Germany an indication of Solms' large silver coin-issuing capability, all out of proportion to its size. Over time, the counts acquired scattered holdings near Frankfurt, in Saxony and in Bohemia. The county underwent numerous divisions from the late Middle Ages well into the 19th century. The first division occurred in 1409, when the lines of Solms-Braunfels and Solms-Lich were founded. All branches of Solms received the mint right from Emperor Karl V in 1552, but not all lines issued coins.

ARMS

Solms - crowned rampant lion left
Greiffenstein - 4 oak leaves in cruciform
Minzenberg - horizontal bar
Sonnenwalde - lion
Wildenfels – rose

REFERENCE

J = Paul Joseph, **Die Münzen und Medaillen des fürstlichen und gräflichen Hauses Solms**, Frankfurt am Main, 1912.

SOLMS-BRAUNFELS

Established in the first division of Solms in 1409, Solms-Braunfels was further divided in 1592 into Solms-Braunfels, Solms-Greiffenstein and Solms-Hungen. Braunfels is located just 1.5 miles (3 km) south of Burgsolms (Hohensolms). Greiffenstein is a small village 7 miles (12 km) northwest of Burgsolms, whereas Hungen is further away, being 12.5 miles (21 km) southeast of Giessen or 22 miles (36 km) east-southeast of Burgsolms. The direct line of Solms-Braunfels became extinct in 1693 and passed to Greiffenstein, which was known as Braunfels from that date onwards count wa.

RULERS

Johann Albrecht I, 1592-1623
jointly with Wilhelm I von Solms-Greiffenstein, 1602-1635
Reinhard von Solms-Hungen, 1610-1630
Johann Albrecht II, 1623-1648
Heinrich Trajectinus, 1648-1693
Wilhelm Moritz von Solms-Greiffenstein, 1693-1724

MINTMASTER INITIALS

Initial	Date	Name
(a)= [mark]	Ca. 1623	

COUNTSHIP

REGULAR COINAGE

KM# 15 ALBUS

Silver **Obv:** Helmeted arms of Solms **Obv. Legend:** SOLMS - GREIFSTEIN **Rev. Legend:** NACH. DEM. F FURTER. SCHLVS. **Rev. Inscription:** Value: I/ALBUS/date

Date	Mintage	VG	F	VF	XF	Unc
1693	—	110	220	375	750	—

KM# 16 ALBUS

Silver **Obv:** Similar to KM#15 **Rev. Legend:** NACH DEM . FRANCFVRTER. SCHLVS. **Note:** Varieties exist.

Date	Mintage	VG	F	VF	XF	Unc
1693	—	110	220	375	750	—

KM# 17 2 ALBUS

Silver **Obv:** Helmeted Solms arms **Obv. Legend:** SOLMS . GREIFFENSTEIN. **Rev. Legend:** NACH. DEM. FRANCFURTER SCHLUS. **Rev. Inscription:** II/ ALBUS/ date **Note:** Varieties exist.

Date	Mintage	VG	F	VF	XF	Unc
1693	—	135	275	475	850	—

KM# 9 15 KREUZER (1/4 Gulden)

Silver **Obv:** Bust right, value "XV" below **Obv. Legend:** Titles of Wilhelm Moritz around **Rev:** Crowned eight-fold arms divide date **Rev. Legend:** Titles continued around

Date	Mintage	VG	F	VF	XF	Unc
1691	—	450	850	1,550	—	—

KM# 12 15 KREUZER (1/4 Gulden)

Silver **Obv:** Bust right, titles of Wilhelm Moritz around **Rev:** Crowned eight-fold arms with central shield divide date, value "XV" in oval below, titles continued

Date	Mintage	VG	F	VF	XF	Unc
1692	—	450	850	1,550	—	—

KM# 3 1/4 THALER
Silver **Obv:** Similar to KM#15 **Rev:** Similar to KM#15
Note: Mining Thaler.

Date	Mintage	VG	F	VF	XF	Unc
1623 (a)	—	—	—	—	—	—

KM# 4 1/2 THALER
Silver **Note:** Mining Thaler. Similar to KM#5

Date	Mintage	VG	F	VF	XF	Unc
1623 (a)	—	2,000	3,500	6,500	—	—

KM# 10 2/3 THALER (Gulden)
Silver **Obv:** Bust right **Obv. Legend:** Titles of Heinrich Trajectinus around **Rev:** Oval eight-fold arms, crown above divides date **Rev. Legend:** Titles continued

Date	Mintage	VG	F	VF	XF	Unc
1691	—	—	—	—	—	—

KM# 11 2/3 THALER (Gulden)
Silver **Obv:** Bust right **Obv. Legend:** Titles of Wilhelm Moritz around **Rev:** Crowned eight-fold arms with central shield divide date **Rev. Legend:** Titles continued

Date	Mintage	VG	F	VF	XF	Unc
1691	—	—	—	—	—	—

KM# 13 2/3 THALER (Gulden)
Silver **Obv:** Similar to KM#11 **Rev:** Arms supported by two griffins, value "2/3" in oval below divides date

Date	Mintage	VG	F	VF	XF	Unc
1692	—	—	—	—	—	—

KM# 6 THALER
Silver **Obv:** Similar to KM#5 **Rev:** Crowned imperial eagle with orb on breast **Rev. Legend:** FERDIN • II • DEI • GR • RO • IMP... **Note:** Dav.#7744.

Date	Mintage	VG	F	VF	XF	Unc
1623//1625 (a)	—	1,850	3,250	6,500	11,500	—

KM# 5 THALER
Silver **Obv:** Three helmets in decoration above HOINGEN, date below **Obv. Legend:** *MO: NO: EX: PRI: SOL: WILH: ET: REINH: CO: SOL: FR(A) **Rev:** Crowned imperial eagle with orb on breast **Rev. Legend:** FERDIN • II • D • G • ROM • IMP... **Note:** Many varieties in abbreviations and punctuation exist. Dav.#7743.

Date	Mintage	VG	F	VF	XF	Unc
1623 (a)	—	1,650	2,750	5,500	10,000	—

SOLMS-HERULETZ

(Neuheroletz)

Established as a separate line from Solms-Lich in 1590, it did not acquire a distinctive name until the count, an officer in the service of the emperor, purchased the confiscated Bohemian lordships of Heruletz and Humpolezin in 1623. Marriage brought other Bohemian properties into the count's holdings. It appears that coinage for this distant branch of the dynasty was all struck in the Lich mint. The line only lasted for two generations and reverted to Solms-Lich upon extinction in 1670.

RULERS
Philipp II, 1590-1631
Philipp Adam, 1631-1670

MINT OFFICIALS' INITIALS

Lich Mint

Initial	Date	Name
(a)= Z/ or		
(b)= m/	1613-14	Georg Arnes (Arends)
(c)= /or /K or /B or tree trunk	1614-21	Ernst Knorr
	1613-21	Hieronymous Pinck, die-cutter

COUNTSHIP

REGULAR COINAGE

KM# 3 PFENNIG
Silver **Ruler:** Philipp II **Obv:** Four-fold arms, SL above **Note:** Uniface schussel type.

Date	Mintage	VG	F	VF	XF	Unc
ND(ca.1612)	—	13.00	27.00	45.00	100	—

KM# 12 PFENNIG
Silver **Ruler:** Philipp II **Obv:** Four-fold arms, P above ote: Similar to KM#3.

Date	Mintage	VG	F	VF	XF	Unc
ND(ca.1615)	—	13.00	27.00	45.00	100	—

KM# 29 PFENNIG
Silver **Ruler:** Philipp II **Obv:** Arms divide date **Note:** Similar to KM#3.

Date	Mintage	VG	F	VF	XF	Unc
(16)Z8	—	—	—	—	—	—

KM# 4 3 KREUZER (Groschen)
Silver **Ruler:** Philipp II **Obv:** Four-fold arms, titles of Philipp around **Obv. Legend:** ...SOLMS. SOL. **Rev:** Crowned imperial eagle, circle with 3 on breast, titles of Matthias, date around **Mint:** Hohensolms

Date	Mintage	VG	F	VF	XF	Unc
161Z	—	45.00	90.00	170	300	—

KM# 6.1 3 KREUZER (Groschen)
Silver **Ruler:** Philipp II **Obv:** First half of date divided by arms **Obv. Legend:** ...SOLMS. LICH. **Mint:** Lich **Note:** Similar to KM#4. Varieties exist.

Date	Mintage	VG	F	VF	XF	Unc
1613 (a)	—	27.00	55.00	90.00	170	—
16/1613 (a)	—	27.00	55.00	90.00	170	—
1613 (b)	—	27.00	55.00	90.00	170	—
1614 (a)	—	27.00	55.00	90.00	170	—
1614 (c)	—	27.00	55.00	90.00	170	—
16/1614 (c)	—	27.00	55.00	90.00	170	—
1616 (c)	—	27.00	55.00	90.00	170	—

KM# 7 3 KREUZER (Groschen)
Silver **Ruler:** Philipp II **Note:** Similar to KM#6.1 but date only in reverse margin. Varieties exist.

Date	Mintage	VG	F	VF	XF	Unc
1614 (c)	—	27.00	55.00	90.00	170	—
1615 (c)	—	27.00	55.00	90.00	170	—
165 (c) Error	—	27.00	55.00	90.00	170	—
1616 (c)	—	27.00	55.00	90.00	170	—
1618 (c)	—	27.00	55.00	90.00	170	—
(16)18	—	27.00	55.00	90.00	170	—
(16)19	—	27.00	55.00	90.00	170	—
ND	—	27.00	55.00	90.00	170	—

KM# 8 3 KREUZER (Groschen)
Silver **Ruler:** Philipp II **Note:** Klippe.

Date	Mintage	VG	F	VF	XF	Unc
1615 (c)	—	—	—	—	—	—

KM# 6.2 3 KREUZER (Groschen)
Silver **Ruler:** Philipp II **Mint:** Lich **Note:** Klippe.

Date	Mintage	VG	F	VF	XF	Unc
1616 (c)	—	—	—	—	—	—

KM# 16 3 KREUZER (Groschen)
Silver **Ruler:** Philipp II **Note:** Similar to KM#15 but date only divided by arms on obverse. Varieties exist.

Date	Mintage	VG	F	VF	XF	Unc
(16)17 (c)	—	33.00	65.00	115	200	—
(16)18 (c)	—	33.00	65.00	115	200	—

KM# 14 3 KREUZER (Groschen)
Silver **Ruler:** Philipp II **Note:** Similar to KM#6.1 but first part of date on reverse, second part on obverse.

Date	Mintage	VG	F	VF	XF	Unc
1617 (c)	—	33.00	65.00	115	200	—

KM# 15 3 KREUZER (Groschen)
Silver **Ruler:** Philipp II **Note:** Similar to KM#6.1 but date on both sides.

Date	Mintage	VG	F	VF	XF	Unc
(16)17 (c)	—	33.00	65.00	115	200	—

KM# 18 3 KREUZER (Groschen)
Silver **Ruler:** Philipp II **Obv:** Similar to KM#16 **Rev. Legend:** Titles of Ferdinand II **Note:** Varieties exist.

Date	Mintage	VG	F	VF	XF	Unc
(16)19	—	20.00	40.00	75.00	135	—
(16)Z0	—	20.00	40.00	75.00	135	—
ND	—	20.00	40.00	75.00	135	—

KM# 21 3 KREUZER (Groschen)
Silver **Ruler:** Philipp II **Note:** Similar to KM#18 but smaller and lighter. Kipper coinage.

Date	Mintage	VG	F	VF	XF	Unc
(16)Z1	—	—	—	—	—	—
(16)ZZ	—	—	—	—	—	—
ND	—	—	—	—	—	—

KM# 22 6 KREUZER
Silver **Ruler:** Philipp II **Obv:** Four-fold arms, date above, titles of Philipp II and 6 K in margin **Rev:** Crowned imperial eagle, orb on breast, titles of Ferdinand II around **Note:** Varieties exist. Kipper coinage.

Date	Mintage	VG	F	VF	XF	Unc
16Z1	—	—	—	—	—	—

KM# 9.1 12 KREUZER (Dreibätzner)
Silver **Ruler:** Philipp II **Obv:** Four-fold arms, titles of Philipp II **Rev:** Crowned imperial eagle, 1Z in orb on breast, titles of Matthias, date in margin

Date	Mintage	VG	F	VF	XF	Unc
1614 (c)	—	—	—	—	—	—

KM# 9.2 12 KREUZER (Dreibätzner)
Silver **Ruler:** Philipp II **Note:** Klippe.

Date	Mintage	VG	F	VF	XF	Unc
1614 (c)	—	—	—	—	—	—

KM# 19 12 KREUZER (Dreibätzner)
Silver **Ruler:** Philipp II **Obv:** Similar to KM#9.1 **Rev:** Titles of Ferdinand II **Note:** Kipper coinage.

Date	Mintage	VG	F	VF	XF	Unc
(16)Z0	—	200	375	600	—	—

KM# 24 1/8 THALER
Silver **Ruler:** Philipp II **Obv:** Oval four-fold arms, date above, titles of Philipp II **Rev:** Crowned imperial eagle, 1/8 in orb on breast, titles of Ferdinand II

Date	Mintage	VG	F	VF	XF	Unc
16Z4	—	—	—	—	—	—

KM# 25 1/4 THALER
Silver **Ruler:** Philipp II **Obv:** Oval four-fold arms, first half of date, titles of Philipp II **Rev:** Crowned imperial eagle, 1/4 in orb on breast, second half of date, titles of Ferdinand II

Date	Mintage	VG	F	VF	XF	Unc
16Z4	—	925	1,600	2,650	—	—

KM# 26 1/2 THALER
Silver **Ruler:** Philipp II **Obv:** Oval four-fold arms divide 1 - 6, three helmets above, titles of Philipp II around **Rev:** Similar to 1/4 Thaler KM#25, but 1/Z in orb on eagle's breast

Date	Mintage	VG	F	VF	XF	Unc
16Z4	—	—	—	—	—	—

KM# 27 1/2 THALER
Silver **Ruler:** Philipp II **Note:** Klippe.

Date	Mintage	VG	F	VF	XF	Unc
16Z4 Rare	—	—	—	—	—	—

SOLMS-HOHENSOLMS

Centered on the ancestral castle of Hohensolms (the modern Burgsolms), the line was originally known as Solms-Lich and Hohensolms from the division of 1409. A second division into Solms-Lich-Hohensolms and Solms-Laubach was effected before Philipp I's death in 1544. Shortly thereafter, in 1562, Hohensolms and Lich were the objects of separate lines. Hohensolms reacquired Lich in 1718 when the latter fell extinct, revising the name to Solms-Hohensolms-Lich. One count became the Danish king's viceroy in Wolfenbüttel during the Thirty Years' War and a later descendant was raised to the rank of prince in 1792. Solms-Hohensolms-Lick was mediatized during the Napoleonic Era, but counts of this line were still in existence in the 20th century. Most of the early 17th century coins for Solms-Hohensolms were struck at the small village of Nieder-Weisel, just to the southeast of Butzbach, itself about 10 miles (16 km) southeast of Wetzlar.

RULERS
Hermann Adolf, 1562-1613
Philipp Reinhard I, 1613-1635
as governor of Braunschweig-Wolfenbüttel for Christian IV of Denmark, 1627-1634
Philipp Reinhard II, 1635-1665
Karl Ludwig, 1665-1668
Johann Heinrich Christian, 1668
Ludwig, 1668-1707

MINT OFFICIALS' INITIALS

Nieder-Weisel Mint

Date	Name
1612-13	Henning Kiessel
1613-15	Hans Ziesler von Molsheim
1612-15	Hans Kapphaus, warden
1615-20	Hans Kapphaus, mintmaster
1620	Hans Jakob Ayrer

Butzbach Mint

Date	Name
1620-22	Hans Jakob Ayrer

Hohensolms Mint

Initial	Date	Name
IB	1675	Johann Bostelmann
ICB	ca. 1675	Johann Christoph Bähr
IA or [symbol]	1676	Jürgen Ahrens (Jörg Arens)
IIF	1690-1719	Johann Jeremias Freitag in Frankfurt am Main
PPP	1676	Peter Paul Peckstein
H	1683	Paul Heuser
	ca. 1691	Wilhelm Lender
FA	1693	Fredrich Arnoldt

COUNTSHIP

REGULAR COINAGE

KM# 12 PFENNIG
Copper-Billon **Note:** Similar to KM#11, but H above arms.

Date	Mintage	VG	F	VF	XF	Unc
ND(1610-15)	—	12.00	24.00	45.00	80.00	—

KM# 13 PFENNIG
Copper-Billon **Note:** Similar to KM#11, but lion above BH.

Date	Mintage	VG	F	VF	XF	Unc
ND(1610-15)	—	12.00	24.00	45.00	80.00	—

KM# 22 PFENNIG
Copper-Billon **Note:** Similar to KM#21, but H above lion arms.

Date	Mintage	VG	F	VF	XF	Unc
ND(1610-15)	—	12.00	24.00	45.00	80.00	—

KM# 4 PFENNIG
Copper-Billon **Note:** Similar to KM#3, but "H" above arms. Varieties exist.

Date	Mintage	VG	F	VF	XF	Unc
ND(1610-15)	—	12.00	24.00	45.00	80.00	—

KM# 5 PFENNIG
Copper-Billon **Note:** Similar to KM#4, but "H" below arms.

Date	Mintage	VG	F	VF	XF	Unc
ND(1610-15)	—	12.00	24.00	45.00	80.00	—

KM# 6 PFENNIG
Copper-Billon **Note:** Similar to KM#4, but "I" above arms.

Date	Mintage	VG	F	VF	XF	Unc
ND(1610-15)	—	12.00	24.00	45.00	80.00	—

KM# 8 PFENNIG
Copper-Billon **Note:** Similar to KM#7, but arms divide B - H.

Date	Mintage	VG	F	VF	XF	Unc
ND(1610-15)	—	12.00	24.00	45.00	80.00	—

KM# 9 PFENNIG

Copper-Billon **Note:** Similar to KM#7, but no letter above arms. Varieties exist.

Date	Mintage	VG	F	VF	XF	Unc
ND(1610-15)	—	12.00	24.00	45.00	80.00	—

KM# 2 PFENNIG

Copper-Billon **Obv:** Crowned oval two-fold arms of Solms and Wildenfels **Note:** Uniface schussel-type.

Date	Mintage	VG	F	VF	XF	Unc
ND(1610-15)	—	12.00	24.00	45.00	80.00	—

KM# 3 PFENNIG

Copper-Billon **Obv:** Two-fold arms of Solms and Wildenfels **Note:** Uniface schussel-type.

Date	Mintage	VG	F	VF	XF	Unc
ND(1610-15)	—	12.00	24.00	45.00	80.00	—

KM# 10 PFENNIG

Copper-Billon **Obv:** Two-fold arms, BH on left, rampant lion left on right **Note:** Uniface Schussel-type.

Date	Mintage	VG	F	VF	XF	Unc
ND(1610-15)	—	12.00	24.00	45.00	80.00	—

KM# 11 PFENNIG

Copper-Billon **Obv:** Two-fold arms, BH above lion left **Note:** Uniface Schussel-type.

Date	Mintage	VG	F	VF	XF	Unc
ND(1610-15)	—	12.00	24.00	45.00	80.00	—

KM# 14 PFENNIG

Copper-Billon **Obv:** Two-folds arms, Minzenberg above lion left, arms divide P - H **Note:** Uniface Schussel-type.

Date	Mintage	VG	F	VF	XF	Unc
ND(1610-15)	—	12.00	24.00	45.00	80.00	—

KM# 15 PFENNIG

Copper-Billon **Obv:** Lion to right, H below head **Note:** Uniface Schussel-type.

Date	Mintage	VG	F	VF	XF	Unc
ND(1610-15)	—	12.00	24.00	45.00	80.00	—

KM# 17 PFENNIG

Copper-Billon **Obv:** Lion right in shield, crown above **Note:** Uniface Schussel-type.

Date	Mintage	VG	F	VF	XF	Unc
ND(1610-15)	—	12.00	24.00	45.00	80.00	—

KM# 20 PFENNIG

Copper-Billon **Obv:** Lion right, H near head **Note:** Uniface Schussel-type.

Date	Mintage	VG	F	VF	XF	Unc
ND(1610-15)	—	12.00	24.00	45.00	80.00	—

KM# 21 PFENNIG

Copper-Billon **Obv:** Lion to left in shield **Note:** Uniface Schussel-type.

Date	Mintage	VG	F	VF	XF	Unc
ND(1610-15)	—	12.00	24.00	45.00	80.00	—

KM# 24 PFENNIG

Copper-Billon **Obv:** Rose arms of Wildenfels **Note:** Uniface schussel-type.

Date	Mintage	VG	F	VF	XF	Unc
ND(1610-15)	—	12.00	24.00	45.00	80.00	—

KM# 25 PFENNIG

Copper-Billon **Obv:** H above rose arms **Note:** Uniface schussel-type.

Date	Mintage	VG	F	VF	XF	Unc
ND(1610-15)	—	12.00	24.00	45.00	80.00	—

KM# 27 PFENNIG

Copper-Billon **Obv:** Maltese cross in shield **Note:** Uniface schussel-type.

Date	Mintage	VG	F	VF	XF	Unc
ND(1610-15)	—	12.00	24.00	45.00	80.00	—

KM# 28 PFENNIG

Copper-Billon **Obv:** H over large crown in circle **Note:** Uniface schussel-type.

Date	Mintage	VG	F	VF	XF	Unc
ND(1610-15)	—	12.00	24.00	45.00	80.00	—

KM# 29 PFENNIG

Copper-Billon **Obv:** Eagle, head to left **Note:** Uniface schussel-type.

Date	Mintage	VG	F	VF	XF	Unc
ND(1610-15)	—	12.00	24.00	45.00	80.00	—

KM# 30 PFENNIG

Copper-Billon **Obv:** Goat in shield divides I - P **Note:** Uniface schussel-type.

Date	Mintage	VG	F	VF	XF	Unc
ND(1610-15)	—	12.00	24.00	45.00	80.00	—

KM# 31 PFENNIG

Copper-Billon **Obv:** Lion rampant left **Note:** Uniface schussel-type.

Date	Mintage	VG	F	VF	XF	Unc
ND(1610-15)	—	13.00	27.00	55.00	90.00	—

KM# 32 PFENNIG

Copper-Billon **Obv:** Lion rampant right **Note:** Uniface schussel-type.

Date	Mintage	VG	F	VF	XF	Unc
ND(1610-15)	—	13.00	27.00	55.00	90.00	—

KM# 33 PFENNIG

Copper-Billon **Obv:** B H, animal head above and below **Note:** Uniface schussel-type.

Date	Mintage	VG	F	VF	XF	Unc
ND(1610-15)	—	13.00	27.00	55.00	90.00	—

KM# 34 PFENNIG

Copper-Billon **Obv:** Three animal heads, one above the other **Note:** Uniface schussel-type.

Date	Mintage	VG	F	VF	XF	Unc
ND(1610-15)	—	13.00	27.00	55.00	90.00	—

KM# 35 PFENNIG

Copper-Billon **Obv:** Three crowns, one above the other **Note:** Uniface schussel-type.

Date	Mintage	VG	F	VF	XF	Unc
ND(1610-15)	—	13.00	27.00	55.00	90.00	—

KM# 7 PFENNIG

Copper-Billon **Obv:** H above two-fold arms of Wildenfels and Solms **Note:** Uniface Schussel-type. Varieties exist.

Date	Mintage	VG	F	VF	XF	Unc
ND(1610-15)	—	12.00	24.00	45.00	80.00	—

KM# 16 PFENNIG

Copper-Billon **Obv:** H above arms with lion to right **Note:** Uniface Schussel-type. Varieties exist.

Date	Mintage	VG	F	VF	XF	Unc
ND(1610-15)	—	12.00	24.00	45.00	80.00	—

KM# 18 PFENNIG

Copper-Billon **Obv:** Shield of lion right, H between paws **Note:** Uniface Schussel-type. Varieties exist.

Date	Mintage	VG	F	VF	XF	Unc
ND(1610-15)	—	12.00	24.00	45.00	80.00	—

KM# 19 PFENNIG

Copper-Billon **Obv:** Lion right in shield **Note:** Uniface Schussel-type. Varieties exist.

Date	Mintage	VG	F	VF	XF	Unc
ND(1610-15)	—	12.00	24.00	45.00	80.00	—

KM# 23 PFENNIG

Copper-Billon **Obv:** Crowned lion left in shield **Note:** Uniface schussel-type. Varieties exist.

Date	Mintage	VG	F	VF	XF	Unc
ND(1610-15)	—	12.00	24.00	45.00	80.00	—

KM# 26 PFENNIG

Copper-Billon **Obv:** Rose in circle **Note:** Uniface schussel-type. Varieties exist.

Date	Mintage	VG	F	VF	XF	Unc
ND(1610-15)	—	12.00	24.00	45.00	80.00	—

KM# 1 PFENNIG

Copper **Obv:** Two small shields of arms, one above two, value "•I•" between two lower arms **Note:** Uniface. Varieties exist.

Date	Mintage	VG	F	VF	XF	Unc
ND(1610-15)	—	13.00	27.00	55.00	90.00	—

KM# 64 12 PFENNIG

Copper **Obv. Inscription:** 12 • /WOLFEB/GARNIS/date. **Note:** Uniface. Varieties exist.

Date	Mintage	VG	F	VF	XF	Unc
1627 Rare	—	—	—	—	—	—

KM# 65 HELLER (Fettmannchen)

Copper **Obv:** Two-fold arms **Obv. Legend:** NVMMVS. CON. SOL. **Rev:** Value: VIII **Rev. Legend:** NVMMVS. COM. SOLM. **Note:** Varieties exist.

Date	Mintage	VG	F	VF	XF	Unc
ND(ca.1627)	—	—	—	—	—	—

KM# 66 GROSCHEN

Silver **Obv:** Crowned cipher (C4) of Christian IV of Denmark **Obv. Legend:** QVID. NON. PRO. RELIGIO(NE). **Rev. Legend:** NACH. REICHS. SCHROT. V. K. **Rev. Inscription:** I/GVTER/GROS(CH)/date **Note:** Varieties exist.

Date	Mintage	VG	F	VF	XF	Unc
1627 Rare	—	—	—	—	—	—

KM# 102 ALBUS

Silver **Obv:** Lion rampant left in shield, crowned helmet above **Obv. Legend:** SOLMS. HOH - EN. SOLMS. **Rev:** Mintmaster's initials **Rev. Legend:** NACH. DEM. SCHLVS. DER. V. STAND. **Rev. Inscription:** I/ALBUS/date

Date	Mintage	VG	F	VF	XF	Unc
1693 FA	—	—	—	—	—	—

KM# 106 ALBUS

Silver **Obv:** Crowned shield of lion rampant left, arms between palm branches **Obv. Legend:** SOLMS - HOCH - SOLMS **Rev. Legend:** NACH DEN FVNF STAENDEN **Rev. Inscription:** I/ALBVS/date

Date	Mintage	VG	F	VF	XF	Unc
1694	—	—	—	—	—	—

KM# 103 2 ALBUS

Silver **Rev:** Similar to Albus KM#102, but value II

Date	Mintage	VG	F	VF	XF	Unc
1693 FA	—	—	—	—	—	—

KM# 104 6 ALBUS

Silver **Obv:** Crowned eight-fold arms **Obv. Legend:** Titles of Ludwig **Rev:** Similar to Albus KM#102, but value VI

Date	Mintage	VG	F	VF	XF	Unc
1693 FA	—	—	—	—	—	—

KM# 43 3 KREUZER (Groschen)

Silver **Note:** Klippe.

Date	Mintage	VG	F	VF	XF	Unc
ND(1612-17)	—	—	—	250	350	—

KM# 40 3 KREUZER (Groschen)

Silver **Obv:** Four-fold arms, titles of Herman Adolf around **Rev:** Crowned imperial eagle, 3 in circle on breast, titles of Rudolf II, date around **Note:** Varieties exist.

Date	Mintage	VG	F	VF	XF	Unc
161Z	—	10.00	20.00	40.00	70.00	—

KM# 41 3 KREUZER (Groschen)

Silver **Obv:** Similar to KM#40 **Rev:** Titles of Matthias **Note:** Varieties exist.

Date	Mintage	VG	F	VF	XF	Unc
1612	—	9.00	17.00	33.00	60.00	—
161Z	—	9.00	17.00	33.00	60.00	—

KM# 42 3 KREUZER (Groschen)

Silver **Obv:** Similar to KM#41, titles of Philipp Reinhard I **Note:** Varieties exist.

Date	Mintage	VG	F	VF	XF	Unc
161Z	—	9.00	17.00	33.00	60.00	—
(1)61Z	—	9.00	17.00	33.00	60.00	—
1615	—	9.00	17.00	33.00	60.00	—
1616	—	9.00	17.00	33.00	60.00	—
1617	—	9.00	17.00	33.00	60.00	—
(16)17	—	9.00	17.00	33.00	60.00	—
ND	—	9.00	17.00	33.00	60.00	—

KM# 46 3 KREUZER (Groschen)

Silver **Obv:** Similar to KM#41 but date above arms

Date	Mintage	VG	F	VF	XF	Unc
1614	—	10.00	20.00	40.00	70.00	—

KM# 48 3 KREUZER (Groschen)

Silver **Obv:** Similar to KM#42, but date divided by arms

Date	Mintage	VG	F	VF	XF	Unc
(16)17	—	10.00	20.00	40.00	70.00	—
(16)18	—	10.00	20.00	40.00	70.00	—

KM# 49 3 KREUZER (Groschen)

Silver **Obv:** Similar to KM#48, but date also in margin

Date	Mintage	VG	F	VF	XF	Unc
(16)17	—	9.00	20.00	40.00	70.00	—

KM# 51 3 KREUZER (Groschen)

Silver **Obv:** Similar to KM#42 **Rev. Legend:** Titles of Ferdinand II

Date	Mintage	VG	F	VF	XF	Unc
(16)19	—	—	—	—	—	—

KM# 57 3 KREUZER (Groschen)

Silver **Note:** Klippe.

Date	Mintage	VG	F	VF	XF	Unc
(16)Z0	—	—	—	—	—	—
(16)Z1	—	—	—	—	—	—

KM# 56 3 KREUZER (Groschen)

Silver **Obv:** Similar to KM#51 **Note:** Reduced size and weight. Varieties exist.

Date	Mintage	VG	F	VF	XF	Unc
(16)Z0	—	9.00	17.00	33.00	60.00	—
(16)Z1	—	9.00	17.00	33.00	60.00	—
(16)ZZ	—	9.00	17.00	33.00	60.00	—

KM# 60 3 KREUZER (Groschen)

Silver **Obv:** Similar to KM#56 **Obv. Legend:** ... BUT **Rev:** Similar to KM#56 **Mint:** Butzbach

Date	Mintage	VG	F	VF	XF	Unc
(16)Z1	—	—	—	—	—	—

KM# 58 12 KREUZER (Dreibätzner)

Silver **Obv:** Four-fold arms, titles of Philipp Reinhard I around **Rev:** Crowned imperial eagle, 1Z in orb on breast, date, titles of Ferdinand II **Note:** Varieties exist.

Date	Mintage	VG	F	VF	XF	Unc
(16)Z0	—	150	300	550	—	—
(16)Z1	—	150	300	550	—	—

KM# 61 12 KREUZER (Dreibätzner)

Silver **Obv:** Similar to KM#58 **Obv. Legend:** ... BUTZB(A) **Rev:** Similar to KM#58 **Mint:** Butzbach

Date	Mintage	VG	F	VF	XF	Unc
(16)Z1	—	—	—	—	—	—

KM# 62 12 KREUZER (Dreibätzner)

Silver **Mint:** Butzbach **Note:** Klippe.

Date	Mintage	VG	F	VF	XF	Unc
(16)Z1	—	—	—	—	—	—

KM# 45 DICKEN (Teston)

Silver **Obv:** Four-fold arms

Date	Mintage	VG	F	VF	XF	Unc
ND(ca.1613-19)	—	—	—	—	—	—

KM# 54 DICKEN (Teston)

Silver **Obv:** Four-fold arms divide date, titles of Philipp Reinhard I **Rev:** Crowned imperial eagle, orb on breast, titles of Ferdinand II

Date	Mintage	VG	F	VF	XF	Unc
1619	—	—	—	—	—	—

KM# 52 DICKEN (Teston)

Silver **Obv:** Crowned eight-fold arms, titles of Philipp Reinhard I **Rev:** Crowned imperial eagle, orb on breast, titles of Matthias, date **Note:** Varieties exist.

Date	Mintage	VG	F	VF	XF	Unc
1619	—	850	1,600	2,700	—	—

KM# 53 DICKEN (Teston)

Silver **Obv:** Similar to KM#52, but date above crown **Rev:** Similar to KM#52 **Note:** Varieties exist.

Date	Mintage	VG	F	VF	XF	Unc
1619	—	850	1,600	2,700	—	—

KM# 68 1/3 THALER (1/2 Gulden)

Silver **Obv:** Bust right, titles of Ludwig **Rev:** Three helmets over eight-fold arms, value (30) below, date divided at top **Rev. Legend:** MONETA...

Date	Mintage	VG	F	VF	XF	Unc
1675	—	—	—	—	—	—

KM# 74 1/3 THALER (1/2 Gulden)

Silver **Obv:** Bust right, value (30) below, titles of Ludwig **Rev:** Crowned eight-fold arms between palm branches, date **Rev. Legend:** MONETA...

Date	Mintage	VG	F	VF	XF	Unc
1676	—	—	—	—	—	—

KM# 90 2/3 THALER (Gulden)

Silver **Obv:** Armored bust right, value (60) below **Obv. Legend:** *LUDWIG • G • ZU • S • H • ZU • M • W • U • S* **Rev:** Crowned arms divide date **Note:** Dav.#984.

Date	Mintage	VG	F	VF	XF	Unc
1671 IA(a)	—	85.00	165	320	525	—

KM# 71 2/3 THALER (Gulden)

Silver **Obv:** Armored bust right, value (60) below **Obv. Legend:** * L * G * Z * (H) * S * H * Z * M * W * V * S * **Rev:** Crowned eight-fold arms, date **Rev. Legend:** MONETA. NOVA. ARGENTEA. **Note:** Varieties exist.

Date	Mintage	VG	F	VF	XF	Unc
ICB	—	90.00	175	325	525	—
1675 IB	—	90.00	175	325	525	—

KM# 87 2/3 THALER (Gulden)

Silver **Obv:** Armored bust right, value (60) below **Obv. Legend:** *LUDWIG • G • ZU • S • H • Z(U) • M • W • U • S* **Rev:** Crowned arms divide date **Note:** Dav.#981.

Date	Mintage	VG	F	VF	XF	Unc
1676 (a)	—	60.00	120	225	375	—
1677 (a)	—	60.00	120	225	375	—

KM# 77 2/3 THALER (Gulden)

Silver **Obv:** Armored bust right in inner circle, value (60) in margin at bottom **Obv. Legend:** * LVTWIG • G • Z • S • (=) H • Z • M • (W) • V • S * **Rev:** Crowned ornate arms, date divided in top margin **Note:** Dav. #970. Varieties exist.

Date	Mintage	VG	F	VF	XF	Unc
1676 (a)	—	80.00	160	300	500	—

KM# 86 2/3 THALER (Gulden)

Silver **Obv:** Armored bust right, date divided below **Obv. Legend:** *LUDWIG • G • Z • S • H • Z • M • W • U • S* **Rev:** Crowned eight-fold arms, palm branch to either side, 2/3 in oval at bottom **Rev. Legend:** MONETA.NOV-A.ARGENTEA **Note:** Dav.#968.

Date	Mintage	VG	F	VF	XF	Unc
1676	—	80.00	160	300	500	—

KM# 78 2/3 THALER (Gulden)

Silver **Obv:** Armored bust right in inner circle **Obv. Legend:** * LVTWIG • G • Z • S • H • Z • M • W • V • S * **Rev:** Crowned arms with palm branches in inner circle **Note:** Dav.#971.

Date	Mintage	VG	F	VF	XF	Unc
1676 (a)	—	80.00	160	300	500	—

KM# 79 2/3 THALER (Gulden)

Silver **Obv:** Armored bust right in inner circle, value (60) in margin below **Obv. Legend:** LVTWIG • G • Z • S - H • Z • M • W • V • S **Rev:** Crowned arms with palm branches in inner circle **Note:** Dav.#972. Varieties exist.

Date	Mintage	VG	F	VF	XF	Unc
1676 (a)	—	100	200	400	725	—

KM# 82 2/3 THALER (Gulden)

Silver **Obv:** Armored bust right, value (60) on shoulder **Obv. Legend:** LUDWIG • G • ZU • S • H • Z(U) • M • W • U • S • **Rev:** Crowned ornate arms, date below **Note:** Dav.#975. Varieties exist.

Date	Mintage	VG	F	VF	XF	Unc
1676 IA	—	60.00	120	225	375	—
1677 IA(a)	—	60.00	120	225	375	—

KM# 83 2/3 THALER (Gulden)

Silver **Obv:** Armored bust right, value (60) on shoulder **Rev:** Ornately-shaped crowned arms divide date **Note:** Dav.#976. Varieties exist.

Date	Mintage	VG	F	VF	XF	Unc
1676 IA(a)	—	70.00	140	275	500	—

KM# 84 2/3 THALER (Gulden)

Silver **Obv:** Crowned ornate eight-fold arms divide date **Rev:** Ornately-shaped crowned arms divide date **Rev. Inscription:** HERR/NACH/DEINEM/WILLEN/60 in sprays **Note:** Dav.#977. Varieties exist.

Date	Mintage	VG	F	VF	XF	Unc
1676	—	65.00	135	275	450	—
1676 IA	—	65.00	135	275	450	—
1676 IA(a)	—	65.00	135	275	450	—

KM# 92 2/3 THALER (Gulden)

Silver **Obv:** Facing bust, value (60) in oval below **Obv. Legend:** *LUDWIG G • Z(U) • S • - H • Z(U) • M • W • V • S • **Rev. Inscription:** HERR./NACH/DEINEM./WILLEN/60 in sprays **Note:** Dav.#978. Varieties exist.

Date	Mintage	VG	F	VF	XF	Unc
ND(1676)	—	275	450	800	—	—

KM# 85 2/3 THALER (Gulden)

Silver **Obv. Legend:** MONETA*NOVA*ARGENTEA*date **Rev. Inscription:** HERRE/NACHDEINE/M WILLEN/60 in sprays **Note:** Dav.#979.

Date	Mintage	VG	F	VF	XF	Unc
1676	—	60.00	120	225	375	—

KM# 80 2/3 THALER (Gulden)

Silver **Obv:** Youthful armored bust right in inner circle **Rev:** With either branches or ornaments to either side of crowned arms in inner circle **Note:** Dav.#973. Varieties exist.

Date	Mintage	VG	F	VF	XF	Unc
1676 LVTWIG	—	65.00	135	250	425	—
1676 LUDWIG	—	65.00	135	250	425	—
1676 PXP	—	65.00	135	250	425	—

KM# 81 2/3 THALER (Gulden)

Silver **Obv:** Older armored bust right **Obv. Legend:** LUDWIG • G • ZU • S • H • Z • M • W • U • S * **Rev:** Ornately-shaped crowned arms divide date **Note:** Dav.#974. Varieties exist.

Date	Mintage	VG	F	VF	XF	Unc
1676 IA	—	60.00	120	225	400	—
1676 (a)	—	60.00	120	225	400	—
1677 IA	—	60.00	120	225	400	—
1677 IA(a)	—	60.00	120	225	400	—

KM# 91 2/3 THALER (Gulden)

Silver **Obv:** Crowned arms divide date **Obv. Legend:** MONETA . NOVA . ARGENTA . **Rev:** Inscription in sprays **Rev. Inscription:** HERR. / NACH / DEINEM. / WILLEN / 60 **Note:** Dav.#980.

Date	Mintage	VG	F	VF	XF	Unc
1677	—	65.00	125	235	385	—

KM# 93 2/3 THALER (Gulden)

Silver **Obv:** Armored bust right **Rev:** Inscription in sprays **Rev. Inscription:** HERR / NACH / DEINEM / WILLEN

Date	Mintage	VG	F	VF	XF	Unc
ND(1677)	—	—	—	—	—	—

KM# 89 2/3 THALER (Gulden)

Silver **Obv:** Legend begins at top **Note:** Similar to KM#81. Dav.#983.

Date	Mintage	VG	F	VF	XF	Unc
1677	—	85.00	165	300	500	—

KM# 94 2/3 THALER (Gulden)

Silver **Obv:** Armored bust right **Obv. Legend:** MONETA NOUA **Note:** Dav.#985.

Date	Mintage	VG	F	VF	XF	Unc
ND(1677) (a)	—	—	—	—	—	—

KM# 95 2/3 THALER (Gulden)

Silver **Obv:** Armored bust right, value (60) on shoulder **Obv. Legend:** *LUDWIG • G • Z • S • H • Z • M • W • V • S* **Rev:** Three helmets above eight-fold arms **Note:** Dav.#986.

Date	Mintage	VG	F	VF	XF	Unc
ND(1677) IIF	—	175	325	600	1,000	—
ND(1677)	—	175	325	600	1,000	—

KM# 96 2/3 THALER (Gulden)

Silver **Obv:** Armored bust in inner circle **Obv. Legend:** *LVDWIG G • Z • S • H • Z • M • W • V • S • **Rev:** Crowned eight-fold arms in inner circle, 60 in oval at bottom **Rev. Legend:** MONETA NOVA ARGENTEA **Note:** Dav.#987.

Date	Mintage	VG	F	VF	XF	Unc
ND(1677)	—	60.00	120	225	375	—

KM# 100 2/3 THALER (Gulden)

Silver **Obv:** Armored bust right, value (60) below **Obv. Legend:** LVDWIG : G : ZV : S = H • ZV : M : W : V : S(ON) : **Rev:** Crowned eight-fold arms in inner circle, 60 in oval at bottom **Rev. Legend:** • MONETA • NOVA • ARGENTEA **Note:** Similar to KM#71. Dav.#988.

Date	Mintage	VG	F	VF	XF	Unc
1686	—	—	—	—	—	—

TRADE COINAGE

FR# 3300 DUCAT

3.5000 g., 0.9860 Gold 0.1109 oz. AGW **Ruler:** Philipp Reinhard I **Obv:** Crowned arms in inner circle **Rev:** Crowned C4 monogram for Christian IV (of Denmark)

Date	Mintage	VG	F	VF	XF	Unc
1627	—	1,500	3,000	6,000	9,800	—

FR# 3299 2 DUCAT

7.0000 g., 0.9860 Gold 0.2219 oz. AGW **Ruler:** Philipp Reinhard I **Obv:** Crowned arms within inner circle **Rev:** Crowned C4 monogram for Christian IV (of Denmark)

Date	Mintage	VG	F	VF	XF	Unc
1627 Rare	—	—	—	—	—	—

SOLMS-LAUBACH

Founded by a younger son of Philipp I of Solms-Lich and Hohensolms prior to 1522 and seated at the town of Laubach some 14 miles (23 km) east-southeast of Giessen, this branch lasted until at least the 20th century. The first division in 1561 resulted in the two lines of Solms-Laubach and Solms-Sonnenwalde. The next division occurred when Solms-Laubach, Solms-Baruth, Solms-Sonnenwalde and Solms-Rödelheim were established in 1600. The first Solms-Laubach died out in 1676 and titles passed to Solms-Wildenfels, from which a second line was constituted in 1696. As was the case with all other branches of Solms, Laubach was mediatized around 1806.

RULERS

Albrecht Otto I, 1600-1610
Albrecht Otto II, 1610-1639, 1610-1631
under guardianship of mother and three uncles
Karl Otto, 1639-1676
Johann Friedrich von Solms-Wildenfels, 1676-1696
Friedrich Ernst, 1696-1723

COUNTY

REGULAR COINAGE

KM# 3 3 KREUZER (Groschen)

Silver **Obv:** Four-fold arms, TUT. AL. OT. etc., around **Rev:** Crowned imperial eagle, 3 in circle on breast, titles of Ferdinand II, date around **Note:** Varieties exist.

Date	Mintage	VG	F	VF	XF	Unc
(16)Z0	—	40.00	80.00	160	275	—
(16)Z1	—	40.00	80.00	160	275	—
(16)ZZ	—	40.00	80.00	160	275	—

KM# 7.1 6 KREUZER

Silver **Obv:** Four-fold arms, date above **Obv. Legend:** TUT. ALB. OT... **Rev:** Crowned imperial eagle, 6 in orb on breast **Rev. Legend:** Titles of Ferdinand II **Note:** Kipper coinage. Varieties exist.

Date	Mintage	VG	F	VF	XF	Unc
16Z1	—	—	—	—	—	—

KM# 7.2 6 KREUZER

Silver **Note:** Klippe.

Date	Mintage	VG	F	VF	XF	Unc
16Z1	—	—	—	—	—	—

KM# 8 6 KREUZER

Silver **Obv:** Similar to KM#7.2 but value "6K" at end of obverse margin **Note:** Varieties exist.

Date	Mintage	VG	F	VF	XF	Unc
16Z1	—	200	400	650	—	—

KM# 9 6 KREUZER

Silver **Obv:** Similar to KM#8 but value "6K" in oval at top **Note:** Varieties exist.

Date	Mintage	VG	F	VF	XF	Unc
16Z1	—	—	—	—	—	—

KM# 4.2 12 KREUZER (Dreibätzner)

Silver

Date	Mintage	VG	F	VF	XF	Unc
(16)Z0	—	—	—	—	—	—

KM# 4.1 12 KREUZER (Dreibätzner)

Silver **Obv:** Four-fold arms **Obv. Legend:** TUT. AL. OT... **Rev:** Crowned imperial eagle, value "1Z" in orb on breast **Rev. Legend:** Titles of Ferdinand II, date around **Note:** Varieties exist.

Date	Mintage	VG	F	VF	XF	Unc
(16)Z0	—	150	285	475	—	—
(16)Z1	—	150	285	475	—	—

KM# 12 12 KREUZER (Dreibätzner)

Silver **Obv:** Similar to KM#4.1 but date above arms

Date	Mintage	VG	F	VF	XF	Unc
16Z1	—	200	400	650	—	—

KM# 14 1/2 THALER

Silver **Obv:** Crowned eight-fold arms **Obv. Legend:** TVT. ALBART. OTT **Rev:** Crowned imperial eagle, orb on breast, titles of Ferdinand II, date

Date	Mintage	VG	F	VF	XF	Unc
16Z3	—	—	—	—	—	—

KM# 15 THALER

Silver **Obv:** Crowned ornate arms **Obv. Legend:** *:TVT: ALB: OTT: COM: IN: SOLMS: D: I: M: W: E: S: **Rev:** Crowned imperial eagle **Rev. Legend:** *FERDINANDVS: II • D:G: ROM. IMP... **Note:** Dav. #7763.

Date	Mintage	VG	F	VF	XF	Unc
16Z3	—	850	1,650	2,750	—	—

SOLMS-LICH

One of the original two divisions of Solms in 1409, with its seat at Lich, just 7 miles (12 km) southeast of Giessen, Solms-Lich was joined with Hohensolms (Burgsolms) until a further division in 1562. The branch of Solms-Heruletz was established from Solms-Lich in 1590, but the parent line fell extinct in 1718.The Lich lands and titles reverted to Solms-Hohensolms in the latter year.

RULERS

Ernst I
With George Eerhard, 1596-1602
Ernst II, 1602-1619
Otto Sebastian, 1619-1640
Ludwig Christoph, 1640-1650
Hermann Adolf Moritz, 1650-1718

Joint Coinage
II - Eberhard (d.1600), Hermann Adolf, Reinhard II, George Eberhard,
Ernest II and Philipp, 1590-1610
III - Otto Sebastian and Ludwig Christoph, under guardianship of Friedrich zu Solms-Rodelheim and Joachim Friedrich zu Mansfeld, 1619-1623

MINT OFFICIALS' INITIALS

Lich Mint

Initial	Date	Name
(a)=	1589-93, 1602-08	Peter Arnsburger
	Ca. 1605	(Amtmann) Sprenger

Södel Mint

Initial	Date	Name
	1612	Georg Kupper
(b)=	1612-19	Hans Schmidt von Bielefeld
	1613-?	Michael Loth von Giessen
(c)=	1620-21	Sebastian Reess
	1621-?	Hartmann Diel

COUNTSHIP

JOINT COINAGE

KM# 18 PFENNIG
Silver **Ruler:** Ernst II **Obv:** 4-fold arms, S D G (SOLI DEO GLORIA) above **Note:** Uniface. Schussel-type.

Date	Mintage	VG	F	VF	XF	Unc
ND(1612)	74,000	9.00	20.00	40.00	80.00	—

KM# 13.2 3 KREUZER (Groschen)
Silver **Ruler:** Ernst II **Note:** Klippe.

Date	Mintage	VG	F	VF	XF	Unc
1611	—	—	—	—	—	—

KM# 13.1 3 KREUZER (Groschen)
Silver **Ruler:** Ernst II **Obv:** 4-fold arms, titles of Ernst II around **Rev:** Crowned imperial eagle, 3 in circle on breast, titles of Rudolf II, date around **Note:** Varieties exist.

Date	Mintage	VG	F	VF	XF	Unc
1611	—	33.00	65.00	135	225	—
1612	—	33.00	65.00	135	225	—
ND	—	33.00	65.00	135	225	—

KM# 19 3 KREUZER (Groschen)
Silver **Ruler:** Ernst II **Rev:** Titles of Matthias in margin **Note:** Similar to KM#13.1. Varieties exist.

Date	Mintage	VG	F	VF	XF	Unc
ND(1612)	—	27.00	55.00	110	200	—
1612	—	27.00	55.00	110	200	—
161Z	—	27.00	55.00	110	200	—
1613	—	27.00	55.00	110	200	—
1613 (b)	—	27.00	55.00	110	200	—
1615 (b)	—	27.00	55.00	110	200	—
(1)615 (b)	—	27.00	55.00	110	200	—
(16)15 (b)	—	27.00	55.00	110	200	—
1616 (b)	—	27.00	55.00	110	200	—
(16)16	—	27.00	55.00	110	200	—
1617 (b)	—	27.00	55.00	110	200	—
(16)17 (b)	—	27.00	55.00	110	200	—
(1)617 (b)	—	27.00	55.00	110	200	—
(16)18 (b)	—	27.00	55.00	110	200	—
1618 (b)	—	27.00	55.00	110	200	—
(16)19 (b)	—	27.00	55.00	110	200	—
(16)19	—	27.00	55.00	110	200	—
ND (b)	—	27.00	55.00	110	200	—

KM# 21 3 KREUZER (Groschen)
Silver **Ruler:** Ernst II **Obv:** First half of date divided by arms **Note:** Similar to KM#19. Varieties exist.

Date	Mintage	VG	F	VF	XF	Unc
16/1613	—	27.00	55.00	110	200	—
1613	—	27.00	55.00	110	200	—
1613 (b)	—	27.00	55.00	110	200	—
1614 (b)	—	27.00	55.00	110	200	—
1616 (b)	—	27.00	55.00	110	200	—
1617 (b)	—	27.00	55.00	110	200	—
16/1617 (b)	—	27.00	55.00	110	200	—
17/1617 (b)	—	27.00	55.00	110	200	—
1618 (b)	—	27.00	55.00	110	200	—

KM# 23 3 KREUZER (Groschen)
Silver **Ruler:** Ernst II **Obv:** First half of date in margin **Note:** Similar to KM#21.

Date	Mintage	VG	F	VF	XF	Unc
1613 (b)	—	33.00	60.00	120	220	—

KM# 20 3 KREUZER (Groschen)
Silver **Ruler:** Ernst II **Note:** Klippe.

Date	Mintage	VG	F	VF	XF	Unc
(16)13 (b)	—	—	—	—	—	—

KM# 38 3 KREUZER (Groschen)
Silver **Ruler:** Ernst II **Note:** Klippe.

Date	Mintage	VG	F	VF	XF	Unc
(16)19	—	—	—	—	—	—

KM# 37 3 KREUZER (Groschen)
Silver **Ruler:** Ernst II **Rev:** Titles of Ferdinand II **Note:** Similar to KM#19. Varieties exist.

Date	Mintage	VG	F	VF	XF	Unc
(16)19	—	—	—	—	—	—
(16)Z0	—	—	—	—	—	—

KM# 41 3 KREUZER (Groschen)
Silver **Ruler:** Ernst II **Note:** Klippe.

Date	Mintage	VG	F	VF	XF	Unc
ND (c)	—	—	—	—	—	—

KM# 40 3 KREUZER (Groschen)
Silver **Ruler:** Ernst II **Obv:** Four-fold arms around ILLUST. TUT. CO. I. SOL. LICH (or variant) **Rev:** Crowned imperial eagle, 3 in circle on breast, titles of Ferdinand II around

Date	Mintage	VG	F	VF	XF	Unc
ND(ca.1620)	—	—	—	—	—	—

KM# 42 3 KREUZER (Groschen)
Silver **Ruler:** Ernst II **Obv:** ILLUS. TUT. CO. SOLMS. LICH (or variant) **Note:** Similar to KM#40. Varieties exist.

Date	Mintage	VG	F	VF	XF	Unc
(16)Z1	—	45.00	85.00	165	300	—
(16)ZZ	—	45.00	85.00	165	300	—

KM# 43 6 KREUZER
Silver **Ruler:** Ernst II **Obv:** Four-fold arms, date above, around ILLUST. TUT. CO(M). SOLMS. LICH 6•K **Rev:** Crowned imperial eagle, orb on breast, titles of Ferdinand II around **Note:** Varieties exist.

Date	Mintage	VG	F	VF	XF	Unc
16Z1	—	—	—	—	—	—

KM# 14 ALBUS
Silver **Ruler:** Ernst II **Obv:** Four-fold arms, titles of Ernst II around **Rev:** NOVVS/ALBVS/date, SOLI DEO GLORIA around **Note:** Varieties exist.

Date	Mintage	VG	F	VF	XF	Unc
1611	—	—	—	—	—	—

KM# 15 12 KREUZER (Dreibätzner)
Silver **Ruler:** Ernst II **Obv:** Four-fold arms, titles of Ernst II around **Rev:** Crowned imperial eagle, 12 in circle on breast, titles of Rudolf II, date around

Date	Mintage	VG	F	VF	XF	Unc
1611	—	1,000	1,800	3,000	—	—

KM# 16 12 KREUZER (Dreibätzner)
Silver **Ruler:** Ernst II **Note:** Klippe.

Date	Mintage	VG	F	VF	XF	Unc
1611	—	—	—	—	—	—

KM# 27 12 KREUZER (Dreibätzner)
Silver **Ruler:** Ernst II **Obv:** Eight-fold arms in ornamented shield, first half of date above, titles of Ernst II around **Rev:** Crowned imperial eagle, 1Z in orb on breast, tail of eagle divides second half of date, titles of Matthias around

Date	Mintage	VG	F	VF	XF	Unc
1614 (b)	—	—	—	—	—	—

KM# 39 12 KREUZER (Dreibätzner)
Silver **Ruler:** Ernst II **Obv:** four-fold arms, around ILLUSTR. TUT. COME. SOLMS. LICH **Rev:** Crowned imperial eagle, 1Z in orb on breast, titles of Ferdinand II, date around **Note:** Varieties exist.

Date	Mintage	VG	F	VF	XF	Unc
(16)19	—	800	1,600	2,700	—	—
(16)Z0	—	800	1,600	2,700	—	—
ND (c)	—	800	1,600	2,700	—	—

KM# 44 12 KREUZER (Dreibätzner)
Silver **Ruler:** Ernst II **Obv:** Date above arms **Note:** Similar to KM#39.

Date	Mintage	VG	F	VF	XF	Unc
16Z1	—	850	1,650	2,850	—	—

KM# 3 DICKEN (Teston)
Silver **Ruler:** Ernst II **Obv:** Oval four-fold arms in ornate frame, date above, MO. ARG. COM... around **Rev:** Crowned imperial eagle, orb on breast, titles of Rudolf II around

Date	Mintage	VG	F	VF	XF	Unc
1601	—	1,095	2,000	3,300	—	—

KM# 5 1/2 THALER
Silver **Obv:** Oval four-fold arms divide date, two helmets above, legend around **Obv. Legend:** MO. ARG. CO - SOLM • LICH **Rev:** Crowned imperial eagle, orb on breast, titles of Rudolf II around

Date	Mintage	VG	F	VF	XF	Unc
1601 Rare	—	—	—	—	—	—

KM# 24 THALER
Silver **Obv:** Helmeted arms **Obv. Legend:** • PHILIPPUS • COMES • IN : SOLMS : LICH **Rev:** Crowned imperial eagle with orb on breast, 1-6-2-3 divided below **Rev. Legend:** • MATTHIAS • I • D : G • RO : IMP... **Note:** Dav. #7747.

Date	Mintage	VG	F	VF	XF	Unc
1613 Rare	—	—	—	—	—	—
1616 Rare	—	—	—	—	—	—

KM# 28 THALER
Silver **Obv:** Crowned imperial eagle with orb on breast, date 1-6-1-4 below tail feathers **Obv. Legend:** ERNESTUS• COM • IN • SOLMS • LICH • L.D.G. **Rev:** Helmeted arms **Rev. Legend:** MATTHIAS • I • D • G • RO • IMP.... **Note:** Dav. #7745.

Date	Mintage	VG	F	VF	XF	Unc
1614 Rare	—	—	—	—	—	—

KM# 48 THALER
Silver **Obv:** Helmeted oval arms **Obv. Legend:** • MO • ARG • CO • SOLM : LICH **Rev:** Crowned imperial eagle with orb on breast, 2-3 next to neck or by claws of eagle **Rev. Legend:** • FERDINAN • II • D : G • ROM • IMP... **Note:** Dav. #7746.

Date	Mintage	VG	F	VF	XF	Unc
16Z3 Rare	—	—	—	—	—	—
ND Rare	—	—	—	—	—	—

KM# 35 2 THALER
Silver **Obv:** Helmeted arms **Obv. Legend:** PHILIPPUS. COMES. IN: SOLMS: LICH **Rev:** Crowned imperial eagle with orb on breast, date divided by tail **Rev. Legend:** MATTHIAS: D: G: RO: IMP... **Note:** Klippe. Dav. #7748.

Date	Mintage	VG	F	VF	XF	Unc
1618 Rare	—	—	—	—	—	—

KM# 53 2 THALER
Silver **Obv:** Helmeted ornate oval arms **Obv. Legend:** PHILIPS • COM • SOLM • LICH **Rev:** Crowned imperial eagle **Rev. Legend:** FERDIN • II • D • G • ROM • IMP... **Note:** Dav. #7752.

Date	Mintage	VG	F	VF	XF	Unc
1624 Rare	—	—	—	—	—	—

KM# 46 2 GULDEN
21.5000 g., Silver **Obv:** Helmeted arms **Obv. Legend:** FERDI. II...REX IZ0 **Note:** Dav, #7750.

Date	Mintage	VG	F	VF	XF	Unc
16ZZ Rare	—	—	—	—	—	—

KM# 49 2 GULDEN
21.5000 g., Silver **Obv:** Helmeted arms **Obv. Legend:** PHILIPS • COM • SOLM • LICH **Note:** Dav.#7751. Similar to Dav. #7753. but Z-3 divided by neck.

Date	Mintage	VG	F	VF	XF	Unc
(16)Z3	—	1,150	2,050	3,400	5,300	—

KM# 52 2 GULDEN
21.5000 g., Silver **Obv:** Helmeted arms **Obv. Legend:** PHILIPS • COM • SOLM • LICH **Rev:** Crowned imperial eagle **Rev. Legend:** FERDIN • II • D • G • ROM • IMP... Z4 **Note:** Dav.#7753.

Date	Mintage	VG	F	VF	XF	Unc
(16)Z4	—	1,150	2,050	3,400	5,300	—

KM# 45 4 GULDEN
24.0000 g., Silver **Obv:** Helmeted arms **Obv. Legend:** PHILIPPUS • COMES • IN : SOLMS: LICH **Rev:** Date divided by necks of crowned imperial eagle **Rev. Legend:** FERDIN II... REX.IV FL **Note:** Dav.#7749

Date	Mintage	VG	F	VF	XF	Unc
16ZZ Rare	—	—	—	—	—	—

TRADE COINAGE

KM# 7 GOLDGULDEN
3.5000 g., 0.9860 Gold 0.1109 oz. AGW **Obv:** Arms in inner circle **Rev:** Crowned imperial eagle in inner circle, titles of Rudolf II **Note:** Fr.#3294.

Date	Mintage	VG	F	VF	XF	Unc
1601 Rare	—	—	—	—	—	—

KM# 30 GOLDGULDEN
3.5000 g., 0.9860 Gold 0.1109 oz. AGW **Obv:** Arms **Rev:** Crowned imperial eagle, titles of Matthias **Note:** Fr.#3295.

Date	Mintage	VG	F	VF	XF	Unc
1615 (b) Rare	—	—	—	—	—	—

KM# 31 GOLDGULDEN
3.5000 g., 0.9860 Gold 0.1109 oz. AGW **Obv:** Arms **Rev:** Crowned imperial eagle **Note:** Fr.#3296.

Date	Mintage	VG	F	VF	XF	Unc
1616	—	1,400	2,700	4,650	7,800	—

KM# 50 GOLDGULDEN
3.5000 g., 0.9860 Gold 0.1109 oz. AGW **Obv:** Arms **Rev:** Crowned imperial eagle, titles of Ferdinand II **Note:** Fr.#3297.

Date	Mintage	VG	F	VF	XF	Unc
1623	—	925	1,850	3,100	5,400	—

KM# 25 DUCAT
3.5000 g., 0.9860 Gold 0.1109 oz. AGW **Obv:** Arms in inner circle **Rev:** Emperor Matthias standing in inner circle **Note:** Fr.#3298.

Date	Mintage	VG	F	VF	XF	Unc
1613	—	1,300	2,600	5,200	8,500	—

KM# 10 6 DUCAT
20.0900 g., 0.9860 Gold 0.6368 oz. AGW **Obv:** Oval four-fold arms divide date, two helmets above, legend around **Obv. Legend:** MO. ARG. CO -SOLM • LICH **Rev:** Crowned imperial eagle, orb on breast, titles of Rudolf II around

Date	Mintage	VG	F	VF	XF	Unc
1601 Rare	—	—	—	—	—	—

SOLMS-ROEDELHEIM

After a short period of joint rule by the four sons of the count of Solms-Laubach, a division of the patrimony was effected in 1607. The third son established a line in Rödelheim, now a suburb to the immediate west of Frankfurt am Main, acquired at some time before the division. That son died without issue and Solms-Rödelheim passed to Solms-Baruth, from which a new line was founded in 1632/1635. However, the sons of the late count were all minors, so a guardianship was set up, followed by brotherly joint rule until about 1665. Although the counts of Solms-Rödelheim were still flourishing in the early 20th century, their lands were mediatized, along with all other branches of Solms, about the year 1806.

RULERS
Friedrich, 1607-1635
Joint Coinage of Johann August, Johann Friedrich, Friedrich Sigismund and Johann George III
1635-1665, first under guardianship, then under joint rule
Johann August, 1660-1680
Ludwig, 1680-1716

MINT OFFICIALS' INITIALS

Initial	Date	Name
MG	1655-57	Martin Ganser
SM	1654-58, 75-76	Sebastian Müller
BM/LBM	1657, 86	Ludwig Balthasar Müller
IIF	1676	Johann Jeremias Freitag, warden

COUNTSHIP

REGULAR COINAGE

KM# 16 KREUZER

Silver **Ruler:** Ludwig **Obv:** Crowned arms of Solms divides S - R, all between two branches **Rev. Inscription:** I/KREU/TZER/date/LBM

Date	Mintage	VG	F	VF	XF	Unc
1686 LBM	—	80.00	165	300	525	—

KM# 3 3 KREUZER (Groschen)

Silver **Ruler:** Friedrich **Obv:** Four-fold arms, titles of Friedrich **Rev:** Crowned imperial eagle, 3 in circle on breast, titles of Ferdinand II, date **Note:** Varieties exist.

Date	Mintage	VG	F	VF	XF	Unc
1622	—	165	325	525	—	—
ND	—	150	300	500	—	—

KM# 4 1/4 THALER

Silver **Ruler:** Friedrich **Obv:** Facing bust, value 1/4 on right, titles of Friedrich **Rev:** Crowned eight-fold arms divide date, titles continue

Date	Mintage	VG	F	VF	XF	Unc
1622	—	—	—	—	—	—

KM# 5 1/4 THALER

Silver **Ruler:** Friedrich **Obv:** Crowned eight-fold arms, titles of Ferdinand II, date **Rev:** Crowned imperial eagle, orb on breast, titles of Ferdinand II, date

Date	Mintage	VG	F	VF	XF	Unc
16ZZ	—	—	—	—	—	—

KM# 11 2/3 THALER (Gulden)

Silver **Ruler:** Johann August **Rev:** Similar to KM#10 but with palm branches at sides of arms **Note:** Dav. #989.

Date	Mintage	VG	F	VF	XF	Unc
1675 SM	—	135	275	525	875	—

KM# 10 2/3 THALER (Gulden)

Silver **Ruler:** Johann August **Obv:** Bust right, titles of Johann August **Rev:** Crowned eight-fold arms, date below, value (60) at bottom **Rev. Legend:** PER ANGUSTA - AD AVGVSTA **Note:** Dav. #989. Varieties exist.

Date	Mintage	VG	F	VF	XF	Unc
1675 SM	—	135	275	525	875	—
1676 SM	—	135	275	525	875	—

KM# 12 2/3 THALER (Gulden)

Silver **Ruler:** Johann August **Rev:** Similar to KM#10 but date divided by arms **Note:** Dav. #990. Varieties exist.

Date	Mintage	VG	F	VF	XF	Unc
1676	—	135	275	—	—	—
1676 SM/IIF	—	135	275	—	—	—

JOINT COINAGE

1635-1665

KM# 7 ALBUS

Silver **Ruler:** Johann August, Johann Friedrich, Friedrich Sigismund, and Johann George III **Obv:** Crowned heart-shaped two-fold arms of Solms and Wildenfels **Obv. Legend:** R. G. S. SOLMS... **Rev:** Value between two branches **Rev. Inscription:** I/ALBVS/date/MG **Note:** Varieties exist.

Date	Mintage	VG	F	VF	XF	Unc
1655 MG	—	55.00	110	200	325	—
1656 MG	—	55.00	110	200	325	—
1657 MG	—	55.00	110	200	325	—
1657 BM	—	55.00	110	200	325	—
1657 SM	—	55.00	110	200	325	—
1658 SM	—	55.00	110	200	325	—

KM# 6 1/2 THALER

Silver **Ruler:** Johann August, Johann Friedrich, Friedrich Sigismund, and Johann George III **Obv:** Crowned eight-fold arms divide date, titles of Friedrich **Rev:** Crowned imperial eagle, orb on breast, titles of Leopold I around

Date	Mintage	F	VF	XF	Unc
1658 SM	—	1,350	2,700	4,700	—	—

TRADE COINAGE

KM# 8 DUCAT

3.5000 g., 0.9860 Gold 0.1109 oz. AGW **Ruler:** Johann August, Johann Friedrich, Friedrich Sigismund, and Johann George III **Obv:** Arms in inner circle **Rev:** Value and date in wreath **Note:** Fr.#3301.

Date	Mintage	VG	F	VF	XF	Unc
1656 Rare	—	—	—	—	—	—

KM# 14 DUCAT

3.5000 g., 0.9860 Gold 0.1109 oz. AGW **Ruler:** Johann August **Obv:** Bust of Johann August right in inner circle **Rev:** Arms in inner circle **Note:** Fr.#3302.

Date	Mintage	VG	F	VF	XF	Unc
1680 Rare	—	—	—	—	—	—

SORAU

The oldest town of Lower Lusatia, Sorau was founded at least by 840 and was the property of the abbey of Fulda until the mid-13th century. It was the seat of the Lords of Döben (Dewin) from 1154 to 1280, then under the Lords of Pack until 1355, at which time it passed to Biberstein. The latter obtained the mint right in 1414. When the Biberstein line died out in 1551, it fell to Brandenburg, which sold it almost immediately to Promnitz. The Lord of Promnitz later struck coins in league with the Elector of Saxony at Sorau during the Kipper Period of the Thirty Years' War.

MINT OFFICIALS

Initial	Date	Name
FS	1621-23	Friedrich von Stierbitz, mintmaster
	1621-23	Sebald Lindelbach, mintmaster
	1621-23	Johann Jacob Huser, mintmaster
	1621-23	Johann Merkel, mintmaster

PROVINCIAL TOWN

STANDARD COINAGE

KM# 1 PFENNIG

Copper **Obv:** Large W, S above divides date **Note:** Uniface. Kipper Coinage. Varieteis exist.

Date	Mintage	VG	F	VF	XF	Unc
1621	—	20.00	40.00	100	200	—
16Z1	—	20.00	40.00	100	200	—
1622	—	20.00	40.00	100	200	—
16ZZ	—	20.00	40.00	100	200	—

KM# 5 PFENNIG

Copper **Obv:** Shield with arrow between 2 star, date above **Note:** Uniface. Kipper Pfennig. Varieties exist.

Date	Mintage	VG	F	VF	XF	Unc
16ZZ	—	22.00	45.00	120	225	—

KM# 8 3 PFENNIG (Drier)

Copper **Obv:** Ornate shield with arrow between 2 stars **Rev:** Large W, S above divides date **Note:** Kipper 3 Pfennig.

Date	Mintage	VG	F	VF	XF	Unc
16ZZ	—	25.00	50.00	135	250	—

KM# 12 3 PFENNIG (Drier)

Copper **Obv:** Ornate shield with arrow between 2 stars **Rev:** Large W with III value below, S above divides date **Note:** Kipper 3 Pfennig. Varieties exist.

Date	Mintage	VG	F	VF	XF	Unc
16ZZ	—	25.00	50.00	135	250	—

KM# 13 3 PFENNIG (Drier)

Copper **Obv:** Oval arms in baroque frame **Rev:** Large W with III value below, S above divides date **Note:** Kipper 3 Pfennig. Varieties exist.

Date	Mintage	VG	F	VF	XF	Unc
1622	—	25.00	50.00	135	250	—

KM# 16 3 KREUZER (Groschen)

Silver **Obv:** 3-fold arms of Promnitz, date divided by orb above, value (3) below, legend **Obv. Legend:** MO•NOVA SORAVI. **Rev:** Crowned imperial eagle, titles of Ferdinand II **Note:** Kipper 3 Kreuzer. Varieties exist.

Date	Mintage	VG	F	VF	XF	Unc
1622 FS Retrograde	—	—	—	—	—	—

KM# 17 3 KREUZER (Groschen)

Silver **Obv:** 3-fold arms of Promnitz, date divided by orb above, value (3) below, legend **Rev:** Bust of Ferdinand II right in circle, titles around **Note:** Kipper 3 Kreuzer. Varieties exist.

Date	Mintage	VG	F	VF	XF	Unc
1622 FS	—	—	—	—	—	—

KM# 19 3 KREUZER (Groschen)

Silver **Obv:** Bust of emperor right, circle around, legend, date **Rev:** Crowned imperial eagle, titles of Ferdinand II **Note:** Kipper 3 Kreuzer. Varieties exist.

Date	Mintage	VG	F	VF	XF	Unc
1622	—	—	—	—	—	—

KM# 20 3 KREUZER (Groschen)

Silver **Obv:** Bust of emperor to right, barely breaks circle at top, value (3) below, titles of Ferdinand II **Rev:** Crowned imperial eagle, Austria arms on breast, titles continued around and dat **Note:** Kipper 3 Kreuzer. Varieties exist.

Date	Mintage	VG	F	VF	XF	Unc
1622	—	—	—	—	—	—
1623	—	—	—	—	—	—

KM# 18 3 KREUZER (Groschen)

Silver **Obv:** Bust of emperor right, head breaks circle, legend, date **Obv. Legend:** MO . NOVA . SORAVIE **Rev:** Crowned imperial eagle, arms of Austria on breast, value (3) below, titles of Ferdinand II **Note:** Kipper 3 Kruezer. Varieties exist.

Date	Mintage	VG	F	VF	XF	Unc
1622	—	—	—	—	—	—
1623	—	—	—	—	—	—

KM# 3 1/24 THALER (Groschen)

Silver **Obv:** 3-fold arms of Promnitz, legend, date **Obv. Legend:** MONETA CIVIT . SORAV **Rev:** Crowned imperial eagle, titles of Ferdinand II **Note:** Kipper 1/24 Thaler.

Date	Mintage	VG	F	VF	XF	Unc
1621	—	—	—	—	—	—

KM# 25.1 1/24 THALER (Groschen)

Silver **Obv:** Promnitz lion rampant left, legend **Obv. Legend:** DO . PROT . NOST. **Rev:** Imperial orb with 24, date above, legend **Rev. Legend:** MO: NO: CIVI . SORA. **Note:** Kipper 1/24 Thaler.

Date	Mintage	VG	F	VF	XF	Unc
1622	—	—	—	—	—	—

KM# 25.2 1/24 THALER (Groschen)

Silver **Obv:** 3-fold arms of Promnitz, legend, date divided at top **Obv. Legend:** MO NOVA SORAVI **Rev:** Imperial orb with 24, titles of Ferdinand II **Note:** Klippe. Varieties exist.

Date	Mintage	VG	F	VF	XF	Unc
1622	—	—	—	—	—	—

SPEYER

(Spires)

City and bishopric spanning the Rhine 15 miles south of Mannheim. The bishopric was founded in the 4th century, destroyed by Barbarians and re-established in 610. The city received the mint right in 1111 and became the site of the imperial mint. It became a free city of the empire in 1294 and was part of France from 1801 to 1814. In 1814 Speyer passed to Bavaria.

BISHOPRIC

RULERS

Eberhard von Dienheim, 1581-1610
Philipp Christof von Sotern, 1610-1652
Lothar Friedrich von Metternich-Burscheid, 1652-1675
Johann Hugh von Orsbeck, 1677-1711

MINT OFFICIALS' INITIALS

Initial	Date	Name
LS	1616-24	Lorenz Schneider at Koblenz
I-A	1624-27	Hans Jakob Ayrer at Koblenz
HL	1625-27	Heinrich Lambert at Koblenz
MS	1627-52	Matthias Stein at Koblenz
MF	ca. 1665-83	Matthias Fischer at Bruchsal
DZ	1678-91	Dietrich Zimmermann at Bruchsal
A	ca. 1680	

ARMS

Cross with middle line between outer line of each arm.

Residence of the bishops was at Bruchsal, about 14 miles (24km) southeast of Speyer, at which place the mint was also located.

REGULAR COINAGE

DAV# 5806 THALER

Silver **Ruler:** Philipp Christof **Subject:** Changing the Name of Udenheim to Phillipsburg **Obv:** Helmeted arms **Obv. Legend:** EP * SPIR * PRAEP * **Rev:** Saint standing **Rev. Legend:** S * PHILIPPVS * PATRONVS *

Date	Mintage	VG	F	VF	XF	Unc
1623	—	2,250	3,750	6,000	9,800	—

DAV# 5807 THALER

Silver **Ruler:** Philipp Christof **Obv. Legend:** ... ARCHI. TREVIR. PRINC. ELECT* **Rev:** Standing saint divides date **Rev. Legend:** EPIS. SPIRENSIS. AD. PRVM. PRAEP. WEISSENB.

Date	Mintage	VG	F	VF	XF	Unc
1623	—	2,250	3,750	6,000	9,800	—

DAV# 5807A THALER

Silver **Ruler:** Philipp Christof **Note:** Klippe.

Date	Mintage	VG	F	VF	XF	Unc
1623 Rare	—	—	—	—	—	—

DAV# 5805 2 THALER

Silver **Ruler:** Philipp Christof **Subject:** Changing the Name of Udenheim to Phillipsburg **Obv:** Helmeted arms **Rev:** Saint standing

Date	Mintage	VG	F	VF	XF	Unc
1623 Rare	—	—	—	—	—	—

TRADE COINAGE

KM# A15 GOLDGULDEN

Gold **Obv:** Crowned 4-fold arms with central shield dividing date **Rev:** Madonna and child on crescent, rays around

Date	Mintage	VG	F	VF	XF	Unc
1632	—	—	—	—	—	—

KM# A16 GOLDGULDEN

Gold **Note:** Klippe.

Date	Mintage	VG	F	VF	XF	Unc
1632	—	—	—	—	—	—

FR# 3304 2 GOLDGULDEN

7.0000 g., 0.9860 Gold 0.2219 oz. AGW **Ruler:** Philipp Christof **Obv:** Helmeted 4-fold arms **Rev:** Madonna and child

Date	Mintage	VG	F	VF	XF	Unc
1612 Rare	—	—	—	—	—	—

FR# 3305 DUCAT

3.5000 g., 0.9860 Gold 0.1109 oz. AGW **Ruler:** Lothar Friedrich **Obv:** Bust right **Rev:** Crowned arms

Date	Mintage	VG	F	VF	XF	Unc
1665	—	1,300	2,600	5,200	8,500	—

CITY

Although the city of Speyer received the mint right in 1111, very few coins were struck on its behalf over the centuries. Special coins were minted for the first and second hundred years of the Protestant Reformation. There are also a few notable countermarked coins dating from the early phase of the Thirty Years' War.

MINT OFFICIAL

LK and L.HEN.K. = Unknown, ca. 1717

TRADE COINAGE

KM# 5 GOLDGULDEN

3.2000 g., 0.9860 Gold 0.1014 oz. AGW **Subject:** Centennial of the Reformation **Obv:** 6-line inscription **Rev:** 8-line inscription with Roman numeral date **Note:** Klippe.

Date	Mintage	VG	F	VF	XF	Unc
ND(1617) Rare	—	—	—	—	—	—

PHILLIPSBURG

TRADE COINAGE

KM# 2 2 GOLDGULDEN

0.9860 Gold **Note:** Klippe. Uniface.

Date	Mintage	VG	F	VF	XF	Unc
1635	—	1,500	3,500	5,500	—	—

KM# 1 2 GOLDGULDEN

0.9860 Gold **Obv:** Madonna and child with rays, crescent moon below, inscription around **Obv. Inscription:** MONETA. NOVA. AVREA. PHILLIPPSBVRG. **Rev:** 10-line inscription **Rev. Inscription:** AO' / 1635.D' / Z4. IANVAR / 1ST, PHILIPS / BVRG DVRCH / D. KAY: OBRISTEN / BAVMBERGER / MIT. STVRM / ER. OBERT. WORD / EN /(Translation: Year 1635, the 24th of January, Phillipsburg was taken by st **Note:** Weight varies: 7.08-7.32 grams.

Date	Mintage	VG	F	VF	XF	Unc
1635 Rare	—	—	—	—	—	—

STADE

First mentioned as early as about 1000AD, Stade is located along the Elbe River about 16 miles (27km) west of Hamburg and downstream from that city. Yet, from the mid-11th century, the town was the site for a mint of the archbishops of Bremen. By 1168, Stade was completely under the control of Bremen, but was given the right to strike its own local coinage beginning in 1272. The city struck a series of issues until the late 17th century. Stade was included in the Duchy of Bremen and Werden from 1644 until 1719, then was made a part of Hannover in the latter year.

RULERS

Austrian until 1643
Swedish, 1644-1719

MINT OFFICIALS' INITALS

Initial	Date	Name
(a)	1614-21	Simon Timpfe, mintmaster
HB (ligature)	ca 1621	unknown
(b) or PT	1638-43	Peter Timpfe, mintmaster
	1649	Heinrich Timke, warden
	1657-60	Johann Schulze, mintmaster
	1660-70	Michael Müller, mintmaster
AH	1670-76	Andreas Hille, mintmaster
IS	1660-80	Jacob Schröder, as warden
	1680-95	as mintmaster
IS	1695-1706	Diedrich Jürgen Schröder, mintmaster

ARMS

Key, as that of Bremen

REFERENCES:

B = Max Bahrfeldt, ***Die Münzen der Stadt Stade***, Vienna, 1879.
S = Hugo Frhr. von Saurma-Jeltsch, *Die Saurmasche Münzsammlung deutscher, schweizerischer und polnischer Gepräge von etwa dem Beginn der Groschenzeit bis zur Kipperperiode,* **Berlin, 1892.**

PROVINCIAL CITY

REGULAR COINAGE

KM# 5 SECHSLING (1/96 Thaler)

Silver **Obv:** Key within circle of branches **Rev:** Value in inner circle, date in legend

Date	Mintage	VG	F	VF	XF	Unc
1676	—	20.00	40.00	80.00	140	—

KM# 6 1/48 THALER (1 Schilling)

Silver **Obv:** Key within circle of branches **Rev:** Value in inner circle, date in legend

Date	Mintage	VG	F	VF	XF	Unc
1676	—	16.00	33.00	65.00	120	—

DAV# 5810 THALER

Silver **Obv:** Supported city arms **Rev:** Crowned double eagle with orb on breast, titles of Matthias

Date	Mintage	VG	F	VF	XF	Unc
1616	—	4,500	6,000	10,000	—	—

KM# 18 THALER

Silver **Obv:** Supported city arms, key left (reversed) on arms **Rev:** 32 in orb on breast of eagle, titles of Ferdinand II **Note:** Dav# 5811.

Date	Mintage	VG	F	VF	XF	Unc
16Z1 HB	—	1,000	1,650	3,000	5,000	—

KM# 19 THALER

Silver **Rev:** 23 in orb on eagle's breast **Note:** Dav# 5811A.

Date	Mintage	VG	F	VF	XF	Unc
1621 HB	—	1,000	1,750	3,200	5,500	—

KM# 24 THALER

Silver **Rev:** Plain orb on eagle's breast, titles of Ferdinand III **Rev. Legend:** ... IMP: S: A: **Note:** Dav# 5812.

Date	Mintage	VG	F	VF	XF	Unc
1640 (b) Rare	—	—	—	—	—	—

DAV# 5814 THALER

Silver **Obv:** Supported city arms, key left (reversed), date in legend **Rev:** Crowned double-headed eagle in inner circle, titles of Leopold I

Date	Mintage	VG	F	VF	XF	Unc
1686	—	1,800	3,000	5,250	8,500	—

DAV# 5809 2 THALER

Silver **Note:** Similar to 1 Thaler, Dav. #5810.

Date	Mintage	VG	F	VF	XF	Unc
1616 Rare	—	—	—	—	—	—

DAV# 5813 2 THALER

Silver **Note:** Similar to 1 Thaler, Dav. #5814.

Date	Mintage	VG	F	VF	XF	Unc
1686 Rare	—	—	—	—	—	—

STOLBERG

The castle of Stolberg, located on the southern slopes of the Harz Mountains, 9 miles (15 km) northeast of Nordhausen, is the ancestral home of the counts of that name. The dynasty has a recognized line of succession from count Heinrich I (1210-1239), but the family claimed descent from Otto Colonna, an Italian noble of the 6th century. The column in the family arms signifies this supposed connection, whether historically accurate or not. Count Heinrich was the younger brother of the count of Hohnstein whose castle lay just 6 miles away. Whatever the origin of the earlier counts of Stolberg, they came to an end and the line founded by Heinrich I began in about 1222. The long series of coins, based on the rich Harz silver mine holdings of the family, began at this time. Various territories, some scattered a distance from the family home, were added to the Stolberg lands and two brothers established separate lines in 1538, Stolberg-Stolberg and Stolberg-Wernigerode. Another brother succeeded to the Dietz portion of Königstein in1574.

RULERS

Wolf Ernst in Stolberg, 1552-1606
Johann in Stolberg, 1606-1612
Heinrich XXII, 1552-1615
Ludwig Georg in Ortenberg, 1572-1618
Christof II in Schwarze (Wernigerode), 1572-1638
Wolfgang Georg in Stolberg, 1612-1631
Heinrich Volrad in Ortenberg, 1618-1641

From 1498 to 1638, various combinations of the above counts-brothers, uncles, nephew and cousins-issued extensive coinages jointly in their names. Because the many counts were rulers in their own right in parts of the Stolberg possessions, their jointly issued coinages are treated together under Stolberg. Individual issues are listed under that particular branch of the countship. The joint issue groupings are given designations to avoid repetition of the names in the following manner:

XII - Wolf Ernst, Johann, Heinrich XXII, Ludwig George Christof II, 1587-1606
XIII - Johann, Heinrich XXII, Ludwig Georg, Christof II, 1606
XIV - Johann and Heinrich XXII, 1607-1612
XV - Heinrich XXII and Wolfgang Georg, 1612-1615
XVI - Christof II and Heinrich Volrad, 1618-1638

MINT OFFICIALS' INITIALS

The output of the Harz silver mines belonging to the counts of Stolberg was often beyond the capacity of their several mints to turn into coins. Production of many coins were frequently farmed out to mints in other territories, such as neighboring Mansfeld, or to city mints in Frankfurt am Main, Augsburg, etc. Sometimes mintmasters and die engravers were invited to work in Stolberg mints on a temporary basis. Over the centuries a bewildering number of people worked in and for Stolberg mints and many left their symbols and initials on the coins.

Erfurt Mint

Mark	Date	Name
(z)=	1605-07	Florian Gruber
	1605	Hans Weber, warden
(bb)=	1607-08	Hieronymus Grunenberger

Frankfurt am Main Mint

Mark	Date	Name
(hh)=	1619? – 1629	Lorenz Schilling

Gedern Mint

Mark	Date	Name
	1622-24	Simon Wefel
	1624-27	Kaspar Pan

Nordhausen Mint

Mark	Date	Name
DZ	1622	Daniel Zunder
	ca.1660	Hans König
	1660-?	Johann Krieg

Ortenberg Mint

Mark	Date	Name
(dd)=	1597-1605?	Daniel Ludwig von Weiersdorf
	1607	Henning Kiesel
	1617-23	Hans Heinrich Schlehenbusch (Schlebusch)
	1621	Jost Arnold
	1621-22	Simon Wefel (Wevel, Wewell)
	1622	Bartholomäus Simon
	1622-23	Hans Georg Dornwaldt

Ranstadt Mint

Mark	Date	Name
	1604-06	Peter Arenburg (Arnburch)
(gg)= or	1605, 1609, 1615-?	Georg Kipper (Kupper)
	1610	Hans Meyer or Schmidt
	1610	Michaël Lodt, warden
(cc)=	1610-12	Daniel Ayrer
(ee)=	1612-14	Paul Lachendress (Lachentriss)
(ff)=	1614	Thomas Isebein
	1615	Hermann Liebert
	1617	Henning Kiesel
	1617-22	Hans Heinrich Schlehenbusch (Schlebusch)
	1622	Simon Wefel (Wevel, Wewell)

Stolberg Mint

Mark	Date	Name
(aa)=	1607	Andreas Lafferts
	1607	Hans Kreuper (Krueper)
GM	1609-12	Georg Meinhart in Eisleben (Mansfeld)
	1619	Thomas N-?, die-cutter
	1621	Baldwin Köln
	1621	Hans Lauch
	1621	Hans Lapp, die-cutter
	1621	Valentin Reich, die-cutter
	1621	Ernst Stam, die-cutter
CZ	1623-26, 1632	Christof Ziegenhorn
UZ / VZ	1644-?	Volkmar Ziegenhorn
IPK	1663	Johann Philipp Koburger in Eisleben (Mansfeld
IA	1668-69	Johann Arensberger von Halberstadt in Rottleberode
	1669	Ernst Kaspar Dürre von Nordhausen, die-cutter
ABK	1669	Anton Bernhard Koburger in Eisleben and Rottleberode
	1623	Bartholomäus Reuke (Renke), warden
IK	1645-60	Johann Krieg
IT	1690-1723	Johann Thun in Gotha
JAS	1692-1706	Julius Angerstein (Sculpsit=engraved), mintmaster and die-cutter in Eisenberg
W/CW	1700-1730	Christian Wermuth, medailleur/die-cutter in Gotha

Wernigerode Mint

Mark	Date	Name
AL	1612-15	Andreas Lafferts
IH	1612	Isaak Henniges (Henniger), die-cutter
CZ	1618-20	Christof Ziegenhorn
BB	1620-21	Braun Block
IK	1620-21	Jürgen Korll (Kröll)
HL (ligature)	1621-22	Hans Lauch
IK	1622-?	Andreas Weber
HB	1659-60	Hans Becker
IB	1671-74	Johann Bostelmann
	1671-74	Johann Arendsburg (Ahrensbergk), warden
	1674	Steffen Berger, die-cutter
	1674	Jürgen Bode, die-cutter
	1674	Johann Fischer, die-cutter
	1674	Gottfried Hasse, die-cutter
	1674	Dittrich Hefering, die-cutter
	1674	Bernt Hermann, die-cutter

ARMS

Stolberg - stag, usually to left, sometimes to right, antlers extend backwards
Wernigerode - one or two fish (trout) standing on tails
Königstein - lion left
Rochefort - eagle
Eppstein - three chevrons
Minzenberg - horizontal bar
Mark - checkerboard in horizontal bar
Agimont - five horizontal bars
Lohra - lion rampant left
Wertheim - top half of eagle above three roses
Breuberg - two horizontal bars
Hohnstein - checkerboard
Klettenberg - stag left, but antlers extend upwards

STOLBERG-STOLBERG

The old line of counts was divided into the senior (Wernigerode) and junior (Stolberg) branches in 1638. The junior branch was divided again in 1704 into Stolberg-Stolberg and Stolberg-Rossla. The two lines issued a large series of coins, mostly as joint issues, throughout the 18th century. There were still counts of Stolberg-Stolberg into the early 20th century.

RULERS

Johann, 1606-1612
Wolfgang Georg, 1612 (1615)-1631
Johann Martin I, 1638-1669
Friedrich Wilhelm, 1669-1684
Christof Ludwig I, 1684-1704

COUNTSHIP

REGULAR COINAGE

KM# 13 1/28 THALER (Groschen)

Silver **Ruler:** Johann **Subject:** Death of Johann **Obv:** Stag left, titles of Johann **Rev:** 5-line inscription with date
Rev. Inscription: OBIIT/30. IVLII/ANNO 1612/ÆTATIS:/63.

Date	Mintage	VG	F	VF	XF	Unc
161Z AL	—	—	—	—	—	—

KM# 18 1/24 THALER (Groschen)

Silver **Ruler:** Wolfgang Georg **Obv:** Stag left in circle **Obv. Legend:** WOLF. GEOR. COM. IN. STO. **Rev:** Imperial orb with 'Z4,' cross on orb divides date and mintmaster's initials at top **Rev. Legend:** KON. WER. ET. HON. **Note:** Varieties exist.

Date	Mintage	VG	F	VF	XF	Unc
1618 CZ	—	—	—	—	—	—
1619 CZ	—	—	—	—	—	—
16Z0 CZ	—	—	—	—	—	—
16Z3 CZ	17,000	—	—	—	—	—
16Z4 CZ	—	—	—	—	—	—
16Z5 CZ	5,994	—	—	—	—	—

KM# 36 12 KREUZER (Schreckenberger)

Silver, 27-28 mm. **Ruler:** Wolfgang Georg **Obv:** Three shields of arms, Stolberg above Wernigerode and Hohnstein, upper arms divide date, value IZ below. **Obv. Legend:** WOLF. GEOR. GR. IN STOLB. K. R. **Rev:** Stag to left in circle, mintmaster's initials between legs **Rev. Legend:** ET. HON. DO. I. EP. M. B. LO. CL. **Note:** Kipper Coinage. F #865.

Date	Mintage	VG	F	VF	XF	Unc
16Z1 HL	—	—	—	—	—	—
16ZZ HL	—	—	—	—	—	—

KM# 74 1/4 THALER

Silver **Ruler:** Johann Martin I **Obv:** Stag left in front of crowned column **Obv. Legend:** IOHAN. MART: COM: IN. STOLB. K. R. W. E. HO. **Rev:** 11-fold arms divide mintmaster's initials, date divided at top **Rev. Legend:** DOM. IN. EPS: MVN: BR: LOR: E. CLETT. **Note:** Varieties exist.

Date	Mintage	VG	F	VF	XF	Unc
1646 IK	—	—	—	—	—	—
1649 IK	—	—	—	—	—	—

KM# 50 1/2 THALER

Silver **Ruler:** Wolfgang Georg **Obv:** 11-fold arms divide mintmaster's initials, 3 ornate helmets above, date divided among crests of helmets **Obv. Legend:** WOLF. GEORG. CO. IN. STOLB. K. **Rev:** Stag left in circle **Rev. Legend:** WERN. ET. HO: DO. IN. EP. MIN. B. LOR. ET. C. **Note:** Varieties exist.

Date	Mintage	VG	F	VF	XF	Unc
16Z4 CZ	—	—	—	—	—	—
16Z5 CZ	—	—	—	—	—	—
16Z6 CZ	—	—	—	—	—	—

KM# 6 THALER

Silver **Ruler:** Johann **Obv:** Crowned stag in frame **Rev:** Helmeted arms dividing date in helmets **Note:** Dav# 7770.

Date	Mintage	VG	F	VF	XF	Unc
1609 GM	Inc. above	300	525	825	1,350	—
1610 GM	4,478	300	525	825	1,350	—
1611 GM	1,484	300	525	825	1,350	—

KM# 5 THALER

Silver **Ruler:** Johann **Obv:** Crowned stag in frame separating date **Rev:** Helmeted arms **Rev. Legend:** DOM: IN. EPST. MVN:... **Note:** Dav# 7768.

Date	Mintage	VG	F	VF	XF	Unc
1609 GM	1,961	425	750	1,300	—	—

KM# 20 THALER

Silver **Ruler:** Wolfgang Georg **Obv:** Helmeted arms, C-Z in field **Obv. Legend:** WOLF. GEORG. COM IN. STOLBER. KON. **Rev:** Stag left **Rev. Legend:** ... LORA. ET. CLE. **Note:** Dav# 7775.

Date	Mintage	VG	F	VF	XF	Unc
1619 CZ	—	265	450	750	1,300	—

KM# 47 THALER

Silver **Ruler:** Wolfgang Georg **Obv:** Helmeted arms, date divided above and C-Z beside **Rev:** Stag left **Rev. Legend:** LOR: ET. CLE(T). **Note:** Dav# 7776.

Date	Mintage	VG	F	VF	XF	Unc
16Z3 CZ	—	265	450	750	1,300	—

DAV# 7782 THALER

Silver **Ruler:** Wolfgang Georg **Obv:** Large shield **Rev:** Crowned imperial eagle **Note:** Dav# 7782.

Date	Mintage	VG	F	VF	XF	Unc
16Z3	—	1,250	2,250	4,500	7,500	—

KM# 52 THALER

Silver **Ruler:** Wolfgang Georg **Rev:** Flowers and grass under stag left **Rev. Legend:** LO. (R). E. C. **Note:** Legend varieties exist. Dav# 7778.

Date	Mintage	VG	F	VF	XF	Unc
16Z4 CZ	—	100	200	425	650	—
16Z5 CZ	—	100	200	425	650	—
16Z6 CZ	—	100	200	425	650	—

KM# 57 THALER

Silver **Ruler:** Wolfgang Georg **Note:** Klippe. Dav# 7778A.

Date	Mintage	VG	F	VF	XF	Unc
16Z5 CZ Rare	—	—	—	—	—	—

KM# 69 THALER

Silver **Ruler:** Johann Martin I **Note:** Dav# 7784. Similar to 2 Thaler, Dav# 7783.

Date	Mintage	VG	F	VF	XF	Unc
1644 UZ Rare	—	—	—	—	—	—

KM# 72 THALER

Silver **Ruler:** Johann Martin I **Obv:** Stag left against a pillar **Obv. Legend:** IOHAN: MART:... **Rev:** Helmeted arms with date divided in helmets and I-K below **Rev. Legend:** ...MVN: BREV(B): LOR: ET. CLETE. **Note:** Dav# 7786.

Date	Mintage	VG	F	VF	XF	Unc
1645 IK	—	145	275	600	1,200	2,000
1646 IK	—	145	275	600	1,200	2,000
1647 IK	—	145	275	600	1,200	2,000
1649 IK	—	145	275	600	1,200	2,000
1650 IK	—	145	275	600	1,200	2,000
1650 IK	—	145	275	600	1,200	2,000
Note: Error: RON for KON in legend						
1652 IK	—	145	275	600	1,200	2,000
1652/3 IK	—	145	275	600	1,200	2,000
1653 IK	—	145	275	600	1,200	2,000
1654 IK	—	145	275	600	1,200	2,000
Note: Legend varieties exist for 1654 date strikes						
1655 IK	—	145	275	600	1,200	2,000
1660 IK	—	145	275	600	1,200	2,000
1663 IK	—	145	275	600	1,200	2,000

KM# 88 THALER

Silver **Ruler:** Johann Martin I **Rev. Legend:** ... MIN: BR:LOR: ET: KLETTENB:. **Note:** Dav# 7786A.

Date	Mintage	VG	F	VF	XF	Unc
1660 IK	—	150	300	650	1,250	—

KM# 90 THALER

Silver **Ruler:** Johann Martin I **Rev. Legend:** ... PREVP: LOR: ET: KLETTEN. **Note:** Dav# 7786B.

Date	Mintage	VG	F	VF	XF	Unc
1663 IK	—	150	300	650	1,250	—

KM# 100 THALER

Silver **Ruler:** Christof Ludwig I **Obv:** Stag left in front of column, trees at sides **Obv. Legend:** CHRISTOPHORVS LUDOVICVS COMES STOLBERGENSIS **Rev:** Helmeted arms, divided date above, JA-S below **Rev. Legend:** KON: ROCH: WER: & HON: DN: EP: MUNZ: BR: AIR: & CL: **Note:** Dav# 7789.

Date	Mintage	VG	F	VF	XF	Unc
1693 JAS Rare	—	—	—	—	—	—
1695 JAS/IT Rare	—	—	—	—	—	—
Note: With edge inscription						

KM# 102 THALER

Silver **Ruler:** Christof Ludwig I **Obv:** Shield of manifold arms, 3 ornate helmets above, legend in Gothic letters with Roman numeral date **Obv. Legend:** CHRISTOPH LUDWIG GRAF ZU STOLBERG. K. R. W. V. H. H. Z. E. M. B. U. L. U. C. ANNO MDCC. **Rev:** Mining scene, "Jehovah" in Hebrew in cloud above, legend in Gothic letters **Rev. Legend:** GOTT SEEGNE DIE STOLLBERGISCHEN BERGWERKE. DENN AN GOTTES SEEGEN IST ALLES GELEGEN. **Note:** Mining Thaler. Dav# 7791.

Date	Mintage	VG	F	VF	XF	Unc
MDCC (1700) IT	—	400	800	1,450	2,750	—

KM# 8 2 THALER

Silver **Ruler:** Johann **Note:** Dav# 7769. Similar to 1 Thaler, Dav. #7770.

Date	Mintage	VG	F	VF	XF	Unc
1609 GM Rare	—	—	—	—	—	—

KM# 21 2 THALER

Silver **Ruler:** Wolfgang Georg **Obv:** Helmeted arms with date in helmets, C-Z divided by shield **Rev:** Stag left **Rev. Legend:** ... LOR. ET. CL **Note:** Dav# 7773.

Date	Mintage	VG	F	VF	XF	Unc
1619 CZ Rare	—	—	—	—	—	—

KM# 22 2 THALER

Silver **Ruler:** Wolfgang Georg **Obv:** Date in legend **Rev. Legend:** ... LOR. ET. CLE*. **Note:** Dav# 7774.

Date	Mintage	VG	F	VF	XF	Unc
1619 CZ Rare	—	—	—	—	—	—

KM# 53 2 THALER

Silver **Ruler:** Wolfgang Georg **Obv:** Stag left in circle **Rev:** Manifold arms divide mintmaster's initials, 3 ornate helmets above, date divided among crests **Note:** Dav# 7777. Varieties exist.

Date	Mintage	VG	F	VF	XF	Unc
1624 CZ	—	1,150	1,900	3,400	5,600	—
1625 CZ	—	1,150	1,900	3,400	5,600	—

KM# 70 2 THALER

Silver **Ruler:** Johann Martin I **Obv:** Manifold arms, 3 ornate helmets above divide mintmaster's initials, date at end of legend **Obv. Legend:** IOHAN: MARTIN: COMES. AN: **Rev:** Stag left in front of column **Rev. Legend:** IN. STOLBERG. KON: RUT: WERN: ET. HONS: **Note:** Dav# 7783. Varieties exist.

Date	Mintage	VG	F	VF	XF	Unc
1644 UZ Rare	—	—	—	—	—	—

KM# 78 2 THALER

Silver **Ruler:** Johann Martin I **Obv:** Stag left in front of column **Rev:** Helmeted arms with date divided in helmets, I-K below **Note:** Dav# 7785.

Date	Mintage	VG	F	VF	XF	Unc
1646 IK	—	900	1,500	2,500	4,150	—
1649 IK	—	900	1,500	2,500	4,150	—
1652 IK	—	900	1,500	2,500	4,150	—
1653 IK	—	900	1,500	2,500	4,150	—
1654 IK	—	900	1,500	2,500	4,150	—
1655 IK	—	900	1,500	2,500	4,150	—
1660 IK	—	900	1,500	2,500	4,150	—

KM# 103 2 THALER

Silver **Ruler:** Christof Ludwig I **Obv:** Shield of manifold arms, 3 ornate helmets above, legend in Gothic letters with Roman numeral date **Obv. Legend:** CHRISTOPH LUDWIG GRAF ZU STOLBERG. K. R. W. V. H. H. Z. E. M. B. U. L. U. C. ANNO MDCC. **Rev:** Mining scene, "Jehovah" in Hebrew in cloud above, legend in Gothic letters **Rev. Legend:** GOTT SEEGNE DIE STOLLBERGISCHEN BERGWERKE. DENN AN GOTTES SEEGEN IST ALLES GELEGEN. **Note:** Struck from Taler dies, KM# 102. Dav# 7790.

Date	Mintage	VG	F	VF	XF	Unc
1700 IT Rare	—	—	—	—	—	—

JOINT COINAGE

Stolberg-Stolberg / Stolberg-Rossla

DAV# 7765 THALER

Silver **Ruler:** Wolf Ernst, Johann, Heinrich XXII, Ludwig Georg, and Christof II **Obv:** Helmeted arms **Obv. Legend:** WOLF. ER. IOHANN. HENR. LVD. GEORG. E. CHRISTOP*. **Rev:** Stag left with date below

Date	Mintage	VG	F	VF	XF	Unc
1605	—	280	500	850	1,350	—

DAV# 7766 THALER

Silver **Ruler:** Johann, Heinrich XXII, Ludwig Georg, and Christof II **Obv:** Helmeted arms with date divided in helmets **Obv. Legend:** IOHANN. HENR. LVD. GROEG. E. CHRISTOP*. **Rev:** Stag left

Date	Mintage	VG	F	VF	XF	Unc
1606 Rare	—	—	—	—	—	—

DAV# 7767 THALER

Silver **Ruler:** Johann and Heinrich **Obv:** Helmeted arms, date **Obv. Legend:** JOHANNES. ET. HEINRICVS. FRATRES **Rev:** Stag left, tree below

Date	Mintage	VG	F	VF	XF	Unc
1608	—	280	500	850	1,350	—
ND	—	280	500	850	1,350	—

DAV# 7771 THALER

Silver **Ruler:** Heinrich XIII and Wolfgang Georg **Obv:** Helmeted arms, A-L in helmets, date **Obv. Legend:** HENRICVS. ET. WOLG: GEORG: COM. IN. STOLB* **Rev:** Stag left before a pillar **Rev. Legend:** KON. RVT. WERN. HONS. DOM. IN. EP: MVN. B. LO. ET. CLET.

Date	Mintage	VG	F	VF	XF	Unc
1612	—	230	425	700	1,100	—

DAV# 7771A THALER

Silver **Ruler:** Heinrich XIII and Wolfgang Georg **Rev:** Without pillar **Rev. Legend:** ...EPS. MVN. B. LO. ET. C.

Date	Mintage	VG	F	VF	XF	Unc
1612	—	230	425	700	1,100	—

DAV# 7771B THALER

Silver **Ruler:** Heinrich XIII and Wolfgang Georg **Rev. Legend:** HONST. DOM. IN. EP. MVN. B. LO. ET. CL.

Date	Mintage	VG	F	VF	XF	Unc
1612	—	230	425	700	1,100	—

DAV# 7772 THALER

Silver **Ruler:** Heinrich XIII and Wolfgang Georg **Rev:** Stag left **Rev. Legend:** WER. HON. DOM. IN. EP. MVN. B. LO: ET: C.

Date	Mintage	VG	F	VF	XF	Unc
1613	—	230	425	700	1,100	—

DAV# 7772A THALER

Silver **Ruler:** Heinrich XIII and Wolfgang Georg **Rev. Legend:** ...HONS... ET. CLET:.

Date	Mintage	VG	F	VF	XF	Unc
1613	—	230	425	700	1,100	—

DAV# 7779 THALER

Silver **Ruler:** Christof II and Heinrich Volrad **Obv:** Stag left in wreath **Obv. Legend:** CHRITS. E. HENRI. VOLR:. **Rev:** Helmeted arms with date below

Date	Mintage	VG	F	VF	XF	Unc
1622 Rare	—	—	—	—	—	—

DAV# 7780 THALER

Silver **Ruler:** Christof II and Heinrich Volrad **Obv:** Stag with date below **Rev:** Crowned double eagle with orb on breast

Date	Mintage	VG	F	VF	XF	Unc
1623 Rare	—	—	—	—	—	—

DAV# 7781 THALER

Silver **Ruler:** Christof II and Heinrich Volrad **Obv:** Helmeted arms, date divided above, C-Z below **Rev:** Stag left with flowers below

Date	Mintage	VG	F	VF	XF	Unc
163Z	—	650	1,250	2,500	4,000	—

TRADE COINAGE

KM# 15 GOLDGULDEN

3.5000 g., 0.9860 Gold 0.1109 oz. AGW **Ruler:** Johann **Subject:** Death of Johann **Obv:** Stag left in inner circle, titles of Johann **Rev:** 5-line inscription with date **Rev. Inscription:** OBIIT/30. IVLII/ANNO 1612/ÆTATIS:/63. **Note:** Struck from same dies as 1/28 Thaler, KM# 13. Fr# 3318.

Date	Mintage	VG	F	VF	XF	Unc
161Z AL	—	850	1,800	3,600	6,000	—

KM# 24 GOLDGULDEN

3.5000 g., 0.9860 Gold 0.1109 oz. AGW **Ruler:** Wolfgang Georg **Obv:** 11-fold arms, titles of Wolfgang Georg **Rev:** Stag left, date divided among legs, titles continued **Note:** Fr# 3320 variety.

Date	Mintage	VG	F	VF	XF	Unc
1619 CZ	—	475	1,100	2,400	4,000	—

KM# 59 GOLDGULDEN

Gold **Ruler:** Wolfgang Georg **Obv:** 11-fold arms, titles of Wolfgang Georg **Rev:** Stag left, half date between legs, titles continued **Note:** Fr# 3320 variety.

Date	Mintage	VG	F	VF	XF	Unc
(16)Z5 CZ	234	475	1,100	2,400	4,000	—

KM# 61 GOLDGULDEN

Gold **Ruler:** Wolfgang Georg **Obv:** 11-fold arms, titles of Wolfgang Georg **Rev:** Stag left, date divided to left and right of stag, titles continued **Note:** Fr# 3320 variety.

Date	Mintage	VG	F	VF	XF	Unc
16Z6 CZ	3,295	475	1,100	2,400	4,000	—

KM# 82 DUCAT

3.5000 g., 0.9860 Gold 0.1109 oz. AGW **Ruler:** Johann Martin I **Obv:** Stag in front of column **Rev:** Value and date in tablet **Note:** Fr# 3323.

Date	Mintage	VG	F	VF	XF	Unc
1647 IK	—	425	825	1,800	3,000	—
1649/7 IK	—	425	825	1,800	3,000	—

KM# 80 2 DUCAT

7.0000 g., 0.9860 Gold 0.2219 oz. AGW **Ruler:** Johann Martin I **Note:** Fr# 3322.

Date	Mintage	VG	F	VF	XF	Unc
1646 IK	—	750	1,500	3,750	6,000	—
1649 IK	—	750	1,500	3,750	6,000	—

KM# 105 10 DUCAT

35.0000 g., 0.9860 Gold 1.1095 oz. AGW 1.1095 oz. AGW, 45 mm. **Ruler:** Christof Ludwig I **Obv:** Shield of manifold arms, 3 ornate helmets above, legend in Gothic letters with Roman numeral date **Obv. Legend:** CHRISTOPH LUDWIG GRAF ZU STOLBERG. K. R. W. V. H. H. Z. E. M. B. U. L. U. C. ANNO MDCC. **Rev:** Mining scene, "Jehovah" in Hebrew in cloud above, legend in Gothic letters **Rev. Legend:** GOTT SEEGNE DIE STOLLBERGISCHEN BERGWERKE. DENN AN GOTTES SEEGEN IST ALLES GELEGEN. **Note:** Struck from Taler dies, KM# 102.

Date	Mintage	VG	F	VF	XF	Unc
1700 IT Rare	—	—	—	—	—	—

JOINT TRADE COINAGE

Stolberg-Stolberg / Stolberg-Rossla

FR# 3316 GOLDGULDEN

3.5000 g., 0.9860 Gold 0.1109 oz. AGW **Obv:** Stag in inner circle **Rev:** Shield of arms in inner circle

Date	Mintage	VG	F	VF	XF	Unc
1607	—	900	1,800	3,750	6,000	—
1609	—	900	1,800	3,750	6,000	—

FR# 3317 GOLDGULDEN

3.5000 g., 0.9860 Gold 0.1109 oz. AGW **Obv:** Stag in front of column in inner circle

Date	Mintage	VG	F	VF	XF	Unc
1612	—	575	1,150	2,500	4,150	—

FR# 3319 GOLDGULDEN

3.5000 g., 0.9860 Gold 0.1109 oz. AGW **Rev:** Shield of arms in inner circle

Date	Mintage	VG	F	VF	XF	Unc
1613 AL	—	800	1,600	3,600	6,000	—
1614 AL	—	800	1,600	3,600	6,000	—
ND AL	—	800	1,600	3,600	6,000	—

FR# 3321 GOLDGULDEN

3.5000 g., 0.9860 Gold 0.1109 oz. AGW **Note:** Titles of Christof II and H. Volrad.

Date	Mintage	VG	F	VF	XF	Unc
1619	—	925	1,850	3,900	6,200	—

STOLBERG-WERNIGERODE

The castle of Wernigerode is situated across the Harz Mountains to the north of Stolberg castle, some 12 miles (20 km) west-southwest of Halberstadt. An early division of the old Stolberg line in 1538 resulted in a separate line in Wernigerode. A second division in 1572 established Stolberg-Ortenberg and Stolberg-Schwarza (Wernigerode) and the latter was divided further into 1876 divided further into the senior branch of Stolberg-Wernigerode and the junior branch of Stolberg-Stolberg.Once again, Stolberg-Wernigerode was the foundation of three separate lines at Gedern, Schwarza and Wernigerode in 1710. The first two fell extinct within a century, but Stolberg-Wernigerode lasted into the 20th century.

RULERS

Heinrich XXI, 1538-1572
Christof II, 1572-1638
Heinrich Ernst I, 1638-1672
Ernst von Stolberg-Wernigerode-Ilsenburg,1672-1710
and Ludwig Christian, 1672-1710

COUNTSHIP

REGULAR COINAGE

KM# 27 8 GUTE GROSCHEN (1/3 Thaler)

Silver **Ruler:** Heinrich Ernst I **Obv:** 5-line inscription with date and mintmaster's initials **Obv. Legend:** HEINR. ERNST. CO. IN. STOL. KON. RI. **Obv. Inscription:** VIII/GUTE/GROSS./ (date)/ (mintmaster's initials) **Rev:** Stag left in circle **Rev. Legend:** WERN. ET. HO. DOM. IN. EP. MIN. B. LOR. ET. CLET. **Note:** Varieties exisit.

Date	Mintage	VG	F	VF	XF	Unc
1671 IB	—	—	—	—	—	—
1672 IB	—	—	—	—	—	—

KM# 31 1/3 THALER (1/2 Gulden)

Silver **Ruler:** Ernst von Stolberg-Wernigerode-Ilsenburg **Obv:** Manifold arms divide mintmaster's initials, crown above divides date, value 1/3 in oval below **Obv. Legend:** ERNST ET LVDO - VICH CHRISTIA' **Rev:** Stag left in circle **Rev. Legend:** CO. IN. S. KO. R. WER. ET. D. IN. EP. M. B. E. LOR. E. CLE. **Note:** Varieties exist.

Date	Mintage	VG	F	VF	XF	Unc
1672 IB	—	25.00	45.00	85.00	175	—
1673 IB	—	25.00	45.00	85.00	175	—

DAV# 7764 THALER

Silver **Obv:** Legend around stag left **Obv. Legend:** LVD. GE. COM. IN. STOLB... **Rev:** Legend around helmeted arms **Rev. Legend:** D. IN. EPST. MINTZ... **Note:** Dav# 7764.

Date	Mintage	VG	F	VF	XF	Unc
1604 Rare	—	—	—	—	—	—

KM# 15 THALER

Silver **Ruler:** Heinrich Ernst I **Obv:** Stag left in circle **Obv. Legend:** HEINR: ERNST. COM: IN. STOLBERG. KON: RV: WERN: E. HONS. **Rev:** Manifold arms divide mintmaster's initials, 3 ornate helmets above, date divided among crests **Rev. Legend:** DOM: IN. EPS: MVN: BREVB: LOR: ET. KLETTEN:. **Note:** Dav# 7787.

Date	Mintage	VG	F	VF	XF	Unc
1659 HB	—	500	975	1,650	2,700	—

KM# 33 THALER

Silver **Ruler:** Heinrich Ernst I **Subject:** Death of Heinrich Ernst I **Obv:** 8-line inscription with Roman numeral dates, below in two upwardly-curved lines HOC ERGASTULO CONFRACTO / SUBLIMIS VIVO **Obv. Legend:** HEINRICH * ERNST * COMES * IN * STOL * KONIG * RIT * WERNIGE ***. **Rev:** Stag left, mintmaster's initials by legs **Rev. Legend:** ET * HOHEN * DO * IN * EPSTEIN * MIN * BREI * EICH * LOR * ET * CLETT *. **Note:** Dav# 7788.

Date	Mintage	VG	F	VF	XF	Unc
1672 IB	—	1,150	2,250	3,750	—	—

KM# 49 THALER

Silver **Ruler:** Ludwig Christian **Subject:** Count Ernst's First Ten Years of Rule **Obv:** Bust to right, titles of Ernst **Rev:** Ornamented 11-fold arms divide date, 3 ornate helmets above **Rev. Legend:** POTITVS. REGIMEN. ANNO. 1672. Æ. TATIS. XXXII.

Date	Mintage	VG	F	VF	XF	Unc
1682	—	—	—	—	—	—

TRADE COINAGE

KM# 5 GOLDGULDEN

3.5000 g., 0.9860 Gold 0.1109 oz. AGW **Ruler:** Christof II **Obv:** Shield of arms **Rev:** Six-line inscription and date **Note:** Fr# 3353.

Date	Mintage	VG	F	VF	XF	Unc
1617	—	575	1,150	2,550	4,150	—

KM# 19 DUCAT

3.5000 g., 0.9860 Gold 0.1109 oz. AGW **Ruler:** Heinrich Ernst I **Obv:** Stag left **Rev:** Crowned shield of arms **Note:** Fr# 3354.

Date	Mintage	VG	F	VF	XF	Unc
1661 HB	—	525	1,050	2,300	3,900	—

STRALSUND

The town of Stralsund, founded about the year 1200 on the mainland opposite the island of Rügen in the Baltic Sea, obtained the rights of a Germanic city in 1234. Stralsund later joined the Hanseatic League and remained strong enough to maintain its independence from the dukes of Pomerania, who struck coins in that place during the 13th century. In 1325, the city purchased the right to coin its own money from the duke and began a series which continued until 1763. The city fell under the rule of Sweden from 1637 until 1815, then passed to Prussia along with the rest of Swedish Pomerania.

MINT OFFICIALS INITIALS OR MARKS

Initials or Marks	Date	Name
	1606-?	Sebastian Schoras
(a)= [mark] or [mark]	1610-23	Matthias Howe, Sr. and Jr.
(c)= [mark]	1623-28	Asmus Riekhof
(d)= [mark] or HP (sometimes in ligature)	1625-35	Hans Puls
(e)= [mark]	1632	Herman Sander (Zander)
(f)= [mark]	1632	Hans Staude
	1633	Heinrich Kleinkamp
CS	1636-62	Casper Sievers
(b)= [mark] or HIH	1662-1705	Heinrich Johann Hille
DHM	1689-91	David Heinrich Mathäus

ARMS

An arrowhead pointed upwards.

REFERENCES

B = P. Bratring, "Über das Münzwesen der Stadt Stralsund in neueren Zeiten," **Berliner Münzblätter**, N.F. 28 (1907), pp. 509ff.
Sch = Wolfgang Schulten, ***Deutsche Münzen aus der Zeit Karls V.***, Frankfurt am Main, 1974.

CITY

REGULAR COINAGE

KM# 2 PFENNIG

Copper **Obv:** City arms divide date **Note:** Uniface.

Date	Mintage	VG	F	VF	XF	Unc
1607 B#14	—	5.00	10.00	22.00	50.00	—

KM# 18 3 PFENNIG (Dreier)

Copper **Obv:** City arms in circle **Obv. Legend:** MONETA NOV STR(AL). **Rev:** 5-line inscription with date **Rev. Inscription:** III/PFEN./NING./SVND/(date) **Note:** Varieties exist.

Date	Mintage	VG	F	VF	XF	Unc
16ZZ B#37a,b	—	—	—	—	—	—
16Z3 B#42	—	—	—	—	—	—

KM# 20 6 PFENNIG (Sechser)

Copper **Obv:** City arms in circle **Obv. Legend:** MON NO STRAL. S. **Rev:** 5-line inscription with date **Rev. Inscription:** VI/PHEN/NING/SVND/(date)

Date	Mintage	VG	F	VF	XF	Unc
16ZZ B#36a	—	8.00	15.00	30.00	65.00	—

KM# 21 6 PFENNIG (Sechser)

Copper **Obv:** City arms in circle **Obv. Legend:** MON NO STRAL. S. **Rev:** 4-line inscription with date **Rev. Inscription:** VI/PHEN./N. SVND/(date)

Date	Mintage	VG	F	VF	XF	Unc
16ZZ B#36b	—	8.00	15.00	30.00	65.00	—

KM# 77 WITTEN (1/2 Schilling)

Silver **Obv:** Shield of city arms in circle **Obv. Legend:** STADT GELDT. **Rev:** 2-line inscription, date in legend **Rev. Legend:** ANNO (date) **Rev. Inscription:** I/WIT.

Date	Mintage	VG	F	VF	XF	Unc
1633 (f) B#65	—	—	—	—	—	—

KM# 125 WITTEN (1/2 Schilling)

Silver **Obv:** City arms in circle **Obv. Legend:** STRAL. STAT. GELDT. **Rev:** Value, 1/WITT within circle, date at end of legend **Rev. Legend:** GOTT MIT UNS **Note:** Prev. KM#30.

Date	Mintage	VG	F	VF	XF	Unc
1657	—	40.00	80.00	160	325	—
1666	—	33.00	65.00	135	275	—
1671	—	24.00	45.00	90.00	200	—
1682	—	17.00	33.00	65.00	135	—
1682 HIH	—	24.00	45.00	90.00	200	—
1685 HIH	—	24.00	45.00	90.00	200	—
1689 HIH	—	—	—	—	—	—
1691 HIH	—	24.00	45.00	90.00	200	—

KM# 83 WITTEN (1/192 Thaler)

Silver **Obv:** Ornately-shaped shield of city arms in circle **Obv. Legend:** STADT. GELDT **Rev:** Value in 2 lines, I/WIT, date in legend **Rev. Legend:** ANNO. (date) **Note:** Prev. KM#7.

Date	Mintage	VG	F	VF	XF	Unc
1637 (f)	—	—	—	—	—	—
1638	—	55.00	110	200	400	—
1667	—	65.00	135	250	475	—

KM# 113 WITTEN (1/192 Thaler)

Silver **Obv:** City arms in inner circle **Note:** Prev. KM#22.

Date	Mintage	VG	F	VF	XF	Unc
1646	—	40.00	80.00	160	325	—
1647 CS	—	40.00	80.00	160	325	—
1648 CS	—	—	—	—	—	—

KM# 190 WITTEN (1/192 Thaler)

Silver **Obv:** City arms above cross **Rev:** Value **Note:** Prev. KM#58.

Date	Mintage	VG	F	VF	XF	Unc
1692 HIH	—	24.00	45.00	90.00	200	—
1694 HI	—	17.00	33.00	65.00	135	—
1696 HIH	—	17.00	33.00	65.00	135	—
1698 HIH	—	17.00	33.00	65.00	135	—

KM# 23 SCHILLING

Silver **Obv:** City arms in circle **Obv. Legend:** MONE: NO. SVNDENS. **Rev:** Cross in circle, date divided in angles **Rev. Legend:** DEV. IN. NO. TV: SALV.

Date	Mintage	VG	F	VF	XF	Unc
16ZZ (a) B#35	—	—	—	—	—	—

KM# 34 SCHILLING

Silver **Obv:** City arms in circle **Obv. Legend:** MO: NO: STRALSVND. **Rev:** Cross in circle, date divided in angles **Rev. Legend:** DEV. IN. NO. TVO: SALV.

Date	Mintage	VG	F	VF	XF	Unc
16Z3 B#41a	—	—	—	—	—	—

KM# 35 SCHILLING

Silver **Obv:** City arms in circle **Obv. Legend:** MO: NO: STRALSVND. **Rev:** Cross in circle, date divided in angles **Rev. Legend:** OL: IN. NO. TV. SALV. DEVS.

Date	Mintage	VG	F	VF	XF	Unc
16Z3 B#41b	—	—	—	—	—	—
16Z7 B#47	—	—	—	—	—	—

KM# 89 SCHILLING

Silver **Obv:** City arms in circle **Obv. Legend:** MONE. NOVA. STRAL. **Rev:** Cross in circle **Rev. Legend:** EIN. SCHIL. SVND. (date)

Date	Mintage	VG	F	VF	XF	Unc
1638 B#75a	—	15.00	30.00	60.00	120	—

KM# 90 SCHILLING

Silver **Obv:** City arms in circle **Obv. Legend:** MONE. NOVA. STRAL. **Rev:** Cross in circle, date divided in angles **Rev. Legend:** EIN. SCHILLING: SVNDIS.

Date	Mintage	VG	F	VF	XF	Unc
1638 B#75b	—	15.00	30.00	60.00	120	—

KM# 4 GROSCHEN (Kreuzgroschen)

Silver **Obv:** City arms in circle **Obv. Legend:** MONET(A) NO. STRALSVN(D). **Rev:** Cross in circle **Rev. Legend:** IN. NOM. TV. SALVA. NOS. DEV(S). **Note:** Varieties exist; U's are engraved instead of V's on some coins.

Date	Mintage	VG	F	VF	XF	Unc
1610 (a) B#23	—	20.00	35.00	55.00	85.00	—
(1)611 (a) B#25	—	20.00	35.00	55.00	85.00	—
(1)61Z (a) B#26	—	20.00	35.00	55.00	85.00	—
(1)613 (a) B#27	—	20.00	35.00	55.00	85.00	—
(1)614 (a) B#28	—	20.00	35.00	55.00	85.00	—

KM# 16 GROSCHEN (Kreuzgroschen)

Silver **Obv:** City arms divide date in circle **Obv. Legend:** MONE. NO. STRALSUND. **Rev:** Cross in circle **Rev. Legend:** IN. NOM. T. SALU. N. DEUS.

Date	Mintage	VG	F	VF	XF	Unc
1614 (a) B#29	—	25.00	40.00	60.00	100	—

KM# 115 1/96 THALER (Sechsling)

Silver **Rev:** Cross pattee **Note:** Prev. KM#23.

Date	Mintage	VG	F	VF	XF	Unc
1646	—	27.00	55.00	110	220	—
1646 CS	—	27.00	55.00	110	220	—
1647	—	27.00	55.00	110	220	—
1647 CS	—	27.00	55.00	110	220	—

KM# 149 1/96 THALER (Sechsling)

Silver **Obv:** City arms in inner circle **Rev:** Value in inner circle, date in legend **Note:** Prev. KM#45.

Date	Mintage	VG	F	VF	XF	Unc
1674 HIH	—	13.00	27.00	55.00	110	—
1682	—	24.00	45.00	90.00	200	—
1685 HIH	—	17.00	33.00	65.00	135	—

KM# 181 1/96 THALER (Sechsling)

Silver **Obv:** City arms above cross, HIH at top **Note:** Prev. KM#70.

Date	Mintage	VG	F	VF	XF	Unc
1685	—	13.00	27.00	55.00	110	—
1691 HIH	—	13.00	27.00	55.00	110	—
1692 HIH	—	33.00	65.00	135	275	—

KM# 130 1/48 THALER (Schilling or 1/2 Groschen)

Silver **Obv:** City arms in ornamented shield **Obv. Legend:** MONETA. NOVA. STRALSVNDENSIS. **Rev:** Imperial orb with 48 in circle divides date near top. **Rev. Legend:** STRAL SVNDISCHE. STAT. GELT.

Date	Mintage	VG	F	VF	XF	Unc
1662 HIH(b) B#111	—	—	—	—	—	—

KM# 142 1/48 THALER (Schilling or 1/2 Groschen)

Silver **Obv:** City arms in oval shield **Rev:** Value, date in legend in circle **Rev. Legend:** 48 EINEN **Note:** Prev. KM#36.

Date	Mintage	VG	F	VF	XF	Unc
1663 HIH	—	13.00	27.00	55.00	110	—
1663 HIH(b)	—	13.00	27.00	55.00	110	—

KM# 143 1/48 THALER (Schilling or 1/2 Groschen)

Silver **Rev:** Date below value in circle **Note:** Prev. KM#37.

Date	Mintage	VG	F	VF	XF	Unc
1663 HIH(b)	—	13.00	27.00	55.00	110	—

KM# 145 1/48 THALER (Schilling or 1/2 Groschen)

Silver **Obv:** City arms in curved shield **Rev:** 48 in orb, date above in inner circle **Note:** Prev. KM#42.

Date	Mintage	VG	F	VF	XF	Unc
1666 HIH(b)	—	17.00	33.00	65.00	135	—

KM# 151 1/48 THALER (Schilling or 1/2 Groschen)

Silver **Obv:** City arms above cross in inner circle **Rev:** Value, date in legend **Rev. Legend:** 48 REICHS **Note:** Prev. KM#46.

Date	Mintage	VG	F	VF	XF	Unc
1674 HIH	—	17.00	33.00	65.00	135	—
1677 HIH	—	13.00	27.00	55.00	110	—
1678 HIH Rare	—	—	—	—	—	—
1681 HIH	—	13.00	27.00	55.00	110	—
1683 HIH	—	13.00	27.00	55.00	110	—
1684 HIH	—	20.00	40.00	80.00	160	—
1685 HIH	—	20.00	40.00	80.00	160	—
1686 HIH	—	20.00	40.00	80.00	160	—
1689 HIH Rare	—	—	—	—	—	—
1691 HIH	—	13.00	27.00	55.00	110	—
1692 HIH	—	20.00	35.00	110	220	—

KM# 171 1/48 THALER (Schilling or 1/2 Groschen)

Silver **Obv:** Legend starts at bottom **Note:** Prev. KM#62.

Date	Mintage	VG	F	VF	XF	Unc
1683 HIH	—	20.00	40.00	80.00	160	—

KM# 132 1/24 THALER (Groschen)

Silver **Obv:** City arms and date in shield **Rev:** Crowned imperial eagle, 24 in circle on breast **Note:** Prev. KM#38.

Date	Mintage	VG	F	VF	XF	Unc
1662 HIH	—	17.00	33.00	65.00	135	—
1662 HIH(b)	—	20.00	40.00	80.00	160	—
1663 HIH(b)	—	—	—	—	—	—
1666 HIH(b)	—	20.00	40.00	80.00	160	—
1667 (b)	—	17.00	33.00	65.00	135	—
1667 HIH	—	17.00	33.00	65.00	135	—
1668	—	—	—	—	—	—

KM# 153 1/24 THALER (Groschen)

Silver **Obv:** City arms above cross in inner circle **Rev:** Value, date in legend **Rev. Legend:** 24 REICHS **Note:** Prev. KM#47.

Date	Mintage	VG	F	VF	XF	Unc
1674 HIH	—	17.00	33.00	65.00	135	—
1677 HIH	—	27.00	55.00	110	220	—
1684 HIH	—	33.00	65.00	135	275	—
1686/4 HIH	—	17.00	33.00	65.00	135	—

KM# 154 1/24 THALER (Groschen)

Silver **Rev:** Legend begins at bottom **Note:** Prev. KM#48.

Date	Mintage	VG	F	VF	XF	Unc
1674 HIH	—	27.00	55.00	110	220	—

KM# 186 1/24 THALER (Groschen)

Silver **Rev:** Value, date in legend at top **Rev. Legend:** 24 EINEN **Note:** Prev. KM#74.

Date	Mintage	VG	F	VF	XF	Unc
1688 HIH	—	17.00	33.00	65.00	135	—
1689 HIH	—	17.00	33.00	65.00	135	—
1691 HIH	—	20.00	40.00	80.00	160	—

KM# 188 1/24 THALER (Groschen)

Silver **Obv:** City arms above cross in round shield **Note:** Prev. KM#75.

Date	Mintage	VG	F	VF	XF	Unc
1691 DHM	—	20.00	40.00	80.00	160	—

KM# 38 1/16 THALER (Düttchen)

Silver **Obv:** City arms above cross in circle **Obv. Legend:** DER. STAD. STRALSVND. GELT. **Rev:** 4-line inscription with date **Rev. Legend:** REICHS. SCHROT. VND KORN. **Rev. Inscription:** 16/REICHS/TALER/(date) **Note:** Klippe.

Date	Mintage	VG	F	VF	XF	Unc
16Z3 (c) B#40a	—	—	—	—	—	—

KM# 37 1/16 THALER (Düttchen)

Silver **Obv:** City arms above cross in circle **Obv. Legend:** DER. STAD. STRALSVND. GELD. **Rev:** 4-line inscription with date **Rev. Legend:** REICHS. SCHROT. VND KORN. **Rev. Inscription:** 16/REICHS/TALER/(date)

Date	Mintage	VG	F	VF	XF	Unc
16Z3 (c) B#40	—	12.00	30.00	45.00	80.00	—
16Z6 (c) B#45	—	12.00	30.00	45.00	80.00	—
16Z7 (c) B#46	—	12.00	30.00	45.00	80.00	—

KM# 46 1/16 THALER (Düttchen)

Silver **Obv:** City arms above cross in circle **Obv. Legend:** DER. STAD. STRALSVND. GELT. **Rev:** 4-line inscription with date **Rev. Legend:** REICHS. SCHROT. VND KORN. **Rev. Inscription:** 16/REICHS/TALER/(date) **Note:** Varieties exist.

Date	Mintage	VG	F	VF	XF	Unc
16Z4 (c) B#43	—	—	—	—	—	—
16Z5 (c) B#44	—	—	—	—	—	—
16Z7 (c) B#46	—	—	—	—	—	—
16Z8 (d) B#51a	—	—	—	—	—	—
1630 (d) B#57	—	—	—	—	—	—
1631 (d) B#59	—	—	—	—	—	—
163Z (d) B#63	—	—	—	—	—	—

KM# 48 1/16 THALER (Düttchen)

Silver **Obv:** City armes above cross in circle **Obv. Legend:** DER. STAD. STRALSVND. (GE). **Rev:** 4-line inscription with date **Rev. Legend:** REICHS. SCHROT. VND KORN. **Rev. Inscription:** 16/REICHS/TALER/(date)

Date	Mintage	VG	F	VF	XF	Unc
16Z8 (d) B#51b	—	—	—	—	—	—
16Z9 (d) B#55	—	—	—	—	—	—

KM# 67 1/16 THALER (Düttchen)

Silver **Obv:** City arms divide date in circle **Obv. Legend:** D. STADT. STRALSVND GELT. **Rev:** 4-line inscription with mintmaster's symbol **Rev. Legend:** REICHS. SCHROT. VND. KORN. **Rev. Inscription:** 16/REICHS/TALER/(mintmaster's symbol)

Date	Mintage	VG	F	VF	XF	Unc
1632 (e)	—	—	—	—	—	—

KM# 117 1/16 THALER (Düttchen)

Silver **Obv:** City arms in oval shield **Rev:** Value in inner circle, date in legend **Note:** Prev. KM#24.

Date	Mintage	VG	F	VF	XF	Unc
1646 CS	—	27.00	55.00	110	220	—

KM# 118 1/16 THALER (Düttchen)

Silver **Obv:** City arms in baroque frame **Obv. Legend:** MONE(TA). NO. CIVIT. STRAL(LS)SVND. **Rev:** 5-line inscription with mintmaster's initials **Rev. Legend:** REICHS. DALER. SILBER. **Rev. Inscription:** XVI. / EINEN / REICHS / DALER / CS **Note:** Prev. KM#25.

Date	Mintage	VG	F	VF	XF	Unc
1646 CS	—	20.00	40.00	80.00	160	—
1647 CS	—	17.00	33.00	65.00	135	—
(1)647 CS	—	20.00	40.00	80.00	160	—
1648 CS	—	27.00	55.00	110	220	—
1658 CS	—	20.00	40.00	80.00	160	—
1659 CS	—	20.00	40.00	80.00	160	—
1660 CS	—	20.00	40.00	80.00	160	—

KM# 128 1/16 THALER (Düttchen)

Silver **Rev:** Value divides CS **Note:** Prev. KM#33.

Date	Mintage	VG	F	VF	XF	Unc
1659 CS	—	33.00	65.00	135	275	—

KM# 25 1/8 THALER (1/2 Reichsort)

Silver **Obv:** City arms above cross in circle **Obv. Legend:** MONETA. NOVA. STRALSV. **Rev:** 5-line inscription with date, top line flanked by two 6-pointed stars **Rev. Inscription:** 1/8 /HALB./REICHS/ORTH/(date)

Date	Mintage	VG	F	VF	XF	Unc
16ZZ (a) B#34	—	—	—	—	—	—

KM# 92 1/8 THALER (4 Schilling)
Silver **Obv:** Round shield of city arms **Rev:** Crowned imperial eagle, 4 in orb on breast **Note:** Prev. KM#10.

Date	Mintage	VG	F	VF	XF	Unc
1638 CS Unique	—	—	—	—	—	—

KM# 27 1/4 THALER (8 Schilling)
Silver, 29 mm. **Obv:** City arms above cross divide date, all in circle **Obv. Legend:** MONETA. NOVA. STRAL. SVNDE. **Rev:** Crowned imperial eagle, 8 in orb on breast **Rev. Legend:** FERDINAN. II. D:G. RO: IM. SE. AVG.

Date	Mintage	VG	F	VF	XF	Unc
16ZZ (a) B#33	—	—	—	—	—	—

KM# 94 1/4 THALER (8 Schilling)
Silver **Obv:** Round shield of city arms **Rev:** Crowned imperial eagle, 8 in orb on breast **Note:** Prev. KM#11.

Date	Mintage	VG	F	VF	XF	Unc
1638 CS/(d) Rare	—	—	—	—	—	—
1639 CS Rare	—	—	—	—	—	—
1640 CS Rare	—	—	—	—	—	—

KM# 155 1/3 THALER (1/2 Gulden)
Silver **Rev:** Cross with triangular tips **Note:** Prev. KM#49.

Date	Mintage	VG	F	VF	XF	Unc
1677 HIH	—	40.00	80.00	160	320	—

KM# 156 1/3 THALER (1/2 Gulden)
Silver **Rev:** Cross Moline **Note:** Prev. KM#50.

Date	Mintage	VG	F	VF	XF	Unc
1677 HIH	—	55.00	110	220	425	—

KM# 173 1/3 THALER (1/2 Gulden)
Silver **Rev:** Greek cross **Note:** Prev. KM#63.

Date	Mintage	VG	F	VF	XF	Unc
1683 HIH	—	65.00	135	275	525	—

KM# 174 1/3 THALER (1/2 Gulden)
Silver **Rev:** Greek cross with trefoils **Note:** Prev. KM#64.

Date	Mintage	VG	F	VF	XF	Unc
1683 HIH	—	80.00	160	325	650	—

KM# 6 1/2 THALER (16 Schilling)
Silver **Obv:** City arms over cross divides date, all in circle **Obv. Legend:** MONETA NOVA. STRALSVNDENSIS. **Rev:** Crowned imperial eagle, 16 in orb on breast **Rev. Legend:** RVDOLPHV. II. D:G. ROMA. IMPE. SE. AVGVS.

Date	Mintage	VG	F	VF	XF	Unc
1610 (a) B#22	—	—	—	—	—	—

KM# 29 1/2 THALER (16 Schilling)
Silver, 34-35 mm. **Obv:** City arms over cross divides date, all in circle **Obv. Legend:** MONETA NOVA. STRALSVNDENSIS. **Rev:** Crowned imperial eagle, 16 in orb on breast **Rev. Legend:** FERDINAN(DVS). II. D:G. RO: IM(P). S(EM). A(VGVS). **Note:** Varieties exist.

Date	Mintage	VG	F	VF	XF	Unc
16ZZ (a) B#32	—	450	800	1,275	1,750	—
16Z3 (c) B#39	—	450	800	1,275	1,750	—
16Z8 (d) B#50	—	450	800	1,275	1,750	—
16Z9/8 (d) B#54	—	450	800	1,275	1,750	—

KM# 85 1/2 THALER (16 Schilling)
Silver **Obv:** City arms in oval frame ornamented with angels facing outwards, all in circle **Obv. Legend:** MONETA. NOVA. CIVITATIS: STRALSVNDENSIS. **Rev:** Crowned imperial eagle, 16 in orb on breast, date at end of legend **Rev. Legend:** FERDINANDUS. II. D:G: ROMA: IMP: SE: AU:

Date	Mintage	VG	F	VF	XF	Unc
1637 CS B#69a	—	—	—	—	—	—

KM# 96 1/2 THALER (16 Schilling)
Silver **Obv:** City arms in oval frame ornamented with angels facing outwards, all in circle **Obv. Legend:** MONETA. NOVA. CIVITATIS: STRALSVNDENSIS. **Rev:** Crowned imperial eagle, 16 in orb on breast, date at end of legend **Rev. Legend:** FERDINANDUS. III. D:G. ROM: IMP: SE. AU.

Date	Mintage	VG	F	VF	XF	Unc
1638 CS B#73	—	—	—	—	—	—

KM# 103 1/2 THALER (16 Schilling)
Silver **Obv:** Oval shield of city arms **Rev:** Crowned imperial eagle, 16 in orb on breast **Note:** Prev. KM#16.

Date	Mintage	VG	F	VF	XF	Unc
1640 CS Rare	—	—	—	—	—	—
164Z CS Rare	—	—	—	—	—	—

KM# 158 2/3 THALER (1 Gulden)
Silver **Obv:** City arms, above value in inner circle, date in legend **Rev:** Cross with triangular tips **Note:** Prev. KM#51.

Date	Mintage	VG	F	VF	XF	Unc
1677 HIH	—	45.00	90.00	200	375	—

KM# 159 2/3 THALER (1 Gulden)
Silver **Rev:** Narrow cross molien with trefoils **Note:** Prev. KM#52.

Date	Mintage	VG	F	VF	XF	Unc
1677 HIH	—	55.00	110	220	425	—
1678 HIH	—	65.00	135	275	525	—
1679 HIH	—	100	200	400	800	—
1680 HIH	—	55.00	110	220	425	—

KM# 160 2/3 THALER (1 Gulden)
Silver **Rev:** Wide cross moline **Note:** Prev. KM#53.

Date	Mintage	VG	F	VF	XF	Unc
1677 HIH	—	55.00	110	220	425	—
1680 HIH	—	55.00	110	220	425	—

KM# 164 2/3 THALER (1 Gulden)
Silver **Rev:** Greek cross **Note:** Prev. KM#55.

Date	Mintage	VG	F	VF	XF	Unc
1680 HIH	—	40.00	80.00	160	300	—
1683 HIH	—	35.00	70.00	140	280	—
1688 HIH	—	50.00	100	200	400	—

KM# 166 2/3 THALER (1 Gulden)
Silver **Rev:** Greek cross, date **Note:** Prev. KM#60.

Date	Mintage	VG	F	VF	XF	Unc
1681 HIH	—	50.00	100	200	400	—
1683 HIH	—	35.00	70.00	140	280	—

KM# 167 2/3 THALER (1 Gulden)
Silver **Rev:** HIH below cross in inner circle, date **Note:** Prev. KM#61.

Date	Mintage	VG	F	VF	XF	Unc
1681 HIH	—	50.00	100	200	400	—
1683 HIH	—	35.00	70.00	140	280	—

KM# 176 2/3 THALER (1 Gulden)
Silver **Rev:** HIH below cross in inner circle **Note:** Prev. KM#65.

Date	Mintage	VG	F	VF	XF	Unc
1683 HIH	—	35.00	70.00	140	280	—

KM# 177 2/3 THALER (1 Gulden)
Silver **Rev:** HIH in oval cartouche below cross in legend **Note:** Prev. KM#66.

Date	Mintage	VG	F	VF	XF	Unc
1683 HIH	—	35.00	70.00	140	280	—

KM# 178 2/3 THALER (1 Gulden)
Silver **Rev:** Greek cross with trefoils, date in legend **Note:** Prev. KM#67.

Date	Mintage	VG	F	VF	XF	Unc
1683 HIH	—	35.00	70.00	140	280	—

KM# 179 2/3 THALER (1 Gulden)

Silver **Obv:** Date added **Rev:** Date removed **Note:** Prev. KM#68.

Date	Mintage	VG	F	VF	XF	Unc
1683 HIH	—	35.00	70.00	140	280	—

KM# 183 2/3 THALER (1 Gulden)

Silver **Obv:** City arms, value within palm branches, date in legend **Rev:** Greek cross **Note:** Prev. KM#72.

Date	Mintage	VG	F	VF	XF	Unc
1687 HIH	—	45.00	90.00	180	360	—
1688 HIH	—	50.00	100	200	400	—

KM# 184 2/3 THALER (1 Gulden)

Silver **Rev:** HIH in oval cartouche below cross in legend **Note:** Prev. KM#73.

Date	Mintage	VG	F	VF	XF	Unc
1687 HIH	—	45.00	90.00	180	360	—

KM# 12 THALER

Silver **Obv:** Ornate shield of city arms in circle, date in outer legend **Rev:** Large cross in cartouche within circle **Note:** Dav. #LS493.

Date	Mintage	VG	F	VF	XF	Unc
1611 (a) Rare	—	—	—	—	—	—

KM# 52 THALER

Silver **Obv:** City arms in wreath **Obv. Legend:** +DEO. OPTIM. MAXIM. IMPEER. ROMANO. FOEDERI. POSTERISQ. **Rev:** 14-line inscription with Roman numeral date **Note:** Under Siege by Wallenstein. Dav. #LS496.

Date	Mintage	VG	F	VF	XF	Unc
MDCXXVIII(1628) Rare	—	—	—	—	—	—

KM# 53 THALER

Silver **Obv:** City arms in wreath **Obv. Legend:** DEO. OPTIM. MAXIM. IMPEER. ROMANO. FOEDERI. POSTERISQ. **Rev:** 14-line inscription with Roman numeral date **Note:** Under Siege by Wallenstein. Dav. #LS500.

Date	Mintage	VG	F	VF	XF	Unc
MDCXXVIII(1628) Rare	—	—	—	—	—	—

KM# 50 THALER

Silver **Obv:** City arms in laurel wreath **Obv. Legend:** DEO. OPTIMI. MAXIM. IMPER. ROMANO. FOEDERI. POSTERISQ. **Rev:** 12-line inscription with Roman numeral date **Rev. Inscription:** MEMORIÆ/URBIS. STRALSUN:/DAE. AN. MDCXXVIII./DIE. XII. MAY. A: MILITE/CÆSARIA: NO. CINCTÆ. ALI/QVOTIES. OPPUGNATÆ./SED. DEI. GRATIA. ET. OPE./INCLYTOR. REGUM. SE/PTENTRIONAL. DIE/XXIII. IULI: OBSIDIO/NE. LIBERATÆ./S: P: Q: S: P: P: **Note:** Dav. #5823.

Date	Mintage	VG	F	VF	XF	Unc
MDCXXVIII(1628)	—	1,250	2,000	3,250	5,000	—

KM# 8 THALER (32 Schilling)

Silver **Obv:** Arrow above cross dividing date **Obv. Legend:** MONETA. NOVA. STRALSVNDENSIS. **Rev:** Crowned imperial eagle with 3Z in orb on breast **Rev. Legend:** RVDOLPHVS. II. D.G. RO. IMP. SEMP. AUGUS. **Note:** Dav. #5816.

Date	Mintage	VG	F	VF	XF	Unc
1610 (a)	—	1,500	2,500	4,400	—	—

KM# 11 THALER (32 Schilling)

Silver **Obv:** Ornament and star above in legend **Obv. Legend:** ...IMP. SEM. AVGVS **Rev:** Different eagle **Note:** Dav. #5817.

Date	Mintage	VG	F	VF	XF	Unc
1611 (a)	—	625	1,150	2,050	—	—

KM# 31 THALER (32 Schilling)

Silver **Obv:** Cross below city arms divides date **Obv. Legend:** MONETA. NOVA. STRALSVNDENSIS. **Rev:** Crowned imperial eagle, 3Z in orb on breast **Rev. Legend:** FERDINANDVS. II. D: G. RO: IMP. SEMP. AVGVS. **Note:** Dav. #5818.

Date	Mintage	VG	F	VF	XF	Unc
16ZZ (a)	—	400	800	1,550	—	—

KM# 32 THALER (32 Schilling)

Silver **Rev:** Without cross on orb **Note:** Dav. #5819.

Date	Mintage	VG	F	VF	XF	Unc
1622 (a)	—	500	950	1,850	—	—

KM# 40 THALER (32 Schilling)

Silver **Obv:** City arms divide date above cross **Obv. Legend:** MONETA. NOVA. STRALSVNDENSIS. **Rev:** Crowned imperial eagle, 3Z in orb on breast **Rev. Legend:** FERDINANDVS. II. D.G. ROM. IMP. SEM. AVG. **Note:** Dav. #5820.

Date	Mintage	VG	F	VF	XF	Unc
16Z3 (c)	—	350	750	1,500	2,750	—

KM# 41 THALER (32 Schilling)

Silver **Obv:** City arms divide date over cross **Obv. Legend:** MONETA. NOVA. STRALSVNDENSIS. **Rev:** Crowned imperial eagle, 3Z in orb on breast **Rev. Legend:** FERDINANDVS. II. D.G. ROM. IMP. SEM. AVG. **Note:** Dav. #5821.

Date	Mintage	VG	F	VF	XF	Unc
1623 (c)	—	350	750	1,500	2,750	—

KM# 42 THALER (32 Schilling)

Silver **Obv:** City arms divide date over cross **Obv. Legend:** MONETA. NOVA. STRALSVNDENSIS. **Rev:** Crowned imperial eagle, 3Z in orb on breast **Rev. Legend:** FERDINANDVS. II. D.G. ROM. IMP. SEM. AVG. **Note:** Klippe. Dav. #5821A.

Date	Mintage	VG	F	VF	XF	Unc
16Z3 (c) Rare	—	—	—	—	—	—

Note: Fritz Rudolf Künker Münzenhandlung Auction 141, 6-08, VF-XF realized approximately $17,040

KM# 51 THALER (32 Schilling)

Silver **Obv:** City arms above cross **Obv. Legend:** MONETA. NOVA. STRALSVNDENSIS. **Rev:** Crowned imperial eagle, 3Z in orb on breast, date divided by tail **Rev. Legend:** FERDINANDVS. II. D. G. ROM. IMP. SEM. A. **Note:** Dav. #5824.

Date	Mintage	VG	F	VF	XF	Unc
16Z8 (c)	—	550	1,000	1,800	3,000	—
16Z9 (d)	—	550	1,000	1,800	3,000	—
1630 (d)	—	550	1,000	1,800	3,000	—

KM# A51 THALER (32 Schilling)

Silver **Obv:** City arms above cross in circle **Obv. Legend:** MONETA. NOVA. STRALSVNDENSIS. **Rev:** Crowned imperial eagle divides date, 3Z in orb on breast **Rev. Legend:** FERDINANDVS. II. DG. ROM. IMP: SEM: AVG. **Note:** Dav. #5824A.

Date	Mintage	VG	F	VF	XF	Unc
16Z8 (c)	—	550	1,000	1,800	3,000	—

KM# 65 THALER (32 Schilling)

Silver **Obv:** City arms above cross **Obv. Legend:** MONETA. NOVA. STRALSVNDENSIS. **Rev:** Crowned imperial eagle, 3Z in orb on breast **Rev. Legend:** FERDINANDVS. II. D.G. ROM. IMP. SEM. AVG. **Note:** Dav. #5825.

Date	Mintage	VG	F	VF	XF	Unc
ND(1630) (d)	—	1,500	2,500	5,000	—	—

KM# 69 THALER (32 Schilling)

Silver **Obv:** Small oval shield of city arms in baroque frame, head and wings of angel above, date below **Obv. Legend:** MONETA. NOVA. CIVITA. STRALSVNDEN. **Rev:** Crowned imperial eagle, 32 in orb on breast **Rev. Legend:** FERDINAND. II. D.G. ROM. IMPER. S. AVG. **Note:** Dav. #5826.

Date	Mintage	VG	F	VF	XF	Unc
1632 (e)	—	1,200	2,250	4,250	—	—

KM# 70 THALER (32 Schilling)

Silver **Obv:** Oval city arms in baroque frame, date divided below **Obv. Legend:** MONETA. NOVA. CIVITA. STRALSVNDEN. **Rev:** Crowned imperial eagle, 32 in orb on breast **Rev. Legend:** FERDINAND. II. D.G. ROM. IMPER. S. AVG. **Note:** Dav. #5827.

Date	Mintage	VG	F	VF	XF	Unc
1632 (e)	—	1,000	2,000	4,000	6,500	—

KM# 71 THALER (32 Schilling)

Silver **Obv:** Oval city arms in baroque frame, date divided below **Obv. Legend:** MONETA. NOVA. CIVITA. STRALSVNDEN. **Rev:** Crowned imperial eagle, 32 in orb on breast **Rev. Legend:** FERDINAND. II. D.G. ROM. IMPER. S. AVG. **Note:** Klippe. Dav. #5827A.

Date	Mintage	VG	F	VF	XF	Unc
1632 (e) Rare	—	—	—	—	—	—

KM# 79 THALER (32 Schilling)

Silver **Obv:** Large oval shield of city arms in baroque frame, small angels at upper left and right, date at end of legend **Obv. Legend:** MONET. NOVA. CIVITAT. STRALSUNDENSIS. **Rev:** Crowned imperial eagle, 32 in orb on breast **Rev. Legend:** FERDINANDUS. II. D.G. ROMA. IMP. SE. AUG. **Note:** Dav. #5828.

Date	Mintage	VG	F	VF	XF	Unc
1633 (f)	—	1,250	2,050	3,150	—	—

KM# 81 THALER (32 Schilling)

Silver **Obv:** Oval shield of city arms in baroque frame, small angels at upper left and right, date at end of legend **Obv. Legend:** MONETA. NOVA. CIVITAT. STRALSVNDENSIS. **Rev:** Crowned imperial eagle, 32 in orb on breast **Rev. Legend:** FERDINANDUS. II. D.G. ROM. IMP. S. AU. **Note:** Dav. #5829.

Date	Mintage	VG	F	VF	XF	Unc
1635 (d)	—	1,000	1,650	2,500	—	—

KM# 87 THALER (32 Schilling)

Silver **Obv:** Oval shield of city arms in baroque frame, small angel supports at left and right, date at end of legend **Obv. Legend:** MON. NOVA. CIVITA. STRALSUNDENSIS. **Rev:** Crowned imperial eagle, 3Z in orb on breast **Rev. Legend:** FERDINANDUS. II. D.G. ROMA. IM. SE. AU. **Note:** Dav. #5830.

Date	Mintage	VG	F	VF	XF	Unc
1637 CS	—	450	900	1,500	—	—

KM# 98 THALER (32 Schilling)

Silver **Obv:** Oval shield of city arms in baroque frame, date at end of legend **Obv. Legend:** MON. NOVA. CIVITA. STRALSVNDEN. **Rev:** Small crown above imperial eagle, 3Z in orb on breast **Rev. Legend:** FERDINANDUS. III. D.G. ROM. IM. SE. AU. **Note:** Prev. KM#13.1. Dav. #5831.

Date	Mintage	VG	F	VF	XF	Unc
1638 CS	—	500	1,000	2,000	3,250	—

KM# 100 THALER (32 Schilling)

Silver **Obv:** Oval city arms in baroque frame supported by ornate angels, date at end of legend **Obv. Legend:** MON. NOVA. CIVIT. STRALSUNDENSIS. **Rev:** Crowned imperial eagle, 3Z in orb on breast **Rev. Legend:** FERDINANDUS. III. D.G. ROMA. IM. SE. A. **Note:** Prev. KM#13.3. Dav. #5831B.

Date	Mintage	VG	F	VF	XF	Unc
1638 CS	—	400	800	1,500	2,500	—
1639 CS	—	400	800	1,500	2,500	—

KM# 99 THALER (32 Schilling)

Silver **Rev:** Large crown above imperial eagle **Note:** Prev. KM#13.2. Dav. #5831A.

Date	Mintage	VG	F	VF	XF	Unc
1638 CS	—	375	750	1,600	2,700	—

KM# 106 THALER (32 Schilling)

Silver **Obv:** Oval shield of city arms in baroque frame, date at end of legend **Obv. Legend:** MON. NOVA. CIVIT. STRAL-SVNDENSIS. **Rev:** Crowned imperial eagle, 32 in orb on breast **Rev. Legend:** FERDINANDUS. III. D.G. ROMANO. IMP. S. A. **Note:** Prev. KM#15. Dav. #5835.

Date	Mintage	VG	F	VF	XF	Unc
1640 CS	—	250	500	1,000	2,000	—
1642 CS	—	500	900	1,750	3,500	—
1644 CS Rare	—	—	—	—	—	—
1645 CS Rare	—	—	—	—	—	—
1646 CS	—	500	900	1,750	3,500	—
1648 CS Rare	—	—	—	—	—	—
1649	—	950	1,800	3,500	6,000	—
1652 CS Rare	—	—	—	—	—	—
1655 CS Rare	—	—	—	—	—	—
1657 CS Rare	—	—	—	—	—	—

KM# 104 THALER (32 Schilling)

Silver **Obv:** City arms within 3 legends, CS in inner circle **Rev:** Crowned imperial eagle, 3Z in orb on breast **Note:** Prev. KM#17. Dav. #5832.

Date	Mintage	VG	F	VF	XF	Unc
1640 CS	—	425	850	1,650	2,750	—

KM# 105 THALER (32 Schilling)

Silver **Obv:** City arms within 3 legends, CS in outer legend **Rev:** Crown above double-headed imperial eagle, value in orb on breast **Note:** Prev. KM#18. Dav. #5833.

Date	Mintage	VG	F	VF	XF	Unc
1640 CS	—	425	850	1,650	2,750	—

KM# 134 THALER (32 Schilling)

Silver **Obv:** City arms in baroque frame, date at end of legend **Obv. Legend:** MONETA. NOVA. CIVITATIS. STRALSVNDEN. **Rev:** Crowned imperial eagle, 32 in orb on breast **Rev. Legend:** LEOPOLDVS. D.G. ROMANORVM. IMPE. SEM. A. **Note:** Dav. #5836. Prev. KM#35.

Date	Mintage	VG	F	VF	XF	Unc
1662 HIH	—	850	1,650	3,250	5,500	—

KM# 13 1-1/2 THALER

Silver **Obv:** Ornate shield of city arms in circle, date in outer legend **Rev:** Large cross in cartouche within circle **Note:** Dav. #LS492. Illustration reduced.

Date	Mintage	VG	F	VF	XF	Unc
1611 (a)	—	2,500	4,150	6,400	—	—

KM# 44 1-1/2 THALER

Silver **Obv:** City arms divide date over cross **Obv. Legend:** MONETA. NOVA. STRALSVNDENSIS. **Rev:** Crowned imperial eagle, 3Z in orb on breast **Rev. Legend:** FERDINANDVS. II. D.G. ROM. IMP. SEM. AVG. **Note:** Klippe. Dav. #5821B. Struck from Thaler dies, KM#41.

Date	Mintage	VG	F	VF	XF	Unc
1623 Rare	—	—	—	—	—	—

KM# 54 1-1/2 THALER

Silver **Obv:** City arms in wreath **Obv. Legend:** +DEO. OPTIM. MAXIM. IMPEER. ROMANO. FOEDERI. POSTERISQ. **Rev:** 14-line inscription with Roman numeral date **Note:** Under Siege by Wallenstein. Dav. #LS495.

Date	Mintage	VG	F	VF	XF	Unc
MDCXXVIII (1628)	—	1,150	1,900	3,000	—	—

KM# 55 1-1/2 THALER

Silver **Obv:** City arms in wreath **Obv. Legend:** DEO. OPTIM. MAXIM. IMPEER. ROMANO. FOEDERI. POSTERISQ. **Rev:** 14-line inscription with Roman numeral date **Note:** Under Siege by Wallenstein. Dav. #LS499.

Date	Mintage	VG	F	VF	XF	Unc
MDCXXVIII (1628) Rare	—	—	—	—	—	—

KM# 73 1-1/2 THALER

Silver **Obv:** Oval city arms in baroque frame, date divided below **Obv. Legend:** MONETA. NOVA. CIVITA. STRALSVNDEN. **Rev:** Crowned imperial eagle, 32 in orb on breast **Rev. Legend:** FERDINAND. II. D.G. ROM. IMPER. S. AVG. **Note:** Struck from Thaler dies, KM#70. Dav. #5827B.

Date	Mintage	VG	F	VF	XF	Unc
1632 (e) Rare	—	—	—	—	—	—

KM# 9 2 THALER

Silver **Note:** Prev. Dav. #5815.

Date	Mintage	VG	F	VF	XF	Unc
1610 (a) Rare	—	—	—	—	—	—

Note: Frankfurter Munzhandlung E. Button #124 3-77 VF realized $9,200

KM# 14 2 THALER

Silver **Obv:** Ornate shield of city arms in circle, date in outer legend **Rev:** Large cross in cartouche within circle **Note:** Dav. #LS491.

Date	Mintage	VG	F	VF	XF	Unc
1611 (a) Rare	—	—	—	—	—	—

KM# 57 2 THALER

Silver **Obv:** City arms in wreath **Obv. Legend:** +DEO. OPTIM. MAXIM. IMPEER. ROMANO. FOEDERI. POSTERISQ. **Rev:** 14-line inscription with Roman numeral date **Note:** Under Siege by Wallenstein. Dav. #LS494.

Date	Mintage	VG	F	VF	XF	Unc
MDCXXVIII (1628)	—	2,500	4,150	6,400	—	—

KM# 58 2 THALER

Silver **Obv:** City arms in wreath **Obv. Legend:** DEO. OPTIM. MAXIM. IMPEER. ROMANO. FOEDERI. POSTERISQ. **Rev:** 14-line inscription with Roman numeral date **Note:** Under Siege by Wallenstein. Dav. #LS498.

Date	Mintage	VG	F	VF	XF	Unc
MDCXXVIII (1628)	—	1,500	2,450	3,750	—	—

KM# 59 2 THALER

Silver **Obv:** City arms in laurel wreath **Obv. Legend:** DEO. OPTIM. MAXIM. IMPER. ROMANO. FOEDERI. POSTERISQ. **Rev:** 12-line inscription with Roman numeral date **Rev. Inscription:** MEMORIÆ/URBIS. STRALSUN:/ DAE. AN. MDCXXVIII./ DIE. XII. MAY. A: MILITE/ CÆSARIA: NO. CINCTÆ. ALI/ QVOTIES. OPPUGNATÆ./ SED. DEI. GRATIA. ET. OPE./ INCLYTOR. REGUM. SE/ PTENTRIONAL. DIE/ XXIII. IULI: OBSIDIO/ NE. LIBERATÆ./ S: P: Q: S: P: P: **Note:** Dav. #5822.

Date	Mintage	VG	F	VF	XF	Unc
MDCXXVIII (1628)	—	2,250	3,750	6,400	9,800	—

KM# 108 2 THALER

Silver **Obv:** Oval city arms in baroque frame with angel supporters, date at end of legend **Obv. Legend:** MON. NOVA. CIVIT. STRALSUNDENSIS. **Rev:** Crowned imperial eagle, 32 in orb on breast **Rev. Legend:** FERDINANDUS. III. D.G. ROMANO. IMP. S.A. **Note:** Struck from Thaler dies, KM#106. Dav. #5834.

Date	Mintage	VG	F	VF	XF	Unc
1642 CS Rare	—	—	—	—	—	—

KM# 61 3 THALER

Silver **Obv:** City arms in wreath **Obv. Legend:** DEO. OPTIM. MAXIM. IMPEER. ROMANO. FOEDERI. POSTERISQ. **Rev:** 14-line inscription with Roman numeral date **Note:** Under siege by Wallenstein. Dav. #LS497.

Date	Mintage	VG	F	VF	XF	Unc
MDCXXVIII(1628) Rare	—	—	—	—	—	—

KM# 15 4 THALER

Silver **Obv:** Ornate shield of city arms in circle, date in outer legend **Rev:** Large cross in cartouche within circle **Note:** Dav. #LS490.

Date	Mintage	VG	F	VF	XF	Unc
1611 (a) Rare	—	—	—	—	—	—

TRADE COINAGE

KM# 64 GOLDGULDEN

Gold **Obv:** Cross below city arms divides date **Obv. Legend:** MO. NO. AVR. STRALSVNDENSIS. **Rev:** Imperial orb in ornamented circle **Rev. Legend:** FERDINAN. II. D.G. ROM. IM. S. A. **Note:** Prev. KM#3.

Date	Mintage	VG	F	VF	XF	Unc
16Z8 HP	—	700	1,500	3,000	5,000	—
16Z9 (d)	—	700	1,500	3,000	5,000	—
1630 (d)	—	700	1,500	3,000	5,000	—
1631 HP	—	700	1,500	3,000	5,000	—

KM# 75 DUCAT

3.5000 g., 0.9860 Gold 0.1109 oz. AGW **Obv:** City arms in wreath **Obv. Legend:** AUREUS. NOVUS. STRALSUNDEN. **Rev:** Crowned imperial eagle **Rev. Legend:** FERDINANDUS. II. D.G. ROM. IM. SE. AU. **Note:** Prev. KM#5.

Date	Mintage	VG	F	VF	XF	Unc
1632	—	265	625	1,050	2,200	—
1633	—	265	625	1,050	2,200	—
1635	—	265	625	1,050	2,200	—
ND(1637) CS	—	265	625	1,050	2,200	—

KM# 102 DUCAT

3.5000 g., 0.9860 Gold 0.1109 oz. AGW **Obv:** City arms divided date in wreath, mintmaster's initials at end of legend, where present **Obv. Legend:** AVREVS. NOVVS. STRALSVNDEN (SIS). **Rev:** Crowned imperial eagle in circle **Rev. Legend:** FERDINANDVS. III. D.G. ROM. IM. S. AV. **Note:** Prev. KM#14.

Date	Mintage	VG	F	VF	XF	Unc
1638	—	240	550	950	2,000	—
1638 CS	—	240	550	950	2,000	—
1640 CS	—	240	550	950	2,000	—
1641 CS	—	240	550	950	2,000	—

KM# 110 DUCAT

3.5000 g., 0.9860 Gold 0.1109 oz. AGW **Obv:** City arms divided mintmaster's initials and date in wreath **Obv. Legend:** AVREVS. NOVVS. STRALSVNDEN. **Rev:** Crowned imperial eagle **Rev. Legend:** FERDINANDVS. III. D.G. ROM. I. S. A. **Note:** Prev. KM#19.

Date	Mintage	VG	F	VF	XF	Unc
1644 CS	—	280	600	1,050	2,150	—

KM# 111 DUCAT
3.5000 g., 0.9860 Gold 0.1109 oz. AGW **Obv:** City arms divide mintmaster's initials and date in wreath **Obv. Legend:** AVREVS. NOVVS. STRALSVNDEN. **Rev:** Crowned imperial eagle, date divided below **Rev. Legend:** FERDINANDUS. III. D.G. ROM. I. S. A. **Note:** Prev. KM#20.

Date	Mintage	VG	F	VF	XF	Unc
1644//1644 CS	—	325	725	1,200	2,400	—

KM# 122 DUCAT
3.5000 g., 0.9860 Gold 0.1109 oz. AGW **Rev:** Crowned imperial eagle, tail divides mintmaster's initials **Note:** Prev. KM#27.

Date	Mintage	VG	F	VF	XF	Unc
1655 CS	—	400	875	1,500	2,950	—

KM# 123 DUCAT
3.5000 g., 0.9860 Gold 0.1109 oz. AGW **Note:** Dated on both sides. Prev. KM#28.

Date	Mintage	VG	F	VF	XF	Unc
1655 CS	—	400	875	1,500	2,950	—

KM# 136 DUCAT
3.5000 g., 0.9860 Gold 0.1109 oz. AGW **Obv:** City arms divide date in wreath **Obv. Legend:** AVREVS. NOVVS. STRALSVNDEN. **Rev:** Crowned imperial eagle in circle **Rev. Legend:** LEOPOL. D.G. ROMANO. IMPE. SEM. A. **Note:** Prev. KM#39.

Date	Mintage	VG	F	VF	XF	Unc
1662 HIH(b)	—	500	1,000	1,900	3,150	—
1664 HIH(b) Rare	—	—	—	—	—	—
1666 HIH(b) Rare	—	—	—	—	—	—

KM# 147 DUCAT
3.5000 g., 0.9860 Gold 0.1109 oz. AGW **Rev:** Date divided by moneyers initials at top of legend **Note:** Prev. KM#44.

Date	Mintage	VG	F	VF	XF	Unc
1671 HIH Rare	—	—	—	—	—	—

KM# 162 DUCAT
3.5000 g., 0.9860 Gold 0.1109 oz. AGW **Obv:** City arms within wreath and circle **Rev:** Date in legend **Note:** Prev. KM#54.

Date	Mintage	VG	F	VF	XF	Unc
1677 HIH	—	375	750	1,500	3,000	—

KM# 169 DUCAT
3.5000 g., 0.9860 Gold 0.1109 oz. AGW **Rev:** Without inner circle **Note:** Prev. KM#56.

Date	Mintage	VG	F	VF	XF	Unc
1681 HIH	—	625	1,250	2,500	4,400	—

KM# 138 6 DUCAT
21.0000 g., 0.9860 Gold 0.6657 oz. AGW **Obv:** Arrow head in oval shield with HH at left in inner circle, date in legend **Rev:** Crowned Imperial eagle in inner circle **Note:** Prev. KM#40. Struck with Thaler dies, KM#134.

Date	Mintage	VG	F	VF	XF	Unc
1662 HIH Rare	—	—	—	—	—	—

KM# 63 10 DUCAT (Portugalöser)
Gold, 57 mm. **Obv:** City arms in wreath **Obv. Legend:** +DEO. OPTIM. MAXIM: IMPER: ROMANO: FOEDERI. POSTERISQ. **Rev:** 14-line inscription with Roman numeral date **Note:** Under siege by Wallenstein. Struck from 2 Thaler dies, KM#57.

Date	Mintage	VG	F	VF	XF	Unc
MDCXXVIII(1628) B#7 Rare	—	—	—	—	—	—

KM# 120 10 DUCAT (Portugalöser)
Gold **Obv:** City arms in oval frame ornamented with angels facing outwards, all in circle, date at end of legend **Obv. Legend:** MON. NOVA. CIVIT. STRALSVNDENSIS. **Rev:** Crowned imperial eagle, 32 in orb on breast **Rev. Legend:** FERDINANDUS. III. D:G. ROMANO. IMP. S. A. **Note:** Struck from Thaler dies, KM#106.

Date	Mintage	VG	F	VF	XF	Unc
1649 CS B#98b Rare	—	—	—	—	—	—

KM# 140 10 DUCAT (Portugalöser)
35.0000 g., 0.9860 Gold 1.1095 oz. AGW **Obv:** Ornate oval arms **Rev:** Crowned imperial eagle, titles of Leopold I **Note:** Prev. KM#41. Struck from Thaler dies, KM#134.

Date	Mintage	VG	F	VF	XF	Unc
1662 HIH Unique	—	—	—	—	—	—

PATTERNS

Including off metal strikes

KM#	Date	Mintage	Identification	Mkt Val
Pn1	1607	—	Pfennig. Silver. KM#2.	—

STRASSBURG

The capital and principal city of Alsace, Strassburg is located very near the Rhine, 55 miles (92 km) southeast of Saarbrucken. It was an early Celtic settlement, then the Roman town of Argentoratum, from which is derived its name as found on many of Strassburg's coins. The first mention of a bishopric existing in the place dates from the 6th century. The city was both home to the bishops and the site of an imperial mint, the latter which functioned from the 9th to the 11th centuries. The bishops had received the right to coin their own money in 873, but it was not until Strassburg was made a free imperial city in the early 13th century that the townspeople came into conflict with them. When bishop Walter von Hohengeroldseck (1260-1263) tried to reassert authority over the town, the populace rose up and soundly defeated him at the Battle of Oberhausbergen in 1262. The power of the bishopric never recovered, then the city grew in importance and Strassburg city received the mint right in 1334, even though coins were struck in its name locally beginning in 1296.Strassburg's coinage continued until beyond the annexation of the city in 1681, whereas issues by the bishops continued until 1773. The bishopric was finally secularized and annexed by France in 1789.

ARMS

Strassburg - diagonal bar from upper left to lower right, often a fleur-de-lis appears on city coinage as well.

Alsace - similar diagonal bar with 6 crowns, 3 on each side along bar.

Lorraine - similar diagonal bar with 3 small eagles within it.

BISHOPRIC

REGULAR COINAGE

MB# 22 PFENNIG
Silver **Ruler:** Karl **Obv:** 4-fold arms with central shield of Lorraine, C above **Note:** Uniface schüssel-type.

Date	Mintage	VG	F	VF	XF	Unc
ND(1592-1607)	—	—	—	—	—	—

MB# 25 PFENNIG
Silver **Ruler:** Karl **Obv:** 4-fold arms with central shield of Lorraine, without C above **Note:** Uniface schüssel-type.

Date	Mintage	VG	F	VF	XF	Unc
ND(1592-1607)	—	—	—	—	—	—

MB# 43 KREUZER
Silver **Ruler:** Karl **Obv:** 4-fold arms with central shield, titles of Karl **Rev:** Crowned imperial eagle, I in orb on breast, titles of Rudolf II

Date	Mintage	VG	F	VF	XF	Unc
ND(1592-1607)	—	20.00	40.00	65.00	125	—

KM# 58 KREUZER
Silver **Ruler:** Franz Egon **Obv:** Arms of Fürstenberg, titles of Franz Egon **Rev:** Arms of Alsace, I.K. above **Note:** Varieties exist.

Date	Mintage	VG	F	VF	XF	Unc
ND(1663-1682)	—	—	—	—	—	—

KM# 94 2 KREUZER
Silver **Ruler:** Leopold Wilhelm **Obv:** Arms of Alsace **Obv. Legend:** MON NOV. ... **Rev:** Inscription in circle, titles of Ferdinand II **Rev. Inscription:** II / KREUTZER **Note:** Varieties exist.

Date	Mintage	VG	F	VF	XF	Unc
ND(1624-32)	—	—	—	—	—	—

KM# 121 3 KREUZER
Silver **Ruler:** Georg **Obv:** 4-fold arms with central shield, titles of Karl, date above arms **Rev:** Crowned imperial eagle, 3 in orb on breast **Note:** Varieties exist.

Date	Mintage	VG	F	VF	XF	Unc
1601	—	—	10.00	20.00	35.00	75.00
1603	—	—	10.00	20.00	35.00	75.00
1604	—	—	10.00	20.00	35.00	75.00
1605	—	—	10.00	20.00	35.00	75.00
1606	—	—	10.00	20.00	35.00	75.00
1607	—	—	10.00	20.00	35.00	75.00

KM# 124 3 KREUZER
Silver **Ruler:** Georg **Obv:** 4-fold arms with central shield, cardinal's hat above arms, no date

Date	Mintage	VG	F	VF	XF	Unc
ND	—	—	—	—	—	—

KM# 138 10 KREUZER
Silver **Ruler:** Franz Egon **Obv:** Bust right, titles of Franz Egon **Rev:** Crowned and mitered 4-fold arms, value (X) above, date below **Note:** Varieties exist.

Date	Mintage	VG	F	VF	XF	Unc
1665	—	12.00	25.00	45.00	85.00	—
1666	—	12.00	25.00	45.00	85.00	—
1667	—	12.00	25.00	45.00	85.00	—

KM# 153.1 12 KREUZER
Silver **Ruler:** Leopold Wilhelm **Obv:** Madonna and child divide date, arms of Alsace below in front, value (XII) at top **Obv. Legend:** MON: NOVA ... **Rev:** Crowned 4-fold arms with central shield

Date	Mintage	VG	F	VF	XF	Unc
1631	—	28.00	50.00	100	200	—

KM# 153.2 12 KREUZER
Silver **Ruler:** Leopold Wilhelm **Obv:** Madonna and child divide date, arms of Alsace below in front, value (XII) at top **Obv. Legend:** MON: NOVA ... **Rev:** Crowned 4-fold arms with central shield **Note:** Klippe.

Date	Mintage	VG	F	VF	XF	Unc
1631	—	28.00	50.00	100	200	—

KM# 156 12 KREUZER
Silver **Ruler:** Franz Egon **Obv:** Bust right, titles of Franz Egon **Rev:** Crowned and mitered 4-fold arms divide date, value (XII) above

Date	Mintage	VG	F	VF	XF	Unc
1666	—	—	—	—	—	—

KM# 194 60 KREUZER
Silver **Ruler:** Wilhelm Egon **Obv:** Bust right, titles of Franz Egon **Rev:** Crowned and mitered 4-fold arms with central shield divide date, crossed sword and crozier behind, titles continued

Date	Mintage	VG	F	VF	XF	Unc
1668	—	—	—	—	—	—

KM# 244 1/3 THALER
Silver **Ruler:** Karl **Obv:** Bust left, date below, titles of Karl **Obv. Legend:** CAROL. D. G. CARD. LOTH. EP. ARGENT. ET. MET **Rev:** 4-fold arms with central shield, cardinal's hat above **Rev. Legend:** ALSAS. LANGRA. ... **Note:** Varieties exist.

Date	Mintage	VG	F	VF	XF	Unc
1602	—	25.00	45.00	75.00	150	—
1603	—	25.00	45.00	75.00	150	—
1604	—	25.00	75.00	75.00	150	—
1605	—	25.00	45.00	75.00	150	—

Date	Mintage	VG	F	VF	XF	Unc
1606	—	25.00	45.00	75.00	150	—
ND	—	25.00	45.00	75.00	150	—

KM# 300 THALER
Silver **Obv:** Crowned imperial eagle **Obv. Legend:** RVDOLP. II. ROM: IMP:... **Rev:** Capped arms **Rev. Legend:** CAROL. D: G: CARD: LOT: EPICS:... **Note:** Dav. #5837.

Date	Mintage	VG	F	VF	XF	Unc
ND Rare	—	—	—	—	—	—

KM# 303 THALER
Silver **Rev:** Six shields with shield of Lorraine at center **Rev. Legend:** CAR. D: G: CARD. LOT. EPS... **Note:** Dav. #5839.

Date	Mintage	VG	F	VF	XF	Unc
1605 Rare	—	—	—	—	—	—

KM# A303 THALER
Silver **Rev. Legend:** ... ARGEN • E • ME •... **Note:** Dav. #5839A.

Date	Mintage	VG	F	VF	XF	Unc
1605 Rare	—	—	—	—	—	—

OBSIDIONAL (SIEGE) COINAGE

KM# 185 40 KREUZER
Silver **Ruler:** Leopold Wilhelm **Obv:** Bust right, titles of Leopold Wilhelm **Rev:** Crowned and mitered 4-fold arms with central shield

Date	Mintage	VG	F	VF	XF	Unc
ND(1632-62)	—	—	—	—	—	—

TRADE COINAGE

KM# 415 1/2 DUCAT
1.7500 g., 0.9860 Gold 0.0555 oz. AGW **Obv:** Bust right, titles of Franz Egon **Rev:** Crowned, mitered four-fold arms with central shield divide date, titles continued **Note:** FR #250.

Date	Mintage	VG	F	VF	XF	Unc
1666	—	—	—	—	—	—

KM# 418 DUCAT
3.5000 g., 0.9860 Gold 0.1109 oz. AGW **Obv:** Madonna and child divide date, arms of Alsace below in front **Rev:** Crowned four-fold arms with central chield **Note:** FR #251.

Date	Mintage	VG	F	VF	XF	Unc
ND(1626-32)	—	600	1,200	2,100	3,300	—

KM# 421 DUCAT
3.5000 g., 0.9860 Gold 0.1109 oz. AGW **Obv:** Madonna and child in inner circle **Rev:** Arms, with lion supporters **Note:** Fr. #238.

Date	Mintage	VG	F	VF	XF	Unc
1632	—	350	800	1,400	2,000	—

KM# 437 4 DUCAT
14.0000 g., 0.9860 Gold 0.4438 oz. AGW **Note:** FR.#236.

Date	Mintage	VG	F	VF	XF	Unc
ND Rare	—	—	—	—	—	—

CITY

REGULAR COINAGE

KM# 36 PFENNIG
Silver **Obv:** Fleur-de-lis 2-stem base like an H flanked by 2 dots **Note:** Uniface.

Date	Mintage	VG	F	VF	XF	Unc
1601	—	—	—	—	—	—

KM# 52 KREUZER
Silver **Obv:** Similar to KM#46.1 but lis on each side in quatrelobe

Date	Mintage	VG	F	VF	XF	Unc
ND	—	—	—	—	—	—

KM# 55 KREUZER
Silver **Rev:** Similar to KM#46.1 but has cross with fleur-de-lis arms in circle

Date	Mintage	VG	F	VF	XF	Unc
ND	—	—	—	—	—	—

KM# 4 KREUZER
Silver **Obv:** City arms in ornate shield, I.K. above **Obv. Legend:** MON: NOV * **Rev:** Fleur-de-lis in circle **Rev. Legend:** GLORIA * IN * EXCELS * DEO *

Date	Mintage	VG	F	VF	XF	Unc
ND	—	—	—	—	—	—

KM# 147 12 KREUZER
Silver **Obv:** Ornate city arms, XII above **Obv. Legend:** MON • NOV • REIP ... **Rev:** Fleur-de-lis in circle **Rev. Legend:** GLORIA ...

Date	Mintage	VG	F	VF	XF	Unc
ND	—	25.00	45.00	90.00	180	—

KM# 150 12 KREUZER
Silver **Obv:** Fleur-de-lis in circle **Obv. Legend:** ASSIS • REIP • ARGENT • DVPLEX **Rev:** Cross within circle **Rev. Legend:** GLORIA * IN * EXCELSIS * DEO *

Date	Mintage	VG	F	VF	XF	Unc
ND(1615-23)	—	28.00	50.00	100	200	—

KM# 159 12 KREUZER
Silver **Obv:** Ornate city arms, XII above **Obv. Legend:** MON. NOV. CIVITAT ... **Rev:** Fleur-de-lis in circle

Date	Mintage	VG	F	VF	XF	Unc
ND	—	25.00	45.00	90.00	180	—

KM# 172 24 KREUZER
Silver **Obv:** Ornate city arms, value (XXIII) above arms **Obv. Legend:** MON • NOV • REIP • ... **Rev:** Fleur-de-lis in circle **Rev. Legend:** GLORIA ...

Date	Mintage	VG	F	VF	XF	Unc
ND	—	35.00	60.00	120	225	—

KM# 178 30 KREUZER
Silver **Obv:** City arms, XXX.K. above **Obv. Legend:** MONETA * NOVA ** **Rev:** Large fleur-de-lis **Rev. Legend:** GLORIA *

Date	Mintage	VG	F	VF	XF	Unc
ND	—	—	—	—	—	—

KM# 197 60 KREUZER
Silver **Obv:** City arms, LX.K. above arms **Obv. Legend:** MONETA * NOVA** **Rev:** Large fleur-de-lis **Rev. Legend:** GLORIA

Date	Mintage	VG	F	VF	XF	Unc
ND	—	50.00	100	200	325	—

KM# 235 1/4 THALER
Silver **Obv:** Ornate city arms with 2 lion supporters **Obv. Legend:** INSIG. REIP. ARGENTORATENSIS **Rev:** Large fleur-de-lis **Rev. Legend:** GLORIA. IN. ALTISSIMIS. DEO.

Date	Mintage	VG	F	VF	XF	Unc
ND	—	—	—	—	—	—

KM# 306 THALER
Silver **Obv:** Legend around lions supporting lis above shield **Obv. Legend:** NVMMVS * REIP *... **Rev:** Legend around ornate fleur-de-lis **Rev. Legend:** * SOLIVS * VIRTVTIS **Note:** Dav.#5842.

Date	Mintage	VG	F	VF	XF	Unc
ND	—	100	200	400	675	—

KM# A306 THALER
28.3000 g., Silver **Note:** Klippe. Struck with 1/2 Thaler dies. Dav.#5842A.

Date	Mintage	VG	F	VF	XF	Unc
ND	—	—	—	—	—	—

KM# 309 THALER
Silver **Obv:** Date divided by lis above shield **Note:** Dav.#5844.

Date	Mintage	VG	F	VF	XF	Unc
1617 Rare	—	—	—	—	—	—

KM# 312.1 THALER
Silver **Subject:** Centennial of Reformation **Rev:** With ornamentation above "PRO" **Note:** Dav.#5846.

Date	Mintage	VG	F	VF	XF	Unc
1617	—	275	575	1,150	2,250	3,500

KM# 312.2 THALER
Silver **Rev:** Without ornamentation above "PRO" **Note:** Dav.#5846A.

Date	Mintage	VG	F	VF	XF	Unc
1617	—	750	1,250	2,500	3,750	—

KM# 312.3 THALER
Silver **Note:** Klippe. Dav.#5846B.

Date	Mintage	VG	F	VF	XF	Unc
1617	—	375	850	1,350	2,250	—

KM# 315 THALER
Silver **Subject:** Peace of Nymegen **Obv:** Date in chronogram **Rev:** Noah's Ark within legend **Note:** Dav.#5847.

Date	Mintage	VG	F	VF	XF	Unc
ND(1679)	—	325	675	1,350	2,250	—

KM# 345 2 THALER
Silver **Obv:** Legend around lions supporting lis above shield **Rev:** Legend around ornate fleur-de-lis **Note:** Dav.#A5841. Similar to 1 Thaler, KM#306.

Date	Mintage	VG	F	VF	XF	Unc
ND Rare	—	—	—	—	—	—

KM# 348 2 THALER
Silver **Subject:** Centennial of Reformation **Note:** Dav.#A5845.

Date	Mintage	VG	F	VF	XF	Unc
1617	—	1,150	2,250	3,750	6,000	—

KM# 354 3 THALER
Silver **Obv:** Legend around lions supporting lis above shield **Rev:** Legend around ornate fleur-de-lis **Note:** Dav.#B5841. Similar to 1 Thaler KM#306.

Date	Mintage	VG	F	VF	XF	Unc
ND Rare	—	—	—	—	—	—

KM# 357 3 THALER
81.8600 g., Silver **Subject:** Centennial of Reformation **Obv:** Shield of arms within inner circle, legends around **Rev:** 10-line inscription **Rev. Inscription:** PRO / RELIGIONIS • / CENTVM • ANTE • / ANNOS • DIVINITVS / RESTITVTÆ • MEMO / RIA • NOVIQVE • SECV • / LI • FELICI • AVSPIGIO / S • P • Q • ARGENTOR • / F • F • A° MDCXVII / CAL • NOVEMB **Note:** Dav.#B5845.

Date	Mintage	VG	F	VF	XF	Unc
1617	—	3,000	6,000	9,000	—	—

KM# 363 5 THALER
Silver **Obv:** Legend around lions supporting lis aabove shield **Rev:** Legend around ornate fleur-de-lis **Note:** Dav.#5841. Similar to 1 Thaler KM#306.

Date	Mintage	VG	F	VF	XF	Unc
ND Rare	—	—	—	—	—	—

KM# 396 6 THALER
Silver **Subject:** Centennial of Reformation **Rev:** With ornamentation above "PRO" **Note:** Dav.#5845. Similar to 1 Thaler KM#312.1.

Date	Mintage	VG	F	VF	XF	Unc
1617 Rare	—	—	—	—	—	—

TRADE COINAGE

KM# 424 DUCAT
Gold **Obv:** Helmeted arms with lion supporters **Rev:** 4-line inscription **Rev. Inscription:** DVCATVS / REIPVBLCÆ ... **Note:** FR#237.

Date	Mintage	VG	F	VF	XF	Unc
ND(1650)	—	225	500	850	1,350	—

KM# 424.1 DUCAT
Gold **Rev:** 4-line inscription in square **Note:** FR#A237.

Date	Mintage	VG	F	VF	XF	Unc
ND(1650)	—	270	600	1,000	1,750	—

KM# 424.2 DUCAT
Gold **Rev:** Inscription within cartouche **Note:** FR#B237.

Date	Mintage	VG	F	VF	XF	Unc
ND(1650)	—	270	600	1,000	1,750	—

KM# 424.3 DUCAT
Gold **Obv:** Oval arms **Rev:** 4-line inscription in open branches **Note:** FR#C237.

Date	Mintage	VG	F	VF	XF	Unc
ND(1650)	—	270	600	1,000	1,750	—

KM# 424.4 DUCAT
Gold **Obv:** Oval arms **Obv. Legend:** GLORIA IN EXCELSIS DEO **Rev:** 4-line inscription within palm branches **Rev. Inscription:** DVCATVS / ... **Note:** FR#D237.

Date	Mintage	VG	F	VF	XF	Unc
ND(1650)	—	270	600	1,000	1,750	—

KM# 427 2 DUCAT
7.0000 g., 0.9860 Gold 0.2219 oz. AGW **Obv:** Helmeted arms with lion supporters **Rev. Inscription:** DVCATVS/REIPVBLCÆ **Note:** FR#252. Similar to 1 Ducat, KM#424.

Date	Mintage	VG	F	VF	XF	Unc
ND(1650) Rare	—	—	—	—	—	—

KM# 430 3 DUCAT
10.5000 g., 0.9860 Gold 0.3328 oz. AGW **Obv:** Helmeted arms with lion supporters **Rev. Inscription:** DVCATVS/CIVITATIS... **Note:** FR#253.

Date	Mintage	VG	F	VF	XF	Unc
ND(1650) Rare	—	—	—	—	—	—

KM# 433 3 DUCAT
10.5000 g., 0.9860 Gold 0.3328 oz. AGW **Obv:** Oval arms **Rev:** 4-line inscription **Note:** FR#254.

Date	Mintage	VG	F	VF	XF	Unc
ND(1681) Rare	—	—	—	—	—	—

KM# 440 4 DUCAT
14.0000 g., 0.9860 Gold 0.4438 oz. AGW **Obv:** Helmeted arms with lion supporters **Rev. Inscription:** DVCATVS / REIPVBLCÆ **Note:** FR#255. Similar to 1 Ducat, KM#424.

Date	Mintage	VG	F	VF	XF	Unc
ND(1650) Rare	—	—	—	—	—	—

KM# 443 6 DUCAT
21.0000 g., 0.9860 Gold 0.6657 oz. AGW **Obv:** Helmeted arms with lion supporters **Rev. Inscription:** DVCATVS / REIPVBLCÆ **Note:** FR#256. Similar to 1 Ducat, KM#424.

Date	Mintage	VG	F	VF	XF	Unc
ND(1650) Rare	—	—	—	—	—	—

SULZ

The counts of this Swabian territory became landgraves of Klettgau in Baden around 1425. They apparently struck no coins until the 17th century when Alwig VII and his brother Karl Ludwig had a small coinage. Maria Anna, daughter and heiress of the last of the line Johann Ludwig (1648-87), married Ferdinand Wilhelm of Schwarzenberg and the lands passed to that house.

RULERS
Ulrich, 1648-50
Johann Ludwig, 1648-87
Maria Anna, 1687-96

MINT OFFICIALS' INITIALS

Initial	Date	Name
PM	1612-21	Possibly Johann Philipp May in Zweibrücken
MS	1622-55	Matthäus Schaffer der Jüngere, die-cutter in Nuremberg
	Ca. 1675	Johann Georg Gilly (Gyllin) in Tiengen

The mint for Sulz usually operated at Tiengen.

ARMS
Old Sulz - 3 points (or pointed mountains)
Klettgau – 3 sheaves
Brandis – knotty pine limb, sometimes with flame at one end
Abbey of Rheinau – curved fish

COUNTSHIP

REGULAR COINAGE

DAV# 7792 THALER
Silver **Obv:** Bust **Rev:** Crowned double eagle with orb, Q-M

Date	Mintage	VG	F	VF	XF	Unc
ND Rare	—	—	—	—	—	—

DAV# 7797 THALER
Silver **Obv:** Crowned arms dividing date **Obv. Legend:** CAROL...

Date	Mintage	VG	F	VF	XF	Unc
1621 Rare	—	—	—	—	—	—

DAV# 7793 THALER
Silver **Obv:** Bust right **Rev:** Crowned double eagle with orb, M-S

Date	Mintage	VG	F	VF	XF	Unc
ND Rare	—	—	—	—	—	—

DAV# 7794 THALER
Silver **Obv:** Crowned bust of Saint right, date in outer legend **Obv. Legend:** Inner: SANCTVS-FINDANVS

Date	Mintage	VG	F	VF	XF	Unc
1622 Rare	—	—	—	—	—	—

DAV# 7795 THALER
Silver **Obv:** Bust right **Rev:** Crowned double eagle, date in legend at top

Date	Mintage	VG	F	VF	XF	Unc
1623 Rare	—	—	—	—	—	—

DAV# 7796 THALER
Silver **Obv:** Crowned arms **Obv. Legend:** CAROLVS LVD...

Date	Mintage	VG	F	VF	XF	Unc
ND Rare	—	—	—	—	—	—

TRADE COINAGE

KM# 20 GOLDGULDEN
Gold **Obv:** Crowned 4-fold arms in ornamented shield, titles of Karl Ludwig Ernst and date in margin **Rev. Designer:** Crowned imperial eagle, orb on breast, titles of Ferdinand II around

Date	Mintage	VG	F	VF	XF	Unc
1622 Rare	—	—	—	—	—	—

Note: Note: Leu Numismatik auction 5-98, XF realized $37,500.

KM# 25 DUCAT
3.5000 g., 0.9860 Gold 0.1109 oz. AGW **Obv:** Imperial eagle with orb on chest **Obv. Legend:** FERDINAND: II: D: G:... **Rev:** Crowned ornate arms **Rev. Legend:** CAR: LV: E: CO: IN: SVLZ:

Date	Mintage	VG	F	VF	XF	Unc
1622 Rare	—	—	—	—	—	—

SWABIAN CIRCLE

An area in Swabia maintained as an imperial administrative district from 1500 to 1806. Constance and Württemberg were the usual administrators over this occasional coin issuer.

IMPERIAL CIRCLE

REGULAR COINAGE

DAV# 7798 THALER
Silver **Obv:** Oval lion arms within branches, date divided below **Rev:** 2 Shields; one with crown and one with mitre **Rev. Legend:** ...LUDOV: DVX WURT: ET... RUDOL: EPISC:... **Note:** Similar to Dav. #7799 with different legend.

Date	Mintage	VG	F	VF	XF	Unc
1694	—	850	1,650	2,750	—	—

DAV# 7799 THALER
Silver **Obv:** Arms in frame and sprays, date divided below **Rev:** 2 Shields; one with crown and one with mitre

Date	Mintage	VG	F	VF	XF	Unc
1694	—	750	1,350	2,250	3,500	5,500

DAV# 7800 THALER
Silver **Obv:** Smaller shield **Rev:** Smaller shields

Date	Mintage	VG	F	VF	XF	Unc
1694	—	750	1,350	2,250	3,750	—

TELGTE

A town in Westphalia 6.5 miles (11km) east-northeast of Münster. A few local issues were reportedly struck in the early period of the Thirty Years' War, but all are very rare.

PROVINCIAL TOWN

REGULAR COINAGE

KM# 1 3 PFENNIG
Copper **Obv:** Tree with 5 branches in circle **Obv. Legend:** STADT - TELGTE (or TELGET) **Rev:** Date; 'III' in double circle

Date	Mintage	VG	F	VF	XF	Unc
1620 Rare	—	—	—	—	—	—

KM# 2 4 PFENNIG
Copper **Obv:** Tree with 5 branches in circle **Obv. Legend:** STADT - TELGTE (or TELGET) **Rev:** Date; II.II in double circle

Date	Mintage	VG	F	VF	XF	Unc
1620 Rare	—	—	—	—	—	—

TEUTONIC ORDER

(Deutscher Orden)

The Order of Knights was founded during the Third Crusade in 1198. They acquired considerable territory by conquest from the heathen Prussians in the late 13th and early 14th centuries. The seat of the Grand Master moved from Acre to Venice and in 1309 to Marienburg, Prussia. The Teutonic Order began striking coins in the late 13th century. In 1355 permission was granted to strike hellers at Mergentheim. However, the bulk of the Order's coinage until 1525 was schillings and half schoters minted in and for Prussia. In 1809 the Order was suppressed and Mergentheim was annexed to Württemberg.

RULERS
Maximilian of Austria, 1588-1618
Karl of Austria, 1618-1624
Johann Eustach von Westernach, 1625-1627
Johann Caspar von Stadion, 1627-1641
Leopold Wilhelm of Austria, 1641-1662
Karl Josef of Austria, 1662-1664
Johann Caspar II von Ampringen, 1664-1684
Ludwig Anton von Pfalz-Neuburg, 1684-1694
Ludwig Franz von Pfalz-Neuburg, 1694-1732

ARMS
Grand Master: Cross, shield w/eagle in ctr., shield is often w/double outline. Later versions include family and territorial arms in angles of cross.
Order Arms: Long cross superimposed, usually on empty shield, sometimes w/eagle in ctr.

MINT OFFICIALS' INITIALS

Initial	Date	Name
CO / CÖ	Ca. 1612-16	Christoph Örber in Hall, Tyrol
	Ca. 1666	Heinrich Moller, die-cutter in Nürnberg
MF	1669-89	Michael Faber in Frankfurt am Main
CB / B	1687-89	Conrad Bechtmann

KNIGHTLY ORDER

REGULAR COINAGE

KM# 45 1/4 THALER
Silver **Note:** Prev. KM#1; Similar to KM#46 but obervse legend broken.

Date	Mintage	VG	F	VF	XF	Unc
1612 CO	—	45.00	85.00	160	300	—
1614 CO	—	—	—	—	—	—

Note: Reported not confirmed

KM# 46 1/4 THALER
Silver **Obv:** Continuous legend **Obv. Legend:** MAXIMIL: DG: ARC: AV:... **Note:** Prev. KM#2.

Date	Mintage	VG	F	VF	XF	Unc
ND CO	—	45.00	85.00	160	300	—

KM# 47 1/4 THALER
Silver **Obv:** Broken legend, supported shield at left **Obv. Legend:** MAX: DG: AR-AV-... **Note:** Prev. KM#3.

Date	Mintage	VG	F	VF	XF	Unc
ND CO	—	45.00	85.00	160	300	—

KM# 52 1/2 THALER
Silver **Note:** Prev. KM#6; Similar to 1 Thaler, Dav. #5851.

Date	Mintage	VG	F	VF	XF	Unc
1612 CO	—	65.00	135	275	475	—
ND CO	—	65.00	135	275	475	—

KM# 53 1/2 THALER
Silver **Obv:** Supported shield at right **Note:** Prev. KM#7.

Date	Mintage	VG	F	VF	XF	Unc
1614 CO	—	65.00	135	275	475	—

KM# 54 1/2 THALER
Silver **Obv:** Supported shield at left **Note:** Prev. KM#8.

Date	Mintage	VG	F	VF	XF	Unc
1616	—	65.00	135	275	475	—
1616 CO	—	65.00	135	275	475	—

DAV# 5848 THALER
Silver **Obv:** Master standing on ground, arms at left, helmet at right **Rev:** Emperor on horseback in circle of shields, date below

Date	Mintage	VG	F	VF	XF	Unc
1603	—	—	170	375	750	1,350

DAV# 5849 THALER
Silver **Rev:** Rear legs of horse lower, date divided by spear and rider's foot

Date	Mintage	VG	F	VF	XF	Unc
1610	—	—	205	400	800	1,500

DAV# 5850 THALER
Silver **Obv:** Feet, arms, and helmet all break legend **Obv. Legend:** ...ADMIN.

Date	Mintage	VG	F	VF	XF	Unc
1611	—	—	205	400	800	1,500

DAV# 5850A THALER
Silver **Obv. Legend:** ...ADM.

Date	Mintage	VG	F	VF	XF	Unc
1611	—	—	205	400	800	1,500

DAV# 5851 THALER
Silver **Obv. Legend:** MAX: DG: AR-AV: D: BV:-M-AG:...

Date	Mintage	VG	F	VF	XF	Unc
1612	—	—	205	400	800	1,500

DAV# 5851A THALER
Silver **Obv. Legend:** ...ARC-AV: D: BV...

Date	Mintage	VG	F	VF	XF	Unc
1612	—	—	205	400	800	1,500

DAV# 5853 THALER
Silver

Date	Mintage	VG	F	VF	XF	Unc
1613	—	—	170	375	750	1,350

DAV# 5855 THALER
Silver **Obv:** Facing bust dividing date **Rev:** Crowned arms

Date	Mintage	VG	F	VF	XF	Unc
1623	—	—	350	750	1,500	3,250

DAV# 5856 THALER
Silver **Obv:** Bust right dividing date

Date	Mintage	VG	F	VF	XF	Unc
1624	—	—	375	750	1,250	2,200

DAV# 5857 THALER
Silver **Obv:** Helmeted arms **Rev:** Madonna and child in radiant oval

Date	Mintage	VG	F	VF	XF	Unc
1625	—	—	275	500	950	2,000

DAV# 5858 THALER

Silver **Subject:** Death of Johann Kaspar I **Obv:** Helmeted arms **Rev:** 6-line inscription

Date	Mintage	VG	F	VF	XF	Unc
1641	—	—	2,000	3,500	6,000	—

DAV# 5859 THALER

Silver **Obv:** Helmeted arms **Rev:** Madonna and child in radiant oval

Date	Mintage	VG	F	VF	XF	Unc
1666	—	—	250	450	850	1,750
1668	—	—	250	450	850	1,750

DAV# 5861 THALER

Silver **Rev:** Madonna and child above arms

Date	Mintage	VG	F	VF	XF	Unc
1673 MF	—	—	500	900	1,600	2,500

DAV# 5862 THALER

Silver **Rev:** Hatted and supported arms

Date	Mintage	VG	F	VF	XF	Unc
1687	—	—	3,500	5,500	7,500	—

DAV# 5852 2 THALER

Silver **Note:** Similar to 1 Thaler, Dav. #5853.

Date	Mintage	VG	F	VF	XF	Unc
1613	—	450	850	1,500	2,500	—

DAV# A5854 2 THALER

Silver **Obv:** Grand Master of the Order standing with sword, date in exergue

Date	Mintage	VG	F	VF	XF	Unc
1614	—	350	650	1,150	2,000	—

DAV# C5854 2 THALER

Silver **Note:** Klippe.

Date	Mintage	VG	F	VF	XF	Unc
1614 Rare	—	—	—	—	—	—

DAV# A5855 2 THALER

Silver **Ruler:** Karl of Austria **Obv:** High-collared bust to right in circle **Obv. Legend:** CAROL • D: G • ARCHIDVX • AVSTRI • ADM • **Rev:** Crown above large manifold arms, small oval mitered arms at left and right, date divided below **Rev. Legend:** M • GEN • PRVS • M • ORD • TEV • EPV • BR • ET • W • **Note:** Klippe.

Date	Mintage	VG	F	VF	XF	Unc
16ZZ Rare	—	—	—	—	—	—

DAV# 5860 2 THALER

Silver **Note:** Similar to 1 Thaler, Dav. #5861.

Date	Mintage	VG	F	VF	XF	Unc
1673 MF	—	1,500	2,500	4,250	—	—

DAV# B5854 3 THALER

86.2000 g., Silver **Obv:** Grand Master of the Order standing holding sword, date in exergue **Rev:** Knight on horseback in circle of shields

Date	Mintage	VG	F	VF	XF	Unc
1614	—	650	1,150	2,000	3,500	—

DAV# D5854 3 THALER

86.2000 g., Silver **Note:** Klippe.

Date	Mintage	VG	F	VF	XF	Unc
1614 Rare	—	—	—	—	—	—

DAV# 5854 5 THALER

Silver **Note:** Similar to 3 Thaler, Dav. #B5854.

Date	Mintage	VG	F	VF	XF	Unc
1614 Rare	—	—	—	—	—	—

TRADE COINAGE

FR# 3379 DUCAT

3.5000 g., 0.9860 Gold 0.1109 oz. AGW **Obv:** Maximilian

Date	Mintage	VG	F	VF	XF	Unc
ND	—	650	1,500	2,900	4,950	—

FR# 3380 DUCAT

3.5000 g., 0.9860 Gold 0.1109 oz. AGW **Obv:** Head of Karl right in inner circle **Rev:** Three shields of arms in inner circle

Date	Mintage	VG	F	VF	XF	Unc
ND	—	600	1,200	2,400	4,200	—

FR# 3382 DUCAT

3.5000 g., 0.9860 Gold 0.1109 oz. AGW **Obv:** Three shields of arms in inner circle **Rev:** Crowned double-headed eagle

Date	Mintage	VG	F	VF	XF	Unc
1626 Rare	—	—	—	—	—	—

FR# 3383 DUCAT

3.5000 g., 0.9860 Gold 0.1109 oz. AGW **Obv:** Crowned arms in inner circle, titles of Johann Kaspar I **Rev:** Madonna and child in inner circle

Date	Mintage	VG	F	VF	XF	Unc
ND Rare	—	—	—	—	—	—

FR# 3386 DUCAT
3.5000 g., 0.9860 Gold 0.1109 oz. AGW **Obv:** Crowned arms in inner circle **Rev:** Madonna and child in inner circle

Date	Mintage	VG	F	VF	XF	Unc
1666	—	400	900	1,900	3,500	—

FR# 3384 DUCAT
3.5000 g., 0.9860 Gold 0.1109 oz. AGW **Obv:** Armored bust of Johann Kaspar II right in inner circle

Date	Mintage	VG	F	VF	XF	Unc
1673 MF	—	600	1,200	2,400	4,200	—

FR# 3388 DUCAT
3.5000 g., 0.9860 Gold 0.1109 oz. AGW **Obv:** Bust of Franz Ludwig right in inner circle **Rev:** Crowned arms in inner circle

Date	Mintage	VG	F	VF	XF	Unc
1696	—	500	1,150	2,200	3,750	—

FR# 3389 DUCAT
3.5000 g., 0.9860 Gold 0.1109 oz. AGW **Ruler:** Ludwig Franz **Obv:** Armored bust right **Rev:** Cruciform arms

Date	Mintage	VG	F	VF	XF	Unc
1699 LPH	—	450	1,050	2,150	3,600	—

FR# 3378 2 DUCAT
7.0000 g., 0.9860 Gold 0.2219 oz. AGW **Obv:** Maximilian standing in inner circle **Rev:** Crowned arms in inner circle

Date	Mintage	VG	F	VF	XF	Unc
ND	—	950	1,900	3,750	6,300	—

FR# 3381 2 DUCAT
7.0000 g., 0.9860 Gold 0.2219 oz. AGW **Obv:** Armored bust of Karl right in inner circle

Date	Mintage	VG	F	VF	XF	Unc
ND	—	1,500	2,800	5,000	8,100	—

FR# 3385 2 DUCAT
7.0000 g., 0.9860 Gold 0.2219 oz. AGW **Obv:** Crowned arms in inner circle **Rev:** Madonna and child in inner circle

Date	Mintage	VG	F	VF	XF	Unc
1666	—	1,500	2,800	5,100	8,400	—

FR# 3379a 3 DUCAT
10.5000 g., 0.9860 Gold 0.3328 oz. AGW **Obv:** Maximilian standing facing with sword **Obv. Legend:** MAX. DGAR: (supported shield)... **Rev:** Equestrian figure right in circle of shields, order arms below

Date	Mintage	VG	F	VF	XF	Unc
1612 Rare	—	—	—	—	—	—

FR# A3379a 3 DUCAT
10.5000 g., 0.9860 Gold 0.3328 oz. AGW **Obv. Legend:** MAX. D (supported shield) G: AR...

Date	Mintage	VG	F	VF	XF	Unc
1612	—	1,200	2,400	4,200	7,200	—

KM# 10 5 DUCAT
17.5000 g., 0.9860 Gold 0.5547 oz. AGW **Obv:** Helmeted ornate arms **Rev:** Madonna with child in flaming oval

Date	Mintage	VG	F	VF	XF	Unc
1666 Rare	—	—	—	—	—	—

KM# 11 5 DUCAT
17.5000 g., 0.9860 Gold 0.5547 oz. AGW **Obv:** Helmeted ornate arms **Rev:** Madonna with child in flaming oval, large flames

Date	Mintage	VG	F	VF	XF	Unc
1668 Rare	—	—	—	—	—	—

KM# 12 6 DUCAT
21.0000 g., 0.9860 Gold 0.6657 oz. AGW **Obv:** Maximilian standing facing with sword **Rev:** Equestrian figure right in circle of shields, arms of the Order below

Date	Mintage	VG	F	VF	XF	Unc
1603 Rare	—	—	—	—	—	—

KM# 13 10 DUCAT
35.0000 g., 0.9860 Gold 1.1095 oz. AGW **Obv:** Maximilian standing facing with sword **Rev:** Equestrian figure right in circle of shields, Order arms below **Note:** Struck with 1 Thaler dies, Dav. #5848.

Date	Mintage	VG	F	VF	XF	Unc
1603 Rare	—	—	—	—	—	—

KM# 14 10 DUCAT
35.0000 g., 0.9860 Gold 1.1095 oz. AGW **Note:** Struck with 1 Thaler dies, Dav. #5850A.

Date	Mintage	VG	F	VF	XF	Unc
1611 Rare	—	—	—	—	—	—

KM# 15 10 DUCAT
35.0000 g., 0.9860 Gold 1.1095 oz. AGW **Obv:** Helmeted ornate arms **Rev:** Madonna with child in flaming oval **Note:** Struck with 1 Thaler dies, Dav. #5859.

Date	Mintage	VG	F	VF	XF	Unc
1666 Rare	—	—	—	—	—	—

THANN

Located just 8 miles (14km) west-northwest of Mühlhausen in Alsace, the town of Thann was raised to the rank of free imperial city in 1383. Bracteats were minted there in the 13th century and it had a proper city coinage during the late 15th to 17th centuries. At the conclusion of the Thirty Years' War in 1648, France acquired the town in the general peace settlement.

ARMS

2-fold, divided vertically, single horizontal bar (usually shaded) on left, pine tree on right.

FREE CITY

REGULAR COINAGE

KM# 1 KREUZER
Silver **Ruler:** (no Ruler Information) **Obv:** City arms in circle **Obv. Legend:** MO. NO. TANNENSIS **Rev:** Cross in circle **Rev. Legend:** SALVE. CRVX. SANC.

Date	Mintage	VG	F	VF	XF	Unc
ND(1622-24)	—	33.00	55.00	95.00	165	—

KM# 2 KREUZER
Silver **Ruler:** (no Ruler Information) **Obv:** City arms in circle, date at end of margin **Obv. Legend:** MO. NO. TANNENSIS **Rev:** Cross in circle **Rev. Legend:** SALVE. CRVX. SANC.

Date	Mintage	VG	F	VF	XF	Unc
1622	—	27.00	45.00	85.00	160	—
1623	—	27.00	45.00	85.00	160	—

KM# 5 2 KREUZER (Halbbatzen)
Silver **Ruler:** (no Ruler Information) **Obv:** City arms, T (Z) S below **Obv. Legend:** MO. NO. TANNENSIS **Rev:** Bust of St. Theobald, date below

Date	Mintage	VG	F	VF	XF	Unc
1622	—	40.00	65.00	120	200	—
1623	—	40.00	65.00	120	200	—
1624	—	40.00	65.00	120	200	—

KM# 7 BATZEN
Silver **Ruler:** (no Ruler Information) **Obv:** City arms in trilobe, date **Obv. Legend:** MO NO... **Rev:** Facing bust of St. Theobald

Date	Mintage	VG	F	VF	XF	Unc
1623	—	45.00	80.00	165	—	—
1624	—	45.00	80.00	165	—	—

KM# 10 2 BATZEN (Doppelbätzner)
Silver **Ruler:** (no Ruler Information) **Obv:** City arms in hexalobe, value (Z) below **Obv. Legend:** MONETA NOVA **Rev:** St. Theobald seated facing forward, date in margin

Date	Mintage	VG	F	VF	XF	Unc
1623	—	65.00	135	275	—	—
1624	—	65.00	135	275	—	—

KM# 11 2 BATZEN (Doppelbätzner)

Silver **Ruler:** (no Ruler Information) **Obv:** City arms in pentalobe, value: (Z) below **Obv. Legend:** MONETA NOVA **Rev:** St. Theobald seated facing, date in margin

Date	Mintage	VG	F	VF	XF	Unc
1624	—	80.00	160	300	—	—

TRIER

The city of Trier, located on the Mosel River just a few miles from the border with Luxembourg, was an important place from Roman times up to the modern era. Tradition holds that the Emperor Claudius founded the city as Augusta Trevirorum (imperial city of the Treviri, a Belgian tribe of that locale). Even today, Trier contains more Roman antiquities than any other city in northern Europe and was one of the earliest centers of Christianity north of the Alps. Some parts of the 4th century basilica built by Valentinian I (364-75) are extant in the present cathedral, which dates from the 11th to 13th centuries. Trier was the western capital of the Roman Empire until it was taken by the Franks in 464. A bishopric was established there at the dawn of the Middle Ages and was raised to an archbishopric under Bishop Hetto (814-47). The earliest archiepiscopal coinage dates from the end of the 10th century. The importance of Trier grew during the High Middle Ages as the city became one of the ecclesiastic electorates of the German Empire under Baldwin of Luxembourg (1307-54). That lofty status was confirmed by the Golden Bull of 1356, which permanently established the seven electorates of the Empire. The wealth, power and prestige of the archbishops continued through the Late Middle Ages and withstood the Protestant Reformation in the 16th century. The economy of Trier was severely circumscribed by the hyper-inflation of the early period of the Thirty Years' War, and the city never regained its former position. Trier was taken by the French in 1794 and the last archbishop fled from his domains. In 1802, the archbishopric was secularized and divided between Nassau and France, but Prussia obtained most of Trier's territory in 1815, following the conclusion of the Napoleonic Wars.

RULERS

Lothar von Metternich, 1599-1623
Philipp Christof von Sötern, 1623-1652
Karl Kaspar von der Leyen, 1652-1676
Johann Hugo von Orsbeck, 1676-1711

MINT OFFICIALS' INITIALS

Initial	Date	Name
AL	1678-83	Adam Longerich
B	?	Philip Christoph Becker, die-cutter
CL	1683-93	Kaspar Longerich
FS	1693-95	Friedrich Schrattauer
GG	1698-1734	Gerhardt Godt
HA	1624-27	Hans Jacob Ayrer
HE	1669-75	Heinrich Eberskirchen
HL	1625-27	Heinrich Lambert
ICB	1659-66	Johann Christoph Buchsmeyer
IL	1680-90	Joseph Longerich
LS	1616-24	Lorenz Schneider
MS	1627-52	Matthias Stein

ARMS

Cross, usually displayed in conjunction with the family arms of the archbishop

REFERENCES

N = Alfred Noss, **Die Münzen von Trier**, v. I, pt. 2, **Beschreibung der Münzen 1307-1556**, Bonn, 1916.
S = Friedrich von Schrötter, **Die Münzen von Trier**, v. II, **Beschreibung der neuzeitlichen Münzen 1556-1794**, Bonn, 1908.
Sch = Wolfgang Schulten, **Deutsche Münzen aus der Zeit Karls V.**, Frankfurt am Main, 1974.

ARCHBISHOPRIC

REGULAR COINAGE

KM# 1 HELLER

Billon **Obv:** Orsbeck arms divide A-L in pearl circle **Note:** Uniface.

Date	Mintage	VG	F	VF	XF	Unc
ND(1678-83) AL	—	9.00	20.00	40.00	80.00	—

KM# 5 PFENNIG

Billon **Obv:** Arms divide last two digits of date, T above arms

Date	Mintage	VG	F	VF	XF	Unc
ND	—	8.00	16.00	30.00	60.00	—
(16)24	—	8.00	16.00	30.00	60.00	—
(16)25	—	8.00	16.00	30.00	60.00	—
(16)26	—	8.00	16.00	30.00	60.00	—
(16)33	—	8.00	16.00	30.00	60.00	—

KM# A5 PFENNIG

Silver **Ruler:** Philipp Christof **Obv:** Shield of Sötern arms superimposed on cross of Trier, all in a circle of pellets **Note:** Uniface schüssel-type.

Date	Mintage	VG	F	VF	XF	Unc
(1623-52)	—	—	—	—	—	—

KM# 2 PFENNIG

Billon **Obv:** Quartered arms with T above **Note:** Uniface.

Date	Mintage	VG	F	VF	XF	Unc
ND	—	8.00	16.00	30.00	60.00	—

KM# 3 PFENNIG

Billon **Obv:** Shield of Trier-Metternich arms with L above

Date	Mintage	VG	F	VF	XF	Unc
ND	—	8.00	16.00	30.00	60.00	—

KM# 4 PFENNIG

Billon **Obv:** L.A.T. above shield

Date	Mintage	VG	F	VF	XF	Unc
ND	—	8.00	16.00	30.00	60.00	—

KM# 6 PFENNIG

Billon **Obv:** Leyen arms on Trier arms in inner circle

Date	Mintage	VG	F	VF	XF	Unc
ND	—	8.00	16.00	30.00	60.00	—

KM# 7 PFENNIG

Billon **Obv:** Quartered shield in inner circle

Date	Mintage	VG	F	VF	XF	Unc
ND	—	8.00	16.00	30.00	60.00	—

KM# 8 PFENNIG

Billon **Obv:** Shield of arms divides C L

Date	Mintage	VG	F	VF	XF	Unc
ND(1683-93) CL	—	8.00	16.00	30.00	60.00	—

KM# 9 PFENNIG

Billon **Obv:** Shield of arms divides F S

Date	Mintage	VG	F	VF	XF	Unc
ND(1693-95) FS	—	8.00	16.00	30.00	60.00	—

KM# 93 4 PFENNIG (1/2 Albus)

Silver **Obv:** Arms in inner circle, titles of Philipp **Rev:** Standing figure

Date	Mintage	VG	F	VF	XF	Unc
1648	—	13.00	27.00	55.00	110	—

KM# 106 4 PFENNIG (1/2 Albus)

Silver **Obv:** Arms in inner circle **Rev:** Standing figure of St. Peter with key and book

Date	Mintage	VG	F	VF	XF	Unc
1652	—	13.00	27.00	55.00	110	—

KM# 107 4 PFENNIG (1/2 Albus)

Silver **Obv:** Shield of arms with date above in inner circle

Date	Mintage	VG	F	VF	XF	Unc
1652	—	9.00	20.00	45.00	90.00	—
1653	—	9.00	20.00	45.00	90.00	—
1654	—	9.00	20.00	45.00	90.00	—
1655	—	9.00	20.00	45.00	90.00	—
1656	—	9.00	20.00	45.00	90.00	—

KM# 121 4 PFENNIG (1/2 Albus)

Silver **Obv:** Oval arms topped by elector's hat **Rev:** Date in legend in Roman numerals

Date	Mintage	VG	F	VF	XF	Unc
ND	—	9.00	20.00	45.00	90.00	—
1657	—	9.00	20.00	45.00	90.00	—
1658	—	9.00	20.00	45.00	90.00	—
1659	—	9.00	20.00	45.00	90.00	—
1660	—	9.00	20.00	45.00	90.00	—
1661	—	9.00	20.00	45.00	90.00	—
1662	—	9.00	20.00	45.00	90.00	—
1663	—	9.00	20.00	45.00	90.00	—
1666	—	9.00	20.00	45.00	90.00	—

KM# 122 4 PFENNIG (1/2 Albus)

Billon

Date	Mintage	VG	F	VF	XF	Unc
1663	—	8.00	20.00	33.00	60.00	—
1664	—	8.00	20.00	33.00	60.00	—
1665	—	8.00	20.00	33.00	60.00	—
1667	—	8.00	20.00	33.00	60.00	—
1668	—	8.00	20.00	33.00	60.00	—
1669	—	8.00	20.00	33.00	60.00	—
1670	—	8.00	20.00	33.00	60.00	—
1672	—	8.00	20.00	33.00	60.00	—
1674	—	8.00	20.00	33.00	60.00	—
1676	—	8.00	20.00	33.00	60.00	—

KM# 123 4 PFENNIG (1/2 Albus)

Billon **Obv:** Halved arms in wreath

Date	Mintage	VG	F	VF	XF	Unc
1665	—	8.00	20.00	33.00	70.00	—

KM# 127 4 PFENNIG (1/2 Albus)

Silver **Rev:** Date in legend in Arabic numerals

Date	Mintage	VG	F	VF	XF	Unc
1667	—	9.00	20.00	45.00	90.00	—
1668	—	9.00	20.00	45.00	90.00	—
1669	—	9.00	20.00	45.00	90.00	—
1670	—	9.00	20.00	45.00	90.00	—
1671	—	9.00	20.00	45.00	90.00	—
1672	—	9.00	20.00	45.00	90.00	—
1673	—	9.00	20.00	45.00	90.00	—
1674	—	9.00	20.00	45.00	90.00	—
1675	—	9.00	20.00	45.00	90.00	—
1676	—	9.00	20.00	45.00	90.00	—

KM# 138 4 PFENNIG (1/2 Albus)

Silver **Obv:** Round arms topped by elector's cap **Rev:** Standing figure of St. Peter with key, date in legend

Date	Mintage	VG	F	VF	XF	Unc
1677	—	13.00	27.00	55.00	110	—
1678	—	13.00	27.00	55.00	110	—
1679	—	13.00	27.00	55.00	110	—
1680	—	13.00	27.00	55.00	110	—
1681	—	13.00	27.00	55.00	110	—

KM# 126 4 PFENNIG (1/2 Albus)

Billon **Obv:** Orsbeck arms on Trier shield in wreath **Rev:** Value and date in wreath

Date	Mintage	VG	F	VF	XF	Unc
1677	—	8.00	20.00	33.00	70.00	—
1679 AL	—	8.00	20.00	33.00	70.00	—
1680	—	8.00	20.00	33.00	70.00	—

KM# 146 4 PFENNIG (1/2 Albus)

Billon **Obv:** Orsbeck arms on Trier shield, date above **Rev:** Value in wreath

Date	Mintage	VG	F	VF	XF	Unc
1680 AL	—	8.00	20.00	33.00	70.00	—

KM# 150 4 PFENNIG (1/2 Albus)

Billon **Rev:** Value: IIII/PFEN/TRIER

Date	Mintage	VG	F	VF	XF	Unc
1681 AL	—	6.00	16.00	33.00	65.00	—
1683 AL	—	6.00	16.00	33.00	65.00	—
1683 CL	—	6.00	16.00	33.00	65.00	—

KM# 154 4 PFENNIG (1/2 Albus)

Silver **Obv:** Arms cover inner circle

Date	Mintage	VG	F	VF	XF	Unc
1682	—	9.00	20.00	40.00	80.00	—
1683	—	9.00	20.00	40.00	80.00	—
1684	—	9.00	20.00	40.00	80.00	—
1686	—	9.00	20.00	40.00	80.00	—
1687	—	9.00	20.00	40.00	80.00	—
1688	—	9.00	20.00	40.00	80.00	—
1689	—	9.00	20.00	40.00	80.00	—

KM# 156 4 PFENNIG (1/2 Albus)

Billon **Rev:** Value: IIII/PHENN/TRIER

Date	Mintage	VG	F	VF	XF	Unc
1683	—	6.00	16.00	33.00	60.00	—

KM# 158 4 PFENNIG (1/2 Albus)

Silver **Obv:** Shield of arms topped by elector's hat, date divided at bottom **Rev:** Bust of St. Peter with key and book in clouds, value below

Date	Mintage	VG	F	VF	XF	Unc
1689	—	16.00	33.00	65.00	135	—

KM# 159 4 PFENNIG (1/2 Albus)

Silver **Obv:** Round arms cover inner circle, date in legend

Date	Mintage	VG	F	VF	XF	Unc
1689	—	16.00	33.00	65.00	135	—

KM# 176 4 PFENNIG (1/2 Albus)
Silver **Rev:** Date divided above St. Peter

Date	Mintage	VG	F	VF	XF	Unc
1691	—	9.00	20.00	38.00	85.00	—
1692	—	9.00	20.00	38.00	85.00	—
1693	—	9.00	20.00	38.00	85.00	—
1694	—	9.00	20.00	38.00	85.00	—
1695	—	9.00	20.00	38.00	85.00	—

KM# 186 1/2 PETERMENGER
Billon **Ruler:** Johann Hugo **Obv:** Date above arms **Rev:** Value: 1/2/PETER/MENGEN

Date	Mintage	VG	F	VF	XF	Unc
1698 GG	—	7.00	13.00	25.00	50.00	—
1699 GG	—	7.00	13.00	25.00	50.00	—
1700 GG	—	7.00	13.00	25.00	50.00	—

KM# A174 60 KREUZER (2/3 Thaler)
Silver **Ruler:** Johann Hugo **Obv:** Bust to right **Obv. Legend:** IOAN. HUGO. D.G. ARCH. TREV: S. R. I. P. E. E. S. **Rev:** Oval 4-fold arms with central shield of Orsbeck in baroque frame, crossed sword and crozier behind, electoral hat above, date at end of legend **Rev. Legend:** MONE. NOVA. TREVI — RENSIS. ANNI. (date) **Note:** Dav# 1024.

Date	Mintage	VG	F	VF	XF	Unc
1690 CL	—	225	450	950	2,200	—

KM# A8 ALBUS (Old Standard)
Silver **Obv:** Standing figure of St. Peter with key and book **Rev:** Quartered arms in inner circle **Mint:** Coblenz

Date	Mintage	VG	F	VF	XF	Unc
ND	—	45.00	80.00	140	225	—

KM# A9 ALBUS (Old Standard)
Silver **Obv:** Standing figure of St. Helena with cross and nail **Mint:** Trier

Date	Mintage	VG	F	VF	XF	Unc
ND	—	45.00	80.00	140	225	—

KM# 10 ALBUS (Old Standard)
Silver **Rev:** Arms divide value **Note:** Klippe.

Date	Mintage	VG	F	VF	XF	Unc
ND	—	—	—	—	—	—

KM# 45 ALBUS (8 Pfennig)
Silver **Obv:** Arms in inner circle **Rev:** Value: VIII/PFENIG/1622, date in inner circle

Date	Mintage	VG	F	VF	XF	Unc
1622	—	33.00	60.00	120	200	—

KM# 46 ALBUS (8 Pfennig)
Silver **Rev:** Value: VIII and date

Date	Mintage	VG	F	VF	XF	Unc
1622	—	33.00	60.00	120	200	—

KM# 44 ALBUS (8 Pfennig)
Silver **Obv:** Standing figure of St. Peter with VIII right in inner circle **Rev:** Date above shield of arms in inner circle **Note:** Kipper 8 Pfennig.

Date	Mintage	VG	F	VF	XF	Unc
1622	—	33.00	60.00	120	200	—

KM# 11 ALBUS (9 Pfennig)
Silver **Obv:** Partial figure of St. Peter in inner circle with key and book **Rev:** Quartered shield of arms in inner circle **Mint:** Coblenz

Date	Mintage	VG	F	VF	XF	Unc
ND	—	33.00	60.00	120	200	—

KM# 12 ALBUS (9 Pfennig)
Silver **Obv:** Smaller figure of St. Peter

Date	Mintage	VG	F	VF	XF	Unc
ND	—	33.00	60.00	120	200	—

KM# 41 ALBUS (9 Pfennig)
Silver **Rev:** Date above shield in inner circle

Date	Mintage	VG	F	VF	XF	Unc
1621	—	33.00	60.00	120	200	—
1622	—	33.00	60.00	120	200	—
1623	—	33.00	60.00	120	200	—

KM# 66 ALBUS (New Standard)
Silver **Obv:** Date above arms in inner circle **Rev:** Standing figure of St. Peter with key **Note:** Large size, approximately 20mm.

Date	Mintage	VG	F	VF	XF	Unc
ND	—	11.00	22.00	45.00	90.00	—
1625	—	—	—	—	—	—

KM# 67 ALBUS (New Standard)
Silver **Note:** Small size, approximately 17mm.

Date	Mintage	VG	F	VF	XF	Unc
1625	—	11.00	22.00	45.00	90.00	—
1627	—	11.00	22.00	45.00	90.00	—

KM# 74 ALBUS (New Standard)
Silver **Obv:** 27 above shield **Note:** Klippe.

Date	Mintage	VG	F	VF	XF	Unc
1627	—	—	—	—	—	—

KM# 72 ALBUS (New Standard)
Silver **Obv:** Oval arms, two-digit date at sides

Date	Mintage	VG	F	VF	XF	Unc
1627	—	11.00	22.00	45.00	90.00	—
1628	—	11.00	22.00	45.00	90.00	—

KM# 75 ALBUS (New Standard)
Silver **Obv:** Flat-topped shield with date above

Date	Mintage	VG	F	VF	XF	Unc
1628	—	11.00	22.00	45.00	90.00	—
1629	—	11.00	22.00	45.00	90.00	—
1630	—	11.00	22.00	45.00	90.00	—

KM# 76 ALBUS (New Standard)
Silver **Obv:** Date above shield **Note:** Klippe.

Date	Mintage	VG	F	VF	XF	Unc
1629	—	—	—	—	—	—

KM# 92 ALBUS (New Standard)
Silver **Obv:** 16 above shield, 47 at sides **Rev:** Standing figure of St. Philip with cross and book

Date	Mintage	VG	F	VF	XF	Unc
1647	—	11.00	27.00	55.00	100	—

KM# 94 ALBUS (New Standard)
Silver **Obv:** 16 above shield, other two digits at sides **Rev:** Standing figure of St. Philip

Date	Mintage	VG	F	VF	XF	Unc
1648	—	9.00	24.00	45.00	90.00	—
1649	—	9.00	24.00	45.00	90.00	—

KM# 100 ALBUS (New Standard)
Silver **Obv:** Date above shield

Date	Mintage	VG	F	VF	XF	Unc
1649	—	9.00	24.00	45.00	90.00	—
1650	—	9.00	24.00	45.00	90.00	—
1651	—	9.00	24.00	45.00	90.00	—
1652	—	9.00	24.00	45.00	90.00	—

KM# 56 3 ALBUS
Billon **Obv:** Standing figure of St. Peter with key, value right **Rev:** Shield of arms with date above in inner circle **Note:** Kipper 3 Albus.

Date	Mintage	VG	F	VF	XF	Unc
1622	—	80.00	135	240	400	—

KM# 48 6 ALBUS
Billon **Obv:** Standing figure of St. Peter with key and book, value right in inner circle **Rev:** Shield of arms with date above in inner circle **Note:** Kipper 6 Albus.

Date	Mintage	VG	F	VF	XF	Unc
1622	—	115	200	325	500	—

KM# 68 1/8 THALER
Silver **Obv:** Bust of Archbishop right in inner circle, date below shoulder **Rev:** Value above arms in inner circle

Date	Mintage	VG	F	VF	XF	Unc
1625 IA	—	450	800	1,350	2,000	—

KM# 77 1/8 THALER
Silver **Obv:** Standing figure of St. Peter with key and book in inner circle, date in Roman numerals in legend **Rev:** Value in four lines in inner circle **Note:** Varieties exist.

Date	Mintage	VG	F	VF	XF	Unc
MDCLIX (1659)	—	85.00	165	300	500	—
MDCLX (1660)	—	85.00	165	300	500	—
MDCLXIII (1663)	—	85.00	165	300	500	—
MDCLXV (1665)	—	85.00	165	300	500	—
MDCLXVIII (1668)	—	85.00	165	300	500	—

KM# 52 1/4 THALER
Silver **Obv:** Bust of Archbishop right in inner circle, date below shoulder **Rev:** Shield of arms in inner circle

Date	Mintage	VG	F	VF	XF	Unc
1624	—	525	950	1,650	2,700	—

KM# 136 1/3 THALER
Silver **Obv:** Bust of Archbishop right in inner circle, value in oval below **Rev:** Crowned heart-shaped arms in inner circle, date in legend

Date	Mintage	VG	F	VF	XF	Unc
1675	—	600	1,200	2,000	3,000	—

KM# 147 1/3 THALER
Silver **Obv:** Bust of Archbishop right in inner circle **Rev:** Crowned oval arms divides date in inner circle, value in oval below

Date	Mintage	VG	F	VF	XF	Unc
1680	—	600	1,200	2,000	3,000	—

KM# 17 1/2 THALER
Silver **Obv:** Standing figure of St. Peter left with key and book in inner circle **Rev:** Shield of arms in inner circle, date in legend

Date	Mintage	VG	F	VF	XF	Unc
1602	—	2,200	3,600	6,000	7,750	—

KM# 18 1/2 THALER
Silver **Obv:** Standing figure of St. Peter right with key above shoulder and book in inner circle **Note:** Klippe.

Date	Mintage	VG	F	VF	XF	Unc
1602	—	2,650	4,300	7,500	—	—

KM# 42 1/2 THALER
Silver **Obv:** Figure of St. Peter walking right with key right and book in inner circle **Rev:** Shield of arms in inner circke, date at top in legend

Date	Mintage	VG	F	VF	XF	Unc
1621	—	1,350	2,400	4,000	6,750	—

KM# 53 1/2 THALER
Silver **Obv:** Bust of Archbishop right in inner circle, date below shoulder **Rev:** Helmeted arms, date divided at top in inner circle

Date	Mintage	VG	F	VF	XF	Unc
1624	—	800	1,350	2,700	4,000	—
1627 MS / IA	—	800	1,350	2,700	4,000	—

KM# 54 1/2 THALER
Silver **Rev:** Without date **Note:** Klippe.

Date	Mintage	VG	F	VF	XF	Unc
1624	—	1,000	1,650	3,300	4,700	—
1627 MS / IA	—	1,000	1,650	3,300	4,700	—

KM# 124 1/2 THALER

Silver **Obv:** Archbishop

Date	Mintage	VG	F	VF	XF	Unc
1666 ICB	—	600	1,200	2,400	4,000	—

KM# 137 2/3 THALER

Silver

Date	Mintage	VG	F	VF	XF	Unc
1675	—	225	450	850	1,900	—

KM# 148 2/3 THALER

Silver **Obv:** Bust of Archbishop right in inner circle **Rev:** Crowned oval arms divide date in inner circle, value in oval below

Date	Mintage	VG	F	VF	XF	Unc
1680 AL	—	525	950	1,650	2,700	—

KM# 174 2/3 THALER

Silver

Date	Mintage	VG	F	VF	XF	Unc
1690 CL	—	200	400	850	2,000	—
1691 CL	—	200	400	850	2,000	—
1692 CL	—	—	—	—	—	—

KM# 173 2/3 THALER

Silver **Note:** Varieties exist, including divided date in legend.

Date	Mintage	VG	F	VF	XF	Unc
1690 CL	—	225	450	950	2,100	—
1691 CL	—	225	450	950	2,100	—

KM# 178 2/3 THALER

Silver

Date	Mintage	VG	F	VF	XF	Unc
1694 FS	—	225	425	900	2,100	—

KM# 73 3/4 THALER

Silver **Obv:** Bust of Archbishop right in inner circle **Rev:** Helmeted arms with date at top in inner circle

Date	Mintage	VG	F	VF	XF	Unc
1627 IA	—	2,700	4,300	6,750	—	—

DAV# 5863 THALER

Silver **Obv:** Standing figure of St. Peter left holding key and book in inner circle **Rev:** Helmeted arms in inner circle, date in legend **Note:** Struck at Coblenz Mint.

Date	Mintage	VG	F	VF	XF	Unc
1600	—	2,400	4,400	7,500	—	—

KM# 14 THALER

Silver **Obv:** Helmeted arms in inner circle **Rev:** Facing figure of St. Helena holding cross and nail in inner circle **Mint:** Trier **Note:** Dav. #5865.

Date	Mintage	VG	F	VF	XF	Unc
ND	—	4,700	7,600	12,000	—	—

KM# 19 THALER

Silver **Obv:** Standing figure of St. Peter left holding key and book in inner circle **Rev:** Helmeted arms in inner circle, date in legend **Mint:** Coblenz **Note:** Dav. #5867.

Date	Mintage	VG	F	VF	XF	Unc
1602	—	4,700	7,600	12,000	—	—

KM# 22 THALER

Silver **Obv:** Helmeted arms in inner circle, two-digit date divided by helmet 6-7 **Rev:** Facing figure of St. Helena holding cross and nail in inner circle **Mint:** Trier **Note:** Dav. #5869.

Date	Mintage	VG	F	VF	XF	Unc
1607	—	4,700	7,600	12,000	—	—

KM# 23 THALER

Silver **Obv:** Full four-digit date divided by helmet **Note:** Varieties exist. Dav. #5871.

Date	Mintage	VG	F	VF	XF	Unc
1608	—	3,500	5,700	8,800	—	—
1609	—	3,500	5,700	8,800	—	—
1610	—	3,500	5,700	8,800	—	—
1611	—	3,500	5,700	8,800	—	—
1612	—	3,500	5,700	8,800	—	—

KM# 25 THALER

Silver **Mint:** Coblenz **Note:** Similar to Dav. #5867, but date divided by helmet on reverse. Varieties exist. Dav. #5873.

Date	Mintage	VG	F	VF	XF	Unc
1609	—	1,600	2,900	6,100	8,800	—
1610	—	1,600	2,900	6,100	8,800	—
1613	—	1,600	2,900	6,100	8,800	—
1615	—	1,600	2,900	6,100	8,800	—

KM# 29 THALER

Silver **Obv:** Helmeted arms in inner circle, date divided by helmet **Rev:** Facing figure of St. Peter holding key and book in inner circle **Mint:** Trier **Note:** Varieties exist. Dav. #5876.

Date	Mintage	VG	F	VF	XF	Unc
1612 Rare	—	—	—	—	—	—

KM# 30 THALER

Silver **Obv:** Obverse of Dav. #5871 **Rev:** Reverse of Dav. #5876 **Note:** Mule. Dav. #5877.

Date	Mintage	VG	F	VF	XF	Unc
1612 Rare	—	—	—	—	—	—

KM# 31 THALER

Silver **Rev:** Radiant Madonna and child in inner circle, date in legend **Mint:** Coblenz **Note:** Dav. #5879.

Date	Mintage	VG	F	VF	XF	Unc
1615 Rare	—	—	—	—	—	—

KM# 33 THALER

Silver **Obv:** Bust of Archbishop right in inner circle **Rev:** Helmeted arms in inner circle, date in legend **Note:** Dav. #5882.

Date	Mintage	VG	F	VF	XF	Unc
1616 LS Rare	—	—	—	—	—	—
1617 LS Rare	—	—	—	—	—	—

KM# 34 THALER

Silver **Note:** Klippe. Dav. #5882A.

Date	Mintage	VG	F	VF	XF	Unc
1616 LS Rare	—	—	—	—	—	—
1617 LS Rare	—	—	—	—	—	—

KM# 35 THALER

Silver **Rev:** Radiant Madonna and child in inner circle, date in legend **Note:** Dav. #5883.

Date	Mintage	VG	F	VF	XF	Unc
1616 Rare	—	—	—	—	—	—

KM# 38 THALER

Silver **Rev:** Helmeted arms in inner circle, two-digit date (17) in legend **Note:** Dav. #5884.

Date	Mintage	VG	F	VF	XF	Unc
1617 Rare	—	—	—	—	—	—

KM# 43 THALER

Silver **Rev:** Date divided below arms in inner circle **Note:** Dav. #5885.

Date	Mintage	VG	F	VF	XF	Unc
1621	—	1,250	2,250	3,500	6,000	—

KM# 59 THALER

Silver **Obv:** Bust of Archbishop right in inner circle, date below shoulder **Rev:** Helmeted arms in inner circle **Note:** Varieties exist. Dav. #5887.

Date	Mintage	VG	F	VF	XF	Unc
1624	—	550	1,150	2,000	4,000	—

KM# 60 THALER

Silver **Note:** Klippe. Dav. #5887A.

Date	Mintage	VG	F	VF	XF	Unc
1624 Rare	—	—	—	—	—	—

Note: Dr. Busso Peus Nachfolger Auction 379, 4-04, XF realized approximately $23,885

KM# 61 THALER

Silver **Rev:** Date divided by helmet **Note:** Dav. #5889.

Date	Mintage	VG	F	VF	XF	Unc
1624	—	775	1,400	2,800	4,900	—

KM# 62 THALER

Silver **Obv:** Bust right with LS and date on shoulder **Note:** Dav. #5890.

Date	Mintage	VG	F	VF	XF	Unc
1624	—	775	1,400	2,800	4,900	—

KM# 69 THALER

Silver **Obv:** Bust of Archbishop right divides date in inner circle **Rev:** Helmeted arms in inner circle **Note:** Dav. #5891.

Date	Mintage	VG	F	VF	XF	Unc
1625 0	—	1,000	1,800	3,250	5,000	—

KM# 70 THALER

Silver **Note:** Klippe. Dav. #5891A.

Date	Mintage	VG	F	VF	XF	Unc
1625 Rare	—	—	—	—	—	—

KM# 109 THALER

Silver **Obv:** Arms topped by elector's hat in inner circle **Rev:** Radiant Madonna and child in inner circle, date in Roman numerals in legend **Note:** Dav. #5894.

Date	Mintage	VG	F	VF	XF	Unc
1657 Rare	—	—	—	—	—	—

KM# 111 THALER

Silver **Obv:** 3/4 right facing bust of Archbishop in inner circle **Rev:** Arms topped by elector's hat in inner circle, date in legend **Note:** Varieties exist. Dav. #5896.

Date	Mintage	VG	F	VF	XF	Unc
1659 ICB Rare	—	—	—	—	—	—

Note: Fritz Rudolf Künker Münzenhandlung Auction 90, 3-03, VF-XF realized approximately $12,715

KM# 112 THALER

Silver **Obv:** 3/4 right facing bust of Archbishop in inner circle **Note:** Dav. #5897.

Date	Mintage	VG	F	VF	XF	Unc
1659 ICB Rare	—	—	—	—	—	—

KM# 125 THALER

Silver **Obv:** Larger head left **Note:** Dav. #5898.

Date	Mintage	VG	F	VF	XF	Unc
1666 ICB Rare	—	—	—	—	—	—

KM# 135 THALER

Silver **Obv:** 3/4 right facing bust of Archbishop in inner circle **Rev:** Heart-shaped arms topped by elector's hat in inner circle, date in legend **Note:** Dav. #5899.

Date	Mintage	VG	F	VF	XF	Unc
1671 Rare	—	—	—	—	—	—

KM# 151 THALER

Silver **Obv:** Bust of Archbishop right in inner circle **Rev:** Helmeted arms in inner circle, date in legend **Note:** Dav. #5901.

Date	Mintage	VG	F	VF	XF	Unc
1681 Rare	—	—	—	—	—	—

KM# 152 THALER

Silver **Obv:** Without inner circle **Note:** Dav. #5902.

Date	Mintage	VG	F	VF	XF	Unc
1681 Rare	—	—	—	—	—	—

KM# A63 1-1/2 THALER

Silver **Ruler:** Lothar **Obv:** 4-fold arms of Trier and Metternich with central shield of Prüm, ornate helmet above with crest of Metternich arms dividing date, titles of Lothar **Rev:** Full-length facing figure of St. Helena with cross **Rev. Legend:** MONETA. NOVA **Note:** S #124a.

Date	Mintage	VG	F	VF	XF	Unc
1611 Rare	—	—	—	—	—	—

KM# 63 1-1/2 THALER

Silver **Obv:** Bust of Archbishop right in inner circle **Rev:** Helmeted arms in inner circle, date divided by helmet **Mint:** Coblenz **Note:** Dav. #A5888.

Date	Mintage	VG	F	VF	XF	Unc
1624 Rare	—	—	—	—	—	—

KM# 64 1-1/2 THALER

Silver **Mint:** Coblenz **Note:** Klippe. Dav. #B5888.

Date	Mintage	VG	F	VF	XF	Unc
1624 Rare	—	—	—	—	—	—

KM# 15 2 THALER

Silver **Obv:** Helmeted arms in inner circle, date divided by helmet **Rev:** Facing figure of St. Helena holding cross and nail in inner circle **Mint:** Trier **Note:** Dav. #B5864

Date	Mintage	VG	F	VF	XF	Unc
ND Rare	—	—	—	—	—	—

KM# 20 2 THALER

Silver **Ruler:** Lothar **Obv:** Standing figure of St. Peter left holding key and book in inner circle **Rev:** Helmeted arms in inner circle, date in legend **Mint:** Coblenz **Note:** Dav. #5866

Date	Mintage	VG	F	VF	XF	Unc
1602 Rare	—	—	—	—	—	—

KM# 21 2 THALER

Silver **Ruler:** Lothar **Obv:** Facing figure of St. Helena holding cross and nail in inner circle **Rev:** Helmeted arms with date above in inner circle **Note:** Dav. #5868.

Date	Mintage	VG	F	VF	XF	Unc
1606 Rare	—	—	—	—	—	—

KM# 24 2 THALER

Silver **Obv:** Helmeted arms in inner circle, date divided by helmet **Rev:** Facing figrue of St. Helena holding cross and nail in inner circle **Mint:** Trier **Note:** Dav. #5870

Date	Mintage	VG	F	VF	XF	Unc
1608 Rare	—	—	—	—	—	—
1609 Rare	—	—	—	—	—	—
1610 Rare	—	—	—	—	—	—

KM# 27 2 THALER

Silver **Mint:** Coblenz **Note:** Klippe. Similar to Dav. #5866, but date divided by helmet on reverse. Dav. #5872.

Date	Mintage	VG	F	VF	XF	Unc
1610 Rare	—	—	—	—	—	—

KM# 28 2 THALER

Silver **Note:** Klippe. Dav. #5870A.

Date	Mintage	VG	F	VF	XF	Unc
1611 Rare	—	—	—	—	—	—

KM# 32 2 THALER

Silver **Obv:** Helmeted arms in inner circle, date divided by helmet **Rev:** Radiant Madonna and child in inner circle, date in legend **Note:** Klippe. Mining 2 Thaler. Dav. #5878.

Date	Mintage	VG	F	VF	XF	Unc
1615	—	6,500	10,000	15,000	—	—

KM# 36 2 THALER

Silver **Note:** Dav. #5880.

Date	Mintage	VG	F	VF	XF	Unc
1616/15 Rare	—	—	—	—	—	—

KM# 37 2 THALER

Silver **Obv:** Bust of Archbishop right in inner circle **Rev:** Helmeted arms in inner circle, date in legend **Note:** Dav. #5881.

Date	Mintage	VG	F	VF	XF	Unc
1616 Rare	—	—	—	—	—	—

KM# 39 2 THALER

Silver **Note:** Klippe. Dav. #5881A.

Date	Mintage	VG	F	VF	XF	Unc
1617 Rare	—	—	—	—	—	—

KM# 55 2 THALER

Silver **Obv:** Bust of Archbishop right in inner circle, date below shoulder **Rev:** Helmeted arms in inner circle **Note:** Dav. #A5886.

Date	Mintage	VG	F	VF	XF	Unc
1624 Rare	—	—	—	—	—	—

KM# A56 2 THALER

Silver **Note:** Klippe. Dav. #B5886.

Date	Mintage	VG	F	VF	XF	Unc
1624 Rare	—	—	—	—	—	—

KM# 57 2 THALER

Silver **Rev:** Date divided by helmet **Note:** Dav. #5888.

Date	Mintage	VG	F	VF	XF	Unc
1624 Rare	—	—	—	—	—	—

KM# 58 2 THALER

Silver **Note:** Klippe. Dav. #5888A.

Date	Mintage	VG	F	VF	XF	Unc
1624 Rare	—	—	—	—	—	—

KM# 110 2 THALER

Silver **Obv:** Arms topped by elector's hat in inner circle **Rev:** Radiant Madonna and child in inner circle, date in roman numerals in legend **Note:** Dav. #5893.

Date	Mintage	VG	F	VF	XF	Unc
1657 Rare	—	—	—	—	—	—

KM# 113 2 THALER

Silver **Note:** Dav. #5895.

Date	Mintage	VG	F	VF	XF	Unc
1659 ICB Rare	—	—	—	—	—	—

KM# 153 2 THALER

Silver **Obv:** Bust of Archbishop right in inner circle **Rev:** Helmeted arms in inner circle, date in legend **Note:** Dav. #5900.

Date	Mintage	VG	F	VF	XF	Unc
1681 Rare	—	—	—	—	—	—

KM# 175 3 THALER

Silver **Obv:** Bust of Archbishop right in inner circle, date below shoulder **Rev:** Helmeted arms in inner circle **Mint:** Coblenz **Note:** Dav. #5886.

Date	Mintage	VG	F	VF	XF	Unc
1624 Rare	—	—	—	—	—	—

TRADE COINAGE

KM# 16 GOLDGULDEN

3.5000 g., 0.9860 Gold 0.1109 oz. AGW **Obv:** Arms topped by Christ on throne **Rev:** Three shields in trefoil with arms at center **Mint:** Coblenz **Note:** Fr#3459.

Date	Mintage	VG	F	VF	XF	Unc
1601	—	500	1,000	2,000	3,200	—
1605	—	500	1,000	2,000	3,200	—
1608	—	500	1,000	2,000	3,200	—
1609	—	500	1,000	2,000	3,200	—
1613	—	500	1,000	2,000	3,200	—
1617	—	500	1,000	2,000	3,200	—
1618	—	500	1,000	2,000	3,200	—
1619	—	500	1,000	2,000	3,200	—
ND	—	500	1,000	2,000	3,200	—

KM# 26 GOLDGULDEN

3.5000 g., 0.9860 Gold 0.1109 oz. AGW **Obv:** St. Helen standing **Rev:** Four shields in quatrefoil with arms at center **Mint:** Trier **Note:** Fr#3462.

Date	Mintage	VG	F	VF	XF	Unc
1608	—	600	1,200	2,250	3,750	—
1610	—	600	1,200	2,250	3,750	—
1611	—	600	1,200	2,250	3,750	—

KM# 40 GOLDGULDEN

3.5000 g., 0.9860 Gold 0.1109 oz. AGW **Obv:** Arms topped by bust of St. Peter **Mint:** Coblenz **Note:** Fr#3460.

Date	Mintage	VG	F	VF	XF	Unc
1619	—	500	1,000	2,500	4,500	—

KM# 85 GOLDGULDEN

3.5000 g., 0.9860 Gold 0.1109 oz. AGW **Obv:** Arms in inner circle **Rev:** Madonna and child in inner circle **Mint:** Philipsburg **Note:** Fr#3463.

Date	Mintage	VG	F	VF	XF	Unc
1632	—	2,400	3,600	6,600	10,000	—

KM# 165 GOLDGULDEN

3.5000 g., 0.9860 Gold 0.1109 oz. AGW **Ruler:** Johann Hugo **Obv:** Bust of St. Peter, value below **Rev:** Three shields of arms **Note:** Fr#3471.

Date	Mintage	VG	F	VF	XF	Unc
1684 CL	—	1,200	2,400	4,800	7,800	—
1694	—	1,200	2,400	4,800	7,800	—
1700	—	1,200	2,400	4,800	7,800	—

KM# 91 1/2 DUCAT

1.7500 g., 0.9860 Gold 0.0555 oz. AGW **Obv:** Bust of Johann Hugo right **Rev:** Crowned arms **Note:** Fr#3469.

Date	Mintage	VG	F	VF	XF	Unc
ND	—	900	1,200	1,800	4,200	—

KM# 108 DUCAT

1.7500 g., 0.9860 Gold 0.0555 oz. AGW **Obv:** Karl Caspar **Note:** Fr#3465.

Date	Mintage	VG	F	VF	XF	Unc
1654	—	900	1,200	2,400	6,000	—
1656	—	900	1,200	2,400	6,000	—

KM# 149 DUCAT

1.7500 g., 0.9860 Gold 0.0555 oz. AGW **Obv:** Johann Hugo **Note:** Fr#3468.

Date	Mintage	VG	F	VF	XF	Unc
1680 AL	—	1,150	2,200	4,400	7,500	—
1684 CL	—	1,150	2,200	4,400	7,500	—
1691	—	1,150	2,200	4,400	7,500	—
1692 CL	—	1,150	2,200	4,400	7,500	—
1699	—	1,150	2,200	4,400	7,500	—

KM# 179 DUCAT

1.7500 g., 0.9860 Gold 0.0555 oz. AGW **Rev:** Three shields of arms **Note:** Fr#3470.

Date	Mintage	VG	F	VF	XF	Unc
1690	—	1,350	2,700	5,400	8,800	—

KM# A114 6 DUCAT

21.0000 g., 0.9860 Gold 0.6657 oz. AGW **Obv:** 3/4 bust of Karl Kaspar right **Rev:** Capped ornate arms **Note:** Struck with 1 Thaler dies, KM#111.

Date	Mintage	VG	F	VF	XF	Unc
1659 Unique	—	—	—	—	—	—

PATTERNS

Including off metal strikes

KM#	Date	Mintage	Identification	Mkt Val
Pn1	1625	—	Thaler. Lead.	1,000
Pn2	1677	—	Petermenger. Gold.	1,200
Pn3	1678	—	Petermenger. Gold.	1,200
Pn4	1681	—	Petermenger. Gold.	1,200
Pn5	1684	—	Petermenger. Gold.	1,200
Pn6	1689	—	3 Petermenger. Gold.	2,250

ULM

A free city on the Danube located about 60 miles southeast of Stuttgart, Ulm is known from documents to have existed at least from the mid-9th century. During the 11th century, Ulm rose to prominence as the chief urban center of Swabia. The city was granted the distinction of a free imperial city in 1155. The right to mint its own coinage was given to the city in 1398. After a period of jointly issued coins with the cities of Ravensburg and Überlingen, Ulm struck a long series on its own beginning in 1546. Local city coinage ended in 1773, but it was not until 1803 that its free status ended, at which time Ulm became part of Bavaria. Ulm passed permanently to Württemberg in 1809.

MINT MARKS

G - Günzburg

MINT OFFICIALS' INITIALS

Initials	Date	Name
	1620-23	Franz Philipp Kling of Augsburg
	1623	Moritz Lang of Augsburg
	June-Oct., 1626	Friedrich held Hagelsheimer
HL	1635-40	Hans Ludwig der Jüngere
MK	1635-40	Marx Kienlin
HLK	1635-40	Ludwig and Kienlin
HL / HLK	1663-70	Hans Ludwig der Jüng-Jüngere and Hans Adam Kielin
M	1671-1704	Johann Bartholomäus Müller

ARMS

2-fold, divided horizontally, upper half usually shaded cross-hatching or other pattern.

FREE CITY

REGULAR COINAGE

KM# 15 THALER

Silver **Obv:** Large Spanish arms **Rev:** Crowned double-headed imperial eagle **Note:** Dav.#5903.

Date	Mintage	VG	F	VF	XF	Unc
1620	—	—	250	500	950	1,750
1623	—	—	275	550	1,000	1,850
1624	—	—	300	600	1,100	2,250

KM# 47 THALER

Silver **Note:** Dav.#5903A. Klippe.

Date	Mintage	VG	F	VF	XF	Unc
1624 Rare	—	—	—	—	—	—

KM# 49 THALER

Silver **Obv:** Angel head above pointed shield, flowers and cornucopia beside, HL below **Rev:** Crown above double-headed imperial eagle **Rev. Legend:** FERDINAND...SEMP.AVG **Note:** Dav.#5904.

Date	Mintage	VG	F	VF	XF	Unc
1635 HL	—	—	650	1,250	2,750	7,500

KM# 50 THALER

Silver **Rev:** Round bottom shield, M below **Note:** Dav.#5904A.

Date	Mintage	VG	F	VF	XF	Unc
1635 M	—	—	600	1,200	2,500	7,000

KM# 51 THALER

Silver **Obv. Legend:** FERDINANDVS...SEMPER.AVGVSTV **Rev:** Altered frame for arms **Note:** Dav.#5905.

Date	Mintage	VG	F	VF	XF	Unc
1635	—	—	1,200	2,500	4,500	—

KM# 52 THALER

Silver **Rev:** Angel head with wings above pointed shield without flower or mint mark below **Note:** Dav.#5906.

Date	Mintage	VG	F	VF	XF	Unc
1635	—	—	750	1,500	3,000	—

KM# 56 THALER

Silver **Obv:** Angel head with wings above straight topped and rounded bottom shield, M below **Rev:** Crown above double-headed imperial eagle **Rev. Legend:** FERDINAND II **Note:** Dav.#5907.

Date	Mintage	VG	F	VF	XF	Unc
1636 M	—	—	1,200	2,500	4,500	—

KM# 57 THALER

Silver **Obv:** Angel head wit wings above highly ornamented oval shield with HL-K below **Note:** Dav.#5908.

Date	Mintage	VG	F	VF	XF	Unc
1636 HLK	—	—	1,800	3,500	6,000	—
1637 HK	—	—	1,800	3,500	6,000	—

KM# 58 THALER

Silver **Rev:** Angel head without wings above highly ornamented oval shield with HL-K below **Note:** Dav.#5908A.

Date	Mintage	VG	F	VF	XF	Unc
1636 HLK	—	—	1,800	3,500	6,000	—

KM# 61 THALER

Silver **Note:** Similar to Thaler, KM# 60. Dav.#5909.

Date	Mintage	VG	F	VF	XF	Unc
1637 Rare	—	—	—	—	—	—
1638 M Rare	—	—	—	—	—	—
1640 HLK Rare	—	—	—	—	—	—

KM# 60 THALER

Silver **Obv:** Angel above oval ornate arms **Rev:** Crown above double-headed imperial eagle **Rev. Legend:** FERDINAND.III... **Note:** Varieties exist. Dav.#5910.

Date	Mintage	VG	F	VF	XF	Unc
1637 M	—	—	2,250	4,250	6,750	—
1638 M	—	—	2,250	4,250	6,750	—
1638 HLK	—	—	2,250	4,250	6,750	—
1639 M	—	—	2,250	4,250	6,750	—
1639 HLK	—	—	2,250	4,250	6,750	—
1640 HLK	—	—	2,250	4,250	6,750	—

TRADE COINAGE

KM# 54 DUCAT

3.5000 g., 0.9860 Gold 0.1109 oz. AGW **Note:** Fr#3480.

Date	Mintage	VG	F	VF	XF	Unc
1635 HL	—	550	1,250	2,500	4,250	—
1635 M	—	550	1,250	2,500	4,250	—
1636 HLK	—	550	1,250	2,500	4,250	—
1636 MK	—	550	1,250	2,500	4,250	—
1637 HLK	—	550	1,250	2,500	4,250	—
1638 HLK	—	550	1,250	2,500	4,250	—
1638 MK	—	550	1,250	2,500	4,250	—
ND	—	550	1,250	2,500	4,250	—

FR# 3482 DUCAT

3.5000 g., 0.9860 Gold 0.1109 oz. AGW **Rev:** 5-line inscription in wreath

Date	Mintage	VG	F	VF	XF	Unc
1639 HLK	—	700	1,500	3,200	5,500	—

KM# 5 2 DUCAT

7.0000 g., 0.9860 Gold 0.2219 oz. AGW **Subject:** Centennial of the Reformation **Note:** Fr#3479.

Date	Mintage	VG	F	VF	XF	Unc
1617	—	1,500	3,000	6,500	12,000	—

KM# 63 2 DUCAT

7.0000 g., 0.9860 Gold 0.2219 oz. AGW **Rev:** 5-line inscription in wreath **Note:** Fr#3481.

Date	Mintage	VG	F	VF	XF	Unc
1639 HLK Rare	—	—	—	—	—	—

PATTERNS

Including off metal strikes

KM#	Date	Mintage	Identification	Mkt Val
Pn1	1617	—	2 Ducat. Silver. KM#5.	125
Pn2	1635	—	Ducat. Copper. KM#54.	100

WALDECK

The former Countship of Waldeck was located in the western part of the German Empire, bordered by the Landgraviate of Hesse-Cassel on the east and south, the Duchy of Westphalia on the west and the Bishopric of Paderborn on the north. Arolsen was the seat of the counts and they traced their line of descent from a branch of the counts of Schwalenberg beginning in the early 11th century. Waldeck underwent several divisions over the centuries, the first such significant occurrence having taken place in 1474 with the establishment of Waldeck-Wildungen and Waldeck-Eisenberg. The latter was further divided into Waldeck-Eisenberg and Waldeck-Neu-Landau in 1539, but the former inherited Wildungen when the elder branch of the family became extinct in 1598. The line at Neu-Landau failed after two generations and reverted to Eisenberg the previous year (1597). A new line at Wildungen was established from Eisenberg in 1598 as well, but this, too, fell extinct in 1692, only ten years after the count having been raised to the rank of prince.

Waldeck-Eisenberg had received the Countship of Pyrmont in 1625 and became known as Waldeck-Pyrmont (see) upon the permanent unification of the two countships in 1668.

RULERS

Johann II of Neu-Landau, 1638-1668
Heinrich Wolrad of Wildungen, 1645-1664
Georg Friedrich of Wildungen, 1664-1692
As Regent for Heinrich Wolrad, 1645-1664
As Count, 1664-1692
Made Prince in 1682

COUNTY / PRINCIPALITY

REGULAR COINAGE

DAV# 7816 THALER

Silver **Subject:** Christian and Wolrad IV **Obv:** Crowned imperial eagle **Obv. Legend:** RUDOLP \ II... **Rev:** Helmeted arms **Rev. Legend:** CHRISTI. ET. WOLRA. CO..

Date	Mintage	VG	F	VF	XF	Unc
1608 Rare	—	—	—	—	—	—

DAV# 7817 THALER

Silver

Date	Mintage	VG	F	VF	XF	Unc
1613 Rare	—	—	—	—	—	—

DAV# 7818 THALER

Silver **Obv:** Date **Obv. Legend:** MATTHIAS. D: G... **Rev. Legend:** CHRISTI: ET. WOLF: FR: COM...

Date	Mintage	VG	F	VF	XF	Unc
1617	—	—	—	—	—	—

DAV# 7819 THALER

Silver **Obv:** Helmeted arms **Obv. Legend:** CHR. ET...I. WALDEC... **Rev:** Date, crowned imperial eagle with orb on breast **Rev. Legend:** FERDINAND: II...

Date	Mintage	VG	F	VF	XF	Unc
16ZZ	—	3,750	6,800	10,500	—	—
1623	—	3,750	6,800	10,500	—	—

DAV# 7820 THALER

Silver **Obv:** Helmeted arms separating J-6 above 2-4 below **Obv. Legend:** CHRIST: ET: WOLRA... **Rev. Legend:** FERDI: II...

Date	Mintage	VG	F	VF	XF	Unc
1624	—	3,750	6,400	9,800	—	—

DAV# 7821 THALER

Silver **Obv:** Helmeted arms divide date below **Obv. Legend:** CHRI: ET: WLRA... **Rev. Legend:** FERDI: II...

Date	Mintage	VG	F	VF	XF	Unc
1625	—	3,750	6,000	9,000	—	—

DAV# 7822 THALER

Silver **Ruler:** Johann II of New-Landau **Subject:** George Friedrich, Johann and Wolrad **Obv:** Helmeted arms **Obv. Legend:** GEORG*FRIDE*JOHAN*WOLRADT... **Rev:** Palm tree with stone dividing date and VF below

Date	Mintage	VG	F	VF	XF	Unc
1653 VF Rare	—	—	—	—	—	—

DAV# 7824 THALER

Silver **Subject:** Christian Ludwig **Obv:** Bust right **Rev:** Palm tree divides date and FW

Date	Mintage	VG	F	VF	XF	Unc
1695 FW Rare	—	—	—	—	—	—

DAV# 7815 2 THALER

Silver **Obv:** Crowned imperial eagle **Obv. Legend:** RUDOLP. II... **Rev:** Helmeted arms **Rev. Legend:** CHRISTI. ET. WOLRA. CO... **Note:** Dav. #7815.

Date	Mintage	VG	F	VF	XF	Unc
1608 Rare	—	—	—	—	—	—

TRADE COINAGE

FR# 3146 DUCAT

3.5000 g., 0.9860 Gold 0.1109 oz. AGW **Ruler:** Georg Friedrich of Wildungen As Regent for Heinrich Wolrad **Subject:** Johann II and Heinrich Wolrad **Obv:** Elaborately helmeted arms in inner circle **Rev:** Luxurious palm tree divides date in inner circle

Date	Mintage	VG	F	VF	XF	Unc
1654 Rare	—	—	—	—	—	—

WEISSENBURG

(Wissembourg)

A town in the Lower Alsace, 42 miles northeast of Strassburg. It grew up around a Benedictine Abbey founded in the 7th century. It became a free imperial city in 1305, but had a very limited coinage. It went with the rest of Alsace to France in 1648 and shared the subsequent adventures of that province.

FREE CITY

REGULAR COINAGE

KM# 5 HELLER

Silver **Obv:** City arms, crown above **Note:** Uniface.

Date	Mintage	Good	VG	F	VF	XF
ND(ca.1622-24)	—	—	—	—	—	—

KM# 25 PFENNIG

Silver **Obv:** City arms divide date, W above **Note:** Uniface.

Date	Mintage	Good	VG	F	VF	XF
1624	—	—	—	—	—	—

KM# 33 GROSCHEN

Silver **Obv:** City arms **Obv. Legend:** CIVIT. WEISSENBVRG. AM. RHEIN. **Rev. Legend:** Titles of Ferdinand II **Rev. Inscription:** +/RAHTS/GELT/

Date	Mintage	Good	VG	F	VF	XF
1627	—	—	33.00	65.00	135	225

KM# 7 KREUZER

Silver **Obv:** City arms, W above **Rev. Inscription:** I/KREVTZ/ER/(date)

Date	Mintage	Good	VG	F	VF	XF
16ZZ	—	—	45.00	85.00	160	275

KM# 27 KREUZER

Silver **Obv:** City arms divide date **Obv. Legend:** WEISSENBVRG. AM. RHEIN. **Rev:** Imperial orb with value I **Rev. Legend:** Titles of Ferdinand II

Date	Mintage	Good	VG	F	VF	XF
1624	—	—	—	—	—	—

KM# 9 2 KREUZERS

Billon **Obv:** Gate arms **Obv. Legend:** MON. NO. IMP. CIV. WISSEMBVRG. **Rev:** Crowned imperial eagle **Rev. Legend:** FERDINAND. II ... **Note:** Prev. KM#3.

Date	Mintage	Good	VG	F	VF	XF
1622	—	—	16.00	33.00	70.00	160

KM# 29 2 KREUZER (Vierer = Halbbatzen)

Silver **Obv:** City arms divide date **Obv. Legend:** WEISSENBVRG. AM. RHEIN. **Rev:** Imperial orb with value Z

Date	Mintage	Good	VG	F	VF	XF
16Z4	—	8.00	16.00	33.00	70.00	160
16Z6	—	8.00	16.00	33.00	70.00	160

KM# 35 2 KREUZER (Vierer = Halbbatzen)

Silver **Obv:** City arms divide date **Rev. Inscription:** Value: II/KREUTZ/ER **Note:** Varieties exist.

Date	Mintage	Good	VG	F	VF	XF
16Z9	—	5.00	11.00	22.00	45.00	100
1630	—	5.00	11.00	22.00	45.00	100
1631	—	5.00	11.00	22.00	45.00	100
163Z	—	5.00	11.00	22.00	45.00	100
1633	—	5.00	11.00	22.00	45.00	100

KM# 3 12 KREUZER (Dreibätzner = Schrechenberger)

Silver **Obv:** City arms divide date **Obv. Legend:** WEISSENBVRG. AM. RHEIN. **Rev:** Crowned imperial eagle, XII in orb on breast **Rev. Legend:** Titles of Ferdinand II **Note:** Varieties exist.

Date	Mintage	Good	VG	F	VF	XF
1616	—	—	—	—	—	—
1618	—	—	—	—	—	—
1622	—	—	55.00	90.00	160	275
1623	—	—	55.00	90.00	160	275
1624	—	—	55.00	90.00	160	275
1626	—	—	55.00	90.00	160	275

KM# 11 12 KREUZER (Dreibätzner = Schrechenberger)

Silver **Obv:** City arms divide date **Obv. Legend:** M. NO. IMP... **Rev:** Crowned imperial eagle, 12 in orb on breast **Rev. Legend:** IN. DEO. SPER. NON. CON. IN. AETER. **Note:** Varieties exist.

Date	Mintage	Good	VG	F	VF	XF
1622	—	—	60.00	100	175	300

KM# 12 12 KREUZER
(Dreibätzner = Schrechenberger)
Silver **Obv:** City arms **Rev:** Crowned imperial eagle
Rev. Legend: Titles of Ferdinand II

Date	Mintage	Good	VG	F	VF	XF
1622	—	—	55.00	90.00	165	300

KM# 13 12 KREUZER
(Dreibätzner = Schrechenberger)
Silver **Obv:** City arms **Rev:** Crowned imperial eagle
Rev. Legend: Titles of Ferdinand II

Date	Mintage	Good	VG	F	VF	XF
ND(1622)	—	—	55.00	90.00	165	300

KM# 31 12 KREUZER
(Dreibätzner = Schrechenberger)
Silver **Obv:** City arms divide date **Obv. Legend:** WEISEMBVRG * AM * RHEIN **Rev:** Value XII above crowned imperial eagle

Date	Mintage	Good	VG	F	VF	XF
1626	—	70.00	120	200	325	—
1628	—	70.00	120	200	325	—

KM# 14 12 KREUZER
(Dreibätzner = Schrechenberger)
Silver **Obv:** 2-towered city gate divides date in circle
Obv. Legend: + WEISSENBVRG * AM * RHEIN: **Rev:** Crowned imperial eagle, orb on breast, (XII) at top **Rev. Legend:** FERDINAND • II • ROM • IMP • SE • AV:

Date	Mintage	Good	VG	F	VF	XF
1626	—	—	—	—	—	—

KM# 30 24 KREUZER
(Sechsbätzner - Doppelschreckenberger)
Silver **Obv:** City arms in ornamented oval frame, date divided above **Obv. Legend:** MON. NOV. IMP... **Rev:** Crowned imperial eagle, 24 in orb on breast **Rev. Legend:** Titles of Ferdinand II

Date	Mintage	Good	VG	F	VF	XF
1624	—	—	—	—	—	—

KM# 15 1/2 THALER
Silver **Obv:** City arms in circle **Obv. Legend:** MON. NOV. IMP...
Rev: Crowned imperial eagle, plain orb on breast
Rev. Legend: Titles of Ferdinand II

Date	Mintage	Good	VG	F	VF	XF
ND(1623-32)	—	—	—	—	—	—

KM# 17 THALER
Silver **Obv:** Gate arms in oval shield in wreath border **Obv. Legend:** ✠ MON * NOV * IMP * CIVIT * WEISSEMBVRG * AM * RHEI * **Rev:** Crowned imperial eagle in wreath border, titles of Ferdinand II **Rev. Legend:** *FERDINANDVS * II * D * G * ROM * IMP * SEM* AVG **Note:** Dav. #5915. Prev. KM#5.

Date	Mintage	Good	VG	F	VF	XF
ND(1623-32) Rare	—	—	—	—	—	—

KM# 19 THALER
Silver **Rev:** Large gate arms **Note:** Dav. #5916. Prev. KM#7.

Date	Mintage	Good	VG	F	VF	XF
ND(1623-32) Rare	—	—	—	—	—	—

Note: Auktionshaus H.D. Rauch GmbH Auction 77, 4-06, near XF realized approximately $59,315

KM# 18 THALER
Silver **Obv:** Without wreath borders **Rev:** Without wreath borders **Note:** Dav. #5917. Prev. KM#6.

Date	Mintage	Good	VG	F	VF	XF
ND(1623-32) Rare	—	—	—	—	—	—

KM# 21 2 THALER
Silver **Obv:** Crowned imperial eagle in wreath border **Rev:** Gate arms on oval shield in wreath border **Note:** Dav. #A5914. Prev. KM#8.

Date	Mintage	Good	VG	F	VF	XF
ND(1623-32) Rare	—	—	—	—	—	—

KM# 23 4 THALER
Silver **Obv:** Gate arms on oval shield in wreath border
Rev: Crowned imperial eagle in wreath border **Note:** Dav. #5914. Prev. KM#9.

Date	Mintage	Good	VG	F	VF	XF
ND(1623-32) Rare	—	—	—	—	—	—

WERDEN & HELMSTAEDT

Abbeys

Bishop Ludger of Münster (791-809) founded the monasteries of Werden and Helmstedt early in his tenure as bishop. Werden is located on the River Ruhr six miles (10 kilometers) south of Essen, whereas Helmstedt is situated 20 miles (34 kilometers) east of Braunschweig in Niedersachsen. The abbot obtained the right to mint coins at Werden and at Lüdinghausen from Emperor Otto II (973-83) in 974, but the earliest known coins of the two monasteries date from the 11th century. A small, but fairly steady, stream of issues were produced from the 16th century through the middle of the 18th century. In 1803, Werden and Helmstedt were secularized and their fifty square miles of territory were annexed to Prussia.

RULERS
Heinrich III Duden, 1573-1601
Conrad II Kloet, 1601-1614
Hugo Preutäus von Assindia, 1614-1646
Heinrich IV Dücker, 1646-1667
Adolf IV von Borken, 1667-1670
Ferdinand von Erwitte, 1670-1706

Arms: (early type) – two crossed crosiers.

(later type) – two crossed crosiers in small shield superimposed on cross in larger shield

Imperial eagle - sometimes included to signify that the abbeys had imperial support and sanction.

CROSS REFERENCES:
G = Hermann Grote, "Die Münzen der Abtei Werden," ***Münzstudien***, v. 3 (1862- 63), pp. 411-445.
S = Hugo Frhr. Von Saurma-Jeltsch, **Die Saurmasche Münzsammlung deutscher, schweizerischer und polnischer Gepräge von etwa dem Beginn der Groschenzeit bis zur Kipperperiode**, Berlin, 1892.
Sch = Wolfgang Schulten, **Deutsche Münzen aus der Zeit Karls V.**, Frankfurt am Main, 1974.

ABBEY

REGULAR COINAGE

KM# 28 THALER
Silver, 47 mm. **Ruler:** Hugo Preutäus von Assindia **Obv:** Cowled bust to right, small date just inside circle to left of back of head, small shield of mitred later arms at bottom **Obv. Legend:** HVGO. D: G. WERDINENSI - VM. ET. HELMONS. ABBAS. **Rev:** Crowned imperial eagle, orb on breast **Rev. Legend:** FERDINANDVS. II. D: G. ROM. IMP. SEMPER. AVGVSTVS. **Note:** Dav#5923, G#29.

Date	Mintage	VG	F	VF	XF	Unc
1636 Rare	—	—	—	—	—	—

KM# 31 THALER
Silver, 46 mm. **Ruler:** Hugo Preutäus von Assindia
Obv: Smaller robed bust to right, small date just inside circle to left of back of head, small shield of mitred later arms at bottom
Obv. Legend: HVGO. D: G. WERDINENS - E. HELMONST. ABBAS. **Rev:** Crowned imperial eagle, orb on breast
Rev. Legend: FERDINAND. I.I.I. D: G. ROM. IMP. SEMP. AVGVST. **Note:** Dav#5924, G#30.

Date	Mintage	VG	F	VF	XF	Unc
1645 Rare	—	—	—	—	—	—

KM# 35 THALER
Silver, 42 mm. **Ruler:** Adolf IV von Borken **Obv:** Shield of early arms superimposed on cross which quarters larger background shield of 4-fold arms, imperial eagle in upper left and lower right quarters, Dücker arms (5 horizontal bars) in upper right
Obv. Legend: HENRICVS. D: G. MONAST: WERDI: ET. HELMON: ABBAS. **Rev:** Crowned imperial eagle, orb on breast
Rev. Legend: FERDINAND. I.I.I. D: G. ROM. IMP. SEMP. AVGVST. **Note:** Dav#5925, G#37.

Date	Mintage	VG	F	VF	XF	Unc
1646 Rare	—	—	—	—	—	—

KM# 36 THALER
Silver, 42 mm. **Ruler:** Heinrich IV Dücker **Obv:** Shield of early arms superimposed on cross which quarters larger background shield of 4-fold arms, imperial eagle in upper left and lower right quarters, Dücker arms (5 horizontal bars) in upper right and lower left, mitre above all divides date **Obv. Legend:** HENRICUS. D. G. MONASTE. WERDI. ET HEL. MON. ABB. **Rev:** Crowned imperial eagle, orb on breast **Rev. Legend:** FERDINAND. I.I.I. D: G. ROM. IMP. SEMP. AVGVST. **Note:** Dav#5925A.

Date	Mintage	VG	F	VF	XF	Unc
1646 Rare	—	—	—	—	—	—

KM# 44 THALER
28.2300 g., Silver, 38x38 mm. **Ruler:** Heinrich IV Dücker
Obv: Bust to right in circle **Obv. Legend:** HENRI: D: G: IMP. MONAS. WERD. ET. HELM. ABBA. **Rev:** Shield of early arms superimposed on cross which quarters larger background shield of 4-fold arms, imperial eagle in upper left and lower right quarters, Dücker arms (5 horizontal bars) in upper right and lower left, mitre above, date at end of legen **Rev. Legend:** DVRI. PATIENTIA. VIGTRIX. **Note:** Klippe; Dav#5926, G#38.

Date	Mintage	VG	F	VF	XF	Unc
1650 Rare	—	—	—	—	—	—

KM# 45 THALER
Silver, 43 mm. **Ruler:** Adolf IV von Borken **Obv:** Shield of early arms superimposed on cross which quarters larger background shield of 4-fold arms, imperial eagle in upper left and lower right quarters, Borken arms (crowned winged heart) in upper ri **Obv. Legend:** MO. ADOLPHI. ABB. WERDIN. ET. HELMSTÆD. **Rev:** Full-length facing figure of St. Ludger holding crozier and model of monastery church, date divided by mitre at top **Rev. Legend:** SANCTVS. LVDGE - RVS. EPISCOP. **Note:** Dav#5927, G#45.

Date	Mintage	VG	F	VF	XF	Unc
1667 Rare	—	—	—	—	—	—

KM# 55 THALER
Silver, 48 mm. **Ruler:** Adolf IV von Borken **Obv:** Shield of early arms superimposed on cross which quarters larger background shield of 4-fold arms, imperial eagle in upper left and lower right quarters, Borken arms (crowned winged heart) in upper right and lower left, mitre above **Obv. Legend:** MON. ADOLPHI. LIB. IMP. - ABB. WERD. &. HELMST. **Rev:** Full-length facing figure of St. Ludger holding crozier and model of monastery church, date divided by mitre at top **Rev. Legend:** SANCTVS. LVDGE - RVS. EPISCOP. **Note:** Dav#5929, G#46.

Date	Mintage	VG	F	VF	XF	Unc
1670 Rare	—	—	—	—	—	—

KM# 61 THALER

Silver, 43 mm. **Ruler:** Ferdinand von Erwitte **Obv:** Four-fold arms, imperial eagle in upper left and lower right quarters, family arms (crowned rampant lion to left on background of 7 horizontal bars) in upper right and lower left, in oval baroque fram **Obv. Legend:** FERDINANDVS: D: G: ABBAS: WERDIN - ET: HELMSTAD. **Rev:** Full-length fcing figure of St. Ludger holding crozier and model of monastery church, mitre above **Rev. Legend:** SANCTVS: LVDGERVS: - EPISCOPVS FVNDATOR. **Note:** Dav#5930, G#48.

Date	Mintage	VG	F	VF	XF	Unc
1696 Rare	—	—	—	—	—	—

KM# 62 THALER

Silver, 42 mm. **Ruler:** Ferdinand von Erwitte **Obv:** Four-fold arms, imperial eagle in upper left and lower right quarters, family arms (crowned rampant lion to left on background of 7 horizontal bars) in upper right and lower left, in round baroque frame, mitre divides date in margin at top **Obv. Legend:** FERDINANDd. D.G. ABBAS. WERDIN. ET. HELMSTAD. **Rev:** Full-length facing figure of St. Mary standing on crescent moon, stars around head, all in circle with arch in it over head **Rev. Legend:** VIRGO IMMACULATA IVGITER SIT PATRONA. **Note:** Dav#5931, G#49.

Date	Mintage	VG	F	VF	XF	Unc
1698	—	875	1,500	2,500	4,050	—

KM# 24 1-1/4 THALER

Silver **Ruler:** Hugo Preutäus von Assindia **Obv:** Ornate shield of 6-fold arms, mitre above **Obv. Legend:** MO. NO. ARG. REV. D. GVGONIS. ABBA. IN. WERDI. ET. HELM. **Rev:** Crowned imperial eagle, orb on breast **Rev. Legend:** FERDINANDVS. II. D: G. RO. IMP. SEMP. AVGVS. **Note:** Klippe, struck from 1/2 Thaler dies, KM#20; G#ex27.

Date	Mintage	VG	F	VF	XF	Unc
ND (1619-37)	—	—	—	—	—	—

KM# 13 1-1/2 THALER

Silver, 45x45 mm. **Ruler:** Hugo Preutäus von Assindia **Obv:** Ornate shield of 6-fold arms, mitre above **Obv. Legend:** MO. NO. ARG. REV. D. HVGONIS. ABB. IN. WERDEN. ET. HELMS. **Rev:** Crowned imperial eagle, orb on breast **Rev. Legend:** MATTHIAS. I. D. ELEC. RO. IMP. SEM. AVGV. **Note:** Klippe; Dav#A5918, G#26.

Date	Mintage	VG	F	VF	XF	Unc
ND (1614-19) Rare	—	—	—	—	—	—

KM# 17 2 THALER

Silver, 41 mm. **Ruler:** Hugo Preutäus von Assindia **Obv:** Two-fold arms divided vertically, later Werden and Helmstedt arms at left, Preutäus arms (3 cloverleafs) at right, mitre above, date downwards along right side of shield **Obv. Legend:** MO. NO. A. R. D. HVGON AB. WERDEN. & HELM. **Rev:** Crowned imperial eagle, orb on breast **Rev. Legend:** MATTH. I. D: G. ELE. ROM IM. SEMPER. AVG. **Note:** Dav#5919.

Date	Mintage	VG	F	VF	XF	Unc
1615 Rare	—	—	—	—	—	—

KM# 18 2 THALER

Silver **Ruler:** Hugo Preutäus von Assindia **Obv:** Two-fold arms divided vertically, later Werden and Helmstedt arms at left, Preutäus arms (3 cloverleafs) at right, mitre above, date downwards along right side of shield **Obv. Legend:** MO. NO. A. R. D. HVGON AB. WERDEN. & HELM. **Rev:** Crowned imperial eagle, orb on breast **Rev. Legend:** MATTH. I. D: G. ELE. ROM. IM. SEMPER. AVG. **Note:** Klippe; Dav#5919A.

Date	Mintage	VG	F	VF	XF	Unc
1616 Rare	—	—	—	—	—	—

KM# 29 2 THALER

Silver **Ruler:** Hugo Preutäus von Assindia **Obv:** Cowled bust to right, small date just inside circle to left of back of head, small shield of mitred later arms at bottom **Obv. Legend:** HVGO. D: G. WERDINENSI - VM. ET. HELMONS. ABBAS. **Rev:** Crowned imperial eagle, orb on breast **Rev. Legend:** FERDINANDVS. II. D: G. ROM. IMP. SEMPER. AVGVSTVS. **Note:** Dav#5922, G#29.

Date	Mintage	VG	F	VF	XF	Unc
1636 Rare	—	—	—	—	—	—
ND Rare	—	—	—	—	—	—

KM# 57 2 THALER

Silver, 48 mm. **Ruler:** Adolf IV von Borken **Obv:** Shield of early arms superimposed on cross which quarters larger background shield of 4-fold arms, imperial eagle in upper left and lower right quarters, Borken arms (crowned winged heart) in upper ri **Obv. Legend:** MON. ADOLPHI. KIB. IMP. - ABB. WERD. &. HELMST. **Rev:** Full-length facing figure of St. Ludger holding crozier and model of monastery church, date divided by mitre at top **Rev. Legend:** SANCTVS. LVDGE - RVS. EPISCOP. **Note:** Dav#5928, G#ex46.

Date	Mintage	VG	F	VF	XF	Unc
1670 Rare	—	—	—	—	—	—

KM# 15 2-1/2 THALER

Silver, 45x45 mm. **Ruler:** Hugo Preutäus von Assindia **Obv:** Ornate shield of 6-fold arms, mitre above **Obv. Legend:** MO. NO. ARG. REV. D. HVGONIS. ABB. IN. WERDEN. ET. HELMS. **Rev:** Crowned imperial eagle, orb on breast **Rev. Legend:** MATTHIAS. I. D. ELEC. RO. IMP. SEM. AVGV. **Note:** Klippe; Dav#5918, G#26.

Date	Mintage	VG	F	VF	XF	Unc
ND (1614-19) Rare	—	—	—	—	—	—

KM# 25 3 THALER

Silver **Ruler:** Hugo Preutäus von Assindia **Obv:** Ornate shield of 6-fold arms, mitre above **Obv. Legend:** MO. NO. ARG. REV. D. HVGONIS. ABBA. IN. WERDI. ET. HELM. **Rev:** Crowned imperial eagle, orb on breast **Rev. Legend:** FERDINANDVS. II. D: G. RO. IMP. SEMP. AVGVS. **Note:** Klippe, struck from 1/2 Thaler dies, KM#20; G#ex27.

Date	Mintage	VG	F	VF	XF	Unc
ND (1619-37) Rare	—	—	—	—	—	—

TRADE COINAGE

KM# 40 DUCAT

3.5000 g., 0.9860 Gold 0.1109 oz. AGW, 24 mm. **Ruler:** Heinrich IV Dücker **Obv:** Shield of early arms superimposed on cross which quarters larger background shield of 4-fold arms, imperial eagle in upper left and lower right quarters, Dücker arms (5 horizontal bars) in upper right **Obv. Legend:** HENRIC9. D. ABBAS. WERD. ET. HELM. **Rev:** Five-line inscription with date between laurel and palm branches **Rev. Inscription:** DVCAT/VS. NOV. 9./ABBATIAE/WERDIN./(date). **Note:** Fr#3510, G#36.

Date	Mintage	VG	F	VF	XF	Unc
1647 Rare	—	—	—	—	—	—

Note: Dr. Busso Peus Nachfolger Auction 385, 11-05, VF realized approximately $14,475; Dr. Busso Peus Nachfolger Auction 383, 4-05, VF realized approximately $20,095; Dr. Busso Peus Nachfolger Auction 383, 4-05, VF realized approximately $8,035

WERNE

A town in Westphalia about 8 miles (13km) west of Hamm. In 1385, Werne received rights as an independant town from the bishop of Münster, but did not strike coins of its own until the early 17th century.

ARMS

Dark horizontal band (cross-hatching on coins) across center of shield, open fields above and below

PROVINCIAL TOWN

REGULAR COINAGE

KM# 1 2 PFENNIG

Copper **Obv:** Town arms in circle, STADT WERNE in legend **Rev:** Value "II" in ornamented circle

Date	Mintage	Good	VG	F	VF	XF
ND(c.1602)	—	55.00	90.00	125	200	—

KM# 2 3 PFENNIG

Copper **Rev:** Value "III" **Note:** Similar to 2 Pfennig KM#1, but date added to obverse legend.

Date	Mintage	Good	VG	F	VF	XF
1602	—	60.00	110	145	235	—

KM# 3 6 PFENNIG

Copper **Rev:** Similar to 2 Pfennig KM#1, but value "VI"

Date	Mintage	Good	VG	F	VF	XF
ND(c.1602)	—	55.00	90.00	125	200	—

KM# 4 12 PFENNIG

Copper **Obv:** Eagle behind town arms in ornamented circle **Rev:** Value "XII" in rectangle, ornaments above and below, M below, all in ornamented circle

Date	Mintage	Good	VG	F	VF	XF
ND(c.1602)	—	60.00	110	145	235	—

KM# 5 12 PFENNIG

Copper **Rev:** Similar to 3 Pfennig, KM#2 but value "XII"

Date	Mintage	Good	VG	F	VF	XF
1602	—	60.00	110	145	235	—

KM# 6 12 PFENNIG

Copper **Rev:** Similar to KM#5 but "W" above value **Note:** Varieties exist.

Date	Mintage	Good	VG	F	VF	XF
1610	—	60.00	110	145	235	—

WESTPHALIA

The Duchy of Westphalia was very early the western part of the old Duchy of Saxony. In 1180, most of Westphalia fell to the archbishops of Cologne who added "Duke of Westphalia" to their titles. When Cologne was secularized in 1801, the duchy was administered by Hesse-Darmstadt until 1814 when it was annexed by Prussia. Coins were struck by the archbishops at the beginning of the 17th century and during the early years of the Thirty Years' War specifically for use in the duchy. For the names of the dukes and archbishops, see Cologne.

MINT OFFICIALS' INITIALS and MARKS

Initial or mark	Date	Name
VF/VFH	1631-50	Urban Felgenhauer (Felgenhewer in Arnsberg
(a) =	1655-?	Jürgen Hartmann in Geseke
(b) =	Ca.1655-68	Unknown, Dorsten mint
(c)=	Ca.1663	?Niessmann, mintmaster in Recklinghausen

KINGDOM

GERMAN STANDARD COINAGE

KM# 53 THALER

Silver **Obv:** Bust right in mantle **Obv. Legend:** ... COL. PR. EL. EP. LEOD. HILD. ADM. BERCH. **Rev:** Capped arms divide date **Rev. Legend:** VTR. BAV. WEST: ANG... COM. PAL. RHE. LAND. LEV. **Note:** Dav.#5149. Prev. Cologne, KM#53.

Date	Mintage	VG	F	VF	XF	Unc
1657 Rare	—	—	—	—	—	—

KM# 54 THALER

Silver **Rev. Legend:** ...BVL. COM. PAL. RHE. LAN: L. **Note:** Dav.#5150. Prev. Cologne, KM#54.

Date	Mintage	VG	F	VF	XF	Unc
1657 Rare	—	—	—	—	—	—

KM# 58 THALER

Silver **Obv. Legend:** ...EP: HIL: LEOD: A: BER: **Rev. Legend:** LAND: LEV: VTR: BA: WEST: AN: B: DVX: CO: PA. RHE: **Note:** Dav.#5151. Prev. Cologne, KM#58.

Date	Mintage	VG	F	VF	XF	Unc
1657 Rare	—	—	—	—	—	—

KM# 59 2 THALER

Silver **Obv:** Bust of Maximillian right **Rev:** Capped arms divide date **Note:** Dav.#5148.

Date	Mintage	VG	F	VF	XF	Unc
1657 Rare	—	—	—	—	—	—

WISMAR

A seaport on the Baltic, the city of Wismar is said to have obtained municipal rights from Mecklenburg in 1229. It was an important member of the Hanseatic League in the 13th and 14th centuries. Their coinage began at the end of the 13th century and terminated in 1854. They belonged to Sweden from 1648 to 1803. A special plate money was struck by the Swedes in 1715 when the town was under siege. In 1803, Sweden sold Wismar to Mecklenburg-Schwerin. The transaction was confirmed in 1815.

RULERS

Swedish, 1648-1803

MINT OFFICIALS' INITIALS

Initial	Date	Name
	1582-1602	Hans Rode, warden
(f)= or JM (ligature)	1594-1600	Jürgen (Georg) Martens der Ältere
(g)=	1601-12	Michael Martens
	1602-06	Andrew Reimers, warden
	1607-19	Cyriacus Klein (Kilian Klehne), warden
	1612	Johann Marten
(h)=	1613-18	Simon Lüdemann
	1618-19	Johann (Hans) Schroeder
	1620-22	Jürgen Martens der Jüngere
(i)=	1622-24	Jacob Mauche (Maucke)
(j)=	1624-37	Johann (Hans) Dase
	1629-30	Hans Jobst (Jost), warden
	1633-45	David Jost, warden
	1636-42	Johann Scheffel, warden
	1643-60	Daniel Hertzberg, warden
(k)=	1647-50	Simon Timpe (Timpffe, Dimpe)
(l)= or BK+	1650-60	Barthold (Balthasar) Krause
(m)= or HS+	1661-70	Henning Stör
	1661-62	Jürgen Maass, warden
(n)=mailed arm holding sword or HR+ plus mailed arm holding sword	1670-74	Hans Ritter (Ridder)
	1671-74	Johann Birek, warden
GS	1675-80	Gregory (Gregor) Sesemann
	1675-80	Heinrich Reimers, warden
IM	1685-1702	Johann Memmies in Rostock

ARMS

2-fold arms divided vertically, half of bull's head of Mecklenburg on left, four alternating light and dark horizontal bars on right. In coin designs, the darker bars are usually designated by cross-hatching or other filler. Some designs show only the four-bar arms in a shield and these are designated "single Wismar arms."

CITY

REGULAR COINAGE

DAV# A5936 THALER (32 Schilling)
Silver **Obv:** St. Laurentius with griddle in right hand and palm spray in left **Rev:** Crown above double-headed imperial eagle, value in orb on breast **Rev. Legend:** RVDOLPHVS...

Date	Mintage	F	VF	XF	Unc
ND(1604-05)	—	775	1,450	2,500	—	—

DAV# 5936 THALER (32 Schilling)
Silver **Obv. Legend:** RUDOL... **Rev:** St. Laurentius with griddle in left hand and palm spray in right

Date	Mintage	VG	F	VF	XF	Unc
ND(1604-05)	—	575	1,050	1,800	—	—

DAV# 5932 THALER (32 Schilling)
Silver **Obv:** Crowned imperial eagle **Rev:** St. Laurentius

Date	Mintage	VG	F	VF	XF	Unc
1606	—	650	1,200	2,050	—	—

DAV# 5933 THALER (32 Schilling)
Silver **Obv:** St. Laurentius with grill, arms in front, date divided above **Rev:** Crowned imperial eagle with orb and 32 on breast

Date	Mintage	VG	F	VF	XF	Unc
1606 (g)	—	650	1,200	2,050	4,750	—
1607 (g)	—	650	1,200	2,050	4,750	—

DAV# 5934 THALER (32 Schilling)
Silver **Obv:** Standing St. above small shield **Obv. Legend:** MONETA NOV*... **Rev:** Crown above double-headed imperial eagle, value in orb on breast **Rev. Legend:** RVDOL: D. II. D. G...

Date	Mintage	VG	F	VF	XF	Unc
1607 (g)	—	650	1,200	2,050	—	—

DAV# 5935 THALER (32 Schilling)
Silver **Obv:** Date divided in field **Obv. Legend:** MONETA NOVA... **Rev:** Crown above double-headed imperial eagle, value in orb on breast **Rev. Legend:** RVDOL: II. D. G.-IMP. SE. A: G: S. **Note:** Varieties exist.

Date	Mintage	VG	F	VF	XF	Unc
1608	—	525	975	1,650	—	—

DAV# 5937 THALER (32 Schilling)
Silver **Obv. Legend:** MATTHIAS*D. G. -ROMAN... **Rev:** Legend, date **Rev. Legend:** Y MONETA*NOVA*...

Date	Mintage	VG	F	VF	XF	Unc
1614 (h)	—	525	975	1,650	—	—

DAV# 5938 THALER (32 Schilling)
Silver **Obv:** Date divided at top **Obv. Legend:** MONETA. NOVA... **Rev. Legend:** MATTHIAS D. G. ROMA...

Date	Mintage	VG	F	VF	XF	Unc
1617 (h)	—	525	975	1,650	—	—

DAV# 5939 THALER (32 Schilling)
Silver **Obv:** Date divided by shield at bottom **Rev:** Crown above double-headed imperial eagle, value in orb on breast **Rev. Legend:** FERDINDNA. II...

Date	Mintage	VG	F	VF	XF	Unc
1622 (i)	—	525	975	1,650	—	—
1623 (i)	—	525	975	1,650	—	—

DAV# 5940 THALER (32 Schilling)
Silver **Obv:** Date divided by St. Laurentius **Rev. Legend:** FERDINAND: II. D. G. RO...

Date	Mintage	VG	F	VF	XF	Unc
1623 (i)	—	525	975	1,650	—	—
1624 (j)	—	525	975	1,650	—	—

DAV# 5941 THALER (32 Schilling)
Silver **Rev:** Date left of St. Laurentius

Date	Mintage	VG	F	VF	XF	Unc
1623	—	525	975	1,650	—	—
1624	—	525	975	1,650	—	—

DAV# 5942 THALER (32 Schilling)
Silver **Obv:** Date divided by St. Laurentius **Rev:** Crowned double-headed imperial eagle, date left of crown

Date	Mintage	VG	F	VF	XF	Unc
1624//16Z4 (j)	—	400	725	1,250	—	—
1624//1625 (j)	—	400	725	1,250	—	—

DAV# 5943 THALER (32 Schilling)
Silver **Obv:** St. Laurentius without date **Rev:** Crowned double-headed imperial eagle

Date	Mintage	VG	F	VF	XF	Unc
1625 (j)	—	425	800	1,400	—	—
16Z6 (j)	—	425	800	1,400	—	—
1627 (j)	—	425	800	1,400	—	—
1628 (j)	—	425	800	1,400	—	—

DAV# 5944 THALER (32 Schilling)
Silver **Rev:** Crown above imperial eagle divides date

Date	Mintage	VG	F	VF	XF	Unc
1629 (j)	—	425	800	1,400	—	—
1630 (j)	—	425	800	1,400	—	—
1631 (j)	—	425	800	1,400	—	—
1632 (j)	—	425	800	1,400	—	—
1635 (j)	—	425	800	1,400	—	—
1637 (j)	—	425	800	1,400	—	—

DAV# 5945 THALER (32 Schilling)
Silver **Obv:** Standing St. above small shield **Rev:** Crowned double-headed imperial eagle, value in orb on breast, date in legend **Rev. Legend:** FERDINAN. III...

Date	Mintage	VG	F	VF	XF	Unc
1640 (j)	—	275	550	1,000	—	—
1641 (j)	—	275	550	1,000	—	—
1645 (j)	—	1,650	3,200	5,500	—	—

DAV# 5946 THALER (32 Schilling)
Silver **Obv:** Standing St. above small shield **Rev:** Crowned double-headed imperial eagle, value in orb on breast
Rev. Legend: FERDINANDUS III. D. Q. ROMA: IMP: S: AU:

Date	Mintage	VG	F	VF	XF	Unc
ND(ca.1640) (j)	—	275	550	1,000	—	—
ND(ca.1645-47) (j)	—	—	—	—	—	—

DAV# LS510 THALER
28.0000 g., Silver **Subject:** Treaty of Pahrenholz **Note:** Similar to 1-1/2 Thaler, Dav. #LS509.

Date	Mintage	VG	F	VF	XF	Unc
ND(1611) Rare	—	—	—	—	—	—

DAV# LS514 THALER
Silver **Obv:** Date below St. Laurentius

Date	Mintage	VG	F	VF	XF	Unc
1617 (h) Rare	—	—	—	—	—	—

DAV# LS509 1-1/2 THALER
43.3000 g., Silver **Subject:** Treaty of Pahrenholz **Obv:** Arms within double legend **Rev:** St. Laurentius with grill and palm spray, shield in front

Date	Mintage	VG	F	VF	XF	Unc
ND(1601)	—	1,350	2,750	5,500	9,000	—

DAV# LS513 1-1/2 THALER
Silver **Rev:** Date below St. Laurentius

Date	Mintage	VG	F	VF	XF	Unc
1617 (h) Rare	—	—	—	—	—	—

DAV# LS508 2 THALER
60.0000 g., Silver **Subject:** Treaty of Pahrenholz **Note:** Similar to 1-1/2 Thaler, Dav. #LS509.

Date	Mintage	VG	F	VF	XF	Unc
ND(1611) Rare	—	—	—	—	—	—

DAV# LS512 2 THALER
Silver **Rev:** Date below St. Laurentius

Date	Mintage	VG	F	VF	XF	Unc
1617 (h) Rare	—	—	—	—	—	—

DAV# LS507 2-1/2 THALER
Silver **Subject:** Treaty of Pahrenholz **Note:** Similar to 1-1/2 Thaler, Dav. #LS509.

Date	Mintage	VG	F	VF	XF	Unc
ND(1611) Rare	—	—	—	—	—	—

DAV# LS506 3 THALER
Silver **Subject:** Treaty of Pahrenholz **Note:** Similar to 1-1/2 Thaler, Dav. #LS509.

Date	Mintage	VG	F	VF	XF	Unc
ND(1611) Rare	—	—	—	—	—	—

DAV# LS511 3 THALER
Silver **Rev:** Date below St. Laurentius

Date	Mintage	VG	F	VF	XF	Unc
1617 (h) Rare	—	—	—	—	—	—

DAV# LS505 4 THALER
Silver **Subject:** Treaty of Pahrenholz **Note:** Similar to 1-1/2 Thaler, Dav. #LS509.

Date	Mintage	VG	F	VF	XF	Unc
ND(1611) Rare	—	—	—	—	—	—

TRADE COINAGE

FR# 3527 GOLDGULDEN
3.5000 g., 0.9860 Gold 0.1109 oz. AGW **Obv:** St. Laurentius standing holding gridiron with left hand

Date	Mintage	VG	F	VF	XF	Unc
(16)16 (h)	—	1,200	2,400	4,800	7,800	—

FR# 3528 GOLDGULDEN
3.5000 g., 0.9860 Gold 0.1109 oz. AGW

Date	Mintage	VG	F	VF	XF	Unc
(16)26 (j)	—	975	2,050	3,550	6,000	—
1629	—	975	2,050	3,550	6,000	—
1632 (j)	—	975	2,050	3,550	6,000	—

SWEDISH ADMINISTRATION

REGULAR COINAGE

KM# 3 4 SCHILLING (1/8 Thaler)
Silver **Obv:** Crowned imperial eagle, 4 in orb on breast **Rev:** St. Laurentius with gridiron in inner circle, shield at bottom

Date	Mintage	VG	F	VF	XF	Unc
1662 HS Rare	—	—	—	—	—	—

KM# 4 8 SCHILLING (1/4 Thaler)
Silver **Obv:** Crowned imperial eagle, 8 in orb on breast **Rev:** St. Laurentius with gridiron in inner circle, shield at bottom

Date	Mintage	VG	F	VF	XF	Unc
1662 HS Rare	—	—	—	—	—	—

KM# 5 16 SCHILLING (1/2 Thaler)
Silver **Obv:** Crowned imperial eagle, 16 in orb on breast
Rev: St. Laurentius with gridiron in inner circle, shield at bottom

Date	Mintage	VG	F	VF	XF	Unc
1668 HS Rare	—	—	—	—	—	—

KM# 6 16 SHILLING (1/3 Thaler)
Silver **Obv:** Shield on cross **Rev:** St. Laurentius with cowl reaching to the feet

Date	Mintage	VG	F	VF	XF	Unc
1671 (n)	—	—	—	—	—	—
1672 (n)	—	45.00	100	200	325	—

KM# 7 16 SHILLING (1/3 Thaler)
Silver **Rev:** St. Laurentius with cowl reaching to the knees

Date	Mintage	VG	F	VF	XF	Unc
1672	—	45.00	100	200	325	—

KM# 8 1/192 THALER (Witten)
Silver **Obv:** Arms in circle **Rev:** 192 in orb in circle
Rev. Legend: FERD. III...

Date	Mintage	VG	F	VF	XF	Unc
1651	—	—	—	—	—	—
1653	—	—	—	—	—	—
ND	—	—	—	—	—	—

KM# 9 1/192 THALER (Witten)
Silver **Obv:** City arms in baroque frame **Obv. Legend:** MO. NO. WISMAR. **Rev:** Imperial orb with 19Z **Rev. Legend:** LEOP. D.G. R. I. S.

Date	Mintage	VG	F	VF	XF	Unc
ND(1661-70) (m)	—	13.00	33.00	50.00	80.00	—
ND(1692-95) IM	—	13.00	33.00	50.00	80.00	—
ND(1692-95) (f)	—	13.00	33.00	50.00	80.00	—

KM# 10 1/192 THALER (Witten)
Silver **Obv:** Arms in shield

Date	Mintage	VG	F	VF	XF	Unc
ND(1671-74) (a)	—	13.00	33.00	50.00	80.00	—
ND(1675-80) GS	—	13.00	33.00	50.00	80.00	—

KM# 11 1/96 THALER (1 Sechsling)

Silver **Obv:** Arms in shield in inner circle **Rev:** 96 in orb in inner circke **Rev. Legend:** FERD. III…

Date	Mintage	VG	F	VF	XF	Unc
ND (c)	—	27.00	45.00	90.00	165	—

KM# 12 1/96 THALER (1 Sechsling)

Silver **Rev. Legend:** LEOP…

Date	Mintage	VG	F	VF	XF	Unc
ND(1661-71) HS	—	—	—	—	—	—
1666	—	—	—	—	—	—
ND(1671-74) (a)	—	13.00	30.00	40.00	70.00	—
ND(1675-80) GS	—	13.00	30.00	45.00	80.00	—
ND(1692-95) (f)	—	13.00	30.00	40.00	70.00	—

KM# 13 1/96 THALER (1 Sechsling)

Silver **Rev. Legend:** LEOPOL…

Date	Mintage	VG	F	VF	XF	Unc
ND (c)	—	13.00	30.00	45.00	80.00	—

KM# 14 1/48 THALER

Silver

Date	Mintage	VG	F	VF	XF	Unc
1661	—	13.00	30.00	45.00	80.00	—

KM# 15 1/48 THALER

Silver **Obv:** City arms in baroque frame **Obv. Legend:** MONETA. NOVA. WISMAR. **Rev:** Imperial orb with 48, date at end of legend **Rev. Legend:** LEOPOL: D:G: R: I: S: A:

Date	Mintage	VG	F	VF	XF	Unc
1663	—	13.00	30.00	50.00	80.00	—
1664	—	13.00	30.00	50.00	80.00	—
1665	—	13.00	30.00	50.00	80.00	—
1666	—	13.00	30.00	50.00	80.00	—
1667	—	13.00	30.00	50.00	80.00	—
1668	—	13.00	30.00	50.00	80.00	—
1669	—	13.00	30.00	50.00	80.00	—
1692	—	13.00	30.00	50.00	80.00	—
1695	—	17.00	35.00	65.00	135	—

KM# 16 1/24 THALER (1 Groschen)

Silver

Date	Mintage	VG	F	VF	XF	Unc
1648	—	—	—	—	—	—
1650 (h)	—	—	—	—	—	—
1650 (c)	—	13.00	33.00	55.00	110	—
1651	—	17.00	35.00	65.00	135	—
1652	—	13.00	33.00	55.00	110	—
1653	—	13.00	33.00	55.00	110	—
1654	—	13.00	33.00	55.00	110	—
1655	—	13.00	33.00	55.00	110	—
1656	—	13.00	33.00	55.00	110	—
1657	—	13.00	33.00	55.00	110	—
1658	—	13.00	33.00	55.00	110	—
1659	—	13.00	33.00	55.00	110	—
1661	—	13.00	33.00	55.00	90.00	—
1662	—	13.00	33.00	55.00	90.00	—
1663	—	13.00	33.00	55.00	90.00	—
1664	—	13.00	33.00	55.00	90.00	—
1665	—	13.00	33.00	55.00	90.00	—
1666	—	13.00	33.00	55.00	90.00	—
1667	—	13.00	33.00	55.00	90.00	—
1668	—	13.00	33.00	55.00	90.00	—
1669	—	13.00	33.00	55.00	90.00	—
1670 (a)	—	17.00	35.00	65.00	135	—
1670 (c)	—	13.00	33.00	55.00	90.00	—

Date	Mintage	VG	F	VF	XF	Unc
1671	—	13.00	33.00	55.00	90.00	—
1672	—	13.00	33.00	55.00	90.00	—

KM# 17 2/3 THALER (1 Gulden)

Silver

Date	Mintage	VG	F	VF	XF	Unc
1684	—	3,300	6,000	8,700	13,500	—

DAV# 5947 THALER (32 Schilling)

Silver **Obv:** St. Laurentius standing with gridiron in inner circle **Rev:** Crowned imperial eagle, 32 in orb on breast in inner circle **Rev. Legend:** FERDINANDUS III…

Date	Mintage	VG	F	VF	XF	Unc
1653 BK	—	2,000	3,250	5,500	7,500	—

DAV# 5948 THALER (32 Schilling)

Silver **Rev. Legend:** LEOPOLDUS…

Date	Mintage	VG	F	VF	XF	Unc
1662 HS	—	2,200	3,500	6,500	—	—
1666 HS	—	2,200	3,500	6,500	—	—
1668 HS Rare	—	—	—	—	—	—
1671/68 HR	—	2,200	3,500	6,500	—	—

DAV# 5949 THALER (32 Schilling)

Silver **Obv:** H-R divided by shield below saint **Rev:** Crowned double-headed imperial eagle, value in orb on breast

Date	Mintage	VG	F	VF	XF	Unc
1673 HR	—	600	1,200	2,500	4,000	—

DAV# 5950 THALER (32 Schilling)

Silver **Obv:** Standing St. above small shield, without inner circle **Rev:** Crowned double-headed imperial eagle, value in orb on breast, without inner circle **Note:** With and without edge inscription.

Date	Mintage	VG	F	VF	XF	Unc
1674 (n)	—	1,000	1,650	5,500	8,500	—

TRADE COINAGE

FR# 3529 DUCAT

3.5000 g., 0.9860 Gold 0.1109 oz. AGW **Obv:** Ornate arms **Obv. Legend:** CIVTATIS + WISMARIEN **Rev:** Crowned imperial eagle **Rev. Legend:** MONETA + AVREA

Date	Mintage	VG	F	VF	XF	Unc
1672 (n)	—	2,000	3,500	6,500	9,500	—
1676 GS	—	2,000	3,500	6,500	9,500	—

WOLFENBUTTEL

City in Brunswick-Wolfenbüttel. Only coinage issued was by besieged Danish forces in 1627.

CITY

REGULAR COINAGE

KM# 5.1 GUTERGROSCHEN

2.1650 g., 0.5000 Silver 0.0348 oz. ASW **Obv:** Value above date in legend **Rev:** Crowned C4 monogram within circle **Note:** Prev. KM#6.1.

Date	Mintage	VG	F	VF	XF	Unc
1627 Rare	—	—	—	—	—	—

KM# 5.2 GUTERGROSCHEN

2.1650 g., 0.5000 Silver 0.0348 oz. ASW **Rev:** Crown breaks inner circle **Note:** Prev. KM#6.2.

Date	Mintage	VG	F	VF	XF	Unc
1627 Rare	—	—	—	—	—	—

KM# 6 THALER

Silver **Ruler:** Philip Reinhard **Obv:** Crowned arms **Obv. Legend:** MONET:R.D.N.VIC:PHIL:REINH:C:S: **Rev:** Crowned C4 monogram, date in legend **Rev. Legend:** *QVID.NON. PRO.RELIGIONE **Note:** Dav. #7758. Specie Thaler.

Date	Mintage	VG	F	VF	XF	Unc
1627	—	600	1,250	2,500	—	—

KM# 7 THALER

Silver **Ruler:** Philip Reinhard **Obv:** Crowned arms **Rev:** Crowned C4 monogram divides date **Note:** Dav. #7759.

Date	Mintage	VG	F	VF	XF	Unc
1627	—	750	1,500	3,000	5,000	7,500

KM# 8 THALER

Silver **Ruler:** Philip Reinhard **Obv:** Crowned shield divides date **Obv. Legend:** *MONET:REGIS.DAN:NORW:VICARII. PHILIP.REINH:COM:S **Rev:** Crowned C4 monogram, legend widely spaced **Note:** Dav. #7760.

Date	Mintage	VG	F	VF	XF	Unc
1627	—	800	1,500	3,000	—	—

KM# 9 2 THALER

Silver **Ruler:** Philip Reinhard **Obv:** Crowned shield **Rev:** Crowned C4 monogram, date in legend **Note:** Dav. #7757. Specie Thaler.

Date	Mintage	VG	F	VF	XF	Unc
1627 Unique	—	—	—	—	—	—

KM# A10 3 THALER

Silver **Ruler:** Philip Reinhard **Obv:** Crowned arms **Obv. Legend:** *MONET: REGIS. DAN: NORW: VICARII. PHILIP. (REIN)H: COM: S. **Rev:** Crowned C4 monogram **Rev. Legend:** *QVID. NON(.)PRO. RELIGION. A(o), date **Note:** Dav. #7756. Specie Thaler.

Date	Mintage	VG	F	VF	XF	Unc
1627 Rare	—	—	—	—	—	—

KM# 3 12 PFENNIG

Copper **Ruler:** Philip Reinhard **Obv:** 12/WOLFEB./GARNIS/ 1627 **Note:** Uniface. Klippe. Approximately 4 grams. Prev. KM#5.

Date	Mintage	VG	F	VF	XF	Unc
1627 Rare	—	—	—	—	—	—

TRADE COINAGE

KM# 10 GOLDGULDEN

3.5000 g., 0.9860 Gold 0.1109 oz. AGW **Ruler:** Philip Reinhard **Obv:** Crowned C4 monogram **Rev:** Value with legend

Date	Mintage	VG	F	VF	XF	Unc
1627 Unique	—	—	—	—	—	—

KM# 11 DUCAT

3.5000 g., 0.9860 Gold 0.1109 oz. AGW **Ruler:** Philip Reinhard **Obv:** Crowned shield **Rev:** Crowned C4 monogram **Note:** Varieties exist. Fr. #3300.

Date	Mintage	VG	F	VF	XF	Unc
1627	—	2,200	4,250	7,000	10,000	—

KM# 12 2 DUCAT

7.0000 g., 0.9860 Gold 0.2219 oz. AGW **Ruler:** Philip Reinhard **Obv:** Crowned shield **Rev:** Crowned C4 monogram **Note:** Varieties exist. Fr. #3299.

Date	Mintage	VG	F	VF	XF	Unc
1627 Rare	—	—	—	—	—	—

WOLGAST

A port city situated at the Baltic coast and the mouth of the Peene River. They received their civic rights in 1247. During the 14th century the dukes of Pomerania struck debased denars at Wolgast. In the late 16th century the city had its own local coinage. When the last duke died in1625, Pomerania became united under Bogislaus XIV, who died in 1637. Coins were probably struck in his name in Wolgast as well as in Stettin.

The Swedes occupied Pomerania during the Thirty-Years War, and Bogislaus was obliged to become an ally. From 1630, Wolgast was a part of Swedish Pomerania until it was ceded to Prussia in 1815. Coins were struck for the Swedish authorities only in 1633, in memory of King Gustavus II Adolphus.

RULERS

Swedish, 1633-1634

CITY

MEDALLIC COINAGE

Largesse Money

KM# M1 1/4 THALER

Silver, 76 mm. **Subject:** Death of Gustavus Adolphus **Obv:** Grapevine growing out of skull resting on ground, two legends around with date **Rev:** Crowned 4-fold arms with central shield, two legens around, date divided by crown

Date	Mintage	VG	F	VF	XF	Unc
1633	—	100	200	400	750	—

Note: Dies possibly also used in Erfurt

KM# M2 1/2 THALER

Silver, 37.5 mm. **Subject:** Death of Gustavus Adolphus **Obv:** Gustavus Adolphus lying in state with battle in backgournd **Rev:** King in chariot crushing enemies below

Date	Mintage	VG	F	VF	XF	Unc
1633	—	250	600	1,000	—	—
1634	—	250	600	1,000	—	—

KM# M3 THALER

Silver **Subject:** Death of Gustavus Adolphus **Obv:** Gustavus Adolphus lying in state with battle in backgournd **Rev:** King in chariot crushing enemies below

Date	Mintage	VG	F	VF	XF	Unc
1633	—	750	1,500	3,000	4,500	—

KM# M15 1-1/2 THALER

Silver **Note:** Similar to 2 Thaler, KM#M4. Dav. #LS275.

Date	Mintage	VG	F	VF	XF	Unc
1633	—	825	1,650	3,150	4,650	—

KM# M4 2 THALER

56.8000 g., Silver **Subject:** Death of Gustavus Adolphus **Obv:** Gustavus Adolphus lying in state with battle in background **Rev:** King in chariot crushing enemies below **Note:** Dav. #LS274.

Date	Mintage	VG	F	VF	XF	Unc
1633	—	825	1,650	3,150	4,650	—

KM# M6 3 THALER

Silver, 60 mm.

Date	Mintage	VG	F	VF	XF	Unc
1633	—	—	—	—	—	—

Note: Reported, not confirmed

KM# M5 3 THALER

83.7000 g., Silver **Subject:** Death of Gustavus Adolphus **Obv:** Gustavus Adolphus lying in state with battle in background **Rev:** King in chariot crushing enemies below **Note:** Dav. #LS273.

Date	Mintage	VG	F	VF	XF	Unc
1633	—	1,300	2,500	5,000	7,500	—

KM# M8 4 THALER

Silver, 60 mm.

Date	Mintage	VG	F	VF	XF	Unc
1633	—	—	—	—	—	—

Note: Reported, not confirmed

KM# M7 4 THALER

116.0000 g., Silver, 76 mm. **Subject:** Death of Gustavus Adolphus **Obv:** Gustavus Adolphus lying in state with battle in background **Rev:** King in chariot crushing enemies below **Note:** Dav. #LS272.

Date	Mintage	VG	F	VF	XF	Unc
1663	—	2,400	4,400	7,000	10,000	—

KM# M9 2 DUCAT

7.0000 g., 0.9860 Gold 0.2219 oz. AGW **Subject:** Death of Gustavus Adolphus **Obv:** Grapevine growing out of skull resting on ground, two legends around with date **Rev:** Crowned 4-fold arms with central shield, two legends around, date divided by crown

Date	Mintage	VG	F	VF	XF	Unc
1633 Rare	—	—	—	—	—	—

KM# M10 4 DUCAT

14.0000 g., 0.9860 Gold 0.4438 oz. AGW **Subject:** Death of Gustavus Adolphus **Obv:** Gustavus Adolphus lying in state with battle in background **Rev:** King in chariot crushing emenies below

Date	Mintage	VG	F	VF	XF	Unc
1633 Rare	—	—	—	—	—	—
1634 Rare	—	—	—	—	—	—

KM# M11 5 DUCAT

17.5000 g., 0.9860 Gold 0.5547 oz. AGW **Subject:** Death of Gustavus Adolphus **Obv:** Gustavus Adolphus lying in state with battle in background **Rev:** King in chariot crushing emenies below

Date	Mintage	VG	F	VF	XF	Unc
1634 Rare	—	—	—	—	—	—

KM# M12 10 DUCAT

35.0000 g., 0.9860 Gold 1.1095 oz. AGW **Subject:** Death of Gustavus Adolphus **Obv:** Gustavus Adolphus lying in state with battle in background **Rev:** King in chariot crushing emenies below

Date	Mintage	VG	F	VF	XF	Unc
1633 Rare	—	—	—	—	—	—

KM# M13 20 DUCAT

70.0000 g., 0.9860 Gold 2.2190 oz. AGW **Subject:** Death of Gustavus Adolphus **Obv:** Gustavus Adolphus lying in state with battle in background **Rev:** King in chariot crushing emenies below

Date	Mintage	VG	F	VF	XF	Unc
1633 Rare	—	—	—	—	—	—

KM# M14 60 DUCAT

210.0000 g., 0.9860 Gold 6.6569 oz. AGW **Subject:** Death of Gustavus Adolphus **Obv:** Gustavus Adolphus lying in state with battle in background **Rev:** King in chariot crushing emenies below

Date	Mintage	VG	F	VF	XF	Unc
1633 Unique	—	—	—	—	—	—

WOLLWARTH

Only one member of this family of free barons, a city councilman of Nuremberg, struck coins in the early 17th century.

RULER

Hans Sigmund von Wöllwarth-Fachsenfeld, 1546-1622

LORDSHIP

STANDARD COINAGE

KM# 1 6 KREUZER (Sechser)

Silver **Ruler:** Hans Sigmund von Wöllwarth-Fachsenfeld **Obv:** Family arms (crescent in shield), helmet above, legend around **Obv. Legend:** HANS * SIGMVND * WELLWARDT. **Rev:** 5-line inscription **Rev. Inscription:** + HERR + / MEINEN. GEIST / BEVELH. ICH / IN. DEIE. HAD (or HED) / (6) **Note:** Varieties exist.

Date	Mintage	VG	F	VF	XF	Unc
ND(ca.1608)	1,160	—	—	—	—	—

WORMS

The site of present-day Worms, located on the Rhine River 25 miles south of Mainz, was occupied before the Roman advance into Germany. An imperial mint was established in the town in the late 9th century and operated through the end of the 11th century. Worms was created a free imperial city in 1156 and obtained the mint right, separate from the bishopric, in 1234. However, most of the city's coinage was produced during the 17th century, with a few commemoratives having been struck also in the early18th century. French forces burned the city to the ground in 1689 and Worms was very slow to recover. It was annexed to France in 1801, but passed along with the episcopal lands to Hesse-Darmstadt in 1815.

RULERS

Philipp I von Rotenstein, 1595-1604
Philipp II Kratz von Scharfenstein, 1604
Wilhelm I von Effern, 1604-1616
Georg Friedrich von Greiffenklau zu Vollraths, 1616-1629
Georg Anton von Rotenstein, 1629-1652

Hugo Eberhard Kratz von Scharfenstein, 1654-1663
Johann Philipp I von Schönborn, 1663-1673
Lothar Friedrich von Metternich, 1673-1675
Damian Hartard von der Leyen, 1675-1678
Karl Heinrich von Metternich, 1679
Franz Emerich Kaspar,
Frhr. von Waldbott-Bassenhein, 1679-1683
Johann Karl, Frhr. von Frankenstein, 1683-1691
Ludwig Anton, Graf von Pfalz-Neuburg, 1691-1694
Franz Ludwig, Graf von Pfalz-Neuburg, 1694-1732

MINTMASTERS INITIALS

Initial	Date	Name
DS	1652-53	Unknown
ET	1644-51	Etherius Hettinger in Mainz
HIA	1624-28	Hans Jakob Ayrer
H ⚒ S	1627-72	Henning Schluter in Goslar and Zellerfeld
(a) = ⚒ or IL	1659-1711	Johannes Linck, die-cutter and warden in Heidelberg
M ⚒ K, MK	1680-82	Unknown
(b) = ⚒		

BISHOPRIC

REGULAR COINAGE

KM# 30 4 KREUZER (Batzen)
Silver **Subject:** Death of Franz Emerich Kaspar **Obv:** Bishop's mitre above 4-fold arms between palm fronds, titles of Franz Emerich Kaspar around **Rev:** 8-line inscription with dates

Date	Mintage	VG	F	VF	XF	Unc
1683	—	—	—	—	—	—

FREE IMPERIAL CITY

REGULAR COINAGE

KM# 86 ALBUS
Silver **Obv:** I/ALB, around RENTEN. GELT. DER., mintmaster's initials **Rev:** City arms, around STATTWORMBS, date **Note:** Varieties exist.

Date	Mintage	VG	F	VF	XF	Unc
1626 HIA	—	8.00	22.00	35.00	70.00	—
1628 HIA	—	8.00	22.00	35.00	70.00	—

KM# 95 ALBUS
Silver **Note:** Joint coinage of Mainz and Hesse-Darmstadt (KM#684), with city arms countermark of Worms on reverse.

Date	Mintage	VG	F	VF	XF	Unc
1638	—	20.00	40.00	85.00	200	—
1639	—	20.00	40.00	85.00	200	—

KM# 100 ALBUS
Silver **Obv:** City arms,legend around **Obv. Legend:** STAAT WORMBS **Rev:** I/ALBVS/date **Note:** Varieties exist.

Date	Mintage	VG	F	VF	XF	Unc
1649 (a)	—	11.00	22.00	38.00	70.00	—
1650 (a)	—	11.00	22.00	38.00	70.00	—
1651 (a)	—	11.00	22.00	38.00	70.00	—
1652 DS	—	11.00	22.00	38.00	70.00	—
1653 DS	—	11.00	22.00	38.00	70.00	—
1654	—	11.00	22.00	38.00	70.00	—
1654 HS	—	11.00	22.00	38.00	70.00	—
1655 HS	—	11.00	22.00	38.00	70.00	—
1656 HS	—	11.00	22.00	38.00	70.00	—
1657	—	11.00	22.00	38.00	70.00	—
1657 HS	—	11.00	22.00	38.00	70.00	—
1658 HS	—	11.00	22.00	38.00	70.00	—

KM# 120 ALBUS
Silver **Obv:** Dragon turned to right over city arms **Rev:** I/ALBVS/date/mintmaster's initials or symbol, all in wreath **Note:** Varieties exist.

Date	Mintage	VG	F	VF	XF	Unc
1680 MK	—	11.00	22.00	38.00	70.00	—
1680 (b)	—	11.00	22.00	38.00	70.00	—
1681 MK	—	11.00	22.00	38.00	70.00	—
1681 (b)	—	11.00	22.00	38.00	70.00	—

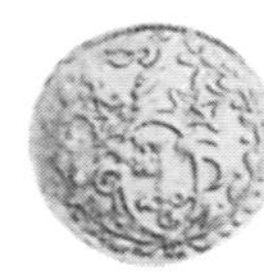

KM# 123 ALBUS
Silver **Obv:** Dragon turned left **Note:** Varieties exist.

Date	Mintage	VG	F	VF	XF	Unc
1681 MK	—	11.00	22.00	38.00	70.00	—
1682 MK	—	11.00	22.00	38.00	70.00	—

KM# 124 KREUZER
Silver **Obv:** City arms in wreath **Rev:** I/KRVTZ, date, mintmaster's initials, all in wreath

Date	Mintage	VG	F	VF	XF	Unc
1681 MK	—	—	—	—	—	—

KM# 125 KREUZER
Silver **Obv:** W above arms **Note:** Varieties exist.

Date	Mintage	VG	F	VF	XF	Unc
1681 MK	—	—	—	—	—	—
1682 MK	—	—	—	—	—	—

KM# 36 3 KREUZER (Groschen)
Silver **Obv:** Crowned imperial eagle, 3 in orb on breast, titles of Matthias **Rev:** City arms, date above **Note:** Varieties exist.

Date	Mintage	VG	F	VF	XF	Unc
1614	—	13.00	27.00	55.00	110	—
1615	—	13.00	27.00	55.00	110	—
1616	—	13.00	27.00	55.00	110	—
1617	—	13.00	27.00	55.00	110	—
1618	—	13.00	27.00	55.00	110	—

KM# 43 3 KREUZER (Groschen)
Silver **Note:** Klippe.

Date	Mintage	VG	F	VF	XF	Unc
1615	—	35.00	60.00	100	200	—

KM# 46 12 KREUZER (Dreibatzner)
Silver **Obv:** City arms **Rev:** Crowned imperial eagle, IZ in orb on breast, date in margin **Note:** Varieties exist.

Date	Mintage	VG	F	VF	XF	Unc
1616	—	45.00	85.00	165	300	—
1617	—	45.00	85.00	165	300	—
1618	—	45.00	85.00	165	300	—
1619	—	45.00	85.00	165	300	—
16Z0	—	45.00	85.00	165	300	—
1620	—	45.00	85.00	165	300	—

KM# 69 12 KREUZER (Dreibatzner)
Silver **Obv:** City arms divide date **Rev:** Dragon standing to right, WORMB...STADT MINTZ around

Date	Mintage	VG	F	VF	XF	Unc
16Z1	—	27.00	55.00	90.00	200	—
16ZZ	—	27.00	55.00	90.00	200	—

KM# 70 12 KREUZER (Dreibatzner)
Silver **Obv:** City arms divide date **Rev:** WORMBS/ISCHE. ST/AT. MVNTZ above heart-shaped baroque frame with IZ

Date	Mintage	VG	F	VF	XF	Unc
16Z1	—	27.00	55.00	90.00	200	—

KM# 71 12 KREUZER (Dreibatzner)
Silver **Obv:** Crowned imperial eagle, orb with 1Z on breast **Rev:** City arms divide S. - M. and date

Date	Mintage	VG	F	VF	XF	Unc
16Z1	—	27.00	55.00	90.00	200	—
16ZZ	—	27.00	55.00	90.00	200	—

KM# 68 12 KREUZER (Dreibatzner)
Silver **Note:** Kipper 12 Kreuzer. Similar to KM#46, arms divide date on obverse.

Date	Mintage	VG	F	VF	XF	Unc
16Z1	—	27.00	55.00	90.00	200	—

KM# 72 12 KREUZER (Dreibatzner)
Silver **Obv:** Similar to KM#71. **Rev:** Similar to KM#70 **Note:** Mule.

Date	Mintage	VG	F	VF	XF	Unc
16Z1	—	27.00	55.00	90.00	200	—

KM# 74 12 KREUZER (Dreibatzner)
Silver **Note:** Similar to KM#69, but dragon to left

Date	Mintage	VG	F	VF	XF	Unc
16ZZ	—	27.00	55.00	90.00	200	—

KM# 75 12 KREUZER (Dreibatzner)
Silver **Obv:** Crowned imperial eagle, 12 in orb on breast, titles of Ferdinand II around **Rev:** City arms divide date **Note:** Varieties exist.

Date	Mintage	VG	F	VF	XF	Unc
1622	—	27.00	55.00	90.00	200	—
16ZZ	—	27.00	55.00	90.00	200	—
16Z3	—	27.00	55.00	90.00	200	—

KM# 38 DICKEN (Teston)
Silver **Obv:** City arms in ornamented shield **Rev:** Crowned double-headed imperial eagle, orb on breast **Note:** Klippe.

Date	Mintage	VG	F	VF	XF	Unc
1614	—	525	1,075	2,000	3,300	—
1616	—	525	1,075	2,000	3,300	—

KM# 37 DICKEN (Teston)
Silver **Obv:** City arms in ornamented shield **Rev:** Crowned double-headed imperial eagle, orb on breast **Note:** Varieties exist.

Date	Mintage	VG	F	VF	XF	Unc
1614	—	60.00	120	225	400	—
1615	—	60.00	120	225	400	—
1616	—	60.00	120	225	400	—
1617	—	60.00	120	225	400	—
1618	—	60.00	120	225	400	—
1619	—	60.00	120	225	400	—
16Z0	—	60.00	120	225	400	—

KM# 56 DICKEN (Teston)
Silver **Note:** Varieties exist.

Date	Mintage	VG	F	VF	XF	Unc
1617	—	525	1,075	2,000	3,300	—

KM# 45 2/3 THALER OF 60 KREUZER (Guldenthaler)
Silver **Obv:** Dragon facing left leaning on city arms, date in field at left **Rev:** Crowned double-headed imperial eagle, value in orb on breast

Date	Mintage	VG	F	VF	XF	Unc
1616	—	—	—	8,750	12,000	—

KM# 78 1/4 THALER
Silver **Obv:** Crowned imperial eagle, orb on breast with 1/4 **Rev:** City arms, date in margin

Date	Mintage	VG	F	VF	XF	Unc
1624 HIA	—	150	250	400	650	—

KM# 40 1/2 THALER
Silver **Obv:** Crowned imperial eagle, orb on breast, date in margin **Rev:** Dragon with city arms

Date	Mintage	VG	F	VF	XF	Unc
1614	—	—	—	—	—	—

KM# 66 4 HELLER
Billon **Obv:** City arms, W above **Rev:** III in ornamented circle or heart shape **Note:** Kipper 4 Heller. Varieties exist.

Date	Mintage	VG	F	VF	XF	Unc
ND(c.1621)	—	60.00	100	190	300	—

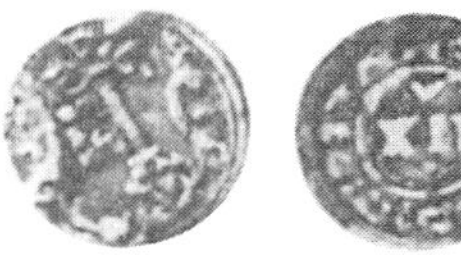

KM# 67 12 HELLER (2-1/2 Pfennig)
Billon **Obv:** City arms, W above **Rev:** XII in ornamented border or heart shape **Note:** Kipper 12 Heller.

Date	Mintage	VG	F	VF	XF	Unc
ND(1621)	—	45.00	85.00	160	275	—

KM# 25 PFENNIG
Silver **Obv:** Shield of city arms divides date (where present), 'W' above, all in circle of pellets **Note:** Uniface schüssel-type.

Date	Mintage	VG	F	VF	XF	Unc
(15)72	—	5.00	10.00	20.00	40.00	—
ND	—	5.00	10.00	20.00	40.00	—

KM# 35 PFENNIG
Silver **Note:** Uniface schussel-type: Double-lined Spanish shield of city arms, W above.

Date	Mintage	VG	F	VF	XF	Unc
ND(1614-18)	—	6.00	20.00	33.00	65.00	—

KM# 44 PFENNIG
Silver **Note:** Similar to KM#25 but arms divide S - G. Known only struck on thick flans of four times normal weight (0.8-1.0 grams).

Date	Mintage	VG	F	VF	XF	Unc
1616	—	6.00	20.00	33.00	65.00	—
1617	—	6.00	20.00	33.00	65.00	—
1620	—	6.00	20.00	33.00	65.00	—

KM# 50 PFENNIG
Silver **Note:** Klippe.

Date	Mintage	VG	F	VF	XF	Unc
1617	—	—	—	—	—	—
1618	—	—	—	—	—	—

KM# 85 PFENNIG
Silver **Obv:** City arms divide R - G (=Rentengeld), W divides date above **Note:** Uniface schussel-type.

Date	Mintage	VG	F	VF	XF	Unc
1626	—	6.00	20.00	33.00	65.00	—

KM# 121 PFENNIG
Silver **Obv:** Key upright (Worms arms) in circle of pellets **Note:** Uniface.

Date	Mintage	VG	F	VF	XF	Unc
ND(c.1681)	—	8.00	22.00	38.00	70.00	—

KM# 122 2 PFENNIG
Silver **Obv:** Key of Worms, W nearby **Note:** Uniface.

Date	Mintage	VG	F	VF	XF	Unc
ND(c.1681)	—	12.00	24.00	45.00	90.00	—

KM# 39 THALER
Silver **Obv:** Arms supported by two dragons, date above **Rev:** Crowned double eagle with orb on breast **Note:** Dav. #5952.

Date	Mintage	VG	F	VF	XF	Unc
1614	—	1,750	3,000	5,000	7,500	—

KM# 47 THALER
Silver **Obv. Legend:** ...IMP. CIVIT. VOR: **Note:** Dav. #5954.

Date	Mintage	VG	F	VF	XF	Unc
1616	—	1,900	3,150	5,300	7,500	—

KM# 51 THALER
Silver **Obv:** Lighthouse and seascape **Rev:** Lit candle and book dividing BIB-LIA, date in chronogram **Note:** Dav. #5955.

Date	Mintage	VG	F	VF	XF	Unc
ND(1617)	—	400	750	1,250	2,000	—

KM# 53 THALER
Silver **Rev:** Without BIB-LIA **Note:** Dav. #5955B.

Date	Mintage	VG	F	VF	XF	Unc
1617	—	900	1,500	3,000	4,500	—

KM# 52 THALER
Silver **Note:** Klippe. Dav. #5955A.

Date	Mintage	VG	F	VF	XF	Unc
1617	—	1,000	1,750	3,200	5,000	—

KM# 65 THALER
Silver **Obv:** Crowned imperial eagle **Rev:** Arms, legend, date **Rev. Legend:** MONETA. NOVA. LIB:S.R: IMP:... **Note:** Dav. #5956.

Date	Mintage	VG	F	VF	XF	Unc
16Z0	—	825	1,400	2,500	3,850	—

KM# 73 THALER
Silver **Obv:** Date in legend **Rev:** Arms supported by two dragons **Rev. Legend:** MON. NOV. LIB-IMP... **Note:** Dav. #5958.

Date	Mintage	VG	F	VF	XF	Unc
16ZZ	—	825	1,400	2,500	3,850	—

KM# 77 THALER
Silver **Obv:** Date divided below by imperial eagle **Rev:** Supported arms **Note:** Dav. #5960.

Date	Mintage	VG	F	VF	XF	Unc
1623	—	825	1,400	2,500	3,850	—

KM# 79 THALER
Silver **Obv:** Crowned imperial eagle **Rev:** Arms, date above in legend **Note:** Dav. #5961.

Date	Mintage	VG	F	VF	XF	Unc
16Z4 HIA	—	450	825	1,550	2,500	—

KM# 80 THALER
Silver **Subject:** 100th Anniversary of the Council of Thirteen **Note:** Similar to 2 Thaler, Dav. #LS517. Dav. #LS518.

Date	Mintage	VG	F	VF	XF	Unc
ND(1625)	—	2,000	3,500	6,000	8,500	—

KM# 89 THALER
Silver **Note:** Klippe. Dav. #5962A.

Date	Mintage	VG	F	VF	XF	Unc
1626	—	1,500	2,500	4,200	6,000	—

KM# 88 THALER
Silver **Rev:** More elaborate shield around arms **Note:** Dav. #5962.

Date	Mintage	VG	F	VF	XF	Unc
1626 HIA	—	450	825	1,550	2,500	—

KM# 90 THALER
Silver **Obv:** Crowned imperial eagle with orb on breast **Rev:** Arms with elaborate shield, date in legend **Note:** Dav. #5962B.

Date	Mintage	VG	F	VF	XF	Unc
1626	—	2,000	3,500	6,000	7,500	—

KM# 109 THALER
Silver **Rev:** Round shield with date above **Note:** Dav. #5963.

Date	Mintage	VG	F	VF	XF	Unc
1660	—	1,200	2,150	3,500	5,000	—

KM# 126 THALER
Silver **Rev:** Arms in frame, date in legend **Note:** Dav. #5964.

Date	Mintage	VG	F	VF	XF	Unc
1681	—	1,200	2,150	3,500	5,000	—

KM# 41 2 THALER
Silver **Obv:** Crowned imperial eagle with orb on breast **Rev:** Arms supported by two dragons, date above **Note:** Dav. #5951.

Date	Mintage	VG	F	VF	XF	Unc
1614	—	5,000	7,000	10,000	13,500	—

KM# 76 2 THALER
Silver **Obv:** Date in legend left of crown **Note:** Dav. #5957.

Date	Mintage	VG	F	VF	XF	Unc
1622	—	5,000	7,000	10,000	13,500	—

KM# A77 2 THALER
Silver **Note:** Similar to 1 Thaler, Dav. #5960. Dav. #5959.

Date	Mintage	VG	F	VF	XF	Unc
1623	—	5,000	7,000	10,000	13,500	—

KM# 81 2 THALER
Silver, 62 mm. **Subject:** 100th Anniversary of the Council of Thirteen **Obv:** Crowned imperial eagle with arms on breast within 13 shields with initials above each one **Rev:** Supported arms above city view **Note:** Dav. #LS517. Illustration reduced.

Date	Mintage	VG	F	VF	XF	Unc
ND(1625)	—	5,000	7,000	10,000	13,500	—

KM# 48 3 THALER
Silver **Obv:** Crowned imperial eagle with orb on breast **Rev:** Arms supported by two dragons, date below **Note:** Dav. #5953.

Date	Mintage	VG	F	VF	XF	Unc
1616	—	6,000	9,000	12,500	16,500	—

KM# 82 3 THALER
Silver **Subject:** 100th Anniversary of the Council of Thirteen **Note:** Similar to 2 Thaler, Dav. #LS517. Dav. #5953.

Date	Mintage	VG	F	VF	XF	Unc
ND(1625)	—	6,000	9,000	12,500	16,500	—

KM# 83 4 THALER
Silver **Subject:** 100th Anniversary of the Council of Thirteen **Note:** Similar to 2 Thaler, Dav. #LS517. Dav. #LS515.

Date	Mintage	VG	F	VF	XF	Unc
ND(1625)	—	7,500	11,500	16,500	22,000	—

TRADE COINAGE

KM# 42 GOLDGULDEN
3.5000 g., 0.9860 Gold 0.1109 oz. AGW **Rev:** Dragon holding arms at right

Date	Mintage	VG	F	VF	XF	Unc
1614	—	250	400	700	1,500	—
1615	—	250	400	700	1,500	—

KM# 49 GOLDGULDEN
3.5000 g., 0.9860 Gold 0.1109 oz. AGW **Rev:** Dragon holding arms at left

Date	Mintage	VG	F	VF	XF	Unc
1616	—	250	400	700	1,500	—
1617	—	250	400	700	1,500	—
1618	—	250	400	700	1,500	—
1619	—	250	400	700	1,500	—
1620	—	250	400	700	1,500	—
1621	—	250	400	700	1,500	—
1622	—	250	400	700	1,500	—

KM# 105 DUCAT
3.5000 g., 0.9860 Gold 0.1109 oz. AGW **Obv:** Crowned imperial eagle in inner circle **Rev:** Dragon holding arms in inner circle

Date	Mintage	VG	F	VF	XF	Unc
1651 ET	—	1,200	2,700	5,400	8,100	—
1655 HS	—	1,200	2,700	5,400	8,100	—

KM# 110 DUCAT
3.5000 g., 0.9860 Gold 0.1109 oz. AGW **Obv:** Bust of Johann Philip left in inner circle **Rev:** Capped arms in inner circle, date in legend

Date	Mintage	VG	F	VF	XF	Unc
1663	—	350	725	1,550	2,650	—
1664	—	350	725	1,550	2,650	—

KM# 116 DUCAT
3.5000 g., 0.9860 Gold 0.1109 oz. AGW **Obv:** Bust of Johann Philip right in inner circle

Date	Mintage	VG	F	VF	XF	Unc
1671	—	350	725	1,550	2,650	—

KM# 54 6 DUCAT
21.2800 g., Gold **Obv:** Lighthouse and seascape **Rev:** Lit candle, book dividing BIB-LIA, date in chronogram **Note:** Struck with 1 Thaler dies, KM#51.

Date	Mintage	VG	F	VF	XF	Unc
ND(1617) Rare	—	—	—	—	—	—

KM# 55 8 DUCAT
26.6500 g., Gold **Note:** Similar to 6 Ducat, KM#54. Struck with 1 Thaler dies, KM#51.

Date	Mintage	VG	F	VF	XF	Unc
ND(1617) Rare	—	—	—	—	—	—

PATTERNS

Including off metal strikes

KM#	Date	Mintage	Identification	Mkt Val
Pn1	1614	—	1/2 Thaler. Gold. KM#40.	—
Pn2	1651 (a)	—	Albus. Gold. KM#100.	—
Pn3	1681	—	Albus. Gold. KM#123.	—

WURTTEMBERG

Located in South Germany, between Baden and Bavaria, Württemberg obtained the mint right in 1374. In 1495 the rulers became dukes. In 1802 the duke exchanged some of his land on the Rhine with France for territories nearer his capital city. Napoleon elevated the duke to the status of elector in 1803 and made him a king in 1806. The kingdom joined the German Empire in 1871 and endured until the king abdicated in 1918.

RULERS

Friedrich I, 1593-1608
Johann Friedrich I, 1608-1628
Ludwig Friedrich von Mömpelgard
Regent and Administrator, 1628-1631
Julius Friedrich von Weiltingen
Regent and Administrator, 1631-1633
Eberhard III, 1633-1674
Wilhelm Ludwig, 1674-1677
Friedrich Karl Administrator, 1677-1693
Eberhard Ludwig, 1693-1733

MINT MARKS

C, CT - Christophstal Mint
F - Freudenstadt Mint
S - Stuttgart Mint
T - Tubingen Mint

MINT OFFICIALS' INITIALS

Christophstal Mint

Initial	Date	Name
DS	1622-28	David Stein
	1604-05	Andreas Hubner
	1605-08	Wolfgang Ulrich Fischer
	1607-08	Jakob Vischer, warden
	1620-22?	Wolfgang Ulrich Fischer
	1622	Andreas Hubner

Stuttgart Mint

Initial	Date	Name
ICM/M	1669-95	Johann Christoph Müller, die-cutter
IDD	?-1694	Johann David Danielder Altere, die-cutter
IIW/wheel	1681-1702	Johann Jakob Wagner
ILW, LW, W, PHM	1694-1707	Philipp Heinrich Müller, die-cutter
(b)=mask	1620-37	Claude Guichard, die-cutter
Rosette	1610-ca. 1634	Francois Guichard, die-cutter
	1596-1606	Hans Kerber
	1601-34	Hans Pfaffenbruch, die-cutter in Koblenz
	1606-15	Wolf Mayer, warden
	1607	Jakob Wichert
	1608-20	Hans Kerber
	1616-35	Matthias Distler, warden
	1618-19	Caspar Guichard, die-cutter
	1620	Wolfgang Ulrich Fischer
	1622	Andreas Hubner
	1622	Valentin Johann Moser
	1622	Johann Schmidt, superintendant
	1622	Albrecht Vayh, superintendant
	1622	Johann Valentin Vay, superintendant
	1638-50	Kaspar Zur Lahn
	1644-49	Gottfried Kuhorst, warden
	1649-65	Christoph Tauchwitz, warden
	1659-63	Georg Pfrundt, die-cutter
	1660-64	Jeremias Pfaffenhauser (Bopfenhauser)
	1664-77	Johann Christoph Holderer
	1665-77	Jeremias Pfaffenhauser, warden
	1673-81	Johann Mayer
	1677-?	Anstett Ulrich Müller, warden
	1691-94	Johann Christoph Müller, warden
	1694-1707	Johann Christoph Pfaffenhauser, warden

Tubingen Mint

Initial	Date	Name
IP	1623-24	Johann Pfister, die-cutter
	1622-23	Franz Kretzmaier, die-cutter
	1622-23	Moritz Salander, die-cutter
	1623	Caspar Zur Lahn, warden

Die-cutters of Various Cities

Date	Name
1579-1616	Francois Briot
1587-1619	Karl Seckler der Jüngere
1597-1609	Josse de Buisson
1602-06	Jean Cassignot
1605-06	Wilhelm Gross
1606-09	Friedrich Daig
1609-10	Johann de Vos of Augsburg
1609-10	Andreas Reichel
1609-10	Andreas Allgewer
1623-66	Paul Zeggin in Munich

ARMS

Württemberg: 3 stag antlers arranged vertically.
Teck (duchy): Field of lozenges (diamond shapes).
Mompelgart (principality): 2 fish standing on tails.

DUCHY

REGULAR COINAGE

KM# 5 HELLER
Silver **Ruler:** Friedrich I **Obv:** Hunting horn divides F-H, stag antler in lower part **Note:** Uniface, coin weight varies 0.15-0.24 grams.

Date	Mintage	VG	F	VF	XF	Unc
ND(1593-1608)	—	17.00	33.00	60.00	120	—

KM# 6 HELLER
Silver **Ruler:** Friedrich I **Obv:** Value I in place of antler

Date	Mintage	VG	F	VF	XF	Unc
ND(1593-1608)	—	17.00	33.00	60.00	120	—

KM# 22 HELLER
Silver **Ruler:** Johann Friedrich I **Obv:** Hunting horn on which superimposed IHF **Note:** Hohl-type; weight varies 0.19-0.42 grams.

Date	Mintage	VG	F	VF	XF	Unc
ND(1608-1628)	—	17.00	33.00	60.00	120	—

KM# 23 HELLER
Silver **Ruler:** Johann Friedrich I **Obv:** Hunting horn, H (=Heller) in center of horn's strap

Date	Mintage	VG	F	VF	XF	Unc
ND(1608-1628)	—	17.00	33.00	60.00	120	—

KM# 24 HELLER
Silver **Ruler:** Johann Friedrich I **Obv:** Shield of Wurttemberg arms, H above **Note:** Schussel-type.

Date	Mintage	VG	F	VF	XF	Unc
ND(1608-1628)	—	17.00	33.00	60.00	120	—

KM# 61 HELLER
Copper **Ruler:** Johann Friedrich I **Obv:** Hunting horn divides date, H in center of horn's strap **Rev:** CCC/XXX/VI **Note:** Kipper Heller. Weight varies 0.19--0.63 grams.

Date	Mintage	VG	F	VF	XF	Unc
1621	—	16.00	30.00	55.00	110	—
1622	—	16.00	30.00	55.00	110	—

KM# 82 HELLER
Copper **Ruler:** Johann Friedrich I **Obv:** Without H

Date	Mintage	VG	F	VF	XF	Unc
1622	—	16.00	30.00	55.00	110	—

KM# 83 HELLER
Copper **Ruler:** Johann Friedrich I **Obv:** Shield of Wurttemberg arms, date above **Rev:** Arms of Teck

Date	Mintage	VG	F	VF	XF	Unc
1622	—	16.00	30.00	55.00	110	—
1623	—	16.00	30.00	55.00	110	—

KM# 255 HELLER
0.1200 g., Silver **Ruler:** Eberhard Ludwig **Note:** Wurttemberg arms in squarish shield between 2 rosettes, H above. Uniface.

Date	Mintage	VG	F	VF	XF	Unc
ND(1693-1733)	—	17.00	33.00	60.00	120	—

KM# 8 PFENNIG
Silver **Ruler:** Friedrich I **Obv:** Shield of Wurttemberg arms, F H above

Date	Mintage	VG	F	VF	XF	Unc
ND(1593-1608)	—	11.00	22.00	45.00	80.00	—

KM# 25 PFENNIG

Silver **Ruler:** Johann Friedrich I **Obv:** Hunting horn with IHF superimposed **Note:** Hohl-type. Weight varies 0.31-0.50 grams.

Date	Mintage	VG	F	VF	XF	Unc
ND(1608-1628)	—	11.00	22.00	45.00	80.00	—

KM# 26 PFENNIG

Silver **Ruler:** Johann Friedrich I **Obv:** Wurttemberg arms in shield, IFH above **Note:** Schussel-type.

Date	Mintage	VG	F	VF	XF	Unc
ND(1608-1628)	—	11.00	22.00	45.00	80.00	—

KM# 175 PFENNIG

Silver **Ruler:** Ludwig Friedrich von Moempelgard Regent and Administrator **Obv:** LFH above arms **Note:** Weight varies 0.31-0.56 grams.

Date	Mintage	VG	F	VF	XF	Unc
ND(1628-1631)	—	11.00	22.00	45.00	80.00	—

KM# 186 PFENNIG

Silver **Ruler:** Julius Friedrich von Weiltingen Regent and Administrator **Obv:** Hunting horn with IHF **Note:** Hohl-type. Weight varies 0.38-0.43 grams.

Date	Mintage	VG	F	VF	XF	Unc
ND(1631-1633)	—	11.00	22.00	45.00	80.00	—

KM# 193 PFENNIG

Silver **Ruler:** Eberhard III **Obv:** Wurttemberg arms, EH above **Note:** Weight varies 0.26-0.54 grams.

Date	Mintage	VG	F	VF	XF	Unc
ND(1633-1674)	—	11.00	22.00	45.00	80.00	—

KM# 194 PFENNIG

Silver **Ruler:** Eberhard III **Obv:** Hunting horn divides E-H

Date	Mintage	VG	F	VF	XF	Unc
ND(1633-1674)	—	11.00	22.00	45.00	80.00	—

KM# 231 PFENNIG

Silver **Ruler:** Wilhelm Ludwig **Obv:** W?rttemberg arms in shield, WLH above **Note:** Weight varies 0.30-0.36 grams.

Date	Mintage	VG	F	VF	XF	Unc
ND(1674-1677)	—	9.00	20.00	40.00	75.00	—

KM# 232 PFENNIG

Silver **Ruler:** Friedrich Karl Administrator **Obv:** W?rttemberg arms in oval baroque frame, FCH above **Note:** Weight varies 0.21-0.37 grams.

Date	Mintage	VG	F	VF	XF	Unc
ND(1677-1693)	—	9.00	20.00	40.00	75.00	—

KM# 233 PFENNIG

Silver **Ruler:** Friedrich Karl Administrator **Obv:** Squarish arms

Date	Mintage	VG	F	VF	XF	Unc
ND(1677-1693)	—	9.00	20.00	40.00	75.00	—

KM# 256 PFENNIG

Silver **Ruler:** Eberhard Ludwig **Obv:** Oval Wurttemberg arms in baroque frame, ELH above **Note:** Uniface; weight varies 0.24-0.39 grams

Date	Mintage	VG	F	VF	XF	Unc
ND(1693-1733)	—	9.00	20.00	40.00	75.00	—

KM# 236 1/6 KREUZER

Copper **Ruler:** Friedrich Karl Administrator **Obv:** Wurttemberg arms in oval baroque frame, H above **Rev. Legend:** VI / EINEN / KREITZER **Note:** Weight varies 0.45-0.70 grams.

Date	Mintage	VG	F	VF	XF	Unc
ND(1680-93)	—	—	—	—	—	—
ND(1680-93) IIW	—	—	—	—	—	—

KM# 248 1/6 KREUZER

Copper **Ruler:** Friedrich Karl Administrator **Obv:** H at top divides date

Date	Mintage	VG	F	VF	XF	Unc
1687 IIW	—	—	—	—	—	—

KM# 257 1/6 KREUZER

Copper **Ruler:** Eberhard Ludwig **Obv:** Squarish shield of arms **Note:** Weight varies 0.45-.070 grams

Date	Mintage	VG	F	VF	XF	Unc
ND(1693-1733)	—	—	—	—	—	—

KM# 216 1/2 KREUZER (4 Pfennig)

0.6400 g., Silver **Obv:** Wurttemberg arms, value 1/2 in circle above **Rev:** Teck arms, date above

Date	Mintage	VG	F	VF	XF	Unc
1654	—	—	—	—	—	—

KM# 241 1/2 KREUZER (4 Pfennig)

Silver **Note:** Wurttemberg arms in oval baroque frame, value 1/2 divides date above. Uniface; weight varies 0.29-0.53 grams.

Date	Mintage	VG	F	VF	XF	Unc
1680	—	6.00	16.00	33.00	60.00	—
1683	—	6.00	16.00	33.00	60.00	—
1684	—	6.00	16.00	33.00	60.00	—
1689	—	6.00	16.00	33.00	60.00	—
1692	—	6.00	16.00	33.00	60.00	—
1693	—	6.00	16.00	33.00	60.00	—

KM# 270 1/2 KREUZER (4 Pfennig)

Silver **Ruler:** Eberhard Ludwig **Obv:** Round Wurttemberg arms in baroque frame, value 1/2 divides date above **Note:** Weight varies 0.23-0.50 grams

Date	Mintage	VG	F	VF	XF	Unc
1695	—	7.00	16.00	33.00	60.00	—
1696	—	7.00	16.00	33.00	60.00	—
1697	—	7.00	16.00	33.00	60.00	—
1698	—	7.00	16.00	33.00	60.00	—
1699	—	7.00	16.00	33.00	60.00	—
1700	—	7.00	16.00	33.00	60.00	—

KM# 62 KREUZER

Silver **Obv:** Bust right **Rev:** Double-cross, arms of Teck in circle in center with value I above, date dividied between ends of cross in upper half **Note:** Weight varies 0.50-0.60 grams.

Date	Mintage	VG	F	VF	XF	Unc
1621	—	24.00	45.00	75.00	125	—

KM# 63 KREUZER

Silver **Obv:** Wurttemberg arms in shield, value I above **Rev:** Arms of Teck, date above **Note:** Weight varies 0.50-0.60 grams.

Date	Mintage	VG	F	VF	XF	Unc
1621	—	20.00	40.00	60.00	110	—

KM# 84 KREUZER

Silver **Obv:** Wurttemberg arms below value **Rev:** Arms of Teck below date

Date	Mintage	VG	F	VF	XF	Unc
(1)622	—	20.00	40.00	60.00	110	—
1622	—	20.00	40.00	60.00	110	—

KM# 120 KREUZER

Silver **Obv:** Bust right **Rev:** Wurttemberg arms divide date, value I above

Date	Mintage	VG	F	VF	XF	Unc
1623	—	24.00	40.00	75.00	125	—

KM# 121 KREUZER

Silver **Obv:** Wurttemberg arms in ornamented shield, date above **Rev:** Teck arms in ornamented shield, value I above

Date	Mintage	VG	F	VF	XF	Unc
1623	—	20.00	40.00	60.00	110	—

KM# 122 KREUZER

Silver **Obv:** Arms divide date

Date	Mintage	VG	F	VF	XF	Unc
1623	—	20.00	40.00	60.00	110	—

KM# 123 KREUZER

Silver **Obv:** Value above arms **Rev:** Date above arms

Date	Mintage	VG	F	VF	XF	Unc
1623	—	20.00	40.00	60.00	110	—

KM# 152 KREUZER

Silver **Obv:** Bust right **Rev:** Shield of arms divided between Wurttemberg and Teck, date above

Date	Mintage	VG	F	VF	XF	Unc
1624	—	22.00	40.00	65.00	120	—
1624 CT	—	22.00	40.00	65.00	120	—
1625	—	22.00	40.00	65.00	120	—

KM# 153 KREUZER

Silver **Rev:** Double-cross, arms of Wurttemberg in circle in center with value I above, date dividied between ends of cross in upper half

Date	Mintage	VG	F	VF	XF	Unc
1624	—	—	—	—	—	—

KM# 200 KREUZER

Silver **Obv:** Oval Wurttemberg arms in baroque frame, date divided at top **Rev:** Oval arms of Teck in baroque frame, value I-K at top **Note:** Weight varies 0.41-.097 grams.

Date	Mintage	VG	F	VF	XF	Unc
1640	—	11.00	22.00	40.00	80.00	—
1641	—	11.00	22.00	40.00	80.00	—
1642	—	11.00	22.00	40.00	80.00	—
1643	—	11.00	22.00	40.00	80.00	—
1644	—	11.00	22.00	40.00	80.00	—
1645	—	11.00	22.00	40.00	80.00	—
1646	—	11.00	22.00	40.00	80.00	—

KM# 207 KREUZER

Silver **Obv:** Arms of Wurttemberg and Teck divided vertically in shield, date above **Rev:** Imperial banner and arms of Mompelgart divided vertically in shield, I.K above **Note:** Weight varies 0.41-0.97 grams.

Date	Mintage	VG	F	VF	XF	Unc
1648	—	—	—	—	—	—

KM# 249 KREUZER

Silver **Rev:** Titles of Friedrich Karl **Note:** Weight varies 0.29-0.84 grams.

Date	Mintage	VG	F	VF	XF	Unc
1687	—	9.00	20.00	40.00	80.00	—
1690	—	9.00	20.00	40.00	80.00	—
1691	—	9.00	20.00	40.00	80.00	—
1692/1	—	9.00	20.00	40.00	80.00	—
1692	—	9.00	20.00	40.00	80.00	—
1693	—	9.00	20.00	40.00	80.00	—

KM# 258 KREUZER

Silver **Ruler:** Eberhard Ludwig **Obv:** Date above divided arms within shield **Rev:** IK above 2-fold arms on shield within inner circle **Note:** Weight varies 0.43-0.71 grams. Varieties exist.

Date	Mintage	VG	F	VF	XF	Unc
1693	—	9.00	20.00	40.00	80.00	—
1694	—	9.00	20.00	40.00	80.00	—
1695	—	9.00	20.00	40.00	80.00	—
1696	—	9.00	20.00	40.00	80.00	—
1697	—	9.00	20.00	40.00	80.00	—
1698	—	9.00	20.00	40.00	80.00	—
1700	—	9.00	20.00	40.00	80.00	—

KM# 65 2 KREUZER (Halbbatzen)

Silver **Note:** Klippe 2 Kreuzer.

Date	Mintage	VG	F	VF	XF	Unc
1621	—	—	—	—	—	—

KM# 64 2 KREUZER (Halbbatzen)

Silver **Obv:** Bust right **Rev:** Wurttemberg arms in shield, value 2 above, date in legend **Note:** Weight varies 0.69-1.43 grams.

Date	Mintage	VG	F	VF	XF	Unc
1621	—	—	—	—	—	—

KM# 125 2 KREUZER (Halbbatzen)

Silver **Obv:** CT above 3 shields **Note:** Weight varies 0.69-1.43 grams.

Date	Mintage	VG	F	VF	XF	Unc
1623 CT	—	16.00	33.00	60.00	120	—

KM# 124 2 KREUZER (Halbbatzen)

Silver **Obv:** 3 small shields of arms, 2 above 1, value 2 between 2 shields above, date dividied by shield at bottom **Rev:** Imperial banner, S below

Date	Mintage	VG	F	VF	XF	Unc
1623 S	—	16.00	33.00	60.00	120	—
1624/3 S	—	16.00	33.00	60.00	120	—
1624 S	—	16.00	33.00	60.00	120	—
1625	—	16.00	33.00	60.00	120	—
1625 S	—	16.00	33.00	60.00	120	—
1628 S	—	16.00	33.00	60.00	120	—

KM# 126 2 KREUZER (Halbbatzen)

Silver **Obv:** CT in center of 3 shields

Date	Mintage	VG	F	VF	XF	Unc
1623 CT	—	16.00	33.00	60.00	120	—
1624 CT	—	16.00	33.00	60.00	120	—
1624 CT	—	16.00	33.00	60.00	120	—
1625 CT/DS	—	—	—	—	—	—
1625/6 CT/DS	—	—	—	—	—	—
1626 CT	—	16.00	33.00	60.00	120	—

KM# 185 2 KREUZER (Halbbatzen)

Silver **Obv:** 4-fold arms in ornamented shield, date above **Rev:** Imperial orb with 2 **Note:** Weight varies 0.97-1.35 grams.

Date	Mintage	VG	F	VF	XF	Unc
1630	—	60.00	115	200	325	—

KM# 187 2 KREUZER (Halbbatzen)
Silver **Obv:** 4-fold arms **Rev:** Imperial orb with 2, cross above divides date **Note:** Weight varies 0.82-1.61 grams.

Date	Mintage	VG	F	VF	XF	Unc
1631	—	60.00	115	200	325	—

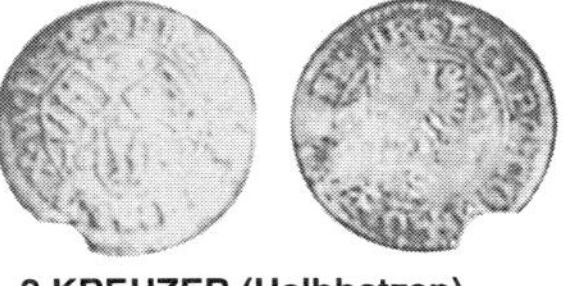

KM# 195 2 KREUZER (Halbbatzen)
Silver **Obv:** 3 small shields of arms, 2 above 1, value 2 between upper shields, date divided by lower shield **Rev:** Imperial banner **Note:** Weight varies 0.82-1.37 grams.

Date	Mintage	VG	F	VF	XF	Unc
1633	—	13.00	30.00	55.00	90.00	—
1634	—	13.00	30.00	55.00	90.00	—
1639	—	13.00	30.00	55.00	90.00	—
1639 S	—	13.00	30.00	55.00	90.00	—
1640 S	—	13.00	30.00	55.00	90.00	—
1641 S	—	13.00	30.00	55.00	90.00	—
1661 S	—	13.00	30.00	55.00	90.00	—
1665 S	—	13.00	30.00	55.00	90.00	—
1668 S	—	13.00	30.00	55.00	90.00	—

KM# 242 2 KREUZER (Halbbatzen)
Silver **Obv:** Titles of Friedrich Karl **Note:** Weight varies 0.99-1.27 grams.

Date	Mintage	VG	F	VF	XF	Unc
1680	—	—	—	—	—	—

KM# 259 2 KREUZER (Halbbatzen)
Silver **Ruler:** Eberhard Ludwig **Obv:** Titles of Eberhard Ludwig **Note:** Weight varies 0.91-1.26 grams.

Date	Mintage	VG	F	VF	XF	Unc
1693	—	13.00	30.00	55.00	90.00	—
1694	—	13.00	30.00	55.00	90.00	—
1694 (wheel)	—	13.00	30.00	55.00	90.00	—
1695	—	13.00	30.00	55.00	90.00	—
1696	—	13.00	30.00	55.00	90.00	—
1697	—	13.00	30.00	55.00	90.00	—

KM# 67 3 KREUZER (Groschen)
Silver **Obv:** Date in legend

Date	Mintage	VG	F	VF	XF	Unc
1621	—	33.00	65.00	120	200	—

KM# 68 3 KREUZER (Groschen)
Silver **Rev:** Date in legend

Date	Mintage	VG	F	VF	XF	Unc
1621	—	33.00	65.00	120	200	—
1622	—	33.00	65.00	120	200	—

KM# 66 3 KREUZER (Groschen)
Silver **Obv:** Bust right **Rev:** Wurttemberg arms in shield, value 3 above **Note:** Kipper 3 Kreuger. Weight varies 0.94-1.39 grams.

Date	Mintage	VG	F	VF	XF	Unc
ND(1621/2)	—	33.00	65.00	120	200	—

KM# 260 4 KREUZER (Batzen)
Silver **Ruler:** Eberhard Ludwig **Obv:** Value above 3 shields, date divided by lower shield **Rev:** Crowned arms within baroque frame **Note:** Weight varies 1.62-2.53 grams.

Date	Mintage	VG	F	VF	XF	Unc
1693 (wheel)	—	22.00	45.00	100	200	—
1694	—	22.00	45.00	100	200	—
1694 (wheel)	—	22.00	45.00	100	200	—
1696	—	22.00	45.00	100	200	—
1698	—	22.00	45.00	100	200	—
1700	—	22.00	45.00	100	200	—

KM# 70 6 KREUZER
Silver **Obv:** Bust right **Rev:** Wurttemberg arms, value 6 above, date in legend

Date	Mintage	VG	F	VF	XF	Unc
1621	—	—	—	—	—	—

KM# 69 6 KREUZER
Silver **Obv:** Wurttemberg arms, value 6 above **Rev:** Arms of Teck, date above **Note:** Weight varies 1.57-2.74 grams Kipper 6 Kreuzer.

Date	Mintage	VG	F	VF	XF	Unc
1621	—	—	—	—	—	—

KM# 85 12 KREUZER (Dreibatzner)
2.4800 g., Silver **Obv:** Bust right, mint mark C in cartouche below in legend **Rev:** Crowned 4-fold arms, value 12 in oval at bottom, date in legend

Date	Mintage	VG	F	VF	XF	Unc
1622 C	—	—	—	—	—	—

KM# 192 15 KREUZER (1/4 Gulden)
Silver **Obv:** Bust right **Rev:** Crowned oval 4-fold arms in baroque frame, date in legend, value (15.K) in legend below

Date	Mintage	VG	F	VF	XF	Unc
1632	—	100	200	375	600	—

KM# 191 15 KREUZER (1/4 Gulden)
Silver **Obv:** 1/2-length figure of Julius Friedrich right **Rev:** 3 small oval arms, 2 above 1, large crown above, date divided by lower arms, value (15.K) in legend at bottom **Note:** Weight varies 4.61-5.53 grams.

Date	Mintage	VG	F	VF	XF	Unc
1632	—	115	225	400	675	—

KM# 196 15 KREUZER (1/4 Gulden)
Silver **Rev:** Date divided at top of arms below crown, value (XV) in legend below **Note:** Weight varies 5.15-5.88 grams.

Date	Mintage	VG	F	VF	XF	Unc
1639	—	90.00	180	325	550	—

KM# 72 24 KREUZER (Sechsbatzner)
Silver **Rev:** Oval arms

Date	Mintage	VG	F	VF	XF	Unc
ND(1621/2)	—	135	275	500	—	—

KM# 71 24 KREUZER (Sechsbatzner)
Silver **Obv:** Bust right **Rev:** Crowned 4-fold arms in squarish shield **Note:** Weight varies 3.68-6.15 grams. Kipper 24 Kreuzer.

Date	Mintage	VG	F	VF	XF	Unc
ND(1621/2)	—	135	275	500	—	—

KM# 91 24 KREUZER (Sechsbatzner)
Silver **Note:** Weight varies 3.68-6.15 grams. Similar to KM#88, but date in obverse legend.

Date	Mintage	VG	F	VF	XF	Unc
(1) 622	—	135	275	500	—	—
1622	—	135	275	500	—	—

KM# 86 24 KREUZER (Sechsbatzner)
Silver **Obv:** Bust right, date below **Rev:** Crowned 4-fold arms in squarish shield divide date

Date	Mintage	VG	F	VF	XF	Unc
1622	—	160	325	550	—	—

KM# 87 24 KREUZER (Sechsbatzner)
Silver **Rev:** Without date

Date	Mintage	VG	F	VF	XF	Unc
1622	—	135	275	500	—	—

KM# 88 24 KREUZER (Sechsbatzner)
Silver **Rev:** Oval arms in baroque frame, without date

Date	Mintage	VG	F	VF	XF	Unc
1622	—	135	275	500	—	—

KM# 89 24 KREUZER (Sechsbatzner)
Silver **Obv:** Date in legend

Date	Mintage	VG	F	VF	XF	Unc
1622	—	135	275	500	—	—

KM# 92 24 KREUZER (Sechsbatzner)
18.0100 g., Silver **Rev:** Date in legend

Date	Mintage	VG	F	VF	XF	Unc
1622	—	135	275	500	—	—
1622 S	—	135	275	500	—	—

KM# 95 24 KREUZER (Sechsbatzner)
Silver **Obv:** Date in legend **Rev:** Squarish arms **Mint:** Christophstal

Date	Mintage	VG	F	VF	XF	Unc
1622 CT	—	135	275	500	—	—

KM# 96 24 KREUZER (Sechsbatzner)
Silver **Rev:** Date divided by arms **Mint:** Christophstal

Date	Mintage	VG	F	VF	XF	Unc
1622 CT	—	160	325	575	—	—

KM# 90 24 KREUZER (Sechsbatzner)
18.0100 g., Silver **Note:** Klippe 24 Kreuzer.

Date	Mintage	VG	F	VF	XF	Unc
1622	—	—	—	—	—	—

KM# 93 24 KREUZER (Sechsbatzner)
5.7900 g., Silver **Note:** Klippe, 24 Kreuzer.

Date	Mintage	VG	F	VF	XF	Unc
1622	—	—	—	—	—	—

KM# 94 24 KREUZER (Sechsbatzner)
Silver **Note:** Similar to KM#88, but mint mark in oval cartouche below bust on obverse.

Date	Mintage	VG	F	VF	XF	Unc
1622 C	—	135	275	400	—	—
1622 F	—	135	275	400	—	—

KM# 98 30 KREUZER (1/2 Gulden)
Silver **Obv:** Oval arms in baroque frame

Date	Mintage	VG	F	VF	XF	Unc
1622 (a)	—	165	325	600	1,000	—
1622 T	—	165	325	600	1,000	—
1623 S	—	165	325	600	1,000	—

KM# 97 30 KREUZER (1/2 Gulden)
Silver **Obv:** Crowned 4-fold arms in squarish shield **Rev:** Stag laying left, value 30 in round cartouche at left, date below **Note:** Kipper, 30 Kreuzer. Weight varies 3.99-5.09 grams.

Date	Mintage	VG	F	VF	XF	Unc
1622 S	—	135	275	475	800	—
1622 CT	—	135	275	475	800	—

KM# 127 30 KREUZER (1/2 Gulden)
Silver **Note:** Klippe 30 Kreuzer.

Date	Mintage	VG	F	VF	XF	Unc
1623 S	—	—	—	—	—	—

KM# 129 60 KREUZER (1 Gulden)
Silver **Obv:** Arms in squarish shield

Date	Mintage	VG	F	VF	XF	Unc
1622	—	135	275	475	800	—
1622 C	—	135	275	475	800	—
1622 S	—	135	275	475	800	—
1623 CT	—	135	275	475	800	—
1623 S	—	135	275	475	800	—

KM# 130 60 KREUZER (1 Gulden)
Silver **Obv:** Date in legend **Rev:** Crowned 4-fold arms in oval baroque frame, date above

Date	Mintage	VG	F	VF	XF	Unc
1622	—	200	400	750	1,000	—
(1)622	—	200	400	750	1,000	—

KM# 132 60 KREUZER (1 Gulden)
Silver **Obv:** Date below bust

Date	Mintage	VG	F	VF	XF	Unc
1622	—	200	400	750	1,200	—

KM# 99 60 KREUZER (1 Gulden)
Silver **Obv:** Crowned 4-fold arms in oval baroque frame **Rev:** Stag laying left, value 60 in cartouche at left, date below **Note:** Kipper 60 Kreuzer. Weight varies 6.98-10.81 grams.

Date	Mintage	VG	F	VF	XF	Unc
1622	—	165	325	600	1,000	—
1622 (a)	—	165	325	600	1,000	—
1622 C	—	165	325	600	1,000	—
1622 CT	—	165	325	600	1,000	—
1622 (a)	—	165	325	600	1,000	—
1623 CT	—	165	325	600	1,000	—
1623 T	—	165	325	600	1,000	—

KM# 131 60 KREUZER (1 Gulden)
Silver **Obv:** Date on obverse only **Note:** Weight varies 6.98-10.81 grams.

Date	Mintage	VG	F	VF	XF	Unc
(1)622	—	200	400	750	1,200	—

KM# 128 60 KREUZER (1 Gulden)
16.0500 g., Silver **Note:** Klippe, 60 Kreuzer.

Date	Mintage	VG	F	VF	XF	Unc
1623 (a)	—	—	—	—	—	—
1623 CT	—	—	—	—	—	—

KM# 172 60 KREUZER (1 Gulden)
Silver **Obv:** Crowned imperial eagle, 60 in orb on breast, date in legend **Rev:** 4-fold arms, 3 ornate helmets above **Note:** Reichs, 60 Kreuzer.

Date	Mintage	VG	F	VF	XF	Unc
1626 CT	—	—	—	—	—	—

KM# 133 120 KREUZER (2 Gulden)
18.3800 g., Silver **Obv:** Crowned 4-fold arms in oval baroque frame **Rev:** 2 stags laying facing center, value 120 in cartouche, date below **Note:** Kipper, 120 Kreuzer.

Date	Mintage	VG	F	VF	XF	Unc
1623 T	—	400	750	1,200	2,150	—

KM# 101 7 SCHILLINGE (1/4 Gulden)
Silver **Obv:** Wurttemberg arms in ornamented shield **Rev:** Teck arms in ornamented shield, date in legend

Date	Mintage	VG	F	VF	XF	Unc
1622	—	325	525	1,000	1,850	—

KM# 102 7 SCHILLINGE (1/4 Gulden)
Silver **Obv:** Wurttemberg arms in baroque frame, date in legend **Rev:** Legend in laurel wreath **Rev. Legend:** VII/SCHIL-/LINDER/S

Date	Mintage	VG	F	VF	XF	Unc
1622 S	—	400	700	1,200	2,150	—

KM# 103 7 SCHILLINGE (1/4 Gulden)
Silver **Obv:** Small oval Wurttemberg arms in baroque frame, date in legend **Rev:** Legend in laurel wreath **Rev. Legend:** VII/SCHIL/LING/ER

Date	Mintage	VG	F	VF	XF	Unc
1622 (a)	—	325	525	1,000	1,850	—

KM# 104 7 SCHILLINGE (1/4 Gulden)
Silver **Rev. Legend:** VII/SCHIL/LING

Date	Mintage	VG	F	VF	XF	Unc
1622 (a)	—	325	525	1,000	1,850	—

KM# 100 7 SCHILLINGE (1/4 Gulden)
Silver **Obv:** Crowned 4-fold arms **Rev:** Stag laying down to left, date below **Note:** Kipper, 7 Schillings.

Date	Mintage	VG	F	VF	XF	Unc
1622	—	325	525	1,000	1,850	—

KM# 105 7 SCHILLINGE (1/4 Gulden)
6.5300 g., Silver **Note:** Klippe, 7 Schillinge.

Date	Mintage	VG	F	VF	XF	Unc
1622 (a)	—	—	—	—	—	—

KM# 73 1/28 THALER (Schilling)
Silver **Obv:** Wurttemberg arms in shield **Rev:** Teck arms in shield, value 28 in legend at top **Note:** Weight varies 0.54-1.49 grams. Kipper 1/28 Thaler.

Date	Mintage	VG	F	VF	XF	Unc
ND(1621/2)	—	135	275	475	725	—

KM# 106 1/28 THALER (Schilling)
Silver **Rev:** Date in legend, value 28 above Teck arms

Date	Mintage	VG	F	VF	XF	Unc
1622	—	135	275	475	725	—
(1)622	—	135	275	475	725	—

KM# 107 1/28 THALER (Schilling)
Silver **Obv:** Hunting horn divides date **Rev:** Ornate round arms of Teck, value 28 in legend at top

Date	Mintage	VG	F	VF	XF	Unc
1622	—	135	275	475	725	—

KM# 108 1/28 THALER (Schilling)
Silver **Obv:** Hunting horn in ornate shield **Rev:** Ornate shiled of Teck arms, value (28) in legend at top, date in legend inscription **Note:** Weight varies 0.54-1.49 grams.

Date	Mintage	VG	F	VF	XF	Unc
1622	—	135	275	475	725	—

KM# 75 1/14 THALER (Doppelschilling)
Silver **Rev:** Date in legend, value 14 at top in legend

Date	Mintage	VG	F	VF	XF	Unc
1621	—	165	325	525	950	—
1622	—	165	325	525	950	—

KM# 74 1/14 THALER (Doppelschilling)
Silver **Obv:** Wurttemberg arms in shield **Rev:** Teck arms in shield, value 14 at top in legend **Note:** Weight varies 0.90-2.41 grams.

Date	Mintage	VG	F	VF	XF	Unc
ND(1621/2)	—	165	325	525	950	—

KM# 109 1/14 THALER (Doppelschilling)
Silver **Rev:** Value 14 above Teck arms

Date	Mintage	VG	F	VF	XF	Unc
1622	—	165	325	525	950	—
(16)23	—	165	325	525	950	—

KM# 110 1/14 THALER (Doppelschilling)
Silver **Rev:** Date divided by arms

Date	Mintage	VG	F	VF	XF	Unc
1622	—	165	325	525	950	—

KM# 111 1/14 THALER (Doppelschilling)
Silver **Obv:** Bust right **Rev:** Wurttemberg arms, value 14 in cartyouche in legend at top, date in legend inscription

Date	Mintage	VG	F	VF	XF	Unc
1622	—	165	325	525	950	—

KM# 134 1/9 THALER
Silver **Obv:** Bust right **Rev:** Crowned 4-fold arms, value 1/9 at bottom, date in legend

Date	Mintage	VG	F	VF	XF	Unc
1623	—	65.00	135	275	475	—
1624/3	—	65.00	135	275	475	—

KM# 177 1/9 THALER
3.4800 g., Silver

Date	Mintage	VG	F	VF	XF	Unc
1626	—	115	220	400	675	—

KM# 135 1/6 THALER
Silver **Note:** Weight varies 4.74-4.96 grams.

Date	Mintage	VG	F	VF	XF	Unc
1623 S	—	135	275	475	850	—
1624/3 S	—	135	275	475	850	—

KM# 178 1/6 THALER
4.7800 g., Silver **Rev:** Oval arms in baroque frame

Date	Mintage	VG	F	VF	XF	Unc
1629	—	200	325	600	1,075	—

KM# 205 1/6 THALER
4.8600 g., Silver **Obv:** 3 ornate helmets, date in legend **Rev:** Crowned oval 4-fold arms in baroque frame, value (1/6) in legend at bottom

Date	Mintage	VG	F	VF	XF	Unc
1647	—	—	—	—	—	—

KM# 12 1/4 THALER
Silver **Obv:** Full-length figure of St. Christopher, child Jesus on shoulder, left arms holding shield with crowned imperial eagle, titles of Rudolf II **Rev:** 4-fold arms, 3 ornate helmets above, date divided near bottom **Note:** Weight varies 7.20-7.35 grams.

Date	Mintage	VG	F	VF	XF	Unc
1606	—	525	850	1,350	—	—

KM# 18 1/4 THALER
Silver **Obv:** Less ornate helmets above arms **Rev:** St. Christopher walking right on ground

Date	Mintage	VG	F	VF	XF	Unc
1607	—	600	1,000	1,650	—	—

KM# 41 1/4 THALER
6.9600 g., Silver

Date	Mintage	VG	F	VF	XF	Unc
1611	—	600	1,000	1,650	—	—

KM# 136 1/4 THALER
Silver **Rev:** Without value **Note:** Weight varies 7.03-7.31 grams.

Date	Mintage	VG	F	VF	XF	Unc
1623 CT	—	400	675	1,200	—	—
1624 CT/IP	—	400	675	1,200	—	—

KM# 203 1/4 THALER
Silver **Obv:** 3 ornate helmets **Rev:** Crowned 4-fold arms in squarish shield, date divided above crown, value (1/4) in legend at bottom **Note:** Weight varies 7.17-7.26 grams.

Date	Mintage	VG	F	VF	XF	Unc
1641 Rare	—	—	—	—	—	—

KM# 208 1/4 THALER
Silver **Obv:** 3 ornately-shaped shields of arms, 2 above 1, crown above, date divided by lower shield, all in laurel wreath, value (1/4) in legend at bottom **Rev:** Imperial banner in laurel wreath

Date	Mintage	VG	F	VF	XF	Unc
1648 Rare	—	—	—	—	—	—

KM# 225 1/4 THALER
Silver **Obv:** Bust right **Rev:** Crowned heart-shaped oval, 4-fold arms divide date

Date	Mintage	VG	F	VF	XF	Unc
1668/59	—	—	—	—	—	—

KM# 244 1/4 THALER
Silver **Rev:** Crowned 4-fold arms in laurel wreath, date divided in legend near top **Note:** Weight varies 7.27-7.32 grams.

Date	Mintage	VG	F	VF	XF	Unc
1681	—	800	1,350	2,350	—	—
1681 M	—	800	1,350	2,350	—	—

KM# 261 1/4 THALER
Silver **Rev:** Crowned 4-fold arms between 2 palm branches, date divided below **Note:** Weight varies 7.29-7.31 grams.

Date	Mintage	VG	F	VF	XF	Unc
1694 IIW	—	165	325	600	1,000	—
1694 IIW (wheel)	—	165	325	600	1,000	—

KM# 276 1/4 THALER
8.6000 g., Silver **Rev:** 4-fold arms, five helmets above, date divided below

Date	Mintage	VG	F	VF	XF	Unc
1699 IIW	—	180	375	675	1,150	—

KM# 179 1/3 THALER
10.0300 g., Silver **Note:** Similar to 1/6 Thaler, KM#135, but value: 1/3 bottom reverse.

Date	Mintage	VG	F	VF	XF	Unc
1629	—	525	925	1,650	—	—

KM# 13 1/2 THALER
6.2000 g., Silver **Note:** Weight varies 14.12-14.60 grams. Similar to 1/4 Thaler, KM#12, but date in legend at bottom on reverse.

Date	Mintage	VG	F	VF	XF	Unc
1606	—	925	1,650	2,850	—	—

KM# 19 1/2 THALER
6.2000 g., Silver **Rev:** St. Christopher walking right on ground **Note:** Similar to 1/4 Thaler, KM#12, but less ornate helmets above arms.

Date	Mintage	VG	F	VF	XF	Unc
1607	—	925	1,650	2,850	—	—

KM# 29 1/2 THALER
Silver **Note:** Weight varies 14.27-14.54 grams.

Date	Mintage	VG	F	VF	XF	Unc
1609	—	1,075	1,800	3,000	—	—
1611	—	1,075	1,800	3,000	—	—

KM# 43 1/2 THALER
Silver **Obv:** Bust right **Rev:** 4-fold arms, three helmets above, date in legend **Note:** Weight varies 14.15-14.73 grams.

Date	Mintage	VG	F	VF	XF	Unc
1612	—	—	—	—	—	—

KM# 46 1/2 THALER
Silver **Rev:** Crowned 4-fold arms, date in legend

Date	Mintage	VG	F	VF	XF	Unc
1613	—	—	—	—	—	—
1621	—	—	—	—	—	—

KM# 76 1/2 THALER
13.1500 g., Silver **Note:** Klippe, 1/2 Thaler.

Date	Mintage	VG	F	VF	XF	Unc
1621	—	—	—	—	—	—

KM# 138 1/2 THALER
Silver **Obv:** Bust right **Rev:** Crowned oval 4-fold arms, date in legend

Date	Mintage	VG	F	VF	XF	Unc
1623 S	—	325	600	1,000	2,000	—
1624/3	—	325	600	1,000	2,000	—
1625	—	325	600	1,000	2,000	—
1626/5	—	325	600	1,000	2,000	—
1626	—	325	600	1,000	2,000	—

KM# 139 1/2 THALER
Silver **Rev:** Crowned 4-fold arms in heart-shaped shield, date in legend

Date	Mintage	VG	F	VF	XF	Unc
1623	—	325	600	1,000	2,000	—
1624 CT	—	325	600	1,000	2,000	—

KM# 137 1/2 THALER
Silver **Obv:** Crowned oval 4-fold arms in baroque frame **Rev:** St. Christopher left, with child Jesus on shoulder divides date **Note:** Exists in numerous multiple weight strikes ranging from 19.85 to 55.19 grams.

Date	Mintage	VG	F	VF	XF	Unc
1623	—	—	—	—	—	—

KM# 151 1/2 THALER
Silver **Note:** Klippe 1/2 Thaler.

Date	Mintage	VG	F	VF	XF	Unc
1624 CT	—	1,000	1,650	2,650	—	—

KM# 164 1/2 THALER
Silver **Rev:** Crowned 4-fold arms in oval baroque frame, mermaid at each side

Date	Mintage	VG	F	VF	XF	Unc
1625 CT/(b)	—	400	675	1,200	2,400	—

KM# 180 1/2 THALER
14.3400 g., Silver

Date	Mintage	VG	F	VF	XF	Unc
1629	—	525	850	1,600	3,000	—

KM# 188 1/2 THALER
14.1700 g., Silver **Obv:** 1/2-length figure of Julius Friedrich right **Rev:** Crowned 4-fold arms, date in legend

Date	Mintage	VG	F	VF	XF	Unc
1631 Rare	—	—	—	—	—	—

KM# 209 1/2 THALER
Silver **Obv:** Facing bust turned slightly right **Rev:** Crowned 4-fold arms in oval baroque frame, angel's head at top and bottom, date divided above crown **Note:** Weight varies 14.32-14.55 grams.

Date	Mintage	VG	F	VF	XF	Unc
1648 Rare	—	—	—	—	—	—

KM# 217 1/2 THALER
Silver **Obv:** Bust right **Rev:** Crowned heart-shaped oval 4-fold arms divide date

Date	Mintage	VG	F	VF	XF	Unc
1659 Rare	—	—	—	—	—	—

KM# 245 1/2 THALER
Silver **Rev:** Crowned 4-fold arms in laurel wreath, date divided in legend neart top **Note:** Weight varies 14.53-14.58 grams.

Date	Mintage	VG	F	VF	XF	Unc
1681 M	—	1,075	2,000	3,700	6,000	—
1681 ICM	—	1,075	2,000	3,700	6,000	—

KM# 263 1/2 THALER
Silver **Rev:** Arms between 2 palm branches **Note:** Weight varies 14.56-14.69 grams.

Date	Mintage	VG	F	VF	XF	Unc
1694 *	—	225	475	850	1,350	—
1694 IDD/IIW	—	225	475	850	1,350	—

KM# 262 1/2 THALER
Silver **Rev:** Crowned 4-fold arms, date divided below **Note:** Weight vareis 14.54-14.62 grams.

Date	Mintage	VG	F	VF	XF	Unc
1694 IDD/IIW	—	225	475	850	1,350	—

KM# 271 1/2 THALER
Silver **Rev:** Roman numeral date below arms **Note:** Weight varies 14.53-14.57 grams.

Date	Mintage	VG	F	VF	XF	Unc
MDCXCV (1695)	—	325	600	1,150	1,900	—

KM# 277 1/2 THALER
Silver **Rev:** 3 helmets above arms

Date	Mintage	VG	F	VF	XF	Unc
1699 IIW	—	—	—	—	—	—

Note: Reported, not confirmed

KM# 10 THALER
Silver **Obv:** St. Christopher with staff and shield, Christ child on shoulder, date in cartouche below **Obv. Legend:** RVDOLPH.II. IMP.AVG... **Rev:** Helmeted arms **Rev. Legend:** FRIDERICVS. D.G... **Note:** Dav. #7826.

Date	Mintage	VG	F	VF	XF	Unc
1605 Rare	—	—	—	—	—	—

KM# 14 THALER
Silver **Obv:** Figure changed, shield held higher **Note:** Dav. #7827.

Date	Mintage	VG	F	VF	XF	Unc
1606	—	1,350	2,250	3,500	7,500	15,500

KM# 20 THALER
Silver **Obv:** Date below St. Christopher, Christ child on left shoulder **Rev:** Date divided by shield below **Note:** Dav. #7828.

Date	Mintage	VG	F	VF	XF	Unc
1607/1607	—	1,350	2,500	4,000	8,000	16,500

KM# 21 THALER
Silver **Obv:** Without date **Note:** Dav. #7828A.

Date	Mintage	VG	F	VF	XF	Unc
1607	—	1,500	2,750	5,000	—	—

KM# 27 THALER
Silver **Obv:** Date divided by shield below **Rev:** St. Christopher with cloak flying behind **Note:** Dav. #7829.

Date	Mintage	VG	F	VF	XF	Unc
1608	—	1,350	3,400	5,300	—	—

KM# 28 THALER
Silver **Obv:** Larger St. Christopher and Christ child **Rev:** Helmeted arms, date in legend **Rev. Legend:** IOHANN:FRID. D.G. DUX... **Note:** Dav. #7831.

Date	Mintage	VG	F	VF	XF	Unc
1608	—	1,200	3,000	4,900	7,500	—
1609	—	1,200	3,000	4,900	7,500	—
1610	—	1,200	3,000	4,900	7,500	—

KM# 30 THALER
Silver **Rev:** Legend without rosettes **Note:** Dav. #7832.

Date	Mintage	VG	F	VF	XF	Unc
1609	—	1,000	2,000	3,300	—	—

KM# 44 THALER
Silver **Obv:** Bust right **Rev:** Helmeted arms, dat at 5 o'clock **Rev. Legend:** COM:MONT:DOM:IN:HEIDENHE **Note:** Dav. #7834.

Date	Mintage	VG	F	VF	XF	Unc
1612	—	600	1,200	2,250	3,750	—

KM# 47 THALER
Silver **Rev:** Legend COM:... begins at 1 o'clock, date at upper left **Note:** Dav. #7837.

Date	Mintage	VG	F	VF	XF	Unc
1613	—	600	1,200	2,250	3,750	—
1614	—	600	1,200	2,250	3,750	—
1615	—	600	1,200	2,250	3,750	—
1616	—	600	1,200	2,250	3,750	—

KM# 52 THALER
Silver **Obv:** Bust right, legend in diamond shape **Rev:** Crowned ams divide date, legend in diamond shape **Note:** Dav. #7838. Klippe Thaler.

Date	Mintage	VG	F	VF	XF	Unc
1617 Rare	—	—	—	—	—	—

KM# 55 THALER
Silver **Obv. Legend:** IOHANN:FRID:... **Rev:** Crowned arms, date in legend **Note:** Dav. #7842.

Date	Mintage	VG	F	VF	XF	Unc
1620	—	425	825	1,500	2,500	—
1621	—	425	825	1,500	2,500	—
1622	—	425	825	1,500	2,500	—

KM# 77 THALER
Silver **Obv. Legend:** IOH:FRI:... **Note:** Dav. #7844.

Date	Mintage	VG	F	VF	XF	Unc
1621	—	425	825	1,500	2,500	—

KM# 112 THALER
Silver **Obv. Legend:** IOHANN:FRID:D:G:DUX... **Note:** Dav. #7848.

Date	Mintage	VG	F	VF	XF	Unc
1622	—	425	825	1,500	2,500	—

KM# 113 THALER
Silver **Note:** Dav. #7848A. Klippe Thaler.

Date	Mintage	VG	F	VF	XF	Unc
1622 Rare	—	—	—	—	—	—

KM# 140 THALER
Silver **Obv. Legend:** FRIDER:D:G:DUX.WIRTENB. ET. TEC **Rev:** Crowned oval arms with mermaids at sides, C-T and cherub head below **Note:** Dav. #7850.

Date	Mintage	VG	F	VF	XF	Unc
1623	—	575	1,150	2,000	3,300	—

KM# 141 THALER
Silver **Obv. Legend:** ...FRID...WIRTEMB: ET. TECC: **Note:** Dav. #7850A.

Date	Mintage	VG	F	VF	XF	Unc
1623	—	575	1,150	2,000	3,300	—

KM# 143 THALER
Silver **Obv. Legend:** IOHAN. FRIDERICH... **Note:** Dav. #7850B.

Date	Mintage	VG	F	VF	XF	Unc
1623	—	575	1,150	2,000	3,300	—

KM# 144 THALER
Silver **Obv:** Without S below bust **Note:** Dav. #7850C.

Date	Mintage	VG	F	VF	XF	Unc
1623	—	575	1,150	2,000	3,300	—

KM# 142 THALER
Silver **Note:** Dav. #7850D. Klippe Thaler.

Date	Mintage	VG	F	VF	XF	Unc
1623 Rare	—	—	—	—	—	—

KM# 145 THALER
Silver **Obv:** Bust right, S behind head **Obv. Legend:** IOHANN: FRID...TECC **Rev:** Crowned, unsupported arms in frame **Rev. Legend:** ...HEIDENHEM **Note:** Dav. #7851.

Date	Mintage	VG	F	VF	XF	Unc
1623	—	500	1,000	1,900	3,150	—
1624	—	500	1,000	1,900	3,150	—

KM# 155 THALER
Silver **Rev:** Mermaid above small oval helmeted arms, C-T below **Note:** Dav. #7853.

Date	Mintage	VG	F	VF	XF	Unc
1624	—	500	1,000	1,900	3,150	—

KM# 156 THALER
Silver **Obv:** New bust right **Obv. Legend:** IOHANN: FRIDER:...TEC **Rev:** Flat topped shield, C-T at sides **Note:** Dav. #7854.

Date	Mintage	VG	F	VF	XF	Unc
1624	—	400	800	1,500	2,500	—

KM# 157 THALER
Silver **Obv:** Bust right **Obv. Legend:** IOHANN:FRID:...TECC **Rev:** Crowned oval supported arms, C-T at sides **Note:** Dav. #7855.

Date	Mintage	VG	F	VF	XF	Unc
1624	—	400	800	1,500	2,500	—

KM# 158 THALER
Silver **Obv:** Bust right **Obv. Legend:** ET.TEC **Note:** Dav. #7856.

Date	Mintage	VG	F	VF	XF	Unc
1624	—	400	800	1,500	2,500	—
1625	—	400	800	1,500	2,500	—

KM# 159 THALER

Silver **Obv. Legend:** IOHANN.FRIDER: D: G: DUX. WIRTEN: **Rev:** Crowned oval arms with or without C-T **Note:** Dav. #7859.

Date	Mintage	VG	F	VF	XF	Unc
1624	—	400	800	1,500	2,500	—
1625	—	400	800	1,500	2,500	—

KM# 165 THALER

Silver **Obv. Legend:** IOHANN: FRID: D: G: DUX. WIRTEMBERG:... **Rev:** Crowned arms with fancy shield **Note:** Dav. #7862.

Date	Mintage	VG	F	VF	XF	Unc
1625	—	400	800	1,500	2,500	—
1626/5	—	400	800	1,500	2,500	—
1626	—	400	800	1,500	2,500	—

KM# 166 THALER

Silver **Obv:** Bust right with angel heads in corners **Rev:** St. Christopher wading in water with staff and Christ child, date in Roman numerals below, arms in 4 corners **Note:** Dav. #7864. Klippe Thaler.

Date	Mintage	VG	F	VF	XF	Unc
1625 Rare	—	—	—	—	—	—

KM# 173 THALER

Silver **Rev:** Crowned supported oval arms **Note:** Dav. #7866.

Date	Mintage	VG	F	VF	XF	Unc
1626	—	400	800	1,500	2,500	—
1627	—	400	800	1,500	2,500	—
1628	—	400	800	1,500	2,500	—

KM# 176 THALER

Silver **Obv:** Bust right **Obv. Legend:** LVDOVIC. FRID: D: G:... **Rev:** Helmeted arms, date divided below **Rev. Legend:** DO: IN.HAIDEN: DVRAT & ADMINISTRATOR **Note:** Dav. #7867.

Date	Mintage	VG	F	VF	XF	Unc
1628 Rare	—	—	—	—	—	—

KM# 181 THALER

Silver **Rev:** Mermaid above helmeted arms, date in legend **Note:** Dav. #7868.

Date	Mintage	VG	F	VF	XF	Unc
1629 Rare	—	—	—	—	—	—

Note: Auktionshaus Meister & Sonntag Auction 4, 10-06, VF-XF realized approximately $15,685

KM# 189 THALER

Silver **Obv:** 1/2 figure right **Obv. Legend:** IVLIVS. FRIDERICVS... **Rev:** Helmeted arms, date **Rev. Legend:** CVRATOR.ET... **Note:** Dav. #7869.

Date	Mintage	VG	F	VF	XF	Unc
1631 Rare	—	—	—	—	—	—

Note: Auktionshaus Meister & Sonntag Auction 4, 10-06, VF-XF realized approximately $15,685

KM# 201 THALER

Silver **Obv:** Facing bust **Obv. Legend:** EBERHARD... **Rev:** Crowned arms with date divided above **Note:** Dav. #7870.

Date	Mintage	VG	F	VF	XF	Unc
1640 Rare	—	—	—	—	—	—
Note: Auktionshaus Meister & Sonntag Auction 4, 10-06, XF realized approximately $20,705						
1644 Rare	—	—	—	—	—	—

KM# 204 THALER

Silver **Obv:** Facing bust with long hair **Rev:** Helmeted arms with date divided in helmets **Note:** Dav. #7871.

Date	Mintage	VG	F	VF	XF	Unc
1645 Rare	—	—	—	—	—	—

KM# 206 THALER

Silver **Obv:** Larger facing bust with mustache and curly hair **Rev:** Crowned oval arms with date below crown **Note:** Dav. #7872.

Date	Mintage	VG	F	VF	XF	Unc
1647 Rare	—	—	—	—	—	—

KM# 218 THALER

Silver **Rev:** Crowned arms divide date below, angel heads above and below arms **Note:** Dav. #7873.

Date	Mintage	VG	F	VF	XF	Unc
1659 Rare	—	—	—	—	—	—
1660 Rare	—	—	—	—	—	—

Note: Fritz Rudolf Künker Münzenhandlung Auction 100, 6-05, XF realized approximately $13,955

KM# 226 THALER

Silver **Obv:** Bust with longer hair right **Rev:** St. Christopher in water with Christ child on right shoulder, shield in front **Note:** Dav. #7874.

Date	Mintage	VG	F	VF	XF	Unc
1669 Rare	—	—	—	—	—	—

KM# 230 THALER

Silver **Obv:** Bust right **Rev:** Capped arms in wreath **Rev. Legend:** 16. OMNIA. CVM. DEO. 70 **Note:** Dav. #7875.

Date	Mintage	VG	F	VF	XF	Unc
1670 Rare	—	—	—	—	—	—

KM# 234 THALER

Silver **Obv. Legend:** WILH.LUD **Rev:** Capped arms in wreath **Rev. Legend:** 16 IN. DEO. SPES. MEA. 77 **Note:** Dav. #7876.

Date	Mintage	VG	F	VF	XF	Unc
1677 ICM Rare	—	—	—	—	—	—

Note: Auktionshaus Meister & Sonntag Auction 4, 10-06, good XF realized approximately $22,590

KM# 235 THALER

Silver **Subject:** Death of Wilhelm Ludwig **Rev:** 11-line inscription **Note:** Dav. #7877.

Date	Mintage	VG	F	VF	XF	Unc
1677 ICM Rare	—	—	—	—	—	—

KM# 243 THALER

Silver **Obv. Legend:** FRID: CAROL D: DG... **Rev:** Capped arms in wreath, 1.6.D.P.F. 80 above **Note:** Dav. #7878.

Date	Mintage	VG	F	VF	XF	Unc
1680 Rare	—	—	—	—	—	—

Note: Auktionshaus Meister & Sonntag Auction 4, 10-06, XF realized approximately $18,195

KM# 264 THALER

Silver **Obv. Legend:** EBERH. LUD.-D.G... **Rev:** Capped arms, date divided below **Rev. Legend:** CUM \ DEO ET DIE **Note:** Dav. #7880.

Date	Mintage	VG	F	VF	XF	Unc
1694 IDD/IIW	—	700	1,350	2,850	4,750	—

KM# 265 THALER

Silver **Rev:** Capped arms in palm sprays **Note:** Dav. #7881.

Date	Mintage	VG	F	VF	XF	Unc
1694 PHM/IIW	—	625	1,250	2,250	3,750	—

KM# 266 THALER

Silver **Rev:** Capped flat topped arms with IL-W at sides, date divided below **Note:** Dav. #7882.

Date	Mintage	VG	F	VF	XF	Unc
1694 PHM/IIW	—	625	1,250	2,250	3,750	—

KM# 272 THALER

Silver **Rev:** Helmeted arms, date in Roman numerals divided below **Note:** Dav. #7884.

Date	Mintage	VG	F	VF	XF	Unc
MDCXCVII (1697) IIW	—	400	750	1,250	2,000	—

KM# 146 1-1/2 THALER

Silver **Obv:** Crowned oval shield **Obv. Legend:** IOHANN FRID: D: G:... **Rev:** St. Christopher holding Christ child dividing date **Note:** Dav. #7852A.

Date	Mintage	VG	F	VF	XF	Unc
1623 Rare	—	—	—	—	—	—

KM# 11 2 THALER

Silver **Note:** Dav. #7825. Similar to 1 Thaler, KM#10.

Date	Mintage	VG	F	VF	XF	Unc
1605 Rare	—	—	—	—	—	—

KM# 40 2 THALER

Silver **Note:** Dav. #7830. Similar to 1 Thaler, KM#28.

Date	Mintage	VG	F	VF	XF	Unc
1610 Rare	—	—	—	—	—	—

KM# 45 2 THALER

Silver **Obv:** Bust right **Obv. Legend:** IOHANN: FRID: D: G:... **Rev:** Helmeted arms **Rev. Legend:** COM: MONT: DOM:... **Note:** Dav. #7833.

Date	Mintage	VG	F	VF	XF	Unc
1612	—	3,000	5,300	8,300	12,000	—

KM# 48 2 THALER

Silver **Note:** Dav. #7836. Similar to 1 Thaler, KM#47.

Date	Mintage	VG	F	VF	XF	Unc
1613	—	3,000	5,300	8,300	12,000	—
1614	—	3,000	5,300	8,300	12,000	—
1615	—	3,000	5,300	8,300	12,000	—
1616	—	3,000	5,300	8,300	12,000	—

KM# 56 2 THALER

Silver **Note:** Dav. #7841. Similar to 1 Thaler, KM#55.

Date	Mintage	VG	F	VF	XF	Unc
1620	—	2,000	3,300	5,800	8,300	—
1621	—	2,000	3,300	5,800	8,300	—
1622	—	2,000	3,300	5,800	8,300	—

KM# 57 2 THALER

Silver **Note:** Dav. #7841A. Klippe 2 Thaler.

Date	Mintage	VG	F	VF	XF	Unc
1620 Rare	—	—	—	—	—	—

KM# 78 2 THALER

Silver **Obv:** Bust right **Obv. Legend:** IOH: FRI: D. G:... **Rev:** Crowned shield **Rev. Legend:** COM: MONT: DOM:... **Note:** Dav. #7843.

Date	Mintage	VG	F	VF	XF	Unc
1621	—	2,000	3,300	5,800	8,300	—

KM# 114 2 THALER

Silver **Obv:** Bust right, S below **Obv. Legend:** IOHANN: FRID:...WIRTEMBERG... **Rev:** Crowned arms **Note:** Dav. #7847.

Date	Mintage	VG	F	VF	XF	Unc
1622	—	2,000	3,300	5,800	8,300	—
1623	—	2,000	3,300	5,800	8,300	—

KM# 115 2 THALER

Silver **Obv. Legend:** ...WIRTEMB:... **Note:** Dav. #7847A.

Date	Mintage	VG	F	VF	XF	Unc
1622	—	2,000	3,300	5,800	8,300	—

KM# 147 2 THALER

Silver **Obv:** Bust right, date below legend **Obv. Legend:** IOH: FRI: D: G:... **Rev:** Helmeted arms **Rev. Legend:** COMES + MONT: DOM:... **Note:** Dav. #7849.

Date	Mintage	VG	F	VF	XF	Unc
1623	—	2,050	3,700	6,200	9,100	—

KM# 149 2 THALER

Silver **Obv:** Crowned oval shield **Obv. Legend:** IOHANN: FRID:... **Rev:** St. Christopher holding Christ child dividing date **Note:** Dav. #7852.

Date	Mintage	VG	F	VF	XF	Unc
1623 Rare	—	—	—	—	—	—

KM# 148 2 THALER

Silver **Note:** Dav. #A7850. Similar to 1 Thaler, KM#140.

Date	Mintage	VG	F	VF	XF	Unc
1623 Rare	—	—	—	—	—	—

KM# 168 2 THALER

Silver **Note:** Dav. #7858A. Klippe 2 Thaler.

Date	Mintage	VG	F	VF	XF	Unc
1624 Rare	—	—	—	—	—	—

KM# 169 2 THALER

Silver **Note:** Dav. #7861. Similar to 1 Thaler, Dav. #7862 but and instead of ET.

Date	Mintage	VG	F	VF	XF	Unc
1625	—	2,400	4,000	7,000	10,000	—

KM# 170 2 THALER

Silver **Note:** Dav. #7863. Klippe. Similar to 1 Thaler, Dav. #166.

Date	Mintage	VG	F	VF	XF	Unc
1625 DS Rare	—	—	—	—	—	—

KM# 167 2 THALER

Silver **Note:** Dav. #7858. Similar to 1 Thaler, KM#159.

Date	Mintage	VG	F	VF	XF	Unc
1625	—	2,400	4,000	7,000	10,000	—

KM# 174 2 THALER

Silver **Note:** Dav. #7865. Similar to 1 Thaler, KM#173.

Date	Mintage	VG	F	VF	XF	Unc
1626	—	2,400	4,000	7,000	10,000	—

KM# 267 2 THALER

Silver **Obv:** Bust right, IDD below **Obv. Legend:** EBERH. LUD... **Rev:** Capped arms, date and IIW below **Note:** Dav. #7879.

Date	Mintage	VG	F	VF	XF	Unc
1694 IDD/IIW Rare	—	—	—	—	—	—

KM# 273 2 THALER

Silver **Note:** Dav. #7883. Similar to 1 Thaler, KM#272.

Date	Mintage	VG	F	VF	XF	Unc
1697 IIW Rare	—	—	—	—	—	—

KM# 49 3 THALER

Silver **Note:** Dav. #7835. Similar to 1 Thaler, KM#37.

Date	Mintage	VG	F	VF	XF	Unc
1613 Rare	—	—	—	—	—	—

KM# 58 3 THALER

Silver **Note:** Dav. #7840. Similar to 1 Thaler, KM#55.

Date	Mintage	VG	F	VF	XF	Unc
1620 Rare	—	—	—	—	—	—
1621 Rare	—	—	—	—	—	—
1622 Rare	—	—	—	—	—	—

KM# 116 3 THALER

Silver **Obv:** Bust right, S below **Obv. Legend:** IOHANN: FRID: D:G:DUX. WIRTEMBERG... **Rev:** Crowned arms, date in legend **Note:** Dav. #7846.

Date	Mintage	VG	F	VF	XF	Unc
1622 S Rare	—	—	—	—	—	—
1623 S Rare	—	—	—	—	—	—

KM# 117 3 THALER

Silver **Obv. Legend:** ...DUX. WIRTEMB: **Note:** Dav. #7846A.

Date	Mintage	VG	F	VF	XF	Unc
1622 Rare	—	—	—	—	—	—

KM# 160 3 THALER

Silver **Note:** Dav. #7857. Similar to 1Thaler, KM#159.

Date	Mintage	VG	F	VF	XF	Unc
1624 Rare	—	—	—	—	—	—

KM# 171 3 THALER

Silver **Note:** Dav. #7860. Similar to 1 Thaler, KM#165.

Date	Mintage	VG	F	VF	XF	Unc
1625 Rare	—	—	—	—	—	—

KM# 59 4 THALER

Silver **Note:** Dav. #7839. Similar to 1 Thaler, KM#55.

Date	Mintage	VG	F	VF	XF	Unc
1620 Rare	—	—	—	—	—	—
1621 Rare	—	—	—	—	—	—

KM# 79 6 THALER

174.6300 g., Silver **Obv:** Bust right **Obv. Legend:** IOHANN: FRID: **Rev:** Crowned arms, date in legend

Date	Mintage	VG	F	VF	XF	Unc
1621 Rare	—	—	—	—	—	—

KM# 150 6 THALER

Silver **Obv:** Bust right, S below **Obv. Legend:** IOHANN: FRID:... **Rev:** Crowned arms, date in legend **Note:** Dav. #7845.

Date	Mintage	VG	F	VF	XF	Unc
1623 S Rare	—	—	—	—	—	—

TRADE COINAGE

KM# 15 GOLDGULDEN

3.5000 g., 0.9860 Gold 0.1109 oz. AGW **Obv:** Armored bust of Friedrich right **Rev:** Arms at center of floriated cross, date in exergue

Date	Mintage	VG	F	VF	XF	Unc
1606	—	1,400	2,800	5,600	9,800	—

KM# 16 GOLDGULDEN

3.5000 g., 0.9860 Gold 0.1109 oz. AGW **Obv:** Bust right in circle **Rev:** Floriated cross, orb at center, small shield of arms in each angle of cross, date in legend

Date	Mintage	VG	F	VF	XF	Unc
1606 Rare	—	—	—	—	—	—
1607 Rare	—	—	—	—	—	—

KM# 31 GOLDGULDEN

3.5000 g., 0.9860 Gold 0.1109 oz. AGW **Obv:** Bust of Johann Friedrich right **Rev:** Crowned double-headed eagle above arms, date in legend

Date	Mintage	VG	F	VF	XF	Unc
1609 Rare	—	—	—	—	—	—

KM# 51 GOLDGULDEN

3.5000 g., 0.9860 Gold 0.1109 oz. AGW **Obv:** Armored bust of Johann Friedrich right **Rev:** Cruciform arms with orb at center, date in legend

Date	Mintage	VG	F	VF	XF	Unc
1614 Rare	—	—	—	—	—	—
1620 Rare	—	—	—	—	—	—
1621 Rare	—	—	—	—	—	—

KM# 17 2 GOLDGULDEN

7.0000 g., 0.9860 Gold 0.2219 oz. AGW **Obv:** Armored bust of Friedrich right **Rev:** Arms at center of floriated cross, date in exergue

Date	Mintage	VG	F	VF	XF	Unc
1606 Rare	—	—	—	—	—	—

KM# 60 2 GOLDGULDEN

7.0000 g., 0.9860 Gold 0.2219 oz. AGW **Obv:** Armored bust of Johann Friedrich right **Rev:** Cruciform arms with orb at center, date in legend **Note:** Thick flan.

Date	Mintage	VG	F	VF	XF	Unc
1620 Rare	—	—	—	—	—	—

KM# 219 1/2 DUCAT

1.7500 g., 0.9860 Gold 0.0555 oz. AGW

Date	Mintage	VG	F	VF	XF	Unc
ND	—	750	1,500	2,700	4,500	—

KM# 220 1/2 DUCAT

1.7500 g., 0.9860 Gold 0.0555 oz. AGW **Obv:** Eberhard

Date	Mintage	VG	F	VF	XF	Unc
1659	—	1,050	2,250	4,150	6,800	—

KM# 250 1/2 DUCAT

1.7500 g., 0.9860 Gold 0.0555 oz. AGW **Obv:** Head of Friedrich Karl right **Rev:** Crowned arms in palms, date divided at top

Date	Mintage	VG	F	VF	XF	Unc
1688	—	975	2,050	3,750	6,000	—

KM# 9 DUCAT

3.5000 g., 0.9860 Gold 0.1109 oz. AGW **Obv:** Armored 1/2 figure of Friedrich right **Rev:** Crowned double-headed eagle above arms, date in legend

Date	Mintage	VG	F	VF	XF	Unc
1601	—	1,700	3,500	6,300	9,800	—
1603 Rare	—	—	—	—	—	—
1605	—	1,700	3,500	6,300	9,800	—

KM# 80 DUCAT

3.5000 g., 0.9860 Gold 0.1109 oz. AGW **Obv:** Armored 1/2 figure of Johann Friedrich right

Date	Mintage	VG	F	VF	XF	Unc
1621 Rare	—	—	—	—	—	—

KM# 197 DUCAT

3.5000 g., 0.9860 Gold 0.1109 oz. AGW **Obv:** Eberhard **Rev:** Crowned arms in cartouche, date divided at top

Date	Mintage	VG	F	VF	XF	Unc
1639	—	1,400	2,800	4,900	8,400	—
1944/39	—	1,400	2,800	4,900	8,400	—
Note: Inverted 6 reads as 9						
1651	—	1,400	2,800	4,900	8,400	—
1659	—	1,400	2,800	4,900	8,400	—
1668	—	1,400	2,800	4,900	8,400	—
1669	—	1,400	2,800	4,900	8,400	—

KM# 246 DUCAT

3.5000 g., 0.9860 Gold 0.1109 oz. AGW **Obv:** Friedrich Karl **Rev:** Crowned arms in branches, date divided at top

Date	Mintage	VG	F	VF	XF	Unc
1681	—	1,400	2,800	4,900	8,400	—
1688	—	1,400	2,800	4,900	8,400	—

KM# 268 DUCAT

3.5000 g., 0.9860 Gold 0.1109 oz. AGW **Obv:** Eberhard Ludwig **Rev:** Date in Roman numerals

Date	Mintage	VG	F	VF	XF	Unc
1694	—	375	800	1,950	3,200	—
1695	—	375	800	1,950	3,200	—
1696	—	375	800	1,950	3,200	—

KM# 274 DUCAT

3.5000 g., 0.9860 Gold 0.1109 oz. AGW **Rev:** Normal date

Date	Mintage	VG	F	VF	XF	Unc
1697	—	375	800	1,950	3,200	—

KM# 190 1-1/4 DUCAT

4.3750 g., 0.9860 Gold 0.1387 oz. AGW **Obv:** Draped bust of Eberhard right in inner circle **Rev:** Crowned oval arms in inner circle, crown divides date at top **Note:** Klippe.

Date	Mintage	VG	F	VF	XF	Unc
1631 Rare	—	—	—	—	—	—

KM# 32 2 DUCAT

7.0000 g., 0.9860 Gold 0.2219 oz. AGW **Obv:** Armored 1/2 figure of Johann Friedrich right **Rev:** Crowned double-headed eagle above arms, date in legend

Date	Mintage	VG	F	VF	XF	Unc
1609 Rare	—	—	—	—	—	—
1615 Rare	—	—	—	—	—	—

KM# 154 2 DUCAT

7.0000 g., 0.9860 Gold 0.2219 oz. AGW **Ruler:** Johann Friedrich I **Obv:** Johann Friedrich

Date	Mintage	VG	F	VF	XF	Unc
1623	—	1,900	3,850	6,600	10,500	—
1624	—	1,900	3,850	6,600	10,500	—

KM# 202 2 DUCAT

7.0000 g., 0.9860 Gold 0.2219 oz. AGW **Obv:** Armored bust of Eberhard facing in inner circle **Rev:** Crowned oval arms in inner circle, date divided near top of arms

Date	Mintage	VG	F	VF	XF	Unc
1640	—	1,900	3,750	6,800	7,500	—
1644/0	—	1,900	3,750	6,800	7,500	—
1648/4	—	1,900	3,750	6,800	7,500	—
1651	—	1,900	3,750	6,800	7,500	—

KM# 215 2 DUCAT

7.0000 g., 0.9860 Gold 0.2219 oz. AGW **Obv:** Older armored bust of Eberhard **Rev:** Palm divides 2 birds and date in inner circle

Date	Mintage	VG	F	VF	XF	Unc
1650	—	1,750	3,500	6,500	11,500	—

KM# 247 2 DUCAT

7.0000 g., 0.9860 Gold 0.2219 oz. AGW **Obv:** Armored bust of Friedrich Karl right **Rev:** Crowned arms in branches, date divided at top

Date	Mintage	VG	F	VF	XF	Unc
1681 Rare	—	—	—	—	—	—
1683 ICM Rare	—	—	—	—	—	—

KM# 269 2 DUCAT

7.0000 g., 0.9860 Gold 0.2219 oz. AGW **Ruler:** Eberhard Ludwig **Obv:** Armored bust right **Rev:** Crowned arms in palm branches, date divided at bottom

Date	Mintage	VG	F	VF	XF	Unc
1694 IIW	—	750	1,550	3,750	6,300	—

KM# 278 2 DUCAT
7.0000 g., 0.9860 Gold 0.2219 oz. AGW **Ruler:** Eberhard Ludwig **Obv:** Armored draped bust right **Obv. Legend:** EBERH: LUD: D: - G: DUX WURTEMB: **Rev:** Helmeted arms **Rev. Legend:** * CUM DEO ET DIE *

Date	Mintage	VG	F	VF	XF	Unc
1699 IIW Rare	—	—	—	—	—	—

KM# 81 2-1/2 DUCAT
8.7500 g., 0.9860 Gold 0.2774 oz. AGW **Obv:** Armored 1/2 figure of Johann Friedrich right **Rev:** Crowned double-headed eagle above arms, date in legend

Date	Mintage	VG	F	VF	XF	Unc
1621 Rare	—	—	—	—	—	—

KM# 279 3 DUCAT
10.5000 g., 0.9860 Gold 0.3328 oz. AGW **Obv:** Armored bust of Eberhard Ludwig right **Rev:** Arms topped by 3 helmets, date divided at bottom

Date	Mintage	VG	F	VF	XF	Unc
1699 IIW Rare	—	—	—	—	—	—

KM# 280 4 DUCAT
14.0000 g., 0.9860 Gold 0.4438 oz. AGW **Ruler:** Eberhard Ludwig **Obv:** Armored bust right **Rev:** Arms topped by 3 helmets, date divided at bottom

Date	Mintage	VG	F	VF	XF	Unc
1699 IIW Rare	—	—	—	—	—	—

KM# 33 5 DUCAT
17.5900 g., 0.9860 Gold 0.5576 oz. AGW **Obv:** St. Christopher standing facing with child and shield **Rev:** Helmeted arms **Note:** Struck with 1/2 Thaler dies, KM#29.

Date	Mintage	VG	F	VF	XF	Unc
1609 Rare	—	—	—	—	—	—

KM# 42 5 DUCAT
17.5900 g., 0.9860 Gold 0.5576 oz. AGW **Note:** Similar to 1/4 Thaler, KM#12 but less ornate helmets above arms and St. Christopher walking right.

Date	Mintage	VG	F	VF	XF	Unc
1611 Rare	—	—	—	—	—	—

KM# 50 5 DUCAT
16.7500 g., 0.9860 Gold 0.5310 oz. AGW **Obv:** Bust right **Rev:** 4-fold arms, 3 helmets above, date in legend

Date	Mintage	VG	F	VF	XF	Unc
1613 Rare	—	—	—	—	—	—

Note: Struck with 1/2 Thaler dies

KM# 210 5 DUCAT
17.3500 g., 0.9860 Gold 0.5500 oz. AGW **Obv:** Facing bust turned slightly right **Rev:** Crowned 4-fold arms in oval baroque frame, angel's head at top and bottom, date divided above crown **Note:** Struck with 1/2 Thaler dies, KM#209.

Date	Mintage	VG	F	VF	XF	Unc
1648 Rare	—	—	—	—	—	—

KM# 119 10 DUCAT
38.0500 g., 0.9860 Gold 1.2062 oz. AGW **Obv:** Bust of Johann Friedrich right **Rev:** Crowned arms **Note:** Struck with 2 Thaler dies, KM#114.

Date	Mintage	VG	F	VF	XF	Unc
1622 S Rare	—	—	—	—	—	—

KM# 275 10 DUCAT
34.6200 g., 0.9860 Gold 1.0974 oz. AGW **Obv:** Bust of Eberhard Ludwig right **Rev:** Capped arms **Note:** Struck with 1 Thaler dies, KM#272.

Date	Mintage	VG	F	VF	XF	Unc
1697 IIW Rare	—	—	—	—	—	—

KM# 161 20 DUCAT
70.0000 g., 0.9860 Gold 2.2190 oz. AGW **Obv:** Bust right, S behind head **Obv. Legend:** IOHANN: FRID... TECC **Rev:** Crowned, unsupported arms in frame **Rev. Legend:** HEIDENHEM **Note:** Struck with 1 Thaler dies.

Date	Mintage	VG	F	VF	XF	Unc
1624 S Rare	—	—	—	—	—	—

KM# 162 20 DUCAT
70.0000 g., 0.9860 Gold 2.2190 oz. AGW **Obv:** Bust of Eberhard Ludwig right **Rev:** Hand from clouds holding imperial banner, legend above **Rev. Legend:** PRO DEO ET IMPERIO

Date	Mintage	VG	F	VF	XF	Unc
ND Rare	—	—	—	—	—	—

KM# 163 30 DUCAT
105.0000 g., 0.9860 Gold 3.3284 oz. AGW **Obv:** Bust of Eberhard Ludwig right **Rev:** Hand from clouds holding imperial banner, legend above **Rev. Legend:** PRO DEO ET IMPERIO

Date	Mintage	VG	F	VF	XF	Unc
ND Rare	—	—	—	—	—	—

PATTERNS

Including off metal strikes

KM#	Date	Mintage	Identification	Mkt Val
Pn1	1601	—	Ducat. Copper. KM#9.	—
PnA2	1622	—	60 Kreuzer. Gold. Weight of 4 Ducat.	—
Pn2	1623	—	2 Thaler. Lead. KM#147.	—
Pn3	1631	—	Thaler. Lead. KM#189.	—
Pn4	1688	—	1/2 Ducat. Silver. KM#250.	150
Pn5	ND(1688)	—	1/2 Ducat. Silver. KM#250.	150
Pn6	1688	—	Ducat. Silver. Weight varies 4.49-7.06 grams, KM#246.	—
Pn7	1697	—	Thaler. Lead. KM#272.	—
Pn8	1697	—	Ducat. Silver. 3.3400 g. KM#274.	—

WURTTEMBERG-OELS

In 1647, Sylvius Nimrod, the elder son of Duke Julius Friedrich of Württemberg-Weiltingen, married Elisabeth Maria, the only child of the last duke of Münsterberg-Öls in Silesia, Karl Friedrich. The duchy of Öls thus passed to the control of a cadet line of the dukes of Württemberg until nearly the end of the 18th century.

The three surviving sons of Sylvius Nimrod lived under the regency of their mother until 1672, as he had died while they were still young, but then they divided their territory and titles. They established the branches of Württemberg-Öls, Württemberg-Öls-Bernstadt and Württemberg-Öls-Juliusburg. The elder line of Württemberg-Öls became extinct after only one generation and the two younger brothers divided those lands as well. When Bernstadt and Juliusburg died out in 1742 and 1745 respectively, all the Öls territories were reconstituted in the remaining member of the family, Karl Christian Erdmann, nephew of the last Bernstadt duke. He died childless in 1792 and Öls passed to Brunswick-Wolfenbüttel by virtue of his marriage to Friederike, daughter of Friedrich August of that duchy.

RULERS

Sylvius Nimrod, 1647-1664
Sylvius Friedrich, 1664-1697
Christian Ulrich von Bernstadt, 1664-1704
Julius Sigismund von Juliusburg, 1664-1684
Karl von Juliusburg und Bernstadt, 1684-1745

MINT OFFICIALS' INITIALS AND SYMBOLS

Initials	Date	Name
IN	1672-1705	Johann Neidhardt, die-cutter in Öls
(a)= and/or SP	1674-1679	Samuel Pfahler, mintmaster in Öls
FCV	1678-1688	Franz Carl Uhle, warden in Öls
T, IIT	1693-1696 (or 1698)	Johann Justus Tolle, warden
LL	1694-1699	Lukas Laurentius, warden in Öls
CVL	1700-1717	Christian von Loh, warden in Öls

ARMS

Württemberg – refer to that state for pertinent arms.
Silesia – eagle with crescent horizontally on breast.
Öls - eagle.

CROSS REFERENCES

F&S = **Ferdinand Friedensburg and Hans Seger,** *Schlesiens Münzen und Medaillen der neueren Zeit*, **Breslau, 1901.** [reprint Frankfurt/Main, 1976].

J&M = **Norbert Jaschke and Fritz P. Maercker,** *Schlesische Münzen und Medaillen,* **Ihringen, 1985.**

B&E = **Christian Binder and Julius Ebner,** *Württembergische Münz- und Medaillen-Kunde,* **vol. 2, Stuttgart, 1912.**

DUCHY

REGULAR COINAGE

KM# 58 GROESCHL (3 Pfennig)
0.7600 g., Silver, 16 mm. **Ruler:** Christian Ulrich in Bernstadt **Obv:** Oval 4-fold arms with central shield of Öls in baroque frame supported by mermaid at right, princely hat divides date above, value '3' in oval at bottom **Rev:** Silesian eagle in oval baroque frame, mintmaster's initials below, where present **Note:** Varieties exist.

Date	Mintage	VG	F	VF	XF	Unc
1691 F&S#2399	—	4.00	10.00	15.00	40.00	—
1694 LL F&S#2401	—	4.00	10.00	15.00	40.00	—
1695 F&S#2403	—	4.00	10.00	15.00	40.00	—
1696 LL F&S#2408	—	4.00	10.00	15.00	40.00	—
1696 F&S#2409	—	4.00	10.00	15.00	40.00	—
1697 LL F&S#2411	—	4.00	10.00	15.00	40.00	—
1698 LL F&S#2414	—	4.00	10.00	15.00	40.00	—
1698 T F&S#2415	—	4.00	10.00	15.00	40.00	—
1699 LL F&S#2416	—	4.00	10.00	15.00	40.00	—
1700 CVL F&S#2420	—	4.00	10.00	15.00	40.00	—

KM# 61 3 KREUZER (Groschen)
1.4500 g., Silver, 21 mm. **Ruler:** Christian Ulrich in Bernstadt **Obv:** Bust to right, value (3) below **Obv. Legend:** (D.G.) CHRIST. (U)(V)LR(IC). (—) (D.G.) DUX. (—) W(URT). T. I. S. O. (&) B. **Rev:** Silesian eagle in circle, princely hat divides date in margin at top **Rev. Legend:** COM(ES). MON(T)(B). DOM. I. HEID(ENH). (STE)(R)(N)(B). & M(ED)(ZB). **Note:** Varieties exist. Weight varies 1.45-1.62g.

Date	Mintage	VG	F	VF	XF	Unc
1695 LL F&S#2402	—	6.00	12.00	25.00	60.00	—
1696 LL F&S#2406	—	6.00	12.00	25.00	60.00	—
1698 LL F&S#2413	—	6.00	12.00	25.00	60.00	—

KM# 9 6 KREUZER
Silver, 27 mm. **Ruler:** Sylvius Friedrich **Obv:** Bust right, value (VI) below **Obv. Legend:** SYLVI9 FRID. D.G. DVX. - WIRT. TEC. I. S. OLS. **Rev:** Silesian eagle in circle, princely hat above, date at end of legend **Rev. Legend:** CO. MONT(B). DO. (I.) HEID. STERN. &. ME(D). **Note:** Weight varies: 2.90-3.25g. Varieties exist.

Date	Mintage	VG	F	VF	XF	Unc
1674	—	8.00	20.00	30.00	70.00	—
1678 SP	—	8.00	20.00	30.00	70.00	—

KM# 10 15 KREUZER

Silver, 30 mm. **Ruler:** Sylvius Friedrich **Obv:** Bust right, value (XV) below **Obv. Legend:** SYLVI9 FRID. D.G. DVX. - WIRT. T. I. S. OLS. **Rev:** Silesian eagle in circle, princely hat above, date at end of legend **Rev. Legend:** CO. MONTB. DO. I. HEID. STERN. &. ME. **Note:** Weight varies: 5.54-6.09g.

Date	Mintage	VG	F	VF	XF	Unc
1674 SP	—	12.00	20.00	30.00	65.00	—
1675 SP	—	12.00	20.00	30.00	65.00	—

DAV# 7885 THALER

Silver **Obv:** Bust right **Obv. Legend:** SYLVI FRID. D: G: DUX... **Rev:** Helmeted arms, date divided above, S-P divided below **Rev. Legend:** CO: MON: DO: I. H-EID:...

Date	Mintage	VG	F	VF	XF	Unc
1671 SP Rare	—	—	—	—	—	—

KM# 11 THALER

Silver **Ruler:** Sylvius Friedrich **Obv. Legend:** SYLVIUS. FRIEDERICUS... **Rev. Legend:** CO. MONTB: DOM: I. HE-ID:... **Note:** Dav#7887.

Date	Mintage	VG	F	VF	XF	Unc
1674 SP(a)	—	700	1,200	2,000	3,400	—

KM# 16 THALER

Silver **Ruler:** Sylvius Friedrich **Obv:** Without inner circle **Obv. Legend:** SYLVI FRID: D: G: DUX:... **Rev. Legend:** CO: MON: DO.I.H-EID: STER: & ME: **Note:** Dav#7889.

Date	Mintage	VG	F	VF	XF	Unc
1675 SP(a)	—	700	1,200	2,000	3,400	—

KM# 17 THALER

Silver **Ruler:** Sylvius Friedrich **Rev:** Changed shield and decoration, larger date **Note:** Dav#7891.

Date	Mintage	VG	F	VF	XF	Unc
1675 SP(a)	—	700	1,200	2,000	3,400	—

KM# 20 THALER

Silver **Ruler:** Sylvius Friedrich **Rev:** Date near top **Rev. Legend:** CO: MONT. DO. I. HE-ID. STER & MEZIB: **Note:** Dav#7893.

Date	Mintage	VG	F	VF	XF	Unc
1676 SP(a)	—	800	1,300	2,200	3,700	—

KM# 24 THALER

Silver **Ruler:** Sylvius Friedrich **Obv. Legend:** SYLVIUS. FRIDERICUS: D • G. DUX WURT. TEC. IN. SIL: OLS **Rev. Legend:** CO: MONTB. DOM. I. HEIDENH: STERNB: & MEZIBOR **Note:** Dav#7894.

Date	Mintage	VG	F	VF	XF	Unc
1677 SP(a)	—	800	1,300	2,200	3,700	—

KM# 25 THALER

Silver **Ruler:** Sylvius Friedrich **Note:** Dav#7894A. 12-sided klippe.

Date	Mintage	VG	F	VF	XF	Unc
1677 SP(a) Rare	—	—	—	—	—	—

KM# 34 THALER

Silver **Ruler:** Sylvius Friedrich **Obv:** Thinner bust right **Rev:** Smaller helmeted arms, date above **Note:** Dav#7895.

Date	Mintage	VG	F	VF	XF	Unc
1678 SP(a) Rare	—	—	—	—	—	—

KM# 42 THALER

Silver **Ruler:** Christian Ulrich in Bernstadt **Obv:** Bust right **Obv. Legend:** CHRISTIAN. ULR. D. G. DUX. W. T. I. S. OLS. & B. **Rev:** Helmeted arms, date divided below **Rev. Legend:** DO. I...MEDZIBOR. **Note:** Dav#7900.

Date	Mintage	VG	F	VF	XF	Unc
1679 FCV Rare	—	—	—	—	—	—

Note: Fritz Rudolf Künker Münzenhandlung Auction 131, 10-07, XF realized approximately $21,245

KM# 48 THALER

Silver **Ruler:** Christian Ulrich in Bernstadt **Obv:** Bust breaks legend at top **Rev:** Capped arms with date below **Rev. Legend:** ...MEDZIB. **Note:** Dav#7901.

Date	Mintage	VG	F	VF	XF	Unc
1681 Rare	—	—	—	—	—	—

Note: Auktionshaus Meister & Sonntag Auction 2, 9-04, nearly XF realized approximately $17,770; Dr. Busso Peus Nachfolger Auction 379, 4-04, XF-VF realized approximately $10,150

KM# 49 THALER

Silver **Ruler:** Christian Ulrich in Bernstadt **Rev:** More scrollwork beside and below shield **Note:** Dav#7901A.

Date	Mintage	VG	F	VF	XF	Unc
1681 Rare	—	—	—	—	—	—

KM# 52 THALER

Silver **Ruler:** Julius Sigismund in Juliusburg **Subject:** Death of Julius Sigismund **Rev:** Tree dividing inscription **Note:** Dav#7904.

Date	Mintage	VG	F	VF	XF	Unc
1684	—	650	1,350	2,750	4,750	—

KM# 56 THALER

Silver **Ruler:** Sylvius Friedrich **Subject:** Death of Elisabeth Maris, Mother of Sylvius Friedrich **Obv:** Bust left, scrollwork at sides **Rev:** 14-line inscription **Note:** Dav#7896.

Date	Mintage	VG	F	VF	XF	Unc
1686 IN	—	—	—	3,500	6,500	—

Note: Fritz Rudolf Künker Münzenhandlung Auction 135, 1-08, XF-Unc realized approximately $14,770

KM# 57 THALER

Silver **Ruler:** Christian Ulrich in Bernstadt **Obv:** Bust right **Obv. Legend:** CHRISTIAN. VLR.-D. G. DUX... **Rev:** Helmeted arms, date above **Rev. Legend:** COM. MONTB. DOM. I. HEID. STERNB. & MEDZIB. **Note:** Dav#7902.

Date	Mintage	VG	F	VF	XF	Unc
1687 Rare	—	—	—	—	—	—

KM# 64 THALER

Silver **Ruler:** Sylvius Friedrich **Obv:** Bust right **Obv. Legend:** D. G. SYLVI FRID. DUX... **Rev:** Crowned arms between palm branches, initials and date below **Note:** Dav#7897.

Date	Mintage	VG	F	VF	XF	Unc
1695 IIT Rare	—	—	—	—	—	—

KM# 65 THALER

Silver **Ruler:** Sylvius Friedrich **Obv:** Bust right without inner circle **Rev:** Helmeted arms, legend, date below **Rev. Legend:** SI DEUS PRO NOBIS AVIS CONTRA NOS **Note:** Dav#7898.

Date	Mintage	VG	F	VF	XF	Unc
1695 IIT Rare	—	—	—	—	—	—

KM# 67 THALER

Silver **Ruler:** Sylvius Friedrich **Subject:** 40th Birthday of Eleonore Charlotte, Wife of Sylvius Friedrich **Obv:** Conjoined busts right **Rev:** DOMINUS-PROVIDEBIT, "Jehovah" in sun above city view, Roman numeral date in exergue **Note:** Dav#7899.

Date	Mintage	VG	F	VF	XF	Unc
1696 IN//IIT Rare	—	—	—	—	—	—

KM# 69 THALER
Silver **Ruler:** Christian Ulrich in Bernstadt **Obv:** Bust right **Rev:** Five crowned shields and four monograms with date in center, initials below **Note:** Dav#7903.

Date	Mintage	F	VF	XF	Unc	BU
1697 IN//LL Rare	—	—	—	—	—	—

KM# 12 2 THALER
Silver **Ruler:** Sylvius Friedrich **Note:** Dav#7886. Similar to Thaler, KM#11.

Date	Mintage	VG	F	VF	XF	Unc
1674 SP(a)	—	1,600	2,900	4,750	7,200	—

KM# 18 2 THALER
Silver **Ruler:** Sylvius Friedrich **Note:** Dav#7888. Similar to 1 Thaler, KM#16.

Date	Mintage	VG	F	VF	XF	Unc
1675 SP(a)	—	1,800	3,150	5,400	8,600	—

KM# 19 2 THALER
Silver **Ruler:** Sylvius Friedrich **Rev:** Larger date, changed shield and decoration **Note:** Dav#7890.

Date	Mintage	VG	F	VF	XF	Unc
1675	—	1,800	3,150	5,400	8,600	—

KM# 21 2 THALER
Silver **Rev:** Date higher **Rev. Legend:** CO. MONT…& MEZIB **Note:** Dav#7892.

Date	Mintage	VG	F	VF	XF	Unc
1676 SP(a)	—	2,150	3,600	5,900	9,000	—

TRADE COINAGE

KM# 45 1/4 DUCAT
0.8750 g., 0.9860 Gold 0.0277 oz. AGW **Ruler:** Christian Ulrich in Bernstadt **Subject:** Death of Anna Elizabeth **Rev:** Bust of Anna Elizabeth right **Note:** Fr#3282.

Date	Mintage	VG	F	VF	XF	Unc
ND(ca.1680)	—	350	700	1,200	2,500	—

KM# 54 1/4 DUCAT
0.8750 g., 0.9860 Gold 0.0277 oz. AGW **Ruler:** Christian Ulrich in Bernstadt **Obv:** Bust of Christian Ulrich right **Rev:** Crowned arms, crown divides date **Note:** Fr#3279.

Date	Mintage	VG	F	VF	XF	Unc
1685	—	190	375	750	1,350	—

KM# 51 1/2 DUCAT
1.7500 g., 0.9860 Gold 0.0555 oz. AGW **Ruler:** Christian Ulrich in Bernstadt **Obv:** Bust of Christian Ulrich right **Rev:** Crowned arms, crown divides date **Note:** Fr#3278.

Date	Mintage	VG	F	VF	XF	Unc
1683	—	300	600	1,200	2,200	—

KM# 70 1/2 DUCAT
1.7500 g., 0.9860 Gold 0.0555 oz. AGW **Ruler:** Christian Ulrich in Bernstadt **Obv:** Bust of Sybil Marie right **Note:** Klippe. Uniface. Fr#3281.

Date	Mintage	VG	F	VF	XF	Unc
ND	—	475	950	1,800	3,050	—

KM# 4 DUCAT
3.5000 g., 0.9860 Gold 0.1109 oz. AGW **Ruler:** Sylvius Friedrich **Subject:** Wedding of Sylvius Friedrich and eleanore Charlotte **Obv:** Bust of Sylvius Friedrich right **Rev:** Bust of Eleanore Charlotte left **Note:** Fr#3275.

Date	Mintage	VG	F	VF	XF	Unc
ND(ca.1672)	—	575	1,150	2,300	3,900	—

KM# 13.1 DUCAT
3.5000 g., 0.9860 Gold 0.1109 oz. AGW **Ruler:** Sylvius Friedrich **Obv:** Bust of Sylvius Friedrich right in inner circle **Rev:** Arms topped by four helmets in inner circle, date divided near top **Note:** Fr#3274.1.

Date	Mintage	VG	F	VF	XF	Unc
1674 SP(a)	—	425	850	1,750	3,200	—
1675 SP(a)	—	425	850	1,750	3,200	—
1676 SP(a)	—	425	850	1,750	3,200	—

KM# 13.2 DUCAT
3.5000 g., 0.9860 Gold 0.1109 oz. AGW **Ruler:** Sylvius Friedrich **Obv:** Bust of Sylvius Friedrich right **Rev:** Helmeted arms in inner circle, date divided near toe **Note:** Fr#3274.2.

Date	Mintage	VG	F	VF	XF	Unc
1675 SP(a)	—	425	850	1,750	3,200	—

KM# 43 DUCAT
3.5000 g., 0.9860 Gold 0.1109 oz. AGW **Ruler:** Christian Ulrich in Bernstadt **Obv:** Bust right in inner circle **Rev:** Arms topped by 4 helmets in inner circle, date divided near top **Note:** Fr#3276.

Date	Mintage	VG	F	VF	XF	Unc
1679	—	650	1,300	2,600	4,550	—
1698	—	650	1,300	2,600	4,550	—

KM# 50 DUCAT
3.5000 g., 0.9860 Gold 0.1109 oz. AGW **Ruler:** Christian Ulrich in Bernstadt **Rev:** Crowned arms in inner circle **Note:** Fr#3277.

Date	Mintage	VG	F	VF	XF	Unc
1681	—	750	1,550	3,050	5,100	—

KM# 68 DUCAT
3.5000 g., 0.9860 Gold 0.1109 oz. AGW **Ruler:** Christian Ulrich in Bernstadt **Rev:** Cruciform arms with shield at center, monograms in angles **Note:** Fr#3280.

Date	Mintage	VG	F	VF	XF	Unc
1696	—	575	1,150	2,300	4,000	—

KM# 71 DUCAT
3.5000 g., 0.9860 Gold 0.1109 oz. AGW **Ruler:** Christian Ulrich in Bernstadt **Subject:** Wedding of Christian Ulrich and Sophia of Mecklenburg **Obv:** Bust of Christian Ulrich right in inner circle **Rev:** Bust of Sophia left in inner circle **Note:** Fr#3283.

Date	Mintage	VG	F	VF	XF	Unc
ND(ca.1700)	—	550	1,150	2,500	4,000	—

KM# 26 2 DUCAT
7.0000 g., 0.9860 Gold 0.2219 oz. AGW **Ruler:** Sylvius Friedrich **Obv:** Bust of Sylvius Friedrich right in inner circle **Rev:** Arms topped by four helmets in inner circle, date divided near top **Note:** Fr#3273.

Date	Mintage	VG	F	VF	XF	Unc
1677 SP(a)	—	1,250	2,500	5,000	8,100	—

WURZBURG

The Bishopric, located in Franconia, was established in 741. The mint right was obtained in the 11th century. The first coins were struck c. 1040. In 1441 the bishops were confirmed as dukes. In 1802 the area was secularized and granted to Bavaria. It was made a grand duchy in 1806 but the 1815 Congress of Vienna returned it to Bavaria.

RULERS
Julius Echter von Mespelbrunn, 1573-1617
Johann Gottfried von Aschhausen, 1617-1622
Philipp Adolph von Ehrenberg, 1623-1631
Franz, Graf von Hatzfeld, 1631-1642
Johann Philipp Franz von Schönborn, 1642-1673
Johann Hartmann von Rosenbach, 1673-1675
Peter Philipp von Dernbach, 1675-1683
Konrad Wilhelm von Wertenau, 1683-1684
Johann Gottfried II von Guttenberg, 1684-1698
Johann Philipp II, Frhr. von Greiffenklau-Vollraths, 1699-1719

MINT MARKS
F - Fürth
N - Nürnberg
W - Würzburg

MINT OFFICIALS' INITIALS

Initial	Date	Name
CM	Ca. 1610	Christian Maler
CS	1620	Conrad Stutz, mintmaster and die-cutter in Furth
CS	1632	In Wurzburg
CW	1617-19	
IL	Ca. 1682	Johann Link
IMW	1693	Johann Michael Wunsch
	1621	Johann Lohrer

MONETARY SYSTEM
3 Drier (Kortling) = 1 Shillinger
7 Shillinger = 15 Kreuzer
28 Shillinger = 1 Guter Gulden
44-4/5 Shillinger = 1 Convention Thaler

BISHOPRIC

REGULAR COINAGE

KM# 45 HELLER
Silver **Obv:** Wurzburg arms divide date, W above **Note:** Uniface.

Date	Mintage	VG	F	VF	XF	Unc
1622	—	13.00	27.00	55.00	100	—

KM# 46 2 HELLER
Silver **Obv:** Wurzburg arms divide date, value li above, W below **Note:** Uniface.

Date	Mintage	VG	F	VF	XF	Unc
1622	—	16.00	33.00	65.00	120	—

KM# 47 3 HELLER
Silver **Obv:** Ornamented Wurzburg arms divide date, W above **Rev:** III in wreath of palm branches

Date	Mintage	VG	F	VF	XF	Unc
1622	—	9.00	20.00	40.00	80.00	—
ND	—	9.00	20.00	40.00	80.00	—

KM# 53 3 HELLER
Silver **Obv:** Wurzburg arms divide date, III above **Note:** Uniface. Varieties exist.

Date	Mintage	VG	F	VF	XF	Unc
16Z3	—	8.00	16.00	33.00	65.00	—
16Z4	—	8.00	16.00	33.00	65.00	—
16Z5	—	8.00	16.00	33.00	65.00	—
16Z9	—	8.00	16.00	33.00	65.00	—

KM# 54 3 HELLER
Silver **Obv:** 2-fold arms of Wurzburg behind arms of Schonborn

Date	Mintage	VG	F	VF	XF	Unc
ND	—	20.00	40.00	65.00	120	—

KM# 166 3 HELLER
Silver **Obv:** Three small shields of arms, value III above

Date	Mintage	VG	F	VF	XF	Unc
1676	—	—	—	—	—	—
1677	—	—	—	—	—	—

KM# 178 3 HELLER
Silver **Obv:** Lower arms of Wertenau divide date, III H. above

Date	Mintage	VG	F	VF	XF	Unc
1683	—	—	—	—	—	—

 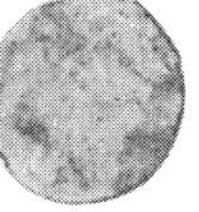

KM# 196 3 HELLER
Silver **Obv:** Lower arms of Guttenberg **Note:** Varieties exist.

Date	Mintage	VG	F	VF	XF	Unc
1685	—	6.00	13.00	27.00	55.00	—
1686	—	6.00	13.00	27.00	55.00	—
1689	—	6.00	13.00	27.00	55.00	—
1693	—	6.00	13.00	27.00	55.00	—
1694	—	6.00	13.00	27.00	55.00	—
1696	—	6.00	13.00	27.00	55.00	—

KM# 211 3 HELLER

Silver **Ruler:** Johann Philipp II von Greifenklau-Vollraths **Obv:** Lower arms of Greiffenklau

Date	Mintage	VG	F	VF	XF	Unc
1699	—	—	—	—	—	—

KM# 72 PFENNIG

Silver **Obv:** 4-fold arms, date **Note:** Uniface.

Date	Mintage	VG	F	VF	XF	Unc
1624	—	—	—	—	—	—

KM# 167 PFENNIG

Silver **Obv:** 2-fold arms divided vertically, Mainz on left, Schonborn on right, A. K. above

Date	Mintage	VG	F	VF	XF	Unc
ND	—	11.00	20.00	40.00	80.00	—

Note: Compare with Pfennig issues of Mainz, KM#97-99

KM# 168 PFENNIG

Silver **Obv:** Small shields of arms, value 1

Date	Mintage	VG	F	VF	XF	Unc
1676	—	11.00	20.00	40.00	80.00	—
1677	—	11.00	20.00	40.00	80.00	—

KM# 179 PFENNIG

Silver **Obv:** 2-fold arms of Wurzburg behind lower arms of Wertenau which divide date

Date	Mintage	VG	F	VF	XF	Unc
1683	—	—	—	—	—	—

KM# 86 3 PFENNIG (Dreier)

Silver **Subject:** Death of Philipp Adolph **Obv:** Arms of Wurzburg and Ehrenberg **Note:** Varieties exist.

Date	Mintage	VG	F	VF	XF	Unc
1631	—	—	—	—	—	—

KM# 33 6 PFENNIG (Sechser)

Silver **Subject:** Death of Julius Echter **Obv:** 4-fold arms, three helmets above **Rev:** 6-line inscription with dates, imperial orb with 6 below **Note:** Varieties exist.

Date	Mintage	VG	F	VF	XF	Unc
1617	—	40.00	65.00	135	225	—

KM# 87 6 PFENNIG (Sechser)

Silver **Subject:** Death of Philipp Adolph **Obv:** Arms of Wurzburg and Ehrenberg **Note:** Varieties exist.

Date	Mintage	VG	F	VF	XF	Unc
1631	—	—	—	—	—	—

KM# 55 1/84 GULDEN (Kortling)

Silver **Obv:** Three small shields of arms, two above one, lower shield divides date **Rev:** Imperial orb with 84 in ornamented rhombus

Date	Mintage	VG	F	VF	XF	Unc
1623	—	6.00	13.00	27.00	55.00	—
16Z4	—	6.00	13.00	27.00	55.00	—

KM# 73 1/84 GULDEN (Kortling)

Silver **Note:** Upper two shields close together, small F above. Varieties exist.

Date	Mintage	VG	F	VF	XF	Unc
16Z4F	—	6.00	13.00	27.00	55.00	—
16Z5F	—	6.00	13.00	27.00	55.00	—
16Z8F	—	6.00	13.00	27.00	55.00	—
16Z9F	—	6.00	13.00	27.00	55.00	—

KM# 108 1/84 GULDEN (Kortling)

Silver **Obv:** Arms of Hatzfeld

Date	Mintage	VG	F	VF	XF	Unc
1635	—	—	—	—	—	—

KM# 132 1/84 GULDEN (Kortling)

Silver **Obv:** Upper left arms of Mainz, lower arms of Schonborn, F in center, crown at top **Note:** Varieties exist.

Date	Mintage	VG	F	VF	XF	Unc
1640F	—	8.00	16.00	33.00	65.00	—
1645F	—	6.00	13.00	27.00	55.00	—
1646F	—	6.00	13.00	27.00	55.00	—
1648F	—	6.00	13.00	27.00	55.00	—
1655F	—	6.00	13.00	27.00	55.00	—
1656F	—	6.00	13.00	27.00	55.00	—
1657F	—	6.00	13.00	27.00	55.00	—
1658F	—	6.00	13.00	27.00	55.00	—
1659F	—	6.00	13.00	27.00	55.00	—
1662F	—	6.00	13.00	27.00	55.00	—
1663F	—	6.00	13.00	27.00	55.00	—
1665F	—	6.00	13.00	27.00	55.00	—
1671F	—	6.00	13.00	27.00	55.00	—

KM# 151 1/84 GULDEN (Kortling)

Silver **Obv:** Upper left arms of Wurzburg, lower arms of Rosenbach

Date	Mintage	VG	F	VF	XF	Unc
1673F	—	13.00	27.00	60.00	120	—
1674F	—	13.00	27.00	60.00	120	—

KM# 162 1/84 GULDEN (Kortling)

Silver **Obv:** Lower arms of Dernbach **Note:** Varieties exist.

Date	Mintage	VG	F	VF	XF	Unc
1675F	—	13.00	22.00	40.00	80.00	—
1676F	—	13.00	22.00	40.00	80.00	—
1677F	—	13.00	22.00	40.00	80.00	—
1679	—	13.00	22.00	40.00	80.00	—
NDF	—	13.00	22.00	40.00	80.00	—

KM# 186 1/84 GULDEN (Kortling)

Silver **Obv:** Lower arms of Guttenberg **Note:** Varieties exist.

Date	Mintage	VG	F	VF	XF	Unc
1684F	—	6.00	13.00	27.00	55.00	—
1685F	—	6.00	13.00	27.00	55.00	—
1686F	—	6.00	13.00	27.00	55.00	—
1687F	—	6.00	13.00	27.00	55.00	—
1688F	—	6.00	13.00	27.00	55.00	—
1689F	—	6.00	13.00	27.00	55.00	—
1690F	—	6.00	13.00	27.00	55.00	—
1693F	—	6.00	13.00	27.00	55.00	—
1694F	—	6.00	13.00	27.00	55.00	—
1695F	—	6.00	13.00	27.00	55.00	—
1696F	—	6.00	13.00	27.00	55.00	—
1697F	—	6.00	13.00	27.00	55.00	—

KM# 212 1/84 GULDEN (Kortling)

Silver **Ruler:** Johann Philipp II von Greifenklau-Vollraths **Obv:** Lower arms of Greifenklau **Rev:** Value on imperial orb within rhombus **Note:** Varieties exist.

Date	Mintage	VG	F	VF	XF	Unc
1699	—	6.00	13.00	27.00	55.00	—

KM# 139 ALBUS (2 Kreuzer)

Silver **Obv:** 4-fold arms with central shield of Schonborn in laurel wreath **Rev:** I/ALBVS/date in laurel wreath **Note:** Varieties exist.

Date	Mintage	VG	F	VF	XF	Unc
1651	—	6.00	13.00	27.00	55.00	—
1653	—	6.00	13.00	27.00	55.00	—
1654	—	6.00	13.00	27.00	55.00	—
1655	—	6.00	13.00	27.00	55.00	—
1656	—	6.00	13.00	27.00	55.00	—

KM# A133 SCHILLING

Silver **Ruler:** Johann Philipp Franz von Schonborn **Obv:** Crowned 2-fold arms behind Schonborn arms **Rev:** St. Kilian standing, sword in right hand, staff in left hand **Rev. Legend:** SANCTVS KILIANVS **Note:** Size varies: 20.9-21mm.

Date	Mintage	VG	F	VF	XF	Unc
1644	—	—	—	—	—	—
1645	—	—	—	—	—	—

KM# 56 SCHILLING (8 Pfennig)

Silver **Obv:** 4-fold arms of Wurzburg and Ehrenberg in circle, date in legend **Rev:** Full-length facing figure of St. Kilian with sword and crozier

Date	Mintage	VG	F	VF	XF	Unc
1623	—	11.00	22.00	45.00	90.00	—
16Z4	—	11.00	22.00	45.00	90.00	—

KM# 77 SCHILLING (8 Pfennig)

Silver **Obv:** Arms pointed at bottom, without inner circle **Note:** Varieties exist.

Date	Mintage	VG	F	VF	XF	Unc
16Z5	—	11.00	22.00	45.00	90.00	—
16Z6	—	11.00	22.00	45.00	90.00	—
16Z8	—	11.00	22.00	45.00	90.00	—
16Z9	—	11.00	22.00	45.00	90.00	—

KM# 109 SCHILLING (8 Pfennig)

Silver **Obv:** Three ornate shields of arms, two above one, lower shield of Hatzfeld divides date **Note:** Varieties exist.

Date	Mintage	VG	F	VF	XF	Unc
1635	—	16.00	30.00	60.00	120	—

KM# 152 SCHILLING (8 Pfennig)

Silver **Obv:** Crowned 4-fold arms of Wurzburg and Rosenbach **Rev:** Standing figure of St. Kilian divides date **Note:** Varieties exist.

Date	Mintage	VG	F	VF	XF	Unc
1650	—	20.00	40.00	75.00	170	—
1651F	—	20.00	40.00	75.00	170	—
1656	—	20.00	40.00	75.00	170	—
1657	—	20.00	40.00	75.00	170	—
1673	—	20.00	40.00	75.00	170	—

KM# 163 SCHILLING (8 Pfennig)

Silver **Obv:** Central shield of Dernbach arms **Note:** Varieties exist.

Date	Mintage	VG	F	VF	XF	Unc
1675	—	11.00	22.00	45.00	90.00	—
1676	—	11.00	22.00	45.00	90.00	—
1677	—	11.00	22.00	45.00	90.00	—
1678	—	11.00	22.00	45.00	90.00	—
1679	—	11.00	22.00	45.00	90.00	—
1680	—	11.00	22.00	45.00	90.00	—
1681	—	11.00	22.00	45.00	90.00	—

KM# 180 SCHILLING (8 Pfennig)

Silver **Obv:** Lower arms of Wertenau, without value

Date	Mintage	VG	F	VF	XF	Unc
1683	—	16.00	30.00	60.00	120	—

KM# 181 SCHILLING (8 Pfennig)

Silver **Obv:** 4-fold arms of Wurzburg and Wertenau

Date	Mintage	VG	F	VF	XF	Unc
1683	—	16.00	30.00	60.00	120	—

KM# 197 SCHILLING (8 Pfennig)

Silver **Obv:** 4-fold arms of Wurzburg and Guttenberg

Date	Mintage	VG	F	VF	XF	Unc
1685	—	—	—	—	—	—

KM# 198 SCHILLING (8 Pfennig)

Silver **Obv:** 4-fold arms of Wurzburg and Wertenau, date divided near bottom **Note:** Varieties exist.

Date	Mintage	VG	F	VF	XF	Unc
1685	—	11.00	22.00	45.00	90.00	—
1686	—	11.00	22.00	45.00	90.00	—
1688	—	11.00	22.00	45.00	90.00	—
1689	—	11.00	22.00	45.00	90.00	—
1690	—	11.00	22.00	45.00	90.00	—
1691	—	11.00	22.00	45.00	90.00	—
1692	—	11.00	22.00	45.00	90.00	—
1693	—	11.00	22.00	45.00	90.00	—
1694	—	11.00	22.00	45.00	90.00	—
(16)95	—	11.00	22.00	45.00	90.00	—
ND	—	11.00	22.00	45.00	90.00	—

KM# 207 SCHILLING (8 Pfennig)

Silver **Obv:** Crowned 2-fold arms of Wurzburg behind Schonborn arms which divide date, lower arms of Guttenberg without value **Note:** Varieties exist.

Date	Mintage	VG	F	VF	XF	Unc
1696	—	11.00	22.00	45.00	90.00	—
1697	—	11.00	22.00	45.00	90.00	—

KM# 213 SCHILLING (8 Pfennig)

Silver **Ruler:** Johann Philipp II von Greifenklau-Vollraths **Obv:** Lower arms of Greifenklau **Rev:** Value on imperial orb within rhombus **Note:** Varieties exist.

Date	Mintage	VG	F	VF	XF	Unc
1699	—	13.00	27.00	60.00	120	—

KM# 48 KREUZER

Copper **Obv:** Ornamented Wurzburg arms, W above **Rev:** 1/KREVT/ZER/date

Date	Mintage	VG	F	VF	XF	Unc
1622	—	9.00	20.00	40.00	80.00	—

KM# 49 KREUZER

Copper **Rev:** I/KREVTZ/ER/date

Date	Mintage	VG	F	VF	XF	Unc
1622	—	9.00	20.00	40.00	80.00	—

KM# 145 KREUZER

Copper **Obv:** 2-fold arms of Mainz and Schonborn enclosed in laurel wreath **Rev:** I/KREVTZ/date enclosed in laurel wreath

Date	Mintage	VG	F	VF	XF	Unc
1661	—	9.00	20.00	40.00	80.00	—

Note: Similar to Mainz, KM#115, but without mintmaster's initials.

KM# 32 3 KREUZER (Groschen)

Silver **Subject:** Death of Julius Echter **Obv:** 4-fold arms, three helmets above **Rev:** 6-line inscription with dates, imperial orb with 3 below **Note:** Varieties exist.

Date	Mintage	VG	F	VF	XF	Unc
1617	—	33.00	60.00	120	220	—

KM# 50 3 KREUZER (Groschen)

Silver **Subject:** Death of Gottfried **Obv:** Four helmets above 4-fold arms with central shield of Aschhausen **Rev:** 6-line inscription with date, small imperial orb with W below

Date	Mintage	VG	F	VF	XF	Unc
1622	—	90.00	200	325	525	—

KM# 120 3 KREUZER (Groschen)

Silver **Subject:** Death of Franz von Hatzfeld **Obv:** Central shield of Hatzfeld

Date	Mintage	VG	F	VF	XF	Unc
1642	—	—	—	—	—	—

KM# 153 3 KREUZER (Groschen)

Silver **Subject:** Death of Johann Philipp I **Obv:** Crowned oval 6-fold arms with central shield of Schonborn **Rev:** 9-line inscription with dates, imperial orb with 3 at bottom, W below **Note:** Varieties exist.

Date	Mintage	VG	F	VF	XF	Unc
1673	—	65.00	135	275	500	—

KM# 164 3 KREUZER (Groschen)

Silver **Subject:** Death of Johann Hartmann **Obv:** Crowned oval 4-fold arms of Wurzburg and Rosenbach **Rev:** 7-line inscription with dates, imperial orb with 3 at bottom

Date	Mintage	VG	F	VF	XF	Unc
1675	—	—	—	—	—	—

KM# 182 3 KREUZER (Groschen)

Silver **Subject:** Death of Peter Philipp **Obv:** Crowned round 4-fold arms of Bamburg and Wurzburg with central shield of Dernbach **Rev:** 9-line inscription with dates, imperial orb with 3 at bottom **Note:** Varieties exist.

Date	Mintage	VG	F	VF	XF	Unc
1683	—	27.00	55.00	110	225	—

Note: This was very likely a joint issue for both bishoprics

KM# 187 3 KREUZER (Groschen)

Silver **Subject:** Death of Konrad Wilhelm **Obv:** Crowned oval 4-fold arms of Wurzburg and Wertenau **Rev:** 6-line inscription with dates, imperial orb with 3 at bottom **Note:** Varieties exist.

Date	Mintage	VG	F	VF	XF	Unc
1684	—	33.00	65.00	135	275	—

KM# 210 3 KREUZER (Groschen)

Silver **Subject:** Death of Johann Gottfried II **Obv:** Crowned round 4-fold arms of Wurzburg and Wertenau **Rev:** 6-line inscription with dates, imperial orb with 3 at bottom

Date	Mintage	VG	F	VF	XF	Unc
1698	—	33.00	65.00	135	275	—

KM# 111 4 KREUZER (Batzen)

Silver **Obv:** Crowned 2-fold arms of Wurzburg behind lower 4-fold arms of Hatzfeld, II - I K above **Rev:** Standing figure of St. Kilian divides date

Date	Mintage	VG	F	VF	XF	Unc
1636	—	27.00	60.00	120	220	—
1637	—	27.00	60.00	120	220	—

KM# 51 12 KREUZER (Schreckenberger)

Silver **Note:** Counterstamp date/W on coin of Brunswick-Wolfenbuttel.

Date	Mintage	VG	F	VF	XF	Unc
16ZZ	—	—	—	—	—	—

Note: Some authorities believe this counterstamp to have been carried out by the Wurzburg city government and not by the bishopric

KM# 5 60 KREUZER (Guldenthaler)

Silver **Obv:** Crowned imperial eagle, orb on breast, titles of Rudolf II **Rev:** St. Kilian divides S - K above 4-fold arms in Spanish shield which divides date **Note:** Dav. #152.

Date	Mintage	VG	F	VF	XF	Unc
1601	—	525	1,200	2,350	3,600	—

KM# 22 60 KREUZER (Guldenthaler)

Silver **Obv:** Larger figure and arms **Rev:** 60 in orb **Note:** Varieties exist. Dav. #152.

Date	Mintage	VG	F	VF	XF	Unc
1613 CM	—	475	1,000	2,200	3,500	—
1615	—	475	1,000	2,200	3,500	—

KM# 40 60 KREUZER (Guldenthaler)

Silver **Obv:** Crowned ornate oval 4-fold arms with center shield **Rev:** St. Kilian divides date, 60 in oval below **Note:** Dav. #154.

Date	Mintage	VG	F	VF	XF	Unc
1619	—	1,200	2,450	4,300	6,750	—

KM# 6 DOUBLE WEIGHT (2 Guldenthalers)

Silver **Obv:** Crowned imperial eagle, 60 in orb on breast, titles of Rudolf II **Rev:** St. Kilian divides S - K above 4-fold arms in Spanish shield which divides date

Date	Mintage	VG	F	VF	XF	Unc
1601	—	—	—	—	—	—

KM# 130 1/28 THALER

Silver **Obv:** Crowned 2-fold arms of Wurzburg behind Schonborn arms which divide date, value Z8 below **Rev:** Full-length facing figure of St. Kilian with sword and crozier **Note:** Varieties exist.

Date	Mintage	VG	F	VF	XF	Unc
1643	—	27.00	55.00	85.00	165	—
1644	—	27.00	55.00	85.00	165	—
1645	—	27.00	55.00	85.00	165	—
1646	—	27.00	55.00	85.00	165	—

KM# 133 1/28 THALER

Silver **Obv:** 4-fold arms of Mainz and Wurzburg with center shield of Schonborn divide date, value Z8 below **Note:** Varieties exist.

Date	Mintage	VG	F	VF	XF	Unc
1648	—	24.00	45.00	75.00	160	—
1649	—	24.00	45.00	75.00	160	—
1650	—	24.00	45.00	75.00	160	—
1651	—	24.00	45.00	75.00	160	—
1656	—	24.00	45.00	75.00	160	—
1657	—	24.00	45.00	75.00	160	—
1658	—	24.00	45.00	75.00	160	—
1659	—	24.00	45.00	75.00	160	—
1661	—	24.00	45.00	75.00	160	—
1668	—	24.00	45.00	75.00	160	—

KM# 57 1/8 THALER

Silver **Obv:** Crowned imperial eagle, 1/8 in orb on breast, titles of Ferdinand II **Rev:** 4-fold arms of Wurzburg and Ehrenberg divide date

Date	Mintage	VG	F	VF	XF	Unc
1623	—	275	525	1,000	1,850	—

KM# 58 1/4 THALER

Silver **Obv:** Crowned imperial eagle, titles of Ferdinand II **Rev:** Crowned 4-fold arms with center shield divide date **Note:** Varieties exist.

Date	Mintage	VG	F	VF	XF	Unc
1623	—	300	600	1,075	2,000	—

KM# 59 1/4 THALER

Silver **Obv:** Half-length figure of St. Kilian divides date, three small shields below **Rev:** Crowned imperial eagle, orb on breast, titles of Ferdinand II **Note:** Varieties exist.

Date	Mintage	VG	F	VF	XF	Unc
1623	—	225	475	950	1,600	—
1624	—	225	475	950	1,600	—
1625	—	225	475	950	1,600	—

KM# 97 1/4 THALER

Silver **Note:** Similar to 1 Thaler, KM#90.

Date	Mintage	VG	F	VF	XF	Unc
1632	—	165	325	675	1,350	—

KM# 177 1/4 THALER

Silver **Obv:** Bust of Peter Philipp right **Rev:** Crowned 4-fold arms of Bamberg and Wurzburg with center shield of Dernbach in crossed palm fronds, date below

Date	Mintage	VG	F	VF	XF	Unc
1681	—	—	—	—	—	—

Note: This may be a joint issue for both Bamberg and Wurzburg

KM# 208 1/4 THALER

Silver **Obv:** Bust of Johann Gottfieid II right **Rev:** Crowned round 4-fold arms of Wurzburg and Guttenberg, date divided at upper left and right

Date	Mintage	VG	F	VF	XF	Unc
1696	—	115	225	475	950	—

KM# 74 1/2 THALER

Silver **Note:** Similar to 1 Thaler, KM#75.

Date	Mintage	VG	F	VF	XF	Unc
16Z4	—	475	1,000	1,800	2,900	—

KM# 85 1/2 THALER

Silver **Note:** Similar to KM#75, but 1/2 in orb on eagle's breast.

Date	Mintage	VG	F	VF	XF	Unc
1630	—	—	—	—	—	—

KM# 88 1/2 THALER

Silver **Note:** Similar to 1 Thaler, KM#90.

Date	Mintage	VG	F	VF	XF	Unc
1631	—	135	275	525	1,075	—
1632	—	135	275	525	1,075	—

KM# 98 1/2 THALER

Silver **Note:** Similar to 1 Thaler, KM#90 but reverse with only volutes beside shield.

Date	Mintage	VG	F	VF	XF	Unc
1632	—	165	325	675	1,350	—

KM# 209 1/2 THALER

Silver **Obv:** Bust of Johann Gottfried II right **Rev:** Three ornate helmets above oval 4-fold arms of Wurzburg and Guttenberg, date at top

Date	Mintage	VG	F	VF	XF	Unc
1696	—	165	325	675	1,350	—

KM# 8 THALER

Silver **Obv:** St. Kilian with sword and scepter behind small oval shield divide date and S-K **Obv. Legend:** RVDOLPHVS. II... **Rev:** Crowned double eagle with orb on breast **Note:** Dav. #5965.

Date	Mintage	VG	F	VF	XF	Unc
1601	—	500	1,000	2,000	4,750	8,500

KM# 23 THALER

Silver **Obv:** Legend, date **Obv. Legend:** MATTHIAS. ROM. IMP. AUG... **Note:** Dav. #5966.

Date	Mintage	VG	F	VF	XF	Unc
1613 Rare	—	—	—	—	—	—

KM# 24 THALER

Silver **Obv:** Crowned imperial eagle, C-M below **Rev:** St. Kilian divides S-K above, date below **Note:** Dav. #5967.

Date	Mintage	VG	F	VF	XF	Unc
1613	—	600	1,150	1,800	3,000	—

KM# 28 THALER

Silver **Rev:** St. Kilian dividing date and S-K at shoulders **Rev. Legend:** IVILIVS D: G: EPISOPVS-WIRTZBUR: G:... **Note:** Dav. #5968.

Date	Mintage	VG	F	VF	XF	Unc
1615	—	600	1,150	1,800	3,000	—

KM# 29 THALER

Silver **Obv:** Bust right with small shield below **Obv. Legend:** PHILIPPUS. ADOLPHUS. D. G. EPIS. **Rev:** Standing saint **Note:** Dav. #5969.

Date	Mintage	VG	F	VF	XF	Unc
ND Rare	—	—	—	—	—	—

KM# 30 THALER

Silver **Obv:** St. Kilian standing with three shields around **Rev:** Crowned imperial eagle with arms on breast **Note:** Dav. #5970.

Date	Mintage	VG	F	VF	XF	Unc
ND	—	1,400	2,250	3,750	6,300	—

KM# 60 THALER

Silver **Obv:** Saint behind shield dividing S-K and date **Obv. Legend:** PHILIP:ADOLP:... **Rev:** Crowned imperial eagle w/orb on breast **Rev. Legend:** FERDINAND: II: D: G:. **Note:** Dav. #5971.

Date	Mintage	VG	F	VF	XF	Unc
1623	—	875	1,650	2,750	4,500	—

KM# 75 THALER

Silver **Obv:** St. Kilian dividing date, three shields in front **Obv. Legend:** PHILIPPVS * ADOLPHVS * EPISCO*... **Rev. Legend:** FERDINANDVS * II * D.G:... **Note:** Dav. #5972.

Date	Mintage	VG	F	VF	XF	Unc
1624	—	700	1,300	2,200	3,600	—
1625	—	700	1,300	2,200	3,600	—

KM# 76 THALER

Silver **Note:** Klippe. Dav. #5972A.

Date	Mintage	VG	F	VF	XF	Unc
1624 Rare	—	—	—	—	—	—

KM# 78 THALER

Silver **Rev. Legend:** PHILIP: ADOLPH: D. G: -EPI. WIRCH:... **Note:** Dav. #5973.

Date	Mintage	VG	F	VF	XF	Unc
1626	—	1,250	2,250	3,750	6,300	—
1628	—	1,250	2,250	3,750	6,300	—
1629	—	1,250	2,250	3,750	6,300	—

KM# 110 THALER

Silver **Obv:** Crowned imperial eagle with Austrian arms on breast, date above **Obv. Legend:** FERDINANDVS. II. D. G... **Rev:** St. Kilian with arms in front **Rev. Legend:** FRANCISC: D: G... **Note:** Dav. #5974.

Date	Mintage	VG	F	VF	XF	Unc
1635 Rare	—	—	—	—	—	—

KM# 112 THALER

Silver **Obv:** Mitred and helmeted arms **Obv. Legend:** ...EPS: BAM:-ET... **Rev:** Saint standing with date divided above **Note:** Varieties exist. Dav. #5975.

Date	Mintage	VG	F	VF	XF	Unc
1636 CS	—	240	475	850	1,450	—
1637	—	240	475	850	1,450	—
1638	—	240	475	850	1,450	—
1639	—	240	475	850	1,450	—

KM# 113 THALER

Silver **Obv:** St. Kilian standing behind arms dividing S-K above **Rev:** Madonna and child in flaming oval above crowned double eagle with shield on breast, date divided at sides **Note:** Dav. #5976.

Date	Mintage	VG	F	VF	XF	Unc
1637	—	400	850	1,500	2,500	—
1638	—	400	850	1,500	2,500	—
1640	—	400	850	1,500	2,500	—
1641	—	400	850	1,500	2,500	—

KM# 131 THALER

Silver **Obv:** Facing bust with crowned shield below **Obv. Legend:** IOHANN. PHILIPP... **Rev:** Madonna standing with child dividing C-S and date **Rev. Legend:** CLYPEVS OMNIBUS... **Note:** Dav. #5978.

Date	Mintage	VG	F	VF	XF	Unc
1643 CS	—	425	775	1,300	2,150	—

KM# 134 THALER

Silver **Obv. Legend:** IO: PHIL. D: G: S. SED... **Note:** Dav. #5979.

Date	Mintage	VG	F	VF	XF	Unc
1649//1643	—	425	775	1,300	2,150	—

KM# 140 THALER

Silver **Obv:** Without inner circle **Rev:** Date divided below **Note:** Dav. #5980.

Date	Mintage	VG	F	VF	XF	Unc
1652	—	240	475	850	1,450	3,250
1659	—	240	475	850	1,450	3,250

KM# 141 THALER

Silver **Obv:** Bust right, shield below **Obv. Legend:** MOG: A: E: S: R: I:-P: G: A: C: P: E: E:... **Note:** Dav. #5981.

Date	Mintage	VG	F	VF	XF	Unc
ND	—	650	1,250	2,500	4,250	—

KM# 154 THALER

Silver **Obv:** Bust right, shield below **Obv. Legend:** IOAN: HARTMAN:... **Rev:** Madonna standing with child on half moon **Rev. Legend:** CLYPEUS OMNIBUS... **Note:** Dav. #5983.

Date	Mintage	VG	F	VF	XF	Unc
ND	—	1,500	2,500	4,250	6,500	—

KM# 155 THALER

Silver **Obv:** Different bust turned more to right **Rev:** Ornament left of halo **Note:** Dav. #5984.

Date	Mintage	VG	F	VF	XF	Unc
ND	—	400	800	1,650	—	—

KM# 156 THALER

Silver **Obv:** Bust right with shield below **Obv. Legend:** PETR. PHILL:... **Note:** Dav. #5985.

Date	Mintage	VG	F	VF	XF	Unc
ND	—	400	800	1,600	2,750	—

KM# 157 THALER

Silver **Obv:** Bust with short hair right **Note:** Dav. #5986.

Date	Mintage	VG	F	VF	XF	Unc
ND	—	400	800	1,600	2,750	—

KM# 176 THALER

Silver **Note:** Dav. #5988.

Date	Mintage	VG	F	VF	XF	Unc
1680	—	420	850	1,750	3,000	—

KM# 175 THALER

Silver **Obv:** Bust divides date **Note:** Cross-reference number Dav. #5987.

Date	Mintage	VG	F	VF	XF	Unc
1680	—	420	850	1,750	3,000	—

KM# 183 THALER

Silver **Obv:** Bust right **Obv. Legend:** CONRAD. WILH. D: G. EPISC... **Rev:** Helmeted arms **Rev. Legend:** CONSULTE. ET. CONSTANTER. **Note:** Dav. #5989.

Date	Mintage	VG	F	VF	XF	Unc
ND Rare	—	—	—	—	—	—

KM# 174 THALER

Silver **Note:** Similar to KM#183 but taller bust with different robes on obverse, and oval arms on reverse, smaller inscriptions with differences on both sides.

Date	Mintage	VG	F	VF	XF	Unc
ND	—	—	—	—	—	—

KM# 188 THALER

Silver **Obv:** Bust right **Obv. Legend:** IOAN GODEFRID. D. G. EPISC... **Rev:** Helmeted arms **Rev. Legend:** SUPER. OMNIA. GERMANA FIDES **Note:** Dav. #5990.

Date	Mintage	VG	F	VF	XF	Unc
ND(1684-98)	—	350	700	2,250	4,350	—

KM# 189 THALER

Silver **Obv:** Larger bust right, I. L. below **Note:** Dav. #5991.

Date	Mintage	VG	F	VF	XF	Unc
ND IL	—	350	700	1,250	2,250	—

KM# 190 THALER

Silver **Obv:** Helmeted arms **Obv. Legend:** IOANNES GODEFRID... **Rev:** St. Kilian standing **Note:** Dav. #5992.

Date	Mintage	VG	F	VF	XF	Unc
ND Rare	—	—	—	—	—	—

KM# 205 THALER

Silver **Obv:** Helmeted arms **Rev:** St. Kilian standing dividing IM-W and date **Note:** Dav. #5993.

Date	Mintage	F	VF	XF	Unc	BU
1693 IMW	—	225	450	950	2,250	—

KM# 206 THALER

Silver **Obv:** Helmeted arms with date divided below **Obv. Legend:** NULLA SALUS BELLO... **Note:** Dav. #5994.

Date	Mintage	F	VF	XF	Unc	BU
1693 IMW	—	250	450	1,000	2,500	—

KM# 221 THALER

Silver **Ruler:** Johann Philipp II von Greifenklau-Vollraths **Obv:** Legend, date, bust right **Obv. Legend:** IOAN. PHILIP... **Rev:** Helmeted arms **Note:** Dav. #2880

Date	Mintage	VG	F	VF	XF	Unc
1700	—	300	800	1,200	2,250	—

KM# 10 2 THALER

Silver **Note:** Similar to 1 Thaler, KM#188.

Date	Mintage	VG	F	VF	XF	Unc
ND Rare	—	—	—	—	—	—

KM# 9 2 THALER

Silver **Note:** Similar to 1 Thaler, KM#8.

Date	Mintage	VG	F	VF	XF	Unc
1601 Rare	—	—	—	—	—	—

TRADE COINAGE

KM# 11 GOLDGULDEN

3.2500 g., 0.7700 Gold 0.0805 oz. AGW **Obv:** St. Kilian divides S - K above small shield with imperial orb; titles of Rudolf II and date in legend **Rev:** 4-fold arms, three ornate helmets above

Date	Mintage	VG	F	VF	XF	Unc
1601	—	1,000	2,000	3,500	5,500	—

KM# 12 GOLDGULDEN

3.2500 g., 0.7700 Gold 0.0805 oz. AGW **Obv:** Date also divided by figure of St. Kilian

Date	Mintage	VG	F	VF	XF	Unc
1608	—	1,200	2,400	4,200	6,600	—

KM# 20 GOLDGULDEN

3.2500 g., 0.7700 Gold 0.0805 oz. AGW **Rev:** Date in legend

Date	Mintage	VG	F	VF	XF	Unc
1611	—	1,200	2,400	4,200	6,600	—

KM# 25 GOLDGULDEN

3.2500 g., 0.7700 Gold 0.0805 oz. AGW **Obv:** 4-fold arms, three helmets above, titles of Matthias **Rev:** St. Kilian divides S - K, small shield with orb below, Roman numeral date in legend

Date	Mintage	VG	F	VF	XF	Unc
1613	—	775	1,500	3,300	5,400	—

KM# 26 GOLDGULDEN

3.2500 g., 0.7700 Gold 0.0805 oz. AGW **Rev:** Arabic date in legend

Date	Mintage	VG	F	VF	XF	Unc
1613	—	775	1,500	3,300	5,400	—
1615	—	775	1,500	3,300	5,400	—

KM# 34 GOLDGULDEN

3.2500 g., 0.7700 Gold 0.0805 oz. AGW **Subject:** Death of Julius Echter **Obv:** 4-fold arms, three helmets above **Rev:** 6-line inscription with dates, without value in orb below

Date	Mintage	VG	F	VF	XF	Unc
1617	—	1,200	2,400	4,200	6,600	—

KM# 35 GOLDGULDEN

3.2500 g., 0.7700 Gold 0.0805 oz. AGW **Obv:** Arms in inner circle **Rev:** Concentric circles with banner at center, S-P bove Q-W at "corners" **Rev. Legend:** AUGUSTUM PATRIAE...

Date	Mintage	VG	F	VF	XF	Unc
ND(1617)	—	675	1,500	3,750	6,000	—

KM# 36 GOLDGULDEN

3.2500 g., 0.7700 Gold 0.0805 oz. AGW **Rev. Legend:** ORE AURO. CORDE...

Date	Mintage	VG	F	VF	XF	Unc
ND	—	675	1,500	3,750	6,000	—

KM# 37 GOLDGULDEN

3.2500 g., 0.7700 Gold 0.0805 oz. AGW

Date	Mintage	VG	F	VF	XF	Unc
1617 CW	—	675	1,500	3,600	5,400	—
1618 CW	—	675	1,500	3,600	5,400	—
1619 CW	—	675	1,500	3,600	5,400	—

KM# 52 GOLDGULDEN

3.2500 g., 0.7700 Gold 0.0805 oz. AGW **Subject:** Death of Johann Gottfried **Obv:** Arms topped by four helmets **Rev:** 6-line inscription

Date	Mintage	VG	F	VF	XF	Unc
1622	—	850	1,750	3,850	6,300	—

KM# 80 GOLDGULDEN

3.2500 g., 0.7700 Gold 0.0805 oz. AGW **Obv:** 4-fold arms topped by three helmets **Rev:** St. Kilian standing half right with crozier dividing S-K

Date	Mintage	VG	F	VF	XF	Unc
ND	—	625	1,400	3,500	5,300	—

KM# 79 GOLDGULDEN

3.2500 g., 0.7700 Gold 0.0805 oz. AGW **Obv:** Half-length bust of St. Kilian slightly to right divides S - K, titles of Ferdinand Ii **Rev:** Three helmets above 4-fold arms in circle

Date	Mintage	VG	F	VF	XF	Unc
1626	—	775	1,700	3,650	5,600	—

KM# 92 GOLDGULDEN

3.2500 g., 0.7700 Gold 0.0805 oz. AGW **Rev:** Legend in wreath

Date	Mintage	VG	F	VF	XF	Unc
ND	—	550	1,200	3,000	4,500	—
1631	—	550	1,200	3,000	4,500	—

KM# 91 GOLDGULDEN

3.2500 g., 0.7700 Gold 0.0805 oz. AGW **Subject:** Death of Philipp Adolph **Rev:** 6-line inscription, orb in cartouche at bottom

Date	Mintage	VG	F	VF	XF	Unc
1631	—	725	1,500	3,300	5,400	—

KM# 121 GOLDGULDEN

3.2500 g., 0.7700 Gold 0.0805 oz. AGW **Subject:** Death of Franz von Hatzfeld **Obv:** Four helmets above 4-fold arms with center shield of Hatzfeld **Rev:** 6-line inscription with date, small imperial orb with W below

Date	Mintage	VG	F	VF	XF	Unc
1642	—	825	1,650	3,300	5,500	—

KM# 122 GOLDGULDEN

3.2500 g., 0.7700 Gold 0.0805 oz. AGW **Obv:** Bust of Johann Philipp right, crowned arms at bottom **Rev:** Radiant "Jehovah" at top, 4-line inscription in branches, arms at bottom

Date	Mintage	VG	F	VF	XF	Unc
ND(1642)	—	525	1,150	2,400	4,150	—

KM# 123 GOLDGULDEN

3.2500 g., 0.7700 Gold 0.0805 oz. AGW **Obv:** Facing bust of Johann Philipp

Date	Mintage	VG	F	VF	XF	Unc
ND(1642)	—	400	850	2,100	3,900	—

KM# 124 GOLDGULDEN

3.2500 g., 0.7700 Gold 0.0805 oz. AGW **Obv:** Arms below mitre **Rev:** Without "Jehovah" at top

Date	Mintage	VG	F	VF	XF	Unc
ND(1642)	—	525	1,150	2,400	4,150	—

KM# 158 GOLDGULDEN

3.2500 g., 0.7700 Gold 0.0805 oz. AGW **Obv:** Bust of Johann Hartman right, crowned arms at bottom

Date	Mintage	VG	F	VF	XF	Unc
ND(1673)	—	1,500	3,000	5,300	9,000	—

KM# 165 GOLDGULDEN

3.2500 g., 0.7700 Gold 0.0805 oz. AGW **Obv:** Bust of Peter Philip right

Date	Mintage	VG	F	VF	XF	Unc
ND(1675)	—	1,150	2,250	4,500	7,500	—

KM# 191 GOLDGULDEN

3.2500 g., 0.7700 Gold 0.0805 oz. AGW **Obv:** Bust of Konrad Wilhelm right, crowned oval 4-fold arms on shoulder

Date	Mintage	VG	F	VF	XF	Unc
ND(1684) Rare	—	—	—	—	—	—

KM# 193 GOLDGULDEN

3.2500 g., 0.7700 Gold 0.0805 oz. AGW **Obv:** Arms topped by three helmets **Rev:** Banner in cartouche in inner circle

Date	Mintage	VG	F	VF	XF	Unc
ND(1684)	—	400	850	2,100	3,900	—

KM# 199 GOLDGULDEN

3.2500 g., 0.7700 Gold 0.0805 oz. AGW **Obv:** Bust of Johann Gottfried II

Date	Mintage	VG	F	VF	XF	Unc
ND(1685)	—	1,200	2,400	5,000	9,000	—

KM# 214 GOLDGULDEN

3.2500 g., 0.7700 Gold 0.0805 oz. AGW **Obv:** Arms **Rev:** Banner in shield

Date	Mintage	VG	F	VF	XF	Unc
ND(1699)	—	325	725	1,500	3,000	—

KM# 215 GOLDGULDEN

3.2500 g., 0.7700 Gold 0.0805 oz. AGW **Obv:** Arms with griffin supporters **Rev:** Arms with three saints above on both sides

Date	Mintage	VG	F	VF	XF	Unc
ND(1699)	—	425	1,000	2,200	4,150	—

KM# 261 GOLDGULDEN

3.2500 g., 0.7700 Gold 0.0805 oz. AGW **Obv:** Crowned and mantled 10-fold arms with center shield of Schonborn, titles of Johann Philipp Franz **Rev:** Altar with arms of Wurzburg on front

Date	Mintage	VG	F	VF	XF	Unc
ND	—	375	825	1,700	3,150	—

KM# 262 GOLDGULDEN

3.2500 g., 0.7700 Gold 0.0805 oz. AGW **Obv:** Legend replaces bishop's name **Obv. Legend:** QVIA TBES DEVS FORTITVDO MEA

Date	Mintage	VG	F	VF	XF	Unc
ND	—	350	750	1,550	2,800	—

KM# 13 2 GOLDGULDEN

6.5000 g., 0.7700 Gold 0.1609 oz. AGW **Obv:** St. Kilian divides S - K and date above small shield with imperial orb, titles of Rudolf II **Rev:** 4-fold arms, three ornate helmets above

Date	Mintage	VG	F	VF	XF	Unc
1608 Rare	—	—	—	—	—	—

KM# 21 2 GOLDGULDEN

6.5000 g., 0.7700 Gold 0.1609 oz. AGW **Rev:** Date in legend

Date	Mintage	VG	F	VF	XF	Unc
1611 Rare	—	—	—	—	—	—

KM# 27 2 GOLDGULDEN

6.5000 g., 0.7700 Gold 0.1609 oz. AGW **Obv:** 4-fold arms, three helmets above, titles of Matthias **Rev:** St. Kilian divides S - K, small shield with orb below, Roman numeral date in legend

Date	Mintage	VG	F	VF	XF	Unc
1613 Rare	—	—	—	—	—	—

KM# 38 2 GOLDGULDEN

6.5000 g., 0.7700 Gold 0.1609 oz. AGW **Subject:** Death of Julius Echter **Obv:** 4-fold arms, three helmets above **Rev:** 6-line inscription iwth dates, without value in orb below

Date	Mintage	VG	F	VF	XF	Unc
1617 Rare	—	—	—	—	—	—

KM# 39 2 GOLDGULDEN

6.5000 g., 0.7700 Gold 0.1609 oz. AGW **Obv:** Arms in inner circle **Rev:** Concentric circles with banner at center and S-P over Q-W at "corners" **Note:** Klippe.

Date	Mintage	VG	F	VF	XF	Unc
ND(1617) Rare	—	—	—	—	—	—

KM# 70 2 GOLDGULDEN

6.5000 g., 0.7700 Gold 0.1609 oz. AGW **Obv:** Arms topped by three helmets **Rev:** St. Kilian standing holding crozier

Date	Mintage	VG	F	VF	XF	Unc
ND(1623) Rare	—	—	—	—	—	—

KM# 71 2 GOLDGULDEN

6.5000 g., 0.7700 Gold 0.1609 oz. AGW **Subject:** New Years Commemorative **Obv:** Three helmets above 4-fold arms, titles of Philipp Adolph around **Rev:** Oval arms of Wurzburg (key) in ornate frame divides S - P/Q - W **Rev. Legend:** OBSEQUIUM PATRIAE...

Date	Mintage	VG	F	VF	XF	Unc
ND Rare	—	—	—	—	—	—

KM# 93 2 GOLDGULDEN

6.5000 g., 0.7700 Gold 0.1609 oz. AGW **Subject:** Death of Philipp Adolph **Obv:** Arms topped by three helmets **Rev:** 6-line inscription, orb in cartouche below

Date	Mintage	VG	F	VF	XF	Unc
1631 Rare	—	—	—	—	—	—

KM# A30 4 GOLDGULDEN

14.0000 g., 0.9860 Gold 0.4438 oz. AGW **Obv:** Crowned imperial eagle, titles of Matthias **Rev:** St. Kilian above arms

Date	Mintage	VG	F	VF	XF	Unc
1615 Rare	—	—	—	—	—	—

KM# 125 DUCAT

3.5000 g., 0.9860 Gold 0.1109 oz. AGW **Obv:** Bust of Johann Philip right, crowned arms at bottom **Rev:** Three peaks below radiant "Jehovah"

Date	Mintage	VG	F	VF	XF	Unc
ND(1642)	—	475	1,000	2,000	3,300	—

KM# 126 DUCAT

3.5000 g., 0.9860 Gold 0.1109 oz. AGW **Obv:** Facing bust of Johann Philip, crowned arms at bottom

Date	Mintage	VG	F	VF	XF	Unc
ND(1642)	—	600	1,200	2,400	4,000	—

KM# 184 DUCAT

3.5000 g., 0.9860 Gold 0.1109 oz. AGW **Obv:** Bust of Conrad Wilhelm right **Rev:** Arms

Date	Mintage	VG	F	VF	XF	Unc
ND(1683)	—	1,300	2,500	4,500	7,500	—

KM# 194 DUCAT

3.5000 g., 0.9860 Gold 0.1109 oz. AGW **Obv:** Bust of Johann Gottfried II right **Rev:** Five ornate helmets above oval 4-fold arms

Date	Mintage	VG	F	VF	XF	Unc
ND	—	1,300	2,500	4,500	7,500	—

KM# 220 DUCAT

3.5000 g., 0.9860 Gold 0.1109 oz. AGW **Ruler:** Johann Philipp II von Greifenklau-Vollraths **Obv:** Bust right **Rev:** Arms topped by three helmets

Date	Mintage	VG	F	VF	XF	Unc
1700	—	525	1,200	2,250	3,750	—

KM# 127 1-1/2 DUCAT

5.2500 g., 0.9860 Gold 0.1664 oz. AGW **Obv:** Facing bust of Johann Philipp **Rev:** Three peaks below radiant "Jehovah"

Date	Mintage	VG	F	VF	XF	Unc
ND(1642)	—	850	1,800	3,600	6,000	—

KM# 128 2 DUCAT

7.0000 g., 0.9860 Gold 0.2219 oz. AGW **Obv:** Bust of Johann Philipp right, crowned arms at bottom **Rev:** Three peaks below radiant "Jehovah"

Date	Mintage	VG	F	VF	XF	Unc
ND(1642)	—	775	1,600	3,300	5,400	—

KM# 129 2 DUCAT
7.0000 g., 0.9860 Gold 0.2219 oz. AGW **Obv:** Bust of Johann Philipp facing half left

Date	Mintage	VG	F	VF	XF	Unc
ND(1642)	—	1,200	2,400	4,800	7,800	—

KM# 31 4 DUCAT
14.0000 g., 0.9860 Gold 0.4438 oz. AGW **Obv:** Large crowned imperial eagle, orb on breast, titles of Rudolf II **Rev:** Larger figure of St. Kilian holding sword and scepter divides S - K, date divided by shield below

Date	Mintage	VG	F	VF	XF	Unc
1615 Rare	—	—	—	—	—	—

KM# 142 5 DUCAT
17.5000 g., 0.9860 Gold 0.5547 oz. AGW **Obv:** Bust of Johann Philipp facing **Rev:** Madonna standing facing with child
Note: Struck with 1 Thaler dies, KM#140.

Date	Mintage	VG	F	VF	XF	Unc
1652 Rare	—	—	—	—	—	—

Note: Hess-Divo Auction 272 10-97 XF realized $10,720

KM# 143 5 DUCAT
17.5000 g., 0.9860 Gold 0.5547 oz. AGW **Obv:** Bust of Johann Philipp, shield below **Obv. Legend:** MOG: A: E: S: R: I: -P: G: A: C: P: E: E:...

Date	Mintage	VG	F	VF	XF	Unc
ND	—	3,000	5,000	7,500	16,000	—

KM# 159 5 DUCAT
17.5000 g., 0.9860 Gold 0.5547 oz. AGW **Obv:** Bust of Johann Hartmann right **Rev:** Madonna standing facing with child, ornament left of halo

Date	Mintage	VG	F	VF	XF	Unc
ND Rare	—	—	—	—	—	—

KM# 160 5 DUCAT
17.5000 g., 0.9860 Gold 0.5547 oz. AGW **Obv:** Bust right with shield below **Obv. Legend:** PETR. PHILL... **Rev:** Madonna and child, ornament left of halo

Date	Mintage	VG	F	VF	XF	Unc
ND Rare	—	—	—	—	—	—

KM# 161 5 DUCAT
17.5000 g., 0.9860 Gold 0.5547 oz. AGW **Obv:** Bust with short hair right

Date	Mintage	VG	F	VF	XF	Unc
ND Rare	—	—	—	—	—	—

KM# 185 5 DUCAT
17.5000 g., 0.9860 Gold 0.5547 oz. AGW **Obv:** Bust right **Obv. Legend:** CONRAD. WILH. D: G: EPISC... **Rev:** Helmeted arms **Rev. Legend:** CONSULTE. ET. CONSTANTER.

Date	Mintage	VG	F	VF	XF	Unc
ND Rare	—	—	—	—	—	—

KM# 195 5 DUCAT
17.5000 g., 0.9860 Gold 0.5547 oz. AGW **Obv:** Bust of Johann Gottfried right **Rev:** Helmeted arms **Note:** Struck with 1 Thaler dies, KM#188.

Date	Mintage	VG	F	VF	XF	Unc
ND Rare	—	—	—	—	—	—

SWEDISH OCCUPATION COINAGE

KM# 96 4 KREUZER (Batzen)
Silver **Obv:** Crowned 4-fold arms with center shield, IIII K above, titles of Gustav Adolph **Rev:** Full-length figure of Christ facing divides date **Note:** Varieties exist.

Date	Mintage	VG	F	VF	XF	Unc
1632	—	33.00	65.00	135	225	—
1634	—	33.00	65.00	135	225	—

KM# 89 THALER
Silver **Obv:** Half-length portrait with sash **Rev:** Crowned shield, legend divides date **Note:** Dav. #4559.

Date	Mintage	VG	F	VF	XF	Unc
1631	—	150	300	550	1,200	—

KM# 90 THALER
Silver **Rev:** Crown divides date at top of shield **Note:** Dav. #4559A.

Date	Mintage	VG	F	VF	XF	Unc
1631	—	120	240	475	1,050	—

KM# 99 THALER
Silver **Rev:** Top of crown divides date above wreaths **Note:** Dav. #4559B.

Date	Mintage	VG	F	VF	XF	Unc
1632	—	110	220	450	1,050	—

KM# 100 THALER
Silver **Obv:** Half-length portrait without sash **Rev:** Legend divides date **Note:** Dav. #4560.

Date	Mintage	VG	F	VF	XF	Unc
1632	—	125	245	500	1,400	—

KM# 101 THALER
Silver **Rev:** Large date above shield dvided by crown **Note:** Dav. #4560A.

Date	Mintage	VG	F	VF	XF	Unc
1632	—	105	210	425	1,200	—

KM# 102 THALER
Silver **Obv:** Half-length portrait without sash **Rev:** Small date above shield dvided by crown **Note:** Dav. #4560B.

Date	Mintage	VG	F	VF	XF	Unc
1632	—	105	210	425	1,200	—

KM# 103 THALER
Silver **Rev:** Punctuated date **Note:** Dav. #4560C.

Date	Mintage	VG	F	VF	XF	Unc
1632	—	125	245	500	1,400	—

KM# 104 THALER
Silver **Rev:** Top of crown divides date **Note:** Dav. #4560D.

Date	Mintage	VG	F	VF	XF	Unc
1632	—	105	210	425	1,200	—

KM# 105 2 THALER
Silver **Note:** Dav. #4558.

Date	Mintage	VG	F	VF	XF	Unc
1632 Unique	—	—	—	—	—	—

KM# 94 DUCAT
3.5000 g., 0.9860 Gold 0.1109 oz. AGW

Date	Mintage	VG	F	VF	XF	Unc
1631	—	250	500	750	1,250	—
1632	—	250	500	750	1,250	—

KM# 106 2 DUCAT
7.0000 g., 0.9860 Gold 0.2219 oz. AGW **Note:** Similar to 1 Ducat, KM#94.

Date	Mintage	VG	F	VF	XF	Unc
1632 Rare	—	—	—	—	—	—

KM# 107 5 DUCAT
17.5000 g., 0.9860 Gold 0.5547 oz. AGW **Note:** Similar to 1 Ducat, KM#94.

Date	Mintage	VG	F	VF	XF	Unc
1632 Rare	—	—	—	—	—	—

KM# 95 10 DUCAT
35.0000 g., 0.9860 Gold 1.1095 oz. AGW **Obv:** Half-length portrait with sash, 10 punched in left of bust **Rev:** Crowned shield, legend divides date

Date	Mintage	VG	F	VF	XF	Unc
1631 Rare	—	—	—	—	—	—

PATTERNS

Including off metal strikes

KM#	Date	Mintage	Identification	Mkt Val
Pn1	16Z4	—	Kortling. Gold. KM#55	—
Pn2	16Z5	—	3 Heller. Gold. KM#53	—
Pn3	ND	—	3 Heller. Gold. KM#54	—
Pn4	16Z5	—	Kortling. Gold. KM#73	—
Pn5	16Z5	—	Schilling. Gold. KM#77	—
Pn6	1691	—	Schilling. Gold. Weight of 1 Ducat, KM#198.	—
Pn7	1699	—	Kortling. Gold. KM#212.	—
Pn8	1699	—	Schilling. Gold. KM#213.	—

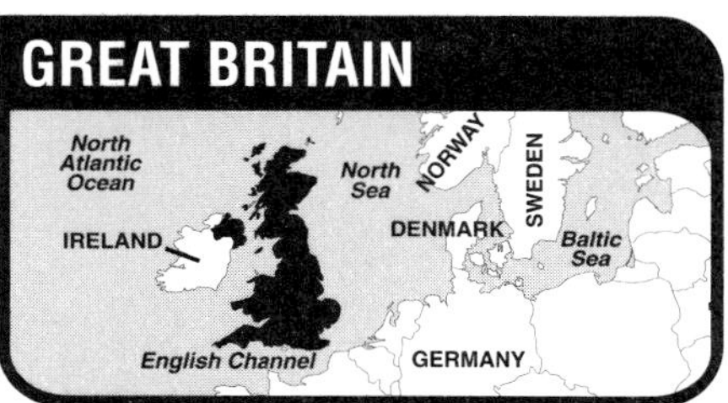

The United Kingdom of Great Britain and Northern Ireland, located off the northwest coast of the European continent, has an area of 94,227 sq. mi. (244,820 sq. km.) and a population of 54 million. Capital: London. The economy is based on industrial activity and trading. Machinery, motor vehicles, chemicals, and textile yarns and fabrics are exported.

After the departure of the Romans, who brought Britain into a more active relationship with Europe, it fell prey to invaders from Scandinavia and the Low Countries who drove the original Britons into Scotland and Wales, and established a profusion of kingdoms that finally united in the 11th century under the Danish King Canute. Norman rule, following the conquest of 1066, stimulated the development of those institutions, which have since distinguished British life. Henry VIII (1509-47) turned Britain from continental adventuring and faced it to the sea - a decision that made Britain a world power during the reign of Elizabeth I (1558-1603). Strengthened by the Industrial Revolution and the defeat of Napoleon, 19th century Britain turned to the remote parts of the world and established a colonial empire of such extent and prosperity that the world has never seen its like. World Wars I and II sealed the fate of the Empire and relegated Britain to a lesser role in world affairs by draining her resources and inaugurating a worldwide movement toward national self-determination in her former colonies.

RULERS
Elizabeth I, 1558-1603
James I, 1603-1625
Charles I, 1625-1649
Commonwealth, 1649-1660
Charles II, 1660-1685
James II, 1685-1688
William and Mary, 1688-1694
William III, 1694-1702

Mint Marks
Under James I, 1603-1625

Mark	Desc.	Date
	Thistle	1603-04
	Lis	1604-05
	Rose	1605-06
	Escallop	1606-07
	Grapes	1607
	Coronet	1607-09
	Key	1609-10
	Bell	1610-11
	Mullet	1611-12
	Tower	1612-13
	Trefoil	1613
	Cinquefoil	1613-15
	Tun	1615-16
	Closed book	161-17
	Crescent	1617-18
	Plain cross	1618-19
	Saltire cross	1619
	Spur rowel	1619-20
	Rose	1620-21
	Thistle	1621-23
	Lis	1623-24
	Trefoil	1624

Under Charles I, 1625-1649

TOWER MINT

Mark	Desc.	Date
	Lis	1625
	Cross Calvary	1625-26
	Negro head	1626-27
	Castle	1627-28
	Anchor	1628-29
	Heart	1629-30
	Plume	1630-31
	Rose	1631-32
	Harp	1632-33
	Portcullis	1633-34
	Bell	1634-35
	Crown	1635-36
	Tun	1636-38
	Anchor	1638-39
	Triangle	1639-40
	Star	1640-41
	Triangle in circle	1641-43

BRIOT'S MINT

Mark	Desc.	Date
	B and flower	1631-32
B	B	1632
	Anchor and B	1638-39
	Anchor and mullet	1638-39

PROVINCIAL MINTS

ABERYSTWYTH MINT

Mark	Desc.	Date
	Open book	1638-42
A	A	1644-46
	Crown	1648-49

BRISTOL MINT

Mark	Desc.	Date
	Cross pattee	1643
	Acorn	1643
	Plume	1643-45
Br	Br	1643-45
	Pellets	1643-45

CHESTER MINT

Mark	Desc.	Date
	Gerb	1644-46

EXETER MINT

Mark	Desc.	Date
	Rose	1643-45
	Castle	1644-46

OXFORD MINT

Mark	Desc.	Date
	Plume	1642-46
	Pellets	1642-46
	Lis	1642-46
	Rosette	1643-45
	Floriated cross	1643-46
	Cross pattee	1644
	Lozenge	1644
	Billet	1644
	Mullet	1644

SALISBURY MINT

Mark	Desc.	Date
	Helmet	1643
	Lis	1643-44
	Bunch of grapes	1643-44
	Bird	1643-44
	Boar's head	1643-44
	Rosette	1643-44

SHREWSBURY MINT

Mark	Desc.	Date
	Plume	1642
	Pellets or pellet	1642

TRURO MINT

Mark	Desc.	Date
	Rose	1642-43

WEYMOUTH MINT

Mark	Desc.	Date
	Castle	1643
	Helmet	1643
	Leopard's head	1643-44
	Two lions	1643-44
	Lis	1643-44
	Bunch of grapes	1643-44
	Bird	1643-44
	Boar's head	1643-44
	Rosette	1643-44

WORCESTER MINT

Mark	Desc.	Date
	Pear	1644-46

YORK MINT

Mark	Desc.	Date
	Lion	1642-44

UNCERTAIN MINT

Mark	Desc.	Date
	Lion rampant	1643-44
	Lis	1644-46
	Plume	1644-46
B	B	1646

Under Parliament

TOWER MINT

Mark	Desc.	Date
(P)	(P)	1643-44

Mark	Desc.	Date
(R)	(R)	1644-45
	Eye	1645
	Sun	1645-46
	Sceptre	1646-48

Commonwealth

Mark	Desc.	Date
	Sun	1649-57
	Anchor	1658-60

Under Charles II

Mark	Desc.	Date
	Crown	1660-62

Under William III

B - Bristol, 1696-1697
C - Chester, 1696-1697
E - Exeter, 1696-1697
N - Norwich, 1696-1697
Y, y - York, 1696-1697

MONETARY SYSTEM

(Until 1970)

4 Farthings = 1 Penny
12 Pence = 1 Shilling
2 Shillings = 1 Florin
5 Shillings = 1 Crown
20 Shillings = 1 Pound (Sovereign)
21 Shillings = 1 Guinea

KINGDOM

PRE-DECIMAL COINAGE

KM# 50 FARTHING

Copper **Ruler:** James I **Obv:** Crown above crossed scepters at center **Rev:** Crowned harp at center **Note:** Normal size. Harrington Issue (1613-14) (Contracted to Lord Harrington.)

Date	Mintage	VG	F	VF	XF	Unc
ND	—	14.00	21.00	50.00	125	—

KM# 49 FARTHING

Copper **Ruler:** James I **Obv:** Crown above crossed scepters at center **Rev:** Crowned harp at center **Note:** Small size. Harrington Issue (1613-14) (Contracted to Lord Harrington.) At one time called "Half Farthings" because of the small size.

Date	Mintage	VG	F	VF	XF	Unc
ND	—	15.00	30.00	100	250	—

KM# 52 FARTHING

Copper **Ruler:** James I **Note:** Lennox Issue (1614-25). (Contract passed to Duke of Lennox.) Oval shape.

Date	Mintage	VG	F	VF	XF	Unc
ND	—	25.00	55.00	125	250	—

KM# 51 FARTHING

Copper **Ruler:** James I **Note:** Lennox Issue (1614-25). (Contract passed to Duke of Lennox.) Varieties exist.

Date	Mintage	VG	F	VF	XF	Unc
ND	—	6.00	15.00	35.00	100	—

KM# 79 FARTHING

Copper **Ruler:** Charles I **Note:** Richmond Issue (1625-34). (Contract passed to Duchess of Richmond.) Oval shape.

Date	Mintage	VG	F	VF	XF	Unc
ND	—	15.00	30.00	90.00	225	—

KM# 78.1 FARTHING

Copper **Ruler:** Charles I **Obv. Legend:** CARO/IACO **Note:** Richmond Issue (1625-34). (Contract passed to Duchess of Richmond.) Round shape.

Date	Mintage	VG	F	VF	XF	Unc
ND	—	6.50	12.00	60.00	120	—

KM# 78.2 FARTHING

Copper **Ruler:** Charles I **Obv. Legend:** CARA... **Note:** Richmond Issue (1625-34). (Contract passed to Duchess of Richmond.)

Date	Mintage	VG	F	VF	XF	Unc
ND	—	50.00	100	215	500	—

Note: Possibly contemporary counterfeits

KM# 78.3 FARTHING

Copper **Ruler:** Charles I **Obv. Legend:** CARO... **Note:** Richmond Issue (1625-34). (Contract passed to Duchess of Richmond.)

Date	Mintage	VG	F	VF	XF	Unc
ND	—	5.00	9.00	40.00	110	—

KM# 174 FARTHING

Copper **Ruler:** Charles I **Obv:** Crown above crossed scepters in inner circle **Rev:** Crowned harp in inner circle **Note:** Maltravers Issue (1634-36). Contract passed to Lord Maltravers. Oval shape.

Date	Mintage	VG	F	VF	XF	Unc
ND	—	25.00	50.00	150	300	—

KM# 173 FARTHING

Copper **Ruler:** Charles I **Obv:** Crown above crossed scepters in inner circle **Rev:** Crowned harp in inner circle **Note:** Maltravers Issue (1634-36). Contract passed to Lord Maltravers. Round shape.

Date	Mintage	VG	F	VF	XF	Unc
ND	—	5.00	9.00	40.00	110	—

KM# 172 FARTHING

Copper **Ruler:** Charles I **Obv:** Apostrophe punctuation **Rev:** Apostrophe punctuation **Note:** Transitional issue (ca.1634)

Date	Mintage	VG	F	VF	XF	Unc
ND	—	12.00	24.00	125	250	—

KM# 177 FARTHING

Copper **Ruler:** Charles I **Obv:** Crown above crossed scepters in inner circle **Note:** Rose Farthing. Varieties exist.

Date	Mintage	VG	F	VF	XF	Unc
ND	—	8.00	15.00	70.00	140	—

KM# 175 FARTHING

Copper **Ruler:** Charles I **Rev:** Crown above double rose in inner circle **Note:** Rose Farthing. Varieties exist. Many specimens found with a wedge of brass in planchet.

Date	Mintage	VG	F	VF	XF	Unc
ND(1635-44)	—	6.00	10.00	40.00	110	—

KM# 176 FARTHING

Copper **Ruler:** Charles I **Rev:** Crown above single rose in inner circle **Note:** Rose Farthing. Varieties exist.

Date	Mintage	VG	F	VF	XF	Unc
ND 1635	—	6.00	10.00	40.00	110	—

KM# 1 1/2 PENNY

Silver **Ruler:** Elizabeth I **Obv:** Portcullis **Rev:** Long cross with large dots in angles **Note:** Sixth Coinage (1601-02).

Date	Mintage	VG	F	VF	XF	Unc
(160)1	—	25.00	45.00	125	250	—
(160)2	—	25.00	45.00	125	250	—

KM# 8 1/2 PENNY

Silver **Ruler:** James I **Rev:** Long cross with small dots in angles **Note:** First Coinage (1603-04).

Date	Mintage	VG	F	VF	XF	Unc
ND	—	15.00	30.00	65.00	160	—

KM# 22 1/2 PENNY

Silver **Ruler:** James I **Obv:** Double rose **Rev:** Thistle **Note:** Second Coinage (1604-19).

Date	Mintage	VG	F	VF	XF	Unc
ND	—	15.00	30.00	60.00	145	—

KM# 54 1/2 PENNY

Silver **Ruler:** James I **Note:** Third Coinage (1619-25).

Date	Mintage	VG	F	VF	XF	Unc
ND	—	15.00	30.00	50.00	120	—

KM# 178 1/2 PENNY

Silver **Ruler:** Charles I **Obv:** Double rose **Rev:** Double rose **Mint:** Tower

Date	Mintage	VG	F	VF	XF	Unc
ND	—	11.00	22.00	65.00	160	—

KM# 179 1/2 PENNY

Silver **Ruler:** Charles I **Rev:** Plumes in crown **Mint:** Aberystwyth

Date	Mintage	VG	F	VF	XF	Unc
ND	—	125	250	850	2,000	—

KM# 2 PENNY

Silver **Ruler:** Elizabeth I **Obv:** Crowned bust of Elizabeth I left in inner circle **Rev:** Shield of arms on long cross **Note:** Sixth Coinage (1601-02).

Date	Mintage	VG	F	VF	XF	Unc
(160)1	—	15.00	60.00	120	300	—
(160)2	—	15.00	60.00	120	300	—

KM# 9 PENNY

Silver **Ruler:** James I **Obv:** Crowned bust of James I right with balue behind in inner circle **Rev:** Shield of arms **Note:** First Coinage (1603-04).

Date	Mintage	VG	F	VF	XF	Unc
ND	—	15.00	30.00	100	250	—

KM# 23 PENNY

Silver **Ruler:** James I **Obv:** Rose in inner circle **Rev:** Thistle in inner circle **Note:** Second Coinage (1604-19). Varieties exist.

Date	Mintage	VG	F	VF	XF	Unc
ND	—	14.00	27.00	70.00	150	—

KM# 55 PENNY

Silver **Ruler:** James I **Note:** Third Coinage (1619-25).

Date	Mintage	VG	F	VF	XF	Unc
ND	—	14.00	27.00	65.00	150	—

KM# 56 PENNY

Silver **Ruler:** Charles I **Rev:** Rose in inner circle **Mint:** Tower **Note:** Varieties exist.

Date	Mintage	VG	F	VF	XF	Unc
ND	—	16.00	29.00	70.00	150	—

KM# 80.1 PENNY

Silver **Ruler:** Charles I **Obv:** Crowned bust of Charles I left with value behind in inner circle **Rev:** Oval shield in inner circle **Note:** Varieties exist.

Date	Mintage	VG	F	VF	XF	Unc
ND(1625-49)	—	10.00	20.00	100	250	—

KM# 80.2 PENNY

Silver **Ruler:** Charles I **Rev:** C R at sides of shield **Note:** Varieties exist.

Date	Mintage	VG	F	VF	XF	Unc
ND(1625-49)	—	9.00	18.00	75.00	180	—

KM# 81 PENNY

Silver **Ruler:** Charles I **Obv:** Older bust of Charles I left with value behind in inner circle **Rev:** Shield of arms in inner circle **Mint:** Tower **Note:** Struck (under Parliament).

Date	Mintage	VG	F	VF	XF	Unc
ND(1625-49)	—	17.00	35.00	100	225	—

KM# 155 PENNY

Silver **Ruler:** Charles I **Obv:** Older bust of Charles I left with value behind **Rev:** Shield of arms in inner circle on long cross **Note:** First Milled Briot Issue (1631-32).

Date	Mintage	VG	F	VF	XF	Unc
ND(1631-32)	—	45.00	95.00	225	550	—

KM# 157 PENNY

Silver **Ruler:** Charles I **Rev:** Without inner circle **Mint:** Aberystwyth

Date	Mintage	VG	F	VF	XF	Unc
ND(1631-32)	—	50.00	100	250	550	—

KM# 160 PENNY

Silver **Ruler:** Charles I **Rev:** Large plumes with bands in inner circle **Mint:** Bristol

Date	Mintage	VG	F	VF	XF	Unc
ND(1631-32)	—	250	550	1,300	3,000	—

KM# 156 PENNY

Silver **Ruler:** Charles I **Rev:** Plumes in crown in inner circle **Mint:** Aberystwyth **Note:** Varieties exist.

Date	Mintage	VG	F	VF	XF	Unc
ND(1631-32)	—	45.00	100	250	550	—

KM# 159 PENNY

Silver **Ruler:** Charles I **Obv:** Crowned bust of Charles I left with value behind in inner circle **Rev:** Plumes in crown in inner circle **Mint:** Oxford **Note:** Varieties exist.

Date	Mintage	VG	F	VF	XF	Unc
ND(1631-32)	—	125	250	700	1,600	—

KM# 270 PENNY

Silver **Ruler:** Charles I **Rev:** Declaration

Date	Mintage	VG	F	VF	XF	Unc
1644	—	150	300	800	2,000	—

KM# 271 PENNY

Silver **Ruler:** Charles I **Obv:** Crowned thin bust of Charles I left with value behind in inner circle **Rev:** Large rose in inner circle **Mint:** Exeter

Date	Mintage	VG	F	VF	XF	Unc
1644	—	225	500	1,400	3,000	—

KM# 158 PENNY

Silver **Ruler:** Charles I **Rev:** Large plumes in crown in inner circle **Mint:** Aberystwyth - Furnace Mint

Date	Mintage	VG	F	VF	XF	Unc
ND(1648-49)	—	425	850	3,000	—	—

KM# 3 2 PENCE (1/2 Groat)

Silver **Ruler:** Elizabeth I **Obv:** Crowned bust left in inner circle **Rev:** Shield of arms on long cross **Note:** Sixth Coinage.

Date	Mintage	Good	VG	F	VF	XF
(160)1	—	—	17.50	35.00	100	225
(160)2	—	—	17.50	35.00	100	225

KM# 10 2 PENCE (1/2 Groat)

0.8300 g., Silver **Ruler:** James I **Obv:** Crowned bust of James I right with value behind within inner circle **Rev:** Shield of arms **Note:** First Coinage (1603-04).

Date	Mintage	VG	F	VF	XF	Unc
ND(1603-04)	—	22.00	45.00	100	200	—

KM# 24 2 PENCE (1/2 Groat)

Silver **Ruler:** James I **Obv:** Crowned rose in inner circle **Rev:** Crowned thistle in inner circle **Note:** Second Coinage (1604-19). Varieties exist.

Date	Mintage	VG	F	VF	XF	Unc
ND	—	15.00	30.00	75.00	150	—

KM# 57 2 PENCE (1/2 Groat)
Silver **Ruler:** James I **Obv:** Large crowned rose in inner circle **Note:** Third Coinage (1619-25).

Date	Mintage	VG	F	VF	XF	Unc
ND	—	15.00	30.00	70.00	150	—

KM# 58 2 PENCE (1/2 Groat)
Silver **Ruler:** James I **Obv:** Crowned rose in inner circle **Rev:** Crowned rose in inner circle **Mint:** Tower **Note:** Varieties exist.

Date	Mintage	VG	F	VF	XF	Unc
ND(1619-25)	—	15.00	30.00	120	300	—

KM# 82 2 PENCE (1/2 Groat)
Silver **Ruler:** Charles I **Obv:** Crowend bust of Charles I left in ruffled collar and mantle, value behind, in inner circle **Rev:** Oval shield of arms **Note:** Varieties exist.

Date	Mintage	VG	F	VF	XF	Unc
ND(1625-49)	—	12.00	30.00	90.00	225	—

KM# 83 2 PENCE (1/2 Groat)
Silver **Ruler:** Charles I **Obv:** Crowend bust of Charles I left in lace collar, value behind in inner circle **Rev:** Oval arms in inner circle **Note:** Varieties exist.

Date	Mintage	VG	F	VF	XF	Unc
ND(1625-49)	—	15.00	30.00	70.00	150	—

KM# 84 2 PENCE (1/2 Groat)
Silver **Ruler:** Charles I **Rev:** Round arms in inner circle **Note:** Varieties exist.

Date	Mintage	VG	F	VF	XF	Unc
ND(1625-49)	—	10.00	30.00	70.00	150	—

KM# 85 2 PENCE (1/2 Groat)
Silver **Ruler:** Charles I **Obv:** Crowned older bust of Charles I left, value behind in inner circle **Rev:** Oval arms in inner circle **Mint:** Tower **Note:** Struck (under Parliament). Varieties exist.

Date	Mintage	VG	F	VF	XF	Unc
ND(1625-49)	—	15.00	30.00	100	250	—

KM# 161 2 PENCE (1/2 Groat)
Silver **Ruler:** Charles I **Obv:** Briot bust of Charles I left, value behind in inner circle **Rev:** Shield of arms on long cross in inner circle **Note:** First Milled Briot Issue (1631-32)

Date	Mintage	VG	F	VF	XF	Unc
ND(1631-32)	—	45.00	90.00	160	400	—

KM# 162 2 PENCE (1/2 Groat)
Silver **Ruler:** Charles I **Obv:** Crowned bust of Charles I with lace collar left with value behind in inner circle **Rev:** Large plumes in crown in inner circle **Mint:** Aberystwyth **Note:** Varieties exist.

Date	Mintage	VG	F	VF	XF	Unc
ND(1631-32)	—	40.00	75.00	325	800	—

KM# 163.1 2 PENCE (1/2 Groat)
Silver **Ruler:** Charles I **Obv:** Crowned bust of Charles with value behind in inner circle **Mint:** Aberystwyth - Furnace Mint

Date	Mintage	VG	F	VF	XF	Unc
ND(1631)	—	200	450	1,000	2,300	—

KM# 163.2 2 PENCE (1/2 Groat)
Silver **Ruler:** Charles I **Mint:** Oxford

Date	Mintage	VG	F	VF	XF	Unc
ND(1631-32)	—	75.00	150	400	950	—

KM# 272.2 2 PENCE (1/2 Groat)
Silver **Ruler:** Charles I **Rev:** Declaration, BR below **Mint:** Bristol

Date	Mintage	VG	F	VF	XF	Unc
ND(1644)	—	300	550	1,250	3,000	—

KM# 163.3 2 PENCE (1/2 Groat)
Silver **Ruler:** Charles I **Rev:** Large plumes divide date **Mint:** Lundy

Date	Mintage	VG	F	VF	XF	Unc
1646	—	225	450	1,100	2,500	—

KM# 273.1 2 PENCE (1/2 Groat)
Silver **Ruler:** Charles I **Rev:** Oval shield in inner circle **Mint:** Exeter

Date	Mintage	VG	F	VF	XF	Unc
1644	—	150	350	850	2,000	—

KM# 273.2 2 PENCE (1/2 Groat)
Silver **Ruler:** Charles I **Mint:** Worcester

Date	Mintage	VG	F	VF	XF	Unc
ND(1644)	—	350	700	1,700	4,000	—

KM# 274 2 PENCE (1/2 Groat)
Silver **Ruler:** Charles I **Obv:** Large rose in inner circle **Mint:** Exeter

Date	Mintage	VG	F	VF	XF	Unc
1644	—	175	350	900	2,000	—

KM# 86 3 PENCE
Silver **Ruler:** Charles I **Obv:** Crowned bust of Charles I left with value behind in inner circle **Rev:** Crowned arms on log cross with inner circle **Mint:** York

Date	Mintage	VG	F	VF	XF	Unc
ND(1625-49)	—	50.00	100	225	500	—

KM# 88 3 PENCE
Silver **Ruler:** Charles I **Rev:** Crowned and garnished arms in inner circle **Mint:** Aberystwyth - Furnace Mint

Date	Mintage	VG	F	VF	XF	Unc
ND(1625-49)	—	125	250	750	1,800	—

KM# 89 3 PENCE
Silver **Ruler:** Charles I **Obv:** Small bust (Rawlins) of Charles I with value behind in inner circle **Rev:** Crowned oval arms in inner circle **Mint:** Oxford

Date	Mintage	VG	F	VF	XF	Unc
ND(1625-49)	—	75.00	150	400	1,000	—

KM# 87 3 PENCE
Silver **Ruler:** Charles I **Obv:** Plumes before face of Charles I **Mint:** Aberystwyth **Note:** Varieties exist.

Date	Mintage	VG	F	VF	XF	Unc
ND(1625-49)	—	30.00	65.00	175	350	—

KM# 275 3 PENCE
Silver **Ruler:** Charles I **Obv:** Crowned bust (Aberystwyth) of Charles I left, plumes in front, value behind, in inner circle **Rev:** Declaration, date above OX **Mint:** Oxford **Note:** Varieties exist.

Date	Mintage	VG	F	VF	XF	Unc
1644	—	40.00	125	400	1,000	—

KM# 277.1 3 PENCE
Silver **Ruler:** Charles I **Obv:** Crowned bust of Charles I left, plumes in front, value behind, in inner circle **Mint:** Bristol **Note:** Varieties exist.

Date	Mintage	VG	F	VF	XF	Unc
1644	—	115	230	550	1,350	—

KM# 278 3 PENCE
Silver **Ruler:** Charles I **Obv:** Crowned bust of Charles I left with value behind, in inner circle **Rev:** Shield of amrs in inner circle on long cross **Mint:** Exeter

Date	Mintage	VG	F	VF	XF	Unc
1644	—	100	225	350	850	—

KM# 279 3 PENCE
Silver **Ruler:** Charles I **Obv:** Crude crowned bust of Charles I left with value behind in inner circle **Rev:** Garnished oval arms in inner circle **Mint:** Worcester

Date	Mintage	VG	F	VF	XF	Unc
ND(1644)	—	250	550	1,000	2,500	—

KM# 280 3 PENCE
Silver **Ruler:** Charles I **Obv:** Crowned bust of Charles I left with value behind, in inner circle **Rev:** Square-topped shield of amrs in inner circle **Mint:** Chester

Date	Mintage	VG	F	VF	XF	Unc
ND(1644)	—	600	1,300	3,500	8,000	—

KM# 277.2 3 PENCE
Silver **Ruler:** Charles I **Mint:** Lundy **Note:** Varieties exist.

Date	Mintage	VG	F	VF	XF	Unc
1645	—	115	230	525	1,300	—
1646	—	60.00	120	360	900	—

KM# 276 3 PENCE
Silver **Ruler:** Charles I **Obv:** Small bust of Charles I left iwth value behind, in inner circle **Rev:** DECLARATION, date below **Mint:** Oxford

Date	Mintage	VG	F	VF	XF	Unc
1646/44	—	65.00	125	400	1,000	—

KM# 91 4 PENCE (Groat)
Silver **Ruler:** Charles I **Rev:** Garnished oval arms with plumes above, in inner circle **Mint:** Aberystwyth - Furnace Mint

Date	Mintage	VG	F	VF	XF	Unc
ND(1625-49)	—	100	200	725	1,350	—

KM# 90 4 PENCE (Groat)
Silver **Ruler:** Charles I **Obv:** Crowned bust of Charles I left, plumes in front, value behind, in inner circle **Rev:** Round arms within wreath in inner circle **Mint:** Aberystwyth **Note:** Varieties exist.

Date	Mintage	VG	F	VF	XF	Unc
ND(1625-49)	—	25.00	50.00	200	650	—

KM# 283.1 4 PENCE (Groat)
Silver **Ruler:** Charles I **Obv:** Bust of Charles I, left **Rev:** Declaration, date and OX below **Mint:** Oxford **Note:** Varieties exist.

Date	Mintage	VG	F	VF	XF	Unc
1644	—	100	200	550	1,300	—

KM# 286.1 4 PENCE (Groat)
Silver **Ruler:** Charles I **Obv:** Crowned bust of Charles I left, value behind in inner circle **Rev:** Declaration, date below **Mint:** Bristol **Note:** Varieties exist.

Date	Mintage	VG	F	VF	XF	Unc
1644	—	150	300	850	2,000	—

KM# 286.2 4 PENCE (Groat)
Silver **Ruler:** Charles I **Obv:** Small plume in front of face **Mint:** Bristol **Note:** Varieties exist.

Date	Mintage	VG	F	VF	XF	Unc
1644	—	150	300	800	1,900	—

KM# 283.2 4 PENCE (Groat)
Silver **Ruler:** Charles I **Obv:** Lion's head on shoulder armor decoration **Mint:** Oxford

Date	Mintage	VG	F	VF	XF	Unc
1644	—	85.00	175	550	1,200	—
1645	—	100	225	550	1,300	—

KM# 284 4 PENCE (Groat)
Silver **Ruler:** Charles I **Obv:** Bust reaches to top of coin **Mint:** Oxford

Date	Mintage	VG	F	VF	XF	Unc
1644	—	100	225	550	1,300	—

KM# 285 4 PENCE (Groat)
Silver **Ruler:** Charles I **Obv:** Bust reaches to bottom of coin **Mint:** Oxford

Date	Mintage	VG	F	VF	XF	Unc
1644	—	100	225	550	1,300	—
1645	—	100	225	550	1,300	—

KM# 288 4 PENCE (Groat)
Silver **Ruler:** Charles I **Obv:** Crowned bust of Charles I left, value behind, in nner circle, date in legend **Rev:** Round arms in inner circle **Mint:** Exeter

Date	Mintage	VG	F	VF	XF	Unc
1644	—	85.00	175	400	950	—

KM# 289 4 PENCE (Groat)
Silver **Ruler:** Charles I **Obv:** Bust of Charles I, left **Mint:** Worcester

Date	Mintage	VG	F	VF	XF	Unc
ND(1644)	—	450	1,000	2,300	—	—

KM# 287 4 PENCE (Groat)
Silver **Ruler:** Charles I **Obv:** Crowned bust (Rawlins) of Charles I left with value behind **Rev:** Declaration in cartouche, date below **Mint:** Oxford

Date	Mintage	VG	F	VF	XF	Unc
1645	—	100	200	550	1,300	—
1646	—	100	200	550	1,300	—

KM# 286.3 4 PENCE (Groat)
Silver **Ruler:** Charles I **Obv:** Small plume in front of face **Mint:** Lundy **Note:** Varieties exist.

Date	Mintage	VG	F	VF	XF	Unc
1645 Rare	—	—	—	—	—	—
1646	—	65.00	125	360	900	—

KM# 4 6 PENCE
Silver **Ruler:** Elizabeth I **Obv:** Crowned bust of Elizabeth I left with rose behind head in inner circle **Rev:** Shield of arms **Note:** Sixth Issue, 1601 - 02 with mint marks numerals "1" and "2".

Date	Mintage	Good	VG	F	VF	XF
1601	—	—	35.00	75.00	325	750
1602	—	—	35.00	75.00	325	750

KM# 12 6 PENCE
Silver **Ruler:** James I **Obv:** Second bust of James I

Date	Mintage	VG	F	VF	XF	Unc
1603	—	40.00	80.00	250	600	—
1604	—	40.00	80.00	250	600	—

KM# 11 6 PENCE
Silver **Ruler:** James I **Obv:** First bust of James I right with value behind head, in inner circle **Note:** First Coinage (1603-04).

Date	Mintage	VG	F	VF	XF	Unc
1603	—	40.00	80.00	250	600	—

KM# 25 6 PENCE
Silver **Ruler:** James I **Obv:** Third bust of James I **Note:** Second Coinage (1604-19).

Date	Mintage	VG	F	VF	XF	Unc
1604	—	35.00	70.00	225	500	—
1605	—	35.00	70.00	225	500	—

KM# 48 6 PENCE
Silver **Ruler:** James I **Obv:** Fourth bust of James I

Date	Mintage	VG	F	VF	XF	Unc
1605	—	35.00	70.00	250	550	—
1606	—	35.00	70.00	250	550	—
1607	—	35.00	70.00	250	550	—
1608	—	35.00	70.00	250	550	—
1609	—	35.00	70.00	250	550	—
1610	—	35.00	70.00	250	550	—
1611	—	35.00	70.00	250	550	—
1612	—	35.00	70.00	250	550	—
1613	—	35.00	70.00	250	550	—
1614	—	35.00	70.00	250	550	—
1615	—	35.00	70.00	250	550	—

KM# 53 6 PENCE
Silver **Ruler:** James I **Obv:** Fifth bust of James I

Date	Mintage	VG	F	VF	XF	Unc
1618 Unique	—	—	—	—	—	—

KM# 77 6 PENCE
Silver **Ruler:** James I **Obv:** Crowned armored bust of James I (Sixth bust) **Rev:** Shield of arms **Note:** Third Coinage (1619-25).

Date	Mintage	VG	F	VF	XF	Unc
1621	—	50.00	95.00	300	700	—
1622	—	50.00	95.00	300	700	—
1623	—	50.00	95.00	300	700	—
1624	—	50.00	95.00	300	700	—

KM# 93 6 PENCE
Silver **Ruler:** Charles I **Obv:** Second bust of Charles I **Mint:** Tower **Note:** Varieties exist.

Date	Mintage	VG	F	VF	XF	Unc
1625	—	80.00	150	500	1,100	—
1626	—	80.00	150	500	1,100	—
1627	—	80.00	150	500	1,100	—
1628	—	80.00	150	500	1,100	—
1629	—	80.00	150	500	1,100	—
1630	—	100	200	700	1,750	—

KM# 94 6 PENCE
Silver **Ruler:** Charles I **Obv:** Third bust of Charles I **Mint:** Tower **Note:** Varieties exist.

Date	Mintage	VG	F	VF	XF	Unc
ND(1625-49)	—	32.50	105	400	950	—

KM# 95 6 PENCE
Silver **Ruler:** Charles I **Obv:** Fourth bust of Charles I **Mint:** Tower **Note:** Varieties exist.

Date	Mintage	VG	F	VF	XF	Unc
ND(1625-49)	—	30.00	85.00	325	750	—

KM# 96 6 PENCE
Silver **Ruler:** Charles I **Obv:** Fifth bust of Charles I **Mint:** Tower **Note:** Varieties exist.

Date	Mintage	VG	F	VF	XF	Unc
ND(1625-49)	—	30.00	90.00	375	900	—

KM# 97 6 PENCE
Silver **Ruler:** Charles I **Obv:** Sixth bust of Charles I **Mint:** Tower **Note:** Struck (under Parliament).

Date	Mintage	VG	F	VF	XF	Unc
ND(1625-49)	—	45.00	150	500	1,250	—

KM# 98 6 PENCE
Silver **Ruler:** Charles I **Obv:** Seventh bust of Charles I **Mint:** Tower **Note:** Struck (under Parliament).

Date	Mintage	VG	F	VF	XF	Unc
ND(1625-49)	—	50.00	105	325	750	—

KM# 92 6 PENCE
Silver **Ruler:** Charles I **Obv:** First bust of Charles I left with value behind head, in inner circle **Mint:** Tower

Date	Mintage	VG	F	VF	XF	Unc
1625	—	65.00	125	450	1,100	—
1626	—	65.00	125	450	1,100	—

KM# 164 6 PENCE
Silver **Ruler:** Charles I **Obv:** Charles I **Note:** First Milled Briot Issue (1631-32).

Date	Mintage	VG	F	VF	XF	Unc
ND	—	100	200	550	1,300	—

KM# 180 6 PENCE
Silver **Ruler:** Charles I **Obv:** Different lace collar on Charles I **Rev:** Cross inside inner collar **Note:** Second Milled Briot Issue (1638-39).

Date	Mintage	VG	F	VF	XF	Unc
ND	—	55.00	115	400	925	—

KM# 181.1 6 PENCE
Silver **Ruler:** Charles I **Obv:** Crowned bust of Charles I **Rev:** Crowned oval arms with crowned C and R at sides **Mint:** York

Date	Mintage	VG	F	VF	XF	Unc
ND(1638-39)	—	200	400	1,000	2,400	—

KM# 181.2 6 PENCE
Silver **Ruler:** Charles I **Rev:** Withour C R at sides of arms **Mint:** York

Date	Mintage	VG	F	VF	XF	Unc
ND(1638-39)	—	200	400	1,000	2,400	—

KM# 182 6 PENCE
Silver **Ruler:** Charles I **Obv:** Crowned bust of Charles I left, plumes in front, value behind **Rev:** Garnished oval arms with plumes at top **Mint:** Aberystwyth

Date	Mintage	VG	F	VF	XF	Unc
ND(1638-39)	—	225	450	1,300	3,000	—

KM# 185 6 PENCE
Silver **Ruler:** Charles I **Obv:** Crowned bust of Charles I left, plumes in front, value behind, in inner circle **Rev:** Garnished oval arms iwth plumes above in inner circle **Mint:** Aberystwyth - Furnace Mint

Date	Mintage	VG	F	VF	XF	Unc
ND(1638-39) Rare	—	—	—	—	—	—

KM# 183 6 PENCE
Silver **Ruler:** Charles I **Obv:** With inner circle **Rev:** Flat-topped arms in inner circle **Mint:** Aberystwyth **Note:** Varieties exist.

Date	Mintage	VG	F	VF	XF	Unc
ND(1638-39)	—	225	450	1,300	3,000	—

KM# 184 6 PENCE
Silver **Ruler:** Charles I **Obv:** Crown breaks inner circle **Rev:** Large oval arms in inner circle, plumes at top **Mint:** Aberystwyth **Note:** Varieties exist.

Date	Mintage	VG	F	VF	XF	Unc
ND(1638-39)	—	225	450	1,300	3,000	—

KM# 203.1 6 PENCE
Silver **Ruler:** Charles I **Rev:** Declaration with three Oxford plumes above and date below **Mint:** Oxford

Date	Mintage	VG	F	VF	XF	Unc
1642	—	200	400	1,100	2,500	—
1643	—	200	400	1,100	2,500	—

KM# 203.2 6 PENCE
Silver **Ruler:** Charles I **Rev:** Three Shrewsbury plumes above **Mint:** Oxford

Date	Mintage	VG	F	VF	XF	Unc
1643	—	150	350	1,000	2,300	—

KM# 241.1 6 PENCE
Silver **Ruler:** Charles I **Obv:** Crude bust of Charles I left with value behind, in inner circle **Rev:** Declaration with plumes above and date below **Mint:** Bristol

Date	Mintage	VG	F	VF	XF	Unc
1643	—	175	400	1,000	2,500	—

KM# 241.2 6 PENCE
Silver **Ruler:** Charles I **Obv:** Plume added in front of face **Mint:** Bristol

Date	Mintage	VG	F	VF	XF	Unc
1644	—	150	300	950	2,300	—

KM# 342 6 PENCE
Silver **Ruler:** Charles I **Obv:** Garnished round arms in inner circle, date divided by rose in legend **Mint:** Exeter

Date	Mintage	VG	F	VF	XF	Unc
1644	—	225	450	1,100	2,500	—

KM# 203.3 6 PENCE
Silver **Ruler:** Charles I **Rev:** Shrewsbury plumes and three lis above **Mint:** Oxford

Date	Mintage	VG	F	VF	XF	Unc
1644	—	275	725	1,800	4,500	—

KM# 343.1 6 PENCE
Silver **Ruler:** Charles I **Obv:** Crowned bust of Charles I left with small plume in front, value behind in inner circle **Rev:** Declaration with plumes above and date below **Mint:** Lundy

Date	Mintage	VG	F	VF	XF	Unc
1645	—	165	400	1,000	2,500	—

KM# 343.2 6 PENCE
Silver **Ruler:** Charles I **Mint:** Lundy

Date	Mintage	VG	F	VF	XF	Unc
1646	—	75.00	160	400	1,000	—

KM# 367 6 PENCE

Silver **Ruler:** Charles I **Obv:** Crude bust of Charles I left with value behind in inner circle **Rev:** Square-topped shield with paws at sides and top **Mint:** Worcester

Date	Mintage	VG	F	VF	XF	Unc
ND(1646)	—	800	2,000	5,000	—	—

KM# 5 SHILLING

Silver **Ruler:** Elizabeth I **Obv:** Crowned bust left in inner circle **Rev:** Shield of arms **Note:** Sixth Issue (1601-02).

Date	Mintage	Good	VG	F	VF	XF
(160)1	—	—	75.00	165	575	1,450
(160)2	—	—	75.00	165	575	1,450

KM# 14 SHILLING

Silver **Ruler:** James I **Obv:** Second bust (pointed beard resting on chest) of James I

Date	Mintage	VG	F	VF	XF	Unc
ND(1604-19)	—	50.00	100	350	850	—

KM# 27 SHILLING

Silver **Ruler:** James I **Obv:** Fourth bust (plain armor) of James I

Date	Mintage	VG	F	VF	XF	Unc
ND	—	45.00	100	350	850	—

KM# 28 SHILLING

Silver **Ruler:** James I **Obv:** Fifth bust (longer hair) of James I

Date	Mintage	VG	F	VF	XF	Unc
ND	—	50.00	100	350	850	—

KM# 13 SHILLING

Silver **Ruler:** James I **Obv:** First bust (square beard) of James I right with value behind head in inner circle **Rev:** Shield of arms in inner circle **Note:** First Coinage. Mint mark: Thistle.

Date	Mintage	VG	F	VF	XF	Unc
ND(1604-19)	—	50.00	175	600	—	—

KM# 26 SHILLING

Silver **Ruler:** James I **Obv:** Third bust (square beard that stands out) of James I **Note:** Second Coinage.

Date	Mintage	VG	F	VF	XF	Unc
ND(1604-19)	—	50.00	100	350	800	—

KM# 59 SHILLING

Silver **Ruler:** James I **Obv:** Sixth bust (longer and very curly hair) of James I **Note:** Third Coinage.

Date	Mintage	VG	F	VF	XF	Unc
ND(1619-25)	—	55.00	125	400	900	—

KM# 60 SHILLING

Silver **Ruler:** James I **Rev:** Plume above shield

Date	Mintage	VG	F	VF	XF	Unc
ND(1619-25)	—	125	250	1,000	2,100	—

KM# 99 SHILLING

Silver **Ruler:** Charles I **Obv:** First bust (large ruffled collar) of Charles I left in inner circle **Rev:** Square-topped shield of arms on long cross in inner circle **Mint:** Tower

Date	Mintage	VG	F	VF	XF	Unc
ND(1625-49)	—	45.00	200	600	1,350	—

KM# 100 SHILLING

Silver **Ruler:** Charles I **Rev:** Without long cross **Mint:** Tower

Date	Mintage	VG	F	VF	XF	Unc
ND(1625-49)	—	75.00	260	650	1,600	—

KM# 101 SHILLING

Silver **Ruler:** Charles I **Obv:** Second bust (tall and thin with scarf covering armor) of Charles I **Rev:** Square-topped shield of arms in inner circle on long cross **Mint:** Tower

Date	Mintage	VG	F	VF	XF	Unc
ND(1625-49)	—	55.00	175	600	1,350	—

KM# 102 SHILLING

Silver **Ruler:** Charles I **Rev:** Without long cross **Mint:** Tower

Date	Mintage	VG	F	VF	XF	Unc
ND(1625-49)	—	60.00	175	750	1,650	—

KM# 103 SHILLING

Silver **Ruler:** Charles I **Obv:** Third bust (more armor shows around scarf) of Charles I **Rev:** Oval arms with C-R above in inner circle **Mint:** Tower

Date	Mintage	VG	F	VF	XF	Unc
ND(1625-49)	—	40.00	150	475	1,150	—

KM# 105 SHILLING

Silver **Ruler:** Charles I **Obv:** Fourth bust (with lace collar) of Charles I **Rev:** Oval arms with C-R at sides in inner circle **Mint:** Tower

Date	Mintage	VG	F	VF	XF	Unc
ND(1625-49)	—	27.50	85.00	300	850	—

KM# 106 SHILLING

Silver **Ruler:** Charles I **Rev:** Plume above shield **Mint:** Tower

Date	Mintage	VG	F	VF	XF	Unc
ND(1625-49)	—	300	650	2,000	5,000	—

KM# 107 SHILLING

Silver **Ruler:** Charles I **Obv:** Without inner circle **Rev:** Round arms without C-R or inner circle **Mint:** Tower

Date	Mintage	VG	F	VF	XF	Unc
ND(1625-49)	—	27.50	85.00	275	825	—

KM# 108 SHILLING

Silver **Ruler:** Charles I **Rev:** Plume above shield **Mint:** Tower

Date	Mintage	VG	F	VF	XF	Unc
ND(1625-49)	—	45.00	200	425	1,050	—

KM# 110 SHILLING

Silver **Ruler:** Charles I **Obv:** Sixth bust (very pointed beard) of Charles I **Mint:** Tower

Date	Mintage	VG	F	VF	XF	Unc
ND(1625-49)	—	25.00	80.00	265	775	—

KM# 109 SHILLING

Silver **Ruler:** Charles I **Obv:** Fifth bust (as Aberystwyth) of Charles I **Rev:** Square-topped shield of arms on long cross in inner circle **Mint:** Tower **Note:** Varieties exist.

Date	Mintage	VG	F	VF	XF	Unc
ND(1625-49)	—	35.00	140	425	1,050	—

KM# 165 SHILLING

Silver **Ruler:** Charles I **Obv:** Early Briot bust of Charles I **Note:** First Milled Briot Issue (1631-32).

Date	Mintage	VG	F	VF	XF	Unc
ND(1625-49)	—	200	400	1,100	2,600	—

KM# 186 SHILLING

Silver **Ruler:** Charles I **Obv:** Late Briot bust of Charles I with collar with lace border **Note:** Second Milled Briot Issue (1638-39).

Date	Mintage	VG	F	VF	XF	Unc
ND(1625-49)	—	75.00	375	700	1,750	—

KM# 111 SHILLING

Silver **Ruler:** Charles I **Obv:** Seventh bust (long and narrow, crude) of Charles I **Mint:** Tower **Note:** Struck under Parliament.

Date	Mintage	VG	F	VF	XF	Unc
ND(1643-44)(P)	—	30.00	90.00	300	825	—

KM# 112 SHILLING

Silver **Ruler:** Charles I **Obv:** Eighth bust (shorter and older) of Charles I **Mint:** Tower **Note:** Struck under Parliament.

Date	Mintage	VG	F	VF	XF	Unc
ND(1644-45)(R)	—	35.00	150	475	1,150	—

KM# 104 SHILLING

Silver **Ruler:** Charles I **Rev:** Plume above shield **Mint:** Tower **Note:** Mint marks: Plume, rose.

Date	Mintage	VG	F	VF	XF	Unc
ND(1625-49)	—	90.00	325	1,000	2,500	—

KM# 193 SHILLING

Silver **Ruler:** Charles I **Rev:** Inner circle added **Mint:** Aberystwyth **Note:** Mint mark: Open book.

Date	Mintage	VG	F	VF	XF	Unc
ND(1638-39)	—	250	550	1,700	4,000	—

KM# 187 SHILLING

Silver **Ruler:** Charles I **Obv:** Crude style **Rev:** Crude style **Note:** Briot Hammered Issue.

Date	Mintage	VG	F	VF	XF	Unc
ND(1638-39)	—	250	500	1,500	3,750	—

KM# 188 SHILLING

Silver **Ruler:** Charles I **Obv:** Crowned bust of Charles I left with lace collar and value behind in inner circle **Rev:** Square-topped shield of arms on long cross in inner circle, EBOR... at top **Mint:** York

Date	Mintage	VG	F	VF	XF	Unc
ND(1638-39)	—	110	300	875	2,000	—

KM# 192 SHILLING

Silver **Ruler:** Charles I **Obv:** Crowned bust of Charles I left, plume in front, small value behind **Rev:** Crowned garnished arms **Mint:** Aberystwyth

Date	Mintage	VG	F	VF	XF	Unc
ND(1638-39)	—	300	600	1,700	4,000	—

KM# 194 SHILLING

Silver **Ruler:** Charles I **Obv:** Large value and inner circle added **Mint:** Aberystwyth

Date	Mintage	VG	F	VF	XF	Unc
ND(1638-39)	—	250	550	1,700	3,500	—

KM# 195 SHILLING

Silver **Ruler:** Charles I **Rev:** Different garnish on shield **Mint:** Aberystwyth

Date	Mintage	VG	F	VF	XF	Unc
ND(1638-39)	—	300	600	1,800	4,000	—

KM# 196 SHILLING

Silver **Ruler:** Charles I **Obv:** Crowned bust of Charles I left, plume in front, value behind in inner circle **Rev:** Garnished oval arms in inner circle, plume above **Mint:** Aberystwyth - Furnace Mint

Date	Mintage	VG	F	VF	XF	Unc
ND(1638-39) Rare	—	—	—	—	—	—

KM# 203 SHILLING

Silver **Ruler:** Charles I **Rev:** Declaration, three plumes above, date below in inner circle **Mint:** Shrewsbury

Date	Mintage	VG	F	VF	XF	Unc
1642	—	850	1,700	4,500	9,500	—

KM# 204 SHILLING

Silver **Ruler:** Charles I **Obv:** Cruder bust without plume in front of face **Mint:** Shrewsbury

Date	Mintage	VG	F	VF	XF	Unc
1642	—	850	1,700	4,500	9,500	—

KM# 205 SHILLING

Silver **Ruler:** Charles I **Obv:** Crowned bust (as Shrewsbury) of Charles I **Mint:** Oxford

Date	Mintage	VG	F	VF	XF	Unc
1642	—	325	600	1,675	4,800	—

KM# 206 SHILLING

Silver **Ruler:** Charles I **Obv:** Small new bust of Charles I **Mint:** Oxford

Date	Mintage	VG	F	VF	XF	Unc
1642	—	200	400	1,200	2,800	—
1643	—	200	400	1,100	2,600	—

KM# 189 SHILLING

Silver **Ruler:** Charles I **Obv:** Plain armor, coarse work **Mint:** York

Date	Mintage	VG	F	VF	XF	Unc
ND(1643-1644)	—	90.00	250	750	2,250	—

KM# 190 SHILLING

Silver **Ruler:** Charles I **Rev:** EBOR below oval shield **Mint:** York

Date	Mintage	VG	F	VF	XF	Unc
ND(1643-1644)	—	90.00	265	800	2,400	—

KM# 242.1 SHILLING

Silver **Ruler:** Charles I **Obv:** Crude bust of Charles I left in inner circle

Date	Mintage	VG	F	VF	XF	Unc
1643	—	80.00	180	550	1,650	—

KM# 242.2 SHILLING

Silver **Ruler:** Charles I **Obv:** Crude bust of Charles I left with bent crown in inner circle **Note:** Varieties exist.

Date	Mintage	VG	F	VF	XF	Unc
1643	—	80.00	225	700	2,200	—
1644	—	80.00	225	700	2,200	—

KM# 242.3 SHILLING

Silver **Ruler:** Charles I **Rev:** Annulets around and in date

Date	Mintage	VG	F	VF	XF	Unc
1646	—	90.00	265	800	2,400	—

KM# 242.4 SHILLING

Silver **Ruler:** Charles I **Obv:** Crowned bust (Oxford) of Charles I left, value behind in inner circle **Rev:** Declaration with plumes above in inner circle **Mint:** Bristol **Note:** Varieties exist.

Date	Mintage	VG	F	VF	XF	Unc
1643	—	200	450	1,250	3,000	—

KM# 242.5 SHILLING

Silver **Ruler:** Charles I **Obv:** Bust of Charles I left **Mint:** Bristol **Note:** Varieties exist.

Date	Mintage	VG	F	VF	XF	Unc
1643	—	125	300	950	2,800	—
1644	—	125	300	950	2,800	—

KM# 242.6 SHILLING

Silver **Ruler:** Charles I **Obv:** Crowned bust of Charles I left, plume in front, value behind, in inner circle **Mint:** Bristol **Note:** Varieties exist.

Date	Mintage	VG	F	VF	XF	Unc
1644	—	250	450	1,200	3,000	—
1645	—	250	450	1,200	3,000	—

KM# 242.7 SHILLING

Silver **Ruler:** Charles I **Obv:** Crowned bust of Charles I with square collar to left without plume in front **Mint:** Bristol **Note:** Varieties exist.

Date	Mintage	VG	F	VF	XF	Unc
1644	—	200	425	1,250	3,300	—
1645	—	200	425	1,250	3,300	—

KM# 242.8 SHILLING

Silver **Ruler:** Charles I **Mint:** Lundy

Date	Mintage	VG	F	VF	XF	Unc
1645 A	—	300	600	1,800	5,400	—

KM# 242.9 SHILLING

Silver **Ruler:** Charles I **Obv:** Small plume added in front of bust of Charles I **Mint:** Lundy

Date	Mintage	VG	F	VF	XF	Unc
1645 A	—	300	600	1,800	5,400	—

KM# 242.10 SHILLING

Silver **Ruler:** Charles I **Rev:** Scroll above declaration **Mint:** Lundy

Date	Mintage	VG	F	VF	XF	Unc
1646	—	125	300	900	2,700	—

KM# 242.11 SHILLING

Silver **Ruler:** Charles I **Obv:** Bust of Charles I left **Mint:** Lundy

Date	Mintage	VG	F	VF	XF	Unc
1646	—	150	325	1,000	3,000	—

KM# 242.12 SHILLING

Silver **Ruler:** Charles I **Rev:** Declaration, plumes above, date below **Mint:** Exeter

Date	Mintage	VG	F	VF	XF	Unc
1645	—	450	1,000	3,000	—	—

KM# 191 SHILLING

Silver **Ruler:** Charles I **Rev:** Crowned oval shield with EBORO below **Mint:** York **Note:** Varieties exist. Mint mark: Lion.

Date	Mintage	VG	F	VF	XF	Unc
ND(1643-44)	—	75.00	200	650	2,000	—

KM# 293 SHILLING

Silver **Ruler:** Charles I **Obv:** Crowned bust (Rawlins) of Charles I **Mint:** Oxford **Note:** Varieties exist.

Date	Mintage	VG	F	VF	XF	Unc
1644	—	200	500	1,350	3,750	—

KM# 292 SHILLING

Silver **Ruler:** Charles I **Obv:** Large, fine style bust of Charles I **Rev:** Declaration, three plumes above in inner circle **Mint:** Oxford

Date	Mintage	VG	F	VF	XF	Unc
1644	—	175	400	1,200	2,900	—
1645	—	175	400	1,200	2,900	—
1646	—	175	400	1,200	2,900	—

KM# 294 SHILLING

Silver **Ruler:** Charles I **Obv:** Small crowned bust of Charles I left with value behind in inner circle **Rev:** Garnished oblong shield of arms in inner circle **Mint:** Truro

Date	Mintage	VG	F	VF	XF	Unc
ND(1644)	—	1,500	3,000	8,500	22,000	—

KM# 295.1 SHILLING

Silver **Ruler:** Charles I **Obv:** Oval arms with scrolls on sides and top in inner circle **Mint:** Truro

Date	Mintage	VG	F	VF	XF	Unc
ND(1644)	—	1,500	3,000	8,500	22,000	—

KM# 295.2 SHILLING

Silver **Ruler:** Charles I **Rev:** Long oval arms with C-R at sides **Mint:** Truro

Date	Mintage	VG	F	VF	XF	Unc
ND(1644)	—	1,500	3,000	8,500	22,000	—

KM# 296 SHILLING

Silver **Ruler:** Charles I **Obv:** Heavier bust of Charles I **Mint:** Truro

Date	Mintage	VG	F	VF	XF	Unc
ND(1644)	—	1,500	3,000	8,500	22,000	—

KM# 297.1 SHILLING

Silver **Ruler:** Charles I **Rev:** Round shield of arms with scrolls on sides and top in inner circle

Date	Mintage	VG	F	VF	XF	Unc
ND(1644)	—	115	350	1,000	3,000	—

KM# 297.2 SHILLING

Silver **Ruler:** Charles I **Rev:** Round arms with scrolls around border in inner circle **Mint:** Exeter

Date	Mintage	VG	F	VF	XF	Unc
1644	—	225	475	1,300	3,300	—
1645	—	225	475	1,300	3,300	—

KM# 297.3 SHILLING

Silver **Ruler:** Charles I **Rev:** Divided date **Mint:** Exeter

Date	Mintage	VG	F	VF	XF	Unc
1644	—	225	475	1,300	3,300	—

KM# 298.1 SHILLING

Silver **Ruler:** Charles I **Rev:** Square-topped shield of arms in inner circle **Mint:** Worcester/Sandsfoot Castle

Date	Mintage	VG	F	VF	XF	Unc
ND(1644)	—	1,200	2,500	5,500	13,000	—

KM# 298.2 SHILLING

Silver **Ruler:** Charles I **Rev:** C-R above shield **Mint:** Worcester/Sandsfoot Castle

Date	Mintage	VG	F	VF	XF	Unc
ND(1644)	—	1,200	2,500	5,500	13,000	—

KM# 299 SHILLING

Silver **Ruler:** Charles I **Rev:** Draped oval arms in inner circle

Date	Mintage	VG	F	VF	XF	Unc
ND(1644)	—	450	875	2,500	7,500	—

KM# 300 SHILLING

Silver **Ruler:** Charles I **Obv:** Crude crowned bust of Charles I **Rev:** Round arms

Date	Mintage	VG	F	VF	XF	Unc
ND(1644)	—	500	1,200	3,600	—	—

KM# 301 SHILLING

Silver **Ruler:** Charles I **Rev:** Square-topped shield of arms with C-R above in inner circle

Date	Mintage	VG	F	VF	XF	Unc
ND(1644)	—	500	1,200	3,600	—	—

KM# 302.1 SHILLING

Silver **Ruler:** Charles I **Obv:** Crowned bust of Charles I right with value behind in inner circle **Rev:** Crowned and draped oval arms in inner circle

Date	Mintage	VG	F	VF	XF	Unc
ND Unique	—	—	—	—	—	—

KM# 302.2 SHILLING

Silver **Ruler:** Charles I **Rev:** Crowned and draped oval arms divide C-R in inner circle

Date	Mintage	VG	F	VF	XF	Unc
ND	—	450	900	2,700	—	—

KM# 6 1/2 CROWN

0.9250 Silver **Ruler:** Elizabeth I **Obv:** Crowned bust left **Rev:** Arms on long cross **Note:** Sixth Issue.

Date	Mintage	Good	VG	F	VF	XF
(160)1	—	—	500	1,100	2,900	7,000
(160)2	—	—	700	1,300	3,000	7,000

KM# A7 1/2 CROWN
1.1250 g., 0.9170 Gold 0.0332 oz. AGW **Ruler:** Elizabeth I **Obv:** Crowned bust left **Rev:** Crowned arms **Note:** Sixth Issue.

Date	Mintage	VG	F	VF	XF	Unc
(160)1	—	800	1,500	3,750	7,500	—
(160)2	—	800	1,500	3,750	7,500	—

KM# 15 1/2 CROWN
0.9250 Silver **Ruler:** James I **Obv:** King James I on horseback right in inner circle **Rev:** Arms in inner circle **Rev. Legend:** EXURGAT DEUS... **Note:** First Coinage (1603-04).

Date	Mintage	VG	F	VF	XF	Unc
ND	—	750	1,500	4,500	9,500	—

KM# 16 1/2 CROWN
1.1250 g., 0.9170 Gold 0.0332 oz. AGW **Ruler:** James I **Obv:** James I

Date	Mintage	VG	F	VF	XF	Unc
ND(1603-04)	—	650	1,200	2,750	5,500	—

KM# 30 1/2 CROWN
1.1250 g., 0.9170 Gold 0.0332 oz. AGW **Ruler:** James I **Obv:** First crowned bust of James I

Date	Mintage	VG	F	VF	XF	Unc
ND(1604-19)	—	175	300	700	—	—

KM# 31 1/2 CROWN
1.1250 g., 0.9170 Gold 0.0332 oz. AGW **Ruler:** James I **Obv:** Third crowned bust of James I

Date	Mintage	VG	F	VF	XF	Unc
ND(1604-19)	—	175	300	700	—	—

KM# 32 1/2 CROWN
1.1250 g., 0.9170 Gold 0.0332 oz. AGW **Ruler:** James I **Obv:** Fifth crowned bust of James I

Date	Mintage	VG	F	VF	XF	Unc
ND(1604-19)	—	150	300	700	—	—

KM# 29 1/2 CROWN
0.9250 Silver **Ruler:** James I **Obv:** King James I on horseback **Rev:** Arms in inner circle **Rev. Legend:** QUAE DEUS... **Note:** Second Coinage (1604-19).

Date	Mintage	VG	F	VF	XF	Unc
ND	—	750	1,500	4,500	9,500	—

KM# 61 1/2 CROWN
Silver **Ruler:** James I **Rev:** Arms in inner circle, bird-headed harp in arms **Note:** Third Coinage (1619-25).

Date	Mintage	VG	F	VF	XF	Unc
ND	—	125	300	1,000	2,400	—

KM# 62 1/2 CROWN
Silver **Ruler:** James I **Rev:** Plumes above shield of arms

Date	Mintage	VG	F	VF	XF	Unc
ND	—	250	550	1,500	3,500	—

KM# 113.1 1/2 CROWN
Silver **Ruler:** Charles I **Obv:** King Charles I on horseback left with sword uplifted in inner circle, rose on flank cloth, ground line **Rev:** Shield of arms on long cross with inner circle **Mint:** Tower

Date	Mintage	VG	F	VF	XF	Unc
ND(1625-49)	—	100	250	750	—	—

KM# 113.2 1/2 CROWN
Silver **Ruler:** Charles I **Obv:** Without rose or ground line **Mint:** Tower

Date	Mintage	VG	F	VF	XF	Unc
ND(1625-49)	—	90.00	200	600	—	—

KM# 114 1/2 CROWN
Silver **Ruler:** Charles I **Rev:** Shield not on cross **Mint:** Tower

Date	Mintage	VG	F	VF	XF	Unc
ND(1625-49)	—	60.00	150	400	—	—

KM# 115.1 1/2 CROWN
Silver **Ruler:** Charles I **Rev:** Plume above shield **Mint:** Tower

Date	Mintage	VG	F	VF	XF	Unc
ND(1625-49)	—	275	600	1,300	—	—

KM# 115.2 1/2 CROWN
Silver **Ruler:** Charles I **Obv:** Rose on flank cloth **Mint:** Tower

Date	Mintage	VG	F	VF	XF	Unc
ND(1625-49)	—	325	675	1,650	—	—

KM# 116.1 1/2 CROWN
Silver **Ruler:** Charles I **Rev:** Arms with C-R at top in inner circle **Mint:** Tower

Date	Mintage	VG	F	VF	XF	Unc
ND(1625-49)	—	50.00	100	350	—	—

KM# 116.2 1/2 CROWN
Silver **Ruler:** Charles I **Rev:** C-R divided by plume **Mint:** Tower

Date	Mintage	VG	F	VF	XF	Unc
ND(1625-49)	—	90.00	175	600	—	—

KM# 117 1/2 CROWN
Silver **Ruler:** Charles I **Rev:** Arms divide C-R **Mint:** Tower

Date	Mintage	VG	F	VF	XF	Unc
ND(1625-49)	—	50.00	100	250	650	—

KM# 118 1/2 CROWN
Silver **Ruler:** Charles I **Rev:** Garnished oval arms with plume above in inner circle **Mint:** Tower

Date	Mintage	VG	F	VF	XF	Unc
ND(1625-49)	—	375	850	2,500	—	—

KM# 119 1/2 CROWN
Silver **Ruler:** Charles I **Obv:** Horse without ornamentation, sword in vertical position **Rev:** Garnished round arms in inner circle **Mint:** Tower

Date	Mintage	VG	F	VF	XF	Unc
ND(1625-49)	—	45.00	95.00	225	650	—

KM# 120.1 1/2 CROWN
Silver **Ruler:** Charles I **Rev:** Plume above shield **Mint:** Tower

Date	Mintage	VG	F	VF	XF	Unc
ND(1625-49)	—	100	200	525	—	—

KM# 120.2 1/2 CROWN
Silver **Ruler:** Charles I **Obv:** Cloak flows from king's shoulder **Mint:** Tower

Date	Mintage	VG	F	VF	XF	Unc
ND(1625-49)	—	45.00	95.00	225	650	—

KM# 120.3 1/2 CROWN
Silver **Ruler:** Charles I **Obv:** Coarse ground below horse **Mint:** Tower

Date	Mintage	VG	F	VF	XF	Unc
ND(1625-49)	—	45.00	95.00	225	650	—

KM# 121 1/2 CROWN
Silver **Ruler:** Charles I **Obv:** Shorter horse, mane flows in front of neck, tail between back legs **Mint:** Tower

Date	Mintage	VG	F	VF	XF	Unc
ND(1625-49)	—	45.00	90.00	225	650	—

KM# 122 1/2 CROWN
Silver **Ruler:** Charles I **Obv:** Coarse style **Mint:** Tower **Note:** Struck under Parliament.

Date	Mintage	VG	F	VF	XF	Unc
ND(1625-49)	—	35.00	75.00	250	700	—

KM# 123 1/2 CROWN
Silver **Ruler:** Charles I **Obv:** Short and awkward horse **Mint:** Tower **Note:** Struck under Parliament.

Date	Mintage	VG	F	VF	XF	Unc
ND(1625-49) Rare	—	—	—	—	—	—

KM# 124 1/2 CROWN
Silver **Ruler:** Charles I **Obv:** Tall horse **Mint:** Tower **Note:** Struck under Parliament.

Date	Mintage	VG	F	VF	XF	Unc
ND(1625-49)	—	35.00	75.00	250	600	—

KM# 166 1/2 CROWN
Silver **Ruler:** Charles I **Obv:** Fine style king on horseback left in inner circle **Rev:** Garnished oval arms with crowned C-R at sides in inner circle **Note:** First Milled Briot Issue.

Date	Mintage	VG	F	VF	XF	Unc
ND(1631-32)	—	300	650	1,900	4,500	—

KM# 197 1/2 CROWN
Silver **Ruler:** Charles I **Rev:** Arms with crowned C-R at sides **Note:** Second Milled Briot Issue.

Date	Mintage	VG	F	VF	XF	Unc
ND(1638-39)	—	225	450	1,100	2,700	—

KM# 198 1/2 CROWN

Silver **Ruler:** Charles I **Obv:** Ground line below horse **Rev:** Garnished square-topped shield in inner circle **Note:** Briot Hammered Issue.

Date	Mintage	VG	F	VF	XF	Unc
ND(1638-39)	—	550	1,100	3,000	7,500	—

KM# 199.1 1/2 CROWN

Silver **Ruler:** Charles I **Obv:** King on horseback with flowing cloak, plume behind, in inner circle **Rev:** Garnished oval arms with large plume above in inner circle **Mint:** Aberystwyth

Date	Mintage	VG	F	VF	XF	Unc
ND(1638-39)	—	550	1,100	4,000	9,000	—

KM# 199.2 1/2 CROWN

Silver **Ruler:** Charles I **Obv:** Ground below horse **Mint:** Aberystwyth

Date	Mintage	VG	F	VF	XF	Unc
ND(1638-39)	—	550	1,100	4,000	9,500	—

KM# 200 1/2 CROWN

Silver **Ruler:** Charles I **Obv:** Lively horse without ground below **Mint:** Aberystwyth

Date	Mintage	VG	F	VF	XF	Unc
ND(1638-39)	—	550	1,100	4,000	9,500	—

KM# 201 1/2 CROWN

Silver **Ruler:** Charles I **Obv:** King on horseback left with plume behind in inner circle **Rev:** Garnished round arms with plume above in inner circle **Mint:** Aberystwyth - Furnace Mint

Date	Mintage	VG	F	VF	XF	Unc
ND(1638-39)	—	1,300	2,800	8,000	—	—

KM# 202 1/2 CROWN

Silver **Ruler:** Charles I **Rev:** Garnished oval arms with plume above in inner circle **Mint:** Shrewsbury

Date	Mintage	VG	F	VF	XF	Unc
ND(1638-39)	—	—	—	—	—	—

KM# 208 1/2 CROWN

Silver **Ruler:** Charles I **Rev:** Declaration, single plume above, date below, in inner circle **Mint:** Shrewsbury

Date	Mintage	VG	F	VF	XF	Unc
1642	—	375	750	2,500	—	—

KM# 209 1/2 CROWN

Silver **Ruler:** Charles I **Obv:** Large plume behind king **Rev:** Three plumes above declaration **Mint:** Shrewsbury

Date	Mintage	VG	F	VF	XF	Unc
1642	—	400	800	2,300	5,500	—

KM# 210 1/2 CROWN

Silver **Ruler:** Charles I **Obv:** Shrewsbury-style horseman **Rev:** One plume above declaration **Mint:** Shrewsbury

Date	Mintage	VG	F	VF	XF	Unc
1642	—	450	850	2,400	5,500	—

KM# 211.1 1/2 CROWN

Silver **Ruler:** Charles I **Rev:** Value 2 and 6 flank plume **Mint:** Shrewsbury

Date	Mintage	VG	F	VF	XF	Unc
1642	—	450	950	2,400	5,500	—

KM# 211.2 1/2 CROWN

Silver **Ruler:** Charles I **Obv:** Ground line below horse **Mint:** Shrewsbury

Date	Mintage	VG	F	VF	XF	Unc
1642	—	450	950	2,400	5,500	—

KM# 212 1/2 CROWN

Silver **Ruler:** Charles I **Rev:** Without value **Mint:** Shrewsbury

Date	Mintage	VG	F	VF	XF	Unc
1642	—	400	850	2,400	5,500	—

KM# 213.1 1/2 CROWN

Silver **Ruler:** Charles I **Rev:** Three thin plumes above declaration **Mint:** Shrewsbury

Date	Mintage	VG	F	VF	XF	Unc
1642	—	350	800	2,200	5,000	—

KM# 213.2 1/2 CROWN

Silver **Ruler:** Charles I **Obv:** Without plume behind king **Mint:** Shrewsbury

Date	Mintage	VG	F	VF	XF	Unc
1642	—	375	750	2,100	5,500	—

KM# 214.1 1/2 CROWN

Silver **Ruler:** Charles I **Obv:** King on horseback left in inner circle **Rev:** Declaration with three plumes above **Mint:** Oxford

Date	Mintage	VG	F	VF	XF	Unc
1642	—	150	300	1,000	2,400	—

KM# 214.2 1/2 CROWN

Silver **Ruler:** Charles I **Obv:** Shrewsbury-style horse with ground line **Mint:** Oxford **Note:** Oxford dies.

Date	Mintage	VG	F	VF	XF	Unc
1642	—	125	300	1,000	2,400	—

KM# 214.3 1/2 CROWN

Silver **Ruler:** Charles I **Obv:** Without ground line **Mint:** Oxford

Date	Mintage	VG	F	VF	XF	Unc
1642	—	125	300	1,000	2,400	—

KM# 215 1/2 CROWN

Silver **Ruler:** Charles I **Mint:** Truro

Date	Mintage	VG	F	VF	XF	Unc
1642	—	850	1,700	4,300	—	—

KM# 216 1/2 CROWN

Silver **Ruler:** Charles I **Obv:** Without weapons below horse **Rev:** Garnished rectangular arms with C-R at sides **Mint:** Truro

Date	Mintage	VG	F	VF	XF	Unc
ND(1642)	—	850	1,700	4,000	—	—

KM# 217 1/2 CROWN

Silver **Ruler:** Charles I **Obv:** New style galloping horse **Mint:** Truro

Date	Mintage	VG	F	VF	XF	Unc
ND(1642)	—	850	1,700	5,350	—	—

KM# 218 1/2 CROWN

Silver **Ruler:** Charles I **Rev:** C-R above arms **Mint:** Truro

Date	Mintage	VG	F	VF	XF	Unc
ND(1642)	—	750	1,600	4,000	—	—

KM# 219 1/2 CROWN

Silver **Ruler:** Charles I **Obv:** Trotting horse **Rev:** C-R divided by arms **Mint:** Truro

Date	Mintage	VG	F	VF	XF	Unc
ND(1642)	—	750	1,400	3,500	8,000	—

KM# 220 1/2 CROWN

Silver **Ruler:** Charles I **Obv:** King on horseback left, sash in bow at back, in inner circle **Rev:** Barrel-like arms divide C-R in inner circle **Mint:** Truro/Exeter

Date	Mintage	VG	F	VF	XF	Unc
ND(1642)	—	275	600	1,500	—	—

KM# 221.1 1/2 CROWN

Silver **Ruler:** Charles I **Rev:** Oval shield with eight scrolls in inner circle **Mint:** Truro/Exeter

Date	Mintage	VG	F	VF	XF	Unc
ND(1642)	—	225	450	1,200	2,900	—

KM# 221.2 1/2 CROWN

Silver **Ruler:** Charles I **Rev:** Oval shield with six scrolls in inner circle **Mint:** Truro/Exeter

Date	Mintage	VG	F	VF	XF	Unc
ND(1642)	—	200	400	1,000	2,300	—

KM# 221.3 1/2 CROWN

Silver **Ruler:** Charles I **Obv:** Sash at king's back flows out to back **Mint:** Truro/Exeter

Date	Mintage	VG	F	VF	XF	Unc
ND(1642)	—	225	450	1,000	2,300	—

KM# 222 1/2 CROWN

Silver **Ruler:** Charles I **Rev:** Garnished barrel-like arms **Mint:** Truro/Exeter

Date	Mintage	VG	F	VF	XF	Unc
ND(1642) Rare	—	—	—	—	—	—

KM# 223.1 1/2 CROWN

Silver **Ruler:** Charles I **Obv:** Briot horseman with ground line below **Rev:** Inverted scrollwork on oval shield **Mint:** Truro/Exeter

Date	Mintage	VG	F	VF	XF	Unc
ND(1642)	—	250	500	1,200	2,900	—

KM# 223.2 1/2 CROWN

Silver **Ruler:** Charles I **Rev:** Upright scrollwork on oval shield **Mint:** Truro/Exeter

Date	Mintage	VG	F	VF	XF	Unc
ND(1642) Rare	—	—	—	—	—	—

KM# 224 1/2 CROWN

Silver **Ruler:** Charles I **Obv:** Briot horseman **Mint:** Truro/Exeter

Date	Mintage	VG	F	VF	XF	Unc
ND(1642)	—	250	500	1,500	—	—

KM# 214.4 1/2 CROWN

Silver **Ruler:** Charles I **Obv:** Oxford-style horse with ground line **Mint:** Oxford

Date	Mintage	VG	F	VF	XF	Unc
1643	—	175	350	950	2,300	—

KM# 214.5 1/2 CROWN

Silver **Ruler:** Charles I **Obv:** Without ground line **Mint:** Oxford

Date	Mintage	VG	F	VF	XF	Unc
1643	—	150	350	950	2,300	—

KM# 214.6 1/2 CROWN

Silver **Ruler:** Charles I **Obv:** Briot-style horse with grass below in inner circle **Mint:** Oxford

Date	Mintage	VG	F	VF	XF	Unc
1643	—	175	350	1,000	2,300	—

KM# 214.7 1/2 CROWN

Silver **Ruler:** Charles I **Rev:** Large center plume above declaration, OX below date **Mint:** Oxford

Date	Mintage	VG	F	VF	XF	Unc
1643	—	175	350	1,000	2,400	—
1643	—	175	350	1,000	2,400	—
1644	—	175	350	1,000	2,400	—

KM# 214.8 1/2 CROWN

Silver **Ruler:** Charles I **Obv:** Choppy ground beneath horse, OX below date **Mint:** Oxford

Date	Mintage	VG	F	VF	XF	Unc
1643	—	175	350	1,000	2,300	—
1643	—	175	350	1,000	2,300	—

KM# 214.9 1/2 CROWN

Silver **Ruler:** Charles I **Obv:** Plain ground beneath horse, OX below date **Mint:** Oxford

Date	Mintage	VG	F	VF	XF	Unc
1644	—	175	350	1,000	2,100	—
1645	—	175	350	1,000	2,100	—

KM# 214.10 1/2 CROWN

Silver **Ruler:** Charles I **Rev:** Small plumes at sides of date, OX below date **Mint:** Oxford

Date	Mintage	VG	F	VF	XF	Unc
1644	—	200	375	1,000	2,200	—

KM# 214.11 1/2 CROWN

Silver **Ruler:** Charles I **Obv:** Larger horse with plain ground beneath, OX below date **Mint:** Oxford

Date	Mintage	VG	F	VF	XF	Unc
1644	—	175	350	1,000	2,200	—
1645	—	175	350	1,000	2,200	—

KM# 214.12 1/2 CROWN

Silver **Ruler:** Charles I **Obv:** Rocky ground beneath horse, OX below date **Mint:** Oxford

Date	Mintage	VG	F	VF	XF	Unc
1644	—	175	350	1,000	2,200	—
1645	—	175	350	1,000	2,200	—

KM# 214.16 1/2 CROWN

Silver **Ruler:** Charles I **Obv:** King on horseback (Oxford), plume behind, in inner circle **Rev:** Declaration, three Bristol plumes above, date below **Mint:** Bristol

Date	Mintage	VG	F	VF	XF	Unc
1643	—	275	550	1,400	3,000	—

KM# 214.17 1/2 CROWN

Silver **Ruler:** Charles I **Rev:** Mint mark: BR. **Mint:** Bristol

Date	Mintage	VG	F	VF	XF	Unc
1643BR.	—	275	550	1,400	3,000	—

KM# 214.18 1/2 CROWN

Silver **Ruler:** Charles I **Obv:** Flat crown on king **Mint:** Bristol

Date	Mintage	VG	F	VF	XF	Unc
1643	—	275	550	1,400	3,000	—

KM# 214.19 1/2 CROWN

Silver **Ruler:** Charles I **Rev:** Mint mark: BR. **Mint:** Bristol

Date	Mintage	VG	F	VF	XF	Unc
1643BR.	—	275	550	1,300	3,000	—
1644BR.	—	275	550	1,300	3,000	—

KM# 306.1 1/2 CROWN

Silver **Ruler:** Charles I **Rev:** Declaration, three plumes above **Mint:** Exeter

Date	Mintage	VG	F	VF	XF	Unc
1644EX	—	800	1,600	5,000	—	—
1645EX	—	800	1,600	5,000	—	—

KM# 306.2 1/2 CROWN

Silver **Ruler:** Charles I **Rev:** EX mint mark also below date **Mint:** Exeter

Date	Mintage	VG	F	VF	XF	Unc
1644	—	700	1,400	4,200	—	—

KM# 307 1/2 CROWN
Silver **Ruler:** Charles I **Obv:** King on horseback left with ground below, in inner circle **Rev:** Square-topped shield of arms divides C-R **Mint:** York

Date	Mintage	VG	F	VF	XF	Unc
ND(1644)	—	175	350	1,100	2,700	—

KM# 308 1/2 CROWN
Silver **Ruler:** Charles I **Rev:** Garnished oval arms in inner circle **Mint:** York

Date	Mintage	VG	F	VF	XF	Unc
ND(1644)	—	200	400	1,200	2,800	—

KM# 310 1/2 CROWN
Silver **Ruler:** Charles I **Obv:** Without ground line **Rev:** Round arms **Mint:** York

Date	Mintage	VG	F	VF	XF	Unc
ND(1644)	—	175	350	1,100	2,600	—

KM# 310a 1/2 CROWN
Base Metal **Ruler:** Charles I **Obv:** EBORO below horse **Mint:** York

Date	Mintage	VG	F	VF	XF	Unc
ND(1644)	—	175	350	1,100	2,600	—

Note: Possibly a contemporary counterfeit

KM# 311 1/2 CROWN
Silver **Ruler:** Charles I **Obv:** Tall horse **Rev:** Crowned square-topped shield divides C-R **Mint:** York

Date	Mintage	VG	F	VF	XF	Unc
ND(1644)	—	175	350	1,000	2,400	—

KM# 312 1/2 CROWN
Silver **Ruler:** Charles I **Obv:** EBORO below horse **Rev:** Crowned oval arms divide crowned C and crowned R **Mint:** York

Date	Mintage	VG	F	VF	XF	Unc
ND(1644)	—	75.00	175	525	—	—

KM# 313 1/2 CROWN
Silver **Ruler:** Charles I **Obv:** EBORO below horse **Rev:** Crowned oval garnished arms with lion's paws at left and right **Mint:** York

Date	Mintage	VG	F	VF	XF	Unc
ND(1644)	—	65.00	175	525	—	—

KM# 314 1/2 CROWN
Silver **Ruler:** Charles I **Obv:** King on horseback left with plume behind and CHST below in inner circle **Rev:** Garnished oval arms in inner circle **Mint:** York

Date	Mintage	VG	F	VF	XF	Unc
ND(1644)	—	300	600	1,800	—	—

KM# 315 1/2 CROWN
Silver **Ruler:** Charles I **Obv:** Without plume or CHST **Rev:** Crowned oval arms in inner circle **Mint:** York

Date	Mintage	VG	F	VF	XF	Unc
ND(1644)	—	375	725	2,150	—	—

KM# 316 1/2 CROWN
Silver **Ruler:** Charles I **Rev:** Crowned square-topped shield with crowned C-R at sides **Mint:** York

Date	Mintage	VG	F	VF	XF	Unc
ND(1644)	—	500	1,000	3,000	—	—

KM# 317.1 1/2 CROWN
Silver **Ruler:** Charles I **Rev:** Declaration, three plumes above and date below **Mint:** York

Date	Mintage	VG	F	VF	XF	Unc
1644	—	500	1,000	5,000	—	—

KM# 317.2 1/2 CROWN
Silver **Ruler:** Charles I **Obv:** W below horse **Mint:** Worcester

Date	Mintage	VG	F	VF	XF	Unc
1644	—	525	1,200	—	—	—

KM# 318.1 1/2 CROWN
Silver **Ruler:** Charles I **Rev:** Crowned square-topped shield of arms **Mint:** Worcester

Date	Mintage	VG	F	VF	XF	Unc
ND(1644)	—	350	850	—	—	—

KM# 318.2 1/2 CROWN
Silver **Ruler:** Charles I **Obv:** Grass added below horse **Mint:** Worcester

Date	Mintage	VG	F	VF	XF	Unc
ND(1644)	—	325	675	2,000	—	—

KM# 319.1 1/2 CROWN
Silver **Ruler:** Charles I **Rev:** Crowned and draped oval arms, LIS in legend **Mint:** Worcester

Date	Mintage	VG	F	VF	XF	Unc
ND(1644)	—	375	750	2,150	—	—

KM# 319.2 1/2 CROWN
Silver **Ruler:** Charles I **Rev. Legend:** FLORENT CONCORDIA REGNA. **Mint:** Worcester

Date	Mintage	VG	F	VF	XF	Unc
ND(1644)	—	300	650	2,000	—	—

KM# 320 1/2 CROWN
Silver **Ruler:** Charles I **Obv:** Tall king on horseback without W below **Rev:** Roses in legend **Mint:** Worcester

Date	Mintage	VG	F	VF	XF	Unc
ND(1644)	—	225	500	1,500	—	—

KM# 321 1/2 CROWN
Silver **Ruler:** Charles I **Rev:** Crowned square-topped shield in inner circle **Mint:** Worcester

Date	Mintage	VG	F	VF	XF	Unc
ND(1644)	—	250	600	1,800	—	—

KM# 322.1 1/2 CROWN
Silver **Ruler:** Charles I **Obv:** Briot-style horseman with sword pointing forward, ground line below **Rev:** Crowned and garnished oval arms, roses in legend **Mint:** Worcester

Date	Mintage	VG	F	VF	XF	Unc
ND(1644)	—	350	900	2,700	—	—

KM# 322.2 1/2 CROWN
Silver **Ruler:** Charles I **Rev:** C-R added at sides of arms **Mint:** Worcester

Date	Mintage	VG	F	VF	XF	Unc
ND(1644)	—	400	900	2,700	—	—

KM# 323 1/2 CROWN
Silver **Ruler:** Charles I **Obv:** Pudgy king on horse of poor style **Rev:** Without C-R at sides of arms **Mint:** Worcester

Date	Mintage	VG	F	VF	XF	Unc
ND(1644)	—	350	900	2,700	—	—

KM# 324 1/2 CROWN
Silver **Ruler:** Charles I **Obv:** Thin king and horse **Rev:** Stars in legend **Mint:** Worcester

Date	Mintage	VG	F	VF	XF	Unc
ND(1644)	—	300	625	1,900	—	—

KM# 325 1/2 CROWN
Silver **Ruler:** Charles I **Rev:** Arms with H C (Hartlebury Castle) at bottom **Mint:** Worcester

Date	Mintage	VG	F	VF	XF	Unc
ND(1644)	—	550	1,100	3,000	—	—

KM# 327 1/2 CROWN
Silver **Ruler:** Charles I **Rev:** Crowned large round shield with coarse garnish **Mint:** Shrewsbury

Date	Mintage	VG	F	VF	XF	Unc
ND(1644)	—	375	750	2,100	—	—

KM# 328 1/2 CROWN
Silver **Ruler:** Charles I **Rev:** Square-topped shield with lion paws at top and sides **Mint:** Shrewsbury

Date	Mintage	VG	F	VF	XF	Unc
ND(1644)	—	425	825	2,500	—	—

KM# 329.1 1/2 CROWN
Silver **Ruler:** Charles I **Rev:** Crowned small oval arms in inner circle **Mint:** Shrewsbury

Date	Mintage	VG	F	VF	XF	Unc
ND(1644)	—	375	750	2,250	—	—

KM# 329.2 1/2 CROWN
Silver **Ruler:** Charles I **Rev. Legend:** FLORENT CONCORDIA REGNA **Mint:** Shrewsbury

Date	Mintage	VG	F	VF	XF	Unc
ND(1644) Rare	—	—	—	—	—	—

KM# 329.3 1/2 CROWN
Silver **Ruler:** Charles I **Obv:** Grass below horse **Mint:** Shrewsbury

Date	Mintage	VG	F	VF	XF	Unc
ND(1644)	—	375	750	2,250	—	—

KM# 329.4 1/2 CROWN
Silver **Ruler:** Charles I **Obv:** Ground below horse **Mint:** Shrewsbury

Date	Mintage	VG	F	VF	XF	Unc
ND(1644)	—	425	825	2,400	—	—

KM# 214.20 1/2 CROWN
Silver **Ruler:** Charles I **Obv:** Shrewsbury plume behind king **Rev:** BR in legend above plumes **Mint:** Bristol

Date	Mintage	VG	F	VF	XF	Unc
1644BR.	—	250	500	1,300	3,000	—

KM# 214.23 1/2 CROWN
Silver **Ruler:** Charles I **Rev:** Declaration: RELIG: PRO: **Mint:** Bristol

Date	Mintage	VG	F	VF	XF	Unc
1644	—	250	500	1,300	3,000	—

KM# 214.21 1/2 CROWN
Silver **Ruler:** Charles I **Obv:** BR. mint mark below horse **Rev:** BR. mint mark below date **Mint:** Bristol

Date	Mintage	VG	F	VF	XF	Unc
1644BR.	—	250	500	1,300	3,000	—
1645BR.	—	250	500	1,300	3,000	—

KM# 214.22 1/2 CROWN
Silver **Ruler:** Charles I **Obv:** BR. mint mark also in legend **Mint:** Bristol

Date	Mintage	VG	F	VF	XF	Unc
1644BR.	—	250	500	1,200	3,000	—
1645BR.	—	250	500	1,200	3,000	—

KM# 303.1 1/2 CROWN
Silver **Ruler:** Charles I **Obv:** Crowned king on galloping horse left, weapons below, in inner circle **Rev:** Oval arms with scrollwork in inner circle, date in legend **Mint:** Exeter

Date	Mintage	VG	F	VF	XF	Unc
1644 Rare	—	—	—	—	—	—

KM# 326.1 1/2 CROWN
Silver **Ruler:** Charles I **Obv:** King on horseback with SA (Sopia) below in inner circle **Rev:** Crowned and garnished oval arms in inner circle **Note:** Possibly struck at Sandsfoot Castle.

Date	Mintage	VG	F	VF	XF	Unc
ND(1644) Rare	—	—	—	—	—	—

KM# 326.2 1/2 CROWN
Silver **Ruler:** Charles I **Obv:** Cannon ball (or large pellet) below horse without SA **Note:** Possibly struck at Sandsfoot Castle.

Date	Mintage	VG	F	VF	XF	Unc
ND(1644)	—	875	2,000	—	—	—

KM# 309 1/2 CROWN
Silver **Ruler:** Charles I **Mint:** York **Note:** Klippe. Similar to KM#300.

Date	Mintage	VG	F	VF	XF	Unc
ND(1644) Rare	—	—	—	—	—	—

KM# 305.1 1/2 CROWN
Silver **Ruler:** Charles I **Obv:** Briot-style horse with ground line beneath **Mint:** Exeter

Date	Mintage	VG	F	VF	XF	Unc
1644	—	225	450	1,100	2,600	—

KM# 305.2 1/2 CROWN
Silver **Ruler:** Charles I **Obv:** Flowing king's sash and horse with twisted tail **Mint:** Exeter

Date	Mintage	VG	F	VF	XF	Unc
1644	—	225	450	1,100	2,600	—
1645	—	225	450	1,100	2,600	—

KM# 304 1/2 CROWN
Silver **Ruler:** Charles I **Obv:** Short king on badly proportioned horse - large front, small back, in inner circle **Mint:** Exeter **Note:** Varieties exist.

Date	Mintage	VG	F	VF	XF	Unc
1644	—	350	725	2,100	—	—
16(ROSE)44	—	350	725	2,100	—	—

KM# 305.3 1/2 CROWN
Silver **Ruler:** Charles I **Rev:** Castle mint mark **Mint:** Exeter

Date	Mintage	VG	F	VF	XF	Unc
1645	—	225	500	1,500	—	—

KM# 305.4 1/2 CROWN
Silver **Ruler:** Charles I **Rev:** EX mint mark in legend **Mint:** Exeter

Date	Mintage	VG	F	VF	XF	Unc
1645EX	—	200	500	1,500	—	—

KM# 303.2 1/2 CROWN
Silver **Ruler:** Charles I **Rev:** Castle mint mark **Mint:** Exeter

Date	Mintage	VG	F	VF	XF	Unc
1645 Rare	—	—	—	—	—	—

KM# 329.5 1/2 CROWN
Silver **Ruler:** Charles I **Obv:** Grass below horse **Rev:** Crowned ornate arms flanked by standing crowned lion and unicorn **Mint:** Shrewsbury

Date	Mintage	VG	F	VF	XF	Unc
1645	—	—	—	—	—	—

KM# 214.13 1/2 CROWN
Silver **Ruler:** Charles I **Obv:** Gravelly ground beneath horse, OX below date f**Mint:** Oxford

Date	Mintage	VG	F	VF	XF	Unc
1645	—	175	350	1,000	2,200	—
1646	—	175	350	1,000	2,200	—

KM# 214.14 1/2 CROWN
Silver **Ruler:** Charles I **Rev:** Dots and annulets among and at sides of plumes and date, OX below date **Mint:** Oxford

Date	Mintage	VG	F	VF	XF	Unc
1645	—	175	350	1,000	2,200	—
1646	—	175	350	1,000	2,200	—

KM# 214.15 1/2 CROWN
Silver **Ruler:** Charles I **Obv:** Grass beneath horse, OX below date **Mint:** Oxford

Date	Mintage	VG	F	VF	XF	Unc
1645	—	175	350	1,000	2,300	—
1646	—	175	350	1,000	2,300	—

KM# 214.24 1/2 CROWN
Silver **Ruler:** Charles I **Rev:** Scrollwork above declaration **Mint:** Bristol **Note:** Late declaration.

Date	Mintage	VG	F	VF	XF	Unc
1646	—	—	—	—	—	—

KM# B7 CROWN
2.2500 g., 0.9170 Gold 0.0663 oz. AGW **Ruler:** Elizabeth I **Obv:** Crowned bust left **Rev:** Crowned arms **Note:** Sixth Issue.

Date	Mintage	VG	F	VF	XF	Unc
(160)1	—	800	1,500	3,750	8,000	—
(160)2	—	800	1,500	3,750	8,000	—

KM# 7 CROWN
Silver **Ruler:** Elizabeth I **Obv:** Crowned bust left **Rev:** Arms on long cross **Note:** Sixth Issue. Dav. #3757.

Date	Mintage	VG	F	VF	XF	Unc
(160)1	—	850	1,800	4,000	8,500	—
(160)2	—	1,000	1,900	4,000	8,500	—

KM# 17 CROWN
Silver **Ruler:** James I **Obv:** James I on horseback right in inner circle **Rev. Legend:** EXURGAT DEUS... **Note:** First Coinage. Dav. #3758.

Date	Mintage	VG	F	VF	XF	Unc
ND(1603-04)	—	700	1,500	3,500	7,500	—

KM# 18 CROWN
2.2500 g., 0.9170 Gold 0.0663 oz. AGW **Ruler:** James I **Obv:** Crowned bust of James I right in inner circle **Rev:** Crowned arms in inner circle

Date	Mintage	VG	F	VF	XF	Unc
ND(1603-04)	—	1,000	1,750	5,500	11,500	—

KM# 34 CROWN
2.2500 g., 0.9170 Gold 0.0663 oz. AGW **Ruler:** James I **Obv:** First crowned bust of James I right in inner circle **Rev:** Crowned square-topped arms **Note:** Britain.

Date	Mintage	VG	F	VF	XF	Unc
ND(1604-19)	—	200	325	750	1,600	—

KM# 33 CROWN
Silver **Ruler:** James I **Obv:** James I on horseback right in inner circle **Rev:** Arms in inner circle **Rev. Legend:** QUAE DEUS... **Note:** Second Coinage Dav. #3759.

Date	Mintage	VG	F	VF	XF	Unc
ND(1604-19)	—	550	1,200	3,500	7,500	—

KM# 35 CROWN
2.2500 g., 0.9170 Gold 0.0663 oz. AGW **Ruler:** James I **Obv:** Third crowned bust of James I right in inner circle **Note:** Britain.

Date	Mintage	VG	F	VF	XF	Unc
ND(1604-19)	—	200	325	750	1,600	—

KM# 36 CROWN
2.2500 g., 0.9170 Gold 0.0663 oz. AGW **Ruler:** James I **Obv:** Fifth crowned bust of James I right in inner circle **Note:** Britain.

Date	Mintage	VG	F	VF	XF	Unc
ND(1604-19)	—	175	300	700	1,500	—

KM# 37 CROWN
2.2500 g., 0.9170 Gold 0.0663 oz. AGW **Ruler:** James I **Obv:** Crowned rose with leaves with I-R at sides **Rev:** Crowned thistle with leaves with I-R at sides **Note:** Thistle.

Date	Mintage	VG	F	VF	XF	Unc
ND(1604-19)	—	200	325	825	1,750	—

KM# 63 CROWN
Silver **Ruler:** James I **Obv:** James I on horseback right in inner circle **Note:** Third Coinage (1619-25). Dav. #3760A.

Date	Mintage	VG	F	VF	XF	Unc
ND(1619-25)	—	400	850	2,100	4,500	—

KM# 64 CROWN

Silver **Ruler:** James I **Rev:** Plume above shield of arms **Note:** Dav. #3760.

Date	Mintage	VG	F	VF	XF	Unc
ND(1619-25)	—	550	1,100	3,000	7,500	—

KM# 128 CROWN

Silver **Ruler:** Charles I **Rev:** Plume divides C-R above oval arms without long cross behind **Note:** Dav. #3762.

Date	Mintage	VG	F	VF	XF	Unc
ND(1625-49)	—	500	900	2,200	5,000	—

KM# 130 CROWN

Silver **Ruler:** Charles I **Rev:** Garnished oval arms without C-R above or cross behind **Note:** Dav. #3764.

Date	Mintage	VG	F	VF	XF	Unc
ND(1625-49)	—	500	850	2,200	5,000	—

KM# 131 CROWN

Silver **Ruler:** Charles I **Rev:** Plume above shield **Note:** Dav. #3764A.

Date	Mintage	VG	F	VF	XF	Unc
ND(1625-49)	—	500	850	2,200	5,000	—

KM# 125 CROWN

Silver **Ruler:** Charles I **Obv:** Charles I on horseback left in inner circle **Mint:** Tower **Note:** Struck at Tower Mint. Dav. #3761.

Date	Mintage	VG	F	VF	XF	Unc
ND(1625-49)	—	500	950	2,200	5,000	—

KM# 126 CROWN

Silver **Ruler:** Charles I **Rev:** Without cross behind shield, plume above shield

Date	Mintage	VG	F	VF	XF	Unc
ND(1625-49)	—	450	900	2,200	—	—

KM# 127 CROWN

Silver **Ruler:** Charles I **Obv:** Small horse with plume on head, king holds sword on shoulder **Rev:** Garnished oval arms on long cross with C-R above in inner circle

Date	Mintage	VG	F	VF	XF	Unc
ND(1625-49)	—	500	900	2,100	4,500	—

KM# 129 CROWN

Silver **Ruler:** Charles I **Rev:** Cross added behind oval arms

Date	Mintage	VG	F	VF	XF	Unc
ND(1632-3)	—	500	1,000	2,300	5,500	—

KM# 132 CROWN

Silver **Ruler:** Charles I **Obv:** Briot-style horseman with ground line below **Rev:** Garnished oval arms in inner circle

Date	Mintage	VG	F	VF	XF	Unc
ND(1625-49)	—	1,225	2,425	6,000	—	—

KM# 133 CROWN

Silver **Ruler:** Charles I **Obv:** Small short horse with king holding sword aloft, in inner circle **Rev:** Garnished oval arms in inner circle **Mint:** Tower **Note:** Mint mark: Eye.

Date	Mintage	VG	F	VF	XF	Unc
ND(1625-49)	—	500	850	2,100	4,500	—

KM# 134 CROWN

Silver **Ruler:** Charles I **Obv:** Large tall horse **Mint:** Tower **Note:** Mint mark: Sun.

Date	Mintage	VG	F	VF	XF	Unc
ND(1625-49)	—	500	950	2,400	5,500	—

KM# 135 CROWN

2.2500 g., 0.9170 Gold 0.0663 oz. AGW **Ruler:** Charles I **Obv:** First crowned bust of Charles I right **Mint:** Tower

Date	Mintage	VG	F	VF	XF	Unc
ND(1625-42)	—	175	275	650	1,350	—

KM# 136 CROWN

2.2500 g., 0.9170 Gold 0.0663 oz. AGW **Ruler:** Charles I **Obv:** Second crowned bust of Charles I left **Mint:** Tower

Date	Mintage	VG	F	VF	XF	Unc
ND(1625-42)	—	150	250	600	1,250	—

KM# 137 CROWN

2.2500 g., 0.9170 Gold 0.0663 oz. AGW **Ruler:** Charles I **Rev:** Crowned oval arms with C-R at sides in inner circle **Mint:** Tower

Date	Mintage	VG	F	VF	XF	Unc
ND(1625-42)	—	150	275	650	1,350	—

KM# 138 CROWN

2.2500 g., 0.9170 Gold 0.0663 oz. AGW **Ruler:** Charles I **Obv:** Third crowned bust of Charles I left in inner circle **Mint:** Tower

Date	Mintage	VG	F	VF	XF	Unc
ND(1625-42)	—	350	600	1,450	3,000	—

KM# 139 CROWN

2.2500 g., 0.9170 Gold 0.0663 oz. AGW **Ruler:** Charles I **Obv:** Fourth crowned bust of Charles I left in inner circle **Mint:** Tower

Date	Mintage	VG	F	VF	XF	Unc
ND(1625-42)	—	175	275	650	1,350	—

KM# 140 CROWN

2.2500 g., 0.9170 Gold 0.0663 oz. AGW **Ruler:** Charles I **Obv:** Fifth crowned bust of Charles I left in inner circle **Mint:** Tower

Date	Mintage	VG	F	VF	XF	Unc
ND(1625-42)	—	275	450	1,000	2,000	—

KM# 141 CROWN

2.2500 g., 0.9170 Gold 0.0663 oz. AGW **Ruler:** Charles I **Obv:** Sixth crowned bust of Charles I left in inner circle **Mint:** Tower

Date	Mintage	VG	F	VF	XF	Unc
ND(1625-42) Unique	—	—	—	—	—	—

KM# 168 CROWN

2.2500 g., 0.9170 Gold 0.0663 oz. AGW **Ruler:** Charles I **Obv:** Finer style crowned bust of Charles I left with value behind head **Rev:** Crowned square-topped arms with C-R at sides **Mint:** Briot **Note:** First milled Briot issue.

Date	Mintage	VG	F	VF	XF	Unc
ND(1631-32)	—	2,000	3,250	9,500	—	—

KM# 167 CROWN

Silver **Ruler:** Charles I **Obv:** Fine style king on horseback with sword pointed aloft, ground below, in inner circle **Rev:** Crowned garnished oval arms divides crowned C and R **Note:** First Milled Briot Issue. Dav. #3763.

Date	Mintage	VG	F	VF	XF	Unc
ND(1631-32)	—	600	1,200	3,000	7,000	—

KM# 225 CROWN

Silver **Ruler:** Charles I **Obv:** King on horseback left with plume behind head, ground line below **Rev:** Declaration with three plumes above and date below **Mint:** Shrewsbury **Note:** Dav. #3767.

Date	Mintage	VG	F	VF	XF	Unc
1642	—	400	800	2,200	5,000	—

KM# 226.1 CROWN

Silver **Ruler:** Charles I **Obv:** Shrewsbury-style horseman **Rev:** Declaration with three plumes above and date below **Mint:** Oxford

Date	Mintage	VG	F	VF	XF	Unc
1642	—	600	1,200	2,600	6,000	—
1643	—	600	1,200	2,600	6,000	—

KM# 226.2 CROWN

Silver **Ruler:** Charles I **Obv:** Grass added to ground line **Mint:** Oxford **Note:** Dav. #3770.

Date	Mintage	VG	F	VF	XF	Unc
1643	—	650	1,300	3,000	7,000	—

KM# 243 CROWN

2.2500 g., 0.9170 Gold 0.0663 oz. AGW **Ruler:** Charles I **Obv:** Fourth crowned bust of Charles I left **Mint:** Tower **Note:** Struck under Parliament, 1643-48.

Date	Mintage	VG	F	VF	XF	Unc
ND(1643-48)	—	550	1,000	2,400	5,000	—

KM# 330 CROWN

Silver **Ruler:** Charles I **Obv:** Rawlins-style horsman with city view of Oxford in background **Rev:** Declaration with scrolls above and below, date and OXON at bottom **Mint:** Oxford **Note:** Dav. #3771.

Date	Mintage	VG	F	VF	XF	Unc
1644 Rare	—	—	—	—	—	—

KM# 331 CROWN

Silver **Ruler:** Charles I **Obv:** King on horseback, facing viewer, in inner circle **Rev:** Garnished oval arms in inner circle **Mint:** Truro

Date	Mintage	VG	F	VF	XF	Unc
ND(1644)	—	250	550	1,400	3,000	—

KM# 332 CROWN

Silver **Ruler:** Charles I **Rev:** 12 evenly spaced scrolls around oval arms **Mint:** Truro

Date	Mintage	VG	F	VF	XF	Unc
ND(1644)	—	250	550	1,400	3,000	—

KM# 333 CROWN

Silver **Ruler:** Charles I **Obv:** King in profile **Mint:** Truro

Date	Mintage	VG	F	VF	XF	Unc
ND(1644)	—	250	550	1,400	3,000	—

KM# 334.1 CROWN

Silver **Ruler:** Charles I **Obv:** King on horseback facing viewer **Rev:** Garnished oval arms in inner circle, date in legend divided by mint mark **Mint:** Exeter

Date	Mintage	VG	F	VF	XF	Unc
1644	—	300	600	1,300	3,000	—

KM# 334.2 CROWN
Silver **Ruler:** Charles I **Rev:** Date in legend left of mint mark **Mint:** Exeter

Date	Mintage	VG	F	VF	XF	Unc
1644	—	300	600	1,300	3,000	—

KM# 334.3 CROWN
Silver **Ruler:** Charles I **Rev:** EX added at top of legend as mint mark **Mint:** Exeter **Note:** Dav. #3765A.

Date	Mintage	VG	F	VF	XF	Unc
1645	—	250	600	1,400	3,000	—

KM# 334.4 CROWN
Silver **Ruler:** Charles I **Obv:** King's sash has loose ends instead of bow **Mint:** Exeter **Note:** Varieties exist.

Date	Mintage	VG	F	VF	XF	Unc
1645	—	350	600	1,300	3,000	—

KM# 38 DOUBLE CROWN
4.5000 g., 0.9170 Gold 0.1327 oz. AGW **Ruler:** James I **Obv:** Third crowned bust of James I right **Rev:** Crowned square-topped arms with I-R at sides

Date	Mintage	VG	F	VF	XF	Unc
ND(1604-19)	—	300	500	1,150	2,500	—

KM# 39 DOUBLE CROWN
4.5000 g., 0.9170 Gold 0.1327 oz. AGW **Ruler:** James I **Obv:** Fourth crowned bust of James I right

Date	Mintage	VG	F	VF	XF	Unc
ND(1604-19)	—	300	500	1,150	2,500	—

KM# 40 DOUBLE CROWN
4.5000 g., 0.9170 Gold 0.1327 oz. AGW **Ruler:** James I **Obv:** Fifth crowned bust of James I right

Date	Mintage	VG	F	VF	XF	Unc
ND(1604-19)	—	275	450	1,000	2,000	—

KM# 142 DOUBLE CROWN
4.5000 g., 0.9170 Gold 0.1327 oz. AGW **Ruler:** Charles I **Obv:** First crowned bust of Charles I **Mint:** Tower

Date	Mintage	VG	F	VF	XF	Unc
ND(1625-42)	—	400	700	1,650	3,500	—

KM# 143 DOUBLE CROWN
4.5000 g., 0.9170 Gold 0.1327 oz. AGW **Ruler:** Charles I **Obv:** Second crowned bust of Charles I **Mint:** Tower

Date	Mintage	VG	F	VF	XF	Unc
ND(1625-42)	—	250	425	1,000	2,000	—

KM# 144 DOUBLE CROWN
4.5000 g., 0.9170 Gold 0.1327 oz. AGW **Ruler:** Charles I **Rev:** Crowned oval shield with C-R at sides **Mint:** Tower

Date	Mintage	VG	F	VF	XF	Unc
ND(1625-42)	—	350	600	1,450	3,000	—

KM# 145 DOUBLE CROWN
4.5000 g., 0.9170 Gold 0.1327 oz. AGW **Ruler:** Charles I **Obv:** Third crowned bust of Charles I left, value behind head, in inner circle **Mint:** Tower

Date	Mintage	VG	F	VF	XF	Unc
ND(1625-42)	—	350	600	1,450	3,000	—

KM# 146 DOUBLE CROWN
4.5000 g., 0.9170 Gold 0.1327 oz. AGW **Ruler:** Charles I **Obv:** Fourth crowned bust of Charles I left, value behind head, in inner circle **Mint:** Tower

Date	Mintage	VG	F	VF	XF	Unc
ND(1625-42)	—	275	500	1,250	2,750	—

KM# 147 DOUBLE CROWN
4.5000 g., 0.9170 Gold 0.1327 oz. AGW **Ruler:** Charles I **Obv:** Fifth crowned bust of Charles I left, value behind head, in inner circle **Mint:** Tower

Date	Mintage	VG	F	VF	XF	Unc
ND(1625-42)	—	400	750	1,700	3,600	—

KM# 148 DOUBLE CROWN
4.5000 g., 0.9170 Gold 0.1327 oz. AGW **Ruler:** Charles I **Obv:** Sixth crowned bust of Charles I left, value behind head, in inner circle **Mint:** Tower

Date	Mintage	VG	F	VF	XF	Unc
ND(1625-42)	—	250	550	1,350	2,850	—

KM# 169 DOUBLE CROWN
4.5000 g., 0.9170 Gold 0.1327 oz. AGW **Ruler:** Charles I **Obv:** Bust of Charles I left **Note:** First milled Briot issue.

Date	Mintage	VG	F	VF	XF	Unc
ND(1631-32)	—	1,250	2,250	5,500	11,500	—

KM# 244 DOUBLE CROWN
4.5000 g., 0.9170 Gold 0.1327 oz. AGW **Ruler:** Charles I **Obv:** Fourth crowned bust of Charles I left, value behind head, in inner circle **Mint:** Tower **Note:** Struck under Parliament.

Date	Mintage	VG	F	VF	XF	Unc
ND(1643-48) Rare	—	650	1,200	2,750	5,500	—

KM# 245 DOUBLE CROWN
4.5000 g., 0.9170 Gold 0.1327 oz. AGW **Ruler:** Charles I **Obv:** Fifth crowned bust of Charles I left, value behind head, in inner circle **Mint:** Tower **Note:** Struck under Parliament.

Date	Mintage	VG	F	VF	XF	Unc
ND(1643-48)	—	500	800	1,850	4,000	—

KM# 246 DOUBLE CROWN
4.5000 g., 0.9170 Gold 0.1327 oz. AGW **Ruler:** Charles I **Obv:** Sixth crowned bust of Charles I left, value behind head, in inner circle **Mint:** Tower **Note:** Struck under Parliament.

Date	Mintage	VG	F	VF	XF	Unc
ND(1643-48)	—	400	700	1,750	3,750	—

KM# 247 DOUBLE CROWN
4.5000 g., 0.9170 Gold 0.1327 oz. AGW **Ruler:** Charles I **Obv:** Seventh crowned bust of Charles I left, value behind head, in inner circle **Mint:** Tower **Note:** Struck under Parliament.

Date	Mintage	VG	F	VF	XF	Unc
ND(1643-48)	—	750	1,350	3,000	—	—

KM# C7 1/2 POUND
5.5750 g., 0.9790 Gold 0.1755 oz. AGW **Ruler:** Elizabeth I **Obv:** Crowned bust left **Rev:** Crowned arms **Note:** Sixth Issue.

Date	Mintage	VG	F	VF	XF	Unc
(160)1	—	950	2,000	5,000	9,500	—
(160)2	—	950	2,000	5,000	9,500	—

KM# 235.5 1/2 POUND
Silver **Ruler:** Charles I **Obv:** Without plume behind or cannon below **Mint:** Shrewsbury **Note:** Dav. #3766.

Date	Mintage	VG	F	VF	XF	Unc
1642	—	700	1,400	3,500	8,500	—

KM# 235.1 1/2 POUND
Silver **Ruler:** Charles I **Obv:** King on horseback left with plume behind in inner circle **Rev:** Declaration with three plumes and value above **Mint:** Shrewsbury **Note:** Dav. #3766A.

Date	Mintage	VG	F	VF	XF	Unc
1642	—	750	1,500	3,500	8,500	—

KM# 235.2 1/2 POUND
Silver **Ruler:** Charles I **Rev:** Two plumes with value **Mint:** Shrewsbury

Date	Mintage	VG	F	VF	XF	Unc
1642	—	800	1,600	3,550	—	—

KM# 235.3 1/2 POUND
Silver **Ruler:** Charles I **Obv:** Ground line below horse **Mint:** Shrewsbury

Date	Mintage	VG	F	VF	XF	Unc
1642	—	800	1,500	3,500	8,500	—

KM# 235.4 1/2 POUND

Silver **Ruler:** Charles I **Obv:** Cannon and weapons below horse **Mint:** Shrewsbury

Date	Mintage	VG	F	VF	XF	Unc
1642	—	800	1,600	3,500	8,500	—

KM# 235.7 1/2 POUND

Silver **Ruler:** Charles I **Obv:** Oxford dies (plumes with bands) **Mint:** Oxford

Date	Mintage	VG	F	VF	XF	Unc
1642	—	700	1,400	3,000	7,500	—
1643	—	700	1,400	3,000	7,500	—

KM# 235.6 1/2 POUND

Silver **Ruler:** Charles I **Mint:** Oxford

Date	Mintage	VG	F	VF	XF	Unc
1642	—	1,250	2,250	6,500	12,500	—

KM# 236 1/2 POUND

Silver **Ruler:** Charles I **Obv:** King on horseback left in inner circle **Rev:** Garnished oval arms in inner circle **Mint:** Truro **Note:** Crown dies struck double thick.

Date	Mintage	VG	F	VF	XF	Unc
ND Rare	—	—	—	—	—	—

KM# D7 POUND

11.1500 g., 0.9790 Gold 0.3509 oz. AGW **Ruler:** Elizabeth I **Obv:** Crowned bust left **Rev:** Crowned arms **Note:** Sixth Issue.

Date	Mintage	VG	F	VF	XF	Unc
(160)1	—	1,600	3,000	7,500	14,000	—
(160)2	—	1,600	3,000	7,500	14,000	—

KM# 237.1 POUND

Silver **Ruler:** Charles I **Obv:** King on horseback, plume behind, in inner circle **Rev:** Declaration, three plumes and value above and date below **Mint:** Shrewsbury

Date	Mintage	VG	F	VF	XF	Unc
1642	—	1,500	3,000	8,000	—	—

KM# 237.2 POUND

Silver **Ruler:** Charles I **Obv:** Shrewsbury horseman with weapons below **Mint:** Shrewsbury

Date	Mintage	VG	F	VF	XF	Unc
1642	—	1,500	3,000	7,500	—	—

KM# 237.3 POUND

Silver **Ruler:** Charles I **Rev:** One plume above value **Mint:** Shrewsbury

Date	Mintage	VG	F	VF	XF	Unc
1642	—	1,500	3,000	8,000	—	—

KM# 238.1 POUND

Silver **Ruler:** Charles I **Obv:** Large horseman above armor and weapons **Rev:** Declaration, three Shrewsbury plumes and value above and date below **Mint:** Oxford

Date	Mintage	VG	F	VF	XF	Unc
1642	—	1,500	3,000	8,500	—	—

KM# 239.1 POUND

Silver **Ruler:** Charles I **Obv:** Shrewsbury horseman above weapons and ground line **Mint:** Oxford

Date	Mintage	VG	F	VF	XF	Unc
1642	—	1,500	3,000	7,500	—	—

KM# 239.2 POUND

Silver **Ruler:** Charles I **Obv:** Cannon added to weapons **Mint:** Oxford

Date	Mintage	VG	F	VF	XF	Unc
1642	—	1,500	3,000	7,500	—	—
1643	—	1,500	3,000	7,500	—	—

KM# 240 POUND

Silver **Ruler:** Charles I **Obv:** Exergue space checkered **Mint:** Oxford

Date	Mintage	VG	F	VF	XF	Unc
1642	—	1,500	3,000	8,000	—	—

KM# 258 POUND

Silver **Ruler:** Charles I **Obv:** Briot-style horseman **Mint:** Oxford

Date	Mintage	VG	F	VF	XF	Unc
1643	—	1,500	3,000	8,500	—	—

KM# 238.2 POUND

Silver **Ruler:** Charles I **Rev:** Three Oxford plumes near value **Mint:** Oxford

Date	Mintage	VG	F	VF	XF	Unc
1643	—	1,500	3,000	8,500	—	—

KM# 340 POUND
Silver **Ruler:** Charles I **Mint:** Oxford

Date	Mintage	VG	F	VF	XF	Unc
1644	—	1,650	3,250	8,500	—	—

ANGEL COINAGE

KM# 43 1/2 ANGEL
2.5000 g., 0.9950 Gold 0.0800 oz. AGW **Ruler:** James I
Obv: St. Michael slaying dragon in inner circle **Rev:** Ship sailing to left with arms

Date	Mintage	VG	F	VF	XF	Unc
ND(1604-19)	—	1,350	2,750	7,500	11,500	—

KM# E7 ANGEL
5.0000 g., 0.9950 Gold 0.1599 oz. AGW **Ruler:** Elizabeth I
Obv: St. Michael slaying dragon **Rev:** Arms on sailing ship
Note: Sixth issue.

Date	Mintage	VG	F	VF	XF	Unc
(160)1	—	60.00	1,200	2,750	5,000	—
(160)2	—	600	1,200	2,750	5,000	—

KM# 44 ANGEL
5.0000 g., 0.9950 Gold 0.1599 oz. AGW **Ruler:** James I

Date	Mintage	VG	F	VF	XF	Unc
ND(1604-19)	—	600	1,250	3,000	6,000	—

KM# 67 ANGEL
5.0000 g., 0.9950 Gold 0.1599 oz. AGW **Ruler:** James I
Rev: Different ship

Date	Mintage	VG	F	VF	XF	Unc
ND(1619-25)	—	750	1,650	4,250	8,500	—

KM# 149.1 ANGEL
5.0000 g., 0.9950 Gold 0.1599 oz. AGW **Ruler:** Charles I
Obv: St. Michael slaying dragon without mark of value in inner circle **Rev:** Ship sailing to left iwth arms in inner circle **Mint:** Tower

Date	Mintage	VG	F	VF	XF	Unc
ND(1625-42)	—	1,400	3,000	6,750	12,500	—

KM# 149.2 ANGEL
5.0000 g., 0.9950 Gold 0.1599 oz. AGW **Ruler:** Charles I
Obv: Mark of value in field at left **Mint:** Tower

Date	Mintage	VG	F	VF	XF	Unc
ND(1625-42)	—	1,400	3,000	6,500	11,500	—

KM# 149.3 ANGEL
5.0000 g., 0.9950 Gold 0.1599 oz. AGW **Ruler:** Charles I
Obv: Mark of value in field at right **Mint:** Tower

Date	Mintage	VG	F	VF	XF	Unc
ND(1625-42)	—	1,300	3,000	6,500	11,500	—

KM# 170 ANGEL
5.0000 g., 0.9950 Gold 0.1599 oz. AGW **Ruler:** Charles I
Mint: Briot **Note:** Smaller planchet and finer style.

Date	Mintage	VG	F	VF	XF	Unc
ND(1631-32) B	—	3,500	6,500	12,500	—	—

RYAL COINAGE

KM# 41 SPUR RYAL
13.0000 g., 0.9950 Gold 0.4159 oz. AGW **Ruler:** James I

Date	Mintage	VG	F	VF	XF	Unc
ND(1604-19)	—	3,000	6,000	15,000	24,000	—

KM# 65 SPUR RYAL
13.0000 g., 0.9950 Gold 0.4159 oz. AGW **Ruler:** James I

Date	Mintage	VG	F	VF	XF	Unc
ND(1619-25)	—	3,000	6,000	14,000	22,000	—

KM# 42 ROSE RYAL
13.0000 g., 0.9950 Gold 0.4159 oz. AGW **Ruler:** James I

Date	Mintage	VG	F	VF	XF	Unc
ND(1604-19)	—	1,800	3,500	8,500	15,000	—

KM# 66.1 ROSE RYAL
13.0000 g., 0.9950 Gold 0.4159 oz. AGW **Ruler:** James I

Date	Mintage	VG	F	VF	XF	Unc
ND(1619-25)	—	2,100	4,000	7,500	11,500	—

KM# 66.2 ROSE RYAL
13.0000 g., 0.9950 Gold 0.4159 oz. AGW **Ruler:** James I
Obv: Plain back on throne

Date	Mintage	VG	F	VF	XF	Unc
ND(1619-25)	—	2,100	4,000	8,000	12,500	—

UNITE COINAGE

KM# 227 1/2 UNITE
4.5000 g., 0.9170 Gold 0.1327 oz. AGW **Ruler:** Charles I **Obv:** Crowned bust of Charles I left in inner circle **Rev:** Declaration in three straight lines, plumes above, date below in inner circle **Mint:** Oxford

Date	Mintage	VG	F	VF	XF	Unc
1642	—	1,150	2,500	6,500	12,500	—

KM# 228 1/2 UNITE
4.5000 g., 0.9170 Gold 0.1327 oz. AGW **Ruler:** Charles I
Rev: Declaration on continuous scroll **Mint:** Oxford

Date	Mintage	VG	F	VF	XF	Unc
1642	—	1,000	2,250	6,000	12,000	—
1643	—	1,000	2,250	6,000	12,000	—

KM# 248.1 1/2 UNITE
4.5000 g., 0.9170 Gold 0.1327 oz. AGW **Ruler:** Charles I
Obv: Bust of Charles I left **Mint:** Oxford

Date	Mintage	VG	F	VF	XF	Unc
1643	—	700	1,550	3,850	7,500	—

KM# 248.2 1/2 UNITE

4.5000 g., 0.9170 Gold 0.1327 oz. AGW **Ruler:** Charles I
Rev: OX below date **Mint:** Oxford

Date	Mintage	VG	F	VF	XF	Unc
1644	—	2,000	3,500	6,500	—	—

KM# 344 1/2 UNITE

4.5000 g., 0.9170 Gold 0.1327 oz. AGW **Ruler:** Charles I
Obv: Crowned bust of Charles I left in inner circle **Rev:** Declaration on continuous scroll, plumes above, date below in inner circle **Mint:** Bristol

Date	Mintage	VG	F	VF	XF	Unc
1645 Rare	—	—	—	—	—	—

KM# 45 UNITE

9.0000 g., 0.9170 Gold 0.2653 oz. AGW **Ruler:** James I
Obv: Second crowned bust of James I right

Date	Mintage	VG	F	VF	XF	Unc
ND(1604-19)	—	400	750	1,550	3,000	—

KM# 46 UNITE

9.0000 g., 0.9170 Gold 0.2653 oz. AGW **Ruler:** James I
Obv: Fourth crowned bust of James I right

Date	Mintage	VG	F	VF	XF	Unc
ND(1604-19)	—	350	650	1,350	2,750	—

KM# 47 UNITE

9.0000 g., 0.9170 Gold 0.2653 oz. AGW **Ruler:** James I
Obv: Fifth crowned bust of James I right

Date	Mintage	VG	F	VF	XF	Unc
ND(1604-19)	—	350	650	1,350	2,750	—

KM# 150 UNITE

9.0000 g., 0.9170 Gold 0.2653 oz. AGW **Ruler:** Charles I
Obv: First crowned bust of Charles I left **Mint:** Tower

Date	Mintage	VG	F	VF	XF	Unc
ND(1625-42)	—	450	900	2,200	4,000	—

KM# 151.1 UNITE

9.0000 g., 0.9170 Gold 0.2653 oz. AGW **Ruler:** Charles I
Obv: Second crowned bust of Charles I left **Mint:** Tower

Date	Mintage	VG	F	VF	XF	Unc
ND(1625-42)	—	450	900	2,200	4,000	—

KM# 151.2 UNITE

9.0000 g., 0.9170 Gold 0.2653 oz. AGW **Ruler:** Charles I
Obv: Anchor below bust **Mint:** Tower

Date	Mintage	VG	F	VF	XF	Unc
ND(1625-42)	—	700	1,500	3,750	7,000	—

KM# 152 UNITE

9.0000 g., 0.9170 Gold 0.2653 oz. AGW **Ruler:** Charles I
Obv: Third crowned bust of Charles I left **Mint:** Tower

Date	Mintage	VG	F	VF	XF	Unc
ND(1625-42)	—	450	900	2,200	4,000	—

KM# 153 UNITE

9.0000 g., 0.9170 Gold 0.2653 oz. AGW **Ruler:** Charles I
Obv: Fourth crowned bust of Charles I left **Mint:** Tower

Date	Mintage	VG	F	VF	XF	Unc
ND(1625-42)	—	450	900	2,200	4,000	—

KM# 154.1 UNITE

9.0000 g., 0.9170 Gold 0.2653 oz. AGW **Ruler:** Charles I
Obv: Sixth crowned bust of Charles I left **Mint:** Tower

Date	Mintage	VG	F	VF	XF	Unc
ND(1625-42)	—	450	900	2,200	4,000	—

KM# 154.2 UNITE

9.0000 g., 0.9170 Gold 0.2653 oz. AGW **Ruler:** Charles I
Mint: Briot **Note:** Mint mark: Anchor.

Date	Mintage	VG	F	VF	XF	Unc
ND(1625-42)	—	3,500	6,500	13,500	—	—

KM# 171 UNITE

9.0000 g., 0.9170 Gold 0.2653 oz. AGW **Ruler:** Charles I
Obv: Charles I left **Mint:** Briot

Date	Mintage	VG	F	VF	XF	Unc
ND(1631-32)	—	1,500	3,000	7,250	11,500	—

KM# 230 UNITE

9.0000 g., 0.9170 Gold 0.2653 oz. AGW **Ruler:** Charles I
Mint: Oxford

Date	Mintage	VG	F	VF	XF	Unc
1642	—	1,300	2,800	7,000	11,000	—
1643	—	1,300	2,800	7,000	11,000	—

KM# 229 UNITE

9.0000 g., 0.9170 Gold 0.2653 oz. AGW **Ruler:** Charles I
Obv: Charles I left **Mint:** Oxford

Date	Mintage	VG	F	VF	XF	Unc
1642	—	1,300	2,800	7,000	11,000	—

KM# 231.1 UNITE

9.0000 g., 0.9170 Gold 0.2653 oz. AGW **Ruler:** Charles I
Rev: Crowned oval arms with C-R at sides **Mint:** Exeter

Date	Mintage	VG	F	VF	XF	Unc
ND(1642-43)	—	13,000	26,000	70,000	—	—

KM# 231.2 UNITE

9.0000 g., 0.9170 Gold 0.2653 oz. AGW **Ruler:** Charles I
Rev: Without C-R at sides of arms **Mint:** Exeter

Date	Mintage	VG	F	VF	XF	Unc
ND(1642-43)	—	13,000	26,000	70,000	—	—

KM# 337 UNITE

9.0000 g., 0.9170 Gold 0.2653 oz. AGW **Ruler:** Charles I
Rev: Crowned oval arms in inner circle **Mint:** Shrewsbury

Date	Mintage	VG	F	VF	XF	Unc
ND(1642) Rare	—	—	—	—	—	—

KM# 253 UNITE
9.0000 g., 0.9170 Gold 0.2653 oz. AGW **Ruler:** Charles I
Obv: Shorter bust **Mint:** Oxford

Date	Mintage	VG	F	VF	XF	Unc
1643	—	1,300	2,600	6,500	11,000	—
1645	—	1,300	2,600	6,500	11,000	—

KM# 249 UNITE
9.0000 g., 0.9170 Gold 0.2653 oz. AGW **Ruler:** Charles I **Obv:** Fourth crowned bust of Charles I left in inner circle **Rev:** Crowned oval arms **Mint:** Tower **Note:** Struck under Parliament.

Date	Mintage	VG	F	VF	XF	Unc
ND(1643-48)	—	600	1,400	3,500	7,000	—

KM# 250 UNITE
9.0000 g., 0.9170 Gold 0.2653 oz. AGW **Ruler:** Charles I **Obv:** Sixth crowned bust of Charles I left in inner circle **Rev:** Cronwed oval arms **Mint:** Tower **Note:** Struck under Parliament.

Date	Mintage	VG	F	VF	XF	Unc
ND(1643-48)	—	600	1,400	4,000	8,000	—

KM# 251 UNITE
9.0000 g., 0.9170 Gold 0.2653 oz. AGW **Ruler:** Charles I **Obv:** Seventh crowned bust of Charles I left in inner circle, crude style **Rev:** Crowned oval arms **Mint:** Tower **Note:** Struck under Parliament.

Date	Mintage	VG	F	VF	XF	Unc
ND(1643-48)	—	600	1,400	4,000	8,000	—

KM# 252 UNITE
9.0000 g., 0.9170 Gold 0.2653 oz. AGW **Ruler:** Charles I
Mint: Oxford

Date	Mintage	VG	F	VF	XF	Unc
1643	—	1,300	2,800	7,000	11,000	—

KM# 254 UNITE
9.0000 g., 0.9170 Gold 0.2653 oz. AGW **Ruler:** Charles I
Mint: Oxford

Date	Mintage	VG	F	VF	XF	Unc
1643	—	1,300	2,700	6,500	11,000	—

KM# 255 UNITE
9.0000 g., 0.9170 Gold 0.2653 oz. AGW **Ruler:** Charles I
Obv: Crude crowned bust of Charles I left, value behind head in inner circle **Rev:** Crowned oval arms with lion claws at sides **Mint:** Worcester

Date	Mintage	VG	F	VF	XF	Unc
ND(1643-44) Rare	—	—	—	—	—	—

KM# 335 UNITE
9.0000 g., 0.9170 Gold 0.2653 oz. AGW **Ruler:** Charles I
Mint: Oxford

Date	Mintage	VG	F	VF	XF	Unc
1644	—	1,300	3,000	7,500	12,000	—

KM# 336 UNITE
9.0000 g., 0.9170 Gold 0.2653 oz. AGW **Ruler:** Charles I
Mint: Oxford

Date	Mintage	VG	F	VF	XF	Unc
1644 Rare	—	—	—	—	—	—

KM# 345 UNITE
9.0000 g., 0.9170 Gold 0.2653 oz. AGW **Ruler:** Charles I
Mint: Oxford

Date	Mintage	VG	F	VF	XF	Unc
1645	—	1,300	3,000	7,000	11,000	—
1646	—	1,300	3,000	7,000	11,000	—

KM# 346 UNITE
9.0000 g., 0.9170 Gold 0.2653 oz. AGW **Ruler:** Charles I
Rev: Declaration in three lines on continuous scroll **Mint:** Bristol

Date	Mintage	VG	F	VF	XF	Unc
1645 Rare	—	—	—	—	—	—

KM# 232 TRIPLE UNITE
27.0000 g., 0.9170 Gold 0.7960 oz. AGW **Ruler:** Charles I
Obv: Crowned half-length figure of Charles I left in inner circle
Rev: Declaration in two wavy lines, plumes and III above, date below in inner circle **Mint:** Shrewsbury

Date	Mintage	VG	F	VF	XF	Unc
1642 Rare	—	—	—	—	—	—

KM# 233 TRIPLE UNITE
27.0000 g., 0.9170 Gold 0.7960 oz. AGW **Ruler:** Charles I
Mint: Oxford

Date	Mintage	VG	F	VF	XF	Unc
1642	—	6,000	12,000	26,000	—	—

KM# 234 TRIPLE UNITE
27.0000 g., 0.9170 Gold 0.7960 oz. AGW **Ruler:** Charles I
Rev: Declaration on continuous scroll

Date	Mintage	VG	F	VF	XF	Unc
1642	—	5,500	11,000	27,000	—	—
1643	—	5,500	11,000	27,000	—	—

KM# 256.1 TRIPLE UNITE
27.0000 g., 0.9170 Gold 0.7960 oz. AGW **Ruler:** Charles I
Obv: Charles I with scarf behind

Date	Mintage	VG	F	VF	XF	Unc
1643	—	6,000	12,000	27,000	—	—

KM# 256.2 TRIPLE UNITE
27.0000 g., 0.9170 Gold 0.7960 oz. AGW **Ruler:** Charles I
Obv: Charles I without scarf behind

Date	Mintage	VG	F	VF	XF	Unc
1643	—	6,000	12,000	27,000	—	—

KM# 257 TRIPLE UNITE
27.0000 g., 0.9170 Gold 0.7960 oz. AGW **Ruler:** Charles I
Rev: OXON below date

Date	Mintage	VG	F	VF	XF	Unc
1643 Rare	—	—	—	—	—	—

KM# 338 TRIPLE UNITE
27.0000 g., 0.9170 Gold 0.7960 oz. AGW **Ruler:** Charles I

Date	Mintage	VG	F	VF	XF	Unc
1644	—	6,000	12,000	27,000	—	—

KM# 339 TRIPLE UNITE
27.0000 g., 0.9170 Gold 0.7960 oz. AGW **Ruler:** Charles I

Date	Mintage	VG	F	VF	XF	Unc
1644	—	6,000	12,000	28,000	—	—

LAUREL COINAGE

KM# 68 1/4 LAUREL
2.2500 g., 0.9170 Gold 0.0663 oz. AGW **Ruler:** James I **Obv:** Second laureate bust of James I left, value behind head, in inner circle **Rev:** Crowned arms in inner circle

Date	Mintage	VG	F	VF	XF	Unc
ND(1619-25)	—	200	325	725	1,250	—

KM# 69 1/4 LAUREL
2.2500 g., 0.9170 Gold 0.0663 oz. AGW **Ruler:** James I **Obv:** Fourth laureate bust of James I

Date	Mintage	VG	F	VF	XF	Unc
ND(1619-25)	—	200	325	725	1,250	—

KM# 70 1/2 LAUREL
4.5000 g., 0.9170 Gold 0.1327 oz. AGW **Ruler:** James I **Obv:** First laureate bust of James I left, value behind head, in inner circle **Rev:** Crowned arms in inner circle

Date	Mintage	VG	F	VF	XF	Unc
ND(1619-25)	—	375	700	1,550	3,000	—

KM# 71 1/2 LAUREL
4.5000 g., 0.9170 Gold 0.1327 oz. AGW **Ruler:** James I **Obv:** Fourth laureate bust of James I **Note:** Mint mark: Rose.

Date	Mintage	VG	F	VF	XF	Unc
ND(1619-25)	—	325	650	1,450	3,000	—

KM# 72 LAUREL
9.0000 g., 0.9170 Gold 0.2653 oz. AGW **Ruler:** James I **Obv:** First laureate bust of James I left, value behind head, in inner circle **Rev:** Crowned arms in inner circle **Note:** Many minor varieties exist.

Date	Mintage	VG	F	VF	XF	Unc
ND(1619-25)	—	450	950	2,000	4,000	—

KM# 73 LAUREL
9.0000 g., 0.9170 Gold 0.2653 oz. AGW **Ruler:** James I **Obv:** Second laureate bust of James I left **Note:** Many minor varieties exist.

Date	Mintage	VG	F	VF	XF	Unc
ND(1619-25)	—	450	950	2,000	4,000	—

KM# 74 LAUREL
9.0000 g., 0.9170 Gold 0.2653 oz. AGW **Ruler:** James I **Obv:** Third laureate bust of James I left **Note:** Many minor varieties exist.

Date	Mintage	VG	F	VF	XF	Unc
ND(1619-25)	—	450	950	2,000	4,000	—

KM# 75 LAUREL
9.0000 g., 0.9170 Gold 0.2653 oz. AGW **Ruler:** James I **Obv:** Fourth laureate bust of James I left **Note:** Many minor varieties exist.

Date	Mintage	VG	F	VF	XF	Unc
ND(1619-25)	—	450	900	2,000	4,000	—

KM# 76 LAUREL
9.0000 g., 0.9170 Gold 0.2653 oz. AGW **Ruler:** James I **Obv:** Fifth laureate bust of James I left **Note:** Many minor varieties exist.

Date	Mintage	VG	F	VF	XF	Unc
ND(1619-25)	—	1,500	3,500	5,000	9,000	—

SOVEREIGN COINAGE

KM# 19 1/2 SOVEREIGN
Gold **Ruler:** James I **Obv:** Crowned bust right **Rev:** Crowned shield, IR flanking

Date	Mintage	VG	F	VF	XF	Unc
ND(1603-04) Rare	—	2,600	4,500	8,500	—	—

KM# 20 SOVEREIGN
11.1500 g., 0.9790 Gold 0.3509 oz. AGW **Ruler:** James I **Obv:** James I in armor

Date	Mintage	VG	F	VF	XF	Unc
ND(1603-04)	—	1,300	2,700	7,500	15,000	—

KM# 21 SOVEREIGN
11.1500 g., 0.9790 Gold 0.3509 oz. AGW **Ruler:** James I **Obv:** James I in ornamented armor

Date	Mintage	VG	F	VF	XF	Unc
ND(1603-04) 1603	—	1,400	2,800	8,000	15,000	—

TRADE COINAGE

Portcullis Series

This series was struck under direct order of Queen Elizabeth I (1558-1603) at the Tower Mint, London, in January 1601. The annulet O on the obverse and reverse is the Tower privy mark for 1600. The issue was intended for trade purposes to be used by merchants trading in the East Indies. Silver fineness of .925; the eight testerns has the same weight as the Spanish eight real piece of the same period but were not widely accepted and thus soon discontinued. Minor varieties exist.

KM# T4.2 8 TESTERNS
27.4000 g., 0.9250 Silver 0.8148 oz. ASW **Rev:** Large end links on chains

Date	Mintage	VG	F	VF	XF	Unc
(160)0	—	1,350	2,450	5,750	10,000	—

SIEGE COINAGE

Carlisle

Carlisle is located in the northwest of England at the border of Scotland. The Siege of Carlisle lasted from October 1644 to June 25, 1645. The seige was in the nature of a blockade, and a lack of food ended the siege. Coins were made in two values with two varieties of each.

KM# 347 SHILLING
Silver **Ruler:** Charles I **Obv:** Large crown above C.R/XII in circle **Rev:** Three-line inscription: OBS: /CARL/1645 in circle

Date	Mintage	VG	F	VF	XF	Unc
1645	—	2,300	6,500	15,000	—	—

KM# 348 SHILLING
Silver **Ruler:** Charles I **Rev:** Two-line inscription: OB CARL/1645 in circle

Date	Mintage	VG	F	VF	XF	Unc
1645	—	2,300	6,500	16,000	—	—

KM# 349 3 SHILLING
Silver **Ruler:** Charles I **Obv:** Large crown above C. R/111 in circle **Rev:** Two-line inscription: OB CARL/1645 in circle

Date	Mintage	VG	F	VF	XF	Unc
1645 Rare	—	—	—	—	—	—

KM# 350 3 SHILLING
Silver **Ruler:** Charles I **Rev:** Three-line inscription: OBS: /CARL/1645 in circle

Date	Mintage	VG	F	VF	XF	Unc
1645	—	1,800	8,000	19,000	—	—

Colchester

Colchester was a Royalist center northeast of London. The Seige lasted from June 3 to August 17, 1648. Siege pieces were struck uniface in gold and silver.

KM# 373 NINEPENCE
Silver **Ruler:** Charles I **Note:** Octagonal planchet. Uniface.

Date	Mintage	VG	F	VF	XF	Unc
ND Rare	—	—	—	—	—	—

KM# 372 NINEPENCE
Silver **Ruler:** Charles I **Obv:** Colchester castle with five towers, script legend around top **Note:** Uniface. Round planchet.

Date	Mintage	VG	F	VF	XF	Unc
ND Rare	—	—	—	—	—	—

KM# 375 SHILLING
Silver **Ruler:** Charles I **Obv:** Colchester castle with five towers, script legend around top **Note:** Octagonal planchet. Uniface. Restrikes exist.

Date	Mintage	VG	F	VF	XF	Unc
ND Rare	—	—	—	—	—	—

KM# 374 SHILLING
Silver **Ruler:** Charles I **Obv:** Colchester castle with five towers, script legend around top **Note:** Uniface.

Date	Mintage	VG	F	VF	XF	Unc
ND Rare	—	—	—	—	—	—

KM# 377 10 SHILLING
Gold **Ruler:** Charles I **Obv:** Colchester gateway divides crowned C-R, date in exergue **Note:** Uniface.

Date	Mintage	VG	F	VF	XF	Unc
1648	—	—	—	—	—	—

KM# 376 10 SHILLING
Gold **Ruler:** Charles I **Obv:** Castle with C-R at sides, date and value in exergue **Mint:** Colchester **Note:** Uniface.

Date	Mintage	VG	F	VF	XF	Unc
1648	—	—	—	—	—	—

Lathom House

Lathom House is located in Lancashire. The siege lasted from 1643 into 1644.

KM# 341 10 SHILLING
Gold **Ruler:** Charles I **Obv:** C-R in dotted circle, value in rectangle

Date	Mintage	VG	F	VF	XF	Unc
ND Unique	—	—	—	—	—	—

Newark

Newark-on-Trent in the Midlands was the scene of a number of sieges. The final surrender was May 6, 1646. All pieces are diamond shaped and these pieces are the most available of a generally difficult series.

KM# 368 6 PENCE
Silver **Ruler:** Charles I

Date	Mintage	VG	F	VF	XF	Unc
1646	—	450	950	1,900	4,500	—

KM# 369.1 9 PENCE
Silver **Ruler:** Charles I **Rev. Legend:** OBS: /NEWARK/...

Date	Mintage	VG	F	VF	XF	Unc
1645	—	450	750	1,600	3,500	—
1646	—	450	750	1,600	3,500	—

KM# 369.2 9 PENCE
Silver **Ruler:** Charles I **Rev:** .../NEWARKE/...

Date	Mintage	VG	F	VF	XF	Unc
1645	—	450	750	1,600	3,500	—

KM# 370 SHILLING
Silver **Ruler:** Charles I **Obv:** Flat arched crown divides C-R, value below **Rev. Legend:** OBS/NEWARKE/1645

Date	Mintage	VG	F	VF	XF	Unc
1645	—	500	850	1,800	4,500	—

KM# 370.1 SHILLING
Silver **Ruler:** Charles I **Obv:** Large high-arched crown divides C-R, value below **Rev. Legend:** OBS/NEWARKE/1645

Date	Mintage	VG	F	VF	XF	Unc
1645	—	400	800	1,700	4,000	—

KM# 370.2 SHILLING
Silver **Ruler:** Charles I **Rev:** .../NEWARK/...

Date	Mintage	VG	F	VF	XF	Unc
1645	—	400	800	1,700	4,000	—
1646	—	400	800	1,700	4,000	—

KM# 371 1/2 CROWN
Silver **Ruler:** Charles I

Date	Mintage	VG	F	VF	XF	Unc
1645	—	550	1,100	2,400	6,000	—
1646	—	500	1,000	2,100	5,000	—

Ponterfract

Called by some the - Key to the North, Pontefract (or Pomfret) was the scene of three sieges during this period. The last began in the fall of 1648 and did not end until March 22, 1649, two months after the execution of Charles I. This series comes in two issues: those issued in the name of Charles I and those issued in the name of Charles II.

KM# 381 SHILLING

Silver **Ruler:** Charles I **Note:** First Issue: In the name of Charles I.

Date	Mintage	VG	F	VF	XF	Unc
1648	—	1,400	2,300	6,000	—	—

KM# 379 SHILLING

Silver **Ruler:** Charles I **Note:** First Issue: In the name of Charles I. Diamond-shaped planchet.

Date	Mintage	VG	F	VF	XF	Unc
1648	—	1,400	2,300	6,000	8,500	—

KM# 380 SHILLING

Silver **Ruler:** Charles I **Note:** First Issue: In the name of Charles I. Octagonal planchet.

Date	Mintage	VG	F	VF	XF	Unc
1648	—	1,400	2,300	6,000	8,500	—

KM# 378 SHILLING

Silver **Ruler:** Charles II **Obv:** Castle **Obv. Legend:** CAROLVS: SECVNDVS: **Rev:** Crowned "CR" **Rev. Legend:** DVM: SPIRO: SPERO **Note:** First Issue: In the name of Charles II.

Date	Mintage	VG	F	VF	XF	Unc
1648	—	1,400	2,300	6,000	8,500	—

KM# 383.1 SHILLING

Silver **Obv:** Crown above HANC DE/US DEDIT/1648 in inner circle **Obv. Legend:** Outer legend: CAROL. II. D. G. MAG. B. F. ET. H. REX. **Rev. Legend:** Outer legend: POST. MORTEM: PATRIS: PRO: FILIO **Note:** Second Issue: In the name of Charles II.

Date	Mintage	VG	F	VF	XF	Unc
1648	—	1,500	2,400	6,000	—	—

KM# 383.2 SHILLING

Silver **Rev:** Cannon at right side **Note:** Second Issue: In the name of Charles II.

Date	Mintage	VG	F	VF	XF	Unc
1648 Unique	—	—	—	—	—	—

KM# 382 SHILLING

Silver **Obv:** Castle gateway with OBS at left, PC above and cannon at right **Obv. Legend:** CAROLUS SECUNDUS 1648 **Rev:** Crown above C-R **Rev. Legend:** DUM SPIRO SPERO **Note:** Second Issue: In the name of Charles II. Octagonal planchet.

Date	Mintage	VG	F	VF	XF	Unc
1648	—	1,300	2,100	5,500	6,500	—

KM# 385 UNITE

Gold **Obv:** Crowned C-R in inner circle **Rev:** Castle with banner from tower dividing P-C, date in legend **Note:** Second Issue: In the name of Charles II. Legend varieties exist.

Date	Mintage	VG	F	VF	XF	Unc
1648 Rare	—	—	—	—	—	—
ND Rare	—	—	—	—	—	—

KM# 384 1/2 CROWN

Silver **Ruler:** Charles I **Obv:** Crude crown above C-R in inner circle **Obv. Legend:** DUN: SPIRO: SPERO **Rev:** Castle gateway with OBS at left, PC above, sword at right **Note:** First Issue: In the name of Charles I.

Date	Mintage	VG	F	VF	XF	Unc
1648 Rare	—	—	—	—	—	—

Scarborough

The siege of Scarborough lasted for a year and was concluded on July 22, 1645. The siege pieces are of diverse weights therefore diverse denominations. Shapes are generally rectangular, square or octagonal. All are uniface.

KM# 351 4 PENCE

Silver **Series:** First **Obv:** Castle walls and gateway with value incuse below **Note:** Uniface.

Date	Mintage	VG	F	VF	XF	Unc
ND Rare	—	—	—	—	—	—

KM# 352 6 PENCE

Silver **Series:** First **Obv:** Castle walls and gateway with value incuse below **Note:** Uniface.

Date	Mintage	VG	F	VF	XF	Unc
ND Rare	—	—	—	—	—	—

KM# 259 6 PENCE

Silver **Series:** Second **Obv:** Castle gateway with value below **Note:** Uniface.

Date	Mintage	VG	F	VF	XF	Unc
ND Rare	—	—	—	—	—	—

KM# 260 7 PENCE

Silver **Series:** Second **Obv:** Castle gateway with value below **Note:** Uniface.

Date	Mintage	VG	F	VF	XF	Unc
ND Rare	—	—	—	—	—	—

KM# 261 10 PENCE

Silver **Series:** Second **Obv:** Castle gateway with value below **Note:** Uniface.

Date	Mintage	VG	F	VF	XF	Unc
ND Rare	—	—	—	—	—	—

KM# 262 11 PENCE

Silver **Series:** Second **Obv:** Castle gateway with value below **Note:** Uniface.

Date	Mintage	VG	F	VF	XF	Unc
ND Rare	—	—	—	—	—	—

KM# 353 SHILLING

Silver **Series:** First **Obv:** Castle walls and gateway with value incuse below **Note:** Uniface.

Date	Mintage	VG	F	VF	XF	Unc
ND Rare	—	—	—	—	—	—

KM# 263 SHILLING

Silver **Series:** Second **Obv:** Castle gateway with value below **Note:** Uniface.

Date	Mintage	VG	F	VF	XF	Unc
ND Rare	—	—	—	—	—	—

KM# 361 1/2 CROWN

Silver **Series:** First **Obv:** Castle walls and gateway with value incuse at side (or below) **Note:** Uniface.

Date	Mintage	VG	F	VF	XF	Unc
ND	—	7,000	10,000	22,000	—	—

KM# 365 CROWN (5 Shillings)

Silver **Series:** First **Obv:** Castle walls and gateway with value incuse below **Note:** Uniface.

Date	Mintage	VG	F	VF	XF	Unc
ND Rare	—	—	—	—	—	—

KM# 264 1 SHILLING 1 PENNY

Silver **Series:** Second **Obv:** Castle gateway with value below **Note:** Uniface.

Date	Mintage	VG	F	VF	XF	Unc
ND	—	6,000	9,000	18,000	—	—

KM# 265 1 SHILLING 2 PENCE

Silver **Series:** Second **Obv:** Castle gateway with value below **Note:** Uniface.

Date	Mintage	VG	F	VF	XF	Unc
ND Rare	—	—	—	—	—	—

KM# 354 1 SHILLING 3 PENCE

Silver **Series:** First **Obv:** Castle walls and gateway with value incuse below **Note:** Uniface.

Date	Mintage	VG	F	VF	XF	Unc
ND	—	6,000	9,500	19,000	—	—

KM# 266 1 SHILLING 3 PENCE

Silver **Series:** Second **Obv:** Castle gateway with value below **Note:** Uniface.

Date	Mintage	VG	F	VF	XF	Unc
ND Rare	—	—	—	—	—	—

KM# 355 1 SHILLING 4 PENCE

Silver **Series:** First **Obv:** Castle walls and gateway with value incuse below **Note:** Uniface.

Date	Mintage	VG	F	VF	XF	Unc
ND Rare	—	—	—	—	—	—

KM# 267 1 SHILLING 4 PENCE

Silver **Series:** Second **Obv:** Castle gateway with value below **Note:** Uniface.

Date	Mintage	VG	F	VF	XF	Unc
ND	—	5,500	8,500	18,000	—	—

KM# 356 1 SHILLING 6 PENCE

Silver **Series:** First **Obv:** Castle walls and gateway with value incuse below **Note:** Uniface.

Date	Mintage	VG	F	VF	XF	Unc
ND Rare	—	—	—	—	—	—

KM# 268 1 SHILLING 6 PENCE

Silver **Series:** Second **Obv:** Castle gateway with value below **Note:** Uniface.

Date	Mintage	VG	F	VF	XF	Unc
ND Rare	—	—	—	—	—	—

KM# 357 1 SHILLING 9 PENCE

Silver **Series:** First **Obv:** Castle walls and gateway with value incuse below **Note:** Uniface.

Date	Mintage	VG	F	VF	XF	Unc
ND Rare	—	—	—	—	—	—

KM# 358 2 SHILLING

Silver **Series:** First **Obv:** Castle walls and gateway with value incuse below **Note:** Uniface.

Date	Mintage	VG	F	VF	XF	Unc
ND Rare	—	—	—	—	—	—

KM# 269 2 SHILLING

Silver **Series:** Second **Obv:** Castle gateway with value below **Note:** Uniface.

Date	Mintage	VG	F	VF	XF	Unc
ND Rare	—	—	—	—	—	—

KM# 359 2 SHILLING 2 PENCE

Silver **Series:** First **Obv:** Castle walls and gateway with value incuse below **Note:** Uniface.

Date	Mintage	VG	F	VF	XF	Unc
ND	—	7,000	9,500	19,000	—	—

KM# 360 2 SHILLING 4 PENCE

Silver **Series:** First **Obv:** Castle walls and gateway with value incuse below **Note:** Uniface.

Date	Mintage	VG	F	VF	XF	Unc
ND Rare	—	—	—	—	—	—

KM# 362 2 SHILLING 10 PENCE

Silver **Series:** First **Obv:** Castle walls and gateway with value incuse below **Note:** Uniface.

Date	Mintage	VG	F	VF	XF	Unc
ND	—	8,500	9,500	20,000	—	—

KM# 363 3 SHILLING

Silver **Series:** First **Obv:** Castle walls and gateway with value incuse below **Note:** Uniface.

Date	Mintage	VG	F	VF	XF	Unc
ND Rare	—	—	—	—	—	—

KM# 364 3 SHILLING 4 PENCE

Silver **Series:** First **Obv:** Castle walls and gateway with value incuse below **Note:** Uniface.

Date	Mintage	VG	F	VF	XF	Unc
ND Rare	—	—	—	—	—	—

KM# 366 5 SHILLING 8 PENCE

Silver **Series:** First **Obv:** Castle walls and gateway with value incuse below **Note:** Uniface.

Date	Mintage	VG	F	VF	XF	Unc
ND Rare	—	—	—	—	—	—

COMMONWEALTH

PRE-DECIMAL COINAGE

KM# 386 1/2 PENNY

Silver **Obv:** Shield with cross of St. George **Rev:** Shield with Irish harp

Date	Mintage	VG	F	VF	XF	Unc
ND	—	20.00	50.00	140	300	—

KM# 387 PENNY

Silver **Obv:** Shield with St. George's cross in branches **Rev:** Two shields with value above

Date	Mintage	VG	F	VF	XF	Unc
ND	—	20.00	40.00	100	250	—

KM# 388 2 PENCE (1/2 Groat)
Silver

Date	Mintage	VG	F	VF	XF	Unc
ND(1649-60)	—	22.00	45.00	100	225	—

KM# 389.1 6 PENCE
Silver **Note:** Mint mark: Sun.

Date	Mintage	VG	F	VF	XF	Unc
1649	—	95.00	175	400	1,000	—
1651/49	—	115	300	850	3,000	—
1651	—	95.00	175	400	1,000	—
1652/49	—	115	300	850	3,000	—
1652/1	—	115	300	850	3,000	—
1652	—	85.00	175	400	1,000	—
1653	—	85.00	175	400	1,000	—
1654/3	—	115	300	850	3,000	—
1654	—	115	300	850	3,000	—
1655	—	125	350	1,000	—	—
1656	—	85.00	175	400	1,000	—
1657/6	—	175	350	850	—	—

KM# 389.2 6 PENCE
Silver **Note:** Mint mark: Anchor. Varieties exist.

Date	Mintage	VG	F	VF	XF	Unc
1658/7	—	350	750	1,800	3,500	—
1658	—	350	750	1,800	3,500	—
1659	—	450	900	2,500	—	—
1660	—	350	750	1,700	3,500	—

KM# E207 6 PENCE
Silver **Obv:** Bust of Cromwell **Rev:** Crowned arms

Date	Mintage	VG	F	VF	XF	Unc
1658	—	—	—	—	—	—

KM# 390.1 SHILLING
Silver **Note:** Mint mark: Sun.

Date	Mintage	VG	F	VF	XF	Unc
1649	—	80.00	300	900	—	—
1651/49	—	85.00	350	950	—	—
1651	—	75.00	250	600	1,900	—
1651	—	125	500	1,350	—	—
Note: "COMONWEALTH" error						
1652/1	—	85.00	275	600	2,000	—
1652	—	75.00	225	600	2,000	—
1652/horizontal 2	—	125	450	1,200	—	—
1652	—	65.00	275	700	3,000	—
Note: "COMMON-WEALTH" error						
1653/2	—	90.00	300	950	—	—
1653	—	75.00	225	600	2,000	—
1653	—	75.00	225	600	2,000	—
Note: "COMMONWEATH" error						
1653	—	150	600	1,600	—	—
Note: "COMMONWEALH" error						
1654/3	—	85.00	250	600	2,000	—
1654	—	75.00	250	600	2,000	—
1655/4	—	150	600	1,600	—	—
1655	—	125	550	1,300	—	—
1656	—	75.00	250	600	2,000	—
1657	—	250	900	2,000	—	—

KM# A207 SHILLING
Silver **Obv:** Bust of Cromwell **Rev:** Crowned arms

Date	Mintage	VG	F	VF	XF	Unc
1658	—	350	850	1,600	3,100	—

KM# 390.2 SHILLING
Silver **Note:** Mint mark: Anchor. Varieties exist.

Date	Mintage	VG	F	VF	XF	Unc
1658/7	—	400	850	2,000	3,500	—
1658	—	400	850	2,000	3,500	—
1659 Rare	—	—	—	—	—	—
1660	—	400	850	2,000	3,500	—

KM# 391.1 1/2 CROWN
Silver **Note:** Mint mark: Sun.

Date	Mintage	VG	F	VF	XF	Unc
1649	—	175	350	1,250	3,100	—
1651	—	150	300	1,200	3,000	—
1652/1	—	125	275	850	2,600	—
1652	—	115	275	850	2,600	—
1653/1	—	100	275	850	2,600	—
1653/2	—	115	275	850	2,600	—
1653	—	110	225	850	2,600	—
1654/3	—	115	275	850	2,600	—
1654	—	135	275	975	2,750	—
1655	—	625	1,250	—	—	—
1656/5	—	135	275	825	2,600	—
1656	—	125	225	775	2,500	—

KM# 391.2 1/2 CROWN
Silver **Note:** Mint mark: Anchor.

Date	Mintage	VG	F	VF	XF	Unc
1658/7	—	750	1,500	3,500	—	—
1658	—	750	1,500	3,500	—	—
1659 Rare	—	—	—	—	—	—
1660	—	750	1,500	3,500	—	—

KM# B207 1/2 CROWN
Silver **Obv:** Bust of Oliver Cromwell left

Date	Mintage	VG	F	VF	XF	Unc
1656	—	—	—	—	—	—
1658	—	550	1,925	2,850	4,750	—

KM# 393.1 CROWN
2.2500 g., 0.9170 Gold 0.0663 oz. AGW **Note:** Mint mark: Sun.

Date	Mintage	VG	F	VF	XF	Unc
1649	—	500	1,100	2,800	5,500	—
1650	—	500	1,100	2,300	4,500	—
1651	—	500	1,100	2,800	5,500	—
1652	—	500	1,100	2,300	4,500	—
1653	—	500	1,100	2,300	4,500	—
1654	—	500	1,100	2,800	5,500	—
1655	—	—	—	—	—	—
1656	—	—	—	—	—	—
1657	—	650	1,750	3,250	6,500	—

KM# 393.2 CROWN
2.2500 g., 0.9170 Gold 0.0663 oz. AGW **Note:** Mint mark: Anchor.

Date	Mintage	VG	F	VF	XF	Unc
1658/7	—	1,400	2,500	6,750	10,000	—
1658	—	1,400	2,450	6,500	9,500	—
1660	—	—	—	—	—	—

KM# 392 CROWN
Silver **Note:** Mint mark: Sun. Dav. #3772. Varieties exist.

Date	Mintage	VG	F	VF	XF	Unc
1649	—	750	1,745	3,850	7,000	—
1651	—	550	1,100	2,500	5,500	—
1652	—	500	950	2,100	5,000	—
1652 Large 2	—	500	950	2,200	5,000	—
1652/1	—	500	950	2,200	5,000	—
1653	—	500	1,000	2,300	5,500	—
1654	—	550	1,100	2,500	5,500	—
1656	—	500	950	2,100	5,000	—
1656/4	—	450	900	2,100	5,000	—

KM# D207 CROWN
Silver **Obv:** Bust of Oliver Cromwell left **Note:** Dav. #3773.

Date	Mintage	VG	F	VF	XF	Unc
1658	—	1,400	2,500	4,000	5,500	—

KM# 394.1 DOUBLE CROWN
4.5000 g., 0.9170 Gold 0.1327 oz. AGW **Note:** Mint mark: Sun.

Date	Mintage	VG	F	VF	XF	Unc
1649	—	600	1,500	3,000	6,000	—
1650	—	550	1,400	3,000	6,000	—
1651	—	550	1,400	3,000	6,000	—
1652	—	600	1,500	3,000	6,000	—
1653	—	550	1,400	3,000	6,000	—
1654	—	600	1,500	3,000	6,000	—
1655	—	—	—	—	—	—
1656	—	600	1,500	3,250	6,000	—
1657	—	600	1,500	3,250	6,000	—

KM# 394.2 DOUBLE CROWN
4.5000 g., 0.9170 Gold 0.1327 oz. AGW **Note:** Mint mark: Anchor.

Date	Mintage	VG	F	VF	XF	Unc
1660	—	2,100	4,000	10,000	14,000	—

UNITE COINAGE

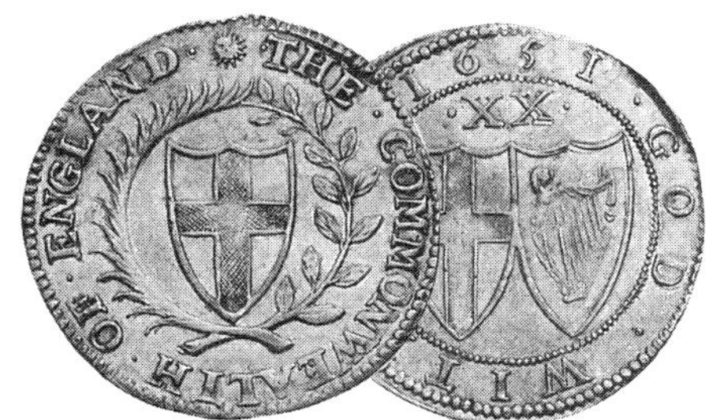

KM# 395.1 UNITE
9.0000 g., 0.9170 Gold 0.2653 oz. AGW **Note:** Mint mark: Sun.

Date	Mintage	VG	F	VF	XF	Unc
1649	—	1,000	2,100	4,500	9,000	—
1650	—	1,000	2,100	4,500	9,000	—
1651	—	950	2,000	4,500	9,000	—
1652	—	1,000	2,100	4,500	9,000	—
1653	—	950	2,000	4,500	9,000	—
1654	—	1,000	2,100	4,500	9,000	—
1655	—	1,000	2,200	5,000	9,000	—
1656	—	1,000	2,200	5,000	9,000	—
1657	—	1,000	2,200	5,000	9,000	—

KM# 395.2 UNITE
9.0000 g., 0.9170 Gold 0.2653 oz. AGW **Note:** Mint mark: Anchor.

Date	Mintage	VG	F	VF	XF	Unc
1658	—	—	—	—	—	—
1660	—	2,700	5,000	13,000	—	—

KINGDOM

HAMMERED COINAGE

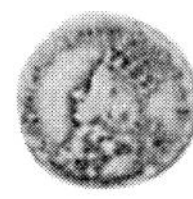
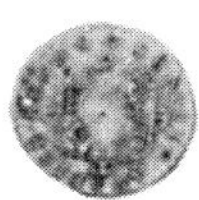

KM# 397 PENNY
Silver **Ruler:** Charles II **Obv:** Value behind head of Charles II **Note:** Second Issue - value added. Varieties exist.

Date	Mintage	VG	F	VF	XF	Unc
ND(1660-62)	—	17.00	35.00	90.00	225	—

KM# 398 PENNY
Silver **Ruler:** Charles II **Obv:** Bust and shield in inner circles **Note:** Third Issue - inner circles added.

Date	Mintage	VG	F	VF	XF	Unc
ND(1660-62)	—	17.50	35.00	105	235	—

KM# 399 2 PENCE (1/2 Groat)
Silver **Ruler:** Charles II **Obv:** Crowned bust of Charles II left **Rev:** Shield of arms on long cross **Note:** First Issue - without inner circles or value.

Date	Mintage	VG	F	VF	XF	Unc
ND(1660-62)	—	20.00	40.00	100	250	—

KM# 400 2 PENCE (1/2 Groat)
Silver **Ruler:** Charles II **Obv:** Value behind head of Charles II **Note:** Second Issue - value added. Varieties exist.

Date	Mintage	VG	F	VF	XF	Unc
ND(1660-62)	—	35.00	75.00	200	500	—

KM# 401 2 PENCE (1/2 Groat)
Silver **Ruler:** Charles II **Rev:** Shield in inner circle **Note:** Third Issue - inner circles added.

Date	Mintage	VG	F	VF	XF	Unc
ND(1660-62)	—	12.50	27.50	95.00	235	—

KM# 281 3 PENCE
Silver **Ruler:** Charles I **Obv:** Crowned bust left of Charles II, value behind head in inner circle **Rev:** Shield in inner circle **Mint:** Chester

Date	Mintage	VG	F	VF	XF	Unc
ND(1660-62)	—	18.50	37.50	100	230	—

KM# 282 3 PENCE
Silver **Ruler:** Charles II **Obv:** Without inner circle, legend begins at bottom-left of bust **Rev:** Without inner circle

Date	Mintage	VG	F	VF	XF	Unc
ND(1660-62)	—	20.00	60.00	150	350	—

KM# 291 4 PENCE (Groat)
Silver **Ruler:** Charles II **Obv:** Without inner circle **Rev:** Without inner circle

Date	Mintage	VG	F	VF	XF	Unc
ND(1660-62)	—	21.00	35.00	95.00	175	—

KM# 290 4 PENCE (Groat)
Silver **Ruler:** Charles II **Obv:** Bust of Charles II and arms in inner circle **Rev:** Square-topped arms in inner circle **Note:** Third Issue.

Date	Mintage	VG	F	VF	XF	Unc
ND(1660-62)	—	17.50	32.50	125	375	—

KM# 402 6 PENCE
Silver **Ruler:** Charles II **Obv:** Charles II, without inner circle or value **Note:** First Issue.

Date	Mintage	VG	F	VF	XF	Unc
ND(1660)	—	100	200	600	1,400	—

KM# 403 6 PENCE
Silver **Ruler:** Charles II **Obv:** Value added behind head of Charles II **Note:** Second Issue. Varieties exist.

Date	Mintage	VG	F	VF	XF	Unc
ND(1660)	—	575	1,125	2,850	—	—

KM# 404 6 PENCE
Silver **Ruler:** Charles II **Obv:** Inner circles added **Note:** Third Issue. Varieties exist.

Date	Mintage	VG	F	VF	XF	Unc
ND(1660)	—	80.00	175	600	1,300	—

KM# 407 SHILLING
Silver **Ruler:** Charles II **Obv:** Inner circles added **Note:** Third Issue. Varieties exist.

Date	Mintage	VG	F	VF	XF	Unc
ND	—	100	225	700	1,500	—

KM# 405 SHILLING
Silver **Ruler:** Charles II **Obv:** Crowned bust of Charles II left, without inner circle or value **Rev:** Shield of arms on long cross **Note:** First Issue. Varieties exist.

Date	Mintage	VG	F	VF	XF	Unc
ND(1660)	—	150	300	800	2,000	—

KM# 406 SHILLING
Silver **Ruler:** Charles II **Obv:** Value added behind head of Charles II **Note:** Second Issue. Varieties exist.

Date	Mintage	VG	F	VF	XF	Unc
ND(1661-62)	—	200	400	1,400	4,200	—

KM# 415 UNITE
9.0000 g., 0.9170 Gold 0.2653 oz. AGW **Ruler:** Charles II **Obv:** Charles II left, without value behind head **Note:** First Issue.

Date	Mintage	VG	F	VF	XF	Unc
ND(1660-62)	—	1,000	2,100	5,500	10,000	—

KM# 416 UNITE
9.0000 g., 0.9170 Gold 0.2653 oz. AGW **Ruler:** Charles II **Obv:** Charles II left, with value behind head

Date	Mintage	VG	F	VF	XF	Unc
ND(1660-62)	—	1,000	2,100	5,000	10,000	—

KM# 408 1/2 CROWN
Silver **Ruler:** Charles II **Obv:** Crowned bust of Charles II left **Rev:** Shield of arms on long cross **Note:** First Issue.

Date	Mintage	VG	F	VF	XF	Unc
ND(1660-85)	—	325	650	1,800	4,500	—

KM# 409 1/2 CROWN
Silver **Ruler:** Charles II **Obv:** Value behind head of Charles II **Note:** Second Issue. Varieties exist.

Date	Mintage	VG	F	VF	XF	Unc
ND(1660-62)	—	540	1,200	3,500	—	—

KM# 410 1/2 CROWN
Silver **Ruler:** Charles II **Obv:** Inner circles added **Note:** Third Issue. Varieties exist.

Date	Mintage	VG	F	VF	XF	Unc
ND(1660-62)	—	135	550	1,200	3,500	—

KM# 411 CROWN

Gold **Ruler:** Charles II **Obv:** Bust of Charles II left **Note:** First Issue.

Date	Mintage	VG	F	VF	XF	Unc
ND(1660-62)	—	650	1,350	3,500	7,500	—

KM# 412 CROWN

Gold **Ruler:** Charles II **Obv:** Bust of Charles II with value behind head left **Note:** Second Issue.

Date	Mintage	VG	F	VF	XF	Unc
ND(1660-62)	—	600	1,100	3,000	7,000	—

KM# 413 DOUBLE CROWN

4.5000 g., 0.9170 Gold 0.1327 oz. AGW **Ruler:** Charles II **Obv:** Bust of Charles II left without value **Note:** First Issue.

Date	Mintage	VG	F	VF	XF	Unc
ND(1660)	—	650	1,400	3,750	7,750	—

KM# 414 DOUBLE CROWN

4.5000 g., 0.9170 Gold 0.1327 oz. AGW **Ruler:** Charles II **Obv:** Bust of Charles II left with value behind head **Note:** Second Issue.

Date	Mintage	VG	F	VF	XF	Unc
ND(1660-62)	—	600	1,200	3,250	7,250	—

PRE-DECIMAL COINAGE

KM# 436.1 FARTHING

Copper **Ruler:** Charles II **Obv:** Bust of Charles II left **Note:** Varieties exist.

Date	Mintage	VG	F	VF	XF	Unc
1672	—	15.00	80.00	300	1,100	—
1673	—	15.00	80.00	300	1,000	—
1674	—	18.00	90.00	325	1,125	—
1675	—	15.00	90.00	325	1,125	—
1679	—	18.00	100	375	1,200	—

KM# 447 FARTHING

Tin with square copper plug **Ruler:** James II **Obv:** Laureate and armored bust of James II right **Rev:** Britannia seated left **Note:** Varieties exist.

Date	Mintage	VG	F	VF	XF	Unc
1684 Rare	—	—	—	—	—	—
1685	—	100	200	750	3,000	—
1686	—	100	225	800	3,000	—
1687 Rare	—	—	—	—	—	—

KM# 436.2 FARTHING

Tin with square copper plug **Ruler:** Charles II **Obv:** Bust of Charles II left **Edge:** Date **Note:** Counterfeits exist.

Date	Mintage	VG	F	VF	XF	Unc
1684	—	75.00	325	1,000	2,200	—
1685 Rare	—	—	—	—	—	—

KM# 461 FARTHING

Tin with square copper plug **Ruler:** William III **Obv:** Draped bust **Note:** Varieties exist.

Date	Mintage	VG	F	VF	XF	Unc
1687	—	70.00	400	1,400	—	—

KM# 466.1 FARTHING

Tin with square copper plug **Ruler:** William and Mary **Obv:** Large armored busts of William and Mary to right **Note:** Varieties exist.

Date	Mintage	VG	F	VF	XF	Unc
1689//90 Rare	—	—	—	—	—	—
Note: 1690 on reverse, 1689 on edge						
1690	—	75.00	250	850	3,500	—
1691	—	75.00	250	850	3,500	—
1692	—	75.00	250	850	3,500	—

KM# 465 FARTHING

Tin with square copper plug **Ruler:** William and Mary **Obv:** Small draped bust of William and Mary right **Rev:** Date in exergue **Edge:** Date

Date	Mintage	VG	F	VF	XF	Unc
1689	—	675	900	—	—	—
1689//90 Rare	—	—	—	—	—	—
Note: 1689 on reverse, 1690 on edge						

KM# 465a FARTHING

Copper **Ruler:** William and Mary **Edge:** Plain

Date	Mintage	VG	F	VF	XF	Unc
1689 Proof	—	—	—	—	—	—

KM# 466.1a FARTHING

Copper **Ruler:** William and Mary **Edge:** Plain

Date	Mintage	VG	F	VF	XF	Unc
1690 Proof	—	—	—	—	—	—

KM# 466.2 FARTHING

Copper **Ruler:** William and Mary **Rev:** Date in exergue **Note:** Varieties exist.

Date	Mintage	VG	F	VF	XF	Unc
1693 Rare	—	—	—	—	—	—
1694	—	25.00	100	400	1,175	—

KM# 466.2a FARTHING

Silver **Ruler:** William and Mary **Note:** Varieties exist.

Date	Mintage	VG	F	VF	XF	Unc
1694 Proof	—	—	—	—	—	—

KM# 483.1 FARTHING

Copper **Ruler:** William III **Obv:** Laureate bust of William III right **Rev:** Britannia seated left, date in exergue **Note:** Varieties exist.

Date	Mintage	VG	F	VF	XF	Unc
1695	—	18.00	65.00	250	1,050	—
1696	—	18.00	65.00	250	1,050	—
1697	—	35.00	70.00	300	1,050	—
1698	—	50.00	350	600	1,350	—
1699	—	18.00	65.00	250	1,050	—
1700	—	15.00	55.00	185	1,050	—

KM# 483.1a FARTHING

Silver **Ruler:** William III

Date	Mintage	VG	F	VF	XF	Unc
1695 Proof	—	—	—	—	—	—
1696 Proof	—	—	—	—	—	—
1697 Proof	—	—	—	—	—	—
1700 Proof	—	—	—	—	—	—

KM# 483.2 FARTHING

Copper **Ruler:** William III **Rev:** Date at end of legend **Note:** Varieties exist.

Date	Mintage	VG	F	VF	XF	Unc
1698	—	18.00	90.00	375	1,250	—
1699	—	18.00	75.00	375	1,250	—

KM# 483.2a FARTHING

Silver **Ruler:** William III

Date	Mintage	VG	F	VF	XF	Unc
1698 Proof	—	—	—	—	—	—
1699 Proof	—	—	—	—	—	—

KM# 437 1/2 PENNY

Copper **Ruler:** Charles II **Obv:** Laureate head of Charles II **Rev:** Date in exergue **Note:** Varieties exist.

Date	Mintage	VG	F	VF	XF	Unc
1672	—	22.00	90.00	400	1,650	—
1673	—	21.00	90.00	375	1,500	—
1675	—	22.00	90.00	650	1,750	—

KM# 448 1/2 PENNY

Tin with square copper plug **Ruler:** James II **Obv:** Laureate head of James II right **Edge:** Date **Note:** Varieties exist.

Date	Mintage	VG	F	VF	XF	Unc
1685	—	90.00	260	1,000	4,500	—
1686	—	110	290	1,025	4,500	—
1687	—	90.00	275	1,000	4,500	—

KM# 467 1/2 PENNY

Tin **Ruler:** William and Mary **Obv:** Small draped busts of William and Mary right **Edge:** Date **Note:** Varieties exist.

Date	Mintage	VG	F	VF	XF	Unc
1689	—	850	1,700	2,700	—	—

KM# 475.1 1/2 PENNY

Tin **Ruler:** William and Mary **Obv:** Large armored busts of William and Mary right **Edge:** Date **Note:** Varieties exist.

Date	Mintage	VG	F	VF	XF	Unc
1690	—	75.00	275	850	4,000	—

KM# 475.2 1/2 PENNY

Tin **Ruler:** William and Mary **Rev:** Date in exergue **Edge:** Date **Note:** Varieties exist.

Date	Mintage	VG	F	VF	XF	Unc
1691	—	70.00	275	850	4,000	—
1691//2	—	—	—	—	—	—
Note: 1691 in exergue, 1692 on edge						
1692	—	70.00	250	825	3,600	—

KM# 475.3 1/2 PENNY

Copper **Ruler:** William and Mary **Rev:** Date in exergue, plain edge **Note:** Varieties exist.

Date	Mintage	VG	F	VF	XF	Unc
1694	—	25.00	80.00	365	1,650	—

KM# A483.1 1/2 PENNY

Copper **Ruler:** William III **Obv:** Laureate head of William III right **Note:** Varieties exist.

Date	Mintage	VG	F	VF	XF	Unc
1695	—	28.00	50.00	225	1,300	—
1696	—	28.00	50.00	200	1,300	—
1697	—	28.00	60.00	200	1,300	—
1698	—	28.00	65.00	250	1,300	—

KM# A483.2 1/2 PENNY

Copper **Ruler:** William III **Rev:** Date in legend **Note:** Varieties exist.

Date	Mintage	VG	F	VF	XF	Unc
1698	—	18.00	70.00	280	1,400	—
1699	—	13.00	55.00	250	1,250	—

KM# 503 1/2 PENNY
Copper **Ruler:** William III **Obv:** Laureate head right **Rev:** Britannia seated left with right hand near knee, date in exergue **Note:** Varieties exist.

Date	Mintage	VG	F	VF	XF	Unc
1699	—	15.00	70.00	235	1,300	—
1700	—	12.00	70.00	240	1,300	—

KM# 396 PENNY
Silver **Ruler:** Charles II **Obv:** Crowned bust of Charles II left **Rev:** Shield of arms on long cross **Note:** First Issue - without inner circles or value. Varieties exist.

Date	Mintage	VG	F	VF	XF	Unc
ND(1660-62)	—	20.00	40.00	100	225	—

KM# 432 PENNY
Silver **Ruler:** Charles II **Obv:** Laureate bust of Charles II right **Rev:** Crowned C, crown divides date **Note:** Varieties exist.

Date	Mintage	VG	F	VF	XF	Unc
1670	—	7.00	15.00	50.00	200	—
1671	—	7.00	15.00	50.00	200	—
1672/1	—	7.00	15.00	50.00	200	—
1673	—	7.00	15.00	50.00	200	—
1674	—	7.00	15.00	50.00	200	—
1675	—	7.00	15.00	50.00	200	—
1676	—	7.00	15.00	50.00	200	—
1677	—	7.00	15.00	50.00	200	—
1678	—	7.00	15.00	50.00	200	—
1679	—	10.00	18.00	50.00	200	—
1680	—	7.00	15.00	50.00	200	—
1680/79	—	7.00	15.00	50.00	200	—
1681	—	8.00	16.00	50.00	200	—
1681/0	—	7.00	15.00	50.00	200	—
1682/1	—	8.00	16.00	50.00	200	—
1682	—	7.00	15.00	50.00	200	—
1683/1	—	7.00	15.00	50.00	200	—
1683/2	—	7.00	15.00	50.00	200	—
1684/3	—	8.00	16.00	50.00	200	—
1684	—	7.00	15.00	75.00	300	—

KM# 449 PENNY
Silver **Ruler:** James II **Obv:** Laureate head of James II right **Rev:** Crowned Roman numeral I, crown divides date

Date	Mintage	VG	F	VF	XF	Unc
1685	—	9.00	17.00	70.00	200	—
1685 Prooflike	—	—	—	—	—	—
1686	—	9.00	17.00	70.00	200	—
1687/6	—	9.00	17.00	70.00	200	—
1687/8	—	11.00	22.00	70.00	200	—
1687	—	9.00	17.00	70.00	200	—
1688/7	—	9.00	17.00	70.00	200	—
1688	—	9.00	17.00	70.00	200	—

KM# 468.1 PENNY
Silver **Ruler:** William and Mary **Obv:** Conjoined busts of William and Mary right, continuous legend **Rev:** Crowned Roman numeral I, date above crown **Note:** Varieties exist.

Date	Mintage	VG	F	VF	XF	Unc
1689	—	85.00	240	800	1,300	—

KM# 468.2 PENNY
Silver **Ruler:** William and Mary **Obv:** Legend broken at top **Note:** Varieties exist.

Date	Mintage	VG	F	VF	XF	Unc
1690	—	18.00	30.00	75.00	300	—
1691/0	—	20.00	40.00	95.00	350	—
1691	—	18.00	40.00	90.00	350	—
1692/1	—	22.50	35.00	90.00	375	—
1692	—	18.00	35.00	90.00	350	—
1693	—	18.00	30.00	80.00	300	—
1694	—	18.00	30.00	65.00	240	—

KM# 499 PENNY
Silver **Ruler:** William III **Obv:** Laureate head right **Rev:** Crowned Roman numeral I, crown divides date **Note:** Varieties exist.

Date	Mintage	VG	F	VF	XF	Unc
1698	—	20.00	42.25	80.00	250	—
1699	—	20.00	42.25	85.00	325	—
1700	—	20.00	42.25	65.00	250	—

KM# 429 2 PENCE (1/2 Groat)
Silver **Ruler:** Charles II **Obv:** Laureate bust of Charles II right **Note:** Varieties exist.

Date	Mintage	VG	F	VF	XF	Unc
1668	—	7.00	15.00	50.00	200	—
1668 Prooflike	—	—	—	—	—	—
1670	—	6.50	12.00	50.00	200	—
1671	—	6.00	10.00	50.00	200	—
1672/1	—	6.00	10.00	50.00	200	—
1673	—	6.00	10.00	50.00	200	—
1674	—	6.00	10.00	50.00	200	—
1675	—	6.00	10.00	50.00	200	—
1676	—	6.00	10.00	50.00	200	—
1677	—	6.00	10.00	50.00	200	—
1678/6	—	6.50	12.00	50.00	200	—
1678	—	6.00	10.00	50.00	200	—
1679	—	5.00	9.00	50.00	200	—
1680/79	—	6.00	10.00	50.00	200	—
1680	—	6.00	10.00	60.00	300	—
1681	—	6.00	10.00	55.00	225	—
1681/0	—	6.00	10.00	60.00	300	—
1682/1	—	6.00	10.00	60.00	300	—
1682	—	6.00	10.00	55.00	225	—
1683/2	—	6.00	10.00	65.00	225	—
1683	—	6.00	10.00	60.00	225	—
1684	—	6.00	10.00	60.00	225	—

KM# 454 2 PENCE (1/2 Groat)
Silver **Ruler:** James II **Obv:** Laureate head of James II left **Rev:** Crowned Roman numeral II, crown divides date **Note:** Varieties exist.

Date	Mintage	VG	F	VF	XF	Unc
1686	—	7.50	15.00	50.00	225	—
1687	—	7.50	15.00	50.00	225	—
1688/7	—	7.50	15.00	50.00	225	—
1688	—	7.50	15.00	50.00	225	—

KM# 469 2 PENCE (1/2 Groat)
Silver **Ruler:** William and Mary **Note:** Varieties exist.

Date	Mintage	VG	F	VF	XF	Unc
1689	—	15.00	40.00	80.00	325	—
1691	—	15.00	40.00	80.00	325	—
1692	—	15.00	35.00	80.00	325	—
1693/2	—	15.00	35.00	80.00	250	—
1693	—	15.00	30.00	60.00	250	—
1694/3	—	12.00	20.00	60.00	200	—
1694	—	18.00	20.00	60.00	200	—

KM# 500.1 2 PENCE (1/2 Groat)
Silver **Ruler:** William III **Obv:** Laureate bust right **Rev:** Crowned 2, large crown nearly touches rim

Date	Mintage	VG	F	VF	XF	Unc
1698	—	20.00	42.25	65.00	250	—

KM# 500.2 2 PENCE
Silver **Ruler:** William III **Obv:** Laureate bust right **Rev:** Crown smaller and lower

Date	Mintage	VG	F	VF	XF	Unc
1699	—	9.00	18.00	120	500	—
1700	—	9.00	18.00	80.00	350	—

KM# 433 3 PENCE
Silver **Ruler:** Charles II **Obv:** Bust of Charles II right **Note:** Varieties exist.

Date	Mintage	VG	F	VF	XF	Unc
1670	—	6.50	12.00	75.00	185	—
1671	—	6.50	12.00	75.00	185	—
1672/1	—	6.50	12.00	75.00	185	—
1673	—	6.00	10.00	60.00	185	—
1674	—	6.00	10.00	60.00	185	—
1675	—	6.50	12.00	75.00	185	—
1676/5	—	6.50	12.00	75.00	185	—
1676	—	6.00	10.00	60.00	185	—
1677	—	6.50	12.00	75.00	185	—
1678	—	6.00	10.00	60.00	185	—
1679	—	6.00	10.00	60.00	185	—
1680	—	6.00	10.00	60.00	185	—
1680/79	—	6.50	12.00	75.00	185	—
1681/0	—	6.50	12.00	75.00	185	—
1681	—	6.00	10.00	65.00	225	—
1682/1	—	6.50	12.00	75.00	200	—
1682	—	6.00	10.00	60.00	185	—
1683	—	6.00	10.00	60.00	185	—
1683/2	—	6.50	12.00	75.00	225	—
1684/3	—	6.50	12.00	75.00	225	—
1684	—	6.00	10.00	60.00	185	—

KM# 450 3 PENCE
Silver **Ruler:** James II **Obv:** Bust of James II left **Note:** Varieties exist.

Date	Mintage	VG	F	VF	XF	Unc
1685	—	6.50	12.00	55.00	215	—
1685 Prooflike	—	—	—	—	—	225
1686	—	6.50	12.00	55.00	215	—
1687/6	—	6.50	12.00	55.00	215	—
1687	—	8.00	15.00	60.00	225	—
1688/7	—	8.00	15.00	60.00	225	—
1688	—	6.50	12.00	55.00	215	—

KM# 470.1 3 PENCE
Silver **Ruler:** William and Mary **Obv:** Conjoined busts of William and Mary right without wreath tie **Rev:** Crowned 3, date above crown **Note:** Varieties exist.

Date	Mintage	VG	F	VF	XF	Unc
1689	—	8.00	26.00	85.00	325	—
1690	—	10.00	25.00	65.00	225	—
1691	—	22.50	45.00	130	400	—

KM# 470.2 3 PENCE
Silver **Ruler:** William and Mary **Obv:** With tie on wreath **Note:** Varieties exist.

Date	Mintage	VG	F	VF	XF	Unc
1691	—	15.00	40.00	130	350	—
1692	—	15.00	40.00	120	350	—
1693	—	15.00	60.00	90.00	300	—
1694	—	15.00	40.00	70.00	225	—
1695/2	—	15.00	40.00	100	200	—

KM# 501 3 PENCE
Silver **Ruler:** William III **Obv:** Laureate bust right **Rev:** Crowned 3, crown divides date **Note:** Varieties exist.

Date	Mintage	VG	F	VF	XF	Unc
1698	—	15.00	30.00	55.00	240	—
1699	—	15.00	30.00	65.00	300	—
1700	—	15.00	30.00	55.00	250	—

KM# 434 4 PENCE (Groat)
Silver **Ruler:** Charles II **Obv:** Bust of Charles II right **Note:** Varieties exist.

Date	Mintage	VG	F	VF	XF	Unc
1670	—	13.00	23.00	90.00	225	—
1671	—	9.00	15.00	65.00	200	—
1672/1	—	9.00	15.00	70.00	225	—
1673	—	9.00	15.00	70.00	225	—
1674/4	—	9.00	15.00	70.00	225	—
1674/574	—	9.00	15.00	70.00	225	—
1674/64	—	9.00	15.00	70.00	225	—
1674	—	9.00	15.00	70.00	225	—
1675/4	—	9.00	15.00	70.00	225	—

Date	Mintage	VG	F	VF	XF	Unc
1675	—	9.00	15.00	70.00	225	—
1676/66	—	9.00	15.00	70.00	225	—
1676/5	—	9.00	15.00	70.00	225	—
1676	—	9.00	15.00	70.00	225	—
1677	—	9.00	15.00	60.00	200	—
1678/6	—	9.00	15.00	60.00	200	—
1678/7	—	9.00	15.00	70.00	225	—
1678	—	9.00	15.00	60.00	200	—
1679	—	9.00	15.00	60.00	200	—
1680	—	9.00	15.00	60.00	200	—
1680/79	—	9.00	15.00	70.00	225	—
1681/0	—	9.00	15.00	70.00	225	—
1681	—	9.00	15.00	60.00	200	—
1682/1	—	9.00	15.00	70.00	225	—
1682	—	9.00	15.00	60.00	200	—
1683	—	9.00	15.00	60.00	200	—
1683/2	—	9.00	15.00	70.00	225	—
1684/3	—	9.00	15.00	60.00	200	—
1684	—	9.00	15.00	70.00	225	—

KM# 455.1 4 PENCE (Groat)
Silver **Ruler:** James II **Obv:** Bust of James II left

Date	Mintage	VG	F	VF	XF	Unc
1686	—	10.00	21.00	75.00	225	—
1687/6	—	10.00	18.00	60.00	225	—
1687/77	—	12.00	21.00	65.00	225	—
1687	—	10.00	18.00	60.00	225	—
1688/7	—	10.00	18.00	75.00	225	—
1688/8688	—	15.00	26.00	75.00	225	—
1688	—	10.00	18.00	75.00	225	—

KM# 455.2 4 PENCE (Groat)
Silver **Ruler:** James II **Rev:** Date above crown

Date	Mintage	VG	F	VF	XF	Unc
1686	—	12.00	22.00	45.00	125	—

KM# 471.1 4 PENCE (Groat)
Silver **Ruler:** William and Mary **Obv:** Conjoined busts of William and Mary without wreath tie **Note:** Varieties exist.

Date	Mintage	VG	F	VF	XF	Unc
1689	—	11.50	30.00	85.00	330	—
1690/1590	—	12.00	25.00	75.00	425	—
1690	—	12.00	25.00	75.00	275	—
1691/0	—	13.00	25.00	90.00	350	—
1691	—	13.00	25.00	90.00	375	—
1694	—	13.00	25.00	75.00	275	—

KM# 471.2 4 PENCE (Groat)
Silver **Ruler:** William and Mary **Obv:** Tie on wreath **Note:** Varieties exist.

Date	Mintage	VG	F	VF	XF	Unc
1692/1	—	13.00	27.50	85.00	325	—
1692	—	13.00	27.50	85.00	325	—
1693/2	—	13.00	25.00	70.00	275	—
1693	—	13.00	25.00	70.00	275	—
1694	—	13.00	25.00	70.00	275	—

KM# 495 4 PENCE (Groat)
Silver **Ruler:** William III **Obv:** Laureate bust right **Rev:** Crown above value divides date

Date	Mintage	VG	F	VF	XF	Unc
1697 Unique	—	—	—	—	—	—
1697 Prooflike	—	—	—	—	—	—
1698	—	15.00	35.00	125	500	—
1699	—	15.00	35.00	200	625	—
1700	—	15.00	35.00	125	500	—

KM# 441 6 PENCE
Silver **Ruler:** Charles II **Obv:** Bust of Charles II right

Date	Mintage	VG	F	VF	XF	Unc
1674	—	35.00	100	425	1,200	—
1675/4	—	35.00	100	425	1,225	—
1675	—	35.00	120	450	1,300	—
1676/5	—	50.00	100	425	1,400	—
1676	—	50.00	120	425	1,400	—
1677	—	35.00	100	425	1,200	—
1678/7	—	35.00	100	425	1,225	—
1679	—	35.00	100	425	1,225	—
1680	—	50.00	150	500	1,550	—
1681	—	35.00	100	450	1,225	—
1682/1	—	35.00	100	450	1,350	—
1682	—	50.00	125	550	1,350	—
1683	—	35.00	100	550	1,350	—
1684	—	50.00	100	550	1,350	—

KM# 456.1 6 PENCE
Silver **Ruler:** James II **Obv:** Bust of James II left **Rev:** Cruciform crowned Type I shields (dip in middle of the shield top)

Date	Mintage	VG	F	VF	XF	Unc
1686	—	55.00	175	625	1,650	—
1687/6	—	55.00	175	625	1,650	—

KM# 456.2 6 PENCE
Silver **Ruler:** James II **Rev:** Type II shields (rise in the middle of shield top)

Date	Mintage	VG	F	VF	XF	Unc
1687/6	—	55.00	175	650	1,250	—
1687	—	55.00	175	600	1,100	—
1688	—	55.00	175	650	1,250	—

KM# 481 6 PENCE
Silver **Ruler:** William and Mary **Obv:** Conjoined bust of William and Mary right **Rev:** Cruciform crowned arms with WM monograms and date numerals in angles **Note:** Varieties exist.

Date	Mintage	VG	F	VF	XF	Unc
1693	—	45.00	200	850	1,900	—
1693 Inverted 3	—	45.00	200	850	1,900	—
1694	—	55.00	220	850	2,000	—

KM# 484.1 6 PENCE
Silver **Ruler:** William III **Obv:** First bust of William III right **Rev:** Cruciform crowned arms with early harp, date divided by crown **Note:** Varieties exist.

Date	Mintage	VG	F	VF	XF	Unc
1695	—	17.00	55.00	175	575	—
1696/5	—	16.00	55.00	175	575	—
1696	—	16.00	55.00	150	525	—

KM# 484.2 6 PENCE
Silver **Ruler:** William III **Obv:** First bust of William III right; B below bust **Rev:** Cruciform crowned arms with early harp, date divided by crown **Mint:** Bristol **Note:** Varieties exist.

Date	Mintage	VG	F	VF	XF	Unc
1696 B	—	17.00	55.00	150	600	—

KM# 484.3 6 PENCE
Silver **Ruler:** William III **Obv:** First bust of William III right; C below bust **Rev:** Cruciform crowned arms with early harp, date divided by crown **Mint:** Chester

Date	Mintage	VG	F	VF	XF	Unc
1696 C	—	25.00	60.00	165	650	—

KM# 484.4 6 PENCE
Silver **Ruler:** William III **Obv:** First bust of William III right; E below bust **Rev:** Cruciform crowned arms iwth early harp, date divided by crown **Mint:** Exeter

Date	Mintage	VG	F	VF	XF	Unc
1696 E	—	20.00	60.00	160	675	—

KM# 484.5 6 PENCE
Silver **Ruler:** William III **Obv:** First bust of William III right; N below bust **Rev:** Cruciform crowned arms with early harp, date divided by crown **Mint:** Norwich

Date	Mintage	VG	F	VF	XF	Unc
1696 N	—	25.00	65.00	175	700	—

KM# 484.6 6 PENCE
Silver **Ruler:** William III **Obv:** First bust of William III right; Y below bust **Rev:** Cruciform crowned arms with early harp, date divided by crown **Mint:** York

Date	Mintage	VG	F	VF	XF	Unc
1696 Y	—	20.00	90.00	400	1,000	—

KM# 484.7 6 PENCE
Silver **Ruler:** William III **Obv:** First bust of William III right; script Y below bust **Rev:** Cruciform crowned arms iwth early harp, date divided by crown **Mint:** York **Note:** Varieties exist.

Date	Mintage	VG	F	VF	XF	Unc
1696	—	14.00	60.00	160	700	—

KM# 484.8 6 PENCE
Silver **Ruler:** William III **Obv:** First bust of William III right **Rev:** Late harp, large crowns **Note:** Varieties exist.

Date	Mintage	VG	F	VF	XF	Unc
1696	—	25.00	85.00	250	675	—

KM# 484.9 6 PENCE
Silver **Ruler:** William III **Obv:** First bust of William III right; B below bust **Rev:** Late harp, large crowns **Mint:** Bristol **Note:** Varieties exist.

Date	Mintage	VG	F	VF	XF	Unc
1696 B	—	30.00	105	350	825	—
1697 B	—	22.50	70.00	160	650	—

KM# 484.10 6 PENCE
Silver **Ruler:** William III **Obv:** First bust of William III right; C below bust **Rev:** Late harp, large crowns **Mint:** Chester

Date	Mintage	VG	F	VF	XF	Unc
1697 C	—	40.00	80.00	200	700	—

KM# 484.11 6 PENCE
Silver **Ruler:** William III **Obv:** First bust of William III right; E below bust **Rev:** Late harp, large crowns **Mint:** Exeter

Date	Mintage	VG	F	VF	XF	Unc
1697 E	—	40.00	80.00	175	650	—

KM# 484.12 6 PENCE
Silver **Ruler:** William III **Obv:** First bust of William III right **Rev:** Late harp, small crowns **Note:** Varieties exist.

Date	Mintage	VG	F	VF	XF	Unc
1697	—	10.00	45.00	120	450	—

KM# 484.13 6 PENCE
Silver **Ruler:** William III **Obv:** First bust of William III right; B below bust **Rev:** Late harp, small crowns **Mint:** Bristol **Note:** Varieties exist.

Date	Mintage	VG	F	VF	XF	Unc
1696 B	—	35.00	100	250	700	—
1697 B	—	24.00	65.00	160	600	—

KM# 484.14 6 PENCE
Silver **Ruler:** William III **Obv:** First bust of William III right; C below bust **Rev:** Late harp, small crowns **Mint:** Chester **Note:** Varieties exist.

Date	Mintage	VG	F	VF	XF	Unc
1696 C	—	30.00	110	425	900	—
1697 C	—	30.00	75.00	185	650	—

KM# 484.15 6 PENCE
Silver **Ruler:** William III **Obv:** First bust of William III right; E below bust **Rev:** Late harp, small crowns **Mint:** Exeter **Note:** Varieties exist.

Date	Mintage	VG	F	VF	XF	Unc
1697 E	—	24.00	65.00	165	625	—

KM# 484.16 6 PENCE
Silver **Ruler:** William III **Obv:** First bust of William III right; N below bust **Rev:** Late harp, small crowns **Mint:** Norwich

Date	Mintage	VG	F	VF	XF	Unc
1696 N	—	30.00	85.00	200	625	—
1697 N	—	30.00	85.00	200	625	—

KM# 484.17 6 PENCE
Silver **Ruler:** William III **Obv:** First bust of William III right; script Y below bust **Rev:** Late harp, small crowns **Mint:** York **Note:** Varieties exist.

Date	Mintage	VG	F	VF	XF	Unc
1697 y	—	40.00	80.00	300	750	—

KM# 489 6 PENCE
Silver **Ruler:** William III **Obv:** Second bust of William III **Note:** Varieties exist.

Date	Mintage	VG	F	VF	XF	Unc
1696	—	100	350	900	1,800	—
1697	—	45.00	200	550	1,700	—

KM# 496.2 6 PENCE
Silver **Ruler:** William III **Obv:** Third bust of William III right; B below bust **Rev:** Cruciform crowned arms, crown divides date, large crowns **Mint:** Bristol

Date	Mintage	VG	F	VF	XF	Unc
1697 B	—	24.00	65.00	165	675	—

KM# 496.3 6 PENCE
Silver **Ruler:** William III **Obv:** Third bust of William III right; C below bust **Rev:** Cruciform crowned arms, crown divides date, large crowns **Mint:** Chester

Date	Mintage	VG	F	VF	XF	Unc
1697 C	—	35.00	90.00	300	800	—

KM# 496.4 6 PENCE
Silver **Ruler:** William III **Obv:** Third bust of William III right; E below bust **Rev:** Cruciform crowned arms, crown divides date, large crowns **Mint:** Exeter

Date	Mintage	VG	F	VF	XF	Unc
1697 E	—	35.00	85.00	275	775	—

KM# 496.5 6 PENCE
Silver **Ruler:** William III **Obv:** Third bust of William III right; E below bust **Rev:** Cruciform crowned arms, crown divides date, small crowns **Note:** Varieties exist.

Date	Mintage	VG	F	VF	XF	Unc
1697 E	—	35.00	80.00	260	725	—

KM# 496.6 6 PENCE
Silver **Ruler:** William III **Obv:** Third bust of William III right; C below bust **Rev:** Cruciform crowned arms, crown divides date, small crowns **Mint:** Chester

Date	Mintage	VG	F	VF	XF	Unc
1697 C	—	40.00	80.00	300	775	—

KM# 496.7 6 PENCE
Silver **Ruler:** William III **Obv:** Third bust of William III right; E below bust **Rev:** Cruciform crowned arms, crown divides date, small crowns **Mint:** Exeter

Date	Mintage	VG	F	VF	XF	Unc
1697 E	—	40.00	80.00	275	750	—

KM# 496.8 6 PENCE
Silver **Ruler:** William III **Obv:** Third bust of William III right; Y below bust **Rev:** Cruciform crowned arms, crown divides date, small crowns **Mint:** York

Date	Mintage	VG	F	VF	XF	Unc
1697 Y	—	40.00	80.00	275	750	—

KM# 496.1 6 PENCE
Silver **Ruler:** William III **Obv:** Third bust right **Rev:** Cruciform crowned arms, crown divides date, large crown **Note:** Varieties exist.

Date	Mintage	VG	F	VF	XF	Unc
1697	—	14.00	40.00	115	450	—
1698	—	25.00	75.00	220	625	—
1699	—	45.00	110	350	1,000	—
1700	—	17.00	90.00	135	500	—

KM# 496.9 6 PENCE
Silver **Ruler:** William III **Obv:** Third bust of William III right **Rev:** Cruciform crowned arms, crown divides date

Date	Mintage	VG	F	VF	XF	Unc
1698	—	30.00	65.00	250	825	—
1699	—	40.00	110	340	925	—

KM# 496.10 6 PENCE
Silver **Ruler:** William III **Rev:** Roses in angles **Note:** Varieties exist.

Date	Mintage	VG	F	VF	XF	Unc
1699	—	35.00	120	350	1,000	—

KM# 496.11 6 PENCE
Silver **Ruler:** William III **Rev:** Plain fields in angles

Date	Mintage	VG	F	VF	XF	Unc
1700 Rare	—	—	—	—	—	—

KM# 418.1 SHILLING
Silver **Ruler:** Charles II **Obv:** First bust of Charles II right **Rev:** Crowned cruciform arms with linked C's in angles, date divided at top **Note:** Varieties exist.

Date	Mintage	VG	F	VF	XF	Unc
1663	—	60.00	140	700	1,700	—

KM# 418.2 SHILLING
Silver **Ruler:** Charles II **Obv:** First bust variety of Charles II - one leaf at top of wreath, three curls behind head

Date	Mintage	VG	F	VF	XF	Unc
1663	—	60.00	140	700	1,700	—
1666 Rare	—	—	—	—	—	—
1668	—	250	445	1,300	3,000	—
1669 Rare	—	—	—	—	—	—
1669/6 Rare	—	—	—	—	—	—

KM# 427.1 SHILLING
Silver **Ruler:** Charles II **Obv:** Second bust of Charles II **Note:** Varieties exist.

Date	Mintage	VG	F	VF	XF	Unc
1666	—	1,100	2,300	6,500	13,000	—
1668/7	—	60.00	160	650	1,750	—
1668	—	40.00	125	500	1,500	—
1669 Rare	—	—	—	—	—	—
1670	—	55.00	160	700	1,850	—
1671	—	60.00	175	750	2,200	—
1672	—	45.00	145	550	1,700	—
1673/2	—	100	200	800	2,500	—
1673	—	65.00	165	700	1,950	—
1674/3	—	70.00	200	800	1,900	—
1674	—	85.00	185	700	2,200	—
1675/4	—	115	350	1,700	3,100	—
1675	—	95.00	260	850	1,500	—
1676/5	—	85.00	250	800	1,450	—
1676	—	55.00	150	550	1,750	—
1677	—	55.00	150	500	1,700	—
1678/7	—	60.00	165	850	1,850	—
1678	—	60.00	165	650	1,800	—
1679/7	—	50.00	155	750	1,800	—
1679	—	50.00	145	575	1,750	—
1680 Rare	—	—	—	—	—	—
1681/0	—	75.00	265	875	2,600	—
1681	—	75.00	275	875	2,550	—
1682/1	—	300	875	2,350	—	—
1683 Rare	—	—	—	—	—	—

KM# 418.3 SHILLING
Silver **Ruler:** Charles II **Obv:** First bust variety of Charles II with elephant below

Date	Mintage	VG	F	VF	XF	Unc
1666	—	190	650	2,250	7,250	—

KM# 426 SHILLING
Silver **Ruler:** Charles II **Obv:** GUINEA head of Charles II right with elephant below **Note:** This obverse die was also used to strike the gold guinea, KM#424.2.

Date	Mintage	VG	F	VF	XF	Unc
1666	—	1,250	3,100	7,000	—	—

KM# 485.1 SHILLING
Silver **Ruler:** William III **Obv:** First bust of William III **Rev:** Lion at center **Note:** Varieties exist.

Date	Mintage	VG	F	VF	XF	Unc
1669 Rare; error	—	—	—	—	—	—
1695	—	14.00	60.00	200	925	—
1696/5	—	—	—	—	—	—
1696	—	14.00	60.00	150	650	—
1697	—	14.00	60.00	150	650	—

KM# 427.2 SHILLING
Silver **Ruler:** Charles II **Obv:** Plume added below bust **Rev:** Plume at center of arms

Date	Mintage	VG	F	VF	XF	Unc
1671	—	165	600	1,300	5,000	—
1673	—	150	550	1,350	5,000	—
1674	—	150	575	1,300	5,000	—
1675	—	165	600	1,450	5,200	—
1676	—	165	600	1,350	5,000	—
1679	—	175	625	1,450	5,000	—
1680/79	—	235	675	1,950	5,700	—
1680	—	185	825	2,300	5,750	—

KM# 427.3 SHILLING
Silver **Ruler:** Charles II **Rev:** Plume at center of arms

Date	Mintage	VG	F	VF	XF	Unc
1674	—	150	600	1,700	5,250	—

KM# 442 SHILLING
Silver **Ruler:** Charles II **Obv:** Third (large) bust of Charles II, ties turn down

Date	Mintage	VG	F	VF	XF	Unc
1674	—	125	400	1,550	4,250	—
1675/3	—	205	425	1,250	4,000	—
1675	—	75.00	375	1,050	2,250	—

KM# 427.4 SHILLING
Silver **Ruler:** Charles II **Obv:** Plume below bust

Date	Mintage	VG	F	VF	XF	Unc
1677	—	300	750	1,825	5,750	—
1679	—	250	625	1,450	5,250	—

KM# 427.5 SHILLING
Silver **Ruler:** Charles II **Obv:** Elephant and castle below bust

Date	Mintage	VG	F	VF	XF	Unc
1681/0	—	1,500	5,000	—	—	—

KM# 446 SHILLING
Silver **Ruler:** Charles II **Obv:** Fourth bust of Charles II, ties turn up

Date	Mintage	VG	F	VF	XF	Unc
1683	—	80.00	300	975	3,400	—
1684	—	75.00	240	850	2,950	—

KM# 451.2 SHILLING
Silver **Ruler:** James II **Rev:** Plume at center of arms

Date	Mintage	VG	F	VF	XF	Unc
1685 Rare	—	—	—	—	—	—

KM# 451.1 SHILLING
Silver **Ruler:** James II **Obv:** Bust of James II left **Note:** Varieties exist.

Date	Mintage	VG	F	VF	XF	Unc
1685	—	75.00	200	675	1,650	—
1686/5	—	75.00	200	775	2,400	—
1686	—	75.00	200	775	2,450	—
1687/6	—	75.00	200	775	2,450	—
1687	—	85.00	350	755	2,650	—
1688/7	—	85.00	350	800	2,600	—
1688	—	75.00	200	800	2,600	—

KM# 480 SHILLING

Silver **Ruler:** William and Mary **Obv:** Conjoined busts of William and Mary right **Rev:** Crowned cruciform arms with WM monograms in angles and numerals of date **Note:** Varieties exist.

Date	Mintage	VG	F	VF	XF	Unc
1692	—	65.00	240	850	2,850	—
1692 inverted 1	—	85.00	300	900	3,000	—
1693	—	55.00	240	825	2,850	—

KM# 497.6 SHILLING

Silver **Ruler:** William III **Obv:** Third bust (short ties) of William III; script y below bust **Mint:** York

Date	Mintage	VG	F	VF	XF	Unc
1696 y Rare	—	—	—	—	—	—
1697 y	—	17.50	70.00	220	850	—

KM# 485.2 SHILLING

Silver **Ruler:** William III **Obv:** First bust of William III; B below bust **Rev:** Lion at center **Mint:** Bristol

Date	Mintage	VG	F	VF	XF	Unc
1696 B	—	14.00	75.00	225	1,050	—
1697 B	—	14.00	75.00	225	1,050	—

KM# 490 SHILLING

Silver **Ruler:** William III **Obv:** Second bust (hair across breast) of William III

Date	Mintage	VG	F	VF	XF	Unc
1696 Unique	—	—	—	—	—	—

KM# 485.3 SHILLING

Silver **Ruler:** William III **Obv:** First bust of William III; C below bust **Rev:** Lion at center **Mint:** Chester **Note:** Varieties exist.

Date	Mintage	VG	F	VF	XF	Unc
1696 C	—	12.50	75.00	225	1,050	—
1697 C	—	9.00	75.00	215	1,000	—

KM# 485.4 SHILLING

Silver **Ruler:** William III **Obv:** First bust of William III; E below bust **Rev:** Lion at center **Mint:** Exeter **Note:** Varieties exist.

Date	Mintage	VG	F	VF	XF	Unc
1696 E	—	14.00	75.00	250	1,150	—
1697 E	—	15.00	75.00	250	1,000	—

KM# 485.5 SHILLING

Silver **Ruler:** William III **Obv:** First bust of William III; N below bust **Rev:** Lion at center **Mint:** Norwich **Note:** Varieties exist.

Date	Mintage	VG	F	VF	XF	Unc
1696 N	—	14.00	75.00	425	1,075	—
1697 N	—	15.00	75.00	425	1,000	—

KM# 485.6 SHILLING

Silver **Ruler:** William III **Obv:** First bust of William III; script Y below bust **Rev:** Lion at center **Mint:** York **Note:** Varieties exist.

Date	Mintage	VG	F	VF	XF	Unc
1696 y	—	12.50	65.00	225	1,050	—
1697 y	—	15.00	60.00	210	900	—

KM# 485.7 SHILLING

Silver **Ruler:** William III **Obv:** First bust of William III; Y below bust **Rev:** Lion at center **Mint:** York **Note:** Varieties exist.

Date	Mintage	VG	F	VF	XF	Unc
1696 Y	—	16.50	70.00	225	1,075	—
1697 Y	—	16.00	65.00	210	950	—

KM# 497.3 SHILLING

Silver **Ruler:** William III **Obv:** Third bust (short ties) of William III; C below bust **Mint:** Chester **Note:** Varieties exist.

Date	Mintage	VG	F	VF	XF	Unc
1696 C	—	65.00	220	725	1,850	—
1697 C	—	18.00	60.00	200	850	—

KM# 497.7 SHILLING

Silver **Ruler:** William III **Obv:** Third bust, long thin ties with y below **Mint:** York **Note:** Varieties exist.

Date	Mintage	VG	F	VF	XF	Unc
1697 y	—	11.00	60.00	200	825	—

KM# 497.9 SHILLING

Silver **Ruler:** William III **Obv:** Third bust (short ties) of William III; C below bust **Mint:** Chester **Note:** Varieties exist.

Date	Mintage	VG	F	VF	XF	Unc
1697 C	—	25.00	180	800	—	—

KM# 497.1 SHILLING

Silver **Ruler:** William III **Obv:** Third bust (short ties) of William III **Note:** Varieties exist.

Date	Mintage	VG	F	VF	XF	Unc
1697	—	16.00	50.00	170	750	—

KM# 497.2 SHILLING

Silver **Ruler:** William III **Obv:** Third bust (short ties) of William III; B below bust **Mint:** Bristol **Note:** Varieties exist.

Date	Mintage	VG	F	VF	XF	Unc
1697 B	—	19.00	85.00	225	925	—

KM# 497.4 SHILLING

Silver **Ruler:** William III **Obv:** Third bust (short ties) of William III; E below bust **Mint:** Exeter

Date	Mintage	VG	F	VF	XF	Unc
1697 E	—	17.50	75.00	215	850	—

KM# 497.5 SHILLING

Silver **Ruler:** William III **Obv:** Third bust (short ties) of William III; N below bust **Mint:** Norwich

Date	Mintage	VG	F	VF	XF	Unc
1697 N	—	17.50	60.00	215	850	—

KM# 497.8 SHILLING

Silver **Ruler:** William III **Obv:** Long, thin ties; B below bust **Mint:** Bristol

Date	Mintage	VG	F	VF	XF	Unc
1697 B	—	1,650	70.00	200	900	—

KM# 497.10 SHILLING

Silver **Ruler:** William III **Obv:** Third bust (short ties) of William III **Rev:** Plumes in angles **Mint:** Chester

Date	Mintage	VG	F	VF	XF	Unc
1698	—	90.00	300	800	2,300	—

KM# 502 SHILLING

Silver **Ruler:** William III **Obv:** Fourth bust (flaming hair) of William III **Note:** Varieties exist.

Date	Mintage	VG	F	VF	XF	Unc
1698	—	37.50	200	700	2,700	—
1699	—	37.50	150	500	1,850	—
1699 Plain edge; Proof	—	—	—	—	—	—

KM# 504.1 SHILLING

Silver **Ruler:** William III **Obv:** Fifth bust (hair high) **Note:** Varieties exist.

Date	Mintage	VG	F	VF	XF	Unc
1699	—	40.00	130	425	1,250	—
1700 Circular 0s	—	13.50	50.00	175	625	—
1700 Oval 0s	—	13.50	50.00	175	625	—

KM# 504.2 SHILLING

Silver **Ruler:** William III **Rev:** Plumes in angles

Date	Mintage	VG	F	VF	XF	Unc
1699	—	35.00	160	650	1,900	—

KM# 504.3 SHILLING

Silver **Ruler:** William III **Obv:** Fifth bust (hair high) of William III **Rev:** Roses in angles

Date	Mintage	VG	F	VF	XF	Unc
1699	—	40.00	125	500	1,800	—

KM# 504.4 SHILLING

Silver **Ruler:** William III **Obv:** Fifth bust (hair high) of William III, plume below bust

Date	Mintage	VG	F	VF	XF	Unc
1700	—	800	3,000	6,000	—	—

KM# 419 1/2 CROWN

Silver **Ruler:** Charles II **Obv:** First bust of Charles II right **Rev:** Crowned cruciform arms with linked C's in angles **Edge:** Regnal year on edge in Roman numerals **Note:** Varieties exist.

Date	Mintage	VG	F	VF	XF	Unc
1663	—	125	250	700	4,000	—

KM# 421 1/2 CROWN

Silver **Ruler:** Charles II **Obv:** Second bust (broader) of Charles II right

Date	Mintage	VG	F	VF	XF	Unc
1664	—	100	225	700	4,500	—

KM# 428.1 1/2 CROWN

Silver **Ruler:** Charles II **Obv:** Third bust (smaller) of Charles II right

Date	Mintage	VG	F	VF	XF	Unc
1666/?	—	650	1,800	—	—	—

KM# 428.2 1/2 CROWN

Silver **Ruler:** Charles II **Rev:** Different die

Date	Mintage	VG	F	VF	XF	Unc
1666/4	—	650	1,800	—	—	—

KM# 428.3 1/2 CROWN

Silver **Ruler:** Charles II **Obv:** Elephant below bust

Date	Mintage	VG	F	VF	XF	Unc
1666	—	600	1,000	2,000	8,000	—

KM# 428.4 1/2 CROWN

Silver **Ruler:** Charles II **Edge:** Regnal year in words **Note:** Varieties exist.

Date	Mintage	VG	F	VF	XF	Unc
1667/4 Rare	—	—	—	—	—	—
1668/4	—	100	325	1,200	3,000	—
1669/4	—	100	325	1,300	3,200	—
1669	—	200	5,500	2,400	6,000	—
1670	—	40.00	130	650	3,750	—

KM# 428.5 1/2 CROWN

Silver **Ruler:** Charles II **Obv:** Variety of the third bust of Charles II **Note:** Varieties exist.

Date	Mintage	VG	F	VF	XF	Unc
1671/0	—	52.50	165	850	4,400	—
1671	—	35.00	130	550	3,950	—
1672	—	50.00	140	750	3,700	—

KM# 438.1 1/2 CROWN

Silver **Ruler:** Charles II **Obv:** Fourth bust of Charles II **Note:** Varieties exist.

Date	Mintage	VG	F	VF	XF	Unc
1672	—	60.00	200	750	3,950	—
1673	—	35.00	130	525	3,750	—
1674/3	—	125	275	1,150	—	—
1674	—	75.00	185	850	—	—
1675	—	50.00	150	575	3,300	—
1676	—	45.00	140	525	2,900	—
1677	—	35.00	140	475	2,700	—
1678	—	100	325	1,225	—	—
1679	—	45.00	140	575	3,200	—
1680	—	100	275	950	—	—
1681/0	—	75.00	260	—	—	—
1681	—	40.00	1,600	675	2,100	—
1682/79	—	145	325	—	—	—
1682/1	—	65.00	200	775	4,250	—
1682	—	50.00	175	675	4,750	—
1683	—	40.00	160	575	3,500	—
1684/3	—	80.00	325	1,200	5,500	—

KM# 438.2 1/2 CROWN
Silver **Ruler:** Charles II **Obv:** Plume below bust

Date	Mintage	VG	F	VF	XF	Unc
1673 Rare	—	—	—	—	—	—
1683 Rare	—	—	—	—	—	—

KM# 438.3 1/2 CROWN
Silver **Ruler:** Charles II **Rev:** Plume at center of cruciform arms

Date	Mintage	VG	F	VF	XF	Unc
1673 Rare	—	—	—	—	—	—

KM# 438.4 1/2 CROWN
Silver **Ruler:** Charles II **Obv:** Elephant and castle below bust **Rev:** Garter star at center of cruciform arms

Date	Mintage	VG	F	VF	XF	Unc
1681 Rare	—	—	—	—	—	—

KM# 452 1/2 CROWN
Silver **Ruler:** James II **Obv:** First bust of James II left **Rev:** Crown above value divides date **Note:** Varieties exist.

Date	Mintage	VG	F	VF	XF	Unc
1685	—	75.00	260	875	3,750	—
1686/5	—	140	360	1,200	4,750	—
1686	—	75.00	260	900	4,000	—
1687/6	—	75.00	300	1,050	4,300	—
1687	—	75.00	275	925	3,300	—

KM# 462 1/2 CROWN
Silver **Ruler:** James II **Obv:** Second bust of James II left, ties at back of head curve upward

Date	Mintage	VG	F	VF	XF	Unc
1687	—	100	275	850	3,350	—
1688	—	90.00	275	850	3,400	—

KM# 472.1 1/2 CROWN
Silver **Ruler:** William and Mary **Obv:** First busts of William and Mary **Note:** Varieties exist.

Date	Mintage	VG	F	VF	XF	Unc
1689	—	45.00	125	500	2,150	—

KM# 472.2 1/2 CROWN
Silver **Ruler:** William and Mary **Obv:** First and fourth quarters quartered with arms of France and England **Note:** Varieties exist.

Date	Mintage	VG	F	VF	XF	Unc
1689	—	45.00	125	525	2,200	—
1690	—	50.00	175	925	4,000	—

KM# 477 1/2 CROWN
Silver **Ruler:** William and Mary **Obv:** Second busts (finer style) of William and Mary right **Rev:** Crowned cruciform arms with WM monograms, date numerals in angles **Note:** Varieties exist.

Date	Mintage	VG	F	VF	XF	Unc
1691	—	45.00	160	700	3,100	—
1692	—	45.00	160	700	3,100	—
1693	—	45.00	160	675	3,100	—
1693 3 over inverted 3	—	50.00	180	750	3,250	—

KM# 491.1 1/2 CROWN
Silver **Ruler:** William III **Obv:** First bust of William III right **Rev:** Crowned cruciform arms with large shields and early harp **Note:** Varieties exist.

Date	Mintage	VG	F	VF	XF	Unc
1696	—	35.00	85.00	300	1,100	—

KM# 491.6 1/2 CROWN
Silver **Ruler:** William III **Obv:** First bust of William III right; script y below bust **Rev:** Crowned cruciform arms with large shields and early harp **Mint:** York **Note:** Varieties exist.

Date	Mintage	VG	F	VF	XF	Unc
1696 y	—	45.00	130	600	1,900	—

KM# 491.7 1/2 CROWN
Silver **Ruler:** William III **Obv:** First bust of William III right **Rev:** Crowned cruciform arms with large shields and ordinary harp **Note:** Varieties exist.

Date	Mintage	VG	F	VF	XF	Unc
1696	—	75.00	150	700	1,800	—
1697/6	—	—	—	—	—	—
1697	—	30.00	90.00	365	1,200	—

KM# 491.9 1/2 CROWN
Silver **Ruler:** William III **Obv:** First bust of William III right; C below bust **Rev:** Crowned cruciform arms with large shields and ordinary harp **Mint:** Chester **Note:** Varieties exist.

Date	Mintage	VG	F	VF	XF	Unc
1696 C	—	75.00	175	800	2,650	—
1697 C	—	55.00	110	550	1,850	—

KM# 491.10 1/2 CROWN
Silver **Ruler:** William III **Obv:** First bust of William III right; E below bust **Rev:** Crowned cruciform arms with large shields and ordinary harp **Mint:** Exeter **Note:** Varieties exist.

Date	Mintage	VG	F	VF	XF	Unc
1696 E	—	40.00	175	800	2,650	—
1697 E	—	35.00	110	500	1,700	—

KM# 491.11 1/2 CROWN
Silver **Ruler:** William III **Obv:** First bust of William III right; N below bust **Rev:** Crowned cruciform arms with large shields and ordinary harp **Mint:** Norwich **Note:** Varieties exist.

Date	Mintage	VG	F	VF	XF	Unc
1696 N	—	100	180	700	2,250	—
1697 N	—	55.00	125	575	1,850	—

KM# 491.13 1/2 CROWN
Silver **Ruler:** William III **Rev:** Crowned cruciform arms with small shields **Note:** Varieties exist.

Date	Mintage	VG	F	VF	XF	Unc
1696	—	35.00	100	400	1,300	—

KM# 491.2 1/2 CROWN
Silver **Ruler:** William III **Obv:** First bust of William III right; B below bust **Rev:** Crowned cruciform arms with large shields and early harp **Mint:** Bristol

Date	Mintage	VG	F	VF	XF	Unc
1696 B	—	30.00	120	440	1,600	—

KM# 491.3 1/2 CROWN
Silver **Ruler:** William III **Obv:** First bust of William III right; C below bust **Rev:** Crowned cruciform arms with large shields and early harp **Mint:** Chester

Date	Mintage	VG	F	VF	XF	Unc
1696 C	—	35.00	120	1,025	1,750	—

KM# 491.4 1/2 CROWN
Silver **Ruler:** William III **Obv:** First bust of William III right; E below bust **Rev:** Crowned cruciform arms with large shields and early harp **Mint:** Exeter

Date	Mintage	VG	F	VF	XF	Unc
1696 E	—	50.00	150	650	2,100	—

KM# 491.5 1/2 CROWN
Silver **Ruler:** William III **Obv:** First bust of William III right; N below bust **Rev:** Crowned cruciform arms with large shields and early harp **Mint:** Norwich

Date	Mintage	VG	F	VF	XF	Unc
1696 N	—	75.00	180	775	2,150	—

KM# 491.14 1/2 CROWN
Silver **Ruler:** William III **Obv:** B below bust **Rev:** Crowned cruciform arms with small shields **Mint:** Bristol

Date	Mintage	VG	F	VF	XF	Unc
1696 B	—	55.00	120	500	1,700	—

KM# 491.15 1/2 CROWN
Silver **Ruler:** William III **Obv:** C below bust **Rev:** Crowned cruciform arms with small shields **Mint:** Chester

Date	Mintage	VG	F	VF	XF	Unc
1696 C	—	80.00	170	625	1,900	—

KM# 491.16 1/2 CROWN
Silver **Ruler:** William III **Obv:** E below bust **Rev:** Crowned cruciform arms with small shields **Mint:** Exeter

Date	Mintage	VG	F	VF	XF	Unc
1696 E	—	100	200	700	1,900	—

KM# 491.17 1/2 CROWN
Silver **Ruler:** William III **Obv:** N below bust **Rev:** Crowned cruciform arms with small shields **Mint:** Norwich

Date	Mintage	VG	F	VF	XF	Unc
1696 N	—	75.00	155	600	2,100	—

KM# 491.18 1/2 CROWN
Silver **Ruler:** William III **Obv:** Script y below bust **Rev:** Crowned cruciform arms with small shields **Mint:** York

Date	Mintage	VG	F	VF	XF	Unc
1696 y	—	55.00	155	650	2,150	—

KM# 492.1 1/2 CROWN
Silver **Ruler:** William III **Obv:** Second bust (two curls on breast, without hair below bust) of William III right

Date	Mintage	VG	F	VF	XF	Unc
1696 Unique	—	—	—	—	—	—

KM# 491.12 1/2 CROWN
Silver **Ruler:** William III **Obv:** First bust of William III right; script y below bust **Rev:** Crowned cruciform arms with large shields and ordinary harp **Mint:** York **Note:** Varieties exist.

Date	Mintage	VG	F	VF	XF	Unc
1697 y	—	45.00	135	525	1,700	—

KM# 491.8 1/2 CROWN
Silver **Ruler:** William III **Obv:** First bust of William III right; B below bust **Rev:** Crowned cruciform arms with large shields and ordinary harp **Mint:** Bristol **Note:** Varieties exist.

Date	Mintage	VG	F	VF	XF	Unc
1697 B	—	40.00	110	500	1,800	—

KM# 492.2 1/2 CROWN
Silver **Ruler:** William III **Obv:** Laureate bust right **Rev:** Crowned cruciform arms **Note:** Varieties exist.

Date	Mintage	VG	F	VF	XF	Unc
1698	—	35.00	115	425	1,500	—
1698/7 Rare	—	—	—	—	—	—
1699	—	50.00	155	550	1,850	—
1700	—	30.00	100	400	1,500	—

KM# 417.2 CROWN
Silver **Ruler:** Charles II **Edge:** Without date

Date	Mintage	VG	F	VF	XF	Unc
1662	—	100	200	800	4,500	—

KM# 417.4 CROWN
Silver **Ruler:** Charles II **Edge:** Without date

Date	Mintage	VG	F	VF	XF	Unc
1662	—	100	200	800	4,500	—

KM# 417.1 CROWN
Silver **Ruler:** Charles II **Obv:** First bust of Charles II right **Note:** Dav. #3774.

Date	Mintage	VG	F	VF	XF	Unc
1662	—	100	200	800	4,500	—

KM# 417.3 CROWN
Silver **Ruler:** Charles II **Obv:** Without rose below bust **Edge:** Dated **Note:** Dav. #3774A.

Date	Mintage	VG	F	VF	XF	Unc
1662	—	100	200	800	4,500	—

KM# 417.5 CROWN
Silver **Ruler:** Charles II **Rev:** Upper and lower shields of arms not quartered **Note:** Dav. #3774B. Varieties exist.

Date	Mintage	VG	F	VF	XF	Unc
1663	—	100	200	800	4,500	—

KM# 422.1 CROWN
Silver **Ruler:** Charles II **Obv:** Second bust (smaller and curved ties on wreath) of Charles II right **Edge:** Regnal year is in Roman numerals **Note:** Dav. #3775. Varieties exist.

Date	Mintage	VG	F	VF	XF	Unc
1664	—	100	200	750	5,000	—
1665/4	—	—	—	—	—	—
1665	—	450	1,000	2,200	—	—
1666	—	100	200	800	5,000	—

KM# 422.2 CROWN
Silver **Ruler:** Charles II **Obv:** Elephant below bust **Note:** Dav. #3775A. Varieties exist.

Date	Mintage	VG	F	VF	XF	Unc
1666	—	200	550	2,200	9,500	—

KM# 422.3 CROWN
Silver **Ruler:** Charles II **Edge:** Regnal year in words **Note:** Dav. #3775B. Varieties exist.

Date	Mintage	VG	F	VF	XF	Unc
1667	—	95.00	175	600	3,500	—
1668/7	—	95.00	175	600	3,500	—
1668	—	80.00	150	600	3,500	—
1669/8	—	200	450	1,300	7,000	—
1669	—	150	350	1,300	7,000	—
1670/69	—	200	450	1,000	5,500	—
1670	—	95.00	175	750	3,500	—
1671	—	80.00	150	750	3,500	—

KM# 435 CROWN
Silver **Ruler:** Charles II **Obv:** Third bust (larger and wider) of Charles II right **Note:** Dav. #3776. Varieties exist.

Date	Mintage	VG	F	VF	XF	Unc
1671	—	80.00	150	600	3,500	—
1672	—	80.00	150	600	3,500	—
1673/2	—	95.00	175	750	3,500	—
1673	—	80.00	150	600	3,500	—
1674 Rare	—	—	—	—	—	—
1675/3	—	450	900	2,200	—	—
1675	—	450	1,000	3,000	—	—
1676	—	75.00	150	450	3,500	—
1677/6	—	80.00	150	675	3,500	—
1677	—	75.00	150	600	3,500	—
1678/7	—	100	225	900	6,000	—
1679	—	75.00	150	700	3,500	—
1680/79	—	95.00	175	800	4,000	—
1680	—	90.00	175	850	4,000	—

KM# 445.1 CROWN
Silver **Ruler:** Charles II **Obv:** Fourth bust (larger and older) of Charles II **Note:** Dav. #3776B.

Date	Mintage	VG	F	VF	XF	Unc
1679	—	75.00	150	700	3,500	—
1680/79	—	85.00	150	750	3,500	—
1680	—	70.00	150	475	3,500	—
1681	—	70.00	150	700	3,500	—
1682/1	—	70.00	150	700	3,500	—
1682	—	250	450	1,350	4,700	—
1683	—	225	400	1,300	5,000	—
1684	—	150	250	775	5,500	—

KM# 445.2 CROWN
Silver **Ruler:** Charles II **Obv:** Elephant and castle below bust **Note:** Dav. #3776A.

Date	Mintage	VG	F	VF	XF	Unc
1681 Rare	—	—	—	—	—	—

KM# 457 CROWN
Silver **Ruler:** James II **Obv:** Laureate first bust of James II left **Rev:** Crowned cruciform arms, date divided at top **Note:** Dav. #3778. Varieties exist.

Date	Mintage	VG	F	VF	XF	Unc
1686	—	200	400	1,400	6,000	—

KM# 463 CROWN
Silver **Ruler:** James II **Obv:** Second bust (narrower) of James II left **Note:** Dav. #3779. Varieties exist.

Date	Mintage	VG	F	VF	XF	Unc
1687	—	125	225	850	2,900	—
1688/7	—	125	225	900	3,000	—
1688	—	125	225	900	3,000	—

KM# 478 CROWN
Silver **Ruler:** William and Mary **Obv:** Conjoined busts of William and Mary right **Note:** Dav. #3780. Varieties exist.

Date	Mintage	VG	F	VF	XF	Unc
1691	—	200	400	1,200	3,350	—
1692	—	200	400	1,200	3,350	—

KM# 486 CROWN
Silver **Ruler:** William III **Obv:** First bust of William III right **Rev:** First harp in left shield **Note:** Dav. #3781. Varieties exist.

Date	Mintage	VG	F	VF	XF	Unc
1695	—	60.00	125	400	1,800	—
1696/5	—	150	300	550	2,000	—
1696	—	60.00	125	350	1,600	—

KM# 493 CROWN
Silver **Ruler:** William III **Obv:** Second bust (two locks of hair across chest without hair below bust) **Note:** Dav. #3781A. Varieties exist.

Date	Mintage	VG	F	VF	XF	Unc
1696 Unique	—	—	—	—	—	—

KM# 494.1 CROWN
Silver **Ruler:** William III **Obv:** Third bust (straight breastplate on chest) of William III right **Rev:** First harp in left shield **Note:** Dav. #3782. Varieties exist.

Date	Mintage	VG	F	VF	XF	Unc
1696	—	60.00	125	350	1,700	—

KM# 494.2 CROWN
Silver **Ruler:** William III **Rev:** Second harp in left shield **Note:** Dav. #3782A.

Date	Mintage	VG	F	VF	XF	Unc
1697	—	400	900	3,000	—	—

KM# 494.3 CROWN
Silver **Ruler:** William III **Rev:** Third harp in left shield **Note:** Dav. #3782B. Varieties exist.

Date	Mintage	VG	F	VF	XF	Unc
1700	—	60.00	125	450	1,800	—

GUINEA COINAGE

KM# 431 1/2 GUINEA
4.1750 g., 0.9170 Gold 0.1231 oz. AGW **Ruler:** Charles II
Obv: Charles II with pointed truncation

Date	Mintage	VG	F	VF	XF	Unc
1669	—	250	650	1,600	5,500	—
1670	—	250	650	1,600	5,000	—
1671	—	300	650	1,700	5,500	—
1672	—	300	650	1,700	5,500	—

KM# 439.1 1/2 GUINEA
4.1750 g., 0.9170 Gold 0.1231 oz. AGW **Ruler:** Charles II
Obv: Rounded truncation

Date	Mintage	VG	F	VF	XF	Unc
1672	—	300	650	1,600	5,500	—
1673	—	350	650	1,700	5,500	—
1674	—	350	650	1,800	6,000	—
1675 Rare	—	—	—	—	—	—
1676	—	300	650	1,600	5,500	—
1677	—	300	650	1,600	5,500	—
1678	—	300	650	1,600	5,500	—
1679	—	250	600	1,600	5,500	—
1680	—	350	650	1,700	5,500	—
1681	—	350	650	1,700	5,500	—
1682	—	350	650	11,700	5,500	—
1683	—	300	650	1,600	5,500	—
1684	—	250	600	1,600	5,500	—

KM# 439.2 1/2 GUINEA
4.1750 g., 0.9170 Gold 0.1231 oz. AGW **Ruler:** Charles II
Obv: Elephant and castle below bust

Date	Mintage	VG	F	VF	XF	Unc
1676 Rare	—	—	—	—	—	—
1677	—	350	900	2,100	6,000	—
1678/7	—	350	800	2,100	6,000	—
1680 Rare	—	—	—	—	—	—
1682	—	350	800	2,100	6,000	—
1683 Rare	—	—	—	—	—	—
1684	—	350	900	2,100	6,000	—

KM# 458.1 1/2 GUINEA
4.1750 g., 0.9170 Gold 0.1231 oz. AGW **Ruler:** James II
Obv: Head of James II left

Date	Mintage	VG	F	VF	XF	Unc
1686	—	250	650	1,700	4,500	—
1687	—	250	700	1,900	5,500	—
1688	—	250	700	1,700	5,500	—

KM# 458.2 1/2 GUINEA
4.1750 g., 0.9170 Gold 0.1231 oz. AGW **Ruler:** James II
Obv: Elephant and castle below bust

Date	Mintage	VG	F	VF	XF	Unc
1686	—	1,200	2,000	5,500	—	—

KM# 473 1/2 GUINEA
4.1750 g., 0.9170 Gold 0.1231 oz. AGW **Ruler:** William and Mary **Obv:** Conjoined heads of William and Mary, right

Date	Mintage	VG	F	VF	XF	Unc
1689	—	250	650	2,100	4,250	—

KM# 476.1 1/2 GUINEA
4.1750 g., 0.9170 Gold 0.1231 oz. AGW **Ruler:** William and Mary **Obv:** Conjoined heads of William and Mary right with hair falling on neck

Date	Mintage	VG	F	VF	XF	Unc
1690	—	300	750	2,100	5,000	—
1691	—	300	750	2,100	5,000	—
1692	—	300	750	2,100	5,000	—
1693/2	—	—	—	—	—	—
1693	—	300	750	2,100	5,000	—
1694	—	300	750	2,100	5,000	—

KM# 476.2 1/2 GUINEA
4.1750 g., 0.9170 Gold 0.1231 oz. AGW **Ruler:** William and Mary **Obv:** Elephant and castle below heads

Date	Mintage	VG	F	VF	XF	Unc
1691	—	300	800	2,200	6,000	—
1692	—	300	800	2,200	6,500	—

KM# 476.3 1/2 GUINEA
4.1750 g., 0.9170 Gold 0.1231 oz. AGW **Ruler:** William and Mary **Obv:** Elephant below heads

Date	Mintage	VG	F	VF	XF	Unc
1692 Rare	—	—	—	—	—	—

KM# 487.1 1/2 GUINEA
4.1750 g., 0.9170 Gold 0.1231 oz. AGW **Ruler:** William III
Obv: Head of William III right

Date	Mintage	VG	F	VF	XF	Unc
1695	—	250	500	1,000	3,500	—

KM# 487.2 1/2 GUINEA
4.1750 g., 0.9170 Gold 0.1231 oz. AGW **Ruler:** William III
Obv: Elephant and castle below head

Date	Mintage	VG	F	VF	XF	Unc
1695	—	250	750	1,325	4,000	—
1696	—	250	750	1,325	4,000	—

KM# 487.3 1/2 GUINEA
4.1750 g., 0.9170 Gold 0.1231 oz. AGW **Ruler:** William III
Obv: Head right **Obv. Legend:** GVLIELMVS • III • DEI • GRA •
Rev: Crowned shields in cruciform, sceptres at angles
Rev. Legend: MAG - BR • FRA - ET • HIB • - REX

Date	Mintage	VG	F	VF	XF	Unc
1697	—	250	550	1,000	3,000	—
1698	—	250	500	950	3,000	—
1699 Rare	—	—	—	—	—	—
1700	—	250	500	950	3,000	—

KM# 487.4 1/2 GUINEA
4.1750 g., 0.9170 Gold 0.1231 oz. AGW **Ruler:** William III
Obv: Elephant and castle below head

Date	Mintage	VG	F	VF	XF	Unc
1698	—	250	550	1,300	5,000	—

KM# 420.1 GUINEA
8.3500 g., 0.9170 Gold 0.2462 oz. AGW **Ruler:** Charles II
Obv: Laureate bust of Charles II right **Rev:** Crowned cruciform arms with scepters

Date	Mintage	VG	F	VF	XF	Unc
1663	—	500	1,100	3,500	9,000	—

KM# 420.2 GUINEA
8.3500 g., 0.9170 Gold 0.2462 oz. AGW **Ruler:** Charles II
Obv: Laureate bust of Charles II right, elephant

Date	Mintage	VG	F	VF	XF	Unc
1663	—	500	1,100	3,000	8,500	—

KM# 423.1 GUINEA

8.3500 g., 0.9170 Gold 0.2462 oz. AGW **Ruler:** Charles II **Obv:** Laureate bust of Charles II right

Date	Mintage	VG	F	VF	XF	Unc
1664	—	500	1,100	3,000	8,000	—

KM# 423.2 GUINEA

8.3500 g., 0.9170 Gold 0.2462 oz. AGW **Ruler:** Charles II **Obv:** Elephant below bust

Date	Mintage	VG	F	VF	XF	Unc
1664 Rare	—	—	—	—	—	—

KM# 424.1 GUINEA

8.3500 g., 0.9170 Gold 0.2462 oz. AGW **Ruler:** Charles II **Obv:** Laureate bust of Charles II right

Date	Mintage	VG	F	VF	XF	Unc
1664	—	400	950	3,000	7,500	—
1665	—	400	900	3,000	7,500	—
1666	—	400	900	3,000	7,500	—
1667	—	400	900	3,000	7,500	—
1668	—	400	900	3,000	7,500	—
1669	—	400	900	3,000	7,500	—
1670	—	400	900	3,000	7,500	—
1671	—	400	900	3,000	7,500	—
1672	—	400	950	3,000	7,500	—
1673	—	450	1,000	3,000	7,500	—

KM# 424.2 GUINEA

8.3500 g., 0.9170 Gold 0.2462 oz. AGW **Ruler:** Charles II **Obv:** Elephant below bust

Date	Mintage	VG	F	VF	XF	Unc
1664	—	550	1,200	3,000	8,000	—
1665	—	450	1,100	3,500	8,000	—
1668	—	—	—	—	—	—

KM# 440.1 GUINEA

8.3500 g., 0.9170 Gold 0.2462 oz. AGW **Ruler:** Charles II **Obv:** Head of Charles II with rounded truncation

Date	Mintage	VG	F	VF	XF	Unc
1672	—	350	850	2,500	6,500	—
1673	—	350	850	2,500	6,500	—
1674	—	350	850	2,600	7,000	—
1675	—	350	850	2,600	6,500	—
1676	—	350	850	2,200	6,500	—
1677	—	350	850	2,200	6,500	—
1678	—	350	850	2,200	6,500	—
1679	—	350	850	2,200	6,500	—
1680	—	350	850	2,200	6,500	—
1681	—	350	850	2,600	6,500	—
1682	—	350	850	2,500	6,500	—
1683	—	350	850	2,200	6,500	—
1684	—	350	850	2,500	6,500	—

KM# 440.2 GUINEA

8.3500 g., 0.9170 Gold 0.2462 oz. AGW **Ruler:** Charles II **Obv:** Elephant and castle below bust

Date	Mintage	VG	F	VF	XF	Unc
1674	—	550	1,200	3,500	10,000	—
1675	—	450	1,100	3,000	9,000	—
1676	—	450	1,100	3,000	9,000	—
1677	—	450	1,100	3,000	9,000	—
1678	—	450	1,100	3,000	9,000	—
1679	—	450	1,100	3,000	9,000	—
1680	—	750	1,200	3,500	10,000	—
1681	—	450	1,100	3,000	9,000	—
1682	—	450	1,100	3,000	9,000	—
1683	—	550	1,200	3,500	10,000	—
1684	—	450	1,100	3,000	9,000	—

KM# 440.3 GUINEA

8.3500 g., 0.9170 Gold 0.2462 oz. AGW **Ruler:** Charles II **Obv:** Elephant below bust

Date	Mintage	VG	F	VF	XF	Unc
1677 Rare	—	—	—	—	—	—
1678 Rare	—	—	—	—	—	—

KM# 453.1 GUINEA

8.3500 g., 0.9170 Gold 0.2462 oz. AGW **Ruler:** James II **Obv:** Head of James II left

Date	Mintage	VG	F	VF	XF	Unc
1685	—	300	800	2,400	6,000	—
1686	—	300	800	2,500	6,000	—

KM# 453.2 GUINEA

8.3500 g., 0.9170 Gold 0.2462 oz. AGW **Ruler:** James II **Obv:** Elephant and castle below bust

Date	Mintage	VG	F	VF	XF	Unc
1685	—	350	850	2,400	6,000	—
1686 Rare	—	—	—	—	—	—

KM# 459.1 GUINEA

8.3500 g., 0.9170 Gold 0.2462 oz. AGW **Ruler:** James II **Obv:** Laureate bust of James II left

Date	Mintage	VG	F	VF	XF	Unc
1686	—	350	850	2,400	5,000	—
1687/6	—	—	—	—	—	—
1687	—	350	850	2,400	5,000	—
1688	—	350	850	2,500	5,000	—

KM# 459.2 GUINEA

8.3500 g., 0.9170 Gold 0.2462 oz. AGW **Ruler:** James II **Obv:** Elephant and castle below bust

Date	Mintage	VG	F	VF	XF	Unc
1686	—	450	900	2,500	6,000	—
1687	—	350	850	2,400	6,000	—
1688	—	350	850	2,400	6,000	—

KM# 474.1 GUINEA

8.3500 g., 0.9170 Gold 0.2462 oz. AGW **Ruler:** William and Mary **Obv:** Conjoined heads of William and Mary right

Date	Mintage	VG	F	VF	XF	Unc
1689	—	350	850	2,600	6,500	—
1690	—	350	850	2,600	6,500	—
1691	—	350	850	2,600	6,500	—
1692	—	350	850	2,600	6,500	—
1693	—	350	850	2,600	6,500	—
1694/3	—	—	—	—	—	—
1694	—	350	850	2,600	6,500	—

KM# 474.2 GUINEA

8.3500 g., 0.9170 Gold 0.2462 oz. AGW **Ruler:** William and Mary **Obv:** Elephant and castle below heads

Date	Mintage	VG	F	VF	XF	Unc
1689	—	350	900	2,700	6,500	—
1690	—	350	900	2,800	7,000	—
1691	—	350	900	2,800	6,500	—
1692	—	350	900	2,800	6,500	—
1693	—	350	900	2,800	6,500	—
1694	—	350	900	2,800	6,500	—

KM# 474.3 GUINEA

8.3500 g., 0.9170 Gold 0.2462 oz. AGW **Ruler:** William and Mary **Obv:** Elephant below heads

Date	Mintage	VG	F	VF	XF	Unc
1692	—	450	1,000	3,500	8,000	—
1693 Rare	—	—	—	—	—	—

KM# 488.1 GUINEA

8.3500 g., 0.9170 Gold 0.2462 oz. AGW **Ruler:** William III **Obv:** Laureate bust of William III right **Rev:** Crowned cruciform arms with scepters in angles, date divided at top

Date	Mintage	VG	F	VF	XF	Unc
1695	—	175	425	1,250	5,000	—
1696	—	175	425	1,400	5,000	—
1697	—	175	425	1,400	5,000	—

KM# 488.2 GUINEA

8.3500 g., 0.9170 Gold 0.2462 oz. AGW **Ruler:** William III **Obv:** Elephant and castle below bust

Date	Mintage	VG	F	VF	XF	Unc
1695 Rare	—	—	—	—	—	—
1696 Rare	—	—	—	—	—	—

KM# 498.2 GUINEA

8.3500 g., 0.9170 Gold 0.2462 oz. AGW **Ruler:** William III **Obv:** Elephant and castle below bust **Rev:** Crowned shields in cruciform, sceptres at angles **Note:** Struck from gold mined in Guinea, now Ghana.

Date	Mintage	VG	F	VF	XF	Unc
1697	—	400	950	4,000	7,000	—
1698	—	400	950	3,000	7,000	—
1699 Rare	—	—	—	—	—	—
1700	—	400	950	4,000	7,000	—

KM# 498.1 GUINEA

8.3500 g., 0.9170 Gold 0.2462 oz. AGW **Ruler:** William III **Obv:** Laureate head right **Obv. Legend:** GVLIELMVS • - III • DEI • GRA • **Rev:** Crowned shields in cruciform, sceptres at angles **Rev. Legend:** MAG - BR • FRA - ET • HIB - REX •

Date	Mintage	VG	F	VF	XF	Unc
1697	—	300	550	1,200	5,000	—
1698	—	300	550	1,100	4,500	—

Date	Mintage	VG	F	VF	XF	Unc
1699	—	300	550	1,350	5,000	—
1700	—	300	550	1,100	4,500	—

KM# 425.1 2 GUINEAS

16.7000 g., 0.9170 Gold 0.4923 oz. AGW **Ruler:** Charles II **Obv:** Laureate bust of Charles II right, pointed truncation **Rev:** Crowned cruciform arms with scepters in angles, date divided at top

Date	Mintage	VG	F	VF	XF	Unc
1664	—	700	1,700	3,500	10,000	—
1665 Rare	—	—	—	—	—	—
1669 Rare	—	—	—	—	—	—
1671	—	700	1,700	3,500	10,000	—

KM# 425.2 2 GUINEAS

16.7000 g., 0.9170 Gold 0.4923 oz. AGW **Ruler:** Charles II **Obv:** Elephant below bust

Date	Mintage	VG	F	VF	XF	Unc
1664	—	350	750	2,250	4,500	—

KM# 443.1 2 GUINEAS

16.7000 g., 0.9170 Gold 0.4923 oz. AGW **Ruler:** Charles II **Obv:** Rounded truncation

Date	Mintage	VG	F	VF	XF	Unc
1675	—	750	1,700	3,500	8,500	—
1676	—	750	1,600	3,000	8,500	—
1677	—	750	1,600	3,000	8,500	—
1678/7	—	—	—	—	—	—
1678	—	750	1,600	3,000	8,500	—
1679	—	750	1,600	3,000	8,500	—
1680	—	750	1,700	3,500	8,500	—
1681	—	750	1,600	3,000	8,500	—
1682	—	750	1,600	3,000	8,500	—
1683	—	750	1,600	3,000	8,500	—
1684	—	900	1,700	3,000	8,500	—

KM# 443.2 2 GUINEAS

16.7000 g., 0.9170 Gold 0.4923 oz. AGW **Ruler:** Charles II **Obv:** Elephant and castle below bust

Date	Mintage	VG	F	VF	XF	Unc
1676	—	850	1,800	3,500	10,000	—
1677	—	850	1,800	3,500	10,000	—
1678/7	—	—	—	—	—	—
1678	—	850	1,800	3,500	10,000	—
1682	—	850	1,800	3,500	10,000	—
1683	—	1,000	1,900	4,000	10,000	—
1684	—	1,000	1,900	4,000	10,000	—

KM# 443.3 2 GUINEAS

16.7000 g., 0.9170 Gold 0.4923 oz. AGW **Ruler:** Charles II **Obv:** Elephant below bust

Date	Mintage	VG	F	VF	XF	Unc
1678 Rare	—	—	—	—	—	—

KM# 464 2 GUINEAS

16.7000 g., 0.9170 Gold 0.4923 oz. AGW **Ruler:** James II **Obv:** Laureate bust of James II left

Date	Mintage	VG	F	VF	XF	Unc
1687	—	1,000	2,200	4,500	11,000	—
1688/7	—	1,000	2,300	5,000	12,000	—

KM# 482.2 2 GUINEAS

16.7000 g., 0.9170 Gold 0.4923 oz. AGW **Ruler:** William and Mary **Obv:** Elephant and castle below heads

Date	Mintage	VG	F	VF	XF	Unc
1691 Rare	—	—	—	—	—	—
1693	—	950	2,100	3,500	9,500	—
1694/3	—	—	—	—	—	—
1694	—	950	2,100	3,500	9,500	—

KM# 482.1 2 GUINEAS

16.7000 g., 0.9170 Gold 0.4923 oz. AGW **Ruler:** William and Mary **Obv:** Conjoined heads of William and Mary right **Rev:** Crowned arms, crown divides date at top

Date	Mintage	VG	F	VF	XF	Unc
1693	—	950	1,900	3,000	8,500	—
1694/3	—	950	1,900	3,000	8,500	—
1694	—	950	1,900	3,000	8,500	—

KM# 430.1 5 GUINEAS

41.7500 g., 0.9170 Gold 1.2308 oz. AGW **Ruler:** Charles II **Obv:** Laureate bust of Charles II right, pointed truncation **Rev:** Crowned cruciform arms with scepters in angles, date divided at top

Date	Mintage	VG	F	VF	XF	Unc
1668	—	1,600	2,700	5,000	15,000	—
1669	—	1,600	2,700	5,500	15,000	—
1670	—	1,600	2,700	5,500	15,000	—
1671	—	1,600	2,700	5,500	15,000	—
1672	—	1,600	2,700	5,500	15,000	—
1673	—	1,600	2,700	5,500	15,000	—
1674	—	1,600	2,700	5,500	15,000	—
1675	—	1,600	2,700	5,500	15,000	—
1676	—	1,600	2,700	5,500	15,000	—
1677	—	1,600	2,700	5,500	15,000	—
1678/7	—	—	—	—	—	—
1678	—	1,600	2,700	5,500	15,000	—

KM# 430.2 5 GUINEAS

41.7500 g., 0.9170 Gold 1.2308 oz. AGW **Ruler:** Charles II **Obv:** Elephant below bust

Date	Mintage	VG	F	VF	XF	Unc
1668	—	1,800	3,000	5,500	16,000	—
1669	—	1,800	3,000	5,500	16,000	—
1675	—	1,800	3,000	5,500	16,000	—
1677/5 Rare	—	—	—	—	—	—

KM# 430.3 5 GUINEAS

41.7500 g., 0.9170 Gold 1.2308 oz. AGW **Ruler:** Charles II **Obv:** Elephant and castle below bust

Date	Mintage	VG	F	VF	XF	Unc
1675	—	1,800	3,000	5,000	—	—
1676	—	1,800	3,000	5,000	—	—
1677	—	1,800	3,000	5,000	—	—
1678/7	—	—	—	—	—	—
1678	—	1,800	3,000	5,000	—	—

KM# 444.1 5 GUINEAS

41.7500 g., 0.9170 Gold 1.2308 oz. AGW **Ruler:** Charles II **Obv:** Rounded truncation

Date	Mintage	VG	F	VF	XF	Unc
1678	—	1,800	3,000	5,000	15,000	—
1679	—	1,800	3,000	5,000	15,000	—
1680	—	1,800	3,000	5,000	15,000	—
1681	—	1,800	3,000	5,000	15,000	—
1682	—	1,800	3,000	5,000	15,000	—
1683	—	1,800	3,000	5,000	15,000	—
1684	—	1,800	3,000	5,000	15,000	—

KM# 444.2 5 GUINEAS

41.7500 g., 0.9170 Gold 1.2308 oz. AGW **Ruler:** Charles II **Obv:** Elephant and castle below bust

Date	Mintage	VG	F	VF	XF	Unc
1680 Rare	—	—	—	—	—	—
1681	—	1,800	3,000	6,000	16,000	—
1682	—	1,800	3,000	6,000	16,000	—
1683	—	1,800	3,000	6,000	16,000	—
1684	—	1,800	3,000	6,000	16,000	—

KM# 460.1 5 GUINEAS

41.7500 g., 0.9170 Gold 1.2308 oz. AGW **Ruler:** James II **Obv:** Laureate bust of James II left

Date	Mintage	VG	F	VF	XF	Unc
1686	—	1,800	3,000	6,500	16,000	—
1687	—	1,800	3,000	6,000	16,000	—
1688	—	1,800	3,000	6,000	16,000	—

KM# 460.2 5 GUINEAS

41.7500 g., 0.9170 Gold 1.2308 oz. AGW **Ruler:** James II **Obv:** Elephant and castle below bust

Date	Mintage	VG	F	VF	XF	Unc
1687	—	1,800	3,000	6,000	16,000	—
1688	—	1,800	3,000	6,500	16,000	—

KM# 479.1 5 GUINEAS

41.7500 g., 0.9170 Gold 1.2308 oz. AGW **Ruler:** William and Mary **Obv:** Conjoined heads of William and Mary right

Date	Mintage	VG	F	VF	XF	Unc
1691	—	1,800	3,500	6,000	15,000	—
1692	—	1,800	3,500	6,000	15,000	—
1693	—	1,800	3,500	6,000	15,000	—
1694	—	1,800	3,500	6,000	15,000	—

KM# 479.2 5 GUINEAS

41.7500 g., 0.9170 Gold 1.2308 oz. AGW **Ruler:** William and Mary **Obv:** Elephant and castle below conjoined busts right

Date	Mintage	VG	F	VF	XF	Unc
1691	—	1,800	3,500	6,000	15,000	—
1692	—	1,800	3,500	6,000	15,000	—
1693	—	1,800	3,500	6,000	15,000	—
1694	—	1,800	3,500	6,000	15,000	—

KM# 505.1 5 GUINEAS

41.7500 g., 0.9170 Gold 1.2308 oz. AGW **Ruler:** William III **Obv:** Laureate bust of William III right **Rev:** Crowned cruciform arms with scepters in angles, date divided at top

Date	Mintage	VG	F	VF	XF	Unc
1699	—	1,800	3,000	5,000	13,000	—
1700	—	1,800	3,000	5,000	13,000	—

KM# 505.2 5 GUINEAS

41.7500 g., 0.9170 Gold 1.2308 oz. AGW **Ruler:** William III **Obv:** Elephant and castle below bust

Date	Mintage	VG	F	VF	XF	Unc
1699	—	1,800	3,000	6,000	14,000	—

PATTERNS

Including off metal strikes

KM#	Date	Mintage	Identification	Mkt Val
PnA1	1601 Rare	—	Penny. Silver. Elizabeth I	
Pn1	ND	—	1/4 Angel. Gold. James I	—
Pn2	ND	—	Double Crown. Gold. Charles I	—
Pn3	ND	—	Double Crown. Gold. Charles I	—
Pn4	ND	—	Angel. Gold. Charles I	—
Pn5	ND	—	Unite. Gold. Charles I	—
Pn6	ND	—	Unite. Silver. Charles I	—
Pn7	ND	—	Unite. Gold. Charles I, value behind head.	—
Pn8	ND	—	Unite. Gold. Charles I	—
Pn9	1630	—	Unite. Gold. Charles I	—
Pn10	1630	—	Unite. Gold. Charles I, bare head	—
Pn11	1630	—	Unite. Silver. Charles I	—

KM#	Date	Mintage	Identification	Mkt Val
Pn12	1630	—	Unite. Gold. Charles I, crowned head.	24,500
Pn13	1630	—	Unite. Silver. Charles I	—
Pn14	1630	—	Unite. Gold. Charles I, bare head to bottom	—
Pn15	1630	—	Unite. Silver. Charles I	—
Pn16	1630	—	Unite. Gold. Charles I, crowned head to bottom	24,500
Pn17	1630	—	Unite. Silver. Charles I	—
PnA18	ND	—	2 Pence. Charles I; by Briot	—
Pn18	1635	—	Unite. Silver. Charles I	—
Pn19	ND	—	Unite. Silver. Charles I	—
Pn20	ND	—	Unite. Gold. Charles I, third bust.	—
Pn21	ND	—	Unite. Gold. Charles I, fourth bust.	—
Pn22	ND	—	3 Unite. Gold. Charles I, crowned bust.	—
Pn23	ND	—	5 Unites. Gold. Charles I	—

Note: Also called the "Juxon Medal."

KM#	Date	Mintage	Identification	Mkt Val
Pn24	1656	—	50 Shilling. Gold. Cromwell, broad sides, thick, lettered edge	—

Note: Stacks 50th Anniversary sale 10-85 nearly mint state realized $31,900

KM#	Date	Mintage	Identification	Mkt Val
Pn25	1656	—	1 Broad. Gold. Cromwell.	12,000
PnA26	1656	—	1/2 Broad. Gold. Cromwell.	17,500

Note: The 1/2 Broad was struck in 1738 from dies made by John Tanner, while other Cromwell patterns were struck from dies made by Thomas Simon contemporary with date

KM#	Date	Mintage	Identification	Mkt Val
Pn26	1656	—	1 Broad. Silver. Cromwell.	—
PnD27	1656	—	1/2 Crown. Silver. Cromwell.	2,200
PnF27	1658	—	1/2 Crown. Gold. Cromwell.	—
PnG27	1658	—	Crown. Gold. Cromwell.	—

Note: Spink London No. 48 Norweb sale part 2 11-85 XF realized $47,850

KM#	Date	Mintage	Identification	Mkt Val
PnE27	1658	—	6 Pence. Silver. Cromwell Care	—
PnA33	1662	—	Crown. Gold. Charles II.	—
PnB33	1663	—	Crown. Silver. Thomas Simon Petition, English lettered edge	—

Note: Stack's sale 12-92 VF realized $34,000

KM#	Date	Mintage	Identification	Mkt Val
PnD33	1663	—	Crown. Silver. Lettered in Latin edge. Thomas Simon	—

Note: Glendining's Willis sale 10-91 VF realized $14,960

KM#	Date	Mintage	Identification	Mkt Val
PnF33	1663	—	Crown. Silver. Lettered in English edge. Thomas Simon	—
PnG33	1663	—	Crown. Silver. Lettered in English edge. Thomas Simon	—
PnC33	1663	—	Crown. Pewter. Plain edge. Thomas Simon Petition	8,500
PnE33	1663	—	Crown. Pewter. Lettered in Latin edge. Thomas Simon	8,000
PnH33	1665	—	Farthing. Gold. Charles II, short hair.	9,000
PnI33	1665	—	Farthing. Gold. Charles II, long hair.	9,000
PnR33	1665	—	Farthing. Silver. Short hair.	850
PnJ33	1672	—	1/2 Penny. Charles II	—
PnK33	1672	—	1/2 Penny. Silver. KM#437	—
PnL33	1673	—	1/2 Penny. Silver. KM#437	—
PnM33	1694	—	1/2 Penny. William and Mary.	—
PnN33	1694	—	1/2 Penny. Silver. KM# 475.3.	—
PnO33	1696	—	1/2 Penny. Silver. KM# 483.1.	—
PnP33	1699	—	1/2 Penny. Silver. KM# 503.	—

MAUNDY SETS

KM#	Date	Mintage	Identification	Issue Price	Mkt Val
MDS1	ND(1660-62) (4)	—	KM#281, 290, 398, 401	—	1,150
MDS2	ND(1662) (4)	—	KM#282, 291, 397, 400	—	1,350
MDS3	1670 (4)	—	KM#429, 432-434	—	900
MDS4	1671 (4)	—	KM#429, 432-434	—	850
MDS5	1672/1 (4)	—	KM#429, 432-434	—	900
MDS6	1673 (4)	—	KM#429, 432-434	—	900
MDS7	1674 (4)	—	KM#429, 432-434	—	900
MDS8	1675 (4)	—	KM#429, 432-434	—	900
MDS9	1676 (4)	—	KM#429, 432-434	—	900
MDS10	1677 (4)	—	KM#429, 432-434	—	875
MDS11	1678 (4)	—	KM#429, 432-434	—	875
MDS12	1679 (4)	—	KM#429, 432-434	—	875
MDS13	1680/79 (4)	—	KM#429, 432-434	—	900
MDS14	1680 (4)	—	KM#429, 432-434	—	950
MDS15	1681/0 (4)	—	KM#429, 432-434	—	1,000
MDS16	1681 (4)	—	KM#429, 432-434	—	950
MDS17	1682/1 (4)	—	KM#429, 432-434	—	1,000
MDS18	1682 (4)	—	KM#429, 432-434	—	900
MDS19	1683/2 (4)	—	KM#429, 432-434	—	975
MDS20	1683 (4)	—	KM#429, 432-434	—	900
MDS21	1684 (4)	—	KM#429, 432-434	—	1,000
MDS22	1686 (4)	—	KM#449, 450, 454, 455.1	—	950
MDS23	1687 (4)	—	KM#449, 450, 454, 455.1	—	950
MDS24	1688 (4)	—	KM#449, 450, 454, 455.1	—	950
MDS25	1689 (4)	—	KM#468.1, 469, 470.1, 471.1	—	2,400

KM#	Date	Mintage	Identification	Issue Price	Mkt Val
MDS26	1691 (4)	—	KM#468.2, 469, 470.1, 471.1	—	1,550
MDS27	1692 (4)	—	KM#468-471	—	1,450
MDS28	1693 (4)	—	KM#468-471	—	1,200
MDS29	1694 (4)	—	KM#468.2, 469, 470.2, 471.1	—	1,050
MDS30	1698 (4)	—	KM#495, 499, 500.1, 501	—	1,325
MDS31	1699 (4)	—	KM#495, 499, 500.1, 501	—	1,850
MDS32	1700 (4)	—	KM#495, 499, 500.2, 501	—	1,450

Hungary is located in central Europe.

The ancient kingdom of Hungary, founded by the Magyars in the 9th century, achieved its greatest extension in the mid-14th century when its dominions touched the Baltic, Black and Mediterranean Seas. After suffering repeated Turkish invasions, Hungary accepted Habsburg rule to escape Turkish occupation, regaining independence in 1867 with the Emperor of Austria as king of a dual Austro-Hungarian monarchy.

MINT MARKS

A, CA, WI - Vienna (Becs)
B, K, KB - Kremnitz (Kormoczbanya)
BP - Budapest
CH - Pressburg (Pozsony)
CM - Kaschau (Kassa)
(c) - castle - Pressburg
(d) - double trefoil - Pressburg
G, GN, NB - Nagybanya
(g) - GC script monogram - Pressburg
GYF - Karlsburg (Gyulafehervar)
HA - Hall
(L) - ICB monogram - Pressburg
(r) - rampant lion left - Pressburg
S - Schmollnitz (Szomolnok)

MINT OFFICIALS' INITIALS

Nagybanya Mint

Initial	Date	Name
IB	1692-98	J. C. Block
ICB	1698-1728	J. C. block
IS	1677-78	
LM	1673-77, 87, 95	Leopold Mittermayer
PO	1684-99	Peter Osterreicher

Pressburg Mint

Initial	Date	Name
(I)	1684-85	Georg Lippai
	1696-99	Christoph Sigmund Hunger
	1674-76	Georg Cetto

MONETARY SYSTEM

Until 1857

2 Poltura = 3 Krajczar
60 Krajczar = 1 Forint (Gulden)
2 Forint = 1 Convention Thaler

KINGDOM

STANDARD COINAGE

KM# 5.2 OBULUS

Silver **Ruler:** Rudolf II **Note:** Thick planchet.

Date	Mintage	VG	F	VF	XF	Unc
1601	—	9.00	18.00	40.25	85.00	—
1607	—	9.00	18.00	40.25	85.00	—

KM# 5.1 OBULUS

Silver **Ruler:** Rudolf II **Obv:** Date above shield of arms **Rev:** Madonna and child divide K-B

Date	Mintage	VG	F	VF	XF	Unc
1601KB	—	9.00	18.00	40.25	85.00	—
1602KB	—	9.00	18.00	40.25	85.00	—
1604KB	—	9.00	18.00	40.25	85.00	—
1606KB	—	9.00	18.00	40.25	85.00	—
1607KB	—	9.00	18.00	40.25	85.00	—
1608KB	—	9.00	18.00	40.25	85.00	—

KM# 22 OBULUS

Silver **Ruler:** Rudolf II **Obv:** Crowned arms, crown divides K-B, shield divides date **Rev:** Radiant Madonna and child

Date	Mintage	VG	F	VF	XF	Unc
1608KB	—	9.00	18.00	40.25	85.00	—
1609KB	—	9.00	18.00	40.25	85.00	—
1610KB	—	9.00	18.00	40.25	85.00	—
1611KB	—	9.00	18.00	40.25	85.00	—
1612KB	—	9.00	18.00	40.25	85.00	—
1613	—	9.00	18.00	40.25	85.00	—

KM# 39 OBULUS

Silver **Obv:** Shield of arms divides K-B, date above **Rev:** Without rays **Note:** Varieties exist.

Date	Mintage	VG	F	VF	XF	Unc
1613KB	—	9.00	18.00	40.25	85.00	—
1614KB	—	9.00	18.00	40.25	85.00	—
1615KB	—	9.00	18.00	40.25	85.00	—
1616KB	—	9.00	18.00	40.25	85.00	—
1617KB	—	9.00	18.00	40.25	85.00	—
1618KB	—	9.00	18.00	40.25	85.00	—
1619KB	—	9.00	18.00	40.25	85.00	—
1621KB	—	9.00	18.00	40.25	85.00	—
1622KB	—	9.00	18.00	40.25	85.00	—
1623KB	—	9.00	18.00	40.25	85.00	—
1625KB	—	9.00	18.00	40.25	85.00	—
1626KB	—	9.00	18.00	40.25	85.00	—
1627KB	—	9.00	18.00	40.25	85.00	—
1629KB	—	9.00	18.00	40.25	85.00	—

KM# 62 OBULUS

Silver **Obv:** Shield of arms divides N-B, date above **Rev:** Madonna and child

Date	Mintage	VG	F	VF	XF	Unc
1619NB	—	9.00	18.00	40.25	85.00	—
1631NB	—	9.00	18.00	40.25	85.00	—
1634NB	—	9.00	18.00	40.25	85.00	—
1638NB	—	9.00	18.00	40.25	85.00	—

KM# 105 OBULUS

Silver **Rev:** Madonna and child divide date

Date	Mintage	VG	F	VF	XF	Unc
1634	—	9.00	18.00	40.25	85.00	—
1635	—	9.00	18.00	40.25	85.00	—
1636	—	9.00	18.00	40.25	85.00	—
1637	—	9.00	18.00	40.25	85.00	—
1638	—	9.00	18.00	40.25	85.00	—
1639	—	9.00	18.00	40.25	85.00	—
1640	—	9.00	18.00	40.25	85.00	—
1641	—	9.00	18.00	40.25	85.00	—
1642	—	9.00	18.00	40.25	85.00	—
1645	—	9.00	18.00	40.25	85.00	—
1647	—	9.00	18.00	40.25	85.00	—
1648	—	9.00	18.00	40.25	85.00	—
1649	—	9.00	18.00	40.25	85.00	—
1654	—	9.00	18.00	40.25	85.00	—
1655	—	9.00	18.00	40.25	85.00	—

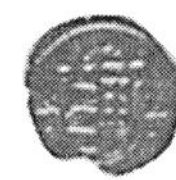

KM# 173 OBULUS

Billon **Ruler:** Leopold I **Obv:** Crowned arms divide K-B **Rev:** Madonna and child divide date **Note:** Varieties exist

Date	Mintage	VG	F	VF	XF	Unc
1662KB	—	9.00	18.00	40.25	85.00	—
1663KB	—	9.00	18.00	40.25	85.00	—
1665KB	—	9.00	18.00	40.25	85.00	—
1674KB	—	9.00	18.00	40.25	85.00	—
1675KB	—	9.00	18.00	40.25	85.00	—
1676KB	—	9.00	18.00	40.25	85.00	—
1679KB	—	9.00	18.00	40.25	85.00	—
1681KB	—	9.00	18.00	40.25	85.00	—
1682KB	—	9.00	18.00	40.25	85.00	—
1684KB	—	9.00	18.00	40.25	85.00	—
1685KB	—	9.00	18.00	40.25	85.00	—
1686KB	—	9.00	18.00	40.25	85.00	—
1687KB	—	9.00	18.00	40.25	85.00	—
1689KB	—	9.00	18.00	40.25	85.00	—
1690KB	—	9.00	18.00	40.25	85.00	—
1691KB	—	9.00	18.00	40.25	85.00	—
1692KB	—	9.00	18.00	40.25	85.00	—
1693KB	—	9.00	18.00	40.25	85.00	—
1695KB	—	9.00	18.00	40.25	85.00	—
1696KB	—	9.00	18.00	40.25	85.00	—
1697KB	—	9.00	18.00	40.25	85.00	—
1699KB	—	9.00	18.00	40.25	85.00	—

KM# 230 DUARIUS

Billon **Obv:** Crowned arms divide C-H in inner circle **Rev:** DVARI/ US/ 1695

Date	Mintage	VG	F	VF	XF	Unc
1695CH	—	12.00	22.50	46.00	90.00	—

KM# 229 DUARIUS

Silver **Obv:** Crowned arms divide K-B in inner circle **Rev:** Madonna and child on right above value and date **Note:** Varities exist

Date	Mintage	VG	F	VF	XF	Unc
1695KB	—	12.00	22.50	46.00	90.00	—
1696KB	—	12.00	22.50	46.00	90.00	—
1697KB	—	12.00	22.50	46.00	90.00	—
1698KB	—	12.00	22.50	46.00	90.00	—
1699KB	—	12.00	22.50	46.00	90.00	—

KM# 243 DUARIUS

Billon **Ruler:** Leopold I **Obv:** Crowned arms divide K-B **Rev:** Madonna and child above value and date

Date	Mintage	VG	F	VF	XF	Unc
1699KB	—	12.00	22.50	46.00	90.00	—
1700KB	—	12.00	22.50	46.00	90.00	—

KM# 244 DUARIUS

Billon

Date	Mintage	VG	F	VF	XF	Unc
1699CH	—	17.00	40.25	80.00	175	—

MB# 260 DENAR

Silver **Ruler:** Rudolf II **Obv:** 4-fold arms with central shield of Austria **Obv. Legend:** RVD • II • RO • I • S • AV • G • H • B • R • **Rev:** Madonna and child divide mintmarks, date in legend **Rev. Legend:** PATR • (date) HVNG • **Note:** Varieties exist. Known struck on thick flan for years 1581-Z, 1585-6, 1588-94, 1596-7, 1600, 1601 with weights 1.80-6.96g (H-1052).

Date	Mintage	VG	F	VF	XF	Unc
1601KB	—	9.00	17.00	40.00	65.00	—
160ZKB	—	9.00	17.00	40.00	65.00	—

KM# 7 DENAR

Silver **Obv:** Shield of arms **Rev:** Madonna and child divide N-B, date in legend

Date	Mintage	VG	F	VF	XF	Unc
1601NB	—	9.00	17.00	40.25	65.00	—

KM# 16 DENAR

Billon **Obv:** Shield of arms in inner circle, small letters in legend **Rev:** Madonna and child divide K-B, date in legend

Date	Mintage	VG	F	VF	XF	Unc
1602KB	—	8.00	17.00	34.50	65.00	—
1603KB	—	8.00	17.00	34.50	65.00	—
1604KB	—	8.00	17.00	34.50	65.00	—
1605KB	—	8.00	17.00	34.50	65.00	—
1606KB	—	8.00	17.00	34.50	65.00	—
1607KB	—	8.00	17.00	34.50	65.00	—
1608KB	—	8.00	17.00	34.50	65.00	—

KM# 23 DENAR

Billon **Obv:** Crowned arms divide K-B in inner circle, date in legend **Rev:** Radiant Madonna and child in inner circle

Date	Mintage	VG	F	VF	XF	Unc
1609KB	—	8.00	17.00	34.50	65.00	—
1610KB	—	8.00	17.00	34.50	65.00	—
1611KB	—	8.00	17.00	34.50	65.00	—

KM# 32 DENAR

Billon **Obv:** Long shield

Date	Mintage	VG	F	VF	XF	Unc
1611	—	8.00	17.00	34.50	65.00	—
1612	—	8.00	17.00	34.50	65.00	—
1613	—	8.00	17.00	34.50	65.00	—

KM# 40.1 DENAR

Billon **Obv:** Shield of arms divides K-B, titles of Matthias **Rev:** Withour rays, date in legend

Date	Mintage	VG	F	VF	XF	Unc
ND	—	6.00	14.00	22.50	46.00	—
1613KB	—	6.00	14.00	22.50	46.00	—
1614KB	—	6.00	14.00	22.50	46.00	—
1615KB	—	6.00	14.00	22.50	46.00	—
1616KB	—	6.00	14.00	22.50	46.00	—
1617KB	—	6.00	14.00	22.50	46.00	—
1618KB	—	6.00	14.00	22.50	46.00	—
1619KB	21,490,000	6.00	14.00	22.50	46.00	—
1620KB	17,315,000	6.00	14.00	22.50	46.00	—

KM# 40.2 DENAR

Billon **Note:** Thick planchet.

Date	Mintage	VG	F	VF	XF	Unc
1615 Rare	—	—	—	—	—	—
1616 Rare	—	—	—	—	—	—
1619 Rare	—	—	—	—	—	—

KM# 43.1 DENAR

Silver **Obv:** Shield of arms divides N-B in inner circle, date in legend, titles as king **Rev:** Madonna and child

Date	Mintage	VG	F	VF	XF	Unc
1614NB	—	6.00	14.00	22.50	46.00	—

KM# 54 DENAR

Silver **Rev:** Madonna and child in inner circle **Note:** Title as emperor. Varieties exist.

Date	Mintage	VG	F	VF	XF	Unc
1615	—	6.00	14.00	22.50	46.00	—
1616	—	6.00	14.00	22.50	46.00	—
1617	—	6.00	14.00	22.50	46.00	—

Date	Mintage	VG	F	VF	XF	Unc
1618	—	—	—	—	—	—
1619	—	—	—	—	—	—

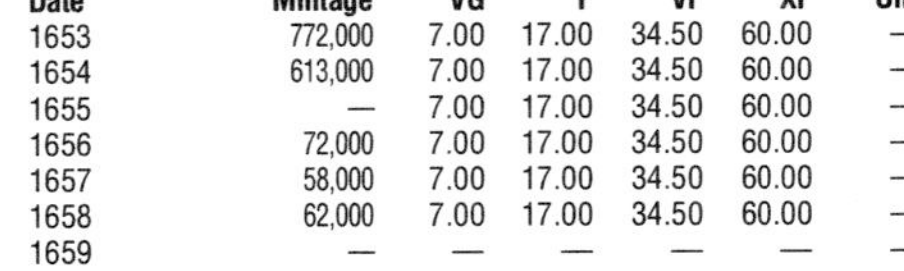

KM# 63 DENAR

Billon **Obv:** Hungarian arms cover entire inner circle

Date	Mintage	VG	F	VF	XF	Unc
1619	21,490,000	6.00	14.00	22.50	46.00	—
1620	17,315,000	6.00	14.00	22.50	46.00	—
1621	—	6.00	14.00	22.50	46.00	—
1622	—	6.00	14.00	22.50	46.00	—
1623	—	6.00	14.00	22.50	46.00	—
1624	—	6.00	14.00	22.50	46.00	—
1625	—	6.00	14.00	22.50	46.00	—

KM# A63 DENAR

Billon **Note:** Mule. KM#63 and Denar of Transylvania.

Date	Mintage	VG	F	VF	XF	Unc
1621	—	—	—	—	—	—

KM# 80 DENAR

Billon **Obv:** Shield of arms in inner circle **Rev:** Madonna and child, date in legend **Note:** Varieties exist.

Date	Mintage	VG	F	VF	XF	Unc
1623	—	6.00	14.00	22.50	46.00	—
1623 PP	—	6.00	14.00	22.50	46.00	—
1624 PP	—	6.00	14.00	22.50	46.00	—

KM# 88 DENAR

Billon **Obv:** Arms divide K-B, date above, in inner circle

Date	Mintage	VG	F	VF	XF	Unc
1625KB	—	6.00	14.00	22.50	46.00	—
1626KB	—	6.00	14.00	22.50	46.00	—
1627KB	—	6.00	14.00	22.50	46.00	—
1628KB	—	6.00	14.00	22.50	46.00	—
1629KB	—	6.00	14.00	22.50	46.00	—
1630KB	—	6.00	14.00	22.50	46.00	—

KM# 95 DENAR

Billon **Rev:** Date in legend

Date	Mintage	VG	F	VF	XF	Unc
1630	34,049,000	6.00	14.00	22.50	46.00	—
1631	16,165,000	6.00	14.00	22.50	46.00	—
1632	10,980,000	6.00	14.00	22.50	46.00	—
1633	11,360,000	6.00	14.00	22.50	46.00	—
1634	—	6.00	14.00	22.50	46.00	—
1635	8,320,000	6.00	14.00	22.50	46.00	—
1636	—	6.00	14.00	22.50	46.00	—
1637	—	6.00	14.00	22.50	46.00	—

KM# 99 DENAR

Silver **Note:** Titles of Ferdinand II. Varieties exist.

Date	Mintage	VG	F	VF	XF	Unc
1631	—	6.00	12.50	22.50	45.00	—
1632	—	6.00	12.50	22.50	45.00	—
1633	—	6.00	12.50	22.50	45.00	—
1634	—	6.00	12.50	22.50	45.00	—
1635	—	6.00	12.50	22.50	45.00	—

KM# 109 DENAR

Billon **Note:** Posthumous issue.

Date	Mintage	VG	F	VF	XF	Unc
1638	—	—	—	—	—	—

KM# 110 DENAR

Silver **Obv:** Shield of arms in inner circle **Rev:** Madonna and child in inner circle, date in legend

Date	Mintage	VG	F	VF	XF	Unc
1638	12,203,000	7.00	17.00	34.50	60.00	—
1639	11,862,000	7.00	17.00	34.50	60.00	—
1640	8,058,000	7.00	17.00	34.50	60.00	—
1641	6,731,000	7.00	17.00	34.50	60.00	—
1642	4,140,000	7.00	17.00	34.50	60.00	—
1643	3,876,000	7.00	17.00	34.50	60.00	—
1644	—	7.00	17.00	34.50	60.00	—
1645	—	7.00	17.00	34.50	60.00	—
1646	—	7.00	17.00	34.50	60.00	—
1647	—	7.00	17.00	34.50	60.00	—
1648	649,000	7.00	17.00	34.50	60.00	—
1649	1,047,000	7.00	17.00	34.50	60.00	—
1650	1,365,000	7.00	17.00	34.50	60.00	—
1651	1,221,000	7.00	17.00	34.50	60.00	—
1652	—	7.00	17.00	34.50	60.00	—
1653	772,000	7.00	17.00	34.50	60.00	—
1654	613,000	7.00	17.00	34.50	60.00	—
1655	—	7.00	17.00	34.50	60.00	—
1656	72,000	7.00	17.00	34.50	60.00	—
1657	58,000	7.00	17.00	34.50	60.00	—
1658	62,000	7.00	17.00	34.50	60.00	—
1659	—	—	—	—	—	—

KM# 125 DENAR

Silver **Obv:** Crowned oval arms in inner circle **Rev:** Radiant Madonna and child, date in legend

Date	Mintage	VG	F	VF	XF	Unc
1640	—	—	—	—	—	—

KM# 144 DENAR

Silver **Note:** Posthumous issue.

Date	Mintage	VG	F	VF	XF	Unc
1658KB	—	—	—	—	—	—
1659KB	—	—	—	—	—	—

KM# 152 DENAR

Billon **Obv:** Shield divides K-B in inner circle **Rev:** Madonna and child in inner circle, date in legend **Note:** Varieties exist.

Date	Mintage	VG	F	VF	XF	Unc
1659	61,000	7.00	17.00	34.50	60.00	—
1660	—	7.00	17.00	34.50	60.00	—
1661	—	7.00	17.00	34.50	60.00	—
1662	—	7.00	17.00	34.50	60.00	—
1674	—	7.00	17.00	34.50	60.00	—
1675	1,464,000	7.00	17.00	34.50	60.00	—
1676	—	7.00	17.00	34.50	60.00	—
1677	1,520,000	7.00	17.00	34.50	60.00	—
1678	1,459,000	7.00	17.00	34.50	60.00	—
1679	1,647,000	7.00	17.00	34.50	60.00	—
1680	1,652,000	7.00	17.00	34.50	60.00	—
1681	1,650,000	7.00	17.00	34.50	60.00	—
1682	—	7.00	17.00	34.50	60.00	—
1683	—	7.00	17.00	34.50	60.00	—

KM# 174 DENAR

Billon **Obv:** Crown above arms **Rev:** Date in legend

Date	Mintage	VG	F	VF	XF	Unc
1662	—	7.00	17.00	34.50	60.00	—
1663	340,000	7.00	17.00	34.50	60.00	—
1664	313,000	7.00	17.00	34.50	60.00	—
1665	174,000	7.00	17.00	34.50	60.00	—
1666	63,000	7.00	17.00	34.50	60.00	—
1667	81,000	7.00	17.00	34.50	60.00	—
1668	137,000	7.00	17.00	34.50	60.00	—
1670	152,000	7.00	17.00	34.50	60.00	—
1671	125,000	7.00	17.00	34.50	60.00	—
1672	143,000	7.00	17.00	34.50	60.00	—
1673	1,027,000	7.00	17.00	34.50	60.00	—
1683	1,809,000	7.00	17.00	34.50	60.00	—
1684	Inc. above	7.00	17.00	34.50	60.00	—
1685	1,428,000	7.00	17.00	34.50	60.00	—
1686	1,869,000	7.00	17.00	34.50	60.00	—
1687	2,055,000	7.00	17.00	34.50	60.00	—
1688	1,933,000	7.00	17.00	34.50	60.00	—
1689	1,676,000	7.00	17.00	34.50	60.00	—
1690	—	7.00	17.00	34.50	60.00	—
1691	1,733,000	7.00	17.00	34.50	60.00	—
1692	—	7.00	17.00	34.50	60.00	—
1693	2,385,000	7.00	17.00	34.50	60.00	—
1694	1,895,000	7.00	17.00	34.50	60.00	—
1695	1,501,000	7.00	17.00	34.50	60.00	—
1696	956,000	7.00	17.00	34.50	60.00	—

KM# 187 DENAR

Billon **Rev:** Head of Madonna divides date

Date	Mintage	VG	F	VF	XF	Unc
1673	—	7.00	17.00	34.50	60.00	—
1674	—	7.00	17.00	34.50	60.00	—
1675	1,464,000	7.00	17.00	34.50	60.00	—
1676	—	7.00	17.00	34.50	60.00	—
1677	—	7.00	17.00	34.50	60.00	—

KM# 221 DENAR

Silver **Ruler:** Leopold I **Obv:** Crowned arms divid N-B in inner circle **Rev:** Madonna and child in inner circle, date in legend

Date	Mintage	VG	F	VF	XF	Unc
1691NB	—	7.00	17.00	34.50	60.00	—
1693NB	—	7.00	17.00	34.50	60.00	—
1700NB	—	7.00	17.00	34.50	60.00	—

KM# 231 DENAR

Silver **Rev:** Date divided at top

Date	Mintage	VG	F	VF	XF	Unc
1695	—	7.00	17.00	34.50	60.00	—
1698	—	7.00	17.00	34.50	60.00	—
1699	—	7.00	17.00	34.50	60.00	—

MB# 264 GROSCHEN (4 DENAR)

Silver **Ruler:** Rudolf II **Obv:** Madonna and child divide mintmarks **Obv. Legend:** RVDOL • II • D • G • RO • IM • S • AV • GE • HV • BO • R • **Rev:** 4-fold arms with central shield of Austria, date at end of legend **Rev. Legend:** MONETA • NOVA • ANNO • DOMINI • **Note:** H#1048. Varieties exist. Known struck on thick flan for years 1584 and 1589, with weights of 24.75 grams and 10.00 grams (H-1047).

Date	Mintage	VG	F	VF	XF	Unc
160Z	—	22.50	46.00	75.00	115	—
1603	—	22.50	46.00	75.00	115	—
1604	—	22.50	46.00	75.00	115	—
1605	—	22.50	46.00	75.00	115	—
1606	—	22.50	46.00	75.00	115	—
1607	—	22.50	46.00	75.00	115	—

KM# 81 GROSCHEN OF 9 DENARE

Silver **Obv:** Ferdinand II

Date	Mintage	VG	F	VF	XF	Unc
1622	—	—	—	—	—	—
1623	—	17.00	34.50	60.00	105	—

KM# 232 POLTURA

Copper **Ruler:** Leopold I **Obv:** Monogram divides date **Rev:** Crowned value within branches **Note:** Without mint mark. City issue. Varieties exist.

Date	Mintage	VG	F	VF	XF	Unc
1695	1,646,000	9.00	17.00	34.50	70.00	—
1696	1,761,000	9.00	17.00	34.50	70.00	—
1697	2,296,000	7.00	14.00	30.00	65.00	—
1698	2,445,000	7.00	14.00	30.00	65.00	—
1699	2,692,000	7.00	14.00	30.00	65.00	—
1700	1,703,000	7.00	14.00	30.00	65.00	—

KM# 245.1 POLTURA

Silver **Ruler:** Leopold I **Obv:** Laureate bust right in inner circle, initials on truncation **Obv. Legend:** LEOPOLD • D • G • ...
Rev: Madonna and child above value and date

Date	Mintage	VG	F	VF	XF	Unc
1696	—	12.00	20.00	34.50	70.00	—
1697	—	12.00	20.00	34.50	70.00	—
1699NB ICB	—	12.00	20.00	34.50	70.00	—
1700NB ICB	—	12.00	20.00	34.50	70.00	—
1700NB	—	12.00	20.00	34.50	70.00	—

KM# 256 3 POLTUREN

Copper **Ruler:** Leopold I **Obv:** Crowned L in branches **Rev:** SC monogram divides date **Note:** Schemnitz issue.

Date	Mintage	VG	F	VF	XF	Unc
1695	—	20.00	40.00	80.00	150	—
1696	—	20.00	40.00	80.00	150	—
1697	—	20.00	40.00	80.00	150	—
1699	—	20.00	40.00	80.00	150	—
1700	—	20.00	40.00	80.00	150	—

KM# 227 KRAJCZAR

Silver **Obv:** Small laureate bust of Leopold I right in inner circle, value below **Rev:** Madonna and child divide N-B in inner circle, date divided at top

Date	Mintage	VG	F	VF	XF	Unc
1694NB	—	7.00	14.00	30.00	60.00	—
1695NB	—	7.00	14.00	30.00	60.00	—

KM# 233 KRAJCZAR

Silver **Obv:** Large laureate bust of Leopold I right in inner circle, value below **Rev:** Madonna and child divide C-M in inner circle, date in legend **Note:** Varieties exist.

Date	Mintage	VG	F	VF	XF	Unc
1695CM	—	7.00	14.00	30.00	60.00	—
1697CM	—	7.00	14.00	30.00	60.00	—
1698CM	—	7.00	14.00	30.00	60.00	—
1699CM	—	7.00	14.00	30.00	60.00	—

KM# 234 KRAJCZAR

Silver **Rev:** Date in legend **Note:** Varieties exist.

Date	Mintage	VG	F	VF	XF	Unc
1695NB PO	—	7.00	14.00	30.00	60.00	—
1699NB ICB	—	7.00	14.00	30.00	60.00	—

KM# 235 KRAJCZAR

Silver **Obv:** Laureate bust of Leopold I right in inner circle, value below **Rev:** Radiant Madonna and child in inner circle, Madonna's head divides date **Note:** Varieties exist.

Date	Mintage	VG	F	VF	XF	Unc
1695CH	—	7.00	14.00	30.00	60.00	—
1698CH	—	7.00	14.00	30.00	60.00	—
1699CH	—	7.00	14.00	30.00	60.00	—
1700CH	—	7.00	14.00	30.00	60.00	—

KM# 241 KRAJCZAR

Silver **Obv:** Large bust **Note:** Varieties exist.

Date	Mintage	VG	F	VF	XF	Unc
1698NB	—	7.00	14.00	30.00	60.00	—
1698NB ICB	—	7.00	14.00	30.00	60.00	—

KM# 188 2 KRAJCZAR

Silver **Obv:** Laureate bust of Leopold I right in inner circle, value below **Rev:** Madonna and child divide K-B in inner circle, date divided at top

Date	Mintage	VG	F	VF	XF	Unc
1673KB	—	12.00	22.50	40.25	70.00	—
1674KB	—	12.00	22.50	40.25	70.00	—

KM# 8 3 KRAJCZAR (Groschen)

Silver **Obv:** Madonna and child diviede N-B in inner circle **Obv. Legend:** RVDOL • II • D • G • RO • IM • S • AV • GE • HVN • B • R • **Rev:** 4-fold arms with central shield of Austria in baroque frame, date at end of legend **Rev. Legend:** MONETA • NOVA • ANNO • DOMINI •

Date	Mintage	VG	F	VF	XF	Unc
1601	—	22.50	46.00	75.00	115	—

KM# 19 3 KRAJCZAR (Groschen)

Silver **Obv:** Retrograde N in mint mark

Date	Mintage	VG	F	VF	XF	Unc
1604NB	—	22.50	45.00	75.00	115	—

KM# 24 3 KRAJCZAR (Groschen)

Silver **Obv:** Crowned arms divide K-B in inner circle **Rev:** Radiant Madonna and child in inner circle, date in legend **Note:** Varieties exist.

Date	Mintage	VG	F	VF	XF	Unc
1609KB	—	20.00	40.00	65.00	100	—
1610KB	—	20.00	40.00	65.00	100	—
1611KB	—	20.00	40.00	65.00	100	—
1612KB	—	20.00	40.00	65.00	100	—
1613KB	—	20.00	40.00	65.00	100	—

KM# 47 3 KRAJCZAR (Groschen)

Silver **Obv:** Without crown above arms **Note:** Varieties exist.

Date	Mintage	VG	F	VF	XF	Unc
1614NB	—	22.50	46.00	75.00	115	—
1615NB	—	22.50	46.00	75.00	115	—
1616NB	—	22.50	46.00	75.00	115	—
1617NB	—	22.50	46.00	75.00	115	—
1618NB	—	22.50	46.00	75.00	115	—
1619NB	—	22.50	46.00	75.00	115	—

KM# 44.1 3 KRAJCZAR (Groschen)

Silver **Obv:** Shield of arms divides K-B in inner circle **Rev:** Madonna and child without rays in inner circle, date in legend

Date	Mintage	VG	F	VF	XF	Unc
1614KB	—	22.50	46.00	75.00	115	—
1615KB	—	22.50	46.00	75.00	115	—

KM# 45 3 KRAJCZAR (Groschen)

Silver **Obv:** Crowned arms divides N-B in inner circle **Rev:** Radiant Madonna and child in inner circle, date in legend

Date	Mintage	VG	F	VF	XF	Unc
1614NB	—	22.50	46.00	75.00	115	—
1615NB	—	22.50	46.00	75.00	115	—

KM# 46 3 KRAJCZAR (Groschen)

Silver **Rev:** Madonna and child without rays in inner circle, date in legend

Date	Mintage	VG	F	VF	XF	Unc
1614	—	22.50	46.00	75.00	115	—

KM# 44.2 3 KRAJCZAR (Groschen)

Silver **Note:** Thick planchet.

Date	Mintage	VG	F	VF	XF	Unc
1615	—	—	—	—	—	—

KM# 82 3 KRAJCZAR (Groschen)

Silver **Obv:** Shield of arms in inner circle **Rev:** Madonna and child in inner circle, date in legend

Date	Mintage	VG	F	VF	XF	Unc
1623CH PP	—	22.50	46.00	75.00	115	—
1624CH PP	—	22.50	46.00	75.00	115	—
1624(d)	—	22.50	46.00	75.00	115	—

KM# 96.1 3 KRAJCZAR (Groschen)

Silver **Obv:** Crowned arms with notched sides divide N-B in inner circle **Rev:** Radiant Madonna and child in inner circle, date in legend

Date	Mintage	VG	F	VF	XF	Unc
1627NB	—	22.50	46.00	75.00	115	—
1630NB	—	22.50	46.00	75.00	115	—

KM# 96.2 3 KRAJCZAR (Groschen)

Silver **Obv:** Crowned arms with straight sides **Note:** Varieties exist.

Date	Mintage	VG	F	VF	XF	Unc
1630	—	22.50	46.00	75.00	115	—
1631	—	22.50	46.00	75.00	115	—

KM# 143 3 KRAJCZAR (Groschen)

Silver **Obv:** Laureate bust of Ferdinand III right in inner circle, value below **Rev:** Crowned double-headed eagle in inner circle, date in legend

Date	Mintage	VG	F	VF	XF	Unc
1657KB	—	22.50	46.00	75.00	115	—

KM# 162 3 KRAJCZAR (Groschen)

Silver **Obv:** Laureate bust of Leopold I right in inner circle, value below **Rev:** Radiant Madonna and child divide K-B in inner circle, date at top **Note:** Varieties exist.

Date	Mintage	VG	F	VF	XF	Unc
1661KB	—	8.00	17.00	34.50	70.00	—
1662KB	—	8.00	17.00	34.50	70.00	—
1663KB	—	8.00	17.00	34.50	70.00	—

KM# 163 3 KRAJCZAR (Groschen)

Silver **Rev:** Date in legend **Note:** Varieties exist.

Date	Mintage	VG	F	VF	XF	Unc
1661KB	—	8.00	17.00	34.50	70.00	—
1665KB	—	8.00	17.00	34.50	70.00	—
1666KB	—	8.00	17.00	34.50	70.00	—
1667KB	—	8.00	17.00	34.50	70.00	—
1668KB	—	8.00	17.00	34.50	70.00	—
1670KB	—	8.00	17.00	34.50	70.00	—
1672KB	—	8.00	17.00	34.50	70.00	—
1673KB	—	8.00	17.00	34.50	70.00	—
1674KB	—	8.00	17.00	34.50	70.00	—
1675KB	—	8.00	17.00	34.50	70.00	—
1676KB	—	8.00	17.00	34.50	70.00	—
1677KB	—	8.00	17.00	34.50	70.00	—
1678KB	—	8.00	17.00	34.50	70.00	—
1679KB	—	8.00	17.00	34.50	70.00	—
1680KB	—	8.00	17.00	34.50	70.00	—
1681KB	—	8.00	17.00	34.50	70.00	—
1682KB	—	8.00	17.00	34.50	70.00	—
1683KB	—	8.00	17.00	34.50	70.00	—
1684KB	—	8.00	17.00	34.50	70.00	—
1685KB	—	8.00	17.00	34.50	70.00	—
1686KB	—	8.00	17.00	34.50	70.00	—
1687KB	—	8.00	17.00	34.50	70.00	—
1688KB	—	8.00	17.00	34.50	70.00	—
1689KB	—	8.00	17.00	34.50	70.00	—
1690KB	—	8.00	17.00	34.50	70.00	—
1691KB	—	8.00	17.00	34.50	70.00	—
1692KB	—	8.00	17.00	34.50	70.00	—
1693KB	—	8.00	17.00	34.50	70.00	—
1694KB	—	8.00	17.00	34.50	70.00	—
1695KB	—	8.00	17.00	34.50	70.00	—
1696KB	—	8.00	17.00	34.50	70.00	—

KM# 194 3 KRAJCZAR (Groschen)

Silver **Ruler:** Leopold I **Obv:** Laureate bust **Rev:** Date divided at top **Note:** Varieties exist.

Date	Mintage	VG	F	VF	XF	Unc
1675CH	—	8.00	17.00	34.50	70.00	—
1695CH	—	8.00	17.00	34.50	70.00	—
1696CH	—	8.00	17.00	34.50	70.00	—
1697CH	—	8.00	17.00	34.50	70.00	—
1698CH	—	8.00	17.00	34.50	70.00	—
1699CH	—	8.00	17.00	34.50	70.00	—

KM# 200 3 KRAJCZAR (Groschen)

Silver **Ruler:** Leopold I **Obv:** Bust right in inner circle **Obv. Legend:** LEOPOLDVS • D • G • ... **Rev:** Radiant Madonna and child divide N-B in inner circle, date in legend **Note:** Varieties exist.

Date	Mintage	VG	F	VF	XF	Unc
1677NB IS	—	8.00	17.00	34.50	70.00	—
1696NB	—	8.00	17.00	34.50	70.00	—
1698NB ICB	—	8.00	17.00	34.50	70.00	—
1699NB ICB	—	8.00	17.00	34.50	70.00	—

KM# 225 3 KRAJCZAR (Groschen)

Silver **Ruler:** Leopold I **Obv:** Bust right in inner circle **Obv. Legend:** LEOPOLD • D • G • R • ... **Rev:** Date divided at top **Note:** Varieties exist.

Date	Mintage	VG	F	VF	XF	Unc
1690NB PO	—	8.00	17.00	34.50	70.00	—
1693NB PO	—	8.00	17.00	34.50	70.00	—
1694NB PO	—	8.00	17.00	34.50	70.00	—
1695NB PO	—	8.00	17.00	34.50	70.00	—
1696NB PO	—	8.00	17.00	34.50	70.00	—
1697NB	—	8.00	17.00	34.50	70.00	—
1698NB PO	—	8.00	17.00	34.50	70.00	—
1699NB PO	—	8.00	17.00	34.50	70.00	—

KM# 236 3 KRAJCZAR (Groschen)

Silver **Ruler:** Leopold I **Obv:** Bust right within inner circle **Obv. Legend:** LEOPOLD • D • G • ... **Rev:** Radiant Madonna and child divides C-M in inner circle, date in legend **Note:** Varieties exist.

Date	Mintage	VG	F	VF	XF	Unc
1695CM	—	8.00	17.00	34.50	70.00	—
1696CM	—	8.00	17.00	34.50	70.00	—

Date	Mintage	VG	F	VF	XF	Unc
1697CM	—	8.00	17.00	34.50	70.00	—
1698CM	—	8.00	17.00	34.50	70.00	—

KM# A236 3 KRAJCZAR (Groschen)

Silver **Rev:** Madonna with child on right

Date	Mintage	VG	F	VF	XF	Unc
1695NB PO	—	8.00	17.00	34.50	70.00	—
1696NB PO	—	8.00	17.00	34.50	70.00	—
1697NB PO	—	8.00	17.00	34.50	70.00	—
1698NB PO	—	8.00	17.00	34.50	70.00	—

KM# 164 6 KRAJCZAR

Silver **Ruler:** Leopold I **Obv:** Laureate bust right in inner circle, value below **Rev:** Radiant Madonna and child divide K-B in inner circle, date divided at top **Note:** Varieties exist.

Date	Mintage	VG	F	VF	XF	Unc
1661KB	—	9.00	20.00	40.25	80.00	—
1667KB	—	9.00	20.00	40.25	80.00	—
1668KB	—	9.00	20.00	40.25	80.00	—
1669/8KB	—	9.00	20.00	40.25	80.00	—
1669KB	—	9.00	20.00	40.25	80.00	—
1670KB	—	9.00	20.00	40.25	80.00	—
1671KB	—	9.00	20.00	40.25	80.00	—
1672KB	—	9.00	20.00	40.25	80.00	—
1673KB	—	9.00	20.00	40.25	80.00	—
1674KB	—	9.00	20.00	40.25	80.00	—
1681KB	—	9.00	20.00	40.25	80.00	—
1682KB	—	9.00	20.00	40.25	80.00	—

KM# 190 6 KRAJCZAR

Silver **Ruler:** Leopold I **Obv:** Bust right in inner circle **Obv. Legend:** LEOPOLDVS • D • G • R • ... **Rev:** Radiant Madonna and child divide N-B in inner circle **Rev. Legend:** PATRONA • HUNGARIÆ • **Note:** Varieties exist.

Date	Mintage	VG	F	VF	XF	Unc
1674NB LM	—	—	—	—	—	—
1676NB LM	—	9.00	20.00	40.25	80.00	—
1677NB IS	—	9.00	20.00	40.25	80.00	—
1677NB LM	—	9.00	20.00	40.25	80.00	—
1678NB IS	—	9.00	20.00	40.25	80.00	—
1680NB	—	9.00	20.00	40.25	80.00	—
1681NB	—	9.00	20.00	40.25	80.00	—
1684NB	—	9.00	20.00	40.25	80.00	—
1685NB PO/CR	—	9.00	20.00	40.25	80.00	—
1685NB PO	—	9.00	20.00	40.25	80.00	—
1686NB PO	—	9.00	20.00	40.25	80.00	—
1691NB PO	—	9.00	20.00	40.25	80.00	—
1692NB PO	—	9.00	20.00	40.25	80.00	—
1693NB PO	—	9.00	20.00	40.25	80.00	—
1694NB	—	9.00	20.00	40.25	80.00	—
1694NB PO	—	9.00	20.00	40.25	80.00	—

KM# 195 6 KRAJCZAR

Silver **Ruler:** Leopold I **Obv:** Bust laureate right **Note:** Varieties exist.

Date	Mintage	VG	F	VF	XF	Unc
1675(g)	—	9.00	20.00	40.25	80.00	—
1676(g)	—	9.00	20.00	40.25	80.00	—
1684(r)	—	9.00	20.00	40.25	80.00	—
1685(r)	—	9.00	20.00	40.25	80.00	—

KM# 165 15 KRAJCZAR

Silver **Ruler:** Leopold I **Obv:** Young laureate bust right in inner circle, value below **Rev:** Radiant Madonna and child above K-B in inner circle, date in legned

Date	Mintage	VG	F	VF	XF	Unc
1661KB	—	12.00	22.50	46.00	90.00	—

KM# 166 15 KRAJCZAR

Silver **Ruler:** Leopold I **Rev:** Madonna's head divides K-B

Date	Mintage	VG	F	VF	XF	Unc
1661KB	—	14.00	30.00	50.00	105	—

KM# 167 15 KRAJCZAR

Silver **Ruler:** Leopold I **Rev:** Date at top

Date	Mintage	VG	F	VF	XF	Unc
1661	—	12.00	22.50	46.00	90.00	—

KM# 175 15 KRAJCZAR

Silver **Ruler:** Leopold I **Obv:** Bust laureate right, legends on scroll **Rev:** Radiant Madonna and child, legends on scroll **Note:** Varieties exist.

Date	Mintage	VG	F	VF	XF	Unc
1661KB	—	12.00	22.50	46.00	90.00	—
1662KB	—	12.00	22.50	46.00	90.00	—
1663KB	—	12.00	22.50	46.00	90.00	—
1664KB	—	12.00	22.50	46.00	90.00	—
1665KB	—	12.00	22.50	46.00	90.00	—
1667KB	—	12.00	22.50	46.00	90.00	—
1674KB	—	12.00	22.50	46.00	90.00	—
1675/4KB	—	12.00	22.50	46.00	90.00	—
1675KB	—	12.00	22.50	46.00	90.00	—
1676KB	—	12.00	22.50	46.00	90.00	—
1677KB	—	12.00	22.50	46.00	90.00	—
1678KB	—	12.00	22.50	46.00	90.00	—
1679KB	—	12.00	22.50	46.00	90.00	—
1680KB	—	12.00	22.50	46.00	90.00	—
1681KB	—	12.00	22.50	46.00	90.00	—
1682KB	—	12.00	22.50	46.00	90.00	—
1683KB	—	12.00	22.50	46.00	90.00	—
1684KB	—	12.00	22.50	46.00	90.00	—
1685KB	—	12.00	22.50	46.00	90.00	—
1686/5KB	—	12.00	22.50	46.00	90.00	—
1686KB	—	12.00	22.50	46.00	90.00	—

KM# 179 15 KRAJCZAR

Silver **Ruler:** Leopold I **Note:** Klippe.

Date	Mintage	VG	F	VF	XF	Unc
1664	—	—	—	—	—	—

KM# 181 15 KRAJCZAR

Silver **Ruler:** Leopold I **Rev:** Madonna's head divides date, solid inner circles

Date	Mintage	VG	F	VF	XF	Unc
1669	—	—	—	—	—	—
1696	—	—	—	—	—	—

KM# 191 15 KRAJCZAR

Silver **Ruler:** Leopold I **Obv:** Bust laureate right **Rev:** Radiant Madonna with child held on left

Date	Mintage	VG	F	VF	XF	Unc
1674NB LM	—	12.00	22.50	46.00	90.00	—
1675NB LM	—	12.00	22.50	46.00	90.00	—
1676NB LM	—	12.00	22.50	46.00	90.00	—
1677NB LM	—	12.00	22.50	46.00	90.00	—
1677NB IS	—	12.00	22.50	46.00	90.00	—
1678NB IS	—	12.00	22.50	46.00	90.00	—
1679NB	—	12.00	22.50	46.00	90.00	—
1680NB	—	12.00	22.50	46.00	90.00	—
1682NB	—	12.00	22.50	46.00	90.00	—
1683NB PO	—	12.00	22.50	46.00	90.00	—
1683NB	—	12.00	22.50	46.00	90.00	—
1684NB PO	—	12.00	22.50	46.00	90.00	—
1684NB	—	12.00	22.50	46.00	90.00	—
1685NB PO	—	12.00	22.50	46.00	90.00	—
1686NB PO	—	12.00	22.50	46.00	90.00	—
1687NB PO	—	12.00	22.50	46.00	90.00	—
1688NB PO	—	12.00	22.50	46.00	90.00	—
1689NB PO	—	12.00	22.50	46.00	90.00	—
1690NB PO	—	12.00	22.50	46.00	90.00	—
1691NB PO	—	12.00	22.50	46.00	90.00	—
1694NB PO	—	12.00	22.50	46.00	90.00	—
1695NB PO	—	12.00	22.50	46.00	90.00	—

KM# 192 15 KRAJCZAR

Silver **Ruler:** Leopold I **Obv:** Bust laureate right **Rev:** Radiant Madonna with child **Note:** Varieties exist.

Date	Mintage	VG	F	VF	XF	Unc
1674(g)	—	12.00	22.50	46.00	90.00	—
1675(g)	—	12.00	22.50	46.00	90.00	—
1676(g)	—	12.00	22.50	46.00	90.00	—
1695CH	—	12.00	22.50	46.00	90.00	—
1696CH CHS	—	12.00	22.50	46.00	90.00	—
1696CH	—	12.00	22.50	46.00	90.00	—

KM# 208 15 KRAJCZAR

Silver **Ruler:** Leopold I **Obv:** Bust laureate right, legend in scroll **Rev:** Radiant Madonna and child, legend in scroll **Note:** Varieties exist.

Date	Mintage	VG	F	VF	XF	Unc
1685KB	—	12.00	22.50	46.00	90.00	—
1686KB	—	12.00	22.50	46.00	90.00	—
1687KB	—	12.00	22.50	46.00	90.00	—
1688KB	—	12.00	22.50	46.00	90.00	—
1689KB	—	12.00	22.50	46.00	90.00	—
1690KB	—	12.00	22.50	46.00	90.00	—

KM# 209 15 KRAJCZAR

Silver **Ruler:** Leopold I **Obv:** Bust laureate right, solid inner circle **Rev:** Radiant Madonna and child, solid inner circle, date in legend **Note:** Varieties exist.

Date	Mintage	VG	F	VF	XF	Unc
1685	—	12.00	22.50	46.00	90.00	—
1690	—	12.00	22.50	46.00	90.00	—
1691	—	12.00	22.50	46.00	90.00	—
1692	—	12.00	22.50	46.00	90.00	—
1693	—	12.00	22.50	46.00	90.00	—
1694	—	12.00	22.50	46.00	90.00	—
1695/4	—	12.00	22.50	46.00	90.00	—
1695	—	12.00	22.50	46.00	90.00	—
1696	—	12.00	22.50	46.00	90.00	—

KM# 237 15 KRAJCZAR

Silver **Ruler:** Leopold I **Obv:** Laureate bust right in inner circle, value below **Rev:** Radiant Madonna and child divides C-M in inner circle, date in legend **Note:** Varieties exist.

Date	Mintage	VG	F	VF	XF	Unc
1695CM	—	—	—	—	—	—
1696CM	—	—	—	—	—	—

KM# A192 15 KRAJCZAR

Silver **Ruler:** Leopold I **Obv:** Bust laureate right **Rev:** Madonna with child on right **Note:** Varieties exist.

Date	Mintage	VG	F	VF	XF	Unc
1696NB PO	—	12.00	22.50	46.00	90.00	—
1696NB	—	12.00	22.50	46.00	90.00	—

Date	Mintage	VG	F	VF	XF	Unc
1697NB PO	—	12.00	22.50	46.00	90.00	—
1698NB PO	—	12.00	22.50	46.00	90.00	—
1699NB ICB	—	12.00	22.50	46.00	90.00	—

MB# 266 1/4 THALER (18 KREUZER)

Silver **Ruler:** Rudolf II **Obv:** Armored bust right, small 4-fold arms and small Madonna and child divide legend **Obv. Legend:** + RVDOL • II • - D • G • RO • IM • S • AV • GER • HV - BO • REX • **Rev:** Crowned imperial eagle holding sword and scepter, imperial orb on breast, date at end of legend **Rev. Legend:** ARC • DVX • AVS • DVX • BVR • MAR • MO • **Note:** H#1046. Varieties exist.

Date	Mintage	VG	F	VF	XF	Unc
1601KB	—	60.00	115	230	400	—
160ZKB	—	60.00	115	230	400	—
1603KB	—	60.00	115	230	400	—
1604KB	—	60.00	115	230	400	—
1607KB	—	60.00	115	230	400	—
1608KB	—	60.00	115	230	400	—

KM# 25 1/4 THALER

Silver **Ruler:** Matthias **Obv:** Crowned bust right in inner circle, designatus legend **Rev:** Crowned arms divide K-B in Order collar and inner circle, date in legend

Date	Mintage	VG	F	VF	XF	Unc
1609KB	—	60.00	115	230	400	—
1610KB	—	60.00	115	230	400	—
1611KB	—	60.00	115	230	400	—

KM# 33.1 1/4 THALER

Silver **Ruler:** Matthias **Obv:** Crowned bust right **Note:** Legend as King of Hungary and Bohemia

Date	Mintage	VG	F	VF	XF	Unc
1611KB	—	60.00	115	230	400	—
1612KB	—	60.00	115	230	400	—
1613KB	—	60.00	115	230	400	—

KM# 33.2 1/4 THALER

Silver **Ruler:** Matthias **Note:** Thick planchet.

Date	Mintage	VG	F	VF	XF	Unc
1612	—	—	—	—	—	—

KM# 48 1/4 THALER

Silver **Ruler:** Matthias **Obv:** Laureate bust right in inner circle **Rev:** Crowned imperial eagle in inner circle, date in legend **Note:** Varieties exist.

Date	Mintage	VG	F	VF	XF	Unc
1614KB	—	46.00	100	190	350	—
1616KB	—	46.00	100	190	350	—
1617KB	—	46.00	100	190	350	—
1618KB	—	46.00	100	190	350	—
1619KB	—	46.00	100	190	350	—

KM# 71 1/4 THALER

Silver **Ruler:** Ferdinand II **Obv:** Laureate bust right

Date	Mintage	VG	F	VF	XF	Unc
1620KB	—	50.00	105	200	350	—
1622KB	—	50.00	105	200	350	—
1630KB	—	50.00	105	200	350	—
1631KB	—	50.00	105	200	350	—
1632KB	—	50.00	105	200	350	—
1633KB	—	50.00	105	200	350	—
1634KB	—	50.00	105	200	350	—
1635KB	—	50.00	105	200	350	—
1636KB	—	50.00	105	200	350	—
1637KB	—	50.00	105	200	350	—

KM# 70 1/4 THALER

Silver **Ruler:** Matthias **Obv:** Bust laureate right
Note: Posthumous issue.

Date	Mintage	VG	F	VF	XF	Unc
1620	—	75.00	145	260	450	—

KM# 103 1/4 THALER

Silver **Ruler:** Ferdinand II **Obv:** Modified laureate bust right in inner circle

Date	Mintage	VG	F	VF	XF	Unc
1633	—	—	—	—	—	—
1634	—	—	—	—	—	—

KM# 116 1/4 THALER

Silver **Ruler:** Ferdinand III **Obv:** Laureate bust right
Note: Varieties exist.

Date	Mintage	VG	F	VF	XF	Unc
1639	—	46.00	90.00	175	290	—
1640	—	46.00	90.00	175	290	—
1641	—	46.00	90.00	175	290	—
1642	—	46.00	90.00	175	290	—
1643	—	46.00	90.00	175	290	—
1644	—	46.00	90.00	175	290	—
1645	—	46.00	90.00	175	290	—
1647	—	46.00	90.00	175	290	—
1648	—	46.00	90.00	175	290	—
1649	—	46.00	90.00	175	290	—
1650	—	46.00	90.00	175	290	—
1651	—	46.00	90.00	175	290	—
1652	—	46.00	90.00	175	290	—
1653	—	46.00	90.00	175	290	—
1654	—	46.00	90.00	175	290	—
1655	—	46.00	90.00	175	290	—
1656	—	46.00	90.00	175	290	—
1657	—	46.00	90.00	175	290	—

KM# 130 1/4 THALER

Silver **Ruler:** Ferdinand III **Obv:** Laureate bust right in inner circle **Rev:** Crowned imperial eagle with N-B divided at bottom in inner circle, date in legend

Date	Mintage	VG	F	VF	XF	Unc
1643NB	—	—	—	—	—	—

KM# 145 1/4 THALER

Silver **Ruler:** Ferdinand III **Obv:** Laureate bust right
Note: Posthumous issue.

Date	Mintage	VG	F	VF	XF	Unc
1658KB	—	22.50	46.00	90.00	175	—
1659KB	—	22.50	46.00	90.00	175	—

KM# 153 1/4 THALER

Silver **Ruler:** Leopold I **Obv:** Young laureate bust right in inner circle **Rev:** Crowned imperial eagle in inner circle, date in legend **Note:** Varieties exist.

Date	Mintage	VG	F	VF	XF	Unc
1659	—	22.50	46.00	90.00	175	—
1660	—	22.50	46.00	90.00	175	—
1661	—	22.50	46.00	90.00	175	—

KM# 176 1/4 THALER

Silver **Ruler:** Leopold I **Obv:** Laureate bust right, date below, legend on scroll **Rev:** Legend on scroll

Date	Mintage	VG	F	VF	XF	Unc
1662	—	22.50	46.00	90.00	175	—
1664	—	22.50	46.00	90.00	175	—
1665	—	22.50	46.00	90.00	175	—
1677	—	22.50	46.00	90.00	175	—
1687	—	22.50	46.00	90.00	175	—

KM# 213 1/4 THALER

Silver **Ruler:** Leopold I **Obv:** Laureate bust right **Rev:** Imperial eagle, crown divides date **Note:** Varieties exist.

Date	Mintage	VG	F	VF	XF	Unc
1688KB	—	22.50	46.00	90.00	175	—
1693KB	—	22.50	46.00	90.00	175	—

KM# 228 1/4 THALER

Silver **Ruler:** Leopold I **Obv:** Laureate bust right flanked by arms and Madonna, value below, all in rhombus **Obv. Legend:** LEOPOLD • - D: G: ... **Rev:** Crowned imperial eagle in diamond, date in legend **Rev. Legend:** ARCHID • - AVST • DVX • ... **Note:** Varieties exist.

Date	Mintage	VG	F	VF	XF	Unc
1694KB	—	14.00	30.00	60.00	115	—
1695KB	—	14.00	30.00	60.00	115	—
1696KB	—	14.00	30.00	60.00	115	—
1698KB	—	14.00	30.00	60.00	115	—
1699KB	—	14.00	30.00	60.00	115	—
1700KB	—	14.00	30.00	60.00	115	—

KM# 238 1/4 THALER

Silver **Ruler:** Leopold I **Rev:** Radiant Madonna and child divided N-B in diamond, date in legend

Date	Mintage	VG	F	VF	XF	Unc
1695NB PO	—	14.00	30.00	60.00	115	—

KM# 250 1/4 THALER

Silver **Ruler:** Leopold I **Obv:** Crowned arms and Madonna and child added at sides of bust **Rev:** Crowned imperial eagle divides N-B in rhombus, date divided at top **Note:** Varieties exist.

Date	Mintage	VG	F	VF	XF	Unc
1700NB	—	14.00	30.00	60.00	115	—

MB# 268 1/2 THALER (36 KREUZER)

Silver **Ruler:** Rudolf II **Obv:** Armored bust right, small 4-fold arms and small Madonna and child divide legend **Obv. Legend:** + RVDOL • II • - D • G • RO • IM • S • AV • GER • HV - BO • REX • **Rev:** Crowned imperial eagle holding sword and scepter, imperial orb on breast, date at end of legend **Rev. Legend:** ARCHI • DVX • AVS • DVX • BVRG • MAR • MORA • **Note:** H#1043. Varieties exist.

Date	Mintage	VG	F	VF	XF	Unc
1601KB	—	75.00	145	260	425	—
1602KB	—	75.00	145	260	425	—
1603KB	—	75.00	145	260	425	—
1604KB	—	75.00	145	260	425	—
1605KB	—	75.00	145	260	425	—
1607KB	—	75.00	145	260	425	—
1608KB	—	75.00	145	260	425	—

KM# 29 1/2 THALER

Silver **Ruler:** Matthias **Note:** Klippe

Date	Mintage	VG	F	VF	XF	Unc
1608NB	—	85.00	175	290	500	—

KM# 26 1/2 THALER
Silver **Ruler:** Matthias **Obv:** Crowned bust right in inner circle, designatus legend **Rev:** Crowned arms divide K-B in Order collar and inner circle, date in legend

Date	Mintage	VG	F	VF	XF	Unc
1609KB	—	75.00	145	260	425	—
1610KB	—	75.00	145	260	425	—
1611	—	75.00	145	260	425	—

KM# 38 1/2 THALER
Silver **Ruler:** Matthias **Obv:** Crowned bust right **Note:** Legend as King of Hungary and Bohemia.

Date	Mintage	VG	F	VF	XF	Unc
161ZKB	—	115	200	375	575	—
1613KB	—	115	200	375	575	—

KM# 49 1/2 THALER
Silver **Ruler:** Matthias **Obv:** Laureate bust right **Rev:** Crowned double-headed eagle **Note:** Varieties exist.

Date	Mintage	VG	F	VF	XF	Unc
1614	—	50.00	100	185	300	—
1615	—	50.00	100	185	300	—
1616	—	50.00	100	185	300	—
1617	—	50.00	100	185	300	—
1618	—	50.00	100	185	300	—
1619	—	50.00	100	185	300	—

KM# 58 1/2 THALER
Silver **Ruler:** Matthias **Rev:** Crowned arms in cartouche divide N-B in inner circle, date in legend

Date	Mintage	VG	F	VF	XF	Unc
1617NB	—	—	—	—	—	—

KM# 72 1/2 THALER
Silver **Ruler:** Matthias **Obv:** Laureate bust right
Note: Posthumous issue.

Date	Mintage	VG	F	VF	XF	Unc
1620KB	—	85.00	175	325	525	—
1622KB	—	85.00	175	325	525	—

KM# 73 1/2 THALER
Silver **Ruler:** Ferdinand II **Obv:** Laureate bust right in inner circle **Rev:** Crowned imperial eagle in inner circle, date in legend **Note:** Varieties exist.

Date	Mintage	VG	F	VF	XF	Unc
1620	—	46.00	90.00	175	290	—
1622	—	46.00	90.00	175	290	—
1623	—	46.00	90.00	175	290	—
1625	—	46.00	90.00	175	290	—
1630	—	46.00	90.00	175	290	—
1631	—	46.00	90.00	175	290	—
1632	—	46.00	90.00	175	290	—
1633	—	46.00	90.00	175	290	—
1634	—	46.00	90.00	175	290	—
1635	—	46.00	90.00	175	290	—
1636	—	46.00	90.00	175	290	—
1637	—	46.00	90.00	175	290	—

KM# 86.1 1/2 THALER
Silver **Ruler:** Ferdinand II **Obv:** Laureate bust right in inner circle

Date	Mintage	VG	F	VF	XF	Unc
1624CH	—	70.00	140	290	450	—

KM# 86.2 1/2 THALER
Silver **Ruler:** Ferdinand II

Date	Mintage	VG	F	VF	XF	Unc
1630NB	—	60.00	115	230	375	—
1633NB	—	60.00	115	230	375	—
1635NB	—	60.00	115	230	375	—

KM# 111 1/2 THALER
Silver **Ruler:** Ferdinand III **Obv:** Laureate bust right in inner circle **Rev:** Crowned imperial eagle with N-B divided at bottom inner circle, date in legend

Date	Mintage	VG	F	VF	XF	Unc
1638NB	—	—	—	—	—	—

KM# 117 1/2 THALER
13.7300 g., Silver **Ruler:** Ferdinand III **Obv:** Laureate armored bust right within inner circle **Obv. Legend:** BOH REX FERDINAND III DG ROIS... **Rev:** Crowned imperial eagle holding shield of arms **Note:** Varieties exist.

Date	Mintage	VG	F	VF	XF	Unc
1639KB	—	46.00	90.00	175	290	—
1640KB	—	46.00	90.00	175	290	—
1641KB	—	46.00	90.00	175	290	—
1642KB	—	46.00	90.00	175	290	—
1643KB	—	46.00	90.00	175	290	—
1644KB	—	46.00	90.00	175	290	—
1645KB	—	46.00	90.00	175	290	—
1646KB	—	46.00	90.00	175	290	—
1647KB	—	46.00	90.00	175	290	—
1648KB	—	46.00	90.00	175	290	—
1649KB	—	46.00	90.00	175	290	—
1650KB	—	46.00	90.00	175	290	—
1651KB	—	46.00	90.00	175	290	—
1652KB	—	46.00	90.00	175	290	—
1653KB	—	46.00	90.00	175	290	—
1654KB	—	46.00	90.00	175	290	—
1655KB	—	46.00	90.00	175	290	—
1656KB	—	46.00	90.00	175	290	—
1657KB	—	46.00	90.00	175	290	—

KM# A146 1/2 THALER
Silver **Ruler:** Ferdinand III **Obv:** • I • K • / • E • M • / date and ornaments **Rev:** Crowned imperial eagle

Date	Mintage	VG	F	VF	XF	Unc
1655	—	—	—	—	—	—

KM# 146 1/2 THALER
Silver **Ruler:** Ferdinand III **Note:** Posthumous issue.

Date	Mintage	VG	F	VF	XF	Unc
1658KB	—	46.00	90.00	175	290	—
1659KB	—	46.00	90.00	175	290	—

KM# 154 1/2 THALER
Silver **Ruler:** Leopold I **Obv:** Young laureate bust right in inner circle **Rev:** Crowned imperial eagle in inner circle, date in legend **Note:** Varieties exist.

Date	Mintage	VG	F	VF	XF	Unc
1659KB	—	46.00	90.00	175	290	—
1660KB	—	46.00	90.00	175	290	—
1661KB	—	46.00	90.00	175	290	—

KM# 168 1/2 THALER
Silver **Ruler:** Leopold I **Obv:** Young laureate bust right in inner circle

Date	Mintage	VG	F	VF	XF	Unc
1661NB	—	46.00	90.00	175	290	—

KM# 169 1/2 THALER
Silver **Ruler:** Leopold I **Note:** Klippe. Varieties exist.

Date	Mintage	VG	F	VF	XF	Unc
1661	—	—	—	—	—	—

KM# 177 1/2 THALER
Silver **Ruler:** Leopold I **Obv:** Laureate bust right, date below, legend on scroll **Rev:** Legend on scroll **Note:** Varieties exist.

Date	Mintage	VG	F	VF	XF	Unc
1662KB	—	40.25	80.00	150	260	—
1663KB	—	40.25	80.00	150	260	—
1665KB	—	40.25	80.00	150	260	—

KM# 185 1/2 THALER
Silver **Ruler:** Leopold I **Note:** Solid inner circle on both sides. Varieties exist.

Date	Mintage	VG	F	VF	XF	Unc
1670	—	40.25	80.00	150	260	—

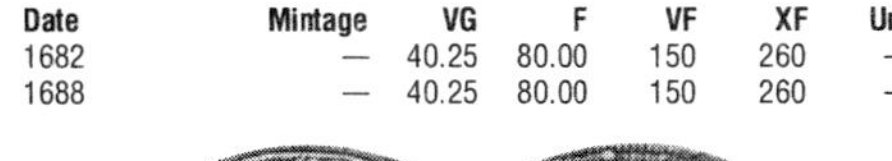

Date	Mintage	VG	F	VF	XF	Unc
1682	—	40.25	80.00	150	260	—
1688	—	40.25	80.00	150	260	—

KM# 220 1/2 THALER

Silver **Ruler:** Leopold I **Obv:** Laureate bust right **Note:** Varieties exist.

Date	Mintage	VG	F	VF	XF	Unc
1690KB	—	34.50	70.00	140	255	—
1691/0KB	—	34.50	70.00	140	255	—
1691KB	—	34.50	70.00	140	255	—
1692KB	—	34.50	70.00	140	255	—
1693KB	—	34.50	70.00	140	255	—
1694KB	—	34.50	70.00	140	255	—
1695KB	—	34.50	70.00	140	255	—
1696KB	—	34.50	70.00	140	255	—
1697KB	—	34.50	70.00	140	255	—
1698KB	—	34.50	70.00	140	255	—
1699KB	—	34.50	70.00	140	255	—

KM# 251 1/2 THALER

Silver **Ruler:** Leopold I **Obv:** Armored bust right **Obv. Legend:** LEOPOLD: - D: G: R: I: S: A: GER: - HV: BO: REX: **Rev:** Crowned arms within Order chain on eagle's breast **Rev. Legend:** ARCHID: AV: DVX: BV: MAR: MOR: ... **Note:** Varieties exist.

Date	Mintage	VG	F	VF	XF	Unc
1700KB	—	34.50	70.00	140	255	—

KM# 12 THALER

Silver **Ruler:** Rudolf II **Obv:** Crowned half figure right holding sceptre **Note:** Dav. #3014.

Date	Mintage	VG	F	VF	XF	Unc
1601NB	—	105	220	375	625	—
160ZNB	—	105	220	375	625	—
1603NB	—	105	220	375	625	—
1604NB	—	105	220	375	625	—

KM# 18 THALER

Silver **Ruler:** Rudolf II **Obv:** Armored bust in ruffled collar right in inner circle **Note:** Dav. #3015.

Date	Mintage	VG	F	VF	XF	Unc
1603	—	125	250	400	700	—
1604	—	125	250	400	700	—
1605	—	125	250	400	700	—
1607	—	125	250	400	700	—
1608	—	125	250	400	700	—

KM# 4 THALER

Silver **Ruler:** Rudolf II **Note:** Klippe. Dav. #3014A.

Date	Mintage	VG	F	VF	XF	Unc
1604 Rare	—	—	—	—	—	—

KM# 20 THALER

Silver **Ruler:** Rudolf II **Note:** Klippe. Dav. #3015A.

Date	Mintage	VG	F	VF	XF	Unc
1604 Rare	—	—	—	—	—	—
1608 Rare	—	—	—	—	—	—

KM# 27 THALER

Silver **Obv:** Crowned bust of Matthias right in inner circle, designatus legend **Rev:** Crowned arms divide K-B in Order collar and inner circle, date in legend **Note:** Dav. #3051.

Date	Mintage	VG	F	VF	XF	Unc
1609KB	22,000	105	220	375	625	—
1610KB	35,000	105	220	375	625	—
1611KB	72,000	105	220	375	625	—
1612KB	43,000	105	220	375	625	—

KM# 34 THALER

Silver **Obv:** Legend as King of Hungary and Bohemia **Note:** Dav. #3053.

Date	Mintage	VG	F	VF	XF	Unc
1611	Inc. above	105	220	375	625	—
1612	Inc. above	105	220	375	625	—
1613	48,000	105	220	375	625	—

KM# 41 THALER

Silver **Obv:** Laureate bust of Matthias right, titles of Holy Roman Emperor **Rev:** Crowned imperial eagle holding sword and sceptre **Note:** Varieties exist. Dav. #3054.

Date	Mintage	VG	F	VF	XF	Unc
1613KB	Inc. above	450	825	1,500	2,500	—
1614KB	—	450	825	1,500	2,500	—
1615/14KB	—	825	1,500	2,500	3,750	—
1615KB	—	450	825	1,500	2,500	—
1616KB	—	450	825	1,500	2,500	—
1617KB	—	450	825	1,500	2,500	—

KM# 59 THALER

Silver **Rev:** Small arms **Note:** Dav. #3056.

Date	Mintage	VG	F	VF	XF	Unc
1617KB	—	95.00	190	325	575	—
1618KB	—	95.00	190	325	575	—
1619KB	37,000	95.00	190	325	575	—
1620KB posthumous	—	95.00	190	325	575	—

KM# 75 THALER

Silver **Note:** Varieties exist. Dav. #3129.

Date	Mintage	VG	F	VF	XF	Unc
1620KB	67,000	65.00	125	200	325	—
1622KB	—	65.00	125	200	325	—
1623KB	—	65.00	125	200	325	—
1630KB	130,000	65.00	125	200	325	—
1631KB	255,000	65.00	125	200	325	—
1631KB Without mint mark	Inc. above	65.00	125	200	325	—
1632KB	181,000	65.00	125	200	325	—
1633KB	80,000	65.00	125	200	325	—
1634KB	—	65.00	125	200	325	—
1635KB	78,000	65.00	125	200	325	—
1636KB	—	65.00	125	200	325	—
1637KB	—	65.00	125	200	325	—

KM# 93 THALER

Silver **Obv:** Bust of Ferdinand II right **Rev:** Bust of Eleonora left **Note:** Show thaler

Date	Mintage	VG	F	VF	XF	Unc
1627	—	105	220	375	625	—

KM# 97.1 THALER

Silver **Obv:** Large bust **Note:** Dav. #3130.

Date	Mintage	VG	F	VF	XF	Unc
1630NB	—	155	325	575	950	—

KM# 97.2 THALER

Silver **Obv:** Smaller bust **Note:** Varieties exist. Dav. #3131.

Date	Mintage	VG	F	VF	XF	Unc
1630NB	—	95.00	190	325	575	—
1631NB	—	95.00	190	325	575	—
1632NB	—	95.00	190	325	575	—
1633NB	—	95.00	190	325	575	—

Date	Mintage	VG	F	VF	XF	Unc
1634NB	—	95.00	190	325	575	—
1635NB	—	95.00	190	325	575	—

KM# 106.1 THALER

Silver **Obv:** Laureate armored bust of Ferdinand II to right breaks top of inner circle **Note:** Dav. #A3132.

Date	Mintage	VG	F	VF	XF	Unc
1636NB	—	195	400	725	1,200	—

KM# 106.2 THALER

Silver **Obv:** Cloaked bust to right breaks top of inner circle **Note:** Varieties exist. Dav. #3132.

Date	Mintage	VG	F	VF	XF	Unc
1637	—	155	325	575	950	—

KM# 107 THALER

Silver **Note:** Dav. #3198.

Date	Mintage	VG	F	VF	XF	Unc
1637KB	—	65.00	125	200	325	—
1638KB	22,000	65.00	125	200	325	—
1639KB	13,000	65.00	125	200	325	—
1640KB	24,000	65.00	125	200	325	—
1641KB	59,000	65.00	125	200	325	—
1642KB	29,000	65.00	125	200	325	—
1643KB	30,000	65.00	125	200	325	—
1644KB	—	65.00	125	200	325	—
1645KB	—	65.00	125	200	325	—
1646KB	—	65.00	125	200	325	—
1647KB	—	65.00	125	200	325	—
1648KB	140,000	65.00	125	200	325	—
1649KB	261,000	65.00	125	200	325	—
1650KB	281,000	65.00	125	200	325	—
1651KB	305,000	65.00	125	200	325	—
1652KB	—	65.00	125	200	325	—
1653KB	367,000	65.00	125	200	325	—
1654KB	385,000	65.00	125	200	325	—
1655KB	—	65.00	125	200	325	—
1656KB	390,000	65.00	125	200	325	—
1657KB	365,000	65.00	125	200	325	—
1658KB posthumous	—	65.00	125	200	325	—
1659KB posthumous	—	65.00	125	200	325	—
1661KB posthumous	—	65.00	125	200	325	—

KM# 108 THALER

Silver **Obv:** Facing bust of Ferdinand III in inner circle **Note:** Dav. #3200.

Date	Mintage	VG	F	VF	XF	Unc
1637NB	—	105	220	375	625	—

KM# 112 THALER

Silver **Obv:** Laureate bust of Ferdinand III in ruffled collar right in inner circle **Note:** Dav. #3201.

Date	Mintage	VG	F	VF	XF	Unc
1638NB	—	575	1,050	1,900	3,150	—

KM# 113.1 THALER

Silver **Obv:** Laureate bust of Ferdinand III in lace collar right in inner circle **Note:** Dav. #3202.

Date	Mintage	VG	F	VF	XF	Unc
1638NB Rare	—	105	220	375	625	—

KM# 113.2 THALER

Silver **Note:** Varieties exist. Dav. #3203.

Date	Mintage	VG	F	VF	XF	Unc
1639NB	—	325	575	950	1,700	—
1640NB	—	325	575	950	1,700	—
1641NB	—	325	575	950	1,700	—
1642NB	—	325	575	950	1,700	—
1643NB	—	325	575	950	1,700	—
1644NB	—	325	575	950	1,700	—
1658NB	—	325	575	950	1,700	—
1659NB	—	325	575	950	1,700	—
1661NB	—	325	575	950	1,700	—

KM# 131 THALER

Silver **Note:** Klippe. Dav. #3203A.

Date	Mintage	VG	F	VF	XF	Unc
1643NB Rare	—	105	220	375	625	—

KM# 140 THALER

Silver **Note:** Klippe. Dav. #3198A.

Date	Mintage	VG	F	VF	XF	Unc
1650KB Rare	—	105	220	375	625	—

KM# 147 THALER

Silver **Subject:** Funeral of Johann Kewiczky, recorder at city of Kaschau **Note:** Struck on the request of the widow, Elisabeth Madarassy. Dav. #3199.

Date	Mintage	VG	F	VF	XF	Unc
1655KB	—	575	1,050	1,900	3,150	—

KM# 148 THALER

Silver **Obv:** Leopold I **Note:** Varieties exist. Dav. #3254.

Date	Mintage	VG	F	VF	XF	Unc
1658KB Reported, not confirmed	337,000	—	—	—	—	—
1659KB	278,000	37.50	80.00	155	300	—
1660KB	282,000	37.50	80.00	155	300	—
1661KB	—	37.50	80.00	155	300	—

KM# 161.1 THALER

Silver **Note:** Klippe. Dav. #3266A.

Date	Mintage	VG	F	VF	XF	Unc
1660NB Rare	—	105	220	375	625	—

KM# 160.1 THALER

Silver **Note:** Dav. #3266.

Date	Mintage	VG	F	VF	XF	Unc
1660NB	—	325	575	950	1,700	—
1661NB	—	325	575	950	1,700	—

KM# 160.2 THALER

Silver **Note:** Dav. #3267.

Date	Mintage	VG	F	VF	XF	Unc
1660NB	—	325	575	950	1,700	—
1662NB	—	325	575	950	1,700	—

KM# 170.1 THALER

Silver **Note:** Dav. #3255.

Date	Mintage	VG	F	VF	XF	Unc
1661KB	—	95.00	190	325	575	—

KM# 178.1 THALER

Silver **Obv:** Bust with lion face on shoulder **Note:** Dav. #3256.

Date	Mintage	VG	F	VF	XF	Unc
1662KB	—	95.00	190	325	575	—
1663KB	28,000	95.00	190	325	575	—

KM# 178.2 THALER

Silver **Obv:** Bust without lion face on shoulder **Note:** Dav. #3257.

Date	Mintage	VG	F	VF	XF	Unc
1662KB	—	95.00	190	325	575	—
1663KB	—	95.00	190	325	575	—

KM# 161.2 THALER

Silver **Note:** Dav. #3267A.

Date	Mintage	VG	F	VF	XF	Unc
1662NB Rare	—	105	220	375	625	—

KM# 160.3 THALER

Silver **Note:** Dav. #3268.

Date	Mintage	VG	F	VF	XF	Unc
1663NB	—	325	575	950	1,700	—
1664NB	—	325	575	950	1,700	—

KM# 161.3 THALER

Silver **Note:** Dav. #3268A.

Date	Mintage	VG	F	VF	XF	Unc
1663NB Rare	—	105	220	375	625	—

KM# 170.2 THALER

Silver **Note:** Varieties exist. Dav. #3258.

Date	Mintage	VG	F	VF	XF	Unc
1664KB	—	95.00	190	325	575	—
1665KB	20,000	95.00	190	325	575	—
1667KB	22,000	95.00	190	325	575	—
1668KB	—	95.00	190	325	575	—
1671KB	1,774	95.00	190	325	575	—
1673KB	1,822	95.00	190	325	575	—

KM# 161.4 THALER

Silver **Note:** Varieties exist. Dav. #3269A.

Date	Mintage	VG	F	VF	XF	Unc
1665NB Rare	—	105	220	375	625	—

KM# 160.4 THALER

Silver **Note:** Dav. #3269.

Date	Mintage	VG	F	VF	XF	Unc
1665NB	—	325	575	950	1,700	—

KM# 160.5 THALER

Silver **Note:** Dav. #3270.

Date	Mintage	VG	F	VF	XF	Unc
1666NB	—	325	575	950	1,700	—

KM# 160.6 THALER

Silver **Note:** Dav. #3271.

Date	Mintage	VG	F	VF	XF	Unc
1667NB	—	325	575	950	1,700	—
1668NB	—	325	575	950	1,700	—
1669NB	—	325	575	950	1,700	—

KM# 180.1 THALER

Silver **Note:** Octagonal klippe. Dav. #3271A.

Date	Mintage	VG	F	VF	XF	Unc
1668NB Rare	—	105	220	375	625	—

KM# 160.7 THALER

Silver **Note:** Dav. #3272.

Date	Mintage	VG	F	VF	XF	Unc
1670NB	—	190	375	700	1,150	—
1671NB	—	190	375	700	1,150	—

KM# 180.2 THALER

Silver **Note:** Dav. #3272A.

Date	Mintage	VG	F	VF	XF	Unc
1670NB Rare	—	105	220	375	625	—

KM# 160.8 THALER

Silver **Note:** Varieties exist. Dav. #3273.

Date	Mintage	VG	F	VF	XF	Unc
1671NB	—	190	375	700	1,150	—
1672NB	—	190	375	700	1,150	—
1673NB	—	190	375	700	1,150	—
1679NB	—	190	375	700	1,150	—

KM# 196 THALER

Silver **Note:** Dav. #3275.

Date	Mintage	VG	F	VF	XF	Unc
1674NB LM	—	325	575	950	1,700	—
1675NB LM	—	325	575	950	1,700	—
1687NB-PO	—	325	575	950	1,700	—
1688NB-PO	—	—	—	—	—	—
1695NB	—	325	575	950	1,700	—

KM# 205 THALER

Silver **Note:** Dav. #3259.

Date	Mintage	VG	F	VF	XF	Unc
1681KB	—	80.00	155	250	450	—
1682KB	—	80.00	155	250	450	—

KM# 214.1 THALER

Silver **Obv:** Laureate bust of Leopold I right in inner circle **Rev:** Crown of imperial eagle divides date **Note:** Dav. #3260.

Date	Mintage	VG	F	VF	XF	Unc
1687KB	19,000	75.00	140	220	375	—
1688KB	25,000	75.00	140	220	375	—
1689KB	43,000	75.00	140	220	375	—
1690KB	—	75.00	140	220	375	—
1691KB	779,000	75.00	140	220	375	—

KM# 214.2 THALER

Silver **Note:** Dav. #3261.

Date	Mintage	VG	F	VF	XF	Unc
1691KB	Inc. above	75.00	140	220	375	—

KM# 214.3 THALER

Silver **Note:** Dav. #3262.

Date	Mintage	VG	F	VF	XF	Unc
1692KB	512,000	75.00	140	220	375	—

KM# 214.4 THALER

Silver **Obv:** With four loops in bow knot **Note:** Dav. #3262A.

Date	Mintage	VG	F	VF	XF	Unc
1692KB	Inc. above	75.00	140	220	375	—

KM# 214.5 THALER

Silver **Obv:** Smaller bust **Note:** Dav. #3262B.

Date	Mintage	VG	F	VF	XF	Unc
1692KB	Inc. above	75.00	140	220	375	—

KM# 214.6 THALER

Silver **Note:** Dav. #3263.

Date	Mintage	VG	F	VF	XF	Unc
1692KB	Inc. above	75.00	140	220	375	—
1693KB	358,000	75.00	140	220	375	—

KM# 214.7 THALER

Silver **Obv:** Smaller bust **Note:** Dav. #3263A.

Date	Mintage	VG	F	VF	XF	Unc
1693KB	Inc. above	75.00	140	220	375	—

KM# 214.8 THALER

Silver **Note:** Dav. #3264.

Date	Mintage	VG	F	VF	XF	Unc
1693KB	—	75.00	140	220	375	—
1694KB	82,000	75.00	140	220	375	—

Date	Mintage	VG	F	VF	XF	Unc
1695KB	443,000	75.00	140	220	375	—
1696KB	324,000	75.00	140	220	375	—
1697KB	214,000	75.00	140	220	375	—
1698KB	364,000	75.00	140	220	375	—
1699KB	440,000	75.00	140	220	375	—

KM# 226 THALER

Silver **Note:** Klippe. Dav. #3264B.

Date	Mintage	VG	F	VF	XF	Unc
1693KB Rare	—	—	—	—	—	—

KM# 240 THALER

Silver **Obv:** Laureate bust of Leopold I right in inner circle **Rev:** Crowned imperial eagle in inner circle, date divided at top **Note:** Dav. #3276.

Date	Mintage	VG	F	VF	XF	Unc
1697CH Rare	—	105	220	375	625	—

KM# 214.9 THALER

Silver **Ruler:** Leopold I **Obv:** Laureate bust right **Obv. Legend:** LEOPOLDUS - D: G: ROM: IMP: S: A: - CE: HV: BO: R: **Rev:** Crown divides date at top **Rev. Legend:** ARCHIDVX • AVS: DVX... **Note:** Dav. #3265.

Date	Mintage	VG	F	VF	XF	Unc
1700KB	337,000	75.00	140	220	375	—

MB# 254 THALER (72 Kreuzer)

Silver **Ruler:** Rudolf II **Obv:** Armored bust right, small 4-fold arms and small Madonna and child divide legend **Obv. Legend:** + RVDOL. II. - D.G. RO. IM. S. AV. GER. HVN - BOE. REX. **Rev:** Crowned imperial eagle holding sword and scepter, imperial orb on breast, date at end of legend **Rev. Legend:** ARCHI. DVX. AVS. DVX. BVRG. MAR. MORA. **Note:** Dav. #8066 (ref. H#1030). Varieties exist.

Date	Mintage	VG	F	VF	XF	Unc
1601KB	—	105	220	375	625	—
160ZKB	—	105	220	375	625	—
1603KB	—	105	220	375	625	—
1604KB	—	105	220	375	625	—
1605KB	—	105	220	375	625	—
1607KB	—	105	220	375	625	—
1608KB	—	105	220	375	625	—

KM# 13 1-1/2 THALER

Silver **Ruler:** Rudolf II **Obv:** Young armored bust of Rudolph II in ruffled collar right in inner circle **Rev:** Crowned imperial eagle with sword and sceptre divide K-B in inner circle, date in legend **Note:** Dav. #3012.

Date	Mintage	VG	F	VF	XF	Unc
1601KB	—	—	—	—	—	—

KM# 141 1-1/2 THALER

Silver **Obv:** Laureate bust of Ferdinand III right in inner circle **Rev:** Crowned imperial eagle in inner circle, date in legend

Date	Mintage	VG	F	VF	XF	Unc
1650	—	—	—	—	—	—

KM# 14.1 2 THALER

Silver **Obv:** Young armored bust of Rudolph II in ruffled collar right in inner circle **Rev:** Crowned imperial eagle with sword and sceptre divide K-B in inner circle, date in legend **Note:** Dav. #3011.

Date	Mintage	VG	F	VF	XF	Unc
1601KB	—	575	950	1,550	2,500	—
1604KB	—	575	950	1,550	2,500	—

KM# 14.2 2 THALER

Silver **Note:** Thicker planchet.

Date	Mintage	VG	F	VF	XF	Unc
1603	—	575	950	1,550	2,500	—

KM# 21 2 THALER

Silver **Note:** Two strikings of Thaler dies on rectangular bar.

Date	Mintage	VG	F	VF	XF	Unc
1608NB	—	575	950	1,550	2,500	—

KM# 28 2 THALER

Silver **Obv:** Crowned bust of Matthias right in inner circle, designatus legend **Rev:** Crowned arms divide K-B in Order collar and inner circle, date in legend **Note:** Dav. #A3050.

Date	Mintage	VG	F	VF	XF	Unc
1609KB	—	1,000	1,700	2,800	4,700	—

KM# 35 2 THALER

Silver **Note:** Legend as King of Hungary and Bohemia. Dav. #A3052.

Date	Mintage	VG	F	VF	XF	Unc
1611KB	—	1,000	1,700	2,800	4,700	—
1612KB	—	1,000	1,700	2,800	4,700	—

KM# 50 2 THALER

Silver **Obv:** Laureate bust of Mathias right in inner circle, titles of Holy Roman Emperor **Rev:** Crowned imperial eagle holding sword and sceptre in inner circle, date in legend **Note:** Varieties exist. Dav. #B3055.

Date	Mintage	VG	F	VF	XF	Unc
1614	—	1,000	1,700	2,800	4,700	—
1616	—	1,000	1,700	2,800	4,700	—

KM# 77 2 THALER

Silver **Obv:** Laureate bust of Ferdinand II right in inner circle **Rev:** Crowned imperial eagle in inner circle, date in legend **Note:** Dav. #3128.

Date	Mintage	VG	F	VF	XF	Unc
1622KB	—	450	825	1,250	2,050	—
1633KB	—	450	825	1,250	2,050	—
1636KB	—	450	825	1,250	2,050	—

KM# 83 2 THALER

Silver **Note:** Dav. #3133.

Date	Mintage	VG	F	VF	XF	Unc
1623 BZ Rare	—	—	—	—	—	—

KM# 132 2 THALER

Silver **Obv:** Portrait and titles of Ferdinand III **Note:** Varieties exist. Dav. #3197.

Date	Mintage	VG	F	VF	XF	Unc
1640KB	—	575	950	1,550	2,500	—
1641KB	—	575	950	1,550	2,500	—
1644KB	—	575	950	1,550	2,500	—
1650KB	—	575	950	1,550	2,500	—
1651KB	—	575	950	1,550	2,500	—
1652KB	—	575	950	1,550	2,500	—
1653KB	—	575	950	1,550	2,500	—
1655KB	—	575	950	1,550	2,500	—

KM# 149 2 THALER

Silver **Note:** Posthumous issue.

Date	Mintage	VG	F	VF	XF	Unc
1658	—	575	950	1,550	2,500	—

KM# 155 2 THALER

Silver **Obv:** Young laureate bust of Leopold I right **Rev:** Crowned imperial eagle **Note:** Dav. #A3254.

Date	Mintage	VG	F	VF	XF	Unc
1659KB Rare	—	—	—	—	—	—

KM# 212 2 THALER

Silver **Obv:** Laureate bust of Leopold I right in inner circle **Rev:** Radiant Madonna and child divide N-B in inner circle, date in legend **Note:** Dav. #3274.

Date	Mintage	VG	F	VF	XF	Unc
1687NB LM Rare	—	—	—	—	—	—
1695NB PO	—	—	—	—	—	—
1695NB LM Rare	—	—	—	—	—	—

KM# 222.1 2 THALER

Silver **Obv:** Older laureate bust of Leopold I **Rev:** Crown divides date **Note:** Dav. #A3261.

Date	Mintage	VG	F	VF	XF	Unc
1691KB Rare	—	—	—	—	—	—

KM# 222.2 2 THALER

Silver **Note:** Varieties exist. Dav. #A3262.

Date	Mintage	VG	F	VF	XF	Unc
1692KB Rare	—	—	—	—	—	—

KM# 15.1 3 THALER

Silver **Obv:** Young armored bust of Rudolph II in ruffled collar right in inner circle **Rev:** Crowned imperial eagle with sword and sceptre divide K-B in inner circle, date in legend **Note:** Dav. #A3011.

Date	Mintage	VG	F	VF	XF	Unc
1601KB	—	1,250	2,200	3,750	6,300	—

KM# 15.2 3 THALER

Silver **Note:** Thicker planchet. Dav. #A3011.

Date	Mintage	VG	F	VF	XF	Unc
1603KB	—	1,250	2,200	3,750	6,300	—

KM# 36 3 THALER

Silver **Obv:** Crowned bust of Matthias right in inner circle, legend as King of Hungary and Bohemia **Rev:** Crowned arms divide K-B in Order collar and inner circle, date in legend **Note:** Dav. #3052.

Date	Mintage	VG	F	VF	XF	Unc
1611KB Rare	—	—	—	—	—	—

KM# 84 3 THALER

Silver **Note:** Thick planchet, 85.20-85.73 grams. Dav. #3127.

Date	Mintage	VG	F	VF	XF	Unc
1623KB Rare	—	—	—	—	—	—
1637KB Rare	—	—	—	—	—	—

KM# 126 3 THALER
Silver **Obv:** Portrait and titles of Ferdinand III **Note:** Varieties exist. Dav. #3196.

Date	Mintage	VG	F	VF	XF	Unc
1641KB	—	1,250	2,200	3,750	6,300	—
1644KB	—	1,250	2,200	3,750	6,300	—
1645KB	—	1,250	2,200	3,750	6,300	—
1647KB	—	1,250	2,200	3,750	6,300	—
1653KB	—	1,250	2,200	3,750	6,300	—
1655KB	—	1,250	2,200	3,750	6,300	—

KM# 30 4 THALER
Silver **Obv:** Crowned bust of Matthias right in inner circle, designatus legend **Rev:** Crowned arms divide K-B in Order collar and inner circle, date in legend **Note:** Dav. #B3050.

Date	Mintage	VG	F	VF	XF	Unc
1610KB Rare	—	—	—	—	—	—

KM# 57 4 THALER
Silver **Obv:** Laureate bust of Matthias right in inner circle **Rev:** Crowned imperial eagle holding sword and sceptre in inner circle, date in legend **Note:** Dav. #A3055.

Date	Mintage	VG	F	VF	XF	Unc
1616KB Rare	—	—	—	—	—	—

KM# 85 4 THALER
Silver **Obv:** Laureate bust of Ferdinand II right in inner circle **Rev:** Crowned imperial eagle in inner circle, date in legend **Note:** Dav. #3126.

Date	Mintage	VG	F	VF	XF	Unc
1623KB Rare	—	—	—	—	—	—
1631KB Rare	—	—	—	—	—	—

KM# 127 4 THALER
Silver **Obv:** Portrait and titles of Ferdinand III **Note:** Dav. #3195.

Date	Mintage	VG	F	VF	XF	Unc
1641KB Rare	—	—	—	—	—	—
1648KB Rare	—	—	—	—	—	—
1651KB Rare	—	—	—	—	—	—
1658KB Rare, posthumous	—	—	—	—	—	—

KM# 31 5 THALER
Silver **Obv:** Crowned bust of Matthias right in inner circle, designatus legend **Rev:** Crowned arms divide K-B in Order collar and inner circle, date in legend

Date	Mintage	VG	F	VF	XF	Unc
1610KB Rare	—	—	—	—	—	—

KM# 142 5 THALER
Silver **Obv:** Laureate bust of Ferdinand III right in inner circle **Rev:** Crowned imperial eagle in inner circle, date in legend **Note:** Varieties exist. Dav. #A3195.

Date	Mintage	VG	F	VF	XF	Unc
1651KB Rare	—	—	—	—	—	—
1654KB Rare	—	—	—	—	—	—

TRADE COINAGE

MB# 258 GOLDGULDEN
3.5000 g., 0.9860 Gold 0.1109 oz. AGW **Ruler:** Rudolf II **Obv:** Madonna and Child on crescent, small shield of Austria arms at bottom **Obv. Legend:** RVDOL. II. D.G. RO. — I. S. AV. GE. HV. B. R. **Rev:** Crowned and armored full-length figure of St. Ladislaus, holding halbert, divides mintmarks, legend ends with date **Rev. Legend:** S. LADISLAVS. — REX. **Note:** Varieties exist; FR#63; (ref. H-1002).

Date	Mintage	VG	F	VF	XF	Unc
1601KB	—	140	280	500	850	—
1602KB	—	140	280	500	850	—
1603KB	—	140	280	500	850	—
1604KB	—	140	280	500	850	—

MB# 304 GOLDGULDEN
3.5000 g., 0.9860 Gold 0.1109 oz. AGW **Ruler:** Rudolf II **Obv:** Crowned and armored full-length figure of St. Ladislaus, holding halbert, divides mintmarks **Obv. Legend:** RVDOL. II. D.G. ROM — IM. S. A. G. H. B. R. **Rev:** Madonna and Child, date at end of legend **Rev. Legend:** PATRONA. HVNGARIÆ. **Note:** Varieties exist; FR#68; (ref. H-1007).

Date	Mintage	VG	F	VF	XF	Unc
1602NB	—	155	325	575	950	—
1603NB	—	155	325	575	950	—
1604NB	—	155	325	575	950	—
1607NB	—	155	325	575	950	—
1608NB	—	155	325	575	950	—

KM# B29 3 GOLDGULDEN
10.5000 g., 0.9860 Gold 0.3328 oz. AGW **Ruler:** Rudolf II **Note:** Struck on thick flan from Goldgulden dies, KM#A29; FR#69; (ref. H-1000).

Date	Mintage	VG	F	VF	XF	Unc
1605CB (cg)	—	2,450	4,550	8,400	13,500	—

KM# 189 1/6 DUCAT
0.5833 g., 0.9860 Gold 0.0185 oz. AGW **Obv:** Leopold I **Rev:** Radiant Madonna and child above arms

Date	Mintage	VG	F	VF	XF	Unc
1673NB LM	—	120	175	325	525	—
1674NB LM	—	120	175	325	525	—
1679NB	—	120	175	325	525	—
1682NB	—	120	175	325	525	—
1685NB	—	120	175	325	525	—
1686NB	—	120	175	325	525	—
1689NB	—	120	175	325	525	—
1690NB	—	120	175	325	525	—
1692NB	—	120	175	325	525	—
1695NB PO	—	120	175	325	525	—
1696NB	—	120	175	325	525	—
1697NB PO	—	120	175	325	525	—
1698NB IB	—	120	175	325	525	—

KM# A16 1/4 DUCAT
0.8750 g., 0.9860 Gold 0.0277 oz. AGW **Obv:** Shield of arms **Rev:** Madonna and child divide N-B, date in legend **Note:** Struck with 1 Denar dies, KM#7.

Date	Mintage	VG	F	VF	XF	Unc
1601NB	—	375	725	1,350	2,300	—
1604NB	—	375	725	1,350	2,300	—

KM# 67 1/4 DUCAT
0.8750 g., 0.9860 Gold 0.0277 oz. AGW **Note:** Similar to 1 Ducat, KM#3.

Date	Mintage	VG	F	VF	XF	Unc
1608	—	350	700	1,250	2,100	—

KM# A50 1/4 DUCAT
0.8750 g., 0.9860 Gold 0.0277 oz. AGW **Obv:** Shield of arms divides N-B, date in legend, titles as king **Rev:** Madonna and child **Note:** Struck with 1 Denar dies, KM#43.

Date	Mintage	VG	F	VF	XF	Unc
1614NB	—	375	775	1,400	2,450	—

KM# 55.1 1/4 DUCAT
0.8750 g., 0.9860 Gold 0.0277 oz. AGW **Obv:** Matthias standing right in inner circle **Rev:** Madonna and child above arms in inner circle

Date	Mintage	VG	F	VF	XF	Unc
1615	—	280	550	1,100	1,950	—

KM# 55.2 1/4 DUCAT
0.8750 g., 0.9860 Gold 0.0277 oz. AGW **Obv:** Without mint mark

Date	Mintage	VG	F	VF	XF	Unc
1615	—	280	550	1,100	1,950	—

KM# A100 1/4 DUCAT
0.8750 g., 0.9860 Gold 0.0277 oz. AGW **Obv:** Ferdinand II **Note:** Struck with 1 Thaler dies, KM#71.

Date	Mintage	VG	F	VF	XF	Unc
1632	—	375	775	140	2,450	—

KM# A104 1/4 DUCAT
0.8750 g., 0.9860 Gold 0.0277 oz. AGW **Note:** Titles of Ferdinand II. Struck with 1 Denar dies, KM#99.

Date	Mintage	VG	F	VF	XF	Unc
1635	—	375	775	1,400	2,450	—

KM# A131 1/4 DUCAT
0.8750 g., 0.9860 Gold 0.0277 oz. AGW **Obv:** Shield of arms in inner circle **Rev:** Madonna and child in inner circle, date in legend **Note:** Struck with 1 Denar dies, KM#110.

Date	Mintage	VG	F	VF	XF	Unc
1639	—	375	775	1,400	2,450	—
1642	—	375	775	1,400	2,450	—

KM# A134 1/4 DUCAT
0.8750 g., 0.9860 Gold 0.0277 oz. AGW **Obv:** Crowned oval arms in inner circle **Rev:** Raidiant Madonna and child, date in legend **Note:** Struck with 1 Denar dies, KM#125.

Date	Mintage	VG	F	VF	XF	Unc
1640	—	—	—	350	700	—
1643	—	—	—	350	700	—

KM# 201 1/4 DUCAT
0.8750 g., 0.9860 Gold 0.0277 oz. AGW **Obv:** Laureate bust of Leopold right in inner circle, value at shoulder **Rev:** Radiant Madonna standing with child above arms, date above

Date	Mintage	VG	F	VF	XF	Unc
1679NB	—	140	210	350	625	—

KM# 207 1/4 DUCAT
0.8750 g., 0.9860 Gold 0.0277 oz. AGW **Rev:** Seated Madonna and child divide mint mark in inner circle, arms below

Date	Mintage	VG	F	VF	XF	Unc
1684	—	105	175	325	550	—
1685	—	105	175	325	550	—
1696	—	105	175	325	550	—

KM# 242 1/4 DUCAT
0.8750 g., 0.9860 Gold 0.0277 oz. AGW **Obv:** Laureate bust of Leopold without value at shoulder **Rev:** Date divided at top

Date	Mintage	VG	F	VF	XF	Unc
1698 ICB	—	140	210	350	625	—

KM# 246 1/4 DUCAT
0.8750 g., 0.9860 Gold 0.0277 oz. AGW **Obv:** Value at shoulder **Rev:** Date at upper left

Date	Mintage	VG	F	VF	XF	Unc
1699 ICB	—	140	210	350	625	—

KM# 156 1/3 DUCAT
1.1666 g., 0.9860 Gold 0.0370 oz. AGW **Obv:** 6-line inscription

Date	Mintage	VG	F	VF	XF	Unc
1655	—	375	775	1,400	2,450	—

KM# 197 1/3 DUCAT
1.1666 g., 0.9860 Gold 0.0370 oz. AGW **Obv:** Leopold I **Rev:** Radiant Madonna and child above arms

Date	Mintage	VG	F	VF	XF	Unc
1675CH (g)	—	210	350	700	1,250	—

KM# A5 1/2 DUCAT
1.7500 g., 0.9860 Gold 0.0555 oz. AGW **Obv:** Shield of arms **Rev:** Madonna and child divide N-B, date in legend **Note:** Struck with 1 Denar dies, KM#7.

Date	Mintage	VG	F	VF	XF	Unc
1604N-B	—	245	375	850	1,400	—

KM# A120 1/2 DUCAT
1.7500 g., 0.9860 Gold 0.0555 oz. AGW **Obv:** 4-line inscription **Rev:** Scale divides date

Date	Mintage	VG	F	VF	XF	Unc
1625	—	245	375	850	1,400	—

KM# A130 1/2 DUCAT
1.7500 g., 0.9860 Gold 0.0555 oz. AGW **Obv:** Shield of arms in inner circle **Rev:** Madonna and child in inner circle, date in legend **Note:** Struck with 1 Denar dies, KM#110.

Date	Mintage	VG	F	VF	XF	Unc
1642K-B	—	280	500	975	1,750	—

KM# C180 1/2 DUCAT
1.7500 g., 0.9860 Gold 0.0555 oz. AGW **Obv:** Crown above arms **Rev:** Date in legend **Note:** Struck with 1 Denar dies, KM#174.

Date	Mintage	VG	F	VF	XF	Unc
1667	—	280	500	1,050	1,750	—

KM# 1.1 DUCAT
3.5000 g., 0.9860 Gold 0.1109 oz. AGW **Obv:** Legend around Madonna and child **Obv. Legend:** RVDOL. II. D.G... **Rev:** St. Ladislaus

Date	Mintage	VG	F	VF	XF	Unc
1601K-B	—	170	230	425	700	—
1602K-B	—	170	230	425	700	—
1603K-B	—	170	230	425	700	—
1604K-B	—	170	230	425	700	—

KM# 1.2 DUCAT
3.5000 g., 0.9860 Gold 0.1109 oz. AGW **Obv:** Roses added to Madonna and child

Date	Mintage	VG	F	VF	XF	Unc
1604K-B	—	170	230	425	700	—
1605K-B	—	170	230	425	700	—
1606K-B	—	170	230	425	700	—
1607K-B	—	170	230	425	700	—
1608K-B	—	170	230	425	700	—

KM# A29 DUCAT

3.5000 g., 0.9860 Gold 0.1109 oz. AGW **Rev:** Crowned imperial eagle **Note:** Klausenberg mint mark: C-B/Castle. Previously KM#29.

Date	Mintage	VG	F	VF	XF	Unc
1604	—	625	1,200	2,100	3,500	—
1605	—	625	1,200	2,100	3,500	—

KM# 37 DUCAT

3.5000 g., 0.9860 Gold 0.1109 oz. AGW **Rev:** Radiant Madonna and child **Note:** Matthias

Date	Mintage	VG	F	VF	XF	Unc
1609K-B	—	175	350	625	1,050	—
1610K-B	—	175	350	625	1,050	—
1611K-B	—	175	350	625	1,050	—
161ZKB	—	175	350	625	1,050	—
1613K-B	—	175	350	625	1,050	—

KM# 42 DUCAT

3.5000 g., 0.9860 Gold 0.1109 oz. AGW **Rev:** Arms added below Madonna and child

Date	Mintage	VG	F	VF	XF	Unc
1613KB	—	175	350	625	1,050	—
1614KB	—	175	350	625	1,050	—
1615KB	—	175	350	625	1,050	—
1616KB	—	175	350	625	1,050	—
1617KB	—	175	350	625	1,050	—
1618KB	—	175	350	625	1,050	—
1619KB	32,000	175	350	625	1,050	—
1620KB	44,000	175	350	625	1,050	—

KM# 51 DUCAT

3.5000 g., 0.9860 Gold 0.1109 oz. AGW

Date	Mintage	VG	F	VF	XF	Unc
1614NB	—	245	425	900	1,700	—

KM# 52 DUCAT

3.5000 g., 0.9860 Gold 0.1109 oz. AGW **Rev:** Madonna with child at left in inner circle

Date	Mintage	VG	F	VF	XF	Unc
1614	—	245	425	900	1,700	—

KM# 56 DUCAT

3.5000 g., 0.9860 Gold 0.1109 oz. AGW **Rev:** Madonna with ornate gown

Date	Mintage	VG	F	VF	XF	Unc
1615	—	245	425	900	1,700	—
1616	—	245	425	900	1,700	—
1619	—	245	425	900	1,700	—

KM# 60 DUCAT

3.5000 g., 0.9860 Gold 0.1109 oz. AGW **Obv:** Matthias standing facing divides mint mark in inner circle **Rev:** Madonna with child at right in inner circle, crowned arms below

Date	Mintage	VG	F	VF	XF	Unc
1617	—	245	425	900	1,700	—

KM# 61 DUCAT

3.5000 g., 0.9860 Gold 0.1109 oz. AGW **Rev:** Madonna with child at left

Date	Mintage	VG	F	VF	XF	Unc
1617	—	245	425	900	1,700	—
1618	—	245	425	900	1,700	—
1619	—	245	425	900	1,700	—

KM# 76 DUCAT

3.5000 g., 0.9860 Gold 0.1109 oz. AGW **Obv:** Ferdinand II standing right divides mint mark in inner circle **Rev:** Madonna and child in inner circle, crowned arms below

Date	Mintage	VG	F	VF	XF	Unc
1620K-B	—	175	350	625	1,050	—

KM# 78 DUCAT

3.5000 g., 0.9860 Gold 0.1109 oz. AGW **Rev:** Radiant Madonna and child

Date	Mintage	VG	F	VF	XF	Unc
1622KB	—	175	325	525	900	—
1623KB	—	175	325	525	900	—
1624KB	—	175	325	525	900	—
1625KB	—	175	325	525	900	—
1626KB	—	175	325	525	900	—
1627KB	—	175	325	525	900	—
1628KB	—	175	325	525	900	—
1629KB	—	175	325	525	900	—
1630KB	—	175	325	525	900	—
1631KB	—	175	325	525	900	—
1632KB	—	175	325	525	900	—
1633KB	—	175	325	525	900	—
1634KB	—	175	325	525	900	—
1635KB	—	175	325	525	900	—
1636KB	—	175	325	525	900	—
1637KB	—	175	325	525	900	—

KM# 98 DUCAT

3.5000 g., 0.9860 Gold 0.1109 oz. AGW **Rev:** Madonna and child in inner circle, crowned arms below

Date	Mintage	VG	F	VF	XF	Unc
1630N-B	—	245	500	975	1,750	—
1631N-B	—	245	500	975	1,750	—
1632N-B	—	245	500	975	1,750	—
1633N-B	—	245	500	975	1,750	—
1634N-B	—	245	500	975	1,750	—
1635N-B	—	245	500	975	1,750	—
1636N-B	—	245	500	975	1,750	—
1637N-B	—	245	500	975	1,750	—

KM# 100 DUCAT

3.5000 g., 0.9860 Gold 0.1109 oz. AGW **Rev:** Crescent below Madonna

Date	Mintage	VG	F	VF	XF	Unc
1632K-B	—	175	350	625	1,050	—

KM# 101 DUCAT

3.5000 g., 0.9860 Gold 0.1109 oz. AGW **Rev:** Cushion beneath Madonna

Date	Mintage	VG	F	VF	XF	Unc
1632N-B	—	280	525	1,050	1,900	—

KM# 104 DUCAT

3.5000 g., 0.9860 Gold 0.1109 oz. AGW **Rev:** Madonna with child at right

Date	Mintage	VG	F	VF	XF	Unc
1633	—	210	375	700	1,250	—

KM# 114 DUCAT

3.5000 g., 0.9860 Gold 0.1109 oz. AGW **Obv:** Ferdinand III **Rev:** Radiant Madonna and child

Date	Mintage	VG	F	VF	XF	Unc
1638K-B	—	175	325	525	900	—
1639K-B	—	175	325	525	900	—
1640K-B	—	175	325	525	900	—
1641K-B	—	175	325	525	900	—
1642K-B	—	175	325	525	900	—
1643K-B	—	175	325	525	900	—
1644K-B	—	175	325	525	900	—
1645K-B	—	175	325	525	900	—
1646K-B	—	175	325	525	900	—
1647K-B	—	175	325	525	900	—
1648K-B	—	175	325	525	900	—
1649K-B	—	175	325	525	900	—
1650K-B	—	175	325	525	900	—
1651K-B	—	175	325	525	900	—
1652K-B	—	175	325	525	900	—
1653K-B	—	175	325	525	900	—
1654K-B	—	175	325	525	900	—
1655K-B	—	175	325	525	900	—
1656K-B	—	175	325	525	900	—
1657K-B	—	175	325	525	900	—
1658K-B posthumous	—	175	325	525	900	—
1659K-B posthumous	—	175	325	525	900	—

KM# 115 DUCAT

3.5000 g., 0.9860 Gold 0.1109 oz. AGW **Rev:** Madonna with ornate gown and child in inner circle, crowned arm below

Date	Mintage	VG	F	VF	XF	Unc
1638NB	—	280	525	1,100	2,050	—

KM# 118 DUCAT

3.5000 g., 0.9860 Gold 0.1109 oz. AGW **Rev:** Madonna with plain gown

Date	Mintage	VG	F	VF	XF	Unc
1639	—	280	525	1,100	2,050	—

KM# 119 DUCAT

3.5000 g., 0.9860 Gold 0.1109 oz. AGW **Rev:** Rays surround Madonna and child

Date	Mintage	VG	F	VF	XF	Unc
1639	—	280	525	1,100	2,050	—
1642	—	280	525	1,100	2,050	—
1643	—	280	525	1,100	2,050	—
1644	—	280	525	1,100	2,050	—

KM# 120 DUCAT

3.5000 g., 0.9860 Gold 0.1109 oz. AGW **Obv:** Ferdinand III standing facing

Date	Mintage	VG	F	VF	XF	Unc
1639	—	280	525	1,100	2,050	—
1641	—	280	525	1,100	2,050	—

KM# 129 DUCAT

3.5000 g., 0.9860 Gold 0.1109 oz. AGW **Rev:** Madonna with child at right

Date	Mintage	VG	F	VF	XF	Unc
1642	—	280	525	1,100	2,050	—

KM# B130 DUCAT

3.5000 g., 0.9860 Gold 0.1109 oz. AGW **Note:** Struck with 1 Dinar dies, KM#26.

Date	Mintage	VG	F	VF	XF	Unc
1642K-B	—	450	900	1,700	2,800	—

KM# 133 DUCAT

3.5000 g., 0.9860 Gold 0.1109 oz. AGW **Rev:** Madonna with ornate gown holds child at left, without rays

Date	Mintage	VG	F	VF	XF	Unc
1644NB	—	280	525	1,100	2,050	—

KM# 134 DUCAT

3.5000 g., 0.9860 Gold 0.1109 oz. AGW **Rev:** Madonna with child at right

Date	Mintage	VG	F	VF	XF	Unc
1644	—	280	525	1,100	2,050	—

KM# 151 DUCAT

3.5000 g., 0.9860 Gold 0.1109 oz. AGW **Ruler:** Leopold I **Obv:** Leopold standing right divides mint mark in inner circle

Obv. Legend: LEOPOLD: D: G: R - S: A: G: H: B: R E X **Rev:** Madonna with child at right **Rev. Legend:** • AR • AV • DV • BV • M • - MOCO • TY • date

Date	Mintage	VG	F	VF	XF	Unc
1658K-B	—	175	325	500	775	—
1659K-B	—	175	325	500	775	—
1660K-B	—	175	325	500	775	—
1661K-B	—	175	325	500	775	—
1662K-B	—	175	325	500	775	—
1663K-B	—	175	325	500	775	—
1664K-B	—	175	325	500	775	—
1665K-B	—	175	325	500	775	—
1666K-B	—	175	325	500	775	—
1667K-B	—	175	325	500	775	—
1668K-B	—	175	325	500	775	—
1669K-B	—	175	325	500	775	—
1670K-B	—	175	325	500	775	—
1671K-B	—	175	325	500	775	—
1672K-B	—	175	325	500	775	—
1673K-B	—	175	325	500	775	—
1674K-B	—	175	325	500	775	—
1675K-B	—	175	325	500	775	—
1676K-B	—	175	325	500	775	—
1677K-B	—	175	325	500	775	—
1678K-B	—	175	325	500	775	—
1679K-B	—	175	325	500	775	—
1680K-B	—	175	325	500	775	—
1681K-B	—	175	325	500	775	—
1682K-B	—	175	325	500	775	—
1683K-B	—	175	325	500	775	—
1684K-B	—	175	325	500	775	—
1685K-B	—	175	325	500	775	—
1686K-B	—	175	325	500	775	—
1687K-B	64,000	175	325	500	775	—
1688K-B	55,000	175	325	500	775	—
1689K-B	55,000	175	325	500	775	—
1690K-B	70,000	175	325	500	775	—
1691K-B	108,000	175	325	500	775	—
1692K-B	—	175	325	500	775	—
1693K-B	83,000	175	325	500	775	—
1694K-B	87,000	175	325	500	775	—
1695K-B	—	175	325	500	775	—
1696K-B	—	175	325	500	775	—
1697K-B	—	175	325	500	775	—
1698K-B	—	175	325	500	775	—
1699K-B	—	175	325	500	775	—
1700K-B	—	175	325	500	775	—

KM# 171 DUCAT

3.5000 g., 0.9860 Gold 0.1109 oz. AGW **Rev:** Radiant Madonna and child in inner circle, crowned arms below

Date	Mintage	VG	F	VF	XF	Unc
1661/0N-B	—	280	525	1,100	2,050	—
1667N-B	—	280	525	1,100	2,050	—
1671N-B	—	280	525	1,100	2,050	—

KM# 186 DUCAT

3.5000 g., 0.9860 Gold 0.1109 oz. AGW **Obv:** Madonna with child at right in inner circle **Rev:** Radiant Madonna with child at left in inner circle, crowned arms below **Note:** Without mint mark.

Date	Mintage	VG	F	VF	XF	Unc
1671	—	175	325	500	775	—

KM# 193 DUCAT

3.5000 g., 0.9860 Gold 0.1109 oz. AGW **Obv:** Laureate bust of Leopold right in inner circle **Rev:** Radiant Madonna and child divides mint mark in inner circle, crowned arms below

Date	Mintage	VG	F	VF	XF	Unc
1674 LM	—	350	850	1,800	3,500	—
1676 LM	—	350	850	1,800	3,500	—
1677 IS	—	350	850	1,800	3,500	—
1677 LM	—	350	850	1,800	3,500	—
1678 IS	—	350	850	1,800	3,500	—

KM# 198 DUCAT

3.5000 g., 0.9860 Gold 0.1109 oz. AGW **Rev:** Radiant Madonna and child in inner circle, 3 shields below

Date	Mintage	VG	F	VF	XF	Unc
1675	—	350	850	1,800	3,500	—

KM# 206 DUCAT

3.5000 g., 0.9860 Gold 0.1109 oz. AGW **Obv:** Leopold standing in finer style

Date	Mintage	VG	F	VF	XF	Unc
1683N-B	—	190	375	700	1,200	—
1687N-B	—	190	375	700	1,200	—
1691N-B	—	190	375	700	1,200	—
1692N-B	—	190	375	700	1,200	—
1694N-B	—	190	375	700	1,200	—
1695N-B	—	190	375	700	1,200	—
1696N-B	—	190	375	700	1,200	—
1697N-B	—	190	375	700	1,200	—
1698N-B	—	190	375	700	1,200	—

KM# 210 DUCAT

3.5000 g., 0.9860 Gold 0.1109 oz. AGW **Rev:** Madonna and child

Date	Mintage	VG	F	VF	XF	Unc
1685K-B	—	175	325	500	775	—

KM# 211 DUCAT

3.5000 g., 0.9860 Gold 0.1109 oz. AGW **Obv:** Leopold standing divides mint mark, moneyers initials

Date	Mintage	VG	F	VF	XF	Unc
1685N-B	—	175	280	425	700	—
1687N-B	—	175	280	425	700	—
1689N-B	—	175	280	425	700	—

KM# A214.1 DUCAT

3.5000 g., 0.9860 Gold 0.1109 oz. AGW **Obv:** Leupold standing divides mint mark, moneyer's initials **Note:** Previous KM#214.1.

Date	Mintage	VG	F	VF	XF	Unc
1689	—	175	280	425	700	—

KM# 223 DUCAT

3.5000 g., 0.9860 Gold 0.1109 oz. AGW **Note:** Octagonal klippe.

Date	Mintage	VG	F	VF	XF	Unc
1691	—	700	1,400	2,800	4,200	—

KM# 224 DUCAT

3.5000 g., 0.9860 Gold 0.1109 oz. AGW **Rev:** Madonna and child divides moneyers initials

Date	Mintage	VG	F	VF	XF	Unc
1691 PO	—	175	280	500	850	—
1695 PO	—	175	280	500	850	—
1696 PO	—	175	280	500	850	—
1697 PO	—	175	280	500	850	—
1698 PO	—	175	280	500	850	—

KM# 239 DUCAT

3.5000 g., 0.9860 Gold 0.1109 oz. AGW **Obv:** Leopold standing right divides mint mark in inner circle

Date	Mintage	VG	F	VF	XF	Unc
1695CH	—	450	900	1,700	2,800	—
1696CH	—	450	900	1,700	2,800	—
1699CH	—	450	900	1,700	2,800	—

KM# A238 DUCAT

3.5000 g., 0.9860 Gold 0.1109 oz. AGW **Obv:** Bust Leopold facing right in inner circle **Rev:** Madonna and child divide date at top

Date	Mintage	VG	F	VF	XF	Unc
1695 C-H Rare	—	—	—	—	—	—

KM# 247 DUCAT

3.5000 g., 0.9860 Gold 0.1109 oz. AGW **Ruler:** Leopold I **Obv:** Initials below Leopold standing

Date	Mintage	VG	F	VF	XF	Unc
1699NB	—	280	550	1,050	1,750	—
1700NB	—	280	550	1,050	1,750	—

KM# 2 2 DUCAT

7.0000 g., 0.9860 Gold 0.2219 oz. AGW **Obv:** Legend around Madonna and child **Obv. Legend:** RVDOL \ II \ D.G... **Rev:** St. Ladislaus

Date	Mintage	VG	F	VF	XF	Unc
1601K-B	—	975	2,100	3,850	6,300	—

KM# 53 2 DUCAT

7.0000 g., 0.9860 Gold 0.2219 oz. AGW **Obv:** Matthias standing right divides mint mark in inner circle **Obv. Legend:** RVDOL • II • D.G... **Rev:** Radiant Madonna and child in inner circle, crowned arms below

Date	Mintage	VG	F	VF	XF	Unc
1614	—	425	850	1,750	3,500	—
1616	—	425	850	1,750	3,500	—
1618	—	425	850	1,750	3,500	—

KM# 79 2 DUCAT

7.0000 g., 0.9860 Gold 0.2219 oz. AGW **Obv:** Ferdinand II standing right in inner circle **Note:** Without mint mark

Date	Mintage	VG	F	VF	XF	Unc
1616	—	425	850	1,750	3,500	—
1622	—	425	850	1,750	3,500	—
1624	—	425	850	1,750	3,500	—

KM# 89 2 DUCAT

7.0000 g., 0.9860 Gold 0.2219 oz. AGW

Date	Mintage	VG	F	VF	XF	Unc
1617NB	—	425	850	1,750	3,500	—

KM# 87 2 DUCAT

7.0000 g., 0.9860 Gold 0.2219 oz. AGW **Obv:** Ferdinand II standing divides mint mark

Date	Mintage	VG	F	VF	XF	Unc
1624K-B	—	350	700	1,400	2,800	—
1625K-B	—	350	700	1,400	2,800	—
1626K-B	—	350	700	1,400	2,800	—
1627K-B	—	350	700	1,400	2,800	—
1628K-B	—	350	700	1,400	2,800	—
1629K-B	—	350	700	1,400	2,800	—
1630K-B	—	350	700	1,400	2,800	—
1631K-B	—	350	700	1,400	2,800	—
1632K-B	—	350	700	1,400	2,800	—
1633K-B	—	350	700	1,400	2,800	—
1634K-B	—	350	700	1,400	2,800	—
1635K-B	—	350	700	1,400	2,800	—
1636K-B	—	350	700	1,400	2,800	—
1637K-B	—	350	700	1,400	2,800	—

KM# 94 2 DUCAT

7.0000 g., 0.9860 Gold 0.2219 oz. AGW

Date	Mintage	VG	F	VF	XF	Unc
1630	—	350	700	1,400	2,800	—

KM# 128 2 DUCAT

7.0000 g., 0.9860 Gold 0.2219 oz. AGW **Obv:** Ferdinand II standing right divides mint mark in inner circle

Date	Mintage	VG	F	VF	XF	Unc
1641KB	—	350	625	1,350	2,600	—
1644KB	—	350	625	1,350	2,600	—
1645KB	—	350	625	1,350	2,600	—
1646KB	—	350	625	1,350	2,600	—
1647KB	—	350	625	1,350	2,600	—
1648KB	—	350	625	1,350	2,600	—
1649KB	—	350	625	1,350	2,600	—
1650KB	—	350	625	1,350	2,600	—
1651KB	—	350	625	1,350	2,600	—
1654KB	—	350	625	1,350	2,600	—

KM# 172 2 DUCAT

7.0000 g., 0.9860 Gold 0.2219 oz. AGW **Obv:** Leopold standing right divides mint mark in inner circle

Date	Mintage	VG	F	VF	XF	Unc
1661	—	500	975	2,100	3,850	—
1667	—	500	975	2,100	3,850	—

KM# B16 3 DUCAT

10.5000 g., 0.9860 Gold 0.3328 oz. AGW **Obv:** Armored 1/2 figure of Rudolph II **Note:** Struck with 1/2 Thaler dies, KM#10.

Date	Mintage	VG	F	VF	XF	Unc
1601KB Rare	—	—	—	—	—	—

KM# A211 3 DUCAT
10.5000 g., 0.9860 Gold 0.3328 oz. AGW **Note:** Leopold I

Date	Mintage	F	VF	XF	Unc	BU
1687	—	1,700	3,150	5,600	9,100	—

KM# A240 3 DUCAT
10.5000 g., 0.9860 Gold 0.3328 oz. AGW **Obv:** Laureate bust of Leopold I right in inner circle **Rev:** Crowned imperial eagle in inner circle, date in legend **Note:** Struck with 1/2 Thaler dies, KM#220.

Date	Mintage	VG	F	VF	XF	Unc
1695KB	—	1,700	3,150	5,600	9,100	—

KM# A102 4 DUCAT
14.0000 g., 0.9860 Gold 0.4438 oz. AGW **Obv:** Laureate bust of Ferdinand right **Rev:** Crowned imperial eagle **Note:** Struck with 1/2 Thaler dies, KM#75. Klippe.

Date	Mintage	VG	F	VF	XF	Unc
1622K-B Rare	—	—	—	—	—	—

KM# B211 4 DUCAT
14.0000 g., 0.9860 Gold 0.4438 oz. AGW **Note:** Leopold I

Date	Mintage	VG	F	VF	XF	Unc
1687NB LM	—	2,450	4,200	7,000	11,000	—

KM# C211 4 DUCAT
14.0000 g., 0.9860 Gold 0.4438 oz. AGW **Note:** Struck with 1/2 Thaler dies, KM#220.

Date	Mintage	VG	F	VF	XF	Unc
1695 PO	—	2,450	4,200	7,000	11,000	—

KM# B1 5 DUCAT
17.5000 g., 0.9860 Gold 0.5547 oz. AGW

Date	Mintage	VG	F	VF	XF	Unc
1601NB Rare	—	—	—	—	—	—

KM# C16 5 DUCAT
17.5000 g., 0.9860 Gold 0.5547 oz. AGW **Obv:** Armored 1/2 figure Rudolph II right **Rev:** Crowned imperial eagle divides mint mark NB **Note:** Struck with 1 Thaler dies, KM#10.

Date	Mintage	VG	F	VF	XF	Unc
1601NB Rare	—	—	—	—	—	—

KM# A53 5 DUCAT
17.5000 g., 0.9860 Gold 0.5547 oz. AGW **Obv:** Standing figure right **Rev:** Madonna and child

Date	Mintage	VG	F	VF	XF	Unc
1614KB	—	2,250	3,850	6,700	11,000	—
1617KB	—	2,250	3,850	6,700	11,000	—

KM# A90 5 DUCAT
17.5000 g., 0.9860 Gold 0.5547 oz. AGW **Rev:** Crowned arms in cartouche divide N-B in inner circle, date in legend **Note:** Struck with 1/2 Thaler dies, KM#58.

Date	Mintage	VG	F	VF	XF	Unc
1617NB Rare	—	—	—	—	—	—

KM# 102 5 DUCAT
17.5000 g., 0.9860 Gold 0.5547 oz. AGW **Obv:** Ferdinand II

Date	Mintage	VG	F	VF	XF	Unc
1622KB	—	2,800	4,200	7,000	12,000	—
1632KB	—	2,800	4,200	7,000	12,000	—

KM# A95 5 DUCAT
17.5000 g., 0.9860 Gold 0.5547 oz. AGW **Obv:** Different laureate bust of Ferdinand II right in inner circle **Note:** Struck with 1/4 Thaler dies, KM#103.

Date	Mintage	VG	F	VF	XF	Unc
1631 Rare	—	—	—	—	—	—

KM# A105 5 DUCAT
17.5000 g., 0.9860 Gold 0.5547 oz. AGW **Obv:** Laureate bust of Ferdinand II right in inner circle **Rev:** Crowned imperial eagle in inner circle, date in legend **Note:** Struck with 1/2 Thaler dies, KM#73.

Date	Mintage	VG	F	VF	XF	Unc
1634KB Rare	—	—	—	—	—	—
1637KB	—	3,500	5,600	9,100	14,000	—

KM# A180 5 DUCAT
17.5000 g., 0.9860 Gold 0.5547 oz. AGW **Obv:** Laureate bust of Leopold in inner circle **Note:** Struck with 1 Thaler dies, KM#170.2.

Date	Mintage	VG	F	VF	XF	Unc
1665	—	2,800	4,200	7,000	12,000	—

KM# 182 5 DUCAT
17.5000 g., 0.9860 Gold 0.5547 oz. AGW **Obv:** Leopold standing **Rev:** Madonna and child

Date	Mintage	VG	F	VF	XF	Unc
1669	—	2,100	3,500	6,000	10,500	—
1674	—	2,100	3,500	6,000	10,500	—

KM# A186 5 DUCAT
17.5000 g., 0.9860 Gold 0.5547 oz. AGW **Obv:** Solid inner circle **Rev:** Solid inner circle **Note:** Struck with 1/2 Thaler dies, KM#185.

Date	Mintage	VG	F	VF	XF	Unc
1670	—	2,800	4,200	7,000	12,000	—

KM# 199 5 DUCAT
17.5000 g., 0.9860 Gold 0.5547 oz. AGW **Obv:** Leopold

Date	Mintage	VG	F	VF	XF	Unc
1675(g)	—	3,500	5,600	9,100	14,000	—

KM# B240 5 DUCAT
17.5000 g., 0.9860 Gold 0.5547 oz. AGW **Obv:** Laureate bust of Leopold I right in inner circle **Rev:** Radiant Madonna and child divide N-B in inner circle, date in legend **Note:** Struck with 2 Thaler dies, KM#212.

Date	Mintage	VG	F	VF	XF	Unc
1695NB-PO	—	3,500	5,600	9,100	14,000	—

KM# C1 10 DUCAT
35.0000 g., 0.9860 Gold 1.1095 oz. AGW **Obv:** Armored 1/2 figure of Rudolph II **Note:** Struck with 1 Thaler dies, KM#12.

Date	Mintage	VG	F	VF	XF	Unc
1601NB Rare	—	—	—	—	—	—

KM# B53 10 DUCAT
35.0000 g., 0.9860 Gold 1.1095 oz. AGW **Obv:** Legend as King of Hungary and Bohemia **Note:** Struck with 1 Thaler dies, KM#34.

Date	Mintage	VG	F	VF	XF	Unc
1612KB Rare	—	—	—	—	—	—

KM# A98 10 DUCAT
35.0000 g., 0.9860 Gold 1.1095 oz. AGW **Obv:** Bust righrt **Rev:** Heraldic double eagle

Date	Mintage	VG	F	VF	XF	Unc
1631NB Rare	—	—	—	—	—	—
1632NB Rare	—	—	—	—	—	—
1635NB Rare	—	—	—	—	—	—

KM# A78 10 DUCAT
35.0000 g., 0.9860 Gold 1.1095 oz. AGW **Obv:** Bust righrt **Rev:** Madonna and child

Date	Mintage	VG	F	VF	XF	Unc
1637KB Rare	—	—	—	—	—	—

KM# 121 10 DUCAT
35.0000 g., 0.9860 Gold 1.1095 oz. AGW **Obv:** Laureate bust of Ferdinand III right **Rev:** Crowned imperial eagle **Note:** Struck with 1 Thaler dies, KM#113.2.

Date	Mintage	VG	F	VF	XF	Unc
1639NB Rare	—	—	—	—	—	—

KM# 123 10 DUCAT
35.0000 g., 0.9860 Gold 1.1095 oz. AGW **Obv:** Laureate bust of Leopold I right **Rev:** Crowned imperial eagle **Note:** Struck with 1 Thaler dies, KM#155.

Date	Mintage	VG	F	VF	XF	Unc
1659KB Rare	—	—	—	—	—	—

KM# B180 10 DUCAT

35.0000 g., 0.9860 Gold 1.1095 oz. AGW **Obv:** Laureate bust of Leopold right 9 **Rev:** Crowned imperial eagle **Note:** Struck with 1 Thaler dies, KM#170.2.

Date	Mintage	VG	F	VF	XF	Unc
1666KB Rare	—	—	—	—	—	—
1668KB Rare	—	—	—	—	—	—

KM# C215 10 DUCAT

35.0000 g., 0.9860 Gold 1.1095 oz. AGW **Obv:** Laureate bust of Leopold right **Rev:** Madonna and child divide NB in flaming oval **Note:** Struck with 1 Thaler dies, KM#196.

Date	Mintage	VG	F	VF	XF	Unc
1687NB Rare	—	—	—	—	—	—

KM# C240 10 DUCAT

35.0000 g., 0.9860 Gold 1.1095 oz. AGW **Note:** Struck with 1 Thaler dies, KM#214.8.

Date	Mintage	VG	F	VF	XF	Unc
1695KB Rare	—	—	—	—	—	—

KM# B78 12 DUCAT

35.0000 g., 0.9860 Gold 1.1095 oz. AGW **Obv:** Bust right **Rev:** Heraldic double eagle **Note:** Struck with 1 Thaler dies, KM#75.

Date	Mintage	VG	F	VF	XF	Unc
1626KB Rare	—	—	—	—	—	—

PATTERNS

Including off metal strikes

KM#	Date	Mintage	Identification	Mkt Val
Pn3	1607	—	Denar. Gold. KM#7	—
Pn4	1608KB	—	Denar. Gold. KM#16.1	—
PnA5	1608	—	Denar. Gold.	—
PnB5	1609KB	—	Denar. Gold. 3.4000 g.	—
Pn5	1610	—	Obol. Gold. KM#22	—
PnA7	1615KB	—	Denar. Gold. 1.1000 g.	—
PnB7	1615NB	—	1/4 Ducat. Silver.	—
PnA8	1620KB	—	Denar. Gold. Weight of 1/4 Ducat.	—
Pn8	1625	—	Denar. Silver. KM#88	—
Pn9	1625	—	Denar. Gold. KM#88	—

PIEFORTS

KM#	Date	Mintage	Identification	Mkt Val
P1	1601	—	Denar. KM#6	—
P2	1607	—	Denar. KM#16	—
P3	1609	—	Denar. KM#23	—
P4	1612	—	Denar. KM#32	—
P5	1615	—	Denar. KM#40	—
P6	1616	—	Denar. KM#40	—
P7	1619	—	Denar. KM#40	—
P8	1625	—	Denar. KM#63	—
P9	1634	—	Denar. KM#95	—
P10	1649	—	Denar. KM#110	—
P11	1650	—	Denar. KM#110	—
P12	1655	—	Denar. KM#110	—
P13	1659	—	Denar. KM#144	—

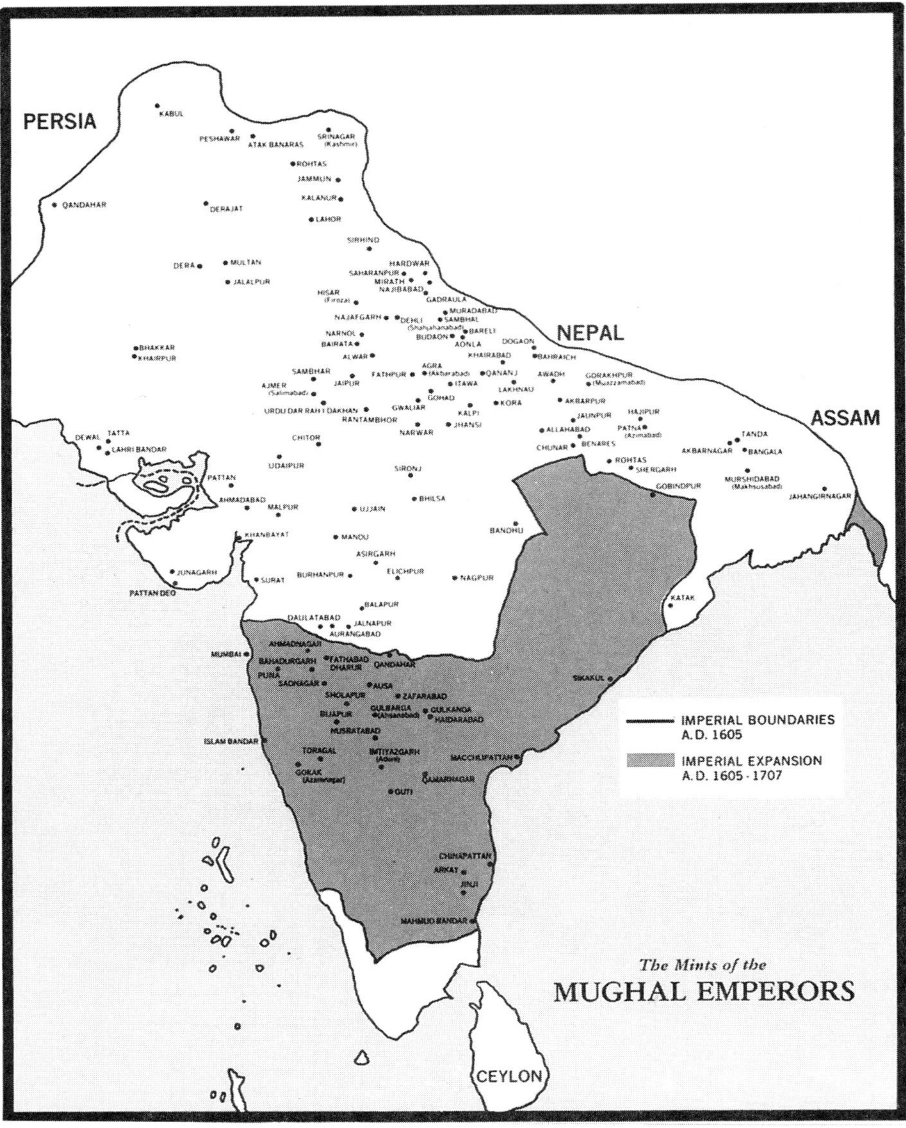

The Lodi Sultanate of Delhi was conquered by Zahir-ud-din Muhammad Babur, a Chagatai Turk descended from Tamerlane, in 1525AD. His son, Nasir-ud-din Muham-mad Humayun, lost the new empire in a series of battles with the Bihari Afghan Sher Shah, who founded the short-lived Suri dynasty. Humayun, with the assistance of the Emperor of Persia, recovered his kingdom from Sher Shah's successors in 1555AD. He did not long enjoy the fruits of victory for his fatal fall down his library steps brought his teenage son Jalal-ud-din Muhammad Akbar to the throne in the following year. During Akbar's long reign of a half century, the Mughal Empire was firmly established throughout much of North India. Under Akbar's son and grandson, the emperors Nur-ud-din Muhammad Jahangir and Shihab-ud-din Muhammad Shah Jahan, the state reached its apogee and art, culture and commerce flourished.

One of the major achievements of the Mughal government was the establishment of a universal silver currency, based on the rupee, a coin of 11.6 grams and as close to pure silver content as the metallurgy of the time was capable of attaining. Supplementary coins were the copper dam and gold mohur. The values of these coin denominations were nominally fixed at 40 dams to 1 rupee, and 8 rupees to 1 mohur; however, market forces determined actual exchange rates.

The maximum expansion of the geographical area under direct Mughal rule was achieved during the reign of Aurangzeb Alamgir. By his death in 1707AD, the whole peninsula, with minor exceptions, the whole subcontinent of India owed fealty to the Mughal emperor.

Aurangzeb's wars, lasting decades, upset the stability and prosperity of the kingdom. The internal dissension and rebellion which resulted brought the eclipse of the empire in succeeding reigns. The Mughal monetary system, especially the silver rupee, supplanted most local currencies throughout India. The number of Mughal mints rose sharply and direct central control declined, so that by the time of the emperor Shah Alam II, many nominally Mughal mints served independent states. The common element in all these coinage issues was the presence of the Mughal emperor's name and titles on the obverse. In the following listings no attempt has been made to solve the problem of separating Mughal from Princely State coins by historical criteria: all Mughal-style coins are considered products of the Mughal empire until the death of Muhammad Shah in 1784AD; thereafter all coins are considered Princely State issues unless there is evidence of the mint being under ever-diminishing Imperial control.

EMPERORS

Akbar, Jalal-ud-din Muhammad

جلال الدین محمد اکبر

AH963-1014/1556-1605AD

Copper Coinage

Persian Word Dates

The copper coins of Akbar issued from AH963 until 1014 were often dated with written Persian words rather than (or in addition to) Arabic numerals. These dates are obviously bulky and crowd one whole face of the flan often with much of the date cut. The pattern of the worded dates follows; with patience the date can be reconstructed even if numerals are missing. The legends read right to left, bottom to top.

Examples:

Two	دو
Seventy and	هفتاد و
Nine hundred and	نهصد و
Year	سنه
AH972	٩٧٢
Ninety	نود
Nine hundred and	نهصد و
Year	سنه
AH990	٩٩٠

Persian Numbers:

يك or يک one	شصت sixty
دو two	هفتاد seventy
ســ or سه three	هشتاد eighty
چهار or چهار four	نود ninety
پنج five	نهصد نهصد nine hundred
شش six	يك هزار one thousand
هفت seven	
هشت eight	ســنـ or سنه year
نـ or نه nine	و and

Silver Coinage

The standard for the Mughal rupee was 11.444 g of .984 Silver with an actual silver weight (ASW) of .362 ounce.

Type 88

In the second half of Akbar's reign the pattern of the silver coinage was changed drastically. The Kalima, the Muslim profession of faith, was dropped from the obverse and the expression *Allahu Akbar Jalla Jalalahu.* "God is great, bright is His glory" (thought to have been meant as a punning reference to the emperor's name) was substituted. Akbar's name and titles were deleted from the reverse, and the mintname with Ilahi year and Persian month placed in center flan.

Type 97

During the last decade of Akbar's reign, his son Salim grew increasingly restive in the desire to assume supreme power. He rebelled outright several times, and, as governor of Allahabad Province, refused to recognize Akbar's suzereignty. The silver coins struck at Allahabad of this period were issued anonymously without following the imperial style, but with a Persian poetic couplet giving mintname and date.

Rebellion Coinage

Akbar's was a conquest state, the major provinces of which were independent kingdoms before incorporation in the Empire. On several occasions coinage was issued by displaced local kings during attempts to re-conquer their kingdoms from Akbar. These issues, coming after the initiation of Mughal-style coinage in their provinces,are listed here.

Gold Coinage

First general issue in gold, the mohur with Hejira dating. All mohurs during Akbar's first thirty years (and some thereafter) carried the Kalima on the obverse and his name and titles on the reverse. They maintained the same weight standard, around 11 grams. Planchets were regularly round except for the rare lozenge-shaped "mehrabi" and some square types after AH987. There was much variety in borders and ornamentation, and some in royal titulature. Representative varieties of various mints are illustrated below.

Heavy "Mohur" Gold Coinage

Between AH986 and 988 gold mohurs were struck at some of the main Mughal mints on square planchets and on a "heavy" weight standard of about 12 grams. This was repeated in the millennial year AH1000 at the travelling camp mint Urdu Zafar Qarin with the striking of heavy mohurs and fractions. A few heavy mohurs on round planchets and with special designs were also struck in the Ilahi dating system, as illustrated.

Jahangir, Nur-ud-din Muhammad,

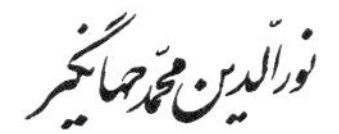

AH1014-1037/1605-1627AD

Copper Coinage

The copper coinage of Jahangir is scarce in comparison with the profuse issues of Akbar. No comprehensive type listing is possible given the few specimens available for study.

Silver Coinage

Type 149

Obv. and rev. form a poetic couplet. Each mint has a distinctive couplet. A typical word from the central portion of the rev. legend is given as identifier for each sub-type in this section.

Type 158

Obv. and rev. form a poetic couplet. Each mint has a distinctive couplet. A typical word from the rev. legend is given as identifier for each sub-type in this section.

Nisar

The nisar was a specially struck coin for ceremonial largesse. Unusual denominations struck by Jahangir were the *Nur Afshan* or "light scattering", and the *Khair-i-qabul* or "acceptable".

Gold Coinage

Type 176

The standard issue mohurs of Jahangir show much variation in execution. Illustrated is a Burhanpur mohur, typical of the average size and design. For comparison sake, two of the very handsomely executed mohurs of Agra are also shown. The design of the Agra mohur tended to be altered frequently, with much variation in border design and calligraphy.

Type 186

Poetic couplets based on Ilahi month names. From the year 1019, at a few mints, a specially composed poetic couplet was employed on the coin for each month. The decorative borders and calligraphy varied monthly. Only a sample illustration is included.

5 Mohurs

Jahangir's treasury stockpiled gold and silver in the form of stamped ingots which were in effect giant coins. 5, 10, 20, 50, 100 and higher mohur denominations are recorded by contemporary observers. In some instances these multiple mohurs were presented to ambassadors, and probably others, and so not all passed away with the Mughal treasury in later reigns. We have illustrated just one such coin.

Dawar Bakhsh, in Lahore

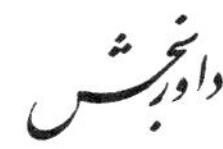

AH1037/1627AD

Shah Jahan, Shihab-ud-din Muhammad,

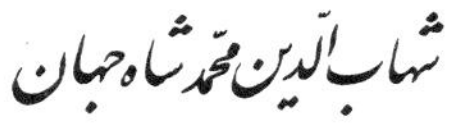

AH1037-1068/1628-1658AD

Copper Coinage

Like the copper coinage of his predecessor Jahangir, Shah Jahan's copper has not survived in sufficient quantities to permit a comprehensive typology. What is listed is a tentative listing.

Silver Coinage

Nazarana

Certain of the previous coin-types of Shah Jahan were specially struck on wide planchets to produce "nazarana" or presentation coins. These are recognizable by the full die impression appearing on wider-than-normal flans.

Murad Bakhsh, Murawwij-ud-din Muhammad, in Gujarat,

AH1068/1658AD

Shah Shuja, in Bengal,

شاه شجاع

AH1068-1070/1657-1660AD

Aurangzeb Alamgir, Muhayyi-ud-din

اورنگ زیب عالمگیر

AH1068-1118/1658-1707AD

Silver Coinage

The standard for the Mughal Rupee was 11.444 g of .984 Silver with an actual silver weight (ASW) of .362 ounce.

Legal Dirham

The "legal dirham" was an exotic coin struck in order to satisfy the strictest interpretations of the Quran in regard to dowry, capitation tax and charity giving. The weight of the coin, at 2.97 g, was intended to equal the dirham of the early Caliphs. The coins are rare, and probably not more than a token number were struck to satisfy the emperor's whim.

MINT NAMES

Adoni (Imtiyazgarh)	ادوني
Advani	ادواني
Agra (Akbarabad)	اگره
Ahmadabad	احمداباد
Ahmadnagar	احمدنگر
Ahsanabad (Gulbarga)	احسن اباد
Ajmer (Salimabad)	اجمير
Ajmer Salimabad	اجمير سليم اباد
Akbarabad (Agra)	اكبراباد
Akbarnagar	اكبرنگر
Akbarpur (Tanda)	اكبرپور
Akbarpur Tanda	اكبرپور تانده
Akhtarnagar (Awadh)	اخترنگر
Alamgirpur (Bhilsa)	عالم گيرپور
Alamgirnagar	عالمگيرنگر
Alinagar (Kalkatta)	علي نگر
Allahabad (Ilahabad)	الله اباد
Alwar	الوار
Anhirwala Pattan	انحيروالا پتن
Anwala (Anola)	انوله
Arkat	اركات
Asadnagar (Aklooj)	
Asafabad (Bareli)	اصف اباد
Asafabad Bareli	اصف اباد بريلي
Asir	اسير
Atak	اتك
Atak Banaras	اتك بنارس
Aurangabad (Khujista Bunyad)	اورنگ اباد
Aurangnagar	اورنگ نگر

Ausa	اوسا
Awadh, Oudh (Khitta)	اوده
Azamnagar (Gokak)	اعظم نگر
Azamnagar Gokak	اعظم نگر گوكاك
Azimabad (Patna)	عظيم اباد
Badakhshan	بدخشان
Bahadarqarh	بهادرگره
Bahraich	بهرايچ بهريچ
Bairata	بيراتة
Bakkar (Bhakkar)	بهكّر بهكهر
Balapur	بالاپور
Balkh	بلخ
Balwantnagar (Jhansi)	بلونت نگر
Bandar Shahi	بندرشاهي
Bandhu (Qila)	بندحو
Bangala	بنگالة
Bankapur	بنكپ بنكاپور
Baramati	بارامتي برامتي
Bareli (Asafabad)	بريلي
Bairata	بيراتة
Berar	برار
Bhakkar	بهكّر بهكهر
Bhalki (?)	
Bharoch (Baroch)	بهروچ
Bhilsa (Alamgirpur)	بهيلسة
Bijapur	بيجاپور
Bikanir	بيكانير
Budaon	بداون
Burhanabad	برهان اباد
Burhanpur	برهانپور
Chinapattan	چيناپتن
Chitor (Akbarpur)	چيتور
Chunar	چنار
Daulatabad (Deogir)	دولت اباد دولتاباد
Dehli (Shahjahanabad)	دهلي
Deogir (Daulatabad)	ديوگير
Derajat	ديرجات
Dewal Bandar	ديول بندر
Dicholi	ديچولي
Dilshadabad	دلشاداباد
Dogaon	دوگاون
Elichpur	ايلچپور
Farkhanda Bunyad (Haidarabad)	فرخنده بنياد
Farrukhabad (Ahmadnagar)	فرخ اباد
Fathabad Dharur	فتح اباد دهرور
Fathnagar	فتحنگر
Fathpur	فتحپور
Firozgarh (Yadgir)	فيروزگره
Firoznagar	فيروزنگر
Gadraula	گدرولة
Gajjikota	گنجيكوت
Garha (Known from rupees of Akbar)	گارحة
Gobindpur	گوبندپور
Gohad	گوهد
Gokak (Azamnagar)	گوكاك
Gokulgarh	گوكل گره
Goraghat	
Gorakhpur (Muazzamabad)	گوركپور
Gulbarga (Ahsanabad)	گلبرگة
Gulkanda (Golkonda)	گلكندة
Gulshanabad (Nasik)	گلشن اباد
Guti	گوتي
Gwalior	گواليار
Hafizabad	هافظاباد
Haidarabad (Farkhanda Bunyad)	حيدراباد
Hajipur	حجيپور
Hardwar (Haridwar) (Tirath)	هاردوار
Hathras	هاتهرس
Hisar (Firoza)	حصر
Hisar Firoza	حصار فيروزة
Hukeri	هوكري
Imtiyazgarh (Adoni)	امتيازگره
Islamabad (Mathura)	اسلام اباد
Islam Bandar (Rajapur)	اسلام بندر
Islamnagar	اسلام نگر
Ismailgahr	اسمعيل گره
Itawa	اتاوه اتاوا
Jahangirnagar (Dacca)	جهانگيرنگر
Jaipur (Sawai)	جي پور
Jalalnagar	جلال نگر
Jalalpur	جلالپور
Jalesar	جليسار
Jallandar	جالندر جلّندر
Jalnapur (Jalna)	جالنة پور
Jaunpur	جونپور
Jinji (Nusratgarh)	جنجي
Jodhpur	جودهپور
Junagarh	جونة گره
Kabul	كابل
Kalanur	كالانور
Kalkatta (Alinagar)	كلكته
Kalpi	كلپي

Kanauj (Qanauj)	قنوج
Kanbayat (Khambayat)	كمبايت
Kanji (Kanchipuram)	كنجي
Kankurti	كانكرتي
Kararabad (Karad)	كراراباد
Karimabad	كريم اباد
Karnatak	كرناتك
Karpa	كرپا
Kashmir (Srinagar)	كشمير
Katak	كتك
Katak Banaras	كتك بنارس
Khairabad	خيراباد
Khairnagar	خيرنگر
Khairpur	خيرپور
Khambayat (Kanbayat)	كمنبايت
Kherawar (?)	
Khujista Bunyad (Aurangabad)	خجسته بنياد
Kishtwar	كشتوار
Koilkunda	كويلكونده
Kolapur	كولاپور كلاپور
Kora	كورا
Lahore	لاهور
Lahri Bandar	لهري بندر
Lakhnau	
Machhlipattan	مچهلي پتن
Madankot	مدنكوت
Mahindurpur (Mahe Indrapur)	مهه اندرپور
Mahmud Bandar	محمودبندر
Mailapur	ميلاپور
Makhsusabad (Murshidabad)	مخصوص اباد
Maliknagar	ملك نگر

Malpur	مالپور
Mandu	مندو
Mangarh (Manghar)	مانگره
Manikpur	مانكپور
Mathura (Islamabad)	متهره
Mirath (Mirtha)	ميرتا ميرتة
Muazzamabad (Gorakhpur)	معظم اباد
Muhammadabad (Udaipur)	محمداباد
Muhammadabad Banaras	محمداباد بنارس
Mulher (Aurangnagar)	ملهر
Multan	ملتان
Mumbai (Bombay)	منبي
Mungir	مهنگير
Muradabad	مراداباد
Murshidabad (Makhsusabad)	مرشداباد
Murtazabad	مرتضاباد
Muzaffargarh	مظفرگره
Nagor	ناگور
Najibabad	نجيباباد
Narnol	نندگانو
Narwar	نرور
Nasirabad (Dharwar)	نصيراباد
Nusratabad (Nasratabad) (Fathpur)	نصرت اباد
Nusratgarh (Jinji)	نصرت گره
Orissa	اوريسة
Patna (Azimabad)	پتنة
Pattan (Anhirwala)	پتن
Pattan Deo (Somnath)	پتن ديو
Peshawar	پشاور
Phonda	پهونده
Punamali	پونامالي

Punch	پونچ
Pune (Muhiabad Poona)	پونه
Purbandar	پوربندر
Purenda	پرينده
Qamarnagar (Qarnool)	قمرنگر
Qanauj (Shahgarh Qanauj)	قنوج
Qandahar	قندهار
Rajapur (Islam Bandar)	راجاپور
Ranthambhor	رنتهور
Ranthor	رنتهور
Rohtas (Rohtak)	رحتاس رهتاس
Saharanpur	سهارنپور
Sahrind (Sarhind)	سرهند سهرند
Saimur	سيمور
Salimabad (Ajmer)	سليم اباد
Sambhal	سنبل
Sambhar	سانبهر
Sangamner	سنگمنر
Sarangpur	سارنگپور
Sarhind (Sahrind)	سرهند سهرند
Satara	ستارا
Shahabad Qanauj	شاه اباد قنوج
Shahgarh Qanauj	شاه گره قنوج
Shahjahanabad (Dehli)	شاه جهان اباد
Shergarh	شيرگره
Sherkot	شيركوت
Sherpur	شيرپور
Sholapur	شولاپور
Sikakul	سيكاكل
Sikandarah	سكندره
Sind	سند
Sironj	سرونج

Sitapur سيتاپور

Srinagar (Kashmir) سرينگر

Surat سورت

Tanda (Akbarpur) تانده

Tarapatri تراپتري

Tatta تته

Tibet-i-Kalan

Toragal تورگل توراگال

Trichanapally

Udaipur (Muhammadabad) اوديپور اديپور

Udgir ادگير

Ujjain اجين

Ujjainpur اجين پور

Umarkot (in Sind) امركوت

Urdu اردو

Urdu Dar Rahi-i-Dakkin اردو دار راه دكين

Urdu Zafar Qarin اردو ظفر قرين

Zafarabad ظفراباد

Zafarnagar ظفرنگر

Zafarpur ظفرپور

Zain-ul-bilad (Zinat-ul-Bilad), (Ahmadabad) زين البلاد

MINT EPITHETS

Mughal mintnames were often accompanied by honorific epithets. Quite often the epithet is visible on the flan when the mintname is absent or cut; in such cases the epithet is the best identification for the coin's mint of issue.

I. Geographical Terms:

بلدات
Baldat
City - Agra, Allahabad, Burhanpur, Bikanir, Patna, Sirhind, Ujjain

بندر
Bandar
Port - Dewal, Lahri, Surat, Machhlipattan

داخل
Dakhil
Breach (in Fort) - Chitor

خطة
Khitta
District - Awadh, Kalpi, Kashmir, Lakhnau

قصبة
Qasba
Town - Panipat, Sherkot

قلعة قلع
Qila
Fort - Agra, Alwar, Bandhu, Gwalior, Punch

قلعة مقام
Qila Muqam
Fort Residence - Gwalior

قطة
Qita
District - Bareli

سركار
Sarkar
County – Lakhnau, Torgal

شهر
Shahr
City - Anhirwala Pattan

سوبة
Suba
Province - Awadh

ترتة
Tirtha
Shrine - Hardwar

II. Poetic Allusion:

اشراف البلاد
Ashraf al-Bilad
Most Noble of Cities - Qandahar/Ahmadshahi

بلدات فخيرة
Baldat-i-Fakhira
Splendid City - Burhanpur

بندر مبارك
Bandar-i-Mubarak
Blessed Port - Surat

دار الامان
Dar-ul-Aman
Seat of Safety - Agra, Jammun, Multan, Sirhind

دار البركات
Dar-ul-Barakat
Seat of Blessings - Nagor

دار الفتح
Dar-ul-Fath
Seat of Conquest - Ujjain

دار الاسلام
Dar-ul-Islam
Seat of Islam - Dogaon, Mandisor

دار الجهاد
Dar-ul-Jihad
Seat of Holy War - Haidarabad

دار الخير
Dar-ul-Khair
Seat of Welfare - Ajmer

دار الخلافة
Dar-ul-Khilafa
Capital (Seat of Caliphate) - Agra, Ahmadabad, Akbarabad, Akbarpur Tanda, Awadh, Bahraich, Daulatabad, Dogaon, Gorakhpur, Gwalior, Jaunpur, Lahore, Lakhnau, Malpur, Shahgarh Qanauj, Shahjahanabad

دار المنصور
Dar-ul-Mansur
Seat of the Victorious - Ajmer, Jodhpur

دار الملك
Dar-ul-Mulk
Capital (Seat of the Kingdom) - Dehli, Fathpur, Kabul

دار السلام
Dar-us-Salam
Seat of Peace – Dogaon, Mandsor

دار السرور
Dar-us-Sarur
Seat of Delight - Burhanpur, Saharanpur

دار السلطنة
Dar-us-Sultanat
Seat of Sovereignty - Ahmadabad, Burhanpur, Fathpur, Kora, Lahore

دار الظفر
Dar-uz-Zafar
Seat of Victory - Advani, Bijapur

دار الضرب
Dar-uz-Zarb
Seat of the Mint - Jaunpur, Kalpi, Patna

فرخنده بنياد
Farkhanda Bunyad
Of Auspicious Foundation - Haidarabad

حضرت
Hazrat
Venerable - Dehli

خجستة بنياد
Khujista Bunyad
Of Fortunate Foundation - Aurangabad

مستقر الخلافة
Mustaqir-ul-Khilafat
Abode of the Caliphate - Akbarabad, Ajmer

مستقر الملك
Mustaqir-ul-Mulk
Abode of the Kingdom - Akbarabad, Azimabad

سواي
Sawai
1-1/4 (A Notch Better) - Jaipur

زين البلاد
Zain-ul-Bilad
Beauty of Cities - Ahmadabad

DATING

The Mughal coins were dated both in the Hejira era and in the regnal era of each emperor. The four-digit Hejira year usually was shown on the obverse, with the one or two-digit regnal (jalus) year on the reverse. Since the regnal and calendar years did not coincide, it was common for two different regnal years to appear on the coins produced during any calendar year. The first jalus year of each reign was usually written as a word, *ahd,* rather than as a numeral.

An exception to the foregoing is that the date on certain coins struck in the Islamic millenial year AH1000 is sometimes represented by the Arabic word *Alf,* meaning,"one thousand". This device was especially used by the Urdu Zafar Qarin Mint.

THE ILAHI ERA

In his 29th regnal year Akbar determined to use a regnal era based on solar years in his administration, instead of the Hejira or Era of the Hegira based on lunar years. The new dating system appeared on the coins the same year, and continued until Akbar's death in Year 50. Mints gradually changed their usage from AH to Ilahi, although some did not convert. During the Ilahi period, many of the mints included the Persian month names as well as year of issue. Use of Ilahi dates continued into the reign of Shah Jahan.

Synchronization of Ilahi, Hejira and AD Eras:

Ilahi	Hejira	AD
Ilahi 30	AH993/4	1585/6
Ilahi 31	AH994/5	1586/7
Ilahi 32	AH995/6	1587/8
Ilahi 33	AH996/7	1588/9
Ilahi 34	AH997/8	1589/90
Ilahi 35	AH998/9	1590/1
Ilahi 36	AH999/1000	1591/2
Ilahi 37	AH1000	1592/3
Ilahi 38	AH1001/2	1593/4
Ilahi 39	AH1002/3	1594/5
Ilahi 40	AH1003/4	1595/6
Ilahi 41	1004/5	1596/7
Ilahi 42	1005/6	1597/8
Ilahi 43	1006/7	1598/9
Ilahi 44	1007/8	1599/1600
Ilahi 45	1008/9	1600/1
Ilahi 46	1009/10	1601/2
Ilahi 47	1010/11	1602/3
Ilahi 48	1011/12	1603/4
Ilahi 49	1012/13	1604/5
Ilahi 50	1013/14	1605/6
Ilahi 51	1014/15	1606/7

Ilahi months:

(1) Farwardin	فروردين فروردي
(2) Ardibihisht	ارديبهشت
(3) Khurdad	خرداد
(4) Tir	تير
(5) Amardad	امرداد
(6) Shahrewar	شهريور
(7) Mihr	مهر
(8) Aban	آبان
(9) Azar	آذر
(10) Di	دي
(11) Bahman	بهمن
(12) Isfandarmuz	اسفندارمز

Standard Coin Pattern

The Mughal Rupees and Mohurs from the time of Aurangzeb (d.1707AD), generally followed a standard pattern of layout.

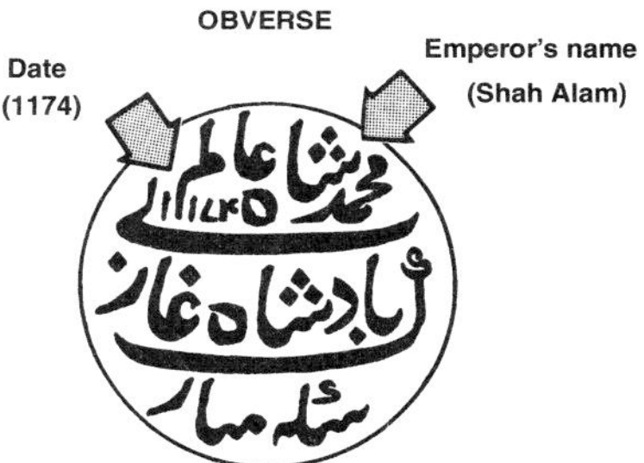

Legend, (read right to left, bottom to top) 'Auspicious coin of the fighter of infidels, the emperor of Shah Alam'.

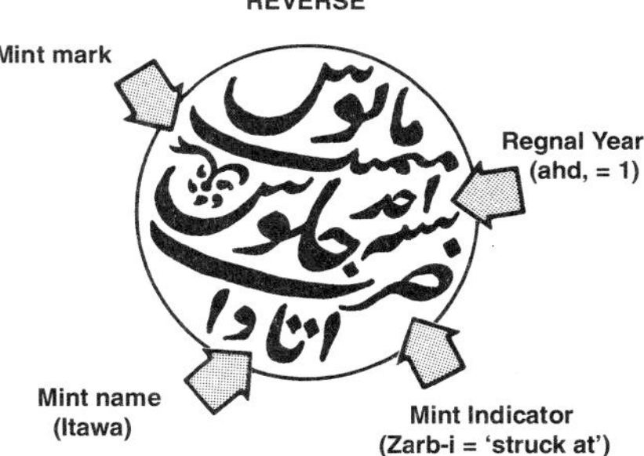

Legend, (read right to left, bottom to top) 'Struck in Itawa in the Year One of the accession associated with prosperity'.

There are many variations of this layout, especially as to the poetic couplet comtaining the king's name on the obverse. In general however the provincial mints and th independent state mints used the simple standard pattern.

LARGESSE COINAGE

نسار

Nisar

The nisar, literally scattering coins, were lightweight silver and gold coins minted especially as largesse money to be scattered amongst the crowd during festival processions and suchlike state occasions. The coins were struck to 1/32 rupee, 1/16 rupee, 1/8 rupee, 1/4 rupee and 1/2 rupee weights. To better to economize, they were very thin with wide flans, appearing more generous than was the case. All coins bore the name nisar, and the different weights should not be considered separate denominations, since this was ceremonial and not circulating currrency. The 1/4 rupee weight is encountered more frequently while specimens struck in the other weights remain quite rare.

TABLE OF PERSO-ARABIC WORDS

Obverse and reverse form a poetic couplet. Each mint has a distinctive couplet. A typical word from the central portion of the reverse legend is given as identifier for each sub-type in this section. These are found on the 1 Rupee, KM#149 series.

Yaft	يافت
Muzaiyan	مزين
Kishwar	كشور
Inayat	عنايات
Firoz	فروز
Fath	فتح
Gardun	گردون
Hamisha	هميشه
Din panah	دين پناه
Sakhat Nurani	ساخت نوراني
Khusro	خسرو
Mihr	مهر
Ruy	روي
Bada bar	بادابر
Ta falak	تا فلك
Ba-sharq wa gharb	بشرق و غرب

EMPIRE

Muhammad Akbar

AH963-1014 / 1556-1605AD

HAMMERED COINAGE

KM# 11.5 DAMRI

Copper **Obv. Inscription:** "One-sixteenth part of a Tanka" **Note:** Weight varies 2.48 - 2.58 grams.

Date	Mintage	Good	VG	F	VF	XF
IE46 (1601-02)	—	2.00	5.00	10.00	17.50	—
IE47 (1602-03)	—	2.00	5.00	10.00	17.50	—
IE49 (1604-05)	—	2.00	5.00	10.00	17.50	—
IE50 (1605-06)	—	2.00	5.00	10.00	17.50	—

Berar

KM# 11.7 DAMRI

Copper **Note:** Weight varies 2.48 - 2.58 grams.

Date	Mintage	Good	VG	F	VF	XF
IE4x (1595-1605)	—	3.50	7.00	12.00	20.00	—

KM# 11.2 DAMRI

Copper **Obv. Inscription:** One-sixteenth part of a Tanka "Akbar Shahi" **Note:** Weight varies 2.48 - 2.58 grams.

Date	Mintage	Good	VG	F	VF	XF
IE45 (1600-01)	—	2.00	4.50	9.00	15.00	—
IE47 (1602-03)	—	2.00	4.50	9.00	15.00	—
IE48 (1603-04)	—	2.00	4.50	9.00	15.00	—

Kabul

KM# 14.1 DAMRI

Copper **Note:** Weight varies 2.48 - 2.58 grams.

Date	Mintage	Good	VG	F	VF	XF
IE46 (1601-02)	—	2.00	4.00	7.00	12.00	—

Ahmadabad

KM# 16.1 DAMRA

Copper **Obv:** Mint name; border of dots **Obv. Legend:** AKBAR SHAHI **Rev:** Ilahi date, Persian month; border of dots **Note:** Weight varies: 4.75-5.50 grams.

Date	Mintage	Good	VG	F	VF	XF
IExx (1585-1607)	—	4.50	9.00	15.00	25.00	—

Ahmadanagar

KM# 16.5 DAMRA

Copper **Obv:** Mint name; border of dots **Rev:** Ilahi date, Persian month; border of dots **Note:** Weight varies 4.97 - 5.17 grams.

Date	Mintage	Good	VG	F	VF	XF
ND(1585-1607)	—	3.50	7.00	12.00	20.00	—

Balapur

KM# 16.11 DAMRA

Copper **Obv:** Mint name, border of dots **Rev:** Ilahi date, Persian month; border of dots **Note:** Weight varies: 4.75-5.50 grams.

Date	Mintage	Good	VG	F	VF	XF
ND(Il 4x)	—	—	—	—	—	—

Berar

KM# 16.6 DAMRA

Copper **Obv:** Mint name; border of dots **Rev:** Ilahi date, Persian month; border of dots **Note:** Weight varies 4.97 - 5.17 grams.

Date	Mintage	Good	VG	F	VF	XF
IE4x (1595-1605)	—	3.50	7.00	12.00	20.00	—

Burhanpur

KM# 16.7 DAMRA

Copper **Obv:** Mint name, border of dots **Rev:** Ilahi date, Persian month; border of dots **Note:** Weight varies 4.97 - 5.17 grams.

Date	Mintage	Good	VG	F	VF	XF
IE45 (1600-01)	—	3.50	7.00	12.00	20.00	—

KM# 16.9 DAMRA

Copper **Obv:** Mint name, border of dots **Rev:** Ilahi date, Persian month; border of dots **Note:** Weight varies: 4.75-5.50 grams.

Date	Mintage	Good	VG	F	VF	XF
IE4x (1595-1605)	—	3.50	7.00	12.00	20.00	—

KM# 16.8 DAMRA

Copper **Obv:** Mint name, dots **Rev:** Mint name **Note:** Weight varies 4.97 - 5.17 grams.

Date	Mintage	Good	VG	F	VF	XF
IE47 (1602-03)	—	5.50	11.00	18.00	30.00	—

KM# 23.7 NISFI

Copper **Obv. Inscription:** "Fourth part of a tanka; Akbar Shahi" **Note:** Weight varies: 9.95-10.35 grams.

Date	Mintage	Good	VG	F	VF	XF
IE45 (1600-01)	—	3.50	7.00	12.00	20.00	—
IE46 (1601-02)	—	3.50	7.00	12.00	20.00	—
IE48 (1603-04)	—	3.50	7.00	12.00	20.00	—

Agra

KM# 23.1 NISFI

Copper **Obv:** Mint name **Rev:** Ilahi date, Persian month **Note:** Weight varies: 9.95-10.35 grams.

Date	Mintage	Good	VG	F	VF	XF
IE45 (1600-01)	—	4.50	9.00	15.00	25.00	—

Ahmadabad

KM# 23.2 NISFI

Copper **Obv:** Mint name **Obv. Inscription:** Tanka; AKBAR SHAHI **Rev:** Ilahi date, Persian month **Note:** Weight varies 9.50-10.30 grams.

Date	Mintage	Good	VG	F	VF	XF
IE4x (1595-1605)	—	3.00	6.00	10.00	17.00	—

Ahmadanagar

KM# 23.9 NISFI

Copper **Obv:** Mint name **Rev:** Ilahi date, Persian month **Note:** Weight varies: 9.95-10.35 grams.

Date	Mintage	Good	VG	F	VF	XF
ND(1585-1607)	—	3.50	7.00	12.00	20.00	—

Atak Banaras

KM# 23.21 NISFI

Copper **Obv:** Mint name **Rev:** Ilahi date, Persian month

Date	Mintage	Good	VG	F	VF	XF
IE48	—	5.00	10.00	20.00	45.00	—

Bairata

KM# 23.10 NISFI

Copper **Obv:** Mint name **Rev:** Ilahi date, Persian month **Note:** Weight varies: 9.95-10.35 grams.

Date	Mintage	Good	VG	F	VF	XF
IE46 (1601-03)	—	3.50	7.00	12.00	20.00	—
IE48 (1603-04)	—	4.50	9.00	15.00	25.00	—

Balapur

KM# 23.11 NISFI

Copper **Obv:** Mint name **Rev:** Ilahi date, Persian month **Note:** Weight varies: 9.95-10.35 grams.

Date	Mintage	Good	VG	F	VF	XF
IE46 (1601-02)	—	4.50	9.00	15.00	25.00	—
IE47 (1602-03)	—	4.50	9.00	15.00	25.00	—

Berar

KM# 23.12 NISFI

Copper **Obv:** Mint name **Rev:** Ilahi date, Persian month **Note:** Weight varies: 9.95-10.35 grams.

Date	Mintage	Good	VG	F	VF	XF
IE38	—	5.00	10.00	20.00	35.00	—
IE46 (1601-02)	—	4.50	9.00	15.00	25.00	—
IE48 (1603-04)	—	3.50	7.00	12.00	20.00	—

Burhanpur

KM# 23.13 NISFI

Copper **Obv:** Mint name **Rev:** Ilahi date, Persian month **Note:** Weight varies: 9.95-10.35 grams.

Date	Mintage	Good	VG	F	VF	XF
IE46 (1601-02)	—	3.50	7.00	12.00	20.00	—
IE47 (1602-03)	—	3.50	7.00	12.00	20.00	—

Gorakhpur

KM# 23.3 NISFI

Copper **Obv:** Mint name **Rev:** Ilahi date, Persian month **Note:** Weight varies: 9.95-10.35 grams.

Date	Mintage	Good	VG	F	VF	XF
IE50 (1605-06)	—	4.50	9.00	15.00	25.00	—

Gwalior, Dar uz-Zarb Khitta

KM# 23.20 NISFI

Copper **Note:** Weight varies: 9.50-10.30 grams. Type 23.

Date	Mintage	Good	VG	F	VF	XF
ND(1595-1607)	—	—	—	—	—	—

Kalpi

KM# 23.14 NISFI

Copper **Obv:** Mint name **Rev:** Ilahi date, Persian month **Note:** Weight varies: 9.95-10.35 grams.

Date	Mintage	Good	VG	F	VF	XF
IExx (1585-1607)	—	3.50	7.00	12.00	20.00	—

Lahore

KM# 23.5 NISFI

Copper **Obv:** Border of dots **Rev:** Border of dots **Note:** Weight varies 9.50-10.30 grams.

Date	Mintage	Good	VG	F	VF	XF
IE4x (1595-1607)	—	2.75	5.50	9.00	15.00	—

Sultanpur

KM# 23.19 NISFI

Copper **Note:** Weight varies: 9.95-10.35 grams.

Date	Mintage	Good	VG	F	VF	XF
ND(1585-1607) Rare	—	—	—	—	—	—

Ujjain

KM# 23.15 NISFI

Copper **Rev:** Ilahi date, Persian month **Note:** Weight varies: 9.95-10.35 grams.

Date	Mintage	Good	VG	F	VF	XF
ND(1585-1607)	—	4.50	9.00	15.00	25.00	—

Ujjainpur

KM# 23.16 NISFI

Copper **Rev:** Ilahi date, Persian month **Note:** Weight varies: 9.95-10.35 grams.

Date	Mintage	Good	VG	F	VF	XF
IE4x (1595-1605)	—	4.50	9.00	15.00	28.00	—

Urdu Zafar Qarin

KM# 25.1 NISFI

Copper **Obv:** Border of dots, AH date **Obv. Inscription:** nisfi **Rev:** Geometric designs **Note:** Without mint name. Weight varies 9.90-10.00 grams. Type 25.

Date	Mintage	Good	VG	F	VF	XF
AH1013	—	5.50	11.00	18.00	30.00	—
AH1031 (sic)	—	5.50	11.00	18.00	30.00	—

Dogaon

KM# 28.19 DAM

Copper **Rev. Inscription:** "Dar-us-Salam" **Note:** Weight varies 19.40-20.80 grams.

Date	Mintage	Good	VG	F	VF	XF
AH1011	—	1.75	3.50	7.00	12.00	—
AH1012	—	1.75	3.50	7.00	12.00	—
AH1013	—	1.75	3.50	7.00	12.00	—

Bairata

KM# 30.1 DAM

Copper **Obv:** Mint and date **Rev. Inscription:** rawani **Note:** Weight varies: 19.9 - 20.7 grams; Type 30.

Date	Mintage	Good	VG	F	VF	XF
AH1010	—	5.50	11.00	18.00	30.00	—

Agra

KM# 32.1 DAM

Copper **Obv:** Mint name; Border of dots **Rev:** Ilahi date, Persian month; Border of dots **Note:** Weight varies 19.40-20.85 grams.

Date	Mintage	Good	VG	F	VF	XF
IE45 (1600-01)	—	1.75	3.50	7.00	12.00	—
IE46 (1601-02)	—	1.75	3.50	7.00	12.00	—
IE47 (1602-03)	—	1.75	3.50	7.00	12.00	—
IE48 (1603-04)	—	1.75	3.50	7.00	12.00	—

Ahmadabad

KM# 32.2 DAM

Copper **Obv. Legend:** TANKA (sic); AKBAR SHAHI **Obv. Inscription:** "Tanka (sic); Akbar Shahi" **Note:** Weight varies: 19.9 - 20.7 grams.

Date	Mintage	Good	VG	F	VF	XF
IE45 (1600-01)	—	1.75	4.50	9.00	15.00	—
IE46 (1601-02)	—	1.75	4.50	9.00	15.00	—
IE47 (1602-03)	—	1.75	4.50	9.00	15.00	—
IE48 (1603-04)	—	1.75	4.50	9.00	15.00	—
IE49 (1604-05)	—	1.75	4.50	9.00	15.00	—
IE50 (1605-06)	—	1.75	4.50	9.00	15.00	—

Atak Banaras

KM# 32.4 DAM

Copper **Note:** Weight varies: 19.9 - 20.7 grams.

Date	Mintage	Good	VG	F	VF	XF
IE48 (1603-04)	—	2.00	4.50	9.00	15.00	—

Bairata

KM# 32.5 DAM

Copper **Obv. Legend:** HALF TANKA; AKBAR SHAHI **Note:** Weight varies: 19.9 - 20.7 grams.

Date	Mintage	Good	VG	F	VF	XF
IE45 (1600-01)	—	1.75	3.50	7.00	12.00	—
IE46 (1601-02)	—	1.75	3.50	7.00	12.00	—
IE47 (1602-03)	—	1.75	3.50	7.00	12.00	—
IE48 (1603-04)	—	1.75	3.50	7.00	12.00	—
IE49 (1604-05)	—	1.75	3.50	7.00	12.00	—

Balapur

KM# 32.32 DAM

Copper **Note:** Weight varies: 19.9 - 20.7 grams.

Date	Mintage	Good	VG	F	VF	XF
IE46 (1601-02)	—	2.75	5.50	9.00	15.00	—
IE47 (1602-03)	—	2.75	5.50	9.00	15.00	—

Berar

KM# 32.34 DAM

Copper **Note:** Weight varies: 19.9 - 20.7 grams.

Date	Mintage	Good	VG	F	VF	XF
IE46 (1601-02)	—	3.50	7.00	12.00	20.00	—
IE47 (1602-03)	—	3.50	7.00	12.00	20.00	—

Burhanpur

KM# 32.7 DAM

Copper **Note:** Weight varies 19.40-20.85 grams.

Date	Mintage	Good	VG	F	VF	XF
IE46 (1601-02)	—	3.50	7.00	12.00	20.00	—
IE49 (1604-05)	—	4.50	9.00	15.00	25.00	—
IE50 (1605-06)	—	4.50	9.00	15.00	25.00	—

Delhi

KM# 32.9 DAM

Copper **Obv:** Without denomination **Note:** Weight varies: 19.9 - 20.7 grams.

Date	Mintage	Good	VG	F	VF	XF
IE45 (1600-01)	—	1.75	3.50	7.00	12.00	—
IE46 (1601-02)	—	1.75	3.50	7.00	12.00	—
IE47 (1602-03)	—	1.75	3.50	7.00	12.00	—

KM# 32.10 DAM

Copper **Obv. Legend:** HALF TANKA; AKBAR SHAHI **Note:** Weight varies: 19.9 - 20.7 grams.

Date	Mintage	Good	VG	F	VF	XF
IE45 (1600-01)	—	2.00	4.00	7.00	12.00	—
IE46 (1601-02)	—	2.00	4.00	7.00	12.00	—
IE47 (1602-03)	—	2.00	4.00	7.00	12.00	—
IE50 (1605-06)	—	2.00	4.00	7.00	12.00	—

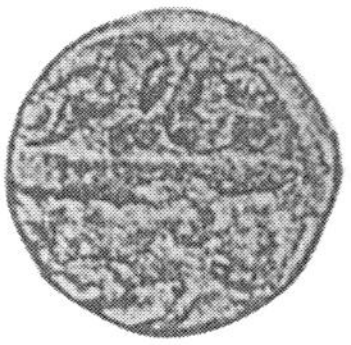
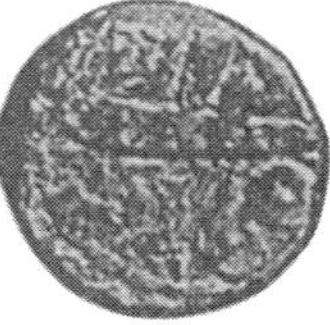

Gobindpur

KM# 32.12 DAM

Copper **Obv. Legend:** TANKA (sic); AKBAR SHAHI **Note:** Weight varies: 19.9 - 20.7 grams.

Date	Mintage	Good	VG	F	VF	XF
IE45 (1600-01)	—	1.75	3.50	7.00	12.00	—
IE46 (1601-02)	—	1.75	3.50	7.00	12.00	—
IE47 (1602-03)	—	1.75	3.50	7.00	12.00	—
IE48 (1603-04)	—	1.75	3.50	7.00	12.00	—

Gorakhpur

KM# 32.13 DAM

Copper **Note:** Weight varies 19.9 - 20.7 grams.

Date	Mintage	Good	VG	F	VF	XF
IE50 (1605-06)	—	2.75	5.50	9.00	15.00	—
IE51 (1606-07)	—	2.75	5.50	9.00	15.00	—

Hisar

KM# 32.15 DAM

Copper **Note:** Weight varies: 19.9 - 20.7 grams.

Date	Mintage	Good	VG	F	VF	XF
IE47 (1602-03)	—	1.75	3.50	7.00	12.00	—
IE48 (1603-04)	—	1.75	3.50	7.00	12.00	—

Khairpur

KM# 32.31 DAM

Copper **Note:** Weight varies: 19.40-20.85 grams.

Date	Mintage	Good	VG	F	VF	XF
IE45 (1600-01)	—	2.00	4.00	7.00	12.00	—

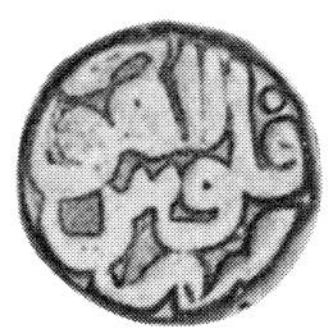

Lahore

KM# 32.17 DAM

Copper **Obv:** Without denomination **Note:** Weight varies: 19.40-20.85 grams.

Date	Mintage	Good	VG	F	VF	XF
IE45 (1600-01)	—	1.75	3.50	7.00	12.00	—
IE46 (1601-02)	—	1.75	3.50	7.00	12.00	—
IE47 (1602-03)	—	1.75	3.50	7.00	12.00	—
IE49 (1604-05)	—	1.75	3.50	7.00	12.00	—
IE50 (1605-06)	—	1.75	3.50	7.00	12.00	—

KM# 32.18 DAM

Copper **Obv. Legend:** "Half Tanka", Akbar Shahi" **Note:** Weight varies: 19.40-20.85 grams.

Date	Mintage	Good	VG	F	VF	XF
IE46 (1601-02)	—	2.00	4.00	7.00	12.00	—
IE49 (1604-05)	—	2.00	4.00	7.00	12.00	—

Mangarh

KM# 32.19 DAM

Copper **Note:** Weight varies: 19.40-20.85 grams.

Date	Mintage	Good	VG	F	VF	XF
IE45 (1600-01)	—	2.75	6.00	12.00	20.00	—
IE47 (1602-03)	—	2.75	6.00	12.00	20.00	—

Narnol

KM# 32.21 DAM

Copper **Obv. Legend:** "Half Tanka" and "Akbar Shahi" **Note:** Weight varies: 19.40-20.85 grams.

Date	Mintage	Good	VG	F	VF	XF
IE47 (1602-03)	—	2.75	5.50	9.00	15.00	—
IE48 (1603-04)	—	2.75	5.50	9.00	15.00	—
IE50 (1605-06)	—	2.75	5.50	9.00	15.00	—

Srinagar

KM# 32.26 DAM

Copper **Note:** Weight varies: 19.40-20.85 grams.

Date	Mintage	Good	VG	F	VF	XF
IE47 (1602-03)	—	2.75	5.50	9.00	15.00	—

Ujjainpur

KM# 32.28 DAM

Copper **Obv. Legend:** "Akbar Shahi" **Note:** Weight varies: 19.40-20.85 grams.

Date	Mintage	Good	VG	F	VF	XF
IE45 (1600-01)	—	2.75	5.50	9.00	15.00	—
IE47 (1602-03)	—	2.75	5.50	9.00	15.00	—
IE5x (1605-06)	—	2.75	5.50	9.00	15.00	—

Urdu Zafar Qarin

KM# 32.29 DAM

Copper **Note:** Weight varies: 19.40-20.85 grams.

Date	Mintage	Good	VG	F	VF	XF
ND(1585-1607)	—	1.75	3.50	7.00	12.00	—
IE47 (1602-03)	—	1.75	3.50	7.00	12.00	—
IE48 (1603-04)	—	1.75	3.50	7.00	12.00	—
IE50(1605-06)	—	1.75	3.50	7.00	12.00	—

KM# 34.2 DAM

Copper **Rev:** Without date **Note:** Weight varies: 19.90-20.60 grams.

Date	Mintage	Good	VG	F	VF	XF
ND(1585-1607)	—	5.50	11.00	18.00	30.00	—

Jaunpur

KM# 35.1 DAM

Copper **Rev:** Geometric design **Note:** Weight varies: 18.40-20.80 grams.

Date	Mintage	Good	VG	F	VF	XF
ND(1585-1607)	—	5.50	11.00	18.00	30.00	—

Ahmadabad

KM# 38.2 TANKA

Copper **Obv:** Border of dots **Obv. Inscription:** "Tanka, Akbar Shahi" **Rev:** Border of dots **Note:** Weight varies: 39.80-41.40 grams.

Date	Mintage	Good	VG	F	VF	XF
IE45 (1600-01)	—	6.00	15.00	30.00	50.00	—
IE46 (1601-02)	—	6.00	15.00	30.00	50.00	—

Bairata

KM# 38.3 TANKA

Copper **Note:** Weight varies: 39.80-41.40 grams.

Date	Mintage	Good	VG	F	VF	XF
IE48 (1603-04)	—	7.50	15.00	25.00	42.50	—
IE50 (1605-06)	—	7.50	15.00	25.00	42.50	—

Gobindpur

KM# 38.5 TANKA

Copper **Note:** Weight varies: 39.80-41.40 grams.

Date	Mintage	Good	VG	F	VF	XF
IE45 (1600-01)	—	7.50	18.00	36.00	60.00	—
IE46 (1601-02)	—	7.50	18.00	36.00	60.00	—
IE47 (1602-03)	—	7.50	18.00	36.00	60.00	—

Agra

KM# 40.1 TANKI

Copper **Obv. Inscription:** "Yak Tnaki", Akbar Shahi" **Rev:** Mint name and Ilahi date, Persian month **Note:** Weight varies: 3.75-3.90 grams.

Date	Mintage	Good	VG	F	VF	XF
IE47 (1602-03)	—	3.00	6.00	10.00	17.00	—

Ahmadabad

KM# 40.4 TANKI

Copper **Note:** Weight varies: 3.75-3.90 grams.

Date	Mintage	Good	VG	F	VF	XF
IExx (1585-1607)	—	3.00	7.00	12.00	20.00	—

Kabul

KM# 40.2 TANKI

Copper **Note:** Weight varies: 3.75-3.90 grams.

Date	Mintage	Good	VG	F	VF	XF
IE47 (1602-03)	—	2.00	4.50	9.00	15.00	—
IE50 (1605-06)	—	2.00	4.50	9.00	15.00	—

Lahore

KM# 40.3 TANKI

Copper **Note:** Weight varies: 3.75-3.90 grams.

Date	Mintage	Good	VG	F	VF	XF
IE46 (1601-02)	—	3.50	7.00	12.00	20.00	—

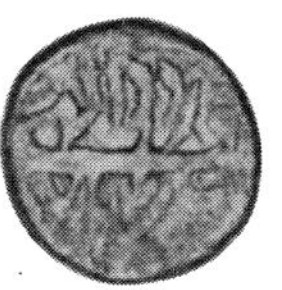

Agra

KM# 41.1 2 TANKI

Copper **Obv:** "Do (2) Tanki" and "Akbar Shahi" **Rev:** Mint name, Ilahi date, Persian month **Note:** Weight varies: 6.80-7.90 grams.

Date	Mintage	Good	VG	F	VF	XF
IE46 (1601-02)	—	2.75	5.50	9.00	15.00	—
IE47 (1602-03)	—	2.75	5.50	9.00	15.00	—
IE48 (1603-04)	—	2.75	5.50	9.00	15.00	—
IE50 (1605-06)	—	2.75	5.50	9.00	15.00	—

Ahmadabad

KM# 41.4 2 TANKI

Copper **Obv:** "Ardibihisht" **Note:** Weight varies: 6.80-7.90 grams.

Date	Mintage	Good	VG	F	VF	XF
IE46 (1601-02)	—	3.50	7.00	12.00	20.00	—
IE47 (1602-03)	—	3.50	7.00	12.00	20.00	—
IE49 (1604-05)	—	3.50	7.00	12.00	20.00	—

Kabul

KM# 41.2 2 TANKI

Copper **Note:** Weight varies: 6.80-7.90 grams.

Date	Mintage	Good	VG	F	VF	XF
IE47 (1602-03)	—	3.50	7.00	12.00	20.00	—

Ujjain

KM# 41.5 2 TANKI

Copper **Note:** Weight varies: 6.80-7.90 grams.

Date	Mintage	Good	VG	F	VF	XF
IE4x (1595-1604)	—	3.50	7.00	12.00	20.00	—

Agra

KM# 42.1 4 TANKI

Copper **Obv:** "Jo (4) Tanki", and "Akbar Shahi" **Rev:** Mint name, Ilahi date, Persian month **Note:** Weight varies: 14.90-15.75 grams.

Date	Mintage	Good	VG	F	VF	XF
IE46 (1601-02)	—	3.50	7.00	12.00	20.00	—

Ahmadabad

KM# 42.2 4 TANKI

Copper **Note:** Weight varies: 14.90-15.75 grams.

Date	Mintage	Good	VG	F	VF	XF
IE46 (1601-02)	—	3.50	7.00	12.00	20.00	—
IE47 (1602-03)	—	3.50	7.00	12.00	20.00	—
IE48 (1603-04)	—	3.50	7.00	12.00	20.00	—
IE49 (1604-05)	—	3.50	7.00	12.00	20.00	—
IE50 (1605-06)	—	3.50	7.00	12.00	20.00	—

Kabul

KM# 42.3 4 TANKI

Copper **Note:** Weight varies: 14.90-15.75 grams.

Date	Mintage	Good	VG	F	VF	XF
IE47 (1602-03)	—	4.50	9.00	15.00	25.00	—

Lahore

KM# 42.4 4 TANKI

Copper **Note:** Weight varies: 14.90-15.75 grams.

Date	Mintage	Good	VG	F	VF	XF
IE46 (1601-02)	—	3.50	7.00	12.00	20.00	—
IE47 (1602-03)	—	3.50	7.00	12.00	20.00	—

Burhanpur

KM# 47.2 TANKA

Copper **Obv:** "Tanka Akbar" **Rev:** Mintname, Ilaha date **Shape:** Square **Note:** Weight varies: 6.35-6.70 grams.

Date	Mintage	Good	VG	F	VF	XF
IE45 (1600-01)	—	3.50	9.00	18.00	30.00	—

Salimabad

KM# 47.3 TANKA

Copper **Note:** Weight varies: 6.35-6.70 grams.

Date	Mintage	Good	VG	F	VF	XF
IE4x (1595-1605)	—	3.50	9.00	18.00	30.00	—

Ujjainpur

KM# 47.1 TANKA

Copper **Note:** Weight varies: 6.35-6.70 grams.

Date	Mintage	Good	VG	F	VF	XF
IE45 (1600-01)	—	3.50	9.00	18.00	30.00	—
IE47 (1602-03)	—	3.50	9.00	18.00	30.00	—

Lahore

KM# 50.2 1/8 RUPEE

1.4300 g., Silver

Date	Mintage	Good	VG	F	VF	XF
IE45 (1600-01)	—	10.00	25.00	40.00	65.00	100

KM# 51.1 1/8 RUPEE

1.4300 g., Silver **Obv:** Similar to 1 Rupee, Type 90 **Rev:** Similar to 1 Rupee, Type 90 **Note:** Without mint name, probably Urdu.

Date	Mintage	Good	VG	F	VF	XF
IExx (1585-1607)	—	6.50	16.50	27.50	42.50	65.00

Ahmadabad

KM# 53.1 1/8 RUPEE

1.4300 g., Silver **Obv:** Similar to 1 Rupee, Type 93 **Rev:** Similar to 1 Rupee, Type 93

Date	Mintage	Good	VG	F	VF	XF
IE4x (1595-1605)	—	6.00	15.00	25.00	40.00	60.00

Lahore

KM# 53.2 1/8 RUPEE

1.4300 g., Silver

Date	Mintage	Good	VG	F	VF	XF
IE45 (1600-01)	—	6.00	15.00	25.00	40.00	60.00

Allahabad

KM# 54.1 1/8 RUPEE
1.4300 g., Silver **Obv:** Similar to 1 Rupee, Type 97 **Rev:** Similar to 1 Rupee, Type 97

Date	Mintage	VG	F	VF	XF	Unc
ND(1585-1607)	—	15.00	25.00	40.00	60.00	—

Lahore

KM# 58.2 1/4 RUPEE
2.8610 g., Silver **Obv:** Similar to 1 Rupee, Type 93 **Rev:** Similar to 1 Rupee, Type 93 **Shape:** Square

Date	Mintage	Good	VG	F	VF	XF
IE45 (1600-01)	—	5.00	12.00	20.00	30.00	50.00
IE46 (1601-02)	—	5.00	12.00	20.00	30.00	50.00
IE47 (1602-03)	—	5.00	12.00	20.00	30.00	50.00
IE48 (1603-04)	—	5.00	12.00	20.00	30.00	50.00
IE49 (1604-05)	—	5.00	12.00	20.00	30.00	50.00
IE50 (1605-06)	—	5.00	12.00	20.00	30.00	50.00

Patna

KM# 64.2 1/2 RUPEE
Silver **Obv:** Similar to 1 Rupee, Type 91 **Rev. Designer:** Similar to 1 Rupee, Type 91 **Shape:** Square **Note:** Weight varies: 5.50-5.80 grams. Without mint name, probably Urdu.

Date	Mintage	Good	VG	F	VF	XF
ND	—	6.50	16.50	27.50	42.50	65.00

Ahmadabad

KM# 66.1 1/2 RUPEE
Silver **Note:** Weight varies: 5.50-5.80 grams.

Date	Mintage	VG	F	VF	XF	Unc
IE47 (1602-03)	—	10.00	16.00	27.50	40.00	—

Burhanpur

KM# 66.6 1/2 RUPEE
Silver **Note:** Weight varies: 5.50-5.80 grams.

Date	Mintage	Good	VG	F	VF	XF
IE45 (1600-01)	—	6.00	10.00	16.00	27.50	40.00
IE48 (1603-04)	—	6.00	10.00	16.00	27.50	40.00

Dewal Bandar

KM# 66.8 1/2 RUPEE
Silver **Note:** Weight varies: 5.50-5.80 grams.

Date	Mintage	Good	VG	F	VF	XF
IE4x (1595-1605)	—	—	—	—	—	—

Kabul

KM# 66.2 1/2 RUPEE
Silver **Note:** Weight varies: 5.50-5.80 grams.

Date	Mintage	Good	VG	F	VF	XF
IE45 (1600-01)	—	5.00	12.00	20.00	32.50	50.00
IE46 (1601-02)	—	5.00	12.00	20.00	32.50	50.00
IE47 (1602-03)	—	5.00	12.00	20.00	32.50	50.00
IE48 (1603-04)	—	5.00	12.00	20.00	32.50	50.00
IE49 (1604-05)	—	5.00	12.00	20.00	32.50	50.00
IE50 (1605-06)	—	5.00	12.00	20.00	32.50	50.00

Lahore

KM# 66.3 1/2 RUPEE
Silver **Note:** Weight varies: 5.50-5.80 grams.

Date	Mintage	Good	VG	F	VF	XF
IE45 (1600-01)	—	5.00	12.00	20.00	32.50	50.00
IE46 (1601-02)	—	5.00	12.00	20.00	32.50	50.00
IE47 (1602-03)	—	5.00	12.00	20.00	32.50	50.00
IE48 (1603-04)	—	5.00	12.00	20.00	32.50	50.00
IE49 (1604-05)	—	5.00	12.00	20.00	32.50	50.00

Patna

KM# 66.4 1/2 RUPEE
Silver **Note:** Weight varies: 5.50-5.80 grams.

Date	Mintage	Good	VG	F	VF	XF
IE47 (1602-03)	—	6.00	15.00	25.00	42.50	65.00
IE48 (1603-04)	—	6.00	15.00	25.00	42.50	65.00

Agra

KM# 67.A1 1/2 RUPEE
Silver **Obv:** Similar to Rupee, Type 94 **Rev:** Similar to Rupee, Type 94 **Note:** Weight varies: 5.50-5.80 grams.

Date	Mintage	Good	VG	F	VF	XF
IE47 (1602-03) Rare; with "Darb"	—	—	—	—	—	—

KM# 67.B1 1/2 RUPEE
Silver **Note:** Weight varies: 5.50-5.80 grams. Similar to 1 Mohur, KM# 115.1.

Date	Mintage	Good	VG	F	VF	XF
IE50 (1605-06)	—	—	—	—	—	—

Ahmedabad

KM# 67.2 1/2 RUPEE
Note: Weight varies: 5.50-5.80 grams

Date	Mintage	Good	VG	'F	VF	XF
IE47(1602-03)	—	8.00	20.00	32.00	55.00	80.00

Lahore

KM# 67.1 1/2 RUPEE Silver **Note:** Weight varies: 5.50-5.80 grams.

Date	Mintage	Good	VG	F	VF	XF
IE48 (1603-04)	—	8.00	20.00	32.00	55.00	80.00
IE49 (1604-05)	—	8.00	20.00	32.00	55.00	80.00
IE50 (1605-06)	—	8.00	20.00	32.00	55.00	80.00

Allahabad

KM# 68.1 1/2 RUPEE
5.7000 g., Silver **Obv:** Similar to Rupee, Type 97 **Rev:** Similar to Rupee, Type 97 **Shape:** Round

Date	Mintage	Good	VG	F	VF	XF
ND(1585-1607)	—	10.00	25.00	40.00	65.00	100

Ujjain

KM# 84.2 RUPEE
Silver **Shape:** Square **Note:** Weight varies: 11.20-11.60 grams. Ilahi date.

Date	Mintage	Good	VG	F	VF	XF
IE46 (1601-02)	—	7.00	10.00	16.00	26.00	40.00

Bangala

KM# 86.1 RUPEE
Silver **Rev:** Poetic couplet, AH date **Shape:** Square **Note:** Weight varies: 11.20-11.60 grams.

Date	Mintage	Good	VG	F	VF	XF
AH1010	—	8.00	13.00	25.00	40.00	60.00
AH1011	—	8.00	13.00	25.00	40.00	60.00
AH1018 Posthumous	—	8.00	13.00	25.00	40.00	60.00

Tatta

KM# 88.7 RUPEE
11.4440 g., Silver **Obv. Inscription:** "... Jalalahu" **Rev:** Mint name, Ilahi date and Persian month **Shape:** Square **Note:** Weight varies: 11.20-11.60 grams.

Date	Mintage	Good	VG	F	VF	XF
IE45 (1600-01)	—	7.00	10.00	16.00	26.00	40.00
IE48 (1603-04)	—	7.00	10.00	16.00	26.00	40.00
IE49 (1604-05)	—	7.00	10.00	16.00	26.00	40.00
IE50 (1605-06)	—	7.00	10.00	16.00	26.00	40.00

Ujjain

KM# 88.8 RUPEE
Silver **Obv. Inscription:** "... Jalalahu" **Rev:** Mint name, Ilahi date and Persian month **Shape:** Square **Note:** Weight varies: 11.20-11.60 grams.

Date	Mintage	Good	VG	F	VF	XF
IE45 (1600-01)	—	6.50	16.00	22.00	32.00	40.00

Tatta

KM# 89.2 RUPEE
Silver **Rev:** Ilahi date, without Persian month **Shape:** Square **Note:** Weight varies: 11.20-11.60 grams.

Date	Mintage	Good	VG	F	VF	XF
IE46 (1601-02)	—	7.00	10.00	16.00	26.00	40.00
IE48 (1603-04)	—	7.00	10.00	16.00	26.00	40.00

KM# 90.1 RUPEE
Silver **Rev:** Ilahi date, Persian month **Shape:** Square **Note:** Weight varies: 11.20-11.60 grams.

Date	Mintage	Good	VG	F	VF	XF
IE45 (1600-01)	—	8.00	12.00	22.00	32.00	50.00
IE47 (1602-03)	—	8.00	12.00	22.00	32.00	50.00
IE48 (1603-04)	—	8.00	12.00	22.00	32.00	50.00

Agra

KM# 93.1 RUPEE
Silver **Obv. Legend:** "...Jalalahu" **Rev:** Ilahi date and Persian month **Note:** Weight varies: 11.20-11.60 grams.

Date	Mintage	Good	VG	F	VF	XF
IE46 (1601-02)	—	8.00	13.00	25.00	38.00	60.00
IE47 (1602-03)	—	8.00	13.00	25.00	38.00	60.00

KM# 93.1A RUPEE
Silver **Obv. Legend:** "...Jalalahu" **Rev:** Ilahi date and Persian month **Note:** Weight varies: 11.20-11.60 grams. Large thin planchet.

Date	Mintage	Good	VG	F	VF	XF
IE47 (1602-03)	—	—	—	—	—	—

Ahmadabad

KM# 93.2 RUPEE
Silver **Obv. Inscription:** "...Jalalahu" **Rev:** Ilahi date and Persian month **Note:** Weight varies: 11.20-11.60 grams.

Date	Mintage	Good	VG	F	VF	XF
IE46 (1601-02)	—	7.00	9.00	13.00	20.00	30.00
IE47 (1602-03)	—	7.00	9.00	13.00	20.00	30.00
IE48 (1603-04)	—	7.00	9.00	13.00	20.00	30.00
IE49 (1604-05)	—	7.00	9.00	13.00	20.00	30.00
IE50 (1605-06)	—	7.00	9.00	13.00	20.00	30.00

Ahmadanagar

KM# 93.3 RUPEE
Silver **Obv. Inscription:** "...Jalalahu" **Rev:** Ilahi date and Persian month **Note:** Weight varies: 11.20-11.60 grams.

Date	Mintage	Good	VG	F	VF	XF
IE46 (1601-02) Rare	—	—	—	—	—	—
IE50 (1605-06) Rare	—	—	—	—	—	—

Akbarnagar

KM# 93.4 RUPEE
Silver **Obv. Inscription:** "...Jalalahu" **Rev:** Ilahi date and Persian month **Note:** Weight varies: 11.20-11.60 grams.

Date	Mintage	Good	VG	F	VF	XF
IE50 (1605-06) Rare	—	—	—	—	—	—

Bairata

KM# 93.20 RUPEE
Silver **Obv. Inscription:** "...Jalalahu" **Rev:** Ilahi date and Persian month **Note:** Weight varies: 11.20-11.60 grams.

Date	Mintage	Good	VG	F	VF	XF
IE49 (1604-05) Rare	—	—	—	—	—	—

Balapur

KM# 93.5 RUPEE
Silver **Obv. Inscription:** "...Jalalahu" **Rev:** Ilahi date and Persian month **Note:** Weight varies: 11.20-11.60 grams.

Date	Mintage	Good	VG	F	VF	XF
IE4x (1595-1605) Rare	—	—	—	—	—	—

Berar

KM# 93.6 RUPEE
Silver **Obv. Inscription:** "...Jalalahu" **Rev:** Ilahi date and Persian month **Note:** Weight varies: 11.20-11.60 grams.

Date	Mintage	Good	VG	F	VF	XF
IE45 (1600-01)	—	7.00	9.00	13.00	20.00	30.00
IE46 (1601-02)	—	7.00	9.00	13.00	20.00	30.00
IE47 (1602-03)	—	7.00	9.00	13.00	20.00	30.00
IE48 (1603-04)	—	7.00	9.00	13.00	20.00	30.00
IE49 (1604-05)	—	7.00	9.00	13.00	20.00	30.00
IE50 (1605-06)	—	7.00	9.00	13.00	20.00	30.00

Burhanpur

KM# 93.7 RUPEE

Silver **Obv. Inscription:** "...Jalalahu" **Rev:** Ilahi date and Persian month **Note:** Weight varies: 11.20-11.60 grams.

Date	Mintage	Good	VG	F	VF	XF
IE45 (1600-01)	—	7.00	9.00	13.00	20.00	30.00
IE46 (1601-02)	—	7.00	9.00	13.00	20.00	30.00
IE47 (1602-03)	—	7.00	9.00	13.00	20.00	30.00
IE48 (1603-04)	—	7.00	9.00	13.00	20.00	30.00
IE49 (1604-05)	—	7.00	9.00	13.00	20.00	30.00
IE50 (1605-06)	—	7.00	9.00	13.00	20.00	30.00

Delhi

KM# 93.8 RUPEE

Silver **Obv. Inscription:** "...Jalalahu" **Rev:** Ilahi date and Persian month **Note:** Weight varies: 11.20-11.60 grams.

Date	Mintage	Good	VG	F	VF	XF
IE45 (1600-01)	—	7.00	9.00	13.00	20.00	30.00
IE47 (1602-03)	—	7.00	9.00	13.00	20.00	30.00
IE49 (1604-05)	—	7.00	9.00	13.00	20.00	30.00
IE50 (1605-06)	—	7.00	9.00	13.00	20.00	30.00

Elichpur

KM# 93.10 RUPEE

Silver **Obv. Inscription:** "...Jalalahu" **Rev:** Ilahi date and Persian month **Note:** Weight varies: 11.20-11.60 grams.

Date	Mintage	Good	VG	F	VF	XF
IE48 (1603-04) Rare	—	—	—	—	—	—
IE50 (1605-06) Rare	—	—	—	—	—	—

Kabul

KM# 93.17 RUPEE

Silver **Obv. Inscription:** "...Jalalahu" **Rev:** Ilahi date and Persian month **Note:** Weight varies: 11.20-11.60 grams.

Date	Mintage	Good	VG	F	VF	XF
IE45 (1600-01)	—	13.00	32.50	55.00	90.00	150

Lahore

KM# 93.11 RUPEE

Silver **Obv. Inscription:** "...Jalalahu" **Rev:** Ilahi date and Persian month **Note:** Weight varies: 11.20-11.60 grams.

Date	Mintage	Good	VG	F	VF	XF
IE45 (1600-01)	—	8.00	12.00	20.00	32.00	50.00
IE46 (1601-02)	—	8.00	12.00	20.00	32.00	50.00
IE47 (1602-03)	—	8.00	12.00	20.00	32.00	50.00
IE48 (1603-04)	—	8.00	12.00	20.00	32.00	50.00
IE49 (1604-05)	—	8.00	12.00	20.00	32.00	50.00

Patna

KM# 93.14 RUPEE

Silver **Obv. Inscription:** "...Jalalahu" **Rev:** Ilahi date and Persian month **Note:** Weight varies: 11.20-11.60 grams.

Date	Mintage	Good	VG	F	VF	XF
IE45 (1600-01)	—	8.00	12.00	20.00	32.00	50.00
IE47 (1602-03)	—	8.00	12.00	20.00	32.00	50.00
IE48 (1603-04)	—	8.00	12.00	20.00	32.00	50.00

Date	Mintage	Good	VG	F	VF	XF
IE49 (1604-05)	—	8.00	12.00	20.00	32.00	50.00
IE50 (1605-06)	—	8.00	12.00	20.00	32.00	50.00

Saimur

KM# 93.21 RUPEE

Silver **Obv. Inscription:** "...Jalalahu" **Rev:** Ilahi date and Persian month **Note:** Weight varies: 11.20-11.60 grams.

Date	Mintage	Good	VG	F	VF	XF
IE47 (1602-03) Rare	—	—	—	—	—	—

Sitapur

KM# 93.18 RUPEE

Silver **Obv. Inscription:** "...Jalalahu" **Rev:** Ilahi date and Persian month **Note:** Weight varies: 11.20-11.60 grams.

Date	Mintage	Good	VG	F	VF	XF
IE49 (1604-05)	—	8.00	15.00	30.00	50.00	80.00

Srinagar

KM# 93.15 RUPEE

Silver **Obv. Inscription:** "...Jalalahu" **Rev:** Ilahi date and Persian month **Note:** Weight varies: 11.20-11.60 grams.

Date	Mintage	Good	VG	F	VF	XF
IE45 (1600-01)	—	8.00	15.00	30.00	50.00	80.00
IE46 (1601-02)	—	8.00	15.00	30.00	50.00	80.00
IE47 (1602-03)	—	8.00	15.00	30.00	50.00	80.00
IE48 (1603-04)	—	8.00	15.00	30.00	50.00	80.00
IE49 (1604-05)	—	8.00	15.00	30.00	50.00	80.00
IE50 (1605-06)	—	8.00	15.00	30.00	50.00	80.00

Ujjain

KM# 93.16 RUPEE

Silver **Obv. Inscription:** "...Jalalahu" **Rev:** Ilahi date and Persian month **Note:** Weight varies: 11.20-11.60 grams.

Date	Mintage	Good	VG	F	VF	XF
IE46 (1601-02) Rare	—	—	—	—	—	—
IE47 (1602-03) Rare	—	—	—	—	—	—
IE48 (1603-04) Rare	—	—	—	—	—	—

Urdu

KM# 93.19 RUPEE

Silver **Obv. Inscription:** "...Jalalahu" **Rev:** Ilahi date and Persian month **Note:** Weight varies: 11.20-11.60 grams.

Date	Mintage	Good	VG	F	VF	XF
IE4x (1595-1605)	—	7.00	17.50	25.00	35.00	50.00

Delhi

KM# 93A.1 RUPEE

Silver **Obv. Inscription:** "...Jalalahu" **Rev:** Ilahi date and Persian month **Note:** Weight varies: 11.20-11.60 grams.

Date	Mintage	Good	VG	F	VF	XF
IE50 (1605-06)	—	—	—	—	—	—

Agra

KM# 94.1 RUPEE

Silver **Obv:** Quatrefoil borders **Obv. Inscription:** "...Jalalahu" **Rev:** Octagonal borders, mint name, Ilahi date and Persian month **Note:** Weight varies: 11.20-11.60 grams. Rare specimens of the Agra rupee bear the word "Rupiya" also.

Date	Mintage	Good	VG	F	VF	XF
IE47 (1602-03)	—	12.00	30.00	60.00	95.00	150
IE48 (1603-04)	—	12.00	30.00	60.00	95.00	150
IE49 (1604-05)	—	12.00	30.00	60.00	95.00	150
IE50 (1605-06)	—	12.00	30.00	60.00	95.00	150

KM# 94.6 RUPEE

11.4440 g., Silver **Note:** With only "Rupiya".

Date	Mintage	Good	VG	F	VF	XF
IE47 Rare	—	—	—	—	—	—

Ahmadabad

KM# 94.2 RUPEE

Silver **Obv:** Quatrefoil borders **Obv. Inscription:** "...Jalalahu" **Rev:** Octagonal borders, mint name, Ilahi date and Persian month **Note:** Weight varies: 11.20-11.60 grams.

Date	Mintage	Good	VG	F	VF	XF
IE47 (1602-03)	—	8.00	14.00	26.00	44.00	70.00

Lahore

KM# 94.3 RUPEE

Silver **Obv:** Quatrefoil borders **Obv. Inscription:** "...Jalalahu" **Rev:** Octagonal borders, mint name, Ilahi date and Persian month **Note:** Weight varies: 11.20-11.60 grams.

Date	Mintage	Good	VG	F	VF	XF
IE47 (1602-03)	—	8.00	14.00	26.00	44.00	70.00
IE48 (1603-04)	—	8.00	14.00	26.00	44.00	70.00
IE49 (1604-05)	—	8.00	14.00	26.00	44.00	70.00
IE50 (1605-06)	—	8.00	14.00	26.00	44.00	70.00

Saimur

KM# 94.5 RUPEE

Silver **Obv:** Quatrefoil borders **Obv. Inscription:** "...Jalalahu" **Rev:** Octagonal borders, mint name, Ilahi date and Persian month **Note:** Weight varies: 11.20-11.60 grams.

Date	Mintage	Good	VG	F	VF	XF
IE47 (1602-03)	—	15.00	40.00	80.00	125	180
IE48 (1603-04)	—	15.00	40.00	80.00	125	180

Sitapur

KM# 94.4 RUPEE

Silver **Obv:** Quatrefoil borders **Obv. Inscription:** "...Jalalahu" **Rev:** Octagonal borders, mint name, Ilahi date and Persian month **Note:** Weight varies: 11.20-11.60 grams.

Date	Mintage	Good	VG	F	VF	XF
IE47 (1602-03)	—	8.00	13.00	24.00	38.00	60.00
IE48 (1603-04)	—	8.00	13.00	24.00	38.00	60.00
IE49 (1604-05)	—	8.00	13.00	24.00	38.00	60.00

Agra

KM# 95.1 RUPEE

11.3400 g., Silver **Obv:** Eight-pointed double star **Rev:** Eight-pointed double star

Date	Mintage	Good	VG	F	VF	XF
IE50 (1605-06) Rare	—	—	—	—	—	—

Bandhu

KM# 96.1 RUPEE

11.4440 g., Silver **Obv:** "Riwaj Sikka Akbar" **Rev:** Mint name **Note:** Mint epithet: "Qila".

Date	Mintage	Good	VG	F	VF	XF
ND(1585-1607) Rare	—	—	—	—	—	—

Agra

KM# 115.1 MOHUR

Gold **Obv:** Persian couplet **Rev:** Persian couplet **Note:** Weight varies: 10.70-11.00 grams.

Date	Mintage	Good	VG	F	VF	XF
IE49 (1604-05) Rare	—	—	—	—	—	—
IE50 (1605-06) Rare	—	—	—	—	—	—

REBELLION COINAGE

Allahabad

KM# 97.1 RUPEE

Silver **Obv:** "Riwaj Sikka Akbar" **Rev:** Mint name **Note:** Weight varies: 11.20-11.60 grams.

Date	Mintage	Good	VG	F	VF	XF
IE45 (1600-01)	—	8.00	12.00	20.00	32.00	50.00
IE46 (1601-02)	—	8.00	12.00	20.00	32.00	50.00
IE47 (1602-03)	—	8.00	12.00	20.00	32.00	50.00
IE48 (1603-04)	—	8.00	12.00	20.00	32.00	50.00
IE49 (1604-05)	—	8.00	12.00	20.00	32.00	50.00

Agra

KM# 103.1 1/2 MOHUR

Gold **Note:** Weight varies: 4.80-5.40 grams.

Date	Mintage	Good	VG	F	VF	XF
IE48 (1603-04)	—	—	300	485	700	1,000
IE50 (1605-06)	—	—	300	485	700	1,000

Lahore

KM# 103.2 1/2 MOHUR

Gold **Note:** Weight varies: 4.80-5.40 grams.

Date	Mintage	Good	VG	F	VF	XF
IE48 (1603-04)	—	—	285	425	625	900

Lahore

KM# 104.1 1/2 MOHUR

Gold **Obv:** Sita and Rama **Rev:** Ilahi date and Persian month **Note:** Weight varies: 4.80-5.40 grams.

Date	Mintage	Good	VG	F	VF	XF
IE50 (1605-06)	—	—	—	—	—	—

Agra

KM# 114.1 MOHUR

Gold **Obv:** Within dotted circles **Obv. Legend:** "...Jalalahu" **Rev:** Mint name and date, within dotted circles **Shape:** Square **Note:** Weight varies: 10.70-11.00 grams.

Date	Mintage	Good	VG	F	VF	XF
IE48 (1603-04)	—	355	410	525	650	900
IE49 (1604-05)	—	355	410	525	650	900

KM# 114.3 MOHUR

Gold **Shape:** Oblong **Note:** Mehrabi. Weight varies: 10.80-11.00 grams.

Date	Mintage	Good	VG	F	VF	XF
IE49 (1604-05) Rare	—	—	—	—	—	—

KM# 114.2 MOHUR

Gold **Obv:** Within 8-pointed doubled star **Obv. Legend:** "...Jalalahu" **Rev:** Mint name and date, within 8-pointed doubled star **Shape:** Square **Note:** Weight varies: 10.70-11.00 grams.

Date	Mintage	Good	VG	F	VF	XF
IE50 (1605-06)	—	365	475	600	800	1,100

Akbarnagar

KM# 114.4 MOHUR

Gold **Obv:** Within dotted circle **Obv. Legend:** "...Jalalahu" **Rev:** Mint name and date, within dotted circle **Shape:** Oblong **Note:** Weight varies: 10.80-11.00 grams.

Date	Mintage	Good	VG	F	VF	XF
IExx (1585-1607)	—	—	235	275	350	500

Burhanpur

KM# 114.5 MOHUR

Gold **Obv:** Within dotted circle **Obv. Legend:** "...Jalalahu" **Rev:** Mint name and date, within dotted circle **Shape:** Oblong **Note:** Weight varies: 10.80-11.00 grams.

Date	Mintage	Good	VG	F	VF	XF
IE48 (1603-04)	—	360	425	550	750	1,000
IE49 (1604-05)	—	360	425	550	750	1,000

Lahore

KM# 114.6 MOHUR

Gold **Obv:** Within dotted circle **Obv. Legend:** "...Jalalahu" **Rev:** Mint name and date, within dotted circle **Shape:** Oblong **Note:** Weight varies: 10.80-11.00 grams.

Date	Mintage	Good	VG	F	VF	XF
IE47 (1602-03)	—	—	350	400	460	550
IE48 (1603-04)	—	—	350	400	460	550
IE49 (1604-05)	—	—	350	400	460	550
IE50 (1605-06)	—	—	350	400	460	550

Sitapur

KM# 114.7 MOHUR

Gold **Obv:** Within dotted circle **Obv. Legend:** "...Jalalahu" **Rev:** Mint name and date, within dotted circle **Shape:** Oblong **Note:** Weight varies: 10.80-11.00 grams.

Date	Mintage	Good	VG	F	VF	XF
IE47 (1602-03) Rare	—	—	—	—	—	—

Agra

KM# 115.2 MOHUR

Gold **Obv:** Short couplet **Rev:** Short couplet **Note:** Weight varies: 10.70-11.00 grams.

Date	Mintage	Good	VG	F	VF	XF
IE50 (1605-06) Rare	—	—	—	—	—	—
IE51 (1606-07) Rare	—	—	—	—	—	—

KM# 115.3 MOHUR

Gold **Obv:** "Dinar-i Jalali" **Note:** Weight varies: 10.70-11.00 grams.

Date	Mintage	Good	VG	F	VF	XF
IE50 (1605-06) Rare	—	—	—	—	—	—

Agra

KM# 118.2 HEAVY 1/2 MOHUR

5.9600 g., Gold **Obv:** Ilahi date, Persian month **Rev:** Hawk to right **Shape:** Square

Date	Mintage	Good	VG	F	VF	XF
IE50 (1605-06) Rare	—	—	—	—	—	—

Agra

KM# 119C.3 HEAVY MOHUR

Gold **Obv:** Hawk left, ornamented field **Rev:** Legend, mint, and date **Rev. Legend:** "Allahu Akbar" **Note:** Weight varies: 11.80-12.20 grams.

Date	Mintage	Good	VG	F	VF	XF
IE47 (1602-03) Rare	—	—	—	—	—	—

KM# 119C.2 HEAVY MOHUR

12.2000 g., Gold **Obv:** Duck, ornamented field

Date	Mintage	Good	VG	F	VF	XF
IE50 (1605-06) Rare	—	—	—	—	—	—

Asir

KM# 119C.1 HEAVY MOHUR

Gold **Obv:** Hawk right **Note:** Weight varies: 11.80-12.20 grams.

Date	Mintage	Good	VG	F	VF	XF
IE45 (1600-01) Rare	—	—	—	—	—	—

Muhammad Jahangir

AH1014-1037 / 1605-1627AD

HAMMERED COINAGE

Delhi

KM# 120.1 1/8 DAM

Copper **Note:** Weight varies: 2.30-2.60 grams.

Date	Mintage	Good	VG	F	VF	XF
AH1021//7	—	4.00	10.00	16.00	24.00	—
AH102x//11	—	4.00	10.00	16.00	24.00	—
AH1023//x	—	4.00	10.00	16.00	24.00	—
AH1029//1x	—	4.00	10.00	16.00	24.00	—

Agra

KM# 122.1 1/4 DAM

Copper **Note:** Weight varies: 4.80-5.20 grams. Varieties exist.

Date	Mintage	Good	VG	F	VF	XF
AH1014//1	—	3.00	7.00	12.00	18.00	—
AH1017//4	—	3.00	7.00	12.00	18.00	—
AH1018//4	—	3.00	7.00	12.00	18.00	—
AH1019//5	—	3.00	7.00	12.00	18.00	—
AH1020//5(sic)	—	3.00	7.00	12.00	18.00	—
AH1020//6	—	3.00	7.00	12.00	18.00	—
AH1021//6(sic)	—	3.00	7.00	12.00	18.00	—
AH1021//7	—	3.00	7.00	12.00	18.00	—

Ahmadabad

KM# 122.4 1/4 DAM

Copper **Note:** Weight varies: 4.80-5.20 grams.

Date	Mintage	Good	VG	F	VF	XF
AH1018//5	—	4.00	10.00	16.00	24.00	—

Ahmadanagar

KM# 122.5 1/4 DAM

Copper **Note:** Weight varies: 4.80-5.20 grams.

Date	Mintage	Good	VG	F	VF	XF
ND	—	4.00	10.00	16.00	24.00	—

Burhanpur

KM# 122.3 1/4 DAM

Copper **Note:** Weight varies: 4.80-5.20 grams.

Date	Mintage	Good	VG	F	VF	XF
ND	—	3.00	7.00	12.00	18.00	—

Delhi

KM# 122.2 1/4 DAM

Copper **Note:** Weight varies: 4.80-5.20 grams.

Date	Mintage	Good	VG	F	VF	XF
AHxxxx//6 Rare	—	—	—	—	—	—

Agra

KM# 124.5 1/2 DAM

Copper **Note:** Weight varies: 9.80-10.50 grams.

Date	Mintage	Good	VG	F	VF	XF
AH1023	—	3.00	7.00	12.00	18.00	—

Ahmadabad

KM# 124.3 1/2 DAM

Copper **Note:** Weight varies: 9.80-10.50 grams.

Date	Mintage	Good	VG	F	VF	XF
AH10xx	—	3.00	7.00	12.00	18.00	—

Ahmadanagar

KM# 124.4 1/2 DAM

Copper **Note:** Weight varies: 9.80-10.50 grams.

Date	Mintage	Good	VG	F	VF	XF
ND Rare	—	—	—	—	—	—

Ajmer

KM# 124.1 1/2 DAM

Copper **Note:** Weight varies: 9.80-10.50 grams.

Date	Mintage	Good	VG	F	VF	XF
AH1023//9 Rare	—	—	—	—	—	—
AH1024//9(sic) Rare	—	—	—	—	—	—

Bairata

KM# 124.6 1/2 DAM

Copper **Note:** Weight varies: 9.80-10.50 grams.

Date	Mintage	Good	VG	F	VF	XF
ND	—	4.00	10.00	16.00	24.00	—
AH1025//11	—	4.00	10.00	16.00	24.00	—

Burhanpur

KM# 124.8 1/2 DAM

Copper **Note:** Weight varies: 9.80-10.50 grams.

Date	Mintage	Good	VG	F	VF	XF
ND(1605) Di	—	4.00	10.00	16.00	24.00	—
ND//3 Di	—	4.00	10.00	16.00	24.00	—

KM# 124.7 1/2 DAM

Copper **Note:** Weight varies: 9.80-10.50 grams.

Date	Mintage	Good	VG	F	VF	XF
ND Azar	—	4.00	10.00	16.00	24.00	—

Qandahar

KM# 124.2 1/2 DAM

Copper **Note:** Weight varies: 9.80-10.50 grams.

Date	Mintage	Good	VG	F	VF	XF
AH1019//5 Rare	—	—	—	—	—	—

Agra

KM# 126.1 DAM

Copper **Note:** Weight varies: 20.20-20.90 grams.

Date	Mintage	Good	VG	F	VF	XF
AH1020//6	—	2.00	5.00	11.00	18.00	—
AH1020//7	—	2.00	5.00	11.00	18.00	—
AH1021//7	—	2.00	5.00	11.00	18.00	—
AH1022//8	—	2.00	5.00	11.00	18.00	—
AH1022//9	—	2.00	5.00	11.00	18.00	—
AH1023//8	—	2.00	5.00	11.00	18.00	—
AH1023//9	—	2.00	5.00	11.00	18.00	—
AH1023//10	—	2.00	5.00	11.00	18.00	—
AH1024//x	—	2.00	5.00	11.00	18.00	—
AH1026//12	—	2.00	5.00	11.00	18.00	—
AH1029//xx	—	2.00	5.00	11.00	18.00	—

KM# 126.1B DAM

Copper **Obv:** "Jahangiri" and regnal year **Rev:** Mint and date

Date	Mintage	Good	VG	F	VF	XF
AH1022/8	—	8.00	15.00	28.00	50.00	—

Ahmadabad

KM# 126.2 DAM

Copper **Obv:** "Jahangiri" and date **Rev:** Mint and Persian month **Note:** Weight varies: 20.20-20.90 grams.

Date	Mintage	Good	VG	F	VF	XF
AH1016//6(sic) Rare	—	—	—	—	—	—
AH1018//4 Rare	—	—	—	—	—	—
AH10xx//6 Rare	—	—	—	—	—	—
AH1025 Rare	—	—	—	—	—	—
AH1026//11 Rare	—	—	—	—	—	—
AH1026//11(sic) Rare	—	—	—	—	—	—
AH1028//31 Rare; error for 13	—	—	—	—	—	—

Ajmer

KM# 126.8 DAM

Copper **Note:** Weight varies: 20.20-20.90 grams.

Date	Mintage	Good	VG	F	VF	XF
AH1024//10	—	3.00	7.00	12.00	18.00	—
AH1024//11	—	3.00	7.00	12.00	18.00	—
AH1025//11	—	3.00	7.00	12.00	18.00	—

Bairata

KM# 126.3 DAM

Copper **Note:** Weight varies: 20.20-20.90 grams.

Date	Mintage	Good	VG	F	VF	XF
AH1015//2	—	2.00	5.00	9.00	15.00	—
AH1017//4	—	2.00	5.00	9.00	15.00	—
AH1018//4	—	2.00	5.00	9.00	15.00	—
AH1018//5	—	2.00	5.00	9.00	15.00	—
AH1019//6	—	2.00	5.00	9.00	15.00	—
AH1019/5	—	2.00	5.00	9.00	15.00	—
AH1020//6	—	2.00	5.00	9.00	15.00	—
AH1021//7	—	2.00	5.00	9.00	15.00	—
AH1022//8	—	2.00	5.00	9.00	15.00	—
AH102x//13	—	2.00	5.00	9.00	15.00	—
AH1028//14	—	2.00	5.00	9.00	15.00	—
AH1030//61(sic) Error for 16	—	2.00	5.00	9.00	15.00	—
AH103x//16	—	2.00	5.00	9.00	15.00	—
AH1034//19(sic)	—	2.00	5.00	9.00	15.00	—
AH1034//20	—	2.00	5.00	9.00	15.00	—
AH1036//18(sic)	—	2.00	5.00	9.00	15.00	—

Burhanpur

KM# 126.10 DAM

Copper **Note:** Weight varies: 20.20-20.90 grams.

Date	Mintage	Good	VG	F	VF	XF
AH1017 Azar	—	—	—	—	—	—

Delhi

KM# 126.4 DAM

Copper **Note:** Weight varies: 20.20-20.90 grams.

Date	Mintage	Good	VG	F	VF	XF
AH103x//21 Rare	—	—	—	—	—	—

Gobindpur

KM# 126.9 DAM

Copper **Note:** Weight varies: 20.20-20.90 grams.

Date	Mintage	Good	VG	F	VF	XF
AH1029//15	—	—	—	—	—	—

Kabul

KM# 126.5 DAM

Copper **Note:** Weight varies: 20.20-20.90 grams.

Date	Mintage	Good	VG	F	VF	XF
AH102x//6 Rare	—	—	—	—	—	—
AH1028//14 Rare	—	—	—	—	—	—

Narnol

KM# 126.6 DAM

Copper **Note:** Weight varies: 20.20-20.90 grams.

Date	Mintage	Good	VG	F	VF	XF
AH102x//7 Rare	—	—	—	—	—	—

Srinagar

KM# 126.11 DAM

Copper **Note:** Weight varies: 20.20-20.90 grams.

Date	Mintage	Good	VG	F	VF	XF
AH1022//8	—	3.00	7.00	12.00	18.00	—

Udaipur

KM# 126.7 DAM

Copper **Note:** Weight varies: 20.20-20.90 grams.

Date	Mintage	Good	VG	F	VF	XF
AH1020//5	—	3.00	7.00	12.00	18.00	—

Ajmir

KM# A127.1 TANKA

40.0000 g., Copper

Date	Mintage	VG	F	VF	XF	Unc
AH1024//10	—	—	—	—	—	—

Ajmir

KM# B127.1 TANKA

40.0000 g., Copper

Date	Mintage	Good	VG	F	VF	XF
ND(1605-27)	—	—	—	—	—	—

Ujjain

KM# 127.1 1/2 FALUS

Copper **Obv:** Emperor's name **Rev:** Mint name **Shape:** Square

Date	Mintage	Good	VG	F	VF	XF
ND	—	2.00	5.00	10.00	15.00	—

Ujjain

KM# 128.1 FALUS

Copper **Shape:** Square

Date	Mintage	Good	VG	F	VF	XF
ND	—	4.00	7.00	12.00	20.00	—
AH102x//14	—	4.00	7.00	12.00	20.00	—
AH102x//15	—	4.00	7.00	12.00	20.00	—
AH1019//14	—	4.00	7.00	12.00	20.00	—

Ahmadabad

KM# 131.3 1/8 RUPEE

1.4300 g., Silver

Date	Mintage	Good	VG	F	VF	XF
AH-	—	13.00	30.00	60.00	95.00	150

Ahmadanagar

KM# 131.4 1/8 RUPEE

1.4300 g., Silver

Date	Mintage	Good	VG	F	VF	XF
AH-	—	13.00	30.00	60.00	95.00	150

Ajmer

KM# 131.1 1/8 RUPEE

1.4300 g., Silver

Date	Mintage	Good	VG	F	VF	XF
AH1031//18	—	13.00	30.00	60.00	95.00	150

Burhanpur

KM# 131.5 1/8 RUPEE

1.4300 g., Silver

Date	Mintage	Good	VG	F	VF	XF
AH1014	—	13.00	30.00	60.00	95.00	150
AH1033	—	13.00	30.00	60.00	95.00	150

Lahore

KM# 131.2 1/8 RUPEE

1.4300 g., Silver

Date	Mintage	Good	VG	F	VF	XF
AH1029//15	—	13.00	30.00	60.00	95.00	150
AH1031//17	—	13.00	30.00	60.00	95.00	150

Burhanpur

KM# A131.3 1/8 RUPEE

1.4300 g., Silver **Shape:** Square

Date	Mintage	Good	VG	F	VF	XF
AH-	—	13.00	30.00	60.00	95.00	150

Jahangirnagar

KM# A131.1 1/8 RUPEE

1.4300 g., Silver **Shape:** Square

Date	Mintage	Good	VG	F	VF	XF
AH-	—	13.00	30.00	60.00	95.00	150

Kabul

KM# A131.2 1/8 RUPEE

1.4300 g., Silver **Shape:** Square

Date	Mintage	Good	VG	F	VF	XF
AHxxxx//7	—	13.00	30.00	60.00	95.00	150

Agra

KM# 132.1 1/4 RUPEE

3.1750 g., Silver **Rev. Inscription:** "Sakhat Nurani" **Note:** Similar to KM#155.1.

Date	Mintage	Good	VG	F	VF	XF
AH1014//1 Rare	—	—	—	—	—	—

Ahmadanagar

KM# 132.3 1/4 RUPEE

3.1750 g., Silver

Date	Mintage	Good	VG	F	VF	XF
AH-	—	—	—	—	—	—

Fathnagar

KM# 132.4 1/4 RUPEE

3.1750 g., Silver

Date	Mintage	Good	VG	F	VF	XF
AH-	—	—	—	—	—	—

Jahangirnagar

KM# 132.5 1/4 RUPEE

3.1750 g., Silver

Date	Mintage	Good	VG	F	VF	XF
AHxxxx//17	—	—	—	—	—	—

Patna

KM# 132.6 1/4 RUPEE

3.1750 g., Silver

Date	Mintage	Good	VG	F	VF	XF
AH1027//13	—	—	—	—	—	—

KM# 132.2 1/4 RUPEE

3.1750 g., Silver **Note:** Similar to 1 Rupee, KM# 145.12.

Date	Mintage	Good	VG	F	VF	XF
AH1027//13 Rare	—	—	—	—	—	—
AH1034//20	—	—	—	—	—	—

Ahmedabad

KM# 133.2 1/2 RUPEE

5.7220 g., Silver **Obv:** Pre-accession name, "Selim Shah", mint name **Note:** Jahangir Regnal year.

Date	Mintage	Good	VG	F	VF	XF
AH101x//2	—	70.00	180	300	420	600

Kabul

KM# 133.1 1/2 RUPEE

5.7220 g., Silver **Obv:** Pre-accession name "Selim Shah", mint name, and AH date **Rev:** Benediction

Date	Mintage	Good	VG	F	VF	XF
AH1014 Rare	—	—	—	—	—	—

KM# 133.3 1/2 RUPEE

5.7220 g., Silver **Obv:** Pre-accession name "Selim Shah" with "Hamisha" couplet

Date	Mintage	Good	VG	F	VF	XF
AH1014	—	—	—	—	—	—

Ahmadanagar

KM# 134.1 1/2 RUPEE

5.7220 g., Silver **Obv:** Kalima

Date	Mintage	Good	VG	F	VF	XF
AH-	—	10.00	20.00	45.00	75.00	120

Elichpur

KM# 134.6 1/2 RUPEE

5.7220 g., Silver **Obv:** Kalima

Date	Mintage	Good	VG	F	VF	XF
AH1015	—	—	—	—	—	—

Fathnagar

KM# 134.3 1/2 RUPEE

5.7220 g., Silver **Obv:** Kalima

Date	Mintage	Good	VG	F	VF	XF
AH- Rare	—	—	—	—	—	—

Lahore

KM# 134.2 1/2 RUPEE

5.7220 g., Silver **Obv:** Kalima

Date	Mintage	Good	VG	F	VF	XF
AH1015//1 Rare	—	—	—	—	—	—

Zafarnagar

KM# 134.4 1/2 RUPEE

5.7220 g., Silver **Obv:** Kalima

Date	Mintage	Good	VG	F	VF	XF
AH- Rare	—	—	—	—	—	—

Kashmir

KM# 135.3 1/2 RUPEE

5.7220 g., Silver **Obv:** Names of "Jahangir" and "Akbar" **Rev:** AH date

Date	Mintage	Good	VG	F	VF	XF
AH1031//17	—	—	—	—	—	—

Lahore

KM# 135.1 1/2 RUPEE

5.7220 g., Silver **Obv:** Names of "Jahangir" and "Akbar" **Rev:** AH date

Date	Mintage	Good	VG	F	VF	XF
AH102x//7 Rare	—	—	—	—	—	—
AH1021//7 Rare	—	—	—	—	—	—
AH1021//8 Rare	—	—	—	—	—	—
AH1022//8 Rare	—	—	—	—	—	—
AH1022//9 Rare	—	—	—	—	—	—
AH1023//9 Rare	—	—	—	—	—	—
AH1023//10 Rare	—	—	—	—	—	—
AH1024//10 Rare	—	—	—	—	—	—
AH1024//11 Rare	—	—	—	—	—	—
AH1025//11 Rare	—	—	—	—	—	—
AH1025//12 Rare	—	—	—	—	—	—
AH1026//12 Rare	—	—	—	—	—	—
AH1026//13 Rare	—	—	—	—	—	—
AH1027//13 Rare	—	—	—	—	—	—
AH1027//14 Rare	—	—	—	—	—	—
AH1028//14 Rare	—	—	—	—	—	—
AH1028//15 Rare	—	—	—	—	—	—
AH1029//15 Rare	—	—	—	—	—	—
AH1029//16 Rare	—	—	—	—	—	—
AH1030//16 Rare	—	—	—	—	—	—
AH1030//17 Rare	—	—	—	—	—	—
AH1031//17 Rare	—	—	—	—	—	—
AH1031//18 Rare	—	—	—	—	—	—
AH1032//18 Rare	—	—	—	—	—	—
AH1032//19 Rare	—	—	—	—	—	—
AH1033//19 Rare	—	—	—	—	—	—
AH1033//20 Rare	—	—	—	—	—	—
AH1034//20 Rare	—	—	—	—	—	—
AH1034//21 Rare	—	—	—	—	—	—
AH1035//21 Rare	—	—	—	—	—	—

Qandahar

KM# 135.2 1/2 RUPEE

5.7220 g., Silver **Obv:** Names of "Jahangir" and "Akbar" **Rev:** AH date

Date	Mintage	Good	VG	F	VF	XF
AH1026//12 Rare	—	—	—	—	—	—
AH1027//13 Rare	—	—	—	—	—	—
AH1028//14 Rare	—	—	—	—	—	—
AH103x//xx Rare	—	—	—	—	—	—

Ahmadabad

KM# 136.6 1/2 RUPEE

5.7220 g., Silver

Date	Mintage	Good	VG	F	VF	XF
AHxxxx	—	—	—	—	—	—

Akbarnagar

KM# 136.3 1/2 RUPEE

5.7220 g., Silver

Date	Mintage	Good	VG	F	VF	XF
AH101x//6	—	—	—	—	—	—

Burhanpur

KM# 136.5 1/2 RUPEE

5.7220 g., Silver **Rev:** AH date and Ilahi month

Date	Mintage	Good	VG	F	VF	XF
AH- Rare	—	—	—	—	—	—

Patna

KM# 136.1 1/2 RUPEE

5.7220 g., Silver **Rev:** AH date and Ilahi month

Date	Mintage	Good	VG	F	VF	XF
AH1021//7 Rare	—	—	—	—	—	—
AH102x//9 Rare	—	—	—	—	—	—
AH102x//10 Rare	—	—	—	—	—	—
AH1025//11 Rare	—	—	—	—	—	—
AH1026//11 Rare	—	—	—	—	—	—
AH1026//12 Rare	—	—	—	—	—	—
AH1027//13 Rare	—	—	—	—	—	—
AH1031//16(sic) Rare	—	—	—	—	—	—
AH1031//17 Rare	—	—	—	—	—	—
AH1032//18 Rare	—	—	—	—	—	—
AH1034//20 Rare	—	—	—	—	—	—
AH1036//22 Rare	—	—	—	—	—	—

Qandahar

KM# 136.4 1/2 RUPEE

5.7220 g., Silver **Rev:** AH date and Ilahi month

Date	Mintage	Good	VG	F	VF	XF
AH1024//11 Rare	—	—	—	—	—	—

Tatta

KM# 136.2 1/2 RUPEE

5.7220 g., Silver **Rev:** AH date and Ilahi month

Date	Mintage	Good	VG	F	VF	XF
AH10xx//15 Rare	—	—	—	—	—	—

Ahmadabad

KM# 137.1 1/2 RUPEE

5.7220 g., Silver **Obv. Legend:** Poetic couplet **Rev. Legend:** Poetic couplet

Date	Mintage	Good	VG	F	VF	XF
AH1022//xx	—	20.00	45.00	95.00	150	240
AH1023//xx	—	20.00	45.00	95.00	150	240
AH1025//xx	—	20.00	45.00	95.00	150	240

Kabul

KM# 137.3 1/2 RUPEE

5.7220 g., Silver **Rev:** AH date and Ilahi month **Note:** Similar to 1 Rupee, KM#149.12.

Date	Mintage	Good	VG	F	VF	XF
ND Rare	—	—	—	—	—	—

Ahmadabad

KM# 138.1 1/2 RUPEE

5.7220 g., Silver **Obv:** Taurus (bull)

Date	Mintage	Good	VG	F	VF	XF
AH1027//13	—	40.00	100	175	250	350

KM# 138.2 1/2 RUPEE

5.7220 g., Silver **Obv:** Leo (lion) **Note:** Zodiac 1/2 Rupees of Agra Mint have been reported, but are believed to be counterfeit.

Date	Mintage	Good	VG	F	VF	XF
AH1027//13	—	40.00	100	150	200	300

Ahmadabad

KM# A139.1 1/2 RUPEE

7.1000 g., Silver **Series:** "Sawai" **Obv:** "Jahangir" and "Akbar" **Rev:** "inayat couplet"

Date	Mintage	Good	VG	F	VF	XF
AHxxxx//3	—	—	—	—	—	—
AHxxxx//6	—	—	—	—	—	—

Agra

KM# 139.2 SULTANI

Silver **Obv:** Kalima **Note:** Weight varies: 6.70-6.85 grams.

Date	Mintage	Good	VG	F	VF	XF
AH101x//4 Rare	—	—	—	—	—	—

Ahmadabad

KM# 139.3 SULTANI

Silver **Obv:** Kalima **Note:** Weight varies: 6.70-6.85 grams.

Date	Mintage	Good	VG	F	VF	XF
AH1016 Rare	—	—	—	—	—	—

Kabul

KM# 139.1 SULTANI

Silver **Obv:** Kalima **Note:** Weight varies: 6.70-6.85 grams.

Date	Mintage	Good	VG	F	VF	XF
AH1014//1	—	18.00	40.00	90.00	140	220
AH1015//1	—	18.00	40.00	90.00	140	220
AH1016//x	—	18.00	40.00	90.00	140	220

Ahmadabad

KM# 140.1 RUPEE

11.4440 g., Silver **Obv:** Pre-accession name, "Selem Shah" in couplet, date **Rev:** Mint name; Royal year of Akbar, "Azur-Isfundarmuz"

Date	Mintage	Good	VG	F	VF	XF
ND(II 50 of Akbar)	—	16.00	40.00	70.00	100	140

KM# 140.2 RUPEE

11.4440 g., Silver **Obv:** Pre-accession name "Selim Shah" in couplet **Rev:** Royal year of Jahangir, "Farwardin-Tir"

Date	Mintage	Good	VG	F	VF	XF
AHxxxx//2	—	12.00	26.00	55.00	88.00	140

Ahmadabad

KM# A141.1 RUPEE

11.4440 g., Silver **Obv:** Kalima **Obv. Inscription:** "Jahangir..."

Date	Mintage	Good	VG	F	VF	XF
AH1015//2	—	—	—	—	—	—

Ahmadanagar

KM# 141.1 RUPEE

11.4440 g., Silver **Obv:** Kalima **Rev:** AH date
Rev. Inscription: "Nur-ud-din Muhammad Jahangir"

Date	Mintage	Good	VG	F	VF	XF
AH1014	—	8.00	15.00	25.00	40.00	65.00
AH1020	—	8.00	15.00	25.00	40.00	65.00
AH1027	—	8.00	15.00	25.00	40.00	65.00

Akbarnagar

KM# 141.2 RUPEE

11.4440 g., Silver **Obv:** Kalima **Rev:** AH date
Rev. Inscription: "Nur-ud-din Muhammad Jahangir"

Date	Mintage	Good	VG	F	VF	XF
AH1014	—	8.00	15.00	25.00	40.00	65.00

Berar

KM# 141.3 RUPEE

11.4440 g., Silver **Obv:** Kalima **Rev:** AH date, bird
Rev. Inscription: "Nur-ud-din Muhammad Jahangir"

Date	Mintage	Good	VG	F	VF	XF
AH1014	—	8.00	20.00	35.00	55.00	80.00

Burhanpur

KM# 141.4 RUPEE

11.4440 g., Silver **Obv:** Kalima **Rev:** AH date
Rev. Inscription: "Nur-ud-din Muhammad Jahangir"

Date	Mintage	Good	VG	F	VF	XF
AH1015//2	—	8.00	15.00	30.00	50.00	80.00

Elichpur

KM# 141.5 RUPEE

11.4440 g., Silver **Obv:** Kalima **Rev:** AH date
Rev. Inscription: "Nur-ud-din Muhammad Jahangir"

Date	Mintage	Good	VG	F	VF	XF
AH1014//x	—	8.00	20.00	35.00	55.00	80.00
AH1015	—	8.00	20.00	35.00	55.00	80.00
AH1015 bird//bird	—	8.00	20.00	35.00	55.00	80.00
AH1015 Erichpur Error	—	8.00	20.00	35.00	55.00	80.00
AH1016//x	—	8.00	20.00	35.00	55.00	80.00
AH1017//4	—	8.00	20.00	35.00	55.00	80.00

Fathnagar

KM# 141.8 RUPEE

11.4440 g., Silver **Obv:** Kalima **Rev:** AH date
Rev. Inscription: "Nur-ud-din Muhammad Jahangir"

Date	Mintage	Good	VG	F	VF	XF
ND	—	8.00	20.00	35.00	55.00	80.00

Jalnapur

KM# 141.6 RUPEE

11.4440 g., Silver **Obv:** Kalima **Rev:** AH date
Rev. Inscription: "Nur-ud-din Muhammad Jahangir"

Date	Mintage	Good	VG	F	VF	XF
AH1014	—	8.00	20.00	35.00	55.00	80.00
AH1015//3 (sic)	—	8.00	20.00	35.00	55.00	80.00
AH1017//x	—	8.00	20.00	35.00	55.00	80.00

Tatta

KM# 141.9 RUPEE

11.4440 g., Silver **Obv:** Kalima **Rev:** AH date
Rev. Inscription: "Nur-ud-din Muhammad Jahangir"

Date	Mintage	Good	VG	F	VF	XF
AH1015//2	—	8.00	20.00	35.00	55.00	80.00
AH1016//2	—	8.00	20.00	35.00	55.00	80.00
AH1016//3	—	8.00	20.00	35.00	55.00	80.00
AH1017//3	—	8.00	20.00	35.00	55.00	80.00
AH1017//4	—	8.00	20.00	35.00	55.00	80.00
AH1018//5	—	8.00	20.00	35.00	55.00	80.00
AH1019//5	—	8.00	20.00	35.00	55.00	80.00
AH1020//6	—	8.00	20.00	35.00	55.00	80.00

Zafarnagar

KM# 141.7 RUPEE

11.4440 g., Silver **Obv:** Kalima **Rev:** AH date
Rev. Inscription: "Nur-ud-din Muhammad Jahangir"

Date	Mintage	Good	VG	F	VF	XF
ND	—	10.00	25.00	45.00	70.00	100

Ahmadanagar

KM# 142.1 RUPEE

11.4440 g., Silver **Obv:** Names of "Jahangir" and "Akbar"
Rev: AH date

Date	Mintage	Good	VG	F	VF	XF
AH1032	—	8.00	14.00	26.00	44.00	70.00
AH1035	—	8.00	14.00	26.00	44.00	70.00
AH1036//xx	—	8.00	14.00	26.00	44.00	70.00
AH1037	—	8.00	14.00	26.00	44.00	70.00

Qandahar

KM# 142.2 RUPEE

11.4440 g., Silver **Obv:** Names of "Jahangir" and "Akbar"
Rev: AH date

Date	Mintage	Good	VG	F	VF	XF
AH1025//11	—	7.00	10.00	16.00	26.00	40.00
AH1025//12	—	7.00	10.00	16.00	26.00	40.00
AH1026//12	—	7.00	10.00	16.00	26.00	40.00
AH1027//13	—	7.00	10.00	16.00	26.00	40.00
AH1026//13	—	7.00	10.00	16.00	26.00	40.00
AH1028//14	—	7.00	10.00	16.00	26.00	40.00
AH1027//14	—	7.00	10.00	16.00	26.00	40.00
AH1029//15	—	7.00	10.00	16.00	26.00	40.00
AH1028//15	—	7.00	10.00	16.00	26.00	40.00
AH1030//16	—	7.00	10.00	16.00	26.00	40.00
AH1029//16	—	7.00	10.00	16.00	26.00	40.00
AH1031//17	—	7.00	10.00	16.00	26.00	40.00
AH1030//17	—	7.00	10.00	16.00	26.00	40.00

Agra

KM# 143.1 RUPEE

11.4440 g., Silver **Obv. Inscription:** ...Sakhat Nurani...
Rev: "Jahangir..."

Date	Mintage	Good	VG	F	VF	XF
AH1016	—	—	—	—	—	—

Burhanpur

KM# 143.3 RUPEE

11.4440 g., Silver **Obv. Inscription:** "...Sakhatnurani..."

Date	Mintage	Good	VG	F	VF	XF
AH1014	—	—	—	—	—	—

Qandahar

KM# 143.2 RUPEE

11.4440 g., Silver **Shape:** Square

Date	Mintage	Good	VG	F	VF	XF
AH1026//11	—	—	—	—	—	—

Agra

KM# A144.1 RUPEE

11.4440 g., Silver **Note:** With Persian Solar months.

Date	Mintage	Good	VG	F	VF	XF
AH1020//6 Khúrdád	—	—	—	—	—	—
AH1020//6 Mihr	—	—	—	—	—	—
AH1020//6 Azar	—	—	—	—	—	—
AH1020//6 Bahman	—	—	—	—	—	—
AH1020//6 Amardád	—	—	—	—	—	—
AH1021//7 Khúrdád	—	—	—	—	—	—
AH1021//7 Mihr	—	—	—	—	—	—
AH1021//7 Amardád	—	—	—	—	—	—
AH1021//7 Farwardín	—	—	—	—	—	—
AH1021//7 Bahman	—	—	—	—	—	—

Agra

KM# 144.1 RUPEE

11.4440 g., Silver **Shape:** Square **Note:** With Persian Solar months.

Date	Mintage	Good	VG	F	VF	XF
AH1020//6 Di	—	50.00	100	200	375	450
AH1020//6 Shahrewar	—	50.00	100	200	375	450
AH1020//6 Aban	—	50.00	100	200	375	450
AH1020//6 Tir	—	50.00	100	200	375	450
AH1020//6 (Ardíbihisht?)	—	50.00	100	200	375	450
AH1021//6(sic) Isfandármuz	—	50.00	100	200	375	450
AH1021//7 Aban	—	50.00	100	200	375	450
AH1021//7 Ardíbihisht	—	50.00	100	200	375	450
AH1021//7 Shahrewar	—	50.00	100	200	375	450
AH1021//7 Tir	—	50.00	100	200	375	450

Agra

KM# 145.1 RUPEE

11.4440 g., Silver **Obv:** "Nur al-Din Jahangir" and "Akbar"
Rev: AH date and/or regnal year

Date	Mintage	Good	VG	F	VF	XF
AH1020//6	—	40.00	100	200	325	450
AH1020//7	—	40.00	100	200	325	450
AH1021//7	—	40.00	100	200	325	450
AH1021//8	—	10.00	25.00	50.00	90.00	150
AH1022//8	—	10.00	25.00	50.00	90.00	150
AH1022//9	—	10.00	25.00	50.00	90.00	150
AH1023//9	—	10.00	25.00	50.00	90.00	150
AH1023//10	—	10.00	25.00	50.00	90.00	150
AH1024/10	—	—	25.00	50.00	90.00	150
AH1024//11	—	10.00	25.00	50.00	90.00	150
AH1025//11	—	10.00	25.00	50.00	90.00	150
AH1025//12	—	10.00	25.00	50.00	90.00	150
AH1026//12	—	10.00	25.00	50.00	90.00	150
AH1026//13	—	10.00	25.00	50.00	90.00	150
AH1027//13	—	10.00	25.00	50.00	90.00	150
AH1028//13(sic)	—	10.00	25.00	50.00	90.00	150

Ahmadabad

KM# 145.2 RUPEE

11.4440 g., Silver **Obv:** "Nur al-Din Jahangir" and "Akbar"
Rev: AH date and/or regnal year

Date	Mintage	Good	VG	F	VF	XF
AH1020//6	—	7.00	9.00	13.00	20.00	30.00
AH1020//7	—	7.00	9.00	13.00	20.00	30.00
AH1021//7	—	7.00	9.00	13.00	20.00	30.00

Date	Mintage	Good	VG	F	VF	XF
AH1021//8	—	7.00	9.00	13.00	20.00	30.00
AH1022//x	—	7.00	9.00	13.00	20.00	30.00
AH1022//8	—	7.00	9.00	13.00	20.00	30.00

Ahmadnagar

KM# 145.19 RUPEE

11.4440 g., Silver **Obv:** "Nur al-Din Jahangir" and "Akbar" **Rev:** AH date and/or regnal year

Date	Mintage	Good	VG	F	VF	XF
AH1037	—	—	—	—	—	—

Note: Mint name appears as "Ahmadanagar"

Akbarnagar

KM# 145.4 RUPEE

11.4440 g., Silver **Obv:** "Nur al-Din Jahangir" and "Akbar" **Rev:** AH date and/or regnal year

Date	Mintage	Good	VG	F	VF	XF
AH1017//x	—	7.00	9.00	13.00	20.00	30.00
AH1021//7	—	7.00	9.00	13.00	20.00	30.00
AH1021//8	—	7.00	9.00	13.00	20.00	30.00
AH1022//8	—	7.00	9.00	13.00	20.00	30.00
AH1022//9	—	7.00	9.00	13.00	20.00	30.00
AH1023//9	—	7.00	9.00	13.00	20.00	30.00
AH1023//10	—	7.00	9.00	13.00	20.00	30.00
AH1024//10	—	7.00	9.00	13.00	20.00	30.00
AH1024//11	—	7.00	9.00	13.00	20.00	30.00
AH1025//xx	—	7.00	9.00	13.00	20.00	30.00
AH10xx//13	—	7.00	9.00	13.00	20.00	30.00
AH10xx//15	—	7.00	9.00	13.00	20.00	30.00
AH10xx//18	—	7.00	9.00	13.00	20.00	30.00
AH10xx//19	—	7.00	9.00	13.00	20.00	30.00
AH10xx//20	—	7.00	9.00	13.00	20.00	30.00
AH10xx//21	—	7.00	9.00	13.00	20.00	30.00
AH10xx//22	—	7.00	9.00	13.00	20.00	30.00

Burhanpur

KM# 145.5 RUPEE

11.4440 g., Silver **Obv:** "Nur al-Din Jahangir" and "Akbar" **Rev:** AH date and/or regnal year

Date	Mintage	Good	VG	F	VF	XF
AH1019//x	—	7.00	10.00	15.00	23.00	35.00
AH1020//6	—	7.00	10.00	15.00	23.00	35.00
AH1020//7	—	7.00	10.00	15.00	23.00	35.00
AH1021//7	—	7.00	10.00	15.00	23.00	35.00
AH1021//8	—	7.00	10.00	15.00	23.00	35.00
AH102x//9	—	7.00	10.00	15.00	23.00	35.00
AH102x//11	—	7.00	10.00	15.00	23.00	35.00
AH102x//14	—	7.00	10.00	15.00	23.00	35.00
AH10xx//15	—	7.00	10.00	15.00	23.00	35.00
AH103x//16	—	7.00	10.00	15.00	23.00	35.00
AH103x//17	—	7.00	10.00	15.00	23.00	35.00
AH103x//18	—	7.00	10.00	15.00	23.00	35.00
AH103x//19	—	7.00	10.00	15.00	23.00	35.00
AH103x//20	—	7.00	10.00	15.00	23.00	35.00
AH1035//21	—	7.00	10.00	15.00	23.00	35.00
AH1037//22(sic)	—	7.00	10.00	15.00	23.00	35.00

Delhi

KM# 145.6 RUPEE

11.4440 g., Silver **Obv:** "Nur al-Din Jahangir" and "Akbar" **Rev:** AH date and/or regnal year

Date	Mintage	Good	VG	F	VF	XF
AH1018//4	—	7.00	10.00	15.00	23.00	35.00
AH1020//6	—	7.00	10.00	15.00	23.00	35.00
AH1020//7	—	7.00	10.00	15.00	23.00	35.00
AH1021//7	—	7.00	10.00	15.00	23.00	35.00
AH1021//8	—	7.00	10.00	15.00	23.00	35.00
AH1022//8	—	7.00	10.00	15.00	23.00	35.00
AH1022//9	—	7.00	10.00	15.00	23.00	35.00
AH1023//9	—	7.00	10.00	15.00	23.00	35.00
AH1023//10	—	7.00	10.00	15.00	23.00	35.00
AH1024//10	—	7.00	10.00	15.00	23.00	35.00
AH1024//11	—	7.00	10.00	15.00	23.00	35.00
AH1025//11	—	7.00	10.00	15.00	23.00	35.00
AH1025//12	—	7.00	10.00	15.00	23.00	35.00
AH1026//12	—	7.00	10.00	15.00	23.00	35.00
AH1027//14	—	7.00	10.00	15.00	23.00	35.00
AH1026//13	—	7.00	10.00	15.00	23.00	35.00
AH1027//13	—	7.00	10.00	15.00	23.00	35.00
AH1028//14	—	7.00	10.00	15.00	23.00	35.00
AH1028//15	—	7.00	10.00	15.00	23.00	35.00
AH1029//15	—	7.00	10.00	15.00	23.00	35.00
AH1029//16	—	7.00	10.00	15.00	23.00	35.00
AH1030//16	—	7.00	10.00	15.00	23.00	35.00
AH1030//17	—	7.00	10.00	15.00	23.00	35.00
AH1031//17	—	7.00	10.00	15.00	23.00	35.00
AH1032//xx	—	7.00	10.00	15.00	23.00	35.00
AH1033//19	—	7.00	10.00	15.00	23.00	35.00
AH1037//23	—	7.00	10.00	15.00	23.00	35.00

Jahangirnagar

KM# 145.7 RUPEE

11.4440 g., Silver **Obv:** "Nur al-Din Jahangir" and "Akbar" **Rev:** AH date and/or regnal year **Note:** Some dates exist with a decorative border.

Date	Mintage	Good	VG	F	VF	XF
ND//7	—	7.00	9.00	13.00	20.00	30.00
ND//9	—	7.00	9.00	13.00	20.00	30.00
ND//10	—	7.00	9.00	13.00	20.00	30.00
ND//11	—	7.00	9.00	13.00	20.00	30.00
ND//12	—	7.00	9.00	13.00	20.00	30.00
ND//13	—	7.00	9.00	13.00	20.00	30.00
ND//14	—	7.00	9.00	13.00	20.00	30.00
ND//15	—	7.00	9.00	13.00	20.00	30.00
ND//16	—	7.00	9.00	13.00	20.00	30.00
ND//17	—	7.00	9.00	13.00	20.00	30.00
ND//18	—	7.00	9.00	13.00	20.00	30.00
ND//19	—	7.00	9.00	13.00	20.00	30.00
ND//20	—	7.00	9.00	13.00	20.00	30.00

Jalesar

KM# 145.8 RUPEE

11.4440 g., Silver **Obv:** "Nur al-Din Jahangir" and "Akbar" **Rev:** AH date and/or regnal year

Date	Mintage	Good	VG	F	VF	XF
AH1031 Rare	—	—	—	—	—	—

Kabul

KM# 145.9 RUPEE

11.4440 g., Silver **Obv:** "Nur al-Din Jahangir" and "Akbar" **Rev:** AH date and/or regnal year

Date	Mintage	Good	VG	F	VF	XF
AH1016//3	—	8.00	12.00	18.00	30.00	55.00
AH1022//8	—	8.00	12.00	18.00	30.00	55.00
AH1023//9	—	8.00	12.00	18.00	30.00	55.00
AH1025//11	—	8.00	12.00	18.00	30.00	55.00
AH1026//11(sic)	—	8.00	12.00	18.00	30.00	55.00
AH1026//12	—	8.00	12.00	18.00	30.00	55.00
AH1027//12(sic)	—	8.00	12.00	18.00	30.00	55.00
AH1027//13	—	8.00	12.00	18.00	30.00	55.00
AH1028//13(sic)	—	8.00	12.00	18.00	30.00	55.00
AH1028//14	—	8.00	12.00	18.00	30.00	55.00
AH1029//14(sic)	—	8.00	12.00	18.00	30.00	55.00
AH103x//21	—	8.00	12.00	18.00	30.00	55.00

Kashmir

KM# 145.10 RUPEE

11.4440 g., Silver **Obv:** "Nur al-Din Jahangir" and "Akbar" **Rev:** AH date and/or regnal year

Date	Mintage	Good	VG	F	VF	XF
AH1021//7	—	8.00	12.00	18.00	30.00	50.00
AH1022//8	—	8.00	12.00	18.00	30.00	50.00
AH1022//9	—	8.00	12.00	18.00	30.00	50.00
AH1023//9	—	8.00	12.00	18.00	30.00	50.00
AH1023//10	—	8.00	12.00	18.00	30.00	50.00
AH1024//10	—	8.00	12.00	18.00	30.00	50.00
AH1024//11	—	8.00	12.00	18.00	30.00	50.00

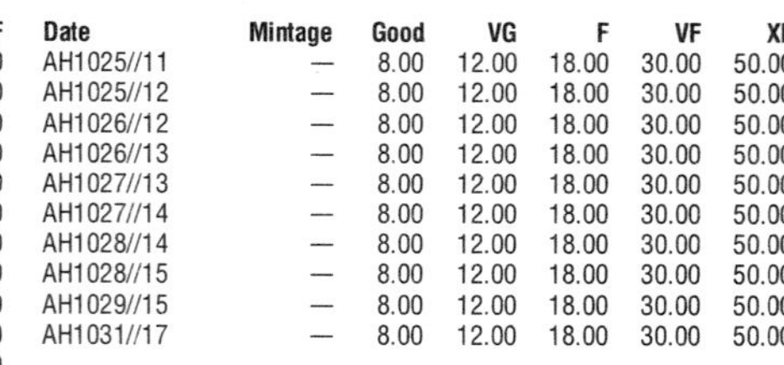

Date	Mintage	Good	VG	F	VF	XF
AH1025//11	—	8.00	12.00	18.00	30.00	50.00
AH1025//12	—	8.00	12.00	18.00	30.00	50.00
AH1026//12	—	8.00	12.00	18.00	30.00	50.00
AH1026//13	—	8.00	12.00	18.00	30.00	50.00
AH1027//13	—	8.00	12.00	18.00	30.00	50.00
AH1027//14	—	8.00	12.00	18.00	30.00	50.00
AH1028//14	—	8.00	12.00	18.00	30.00	50.00
AH1028//15	—	8.00	12.00	18.00	30.00	50.00
AH1029//15	—	8.00	12.00	18.00	30.00	50.00
AH1031//17	—	8.00	12.00	18.00	30.00	50.00

Katak

KM# 145.18 RUPEE

11.4440 g., Silver **Obv:** "Nur al-Din Jahangir" and "Akbar" **Rev:** AH date and/or regnal year

Date	Mintage	Good	VG	F	VF	XF
AH1027 Rare	—	—	—	—	—	—

Kishtwar

KM# 145.20 RUPEE

11.4440 g., Silver **Obv:** "Nur al-Din Jahangir" and "Akbar" **Rev:** AH date and/or regnal year

Date	Mintage	Good	VG	F	VF	XF
AH1024//10	—	—	—	—	—	—

Lahore

KM# 145.11 RUPEE

11.4440 g., Silver **Obv:** "Nur al-Din Jahangir" and "Akbar" **Rev:** AH date and/or regnal year

Date	Mintage	Good	VG	F	VF	XF
ND//5	—	7.00	10.00	15.00	23.00	40.00
ND//6	—	7.00	10.00	15.00	23.00	40.00
ND//7	—	7.00	10.00	15.00	23.00	40.00
ND//8	—	7.00	10.00	15.00	23.00	40.00
ND//9	—	7.00	10.00	15.00	23.00	40.00
ND//10	—	7.00	10.00	15.00	23.00	40.00
ND//11	—	7.00	10.00	15.00	23.00	40.00

Patna

KM# 145.12 RUPEE

11.4440 g., Silver **Obv:** "Nur al-Din Jahangir" and "Akbar" **Rev:** AH date and/or regnal year

Date	Mintage	Good	VG	F	VF	XF
AH1020//6	—	7.00	9.00	13.00	20.00	30.00
AH1021//7	—	7.00	9.00	13.00	20.00	30.00
AH1021//7	—	7.00	9.00	13.00	20.00	30.00
AH1021//8	—	7.00	9.00	13.00	20.00	30.00
AH1022//8	—	7.00	9.00	13.00	20.00	30.00
AH1022//9	—	7.00	9.00	13.00	20.00	30.00
AH1023//9	—	7.00	9.00	13.00	20.00	30.00
AH1023//10	—	7.00	9.00	13.00	20.00	30.00
AH1024//10	—	7.00	9.00	13.00	20.00	30.00
AH1024//11	—	7.00	9.00	13.00	20.00	30.00
AH1025//11	—	7.00	9.00	13.00	20.00	30.00
AH1025//12	—	7.00	9.00	13.00	20.00	30.00
AH1026//12	—	7.00	9.00	13.00	20.00	30.00
AH1026//13	—	7.00	9.00	13.00	20.00	30.00
AH1027//13	—	7.00	9.00	13.00	20.00	30.00
AH1027//14	—	7.00	9.00	13.00	20.00	30.00
AH1028//14	—	7.00	9.00	13.00	20.00	30.00
AH1028//15	—	7.00	9.00	13.00	20.00	30.00
AH1029//15	—	7.00	9.00	13.00	20.00	30.00
AH1029//16	—	7.00	9.00	13.00	20.00	30.00
AH1030//16	—	7.00	9.00	13.00	20.00	30.00
AH1030//17	—	7.00	9.00	13.00	20.00	30.00
AH1031//16	—	7.00	9.00	13.00	20.00	30.00
AH1031//17	—	7.00	9.00	13.00	20.00	30.00
AH1031//18	—	7.00	9.00	13.00	20.00	30.00
AH1032//18	—	7.00	9.00	13.00	20.00	30.00
AH1032//19	—	7.00	9.00	13.00	20.00	30.00
AH1033//19	—	7.00	9.00	13.00	20.00	30.00
AH1033//20	—	7.00	9.00	13.00	20.00	30.00
AH1034//20	—	7.00	9.00	13.00	20.00	30.00
AH1034//21	—	7.00	9.00	13.00	20.00	30.00
AH1035//21	—	7.00	9.00	13.00	20.00	30.00
AH1035//22	—	7.00	9.00	13.00	20.00	30.00
AH1036//22	—	7.00	9.00	13.00	20.00	30.00
AH1037//22(sic)	—	7.00	9.00	13.00	20.00	30.00

Qandahar

KM# 145.13 RUPEE

11.4440 g., Silver **Obv:** "Nur al-Din Jahangir" and "Akbar" **Rev:** AH date and/or regnal year

Date	Mintage	Good	VG	F	VF	XF
AH1020//x	—	7.00	9.00	13.00	20.00	30.00
AH1022//8	—	7.00	9.00	13.00	20.00	30.00
AH1023//9	—	7.00	9.00	13.00	20.00	30.00
AH1024//10	—	7.00	9.00	13.00	20.00	30.00
AH1025//11	—	7.00	9.00	13.00	20.00	30.00
AH1029//19	—	7.00	9.00	13.00	20.00	30.00

Rohtas

KM# 145.14 RUPEE

11.4440 g., Silver **Obv:** "Nur al-Din Jahangir" and "Akbar" **Rev:** AH date and/or regnal year

Date	Mintage	Good	VG	F	VF	XF
AH1034//19 Rare	—	—	—	—	—	—
ND//20 Rare	—	—	—	—	—	—

Surat

KM# 145.15 RUPEE

11.4440 g., Silver **Obv:** "Nur al-Din Jahangir" and "Akbar" **Rev:** AH date and/or regnal year

Date	Mintage	Good	VG	F	VF	XF
AH1029//15 Rare	—	—	—	—	—	—
AH103x//17 Rare	—	—	—	—	—	—

Tatta

KM# 145.17 RUPEE

11.4440 g., Silver **Obv:** "Nur al-Din Jahangir" and "Akbar" **Rev:** AH date and/or regnal year

Date	Mintage	Good	VG	F	VF	XF
AH10xx//3	—	7.00	9.00	13.00	20.00	30.00
AH1020//6	—	7.00	9.00	13.00	20.00	30.00
AH1020//7	—	7.00	9.00	13.00	20.00	30.00
AH1021//7	—	7.00	9.00	13.00	20.00	30.00
AH1021//8	—	7.00	9.00	13.00	20.00	30.00
AH1022//8	—	7.00	9.00	13.00	20.00	30.00
AH1022//9	—	7.00	9.00	13.00	20.00	30.00
AH1023//9	—	7.00	9.00	13.00	20.00	30.00
AH1023//10	—	7.00	9.00	13.00	20.00	30.00
AH1024//10	—	7.00	9.00	13.00	20.00	30.00
AH1024//11	—	7.00	9.00	13.00	20.00	30.00
AH1025//11	—	7.00	9.00	13.00	20.00	30.00
AH1025//12	—	7.00	9.00	13.00	20.00	30.00
AH1026//12	—	7.00	9.00	13.00	20.00	30.00
AH1026//13	—	7.00	9.00	13.00	20.00	30.00
AH1027//13	—	7.00	9.00	13.00	20.00	30.00
AH1027//14	—	7.00	9.00	13.00	20.00	30.00
AH1028//14	—	7.00	9.00	13.00	20.00	30.00
AH1028//15	—	7.00	9.00	13.00	20.00	30.00
AH1029//15	—	7.00	9.00	13.00	20.00	30.00
AH1029//16	—	7.00	9.00	13.00	20.00	30.00
AH10xx//17	—	7.00	9.00	13.00	20.00	30.00
AH10xx//18	—	7.00	9.00	13.00	20.00	30.00
AH10xx//19	—	7.00	9.00	13.00	20.00	30.00
AH10xx//20	—	7.00	9.00	13.00	20.00	30.00
AH1035//21	—	7.00	9.00	13.00	20.00	30.00
AH1037//22	—	7.00	9.00	13.00	20.00	30.00

Ujjain

KM# 145.16 RUPEE

11.4440 g., Silver **Obv:** "Nur al-Din Jahangir" and "Akbar" **Rev:** AH date and/or regnal year

Date	Mintage	Good	VG	F	VF	XF
AH10xx//15 Rare	—	—	—	—	—	—

Agra

KM# 147.1 RUPEE

Silver **Shape:** Square **Note:** Weight varies: 11.20-11.50 grams.

Date	Mintage	Good	VG	F	VF	XF
AH1020//6	—	60.00	150	250	350	500
AH1020//7	—	60.00	150	250	350	500
AH1021//7	—	60.00	150	250	350	500
AH1021//8	—	30.00	60.00	120	190	300
AH1022//8	—	30.00	60.00	120	190	300
AH1023//9	—	30.00	60.00	120	190	300
AH1023//10	—	30.00	60.00	120	190	300
AH1024//9	—	30.00	60.00	120	190	300
AH1024//10	—	30.00	60.00	120	190	300
AH1024//11	—	30.00	60.00	120	190	300
AH1025//11	—	30.00	60.00	120	190	300
AH1025//12	—	30.00	60.00	120	190	300
AH1026//12	—	30.00	60.00	120	190	300
AH1026//13	—	30.00	60.00	120	190	300
AH1027//13	—	30.00	60.00	120	190	300
AH1028//1x	—	30.00	60.00	120	190	300

Surat

KM# 148.1 RUPEE

11.4440 g., Silver

Date	Mintage	Good	VG	F	VF	XF
AH102x//8	—	8.00	20.00	30.00	50.00	80.00
AH1023//9	—	8.00	20.00	30.00	50.00	80.00
AH103x//15	—	8.00	20.00	30.00	50.00	80.00
AH1030//16	—	8.00	20.00	30.00	50.00	80.00
AH1030//17	—	8.00	20.00	30.00	50.00	80.00
AH1031//17	—	8.00	20.00	30.00	50.00	80.00
AH1031//18	—	8.00	20.00	30.00	50.00	80.00
AH1032//18	—	8.00	20.00	30.00	50.00	80.00
AH1032//19	—	8.00	20.00	30.00	50.00	80.00
AH1033//18(sic)	—	8.00	20.00	30.00	50.00	80.00

Agra

KM# 149.1 RUPEE

11.4440 g., Silver **Rev:** "Yaft"

Date	Mintage	Good	VG	F	VF	XF
AH1030//16	—	8.00	13.00	24.00	38.00	60.00
AH1031//17	—	8.00	13.00	24.00	38.00	60.00
AH1031//18	—	8.00	13.00	24.00	38.00	60.00
AH1032//18	—	8.00	13.00	24.00	38.00	60.00
AH103x//19	—	8.00	13.00	24.00	38.00	60.00
AH1034//20	—	8.00	13.00	24.00	38.00	60.00
AH1034//21	—	8.00	13.00	24.00	38.00	60.00
AH1035//21	—	8.00	13.00	24.00	38.00	60.00
AH1036//2x	—	8.00	13.00	24.00	38.00	60.00

Ahmadabad

KM# 149.4 RUPEE

11.4440 g., Silver **Rev. Inscription:** "Inayat"

Date	Mintage	Good	VG	F	VF	XF
AH1016//3	—	7.00	10.00	16.00	26.00	40.00
AH1022//8	—	7.00	10.00	16.00	26.00	40.00
AH1027//13	—	7.00	10.00	16.00	26.00	40.00
AH1027//14	—	7.00	10.00	16.00	26.00	40.00
AH1028//14	—	7.00	10.00	16.00	26.00	40.00
AH1028//15	—	7.00	10.00	16.00	26.00	40.00
AH1029//15	—	7.00	10.00	16.00	26.00	40.00
AH1029//16	—	7.00	10.00	16.00	26.00	40.00
AH1030//15	—	7.00	10.00	16.00	26.00	40.00
AH1030//16	—	7.00	10.00	16.00	26.00	40.00
AH1030//17	—	7.00	10.00	16.00	26.00	40.00
AH1031//61 (error for 16)	—	7.00	10.00	16.00	26.00	40.00
AH1031//16	—	7.00	10.00	16.00	26.00	40.00
AH1031//17	—	7.00	10.00	16.00	26.00	40.00
AH1032//18	—	7.00	10.00	16.00	26.00	40.00
AH1032//19	—	7.00	10.00	16.00	26.00	40.00
AH1033//19	—	7.00	10.00	16.00	26.00	40.00

KM# 149.2 RUPEE

11.4440 g., Silver **Rev. Inscription:** "Muzaiyan"

Date	Mintage	Good	VG	F	VF	XF
AH1022//8	—	7.00	10.00	16.00	26.00	40.00
AH1022//9	—	7.00	10.00	16.00	26.00	40.00
AH1023//9	—	7.00	10.00	16.00	26.00	40.00
AH1023//10	—	7.00	10.00	16.00	26.00	40.00
AH1024//10	—	7.00	10.00	16.00	26.00	40.00
AH1024//11	—	7.00	10.00	16.00	26.00	40.00
AH1025//11	—	7.00	10.00	16.00	26.00	40.00
AH1025//12	—	7.00	10.00	16.00	26.00	40.00
AH1026//12	—	7.00	10.00	16.00	26.00	40.00

KM# 149.2A RUPEE

11.4440 g., Silver **Note:** "Hamisha" couplet.

Date	Mintage	Good	VG	F	VF	XF
AH1027//12	—	—	—	—	—	—

KM# 149.3 RUPEE

11.4440 g., Silver **Rev:** "Kishwar" **Note:** Struck from gold mohur dies.

Date	Mintage	Good	VG	F	VF	XF
AH1027//12(sic)	—	8.00	13.00	24.00	38.00	60.00
AH1029//14(sic)	—	8.00	13.00	24.00	38.00	60.00

Ajmer

KM# 149.5 RUPEE

11.4440 g., Silver **Rev. Inscription:** "Firoz"

Date	Mintage	Good	VG	F	VF	XF
AH1023//9	—	8.00	15.00	30.00	50.00	80.00
AH1023//10	—	8.00	15.00	30.00	50.00	80.00
AH1024//10	—	8.00	15.00	30.00	50.00	80.00
AH1025//11	—	8.00	15.00	30.00	50.00	80.00

KM# 149.6 RUPEE

11.4440 g., Silver **Rev:** "Fath"

Date	Mintage	Good	VG	F	VF	XF
AH1024//10	—	9.00	16.00	33.00	57.00	90.00

Akbarnagar

KM# 149.7 RUPEE

11.4440 g., Silver **Rev:** "Gardun"

Date	Mintage	Good	VG	F	VF	XF
AH1019//x	—	7.00	10.00	16.00	26.00	40.00
AH1020//x	—	7.00	10.00	16.00	26.00	40.00

Allahabad

KM# 149.8 RUPEE

11.4440 g., Silver **Rev:** "Hamisha"

Date	Mintage	Good	VG	F	VF	XF
AH10xx//15	—	8.00	13.00	24.00	38.00	60.00
AH1032//1x	—	8.00	13.00	24.00	38.00	60.00
AH1034//19(sic)	—	8.00	13.00	24.00	38.00	60.00
AH1035//21	—	8.00	13.00	24.00	38.00	60.00
AH1037//22(sic)	—	8.00	13.00	24.00	38.00	60.00

Burhanpur

KM# 149.10 RUPEE

11.4440 g., Silver **Rev. Inscription:** "Din Panah"

Date	Mintage	Good	VG	F	VF	XF
AH1014//(1)	—	7.00	10.00	15.00	23.00	40.00
AH1017//3	—	7.00	10.00	15.00	23.00	40.00
AH101x//4	—	7.00	10.00	15.00	23.00	40.00
AH101x//5	—	7.00	10.00	15.00	23.00	40.00

Jalnapur

KM# 149.11 RUPEE

11.4440 g., Silver **Rev:** "Sakhat Nurani"

Date	Mintage	Good	VG	F	VF	XF
ND Rare	—	—	—	—	—	—

Kabul

KM# 149.12 RUPEE

11.4440 g., Silver

Date	Mintage	Good	VG	F	VF	XF
AH1023//9	—	13.00	32.00	65.00	100	160
AH1024//10	—	13.00	32.00	65.00	100	160
AH103x//17	—	13.00	32.00	65.00	100	160
AH103x//18	—	13.00	32.00	65.00	100	160
AH1033//19	—	13.00	32.00	65.00	100	160
AH1034//19(sic)	—	13.00	32.00	65.00	100	160
AH1034//20	—	13.00	32.00	65.00	100	160
AH1036//21(sic)	—	13.00	32.00	65.00	100	160

KM# 149.13 RUPEE

11.4440 g., Silver **Rev:** "Khusro"

Date	Mintage	Good	VG	F	VF	XF
AH1024//9(sic)	—	8.00	13.00	24.00	38.00	60.00
AH1034//19(sic)	—	8.00	13.00	24.00	38.00	60.00

KM# 149.12A RUPEE

11.4440 g., Silver **Obv:** "Ilhahi" and month "Tir" in loop of "Kabul"

Date	Mintage	Good	VG	F	VF	XF
AHxxxx//16 Rare	—	—	—	—	—	—

KM# 149.12B RUPEE

11.4440 g., Silver **Note:** "Inayat" couplet.

Date	Mintage	Good	VG	F	VF	XF
AH103x//21	—	—	—	—	—	—

Katak

KM# 149.18 RUPEE

11.4440 g., Silver **Note:** Couplet and month "Tir".

Date	Mintage	Good	VG	F	VF	XF
AH1035	—	—	—	—	—	—

Lahore

KM# 149.14 RUPEE

11.4440 g., Silver **Rev:** "Hamisha" at top

Date	Mintage	Good	VG	F	VF	XF
AH1025//11	—	7.00	10.00	16.00	26.00	40.00
AH1025//12	—	7.00	10.00	16.00	26.00	40.00
AH1026//12	—	7.00	10.00	16.00	26.00	40.00
AH1026//13	—	7.00	10.00	16.00	26.00	40.00
AH1027//13	—	7.00	10.00	16.00	26.00	40.00
AH1027//14	—	7.00	10.00	16.00	26.00	40.00
AH1028//14	—	7.00	10.00	16.00	26.00	40.00
AH1029//1x	—	7.00	10.00	16.00	26.00	40.00
AH1028//15	—	7.00	10.00	16.00	26.00	40.00

KM# 149.15 RUPEE

11.4440 g., Silver **Rev:** "Ruy"

Date	Mintage	Good	VG	F	VF	XF
AH1029//14(sic)	—	8.00	12.00	20.00	32.00	50.00
AH1029//15	—	8.00	12.00	20.00	32.00	50.00

KM# 149.16 RUPEE

11.4440 g., Silver **Rev:** "Bada bar"

Date	Mintage	Good	VG	F	VF	XF
AH1029//15	—	7.00	10.00	16.00	26.00	40.00
AH1029//16	—	7.00	10.00	16.00	26.00	40.00
AH1030//16	—	7.00	10.00	16.00	26.00	40.00
AH1030//17	—	7.00	10.00	16.00	26.00	40.00
AH1031//16	—	7.00	10.00	16.00	26.00	40.00
AH1031//17	—	7.00	10.00	16.00	26.00	40.00
AH1031//18	—	7.00	10.00	16.00	26.00	40.00
AH1032//18	—	7.00	10.00	16.00	26.00	40.00
AH1032//19	—	7.00	10.00	16.00	26.00	40.00
AH1033//19	—	7.00	10.00	16.00	26.00	40.00
AH1033//20	—	7.00	10.00	16.00	26.00	40.00
AH1034//20	—	7.00	10.00	16.00	26.00	40.00
AH1034//21	—	7.00	10.00	16.00	26.00	40.00
AH1035//21	—	7.00	10.00	16.00	26.00	40.00
AH1035//22	—	7.00	10.00	16.00	26.00	40.00
AH1036//22	—	7.00	10.00	16.00	26.00	40.00
AH1036//23	—	7.00	10.00	16.00	26.00	40.00
AH1037//2x	—	7.00	10.00	16.00	26.00	40.00

Mandu

KM# 149.19A RUPEE

11.4440 g., Silver **Note:** "Z nam--jahangir" couplet.

Date	Mintage	Good	VG	F	VF	XF
AH1026//12	—	—	—	—	—	—

KM# 149.19 RUPEE

11.4440 g., Silver **Note:** "Fath-i-dakkam" couplet.

Date	Mintage	Good	VG	F	VF	XF
AH1026//12	—	—	—	—	—	—

Orissa

KM# 149.20 RUPEE

11.4440 g., Silver

Date	Mintage	Good	VG	F	VF	XF
AH1023//9	—	—	—	—	—	—

Urdu Dar Rah-i-Dakhan

KM# 149.17 RUPEE

11.4440 g., Silver

Date	Mintage	Good	VG	F	VF	XF
AH1025//11 Rare	—	—	—	—	—	—

Agra

KM# 150.9 ZODIAC RUPEE

11.4440 g., Silver **Obv:** Cancer (crab) **Rev:** Names of "Jahangir" and "Akbar"

Date	Mintage	Good	VG	F	VF	XF
AH1027//13	—	60.00	140	240	350	500
AH1029//15	—	60.00	140	240	350	500

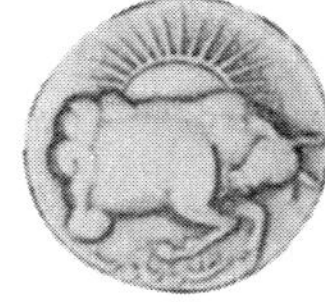

KM# 150.4 ZODIAC RUPEE

11.4440 g., Silver **Obv:** Taurus (bull) to right **Rev:** Names of "Jahangir" and "Akbar" **Note:** Struck from gold mohur dies.

Date	Mintage	Good	VG	F	VF	XF
AH1028//13(sic)	—	60.00	140	240	350	500
AH1029//15	—	60.00	140	240	350	500
AH1029//16	—	60.00	140	240	350	500
AH1030//16	—	60.00	140	240	350	500

KM# 150.6 ZODIAC RUPEE

11.4440 g., Silver **Obv:** Gemini (twins) **Rev:** Names of "Jahangir" and "Akbar" **Note:** Struck from gold mohur dies.

Date	Mintage	Good	VG	F	VF	XF
AH1028//14	—	60.00	140	240	350	500
AH1029//15	—	60.00	140	240	350	500
AH1033//19	—	60.00	140	240	350	500

KM# 150.12 ZODIAC RUPEE

11.4440 g., Silver **Obv:** Capricorn (goat) to left **Rev:** Names of "Jahangir" and "Akbar" **Note:** Struck from gold mohur dies.

Date	Mintage	Good	VG	F	VF	XF
AH1029//14(sic)	—	75.00	180	300	450	650

KM# 150.1 ZODIAC RUPEE

11.4440 g., Silver **Obv:** Aries (ram) to left **Rev:** Names of "Jahangir" and "Akbar" **Note:** Struck from gold mohur dies.

Date	Mintage	Good	VG	F	VF	XF
AH1030//16	—	55.00	130	225	350	500

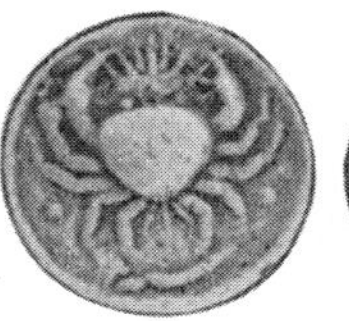

Ahmadabad

KM# 150.10 ZODIAC RUPEE

11.4440 g., Silver **Obv:** Cancer (crab) **Rev:** Names of "Jahangir" and "Akbar"

Date	Mintage	Good	VG	F	VF	XF
AH1027//13	—	60.00	140	240	350	500

KM# 150.11 ZODIAC RUPEE

11.4440 g., Silver **Obv:** Leo (lion) to left **Rev:** Names of "Jahangir" and "Akbar"

Date	Mintage	Good	VG	F	VF	XF
AH1027//13	—	50.00	120	200	275	400

KM# 150.2 ZODIAC RUPEE

11.4440 g., Silver **Obv:** Aries (ram) to left **Rev:** Names of "Jahangir" and "Akbar"

Date	Mintage	Good	VG	F	VF	XF
AH1027//13	—	75.00	180	300	450	650

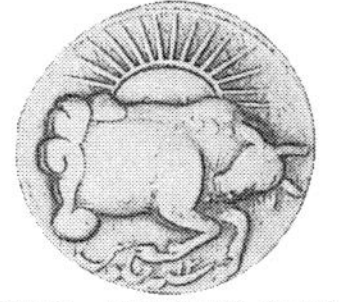

KM# 150.5 ZODIAC RUPEE

11.4440 g., Silver **Obv:** Taurus (bull) to right **Rev:** Names of "Jahangir" and "Akbar"

Date	Mintage	Good	VG	F	VF	XF
AH1027//13	—	50.00	120	200	275	400

KM# 150.7 ZODIAC RUPEE

11.4440 g., Silver **Obv:** Gemini (twins) **Rev:** Names of "Jahangir" and "Akbar"

Date	Mintage	Good	VG	F	VF	XF
AH1027//13	—	75.00	180	300	450	650

Fathpur

KM# 150.3 ZODIAC RUPEE

11.4440 g., Silver **Obv:** Aries (ram) to left **Rev:** Names of "Jahangir" and "Akbar" **Note:** Weight varies 13.4 - 13.7 grams; Struck from gold mohur dies.

Date	Mintage	Good	VG	F	VF	XF
AH1028//14 Rare	—	—	—	—	—	—

KM# 150.13 ZODIAC RUPEE

11.4440 g., Silver **Obv:** Capricorn (goat) to left **Rev:** Names of "Jahangir" and "Akbar" **Note:** Weight varies 13.4 - 13.7 grams; Struck from gold mohur dies.

Date	Mintage	Good	VG	F	VF	XF
AH1028//14 Rare	—	—	—	—	—	—

Kashmir

KM# 150.8 ZODIAC RUPEE

11.4440 g., Silver **Obv:** Gemini (twins) **Rev:** Names of "Jahangir" and "Akbar" **Note:** Weight varies 13.4 - 13.7 grams.

Date	Mintage	Good	VG	F	VF	XF
AH10xx//15 Rare	—	—	—	—	—	—

Agra

KM# 152.1 HEAVY RUPEE

Silver **Series:** "JAHANGIRI" **Obv:** Kalima, AH date **Rev. Legend:** "Nur-ud'din Muhammad Jahangir" **Note:** First Issue: 20 percent overweight. Weight varies: 13.40-13.70 grams.

Date	Mintage	Good	VG	F	VF	XF
AH1014//1	—	22.50	55.00	90.00	150	225
AH1015//1	—	22.50	55.00	90.00	150	225
AH1015//2	—	22.50	55.00	90.00	150	225
AH1016//x	—	22.50	55.00	90.00	150	225

Ahmadabad

KM# 152.2 HEAVY RUPEE

Silver **Series:** "JAHANGIRI" **Obv:** Kalima, AH date **Rev. Legend:** "Nur-ud'din Muhammad Jahangir" **Note:** Weight varies: 13.40-13.70 grams.

Date	Mintage	Good	VG	F	VF	XF
AH1014//1	—	22.50	55.00	90.00	150	225
AH1015//1	—	22.50	55.00	90.00	150	225
AH1016//2	—	22.50	55.00	90.00	150	225
AH1016//3	—	22.50	55.00	90.00	150	225
AH1017//3	—	22.50	55.00	90.00	150	225

Burhanpur

KM# 152.3 HEAVY RUPEE

Silver **Series:** "JAHANGIRI" **Obv:** Kalima, AH date **Rev. Legend:** "Nur-ud'din Muhammad Jahangir" **Note:** Weight varies: 13.40-13.70 grams.

Date	Mintage	Good	VG	F	VF	XF
AHxxxx//2	—	32.50	80.00	135	225	325

Delhi

KM# 152.8 HEAVY RUPEE

Silver **Series:** "JAHANGIRI" **Obv:** Kalima, AH date **Rev. Legend:** "Nur-ud'din Muhammad Jahangir" **Note:** Weight varies: 13.40-13.70 grams.

Date	Mintage	Good	VG	F	VF	XF
AH1016//2 Rare	—	—	—	—	—	—

Jalnapur

KM# 152.9 HEAVY RUPEE

Silver **Series:** "JAHANGIRI" **Obv:** Kalima, AH date **Rev. Legend:** "Nur-ud'din Muhammad Jahangir" **Note:** Weight varies: 13.40-13.70 grams.

Date	Mintage	Good	VG	F	VF	XF
ND Rare	—	—	—	—	—	—

Lahore

KM# 152.4 HEAVY RUPEE

Silver **Series:** "JAHANGIRI" **Obv:** Kalima, AH date **Rev. Legend:** "Nur-ud'din Muhammad Jahangir" **Note:** Weight varies: 13.40-13.70 grams.

Date	Mintage	Good	VG	F	VF	XF
AH1015//1	—	22.50	55.00	90.00	150	225
AH1019//5	—	22.50	55.00	90.00	150	225

Patna

KM# 152.5 HEAVY RUPEE

Silver **Series:** "JAHANGIRI" **Obv:** Kalima, AH date **Rev. Legend:** "Nur-ud'din Muhammad Jahangir" **Note:** Weight varies: 13.40-13.70 grams.

Date	Mintage	Good	VG	F	VF	XF
AH1014//1	—	22.50	55.00	90.00	150	225
AH1015//1	—	22.50	55.00	90.00	150	225
AH1015//2	—	22.50	55.00	90.00	150	225
AH1016//2	—	22.50	55.00	90.00	150	225
AH1016//3	—	22.50	55.00	90.00	150	225
AH1017//3	—	22.50	55.00	90.00	150	225
AH1018//5	—	22.50	55.00	90.00	150	225
AH1019//5	—	22.50	55.00	90.00	150	225

Qandahar

KM# 152.6 HEAVY RUPEE

Silver **Series:** "JAHANGIRI" **Obv:** Kalima, AH date **Rev. Legend:** "Nur-ud'din Muhammad Jahangir" **Note:** Weight varies: 13.40-13.70 grams.

Date	Mintage	Good	VG	F	VF	XF
AH1020//6	—	30.00	75.00	125	200	265
AH1021//7	—	30.00	75.00	125	200	265

Tatta

KM# 152.7 HEAVY RUPEE

Silver **Series:** "JAHANGIRI" **Obv:** Kalima, AH date **Rev. Legend:** "Nur-ud'din Muhammad Jahangir" **Note:** Weight varies: 13.40-13.70 grams.

Date	Mintage	Good	VG	F	VF	XF
AH1015//2	—	30.00	75.00	125	200	265
AH1016//2	—	30.00	75.00	125	200	265
AH1016//3	—	30.00	75.00	125	200	265
AH1017//3	—	30.00	75.00	125	200	265
AH1017//4	—	30.00	75.00	125	200	265
AH1018//4	—	30.00	75.00	125	200	265
AH1018//5	—	30.00	75.00	125	200	265
AH1019//5	—	30.00	75.00	125	200	265
AH1019//6	—	30.00	75.00	125	200	265
AH1020//6	—	30.00	75.00	125	200	265

Lahore

KM# 154.1 HEAVY RUPEE

13.6200 g., Silver **Series:** "JAHANGIRI" **Obv:** Kalima and mint name **Shape:** Square **Note:** First Issue: 20 percent overweight. Weight varies: 13.40-13.70 grams.

Date	Mintage	Good	VG	F	VF	XF
AH1015//2	—	45.00	110	185	275	400
AH1016//2	—	45.00	110	185	275	400
AH1016//3	—	45.00	110	185	275	400

Agra

KM# A155.1 HEAVY RUPEE

Silver **Series:** "JAHANGIRI" **Obv:** Similar to Mohur KM#186 **Rev:** Similar to Mohur KM#186 **Note:** Weight varies 13.4 - 13.8 grams; "Azar" couplet.

Date	Mintage	Good	VG	F	VF	XF
AH1019//5	—	—	—	—	—	—

Agra

KM# 155.1 HEAVY RUPEE

Silver **Series:** "JAHANGIRI" **Rev:** "Sakhat Nurani" **Note:** Weight varies: 13.40-13.70 grams. Obverse and reverse form a poetic couplet, distinguished by certain words in the reverse legend.

Date	Mintage	Good	VG	F	VF	XF
AH1014//1	—	16.00	40.00	60.00	90.00	120
AH1015//1	—	16.00	40.00	60.00	90.00	120
AH1015//2	—	16.00	40.00	60.00	90.00	120

KM# 155.1A HEAVY RUPEE

Silver **Series:** "JAHANGIRI" **Note:** Weight varies 13.4 - 13.8 grams; "Khursu" couplet.

Date	Mintage	Good	VG	F	VF	XF
AH1018//4	—	—	—	—	—	—

Akbarnagar

KM# 155.2A HEAVY RUPEE

Silver **Series:** "JAHANGIRI" **Note:** Weight varies 13.4 - 13.8 grams; "Gardun" couplet.

Date	Mintage	Good	VG	F	VF	XF
AHxxxx	—	—	—	—	—	—

KM# 155.2 HEAVY RUPEE

Silver **Series:** "JAHANGIRI" **Rev:** "Sakhat Nurani" **Note:** Weight varies: 13.40-13.70 grams. Obverse and reverse form a poetic couplet, distinguished by certain words in the reverse legend.

Date	Mintage	Good	VG	F	VF	XF
AH1014//x	—	20.00	50.00	75.00	100	140
AH1015//x	—	20.00	50.00	75.00	100	140
AH1016//x	—	20.00	50.00	75.00	100	140

Delhi

KM# 155.7 HEAVY RUPEE

Silver **Series:** "JAHANGIRI" **Rev:** "Ta falak" **Note:** Weight varies: 13.40-13.70 grams. Obverse and reverse form a poetic couplet, distinguished by certain words in the reverse legend.

Date	Mintage	Good	VG	F	VF	XF
AH1014//x	—	16.00	40.00	60.00	90.00	130

Kashmir

KM# 155.3 HEAVY RUPEE

Silver **Series:** "JAHANGIRI" **Rev:** "Sakhat Nurani" **Note:** Weight varies: 13.40-13.70 grams. Obverse and reverse form a poetic couplet, distinguished by certain words in the reverse legend.

Date	Mintage	Good	VG	F	VF	XF
AH1017//x	—	25.00	60.00	100	150	200
AH1017//x	—	25.00	60.00	100	150	200
AH1018//x	—	25.00	60.00	100	150	200
AH1019//x	—	25.00	60.00	100	150	200
AH1020//x	—	25.00	60.00	100	150	200

Lahore

KM# 155.4 HEAVY RUPEE

Silver **Series:** "JAHANGIRI" **Rev:** "Sakhat Nurani" **Note:** Weight varies: 13.40-13.70 grams. Obverse and reverse form a poetic couplet, distinguished by certain words in the reverse legend.

Date	Mintage	Good	VG	F	VF	XF
AH1014//1	—	16.00	40.00	60.00	90.00	120
AH1015//1	—	16.00	40.00	60.00	90.00	120

KM# 155.6 HEAVY RUPEE

Silver **Series:** "JAHANGIRI" **Rev:** "Ta falak" **Note:** Weight varies: 13.40-13.70 grams. Obverse and reverse form a poetic couplet, distinguished by certain words in the reverse legend.

Date	Mintage	Good	VG	F	VF	XF
AH1017//3	—	16.00	40.00	60.00	90.00	130
AH1017//4	—	16.00	40.00	60.00	90.00	130
AH1018//4	—	16.00	40.00	60.00	90.00	130
AH1018//5	—	16.00	40.00	60.00	90.00	130
AH1019//5	—	16.00	40.00	60.00	90.00	130

Qandahar

KM# 155.5 HEAVY RUPEE

Silver **Series:** "JAHANGIRI" **Rev:** "Sakhat Nurani" **Note:** Weight varies: 13.40-13.70 grams. Obverse and reverse form a poetic couplet, distinguished by certain words in the reverse legend.

Date	Mintage	Good	VG	F	VF	XF
AH1020//6	—	20.00	50.00	75.00	100	140
AH1021//7	—	20.00	50.00	75.00	100	140

Date	Mintage	Good	VG	F	VF	XF
AH1021//8	—	20.00	50.00	75.00	100	140
AH1022//8	—	20.00	50.00	75.00	100	140

Lahore

KM# 156.1 HEAVY RUPEE

Silver **Series:** "JAHANGIRI" **Note:** Weight varies: 13.40-13.70 grams. Obverse and reverse form a poetic couplet incorporating the Ilahi month name. Couplet changed monthly.

Date	Mintage	Good	VG	F	VF	XF
AH1019//5	—	25.00	60.00	90.00	130	180

Lahore

KM# A157.1 HEAVY RUPEE

Silver **Series:** "JAHANGIRI" **Note:** Weight varies 13.4 - 13.8 grams.

Date	Mintage	Good	VG	F	VF	XF
AH1020//6 Farwardín	—	—	—	—	—	—

Lahore

KM# B157.1 HEAVY RUPEE

Silver **Series:** "JAHANGIRI" **Obv:** Inscription in octagonal star **Rev:** Inscription in octagonal star **Note:** Weight varies 13.4 - 13.8 grams; square.

Date	Mintage	Good	VG	F	VF	XF
AH1020//6 Ardíbihisht	—	—	—	—	—	—

Lahore

KM# 157.1 HEAVY RUPEE

Silver **Series:** "JAHANGIRI" **Rev:** "Sakhat Nurani" **Shape:** Square **Note:** Weight varies: 13.40-13.70 grams. Obverse and reverse form a poetic couplet.

Date	Mintage	Good	VG	F	VF	XF
AH1015//2	—	30.00	75.00	150	275	400
AH1016//2	—	30.00	75.00	150	275	400
AH1016//3	—	30.00	75.00	150	275	400
AH1017//3	—	30.00	75.00	150	275	400

Ahmadabad

KM# 158.3 HEAVY RUPEE

Silver **Series:** "SAWAI" **Obv:** Names of "Jahangir" and "Akbar" **Rev:** "Inayat" couplet **Note:** Weight varies: 14.00-14.40 grams. Obverse and reverse form a poetic couplet. Each mint has a distinctive couplet. A typical word from the reverse legend is given as identifier for er each sub-type in this section.

Date	Mintage	Good	VG	F	VF	XF
AH1016//3	—	16.00	40.00	60.00	90.00	130
AH1017//3	—	16.00	40.00	60.00	90.00	130
AH1017//4	—	16.00	40.00	60.00	90.00	130
AH1018//4	—	16.00	40.00	60.00	90.00	130
AH1018//5	—	16.00	40.00	60.00	90.00	130
AH1019//5	—	16.00	40.00	60.00	90.00	130
AH1019//6	—	16.00	40.00	60.00	90.00	130

Burhanpur

KM# 158.4 HEAVY RUPEE

Silver **Series:** "SAWAI" **Obv:** "Jahangir" and "Akbar" **Rev:** "Din panah" **Note:** Weight varies: 14.00-14.40 grams. Obverse and reverse form a poetic couplet. Each mint has a distinctive couplet. A typical word from the reverse legend is given as identifier for er each sub-type in this section.

Date	Mintage	Good	VG	F	VF	XF
AH1019	—	20.00	50.00	75.00	110	150

Kabul

KM# 158.1 HEAVY RUPEE

13.9000 g., Silver **Series:** "SAWAI" **Obv:** "Jahangir" and "Akbar" **Rev:** "Khusru" **Note:** Second Issue: 25 percent overweight. Weight varies: 14.00-14.40 grams. Obverse and reverse form a poetic couplet. Each mint has a distinctive couplet. A typical word from the reverse legend is given as identifier for er each sub-type in this section.

Date	Mintage	Good	VG	F	VF	XF
AH1017//3	—	16.00	40.00	60.00	90.00	130
AH1017//4	—	16.00	40.00	60.00	90.00	130

Date	Mintage	Good	VG	F	VF	XF
AH1018//4	—	16.00	40.00	60.00	90.00	130
AH1018//5	—	16.00	40.00	60.00	90.00	130
AH1019//5	—	16.00	40.00	60.00	90.00	130

KM# 158.2 HEAVY RUPEE

Silver **Series:** "SAWAI" **Obv:** Names of "Jahangir" and "Akbar" **Rev:** "Khusru" **Note:** Weight varies: 14.00-14.40 grams. Obverse and reverse form a poetic couplet. Each mint has a distinctive couplet. A typical word from the reverse legend is given as identifier for er each sub-type in this section.

Date	Mintage	Good	VG	F	VF	XF
AH1017//3	—	20.00	50.00	75.00	110	150
AH1018//4	—	20.00	50.00	75.00	110	150
AH1020//6	—	20.00	50.00	75.00	110	150

Lahore

KM# 158.5 HEAVY RUPEE

Silver **Series:** "SAWAI" **Obv:** "Jahangir" and "Akbar" **Rev:** "Ta falak" **Note:** Weight varies: 14.00-14.40 grams. Obverse and reverse form a poetic couplet. Each mint has a distinctive couplet. A typical word from the reverse legend is given as identifier for er each sub-type in this section.

Date	Mintage	Good	VG	F	VF	XF
AH1017//3	—	16.00	40.00	60.00	90.00	130
AH1017//4	—	16.00	40.00	60.00	90.00	130
AH1018//4	—	16.00	40.00	60.00	90.00	130
AH1018//5	—	16.00	40.00	60.00	90.00	130
AH1019//5	—	16.00	40.00	60.00	90.00	130

Patna

KM# 158.6 HEAVY RUPEE

Silver **Series:** "SAWAI" **Obv:** "Jahangir" and "Akbar" **Rev:** "Khusru" **Note:** Weight varies: 14.00-14.40 grams. Obverse and reverse form a poetic couplet. Each mint has a distinctive couplet. A typical word from the reverse legend is given as identifier for er each sub-type in this section.

Date	Mintage	Good	VG	F	VF	XF
AH1017//3	—	20.00	50.00	75.00	110	150
AH1019//6	—	20.00	50.00	75.00	110	150
AH1020//6	—	20.00	50.00	75.00	110	150

Akbarnagar

KM# A159.1 HEAVY RUPEE

Silver **Series:** "Sawai" **Note:** "Gardun" couplet; weight varies 14.0 - 14.4 grams.

Date	Mintage	Good	VG	F	VF	XF
AH1017//4	—	—	—	—	—	—

Agra

KM# 159.2 HEAVY RUPEE

Silver **Series:** "SAWAI" **Note:** Obverse and reverse form a poetic couplet incorporating the Ilahi month. Couplet changed monthly; Weight varies 14.0 - 14.4 grams.

Date	Mintage	Good	VG	F	VF	XF
AH1019//5	—	32.00	80.00	160	300	440

Lahore

KM# 159.1 HEAVY RUPEE

Silver **Note:** Obverse and reverse form a poetic couplet incorporating the Ilahi month. Couplet changed monthly; Weight varies 14.0 - 14.4 grams.

Date	Mintage	Good	VG	F	VF	XF
AH1019//5	—	25.00	60.00	90.00	150	220
AH1019//6	—	25.00	60.00	90.00	150	220
AH1020//6	—	25.00	60.00	90.00	150	220

Agra

KM# 160.1 HEAVY RUPEE

Silver **Shape:** Square **Note:** Weight varies: 14.00-14.40 grams.The circlular and square rupees were struck at Agra in alternate months.

Date	Mintage	Good	VG	F	VF	XF
AH1019//5	—	32.00	80.00	160	300	440
AH1020//6	—	32.00	80.00	160	300	440

Lahore

KM# 160.2 HEAVY RUPEE

Silver **Series:** "Sawai" **Shape:** Square **Note:** Weight varies: 14.00-14.40 grams.

Date	Mintage	Good	VG	F	VF	XF
AH1019//5 Isfandármuz	—	30.00	75.00	150	275	400

Date	Mintage	Good	VG	F	VF	XF
AH1020//6 Ardíbihisht	—	30.00	75.00	150	275	400
AHxxxx//6 Tír	—	30.00	75.00	150	275	400

Patna

KM# A167.1 1/4 RUPEE

2.8610 g., Silver **Obv. Inscription:** "...Jahangir" **Rev. Inscription:** "...Nur Jahan"

Date	Mintage	Good	VG	F	VF	XF
AH1037//23	—	—	—	—	—	—

Agra

KM# 167.4 1/2 RUPEE

5.7220 g., Silver **Obv. Inscription:** "...Jahangir" **Rev. Inscription:** "...Nur Jahan"

Date	Mintage	Good	VG	F	VF	XF
AH1036//2x	—	—	—	—	—	—

Ahmadabad

KM# 167.3 1/2 RUPEE

5.7220 g., Silver **Obv. Inscription:** "...Jahangir" **Rev. Inscription:** "...Nur Jahan"

Date	Mintage	Good	VG	F	VF	XF
AH1034//x Rare	—	—	—	—	—	—

Patna

KM# 167.1 1/2 RUPEE

5.7220 g., Silver **Obv. Inscription:** "...Jahangir" **Rev. Inscription:** "...Nur Jahan"

Date	Mintage	Good	VG	F	VF	XF
AH1037//22(sic) Rare	—	—	—	—	—	—

Surat

KM# 167.2 1/2 RUPEE

5.7220 g., Silver **Obv. Inscription:** "...Jahangir" **Rev. Inscription:** "...Nur Jahan"

Date	Mintage	Good	VG	F	VF	XF
AH1034//2x Rare	—	—	—	—	—	—
AH1035//x Rare	—	—	—	—	—	—
AH1036//x Rare	—	—	—	—	—	—

Agra

KM# 168.1 RUPEE

11.4440 g., Silver **Obv. Inscription:** "...Jahangir" **Rev. Inscription:** "...Nur Jahan"

Date	Mintage	Good	VG	F	VF	XF
AH1034//19(sic)	—	13.00	30.00	60.00	95.00	150
AH1034//20	—	13.00	30.00	60.00	95.00	150
AH1034//21	—	13.00	30.00	60.00	95.00	150
AH1035//21	—	13.00	30.00	60.00	95.00	150
AH1035//22	—	13.00	30.00	60.00	95.00	150
AH1036//22	—	13.00	30.00	60.00	95.00	150
AH1037//22(sic)	—	13.00	30.00	60.00	95.00	150

Ahmadabad

KM# 168.2 RUPEE

11.4440 g., Silver **Obv. Inscription:** "...Jahangir" **Rev. Inscription:** "...Nur Jahan"

Date	Mintage	Good	VG	F	VF	XF
AH1033//19	—	10.00	20.00	45.00	75.00	120
AH1034//xx	—	10.00	20.00	45.00	75.00	120
AH1036//21(sic)	—	10.00	20.00	45.00	75.00	120
AH1036//22	—	10.00	20.00	45.00	75.00	120
AH1036//23	—	10.00	20.00	45.00	75.00	120
AH1037//2x	—	10.00	20.00	45.00	75.00	120

Akbarnagar

KM# 168.3 RUPEE

11.4440 g., Silver **Obv. Inscription:** "...Jahangir" **Rev. Inscription:** "...Nur Jahan"

Date	Mintage	Good	VG	F	VF	XF
AH1037//22(sic)	—	15.00	40.00	90.00	140	220

Allahabad

KM# 168.7 RUPEE

11.4440 g., Silver **Obv. Inscription:** "...Jahangir" **Rev. Inscription:** "...Nur Jahan"

Date	Mintage	Good	VG	F	VF	XF
AH1037//22(sic) Rare	—	—	—	—	—	—

Lahore

KM# 168.4 RUPEE

11.4440 g., Silver **Obv. Inscription:** "...Jahangir" **Rev. Inscription:** "...Nur Jahan"

Date	Mintage	Good	VG	F	VF	XF
AH1034//19(sic)	—	15.00	40.00	80.00	125	180
AH1034//20	—	15.00	40.00	80.00	125	180
AH1035//20	—	15.00	40.00	80.00	125	180

Patna

KM# 168.5 RUPEE

11.4440 g., Silver **Obv. Inscription:** "...Jahangir" **Rev. Inscription:** "...Nur Jahan"

Date	Mintage	Good	VG	F	VF	XF
AH1037//22(sic)	—	15.00	40.00	80.00	125	180

Surat

KM# 168.6 RUPEE

11.4440 g., Silver **Obv. Inscription:** "...Jahangir" **Rev. Inscription:** "...Nur Jahan"

Date	Mintage	Good	VG	F	VF	XF
AH1033//19	—	10.00	20.00	45.00	75.00	120
AH1033//91 Error for 19	—	10.00	20.00	45.00	75.00	120
AH1034//20	—	10.00	20.00	45.00	75.00	120
AH1035//20	—	10.00	20.00	45.00	75.00	120
AH1035//21	—	10.00	20.00	45.00	75.00	120
AH1036//21	—	10.00	20.00	45.00	75.00	120
AH1036//22	—	10.00	20.00	45.00	75.00	120
AH1037//22(sic)	—	10.00	20.00	45.00	75.00	120

Lahore

KM# 169.1 RUPEE

11.4440 g., Silver **Rev:** Couplet with inscription **Rev. Inscription:** "Fazudah nur Jahan"

Date	Mintage	Good	VG	F	VF	XF
AH1035//21	—	—	—	—	—	—

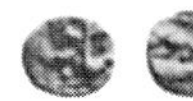

Fathpur

KM# 170.1 1/30 MOHUR

0.3600 g., Gold

Date	Mintage	Good	VG	F	VF	XF
AH10xx//xx Rare	—	—	—	—	—	—

KM# 172.1 1/4 MOHUR

2.7000 g., Gold **Note:** "Shahi". Without mint name, probably Ajmer.

Date	Mintage	Good	VG	F	VF	XF
AH102x//x Rare	—	—	—	—	—	—

Ajmer

KM# 172.2 1/4 MOHUR

2.7000 g., Gold **Obv:** Date **Rev:** "Ya'Muinu" and regnal year

Date	Mintage	VG	F	VF	XF	Unc
AH1024//10 Rare	—	—	—	—	—	—

Mandu

KM# 172.3 1/4 MOHUR

2.7000 g., Gold **Obv:** "Jahangir" and regnal year **Rev:** Mint name, AH date

Date	Mintage	VG	F	VF	XF	Unc
AH1026/12 Rare	—	—	—	—	—	—

Shikargarh

KM# 172.4 1/4 MOHUR

2.7000 g., Gold **Obv:** "Jahangir" and regnal year **Rev:** Mint name, AH date

Date	Mintage	Good	VG	F	VF	XF
AH1026//20 Rare	—	—	—	—	—	—

Agra

KM# A173.1 HEAVY 1/4 MOHUR

3.2000 g., Gold **Obv. Legend:** ...Sakhat nurani **Note:** Previous KM#173.1.

Date	Mintage	Good	VG	F	VF	XF
AH1014//1 Rare	—	—	—	—	—	—

Agra

KM# 173.1 1/2 MOHUR

5.3800 g., Gold **Note:** Previous KM#A173.1.

Date	Mintage	Good	VG	F	VF	XF
AH102x//8 Rare	—	—	—	—	—	—

Agra

KM# 174.1 MOHUR

Gold **Obv:** Kalima, mint name, date **Rev:** Jahangir's full name **Note:** Weight varies: 10.80-10.90 grams.

Date	Mintage	Good	VG	F	VF	XF
AH1014//1 Rare	—	—	—	—	—	—
AH1015//1 Rare	—	—	—	—	—	—
AH1015//2 Rare	—	—	—	—	—	—

Agra

KM# 175.1 MOHUR

Gold **Obv:** Names of "Jahangir" and "Akbar" **Rev:** AH date and mint name **Note:** Weight varies: 10.80-10.90 grams.

Date	Mintage	Good	VG	F	VF	XF
AH1020//6 Rare	—	—	—	—	—	—

Agra

KM# 176.1 MOHUR

Gold **Obv:** Names of "Jahangir" and "Akbar" **Rev:** Mint name, AH date, Ilahi month **Note:** Weight varies: 10.60-10.90 grams.

Date	Mintage	Good	VG	F	VF	XF
AH1020/6	—	375	525	700	900	1,300
AH1020/7	—	375	525	700	900	1,300
Note: Ilahi month Ardibihisht (2)						
AH1021/7	—	375	525	700	900	1,300
AH1021/8	—	375	525	700	900	1,300
AH1022/8	—	375	525	700	900	1,300
AH1023/8	—	375	525	700	900	1,300
AH1022//9	—	375	525	700	900	1,300
AH1023//9	—	375	525	700	900	1,300
AH1023//10	—	375	525	700	900	1,300
AH1024//10	—	375	525	700	900	1,300
AH1024//11	—	375	525	700	900	1,300
AH1025//11	—	375	525	700	900	1,300
AH1025//12	—	375	525	700	900	1,300
AH1026//12	—	375	525	700	900	1,300
AH1026//13	—	375	525	700	900	1,300
AH1027//13	—	375	525	700	900	1,300

Date	Mintage	Good	VG	F	VF	XF
Note: Ilahi month Azar (9)						
AH1031//17	—	375	525	700	900	1,300

Ahmadanagar

KM# 176.2 MOHUR

Gold **Obv:** Names of "Jahangir" and "Akbar" **Rev:** Mint name, AH date, Ilahi month **Note:** Weight varies: 10.60-10.90 grams.

Date	Mintage	Good	VG	F	VF	XF
AH-	—	255	410	525	650	900

Burhanpur

KM# 176.3 MOHUR

Gold **Obv:** Names of "Jahangir" and "Akbar" **Rev:** Mint name, AH date, Ilahi month **Note:** Weight varies: 10.60-10.90 grams.

Date	Mintage	Good	VG	F	VF	XF
AH1023//8(sic)	—	355	410	525	650	900
AH102x//12	—	355	410	525	650	900
AHxxxx//14	—	355	410	525	650	900
AH10xx//15	—	355	410	525	650	900
AH103x//16	—	355	410	525	650	900
AH103x//17	—	355	410	525	650	900
Note: Ilahi month Farwardin						
AH103x//18	—	355	410	525	650	900
AH1037//22(sic)	—	355	410	525	650	900

Jahangirnagar

KM# 176.4 MOHUR

Gold **Obv:** Names of "Jahangir" and "Akbar" **Rev:** Mint name, AH date, Ilahi month **Note:** Weight varies: 10.60-10.90 grams.

Date	Mintage	Good	VG	F	VF	XF
ND//19	—	355	410	525	650	900

Patna

KM# 176.5 MOHUR

Gold **Obv:** Names of "Jahangir" and "Akbar" **Rev:** Mint name, AH date, Ilahi month **Note:** Weight varies: 10.60-10.90 grams.

Date	Mintage	Good	VG	F	VF	XF
AH1027//13	—	355	410	525	650	900
AH1035//20(sic)	—	355	410	525	650	900

Tatta

KM# 176.6 MOHUR

Gold **Obv:** Names of "Jahangir" and "Akbar" **Rev:** Mint name, AH date, Ilahi month **Note:** Weight varies: 10.60-10.90 grams.

Date	Mintage	Good	VG	F	VF	XF
AH1027//13 Rare	—	—	—	—	—	—
AH1031//16(sic) Rare	—	—	—	—	—	—
AH1031//17 Rare	—	—	—	—	—	—
AH1032//18 Rare	—	—	—	—	—	—
AH1036//22 Rare	—	—	—	—	—	—

Agra

KM# 177.1 MOHUR

Gold **Obv:** Legend in cartouche within square **Rev:** Legend in cartouche within square **Shape:** Square **Note:** Weight varies: 10.60-10.90 grams. Similar to 1 Rupee, KM#160.1.

Date	Mintage	Good	VG	F	VF	XF
AH1019//5	—	400	700	1,000	1,500	2,200
AH1019//6	—	400	700	1,000	1,500	2,200
AH1020//6	—	400	700	1,000	1,500	2,200
AH1022//x	—	400	700	1,000	1,500	2,200
AH102x//12	—	400	700	1,000	1,500	2,200

Agra

KM# 178.9 MOHUR

Gold **Rev:** "Sakhat Nurani" **Note:** Weight varies: 10.60-10.90 grams.

Date	Mintage	VG	F	VF	XF	Unc
AH1014//1 Rare	—	—	—	—	—	—

KM# 178.1 MOHUR

Gold **Rev:** "Yaft" **Note:** Weight varies: 10.60-10.90 grams. Obverse and reverse form a poetic couplet, wording individual to mints.

Date	Mintage	Good	VG	F	VF	XF
AH1035//21 Rare	—	—	—	—	—	—

Ahmadabad

KM# 178.2 MOHUR

Gold **Rev:** "Ba-sharq wa gharb" **Note:** Weight varies: 10.60-10.90 grams. Obverse and reverse form a poetic couplet, wording individual to mints.

Date	Mintage	Good	VG	F	VF	XF
AH1028//14	—	400	600	800	1,200	2,000
AH1028//15	—	400	600	800	1,200	2,000
AH1029//15	—	400	600	800	1,200	2,000
AH1030//15(sic)	—	400	600	800	1,200	2,000
AH1033//18(sic)	—	400	600	800	1,200	2,000

Ajmir

KM# 178.3 MOHUR

Gold **Rev:** "Din panah" **Note:** Weight varies: 10.60-10.90 grams. Obverse and reverse form a poetic couplet, wording individual to mints.

Date	Mintage	Good	VG	F	VF	XF
AH1023//9	—	400	600	800	1,200	2,000
AH1023//10	—	400	600	800	1,200	2,000
AH1024//10	—	400	600	800	1,200	2,000
AH1025//11	—	400	600	800	1,200	2,000

Delhi

KM# 178.4 MOHUR

Gold **Rev:** "Fazl" **Note:** Weight varies: 10.60-10.90 grams. Obverse and reverse form a poetic couplet, wording individual to mints.

Date	Mintage	Good	VG	F	VF	XF
AH1035//21	—	235	275	400	550	700

Kabul

KM# 178.8 MOHUR

Gold **Note:** Weight varies: 10.60-10.90 grams. Obverse and reverse form a poetic couplet, wording individual to mints. Similar to 1 rupee, KM#149.12; Previous KM#178.1.

Date	Mintage	Good	VG	F	VF	XF
ND Rare	—	—	—	—	—	—

Lahore

KM# 178.7 MOHUR

Gold **Note:** Weight varies: 10.60-10.90 grams. Obverse and reverse form a poetic couplet, wording individual to mints.

Date	Mintage	Good	VG	F	VF	XF
AH1032//17(sic)	—	400	600	800	1,200	2,000

KM# 178.5 MOHUR

Gold **Rev:** "Bada bar" **Note:** Weight varies: 10.60-10.90 grams. Obverse and reverse form a poetic couplet, wording individual to mints.

Date	Mintage	Good	VG	F	VF	XF
AH1036//22	—	400	600	800	1,200	2,000

Mandu

KM# 178.6 MOHUR

Gold **Rev:** "Bada bar" **Note:** Weight varies: 10.60-10.90 grams. Obverse and reverse form a poetic couplet, wording individual to mints.

Date	Mintage	Good	VG	F	VF	XF
AH1026//12 Rare	—	—	—	—	—	—

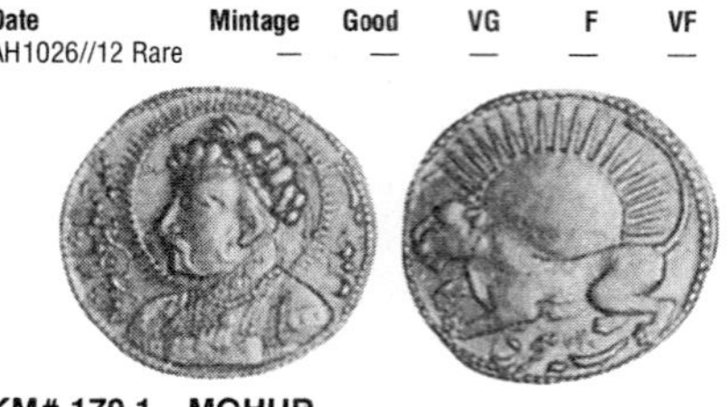

KM# 179.1 MOHUR

Gold **Obv:** Jahangir left, hand on book **Rev:** Lion left **Note:** Weight varies: 10.80-10.90 grams.

Date	Mintage	Good	VG	F	VF	XF
AH1020//6	—	—	4,000	6,000	8,000	12,000

KM# 179.3 MOHUR

Gold **Obv:** Jahangir left, holding fruit **Rev:** Lion right **Note:** Weight varies: 10.80-10.90 grams.

Date	Mintage	Good	VG	F	VF	XF
AH1020//6 Rare	—	—	—	—	—	—

KM# 179.2 MOHUR

Gold **Obv:** Jahangir left, hand on book **Rev:** Lion right **Note:** Weight varies: 10.80-10.90 grams.

Date	Mintage	Good	VG	F	VF	XF
AH1020//6	—	—	4,000	6,000	8,000	12,000

KM# 179.4 MOHUR

Gold **Obv:** Jahangir left, holding goblet **Rev:** Lion right **Note:** Weight varies: 10.80-10.90 grams.

Date	Mintage	Good	VG	F	VF	XF
AH1020//6 Rare	—	—	—	—	—	—

Ajmer

KM# 179.5 MOHUR

Gold **Obv:** Jahangir seated left, holding goblet with legend around **Rev:** Lion right with legend around **Note:** Weight varies: 10.80-10.90 grams.

Date	Mintage	Good	VG	F	VF	XF
AH1023//8(sic)	—	—	1,200	2,750	5,000	8,000

KM# 179.6 MOHUR

Gold **Obv:** Jahangir seated left, holding goblet **Rev:** Sun, legend around **Note:** Weight varies: 10.80-10.90 grams.

Date	Mintage	Good	VG	F	VF	XF
AH1023//9	—	—	1,200	2,750	5,000	8,000

Agra

KM# 180.1 ZODIAC MOHUR

Gold **Obv:** Aries (ram) left **Note:** Weight varies: 10.70-10.90 grams.

Date	Mintage	Good	VG	F	VF	XF
AH1028//14	—	—	1,000	1,600	3,000	6,000
AH1028//15	—	—	1,000	1,600	3,000	6,000
AH1029//15	—	—	1,000	1,600	3,000	6,000
AH1029//16	—	—	1,000	1,600	3,000	6,000
AH1030//16	—	—	1,000	1,600	3,000	6,000
AH1032//18	—	—	1,000	1,600	3,000	6,000

KM# 180.4 ZODIAC MOHUR

Gold **Obv:** Taurus (bull) left **Note:** Weight varies: 10.70-10.90 grams.

Date	Mintage	Good	VG	F	VF	XF
AH1028//14	—	—	1,000	1,250	2,500	4,000
AH1028//15	—	—	1,000	1,250	2,500	4,000
AH1029//15	—	—	1,000	1,250	2,500	4,000
AH1033//19	—	—	1,000	1,250	2,500	4,000

KM# 180.6 ZODIAC MOHUR

Gold **Obv:** Gemini (twins) left leg raised **Note:** Weight varies: 10.80-10.90 grams.

Date	Mintage	Good	VG	F	VF	XF
AH1028//1x	—	—	1,200	1,500	2,750	5,000
AH1029//15	—	—	1,200	1,500	2,750	5,000
AH1029//16	—	—	1,200	1,500	2,750	5,000
AH1030//16	—	—	1,200	1,500	2,750	5,000
AH1030//17	—	—	1,200	1,500	2,750	5,000
AH1031//17	—	—	1,200	1,500	2,750	5,000
AH1031//18	—	—	1,200	1,500	2,750	5,000
AH1032//18	—	—	1,200	1,500	2,750	5,000
AH1032//19	—	—	1,200	1,500	2,750	5,000
AH1033//19	—	—	1,200	1,500	2,750	5,000

KM# 180.8 ZODIAC MOHUR

Gold **Obv:** Cancer (crab) **Note:** Weight varies: 10.80-10.90 grams.

Date	Mintage	Good	VG	F	VF	XF
AH1028//14	—	—	4,000	6,000	8,000	10,000
AH1027//13	—	—	4,000	6,000	8,000	10,000
AH1028//15	—	—	4,000	6,000	8,000	10,000
AH1029//15	—	—	4,000	6,000	8,000	10,000
AH1029//16	—	—	4,000	6,000	8,000	10,000
AH1030//16	—	—	4,000	6,000	8,000	10,000
AH1030//17	—	—	4,000	6,000	8,000	10,000
AH1031//17	—	—	4,000	6,000	8,000	10,000
AH1033//19	—	—	4,000	6,000	8,000	10,000

KM# 180.9 ZODIAC MOHUR

Gold **Obv:** Leo (lion) right **Note:** Weight varies: 10.80-10.90 grams.

Date	Mintage	Good	VG	F	VF	XF
AH1028//14	—	—	900	1,500	2,750	5,000
AH1028//15	—	—	900	1,500	2,750	5,000
AH1029//15	—	—	900	1,500	2,750	5,000
AH1031//17	—	—	900	1,500	2,750	5,000
AH1033//18(sic)	—	—	900	1,500	2,750	5,000

KM# 180.11 ZODIAC MOHUR

Gold **Obv:** Virgo (maiden) left **Note:** Weight varies: 10.80-10.90 grams.

Date	Mintage	Good	VG	F	VF	XF
AH1028//14	—	—	1,000	1,600	3,000	6,000
AH1028//15	—	—	1,000	1,600	3,000	6,000
AH1029//15	—	—	1,000	1,600	3,000	6,000
AH1031//16(sic)	—	—	1,000	1,600	3,000	6,000
AH1031//17	—	—	1,000	1,600	3,000	6,000
AH1033//19	—	—	1,000	1,600	3,000	6,000

Note: Other depictions exist, of crude workmanship and possibly spurious

KM# 180.13 ZODIAC MOHUR

Gold **Obv:** Libra (scales) **Note:** Weight varies: 10.80-10.90 grams.

Date	Mintage	Good	VG	F	VF	XF
AH1028//14	—	—	1,250	1,650	2,750	4,000
AH1029//14	—	—	1,250	1,650	2,750	4,000
AH1029//15	—	—	1,250	1,650	2,750	4,000
AH1030//16	—	—	1,250	1,650	2,750	4,000
AH1030//17	—	—	1,250	1,650	2,750	4,000
AH1031//17	—	—	1,250	1,650	2,750	4,000
AH1031//18	—	—	1,250	1,650	2,750	4,000
AH1032//18	—	—	1,250	1,650	2,750	4,000
AH1032//19	—	—	1,250	1,650	2,750	4,000
AH1033//19	—	—	1,250	1,650	2,750	4,000
AH1034//19(sic)	—	—	1,250	1,650	2,750	4,000

KM# 180.19 ZODIAC MOHUR

Gold **Obv:** Capricornus (goat) left **Rev:** Poetic couplet **Note:** Weight varies: 10.80-10.90 grams.

Date	Mintage	Good	VG	F	VF	XF
AH1028//14	—	—	900	1,500	2,750	4,000
AH1028//15	—	—	900	1,500	2,750	4,000
AH1029//15	—	—	900	1,500	2,750	4,000
AH1029//16	—	—	900	1,500	2,750	4,000
AH1030//16	—	—	900	1,500	2,750	4,000
AH1030//17	—	—	900	1,500	2,750	4,000
AH1031//17	—	—	900	1,500	2,750	4,000
AH1031//18	—	—	900	1,500	2,750	4,000
AH1032//18	—	—	900	1,500	2,750	4,000
AH1032//19	—	—	900	1,500	2,750	4,000
AH1033//19	—	—	900	1,500	2,750	4,000
AH1034//29(sic)	—	—	900	1,500	2,750	4,000

KM# 180.20 ZODIAC MOHUR

Gold **Obv:** Pisces (fish) **Rev:** Poetic couplet **Note:** Weight varies: 10.80-10.90 grams.

Date	Mintage	Good	VG	F	VF	XF
AH1028//13(sic)	—	—	1,500	2,000	3,000	5,000
AH1031//17	—	—	1,500	2,000	3,000	5,000
AH1031//18	—	—	1,500	2,000	3,000	5,000
AH1032//18	—	—	1,500	2,000	3,000	5,000
AH1033//18(sic)	—	—	1,500	2,000	3,000	5,000

KM# 180.17 ZODIAC MOHUR

Gold **Obv:** Sagittarius (archer) **Note:** Weight varies: 10.80-10.90 grams.

Date	Mintage	Good	VG	F	VF	XF
AH1029//14(sic)	—	—	1,200	1,700	2,750	4,000
AH1029//15	—	—	1,200	1,700	2,750	4,000
AH1029//16	—	—	1,200	1,700	2,750	4,000
AH1030//16	—	—	1,200	1,700	2,750	4,000
AH1030//17	—	—	1,200	1,700	2,750	4,000
AH1031//17	—	—	1,200	1,700	2,750	4,000
AH1031//18	—	—	1,200	1,700	2,750	4,000
AH1032//18	—	—	1,200	1,700	2,750	4,000
AH1032//19	—	—	1,200	1,700	2,750	4,000
AH1033//19	—	—	1,200	1,700	2,750	4,000
AH1033//20	—	—	1,200	1,700	2,750	4,000
AH1034//20	—	—	1,200	1,700	2,750	4,000
AH1034//29(sic)	—	—	1,200	1,700	2,750	4,000

KM# 180.14 ZODIAC MOHUR

Gold **Obv:** Scorpio (scorpion) left **Note:** Weight varies: 10.80-10.90 grams.

Date	Mintage	Good	VG	F	VF	XF
AH1028//15	—	—	1,300	1,750	3,500	6,000
AH1029//15	—	—	1,300	1,750	3,500	6,000
AH1029//16	—	—	1,300	1,750	3,500	6,000
AH1030//16	—	—	1,300	1,750	3,500	6,000
AH1030//17	—	—	1,300	1,750	3,500	6,000
AH1031//17	—	—	1,300	1,750	3,500	6,000
AH1033//18(sic)	—	—	1,300	1,750	3,500	6,000

KM# 180.15 ZODIAC MOHUR

Gold **Obv:** Scorpio (scorpion) right **Note:** Weight varies: 10.80-10.90 grams.

Date	Mintage	Good	VG	F	VF	XF
AH1031//16(sic)	—	—	1,300	1,750	3,500	6,000
AH1031//17	—	—	1,300	1,750	3,500	6,000
AH1031//18	—	—	1,300	1,750	3,500	6,000
AH1032//17(sic)	—	—	1,300	1,750	3,500	6,000

KM# 180.5 ZODIAC MOHUR

Gold **Obv:** Taurus (bull) right **Note:** Weight varies: 10.70-10.90 grams.

Date	Mintage	Good	VG	F	VF	XF
AH1030//16	—	—	1,000	1,250	2,500	4,000
AH1031//16(sic)	—	—	1,000	1,250	2,500	4,000
AH1031//17	—	—	1,000	1,250	2,500	4,000
AH1031//18	—	—	1,000	1,250	2,500	4,000
AH1032//18	—	—	1,000	1,250	2,500	4,000

KM# 180.10 ZODIAC MOHUR

Gold **Obv:** Leo (lion) left **Note:** Weight varies: 10.80-10.90 grams.

Date	Mintage	Good	VG	F	VF	XF
AH1031//17	—	—	1,000	1,600	3,000	5,000

Ajmer

KM# 180.21 ZODIAC MOHUR

Gold **Obv:** Aquarius (water bearer) **Rev:** Poetic couplet **Note:** Weight varies: 10.80-10.90 grams.

Date	Mintage	Good	VG	F	VF	XF
AH1032//18 Rare	—	—	—	—	—	—

KM# 180.7 ZODIAC MOHUR

Gold **Obv:** Gemini (twins) right leg raised **Note:** Weight varies: 10.80-10.90 grams.

Date	Mintage	Good	VG	F	VF	XF
AH1033//18	—	—	1,000	2,000	3,500	6,000

Fathpur

KM# 180.2 ZODIAC MOHUR

Gold **Obv:** Aries (ram) left **Note:** Weight varies: 10.70-10.90 grams.

Date	Mintage	Good	VG	F	VF	XF
AH1028//13 Rare	—	—	—	—	—	—

Lahore

KM# 180.16 ZODIAC MOHUR

Gold **Obv:** Scorpio (scorpion) right **Note:** Weight varies: 10.80-10.90 grams.

Date	Mintage	Good	VG	F	VF	XF
AH1032//17(sic) Rare	—	—	—	—	—	—

KM# 180.12 ZODIAC MOHUR

Gold **Note:** Different portrayal of Virgo. Weight varies: 10.80-10.90 grams.

Date	Mintage	Good	VG	F	VF	XF
AH1032//17(sic) Rare	—	—	—	—	—	—

KM# 180.18 ZODIAC MOHUR

Gold **Obv:** Smaller Sagittarius (archer) **Rev:** Poetic couplet **Note:** Weight varies: 10.80-10.90 grams.

Date	Mintage	Good	VG	F	VF	XF
AH1035//20	—	—	—	—	—	—
AH1036//21(sic) Rare	—	—	—	—	—	—

Urdu

KM# 180.3 ZODIAC MOHUR

Gold **Obv:** Aries (ram) right **Note:** Weight varies: 10.70-10.90 grams.

Date	Mintage	Good	VG	F	VF	XF
AH1036//22	—	—	1,000	2,000	3,500	6,000

Burhanpur

KM# 182.1 HEAVY MOHUR

Gold **Subject:** "Nur Jahani" **Obv:** Kalima **Note:** First Issue: 20 percent overweight. Weight varies: 12.80-1300 grams.

Date	Mintage	Good	VG	F	VF	XF
AH1014(1)	—	—	450	900	1,300	2,500

Lahore

KM# 182.2 HEAVY MOHUR

Gold **Obv:** Kalima **Note:** Weight varies: 12.80-1300 grams.

Date	Mintage	Good	VG	F	VF	XF
AH1015//1	—	—	450	900	1,300	2,500

Agra

KM# 183.1 HEAVY MOHUR

Gold **Rev:** "Sakhat Nurani" **Note:** Poetic couplets on obverse and reverse. Weight varies: 12.80-13.00 grams.

Date	Mintage	Good	VG	F	VF	XF
AH1014//1	—	500	675	900	1,300	1,800

Date	Mintage	Good	VG	F	VF	XF
AH1015//1	—	500	675	900	1,300	1,800
AH1015//2	—	500	675	900	1,300	1,800

Lahore

KM# 183.2 HEAVY MOHUR

Gold **Rev:** "Sakhat Nurani" **Note:** Poetic couplets on obverse and reverse. Weight varies: 12.80-13.00 grams.

Date	Mintage	Good	VG	F	VF	XF
AH1014(1)	—	500	675	900	1,300	1,800
AH1015//1	—	500	675	900	1,300	1,800

KM# 183.3 HEAVY MOHUR

13.0300 g., Gold **Rev:** "Khusru" **Note:** Weight varies: 12.95-13.10 grams.

Date	Mintage	Good	VG	F	VF	XF
AH1017//3	—	550	800	1,100	1,500	2,000
AH1017//4	—	550	800	1,100	1,500	2,000
AH1018//4	—	550	800	1,100	1,500	2,000

Lahore

KM# 184.1 HEAVY MOHUR

Gold **Rev:** "Sakhat Nurani" **Shape:** Square **Note:** Poetic couplets on obverse and reverse. Weight varies: 12.90-13.00 grams.

Date	Mintage	Good	VG	F	VF	XF
AH1015//1	—	—	1,000	1,500	2,250	3,300
AH1015//2	—	—	1,000	1,500	2,250	3,300
AH1016//2	—	—	1,000	1,500	2,250	3,300
AH1016//3	—	—	1,000	1,500	2,250	3,300

Agra

KM# 185.1 HEAVY MOHUR

Gold **Rev:** "Khusru" **Note:** Second Issue: 25 percent overweight. Poetic couplets on obverse and reverse. Weight varies: 13.55-13.70 grams.

Date	Mintage	Good	VG	F	VF	XF
AH1017//3 Rare	—	—	—	—	—	—
AH1017//4 Rare	—	—	—	—	—	—
AH1018//4 Rare	—	—	—	—	—	—
AH1018//5 Rare	—	—	—	—	—	—

Agra

KM# 186.1 HEAVY MOHUR

Gold **Note:** Poetic couplets based on Ilahi month names. From the year 1019, at a few mints, a specially composed poetic couplet was employed on the coin for each month. The decorative borders and calligraphy varied monthly. Only a sample illustration is included here. Weight varies: 13.55-13.70 grams.

Date	Mintage	Good	VG	F	VF	XF
AH1019//5 Azar	—	365	475	600	800	1,100
AH1019//6	—	365	475	600	800	1,100
AH1020//6	—	365	475	600	800	1,100

Note: Some specimens of the type dated AH1020/6 are reported to be of normal weight

KM# 186.2 HEAVY MOHUR

Gold **Note:** Weight varies 13.55 - 13.75 grams.

Date	Mintage	Good	VG	F	VF	XF
AH1019//5 Mihr	—	365	475	600	800	1,100

Agra

KM# 187.1 HEAVY MOHUR

Gold **Shape:** Square **Note:** Weight varies: 13.55-13.70 grams.

Date	Mintage	Good	VG	F	VF	XF
AH1017//3	—	—	1,000	1,700	2,500	3,500
AH1019//5	—	—	1,000	1,700	2,500	3,500

Agra

KM# 188.1 5 MOHURS

54.6300 g., Gold

Date	Mintage	Good	VG	F	VF	XF
AH1028//14 Rare	—	—	—	—	—	—

Ahmadabad

KM# 190.1 MOHUR

Gold **Obv. Inscription:** "...Jahangir" **Rev. Inscription:** "...Nur Jahan" **Note:** Weight varies: 10.80-10.90 grams.

Date	Mintage	Good	VG	F	VF	XF
AH1034//19(sic)	—	400	500	625	800	1,000
AH1037//2x	—	400	500	625	800	1,000

Surat

KM# 190.2 MOHUR

Gold **Obv. Inscription:** "...Jahangir" **Rev. Inscription:** "...Nur Jahan" **Note:** Weight varies: 10.80-10.90 grams.

Date	Mintage	Good	VG	F	VF	XF
AH1036//2x	—	400	500	625	800	1,000

Kashmir

KM# 192.1 ZODIAC MOHUR

Gold **Obv:** Cancer (crab) **Rev. Inscription:** "Jahangir...Nur Jahan" **Note:** Weight varies: 10.80-10.90 grams.

Date	Mintage	Good	VG	F	VF	XF
AH1034//20 Rare	—	—	—	—	—	—

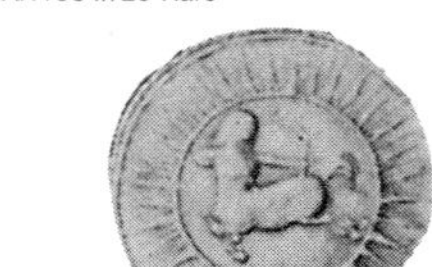

Lahore

KM# 192.2 ZODIAC MOHUR

Gold **Obv:** Sagittarius (archer) **Rev. Inscription:** "Jahangir...Nur Jahan" **Note:** Weight varies: 10.80-10.90 grams.

Date	Mintage	Good	VG	F	VF	XF
AH1035//20(sic) Rare	—	—	—	—	—	—

KM# 192.3 ZODIAC MOHUR

Gold **Obv:** Capricorn (goat) **Rev. Inscription:** "Jahangir...Nur Jahan" **Note:** Weight varies: 10.80-10.90 grams.

Date	Mintage	Good	VG	F	VF	XF
AH1036//21(sic) Rare	—	—	—	—	—	—

KM# 192.4 ZODIAC MOHUR

Gold **Obv:** Pisces (fish) **Rev. Inscription:** "Jahangir...Nur Jahan" **Note:** Weight varies: 10.80-10.90 grams.

Date	Mintage	Good	VG	F	VF	XF
AH1036//21(sic) Rare	—	—	—	—	—	—

Agra

KM# 189.1 NAZARANA 1000 MOHURS

11.9358 g., Gold, 210 mm. **Obv. Inscription:** "...Jahangir" **Rev. Inscription:** Dar-ul-Kalifa

Date	Mintage	Good	VG	F	VF	XF
AH1022//8 Unique	—	—	—	—	—	—

LARGESSE COINAGE

Agra

KM# A161.1 NISAR

0.6000 g., Silver **Obv. Inscription:** "Jahangir Bad Shah"

Date	Mintage	Good	VG	F	VF	XF
AH1033//19	—	—	—	—	—	—
AH1034//19	—	—	—	—	—	—

Patna

KM# B161.1 NISAR

0.9000 g., Silver **Obv. Inscription:** "Nisar Jahangir"

Date	Mintage	Good	VG	F	VF	XF
AH1034	—	—	—	—	—	—

Agra

KM# C161.1 NISAR

1.2000 g., Silver **Obv. Inscription:** "Nisar Jahangir"

Date	Mintage	Good	VG	F	VF	XF
AHxxxx//3	—	—	—	—	—	—

Agra

KM# D161.1 NISAR

1.7000 g., Silver **Obv. Inscription:** "Nisar Jahangir" **Rev. Inscription:** "Dar al-Khilafa"

Date	Mintage	VG	F	VF	XF	Unc
AH1032//18	—	—	—	—	—	—

Agra

KM# E161.1 NISAR

1.4000 g., Silver **Obv. Inscription:** "Jahangir Bad Shah Ghazi"

Date	Mintage	Good	VG	F	VF	XF
AH1033	—	—	—	—	—	—

Ajmir

KM# E161.2 NISAR

1.5000 g., Silver **Obv. Inscription:** "Jahangir Bad Shah Ghazi"

Date	Mintage	Good	VG	F	VF	XF
AH1032//18	—	—	—	—	—	—

Burhanpur

KM# F161.1 NISAR

1.4000 g., Silver **Obv. Inscription:** "Nisar Jahangir" **Shape:** Square

Date	Mintage	Good	VG	F	VF	XF
AHxxxx//x Azar	—	—	—	—	—	—
AHxxxx//x Di	—	—	—	—	—	—

Kabul

KM# G161.1 NISAR

1.4000 g., Silver **Obv. Inscription:** "Jahangir Shahi"

Date	Mintage	Good	VG	F	VF	XF
AHxxxx//8(?)	—	—	—	—	—	—

Lahore

KM# H161.1 NISAR

Silver Obv. Inscription: "Jahangir Bad Shah" Note: Weight varies 1.0 - 1.2 grams.

Date	Mintage	Good	VG	F	VF	XF
AH1033//18 (sic)	—	—	—	—	—	—
AH1034//19	—	—	—	—	—	—
AH1036//21	—	—	—	—	—	—

Kashmir

KM# J161.1 NISAR

2.7000 g., Silver **Obv. Inscription:** "Jahangir Shah"

Date	Mintage	Good	VG	F	VF	XF
AH1032//19	—	—	—	—	—	—

Lahore

KM# K161.1 NISAR

5.7000 g., Silver **Obv. Inscription:** "Jahangir Shah Akbar Shah"

Date	Mintage	Good	VG	F	VF	XF
AH1031//17	—	—	—	—	—	—

KM# K161.2 NISAR

5.7000 g., Silver **Obv. Inscription:** "Jahangir Shah Akbar Shah"

Date	Mintage	Good	VG	F	VF	XF
AH1033//18	—	—	—	—	—	—

Ajmer

KM# 161.1 NISAR

0.9000 g., Silver **Note:** 1/12 rupee weight varies .80 - .90 grams.

Date	Mintage	Good	VG	F	VF	XF
AH1014 Rare	—	—	—	—	—	—
AH1024//10 Rare	—	—	—	—	—	—

Kashmir

KM# 161.2 NISAR

Silver **Obv. Inscription:** "Jahangir Shah Akbar Shah"
Note: Weight varies 1.0 - 1.7 grams.

Date	Mintage	Good	VG	F	VF	XF
AH1037//22(sic)	—	—	—	—	—	—

Kashmir

KM# 162.1 NISAR

1.1300 g., Silver **Shape:** Square **Note:** 1/8 rupee weight.

Date	Mintage	Good	VG	F	VF	XF
AH1023//10 Rare	—	—	—	—	—	—

Agra

KM# 163.1 NISAR

2.7000 g., Silver **Obv. Inscription:** "Nisar Jahangiri"
Rev. Inscription: Epithet: "Dar al-Khilafa" **Note:** Weight varies: 2.46-2.80 grams, (1/4 rupee weight).

Date	Mintage	Good	VG	F	VF	XF
AH1028//14	—	35.00	90.00	135	225	400
AH1029//14 (sic)	—	35.00	90.00	135	225	400

KM# 163.9 NISAR

Silver **Obv. Legend:** "Jalus Nisar Jahangiri" **Note:** Weight varies 2.5 - 2.9 grams.

Date	Mintage	Good	VG	F	VF	XF
AH1037//18	—	—	—	—	—	—

Ahmadabad

KM# 163.2 NISAR

Silver **Obv. Inscription:** "Nisar Jahangir" **Note:** Weight varies: 2.46-2.80 grams, (1/4 rupee weight). Large flan.

Date	Mintage	Good	VG	F	VF	XF
AH1027//12	—	40.00	100	150	250	450
AH1027//13	—	40.00	100	150	250	450

KM# 163.4 NISAR

Silver **Obv. Inscription:** "Nisar Jahangir" **Note:** Weight varies: 2.5-2.90 grams, (1/4 rupee weight). Small flan.

Date	Mintage	Good	VG	F	VF	XF
AH1034//19(sic)	—	35.00	90.00	135	225	400

Akbarnagar

KM# 163.7 NISAR

Silver **Rev. Inscription:** "Jahangir Shah" **Note:** Weight varies: 2.50-2.90 grams.

Date	Mintage	Good	VG	F	VF	XF
AH1033//19	—	—	150	200	350	550

Burhanpur

KM# 163.6 NISAR

Silver **Obv. Inscription:** "Nisar Jahangiri" **Note:** Weight varies: 2.50-2.80 grams.

Date	Mintage	Good	VG	F	VF	XF
AH102x//6	—	—	—	—	—	—
AH(10)31//21 (error for 16)	—	—	—	—	—	—

KM# 163.3 NISAR

Silver **Obv. Inscription:** "Nisar Jahangiri" **Note:** Weight varies: 2.50-2.80 grams. Large flan.

Date	Mintage	Good	VG	F	VF	XF
AH1031//16(sic) Rare	—	—	—	—	—	—

Lahore

KM# 163.8 NISAR

2.5000 g., Silver **Obv. Inscription:** "Jalus Nisar Jahangiri"

Date	Mintage	Good	VG	F	VF	XF
AH1029//14	—	—	—	—	—	—

KM# 163.5 NISAR

2.7000 g., Silver **Obv. Inscription:** "Nisar Jahangiri"
Note: Weight varies: 2.50-2.80 grams.

Date	Mintage	Good	VG	F	VF	XF
AH1029//14(sic)	—	—	—	—	—	—
AH1029//15	—	—	—	—	—	—

Ahmadabad

KM# A164.1 NISAR

0.7000 g., Silver **Rev. Inscription:** "Khair-i-qabul"

Date	Mintage	Good	VG	F	VF	XF
AH1033//19	—	—	—	—	—	—

KM# B164.1 NISAR

Silver **Obv. Inscription:** "Jahangir Bad Shah Ghazi" **Rev. Inscription:** "Khair-i-qabul" **Note:** Weight varies 1.3 - 1.4 grams.

Date	Mintage	Good	VG	F	VF	XF
AH1014	—	—	—	—	—	—
AH1015//2	—	—	—	—	—	—
AH1016//3	—	—	—	—	—	—
AH1020	—	—	—	—	—	—

Lahore

KM# 164.1 NISAR

Silver **Obv. Inscription:** "Jahangir Shah Akbar Shah" **Rev. Inscription:** "Khair-i-qabaul" **Note:** Weight varies: 1.30-1.40 grams.

Date	Mintage	Good	VG	F	VF	XF
AH1029//15 Rare	—	—	—	—	—	—
AHxxxx//29 Rare	—	—	—	—	—	—

Agra

KM# 165.1 NISAR

Silver **Rev. Inscription:** "Nur Afshan" **Note:** Weight varies: 0.58-0.65 grams, 1/12 rupee weight.

Date	Mintage	Good	VG	F	VF	XF
AH1019//5 Rare	—	—	—	—	—	—
AH1025//11 Rare	—	—	—	—	—	—
AH1031//16 (sic) Rare	—	—	—	—	—	—

Lahore

KM# 165.2 NISAR

0.6000 g., Silver **Note:** Weight varies: 0.58-0.65 grams, 1/12 rupee weight.

Date	Mintage	Good	VG	F	VF	XF
AH1033//18(sic)	—	—	—	—	—	—
AH103x//20	—	—	—	—	—	—

Ajmir

KM# 166.1 NISAR

1.1000 g., Gold **Obv. Inscription:** "Nisar Jahangir Shahi"

Date	Mintage	Good	VG	F	VF	XF
AHxxxx//7	—	—	—	—	—	—

Dawar Bakhsh

In Lahore, AH1037 / 1627AD

HAMMERED COINAGE

Lahore

KM# 195.1 RUPEE

10.9500 g., Silver

Date	Mintage	Good	VG	F	VF	XF
AH1037//1	—	160	400	500	700	1,000

Muhammad Shah Jahan

AH1037-1068 / 1628-1658AD

HAMMERED COINAGE

Kabul

KM# 197.2 RUPEE

11.4440 g., Silver **Obv:** Pre-accession name of "Khurram"

Date	Mintage	Good	VG	F	VF	XF
ND	—	—	—	—	—	—

Lahore

KM# 197.1 RUPEE

11.4440 g., Silver **Obv:** Pre-accession name of "Khurram"
Note: In pre-accession name: "Khurram". Weight varies: 11.00-11.15 grams; Previous KM#220.1.

Date	Mintage	Good	VG	F	VF	XF
AH1037//1 Rare	—	—	—	—	—	—

Lahore

KM# 198 NISAR

2.9000 g., Silver **Obv:** Pre-accession name of "Khurram"
Note: Pre-Accession Largesse

Date	Mintage	Good	VG	F	VF	XF
AH1037//(I) Ahad; Rare	—	—	—	—	—	—

KM# 199.1 1/16 DAM

Copper **Note:** Without mint name or mint name off flan; weight varies 1.2 - 1.3 grams.

Date	Mintage	Good	VG	F	VF	XF
ND	—	—	—	—	—	—

Akbarabad

KM# 200.1 1/8 DAM

Copper **Note:** Weight varies: 2.00-2.40 grams.

Date	Mintage	Good	VG	F	VF	XF
AH104x//8	—	5.50	9.00	15.00	25.00	—
AH1044//7	—	5.50	9.00	15.00	25.00	—
AH105x//14	—	5.50	9.00	15.00	25.00	—
AH105x//15	—	5.50	9.00	15.00	25.00	—
AH105x//19	—	5.50	9.00	15.00	25.00	—

Allahabad

KM# 200.5 1/8 DAM

Copper **Note:** Weight varies 4.8 - 5.1 grams.

Date	Mintage	Good	VG	F	VF	XF
AH1044//7	—	—	—	—	—	—

Bairata

KM# 200.2 1/8 DAM Copper **Note:** Weight varies: 2.00-2.40 grams.

Date	Mintage	Good	VG	F	VF	XF
AH104x//7	—	5.50	9.00	15.00	25.00	—
AH1045//x	—	5.50	9.00	15.00	25.00	—

Delhi

KM# 200.3 1/8 DAM

Copper **Note:** Weight varies: 2.00-2.40 grams.

Date	Mintage	Good	VG	F	VF	XF
AH104x//7	—	5.50	9.00	15.00	25.00	—
AH104x//9	—	5.50	9.00	15.00	25.00	—
AH104x//12	—	5.50	9.00	15.00	25.00	—
AH1051//1x	—	5.50	9.00	15.00	25.00	—
AH10xx//16	—	5.50	9.00	15.00	25.00	—

Narnol

KM# 200.4 1/8 DAM

Copper **Note:** Weight varies: 2.00-2.40 grams.

Date	Mintage	Good	VG	F	VF	XF
AH10xx//1x Rare	—	—	—	—	—	—

Ujjain

KM# 201.1 1/2 FALUS

Copper **Obv:** Emperor's name **Rev:** Mint **Shape:** Square
Note: Weight varies 3.0 - 3.4 grams.

Date	Mintage	Good	VG	F	VF	XF
ND(1628-58)	—	—	—	—	—	—

Ahmadabad

KM# 202.2 1/4 DAM

Copper **Note:** Weight varies: 4.80-5.10 grams.

Date	Mintage	Good	VG	F	VF	XF
ND	—	5.50	9.00	15.00	25.00	—
AH104x//4	—	5.50	9.00	15.00	25.00	—

Ahmadanagar

KM# 202.3 1/4 DAM

Copper **Note:** Weight varies 4.8 - 5.1 grams.

Date	Mintage	Good	VG	F	VF	XF
ND	—	—	—	—	—	—

Surat
KM# 202.1 1/4 DAM
Copper **Note:** Weight varies: 4.80-5.10 grams.

Date	Mintage	Good	VG	F	VF	XF
AH106x//29 Rare	—	—	—	—	—	—

Ujjain
KM# 203.1 FALUS
7.0000 g., Silver **Shape:** Square

Date	Mintage	Good	VG	F	VF	XF
ND Rare	—	—	—	—	—	—

Ujjain
KM# A204.1 FALUS
6.7000 g., Copper **Series:** Malwa **Shape:** Square

Date	Mintage	Good	VG	F	VF	XF
ND	—	5.50	11.00	15.00	20.00	—

Ahmadabad
KM# 204.1 1/2 DAM
Copper **Note:** Weight varies: 9.80-10.40 grams.

Date	Mintage	Good	VG	F	VF	XF
AH104x//6	—	4.50	9.00	15.00	25.00	—
AH1044//7	—	4.50	9.00	15.00	25.00	—
AH1044//8	—	4.50	9.00	15.00	25.00	—
AH1046//9	—	4.50	9.00	15.00	25.00	—
AH1046//10	—	4.50	9.00	15.00	25.00	—

Bairata
KM# 204.3 1/2 DAM
Copper **Note:** Weight varies: 9.80-10.40 grams.

Date	Mintage	Good	VG	F	VF	XF
AH1048//1x	—	5.50	11.00	18.00	30.00	—

Lakhnau
KM# 204.2 1/2 DAM
Copper **Note:** Weight varies: 9.80-10.40 grams.

Date	Mintage	Good	VG	F	VF	XF
AH1049//1x Rare	—	—	—	—	—	—

Patna
KM# 204.5 1/2 DAM
Copper **Note:** Weight varies: 9.80-10.40 grams.

Date	Mintage	Good	VG	F	VF	XF
ND	—	8.00	15.00	25.00	35.00	—

Surat
KM# 204.4 1/2 DAM
Copper **Note:** Weight varies: 9.80-10.40 grams.

Date	Mintage	Good	VG	F	VF	XF
AH106x//29	—	5.50	11.00	18.00	30.00	—

Akbarabad
KM# 205.1 1/2 DAM
Copper **Note:** Weight varies: 9.80-10.40 grams.

Date	Mintage	Good	VG	F	VF	XF
AH1041//4	—	5.50	11.00	18.00	30.00	—

Narnol
KM# A206.1 FALUS
13.7000 g., Copper

Date	Mintage	Good	VG	F	VF	XF
ND	—	—	—	—	—	—

Agra
KM# 206.13 DAM
Copper **Note:** Weight varies: 19.00-20.80 grams.

Date	Mintage	Good	VG	F	VF	XF
AH104x//8	—	5.50	11.00	18.00	30.00	—

Ahmadabad
KM# 206.9 DAM
Copper **Obv:** Emperor's name, regnal year **Rev:** Mint and date **Note:** Weight varies: 19.00-20.80 grams.

Date	Mintage	Good	VG	F	VF	XF
AH1044//7	—	4.00	9.00	17.50	32.00	—
AH1044//8	—	4.00	9.00	17.50	32.00	—
AH1045//8	—	4.00	9.00	17.50	32.00	—
AH1051//13(sic)	—	4.00	9.00	17.50	32.00	—
AH1051//15	—	4.00	9.00	17.50	32.00	—

Akbarabad
KM# 206.1 DAM
Copper **Note:** Mint epithet: "Dar-ul-Khilafat". Weight varies: 19.00-20.80 grams.

Date	Mintage	Good	VG	F	VF	XF
AH1041//4	—	3.00	6.00	10.00	16.00	—
AH1044//7	—	3.00	6.00	10.00	16.00	—
AH1045//8	—	3.00	6.00	10.00	16.00	—
AH1045//9	—	3.00	6.00	10.00	16.00	—
AH1046//9	—	3.00	6.00	10.00	16.00	—
AH1046//10	—	3.00	6.00	10.00	16.00	—
AH1050//13	—	3.00	6.00	10.00	16.00	—
AH1052//16	—	3.00	6.00	10.00	16.00	—
AH1053/16	—	3.00	6.00	10.00	16.00	—
AH1055//1x	—	3.00	6.00	10.00	16.00	—

Akbarnagar
KM# A206.8 DAM
21.6100 g., Copper

Date	Mintage	Good	VG	F	VF	XF
AH1067//31	—	—	—	—	—	—

Allahabad
KM# 206.8 DAM
Copper **Note:** Weight varies: 19.00-20.80 grams.

Date	Mintage	Good	VG	F	VF	XF
AH1051//15	—	7.50	15.00	22.50	35.00	—
AH1052	—	7.50	15.00	22.50	35.00	—

Bairata
KM# 206.2 DAM
Copper **Note:** Weight varies: 19.00-20.80 grams.

Date	Mintage	Good	VG	F	VF	XF
AH1037//(1) Ahad	—	2.75	5.50	9.00	15.00	—
AH1038//2	—	2.75	5.50	9.00	15.00	—
AH1039//x	—	2.75	5.50	9.00	15.00	—
AH1040//x	—	2.75	5.50	9.00	15.00	—
AH1042//x	—	2.75	5.50	9.00	15.00	—
AH1044//x	—	2.75	5.50	9.00	15.00	—
AH1045//x	—	2.75	5.50	9.00	15.00	—
AH1048//1x	—	2.75	5.50	9.00	15.00	—
AH1065//29	—	2.75	5.50	9.00	15.00	—

Daulatabad
KM# 206.14 DAM
Copper **Note:** Weight varies: 19.00-20.80 grams.

Date	Mintage	Good	VG	F	VF	XF
ND	—	5.50	11.00	18.00	30.00	—

Dogaon
KM# 206.3 DAM
Copper **Note:** Weight varies: 19.00-20.80 grams.

Date	Mintage	Good	VG	F	VF	XF
AH104x//10	—	3.00	6.00	10.00	16.00	—
AH105x//15	—	3.00	6.00	10.00	16.00	—

Kashmir
KM# 206.10 DAM
Copper **Note:** Weight varies: 19.00-20.80 grams.

Date	Mintage	Good	VG	F	VF	XF
AH1043//x	—	2.25	4.50	7.00	12.00	—
AHxxxx//29	—	2.25	4.50	7.00	12.00	—

Lakhnau
KM# 206.4 DAM
Copper **Note:** Weight varies: 19.00-20.80 grams.

Date	Mintage	Good	VG	F	VF	XF
AH1041//7	—	2.50	5.00	8.50	14.00	—

Multan
KM# 206.15 DAM
Copper **Note:** Weight varies: 19.00-20.80 grams.

Date	Mintage	Good	VG	F	VF	XF
AH104x//4	—	3.00	6.00	10.00	16.00	—

Narnol
KM# 206.12 DAM
Copper **Note:** Weight varies: 19.00-20.80 grams.

Date	Mintage	Good	VG	F	VF	XF
ND	—	3.00	6.00	10.00	16.00	—
AH106x//31	—	3.00	6.00	10.00	16.00	—

Patna
KM# 206.11 DAM
Copper **Note:** Weight varies: 19.00-20.80 grams.

Date	Mintage	Good	VG	F	VF	XF
AH10xx//x	—	2.25	4.50	7.00	12.00	—

Shahjahanabad
KM# 206.5 DAM
Copper **Note:** Weight varies: 19.00-20.80 grams.

Date	Mintage	Good	VG	F	VF	XF
ND	—	2.25	4.50	7.00	12.00	—

Surat
KM# 206.6 DAM
Copper **Note:** Weight varies: 19.00-20.80 grams.

Date	Mintage	Good	VG	F	VF	XF
AH104x//7	—	3.00	6.00	10.00	16.00	—
AH104x/9	—	3.00	6.00	10.00	16.00	—
AH106x//29	—	3.00	6.00	10.00	16.00	—
AH1067//30	—	3.00	6.00	10.00	16.00	—
AH106x//32	—	3.00	6.00	10.00	16.00	—

Udaipur
KM# 206.7 DAM
Copper **Note:** Weight varies: 19.00-20.80 grams.

Date	Mintage	Good	VG	F	VF	XF
AH10xx//3 Rare	—	—	—	—	—	—

Lakhnau
KM# 208.1 2 DAMS
Copper **Note:** Weight varies: 40.00-41.50 grams.

Date	Mintage	Good	VG	F	VF	XF
AH104x//5 Rare	—	—	—	—	—	—

Akbarabad

KM# 210.1 1/16 RUPEE

0.7150 g., Silver

Date	Mintage	Good	VG	F	VF	XF
AH1039//2	—	—	70.00	135	225	325

Aurangnabar

KM# 210.2 1/16 RUPEE

0.7150 g., Silver

Date	Mintage	Good	VG	F	VF	XF
ND Rare	—	—	—	—	—	—

Burhanpur

KM# 210.3 1/16 RUPEE

0.7150 g., Silver

Date	Mintage	Good	VG	F	VF	XF
AHxxxx Rare	—	—	—	—	—	—

Kabul

KM# 210.4 1/16 RUPEE

0.7150 g., Silver

Date	Mintage	Good	VG	F	VF	XF
AHxxxx Rare	—	—	—	—	—	—

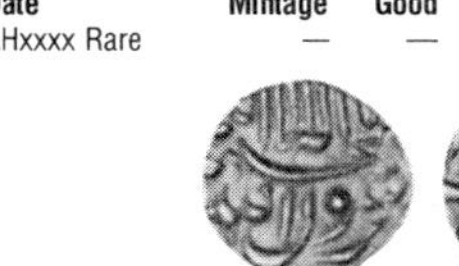 

KM# 211.1 1/8 RUPEE

1.4300 g., Silver

Date	Mintage	Good	VG	F	VF	XF
AH104x//5	—	—	45.00	85.00	140	200

Akbarabad

KM# 211.2 1/8 RUPEE

1.4300 g., Silver

Date	Mintage	Good	VG	F	VF	XF
AH1064//2x	—	—	10.00	20.00	40.00	65.00

Burhanpur

KM# 211.3 1/8 RUPEE

1.4300 g., Silver **Obv:** Inscription in square outlined with dots

Date	Mintage	Good	VG	F	VF	XF
AH1058	—	—	—	—	—	—

Patna

KM# 211.4 1/8 RUPEE

1.4300 g., Silver **Obv:** Inscription in outlined square

Date	Mintage	Good	VG	F	VF	XF
AHxxxx//25	—	—	—	—	—	—

Ujjain

KM# A212.1 1/8 RUPEE

1.4300 g., Silver **Shape:** Square

Date	Mintage	Good	VG	F	VF	XF
ND	—	—	—	—	—	—

KM# 212.2 1/4 RUPEE

2.8610 g., Silver **Obv:** Central inscription within square **Rev:** Central inscription within square

Date	Mintage	Good	VG	F	VF	XF
AH1040//x	—	15.00	37.50	75.00	125	175
AH1065//29	—	15.00	37.50	75.00	125	175
AH1069//32	—	15.00	37.50	75.00	125	175

KM# 212.1 1/4 RUPEE

2.8610 g., Silver **Obv:** Central inscription within quatrefoil **Rev:** Central inscription within quatrefoil

Date	Mintage	Good	VG	F	VF	XF
AH1053//1x	—	—	37.50	75.00	125	175

Burhanpur

KM# 212.4 1/4 RUPEE

2.8610 g., Silver

Date	Mintage	Good	VG	F	VF	XF
AHxxxx//(1) Ahad	—	—	—	—	—	—

Daulatabad

KM# 212.3 1/4 RUPEE

2.8610 g., Silver **Obv:** Central legend within quatrefoil **Rev:** Central legend within quatrefoil **Note:** Similar to 1/2 Rupee, KM#213.

Date	Mintage	Good	VG	F	VF	XF
AH104x//5 Rare	—	—	—	—	—	—

Golkonda

KM# 212.5 1/4 RUPEE

2.8610 g., Silver **Note:** Similar to Rupee KM#223.

Date	Mintage	VG	F	VF	XF	Unc
ND	—	—	—	—	—	—

Surat

KM# 212.6 1/4 RUPEE

2.8610 g., Silver

Date	Mintage	Good	VG	F	VF	XF
AHxxxx	—	—	—	—	—	—

Akbarabad

KM# A213 1/4 RUPEE

2.8100 g., Silver **Note:** Without epithet or "Nisar"

Date	Mintage	Good	VG	F	VF	XF
AH1049//13 Rare	—	—	—	—	—	—

Ahmadabad

KM# B213.1 1/4 RUPEE

2.8610 g., Silver **Obv:** Inscription in square area

Date	Mintage	Good	VG	F	VF	XF
AHxxxx	—	—	—	—	—	—

Burhanpur

KM# B213.2 1/4 RUPEE

2.8610 g., Silver **Obv:** Inscription in square outlined with dots

Date	Mintage	Good	VG	F	VF	XF
AH1063	—	—	—	—	—	—
AH1068	—	—	—	—	—	—

Patna

KM# B213.3 1/4 RUPEE

2.8610 g., Silver **Obv:** Inscription in square area

Date	Mintage	Good	VG	F	VF	XF
AH1044//7	—	—	—	—	—	—
AHxxxx//16	—	—	—	—	—	—
AHxxxx//19	—	—	—	—	—	—

Surat

KM# B213.4 1/4 RUPEE

2.8610 g., Silver **Obv:** Inscription in square area

Date	Mintage	Good	VG	F	VF	XF
AHxxxx	—	—	—	—	—	—

Ujjain

KM# B213.5 1/4 RUPEE

2.8610 g., Silver **Obv:** Inscription in square area

Date	Mintage	Good	VG	F	VF	XF
AHxxxx	—	—	—	—	—	—

Allahabad

KM# C213.1 1/4 RUPEE

2.8610 g., Silver **Obv:** Inscription in square area **Obv. Inscription:** "Shah Jahan Bad Shah Ghazi" **Rev:** Inscription in square area with mint name and AH date

Date	Mintage	Good	VG	F	VF	XF
AH1045//8	—	—	—	—	—	—

Surat

KM# D213.1 1/2 RUPEE

5.7220 g., Silver **Note:** Similar to Rupee KM#221.1.

Date	Mintage	Good	VG	F	VF	XF
AHxxxx	—	—	—	—	—	—

Ahmadabad

KM# 213.1 1/2 RUPEE

5.7220 g., Silver **Obv:** AH date

Date	Mintage	Good	VG	F	VF	XF
AH1037//(1) Ahad	—	—	37.50	75.00	125	175

Akbarabad

KM# 213.5 1/2 RUPEE

5.7220 g., Silver

Date	Mintage	Good	VG	F	VF	XF
AHxxxx//2	—	—	—	—	—	—
AH1039//3	—	—	—	—	—	—

Akbarnagar

KM# 213.6 1/2 RUPEE

5.7220 g., Silver

Date	Mintage	Good	VG	F	VF	XF
AHxxxx//5	—	—	—	—	—	—
AH1044//7	—	—	—	—	—	—

Bhakkar

KM# 213.7 1/2 RUPEE

5.7220 g., Silver

Date	Mintage	Good	VG	F	VF	XF
AHxxxx	—	—	—	—	—	—

Burhanpur

KM# 213.8 1/2 RUPEE

5.7220 g., Silver

Date	Mintage	Good	VG	F	VF	XF
AHxxxx	—	—	—	—	—	—

Daulatabad

KM# 213.9 1/2 RUPEE

5.7220 g., Silver

Date	Mintage	Good	VG	F	VF	XF
AH1037//(1)	—	—	—	—	—	—

Goraghat

KM# 213.10 1/2 RUPEE

5.7220 g., Silver

Date	Mintage	Good	VG	F	VF	XF
ND	—	—	—	—	—	—

Patna

KM# 213.3 1/2 RUPEE

5.7220 g., Silver **Obv:** AH date

Date	Mintage	Good	VG	F	VF	XF
AH1038//2	—	15.00	37.50	75.00	125	175
AH1039//2	—	15.00	37.50	75.00	125	175
AH1039//3	—	15.00	37.50	75.00	125	175
AH1040//4	—	15.00	37.50	75.00	125	175
AH1042//5	—	15.00	37.50	75.00	125	175

Surat

KM# 213.2 1/2 RUPEE

5.7220 g., Silver **Obv:** AH date

Date	Mintage	Good	VG	F	VF	XF
AH1037//(1) Ahad	—	5.50	13.50	20.00	35.00	50.00
AH1038//(1) Ahad	—	5.50	13.50	20.00	35.00	50.00
AH1040//3	—	5.50	13.50	20.00	35.00	50.00
AH1042	—	5.50	13.50	20.00	35.00	50.00

Ujjain

KM# 213.4 1/2 RUPEE

5.7220 g., Silver **Obv:** AH date

Date	Mintage	Good	VG	F	VF	XF
AH104x//4	—	—	—	—	—	—

Akbarabad

KM# A214.1 1/2 RUPEE

5.7220 g., Silver **Note:** Similar to Rupee, KM#227.10.

Date	Mintage	Good	VG	F	VF	XF
ND	—	—	—	—	—	—

Gulkanda

KM# 214.1 1/2 RUPEE

5.7220 g., Silver **Note:** Crude calligraphy.

Date	Mintage	Good	VG	F	VF	XF
AH104x//5	—	11.00	28.50	50.00	85.00	125

Ahmadnagar

KM# 215.1 1/2 RUPEE

5.7220 g., Silver **Obv:** Ilahi month **Rev:** AH date

Date	Mintage	Good	VG	F	VF	XF
AH1042//x	—	11.00	28.50	50.00	85.00	125

Patna

KM# 215.2 1/2 RUPEE

5.7220 g., Silver **Obv:** Ilahi month **Rev:** AH date **Note:** Struck on large planchet.

Date	Mintage	Good	VG	F	VF	XF
AH1038//2 Rare	—	—	—	—	—	—

Surat

KM# 216.1 1/2 RUPEE

5.7220 g., Silver **Obv:** Central legend within circle **Rev:** Central legend within circle

Date	Mintage	Good	VG	F	VF	XF
AH1067//31	—	11.00	28.50	50.00	85.00	125

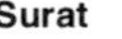

Surat

KM# 217.1 1/2 RUPEE

5.7220 g., Silver **Obv:** Inscription within quatrefoil **Rev:** Inscription within quatrefoil

Date	Mintage	Good	VG	F	VF	XF
AH1057//20	—	11.00	28.50	50.00	85.00	125
AH1057//21	—	11.00	28.50	50.00	85.00	125

Ahmadabad

KM# 218.1 1/2 RUPEE

5.7220 g., Silver **Obv:** Inscription within square **Rev:** Inscription within square **Note:** Similar to Rupee, Type 235.

Date	Mintage	Good	VG	F	VF	XF
AH1044//8	—	9.00	22.50	42.50	70.00	100
AH104x//12	—	9.00	22.50	42.50	70.00	100
AH105x//17	—	9.00	22.50	42.50	70.00	100

Akbarabad

KM# 218.2 1/2 RUPEE

5.7220 g., Silver **Obv:** Inscription within square **Rev:** Inscription within square

Date	Mintage	Good	VG	F	VF	XF
AH1042//5	—	9.00	22.50	42.50	70.00	100

Akbarnagar

KM# 218.3 1/2 RUPEE

5.7220 g., Silver **Obv:** Inscription within square **Rev:** Inscription within square

Date	Mintage	Good	VG	F	VF	XF
AH1045//8	—	9.00	22.50	42.50	70.00	100

Daulatabad

KM# 218.4 1/2 RUPEE

5.7220 g., Silver **Obv:** Inscription within square **Rev:** Inscription within square

Date	Mintage	Good	VG	F	VF	XF
AH1043//x	—	9.00	22.50	42.50	70.00	100
AH1044//x	—	9.00	22.50	42.50	70.00	100
AH1061//24	—	9.00	22.50	42.50	70.00	100

Junagar

KM# 218.15 1/2 RUPEE

5.7220 g., Silver **Obv:** Inscription within square **Rev:** Inscription within square

Date	Mintage	Good	VG	F	VF	XF
AH1049//13	—	9.00	22.50	42.50	70.00	100
AH1053//xx	—	9.00	22.50	42.50	70.00	100
AH1057//xx	—	9.00	22.50	42.50	70.00	100

Kabul

KM# 218.5 1/2 RUPEE

5.7220 g., Silver **Obv:** Inscription within square **Rev:** Inscription within square

Date	Mintage	Good	VG	F	VF	XF
AH1053//17	—	9.00	22.50	42.50	70.00	100

Kambayat

KM# 218.13 1/2 RUPEE

5.7220 g., Silver **Obv:** Inscription within square **Rev:** Inscription within square

Date	Mintage	Good	VG	F	VF	XF
ND	—	9.00	22.50	42.50	70.00	100

Lahore

KM# 218.6 1/2 RUPEE

5.7220 g., Silver **Obv:** Inscription within square **Rev:** Inscription within square

Date	Mintage	Good	VG	F	VF	XF
AH1054//1x	—	9.00	22.50	42.50	70.00	100

Patna

KM# 218.14 1/2 RUPEE

5.7220 g., Silver **Obv:** Inscription within square **Rev:** Inscription within square **Shape:** Square

Date	Mintage	Good	VG	F	VF	XF
AH10xx//3 Rare	—	—	—	—	—	—

KM# 218.7 1/2 RUPEE

5.7220 g., Silver **Obv:** Inscription within square **Rev:** Inscription within square

Date	Mintage	Good	VG	F	VF	XF
AH1044//7	—	9.00	22.50	42.50	70.00	100
AH1045//8	—	9.00	22.50	42.50	70.00	100
AH104x//10	—	9.00	22.50	42.50	70.00	100
AH104x//12	—	9.00	22.50	42.50	70.00	100
AH1054//18	—	9.00	22.50	42.50	70.00	100
AH105x//20	—	9.00	22.50	42.50	70.00	100

Pattan Deo

KM# 218.11 1/2 RUPEE

5.7220 g., Silver **Obv:** Inscription within square **Rev:** Inscription within square

Date	Mintage	Good	VG	F	VF	XF
AH1047//10 Rare	—	—	—	—	—	—

Surat

KM# 218.8 1/2 RUPEE

5.7220 g., Silver **Obv:** Inscription within square **Rev:** Inscription within square

Date	Mintage	Good	VG	F	VF	XF
AH1044//7	—	5.50	13.50	20.00	35.00	50.00
AH1044//8	—	5.50	13.50	20.00	35.00	50.00
AH1045//8	—	5.50	13.50	20.00	35.00	50.00
AH104x//10	—	5.50	13.50	20.00	35.00	50.00
AH1047//9(sic)	—	5.50	13.50	20.00	35.00	50.00
AH1048//12	—	5.50	13.50	20.00	35.00	50.00
AH1049//12	—	5.50	13.50	20.00	35.00	50.00
AH105x//15	—	5.50	13.50	20.00	35.00	50.00
AH105x//16	—	5.50	13.50	20.00	35.00	50.00
AH1055//18	—	5.50	13.50	20.00	35.00	50.00
AH1055//19	—	5.50	13.50	20.00	35.00	50.00
AH105x//21	—	5.50	13.50	20.00	35.00	50.00
AH105x//22	—	5.50	13.50	20.00	35.00	50.00
AH10xx//23	—	9.00	13.50	20.00	35.00	50.00
AH106x//24	—	5.50	13.50	20.00	35.00	50.00
AH106x//25	—	5.50	13.50	20.00	35.00	50.00
AH1065//29	—	5.50	13.50	20.00	35.00	50.00
AH1067//30	—	5.50	13.50	20.00	35.00	50.00
AH106x//31	—	5.50	13.50	20.00	35.00	50.00

Ujjain

KM# 218.9 1/2 RUPEE

5.7220 g., Silver **Obv:** Inscription within square **Rev:** Inscription within square

Date	Mintage	Good	VG	F	VF	XF
ND	—	9.00	22.50	42.50	70.00	100

Zafarnagar

KM# 218.12 1/2 RUPEE

5.7220 g., Silver **Obv:** Inscription within square **Rev:** Inscription within square

Date	Mintage	Good	VG	F	VF	XF
AH1043//x	—	9.00	22.50	42.50	70.00	100

Daulatabad

KM# 219.1 1/2 RUPEE

5.7220 g., Silver **Obv:** Inscription within foliated eightfoil **Rev:** Inscription within foliated eightfoil **Note:** Similar to 1 Rupee, KM#232.1.

Date	Mintage	Good	VG	F	VF	XF
AH1068//31	—	5.50	12.00	25.00	40.00	60.00

Burhanpur

KM# A220 1/2 RUPEE

5.7220 g., Silver **Obv:** Inscription in square outlined with dots

Date	Mintage	Good	VG	F	VF	XF
AH1052	—	—	—	—	—	—

Badakhshan

KM# 220.1 SHAHRUKHI

4.3000 g., Silver **Obv:** Inscription in square

Date	Mintage	Good	VG	F	VF	XF
ND	—	—	—	—	—	—

Surat

KM# 221.1 RUPEE

11.4440 g., Silver **Obv:** Date **Rev:** "Shah Jahan" with "raij" at top **Note:** Legend varieties exist.

Date	Mintage	Good	VG	F	VF	XF
AH1037//(1) Ahad	—	10.00	25.00	45.00	75.00	120

KM# 221.2 RUPEE

Silver **Obv:** Date **Rev:** With "Shah Jahan" at top of legend **Note:** Weight varies: 11.00-11.15 grams.

Date	Mintage	Good	VG	F	VF	XF
AH1037//(1) Ahad	—	14.00	35.00	65.00	100	150

Agra

KM# 222.1 RUPEE

11.4440 g., Silver **Obv:** AH date **Note:** Mint epithet: "Dar-ul-Khilafat".

Date	Mintage	Good	VG	F	VF	XF
AH1037//(1) Ahad	—	8.00	12.00	20.00	32.00	50.00
AH1038//(1) Ahad	—	8.00	12.00	20.00	32.00	50.00
AH1038//2	—	8.00	12.00	20.00	32.00	50.00

Ahmadabad

KM# 222.2 RUPEE

11.4440 g., Silver **Obv:** AH date

Date	Mintage	Good	VG	F	VF	XF
AH1037//(1) Ahad	—	8.00	12.00	20.00	32.00	50.00
AH1038//(1) Ahad	—	8.00	12.00	20.00	32.00	50.00
AH1038//2	—	8.00	12.00	20.00	32.00	50.00

Akbarnagar

KM# 222.3 RUPEE

11.4440 g., Silver **Obv:** AH date

Date	Mintage	Good	VG	F	VF	XF
AH1037//(1) Ahad	—	8.00	12.00	20.00	32.00	50.00
AH1038//(1) Ahad	—	8.00	12.00	20.00	32.00	50.00
AH1038//2	—	8.00	12.00	20.00	32.00	50.00

Allahabad

KM# 222.4 RUPEE

11.4440 g., Silver **Obv:** AH date

Date	Mintage	Good	VG	F	VF	XF
AH1038//(1) Ahad	—	8.00	12.00	20.00	32.00	50.00
AH1038//2	—	8.00	12.00	20.00	32.00	50.00

Burhanpur

KM# 222.5 RUPEE

11.4440 g., Silver **Obv:** AH date

Date	Mintage	Good	VG	F	VF	XF
AH1037//(1) Ahad	—	8.00	12.00	20.00	32.00	50.00
AH1038//(1) Ahad	—	8.00	12.00	20.00	32.00	50.00
AH1038//2	—	8.00	12.00	20.00	32.00	50.00

Darur

KM# 222.17 RUPEE

11.4440 g., Silver **Obv:** AH date **Note:** Mint epithet: Fathabad.

Date	Mintage	Good	VG	F	VF	XF
AH1041//4 Rare	—	—	—	—	—	—

Daulatabad

KM# 222.6 RUPEE
11.4440 g., Silver **Obv:** AH date

Date	Mintage	Good	VG	F	VF	XF
AH1037//(1) Ahad	—	8.00	12.00	20.00	32.00	50.00

Delhi

KM# 222.7 RUPEE
11.4440 g., Silver **Obv:** AH date

Date	Mintage	Good	VG	F	VF	XF
AH1037//(1) Ahad	—	8.00	12.00	20.00	32.00	50.00
AH1038//(1) Ahad	—	8.00	12.00	20.00	32.00	50.00
AH1038//2	—	8.00	12.00	20.00	32.00	50.00

Fathpur

KM# 222.8 RUPEE
11.4440 g., Silver **Obv:** AH date **Note:** Mint epithet: "Dar-us-Sultanat".

Date	Mintage	Good	VG	F	VF	XF
AH1038//(1) Ahad	—	8.00	13.00	24.00	38.00	60.00

Goraghat

KM# 222.20 RUPEE
11.4440 g., Silver

Date	Mintage	Good	VG	F	VF	XF
AH1037//(1) Ahad; Rare	—	—	—	—	—	—

Kabul

KM# 222.9 RUPEE
11.4440 g., Silver **Obv:** AH date

Date	Mintage	Good	VG	F	VF	XF
AH1040//x	—	8.00	12.00	20.00	32.00	50.00
AH1041//4	—	8.00	12.00	20.00	32.00	50.00
AH1041//5	—	8.00	12.00	20.00	32.00	50.00
AH104x//6	—	8.00	12.00	20.00	32.00	50.00
AH105x//16	—	8.00	12.00	20.00	32.00	50.00
AH105x19	—	8.00	12.00	20.00	32.00	50.00

Lahore

KM# 222.10 RUPEE
11.4440 g., Silver **Obv:** AH date **Note:** Mint epithet: "Dar-us-Sultanat".

Date	Mintage	Good	VG	F	VF	XF
AH1037//(1) Ahad	—	8.00	12.00	20.00	32.00	50.00
AH1038//(1) Ahad	—	8.00	12.00	20.00	32.00	50.00
AH1038//2	—	8.00	12.00	20.00	32.00	50.00

Multan

KM# 222.11 RUPEE
11.4440 g., Silver **Obv:** AH date

Date	Mintage	Good	VG	F	VF	XF
AH1037//(1) Ahad	—	8.00	12.00	20.00	32.00	50.00
AH1038//(1) Ahad	—	8.00	12.00	20.00	32.00	50.00
AH1038//2	—	8.00	12.00	20.00	32.00	50.00
AH1039//2	—	8.00	12.00	20.00	32.00	50.00

Patna

KM# 222.12 RUPEE
11.4440 g., Silver **Obv:** AH date

Date	Mintage	Good	VG	F	VF	XF
AH1037/(/1) Ahad	—	8.00	12.00	20.00	32.00	50.00
AH1037//2(sic)	—	8.00	12.00	20.00	32.00	50.00
AH1038//x	—	8.00	12.00	20.00	32.00	50.00

Surat

KM# 222.13 RUPEE
11.4440 g., Silver **Obv:** AH date

Date	Mintage	Good	VG	F	VF	XF
AH1037//(1) Ahad	—	8.00	12.00	20.00	32.00	50.00
AH1038//(1) Ahad	—	8.00	12.00	20.00	32.00	50.00
AH1038//2	—	8.00	12.00	20.00	32.00	50.00
AH1040//x	—	8.00	12.00	20.00	32.00	50.00
AH1041//x	—	8.00	12.00	20.00	32.00	50.00
AH1042//x	—	8.00	12.00	20.00	32.00	50.00
AH1043//x	—	8.00	12.00	20.00	32.00	50.00
AH1046//x	—	8.00	12.00	20.00	32.00	50.00

KM# 222.19 RUPEE
11.4440 g., Silver **Obv:** AH date **Rev:** Regnal year expressed as numeral "1"

Date	Mintage	Good	VG	F	VF	XF
AH1037//(1) Ahad Rare	—	—	—	—	—	—

Tatta

KM# 222.14 RUPEE
11.4440 g., Silver **Obv:** AH date **Rev:** Regnal year expressed as numeral "1"

Date	Mintage	Good	VG	F	VF	XF
AH1038//(1) Ahad	—	8.00	13.00	24.00	38.00	60.00
AH1051//14	—	8.00	13.00	24.00	38.00	60.00
AH1053//16	—	8.00	13.00	24.00	38.00	60.00

Ujjain

KM# 222.15 RUPEE
11.4440 g., Silver **Obv:** Mint epithet Baldat

Date	Mintage	Good	VG	F	VF	XF
AH1039//2	—	8.00	14.00	26.00	44.00	70.00

KM# 222.16 RUPEE
11.4440 g., Silver **Obv:** Without mint epithet

Date	Mintage	Good	VG	F	VF	XF
AH1040//4	—	8.00	12.00	20.00	32.00	50.00
AH1041//5	—	8.00	12.00	20.00	32.00	50.00

Urdu Zafar Qarin

KM# 222.21 RUPEE
11.4440 g., Silver

Date	Mintage	Good	VG	F	VF	XF
AH1038//(1) Ahad	—	—	—	—	—	—

Zafarnagar

KM# 222.18 RUPEE
11.4440 g., Silver

Date	Mintage	Good	VG	F	VF	XF
AH1038//(1) Ahad	—	—	—	—	—	—
AH1039//x	—	—	—	—	—	—

Gulkanda

KM# 223.1 RUPEE
11.4440 g., Silver **Obv:** Inscription in crude calligraphy **Rev:** Inscription in crude calligraphy

Date	Mintage	Good	VG	F	VF	XF
ND	—	7.00	10.00	16.00	26.00	40.00

Akbarabad

KM# A224.1 RUPEE
11.4440 g., Silver **Obv:** Mint name in circle **Obv. Inscription:** "Kalima" **Rev:** Inscription with titles similar to Rupee, KM#224 series

Date	Mintage	VG	F	VF	XF	Unc
AH1040//4	—	—	—	—	—	—

Agra

KM# 224.20 RUPEE
11.4440 g., Silver

Date	Mintage	Good	VG	F	VF	XF
AH1038//2 Rare	—	—	—	—	—	—

Ahmadabad

KM# 224.1 RUPEE
11.4440 g., Silver

Date	Mintage	Good	VG	F	VF	XF
AH1039//2	—	7.00	10.00	15.00	23.00	35.00
AH1040//3	—	7.00	10.00	15.00	23.00	35.00
AH1040//4	—	7.00	10.00	15.00	23.00	35.00
AH1041//4	—	7.00	10.00	15.00	23.00	35.00
AH1042//5	—	7.00	10.00	15.00	23.00	35.00

Ahmadnagar

KM# 224.2 RUPEE
11.4440 g., Silver

Date	Mintage	Good	VG	F	VF	XF
AH1038//2	—	7.00	10.00	15.00	23.00	35.00
AH1039//3	—	7.00	10.00	15.00	23.00	35.00
AH1041//x	—	7.00	10.00	15.00	23.00	35.00
AH1042//x	—	7.00	10.00	15.00	23.00	35.00

Ajmer

KM# 224.3 RUPEE
11.4440 g., Silver

Date	Mintage	Good	VG	F	VF	XF
AH1041//x Rare	—	—	—	—	—	—

Akbarabad

KM# 224.4 RUPEE
11.4440 g., Silver **Note:** Mint epithet: "Dar-ul-Khilatat".

Date	Mintage	Good	VG	F	VF	XF
AH1038//(1) Ahad	—	7.00	10.00	15.00	23.00	35.00
AH1038//2	—	7.00	10.00	15.00	23.00	35.00
AH1039//2	—	7.00	10.00	15.00	23.00	35.00
AH1041//4	—	7.00	10.00	15.00	23.00	35.00
AH10xx//5	—	7.00	10.00	15.00	23.00	35.00

Akbarnagar

KM# 224.5 RUPEE
11.4440 g., Silver

Date	Mintage	Good	VG	F	VF	XF
AH1038//2	—	7.00	10.00	15.00	23.00	35.00
AH1039//3	—	7.00	10.00	15.00	23.00	35.00
AH104x//4	—	7.00	10.00	15.00	23.00	35.00
AH1042//5	—	7.00	10.00	15.00	23.00	35.00
AH1042//6	—	7.00	10.00	15.00	23.00	35.00
AH1043//7	—	7.00	10.00	15.00	23.00	35.00
AH1044//7	—	7.00	10.00	15.00	23.00	35.00

Allahabad

KM# 224.6 RUPEE
11.4440 g., Silver

Date	Mintage	Good	VG	F	VF	XF
AH1038//2	—	7.00	10.00	15.00	23.00	35.00
AH1039//2	—	7.00	10.00	15.00	23.00	35.00
AH1039//3	—	7.00	10.00	15.00	23.00	35.00
AH1040//3	—	7.00	10.00	15.00	23.00	35.00
AH1040//4	—	7.00	10.00	15.00	23.00	35.00
AH1041//4	—	7.00	10.00	15.00	23.00	35.00
AH1041//5	—	7.00	10.00	15.00	23.00	35.00

Bhakkar

KM# 224.7 RUPEE

11.4440 g., Silver **Note:** Mint name spelled Bakkar.

Date	Mintage	Good	VG	F	VF	XF
AH1040/4	—	7.00	10.00	16.00	26.00	40.00
AH1041//4	—	7.00	10.00	16.00	26.00	40.00
AH1041//5	—	7.00	10.00	16.00	26.00	40.00
AH1042//5	—	7.00	10.00	16.00	26.00	40.00

Burhanpur

KM# 224.8 RUPEE

11.4440 g., Silver

Date	Mintage	Good	VG	F	VF	XF
AH103x//(1) Ahad	—	7.00	9.00	13.00	20.00	30.00
AH1038//2	—	7.00	9.00	13.00	20.00	30.00
AH1039//2	—	7.00	9.00	13.00	20.00	30.00
AH1039//3	—	7.00	9.00	13.00	20.00	30.00
AH1040//3	—	7.00	9.00	13.00	20.00	30.00

Delhi

KM# 224.9 RUPEE

11.4440 g., Silver

Date	Mintage	Good	VG	F	VF	XF
AH103x//(1) Ahad	—	7.00	9.00	12.00	16.00	25.00
AH1038//2	—	7.00	9.00	12.00	16.00	25.00
AH1039//2	—	7.00	9.00	12.00	16.00	25.00
AH1039//3	—	7.00	9.00	12.00	16.00	25.00
AH1040//3	—	7.00	9.00	12.00	16.00	25.00
AH1040//4	—	7.00	9.00	12.00	16.00	25.00

Jahangirnagar

KM# 224.10 RUPEE

11.4440 g., Silver **Obv:** Emperor's name and titles, date **Rev:** Kalima, mint and regnal year

Date	Mintage	Good	VG	F	VF	XF
AH103x//(1) Ahad	—	7.00	9.00	12.00	16.00	25.00
AH1038//2	—	7.00	9.00	12.00	16.00	25.00
AH1039//2	—	7.00	9.00	12.00	16.00	25.00
AH1039//3	—	7.00	9.00	12.00	16.00	25.00
AH1040//3	—	7.00	9.00	12.00	16.00	25.00
AH1040//4	—	7.00	9.00	12.00	16.00	25.00
AH1041//4	—	7.00	9.00	12.00	16.00	25.00
AH1041//5	—	7.00	9.00	12.00	16.00	25.00
AH1042//5	—	7.00	9.00	12.00	16.00	25.00
AH1042//6	—	7.00	9.00	12.00	16.00	25.00
AH1043//6	—	7.00	9.00	12.00	16.00	25.00
AH1043//7	—	7.00	9.00	12.00	16.00	25.00

Kabul

KM# 224.11 RUPEE

11.4440 g., Silver

Date	Mintage	Good	VG	F	VF	XF
AH1038//2	—	8.00	12.00	20.00	32.00	50.00
AH104x//6	—	8.00	12.00	20.00	32.00	50.00
AH104x//8	—	8.00	12.00	20.00	32.00	50.00
AH1047//10	—	8.00	12.00	20.00	32.00	50.00
AH105x//17	—	8.00	12.00	20.00	32.00	50.00

Kashmir

KM# 224.12 RUPEE

11.4440 g., Silver **Obv:** Ilahi month and regnal year **Rev:** AH date

Date	Mintage	Good	VG	F	VF	XF
AH104x//4	—	8.00	12.00	20.00	32.00	50.00
AH1041//5	—	8.00	12.00	20.00	32.00	50.00
AH1042//x	—	8.00	12.00	20.00	32.00	50.00

Katak

KM# 224.13 RUPEE

11.4440 g., Silver **Obv:** Ilahi month and regnal year **Rev:** AH date

Date	Mintage	Good	VG	F	VF	XF
AH1037//(1) Ahad	—	8.00	13.00	24.00	38.00	60.00
AH10xx//3	—	8.00	13.00	24.00	38.00	60.00
AH104x//5	—	8.00	13.00	24.00	38.00	60.00
AH104x//8	—	8.00	13.00	24.00	38.00	60.00

Lahore

KM# 224.14 RUPEE

11.4440 g., Silver **Obv:** Ilahi month and regnal year **Rev:** AH date

Date	Mintage	Good	VG	F	VF	XF
AH1038//2	—	7.00	9.00	13.00	20.00	30.00
AH1039//2	—	7.00	9.00	13.00	20.00	30.00

Multan

KM# 224.15 RUPEE

11.4440 g., Silver **Obv:** Ilahi month and regnal year **Rev:** AH date

Date	Mintage	Good	VG	F	VF	XF
AH1038//2	—	7.00	9.00	13.00	20.00	30.00
AH1039//2	—	7.00	9.00	13.00	20.00	30.00
AH1039//3	—	7.00	9.00	13.00	20.00	30.00

Nagar

KM# 224.21 RUPEE

11.4440 g., Silver **Obv:** Ilahi month and regnal year **Rev:** AH date

Date	Mintage	Good	VG	F	VF	XF
AH1040//3	—	7.00	10.00	16.00	26.00	40.00
AH1040//4	—	7.00	10.00	16.00	26.00	40.00
AH1043//5(sic)	—	7.00	10.00	16.00	26.00	40.00

Patna

KM# 224.16 RUPEE

11.4440 g., Silver **Obv:** Ilahi month and regnal year **Rev:** AH date

Date	Mintage	Good	VG	F	VF	XF
AH1037//2(sic)	—	7.00	10.00	15.00	23.00	35.00
AH1038//2	—	7.00	10.00	15.00	23.00	35.00
AH1039//2	—	7.00	10.00	15.00	23.00	35.00
AH1039//3	—	7.00	10.00	15.00	23.00	35.00
AH1040//3	—	7.00	10.00	15.00	23.00	35.00

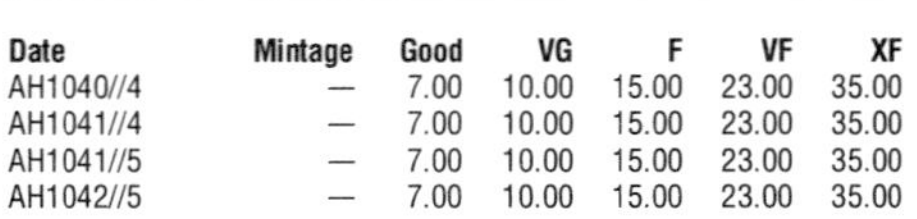

Date	Mintage	Good	VG	F	VF	XF
AH1040//4	—	7.00	10.00	15.00	23.00	35.00
AH1041//4	—	7.00	10.00	15.00	23.00	35.00
AH1041//5	—	7.00	10.00	15.00	23.00	35.00
AH1042//5	—	7.00	10.00	15.00	23.00	35.00

Qandahar

KM# 224.17 RUPEE

11.4440 g., Silver **Obv:** Ilahi month and regnal year **Rev:** AH date

Date	Mintage	Good	VG	F	VF	XF
AH104x//5 Rare	—	—	—	—	—	—
AH104x//11	—	8.00	14.00	26.00	44.00	70.00

Surat

KM# 224.23 RUPEE

11.4440 g., Silver **Obv:** Ilahi month and regnal year **Rev:** AH date

Date	Mintage	Good	VG	F	VF	XF
AH104x//4 Rare	—	—	—	—	—	—

Tatta

KM# 224.18 RUPEE

11.4440 g., Silver **Obv:** Ilahi month and regnal year **Rev:** AH date

Date	Mintage	Good	VG	F	VF	XF
AH1038//(1) Ahad	—	7.00	9.00	12.00	20.00	30.00
AH1038//2	—	7.00	9.00	12.00	20.00	30.00
AH1039//2	—	7.00	9.00	12.00	20.00	30.00
AH1039//3	—	7.00	9.00	12.00	20.00	30.00
AH1040//3	—	7.00	9.00	12.00	20.00	30.00
AH1040//4	—	7.00	9.00	12.00	20.00	30.00
AH1041//4	—	7.00	9.00	12.00	20.00	30.00
AH1041//5	—	7.00	9.00	12.00	20.00	30.00
AH1042//5	—	7.00	9.00	12.00	20.00	30.00
AH1042//6	—	7.00	9.00	12.00	20.00	30.00
AH1043//6	—	7.00	9.00	12.00	20.00	30.00
AH1043//7	—	7.00	9.00	12.00	20.00	30.00
AH1044//7	—	7.00	9.00	12.00	20.00	30.00
AH1044//8	—	7.00	9.00	12.00	20.00	30.00
AH1045//8	—	7.00	9.00	12.00	20.00	30.00
AH1045//9	—	7.00	9.00	12.00	20.00	30.00
AH1046//9	—	7.00	9.00	12.00	20.00	30.00
AH1046//10	—	7.00	9.00	12.00	20.00	30.00
AH1047//10	—	7.00	9.00	12.00	20.00	30.00
AH1047//11	—	7.00	9.00	12.00	20.00	30.00
AH1048//11	—	7.00	9.00	12.00	20.00	30.00
AH1048//12	—	7.00	9.00	12.00	20.00	30.00
AH1049//12	—	7.00	9.00	12.00	20.00	30.00
AH1049//13	—	7.00	9.00	12.00	20.00	30.00
AH1050//13	—	7.00	9.00	12.00	20.00	30.00
AH1050//14	—	7.00	9.00	12.00	20.00	30.00
AH1051//14	—	7.00	9.00	12.00	20.00	30.00
AH1051//15	—	7.00	9.00	12.00	20.00	30.00
AH1052//15	—	7.00	9.00	12.00	20.00	30.00
AH1052//16	—	7.00	9.00	12.00	20.00	30.00
AH1053//16	—	7.00	9.00	12.00	20.00	30.00
AH1053//17	—	7.00	9.00	12.00	20.00	30.00
AH1054//17	—	7.00	9.00	12.00	20.00	30.00
AH1054//18	—	7.00	9.00	12.00	20.00	30.00
AH1055//18	—	7.00	9.00	12.00	20.00	30.00
AH1055//19	—	7.00	9.00	12.00	20.00	30.00
AH1056//19	—	7.00	9.00	12.00	20.00	30.00
AH1056//20	—	7.00	9.00	12.00	20.00	30.00
AH1057//20	—	7.00	9.00	12.00	20.00	30.00
AH1057//21	—	7.00	9.00	12.00	20.00	30.00
AH1058//21	—	7.00	9.00	12.00	20.00	30.00
AH1058//22	—	7.00	9.00	12.00	20.00	30.00
AH1059//22	—	7.00	9.00	12.00	20.00	30.00
AH1059//23	—	7.00	9.00	12.00	20.00	30.00
AH1060//23	—	7.00	9.00	12.00	20.00	30.00
AH1060//24	—	7.00	9.00	12.00	20.00	30.00
AH1061//24	—	7.00	9.00	12.00	20.00	30.00
AH1061//25	—	7.00	9.00	12.00	20.00	30.00
AH1062//25	—	7.00	9.00	12.00	20.00	30.00
AH1062//26	—	7.00	9.00	12.00	20.00	30.00
AH1063//26	—	7.00	9.00	12.00	20.00	30.00
AH1063//27	—	7.00	9.00	12.00	20.00	30.00
AH1064//27	—	7.00	9.00	12.00	20.00	30.00
AH1064//28	—	7.00	9.00	12.00	20.00	30.00
AH1065//28	—	7.00	9.00	12.00	20.00	30.00
AH1065//29	—	7.00	9.00	12.00	20.00	30.00
AH1066//29	—	7.00	9.00	12.00	20.00	30.00
AH1066//30	—	7.00	9.00	12.00	20.00	30.00
AH1067//30	—	7.00	9.00	12.00	20.00	30.00
AH1067//31	—	7.00	9.00	12.00	20.00	30.00
AH1068//31	—	7.00	9.00	12.00	20.00	30.00
AH1068//32	—	7.00	9.00	12.00	20.00	30.00
AH1069//32	—	7.00	9.00	12.00	20.00	30.00
AH1069//33	—	7.00	9.00	12.00	20.00	30.00

Ujjain

KM# 224.22 RUPEE

11.4440 g., Silver **Obv:** Ilahi month and regnal year **Rev:** AH date

Date	Mintage	Good	VG	F	VF	XF
AH104x//4	—	7.00	10.00	16.00	26.00	40.00

Zafarnagar

KM# 224.19 RUPEE

11.4440 g., Silver **Obv:** Ilahi month and regnal year **Rev:** AH date

Date	Mintage	Good	VG	F	VF	XF
AH10xx//3	—	8.00	13.00	24.00	38.00	60.00
AH1041//4	—	8.00	13.00	24.00	38.00	60.00
AH1041//5	—	8.00	13.00	24.00	38.00	60.00
AH1042//5	—	8.00	13.00	24.00	38.00	60.00
AH104x//6	—	8.00	13.00	24.00	38.00	60.00
AH1046//x	—	8.00	13.00	24.00	38.00	60.00

Akbarabad

KM# 225.1 RUPEE

11.4440 g., Silver **Shape:** Square

Date	Mintage	Good	VG	F	VF	XF
AH1038//2	—	80.00	200	400	700	1,000

Akbarabad

KM# 226.1 RUPEE

11.4440 g., Silver **Obv:** Names of four Caliphs above Kalima

Date	Mintage	Good	VG	F	VF	XF
AH1039//2	—	8.00	13.00	24.00	38.00	60.00
AH1039//3	—	8.00	13.00	24.00	38.00	60.00
AH1040//3	—	8.00	13.00	24.00	38.00	60.00
AH1040//4	—	8.00	13.00	24.00	38.00	60.00
AH1041//4	—	8.00	13.00	24.00	38.00	60.00
AH1041//5	—	8.00	13.00	24.00	38.00	60.00
AH1042//x	—	8.00	13.00	24.00	38.00	60.00

Bhilsa

KM# 226.3 RUPEE

11.4440 g., Silver **Obv:** Names of four Caliphs above Kalima

Date	Mintage	Good	VG	F	VF	XF
AH1042//6	—	8.00	15.00	30.00	50.00	80.00

Burhanpur

KM# 226.2 RUPEE

11.4440 g., Silver **Obv:** Names of four Caliphs above Kalima

Date	Mintage	Good	VG	F	VF	XF
AH1040//3	—	8.00	12.00	20.00	32.00	50.00
AH1040//4	—	8.00	12.00	20.00	32.00	50.00
AH1041//4	—	8.00	12.00	20.00	32.00	50.00
AH1041//5	—	8.00	12.00	20.00	32.00	50.00
AH1042//5	—	8.00	12.00	20.00	32.00	50.00
AH1044//x	—	8.00	12.00	20.00	32.00	50.00

Akbarabad

KM# A227 RUPEE

Silver **Obv:** Kalima within circle **Rev:** Emperor's full name and title in square

Date	Mintage	Good	VG	F	VF	XF
AH1042/5	—	7.00	10.00	16.00	26.00	40.00

Ahmadnagar

KM# 227.1 RUPEE

11.4440 g., Silver **Obv:** Kalima within circle **Rev:** Emperor's fullname and title in legend, layouts vary

Date	Mintage	Good	VG	F	VF	XF
AH10xx//3	—	8.00	12.00	20.00	32.00	50.00
AH1044//8	—	8.00	12.00	20.00	32.00	50.00

Akbarabad

KM# 227.2 RUPEE

11.4440 g., Silver **Obv:** Kalima within circle **Rev:** Emperor's full name and title in legend, layouts vary

Date	Mintage	Good	VG	F	VF	XF
AH1039//2	—	7.00	10.00	16.00	26.00	40.00
AH1039//3	—	7.00	10.00	16.00	26.00	40.00
AH1040//3	—	7.00	10.00	16.00	26.00	40.00
AH1040//4	—	7.00	10.00	16.00	26.00	40.00
AH1041//4	—	7.00	10.00	16.00	26.00	40.00
AH1041//5	—	7.00	10.00	16.00	26.00	40.00
AH1042//5	—	7.00	10.00	16.00	26.00	40.00
AH1042//6	—	7.00	10.00	16.00	26.00	40.00
AH1043//6	—	7.00	10.00	16.00	26.00	40.00
AH1045//8	—	7.00	10.00	16.00	26.00	40.00

KM# 227.9 RUPEE

11.4440 g., Silver **Obv:** KM#235.3 **Rev:** KM#227.2 **Note:** Mule.

Date	Mintage	VG	F	VF	XF	Unc
AH1041//5	—	—	—	—	—	—
AH1042//5	—	—	—	—	—	—

KM# 227.10 RUPEE

11.4440 g., Silver **Obv:** KM#227.2 **Rev:** KM#235.3 **Note:** Mule.

Date	Mintage	Good	VG	F	VF	XF
AH1042//x	—	—	—	—	—	—

Allahabad

KM# 227.3 RUPEE

11.4440 g., Silver **Obv:** Kalima within circle **Rev:** Emperor's full name and title in legend; layouts vary

Date	Mintage	Good	VG	F	VF	XF
AH1040//3	—	8.00	12.00	20.00	32.00	50.00

Bhakkar

KM# 227.4 RUPEE

11.4440 g., Silver **Obv:** Kalima within circle **Rev:** Emperor's full name and title in legend; layouts vary

Date	Mintage	Good	VG	F	VF	XF
AH1040//3	—	8.00	12.00	20.00	32.00	50.00
AH1042//5	—	8.00	12.00	20.00	32.00	50.00
AH1042//6	—	8.00	12.00	20.00	32.00	50.00

Burhanpur

KM# 227.5 RUPEE

11.4440 g., Silver **Obv:** Kalima within circle **Rev:** Emperor's full name and title in legend; layouts vary

Date	Mintage	Good	VG	F	VF	XF
AH1040//3	—	8.00	12.00	20.00	32.00	50.00
AH1042//x	—	8.00	12.00	20.00	32.00	50.00

Delhi

KM# 227.6 RUPEE

11.4440 g., Silver **Obv:** Kalima within circle **Rev:** Emperor's full name and title in legend; layouts vary

Date	Mintage	Good	VG	F	VF	XF
AH1040//4	—	7.00	10.00	15.00	23.00	35.00
AH1041//4	—	7.00	10.00	15.00	23.00	35.00
AH1041//5	—	7.00	10.00	15.00	23.00	35.00
AH1042//5	—	7.00	10.00	15.00	23.00	35.00
AH1042//6	—	7.00	10.00	15.00	23.00	35.00
AH1043//6	—	7.00	10.00	15.00	23.00	35.00
AH1043//7	—	7.00	10.00	15.00	23.00	35.00
AH1044//7	—	7.00	10.00	15.00	23.00	35.00

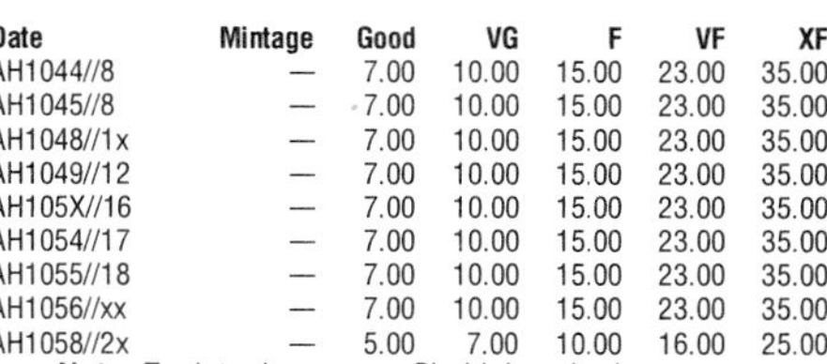

Date	Mintage	Good	VG	F	VF	XF
AH1044//8	—	7.00	10.00	15.00	23.00	35.00
AH1045//8	—	7.00	10.00	15.00	23.00	35.00
AH1048//1x	—	7.00	10.00	15.00	23.00	35.00
AH1049//12	—	7.00	10.00	15.00	23.00	35.00
AH105X//16	—	7.00	10.00	15.00	23.00	35.00
AH1054//17	—	7.00	10.00	15.00	23.00	35.00
AH1055//18	—	7.00	10.00	15.00	23.00	35.00
AH1056//xx	—	7.00	10.00	15.00	23.00	35.00
AH1058//2x	—	5.00	7.00	10.00	16.00	25.00

Note: For later issues see Shahjahanabad.

Lahore

KM# 227.7 RUPEE

11.4440 g., Silver **Obv:** Kalima within circle **Rev:** Emperor's full name and title in legend; layouts vary

Date	Mintage	Good	VG	F	VF	XF
AH1039//3	—	7.00	10.00	16.00	26.00	40.00
AH1040//3	—	7.00	10.00	16.00	26.00	40.00
AH1040//4	—	7.00	10.00	16.00	26.00	40.00
AH1041//4	—	7.00	10.00	16.00	26.00	40.00
AH1041//5	—	7.00	10.00	16.00	26.00	40.00
AH1042//5	—	7.00	10.00	16.00	26.00	40.00

Multan

KM# 227.8 RUPEE

11.4440 g., Silver **Obv:** Kalima within circle **Rev:** Emperor's full name and title in legend; layouts vary

Date	Mintage	Good	VG	F	VF	XF
AH1039//3	—	7.00	10.00	15.00	23.00	35.00
AH1040//3	—	7.00	10.00	15.00	23.00	35.00
AH1041//4	—	7.00	10.00	15.00	23.00	35.00
AH1041//5	—	7.00	10.00	15.00	23.00	35.00
AH1042//5	—	7.00	10.00	15.00	23.00	35.00
AH1043//6	—	7.00	10.00	15.00	23.00	35.00

Akbarabad

KM# 228.1 RUPEE

11.4440 g., Silver **Obv:** Central inscription within circle **Rev:** Central inscription within circle

Date	Mintage	Good	VG	F	VF	XF
AH1047//10	—	8.00	15.00	30.00	50.00	80.00

Bhakkar

KM# 228.2 RUPEE

11.4440 g., Silver **Obv:** Central inscription within circle **Rev:** Central inscription within circle **Note:** Mint name spelled Bakkar.

Date	Mintage	Good	VG	F	VF	XF
AH1042//5	—	8.00	13.00	24.00	38.00	60.00
AH1042//6	—	8.00	13.00	24.00	38.00	60.00
AH1043//6	—	8.00	13.00	24.00	38.00	60.00

Qandahar

KM# 228.3 RUPEE

11.4440 g., Silver **Obv:** Central inscription within circle **Rev:** Central inscription within circle

Date	Mintage	Good	VG	F	VF	XF
AH1048//11	—	9.00	16.00	33.00	57.00	90.00
AH1048//12	—	9.00	16.00	33.00	57.00	90.00

Shahjahanabad

KM# 228.4 RUPEE

11.4440 g., Silver **Obv:** Central inscription within circle **Rev:** Central inscription within circle **Note:** For earlier issues see Dehli.

Date	Mintage	Good	VG	F	VF	XF
AH1058//22	—	8.00	14.00	26.00	44.00	70.00
AH1060//24	—	8.00	14.00	26.00	44.00	70.00
AH106x//25	—	8.00	14.00	26.00	44.00	70.00
AH1062//2x	—	8.00	14.00	26.00	44.00	70.00
AH106x//27	—	8.00	14.00	26.00	44.00	70.00
AH1065//28	—	8.00	14.00	26.00	44.00	70.00
AH1065//29	—	8.00	14.00	26.00	44.00	70.00
AH1066//29	—	8.00	14.00	26.00	44.00	70.00
AH1066//30	—	8.00	14.00	26.00	44.00	70.00
AH106x//31	—	8.00	14.00	26.00	44.00	70.00

Surat

KM# 228.5 RUPEE

11.4440 g., Silver **Obv:** Central inscription within circle **Rev:** Central inscription within circle

Date	Mintage	Good	VG	F	VF	XF
AH10xx//3	—	8.00	13.00	24.00	38.00	60.00
AH1067//31	—	8.00	13.00	24.00	38.00	60.00
AH1068//31	—	8.00	13.00	24.00	38.00	60.00

Akbarabad

KM# 229.1 RUPEE

11.4440 g., Silver **Obv:** Central inscription within foliated quatrefoil

Date	Mintage	Good	VG	F	VF	XF
AH104x//4	—	8.00	13.00	24.00	38.00	60.00
AH1041//5	—	8.00	13.00	24.00	38.00	60.00
AH1042//5	—	8.00	13.00	24.00	38.00	60.00
AH1042//6	—	8.00	13.00	24.00	38.00	60.00

Burhanpur

KM# 229.2 RUPEE

11.4440 g., Silver **Obv:** Central inscription within foliated quatrefoil

Date	Mintage	Good	VG	F	VF	XF
AH103x//2	—	8.00	14.00	26.00	44.00	70.00
AH1040//3	—	8.00	14.00	26.00	44.00	70.00
AH104x//4	—	8.00	14.00	26.00	44.00	70.00

KM# 229.4 RUPEE

11.4440 g., Silver **Obv:** Central inscription without foliated quatrefoil

Date	Mintage	Good	VG	F	VF	XF
AH1040//x	—	—	—	—	—	—

Shahjahanabad

KM# 229.3 RUPEE

11.4440 g., Silver **Obv:** Central inscription within foliated quatrefoil **Rev:** Central inscription within circle

Date	Mintage	Good	VG	F	VF	XF
AH1060//24 Rare	—	—	—	—	—	—
AH1061//24 Rare	—	—	—	—	—	—

Akbarabad

KM# 230.1 RUPEE

11.4440 g., Silver **Obv:** Central inscription within foliated quatrefoil **Rev:** Central inscription within foliated quatrefoil

Date	Mintage	Good	VG	F	VF	XF
AH1043//6	—	8.00	14.00	26.00	44.00	70.00
AH104x//7	—	8.00	14.00	26.00	44.00	70.00

Shahjahanabad

KM# 230.2 RUPEE

11.4440 g., Silver **Obv:** Central inscription within foliated quatrefoil **Rev:** Central inscription within foliated quatrefoil **Note:** For earlier issues see Dehli.

Date	Mintage	Good	VG	F	VF	XF
AH1058//22	—	8.00	14.00	26.00	44.00	70.00
AH1059//22	—	8.00	14.00	26.00	44.00	70.00

Surat

KM# 230.3 RUPEE

11.4440 g., Silver **Obv:** Central inscription within foliated quatrefoil **Rev:** Central inscription within foliated quatrefoil

Date	Mintage	Good	VG	F	VF	XF
AH1051//1x	—	8.00	12.00	20.00	32.00	50.00
AH1054//1x	—	8.00	12.00	20.00	32.00	50.00
AH1057//20	—	8.00	12.00	20.00	32.00	50.00
AH1057//21	—	8.00	12.00	20.00	32.00	50.00
AH1057//22 (sic)	—	8.00	12.00	20.00	32.00	50.00

Akbarabad

KM# 231.1 RUPEE

11.4440 g., Silver **Obv:** Central inscription within sixfoil

Date	Mintage	Good	VG	F	VF	XF
AH1040//3	—	8.00	12.00	20.00	32.00	50.00
AH1040//4	—	8.00	12.00	20.00	32.00	50.00
AH1041//4	—	8.00	12.00	20.00	32.00	50.00
AH1041//5	—	8.00	12.00	20.00	32.00	50.00

Burhanpur

KM# 231.2 RUPEE

11.4440 g., Silver **Obv:** Central within sixfoil

Date	Mintage	Good	VG	F	VF	XF
AH1040//3	—	8.00	15.00	30.00	50.00	80.00

Ahmadabad

KM# 232.3 RUPEE

11.4440 g., Silver **Obv:** Central inscription within foliated eightfoil **Rev:** Central inscription within foliated eightfoil

Date	Mintage	Good	VG	F	VF	XF
AH1067//31	—	8.00	13.00	24.00	38.00	60.00
AH1068//31	—	8.00	13.00	24.00	38.00	60.00

Akbarabad

KM# 232.4 RUPEE

11.4440 g., Silver **Obv:** Central inscription within foliated eightfoil **Rev:** Central inscription within foliated eightfoil **Note:** Mint epithet: "Dar-ul Khilafat"

Date	Mintage	Good	VG	F	VF	XF
AH1068//31	—	8.00	12.00	20.00	32.00	50.00
AH1068//32	—	8.00	12.00	20.00	32.00	50.00
AH1069//32	—	8.00	12.00	20.00	32.00	50.00

Daulatabad

KM# 232.1 RUPEE

11.4440 g., Silver **Obv:** Central inscription within foliated eightfoil **Rev:** Central inscription within foliated eightfoil

Date	Mintage	Good	VG	F	VF	XF
AH1067//31	—	9.00	16.00	33.00	57.00	90.00
AH1068//31	—	9.00	16.00	33.00	57.00	90.00
AH1068//32	—	9.00	16.00	33.00	57.00	90.00

Shahjahanabad

KM# 232.2 RUPEE

11.4440 g., Silver **Obv:** Central inscription within foliated eightfoil **Rev:** Central inscription within foliated eightfoil

Date	Mintage	Good	VG	F	VF	XF
AH1065//29	—	8.00	14.00	26.00	44.00	70.00
AH1067//31	—	8.00	14.00	26.00	44.00	70.00
AH1068//31	—	8.00	14.00	26.00	44.00	70.00
AH1069//32	—	8.00	14.00	26.00	44.00	70.00

Akbarabad

KM# 233.1 RUPEE

11.4440 g., Silver **Obv:** Central inscription within foliated lozenge

Date	Mintage	Good	VG	F	VF	XF
AH1039//2	—	8.00	14.00	26.00	44.00	70.00
AH1041//4	—	8.00	14.00	26.00	44.00	70.00
AH1041//5	—	8.00	14.00	26.00	44.00	70.00
AH1042//2 (sic)	—	8.00	14.00	26.00	44.00	70.00
AH1042//5	—	8.00	14.00	26.00	44.00	70.00
AH1042//6	—	8.00	14.00	26.00	44.00	70.00
AH1043//6	—	8.00	14.00	26.00	44.00	70.00

Akbarabad

KM# 234.1 RUPEE

11.4440 g., Silver **Obv:** Central inscription within lozenge **Rev:** Central inscription within lozenge

Date	Mintage	Good	VG	F	VF	XF
AH1042//6	—	9.00	16.00	33.00	57.00	90.00
AH1043//6	—	9.00	16.00	33.00	57.00	90.00
AH1043//7	—	9.00	16.00	33.00	57.00	90.00

Ahmadabad

KM# 235.1 RUPEE

11.4440 g., Silver **Obv:** Central inscription within square, knots at corners **Rev:** Central inscription within square, knots at corners

Date	Mintage	Good	VG	F	VF	XF
AH1043//6	—	7.00	9.00	13.00	20.00	30.00
AH1043//7	—	7.00	9.00	13.00	20.00	30.00
AH1044//7	—	7.00	9.00	13.00	20.00	30.00
AH1044//8	—	7.00	9.00	13.00	20.00	30.00
AH1045//8	—	7.00	9.00	13.00	20.00	30.00
AH1045//9	—	7.00	9.00	13.00	20.00	30.00
AH1046//9	—	7.00	9.00	13.00	20.00	30.00
AH1046//10	—	7.00	9.00	13.00	20.00	30.00
AH1047//10	—	7.00	9.00	13.00	20.00	30.00
AH1047//11	—	7.00	9.00	13.00	20.00	30.00
AH1048//11	—	7.00	9.00	13.00	20.00	30.00
AH1048//12	—	7.00	9.00	13.00	20.00	30.00
AH1049//12	—	7.00	9.00	13.00	20.00	30.00
AH1049//13	—	7.00	9.00	13.00	20.00	30.00
AH1050//13	—	7.00	9.00	13.00	20.00	30.00
AH1650//14	—	7.00	9.00	13.00	20.00	30.00
AH1053//16	—	7.00	9.00	13.00	20.00	30.00
AH1053//17	—	7.00	9.00	13.00	20.00	30.00
AH1054//17	—	7.00	9.00	13.00	20.00	30.00
AH1054//18	—	7.00	9.00	13.00	20.00	30.00
AH1055//18	—	7.00	9.00	13.00	20.00	30.00
AH1055//19	—	7.00	9.00	13.00	20.00	30.00
AH1056//19	—	7.00	9.00	13.00	20.00	30.00
AH1056//20	—	7.00	9.00	13.00	20.00	30.00
AH1057//20	—	7.00	9.00	13.00	20.00	30.00
AH1057//21	—	7.00	9.00	13.00	20.00	30.00
AH1058//21	—	7.00	9.00	13.00	20.00	30.00
AH1061//24	—	7.00	9.00	13.00	20.00	30.00
AH1063//27	—	7.00	9.00	13.00	20.00	30.00
AH1065//29	—	7.00	9.00	13.00	20.00	30.00
AH1066//29	—	7.00	9.00	13.00	20.00	30.00
AH1067//3x	—	7.00	9.00	13.00	20.00	30.00
AH1069//32	—	7.00	9.00	13.00	20.00	30.00
AH106x//33	—	7.00	9.00	13.00	20.00	30.00

Ahmadnagar

KM# 235.2 RUPEE

11.4440 g., Silver **Obv:** Central inscription within square, knots at corners **Rev:** Central inscription within square, knots at corners

Date	Mintage	Good	VG	F	VF	XF
AH1043//x	—	7.00	10.00	16.00	26.00	40.00
AH1044//7	—	7.00	10.00	16.00	26.00	40.00
AH1053//xx	—	7.00	10.00	16.00	26.00	40.00
AH1055//1x	—	7.00	10.00	16.00	26.00	40.00
AH1058//21	—	7.00	10.00	16.00	26.00	40.00
AH105x//22	—	7.00	10.00	16.00	26.00	40.00
AH1061//24	—	7.00	10.00	16.00	26.00	40.00
AH1061//25	—	7.00	10.00	16.00	26.00	40.00
AH1062//25	—	7.00	10.00	16.00	26.00	40.00
AH1062//26	—	7.00	10.00	16.00	26.00	40.00
AH1063//26	—	7.00	10.00	16.00	26.00	40.00
AH1063//27	—	7.00	10.00	16.00	26.00	40.00
AH1066//29	—	7.00	10.00	16.00	26.00	40.00
AH1067//30	—	7.00	10.00	16.00	26.00	40.00
AH1067//31	—	7.00	10.00	16.00	26.00	40.00
AH1068//31	—	7.00	10.00	16.00	26.00	40.00
AH1068//32	—	7.00	10.00	16.00	26.00	40.00
AH1069//32	—	7.00	10.00	16.00	26.00	40.00
AH1069//33	—	7.00	10.00	16.00	26.00	40.00

Akbarabad

KM# 235.3 RUPEE

11.4440 g., Silver **Obv:** Central inscription within square, knots at corners **Rev:** Central inscription within square, knots at corners

Date	Mintage	Good	VG	F	VF	XF
AH1041//4	—	7.00	9.00	13.00	20.00	30.00
AH1041//5	—	7.00	9.00	13.00	20.00	30.00
AH1042//5	—	7.00	9.00	13.00	20.00	30.00
AH1042//6	—	7.00	9.00	13.00	20.00	30.00
AH1043//6	—	7.00	9.00	13.00	20.00	30.00
AH1043//7	—	7.00	9.00	13.00	20.00	30.00
AH1044//7	—	7.00	9.00	13.00	20.00	30.00
AH1044//8	—	7.00	9.00	13.00	20.00	30.00
AH1045//8	—	7.00	9.00	13.00	20.00	30.00
AH1045//9	—	7.00	9.00	13.00	20.00	30.00
AH1046//9	—	7.00	9.00	13.00	20.00	30.00
AH1046//10	—	7.00	9.00	13.00	20.00	30.00
AH1047//10	—	7.00	9.00	13.00	20.00	30.00
AH1047//11	—	7.00	9.00	13.00	20.00	30.00
AH1048//11	—	7.00	9.00	13.00	20.00	30.00
AH1048//12	—	7.00	9.00	13.00	20.00	30.00
AH1049//12	—	7.00	9.00	13.00	20.00	30.00
AH1049//13	—	7.00	9.00	13.00	20.00	30.00
AH1050//13	—	7.00	9.00	13.00	20.00	30.00
AH1050//14	—	7.00	9.00	13.00	20.00	30.00
AH1051//14	—	7.00	9.00	13.00	20.00	30.00
AH1051//15	—	7.00	9.00	13.00	20.00	30.00
AH1052//15	—	7.00	9.00	13.00	20.00	30.00
AH1052//16	—	7.00	9.00	13.00	20.00	30.00
AH1053//17	—	7.00	9.00	13.00	20.00	30.00
AH1054//17	—	7.00	9.00	13.00	20.00	30.00
AH1054//18	—	7.00	9.00	13.00	20.00	30.00
AH1055//18	—	7.00	9.00	13.00	20.00	30.00
AH1055//19	—	7.00	9.00	13.00	20.00	30.00
AH1056//19	—	7.00	9.00	13.00	20.00	30.00
AH1056//20	—	7.00	9.00	13.00	20.00	30.00
AH1057//20	—	7.00	9.00	13.00	20.00	30.00
AH1057//21	—	7.00	9.00	13.00	20.00	30.00
AH1058//21	—	7.00	9.00	13.00	20.00	30.00
AH1058//22	—	7.00	9.00	13.00	20.00	30.00
AH1059//22	—	7.00	9.00	13.00	20.00	30.00
AH1059//23	—	7.00	9.00	13.00	20.00	30.00
AH1060//23	—	7.00	9.00	13.00	20.00	30.00
AH1061//24	—	7.00	9.00	13.00	20.00	30.00
AH1060//24	—	7.00	9.00	13.00	20.00	30.00
AH1061//25	—	7.00	9.00	13.00	20.00	30.00
AH1062//25	—	7.00	9.00	13.00	20.00	30.00
AH1062//26	—	7.00	9.00	13.00	20.00	30.00
AH1063//26	—	7.00	9.00	13.00	20.00	30.00
AH1063//27	—	7.00	9.00	13.00	20.00	30.00
AH1064//27	—	7.00	9.00	13.00	20.00	30.00
AH1064//28	—	7.00	9.00	13.00	20.00	30.00
AH1065//29	—	7.00	9.00	13.00	20.00	30.00

Akbarnagar

KM# 235.4 RUPEE

11.4440 g., Silver **Obv:** Central inscription within square, knots at corners **Rev:** Central inscription within square, knots at corners

Date	Mintage	Good	VG	F	VF	XF
AH1044//7	—	7.00	9.00	13.00	20.00	30.00
AH1044//8	—	7.00	9.00	13.00	20.00	30.00
AH1045//8	—	7.00	9.00	13.00	20.00	30.00
AH1045//9	—	7.00	9.00	13.00	20.00	30.00
AH1046//9	—	7.00	9.00	13.00	20.00	30.00
AH1046//10	—	7.00	9.00	13.00	20.00	30.00
AH1047//10	—	7.00	9.00	13.00	20.00	30.00
AH1047//11	—	7.00	9.00	13.00	20.00	30.00
AH1048//11	—	7.00	9.00	13.00	20.00	30.00
AH1048//12	—	7.00	9.00	13.00	20.00	30.00
AH1049//12	—	7.00	9.00	13.00	20.00	30.00
AH1049//13	—	7.00	9.00	13.00	20.00	30.00
AH1050//13	—	7.00	9.00	13.00	20.00	30.00
AH1050//14	—	7.00	9.00	13.00	20.00	30.00
AH1051//14	—	7.00	9.00	13.00	20.00	30.00
AH1051//15	—	7.00	9.00	13.00	20.00	30.00
AH1052//15	—	7.00	9.00	13.00	20.00	30.00
AH1052//16	—	7.00	9.00	13.00	20.00	30.00
AH1055//19	—	7.00	9.00	13.00	20.00	30.00
AH1056//19	—	7.00	9.00	13.00	20.00	30.00
AH1056//20	—	7.00	9.00	13.00	20.00	30.00
AH1057//20	—	7.00	9.00	13.00	20.00	30.00
AH1057//21	—	7.00	9.00	13.00	20.00	30.00
AH1058//21	—	7.00	9.00	13.00	20.00	30.00
AH1058//22	—	7.00	9.00	13.00	20.00	30.00
AH1059//22	—	7.00	9.00	13.00	20.00	30.00
AH1059//23	—	7.00	9.00	13.00	20.00	30.00
AH1060//23	—	7.00	9.00	13.00	20.00	30.00
AH1060//24	—	7.00	9.00	13.00	20.00	30.00
AH1062//26	—	7.00	9.00	13.00	20.00	30.00
AH1063//26	—	7.00	9.00	13.00	20.00	30.00
AH1063//27	—	7.00	9.00	13.00	20.00	30.00
AH1064//27	—	7.00	9.00	13.00	20.00	30.00
AH1064//28	—	7.00	9.00	13.00	20.00	30.00
AH1065//28	—	7.00	9.00	13.00	20.00	30.00
AH1065//29	—	7.00	9.00	13.00	20.00	30.00
AH1066//29	—	7.00	9.00	13.00	20.00	30.00
AH1066//30	—	7.00	9.00	13.00	20.00	30.00
AH1067//30	—	7.00	9.00	13.00	20.00	30.00
AH1067//31	—	7.00	9.00	13.00	20.00	30.00
AH1068//31	—	7.00	9.00	13.00	20.00	30.00
AH1068//32	—	7.00	9.00	13.00	20.00	30.00

Allahabad

KM# 235.5 RUPEE

11.4440 g., Silver **Obv:** Central inscription within square, knots at corners **Rev:** Central inscription within square, knots at corners

Date	Mintage	Good	VG	F	VF	XF
AH1042//6	—	7.00	10.00	15.00	23.00	35.00
AH1043//6	—	7.00	10.00	15.00	23.00	35.00
AH1043//7	—	7.00	10.00	15.00	23.00	35.00
AH1044//7	—	7.00	10.00	15.00	23.00	35.00
AH1045//8	—	7.00	10.00	15.00	23.00	35.00
AH1045//9	—	7.00	10.00	15.00	23.00	35.00
AH1046//10	—	7.00	10.00	15.00	23.00	35.00
AH1047//10	—	7.00	10.00	15.00	23.00	35.00
AH1048//12	—	7.00	10.00	15.00	23.00	35.00
AH1049//12	—	7.00	10.00	15.00	23.00	35.00
AH1050//14	—	7.00	10.00	15.00	23.00	35.00
AH0151//14 (error for 1051)	—	7.00	10.00	15.00	23.00	35.00
AH1051//14	—	7.00	10.00	15.00	23.00	35.00
AH1051//15	—	7.00	10.00	15.00	23.00	35.00
AH1052//15	—	7.00	10.00	15.00	23.00	35.00
AH1052//16	—	7.00	10.00	15.00	23.00	35.00
AH1054//17	—	7.00	10.00	15.00	23.00	35.00
AH1054//18	—	7.00	10.00	15.00	23.00	35.00
AH1057//20	—	7.00	10.00	15.00	23.00	35.00
AH1062//26	—	7.00	10.00	15.00	23.00	35.00

Aurangabad

KM# 235.6 RUPEE

11.4440 g., Silver **Obv:** Central inscription within square, knots at corners **Rev:** Central inscription within square, knots at corners

Date	Mintage	Good	VG	F	VF	XF
AH104x//12 Rare	—	—	—	—	—	—

Aurangnagar

KM# 235.30 RUPEE

11.4440 g., Silver **Obv:** Central inscription within square, knots at corners **Rev:** Central inscription within square, knots at corners

Date	Mintage	Good	VG	F	VF	XF
AH1048//xx	—	—	—	—	—	—

Ausa

KM# 235.31 RUPEE

11.4440 g., Silver **Obv:** Central inscription within square, knots at corners **Rev:** Central inscription within square, knots at corners

Date	Mintage	Good	VG	F	VF	XF
AHxxxx//11	—	—	—	—	—	—

Balkh

KM# 235.29 RUPEE

11.4440 g., Silver **Obv:** Central inscription within square, knots at corners **Rev:** Central inscription within square, knots in corners **Shape:** Square

Date	Mintage	Good	VG	F	VF	XF
ND(ca.1056-57) Rare	—	—	—	—	—	—

Bhakkar

KM# 235.7 RUPEE

11.4440 g., Silver **Obv:** Central inscription within square, knots at corners **Rev:** Central inscription within square, knots at corners

Date	Mintage	Good	VG	F	VF	XF
AH1043//7	—	7.00	10.00	15.00	23.00	35.00
AH1044//7	—	7.00	10.00	15.00	23.00	35.00
AH1044//8	—	7.00	10.00	15.00	23.00	35.00
AH1045//9	—	7.00	10.00	15.00	23.00	35.00
AH1046//9	—	7.00	10.00	15.00	23.00	35.00
AH104x//10	—	7.00	10.00	15.00	23.00	35.00
AH1047//11	—	7.00	10.00	15.00	23.00	35.00
AH1048//12	—	7.00	10.00	15.00	23.00	35.00
AH10xx//13	—	7.00	10.00	15.00	23.00	35.00
AH1052//15	—	7.00	10.00	15.00	23.00	35.00
AH1052//16	—	7.00	10.00	15.00	23.00	35.00
AH1054//17	—	7.00	10.00	15.00	23.00	35.00
AH105x//18	—	7.00	10.00	15.00	23.00	35.00
AH1056//20	—	7.00	10.00	15.00	23.00	35.00
AH1057//20	—	7.00	10.00	15.00	23.00	35.00
AH1057//21	—	7.00	10.00	15.00	23.00	35.00
AH1058//21	—	7.00	10.00	15.00	23.00	35.00
AH1058//22	—	7.00	10.00	15.00	23.00	35.00
AH1059/22	—	7.00	10.00	15.00	23.00	35.00
AH1059//23	—	7.00	10.00	15.00	23.00	35.00
AH1060//24	—	7.00	10.00	15.00	23.00	35.00
AH1061//25	—	7.00	10.00	15.00	23.00	35.00
AH1062//25	—	7.00	10.00	15.00	23.00	35.00
AH1062//26	—	7.00	10.00	15.00	23.00	35.00
AH1063//26	—	7.00	10.00	15.00	23.00	35.00
AH1065//29	—	7.00	10.00	15.00	23.00	35.00
AH1066//29	—	7.00	10.00	15.00	23.00	35.00
AH1066//30	—	7.00	10.00	15.00	23.00	35.00
AH1067//30	—	7.00	10.00	15.00	23.00	35.00
AH1067//31	—	7.00	10.00	15.00	23.00	35.00
AH1068//31	—	7.00	10.00	15.00	23.00	35.00
AH1068//32	—	7.00	10.00	15.00	23.00	35.00

Bhilsa

KM# 235.8 RUPEE

11.4440 g., Silver **Obv:** Central inscription within square, knots at corners **Rev:** Central inscription within square, knots at corners

Date	Mintage	Good	VG	F	VF	XF
AH104x//12	—	7.00	10.00	16.00	26.00	40.00
AH1049//13	—	7.00	10.00	16.00	26.00	40.00
AH1049//14(sic)	—	7.00	10.00	16.00	26.00	40.00
AH1051//15	—	7.00	10.00	16.00	26.00	40.00
AH1052//15	—	7.00	10.00	16.00	26.00	40.00
AH105x//16	—	7.00	10.00	16.00	26.00	40.00
AH1054//xx	—	7.00	10.00	16.00	26.00	40.00
AH105x//18	—	7.00	10.00	16.00	26.00	40.00
AH1055//19	—	7.00	10.00	16.00	26.00	40.00
AH1056//19	—	7.00	10.00	16.00	26.00	40.00
AH1056/20	—	7.00	10.00	16.00	26.00	40.00
AH1057//20	—	7.00	10.00	16.00	26.00	40.00
AH1057//21	—	7.00	10.00	16.00	26.00	40.00
AH1058//21	—	7.00	10.00	16.00	26.00	40.00
AH1058//22	—	7.00	10.00	16.00	26.00	40.00
AH1059//22	—	7.00	10.00	16.00	26.00	40.00
AH1059//23	—	7.00	10.00	16.00	26.00	40.00
AH1060//23	—	7.00	10.00	16.00	26.00	40.00
AH1061//25	—	7.00	10.00	16.00	26.00	40.00
AH1062//26	—	7.00	10.00	16.00	26.00	40.00
AH1063//26	—	7.00	10.00	16.00	26.00	40.00
AH1063//27	—	7.00	10.00	16.00	26.00	40.00
AH1064//27	—	7.00	10.00	16.00	26.00	40.00
AH1064//28	—	7.00	10.00	16.00	26.00	40.00
AH1065//28	—	7.00	10.00	16.00	26.00	40.00
AH1065//29	—	7.00	10.00	16.00	26.00	40.00
AH1066//29	—	7.00	10.00	16.00	26.00	40.00

Burhanpur

KM# 235.33 RUPEE

11.4440 g., Silver **Obv:** Central inscription within square **Obv. Legend:** Khallada Allah Mulkahu **Rev:** Central inscription within square

Date	Mintage	Good	VG	F	VF	XF
AH1040//4	—	7.00	10.00	15.00	23.00	35.00
AH10xx//5	—	7.00	10.00	15.00	23.00	35.00

KM# 235.36 RUPEE

11.4440 g., Silver **Obv:** Legend at left **Obv. Legend:** "May God preserve the kingdom"

Date	Mintage	Good	VG	F	VF	XF
AH1040//3	—	—	—	—	—	—

Date	Mintage	Good	VG	F	VF	XF
AH1040//4	—	—	—	—	—	—
AH1042//5	—	—	—	—	—	—

KM# 235.9 RUPEE

11.4440 g., Silver **Obv:** Central inscription within square, knots at corners **Rev:** Central inscription within square, knots at corners

Date	Mintage	Good	VG	F	VF	XF
AH1042//5	—	7.00	10.00	15.00	23.00	35.00
AH1043//6	—	7.00	10.00	15.00	23.00	35.00
AH1043//7	—	7.00	10.00	15.00	23.00	35.00
AH1044//7	—	7.00	10.00	15.00	23.00	35.00
AH1044//8	—	7.00	10.00	15.00	23.00	35.00
AH1045//8	—	7.00	10.00	15.00	23.00	35.00
AH1045//9	—	7.00	10.00	15.00	23.00	35.00
AH1046//9	—	7.00	10.00	15.00	23.00	35.00
AH1046//10	—	7.00	10.00	15.00	23.00	35.00
AH1047//10	—	7.00	10.00	15.00	23.00	35.00
AH1047//11	—	7.00	10.00	15.00	23.00	35.00
AH1648//11	—	7.00	10.00	15.00	23.00	35.00
AH1048//12	—	7.00	10.00	15.00	23.00	35.00
AH1049//1x	—	7.00	10.00	15.00	23.00	35.00
AH1051//1x	—	7.00	10.00	15.00	23.00	35.00
AH1052//1x	—	7.00	10.00	15.00	23.00	35.00
AH1053//xx	—	7.00	10.00	15.00	23.00	35.00
AH1054//1x	—	7.00	10.00	15.00	23.00	35.00
AH1055//xx	—	7.00	10.00	15.00	23.00	35.00
AH1056//xx	—	7.00	10.00	15.00	23.00	35.00
AH1060//24	—	7.00	10.00	15.00	23.00	35.00
AH1061//24	—	7.00	10.00	15.00	23.00	35.00
AH1061//25	—	7.00	10.00	15.00	23.00	35.00
AH1064//2x	—	7.00	10.00	15.00	23.00	35.00
AH1068//31	—	7.00	10.00	15.00	23.00	35.00
AH1068//32	—	7.00	10.00	15.00	23.00	35.00

Daulatabad

KM# 235.10 RUPEE

11.4440 g., Silver **Obv:** Central inscription within square, knots at corners **Rev:** Central inscription within square, knots at corners

Date	Mintage	Good	VG	F	VF	XF
AH1043//x	—	7.00	10.00	15.00	23.00	35.00
AH1045//x	—	7.00	10.00	15.00	23.00	35.00
AH1047//x	—	7.00	10.00	15.00	23.00	35.00
AH1050//14	—	7.00	10.00	15.00	23.00	35.00
AH1053//1x	—	7.00	10.00	15.00	23.00	35.00
AH1054//17	—	7.00	10.00	15.00	23.00	35.00
AH1054//18	—	7.00	10.00	15.00	23.00	35.00
AH1055//18	—	7.00	10.00	15.00	23.00	35.00
AH1055//19	—	7.00	10.00	15.00	23.00	35.00
AH1056//19	—	7.00	10.00	15.00	23.00	35.00
AH1056//20	—	7.00	10.00	15.00	23.00	35.00
AH1057//20	—	7.00	10.00	15.00	23.00	35.00
AH1057//21	—	7.00	10.00	15.00	23.00	35.00
AH1058//21	—	7.00	10.00	15.00	23.00	35.00
AH1058//22	—	7.00	10.00	15.00	23.00	35.00
AH1059//22	—	7.00	10.00	15.00	23.00	35.00
AH1059//23	—	7.00	10.00	15.00	23.00	35.00
AH1060//23	—	7.00	10.00	15.00	23.00	35.00
AH1060//24	—	7.00	10.00	15.00	23.00	35.00
AH1061//24	—	7.00	10.00	15.00	23.00	35.00
AH1061//25	—	7.00	10.00	15.00	23.00	35.00
AH1062//25	—	7.00	10.00	15.00	23.00	35.00
AH1062//26	—	7.00	10.00	15.00	23.00	35.00
AH1063//27	—	7.00	10.00	15.00	23.00	35.00
AH1064//27	—	7.00	10.00	15.00	23.00	35.00
AH1064//28	—	7.00	10.00	15.00	23.00	35.00
AH1065//28	—	7.00	10.00	15.00	23.00	35.00
AH1065//29	—	7.00	10.00	15.00	23.00	35.00
AH1066//29	—	7.00	10.00	15.00	23.00	35.00
AH1066//30	—	7.00	10.00	15.00	23.00	35.00
AH1067//30	—	7.00	10.00	15.00	23.00	35.00
AH1067//31	—	7.00	10.00	15.00	23.00	35.00

Golkonda

KM# 235.34 RUPEE

11.4440 g., Silver **Obv:** Central inscription within square, knots at corners **Rev:** Central inscription within square, knots at corners

Date	Mintage	Good	VG	F	VF	XF
AH1045//9	—	—	—	—	—	—

Jahangirnagar

KM# 235.11 RUPEE

11.4440 g., Silver **Obv:** Central inscription within square, knots at corners **Rev:** Central inscription within square, knots at corners

Date	Mintage	Good	VG	F	VF	XF
AH1043//7	—	7.00	10.00	16.00	26.00	40.00
AH1044//7	—	7.00	10.00	16.00	26.00	40.00
AH1044//8	—	7.00	10.00	16.00	26.00	40.00
AH1045//9	—	7.00	10.00	16.00	26.00	40.00
AH1046//9	—	7.00	10.00	16.00	26.00	40.00
AH1046//10	—	7.00	10.00	16.00	26.00	40.00
AH1047//10	—	7.00	10.00	16.00	26.00	40.00
AH1047//11	—	7.00	10.00	16.00	26.00	40.00
AH1048//11	—	7.00	10.00	16.00	26.00	40.00
AH1048//12	—	7.00	10.00	16.00	26.00	40.00
AH1049//12	—	7.00	10.00	16.00	26.00	40.00
AH1049//13	—	7.00	10.00	16.00	26.00	40.00
AH1051//14	—	7.00	10.00	16.00	26.00	40.00
AH1051//15	—	7.00	10.00	16.00	26.00	40.00
AH1052//15	—	7.00	10.00	16.00	26.00	40.00
AH1052//16	—	7.00	10.00	16.00	26.00	40.00
AH1054//1x	—	5.00	7.50	11.00	18.00	24.00
AH106x//31	—	5.00	7.50	11.00	18.00	24.00

Junagadh

KM# 235.12 RUPEE

11.4440 g., Silver **Obv:** Central inscription within square, knots at corners **Rev:** Central inscription within square, knots at corners

Date	Mintage	Good	VG	F	VF	XF
AH1045//8	—	7.00	10.00	15.00	23.00	35.00
AH1047//1x	—	7.00	10.00	15.00	23.00	35.00
AH1049//12	—	7.00	10.00	15.00	23.00	35.00
AH1049//13	—	7.00	10.00	15.00	23.00	35.00
AH1050//14	—	7.00	10.00	15.00	23.00	35.00
AH1051//14	—	7.00	10.00	15.00	23.00	35.00
AH1051//15	—	7.00	10.00	15.00	23.00	35.00
AH1052//15	—	7.00	10.00	15.00	23.00	35.00
AH1052//16	—	7.00	10.00	15.00	23.00	35.00
AH1053//16	—	7.00	10.00	15.00	23.00	35.00
AH1053//17	—	7.00	10.00	15.00	23.00	35.00
AH1054//17	—	7.00	10.00	15.00	23.00	35.00
AH1054//18	—	7.00	10.00	15.00	23.00	35.00
AH1055//18	—	7.00	10.00	15.00	23.00	35.00
AH1055//19	—	7.00	10.00	15.00	23.00	35.00
AH1056//19	—	7.00	10.00	15.00	23.00	35.00
AH1056//20	—	7.00	10.00	15.00	23.00	35.00
AH1057//2x	—	7.00	10.00	15.00	23.00	35.00
AH1059//2x	—	7.00	10.00	15.00	23.00	35.00
AH1060//23	—	7.00	10.00	15.00	23.00	35.00
AH1060//24	—	7.00	10.00	15.00	23.00	35.00
AH1061//24	—	7.00	10.00	15.00	23.00	35.00
AH1061//25	—	7.00	10.00	15.00	23.00	35.00
AH1062//25	—	7.00	10.00	15.00	23.00	35.00
AH1062//26	—	7.00	10.00	15.00	23.00	35.00
AH1063//26	—	7.00	10.00	15.00	23.00	35.00
AH1063//27	—	7.00	10.00	15.00	23.00	35.00
AH1064//27	—	7.00	10.00	15.00	23.00	35.00
AH1064//28	—	7.00	10.00	15.00	23.00	35.00
AH1065//28	—	7.00	10.00	15.00	23.00	35.00
AH1065//29	—	7.00	10.00	15.00	23.00	35.00
AH1066//29	—	7.00	10.00	15.00	23.00	35.00
AH1066//30	—	7.00	10.00	15.00	23.00	35.00
AH1067//30	—	7.00	10.00	15.00	23.00	35.00
AH1067//31	—	7.00	10.00	15.00	23.00	35.00
AH1068//31	—	7.00	10.00	15.00	23.00	35.00
AH1068//32	—	7.00	10.00	15.00	23.00	35.00
AH1069//3x	—	7.00	10.00	15.00	23.00	35.00

Kabul

KM# 235.13 RUPEE

11.4440 g., Silver **Obv:** Central inscription within square, knots at corners **Rev:** Central inscription within square, knots at corners

Date	Mintage	Good	VG	F	VF	XF
AH1047//10	—	8.00	14.00	26.00	44.00	70.00
AH1047//11	—	8.00	14.00	26.00	44.00	70.00
AH1048//11	—	8.00	14.00	26.00	44.00	70.00
AH10xx//14	—	8.00	14.00	26.00	44.00	70.00
AH1052//16	—	8.00	14.00	26.00	44.00	70.00
AH1053//16	—	8.00	14.00	26.00	44.00	70.00
AH1053//17	—	8.00	14.00	26.00	44.00	70.00
AH1054//17	—	8.00	14.00	26.00	44.00	70.00
AH1062//25	—	8.00	14.00	26.00	44.00	70.00
AH1065//28	—	8.00	14.00	26.00	44.00	70.00
AH1067//30	—	8.00	14.00	26.00	44.00	70.00

Kalpi

KM# 235.35 RUPEE

11.4440 g., Silver **Obv:** Central inscription in square, knots at corners **Rev:** Central inscription in square, knots at corners

Date	Mintage	Good	VG	F	VF	XF
AHxxxx//27	—	—	—	—	—	—

Kashmir

KM# 235.14 RUPEE

11.4440 g., Silver **Obv:** Central inscription within square, knots at corners **Rev:** Central inscription within square, knots at corners

Date	Mintage	Good	VG	F	VF	XF
AH104x//12	—	8.00	12.00	20.00	32.00	50.00
AH1051//14	—	8.00	12.00	20.00	32.00	50.00
AH1052//15	—	8.00	12.00	20.00	32.00	50.00
AH1052//16	—	8.00	12.00	20.00	32.00	50.00
AH1053//16	—	8.00	12.00	20.00	32.00	50.00
AH105x//17	—	8.00	12.00	20.00	32.00	50.00
AH1055//18	—	8.00	12.00	20.00	32.00	50.00
AH1059//2x	—	8.00	12.00	20.00	32.00	50.00
AH1065//2x	—	8.00	12.00	20.00	32.00	50.00

Katak

KM# 235.15 RUPEE

11.4440 g., Silver **Obv:** Central inscription within square, knots at corners **Rev:** Central inscription within square, knots at corners

Date	Mintage	Good	VG	F	VF	XF
AH10xx//13	—	7.00	10.00	16.00	26.00	40.00
AH105x//14	—	7.00	10.00	16.00	26.00	40.00
AH1052//1x	—	7.00	10.00	16.00	26.00	40.00
AH1054//18	—	7.00	10.00	16.00	26.00	40.00
AH105x//81(sic)	—	7.00	10.00	16.00	26.00	40.00
AH10xx//22	—	7.00	10.00	16.00	26.00	40.00
AH10xx//23	—	7.00	10.00	16.00	26.00	40.00
AH1062//26	—	7.00	10.00	16.00	26.00	40.00
AH1064//27	—	7.00	10.00	16.00	26.00	40.00
AH1064//28	—	7.00	10.00	16.00	26.00	40.00
AH1065//28	—	7.00	10.00	16.00	26.00	40.00
AH1065//29	—	7.00	10.00	16.00	26.00	40.00
AH1066//29	—	7.00	10.00	16.00	26.00	40.00
AH1066//30	—	7.00	10.00	16.00	26.00	40.00
AH1067//30	—	7.00	10.00	16.00	26.00	40.00
AH1067//31	—	7.00	10.00	16.00	26.00	40.00
AH1068//31	—	7.00	10.00	16.00	26.00	40.00
AH1068//32	—	7.00	10.00	16.00	26.00	40.00
AH1069//32	—	7.00	10.00	16.00	26.00	40.00

Khambayat

KM# 235.16 RUPEE

11.4440 g., Silver **Obv:** Central inscription within square, knots at corners **Rev:** Central inscription within square, knots at corners

Date	Mintage	Good	VG	F	VF	XF
AH104x//8	—	7.00	10.00	16.00	26.00	40.00
AH1046/10	—	7.00	10.00	16.00	26.00	40.00
AH1057//20	—	7.00	10.00	16.00	26.00	40.00
AH1057//12(sic)	—	7.00	10.00	16.00	26.00	40.00
AH1058//20	—	7.00	10.00	16.00	26.00	40.00
AH105x//21	—	7.00	10.00	16.00	26.00	40.00
AH10xx//23	—	7.00	10.00	16.00	26.00	40.00
AH1060//2x	—	7.00	10.00	16.00	26.00	40.00
AH1061//24	—	7.00	10.00	16.00	26.00	40.00
AH1061//25	—	7.00	10.00	16.00	26.00	40.00
AH1062//25	—	7.00	10.00	16.00	26.00	40.00
AH1062//26	—	7.00	10.00	16.00	26.00	40.00
AH1063//26	—	7.00	10.00	16.00	26.00	40.00
AH1063//27	—	7.00	10.00	16.00	26.00	40.00
AH1064//27	—	7.00	10.00	16.00	26.00	40.00
AH1064//28	—	7.00	10.00	16.00	26.00	40.00
AH1065//28	—	7.00	10.00	16.00	26.00	40.00
AH1065//29	—	7.00	10.00	16.00	26.00	40.00
AH1067//3x	—	7.00	10.00	16.00	26.00	40.00
AH1068//31	—	7.00	10.00	16.00	26.00	40.00
AH1068//32	—	7.00	10.00	16.00	26.00	40.00
AH1069//32	—	7.00	10.00	16.00	26.00	40.00

Lahore

KM# 235.17 RUPEE

11.4440 g., Silver **Obv:** Central inscription within square, knots at corners **Rev:** Central inscription within square, knots at corners

Date	Mintage	Good	VG	F	VF	XF
AH1042//6	—	7.00	9.00	13.00	20.00	30.00
AH1043//6	—	7.00	9.00	13.00	20.00	30.00
AH1043//7	—	7.00	9.00	13.00	20.00	30.00
AH1044//7	—	7.00	9.00	13.00	20.00	30.00
AH1044//8	—	7.00	9.00	13.00	20.00	30.00
AH1045//8	—	7.00	9.00	13.00	20.00	30.00
AH1045//9	—	7.00	9.00	13.00	20.00	30.00
AH1046//9	—	7.00	9.00	13.00	20.00	30.00
AH1046//10	—	7.00	9.00	13.00	20.00	30.00
AH1047//10	—	7.00	9.00	13.00	20.00	30.00
AH1047//11	—	7.00	9.00	13.00	20.00	30.00
AH1048//11	—	7.00	9.00	13.00	20.00	30.00
AH1048//12	—	7.00	9.00	13.00	20.00	30.00
AH1049//12	—	7.00	9.00	13.00	20.00	30.00
AH1049//13	—	7.00	9.00	13.00	20.00	30.00
AH1050//13	—	7.00	9.00	13.00	20.00	30.00
AH1050//14	—	7.00	9.00	13.00	20.00	30.00
AH1051//14	—	7.00	9.00	13.00	20.00	30.00
AH1051//15	—	7.00	9.00	13.00	20.00	30.00
AH1052//15	—	7.00	9.00	13.00	20.00	30.00
AH1052//16	—	7.00	9.00	13.00	20.00	30.00
AH1053//16	—	7.00	9.00	13.00	20.00	30.00
AH1053//17	—	7.00	9.00	13.00	20.00	30.00
AH1054//17	—	7.00	9.00	13.00	20.00	30.00
AH1054//18	—	7.00	9.00	13.00	20.00	30.00
AH1055//18	—	7.00	9.00	13.00	20.00	30.00
AH1055//19	—	7.00	9.00	13.00	20.00	30.00
AH1056//19	—	7.00	9.00	13.00	20.00	30.00
AH1056//20	—	7.00	9.00	13.00	20.00	30.00
AH1057//20	—	7.00	9.00	13.00	20.00	30.00
AH1057//21	—	7.00	9.00	13.00	20.00	30.00
AH1058//21	—	7.00	9.00	13.00	20.00	30.00
AH1058//22	—	7.00	9.00	13.00	20.00	30.00
AH1059//22	—	7.00	9.00	13.00	20.00	30.00
AH1059//23	—	7.00	9.00	13.00	20.00	30.00
AH1060//23	—	7.00	9.00	13.00	20.00	30.00
AH1060//24	—	7.00	9.00	13.00	20.00	30.00
AH1061//24	—	7.00	9.00	13.00	20.00	30.00
AH1061//25	—	7.00	9.00	13.00	20.00	30.00
AH1062//25	—	7.00	9.00	13.00	20.00	30.00
AH1062//26	—	7.00	9.00	13.00	20.00	30.00
AH1063//26	—	7.00	9.00	13.00	20.00	30.00
AH1063//27	—	7.00	9.00	13.00	20.00	30.00
AH1064//27	—	7.00	9.00	13.00	20.00	30.00
AH1064//28	—	7.00	9.00	13.00	20.00	30.00
AH1065//28	—	7.00	9.00	13.00	20.00	30.00
AH1065//29	—	7.00	9.00	13.00	20.00	30.00
AH1066//29	—	7.00	9.00	13.00	20.00	30.00
AH1066//30	—	7.00	9.00	13.00	20.00	30.00
AH1067//30	—	7.00	9.00	13.00	20.00	30.00
AH1067//31	—	7.00	9.00	13.00	20.00	30.00
AH1068//31	—	7.00	9.00	13.00	20.00	30.00
AH1068//32	—	7.00	9.00	13.00	20.00	30.00
AH1069//32	—	7.00	9.00	13.00	20.00	30.00
AH1069//33	—	7.00	9.00	13.00	20.00	30.00

Lakhnau

KM# 235.18 RUPEE

11.4440 g., Silver **Obv:** Central inscription within square, knots at corners **Rev:** Central inscription within square, knots at corners

Date	Mintage	Good	VG	F	VF	XF
AH1045//x	—	8.00	13.00	24.00	38.00	60.00
AH1049//11(sic)	—	8.00	13.00	24.00	38.00	60.00
AH10xx//13	—	8.00	13.00	24.00	38.00	60.00
AH1050//14	—	8.00	13.00	24.00	38.00	60.00
AH1055//19	—	8.00	13.00	24.00	38.00	60.00
AH1056//19	—	8.00	13.00	24.00	38.00	60.00
AH1065//29	—	8.00	13.00	24.00	38.00	60.00
AH1068//31	—	8.00	13.00	24.00	38.00	60.00

Multan

KM# 235.19 RUPEE

11.4440 g., Silver **Obv:** Central inscription within square, knots at corners **Rev:** Central inscription within square, knots at corners

Date	Mintage	Good	VG	F	VF	XF
AH1042//5	—	7.00	9.00	13.00	20.00	30.00
AH1042//6	—	7.00	9.00	13.00	20.00	30.00
AH1043//6	—	7.00	9.00	13.00	20.00	30.00
AH1043//7	—	7.00	9.00	13.00	20.00	30.00
AH1044//7	—	7.00	9.00	13.00	20.00	30.00
AH1044//8	—	7.00	9.00	13.00	20.00	30.00
AH1045//8	—	7.00	9.00	13.00	20.00	30.00
AH1045//9	—	7.00	9.00	13.00	20.00	30.00
AH1046//9	—	7.00	9.00	13.00	20.00	30.00
AH1046//10	—	7.00	9.00	13.00	20.00	30.00
AH1047//10	—	7.00	9.00	13.00	20.00	30.00
AH1047//11	—	7.00	9.00	13.00	20.00	30.00
AH1048//11	—	7.00	9.00	13.00	20.00	30.00
AH1048//12	—	7.00	9.00	13.00	20.00	30.00
AH1049//12	—	7.00	9.00	13.00	20.00	30.00
AH1049//13	—	7.00	9.00	13.00	20.00	30.00
AH1050//13	—	7.00	9.00	13.00	20.00	30.00
AH1050//14	—	7.00	9.00	13.00	20.00	30.00
AH1051//14	—	7.00	9.00	13.00	20.00	30.00
AH1051//15	—	7.00	9.00	13.00	20.00	30.00
AH1052//15	—	7.00	9.00	13.00	20.00	30.00
AH1052//16	—	7.00	9.00	13.00	20.00	30.00
AH1653//16	—	7.00	9.00	13.00	20.00	30.00
AH1053//17	—	7.00	9.00	13.00	20.00	30.00
AH1054//17	—	7.00	9.00	13.00	20.00	30.00
AH1054//18	—	7.00	9.00	13.00	20.00	30.00
AH1055//18	—	7.00	9.00	13.00	20.00	30.00
AH1055//19	—	7.00	9.00	13.00	20.00	30.00
AH1056//19	—	7.00	9.00	13.00	20.00	30.00
AH1056//20	—	7.00	9.00	13.00	20.00	30.00
AH1057//20	—	7.00	9.00	13.00	20.00	30.00
AH1057//21	—	7.00	9.00	13.00	20.00	30.00
AH1058//21	—	7.00	9.00	13.00	20.00	30.00
AH1058//22	—	7.00	9.00	13.00	20.00	30.00
AH1059//22	—	7.00	9.00	13.00	20.00	30.00
AH1059//23	—	7.00	9.00	13.00	20.00	30.00
AH1060//23	—	7.00	9.00	13.00	20.00	30.00
AH1060//24	—	7.00	9.00	13.00	20.00	30.00
AH1061//24	—	7.00	9.00	13.00	20.00	30.00
AH1061//25	—	7.00	9.00	13.00	20.00	30.00
AH1062//25	—	7.00	9.00	13.00	20.00	30.00
AH1062//26	—	7.00	9.00	13.00	20.00	30.00
AH1063//26	—	7.00	9.00	13.00	20.00	30.00
AH1063//27	—	7.00	9.00	13.00	20.00	30.00
AH1064//27	—	7.00	9.00	13.00	20.00	30.00
AH1064//28	—	7.00	9.00	13.00	20.00	30.00
AH1065//28	—	7.00	9.00	13.00	20.00	30.00
AH1065//29	—	7.00	9.00	13.00	20.00	30.00
AH1066//29	—	7.00	9.00	13.00	20.00	30.00
AH1066//30	—	7.00	9.00	13.00	20.00	30.00
AH1067//30	—	7.00	9.00	13.00	20.00	30.00
AH1067//31	—	7.00	9.00	13.00	20.00	30.00
AH1068//31	—	7.00	9.00	13.00	20.00	30.00
AH1068//32	—	7.00	9.00	13.00	20.00	30.00
AH1069//32	—	7.00	9.00	13.00	20.00	30.00
AH1069//33	—	7.00	9.00	13.00	20.00	30.00

Patna

KM# 235.20 RUPEE

11.4440 g., Silver **Obv:** Central inscription within square, knots at corners **Rev:** Central inscription within square, knots at corners

Date	Mintage	Good	VG	F	VF	XF
AH1042//5	—	7.00	9.00	13.00	20.00	30.00
AH1042//6	—	7.00	9.00	13.00	20.00	30.00
AH1043//6	—	7.00	9.00	13.00	20.00	30.00
AH1043//7	—	7.00	9.00	13.00	20.00	30.00
AH1044//7	—	7.00	9.00	13.00	20.00	30.00
AH1044//8	—	7.00	9.00	13.00	20.00	30.00
AH1045//8	—	7.00	9.00	13.00	20.00	30.00
AH1045//9	—	7.00	9.00	13.00	20.00	30.00
AH1046//9	—	7.00	9.00	13.00	20.00	30.00
AH1046//10	—	7.00	9.00	13.00	20.00	30.00
AH1047//10	—	7.00	9.00	13.00	20.00	30.00
AH1047//11	—	7.00	9.00	13.00	20.00	30.00
AH1048//11	—	7.00	9.00	13.00	20.00	30.00
AH1048//12	—	7.00	9.00	13.00	20.00	30.00
AH1049//12	—	7.00	9.00	13.00	20.00	30.00
AH1049//13	—	7.00	9.00	13.00	20.00	30.00
AH1050//13	—	7.00	9.00	13.00	20.00	30.00
AH1050//14	—	7.00	9.00	13.00	20.00	30.00
AH1051//14	—	7.00	9.00	13.00	20.00	30.00
AH105x//15	—	7.00	9.00	13.00	20.00	30.00
AH1053//16	—	7.00	9.00	13.00	20.00	30.00
AH105x//17	—	7.00	9.00	13.00	20.00	30.00
AH1055//18	—	7.00	9.00	13.00	20.00	30.00
AH105x//19	—	7.00	9.00	13.00	20.00	30.00
AH105x//20	—	7.00	9.00	13.00	20.00	30.00
AH105x//21	—	7.00	9.00	13.00	20.00	30.00
AH105x//22	—	7.00	9.00	13.00	20.00	30.00
AH10xx//23	—	7.00	9.00	13.00	20.00	30.00
AH1061//24	—	7.00	9.00	13.00	20.00	30.00
AH106x//25	—	7.00	9.00	13.00	20.00	30.00
AH106x//26	—	7.00	9.00	13.00	20.00	30.00
AH1063//27	—	7.00	9.00	13.00	20.00	30.00
AH1064//27	—	7.00	9.00	13.00	20.00	30.00
AH1064//28	—	7.00	9.00	13.00	20.00	30.00
AH1065//29	—	7.00	9.00	13.00	20.00	30.00
AH1066//29	—	7.00	9.00	13.00	20.00	30.00
AH1066//30	—	7.00	9.00	13.00	20.00	30.00
AH1067//30	—	7.00	9.00	13.00	20.00	30.00
AH1067//31	—	7.00	9.00	13.00	20.00	30.00
AH1068//31	—	7.00	9.00	13.00	20.00	30.00
AH1068//32	—	7.00	9.00	13.00	20.00	30.00
AH1069//32	—	7.00	9.00	13.00	20.00	30.00
AH1069//33	—	7.00	9.00	13.00	20.00	30.00

Pattan Deo

KM# 235.21 RUPEE

11.4440 g., Silver **Obv:** Central inscription within square, knots at corners **Rev:** Central inscription within square, knots at corners

Date	Mintage	Good	VG	F	VF	XF
AH1047//10	—	30.00	60.00	120	190	300

Qandahar

KM# 235.22 RUPEE

11.4440 g., Silver **Obv:** Central inscription within square, knots at corners **Rev:** Central inscription within square, knots at corners

Date	Mintage	Good	VG	F	VF	XF
ND(1628)	—	7.00	10.00	16.00	26.00	40.00
AH1042//5	—	7.00	10.00	16.00	26.00	40.00
AH1044//5	—	7.00	10.00	16.00	26.00	40.00
AH1044//8	—	7.00	10.00	16.00	26.00	40.00
AH1051//15	—	7.00	10.00	16.00	26.00	40.00
AH1056//20	—	7.00	10.00	16.00	26.00	40.00

KM# 235.32 RUPE

11.4440 g., Silver **Obv:** Central inscription within square, knots at corners **Rev:** Central inscription within square, knots at corners

Date	Mintage	Good	VG	F	VF	XF
AH1048//12	—	7.00	10.00	16.00	26.00	40.00
AH1049//12	—	7.00	10.00	16.00	26.00	40.00
AH1050//13	—	7.00	10.00	16.00	26.00	40.00
AH1050//14	—	7.00	10.00	16.00	26.00	40.00
AH1051//14	—	7.00	10.00	16.00	26.00	40.00
AH1051//15	—	7.00	10.00	16.00	26.00	40.00
AH1052//16	—	7.00	10.00	16.00	26.00	40.00
AH1053//16	—	7.00	10.00	16.00	26.00	40.00
AH1053//17	—	7.00	10.00	16.00	26.00	40.00
AH1054//17	—	7.00	10.00	16.00	26.00	40.00
AH1054//18	—	7.00	10.00	16.00	26.00	40.00
AH1055//18	—	7.00	10.00	16.00	26.00	40.00
AH1055//19	—	7.00	10.00	16.00	26.00	40.00
AH1056//19	—	7.00	10.00	16.00	26.00	40.00
AH1056//20	—	7.00	10.00	16.00	26.00	40.00
AH1056//21 (sic)	—	7.00	10.00	16.00	26.00	40.00
AH1057//21	—	7.00	10.00	16.00	26.00	40.00
AH1058//21	—	7.00	10.00	16.00	26.00	40.00

Sironj

KM# 235.27 RUPEE

11.4440 g., Silver **Obv:** Central inscription within square, knots at corners **Rev:** Central inscription within square, knots at corners

Date	Mintage	Good	VG	F	VF	XF
AH1065//2x Rare	—	—	—	—	—	—
AH106x//31 Rare	—	—	—	—	—	—

Surat

KM# 235.23 RUPEE

11.4440 g., Silver **Obv:** Central inscription within square, knots at corners **Rev:** Central inscription within square, knots at corners

Date	Mintage	Good	VG	F	VF	XF
AH1042//6	—	7.00	9.00	13.00	20.00	30.00
AH1043//6	—	7.00	9.00	13.00	20.00	30.00
AH1043//7	—	7.00	9.00	13.00	20.00	30.00
AH1044//7	—	7.00	9.00	13.00	20.00	30.00
AH1044//8	—	7.00	9.00	13.00	20.00	30.00
AH1045//8	—	7.00	9.00	13.00	20.00	30.00
AH1045//9	—	7.00	9.00	13.00	20.00	30.00
AH1046//9	—	7.00	9.00	13.00	20.00	30.00

Date	Mintage	Good	VG	F	VF	XF
AH1046//10	—	7.00	9.00	13.00	20.00	30.00
AH1047//10	—	7.00	9.00	13.00	20.00	30.00
AH1047//11	—	7.00	9.00	13.00	20.00	30.00
AH1048//11	—	7.00	9.00	13.00	20.00	30.00
AH1048//12	—	7.00	9.00	13.00	20.00	30.00
AH1049//12	—	7.00	9.00	13.00	20.00	30.00
AH1049//13	—	7.00	9.00	13.00	20.00	30.00
AH1050//13	—	7.00	9.00	13.00	20.00	30.00
AH1050//14	—	7.00	9.00	13.00	20.00	30.00
AH1051//14	—	7.00	9.00	13.00	20.00	30.00
AH1051//15	—	7.00	9.00	13.00	20.00	30.00
AH1052//15	—	7.00	9.00	13.00	20.00	30.00
AH1052//16	—	7.00	9.00	13.00	20.00	30.00
AH1053//16	—	7.00	9.00	13.00	20.00	30.00
AH1053//17	—	7.00	9.00	13.00	20.00	30.00
AH1054//17	—	7.00	9.00	13.00	20.00	30.00
AH1054//18	—	7.00	9.00	13.00	20.00	30.00
AH1055//18	—	7.00	9.00	13.00	20.00	30.00
AH1055//19	—	7.00	9.00	13.00	20.00	30.00
AH1056//19	—	7.00	9.00	13.00	20.00	30.00
AH1056//20	—	7.00	9.00	13.00	20.00	30.00
AH1057//20	—	7.00	9.00	13.00	20.00	30.00
AH1057//21	—	7.00	9.00	13.00	20.00	30.00
AH1058//21	—	7.00	9.00	13.00	20.00	30.00
AH1058//12 (error for 22)	—	7.00	12.00	20.00	30.00	55.00
AH1058//22	—	7.00	9.00	13.00	20.00	30.00
AH1059//22	—	7.00	9.00	13.00	20.00	30.00
AH1059//23	—	7.00	9.00	13.00	20.00	30.00
AH1006//23 (error for 1060)	—	7.00	12.00	20.00	30.00	55.00
AH1060//23	—	7.00	9.00	13.00	20.00	30.00
AH1060//24	—	7.00	9.00	13.00	20.00	30.00
AH1061//24	—	7.00	9.00	13.00	20.00	30.00
AH1061//25	—	7.00	9.00	13.00	20.00	30.00
AH1062//25	—	7.00	9.00	13.00	20.00	30.00
AH1062/26	—	7.00	9.00	13.00	20.00	30.00
AH1063//26	—	7.00	9.00	13.00	20.00	30.00
AH1063//27	—	7.00	9.00	13.00	20.00	30.00
AH1064//27	—	7.00	9.00	13.00	20.00	30.00
AH1064//28	—	7.00	9.00	13.00	20.00	30.00
AH1065//28	—	7.00	9.00	13.00	20.00	30.00
AH1065//29	—	7.00	9.00	13.00	20.00	30.00
AH1066//29	—	7.00	9.00	13.00	20.00	30.00
AH1066//30	—	7.00	9.00	13.00	20.00	30.00
AH1067//30	—	7.00	9.00	13.00	20.00	30.00
AH1067//31	—	7.00	9.00	13.00	20.00	30.00
AH1068//31	—	7.00	9.00	13.00	20.00	30.00
AH1068//32	—	7.00	9.00	13.00	20.00	30.00
AH1069//32	—	7.00	9.00	13.00	20.00	30.00

Tatta

KM# 235.28 RUPEE

11.4440 g., Silver **Obv:** Central inscription within square, knots at corners **Rev:** Central inscription within square, knots at corners

Date	Mintage	Good	VG	F	VF	XF
AH1062//2x	—	—	—	—	—	—

Ujjain

KM# 235.24 RUPEE

11.4440 g., Silver **Obv:** Central inscription within square, knots at corners **Rev:** Central inscription within square, knots at corners

Date	Mintage	Good	VG	F	VF	XF
AH10xx//3	—	7.00	10.00	16.00	26.00	40.00
AH104x//5	—	7.00	10.00	16.00	26.00	40.00
AH1046//x	—	7.00	10.00	16.00	26.00	40.00
AH10xx//13	—	7.00	10.00	16.00	26.00	40.00
AH105x//14	—	7.00	10.00	16.00	26.00	40.00
AH1054//18	—	7.00	10.00	16.00	26.00	40.00
AH106x//31	—	7.00	10.00	16.00	26.00	40.00

Zafarabad

KM# 235.25 RUPEE

11.4440 g., Silver **Obv:** Central inscription within square, knots at corners **Rev:** Central inscription within square, knots at corners

Date	Mintage	Good	VG	F	VF	XF
AH1067//31	—	8.00	15.00	30.00	50.00	80.00
AH1068//31	—	8.00	15.00	30.00	50.00	80.00
AH1068//32	—	8.00	15.00	30.00	50.00	80.00
AH1069//32	—	8.00	15.00	30.00	50.00	80.00

Zafarnagar

KM# 235.26 RUPEE

11.4440 g., Silver **Obv:** Central inscription within square, knots at corners **Rev:** Central inscription within square, knots at corners

Date	Mintage	Good	VG	F	VF	XF
AH1043//x	—	9.00	16.00	32.00	56.00	90.00
AH1044//x	—	9.00	16.00	32.00	56.00	90.00
AH104x//12	—	9.00	16.00	32.00	56.00	90.00

Ahmadabad

KM# 236.1 RUPEE

Silver **Shape:** Square **Note:** Weight varies: 10.80-11.20 grams.

Date	Mintage	Good	VG	F	VF	XF
AH104x//6 Rare	—	—	—	—	—	—

Lahore

KM# 236.4 RUPEE

Silver **Shape:** Square **Note:** Weight varies: 10.80-11.20 grams.

Date	Mintage	Good	VG	F	VF	XF
AH1040//4 Rare	—	—	—	—	—	—

Multan

KM# 236.2 RUPEE

Silver **Shape:** Square **Note:** Weight varies: 10.80-11.20 grams.

Date	Mintage	Good	VG	F	VF	XF
AH1042//6 Rare	—	—	—	—	—	—
AH1047 Rare	—	—	—	—	—	—

Surat

KM# 236.3 RUPEE

11.4440 g., Silver **Shape:** Square

Date	Mintage	Good	VG	F	VF	XF
AHxxxx//x	—	20.00	45.00	95.00	150	240

Akbarabad

KM# 249.1 NAZARANA RUPEE

Silver **Note:** Weight varies: 10.15-10.40 grams.

Date	Mintage	Good	VG	F	VF	XF
AH1054//18 Rare	—	—	—	—	—	—

Agra

KM# 252.1 1/4 MOHUR

Gold **Note:** Weight varies: 2.60-2.75 grams.

Date	Mintage	Good	VG	F	VF	XF
AH1037//(1) Ahad	—	—	120	300	450	650

Tatta

KM# 253.1 1/2 MOHUR

Gold **Note:** Similar to 1 Rupee, KM#224.18; Weight varies 5.4 - 5.5 grams.

Date	Mintage	Good	VG	F	VF	XF
AH1039//2 Rare	—	—	—	—	—	—

Agra

KM# 254.1 MOHUR

Gold **Obv:** Within dotted borders; Kalima, mint name, AH date **Rev:** Within dotted borders; Emperor's full name and titles **Note:** Weight varies: 10.80-11.00 grams. Mint epithet: "Dar-ul-Khilafat".

Date	Mintage	Good	VG	F	VF	XF
AH1037//(1) Ahad	—	—	380	450	550	700
AH1038//(1) Ahad	—	—	380	450	550	700

Burhanpur

KM# 254.2 MOHUR

Gold **Obv:** Within dotted borders; Kalima, mint name, AH dates **Rev:** Within dotted borders; Emperor's full name and titles **Note:** Weight varies: 10.80-11.00 grams.

Date	Mintage	Good	VG	F	VF	XF
AH1037//(1) Ahad	—	—	380	450	550	700
AH1038//(1) Ahad	—	—	380	450	550	700
AH1038//2	—	—	380	450	550	700

Gulkanda

KM# 254.3 MOHUR

Gold **Obv:** Within dotted borders; Kalima, mint name, AH dates **Rev:** Within dotted borders; Emperor's full name and titles **Note:** Weight varies: 10.80-11.00 grams.

Date	Mintage	Good	VG	F	VF	XF
ND	—	—	380	450	550	700

Kabul

KM# 254.4 MOHUR

Gold **Obv:** Within dotted borders; Kalima, mint name, AH dates **Rev:** Within dotted borders; Emperor's full name and titles **Note:** Weight varies: 10.80-11.00 grams.

Date	Mintage	Good	VG	F	VF	XF
AH1039//3	—	350	425	500	625	800
AH1040//4	—	350	425	500	625	800

Kashmir

KM# 254.7 MOHUR

Gold **Obv:** Kalima, AH date and mint name within dotted border **Rev:** Emperor's full name and titles within dotted border **Note:** Weight varies 10.8 - 11 grams.

Date	Mintage	Good	VG	F	VF	XF
ND	—	350	425	500	625	800

Lahore

KM# 254.5 MOHUR

Gold **Obv:** Within dotted borders; Kalima, mint name, AH dates **Rev:** Within dotted borders; Emperor's full name and titles **Note:** Weight varies: 10.80-11.00 grams.

Date	Mintage	Good	VG	F	VF	XF
AH1037//(1) Ahad	—	—	380	450	550	700

Surat

KM# 254.6 MOHUR

Gold **Obv:** Within dotted borders; Kalima, mint name, AH date **Rev:** Within dotted borders; Emperor's full name and titles **Note:** Weight varies: 10.80-11.00 grams.

Date	Mintage	Good	VG	F	VF	XF
AH1037//(1) Ahad	—	—	380	450	550	700
AH1038//(1) Ahad	—	—	380	450	550	700

Ahmadabad

KM# 255.1 MOHUR

Gold **Obv:** Kalima, mint name, Ilahi month **Rev:** AH date **Note:** Weight varies: 10.80-11.00 grams.

Date	Mintage	Good	VG	F	VF	XF
AH1038//2	—	—	365	430	525	650
AH1039//2	—	—	365	430	525	650
AH1039//3	—	—	365	430	525	650
AH1040//4	—	—	365	430	525	650
AH1041//4	—	—	365	430	525	650
AH1041//5	—	—	365	430	525	650
AH1042//x	—	—	365	430	525	650

Akbarabad

KM# 255.8 MOHUR

Gold **Obv:** Kalima, mint name, Ilahi month **Rev:** AH date **Note:** Weight varies: 10.80-11.00 grams. Mint epithet: "Dar-ul-Khilafat".

Date	Mintage	Good	VG	F	VF	XF
AH1037//(1) Ahad	—	—	380	450	550	700
AH1038//(1) Ahad	—	—	380	450	550	700
AH1038//2	—	—	380	450	550	700

Burhanpur

KM# 255.2 MOHUR

Gold **Obv:** Kalima, mint name, Ilahi month **Rev:** AH date **Note:** Weight varies: 10.80-11.00 grams.

Date	Mintage	Good	VG	F	VF	XF
AH1038//2	—	—	380	450	550	700

Jahangirnagar

KM# 255.3 MOHUR

Gold **Obv:** Kalima, mint name, Ilahi month **Rev:** AH date **Note:** Struck at Jahangirnagar. Weight varies: 10.80-11.00 grams.

Date	Mintage	Good	VG	F	VF	XF
AH1042//6	—	—	380	450	550	700

Katak

KM# 255.9 MOHUR

Gold **Obv:** Kalima, mint name, Ilahi month **Rev:** AH date **Note:** Weight varies: 10.80-11.00 grams.

Date	Mintage	Good	VG	F	VF	XF
AH1046 "Aban"; Rare	—	—	—	—	—	—
AH1049 "Shawwal"; Rare	—	—	—	—	—	—

Lahore

KM# 255.4 MOHUR

Gold **Obv:** Kalima, mint name, Ilahi month **Rev:** AH date **Note:** Weight varies: 10.80-11.00 grams.

Date	Mintage	Good	VG	F	VF	XF
AH1039//2	—	—	380	450	550	700

Patna

KM# 255.5 MOHUR

Gold **Obv:** Kalima, mint name, Ilahi month **Rev:** AH date **Note:** Weight varies: 10.80-11.00 grams.

Date	Mintage	Good	VG	F	VF	XF
AH1039//2	—	—	380	450	550	700
AH1041//5	—	—	380	450	550	700

Surat

KM# 255.6 MOHUR

Gold **Obv:** Regnal years only **Rev:** AH date **Note:** Weight varies: 10.80-11.00 grams.

Date	Mintage	Good	VG	F	VF	XF
AHxxxx//2	—	—	380	450	550	700
AH104x//4	—	—	380	450	550	700
AH104x//5	—	—	380	450	550	700

Tatta

KM# 255.7 MOHUR

Gold **Obv:** Regnal years only **Rev:** AH date **Note:** Weight varies: 10.80-11.00 grams.

Date	Mintage	Good	VG	F	VF	XF
AH1047//10	—	—	380	450	550	700
AH1066//30	—	—	380	450	550	700

Burhanpur

KM# A256.1 MOHUR

Gold **Obv:** Inscription without quatrefoil **Obv. Inscription:** "Kalima" **Rev:** Emperor's full name and titles, AH date **Note:** Weight varies 10.8 - 11 grams

Date	Mintage	Good	VG	F	VF	XF
AH1040//3	—	355	410	525	650	900

Akbarabad

KM# 256.1 MOHUR

Gold **Obv:** Within dotted borders; Kalima within quatrefoil **Rev:** Within dotted border; Emperor's full name and titles, date **Note:** Weight varies: 10.80-11.00 grams.

Date	Mintage	Good	VG	F	VF	XF
AH1041//4	—	355	410	525	650	900
AH1042//5	—	355	410	525	650	900
AH1042//6	—	355	410	525	650	900
AH1043//6	—	355	410	525	650	900

Burhanpur

KM# 256.2 MOHUR

Gold **Obv:** Within dotted borders; Kalima within quatrefoil **Rev:** Within dotted border; Emperor's full name and titles, date **Note:** Weight varies: 10.80-11.00 grams.

Date	Mintage	Good	VG	F	VF	XF
AH1040//3	—	355	410	525	650	900

Burhanpur

KM# 257.2 MOHUR

Gold **Obv:** Kalima within small circle **Note:** Weight varies: 10.80-11.00 grams.

Date	Mintage	Good	VG	F	VF	XF
AH1039//2	—	355	410	525	650	900

Lahore

KM# 257.1 MOHUR

Gold **Obv:** Kalima within duofoil, AH date **Note:** Weight varies: 10.80-11.00 grams.

Date	Mintage	Good	VG	F	VF	XF
AH1042//5	—	350	410	525	650	900

Akbarabad

KM# 258.1 MOHUR

Gold **Obv:** Kalima within quatrefoil **Rev:** "Shah Jahan Badshah Ghazi" within quatrefoil, AH date **Note:** Weight varies: 10.80-11.00 grams.

Date	Mintage	Good	VG	F	VF	XF
AH1043//6	—	—	350	410	480	600
AH1044//7	—	—	350	410	480	600
AH1044//8	—	—	350	410	480	600
AH1045//8	—	—	350	410	480	600
AH1045//9	—	—	350	410	480	600
AH1046//9	—	—	350	410	480	600
AH1047//10	—	—	350	410	480	600
AH1047//11	—	—	350	410	480	600
AH1048//11	—	—	350	410	480	600
AH1048//12	—	—	350	410	480	600
AH1049//13	—	—	350	410	480	600
AH1050//13	—	—	350	410	480	600
AH1051//15	—	—	350	410	480	600
AH1052//16	—	—	350	410	480	600
AH1053//16	—	—	350	410	480	600
AH1053//17	—	—	350	410	480	600
AH1054//17	—	—	350	410	480	600
AH1054//18	—	—	350	410	480	600
AH1055//18	—	—	350	410	480	600
AH1057//20	—	—	350	410	480	600
AH1057//21	—	—	350	410	480	600
AH1059//22	—	—	350	410	480	600
AH1059//23	—	—	350	410	480	600
AH1060//23	—	—	350	410	480	600
AH1061//25	—	—	350	410	480	600
AH1060//24	—	—	350	410	480	600
AH1062//26	—	—	350	410	480	600
AH1062//27 (sic)	—	—	350	410	480	600

KM# 258.2 MOHUR

Gold **Obv:** Kalima within quatrefoil, date **Rev:** "Shah Jahan Badshah Ghazi" within quatrefoil, AH date **Note:** Weight varies: 10.80-11.00 grams.

Date	Mintage	Good	VG	F	VF	XF
AH1051//15	—	—	380	450	550	700
AH1062//26	—	—	380	450	550	700
AH1064//28	—	—	380	450	550	700

Daulatabad

KM# 258.4 MOHUR

Gold **Rev:** AH Date **Note:** Weight varies: 10.80-11.00 grams.

Date	Mintage	Good	VG	F	VF	XF
AH1050//1x	—	—	380	450	550	700
AH1051//14	—	—	380	450	550	700

KM# 258.3 MOHUR

Gold **Obv:** Kalima within quatrefoil, date **Rev:** "Shah Jahan Bad Shah Ghazi" within quatrefoil, AH date **Note:** Weight varies: 10.80-11.00 grams.

Date	Mintage	Good	VG	F	VF	XF
AH1052//15	—	—	365	425	525	650
AH1061//24	—	—	365	425	525	650
AH1062//25	—	—	365	425	525	650
AH1063//27	—	—	365	425	525	650
AH1064//27	—	—	365	425	525	650
AH1065//29	—	—	365	425	525	650
AH1066//30	—	—	365	425	525	650
AH1067//30	—	—	365	425	525	650
AH1067//31	—	—	365	425	525	650

Akbarabad

KM# A259.1 MOHUR

Gold **Obv:** Inscription within eightfoil **Rev:** Inscription within eightfoil, AH date **Note:** Weight varies 10.8 - 11 grams.

Date	Mintage	Good	VG	F	VF	XF
AH1043//1x Rare	—	—	—	—	—	—

Daulatabad

KM# A259.2 MOHUR

Gold **Obv:** Inscription within eightfoil **Rev:** Inscription within eightfoil, AH date **Note:** Weight varies 10.8 - 11 grams.

Date	Mintage	Good	VG	F	VF	XF
AH103x//2 Rare	—	—	—	—	—	—

Akbarabad

KM# 259.5 MOHUR

11.4440 g., Gold **Obv:** Inscription within lozenge **Rev:** Inscription within lozenge

Date	Mintage	Good	VG	F	VF	XF
AH1043	—	—	—	—	—	—

KM# 259.1 MOHUR

Gold **Obv:** Inscription within eightfoil **Rev:** AH date, inscription within eightfoil **Note:** Weight varies: 10.80-11.00 grams.

Date	Mintage	Good	VG	F	VF	XF
AH10xx//31	—	350	410	525	650	900
AH1068//32	—	350	410	525	650	900
AH1069//32	—	350	410	525	650	900

Daulatabad

KM# 259.2 MOHUR

Gold **Obv:** Inscription within eightfoil, AH date **Rev:** Inscription within eightfoil **Note:** Weight varies: 10.80-11.00 grams.

Date	Mintage	Good	VG	F	VF	XF
AH1068//31	—	350	410	525	650	900
AH1068//32	—	350	410	525	650	900
AH1069//32	—	350	410	525	650	900

Kabul

KM# 259.3 MOHUR

Gold **Obv:** Inscription within eightfoil, AH date **Rev:** Inscription within eightfoil **Note:** Weight varies: 10.80-11.00 grams.

Date	Mintage	Good	VG	F	VF	XF
AH1067//31	—	350	410	525	650	900

Shahjahanabad

KM# 259.4 MOHUR

Gold **Obv:** Inscription within eightfoil, AH date **Rev:** Inscription within eightfoil **Rev. Inscription:** "dar al-khilafa" **Note:** Weight varies 10.8 - 11 grams.

Date	Mintage	Good	VG	F	VF	XF
AH1069	—	—	—	—	—	—

Ahmadabad

KM# 260.1 MOHUR

Gold **Obv:** Inscription within square, with knots at corners; Kalima, AH date **Rev:** Inscription within square, with knots at corners;"Shah Jahan Bad Shah Ghazi" **Note:** Weight varies: 10.80-11.00 grams.

Date	Mintage	Good	VG	F	VF	XF
AH1044//8	—	—	365	425	525	650
AH1045//8	—	—	365	425	525	650
AH1046//9	—	—	365	425	525	650
AH1052//16	—	—	365	425	525	650
AH1067//30	—	—	365	425	525	650

Akbarabad

KM# 260.24 MOHUR

Gold, 27.5 mm. **Obv:** Inscription within square, with knots at corners; Kalima, AH date **Rev:** Mint epithet: "May Gopd preserve the kingdom" in right margin **Note:** Weight varies: 10.80-11.00 grams.

Date	Mintage	Good	VG	F	VF	XF
AH1038//2 Rare	—	—	—	—	—	—

KM# 260.2 MOHUR

Gold **Obv:** Inscription within square, with knots at corners; Kalima, AH date **Rev:** Inscription within square, with knots at corners;"Shah Jahan Bad Shah Ghazi" **Note:** Weight varies: 10.80-11.00 grams.

Date	Mintage	Good	VG	F	VF	XF
AH1046//9	—	—	380	450	550	700
AH1056//19	—	—	380	450	550	700

Allahabad

KM# 260.3 MOHUR

Gold **Obv:** Legend within square, with knots at corners; Kalima, AH date **Rev:** Legend within square, with knots at corners; "Shah Jahan Bad Shah Ghazi" **Note:** Weight varies: 10.80-11.00 grams.

Date	Mintage	Good	VG	F	VF	XF
AH1045//9	—	—	365	425	525	650
AH1046//9	—	—	365	425	525	650

Date	Mintage	Good	VG	F	VF	XF
AH1046//10	—	—	365	425	525	650
AH1052//15	—	—	365	425	525	650
AH1055//18	—	—	365	425	525	650
AH1057//21	—	—	365	425	525	650
AH1058//21	—	—	365	425	525	650

Aurangabad

KM# 260.4 MOHUR

Gold **Obv:** Legend within square, with knots at corners; Kalima, AH date **Rev:** Legend within square, with knots at corners; "Shah Jahan Bad Shah Ghazi" **Note:** Weight varies: 10.80-11.00 grams.

Date	Mintage	Good	VG	F	VF	XF
AH1049//13	—	—	380	450	550	700

Aurangnagar

KM# 260.23 MOHUR

Gold **Obv:** Legend within square, with knots at corners; Kalima, AH date **Rev:** Legend within square, with knots at corners; "Shah Jahan Bad Shah Ghazi" **Note:** Weight varies: 10.80-11.00 grams.

Date	Mintage	Good	VG	F	VF	XF
AH1048//11 Rare	—	—	—	—	—	—

Balkh

KM# 260.16 MOHUR

Gold **Obv:** Legend within square, with knots at corners; Kalima, AH date **Rev:** Legend within square, with knots at corners; "Shah Jahan Bad Shah Ghazi" **Note:** Weight varies: 10.80-11.00 grams.

Date	Mintage	Good	VG	F	VF	XF
AH1056//20 Rare	—	—	—	—	—	—
AH1056//1057 Rare	—	—	—	—	—	—
AH1057//20 Rare	—	—	—	—	—	—

Bhilsa

KM# 260.5 MOHUR

Gold **Obv:** Legend within square, with knots at corners; Kalima, AH date **Rev:** Legend within square, with knots at corners; "Shah Jahan Bad Shah Ghazi" **Note:** Weight varies: 10.80-11.00 grams.

Date	Mintage	Good	VG	F	VF	XF
AH1059//2x	—	—	380	450	550	700
AH106x//24	—	—	380	450	550	700
AH1065//29	—	—	380	450	550	700

Burhanpur

KM# 260.6 MOHUR

Gold **Obv:** Inscription within square, with knots at corners; Kalima, AH date **Rev:** Inscription within square, with knots at corners; "Shah Jahan Bad Shah Ghazi" **Note:** Weight varies: 10.80-11.00 grams.

Date	Mintage	Good	VG	F	VF	XF
AH1040//4	—	—	350	410	480	600
AH1041//4	—	—	350	410	480	600
AH1042//x	—	—	350	410	480	600
AH1043//6	—	—	350	410	480	600
AH1043//7	—	—	350	410	480	600
AH1048//xx	—	—	350	410	480	600
AH1049//12	—	—	350	410	480	600
AH1050//xx	—	—	350	410	480	600
AH1051//15	—	—	350	410	480	600
AH1052//15	—	—	350	410	480	600
AH1052//16	—	—	350	410	480	600
AH1053//16	—	—	350	410	480	600
AH1053//17	—	—	350	410	480	600
AH1054//17	—	—	350	410	480	600
AH1054//18	—	—	350	410	480	600
AH1055//18	—	—	350	410	480	600
AH1055//19	—	—	350	410	480	600
AH1056//19	—	—	350	410	480	600
AH1057//20	—	—	350	410	480	600
AH1057//21	—	—	350	410	480	600
AH1058//21	—	—	350	410	480	600
AH1058//22	—	—	350	410	480	600
AH1059//22	—	—	350	410	480	600
AH1059//23	—	—	350	410	480	600
AH1060//23	—	—	350	410	480	600
AH1060//24	—	—	350	410	480	600
AH1061//24	—	—	350	410	480	600
AH1061//25	—	—	350	410	480	600
AH1063//26	—	—	350	410	480	600
AH1063//27	—	—	350	410	480	600

KM# 260.26 MOHUR

Gold **Obv:** Inscription within square, with knots at corners; Kalima, AH date **Rev:** Inscription within square, with knots at corners; mint epithet: "May God preserve the kingdom" in right margin **Rev. Inscription:** "Shah Jahan Bad Shah Ghazi" **Note:** Weight varies: 10.80-11.00 grams.

Date	Mintage	Good	VG	F	VF	XF
AH1040//4 Rare	—	—	—	—	—	—
AH1041//4 Rare	—	—	—	—	—	—
AH1041//5 Rare	—	—	—	—	—	—

KM# 260.25 MOHUR

Gold **Obv:** Inscription within square, Kalima, AH date **Rev:** Inscription within square of dots **Rev. Inscription:** "Shah Jahan Bad Shah Ghazi" **Note:** Weight varies 10.8 - 11 grams.

Date	Mintage	Good	VG	F	VF	XF
AH1047//xx	—	—	380	450	550	700
AH1056//20	—	—	380	450	550	700
AH1068//32	—	—	380	450	550	700

Daulatabad

KM# 260.21 MOHUR

Gold **Obv:** Inscription within square, with knots at corners; Kalima, AH date **Rev:** Inscription within square, with knots at corners **Rev. Inscription:** "Shah Jahan Bad Shah Ghazi" **Note:** Weight varies: 10.80-11.00 grams.

Date	Mintage	Good	VG	F	VF	XF
AH1043//x Rare	—	—	—	—	—	—
AH1061//23(sic) Rare	—	—	—	—	—	—

Gulkanda

KM# 260.17 MOHUR

Gold **Obv:** Inscription within square, with knots at corners; Kalima, AH date **Rev:** Inscription within square, with knots at corners **Rev. Inscription:** "Shah Jahan Bad Shah Ghazi" **Note:** Weight varies: 10.80-11.00 grams.

Date	Mintage	Good	VG	F	VF	XF
AH1045//9	—	—	380	450	550	700

Junagarh

KM# 260.7 MOHUR

Gold **Obv:** Inscription within square, with knots at corners; Kalima, AH date **Rev:** Inscription within square, with knots at corners **Rev. Inscription:** "Shah Jahan Bad Shah Ghazi" **Note:** Weight varies: 10.80-11.00 grams.

Date	Mintage	Good	VG	F	VF	XF
AH1044//7	—	—	380	450	550	700

Kabul

KM# 260.8 MOHUR

Gold **Obv:** Inscription within square, with knots at corners; Kalima, AH date **Rev:** Inscription within square, with knots at corners **Rev. Inscription:** "Shah Jahan Bad Shah Ghazi" **Note:** Weight varies: 10.80-11.00 grams.

Date	Mintage	Good	VG	F	VF	XF
AH1048//11	—	—	380	450	550	700
AH106x//25	—	—	380	450	550	700

Kashmir

KM# 260.9 MOHUR

Gold **Obv:** Inscription within square, with knots at corners; Kalima, AH date **Rev:** Inscription within square, with knots at corners **Rev. Inscription:** "Shah Jahan Bad Shah Ghazi" **Note:** Weight varies: 10.80-11.00 grams.

Date	Mintage	Good	VG	F	VF	XF
AH105x//19	—	—	380	450	550	700
AH105x//22	—	—	380	450	550	700
AH1065//2x	—	—	380	450	550	700
AH1068//31	—	—	380	450	550	700

Katak

KM# 260.22 MOHUR

Gold **Obv:** Inscription within square, with knots at corners; Kalima, AH date **Rev:** Inscription within square, with knots at corners **Rev. Inscription:** "Shah Jahan Bad Shah Ghazi" **Note:** Weight varies: 10.80-11.00 grams.

Date	Mintage	Good	VG	F	VF	XF
AH1054//1x	—	360	425	550	750	1,000

Khambayat

KM# 260.10 MOHUR

Gold **Obv:** Inscription within square, with knots at corners; Kalima, AH date **Rev:** Inscription within square, with knots at corners; "Shah Jahan Badshah Ghazi" **Rev. Inscription:** "Shah Jahan Bad Shah Ghazi" **Note:** Weight varies: 10.80-11.00 grams.

Date	Mintage	Good	VG	F	VF	XF
AH1060//24	—	—	380	450	550	700
AH1064//27	—	—	380	450	550	700
AH1067//30	—	—	380	450	550	700

Lahore

KM# 260.11 MOHUR

Gold **Obv:** Inscription within square, with knots at corners; Kalima, AH date **Rev:** Inscription within square, with knots at corners **Rev. Inscription:** "Shah Jahan Bad Shah Ghazi" **Note:** Weight varies: 10.80-11.00 grams.

Date	Mintage	Good	VG	F	VF	XF
AH1046//9	—	—	365	425	525	650
AH1047//10	—	—	365	425	525	650
AH1048//12	—	—	365	425	525	650
AH1052//16	—	—	365	425	525	650
AH1053//17	—	—	365	425	525	650
AH1057//21	—	—	365	425	525	650
AH1058//22	—	—	365	425	525	650
AH1062//25	—	—	365	425	525	650
AH1062//26	—	—	365	425	525	650

Lakhnau

KM# 260.12 MOHUR

Gold **Obv:** Inscription within square, with knots at corners; Kalima, AH date **Rev:** Inscription within square, with knots at corners; "Shah Jahan Badshah Ghazi" **Note:** Struck at Lakhnau. Weight varies: 10.80-11.00 grams.

Date	Mintage	Good	VG	F	VF	XF
AH1051//15	—	—	380	450	550	700

Multan

KM# 260.13 MOHUR

Gold **Obv:** Inscription within square, with knots at corners; Kalima, AH date **Rev:** Inscription within square, with knots at corners **Rev. Inscription:** "Shah Jahan Bad Shah Ghazi" **Note:** Weight varies: 10.80-11.00 grams.

Date	Mintage	Good	VG	F	VF	XF
AH1043//6	—	—	365	425	525	650
AH1044//7	—	—	365	425	525	650
AH1059//22	—	—	365	425	525	650
AH1064//28	—	—	365	425	525	650
AH1066//29	—	—	365	425	525	650
AH1066//30	—	—	365	425	525	650
AH1068//31	—	—	365	425	525	650
AH1068//32	—	—	365	425	525	650
AH1069//33	—	—	365	425	525	650

Patna

KM# 260.14 MOHUR

Gold **Obv:** Inscription within square, with knots at corners; Kalima, AH date **Rev:** Inscription within square, with knots at corners **Rev. Inscription:** "Shah Jahan Bad Shah Ghazi" **Note:** Weight varies: 10.80-11.00 grams.

Date	Mintage	Good	VG	F	VF	XF
AH1042//6	—	—	365	425	525	650
AH1045//8	—	—	365	425	525	650
AH1047//11	—	—	365	425	525	650
AH10xx//13	—	—	365	425	525	650
AH105x//15	—	—	365	425	525	650
AH105x//16	—	—	365	425	525	650
AH105x//17	—	—	365	425	525	650
AH105x//21	—	—	365	425	525	650
AH106x//25	—	—	365	425	525	650

Pattan Deo

KM# 260.19 MOHUR

Gold **Obv:** Inscription within square, with knots at corners; Kalima, AH date **Rev:** Inscription within square, with knots at corners **Rev. Inscription:** "Shah Jahan Bad Shah Ghazi" **Note:** Weight varies: 10.80-11.00 grams.

Date	Mintage	Good	VG	F	VF	XF
AH1047//1x	—	365	425	550	750	1,100

Qandahar

KM# 260.18 MOHUR

Gold **Obv:** Inscription within square, with knots at corners; Kalima, AH date **Rev:** Inscription within square, with knots at corners **Rev. Inscription:** "Shah Jahan Bad Shah Ghazi" **Note:** Weight varies: 10.80-11.00 grams.

Date	Mintage	Good	VG	F	VF	XF
AH105x//18	—	—	380	450	550	700

Surat

KM# 260.15 MOHUR

Gold **Obv:** Inscription within square, with knots at corners; Kalima, AH date **Rev:** Inscription within square, with knots at corners **Rev. Inscription:** "Shah Jahan Bad Shah Ghazi" **Note:** Weight varies: 10.80-11.00 grams.

Date	Mintage	Good	VG	F	VF	XF
AH1043//6	—	—	365	425	525	650
AH1045//8	—	—	365	425	525	650
AH1045//9	—	—	365	425	525	650
AH1046//9	—	—	365	425	525	650
AH1047//11	—	—	365	425	525	650

Date	Mintage	Good	VG	F	VF	XF
AH1048//11	—	—	365	425	525	650
AH1069//32	—	—	365	425	525	650

Ujjain

KM# 260.20 MOHUR

Gold **Obv:** Inscription within square, with knots at corners; Kalima, AH date **Rev:** Inscription within square, with knots at corners **Rev. Inscription:** "Shah Jahan Bad Shah Ghazi" **Note:** Weight varies: 10.80-11.00 grams.

Date	Mintage	Good	VG	F	VF	XF
AH106x//25	—	—	380	450	550	700

Delhi

KM# 261.2 MOHUR

Gold **Obv:** Inscription, Kalima in circle, date **Rev:** Ruler's name and titles, mint name **Note:** Weight varies: 10.80-11.00 grams.

Date	Mintage	Good	VG	F	VF	XF
AH1047//1x	—	—	380	450	550	700
AH1054//17	—	—	380	450	550	700

Shahjahanabad

KM# 262.1 MOHUR

Gold **Obv:** Within dotted borders; Kalima within circle, AH date **Rev:** Within dotted borders; inscription within circle **Rev. Inscription:** "Shah Jahan Bad Shah Ghazi" **Note:** Weight varies: 10.80-11.00 grams.

Date	Mintage	Good	VG	F	VF	XF
AH10xx//25	—	350	400	475	575	750
AH106x//26	—	350	400	475	575	750
AH1065//29	—	350	400	475	575	750
AH1066//xx	—	350	400	475	575	750
AH1067//30	—	350	400	475	575	750

Surat

KM# 262.2 MOHUR

Gold **Obv:** Within dotted borders; Kalima within circle, AH date **Rev:** Within dotted borders; inscription within circle **Rev. Inscription:** "Shah Jahan Bad Shah Ghazi" **Note:** Weight varies: 10.80-11.00 grams.

Date	Mintage	Good	VG	F	VF	XF
AH1068//31	—	350	400	475	575	750

KM# 264.2 MOHUR

Gold **Obv:** Kalima within square **Rev:** Inscription within square, AH date **Rev. Inscription:** "Shah Jahan Bad Shah Ghazi" **Note:** Weight varies: 10.80-11.00 grams. Square.

Date	Mintage	Good	VG	F	VF	XF
AH104x//6 Rare	—	—	—	—	—	—

Akbarabad

KM# 264.1 MOHUR

Gold **Obv:** inscription, Kalima within square **Rev:** Inscription within square, AH date **Rev. Inscription:** "Shah Jahan Bad Shah Ghazi" **Note:** Weight varies: 10.80-11.00 grams. Square.

Date	Mintage	Good	VG	F	VF	XF
AH1057//21	—	350	400	475	575	750

Gulkanda

KM# 263.1 MOHUR

Gold **Note:** Weight varies: 10.80-11.00 grams. Crude calligraphy.

Date	Mintage	Good	VG	F	VF	XF
ND	—	—	380	450	550	700

Akbarabad

KM# A264.1 MOHUR

Gold **Obv:** Inscription with names of four caliphs above Kalima **Rev:** Ruler's name, mint name **Note:** Weight varies 10.8 - 11 grams; similar to Rupee, KM#226.1.

Date	Mintage	Good	VG	F	VF	XF
AH1039//2	—	—	—	—	—	—

Akbarabad

KM# B264.2 MOHUR

Gold **Obv:** Inscription in wavy pentagon **Obv. Inscription:** "Kalima" **Rev:** Ruler's titles in oblong outline **Note:** Weight varies 10.8 - 11 grams.

Date	Mintage	Good	VG	F	VF	XF
AH1040//4	—	—	—	—	—	—

Akbarabad

KM# 265 MOHUR

Gold **Obv:** Kalima within quatrefoil **Rev:** "Shah Jahan Badshah Ghazi" within quatrefoil, AH date **Shape:** Square **Note:** Weight varies: 10.80-11.00 grams.

Date	Mintage	Good	VG	F	VF	XF
AH1057//21	—	—	—	—	—	—

KM# 266.1 HEAVY MOHUR

Gold **Obv:** Inscription within square with knots at corners **Rev:** Inscription within square with knots at corners **Shape:** Square **Note:** Weight varies: 12.00-12.20 grams.

Date	Mintage	Good	VG	F	VF	XF
ND	—	375	475	650	850	1,200

Shahjahanabad

KM# 268.1 NAZARANA 200 MOHURS

2177.0000 g., Gold, 102 mm.

Date	Mintage	Good	VG	F	VF	XF
AH1064//28 Unique	—	—	—	—	—	—

Lahore

KM# A268.1 NAZARANA 100 MOHURS

1094.5000 g., Gold **Rev. Inscription:** Dar-us-Sultana. **Note:** Illustration reduced, actual size 94mm.

Date	Mintage	Good	VG	F	VF	XF
AH1048//12 Unique	—	—	—	—	—	—

LARGESSE COINAGE

Lahore

KM# 237.1 NISAR

2.8500 g., Silver

Date	Mintage	Good	VG	F	VF	XF
AH1037	—	60.00	150	175	225	300

Lahore

KM# 238.1 NISAR

5.7000 g., Silver **Obv. Inscription:** "Z nam Shah Jahan Bad Shah" **Rev. Inscription:** "Sahib-i-qiran sani" **Note:** 1/2 Rupee weight.

Date	Mintage	Good	VG	F	VF	XF
AH1037//(1) Ahad	—	60.00	150	175	225	300
AH1039//3	—	60.00	150	175	225	300

Ahmadabad

KM# A239.1 NISAR

0.7000 g., Silver **Obv. Inscription:** "Nizar Shah Jahan"

Date	Mintage	Good	VG	F	VF	XF
1063//27	—	—	—	—	—	—

Akbarabad

KM# A239.2 NISAR

Silver **Obv:** Inscription **Rev:** Inscription **Note:** Weight varies .6 - .7 grams.

Date	Mintage	Good	VG	F	VF	XF
AH1039//2 Rare	—	—	—	—	—	—

Burhanpur

KM# A239.3 NISAR

Silver **Obv. Inscription:** "Shah Jahan Bad Shah" **Note:** Weight varies .6 - .7 grams

Date	Mintage	VG	F	VF	XF	Unc
AH1040	—	—	—	—	—	—

Shahjahanabad

KM# B239.1 NISAR

1.4000 g., Silver **Obv. Inscription:** "Shah Jahan Bad Shah Ghazi" **Note:** Square.

Date	Mintage	Good	VG	F	VF	XF
AH1059//23	—	—	—	—	—	—

Agra

KM# 239.2 NISAR

1.4000 g., Silver **Obv. Inscription:** "Shah Jahan Bad Shah Ghazi"

Date	Mintage	Good	VG	F	VF	XF
AHxxxx	—	—	—	—	—	—

Ahmadabad

KM# 239.3 NISAR

Silver **Obv. Inscription:** "Nisar Shah Jahan Bad Shah" **Note:** Weight varies 1.2 - 1.4 grams.

Date	Mintage	Good	VG	F	VF	XF
AH1052//15	—	—	—	—	—	—
AH1062	—	—	—	—	—	—
AH1063//27	—	—	—	—	—	—

Akbarabad

KM# 239.4 NISAR

Silver **Obv. Inscription:** "Nisar Shah Jahan Bad Shah Ghazi" **Note:** Weight varies 1.1 - 1.3 grams.

Date	Mintage	Good	VG	F	VF	XF
AH1043//6	—	—	—	—	—	—
AH1049//13	—	—	—	—	—	—
AH1052//16	—	—	—	—	—	—

Akbarnagar

KM# 239.5 NISAR

1.4000 g., Silver **Obv. Inscription:** "Nisar Shah Jahani"

Date	Mintage	Good	VG	F	VF	XF
AH1056	—	—	—	—	—	—

Allahabad

KM# 239.6 NISAR

1.4000 g., Silver **Obv. Inscription:** "Shah Jahan Bad Shah Ghazi"

Date	Mintage	Good	VG	F	VF	XF
AH1045//8	—	—	—	—	—	—

Bhilsa

KM# 239.7 NISAR

1.5000 g., Silver **Obv. Inscription:** "(Shah Jahan) Bad Shah Ghazi"

Date	Mintage	Good	VG	F	VF	XF
AHxxxx	—	—	—	—	—	—

Burhanpur

KM# 239.8 NISAR

1.5000 g., Silver **Obv. Inscription:** "Nisar Shah Jahan Bad Shah Ghazi"

Date	Mintage	Good	VG	F	VF	XF
AH1040//3	—	—	—	—	—	—

Daulatabad

KM# 239.9 NISAR

1.4000 g., Silver **Obv. Inscription:** "Nisar Shah Jahan Bad Shah Ghazi"

Date	Mintage	Good	VG	F	VF	XF
AH1045	—	—	—	—	—	—
AH1047	—	—	—	—	—	—

Ujjain

KM# 239.1 NISAR

1.3000 g., Silver **Obv:** Inscription **Rev:** Inscription **Note:** 1/8 Rupee weight.

Date	Mintage	Good	VG	F	VF	XF
ND Rare	—	—	—	—	—	—

Agra

KM# 240.1 NISAR

Silver **Obv. Inscription:** "Nisar Shah Jahan Bad Shah Ghazi" **Note:** 1/4 Rupee weight varies 2.65 - 2.9 grams; Mint epithet: "Dar-ul-Khilafat". For later issues see Akbarabad.

Date	Mintage	Good	VG	F	VF	XF
AH1037//(1) Ahad	—	—	110	185	250	360
AH1038//(1) Ahad	—	—	110	185	250	360
AH1038//2	—	—	110	185	250	360

Ahmadabad

KM# 240.6 NISAR

2.8000 g., Silver **Obv. Inscription:** "Nisar Shah Jahan" **Note:** 1/4 Rupee weight.

Date	Mintage	Good	VG	F	VF	XF
AH1054//1x	—	35.00	85.00	125	190	275
AH1069//33	—	35.00	85.00	125	190	275

Akbarabad

KM# 240.2 NISAR

Silver **Obv. Inscription:** "Nisar Shah Jahan Bad Shah Ghazi" **Rev. Inscription:** "dar al-khilafa" **Note:** 1/4 Rupee weight. Weight varies: 2.65-2.90 grams. Mint epithet: "Dar-ul-Khilafat".

Date	Mintage	Good	VG	F	VF	XF
AH1039//2	—	45.00	110	175	250	360
AH1041//5	—	45.00	110	175	250	360
AH1042//5	—	45.00	110	175	250	360
AH1042//6	—	45.00	110	175	250	360
AH1043//6	—	45.00	110	175	250	360
AH1043//7	—	45.00	110	175	250	360
AH1044//7	—	45.00	110	175	250	360
AH1044//8	—	45.00	110	175	250	360
AH1045//8	—	45.00	110	175	250	360
AH1045//9	—	45.00	110	175	250	360
AH1046//9	—	45.00	110	175	250	360
AH1046//10	—	45.00	110	175	250	360
AH1047//10	—	45.00	110	175	250	360
AH1047//11	—	45.00	110	175	250	360
AH1048//11	—	45.00	110	175	250	360
AH1052//16	—	45.00	110	175	250	360
AH1054//17	—	45.00	110	175	250	360
AH1054//18	—	45.00	110	175	250	360
AH1056//20	—	45.00	110	175	250	360
AH1060//24	—	45.00	110	175	250	360
AH1064//28	—	45.00	110	175	250	360

KM# 240.7 NISAR

2.8000 g., Silver **Obv. Inscription:** "Shah Jahan Bad Shah Ghazi"

Date	Mintage	Good	VG	F	VF	XF
AH1049//13	—	—	—	—	—	—

Akbarnagar

KM# 240.8 NISAR

2.8000 g., Silver **Obv. Inscription:** "Nisar Shah Jahani"

Date	Mintage	Good	VG	F	VF	XF
AH1056//20	—	—	—	—	—	—
AH1061//25	—	—	—	—	—	—

Burhanpur

KM# 240.9 NISAR

Silver **Obv. Inscription:** "Nisar Shah Jahan Bad Shah Ghazi" **Note:** Weight varies 2.6 - 2.9 grams.

Date	Mintage	Good	VG	F	VF	XF
AH1040//3	—	—	—	—	—	—
AH1041//5	—	—	—	—	—	—

Daulatabad

KM# 240.10 NISAR

2.7000 g., Silver **Obv. Inscription:** "Nisar Shah Jahan Bad Shah Ghazi"

Date	Mintage	Good	VG	F	VF	XF
AH1045//9	—	—	—	—	—	—

Jahangirnagar

KM# 240.11 NISAR

2.8000 g., Silver **Obv. Inscription:** "Nisar Shah Jahani"

Date	Mintage	Good	VG	F	VF	XF
AHxxxx//22	—	—	—	—	—	—

Kabul

KM# 240.12 NISAR

2.8000 g., Silver **Obv. Inscription:** "Nisar Shah Jahan Bad Shah Ghazi"

Date	Mintage	Good	VG	F	VF	XF
AH1059 (?)	—	—	—	—	—	—

Kashmir

KM# 240.3 NISAR

Silver **Obv. Inscription:** "Nisar Shah Jahan Bad Shah Ghazi" **Note:** 1/4 Rupee weight. Weight varies: 2.65-2.90 grams.

Date	Mintage	Good	VG	F	VF	XF
AHxxxx//13 Rare	—	—	—	—	—	—

Lahore

KM# 240.5 NISAR

Silver **Obv. Legend:** "Nisar Shah Jahan Bad Shah Ghazi" **Note:** 1/4 Rupee weight. Weight varies: 2.65-2.90 grams. Without epithet.

Date	Mintage	Good	VG	F	VF	XF
AH1044//7	—	35.00	85.00	125	190	275

KM# 240.13 NISAR

Silver **Obv. Inscription:** "Nisar Shah Jahan Bad Shah Ghazi" **Rev. Inscription:** "dar al-Zarb" **Note:** Weight varies 2.1 - 2.9 grams.

Date	Mintage	Good	VG	F	VF	XF
AH1047//11	—	—	—	—	—	—

KM# 240.4 NISAR

Silver **Obv. Inscription:** "Shah Jahan" **Rev. Inscription:** "Dar-al-Sultana" **Note:** 1/4 Rupee weight. Weight varies: 2.65-2.90 grams.

Date	Mintage	Good	VG	F	VF	XF
AH1048//12	—	35.00	85.00	125	190	275
AH1049//12	—	35.00	85.00	125	190	275
AH1049//13	—	35.00	85.00	125	190	275
AH1050//13	—	35.00	85.00	125	190	275
AH1050//14	—	35.00	85.00	125	190	275
AH1051//14	—	35.00	85.00	125	190	275
AH1051//15	—	35.00	85.00	125	190	275
AH1052//15	—	35.00	85.00	125	190	275
AH1053//17	—	35.00	85.00	125	190	275
AH106x//30	—	35.00	85.00	125	190	275
AH1068//32	—	35.00	85.00	125	190	275

Urdu Zafar Qarin

KM# 240.14 NISAR

Silver **Note:** Weight varies 2.1 - 2.9 grams.

Date	Mintage	Good	VG	F	VF	XF
ND	—	—	—	—	—	—

Kashmir

KM# 241.1 NISAR

Silver **Obv. Legend:** SHAH JAHAN **Note:** Weight varies: 5.60-5.80 g (1/2 Rupee weight).

Date	Mintage	VG	F	VF	XF	Unc
AH1048//13	—	110	185	250	360	—

Shahjahanabad

KM# 242.1 NISAR

Silver **Obv. Legend:** "Nisar Sahib Qiran Sani Shah Jahan Bad Shah Ghazi" **Note:** 1/2 Rupee weight. Weight varies: 5.60-5.80 grams. Mint epithet: Dar-ul-Khilafat".

Date	Mintage	Good	VG	F	VF	XF
AH1060//24	—	35.00	85.00	125	190	275
AH1063//26	—	35.00	85.00	125	190	275

Akbarabad

KM# 243.1 NISAR

Silver **Obv. Legend:** "Sahib Qiran" **Note:** 1/16 Rupee weight. Weight varies: 0.55-0.75 grams.

Date	Mintage	Good	VG	F	VF	XF
AH1047//11 Rare	—	—	—	—	—	—

Akbarabad

KM# 244.3 NISAR

1.1000 g., Silver **Obv. Legend:** "Nisar Sahib Qiran Sani" **Note:** 1/8 Rupee weight.

Date	Mintage	Good	VG	F	VF	XF
AH1064//2x Rare	—	—	—	—	—	—
AH106x//29 Rare	—	—	—	—	—	—

Akbarnagar

KM# 244.4 NISAR

Silver **Obv. Inscription:** "Sahib Qiran Sani" **Note:** Weight varies 1.1 - 1.4 grams.

Date	Mintage	Good	VG	F	VF	XF
AH1055//19	—	—	—	—	—	—

KM# 244.1 NISAR

Silver **Obv. Inscription:** "Nisar Sahib Qiran Sani" **Note:** 1/8 Rupee weight. Weight varies: 1.30-1.45 grams.

Date	Mintage	Good	VG	F	VF	XF
AH1064//28 Rare	—	—	—	—	—	—
AH1068//32 Rare	—	—	—	—	—	—

Shahjahanabad

KM# 244.2 NISAR

Silver **Obv. Inscription:** "Nisar Sahib Qiran Sani" **Rev. Inscription:** "dar al-khilafa" **Note:** 1/8 Rupee weight. Weight varies: 1.30-1.45 grams.

Date	Mintage	Good	VG	F	VF	XF
AH1067//3x Rare	—	—	—	—	—	—
AH106x//32 (sic) Rare	—	—	—	—	—	—

Akbarabad

KM# A246.1 NISAR

Silver **Note:** Weight varies 2.55 - 2.9 grams; without epithet.

Date	Mintage	Good	VG	F	VF	XF
AH1047//11	—	—	—	—	—	—

Akbarabad

KM# 246.7 NISAR

2.8000 g., Silver **Obv. Inscription:** "Sahib Qiran Sani"

Date	Mintage	Good	VG	F	VF	XF
AH1047//10	—	—	—	—	—	—

KM# 246.1 NISAR

Silver **Obv. Inscription:** "Nisar Sahib Qiran sani" **Rev. Inscription:** "dar al-khilafa" **Note:** Weight varies: 2.55-2.90 grams. 1/4 Rupee weight. For earlier issues see Agra.

Date	Mintage	Good	VG	F	VF	XF
AH1048//11	—	45.00	110	185	300	425
AH1053//17	—	45.00	110	185	300	425
AH1054//17	—	45.00	110	185	300	425
AH1058//21	—	45.00	110	185	300	425
AH1060//23	—	45.00	110	185	300	425
AH1060//24	—	45.00	110	185	300	425
AH1064//28	—	45.00	110	185	300	425
AH1068//31	—	45.00	110	185	300	425
AH1069//33	—	45.00	110	185	300	425

Akbarnagar

KM# 246.2 NISAR

Silver **Obv. Inscription:** "Nisar Sahib Qiran Sani" **Note:** Weight varies: 2.55-2.90 grams. 1/4 Rupee weight.

Date	Mintage	Good	VG	F	VF	XF
AH1065//29	—	55.00	140	225	335	475
AH1066//29	—	55.00	140	225	335	475
AH1068//32	—	55.00	140	225	335	475

Kabul

KM# 246.3 NISAR

Silver **Obv. Inscription:** "Sahib Qiran" **Note:** Weight varies: 2.55-2.90 grams. 1/4 Rupee weight.

Date	Mintage	Good	VG	F	VF	XF
AH1049//9 (sic) Rare	—	—	—	—	—	—
AH1049//12 Rare	—	—	—	—	—	—

Kashmir

KM# 246.4 NISAR

Silver **Obv. Inscription:** "Nisar Sahib Qiran Sani" **Note:** Weight varies: 2.55-2.90 grams. 1/4 Rupee weight.

Date	Mintage	Good	VG	F	VF	XF
AH1050//13 Rare	—	—	—	—	—	—
AH1061//25 Rare	—	—	—	—	—	—
AH1064//27 Rare	—	—	—	—	—	—

Lahore

KM# 246.5 NISAR

Silver **Obv. Inscription:** "Nisar Sahib Qiran Sani" **Rev. Inscription:** "dar al-Saltana" **Note:** Weight varies: 2.55-2.90 grams. 1/4 Rupee weight.

Date	Mintage	Good	VG	F	VF	XF
AH1052//15	—	55.00	140	225	335	475
AH1055//18	—	55.00	140	225	335	475
AH105x//19	—	55.00	140	225	335	475
AH1056//20	—	55.00	140	225	335	475
AH1057//20	—	55.00	140	225	335	475
AH1058//2x	—	55.00	140	225	335	475
AH1061//24	—	55.00	140	225	335	475
AH1062//2x	—	55.00	140	225	335	475
AH1062//26	—	55.00	140	225	335	475
AH1063//26	—	55.00	140	225	335	475

Shahjahanabad

KM# 246.6 NISAR

Silver **Obv. Inscription:** "Nisar Sahib Qiran Sani" **Note:** Weight varies: 2.55-2.90 grams. 1/4 Rupee weight. For earlier issues see Dehli.

Date	Mintage	Good	VG	F	VF	XF
AH1060//24	—	55.00	110	185	300	425
AH1061//24	—	55.00	110	185	300	425
AH1061//25	—	55.00	110	185	300	425
AH1062//25	—	55.00	110	185	300	425
AH1062//26	—	55.00	110	185	300	425
AH1063//26	—	55.00	110	185	300	425
AH1063//27	—	55.00	110	185	300	425
AH1066//29	—	55.00	110	185	300	425
AH1066//30	—	55.00	110	185	300	425
AH1067//30	—	55.00	110	185	300	425
AH1067//31	—	55.00	110	185	300	425

Akbarabad

KM# 247.3 NISAR

Silver **Obv. Inscription:** "Jalus Nisar Sahib Qiran Sani" **Rev. Inscription:** "dar al-khilafa" **Note:** Weight varies: 5.50-5.80 grams. 1/2 Rupee weight.

Date	Mintage	Good	VG	F	VF	XF
AH1046//10	—	52.50	130	210	300	420
AH1046//9	—	52.50	130	210	300	420
AH1054//(18)	—	52.50	130	210	300	420

KM# 247.4 NISAR

5.5000 g., Silver **Obv. Inscription:** "Sahib Qiran Sani Shah Jahan Bad Shah Ghazi" **Rev. Inscription:** "dar al-Khilafa"

Date	Mintage	Good	VG	F	VF	XF
AH1047	—	—	—	—	—	—

KM# 247.5 NISAR

5.3000 g., Silver **Obv. Inscription:** "Nisar Shah Qiran Sani Shah Jahan Bad Shah Ghazi" **Rev. Inscription:** "dar al-Khilafa"

Date	Mintage	Good	VG	F	VF	XF
AH1054//18	—	—	—	—	—	—

KM# 247.6 NISAR

Silver **Obv. Inscription:** "Nisar Sahib Qiran Sani" **Rev. Inscription:** "dar al-Khilafa" **Note:** Weight varies 5.4 - 5.7 grams.

Date	Mintage	Good	VG	F	VF	XF
AH1069//33 (sic)	—	—	—	—	—	—

Daulatabad

KM# 247.7 NISAR

5.6000 g., Silver **Obv. Inscription:** "Nisar Sahib Qiran Sani"

Date	Mintage	Good	VG	F	VF	XF
AH1045//8	—	—	—	—	—	—

Lahore

KM# 247.1 NISAR

Silver **Obv. Inscription:** "Sahib Qiran Sani" **Note:** Weight varies: 5.50-5.80 grams. 1/2 Rupee weight. Mint epithet: "Dar-us-Sultanat".

Date	Mintage	Good	VG	F	VF	XF
AH1048//13	—	52.50	130	210	300	420
AH1051//15	—	52.50	130	210	300	420
AH1055//19	—	52.50	130	210	300	420

Shahjahanabad

KM# 247.2 NISAR

Silver **Obv. Inscription:** "Nisar Sahib Qiran Sani" **Rev. Inscription:** "dar al-khilafa" **Note:** Weight varies: 5.50-5.80 grams. 1/2 Rupee weight. For earlier issues see Dehli.

Date	Mintage	Good	VG	F	VF	XF
AH1047//11	—	55.00	135	225	330	450
AH1066//29	—	55.00	135	225	330	450

Akbarabad

KM# 248.1 NISAR

Gold **Obv. Legend:** "Sahib Qiran" **Note:** Previous KM#A267.1; Weight varies: 2.50-2.85 grams.

Date	Mintage	Good	VG	F	VF	XF
AH1068//31	—	—	—	—	—	—

Shahjahanabad

KM# 248.2 NISAR

Gold **Obv. Legend:** "Sahib Qiran" **Note:** Previous KM#A267.2; Weight varies: 2.50-2.85 grams.

Date	Mintage	Good	VG	F	VF	XF
AH1069//3x	—	—	—	—	—	—

Agra

KM# A249.1 NISAR

Gold **Obv. Legend:** "Shah Jahan" **Note:** Previous KM#267.1; Weight varies: 2.50-2.85 grams.

Date	Mintage	Good	VG	F	VF	XF
AH1037//1	—	—	—	—	—	—

Akbarabad

KM# A249.2 NISAR

Gold **Obv. Legend:** "Shah Jahan" **Note:** Previous KM#267.2; Weight varies: 2.50-2.85 grams.

Date	Mintage	Good	VG	F	VF	XF
AH1042//5	—	—	—	—	—	—
AH1047//1x	—	—	—	—	—	—
AH1048//11	—	—	—	—	—	—

Akbarabad

KM# 267.1 NISAR

Gold **Obv. Legend:** Shah Jahan **Note:** Weight varies 2.5-2.85 grams (1/4 Mohur weight).

Date	Mintage	Good	VG	F	VF	XF
AH1037//(1) Ahad Rare	—	—	—	—	—	—

KM# 267.2 NISAR

Gold **Obv. Legend:** Shah Jahan **Note:** Weight varies 2.5-2.85 grams (1/4 Mohur weight).

Date	Mintage	Good	VG	F	VF	XF
AH1042//5 Rare	—	—	—	—	—	—
AH1047//11 Rare	—	—	—	—	—	—
AH1048//11 Rare	—	—	—	—	—	—

Akbarabad

KM# A267.1 NISAR

Gold **Obv. Legend:** Sahib Qiran **Note:** Weight varies 2.5-2.85 grams (1/4 Mohur weight).

Date	Mintage	Good	VG	F	VF	XF
AH1068//31 Rare	—	—	—	—	—	—

Shahjahanabad

KM# A267.2 NISAR

Gold **Obv. Legend:** Sahib Qiran **Note:** Weight varies 2.5-2.85 grams (1/4 Mohur weight).

Date	Mintage	Good	VG	F	VF	XF
AH1069 Rare	—	—	—	—	—	—

Shah Shuja, in Bengal

AH1068-1070 / 1657-1660AD

HAMMERED COINAGE

Akbarnagar

KM# A274.1 1/2 RUPEE

5.7220 g., Silver **Note:** Similar to Rupee, KM#275.1.

Date	Mintage	Good	VG	F	VF	XF
AHxxxx//(1) Ahad	—	—	—	—	—	—

Akbarnagar

KM# 274.1 1/2 RUPEE

5.7220 g., Silver **Note:** Similar to Rupee, KM#276.1.

Date	Mintage	Good	VG	F	VF	XF
AH1068//(1) Ahad	—	—	—	—	—	—

Akbarnagar

KM# 275.1 RUPEE

11.4440 g., Silver **Obv:** Inscription in outlined square **Obv. Inscription:** "Kalima" **Rev:** Ruler's name and titles in 4-line inscription

Date	Mintage	Good	VG	F	VF	XF
AH1068//(1) Ahad	—	180	450	650	900	1,300

Patna

KM# 276.1 RUPEE

11.4440 g., Silver **Obv:** Inscription in outlined square **Obv. Inscription:** "Kalima" **Rev:** Inscription with ruler's name in lower part of outlined square

Date	Mintage	Good	VG	F	VF	XF
AH1068//(1) Ahad	—	160	400	500	750	1,000

Akbarnagar

KM# 277.1 RUPEE

11.4440 g., Silver **Obv:** Inscription in outlined square **Obv. Inscription:** "Kalima" **Rev:** Inscription with ruler's name in upper part of Outlined square

Date	Mintage	Good	VG	F	VF	XF
AH1068//(1) Ahad Unique	—	—	—	—	—	—

Katak

KM# 277.2 RUPEE

11.4440 g., Silver

Date	Mintage	Good	VG	F	VF	XF
AH1068//(1) Ahad	—	—	—	—	—	—

Akbarnagar

KM# A278.1 1/4 RUPEE

2.7000 g., Silver **Note:** Similar to Nisar, KM#278.1.

Date	Mintage	Good	VG	F	VF	XF
AH1068//(1) Ahad	—	—	—	—	—	—

LARGESSE COINAGE

Akbarnagar

KM# 278 NISAR

5.7200 g., Silver

Date	Mintage	Good	VG	F	VF	XF
AH1068//(1)	—	—	600	800	1,000	1,350

KM# 278.1 NISAR

5.7200 g., Silver **Note:** Type 278.

Date	Mintage	Good	VG	F	VF	XF
AH1068	—	—	600	800	1,000	1,200

Muhammad Murad Bakhsh

In Gujarat; AH 1068 / 1658AD

HAMMERED COINAGE

Surat

KM# A269.1 1/2 DAM

Copper **Note:** Weight varies 10.2 - 10.8 grams.

Date	Mintage	Good	VG	F	VF	XF
AH(1068)//(1) Ahad	—	—	—	—	—	—

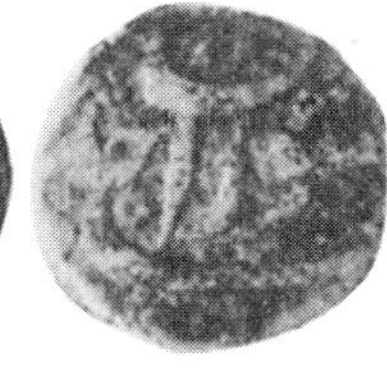

Surat

KM# 269.1 DAM

Copper **Note:** Weight varies: 20.40-21.60 grams.

Date	Mintage	Good	VG	F	VF	XF
AH(1068)//(1) Ahad Rare	—	—	—	—	—	—

Ahmadabad

KM# A270.1 1/4 RUPEE

2.8610 g., Silver **Obv:** Central inscription within square **Rev:** Central inscription within square

Date	Mintage	Good	VG	F	VF	XF
AH1068//(1) Ahad Rare	—	—	—	—	—	—

Surat

KM# A270.2 1/4 RUPEE

2.8610 g., Silver **Obv:** Central inscription within square **Rev:** Central inscription within square

Date	Mintage	Good	VG	F	VF	XF
AH1068//(1) Ahad Rare	—	—	—	—	—	—

Ahmadabad

KM# 270.1 1/2 RUPEE

5.7220 g., Silver **Obv:** Central inscription within square **Rev:** Central inscription within square

Date	Mintage	Good	VG	F	VF	XF
AH1068//(1) Ahad Rare	—	—	—	—	—	—

Khambayat
KM# 270.3 1/2 RUPEE

5.7220 g., Silver **Obv:** Central inscription within square **Rev:** Central inscription within square

Date	Mintage	Good	VG	F	VF	XF
AHxxxx	—	—	—	—	—	—

Surat
KM# 270.2 1/2 RUPEE

5.7220 g., Silver **Obv:** Central inscription within square **Rev:** Central inscription within square

Date	Mintage	Good	VG	F	VF	XF
AH1068//(1) Ahad Rare	—	—	—	—	—	—

Surat
KM# A271.1 1/2 RUPEE

5.7220 g., Silver **Note:** Similar to Rupee, KM#271.1.

Date	Mintage	Good	VG	F	VF	XF
AHxxxx//(1)	—	—	—	—	—	—

Surat
KM# 271.1 RUPEE

11.4440 g., Silver

Date	Mintage	Good	VG	F	VF	XF
AH1068//(1) Ahad Rare	—	—	—	—	—	—

Khambayat
KM# A272.2 RUPEE

11.4440 g., Silver **Obv:** Central inscription within squares; ruler's name excludes "Muhammad" **Rev:** Central inscription within squares **Note:** Previous KM#272.2; Varieties exist.

Date	Mintage	Good	VG	F	VF	XF
AH1068//(1) Ahad	—	20.00	50.00	65.00	80.00	120

Ahmadabad
KM# 272.1 RUPEE

11.4440 g., Silver **Obv:** Central inscription within squares, ruler's name includes "Muhammad" **Rev:** Central inscription within squares

Date	Mintage	Good	VG	F	VF	XF
AH1068//(1) Ahad	—	16.00	40.00	50.00	70.00	90.00

Surat
KM# 272.3 RUPEE

11.4440 g., Silver **Obv:** Central inscription within squares **Rev:** Central inscription within squares

Date	Mintage	Good	VG	F	VF	XF
AH1068//(1) Ahad	—	16.00	40.00	50.00	70.00	90.00

Ahmadabad
KM# 273.1 MOHUR

Gold **Note:** Weight varies 10.8 - 11 grams.

Date	Mintage	Good	VG	F	VF	XF
AH1068//(1) Ahad	—	—	1,200	2,000	3,250	5,000

Khambayat
KM# 273.2 MOHUR

Gold **Note:** Weight varies 10.8 - 11 grams.

Date	Mintage	Good	VG	F	VF	XF
AH1068//(1) Ahad	—	—	1,200	2,000	3,250	5,000

Muhayyi-ud-din Aurangzeb Alamgir
AH1068-1118 / 1658-1707AD
HAMMERED COINAGE

Surat
KM# 273.3 MOHUR

Gold Weight varies: 10.8-11.0 grams. **Obv:** Name and titles in square, mint in left segment **Rev:** Kalima in square, date

Date	Mintage	VG	F	VF	XF	Unc
AH1068/(1) Ahad	—	375	550	875	1,200	—

Lahore
KM# 280.1 1/8 PAISA

Copper **Note:** Type 280. Weight varies 1.90-2.20 grams.

Date	Mintage	Good	VG	F	VF	XF
AH1075	—	3.50	7.00	12.00	20.00	—

Narnol
KM# 280.2 1/8 PAISA

Copper **Note:** Weight varies 1.9 - 2.2 grams.

Date	Mintage	Good	VG	F	VF	XF
ND(1658-1707)	—	2.50	6.00	12.00	20.00	—

Haidarabad
KM# 281.3 1/4 PAISA

Copper **Note:** Weight varies 3.90-4.05 grams.

Date	Mintage	Good	VG	F	VF	XF
ND(1658-1707)	—	5.50	11.00	18.00	30.00	—

Multan
KM# 282.1 1/4 PAISA

Copper **Note:** Weight varies 3.90-4.05 grams.

Date	Mintage	Good	VG	F	VF	XF
AH1073//x	—	5.50	11.00	18.00	30.00	—

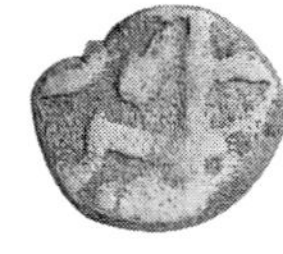

Surat
KM# 282.2 1/4 PAISA

Copper **Note:** Weight varies 3.90-4.05 grams.

Date	Mintage	Good	VG	F	VF	XF
ND(1658-1707)	—	5.50	11.00	18.00	30.00	—

Bijapur
KM# 283.7 1/2 PAISA

Copper **Note:** Weight varies 6.15-7.05 grams.

Date	Mintage	Good	VG	F	VF	XF
AHxxxx//x	—	—	—	—	—	—

Burhanpur
KM# 283.6 1/2 PAISA

Copper **Note:** Weight varies 6.15-7.05 grams.

Date	Mintage	Good	VG	F	VF	XF
AHxxxx//19 Rare	—	—	—	—	—	—
AHxxxx//21 Rare	—	—	—	—	—	—
AHXXXX//31 Rare	—	—	—	—	—	—
No date	—	18.00	40.00	60.00	100	—

Haidarabad (Farkhanda Bunyad)
KM# 283.1 1/2 PAISA

Copper **Note:** Weight varies 6.15-7.05 grams.

Date	Mintage	Good	VG	F	VF	XF
AH1xxx//32	—	4.00	8.50	14.00	20.00	—
AH1103//35	—	4.00	8.50	14.00	20.00	—
AH1106//38	—	4.00	8.50	14.00	20.00	—
AH1108//4x	—	4.00	8.50	14.00	20.00	—
AH1109//41	—	4.00	8.50	14.00	20.00	—
AH1112//45	—	4.00	8.50	14.00	20.00	—

Kabul
KM# 283.10 1/2 PAISA

Copper **Note:** Weight varies 6.15 - 7.05 grams.

Date	Mintage	Good	VG	F	VF	XF
AH1074	—	2.75	5.50	9.00	15.00	—

KM# 283.11 1/2 PAISA

Copper **Note:** Weight varies 6.15 - 7.05 grams.

Date	Mintage	Good	VG	F	VF	XF
AH1074	—	—	—	—	—	—

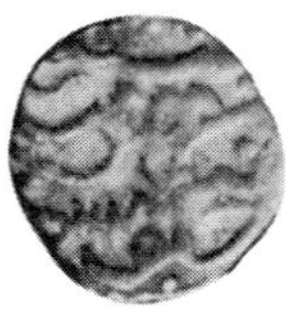
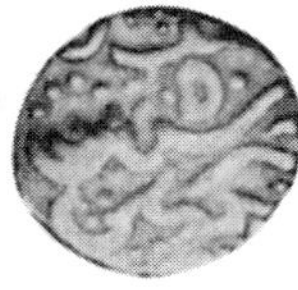

Macchlipattan
KM# 283.2 1/2 PAISA

Copper **Obv. Inscription:** "Mubarak julus sanah" **Rev. Inscription:** "Zarb bandar machhlipatan sanah" **Note:** Weight varies 6.15-7.05 grams.

Date	Mintage	Good	VG	F	VF	XF
AH1110//42	—	5.50	11.00	25.00	40.00	—
AH1111//43	—	6.00	12.00	30.00	50.00	—
AH1111//44	—	5.50	11.00	25.00	40.00	—
AH1112//45	—	6.00	12.00	30.00	50.00	—

Shahjahanabad
KM# 283.3 1/2 PAISA

Copper **Note:** Weight varies 6.15-7.05 grams.

Date	Mintage	Good	VG	F	VF	XF
AH1074//6	—	2.75	5.50	9.00	15.00	—

Sholapur
KM# 283.4 1/2 PAISA

Copper **Note:** Weight varies 6.15-7.05 grams.

Date	Mintage	Good	VG	F	VF	XF
ND(1658-1707)	—	2.75	5.50	12.00	20.00	—

Surat
KM# 283.8 1/2 PAISA

Copper **Note:** Weight varies 6.15 - 7.05 grams.

Date	Mintage	Good	VG	F	VF	XF
AH1093	—	2.75	5.50	9.00	15.00	—

Surat
KM# 284.1 1/2 DAM

Copper **Obv. Inscription:** "Julus sanah mubarak" **Note:** Weight varies 9.50-10.30 grams.

Date	Mintage	Good	VG	F	VF	XF
year 1	—	5.00	12.00	25.00	45.00	—
AH107x//3	—	5.00	12.00	25.00	45.00	—
AH1073//5	—	5.00	12.00	25.00	45.00	—
AH107x//7	—	5.00	12.00	25.00	45.00	—
AH177x//11	—	5.00	12.00	25.00	45.00	—
AH108x//13	—	5.00	12.00	25.00	45.00	—
AH1082//1x	—	5.00	12.00	25.00	45.00	—
AH1083//15	—	5.00	12.00	25.00	45.00	—
AH1086//1x	—	5.00	12.00	25.00	45.00	—
AH1088//2x	—	5.00	12.00	25.00	45.00	—

Ahmadabad

KM# 285.12 PAISA

Copper **Note:** Weight varies 12.30-14.10 grams.

Date	Mintage	Good	VG	F	VF	XF
AH1100//xx	—	5.50	11.00	18.00	30.00	—

Ahmadanagar

KM# 285.18 PAISA

Copper **Note:** Weight varies 12.3 - 14.1 grams.

Date	Mintage	Good	VG	F	VF	XF
AH109x//26	—	3.50	7.00	12.00	20.00	—

Akbarabad

KM# 285.1 PAISA

Copper **Note:** Weight varies 12.3 - 14.1 grams.

Date	Mintage	Good	VG	F	VF	XF
AH1074//7	—	3.50	7.00	12.00	20.00	—
AH1075//8	—	3.50	7.00	12.00	20.00	—

Azamnagar

KM# 285.19 PAISA

Copper **Note:** Weight varies 12.3 - 14.1 grams.

Date	Mintage	Good	VG	F	VF	XF
AH1099//32	—	5.50	7.00	12.00	20.00	—
AH110x//33	—	5.50	7.00	12.00	20.00	—

Azimabad

KM# 285.20 PAISA

Copper **Note:** Weight varies 12.3 - 14.1 grams.

Date	Mintage	Good	VG	F	VF	XF
AH1110//xx	—	3.50	7.00	12.00	20.00	—

Bairata

KM# 285.2 PAISA

Copper **Note:** Weight varies 12.3 - 14.1 grams.

Date	Mintage	Good	VG	F	VF	XF
ND(1658-1707)	—	3.50	7.00	12.00	20.00	—

Banaras

KM# 285.25 PAISA

Copper **Note:** Weight varies 12.30-14.10 grams.

Date	Mintage	Good	VG	F	VF	XF
ND(1658-1707)	—	—	—	—	—	—

Bijapur

KM# 285.21 PAISA

Copper **Note:** Weight varies 12.3 - 14.1 grams.

Date	Mintage	Good	VG	F	VF	XF
ND(1658-1707)	—	5.50	11.00	18.00	30.00	—

Burhanpur

KM# 285.22 PAISA

Copper **Note:** Weight varies 12.3 - 14.1 grams.

Date	Mintage	Good	VG	F	VF	XF
AH108x//21	—	5.50	11.00	18.00	30.00	—

Chinapattan

KM# 285.23 PAISA

Copper **Note:** Weight varies 12.3 - 14.1 grams.

Date	Mintage	Good	VG	F	VF	XF
ND(1658-1707)	—	5.50	11.00	20.00	35.00	—

Haidarabad (Farkhanda Bunyad)

KM# 285.3 PAISA

Copper **Note:** Weight varies 12.3 - 14.1 grams.

Date	Mintage	Good	VG	F	VF	XF
AH1xxx//32	—	2.75	5.50	9.00	15.00	—
AH1102//3x	—	2.75	5.50	9.00	15.00	—
AH1103//3x	—	2.75	5.50	9.00	15.00	—
AH1106//38	—	2.75	5.50	9.00	15.00	—
AH1106//39	—	2.75	5.50	9.00	15.00	—
AH1107//39	—	2.75	5.50	9.00	15.00	—
AH1107//40	—	2.75	5.50	9.00	15.00	—
AH1108//4x	—	2.75	5.50	9.00	15.00	—
AH1109//41	—	2.75	5.50	9.00	15.00	—
AH1111//43	—	2.75	5.50	9.00	15.00	—
AH1111//44	—	2.75	5.50	9.00	15.00	—
AH1112//44	—	2.75	5.50	9.00	15.00	—
AH1112//45	—	2.75	5.50	9.00	15.00	—

Kabul

KM# 285.13 PAISA

Copper **Note:** Weight varies 12.3 - 14.1 grams.

Date	Mintage	Good	VG	F	VF	XF
ND(1658-1707)	—	5.50	11.00	18.00	30.00	—

Katak

KM# 285.4 PAISA

Copper **Note:** Weight varies 12.3 - 14.1 grams.

Date	Mintage	Good	VG	F	VF	XF
AH108x//16	—	5.50	11.00	18.00	30.00	—

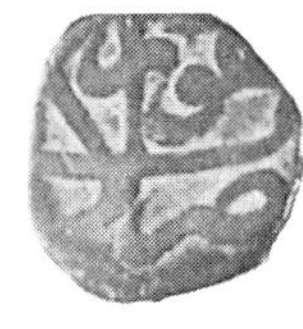 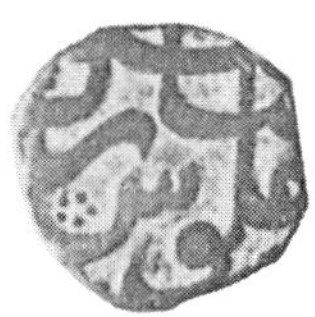

Lahore

KM# 285.5 PAISA

Copper **Note:** Weight varies 12.30-14.10 grams.

Date	Mintage	Good	VG	F	VF	XF
AH1074//7	—	10.00	20.00	35.00	55.00	—
AH1075//x	—	10.00	20.00	35.00	55.00	—
AH1079//11	—	10.00	20.00	35.00	55.00	—
AH108x//17	—	10.00	20.00	35.00	55.00	—
AH1084//16	—	10.00	20.00	35.00	55.00	—
AH1092//24	—	10.00	20.00	35.00	55.00	—
AH110x//39	—	10.00	20.00	35.00	55.00	—

Lakhnau

KM# 285.14 PAISA

Copper **Note:** Weight varies 12.3 - 14.1 grams.

Date	Mintage	Good	VG	F	VF	XF
AH1095//2x	—	4.50	9.00	15.00	25.00	—

 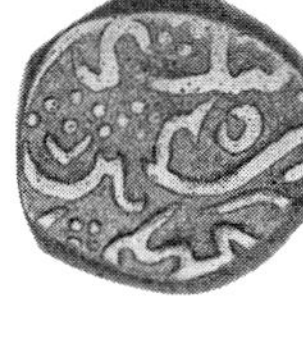

Macchlipattan

KM# 285.6 PAISA

Copper **Obv. Inscription:** "Mubarak julus sanah"
Rev. Inscription: "Zarb bandar machhlipatan sanah"
Note: Weight varies 12.30-14.10 grams.

Date	Mintage	Good	VG	F	VF	XF
AH1079//11	—	2.25	5.00	12.00	25.00	—
AH1087//18	—	2.25	5.00	12.00	25.00	—
AH110x//34	—	2.25	5.00	12.00	25.00	—
AH110x//41	—	2.25	5.00	12.00	25.00	—
AH1110//42	—	2.25	5.00	12.00	25.00	—
AH1111//43	—	2.25	5.00	12.00	25.00	—
AH1111//44	—	2.25	5.00	12.00	25.00	—
AH1112//44	—	2.25	5.00	12.00	25.00	—

Muazzamabad

KM# 285.15 PAISA

Copper **Note:** Struck at Mu'azzamabad Mint.

Date	Mintage	Good	VG	F	VF	XF
AH10xx//12	—	5.50	11.00	18.00	30.00	—

Multan

KM# 285.7 PAISA

Copper **Obv:** Emperor's name and titles, date **Rev:** Mint and regnal year **Note:** Weight varies 12.3 - 14.1 grams.

Date	Mintage	Good	VG	F	VF	XF
AH1107//39	—	5.50	11.00	18.00	30.00	—
AH1107//40	—	5.50	11.00	18.00	30.00	—
AH1108//40	—	5.50	11.00	18.00	30.00	—

Narnol

KM# 285.8 PAISA

Copper **Obv:** Emperor's name **Rev:** Mint **Note:** Weight varies 12.3 - 14.1 grams.

Date	Mintage	Good	VG	F	VF	XF
AH1075//7	—	3.50	7.00	12.50	20.00	—
AH107x//8	—	3.50	7.00	12.50	20.00	—
AH109x//xx	—	3.50	7.00	12.50	20.00	—
ND(1658-1707)	—	3.50	7.00	12.50	20.00	—

Nusratabad

KM# 285.29 PAISA

Copper **Note:** Weight varies 12.3 - 14.1 grams.

Date	Mintage	Good	VG	F	VF	XF
AH1101//33 Rare	—	—	—	—	—	—

Patna

KM# 285.28 PAISA

Copper **Note:** Weight varies 12.3 - 14.1 grams.

Date	Mintage	Good	VG	F	VF	XF
AHxxxx//x	—	—	—	—	—	—

Sakkhar

KM# 285.26 PAISA

Copper **Note:** Weight varies 12.3 - 14.1 grams.

Date	Mintage	Good	VG	F	VF	XF
AHxxxx//x	—	—	—	—	—	—

Shahjahanabad

KM# 285.9 PAISA

Copper **Note:** Weight varies 12.3 - 14.1 grams.

Date	Mintage	Good	VG	F	VF	XF
AH1068//(1) Ahad	—	2.75	5.50	9.00	15.00	—
AH1072//5	—	2.75	5.50	9.00	15.00	—
AH1074//6	—	2.75	5.50	9.00	15.00	—
AH1075//7	—	2.75	5.50	9.00	15.00	—
AH1075//8	—	2.75	5.50	9.00	15.00	—
AH1076//8	—	2.75	5.50	9.00	15.00	—
AH10xx//9	—	2.75	5.50	9.00	15.00	—
AH1078//10	—	2.75	5.50	9.00	15.00	—
AH1079//11	—	2.75	5.50	9.00	15.00	—
AH1080//12	—	2.75	5.50	9.00	15.00	—
AH1081//14	—	2.75	5.50	9.00	15.00	—
AH1084//16	—	2.75	5.50	9.00	15.00	—

Sholapur

KM# 285.10 PAISA

Copper **Note:** Weight varies 12.3 - 14.1 grams.

Date	Mintage	Good	VG	F	VF	XF
AHxxxx//4	—	3.50	7.50	12.50	20.00	—
AHxxxx//30	—	3.50	7.50	12.50	20.00	—
AHxxxx//32	—	3.50	7.50	12.50	20.00	—
AHxxxx//34	—	3.50	7.50	12.50	20.00	—

Surat

KM# 285.11 PAISA

Copper **Obv:** Emperor's name **Rev:** Mint and date **Note:** Weight varies 12.30-14.10 grams.

Date	Mintage	Good	VG	F	VF	XF
AH1079//12	—	2.75	5.50	9.00	15.00	—
AH1082//14	—	2.75	5.50	9.00	15.00	—
AH1083//15	—	2.75	5.50	9.00	15.00	—
AH1088//2x	—	2.75	5.50	9.00	15.00	—
AH1089//22	—	2.75	5.50	9.00	15.00	—
AH1091	—	2.75	5.50	9.00	15.00	—
AH109x//24	—	2.75	5.50	9.00	15.00	—
AH109x//26	—	2.75	5.50	9.00	15.00	—
AH1095//27	—	2.75	5.50	9.00	15.00	—
AH1098//3x	—	2.75	5.50	9.00	15.00	—
AH1105//3x	—	2.75	5.50	9.00	15.00	—
AH11xx//42	—	2.75	5.50	9.00	15.00	—
AH1111//44	—	2.75	5.50	9.00	15.00	—
AH1115//4x	—	2.75	5.50	9.00	15.00	—

Zafarabad

KM# 285.24 PAISA

11.4000 g., Copper **Note:** Weight varies 12.3 - 14.1 grams.

Date	Mintage	Good	VG	F	VF	XF
ND(1658-1707)	—	5.50	11.00	18.00	30.00	—

Bairata

KM# 286.6 DAM

Copper **Note:** Weight varies 17.00-18.60 grams.

Date	Mintage	Good	VG	F	VF	XF
AH110x//xx	—	3.50	7.00	12.00	20.00	—

Elichpur

KM# 286.1 DAM

Copper **Note:** Weight varies 19.7 - 20.2 grams.

Date	Mintage	Good	VG	F	VF	XF
AH1078//1x	—	2.00	4.00	7.00	12.00	—

Lakhnau

KM# 286.7 DAM

19.9500 g., Copper **Note:** Weight varies 19.50-20.20 grams.

Date	Mintage	Good	VG	F	VF	XF
AH1085//9	—	3.50	7.00	12.00	20.00	—
AH1095//19	—	3.50	7.00	12.00	20.00	—

Narnol

KM# 286.2 DAM

Copper **Note:** Weight varies 19.7 - 20.2 grams.

Date	Mintage	Good	VG	F	VF	XF
AH108x//21	—	3.50	7.00	12.00	20.00	—

Shahjahanabad

KM# 286.3 DAM

Copper **Note:** Weight varies 19.7 - 20.2 grams.

Date	Mintage	Good	VG	F	VF	XF
AH1069//(1) Ahad	—	2.75	5.50	9.00	15.00	—
AH1069//2	—	2.75	5.50	9.00	15.00	—
AH107x//3	—	2.75	5.50	9.00	15.00	—
AH1071//4	—	2.75	5.50	9.00	15.00	—

Surat

KM# 286.4 DAM

Copper, 20.8 mm. **Note:** Weight varies 19.7 - 20.2 grams.

Date	Mintage	Good	VG	F	VF	XF
AH106x//(1) Ahad	—	2.75	5.50	9.00	15.00	—
AH107x//3	—	2.75	5.50	9.00	15.00	—
AH107x//4	—	2.75	5.50	9.00	15.00	—
AH107x//5	—	2.75	5.50	9.00	15.00	—
AH1075//7	—	2.75	5.50	9.00	15.00	—
AH1075//8	—	2.75	5.50	9.00	15.00	—
AH107x//9	—	2.75	5.50	9.00	15.00	—
AH107x//10	—	2.75	5.50	9.00	15.00	—
AH107x//11	—	2.75	5.50	9.00	15.00	—
AH108x//13	—	2.75	5.50	9.00	15.00	—
AH1083//15	—	2.75	5.50	9.00	15.00	—
AH//29	—	4.00	8.50	17.50	30.00	—
ND	—	2.75	5.50	9.00	15.00	—

Zafarabad

KM# 286.5 DAM

Copper **Note:** Weight varies 19.7 - 20.2 grams.

Date	Mintage	Good	VG	F	VF	XF
ND	—	3.50	7.00	12.00	20.00	—

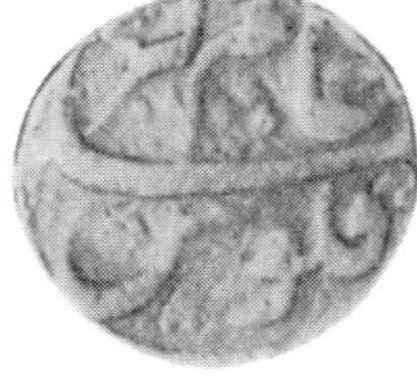
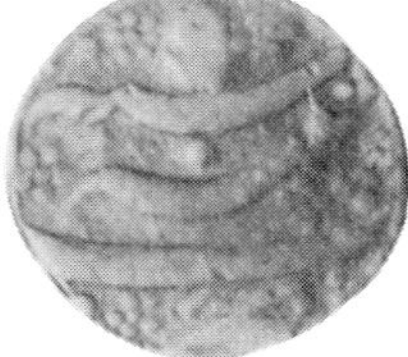

Patna

KM# 288.1 2 DAM

43.4000 g., Copper **Obv. Legend:** FALUS ALAMGIR SHAHI **Note:** Weight varies 42.90-43.41 grams.

Date	Mintage	Good	VG	F	VF	XF
AH107x//6	—	10.00	20.00	35.00	60.00	—
AH107x//6	—	10.00	20.00	35.00	60.00	—
AH107x//9	—	10.00	20.00	35.00	60.00	—

Lahore

KM# 289.1 1/32 RUPEE

0.3580 g., Silver **Obv:** Legend is a poetic couplet

Date	Mintage	Good	VG	F	VF	XF
AH1105//3x	—	10.00	20.00	35.00	50.00	—
AH1109//42	—	10.00	20.00	35.00	50.00	—

Ujjain

KM# 289.2 1/32 RUPEE

0.3580 g., Silver

Date	Mintage	Good	VG	F	VF	XF
AH108x//21	—	—	—	—	—	—

Akbarnagar

KM# 290.3 1/16 RUPEE

0.7150 g., Silver **Obv:** Legend is a poetic couplet

Date	Mintage	Good	VG	F	VF	XF
AH1081//1x	—	5.00	12.00	25.00	45.00	70.00

Gulkanda

KM# 290.1 1/16 RUPEE

0.7150 g., Silver

Date	Mintage	Good	VG	F	VF	XF
AH1076//1x	—	—	12.00	25.00	45.00	70.00
AH108x//15	—	—	12.00	25.00	45.00	70.00

Sholapur

KM# 290.4 1/16 RUPEE

0.7150 g., Silver

Date	Mintage	Good	VG	F	VF	XF
AHxxxx//x	—	—	—	—	—	—

Surat

KM# 290.5 1/16 RUPEE

0.7150 g., Silver

Date	Mintage	Good	VG	F	VF	XF
AHxxxx//x	—	—	—	—	—	—

Ujjain

KM# 290.6 1/16 RUPEE

0.7150 g., Silver **Rev:** Inscription and mint name **Rev. Inscription:** "dar al-Fath"

Date	Mintage	Good	VG	F	VF	XF
AH1084//17	—	—	—	—	—	—
AH1109	—	—	—	—	—	—

Zafarabad

KM# 290.2 1/16 RUPEE

0.7150 g., Silver **Obv:** Mihr

Date	Mintage	Good	VG	F	VF	XF
AH1079//12	—	5.00	12.00	25.00	45.00	70.00

Jahangirnagar

KM# 291.1 1/16 RUPEE

0.7150 g., Silver **Obv. Legend:** SIKKA ALAMGIR SHAHI

Date	Mintage	Good	VG	F	VF	XF
AH1071//x Rare	—	—	—	—	—	—

Burhanpur

KM# A292.1 1/8 RUPEE

1.4300 g., Silver **Obv:** Couplet legend. **Shape:** Square.

Date	Mintage	Good	VG	F	VF	XF
ND(1658-1707)	—	—	—	—	—	—

KM# A292.3 1/8 RUPEE

Silver

Date	Mintage	Good	VG	F	VF	XF
AHxxxx	—	20.00	45.00	85.00	—	—

Ujjain

KM# A292.2 1/8 RUPEE

1.4305 g., Silver **Shape:** Square

Date	Mintage	Good	VG	F	VF	XF
AH1079//10	—	—	—	—	—	—
AH1084//17	—	—	—	—	—	—
AH1086//18	—	—	—	—	—	—

Akbarnagar

KM# 292.3 1/8 RUPEE

1.4300 g., Silver **Obv:** Legend is a couplet

Date	Mintage	Good	VG	F	VF	XF
AH108x//16	—	8.00	20.00	45.00	85.00	135

Burhanpur

KM# 292.4 1/8 RUPEE

Silver **Obv:** Inscription **Rev:** Inscription **Note:** Weight varies 1.38-1.45 grams.

Date	Mintage	Good	VG	F	VF	XF
ND	—	—	20.00	45.00	85.00	135

Gulkanda

KM# 292.1 1/8 RUPEE

Silver **Note:** Weight varies 1.38-1.45 grams.

Date	Mintage	Good	VG	F	VF	XF
AH1076//20 (sic)	—	8.00	20.00	45.00	85.00	135

Sholapur

KM# 292.6 1/8 RUPEE

1.4305 g., Silver

Date	Mintage	Good	VG	F	VF	XF
AH1071	—	—	—	—	—	—

Surat

KM# 292.7 1/8 RUPEE

1.4305 g., Silver

Date	Mintage	Good	VG	F	VF	XF
AHxxxx//35	—	—	—	—	—	—

Ujjain

KM# 292.5 1/8 RUPEE

1.4300 g., Silver **Obv:** Inscription **Rev:** Inscription **Shape:** Round **Note:** Weight varies 1.38-1.45 grams.

Date	Mintage	Good	VG	F	VF	XF
ND	—	8.00	20.00	45.00	85.00	135

Zafarabad

KM# 292.8 1/8 RUPEE

1.4305 g., Silver

Date	Mintage	Good	VG	F	VF	XF
AH1079//12	—	—	—	—	—	—

Burhanpur

KM# A293.1 1/4 RUPEE

2.8610 g., Silver **Obv:** Inscription **Rev:** Inscription **Shape:** Square **Note:** Weight varies: 2.75-2.90 grams.

Date	Mintage	Good	VG	F	VF	XF
ND Rare	—	—	—	—	—	—

Ujjain

KM# A293.2 1/4 RUPEE

2.8610 g., Silver **Rev:** Inscription and mint name **Rev. Inscription:** "dar al-Fath" **Note:** Square.

Date	Mintage	Good	VG	F	VF	XF
AH1082//15	—	—	—	—	—	—
AH1109	—	—	—	—	—	—

Burhanpur

KM# B293.1 1/4 RUPEE

2.8610 g., Silver **Obv. Inscription:** "...Muhi al-Din"

Date	Mintage	Good	VG	F	VF	XF
AHxxxx//(1) Ahad	—	—	—	—	—	—

Patna

KM# B293.2 1/4 RUPEE

2.8610 g., Silver **Obv. Inscription:** "...Muhi al-Din"

Date	Mintage	Good	VG	F	VF	XF
AHxxxx//(1) Ahad	—	—	—	—	—	—

Gulkanda

KM# C293.1 1/4 RUPEE

Silver **Note:** Similar to Rupee, KM#299.1.

Date	Mintage	Good	VG	F	VF	XF
AH1069//(1) Ahad	—	—	—	—	—	—

Ajmir

KM# 293.11 1/4 RUPEE

2.8610 g., Silver

Date	Mintage	Good	VG	F	VF	XF
AH1111	—	—	—	—	—	—

Akbarabad

KM# 293.2 1/4 RUPEE

2.8610 g., Silver

Date	Mintage	Good	VG	F	VF	XF
AH1079//1x	—	6.00	15.00	35.00	75.00	125
AH1107//xx	—	6.00	15.00	35.00	75.00	125
AH111x//45	—	6.00	15.00	35.00	75.00	125

Akbarnagar

KM# 293.6 1/4 RUPEE

2.8610 g., Silver

Date	Mintage	Good	VG	F	VF	XF
AHxxxx//5	—	6.00	15.00	35.00	75.00	125
AH108x//14	—	6.00	15.00	35.00	75.00	125
AH109x//24	—	6.00	15.00	35.00	75.00	125

Aurangabad

KM# 293.12 1/4 RUPEE

2.8610 g., Silver **Rev:** Inscription with mint name at top

Date	Mintage	Good	VG	F	VF	XF
AH1081	—	—	—	—	—	—

KM# 293.13 1/4 RUPEE

2.8610 g., Silver **Rev:** Inscription with mint name at bottom

Date	Mintage	Good	VG	F	VF	XF
AH1092	—	—	—	—	—	—
AH1093	—	—	—	—	—	—

Bijapur

KM# 293.14 1/4 RUPEE

2.8610 g., Silver **Rev:** Inscription and mint name **Rev. Inscription:** "dar al-Zafar"

Date	Mintage	Good	VG	F	VF	XF
AHxxxx//x	—	—	—	—	—	—

Burhanpur

KM# 293.3 1/4 RUPEE

2.8610 g., Silver

Date	Mintage	Good	VG	F	VF	XF
AH107x//3	—	6.00	15.00	35.00	75.00	125
AH1072	—	6.00	15.00	35.00	75.00	125
AHxxxx//25	—	6.00	15.00	35.00	75.00	125

Gulkanda

KM# 293.1 1/4 RUPEE

2.8610 g., Silver

Date	Mintage	Good	VG	F	VF	XF
AH107x//5	—	6.00	15.00	35.00	75.00	125
AH1076//8	—	6.00	15.00	35.00	75.00	125
AHxxxx//11	—	6.00	15.00	35.00	75.00	125
AHxxxx//13	—	6.00	15.00	35.00	75.00	125
AH108x//20	—	6.00	15.00	35.00	75.00	125
AHxxxx//21	—	6.00	15.00	35.00	75.00	125
AHxxxx//23	—	6.00	15.00	35.00	75.00	125
AH109x//27	—	6.00	15.00	35.00	75.00	125
AH1076//27 (sic)	—	6.00	15.00	35.00	75.00	125

Kabul

KM# 293.8 1/4 RUPEE

2.8610 g., Silver

Date	Mintage	Good	VG	F	VF	XF
AH107x//5 Rare	—	—	—	—	—	—

KM# 293.15 1/4 RUPEE

2.8610 g., Silver **Rev. Inscription:** "dar al-Mulk"

Date	Mintage	Good	VG	F	VF	XF
AH1096	—	—	—	—	—	—

Khambayat

KM# 293.7 1/4 RUPEE

2.8610 g., Silver

Date	Mintage	Good	VG	F	VF	XF
AH1090//22	—	6.00	15.00	35.00	75.00	125

Khujista Bunyad

KM# 293.9 1/4 RUPEE

Silver **Note:** Weight varies 2.75-2.90 grams.

Date	Mintage	Good	VG	F	VF	XF
AH1112//4x	—	—	—	—	—	—

Sholapur

KM# 293.16 1/4 RUPEE

2.8610 g., Silver

Date	Mintage	Good	VG	F	VF	XF
AH1095//2x	—	—	—	—	—	—

Surat

KM# 293.17 1/4 RUPEE

2.8610 g., Silver **Note:** Weight varies 2.75-2.90 grams.

Date	Mintage	Good	VG	F	VF	XF
AH1098	—	—	—	—	—	—

Ujjain

KM# 293.5 1/4 RUPEE

Silver **Obv:** Inscription **Rev. Inscription:** Dar-ul Fath **Note:** Weight varies 2.75-2.90 grams.

Date	Mintage	Good	VG	F	VF	XF
AH1088//21	—	6.00	15.00	35.00	75.00	125

Aurangabad

KM# A294.1 1/2 RUPEE

5.7220 g., Silver **Obv. Inscription:** "Muhi al-Din"

Date	Mintage	Good	VG	F	VF	XF
AH1071//3	—	—	—	—	—	—

Kabul

KM# A294.2 1/2 RUPEE

5.7220 g., Silver **Obv:** Short inscription **Obv. Legend:** "Muhi al-Din"

Date	Mintage	Good	VG	F	VF	XF
AH1072//5	—	—	—	—	—	—

Patna

KM# A294.3 1/2 RUPEE

5.7220 g., Silver **Obv. Inscription:** "Muhi al-Din"

Date	Mintage	Good	VG	F	VF	XF
AH1071//(1) (sic) Ahad	—	—	—	—	—	—
AHxxxx//3	—	—	—	—	—	—
AH1072//4	—	—	—	—	—	—

Ahmadabad

KM# 294.1 1/2 RUPEE

Silver **Note:** Weight varies: 5.50-5.80 grams.

Date	Mintage	Good	VG	F	VF	XF
AH1075//7	—	6.00	15.00	35.00	75.00	125
AH1079//12	—	6.00	15.00	35.00	75.00	125
AH10xx//18	—	6.00	15.00	35.00	75.00	125
AH109x//23	—	6.00	15.00	35.00	75.00	125
AH1091//23	—	6.00	15.00	35.00	75.00	125
AH1103//3x	—	6.00	15.00	35.00	75.00	125
AH1109	—	6.00	15.00	35.00	75.00	125

Akbarabad

KM# 294.12 1/2 RUPEE

5.7220 g., Silver

Date	Mintage	Good	VG	F	VF	XF
AH1077//9	—	10.00	25.00	50.00	90.00	150
AH1078//11	—	10.00	25.00	50.00	90.00	150
AH1080//13	—	10.00	25.00	50.00	90.00	150

Akbarnagar

KM# 294.24 1/2 RUPEE

5.7220 g., Silver

Date	Mintage	Good	VG	F	VF	XF
AHxxxx//11	—	—	—	—	—	—
AH10xx//15	—	—	—	—	—	—
AH1096//29	—	—	—	—	—	—

Allahabad

KM# 294.14 1/2 RUPEE

5.7220 g., Silver

Date	Mintage	Good	VG	F	VF	XF
AH1080//13	—	—	—	—	—	—
AH1081//13	—	—	—	—	—	—

Aurangabad

KM# 294.25 1/2 RUPEE

5.7220 g., Silver **Rev:** Inscription with mint name at top

Date	Mintage	Good	VG	F	VF	XF
AH1086//19	—	—	—	—	—	—

Bijapur

KM# 294.2 1/2 RUPEE

5.7220 g., Silver

Date	Mintage	Good	VG	F	VF	XF
AH1089//22	—	10.00	25.00	50.00	90.00	150
AH1091//23	—	10.00	25.00	50.00	90.00	150
AH1091//26 (sic)	—	10.00	25.00	50.00	90.00	150
AH109x//31	—	10.00	25.00	50.00	90.00	150

Burhanpur

KM# 294.15 1/2 RUPEE

5.7220 g., Silver

Date	Mintage	Good	VG	F	VF	XF
AH1098	—	—	—	—	—	—
AH111x//42	—	—	—	—	—	—
AH1111//4x	—	—	—	—	—	—

Gulbarga

KM# 294.26 1/2 RUPEE

5.7220 g., Silver

Date	Mintage	Good	VG	F	VF	XF
AH1102//3x	—	—	—	—	—	—
AH1110//42	—	—	—	—	—	—

KM# 294.7 1/2 RUPEE

5.7220 g., Silver

Date	Mintage	Good	VG	F	VF	XF
AH111x//43 Rare	—	—	—	—	—	—

Gulkanda

KM# 294.27 1/2 RUPEE

5.7220 g., Silver **Note:** Similar to Rupee, KM#299.1.

Date	Mintage	Good	VG	F	VF	XF
AH1069//(1) Ahad	—	—	—	—	—	—

KM# 294.3 1/2 RUPEE
5.7220 g., Silver

Date	Mintage	Good	VG	F	VF	XF
AHxxxx//4	—	6.00	15.00	35.00	75.00	125
AHxxxx//5	—	6.00	15.00	35.00	75.00	125
AH107x//7	—	6.00	15.00	35.00	75.00	125
AH1076//9	—	6.00	15.00	35.00	75.00	125
AH107x//11	—	6.00	15.00	35.00	75.00	125
AH10xx//12	—	6.00	15.00	35.00	75.00	125
AH108x//13	—	6.00	15.00	35.00	75.00	125
AHxxxx//17	—	6.00	15.00	35.00	75.00	125
AHxxxx//18	—	6.00	15.00	35.00	75.00	125
AH108x//20	—	6.00	15.00	35.00	75.00	125
AH108x//21	—	6.00	15.00	35.00	75.00	125
AH10xx//22	—	6.00	15.00	35.00	75.00	125
AHxxxx//24	—	6.00	15.00	35.00	75.00	125
AHxxxx//25	—	6.00	15.00	35.00	75.00	125
AH109x//25	—	6.00	15.00	35.00	75.00	125
AH1076//28	—	6.00	15.00	35.00	75.00	125
AH10xx//30	—	6.00	15.00	35.00	75.00	125

Haidarabad

KM# 294.28 1/2 RUPEE
5.7220 g., Silver

Date	Mintage	Good	VG	F	VF	XF
AHxxxx//32	—	—	—	—	—	—

Hukeri

KM# 294.10 1/2 RUPEE
5.7220 g., Silver

Date	Mintage	Good	VG	F	VF	XF
AH1110//4x Rare	—	—	—	—	—	—

Islamnagar

KM# 294.29 1/2 RUPEE
5.7220 g., Silver

Date	Mintage	Good	VG	F	VF	XF
AHxxxx//x	—	—	—	—	—	—

Itawa

KM# 294.30 1/2 RUPEE
5.7220 g., Silver

Date	Mintage	Good	VG	F	VF	XF
AH1108//40	—	—	—	—	—	—

Kabul

KM# 294.31 1/2 RUPEE
5.7220 g., Silver

Date	Mintage	Good	VG	F	VF	XF
AHxxxx//8	—	—	—	—	—	—

Katak

KM# 294.13 1/2 RUPEE
5.7220 g., Silver

Date	Mintage	Good	VG	F	VF	XF
AH1080//1x	—	12.00	30.00	60.00	125	200

Khambayat

KM# 294.4 1/2 RUPEE
5.7220 g., Silver

Date	Mintage	Good	VG	F	VF	XF
AH108x//15	—	6.00	15.00	35.00	75.00	125
AH1085//18	—	6.00	15.00	35.00	75.00	125
AH1086	—	6.00	15.00	35.00	75.00	125
AH1087//19	—	6.00	15.00	35.00	75.00	125
AH1087//2x	—	6.00	15.00	35.00	75.00	125
AH1089//2x	—	6.00	15.00	35.00	75.00	125
AH1091//24	—	6.00	15.00	35.00	75.00	125
AH1095//27	—	6.00	15.00	35.00	75.00	125
AH1098//30	—	6.00	15.00	35.00	75.00	125
AH1100//3x	—	6.00	15.00	35.00	75.00	125
AH1102//34	—	6.00	15.00	35.00	75.00	125
AH1104//3x	—	6.00	15.00	35.00	75.00	125

Macchlipattan

KM# 294.32 1/2 RUPEE
5.7220 g., Silver

Date	Mintage	Good	VG	F	VF	XF
AH1100	—	—	—	—	—	—

Patna

KM# 294.11 1/2 RUPEE
5.7220 g., Silver

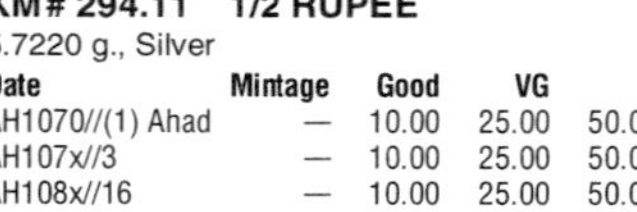

Date	Mintage	Good	VG	F	VF	XF
AH1070//(1) Ahad	—	10.00	25.00	50.00	90.00	150
AH107x//3	—	10.00	25.00	50.00	90.00	150
AH108x//16	—	10.00	25.00	50.00	90.00	150
AH1089//22	—	10.00	25.00	50.00	90.00	150

Sangamner

KM# 294.22 1/2 RUPEE
Silver **Note:** Struck at Sangamner Mint.

Date	Mintage	Good	VG	F	VF	XF
AHxxxx//x	—	—	—	—	—	—

Sholapur

KM# 294.21 1/2 RUPEE
5.7220 g., Silver

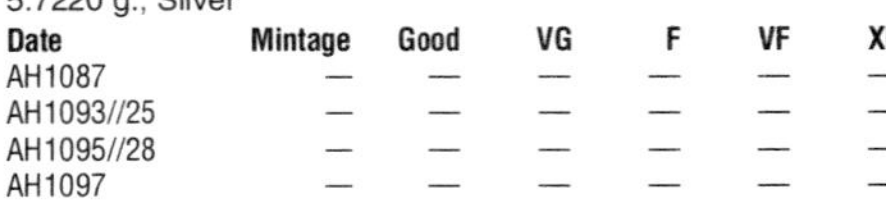

Date	Mintage	Good	VG	F	VF	XF
AH1087	—	—	—	—	—	—
AH1093//25	—	—	—	—	—	—
AH1095//28	—	—	—	—	—	—
AH1097	—	—	—	—	—	—

Surat

KM# 294.6 1/2 RUPEE
Silver **Rev:** Without mint epithet **Note:** Weight varies 5.50-5.80 grams.

Date	Mintage	Good	VG	F	VF	XF
AH107x//3	—	4.00	6.00	12.00	20.00	30.00
AH1072//x	—	4.00	6.00	12.00	20.00	30.00
AH1075//8	—	4.00	6.00	12.00	20.00	30.00
AH1078//1x	—	4.00	6.00	12.00	20.00	30.00
AH1079//11	—	4.00	6.00	12.00	20.00	30.00
AH1079//12	—	4.00	6.00	12.00	20.00	30.00
AH108x//13	—	4.00	6.00	12.00	20.00	30.00
AH1080//12	—	4.00	6.00	12.00	20.00	30.00
AH108x//18	—	4.00	6.00	12.00	20.00	30.00
AH1089//21	—	4.00	6.00	12.00	20.00	30.00
AH1089//22	—	4.00	6.00	12.00	20.00	30.00
AH1090//22	—	4.00	6.00	12.00	20.00	30.00
AH1090//23	—	4.00	6.00	12.00	20.00	30.00
AH1091//23	—	4.00	6.00	12.00	20.00	30.00
AH1091//24	—	4.00	6.00	12.00	20.00	30.00
AH1092//24	—	4.00	6.00	12.00	20.00	30.00
AH1092//25	—	4.00	6.00	12.00	20.00	30.00
AH1093//25	—	4.00	6.00	12.00	20.00	30.00
AH1093//26	—	4.00	6.00	12.00	20.00	30.00
AH1094//26	—	4.00	6.00	12.00	20.00	30.00
AH1094//27	—	4.00	6.00	12.00	20.00	30.00
AH1095//27	—	4.00	6.00	12.00	20.00	30.00
AH1095//28	—	4.00	6.00	12.00	20.00	30.00
AH1096//28	—	4.00	6.00	12.00	20.00	30.00
AH1096//29	—	4.00	6.00	12.00	20.00	30.00
AH1097//29	—	4.00	6.00	12.00	20.00	30.00
AH109x//30	—	4.00	6.00	12.00	20.00	30.00
AH109x//31	—	4.00	6.00	12.00	20.00	30.00
AH10xx//32	—	4.00	6.00	12.00	20.00	30.00
AH1102//34	—	4.00	6.00	12.00	20.00	30.00
AH1102//35	—	4.00	6.00	12.00	20.00	30.00
AH1103//35	—	4.00	6.00	12.00	20.00	30.00
AH1103//36	—	4.00	6.00	12.00	20.00	30.00
AH1104//36	—	4.00	6.00	12.00	20.00	30.00
AH1104//37	—	4.00	6.00	12.00	20.00	30.00
AH1105//37	—	4.00	6.00	12.00	20.00	30.00
AH1105//38	—	4.00	6.00	12.00	20.00	30.00
AH1106//38	—	4.00	6.00	12.00	20.00	30.00
AH1106//39	—	4.00	6.00	12.00	20.00	30.00
AH1107//39	—	4.00	6.00	12.00	20.00	30.00
AH1108//40	—	4.00	6.00	12.00	20.00	30.00
AH1109//41	—	4.00	6.00	12.00	20.00	30.00
AH1110//42	—	4.00	6.00	12.00	20.00	30.00
AH1110//4x	—	4.00	6.00	12.00	20.00	30.00
AH1111//43	—	4.00	6.00	12.00	20.00	30.00
AH1111//44	—	4.00	6.00	12.00	20.00	30.00
AH1112//44	—	4.00	6.00	12.00	20.00	30.00

KM# 294.5 1/2 RUPEE
5.7220 g., Silver **Note:** Mint epithet: "Bandar-i-Mubarak".

Date	Mintage	Good	VG	F	VF	XF
AH1070//1 sic	—	18.00	30.00	60.00	125	200

Tatta

KM# 294.16 1/2 RUPEE
5.7220 g., Silver

Date	Mintage	Good	VG	F	VF	XF
AHxxxx//20	—	—	—	—	—	—

Ujjain

KM# 294.33 1/2 RUPEE
5.7220 g., Silver **Rev:** Inscription with mint name at bottom

Date	Mintage	Good	VG	F	VF	XF
AHxxxx//3	—	—	—	—	—	—

KM# 294.34 1/2 RUPEE
5.7220 g., Silver **Rev:** Inscription with mint name at top **Rev. Inscription:** "dar al-Fath"

Date	Mintage	Good	VG	F	VF	XF
AH1078//11	—	—	—	—	—	—
AH1084//17	—	—	—	—	—	—

Jahangirnagar

KM# 295.2 1/2 RUPEE
5.7220 g., Silver **Obv:** Central inscription in square **Rev:** Central inscription in square

Date	Mintage	Good	VG	F	VF	XF
AH1082//15	—	—	—	—	—	—

Junagarh

KM# 295.1 1/2 RUPEE
5.7220 g., Silver **Obv:** Central inscription within square **Rev:** Central inscription within square

Date	Mintage	Good	VG	F	VF	XF
AH1074	—	22.00	55.00	90.00	150	225
AH1077	—	22.00	55.00	90.00	150	225
AH1095//28	—	22.00	55.00	90.00	—	225

Surat

KM# 296.1 1/2 RUPEE
5.7220 g., Silver

Date	Mintage	Good	VG	F	VF	XF
AHxxxx//(1) Ahad	—	—	—	—	—	—

Ahmadanagar

KM# 297.1 RUPEE
11.4440 g., Silver **Obv:** Ruler's full name and titles

Date	Mintage	Good	VG	F	VF	XF
AH1070//(1) Ahad	—	8.00	13.00	24.00	38.00	60.00
AH1072	—	8.00	13.00	24.00	38.00	60.00
AH1074//x	—	8.00	13.00	24.00	38.00	60.00
AH1075//7	—	8.00	13.00	24.00	38.00	60.00
AH1075//8	—	8.00	13.00	24.00	38.00	60.00
AH1079//12	—	8.00	13.00	24.00	38.00	60.00
AH1086//18	—	8.00	13.00	24.00	38.00	60.00
AH1087//18 (sic)	—	8.00	13.00	24.00	38.00	60.00
AH10xx//21	—	8.00	13.00	24.00	38.00	60.00

Akbarabad

KM# 297.11 RUPEE
11.4440 g., Silver **Obv:** Ruler's full name and titles

Date	Mintage	Good	VG	F	VF	XF
AH1069//(1) Ahad Rare	—	—	—	—	—	—

Akbarnagar

KM# 297.12 RUPEE
11.4440 g., Silver

Date	Mintage	Good	VG	F	VF	XF
AH10xx//(1) Ahad Rare	—	—	—	—	—	—

Aurangabad

KM# 297.2 RUPEE
11.4440 g., Silver **Obv:** Ruler's full name and titles

Date	Mintage	Good	VG	F	VF	XF
AH1071//3	—	8.00	15.00	30.00	50.00	80.00

Burhanpur

KM# 297.3 RUPEE
11.4440 g., Silver **Obv:** Ruler's full name and titles

Date	Mintage	Good	VG	F	VF	XF
AHxxxx//(1) Ahad Rare	—	—	—	—	—	—

Kabul

KM# 297.4 RUPEE
11.4440 g., Silver **Obv:** Ruler's full name and titles

Date	Mintage	Good	VG	F	VF	XF
AH1069//(1) Ahad	—	8.00	15.00	30.00	50.00	80.00
AH1070//x	—	8.00	15.00	30.00	50.00	80.00
AH107x//3	—	8.00	15.00	30.00	50.00	80.00
AH107x//4	—	8.00	15.00	30.00	50.00	80.00
AH107x//5	—	8.00	15.00	30.00	50.00	80.00
AH107x//6	—	8.00	15.00	30.00	50.00	80.00
AH1078//11	—	8.00	15.00	30.00	50.00	80.00

Multan

KM# 297.5 RUPEE
11.4440 g., Silver **Obv:** Ruler's full name and titles

Date	Mintage	Good	VG	F	VF	XF
AH1069//(1) Ahad	—	8.00	15.00	30.00	50.00	80.00

Patna

KM# 297.6 RUPEE
11.4440 g., Silver **Obv:** Ruler's full name and titles

Date	Mintage	Good	VG	F	VF	XF
AH1070//(1) Ahad	—	8.00	13.00	24.00	38.00	60.00
AH1070//2	—	8.00	13.00	24.00	38.00	60.00
AH1071//3	—	8.00	13.00	24.00	38.00	60.00

Date	Mintage	Good	VG	F	VF	XF
AH1071//4	—	8.00	13.00	24.00	38.00	60.00
AH1072//4	—	8.00	13.00	24.00	38.00	60.00

Shahjahanabad

KM# 297.7 RUPEE

11.4440 g., Silver **Obv:** Ruler's full name and titles

Date	Mintage	Good	VG	F	VF	XF
AH1069//(1) Ahad	—	9.00	16.00	32.00	56.00	90.00
AH1071//4	—	9.00	16.00	32.00	56.00	90.00

Tatta

KM# 297.8 RUPEE

11.4440 g., Silver **Obv:** Ruler's full name and titles

Date	Mintage	Good	VG	F	VF	XF
AH1069//(1) Ahad	—	8.00	13.00	24.00	38.00	60.00
AH1070//(1) Ahad	—	8.00	13.00	24.00	38.00	60.00
AH1070//3	—	8.00	13.00	24.00	38.00	60.00
AH1071//3	—	8.00	13.00	24.00	38.00	60.00
AH1071//4	—	8.00	13.00	24.00	38.00	60.00
AH1072//4	—	8.00	13.00	24.00	38.00	60.00

Ujjain

KM# 297.9 RUPEE

11.4440 g., Silver **Obv:** Ruler's full name and titles

Date	Mintage	Good	VG	F	VF	XF
AH1070	—	9.00	16.00	32.00	56.00	90.00
AH1072//4	—	9.00	16.00	32.00	56.00	90.00

Zafarabad

KM# 297.10 RUPEE

11.4440 g., Silver **Obv:** Ruler's full name and titles

Date	Mintage	Good	VG	F	VF	XF
AH1069//(1) Ahad	—	9.00	17.00	36.00	64.00	100
AH1069//2	—	9.00	17.00	36.00	64.00	100
AH1070//3	—	9.00	17.00	36.00	64.00	100
AH1070//2	—	9.00	17.00	36.00	64.00	100
AH1071//3	—	9.00	17.00	36.00	64.00	100
AH1071//4	—	9.00	17.00	36.00	64.00	100

Akbarabad

KM# 298.1 RUPEE

11.4440 g., Silver **Obv:** Ruler's full name and titles, central inscription within square **Rev:** Mint name within square

Date	Mintage	Good	VG	F	VF	XF
AH1069//(1) Ahad	—	7.00	10.00	16.00	26.00	40.00
AH1070//1	—	7.00	10.00	16.00	26.00	40.00
AH1070//3	—	7.00	10.00	16.00	26.00	40.00
AH1071//3	—	7.00	10.00	16.00	26.00	40.00
AH1071//4	—	7.00	10.00	16.00	26.00	40.00
AH1072//4	—	7.00	10.00	16.00	26.00	40.00
AH1072//5	—	7.00	10.00	16.00	26.00	40.00
AH1073//5	—	7.00	10.00	16.00	26.00	40.00
AH1073//6	—	7.00	10.00	16.00	26.00	40.00
AH1074//6	—	7.00	10.00	16.00	26.00	40.00
AH1074//7	—	7.00	10.00	16.00	26.00	40.00
AH1075//7	—	7.00	10.00	16.00	26.00	40.00
AH1075//8	—	7.00	10.00	16.00	26.00	40.00
AH1076//8	—	7.00	10.00	16.00	26.00	40.00
AH1076//9	—	7.00	10.00	16.00	26.00	40.00
AH1077//9	—	7.00	10.00	16.00	26.00	40.00
AH1077//10	—	7.00	10.00	16.00	26.00	40.00
AH1078//10	—	7.00	10.00	16.00	26.00	40.00
AH1080//xx	—	7.00	10.00	16.00	26.00	40.00
AH1081//13	—	7.00	10.00	16.00	26.00	40.00
AH1081//14	—	7.00	10.00	16.00	26.00	40.00
AH1082//14	—	7.00	10.00	16.00	26.00	40.00
AH1082//15	—	7.00	10.00	16.00	26.00	40.00
AH1083//15	—	7.00	10.00	16.00	26.00	40.00

Date	Mintage	Good	VG	F	VF	XF
AH1083//16	—	7.00	10.00	16.00	26.00	40.00
AH1084//16	—	7.00	10.00	16.00	26.00	40.00
AH1084//17	—	7.00	10.00	16.00	26.00	40.00
AH1085//17	—	7.00	10.00	16.00	26.00	40.00
AH1085//18	—	7.00	10.00	16.00	26.00	40.00
AH1086//18	—	7.00	10.00	16.00	26.00	40.00
AH1086//19	—	7.00	10.00	16.00	26.00	40.00
AH1087//19	—	7.00	10.00	16.00	26.00	40.00
AH1087//20	—	7.00	10.00	16.00	26.00	40.00
AH1088//20	—	7.00	10.00	16.00	26.00	40.00
AH1088//21	—	7.00	10.00	16.00	26.00	40.00
AH1089//21	—	7.00	10.00	16.00	26.00	40.00
AH1089//22	—	7.00	10.00	16.00	26.00	40.00
AH1090//22	—	7.00	10.00	16.00	26.00	40.00
AH1090//23	—	7.00	10.00	16.00	26.00	40.00
AH1091//23	—	7.00	10.00	16.00	26.00	40.00
AH1091//24	—	7.00	10.00	16.00	26.00	40.00
AH1092//24	—	7.00	10.00	16.00	26.00	40.00
AH1092//25	—	7.00	10.00	16.00	26.00	40.00
AH1094//26	—	7.00	10.00	16.00	26.00	40.00
AH1094//27	—	7.00	10.00	16.00	26.00	40.00
AH1095//27	—	7.00	10.00	16.00	26.00	40.00
AH1095//28	—	7.00	10.00	16.00	26.00	40.00
AH1096//28	—	7.00	10.00	16.00	26.00	40.00
AH1096//29	—	7.00	10.00	16.00	26.00	40.00
AH1097//29	—	7.00	10.00	16.00	26.00	40.00

Junagadh

KM# 298.3 RUPEE

11.4440 g., Silver **Obv:** Ruler's full name and titles, central inscription within square **Rev:** Mint name in square

Date	Mintage	Good	VG	F	VF	XF
AH1080 Rare	—	—	—	—	—	—
AH1086 Rare	—	—	—	—	—	—

Shahjahanabad

KM# 298.2 RUPEE

11.4440 g., Silver **Obv:** Ruler's full name and titles, central inscription within square **Rev:** Mint name in square **Rev. Inscription:** "dar al-Khilafa"

Date	Mintage	Good	VG	F	VF	XF
AH1070//(1) Ahad Rare	—	—	—	—	—	—

Gulkanda

KM# 299.1 RUPEE

11.4440 g., Silver **Obv:** Legend is crude, clumsy, idiosyncratic execution **Rev:** Legend is crude, clumsy, idosyncratic execution

Date	Mintage	Good	VG	F	VF	XF
AH1069//(1) Ahad	—	8.00	14.00	26.00	45.00	70.00

Advani

KM# 300.1 RUPEE

Silver **Obv. Inscription:** Poetic couplet **Note:** Weight varies 11.00-11.60 grams.

Date	Mintage	Good	VG	F	VF	XF
AHxxxx//30	—	9.00	16.00	32.00	56.00	90.00

Ahmadabad

KM# 300.2 RUPEE

Silver **Obv:** Poetic couplet **Rev:** Inscription **Note:** Weight varies 11.00-11.60 grams.

Date	Mintage	Good	VG	F	VF	XF
AH1069//(1) Ahad	—	7.00	9.00	12.00	17.50	27.50
AH1070//2	—	7.00	9.00	12.00	17.50	27.50
AH1070//3	—	7.00	9.00	12.00	17.50	27.50
AH1071//3	—	7.00	9.00	12.00	17.50	27.50
AH1071//4	—	7.00	9.00	12.00	17.50	27.50
AH1072//4	—	7.00	9.00	12.00	17.50	27.50
AH1072//5	—	7.00	9.00	12.00	17.50	27.50
AH1073//5	—	7.00	9.00	12.00	17.50	27.50
AH1073//6	—	7.00	9.00	12.00	17.50	27.50
AH1074//6	—	7.00	9.00	12.00	17.50	27.50
AH1074//7	—	7.00	9.00	12.00	17.50	27.50
AH1075//7	—	7.00	9.00	12.00	17.50	27.50
AH1075//8	—	7.00	9.00	12.00	17.50	27.50
AH1076//8	—	7.00	9.00	12.00	17.50	27.50
AH1076//9	—	7.00	9.00	12.00	17.50	27.50
AH1077//9	—	7.00	9.00	12.00	17.50	27.50
AH1079//11	—	7.00	9.00	12.00	17.50	27.50
AH1079//12	—	7.00	9.00	12.00	17.50	27.50
AH108x//15	—	7.00	9.00	12.00	17.50	27.50
AH1080//12	—	7.00	9.00	12.00	17.50	27.50
AH1085//17	—	7.00	9.00	1.00	17.50	27.50
AH1085//18	—	7.00	9.00	12.00	17.50	27.50
AH1086//18	—	7.00	9.00	12.00	17.50	27.50
AH1086//19	—	7.00	9.00	12.00	17.50	27.50
AH1087//19	—	7.00	9.00	12.00	17.50	27.50
AH1087//20	—	7.00	9.00	12.00	17.50	27.50
AH1090//23	—	7.00	9.00	12.00	17.50	27.50
AH1091//23	—	7.00	9.00	12.00	17.50	27.50
AH1095//27	—	7.00	9.00	12.00	17.50	27.50
AH1095//28	—	7.00	9.00	12.00	17.50	27.50
AH1096//28	—	7.00	9.00	12.00	17.50	27.50
AH1096//29	—	7.00	9.00	12.00	17.50	27.50
AH1097//29	—	7.00	9.00	12.00	17.50	27.50
AH1099//30	—	7.00	9.00	12.00	17.50	27.50
AH1099//31	—	7.00	9.00	12.00	17.50	27.50
AH1101//34	—	7.00	9.00	12.00	17.50	27.50
AH1102//34	—	7.00	9.00	12.00	17.50	27.50
AH1108//40	—	7.00	9.00	12.00	17.50	27.50
AH1108//41	—	7.00	9.00	12.00	17.50	27.50
AH1109//41	—	7.00	9.00	12.00	17.50	27.50
AH1111//43	—	7.00	9.00	12.00	17.50	27.50
AH1111//44	—	7.00	9.00	12.00	17.50	27.50
AH1112//4x	—	7.00	9.00	12.00	17.50	27.50

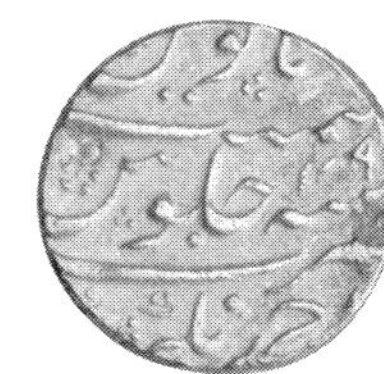

Ahmadanagar

KM# 300.3 RUPEE

Silver **Note:** Weight varies 11.00-11.60 grams.

Date	Mintage	Good	VG	F	VF	XF
AH1072//8	—	7.00	9.00	12.00	17.50	27.50
AH1074//6	—	7.00	9.00	12.00	17.50	27.50
AH1079//12	—	7.00	9.00	12.00	17.50	27.50
AH108x//19	—	7.00	9.00	12.00	17.50	27.50
AH1090//22	—	7.00	9.00	12.00	17.50	27.50
AH1091//23	—	7.00	9.00	12.00	17.50	27.50
AH109x//27	—	7.00	9.00	12.00	17.50	27.50
AH1095//28	—	7.00	9.00	12.00	17.50	27.50
AH1096//28	—	7.00	9.00	12.00	17.50	27.50
AH1096//29	—	7.00	9.00	12.00	17.50	27.50
AH1097//29	—	7.00	9.00	12.00	17.50	27.50
AH1097//30	—	7.00	9.00	12.00	17.50	27.50
AH1098//30	—	7.00	9.00	12.00	17.50	27.50
AH1098//31	—	7.00	9.00	12.00	17.50	27.50
AH1099//31	—	7.00	9.00	12.00	17.50	27.50
AH1099//32	—	7.00	9.00	12.00	17.50	27.50
AH1100//32	—	7.00	9.00	12.00	17.50	27.50
AH1100//33	—	7.00	9.00	12.00	17.50	27.50
AH1101//32	—	7.00	9.00	12.00	17.50	27.50
AH1108//40	—	7.00	9.00	12.00	17.50	27.50
AH1108//41	—	7.00	9.00	12.00	17.50	27.50

Ahsanabad

KM# 300.4 RUPEE

Silver **Note:** Weight varies 11.00-11.60 grams.

Date	Mintage	Good	VG	F	VF	XF
AH1112//45	—	8.00	12.00	20.00	30.00	50.00

Ajmer

KM# 300.5 RUPEE

Silver **Obv:** Inscription, date **Rev. Inscription:** Dar-ul-Khair **Note:** Weight varies 11.00-11.60 grams.

Date	Mintage	Good	VG	F	VF	XF
AH1097//29	—	7.00	9.00	12.00	20.00	32.50
AH1098//30	—	7.00	9.00	12.00	20.00	32.50
AH1098//31	—	7.00	9.00	12.00	20.00	32.50
AH1100//32	—	7.00	9.00	12.00	20.00	32.50
AH1101//33	—	7.00	9.00	12.00	20.00	32.50
AH1101//34	—	7.00	9.00	12.00	20.00	32.50
AH1103//35	—	7.00	9.00	12.00	20.00	32.50
AH1104//36	—	7.00	9.00	12.00	20.00	32.50
AH1104//37	—	7.00	9.00	12.00	20.00	32.50
AH1105//37	—	7.00	9.00	12.00	20.00	32.50
AH1105//38	—	7.00	9.00	12.00	20.00	32.50
AH1106//38	—	7.00	9.00	12.00	20.00	32.50
AH1106//39	—	7.00	9.00	12.00	20.00	32.50
AH1107//39	—	7.00	9.00	12.00	20.00	32.50
AH1107//40	—	7.00	9.00	12.00	20.00	32.50
AH1108//40	—	7.00	9.00	12.00	20.00	32.50
AH1108//41	—	7.00	9.00	12.00	20.00	32.50
AH1109//41	—	7.00	9.00	12.00	20.00	32.50
AH1109//42	—	7.00	9.00	12.00	20.00	32.50
AH1110//42	—	7.00	9.00	12.00	20.00	32.50
AH1110//43	—	7.00	9.00	12.00	20.00	32.50
AH1111//43	—	7.00	9.00	12.00	20.00	32.50
AH1111//44	—	7.00	9.00	12.00	20.00	32.50
AH1112//44	—	7.00	9.00	12.00	20.00	32.50
AH1112//45	—	7.00	9.00	12.00	20.00	32.50

Akbarabad

KM# 300.6 RUPEE

Silver **Obv:** Mustagir-ul-Khirafa **Rev. Inscription:** Inscription **Note:** Weight varies 11.00-11.60 grams.

Date	Mintage	Good	VG	F	VF	XF
AH109x//28	—	7.00	9.00	12.00	17.50	27.50
AH1096//29	—	7.00	9.00	12.00	17.50	27.50
AH1097//29	—	7.00	9.00	12.00	17.50	27.50
AH1097//30	—	7.00	9.00	12.00	17.50	27.50
AH1098//30	—	7.00	9.00	12.00	17.50	27.50
AH1098//31	—	7.00	9.00	12.00	17.50	27.50
AH1099//31	—	7.00	9.00	12.00	17.50	27.50
AH1099//32	—	7.00	9.00	12.00	17.50	27.50
AH1101//33	—	7.00	9.00	12.00	17.50	27.50
AH1101//34 (sic)	—	7.00	9.00	12.00	17.50	27.50
AH1102//34	—	7.00	9.00	12.00	17.50	27.50
AH1102//35	—	7.00	9.00	12.00	17.50	27.50
AH1103//35	—	7.00	9.00	12.00	17.50	27.50
AH1103//36	—	7.00	9.00	12.00	17.50	27.50
AH1104//36	—	7.00	9.00	12.00	17.50	27.50
AH110x//38	—	7.00	9.00	12.00	17.50	27.50
AH1106//39	—	7.00	9.00	12.00	17.50	27.50
AH1107//39	—	7.00	9.00	12.00	17.50	27.50
AH1108//40	—	7.00	9.00	12.00	17.50	27.50
AH1108//41	—	7.00	9.00	12.00	17.50	27.50
AH1109//41	—	7.00	9.00	12.00	17.50	27.50
AH1109//42	—	7.00	9.00	12.00	17.50	27.50
AH1110//43	—	7.00	9.00	12.00	17.50	27.50
AH1111//43	—	7.00	9.00	12.00	17.50	27.50
AH1111//44	—	7.00	9.00	12.00	17.50	27.50
AH1112//44	—	7.00	9.00	12.00	17.50	27.50
AH1112//45	—	7.00	9.00	12.00	17.50	27.50

Akbarnagar

KM# 300.7 RUPEE

Silver **Note:** "Mihr" couplet; Weight varies 11.00-11.60 grams.

Date	Mintage	Good	VG	F	VF	XF
AH1070//3	—	7.00	9.00	12.00	17.50	27.50
AH1071//3	—	7.00	9.00	12.00	17.50	27.50
AH1071//4	—	7.00	9.00	12.00	17.50	27.50
AH1072//4	—	7.00	9.00	12.00	17.50	27.50
AH1072//5	—	7.00	9.00	12.00	17.50	27.50
AH1073//5	—	7.00	9.00	12.00	17.50	27.50
AH1073//6	—	7.00	9.00	12.00	17.50	27.50
AH1074//6	—	7.00	9.00	12.00	17.50	27.50
AH1074//7	—	7.00	9.00	12.00	17.50	27.50
AH1075//7	—	7.00	9.00	12.00	17.50	27.50
AH1075//8	—	7.00	9.00	12.00	17.50	27.50
AH1076//8	—	7.00	9.00	12.00	17.50	27.50
AH1076//9	—	7.00	9.00	12.00	17.50	27.50
AH1078//10	—	7.00	9.00	12.00	17.50	27.50
AH1078//11	—	7.00	9.00	12.00	17.50	27.50
AH1079//11	—	7.00	9.00	12.00	17.50	27.50
AH1079//12	—	7.00	9.00	12.00	17.50	27.50
AH1080//13(sic)	—	7.00	9.00	12.00	17.50	27.50
AH1081//12	—	7.00	9.00	12.00	17.50	27.50
AH1081//13	—	7.00	9.00	12.00	17.50	27.50
AH1081//14	—	7.00	9.00	12.00	17.50	27.50
AH1082//14	—	7.00	9.00	12.00	17.50	27.50
AH1082//15	—	7.00	9.00	12.00	17.50	27.50
AH1083//15	—	7.00	9.00	12.00	17.50	27.50
AH1083//16	—	7.00	9.00	12.00	17.50	27.50
AH108x//18	—	7.00	9.00	12.00	17.50	27.50
AH108x//20	—	7.00	9.00	12.00	17.50	27.50
AH108x//21	—	7.00	9.00	12.00	17.50	27.50
AH1090//22	—	7.00	9.00	12.00	17.50	27.50
AH1090//23	—	7.00	9.00	12.00	17.50	27.50
AH1091//23	—	7.00	9.00	12.00	17.50	27.50
AH1091//24	—	7.00	9.00	12.00	17.50	27.50
AH1092//24	—	7.00	9.00	12.00	17.50	27.50
AH1092//25	—	7.00	9.00	12.00	17.50	27.50
AH1093//25	—	7.00	9.00	12.00	17.50	27.50
AH1094//26	—	7.00	9.00	12.00	17.50	27.50
AH1094//27	—	7.00	9.00	12.00	17.50	27.50
AH1093//26	—	7.00	9.00	12.00	17.50	27.50
AH1095//27	—	7.00	9.00	12.00	17.50	27.50
AH1095//28	—	7.00	9.00	12.00	17.50	27.50
AH1096//28	—	7.00	9.00	12.00	17.50	27.50
AH1096//29	—	7.00	9.00	12.00	17.50	27.50
AH1097//29	—	7.00	9.00	12.00	17.50	27.50
AH1097//30	—	7.00	9.00	12.00	17.50	27.50
AH1098//30	—	7.00	9.00	12.00	17.50	27.50
AH1098//31	—	7.00	9.00	12.00	17.50	27.50
AH1099//31	—	7.00	9.00	12.00	17.50	27.50
AH1099//32	—	7.00	9.00	12.00	17.50	27.50
AH1100//32	—	7.00	9.00	12.00	17.50	27.50
AH1100//33	—	7.00	9.00	12.00	17.50	27.50
AH1101//33	—	7.00	9.00	12.00	17.50	27.50
AH1101//34	—	7.00	9.00	12.00	17.50	27.50
AH1102//34	—	7.00	9.00	12.00	17.50	27.50
AH1102//35	—	7.00	9.00	12.00	17.50	27.50
AH1103//35	—	7.00	9.00	12.00	17.50	27.50
AH1103//36	—	7.00	9.00	12.00	17.50	27.50
AH1104//36	—	7.00	9.00	12.00	17.50	27.50
AH1104//37	—	7.00	9.00	12.00	17.50	27.50
AH1105//37	—	7.00	9.00	12.00	17.50	27.50
AH1105//38	—	7.00	9.00	12.00	17.50	27.50
AH1106//38	—	7.00	9.00	12.00	17.50	27.50
AH1107//39	—	7.00	9.00	12.00	17.50	27.50
AH1108//40	—	7.00	9.00	12.00	17.50	27.50
AH1108//41	—	7.00	9.00	12.00	17.50	27.50
AH1112//45	—	7.00	9.00	12.00	17.50	27.50

KM# 300.100 RUPEE

11.4440 g., Silver **Note:** "Badr" couplet

Date	Mintage	Good	VG	F	VF	XF
AH1109//42	—	7.00	10.00	16.00	28.00	40.00
AH1110//42	—	7.00	10.00	16.00	28.00	40.00
AH1111//43	—	7.00	10.00	16.00	28.00	40.00
AH1111//44	—	7.00	10.00	16.00	28.00	40.00
AH1112//45	—	7.00	10.00	16.00	28.00	40.00

Alamgirpur

KM# 300.8 RUPEE

Silver **Obv:** Mint name at right **Note:** Struck at Alamgirpur Mint.

Date	Mintage	Good	VG	F	VF	XF
AH1071//3	—	8.00	12.00	20.00	32.00	50.00

KM# 300.9 RUPEE

11.4440 g., Silver **Rev:** Mint name at top

Date	Mintage	Good	VG	F	VF	XF
AH1072//x	—	7.00	9.00	13.50	22.50	35.00
AH1073//5	—	7.00	9.00	13.50	22.50	35.00
AH1073//6	—	7.00	9.00	13.50	22.50	35.00
AH1074//6	—	7.00	9.00	13.50	22.50	35.00
AH1074//7	—	7.00	9.00	13.50	22.50	35.00
AH1075//7	—	7.00	9.00	13.50	22.50	35.00
AH1075//8	—	7.00	9.00	13.50	22.50	35.00
AH1076//8	—	7.00	9.00	13.50	22.50	35.00
AH1076//9	—	7.00	9.00	13.50	22.50	35.00
AH1077//9	—	7.00	9.00	13.50	22.50	35.00
AH1077//10	—	7.00	9.00	13.50	22.50	35.00
AH1078//10	—	7.00	9.00	13.50	22.50	35.00
AH1078//11	—	7.00	9.00	13.50	22.50	35.00
AH1079//11	—	7.00	9.00	13.50	22.50	35.00
AH1079//12	—	7.00	9.00	13.50	22.50	35.00
AH1081//14	—	7.00	9.00	13.50	22.50	35.00
AH1082//14	—	7.00	9.00	13.50	22.50	35.00
AH1082//15	—	7.00	9.00	13.50	22.50	35.00
AH1083//15	—	7.00	9.00	13.50	22.50	35.00
AH1083//16	—	7.00	9.00	13.50	22.50	35.00
AH1084//16	—	7.00	9.00	13.50	22.50	35.00
AH1084//17	—	7.00	9.00	13.50	22.50	35.00
AH1085//17	—	7.00	9.00	13.50	22.50	35.00
AH1085//18	—	7.00	9.00	13.50	22.50	35.00
AH1086//18	—	7.00	9.00	13.50	22.50	35.00
AH1086//19	—	7.00	9.00	13.50	22.50	35.00
AH1087//19	—	7.00	9.00	13.50	22.50	35.00
AH1087//20	—	7.00	9.00	13.50	22.50	35.00
AH1088//20	—	7.00	9.00	13.50	22.50	35.00
AH1088//21	—	7.00	9.00	13.50	22.50	35.00
AH1090//23	—	7.00	9.00	13.50	22.50	35.00
AH1095//27	—	7.00	9.00	13.50	22.50	35.00
AH1096//xx	—	7.00	9.00	13.50	22.50	35.00
AH1105//4x	—	7.00	9.00	13.50	22.50	35.00

KM# 300.101 RUPEE

11.4440 g., Silver **Rev:** Mint name at top **Note:** "Mihr" couplet.

Date	Mintage	Good	VG	F	VF	XF
AH1081//14	—	—	—	—	—	—

KM# 300.10 RUPEE

Silver **Rev:** Mint name at bottom **Note:** Weight varies 11.00-11.60 grams.

Date	Mintage	Good	VG	F	VF	XF
AH1089//xx	—	7.00	9.00	13.50	22.50	35.00
AH1090//22	—	7.00	9.00	13.50	22.50	35.00
AH1090//23	—	7.00	9.00	13.50	22.50	35.00
AH1091//23	—	7.00	9.00	13.50	22.50	35.00
AH1091//24	—	7.00	9.00	13.50	22.50	35.00
AH1092//24	—	7.00	9.00	13.50	22.50	35.00
AH1093//25	—	7.00	9.00	13.50	22.50	35.00
AH1092//25	—	7.00	9.00	13.50	22.50	35.00
AH1094//26	—	7.00	9.00	13.50	22.50	35.00
AH1094//27	—	7.00	9.00	13.50	22.50	35.00
AH1093//26	—	7.00	9.00	13.50	22.50	35.00
AH1095//27	—	7.00	9.00	13.50	22.50	35.00
AH1095//28	—	7.00	9.00	13.50	22.50	35.00
AH1096//28	—	7.00	9.00	13.50	22.50	35.00
AH1096//29	—	7.00	9.00	13.50	22.50	35.00
AH1097//29	—	7.00	9.00	13.50	22.50	35.00
AH1098//30	—	7.00	9.00	13.50	22.50	35.00
AH1098//31	—	7.00	9.00	13.50	22.50	35.00
AH1099//31	—	7.00	9.00	13.50	22.50	35.00
AH1099//32	—	7.00	9.00	13.50	22.50	35.00
AH1100//32	—	7.00	9.00	13.50	22.50	35.00
AH1100//33	—	7.00	9.00	13.50	22.50	35.00
AH1101//33	—	7.00	9.00	13.50	22.50	35.00
AH1101//34	—	7.00	9.00	13.50	22.50	35.00
AH1102//34	—	7.00	9.00	13.50	22.50	35.00
AH1102//35	—	7.00	9.00	13.50	22.50	35.00
AH1103//35	—	7.00	9.00	13.50	22.50	35.00
AH1103//36	—	7.00	9.00	13.50	22.50	35.00
AH1104//36	—	7.00	9.00	13.50	22.50	35.00
AH1104//37	—	7.00	9.00	13.50	22.50	35.00
AH1105//37	—	7.00	9.00	13.50	22.50	35.00
AH1105//38	—	7.00	9.00	13.50	22.50	35.00
AH1106//38	—	7.00	9.00	13.50	22.50	35.00
AH110x//39	—	7.00	9.00	13.50	22.50	35.00
AH1107//4x	—	7.00	9.00	13.50	22.50	35.00
AHxxxx//41	—	7.00	9.00	13.50	22.50	35.00
AH1109//42	—	7.00	9.00	13.50	22.50	35.00
AH1111//44	—	7.00	9.00	13.50	22.50	35.00
AH1112//45	—	7.00	9.00	13.50	22.50	35.00

Allahabad

KM# 300.11 RUPEE

Silver **Rev:** Epithet Balda + "mihr" couplet, and mint name at top **Note:** Weight varies: 11.00-11.60 grams.

Date	Mintage	Good	VG	F	VF	XF
AH1070//(1) Ahad	—	7.00	10.00	15.00	25.00	40.00
AH1070//3	—	7.00	10.00	15.00	25.00	40.00
AH1071//3	—	7.00	10.00	15.00	25.00	40.00
AH1071//4	—	7.00	10.00	15.00	25.00	40.00
AH1072//4	—	7.00	10.00	15.00	25.00	40.00
AH1086//xx	—	7.00	10.00	15.00	25.00	40.00

KM# 300.102 RUPEE

11.4440 g., Silver **Rev:** Mint name at bottom **Note:** "Mihr" couplet.

Date	Mintage	Good	VG	F	VF	XF
AH1073//6	—	7.00	10.00	16.00	26.00	40.00

KM# 300.12 RUPEE

Silver **Obv:** Inscription **Rev:** "badr" couplets, mint name at bottom **Note:** Weight varies 11.00-11.60 grams.

Date	Mintage	Good	VG	F	VF	XF
AH1074//6	—	7.00	9.00	12.00	17.50	27.50
AH1074//7	—	7.00	9.00	12.00	17.50	27.50
AH1075//7	—	7.00	9.00	12.00	17.50	27.50
AH1075//8	—	7.00	9.00	12.00	17.50	27.50
AH1076//8	—	7.00	9.00	12.00	17.50	27.50
AH1076//9	—	7.00	9.00	12.00	17.50	27.50
AH1077//9	—	7.00	9.00	12.00	17.50	27.50
AH1077//10	—	7.00	9.00	12.00	17.50	27.50
AH1078//10	—	7.00	9.00	12.00	17.50	27.50
AH10xx//12	—	7.00	9.00	12.00	17.50	27.50
AH1085//18	—	7.00	9.00	12.00	17.50	27.50
AH1087//19	—	7.00	9.00	12.00	17.50	27.50
AH1091//24	—	7.00	9.00	12.00	17.50	27.50
AH1094//27	—	7.00	9.00	12.00	17.50	27.50
AH1095//27	—	7.00	9.00	12.00	17.50	27.50
AH1095//28	—	7.00	9.00	12.00	17.50	27.50
AH1098//30	—	7.00	9.00	12.00	17.50	27.50
AH1098//31	—	7.00	9.00	12.00	17.50	27.50
AH1099//31	—	7.00	9.00	12.00	17.50	27.50
AH1099//32	—	7.00	9.00	12.00	17.50	27.50
AH1103//35	—	7.00	9.00	12.00	17.50	27.50
AH1105//38	—	7.00	9.00	12.00	17.50	27.50
AH1106//38	—	7.00	9.00	12.00	17.50	27.50
AH1106//39	—	7.00	9.00	12.00	17.50	27.50
AH1107//39	—	7.00	9.00	12.00	17.50	27.50

Date	Mintage	Good	VG	F	VF	XF
AH1107//40	—	7.00	9.00	12.00	17.50	27.50
AH1109//41	—	7.00	9.00	12.00	17.50	27.50
AH1111//43	—	7.00	9.00	12.00	17.50	27.50
AH1111//44	—	7.00	9.00	12.00	17.50	27.50
AH111x//45	—	7.00	9.00	12.00	17.50	27.50
AH1112//44	—	7.00	9.00	12.00	17.50	27.50

Atak

KM# 300.103 RUPEE

Silver **Note:** Weight varies 11.00-11.60 grams.

Date	Mintage	Good	VG	F	VF	XF
AH1108//xx	—	9.00	16.00	32.00	56.00	90.00

Aurangabad

KM# 300.13 RUPEE

Silver **Rev:** Mint name at top **Note:** Weight varies: 11.00-11.60 grams.

Date	Mintage	Good	VG	F	VF	XF
AH1071//3	—	7.00	9.00	13.00	20.00	30.00
AH1071//4	—	7.00	9.00	13.00	20.00	30.00
AH1072//4	—	7.00	9.00	13.00	20.00	30.00
AH1072//5	—	7.00	9.00	13.00	20.00	30.00
AH1073//5	—	7.00	9.00	13.00	20.00	30.00
AH1073//6	—	7.00	9.00	13.00	20.00	30.00
AH1074//6	—	7.00	9.00	13.00	20.00	30.00
AH1074//7	—	7.00	9.00	13.00	20.00	30.00
AH1075//7	—	7.00	9.00	13.00	20.00	30.00
AH1075//8	—	7.00	9.00	13.00	20.00	30.00
AH1076//8	—	7.00	9.00	13.00	20.00	30.00
AH1076//9	—	7.00	9.00	13.00	20.00	30.00
AH1077//9	—	7.00	9.00	13.00	20.00	30.00
AH1077//10	—	7.00	9.00	13.00	20.00	30.00
AH1079//12	—	7.00	9.00	13.00	20.00	30.00
AH1080//13	—	7.00	9.00	13.00	20.00	30.00
AH1081//13	—	7.00	9.00	13.00	20.00	30.00
AH1081//14	—	7.00	9.00	13.00	20.00	30.00
AH1082//14	—	7.00	9.00	13.00	20.00	30.00
AH1082//15	—	7.00	9.00	13.00	20.00	30.00
AH1083//15	—	7.00	9.00	13.00	20.00	30.00
AH1083//16	—	7.00	9.00	13.00	20.00	30.00
AH1084//16	—	7.00	9.00	13.00	20.00	30.00
AH1086//18	—	7.00	9.00	13.00	20.00	30.00
AH1086//19	—	7.00	9.00	13.00	20.00	30.00
AH1087//19	—	7.00	9.00	13.00	20.00	30.00
AH1087//20	—	7.00	9.00	13.00	20.00	30.00
AH1088//20	—	7.00	9.00	13.00	20.00	30.00
AH1090//xx	—	7.00	9.00	13.00	20.00	30.00
AH1092//25	—	7.00	9.00	13.00	20.00	30.00
AH1093//26	—	7.00	9.00	13.00	20.00	30.00
AH1099//30	—	7.00	9.00	13.00	20.00	30.00

KM# 300.14 RUPEE

Silver **Rev:** Mint name at bottom **Note:** Weight varies: 11.00-11.60 grams. For later issues see Khujista Bunyad.

Date	Mintage	Good	VG	F	VF	XF
AH1091//24	—	7.00	9.00	13.00	20.00	30.00
AH1093//25	—	7.00	9.00	13.00	20.00	30.00
AH1094//27	—	7.00	9.00	13.00	20.00	30.00
AH1093//26	—	7.00	9.00	13.00	20.00	30.00
AH1096//xx	—	7.00	9.00	13.00	20.00	30.00
AH1097//30	—	7.00	9.00	13.00	20.00	30.00
AH1098//30	—	7.00	9.00	13.00	20.00	30.00
AH1098//31	—	7.00	9.00	13.00	20.00	30.00
AH1099//31	—	7.00	9.00	13.00	20.00	30.00

Azamnagar

KM# 300.15 RUPEE

Silver **Note:** Weight varies 11.00-11.60 grams.

Date	Mintage	Good	VG	F	VF	XF
AH1110//4x	—	8.00	14.00	26.00	45.00	70.00

Bankapur

KM# 300.18 RUPEE

Silver **Note:** Weight varies 11.00-11.60 grams.

Date	Mintage	Good	VG	F	VF	XF
AHxxxx//44	—	9.00	16.00	32.00	56.00	90.00

Bareli

KM# 300.19 RUPEE

Silver **Obv:** Inscription, date **Rev:** Inscription **Note:** Weight varies 11.00-11.60 grams.

Date	Mintage	Good	VG	F	VF	XF
AH1097//29	—	7.00	9.00	12.00	17.50	27.50
AH1097//30	—	7.00	9.00	12.00	17.50	27.50
AH1098//30	—	7.00	9.00	12.00	17.50	27.50
AH1098//31	—	7.00	9.00	12.00	17.50	27.50
AH1099//31	—	7.00	9.00	12.00	17.50	27.50
AH1099//32	—	7.00	9.00	12.00	17.50	27.50
AH1100//32	—	7.00	9.00	12.00	17.50	27.50
AH1100//33	—	7.00	9.00	12.00	17.50	27.50
AH1101//33	—	7.00	9.00	12.00	17.50	27.50
AH1101//34	—	7.00	9.00	12.00	17.50	27.50
AH1102//34	—	7.00	9.00	12.00	17.50	27.50
AH1102//35	—	7.00	9.00	12.00	17.50	27.50
AH1103//35	—	7.00	9.00	12.00	17.50	27.50
AH1103//36	—	7.00	9.00	12.00	17.50	27.50
AH1107//39	—	7.00	9.00	12.00	17.50	27.50
AH1107//40	—	7.00	9.00	12.00	17.50	27.50
AH1108//40	—	7.00	9.00	12.00	17.50	27.50
AH1108//41	—	7.00	9.00	12.00	17.50	27.50
AH1109//41	—	7.00	9.00	12.00	17.50	27.50
AH1109//42	—	7.00	9.00	12.00	17.50	27.50
AH1110//42	—	7.00	9.00	12.00	17.50	27.50
AH1110//43	—	7.00	9.00	12.00	17.50	27.50
AH1111//43	—	7.00	9.00	12.00	17.50	27.50
AH1111//44	—	7.00	9.00	12.00	17.50	27.50
AH1112//44	—	7.00	9.00	12.00	17.50	27.50
AH1112//45	—	7.00	9.00	12.00	17.50	27.50

Bhakkar

KM# 300.20 RUPEE

Silver **Note:** Weight varies 11.00-11.60 grams.

Date	Mintage	Good	VG	F	VF	XF
AH1081//13	—	8.00	12.00	20.00	32.00	50.00
AH1083//15	—	8.00	12.00	20.00	32.00	50.00
AH1083//16	—	8.00	12.00	20.00	32.00	50.00
AH1088//21	—	8.00	12.00	20.00	32.00	50.00
AH1091//24	—	8.00	12.00	20.00	32.00	50.00
AH1094//27	—	8.00	12.00	20.00	32.00	50.00
AH1095//27	—	8.00	12.00	20.00	32.00	50.00
AH1097//30	—	8.00	12.00	20.00	32.00	50.00
AH1108//41	—	8.00	12.00	20.00	32.00	50.00

KM# 300.104 RUPEE

11.4440 g., Silver **Rev:** Inscription and mint name **Rev. Inscription:** "wala julus"

Date	Mintage	Good	VG	F	VF	XF
AH1083//15	—	8.00	13.00	24.00	38.00	60.00
AH1086//18	—	8.00	13.00	24.00	38.00	60.00

Bhilsa

KM# 300.21 RUPEE

Silver **Rev:** Mint name at bottom **Note:** Weight varies: 11.00-11.60 grams; "Mihr" couplet. For later issues see Alamgirpur.

Date	Mintage	Good	VG	F	VF	XF
AH1069//(1) Ahad	—	8.00	14.00	26.00	45.00	70.00
AHxxxx//3	—	8.00	14.00	26.00	45.00	70.00

Bijapur

KM# 300.22 RUPEE

Silver **Rev:** Without mint epithet **Note:** Weight varies: 11.00-11.60 grams.

Date	Mintage	Good	VG	F	VF	XF
AH1091//23	—	7.00	10.00	15.00	25.00	40.00
AH1091//24	—	7.00	10.00	15.00	25.00	40.00
AH1092//2x	—	7.00	10.00	15.00	25.00	40.00
AH109x//26	—	7.00	10.00	15.00	25.00	40.00
AH1100//32	—	7.00	10.00	15.00	25.00	40.00
AH1106//38	—	7.00	10.00	15.00	25.00	40.00
AH1108//41	—	7.00	10.00	15.00	25.00	40.00
AH1109//42	—	7.00	10.00	15.00	25.00	40.00
AH1111//43	—	7.00	10.00	15.00	25.00	40.00
AH1112//44	—	7.00	10.00	15.00	25.00	40.00
AH1112//45	—	7.00	10.00	15.00	25.00	40.00

KM# 300.23 RUPEE

Silver **Obv:** Inscription **Rev. Inscription:** Dar-uz-Zafar **Note:** Weight varies 11.00-11.60 grams. Mint name exist in various arrangements.

Date	Mintage	Good	VG	F	VF	XF
AH1097//30	—	7.00	9.00	12.00	17.50	27.50
AH1098//30	—	7.00	9.00	12.00	17.50	27.50
AH1098//31	—	7.00	9.00	12.00	17.50	27.50
AH1099//31	—	7.00	9.00	12.00	17.50	27.50
AH1099//32	—	7.00	9.00	12.00	17.50	27.50
AH1100//32	—	7.00	9.00	12.00	17.50	27.50
AH1100//33	—	7.00	9.00	12.00	17.50	27.50
AH1101//33	—	7.00	9.00	12.00	17.50	27.50
AH1101//34	—	7.00	9.00	12.00	17.50	27.50
AH1102//34	—	7.00	9.00	12.00	17.50	27.50
AH1102//35	—	7.00	9.00	12.00	17.50	27.50
AH1103//35	—	7.00	9.00	12.00	17.50	27.50
AH1103//36	—	7.00	9.00	12.00	17.50	27.50
AH1104//36	—	7.00	9.00	12.00	17.50	27.50
AH1104//37	—	7.00	9.00	12.00	17.50	27.50
AH1105//37	—	7.00	9.00	12.00	17.50	27.50
AH1105//38	—	7.00	9.00	12.00	17.50	27.50
AH1106//38	—	7.00	9.00	12.00	17.50	27.50
AH1106//39	—	7.00	9.00	12.00	17.50	27.50
AH1107//39	—	7.00	9.00	12.00	17.50	27.50
AH1107//40	—	7.00	9.00	12.00	17.50	27.50
AH1108//40	—	7.00	9.00	12.00	17.50	27.50
AH1108//41	—	7.00	9.00	12.00	17.50	27.50
AH1109//42	—	7.00	9.00	12.00	17.50	27.50
AH1110//43	—	7.00	9.00	12.00	17.50	27.50
AH1111//43	—	7.00	9.00	12.00	17.50	27.50
AH1111//44	—	7.00	9.00	12.00	17.50	27.50
AH1112//44	—	7.00	9.00	12.00	17.50	27.50
AH1112//45	—	7.00	9.00	12.00	17.50	27.50

Burhanpur

KM# 300.105 RUPEE

11.4440 g., Silver **Note:** "Mihr" couplet.

Date	Mintage	Good	VG	F	VF	XF
AHxxxx//4	—	8.00	12.00	20.00	32.00	50.00
AH1086//xx	—	8.00	12.00	20.00	32.00	50.00
AH1088//xx	—	8.00	12.00	20.00	32.00	50.00
AHxxxx//31	—	8.00	12.00	20.00	32.00	50.00
AHxxxx//34	—	8.00	12.00	20.00	32.00	50.00
AHxxxx//39	—	8.00	12.00	20.00	32.00	50.00

KM# 300.24 RUPEE

Silver **Note:** "Badr" couplet; Weight varies 11.00-11.60 grams.

Date	Mintage	Good	VG	F	VF	XF
AH107x//3	—	7.00	9.00	12.00	17.50	27.50
AH107x//7	—	7.00	9.00	12.00	17.50	27.50
AH1078//10	—	7.00	9.00	12.00	17.50	27.50
AH108x//15	—	7.00	9.00	12.00	17.50	27.50
AH1085//18	—	7.00	9.00	12.00	17.50	27.50
AH1086//18	—	7.00	9.00	12.00	17.50	27.50
AH1086//19	—	7.00	9.00	12.00	17.50	27.50
AH1087//19	—	7.00	9.00	12.00	17.50	27.50
AH1087//20	—	7.00	9.00	12.00	17.50	27.50
AH1088//20	—	7.00	9.00	12.00	17.50	27.50
AH1088//21	—	7.00	9.00	12.00	17.50	27.50
AH1089//21	—	7.00	9.00	12.00	17.50	27.50
AH1089//22	—	7.00	9.00	12.00	17.50	27.50
AH1090//22	—	7.00	9.00	12.00	17.50	27.50
AH1090//23	—	7.00	9.00	12.00	17.50	27.50
AH1091//23	—	7.00	9.00	12.00	17.50	27.50
AH1091//24	—	7.00	9.00	12.00	17.50	27.50
AH1092//24	—	7.00	9.00	12.00	17.50	27.50
AH1092//25	—	7.00	9.00	12.00	17.50	27.50
AH1093//25	—	7.00	9.00	12.00	17.50	27.50
AH1096//29	—	7.00	9.00	12.00	17.50	27.50
AH1093//28	—	7.00	9.00	12.00	17.50	27.50
AH1097//29	—	7.00	9.00	12.00	17.50	27.50
AH1097//30	—	7.00	9.00	12.00	17.50	27.50
AH1098//30	—	7.00	9.00	12.00	17.50	27.50
AH1098//31	—	7.00	9.00	12.00	17.50	27.50
AH1099//31	—	7.00	9.00	12.00	17.50	27.50
AH1099//32	—	7.00	9.00	12.00	17.50	27.50
AH1100//32	—	7.00	9.00	12.00	17.50	27.50
AH1100//33	—	7.00	9.00	12.00	17.50	27.50
AH1101//33	—	7.00	9.00	12.00	17.50	27.50
AH1101//34	—	7.00	9.00	12.00	17.50	27.50
AH1102//34	—	7.00	9.00	12.00	17.50	27.50
AH1102//35	—	7.00	9.00	12.00	17.50	27.50

Date	Mintage	Good	VG	F	VF	XF
AH1103//36	—	7.00	9.00	12.00	17.50	27.50
AH110x//38	—	7.00	9.00	12.00	17.50	27.50
AH1107//39	—	7.00	9.00	12.00	17.50	27.50
AH1107//40	—	7.00	9.00	12.00	17.50	27.50
AH1108//40	—	7.00	9.00	12.00	17.50	27.50
AH1108//41	—	7.00	9.00	12.00	17.50	27.50
AH1109//41	—	7.00	9.00	12.00	17.50	27.50
AH1109//42	—	7.00	9.00	12.00	17.50	27.50
AH1110//42	—	7.00	9.00	12.00	17.50	27.50
AH1110//43	—	7.00	9.00	12.00	17.50	27.50
AH1111//43	—	7.00	9.00	12.00	17.50	27.50
AH1111//44	—	7.00	9.00	12.00	17.50	27.50
AH1112//44	—	7.00	9.00	12.00	17.50	27.50

Dicholi

KM# 300.106 RUPEE

Silver **Note:** Weight varies 11.00-11.60 grams.

Date	Mintage	Good	VG	F	VF	XF
AHxxxx//35	—	—	—	—	—	—
AHxxxx//41	—	—	—	—	—	—

Gulbarga

KM# 300.27 RUPEE

Silver **Note:** Weight varies: 11.00-11.60 grams. For later issues see Ahsanabad.

Date	Mintage	Good	VG	F	VF	XF
AH1096//xx	—	7.00	9.00	12.00	20.00	30.00
AH1097//30	—	7.00	9.00	12.00	20.00	30.00
AH1098//30	—	7.00	9.00	12.00	20.00	30.00
AH1098//31	—	7.00	9.00	12.00	20.00	30.00
AH1099//31	—	7.00	9.00	12.00	20.00	30.00
AH1099//32	—	7.00	9.00	12.00	20.00	30.00
AH1101//33	—	7.00	9.00	12.00	20.00	30.00
AH1101//34	—	7.00	9.00	12.00	20.00	30.00
AH1102//34	—	7.00	9.00	12.00	20.00	30.00
AH1102//35	—	7.00	9.00	12.00	20.00	30.00
AH1103//35	—	7.00	9.00	12.00	20.00	30.00
AH1103//36	—	7.00	9.00	12.00	20.00	30.00
AH1104//36(sic)	—	7.00	9.00	12.00	20.00	30.00
AH1104//38	—	7.00	9.00	12.00	20.00	30.00
AH1104//37	—	7.00	9.00	12.00	20.00	30.00
AH1105//37	—	7.00	9.00	12.00	20.00	30.00
AH1105//38	—	7.00	9.00	12.00	20.00	30.00
AH1106//38	—	7.00	9.00	12.00	20.00	30.00
AH1106//39	—	7.00	9.00	12.00	20.00	30.00
AH1107//39	—	7.00	9.00	12.00	20.00	30.00
AH110x//40	—	7.00	9.00	12.00	20.00	30.00

Gulkanda

KM# 300.28 RUPEE

Silver **Note:** Weight varies: 11.00-11.60 grams.

Date	Mintage	Good	VG	F	VF	XF
AH107x//3	—	7.00	10.00	16.00	26.00	40.00
AH1071//4	—	7.00	10.00	16.00	26.00	40.00
AH107x//5	—	7.00	10.00	16.00	26.00	40.00
AH107x//6	—	7.00	10.00	16.00	26.00	40.00
AH107x//7	—	7.00	10.00	16.00	26.00	40.00
AH1076//8	—	7.00	10.00	16.00	26.00	40.00
AH1076//11	—	7.00	10.00	16.00	26.00	40.00
AHxxxx//12	—	7.00	10.00	16.00	26.00	40.00
AHxxxx//13	—	7.00	10.00	16.00	26.00	40.00
AH1076//14	—	7.00	10.00	16.00	26.00	40.00
AH1072//14(sic)	—	7.00	10.00	16.00	26.00	40.00
AH1072//16(sic)	—	7.00	10.00	16.00	26.00	40.00
AH1076//15	—	7.00	10.00	16.00	26.00	40.00
AH1084//16	—	7.00	10.00	16.00	26.00	40.00
AHxxxx//19	—	7.00	10.00	16.00	26.00	40.00
AH1072//18(sic)	—	7.00	10.00	16.00	26.00	40.00
AH1076//20	—	7.00	10.00	16.00	26.00	40.00
AHxxxx//22	—	7.00	10.00	16.00	26.00	40.00
AH1076//23(sic)	—	7.00	10.00	16.00	26.00	40.00
AHxxxx//27	—	7.00	10.00	16.00	26.00	40.00
AHxxxx//28	—	7.00	10.00	16.00	26.00	40.00
AH1076//30(sic)	—	7.00	10.00	16.00	26.00	40.00
AH1097//29	—	7.00	10.00	16.00	26.00	40.00
AH1096//30(sic)	—	7.00	10.00	16.00	26.00	40.00
AH1098//30	—	7.00	10.00	16.00	26.00	40.00
AH1098//31	—	7.00	10.00	16.00	26.00	40.00

Guti

KM# 300.29 RUPEE

Silver **Note:** Weight varies: 11.00-11.60 grams.

Date	Mintage	Good	VG	F	VF	XF
AH1107//41(sic)	—	9.00	16.00	32.00	56.00	90.00

Gwalior

KM# 300.30 RUPEE

Silver **Note:** Weight varies: 11.00-11.60 grams.

Date	Mintage	Good	VG	F	VF	XF
AH1096//29	—	7.00	10.00	16.00	26.00	40.00
AH1097//29	—	7.00	10.00	16.00	26.00	40.00
AH1097//30	—	7.00	10.00	16.00	26.00	40.00
AH1098//30	—	7.00	10.00	16.00	26.00	40.00
AH1098//31	—	7.00	10.00	16.00	26.00	40.00
AH1099//31	—	7.00	10.00	16.00	26.00	40.00
AH1099//32	—	7.00	10.00	16.00	26.00	40.00
AH1100//32	—	7.00	10.00	16.00	26.00	40.00
AH1100//33	—	7.00	10.00	16.00	26.00	40.00
AH1101//33	—	7.00	10.00	16.00	26.00	40.00
AH1011//33 (Error for 1101)	—	7.00	10.00	16.00	26.00	40.00

Haidarabad

KM# 300.31 RUPEE

Silver **Obv:** Inscription **Rev. Inscription:** Dar-ul-Jihad **Note:** Weight varies 11.00-11.60 grams.

Date	Mintage	Good	VG	F	VF	XF
AH1098//xx	—	7.00	9.00	12.00	20.00	30.00
AH1099//31	—	7.00	9.00	12.00	20.00	30.00
AH1099//32	—	7.00	9.00	12.00	20.00	30.00
AH1100//32	—	7.00	9.00	12.00	20.00	30.00
AH1100//33	—	7.00	9.00	12.00	20.00	30.00
AH1105//38	—	7.00	9.00	12.00	20.00	30.00
AH1106//38	—	7.00	9.00	12.00	20.00	30.00
AH1106//39	—	7.00	9.00	12.00	20.00	30.00
AH1107//39	—	7.00	9.00	12.00	20.00	30.00
AH1111//43	—	7.00	9.00	12.00	20.00	30.00
AH1111//44	—	7.00	9.00	12.00	20.00	30.00
AH1112//44	—	7.00	9.00	12.00	20.00	30.00
AH1112//45	—	7.00	9.00	12.00	20.00	30.00

Hukeri

KM# 300.33 RUPEE

Silver **Note:** Weight varies 11.00-11.60 grams.

Date	Mintage	Good	VG	F	VF	XF
AH1110//xx Rare	—	—	—	—	—	—

Imtiyazgarh

KM# 300.34 RUPEE

Silver **Rev:** Without mint epithet **Note:** Weight varies: 11.00-11.60 grams.

Date	Mintage	Good	VG	F	VF	XF
AH111x//43	—	9.00	16.00	32.00	56.00	90.00

Islam Bandar

KM# 300.37 RUPEE

Silver

Date	Mintage	Good	VG	F	VF	XF
AHxxxx//4x Rare	—	—	—	—	—	—

Islamabad

KM# 300.35 RUPEE

Silver **Rev:** Mint name at top **Note:** Weight varies: 11.00-11.60 grams.

Date	Mintage	Good	VG	F	VF	XF
AH107x//3	—	8.00	12.00	20.00	32.00	50.00
AH1072//4	—	8.00	12.00	20.00	32.00	50.00
AH1074//7	—	8.00	12.00	20.00	32.00	50.00
AH1076//8	—	8.00	12.00	20.00	32.00	50.00
AH1076//9	—	8.00	12.00	20.00	32.00	50.00
AH1077//x	—	8.00	12.00	20.00	32.00	50.00
AH1078	—	8.00	12.00	20.00	32.00	50.00
AH1079//12	—	8.00	12.00	20.00	32.00	50.00

KM# 300.36 RUPEE

Silver **Rev:** Mint name at bottom **Note:** Weight varies: 11.00-11.60 grams.

Date	Mintage	Good	VG	F	VF	XF
AH1094//27	—	7.00	10.00	16.00	26.00	40.00
AH1098//30	—	7.00	10.00	16.00	26.00	40.00
AH1098//3x	—	7.00	10.00	16.00	26.00	40.00
AH1099//3x	—	7.00	10.00	16.00	26.00	40.00
AH1103//35	—	7.00	10.00	16.00	26.00	40.00
AH1106//38	—	7.00	10.00	16.00	26.00	40.00
AH1106//39	—	7.00	10.00	16.00	26.00	40.00
AH1107//40	—	7.00	10.00	16.00	26.00	40.00
AH1108//40	—	7.00	10.00	16.00	26.00	40.00
AH1109//41	—	7.00	10.00	16.00	26.00	40.00
AH1111//xx	—	7.00	10.00	16.00	26.00	40.00
AH1112//45	—	7.00	10.00	16.00	26.00	40.00

Islamnagar

KM# 300.38 RUPEE

Silver **Note:** Weight varies 11.00-11.60 grams.

Date	Mintage	Good	VG	F	VF	XF
AH1077//10 Rare	—	—	—	—	—	—
AH1078//11 Rare	—	—	—	—	—	—
AH107x//12 Rare	—	—	—	—	—	—
AH1080//12 Rare	—	—	—	—	—	—

Itawa

KM# 300.39 RUPEE

Silver **Obv:** Inscription **Rev:** Inscription **Note:** Weight varies 11.00-11.60 grams.

Date	Mintage	Good	VG	F	VF	XF
AH1096//29	—	7.00	9.00	12.00	17.50	27.50
AH1097//29	—	7.00	9.00	12.00	17.50	27.50
AH1098//30	—	7.00	9.00	12.00	17.50	27.50
AH1098//31	—	7.00	9.00	12.00	17.50	27.50
AH1099//31	—	7.00	9.00	12.00	17.50	27.50
AH1099//32	—	7.00	9.00	12.00	17.50	27.50
AH1100//32	—	7.00	9.00	12.00	17.50	27.50
AH1100//33	—	7.00	9.00	12.00	17.50	27.50
AH1101//33	—	7.00	9.00	12.00	17.50	27.50
AH1101//34	—	7.00	9.00	12.00	17.50	27.50
AH1102//34	—	7.00	9.00	12.00	17.50	27.50
AH1102//35	—	7.00	9.00	12.00	17.50	27.50
AH1103//35	—	7.00	9.00	12.00	17.50	27.50
AH1103//36	—	7.00	9.00	12.00	17.50	27.50
AH1104//36	—	7.00	9.00	12.00	17.50	27.50
AH1104//37	—	7.00	9.00	12.00	17.50	27.50
AH1105//37	—	7.00	9.00	12.00	17.50	27.50
AH1105//38	—	7.00	9.00	12.00	17.50	27.50
AH1106//38	—	7.00	9.00	12.00	17.50	27.50
AH1106//39	—	7.00	9.00	12.00	17.50	27.50
AH1107//39	—	7.00	9.00	12.00	17.50	27.50
AH1107//40	—	7.00	9.00	12.00	17.50	27.50
AH1108//40	—	7.00	9.00	12.00	17.50	27.50
AH1108//41	—	7.00	9.00	12.00	17.50	27.50
AH1109//41	—	7.00	9.00	12.00	17.50	27.50
AH1110//42	—	7.00	9.00	12.00	17.50	27.50
AH1111//43	—	7.00	9.00	12.00	17.50	27.50
AH1111//44	—	7.00	9.00	12.00	17.50	27.50
AH1112//44	—	7.00	9.00	12.00	17.50	27.50
AH1112//45	—	7.00	9.00	12.00	17.50	27.50

Jahangirnagar

KM# 300.107 RUPEE

11.4440 g., Silver **Rev:** Mint name at top **Note:** "Mihr" couplet.

Date	Mintage	Good	VG	F	VF	XF
AH1070//3	—	—	—	—	—	—
AH1071//3	—	—	—	—	—	—
AHxxxx//4	—	—	—	—	—	—

KM# 300.108 RUPEE

11.4440 g., Silver **Rev:** Mint name at bottom **Note:** "Mihr" couplet.

Date	Mintage	Good	VG	F	VF	XF
AHxxxx//5	—	7.00	10.00	15.00	25.00	40.00
AH1073//6	—	7.00	10.00	15.00	25.00	40.00
AH1102//35	—	7.00	10.00	15.00	25.00	40.00

KM# 300.40 RUPEE
Silver **Obv:** Inscription **Rev:** Inscription **Note:** Weight varies 11.00-11.60 grams.

Date	Mintage	Good	VG	F	VF	XF
AH107x//10	—	7.00	9.00	12.00	17.50	27.50
AH108x//20	—	7.00	9.00	12.00	17.50	27.50
AH1092//24	—	7.00	9.00	12.00	17.50	27.50
AH1092//25	—	7.00	9.00	12.00	17.50	27.50
AH1093//25	—	7.00	9.00	12.00	17.50	27.50
AH1094//26	—	7.00	9.00	12.00	17.50	27.50
AH1094//27	—	7.00	9.00	12.00	17.50	27.50
AH1093//26	—	7.00	9.00	12.00	17.50	27.50
AH1095//27	—	7.00	9.00	12.00	17.50	27.50
AH1095//28	—	7.00	9.00	12.00	17.50	27.50
AH1096//28	—	7.00	9.00	12.00	17.50	27.50
AH109x//30	—	7.00	9.00	12.00	17.50	27.50
AH109x//31	—	7.00	9.00	12.00	17.50	27.50
AH1099//32	—	7.00	9.00	12.00	17.50	27.50
AH1100//32	—	7.00	9.00	12.00	17.50	27.50
AH1100//33	—	7.00	9.00	12.00	17.50	27.50
AH1101//33	—	7.00	9.00	12.00	17.50	27.50
AH1101//34	—	7.00	9.00	12.00	17.50	27.50
AH1102//34	—	7.00	9.00	12.00	17.50	27.50
AH1102//35	—	7.00	9.00	12.00	17.50	27.50
AH1103//35	—	7.00	9.00	12.00	17.50	27.50
AH1103//36	—	7.00	9.00	12.00	17.50	27.50
AH1104//36	—	7.00	9.00	12.00	17.50	27.50
AH1104//37	—	7.00	9.00	12.00	17.50	27.50
AH1105//37	—	7.00	9.00	12.00	17.50	27.50
AH1105//38	—	7.00	9.00	12.00	17.50	27.50
AH1106//38	—	7.00	9.00	12.00	17.50	27.50
AH1106//39	—	7.00	9.00	12.00	17.50	27.50
AH1107//39	—	7.00	9.00	12.00	17.50	27.50
AH1107//40	—	7.00	9.00	12.00	17.50	27.50
AH1108//40	—	7.00	9.00	12.00	17.50	27.50
AH1108//41	—	7.00	9.00	12.00	17.50	27.50
AH1109//41	—	7.00	9.00	12.00	17.50	27.50
AH1109//42	—	7.00	9.00	12.00	17.50	27.50
AH1110//42	—	7.00	9.00	12.00	17.50	27.50
AH1110//43	—	7.00	9.00	12.00	17.50	27.50
AH1111//43	—	7.00	9.00	12.00	17.50	27.50
AH1111//44	—	7.00	9.00	12.00	17.50	27.50
AH1112//45	—	7.00	9.00	12.00	17.50	27.50

Jaunpur

KM# 300.41 RUPEE
Silver **Note:** Weight varies: 11.00-11.60 grams.

Date	Mintage	Good	VG	F	VF	XF
AH1097//30	—	8.00	13.00	24.00	38.00	60.00
AH1099//31	—	8.00	13.00	24.00	38.00	60.00
AH1099//32	—	8.00	13.00	24.00	38.00	60.00
AH1101//3x	—	8.00	13.00	24.00	38.00	60.00

Jinji

KM# 300.42 RUPEE
Silver **Note:** Weight varies: 11.00-11.60 grams.

Date	Mintage	Good	VG	F	VF	XF
AH1106//42	—	8.00	15.00	30.00	50.00	80.00
AH1109//xx	—	8.00	15.00	30.00	50.00	80.00

Junagadh

KM# 300.43 RUPEE
Silver **Note:** Weight varies 11.00-11.60 grams.

Date	Mintage	Good	VG	F	VF	XF
AH1099//31	—	7.00	9.00	12.00	20.00	30.00
AH1099//32	—	7.00	9.00	12.00	20.00	30.00
AH1100//32	—	7.00	9.00	12.00	20.00	30.00
AH1100//33	—	7.00	9.00	12.00	20.00	30.00
AH1101//33	—	7.00	9.00	12.00	20.00	30.00
AH1101//34	—	7.00	9.00	12.00	20.00	30.00
AH1102//34	—	7.00	9.00	12.00	20.00	30.00
AH1102//35	—	7.00	9.00	12.00	20.00	30.00
AH1103//35	—	7.00	9.00	12.00	20.00	30.00
AH1103//36	—	7.00	9.00	12.00	20.00	30.00
AH1104//36	—	7.00	9.00	12.00	20.00	30.00
AH1104//37	—	7.00	9.00	12.00	20.00	30.00
AH1105//37	—	7.00	9.00	12.00	20.00	30.00
AH1105//38	—	7.00	9.00	12.00	20.00	30.00
AH1106//38	—	7.00	9.00	12.00	20.00	30.00
AH1108//40	—	7.00	9.00	12.00	20.00	30.00
AH1108//41	—	7.00	9.00	12.00	20.00	30.00
AH1109//41	—	7.00	9.00	12.00	20.00	30.00

Date	Mintage	Good	VG	F	VF	XF
AH1109//42	—	7.00	9.00	12.00	20.00	30.00
AH1110//42	—	7.00	9.00	12.00	20.00	30.00
AH1110//43	—	7.00	9.00	12.00	20.00	30.00
AH1111//43	—	7.00	9.00	12.00	20.00	30.00

Kabul

KM# 300.109 RUPEE
11.4440 g., Silver **Rev:** Without mint epithet **Note:** "Mihr" couplet.

Date	Mintage	Good	VG	F	VF	XF
AH1082//15	—	7.00	10.00	16.00	26.00	40.00
AH1083//16	—	7.00	10.00	16.00	26.00	40.00
AH1085//18	—	7.00	10.00	16.00	26.00	40.00
AH1088//21	—	7.00	10.00	16.00	26.00	40.00

KM# 300.44 RUPEE
Silver **Rev:** Without mint epithet **Note:** "Badr" couplet; Weight varies: 11.00-11.60 grams.

Date	Mintage	Good	VG	F	VF	XF
AH1082//14	—	7.00	10.00	16.00	26.00	40.00
AH1082//15	—	7.00	10.00	16.00	26.00	40.00
AH1083//15	—	7.00	10.00	16.00	26.00	40.00
AH1086//18	—	7.00	10.00	16.00	26.00	40.00
AH108x//20	—	7.00	10.00	16.00	26.00	40.00
AH1089//xx	—	7.00	10.00	16.00	26.00	40.00
AH1092//24	—	7.00	10.00	16.00	26.00	40.00
AH109x//27	—	7.00	10.00	16.00	26.00	40.00
AH1101//34	—	7.00	10.00	16.00	26.00	40.00

KM# 300.45 RUPEE
Silver **Obv:** Inscription **Rev. Inscription:** Dar-ul-Mulk and mint name **Note:** Weight varies 11.00-11.60 grams.

Date	Mintage	Good	VG	F	VF	XF
AH1094//27	—	7.00	9.00	12.00	20.00	30.00
AH1096//29	—	7.00	9.00	12.00	20.00	30.00
AH1098//30	—	7.00	9.00	12.00	20.00	30.00
AH1098//31	—	7.00	9.00	12.00	20.00	30.00
AH1099//31	—	7.00	9.00	12.00	20.00	30.00
AH1099//32	—	7.00	9.00	12.00	20.00	30.00
AH1100//32	—	7.00	9.00	12.00	20.00	30.00
AH110x//33	—	7.00	9.00	12.00	20.00	30.00
AH1101//XX	—	7.00	9.00	12.00	20.00	30.00
AH1102//34	—	7.00	9.00	12.00	20.00	30.00
AH1102//35	—	7.00	9.00	12.00	20.00	30.00
AH1104//36	—	7.00	9.00	12.00	20.00	30.00
AH110X//37	—	7.00	9.00	12.00	20.00	30.00
AH1105//xx	—	7.00	9.00	12.00	20.00	30.00
AH1106//38	—	7.00	9.00	12.00	20.00	30.00
AH1106//39	—	7.00	9.00	12.00	20.00	30.00
AH1107//39	—	7.00	9.00	12.00	20.00	30.00
AH1107//40	—	7.00	9.00	12.00	20.00	30.00
AH1110//42	—	7.00	9.00	12.00	20.00	30.00
AH1111//43	—	7.00	9.00	12.00	20.00	30.00
AH1111//44	—	7.00	9.00	12.00	20.00	30.00
AH1112//44	—	7.00	9.00	12.00	20.00	30.00

Kanji

KM# 300.46 RUPEE
Silver **Note:** Weight varies: 11.00-11.60 grams.

Date	Mintage	Good	VG	F	VF	XF
AH1xxx//32	—	8.00	14.00	26.00	45.00	70.00
AH1105	—	8.00	14.00	26.00	45.00	70.00
AH1106//38	—	8.00	14.00	26.00	45.00	70.00
AH1106//39	—	8.00	14.00	26.00	45.00	70.00
AH1106//40(sic)	—	8.00	14.00	26.00	45.00	70.00
AH1106//41(sic)	—	8.00	14.00	26.00	45.00	70.00
AH1106//42(sic)	—	8.00	14.00	26.00	45.00	70.00
AH11xx//45	—	8.00	14.00	26.00	45.00	70.00

Karappa

KM# 300.97 RUPEE
Silver **Note:** Weight varies: 11.00-11.60 grams.

Date	Mintage	Good	VG	F	VF	XF
AHxxxx//32 Rare	—	—	—	—	—	—
AH11xx//34 Rare	—	—	—	—	—	—
AH11xx//37 Rare	—	—	—	—	—	—

Karnatik

KM# 300.47 RUPEE
Silver **Note:** Weight varies: 11.00-11.60 grams.

Date	Mintage	Good	VG	F	VF	XF
AH1xxx//32 Rare	—	—	—	—	—	—

KM# 300.110 RUPEE
11.4440 g., Silver **Rev. Inscription:** "dar al-Zafar Bijapur"

Date	Mintage	Good	VG	F	VF	XF
AH1110//43 Rare	—	—	—	—	—	—

Kashmir

KM# 300.48 RUPEE
Silver **Obv:** Couplet in three lines **Note:** Weight varies 11.00-11.60 grams.

Date	Mintage	Good	VG	F	VF	XF
AH107x//4	—	7.00	11.00	18.50	32.50	50.00
AHxxxx//9	—	7.00	11.00	18.50	32.50	50.00
AH107x//10	—	7.00	11.00	18.50	32.50	50.00
AH1089//21	—	7.00	11.00	18.50	32.50	50.00
AH1096//xx	—	7.00	11.00	18.50	32.50	50.00
AH109x//30	—	7.00	11.00	18.50	32.50	50.00
AH1xxx//32	—	7.00	11.00	18.50	32.50	50.00
AH1105//3x	—	7.00	11.00	18.50	32.50	50.00
AH1106//39	—	7.00	11.00	18.50	32.50	50.00
AH1108//40	—	7.00	11.00	18.50	32.50	50.00
AH1108//41	—	7.00	11.00	18.50	32.50	50.00
AH1109//41	—	7.00	11.00	18.50	32.50	50.00
AH1109//42	—	7.00	11.00	18.50	32.50	50.00
AH1110//42	—	7.00	11.00	18.50	32.50	50.00
AH111x//43	—	7.00	11.00	18.50	32.50	50.00
AH111x//44	—	7.00	11.00	18.50	32.50	50.00
AH111x//45	—	7.00	11.00	18.50	32.50	50.00

Katak

KM# 300.50 RUPEE
Silver **Obv:** Inscription **Rev:** Mint name at bottom **Note:** "Badr" couplet; Weight varies 11.00-11.60 grams.

Date	Mintage	Good	VG	F	VF	XF
AHxxxx//2	—	7.00	9.00	12.00	20.00	30.00
AH107x//3	—	7.00	9.00	12.00	20.00	30.00
AH1072//4	—	7.00	9.00	12.00	20.00	30.00
AH1073//5	—	7.00	9.00	12.00	20.00	30.00
AH107x//7	—	7.00	9.00	12.00	20.00	30.00
AH107x//9	—	7.00	9.00	12.00	20.00	30.00
AH1082//15	—	7.00	9.00	12.00	20.00	30.00
AH1085//18	—	7.00	9.00	12.00	20.00	30.00
AH108x//19	—	7.00	9.00	12.00	20.00	30.00
AH108x//20	—	7.00	9.00	12.00	20.00	30.00
AH1088//21	—	7.00	9.00	12.00	20.00	30.00
AH1089//22	—	7.00	9.00	12.00	20.00	30.00
AH109x//23	—	7.00	9.00	12.00	20.00	30.00
AH1092//25	—	7.00	9.00	12.00	20.00	30.00
AH1094//26	—	7.00	9.00	12.00	20.00	30.00
AH1094//27	—	7.00	9.00	12.00	20.00	30.00
AH1095//27	—	7.00	9.00	12.00	20.00	30.00
AH1095//28	—	7.00	9.00	12.00	20.00	30.00
AH1097//30	—	7.00	9.00	12.00	20.00	30.00
AH1099//31	—	7.00	9.00	12.00	20.00	30.00
AH1099//32	—	7.00	9.00	12.00	20.00	30.00
AH110x//33	—	7.00	9.00	12.00	20.00	30.00
AH1100//32	—	7.00	9.00	12.00	20.00	30.00
AH1102//35	—	7.00	9.00	12.00	20.00	30.00
AH1103//35	—	7.00	9.00	12.00	20.00	30.00
AH1103//36	—	7.00	9.00	12.00	20.00	30.00
AH1104//36	—	7.00	9.00	12.00	20.00	30.00
AH1104//37	—	7.00	9.00	12.00	20.00	30.00
AH1105//37	—	7.00	9.00	12.00	20.00	30.00
AH1105//38	—	7.00	9.00	12.00	20.00	30.00
AH1106//38	—	7.00	9.00	12.00	20.00	30.00
AH1106//39	—	7.00	9.00	12.00	20.00	30.00
AH1107//39	—	7.00	9.00	12.00	20.00	30.00
AH1107//40	—	7.00	9.00	12.00	20.00	30.00
AH1108//40	—	7.00	9.00	12.00	20.00	30.00
AH1108//41	—	7.00	9.00	12.00	20.00	30.00
AH1109//41	—	7.00	9.00	12.00	20.00	30.00
AH1109//42	—	7.00	9.00	12.00	20.00	30.00
AH1110//42	—	7.00	9.00	12.00	20.00	30.00
AH1110//43	—	7.00	9.00	12.00	20.00	30.00
AH1112//44	—	7.00	9.00	12.00	20.00	30.00
AH1112//45	—	7.00	9.00	12.00	20.00	30.00

KM# 300.49 RUPEE
Silver **Rev:** Mint name at top **Note:** "Mihr" couplet; Weight varies: 11.00-11.60 grams.

Date	Mintage	Good	VG	F	VF	XF
AH1070//(1) Ahad	—	8.00	12.00	20.00	32.00	50.00
AH1071//3	—	8.00	12.00	20.00	32.00	50.00
AHxxxx//4	—	8.00	12.00	20.00	32.00	50.00
AH1072//5	—	8.00	12.00	20.00	32.00	50.00
AH1073//5	—	8.00	12.00	20.00	32.00	50.00
AHxxxx//18	—	8.00	12.00	20.00	32.00	50.00
AHxxxx//25	—	8.00	12.00	20.00	32.00	50.00
AHxxxx//33	—	8.00	12.00	20.00	32.00	50.00
AHxxxx//36	—	8.00	12.00	20.00	32.00	50.00
AHxxxx//43	—	8.00	12.00	20.00	32.00	50.00

Khambayat

KM# 300.51 RUPEE

Silver **Obv:** Inscription **Rev:** Mint name at bottom **Note:** "Badr" couplet; Weight varies 11.00-11.60 grams.

Date	Mintage	Good	VG	F	VF	XF
AH1070//(1) Ahad	—	7.00	9.00	12.00	17.50	27.50
AH1072//4	—	7.00	9.00	12.00	17.50	27.50
AH1072//5	—	7.00	9.00	12.00	17.50	27.50
AH1073//5	—	7.00	9.00	12.00	17.50	27.50
AH1073//6	—	7.00	9.00	12.00	17.50	27.50
AH1074//6	—	7.00	9.00	12.00	17.50	27.50
AH1074//7	—	7.00	9.00	12.00	17.50	27.50
AH1075//7	—	7.00	9.00	12.00	17.50	27.50
AH1075//8	—	7.00	9.00	12.00	17.50	27.50
AH1076//8	—	7.00	9.00	12.00	17.50	27.50
AH1076//7	—	7.00	9.00	12.00	17.50	27.50
AH1077//x	—	7.00	9.00	12.00	17.50	27.50
AH1078//10	—	7.00	9.00	12.00	17.50	27.50
AH1078//11	—	7.00	9.00	12.00	17.50	27.50
AH1079//11	—	7.00	9.00	12.00	17.50	27.50
AH1079//12	—	7.00	9.00	12.00	17.50	27.50
AH1080//12	—	7.00	9.00	12.00	17.50	27.50
AH1080//13	—	7.00	9.00	12.00	17.50	27.50
AH1081//13	—	7.00	9.00	12.00	17.50	27.50
AH1081//14	—	7.00	9.00	12.00	17.50	27.50
AH1082//14	—	7.00	9.00	12.00	17.50	27.50
AH1082//15	—	7.00	9.00	12.00	17.50	27.50
AH1083//15	—	7.00	9.00	12.00	17.50	27.50
AH1083//16	—	7.00	9.00	12.00	17.50	27.50
AH1084//16	—	7.00	9.00	12.00	17.50	27.50
AH1084//17	—	7.00	9.00	12.00	17.50	27.50
AH1085//17	—	7.00	9.00	12.00	17.50	27.50
AH1085//18	—	7.00	9.00	12.00	17.50	27.50
AH1086//18	—	7.00	9.00	12.00	17.50	27.50
AH1086//19	—	7.00	9.00	12.00	17.50	27.50
AH1087//19	—	7.00	9.00	12.00	17.50	27.50
AH1087//20	—	7.00	9.00	12.00	17.50	27.50
AH1088//20	—	7.00	9.00	12.00	17.50	27.50
AH1088//21	—	7.00	9.00	12.00	17.50	27.50
AH1089//21	—	7.00	9.00	12.00	17.50	27.50
AH1089//22	—	7.00	9.00	12.00	17.50	27.50
AH1090//22	—	7.00	9.00	12.00	17.50	27.50
AH1090//23	—	7.00	9.00	12.00	17.50	27.50
AH1091//23	—	7.00	9.00	12.00	17.50	27.50
AH1091//24	—	7.00	9.00	12.00	17.50	27.50
AH1092//24	—	7.00	9.00	12.00	17.50	27.50
AH1092//25	—	7.00	9.00	12.00	17.50	27.50
AH1093//25	—	7.00	9.00	12.00	17.50	27.50
AH1094//26	—	7.00	9.00	12.00	17.50	27.50
AH1094//27	—	7.00	9.00	12.00	17.50	27.50
AH1093//26	—	7.00	9.00	12.00	17.50	27.50
AH1095//27	—	7.00	9.00	12.00	17.50	27.50
AH1095//28	—	7.00	9.00	12.00	17.50	27.50
AH1096//28	—	7.00	9.00	12.00	17.50	27.50
AH1096//29	—	7.00	9.00	12.00	17.50	27.50
AH1097//29	—	7.00	9.00	12.00	17.50	27.50
AH1097//30	—	7.00	9.00	12.00	17.50	27.50
AH1098//30	—	7.00	9.00	12.00	17.50	27.50
AH1098//31	—	7.00	9.00	12.00	17.50	27.50
AH1099//31	—	7.00	9.00	12.00	17.50	27.50
AH1099//32	—	7.00	9.00	12.00	17.50	27.50
AH1100//32	—	7.00	9.00	12.00	17.50	27.50
AH1100//33	—	7.00	9.00	12.00	17.50	27.50
AH1101//33	—	7.00	9.00	12.00	17.50	27.50
AH1101//34	—	7.00	9.00	12.00	17.50	27.50
AH1102//34	—	7.00	9.00	12.00	17.50	27.50
AH1102//35	—	7.00	9.00	12.00	17.50	27.50
AH1103//35	—	7.00	9.00	12.00	17.50	27.50
AH1104//36	—	7.00	9.00	12.00	17.50	27.50
AH1105//37	—	7.00	9.00	12.00	17.50	27.50
AH1106//38	—	7.00	9.00	12.00	17.50	27.50
AH1107//40	—	7.00	9.00	12.00	17.50	27.50
AH1109//41	—	7.00	9.00	12.00	17.50	27.50
AH1109//43 (sic)	—	7.00	9.00	12.00	17.50	27.50
AH1110//42	—	7.00	9.00	12.00	17.50	27.50
AH1111//43	—	7.00	9.00	12.00	17.50	27.50
AH1112//44	—	7.00	9.00	12.00	17.50	27.50

KM# 300.95 RUPEE

Silver **Rev:** Mint name at top **Note:** Weight varies: 11.00-11.60 grams.

Date	Mintage	Good	VG	F	VF	XF
AH1070//(1) Ahad	—	9.00	16.00	32.00	56.00	90.00

KM# 300.111 RUPEE

11.4440 g., Silver **Rev:** Mint name at bottom **Note:** "Mihr" couplet.

Date	Mintage	Good	VG	F	VF	XF
AH1109//41	—	7.00	10.00	15.00	23.00	35.00

Khujista Bunyad

KM# 300.52 RUPEE

Silver **Obv:** Inscription **Rev:** Inscription **Note:** Weight varies 11.00-11.60 grams.

Date	Mintage	Good	VG	F	VF	XF
AH1091//23	—	7.00	9.00	12.00	20.00	30.00
AH1091//24	—	7.00	9.00	12.00	20.00	30.00
AH1094//26	—	7.00	9.00	12.00	20.00	30.00
AH1096//28	—	7.00	9.00	12.00	20.00	30.00
AH1100//32	—	7.00	9.00	12.00	20.00	30.00
AH1100//33	—	7.00	9.00	12.00	20.00	30.00
AH1101//33	—	7.00	9.00	12.00	20.00	30.00
AH1101//34	—	7.00	9.00	12.00	20.00	30.00
AH1102//34	—	7.00	9.00	12.00	20.00	30.00
AH1102//35	—	7.00	9.00	12.00	20.00	30.00
AH1103//35	—	7.00	9.00	12.00	20.00	30.00
AH1106//38	—	7.00	9.00	12.00	20.00	30.00
AH1106//39	—	7.00	9.00	12.00	20.00	30.00
AH1107//39	—	7.00	9.00	12.00	20.00	30.00
AH1107//40	—	7.00	9.00	12.00	20.00	30.00
AH1108//40	—	7.00	9.00	12.00	20.00	30.00
AH1108//41	—	7.00	9.00	12.00	20.00	30.00
AH1109//41	—	7.00	9.00	12.00	20.00	30.00
AH1109//42	—	7.00	9.00	12.00	20.00	30.00
AH1110//42	—	7.00	9.00	12.00	20.00	30.00
AH1110//43	—	7.00	9.00	12.00	20.00	30.00
AH1111//43	—	7.00	9.00	12.00	20.00	30.00
AH1111//44	—	7.00	9.00	12.00	20.00	30.00
AH1112//44	—	7.00	9.00	12.00	20.00	30.00

Lahore

KM# 300.112 RUPEE

11.4440 g., Silver **Rev. Inscription:** "dar al-Sultanat" **Note:** "Mihr" couplet.

Date	Mintage	Good	VG	F	VF	XF
AH1070//(1) Ahad	—	8.00	12.00	20.00	32.00	50.00
AH1069//(1) Ahad	—	8.00	12.00	20.00	32.00	50.00
AH1070//2	—	8.00	12.00	20.00	32.00	50.00
AH1071//3	—	8.00	12.00	20.00	32.00	50.00
AH1071//4	—	8.00	12.00	20.00	32.00	50.00
AH1072//4	—	8.00	12.00	20.00	32.00	50.00
AHxxxx//5	—	8.00	12.00	20.00	32.00	50.00
AHxxxx//6	—	8.00	12.00	20.00	32.00	50.00
AH1085//18	—	8.00	12.00	20.00	32.00	50.00
AH1109//42	—	8.00	12.00	20.00	32.00	50.00

KM# 300.53 RUPEE

Silver **Obv:** Inscription **Rev. Inscription:** "Dar-us-Sultanat", mint name **Note:** "Badr couplet"; Weight varies 11.00-11.60 grams.

Date	Mintage	Good	VG	F	VF	XF
AH1072//5	—	7.00	9.00	12.00	17.50	27.50
AH1073//5	—	7.00	9.00	12.00	17.50	27.50
AH1074//6	—	7.00	9.00	12.00	17.50	27.50
AH1076//8	—	7.00	9.00	12.00	17.50	27.50
AH1076//9	—	7.00	9.00	12.00	17.50	27.50
AH1077//9	—	7.00	9.00	12.00	17.50	27.50
AH1077//10	—	7.00	9.00	12.00	17.50	27.50
AH1078//10	—	7.00	9.00	12.00	17.50	27.50
AH1078//11	—	7.00	9.00	12.00	17.50	27.50
AH1079//11	—	7.00	9.00	12.00	17.50	27.50
AH1079//12	—	7.00	9.00	12.00	17.50	27.50
AH1080//12	—	7.00	9.00	12.00	17.50	27.50
AH1080//13	—	7.00	9.00	12.00	17.50	27.50
AH1081//13	—	7.00	9.00	12.00	17.50	27.50
AH1081//14	—	7.00	9.00	12.00	17.50	27.50
AH1083//16	—	7.00	9.00	12.00	17.50	27.50
AH1085//17	—	7.00	9.00	12.00	17.50	27.50
AH1087//19	—	7.00	9.00	12.00	17.50	27.50
AH1088//20	—	7.00	9.00	12.00	17.50	27.50
AH1089//21	—	7.00	9.00	12.00	17.50	27.50
AH1090//22	—	7.00	9.00	12.00	17.50	27.50
AH1090//23	—	7.00	9.00	12.00	17.50	27.50
AH1091//23	—	7.00	9.00	12.00	17.50	27.50
AH1092//24	—	7.00	9.00	12.00	17.50	27.50
AH1093//25	—	7.00	9.00	12.00	17.50	27.50
AH1094//26	—	7.00	9.00	12.00	17.50	27.50
AH1094//27	—	7.00	9.00	12.00	17.50	27.50
AH1095//28	—	7.00	9.00	12.00	17.50	27.50
AH1096//29	—	7.00	9.00	12.00	17.50	27.50
AH1097//29	—	7.00	9.00	12.00	17.50	27.50
AH1097//30	—	7.00	9.00	12.00	17.50	27.50
AH1098//30	—	7.00	9.00	12.00	17.50	27.50
AH1098//31	—	7.00	9.00	12.00	17.50	27.50
AH1099//31	—	7.00	9.00	12.00	17.50	27.50
AH1099//32	—	7.00	9.00	12.00	17.50	27.50
AH1100//32	—	7.00	9.00	12.00	17.50	27.50
AH1100//33	—	7.00	9.00	12.00	17.50	27.50
AH1101//33	—	7.00	9.00	12.00	17.50	27.50
AH1101//34	—	7.00	9.00	12.00	17.50	27.50
AH1102//34	—	7.00	9.00	12.00	17.50	27.50
AH1103//35	—	7.00	9.00	12.00	17.50	27.50
AH1103//36	—	7.00	9.00	12.00	17.50	27.50
AH1104//36	—	7.00	9.00	12.00	17.50	27.50
AH1104//37	—	7.00	9.00	12.00	17.50	27.50
AH1105//37	—	7.00	9.00	12.00	17.50	27.50
AH1105//38	—	7.00	9.00	12.00	17.50	27.50
AH1106//38	—	7.00	9.00	12.00	17.50	27.50
AH1106//39	—	7.00	9.00	12.00	17.50	27.50
AH1107//39	—	7.00	9.00	12.00	17.50	27.50
AH1107//40	—	7.00	9.00	12.00	17.50	27.50
AH1108//40	—	7.00	9.00	12.00	17.50	27.50
AH1108//41	—	7.00	9.00	12.00	17.50	27.50
AH1109//41	—	7.00	9.00	12.00	17.50	27.50
AH1109//42	—	7.00	9.00	12.00	17.50	27.50
AH1110//42	—	7.00	9.00	12.00	17.50	27.50
AH1110//43	—	7.00	9.00	12.00	17.50	27.50
AH1111//43	—	7.00	9.00	12.00	17.50	27.50
AH1111//44	—	7.00	9.00	12.00	17.50	27.50
AH1112//44	—	7.00	9.00	12.00	17.50	27.50
AH1112//45	—	7.00	9.00	12.00	17.50	27.50

Lakhnau

KM# 300.54 RUPEE

Silver **Obv:** Inscription **Rev:** Inscription **Note:** Weight varies 11.00-11.60 grams.

Date	Mintage	Good	VG	F	VF	XF
AH1081//14	—	7.00	9.00	12.00	17.50	27.50
AH1084//16	—	7.00	9.00	12.00	17.50	27.50
AH1084//17	—	7.00	9.00	12.00	17.50	27.50
AH1085//17	—	7.00	9.00	12.00	17.50	27.50
AH1085//18	—	7.00	9.00	12.00	17.50	27.50
AH1087//19	—	7.00	9.00	12.00	17.50	27.50
AH1087//20	—	7.00	9.00	12.00	17.50	27.50
AH1088//20	—	7.00	9.00	12.00	17.50	27.50
AH1088//21	—	7.00	9.00	12.00	17.50	27.50
AH1089//21	—	7.00	9.00	12.00	17.50	27.50
AH1091//23	—	7.00	9.00	12.00	17.50	27.50
AH11xx//25	—	7.00	9.00	12.00	17.50	27.50
AH1095//27	—	7.00	9.00	12.00	17.50	27.50
AH1095//28	—	7.00	9.00	12.00	17.50	27.50
AH1097//29	—	7.00	9.00	12.00	17.50	27.50
AH1098//30	—	7.00	9.00	12.00	17.50	27.50
AH1098//31	—	7.00	9.00	12.00	17.50	27.50
AH1099//32	—	7.00	9.00	12.00	17.50	27.50
AH1100//32	—	7.00	9.00	12.00	17.50	27.50
AH1101//33	—	7.00	9.00	12.00	17.50	27.50
AH1102//34	—	7.00	9.00	12.00	17.50	27.50
AH1103//35	—	7.00	9.00	12.00	17.50	27.50
AH110x//36	—	7.00	9.00	12.00	17.50	27.50
AH11xx//38	—	7.00	99.00	12.00	17.50	27.50
AH11xx//39	—	7.00	9.00	12.00	17.50	27.50
AH11xx//40	—	7.00	9.00	12.00	17.50	27.50
AH11xx//41	—	7.00	9.00	12.00	17.50	27.50
AH11xx//42	—	7.00	9.00	12.00	17.50	27.50
AH1110//43	—	7.00	9.00	12.00	17.50	27.50
AH11xx//44	—	7.00	9.00	12.00	17.50	27.50
AH11xx//45	—	7.00	9.00	12.00	17.50	27.50
AH1113//46	—	7.00	9.00	12.00	17.50	27.50

Macchlipattan

KM# 300.55 RUPEE

Silver **Note:** Weight varies 11.00-11.60 grams.

Date	Mintage	Good	VG	F	VF	XF
AH1099//31	—	7.00	10.00	16.00	28.00	40.00
AH1099//32	—	7.00	10.00	16.00	28.00	40.00
AH10100//32(sic)	—	7.00	10.00	16.00	28.00	40.00
AH1100//32	—	7.00	10.00	16.00	28.00	40.00
AH1100//33	—	7.00	10.00	16.00	28.00	40.00
AH1111//43	—	7.00	10.00	16.00	28.00	40.00
AH1111//44	—	7.00	10.00	16.00	28.00	40.00
AH1112//44	—	7.00	10.00	16.00	28.00	40.00
AH1112//45	—	7.00	10.00	16.00	28.00	40.00

Makhsusabad

KM# 300.58 RUPEE

Silver **Obv:** Inscription, date **Rev:** Inscription **Note:** Weight varies 11.00-11.60 grams. For later isues see Murshidabad, KM#300.65.

Date	Mintage	Good	VG	F	VF	XF
AH1111//44	—	8.00	15.00	30.00	50.00	80.00

Muazzamabad

KM# 300.60 RUPEE

Silver **Note:** Weight varies: 11.00-11.60 grams.

Date	Mintage	Good	VG	F	VF	XF
AH1096//29	—	8.00	14.00	26.00	26.00	70.00
AH1097//29	—	8.00	14.00	26.00	26.00	70.00
AH1097//30	—	8.00	14.00	26.00	26.00	70.00
AH1098//30	—	8.00	14.00	26.00	26.00	70.00
AH1098//31	—	8.00	14.00	26.00	26.00	70.00
AH1099//31	—	8.00	14.00	26.00	26.00	70.00
AH1099//32	—	8.00	14.00	26.00	26.00	70.00
AH1100//32	—	8.00	14.00	26.00	26.00	70.00
AH1100//33	—	8.00	14.00	26.00	26.00	70.00
AH110x//34	—	8.00	14.00	26.00	26.00	70.00

Muhammadabad

KM# 300.61 RUPEE

Silver **Note:** Weight varies: 11.00-11.60 grams.

Date	Mintage	Good	VG	F	VF	XF
AHxxxx//28 Rare	—	—	—	—	—	—
AH1096//29 Rare	—	—	—	—	—	—
AH1099//31 Rare	—	—	—	—	—	—
AH1102//34 Rare	—	—	—	—	—	—

Mulher

KM# 300.59 RUPEE

Silver **Note:** Weight varies: 11.00-11.60 grams.

Date	Mintage	Good	VG	F	VF	XF
AH1095//28 Rare	—	—	—	—	—	—
AH1098//30 Rare	—	—	—	—	—	—

Multan

KM# 300.62 RUPEE

Silver **Rev:** "Dar-ul-Aman" with mint name at top **Note:** "Mihr" couplet; Weight varies: 11.00-11.60 grams.

Date	Mintage	Good	VG	F	VF	XF
AH1070//(1) Ahad	—	7.00	9.00	13.00	20.00	30.00
AH1070//2	—	7.00	9.00	13.00	20.00	30.00
AH1070//3	—	7.00	9.00	13.00	20.00	30.00
AH1071//3	—	7.00	9.00	13.00	20.00	30.00
AH1071//4	—	7.00	9.00	13.00	20.00	30.00
AH1072//4	—	7.00	9.00	13.00	20.00	30.00
AH1072//5	—	7.00	9.00	13.00	20.00	30.00
AH1073//5	—	7.00	9.00	13.00	20.00	30.00

KM# 300.63 RUPEE

Silver **Obv:** Inscription **Rev:** Inscription, without mint epithet, mint name at bottom **Note:** Weight varies 11.00-11.60 grams.

Date	Mintage	Good	VG	F	VF	XF
AH1072//4	—	7.00	9.00	12.00	17.50	27.50
AH1073//5	—	7.00	9.00	12.00	17.50	27.50
AH1074//6	—	7.00	9.00	12.00	17.50	27.50
AH1074//7	—	7.00	9.00	12.00	17.50	27.50
AH1075//7	—	7.00	9.00	12.00	17.50	27.50
AH1075//8	—	7.00	9.00	12.00	17.50	27.50
AH1076//8	—	7.00	9.00	12.00	17.50	27.50
AH1076//9	—	7.00	9.00	12.00	17.50	27.50
AH1077//9	—	7.00	9.00	12.00	17.50	27.50
AH1077//10	—	7.00	9.00	12.00	17.50	27.50
AH1078//11	—	7.00	9.00	12.00	17.50	27.50
AH1079//10	—	7.00	9.00	12.00	17.50	27.50
AH1079//11	—	7.00	9.00	12.00	17.50	27.50
AH1079//12	—	7.00	9.00	12.00	17.50	27.50
AH1080//12	—	7.00	9.00	12.00	17.50	27.50
AH1080//13	—	7.00	9.00	12.00	17.50	27.50
AH1081//13	—	7.00	9.00	12.00	17.50	27.50
AH1081//14	—	7.00	9.00	12.00	17.50	27.50
AH1082//14	—	7.00	9.00	12.00	17.50	27.50
AH1082//15	—	7.00	9.00	12.00	17.50	27.50
AH1083//15	—	7.00	9.00	12.00	17.50	27.50
AH1083//16	—	7.00	9.00	12.00	17.50	27.50
AH1084//16	—	7.00	9.00	12.00	17.50	27.50
AH1084//17	—	7.00	9.00	12.00	17.50	27.50
AH1085//17	—	7.00	9.00	12.00	17.50	27.50
AH1085//18	—	7.00	9.00	12.00	17.50	27.50
AH1086//19	—	7.00	9.00	12.00	17.50	27.50
AH1087//20	—	7.00	9.00	12.00	17.50	27.50
AH1088//20	—	7.00	9.00	12.00	17.50	27.50
AH1088//21	—	7.00	9.00	12.00	17.50	27.50
AH1089//21	—	7.00	9.00	12.00	17.50	27.50
AH1089//22	—	7.00	9.00	12.00	17.50	27.50
AH1090//22	—	7.00	9.00	12.00	17.50	27.50
AH1090//23	—	7.00	9.00	12.00	17.50	27.50
AH1091//23	—	7.00	9.00	12.00	17.50	27.50
AH1091//24	—	7.00	9.00	12.00	17.50	27.50
AH1092//24	—	7.00	9.00	12.00	17.50	27.50
AH1092//25	—	7.00	9.00	12.00	17.50	27.50
AH1093//25	—	7.00	9.00	12.00	17.50	27.50
AH1093//26	—	7.00	9.00	12.00	17.50	27.50
AH1094//26	—	7.00	9.00	12.00	17.50	27.50
AH1094//27	—	7.00	9.00	12.00	17.50	27.50
AH1095//27	—	7.00	9.00	12.00	17.50	27.50
AH1095//28	—	7.00	9.00	12.00	17.50	27.50
AH1096//28	—	7.00	9.00	12.00	17.50	27.50
AH1096//29	—	7.00	9.00	12.00	17.50	27.50
AH1097//29	—	7.00	9.00	12.00	17.50	27.50
AH1097//30	—	7.00	9.00	12.00	17.50	27.50
AH1098//30	—	7.00	9.00	12.00	17.50	27.50
AH1098//31	—	7.00	9.00	12.00	17.50	27.50
AH1099//31	—	7.00	9.00	12.00	17.50	27.50
AH1099//32	—	7.00	9.00	12.00	17.50	27.50
AH1100//32	—	7.00	9.00	12.00	17.50	27.50
AH1100//33	—	7.00	9.00	12.00	17.50	27.50
AH1101//33	—	7.00	9.00	12.00	17.50	27.50
AH1101//34	—	7.00	9.00	12.00	17.50	27.50
AH1102//34	—	7.00	9.00	12.00	17.50	27.50
AH1102//35	—	7.00	9.00	12.00	17.50	27.50
AH1103//35	—	7.00	9.00	12.00	17.50	27.50
AH1103//36	—	7.00	9.00	12.00	17.50	27.50
AH1104//36	—	7.00	9.00	12.00	17.50	27.50
AH1104//37	—	7.00	9.00	12.00	17.50	27.50
AH1105//37	—	7.00	9.00	12.00	17.50	27.50
AH1105//38	—	7.00	9.00	12.00	17.50	27.50
AH1106//38	—	7.00	9.00	12.00	17.50	27.50
AH1106//39	—	7.00	9.00	12.00	17.50	27.50
AH1107//39	—	7.00	9.00	12.00	17.50	27.50
AH1107//40	—	7.00	9.00	12.00	17.50	27.50
AH1108//40	—	7.00	9.00	12.00	17.50	27.50
AH1108//41	—	7.00	9.00	12.00	17.50	27.50
AH1109//41	—	7.00	9.00	12.00	17.50	27.50
AH1109//42	—	7.00	9.00	12.00	17.50	27.50
AH1110//42	—	7.00	9.00	12.00	17.50	27.50
AH1110//43	—	7.00	9.00	12.00	17.50	27.50
AH1111//43	—	7.00	9.00	12.00	17.50	27.50
AH1111//44	—	7.00	9.00	12.00	17.50	27.50
AH1112//44	—	7.00	9.00	12.00	17.50	27.50

Muradabad

KM# 300.64 RUPEE

Silver **Rev:** Without mint epithet; mint name at bottom **Note:** Weight varies: 11.00-11.60 grams.

Date	Mintage	Good	VG	F	VF	XF
AH1097//29 Rare	—	—	—	—	—	—

Narnol

KM# 300.66 RUPEE

Silver **Rev:** Without mint epithet; mint name at bottom **Note:** Weight varies: 11.00-11.60 grams.

Date	Mintage	Good	VG	F	VF	XF
AH1098//30	—	7.00	10.00	16.00	26.00	40.00
AH1098//31	—	7.00	10.00	16.00	26.00	40.00
AH1099//31	—	7.00	10.00	16.00	26.00	40.00
AH1099//32	—	7.00	10.00	16.00	26.00	40.00
AH1100//32	—	7.00	10.00	16.00	26.00	40.00
AH1100//33	—	7.00	10.00	16.00	26.00	40.00
AH1101//33	—	7.00	10.00	16.00	26.00	40.00
AH1101//34	—	7.00	10.00	16.00	26.00	40.00
AH1102//34	—	7.00	10.00	16.00	26.00	40.00

Nasirabad

KM# 300.67 RUPEE

Silver **Rev:** Without mint epithet; mint name at bottom **Note:** Weight varies: 11.00-11.60 grams.

Date	Mintage	Good	VG	F	VF	XF
AH1101//3x Rare	—	—	—	—	—	—
AH1102//34 Rare	—	—	—	—	—	—
AH1102//35 Rare	—	—	—	—	—	—
AH1102//36 (sic) Rare	—	—	—	—	—	—
AH1109//4x Rare	—	—	—	—	—	—
AH1110//32(sic) Rare	—	—	—	—	—	—
AH1110//35(sic) Rare	—	—	—	—	—	—
AH1112//4x Rare	—	—	—	—	—	—

Nusratabad

KM# 300.68 RUPEE

Silver **Note:** Weight varies 11.00-11.60 grams.

Date	Mintage	Good	VG	F	VF	XF
AH1xxx//32	—	8.00	12.00	20.00	32.00	50.00
AH1101//33	—	8.00	12.00	20.00	32.00	50.00
AH1106//38	—	8.00	12.00	20.00	32.00	50.00
AHxxxx//40	—	8.00	12.00	20.00	32.00	50.00
AH1109//41	—	8.00	12.00	20.00	32.00	50.00
AH1112//44	—	8.00	12.00	20.00	32.00	50.00

Nusratgarh

KM# 300.69 RUPEE

Silver **Rev:** Without mint epithet; mint name at bottom **Note:** Weight varies: 11.00-11.60 grams.

Date	Mintage	Good	VG	F	VF	XF
AH1110//42	—	8.00	15.00	30.00	50.00	80.00
AH1110//43	—	8.00	15.00	30.00	50.00	80.00
AH1111//43	—	8.00	15.00	30.00	50.00	80.00
AH111x//44	—	8.00	15.00	30.00	50.00	80.00

Patna

KM# 300.71 RUPEE

Silver **Note:** Weight varies 11.00-11.60 grams. For later issues see Azimabad, KM#300.16.

Date	Mintage	Good	VG	F	VF	XF
AH1069//(1) Ahad	—	7.00	9.00	12.00	17.50	27.50
AH1070//1	—	7.00	9.00	12.00	17.50	27.50
AH1070//3	—	7.00	9.00	12.00	17.50	27.50
AH107x//4	—	7.00	9.00	12.00	17.50	27.50
AH107x//5	—	7.00	9.00	12.00	17.50	27.50
AH1074//6	—	7.00	9.00	12.00	17.50	27.50
AH107x//7	—	7.00	9.00	12.00	17.50	27.50
AH107x//9	—	7.00	9.00	12.00	17.50	27.50
AH10xx//12	—	7.00	9.00	12.00	17.50	27.50
AH1080//13	—	7.00	9.00	12.00	17.50	27.50
AH1081//13	—	7.00	9.00	12.00	17.50	27.50
AH1081//14	—	7.00	9.00	12.00	17.50	27.50
AH108x//15	—	7.00	9.00	12.00	17.50	27.50
AH108x//18	—	7.00	9.00	12.00	17.50	27.50
AH108x//21	—	7.00	9.00	12.00	17.50	27.50
AH1089//22	—	7.00	9.00	12.00	17.50	27.50
AH1090//22	—	7.00	9.00	12.00	17.50	27.50
AH1090//23	—	7.00	9.00	12.00	17.50	27.50
AH1091//23	—	7.00	9.00	12.00	17.50	27.50
AH1091//24	—	7.00	9.00	12.00	17.50	27.50
AH1092//24	—	7.00	9.00	12.00	17.50	27.50
AH1092//25	—	7.00	9.00	12.00	17.50	27.50
AH1093//25	—	7.00	9.00	12.00	17.50	27.50
AH1093//26	—	7.00	9.00	12.00	17.50	27.50
AH1094//26	—	7.00	9.00	12.00	17.50	27.50
AH1094//27	—	7.00	9.00	12.00	17.50	27.50
AH1095//27	—	7.00	9.00	12.00	17.50	27.50
AH1095//28	—	7.00	9.00	12.00	17.50	27.50
AH1096//28	—	7.00	9.00	12.00	17.50	27.50
AH1096//29	—	7.00	9.00	12.00	17.50	27.50
AH1097//29	—	7.00	9.00	12.00	17.50	27.50
AH1097//30	—	7.00	9.00	12.00	17.50	27.50
AH1098//30	—	7.00	9.00	12.00	17.50	27.50
AH1098//31	—	7.00	9.00	12.00	17.50	27.50
AH1099//31	—	7.00	9.00	12.00	17.50	27.50
AH1099//32	—	7.00	9.00	12.00	17.50	27.50
AH1100//32	—	7.00	9.00	12.00	17.50	27.50
AH1100//33	—	7.00	9.00	12.00	17.50	27.50
AH1101//33	—	7.00	9.00	12.00	17.50	27.50
AH1101//34	—	7.00	9.00	12.00	17.50	27.50
AH1102//34	—	7.00	9.00	12.00	17.50	27.50
AH1102//35	—	7.00	9.00	12.00	17.50	27.50
AH1103//35	—	7.00	9.00	12.00	17.50	27.50
AH1103//36	—	7.00	9.00	12.00	17.50	27.50
AH1104//36	—	7.00	9.00	12.00	17.50	27.50
AH1104//37	—	7.00	9.00	12.00	17.50	27.50
AH1105//37	—	7.00	9.00	12.00	17.50	27.50

Date	Mintage	Good	VG	F	VF	XF
AH1105//38	—	7.00	9.00	12.00	17.50	27.50
AH1106//38	—	7.00	9.00	12.00	17.50	27.50
AH1106//39	—	7.00	9.00	12.00	17.50	27.50
AH1107//40	—	7.00	9.00	12.00	17.50	27.50
AH1108//41	—	7.00	9.00	12.00	17.50	27.50
AH1109//41	—	7.00	9.00	12.00	17.50	27.50
AH1109//42	—	7.00	9.00	12.00	17.50	27.50
AH1110//42	—	7.00	9.00	12.00	17.50	27.50
AH1110//43	—	7.00	9.00	12.00	17.50	27.50
AH1111//43	—	7.00	9.00	12.00	17.50	27.50
AH1111//44	—	7.00	9.00	12.00	17.50	27.50
AH1112//44	—	7.00	9.00	12.00	17.50	27.50

Phonda

KM# 300.72 RUPEE

Silver **Rev:** Without mint epithet; mint name at bottom **Note:** Weight varies: 11.00-11.60 grams.

Date	Mintage	Good	VG	F	VF	XF
AHxxxx//43 Rare	—	—	—	—	—	—

Punamali

KM# 300.73 RUPEE

Silver **Rev:** Without mint epithet; mint name at bottom **Note:** Weight varies: 11.00-11.60 grams.

Date	Mintage	Good	VG	F	VF	XF
AH1112//44 Rare	—	—	—	—	—	—
AH1111//45 (sic) Rare	—	—	—	—	—	—

Pune

KM# 300.74 RUPEE

Silver **Rev:** Without mint epithet; mint name at bottom **Note:** Weight varies: 11.00-11.60 grams.

Date	Mintage	Good	VG	F	VF	XF
AH1111/4x Rare	—	—	—	—	—	—
AH111x/45 Rare	—	—	—	—	—	—

Qamarnagar

KM# 300.75 RUPEE

Silver **Rev:** Without mint epithet; mint name at bottom **Note:** Weight varies: 11.00-11.60 grams.

Date	Mintage	Good	VG	F	VF	XF
AHxxxx//4x	—	9.00	16.00	32.00	56.00	90.00

Ranthambhor

KM# 300.76 RUPEE

Silver **Rev:** Without mint epithet; mint name at bottom **Note:** Weight varies: 11.00-11.60 grams.

Date	Mintage	Good	VG	F	VF	XF
AH1097//30 Rare	—	—	—	—	—	—
AH1098//30 Rare	—	—	—	—	—	—
AH1098//31 Rare	—	—	—	—	—	—
AH1099//31 Rare	—	—	—	—	—	—
AH1099//32 Rare	—	—	—	—	—	—
AH1100//32 Rare	—	—	—	—	—	—

Saharanpur

KM# 300.77 RUPEE

Silver **Rev:** Without mint epithet; mint name at bottom **Note:** Struck at Saharanpur. Weight varies: 11.00-11.60 grams.

Date	Mintage	Good	VG	F	VF	XF
AH109x//28	—	9.00	16.00	32.00	56.00	90.00
AH1097//30	—	9.00	16.00	32.00	56.00	90.00

Sahrind

KM# 300.78 RUPEE

Silver **Obv:** Inscription, date **Rev:** Inscription **Note:** Weight varies 11.00-11.60 grams.

Date	Mintage	Good	VG	F	VF	XF
AH1098//30	—	7.00	9.00	12.00	17.50	27.50
AH1098//31	—	7.00	9.00	12.00	17.50	27.50
AH1099//31	—	7.00	9.00	12.00	17.50	27.50
AH1099//32	—	7.00	9.00	12.00	17.50	27.50
AH1100//32	—	7.00	9.00	12.00	17.50	27.50
AH1100//33	—	7.00	9.00	12.00	17.50	27.50
AH1101//33	—	7.00	9.00	12.00	17.50	27.50
AH1101//34	—	7.00	9.00	12.00	17.50	27.50
AH1102//34	—	7.00	9.00	12.00	17.50	27.50
AH1102//35	—	7.00	9.00	12.00	17.50	27.50
AH1103//35	—	7.00	9.00	12.00	17.50	27.50
AH1103//36	—	7.00	9.00	12.00	17.50	27.50
AH1104//36	—	7.00	9.00	12.00	17.50	27.50
AH1104//37	—	7.00	9.00	12.00	17.50	27.50
AH1105//37	—	7.00	9.00	12.00	17.50	27.50
AH1105//38	—	7.00	9.00	12.00	17.50	27.50
AH1106//38	—	7.00	9.00	12.00	17.50	27.50
AH1106//39	—	7.00	9.00	12.00	17.50	27.50
AH1107//39	—	7.00	9.00	12.00	17.50	27.50
AH1107//40	—	7.00	9.00	12.00	17.50	27.50
AH1108//40	—	7.00	9.00	12.00	17.50	27.50
AH1108//41	—	7.00	9.00	12.00	17.50	27.50
AH1109//41	—	7.00	9.00	12.00	17.50	27.50
AH1109//42	—	7.00	9.00	12.00	17.50	27.50
AH1110//42	—	7.00	9.00	12.00	17.50	27.50
AH1110//43	—	7.00	9.00	12.00	17.50	27.50
AH1111//43	—	7.00	9.00	12.00	17.50	27.50
AH1111//44	—	7.00	9.00	12.00	17.50	27.50
AH1112//44	—	7.00	9.00	12.00	17.50	27.50

Sambhar

KM# 300.79 RUPEE

Silver **Rev:** Without mint epithet; mint name at bottom **Note:** Weight varies: 11.00-11.60 grams.

Date	Mintage	Good	VG	F	VF	XF
AH1098//31 Rare	—	—	—	—	—	—
AH1099//31 Rare	—	—	—	—	—	—
AH1099//32 Rare	—	—	—	—	—	—
AH1100//32 Rare	—	—	—	—	—	—
AH1101//33 Rare	—	—	—	—	—	—

Sarangpur

KM# 300.98 RUPEE

Silver **Rev:** Without mint epithet; mint name at bottom **Note:** Weight varies: 11.00-11.60 grams.

Date	Mintage	Good	VG	F	VF	XF
AHxxxx//x	—	—	—	—	—	—

Shahjahanabad

KM# 300.113 RUPEE

11.4440 g., Silver **Rev:** Inscription and mint name **Rev. Inscription:** "Dar al-Khilafa" **Note:** "Mihr" couplet.

Date	Mintage	Good	VG	F	VF	XF
AH1069//(1) Ahad	—	—	—	—	—	—

KM# 300.81 RUPEE

Silver **Obv:** Inscription **Rev. Inscription:** Dar-ul-Khilafat and mint name **Note:** "Badr" couplet; Weight varies 11.00-11.60 grams.

Date	Mintage	Good	VG	F	VF	XF
AH1069//2	—	7.00	9.00	12.00	17.50	27.50
AH1070//2	—	7.00	9.00	12.00	17.50	27.50
AH1070//3	—	7.00	9.00	12.00	17.50	27.50
AH1071//3	—	7.00	9.00	12.00	17.50	27.50
AH1071//4	—	7.00	9.00	12.00	17.50	27.50
AH1072//4	—	7.00	9.00	12.00	17.50	27.50
AH1072//5	—	7.00	9.00	12.00	17.50	27.50
AH1073//5	—	7.00	9.00	12.00	17.50	27.50
AH1073//6	—	7.00	9.00	12.00	17.50	27.50
AH1074//6	—	7.00	9.00	12.00	17.50	27.50
AH1074//7	—	7.00	9.00	12.00	17.50	27.50
AH1075//7	—	7.00	9.00	12.00	17.50	27.50
AH1075//8	—	7.00	9.00	12.00	17.50	27.50
AH1076//8	—	7.00	9.00	12.00	17.50	27.50
AH1076//9	—	7.00	9.00	12.00	17.50	27.50
AH1077//9	—	7.00	9.00	12.00	17.50	27.50
AH1077//10	—	7.00	9.00	12.00	17.50	27.50
AH1078//10	—	7.00	9.00	12.00	17.50	27.50
AH1078//11	—	7.00	9.00	12.00	17.50	27.50
AH1079//11	—	7.00	9.00	12.00	17.50	27.50
AH1079//12	—	7.00	9.00	12.00	17.50	27.50
AH1080//12	—	7.00	9.00	12.00	17.50	27.50
AH1080//13	—	7.00	9.00	12.00	17.50	27.50
AH1081//13	—	7.00	9.00	12.00	17.50	27.50
AH1081//14	—	7.00	9.00	12.00	17.50	27.50
AH1082//14	—	7.00	9.00	12.00	17.50	27.50
AH1082//15	—	7.00	9.00	12.00	17.50	27.50
AH1083//15	—	7.00	9.00	12.00	17.50	27.50
AH1083//16	—	7.00	9.00	12.00	17.50	27.50
AH1084//16	—	7.00	9.00	12.00	17.50	27.50
AH1084//17	—	7.00	9.00	10.00	17.50	27.50
AH1085//17	—	7.00	9.00	10.00	17.50	27.50
AH1085//18	—	7.00	9.00	10.00	17.50	27.50
AH1086//18	—	7.00	9.00	10.00	17.50	27.50
AH1086//19	—	7.00	9.00	10.00	17.50	27.50
AH1087//19	—	7.00	9.00	10.00	17.50	27.50
AH1087//20	—	7.00	9.00	10.00	17.50	27.50
AH1088//20	—	7.00	9.00	10.00	17.50	27.50
AH1088//21	—	7.00	9.00	10.00	17.50	27.50
AH1089//21	—	7.00	9.00	10.00	17.50	27.50
AH1089//22	—	7.00	9.00	10.00	17.50	27.50
AH1090//22	—	7.00	9.00	10.00	17.50	27.50
AH1090//23	—	7.00	9.00	10.00	17.50	27.50
AH1091//23	—	7.00	9.00	10.00	17.50	27.50
AH1091//24	—	7.00	9.00	10.00	17.50	27.50
AH1092//24	—	7.00	9.00	12.00	17.50	27.50
AH1092//25	—	7.00	9.00	12.00	17.50	27.50
AH1093//25	—	7.00	9.00	12.00	17.50	27.50
AH1094//26	—	7.00	9.00	12.00	17.50	27.50
AH1094//27	—	7.00	9.00	12.00	17.50	27.50
AH1093//26	—	7.00	99.00	12.00	17.50	27.50
AH1095//27	—	7.00	9.00	12.00	17.50	27.50
AH1095//28	—	7.00	9.00	12.00	17.50	27.50
AH1096//28	—	7.00	9.00	12.00	17.50	27.50
AH1096//29	—	7.00	9.00	12.00	17.50	27.50
AH1097//29	—	7.00	9.00	12.00	17.50	27.50
AH1097//30	—	7.00	9.00	12.00	17.50	27.50
AH1098//30	—	7.00	9.00	12.00	17.50	27.50
AH1098//31	—	7.00	9.00	12.00	17.50	27.50
AH1099//31	—	7.00	9.00	12.00	17.50	27.50
AH1099//32	—	7.00	9.00	12.00	17.50	27.50
AH1100//32	—	7.00	9.00	12.00	17.50	27.50
AH1100//33	—	7.00	9.00	12.00	17.50	27.50
AH1101//33	—	7.00	9.00	12.00	17.50	27.50
AH1101//34	—	7.00	9.00	12.00	17.50	27.50
AH1102//34	—	7.00	9.00	12.00	17.50	27.50
AH1102//35	—	7.00	9.00	12.00	17.50	27.50
AH1103//35	—	7.00	9.00	12.00	17.50	27.50
AH1103//36	—	7.00	9.00	12.00	17.50	27.50
AH1104//36	—	7.00	9.00	12.00	17.50	27.50
AH1104//37	—	7.00	9.00	12.00	17.50	27.50
AH1105//37	—	7.00	9.00	12.00	17.50	27.50
AH1105//38	—	7.00	9.00	12.00	17.50	27.50
AH1106//38	—	7.00	9.00	12.00	17.50	27.50
AH1106//39	—	7.00	9.00	12.00	17.50	27.50
AH1107//39	—	7.00	9.00	12.00	17.50	27.50
AH1107//40	—	7.00	9.00	12.00	17.50	27.50
AH1108//40	—	7.00	9.00	12.00	17.50	27.50
AH1108//41	—	7.00	9.00	12.00	17.50	27.50
AH1109//41	—	7.00	9.00	12.00	17.50	27.50
AH1109//42	—	7.00	9.00	12.00	17.50	27.50
AH1110//42	—	7.00	9.00	12.00	17.50	27.50
AH1110//43	—	7.00	9.00	12.00	17.50	27.50
AH1111//43	—	7.00	9.00	12.00	17.50	27.50
AH1111//44	—	7.00	9.00	12.00	17.50	27.50
AH1112//44	—	7.00	9.00	12.00	17.50	27.50

Sholapur

KM# 300.99 RUPEE

Silver **Rev:** Mint name in middle **Note:** Weight varies: 11.00-11.60 grams.

Date	Mintage	Good	VG	F	VF	XF
AH1079//13(sic) Rare	—	—	—	—	—	—
AH1089//21 Rare	—	—	—	—	—	—
AH1090//23 Rare	—	—	—	—	—	—
AH1096//29 Rare	—	—	—	—	—	—

KM# 300.82 RUPEE

Silver **Note:** Weight varies 11.00-11.60 grams.

Date	Mintage	Good	VG	F	VF	XF
AH1085//18	—	7.00	10.00	15.00	23.00	35.00
AH1087//20	—	7.00	10.00	15.00	23.00	35.00
AH1089//21	—	7.00	10.00	15.00	23.00	35.00
AH1089//22	—	7.00	10.00	15.00	23.00	35.00
AH1090//22	—	7.00	10.00	15.00	23.00	35.00
AH1090//23	—	7.00	10.00	15.00	23.00	35.00
AH1091//23	—	7.00	10.00	15.00	23.00	35.00
AH1091//24	—	7.00	10.00	15.00	23.00	35.00
AH1092//24	—	7.00	10.00	15.00	23.00	35.00
AH1092//25	—	7.00	10.00	15.00	23.00	35.00
AH1093//25	—	7.00	10.00	15.00	23.00	35.00
AH1094//26	—	7.00	10.00	15.00	23.00	35.00
AH1094//27	—	7.00	10.00	15.00	23.00	35.00
AH1093//26	—	7.00	10.00	15.00	23.00	35.00
AH1095//27	—	7.00	10.00	15.00	23.00	35.00
AH1095//28	—	7.00	10.00	15.00	23.00	35.00
AH1096//28	—	7.00	10.00	15.00	23.00	35.00
AH1096//29	—	7.00	10.00	15.00	23.00	35.00
AH1097//29	—	7.00	10.00	15.00	23.00	35.00
AH1097//30	—	7.00	10.00	15.00	23.00	35.00
AH1098//30	—	7.00	10.00	15.00	23.00	35.00
AH1098//31	—	7.00	10.00	15.00	23.00	35.00
AH1100//32	—	7.00	10.00	15.00	23.00	35.00
AH1100//33	—	7.00	10.00	15.00	23.00	35.00
AH1101//3x	—	7.00	10.00	15.00	23.00	35.00
AH1108//41	—	7.00	10.00	15.00	23.00	35.00
AH1100//42	—	7.00	10.00	15.00	23.00	35.00
AH1111//4x	—	7.00	10.00	15.00	23.00	35.00

Sikakul

KM# 300.83 RUPEE

Silver **Rev:** Mint name in middle **Note:** Weight varies: 11.00-11.60 grams.

Date	Mintage	Good	VG	F	VF	XF
AH109x//23	—	8.00	15.00	30.00	50.00	80.00
AH1100//32	—	8.00	15.00	30.00	50.00	80.00
AH110x//36	—	8.00	15.00	30.00	50.00	80.00

Sikandarah

KM# 300.84 RUPEE

Silver **Rev:** Mint name in middle **Note:** Weight varies: 11.00-11.60 grams.

Date	Mintage	Good	VG	F	VF	XF
AH1xxx//32 Rare	—	—	—	—	—	—

Surat

KM# 300.85 RUPEE

Silver **Rev:** "Bandar-i-Mubarak" and mint name **Note:** Weight varies: 11.00-11.60 grams.

Date	Mintage	Good	VG	F	VF	XF
AH1069//(1) Ahad	—	8.00	15.00	30.00	50.00	80.00
AH1070//(1) Ahad	—	8.00	15.00	30.00	50.00	80.00
AH1070//2	—	8.00	15.00	30.00	50.00	80.00
AH1071//x	—	8.00	15.00	30.00	50.00	80.00
AH1090//22	—	8.00	15.00	30.00	50.00	80.00
AH1093//25	—	8.00	15.00	30.00	50.00	80.00
AH1094//26	—	8.00	15.00	30.00	50.00	80.00

KM# 300.86 RUPEE
Silver **Obv:** Inscription **Rev:** Inscription, without mint epithet **Note:** Weight varies 11.00-11.60 grams.

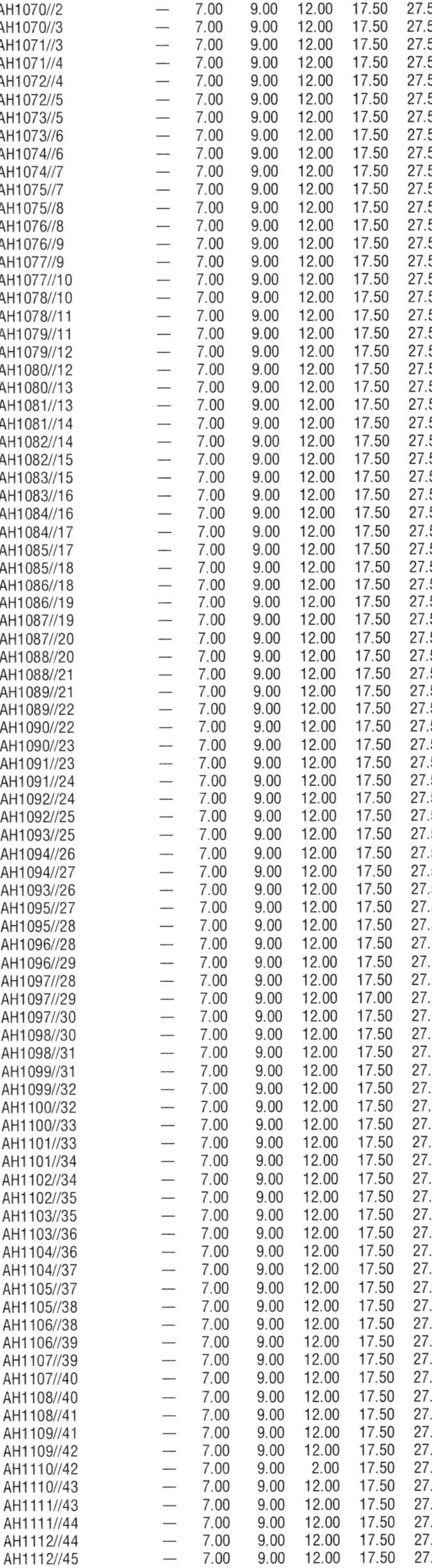

Date	Mintage	Good	VG	F	VF	XF
AH1070//2	—	7.00	9.00	12.00	17.50	27.50
AH1070//3	—	7.00	9.00	12.00	17.50	27.50
AH1071//3	—	7.00	9.00	12.00	17.50	27.50
AH1071//4	—	7.00	9.00	12.00	17.50	27.50
AH1072//4	—	7.00	9.00	12.00	17.50	27.50
AH1072//5	—	7.00	9.00	12.00	17.50	27.50
AH1073//5	—	7.00	9.00	12.00	17.50	27.50
AH1073//6	—	7.00	9.00	12.00	17.50	27.50
AH1074//6	—	7.00	9.00	12.00	17.50	27.50
AH1074//7	—	7.00	9.00	12.00	17.50	27.50
AH1075//7	—	7.00	9.00	12.00	17.50	27.50
AH1075//8	—	7.00	9.00	12.00	17.50	27.50
AH1076//8	—	7.00	9.00	12.00	17.50	27.50
AH1076//9	—	7.00	9.00	12.00	17.50	27.50
AH1077//9	—	7.00	9.00	12.00	17.50	27.50
AH1077//10	—	7.00	9.00	12.00	17.50	27.50
AH1078//10	—	7.00	9.00	12.00	17.50	27.50
AH1078//11	—	7.00	9.00	12.00	17.50	27.50
AH1079//11	—	7.00	9.00	12.00	17.50	27.50
AH1079//12	—	7.00	9.00	12.00	17.50	27.50
AH1080//12	—	7.00	9.00	12.00	17.50	27.50
AH1080//13	—	7.00	9.00	12.00	17.50	27.50
AH1081//13	—	7.00	9.00	12.00	17.50	27.50
AH1081//14	—	7.00	9.00	12.00	17.50	27.50
AH1082//14	—	7.00	9.00	12.00	17.50	27.50
AH1082//15	—	7.00	9.00	12.00	17.50	27.50
AH1083//15	—	7.00	9.00	12.00	17.50	27.50
AH1083//16	—	7.00	9.00	12.00	17.50	27.50
AH1084//16	—	7.00	9.00	12.00	17.50	27.50
AH1084//17	—	7.00	9.00	12.00	17.50	27.50
AH1085//17	—	7.00	9.00	12.00	17.50	27.50
AH1085//18	—	7.00	9.00	12.00	17.50	27.50
AH1086//18	—	7.00	9.00	12.00	17.50	27.50
AH1086//19	—	7.00	9.00	12.00	17.50	27.50
AH1087//19	—	7.00	9.00	12.00	17.50	27.50
AH1087//20	—	7.00	9.00	12.00	17.50	27.50
AH1088//20	—	7.00	9.00	12.00	17.50	27.50
AH1088//21	—	7.00	9.00	12.00	17.50	27.50
AH1089//21	—	7.00	9.00	12.00	17.50	27.50
AH1089//22	—	7.00	9.00	12.00	17.50	27.50
AH1090//22	—	7.00	9.00	12.00	17.50	27.50
AH1090//23	—	7.00	9.00	12.00	17.50	27.50
AH1091//23	—	7.00	9.00	12.00	17.50	27.50
AH1091//24	—	7.00	9.00	12.00	17.50	27.50
AH1092//24	—	7.00	9.00	12.00	17.50	27.50
AH1092//25	—	7.00	9.00	12.00	17.50	27.50
AH1093//25	—	7.00	9.00	12.00	17.50	27.50
AH1094//26	—	7.00	9.00	12.00	17.50	27.50
AH1094//27	—	7.00	9.00	12.00	17.50	27.50
AH1093//26	—	7.00	9.00	12.00	17.50	27.50
AH1095//27	—	7.00	9.00	12.00	17.50	27.50
AH1095//28	—	7.00	9.00	12.00	17.50	27.50
AH1096//28	—	7.00	9.00	12.00	17.50	27.50
AH1096//29	—	7.00	9.00	12.00	17.50	27.50
AH1097//28	—	7.00	9.00	12.00	17.50	27.50
AH1097//29	—	7.00	9.00	12.00	17.00	27.50
AH1097//30	—	7.00	9.00	12.00	17.50	27.50
AH1098//30	—	7.00	9.00	12.00	17.50	27.50
AH1098//31	—	7.00	9.00	12.00	17.50	27.50
AH1099//31	—	7.00	9.00	12.00	17.50	27.50
AH1099//32	—	7.00	9.00	12.00	17.50	27.50
AH1100//32	—	7.00	9.00	12.00	17.50	27.50
AH1100//33	—	7.00	9.00	12.00	17.50	27.50
AH1101//33	—	7.00	9.00	12.00	17.50	27.50
AH1101//34	—	7.00	9.00	12.00	17.50	27.50
AH1102//34	—	7.00	9.00	12.00	17.50	27.50
AH1102//35	—	7.00	9.00	12.00	17.50	27.50
AH1103//35	—	7.00	9.00	12.00	17.50	27.50
AH1103//36	—	7.00	9.00	12.00	17.50	27.50
AH1104//36	—	7.00	9.00	12.00	17.50	27.50
AH1104//37	—	7.00	9.00	12.00	17.50	27.50
AH1105//37	—	7.00	9.00	12.00	17.50	27.50
AH1105//38	—	7.00	9.00	12.00	17.50	27.50
AH1106//38	—	7.00	9.00	12.00	17.50	27.50
AH1106//39	—	7.00	9.00	12.00	17.50	27.50
AH1107//39	—	7.00	9.00	12.00	17.50	27.50
AH1107//40	—	7.00	9.00	12.00	17.50	27.50
AH1108//40	—	7.00	9.00	12.00	17.50	27.50
AH1108//41	—	7.00	9.00	12.00	17.50	27.50
AH1109//41	—	7.00	9.00	12.00	17.50	27.50
AH1109//42	—	7.00	9.00	12.00	17.50	27.50
AH1110//42	—	7.00	9.00	2.00	17.50	27.50
AH1110//43	—	7.00	9.00	12.00	17.50	27.50
AH1111//43	—	7.00	9.00	12.00	17.50	27.50
AH1111//44	—	7.00	9.00	12.00	17.50	27.50
AH1112//44	—	7.00	9.00	12.00	17.50	27.50
AH1112//45	—	7.00	9.00	12.00	17.50	27.50

Tatta

KM# 300.87 RUPEE
Silver **Note:** "Badr" couplet; Weight varies 11.00-11.60 grams.

Date	Mintage	Good	VG	F	VF	XF
AH1072//4	—	7.00	9.00	12.00	17.50	27.50
AH1072//5	—	7.00	9.00	12.00	17.50	27.50
AH1073//5	—	7.00	9.00	12.00	17.50	27.50
AH1073//6	—	7.00	9.00	12.00	17.50	27.50
AH1074//6	—	7.00	9.00	12.00	17.50	27.50
AH107x//7	—	7.00	9.00	12.00	17.50	27.50
AH107x//9	—	7.00	9.00	12.00	17.50	27.50
AH1076//8	—	7.00	9.00	12.00	17.50	27.50
AH107x//10	—	7.00	9.00	12.00	17.50	27.50
AH1079//11	—	7.00	9.00	12.00	17.50	27.50
AH1079//12	—	7.00	9.00	12.00	17.50	27.50
AH1080//12	—	7.00	9.00	12.00	17.50	27.50
AH1080//13	—	7.00	9.00	12.00	17.50	27.50
AH1081//13	—	7.00	9.00	12.00	17.50	27.50
AH1081//14	—	7.00	9.00	12.00	17.50	27.50
AH1082//14	—	7.00	9.00	12.00	17.50	27.50
AH1083//16	—	7.00	9.00	12.00	17.50	27.50
AH1084//16	—	7.00	9.00	12.00	17.50	27.50
AH1084//17	—	7.00	9.00	12.00	17.50	27.50
AH1085//17	—	7.00	9.00	12.00	17.50	27.50
AH1085//18	—	7.00	9.00	12.00	17.50	27.50
AH1086//18	—	7.00	9.00	12.00	17.50	27.50
AH1086//19	—	7.00	9.00	12.00	17.50	27.50
AH1087//19	—	7.00	9.00	12.00	17.50	27.50
AH1087//20	—	7.00	9.00	12.00	17.50	27.50
AH1088//20	—	7.00	9.00	12.00	17.50	27.50
AH1088//21	—	7.00	9.00	12.00	17.50	27.50
AH1089//21	—	7.00	9.00	12.00	17.50	27.50
AH1089//22	—	7.00	9.00	12.00	17.50	27.50
AH1090//22	—	7.00	9.00	12.00	17.50	27.50
AH1090//23	—	7.00	9.00	12.00	17.50	27.50
AH1091//23	—	7.00	9.00	12.00	17.50	27.50
AH1091//24	—	7.00	9.00	12.00	17.50	27.50
AH1092//24	—	7.00	9.00	12.00	17.50	27.50
AH1092//25	—	7.00	9.00	12.00	17.50	27.50
AH1093//25	—	7.00	9.00	12.00	17.50	27.50
AH1094//26	—	7.00	9.00	12.00	17.50	27.50
AH1094//27	—	7.00	9.00	12.00	17.50	27.50
AH1093//26	—	7.00	9.00	12.00	17.50	27.50
AH1095//27	—	7.00	9.00	12.00	17.50	27.50
AH1095//28	—	7.00	9.00	12.00	17.50	27.50
AH1097//29	—	7.00	9.00	12.00	17.50	27.50
AH1098//30	—	7.00	9.00	12.00	17.50	27.50
AH1098//31	—	7.00	9.00	12.00	17.50	27.50
AH1099//31	—	7.00	9.00	12.00	17.50	27.50
AH1100//32	—	7.00	9.00	12.00	17.50	27.50
AH1100//33	—	7.00	9.00	12.00	17.50	27.50
AH1101//34	—	7.00	9.00	12.00	17.50	27.50
AH1102//34	—	7.00	9.00	12.00	17.50	27.50
AH1103//35	—	7.00	9.00	12.00	17.50	27.50
AH1104//36	—	7.00	9.00	12.00	17.50	27.50
AH1105//37	—	7.00	9.00	12.00	17.50	27.50
AH1105//38	—	7.00	9.00	12.00	17.50	27.50
AH1106//38	—	7.00	9.00	12.00	17.50	27.50
AH1107//40	—	7.00	9.00	12.00	17.50	27.50
AH1108//40	—	7.00	9.00	12.00	17.50	27.50
AH1108//41	—	7.00	9.00	12.00	17.50	27.50
AH1109//xx	—	7.00	9.00	12.00	17.50	27.00
AH1110//42	—	7.00	9.00	12.00	17.50	27.50
AH1110//43	—	7.00	9.00	12.00	17.50	27.50
AH1111//4x	—	7.00	9.00	12.00	17.50	27.50
AH1112//44	—	7.00	9.00	12.00	17.50	27.50

KM# 300.114 RUPEE
11.4440 g., Silver **Note:** "Mihr" couplet.

Date	Mintage	Good	VG	F	VF	XF
AHxxxx//8	—	7.00	10.00	16.00	26.00	40.00
AHxxxx//10	—	7.00	10.00	16.00	26.00	40.00
AHxxxx//11	—	7.00	10.00	16.00	26.00	40.00
AH1086//18	—	7.00	10.00	16.00	26.00	40.00
AHxxxx//19	—	7.00	10.00	16.00	26.00	40.00

Trichanapally

KM# 300.115 RUPEE
11.4440 g., Silver

Date	Mintage	Good	VG	F	VF	XF
AH1106//39	—	—	—	—	—	—

Udgir

KM# 300.89 RUPEE
Silver **Note:** "Dar-uz-Zafar Qila". Weight varies: 11.00-11.60 grams.

Date	Mintage	Good	VG	F	VF	XF
AH1098//xx Rare	—	—	—	—	—	—

Ujjain

KM# 300.90 RUPEE
Silver **Rev:** "Dar al-Fath" and mint name at top **Note:** "Dar-ul-Fath". Weight varies: 11.00-11.60 grams.

Date	Mintage	Good	VG	F	VF	XF
AH1070//(1) Ahad	—	7.00	9.00	13.50	22.50	35.00
AHxxxx//3	—	7.00	9.00	13.50	22.50	35.00
AH1072	—	7.00	9.00	13.50	22.50	35.00
AH1073//5	—	7.00	9.00	13.50	22.50	35.00
AH1075	—	7.00	9.00	13.50	22.50	35.00
AH1077//x	—	7.00	9.00	13.50	22.50	35.00
AH1082//14	—	7.00	9.00	13.50	22.50	35.00
AH1087//19	—	7.00	9.00	13.50	22.50	35.00

KM# 300.91 RUPEE
Silver **Rev:** "Dar al-Fath" and mint name at bottom **Note:** Weight varies 11.00-11.60 grams.

Date	Mintage	Good	VG	F	VF	XF
AH1072//4	—	7.00	9.00	13.50	22.50	35.00
AH1072//5	—	7.00	9.00	13.50	22.50	35.00
AH1073//5	—	7.00	9.00	13.50	22.50	35.00
AH1078//11	—	7.00	9.00	13.50	22.50	35.00
AH1082//15	—	7.00	9.00	13.50	22.50	35.00
AH1088//21	—	7.00	9.00	13.50	22.50	35.00
AH1099//xx	—	7.00	9.00	13.50	22.50	35.00
AH1100//32	—	7.00	9.00	13.50	22.50	35.00
AH1103//35	—	7.00	9.00	13.50	22.50	35.00
AH110x//40	—	7.00	9.00	13.50	22.50	35.00
AH1108//41	—	7.00	9.00	13.50	22.50	35.00
AH1109//41	—	7.00	9.00	13.50	22.50	35.00
AH110x//44	—	7.00	9.00	13.50	22.50	35.00
AH1112//45	—	7.00	9.00	13.50	22.50	35.00

KM# 300.92 RUPEE
Silver **Obv:** Without mint epithet **Note:** Weight varies: 11.00-11.60 grams.

Date	Mintage	Good	VG	F	VF	XF
AH1095	—	7.00	10.00	15.00	25.00	40.00
AH1097//29	—	7.00	10.00	15.00	25.00	40.00
AH1101//xx	—	7.00	10.00	15.00	25.00	40.00

Zafarabad

KM# 300.93 RUPEE
Silver **Obv:** Inscription **Rev:** Inscription **Note:** "Badr" couplet; Weight varies 11.00-11.60 grams.

Date	Mintage	Good	VG	F	VF	XF
AHxxxx//(1) Ahad	—	7.00	11.00	18.00	30.00	50.00
AH107x//3	—	7.00	11.00	18.00	30.00	50.00
AH1074//6	—	7.00	11.00	18.00	30.00	50.00
AH1074//7	—	7.00	11.00	18.00	30.00	50.00
AH1075//7	—	7.00	11.00	18.00	30.00	50.00
AH1075//8	—	7.00	11.00	18.00	30.00	50.00
AH1075//9(sic)	—	7.00	11.00	18.00	30.00	50.00
AH1078//11	—	7.00	11.00	18.00	30.00	50.00
AH1079//11	—	7.00	11.00	18.00	30.00	50.00
AH1079//12	—	7.00	11.00	18.00	30.00	50.00
AH1080//12	—	7.00	11.00	18.00	30.00	50.00
AH1080//13	—	7.00	11.00	18.00	30.00	50.00
AH108x//14	—	7.00	11.00	18.00	30.00	50.00
AH108x//18	—	7.00	11.00	18.00	30.00	50.00
AH108x//19	—	7.00	11.00	18.00	30.00	50.00
AH108x//21	—	7.00	11.00	18.00	30.00	50.00
AH10xx//22	—	7.00	11.00	18.00	30.00	50.00
AH1093//25	—	7.00	11.00	18.00	30.00	50.00
AH1093//26	—	7.00	11.00	18.00	30.00	50.00
AH1094//26	—	7.00	11.00	18.00	30.00	50.00
AH1094//27	—	7.00	11.00	18.00	30.00	50.00
AH109x//28	—	7.00	11.00	18.00	30.00	50.00
AH1098//30	—	7.00	11.00	18.00	30.00	50.00
AH1098//31	—	7.00	11.00	18.00	30.00	50.00
AH1099//31	—	7.00	11.00	18.00	30.00	50.00
AH1099//32	—	7.00	11.00	18.00	30.00	50.00

Date	Mintage	Good	VG	F	VF	XF
AH1100//32	—	7.00	11.00	18.00	30.00	50.00
AH1100//33	—	7.00	11.00	18.00	30.00	50.00
AH110x//35	—	7.00	11.00	18.00	30.00	50.00
AH1104//37	—	7.00	11.00	18.00	30.00	50.00
AH1106//39	—	7.00	11.00	18.00	30.00	50.00
AH1108//40	—	7.00	11.00	18.00	30.00	50.00
AH1108//41	—	7.00	11.00	18.00	30.00	50.00
AH1112//45	—	7.00	11.00	18.00	30.00	50.00

KM# 300.116 RUPEE

11.4440 g., Silver **Note:** "Mihr" couplet.

Date	Mintage	Good	VG	F	VF	XF
AH1074//6	—	8.00	12.00	20.00	32.00	50.00
AH1075//8	—	8.00	12.00	20.00	32.00	50.00
AH1079//12	—	8.00	12.00	20.00	32.00	50.00
AH1080//12	—	8.00	12.00	20.00	32.00	50.00
AHxxxx//17	—	8.00	12.00	20.00	32.00	50.00
AHxxxx//22	—	8.00	12.00	20.00	32.00	50.00
AH1099//31	—	8.00	12.00	20.00	32.00	50.00

Zafarpur

KM# 300.94 RUPEE

Silver **Note:** Weight varies: 11.00-11.60 grams.

Date	Mintage	Good	VG	F	VF	XF
AH109x//28	—	8.00	13.00	24.00	38.00	60.00
AH1097//30	—	8.00	13.00	24.00	38.00	60.00
AH1098//30	—	8.00	13.00	24.00	38.00	60.00
AH1098//31	—	8.00	13.00	24.00	38.00	60.00
AH1099//31	—	8.00	13.00	24.00	38.00	60.00
AH1099//32	—	8.00	13.00	24.00	38.00	60.00
AH1100//32	—	8.00	13.00	24.00	38.00	60.00
AH1100//33	—	8.00	13.00	24.00	38.00	60.00
AH1101//33	—	8.00	13.00	24.00	38.00	60.00
AH1101//34	—	8.00	13.00	24.00	38.00	60.00
AH1102//34	—	8.00	13.00	24.00	38.00	60.00

Jahangirnagar

KM# 301.1 RUPEE

Silver **Obv:** Couplet with ruler's name within square **Rev:** Inscription within square **Rev. Inscription:** "Jalus (maimanat manus)" **Note:** Weight varies: 11.00-11.60 grams.

Date	Mintage	Good	VG	F	VF	XF
AH1081//14	—	30.00	70.00	150	225	350
AH1087//20	—	30.00	70.00	150	225	350

Junagadh

KM# 301.2 RUPEE

Silver **Obv:** Couplet with ruler's name within square **Rev:** Inscription within square **Rev. Legend:** "Jalus (maimamat manus)" **Note:** Two obverse varieties exist; Weight varies: 11.00-11.60 grams.

Date	Mintage	Good	VG	F	VF	XF
AH1071//3	—	7.00	9.00	15.00	25.00	40.00
AH1071//4	—	7.00	9.00	15.00	25.00	40.00
AH1072//4	—	7.00	9.00	15.00	25.00	40.00
AH107x//5	—	7.00	9.00	15.00	25.00	40.00
AH107x//8	—	7.00	9.00	15.00	25.00	40.00
AH1075//x	—	7.00	9.00	15.00	25.00	40.00
AH107x//9	—	7.00	9.00	15.00	25.00	40.00
AH1077//x	—	7.00	9.00	15.00	25.00	40.00
AH1078//10	—	7.00	9.00	15.00	25.00	40.00
AH1078//11	—	7.00	9.00	15.00	25.00	40.00
AH1079//11	—	7.00	9.00	15.00	25.00	40.00
AH1079//12	—	7.00	9.00	15.00	25.00	40.00
AH1080//12	—	7.00	9.00	15.00	25.00	40.00
AH1080//13	—	7.00	9.00	15.00	25.00	40.00
AH1081//13	—	7.00	9.00	15.00	25.00	40.00
AH1081//14	—	7.00	9.00	15.00	25.00	40.00
AH1082//14	—	5.50	9.00	15.00	25.00	40.00
AH1082//15	—	7.00	9.00	15.00	25.00	40.00
AH1083//15	—	7.00	9.00	15.00	25.00	40.00
AH108x//18	—	7.00	9.00	15.00	25.00	40.00
AH109x//23	—	7.00	9.00	15.00	25.00	40.00
AH109x//24	—	7.00	9.00	15.00	25.00	40.00
AH1093//xx	—	7.00	9.00	15.00	25.00	40.00
AH1094//27	—	7.00	9.00	15.00	25.00	40.00
AH1094//26	—	7.00	9.00	15.00	25.00	40.00
AH1095//27	—	7.00	9.00	15.00	25.00	40.00
AH1095//28	—	7.00	9.00	15.00	25.00	40.00
AH1096//28	—	7.00	9.00	15.00	25.00	40.00
AH1096//29	—	7.00	9.00	15.00	25.00	40.00

Date	Mintage	Good	VG	F	VF	XF
AH1097//29	—	7.00	9.00	15.00	25.00	40.00
AH109x//31	—	7.00	9.00	15.00	25.00	40.00
AH1108//41	—	7.00	9.00	15.00	25.00	40.00

Bhakkar

KM# 302.1 RUPEE

Silver **Obv:** Poetic couplet **Rev:** Poetic couplet **Note:** Weight varies: 11.00-11.60 grams.

Date	Mintage	Good	VG	F	VF	XF
AH1071//3	—	8.00	12.00	20.00	32.00	50.00
AH1071//4	—	8.00	12.00	20.00	32.00	50.00
AH1072//4	—	8.00	12.00	20.00	32.00	50.00
AH1072//5	—	8.00	12.00	20.00	32.00	50.00
AH1073//5	—	8.00	12.00	20.00	32.00	50.00
AH1075//7	—	8.00	12.00	20.00	32.00	50.00
AH1075//8	—	8.00	12.00	20.00	32.00	50.00
AH1076//8	—	8.00	12.00	20.00	32.00	50.00
AH1076//9	—	8.00	12.00	20.00	32.00	50.00
AH1077//9	—	8.00	12.00	20.00	32.00	50.00
AH1077//10	—	8.00	12.00	20.00	32.00	50.00
AH1078//10	—	8.00	12.00	20.00	32.00	50.00

KM# 302.2 RUPEE

11.4440 g., Silver **Obv. Inscription:** "Alanagir Shah Aurangzeb" **Rev:** Mint name, date formula

Date	Mintage	Good	VG	F	VF	XF
AH1084//16	—	—	—	—	—	—

Shahjahanabad

KM# 304.1 200 RUPEES

2275.0000 g., Silver **Obv:** Ruler's name and titles within square, poetic couplet around **Note:** " Dar-ul-Khilafat"

Date	Mintage	Good	VG	F	VF	XF
AH1083//15 Unique	—	—	—	—	—	—

Akbarabad

KM# 307.1 LEGAL DIRHAM

Silver **Note:** Square. Weight varies: 2.80-3.25 grams.

Date	Mintage	Good	VG	F	VF	XF
AH1091//24 Rare	—	—	—	—	—	—

Allahabad

KM# 307.2 LEGAL DIRHAM

Silver **Note:** Square. Weight varies: 2.80-3.25 grams.

Date	Mintage	Good	VG	F	VF	XF
AH1092//24 Rare	—	—	—	—	—	—
AH1105//37 Rare	—	—	—	—	—	—

Katak

KM# 307.3 LEGAL DIRHAM

Silver **Note:** Square. Weight varies: 2.80-3.25 grams.

Date	Mintage	Good	VG	F	VF	XF
AHxxxx//29 Rare	—	—	—	—	—	—
AHxxxx//30 Rare	—	—	—	—	—	—

Lahore

KM# 307.4 LEGAL DIRHAM

Silver **Note:** Square. Weight varies: 2.80-3.25 grams.

Date	Mintage	Good	VG	F	VF	XF
AH1091//23 Rare	—	—	—	—	—	—
AH1092//24 Rare	—	—	—	—	—	—

Multan

KM# 307.5 LEGAL DIRHAM

Silver **Note:** Square. Weight varies: 2.80-3.25 grams.

Date	Mintage	Good	VG	F	VF	XF
AH1091//xx Rare	—	—	—	—	—	—
AH1093//xx Rare	—	—	—	—	—	—
AH1094//xx Rare	—	—	—	—	—	—

Patna

KM# 307.6 LEGAL DIRHAM

Silver **Note:** Square. Weight varies: 2.80-3.25 grams.

Date	Mintage	Good	VG	F	VF	XF
AHxxxx//24 Rare	—	—	—	—	—	—

Shahjahanabad

KM# 307.7 LEGAL DIRHAM

Silver **Note:** Square. Weight varies: 2.80-3.25 grams.

Date	Mintage	Good	VG	F	VF	XF
ND	—	—	—	—	—	—

Akbarabad

KM# 308.1 LEGAL DIRHAM

2.9700 g., Silver

Date	Mintage	Good	VG	F	VF	XF
AH1093//26 Rare	—	—	—	—	—	—
AH1106 Rare	—	—	—	—	—	—
AH111x//x Rare	—	—	—	—	—	—

Shahjahanabad

KM# 308.2 LEGAL DIRHAM

2.9700 g., Silver

Date	Mintage	Good	VG	F	VF	XF
AH109x//25	—	—	—	—	—	—

Bijapur

KM# 309.1 1/4 MOHUR

Gold **Note:** "Dar-ul Zafar". Weight varies: 2.70-2.75 grams.

Date	Mintage	Good	VG	F	VF	XF
AHxxxx//9	—	—	500	700	1,000	1,500

Surat

KM# 309A 1/2 MOHUR

Gold

Date	Mintage	Good	VG	F	VF	XF
AHxxxx//17	—	—	500	700	1,000	1,500

Akbarnagar

KM# 310.1 MOHUR

Gold **Obv:** Ruler's titles **Note:** Weight varies: 10.80-11.00 grams.

Date	Mintage	Good	VG	F	VF	XF
AH1074//6 Rare	—	—	—	—	—	—
AHxxxx//13 Rare	—	—	—	—	—	—
AHxxxx//14 Rare	—	—	—	—	—	—
AH1082//15 Rare	—	—	—	—	—	—
AH1090//22 Rare	—	—	—	—	—	—
AH1090//23 Rare	—	—	—	—	—	—
AHxxxx//27 Rare	—	—	—	—	—	—
AHxxxx//28 Rare	—	—	—	—	—	—
AH11xx//33 Rare	—	—	—	—	—	—

Kabul

KM# 314.1 MOHUR

Gold **Note:** Weight varies: 10.80-11.00 grams.

Date	Mintage	Good	VG	F	VF	XF
AHxxxx//3	—	—	—	—	—	—
AHxxxx//4	—	—	—	—	—	—
AHxxxx//5	—	—	—	—	—	—
AHxxxx//6	—	—	—	—	—	—
AHxxxx//7	—	—	—	—	—	—
AH1074//7	—	—	—	—	—	—
AHxxxx//8	—	—	—	—	—	—

Patna

KM# 314.2 MOHUR

Gold **Note:** Weight varies 10.8 - 11 grams.

Date	Mintage	Good	VG	F	VF	XF
AH1070//3(?)	—	—	—	—	—	—

Ahmadabad

KM# 315.1 MOHUR

Gold **Note:** Weight varies: 10.80-11.00 grams.

Date	Mintage	Good	VG	F	VF	XF
AH1073//5	—	—	350	400	480	600
AH1074//7	—	—	350	400	480	600
AH1075//7	—	—	350	400	480	600
AH1075//8	—	—	350	400	480	600
AH1076//8	—	—	350	400	480	600
AH1076//9	—	—	350	400	480	600
AH1077//9	—	—	350	400	480	600
AH1077//10	—	—	350	400	480	600
AH1078//10	—	—	350	400	480	600
AH1078//11	—	—	350	400	480	600
AH1079//11	—	—	350	400	480	600
AH1079//12	—	—	350	400	480	600
AH1080//12	—	—	350	400	480	600
AH1080//13	—	—	350	400	480	600

Date	Mintage	Good	VG	F	VF	XF
AH1081//13	—	—	350	400	480	600
AH1081//14	—	—	350	400	480	600
AH1082//14	—	—	350	400	480	600
AH1082//15	—	—	350	400	480	600
AH1083//15	—	—	350	400	480	600
AH1083//16	—	—	350	400	480	600
AH1084//16	—	—	350	400	480	600
AH1084//17	—	—	350	400	480	600
AH1085//17	—	—	350	400	480	600
AH1085//18	—	—	350	400	480	600
AH1086//18	—	—	350	400	480	600
AH1086//19	—	—	350	400	480	600
AH1087//19	—	—	350	400	480	600
AH1087//20	—	—	350	400	480	600
AH1088//20	—	—	350	400	480	600
AH1088//21	—	—	350	400	480	600
AH1089//21	—	—	350	400	480	600
AH1089//22	—	—	350	400	480	600
AH1090//22	—	—	350	400	480	600
AH1090//23	—	—	350	400	480	600
AH1091//23	—	—	350	400	480	600
AH1091//24	—	—	350	400	480	600
AH1092//24	—	—	350	400	480	600
AH1092//25	—	—	350	400	480	600
AH1093//25	—	—	350	400	480	600
AH1093//26	—	—	350	400	480	600
AH1094//26	—	—	350	400	480	600
AH1094//27	—	—	350	400	480	600
AH1095//27	—	—	350	400	480	600
AH1095//28	—	—	350	400	480	600
AH1096//28	—	—	350	400	480	600
AH1096//29	—	—	350	400	480	600
AH1097//29	—	—	350	400	480	600
AH1097//30	—	—	350	400	480	600
AH1098//30	—	—	350	400	480	600
AH1098//31	—	—	350	400	480	600
AH1099//31	—	—	350	400	480	600
AH1092//32	—	—	350	400	480	600
AH1100//32	—	—	350	400	480	600
AH1100//33	—	—	350	400	480	600
AH1101//33	—	—	350	400	480	600
AH1101//34	—	—	350	400	480	600
AH1102//34	—	—	350	400	480	600
AH1102//35	—	—	350	400	480	600
AH1103//35	—	—	350	400	480	600
AH1103//36	—	—	350	400	480	600
AH1104//36	—	—	350	400	480	600
AH1104//37	—	—	350	400	480	600
AH1105//37	—	—	350	400	480	600
AH1105//38	—	—	350	400	480	600
AH1106//38	—	—	350	400	480	600
AH1106//39	—	—	350	400	480	600
AH1107//39	—	—	350	400	480	600
AH1107//40	—	—	350	400	480	600
AH1108//40	—	—	350	400	480	600
AH1108//41	—	—	350	400	480	600
AH1109//41	—	—	350	400	480	600
AH1109//42	—	—	350	400	480	600
AH1110//42	—	—	350	400	480	600
AH1110//43	—	—	350	400	480	600
AH1111//43	—	—	350	400	480	600
AH1111//44	—	—	350	400	480	600
AH1112//44	—	—	350	400	480	600

Ahmadanagar

KM# 315.2 MOHUR

Gold **Note:** Weight varies 10.80-11.00 grams.

Date	Mintage	Good	VG	F	VF	XF
AH1080//13	—	—	350	410	480	600
AHxxxx//14	—	—	350	410	480	600
AH1097//29	—	—	350	410	480	600
AH1098//30	—	—	350	410	480	600
AH1099//31	—	—	350	410	480	600
AH1100//32	—	—	350	410	480	600
AH1112//44	—	—	350	410	480	600

Ajmir

KM# 315.4 MOHUR

Gold **Note:** Weight varies: 10.80-11.00 grams.

Date	Mintage	Good	VG	F	VF	XF
AH1109//42 Rare	—	—	—	—	—	—

Akbarabad

KM# 315.5 MOHUR

Gold **Note:** Without mint epithet. Weight varies: 10.80-11.00 grams.

Date	Mintage	Good	VG	F	VF	XF
AH1070//(1) Ahad	—	—	350	400	460	550
AH1070//2	—	—	350	400	460	550
AH1071//4	—	—	350	400	460	550
AH1072//4	—	—	350	400	460	550
AH1075//7	—	—	350	400	460	550
AH1078//11	—	—	350	400	460	550
AH1080//13	—	—	350	400	460	550
AH1084//16	—	—	350	400	460	550
AH1086//18	—	—	350	400	460	550
AH1086//19	—	—	350	400	460	550
AH1087//19	—	—	350	400	460	550
AH1089//21	—	—	350	400	460	550
AH1089//22	—	—	350	400	460	550
AH1090//23	—	—	350	400	460	550
AH1091//23	—	—	350	400	460	550
AH1091//24	—	—	350	400	460	550
AH1099//31	—	—	350	400	460	550

KM# 315.6 MOHUR

Gold **Obv:** Inscription **Rev. Inscription:** Mustagir-ul-Mulk **Note:** Weight varies 10.80-11.00 grams.

Date	Mintage	Good	VG	F	VF	XF
AH1096//29	—	—	350	400	460	550
AH1097//29	—	—	350	400	460	550
AH1097//30	—	—	350	400	460	550
AH1098//30	—	—	350	400	460	550
AH1098//31	—	—	350	400	460	550
AH1099//31	—	—	350	400	460	550
AH1099//32	—	—	350	400	460	550
AH1100//32	—	—	350	400	460	550
AH1103//3x	—	—	350	400	460	550
AH1105//37	—	—	350	400	460	550
AH1105//38	—	—	350	400	460	550
AH1107//39	—	—	350	400	460	550
AH1109//41	—	—	350	400	460	550
AH1109//42	—	—	350	400	460	550

Alamgirpur

KM# 315.7 MOHUR

Gold **Rev:** Mint name at top **Note:** Weight varies: 10.80-11.00 grams.

Date	Mintage	Good	VG	F	VF	XF
AH1071//2	—	—	350	410	480	600
AH1071//4	—	—	350	410	480	600
AH1077//10	—	—	350	410	480	600
AH1082//xx	—	—	350	410	480	600
AH1084//17	—	—	350	410	480	600
AH1085//18	—	—	350	410	480	600
AH111x//43	—	—	350	410	480	600

KM# 315.66 MOHUR

Gold **Rev:** Mint name at bottom **Note:** Weight varies 10.8 - 11 grams.

Date	Mintage	Good	VG	F	VF	XF
AH1106//3x	—	350	410	525	650	900

Allahabad

KM# 315.9 MOHUR

Gold **Obv:** Inscription **Rev:** Inscription, mint name below **Note:** Weight varies 10.80-11.00 grams.

Date	Mintage	Good	VG	F	VF	XF
AH1072//4	—	—	350	400	460	550
AH1074//7	—	—	350	400	460	550
AH1076//8	—	—	350	400	460	550
AH1076//9	—	—	350	400	460	550
AH1078//11	—	—	350	400	460	550
AH1079//12	—	—	350	400	460	550
AH1080//13	—	—	350	400	460	550
AH1081//13	—	—	350	400	460	550
AH1084//17	—	—	350	400	460	550
AH1085//18	—	—	350	400	460	550
AH1088//21	—	—	350	400	460	550
AH1099//31	—	—	350	400	460	550
AH1099//32	—	—	350	400	460	550
AH1110//xx	—	—	350	400	460	550
AH1104//36	—	—	350	400	460	550
AH1108//40	—	—	350	400	460	550
AH1109//42	—	—	350	400	460	550

Date	Mintage	Good	VG	F	VF	XF
AH1111//4x	—	—	350	400	460	550
AH1112//45	—	—	350	400	460	550

Aurangabad

KM# 315.10 MOHUR

Gold **Note:** Mint name above. Weight varies: 10.80-11.00 grams.

Date	Mintage	Good	VG	F	VF	XF
AH1070//3	—	—	350	400	460	550
AH1073//5	—	—	350	400	460	550
AH1073//6	—	—	350	400	460	550
AH1074//6	—	—	350	400	460	550
AH1074//7	—	—	350	400	460	550
AH1075//7	—	—	350	400	460	550
AH1075//8	—	—	350	400	460	550
AH1076//8	—	—	350	400	460	550
AH1077//9	—	—	350	400	460	550
AH1077//10	—	—	350	400	460	550
AH1078//10	—	—	350	400	460	550
AH1078//11	—	—	350	400	460	550
AH1079//11	—	—	350	400	460	550
AH1079//12	—	—	350	400	460	550
AH1080//12	—	—	350	400	460	550
AH1081//14	—	—	350	400	460	550
AH1082//14	—	—	350	400	460	550
AH1082//15	—	—	350	400	460	550
AH1084//16	—	—	350	400	460	550
AH1084//17	—	—	350	400	460	550
AH1085//xx	—	—	350	400	460	550
AH1086//18	—	—	350	400	460	550
AH1086//19	—	—	350	400	460	550
AH1087//19	—	—	350	400	460	550
AH1087//20	—	—	350	400	460	550
AH1088//20	—	—	350	400	460	550
AH1088//21	—	—	350	400	460	550
AH1089//21	—	—	350	400	460	550
AH1093	—	—	350	400	460	550
AH1098//30	—	—	350	400	460	500
AH1098//31	—	—	350	400	460	550
AH1099	—	—	350	400	460	550
AH1100//32	—	—	350	400	460	550

KM# 315.11 MOHUR

Gold **Obv:** Emperor's name and titles, date **Rev:** Mint and regnal year **Note:** Mint name below. Weight varies: 10.80-11.00 grams.

Date	Mintage	Good	VG	F	VF	XF
AH1089//22	—	—	365	425	525	650
AH1091//23	—	—	365	425	525	650
AH1091//24	—	—	365	425	525	650
AH1092//24	—	—	365	425	525	650
AH1092//25	—	—	365	425	525	650
AH1093//27	—	—	365	425	525	650
AH1095//28	—	—	365	425	525	650
AH1096//28	—	—	365	425	525	650
AH1096//29	—	—	365	425	525	650
AH1097//29	—	—	365	425	525	650

Bhakkar

KM# 315.14 MOHUR

Gold

Date	Mintage	Good	VG	F	VF	XF
AH1112//44	—	350	410	525	615	800

Bijapur

KM# 315.15 MOHUR

Gold **Obv:** Inscription **Rev. Inscription:** Dar-uz-Zafar **Note:** Arrangement of the mint name varies. Weight varies 10.80-11.00 grams.

Date	Mintage	Good	VG	F	VF	XF
AH1101//33	—	—	350	400	460	550
AH1102//34	—	—	350	400	460	550
AH1103//35	—	—	350	400	460	550
AH1103//36	—	—	350	400	460	550

Date	Mintage	Good	VG	F	VF	XF
AH1104//36	—	—	350	400	460	550
AH1105//37	—	—	350	400	460	550
AH1106//38	—	—	350	400	460	550
AH1107//39	—	—	350	400	460	550
AH1107//40	—	—	350	400	460	550
AH1106//39	—	—	350	400	460	550
AH1108//40	—	—	350	400	460	550
AH1108//41	—	—	350	400	460	550
AH1109//41	—	—	350	400	460	550
AH1109//42	—	—	350	400	460	550
AH1110//42	—	—	350	400	460	550
AH1110//43	—	—	350	400	460	550
AH1111//43	—	—	350	400	460	550
AH1111//44	—	—	350	400	460	550
AH1112//44	—	—	350	400	460	550
AH1112//45	—	—	350	400	460	550

Burhanpur

KM# 315.16 MOHUR

Gold **Note:** Weight varies 10.80-11 grams.

Date	Mintage	Good	VG	F	VF	XF
AH1069//2	—	—	350	400	460	550
AH1077//10	—	—	350	400	460	550
AH1085//18	—	—	350	400	460	550
AH1089//21	—	—	350	400	460	550
AH1089//22	—	—	350	400	460	550
AH109x//24	—	—	350	400	460	550
AH1092//23	—	—	350	400	460	550
AH109x//25	—	—	350	400	460	550
AH109x//28	—	—	350	400	460	550
AH109x//29	—	—	350	400	460	550
AH1098//30	—	—	350	400	460	550
AH1xxx//32	—	—	350	400	460	550
AH1100//3x	—	—	350	400	460	550
AH1103//36	—	—	350	400	460	550
AHxxxx//37	—	—	350	400	460	550
AH1105//38	—	—	350	400	460	550
AH1109//41	—	—	350	400	460	550
AH1110//42	—	—	350	400	460	550
AH1111//43	—	—	350	400	460	550
AH1111//44	—	—	350	400	460	550
AH1112//44	—	—	350	400	460	550

KM# 315.57 MOHUR

Gold **Rev. Inscription:** "Baldat-i-Fakhira" **Note:** Weight varies 10.8 - 11 grams.

Date	Mintage	Good	VG	F	VF	XF
AHxxxx//3	—	—	—	—	—	—

Golkonda

KM# 315.18 MOHUR

Gold **Note:** Weight varies: 10.80-11.00 grams.

Date	Mintage	Good	VG	F	VF	XF
AH1086//19	—	—	350	400	460	550
AH1086//20(sic)	—	—	350	400	460	550
AH1086//22(sic)	—	—	350	400	460	550
AH1086//23 (sic)	—	—	350	400	460	550
AH1086//25 (sic)	—	—	350	400	460	550
AH1086//30(sic)	—	—	350	400	460	550
AH1086//31(sic)	—	—	350	400	460	550

Gulbarga

KM# 315.19 MOHUR

Gold **Note:** Weight varies: 10.80-11.00 grams.

Date	Mintage	Good	VG	F	VF	XF
AH1096//2x	—	—	350	410	480	600
AH1097//30	—	—	350	410	480	600
AH1098//30	—	—	350	410	480	600
AH1098//31	—	—	350	410	480	600
AH1099//32	—	—	350	410	480	600
AH1100//33	—	—	350	410	480	600
AH1101//33	—	—	350	410	480	600
AH1104//3x	—	—	350	410	480	600
AH1105//39	—	—	350	410	480	600
AH1106//40 (sic)	—	—	350	410	480	600
AH1107//xx	—	—	350	410	480	600
AH1108//41 (sic)	—	—	350	410	480	600
AH1109//42	—	—	350	410	480	600
AH1110//42	—	—	350	410	480	600
AH1110//43	—	—	350	410	480	600

Gwalior

KM# 315.59 MOHUR

Gold **Note:** Weight varies 10.8 - 11 grams.

Date	Mintage	Good	VG	F	VF	XF
AH1100//33	—	350	410	525	650	900

Haidarabad

KM# 315.20 MOHUR

Gold **Obv:** Inscription **Rev. Inscription:** Dar-ul-Jihad, mint name **Note:** Weight varies 10.80-11.00 grams.

Date	Mintage	Good	VG	F	VF	XF
AH1099//32	—	—	350	400	460	550
AH1100//3x	—	—	350	400	460	550
AH110x//34	—	—	350	400	460	550
AH1102//35	—	—	350	400	460	550
AH1105//38	—	—	350	400	460	550
AH1106//38	—	—	350	400	460	550
AH1107//39	—	—	350	400	460	550
AH1108//41	—	—	350	400	460	550
AH1110//43	—	—	350	400	460	550
AH1111//43	—	—	350	400	460	550
AH1111//44	—	—	350	400	460	550
AH1112//44	—	—	350	400	460	550
AH1112//45	—	—	350	400	460	550

Islamabad

KM# 315.21 MOHUR

Gold **Note:** Weight varies: 10.80-11.00 grams.

Date	Mintage	Good	VG	F	VF	XF
AH1079//11	—	—	350	400	460	550
AH1098//30	—	—	350	400	460	550
AH1102//3x	—	—	350	400	460	550
AH110x//38	—	—	350	400	460	550
AH1112//44	—	—	350	400	460	550

Itawa

KM# 315.22 MOHUR

Gold **Note:** Weight varies 10.80-11.00 grams.

Date	Mintage	Good	VG	F	VF	XF
AH1106//38	—	—	350	400	460	550
AH1106//39	—	—	350	400	460	550
AH1107//39	—	—	350	400	460	550
AH1109//41	—	—	350	400	460	550
AH1109//42	—	—	350	400	460	550
AH1111/44	—	—	350	400	460	550
AH1112//44	—	—	350	400	460	550

KM# 315.60 MOHUR

Gold **Note:** Weight varies 10.8 - 11 grams.

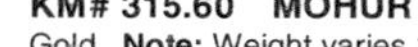

Date	Mintage	Good	VG	F	VF	XF
AH1111//43	—	—	365	425	525	650

Jahangirnagar

KM# 315.23 MOHUR

Gold **Note:** Weight varies: 10.80-11.00 grams.

Date	Mintage	Good	VG	F	VF	XF
AH1107//40	—	—	350	410	480	600
AH1111//44	—	—	350	410	480	600
AH1112//45	—	—	350	410	480	600

Kabul

KM# 315.24 MOHUR

Gold **Note:** Without mint epithet. Weight varies: 10.80-11.00 grams.

Date	Mintage	Good	VG	F	VF	XF
AH1071//3	—	—	350	420	480	600
AH10xx//4	—	—	350	420	480	600

Date	Mintage	Good	VG	F	VF	XF
AH108x//15	—	—	350	420	480	600
AH(10)85//17	—	—	350	420	480	600
AH1085//17	—	—	350	420	480	600
AH109x//23	—	—	350	420	480	600
AH109x//26	—	—	350	420	480	600

KM# 315.61 MOHUR

Gold **Rev:** Mint name **Rev. Inscription:** "Dar al-Mulk" **Note:** "Badr" couplet; Weight varies 10.8 - 11 grams.

Date	Mintage	Good	VG	F	VF	XF
AH1110//xx	—	—	380	450	550	700

KM# 315.25 MOHUR

Gold **Obv:** Inscription **Rev. Inscription:** Dar-ul-Mulk, mint name **Note:** "Mihr" couplet; Weight varies 10.8 - 11 grams.

Date	Mintage	Good	VG	F	VF	XF
AHxxxx//32	—	—	350	410	480	600
AH1104//36	—	—	350	410	480	600
AHxxxx//38	—	—	350	410	480	600
AH1106//39	—	—	350	410	480	600
AH1107//40	—	—	350	410	480	600
AH1108//40	—	—	350	410	480	600
AH1110//42	—	—	350	410	480	600
AH1111//43	—	—	350	410	480	600
AH1111//44	—	—	350	410	480	600

Kanbayat

KM# 315.26 MOHUR

Gold **Note:** Mint name above. Weight varies: 10.80-11.00 grams.

Date	Mintage	Good	VG	F	VF	XF
AH1069//(1) Ahad	—	400	500	650	850	1,100

KM# 315.27 MOHUR

Gold **Note:** Mint name below. Weight varies: 10.80-11.00 grams.

Date	Mintage	Good	VG	F	VF	XF
AH1072//4	—	—	350	400	460	550
AH1074//7	—	—	350	400	460	550
AH1077//9	—	—	350	400	460	550
AH1082//14	—	—	350	400	460	550
AH1084//16	—	—	350	400	460	550
AH1086//1x	—	—	350	400	460	550
AH1090//xx	—	—	350	400	460	550
AH1091//xx	—	—	350	400	460	550
AH1092//24	—	—	350	400	460	550
AH1100//33	—	—	350	400	460	550
AH1106//38	—	—	350	400	460	550
AH1109//41	—	—	350	400	460	550
AH1112//xx	—	—	350	400	460	550

Kashmir

KM# 315.28 MOHUR

Gold **Note:** Weight varies: 10.80-11.00 grams.

Date	Mintage	Good	VG	F	VF	XF
AHxxxx//2 Rare	—	—	—	—	—	—
AHxxxx//15 Rare	—	—	—	—	—	—
AHxxxx//32 Rare	—	—	—	—	—	—

Katak

KM# 315.29 MOHUR

Gold **Obv:** Ruler's name and titles, date **Rev:** Mint and regnal year **Note:** Weight varies: 10.80-11.00 grams.

Date	Mintage	Good	VG	F	VF	XF
AH10xx//31	—	365	475	600	800	1,100
AH1099//32	—	365	475	600	800	1,100
AH11xx//33	—	365	475	600	800	1,100
AHxxxx//39	—	365	475	600	800	1,100
AHxxxx//44	—	365	475	600	800	1,100

Khujista Bunyad

KM# 315.30 MOHUR

Gold **Note:** Weight varies 10.80-11.00 grams.

Date	Mintage	Good	VG	F	VF	XF
AH1xxx//32	—	—	365	425	525	650
AH1101//33	—	—	365	425	525	650

Date	Mintage	Good	VG	F	VF	XF
AH1102//34	—	—	365	425	525	650
AH1102//35	—	—	365	425	525	650
AH1104//36	—	—	365	425	525	650
AH110x//37	—	—	365	425	525	650
AH1106//38	—	—	365	425	525	650
AH1107//39	—	—	365	425	525	650
AH1108//40	—	—	365	425	525	650
AH1108//41	—	—	365	425	525	650
AH1109//41	—	—	365	425	525	650
AH1109//42	—	—	365	425	525	650
AH1110//42	—	—	365	425	525	650
AH1110//43	—	—	365	425	525	650
AH1111//44	—	—	365	425	525	650
AH1112//43	—	—	365	425	525	650
AH1112//44	—	—	365	425	525	650
AH1112//45	—	—	365	425	525	650

Lahore

KM# 315.31 MOHUR

Gold **Obv:** Inscription **Rev. Inscription:** Dar-us-Sultanat **Note:** Weight varies 10.80-11.00 grams.

Date	Mintage	Good	VG	F	VF	XF
AH1097//29	—	—	350	400	460	550
AH1105//37	—	—	350	400	460	550
AH1106//38	—	—	350	400	460	550
AH1106//39	—	—	350	400	460	550
AH1107//39	—	—	350	400	460	550
AH1108//41	—	—	350	400	460	550
AH1108//40	—	—	350	400	460	550
AH1109//41	—	—	350	400	460	550
AH1110//43	—	—	350	400	460	550
AH1112//44	—	—	350	400	460	550
AH1112//45	—	—	350	400	460	550

Lakhnau

KM# 315.32 MOHUR

Gold **Obv:** Emperor's name and titles, date **Rev:** Mint and regnal year **Note:** Weight varies: 10.80-11.00 grams.

Date	Mintage	Good	VG	F	VF	XF
AH1082//14	—	—	380	450	550	700
AH1084//16	—	—	380	450	550	700
AH1084//61 (error for 16)	—	—	380	450	550	700
AH1090//2x	—	—	380	450	550	700
AH1097//29	—	—	380	450	550	700

Macchlipattan

KM# 315.62 MOHUR

Gold **Note:** Weight varies 10.8 - 11 grams.

Date	Mintage	Good	VG	F	VF	XF
AH1105//37	—	350	410	525	625	900

Mu-azzamadad

KM# 315.33 MOHUR

Gold **Note:** Weight varies: 10.80-11.00 grams.

Date	Mintage	Good	VG	F	VF	XF
AHxxxx//39	—	365	475	600	800	1,100

Muhammadabad

KM# 315.34 MOHUR

Gold **Note:** Weight varies: 10.80-11.00 grams.

Date	Mintage	Good	VG	F	VF	XF
AH1099//31	—	400	500	650	850	1,100
AH1100//32	—	400	500	650	850	1,100

Multan

KM# 315.35 MOHUR

Gold **Note:** Mint epithet: "Dar-ul-Aman". Weight varies: 10.80-11.00 grams.

Date	Mintage	Good	VG	F	VF	XF
AH1069//2	—	—	350	380	430	500
AH1070//3	—	—	350	380	430	500
AH1071//3	—	—	350	380	430	500
AH1072//4	—	—	350	380	430	500
AH1073//x	—	—	350	380	430	500
AH1080//12	—	—	350	380	430	500
AH1091//24	—	—	350	380	430	500
AH1096//29	—	—	350	380	430	500

KM# 315.53 MOHUR

Gold **Obv:** Four-line couplet **Rev:** Date and Regnal Year **Note:** Mint epithet: "Dar-ul-Aman". Weight varies: 10.80-11.00 grams; Previous KM#315.35A.

Date	Mintage	Good	VG	F	VF	XF
AH1069//(1) Ahad Rare	—	—	—	—	—	—

KM# 315.36 MOHUR

Gold **Obv:** Inscription **Rev:** Inscription, without mint epithet, mint name at bottom **Note:** Weight varies 10.80 - 11.00 grams.

Date	Mintage	Good	VG	F	VF	XF
AH1072//4	—	—	350	400	460	550
AH1072//5	—	—	350	400	460	550
AH1073//5	—	—	350	400	460	550
AH1073//6	—	—	350	400	460	550
AH1074//6	—	—	350	400	460	550
AH1074//7	—	—	350	400	460	550
AH1075//7	—	—	350	400	460	550
AH1075//8	—	—	350	400	460	550
AH1076//8	—	—	350	400	460	550
AH1076//9	—	—	350	400	460	550
AH1077//9	—	—	350	400	460	550
AH1077//10	—	—	350	400	460	550
AH1078//10	—	—	350	400	460	550
AH1078//11	—	—	350	400	460	550
AH1079//11	—	—	350	400	460	550
AH1079//12	—	—	350	400	460	550
AH1081//13	—	—	350	400	460	550
AH1081//14	—	—	350	400	460	550
AH1082//14	—	—	350	400	460	550
AH1082//15	—	—	350	400	460	550
AH1083//15	—	—	350	400	460	550
AH1083//16	—	—	350	400	460	550
AH1084//17	—	—	350	400	460	550
AH1086//18	—	—	350	400	460	550
AH1087//19	—	—	350	400	460	550
AH1087//20	—	—	350	400	460	550
AH1088//20	—	—	350	400	460	550
AH1094//26	—	—	350	400	460	550
AH1100//32	—	—	350	400	460	550
AH1112//44	—	—	350	400	460	550

Narnol

KM# 315.38 MOHUR

Gold **Obv:** Four-line couplet **Rev:** Date and Regnal Year **Note:** Weight varies: 10.80-11.00 grams.

Date	Mintage	Good	VG	F	VF	XF
AH1102//3x	—	350	410	525	650	900

Nusratabad

KM# 315.39 MOHUR

Gold **Note:** Weight varies 10.80 - 11.00 grams.

Date	Mintage	Good	VG	F	VF	XF
AH1101//34	—	—	380	450	550	700
AHxxxx//38	—	—	380	450	550	700
AH11xx//42	—	—	380	450	550	700

Patna

KM# 315.40 MOHUR

Gold **Note:** Struck at Patna. Weight varies: 10.80-11.00 grams.

Date	Mintage	Good	VG	F	VF	XF
AH107x//8	—	—	350	400	460	550
AHxxxx//18	—	—	350	400	460	550
AH1090//22	—	—	350	400	460	550
AH1102//3x	—	—	350	400	460	550
AH1103//36	—	—	350	400	460	550
AH1104//36	—	—	350	400	460	550
AH1105//37	—	—	350	400	460	550
AH1105//38	—	—	350	400	460	550
AH1106//38	—	—	350	400	460	550
AH1109//41	—	—	350	400	460	550
AH1109//42	—	—	350	400	460	550
AH1110//43	—	—	350	400	460	550

Shahjahanabad

KM# 315.55 MOHUR

Gold **Note:** Weight varies: 10.80-11.00 grams.

Date	Mintage	Good	VG	F	VF	XF
AH1069//(1) Ahad Rare	—	—	—	—	—	—

KM# 315.42 MOHUR

Gold **Obv:** Inscription **Rev. Inscription:** Dar-ul-Khilafat, mint name **Note:** "Badr" couplet; Weight varies 10.80 - 11.00 grams.

Date	Mintage	Good	VG	F	VF	XF
AH1069//(1) Ahad	—	—	350	400	465	550
AH1070//3	—	—	350	400	465	550
AH1071//3	—	—	350	400	465	550
AH107x//4	—	—	350	400	465	550
AH1072//5	—	—	350	400	465	550
AH1073//5	—	—	350	400	465	550
AH1073//6	—	—	350	400	465	550
AH1074//6	—	—	350	400	465	550
AH1075//7	—	—	350	400	465	550
AH1076//8	—	—	350	400	465	550
AH1080//12	—	—	350	400	465	550
AH1082//14	—	—	350	400	465	550
AH1082//15	—	—	350	400	465	550
AH1083//15	—	—	350	400	465	550
AH1083//16	—	—	350	400	465	550
AH1084//16	—	—	350	400	465	550
AH1084/17	—	—	350	400	465	550
AH1086//19	—	—	350	400	465	550
AH1087//19	—	—	350	400	465	550
AH1088//xx	—	—	350	400	465	550
AH1089//21	—	—	350	400	465	550
AH1090//22	—	—	350	400	465	550
AH1090//23	—	—	350	400	465	550
AH1091//23	—	—	350	400	465	550
AH1091//24	—	—	350	400	465	550
AH1093//25	—	—	350	400	465	550
AH1094//27	—	—	350	400	465	550
AH1095//27	—	—	350	400	465	550
AH1096//28	—	—	350	400	465	550
AH1096//29	—	—	350	400	465	550
AH1097//29	—	—	350	400	465	550
AH1097//30	—	—	350	400	465	550
AH1098//31	—	—	350	400	465	550
AH1099//31	—	—	350	400	465	550
AH1099//32	—	—	350	400	465	550
AH1100//32	—	—	350	400	465	550
AH1100//33	—	—	350	400	465	550
AH1101//33	—	—	350	400	465	550
AH1101//34	—	—	350	400	465	550
AH1102//34	—	—	350	400	465	550
AH1103//35	—	—	350	400	465	550
AH1104//37	—	—	350	400	465	550
AH1105//37	—	—	350	400	465	550
AH1106//38	—	—	350	400	465	550
AH1106//39	—	—	350	400	465	550
AH1107//39	—	—	350	400	465	550
AH1107//40	—	—	350	400	465	550
AH1108//40	—	—	350	400	465	550
AH1108//41	—	—	350	400	465	550
AH1109//41	—	—	350	400	465	550
AH1109//42	—	—	350	400	465	550
AH1110//42	—	—	350	400	465	550
AH1110//43	—	—	350	400	465	550
AH1111//42	—	—	350	400	465	550
AH1112//44	—	—	350	400	465	550
AH1112//45	—	—	350	400	465	550

KM# 315.42A MOHUR

Gold

Date	Mintage	Good	VG	F	VF	XF
AH1069//(1) Ahad	—	—	—	5,000	7,000	10,000

KM# 315.63 MOHUR

Gold **Rev:** Mint name **Rev. Inscription:** "Dar al-Khilafat" **Note:** "Badr" couplet; Weight varies 10.8 - 11 grams.

Date	Mintage	Good	VG	F	VF	XF
AHxxxx//12	—	—	—	—	—	—

Sholapur

KM# 315.43 MOHUR

Gold **Note:** Weight varies: 10.80-11.00 grams.

Date	Mintage	Good	VG	F	VF	XF
AH1080//12	—	—	350	400	460	550
AH1080//13	—	—	350	400	460	550
AH1081//13	—	—	350	400	460	550
AH1081//14	—	—	350	400	460	550
AH1082//14	—	—	350	400	460	550
AH1082//15	—	—	350	400	460	550
AH1083//15	—	—	350	400	460	550
AH1085//18	—	—	350	400	460	550
AH1087//19	—	—	350	400	460	550
AH1087//20	—	—	350	400	460	550
AH1094//27	—	—	350	400	460	550
AH1097//29	—	—	350	400	460	550

Surat

KM# 315.44 MOHUR

Gold **Rev:** Inscription and mint name **Rev. Inscription:** "Bandar-i-Mubarak". **Note:** "Badr" couplet; Weight varies: 10.80-11.00 grams.

Date	Mintage	Good	VG	F	VF	XF
AH1070//(1) Ahad	—	—	380	450	550	700

KM# 315.45 MOHUR

Gold **Note:** Without mint epithet. Weight varies: 10.80-11.00 grams.

Date	Mintage	Good	VG	F	VF	XF
AH1071//3	—	—	350	400	460	550
AH1073//5	—	—	350	400	460	550
AH1073//6	—	—	350	400	460	550
AH1074//6	—	—	350	400	460	550
AH1074//7	—	—	350	400	460	550
AH1075//7	—	—	350	400	460	550
AH1075//8	—	—	350	400	460	550
AH1077//x	—	—	350	400	460	550
AH1079//11	—	—	350	400	460	550
AH1079//12	—	—	350	400	460	550
AH1080//12	—	—	350	400	460	550
AH1082//14	—	—	350	400	460	550
AH1083//15	—	—	350	400	460	550
AH1083//16	—	—	350	400	460	550
AH1084//16	—	—	350	400	460	550
AH1084//17	—	—	350	400	460	550
AH1085//17	—	—	350	400	460	550
AHxxxx//18	—	—	350	400	460	550
AH1089//22	—	—	350	400	460	550
AH1090//23	—	—	350	400	460	550
AH1091//23	—	—	350	400	460	550
AH1091//24	—	—	350	400	460	550
AH1092//24	—	—	350	400	460	550
AH1092//25	—	—	350	400	460	550
AH1093//25	—	—	350	400	460	550
AH1094//26	—	—	350	400	460	550
AH1094//27	—	—	350	400	460	550
AH1093//26	—	—	350	400	460	550
AH1095//27	—	—	350	400	460	550
AH1095//28	—	—	350	400	460	550
AH1096//28	—	—	350	400	460	550
AH1096//29	—	—	350	400	460	550
AH1097//29	—	—	350	400	460	550
AH1097//30	—	—	350	400	460	550
AH1098//30	—	—	350	400	460	550
AH1098//31	—	—	350	400	460	550
AH1xxx//32	—	—	350	400	460	550
AH1099//xx	—	—	350	400	460	550
AH1101//3x	—	—	350	400	460	550
AH1102//35	—	—	350	400	460	550
AH1104//36	—	—	350	400	460	550
AH1104//37	—	—	350	400	460	550
AH1105//37	—	—	350	400	460	550
AH1105//38	—	—	350	400	460	550
AH1106//38	—	—	350	400	460	550
AH1107//39	—	—	350	400	460	550
AH1107//40	—	—	350	400	460	550
AH1109//41	—	—	350	400	460	550
AH1109//42	—	—	350	400	460	550
AH1110//42	—	—	350	400	460	550
AH1110//43	—	—	350	400	460	550
AH1111//43	—	—	350	400	460	550
AH1111//44	—	—	350	400	460	550
AH1112//44	—	—	350	400	460	550
AH1112//45	—	—	350	400	460	550

Tatta

KM# 315.46 MOHUR

Gold **Obv:** Inscription **Rev:** Inscription **Note:** "Mihr" couplet; Weight varies 10.80 to 11.00 grams.

Date	Mintage	Good	VG	F	VF	XF
AH1071//4	—	—	350	400	460	550
AH1072//5	—	—	350	400	460	550
AH107x//6	—	—	350	400	460	550
AH1075//8	—	—	350	400	460	550
AH107x//9	—	—	350	400	460	550
AHxxxx//17	—	—	350	400	460	550
AH1088//21	—	—	350	400	460	550
AH1102//35	—	—	350	400	460	550
AH1112//45	—	—	350	400	460	550

KM# 315.64 MOHUR

Gold **Note:** "Badr" couplet; Weight varies 10.8 - 11 grams.

Date	Mintage	Good	VG	F	VF	XF
AH1073//5	—	—	350	410	480	600

Tibet-i-Kalan

KM# 315.65 MOHUR

Gold **Note:** Weight varies 10.8 - 11 grams.

Date	Mintage	Good	VG	F	VF	XF
AH1076//8	—	—	—	—	—	—

Toragal

KM# 315.47 MOHUR

Gold **Note:** Weight varies: 10.80-11.00 grams.

Date	Mintage	Good	VG	F	VF	XF
AH1110//xx Rare	—	—	—	—	—	—
AH111x//50 Rare	—	—	—	—	—	—

Ujjain

KM# 315.48 MOHUR

Gold **Obv:** Inscription **Rev. Inscription:** Dar-ul-Fath **Note:** Weight varies 10.80 - 11.00 grams.

Date	Mintage	Good	VG	F	VF	XF
AH1073//x	—	—	350	400	460	550
AH1105//37	—	—	350	400	460	550
AH1105//38	—	—	350	400	460	550
AH1106//39	—	—	350	400	460	550
AH1112//xx	—	—	350	400	460	550

Zafarabad

KM# 315.49 MOHUR

Gold **Note:** Weight varies 10.80 - 11.00 grams.

Date	Mintage	Good	VG	F	VF	XF
AH1074//6	—	—	350	410	480	600
AH1075//8	—	—	350	410	480	600
AH1080//13	—	—	350	410	480	600
AH108x//14	—	—	350	410	480	600
AH108x//17	—	—	350	410	480	600
AH108x//18	—	—	350	410	480	600
AH10xx//22	—	—	350	410	480	600
AH1097//29	—	—	350	410	480	600
AH1097//30	—	—	350	410	480	600
AH1098//30	—	—	350	410	480	600
AH1098//31	—	—	350	410	480	600
AH1099//31	—	—	350	410	480	600
AH1101//33	—	—	350	410	480	600

Zafarpur

KM# 315.50 MOHUR

Gold **Note:** Weight varies: 10.80-11.00 grams.

Date	Mintage	Good	VG	F	VF	XF
AH1098//31	—	350	410	525	650	900

Akbarnagar

KM# 320.1 MOHUR

Gold **Obv:** Central inscription with ruler's name and titles in outlined square **Rev:** Mint name appears on top or bottom of inscription within outlined square **Note:** Weight varies: 10.80-11.00 grams.

Date	Mintage	Good	VG	F	VF	XF
AH1070//3	—	370	480	650	850	1,200
AH1073//5	—	370	480	650	850	1,200
AH1074//6	—	370	480	650	850	1,200
AH10xx//12	—	370	480	650	850	1,200

Patna

KM# 320.3 MOHUR

Gold **Obv:** Central inscription with ruler's name and titles in outlined square **Rev:** Central inscription in outlined square **Note:** Weight varies: 10.80-11.00 grams.

Date	Mintage	Good	VG	F	VF	XF
AH1070//3	—	385	580	850	1,050	1,400

Jahangirnagar

KM# 323.1 MOHUR

Gold **Obv:** Central inscription with ruler's name and titles in outlined square, couplet **Rev:** Central inscription outlined in square **Note:** Weight varies: 10.80-11.00 grams.

Date	Mintage	Good	VG	F	VF	XF
AH108x//15	—	375	525	700	950	1,300
AH1082//14	—	375	525	700	950	1,300
AH1085//18	—	375	525	700	950	1,300

Junagarh

KM# 323.2 MOHUR

Gold **Note:** Weight varies: 10.80-11.00 grams; previous KM#320.2.

Date	Mintage	Good	VG	F	VF	XF
AHxxxx//x	—	350	410	525	650	900

Nasirabad

KM# 325.1 1/2 PAGODA

1.7000 g., Gold

Date	Mintage	Good	VG	F	VF	XF
AH1102 Rare	—	—	—	—	—	—

Chinapattan

KM# 326.1 NISAR OR PAGODA

2.9800 g., Gold **Note:** Weight varies 3 - 3.3 grams.

Date	Mintage	Good	VG	F	VF	XF
AH1103//35 Rare	—	—	—	—	—	—
AH1111//4x Rare	—	—	—	—	—	—

Nasirabad

KM# 326.2 NISAR OR PAGODA

Gold **Note:** Weight varies 3 - 3.3 grams.

Date	Mintage	Good	VG	F	VF	XF
AH1100//33	—	250	350	500	700	1,000

LARGESSE COINAGE

Akbarabad

KM# A306.1 NISAR

Silver **Obv. Inscription:** "Nisar Alamgir" **Note:** Weight varies .30 - .40 grams.

Date	Mintage	Good	VG	F	VF	XF
AHxxxx//x	—	—	—	—	—	—

Lahore

KM# A306.2 NISAR

Silver **Obv. Inscription:** "Alamgir" **Note:** Weight varies .30 - .40 grams.

Date	Mintage	Good	VG	F	VF	XF
AH1109//42	—	—	—	—	—	—

Ahmadabad

KM# B306.1 NISAR

Silver **Obv. Inscription:** "Almagir" **Note:** Weight varies .60 - .70 grams.

Date	Mintage	Good	VG	F	VF	XF
AHxxxx//14	—	—	—	—	—	—

Akbarabad

KM# B306.3 NISAR

Silver **Obv. Inscription:** "Nisar Bad Shah 'Alamgir" **Rev:** Inscription and mint name **Rev. Inscription:** "Mustagir al-Khilafa" **Note:** Weight varies .60 - .70 grams.

Date	Mintage	Good	VG	F	VF	XF
AHxxxx//x	—	—	—	—	—	—

KM# B306.2 NISAR

Silver **Obv. Inscription:** "Nisar 'Alamgiri" **Note:** Weight varies .60 - .70 grams.

Date	Mintage	Good	VG	F	VF	XF
AH1089//22	—	—	—	—	—	—

Jahangirnagar

KM# B306.6 NISAR

Silver **Obv. Inscription:** "Sikka 'Alamgir Shah" **Note:** Weight varies .60 - .70 grams.

Date	Mintage	Good	VG	F	VF	XF
AH1071	—	—	—	—	—	—

Lahore

KM# B306.7 NISAR

Silver **Obv. Inscription:** "Alamgir Bad Shah" **Note:** Weight varies .60 - .70 grams.

Date	Mintage	Good	VG	F	VF	XF
AHxxxx//26	—	—	—	—	—	—

Shahjahanabad

KM# B306.8 NISAR

Silver **Obv. Inscription:** "Nisar 'Alamgir Bad Shah" **Rev:** Mint **Rev. Inscription:** "dar al-Khilafa" **Note:** Weight varies 0.60-0.70 grams.

Date	Mintage	Good	VG	F	VF	XF
AHxxxx//x	—	—	—	—	—	—

Akbarabad

KM# C306.1 NISAR

Silver **Obv. Inscription:** "Alamgir Bad Shah Ghazi" **Note:** Weight varies 1.1 - 1.5 grams.

Date	Mintage	Good	VG	F	VF	XF
AH1071	—	—	—	—	—	—
AH1074	—	—	—	—	—	—

KM# C306.2 NISAR

Silver **Obv. Inscription:** "Nisar 'Alamgir" **Note:** Weight varies 1.1 - 1.5 grams.

Date	Mintage	Good	VG	F	VF	XF
AH1081//14	—	—	—	—	—	—

Akbarnagar

KM# C306.3 NISAR

Silver **Obv. Inscription:** "Nisar Bad Shah" **Rev:** Mint name **Rev. Inscription:** "Alamgir Shah" **Note:** Weight varies 1.1 - 1.5 grams.

Date	Mintage	Good	VG	F	VF	XF
AHxxxx//3	—	—	—	—	—	—

Allahabad

KM# C306.4 NISAR

Silver **Obv. Inscription:** "Nisar 'Alamgir Bad Shah Ghazi" **Note:** Weight varies 1.1 - 1.5 grams.

Date	Mintage	Good	VG	F	VF	XF
AH1070	—	—	—	—	—	—
AH1173/6	—	—	—	—	—	—

Bijapur

KM# C306.5 NISAR

Silver **Obv. Inscription:** "Alamgir..." **Note:** Weight varies 1.1 - 1.5 grams.

Date	Mintage	Good	VG	F	VF	XF
AHxxxx//x	—	—	—	—	—	—

Lahore

KM# C306.6 NISAR

Silver **Obv. Inscription:** "Alamgir Bad Shah" **Note:** Weight varies 1.1 - 1.5 grams.

Date	Mintage	Good	VG	F	VF	XF
AH1086//19	—	—	—	—	—	—
AH1112//45	—	—	—	—	—	—

KM# C306.7 NISAR

Silver **Obv. Inscription:** "Nisar 'Alamgir Bad Shah" **Note:** Weight varies 1.1 - 1.5 grams.

Date	Mintage	Good	VG	F	VF	XF
AHxxxx//35	—	—	—	—	—	—

Macchlipattan

KM# C306.8 NISAR

Silver **Obv. Inscription:** "Alamgir Bad Shah Sanah" **Note:** Weight varies 1.1 - 1.5 grams.

Date	Mintage	Good	VG	F	VF	XF
AH1113//42	—	—	—	—	—	—

Shahjahanabad

KM# C306.9 NISAR

Silver **Obv. Inscription:** "Nisar 'Alamgir Bad Shah Ghazi" **Note:** Weight varies 1.1 - 1.5 grams.

Date	Mintage	Good	VG	F	VF	XF
AH1089	—	—	—	—	—	—

Ahmadabad

KM# D306.1 NISAR

Silver **Obv. Inscription:** "Aurangzeb Bad Shah Ghazi" **Note:** Weight varies 2.5 - 2.9 grams.

Date	Mintage	Good	VG	F	VF	XF
AHxxxx//(1) Ahad	—	—	—	—	—	—

Akbarabad

KM# D306.3 NISAR

Silver **Obv. Inscription:** "Nisar 'Alamgir Bad Shah Ghazi" **Rev:** Mint name **Rev. Inscription:** "Jalus Maimanat Manus" **Note:** Weight varies 2.5 - 2.9 grams.

Date	Mintage	Good	VG	F	VF	XF
AHxxxx//x	—	—	—	—	—	—

KM# D306.4 NISAR

Silver **Obv. Inscription:** "Nisar 'Alamgir Bad Shah Ghazi" **Rev:** With mint name in inscription, but without "jalus...." **Note:** Weight varies 2.5 - 2.9 grams.

Date	Mintage	Good	VG	F	VF	XF
AH1071//4	—	—	—	—	—	—
AH1073//6	—	—	—	—	—	—
AH1076//8	—	—	—	—	—	—
AH1076//9	—	—	—	—	—	—
AH1077	—	—	—	—	—	—
AH1080//12	—	—	—	—	—	—
AH1081//14	—	—	—	—	—	—
AH1089//22	—	—	—	—	—	—
AH1092//25	—	—	—	—	—	—

KM# D306.5 NISAR

Silver **Rev. Inscription:** "dar al-Khilafa" **Note:** Weight varies 2.5 - 2.9 grams.

Date	Mintage	Good	VG	F	VF	XF
AH1098//31	—	—	—	—	—	—
AH1101//3x	—	—	—	—	—	—

Akbarnagar

KM# D306.6 NISAR

Silver **Note:** Weight varies 2.5 - 2.9 grams.

Date	Mintage	Good	VG	F	VF	XF
AHxxxx//15	—	—	—	—	—	—
AHxxxx//32	—	—	—	—	—	—

Alamgirpur

KM# D306.7 NISAR

Silver **Obv. Inscription:** "Nisar Bad Shah 'Alamgir" **Note:** Weight varies 2.5 - 2.9 grams.

Date	Mintage	Good	VG	F	VF	XF
AH1089//21	—	—	—	—	—	—

KM# D306.8 NISAR

Silver **Obv. Inscription:** "Nisar Aurangzeb 'Alamgir" **Note:** Weight varies 2.5 - 2.9 grams.

Date	Mintage	Good	VG	F	VF	XF
AH1102	—	—	—	—	—	—

Itawa

KM# D306.9 NISAR

Silver **Note:** Weight varies 2.5-2.9 grams.

Date	Mintage	Good	VG	F	VF	XF
AH1097//29	—	—	—	—	—	—

Jahangirnagar

KM# D306.10 NISAR

Silver **Obv. Inscription:** "Nisar Bad Shah 'Alamgir" **Note:** Weight varies 2.5 - 2.9 grams.

Date	Mintage	Good	VG	F	VF	XF
AHxxxx//19	—	—	—	—	—	—
AH1090	—	—	—	—	—	—

Shahjahanabad

KM# D306.11 NISAR

Silver **Obv. Inscription:** "Nisar 'Alamgir Bad Shah Ghazi **Rev:** Mint name **Rev. Inscription:** "dar al-Khilafa" **Note:** Weight varies 2.5 - 2.9 grams.

Date	Mintage	Good	VG	F	VF	XF
AH1070//3	—	—	—	—	—	—
AH1071//4	—	—	—	—	—	—
AH1074//7	—	—	—	—	—	—
AH1076//8	—	—	—	—	—	—
AH1077//10	—	—	—	—	—	—
AH1078//10	—	—	—	—	—	—
AHxxxx//11	—	—	—	—	—	—
AH1080//12	—	—	—	—	—	—
AH1082//14	—	—	—	—	—	—
AH1083//16	—	—	—	—	—	—
AH1102//3x	—	—	—	—	—	—
AH1103//36	—	—	—	—	—	—

Akbarabad

KM# 306.1 NISAR

Silver **Obv. Inscription:** "Nisar 'Alamgir Bad Shah Ghazi" **Rev:** Mint name and AH date in inscription **Note:** Weight varies: 5.6 - 5.8 grams.

Date	Mintage	Good	VG	F	VF	XF
AH1078//11	—	—	35.00	60.00	100	160
AH1080//12	—	—	35.00	60.00	100	160
AH1081//13	—	—	35.00	60.00	100	160

KM# 306.2 NISAR

Silver **Rev:** Mint epithet: "Mustaqir-ul-Khilafat" **Note:** Weight varies: 0.35-2.90 grams.

Date	Mintage	Good	VG	F	VF	XF
AH1098//31	—	—	—	—	—	—

Akbarnagar

KM# 306.4 NISAR

Silver **Note:** Weight varies: 0.35-2.90 grams.

Date	Mintage	Good	VG	F	VF	XF
AH1073//6	—	—	55.00	90.00	150	250
AHxxxx//15	—	—	55.00	90.00	150	250
AHxxxx//32	—	—	55.00	90.00	150	250

Alamgirpur

KM# 306.8 NISAR

Silver **Note:** Weight varies: 0.35-2.90 grams.

Date	Mintage	Good	VG	F	VF	XF
AH1102//xx	—	—	—	—	—	—

Allahabad

KM# 306.10 NISAR

Silver **Obv. Inscription:** "Nisar 'Alamgir Bad Shah Ghazi" **Note:** Weight varies 5.60 - 5.80 grams.

Date	Mintage	Good	VG	F	VF	XF
AH1082//14	—	—	—	—	—	—

Itawa

KM# 306.9 NISAR

Silver **Note:** Weight varies: 0.35-2.90 grams.

Date	Mintage	Good	VG	F	VF	XF
AH1112//4x	—	—	—	—	—	—

Jahangirnagar

KM# 306.5 NISAR

Silver **Note:** Weight varies: 0.35-2.90 grams.

Date	Mintage	Good	VG	F	VF	XF
AHxxxx//19	—	—	55.00	90.00	150	250

Lahore

KM# 306.6 NISAR

Silver **Note:** Weight varies: 5.60-5.80 grams (1/2 Rupee weight).

Date	Mintage	Good	VG	F	VF	XF
AHxxxx//26	—	16.00	40.00	65.00	110	180
AHxxxx//35	—	16.00	40.00	65.00	110	180
AH1112//45	—	16.00	40.00	65.00	110	180

Shahjahanabad

KM# 306.7 NISAR

Silver **Note:** Mint epithet: "Dar-ul- Khalifat". Weight varies: 5.60-5.80 grams (1/2 Rupee weight).

Date	Mintage	Good	VG	F	VF	XF
AH1070//3	—	16.00	40.00	65.00	110	180
AH1071//4	—	16.00	40.00	65.00	110	180
AH1074//7	—	16.00	40.00	65.00	110	180
AH1076//8	—	16.00	40.00	65.00	110	180
AH1077//10	—	16.00	40.00	65.00	110	180
AH1078//10	—	16.00	40.00	65.00	110	180
AH1078//11	—	16.00	40.00	65.00	110	180
AH1079//11	—	16.00	40.00	65.00	110	180
AH1079//12	—	16.00	40.00	65.00	110	180
AH1080//12	—	16.00	40.00	65.00	110	180
AH1082//14	—	16.00	40.00	65.00	110	180
AH1083//1x	—	16.00	40.00	65.00	110	180
AH108x//17	—	16.00	40.00	65.00	110	180

Shahjahanabad

KM# A307.1 NISAR

2.7200 g., Gold

Date	Mintage	Good	VG	F	VF	XF
AH1072//5 Rare	—	—	—	—	—	—

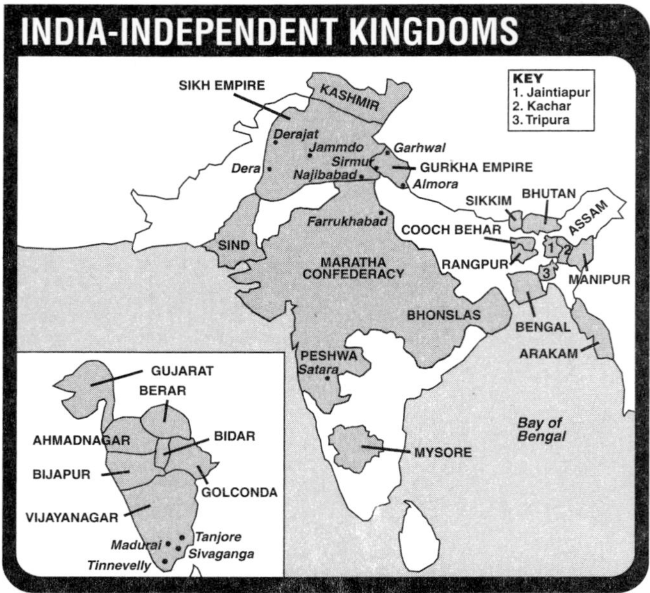

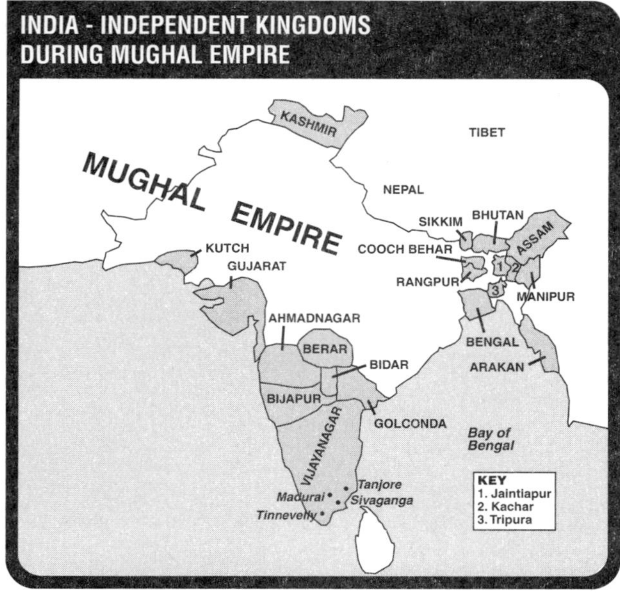

ARAKAN

A coastal region of Burma on the Bay of Bengal. The Buddhist Arakanese trace their history back 4500 years.

Arakan surrendered to the Burmese King Bodawpaya in 1784 and coins were issued by the king's governor in Arakan, bearing the following inscription: Amarapura, Kingdom of the Lord of Many White Elephants.

RULERS

Min Raza Gyi, Naradibbati, BE955-974/1593-1612AD
Min Khamaung, Waradhamma Raza, Hussein Shah, BE974-984/1612-1622AD
Thirithudhamma, BE984-1000/1622-1638AD
Narabadigyi, BE1000-1007/1638-1645AD
Thado, BE1007-1014/1645-1652AD
Sanda Thudhamma, BE1014-1047/1652-1685AD
Waradhamma Raza, BE1047-1059/1685-1697AD
Kalamandat, BE1059-1072/1697-1710AD

KINGDOM

Min Raza Gyu, Naradibbati
BE955-974/1593-1612AD

HAMMERED COINAGE

KM# 5 TANKAH

Silver **Note:** Varieties exist. Weight varies: 10.00-10.30 grams.

Date	Mintage	Good	VG	F	VF	XF
ND(1593-1612)	—	85.00	170	280	400	—

KM# 6.1 TANKAH

Silver **Rev. Inscription:** Selim Shah... **Note:** Weight varies: 10.00-10.30 grams.

Date	Mintage	Good	VG	F	VF	XF
BE963 (1601)	—	100	200	350	500	—

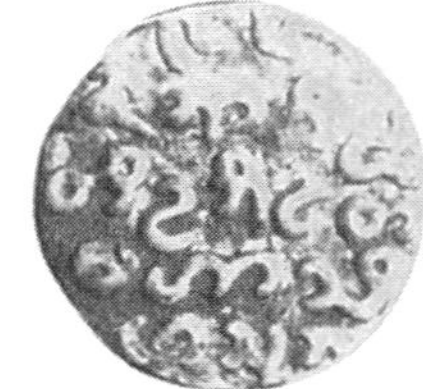

KM# 6.2 TANKAH

Silver **Rev. Inscription:** Halal Shah... **Note:** Weight varies: 10.00-10.30 grams.

Date	Mintage	Good	VG	F	VF	XF
BE974 (1612)	—	85.00	170	280	400	—

Min Khamaung, Waradhamma Raza, Hussein Shah
BE974-984/1612-22AD

HAMMERED COINAGE

KM# 7 TANKAH

Silver **Rev. Inscription:** Hussein Shah... **Note:** Weight varies: 9.98-10.06 grams. Varieties exist.

Date	Mintage	Good	VG	F	VF	XF
BE974 (1612)	—	125	250	420	600	—

Thirithudhamma
BE984-1000/1622-38AD

HAMMERED COINAGE

KM# 8.1 TANKAH

Silver **Note:** Weight varies: 9.95-10.15 grams. Varieties exist.

Date	Mintage	Good	VG	F	VF	XF
BE984 (1622)	—	42.00	85.00	140	200	—

KM# 8.2 TANKAH

Silver **Obv:** Legend within dotted border **Note:** Weight varies: 9.95-10.15 grams.

Date	Mintage	Good	VG	F	VF	XF
BE98x (1626) Rare	—	—	—	—	—	—

KM# 9 TANKAH

Silver **Subject:** Coronation **Note:** Weight varies: 9.95-10.15 grams.

Date	Mintage	Good	VG	F	VF	XF
BE996 (1634) Rare	—	—	—	—	—	—

Narabadigyi
BE1000-07/1638-45AD

HAMMERED COINAGE

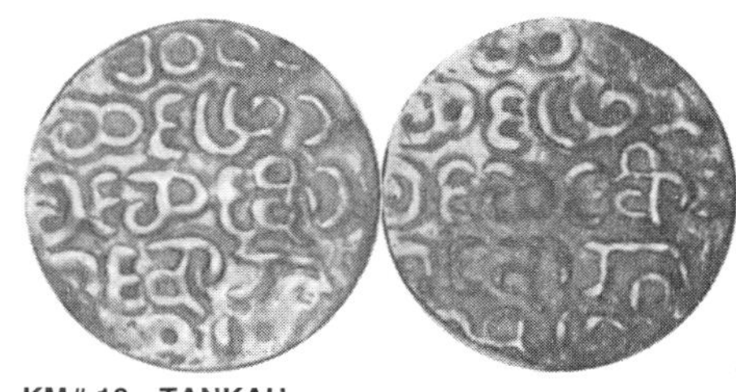

KM# 10 TANKAH

Silver **Note:** Weight varies: 10.12-10.30 grams.

Date	Mintage	Good	VG	F	VF	XF
BE1000 (1638)	—	30.00	60.00	100	150	—

Thado
BE1007-14/1645-52AD

HAMMERED COINAGE

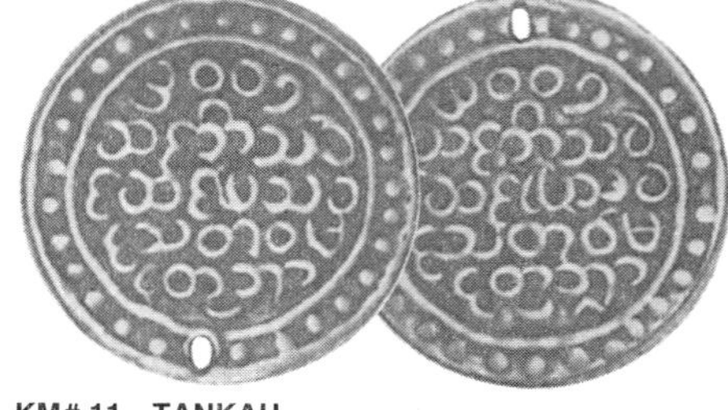

KM# 11 TANKAH

Silver **Note:** Weight varies: 9.37-10.33 grams.

Date	Mintage	Good	VG	F	VF	XF
BE1005/7 (1645)	—	50.00	100	175	250	—

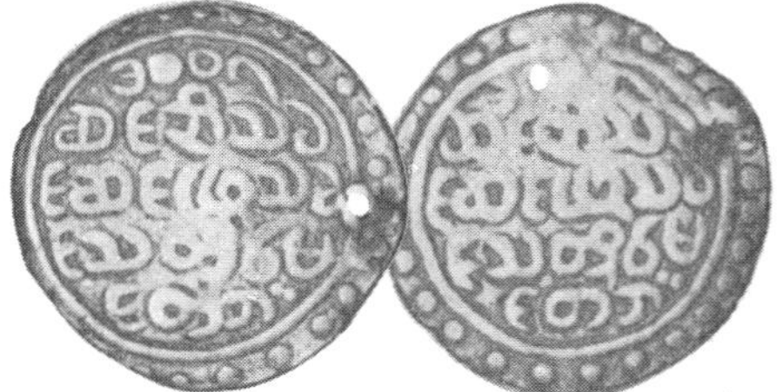

KM# 12.1 TANKAH

Silver **Note:** Weight varies: 9.37-10.33 grams.

Date	Mintage	Good	VG	F	VF	XF
BE1007 (1645)	—	20.00	42.00	70.00	100	—

KM# 12.2 TANKAH

Silver **Note:** Weight varies: 9.37-10.33 grams. Broad flan.

Date	Mintage	Good	VG	F	VF	XF
BE1007 (1645)	—	42.00	84.00	140	200	—

Sanda Thudhamma
BE1014-47/1652-85AD
HAMMERED COINAGE

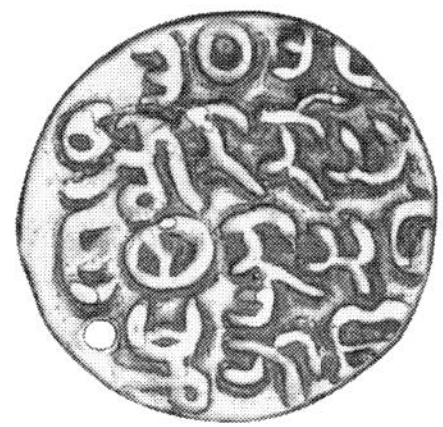

KM# 13 TANKAH

Silver **Note:** Weight varies: 8.84-10.32 grams.

Date	Mintage	Good	VG	F	VF	XF
BE1014 (1652)	—	18.00	336	62.00	90.00	—

KM# 14 TANKAH

Silver **Rev:** Legend divided **Note:** Weight varies: 8.84-10.32 grams.

Date	Mintage	Good	VG	F	VF	XF
BE1014 (1652)	—	25.00	50.00	85.00	125	—

Waradhamma Raza
BE1047-59/1685-97AD
HAMMERED COINAGE

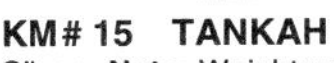

KM# 15 TANKAH

Silver **Note:** Weight varies: 8.84-10.32 grams.

Date	Mintage	Good	VG	F	VF	XF
BE1047 (1685)	—	30.00	60.00	100	150	—

Kalamandat
BE1059-72/1697-1710AD
HAMMERED COINAGE

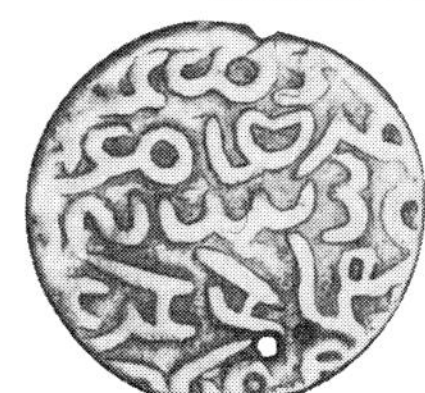
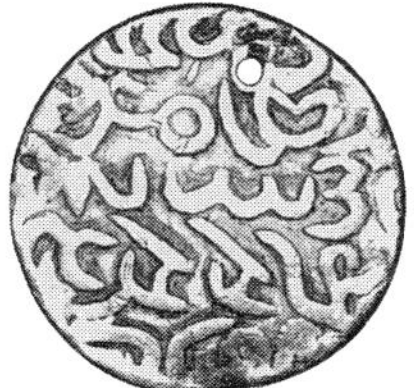

KM# 16 TANKAH

Silver **Note:** Weight varies: 9.84-10.04 grams. Varieties exist.

Date	Mintage	Good	VG	F	VF	XF
BE1059 (1697)	—	50.00	100	175	250	—

ASSAM

It was in the 13th century that a tribal leader called Sukapha, with about 9,000 followers, left their traditional home in the Shan States of Northern Burma, and carved out the Ahom Kingdom in upper Assam.

The Ahom Kingdom gradually increased in power and extent over the following centuries, particularly during the reign of King Suhungmung (1497-1539). This king also took on a Hindu title, Svarga Narayan, which shows the increasing influence of the Brahmins over the court. Although several of the other Hindu states in north-east India started a silver coinage during the 16th century, it was not until the mid-17th century that the Ahoms first struck coin.

From the time of Kusain Shah's invasion of Cooch Behar in 1494AD the Muslims had cast acquisitive eyes towards the valley of the Brahmaputra, but the Ahoms managed to preserve their independence. In 1661 Aurangzeb's governor in Bengal, Mir Jumla, made a determined effort to bring Assam under Mughal rule. Cooch Behar was annexed without difficulty, and in March 1662 Mir Jumla occupied Gargaon, the Ahom capital, without opposition. However, during the rainy season the Muslim forces suffered severely from disease, lack of food and from the occasional attacks from the Ahom forces, who had tactically withdrawn from the capital together with the king. After the end of the monsoon a supply line was opened with Bengal again, but morale in the Muslim army was low, so Mir Jumla was forced to agree to peace terms somewhat less onerous than the Mughals liked to impose on subjugated states. The Ahoms agreed to pay tribute, but the Ahom kingdom remained entirely independent of Mughal control, and never again did a Muslim army venture into upper Assam.

RULERS

Ruler's names, where present on the coins, usually appear on the obverse (dated) side, starting either at the end of the first line, after <I>Shri, </I>or in the second line. Most of the Ahom rulers after the adoption of Hinduism in about 1500AD had both an Ahom and a Hindu name.

HINDU NAME	AHOM NAME	Dates
Khora Raja	Sukhampa	SE1474-1525/1552-1603AD
Pratap Singh or Burha Raja	Susengpha	SE1525-1563/1603-1641AD
Jayaditya or Bhaga Raja	Surampha	SE1563-1566/1641-1644AD
Nariya Raja	Sutyinpha	SE1566-1570/1644-1648AD
Jayadhvaja Simha or Surga Narayana	Sutamla	SE1570-1585/1648-1663AD
Chakradhvaja Simha	Supungmung	SE1585-1592/1663-1670AD
Udayaditya	Sunyatpha	SE1592-1594/1670-1672AD
Ramadhvaja Simha	Suklampha	SE1594-1596/1672-1675AD
Chamaguriya Raja	Suhung	SE1596-7/1675AD
Gobar Raja		SE1597/1675AD
Dihingia Raja II	Suhung	SE1597-1599/1675-1677AD
Parvatia Raja	Sudaipha	SE1599-1601/1677-1679AD
Ratnadhvaja Simha	Sulikpha	SE1601-1603/1679-1681AD
Gadadhara Simha	Supatpha	SE1603-1618/1681-1696AD
Rudra Simha	Sukhrungpha	SE1618-1636/1696-1714/AD

COINAGE

It is frequently stated that coins were first struck in Assam during the reign of King Suklenmung (1539-1552), but this is merely due to a misreading of the Ahom legend on the coins of King Supungmung (1663-70). The earliest Ahom coins known, therefore, were struck during the reign of King Jayadhvaja Simha (1648-1663). Although the inscription and general design of these first coins of the Ahom Kingdom were copied from the coins of Cooch Behar, the octagonal shape was entirely Ahom, and according to tradition was chosen because of the belief that the Ahom country was eight sided. Apart from the unique shape, the coins were of similar fabric and weight standard to the Moghul rupee.

The earliest coins had inscriptions in Sanskrit using the Bengali script, but the retreat of the Moghul army under Mir Jumla in 1663 seems to have led to a revival of Ahom nationalism that may account for the fact that most of the coins struck between 1663 and 1696 had inscriptions in the old Ahom script, with invocations to Ahom deities.

Up to this time all the coins, following normal practice in Northeast India, were merely dated to the coronation year of the ruler, but Rudra Simha (1696-1714) insti-tuted the practice of dating coins to the year of issue. This ruler was a fervent Hindu, and reinstated Sanskrit inscriptions on the coins. After this the Ahom script was used on a few rare ceremonial issues.

The majority of coins issued were of silver, with binary subdivions down to a fraction of 1/32nd rupee. Cowrie shells were used for small change. Gold coins were struck throughout the period, often using the same dies as were used for the silver coins. A few copper coins were struck during the reign of Brajanatha Simha (1818-19), but these are very rare.

NUMERALS

The early coinage is usually dated in the Saka era using Bengali numerals while later issues use modified numerals called Assamese.

MINT NAMES

گرگاو

Gargaon

رنگپور

Rangpur

REGNAL YEARS

Some of the earliest dated coins have the regnal years in written characters. These listings will have the numerical regnal years in parenthesis in the following listings.

Written	Numeric	Symbol
RAITYEO	13	
PLEKNGI	15	
KAPSAN	21	
KHUCHNGI for KHUTNGI	27	
RAISAN	33	
KATKEU	36	
RAISINGA	43	

KINGDOM

Jayadhvaja Simha (Sutamla)

SE1570-1585 / 1648-1663AD

HAMMERED COINAGE

KM# 1 RUPEE

Silver

Date	Mintage	Good	VG	F	VF	XF
SE1570	—	60.00	150	250	350	500

KM# 2 RUPEE

Silver **Obv. Inscription:** "Deva" included

Date	Mintage	Good	VG	F	VF	XF
SE1570	—	60.00	150	250	350	500

KM# 3 RUPEE

Silver **Rev. Inscription:** Different style

Date	Mintage	Good	VG	F	VF	XF
SE1570	—	60.00	150	250	350	500

KM# 4 RUPEE

Silver **Rev. Inscription:** Chinese "Ysang Pao"

Date	Mintage	Good	VG	F	VF	XF
SE1570	—	120	300	600	750	1,250

Note: The Chinese inscription may be translated as "Tibetan Coin", so this coin may have been intended as a trade coin for use in Tibet

KM# 5 MOHUR

11.2000 g., Gold **Shape:** Octagonal **Note:** Similar to KM#1, Rupee.

Date	Mintage	Good	VG	F	VF	XF
SE1570 (1648) Rare	—	—	275	500	800	1,350

KM# A6 MOHUR

11.2000 g., Gold **Note:** Similar to KM#2, Rupee.

Date	Mintage	Good	VG	F	VF	XF
SE1570 (1648) Rare	—	—	275	500	800	1,350

Chakradhvaja Simha (Supungmung)

SE1585-1592 / 1663-1670AD

HAMMERED COINAGE

KM# 8 RUPEE

Silver **Obv:** Sanskrit legend **Rev:** Sanskrit legend

Date	Mintage	Good	VG	F	VF	XF
SE1585	—	30.00	60.00	120	200	300

KM# 9 RUPEE

Silver **Obv. Inscription:** Ahomese **Rev. Inscription:** Ahomese

Date	Mintage	Good	VG	F	VF	XF
ND//(15)	—	32.00	80.00	160	250	360

KM# 10 RUPEE

Silver **Obv:** Without lion

Date	Mintage	Good	VG	F	VF	XF
ND//(15)	—	25.00	55.00	110	175	270

KM# 11 RUPEE

Silver **Obv:** Lion at left

Date	Mintage	Good	VG	F	VF	XF
ND//(15)	—	25.00	55.00	110	175	270

KM# 12 RUPEE

Silver **Obv:** Lion at bottom

Date	Mintage	Good	VG	F	VF	XF
ND//(15)	—	25.00	55.00	110	175	270

KM# 13 RUPEE

Silver **Rev:** Crescents in border

Date	Mintage	Good	VG	F	VF	XF
ND//(15)	—	25.00	55.00	110	175	270

KM# 16 MOHUR

Gold **Obv:** Without lion **Note:** Similar to Rupee, KM#10.

Date	Mintage	Good	VG	F	VF	XF
ND//(15)	—	700	1,000	1,400	2,000	2,800

KM# 18 MOHUR

Gold **Obv:** Lion at bottom **Note:** Similar to Rupee, KM#12.

Date	Mintage	Good	VG	F	VF	XF
ND//(15)	—	700	1,000	1,400	2,000	2,800

KM# 19 MOHUR

Gold **Rev:** Crescents in border **Note:** Similar to Rupee, KM#13.

Date	Mintage	Good	VG	F	VF	XF
ND//(15)	—	700	1,000	1,400	2,000	2,800

Udayaditya (Sunyatpha)

SE1592-1594 / 1670-1672AD

HAMMERED COINAGE

KM# 21 RUPEE

Silver

Date	Mintage	Good	VG	F	VF	XF
ND//(21)	—	64.00	160	320	500	720

KM# 23 MOHUR

Gold **Obv:** Bird at bottom

Date	Mintage	Good	VG	F	VF	XF
ND//(21)	—	1,100	1,500	2,200	3,000	4,200

Dihingia Raja

SE1597-1599 / 1675-1677AD

HAMMERED COINAGE

KM# 25 RUPEE

Silver

Date	Mintage	Good	VG	F	VF	XF
ND//(27)	—	65.00	165	330	550	775

KM# 26 RUPEE

Silver

Date	Mintage	Good	VG	F	VF	XF
ND//(27)	—	65.00	165	330	550	775

Gadadhara Simha (Supatpha)

SE1603-1618 / 1681-1696AD

HAMMERED COINAGE

KM# 28 RUPEE

Silver **Obv:** Without animals **Rev:** Without animals

Date	Mintage	Good	VG	F	VF	XF
ND//(33)	—	12.00	26.00	55.00	90.00	140

KM# 29 RUPEE

Silver **Rev:** Lion

Date	Mintage	Good	VG	F	VF	XF
ND//(33)	—	12.00	26.00	55.00	90.00	140

KM# 30 RUPEE

Silver **Rev:** Lion and bird

Date	Mintage	Good	VG	F	VF	XF
ND//(33)	—	12.00	26.00	55.00	90.00	140

KM# 31 RUPEE

Silver **Rev:** Lion and two birds

Date	Mintage	Good	VG	F	VF	XF
ND//(33)	—	12.00	26.00	55.00	90.00	140

KM# 32 RUPEE

Silver **Obv:** Lion **Rev:** Bird preening itself

Date	Mintage	Good	VG	F	VF	XF
ND//(33)	—	12.00	26.00	55.00	90.00	140

KM# 33 RUPEE
Silver **Rev:** Bird preening itself facing right

Date	Mintage	Good	VG	F	VF	XF
ND//(33)	—	12.00	26.00	55.00	90.00	140

KM# 34 RUPEE
Silver **Rev:** Bird at top

Date	Mintage	Good	VG	F	VF	XF
ND//(33)	—	13.00	32.00	65.00	100	160

Rudra Simha (Sukhrungpha)
SE1618-1636 / 1696-1714AD
HAMMERED COINAGE

KM# 36 1/4 RUPEE
Silver **Note:** Weight varies 2.67 - 2.9 grams.

Date	Mintage	Good	VG	F	VF	XF
SE1619	—	32.00	80.00	160	250	360

KM# 38 1/2 RUPEE
Silver **Note:** Weight varies 5.35 - 5.8 grams.

Date	Mintage	Good	VG	F	VF	XF
ND(1696-1714)	—	20.00	45.00	95.00	150	240

KM# 40 RUPEE
Silver **Obv:** Inscription **Rev:** Inscription **Note:** Weight varies: 10.70-11.60 grams.

Date	Mintage	Good	VG	F	VF	XF
SE1618	—	7.00	11.00	18.00	30.00	46.00
SE1620	—	7.00	11.00	18.00	30.00	46.00
SE1621	—	7.00	11.00	18.00	30.00	46.00
SE1622	—	7.00	11.00	18.00	30.00	46.00

KM# 41 RUPEE
Silver **Note:** Weight varies: 10.70-11.60 grams.

Date	Mintage	Good	VG	F	VF	XF
SE1619	—	13.00	65.00	130	200	320

KM# 43 1/4 MOHUR
Gold **Note:** Weight varies 2.67 - 2.9 grams.

Date	Mintage	Good	VG	F	VF	XF
SE1619	—	300	425	550	750	1,000

KM# 44 1/2 MOHUR
Gold **Note:** Weight varies 5.35 - 5.7 grams.

Date	Mintage	Good	VG	F	VF	XF
ND(1696-1714)	—	300	420	530	700	900

KM# 45 MOHUR
Gold **Obv:** Inscription **Rev:** Inscription **Note:** Weight varies: 10.70-11.40 grams.

Date	Mintage	Good	VG	F	VF	XF
SE1620	—	350	420	530	700	900

BAGLANA
KINGDOM
HAMMERED COINAGE

Mulher

KM# 1 1/2 MAHMUDI
Silver Weight varies 2.70-2.80g. **Obv:** Akbar's name and titles, date **Rev:** Kalima in square **Note:** In name of Mughal Akbar, continued into 19th c. with posthumous dates. Prev. India-Mughal Empire, KM# 71.1.

Date	Mintage	Good	VG	F	VF	XF
ND(1578-1810)	—	—	12.00	20.00	32.50	50.00

Mulher

KM# 2 MAHMUDI
Silver Weight varies, 5.40-5.60g **Obv:** Akbar's name and titles, date **Rev:** Kalima in square **Note:** In name of Mughal Akbar, continued into 19th c. with posthumous dates. Prev. India-Mughal Empire, KM# 72.1.

Date	Mintage	Good	VG	F	VF	XF
AH1010	—	—	10.00	16.00	27.50	40.00
AH1011	—	—	10.00	16.00	27.50	40.00
AH1012	—	—	10.00	16.00	27.50	40.00
AH1013	—	—	10.00	16.00	27.50	—
AH1014	—	—	10.00	16.00	27.50	40.00
AH1015	—	—	10.00	16.00	27.50	40.00
AH1016	—	—	10.00	16.00	27.50	40.00
AH1017	—	—	10.00	16.00	27.50	40.00
AH1018	—	—	10.00	16.00	27.50	40.00
AH1019	—	—	10.00	16.00	27.50	40.00
AH1020	—	—	10.00	16.00	27.50	40.00
AH1021	—	—	10.00	16.00	27.50	40.00
AH1022	—	—	10.00	16.00	27.50	40.00
AH1023	—	—	10.00	16.00	27.50	40.00
AH1024	—	—	10.00	16.00	27.50	40.00
AH1025	—	—	10.00	16.00	27.50	40.00
AH1026	—	—	10.00	16.00	27.50	40.00
AH1027	—	—	10.00	16.00	27.50	40.00
AH1028	—	—	10.00	16.00	27.50	40.00
AH1029	—	—	10.00	16.00	27.50	40.00

COOCH BEHAR

During the 15th century, the area that was to become Cooch Behar was ruled by the powerful Hindu kings of Kamata, who were defeated by Sultan Ala al din Husain, Shah of Bengal in 1494AD. In 1511AD the kingdom of Cooch Behar was established by Chandan, a chieftain of the Koch tribe.

Chandan was succeeded about 1522 by Visvasimha, who consolidated the kingdom, and set up his capital at the present town of Cooch Behar. It was he who laid the foundations of the prosperity of the area by developing the Tibetan trade routes through Bhutan. Visvasimha is said to have abdicated about 1555AD to become an ascetic, and was succeeded by his son Nara Narayan, under whose reign the state reached the zenith of its power.

From the solid basis set up by his father, Nara Narayan set out, assisted by his brother Sukladhvaja, to extend the borders of his kingdom. Over the next quarter century he proceeded to subdue part of the Assam Valley, Kachar, Manipur, the Khasi and Jaintia Hills and part of Tripura and Sylhet. Nara Narayan was the first king of Cooch Behar to strike coins, and the varied style may indicate that he set up several mints over his empire. The style of one piece is very similar to that of later pieces struck by the Rajas of Jaintiapur, which suggests Jaintiapur as the mint for this variety, but no other varieties have been assigned to specific mints.

After the death of Sukladhvaja, who was a great general, the military strength of the kingdom waned. Nara Narayan quarrelled with Sukladhvaja's son Raghu Deva, and the latter set himself up as ruler of the eastern part of the kingdom in 1581, initially under the suzerainty of his uncle, but after Nara Narayan's death, as full independent ruler.

Nara Narayan's son, Lakshmi Narayan inherited the western part of the kingdom, but no attempt was made to consolidate the conquests made by his father, and Kachar, Tripura and other states reverted to their former fully independent state. Lakshmi Narayan was a weak, peace loving king who preferred to declare himself a vassal of the Mughal Emperor in 1596, rather than make any attempt to preserve his independence. In accepting any attempt to preserve his independence. In accepting Mughal suzeraincy, he gravely offended his subjects, who rose in revolt. The Mughals assisted Lakshmi Narayan quell the rebellion, and in 1603 a treaty was signed under which Lakshmi Narayan agreed never again to strike full rupees and to abandon certain other royal prerogatives. The Eastern Kingdom under Raghu Deva and his son Parikshit refused to bow to Mughal domination in the same way, and in 1612 the Mughals invaded and destroyed their kingdom.

After Lakshmi Narayan's death in 1627, the new ruler Vira Narayan exhibited a certain degree of independence by striking full rupees and retaking the former Eastern Cooch Behar Kingdom from the Mughals. By this time, however, a powerful leader had emerged in Bhutan, and trade was disrupted by wars between Bhutan and Tibet, causing a reduction in the number of coins struck.

The Mughals soon recaptured the eastern territories, but the next ruler, Prana Narayan, was able to reopen trade links with Tibet through Bhutan. In 1661 Prana Narayan was expelled from his capital by the Mughal governor of Bengal, Mir Jumia, and sought refuge in Bhutan. At this time, Mir Jumia struck coins in Cooch Behar in the name of the Mughal Emperor Aurangzeb, but while Mir Jumia was stuck in Assam during the monsoon of 1663, Prana Narayan managed to regain control of his kingdom paying tribute to the Mughal Emperor.

For the next century Cooch Behar was relatively peaceful until there was a dispute over the succession in 1772. After a confusing period during which the Bhutanese installed their own nominated ruler and captured Dhairyendra Narandra, the Chief Minister appealed to the British for assistance. With an eye on the potentially lucrative Tibetan trade, which had increased somewhat in volume since Prithvi Narayan's rise to power in Nepal, the British agreed to support Darendra Narayan, so long as British suzerainty was acknowledged.

RULERS

Lakshmi Narayan, CB77-117/
SE1509-1549/1587-1627AD
Raghu Deva, CB71-93/
SE1503-1525/1581-1603AD
Parikshit Narayan, C93-102/
SE1525-1534/1603-1612AD
Vira Narayan, CB117-123/
SE1549-1555/1627-1633AD
Prana Narayan, CB123-156/
SE1555-1588/1633-1666AD
Aurangzeb, during Mughal occupation,
CB151-153/SE1583-1585/1661-1663AD
Mada narayan, CB156-171/
SE1588-1603/1666-1681AD
Vasudeva Narayan, CB171-173/
SE1603-1605/1681-1683AD
Mahendra Narayan, CB173-185/
SE1605-1617/1683-1695AD
Rupa Narayan, CB185-205/
SE1617-1637/1695-1715AD

DATING

The coins are dated in either the Saka era (Saka yr. + 78 = AD year) or the Cooch Behar era (CB yr. + 1510 = AD year) calculated from the year of the founding of the kingdom by Chandan in 1511AD. Some coins have dates in both eras, but as the Saka always refers back to the accession year, and the Cooch Behar year seems to show the actual date of striking, the two years seems to show the actual date of striking, the two years do not necessarily correspond to the same AD year.

Unfortunately the dies for the half rupees were usually rather broader than the flans, so the year is only rarely visible.

KINGDOM

Parikshit Narayan
SE1525-1534 / 1603-1612AD
STANDARD COINAGE

KM# 59 RUPEE
Silver

Date	Mintage	Good	VG	F	VF	XF
SE1525 (1603)	—	32.00	80.00	160	250	360

Vira Narayan
SE1549-1555 / 1627-1633AD
STANDARD COINAGE

KM# 64 1/2 RUPEE
4.9000 g., Silver

Date	Mintage	Good	VG	F	VF	XF
SE1548 CB117 (1627)	—	40.00	90.00	180	360	—

KM# 66 RUPEE
10.2000 g., Silver

Date	Mintage	Good	VG	F	VF	XF
SE1548 CB117 (1627)	—	60.00	150	250	350	500

Prana Narayan
SE1555-1588 / 1633-1666AD
STANDARD COINAGE

KM# 72 1/2 RUPEE
4.7000 g., Silver **Note:** Several varieties of ornamentation exist. The date is rarely visible. Prices given are for invisible or incomplete dates - pieces with clear dates are worth slightly more. Some pieces may exist with a date in the Saka era, but no clear specimens have been noted.

Date	Mintage	Good	VG	F	VF	XF
CB129 (1639)	—	5.00	13.00	26.00	45.00	—
CB131 (1641)	—	5.00	13.00	26.00	45.00	—
CB141 (1651)	—	5.00	13.00	26.00	45.00	—
CB151 (1661)	—	5.00	13.00	26.00	45.00	—

KM# 74 RUPEE
9.4000 g., Silver

Date	Mintage	Good	VG	F	VF	XF
SE1554 (1632)	—	—	—	—	—	—
SE1555 (1633)	—	10.00	20.00	45.00	75.00	120

BRITISH PROTECTORATE

Prana Narayan
SE1555-1588 / 1633-1666AD
STANDARD COINAGE

KM# 75 RUPEE
9.4000 g., Silver

Date	Mintage	Good	VG	F	VF	XF
CB130 (1640)	—	32.00	80.00	160	250	360
CB140 (1650)	—	32.00	80.00	160	250	360

KM# 79 1/2 MOHUR
6.9000 g., Gold

Date	Mintage	Good	VG	F	VF	XF
NS753 (1633)	—	1,100	1,500	2,200	3,000	4,200

Aurangzeb
Mughal Occupation, SE1583-1585 / 1661-1663AD
STANDARD COINAGE

KM# 85 1/2 RUPEE
Silver **Note:** See Mughal Empire, KM#296.1.

Date	Mintage	Good	VG	F	VF	XF
ND(1661-63) Rare	—	—	—	—	—	—

Note: Struck during the Mughal occupation between 1661 and 1663AD

Mada Narayan
SE1588-1603 / 1666-1681AD
STANDARD COINAGE

KM# 91 1/2 RUPEE
Silver **Note:** The dates are very rarely legible. Some pieces may be dated with SE dates, but no clear pieces have been noted.

Date	Mintage	Good	VG	F	VF	XF
CB16x (1670-79)	—	5.00	7.50	13.50	20.00	—
CB170 (1680)	—	5.00	7.50	13.50	20.00	—
CB171 (1681)	—	5.00	7.50	13.50	20.00	—

Vasudeva Narayan
SE1603-1605 / 1681-1683AD
STANDARD COINAGE

KM# 97 1/2 RUPEE
Silver

Date	Mintage	Good	VG	F	VF	XF
ND(1681-83)	—	10.00	20.00	45.00	65.00	—

Rupa Narayan
SE1617-1637 / 1695-1715AD
STANDARD COINAGE

KM# 109 1/2 RUPEE
Silver

Date	Mintage	Good	VG	F	VF	XF
ND(1695-1715)	—	4.00	6.50	10.00	15.00	—

DECCAN SULTANATES

In 1347 an officer in the service of Muhammad bin Tughluq, the Dehli sultan, occupied the fortress of Daulatabad in the Western Deccan and declared his independence of the Dehli Sultanate. It was from such small beginnings that the sprawling Bahmani kingdom of the Deccan arose. A hundred years later the Bahmanis also began to disintegrate under the disastrous leadership of Sultan Mahmud Shah (1482-1518). In their place five regional kingdoms arose, each founded by an officer or provincial governor in the service of Mahmud. The comparative vigor of these individual sultanates may to some extent be measured by the size and quality of their coinage. The Adil Shah dynasty of Bijapur, the Nizam Shahs of Ahmadnagar, and the Qutb Shahs of Golkonda (Hyderabad) all minted fairly prolifically although mostly in copper. Coins of the Barid Shahs of Bidar are few and far between, and no coins of the Imad Shahs of Berar are known. The Barid Shahs were absorbed by Bijapur, the Imad Shahs by Ahmadnagar, and the others were all annexed by the Mughals between 1596 and1687.

Further details on the coins of the Nizam Shahi dynasty of Ahmadnagar, the Barid Shahi dynasty of Bidar, the Adil Shahi dynasty of Bijapur, and the Qutb Shahi dynasty of Golkonda may be found in the *Standard Catalogue of Sultanate Coins of India*, by Dilip Rajgor, Bombay, India 1991.

AHMADNAGAR

Nizam Shahs

The Nizam Shahi dynasty owed its origin as an independent kingdom to Malik Ahmad, the Bahmani governor of Junnar. In 1490, Malik Ahmad revolted against his superiors by defeating Mahmud Bahmani's army. He then assumed the name of Ahmad Nizam Shah, from which name the dynasty itself became known.About 1574 Ahmadnagar annexed Berar and the short-lived Imad Shahi dynasty came to an end. Ahmadnagar came under increasing Mughal pressure after 1596 and was annexed by Shah Jahan in 1637.

RULERS

(after 1556AD)

Murtaza II as Mughal vassal, AH1009-1019/1600-1610AD
Burhan III, as Mughal vassal, AH1019-1041/1610-1631AD
Hosayn III, AH1041-1043/1631-1633AD
Murtaza III, AH1043-1046/1633-1636AD
(conquest, annexation by Mughal Emperor Aurangzeb)

MINTS

Ahmadnagar
Burhanabad
Parenda

INDEPENDENT KINGDOM

Murtaza II as Mughal Vassal
AH1009-1019/1600-1610AD
HAMMERED COINAGE

Burhanabad

KM# 9 1/3 FALUS
Copper **Rev. Inscription:** "Dar-us-Sultanate" **Note:** Weight varies: 4.00-5.00 grams. Prev. KM #11.1.

Date	Mintage	Good	VG	F	VF	XF
ND(1600-10)	—	12.00	30.00	60.00	100	—

Ahmadnagar

KM# 10.1 1/2 FALUS
Copper **Obv:** King's name, mint name **Note:** Fine style. Weight varies: 9.00-10.00 grams. Size varies: 15-17 mm. Prev. KM # 11.3.

Date	Mintage	Good	VG	F	VF	XF
AH1011 (1602)	—	3.00	7.50	15.00	25.00	—
AH1013 (1604)	—	3.00	7.50	15.00	25.00	—
AH1017 (1608)	—	3.00	7.50	15.00	25.00	—
AH1018 (1609)	—	3.00	7.50	15.00	25.00	—

Burhanabad

KM# 10.2 1/2 FALUS
Copper **Rev. Inscription:** "Dar-us-Sultanate" **Note:** Weight varies: 6.80-7.20grams. Prev. KM #11.2.

Date	Mintage	Good	VG	F	VF	XF
AH1012 (1603)	—	3.00	7.50	15.00	25.00	—

Parenda

KM# 10.3 1/2 FALUS
Copper **Note:** Weight varies: 6.80-7.20 grams. Prev. KM #12.2.

Date	Mintage	Good	VG	F	VF	XF
ND(1600-10)	—	3.00	7.50	15.00	25.00	—

Daulatabad

KM# 15.3 2/3 FALUS

9.3300 g., Copper **Obv:** King's name **Rev:** Mint name **Note:** Fine style. Weight varies: 9.20-9.60 grams. Size varies: 17-18 mm.

Date	Mintage	Good	VG	F	VF	XF
AH1031 (1622)	—	3.50	4.50	6.50	10.00	—
AH1037 (1627)	—	3.50	4.50	6.50	10.00	—

Parenda

KM# 11 2/3 FALUS

Copper **Note:** Weight varies: 9.00-10.00 grams. Prev. KM # 12.3.

Date	Mintage	Good	VG	F	VF	XF
AH1009 (1600)	—	4.00	10.00	20.00	35.00	—

Ahmadnagar

KM# 12.1 FALUS

Copper **Note:** Weight varies: 14.00-15.00 grams. Prev. KM#11.4.

Date	Mintage	Good	VG	F	VF	XF
AH1011 (1602)	—	3.50	9.00	18.00	30.00	—
AH1013 (1604)	—	3.50	9.00	18.00	30.00	—
AH1017 (1608)	—	3.50	9.00	18.00	30.00	—

Daulatabad

KM# 15.4 FALUS

Copper **Note:** Fine style. Weight varies: 13.70-14.50 grams. Size varies: 18-20 mm.

Date	Mintage	Good	VG	F	VF	XF
AH1037 (1628)	—	3.00	4.00	6.00	8.50	—

Parenda

KM# 12.2 FALUS

Copper **Note:** Weight varies: 14.00-15.00 grams. Prev. KM #12.4.

Date	Mintage	Good	VG	F	VF	XF
ND(1600-1610)	—	3.00	7.50	15.00	25.00	—

Burhan III as Mughal Vassal

AH1019-1041/1610-1631AD

HAMMERED COINAGE

Parenda

KM# 13.3 1/2 FALUS

Copper **Note:** Fine style. Weight varies: 7.00-8.00 grams. Prev. KM # 15.2.

Date	Mintage	Good	VG	F	VF	XF
AH1027 (1618)	—	3.50	9.00	18.00	30.00	—

BIDAR

Barid Shahs

For all practical purposes the Barid Shahi sultans established their kingdom at Bidar about 1492 when Qasim Barid, minister of Mahmud Bahmani, asserted his independence. Beyond a few majestic buildings at Bidar, the capital, and an impressive fortress, the dynasty left little impression on the Deccan. About 1619 the kingdom was absorbed by Bijapur.

RULERS

(after 1556AD)

Mirza 'Ali III, AH1009-c.1018/1601-c.1609AD
Amir III, AH1018-1028/c.1609-1618AD
Kingdom annexed by Adil Shahs of Bijapur, AH1028/1619AD

FALUS

The Barid Shahs of Bidar based on the traditional *gani* weighing around 15 grams, maintained a copper coinage on a weight standard different from that of the neighboring Adil Shahs of Bijapur who eventually absorbed their principality. Their coins are generally scarce or rare, and are without mintname although struck at Bidar.

DECCAN SULTANATE

Amir III

c.AH1018-1028/1609-1618AD

HAMMERED COINAGE

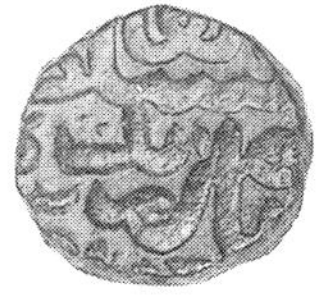

KM# 14 2/3 GANI

Copper **Note:** Weight varies: 10.00-12.00 grams. Size varies: 18-19 mm. Prev. KM#14.2.

Date	Mintage	Good	VG	F	VF	XF
ND(1609-18)	—	200	50.00	100	175	—

KM# 15 GANI

Copper **Note:** Weight varies: 15.00-18.00 grams. Size varies: 20-22 mm. Prev. KM#14.3.

Date	Mintage	Good	VG	F	VF	XF
ND(1609-18)	—	10.00	24.00	48.00	80.00	—
AH1018	—	24.00	60.00	120	200	—

BIJAPUR

Adil Shahs

The Adil Shahi dynasty of Bijapur was named after its founder, Yusuf Adil Khan, the Bahmani governor of the region. In 1489, reacting to Bahmani weakness and to the outrageous leadership of Mahmud Shah, Yusuf Adil Khan asserted his independence. If the records can be trusted, Yusuf was a scion of the Turkish royal house who had fled to India only to be sold as a slave in Bidar to a minister of the Bahmani ruler. Remarkably, he worked his way up from so unpromising a situation to the position of a regional governor, and then sultan, over what was destined to become the most prominent of the five Muslim sultanates of the Deccan. Bijapur became famed as a center of Sufism, a form of Muslim mysticism and sensitivity, and was renowned for the elegance of its city and its architecture. Even its coinage had a distinctive quality. In the copper series some of the calligraphy is conspicuously superior to that of Bijapur's neighbors and its silver larins are almost unique. The dynasty flourished for almost two centuries until, in 1686, the city of Bijapur and its surrounding areas were annexed by the Mughal emperor Aurangzeb.

RULERS

(after 1556AD)

Ibrahim II, AH988-1037/1580-1627AD
Muhammad, AH1037-1068/1627-1657AD
'Ali II, AH1068-1083/1657-1672AD
Sultan Sikander, AH1083-1097/1672-1686AD
Conquered and annexed by Mughal
Emperor Aurangzeb Alamgir, AH1097/1686AD

MINT

Daboli

FALUS

Many Islamic copper coins were known as "falus" irrespective of weight. The Adil Shahi copper coinage appears to have been based on a unit of around 12 grams - the normal tola weight - with fractional units.

DECCAN SULTANATE

Ibrahim II

AH988-1037/1580-1627AD

HAMMERED COINAGE

KM# 8 1/3 FALUS

Copper **Obv:** "Ghulam" with two vertical strokes forming a "V"; circle of large dots **Rev:** King's name; circle of large dots **Note:** Type 3. Weight varies: 3.50-4.00 grams. Size varies: 13-15 mm. Prev. KM#3.1.

Date	Mintage	Good	VG	F	VF	XF
ND(1580-1627)	—	3.50	9.00	18.00	30.00	—

KM# 13 1/3 FALUS

Copper **Obv:** Vertical strokes upright; scalloped circle of small dots **Rev:** King's name; scalloped circle of small dots **Note:** Type 4. Weight varies: 3.60-4.00 grams. Size varies: 12-14 mm. Finer style. Prev. KM#4.1.

Date	Mintage	Good	VG	F	VF	XF
ND(1580-1627)	—	3.50	9.00	18.00	30.00	—

KM# 16 HEAVY 1/2 FALUS

Copper **Shape:** square **Note:** Weight varies: 7.5 - 7.6 grams. Prev. KM#A5.

Date	Mintage	Good	VG	F	VF	XF
AH1022 Rare	—	—	—	—	—	—

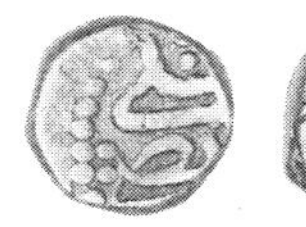

KM# 9 2/3 FALUS

Copper **Obv:** "Ghulam" with two vertical strokes forming a "V"; circle of large dots **Rev:** King's name; circle of large dots **Note:** Type 3. Weight varies: 7.50-8.00 grams. Size varies: 14-16 mm. Thick flan. Prev. KM#3.2.

Date	Mintage	Good	VG	F	VF	XF
ND(1580-1627)	—	1.80	6.00	12.00	20.00	—

KM# 14 2/3 FALUS

Copper **Obv:** Vertical strokes upright; scalloped circle of small dots **Rev:** King's name; scalloped circle of small dots **Note:** Type 4. Weight varies: 7.50-8.00 grams. Size varies: 16-18 mm. Finer style. Prev. KM#4.2.

Date	Mintage	Good	VG	F	VF	XF
ND(1580-1627)	—	1.80	6.00	12.00	20.00	—

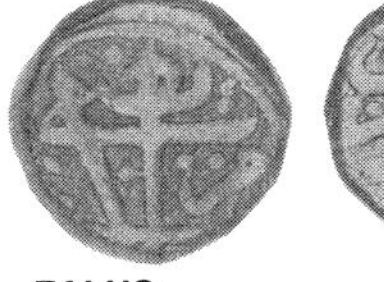

KM# 10 FALUS

Copper **Obv:** "Ghulam" with two vertical strokes forming a "V"; circle of large dots **Rev:** King's name; circle of large dots **Note:** Type 3. Weight varies: 11.60-12.00 grams. Size varies: 17-20 mm. Prev. KM#3.3.

Date	Mintage	Good	VG	F	VF	XF
ND(1580-1627)	—	4.80	12.00	24.00	40.00	—

KM# 15 FALUS

Copper **Obv:** Vertical strokes upright; scalloped circle of small dots **Rev:** King's name; scalloped circle of small dots **Note:** Type 4. Weight varies: 11.00-12.00 grams. Size varies: 19-20 mm. Finer style. Prev. KM#4.3.

Date	Mintage	Good	VG	F	VF	XF
ND(1580-1627)	—	3.00	7.50	15.00	25.00	—

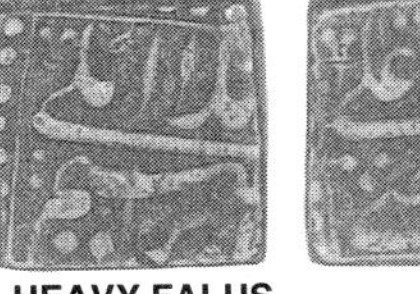

KM# 17 HEAVY FALUS

Copper **Note:** Type 5. Weight varies: 15.00-15.20 grams. Size varies: 17-18 mm. Square. Prev. KM#5.1.

Date	Mintage	Good	VG	F	VF	XF
AH1022 (1613) Rare	—	—	—	—	—	—

Muhammad
AH1037-1068/1627-1657AD
HAMMERED COINAGE

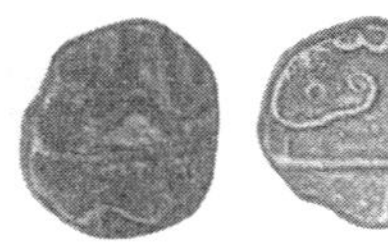

KM# 18 1/3 FALUS
Copper **Rev:** Couplet including King's name, large letters
Note: Type 6. Weight varies: 3.40-4.00 grams. Size varies: 13-15 mm. Prev. KM#6.1.

Date	Mintage	Good	VG	F	VF	XF
ND(1627-57)	—	4.80	12.00	24.00	40.00	—

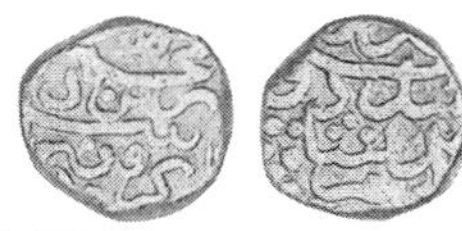

KM# 22 1/3 FALUS
Copper **Obv:** Couplet including king's name, smaller letters and finer style; circle of dots and rosette **Rev:** Circle of dots and rosette **Note:** Type 7. Weight varies: 3.60-4.00 grams. Size varies: 13-15 mm. Prev. KM#7.1.

Date	Mintage	Good	VG	F	VF	XF
ND(1627-57)	—	6.80	17.00	34.00	85.00	—

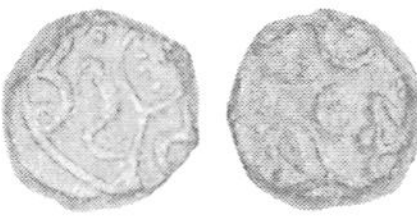

KM# 25 1/3 FALUS
Copper **Obv:** Dotted leaf, legend around within solid circle **Rev:** Dotted leaf, legend around within solid circle **Note:** Type 8. Weight varies: 3.50-4.00 grams. Size varies: 13-15 mm. Prev. KM#8.1.

Date	Mintage	Good	VG	F	VF	XF
ND(1627-57)	—	3.60	9.00	18.00	30.00	—

KM# 19 2/3 FALUS
Copper **Rev:** Couplet including King's name, large letters
Note: Type 6. Weight varies: 7.60-8.00grams. Size varies: 15-17 mm. Prev. KM#6.2.

Date	Mintage	Good	VG	F	VF	XF
ND(1627-57)	—	4.80	12.00	24.00	40.00	—

KM# 23 2/3 FALUS
Copper **Obv:** Couplet including king's name, smaller letters and finer style; circle of dots and rosette **Rev:** Circle of dots and rosette **Note:** Type 7. Weight varies: 7.60-8.00 grams. Size varies: 15-17 mm. Prev. KM#7.2.

Date	Mintage	Good	VG	F	VF	XF
ND(1627-57)	—	10.00	25.00	50.00	85.00	—

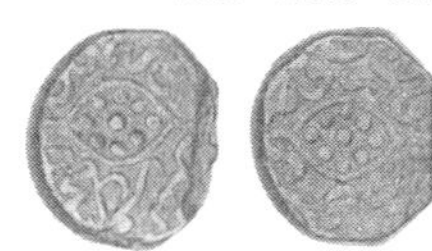

KM# 26 2/3 FALUS
Copper **Obv:** Dotted leaf, legend around within solid circle **Rev:** Dotted leaf, legend around within solid circle **Note:** Type 8. Weight varies: 7.40-8.00 grams. Size varies: 16-18 mm. Prev. KM#8.2.

Date	Mintage	Good	VG	F	VF	XF
ND(1627-57)	—	6.00	15.00	30.00	50.00	—

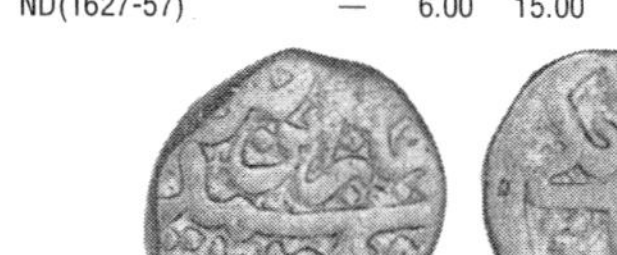

KM# 20 FALUS
Copper **Rev:** Couplet including King's name, large script
Note: Type 6. Weight varies: 11.20-12.00 grams. Size varies: 18-20 mm. Prev. KM#6.3.

Date	Mintage	Good	VG	F	VF	XF
ND(1627-57)	—	6.00	15.00	30.00	50.00	—

KM# 24 FALUS
Copper **Obv:** Couplet including king's name, smaller script and finer style; circle of dots and rosette **Rev:** Circle of dots and rosette
Note: Type 7. Weight varies: 11.20-12.00 grams. Size varies: 18-20 mm. Prev. KM#7.3.

Date	Mintage	Good	VG	F	VF	XF
ND(1627-57)	—	8.00	20.00	40.00	70.00	—

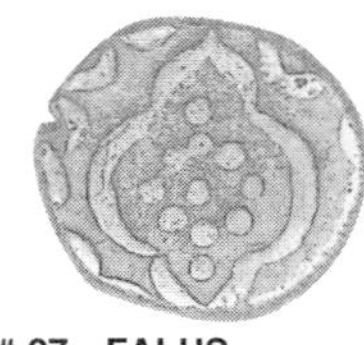
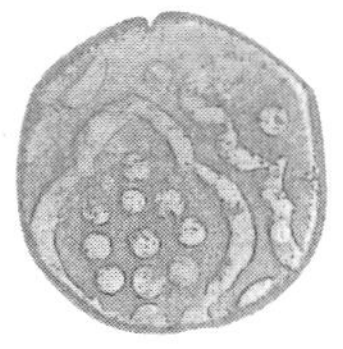

KM# 27 FALUS
Copper **Obv:** Dotted leaf, legend around within solid circle
Rev: Dotted leaf, legend around within solid circle **Note:** Type 8. Weight varies: 11.20-12.00 grams. Size varies: 18-20 mm. Crude issues are believed to be later imitations. Prev. KM#8.3.

Date	Mintage	Good	VG	F	VF	XF
ND(1627-57)	—	6.00	15.00	30.00	50.00	—

Daboli

KM# 33 LARIN
Silver **Obv. Inscription:** Sultan Muhammad 'Adil Shah
Note: Type 9. Weight varies: 4.20-4.90 grams. Size varies: 50-60 mm long. Prev. KM#9.1.

Date	Mintage	Good	VG	F	VF	XF
ND(1627-57)	—	8.00	20.00	40.00	65.00	—
Note: Date off flan						
AH1037	—	18.00	45.00	90.00	150	—

Daboli

KM# 30 PAGODA
3.4000 g., Gold **Obv:** Persian couplet **Rev:** Persian couplet
Note: Prev. KM#9A.1

Date	Mintage	Good	VG	F	VF	XF
ND(1627-57)	—	—	160	250	300	385

'Ali 'Adil Shah II
AH1068-1083/1657-1672AD
HAMMERED COINAGE

KM# 36 1/3 FALUS
Copper **Obv:** Dotted circular border **Rev:** King's name, dotted circular border **Note:** Type 10. Weight varies: 3.80-4.20 grams. Size varies: 13-14 mm. Prev. KM#10.1

Date	Mintage	Good	VG	F	VF	XF
ND(1657-72)	—	3.60	9.00	18.00	30.00	—

KM# 37 2/3 FALUS
Copper **Obv:** King's name; dotted circular border **Rev:** Dotted circular border **Note:** Type 10. Weight varies: 7.50-8.00 grams. Size varies: 15-16 mm. Prev. KM#10.2.

Date	Mintage	Good	VG	F	VF	XF
ND(1657-72)	—	3.60	9.00	18.00	30.00	—

KM# 38 FALUS
Copper **Obv:** King's name; dotted circular border **Rev:** Dotted circular border **Note:** Type 10. Weight varies: 11.20-12.00 grams. Size varies: 17-18 mm. Prev. KM#10.3.

Date	Mintage	Good	VG	F	VF	XF
ND(1657-72)	—	3.00	7.50	15.00	25.00	—

Daboli

KM# 40 LARIN
Silver **Obv. Inscription:** 'Ali 'Adil Shah **Note:** Weight varies: 4.50-4.90 grams. Size varies: 40-45 mm long. Prev. KM#11.1

Date	Mintage	Good	VG	F	VF	XF
AH1066	—	9.00	22.50	45.00	75.00	—
Note: error for 1077						
AH1067	—	9.00	22.50	45.00	75.00	—
ND(1657-72)	—	5.50	13.50	27.00	45.00	—
Note: Date off flan						
AH1069	—	9.00	22.50	45.00	75.00	—
AH1071	—	9.00	22.50	45.00	75.00	—
AH1072	—	9.00	22.50	45.00	75.00	—
AH1075	—	9.00	22.50	45.00	75.00	—
AH1077	—	9.00	22.50	45.00	75.00	—
AH1082	—	9.00	22.50	45.00	75.00	—

Sultan Sikander
AH1083-1097/1672-1686AD
HAMMERED COINAGE

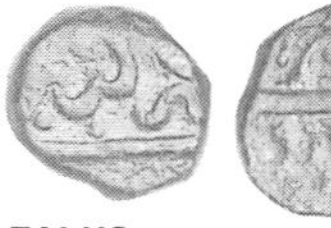

KM# 42 1/3 FALUS
Copper **Obv:** King's name **Note:** Type 12. Weight varies: 3.60-4.00 grams. Size varies: 13-15 mm. Prev. KM#12.1

Date	Mintage	Good	VG	F	VF	XF
ND(1672-86)	—	6.00	15.00	30.00	50.00	—

KM# 44 FALUS
Copper **Obv:** King's name **Rev. Inscription:** Khusro giti
Note: Type 12. Weight varies: 11.20-1200 grams. Size varies: 18-20 mm. Fine style. Prev. KM#12.3.

Date	Mintage	Good	VG	F	VF	XF
AH1086 (1675)	—	3.00	7.50	15.00	25.00	—
AH1087 (1676)	—	3.00	7.50	15.00	25.00	—

KM# 48 FANAM
0.3800 g., Gold, 5 mm. **Obv:** Sultan's name **Rev:** Date
Note: Type 13. Prev. KM#13.

Date	Mintage	Good	VG	F	VF	XF
AH1087 (1676)	—	—	70.00	140	200	260

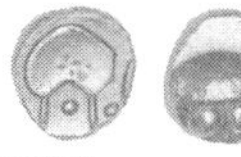

KM# 46 1/2 PAGODA
1.7000 g., Gold, 10 mm. **Note:** With Arabic "S" on top of shaft. Prev. KM#14.

Date	Mintage	Good	VG	F	VF	XF
ND(1672-86)	—	—	160	250	300	385

KM# 49 1/2 PAGODA
1.7000 g., Gold **Note:** Similar to 1/2 Pagoda, KM# 46 but without Arabic "S" on top of shaft.

Date	Mintage	Good	VG	F	VF	XF
ND(1672-86)	—	—	100	150	180	230

KM# 47 PAGODA
3.4000 g., Gold, 18 mm. **Note:** With Arabic "S" on top of shaft. Prev. KM#15.

Date	Mintage	Good	VG	F	VF	XF
ND(1672-86)	—	—	160	250	300	385

KM# 50 PAGODA
3.4000 g., Gold **Note:** Similar to Pagoda, KM#47 but without Arabic "S" on top of shaft.

Date	Mintage	Good	VG	F	VF	XF
ND(1672-86)	—	—	110	160	200	250

GOLKONDA

Qutb Shahs

The Qutb Shahi kingdom of Golkonda was the last of the five Deccani sultanates to break free of the Bahmanis and the last to fall to the Mughal army. The dynasty was founded in 1518 by an officer who came to be known as Quli Qutb Shah, whose long and prosperous reign laid a solid foundation for his successors. Early in his reign he moved his capital to Golkonda from Warangal, once capital of the old Hindu Kakatiya kingdom which had fallen to the Tughluqs of Delhi. Here at Golkonda the Qutb Shahs built a powerful fortress seven miles in circumference, and from here they governed the area until increasing Mughal pressures led to its annexation by Aurangzeb in 1687. Within fifty years, in the twilight of Mughal fortunes, regionalism again asserted itself and Golkonda became the citadel of Nizam-ul Mulk, the founder of Hyderabad State.

RULERS

(after 1556AD)

Muhammad Quli, AH988-1020/1580-1612AD
Sultan Muhammad, AH1020-1035/1612-1626AD
Abdullah, AH1035-1083/1626-1672AD
Abu'l Hasan, AH1083-1098/1672-1686AD
Conquered and annexed by Mughal
Emperor Aurangzeb Alamgir, AH1098/1686AD

NOTE: The only known coins of the Qutb Shahs are copper. While weight systems vary between rulers, and even within a single reign, the coins in any one system clearly comprise a basic unit and its fractions - two thirds, one-half and one-third - by weight. Further details may be found in QUTUB SHAHI COINS IN THE ANDHRA PRADESH GOVERNMENT MUSEUM, by Muhammad Abdul Wali Khan, Hyderabad, India, 1961.

COPPER COINAGE

Around 1604AD copper coins began to be struck in the name of Muhammad Quli on a heavier weight standard (17-18 grams) from a new mint, Hyderabad. All are on round planchets and most carry the apparently frozen date AH1012.

Sultan Muhammad continued his predecessor's copper coinage type from Hyderabad, with the apparently frozen date AH1025 (1585AD). Fractions are extremely rare.

The decline of the Qutb Shahi kingdom can be seen in the changes in Abdullah's copper coinage which began with coins bearing his name and titles on a relatively heavy weight standard, declining into lighter, cruder coins and ending in anonymous issues bearing a pathetic, fatalistic verse.

DECCAN SULTANATE

Muhammad Quli
AH988-1020/1580-1612AD

HAMMERED COINAGE

Hyderabad

KM# 8.1 1/3 FALUS

Copper **Obv:** King's name **Rev:** Mint name, date **Note:** Size varies: 16-18 mm. Weight varies: 5.60-6.00 grams.

Date	Mintage	Good	VG	F	VF	XF
AH1012 (1603)	—	9.00	22.50	45.00	75.00	—

Hyderabad

KM# 8.2 1/2 FALUS

Copper **Note:** Size varies: 18-20 mm. Weight varies: 8.50-9.00 grams.

Date	Mintage	Good	VG	F	VF	XF
AH1012 (1603)	—	6.00	15.00	30.00	50.00	—

Hyderabad

KM# 8.3 3/4 FALUS

Copper **Note:** Size varies: 19-22 mm. Weight varies: 11.00-12.00 grams.

Date	Mintage	Good	VG	F	VF	XF
AH1012 (1603)	—	7.20	18.00	36.00	60.00	—

Hyderabad

KM# 8.4 FALUS

Copper **Note:** Weight varies: 17.00-18.00 grams. Size varies: 20-24 mm.

Date	Mintage	Good	VG	F	VF	XF
AH1012 (1603)	—	12.00	30.00	62.00	90.00	—

Sultan Muhammad
AH1020-1035/1612-1626AD

HAMMERED COINAGE

Hyderabad Shahr

KM# 10.1 1/3 FALUS

6.0000 g., Copper, 16 mm. **Obv:** King's name **Rev:** Mint name, date **Rev. Inscription:** "Dar-us-Sultanat"

Date	Mintage	Good	VG	F	VF	XF
AH1025 (1616)	—	18.00	45.00	90.00	150	—

Hyderabad Shahr

KM# 10.3 FALUS

Copper **Rev. Inscription:** "Dar-us-Sultanat" **Note:** Weight varies: 17.50-18.00 grams. Size varies: 20-24 mm.

Date	Mintage	Good	VG	F	VF	XF
AH1025 (1616)	—	30.00	75.00	150	250	—

Abdullah
AH1035-1083/1626-1672AD

NAMED COINAGE

Hyderabad

KM# 12.1 1/2 FALUS

6.5000 g., Copper, 16 mm. **Obv:** King's name, "Sultan Badshah Ghazi"; eight-foil lozenge in center **Rev:** Mint name, eight-foil lozenge in center **Rev. Inscription:** "Dar-us-Sultanat"

Date	Mintage	Good	VG	F	VF	XF
ND(1626-72)	—	6.00	15.00	30.00	50.00	—

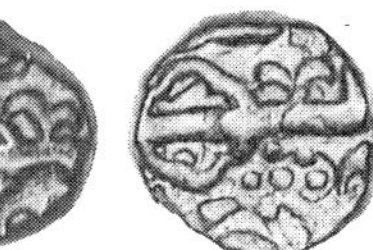

Hyderabad

KM# 12.2 2/3 FALUS

Copper **Rev. Inscription:** "Dar-us-Sultanat" **Note:** Weight varies: 8.40-9.20 grams. Size varies: 16-18 mm.

Date	Mintage	Good	VG	F	VF	XF
ND(1626-72)	—	6.00	15.00	30.00	50.00	—

KM# 14.2 2/3 FALUS

Copper **Obv:** King's name, "Sultan Badshah Ghazi" **Rev. Inscription:** "Dar-us-Sultanat" **Note:** Weight varies: 7.00-8.00 grams. Size varies: 16-18 mm.

Date	Mintage	Good	VG	F	VF	XF
ND(1626-72)	—	3.60	9.00	18.00	30.00	—

Hyderabad

KM# 12.3 FALUS

Copper **Rev. Inscription:** "Dar-us-Sultanat" **Note:** Weight varies: 12.80-13.60 grams. Size varies: 20-22 mm.

Date	Mintage	Good	VG	F	VF	XF
ND(1626-72)	—	5.20	13.50	27.00	45.00	—

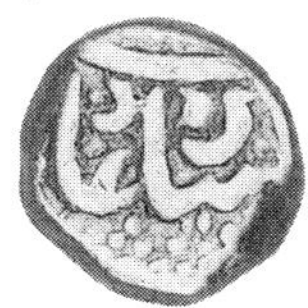

KM# 14.3 FALUS

Copper **Rev. Inscription:** "Dar-us-Sultanat" **Note:** Weight varies: 11.00-12.00 grams. Size varies: 18-20 mm.

Date	Mintage	Good	VG	F	VF	XF
ND(1626-72)	—	2.40	6.00	12.00	20.00	—

Hyderabad

KM# 12.4 DOUBLE FALUS

24.0000 g., Copper, 26 mm. **Rev. Inscription:** "Dar-us-Sultanat"

Date	Mintage	Good	VG	F	VF	XF
ND(1626-72)	—	30.00	75.00	150	250	—

ANONYMOUS COINAGE

Hyderabad

KM# 16.1 1/3 FALUS

3.0000 g., Copper, 15 mm. **Obv:** Persian legend **Obv. Inscription:** "It has ended peacefully and auspiciously" **Rev:** Mint name

Date	Mintage	Good	VG	F	VF	XF
ND(1626-72)	—	9.00	22.50	45.00	75.00	—

Hyderabad

KM# 16.2 2/3 FALUS

Copper **Note:** Weight varies: 7.40-8.20 grams. Size varies: 16-18 mm.

Date	Mintage	Good	VG	F	VF	XF
ND(1626-72)	—	6.00	15.00	30.00	50.00	—

KM# 18.3 2/3 FALUS

Copper **Note:** Struck at Hyderabad. Weight varies: 6.00-7.40 grams. Size varies: 16-19 mm.

Date	Mintage	Good	VG	F	VF	XF
AH1068 (1657)	—	1.80	4.50	9.00	15.00	—

Hyderabad

KM# 16.3 FALUS

Copper **Note:** Weight varies: 11.00-12.20 grams. Size varies: 18-21 mm.

Date	Mintage	Good	VG	F	VF	XF
ND(1626-72)	—	4.80	12.00	24.00	40.00	—

KM# 18.4 FALUS

Copper **Note:** Weight varies: 10.30-11.00 grams. Size varies: 19-22 mm.

Date	Mintage	Good	VG	F	VF	XF
AH1068	—	1.50	3.75	7.50	12.50	—
AH1028 Error	—	3.00	7.50	15.00	25.00	—

Muhammadnagar

KM# 20.1 FALUS

Copper, 21 mm. **Obv:** "Sultan Abdullah Badshah" **Rev:** Mint name **Note:** Weight varies: 10.60-10.70 grams.

Date	Mintage	Good	VG	F	VF	XF
ND(1626-72)	—	12.00	30.00	60.00	100	—

Abu'l Hasan
AH1083-1098/1672-1686AD

ANONYMOUS COINAGE

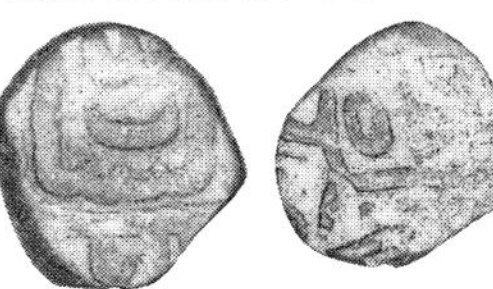

Hyderabad

KM# 22.2 2/3 FALUS

Copper **Obv:** Date, Persian legend **Obv. Legend:** "It has ended peacefully and auspiciously" **Rev:** Mint name **Rev. Inscription:** "Dar-us-Sultanat" **Note:** Weight varies: 6.70-7.00 grams. Size varies: 15-18 mm.

Date	Mintage	Good	VG	F	VF	XF
AH1095 (1683)	—	4.00	10.00	20.00	35.00	—

Hyderabad

KM# 22.3 FALUS

Copper **Rev. Inscription:** "Dar-us-Sultanat" **Note:** Weight varies: 10.00-11.00 grams. Size varies: 18-22 mm.

Date	Mintage	Good	VG	F	VF	XF
AH1095 (1683)	—	3.60	9.00	18.00	30.00	—

JAINTIAPUR

The territory ruled over by the Jaintia Rajas consisted of the Jaintia Hills, and a section of the adjoining plains to the north of Sylhet.

In the Cooch Behar chronicle it is recorded that when Nara Narayan defeated the Jaintia Raja about 1564AD, one of the conditions imposed on the defeated monarch was that he should never put his own name on his coins, but only that of his capital city. Whether this is the true reason is open to debate, but virtually all the coins of Jaintiapur are anonymous, and merely bear the accession year of the ruler during whose reign they were issued.

The earliest known coins of Jaintiapur are dated 1633AD, and are clearly copied in general design and weight standard from the coins of Cooch Behar. During the 18th century the right to strike coins was sold by the Raja to the highest bidder, and this resulted in a serious debasement of the coinage, which therefore never circulated outside the confines of the State.

Independence was retained until 1835AD, when the administration was finally taken over by the British.

RULERS

Local traditions have preserved the names of the Jaintia Kings since the kingdom was founded, but few reliable dated are known for the early Kings.

Dhan Manik, c1602
Jasa Manik, c1606/18
Sundar Ray, or
Chota Parbat Ray, SE1555-1569/1633-1647AD
Jasamanta Ray, SE1569-1582/1647-1660AD
Ban Simha, SE1582-1591/1660-1669AD
Pratap Simha, SE1591-1592/1669-1670AD
Lakshmi Narayan, SE1592-1625/1670-1703AD

KINGDOM

Sundar Ray or Chota Parbat Ray

SE1555-1569 / 1633-1647AD

HAMMERED COINAGE

Anonymous

KM# 100 RUPEE

9.2000 g., Silver

Date	Mintage	Good	VG	F	VF	XF
SE1555	—	65.00	165	330	550	775

Ban Simha

SE1582-1591 / 1660-1669 AD

HAMMERED COINAGE

Anonymous

KM# 120 RUPEE

9.2000 g., Silver

Date	Mintage	Good	VG	F	VF	XF
SE1582	—	65.00	165	330	550	775

Pratap Simha

SE1591-1592 / 1669-1670 AD

HAMMERED COINAGE

Anonymous

KM# 130 RUPEE

9.2000 g., Silver

Date	Mintage	Good	VG	F	VF	XF
SE1591	—	80.00	200	400	650	925

Lakshmi Narayan

SE1592-1625 / 1670-1703AD

HAMMERED COINAGE

Anonymous

KM# 140 RUPEE

9.2000 g., Silver

Date	Mintage	Good	VG	F	VF	XF
SE1592	—	32.00	80.00	160	250	360

KACHAR

The Kacharis are probably the original inhabitants of the Assam Valley, and in the 13th century ruled much of the south bank of the Brahmaputra from their capital at Dimapur.

Around 1530 the Ahoms inflicted several crushing defeats on the Kacharis, Dimapur was sacked, and the Kacharis were forced to retreat further south and set up a new capital at Maibong.

Very little is known about this obscure state, and the only time that coins were struck in any quantity was during the late 16th and early 17th centuries. One coin, indeed, proudly announces the conquest of Sylhet, but the military prowess seems to have been short lived, and the small kingdom was only saved from Muslim domination by its isolation and lack of economic worth.

A few coins were struck during the 18th and 19th centuries, but this was probably merely as a demonstration of independence, rather than for any economic reason.

In 1819, the last Kachari ruler, Govind Chandra was ousted by the Manipuri ruler Chaurajit Simha, and during the Burmese occupation of Manipur and Assam, the Manipuris remained in control of Kachar. In 1824, Govind Chandra was restored to his throne by the British, and ruled under British suzerainty. By all accounts his administration was not a success, and in 1832, soon after Govind Chandra had been murdered, the British took over the administration of the State in "compliance with the frequent and earnestly expressed wishes of the people.

The earliest coins of Kachar were clearly copied from the contemporary coins of Cooch Behar, with weight standard also copied from the Bengali standard. The flans are, however, even broader than those of the Cooch Behar coins, making the coins very distinctive.

A number of spectacular gold and silver coins, purporting to come from Kachar, appeared in Calcutta during the 1960's, but as their authenticity has been doubted, they have been omitted from this listing.

RULERS

A list of the Kings of Kachar has been preserved in local traditions, but is rather unreliable. The following list has been compiled from this traditional list, together with names and dates obtained from other sources, but may not be completely accurate.

Yaso Narayan, SE1505-1523/1583-1601AD
Pratap Narayan, SE1523-1533/1601-after 1611AD
Nar Narayan, SEc.1537/c.1615AD
Bhim Darpa, SEc.1540/c.1618AD
Indra Ballabh, SEc.1550/c.1628AD
Bir Darpa, SEc.1566-1603/c.1644-1681AD
Garur Dhvaja, SE1603-1617/1681-1695AD
Makar Dhvaja, SE1617-/1695-AD
Udayaditya, SEc.1622/c.1700AD
Tamradhvaja, SEc.1622-1630/c.1700-1708AD

KINGDOM

Pratap Narayan

SE1523-1533 / 1601-1611AD

HAMMERED COINAGE

KM# 114 1/4 RUPEE

Silver **Note:** Varieties exist.

Date	Mintage	Good	VG	F	VF	XF
ND(1601-11) (1601)	—	100	250	500	800	1,150

KM# 116 RUPEE

Silver

Date	Mintage	Good	VG	F	VF	XF
SE1523 (1601)	—	180	450	900	1,500	2,100

KM# 117 RUPEE

Silver **Subject:** Victory over Sylhet

Date	Mintage	Good	VG	F	VF	XF
SE1524 (1602)	—	120	300	600	1,000	1,450

KM# 122 MOHUR

Gold **Note:** Similar to 1 Rupee, KM#117.

Date	Mintage	Good	VG	F	VF	XF
SE1524 (1602)	—	—	—	—	—	—

Note: Reported, not confirmed

Bir Darpa

SE1566-1603 / 1644-1681AD

HAMMERED COINAGE

KM# 127 1/4 RUPEE

Silver

Date	Mintage	Good	VG	F	VF	XF
ND(1644-81) (1644)	—	100	250	500	850	1,200

KM# 130 MOHUR

Gold

Date	Mintage	Good	VG	F	VF	XF
SE1565 (1644)	—	—	1,700	2,400	3,500	—

Tamradhvaja

SE c.1622-1630 / c.1700-1708AD

HAMMERED COINAGE

KM# 132 1/4 RUPEE

Silver **Obv:** Inscription within circle **Rev:** Inscription within circle

Date	Mintage	Good	VG	F	VF	XF
ND(ca.1700-08)	—	120	300	600	1,000	1,450

KUTCH

State located in northwest India, consisting of a peninsula north of the Gulf of Kutch.

The rulers of Kutch were Jareja Rajputs who, coming from Tatta in Sind, conquered Kutch in the 14th or 15th centuries. The capital city of Bhuj is thought to date from the mid-16th century. In 1617, after Akbar's conquest of Gujerat and the fall of the Gujerat sultans, the Kutch ruler, Rao Bharmal I (1586-1632) visited Jahangir and established a relationship which was sufficiently warm as to leave Kutch virtually independent throughout the Mughal period. Early in the 19th century internal disorder and the existence of rival claimants to the throne resulted in British intrusion into the state's affairs. Rao Bharmalji II was deposed in favor of Rao Desalji II who proved much more amenable to the Government of India's wishes. He and his successors continued to rule in a manner considered by the British to be most enlightened and, as a result, Maharao Khengarji III was created a Knight Grand Commander of the Indian Empire. In view of its geographical isolation Kutch came under the direct control of the Central Government at India's independence.

First coinage was struck in 1617AD.

RULERS

Raos

राउ श्री भाराजी

Bharmalji I, 1586-1632AD

रा उ श्री पा ज जी

Ra-o Sri Bha-ra-jl
Bhorajji, 1632-1645AD

रा उ श्री षं गा र जी

Ra-o Sri Bho-j-ji
Khengarji II, 1645-1654AD

रा उ श्री त मा ढी जी

Ra-o Sri Shen-ga-r-ji
Tamachiji

रा उ श्री रा य ध पा जी

Ra-o Sri T(a)-ma-chi-ji
Rayadhanji I, 1666-1698AD

रा उ श्री प्रा ग जी

Ra-o Sri Ra-y(a)-dh(a)-n-ji
Pragmalji I, 1698-1715AD

MINT

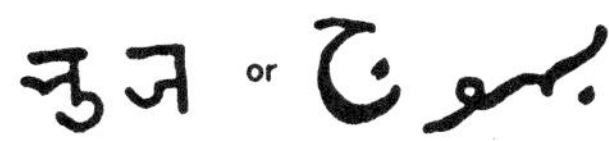

Bhuj (Devanagari) (Persian)

MONETARY SYSTEM

1/2 Trambiyo = 1 Babukiya
2 Tramiyo = 1 Dokda
3 Trambiyo = 1 Dhinglo
2 Dhinglo = 1 Dhabu
2 Dhabu = 1 Payalo
2 Payalo = 1 Adlinao
2 Adlina = 1 Kori

NOTE: All coins through Bharmalji II bear a common type, derived from the Gujarati coinage of Muzaffar III (late 16th century AD), and bear a stylized form of the date AH978 (1570AD). The silver issues of Bharmalji II also have the fictitious date AH1165. The rulers name appears in the Devanagri script on the obverse.

NOTE: Br#'s are in reference to *Coinage of Kutch* by Richard K. Bright.

KINGDOM

Bhorajji (Bhojraji)

AH1042-1055 / 1632-1645AD

HAMMERED COINAGE

KM# 9 DOKDO
Copper **Note:** Br.#7.

Date	Mintage	Good	VG	F	VF	XF
ND(1632-45)	—	—	25.00	35.00	50.00	70.00

KM# 10 DHINGLO
12.0000 g., Copper **Rev:** Inscription in Nagari below **Rev. Inscription:** "Rao Sri Bharaji" **Note:** Br.#8.

Date	Mintage	Good	VG	F	VF	XF
ND(1632-45)	—	4.80	12.00	24.00	40.00	—

KM# 11 1/2 KORI
2.5000 g., Silver **Obv:** Katar **Rev:** Trident, inscription in Nagari **Rev. Inscription:** "Rao Sri Bhojji" **Note:** Br.#9.

Date	Mintage	Good	VG	F	VF	XF
ND(1632-45)	—	3.60	12.00	27.00	54.00	90.00

KM# 12 KORI
4.5500 g., Silver **Note:** Br.#10.

Date	Mintage	Good	VG	F	VF	XF
AH978 Frozen date	—	3.00	7.20	18.00	36.00	60.00

Khengarji II

AH1055-1065 / 1645-1654AD

HAMMERED COINAGE

KM# 14 1/2 TRAMBIYO
1.1000 g., Copper **Obv:** Katar **Rev:** Trident, inscription in Nagari **Rev. Inscription:** "Rao Sri Shengarji" **Note:** Br.#A11. Size varies: 8-9 mm.

Date	Mintage	Good	VG	F	VF	XF
ND(1645-54)	—	2.40	8.00	20.00	40.00	—

KM# 16 DOKDO
9.2000 g., Copper **Note:** Br.#12.

Date	Mintage	Good	VG	F	VF	XF
ND(1645-54)	—	2.75	9.00	22.50	45.00	—

KM# 18 1/4 KORI
1.1000 g., Silver **Obv:** Katar **Rev:** Trident, inscription in Nagari **Rev. Inscription:** "Rao Sri Shengarji" **Note:** Br.#A14. Size varies: 8-10 mm.

Date	Mintage	Good	VG	F	VF	XF
ND(1645-54)	—	12.00	30.00	75.00	150	250

KM# 19 1/2 KORI
2.5000 g., Silver, 12.7 mm. **Obv:** Katar **Rev:** Trident, "Rao Sri Shengarji" in Nagari **Note:** Br.#14.

Date	Mintage	Good	VG	F	VF	XF
ND(1645-54)	—	4.50	15.00	37.50	75.00	125

KM# 20 KORI
4.5500 g., Silver **Note:** Br.#15.

Date	Mintage	Good	VG	F	VF	XF
AH(9)78 Frozen date	—	3.00	9.00	22.50	45.00	75.00

Tamachiji

AH1066-1077 / 1655-1666AD

HAMMERED COINAGE

KM# 24 DOKDA
8.6000 g., Copper **Note:** Br.#17.

Date	Mintage	Good	VG	F	VF	XF
ND(1655-66)	—	3.00	10.00	25.00	50.00	—

KM# 26 1/4 KORI
1.2000 g., Silver **Obv:** Katar **Rev:** Inscription in Nagari **Rev. Inscription:** "Rao Sri Tmachiji" **Note:** Br.#A19. Size varies: 8-10 mm.

Date	Mintage	Good	VG	F	VF	XF
ND(1655-66)	—	6.00	20.00	50.00	100	165

KM# 27 1/2 KORI
2.1300 g., Silver, 11.9 mm. **Obv:** Katar **Rev:** Inscription in Nagari **Rev. Inscription:** "Rao Sri Tmachiji" **Note:** Br.#19.

Date	Mintage	Good	VG	F	VF	XF
ND(1655-66)	—	4.50	14.50	36.00	72.00	120

KM# 28 KORI
4.4000 g., Silver **Note:** Br.#20.

Date	Mintage	Good	VG	F	VF	XF
AH(9)78 Frozen date	—	3.00	10.00	25.00	50.00	85.00

Rayadhanji I

AH1077-1110 / 1666-98AD

HAMMERED COINAGE

KM# 31 TRAMBIYO
4.2000 g., Copper, 14 mm. **Obv:** Katar **Rev:** Inscription in Nagari **Rev. Inscription:** "Rao Sri Raydhnji" **Note:** Br.#21.

Date	Mintage	Good	VG	F	VF	XF
ND(1666-98)	—	3.60	9.00	18.00	30.00	—

KM# 33 DHINGLO
Copper, 22 mm. **Obv:** Katar **Rev:** Inscription in Nagari **Rev. Inscription:** "Rao Sri Raydhnji" **Note:** Br.#23. Weight varies: 12.00-12.50 grams.

Date	Mintage	Good	VG	F	VF	XF
ND(1666-98)	—	2.40	6.00	12.00	20.00	—

KM# 32 DOKDA
8.0000 g., Copper **Note:** Br.#22.

Date	Mintage	Good	VG	F	VF	XF
ND(1666-98)	—	3.60	9.00	18.00	30.00	—

KM# 35 1/2 KORI
2.2000 g., Silver **Note:** Br.#24.

Date	Mintage	Good	VG	F	VF	XF
ND(1666-98)	—	3.60	12.00	30.00	60.00	100

KM# 36 KORI
4.5500 g., Silver, 15 mm. **Obv:** Katar **Rev:** Inscription in Nagari **Rev. Inscription:** "Rao Sri Raydhnji" **Note:** Br.#25.

Date	Mintage	Good	VG	F	VF	XF
AH(9)78 Frozen date	—	3.00	6.00	15.00	30.00	50.00

Pragmalji I

AH1110-1127 / 1698-1715AD

HAMMERED COINAGE

KM# 39 DOKDO
Copper **Obv:** Inscription, date **Rev:** Inscription **Note:** Br.#27.

Date	Mintage	Good	VG	F	VF	XF
ND(1698-1715)	—	1.20	4.00	10.00	20.00	—

KM# 40 DHINGLO
11.8000 g., Copper **Obv:** Inscription **Rev:** Inscription, scissors **Note:** Br.#28.

Date	Mintage	Good	VG	F	VF	XF
ND(1698-1715)	—	1.50	5.00	12.50	25.00	—

KM# 43 KORI
4.5000 g., Silver **Obv:** Inscription, date **Rev:** Inscription **Note:** Br.#30.

Date	Mintage	Good	VG	F	VF	XF
AH(9)78 Frozen	—	3.00	8.00	20.00	40.00	65.00

Gohadaji I

AH1127-1132 / 1715-1719AD

HAMMERED COINAGE

KM# 45 KORI
4.5000 g., Silver, 15 mm. **Obv:** Inscription, trident **Rev. Inscription:** Rao Sri Gohodji (Nagari in small characters) **Note:** Br.#35.

Date	Mintage	Good	VG	F	VF	XF
AH978 Frozen; Rare	—	—	—	—	—	—

MADURAI

Nayakas

Located in South India approximately 180 miles north of the southernmost tip. It is noted for its great temple with colonnades and nine massive gate towers (gopuras) adorned with elaborate carvings and enclosing a quadrangle, the "Tank of the Golden Lilies". It was the capital of the Pandya dynasty from 5th century B.C. to the end of the 11th century A.D. It came under Vijayanagar control in the 14th century A.D.; and then under the Nayak dynasty from about the middle of the 16th century to 1735AD when it was taken by the Nawab of the Carnatic. Later, in 1801, it came under the rule of the British East India Company.

KINGDOM

HAMMERED COINAGE

KM# 2 KASU
Copper **Obv:** Inscription in two lines **Obv. Inscription:** "Tiru Vengala" **Rev:** Inscription in two lines **Rev. Inscription:** "Mudu Krishna" **Note:** Struck in the name of Muttu Krishnappa Nayaka.

Date	Mintage	Good	VG	F	VF	XF
ND(1601-09)	—	0.75	2.50	6.00	12.00	—

KM# 1 KASU
Copper **Obv:** Venkatesvara standing, altar at left, banner to right **Rev. Inscription:** "Vemkatapa" **Note:** Struck in the name of Venkata(pati)raya (Vi jayanagar).

Date	Mintage	Good	VG	F	VF	XF
ND(1630-41)	—	0.75	2.50	6.00	12.00	—

MARATHA CONFEDERACY

INDEPENDENT KINGDOM

Aurangzeb Alamgir

AH1068-1119 / 1658-1707AD

HAMMERED COINAGE

Nipani

KM# 200 1/4 RUPEE

Silver **Obv. Inscription:** Aurangzeb Alamgir **Note:** Weight varies: 2.68-2.90 grams.

Date	Mintage	VG	F	VF	XF	Unc
ND(1658-1707)	—	7.50	12.50	20.00	35.00	—

Chikodi

KM# 95 1/2 RUPEE

Silver **Obv. Inscription:** Mughal Emperor Aurangzeb **Note:** Weight varies 5.35-5.80 grams.

Date	Mintage	VG	F	VF	XF	Unc
ND(1658-1707)	—	4.25	8.50	14.00	20.00	—

Nipani

KM# 201 1/2 RUPEE

Silver, 17-18 mm. **Obv. Inscription:** Aurangzeb Alamgir **Note:** Size varies. Weight varies: 5.35-5.80 grams.

Date	Mintage	VG	F	VF	XF	Unc
ND(1658-1707)	—	8.00	13.50	18.50	30.00	—

Chikodi

KM# 96 RUPEE

Silver **Obv. Inscription:** Mughal Emperor Aurangzeb **Note:** Weight varies: 10.70-11.60 grams.

Date	Mintage	VG	F	VF	XF	Unc
ND(1658-1707)	—	5.50	11.00	17.50	25.00	—

Nipani

KM# 202 RUPEE

Silver, 23-24 mm. **Obv. Inscription:** Aurangzeb Alamgir **Note:** Size varies. Weight varies: 10.70-11.60 grams.

Date	Mintage	VG	F	VF	XF	Unc
ND(1658-1707)	—	11.50	18.50	30.00	50.00	—

TRIPURA

Hill Tipperah

Tripura was a Hindu Kingdom consisting of a strip of the fertile plains east of Bengal, and a large tract of hill territory beyond, which had a reputation for providing wild elephants.

At times when Bengal was weak, Tripura rose to prominence and extended its rule into the plains, but when Bengal was strong the kingdom consisted purely of the hill area, which was virtually impregnable and not of enough economic worth to encourage the Muslims to conquer it. In this way Tripura was able to maintain its full independence until the 19th century.

The origins of the Kingdom are veiled in legend, but the first coins were struck during the reign of Ratna Manikya (1464-89) and copied the weight and fabric of the contemporary issues of the Sultans of Bengal. He also copied the lion design that had appeared on certain rare tangkas of Nasir-ud-din Mahmud Shah I dated AH849 (1445AD). In other respects the designs were purely Hindu, and the lion was retained on most of the later issues as a national emblem.

Tripura rose to a political zenith during the 16th century, while Muslim rule in Bengal was weak, and several coins were struck to commemorate successful military campaigns from Chittagong in the south to Sylhetin the north. These conquests were not sustained, and in the early 17th century the Mughal army was able to inflict severe defeats on Tripura, which was forced to pay tribute.

In about 1733AD all the territory in the plains was annexed by the Mughals, and the Raja merely managed his estate there as a zemindar, although he still retained control as independent King of his hill territory.

The situation remained unchanged when the British took over the administration of Bengal in 1765, and it was only in 1871 that the British appointed an agent in the hills, and began to assist the Maharaja in the administration of his hill territory, which became known as the State of Hill Tipperah.

After the middle of the 18th century, coins were not struck for monetary reasons, but merely for ceremonial use at coronations and other ceremonies, and to keep up the treasured right of coinage.

The coins of Tripura are unusual in that the majority have the name of the King together with that of his Queen, and is the only coinage in the world where this was done consistently.

In common with most other Hindu coinages of northeast India, the coins bear fixed dates. Usually the date used was that of the coronation ceremony, but during the 16th century, coins which were struck with a design commemorating a particular event, bore the date of that event, which can be useful as a historical source, where other written evidence is virtually non-existent.

All modern Tripura coins were presentation pieces, more medallic than monetary in nature. They were struck in very limited numbers and although not intended for local circulation as money, they are often encountered in worn condition.

RULERS

Yaso Manikya
Sec1521-22, c1522-48/
C1599-1600, c1600-26AD
Queens of Yaso Manikya
Queen Lakshmi
Queen Gauri

Isvara Manikya
Sec1522/c1600AD

Kalyana Manikya
Sec1548-82/c1626-60AD
Queen of Kalyana Manikya
Queen Kalavati

Govinda Manikya
Queen of Govinda Manikya
Queen Gunavati

Chattra Manikya
Sec1583-89/c1661-67AD

Rama Manikya
Sec1598-1603/c1676-81AD
Queen of Rama Manikya
Queen Ratnavati

Ratna Manikya II

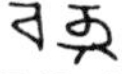

Sec1607-15, c1617-34/
1685-93, c1695-1712AD
Queens of Ratna Manikya II
Queen Satyavati
Queen Bhagavati

Narendra Manikya
Sec1615-1617/c1693-1695AD

DATING

While the early coinage is dated in the Saka Era (SE) the later issues are dated in the Tripurabda era (TE). To convert, TE date plus 590 = AD date. The dates appear to be accession years.

KINGDOM

Dharma Manikya with Selim

SE1523 / 1601AD

HAMMERED COINAGE

KM# 118 TANKA

Silver

Date	Mintage	VG	F	VF	XF	Unc
SEca1523 (1601)	—	300	500	750	1,000	—

Kalyana Manikya

SEc.1548-1582 / c.1626-1660AD

HAMMERED COINAGE

KM# 122 1/4 RUPEE

2.6000 g., Silver

Date	Mintage	VG	F	VF	XF	Unc
SE1548 (1626)	—	30.00	50.00	125	175	—

KM# 123 1/2 RUPEE

5.2000 g., Silver

Date	Mintage	VG	F	VF	XF	Unc
SE1548 (1626)	—	32.50	55.00	125	175	—

KM# 124 RUPEE

10.5000 g., Silver

Date	Mintage	VG	F	VF	XF	Unc
SE1548 (1626)	—	55.00	90.00	150	200	—

KM# 127 MOHUR

Gold

Date	Mintage	VG	F	VF	XF	Unc
SE1548 (1626) Rare	—	—	—	—	—	—

Chattra Manikya

SEc1583-1589 / c 1661-1667AD

HAMMERED COINAGE

KM# 143 1/4 RUPEE

2.6000 g., Silver

Date	Mintage	VG	F	VF	XF	Unc
SE1583 (1661)	—	60.00	100	150	200	—

KM# 145 RUPEE

10.5000 g., Silver **Rev:** Inscription without Queen's name

Date	Mintage	VG	F	VF	XF	Unc
SE1583 (1661)	—	90.00	150	200	300	—

Govinda Manikya

SEc.1582, 1589-1598 / c.1660, 1667-1676AD

HAMMERED COINAGE

KM# 131 1/8 RUPEE

1.3000 g., Silver **Obv:** Lion right

Date	Mintage	VG	F	VF	XF	Unc
ND (1660)	—	10.00	17.50	30.00	45.00	—

KM# 132 1/8 RUPEE

1.3000 g., Silver **Obv:** Lion left

Date	Mintage	VG	F	VF	XF	Unc
ND (1660)	—	6.00	10.00	20.00	30.00	—

KM# 133 1/4 RUPEE
2.6000 g., Silver

Date	Mintage	VG	F	VF	XF	Unc
SE1582 (1660)	—	10.00	17.50	30.00	45.00	—

KM# 135 RUPEE
10.5000 g., Silver **Rev. Legend:** "Queen Gunavati..."

Date	Mintage	VG	F	VF	XF	Unc
SE1582 (1660)	—	45.00	70.00	100	150	—

Rama Manikya
SEc.1598-1603 / c.1676-1681AD
HAMMERED COINAGE

KM# 153 1/4 RUPEE
2.6000 g., Silver

Date	Mintage	VG	F	VF	XF	Unc
SE1598 (1676)	—	18.50	30.00	100	150	—

KM# 155 RUPEE
10.5000 g., Silver **Rev. Inscription:** *Srimati Ratnavati Maha Devi*

Date	Mintage	VG	F	VF	XF	Unc
SE1598 (1676)	—	45.00	70.00	135	190	—

KM# 158 RUPEE
10.5000 g., Gold

Date	Mintage	VG	F	VF	XF	Unc
SE1598 (1676)	—	700	1,000	1,500	2,000	—

Ratna Manikya II
SE1607-1615 / c.1695-1712AD
HAMMERED COINAGE

KM# 161 1/16 RUPEE
0.6500 g., Silver

Date	Mintage	VG	F	VF	XF	Unc
ND (1681)	—	10.00	17.50	30.00	45.00	—

KM# 164 1/4 RUPEE
2.6000 g., Silver

Date	Mintage	VG	F	VF	XF	Unc
SE1607 (1685)	—	10.00	17.50	30.00	45.00	—

KM# 166 RUPEE
10.5000 g., Silver **Rev:** Inscription without Queen's name

Date	Mintage	VG	F	VF	XF	Unc
SE1607 (1685)	—	20.00	30.00	45.00	65.00	—

KM# 167 RUPEE
10.5000 g., Silver **Rev. Legend:** "Queen Satyavati..."

Date	Mintage	VG	F	VF	XF	Unc
SE1607 (1685)	—	20.00	30.00	45.00	65.00	—

KM# 168 RUPEE
10.5000 g., Silver **Rev. Legend:** "Queen Bhagyavati..."

Date	Mintage	VG	F	VF	XF	Unc
SE1607 (1685)	—	100	150	200	300	—

KM# 162 1/16 MOHUR
0.6500 g., Gold

Date	Mintage	VG	F	VF	XF	Unc
ND (1685)	—	100	175	300	500	—

Narendra Manikya
SEc.1615-1617 / c.1693-1695AD
HAMMERED COINAGE

KM# 175 1/8 RUPEE
Silver

Date	Mintage	VG	F	VF	XF	Unc
(1692)	—	100	175	300	425	—

KM# 178 RUPEE
10.5000 g., Silver

Date	Mintage	VG	F	VF	XF	Unc
SE1615 (1693)	—	100	175	300	425	—

KM# 180 MOHUR
10.0000 g., Gold

Date	Mintage	VG	F	VF	XF	Unc
SE1615 (1693) Rare	—	—	—	—	—	—

VIJAYANAGAR

The Vijayanagar kingdom was founded by two brothers, Harihari and Bukka, from the Telangana region of present day Andhra Pradesh in East Central India. They had previously served the raja of Warangal until they were captured and transported to Delhi where they were reputed to have become converts to Islam. They then revolted and, returning to the Hindu fold, in 1336 founded the kingdom as a bulwark against further Muslim inroads into the South. Vijayanagar (literally, City of Victory) grew into the most remarkable of all the medieval Hindu kingdoms. Some 19 square miles in area, Vijayanage itself - the capital after which the empire was named – sat on the southern bank of the Kristna river, not far from modern Hospet in Mysore State. Contemporary observers compared the city both in size and stature to ancient Rome.

Even to this day, the ruins of this remarkable capital are among the most impressive anywhere in India. Resplendent with intricate stone carving, fine temples and broad public ways, it was a city whose wealth knew no equal in South or Central India. Its sovereignty extended over virtually the whole of South India. The rulers, or rayas, of Vijayanagar were patrons of the arts and under their authority art, architecture and literature flourished. Its Hinduism was eclectic, Vaishnavite in sentiment and vibrant in expression. It was a wealthy city, whose vices were the vices of the rich. Its coinage was predominantly in gold and, like its culture, distinctly South Indian in style.

After the period of the 2 chiefs Harihari (1336-1354) and Bukka (1354-1377), Vijayanagar history fell into 4 periods, viz., the Sangama dynasty (1377-1485), the Saluva dynasty (1486-ca.1503), the Tuluva dynasty(ca. 1503-1570), and the Aravidu (or Karnata) dynasty (1570-ca. 1646). For over 2 centuries the Vijayanagar kingdom was more or less in a constant state of war against the Bahmanis and their successor sultanates in the Deccan. And for those two hundred years Vijayanagar effectively halted Muslim attempts to encroach southwards. This was the empire's golden age as Vijayanagar grew to be the one real center in India for Hindu self-expression within a context of political self-determination. Vassal to none, Vijayanagar held the south of India as a constant rebuke to Muslim expansionism.

Then, in 1565, disaster struck. The sultanates of Ahmadnagar, Bijapur, Bidar and Golkonda combined forces to bring about the destruction of Vijayanagar. Vijayanagar was well equipped for this confrontation, putting perhaps as many as a million men on the field. But, by one of those quirks in the fortunes of war, the Vijayanagar commander, Ramaraja (who was also the regent and controlling noble of the kingdom), was cut off from his troops, dragged down from his elephant, and at once beheaded. His army immediately panicked and their strategy fell apart. This battle, remembered as the battle of Talikota, was followed by a complete rout of the forces of Vijayanagar and by the plunder and destruction of their capital city.

The nominal king, in whose place Ramaraja had ruled, fled to Penukonda. There on this rocky hill further south he re-established the dynasty. Five years later he was overthrown by Tirumala, his brother, and the Karnata dynasty was inaugurated. A few years later the capital was shifted to Chandragiri, under Venkata I. Here, for a while, the truncated kingdom seemed to regain some of its lost vigor. But after Venkata's death even this dynasty disintegrated and the remnants of this once-proud empire were reduced to the status of local chiefs. Yet, in spite of Muslim encroachment into the Deccan, first by the Adil Shahis of Bijapur and the Qutb Shahis of Golkonda, and by the Mughal armies under Aurangzeb, these chieftains continued to exercise a considerable degree of local independence.

But Vijayanagar was gone, and in its passing the brightest star of Hindu art, architecture, philosophy and culture was extinguished. Never again would there rise a Hindu kingdom comparable to Vijayanagar, and never again until Indian Independence, would South India be so free of foreign domination.

RULERS

Aravidu Dynasty

Venkata(pati)raya II, 1586-1614AD — वेंकटराय

Rama Devaraya II, 1614-1630AD — रगराय

Venkata(pati)raya III, 1630-1641AD — वेंकटराय

Rama Deva Raya III, 1642-1649; 1679AD

KINGDOM
ANONYMOUS HAMMERED COINAGE
1642-1757AD

KM# 8 PAGODA
3.4000 g., Gold **Obv:** Venkatesvara kneeling **Note:** Uniface.

Date	Mintage	VG	F	VF	XF	Unc
ND	—	50.00	60.00	75.00	125	—

KM# 9 PAGODA
3.4000 g., Gold **Obv:** Sri-devi Venkatesvara and Bhu-devi standing

Date	Mintage	VG	F	VF	XF	Unc
ND	—	50.00	65.00	85.00	135	—

Rama Devaraya II
HAMMERED COINAGE

KM# 5 DAM
3.5000 g., Copper **Obv:** Elephant left **Rev:** Inscription in three lines **Rev. Inscription:** "Sri Chalama Rama"

Date	Mintage	Good	VG	F	VF	XF
ND(1614-30)	—	6.00	15.00	30.00	50.00	—

Venkata(pati)raya III
HAMMERED COINAGE

KM# 6 DAM
3.5000 g., Copper **Obv:** Two animals **Rev:** Inscription in two lines **Rev. Inscription:** "Chalama Venkata"

Date	Mintage	Good	VG	F	VF	XF
ND(1630-41)	—	7.20	18.00	36.00	60.00	—

KM# 7 1/2 PAGODA
1.7000 g., Gold **Obv:** Venkatesvara standing in archway **Rev:** Inscription in three lines **Rev. Inscription:** "Sri Venkatesvara Yanamah"

Date	Mintage	Good	VG	F	VF	XF
ND(1630-41)	—	—	—	60.00	75.00	110

INDIA - BRITISH

The civilization of India, which began about 2500 B.C., flourished under a succession of empires - notably those of the Mauryas, the Kushans, the Guptas, the Delhi Sultans and the Mughals – until undermined in the 18th and 19th centuries by European colonial powers.

The Portuguese were the first to arrive, off Calicut in May 1498. It wasn't until 1612, after the Portuguese and Spanish power had begun to wane, that the British East India Company established its initial settlement at Surat. Britain could not have chosen a more propitious time as the central girdle of petty states, and the southern Vijayanagar Empire were crumbling and ripe for foreign exploitation. By the end of the century, English traders were firmly established in Bombay, Madras, Calcutta and lesser places elsewhere, and Britain was implementing its announced policy to create such civil and military institutions as may be the foundation of secure English domination for all time'. By 1757, following the successful conclusion of a war of colonial rivalry with France during which the military victories of Robert Clive, a young officer with the British East India Company, made him a powerful man in India, the British were firmly settled in India not only as traders but as conquerors. During the next 60 years, the British East India Company acquired dominion over most of India by bribery and force, and governed it directly or through puppet princelings.

COLONY

TRADE COINAGE

"Portcullis" Issue

The "portcullis" coinage was struck at the Tower Mint for the maiden voyage of the incorporated "Company of Merchants of London" trading into the East Indies. They were struck to the weights of the Spanish 1, 2, 4, and 8 Reales. These issues include a "0" mintmark.

KM# T1.1 TESTERN

3.4200 g., 0.9250 Silver 0.1017 oz. ASW **Ruler:** Elizabeth I **Issuer:** East India Company **Obv:** Crowned arms between crowned "E" and crowned "R" **Obv. Legend:** :ELIZABETH • D:G: ANG: FR: ET • REGINA • **Rev:** Crowned portcullis **Rev. Legend:** :POSVI • DEVM • ADIVTOREM • MEVM • **Mint:** Tower

Date	Mintage	Good	VG	F	VF	XF
ND(1600-01)O	—	900	1,800	3,200	5,500	7,500

KM# T1.2 TESTERN

3.4200 g., 0.9250 Silver 0.1017 oz. ASW **Ruler:** Elizabeth I **Issuer:** East India Company **Obv:** Crowned arms between crowned "E" and crowned "R" **Obv. Legend:** :ELIZABETH • D:G: ANG: FR: ET • HIB: REGIN' • **Rev:** Crowned portcullis **Rev. Legend:** :POSVI • DEVM • ADIVTOREM • MEVM • **Mint:** Tower

Date	Mintage	Good	VG	F	VF	XF
ND(1600-01)O	—	1,000	2,000	3,500	6,000	8,000

KM# T2.1 2 TESTERNS

6.8500 g., 0.9250 Silver 0.2037 oz. ASW **Ruler:** Elizabeth I **Issuer:** East India Company **Obv:** Crowned arms between crowned "E" and crowned "R" **Obv. Legend:** ELIZABETH • D:G: ANG: FR: ET • HIB: REGINA • **Rev:** Crowned portcullis **Rev. Legend:** :POSVI • DEVM • ADIVTOREM • MEVM • **Mint:** Tower

Date	Mintage	Good	VG	F	VF	XF
ND(1600-01)O	—	600	1,200	2,500	4,000	6,500

KM# T2.2 2 TESTERNS

6.8500 g., 0.9250 Silver 0.2037 oz. ASW **Ruler:** Elizabeth I **Issuer:** East India Company **Obv:** Crowned arms between crowned "E" and crowned "R" **Obv. Legend:** ELIZABETH • D:G: ANG: FR: ET • HIB: REGIN' • **Rev:** Crowned portcullis **Rev. Legend:** :POSVI • DEVM • ADIVTOREM • MEVM • **Mint:** Tower

Date	Mintage	VG	F	VF	XF	Unc
ND(1600-01)O	—	1,500	2,750	4,500	7,000	—

KM# T2.3 2 TESTERNS

6.8500 g., 0.9250 Silver 0.2037 oz. ASW **Ruler:** Elizabeth I **Issuer:** East India Company **Obv:** Crowned arms between crowned "E" and crowned "R" **Obv. Legend:** ELIZABETH • D:G: ANG: FR: ET • HIB: REGI' • **Rev:** Crowned portcullis **Rev. Legend:** :POSVI • DEVM • ADIVTOREM • MEVM • **Mint:** Tower

Date	Mintage	Good	VG	F	VF	XF
ND(1600-01)O	—	800	1,650	3,000	5,000	7,500

KM# T3.1 4 TESTERNS

13.7000 g., 0.9250 Silver 0.4074 oz. ASW **Ruler:** Elizabeth I **Issuer:** East India Company **Obv:** Crowned arms between crowned "E" and crowned "R" **Obv. Legend:** :ELIZABETH • D:G' ANG'• FRA'• ET • HIBER'• REGINA **Rev:** Crowned portcullis **Rev. Legend:** :POSVI • DEVM • ADIVTOREM • MEVM • **Mint:** Tower

Date	Mintage	Good	VG	F	VF	XF
ND(1600-01)O	—	1,000	2,000	3,500	6,000	9,000

KM# T3.2 4 TESTERNS

13.7000 g., 0.9250 Silver 0.4074 oz. ASW **Ruler:** Elizabeth I **Issuer:** East India Company **Obv:** Crowned arms between crowned "E" and crowned "R" **Obv. Legend:** :ELIZABETH • D:G' ANG'• FRA'• ET• HIBER'• REGI'• **Rev:** Crowned portcullis **Rev. Legend:** :POSVI • DEVM • ADIVTOREM • MEVM **Mint:** Tower

Date	Mintage	Good	VG	F	VF	XF
ND(1600-01)O	—	1,150	2,200	3,750	6,500	9,500

KM# T4.1 8 TESTERNS

27.4000 g., 0.9250 Silver 0.8148 oz. ASW **Ruler:** Elizabeth I **Issuer:** East India Company **Obv:** Crowned arms between high crowned "E" and high crowned "R" **Obv. Legend:** ELIZABETH • D:G: ANG: FR ET • HIB: REGINA • **Rev:** Crowned portcullis with curved chains at left and right **Rev. Legend:** :POSVI • DEVM • ADIVTOREM • MEVM • **Mint:** Tower

Date	Mintage	Good	VG	F	VF	XF
ND(1600-01)O	—	3,000	6,000	9,500	16,500	25,000

KM# T4.2 8 TESTERNS

27.4000 g., 0.9250 Silver 0.8148 oz. ASW, 39 mm. **Ruler:** Elizabeth I **Issuer:** East India Company **Obv:** Crowned arms between Crowned "E" and crowned "R" **Obv. Legend:** ELIZABETH • D:G: ANG: FR: ET • HIB: REGINA **Rev:** Crowned portcullis with angular chains at left and right. **Rev. Legend:** :POSVI • DEVM • ADIVTOREM • MEVM • **Mint:** Tower

Date	Mintage	Good	VG	F	VF	XF
ND(1600-01)	—	3,200	6,250	9,750	17,000	25,000

BOMBAY PRESIDENCY

Following a naval victory over the Portuguese on December 24, 1612 negotiations were started that developed into the opening of the first East India Company factory in Surat in 1613. Silver coins for the New World as well as various other foreign coins were used in early trade. Within the decade the Mughal mint at Surat was melting all of these foreign coins and re-minting them as various denominations of Mughal coinage.

Bombay became an English holding as part of the dowry of Catherine of Braganza, Princess of Portugal when she was betrothed to Charles II of England. Also included in the dowry was Tangier and $500,000. With this acquisition the trading center of the Indian West Coast moved from Surat to Bombay.

Possession of Bombay Island took place on February 8, 1665 and by 1672 the East India Company had a mint in Bombay to serve their trading interests. European designed coins were struck here until 1717. Experimental issues of Mughal style rupees with regnal years pertaining to the reigns of James II and William and Mary were made in 1693-94.

MINTS

Ahmadabad	احمداباد
Bombay (Mumbai)	منبي
Surat	سورت
Tellicherry	تلجري تالچري

MONETARY SYSTEM

3 Pies = 1 Pice (Paisa)
11 Tinnys (Bujruk) = 1 Copperoon (Pice)
48 Copperoons = 1 Anglina (Rupee)

BRITISH COLONY

CAST COINAGE

KM# 130 TINNY (Bujruk)

1.5600 g., Cast Tin **Obv:** U.E.I.Co. bale mark **Rev:** 1/72 (first issue) **Note:** P227.

Date	Mintage	Good	VG	F	VF	XF
(16)72	—	10.00	18.50	28.50	40.00	—

KM# 138 TINNY (Bujruk)

2.7100 g., Cast Tin **Obv:** U.E.I.Co. arms **Rev:** 2/75 (second issue) **Note:** P228.

Date	Mintage	Good	VG	F	VF	XF
(16)75	—	30.00	45.00	75.00	110	—

KM# 131 PICE

13.0000 g., Copper **Obv:** Honorable English Co. of the East Indies arms **Obv. Legend:** HON: SOC: ANG: IND: ORI **Rev:** Inscription, legend in outer circle **Rev. Legend:** A: DEO: PAX: & INCREMENTUM: **Rev. Inscription:** MON: BOMBAYA ANGLIC REGINS Ao7o **Mint:** Bombay **Note:** P78.

Date	Mintage	Good	VG	F	VF	XF
ND(1672)/7	—	30.00	45.00	65.00	90.00	—
Note: Ao7o = 1672						
ND(1673)/8	—	30.00	45.00	65.00	90.00	—

Date	Mintage	Good	VG	F	VF	XF
Note: Ao8o = 1673						
ND(1674)/9	—	30.00	45.00	65.00	90.00	—
Note: Ao9o = 1674						

KM# 133 PICE

13.0000 g., Copper **Rev:** Inscription: MON. BOMBAY ANGLIC REGIMS Ao7o **Mint:** Bombay

Date	Mintage	Good	VG	F	VF	XF
ND(1672)/7 (1672)	—	20.00	30.00	50.00	80.00	—

KM# 132 PICE

13.0000 g., Copper **Rev. Legend:** MON: BMBAYA ANGLIC REGIMS Ao7o **Mint:** Bombay **Note:** P80.

Date	Mintage	Good	VG	F	VF	XF
ND(1672)/7 (1672)	—	30.00	45.00	65.00	90.00	—

KM# 136 PICE

13.0000 g., Copper **Rev. Legend:** A DEO PAX & INCREMENTVM 74 **Mint:** Bombay **Note:** P81.

Date	Mintage	Good	VG	F	VF	XF
(16)73/8	—	—	—	—	—	—
Note: Ao8o appears as Ao&o with the & inverted						
(16)74/9	—	30.00	45.00	65.00	90.00	—

KM# A143 PICE

13.0000 g., Copper **Rev:** Date: Ao9o **Mint:** Bombay

Date	Mintage	Good	VG	F	VF	XF
(16)74	—	30.00	45.00	65.00	90.00	—

KM# 141 PICE

13.0000 g., Copper **Rev:** Inscription: MONETA BOMBAYES ANGLICI REGIMs ANDOR **Rev. Legend:** A DEO PAX ET INCREMENTVM 78 **Mint:** Bombay **Note:** P87.

Date	Mintage	Good	VG	F	VF	XF
(16)78	—	30.00	45.00	65.00	90.00	—

KM# 142 PICE

13.0000 g., Copper **Rev:** Inscription: MONETA BOMBAYES ANGLICI REGIMS ANoDo **Mint:** Bombay **Note:** P89.

Date	Mintage	Good	VG	F	VF	XF
(16)78	—	30.00	45.00	65.00	90.00	—

KM# 145 PICE

13.0000 g., Copper **Rev:** Inscription: MOET BOMBAY ANGLIC REGIMs AoD9(Arabic)2 **Rev. Legend:** HON SOC ANG IND ORI **Mint:** Bombay **Note:** P90.

Date	Mintage	Good	VG	F	VF	XF
(16)92	—	30.00	45.00	65.00	90.00	—

KM# 146 PICE

13.0000 g., Copper **Rev:** Inscription: MOET BOMBAY ANGII hGEIM AoD9(Arabic)2 **Mint:** Bombay **Note:** P93.

Date	Mintage	Good	VG	F	VF	XF
(16)92	—	30.00	45.00	65.00	90.00	—

HAMMERED COINAGE

KM# 134 1/2 RUPEE

5.7500 g., Silver **Obv:** Honorable English Co. of the East Indies arms **Obv. Legend:** HON: SOC: ANG: IND: ORI **Rev:** Inscription: MON: BOMBAYr ANGELIC REGIMs Ao7o **Rev. Legend:** A: DEO: PAX: SS: INCREMENTVM in outer circle **Mint:** Bombay **Note:** P13; The authenticity of KM#134 is questionable.

Date	Mintage	VG	F	VF	XF	Unc
ND(1672)7	—	—	—	—	—	—
Note: The authenticity of KM#134 is questionable.						

KM# 139 1/2 RUPEE

5.7500 g., Silver **Obv:** Honorable English Co. of the East Indies arms **Rev. Legend:** MONETA BOMBAIENSIS **Rev. Inscription:** PAX / DEO **Mint:** Bombay **Note:** P18; The authenticity of KM#139 is questionable.

Date	Mintage	VG	F	VF	XF	Unc
ND(1676)	—	—	—	—	—	—

KM# 147 1/2 RUPEE

5.7500 g., Silver **Obv:** Persian inscription: "Coin struck during the reign of King William and Queen Mary" **Rev:** Persian inscription: In their 5th regnal year; Coin of the English Company **Mint:** Bombay **Note:** P29.

Date	Mintage	VG	F	VF	XF	Unc
1693/5 (1693) Rare	—	—	—	—	—	—

KM# 135 RUPEE (Anglina)

11.4800 g., Silver **Obv:** Honorable English Co. of the East Indies arms **Obv. Legend:** HON: SOC: ANG: IND: ORI **Rev:** Inscription: MON: BOMBAYr ANGLIC REGIMs Ao7o **Rev. Legend:** A: DEO: PAX: SS: INCREMENTVM: **Mint:** Bombay **Note:** P12.

Date	Mintage	VG	F	VF	XF	Unc
ND(1672)7	—	800	2,000	4,000	6,000	—
Note: Ao7o = 1672						

KM# 137 RUPEE (Anglina)

11.6200 g., Silver **Obv. Legend:** HON: SOC: ANG: IND: ORI **Rev:** Crowned, linked C's **Rev. Legend:** A: DEO: PAX: ET: INCREMENTVM: **Mint:** Bombay **Note:** P14.

Date	Mintage	VG	F	VF	XF	Unc
1674 (1675)	—	800	2,000	4,000	6,000	—

KM# 140 RUPEE (Anglina)

11.7500 g., Silver **Obv:** Honorable English Co. of the East Indies arms **Rev. Legend:** MONETA • BOMBAIENSIS **Rev. Inscription:** PAX / DEO **Mint:** Bombay **Note:** P16.

Date	Mintage	VG	F	VF	XF	Unc
ND(1676)	—	500	1,200	2,500	3,500	—

KM# 143 RUPEE (Anglina)

11.7500 g., Silver **Obv:** Rosettes in H.E. Co. arms, between ships **Mint:** Bombay **Note:** Varieties exist.

Date	Mintage	VG	F	VF	XF	Unc
1687	—	—	—	—	—	—

KM# 144 RUPEE (Anglina)

Silver **Obv:** Persian inscription: Struck in the name of King James II **Rev:** Persian inscription: "Regnal year 4..." **Mint:** Bombay **Note:** P10; Weight varies: 10.70-11.60 grams.

Date	Mintage	VG	F	VF	XF	Unc
ND(1687)/4 Rare	—	—	—	—	—	—

KM# 148.1 RUPEE (Anglina)

Silver **Obv:** Persian inscription: "Coin struck during the reign of King William and Queen Mary" **Rev:** Persian inscription: "in their 4-6 regnal year" **Mint:** Bombay **Note:** Weight varies: 10.70-11.60 grams.

Date	Mintage	VG	F	VF	XF	Unc
ND(1692)/4	—	750	1,250	1,750	2,500	—

KM# 148.2 RUPEE (Anglina)

Silver **Obv:** Inscription: Finer style **Rev:** Inscription: Finer style **Mint:** Bombay **Note:** P27; Weight varies: 10.70-11.60 grams.

Date	Mintage	VG	F	VF	XF	Unc
ND(1693)/5	—	350	550	850	1,250	—
ND(1694)/6	—	350	550	850	1,250	—

PATTERNS

Including off metal strikes

KM#	Date	Mintage	Identification	Mkt Val
Pn1	1677	—	Rupee. Silver. Pr19; English manufacture.	—
Pn2	1678	—	Rupee. Silver. Pr20; English manufacture.	—
Pn3	1678	—	Rupee. Pewter. Pr22; English manufacture.	—
Pn4	1678	—	Rupee. Silver. Pr25.	—

MADRAS PRESIDENCY

English trade was begun on the east coast of India in 1611. The first factory was at Mazulipatam and was maintained intermittently until modern times.

Madras was founded in 1639 and Fort St. George was made the chief factory on the east coast in 1641. A mint was established at Fort St. George where coins of the style of Vijayanagar were struck.

The Madras mint began minting copper coins after the renovation. In 1689 silver fanams were authorized to be struck by the new Board of Directors.

In 1692 the Mughal Emperor Aurangzeb gave permission for Mughal type rupees to be struck at Madras. These circulated locally and were also sent to Bengal. The chief competition for the Madras coins were the Arcot rupees. Some of the bulk coins from Madras were sent to the Nawabs mint to be made into Arcot rupees.

MONETARY SYSTEM

36 Fanam = 1 Pagoda (1688-1802)

MINT

چيناپتن

Chinapatton

Masulipatnam (Machilipatnam)

BRITISH COLONY

HAMMERED COINAGE

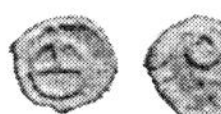

KM# 281 CASH

0.5300 g., Copper **Obv:** Bale mark **Rev:** Inscription: Telugu in two lines **Note:** P89; Size varies: 6.50-7.00mm.

Date	Mintage	Good	VG	F	VF	XF
ND(1660-78)	—	9.00	15.00	25.00	50.00	—

KM# 282 CASH

Copper **Obv:** Bull walking left **Rev:** "65" in beaded circle **Note:** P1.

Date	Mintage	Good	VG	F	VF	XF
(16)65	—	—	—	—	—	—

KM# 286 CASH

0.5900 g., Copper, 7.50 mm. **Obv:** Bale mark in dotted circle **Note:** P91.

Date	Mintage	Good	VG	F	VF	XF
1678	—	9.00	15.00	25.00	50.00	—

KM# 287 CASH

0.8800 g., Copper, 8.0 mm. **Obv:** Bale markwith date "78" in bottom half in beaded circle **Note:** P92.

Date	Mintage	Good	VG	F	VF	XF
(16)78	—	9.00	15.00	25.00	50.00	—

KM# 292 CASH

0.8800 g., Copper, 8.0 mm. **Obv:** Date in two lines in beaded circle **Rev:** Inscription, Telugu in two lines in beaded circle **Note:** P93.

Date	Mintage	Good	VG	F	VF	XF
1698	—	9.00	15.00	25.00	50.00	—

KM# 283 1/2 DUDU (5 Cash)

3.1500 g., Copper **Obv:** Bale mark with CC/E **Rev:** Inscription

Date	Mintage	Good	VG	F	VF	XF
ND(ca.1600)	—	—	—	—	—	—

KM# 284 1/2 DUDU (5 Cash)

3.1500 g., Copper **Obv:** Bale mark with CC/E **Rev:** Inscription

Date	Mintage	Good	VG	F	VF	XF
ND(ca.1600)	—	—	—	—	—	—

KM# 285 1/2 DUDU (5 Cash)

3.1500 g., Copper **Obv:** Bale mark with CC/E **Rev:** Inscription

Date	Mintage	Good	VG	F	VF	XF
ND(ca.1600)	—	—	—	—	—	—

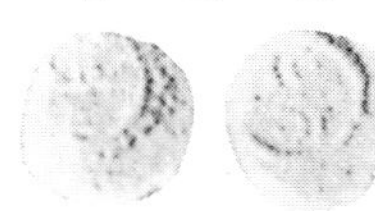

KM# 290 1/2 DUDU (5 Cash)

4.4300 g., Copper **Obv:** Bale mark with CC/E or GC/E **Rev:** Date in 2 lines

Date	Mintage	Good	VG	F	VF	XF
1691	—	7.00	11.00	22.00	35.00	—

KM# 300 1/2 DUDU (5 Cash)

4.4300 g., Copper **Obv:** Bale mark with CC/E or GC/E **Rev:** Date with wavy lines above and below **Note:** Type of Dudu; weight of 1/2 Dudu.

Date	Mintage	Good	VG	F	VF	XF
1700	—	10.00	20.00	35.00	55.00	—

KM# 291 DUDU (10 Cash)

Copper, 16.9 mm. **Obv:** Bale mark with CC/E or GC/E **Rev:** Date with wavy lines above and below **Note:** Weight varies 8.21-8.35 grams.

Date	Mintage	Good	VG	F	VF	XF
1693	—	3.50	9.00	15.00	25.00	—
1695	—	3.50	9.00	15.00	25.00	—
1700	—	3.50	9.00	15.00	25.00	—

KM# 297 1/2 FANAM

0.5100 g., Silver **Obv:** Large deity Vishnu **Rev:** Bead at left and right of interlocked C's **Note:** P17.

Date	Mintage	Good	VG	F	VF	XF
ND(1690-1763)	—	12.00	30.00	60.00	100	165

KM# 293 FANAM

1.2300 g., Silver **Obv:** Small Vishnu ideity **Rev:** 1 before interlocked C's

Date	Mintage	Good	VG	F	VF	XF
ND(1689)	—	5.50	18.00	45.00	90.00	150

KM# 298 FANAM

1.0300 g., Silver **Obv:** Large deity Vishnu **Rev:** Bead at left and right of interlocked C's **Note:** P16.

Date	Mintage	Good	VG	F	VF	XF
ND(1690-1763)	—	4.50	15.00	37.50	75.00	125

KM# 296 2 FANAM

2.4600 g., Silver **Obv:** Large deity Vishnu **Rev:** Bead at left and right of interlocked C's

Date	Mintage	Good	VG	F	VF	XF
ND(1690-1763)	—	3.50	12.00	30.00	60.00	100

KM# A289 RUPEE

11.5900 g., Silver **Obv:** Inscription in Persian **Obv. Inscription:** "Aurangzeb Alamgir..." **Rev:** Inscription in Persian **Mint:** Chinapattan **Note:** It has been determined that the AH date is lacking for all but AH1103//38. Prev. KM#300.25.

Date	Mintage	Good	VG	F	VF	XF
AH1103//38	—	24.00	60.00	120	200	300
AH-//38	—	8.00	18.00	35.00	65.00	100
AH-//39	—	8.00	18.00	35.00	65.00	100
AH-//40	—	8.00	18.00	35.00	65.00	100
AH-//41	—	8.00	18.00	35.00	65.00	100
AH-//42	—	8.00	18.00	35.00	65.00	100
AH-//43	—	8.00	18.00	35.00	65.00	100
AH-//44	—	8.00	18.00	35.00	65.00	100
AH-//45	—	8.00	18.00	35.00	65.00	100

HAMMERED COINAGE

Pagoda Series

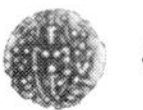 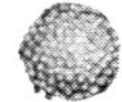

KM# A288 1/4 PAGODA

0.8370 g., Gold **Obv:** Single standing deity Vishnu **Rev:** Granulated **Mint:** Madras **Note:** Single swami type. Fr. #1574.

Date	Mintage	Good	VG	F	VF	XF
ND(c.1678-1740)	—	—	40.00	100	175	250

KM# B280 1/2 PAGODA

1.7250 g., Gold, 9.3 mm. **Obv:** 3 full swami **Rev:** Granulated **Mint:** Fort St. George **Note:** P. #4. Fr. #1573.

Date	Mintage	Good	VG	F	VF	XF
ND(1691-1740)	—	—	65.00	100	175	250

KM# 280 PAGODA

3.4500 g., Gold, 13 mm. **Obv:** Large crude deity Vishnu **Mint:** Fort St. George **Note:** P. #1. Fr. #1572.

Date	Mintage	Good	VG	F	VF	XF
ND(c.1643-77)	—	—	110	130	175	—

KM# 288 PAGODA

3.4300 g., Gold **Obv:** Single standing deity Vishnu **Rev:** Granulated **Mint:** Fort St. George **Note:** Struck at Madras Mint. P. #2. Fr. #1572.

Date	Mintage	Good	VG	F	VF	XF
ND(c.1678-1740)	—	BV	BV	110	130	175

KM# 289 PAGODA

3.4000 g., Gold **Obv:** 3 full length dieties **Rev:** Granulated **Mint:** Fort St. George **Note:** Struck at Madras Mint. P3A.

Date	Mintage	VG	F	VF	XF	Unc
ND(c.1691-1740)	—	60.00	100	135	175	—

INDIA-DANISH, TRANQUEBAR

Danish India or Tranquebar is a town and former Danish colony on the southeast coast of India. In Danish times, 1620-1845, it was a factory site and seaport operated by the Danish Asiatic Company. Tranquebar and the other Danish settlements in India were sold to the British East India Company in 1845.

RULER

Danish, until 1845

ADMINISTRATION OF TRANQUEBAR

Danish East India Company (DOC)
1620-(1650)
Danish Crown
ca.1630-1670
Christian IV, 1588-1648
Danish East India Company (DOC)
1670-1729

MONETARY SYSTEM

80 Kas (Cash) = Royaliner (Fano or
8 Royaliner = 1 Rupee
18 Royaliner = 1 Speciesdaler

Danish East India Co.

Lead Cash (Kas)

The lead cash (Kas) of Danish India were struck in many varieties. The following listings are representative only.

DANISH COLONY

CAST COINAGE

KM# 1 CASH

Lead **Ruler:** Christian IV **Obv:** R C4 P **Rev:** Walls of forts outline

Date	Mintage	Good	VG	F	VF	XF
ND	—	30.00	50.00	150	300	—

KM# 2 CASH

Lead **Ruler:** Christian IV **Obv:** DA/NSBO/RG in three lines

Date	Mintage	Good	VG	F	VF	XF
ND	—	—	200	500	1,000	—

KM# 3 CASH

Lead **Ruler:** Christian IV **Obv:** DAN/NSBO/RG in three lines **Rev:** BEW/INTHE/BER in three lines

Date	Mintage	Good	VG	F	VF	XF
ND	—	60.00	200	450	900	—

KM# 4 CASH

Lead **Ruler:** Christian IV **Obv:** Similar to KM#3 **Rev:** TRA/NGEB/ARI in three lines

Date	Mintage	Good	VG	F	VF	XF
ND	—	200	600	800	1,200	—

KM# 5 CASH

Lead **Ruler:** Christian IV **Obv:** Similar to KM#3 **Rev:** T/DOC/B in three lines

Date	Mintage	Good	VG	F	VF	XF
ND	—	40.00	75.00	150	300	—

KM# 6 CASH

Lead **Ruler:** Christian IV **Obv:** Similar to KM#3 **Rev:** FOR/TVNA in two lines

Date	Mintage	Good	VG	F	VF	XF
ND	—	—	—	800	1,600	—

KM# 7 CASH

Lead **Ruler:** Christian IV **Obv:** DANN/ISBOR/G in three lines **Rev:** CHRIS/TIANS/HAFN in three lines

Date	Mintage	Good	VG	F	VF	XF
ND	—	40.00	75.00	200	400	—

KM# 8 CASH

Lead **Ruler:** Christian IV **Obv:** DAN/NISB/ORG in three lines **Rev:** PER/LEN in two lines

Date	Mintage	Good	VG	F	VF	XF
ND	—	25.00	50.00	120	300	—

KM# 9 CASH

Lead **Ruler:** Christian IV **Rev:** IVP/TER in two lines

Date	Mintage	Good	VG	F	VF	XF
ND	—	25.00	50.00	120	300	—

KM# 10 CASH

Lead **Ruler:** Christian IV **Rev:** KE/DA in two lines

Date	Mintage	Good	VG	F	VF	XF
ND	—	25.00	50.00	120	300	—

KM# 11 CASH

Lead **Ruler:** Christian IV **Rev:** VOCD

Date	Mintage	Good	VG	F	VF	XF
ND	—	20.00	40.00	80.00	160	—

KM# 12 CASH

Lead **Ruler:** Christian IV **Obv:** Similar to KM#8 **Rev:** AM/AGE/R in three lines

Date	Mintage	Good	VG	F	VF	XF
ND	—	20.00	40.00	100	240	—

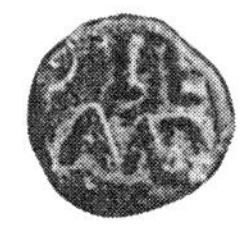

KM# 13 CASH

Lead **Ruler:** Christian IV **Obv:** Similar to KM#8 **Rev:** SIE/LAND in two lines

Date	Mintage	Good	VG	F	VF	XF
ND	—	20.00	40.00	100	240	—

KM# 14 CASH

Lead **Ruler:** Christian IV **Rev:** St. /AN/NA in three lines

Date	Mintage	Good	VG	F	VF	XF
ND	—	20.00	40.00	100	200	—

KM# 15 CASH

Lead **Ruler:** Christian IV **Rev:** CHA/RIT/AS in three lines

Date	Mintage	Good	VG	F	VF	XF
ND	—	20.00	40.00	100	240	—

KM# 16 CASH

Lead **Ruler:** Christian IV **Obv:** DA/NISB/ORG in three lines **Rev:** ST./IACO/B. in three lines

Date	Mintage	Good	VG	F	VF	XF
ND	—	18.00	30.00	100	300	—

KM# 17 CASH

Lead **Ruler:** Christian IV **Rev:** SVN/DE/BYE in three lines

Date	Mintage	Good	VG	F	VF	XF
ND	—	40.00	100	200	400	—

KM# 18 CASH

Lead **Ruler:** Christian IV **Rev:** VAL/DE/BYE in three lines

Date	Mintage	Good	VG	F	VF	XF
ND	—	40.00	100	200	400	—

KM# 19 CASH

Lead **Ruler:** Christian IV **Obv:** DAN/NIS/BORG in three lines **Rev:** AAL/BORG in two lines

Date	Mintage	Good	VG	F	VF	XF
ND	—	30.00	60.00	120	300	—

KM# 20 CASH

Lead **Ruler:** Christian IV **Obv:** Similar to KM#19 **Rev:** STE/GE in two lines

Date	Mintage	Good	VG	F	VF	XF
ND	—	18.00	30.00	100	300	—

KM# 21 CASH

Lead **Ruler:** Christian IV **Obv:** Similar to KM#19 **Rev:** SKA/GEN in two lines

Date	Mintage	Good	VG	F	VF	XF
ND	—	20.00	40.00	100	200	—

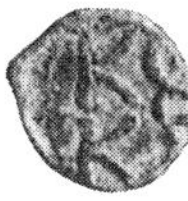

KM# 22 CASH

Lead **Ruler:** Christian IV **Obv:** Similar to KM#19 **Rev:** KO/KE in two lines

Date	Mintage	Good	VG	F	VF	XF
ND	—	25.00	40.00	120	250	—

KM# 23 CASH

Lead **Ruler:** Christian IV **Obv:** Horizontal line divides DANS/BORG **Rev:** NY/BE in two lines

Date	Mintage	Good	VG	F	VF	XF
ND	—	20.00	40.00	100	220	—

KM# 24 CASH

Lead **Ruler:** Christian IV **Rev:** D/SOL in two lines

Date	Mintage	Good	VG	F	VF	XF
ND	—	25.00	40.00	120	250	—

KM# 25 CASH

Lead **Ruler:** Christian IV **Rev:** LES/O in two lines

Date	Mintage	Good	VG	F	VF	XF
ND	—	20.00	40.00	100	220	—

KM# 26.1 CASH

Lead **Ruler:** Christian IV **Obv:** Crowned C4 monogram **Rev:** FOR/TVN in two lines

Date	Mintage	Good	VG	F	VF	XF
ND	—	15.00	30.00	60.00	200	—

KM# 26.2 CASH

Lead **Ruler:** Christian IV **Obv:** Similar to KM#26, but 4 turned 45 degrees

Date	Mintage	Good	VG	F	VF	XF
ND Rare	—	—	—	—	—	—

KM# 26.3 CASH

Lead **Ruler:** Christian IV **Obv:** Similar to KM#26, but retrograde 4

Date	Mintage	Good	VG	F	VF	XF
ND Rare	—	—	—	—	—	—

KM# 27 CASH

Lead **Ruler:** Christian IV **Obv:** Similar to KM#26 **Rev:** HO/PO in two lines

Date	Mintage	Good	VG	F	VF	XF
ND	—	15.00	30.00	70.00	160	—

KM# 28 CASH

Lead **Ruler:** Christian IV **Rev:** IHS inscription

Date	Mintage	Good	VG	F	VF	XF
ND	—	20.00	40.00	100	220	—

KM# A29 CASH

Lead **Ruler:** Christian IV **Obv:** IHS inscription **Rev:** Similar to KM 29, GUD inscription

Date	Mintage	Good	VG	F	VF	XF
ND Rare	—	—	—	—	—	—

KM# 29 CASH

Lead **Ruler:** Christian IV **Rev:** GVD (Danish for God)

Date	Mintage	Good	VG	F	VF	XF
ND	—	20.00	40.00	100	220	—

KM# 30 CASH

Lead **Ruler:** Christian IV **Rev:** IEHO/VAH in two lines

Date	Mintage	Good	VG	F	VF	XF
ND	—	20.00	40.00	100	220	—

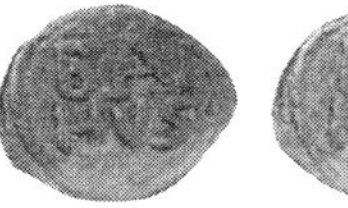

KM# 31 CASH

Lead **Ruler:** Christian IV **Obv:** Similar to KM#30 **Rev:** BA/HVS in two lines

Date	Mintage	Good	VG	F	VF	XF
ND	—	15.00	30.00	75.00	200	—

KM# 32 CASH

Lead **Ruler:** Christian IV **Obv:** Three-diamond crown above C4 monogram **Rev:** KAS

Date	Mintage	Good	VG	F	VF	XF
ND	—	10.00	25.00	60.00	160	—

KM# 33 CASH

Lead **Ruler:** Christian IV **Rev:** D/CAS/1644 in three lines

Date	Mintage	Good	VG	F	VF	XF
1644	—	20.00	40.00	100	250	—

KM# 34 CASH

Lead **Ruler:** Christian IV **Rev:** CH/CAS (S retrograd)/1645

Date	Mintage	Good	VG	F	VF	XF
1645	—	20.00	40.00	100	250	—

KM# 35 CASH

Lead **Ruler:** Christian IV **Obv:** Similar to KM#34 **Rev:** TR/CAS/1645 in three lines

Date	Mintage	Good	VG	F	VF	XF
1645	—	30.00	70.00	150	300	—

KM# 36 CASH

Lead **Ruler:** Christian IV **Rev:** St/MICA/EL in three lines

Date	Mintage	Good	VG	F	VF	XF
ND	—	20.00	10.00	100	250	—

KM# 37 CASH

Lead **Ruler:** Christian IV **Rev:** PE/JT in two lines

Date	Mintage	Good	VG	F	VF	XF
ND	—	15.00	30.00	80.00	200	—

KM# 38 CASH

Lead **Ruler:** Christian IV **Rev:** DAN/MAR/CK in three lines

Date	Mintage	Good	VG	F	VF	XF
ND	—	15.00	30.00	100	200	—

KM# 39 CASH

Lead **Ruler:** Christian IV **Rev:** IHS/date in two lines

Date	Mintage	Good	VG	F	VF	XF
1646	—	30.00	60.00	140	300	—

KM# 40 CASH

Lead **Ruler:** Christian IV **Rev:** SPSP/1646DB (4 and D retrograde)

Date	Mintage	Good	VG	F	VF	XF
1646	—	25.00	60.00	140	300	—

KM# 41 CASH

Lead **Ruler:** Christian IV **Rev:** IeHO/VS/Dan=/1647 in four lines

Date	Mintage	Good	VG	F	VF	XF
1647	—	20.00	50.00	120	250	—

KM# 42 CASH

Lead **Ruler:** Christian IV **Obv:** Similar to KM#41 **Rev:** WB/1647

Date	Mintage	Good	VG	F	VF	XF
1647	—	20.00	40.00	100	250	—

KM# 43 CASH

Lead **Ruler:** Christian IV **Obv:** Crowned C4 **Rev:** DB/1648 in two lines

Date	Mintage	Good	VG	F	VF	XF
1648	—	20.00	50.00	100	250	—

KM# 44 CASH

Lead **Ruler:** Christian IV **Obv:** Crowned C4 (4 retrograde)

Date	Mintage	Good	VG	F	VF	XF
1648	—	15.00	25.00	70.00	160	—

KM# 45 CASH

Lead **Ruler:** Christian IV **Rev:** DBS with • + • above S

Date	Mintage	Good	VG	F	VF	XF
1648	—	15.00	30.00	80.00	170	—

KM# 46 CASH

Lead **Ruler:** Christian IV **Obv:** C4 **Rev:** Outlined castle gate with three turrets **Note:** Weight about 8.0 grams.

Date	Mintage	Good	VG	F	VF	XF
ND	—	35.00	70.00	150	300	—

KM# 47.1 CASH

Lead **Ruler:** Christian IV **Note:** Weight about 4.0 grams.

Date	Mintage	Good	VG	F	VF	XF
ND	—	20.00	35.00	100	200	—

KM# 47.2 CASH

Lead **Ruler:** Christian IV **Note:** Weight about 8.0 grams.

Date	Mintage	Good	VG	F	VF	XF
ND Rare	—	—	—	—	—	—

KM# 48 CASH

Lead **Ruler:** Christian IV **Note:** Weight about 2.0 grams.

Date	Mintage	Good	VG	F	VF	XF
ND	—	10.00	20.00	50.00	100	—

KM# 49 CASH

Lead **Ruler:** Frederik III **Obv:** Crowned F **Rev:** 3RD

Date	Mintage	Good	VG	F	VF	XF
ND	—	35.00	50.00	140	300	—

KM# 50 CASH

Lead **Ruler:** Frederik III **Obv:** Crowned F3 monogram **Rev:** DB/1650 **Note:** Weight about 2.0 grams.

Date	Mintage	Good	VG	F	VF	XF
1650	—	20.00	40.00	80.00	200	—

KM# 51 CASH

Lead **Ruler:** Frederik III **Obv:** Similar to KM#50 **Rev:** CH/1650

Date	Mintage	Good	VG	F	VF	XF
1650	—	20.00	40.00	80.00	220	—

KM# 52 CASH

Lead **Ruler:** Frederik III **Obv:** Similar to KM#50 **Rev:** S/PP/50

Date	Mintage	Good	VG	F	VF	XF
1650	—	20.00	40.00	80.00	200	—

KM# 53 CASH

Lead **Ruler:** Frederik III **Obv:** Similar to KM#50 **Rev:** D:B.

Date	Mintage	Good	VG	F	VF	XF
ND	—	20.00	40.00	80.00	200	—

KM# 54 CASH

Lead **Ruler:** Frederik III **Obv:** Similar to KM#50 **Rev:** HAAB (Danish for hope)

Date	Mintage	Good	VG	F	VF	XF
ND	—	20.00	40.00	80.00	200	—

KM# 55 CASH

Lead **Ruler:** Frederik III **Obv:** Similar to KM#50 **Rev:** Cross in circle

Date	Mintage	Good	VG	F	VF	XF
ND	—	20.00	30.00	70.00	150	—

KM# 56 CASH

Lead **Ruler:** Frederik III **Obv:** Similar to KM#50 **Rev:** NOR

Date	Mintage	Good	VG	F	VF	XF
ND	—	20.00	30.00	70.00	150	—

KM# 57 CASH

Lead **Ruler:** Frederik III **Obv:** Similar to KM#50 **Rev:** S/PP/50

Date	Mintage	Good	VG	F	VF	XF
1650	—	25.00	40.00	80.00	200	—

KM# 58 CASH

Lead **Ruler:** Frederik III **Obv:** Similar to KM#50 **Rev:** NOR

Date	Mintage	Good	VG	F	VF	XF
ND Rare	—	—	—	—	—	—

KM# 59 CASH

Lead **Ruler:** Frederik III **Obv:** Similar to KM#50 **Rev:** DB/1652

Date	Mintage	Good	VG	F	VF	XF
1652	—	20.00	30.00	80.00	200	—

KM# 60 CASH

Lead **Ruler:** Frederik III **Obv:** Crowned F3 monogram **Rev:** PAX

Date	Mintage	Good	VG	F	VF	XF
ND	—	35.00	50.00	100	250	—

KM# 69 CASH

Lead **Ruler:** Frederik III **Obv:** Similar to KM#61 **Rev:** Norse lion right

Date	Mintage	Good	VG	F	VF	XF
ND	—	20.00	35.00	75.00	200	—

KM# 65 CASH

Lead **Ruler:** Frederik III **Obv:** Crowned F3 **Rev:** Horseman above C

Date	Mintage	Good	VG	F	VF	XF
ND	—	15.00	25.00	70.00	160	—

KM# 61 CASH

Lead **Ruler:** Frederik III **Obv:** Crowned F3 monogram **Rev:** CAS

Date	Mintage	Good	VG	F	VF	XF
ND	—	35.00	50.00	100	250	—

KM# 62 CASH

Lead **Ruler:** Frederik III **Obv:** Similar to KM#61 **Rev:** Crown

Date	Mintage	Good	VG	F	VF	XF
ND	—	20.00	30.00	80.00	200	—

KM# 63 CASH

Lead **Ruler:** Frederik III **Obv:** Similar to KM#61 **Rev:** Three crowns

Date	Mintage	Good	VG	F	VF	XF
ND	—	20.00	30.00	80.00	200	—

KM# 64 CASH

Lead **Ruler:** Frederik III **Obv:** Similar to KM#61 **Rev:** Horse

Date	Mintage	Good	VG	F	VF	XF
ND	—	25.00	40.00	90.00	230	—

KM# 66 CASH

Lead **Ruler:** Frederik III **Obv:** Similar to KM#61 **Rev:** Crowned codfish

Date	Mintage	Good	VG	F	VF	XF
ND	—	25.00	50.00	100	250	—

KM# 67 CASH

Lead **Ruler:** Frederik III **Rev:** Crowned codfish, A

Date	Mintage	Good	VG	F	VF	XF
ND	—	15.00	25.00	70.00	160	—

KM# 68 CASH

Lead **Ruler:** Frederik III **Rev:** Crowned codfish, N

Date	Mintage	Good	VG	F	VF	XF
ND	—	20.00	40.00	100	220	—

KM# 70 CASH

Lead **Ruler:** Frederik III **Obv:** Similar to KM#61 **Rev:** Nettle leaf

Date	Mintage	Good	VG	F	VF	XF
ND	—	20.00	50.00	120	250	—

KM# 71 CASH

Lead **Ruler:** Frederik III **Rev:** Nettle leaf, O

Date	Mintage	Good	VG	F	VF	XF
ND	—	20.00	30.00	80.00	200	—

KM# 72 CASH

Lead **Ruler:** Frederik III **Rev:** Lamb right

Date	Mintage	Good	VG	F	VF	XF
ND	—	20.00	30.00	70.00	220	—

KM# 73 CASH

Lead **Ruler:** Frederik III **Obv:** Similar to KM#65 **Rev:** Lamb left, b

Date	Mintage	Good	VG	F	VF	XF
ND	—	10.00	20.00	60.00	140	—

KM# 74 CASH

Lead **Ruler:** Frederik III **Rev:** Lamb left, F

Date	Mintage	Good	VG	F	VF	XF
ND	—	20.00	30.00	80.00	160	—

KM# 75 CASH

Lead **Ruler:** Frederik III **Rev:** The Wendish Wyvern (crowned swan) right

Date	Mintage	Good	VG	F	VF	XF
ND	—	20.00	30.00	80.00	200	—

KM# 76 CASH

Lead **Ruler:** Frederik III **Obv:** Similar to KM#75 **Rev:** Cross

Date	Mintage	Good	VG	F	VF	XF
ND	—	20.00	30.00	80.00	200	—

KM# 77 CASH

Lead **Ruler:** Frederik III **Rev:** Cross, 'e' in lower left quadrant

Date	Mintage	Good	VG	F	VF	XF
ND	—	20.00	30.00	80.00	200	—

KM# 78 CASH

Lead **Ruler:** Frederik III **Obv:** Similar to KM#74 **Rev:** Cross divides JO

Date	Mintage	Good	VG	F	VF	XF
ND	—	35.00	60.00	140	280	—

KM# 79 CASH

Lead **Ruler:** Frederik III **Rev:** Elephant left

Date	Mintage	Good	VG	F	VF	XF
ND	—	15.00	25.00	70.00	160	—

KM# 80 CASH

Lead **Ruler:** Frederik III **Obv:** Similar to KM#79 **Rev:** Norse lion left

Date	Mintage	Good	VG	F	VF	XF
ND	—	20.00	35.00	80.00	200	—

KM# 81 CASH

Lead **Ruler:** Frederik III **Rev:** Norse lion left, E

Date	Mintage	Good	VG	F	VF	XF
ND	—	15.00	25.00	70.00	160	—

KM# 82 CASH

Lead **Ruler:** Frederik III **Rev:** Norse lion left, DC

Date	Mintage	Good	VG	F	VF	XF
ND	—	20.00	30.00	80.00	200	—

KM# 83 CASH

Lead **Ruler:** Frederik III **Obv:** Similar to KM#82 **Rev:** Norse lion left above I

Date	Mintage	Good	VG	F	VF	XF
ND	—	20.00	60.00	130	250	—

KM# 84 CASH

Lead **Ruler:** Frederik III **Rev:** Slesvig lion right above I

Date	Mintage	Good	VG	F	VF	XF
ND	—	20.00	35.00	80.00	200	—

KM# 85 CASH

Lead **Ruler:** Frederik III **Rev:** Gothic lion left, nine hearts

Date	Mintage	Good	VG	F	VF	XF
ND	—	15.00	25.00	70.00	160	—

KM# 86 CASH

Lead **Ruler:** Frederik III **Obv:** Similar to KM#81 **Rev:** Nine hearts

Date	Mintage	Good	VG	F	VF	XF
ND	—	15.00	25.00	70.00	160	—

KM# 87 CASH

Lead **Ruler:** Frederik III **Rev:** Flower

Date	Mintage	Good	VG	F	VF	XF
ND	—	15.00	25.00	80.00	200	—

KM# 88 CASH

Lead **Ruler:** Frederik III **Rev:** Flower above 76

Date	Mintage	Good	VG	F	VF	XF
ND	—	15.00	25.00	80.00	200	—

KM# 89 CASH

Lead **Ruler:** Frederik III **Rev:** Swan right, S

Date	Mintage	Good	VG	F	VF	XF
ND	—	20.00	50.00	120	240	—

KM# 90 CASH

Lead **Ruler:** Christian V **Obv:** C5 monogram **Rev:** DC

Note: Weight about 2.3 grams.

Date	Mintage	Good	VG	F	VF	XF
ND	—	6.00	15.00	40.00	100	—

KM# 91 CASH

Lead **Ruler:** Christian V **Obv:** Crowned C5 monogram

Date	Mintage	Good	VG	F	VF	XF
ND	—	8.00	15.00	40.00	100	—

KM# 92 CASH

Lead **Ruler:** Christian V **Obv:** Crowned DOC **Note:** Varieties exist.

Date	Mintage	Good	VG	F	VF	XF
ND	—	7.00	15.00	40.00	100	—

KM# 93.1 CASH

Lead **Ruler:** Christian V **Obv:** Crowned C5 monogram **Rev:** Crowned DOC, small letters **Note:** Weight about 4.6 grams.

Date	Mintage	Good	VG	F	VF	XF
ND	—	10.00	20.00	40.00	100	—

KM# 93.2 CASH

Lead **Ruler:** Christian V **Obv:** Crowned C5 monogram **Rev:** Crowned DOC, large letters **Note:** Varieties exist.

Date	Mintage	Good	VG	F	VF	XF
ND	—	12.00	20.00	45.00	110	—

KM# 95.1 CASH

Lead **Ruler:** Christian V **Rev:** Crowned DOC above K, small letters

Date	Mintage	Good	VG	F	VF	XF
ND	—	20.00	30.00	80.00	170	—

Note: "K" and "WHVK" = W.H. von Kalnien.

KM# 95.2 CASH

Lead **Ruler:** Christian V **Obv:** Similar to KM#95 **Rev:** Crowned DOC above K, large letters

Date	Mintage	Good	VG	F	VF	XF
ND	—	15.00	25.00	60.00	140	—

Note: "K" and "WHVK" = W.H. von Kalnien.

KM# 97 CASH

Lead **Ruler:** Christian V **Obv:** Crowned C5 divides date **Rev:** Crowned DOC above WHVK

Date	Mintage	Good	VG	F	VF	XF
1687	—	20.00	35.00	80.00	200	—

Note: "K" and "WHVK" = W.H. von Kalnien.

KM# 98 CASH

Lead **Ruler:** Christian V **Obv:** Similar to KM#97, with rosettes **Note:** Previously KM#98.1

Date	Mintage	Good	VG	F	VF	XF
1687	—	30.00	50.00	130	260	—

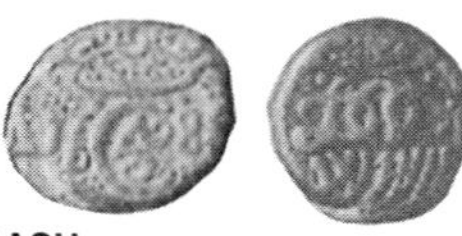

KM# 99 CASH

Lead **Ruler:** Christian V **Note:** Previously KM#98.2

Date	Mintage	Good	VG	F	VF	XF
1688	—	12.00	20.00	50.00	140	—

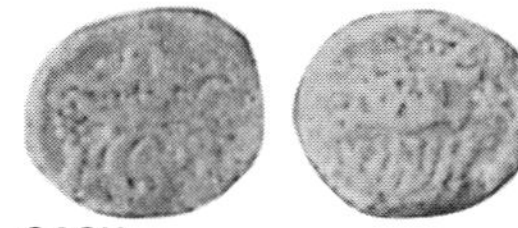

KM# 100 CASH

Lead **Ruler:** Christian V **Obv:** Similar to KM#99 **Rev:** Crowned *DOC* above WHVK

Date	Mintage	Good	VG	F	VF	XF
1688	—	15.00	25.00	60.00	150	—

Note: "K" and "WHVK" = W.H. von Kalnien.

HAMMERED COINAGE

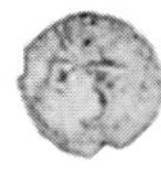

KM# 110 CASH

1.0000 g., Copper **Ruler:** Christian IV **Obv:** Crowned F3 monogram **Rev:** Norse lion on battle axe to left **Note:** Previously KM#118.1. Varieties exists.

Date	Mintage	Good	VG	F	VF	XF
ND	—	6.00	15.00	40.00	100	—

KM# 111 CASH

2.3000 g., Copper **Ruler:** Frederik III **Obv:** Crowned F3 monogram in half circle, ANO 1667 below **Rev:** Norse lion on battle axe to left in beaded circle **Note:** Previously KM#125.

Date	Mintage	Good	VG	F	VF	XF
1667	—	15.00	25.00	70.00	160	—

KM# 119 CASH

1.0000 g., Copper **Ruler:** Christian V **Obv:** Crowned double C5 monogram divides last two digits of date **Rev:** Crowned DOC monogram divides W H, VK below

Date	Mintage	Good	VG	F	VF	XF
(16)89	—	5.00	10.00	20.00	60.00	—
(16)90	—	5.00	10.00	30.00	90.00	—
(16)91	—	7.00	15.00	40.00	100	—

KM# 120 CASH

1.0000 g., Copper **Ruler:** Christian V **Obv:** Crowned double C5 monogram **Rev:** Crowned DOC monogram divides 1 6, two digits below **Note:** Monogram varieties exist.

Date	Mintage	Good	VG	F	VF	XF
1692	—	5.00	10.00	30.00	100	—
1694	—	5.00	10.00	20.00	60.00	—
1697	—	5.00	10.00	25.00	80.00	—

Note: Varieties exist

KM# 117 CASH

1.0000 g., Copper **Ruler:** Christian V **Obv:** Crowned C5 monogram. **Note:** Uniface. Previously KM#A122.

Date	Mintage	Good	VG	F	VF	XF
ND	—	10.00	20.00	40.00	100	—

KM# 121 CASH

Copper **Ruler:** Frederik IV **Issuer:** Danish East India Company **Obv:** Crowned double F4 monogram **Rev:** Crowned DOC monogram **Note:** Previously KM#122.

Date	Mintage	Good	VG	F	VF	XF
	—	10.00	20.00	40.00	100	—

Note: Posthumous issue, struck in 1700 and after.

KM# 122 CASH

Copper **Ruler:** Frederik IV **Issuer:** Danish East India Company **Obv:** Crowned F4 monogram using one vertical for both **Rev:** Crowned DOC monogram **Note:** Previously KM#123.1. Weight varies: 0.40-1.65 grams.

Date	Mintage	Good	VG	F	VF	XF
	—	5.00	8.00	20.00	40.00	—

Note: Posthumous issue, struck in 1700 and after.

KM# 123 CASH

Copper **Ruler:** Frederik IV **Issuer:** Danish East India Company **Rev:** Inverted DOC monogram **Note:** Previously KM#123.2.

Date	Mintage	Good	VG	F	VF	XF
	—	20.00	50.00	100	200	—

Note: Posthumous issue, struck in 1700 and after.

KM# 124 CASH

Copper **Ruler:** Frederik IV **Issuer:** Danish East India Company **Obv:** Crowned F4 monogram **Rev:** Crowned DOC monogram

Date	Mintage	Good	VG	F	VF	XF
	—	10.00	20.00	40.00	100	—

Note: Posthumous issue, struck in 1700 and after.

KM# A135 2 CASH

1.6000 g., Copper **Ruler:** Frederik IV **Issuer:** Danish East India Company **Obv:** Crowned double F4 monogram **Rev:** DOC monogram, 2 KAS below

Date	Mintage	Good	VG	F	VF	XF
ND	—	10.00	20.00	40.00	100	—

Note: Posthumous issue, struck in 1700 and after.

KM# 126.1 4 CASH

4.8000 g., Copper **Ruler:** Frederik IV **Issuer:** Danish East India Company **Obv:** Crowned double F4 monogram **Rev:** DOC monogram, 4 KAS below

Date	Mintage	Good	VG	F	VF	XF
ND	—	100	200	500	1,000	—

Note: Posthumous issue, struck in 1700 and after.

KM# 126.2 4 CASH

4.8000 g., Copper **Ruler:** Frederik IV **Issuer:** Danish East India Company **Rev:** 4 CAS below monogram

Date	Mintage	Good	VG	F	VF	XF
ND Rare	—	—	—	—	—	—

Note: Posthumous issue, struck in 1700 and after.

KM# 127 10 CASH

10.0000 g., Copper **Ruler:** Frederik IV **Issuer:** Danish East India Company **Obv:** Crowned double F4 monogram **Rev:** Crowned DAC monogram, 10 and Kass below

Date	Mintage	Good	VG	F	VF	XF
ND	—	100	300	800	1,400	—

Note: Posthumous issue, struck in 1700 and after.

INDIA-DUTCH

The Netherlands, operating as the United East India Company of the Netherlands, were the real successors to the Portuguese in India. They maintained a number of thriving establishments on the subcontinent until 1795, when Robert Clive, founder of the empire of British India, completed Britain's conquest of Bengal. Thereafter the Dutch holdings were gradually ceded to Britain, the most important to numismatics being Cochin, ceded in 1814; Negapatnam, ceded in 1784; Pulicat, ceded in 1824; and Tuticorin, ceded in 1795.

MINT MARK

NOTE: On Princely style coins the Dutch East India Company often used the mint mark: Lazy J (possibly a Kris: Malay knife).

COLONY

HAMMERED COINAGE

KM# 2 BAZARUK

Tin **Obv:** VOC monogram **Rev:** Cauri shell **Mint:** Cochin

Date	Mintage	Good	VG	F	VF	XF
ND(1663-1724)	—	—	—	—	—	—

KM# 4 1/2 RASI

Copper **Mint:** Cochin **Note:** Struck for trade with Muscat. Weight varies 5.42-5.89 grams. Similar to 1 Rasi, KM#5.

Date	Mintage	Good	VG	F	VF	XF
	—	20.00	35.00	75.00	150	—

KM# 5 RASI

Copper **Mint:** Cochin **Note:** Weight varies 10.84-11.79 grams. Struck for trade with Muscat.

Date	Mintage	Good	VG	F	VF	XF
	—	5.00	10.00	20.00	40.00	—

KM# 40 FANAM

Gold **Obv:** Degenerated Kali **Rev:** Similar to 1 Cash, KM#35; Arabic legend **Rev. Legend:** "In the name of Sultan Abd'allah" **Mint:** Pulicat

Date	Mintage	VG	F	VF	XF	Unc
ND(1646-1781) Rare	—	—	—	—	—	—

KM# 10 PAGODA

Gold **Obv:** Facing figures of three gods with two pointed crowns **Rev:** Granular dots **Mint:** Masulipatnam

Date	Mintage	VG	F	VF	XF	Unc
ND(1646-1747) Rare	—	—	—	—	—	—

Note: Copied by the British (Madras KM#3a) and the Nawab of Arcot (KM#13)

KM# 41 PAGODA

Gold **Obv:** Facing figure of God Ganesh **Rev:** Three-line Nagari inscription **Mint:** Pulicat

Date	Mintage	VG	F	VF	XF	Unc
ND(1646-1781) Unique	—	—	—	—	—	—

KM# 21 PAGODA
Gold **Obv:** Facing god, lazy "J" at right **Rev:** Granulated **Mint:** Negapatnam

Date	Mintage	VG	F	VF	XF	Unc
ND(1662-1749) Rare	—	—	—	—	—	—

CAST COINAGE

KM# 14.1 CASH
Lead **Obv:** N/VOC monogram **Rev:** Legend in two lines **Rev. Legend:** Tamil "Nakapattanam" **Mint:** Negapatnam

Date	Mintage	Good	VG	F	VF	XF
ND	—	20.00	30.00	42.50	60.00	—

KM# 14.2 CASH
Lead **Obv:** Retrograde N **Mint:** Negapatnam

Date	Mintage	Good	VG	F	VF	XF
ND	—	—	—	—	—	—

HAMMERED COINAGE

KM# 30 FANAM
Silver **Obv:** Degenerated Kali **Rev:** "OC" above lazy "J" above three rows of four dots each **Mint:** Negapatnam **Note:** This series for circulation in Ceylon.

Date	Mintage	VG	F	VF	XF	Unc
ND(ca.1675)	—	27.50	40.00	55.00	80.00	—

KM# 31 FANAM
Gold **Obv:** Degenerated Kali **Rev:** "OC" above lazy "J" above three rows of four dots each **Mint:** Negapatnam **Note:** This series for circulation in Ceylon. Weight varies: 0.33-0.37 grams.

Date	Mintage	VG	F	VF	XF	Unc
ND(ca.1675)	—	17.50	25.00	35.00	50.00	—

KM# 13 CASH
Copper **Obv:** N above VOC monogram **Rev:** Nagari legend in two lines **Mint:** Negapatnam

Date	Mintage	Good	VG	F	VF	XF
ND(1662-74)	—	—	—	—	—	—

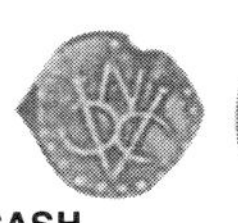 

KM# 15.1 CASH
Copper **Mint:** Negapatnam

Date	Mintage	Good	VG	F	VF	XF
ND	—	15.00	22.50	32.50	45.00	—

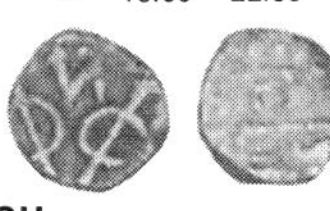

KM# 15.2 CASH
Copper **Obv:** Retrograde "N"/VOC monogram **Mint:** Negapatnam

Date	Mintage	Good	VG	F	VF	XF
ND	—	50.00	70.00	100	—	—

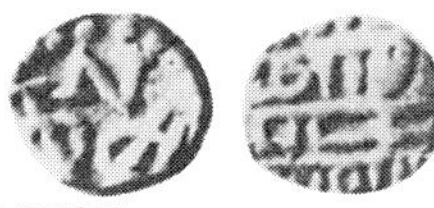

KM# 16.1 2 CASH
Copper **Rev:** Legend in three lines **Rev. Inscription:** Tamil "Nakapattanam" **Mint:** Negapatnam

Date	Mintage	Good	VG	F	VF	XF
ND	—	10.00	15.00	20.00	30.00	—

KM# 16.2 2 CASH
Copper **Obv:** Retrograde N/VOC monogram **Mint:** Negapatnam

Date	Mintage	Good	VG	F	VF	XF
ND	—	—	—	—	—	—

KM# 18 4 CASH
Copper **Obv:** N/VOC monogram/IV **Mint:** Negapatnam

Date	Mintage	Good	VG	F	VF	XF
ND 1 known	—	—	—	—	—	—

KM# 17 4 CASH
Copper **Obv:** N/VOC monogram/4 **Rev:** Inscription in two lines **Rev. Inscription:** Tamil "Nakapattanam" **Mint:** Negapatnam

Date	Mintage	Good	VG	F	VF	XF
ND	—	17.50	25.00	45.00	75.00	—

KM# 19 10 CASH
Copper **Obv:** N/VOC monogram/10 **Rev. Inscription:** Tamil "Nakapattanam" **Mint:** Negapatnam

Date	Mintage	Good	VG	F	VF	XF
ND Rare	—	—	—	—	—	—

KM# 20 15 CASH
Copper **Obv:** N/VOC monogram/15 **Rev. Inscription:** Tamil "Nakapattanam" **Mint:** Negapatnam

Date	Mintage	Good	VG	F	VF	XF
ND Rare	—	—	—	—	—	—

KM# 25 1/2 DUIT
Copper **Obv:** Facing figure of God Kali **Rev. Inscription:** Tamil "Nakapattanam" **Mint:** Negapatnam **Note:** This series for circulation in Ceylon. Weight varies: 1.60-1.80 grams.

Date	Mintage	Good	VG	F	VF	XF
ND(1695)	—	40.00	55.00	80.00	—	—

KM# 26 DUIT
Copper **Obv:** Facing figure of God Kali **Rev:** Inscription in two lines **Rev. Inscription:** Tamil "Nakapattanam" **Mint:** Negapatnam **Note:** This series for circulation in Ceylon. Weight varies: 2.60-3.60 grams.

Date	Mintage	Good	VG	F	VF	XF
ND(1695)	—	20.00	30.00	40.00	55.00	—

KM# 27 STUIVER
Copper **Obv:** 1 ST in sprays **Rev:** 1 ST in sprays **Mint:** Negapatnam **Note:** This series for circulation in Ceylon. Also struck in Ceylon but with different sprays.

Date	Mintage	Good	VG	F	VF	XF
ND(1675)	—	4.00	7.00	10.00	15.00	—

KM# 28 STUIVER
Copper **Obv:** Facing figure of God Kali **Rev:** Inscription in two lines **Rev. Inscription:** Tamil "Nakapattanam" **Mint:** Negapatnam **Note:** This series for circulation in Ceylon. Weight varies: 25.70-28.20 grams.

Date	Mintage	Good	VG	F	VF	XF
ND	—	27.50	40.00	55.00	80.00	—

KM# 29 2 STUIVERS
Copper **Obv:** Facing figure of God Kali **Rev:** Inscription in two lines **Rev. Inscription:** Tamil "Nakapattanam" **Mint:** Negapatnam **Note:** This series for circulation in Ceylon. Weight varies: 53.60-57.10 grams.

Date	Mintage	Good	VG	F	VF	XF
ND(1695)	—	65.00	100	130	175	—

HAMMERED COINAGE

First Series

KM# 34 CASH
Copper **Obv:** P/VOC monogram **Rev:** Two-line Nandi-Nagara inscription **Mint:** Pulicat

Date	Mintage	Good	VG	F	VF	XF
ND(1615-46)	—	17.50	25.00	35.00	50.00	—

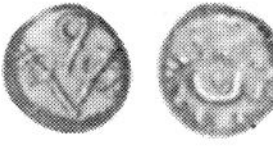

KM# 35.1 CASH
Copper **Rev:** Arabic inscription "in the name of Sultan Abd'allah" **Mint:** Pulicat

Date	Mintage	VG	F	VF	XF	Unc
ND(1646-)	—	7.50	12.50	18.00	28.00	—

KM# 35.2 CASH
Copper **Obv:** Retrograde P **Mint:** Pulicat

Date	Mintage	VG	F	VF	XF	Unc
ND(1646-)	—	15.00	20.00	30.00	45.00	—

KM# 36.1 2 CASH
Copper **Obv:** VOC monogram with P above **Rev:** Two-line Nandi-Nagara inscription **Mint:** Pulicat

Date	Mintage	Good	VG	F	VF	XF
ND(1615-46) Rare	—	—	—	—	—	—

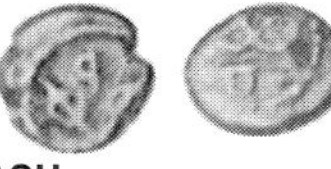

KM# 36.2 2 CASH
Copper **Obv:** P/VOC monogram **Rev:** Arabic inscription "in the name of Sultan Abd'allah" **Mint:** Pulicat

Date	Mintage	Good	VG	F	VF	XF
ND(1646-)	—	17.50	25.00	35.00	50.00	—

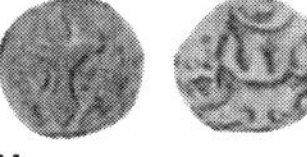

KM# 37 2 CASH
Copper **Obv:** II/VOC monogram **Rev:** Similar to 1 Cash, KM#35 **Mint:** Pulicat

Date	Mintage	VG	F	VF	XF	Unc
ND(1646-)	—	17.50	25.00	35.00	50.00	—

KM# 38 4 CASH
Copper **Obv. Inscription:** PAL/IIII/VOC **Rev:** Similar to 1 Cash, KM#35 **Mint:** Pulicat

Date	Mintage	VG	F	VF	XF	Unc
ND(1646-)	—	37.50	60.00	100	160	—

KM# 39 8 CASH
Copper **Obv. Inscription:** PAL/VIII/VOC **Rev:** Similar to 1 Cash, KM#35 **Mint:** Pulicat

Date	Mintage	VG	F	VF	XF	Unc
ND(1646-)	—	80.00	110	150	225	—

HAMMERED COINAGE

Second Series

KM# 42 5 CASH
Copper **Obv:** V/VOC monogram **Rev:** Similar to 1 Cash, KM#35 **Mint:** Pulicat **Note:** Struck for circulatin in Ceylon.

Date	Mintage	VG	F	VF	XF	Unc
ND(1646-74)	—	37.50	60.00	100	160	—

KM# 43 10 CASH
Copper **Obv:** X/VOC monogram **Rev:** Similar to 1 Cash, KM#35 **Mint:** Pulicat **Note:** Struck for circulatin in Ceylon.

Date	Mintage	VG	F	VF	XF	Unc
ND(1646-74)	—	17.50	30.00	50.00	80.00	—

INDIA-FRENCH

It was not until 1664, during the reign of Louis XIV, that the Compagnie des Indes Orientales was formed for the purpose of obtaining holdings on the subcontinent of India. Between 1666 and 1721, French settlements were established at Arcot, Mahe, Surat, Pondichery, Masulipatam, Karikal, Yanam, Murshidabad, Chandernagore, Balasore and Calicut. War with Britain reduced the French holdings to Chandernagore, Pondichery, Karikal, Yanam and Mahe. Chandernagore voted in 1949 to join India and became part of the Republic of India in 1950. Pondichery, Karikal, Yanam and Mahe formed the Pondichery union territory and joined the republic of India in 1954.

RULER
French, until 1954

MINTS

Pondichery

A city south of Madras on the southeast coast which became the site of the French Mint from 1700-1841. Pondichery was settled by the French in 1683. It became their main Indian possession even though it was occupied by the Dutch in 1693-98 and several times by the British from 1761-1816.

Surat

MONETARY SYSTEM
Cache Kas or Cash
Doudou = 4 Caches
Biche = 1 Pice
2 Royalins = 1 Fanon Pondichery
5 Heavy Fanons = 1 Rupee Mahe
64 Biches = 1 Rupee

PONDICHERY

HAMMERED COINAGE

KM# 40 FANON
0.9480 Silver **Obv:** Lis **Obv. Legend:** PONDICHERY **Rev:** Lis in center of outlined cross **Note:** Weight varies 2.50-2.70 grams. Size varies 13-15 mm.

Date	Mintage	VG	F	VF	XF	Unc
1700	—	25.00	45.00	125	200	—

INDIA-PORTUGUESE

Vasco da Gama, the Portuguese explorer, first visited India in 1498. Portugal seized control of a number of islands and small enclaves on the west coast of India, and for the next hundred years enjoyed a monopoly on trade. With the arrival of powerful Dutch and English fleets in the first half of the 17th century, Portuguese power in the area declined until virtually all of India that remained under Portuguese control were the west coast enclaves of Goa, Damao and Diu. They were forcibly annexed by India in 1962.

RULER
Portuguese, until 1961

DENOMINATION
The denomination of most copper coins appears in numerals on the reverse, though 30 Reis is often given as "1/2 T", and 60 Reis as "T" (T = Tanga). The silver coins have the denomination in words, usually on the obverse until 1850, then on the reverse.

BACAIM

(Bessein)

Located less than 30 miles north of Bombay on the Gulf of Cambay. In 1611 the Portuguese opened a mint at Bacaim. The greatest minting activity was between 1678 and 1697. Many issues for Bacaim were in conjunction with other Portuguese settlements. The British took Bacaim in 1780.

MINT MARK
B - Bacain

MONETARY SYSTEM
375 Bazarucos = 1 Pardao
2 Pardaos = 1 Rupia

COLONY

HAMMERED COINAGE

KM# 1 XERAFIM
10.4800 g., Silver **Subject:** Alfonso VI **Obv:** Crowned arms divide FB in inner circle **Rev:** Numerals of date in angles of cross

Date	Mintage	Good	VG	F	VF	XF
1661	—	200	375	650	1,200	—
1662	—	200	375	650	1,200	—
1663	—	200	375	650	1,200	—
1664	—	200	375	650	1,200	—

BACAIM & CHAUL

These two Portuguese settlements flanked the city of Bombay and minted coins as a joint venture in the 1650's after minting permission was granted in 1646. These coins are identified by the coat of arms being flanked by B-C or C-B.

COLONY

HAMMERED COINAGE

KM# 4 4 BAZARUCOS
4.2200 g., Copper **Subject:** John IV **Obv:** Crowned arms flanked by C & B **Rev:** Numerals in angles of cross; all in dotted circles

Date	Mintage	Good	VG	F	VF	XF
1654	—	40.00	80.00	145	300	—

KM# 2 TANGA
2.1000 g., Silver **Subject:** John IV **Obv:** Crowned arms flanked by C and B **Rev:** St. John standing left divides S and T; date divided at bottom

Date	Mintage	Good	VG	F	VF	XF
1653	—	60.00	125	225	450	—

KM# 1 2 TANGAS
4.2000 g., Silver **Subject:** John IV **Obv:** Crowned arms divide B and C in dotted circle **Rev:** Gridiron of St. Lawrence divides date in dotted circle

Date	Mintage	Good	VG	F	VF	XF
1645	—	65.00	135	250	475	—

Note: Exists overstruck on Goa 2 Tanga, KM#68.

KM# 3 2 TANGAS
4.2400 g., Silver **Obv:** Crowned arms divide C and B in dotted circle **Rev:** St. John standing left divides S and T; date divided at bottom

Date	Mintage	Good	VG	F	VF	XF
1653	—	50.00	110	200	425	—

COCHIN

(Cochim)

Cochim was the first European settlement in India. Vasco da Gama founded a trading factory for the Portuguese at this location in 1502. Alfonso d'Albuquerque (who was to be the second governor of Portuguese settlements in India, 1509-1515) built a fort here in 1503. This location was an important Portuguese center until the British withdrew when the Dutch attacked in 1663. The town was retaken by the British in 1795.

COLONY

HAMMERED COINAGE

KM# 15 XERAFIM
10.2300 g., Silver **Obv:** Crowned arms divides CO in inner circle **Rev:** Numerals of date in angles of cross

Date	Mintage	Good	VG	F	VF	XF
1661	—	400	750	1,250	2,000	—

DAMAO

(Daman)

A city located 100 miles north of Bombay. It was captured by the Portuguese in 1559. A mint was opened in Damao in 1611. This mint continued in operation until 1854. While important to early Portuguese trade, Damao dwindled as time passed. It was annexed to India in 1962.

MONETARY SYSTEM
375 Bazacucos = 300 Reis
300 Reis = 1 Pardao
60 Reis = 1 Tanga
2 Pardao (Xerafins) = 1 Rupia

COLONY

CAST COINAGE

KM# 5 BAZARUCO
1.8000 g., Tin

Date	Mintage	Good	VG	F	VF	XF
ND	—	15.00	28.00	50.00	100	—

HAMMERED COINAGE

KM# 1 BAZARUCO
2.8000 g., Copper **Subject:** Philip II **Obv:** Large crowned arms divide IB; all in beaded circle **Rev:** Cross with stars in angles in beaded circle

Date	Mintage	Good	VG	F	VF	XF
ND(1598-1621)	—	18.00	30.00	55.00	110	—

KM# 2 BAZARUCO
2.7000 g., Copper **Obv:** Small crowned arms divide IB without outer circle **Rev:** Cross with stars in angles in beaded circle

Date	Mintage	Good	VG	F	VF	XF
ND(1598-1621)	—	12.00	25.00	50.00	100	—

KM# 3 BAZARUCO
2.4000 g., Copper **Obv:** Small crowned arms divide BI in beaded circle **Rev:** Cross with stars in angles in beaded circle

Date	Mintage	Good	VG	F	VF	XF
ND(1598-1621)	—	—	—	—	—	—

KM# 4 3 BAZARUCOS
9.0000 g., Copper **Obv:** Crowned arms divide IIIB in circle **Rev:** Cross with stars in angles in beaded circle

Date	Mintage	Good	VG	F	VF	XF
ND(1598-1621)	—	60.00	120	200	400	—

KM# 6 5 BAZARUCOS
14.6000 g., Copper **Subject:** Philip II **Obv:** Crowned arms in inner circle divide VB; legend in outer circle **Rev:** Cross with stars in angles in inner circle; legend in outer circle

Date	Mintage	Good	VG	F	VF	XF
1611	—	80.00	160	285	550	—

DIU

A district in Western India formerly belonging to Portugal. It is 170 miles northwest of Bombay on the Kathiawar peninsula. The Portuguese settled here and built a fort in 1535. A mint was opened in 1685 and was closed in 1859. As with Damao, the importance of Diu diminished with the passage of time. It was annexed to India in 1962.

MONETARY SYSTEM

750 Bazarucos = 600 Reis
40 Atia = 10 Tanga = 1 Rupia

COLONY

HAMMERED COINAGE

KM# 1 1/2 BAZARUCO

2.8000 g., Copper **Obv:** Crowned arms divide DO **Rev:** Numerals of date in angles of cross potent

Date	Mintage	Good	VG	F	VF	XF
1686	—	10.00	20.00	35.00	60.00	—
1698	—	10.00	20.00	35.00	60.00	—

KM# 2 BAZARUCO

4.5700 g., Copper **Subject:** Peter, as Prince Regent **Obv:** Crowned arms divide DO **Rev:** Numerals of date in angles of cross potent

Date	Mintage	Good	VG	F	VF	XF
1668	—	15.00	30.00	50.00	95.00	—
1670	—	8.50	17.50	27.50	48.00	—
1670 Retrograde 7	—	15.00	25.00	40.00	70.00	—
1678	—	8.50	17.50	27.50	48.00	—
1678	—	10.00	20.00	35.00	60.00	—
1680 Large 8	—	8.50	17.50	30.00	55.00	—
1680 Small 8	—	10.00	20.00	35.00	60.00	—
1682	—	10.00	20.00	35.00	60.00	—

KM# 6 BAZARUCO

7.5000 g., Copper **Subject:** Peter II **Obv:** Crowned medium arms divide DO **Rev:** Numerals of date in angles of cross potent

Date	Mintage	Good	VG	F	VF	XF
1686	—	8.50	17.50	27.50	48.00	—
1688	—	10.00	20.00	35.00	60.00	—
1689	—	8.50	17.50	27.50	48.00	—
1697	—	8.50	17.50	30.00	55.00	—
1698	—	8.50	17.50	30.00	55.00	—

KM# 10 BAZARUCO

6.9700 g., Copper **Obv:** Crowned small arms **Rev:** Numerals of date in angles of cross

Date	Mintage	Good	VG	F	VF	XF
1699	—	10.00	20.00	35.00	60.00	—

KM# 11 BAZARUCO

7.5000 g., Copper **Obv:** Crowned large arms divide D (retrograde), O in beaded circle **Rev:** Numerals of date in angles of cross potent

Date	Mintage	Good	VG	F	VF	XF
1700	—	10.00	20.00	35.00	60.00	—

KM# 3 2 BAZARUCOS

6.2000 g., Copper **Subject:** Peter, as Prince Regent **Obv:** Crowned small arms divide DO in inner circle **Rev:** Numerals of date in angles of cross potent

Date	Mintage	Good	VG	F	VF	XF
1679	—	20.00	50.00	90.00	180	—

KM# 7 2 BAZARUCOS

6.8000 g., Copper **Subject:** Peter II **Obv:** Crowned small arms divide DO in plain circle **Rev:** Numerals of date in angles of cross potent

Date	Mintage	Good	VG	F	VF	XF
1686	—	15.00	30.00	50.00	110	—

KM# 12 2 BAZARUCOS

8.2000 g., Copper **Obv:** Crowned large arms divide DO in plain circle **Rev:** Numerals of date in angles of cross potent

Date	Mintage	Good	VG	F	VF	XF
1700	—	12.50	25.00	45.00	100	—

KM# 4 1/2 XERAFIM

5.8900 g., Silver **Ruler:** Peter II **Obv:** Crude crowned arms in branches **Rev:** Voided floreated cross

Date	Mintage	Good	VG	F	VF	XF
ND(1683-1706)	—	80.00	160	285	475	—

KM# A4 1/2 XERAFIM

5.0000 g., Silver **Subject:** Peter II **Obv:** Crowned arms divide DO in circle **Rev:** Numerals of date in angles of cross in circle

Date	Mintage	Good	VG	F	VF	XF
1684	—	175	325	575	1,000	—
1690	—	175	325	575	1,000	—
1691	—	175	325	575	1,000	—
1692	—	175	325	575	1,000	—
1694	—	175	325	575	1,000	—
1697	—	175	325	575	1,000	—

KM# 5 XERAFIM

11.4700 g., Silver **Ruler:** Peter II **Obv:** Crowned arms in branches **Rev:** Voided floreated cross

Date	Mintage	Good	VG	F	VF	XF
ND(1683-1706)	—	65.00	125	225	375	—

KM# 8 XERAFIM

10.6300 g., Silver **Ruler:** Peter II **Obv:** Crowned arms divide DO within circle **Rev:** Numerals of date in angles of cross within circle

Date	Mintage	Good	VG	F	VF	XF
1684	—	70.00	150	250	500	—
1686	—	70.00	150	250	500	—
1688	—	70.00	150	250	500	—
1690	—	65.00	135	235	450	—
1691	—	70.00	150	250	500	—
1692	—	70.00	150	250	500	—
1693	—	70.00	150	250	500	—
1694	—	70.00	150	250	500	—
1695	—	70.00	150	250	500	—
1696	—	65.00	135	235	450	—
1697	—	65.00	135	235	450	—
1698	—	70.00	150	250	500	—
1699	—	65.00	135	235	450	—
1700	—	70.00	150	250	500	—

KM# 9 2 XERAFINS

21.3600 g., Silver **Subject:** Peter II **Obv:** Crowned arms divide OD (retrograde) in plain circle **Rev:** Numerals of date in angles of cross in plain circle

Date	Mintage	Good	VG	F	VF	XF
1688	—	250	450	750	1,450	—

GOA

Goa was the capitol of Portuguese India and is located 250 miles south of Bombay on the west coast of India. It was taken by Albuquerque in 1510. A mint was established immediately and operated until closed by the British in 1869. Later coins were struck at Calcutta and Bombay. Goa was annexed by India in 1962.

MONETARY SYSTEM

375 Bazarucos = 300 Reis
240 Reis = 1 Pardao
2 Xerafim = 1 Rupia

NOTE: The silver Xerafim was equal to the silver Pardao, but the gold Xerafim varied according to fluctuations in the gold/silver ratio.

COLONY

CAST COINAGE

KM# 51 BAZARUCO

3.1000 g., Tin **Obv:** Crowned simple arms divide GA in plain circle **Rev:** Astrolabe in plain circle

Date	Mintage	Good	VG	F	VF	XF
ND(1598-1621)	—	20.00	40.00	65.00	130	—

KM# 52 BAZARUCO

2.1000 g., Tin **Obv:** Crowned arms divide GA in plain circle **Rev:** Cross with stars in angles in plain circle

Date	Mintage	Good	VG	F	VF	XF
ND(1598-1621)	—	10.00	20.00	35.00	85.00	—

HAMMERED COINAGE

KM# 48 1/4 BAZARUCO

1.2000 g., Copper **Obv:** Arms in circle **Rev:** Astrolabe in circle

Date	Mintage	Good	VG	F	VF	XF
ND(1598-1621)	—	20.00	35.00	70.00	175	—

KKM# 50 BAZARUCO

3.1000 g., Copper **Subject:** Philip II **Obv:** Crowned arms divide GA in circle **Rev:** Globe in beaded circle

Date	Mintage	Good	VG	F	VF	XF
ND(1598-1621)	—	22.00	45.00	75.00	120	—

KM# 42 2 BAZARUCOS

6.9000 g., Copper **Obv:** F **Rev:** R

Date	Mintage	Good	VG	F	VF	XF
ND	—	8.00	16.00	28.00	45.00	—

KM# 43 2 BAZARUCOS

9.1000 g., Copper **Obv:** Retrograde K **Rev:** Retrograde R

Date	Mintage	Good	VG	F	VF	XF
ND	—	10.00	20.00	35.00	55.00	—

KM# 53 10 BAZARUCOS

0.2800 g., Silver **Subject:** Philip II **Obv:** Crowned arms divide GA in circle

Date	Mintage	Good	VG	F	VF	XF
ND Rare	—	—	—	—	—	—

KM# 54 30 BAZARUCOS
0.7700 g., Silver **Obv:** Crowned arms divide GA in circle **Rev:** 30 in circle

Date	Mintage	Good	VG	F	VF	XF
ND Rare	—	—	—	—	—	—

KM# 44 1/2 TANGA (30 Reis)
1.8000 g., Silver **Obv:** Crowned arms divide GA in circle **Rev:** Standing figure of St. Philip divides MA

Date	Mintage	Good	VG	F	VF	XF
ND	—	40.00	80.00	145	225	—

KM# 55 1/2 TANGA (30 Reis)
1.4900 g., Silver **Subject:** Philip II **Obv:** Crowned arms divide MT in inner circle **Rev:** Latin cross in inner circle

Date	Mintage	Good	VG	F	VF	XF
ND Rare	—	—	—	—	—	—

KM# 58 1/2 TANGA (30 Reis)
1.0200 g., Silver **Subject:** Philip III **Obv:** Crowned arms divide GA in circle **Rev:** Standing figure of St. Philip with cross at left, F at right

Date	Mintage	Good	VG	F	VF	XF
ND	—	100	200	325	550	—

KM# 59 1/2 TANGA (30 Reis)
0.9800 g., Silver **Rev:** MTA monogram in circle

Date	Mintage	Good	VG	F	VF	XF
ND	—	50.00	100	200	350	—

KM# 64 1/2 TANGA (30 Reis)
0.9000 g., Silver **Subject:** John IV **Obv:** Crowned arms divide AD in circle **Rev:** MTA monogram in circle

Date	Mintage	Good	VG	F	VF	XF
ND	—	125	250	400	725	—

KM# 69 1/2 TANGA (30 Reis)
1.0400 g., Silver **Obv:** Standing figure of St. John divides SI and date

Date	Mintage	Good	VG	F	VF	XF
ND	—	85.00	165	325	—	—

KM# 75 1/2 TANGA (30 Reis)
0.9000 g., Silver **Subject:** Peter as Prince Regent **Obv:** Crowned arms divide GA in circle **Rev:** Numerals of date in angles of cross

Date	Mintage	Good	VG	F	VF	XF
1678	—	150	300	500	825	—

KM# 79 1/2 TANGA (30 Reis)
0.9400 g., Silver **Subject:** Peter II **Rev:** Numerals of date in angles of cross in circle

Date	Mintage	Good	VG	F	VF	XF
1691	—	100	200	350	650	—

KM# 45 TANGA (60 Reis)
3.7000 g., Silver **Obv:** Crowned arms divide GA in beaded circle **Rev:** Standing figure of St. Philip divides TA in circle

Date	Mintage	Good	VG	F	VF	XF
ND	—	70.00	145	265	400	—

KM# 56 TANGA (60 Reis)
3.0000 g., Silver **Subject:** Philip II **Obv:** Crowned arms divide IT in inner circle **Rev:** Latin cross on mound in inner circle

Date	Mintage	Good	VG	F	VF	XF
ND Rare	—	—	—	—	—	—

KM# 63 TANGA (60 Reis)
2.1700 g., Silver **Subject:** Philip III **Obv:** Crowned arms divide GA in circle **Rev:** Standing figure of St. Philip divides date and SF

Date	Mintage	Good	VG	F	VF	XF
1634	—	85.00	175	325	550	—
1640	—	50.00	100	200	375	—
1641	—	50.00	100	200	375	—

KM# 65 TANGA (60 Reis)
2.2000 g., Silver **Obv:** Crowned arms divide GA **Rev:** Gridiron of St. Lawrence divides date; crown below

Date	Mintage	Good	VG	F	VF	XF
1640	—	40.00	85.00	175	325	—

KM# 70 TANGA (60 Reis)
1.5500 g., Silver **Subject:** John IV **Obv:** Crowned arms divide GA in circle **Rev:** Standing figure of St. John divides SI and date

Date	Mintage	Good	VG	F	VF	XF
1644	—	70.00	145	265	450	—

KM# 71 TANGA (60 Reis)
1.9400 g., Silver **Rev:** Numerals of date in angles of cross in circle

Date	Mintage	Good	VG	F	VF	XF
1650	—	40.00	80.00	150	275	—
1654	—	60.00	120	225	425	—
1655	—	60.00	120	225	425	—

KM# 74 TANGA (60 Reis)
1.9800 g., Silver **Subject:** Alfonso VI

Date	Mintage	Good	VG	F	VF	XF
1661	—	100	200	350	650	—
1662	—	100	200	350	600	—
1663	—	100	200	350	650	—
1664	—	100	200	350	650	—
1676	—	40.00	80.00	135	270	—
1677	—	40.00	80.00	135	270	—
1681	—	40.00	80.00	135	270	—
1682	—	40.00	80.00	135	270	—
1683	—	45.00	90.00	155	300	—
1684	—	35.00	70.00	120	250	—
1686	—	35.00	70.00	120	250	—
1687	—	30.00	60.00	100	220	—
1691	—	30.00	60.00	100	220	—
1692	—	30.00	60.00	100	220	—
1698	—	35.00	70.00	120	250	—

KM# 66 2 TANGAS
4.2500 g., Silver **Subject:** John IV **Obv:** Crowned arms divide GA in circle **Rev:** Standing figure of St. Philip divides SF and date

Date	Mintage	Good	VG	F	VF	XF
1640	—	75.00	135	225	375	—
1641	—	65.00	125	200	350	—

KM# 68 2 TANGAS
4.4000 g., Silver **Rev:** Standing figure of St. John divides SI and date

Date	Mintage	Good	VG	F	VF	XF
1642	—	45.00	90.00	165	300	—
1643	—	45.00	90.00	165	300	—
1649	—	50.00	100	180	325	—
1650	—	30.00	65.00	120	220	—
1651	—	35.00	75.00	135	250	—
1652	—	25.00	55.00	110	205	—
1653	—	50.00	100	120	325	—
1655	—	50.00	100	120	325	—
1656	—	50.00	100	120	325	—

KM# A68 2 TANGAS
4.4000 g., Silver **Rev:** Gridiron of St. Lawrence divides date, crown below

Date	Mintage	Good	VG	F	VF	XF
1645	—	60.00	120	240	400	—

KM# 72 1/2 XERAFIM (150 Reis)
5.3400 g., Silver **Subject:** John IV **Obv:** Crowned arms divide GA in circle **Rev:** Numerals of date in angles of cross in circle

Date	Mintage	Good	VG	F	VF	XF
1650	—	50.00	100	200	375	—
1665	—	200	400	750	1,400	—
1666	—	250	525	950	1,700	—
1668	—	250	525	950	1,700	—
1672	—	50.00	100	200	375	—
1673	—	35.00	65.00	135	275	—
1680	—	35.00	65.00	135	275	—
1681	—	30.00	60.00	120	220	—
1682	—	30.00	60.00	120	220	—
1683	—	30.00	60.00	120	220	—
1684	—	30.00	60.00	120	220	—
1685	—	20.00	40.00	85.00	180	—
1686	—	22.50	45.00	100	205	—
1688	—	20.00	40.00	85.00	180	—
1690	—	20.00	40.00	85.00	180	—
1693	—	20.00	40.00	85.00	180	—
1694	—	20.00	40.00	85.00	180	—
1697	—	20.00	40.00	85.00	180	—
1699	—	20.00	40.00	85.00	180	—
1700	—	25.00	50.00	110	220	—

KM# A45 XERAFIM
19.2000 g., Silver **Obv:** Crowned arms divide GA in circle **Rev:** Standing figure of St. Philip right divides SF

Date	Mintage	Good	VG	F	VF	XF
ND Rare	—	—	—	—	—	—

KM# 67 XERAFIM
11.0000 g., Silver **Subject:** John IV **Obv:** Crowned arms divide GA in inner circle **Rev:** Standing figure of St. Philip left divides SF and date

Date	Mintage	Good	VG	F	VF	XF
ND	—	200	400	750	1,400	—
1641	—	300	650	1,150	1,950	—
1642	—	125	275	525	1,000	—
1643	—	200	400	750	1,400	—
1644	—	200	400	750	1,400	—
1649	—	125	275	525	1,000	—

KM# 73 XERAFIM

10.4400 g., Silver **Obv:** Crowned arms divide GA in inner circle **Rev:** Numerals of date in angles of cross in circle

Date	Mintage	Good	VG	F	VF	XF
1650	—	60.00	125	300	550	—
1651	—	60.00	125	300	550	—
1652	—	75.00	150	325	600	—
1653	—	65.00	135	310	575	—
1654	—	50.00	110	275	525	—
1655	—	50.00	110	275	525	—
1656	—	50.00	110	275	525	—
1657	—	50.00	110	275	525	—
1659	—	250	450	750	1,400	—
1664	—	250	450	750	1,400	—
1668	—	250	450	750	1,400	—
1669	—	45.00	90.00	200	375	—
1671	—	35.00	75.00	150	300	—
1672	—	35.00	75.00	150	300	—
1673	—	35.00	75.00	150	300	—
1675	—	35.00	75.00	150	300	—
1676	—	35.00	75.00	150	300	—
1678	—	35.00	75.00	150	300	—
1681	—	30.00	65.00	125	275	—
1682	—	30.00	65.00	125	275	—
1683	—	30.00	65.00	125	275	—

KM# 76 XERAFIM

0.6800 g., Gold **Subject:** Alfonso VI **Obv:** Crowned arms divide GA in inner circle **Rev:** Numerals of date in angles of cross in inner circle

Date	Mintage	Good	VG	F	VF	XF
1678	—	700	1,200	2,000	4,200	—
1679	—	700	1,200	2,000	4,200	—
1680	—	700	1,200	2,000	4,200	—

KM# 77 XERAFIM

10.5700 g., Silver **Subject:** Peter II

Date	Mintage	Good	VG	F	VF	XF
1683	—	45.00	90.00	165	325	—
1684	—	32.50	75.00	125	250	—
1685	—	32.50	75.00	125	250	—
1686	—	30.00	60.00	60.00	220	—
1687	—	30.00	60.00	60.00	220	—
1688	—	30.00	60.00	60.00	220	—
1689	—	30.00	60.00	60.00	220	—
1690	—	30.00	60.00	60.00	220	—
1691	—	30.00	60.00	60.00	220	—
1700	—	40.00	85.00	85.00	290	—

KM# 60 1/2 PATACAO

8.6300 g., Silver **Subject:** Philip III **Obv:** Crowned arms divide GA in inner circle **Rev:** Cross fleury in inner circle

Date	Mintage	Good	VG	F	VF	XF
1630 Rare	—	—	—	—	—	—

KM# 61 PATACAO

17.2900 g., Silver **Subject:** Philip III **Obv:** Crowned arms divide GA in inner circle, date below **Rev:** Cross fleury in inner circle

Date	Mintage	Good	VG	F	VF	XF
1630 Rare	—	—	—	—	—	—
1631 Rare	—	—	—	—	—	—

KM# 78 2 XERAFINS

21.0000 g., Silver **Subject:** Peter II **Obv:** Crowned arms divide GA in circle **Rev:** Numerals of date in angles of cross in circle
Note: This issue is often encountered with various local countermarks.

Date	Mintage	Good	VG	F	VF	XF
1685	—	85.00	175	325	600	—
1686	—	85.00	175	325	600	—
1694	—	85.00	175	325	600	—
1700	—	100	200	350	650	—

KM# 46 5 XERAFINS

3.3800 g., Gold **Rev:** Standing figure of St. Thomas left divides S and T

Date	Mintage	Good	VG	F	VF	XF
ND Rare	—	—	—	—	—	—

KM# 57 5 XERAFINS

3.4600 g., Gold **Subject:** Philip II **Obv:** Crowned arms divide GA in inner circle; legend around border **Rev:** Standing figure of St. Thomas left in inner circle; legend around border

Date	Mintage	Good	VG	F	VF	XF
1616 Rare	—	—	—	—	—	—

Note: Hess-Divo Romanones Auction 269 10-96 GVF realized $19,055

KM# 62 5 XERAFINS

3.6000 g., Gold **Subject:** Philip III

Date	Mintage	Good	VG	F	VF	XF
1632	—	550	1,400	3,000	5,100	—
1633	—	550	1,400	3,000	5,100	—
1634	—	550	1,400	3,000	5,100	—
1635	—	550	1,400	3,000	5,100	—
1650 Rare	—	—	—	—	—	—
1651 Rare	—	—	—	—	—	—

Note: Hess-Divo Romanones Auction 269 10-96 VF realized $13,255

Date	Mintage	Good	VG	F	VF	XF
1660 Rare	—	—	—	—	—	—
1670 Rare	—	—	—	—	—	—
1677 Rare	—	—	—	—	—	—
1678 Rare	—	—	—	—	—	—
1680 Rare	—	—	—	—	—	—
1681 Rare	—	—	—	—	—	—
1682 Rare	—	—	—	—	—	—
	—	475	1,200	2,400	4,800	—

TOKEN COINAGE

KM# Tn1 BAZARUCO

7.2900 g., Copper **Obv:** Crowned arms between symbols, date below **Rev:** Cross in inner circle; legend around border
Note: Antonio Telles de Menezes, issuer of this token was captain of Diu and later Governor of all Portuguese India (1639-1640). Many varieties exist in the legends and shield.

Date	Mintage	Good	VG	F	VF	XF
1626	—	25.00	50.00	100	185	—
1627	—	25.00	50.00	100	185	—
1628	—	25.00	50.00	100	185	—

IRAN

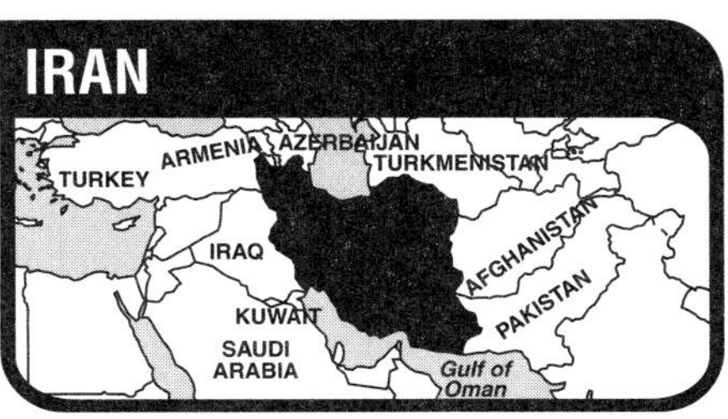

Iran (historically known as Persia until 1931AD) is one of the world's most ancient and resilient nations. Strategically astride the lower land gate to Asia, it has been conqueror and conquered, sovereign nation and vassal state, ever emerging from its periods of glory or travail with its culture and political individuality intact. Iran (Persia) was a powerful empire under Cyrus the Great (600-529 B.C.), its borders extending from the Indus to the Nile. It has also been conquered by the predatory empires of antique and recent times - Assyrian, Medean, Macedonian, Seljuq, Turk, Mongol - and more recently been coveted by Russia, the Third Reich and Great Britain. Revolts against the absolute power of the Persian shahs resulted in the establishment of a constitutional monarchy in1906.

RULERS

Abbas I, AH997-1039/1588-1629AD
Safi I, AH1038-52/1629-42AD
Abbas II, AH1052-77/1642-66AD
Safi II, AH1077-79/1666-68AD
Sulayman I, AH1079-1105/1668-94AD
Husayn I, AH1105-35/1694-1722AD

MINT NAMES

Abu Shahr (Bushire)	ابو سهر
Ardanush	اردنوش
Ardebil (Ardabil)	اردبيل
Astarabad (Iran)	استراباد
Baghdad (Iraq)	بغداد
Bandar Abbas	بندر عباس
Bandar Abu Shahr	بندر ابو شهر
Basra (al-Basrah, Iraq)	البصرة
Behbahan (Bihbihan)	بهبهان
Bahkar (Afghanistan)	بكهر بكّر
Borujerd	بروجرد
Dadiyan	داديان
Darband	دربند
Dawraq	دورق
Dehdasht	دهدشت
Dezful	دزفول

Eravan (Iravan, Armenia)	ايروان
Farahabad	فرح اباد
Fuman	فومان
Ganjeh (Ganja, Azerbaijan)	گنجه
Gilan	گنلان
Hamadan	همدان
Herat, (Afghanistan)	هرات هراة
Huwayza	حويزة
Iravan (Yeravan, Armenia)	ايروان
Isfahan (Esfahan)	اصفهان
Jelou (Army Mint)	جلو
Kashan	كاشان
Kirman (Kerman)	كرمان
Kirmanshahan (Kermanshah)	كرمانساهان
Khoy (Khoi, Khuy)	خوي
Lahijan	لاهيجان
Lahore (Afghanistan)	لاهور
Maragheh	مراغة
Mashhad (Meshad Iman Rida)	مشهد امام رضى
Mazandaran	مازندران
Nahawand	نهاوند
Nakhjawan (Azerbaijan)	نخجوان
Naseri	ناصري
Nimruz	نمرز نيمروز
Nukhwi	نخوي
Panahabad (Azerbaijan)	پناه اباد
Peshawar (Afghanistan)	پشاور
Qandahar (Kandahar, Afghanistan)	قندهار
Qazvin	قزوين
Qomm (Kumm, Qumm)	قم
Ra'nash (Ramhurmuz)	رعنش
Rasht	رشت
Rekab (Rikab)	ركاب
Reza'iyeh (Army Mint)	رضائية
Sarakhs	سرخس
Sari	ساري
Sawuj Balagh	ساوج بلاق
Shamakha (Shemakhi, Shimakhi, Azerbaijan)	شماخي شماخه
Shiraz	شيراز
Shirwan (Azerbaijan)	شيروان شروان
Shushtar	شوستر
Simnan (Semnan)	سمنان
Sind (Afghanistan)	سند
Sultanabad	سلطاناباد
Tabaristan (Tabarestan, region N.W. of Iran)	طبرستان
Tabriz	تبريز
Tehran	طهران
Tiflis (Georgia)	تفليس
Tuyserkan	توي سركان
Urumi (Reza'iyeh)	ارمية
Yazd	يزد
Zanjan	زنجان
Zegam	زگام

MONETARY SYSTEM

The Shahi was a fixed unit, first coined in AD1501, equal to 50 Dinars. The Toman, introduced as a unit of account about AH1240 (1824AD) was always fixed at 10,000 Dinars. The value of the Rupee for this period is not known with certainty.

SILVER and GOLD COINAGE

The precious metal monetary system of Qajar Persia prior to the reforms of 1878 was the direct descendant of the Mongol system introduced by Ghazan Mahmud in 1297AD, and was the last example of a medieval Islamic coinage. It is not a modern system, and cannot be understood as such. It is not possible to list types, dates, and mints as for other countries, both because of the nature of the coinage, and because very little research has been done on the series. The following comments should help elucidate its nature.

DENOMINATIONS

In addition to the primary denominations, noted in the last paragraph, fractional pieces were coined, valued at one-eighth, one-fourth, and one-half the primary denomination, usually in much smaller quantities. These were ordinarily struck from the same dies as the larger pieces, sometimes on broad, thin flans, sometimes on thick, dumpy flans. On the smaller coins, the denomination can best be determined only by weighing the coin. The denomination is almost never expressed on the coin!

KINGDOM

Anonymous

HAMMERED COINAGE

Ardebil

KM# 150 FALUS

10.8200 g., Copper **Obv:** Fish in sprays **Rev:** Inscription with value, mint name and date

Date	Mintage	Good	VG	F	VF	XF
AH1052	—	11.50	27.50	45.00	—	—

Eravan

KM# 124 FALUS

11.1900 g., Copper **Obv:** Duck right, branches behind **Rev:** Inscription with value, mint name and date

Date	Mintage	Good	VG	F	VF	XF
AH1040	—	8.00	20.00	35.00	—	—

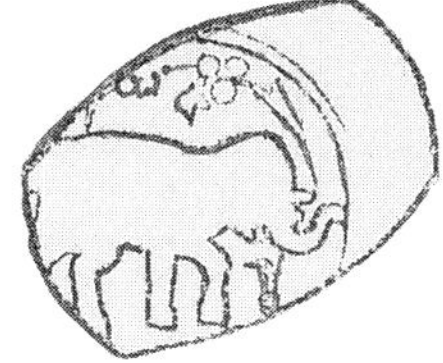

KM# 152 FALUS

10.4200 g., Copper **Obv:** Elephant right, branch behind **Rev:** Inscription with value, mint name and AH date

Date	Mintage	Good	VG	F	VF	XF
AH1057	—	8.00	20.00	35.00	—	—

KM# 154 FALUS

10.5900 g., Copper **Obv:** Lion right, facing **Rev:** Inscription with value, mint name and AH date

Date	Mintage	Good	VG	F	VF	XF
AH1060	—	8.00	20.00	35.00	—	—

KM# B208 FALUS

7.9700 g., Copper **Obv:** Lion left, rayed sunface behind **Rev:** Inscription with value, mint name and AH date

Date	Mintage	Good	VG	F	VF	XF
AH1084	—	8.00	20.00	35.00	—	—

KM# 208 FALUS

8.1300 g., Copper **Obv:** Sheep resting amongst bushes **Rev:** Inscription with value, mint name and AH date

Date	Mintage	Good	VG	F	VF	XF
AH1095	—	8.00	20.00	35.00	—	—

KM# 209 FALUS

9.8500 g., Copper **Obv:** Bird left in bushes **Rev:** Inscription with value, mint name and AH date

Date	Mintage	Good	VG	F	VF	XF
AH1104	—	10.00	25.00	40.00	—	—

KM# 245 FALUS

8.5400 g., Copper **Obv:** Peacock left **Rev:** Inscription with value, mint name and AH date

Date	Mintage	Good	VG	F	VF	XF
AH1108	—	10.00	25.00	40.00	—	—

Ganjah

KM# 126 FALUS

8.9100 g., Copper **Obv:** Goat right, branches behind **Rev:** Inscription with value, mint name and date

Date	Mintage	Good	VG	F	VF	XF
AH1042	—	7.50	18.50	30.00	—	—

KM# A208 FALUS

8.1400 g., Copper **Obv:** Lion (?) left, branches above **Rev:** Inscription with value, mint name and AH date

Date	Mintage	Good	VG	F	VF	XF
AH1081	—	7.50	18.50	30.00	—	—

KM# C208 FALUS

7.7000 g., Copper **Obv:** Lion (?) right, branches above **Rev:** Inscription with mint name and AH date

Date	Mintage	Good	VG	F	VF	XF
AH1088	—	7.50	18.50	30.00	—	—

KM# 241 FALUS

10.6000 g., Copper **Obv:** Lion left **Rev:** Inscription with mint name and AH date

Date	Mintage	Good	VG	F	VF	XF
AH1106	—	7.50	18.50	30.00	—	—

KM# 244 FALUS

4.4600 g., Copper **Obv:** Stag right **Rev:** Inscription with value, mint name and AH date

Date	Mintage	Good	VG	F	VF	XF
AH1108	—	7.50	18.50	30.00	—	—

Hamadan

KM# 128 FALUS

10.7400 g., Copper **Obv:** Bird perched at left, branches behind **Rev:** Inscription with value, mint name and date

Date	Mintage	Good	VG	F	VF	XF
AH1048	—	6.00	15.00	25.00	—	—

KM# D209 FALUS

10.5200 g., Copper **Obv:** Brahma bull left **Rev:** Inscription with value, mint name and AH date

Date	Mintage	Good	VG	F	VF	XF
AH1099	—	6.00	15.00	25.00	—	—

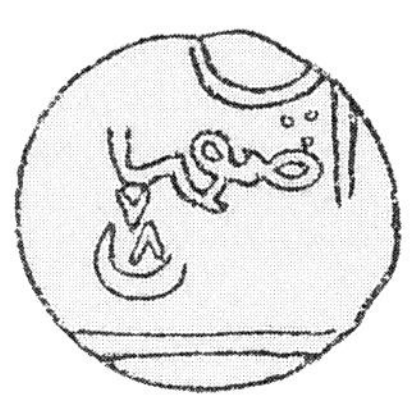

Isfahan

KM# 195 FALUS

7.7100 g., Copper **Obv:** Stag left, branches above **Rev:** Inscription with value, mint name and AH date

Date	Mintage	Good	VG	F	VF	XF
AH1078	—	6.00	15.00	25.00	—	—

Qandahar

KM# 81 FALUS

Copper **Obv:** Sun over lion walking left

Date	Mintage	Good	VG	F	VF	XF
AH1058	—	9.00	15.00	25.00	45.00	—

KM# 82 FALUS

Copper **Obv:** Lion left seizing stag right **Note:** Type 82.

Date	Mintage	Good	VG	F	VF	XF
AH1059	—	11.50	18.50	30.00	55.00	—

KM# 83 FALUS

Copper **Obv:** Sun over lion walking left **Note:** Type 83.

Date	Mintage	Good	VG	F	VF	XF
AH107x	—	9.00	15.00	25.00	45.00	—
AH1085	—	9.00	15.00	25.00	45.00	—
AH1086	—	9.00	15.00	25.00	45.00	—

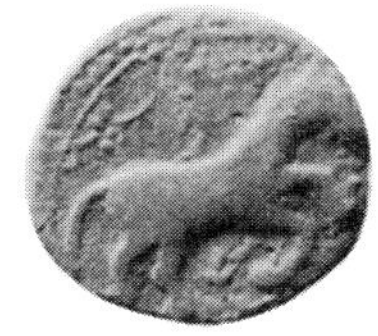

KM# 84 FALUS

Copper **Obv:** Horse galloping right **Note:** Type 84.

Date	Mintage	Good	VG	F	VF	XF
AH1080	—	11.50	18.50	30.00	55.00	—

KM# 85 FALUS

Copper **Obv:** Horse galloping left **Note:** Type 85.

Date	Mintage	Good	VG	F	VF	XF
AH1080	—	11.50	18.50	30.00	55.00	—

KM# 86 FALUS

Copper **Obv:** Camel left **Note:** Type 86.

Date	Mintage	Good	VG	F	VF	XF
AH1082	—	12.50	20.00	35.00	65.00	—

KM# 87 FALUS

Copper **Obv:** Camel right **Note:** Type 87.

Date	Mintage	Good	VG	F	VF	XF
AH1082	—	11.50	18.50	30.00	55.00	—
AH1083	—	11.50	18.50	30.00	55.00	—

KM# 88 FALUS
Copper **Obv:** Flowers at left, two-bladed sabre at center **Note:** Type 88.

Date	Mintage	Good	VG	F	VF	XF
AH1097	—	11.50	18.50	30.00	55.00	—
ND Date effaced	—	9.00	15.00	25.00	45.00	—

KM# 89 FALUS
Copper **Obv:** Sun over lion walking right **Note:** Type 89.

Date	Mintage	Good	VG	F	VF	XF
AH1107	—	9.00	15.00	25.00	45.00	—

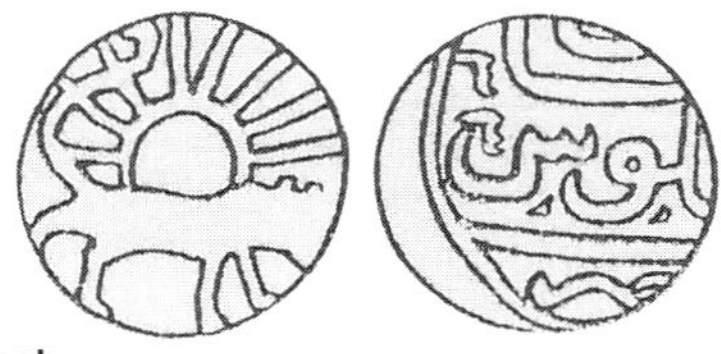

Ra'nash

KM# A112 FALUS
8.6500 g., Copper **Obv:** Rayed sun behind lion at right **Rev:** Inscription with value, mint name and date

Date	Mintage	Good	VG	F	VF	XF
AH1033	—	17.50	42.50	70.00	—	—

KM# 158 FALUS
10.3900 g., Copper **Obv:** Bird standing left, branches behind **Rev:** Value, mint name

Date	Mintage	Good	VG	F	VF	XF
AH1076	—	8.00	20.00	35.00	—	—

Rasht

KM# 151 FALUS
10.7300 g., Copper **Obv:** Peacock right **Rev:** Inscription with value, mint name and AH date

Date	Mintage	Good	VG	F	VF	XF
AH1054	—	10.00	25.00	40.00	—	—

Shamakha

KM# D208 FALUS
5.6600 g., Copper **Obv:** Two upright animals facing each other **Rev:** Inscription with value, mint name and AH date

Date	Mintage	Good	VG	F	VF	XF
AH1091	—	8.00	20.00	35.00	—	—

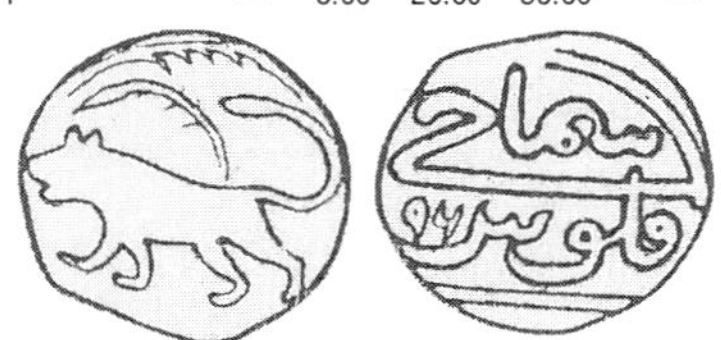

KM# B209 FALUS
8.4500 g., Copper **Obv:** Lion left, branch above **Rev:** Inscription with value, mint name and AH date

Date	Mintage	Good	VG	F	VF	XF
AH1096	—	8.00	20.00	35.00	—	—

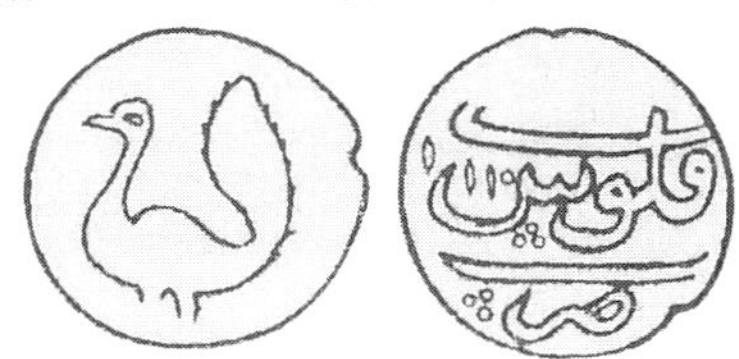

KM# 247 FALUS
10.2100 g., Copper **Obv:** Peacock left **Rev:** Inscription with value, mint name and AH date

Date	Mintage	Good	VG	F	VF	XF
AH1110	—	8.00	20.00	35.00	—	—

Tabriz

KM# 127 FALUS
10.9500 g., Copper **Obv:** Peacock right, branches behind **Rev:** Inscription with value, mint name and date

Date	Mintage	Good	VG	F	VF	XF
AH1048	—	11.00	27.50	45.00	—	—

KM# 129 FALUS
10.5700 g., Copper **Obv:** Elephant right, branches behind **Rev:** Inscription with value, mint name and date

Date	Mintage	Good	VG	F	VF	XF
AH1051	—	10.00	25.00	40.00	—	—

KM# 101 FALUS
Copper **Obv:** Elephant right **Note:** Type 101.

Date	Mintage	Good	VG	F	VF	XF
AH1051	—	18.00	30.00	50.00	90.00	—

KM# 155 FALUS
9.5500 g., Copper **Obv:** Bird attacking animal right **Rev:** Inscription with value, mint name and AH date

Date	Mintage	Good	VG	F	VF	XF
AH1062	—	7.50	18.50	30.00	—	—

KM# 156 FALUS
9.8100 g., Copper **Obv:** Peacock right **Rev:** Inscription with value, mint name and AH date

Date	Mintage	Good	VG	F	VF	XF
AH1069	—	6.00	15.00	25.00	—	—

KM# 157 FALUS
9.7800 g., Copper **Obv:** Bramabull right **Rev:** Value, mint name

Date	Mintage	Good	VG	F	VF	XF
AH1072	—	6.00	15.00	25.00	—	—

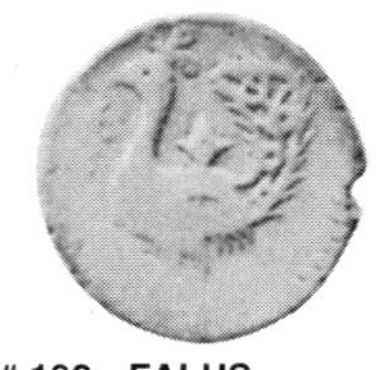

KM# 102 FALUS
Copper **Obv:** Peacock left **Note:** Type 102.

Date	Mintage	Good	VG	F	VF	XF
AH1081	—	18.00	30.00	55.00	90.00	—

KM# 103 FALUS
Copper **Obv:** Lion left and sun **Note:** Type 103.

Date	Mintage	Good	VG	F	VF	XF
AH(10)85	—	15.00	25.00	40.00	70.00	—

KM# 104 FALUS
Copper **Obv:** Brahma bull right, branch below in wreath border **Note:** Type 104.

Date	Mintage	Good	VG	F	VF	XF
AH1095	—	15.00	25.00	40.00	70.00	—

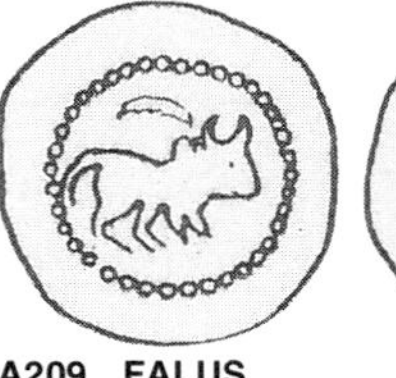

KM# A209 FALUS
10.8700 g., Copper **Obv:** Brama bull right **Rev:** Inscription with value, mint name and AH date

Date	Mintage	Good	VG	F	VF	XF
AH1095	—	6.00	15.00	25.00	—	—

KM# 246 FALUS
10.4700 g., Copper **Obv:** Large animal right, palm tree behind **Rev:** Inscription with value, mint name and AH date

Date	Mintage	Good	VG	F	VF	XF
AH1108	—	6.00	15.00	25.00	—	—

KM# 105 FALUS
Copper **Obv:** Brahma bull right, fish below **Note:** Type 105.

Date	Mintage	Good	VG	F	VF	XF
AH1112	—	15.00	25.00	40.00	70.00	—

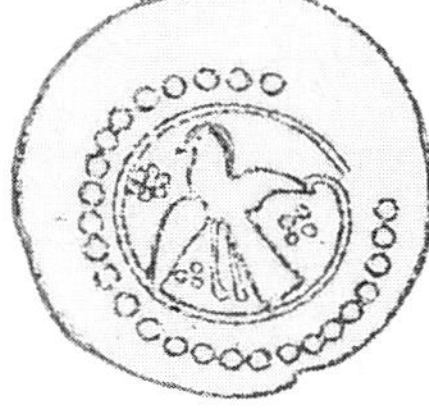

Urumi

KM# 153 FALUS
8.3200 g., Copper **Obv:** Dove in flight **Rev:** Mint name

Date	Mintage	Good	VG	F	VF	XF
AH1058	—	11.50	27.50	45.00	—	—

KM# C209 FALUS
15.8100 g., Copper **Obv:** Lion left, rayed sunface behind **Rev:** Inscription with value, mint name and AH date

Date	Mintage	Good	VG	F	VF	XF
AH1098	—	11.50	27.50	45.00	—	—

Abbas I

AH997-1039 / 1588-1629AD

The enthronement of Shah Abbas I occurred in the last part of the month of Dhu'l-Hijja 995, but his official date of accession is reckoned as AH996, which commenced a few days later. Abbas rescued the Iranian empire from the throes of Turkish and Uzbek invasions, bringing it to its apogee under Safavid rule. He died of natural causes on the 19th of January, 1629.

There were many coin types for the reign, but they have never been properly studied. The last type was introduced in AH1011 (1602-03), and consists of the short legend on the obverse, *Abbas bande-ye Shah-e Velayat*, "Abbas, servant of the king of velayat", plus date and mint. The term, "king of the velayat", is an epithet of the fourth caliph, Ali, son of Abu Talib, who ruled from 656-661AD. This type has been designated Type D in the listing. Coins of Type D are generally well struck, though often off-center. Prices are for attractively struck pieces with minimal weak areas.

Type M. A local type of Mazandaran mint, with obverse legend the distich, *Az bahr-e khayr in sekke-ra kalb-e Ali Abbas zad*, "For the sake of goodness, Abbas, the dog of Ali, struck this coin". The mint name is often omitted from the die.

Gold coins of Type D remain elusive, and none are attested dated after AH1019. The resumption of regular gold coinage does not seem to have begun until AH1127, more than a century later. A few gold coins of intermediary years are assumed to be presentation prestige issues. Imported Ottoman sultanis and Venetian ducats, which shared a common standard with the ashrafi, were in general use.

NOTE: For mints known from dated specimens, specimens with dates off flan or undated specimens are worth about 50% less than dated specimens. The same applies to other denominations of this reign. This applies to all types of the 18th century. Coins lacking both date and mints are of still less value, generally about 40-50% of the most common date and mint of the type.

HAMMERED COINAGE

Ardebil

KM# 112.1 SHAHI (50 Dinars)

1.9200 g., Silver

Date	Mintage	VG	F	VF	XF	Unc
AH1025	—	12.00	30.00	45.00	65.00	—

Eravan

KM# 112.3 SHAHI (50 Dinars)

1.9200 g., Silver

Date	Mintage	VG	F	VF	XF	Unc
AH1024	—	12.00	30.00	45.00	65.00	—

Farahabad

KM# 112.2 SHAHI (50 Dinars)

1.9200 g., Silver

Date	Mintage	VG	F	VF	XF	Unc
ND	—	18.00	42.00	75.00	100	—

Herat

KM# 112.4 SHAHI (50 Dinars)

1.9200 g., Silver

Date	Mintage	VG	F	VF	XF	Unc
ND	—	18.00	42.00	70.00	95.00	—

Isfahan

KM# 112.5 SHAHI (50 Dinars)

1.9200 g., Silver

Date	Mintage	VG	F	VF	XF	Unc
AH1011	—	7.00	18.00	33.00	55.00	—
AH1022	—	7.00	18.00	33.00	55.00	—
AH1033	—	7.00	18.00	33.00	55.00	—
AH1034	—	7.00	18.00	33.00	55.00	—

Rasht

KM# 112.6 SHAHI (50 Dinars)

1.9200 g., Silver

Date	Mintage	VG	F	VF	XF	Unc
AH1022	—	6.00	18.00	33.00	55.00	—
AH1024	—	11.00	33.50	50.00	70.00	—
AH1030	—	6.00	18.00	33.00	55.00	—

Tabriz

KM# 112.7 SHAHI (50 Dinars)

1.9200 g., Silver

Date	Mintage	VG	F	VF	XF	Unc
AH1028	—	7.00	18.00	33.00	55.00	—

Urdu

KM# 112.8 SHAHI (50 Dinars)

1.9200 g., Silver

Date	Mintage	VG	F	VF	XF	Unc
ND	—	18.00	42.00	70.00	95.00	—

Baghdad

KM# 113.1 2 SHAHI (Mahmudi)

3.8400 g., Silver

Date	Mintage	VG	F	VF	XF	Unc
ND	—	14.00	36.00	48.00	65.00	—

Behbehán

KM# 113.2 2 SHAHI (Mahmudi)

3.8400 g., Silver

Date	Mintage	VG	F	VF	XF	Unc
AH1018	—	12.00	30.00	48.00	70.00	—
AH1029	—	12.00	30.00	48.00	70.00	—

Dawraq

KM# 113.3 2 SHAHI (Mahmudi)

3.8400 g., Silver

Date	Mintage	VG	F	VF	XF	Unc
AH1015	—	7.00	18.00	30.00	55.00	—

Isfahan

KM# 113.4 2 SHAHI (Mahmudi)

3.8400 g., Silver

Date	Mintage	VG	F	VF	XF	Unc
AH1023	—	7.00	18.00	33.00	55.00	—
AH102(4)	—	7.00	18.00	27.50	48.00	—
AH1034	—	10.00	25.00	36.00	55.00	—

Mashhad

KM# 113.5 2 SHAHI (Mahmudi)

3.8400 g., Silver

Date	Mintage	VG	F	VF	XF	Unc
AH10(2)7	—	10.00	25.00	36.00	55.00	—

Ramhurmuz

KM# 113.6 2 SHAHI (Mahmudi)

3.8400 g., Silver

Date	Mintage	VG	F	VF	XF	Unc
AH1031	—	12.00	30.00	48.00	70.00	—

Tabriz

KM# 127.7 2 SHAHI (Mahmudi)

3.8400 g., Silver

Date	Mintage	VG	F	VF	XF	Unc
AH1035	—	—	—	—	—	—

Hamadan

KM# 142.10 ABBASI (Heavy Standard - type 142)

7.6800 g., Silver **Note:** Type C.

Date	Mintage	VG	F	VF	XF	Unc
AH1050	—	—	—	—	—	—

Ardebil

KM# 114.1 ABBASI

7.6800 g., Silver

Date	Mintage	VG	F	VF	XF	Unc
AH1017	—	6.00	15.00	25.00	42.00	—
AH1028	—	6.00	15.00	25.00	42.00	—
AH1029	—	6.00	15.00	25.00	42.00	—
AH1030	—	6.00	15.00	22.50	39.00	—
AH1032	—	6.00	15.00	25.00	42.00	—
AH1035	—	6.00	15.00	25.00	42.00	—
AH1036	—	6.00	15.00	25.00	42.00	—
AH1037	—	6.00	15.00	25.00	42.00	—
AH1038	—	6.00	15.00	25.00	42.00	—

Astarabad

KM# 114.2 ABBASI

7.6800 g., Silver

Date	Mintage	VG	F	VF	XF	Unc
ND	—	10.00	25.00	39.00	55.00	—

Baghdad

KM# 114.3 ABBASI

7.6800 g., Silver

Date	Mintage	VG	F	VF	XF	Unc
AH1031	—	14.00	36.00	48.00	70.00	—
AH1032	—	14.00	36.00	48.00	70.00	—
AH1033	—	14.00	36.00	48.00	70.00	—
AH1035	—	14.00	36.00	48.00	70.00	—

KM# 130.1 ABBASI

7.6800 g., Silver **Note:** Type A.

Date	Mintage	VG	F	VF	XF	Unc
AH1038	—	—	—	—	—	—

Behbehán

KM# 114.4 ABBASI

7.6800 g., Silver

Date	Mintage	VG	F	VF	XF	Unc
AH1029	—	12.00	36.00	55.00	70.00	—
AH1031	—	12.00	36.00	55.00	70.00	—

Dawraq

KM# 114.5 ABBASI

7.6800 g., Silver

Date	Mintage	VG	F	VF	XF	Unc
AH1032	—	8.00	25.00	42.00	65.00	—
AH1038	—	8.00	25.00	42.00	65.00	—

Dezful

KM# 114.6 ABBASI

7.6800 g., Silver

Date	Mintage	VG	F	VF	XF	Unc
AH1031	—	10.00	25.00	42.00	65.00	—

Eravan

KM# 114.7 ABBASI

7.6800 g., Silver

Date	Mintage	VG	F	VF	XF	Unc
AH1021	—	7.00	18.00	27.50	42.00	—
AH1024	—	7.00	18.00	27.50	42.00	—
AH1026	—	6.00	15.00	22.50	39.00	—
AH1027	—	6.00	12.00	18.00	33.00	—
AH1030	—	5.00	12.00	18.00	33.00	—
AH1031	—	6.00	12.00	18.00	33.00	—
AH1032	—	5.00	12.00	18.00	33.00	—
AH1033	—	5.00	12.00	18.00	33.00	—
AH1034	—	5.00	12.00	18.00	33.00	—
AH1035	—	5.00	12.00	18.00	33.00	—
AH1036	—	5.00	12.00	18.00	33.00	—
AH1037	—	5.00	12.00	18.00	33.00	—

KM# 130.3 ABBASI

7.6800 g., Silver **Note:** Type A.

Date	Mintage	VG	F	VF	XF	Unc
AH1038	—	—	—	—	—	—

Farahabad

KM# 114.8 ABBASI

7.6800 g., Silver

Date	Mintage	VG	F	VF	XF	Unc
ND	—	17.00	39.00	65.00	90.00	—
AH1027	—	17.00	39.00	65.00	90.00	—

Ganjah

KM# 130.2 ABBASI

7.6800 g., Silver **Note:** Type A.

Date	Mintage	VG	F	VF	XF	Unc
AH1038	—	—	—	—	—	—

KM# 114.9 ABBASI

7.6800 g., Silver

Date	Mintage	VG	F	VF	XF	Unc
AH1019	—	10.00	25.00	36.00	55.00	—
AH1020	—	10.00	25.00	36.00	55.00	—
AH1029	—	7.00	18.00	27.50	45.00	—
AH1031	—	7.00	18.00	27.50	45.00	—
AH1032	—	7.00	18.00	27.50	45.00	—
AH1036	—	7.00	18.00	27.50	45.00	—

Hamadan

KM# 114.22 ABBASI

7.6800 g., Silver

Date	Mintage	VG	F	VF	XF	Unc
AH1019	—	—	—	—	—	—

Isfahan

KM# 114.10 ABBASI

7.6800 g., Silver

Date	Mintage	VG	F	VF	XF	Unc
AH1017	—	7.00	18.00	27.50	42.00	—
AH1018	—	7.00	18.00	27.50	42.00	—
AH1022	—	7.00	15.00	25.00	39.00	—
AH1024	—	7.00	15.00	25.00	39.00	—
AH1025	—	7.00	15.00	25.00	39.00	—
AH1028	—	6.00	15.00	25.00	39.00	—
AH1030	—	6.00	15.00	25.00	39.00	—
AH1033	—	7.00	15.00	25.00	39.00	—

KM# 130.4 ABBASI

7.6800 g., Silver **Note:** Type A.

Date	Mintage	VG	F	VF	XF	Unc
AH1038	—	—	—	—	—	—

Qazvin

KM# 114.11 ABBASI

7.6800 g., Silver

Date	Mintage	VG	F	VF	XF	Unc
AH1014(?)	—	7.00	18.00	27.50	42.00	—
AH1025	—	7.00	15.00	22.50	39.00	—
AH1027	—	6.00	15.00	22.50	39.00	—
AH1028	—	6.00	15.00	22.50	39.00	—
AH1030	—	6.00	15.00	22.50	39.00	—
AH1037	—	7.00	15.00	22.50	39.00	—

Ramhurmuz

KM# 114.12 ABBASI

7.6800 g., Silver

Date	Mintage	VG	F	VF	XF	Unc
AH1021	—	12.00	30.00	48.00	70.00	—

Rasht

KM# 114.13 ABBASI

7.6800 g., Silver

Date	Mintage	VG	F	VF	XF	Unc
AH1027	—	7.00	18.00	27.50	45.00	—
AH1031	—	7.00	18.00	27.50	45.00	—

Shamakha

KM# 114.21 ABBASI

7.6800 g., Silver

Date	Mintage	VG	F	VF	XF	Unc
AH1015	—	—	—	—	—	—

Shushtar

KM# 114.15 ABBASI

7.6800 g., Silver

Date	Mintage	VG	F	VF	XF	Unc
AH1031	—	8.00	20.00	33.00	55.00	—
AH1034	—	8.00	20.00	33.00	55.00	—

Tabriz

KM# 114.16 ABBASI

7.6800 g., Silver

Date	Mintage	VG	F	VF	XF	Unc
AH1017	—	7.00	18.00	27.50	42.00	—
AH1019	—	7.00	18.00	27.50	42.00	—
AH1021	—	7.00	18.00	27.50	42.00	—
AH1022	—	7.00	18.00	27.50	42.00	—
AH1024	—	7.00	18.00	27.50	42.00	—
AH1026	—	4.00	11.00	16.00	33.00	—
AH1027	—	4.00	11.00	16.00	33.00	—
AH1028	—	4.00	11.00	16.00	33.00	—
AH1030	—	4.00	11.00	16.00	33.00	—
AH1031	—	4.00	11.00	16.00	33.00	—
AH1032	—	4.00	11.00	16.00	33.00	—
AH1033//1032	—	4.00	11.00	16.00	33.00	—
AH1035	—	4.00	11.00	16.00	33.00	—
AH1036	—	4.00	11.00	16.00	33.00	—
AH1037	—	4.00	11.00	16.00	33.00	—
AH1038	—	4.00	11.00	16.00	33.00	—

KM# 130.5 ABBASI

7.6800 g., Silver **Note:** Type A.

Date	Mintage	VG	F	VF	XF	Unc
AH1038	—	—	—	—	—	—

Tehran

KM# 114.17 ABBASI

7.6800 g., Silver

Date	Mintage	VG	F	VF	XF	Unc
AH1011	—	27.50	42.00	70.00	95.00	—

Tiflis

KM# 114.18 ABBASI

7.6800 g., Silver

Date	Mintage	VG	F	VF	XF	Unc
AH1028	—	12.00	30.00	42.00	65.00	—
AH1038	—	12.00	30.00	42.00	65.00	—

KM# 130.6 ABBASI

7.6800 g., Silver **Note:** Type A.

Date	Mintage	VG	F	VF	XF	Unc
AH1039	—	—	—	—	—	—

Urdu

KM# 114.19 ABBASI

7.6800 g., Silver

Date	Mintage	VG	F	VF	XF	Unc
AH1014	—	10.00	25.00	36.00	55.00	—
AH1020	—	10.00	25.00	36.00	55.00	—
AH1023	—	10.00	25.00	39.00	60.00	—
AH1032	—	7.00	18.00	30.00	48.00	—
AH1035	—	7.00	18.00	27.50	45.00	—

Zegam

KM# 114.20 ABBASI

7.6800 g., Silver

Date	Mintage	VG	F	VF	XF	Unc
ND	—	14.00	36.00	50.00	70.00	—

KM# 118.2 ABBASI (type 118)

7.6800 g., Silver **Note:** Without mint name.

Date	Mintage	VG	F	VF	XF	Unc
AH1033	—	7.00	18.00	27.50	48.00	—

Mazandaran

KM# 118.1 ABBASI (type 118)

7.6800 g., Silver

Date	Mintage	VG	F	VF	XF	Unc
AH1037	—	7.00	18.00	30.00	55.00	—

Mashhad

KM# 108 ASHRAFI (Heavy Standard)

3.9000 g., Gold **Rev:** Mintname and epithet in central cartouche

Date	Mintage	VG	F	VF	XF	Unc
AH1014	—	140	170	220	300	—

Qazvín

KM# B116 ASHRAFI (Heavy Standard)

3.9000 g., Gold

Date	Mintage	VG	F	VF	XF	Unc
AH1019	—	160	200	280	400	—

Safi I

AH1038-1952 / 1629-1642AD

Safi I succeeded his grandfather on 23 Jumada II 1038 (February 16, 1629). His rule saw the beginning of a long decline in Safavid power. Baghdad was permanently lost to the Turks during this reign. Safi died on the 12th of May, 1642.

There is no gold coinage known for this reign. There are three types for the silver coinage.

Silver coin types for this reign:

A. Obverse, *Safi bande-ye shah-e velâyat* (known only for the full abbasi).

B. Reverse, *hast az jan gholam-e Shah Safi*, "From his soul, he is the slave of Shah Safi", (reference to the eponymous founder of the Safavid line in the 14th century), plus mint and date.

C. Legend as B but with mint name enclosed within a circle.

H. There is also a local type of Huwayza and other mints in Khuzestan province, derived from Type B of Abbas I, but with the normal inscription of Safi I,as on Type A. There is just one denomination, equivalent to the 2 Shahi, but generally known in commercial records as mahmudi (mahmoodee) or huwayzi.

HAMMERED COINAGE

Local Type of Khuzistan

Dawraq

KM# 147.1 2 SHAHI (Mahmudi)

Silver **Note:** 3.84 grams or less.

Date	Mintage	VG	F	VF	XF	Unc
ND	—	5.00	12.00	25.00	36.00	—

Huwayza

KM# 147.2 2 SHAHI (Mahmudi)

Silver **Note:** 3.84 grams or less.

Date	Mintage	VG	F	VF	XF	Unc
ND	—	5.00	12.00	17.00	27.50	—

HAMMERED COINAGE

Ardebil

KM# 132.1 SHAHI (50 Dinars)

1.9200 g., Silver **Note:** Type B.

Date	Mintage	VG	F	VF	XF	Unc
AH1045	—	7.00	18.00	30.00	48.00	—
AH1046	—	7.00	18.00	30.00	48.00	—

Farahabad

KM# 132.2 SHAHI (50 Dinars)

1.9200 g., Silver **Note:** Type B.

Date	Mintage	VG	F	VF	XF	Unc
AH1049	—	14.00	36.00	55.00	80.00	—

KM# 132.3 SHAHI (50 Dinars)

1.9200 g., Silver **Note:** Type B.

Date	Mintage	VG	F	VF	XF	Unc
AH1040	—	7.00	18.00	27.50	42.00	—

Hamadan

KM# 132.4 SHAHI (50 Dinars)

1.9200 g., Silver **Note:** Type B.

Date	Mintage	VG	F	VF	XF	Unc
AH1039	—	7.00	18.00	30.00	48.00	—

Isfahan

KM# 132.5 SHAHI (50 Dinars)

1.9200 g., Silver **Note:** Type B.

Date	Mintage	VG	F	VF	XF	Unc
AH1040	—	6.00	15.00	25.00	36.00	—
AH1042	—	6.00	15.00	25.00	36.00	—

Rasht

KM# 132.6 SHAHI (50 Dinars)

1.9200 g., Silver **Note:** Type B.

Date	Mintage	VG	F	VF	XF	Unc
AHxxxx	—	7.00	18.00	27.50	42.00	—

Shiraz

KM# 132.7 SHAHI (50 Dinars)

1.9200 g., Silver **Note:** Type B.

Date	Mintage	VG	F	VF	XF	Unc
AHxxxx	—	6.00	18.00	27.50	42.00	—

Tabriz

KM# 132.8 SHAHI (50 Dinars)

1.9200 g., Silver **Note:** Type B.

Date	Mintage	VG	F	VF	XF	Unc
AH1044	—	—	—	—	—	—

Shamakha

KM# 140.1 SHAHI (50 Dinars - type 140)

1.9200 g., Silver **Note:** Type C.

Date	Mintage	VG	F	VF	XF	Unc
ND	—	7.00	18.00	27.50	39.00	—

Tiflis

KM# 140.2 SHAHI (50 Dinars - type 140)

1.9200 g., Silver **Note:** Type C.

Date	Mintage	VG	F	VF	XF	Unc
AH1052	—	8.00	20.00	35.00	50.00	—

Ardebil

KM# 133.1 2 SHAHI (Mahmudi)

3.8400 g., Silver **Note:** Type B.

Date	Mintage	VG	F	VF	XF	Unc
AH1045	—	12.00	30.00	45.00	60.00	—

Baghdad

KM# 133.2 2 SHAHI (Mahmudi)

3.8400 g., Silver **Note:** Type B.

Date	Mintage	VG	F	VF	XF	Unc
AH1038	—	15.00	36.00	55.00	80.00	—
AH1042	—	14.00	36.00	55.00	80.00	—
AH1047	—	14.00	36.00	55.00	80.00	—

Dawraq

KM# 133.3 2 SHAHI (Mahmudi)

3.8400 g., Silver **Note:** Type B.

Date	Mintage	VG	F	VF	XF	Unc
AH1047	—	12.00	30.00	48.00	65.00	—

Dehdasht

KM# 133.4 2 SHAHI (Mahmudi)

3.8400 g., Silver **Note:** Type B.

Date	Mintage	VG	F	VF	XF	Unc
AH1044	—	14.00	36.00	55.00	85.00	—

KM# 133.5 2 SHAHI (Mahmudi)

3.8400 g., Silver **Note:** Type B.

Date	Mintage	VG	F	VF	XF	Unc
AH1041	—	12.00	30.00	45.00	60.00	—

Isfahan

KM# 133.6 2 SHAHI (Mahmudi)

3.8400 g., Silver **Note:** Type B.

Date	Mintage	VG	F	VF	XF	Unc
AH1038	—	8.00	22.50	30.00	42.00	—
AH1042	—	8.00	22.50	30.00	42.00	—

Kashan

KM# 133.7 2 SHAHI (Mahmudi)

3.8400 g., Silver **Note:** Type B.

Date	Mintage	VG	F	VF	XF	Unc
AH1038	—	10.00	25.00	36.00	48.00	—

KM# 133.8 2 SHAHI (Mahmudi)

3.8400 g., Silver **Note:** Type B.

Date	Mintage	VG	F	VF	XF	Unc
AH1038	—	7.00	18.00	27.50	39.00	—

Rasht

KM# 133.9 2 SHAHI (Mahmudi)

3.8400 g., Silver **Note:** Type B.

Date	Mintage	VG	F	VF	XF	Unc
AH1038	—	8.00	22.50	30.00	42.00	—
AH1040	—	8.00	22.50	30.00	42.00	—

Tehran

KM# 133.10 2 SHAHI (Mahmudi)

3.8400 g., Silver **Note:** Type B.

Date	Mintage	VG	F	VF	XF	Unc
ND	—	10.00	25.00	36.00	48.00	—

Tiflis

KM# 141 2 SHAHI (Mahmudi - type 141)

3.8400 g., Silver **Note:** Type C.

Date	Mintage	VG	F	VF	XF	Unc
AH1052	—	18.00	42.00	60.00	95.00	—

Ardanush

KM# 134.2 ABBASI (Heavy Standard)

7.6800 g., Silver **Note:** Type B.

Date	Mintage	VG	F	VF	XF	Unc
AH1043	—	27.50	48.00	70.00	110	—

Ardebil

KM# 134.1 ABBASI (Heavy Standard)

7.6800 g., Silver **Note:** Type B.

Date	Mintage	VG	F	VF	XF	Unc
AH1039	—	6.00	15.00	25.00	36.00	—
AH1040	—	6.00	15.00	25.00	36.00	—
AH1041	—	6.00	15.00	25.00	36.00	—
AH1042	—	5.00	12.00	25.00	36.00	—
AH1045	—	6.00	15.00	25.00	36.00	—
AH1046	—	6.00	15.00	25.00	36.00	—

Baghdad

KM# 134.3 ABBASI (Heavy Standard)

7.6800 g., Silver **Note:** Type B. Illustration reduced.

Date	Mintage	VG	F	VF	XF	Unc
AH1038	—	10.00	25.00	39.00	60.00	—
AH1040	—	10.00	25.00	39.00	60.00	—
AH1044	—	10.00	25.00	39.00	60.00	—
AH1045	—	10.00	25.00	39.00	60.00	—
AH1046	—	10.00	25.00	39.00	60.00	—
AH1047	—	10.00	25.00	39.00	60.00	—

Dehdasht

KM# 134.4 ABBASI (Heavy Standard)

7.6800 g., Silver **Note:** Type B.

Date	Mintage	VG	F	VF	XF	Unc
AH1044	—	22.50	36.00	60.00	90.00	—

Eravan

KM# 134.5 ABBASI (Heavy Standard)
7.6800 g., Silver **Note:** Type B.

Date	Mintage	VG	F	VF	XF	Unc
AH1038	—	5.00	12.00	18.00	30.00	—
AH1039	—	5.00	12.00	18.00	30.00	—
AH1040	—	5.00	12.00	18.00	30.00	—
AH1041	—	5.00	12.00	18.00	30.00	—
AH1042	—	5.00	12.00	18.00	30.00	—
AH1043	—	5.00	12.00	18.00	30.00	—
AH1044	—	5.00	12.00	18.00	30.00	—
AH1045	—	5.00	12.00	18.00	30.00	—
AH1046	—	5.00	12.00	18.00	30.00	—
AH1047	—	5.00	12.00	18.00	27.50	—
AH1048	—	6.00	15.00	22.50	33.50	—
AH1049	—	6.00	15.00	22.50	33.50	—

KM# 134.6 ABBASI (Heavy Standard)
7.6800 g., Silver **Note:** Type B.

Date	Mintage	VG	F	VF	XF	Unc
AH1038	—	5.00	12.00	18.00	30.00	—
AH1039	—	5.00	12.00	18.00	30.00	—
AH1040	—	5.00	12.00	18.00	30.00	—
AH1041	—	5.00	12.00	18.00	30.00	—
AH1042	—	5.00	12.00	18.00	30.00	—
AH1044	—	5.00	12.00	18.00	30.00	—
AH1045	—	5.00	12.00	18.00	30.00	—
AH1047	—	6.00	15.00	22.50	33.50	—
AH1048	—	6.00	15.00	22.50	33.50	—

Hamadan

KM# 134.7 ABBASI (Heavy Standard)
7.6800 g., Silver **Note:** Type B.

Date	Mintage	VG	F	VF	XF	Unc
AH1038	—	6.00	15.00	25.00	36.00	—
AH1039	—	6.00	15.00	25.00	36.00	—
AH1049	—	6.00	15.00	25.00	36.00	—
AH1050	—	6.00	15.00	25.00	36.00	—

Herat

KM# 134.8 ABBASI (Heavy Standard)
7.6800 g., Silver **Note:** Type B.

Date	Mintage	VG	F	VF	XF	Unc
ND	—	22.50	36.00	55.00	85.00	—

Isfahan

KM# 134.9 ABBASI (Heavy Standard)
7.6800 g., Silver **Note:** Type B.

Date	Mintage	VG	F	VF	XF	Unc
AH1038	—	5.00	12.00	18.00	30.00	—
AH1039	—	5.00	12.00	18.00	30.00	—
AH1040	—	5.00	12.00	18.00	30.00	—
AH1041	—	5.00	12.00	18.00	30.00	—
AH1042	—	5.00	12.00	18.00	30.00	—
AH1044	—	5.00	12.00	18.00	30.00	—
AH1048	—	5.00	12.00	18.00	30.00	—

Kashan

KM# 134.10 ABBASI (Heavy Standard)
7.6800 g., Silver **Note:** Type B.

Date	Mintage	VG	F	VF	XF	Unc
AH1038	—	7.00	18.00	27.50	36.00	—
AH1040	—	7.00	18.00	27.50	36.00	—

Nakhchawan

KM# 134.11 ABBASI (Heavy Standard)
7.6800 g., Silver **Note:** Type B.

Date	Mintage	VG	F	VF	XF	Unc
ND	—	7.00	18.00	30.00	48.00	—

Qazvín

KM# 134.12 ABBASI (Heavy Standard)
7.6800 g., Silver **Note:** Type B.

Date	Mintage	VG	F	VF	XF	Unc
AH1038	—	5.00	12.00	18.00	30.00	—
AH1039	—	5.00	12.00	18.00	30.00	—
AH1040	—	5.00	12.00	18.00	30.00	—
AH1042	—	5.00	12.00	18.00	30.00	—
AH1045	—	7.00	12.00	18.00	30.00	—
AH1046	—	6.00	15.00	22.50	33.50	—
AH1047	—	6.00	15.00	22.50	33.50	—

Rasht

KM# 134.13 ABBASI (Heavy Standard)
7.6800 g., Silver **Note:** Type B.

Date	Mintage	VG	F	VF	XF	Unc
AH1038	—	6.00	15.00	22.50	33.50	—
AH1039	—	6.00	15.00	22.50	33.50	—
AH1049	—	7.00	18.00	27.50	42.00	—

Shamakha

KM# 134.14 ABBASI (Heavy Standard)
7.6800 g., Silver **Note:** Type B.

Date	Mintage	VG	F	VF	XF	Unc
AH1038	—	6.00	15.00	22.50	33.50	—
AH1040	—	6.00	15.00	22.50	33.50	—
AH1041	—	6.00	15.00	22.50	33.50	—
AH1042	—	6.00	15.00	22.50	33.50	—
AH1043	—	7.00	18.00	27.50	36.00	—
AH1050	—	7.00	18.00	27.50	36.00	—

Shiraz

KM# 134.21 ABBASI (Heavy Standard)
7.8600 g., Silver **Note:** Type B.

Date	Mintage	VG	F	VF	XF	Unc
AH103x	—	—	—	—	—	—
AH1041	—	—	—	—	—	—

Shushtar

KM# 134.15 ABBASI (Heavy Standard)
7.6800 g., Silver **Note:** Type B.

Date	Mintage	VG	F	VF	XF	Unc
AH1042	—	7.00	18.00	27.50	36.00	—

Tabriz

KM# 134.16 ABBASI (Heavy Standard)
7.6800 g., Silver **Note:** Type B.

Date	Mintage	VG	F	VF	XF	Unc
AH1038	—	4.00	11.00	15.00	25.00	—
AH1039	—	4.00	11.00	15.00	25.00	—
AH1040	—	4.00	11.00	15.00	25.00	—
AH1041	—	4.00	11.00	15.00	25.00	—
AH1042	—	4.00	11.00	15.00	25.00	—
AH1043	—	4.00	11.00	15.00	25.00	—
AH1044	—	4.00	11.00	15.00	25.00	—
AH1045	—	4.00	11.00	15.00	25.00	—
AH1046	—	5.00	12.00	18.00	27.50	—
AH1047	—	5.00	12.00	18.00	27.50	—
AH1048	—	5.00	12.00	18.00	27.50	—
AH1049	—	6.00	15.00	22.50	33.50	—
AH1050	—	6.00	15.00	22.50	33.50	—

Tehran

KM# 134.17 ABBASI (Heavy Standard)
7.6800 g., Silver **Note:** Type B.

Date	Mintage	VG	F	VF	XF	Unc
AH1041	—	18.00	33.00	48.00	70.00	—

Tiflis

KM# 134.18 ABBASI (Heavy Standard)
7.6800 g., Silver **Note:** Type B.

Date	Mintage	VG	F	VF	XF	Unc
AH1039	—	7.00	18.00	30.00	48.00	—
AH1040	—	7.00	18.00	30.00	48.00	—
AH1041	—	7.00	18.00	30.00	48.00	—
AH1043	—	7.00	18.00	30.00	48.00	—
AH1045	—	7.00	18.00	30.00	48.00	—
AH1046	—	7.00	18.00	30.00	48.00	—

Urdu

KM# 134.19 ABBASI (Heavy Standard)
7.6800 g., Silver **Note:** Type B.

Date	Mintage	VG	F	VF	XF	Unc
AH1045	—	12.00	27.50	42.00	60.00	—

Yazd

KM# 134.20 ABBASI (Heavy Standard)
7.6800 g., Silver **Note:** Type B.

Date	Mintage	VG	F	VF	XF	Unc
AH1039	—	7.00	18.00	30.00	38.50	—
AH1040	—	7.00	18.00	30.00	38.50	—

Ardebil

KM# 142.1 ABBASI (Heavy Standard - type 142)
7.6800 g., Silver **Note:** Type C.

Date	Mintage	VG	F	VF	XF	Unc
AH1052	—	8.00	20.00	36.00	55.00	—

Eravan

KM# 142.2 ABBASI (Heavy Standard - type 142)
7.6800 g., Silver **Note:** Type C.

Date	Mintage	VG	F	VF	XF	Unc
AH1050	—	7.00	18.00	30.00	45.00	—
AH1051	—	7.00	18.00	30.00	45.00	—
AH1052	—	7.00	18.00	30.00	45.00	—

Ganjah

KM# 142.3 ABBASI (Heavy Standard - type 142)
7.6800 g., Silver **Note:** Type C.

Date	Mintage	VG	F	VF	XF	Unc
AH1050	—	8.00	20.00	33.00	48.00	—
AH1052	—	8.00	20.00	33.00	48.00	—

Isfahan

KM# 142.7 ABBASI (Heavy Standard - type 142)
7.6800 g., Silver **Note:** Type C.

Date	Mintage	VG	F	VF	XF	Unc
AH1051	—	—	—	—	—	—
AH1052	—	—	—	—	—	—

Rasht

KM# 142.9 ABBASI (Heavy Standard - type 142)
7.6800 g., Silver **Note:** Type C.

Date	Mintage	VG	F	VF	XF	Unc
AH1050	—	—	—	—	—	—
AH1051	—	—	—	—	—	—

Shamakha

KM# 142.8 ABBASI (Heavy Standard - type 142)
7.6800 g., Silver **Note:** Type C.

Date	Mintage	VG	F	VF	XF	Unc
ND	—	—	—	—	—	—

Tabriz

KM# 142.4 ABBASI (Heavy Standard - type 142)
7.6800 g., Silver **Note:** Type C.

Date	Mintage	VG	F	VF	XF	Unc
AH1050	—	10.00	25.00	36.00	55.00	—
AH1051	—	7.00	18.00	30.00	45.00	—
AH1052	—	7.00	18.00	30.00	45.00	—

Tiflis

KM# 142.5 ABBASI (Heavy Standard - type 142)
7.6800 g., Silver **Note:** Type C.

Date	Mintage	VG	F	VF	XF	Unc
AH1051	—	12.00	30.00	45.00	70.00	—
AH1052	—	12.00	30.00	45.00	70.00	—

Zegam

KM# 142.6 ABBASI (Heavy Standard - type 142)
7.6800 g., Silver **Note:** Type C.

Date	Mintage	VG	F	VF	XF	Unc
ND	—	12.00	30.00	55.00	80.00	—

Nimruz

KM# 134.22 ABBASI
7.6800 g., Silver **Note:** Type B.

Date	Mintage	VG	F	VF	XF	Unc
ND	—	—	—	—	—	—

Zegam

KM# 134.23 ABBASI
7.6800 g., Silver **Note:** Type B.

Date	Mintage	VG	F	VF	XF	Unc
AH1045	—	—	—	—	—	—

Eravan

KM# 145 5 SHAHI
9.6100 g., Silver **Note:** Type A.

Date	Mintage	VG	F	VF	XF	Unc
AHxxxx	—	18.00	42.00	55.00	85.00	—

Abbas II

AH1052-1077 / 1642-1666AD

Abbas II, son of Safi I, was enthroned on 16 Safar 1052 (May 16, 1642). He died on the 25th of September, 1666. Silver coins were first struck to a standard of 2000 nokhod to the toman (Type A), then to a reduced standard of 1925 nokhod.

Types for this reign:

A. Same as Type D of Abbas I. When the date is not visible, Type A of Abbas II can only be distinguished from Type D of Abbas I by style and calligraphy.

B. Obverse couplet, *be-giti sekke-ye Sahebqerani /zad az toufiq-e haqq Abbas-e thani,* "In the world, Abbas the second, by the favor of God, struck the Sahebqerani coin". There are two versions of the type. On B1, struck AH1054-1064, the date appears normally above the second line of the obverse, usually somewhat towards the right. On B2, struck AH1063-1068, the date appears in the third line, usually to the left. The calligraphy is *naskhi*(upright).

C. Same as B, but with *nasta'liq* calligraphy (flowing). Subtype C1 has the date to the lower left in the third line of the obverse, C2 has the date as on B1. The principal denomination was changed from the abbasi to the panjshahi (5 shahi).

D. Obverse couplet, Be-giti ankeh sekke-ye sahebqerani zad / za toufiq-e khoda kalb-e Ali Abbas-e thani zad, "Whatever Sahebqerani coin has been struck in the world, Abbas the second struck (it), by the grace of God". This type was used only for large multiples of the shahi, as presentation coins.

HA. Design as previous Huwayza issues, but with the legend of Type A.

HB. Similar design, but legend of Type B.

NOTE: Gold coins of this reign are extremely rare. The type is R1 and R2, similar to B1 and B2, respectively. The weights are sometimes quite off the standard of 3.5 g for the ashrafi, further evidence that there were largesse or prestige coins not intended for normal circulation.

HAMMERED COINAGE

Local Type of Khuzistan

Dawraq

KM# 187.1 MAHMUDI
3.5000 g., Silver **Note:** Type HA.

Date	Mintage	VG	F	VF	XF	Unc
ND	—	6.00	15.00	25.00	36.00	—

Dezful

KM# 187.2 MAHMUDI

3.5000 g., Silver **Note:** Type HA.

Date	Mintage	VG	F	VF	XF	Unc
ND	—	6.00	15.00	25.00	36.00	—

Huwayza

KM# 187.3 MAHMUDI

3.5000 g., Silver **Note:** Type HA.

Date	Mintage	VG	F	VF	XF	Unc
AH1053	—	8.00	22.50	30.00	48.00	—
AH1054	—	8.00	22.50	30.00	48.00	—
AH1055	—	8.00	22.50	30.00	48.00	—
ND	—	1.75	4.00	9.00	25.00	—

Dawraq

KM# 188.1 MAHMUDI (type 188)

3.5000 g., Silver **Note:** Type HB.

Date	Mintage	VG	F	VF	XF	Unc
AH1061	—	10.00	25.00	42.00	60.00	—

Huwayza

KM# 188.2 MAHMUDI (type 188)

3.5000 g., Silver **Note:** Type HB.

Date	Mintage	VG	F	VF	XF	Unc
AH1063	—	7.00	18.00	27.50	42.00	—
AH1064	—	5.00	12.00	18.00	30.00	—
AH1066	—	7.00	18.00	27.50	36.00	—
AH1067	—	7.00	18.00	27.50	36.00	—
AH1072	—	7.00	18.00	27.50	36.00	—
AH1076	—	7.00	18.00	27.50	36.00	—
AH1077	—	7.00	18.00	27.50	36.00	—

Ramhurmuz

KM# 188.3 MAHMUDI (type 188)

3.5000 g., Silver **Note:** Type HB.

Date	Mintage	VG	F	VF	XF	Unc
AH1056	—	10.00	25.00	36.00	55.00	—

HAMMERED COINAGE

Tabriz

KM# 166 1/2 SHAHI (25 Dinars)

0.9600 g., Silver **Note:** Type B2.

Date	Mintage	VG	F	VF	XF	Unc
AH1064	—	27.50	60.00	80.00	110	—

Isfahan

KM# 161 SHAHI (50 Dinars)

1.9200 g., Silver **Note:** Type A.

Date	Mintage	VG	F	VF	XF	Unc
AH1053	—	12.00	30.00	42.00	60.00	—

Ganjah

KM# 167.21 SHAHI (50 Dinars - type 167)

1.8400 g., Silver **Note:** Type B2.

Date	Mintage	VG	F	VF	XF	Unc
AH1064	—	8.00	20.00	33.00	48.00	—

Isfahan

KM# 167.11 SHAHI (50 Dinars - type 167)

1.8400 g., Silver **Note:** Type B1.

Date	Mintage	VG	F	VF	XF	Unc
AH1057	—	10.00	25.00	33.00	48.00	—

Mashhad

KM# 167.12 SHAHI (50 Dinars - type 167)

1.8400 g., Silver **Note:** Type B1.

Date	Mintage	VG	F	VF	XF	Unc
AH1060	—	10.00	25.00	33.00	48.00	—

Rasht

KM# 167.13 SHAHI (50 Dinars - type 167)

1.8400 g., Silver **Note:** Type B1.

Date	Mintage	VG	F	VF	XF	Unc
AHxxxx	—	7.00	18.00	25.00	36.00	—

Shamakha

KM# 167.14 SHAHI (50 Dinars - type 167)

1.8400 g., Silver **Note:** Type B1.

Date	Mintage	VG	F	VF	XF	Unc
AH1061	—	10.00	25.00	33.00	48.00	—

Tabriz

KM# 167.15 SHAHI (50 Dinars - type 167)

1.8400 g., Silver **Note:** Type B1.

Date	Mintage	VG	F	VF	XF	Unc
AH1057	—	7.00	18.00	25.00	36.00	—
AH1059	—	7.00	18.00	25.00	36.00	—

KM# 167.22 SHAHI (50 Dinars - type 167)

1.8400 g., Silver **Note:** Type B2.

Date	Mintage	VG	F	VF	XF	Unc
AH1064	—	8.00	20.00	33.00	48.00	—

Unknown

KM# 174 SHAHI (50 Dinars - type 174)

1.8400 g., Silver **Note:** Type C1 or C2.

Date	Mintage	VG	F	VF	XF	Unc
AHxxxx	—	7.00	18.00	30.00	42.00	—

Eravan

KM# 202.1 2 SHAHI (Mahmudi)

3.6900 g., Silver

Date	Mintage	VG	F	VF	XF	Unc
AH1078	—	—	—	—	—	—

Isfahan

KM# 162.1 2 SHAHI (Mahmudi)

3.8400 g., Silver **Note:** Type A.

Date	Mintage	VG	F	VF	XF	Unc
AH1053	—	14.00	36.00	55.00	80.00	—

Tiflis

KM# 162.2 2 SHAHI (Mahmudi)

3.8400 g., Silver **Note:** Type A.

Date	Mintage	VG	F	VF	XF	Unc
AH1052	—	—	—	—	—	—

KM# 202.2 2 SHAHI (Mahmudi)

3.6900 g., Silver

Date	Mintage	VG	F	VF	XF	Unc
AHxxxx	—	—	—	—	—	—

Ardebil

KM# 168.11 2 SHAHI (Mahmudi - type 168)

3.6900 g., Silver **Note:** Type B1.

Date	Mintage	VG	F	VF	XF	Unc
AH1059	—	10.00	25.00	36.00	48.00	—
AH1064	—	10.00	25.00	36.00	48.00	—

Eravan

KM# 168.12 2 SHAHI (Mahmudi - type 168)

3.6900 g., Silver **Note:** Type B1.

Date	Mintage	VG	F	VF	XF	Unc
AH1058	—	8.00	22.50	33.00	45.00	—

Kashan

KM# 168.13 2 SHAHI (Mahmudi - type 168)

3.6900 g., Silver **Note:** Type B1.

Date	Mintage	VG	F	VF	XF	Unc
AH1056	—	10.00	25.00	36.00	48.00	—

Mashhad

KM# 168.14 2 SHAHI (Mahmudi - type 168)

3.6900 g., Silver **Note:** Type B1.

Date	Mintage	VG	F	VF	XF	Unc
AH1061	—	11.00	27.50	42.00	60.00	—

Qazvín

KM# 168.21 2 SHAHI (Mahmudi - type 168)

3.6900 g., Silver **Note:** Type B2.

Date	Mintage	VG	F	VF	XF	Unc
AH1065	—	18.00	42.00	60.00	85.00	—

Shamakha

KM# 168.22 2 SHAHI (Mahmudi - type 168)

3.6900 g., Silver **Note:** Type B2.

Date	Mintage	VG	F	VF	XF	Unc
AH1065	—	14.00	36.00	50.00	70.00	—

Shushtar

KM# 168.15 2 SHAHI (Mahmudi - type 168)

3.6900 g., Silver **Note:** Type B1.

Date	Mintage	VG	F	VF	XF	Unc
AHxxxx	—	7.00	18.00	30.00	42.00	—
AH1056	—	7.00	18.00	30.00	42.00	—
AH1063	—	7.00	18.00	30.00	42.00	—

Tiflis

KM# 168.16 2 SHAHI (Mahmudi - type 168)

3.6900 g., Silver **Note:** Type B1.

Date	Mintage	VG	F	VF	XF	Unc
AH1054	—	11.00	27.50	42.00	60.00	—
AH1061	—	11.00	27.50	42.00	60.00	—

Ardebil

KM# 163.1 ABBASI

7.6800 g., Silver **Note:** Type A.

Date	Mintage	VG	F	VF	XF	Unc
AH1052	—	8.00	20.00	36.00	55.00	—
AH1053	—	8.00	20.00	36.00	55.00	—

Dadiyan

KM# 163.13 ABBASI

7.6800 g., Silver **Note:** Type A.

Date	Mintage	VG	F	VF	XF	Unc
AH1053	—	—	—	—	—	—

Eravan

KM# 163.2 ABBASI

7.6800 g., Silver **Note:** Type A.

Date	Mintage	VG	F	VF	XF	Unc
AH1052	—	6.00	15.00	25.00	36.00	—
AH1053	—	6.00	15.00	25.00	36.00	—

Ganjah

KM# 163.3 ABBASI

7.6800 g., Silver **Note:** Type A.

Date	Mintage	VG	F	VF	XF	Unc
AH1052	—	8.00	20.00	33.00	48.00	—
AH1053	—	8.00	20.00	33.00	48.00	—
AH1054	—	8.00	20.00	33.00	48.00	—

Hamadan

KM# 163.10 ABBASI

7.6800 g., Silver **Note:** Type A.

Date	Mintage	VG	F	VF	XF	Unc
AH1053	—	—	—	—	—	—

Isfahan

KM# 163.4 ABBASI

7.6800 g., Silver **Note:** Type A.

Date	Mintage	VG	F	VF	XF	Unc
AH1052	—	7.00	18.00	30.00	42.00	—
AH1053	—	7.00	18.00	30.00	42.00	—

Mashhad

KM# 163.11 ABBASI

7.6800 g., Silver **Note:** Type A.

Date	Mintage	VG	F	VF	XF	Unc
AH1052	—	—	—	—	—	—
AH1054	—	—	—	—	—	—

Nimruz

KM# 163.5 ABBASI

7.6800 g., Silver **Note:** Type A.

Date	Mintage	VG	F	VF	XF	Unc
AH1054 (sic)	—	18.00	42.00	65.00	95.00	—

Qazvin

KM# 163.12 ABBASI

7.6800 g., Silver **Note:** Type A.

Date	Mintage	VG	F	VF	XF	Unc
AH1052	—	—	—	—	—	—
AH1053	—	—	—	—	—	—

Rasht

KM# 163.6 ABBASI

7.6800 g., Silver **Note:** Type A.

Date	Mintage	VG	F	VF	XF	Unc
AH1052	—	10.00	25.00	36.00	50.00	—
AH1054	—	10.00	25.00	36.00	50.00	—

Shamakha

KM# 163.7 ABBASI

7.6800 g., Silver **Note:** Type A.

Date	Mintage	VG	F	VF	XF	Unc
AH1052	—	8.00	20.00	33.00	48.00	—
AH1053	—	8.00	20.00	33.00	48.00	—

Tabriz

KM# 163.8 ABBASI

7.6800 g., Silver **Note:** Type A.

Date	Mintage	VG	F	VF	XF	Unc
AH1052	—	6.00	15.00	25.00	36.00	—
AH1053	—	6.00	15.00	25.00	36.00	—
	—	6.00	15.00	25.00	36.00	—

Tiflis

KM# 163.9 ABBASI

7.6800 g., Silver **Note:** Type A.

Date	Mintage	VG	F	VF	XF	Unc
AH1052	—	10.00	25.00	36.00	55.00	—
AH1053	—	10.00	25.00	36.00	55.00	—
AH1054	—	10.00	25.00	36.00	55.00	—

Ardebil

KM# 169.1 ABBASI (type 169)

7.3900 g., Silver **Note:** Type B1.

Date	Mintage	VG	F	VF	XF	Unc
AH1054	—	4.00	10.00	15.00	25.00	—
AH1055	—	4.00	10.00	18.00	28.00	—
AH1056	—	4.00	10.00	18.00	28.00	—
AH1057	—	4.00	10.00	18.00	28.00	—
AH1059	—	4.00	10.00	18.00	28.00	—
AH1059/8	—	4.00	10.00	18.00	28.00	—
AH1063	—	4.00	10.00	18.00	28.00	—
AH1064	—	5.00	12.50	18.00	28.00	—

KM# 169.21 ABBASI (type 169)

7.3900 g., Silver **Note:** Type B2.

Date	Mintage	VG	F	VF	XF	Unc
AH1067	—	6.00	15.00	22.50	33.50	—

Dadiyan

KM# 169.2 ABBASI (type 169)

7.3900 g., Silver **Note:** Type B1.

Date	Mintage	VG	F	VF	XF	Unc
ND	—	15.00	35.00	45.00	60.00	—

Dawraq

KM# 169.22 ABBASI (type 169)

7.3900 g., Silver **Note:** Type B2.

Date	Mintage	VG	F	VF	XF	Unc
AH1063	—	12.00	30.00	42.00	55.00	—

Eravan

KM# 169.3 ABBASI (type 169)

7.3900 g., Silver **Note:** Type B1.

Date	Mintage	VG	F	VF	XF	Unc
AH1054	—	4.00	11.00	16.00	25.00	—
AH1055	—	4.00	11.00	16.00	25.00	—
AH1056	—	4.00	11.00	16.00	25.00	—
AH1057	—	4.00	11.00	16.00	25.00	—
AH1058	—	4.00	11.00	16.00	25.00	—
AH1059	—	4.00	11.00	16.00	25.00	—
AH1060	—	4.00	11.00	16.00	25.00	—
AH1061	—	4.00	11.00	16.00	25.00	—
AH1062	—	5.00	12.00	18.00	30.00	—
AH1063	—	5.00	12.00	18.00	30.00	—
AH1064	—	5.00	12.00	18.00	30.00	—

KM# 169.23 ABBASI (type 169)

7.3900 g., Silver **Note:** Type B2.

Date	Mintage	VG	F	VF	XF	Unc
AH1064	—	5.00	12.00	18.00	30.00	—
AH1065	—	5.00	12.00	18.00	30.00	—
AH1066	—	5.00	12.00	18.00	30.00	—
AH1067	—	5.00	12.00	18.00	30.00	—
AH1068	—	6.00	15.00	22.50	33.50	—

Ganjah

KM# 169.4 ABBASI (type 169)

7.3900 g., Silver **Note:** Type B1.

Date	Mintage	VG	F	VF	XF	Unc
AH1054	—	5.00	12.00	18.00	30.00	—
AH1055	—	5.00	12.00	18.00	30.00	—
AH1056	—	5.00	12.00	18.00	30.00	—
AH1057	—	5.00	12.00	18.00	30.00	—
AH1058	—	5.00	12.00	18.00	30.00	—
AH1059	—	5.00	12.00	18.00	30.00	—
AH1060	—	5.00	12.00	18.00	30.00	—
AH1061	—	5.00	12.00	18.00	30.00	—
AH1062	—	5.00	12.00	18.00	30.00	—
AH1063	—	5.00	12.00	18.00	30.00	—

KM# 169.24 ABBASI (type 169)

7.3900 g., Silver **Note:** Type B2.

Date	Mintage	VG	F	VF	XF	Unc
AH1064	—	5.00	12.00	18.00	30.00	—
AH1066	—	5.00	12.00	18.00	30.00	—
AH1067	—	5.00	12.00	18.00	30.00	—
AH1068	—	6.00	15.00	22.50	33.50	—

Hamadan

KM# 169.5 ABBASI (type 169)

7.3900 g., Silver **Note:** Type B1.

Date	Mintage	VG	F	VF	XF	Unc
AH1054	—	7.00	18.00	30.00	42.00	—
AH1056	—	7.00	18.00	30.00	42.00	—
AH1061	—	7.00	18.00	30.00	42.00	—

KM# 169.25 ABBASI (type 169)

7.3900 g., Silver **Note:** Type B2.

Date	Mintage	VG	F	VF	XF	Unc
AH1066	—	10.00	25.00	36.00	50.00	—

Herat

KM# 169.17 ABBASI (type 169)

7.3900 g., Silver **Note:** Type B1.

Date	Mintage	VG	F	VF	XF	Unc
AH1060	—	—	—	—	—	—

Isfahan

KM# 169.6 ABBASI (type 169)

7.3900 g., Silver **Note:** Type B1.

Date	Mintage	VG	F	VF	XF	Unc
AH1054	—	5.00	12.00	18.00	30.00	—
AH1055	—	5.00	12.00	18.00	30.00	—
AH1057	—	6.00	15.00	22.50	33.50	—
AH1058	—	5.00	12.00	18.00	30.00	—
AH1063	—	5.00	13.00	20.00	33.00	—
AH1025	—	6.00	15.00	22.50	33.50	—

Note: Error for 1065 with retrograde 6

Kashan

KM# 169.7 ABBASI (type 169)

7.3900 g., Silver **Note:** Type B1.

Date	Mintage	VG	F	VF	XF	Unc
AH1054	—	6.00	15.00	22.50	33.50	—
AH1055	—	6.00	15.00	22.50	33.50	—
AH1056	—	6.00	15.00	22.50	33.50	—
AH1060	—	7.00	18.00	27.50	36.00	—
AH1063	—	7.00	18.00	27.50	42.00	—
AH1064	—	8.00	20.00	30.00	42.00	—

Mashhad

KM# 169.8 ABBASI (type 169)

7.3900 g., Silver **Note:** Type B1.

Date	Mintage	VG	F	VF	XF	Unc
AH1054	—	7.00	18.00	27.50	36.00	—
AH1056	—	7.00	18.00	27.50	39.00	—
AH1058	—	7.00	18.00	27.50	36.00	—
AH1059	—	7.00	18.00	27.50	36.00	—
AH1061	—	7.00	18.00	27.50	36.00	—

Qandahar

KM# 169.16 ABBASI (type 169)

7.3900 g., Silver **Note:** Type B1.

Date	Mintage	VG	F	VF	XF	Unc
AH1059	—	—	—	—	—	—

KM# 169.30 ABBASI (type 169)

7.3900 g., Silver **Note:** Type B2.

Date	Mintage	VG	F	VF	XF	Unc
AH1059	—	—	—	—	—	—

Qazvin

KM# 169.31 ABBASI (type 169)

7.3900 g., Silver **Note:** Type B2.

Date	Mintage	VG	F	VF	XF	Unc
AH1053	—	—	—	—	—	—
AH1055	—	—	—	—	—	—

KM# 169.14 ABBASI (type 169)

7.3900 g., Silver **Note:** Type B1.

Date	Mintage	VG	F	VF	XF	Unc
AH1055	—	—	—	—	—	—
AH1056	—	—	—	—	—	—
AH1060	—	—	—	—	—	—

Rasht

KM# 169.9 ABBASI (type 169)

7.3900 g., Silver **Note:** Type B1.

Date	Mintage	VG	F	VF	XF	Unc
AH1056	—	10.00	25.00	36.00	48.00	—
AH1057	—	10.00	25.00	36.00	48.00	—

Shamakha

KM# 169.10 ABBASI (type 169)

7.3900 g., Silver **Note:** Type B1.

Date	Mintage	VG	F	VF	XF	Unc
AH1054	—	5.00	12.00	18.00	30.00	—
AH1055	—	5.00	12.00	22.50	33.50	—
AH1057	—	6.00	15.00	22.50	33.50	—
AH1061	—	6.00	15.00	20.00	33.50	—
AH1062	—	6.00	15.00	22.50	33.50	—

KM# 169.26 ABBASI (type 169)

7.3900 g., Silver **Note:** Type B2.

Date	Mintage	VG	F	VF	XF	Unc
AH1065	—	8.00	20.00	33.00	48.00	—

Shushtar

KM# 169.11 ABBASI (type 169)

7.3900 g., Silver **Note:** Type B1.

Date	Mintage	VG	F	VF	XF	Unc
AH1056	—	6.00	15.00	22.50	33.50	—

KM# 169.27 ABBASI (type 169)

7.3900 g., Silver **Note:** Type B2.

Date	Mintage	VG	F	VF	XF	Unc
AH1063	—	10.00	25.00	36.00	48.00	—

Tabriz

KM# 169.12 ABBASI (type 169)

7.3900 g., Silver **Note:** Type B1.

Date	Mintage	VG	F	VF	XF	Unc
AH1054	—	4.00	11.00	16.00	25.00	—
AH1055	—	4.00	11.00	16.00	25.00	—
AH1056	—	4.00	11.00	16.00	25.00	—
AH1057	—	4.00	11.00	16.00	25.00	—
AH1058	—	4.00	11.00	16.00	25.00	—
AH1059	—	4.00	11.00	16.00	25.00	—
AH1059/6	—	4.00	11.00	16.00	25.00	—
AH1060	—	4.00	11.00	16.00	25.00	—
AH1061	—	4.00	11.00	16.00	25.00	—
AH1062	—	4.00	11.00	16.00	25.00	—
AH1063	—	4.00	11.00	16.00	25.00	—
AH1064	—	5.00	12.00	18.00	30.00	—

KM# 169.28 ABBASI (type 169)

7.3900 g., Silver **Note:** Type B2.

Date	Mintage	VG	F	VF	XF	Unc
AH1063	—	4.00	11.00	16.00	25.00	—
AH1064	—	4.00	11.00	16.00	25.00	—
AH1065	—	4.00	11.00	16.00	25.00	—
AH1066	—	4.00	11.00	16.00	25.00	—
AH1067	—	4.00	11.00	16.00	25.00	—
AH1068	—	6.00	15.00	22.50	33.50	—

Tiflis

KM# 169.13 ABBASI (type 169)

7.3900 g., Silver **Note:** Type B1.

Date	Mintage	VG	F	VF	XF	Unc
AH1054	—	7.00	18.00	27.50	36.00	—
AH1055	—	7.00	18.00	27.50	36.00	—
AH1056	—	7.00	18.00	27.50	36.00	—
AH1058	—	7.00	18.00	27.50	36.00	—
AH1059	—	7.00	18.00	27.50	36.00	—
AH1060	—	5.00	12.00	18.00	30.00	—
AH1061	—	5.00	12.00	18.00	30.00	—
AH1062	—	5.00	12.00	18.00	30.00	—
AH1063	—	5.00	12.00	18.00	30.00	—
AH1064	—	5.00	13.00	20.00	33.00	—

KM# 169.29 ABBASI (type 169)

7.3900 g., Silver **Note:** Type B2.

Date	Mintage	VG	F	VF	XF	Unc
AH1063	—	5.00	12.00	18.00	30.00	—
AH1064	—	5.00	12.00	18.00	30.00	—
AH1065	—	5.00	12.00	18.00	30.00	—
AH1065//1064	—	7.00	18.00	27.50	39.00	—
AH1066	—	5.00	12.00	18.00	30.00	—
AH1067	—	5.00	12.00	18.00	30.00	—

Urdu

KM# 169.15 ABBASI (type 169)

7.3900 g., Silver **Note:** Type B1.

Date	Mintage	VG	F	VF	XF	Unc
AH1058	—	—	—	—	—	—
AH1059	—	—	—	—	—	—

Zegam

KM# 169.18 ABBASI (type 169)

7.3900 g., Silver **Note:** Type B1.

Date	Mintage	VG	F	VF	XF	Unc
ND	—	—	—	—	—	—

Ardebil

KM# 176.1 5 SHAHI

9.2400 g., Silver **Note:** Type C1.

Date	Mintage	VG	F	VF	XF	Unc
AH1067	—	7.00	18.00	27.50	42.00	—
AH1068	—	7.00	18.00	27.50	42.00	—
AH1070	—	8.00	20.00	30.00	48.00	—

KM# 176.31 5 SHAHI

9.2400 g., Silver **Note:** Type C1.

Date	Mintage	VG	F	VF	XF	Unc
AH1075	—	8.00	20.00	33.00	48.00	—

Eravan

KM# 176.2 5 SHAHI

9.2400 g., Silver **Note:** Type C1.

Date	Mintage	VG	F	VF	XF	Unc
AH1067	—	7.00	18.00	27.50	42.00	—
AH1068	—	7.00	18.00	27.50	42.00	—

KM# 176.32 5 SHAHI

9.2400 g., Silver **Note:** Type C2.

Date	Mintage	VG	F	VF	XF	Unc
AH1069	—	6.00	15.00	22.50	36.00	—
AH1070	—	6.00	15.00	22.50	36.00	—
AH1071	—	6.00	15.00	22.50	36.00	—
AH1072	—	6.00	15.00	22.50	36.00	—
AH1073	—	6.00	15.00	22.50	36.00	—
AH1074	—	6.00	15.00	22.50	36.00	—
AH1076	—	6.00	15.00	22.50	36.00	—
AH1077	—	10.00	25.00	36.00	55.00	—

Ganjah

KM# 176.3 5 SHAHI

9.2400 g., Silver **Note:** Type C2.

Date	Mintage	VG	F	VF	XF	Unc
AH1067	—	7.00	18.00	27.50	42.00	—
AH1069	—	7.00	18.00	27.50	42.00	—

KM# 176.33 5 SHAHI

9.2400 g., Silver **Note:** Type C2.

Date	Mintage	VG	F	VF	XF	Unc
AH1071	—	8.00	20.00	33.00	48.00	—
AH1074	—	8.00	20.00	33.00	48.00	—
AH1075	—	8.00	20.00	33.00	48.00	—

Isfahan

KM# 176.34 5 SHAHI

9.2400 g., Silver **Note:** Type C2.

Date	Mintage	VG	F	VF	XF	Unc
AH1067	—	10.00	25.00	39.00	60.00	—
AH1071	—	8.00	20.00	33.00	48.00	—

Kashan

KM# 176.35 5 SHAHI

9.2400 g., Silver **Note:** Type C2.

Date	Mintage	VG	F	VF	XF	Unc
AH1073	—	10.00	25.00	36.00	55.00	—

Mashhad

KM# 176.36 5 SHAHI

9.2400 g., Silver **Note:** Type C2.

Date	Mintage	VG	F	VF	XF	Unc
ND	—	7.00	18.00	30.00	48.00	—

Qazvín

KM# 176.37 5 SHAHI

9.2400 g., Silver **Note:** Type C2.

Date	Mintage	VG	F	VF	XF	Unc
AH1072	—	12.00	30.00	42.00	60.00	—

Shamakha

KM# 176.38 5 SHAHI

9.2400 g., Silver **Note:** Type C2.

Date	Mintage	VG	F	VF	XF	Unc
AH1069	—	7.00	18.00	27.50	48.00	—
AH1071	—	7.00	17.00	25.00	42.00	—
AH1072	—	7.00	17.00	25.00	42.00	—
AH1073	—	7.00	17.00	25.00	42.00	—
AH1074	—	7.00	17.00	25.00	42.00	—
AH1075	—	7.00	17.00	25.00	42.00	—
AH1076	—	7.00	17.00	25.00	42.00	—

Shushtar

KM# 176.39 5 SHAHI

9.2400 g., Silver **Note:** Type C2.

Date	Mintage	VG	F	VF	XF	Unc
AH1068	—	6.00	15.00	22.50	36.00	—
AHxxxx	—	6.00	15.00	22.50	36.00	—

Tabriz

KM# 176.4 5 SHAHI

9.2400 g., Silver **Note:** Type C1.

Date	Mintage	VG	F	VF	XF	Unc
AH1067	—	7.00	18.00	27.50	42.00	—

KM# 176.21 5 SHAHI

9.2400 g., Silver **Note:** Type C - Special.

Date	Mintage	VG	F	VF	XF	Unc
AH1068	—	14.00	36.00	55.00	85.00	—
AH1069	—	14.00	36.00	55.00	85.00	—

KM# 176.40 5 SHAHI

9.2400 g., Silver **Note:** Type C2.

Date	Mintage	VG	F	VF	XF	Unc
AH1069	—	6.00	15.00	22.50	36.00	—
AH1070	—	6.00	15.00	22.50	36.00	—
AH1071	—	6.00	15.00	22.50	36.00	—
AH1072	—	6.00	15.00	22.50	36.00	—
AH1073	—	6.00	15.00	22.50	36.00	—
AH1076	—	6.00	15.00	22.50	36.00	—

Tiflis

KM# 176.41 5 SHAHI

9.2400 g., Silver **Note:** Type C2.

Date	Mintage	VG	F	VF	XF	Unc
AH1069	—	7.00	17.00	25.00	42.00	—
AH1070	—	7.00	17.00	25.00	42.00	—
AH1071	—	6.00	15.00	22.50	36.00	—
AH1072	—	6.00	15.00	22.50	36.00	—
AH1073	—	6.00	15.00	22.50	36.00	—
AH1074	—	6.00	15.00	22.50	36.00	—
AH1075	—	6.00	15.00	22.50	36.00	—
AH1076	—	6.00	15.00	22.50	36.00	—

Urdu

KM# 180 2-1/2 ABBASI (10 Shahi)

18.4800 g., Silver **Note:** Type D (Kalb).

Date	Mintage	VG	F	VF	XF	Unc
AHxxxx Rare	—	—	—	—	—	—

Kashan

KM# 178 5 ABBASI (20 Shahi)

36.9600 g., Silver **Note:** Type C1.

Date	Mintage	VG	F	VF	XF	Unc
AH1068 Rare	—	—	—	—	—	—

Urdu

KM# 181 5 ABBASI (20 Shahi - type 181)

36.9600 g., Silver **Note:** Type D (Kalb).

Date	Mintage	VG	F	VF	XF	Unc
AHxxxx Rare	—	—	—	—	—	—

Ardebil

KM# 184 1/2 ASHRAFI

1.7500 g., Gold **Obv:** Date above second line **Note:** Type R1.

Date	Mintage	VG	F	VF	XF	Unc
AH1072 Rare	—	—	—	—	—	—

Isfahan

KM# 185 ASHRAFI

3.5000 g., Gold **Obv:** Date in third line **Note:** Type R2.

Date	Mintage	VG	F	VF	XF	Unc
AH1081 Rare	—	—	—	—	—	—

Note: Error for 1071?

Safi II

AH1077-1079 / 1666-1668AD

Safi II, son of Abbas II, acceded to the throne on 3 Rabi' II 1077 (October 2, 1666), but quickly fell deathly ill. After his miraculous recovery, he was re-enthroned as Sulayman I on 19 Shawwal 1079 (March 20, 1669). He died on the 29th of January, 1694.

Types for this reign:

A. Obverse couplet, *za ba'd-e hasti-ye Abbas-e thani / Safi zad sekke-ye sahebqerani*, "After the existence of Abbas the second, Safi struck the sahebqerani coin".

B. Obverse couplet, *az baraye sarf-e zovar-e emam-e ons o jan / tazeh az nam-e safi shod sekke-ye sahebqerani*, @05"For the expenditures of the pilgrims to the Imam of bold and soul, the sahebqerani coin was renewed with the name of Safi". Used only for large multiples.

HAMMERED COINAGE

Dawraq

KM# 207.1 MAHMUDI

Silver **Note:** Type H; About 3.60 grams.

Date	Mintage	VG	F	VF	XF	Unc
ND	—	19.00	48.00	65.00	85.00	—

Huwayza

KM# 207.2 MAHMUDI

Silver **Note:** Type H; About 3.60 grams.

Date	Mintage	VG	F	VF	XF	Unc
ND	—	12.00	30.00	39.00	60.00	—

Isfahan

KM# 201.1 SHAHI (50 Dinars)

1.8400 g., Silver **Note:** Type A.

Date	Mintage	VG	F	VF	XF	Unc
AH1078	—	18.00	42.00	65.00	110	—

Tabriz

KM# 201.2 SHAHI (50 Dinars)

1.8400 g., Silver **Note:** Type A.

Date	Mintage	VG	F	VF	XF	Unc
AH1078	—	18.00	42.00	65.00	110	—

Eravan

KM# 203.1 ABBASI

7.3900 g., Silver **Note:** Type A.

Date	Mintage	VG	F	VF	XF	Unc
AH1079	—	18.00	42.00	65.00	100	—

Tabriz

KM# 203.2 ABBASI

7.3900 g., Silver **Note:** Type A.

Date	Mintage	VG	F	VF	XF	Unc
AH1077	—	18.00	42.00	65.00	100	—

Tiflis

KM# 203.3 ABBASI

7.3900 g., Silver **Note:** Type A.

Date	Mintage	VG	F	VF	XF	Unc
AH1078	—	14.00	36.00	60.00	95.00	—
AH1079	—	14.00	36.00	60.00	95.00	—

Isfahan

KM# 205 5 ABBASI (20 Shahi)

36.9500 g., Silver **Note:** Type B.

Date	Mintage	VG	F	VF	XF	Unc
AH1078	—	—	350	475	900	—

Sulayman I

AH1079-1105 / 1668-1694AD

Silver coin types for this reign:

A. Obverse couplet, *bahr-e tahsil-e rezaye moqtadaye ons o jan / sekke-ye khayarat bar zar zad Soleiman-e jahan*, "For obtaining the acquiescence of the one followed in body and soul (i.e., Ali), the Solomon of the world struck the coin of benevolence in precious metal".

B. Obverse, date, mint and the phrase, *Soleiman bande-ye shah-e velayat* (cf. Type D of Abbas I). Flowing calligraphy. The quality of production sank to an all time low during the currency of this type (1081-1095). Nearly all pieces show significant weakness of strike.

C. As B, but upright calligraphy. This type was usually well struck, though quality control declined after about AH1100.

H. As Type HA of Abbas I, but with the phrase of Type B. The undated pieces are believed to have been struck after AH1092.

During this reign, a large number of presentation coins were struck in various denominations, principally 10 and 20 shahi in silver, and 10 ashrafi in gold. These were presented to high officials and foreign dignitaries, who were expected to wear them on their clothing during official functions. As a result, they are almost invariably found holed, mounted, or otherwise damaged. Only a small selection are catalogued here.

HAMMERED COINAGE

Local Type of Khuzistan

Huwayza

KM# 235 MAHMUDI

Silver **Note:** Type H; Weight varies: 3.00-3.50 grams. Sometimes debased.

Date	Mintage	VG	F	VF	XF	Unc
ND	—	1.75	5.00	10.00	25.00	—
AH1084	—	1.75	5.00	10.00	25.00	—
AH1085	—	1.75	5.00	10.00	25.00	—
AH1086	—	1.75	5.00	10.00	25.00	—
AH1087	—	1.75	5.00	10.00	25.00	—
AH1088	—	1.75	5.00	10.00	25.00	—
AH1089	—	1.75	5.00	10.00	25.00	—
AH1090	—	1.75	5.00	10.00	25.00	—
AH1091	—	1.75	5.00	10.00	25.00	—
AH1092	—	1.75	5.00	10.00	25.00	—

Note: Symbol in place of date.

HAMMERED COINAGE

Qazvín

KM# 210 1/2 SHAHI (25 Dinars)

0.9600 g., Silver **Note:** Type A.

Date	Mintage	VG	F	VF	XF	Unc
AHxxxx	—	14.00	36.00	48.00	65.00	—

Unknown

KM# 211 SHAHI (50 Dinars)

1.8400 g., Silver **Note:** Type B.

Date	Mintage	VG	F	VF	XF	Unc
AHxxxx	—	7.00	18.00	27.50	36.00	—

Ardebil

KM# 218.1 SHAHI (50 Dinars - type 218)

1.8400 g., Silver **Note:** Type B.

Date	Mintage	VG	F	VF	XF	Unc
AH1088	—	12.00	30.00	42.00	60.00	—

Eravan

KM# 218.2 SHAHI (50 Dinars - type 218)

1.8400 g., Silver **Note:** Type B.

Date	Mintage	VG	F	VF	XF	Unc
AH1083	—	12.00	30.00	42.00	60.00	—

Tabriz

KM# 218.3 SHAHI (50 Dinars - type 218)

1.8400 g., Silver **Note:** Type B.

Date	Mintage	VG	F	VF	XF	Unc
AH1082	—	12.00	30.00	42.00	60.00	—

Tiflis

KM# 218.4 SHAHI (50 Dinars - type 218)

1.8400 g., Silver **Note:** Type B.

Date	Mintage	VG	F	VF	XF	Unc
AH1094	—	12.00	30.00	42.00	60.00	—

Ardebil

KM# 224.1 SHAHI (50 Dinars - type 224)

1.8400 g., Silver **Note:** Type C.

Date	Mintage	VG	F	VF	XF	Unc
AH1104	—	13.00	33.00	48.00	65.00	—

Eravan

KM# 224.2 SHAHI (50 Dinars - type 224)

1.8400 g., Silver **Note:** Type C.

Date	Mintage	VG	F	VF	XF	Unc
AH1103	—	10.00	25.00	36.00	48.00	—
AH1105	—	10.00	25.00	36.00	48.00	—

Ganjah

KM# 224.3 SHAHI (50 Dinars - type 224)

1.8400 g., Silver **Note:** Type C.

Date	Mintage	VG	F	VF	XF	Unc
AH1102	—	10.00	25.00	36.00	48.00	—
AH1103	—	10.00	25.00	36.00	48.00	—
AH1104	—	10.00	25.00	36.00	48.00	—

Isfahan

KM# 224.4 SHAHI (50 Dinars - type 224)

1.8400 g., Silver **Note:** Type C.

Date	Mintage	VG	F	VF	XF	Unc
AH1095	—	7.00	18.00	25.00	36.00	—
AH1096	—	7.00	18.00	25.00	36.00	—
AH1098	—	7.00	18.00	25.00	36.00	—
AH1099	—	7.00	18.00	25.00	36.00	—
AH1100	—	7.00	18.00	25.00	36.00	—
AH1104	—	7.00	18.00	25.00	36.00	—
AH1105	—	10.00	25.00	36.00	48.00	—

Nakhchawan

KM# 224.5 SHAHI (50 Dinars - type 224)

1.8400 g., Silver **Note:** Type C.

Date	Mintage	VG	F	VF	XF	Unc
AH1096	—	7.00	18.00	25.00	36.00	—
AH1097	—	7.00	18.00	25.00	36.00	—
AH1099	—	7.00	18.00	25.00	36.00	—
AH1102	—	7.00	18.00	25.00	36.00	—

Rasht

KM# 224.6 SHAHI (50 Dinars - type 224)

1.8400 g., Silver **Note:** Type C.

Date	Mintage	VG	F	VF	XF	Unc
AH1097	—	10.00	25.00	36.00	48.00	—
AH1098	—	10.00	25.00	36.00	48.00	—
AH1100	—	10.00	25.00	36.00	48.00	—

Tabriz

KM# 224.7 SHAHI (50 Dinars - type 224)

1.8400 g., Silver **Note:** Type C.

Date	Mintage	VG	F	VF	XF	Unc
AH1098	—	7.00	18.00	25.00	36.00	—
AH1099	—	7.00	18.00	25.00	36.00	—
AH1101	—	7.00	18.00	25.00	36.00	—

Isfahan

KM# 212 2 SHAHI (Mahmudi)

3.6900 g., Silver **Note:** Type A.

Date	Mintage	VG	F	VF	XF	Unc
AH1079	—	25.00	55.00	70.00	110	—

Eravan

KM# 219.1 2 SHAHI (Mahmudi - type 219)

3.6900 g., Silver **Note:** Type B.

Date	Mintage	VG	F	VF	XF	Unc
AH1083	—	15.00	37.50	55.00	75.00	—

Ganjah

KM# 219.4 2 SHAHI (Mahmudi - type 219)

3.6900 g., Silver **Note:** Type B.

Date	Mintage	VG	F	VF	XF	Unc
AH1091	—	—	—	—	—	—

Tabriz

KM# 219.2 2 SHAHI (Mahmudi - type 219)

3.6900 g., Silver **Note:** Type B.

Date	Mintage	VG	F	VF	XF	Unc
AH1081	—	12.00	30.00	45.00	60.00	—

Tiflis

KM# 219.3 2 SHAHI (Mahmudi - type 219)

3.6900 g., Silver **Note:** Type B.

Date	Mintage	VG	F	VF	XF	Unc
AH1086	—	12.00	30.00	45.00	60.00	—

Eravan

KM# 225.1 2 SHAHI (Mahmudi - type 225)

3.6900 g., Silver **Note:** Type C.

Date	Mintage	VG	F	VF	XF	Unc
AH1104	—	12.00	30.00	42.00	55.00	—
AH1105	—	12.00	30.00	42.00	55.00	—

Ganjah

KM# 225.2 2 SHAHI (Mahmudi - type 225)

3.6900 g., Silver **Note:** Type C.

Date	Mintage	VG	F	VF	XF	Unc
AH1103	—	12.00	30.00	42.00	55.00	—
AH1105	—	12.00	30.00	42.00	55.00	—

Hamadan

KM# 225.3 2 SHAHI (Mahmudi - type 225)

3.6900 g., Silver **Note:** Type C.

Date	Mintage	VG	F	VF	XF	Unc
AH1097	—	14.00	36.00	48.00	65.00	—

Isfahan

KM# 225.4 2 SHAHI (Mahmudi - type 225)

3.6900 g., Silver **Note:** Type C.

Date	Mintage	VG	F	VF	XF	Unc
AH1095	—	7.00	18.00	30.00	42.00	—
AH1096	—	7.00	18.00	30.00	42.00	—
AH1099	—	7.00	18.00	30.00	42.00	—

Mashhad

KM# 225.9 2 SHAHI (Mahmudi - type 225)

3.6900 g., Silver **Note:** Type C.

Date	Mintage	VG	F	VF	XF	Unc
AH1099	—	—	—	—	—	—

Nakhchawan

KM# 225.5 2 SHAHI (Mahmudi - type 225)

3.6900 g., Silver **Note:** Type C.

Date	Mintage	VG	F	VF	XF	Unc
AH1097	—	8.00	22.50	36.00	50.00	—
AH1101	—	8.00	22.50	36.00	50.00	—

Qazvín

KM# 225.6 2 SHAHI (Mahmudi - type 225)

3.6900 g., Silver **Note:** Type C.

Date	Mintage	VG	F	VF	XF	Unc
AH1097	—	12.00	30.00	42.00	55.00	—

Rasht

KM# 225.7 2 SHAHI (Mahmudi - type 225)

3.6900 g., Silver **Note:** Type C.

Date	Mintage	VG	F	VF	XF	Unc
AH1097	—	10.00	25.00	36.00	48.00	—
AH1098	—	10.00	25.00	36.00	48.00	—

Tabriz

KM# 225.8 2 SHAHI (Mahmudi - type 225)

3.6900 g., Silver **Note:** Type C.

Date	Mintage	VG	F	VF	XF	Unc
AH1098	—	10.00	25.00	36.00	48.00	—

Ardebil

KM# 213.1 ABBASI

7.3900 g., Silver **Note:** Type A.

Date	Mintage	VG	F	VF	XF	Unc
AH1081	—	12.00	30.00	42.00	60.00	—

Ganjah

KM# 213.2 ABBASI

7.3900 g., Silver **Note:** Type A.

Date	Mintage	VG	F	VF	XF	Unc
AH1080	—	12.00	30.00	42.00	60.00	—

Qazvín

KM# 213.3 ABBASI

7.3900 g., Silver **Note:** Type A.

Date	Mintage	VG	F	VF	XF	Unc
AH1080	—	12.00	30.00	42.00	60.00	—

Shamakha

KM# 213.4 ABBASI

7.3900 g., Silver **Note:** Type A.

Date	Mintage	VG	F	VF	XF	Unc
ND	—	12.00	30.00	42.00	60.00	—

Tiflis

KM# 213.5 ABBASI

7.3900 g., Silver **Note:** Type A.

Date	Mintage	VG	F	VF	XF	Unc
AH1080	—	12.00	30.00	42.00	60.00	—

Ardebil

KM# 220.1 ABBASI (type 220)

7.3900 g., Silver **Note:** Type B.

Date	Mintage	VG	F	VF	XF	Unc
AH1082	—	6.00	15.00	22.50	36.00	—
AH1089	—	6.00	15.00	22.50	36.00	—

Eravan

KM# 220.2 ABBASI (type 220)

7.3900 g., Silver **Note:** Type B.

Date	Mintage	VG	F	VF	XF	Unc
AH1082	—	6.00	15.00	22.50	36.00	—
AH1083	—	6.00	15.00	22.50	36.00	—
AH1084	—	6.00	15.00	22.50	36.00	—
AH1086	—	6.00	15.00	22.50	36.00	—
AH1087	—	6.00	15.00	22.50	36.00	—
AH1088	—	6.00	15.00	22.50	36.00	—

Ganjah

KM# 220.3 ABBASI (type 220)

7.3900 g., Silver **Note:** Type B.

Date	Mintage	VG	F	VF	XF	Unc
AH1081	—	10.00	25.00	36.00	48.00	—
AH1090	—	7.00	18.00	27.50	42.00	—

Mashhad

KM# 220.4 ABBASI (type 220)

7.3900 g., Silver **Note:** Type B.

Date	Mintage	VG	F	VF	XF	Unc
AH1082	—	10.00	25.00	36.00	48.00	—

Qazvín

KM# 220.5 ABBASI (type 220)

7.3900 g., Silver **Note:** Type B.

Date	Mintage	VG	F	VF	XF	Unc
AH108x	—	7.00	18.00	27.50	43.25	—

Shamakha

KM# 220.6 ABBASI (type 220)

7.3900 g., Silver **Note:** Type B.

Date	Mintage	VG	F	VF	XF	Unc
AH1087	—	7.00	18.00	27.50	42.00	—

Tabriz

KM# 220.7 ABBASI (type 220)

7.3900 g., Silver **Note:** Type B.

Date	Mintage	VG	F	VF	XF	Unc
AH1081	—	6.00	15.00	22.50	36.00	—
AH1082	—	6.00	15.00	22.50	36.00	—
AH1087	—	6.00	15.00	22.50	36.00	—

Tiflis

KM# 220.8 ABBASI (type 220)

7.3900 g., Silver **Note:** Type B.

Date	Mintage	VG	F	VF	XF	Unc
AH1085	—	5.00	15.00	22.50	36.00	—
AH1086	—	5.00	15.00	22.50	36.00	—
AH1087	—	5.00	15.00	22.50	36.00	—
AH1088	—	5.00	15.00	22.50	36.00	—
AH1090	—	5.00	15.00	22.50	36.00	—
AH1091	—	5.00	15.00	22.50	36.00	—
AH1092	—	5.00	15.00	22.50	36.00	—

Ardebil

KM# 226.1 ABBASI (type 226)

7.3900 g., Silver **Note:** Type C.

Date	Mintage	VG	F	VF	XF	Unc
AH1104	—	7.00	18.00	27.50	42.00	—

Eravan

KM# 226.2 ABBASI (type 226)

7.3900 g., Silver **Note:** Type C.

Date	Mintage	VG	F	VF	XF	Unc
AH1103	—	4.00	8.00	12.00	25.00	—
AH1104	—	4.00	8.00	12.00	25.00	—
AH1105	—	4.00	8.00	12.00	25.00	—

Ganjah

KM# 226.3 ABBASI (type 226)

7.3900 g., Silver **Note:** Type C.

Date	Mintage	VG	F	VF	XF	Unc
AH1103	—	4.00	8.00	12.00	25.00	—
AH1104	—	4.00	8.00	12.00	25.00	—
AH1105	—	4.00	8.00	12.00	25.00	—

Hamadan

KM# 226.4 ABBASI (type 226)

7.3900 g., Silver **Note:** Type C.

Date	Mintage	VG	F	VF	XF	Unc
AH1096	—	6.00	15.00	20.00	33.00	—

Isfahan

KM# 226.5 ABBASI (type 226)

7.3900 g., Silver **Note:** Type C.

Date	Mintage	VG	F	VF	XF	Unc
AH1095	—	5.00	12.00	18.00	30.00	—
AH1096	—	4.00	8.00	12.00	25.00	—
AH1097	—	4.00	8.00	12.00	25.00	—
AH1098	—	4.00	8.00	12.00	25.00	—
AH1099	—	4.00	8.00	12.00	25.00	—
AH1100	—	4.00	8.00	12.00	25.00	—
AH1102	—	5.00	12.00	18.00	30.00	—
AH1103	—	4.00	8.00	12.00	25.00	—
AH1104	—	4.00	8.00	12.00	25.00	—
AH1105	—	4.00	8.00	12.00	25.00	—

Kashan

KM# 226.6 ABBASI (type 226)

7.3900 g., Silver **Note:** Type C.

Date	Mintage	VG	F	VF	XF	Unc
AH1096	—	6.00	15.00	20.00	33.00	—
AH1097	—	6.00	15.00	20.00	33.00	—

Mashhad

KM# 226.7 ABBASI (type 226)

7.3900 g., Silver **Note:** Type C.

Date	Mintage	VG	F	VF	XF	Unc
AH1095	—	7.00	18.00	27.50	39.00	—
AH1096	—	6.00	15.00	20.00	33.00	—
AH1098	—	6.00	15.00	20.00	33.00	—
AH(110)4	—	7.00	18.00	27.50	42.00	—

Note: Only final digit engraved

Nakhchawan

KM# 226.8 ABBASI (type 226)

7.3900 g., Silver **Note:** Type C.

Date	Mintage	VG	F	VF	XF	Unc
AH1096	—	4.00	8.00	12.00	25.00	—
AH1097	—	4.00	8.00	12.00	25.00	—
AH1098	—	4.00	8.00	12.00	25.00	—
AH1099	—	4.00	8.00	12.00	25.00	—
AH1100	—	4.00	8.00	12.00	25.00	—
AH1101	—	4.00	8.00	12.00	25.00	—
AH1102	—	4.00	8.00	12.00	25.00	—
AH1103	—	4.00	8.00	12.00	25.00	—
AH1104	—	4.00	8.00	12.00	25.00	—
AH1105	—	4.00	8.00	12.00	25.00	—

Qazvín

KM# 226.9 ABBASI (type 226)

7.3900 g., Silver **Note:** Type C.

Date	Mintage	VG	F	VF	XF	Unc
AH1096	—	5.00	12.00	18.00	30.00	—
AH1097	—	5.00	12.00	18.00	30.00	—

Date	Mintage	VG	F	VF	XF	Unc
AH1099	—	5.00	12.00	18.00	30.00	—
AH1105	—	5.00	12.00	18.00	30.00	—

Rasht

KM# 226.10 ABBASI (type 226)
7.3900 g., Silver **Note:** Type C.

Date	Mintage	VG	F	VF	XF	Unc
AH1095	—	6.00	15.00	25.00	36.00	—
AH1097	—	4.00	8.00	12.00	25.00	—
AH1098	—	4.00	8.00	12.00	25.00	—
AH1100	—	4.00	8.00	12.00	25.00	—
AH1105	—	4.00	10.00	15.00	27.50	—

Shamakha

KM# 226.11 ABBASI (type 226)
7.3900 g., Silver **Note:** Type C.

Date	Mintage	VG	F	VF	XF	Unc
AH1104	—	7.00	18.00	27.50	42.00	—

Tabriz

KM# 226.12 ABBASI (type 226)
7.3900 g., Silver **Note:** Type C.

Date	Mintage	VG	F	VF	XF	Unc
AH1096	—	4.00	8.00	12.00	25.00	—
AH1097	—	4.00	8.00	12.00	25.00	—
AH1098	—	4.00	8.00	12.00	25.00	—
AH1099	—	4.00	8.00	12.00	25.00	—
AH1100	—	4.00	8.00	12.00	25.00	—
AH1101	—	4.00	8.00	12.00	25.00	—
AH1102	—	4.00	8.00	12.00	25.00	—
AH1103	—	4.00	8.00	12.00	25.00	—
AH1104	—	4.00	8.00	12.00	25.00	—
AH1105	—	4.00	8.00	12.00	25.00	—

Tiflis

KM# 226.13 ABBASI (type 226)
7.3900 g., Silver **Note:** Type C.

Date	Mintage	VG	F	VF	XF	Unc
AH1103	—	6.00	15.00	25.00	39.00	—
AH1104	—	6.00	15.00	25.00	39.00	—
AH1105	—	6.00	15.00	25.00	39.00	—

Isfahan

KM# 214 2-1/2 ABBASI (10 Shahi)
18.4800 g., Silver **Note:** Type A.

Date	Mintage	VG	F	VF	XF	Unc
AH1079	—	60.00	120	210	350	—
AH1081	—	60.00	120	210	350	—
AH1082	—	60.00	120	210	350	—
AH1087	—	60.00	120	210	350	—
AH1090	—	60.00	120	210	350	—
AH1093	—	60.00	120	210	350	—
AH1094	—	60.00	120	210	350	—

Isfahan

KM# 227 2-1/2 ABBASI (10 Shahi - type 227)
18.4800 g., Silver

Date	Mintage	VG	F	VF	XF	Unc
AH1094	—	90.00	180	240	550	—
AH1096	—	90.00	180	240	550	—

Isfahan

KM# 215.1 5 ABBASI (20 Shahi)
36.9500 g., Silver

Date	Mintage	VG	F	VF	XF	Unc
AH1083	—	150	240	350	775	—
AH1084	—	150	240	350	775	—
AH1090	—	150	240	350	775	—
AH1091	—	150	240	350	775	—

Qazvín

KM# 215.2 5 ABBASI (20 Shahi)
36.9500 g., Silver **Note:** Struck at Qazvín.

Date	Mintage	VG	F	VF	XF	Unc
AH1085	—	150	300	425	900	—

Isfahan

KM# 228 5 ABBASI (20 Shahi - type 228)
36.9500 g., Silver **Rev:** Without border inscription

Date	Mintage	VG	F	VF	XF	Unc
AH1096	—	180	300	475	1,200	—

Isfahan

KM# 229 5 ABBASI (20 Shahi - type 229)
36.9500 g., Silver **Rev:** With border inscription

Date	Mintage	VG	F	VF	XF	Unc
AH1099	—	180	300	475	1,200	—

Isfahan

KM# 230.1 7 1/2 ABBASI
56.3700 g., Gold **Obv. Inscription:** "Shi'a Kalima"

Date	Mintage	VG	F	VF	XF	Unc
AH1096 Rare	—	—	—	—	—	—

Ganjah

KM# 231 1/4 ASHRAFI
0.8800 g., Gold **Note:** Type C.

Date	Mintage	VG	F	VF	XF	Unc
AHxxxx Rare	—	—	—	—	—	—

Isfahan

KM# 232 ASHRAFI
3.5000 g., Gold

Date	Mintage	VG	F	VF	XF	Unc
AH1095	—	250	400	550	800	—

Husayn I

AH1105-1135 / 1694-1722AD

Husayn, son of Sulayman I, was enthroned on 14 Dhu'l-Hijja 1105 (August 6, 1694), and abdicated under pressure from the Afghan invaders on 11 Muharram 1135 (October 23, 1722). He was murdered by his Afghan mentors in AH1142 (1729AD). He is sometimes known as Husayn I, to distinguish him from a pretender who set himself up in the mid-18th century, but struck no coins.

Silver types for this reign:

A. Obverse couplet, *zad za toufiq-e haqq be-chehre-ye zar / seeke-ye soltan Hosein-e din-parvar,* "Upon the face of precious metal, by the grace of God, was imprinted the stamp of Sultan Husayn, the nurturer of the religion". Used AH1105-1107 only. Struck to the 1925 nokhod standard in use since AH1054.

B. Obverse couplet, *gasht saheb-e sekke az toufiq-e rab ol-mashreqein / dar jahan kalb-e amir ol-mo'menin soltan Hosayn,* "In this world, the dog of the commander of the believers (i.e., Ali ibn Abi Talib), Sultan Husayn, became master of the die, by the grace of the Lord of the Two Easts". Used AH1107-1123.

NOTE: Because the mint is normal at the bottom of the die and the date near the top, specimens with date and mint of Types A and B are relatively scarce, especially for the smaller denominations.

C. Obverse, mint and date, plus the formula *bande-ye shah-e velayat Hosein* (cf. Type D of Abbas I). Struck to the standard of 1800 nokhod (abbasi = 6.91 g).

D. As Type C, but to the standard of 1400 nokhod (abbasi = 5.34 g). During the siege of Isfahan, in AH1134 (1721-22AD), the Isfahan abbasi was reduced to the 1200 nokhod standard (abbasi = 4.61 g). The 1400 standard was retained at all other mints.

E. Obverse, mint and date, plus the formula *kalb-e astan-e Ali Hosein,* "Husayn, the dog on the doorstep of Ali". Used only at Mashhad. Struck in AH1123 to the 1800 nokhod standard and from AH1130-1137 to the 1400 standard. Issues of AH1135-1137 were orderd by Shah Mahmud Sistani, who later in AH1137-1138, struck coins in his own name.

As in the previous reign, there are a great variety of presentation pieces, few of which have been published. Only a small number are listed here. Most are extremely rare.

HAMMERED COINAGE

Local Type of Khuzistan

Huwayza

KM# 295 2 SHAHI (Mahmudi)
Silver **Note:** Type H. About 3.00 grams.

Date	Mintage	VG	F	VF	XF	Unc
AH1108	—	18.50	55.00	75.00	100	—

HAMMERED COINAGE

Isfahan

KM# 255 PUL (1/2 Shahi)
0.9200 g., Silver **Note:** Type B.

Date	Mintage	VG	F	VF	XF	Unc
AH111x	—	25.00	48.00	60.00	70.00	—

KM# 256 SHAHI (50 Dinars)
1.8400 g., Silver **Note:** Type B.

Date	Mintage	VG	F	VF	XF	Unc
AH1108	—	12.00	30.00	42.00	60.00	—
AH1109	—	10.00	25.00	36.00	48.00	—
AH1110	—	12.00	30.00	42.00	60.00	—
AH1110	—	10.00	25.00	36.00	48.00	—
AH1112	—	10.00	25.00	36.00	48.00	—

Eravan

KM# 256.1 SHAHI (50 Dinars)
1.8400 g., Silver **Note:** Type B.

Date	Mintage	VG	F	VF	XF	Unc
AH1108	—	12.00	30.00	42.00	60.00	—

Ganjah

KM# 256.2 SHAHI (50 Dinars)
1.8400 g., Silver **Note:** Type B.

Date	Mintage	VG	F	VF	XF	Unc
AH1110	—	12.00	30.00	42.00	60.00	—

Isfahan

KM# 251 SHAHI (50 Dinars)
1.8400 g., Silver **Note:** Type A.

Date	Mintage	VG	F	VF	XF	Unc
AH1106	—	14.00	36.00	48.00	60.00	—

KM# 256.3 SHAHI (50 Dinars)
1.8400 g., Silver **Note:** Type B.

Date	Mintage	VG	F	VF	XF	Unc
AH1109	—	10.00	25.00	36.00	48.00	—

Date	Mintage	VG	F	VF	XF	Unc
AH1110	—	10.00	25.00	36.00	48.00	—
AH1112	—	10.00	25.00	36.00	48.00	—

Eravan

KM# 252 2 SHAHI (Mahmudi)
3.6900 g., Silver **Note:** Type A.

Date	Mintage	VG	F	VF	XF	Unc
AH1106	—	19.00	48.00	65.00	80.00	—

KM# 257.3 2 SHAHI (Mahmudi)
3.6900 g., Silver **Note:** Type B.

Date	Mintage	VG	F	VF	XF	Unc
1107	—	30.00	42.00	55.00	70.00	—

Isfahan

KM# 257.1 2 SHAHI (Mahmudi)
3.6900 g., Silver **Note:** Type B.

Date	Mintage	VG	F	VF	XF	Unc
AH1112	—	30.00	42.00	55.00	70.00	—

Tiflis

KM# 257.2 2 SHAHI (Mahmudi)
3.6900 g., Silver **Note:** Type B.

Date	Mintage	VG	F	VF	XF	Unc
AH1107	—	12.00	30.00	42.00	55.00	—

Eravan

KM# 253.1 ABBASI
9.2400 g., Silver **Note:** Type A.

Date	Mintage	VG	F	VF	XF	Unc
AH1106	—	7.00	18.00	30.00	42.00	—
AH1107	—	7.00	18.00	30.00	42.00	—

Ganjah

KM# 253.2 ABBASI
9.2400 g., Silver **Note:** Type A.

Date	Mintage	VG	F	VF	XF	Unc
AH1105	—	10.00	25.00	36.00	48.00	—

Isfahan

KM# 253.3 ABBASI
9.2400 g., Silver **Note:** Type A.

Date	Mintage	VG	F	VF	XF	Unc
AH1106	—	6.00	15.00	25.00	36.00	—
AH1107	—	6.00	15.00	25.00	36.00	—

Nakhchawan

KM# 253.4 ABBASI
9.2400 g., Silver **Note:** Type A.

Date	Mintage	VG	F	VF	XF	Unc
AH1106	—	7.00	18.00	30.00	42.00	—
AH1107	—	7.00	18.00	30.00	42.00	—

Qazvín

KM# 253.5 ABBASI
9.2400 g., Silver **Note:** Type A.

Date	Mintage	VG	F	VF	XF	Unc
AH1105	—	9.00	22.50	33.00	45.00	—

Rasht

KM# 253.6 ABBASI
9.2400 g., Silver **Note:** Type A.

Date	Mintage	VG	F	VF	XF	Unc
AH1105	—	10.00	25.00	36.00	48.00	—

Tabriz

KM# 253.7 ABBASI
9.2400 g., Silver **Note:** Type A.

Date	Mintage	VG	F	VF	XF	Unc
AH1106	—	6.00	15.00	25.00	36.00	—
AH1107	—	6.00	15.00	25.00	36.00	—

Tiflis

KM# 253.8 ABBASI
9.2400 g., Silver **Note:** Type A.

Date	Mintage	VG	F	VF	XF	Unc
AH1106	—	6.00	15.00	25.00	36.00	—
AH1107	—	6.00	15.00	25.00	36.00	—

Eravan

KM# 258.1 ABBASI (type 258)
9.2400 g., Silver **Note:** Type B.

Date	Mintage	VG	F	VF	XF	Unc
AH1108	—	5.00	12.00	18.00	30.00	—
AH1109	—	5.00	12.00	18.00	30.00	—
AH1110	—	5.00	12.00	18.00	30.00	—
AH1111	—	5.00	12.00	18.00	30.00	—
AH1112	—	5.00	12.00	18.00	30.00	—

Ganjah

KM# 258.2 ABBASI (type 258)
9.2400 g., Silver **Note:** Type B.

Date	Mintage	VG	F	VF	XF	Unc
AH1107	—	6.00	15.00	20.00	33.00	—
AH1108	—	6.00	15.00	20.00	33.00	—
AH1110	—	6.00	15.00	20.00	33.00	—
AH1111	—	6.00	15.00	20.00	33.00	—
AH1112	—	6.00	15.00	20.00	33.00	—

Isfahan

KM# 258.4 ABBASI (type 258)
9.2400 g., Silver **Note:** Type B.

Date	Mintage	VG	F	VF	XF	Unc
AH1107	—	5.00	12.00	18.00	30.00	—
AH1108	—	5.00	12.00	18.00	30.00	—
AH1109	—	5.00	12.00	18.00	30.00	—
AH1111	—	5.00	12.00	18.00	30.00	—
AH1112	—	5.00	12.00	18.00	30.00	—

Nakhchawan

KM# 258.5 ABBASI (type 258)
9.2400 g., Silver **Note:** Type B.

Date	Mintage	VG	F	VF	XF	Unc
AH1107	—	7.00	18.00	30.00	42.00	—
AH1108	—	7.00	18.00	30.00	42.00	—
AH1110	—	7.00	18.00	30.00	42.00	—
AH1111	—	7.00	18.00	30.00	42.00	—

Rasht

KM# 258.6 ABBASI (type 258)
9.2400 g., Silver **Note:** Type B.

Date	Mintage	VG	F	VF	XF	Unc
AH1109	—	7.00	18.00	30.00	42.00	—

Tabriz

KM# 258.7 ABBASI (type 258)
9.2400 g., Silver **Note:** Type B.

Date	Mintage	VG	F	VF	XF	Unc
AH1108	—	5.00	12.00	18.00	30.00	—
AH1110	—	5.00	12.00	18.00	30.00	—

Tiflis

KM# 258.8 ABBASI (type 258)
9.2400 g., Silver **Note:** Type B.

Date	Mintage	VG	F	VF	XF	Unc
AH1107	—	5.00	12.00	18.00	30.00	—
AH1108	—	5.00	12.00	18.00	30.00	—
AH1109	—	5.00	12.00	18.00	30.00	—
AH1110	—	5.00	12.00	18.00	30.00	—
AH1111	—	5.00	12.00	18.00	30.00	—
AH1112	—	5.00	12.00	18.00	30.00	—

Eravan

KM# 259.1 5 SHAHI
9.2400 g., Silver **Note:** Type B.

Date	Mintage	VG	F	VF	XF	Unc
AH1108	—	12.00	30.00	48.00	65.00	—

Ganjah

KM# 259.2 5 SHAHI
9.2400 g., Silver **Note:** Type B.

Date	Mintage	VG	F	VF	XF	Unc
AH1107	—	10.00	25.00	42.00	60.00	—
AH1108	—	10.00	25.00	42.00	60.00	—

Isfahan

KM# 259.3 5 SHAHI
9.2400 g., Silver **Note:** Type B.

Date	Mintage	VG	F	VF	XF	Unc
AH1107	—	10.00	25.00	42.00	60.00	—

Tabriz

KM# 259.4 5 SHAHI
9.2400 g., Silver **Note:** Type B.

Date	Mintage	VG	F	VF	XF	Unc
AH1107	—	12.00	30.00	48.00	65.00	—

Isfahan

KM# 261 5 ABBASI (20 Shahi)
36.9600 g., Silver **Note:** Type B.

Date	Mintage	VG	F	VF	XF	Unc
AH1109 Rare	—	—	—	—	—	—

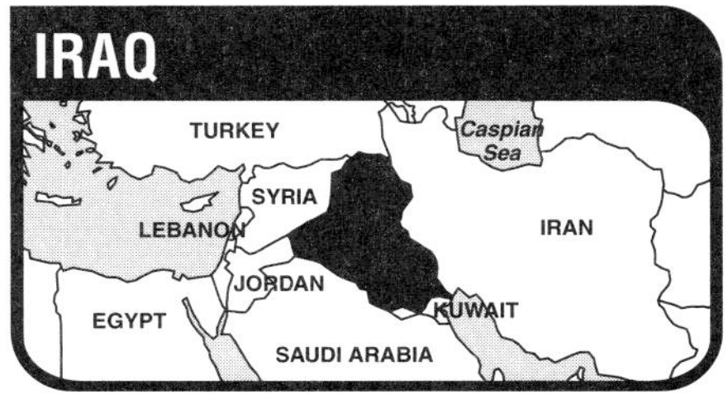

Iraq, historically known as Mesopotamia, is located in the Near East and is bordered by Kuwait, Iran, Turkey, Syria, Jordan and Saudi Arabia. Mesopotamia was the site of a number of flourishing civilizations of antiquity - Sumeria, Assyria, Babylonia, Parthia, Persia and the Biblical cities of Ur, Nineveh and Babylon. Desired because of its favored location, which embraced the fertile alluvial plains of the Tigris and Euphrates Rivers, Mesopotamia - 'land between the rivers'- was conquered by Cyrus the Great of Persia, Alexander of Macedonia and by Arabs who made the legendary city of Baghdad the capital of the ruling caliphate. Suleiman the Magnificent conquered Mesopotamia for Turkey in 1534, and it formed part of the Ottoman Empire until 1623, and from 1638 to 1917

RULER
Ottoman, until 1917

MESOPOTAMIA

Ottoman Empire

MONETARY SYSTEM
40 Para = 1 Piastre (Kurus)

MINT NAMES

بغداد
Baghdad

البصرة
al-Basrah (Basra)

الحلة
al-Hille

Mehmed III

AH1003-1012 / 1595-1603AD

HAMMERED COINAGE

KM# 2 DIRHEM (Shahi)
4.6200 g., Silver

Date	Mintage	VG	F	VF	XF	Unc
AH100(3)	—	—	—	—	—	—

KM# 3 DIRHEM (Shahi)
3.0000 g., Silver

Date	Mintage	VG	F	VF	XF	Unc
AH1003	—	30.00	60.00	100	175	—

KM# 5 ALTIN
3.4500 g., Gold **NOTE:** 2 varieties exist.

Date	Mintage	VG	F	VF	XF	Unc
AH1003	—	75.00	150	250	350	—

KM# 6 SULTANI
3.5000 g., Gold

Date	Mintage	VG	F	VF	XF	Unc
AH1003 Rare	—	—	—	—	—	—

Ahmed I

AH1012-1026 / 1603-1617AD

HAMMERED COINAGE

KM# 8 DIRHEM (Shahi)
Silver **Obv:** 5-line inscription **Note:** Weight varies 4.07 - 4.82 grams.

Date	Mintage	VG	F	VF	XF	Unc
AH1012	—	—	—	—	—	—

KM# 9 SULTANI
3.3500 g., Gold

Date	Mintage	VG	F	VF	XF	Unc
AH1012	—	100	150	250	350	—

Mustafa I

AH1026-1027/1617-1618AD

HAMMERED COINAGE

KM# 10 MANGIR
1.0400 g., Copper, 14 mm. **Obv:** Toughra **Rev:** Mint name in ornament

Date	Mintage	VG	F	VF	XF	Unc
ND	—	—	—	—	—	—

Osman II

AH1027-1031 / 1618-1622AD

HAMMERED COINAGE

KM# 12 DIRHEM (Shahi)
Silver **Obv:** 5-line inscription **Note:** Weight varies 4.26 - 4.70 grams.

Date	Mintage	VG	F	VF	XF	Unc
AHxxxx	—	—	—	—	—	—

Murad IV

AH1032-1049 / 1623-1640AD

HAMMERED COINAGE

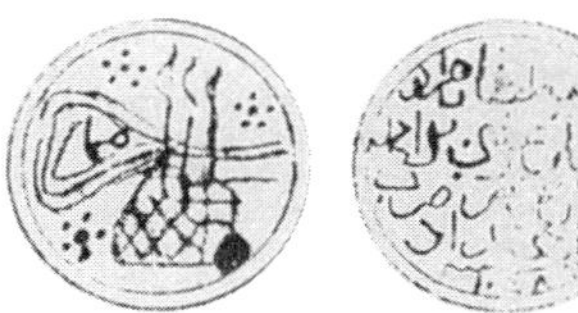

KM# 15 DIRHEM (Shahi)
2.9600 g., Silver **Obv:** Toughra **Rev:** 5-line inscription

Date	Mintage	VG	F	VF	XF	Unc
AH1048	—	50.00	75.00	100	150	—

KM# 17 SULTANI
Gold

Date	Mintage	Good	VG	F	VF	XF
AH1043 Rare	—	—	—	—	—	—

KM# 18 SULTANI
3.4500 g., Gold

Date	Mintage	VG	F	VF	XF	Unc
AH1049	—	—	—	—	—	—

KM# 32 SULTANI
3.1000 g., Gold

Date	Mintage	VG	F	VF	XF	Unc
AH1058	—	—	—	—	—	—

Ibrahim

AH1049-1058 / 1640-1648AD

HAMMERED COINAGE

KM# 19 MANGIR
1.8200 g., Copper **Obv:** Ornaments **Note:** Prev. KM#24.

Date	Mintage	VG	F	VF	XF	Unc
AH1049	—	20.00	30.00	50.00	75.00	—

KM# A20 MANGIR
1.6500 g., Copper

Date	Mintage	VG	F	VF	XF	Unc
AH1058	—	—	—	—	—	—

KM# B20 AKCE
Silver

Date	Mintage	VG	F	VF	XF	Unc
AH1049	—	—	—	—	—	—

KM# 20 1/2 DIRHEM (1/2 Shahi)
1.8000 g., Silver

Date	Mintage	VG	F	VF	XF	Unc
AHxx4x	—	—	—	—	—	—

KM# 22 DIRHEM (Shahi)
2.7500 g., Silver

Date	Mintage	VG	F	VF	XF	Unc
AH10xx	—	—	—	—	—	—

KM# 23 DIRHEM (Shahi)
Silver **Obv:** Toughra **Note:** Five varieties exist.

Date	Mintage	VG	F	VF	XF	Unc
AH1049	—	7.00	12.00	20.00	40.00	—

Note: Five varieties exist

Mehmed IV

AH1058-1099 / 1648-1687AD

HAMMERED COINAGE

KM# 25 MANGIR
0.9000 g., Copper, 15 mm. **Obv:** Ornament **Rev:** Mint name

Date	Mintage	VG	F	VF	XF	Unc
AH1058 Rare	—	—	—	—	—	—

KM# 33 DIRHEM (Shahi)
2.9200 g., Gold

Date	Mintage	VG	F	VF	XF	Unc
AH1058	—	150	200	300	450	—

KM# 26 DIRHEM (Shahi)
Silver **Obv:** 4-line inscription **Rev:** 5-line inscription **Note:** Weight varies: 2.59-2.90 grams.

Date	Mintage	VG	F	VF	XF	Unc
AH1058	—	20.00	30.00	40.00	60.00	—

KM# 27 DIRHEM (Shahi)
Silver **Obv:** Toughra **Rev:** 5-line inscription **Note:** Weight varies: 2.77-2.90 grams.

Date	Mintage	VG	F	VF	XF	Unc
AH1058	—	20.00	30.00	40.00	60.00	—

KM# 28 DIRHEM (Shahi)
Silver **Rev. Legend:** Around inner circle with mintname **Note:** Weight varies: 2.77-2.90 grams.

Date	Mintage	VG	F	VF	XF	Unc
AH1058	—	20.00	30.00	45.00	65.00	—

KM# 29 DIRHEM (Shahi)
Silver **Obv:** 3-line inscription **Rev:** 3-line inscripton **Note:** Weight varies: 2.77-2.90 grams.

Date	Mintage	VG	F	VF	XF	Unc
AH1059	—	15.00	25.00	30.00	55.00	—

KM# 30 DIRHEM (Shahi)
Silver **Rev:** 4-line inscripton **Note:** Weight varies: 2.77-2.90 grams.

Date	Mintage	VG	F	VF	XF	Unc
AH1062	—	40.00	60.00	100	150	—

Suleyman II

AH1099-1102 / 1687-1691AD

HAMMERED COINAGE

KM# 34 MANGIR
0.8000 g., Copper **Obv:** Ornament **Rev:** Mint name

Date	Mintage	VG	F	VF	XF	Unc
AH(1)099	—	—	—	—	—	—

KM# 36 DIRHEM (Shahi)
2.8500 g., Silver **Obv:** Toughra **Rev:** 4-line inscription

Date	Mintage	VG	F	VF	XF	Unc
AH1099 Rare	—	—	—	—	—	—

KM# 37 LARIN
Silver

Date	Mintage	VG	F	VF	XF	Unc
ND Rare	—	—	—	—	—	—

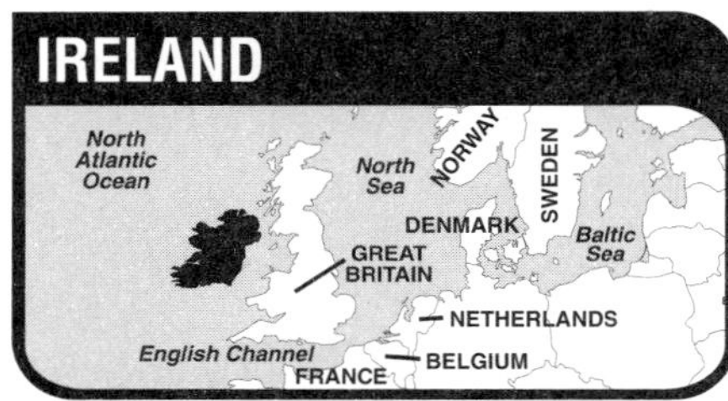

Ireland, the island located in the Atlantic Ocean west of Great Britain, was settled by a race of tall, red-haired Celts from Gaul about 400 BC. They assimilated the native Erainn and Picts and established a Gaelic civilization. After the arrival of St. Patrick in 432 AD, Ireland evolved into a center of Latin learning, which sent missionaries to Europe and possibly North America. In 1154, Pope Adrian IV gave all of Ireland to English King Henry II to administer as a Papal fief. Because of the enactment of anti-Catholic laws and the awarding of vast tracts of Irish land to Protestant absentee landowners, English control did not become reasonably absolute until 1800 when England and Ireland became the "United Kingdom of Great Britain and Ireland". Religious freedom was restored to the Irish in 1829, but agitation for political autonomy continued until the Irish Free State was established as a Dominion on Dec. 6, 1921 while Northern Ireland remained under the British rule.

RULER
British to 1921

MONETARY SYSTEM
4 Farthings = 1 Penny
12 Pence = 1 Shilling
5 Shillings = 1 Crown

UNITED KINGDOM

STANDARD COINAGE

KM# 20.1 FARTHING
Tin Plated Copper **Obv:** Crown on crossed sceptres, titles of James I **Rev:** Crowned harp **Note:** Small "Harrington" Issue. No mintmark.

Date	Mintage	VG	F	VF	XF	Unc
ND(1613)	—	40.00	9.00	375	750	—

KM# 20.2 FARTHING
Tin Plated Copper **Obv:** Crown on crossed sceptres, titles of James I **Rev:** Crowned harp **Note:** Small "Harrington" Issue; mintmark: A.

Date	Mintage	VG	F	VF	XF	Unc
ND(1613)	—	40.00	90.00	375	750	—

KM# 20.3 FARTHING
Tin Plated Copper **Obv:** Crown on crossed sceptres, titles of James I **Rev:** Crowned harp **Note:** Small "Harrington" Issue; mintmark: B.

Date	Mintage	VG	F	VF	XF	Unc
ND(1613)	—	40.00	90.00	375	750	—

KM# 20.4 FARTHING
Tin Plated Copper **Obv:** Crown on crossed sceptres, titles of James I **Rev:** Crowned harp **Note:** Small "Harrington" Issue; mintmark: C.

Date	Mintage	VG	F	VF	XF	Unc
ND(1613)	—	40.00	90.00	375	750	—

KM# 20.5 FARTHING
Tin Plated Copper **Obv:** Crown on crossed sceptres, titles of James I **Rev:** Crowned harp **Note:** Small "Harrington" Issue; mintmark: D.

Date	Mintage	VG	F	VF	XF	Unc
ND(1613)	—	40.00	90.00	375	750	—

KM# 20.6 FARTHING
Tin Plated Copper **Obv:** Crown on crossed sceptres, titles of James I **Rev:** Crowned harp **Note:** Small "Harrington" Issue; mintmark: F.

Date	Mintage	VG	F	VF	XF	Unc
ND(1613)	—	40.00	90.00	375	750	—

KM# 20.7 FARTHING
Tin Plated Copper **Obv:** Crown on crossed sceptres, titles of James I **Rev:** Crowned harp **Note:** Small "Harrington" Issue; mintmark: L.

Date	Mintage	VG	F	VF	XF	Unc
ND(1613)	—	40.00	90.00	375	750	—

KM# 20.8 FARTHING
Tin Plated Copper **Obv:** Crown on crossed sceptres, titles of James I **Rev:** Crowned harp **Note:** Small "Harrington" Issue; mintmark: Crescent.

Date	Mintage	VG	F	VF	XF	Unc
ND(1613)	—	40.00	90.00	375	750	—

KM# 20.9 FARTHING
Tin Plated Copper **Obv:** Crown on crossed sceptres, titles of James I **Rev:** Crowned harp **Note:** Small "Harrington" Issue; mintmark: Ermine.

Date	Mintage	VG	F	VF	XF	Unc
ND(1613)	—	40.00	90.00	375	750	—

KM# 20.10 FARTHING
Tin Plated Copper **Obv:** Crown on crossed sceptres, titles of James I **Rev:** Crowned harp **Note:** Small "Harrington" Issue; mintmark: Millrind.

Date	Mintage	VG	F	VF	XF	Unc
ND(1613)	—	40.00	90.00	375	750	—

KM# 20.11 FARTHING
Tin Plated Copper **Obv:** Crown on crossed sceptres, titles of James I **Rev:** Crowned harp **Note:** Small "Harrington" Issue; mintmark: Mullet.

Date	Mintage	VG	F	VF	XF	Unc
ND(1613)	—	40.00	90.00	375	750	—

KM# 20.12 FARTHING
Tin Plated Copper **Obv:** Crown on crossed sceptres, titles of James I **Rev:** Crowned harp **Note:** Small "Harrington" Issue; mintmark: Pellet.

Date	Mintage	VG	F	VF	XF	Unc
ND(1613)	—	40.00	90.00	375	750	—

KM# 20.13 FARTHING
Tin Plated Copper **Obv:** Crown on crossed sceptres, titles of James I **Rev:** Crowned harp **Note:** Small "Harrington" Issue; mintmark: Trefoil.

Date	Mintage	VG	F	VF	XF	Unc
ND(1613)	—	40.00	90.00	375	750	—

KM# 21.1 FARTHING
Copper **Obv:** Crown on crossed sceptres, titles of James I **Rev:** Crowned harp **Note:** Normal "Harrington" Issue; mintmark: Cinquefoil.

Date	Mintage	VG	F	VF	XF	Unc
ND(1613)	—	18.00	37.50	95.00	190	—

KM# 21.2 FARTHING
Copper **Obv:** Crown on crossed sceptres, titles of James I **Rev:** Crowned harp **Note:** Normal "Harrington" Issue; mintmark: Lis.

Date	Mintage	VG	F	VF	XF	Unc
ND(1613)	—	18.00	37.50	95.00	190	—

KM# 21.3 FARTHING

Copper **Obv:** Crown on crossed sceptres, titles of James I **Rev:** Crowned harp **Note:** Normal "Harrington" Issue; mintmark: Martlet.

Date	Mintage	VG	F	VF	XF	Unc
ND(1613)	—	18.00	37.50	95.00	190	—

KM# 21.4 FARTHING

Copper **Obv:** Crown on crossed sceptres, titles of James I **Rev:** Crowned harp **Note:** Normal "Harrington" Issue; mintmark: Mullet.

Date	Mintage	VG	F	VF	XF	Unc
ND(1613)	—	18.00	37.50	95.00	190	—

KM# 21.5 FARTHING

Copper **Obv:** Crown on crossed sceptres, titles of James I **Rev:** Crowned harp **Note:** Normal "Harrington" Issue; mintmark: Saltire.

Date	Mintage	VG	F	VF	XF	Unc
ND(1613)	—	18.00	37.50	959	190	—

KM# 21.6 FARTHING

Copper **Obv:** Crown on crossed sceptres, titles of James I **Rev:** Crowned harp **Note:** Normal "Harrington" Issue; mintmark: Trefoil.

Date	Mintage	VG	F	VF	XF	Unc
ND(1613)	—	18.00	37.50	95.00	190	—

KM# 22.1 FARTHING

Copper **Obv:** Crown on crossed sceptres, titles of James I **Rev:** Crowned harp **Note:** Lennox Issue; Mint mark: Annulet with 6 or 7 harp strings.

Date	Mintage	VG	F	VF	XF	Unc
ND(1613)	—	7.50	18.00	37.50	75.00	—

KM# 22.2 FARTHING

Copper **Obv:** Crown on crossed sceptres, titles of James I **Rev:** Crowned harp **Note:** Lennox Issue; Mint mark: Ball.

Date	Mintage	VG	F	VF	XF	Unc
ND(1613)	—	7.50	18.00	37.50	75.00	—

KM# 22.3 FARTHING

Copper **Obv:** Crown on crossed sceptres, titles of James I **Rev:** Crowned harp **Note:** Lennox Issue; Mint mark: Bell.

Date	Mintage	VG	F	VF	XF	Unc
ND(1613)	—	7.50	18.00	37.50	75.00	—

KM# 22.4 FARTHING

Copper **Obv:** Crown on crossed sceptres, titles of James I **Rev:** Crowned harp **Note:** Lennox Issue; Mint mark: Coronet.

Date	Mintage	VG	F	VF	XF	Unc
ND(1613)	—	7.50	18.00	37.50	75.00	—

KM# 22.5 FARTHING

Copper **Obv:** Crown on crossed sceptres, titles of James I **Rev:** Crowned harp **Note:** Lennox Issue; Mint mark: Crescent.

Date	Mintage	VG	F	VF	XF	Unc
ND(1613)	—	7.50	18.00	37.50	75.00	—

KM# 22.6 FARTHING

Copper **Obv:** Crown on crossed sceptres, titles of James I **Rev:** Crowned harp **Note:** Lennox Issue; Mint mark: Cross.

Date	Mintage	VG	F	VF	XF	Unc
ND(1613)	—	7.50	18.00	37.50	75.00	—

KM# 22.7 FARTHING

Copper **Obv:** Crown on crossed sceptres, titles of James I **Rev:** Crowned harp **Note:** Lennox Issue; Mint mark: Dagger.

Date	Mintage	VG	F	VF	XF	Unc
ND(1613)	—	7.50	18.00	37.50	75.00	—

KM# 22.8 FARTHING

Copper **Obv:** Crown on crossed sceptres, titles of James I **Rev:** Crowned harp **Note:** Lennox Issue; Mint mark: Double rose.

Date	Mintage	VG	F	VF	XF	Unc
ND(1613)	—	7.50	18.00	37.50	75.00	—

KM# 22.9 FARTHING

Copper **Obv:** Crown on crossed sceptres, titles of James I **Rev:** Crowned harp **Note:** Lennox Issue; Mint mark: Eagle's head.

Date	Mintage	VG	F	VF	XF	Unc
ND(1613)	—	7.50	18.00	37.50	75.00	—

KM# 22.10 FARTHING

Copper **Obv:** Crown on crossed sceptres, titles of James I **Rev:** Crowned harp **Note:** Lennox Issue; Mint mark: Flower.

Date	Mintage	VG	F	VF	XF	Unc
ND(1613)	—	7.50	18.00	37.50	75.00	—

KM# 22.11 FARTHING

Copper **Obv:** Crown on crossed sceptres, titles of James I **Rev:** Crowned harp **Note:** Lennox Issue; Mint mark: Grapes.

Date	Mintage	VG	F	VF	XF	Unc
ND(1613)	—	7.50	18.00	37.50	75.00	—

KM# 22.12 FARTHING

Copper **Obv:** Crown on crossed sceptres, titles of James I **Rev:** Crowned harp **Note:** Lennox Issue; Mint mark: Keg.

Date	Mintage	VG	F	VF	XF	Unc
ND(1613)	—	7.50	18.00	37.50	75.00	—

KM# 22.13 FARTHING

Copper **Obv:** Crown on crossed sceptres, titles of James I **Rev:** Crowned harp **Note:** Lennox Issue; Mint mark: Key.

Date	Mintage	VG	F	VF	XF	Unc
ND(1613)	—	7.50	18.00	37.50	75.00	—

KM# 22.14 FARTHING

Copper **Obv:** Crown on crossed sceptres, titles of James I **Rev:** Crowned harp **Note:** Lennox Issue; Mint mark: Lion.

Date	Mintage	VG	F	VF	XF	Unc
ND(1613)	—	7.50	18.00	37.50	75.00	—

KM# 22.15 FARTHING

Copper **Obv:** Crown on crossed sceptres, titles of James I **Rev:** Crowned harp **Note:** Lennox Issue; Mint mark: 3 Lis.

Date	Mintage	VG	F	VF	XF	Unc
ND(1613)	—	7.50	18.00	37.50	75.00	—

KM# 22.16 FARTHING

Copper **Obv:** Crown on crossed sceptres, titles of James I **Rev:** Crowned harp **Note:** Lennox Issue; Mint mark: Lombardic A.

Date	Mintage	VG	F	VF	XF	Unc
ND(1613)	—	7.50	18.00	37.50	75.00	—

KM# 22.17 FARTHING

Copper **Obv:** Crown on crossed sceptres, titles of James I **Rev:** Crowned harp **Note:** Lennox Issue; Mint mark: Mascle.

Date	Mintage	VG	F	VF	XF	Unc
ND(1613)	—	7.50	18.00	37.50	75.00	—

KM# 22.18 FARTHING

Copper **Obv:** Crown on crossed sceptres, titles of James I **Rev:** Crowned harp **Note:** Lennox Issue; Mint mark: Mussel.

Date	Mintage	VG	F	VF	XF	Unc
ND(1613)	—	7.50	18.00	37.50	75.00	—

KM# 22.19 FARTHING

Copper **Obv:** Crown on crossed sceptres, titles of James I **Rev:** Crowned harp **Note:** Lennox Issue; Mint mark: Quatrefoil.

Date	Mintage	VG	F	VF	XF	Unc
ND(1613)	—	7.50	18.00	37.50	75.00	—

KM# 22.20 FARTHING

Copper **Obv:** Crown on crossed sceptres, titles of James I **Rev:** Crowned harp **Note:** Lennox Issue; Mint mark: Rose.

Date	Mintage	VG	F	VF	XF	Unc
ND(1613)	—	7.50	18.00	37.50	75.00	—

KM# 22.21 FARTHING

Copper **Obv:** Crown on crossed sceptres, titles of James I **Rev:** Crowned harp **Note:** Lennox Issue; Mint mark: Star.

Date	Mintage	VG	F	VF	XF	Unc
ND(1613)	—	7.50	18.00	37.50	75.00	—

KM# 22.22 FARTHING

Copper **Obv:** Crown on crossed sceptres, titles of James I **Rev:** Crowned harp **Note:** Lennox Issue; Mint mark: Stirrup.

Date	Mintage	VG	F	VF	XF	Unc
ND(1613)	—	7.50	18.00	37.50	75.00	—

KM# 22.23 FARTHING

Copper **Obv:** Crown on crossed sceptres, titles of James I **Rev:** Crowned harp **Note:** Lennox Issue; Mint mark: Thistle.

Date	Mintage	VG	F	VF	XF	Unc
ND(1613)	—	7.50	18.00	37.50	75.00	—

KM# 22.24 FARTHING

Copper **Obv:** Crown on crossed sceptres, titles of James I **Rev:** Crowned harp **Note:** Lennox Issue; Mint mark: Trefoil.

Date	Mintage	VG	F	VF	XF	Unc
ND(1613)	—	7.50	18.00	37.50	75.00	—

KM# 22.25 FARTHING

Copper **Obv:** Crown on crossed sceptres, titles of James I **Rev:** Crowned harp **Note:** Lennox Issue; Mint mark: Triangle.

Date	Mintage	VG	F	VF	XF	Unc
ND(1613)	—	7.50	18.00	37.50	75.00	—

KM# 23 FARTHING

Copper **Obv:** Crown on crossed sceptres, legend begins at lower left. **Rev:** Crowned harp **Note:** Oval planchet; Mint mark: Cross.

Date	Mintage	VG	F	VF	XF	Unc
ND(1613)	—	18.00	37.50	115	225	—

KM# 25.1 FARTHING

Copper **Obv:** Single arched crown on crossed sceptres, titles of Charles I. **Rev:** Crowned harp **Note:** Richmond Issue.

Date	Mintage	VG	F	VF	XF	Unc
ND(1625-44)	—	7.50	18.00	37.50	75.00	—

KM# 25.2 FARTHING

Copper **Obv:** Single arched crown on crossed sceptres, titles of Charles I. **Rev:** Crowned harp **Note:** Richmond Issue; Mint mark: Annulet.

Date	Mintage	VG	F	VF	XF	Unc
ND(1625-44)	—	7.50	18.00	37.50	75.00	—

KM# 25.3 FARTHING

Copper **Obv:** Single arched crown on crossed sceptres, titles of Charles I. **Rev:** Crowned harp **Note:** Richmond Issue; Mint mark: Bell.

Date	Mintage	VG	F	VF	XF	Unc
ND(1625-44)	—	7.50	18.00	37.50	75.00	—

KM# 25.4 FARTHING

Copper **Obv:** Single arched crown on crossed sceptres, titles of Charles I. **Rev:** Crowned harp **Note:** Richmond Issue; Mint mark: Book.

Date	Mintage	VG	F	VF	XF	Unc
ND(1625-44)	—	7.50	18.00	37.50	75.00	—

KM# 25.5 FARTHING

Copper **Obv:** Single arched crown on crossed sceptres, titles of Charles I. **Rev:** Crowned harp **Note:** Richmond Issue; Mint mark: Cinquefoil.

Date	Mintage	VG	F	VF	XF	Unc
ND(1625-44)	—	7.50	18.00	37.50	75.00	—

KM# 25.6 FARTHING

Copper **Obv:** Single arched crown on crossed sceptres, titles of Charles I. **Rev:** Crowned harp **Note:** Richmond Issue; Mint mark: Coronet.

Date	Mintage	VG	F	VF	XF	Unc
ND(1625-44)	—	7.50	18.00	37.50	75.00	—

KM# 25.7 FARTHING

Copper **Obv:** Single arched crown on crossed sceptres, titles of Charles I. **Rev:** Crowned harp **Note:** Richmond Issue; Mint mark: Crescent.

Date	Mintage	VG	F	VF	XF	Unc
ND(1625-44)	—	7.50	18.00	37.50	75.00	—

KM# 25.8 FARTHING

Copper **Obv:** Single arched crown on crossed sceptres, titles of Charles I. **Rev:** Crowned harp **Note:** Richmond Issue; Mint mark: Cross with pellets

Date	Mintage	VG	F	VF	XF	Unc
ND(1625-44)	—	7.50	18.00	37.50	75.00	—

KM# 25.9 FARTHING

Copper **Obv:** Single arched crown on crossed sceptres, titles of Charles I. **Rev:** Crowned harp **Note:** Richmond Issue; Mint mark: Dagger.

Date	Mintage	VG	F	VF	XF	Unc
ND(1625-44)	—	7.50	18.00	37.50	75.00	—

KM# 25.10 FARTHING

Copper **Obv:** Single arched crown on crossed sceptres, titles of Charles I. **Rev:** Crowned harp **Note:** Richmond Issue; Mint mark: Ermine.

Date	Mintage	VG	F	VF	XF	Unc
ND(1625-44)	—	7.50	18.00	37.50	75.00	—

KM# 25.11 FARTHING

Copper **Obv:** Single arched crown on crossed sceptres, titles of Charles I. **Rev:** Crowned harp **Note:** Richmond Issue; Mint mark: Eye.

Date	Mintage	VG	F	VF	XF	Unc
ND(1625-44)	—	7.50	18.00	37.50	75.00	—

KM# 25.12 FARTHING

Copper **Obv:** Single arched crown on crossed sceptres, titles of Charles I. **Rev:** Crowned harp **Note:** Richmond Issue; Mint mark: Fish-hook.

Date	Mintage	VG	F	VF	XF	Unc
ND(1625-44)	—	7.50	18.00	37.50	75.00	—

KM# 25.13 FARTHING

Copper **Obv:** Single arched crown on crossed sceptres, titles of Charles I. **Rev:** Crowned harp **Note:** Richmond Issue; Mint mark: Fleece.

Date	Mintage	VG	F	VF	XF	Unc
ND(1625-44)	—	7.50	18.00	37.50	75.00	—

KM# 25.14 FARTHING

Copper **Obv:** Single arched crown on crossed sceptres, titles of Charles I. **Rev:** Crowned harp **Note:** Richmond Issue; Mint mark: Gauntlet.

Date	Mintage	VG	F	VF	XF	Unc
ND(1625-44)	—	7.50	18.00	37.50	75.00	—

KM# 25.15 FARTHING

Copper **Obv:** Single arched crown on crossed sceptres, titles of Charles I. **Rev:** Crowned harp **Note:** Richmond Issue; Mint mark: Grapes.

Date	Mintage	VG	F	VF	XF	Unc
ND(1625-44)	—	7.50	18.00	37.50	75.00	—

KM# 25.16 FARTHING

Copper **Obv:** Single arched crown on crossed sceptres, titles of Charles I. **Rev:** Crowned harp **Note:** Richmond Issue; Mint mark: Halberd.

Date	Mintage	VG	F	VF	XF	Unc
ND(1625-44)	—	7.50	18.00	37.50	75.00	—

KM# 25.17 FARTHING

Copper **Obv:** Single arched crown on crossed sceptres, titles of Charles I. **Rev:** Crowned harp **Note:** Richmond Issue; Mint mark: Harp.

Date	Mintage	VG	F	VF	XF	Unc
ND(1625-44)	—	7.50	18.00	37.50	75.00	—

KM# 25.18 FARTHING

Copper **Obv:** Single arched crown on crossed sceptres, titles of Charles I. **Rev:** Crowned harp **Note:** Richmond Issue; Mint mark: Heart.

Date	Mintage	VG	F	VF	XF	Unc
ND(1625-44)	—	7.50	18.00	37.50	75.00	—

KM# 25.19 FARTHING

Copper **Obv:** Single arched crown on crossed sceptres, titles of Charles I. **Rev:** Crowned harp **Note:** Richmond Issue; Mint mark: Horse shoe.

Date	Mintage	VG	F	VF	XF	Unc
ND(1625-44)	—	7.50	18.00	37.50	75.00	—

KM# 25.20 FARTHING

Copper **Obv:** Single arched crown on crossed sceptres, titles of Charles I. **Rev:** Crowned harp **Note:** Richmond Issue; Mint mark: Key.

Date	Mintage	VG	F	VF	XF	Unc
ND(1625-44)	—	7.50	18.00	37.50	75.00	—

KM# 25.21 FARTHING

Copper **Obv:** Single arched crown on crossed sceptres, titles of Charles I. **Rev:** Crowned harp **Note:** Richmond Issue; Mint mark: Leaf.

Date	Mintage	VG	F	VF	XF	Unc
ND(1625-44)	—	7.50	18.00	37.50	75.00	—

KM# 25.22 FARTHING

Copper **Obv:** Single arched crown on crossed sceptres, titles of Charles I. **Rev:** Crowned harp **Note:** Richmond Issue; Mint mark: Lion.

Date	Mintage	VG	F	VF	XF	Unc
ND(1625-44)	—	7.50	18.00	37.50	75.00	—

KM# 25.23 FARTHING

Copper **Obv:** Single arched crown on crossed sceptres, titles of Charles I. **Rev:** Crowned harp **Note:** Richmond Issue; Mint mark: Lis.

Date	Mintage	VG	F	VF	XF	Unc
ND(1625-44)	—	7.50	18.00	37.50	75.00	—

KM# 25.24 FARTHING

Copper **Obv:** Single arched crown on crossed sceptres, titles of Charles I. **Rev:** Crowned harp **Note:** Richmond Issue; Mint mark: Demi-lis.

Date	Mintage	VG	F	VF	XF	Unc
ND(1624-44)	—	7.50	18.00	37.50	75.00	—

KM# 25.25 FARTHING

Copper **Obv:** Single arched crown on crossed sceptres, titles of Charles I. **Rev:** Crowned harp **Note:** Richmond Issue; Mint mark: 3 Lis.

Date	Mintage	VG	F	VF	XF	Unc
ND(1625-44)	—	7.50	18.00	37.50	75.00	—

KM# 25.26 FARTHING

Copper **Obv:** Single arched crown on crossed sceptres, titles of Charles I. **Rev:** Crowned harp **Note:** Richmond Issue; Mint mark: Martlet.

Date	Mintage	VG	F	VF	XF	Unc
ND(1625-44)	—	7.50	18.00	37.50	75.00	—

KM# 25.27 FARTHING

Copper **Obv:** Single arched crown on crossed sceptres, titles of Charles I. **Rev:** Crowned harp **Note:** Richmond Issue; Mint mark: Mascle.

Date	Mintage	VG	F	VF	XF	Unc
ND(1625-44)	—	7.50	18.00	37.50	75.00	—

KM# 25.28 FARTHING

Copper **Obv:** Single arched crown on crossed sceptres, titles of Charles I. **Rev:** Crowned harp **Note:** Richmond Issue; Mint mark: Musket.

Date	Mintage	VG	F	VF	XF	Unc
ND(1625-44)	—	7.50	18.00	37.50	75.00	—

KM# 25.29 FARTHING

Copper **Obv:** Single arched crown on crossed sceptres, titles of Charles I. **Rev:** Crowned harp **Note:** Richmond Issue; Mint mark: 2 Muskets.

Date	Mintage	VG	F	VF	XF	Unc
ND(1625-44)	—	7.50	18.00	37.50	75.00	—

KM# 25.30 FARTHING

Copper **Obv:** Single arched crown on crossed sceptres, titles of Charles I. **Rev:** Crowned harp **Note:** Richmond Issue; Mint mark: Nautilus.

Date	Mintage	VG	F	VF	XF	Unc
ND(1625-44)	—	7.50	18.00	37.50	75.00	—

KM# 25.31 FARTHING

Copper **Obv:** Single arched crown on crossed sceptres, titles of Charles I. **Rev:** Crowned harp **Note:** Richmond Issue; Mint mark: Rose.

Date	Mintage	VG	F	VF	XF	Unc
ND(1625-44)	—	7.50	18.00	37.50	75.00	—

KM# 25.32 FARTHING

Copper **Obv:** Single arched crown on crossed sceptres, titles of Charles I. **Rev:** Crowned harp **Note:** Richmond Issue; Mint mark: Shield.

Date	Mintage	VG	F	VF	XF	Unc
ND(1625-44)	—	7.50	18.00	37.50	75.00	—

KM# 25.33 FARTHING

Copper **Obv:** Single arched crown on crossed sceptres, titles of Charles I. **Rev:** Crowned harp **Note:** Richmond Issue; Mint mark: Spearhead.

Date	Mintage	VG	F	VF	XF	Unc
ND(1625-44)	—	7.50	18.00	37.50	75.00	—

KM# 25.34 FARTHING

Copper **Obv:** Single arched crown on crossed sceptres, titles of Charles I. **Rev:** Crowned harp **Note:** Richmond Issue; Mint mark: Tower.

Date	Mintage	VG	F	VF	XF	Unc
ND(1625-44)	—	7.50	18.00	37.50	75.00	—

KM# 25.35 FARTHING

Copper **Obv:** Single arched crown on crossed sceptres, titles of Charles I. **Rev:** Crowned harp **Note:** Richard Issue; Mint mark: Trefoil.

Date	Mintage	VG	F	VF	XF	Unc
ND(1625-44)	—	7.50	18.00	37.50	75.00	—

Note: Varieties exist

KM# 25.36 FARTHING

Copper **Obv:** Single arched crown on crossed sceptres, titles of Charles I **Rev:** Crowned harp **Note:** Richmond Issue. Mint mark: Woolpack.

Date	Mintage	VG	F	VF	XF	Unc
ND(1625-44)	—	7.50	18.00	37.50	75.00	—

KM# 26.1 FARTHING

Copper **Obv:** Double-arched crown **Note:** Transitional Issue; Mint mark: Harp.

Date	Mintage	VG	F	VF	XF	Unc
ND(1625-44)	—	18.00	37.50	115	225	—

KM# 26.2 FARTHING

Copper **Obv:** Double-arched crown **Note:** Transitional Issue; Mint mark: Quatrefoil.

Date	Mintage	VG	F	VF	XF	Unc
ND(1625-44)	—	18.00	37.50	115	225	—

KM# 27.1 FARTHING

Copper **Obv:** Crown on crossed sceptres within inner circle **Rev:** Crowned harp within inner circle **Note:** "Maltravers" Issue; Mint mark: Bell with 5 or 6 harp strings.

Date	Mintage	VG	F	VF	XF	Unc
ND(1625-44)	—	7.50	18.00	37.50	75.00	—

KM# 27.2 FARTHING

Copper **Obv:** Crown on crossed sceptres within inner circle **Rev:** Crowned harp within inner circle **Note:** "Maltravers" Issue; Mint mark: Billet.

Date	Mintage	VG	F	VF	XF	Unc
ND(1625-44)	—	7.50	18.00	37.50	75.00	—

KM# 27.3 FARTHING

Copper **Obv:** Crown on crossed sceptres within inner circle **Rev:** Crowned harp within inner circle **Note:** "Maltravers" Issue; Mint mark: Cross.

Date	Mintage	VG	F	VF	XF	Unc
ND(1625-44)	—	7.50	18.00	37.50	75.00	—

KM# 27.4 FARTHING

Copper **Obv:** Crown on crossed sceptres within inner circle **Rev:** Crowned harp within inner circle **Note:** "Maltravers" Issue; Mint mark: Harp.

Date	Mintage	VG	F	VF	XF	Unc
ND(1625-44)	—	7.50	18.00	37.50	75.00	—

KM# 27.5 FARTHING

Copper **Obv:** Crown on crossed sceptres within inner circle **Rev:** Crowned harp within inner circle **Note:** "Maltravers" Issue; Mint mark: Lis.

Date	Mintage	VG	F	VF	XF	Unc
ND(1625-44)	—	7.50	18.00	37.50	75.00	—

KM# 27.6 FARTHING

Copper **Obv:** Crown on crossed sceptres within inner circle **Rev:** Crowned harp within inner circle **Note:** "Maltravers" Issue; Mint mark: Martlet.

Date	Mintage	VG	F	VF	XF	Unc
ND(1625-44)	—	7.50	18.00	37.50	75.00	—

KM# 27.7 FARTHING

Copper **Obv:** Crown on crossed sceptres within inner circle **Rev:** Crowned harp within inner circle **Note:** "Maltravers" Issue; Mint mark: Portcullis.

Date	Mintage	VG	F	VF	XF	Unc
ND(1625-44)	—	7.50	18.00	37.50	75.00	—

KM# 27.8 FARTHING

Copper **Obv:** Crown on crossed sceptres within inner circle **Rev:** Crowned harp within inner circle **Note:** "Maltravers" Issue; Mint mark: Rose.

Date	Mintage	VG	F	VF	XF	Unc
ND(1625-44)	—	7.50	18.00	37.50	75.00	—

Note: Varieties exist

KM# 28.1 FARTHING

Copper **Note:** "Maltravers" Issue; Mint mark: Crescent; oval planchet.

Date	Mintage	VG	F	VF	XF	Unc
ND(1625-44)	—	18.00	35.00	110	220	—

KM# 27.9 FARTHING

Copper **Obv:** Crown on crossed sceptres within inner circle **Rev:** Crowned harp within inner circle **Note:** "Maltravers" Issue; mint mark: Woolpack.

Date	Mintage	VG	F	VF	XF	Unc
ND(1625-44)	—	7.50	18.00	37.50	75.00	—

KM# 28.2 FARTHING

Copper **Note:** "Maltravers" Issue; Mint mark: Cross; oval planchet.

Date	Mintage	VG	F	VF	XF	Unc
ND(1625-44)	—	18.00	35.00	110	220	—

KM# 28.3 FARTHING

Copper **Note:** "Maltravers" Issue; Mint mark: Demi-lis; oval planchet.

Date	Mintage	VG	F	VF	XF	Unc
ND(1625-44)	—	18.00	35.00	110	220	—

KM# 28.4 FARTHING

Copper **Note:** "Maltravers" Issue; Mint mark: Martlet; oval planchet.

Date	Mintage	VG	F	VF	XF	Unc
ND(1625-44)	—	18.00	35.00	110	220	—

KM# 28.5 FARTHING

Copper **Note:** "Maltravers" Issue; Mint mark: Rose; oval planchet.

Date	Mintage	VG	F	VF	XF	Unc
ND(1625-44)	—	18.00	35.00	110	220	—

KM# 28.6 FARTHING

Copper **Note:** "Maltravers" Issue; Mint mark: Scroll; oval planchet.

Date	Mintage	VG	F	VF	XF	Unc
ND(1625-44)	—	18.00	35.00	110	220	—

KM# 28.7 FARTHING

Copper **Note:** "Maltravers" Issue; Mint mark: 9; oval planchet.

Date	Mintage	VG	F	VF	XF	Unc
ND(1625-44)	—	18.00	35.00	110	220	—

Note: Varieties exist

KM# 29 FARTHING

Copper **Obv:** Double-arched crown **Note:** "Maltravers" Issue; Mint mark: Lis; oval planchet.

Date	Mintage	VG	F	VF	XF	Unc
ND(1625-44)	—	25.00	47.00	145	300	—

KM# 30.1 FARTHING

Copper **Rev:** Crowned rose **Note:** "Rose" Issue; Mint mark: Crescent.

Date	Mintage	VG	F	VF	XF	Unc
ND(1625-44)	—	7.50	18.00	37.50	75.00	—

KM# 30.2 FARTHING

Copper **Rev:** Crowned rose **Note:** "Rose" Issue; Mint mark: Cross.

Date	Mintage	VG	F	VF	XF	Unc
ND(1625-44)	—	7.50	18.00	37.50	75.00	—

KM# 30.3 FARTHING

Copper **Rev:** Crowned rose **Note:** "Rose" Issue; Mint mark: Lis.

Date	Mintage	VG	F	VF	XF	Unc
ND(1625-44)	—	7.50	18.00	37.50	75.00	—

KM# 30.4 FARTHING

Copper **Rev:** Crowned rose **Note:** "Rose" Issue; Mint mark: Martlet.

Date	Mintage	VG	F	VF	XF	Unc
ND(1625-44)	—	7.50	18.00	37.50	75.00	—

KM# 30.5 FARTHING

Copper **Rev:** Crowned rose **Note:** "Rose" Issue; Mint mark: Mullet.

Date	Mintage	VG	F	VF	XF	Unc
ND(1625-44)	—	7.50	18.00	37.50	75.00	—

Note: Varieties exist

KM# 31.1 FARTHING

Copper **Obv:** Single-arched crown **Note:** "Rose" Issue; Mint mark: Crescent.

Date	Mintage	VG	F	VF	XF	Unc
ND(1625-44)	—	7.50	18.00	37.50	75.00	—

KM# 31.2 FARTHING

Copper **Obv:** Single-arched crown **Note:** "Rose" Issue; Mint mark: Mullet.

Date	Mintage	VG	F	VF	XF	Unc
ND(1625-44)	—	7.50	18.00	37.50	75.00	—

Note: Varieties exist

KM# 32 FARTHING

Copper **Obv:** Sceptres below crown **Note:** "Rose" Issue; Mint mark: Mullet.

Date	Mintage	VG	F	VF	XF	Unc
ND(1625-44)	—	13.00	22.50	70.00	140	—

KM# 85 FARTHING

Copper **Obv:** Crown over crossed sceptres, titles of Charles II **Rev:** Crowned harp **Note:** Armstrong Issue; Mint mark: Plumes.

Date	Mintage	VG	F	VF	XF	Unc
ND(1660-1)	—	37.50	75.00	190	400	—

KM# 86.1 FARTHING

Copper **Obv:** St. Patrick with cross driving out snakes, church at right **Rev:** Crown above King David playing harp **Note:** St. Patrick's Issue; Mint mark: Annulet

Date	Mintage	VG	F	VF	XF	Unc
ND(ca. 1678)	—	100	300	900	2,000	—

KM# 86.2 FARTHING

Copper **Obv:** St. Patrick with cross driving out snakes, church at right **Rev:** Crown above King David playing harp **Note:** St. Patrick's Issue; Mint mark: Martlet.

Date	Mintage	VG	F	VF	XF	Unc
ND	—	150	400	1,000	2,500	—

Note: Varieties exist

KM# 86.2a FARTHING

Silver **Obv:** St. Patrick with cross driving out snakes, church at right **Rev:** Crown above King David playing harp **Note:** St. Patrick's Issue.

Date	Mintage	VG	F	VF	XF	Unc
ND Rare	—	—	—	3,800	—	—

KM# 86.2b FARTHING
Gold **Obv:** St. Patrick with cross driving out snakes, church at right **Rev:** Crown above King David playing harp **Note:** St. Patrick's Issue.

Date	Mintage	VG	F	VF	XF	Unc
ND Rare	—	—	—	—	—	—

KM# 86.3 FARTHING
Copper **Obv:** St. Patrick with cross driving out snakes, church at right **Rev:** Crown above King David playing harp **Note:** St. Patrick's Issue. At least 180 die varieties.

Date	Mintage	VG	F	VF	XF	Unc
ND	—	150	400	1,000	3,000	—

KM# 5.1 1/2 PENNY
Copper **Obv:** Shield of arms in inner circle, titles of Elizabeth I **Rev:** Crowned harp divides date in inner circle **Note:** Mint mark: Star.

Date	Mintage	VG	F	VF	XF	Unc
1601	—	27.50	65.00	160	320	—

KM# 5.2 1/2 PENNY
Copper **Obv:** Shield of arms in inner circle, titles of Elizabeth I **Rev:** Crowned harp divides date in inner circle **Note:** Mint mark: Trefoil.

Date	Mintage	VG	F	VF	XF	Unc
1601	—	27.50	65.00	160	320	—

KM# 5.3 1/2 PENNY
Copper **Obv:** Shield of arms in inner circle, titles of Elizabeth I **Rev:** Crowned harp divides date in inner circle **Note:** Mint mark: Martlet.

Date	Mintage	VG	F	VF	XF	Unc
1602	—	27.50	65.00	185	375	—

KM# 87 1/2 PENNY
Copper **Obv:** St. Patrick holding cross and crozier preaching to multitude, arms of Dublin at right **Rev:** King David playing harp, crown above **Note:** St. Patrick issue. Varieties, including off-metal strikes in silver and gold exist.

Date	Mintage	VG	F	VF	XF	Unc
ND(ca. 1678)	—	350	850	2,000	—	—

KM# 90.1 1/2 PENNY
Copper **Obv:** Laureate and draped bust right, large letters **Rev:** Crowned harp, large letters **Note:** Armstrong and Legg issue.

Date	Mintage	VG	F	VF	XF	Unc
1680	—	13.00	25.00	100	250	—
1681	—	8.00	19.00	75.00	190	—
1682 Rare	—	—	—	—	—	—

KM# 90.1a 1/2 PENNY
Silver **Obv:** Large letters **Rev:** Large letters **Note:** Armstrong and Legg issue.

Date	Mintage	VG	F	VF	XF	Unc
1680 Proof, Rare	—	—	—	—	—	—

KM# 90.2 1/2 PENNY
Copper **Obv:** I in circle on King's shoulder **Rev:** Large letters **Note:** Armstrong and Legg issue.

Date	Mintage	VG	F	VF	XF	Unc
1680 Rare	—	—	—	—	—	—

KM# 91 1/2 PENNY
Copper **Obv:** Laureate and draped bust right, small letters **Rev:** Crowned harp, small letters **Note:** Armstrong and Legg issue.

Date	Mintage	VG	F	VF	XF	Unc
1681 Unique	—	—	—	—	—	—
1682	—	8.00	19.00	75.00	190	—
1683	—	13.00	25.00	100	220	—
1684	—	50.00	120	280	600	—

KM# 91a 1/2 PENNY
Silver **Obv:** Small letters **Rev:** Small letters **Note:** Armstrong and Legg issue.

Date	Mintage	VG	F	VF	XF	Unc
1681 Proof, Rare	—	—	—	—	—	—

KM# 92 1/2 PENNY
Copper **Obv:** Laureate and draped bust of James II right **R ev:** Crowned harp divides date

Date	Mintage	VG	F	VF	XF	Unc
1685	—	15.00	37.50	150	350	—
1686	—	13.00	25.00	115	280	—
1687 Rare	—	—	—	—	—	—
1688	—	19.00	37.50	190	450	—

KM# 92a 1/2 PENNY
Silver **Obv:** Laureate and draped bust of James II right **Rev:** Crowned harp divides date

Date	Mintage	VG	F	VF	XF	Unc
1686	—	—	—	—	—	—

KM# 109 1/2 PENNY
Copper **Obv:** Conjoined busts of William and Mary right **Rev:** Crowned harp divides date

Date	Mintage	VG	F	VF	XF	Unc
1692	—	9.00	19.00	95.00	250	—
1693	—	8.00	16.00	75.00	220	—
1694	—	9.00	19.00	95.00	250	—

KM# 109a 1/2 PENNY
Silver **Obv:** Conjoined busts of William and Mary right **Rev:** Crowned harp divides date

Date	Mintage	VG	F	VF	XF	Unc
1693 Proof, rare	—	—	—	—	—	—

KM# 110 1/2 PENNY
Copper **Obv:** Laureate and draped bust of William III **Rev:** Crowned harp divides date

Date	Mintage	VG	F	VF	XF	Unc
1696	—	25.00	47.00	220	750	—

Note: Reverse legend varieties exist

KM# 110a 1/2 PENNY
Silver **Obv:** Laureate and draped bust of William III **Rev:** Crowned harp divides date

Date	Mintage	VG	F	VF	XF	Unc
1696 Proof, Rare	—	—	—	—	—	—

KM# 110b 1/2 PENNY
Silver Gilt **Obv:** Laureate and draped bust of William III **Rev:** Crowned harp divides date

Date	Mintage	VG	F	VF	XF	Unc
1696 Proof, 3 known	—	—	—	—	—	—

KM# 111 1/2 PENNY
Copper **Obv:** Crude undraped bust **Rev:** Crowned harp divides date

Date	Mintage	VG	F	VF	XF	Unc
1696	—	75.00	155	650	1,400	—

KM# 6.1 PENNY
Copper **Obv:** Shield of arms in inner circle, titles of Elizabeth I **Rev:** Crowned harp divides date in inner circle **Note:** Mint mark: Star.

Date	Mintage	VG	F	VF	XF	Unc
1601	—	25.00	50.00	95.00	190	—
ND Rare	—	—	—	—	—	—

KM# 6.2 PENNY
Copper **Obv:** Shield of arms in inner circle, titles of Elizabeth I **Rev:** Crowned harp divides date in inner circle **Note:** Mint mark: Trefoil.

Date	Mintage	VG	F	VF	XF	Unc
1601	—	25.00	50.00	95.00	190	—

KM# 6.3 PENNY
Copper **Obv:** Shield of arms in inner circle, titles of Elizabeth I **Rev:** Crowned harp divides date in inner circle **Note:** Mint mark: Martlet.

Date	Mintage	VG	F	VF	XF	Unc
1602	—	25.00	50.00	105	220	—

KM# 7.1 3 PENCE
Base Silver **Obv:** Shield of arms in inner circle, titles of Elizabeth I **Rev:** Crowned harp divides date in inner circle **Note:** Mint mark: Martlet.

Date	Mintage	VG	F	VF	XF	Unc
ND(1601-02)	—	125	325	625	1,400	—

KM# 7.2 3 PENCE
Base Silver **Obv:** Shield of arms in inner circle, titles of Elizabeth I **Rev:** Crowned harp divides date in inner circle **Note:** Mint mark: Star

Date	Mintage	VG	F	VF	XF	Unc
ND	—	125	325	625	1,400	—

KM# 7.3 3 PENCE
Base Silver **Obv:** Shield of arms in inner circle, titles of Elizabeth I **Rev:** Crowned harp divides date in inner circle **Note:** Mint mark: Trefoil.

Date	Mintage	VG	F	VF	XF	Unc
ND	—	125	325	625	1,400	—

KM# 8.1 6 PENCE
Base Silver **Obv:** Shield of arms in inner circle, titles of Elizabeth I **Rev:** Crowned harp divides date in inner circle **Note:** Mint mark: Martlet.

Date	Mintage	VG	F	VF	XF	Unc
ND(1601-02)	—	43.75	125	375	825	—

KM# 8.2 6 PENCE
Base Silver **Obv:** Shield of arms in inner circle, titles of Elizabeth I **Rev:** Crowned harp divides date in inner circle **Note:** Mint mark: Star.

Date	Mintage	VG	F	VF	XF	Unc
ND	—	43.75	125	375	825	—

KM# 8.3 6 PENCE
Base Silver **Obv:** Shield of arms in inner circle, titles of Elizabeth I **Rev:** Crowned harp divides date in inner circle **Note:** Mint mark: Trefoil.

Date	Mintage	VG	F	VF	XF	Unc
ND	—	43.75	125	375	825	—

KM# 10.1 6 PENCE
Silver **Obv:** Crowned first bust of James I right in inner circle **Obv. Legend:** IACOBVS. D. G. Ang... **Rev:** Crowned harp in inner circle **Rev. Legend:** TVEATVR... **Note:** Mint mark: bell.

Date	Mintage	VG	F	VF	XF	Unc
ND(1603-04)	—	37.50	100	250	525	—

KM# 10.2 6 PENCE
Silver **Obv:** Crowned first bust of James I right in inner circle **Obv. Legend:** IACOBVS. D. G. Ang... **Rev:** Crowned harp in inner circle **Rev. Legend:** TUEATUR... **Note:** Mint mark: Martlet.

Date	Mintage	VG	F	VF	XF	Unc
ND	—	30.00	80.00	200	425	—

KM# 11.1 6 PENCE
Silver **Obv:** Crowned first bust of James I right in inner circle **Obv. Legend:** MAG BRIT... **Rev:** Crowned harp in inner circle **Rev. Legend:** TVEATVR... **Note:** Mint mark: Martlet.

Date	Mintage	VG	F	VF	XF	Unc
ND(1603-4)	—	37.50	100	280	600	—

KM# 11.2 6 PENCE
Silver **Obv:** Crowned first bust of James I right in inner circle **Obv. Legend:** MAG BRIT... **Rev:** Crowned harp in inner circle **Rev. Legend:** TVEATVR... **Note:** Mint mark: Rose.

Date	Mintage	VG	F	VF	XF	Unc
ND(1604-7)	—	37.50	100	280	600	—

KM# 11.3 6 PENCE
Silver **Obv:** Crowned first bust of James I right in inner circle **Obv. Legend:** MAG BRIT... **Rev:** Crowned harp in inner circle **Rev. Legend:** TVEATVR... **Note:** Mint mark: Scallop shell.

Date	Mintage	VG	F	VF	XF	Unc
ND	—	43.75	100	325	625	—

KM# 9.1 SHILLING
Base Silver **Note:** Mint mark: Martlet.

Date	Mintage	VG	F	VF	XF	Unc
ND(1601-02)	—	65.00	125	475	875	—

KM# 9.2 SHILLING
Base Silver **Note:** Mint mark: Star.

Date	Mintage	VG	F	VF	XF	Unc
ND	—	65.00	125	475	875	—

KM# 9.3 SHILLING
Base Silver **Note:** Mint mark: Trefoil.

Date	Mintage	VG	F	VF	XF	Unc
ND	—	65.00	125	475	875	—

KM# 12 SHILLING
Silver **Obv:** Crowned first bust of James I, short square-cut beard **Obv. Legend:** IACOBVS. D.G. Ang. SCO... **Note:** Mint mark: Bell.

Date	Mintage	VG	F	VF	XF	Unc
ND(1603-4)	—	37.50	100	280	600	—

KM# 13 SHILLING
Silver **Obv:** Second bust - pointed beard **Note:** Mint mark: Martlet.

Date	Mintage	VG	F	VF	XF	Unc
ND	—	37.50	105	375	750	—

KM# 14.1 SHILLING
Silver **Obv:** Third bust - longer square-cut beard **Obv. Legend:** IACOBVS. D. G. MAG. BRIT. FRA... **Note:** Mint mark: Martlet

Date	Mintage	VG	F	VF	XF	Unc
ND	—	37.50	100	280	600	—

KM# 14.2 SHILLING
Silver **Obv:** Third bust - longer square-cut beard **Obv. Legend:** IACOBVS. D. G. MAG. BRIT. FRA... **Note:** Mint mark: Rose.

Date	Mintage	VG	F	VF	XF	Unc
ND rose/martlet	—	37.50	100	280	600	—
ND	—	37.50	100	280	600	—

KM# 14.3 SHILLING
Silver **Obv:** Third bust - longer square-cut beard **Obv. Legend:** IACOBVS. D. G. MAG. BRIT. FRA... **Note:** Mint mark: Scallop shell.

Date	Mintage	VG	F	VF	XF	Unc
ND	—	37.50	100	280	600	—

KM# 15.1 SHILLING
Silver **Obv:** Fourth bust - long beard **Note:** Mint mark: Scallop shell

Date	Mintage	VG	F	VF	XF	Unc
ND	—	65.00	125	475	1,000	—

KM# 15.2 SHILLING
Silver **Obv:** Fourth bust - long beard **Note:** Mint mark: Rose.

Date	Mintage	VG	F	VF	XF	Unc
ND	—	50.00	100	375	800	—

GREAT REBELLION

Public dissension had been accumulating through the early part of the 17th century until rebellion broke out in Ireland in October, 1641. During the next 8 years various issues of coins were produced. They fall into 3 basic categories: Issues of the Lords Justices (representing the Crown), Issues of the Catholic Confederacy (representing the people) and Local Issues of the Cities of Refuge.

LORDS JUSTICES COINAGE

Inchiquin Money

These pieces are struck from cut pieces of flattened plate.

KM# 35 GROAT
1.9400 g., Silver **Obv:** Weight in double circle **Rev:** Weight in double circle

Date	Mintage	VG	F	VF	XF	Unc
ND(1642) Rare	—	—	—	—	—	—

KM# 36 6 PENCE
2.9800 g., Silver **Obv:** Weight in double circle **Rev:** Weight in double circle

Date	Mintage	VG	F	VF	XF	Unc
ND(1642) Rare	—	—	—	—	—	—

KM# 37 9 PENCE
4.4100 g., Silver **Obv:** Weight in triple circle, outer circle beaded **Rev:** Weight in triple circle, outer circle beaded

Date	Mintage	VG	F	VF	XF	Unc
ND(1642)	—	5,000	7,500	—	—	—

KM# 38 SHILLING
6.0300 g., Silver **Obv:** Weight in triple beaded circle **Rev:** Weight in triple beaded circle

Date	Mintage	VG	F	VF	XF	Unc
ND(1642)	—	2,250	4,500	8,500	—	—

KM# 40 1/2 CROWN
15.0300 g., Silver **Obv:** Weight in double circle **Rev:** Weight in double circle

Date	Mintage	VG	F	VF	XF	Unc
ND(1642)	—	1,650	3,250	5,750	—	—

KM# 41 CROWN
30.0700 g., Silver **Obv:** Weight in double circle, outer circle beaded **Rev:** Weight in double circle, outer circle beaded **Note:** Dav. #3790.

Date	Mintage	VG	F	VF	XF	Unc
ND(1642)	—	1,250	2,500	5,000	—	—

Annulets Coinage

KM# 43 3 PENCE
1.4900 g., Silver **Obv:** Weight in circle **Rev:** 3 annulets in double circle

Date	Mintage	VG	F	VF	XF	Unc
ND(1642) 4 known	—	5,000	8,000	12,000	—	—

KM# 44 4 PENCE (Groat)
1.9400 g., Silver **Obv:** Weight in double circle **Rev:** 4 annulets in double circle

Date	Mintage	VG	F	VF	XF	Unc
ND(1642)	—	5,500	8,500	12,500	—	—

KM# 45 6 PENCE
2.9800 g., Silver **Obv:** Weight in double circle **Rev:** 6 annulets in double circle

Date	Mintage	VG	F	VF	XF	Unc
ND(1642) Rare	—	2,750	4,500	7,500	—	—

KM# 46 9 PENCE

4.4100 g., Silver **Obv:** Weight in double circle **Rev:** 9 annulets in double circle

Date	Mintage	VG	F	VF	XF	Unc
ND(1642) Rare	—	—	—	—	—	—

"Dublin" Money

KM# 53 1/2 CROWN

Silver **Obv:** Value in circle **Rev:** Value in circle

Date	Mintage	VG	F	VF	XF	Unc
ND(1643)	—	1,750	3,500	6,000	—	—

KM# 54 CROWN

30.0000 g., Silver **Obv:** Value in circle **Rev:** Value in circle
Note: Dav. #3791.

Date	Mintage	VG	F	VF	XF	Unc
ND(1643)	—	2,250	4,250	8,500	—	—

KM# 55 CROWN

30.0000 g., Silver **Obv:** Value in circle **Rev:** Value in circle
Note: Smaller dies. Dav. #3791.

Date	Mintage	VG	F	VF	XF	Unc
ND(1643)	—	2,500	5,000	9,000	—	—

Note: 19th century copies exist of some of the preceeding silver siege issues.

"Ormonde" Money

The Earl of Ormonde was Lieutenant of Ireland from 1643 to 1649.

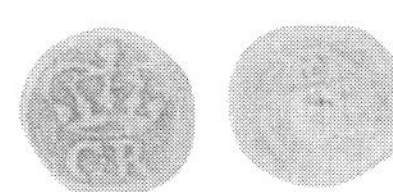

KM# 56 2 PENCE (1/2 Groat)

0.9100 g., Silver **Obv:** Crown above C-R **Rev:** Value in circle

Date	Mintage	VG	F	VF	XF	Unc
ND(1643-44)	—	300	600	1,200	2,000	—

Note: Varieties exist

KM# 57 3 PENCE

1.4300 g., Silver **Obv:** Crown above C-R **Rev:** Value in circle

Date	Mintage	VG	F	VF	XF	Unc
ND(1643-44)	—	250	500	1,000	1,750	—

Note: Varieties exist

KM# 58 4 PENCE (Groat)

1.9400 g., Silver **Obv:** Crown above C-R **Rev:** Value in circle

Date	Mintage	VG	F	VF	XF	Unc
ND(1643-44)	—	150	300	500	900	—

Note: Varieties exist

KM# 59 6 PENCE

2.9800 g., Silver **Obv:** Crown above C-R **Rev:** Value in circle

Date	Mintage	VG	F	VF	XF	Unc
ND(1643-44)	—	115	225	450	850	—

Note: Varieties exist

KM# 60 SHILLING

Silver **Obv:** Crown above C-R **Rev:** Value in circle

Date	Mintage	VG	F	VF	XF	Unc
ND(1643-44)	—	150	300	650	1,150	—

Note: Varieties exist

KM# 61 1/2 CROWN

14.7100 g., Silver **Obv:** Crown above C-R **Rev:** Value in circle

Date	Mintage	VG	F	VF	XF	Unc
ND(1643-44)	—	250	500	900	1,600	—

Note: Varieties exist

KM# 63 CROWN

Silver **Obv:** Crown above C-R **Rev:** Value in circle with ornamental S

Date	Mintage	VG	F	VF	XF	Unc
ND(1643-44)	—	400	750	1,250	3,000	—

Note: Varieties exist

KM# 64 CROWN

Silver **Obv:** Crown above C-R **Rev:** Value in circle with plain S
Note: Dav. #3792

Date	Mintage	VG	F	VF	XF	Unc
ND(1643-44)	—	350	700	1,150	2,750	—

Note: Varieties exist. Contemporary copies, in silver with copper cores, exist for the crown and half crown and has been suggested as an an attempt to conserve silver by the official mint. Copies made in the last century are easily distinguishable by their neatness of strike

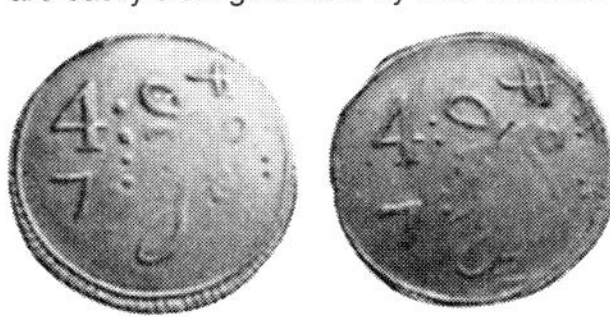

KM# 67 PISTOLE

6.6100 g., Gold **Obv:** 4 DWTT. 7 GR. in circle **Rev:** 4 DWTT. 7 GR. in circle

Date	Mintage	VG	F	VF	XF	Unc
ND(1646) Rare	10	—	—	—	—	—

Note: Whyte's Millennial collection sale 4-2000, VF realized $135,650

KM# A68 2 PISTOLE

13.2200 g., Gold **Obv:** 8 DWTT. 14 GR. in circle **Rev:** 8 DWTT. 14 GR. in circle

Date	Mintage	VG	F	VF	XF	Unc
ND(1646) Rare	2	—	—	—	—	—

Charles II Issue

Issued upon the execution of Charles I in 1649 by the royalist Marquis of Ormond to proclaim Charles II as King of Ireland.

KM# 83 1/2 CROWN

14.7100 g., Silver **Obv:** Crown in inner circle **Rev:** Value in inner circle

Date	Mintage	VG	F	VF	XF	Unc
ND(1649) Rare	—	—	—	—	—	—

Note: Dix-Noonan-Webb Auction 78, 6-2008, about VF realized approximately $16,030.

KM# 84 CROWN
Silver **Obv:** Crown in inner circle **Rev:** Value in inner circle
Note: Dav. #3794.

Date	Mintage	VG	F	VF	XF	Unc
ND(1649)	5	—	—	—	—	—

Note: Dix-Noonan-Webb Auction 78, 6-2008, about VF realized approximately $10,165.

Kilkenny Issues

KM# 47 FARTHING
2.2000 g., Bronze **Obv:** Crown on crossed scepters without inner circle **Rev:** Crowned harp

Date	Mintage	VG	F	VF	XF	Unc
ND(1642-43)	—	350	950	1,850	—	—

KM# 48 FARTHING
2.2000 g., Bronze **Obv:** KILKENNY stamped in long rectangle on blank plachet **Note:** Uniface.

Date	Mintage	VG	F	VF	XF	Unc
ND Rare	—	—	—	—	—	—

KM# 49 1/2 PENNY
4.8600 g., Bronze **Obv:** Crown on crossed sceptres in inner circle **Rev:** Crowned harp divides C-R in inner circle

Date	Mintage	VG	F	VF	XF	Unc
ND(1642-43)	—	250	700	1,450	—	—

Note: Contemporary counterfeits of the 1/2 penny are often encountered

KM# 51.1 1/2 CROWN
14.3900 g., Silver **Obv:** Similar to KM#51.2 but with cross on flank cloth

Date	Mintage	VG	F	VF	XF	Unc
ND	—	385	750	1,650	2,800	—

KM# 51.2 1/2 CROWN
14.3900 g., Silver **Obv:** Without cross on flank cloth

Date	Mintage	VG	F	VF	XF	Unc
ND	—	500	1,200	2,400	4,000	—

Rebel Money

KM# 65 1/2 CROWN
12.1800 g., Silver **Obv:** Cross in inner circle, star in outer circle **Rev:** Value in inner circle

Date	Mintage	VG	F	VF	XF	Unc
ND(1643-44)	—	1,750	3,250	7,000	—	—

KM# 66 CROWN
24.3600 g., Silver **Obv:** Cross in inner circle **Rev:** Value VS in inner circle **Note:** Dav. #3793.

Date	Mintage	VG	F	VF	XF	Unc
ND(1643-44)	—	1,500	3,000	6,500	—	—

LOCAL COINAGE

Bandon

KM# 68 FARTHING
1.9400 g., Copper **Issuer:** Bandon **Obv:** BB in circle (BB = Bandon Bridge) **Rev:** 3 castles, 1 above 2 in circle

Date	Mintage	VG	F	VF	XF	Unc
ND Rare	2	—	—	—	—	—

KM# 69 FARTHING
1.9400 g., Copper **Issuer:** Bandon **Obv:** BB i **Rev:** BB (or EE) back to back

Date	Mintage	VG	F	VF	XF	Unc
ND	—	—	—	—	—	—

Cork

KM# 70 FARTHING
2.2700 g., Copper **Issuer:** Cork **Obv:** CORK (or CORKE) in dotted circle **Rev:** Castle in dotted circle

Date	Mintage	VG	F	VF	XF	Unc
ND	—	1,000	2,000	4,000	7,500	—

KM# 72 FARTHING
2.2700 g., Copper **Issuer:** Cork **Note:** CORK (or CORKE) countermarked on foreign copper coins.

Date	Mintage	VG	F	VF	XF	Unc
ND	—	525	875	2,100	—	—

KM# 73 1/2 PENNY
5.4400 g., Copper **Issuer:** Cork **Obv:** CORK in circle **Rev:** Castle

Date	Mintage	VG	F	VF	XF	Unc
ND	—	3,000	6,000	10,000	—	—

KM# 80 6 PENCE
2.2000 g., Silver **Issuer:** Cork **Obv:** CORK/1647 in circle **Rev:** Value in circle

Date	Mintage	VG	F	VF	XF	Unc
1647	—	1,200	2,500	4,500	—	—

KM# 81 SHILLING
4.4100 g., Silver **Issuer:** Cork **Obv:** CORK/1647 in circle **Rev:** Value in circle

Date	Mintage	VG	F	VF	XF	Unc
1647	—	—	6,000	12,500	—	—

Note: There are modern cast counterfeits of these silver coins

KM# 82 SHILLING
4.4100 g., Silver **Issuer:** Cork **Note:** CORKE (or CORK) countermarked on Elizabethan Shillings.

Date	Mintage	VG	F	VF	XF	Unc
ND	—	—	—	—	—	—

Kinsale

KM# 74 FARTHING
2.2700 g., Copper **Issuer:** Kinsale **Obv:** K-S in circle **Rev:** Checkered shield of arms

Date	Mintage	VG	F	VF	XF	Unc
ND	—	400	800	1,600	—	—

KM# 75 SHILLING
Copper **Issuer:** Kilkenny **Note:** Castle with K below countermarked on Charles I Kilkenny 1/2 Penny.

Date	Mintage	VG	F	VF	XF	Unc
ND	—	850	1,750	3,250	—	—

KM# 76 SHILLING
Copper **Issuer:** Kilkenny **Note:** 5 castles in rosette form countermarked on Charles I Kilkenny 1/2 Penny

Date	Mintage	VG	F	VF	XF	Unc
ND	—	1,200	2,500	4,500	—	—

Youghal

KM# 78 FARTHING
0.9700 g., Copper **Issuer:** Youghal **Obv:** Bird above Y.T/1646 in circle **Rev:** Ship in circle

Date	Mintage	VG	F	VF	XF	Unc
1646	—	1,750	3,500	7,000	—	—

KM# 79 FARTHING
0.5800 g., Copper **Issuer:** Youghal **Obv:** Y. T in circle **Rev:** Fish in circle

Date	Mintage	VG	F	VF	XF	Unc
ND Rare	—	—	—	—	—	—

CIVIL WAR

After leaving the throne of England James II gathered popular support in Ireland. He landed in Ireland in March, 1689 and proceeded to raise an army. Adequate funds were not available to him so a plan was devised whereby base metal coins could be exchanged for silver following the war. Metal for the new coinage came from church bells, cannon (hence gun money) and any other compatible metal.

A unique feature of these coins is that they are dated by month as well as year. England was still on the Julian calendar and the new year began on March 25. Therefore March, 1689 and March, 1690 are the same month and December and January follow each other in 1689.

"Gun Money" comes in 2 issues: The first authorized in June, 1689 and consisting of 6 pence, shillings and 1/2 crowns. The second issue was authorized in April and June of 1690 and the crown denomination was added. The original values were reduced in size and many pieces of the second issue were struck over those of the first issue.

NOTE: Varieties of spelling, punctuation and placement of design elements exist. Not all have been listed.

GUN MONEY COINAGE

Pewter Money

KM# 96 1/2 PENNY

Pewter **Obv:** Head of James II left

Date	Mintage	VG	F	VF	XF	Unc
1689	—	190	375	825	1,900	—
1690	—	95.00	190	450	1,000	—

KM# 96a 1/2 PENNY

Silver **Obv:** Head of James II left **Edge:** Reeded

Date	Mintage	VG	F	VF	XF	Unc
1690 Proof	—	—	—	—	—	—

KM# 96b 1/2 PENNY

Silver **Obv:** Head of James II left **Edge:** Plain

Date	Mintage	VG	F	VF	XF	Unc
1690 Proof	—	—	—	—	—	—

KM# 104 1/2 PENNY

Pewter **Obv:** Small laureate head, leaf below **Note:** Brass plug through planchet.

Date	Mintage	VG	F	VF	XF	Unc
1690	—	65.00	150	375	825	—

KM# 97 PENNY

Pewter **Obv:** Laureate head of James II left **Rev:** Crowned harp, date at top

Date	Mintage	VG	F	VF	XF	Unc
1689	—	—	—	—	—	—
1690	—	250	500	1,250	2,800	—

KM# 105 PENNY

Pewter **Obv:** Small laureate head of James II left, value behind **Rev:** Crowned harp divides date

Date	Mintage	VG	F	VF	XF	Unc
1690	—	190	400	1,000	2,000	—

KM# 98 4 PENCE (Groat)

Pewter **Obv:** Laureate bust of James II left **Rev:** Crowned harp divides value, date at top

Date	Mintage	VG	F	VF	XF	Unc
1689 Rare	—	—	—	—	—	—

KM# A106 1/2 CROWN

Pewter **Obv:** Laureate head of James II left **Rev:** Crowned divides ornate JR

Date	Mintage	VG	F	VF	XF	Unc
1690 Rare	—	—	—	—	—	—

Note: Struck with dies of 1/2 Crown, KM#95

KM# 106.1 CROWN

Pewter With Brass **Edge:** Lettered **Note:** Plug pressed in planchet.

Date	Mintage	VG	F	VF	XF	Unc
1690	—	575	1,150	2,250	5,000	—
1690 Proof, Rare	—	—	—	—	—	—

KM# 106.2 CROWN

Pewter With Brass **Edge:** Plain **Note:** Plug pressed in planchet.

Date	Mintage	VG	F	VF	XF	Unc
1690	—	—	—	—	—	—
1690 Proof, Rare	—	—	—	—	—	—

GUN MONEY COINAGE

A unique feature of these coins is that they are dated by month as well as year. England was still on the Julian calendar and the new year began on March 25. Therefore March, 1689 and March 1690 are the same month and December and January follow each other in 1689.

KM# 93 SIXPENCE

Brass **Obv:** Head of James II left

Date	Mintage	VG	F	VF	XF	Unc
1689 Jan	—	19.00	31.25	65.00	105	—
1689 Feb	—	19.00	31.25	65.00	105	—
1689 Mar	—	19.00	31.25	65.00	105	—
1689 June	—	19.00	31.25	65.00	105	—
1689 Jvne	—	19.00	31.25	65.00	105	—
1689 July	—	19.00	31.25	65.00	105	—
1689 Aug	—	19.00	31.25	65.00	105	—
1689 Augt	—	19.00	31.25	65.00	105	—
1689 Sep	—	19.00	31.25	65.00	105	—
1689 Sepr	—	19.00	31.25	65.00	105	—
1689 7ber	—	37.50	75.00	200	400	—
1689 Oct	—	—	—	—	—	—
1689 Nov	—	19.00	31.25	65.00	105	—
1689 Dec	—	19.00	31.25	65.00	105	—
1690 Mar	—	19.00	31.25	65.00	105	—
1690 April	—	19.00	31.25	65.00	105	—
1690 May	—	19.00	31.25	65.00	105	—

KM# 93a SIXPENCE

Silver **Obv:** Head of James II left

Date	Mintage	VG	F	VF	XF	Unc
1689 Jan Proof, Rare	—	—	—	—	—	—
1689 Feb Proof	—	Value: 2,000				
1689 July Proof	—	—	—	—	—	—
1689 Aug Proof	—	—	—	—	—	—
1689 Sepr Proof	—	—	—	—	—	—

KM# 93b SIXPENCE

Gold **Obv:** Head of James II left

Date	Mintage	VG	F	VF	XF	Unc
1689 Feb Proof, Rare	—	—	—	—	—	—

Note: Gold strikings not contemporary

KM# 94 SHILLING

Brass **Obv:** Head of James II left **Note:** Large size.

Date	Mintage	VG	F	VF	XF	Unc
1689 Jan	—	19.00	31.25	65.00	100	—
1689 Feb	—	19.00	31.25	65.00	100	375
1689 Mar	—	19.00	31.25	65.00	100	—
1689 July	—	19.00	31.25	65.00	100	—
1689 Aug	—	19.00	31.25	65.00	100	—
1689 Augt	—	19.00	31.25	65.00	100	—
1689 Sep	—	19.00	31.25	65.00	100	—
1689 Sepr	—	19.00	31.25	65.00	100	—
1689 Sept	—	19.00	31.25	65.00	100	—
1689 Septr	—	19.00	31.25	65.00	100	450
1689 Oct	—	19.00	31.25	65.00	100	—
1689 OCT	—	19.00	31.25	65.00	100	—
1689 OCTR	—	19.00	31.25	65.00	100	—
1689 OCTr	—	19.00	31.25	65.00	100	—
1689 8BER	—	19.00	34.50	90.00	190	—
1689 8Ber	—	19.00	34.50	90.00	190	—
1689 8BR	—	19.00	34.50	90.00	190	—
1689 8br	—	19.00	34.50	90.00	190	—
1689 Nov	—	19.00	31.25	65.00	100	—
1689 novr	—	19.00	31.25	65.00	100	—
1689 9	—	19.00	34.50	90.00	190	—
1689 9r	—	19.00	31.25	65.00	100	—
1689 Dec	—	19.00	31.25	65.00	100	—
1689 Decr	—	19.00	31.25	65.00	100	—
1689 10r	—	19.00	31.25	65.00	100	—
1690 Mar	—	19.00	31.25	65.00	100	—
1690 Apr	—	19.00	31.25	65.00	100	—

KM# 94a SHILLING

Silver **Obv:** Head of James II left **Note:** Large size.

Date	Mintage	VG	F	VF	XF	Unc
1689 Jan Proof, Rare	—	—	—	—	—	—
1689 Feb Proof, Rare	—	—	—	—	—	—
1689 Mar Proof, Rare	—	—	—	—	—	—
1689 July Proof, Rare	—	—	—	—	—	—
1689 Aug Proof, Rare	—	—	—	—	—	—
1689 Augt Proof, Rare	—	—	—	—	—	—
1689 Sepr Proof, Rare	—	—	—	—	—	—
1689 Sept Proof, Rare	—	—	—	—	—	—
1689 Septr Proof, Rare	—	—	—	—	—	—
1690 Mar Proof, Rare	—	—	—	—	—	—
1690 Apr Proof, Rare	—	—	—	—	—	—

KM# 100 SHILLING

Brass **Obv:** Head of James II left **Note:** Small size.

Date	Mintage	VG	F	VF	XF	Unc
1690 Apr	—	19.00	31.25	65.00	125	—
1690 May	—	19.00	31.25	65.00	100	375
1690 MAY	—	19.00	31.25	65.00	100	—
1690 June	—	19.00	31.25	65.00	100	—
1690 Sep	—	31.25	65.00	125	250	—

KM# 100a SHILLING

Silver **Obv:** Head of James II left **Note:** Small size.

Date	Mintage	VG	F	VF	XF	Unc
1690 May Proof	—	Value: 2,250				
1690 June Proof, Rare	—	—	—	—	—	—

KM# 100b SHILLING

Gold **Obv:** Head of James II left **Note:** Small size.

Date	Mintage	VG	F	VF	XF	Unc
1690 June Proof, Rare	—	—	—	—	—	—

Note: Gold strikings not contemporary

KM# 95 1/2 CROWN

Brass **Obv:** Head of James II left

Date	Mintage	VG	F	VF	XF	Unc
1689 Jan	—	19.00	31.25	65.00	125	—
1689 jan	—	19.00	31.25	65.00	125	—
1689 Feb	—	19.00	31.25	65.00	125	—
1689 Mar	—	19.00	31.25	70.00	150	—
1689 July	—	19.00	37.50	105	170	—
1689 Aug	—	19.00	31.25	65.00	125	—
1689 Augt	—	19.00	31.25	65.00	125	—
1689 Sep	—	—	—	—	—	—
1689 Sepr	—	19.00	31.25	70.00	150	—
1689 Sept	—	19.00	31.25	70.00	150	—
1689 Septr	—	19.00	31.25	70.00	150	—
1689 Oct	—	19.00	31.25	70.00	150	—
1689 OCTR	—	19.00	31.25	65.00	125	—
1689 Octr	—	19.00	31.25	65.00	125	—
1689 OCT	—	19.00	31.25	65.00	125	—
1689 8r	—	50.00	100	250	525	—

Date	Mintage	VG	F	VF	XF	Unc
1689 8BER	—	50.00	100	250	525	—
1689 Nov	—	19.00	31.25	65.00	125	—
1689 Novr	—	19.00	31.25	65.00	125	—
1689 Dec	—	19.00	31.25	65.00	125	—
1689 Decr	—	19.00	31.25	65.00	125	—
1689 10r	—	65.00	125	280	625	—
1690 Mar	—	19.00	31.25	70.00	150	—
1690 Apr	—	19.00	31.25	65.00	125	575
1690 May	—	19.00	37.50	105	230	—

KM# 95a 1/2 CROWN

Silver **Obv:** Head of James II left

Date	Mintage	VG	F	VF	XF	Unc
1689 jan Proof, Rare	—	—	—	—	—	—
1689 Jan Proof, Rare	—	—	—	—	—	—
1689 Feb Proof, Rare	—	—	—	—	—	—
1689 Mar Proof, Rare	—	—	—	—	—	—
1689 Aug Proof, Rare	—	—	—	—	—	—
1689 Augt Proof,f Rare	—	—	—	—	—	—
1689 Sepr Proof, Rare	—	—	—	—	—	—
1689 Sept Proof, Rare	—	—	—	—	—	—
1689 Septr Proof, Rare	—	—	—	—	—	—
1689 Nov Proof, Rare	—	—	—	—	—	—
1689 Novr Proof, Rare	—	—	—	—	—	—
1690 Mar Proof, Rare	—	—	—	—	—	—
1690 Apr Proof, Rare	—	—	—	—	—	—

KM# 101a 1/2 CROWN

Silver **Obv:** Head of James II left **Note:** Small size.

Date	Mintage	VG	F	VF	XF	Unc
1690 May Proof, Rare	—	—	—	—	—	—

KM# 101b 1/2 CROWN

Gold **Obv:** Head of James II left **Note:** Small size.

Date	Mintage	VG	F	VF	XF	Unc
1690 May Proof, Rare	—	—	—	—	—	—

KM# 101 1/2 CROWN

Brass **Obv:** Head of James II left **Note:** Small size.

Date	Mintage	VG	F	VF	XF	Unc
1690 Apr Rare	—	—	—	—	—	—
1690 May	—	19.00	31.25	65.00	100	750
1690 May	—	19.00	31.25	65.00	100	—
1690 Jun	—	19.00	31.25	65.00	120	—
1690 June	—	19.00	31.25	65.00	120	950
1690 Jnue (error)	—	25.00	50.00	120	250	—
1690 July	—	19.00	31.25	65.00	150	—
1690 Aug	—	25.00	50.00	125	280	—
1690 Oct Rare	—	—	—	—	—	—

KM# 95b 1/2 CROWN

Gold **Obv:** Head of James II left

Date	Mintage	VG	F	VF	XF	Unc
1690 Apr Proof, Rare	—	—	—	—	—	—

KM# 102 CROWN

Brass **Obv:** Sword points to E in REX **Note:** Overstruck on large size 1/2 Crown.

Date	Mintage	VG	F	VF	XF	Unc
1690	—	100	750	800	1,600	—

KM# 103.1 CROWN

Brass **Obv:** Sword points between REX and IAC **Note:** Overstruck on large size 1/2 Crown.

Date	Mintage	VG	F	VF	XF	Unc
1690	—	25.00	75.00	400	800	1,800

Note: Legend varieties exist

KM# 103.1a CROWN

Silver **Note:** Overstruck on large size 1/2 Crown.

Date	Mintage	VG	F	VF	XF	Unc
1690 Proof, Rare	—	—	—	—	—	—

KM# 103.1b CROWN

Gold **Note:** Overstruck on large size 1/2 Crown.

Date	Mintage	VG	F	VF	XF	Unc
1690 Proof, Rare	—	—	—	—	—	—

KM# 103.2 CROWN

Brass **Rev. Legend:** ...VICTO/ RE... **Note:** Overstruck on large size 1/2 Crown.

Date	Mintage	VG	F	VF	XF	Unc
1690	—	25.00	35.00	400	800	—

KM# 103.3 CROWN

Brass **Rev. Legend:** ...RIX... **Note:** Overstruck on large size 1/2 Crown.

Date	Mintage	VG	F	VF	XF	Unc
1690	—	25.00	75.00	400	800	—

SIEGE COINAGE

Siege of Limerick

KM# 107.1 FARTHING

Brass **Obv:** Laureate bust of James II left. **Rev:** Hibernia seated left, harp at right, retrograde N in HIBERNIA **Note:** Struck over small "Gun Money" Shillings.

Date	Mintage	VG	F	VF	XF	Unc
1691	—	31.25	65.00	105	250	—

KM# 107.2 FARTHING

Brass **Obv:** Laureate bust of James II left. **Rev:** Hibernia seated left, harp at right, normal N in HIBERNIA **Note:** Struck over small "Gun Money" Shillings.

Date	Mintage	VG	F	VF	XF	Unc
1691	—	55.00	125	190	450	—

KM# 108 1/2 PENNY

Brass **Obv:** Laureate bust of James II left. **Rev:** Hibernia seated left, harp at right, retrogradel N in HIBERNIA **Note:** Struck over large "Gun Money" Shillings.

Date	Mintage	VG	F	VF	XF	Unc
1691	—	19.00	37.50	95.00	190	—

PATTERNS

Including off metal strikes

KM#	Date	Mintage	Identification	Mkt Val
Pn1	1689	—	1/2 Penny. Copper. Lion on crown above harp. KM96. 2 examples are known, one at the National Museum of Ireland and the other in private hands.	—
Pn2	1689	—	Penny. Pewter. 8.4200 g. KM97. Unique example is in the National Museum of Ireland.	600
Pn3	1689	—	4 Pence. Pewter. 3.3700 g. KM98.	1,200
Pn4	1690	—	1/2 Penny. Silver. Milled edge. KM96.	1,000
Pn5	1690	—	1/2 Penny. Silver. Plain edge. KM96.	—
Pn6	1690	—	1/2 Penny. Pewter. Plugged, KM104.	—
Pn7	1690	—	Penny. Pewter. 8.4200 g. KM105.	600
Pn8	1690	—	Crown. White Metal. 18.3400 g. KM106.	—
Pn9	1690	—	Crown. White Metal. 18.3400 g. With brass plug, KM106.	—
Pn10	1690	—	Crown. Tin. Plain edge. KM106.	—
Pn11	1690	—	Crown. Silver. Lettered edge. KM106.	6,000
Pn12	1690	—	Crown. Silver. Gun money, small legends, KM103.	—

KM#	Date	Mintage	Identification	Mkt Val
Pn13	1690	—	Crown. Silver. Gun money, large legends, KM103.	—
Pn14	1690	—	Crown. Gold. Gun money, small legends, KM103.	—
Pn15	1690	—	Crown. Gold. Gun money, large legends, KM103.	—
Pn16	1690	—	Crown. Gold. Lettered edge. KM103.	—
Pn17	ND	—	Farthing. Bath Metal. Bust. Seated woman holding orb, leaning on shield.	—

a map of the ITALIAN STATES
SWITZERLAND
SAVOY
Chambery
PIEDMONT
Cisterna
Carmagnola
FRANCE
LOMBARDY
Milan
Vercelli
Passerano
Campi
Tassarolo
Arquata
Genoa
Belgioioso
VENETIA
Porcia
Gazzoldo
PARMA
MODENA
Bologna
Forli
Pesaro
Fosdinovo
Massa Di Lunigiana
Leghorn
Orciano
Siena
Ancona
Gubbio
Camerino
TUSCANY
Castro
PAPAL STATES
Vasto
KINGDOM
OF THE TWO
SICILIES
Belmonte
San Georgio
Reggio
Ventimiglia
SICILY
CORSICA
SARDINIA

ITALIAN STATES

ALBERA

A feudal fief in Piedmont with an unauthorized coinage in 1678 at the Genoa Mint by a member of the Vescova family.

RULER
Carlo Settola, 1653--

FEUDAL FIEF

HAMMERED COINAGE

KM# 1 27 MILANESE SOLDI
7.3900 g., Silver, 33 mm. **Obv:** Arms supported by angels **Rev:** Saint offering a blessing

Date	Mintage	VG	F	VF	XF	Unc
ND Rare	—	—	—	—	—	—

KM# 2 54 MILANESE SOLDI
13.7600 g., Silver, 34 mm. **Obv:** Arms supported by angels **Rev:** Saint offering a blessing

Date	Mintage	VG	F	VF	XF	Unc
ND Rare	—	—	—	—	—	—

ARQUATA

RULERS
Filippo Spinola, 1641-1667
Guilio Spinola, Marquis 1661-1691
Gerardo Spinola, 1682-1694

STATE

STANDARD COINAGE

KM# A2 LUIGINO
Silver **Ruler:** Filippo Spinola **Obv:** Female bust right **Obv. Legend:** PVLCRAA. VERT. IMAGO. DOM **Rev:** Crowned shield of 3 lis **Rev. Legend:** DEVS. MEVS. ET. OMNIA. IN. SECV. SE.

Date	Mintage	VG	F	VF	XF	Unc
1666	—	—	—	375	—	—

KM# 2 LUIGINO
Billon **Note:** Weight varies: 2.14-2.41 grams. Anonymous for the Levant

Date	Mintage	VG	F	VF	XF	Unc
1668	—	42.00	90.00	200	325	—
1669	—	42.00	90.00	200	325	—

KM# 6 LUIGINO
2.5100 g., Silver **Ruler:** Gerardo Spinola **Obv:** Bust of Gerardo left **Rev:** Double eage with supported arms, date in legend

Date	Mintage	VG	F	VF	XF	Unc
1682	—	175	350	625	1,050	—

KM# 7 1/8 SCUDO
5.1200 g., Silver **Ruler:** Gerardo Spinola **Obv:** Bust of Gerardo left **Rev:** Crowned arms in branches, date in legend

Date	Mintage	VG	F	VF	XF	Unc
ND	—	210	375	700	1,200	—

KM# 1 1/4 SCUDO
7.7000 g., Silver **Ruler:** Filippo Spinola **Obv:** Bust of Filippo right **Rev:** Crowned eagle with arms

Date	Mintage	VG	F	VF	XF	Unc
1644 Rare	—	—	—	—	—	—

KM# 3 1/4 SCUDO
7.7000 g., Silver **Ruler:** Guilio Spinola **Obv:** Bust of Guilio left **Rev:** Crowned Spinola arms in branches

Date	Mintage	VG	F	VF	XF	Unc
1681	—	280	525	975	1,750	—

KM# 4 1/4 SCUDO
7.7000 g., Silver **Ruler:** Gerardo Spinola **Obv:** Bust of Gerardo left

Date	Mintage	VG	F	VF	XF	Unc
ND Rare	—	—	—	—	—	—

KM# 5 1/2 DOPPIA
3.5000 g., 0.9860 Gold 0.1109 oz. AGW **Ruler:** Guilio Spinola **Obv:** Bust of Guilio left in inner circle **Rev:** Crowned Spinola arms, date in legend

Date	Mintage	VG	F	VF	XF	Unc
1681	—	2,250	4,500	9,000	15,000	—

KM# 8 DOPPIA
7.0000 g., 0.9860 Gold 0.2219 oz. AGW **Ruler:** Gerardo Spinola **Obv:** Bust of Gerardo left **Rev:** Crowned arms in branches, date in legend

Date	Mintage	VG	F	VF	XF	Unc
1682	—	3,000	6,000	12,000	22,500	—

BOZZOLO

Bozzolo is located a little west of Mantua. Charles V granted the mint right in 1497. Bozzolo was given to the Gonzaga family by the Emperor Rudolph in 1593, and Guilio Cesare was created prince of Bozzolo. Guilio was succeeded by his 13-year-old nephew, Scipione who ruled under the regency of his mother Isabella until 1613. Scipione became duke of Sabbioneta in 1636. The mint was closed at his death in 1670.

RULERS
Guilio Cesare Gonzaga, 1593-1609
Scipione Gonzaga, 1609-1670

Reference:
V = Alberto Varesi, ***Monete Italiane Regionali: Lombardia, Zecche Minori. Pavia***, 1995.

PRINCIPALITY

STANDARD COINAGE

KM# 5 SESINO
Billon **Obv:** Head right, PRINCEPS **Rev:** Sun **Note:** Weight varies: 0.75-1.25 grams.

Date	Mintage	Good	VG	F	VF	XF
ND	—	18.00	36.00	80.00	155	260

KM# 6 SESINO
Billon **Obv:** Head right, I.C. PRIN **Rev:** St. Peter **Note:** Weight varies: 0.75-1.25 grams.

Date	Mintage	Good	VG	F	VF	XF
ND	—	8.00	18.00	39.00	85.00	165

KM# 7 SESINO
Billon **Obv:** Head right, PRINCEPS **Note:** Weight varies: 0.75-1.25 grams.

Date	Mintage	Good	VG	F	VF	XF
ND	—	8.00	18.00	39.00	85.00	165

KM# 8 SESINO
Billon **Obv:** Head right, IVLI **Rev:** St. Andrew **Note:** Weight varies: 0.75-1.25 grams.

Date	Mintage	Good	VG	F	VF	XF
ND	—	12.00	25.00	50.00	110	230

KM# 9 SESINO
Billon **Obv:** Cross with four eagles **Rev:** Large crowned F **Note:** Weight varies: 0.75-1.25 grams.

Date	Mintage	Good	VG	F	VF	XF
ND	—	7.00	17.00	36.50	70.00	130

KM# 10 SESINO
Billon **Obv:** Eagle, SCIP **Rev:** St. Peter **Note:** Weight varies: 0.75-1.25 grams.

Date	Mintage	Good	VG	F	VF	XF
ND	—	11.00	22.50	45.50	100	195

KM# 72 SESINO
Billon **Obv:** Cross with three stars **Rev:** Madonna and child **Note:** Weight varies: 0.75-1.25 grams.

Date	Mintage	Good	VG	F	VF	XF
1660	—	7.00	17.00	36.50	70.00	130

KM# 73 SESINO
Billon **Obv:** Madonna and child **Rev:** Cross, BOZ **Note:** Weight varies: 0.75-1.25 grams.

Date	Mintage	Good	VG	F	VF	XF
ND	—	22.50	42.00	90.00	175	325

KM# 74 SESINO
Billon **Rev:** Ornate cross **Note:** Weight varies: 0.75-1.25 grams.

Date	Mintage	Good	VG	F	VF	XF
ND	—	7.00	17.00	36.50	70.00	130

KM# 75 SESINO
Billon **Obv:** Flame **Rev:** Large L **Note:** Weight varies: 0.75-1.25 grams.

Date	Mintage	Good	VG	F	VF	XF
ND	—	11.00	22.50	45.50	100	195

KM# 76 SESINO
Billon **Obv:** Bust right **Rev:** Large star with 16 points **Note:** Weight varies: 0.75-1.25 grams.

Date	Mintage	Good	VG	F	VF	XF
ND	—	7.00	17.00	36.50	70.00	130

KM# 77 SESINO
Billon **Obv:** Crowned arms **Rev:** John the Baptist **Note:** Weight varies: 0.75-1.25 grams.

Date	Mintage	Good	VG	F	VF	XF
ND	—	8.00	18.00	39.00	85.00	165

KM# 78 SESINO
Billon **Obv:** Bust right, SCIP **Rev:** Crowned arms, MAR **Note:** Weight varies: 0.75-1.25 grams.

Date	Mintage	Good	VG	F	VF	XF
ND	—	7.00	17.00	36.50	80.00	145

KM# 79 SESINO
Billon **Rev:** Crowned arms, SCIP **Note:** Weight varies: 0.75-1.25 grams.

Date	Mintage	Good	VG	F	VF	XF
ND	—	7.00	17.00	36.50	80.00	145

KM# 80 SESINO
Billon **Obv:** Head left **Rev:** Crowned eagle, SAC **Note:** Weight varies: 0.75-1.25 grams.

Date	Mintage	Good	VG	F	VF	XF
ND	—	7.00	17.00	36.50	80.00	145

KM# 81 SESINO
Billon **Obv:** Head right **Rev:** Crowned eagle, BOZ **Note:** Weight varies: 0.75-1.25 grams.

Date	Mintage	Good	VG	F	VF	XF
ND	—	7.00	17.00	36.50	80.00	145

KM# 82 SESINO
Billon **Rev:** Crowned eagle, SABL **Note:** Weight varies: 0.75-1.25 grams.

Date	Mintage	Good	VG	F	VF	XF
ND	—	7.00	17.00	36.50	80.00	145

KM# 83 SESINO
Billon **Obv:** Crowned eagle **Rev:** Bust left **Note:** Weight varies: 0.75-1.25 grams.

Date	Mintage	Good	VG	F	VF	XF
ND	—	7.00	17.00	36.50	80.00	145

KM# 84 SESINO
Billon **Obv:** Cross on shield with three stars **Rev:** Madonna in nimbus **Note:** Weight varies: 0.75-1.25 grams.

Date	Mintage	Good	VG	F	VF	XF
ND	—	8.00	18.00	39.00	85.00	165

KM# 85 SESINO
Billon **Obv:** Head right **Rev:** Cross with eagle and lion **Note:** Weight varies: 0.75-1.25 grams.

Date	Mintage	Good	VG	F	VF	XF
ND	—	8.00	18.00	39.00	85.00	165

KM# 86 SESINO
Billon **Obv:** Crowned arms **Rev:** Madonna and child **Note:** Weight varies: 0.75-1.25 grams.

Date	Mintage	Good	VG	F	VF	XF
ND	—	8.00	18.00	39.00	85.00	165

KM# 11 BAGATTINO
Billon **Obv:** Head right **Rev:** Eagle, value **Note:** Weight varies: 0.40-0.80 grams.

Date	Mintage	Good	VG	F	VF	XF
ND	—	12.00	25.00	50.00	100	195

KM# 12 BAGATTINO
Billon **Obv:** Medici arms **Rev:** John the Baptist **Note:** Weight varies: 0.40-0.80 grams.

Date	Mintage	Good	VG	F	VF	XF
ND	—	18.00	36.00	65.00	115	240

KM# 38 QUATTRINO
Billon **Obv:** Mountain, FIDES **Rev:** Foliate cross **Note:** Weight varies: 0.46-1.11 grams.

Date	Mintage	Good	VG	F	VF	XF
1605	—	22.50	42.00	100	165	295

KM# 39 QUATTRINO
Billon **Obv:** Head right, IVL **Rev:** Crowned arms with large star **Note:** Weight varies: 0.46-1.11 grams.

Date	Mintage	Good	VG	F	VF	XF
ND	—	12.00	25.00	45.50	85.00	165

KM# 40 QUATTRINO
Billon **Obv:** Head right, PRINCEPS **Rev:** Crowned arms with star, ME. DVCAT. **Note:** Weight varies: 0.46-1.11 grams.

Date	Mintage	Good	VG	F	VF	XF
ND	—	12.00	25.00	45.50	85.00	165

KM# 41 QUATTRINO
Billon **Obv:** Head left **Rev:** Crowned arms with star **Note:** Weight varies: 0.46-1.11 grams.

Date	Mintage	Good	VG	F	VF	XF
ND	—	12.00	25.00	45.50	85.00	165

KM# 42 QUATTRINO
Billon **Obv:** Crowned arms **Rev:** Madonna and child, ESTO **Note:** Weight varies: 0.46-1.11 grams.

Date	Mintage	Good	VG	F	VF	XF
ND	—	12.00	25.00	45.50	85.00	165

KM# 43 QUATTRINO
Billon **Obv:** Head right **Rev:** Large star **Note:** Weight varies: 0.46-1.11 grams.

Date	Mintage	Good	VG	F	VF	XF
ND	—	12.00	25.00	45.50	85.00	165

KM# 70 QUATTRINO
Billon **Obv:** BOZALI/ PRI/ NCEPS/ date **Rev:** Rampant lion **Note:** Weight varies: 0.46-1.11 grams.

Date	Mintage	Good	VG	F	VF	XF
1657	—	8.00	18.00	39.00	65.00	115
1665	—	8.00	18.00	39.00	65.00	115
1667	—	8.00	18.00	39.00	65.00	115

KM# 13 PARPAGLIOLA
1.7800 g., Billon **Obv:** Crowned arms **Rev:** Woman with vase

Date	Mintage	Good	VG	F	VF	XF
ND	—	18.00	36.00	80.00	130	260

KM# 14 CAVALOTTO
Billon **Obv:** Pegasus **Rev:** St. Catharine standing **Note:** Weight varies: 1.70-2.50 grams.

Date	Mintage	Good	VG	F	VF	XF
ND	—	25.00	48.00	105	195	325

KM# 15 FIORINO
4.6700 g., Billon

Date	Mintage	Good	VG	F	VF	XF
ND	—	150	250	550	1,000	1,750

KM# 16 SOLDO
1.6500 g., Billon **Obv:** Crowned arms **Rev:** Cross in ornate frame

Date	Mintage	Good	VG	F	VF	XF
ND	—	12.00	25.00	39.00	85.00	165

KM# 17 3 SOLDI
Billon **Obv:** Bust right, 3 below, SCIP **Rev:** Crowned quartered arms **Note:** Weight varies: 1.14-1.75 grams.

Date	Mintage	Good	VG	F	VF	XF
ND	—	22.50	42.00	100	210	375

KM# 18 3 SOLDI
Billon **Obv:** Crowned quartered arms **Rev:** Crowned double eagle, 3 below **Note:** Weight varies: 1.14-1.75 grams.

Date	Mintage	Good	VG	F	VF	XF
ND	—	12.00	25.00	39.00	85.00	165

KM# 19 3 SOLDI
Billon **Obv:** Bust right, 3 below, SCI **Rev:** Three shields in triangle **Note:** Weight varies: 1.14-1.75 grams.

Date	Mintage	Good	VG	F	VF	XF
ND	—	12.00	25.00	39.00	85.00	165

KM# 20 3 SOLDI
Billon **Obv:** Crowned double eagle, 3 below, SVBPEN **Note:** Weight varies: 1.14-1.75 grams.

Date	Mintage	Good	VG	F	VF	XF
ND	—	22.50	42.00	100	210	375

KM# 21 3 SOLDI
Billon **Obv:** Bust left **Rev:** Crowned double eagle, 3 below **Note:** Weight varies: 1.14-1.75 grams.

Date	Mintage	Good	VG	F	VF	XF
ND	—	18.00	36.00	80.00	165	295

KM# 22 3 SOLDI
Billon **Rev:** Crowned double eagle, 3 below cross **Note:** Weight varies: 1.14-1.75 grams.

Date	Mintage	Good	VG	F	VF	XF
ND	—	18.00	36.00	80.00	165	295

KM# 23 3 SOLDI
Billon **Rev:** Without 3 **Note:** Weight varies: 1.14-1.75 grams.

Date	Mintage	Good	VG	F	VF	XF
ND	—	12.00	25.00	50.00	100	195

KM# 24 3 SOLDI
Billon **Obv:** Crowned arms **Rev:** Pisside **Note:** Weight varies: 1.14-1.75 grams.

Date	Mintage	Good	VG	F	VF	XF
ND	—	12.00	25.00	45.50	85.00	165

KM# 25 5 SOLDI
Billon **Obv:** Bust right **Rev:** St. Nicholas standing **Note:** Weight varies: 1.79-2.49 grams.

Date	Mintage	Good	VG	F	VF	XF
ND	—	25.00	48.00	110	215	400

KM# 26 8 SOLDI
3.7500 g., Billon **Obv:** Crowned arms in cartouche **Rev:** St. Peter with keys

Date	Mintage	Good	VG	F	VF	XF
ND	—	42.00	70.00	130	260	450

KM# 64 8 SOLDI
3.7500 g., Billon **Obv:** Draped bust left **Rev:** Crowned quartered arms

Date	Mintage	Good	VG	F	VF	XF
ND Rare	—	—	—	—	—	—

KM# 65 8 SOLDI
3.7500 g., Billon **Obv:** Armored bust, date before, VIII below **Rev:** Crowned oval arms

Date	Mintage	Good	VG	F	VF	XF
1641	—	48.00	90.00	165	285	500

KM# 66 8 SOLDI
3.7500 g., Billon **Obv:** *80*SCIPION in six lines **Rev:** Sun with rays

Date	Mintage	Good	VG	F	VF	XF
ND	—	25.00	48.00	100	165	325

KM# 27 10 SOLDI
2.7100 g., Billon **Obv:** Bust right **Rev:** Five-line inscription

Date	Mintage	Good	VG	F	VF	XF
ND	—	30.00	60.00	130	230	400

KM# 28 10 SOLDI
2.7100 g., Billon **Obv:** Cross with four stars **Rev:** Madonna and child

Date	Mintage	Good	VG	F	VF	XF
ND	—	18.00	36.00	65.00	130	260

KM# 29 15-1/2 SOLDI
4.0300 g., Billon **Obv:** Bust right **Rev:** Crowned double eagle with quartered arms

Date	Mintage	Good	VG	F	VF	XF
ND Rare	—	—	—	—	—	—

KM# 30 30 SOLDI
5.3500 g., Billon **Obv:** Bust right **Rev:** St. Catharine with palms, XX* below

Date	Mintage	Good	VG	F	VF	XF
ND Rare	—	—	—	—	—	—

KM# 49 LIRA
Silver **Obv:** Bust right **Rev:** Figure of Hope **Note:** Weight varies: 4.00-6.75 grams.

Date	Mintage	Good	VG	F	VF	XF
1614	—	300	450	900	1,350	3,000

KM# 50 LIRA
Silver **Obv:** Bust left **Note:** Weight varies: 4.00-6.75 grams.

Date	Mintage	Good	VG	F	VF	XF
1618	—	375	600	1,150	1,900	3,550

KM# 51 LIRA
Silver **Obv:** Crowned quartered arms **Rev:** St. Peter with keys **Note:** Weight varies: 4.00-6.75 grams.

Date	Mintage	Good	VG	F	VF	XF
ND	—	125	275	450	—	—

KM# 31 TESTONE
Silver **Obv:** Bust right **Rev:** St. Peter kneeling left **Note:** Weight varies: 8.50-8.70 grams.

Date	Mintage	Good	VG	F	VF	XF
ND Rare	—	—	—	—	—	—

KM# 32 1/4 TALLERO
Silver **Obv:** Half figure right **Rev:** Crowned double eagle **Note:** Weight varies: 6.46-6.85 grams.

Date	Mintage	Good	VG	F	VF	XF
ND Rare	—	—	—	—	—	—

KM# 33 TALLERO
Silver **Obv:** Armed half figure right **Rev:** Four arms in frame **Note:** Weight varies: 21.00-27.00 grams. Dav. #3849.

Date	Mintage	Good	VG	F	VF	XF
ND Rare	—	—	—	—	—	—

KM# 44 TALLERO
Silver **Obv:** Confronted busts **Rev:** Rampant lion **Note:** Weight varies: 21.00-27.00 grams. Dav. #3850.

Date	Mintage	Good	VG	F	VF	XF
1613 Rare	—	—	—	—	—	—

KM# 45 TALLERO
Silver **Obv:** Armed half figure right **Rev:** Two shields of Gonzaga arms **Note:** Weight varies: 21.00-27.00 grams. Dav. #3853.

Date	Mintage	Good	VG	F	VF	XF
ND Rare	—	—	—	—	—	—

KM# 46 TALLERO
Silver **Obv:** Half figure right, 80 below **Rev:** Crowned double eagle with arms **Note:** Weight varies: 21.00-27.00 grams. Dav. #3854.

Date	Mintage	Good	VG	F	VF	XF
ND	—	1,050	1,750	3,500	6,100	10,500

KM# 47 TALLERO
Silver **Obv:** Bust right, C.80.C below **Rev:** Crowned quartered arms **Note:** Weight varies: 21.00-27.00 grams. Dav. #3855.

Date	Mintage	Good	VG	F	VF	XF
ND	—	1,050	1,750	3,500	6,100	—

KM# 55 TALLERO
Silver **Obv:** Warrior behind shield **Rev:** Rampant lion **Note:** Weight varies: 21.00-27.00 grams. Dav. #3856.

Date	Mintage	Good	VG	F	VF	XF
1638	—	220	450	800	1,650	—
1659	—	220	450	800	1,650	—

KM# 88 TALLERO
Silver **Obv:** Warrior behind shield **Obv. Legend:** SCIP. G. DVX... **Rev:** Rampant lion **Rev. Legend:** VICIT. LEO. DETRIBV... **Note:** Weight varies: 21.00-27.00 grams. Dav. #3858.

Date	Mintage	Good	VG	F	VF	XF
1659 Rare	—	—	—	—	—	—

KM# 34 1/2 DUCATONE
13.1600 g., Silver **Obv:** Laureate head right **Rev:** Ornate cross

Date	Mintage	Good	VG	F	VF	XF
ND Rare	—	—	—	—	—	—

KM# 35 DUCATONE
Silver **Obv:** Bust of Giulio right **Rev:** Crowned quartered arms in Order chain **Note:** Weight varies: 31.00-32.00 grams. Dav. #3848.

Date	Mintage	Good	VG	F	VF	XF
ND Rare	—	—	—	—	—	—

KM# 48.1 DUCATONE
Silver **Obv:** Bust left, GASP below **Rev:** Christ giving keys to St. Peter **Note:** Weight varies: 31.00-32.00 grams. Dav. #3851.

Date	Mintage	Good	VG	F	VF	XF
1613	—	800	1,500	2,900	5,300	8,800

KM# 48.2 DUCATONE
Silver **Obv:** Bust left, G. MOLO **Note:** Weight varies: 31.00-32.00 grams. Dav. #3852.

Date	Mintage	Good	VG	F	VF	XF
1617	—	800	1,500	2,900	5,300	8,800

KM# 48.3 DUCATONE
Silver **Obv. Legend:** SCIP: D: G: DVX: SABL:... **Rev. Legend:** TV ES PETRVS:-PRAESIDIVM... **Note:** Weight varies: 31.00-32.00 grams. Dav. #3857.

Date	Mintage	Good	VG	F	VF	XF
1639	—	300	525	975	1,750	3,500

KM# 48.4 DUCATONE
Silver **Obv:** Different bust **Rev:** Legend without space after PETRVS: **Note:** Weight varies: 31.00-32.00 grams. Dav. #3859.

Date	Mintage	Good	VG	F	VF	XF
1665	—	300	525	975	1,750	3,500
1666	—	300	525	975	1,750	3,500

KM# 57 DUCATONE
Silver **Rev:** Crowned quartered arms **Note:** Weight varies: 31.00-32.00 grams. Dav. #3860.

Date	Mintage	Good	VG	F	VF	XF
ND Rare	—	1,300	2,200	4,400	7,900	13,000

KM# 58 DUCATONE
Silver **Rev:** Star with 16 points **Note:** Weight varies: 31.00-32.00 grams. Dav. #3861.

Date	Mintage	Good	VG	F	VF	XF
ND Rare	—	1,050	1,750	3,500	6,100	11,500

KM# 87 2 DUCATONE
63.8000 g., Silver **Obv:** Bust left **Rev:** Christ giving keys to St. Peter **Note:** Dav. #A3859.

Date	Mintage	Good	VG	F	VF	XF
1666 Rare	—	—	—	—	—	—

KM# 52 DOPPIA
7.0000 g., 0.9860 Gold 0.2219 oz. AGW **Obv:** Crowned arms in inner circle **Rev:** Figure of crowned female

Date	Mintage	VG	F	VF	XF	Unc
1618	—	3,750	6,800	11,500	19,000	—

KM# 53 DOPPIA
7.0000 g., 0.9860 Gold 0.2219 oz. AGW **Obv:** Bust of Scipio left in inner circle **Rev:** Two shields in inner circle

Date	Mintage	VG	F	VF	XF	Unc
ND Rare	—	—	—	—	—	—

KM# 54 DOPPIA
7.0000 g., 0.9860 Gold 0.2219 oz. AGW **Rev:** Crowned arms in inner circle

Date	Mintage	VG	F	VF	XF	Unc
ND Rare	—	—	—	—	—	—

KM# 59 4 DOPPIE
26.0700 g., Gold **Obv:** Bust left **Rev:** Christ giving keys to St. Peter

Date	Mintage	VG	F	VF	XF	Unc
1639 Rare	—	—	—	—	—	—

KM# 60 6 DOPPIE
Gold **Obv:** Bust left **Rev:** Christ giving keys to St. Peter **Note:** Weight varies: 39.11-39.36 grams.

Date	Mintage	VG	F	VF	XF	Unc
1639 Rare	—	—	—	—	—	—

KM# 61 6 DOPPIE
Gold **Rev:** Crowned quartered arms **Note:** Weight varies: 39.11-39.36 grams.

Date	Mintage	VG	F	VF	XF	Unc
ND Rare	—	—	—	—	—	—

KM# 37 DUCAT
3.5000 g., 0.9860 Gold 0.1109 oz. AGW **Obv:** Soldier standing **Rev:** Four-line inscription in tablet

Date	Mintage	VG	F	VF	XF	Unc
ND	—	1,500	2,700	4,900	10,500	—

PATTERNS

Including off metal strikes

KM#	Date	Mintage	Identification	Mkt Val
Pn1	ND(1593-1609)	—	5 Doppie. Bronze. MB#1.	—

CAMPI

An ancient feudal enclave in the Valle di Trebbia ruled by the Scotti dynasty. Emperor Ferdinand III conveyed the right to strike coinage on the rulers in 1654.

RULERS
Carlo Centurioni, 1654-1663
Giovanni Battista Centurioni, 1663-1715
Giulia Maria Serra, 1663-?

Reference:
V = Alberto Varesi, ***Monete Italiane Regionali: Piemonte, Sardegna, Liguria, Isola di Corsica.*** Pavia, 1996.

FEUDAL LORDSHIP

STANDARD COINAGE

KM# 3.1 LUIGINO
Billon **Obv:** Bust of princess to right **Obv. Legend:** IVLIA. M. PRINCIP. CAMP(I). **Rev:** Crowned shield of French arms divide date **Rev. Legend:** C(-)E(-)NTVPLV(M). GERMIN(_)(A). (-) B (-)(V). **Note:** Weight varies: 1.50-2.70 grams. 20-21mm. Struck in the name of the princess for the Levant. 14 varieties are known to exist. V#116.

Date	Mintage	VG	F	VF	XF	Unc
1668	—	55.00	115	275	475	—

KM# 7 LUIGINO
Billon **Obv:** Bust of princess to right **Obv. Legend:** IVL. M. S. R. I. PRINC. SOW. DOM. **Rev:** Crowned shield of French arms divide date **Rev. Legend:** MELLIBAT. EXLILLIIS. **Note:** Weight varies: 1.50-2.70 grams. Ref. V#118.

Date	Mintage	VG	F	VF	XF	Unc
1669	—	80.00	175	350	625	—

KM# 3.2 LUIGINO
Billon **Ruler:** Giovanni Battista Centurioni Scotti **Obv:** Bust of princess to right **Obv. Legend:** IVLIA. M. PRINCIP. CAMP(I). **Rev:** Crowned shield of French arms divide date **Rev. Legend:** PVLCRA. GERMINAT. BON. **Note:** V#117.

Date	Mintage	VG	F	VF	XF	Unc
1669	—	65.00	140	275	500	—

KM# 2 TESTONE
7.9800 g., Silver **Ruler:** Carlo Centurioni Scotti **Obv:** Armored long-haired bust to right **Obv. Legend:** CAROLVS. CENTVR. MAR. CAMPI. **Rev:** Crowned family arms superimposed on imperial eagle, date at end of legend **Rev. Legend:** ET. SAC. ROM. IMP. PRINCEPS. **Note:** Ref. V#112. Size varies: 29-30mm.

Date	Mintage	VG	F	VF	XF	Unc
1662 Rare	—	—	—	—	—	—

KM# 4 TESTONE
Silver **Ruler:** Giovanni Battista Centurioni Scotti **Obv:** Accolated busts to right **Obv. Legend:** IO. BAPT. CENTVRIO. ET. IVL. M. MAR. CAM. **Rev:** Crowned family arms superimposed on crowned imperial eagle, date at end of legend **Rev. Legend:** ET. SAC. ROM. IMP. PRINCEPES. **Note:** Weight varies: 7.96-13.10 grams. Size varies 31-32mm. Ref. V#115.

Date	Mintage	VG	F	VF	XF	Unc
1672 Rare	—	—	—	—	—	—

KM# 5 1/2 DOPPIA (Mezza Doppia)
3.2300 g., Gold, 21 mm. **Ruler:** Giovanni Battista Centurioni Scotti **Obv:** Bust of Giovanni Baptiste right **Obv. Legend:** IO. BAP. CENTVR. MAR. CAMPI. **Rev:** Shield of family arms superimposed on crowned imperial eagle, date at end of legend **Rev. Legend:** ET. SAC. ROM. IMP. PRIN. AN. **Note:** Fr. #152. Ref. V#113.

Date	Mintage	VG	F	VF	XF	Unc
1668 Rare	—	—	—	—	—	—

KM# 1 DOPPIA
6.5300 g., Gold **Ruler:** Carlo Centurioni Scotti **Obv:** Armored long-haired bust to right **Obv. Legend:** CAROLVS. CENTVR. MAR. CAMPI. **Rev:** Crowned family arms superimposed on imperial eagle, date at end of legend **Rev. Legend:** ET. SAC. ROM. IMP. PRINCEPS. **Note:** Fr. #151. Ref. V#111. Size varies: 29-30mm.

Date	Mintage	VG	F	VF	XF	Unc
1661	—	3,500	8,275	14,000	27,500	—
1662	—	3,500	8,275	14,000	27,500	—

KM# 6 DOPPIA
6.5300 g., Gold **Ruler:** Giovanni Battista Centurioni Scotti **Obv:** Accolated busts to right **Obv. Legend:** IO. BAPT. CENTVRIO. ET. IVL. M. MAR. CAM. **Rev:** Crowned family arms superimposed on crowned imperial eagle, date at end of legend. **Rev. Legend:** ET. SAC. ROM. IMP. PRINCEPES. **Note:** Fr. #153. Ref. V#114. Size varies, 31-32mm.

Date	Mintage	VG	F	VF	XF	Unc
1668 Rare	—	—	—	—	—	—

Note: Superior Pipito sale 12-87 VF realized $30,250

CASALE

Of very ancient origin, the city of Casale, 40 miles (67 kilometers) southwest of Milan, became the capital of Monferrat, a marquisate erected in 967 by Emperor Otto I (936-73). The first ruling dynasty of the Aleramidi died out in 1305 and Casale passed to the Paleologi, which in turn became extinct in the male line in 1533. The marchese was raised to the rank of Prince of the Empire in 1464. Emperor Carlo V (1516-56) assigned the succession of Casale to the Gonzaga Duke of Mantua (which see), who married the daughter of the last Paleologo marchese. Austrian and Spanish forces besieged the French defenders in the city from 1628 to 1630, resulting in several issues of obsidional coinage. When a later Gonzaga ruler was accused of a felony in 1703, Emperor Leopold I (1658-1705) transferred Casale to Savoy, an act which was finalized as a part of the Treaty of Utrecht in 1713.

RULER
Vincenzo I Gonzaga, 1587-1612
Francesco IV Gonzaga, 1612 (Feb-Dec)
Ferdinando Gonzaga, 1612-1626
Vincenzo II Gonzaga, 1627 (May-Dec)
Carlo I Gonzaga, 1627-1637
Carlo II Gonzaga, 1637-1665
Maria, regent 1637-1647
Ferdinando Carlo Gonzaga, 1669-1707

MINT OFFICIALS' INITIALS

Initial	Date	Name
GC	Ca. 1617-1622	Ciulio Campo, die-cutter

ARMS
2-fold, divided horizontally, upper half shaded (early type)

Reference:
V = Alberto Varesi, ***Monete Italiane Regionali: Piemonte, Sardegna, Liguria, Isola di Corsica***. Pavia, 1996.

DUCHY

STANDARD COINAGE

KM# 8 QUATTRINO
Billon **Obv:** Bust right **Rev:** St. Catherine **Note:** Weight varies: 0.40-0.60 grams.

Date	Mintage	VG	F	VF	XF	Unc
1602	—	20.00	35.00	65.00	150	—
1603	—	20.00	35.00	65.00	150	—
1604	—	20.00	35.00	65.00	150	—
1605	—	20.00	35.00	65.00	150	—
1606	—	20.00	35.00	65.00	150	—
1608	—	20.00	35.00	65.00	150	—
1609	—	20.00	35.00	65.00	150	—

KM# 9 QUATTRINO
Billon **Obv:** SIC in half moon **Rev:** Symbol **Note:** Weight varies: 0.40-0.60 grams.

Date	Mintage	VG	F	VF	XF	Unc
ND	—	20.00	35.00	65.00	150	—

KM# 10 QUATTRINO
Billon **Obv:** Eagle **Rev:** Sun with rays **Note:** Weight varies: 0.40-0.60 grams.

Date	Mintage	VG	F	VF	XF	Unc
ND	—	20.00	35.00	65.00	150	—

KM# 11 QUATTRINO
Billon **Obv:** F-D-M-M **Rev:** Jerusalem cross **Note:** Weight varies: 0.40-0.60 grams.

Date	Mintage	VG	F	VF	XF	Unc
ND	—	20.00	35.00	65.00	150	—

KM# 66 SOLDO
Billon **Obv:** Bust left **Rev:** Sun in rays **Note:** Weight varies: 1.58-2.86 grams.

Date	Mintage	VG	F	VF	XF	Unc
1661	—	15.00	25.00	50.00	100	—

KM# 33 2 SOLDI
0.6100 g., Billon **Ruler:** Ferdinand Gonzaga **Obv:** Monferrato arms, FER **Rev:** Radiant sun

Date	Mintage	VG	F	VF	XF	Unc
ND(1612-26)	—	20.00	35.00	75.00	165	—

KM# 32 1/2 BIANCO
0.7000 g., Billon **Ruler:** Ferdinand Gonzaga **Obv:** Radiant sun **Rev:** Jerusalem cross

Date	Mintage	VG	F	VF	XF	Unc
ND(1612-26)	—	30.00	60.00	120	200	—

KM# 15 GROSSO
Billon **Obv. Inscription:** FIDES on mountain - VIN **Rev:** Ornate cross **Note:** Weight varies: 0.89-1.20 grams.

Date	Mintage	VG	F	VF	XF	Unc
1604	—	15.00	25.00	45.00	85.00	—
1607	—	15.00	25.00	45.00	85.00	—
1608	—	15.00	25.00	45.00	85.00	—
1609	—	15.00	25.00	45.00	85.00	—
1610	—	15.00	25.00	45.00	85.00	—
1611	—	15.00	25.00	45.00	85.00	—
ND	—	15.00	25.00	45.00	85.00	—

KM# 17 GROSSO
Billon **Obv. Legend:** FRAN IIII **Note:** Weight varies: 0.89-1.20 grams.

Date	Mintage	VG	F	VF	XF	Unc
1612	—	20.00	40.00	95.00	250	—
1613	—	20.00	40.00	95.00	250	—

KM# 47 GROSSO
Billon **Obv:** Four-line legend in cartouche, CAR **Note:** Weight varies: 0.89-1.20 grams.

Date	Mintage	VG	F	VF	XF	Unc
ND	—	20.00	35.00	65.00	150	—

KM# 69 GROSSO
Billon **Obv. Inscription:** FIDES on mountain, FERD CAR **Note:** Weight varies: 1.66-3.24 grams.

Date	Mintage	VG	F	VF	XF	Unc
ND	—	18.00	32.00	60.00	135	—

KM# 61 QUARTO
Billon **Obv. Legend:** CAROLVS **Obv. Inscription:** FIDES on mountain **Rev:** Jerusalem cross **Note:** Weight varies: 0.95-1.37 grams.

Date	Mintage	VG	F	VF	XF	Unc
ND	—	30.00	60.00	125	375	—

KM# 70 QUARTO
Billon **Obv:** Crowned eagle **Obv. Legend:** FER CAR **Rev:** Sun **Note:** Weight varies: 0.95-1.37 grams.

Date	Mintage	VG	F	VF	XF	Unc
ND	—	25.00	50.00	100	200	—

KM# 85 MADONNINA
1.9500 g., Silver **Obv. Inscription:** Five lines **Rev:** Madonna and child

Date	Mintage	VG	F	VF	XF	Unc
ND	—	25.00	40.00	75.00	150	—

KM# 34 3 GROSSI
Billon **Obv. Inscription:** FIDES on mountain **Rev:** Crowned Paleologus arms **Note:** Weight varies: 2.15-2.70 grams.

Date	Mintage	VG	F	VF	XF	Unc
1621	—	25.00	40.00	85.00	175	—
1622	—	25.00	40.00	85.00	175	—
1626	—	25.00	40.00	85.00	175	—
ND	—	25.00	40.00	85.00	175	—

KM# 35 3 GROSSI
Billon **Obv:** Crowned eagle **Rev. Inscription:** CAS/ALE in circle **Note:** Weight varies: 2.15-2.70 grams.

Date	Mintage	VG	F	VF	XF	Unc
ND	—	40.00	90.00	185	325	—

KM# 30 6 GROSSI
Billon **Ruler:** Ferdinand Gonzaga **Obv:** Five-line legend on ornate cartouche **Rev:** Madonna and child, CASALE below **Rev. Legend:** DIVAE VIRGINIS CRETAE **Note:** Weight varies: 1.75-2.25 grams.

Date	Mintage	VG	F	VF	XF	Unc
ND(1612-26)	—	30.00	60.00	120	200	—

KM# 5 PARPAGLIOLA
Billon **Obv:** Eagle, VINC **Rev:** St. Francis **Note:** Weight varies: 1.58-2.86 grams.

Date	Mintage	VG	F	VF	XF	Unc
1601	—	15.00	25.00	50.00	100	—
1602	—	15.00	25.00	50.00	100	—
1605	—	15.00	25.00	50.00	100	—
1608	—	15.00	25.00	50.00	100	—
1609	—	15.00	25.00	50.00	100	—

KM# 20 PARPAGLIOLA
Billon **Obv:** Crowned eagle **Obv. Legend:** FRAN **Rev:** St. Francis **Note:** Weight varies: 1.58-2.86 grams.

Date	Mintage	VG	F	VF	XF	Unc
1612	—	20.00	35.00	65.00	150	—
1613	—	20.00	35.00	65.00	150	—

KM# 24 PARPAGLIOLA
Billon **Obv:** Crowned eagle **Obv. Legend:** FERD **Rev:** St. Francis **Note:** Weight varies: 1.58-2.86 grams.

Date	Mintage	VG	F	VF	XF	Unc
1613	—	15.00	25.00	50.00	100	—
1614	—	15.00	25.00	50.00	100	—
1615	—	15.00	25.00	50.00	100	—
1616	—	15.00	25.00	50.00	100	—
1617	—	15.00	25.00	50.00	100	—
1618	—	15.00	25.00	50.00	100	—
1619	—	15.00	25.00	50.00	100	—
1620	—	15.00	25.00	50.00	100	—
1623	—	15.00	25.00	50.00	100	—
1624	—	15.00	25.00	50.00	100	—

KM# 51 PARPAGLIOLA
Billon **Obv:** Crowned eagle **Obv. Legend:** CAR **Rev:** St. Evasius **Note:** Weight varies: 1.58-2.86 grams.

Date	Mintage	VG	F	VF	XF	Unc
1629	—	20.00	35.00	65.00	150	—
1632	—	20.00	35.00	65.00	150	—

KM# 65 PARPAGLIOLA
Billon **Obv:** Crowned eagle **Obv. Legend:** CAR II **Note:** Weight varies: 1.58-2.86 grams.

Date	Mintage	VG	F	VF	XF	Unc
1661	—	15.00	25.00	50.00	100	—

KM# 80 PARPAGLIOLA
Billon **Obv:** Crowned eagle **Obv. Legend:** FER CAR... **Rev:** St. Evasius **Note:** Weight varies: 1.58-2.86 grams.

Date	Mintage	VG	F	VF	XF	Unc
1684	—	15.00	25.00	50.00	100	—
1693	—	15.00	25.00	50.00	100	—

KM# 31 7 SOLDI
1.5000 g., Billon **Ruler:** Ferdinand Gonzaga **Obv:** Monferrato arms, FERD **Rev:** Radiant sun, NON, 7

Date	Mintage	VG	F	VF	XF	Unc
ND(1612-26)	—	15.00	25.00	50.00	100	—

KM# 19 1-1/2 REALES (18 Grossi)
Billon **Ruler:** Ferdinand Gonzaga **Obv. Legend:** FERD... **Rev:** Foliated cross **Note:** Weight varies: 0.89-1.20 grams.

Date	Mintage	VG	F	VF	XF	Unc
1612	—	18.00	30.00	55.00	125	—
1613	—	18.00	30.00	55.00	125	—
1615	—	18.00	30.00	55.00	125	—
1619	—	18.00	30.00	55.00	125	—
1620	—	18.00	30.00	55.00	125	—
1623	—	18.00	30.00	55.00	125	—

KM# 29 1-1/2 REALES (18 Grossi)
Billon **Ruler:** Ferdinand Gonzaga **Obv. Inscription:** Four-lines in cartouche, FER **Rev:** Jerusalem cross **Note:** Weight varies: 0.89-1.20 grams.

Date	Mintage	VG	F	VF	XF	Unc
ND(1612-26)	—	18.00	30.00	55.00	125	—

KM# 36 1-1/2 REALES (18 Grossi)
3.7000 g., Silver **Note:** Similar to 4 Reales, KM# 41.

Date	Mintage	VG	F	VF	XF	Unc
1621	—	65.00	120	200	375	—
1622	—	65.00	120	200	375	—

KM# 67 2 REALES
Billon **Obv:** Similar to 4 Reales, KM# 41. **Rev:** Madonna and child **Note:** Weight varies: 3.25-4.11 grams.

Date	Mintage	VG	F	VF	XF	Unc
1662	—	75.00	150	265	450	—

KM# 41 4 REALES
Billon **Obv. Inscription:** FERDIN... **Note:** Weight varies: 6.67-7.42 grams.

Date	Mintage	VG	F	VF	XF	Unc
1623	—	100	200	300	550	—
1626	—	100	200	300	550	—

KM# 68 4 REALES
Billon **Obv. Inscription:** CARO II... **Note:** Weight varies: 6.67-7.42 grams.

Date	Mintage	VG	F	VF	XF	Unc
1662	—	100	200	350	575	—

KM# 43 1/8 TALLERO
3.5000 g., Silver **Obv:** Bust right **Obv. Legend:** VICENTIVS **Rev:** Crowned eagle with arms

Date	Mintage	VG	F	VF	XF	Unc
ND(1587-1612)	—	—	—	—	—	—

KM# 44 1/2 TALLERO
10.3000 g., Silver **Obv:** Bust right **Obv. Legend:** VINCENTIVS **Rev:** Crowned eagle with Austriaco arms

Date	Mintage	VG	F	VF	XF	Unc
ND(1587-1612)	—	—	—	—	—	—

KM# 45 1/2 TALLERO
10.7300 g., Silver **Obv:** Crowned arms **Rev:** Short cross with cross in angles

Date	Mintage	VG	F	VF	XF	Unc
ND(1612-26)	—	—	—	—	—	—

KM# 18 TALLERO
Silver **Obv:** Bust of Vincenzo right **Rev:** Crowned eagle with arms on breast **Note:** Dav. #3867. Weight varies: 27.00-29.00 grams.

Date	Mintage	VG	F	VF	XF	Unc
ND(1587-1612)	—	400	800	1,500	2,500	—

KM# 71 TALLERO
Silver **Obv:** Crowned arms **Obv. Legend:** FERDINANDVS • D • G •... **Rev:** Short cross with crosses in angles **Note:** Dav. #3870. Weight varies: 27.00-29.00 grams.

Date	Mintage	VG	F	VF	XF	Unc
ND(1612-26)	—	750	1,250	2,200	4,250	—

KM# 72 1/4 DUCATONE
6.4000 g., Silver **Obv:** Five lines in cartouche **Obv. Legend:** FERDIN

Date	Mintage	VG	F	VF	XF	Unc
ND(1612-26)	—	1,150	2,250	4,500	8,300	—

KM# 37 1/4 DUCATONE
7.7700 g., Silver **Obv:** Bust right **Obv. Legend:** FERD **Rev:** St. George and dragon

Date	Mintage	VG	F	VF	XF	Unc
1621	—	650	1,250	2,500	5,000	—

KM# 38 1/2 DUCATONE
15.4000 g., Silver **Obv:** Bust right **Obv. Legend:** FERD **Rev:** St. George and dragon

Date	Mintage	VG	F	VF	XF	Unc
1621	—	650	1,250	2,500	5,000	—

KM# 6 DUCATONE
31.5000 g., Silver **Obv:** Bust of Vincenzo I right **Rev:** St. George and dragon, date in legend **Note:** Dav. #3862.

Date	Mintage	VG	F	VF	XF	Unc
1601	—	300	700	1,250	2,250	—

KM# 12 DUCATONE
31.5000 g., Silver **Obv:** Bust of Vincenzo I right **Rev:** St. George and dragon, date below horse **Note:** Dav. #3863.

Date	Mintage	VG	F	VF	XF	Unc
1603	—	300	700	1,250	2,250	—

KM# 13 DUCATONE
31.5000 g., Silver **Obv:** Bust of Vincenzo I left, date below **Rev:** St. George and dragon **Note:** Dav. #3864.

Date	Mintage	VG	F	VF	XF	Unc
1603	—	500	900	1,850	3,000	—

KM# 14 DUCATONE
31.5000 g., Silver **Obv:** Bust of Vincenzo I left, without date **Rev:** St. George and dragon, date below horse **Note:** Dav. #3865.

Date	Mintage	VG	F	VF	XF	Unc
1603	—	400	800	1,650	2,750	—

KM# 16 DUCATONE
31.5000 g., Silver **Obv:** Bust of Vincenzo I left, date below **Rev:** St. George on smaller horse, date above dragon **Note:** Dav. #3866.

Date	Mintage	VG	F	VF	XF	Unc
1604	—	400	800	1,650	2,750	—
1606	—	400	800	1,650	2,750	—

KM# 25 DUCATONE
31.5000 g., Silver **Obv:** Bust of Ferdinand right **Rev:** St. George and dragon **Note:** Dav. #3868.

Date	Mintage	VG	F	VF	XF	Unc
1617	—	350	750	1,500	2,500	—
1622	—	350	750	1,500	2,500	—

KM# 26 DUCATONE
31.5000 g., Silver **Obv:** Bust left **Note:** Dav. #3869.

Date	Mintage	VG	F	VF	XF	Unc
1617	—	850	1,650	2,750	4,500	—

KM# 50 DUCATONE OSSIDIONALI
Silver **Obv:** Four-line inscription in cartouche, R XII above **Rev:** Crowned complex arms in chain **Note:** Dav. #3871. Weight varies: 23.00-24.00 grams.

Date	Mintage	VG	F	VF	XF	Unc
1628	—	2,500	5,000	8,800	14,000	—

KM# 52 1/4 SCUDO
7.2600 g., Billon **Obv:** Bust right, CAROLVS **Rev:** Arms in collar

Date	Mintage	VG	F	VF	XF	Unc
1629	—	—	—	—	—	—
1630	—	—	—	—	—	—

KM# 21 DOPPIA
7.0000 g., 0.9860 Gold 0.2219 oz. AGW **Obv:** Facing busts of Francesco and Margaret, date below **Rev:** Large, complex flower in inner circle

Date	Mintage	VG	F	VF	XF	Unc
1612	—	6,300	8,800	15,000	27,500	—

KM# 22 DOPPIA
7.0000 g., 0.9860 Gold 0.2219 oz. AGW **Obv:** Cross in inner circle **Rev:** Arms on mountain

Date	Mintage	VG	F	VF	XF	Unc
1612	—	3,150	5,600	10,500	20,000	—

KM# 27 DOPPIA
7.0000 g., 0.9860 Gold 0.2219 oz. AGW **Obv:** Ferdinand

Date	Mintage	VG	F	VF	XF	Unc
1617	—	1,250	2,500	5,000	7,500	—
ND	—	1,250	2,500	4,400	6,900	—

KM# 46 DOPPIA
7.0000 g., 0.9860 Gold 0.2219 oz. AGW **Obv:** Bust of Vincenzo left in inner circle

Date	Mintage	VG	F	VF	XF	Unc
ND	—	1,900	3,750	7,500	12,000	—

KM# 60 DOPPIA
7.0000 g., 0.9860 Gold 0.2219 oz. AGW **Obv:** Bust of Carlo left in inner circle

Date	Mintage	VG	F	VF	XF	Unc
1632	—	1,250	2,500	5,600	11,500	—

KM# 62 DOPPIA
7.0000 g., 0.9860 Gold 0.2219 oz. AGW **Obv:** Facing busts of Carlo II and Maria

Date	Mintage	VG	F	VF	XF	Unc
ND	—	1,550	3,150	8,100	15,000	—

KM# 7 2 DOPPIE
0.9860 Gold **Obv:** Bust of Vincenzo right **Rev:** Crowned complex arms **Note:** Weight varies: 11.71-13.10 grams.

Date	Mintage	VG	F	VF	XF	Unc
1601	—	1,900	3,750	7,500	15,000	—

KM# 28 2 DOPPIE
14.0000 g., 0.9860 Gold 0.4438 oz. AGW **Obv:** Ferdinand left **Rev:** Crowned arms in order collar in inner circle

Date	Mintage	VG	F	VF	XF	Unc
1617	—	1,000	2,000	5,600	10,000	—

KM# 39 2 DOPPIE
14.0000 g., 0.9860 Gold 0.4438 oz. AGW **Obv:** Ferdinand right **Rev:** Without collar

Date	Mintage	VG	F	VF	XF	Unc
1621	—	1,000	2,000	5,600	10,000	—

KM# 40 2 DOPPIE
14.0000 g., 0.9860 Gold 0.4438 oz. AGW **Obv:** Ferdinand right

Date	Mintage	VG	F	VF	XF	Unc
ND Rare	—	—	—	—	—	—

KM# 48 2 DOPPIE
14.0000 g., 0.9860 Gold 0.4438 oz. AGW **Obv:** Bust of Vincenzo left in inner circle

Date	Mintage	VG	F	VF	XF	Unc
1627	—	2,500	5,000	10,000	16,500	—

KM# 53 2 DOPPIE
14.0000 g., 0.9860 Gold 0.4438 oz. AGW **Obv:** Bust of Carlo left in inner circle

Date	Mintage	VG	F	VF	XF	Unc
1629	—	2,500	5,000	10,000	16,500	—

Date	Mintage	VG	F	VF	XF	Unc
1631	—	2,500	5,000	10,000	16,500	—
1636	—	2,500	5,000	10,000	16,500	—

KM# 63 2 DOPPIE

14.0000 g., 0.9860 Gold 0.4438 oz. AGW **Obv:** Facing busts of Carlo II and Maria

Date	Mintage	VG	F	VF	XF	Unc
ND Rare	—	—	—	—	—	—

KM# 73 2 DOPPIE

14.0000 g., 0.9860 Gold 0.4438 oz. AGW **Obv:** Bust of Ferdinand Carlo left in inner circle

Date	Mintage	VG	F	VF	XF	Unc
ND Rare	—	—	—	—	—	—

KM# 74 5 DOPPIE

35.0000 g., 0.9860 Gold 1.1095 oz. AGW **Obv:** Bust of Ferdinand right in inner circle **Rev:** Reclining stag to left holding shield of arms

Date	Mintage	VG	F	VF	XF	Unc
ND Rare	—	—	—	—	—	—

NECESSITY COINAGE

KM# 55 FIORINO

2.0500 g., Bronze **Obv:** Similar to 5 Fiorino, KM#56 **Rev:** Two palms within border

Date	Mintage	VG	F	VF	XF	Unc
1630	—	600	1,200	2,400	4,000	—

KM# 56 5 FIORINO

5.0000 g., Bronze **Rev:** Trophy and siren

Date	Mintage	VG	F	VF	XF	Unc
1630	—	1,000	2,000	3,500	6,000	—

KM# 57 10 FIORINO

Bronze **Note:** Weight varies: 10.00-11.00 grams.

Date	Mintage	VG	F	VF	XF	Unc
1630	—	850	1,750	3,000	5,000	—

KM# 58 20 FIORINO

Bronze **Rev:** Justice and Strength **Note:** Weight varies: 19.00-21.00 grams.

Date	Mintage	VG	F	VF	XF	Unc
1630	—	1,000	2,000	3,250	5,500	—

CASTIGLIONE DEI GATTI

RULERS

Ercole and Cornelius Pepoli, ca. 1700
Alessandro and Sicinio Pepoli, 1703-1713

Arms

Checkerboard

Reference

V = Alberto Varesi, ***Monete Italiane Regionali: Emilia***. Pavia, 1998.

COUNTSHIP

TRADE COINAGE

FR# 207 DUCAT

3.5000 g., 0.9860 Gold 0.1109 oz. AGW **Ruler:** Hercules and Cornelius Pepoli **Obv:** 5-line inscription on ornamental tablet **Obv. Legend:** HERCULES ET... **Rev:** Eagle with crowned arms on breast

Date	Mintage	VG	F	VF	XF	Unc
ND	—	2,500	4,500	8,500	14,000	—

CASTIGLIONE DELLE STIVIERE

Castiglione, a principality in Mantua, came into possession of the Gonzaga family in 1404 and was given to one of the Cadel lines. It passed into Spanish and finally into imperial possession in 1772.

RULERS

Francesco Gonzaga, 1593-1616
Ferdinand Gonzaga, 1616-1678
Carlo, 1678-1680
Ferdinand II, 1680-1723

PRINCIPALITY

STANDARD COINAGE

KM# 5 SESINO

Billon **Obv:** Arms in cartouche **Rev:** SESIN/ VS/ CASTI **Note:** Weight varies: 0.55-1.05 grams.

Date	Mintage	VG	F	VF	XF	Unc
ND	—	18.00	35.00	70.00	125	—

KM# 6 SESINO

Billon **Obv:** Crowned eagle **Rev:** St. Aloysius **Note:** Weight varies: 0.55-1.05 grams.

Date	Mintage	VG	F	VF	XF	Unc
ND	—	18.00	35.00	70.00	125	—

KM# 92 SESINO

Billon **Obv:** Bust left **Rev:** Sun with rays **Note:** Weight varies: 0.55-1.05 grams.

Date	Mintage	VG	F	VF	XF	Unc
1683	—	25.00	43.75	80.00	150	—

KM# 93 SESINO

Billon **Obv:** Bust right, FER **Rev:** SESIN/ VS/ CASTI **Note:** Weight varies: 0.55-1.05 grams.

Date	Mintage	VG	F	VF	XF	Unc
ND	—	18.00	35.00	70.00	125	—

KM# 95 SESINO

Billon **Obv:** FER/ II/ SR **Rev:** PRI/ CAS/ ETC **Note:** Weight varies: 0.55-1.05 grams.

Date	Mintage	VG	F	VF	XF	Unc
ND	—	25.00	43.75	80.00	150	—

KM# 96 SESINO

Billon **Obv:** Bust right, FER **Rev:** MEDV/ MAR/ ETC **Note:** Weight varies: 0.55-1.05 grams.

Date	Mintage	VG	F	VF	XF	Unc
ND	—	25.00	43.75	80.00	150	—

KM# 97 SESINO

Billon **Rev. Legend:** MAR/ ME.DV/ ETC. **Note:** Weight varies: 0.55-1.05 grams.

Date	Mintage	VG	F	VF	XF	Unc
ND	—	25.00	43.75	80.00	150	—

KM# 98 SESINO

Billon **Obv:** Medici arms **Obv. Legend:** FERD... **Rev:** John the Baptist **Note:** Weight varies: 0.55-1.05 grams.

Date	Mintage	VG	F	VF	XF	Unc
ND	—	25.00	43.75	80.00	150	—

KM# 94 SESINO

Billon **Rev:** PRI/CAST/ETC. **Note:** Weight varies: 0.55-1.05 grams.

Date	Mintage	VG	F	VF	XF	Unc
1688	—	25.00	43.75	80.00	150	—

KM# 7 QUATTRINO

Billon **Obv:** Head left **Obv. Legend:** FERDIN... **Rev:** St. Peter standing **Note:** Weight varies: 0.50-0.65 grams.

Date	Mintage	VG	F	VF	XF	Unc
ND	—	25.00	43.75	80.00	155	—

KM# 8 QUATTRINO

Billon **Obv:** Crowned eagle **Rev:** St. Nazarius standing with palms **Note:** Weight varies: 0.50-0.65 grams.

Date	Mintage	VG	F	VF	XF	Unc
ND	—	13.00	25.00	50.00	100	—

KM# 9 QUATTRINO

Billon **Obv:** Eagle in shield **Rev:** St. Sirius standing **Note:** Weight varies: 0.50-0.65 grams.

Date	Mintage	VG	F	VF	XF	Unc
ND	—	50.00	100	220	450	—

KM# 10 QUATTRINO

Billon **Obv:** Large F in legend **Obv. Legend:** FERD... **Rev:** Flame **Note:** Weight varies: 0.50-0.65 grams.

Date	Mintage	VG	F	VF	XF	Unc
ND	—	13.00	25.00	50.00	100	—

KM# 11 QUATTRINO

Billon **Obv:** Crowned arms in cartouche **Rev:** St. John standing **Note:** Weight varies: 0.50-0.65 grams.

Date	Mintage	VG	F	VF	XF	Unc
ND	—	13.00	25.00	50.00	100	—

KM# 12 QUATTRINO

Billon **Obv:** Medici arms, 68 **Rev:** John the Baptist **Note:** Weight varies: 0.50-0.65 grams.

Date	Mintage	VG	F	VF	XF	Unc
ND	—	13.00	25.00	50.00	100	—

KM# 13 QUATTRINO

Billon **Obv:** Large L, 65 **Obv. Legend:** FER... **Rev:** St. Vultus **Note:** Weight varies: 0.50-0.65 grams.

Date	Mintage	VG	F	VF	XF	Unc
ND	—	13.00	25.00	50.00	100	—

KM# 14 QUATTRINO

Billon **Obv:** Eagle **Rev:** St. Peter **Note:** Weight varies: 0.50-0.65 grams.

Date	Mintage	VG	F	VF	XF	Unc
ND	—	25.00	43.75	80.00	155	—

KM# 15 QUATTRINO

Billon **Obv:** Rampant lion **Rev:** St. Paternianus **Note:** Weight varies: 0.50-0.65 grams.

Date	Mintage	VG	F	VF	XF	Unc
ND	—	31.25	65.00	125	250	—

KM# 16 QUATTRINO

Billon **Obv:** Papal arms **Rev:** Figure and cross **Note:** Weight varies: 0.50-0.65 grams.

Date	Mintage	VG	F	VF	XF	Unc
ND	—	13.00	25.00	50.00	100	—

KM# 17 QUATTRINO

Billon **Obv:** Eagle **Rev. Legend:** MEDVLARIVM **Note:** Weight varies: 0.50-0.65 grams.

Date	Mintage	VG	F	VF	XF	Unc
ND	—	25.00	43.75	80.00	155	—

KM# 18 QUATTRINO

Billon **Obv:** Bust right **Obv. Legend:** FER... **Rev:** MARCHIO MEDOLANI **Note:** Weight varies: 0.50-0.65 grams.

Date	Mintage	VG	F	VF	XF	Unc
ND	—	15.00	31.25	65.00	125	—

KM# 19 QUATTRINO

Billon **Rev:** MARCHIO **Note:** Weight varies: 0.50-0.65 grams.

Date	Mintage	VG	F	VF	XF	Unc
ND	—	13.00	25.00	50.00	100	—

KM# 20 QUATTRINO

Billon **Obv:** Crowned cross **Rev:** Quartered arms **Note:** Weight varies: 0.50-0.65 grams.

Date	Mintage	VG	F	VF	XF	Unc
ND	—	25.00	43.75	80.00	155	—

KM# 21 PARPAGLIOLA

Billon **Obv:** Arms of Savoy **Rev:** Cross of St. Lazaras **Note:** Weight varies: 0.60-1.18 grams.

Date	Mintage	VG	F	VF	XF	Unc
ND	—	31.25	50.00	95.00	190	—

KM# 22 PARPAGLIOLA

Billon **Obv:** Arms of Gonzaga **Rev:** Pisside **Note:** Weight varies: 0.60-1.18 grams.

Date	Mintage	VG	F	VF	XF	Unc
ND	—	43.75	95.00	190	375	—

KM# 23 PARPAGLIOLA

Billon **Obv:** Arms and four eagles **Rev:** Ornate cross **Note:** Weight varies: 0.60-1.18 grams.

Date	Mintage	VG	F	VF	XF	Unc
ND	—	37.50	75.00	155	325	—

KM# 24 PARPAGLIOLA

Billon **Obv:** Crowned eagle **Rev:** Madonna and child **Note:** Weight varies: 0.60-1.18 grams.

Date	Mintage	VG	F	VF	XF	Unc
ND	—	20.00	30.00	60.00	100	—

KM# 25 PARPAGLIOLA

Billon **Obv:** Crowned arms **Rev:** PRVDE-NTIA **Note:** Weight varies: 0.60-1.18 grams.

Date	Mintage	VG	F	VF	XF	Unc
ND	—	25.00	37.50	75.00	125	—

KM# 26 PARPAGLIOLA

Billon **Rev:** FORTITVDO **Note:** Weight varies: 0.60-1.18 grams.

Date	Mintage	VG	F	VF	XF	Unc
ND	—	25.00	37.50	75.00	125	—

KM# 27 PARPAGLIOLA

Billon **Rev:** St. Nazarius **Note:** Weight varies: 0.60-1.18 grams.

Date	Mintage	VG	F	VF	XF	Unc
ND	—	19.00	31.25	65.00	115	—

KM# 28 MURAIOLA

Billon **Obv:** Bust of Pope right **Rev:** St. Antonius **Note:** Weight varies: 0.82-2.10 grams.

Date	Mintage	VG	F	VF	XF	Unc
ND	—	31.25	43.75	90.00	150	—

KM# 29 MURAIOLA

Billon **Rev:** St. Martin **Note:** Weight varies: 0.82-2.10 grams.

Date	Mintage	VG	F	VF	XF	Unc
ND	—	31.25	43.75	90.00	150	—

KM# 30 MURAIOLA

Billon **Obv:** Bust right, FER **Rev:** Pesside, QVOS **Note:** Weight varies: 0.82-2.10 grams.

Date	Mintage	VG	F	VF	XF	Unc
ND	—	31.25	43.75	90.00	150	—

KM# 31 MURAIOLA

Billon **Rev:** Pesside, TVRRIS **Note:** Weight varies: 0.82-2.10 grams.

Date	Mintage	VG	F	VF	XF	Unc
ND	—	31.25	43.75	90.00	150	—

KM# 32 MURAIOLA

Billon **Obv:** Crowned cross in shield **Rev:** Crown with CC's **Note:** Weight varies: 0.82-2.10 grams.

Date	Mintage	VG	F	VF	XF	Unc
ND	—	31.25	43.75	90.00	150	—

KM# 33 MURAIOLA

Billon **Rev:** Tower **Note:** Weight varies: 0.82-2.10 grams.

Date	Mintage	VG	F	VF	XF	Unc
ND	—	31.25	43.75	90.00	150	—

KM# 34 MURAIOLA
Billon **Obv:** Cross in shield, three *'s **Rev:** Madonna and child **Note:** Weight varies: 0.82-2.10 grams.

Date	Mintage	VG	F	VF	XF	Unc
ND	—	31.25	43.75	90.00	150	—

KM# 35 MURAIOLA
Billon **Obv:** Arms of Farnese **Rev:** St. Ignatius **Note:** Weight varies: 0.82-2.10 grams.

Date	Mintage	VG	F	VF	XF	Unc
ND	—	31.25	43.75	90.00	150	—

KM# 36 GIORGINO
Billon **Obv:** Bust right **Obv. Legend:** FER... **Rev:** Kneeling saint **Rev. Legend:** PROTECTO **Note:** Weight varies: 1.90-2.05 grams.

Date	Mintage	VG	F	VF	XF	Unc
ND	—	31.25	70.00	125	230	—

KM# 37 GIORGINO
Billon **Rev:** Kneeling saint **Rev. Legend:** S. NICOL **Note:** Weight varies: 1.90-2.05 grams.

Date	Mintage	VG	F	VF	XF	Unc
ND	—	37.50	75.00	155	280	—

KM# 38 GIORGINO
Billon **Rev:** Kneeling saint **Rev. Legend:** S. MARTINVS **Note:** Weight varies: 1.90-2.05 grams.

Date	Mintage	VG	F	VF	XF	Unc
ND	—	65.00	125	220	375	—

KM# 85 FRAZIONE DI LIRA
Billon **Obv:** Arms with two crowns, CAROLVS **Rev:** St. Nicolaus **Note:** Weight varies: 1.40-2.32 grams.

Date	Mintage	VG	F	VF	XF	Unc
1678	—	70.00	135	235	400	—

KM# 86 FRAZIONE DI LIRA
Billon **Obv:** Crowned CG monogram **Obv. Legend:** PRINC... **Rev:** St. Aloysius **Note:** Weight varies: 1.40-2.32 grams.

Date	Mintage	VG	F	VF	XF	Unc
ND	—	31.25	50.00	95.00	155	—

KM# 39 CAVALOTTO
2.5000 g., Billon **Obv:** Quartered arms **Rev:** Horse right

Date	Mintage	VG	F	VF	XF	Unc
ND	—	110	235	475	875	—

KM# 40 CAVALOTTO
2.5000 g., Billon **Obv:** Crowned arms **Rev:** Pisside

Date	Mintage	VG	F	VF	XF	Unc
ND	—	55.00	110	215	450	—

KM# 41 1/2 SOLDO
Copper **Obv:** Crowned FG monogram **Rev:** Rampant dog **Note:** Weight varies: 0.78-0.87 grams.

Date	Mintage	VG	F	VF	XF	Unc
ND	—	35.00	60.00	110	185	—

KM# 42 SOLDO
Copper **Obv:** Crowned FG monogram **Rev:** Rampant dog **Note:** Weight varies: 1.15-1.65 grams.

Date	Mintage	VG	F	VF	XF	Unc
ND	—	30.00	60.00	115	190	—

KM# 43 SOLDO
Copper **Obv:** Crowned snake **Rev:** St. Peter standing **Note:** Weight varies: 1.15-1.65 grams.

Date	Mintage	VG	F	VF	XF	Unc
ND	—	30.00	55.00	100	150	—

KM# 44 SOLDO
Copper **Obv:** Crowned eagle **Rev:** Kneeling saint **Note:** Weight varies: 1.15-1.65 grams.

Date	Mintage	VG	F	VF	XF	Unc
ND	—	45.00	90.00	180	300	—

KM# 87 SOLDO
Copper **Obv:** Crowned CG monogram **Obv. Legend:** PRINC... **Rev:** Dog **Note:** Weight varies: 1.15-1.65 grams.

Date	Mintage	VG	F	VF	XF	Unc
ND	—	30.00	60.00	115	190	—

KM# 88 SOLDO
Copper **Obv:** Arms **Obv. Legend:** CAR **Rev:** St. Hilarius **Note:** Weight varies: 1.15-1.65 grams.

Date	Mintage	VG	F	VF	XF	Unc
ND	—	45.00	90.00	180	300	—

KM# 75 3 SOLDI
2.1000 g., Billon **Obv:** Crowned eagle **Rev:** Three shields, 3 below

Date	Mintage	VG	F	VF	XF	Unc
ND	—	90.00	170	300	500	—

KM# 76 4 SOLDI
Billon **Obv:** Bust left **Obv. Legend:** FERD... **Rev:** Crowned quartered arms **Note:** Weight varies: 1.60-2.25 grams.

Date	Mintage	VG	F	VF	XF	Unc
1666	—	55.00	100	190	300	—

KM# 77 4 SOLDI
Billon **Obv:** Crowned quartered arms **Rev:** Woman standing **Note:** Weight varies: 1.60-2.25 grams.

Date	Mintage	VG	F	VF	XF	Unc
ND	—	40.00	65.00	120	275	—

KM# 78 5 SOLDI
Billon **Obv:** Crowned arms **Obv. Legend:** FER... **Rev:** Half figure of the Virgin **Note:** Weight varies: 1.65-2.05 grams.

Date	Mintage	VG	F	VF	XF	Unc
ND	—	40.25	65.00	100	190	—

KM# 79 8 SOLDI
Billon **Obv:** Head left **Rev:** Crowned eagle and serpent **Note:** Weight varies: 1.47-2.75 grams.

Date	Mintage	VG	F	VF	XF	Unc
1666	—	115	200	350	—	—

KM# 80 8 SOLDI
Billon **Note:** Weight varies: 1.47-2.75 grams.

Date	Mintage	VG	F	VF	XF	Unc
ND	—	46.00	75.00	115	215	—

KM# 90 25 SOLDI
Silver **Rev:** Gonzaga and Pico arms **Note:** Weight varies: 4.50-5.15 grams.

Date	Mintage	VG	F	VF	XF	Unc
1682	—	—	—	—	—	—
1685	—	80.00	19.00	325	575	—

KM# 91 25 SOLDI
Silver **Obv:** Bust right **Rev:** Crowned imperial eagle, arms in center **Note:** Weight varies: 4.50-5.15 grams.

Date	Mintage	VG	F	VF	XF	Unc
ND	—	43.75	95.00	190	350	—

KM# 45 BIANCO
Billon **Obv:** Crowned Gonzaga arms **Rev:** Cross with four flowerettes **Note:** Weight varies: 2.68-3.09 grams.

Date	Mintage	VG	F	VF	XF	Unc
ND	—	265	350	525	—	—

KM# 46 LIRA
Silver **Obv:** Bust right, FRANC **Rev:** Crowned quartered arms **Note:** Weight varies: 4.79-4.90 grams.

Date	Mintage	VG	F	VF	XF	Unc
1614	—	190	350	575	—	—

KM# 47 LIRA
Silver **Obv:** Crowned eagle **Rev:** Steer head, CASTIONE **Note:** Weight varies: 4.79-4.90 grams.

Date	Mintage	VG	F	VF	XF	Unc
ND	—	60.00	120	275	—	—

KM# 48 LIRA
Silver **Rev:** Steer head, MARCHIO **Note:** Weight varies: 4.79-4.90 grams.

Date	Mintage	VG	F	VF	XF	Unc
ND	—	90.00	180	425	—	—

KM# 60 LIRA
Silver **Obv:** Crowned arms **Obv. Legend:** FERDINANDVS... **Rev:** St. Aloysius **Note:** Weight varies: 4.79-4.90 grams.

Date	Mintage	VG	F	VF	XF	Unc
ND	—	60.00	120	225	425	—

KM# 49 LIRA
Silver **Obv:** Rampant lion, FRAN... **Rev:** Steer head **Note:** Weight varies: 4.79-4.90 grams.

Date	Mintage	VG	F	VF	XF	Unc
ND	—	90.00	180	425	—	—

KM# A49 PIASTRE
Silver **Obv:** Bust of Francesco right **Rev:** Crowned eagle **Note:** Dav. #3872.

Date	Mintage	VG	F	VF	XF	Unc
ND	—	1,950	3,300	5,500	8,300	—

KM# 61 1/4 SCUDO
7.3400 g., Silver **Obv:** Bust right **Obv. Legend:** FERDINANDVS... **Rev:** Three shields crowned in triangle

Date	Mintage	VG	F	VF	XF	Unc
ND	—	1,400	2,500	4,400	6,600	—

KM# 62 1/2 SCUDO
Silver **Obv:** Bust right **Rev:** Three shields crowned in triangle **Note:** Weight varies: 15.51-16.31 grams.

Date	Mintage	VG	F	VF	XF	Unc
ND	—	1,100	2,200	3,850	6,100	—

KM# 63 2/3 SCUDO
Silver **Obv:** Bust right, 2/3 below **Obv. Legend:** FERD... **Rev:** Crowned eagle **Note:** Weight varies: 16.97-17.27 grams.

Date	Mintage	VG	F	VF	XF	Unc
ND	—	1,500	2,750	4,700	7,200	—

KM# 99 2/3 SCUDO
Silver **Obv:** Bust right **Obv. Legend:** FERD... **Rev:** Crowned double eagle **Note:** Weight varies: 16.97-17.27 grams.

Date	Mintage	VG	F	VF	XF	Unc
1689 Rare	—	—	—	—	—	—

KM# 50 SCUDO
26.2500 g., Silver **Obv:** Armored bust right, FRANCISCVS... **Rev:** Crowned multiple arms **Note:** Dav. #3874.

Date	Mintage	VG	F	VF	XF	Unc
ND Rare	—	—	—	—	—	—

KM# 51 TALLERO
31.6700 g., Silver **Obv:** Armored bust right, FRANCISCVS **Rev:** Helmeted figure standing **Note:** Dav. #3873.

Date	Mintage	VG	F	VF	XF	Unc
ND Rare	—	—	—	—	—	—

KM# 52 1/8 DOPPIA
0.8750 g., 0.9860 Gold 0.0277 oz. AGW **Obv:** Rampant lion in inner circle **Rev:** Crowned bullhead in inner circle

Date	Mintage	VG	F	VF	XF	Unc
ND	—	725	1,700	2,750	3,900	—

KM# 53 1/2 DOPPIA
3.5000 g., 0.9860 Gold 0.1109 oz. AGW **Obv:** Bust of Francesco right **Rev:** Crowned arms in order collar

Date	Mintage	VG	F	VF	XF	Unc
ND	—	1,000	2,250	5,600	10,500	—

KM# 54 5 DOPPIE
35.0000 g., 0.9860 Gold 1.1095 oz. AGW **Obv:** Bust of Francesco right in inner circle, date below **Rev:** Crowned arms in inner circle

Date	Mintage	VG	F	VF	XF	Unc
1614 Rare	—	—	—	—	—	—

KM# 65 FLORIN
3.5000 g., 0.9860 Gold 0.1109 oz. AGW **Obv:** Eagle in inner circle **Rev:** Soldier standing in inner circle

Date	Mintage	VG	F	VF	XF	Unc
1639 Rare	—	—	—	—	—	—

KM# 69 FLORIN
3.5000 g., 0.9860 Gold 0.1109 oz. AGW **Obv:** Rampant lion in inner circle

Date	Mintage	VG	F	VF	XF	Unc
ND Rare	—	—	—	—	—	—

KM# 70 FLORIN
3.5000 g., 0.9860 Gold 0.1109 oz. AGW **Obv:** Knight standing **Rev:** Five-line legend in cartouche

Date	Mintage	VG	F	VF	XF	Unc
1655	—	1,250	2,500	4,400	8,800	—

KM# 66 FLORIN
3.5000 g., 0.9860 Gold 0.1109 oz. AGW **Obv:** St. Nazarius standing in inner circle **Rev:** Value in inner circle

Date	Mintage	VG	F	VF	XF	Unc
ND Rare	—	—	—	—	—	—

KM# 67 FLORIN
3.5000 g., 0.9860 Gold 0.1109 oz. AGW **Obv:** St. Francis standing in inner circle

Date	Mintage	VG	F	VF	XF	Unc
ND Rare	—	—	—	—	—	—

KM# 68 FLORIN
3.5000 g., 0.9860 Gold 0.1109 oz. AGW **Obv:** Madonna and child facing in inner circle

Date	Mintage	VG	F	VF	XF	Unc
ND Rare	—	—	—	—	—	—

CISTERNA

An ancient feudatory centered on Alessandria, to the southwest of Milan. Emperor Henry III (1039-56) assigned Cisterna to Vescovo d'Asti in 1041. In the 15th century, it passed from the Garretti family to Domenico and Antonio Paletta, who ceded their rights in Cisterna to Antonio della Rovere, the nephew of Pope Sixtus IV (1471-84). Finally, Cisterna was sold in 1665 to Giacomo Dal Pozzo, the Marchese di Voghera (near Pavia). The place already having received the mint right in 1660, Cisterna was erected into a principality by imperial decree in 1670.

RULER

Giacomo Dal Pozzo, 1665-1696

Reference

V = Alberto Varesi, ***Monete Italiane Regionali: Piemonte, Sardegna, Liguria, Isola di Corsica***. Pavia, 1996.

PRINCIPALITY

STANDARD COINAGE

KM# 1 SOLDINO

1.7200 g., Copper, 17 mm. **Obv:** Bust right, date below **Obv. Legend:** I. AP... E. EG. **Rev:** Ornate cross with lily ends **Rev. Legend:** CIST. ET. BELG. PRINC. **Note:** Ref. V#408.

Date	Mintage	F	VF	XF	Unc	BU
1675	—	900	1,650	2,500	3,750	—

KM# 2 1/2 SCUDO (Mezzo Scudo)

13.0000 g., Silver **Obv:** Draped bust right **Obv. Legend:** I. A. PVT. CIST. ET. BELG. PRIN. **Rev:** Crowned 4-fold arms with central shield, date at end of legend **Rev. Legend:** qVI. BIBET. SITIET. ITERVM. **Note:** Ref. V#407. Size varies: 31-33 mm

Date	Mintage	VG	F	VF	XF	Unc
1677	—	2,050	3,400	4,550	6,500	8,800

KM# 3 SCUDO

Silver **Obv:** Bust right, date at top in legend **Obv. Legend:** IA. A. PVT. PRIN. 1677 CIS. ET. B. D. **Rev:** 2 ornate crossed keys with small oval shield of family arms in center, small crowned shield of arms in each angle **Rev. Legend:** A. DNO - FACT - ISTVD. **Note:** Dav. #3875. Ref. V#406. Size varies: 40-41 mm.

Date	Mintage	VG	F	VF	XF	Unc
1677 Rare	—	—	—	—	—	—

KM# 4 2 DOPPIE

14.0000 g., 0.9860 Gold 0.4438 oz. AGW **Obv:** Draped bust of Giacomo right **Obv. Legend:** I. A. PVT. CIST. ET. BELG. PRIN. **Rev:** Crowned 4-fold arms with central shield, date at end of legend **Rev. Legend:** qVI. BIBET. SITIET. ITERVM. **Note:** Fr.#213. Ref. V#405. Size varies: 31-33 mm.

Date	Mintage	VG	F	VF	XF	Unc
1677 Rare	—	—	—	—	—	—

KM# 5 10 SCUDI

32.9700 g., Gold **Obv:** Bust right, date at top in legend **Obv. Legend:** IA. A. PVT. PRIN. 1677 CIS. ET. B. D. **Rev:** 2 ornate crossed keys with small oval shield of family arms in center, small crowned shield of arms in each angle **Rev. Legend:** A. DNO - FACT - EST - ISTVD. **Note:** Fr.#212. Ref. V#404. Size varies: 40-41 mm.

Date	Mintage	VG	F	VF	XF	Unc
1677 Rare	—	—	—	—	—	—

COMPIANO

A commune in the province of Parma approximately eight miles N.W. of Emilia ruled by the Landi Family until 1862. The Landi's also held the commune de Bardi and the principality of Borgotaro. During the hundreds of years that the Landi Family ruled, Compiano developed as a progressive center with a public school system and eventually coinage. Granted the mintage right in 1551, the Landi Family did not strike coins until the rule of Frederico Landi, 1590-1630, after which the mint was closed.

RULER

Frederico Landi of Borgotera, Cena, Bardi and Compiano, 1590-1627

STATE

STANDARD COINAGE

KM# 5 SESTINO

Billon **Obv:** Bust of Federico right **Rev:** Laurel branch **Note:** Weight varies: 0.53-0.72 grams.

Date	Mintage	VG	F	VF	XF	Unc
ND	—	60.00	105	180	300	—

KM# 6 SESTINO

Billon **Rev:** Rock **Note:** Weight varies: 0.46-0.84 grams.

Date	Mintage	VG	F	VF	XF	Unc
ND	—	75.00	135	270	450	—

KM# 16 SESTINO

Billon **Ruler:** Federico Landi **Obv:** Bust right **Rev:** Crossed palm branches **Note:** Weight varies 0.52-0.71g

Date	Mintage	VG	F	VF	XF	Unc
ND	—	70.00	120	240	425	—

KM# 17 2 SOLDI

Billon **Ruler:** Federico Landi **Obv:** Bust right **Rev:** Standing figure of John the Baptist **Note:** Weight varies 1.12-1.60g

Date	Mintage	VG	F	VF	XF	Unc
ND	—	150	300	600	975	—

KM# 7 5 SOLDI

Billon **Obv:** Bust of Federico right **Rev:** Standing figure of St. Terentius **Note:** Weight varies: 1.12-2.12 grams.

Date	Mintage	VG	F	VF	XF	Unc
ND	—	115	225	450	750	—

KM# 8 15 SOLDI

4.9000 g., Silver **Obv:** Bust of Federico right **Rev:** Crowned double eagle with arms

Date	Mintage	VG	F	VF	XF	Unc
ND	—	—	—	—	—	—

KM# 9 LIRA

Silver **Obv:** Bust of Federico right **Rev:** John the Baptist

Date	Mintage	VG	F	VF	XF	Unc
1622	—	—	—	—	—	—

KM# 10 LIRA

5.9000 g., Silver

Date	Mintage	VG	F	VF	XF	Unc
ND	—	—	—	—	—	—

KM# 11 DUCATONE

Silver **Obv:** Bust of Federico right **Rev:** St. Francis kneeling, date below **Note:** Weight varies: 30.00-31.00 grams. Dav. #3847.

Date	Mintage	VG	F	VF	XF	Unc
1622	—	1,500	3,000	5,100	9,000	—

KM# 12 DOPPIA

7.0000 g., 0.9860 Gold 0.2219 oz. AGW **Obv:** Bust of Federico right **Rev:** Crowned arms in Order collar

Date	Mintage	VG	F	VF	XF	Unc
ND	—	3,600	6,000	9,000	16,000	—

KM# 13 2 DOPPIE

14.0000 g., 0.9860 Gold 0.4438 oz. AGW **Obv:** Bust of Federico right in inner circle **Rev:** St. John standing facing in inner circle, date in exergue

Date	Mintage	VG	F	VF	XF	Unc
1623 Rare	—	—	—	—	—	—

KM# 14 2 DOPPIE

14.0000 g., 0.9860 Gold 0.4438 oz. AGW **Rev:** Crowned arms in Order collar in inner circle

Date	Mintage	VG	F	VF	XF	Unc
ND	—	4,200	7,200	11,500	21,000	—

KM# 15 5 DOPPIE

0.9860 Gold **Obv:** Bust of Federico **Rev:** St. Francis kneeling

Date	Mintage	VG	F	VF	XF	Unc
1622 Rare	—	—	—	—	—	—

CORREGGIO

First mentioned in the 10th century, the town of Correggio is located about 8 miles (14 kilometers) northeast of Reggio nell' Emilia and a like distance northwest of Modena. The local lords of the place trace back to a certain Frogerio and his descendants were raised to the rank of count in 1452, reconfirmed by Emperor Carol V in 1520. The title of Prince of the Empire was bestowed on the count by Emperor Mattia (Mathias) in 1616. However, cordial relations with the imperial court did not last as the prince abused his right to strike coins. After years of issuing substandard coinage in spite of warnings and investigations, the prince was deposed in 1631 and the principality was sold to Modena in 1635. The last territorial prince died impoverished in 1645 at the age of 70, although the line itself did not become extinct until 1711.

RULERS

Camillo, 1546-1597;
As Camillo d'Austria, 1597-1605
Giovanni Siro, 1597-1631, Prince in 1616

Reference:

V = Alberto Varesi, ***Monete Italiane Regionali: Emelia***. Pavia, 1998.

PRINCIPALITY

STANDARD COINAGE

DAV# 3881 SCUDO

Silver **Obv:** Bust of Siro right, 1620 below **Rev:** Crowned arms **Rev. Legend:** ANTIQVISS. FAM. AVS. INSIGN

Date	Mintage	Good	VG	F	VF	XF
1620 Rare	—	—	—	—	—	—

DAV# 3887 SCUDO

Silver **Obv:** Ornate cross, SCP below **Obv. Legend:** SI. PRO... **Rev:** Arms, 140 below **Rev. Legend:** SANCTVS. MARCVS...

Date	Mintage	Good	VG	F	VF	XF
ND Rare	—	—	—	—	—	—

DAV# 3876 TALLERO

Silver **Obv:** Date divided by shield **Obv. Legend:** *MO* NO* CAM*... **Rev. Legend:** *CONFIDENS* DNO* NON*...

Date	Mintage	Good	VG	F	VF	XF
1603	—	200	400	800	1,400	—
ND	—	200	400	800	1,400	—

DAV# 3877 TALLERO

Silver **Obv:** SO-70 divided by shield

Date	Mintage	Good	VG	F	VF	XF
ND	—	200	400	800	1,400	—

DAV# 3879 TALLERO

Silver **Obv. Legend:** *CAM* AVST* CIVIT* -CORR*... **Rev. Legend:** MONE* NVOVA* FATTA* PER*...

Date	Mintage	Good	VG	F	VF	XF
ND	—	200	400	800	1,400	—

DAV# 3880 TALLERO

Silver **Obv:** Crowned arms **Obv. Legend:** *MONETA*NOVA*... **Rev. Legend:** *CONFIDENS*DNO NON*MOVETVR*

Date	Mintage	Good	VG	F	VF	XF
ND Rare	—	—	—	—	—	—

DAV# 3882 DUCATONE

Silver **Obv:** Bust of Siro right **Rev:** Crowned arms

Date	Mintage	Good	VG	F	VF	XF
1627 Rare	—	—	—	—	—	—

DAV# 3883 DUCATONE

Silver **Obv:** Bust right **Rev:** Narrow crowned arms

Date	Mintage	Good	VG	F	VF	XF
1628 Rare	—	—	—	—	—	—

Note: Numismatica Ars Classica Auction 32, 1-06, nearly XF realized approximately $16,670

DAV# 3885 DUCATONE

Silver **Obv:** Bust left **Rev:** Crowned plain arms **Note:** Legend varieties exist.

Date	Mintage	Good	VG	F	VF	XF
ND Rare	—	—	—	—	—	—

DAV# 3886 DUCATONE

Silver **Obv:** Bust right **Rev:** Crowned arms in Order chain **Note:** Varieteies in arms exist.

Date	Mintage	Good	VG	F	VF	XF
ND	—	900	1,650	3,000	4,950	—

TRADE COINAGE

FR# 221 DUCAT
3.5000 g., 0.9860 Gold 0.1109 oz. AGW **Obv:** Knight standing **Rev:** Arms

Date	Mintage	VG	F	VF	XF	Unc
ND	—	425	725	1,150	2,400	—

FR# 222 DUCAT
3.5000 g., 0.9860 Gold 0.1109 oz. AGW **Obv:** Ruler standing **Rev:** Double eagle

Date	Mintage	VG	F	VF	XF	Unc
ND	—	750	1,500	3,000	5,300	—

FR# 223 DUCAT
3.5000 g., 0.9860 Gold 0.1109 oz. AGW **Rev:** Madonna

Date	Mintage	VG	F	VF	XF	Unc
ND	—	425	725	1,150	2,400	—

FR# 224 DUCAT
3.5000 g., 0.9860 Gold 0.1109 oz. AGW **Obv:** Knight standing **Rev:** Four-line inscription in tablet

Date	Mintage	VG	F	VF	XF	Unc
1609	—	750	1,500	3,000	5,300	—

CREMONA

Founded by the Romans in 218BC, Cremona is situated in Lombardy, 45 miles (75 kilometers) southeast of Milan. In the Middle Ages, from about the 9th through 12th centuries, the city was controlled almost exclusively by the local bishops. During the 13th century and into the early 14th century, Cremona was caught up in the struggle between the Guelfs and Ghibellines, which was actually a long drawn out conflict between competing dynasties in Germany for the imperial throne. In 1334, the city submitted to rule by the Visconti of Milan, but gradually local leaders regained control until Cremona was reunited with Milan in 1420. Except for a brief period (1499-1509), when the city was attached to Venice, its fortunes followed those of Milan. Cremona was besieged by French, Papal and Venetian forces in 1526.

RULER
Francesco II Sforza, 1521-1535

Reference:
V = Alberto Varesi, ***Monete Italiane Regionali: Lombardia, Zecche Minori***. Pavia, 1995.

CITY

STANDARD COINAGE

KM# 1 SCUDO (Scudo d'Oro)
3.4300 g., Gold **Ruler:** Francesco II Sforza **Obv:** Crowned serpent in circle (Sforza arms), date at end of legend **Obv. Legend:** FR. II. SF. MEDIOLA. DVCE. **Rev:** Seated figure of St. Omobono offering help to a poor youth at left **Rev. Legend:** S. HOMOBO. PAVPERTATI. CREMONEN. **Note:** FR. #226. Ref. V#308. Size varies: 22-23mm.

Date	Mintage	VG	F	VF	XF	Unc
1527 Rare	—	—	—	—	—	—

CUNEO

STATE

SIEGE COINAGE

KM# 1 LIRA
Billon **Obv:** Arms **Rev:** Column and banner **Note:** Weight varies: 10.72-11.82 grams.

Date	Mintage	VG	F	VF	XF	Unc
1641 Rare	—	—	—	—	—	—

Note: Fritz Rudolf Künker Münzenhandlung Auction 116, 9-06, VF realized approximately $20,335

KM# 2 DOPPIA
7.0000 g., 0.9860 Gold 0.2219 oz. AGW **Obv:** Arms in inner circle **Rev:** Flag and column crossed in inner circle, date at bottom in legend

Date	Mintage	VG	F	VF	XF	Unc
1641 Rare	—	—	—	—	—	—

KM# 3 5 DOPPIE
35.0000 g., 0.9860 Gold 1.1095 oz. AGW **Obv:** Arms in inner circle **Rev:** Flag and column crossed in inner circle, date at bottom in legend **Note:** Varieties exist.

Date	Mintage	VG	F	VF	XF	Unc
1641 Rare	—	—	—	—	—	—

DESANA

Countship

The town of Desana in Piedmont, less than five miles (7.5 kilometers) southwest of Vercelli, was under the control of the bishop of that city from 1003. Teodosio II of Montferrat was proclaimed lord of the town in 1411 and persuaded the town council to cede power to Ludovico (I) Tizzone. Ludovico II received the mint right in 1482 and was raised to the rank of count in 1510. Because the count had sided with Emperor Carlo V, King Francis II of France took the feudal lordship away from the Tizzone family and conferred it upon François de Mareuil in 1515. The latter then ceded the rights over Desana to Pierre de Beraud the next year, who in turn sold half of the countship to Filippo Tornielli. The count then sold Desana to Duke Carlo III of Savoy, who restored it to the Tizzone family in 1529. The widow of the last count sold the countship to Duke Vittorio Amadeo II of Savoy in 1693.

RULERS
Antonio Maria II Tizzone, 1598-1641
Carlo Giuseppe Francesco Tizzone, 1641-1676

Arms:
5 diagonal firebrands (Italian = tizzone)

Reference:
Alberto Varesi, ***Monete Italiane Regionali: Piemonte, Sardegna, Liguria, Isola di Corsica***. *Pavia, 1996.*

COUNTSHIP

STANDARD COINAGE

KM# 2 TRILLINA
1.0000 g., Billon, 16 mm. **Ruler:** Antonio Maria II **Obv:** Crowned "T.11" in circle **Obv. Legend:** MONETA. CAESARI. **Rev:** Floriated cross in circle **Rev. Legend:** CRVX. SANTA. ET. BEN. **Note:** Varesi 585.

Date	Mintage	VG	F	VF	XF	Unc
ND(1618-30)	—	75.00	140	300	500	—

KM# 75 TRILLINA
Billon, 14-15 mm. **Ruler:** Carlo **Obv:** Oval shield of four-fold arms **Obv. Legend:** CAR. IOS. TICO. D. **Rev:** Crown above PHI **Rev. Legend:** CIAN. SAC. RO. IMP. **Note:** Weight varies: 1.08-1.20 grams. Prev KM# 15. Varesi 600.

Date	Mintage	VG	F	VF	XF	Unc
ND(1641-76)	—	40.00	80.00	170	275	—

KM# 76 TRILLINA
Billon, 14-15 mm. **Ruler:** Carlo **Obv:** Crown over PTI **Obv. Legend:** ...EX. A...E. **Rev:** Nimbate facing bust divides S - A **Rev. Legend:** ME... NIDX. **Note:** Weight varies: 1.08-1.20 grams. Varesi 601.

Date	Mintage	VG	F	VF	XF	Unc
ND(1641-76)	—	80.00	165	325	550	—

KM# 82 SOLDINO
Billon, 16-17 mm. **Ruler:** Carlo **Obv:** Bust to right, date below, where present **Obv. Legend:** CAROLVS. - IO. COM. **Rev:** Floriated cross **Rev. Legend:** VIC. PERP. S. R. IMP. **Note:** Weight varies: 1.27-1.88 grams. Prev KM# 95. Varesi 598.

Date	Mintage	VG	F	VF	XF	Unc
1672	—	55.00	110	225	350	—
ND(1641-76)	—	55.00	110	225	350	—

KM# 83 SOLDINO
Billon, 16-17 mm. **Ruler:** Carlo **Obv:** Bust to right, date below **Obv. Legend:** CAROL. - TI. C. D. SA. **Rev:** Floriated cross **Rev. Legend:** MARC. MEDIOL. **Note:** Weight varies: 1.27-1.88 grams. Prev KM# 96. Varesi 599.

Date	Mintage	VG	F	VF	XF	Unc
1676	—	55.00	110	225	350	—

KM# 5 QUATTRINO
Billon, 14-15 mm. **Ruler:** Antonio Maria II **Obv:** Armored bust to right **Obv. Legend:** ANT. MAR. TIT. BL. COM. **Rev:** Ornate shield of crowned arms **Rev. Legend:** DECIAN. VIC. IMP. PER. **Note:** Weight varies: 0.42-0.65 grams. Varesi 586.

Date	Mintage	VG	F	VF	XF	Unc
ND(1618-30)	—	40.00	80.00	200	330	—

KM# 6 QUATTRINO
Billon, 14-15 mm. **Ruler:** Antonio Maria II **Obv:** Head left **Obv. Legend:** ANT. MAR. TIT. BL. COM. DEC. V. IMP. **Rev:** Ornate cross **Rev. Legend:** IN. HOC. SIGNO. CONFIDO. **Note:** Weight varies: 0.42-0.65 grams. Varesi 587.

Date	Mintage	VG	F	VF	XF	Unc
ND(1618-30)	—	40.00	80.00	200	330	—

KM# 7 QUATTRINO
Billon, 14-15 mm. **Ruler:** Antonio Maria II **Obv:** Head to left **Obv. Legend:** ANT. MAR. TIT. BL. COM. DEC. V. IMP. **Rev:** Bear walking to left **Rev. Legend:** AB. INVIDIS. ERIPE. ME. D. **Note:** Weight varies: 0.42-0.65 grams. Varesi 588.

Date	Mintage	VG	F	VF	XF	Unc
ND(1618-30)	—	40.00	80.00	200	330	—

KM# 8 QUATTRINO
Billon, 14-15 mm. **Ruler:** Antonio Maria II **Obv:** Crowned MA monogram superimposed on two crossed palm branches **Obv. Legend:** TIT. BLA. COMES. **Rev:** Crowned arms **Rev. Legend:** COMES. DECIANE. **Note:** Weight varies: 0.42-0.65 grams. Varesi 589.

Date	Mintage	VG	F	VF	XF	Unc
ND(1618-30)	—	40.00	80.00	200	330	—

KM# 9 QUATTRINO
Billon, 14-15 mm. **Ruler:** Antonio Maria II **Obv:** Crowned MA monogram superimposed on two crossed palm branches **Obv. Legend:** TIT. BLA. COM. DEC. **Rev:** Cross with lily ends **Rev. Legend:** IN. HOC. SIGNO. CONFIDO. **Note:** Weight varies: 0.42-0.65 grams. Varesi 590.

Date	Mintage	VG	F	VF	XF	Unc
ND(1618-30)	—	40.00	80.00	200	330	—

KM# 10 QUATTRINO
Billon, 14-15 mm. **Ruler:** Antonio Maria II **Obv:** Crowned MA monogram superimposed on two crossed palm branches **Obv. Legend:** TIT. BLA. COM. DEC. **Rev:** Bear walking to left **Rev. Legend:** AB. INVID. VT. AB. VRSO. ERIP. N. D. **Note:** Weight varies: 0.42-0.65 grams. Varesi 591.

Date	Mintage	VG	F	VF	XF	Unc
ND(1618-30)	—	75.00	140	325	550	—

KM# 77 QUATTRINO
Copper, 15-16 mm. **Ruler:** Carlo **Obv:** High-collared bust to right **Obv. Legend:** CAR. GIOS. TICONE. CONT. **Rev:** Round four-fold arms **Rev. Legend:** DESANA. VIC. IMP. PERPETVO. **Note:** Weight varies: 1.32-2.47 grams. Prev KM# 85. Varesi 602.

Date	Mintage	VG	F	VF	XF	Unc
ND(1641-76)	—	55.00	110	225	350	—

KM# 51 KREUZER
Billon, 18 mm. **Ruler:** Carlo **Obv:** Shield of two-fold arms, displayed eagle above **Obv. Legend:** CAROLO. GIOS. TIZ. B. A. **Rev:** Cross in circle, date (?) at end of legend **Rev. Legend:** S. THEODOLVS. **Note:** Weight varies: 1.48-1.49 grams. Previous KM# 79. Varesi 597. The date is questionable.

Date	Mintage	VG	F	VF	XF	Unc
"1628"	—	80.00	165	325	550	—

KM# 11 2 KREUZER
0.8800 g., Billon, 19 mm. **Ruler:** Antonio Maria II **Obv:** Crowned shield of four-fold arms with central shield **Obv. Legend:** ANT. MAR. TIT. BLAN. COM. DEC. **Rev:** Crowned imperial eagle, '2' in orb on breast **Rev. Legend:** SAC. ROM. IMP. VIC. PERPE. **Note:** Prev KM# 77. Varesi 579.

Date	Mintage	VG	F	VF	XF	Unc
ND(1618-30)	—	200	385	875	1,400	—

KM# 12 3 KREUZER
1.3600 g., Billon, 19 mm. **Ruler:** Antonio Maria II **Obv:** Shield of four-fold arms **Obv. Legend:** ANT. MAR. TITIO. COM. DEC. **Rev:** Crowned imperial eagle, '3' in circle on breast **Rev. Legend:** SAC. ROM. IMP. VICA. PERPE. **Note:** Prev KM# 76. Varesi 578.

Date	Mintage	VG	F	VF	XF	Unc
ND(1618-30)	—	150	275	550	825	—

KM# 53 SOLDO
Billon, 18-19 mm. **Ruler:** Antonio Maria II **Obv:** Small shield of two-fold arms divides L-V, small imperial eagle above, all in quatrefoil **Obv. Legend:** MONETA. DECIEN. **Rev:** 3/4-length facing figure of St. Ludger **Rev. Legend:** SACT - LVDIGA. **Note:** Weight varies: 0.63-1.29 grams. Prev KM# 11. Varesi 582.

Date	Mintage	VG	F	VF	XF	Unc
ND(1630-41)	—	150	275	650	1,000	—

KM# 54 SOLDO
Billon, 18-19 mm. **Ruler:** Antonio Maria II **Obv:** Crowned imperial eagle over small shield of arms **Obv. Legend:** MON. NOV. COM. DEC. **Rev:** Facing bust of St. Leonard **Rev. Legend:** SANCTVS. LEONAR. **Note:** Weight varies: 0.63-1.29 grams. Prev KM# 12. Varesi 583. Imitation of Luzern (Switz.) Schilling, KM# 25.

Date	Mintage	VG	F	VF	XF	Unc
ND(1630-41)	—	80.00	165	325	550	—

KM# 55 SOLDO
Billon, 18-19 mm. **Ruler:** Antonio Maria II **Obv:** Crowned imperial eagle over small shield of arms **Obv. Legend:** MONETA. DECIAN. **Rev:** Facing bust of St. Leonard **Rev. Legend:** SANCTVS. LEONAR. **Note:** Weight varies: 0.63-1.29 grams. Previous KM# 13. Varesi 583/1. Imitation of Luzern (Switz.) Schilling, KM# 25.

Date	Mintage	VG	F	VF	XF	Unc
ND(1630-41)	—	90.00	195	425	660	—

KM# 56 SOLDO
Billon, 18-19 mm. **Ruler:** Antonio Maria II **Obv:** Crowned imperial eagle over small shield of arms **Obv. Legend:** MONETA - DECIAN. **Rev:** Full-length facing figure of St. Martin **Rev. Legend:** SANCTV - MARINV. **Note:** Weight varies: 0.63-1.29 grams. Previous KM# 14. Varesi 584.

Date	Mintage	VG	F	VF	XF	Unc
ND(1630-41) Rare	—	—	—	—	—	—

KM# 13 PARPAGLIOLA
2.3000 g., Silver Wash On Copper, 20 mm. **Ruler:** Antonio Maria II **Obv:** Crowned shield of four-fold arms, quartered with eagle and head of dolphin **Obv. Legend:** MEDIO - ANT. D. **Rev:** Standing figure of Providence **Rev. Legend:** PROVIDENTIA. **Note:** Varesi 580.

Date	Mintage	VG	F	VF	XF	Unc
ND(1618-30)	—	125	220	475	700	—

KM# 14 PARPAGLIOLA
1.3600 g., Silver Wash On Copper, 19 mm. **Ruler:** Antonio Maria II **Obv:** Crowned shield of four-fold arms, quartered with firebrands and coiled adder **Obv. Legend:** MEDD - LANI. D. **Rev:** Standing figure of Providence **Rev. Legend:** PROVIDENTIA. **Note:** Varesi 581.

Date	Mintage	VG	F	VF	XF	Unc
ND(1618-30)	—	125	220	475	700	—

KM# 49 30 KREUZER
3.2500 g., Billon, 24-25 mm. **Ruler:** Antonio Maria II **Obv:** Arms of Bern in baroque frame, date at end of legend **Obv. Legend:** MONE. NOV. T. B. DESANENSIS. **Rev:** Imperial eagle in circle **Rev. Legend:** +BERTH. D. TERR. IM. FVNDATOR. **Note:** Previous KM# 75. Varesi 577. Imitation of Bern (Switz.) 1/2 Dicken, KM# A20.

Date	Mintage	VG	F	VF	XF	Unc
16ZZ Rare	—	—	—	—	—	—

KM# 15 4 GROSSI
Billon, 23-24 mm. **Ruler:** Antonio Maria II **Obv:** Two adjacent shields of arms, crown above, value 'IIII' below, all in circle **Obv. Legend:** ANT. MAR. TIT. BLAN. COM. D. V. IM. P. **Rev:** Bust of St. Ladislaus right in circle **Rev. Legend:** SANCTVS. LADISLAVS. REX. **Note:** Weight varies: 3.55-3.74 grams. Previous KM# 74. Varesi 576. Imitation of an issue of Lithuania.

Date	Mintage	VG	F	VF	XF	Unc
ND(1618-30)	—	275	440	950	1,600	—

KM# 50 FIORINO (12 Grossi)
Billon, 24 mm. **Ruler:** Antonio Maria II **Obv:** Oval two-fold arms in baroque frame, value 'XII.G.' in exergue **Obv. Legend:** MONETA. NOVA. M. T. B. COMES. D. **Rev:** Bust of St. Stephen to left, date in exerque **Rev. Legend:** S. STEPHANVS. PROTHOM. **Note:** Weight varies: 3.55-6.59 grams. Previous KM# 65. Varesi 565. Imitation of Metz 12 Groschen, KM# 2.

Date	Mintage	VG	F	VF	XF	Unc
1622	—	550	825	1,600	2,750	—

KM# 16 FIORINO
Billon, 29 mm. **Ruler:** Antonio Maria II **Obv:** Lion rampant to left in circle **Obv. Legend:** MONETA. NOVA. ARGENTEA. D. T. D. **Rev:** Full-length facing figure of Madonna and Child, crescent below. rays around **Rev. Legend:** SANCTA. MAR - IA. VIRGO. **Note:** Weight varies: 3.55-6.59 grams. Prev KM# 66. Varesi 566.

Date	Mintage	VG	F	VF	XF	Unc
ND(1618-30) Rare	—	—	—	—	—	—

KM# 17 FIORINO
Billon, 27-28 mm. **Ruler:** Antonio Maria II **Obv:** Shield of four-fold arms with central shield, all in circle **Obv. Legend:** ANT. MAR. TIT. BLA. COM. DEC. VIC. I. P. **Rev:** Bust of St. Leonard to right in circle **Rev. Legend:** DIVVS. LEONARDVS. EPISC. PROTEC. **Note:** Weight varies: 3.55-6.59 grams. Prev KM# 67. Varesi 567. Imitation of teston of Hanau-Lichtenberg, KM# 30.

Date	Mintage	VG	F	VF	XF	Unc
ND(1618-30)	—	775	1,100	2,750	4,500	—

KM# 18 FIORINO
Billon, 28 mm. **Ruler:** Antonio Maria II **Obv:** Crowned shield of four-fold arms in circle **Obv. Legend:** ANT. MAR. TIT. BLA. COM. DEC. VIC. IMP. P. **Rev:** Crowned imperial eagle in circle **Rev. Legend:** SVB. VMBRA. ALAR. TVAR. PROTEGOR. **Note:** Weight varies: 3.55-6.59 grams. Prev KM# 69. Varesi 570. Imitation of Campen 6 Stuivers, KM# 7ff.

Date	Mintage	VG	F	VF	XF	Unc
ND(1618-30)	—	325	550	1,100	1,650	—

KM# 19 FIORINO
Billon, 28 mm. **Ruler:** Antonio Maria II **Obv:** Large five-petaled rose in circle **Obv. Legend:** ANT. MAR. TIT. BL. COM. DEC. VIC. IMP. P. **Rev:** Crowned imperial eagle, '12' in circle on breast **Rev. Legend:** SVB. VMBRA. ALAR. TVAR. PROTEC. **Note:** Weight varies: 3.55-6.59 grams. Prev KM# 70. Varesi 571. Imitation of Hagenau 12 Kreuzer, KM# 37.

Date	Mintage	VG	F	VF	XF	Unc
ND(1618-30) Rare	—	—	—	—	—	—

KM# 20 FIORINO
Billon, 26-27 mm. **Ruler:** Antonio Maria II **Obv:** Large lily in circle **Obv. Legend:** MON. ARGENTEA. COM. D. VIC. IM. P. **Rev:** Cross with floriated ends in circle **Rev. Legend:** IN HOC. SIGNO VINCES. **Note:** Weight varies: 3.55-6.59 grams. Prev KM# 71. Varesi 572. Imitation of Strassburg (city) 12 Kreuzer.

Date	Mintage	VG	F	VF	XF	Unc
ND(1618-30)	—	750	1,100	2,750	4,500	—

KM# 21 FIORINO
Billon, 26-27 mm. **Ruler:** Antonio Maria II **Obv:** Large lily in circle, value (XI) at top in margin **Obv. Legend:** MONE. NOVA. ARGENT. CO. DEC. **Rev:** Cross with floriated ends in circle **Rev. Legend:** GLORIA. IN EXCELSIS. DE. **Note:** Weight varies: 3.55-6.59 grams. Prev KM# 72. Varesi 573. Imitation of Strassburg (city) 12 Kreuzer.

Date	Mintage	VG	F	VF	XF	Unc
ND(1618-30) Rare	—	—	—	—	—	—

KM# 22 FIORINO
Billon, 26-27 mm. **Ruler:** Antonio Maria II **Obv:** Large lily in circle **Obv. Legend:** SICVT. LILIVM. INTER. SPINAS. **Rev:** Cross with floriated ends in circle **Rev. Legend:** MON. ARG. COM. DEC. VIC. IMP. PER. **Note:** Weight varies: 3.55-6.59 grams. Prev KM# 73. Varesi 574. Imitation of Strassburg (city) 12 Kreuzer.

Date	Mintage	VG	F	VF	XF	Unc
ND(1618-30) Rare	—	—	—	—	—	—

KM# 47 FIORINO
Billon, 31 mm. **Ruler:** Antonio Maria II **Obv:** Crowned imperial eagle in circle **Obv. Legend:** ANT. MAR. TIT. BL. COM. DEC. VI. IMP. P. P. **Rev:** Half-length figure of St. Charles Borromeo to right divides date **Rev. Legend:** S. CAROL. BOROM. AR. ME. P. M. **Note:** Weight varies: 3.55-6.59 grams. Prev KM# 60. Varesi 568.

Date	Mintage	VG	F	VF	XF	Unc
1619 Rare	—	—	—	—	—	—

KM# 48 FIORINO
Billon, 27 mm. **Ruler:** Antonio Maria II **Obv:** Crowned shield of four-fold arms in circle **Obv. Legend:** ANT. MAR. TIT. BLA. COM. DE. VIC. IMP. P. **Rev:** Crowned imperial eagle, '12' in circle on breast **Rev. Legend:** SVB. VMBRA. ALAR. TVAR. PROTEG. **Note:** Weight varies: 3.55-6.59 grams. Prev KM# 68. Varesi 569.

Date	Mintage	VG	F	VF	XF	Unc
1621	—	500	825	1,650	2,500	—
ND	—	500	825	1,650	2,500	—

KM# 57 FIORINO
Billon, 28-29 mm. **Ruler:** Antonio Maria II **Obv:** Shield with crowned displayed eagle, ornate crowned helmet above **Obv. Legend:** ANT. MAR. TIT. COM. DEC. VI. IMP. P. **Rev:** Crowned imperial eagle with shield of Austrian arms on breast **Rev. Legend:** SVB. VMBRA. ALAR. TVAR. PROTEGOR. **Note:** Weight varies: 3,55-6.59 grams. Previous KM# 78. Varesi 575.

Date	Mintage	VG	F	VF	XF	Unc
ND(1630-41)	—	500	825	1,650	2,500	—

KM# 23 3 BIANCHI
Silver, 29-30 mm. **Ruler:** Antonio Maria II **Obv:** Imperial eagle above small shield of Tizzone arms **Obv. Legend:** MON. NOV. COM. DECI. **Rev:** Bust of St. Leonard to right **Rev. Legend:** SACTVS - LEONARDVS. **Note:** Weight varies: 7.14-8.07 grams. Prev KM# 22. Varesi 563. Imitation of Luzern (Switz.) Dicken, KM# 16.

Date	Mintage	VG	F	VF	XF	Unc
ND(1618-30)	—	750	1,100	2,750	3,500	—

KM# 58 3 BIANCHI
Silver, 29-30 mm. **Ruler:** Antonio Maria II **Obv:** Imperial eagle in circle **Obv. Legend:** MONETA. COM. DEC. VICARII. IMP. PE. **Rev:** Lion emerging to left from castle tower at right **Rev. Legend:** IN. FORTITVDINE. MEA. **Note:** Weight varies: 7.14-8.07 grams. Prev KM# 21. Varesi 564.

Date	Mintage	VG	F	VF	XF	Unc
ND(1630-41)	—	800	1,100	2,900	3,850	—

KM# 81 1/4 TALLERO (15 Quattrini)
7.2500 g., Silver, 29 mm. **Ruler:** Carlo **Obv:** Armored bust to right, value (XV) below **Obv. Legend:** CAROLVS. TIT. D.G. COM. DECIANÆ. **Rev:** Imperial eagle with shield of Tizzone arms on breast, large crown above divides date **Rev. Legend:** MONETA. NOVA. ARGENTEA. **Note:** Prev KM# 91. Varesi 595.

Date	Mintage	VG	F	VF	XF	Unc
1669 Rare	—	—	—	—	—	—

KM# 24 TESTONE
Silver, 28-30 mm. **Ruler:** Antonio Maria II **Obv:** Bust to right in circle **Obv. Legend:** ANT. MAR. TIT. BLA. COM. DEC. VIL. IMPE. **Rev:** Full-length facing female figure, right hand resting on column **Rev. Legend:** FORTITV. ILLIVS. DEXT. EIVS. **Note:** Weight varies: 4.49-6.67 grams. Prev KM# 16. Varesi 558.

Date	Mintage	VG	F	VF	XF	Unc
ND(1618-30)	—	650	1,000	2,500	3,850	—

KM# 25 TESTONE
Silver, 28-30 mm. **Ruler:** Antonio Maria II **Obv:** Bust with high collar to right **Obv. Legend:** ANT. MAR. TIT. COM. DEC. PRO. IMP. **Rev:** Crowned four-fold arms with oval central shield of Tizzone arms in baroque frame **Rev. Legend:** SACRIQVE. ROM. IMP. VICARIVS. PERP. **Note:** Weight varies: 4.49-6.67 grams. Prev KM# 17. Varesi 559.

Date	Mintage	VG	F	VF	XF	Unc
ND(1618-30) Rare	—	—	—	—	—	—

KM# 26 TESTONE
Silver, 28-30 mm. **Ruler:** Antonio Maria II **Obv:** Half-length armored figure to right in circle **Obv. Legend:** ANT. MAR. TIT. COM. DEC. VIC. IMP. PERP. **Rev:** Crowned imperial eagle with oval shield of Austrian arms on breast **Rev. Legend:** VIRTVTE. CAESAREA. DVCE. **Note:** Weight varies: 4.49-6.67 grams. Prev KM# 18. Varesi 560.

Date	Mintage	VG	F	VF	XF	Unc
ND(1618-30)	—	300	550	1,400	2,200	—

KM# 27 TESTONE
Billon, 28-30 mm. **Ruler:** Antonio Maria II **Subject:** To the memory of Antonio Maria II's father, Delfino **Obv:** Half-length armored figure to right in circle **Obv. Legend:** DELPHINVS. PAT. ANT. MAR. TIT. BL. CO. DE. **Rev:** Crowned imperial eagle with oval shield of Austrian arms on breast **Rev. Legend:** ET. SACRI. ROMANI. IMPER. VICARII. PE. **Note:** Weight varies: 4.49-6.67 grams. Prev KM# 19. Varesi 561.

Date	Mintage	VG	F	VF	XF	Unc
ND(1618-30)	—	300	550	1,400	2,200	—

KM# 59 TESTONE
7.2400 g., Silver, 29 mm. **Ruler:** Antonio Maria II **Obv:** High-collared bust to right **Obv. Legend:** ANT. MAR. TIT. COM. DEC. PRO. IMP. **Rev:** Crowned displayed eagle **Rev. Legend:** SVM. (sic) VMBRA. ALAR. TVAR. PROTEGOR. **Note:** Prev KM# 20. Varesi 562.

Date	Mintage	VG	F	VF	XF	Unc
ND(1630-41)	—	900	1,650	3,800	5,500	—

KM# 80 TESTONE
Silver, 30-31 mm. **Ruler:** Carlo **Obv:** Draped bust to right in circle, date at end of legend **Obv. Legend:** FRAN. TIT. M. ROD. C. DE. CS. R. I. VI. **Rev:** Virgin Mary at right in adoration of baby Jesus at left **Rev. Legend:** QVÆ. SOLA. VIRGO. PARTVRIT. **Note:** Weight varies: 7.54-7.82 grams. Prev KM# 90. Varesi 596.

Date	Mintage	VG	F	VF	XF	Unc
1667	—	750	1,100	2,850	4,500	—

KM# 29 TALLERO
Billon, 39 mm. **Ruler:** Antonio Maria II **Subject:** In memory of Antonio Maria II's father, Delfino **Obv:** Half-length armored figure of Delfino to right **Obv. Legend:** DELPHINVS. PAT. ANT. MAR. TIT. BL. COM. DEC. **Rev:** Crowned imperial eagle, shield of Austrian arms on breast **Rev. Legend:** ET. SACRI. ROMANI. IMPER. VICARII. PERPE. **Note:** Weight varies: 17.90-19.04 grams. Prev KM# 24. Not in Dav. Varesi 548.

Date	Mintage	VG	F	VF	XF	Unc
ND(1618-30)	—	650	1,000	2,350	3,600	—

KM# 28 TALLERO
Silver Or Billon, 39-40 mm. **Ruler:** Antonio Maria II **Subject:** In memory of Antonio Maria II's father, Delfino **Obv:** High-collared bust of Delfino to right **Obv. Legend:** DELPHINVS. PATER. ANTO. MAR. TIT. BL. COM. D. **Rev:** Crowned shield of manifold arms with central shield of displayed eagle, garland around. **Rev. Legend:** SACRIQVE. ROM. IMPER. VICARIVS. PERPET. **Note:** Weight varies: 27.20-28.97 grams. Prev. KM# 23. Dav. 3888. Varesi 547.

Date	Mintage	VG	F	VF	XF	Unc
ND(1618-30)	—	900	1,650	4,000	6,600	—

KM# 30 TALLERO
26.1700 g., Silver, 40 mm. **Ruler:** Antonio Maria II **Obv:** Half-length armored figure to right **Obv. Legend:** ANT. MAR. TIT. COM. DEC. PRO. IMP. **Rev:** Crowned imperial eagle, shield of Tizzone arms on breast **Rev. Legend:** SACRIQVE. ROM. IM. VICARIVS. PERPETVVS. **Note:** Prev. KM# 24a. Dav. #3889. Varesi 549.

Date	Mintage	VG	F	VF	XF	Unc
ND(1618-30)	—	1,250	2,200	5,000	8,275	—

KM# 31 TALLERO
26.4500 g., Silver, 40 mm. **Ruler:** Antonio Maria II **Obv:** Half-length armored figure to right holding scepter over right shoulder **Obv. Legend:** ANTONIVS. MARIA. TITIO. COMES. DECIANE. **Rev:** Crowned imperial eagle, small shield of arms on breast **Rev. Legend:** SACRIQVE. ROM. IMP. VICARIVS. PERPETVVS. **Note:** Prev. KM# 26. Dav. #3890. Varesi 550.

Date	Mintage	VG	F	VF	XF	Unc
ND(1618-30) Rare	—	—	—	—	—	—

KM# 32 TALLERO

28.7500 g., Silver, 40 mm. **Ruler:** Antonio Maria II **Obv:** Crowned oval three-fold arms in baroque frame **Obv. Legend:** ANT. MAR. TIT. BLANC. COM. DEC. VIC. IMP. P. **Rev:** Seated facing figure of St. Ubertus on throne **Rev. Legend:** SANCTVS. VBERTVS. EPISC. PROTECTOR. **Note:** Prev. KM# 27. Dav. #3891. Varesi 551. Imitation of Salzburg Thaler, KM# 38ff.

Date	Mintage	VG	F	VF	XF	Unc
ND(1618-30)	—	850	1,400	2,850	4,950	—

KM# 33 TALLERO

28.5000 g., Silver, 40 mm. **Ruler:** Antonio Maria II **Obv:** Crowned oval three-fold arms in baroque frame **Obv. Legend:** ANT. MAR. TIT. BLAN. COM. DEC. VIC. IMP. P. **Rev:** St. George on horseback to right slaying dragon below **Rev. Legend:** SANCTVS. GEORGIVS. PROTECT. DECIA. **Note:** Prev. KM# 29. Dav. #3892. Varesi 552. Mule of KM# 32 obv. and KM# 34 rev.

Date	Mintage	VG	F	VF	XF	Unc
ND(1618-30) Rare	—	—	—	—	—	—

KM# 34 TALLERO

26.6700 g., Silver, 40 mm. **Ruler:** Antonio Maria II **Obv:** Shield of four-fold arms, two ornate helmets above, 'AM 97' at top **Obv. Legend:** ANT. MAR. TIT. BLA. COM. DEC. V. IMP. P. **Rev:** St. George on horseback to right slaying dragon below **Rev. Legend:** SANCTVS. GEORGIVS. PROTECT. DECIA. **Note:** Previous KM# 28. Dav. #3893. Varesi 553. Imitation of Mansfeld-Friedeburg Thaler, Dav. #9510.

Date	Mintage	VG	F	VF	XF	Unc
ND(1618-30)	—	900	1,650	4,000	6,600	—

KM# 35 TALLERO

25.8000 g., Silver, 38-39 mm. **Ruler:** Antonio Maria II **Obv:** Crowned 4-fold arms with central shield of Tizzone in baroque frame **Obv. Legend:** CESARIE. MAIESTATIS. ROMANOROM. IMPERIO. **Rev:** St. George on horseback to right slaying dragon below **Rev. Legend:** SANCTVS. GEORGIVS. PROTECT. DECIA. **Note:** Previous KM# 31. Dav. #3894. Varesi 555. Mule of two rev. dies-KM# 60 and KM# 34.

Date	Mintage	VG	F	VF	XF	Unc
ND(1618-30)	—	1,250	2,200	4,500	6,750	—

KM# 60 TALLERO

23.9100 g., Silver, 39-40 mm. **Ruler:** Antonio Maria II **Obv:** Half-length armored figure to right **Obv. Legend:** MONETA. NOVA. ANT. MAR. TI. COM. DEC. PRO. VI. **Rev:** Crowned four-fold arms with central shield of Tizzone in baroque frame **Rev. Legend:** CESARIE. MAIESTATIS. ROMANOROM. IMPERIO. **Note:** Previous KM# 32. Dav. #3895. Varesi 554.

Date	Mintage	VG	F	VF	XF	Unc
ND(1630-41) Rare	—	—	—	—	—	—

KM# 61 TALLERO

24.1000 g., Silver, 39-40 mm. **Ruler:** Antonio Maria II **Obv:** Half-length armored figure to right **Obv. Legend:** ANT. MAR. TIT. COM. DEC. PRO. IMPE. **Rev:** Crowned four-fold arms with central shield of Tizzone in baroque frame **Rev. Legend:** CESARIE. MAIESTATIS. ROMANOROM. IMPERIO. **Note:** Prev. KM# 34. Dav. #3896. Varesi 554/1.

Date	Mintage	VG	F	VF	XF	Unc
ND(1630-41)	—	1,500	2,500	5,500	9,000	—

KM# 62 TALLERO

27.5000 g., Silver, 40-41 mm. **Ruler:** Antonio Maria II **Obv:** Large half-length armored figure to right **Obv. Legend:** MONETA. NOVA. ANT. MAR. TI. COM. DEC. PRO. VI. **Rev:** Crowned imperial eagle, shield of Tizzone arms on breast, 'R XI III' in margin at bottom **Rev. Legend:** SACRO. ROM. IMP. - VICAR. PERPET. **Note:** Prev. KM# 33. Dav. #3897. Varesi 556.

Date	Mintage	VG	F	VF	XF	Unc
ND(1630-41) Rare	—	—	—	—	—	—

KM# 63 TALLERO

27.9600 g., Silver, 39-40 mm. **Ruler:** Antonio Maria II **Obv:** Crowned half-length armored figure to left, holding scepter over left shoulder **Obv. Legend:** FERDI. D.G. RO. VNG. BOE. DAL. CR. REX. **Rev:** Displayed eagle with shield of Tizzone arms on breast **Rev. Legend:** NVMVS. ARG. IMP. COMITIS. DECIANE. **Note:** Prev. KM# 35. Dav. #3898. Varesi 557.

Date	Mintage	VG	F	VF	XF	Unc
ND(1630-41) Rare	—	—	—	—	—	—

KM# 36 FIORINO D'ORO

Gold, 21-22 mm. **Ruler:** Antonio Maria II **Obv:** Half-length facing armored figure turned slightly to right, holding scepter over right shoulder **Obv. Legend:** ANT. MAR. TIT. BL. COM. DEC. VIC. IM. PER. **Rev:** Crowned imperial eagle, round shield of Austrian arms on breast **Rev. Legend:** SVB. VMBRA. AL - TVAR. PROTEG. **Note:** Weight varies: 2.59-3.15 grams. Previous KM# 45. Fr. #244. Varesi 534.

Date	Mintage	VG	F	VF	XF	Unc
ND(1618-30) Rare	—	—	—	—	—	—

KM# 37 FIORINO D'ORO

Gold, 21-22 mm. **Ruler:** Antonio Maria II **Obv:** Half-length facing armored figure turned slightly to right, holding scepter over right shoulder **Obv. Legend:** ANT. MAR. TIT. BL. COM. DEC. VIC. IM. PER. **Rev:** Crowned imperial eagle, round shield of Austrian arms on breast **Rev. Legend:** LVX. MEA. LVCEM. AB. ALIA. NON. MVTVAT. **Note:** Weight varies: 2.59-3.15 grams. Previous KM# 46. Fr. #244a. Varesi 535.

Date	Mintage	VG	F	VF	XF	Unc
ND(1618-30)	—	1,000	1,900	3,850	5,500	—

KM# 38 FIORINO D'ORO

Gold, 21-22 mm. **Ruler:** Antonio Maria II **Obv:** Crowned imperial eagle, round shield of Austria arms on breast **Obv. Legend:** LVX. MEA. LVCEM. AB. ALIA. NON. MVTVAT. **Rev:** Facing figure of St. Peter standing behind shield of arms below **Rev. Legend:** SANT. PETRVS. - PROP. DECIA. **Note:** Weight varies: 2.59-3.15 grams. Previous KM# 47. Fr. #245. Varesi 536.

Date	Mintage	VG	F	VF	XF	Unc
ND(1618-30) Rare	—	—	—	—	—	—

KM# 39 FIORINO D'ORO

Gold, 21-22 mm. **Ruler:** Antonio Maria II **Obv:** Crowned imperial eagle in circle **Obv. Legend:** MONETA. NOVA. AVREA. **Rev:** Small shield of arms, ornate helmet above **Rev. Legend:** NON. EST. CONS. ADVERS. DNM. **Note:** Weight varies: 2.59-3.15 grams. Previous KM# 48. Fr. #246. Varesi 537.

Date	Mintage	VG	F	VF	XF	Unc
ND(1618-30)	—	1,000	1,900	3,850	5,500	—

KM# 40 SCUDO D'ORO

3.0200 g., Gold, 22 mm. **Ruler:** Antonio Maria II **Obv:** Crowned shield of four-fold arms with central shield of Tizzone **Obv. Legend:** MONE. AVREA. FI. DECI. CVSSA. **Rev:** Cross with lily ends in circle **Rev. Legend:** IN. HOC. SIGNO VINCES. **Note:** Previous KM# 36. Fr. #248. Varesi 540.

Date	Mintage	VG	F	VF	XF	Unc
ND(1618-30)	—	1,250	2,200	4,500	7,000	—

KM# 65 SCUDO D'ORO

Gold, 20 mm. **Ruler:** Antonio Maria II **Obv:** Crowned shield of 4-fold arms with central shield of Tizzone **Obv. Legend:** ANT. MAR. TITI. COM. DEC. V. I. P. **Rev:** Seated facing figure of St. Catherine holding palm frond and wheel **Rev. Legend:** SANCTA - CATERINA. **Note:** Weight varies: 3.02-3.07 grams. Previous KM# 52. Fr. #251. Varesi 542.

Date	Mintage	VG	F	VF	XF	Unc
ND(1630-41) Rare	—	—	—	—	—	—

KM# 66 SCUDO D'ORO

Gold, 20 mm. **Ruler:** Antonio Maria II **Obv:** Displayed eagle in circle **Obv. Legend:** +MONETA. NOVA. AVREA. **Rev:** Full-length figure of St. Lawrence, turned slightly to right, holding grill and book **Rev. Legend:** SANCTVS - LAVRENTIVS. **Note:** Weight varies: 3.02-3.07 grams. Previous KM# 53. Fr. #252. Varesi 543.

Date	Mintage	VG	F	VF	XF	Unc
ND(1630-41) Rare	—	—	—	—	—	—

KM# 67 SCUDO D'ORO

Gold, 20 mm. **Ruler:** Antonio Maria II **Obv:** Imperial eagle in circle **Obv. Legend:** +SVB. VMBRA. ALARVM. TVARVM. **Rev:** Full-length facing figure of St. Louis **Rev. Legend:** SANCTVS - LVDOVICVS. **Note:** Weight varies: 3.02-3.07 grams. Previous KM# 54. Fr. #253. Varesi 544.

Date	Mintage	VG	F	VF	XF	Unc
ND(1630-41) Rare	—	—	—	—	—	—

KM# 68 SCUDO D'ORO

3.0700 g., Gold, 22 mm. **Ruler:** Antonio Maria II **Obv:** Crowned imperial eagle, orb on breast **Obv. Legend:** MONETA. NOVA. AVREA. **Rev:** Small shield of arms with displayed eagle, ornate helmet above **Rev. Legend:** SIT. NOMEN. DOMINI. BENEDI. **Note:** Previous KM# 49. Varesi 545.

Date	Mintage	VG	F	VF	XF	Unc
ND(1630-41) Rare	—	—	—	—	—	—

KM# 64 DUCATO D'ORO

3.0200 g., Gold, 20 mm. **Ruler:** Antonio Maria II **Obv:** Crowned shield of 4-fold arms with central shield of Tizzone **Obv. Legend:** ANT. MAR. TITI. COM. DEC. V. I. P. **Rev:** Crowned imperial eagle, shield of Austrian arms on breast **Rev. Legend:** VIRTVTE. CAESAREA. DVCE. **Note:** Previous KM# 37. Varesi 541.

Date	Mintage	VG	F	VF	XF	Unc
ND(1630-41)	—	1,350	2,200	5,000	7,700	—

KM# 1 DUCATO

3.3600 g., Gold, 22 mm. **Ruler:** Antonio Maria II **Obv:** Full-length armored figure of count, holdling sword over right shoulder, divides date **Obv. Legend:** DOM. ANT. MA. TIT. COM. DECI. **Rev:** Square tablet in ornamented frame with 5-line inscription **Rev. Inscription:** MO. NOV./AV. DO. AN./MAR. TIT./COM. DEC./PRO. IMP. **Note:** Previous KM# 50. Fr. #249. Varesi 538.

Date	Mintage	VG	F	VF	XF	Unc
1603 Rare	—	—	—	—	—	—

KM# 69 DUCATO

3.4200 g., Gold, 23 mm. **Ruler:** Antonio Maria II **Obv:** Crowned shield of 4-fold arms with central shield of Tizzone arms **Obv. Legend:** CONCORDIA. PAR. RES. CRESCV. **Rev:** Crowned imperial eagle in circle **Rev. Legend:** SVB. VMBRA. ALARVM. TVARVM. **Note:** Prev. KM# 38. Fr. #247. Varesi 546.

Date	Mintage	VG	F	VF	XF	Unc
ND(1630-41) Rare	—	—	—	—	—	—

KM# 70 DUCATO

3.2700 g., Gold, 21-22 mm. **Ruler:** Antonio Maria II **Obv:** Full-length armored figure of count turned slightly to right, 2 small crowned shields of arms at left and right **Obv. Legend:** ANT. MAR. TITI. COM. DEC. VI. **Rev:** Square tablet in ornamented frame with 5-line inscription **Rev. Inscription:** LVX. ET I/AM. IN TE/NEBRIS/POSITA/LVCET. **Note:** Fr. #250. Varesi 539.

Date	Mintage	VG	F	VF	XF	Unc
ND(1630-41) Rare	—	—	—	—	—	—

KM# 71 DUCATO

3.3100 g., Gold **Ruler:** Antonio Maria II **Obv:** Full-length armored figure turned slightly to right **Obv. Legend:** ANT. MAR. TITI. COM. CEC. VI. **Rev:** Square tablet in ornamented frame with 5-line inscription **Rev. Inscription:** LVX. ET I/AM. IN TE/NEBRIS/POSITA/LVCET. **Note:** Prev. KM# 51. Varesi 539/1.

Date	Mintage	VG	F	VF	XF	Unc
ND(1630-41)	—	1,000	1,900	3,750	5,500	—

KM# 78 DUCATO

Gold, 22-23 mm. **Ruler:** Carlo **Obv:** Full-length armored figure of count to right holding sword with point down **Obv. Legend:** VIRTVS. VNIT - A. - FORTIOR. EST. **Rev:** Square tablet in ornamented frame with 5-line inscription **Rev. Inscription:** LEOPOL./I. IMP. FI./FERD. CO./DEC. FEL./PERPET. **Note:** Weight varies: 3.01-3.16 grams. Prev. KM# 86. Fr. #254. Varesi 592.

Date	Mintage	VG	F	VF	XF	Unc
ND(1641-76) Rare	—	—	—	—	—	—

KM# 79 DUCATO

Gold, 22-23 mm. **Ruler:** Carlo **Obv:** Full-length armored figure of count to right holding sword with point down **Obv. Legend:** VIRTVS. VNIT - A. - FORTIOR. EST. **Rev:** Square tablet in ornamented frame with 5-line inscription **Rev. Inscription:** NON. TIM/EBO. MAL/A. QVIAT/V. DOM. M/ECVM. ES. **Note:** Weight varies: 3.01-3.16 grams. Prev. KM# 87. Fr. #255. Varesi 593-4.

Date	Mintage	VG	F	VF	XF	Unc
ND(1641-76)	—	1,000	2,000	3,500	5,500	—

KM# 41 DOPPIA

Gold, 25-27 mm. **Ruler:** Antonio Maria II **Obv:** High-collared armored bust to right **Obv. Legend:** ANT. MAR. TIT. COM. DEC. PRO. IMP. **Rev:** Crowned shield of 4-fold arms witih central shield of Tizzone arms **Rev. Legend:** SOLI. DEO. HONOR. ET. GLORIA. **Note:** Weight varies: 6.40-6.57 grams. Prev. KM# 39. Fr. #238. Varesi 531.

Date	Mintage	VG	F	VF	XF	Unc
ND(1618-30)	—	2,000	4,000	7,500	12,000	—

KM# 42 DOPPIA

Gold, 25-27 mm. **Ruler:** Antonio Maria II **Obv:** High-collared armored bust to right. **Obv. Legend:** ANT. MARIA. TIT. BLA. COM. **Rev:** Crowned shield of manifold arms in baroque frame, FLOR. AVR in exergue **Rev. Legend:** DECI. VIC. - IMP. PER. **Note:** Weight varies: 6.40-6.57 grams. Prev. KM# 40. Varesi 532.

Date	Mintage	VG	F	VF	XF	Unc
ND(1618-30) Rare	—	—	—	—	—	—

Note: Numismatica Ars Classica Auction 35, 12-06, VF realized approximately $11,995

KM# 43 DOPPIA

Gold, 25-27 mm. **Ruler:** Antonio Maria II **Obv:** Head to right **Obv. Legend:** ANT. MAR. TIT. BL. COM. DEC. VIC. IMP. P. **Rev:** Standing figure of St. Dorothea holding flower **Rev. Legend:** SANCTA. - DOROTHEA. **Note:** Weight varies: 6.40-6.57 grams. Prev. KM# 41. Fr. #243. Varesi 533.

Date	Mintage	VG	F	VF	XF	Unc
ND(1618-30)	—	2,250	4,250	8,500	13,800	—

KM# 72 DOPPIA
Gold, 25-27 mm. **Ruler:** Antonio Maria II **Obv:** High-collared bearded bust to right **Obv. Legend:** ANT. MAR. TIT. COM. DEC. PRO. IMP. **Rev:** Crowned shield of 4-fold arms with central shield of Tizzone arms **Rev. Legend:** SOLI. DEO. HONOR. ET. GLORIA. **Note:** Weight varies: 6.40-6.57 grams. Fr. #241. Varesi 531/1.

Date	Mintage	VG	F	VF	XF	Unc
ND(1630-41) Rare	—	—	—	—	—	—

KM# 44 2 DOPPIE
Gold, 28-31 mm. **Ruler:** Antonio Maria II **Obv:** High-collared armored bust to right **Obv. Legend:** ANT. MAR. TIT. COM. DEC. PRO. IMP. **Rev:** Crowned shield of 4-fold arms with central shield of Tizzone arms **Rev. Legend:** SACRIQVE. ROM. IMP. VICARIVS. PERP. **Note:** Weight varies: 13.00-13.05 grams. Prev. KM# 42. Fr. #237. Varesi 529.

Date	Mintage	VG	F	VF	XF	Unc
ND(1618-30)	—	2,500	4,500	8,500	16,000	—

KM# 45 2 DOPPIE
Gold, 28-31 mm. **Ruler:** Antonio Maria II **Obv:** Head to right **Obv. Legend:** ANT. MAR. TIT. BLA. COM. DEC. VIC. IMP. PE. **Rev:** Standing female figure resting right hand on column **Rev. Legend:** FORTITV. ILLUS. DEXT. EIVS. **Note:** Weight varies: 13.00-13.05 grams. Prev. KM# 44. Fr. #242. Varesi 530.

Date	Mintage	VG	F	VF	XF	Unc
ND(1618-30) Rare	—	—	—	—	—	—

KM# 73 2 DOPPIE
Gold, 28-31 mm. **Ruler:** Antonio Maria II **Obv:** High-collared bearded bust to right **Obv. Legend:** ANT. MAR. TIT. COMES. DEC. PRO. IMP. **Rev:** Crowned shield of 4-fold arms with central shield of Tizzone arms **Rev. Legend:** SACRIQVE. ROM. IMP. VICARIVS. PERP. **Note:** Weight varies: 13.00-13.05 grams. Prev. KM# 43. Fr. #240. Varesi 529/1.

Date	Mintage	VG	F	VF	XF	Unc
ND(1630-41) Rare	—	—	—	—	—	—

GAZZOLDO

Paolo, Matti, Ercole, and Francesco were counts of the Ippoliti family.

RULERS
Francesco, 1616-1632
Hannibal Degli Ippoliti, 1632-1666

COUNTY

STANDARD COINAGE

KM# 5 BOLOGNESE MARAIOLA
Billon **Subject:** Of the 4 Brothers **Obv:** Standing saint **Rev:** Bust of St. Gregory right **Note:** Weight varies: 1.64-2.10 grams.

Date	Mintage	VG	F	VF	XF	Unc
ND	—	245	500	975	1,950	—

KM# 6 BOLOGNESE MARAIOLA
Billon **Subject:** Of the 3 Brothers **Note:** Weight varies: 1.89-2.49 grams.

Date	Mintage	VG	F	VF	XF	Unc
ND	—	280	550	1,100	2,100	—

KM# 7 SESTINO
1.2600 g., Billon **Obv:** Head of Francisco left **Rev:** St. Nicolaus standing

Date	Mintage	VG	F	VF	XF	Unc
ND	—	175	350	775	1,700	—

KM# 11 1/2 TALLERO
Silver **Obv:** Bust of Hannibal left, date below **Rev:** Phoenix below rayed sunface **Note:** Weight varies: 12.85-15.33 grams.

Date	Mintage	VG	F	VF	XF	Unc
1663	—	750	1,350	3,000	5,300	—

KM# 10 2 DOPPIE
14.0000 g., 0.9860 Gold 0.4438 oz. AGW **Obv:** Armored bust of Hannibal left **Rev:** St. Hippolitus standing facing in inner circle

Date	Mintage	VG	F	VF	XF	Unc
1662	—	3,500	5,000	8,500	16,000	—
1663	—	3,500	5,000	8,500	16,000	—

GENOA

A seaport in Liguria, Genoa was a dominant republic and colonial power in the Middle Ages. In 1798 Napoleon remodeled it into the Ligurian Republic, and in 1805 it was incorporated in the Kingdom of Napoleon. Following a brief restoration of the republic, it was absorbed by the Kingdom of Sardinia in 1815.

RULER
Conrad II, 1554-1637

MINT MARKS

During the occupation by the French forces regular French coins, 1/2, 1, 2, 5, 20 and 40 Francs were struck between 1813 and 1814 with the mint mark C.L.

After Sardinia absorbed Genoa in 1815, regular Sardinian coins were struck until 1860 with a fouled anchor mint mark.

MINT OFFICIALS' INITIALS

Initials	Date	Name
HP	1607	Hieronimus Palvis
MC	1610	Michael Cavus
IZ	1615	Joseph Zinus
(IB) DN	1618	John Baptist Damian Novarius
GF	1619	Georgius de Franchis
(IB) SVS	1634	John Benedictus Seminus
IBN	1647	John Baptist Nascius
IAB	1652	Johannes Anthonius Buronus
AB	1661	Augustinus Boniventus
ISS	1668	Johannes Stephanus Spinola
GSS	1668	Giovanni Stefano Spinola
(GBT) IBT	1672	Iohn Baptista Turris
(GLM) ILM	1674	Johannes Lucas Maiolus
ITC	1687	Io. Thomas Caminata

MONETARY SYSTEM
12 Denari = 1 Soldo
20 Soldi = 10 Parpagliola =
5 Cavallotti = 1 Lira (Madonnina)

REPUBLIC

STANDARD COINAGE

KM# 9 MINUTO
Copper **Obv:** Castle **Rev:** Cross

Date	Mintage	Good	VG	F	VF	XF
ND(1576-1602) PP	—	8.00	18.00	37.50	75.00	—
ND(1582-1608) IV	—	8.00	18.00	37.50	75.00	—
ND(1607-09) HP	—	8.00	18.00	37.50	75.00	—
ND(1615-18) IZ	—	8.00	18.00	37.50	75.00	—
ND(1619-21) GF	—	8.00	18.00	37.50	75.00	—

KM# 77 MINUTO
Copper **Obv:** Bust of Madonna and child **Obv. Legend:** E R E **Rev:** Cross **Rev. Legend:** D G R G

Date	Mintage	Good	VG	F	VF	XF
ND(1638-1752)	—	10.00	19.00	42.00	85.00	—
1643	—	10.00	19.00	42.00	85.00	—
1671	—	10.00	19.00	42.00	85.00	—

KM# 141 3 DENARI
3.8000 g., Billon **Obv:** Oval shield **Rev:** Legend

Date	Mintage	Good	VG	F	VF	XF
1671 ISS	—	25.00	36.00	75.00	150	—

KM# 20 4 DENARI
Billon **Ruler:** Conrad II **Obv:** Castle in shield **Obv. Legend:** DVX GBV RP GENV **Rev:** Cross with date in angles **Rev. Legend:** CONRA II RO REX

Date	Mintage	Good	VG	F	VF	XF
1601 IV	—	6.00	12.00	30.00	70.00	—
1602 IV	—	6.00	12.00	30.00	70.00	—
1603 IV	—	6.00	12.00	30.00	70.00	—
1605 IV	—	6.00	12.00	30.00	70.00	—
1606 IV	—	6.00	12.00	30.00	70.00	—
1607 HP	—	6.00	12.00	30.00	70.00	—
1608	—	6.00	12.00	30.00	70.00	—
1608 IA	—	6.00	12.00	30.00	70.00	—
1609 HP	—	6.00	12.00	30.00	70.00	—
1610 MC	—	6.00	12.00	30.00	70.00	—
1611 MC	—	6.00	12.00	30.00	70.00	—
1612 MC	—	6.00	12.00	30.00	70.00	—
1613 MC	—	6.00	12.00	30.00	70.00	—
1615 IZ	—	6.00	12.00	30.00	70.00	—
1616 IZ	—	6.00	12.00	30.00	70.00	—
1617 IZ	—	6.00	12.00	30.00	70.00	—
1618	—	6.00	12.00	30.00	70.00	—
1619	—	6.00	12.00	30.00	70.00	—
1621	—	6.00	12.00	30.00	70.00	—
1625	—	6.00	12.00	30.00	70.00	—
1626	—	6.00	12.00	30.00	70.00	—

KM# 161 4 DENARI
Billon **Obv:** Bust of Madonna and child **Rev:** Cross

Date	Mintage	Good	VG	F	VF	XF
1700 OM	—	—	—	—	—	—

KM# 142 6 DENARI
4.5000 g., Copper **Obv:** Oval shield **Rev:** Legend

Date	Mintage	Good	VG	F	VF	XF
1671 SS	—	30.00	42.00	90.00	180	—

KM# 42.1 8 DENARI
Billon **Ruler:** Conrad II **Obv:** Castle **Obv. Legend:** DVX GVB REIP GENV **Rev:** Stars flank shield **Rev. Legend:** CONRA II RO REX **Note:** Weight varies: 0.70-0.90 grams.

Date	Mintage	Good	VG	F	VF	XF
1619	—	8.00	18.00	37.50	85.00	—
1625	—	8.00	18.00	37.50	85.00	—
1626	—	8.00	18.00	37.50	85.00	—
1627	—	8.00	18.00	37.50	85.00	—

KM# 42.2 8 DENARI
Billon **Rev:** Three stars surround shield **Note:** Weight varies: 0.70-0.90 grams.

Date	Mintage	Good	VG	F	VF	XF
1626	—	8.00	18.00	37.50	85.00	—
1627	—	8.00	18.00	37.50	85.00	—
1628	—	8.00	18.00	37.50	85.00	—
1629	—	8.00	18.00	37.50	85.00	—
1630	—	8.00	18.00	37.50	85.00	—
1631	—	8.00	18.00	37.50	85.00	—
1633	—	8.00	18.00	37.50	85.00	—

KM# 115 8 DENARI
Billon **Obv:** Three stars surround shield **Rev:** Bust of Madonna and child

Date	Mintage	Good	VG	F	VF	XF
1653	—	8.00	18.00	37.50	85.00	—
1654	—	8.00	18.00	37.50	85.00	—
1656	—	8.00	18.00	37.50	85.00	—
1699 OM	—	8.00	18.00	37.50	85.00	—
1700 OM	—	8.00	18.00	37.50	85.00	—

KM# 140 12 DENARI (Soldo)
9.2500 g., Copper **Obv:** Crowned shield **Obv. Legend:** DVX ET GVBERNATORES **Rev:** Date, denomination **Rev. Legend:** REIPVBLICE GENV

Date	Mintage	Good	VG	F	VF	XF
1670 ISS	—	36.00	60.00	115	225	—
1671 ISS	—	36.00	60.00	115	225	—

KM# 71 20 DENARI (Soldo)
2.9600 g., Billon **Ruler:** Conrad II **Obv:** Castle, date and 20 below **Obv. Legend:** DVX ET GVB REIP GEN **Rev:** Oval shield **Rev. Legend:** CONRADVS II RO RX

Date	Mintage	Good	VG	F	VF	XF
1631	—	14.00	25.00	55.00	100	—
1632	—	14.00	25.00	55.00	100	—
1633	—	14.00	25.00	55.00	100	—
1634	—	14.00	25.00	55.00	100	—
1635 IBS	—	14.00	25.00	55.00	100	—
1635	—	14.00	25.00	55.00	100	—

KM# 109 20 DENARI (Soldo)
2.9600 g., Billon **Obv:** Crowned oval shield **Obv. Legend:** DVX ET GVB REIP GEN **Rev:** Madonna and child, date and 20 below **Rev. Legend:** ET REGE EOS

Date	Mintage	Good	VG	F	VF	XF
1643	—	11.00	22.50	45.00	90.00	—
1644	—	11.00	22.50	45.00	90.00	—
1645	—	11.00	22.50	45.00	90.00	—

KM# 143 30 DENARI
Silver **Obv:** Oval shield **Rev. Legend:** DENARI TRENTA

Date	Mintage	VG	F	VF	XF	Unc
1671	—	42.00	65.00	130	265	—

KM# 22 SOLDINO
Billon **Obv:** Castle in arches **Obv. Legend:** DVX ET GBV RIED GENV **Rev:** Cross in arches **Rev. Legend:** CONRADVS II RO REX

Date	Mintage	Good	VG	F	VF	XF
1601 IV	—	18.00	30.00	60.00	105	—
1602 IV	—	18.00	30.00	60.00	105	—
1605 IV	—	18.00	30.00	60.00	105	—
1611 MC	—	18.00	30.00	60.00	105	—
1612 MC	—	18.00	30.00	60.00	105	—
1615 IZ	—	18.00	30.00	60.00	105	—
1616 IZ	—	18.00	30.00	60.00	105	—
1618 IZ	—	18.00	30.00	60.00	105	—

KM# 144 2-1/2 SOLIDI
0.5500 g., Silver **Obv:** Oval shield **Rev:** Legend

Date	Mintage	Good	VG	F	VF	XF
1671	—	48.00	70.00	135	280	—

KM# 88 5 SOLDI
Billon **Obv:** Crowned oval shield **Obv. Legend:** DVX ET GVB REIP GEN **Rev:** Bust of Madonna, V below **Rev. Legend:** ET REG EOS

Date	Mintage	Good	VG	F	VF	XF
1639 IBS	—	8.00	18.00	42.00	75.00	—
1641	—	8.00	18.00	42.00	75.00	—
1642 CS	—	8.00	18.00	42.00	75.00	—
1648 IBN	—	8.00	18.00	42.00	75.00	—

KM# 120 5 SOLDI
Billon **Obv:** Crowned shield **Rev:** Shield with LIBERT on band across **Rev. Legend:** IN AETERNUM VIVET

Date	Mintage	Good	VG	F	VF	XF
1663 AB	—	18.00	36.00	75.00	135	—

KM# 145 5 SOLDI
Billon **Rev:** St. John

Date	Mintage	Good	VG	F	VF	XF
1671	—	8.00	18.00	42.00	75.00	—
1672	—	8.00	18.00	42.00	75.00	—
1673	—	8.00	18.00	42.00	75.00	—
1674	—	8.00	18.00	42.00	75.00	—
1675	—	8.00	18.00	42.00	75.00	—

KM# 117 8 SOLDI
2.2000 g., Silver **Obv:** Cross with four stars **Rev:** Madonna and child, VIII below

Date	Mintage	VG	F	VF	XF	Unc
1653 IAB	—	12.00	24.00	49.50	90.00	—
1654 IAB	—	12.00	24.00	49.50	90.00	—
1655 IAB	—	12.00	24.00	49.50	90.00	—
1656 IAB	—	12.00	24.00	49.50	90.00	—

KM# 89 10 SOLDI (1/2 Lire)
Billon **Obv:** Crowned oval shield **Obv. Legend:** DVX ET GVB GVB REIP **Rev:** Bust of the Madonna, X below **Rev. Legend:** ET REGE EOS

Date	Mintage	Good	VG	F	VF	XF
1639 IBS	—	15.00	30.00	60.00	105	—
1640 IBS	—	15.00	30.00	60.00	105	—
1641 CS	—	15.00	30.00	60.00	105	—
1642 CS	—	15.00	30.00	60.00	105	—
1643 CS	—	15.00	30.00	60.00	105	—

Date	Mintage	Good	VG	F	VF	XF
1644 CS	—	15.00	30.00	60.00	105	—
1649 IBN	—	15.00	30.00	60.00	105	—

KM# 146 10 SOLDI (1/2 Lire)

Billon **Rev:** St. John

Date	Mintage	VG	F	VF	XF	Unc
1671	—	15.00	30.00	60.00	105	—
1672	—	15.00	30.00	60.00	105	—
1673	—	15.00	30.00	60.00	105	—
1674	—	15.00	30.00	60.00	105	—
1675	—	15.00	30.00	60.00	105	—
1679	—	15.00	30.00	60.00	105	—

KM# 103 20 SOLDI (Lira)

6.3000 g., Silver **Obv:** Crowned shield **Rev:** Madonna and child, 20 below

Date	Mintage	VG	F	VF	XF	Unc
1641 CS	—	27.50	55.00	115	240	—
1643 CS	—	27.50	55.00	115	240	—
1648 CS	—	27.50	55.00	115	240	—

KM# 147 20 SOLDI (Lira)

6.3000 g., Silver **Obv:** Crowned shield **Rev:** St. John, 20 below

Date	Mintage	VG	F	VF	XF	Unc
1671 ISS	—	24.00	48.00	105	225	—
1672	—	24.00	48.00	105	225	—
1673	—	24.00	48.00	105	225	—
1675	—	24.00	48.00	105	225	—
1679	—	24.00	48.00	105	225	—
1687	—	24.00	48.00	105	225	—

KM# 70 CAVALOTTO

Silver **Ruler:** Conrad II **Obv:** Castle in three arches **Obv. Legend:** DVX ET GVBER REIP GENV **Rev:** St. Bernard standing **Rev. Legend:** NON OBLIVISCAR TVI **Note:** Weight varies: 2.76-3.00 grams.

Date	Mintage	VG	F	VF	XF	Unc
1630	—	45.00	85.00	150	270	—

KM# 132 CAVALOTTO

2.8500 g., Billon **Obv:** Castle **Obv. Legend:** REIPVBLICAE GEN **Rev:** Shield **Rev. Legend:** DVX ET GVBERNATORES

Date	Mintage	VG	F	VF	XF	Unc
1669 ISS	—	37.50	70.00	130	250	—
1670 ISS	—	37.50	70.00	130	250	—

KM# 148 2 LIRE

10.0000 g., Silver **Obv:** Griffins support crowned shield **Rev:** St. John

Date	Mintage	VG	F	VF	XF	Unc
1671 ISS	—	50.00	75.00	150	280	—
1672 ISS	—	50.00	75.00	150	280	—
1675 ILM	—	50.00	75.00	150	280	—
1676 GLM	—	50.00	75.00	150	280	—
1677 GLM	—	50.00	75.00	150	280	—
1679 GLM	—	50.00	75.00	150	280	—
1684 PBM	—	50.00	75.00	150	280	—
1685 PBM	—	50.00	75.00	150	280	—
1687 ILM	—	50.00	75.00	150	280	—

KM# 150 2 LIRE

10.0000 g., Silver **Obv:** Griffins support crowned arms **Obv. Legend:** DVX ET GVBER REIPV GENVEN **Rev:** St. John **Rev. Legend:** NON SVRREXIT MAIOR

Date	Mintage	VG	F	VF	XF	Unc
1672 ISS	—	55.00	100	225	375	—
1673 GBT	—	55.00	100	225	375	—
1675 ILM	—	55.00	100	225	375	—
1676 GLM	—	55.00	100	225	375	—
1678 GLM	—	55.00	100	225	375	—
1679 GLM	—	55.00	100	225	375	—

KM# 121 REAL

Silver **Obv:** Palm fronds flank crowned shield with LIBERTAS in banner across **Obv. Legend:** DVX ET GVB REIP GENV **Rev:** St. George slaying dragon

Date	Mintage	VG	F	VF	XF	Unc
1666	—	600	1,150	2,100	3,600	—

KM# 122 2 REALI

Silver **Obv:** Crowned shield **Rev:** St. George slaying dragon

Date	Mintage	VG	F	VF	XF	Unc
1666	—	900	1,800	3,300	5,400	—

KM# 123 4 REALI

Silver **Obv:** Palm fronds flank cronwed shield with LIBERTAS in banner across **Obv. Legend:** DVX ET VB REIP GENV **Rev:** St. George slaying dragon **Note:** Weight varies: 12.30-12.50 grams.

Date	Mintage	VG	F	VF	XF	Unc
1666	—	1,500	3,000	5,400	9,000	—

KM# 124 8 REALI

Silver **Obv:** Palm fronds flank crowned shield with LIBERTAS in banner across **Obv. Legend:** DVX ET VB REIP GENV **Rev:** St. George slaying dragon

Date	Mintage	VG	F	VF	XF	Unc
1666 Rare	—	—	—	—	—	—

KM# 23 1/2 DUCATONE

15.8000 g., Silver **Obv:** Doge kneeling before Christ **Obv. Legend:** DVX ET GVB REIP GENVEN **Rev:** Griffins support crowned shield **Rev. Legend:** CONRADVS II RO REX

Date	Mintage	VG	F	VF	XF	Unc
1601 IV	—	1,800	3,350	5,400	9,000	—
1605 IV	—	1,800	3,350	5,400	9,000	—
1615 IZ	—	1,800	3,350	5,400	9,000	—

KM# 24 DUCATONE

32.2500 g., Silver **Obv:** Savior blessing kneeling Doge and attendants **Obv. Legend:** DVX ET GVB REIP GEN **Rev:** Crowned and supported city arms **Rev. Legend:** CONRADVS II RO REX **Note:** Dav. #3899.

Date	Mintage	VG	F	VF	XF	Unc
1601 IV	—	2,400	4,800	7,800	11,500	—
1607 HP	—	2,400	4,800	7,800	11,500	—

KM# 50 1/8 SCUDO

4.5000 g., Silver **Ruler:** Conrad II **Obv:** Stars flank castle, cross above **Obv. Legend:** DVX ET GVB REIP GEN **Rev:** Oval shield **Rev. Legend:** CONRADVS II RO REX

Date	Mintage	VG	F	VF	XF	Unc
1621 GF	—	37.50	70.00	125	250	—

KM# 54 1/8 SCUDO

4.5000 g., Silver **Rev:** Cross with stars in angles

Date	Mintage	VG	F	VF	XF	Unc
1622 GF	—	30.00	55.00	100	205	—
1623 GF	—	30.00	55.00	100	205	—
1624 GF	—	30.00	55.00	100	205	—
1625	—	30.00	55.00	100	205	—
1626	—	30.00	55.00	100	205	—
1627	—	30.00	55.00	100	205	—
1628	—	30.00	55.00	100	205	—
1630	—	30.00	55.00	100	205	—
1633	—	30.00	55.00	100	205	—

KM# 57 1/8 SCUDO

4.5000 g., Silver **Rev:** Cross with stars in angles **Rev. Legend:** IN HOC SALVS MUNDI

Date	Mintage	VG	F	VF	XF	Unc
1624	—	33.00	60.00	105	225	—

KM# 75 1/8 SCUDO (Stretto)

4.5000 g., Silver **Rev:** Cross with stars in angles **Rev. Legend:** IN HOC SALVS MUNDI

Date	Mintage	VG	F	VF	XF	Unc
1635	—	33.00	60.00	105	225	—

KM# 104 1/8 SCUDO (Stretto)

4.5000 g., Silver **Obv:** Cross **Rev:** Madonna and child

Date	Mintage	VG	F	VF	XF	Unc
1641 IBS	—	21.00	42.00	85.00	150	—
1650 IBN	—	21.00	42.00	85.00	150	—
1653 IAB	—	21.00	42.00	85.00	150	—
1654 IAB	—	21.00	42.00	85.00	150	—
1655 IAB	—	21.00	42.00	85.00	150	—
1658 IBN	—	21.00	42.00	85.00	150	—
1661 AB	—	21.00	42.00	85.00	150	—
1662 AB	—	21.00	42.00	85.00	150	—
1664 AB	—	21.00	42.00	85.00	150	—
1665 AB	—	21.00	42.00	85.00	150	—
1668 ISS	—	21.00	42.00	85.00	150	—
1670 ISS	—	21.00	42.00	85.00	150	—

KM# 119 1/8 SCUDO (Largo)

4.5000 g., Silver **Obv:** Cross **Rev:** Madonna and child

Date	Mintage	VG	F	VF	XF	Unc
1661 AB	—	22.50	45.00	90.00	165	—
1664 AB	—	22.50	45.00	90.00	165	—
1668 AB	—	22.50	45.00	90.00	165	—
1693 ITC	—	22.50	45.00	90.00	165	—

KM# 29 1/4 SCUDO

Silver **Ruler:** Conrad II **Obv:** Stars flank crowned castle, date below **Rev:** Cross with stars in angles **Note:** Weight varies: 8.70-9.50 grams.

Date	Mintage	VG	F	VF	XF	Unc
1604 IV	—	65.00	130	255	425	—
1610 MC	—	65.00	130	255	425	—
1611 MC	—	65.00	130	255	425	—
1612 MC	—	65.00	130	255	425	—
1613 MC	—	65.00	130	255	425	—
1614 MC	—	65.00	130	255	425	—
1615 IZ	—	65.00	130	255	425	—
1616 IZ	—	65.00	130	255	425	—
1617 IZ	—	65.00	130	255	425	—
1618 DN	—	65.00	130	255	425	—
1622 GF	—	65.00	130	255	425	—
1623 GF	—	65.00	130	255	425	—
1624 GF	—	65.00	130	255	425	—
1625	—	65.00	130	255	425	—
1626	—	65.00	130	255	425	—
1627	—	65.00	130	255	425	—
1628	—	65.00	130	255	425	—
1630	—	65.00	130	255	425	—
1633	—	65.00	130	255	425	—
1634 IBS	—	65.00	130	255	425	—
1635 IBS	—	65.00	130	255	425	—
1636	—	65.00	130	255	425	—

KM# 80 1/4 SCUDO (Stretto)

Silver **Obv:** Cross **Rev:** Madonna and child **Note:** Weight varies: 8.70-9.50 grams.

Date	Mintage	VG	F	VF	XF	Unc
1638 IBS	—	60.00	115	245	425	—
1639 IBS	—	60.00	115	245	425	—
1640 IBS	—	60.00	115	245	425	—
1648 IBN	—	60.00	115	245	425	—
1649 IBN	—	60.00	115	245	425	—
1651 IBN	—	60.00	115	245	425	—
1653 IAB	—	60.00	115	245	425	—
1654 IAB	—	60.00	115	245	425	—
1655 IAB	—	60.00	115	245	425	—
1658 IBN	—	60.00	115	245	425	—
1661 AB	—	60.00	115	245	425	—
1663 AB	—	60.00	115	245	425	—
1664 AB	—	60.00	115	245	425	—
1665 AB	—	60.00	115	245	425	—
1666 AB	—	60.00	115	245	425	—
1667 AB	—	60.00	115	245	425	—
1668 AB	—	60.00	115	245	425	—
1668 ISS	—	60.00	115	245	425	—
1670 ISS	—	60.00	115	245	425	—
1672 IBT	—	60.00	115	245	425	—
1673 IBT	—	60.00	115	245	425	—
1676 ILM	—	60.00	115	245	425	—
1677 ILM	—	60.00	115	245	425	—
1680 SM	—	60.00	115	245	425	—
1682 SM	—	60.00	115	245	425	—
1684 SM	—	60.00	115	245	425	—
1685 ILM	—	60.00	115	245	425	—
1687 GLM	—	60.00	115	245	425	—
1689 ILM	—	100	195	425	650	—
1691 ITC	—	60.00	115	245	425	—
1692 ITC	—	60.00	115	245	425	—
1694 ITC	—	60.00	115	245	425	—
1698 ITC	—	60.00	115	245	425	—
1699 IBM	—	60.00	115	245	425	—

KM# 108 1/4 SCUDO (Largo)

Silver **Obv:** Cross **Rev:** Madonna and child **Note:** Weight varies: 8.70-9.50 grams.

Date	Mintage	VG	F	VF	XF	Unc
1642 CS	—	70.00	145	270	475	—
1650 IBN	—	70.00	145	270	475	—
1651 IBN	—	70.00	145	270	475	—
1652 IAB	—	70.00	145	270	475	—
1653 IAB	—	70.00	145	270	475	—
1654 IAB	—	70.00	145	270	475	—
1661 AB	—	70.00	145	270	475	—
1664 AB	—	70.00	145	270	475	—
1665 AB	—	70.00	145	270	475	—
1666 AB	—	70.00	145	270	475	—
1670 ISS	—	70.00	145	270	475	—
1673 IBT	—	70.00	145	270	475	—
1680 SM	—	70.00	145	270	475	—
1682 SM	—	70.00	145	270	475	—
1691 ITC	—	70.00	145	270	475	—
1692 ITC	—	70.00	145	270	475	—
1693 ITC	—	70.00	145	270	475	—

KM# 26 1/2 SCUDO

Silver **Ruler:** Conrad II **Obv:** Stars flank castle, II below **Obv. Legend:** DVX ET GVB REIP GENV **Rev:** Cross with stars in angles **Rev. Legend:** CONRADVS II **Note:** Weight varies: 18.40-18.60 grams.

Date	Mintage	VG	F	VF	XF	Unc
1603 IV	—	80.00	155	325	575	—
1604 IV	—	80.00	155	325	575	—
1607 HP	—	80.00	155	325	575	—
1608 HP	—	80.00	155	325	575	—
1609 HP	—	80.00	155	325	575	—
1610 MC	—	80.00	155	325	575	—
1611 MC	—	80.00	155	325	575	—
1613 MC	—	80.00	155	325	575	—
1614 MC	—	80.00	155	325	575	—
1615 IZ	—	80.00	155	325	575	—
1618 DN	—	80.00	155	325	575	—
1622 GF	—	80.00	155	325	575	—
1623 GF	—	80.00	155	325	575	—
1624 GF	—	80.00	155	325	575	—
1625	—	80.00	155	325	575	—
1626	—	80.00	155	325	575	—
1627	—	80.00	155	325	575	—
1628	—	80.00	155	325	575	—
1629	—	80.00	155	325	575	—
1630	—	80.00	155	325	575	—
1633	—	80.00	155	325	575	—
1634 IBS	—	80.00	155	325	575	—
1635 IBS	—	80.00	155	325	575	—
1636	—	80.00	155	325	575	—

KM# 81.1 1/2 SCUDO (Stretto)

Silver **Obv:** Cross **Rev:** Madonna and child **Note:** Weight varies: 18.4-18.6 grams.

Date	Mintage	VG	F	VF	XF	Unc
1638 IBS	—	55.00	110	200	385	—
1639 IBS	—	55.00	110	200	385	—
1642 CS	—	55.00	110	200	385	—
1643 CS	—	55.00	110	200	385	—
1646 CS	—	55.00	110	200	385	—
1649 IBN	—	55.00	110	200	385	—
1651 IBN	—	55.00	110	200	385	—
1653 IAB	—	55.00	110	200	385	—
1654 IAB	—	55.00	110	200	385	—
1656 IAB	—	55.00	110	200	385	—
1661 AB	—	55.00	110	200	385	—
1664 AB	—	55.00	110	200	385	—
1665 AB	—	55.00	110	200	385	—
1666 AB	—	55.00	110	200	385	—

Date	Mintage	VG	F	VF	XF	Unc
1667 AB	—	55.00	110	200	385	—
1668 AB	—	55.00	110	200	385	—
1668 ISS	—	55.00	110	200	385	—
1670 ISS	—	55.00	110	200	385	—
1671 ISS	—	55.00	110	200	385	—
1672 IBT	—	55.00	110	200	385	—
1672 ISS	—	55.00	110	200	385	—
1673 IBT	—	55.00	110	200	385	—
1674 ILM	—	55.00	110	200	385	—
1675 ILM	—	55.00	110	200	385	—
1676 ILM	—	55.00	110	200	385	—
1677 ILM	—	55.00	110	200	385	—
1679 ILM	—	55.00	110	200	385	—
1679 SM	—	55.00	110	200	385	—
1680 SM	—	55.00	110	200	385	—
1681 SM	—	55.00	110	200	385	—
1682 SM	—	55.00	110	200	385	—
1683 SM	—	55.00	110	200	385	—
1685 ILM	—	55.00	110	200	385	—
1686 ILM	—	55.00	110	200	385	—
1687 ILM	—	55.00	110	200	385	—
1689 ILM	—	55.00	110	200	385	—
1690 ILM	—	55.00	110	200	385	—
1691 ITC	—	55.00	110	200	385	—
1692 ITC	—	55.00	110	200	385	—
1693 ITC	—	55.00	110	200	385	—
1694 ITC	—	55.00	110	200	385	—
1695 ITC	—	55.00	110	200	385	—
1696 ITC	—	55.00	110	200	385	—
1697 ITC	—	55.00	110	200	385	—
1698 IBM	—	55.00	110	200	385	—
1699 IBM	—	55.00	110	200	385	—
1700 IBM	—	55.00	110	200	385	—

KM# 81.2 1/2 SCUDO (Largo)

Silver **Note:** Weight varies: 18.4-18.6 grams.

Date	Mintage	VG	F	VF	XF	Unc
1642 CS	—	60.00	120	220	400	—
1648 IBN	—	60.00	120	220	400	—
1649 IBN	—	60.00	120	220	400	—
1650 IBN	—	60.00	120	220	400	—
1651 IBN	—	60.00	120	220	400	—
1652 IAB	—	60.00	120	220	400	—
1653 IAB	—	60.00	120	220	400	—
1654 IAB	—	60.00	120	220	400	—
1655 IAB	—	60.00	120	220	400	—
1662 AB	—	60.00	120	220	400	—
1664 AB	—	60.00	120	220	400	—
1665 AB	—	60.00	120	220	400	—
1666 AB	—	60.00	120	220	400	—
1668 AB	—	60.00	120	220	400	—
1670 ISS	—	60.00	120	220	400	—
1671 ISS	—	60.00	120	220	400	—
1672 IBT	—	60.00	120	220	400	—
1673 IBT	—	60.00	120	220	400	—
1679 SM	—	60.00	120	220	400	—
1680 SM	—	60.00	120	220	400	—
1682 SM	—	60.00	120	220	400	—
1683 SM	—	60.00	120	220	400	—
1691 ITC	—	60.00	120	220	400	—
1692 ITC	—	60.00	120	220	400	—
1693 ITC	—	60.00	120	220	400	—
1694 ITC	—	60.00	120	220	400	—
1695 ITC	—	60.00	120	220	400	—
1698 IBM	—	60.00	120	220	400	—
1699 IBM	—	60.00	120	220	400	—

KM# 25 SCUDO (Stretto)

Silver **Obv:** Crowned porta, crosses at sides, date below **Rev:** Cross with stars in angles **Note:** Weight varies: 35.0-38.0 grams. Dav. #3900.

Date	Mintage	VG	F	VF	XF	Unc
1602 IV	—	85.00	175	325	650	—
1603 IV	—	85.00	175	325	650	—
1604 IV	—	85.00	175	325	650	—
1607 HP	—	85.00	175	325	650	—
1608 HP	—	85.00	175	325	650	—
1609 HP	—	85.00	175	325	650	—
1610 MC	—	85.00	175	325	650	—
1611 MC	—	85.00	175	325	650	—
1612 MC	—	85.00	175	325	650	—
1613 MC	—	85.00	175	325	650	—
1614 MC	—	85.00	175	325	650	—
1615 IZ	—	85.00	175	325	650	—
1616 IZ	—	85.00	175	325	650	—
1618 DN	—	85.00	175	325	650	—
1622 GF	—	85.00	175	325	650	—
1623 GF	—	85.00	175	325	650	—
1624 GF	—	85.00	175	325	650	—
1625	—	85.00	175	325	650	—
1626	—	85.00	175	325	650	—
1627	—	85.00	175	325	650	—
1628	—	85.00	175	325	650	—
1629	—	85.00	175	325	650	—
1630	—	85.00	175	325	650	—
1631	—	85.00	175	325	650	—
1632	—	85.00	175	325	650	—
1633	—	85.00	175	325	650	—
1634 IBS	—	85.00	175	325	650	—
1635 IBS	—	85.00	175	325	650	—
1636 IBS	—	85.00	175	325	650	—
1637 IBS	—	85.00	175	325	650	—

KM# 56 SCUDO (Stretto)

Silver **Ruler:** Conrad II **Obv:** Stars flank crowned castle **Obv. Legend:** DVX ET GVB REIP GEN **Rev:** Cross with stars in angles **Rev. Legend:** IN HOC SALVS MUNDI **Note:** Weight varies: 35.0-38.0 grams.

Date	Mintage	VG	F	VF	XF	Unc
1624	—	90.00	170	350	700	—

KM# 79 SCUDO (Stretto)

Silver **Obv:** Cross with four stars in angles **Rev:** Virgin and child on cloud **Note:** Dav. #3901. Illustration reduced.

Date	Mintage	VG	F	VF	XF	Unc
1637 IBS	—	75.00	140	275	600	—
1638 IBS	—	75.00	140	275	600	—
1639 IBS	—	75.00	140	275	600	—
1640 IBS	—	75.00	140	275	600	—
1641 IBS	—	75.00	140	275	600	—
1642 CS	—	75.00	140	275	600	—
1644 CS	—	75.00	140	275	600	—
1646 CS	—	75.00	140	275	600	—
1647 IBN	—	75.00	140	275	600	—
1648 IBN	—	75.00	140	275	600	—
1649 IBN	—	75.00	140	275	600	—
1650 IBN	—	75.00	140	275	600	—
1651 IBN	—	75.00	140	275	600	—
1652 IAB	—	75.00	140	275	600	—
1653 IAB	—	75.00	140	275	600	—
1654 IAB	—	75.00	140	275	600	—
1655 IAB	—	75.00	140	275	600	—
1656 IAB	—	75.00	140	275	600	—
1661 AB	—	75.00	140	275	600	—
1662 AB	—	75.00	140	275	600	—
1664 AB	—	75.00	140	275	600	—
1665 AB	—	75.00	140	275	600	—
1666 AB	—	75.00	140	275	600	—
1667 AB	—	75.00	140	275	600	—
1668 AB	—	75.00	140	275	600	—
1668 ISS	—	75.00	140	275	600	—
1668 GSS	—	75.00	140	275	600	—
1669 ISS	—	75.00	140	275	600	—
1670 ISS	—	75.00	14.00	275	600	—
1671 ISS	—	75.00	140	275	600	—
1672 ISS	—	75.00	140	275	600	—
1672 IBT	—	75.00	140	275	600	—
1673 IBT	—	75.00	140	275	600	—
1674 ILM	—	75.00	140	275	600	—
1675 ILM	—	75.00	140	275	600	—
1676 ILM	—	75.00	140	275	600	—
1679 ILM	—	75.00	140	275	600	—
1679 SM	—	75.00	140	275	600	—

Note: Ira & Larry Goldberg Coins & Collectibles Auction 46 - The Millennia Collection, 5-08, MS-64 realized $7,250

Date	Mintage	VG	F	VF	XF	Unc
1680 SM	—	75.00	140	275	600	—
1681 SM	—	75.00	140	275	600	—
1682 SM	—	75.00	140	275	600	—
1683 PBM	—	75.00	140	275	600	—
1683 SM	—	75.00	140	275	600	—
1684 SM	—	75.00	140	275	600	—
1684 PBM	—	75.00	140	275	600	—
1685 ILM	—	65.00	140	275	600	—
1687 ILM	—	75.00	140	275	600	—
1688 ILM	—	75.00	140	275	600	—
1689 ILM	—	75.00	140	275	600	—

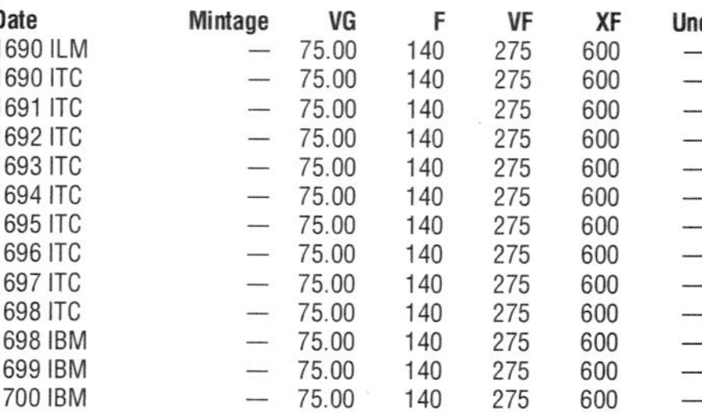

Date	Mintage	VG	F	VF	XF	Unc
1690 ILM	—	75.00	140	275	600	—
1690 ITC	—	75.00	140	275	600	—
1691 ITC	—	75.00	140	275	600	—
1692 ITC	—	75.00	140	275	600	—
1693 ITC	—	75.00	140	275	600	—
1694 ITC	—	75.00	140	275	600	—
1695 ITC	—	75.00	140	275	600	—
1696 ITC	—	75.00	140	275	600	—
1697 ITC	—	75.00	140	275	600	—
1698 ITC	—	75.00	140	275	600	—
1698 IBM	—	75.00	140	275	600	—
1699 IBM	—	75.00	140	275	600	—
1700 IBM	—	75.00	140	275	600	—

KM# 113 SCUDO (Largo)

38.0000 g., Silver **Obv:** Ornate cross with cherub heads and wings in angles **Obv. Legend:** GVBERNATORES * REIP * GENV + DVX * ET * **Rev:** Madonna and child on cloud, two cherubs above **Rev. Legend:** * ET * REGE *.... **Note:** Dav. #LS555. **Note:** Illustration reduced.

Date	Mintage	VG	F	VF	XF	Unc
1649 IBN	—	550	1,150	2,250	4,500	—
1650 IBN	—	550	1,150	2,250	4,500	—
1652 IAB	—	550	1,150	2,250	4,500	—
1653 IAB	—	550	1,150	2,250	4,500	—
1656 IAB	—	550	1,150	2,250	4,500	—
1664 AB	—	550	1,150	2,250	4,500	—
1666 AB	—	550	1,150	2,250	4,500	—
1670 ISS	—	550	1,150	2,250	4,500	—
1676 ILM	—	550	1,150	2,250	4,500	—
1680 SM	—	550	1,150	2,250	4,500	—
1681 SM	—	550	1,150	2,250	4,500	—
1682 SM	—	550	1,150	2,250	4,500	—
1683 SM	—	550	1,150	2,250	4,500	—
1684 PBM	—	550	1,150	2,250	4,500	—
1689 GLM	—	550	1,150	2,250	4,500	—
1691 ITC	—	550	1,150	2,250	4,500	—
1692 ITC	—	550	1,150	2,250	4,500	—
1693 ITC	—	550	1,150	2,250	4,500	—
1694 ITC	—	550	1,150	2,250	4,500	—
1698 IBM	—	550	1,150	2,250	4,500	—
1699 IBM	—	550	1,150	2,250	4,500	—
1700 IBM	—	550	1,150	2,250	4,500	—

KM# 74 1-1/2 SCUDI

47.0000 g., Silver **Note:** Similar to 2 Scudos, Dav. #1364. Dav. #LS554.

Date	Mintage	VG	F	VF	XF	Unc
1634 IBS	—	650	1,250	2,500	5,000	—
1641	—	650	1,250	2,500	5,000	—

KM# 31 2 SCUDI

76.0000 g., Silver **Obv:** Ring above cipher supported by two griffins, cherub winged head below **Rev:** Cross with winged cherub heads in angles **Note:** Dav. #LS542.

Date	Mintage	VG	F	VF	XF	Unc
1607 HP Rare	—	—	—	—	—	—
1608 HP Rare	—	—	—	—	—	—
1610 MC Rare	—	—	—	—	—	—
1611 MC Rare	—	—	—	—	—	—
1612 MC Rare	—	—	—	—	—	—
1613 MC Rare	—	—	—	—	—	—
1614 MC Rare	—	—	—	—	—	—

KM# 40 2 SCUDI

76.0000 g., Silver **Obv:** Cross above crown breaks legend **Note:** Dav. #LS545. Illustration reduced.

Date	Mintage	VG	F	VF	XF	Unc
1615 IZ Rare	—	—	—	—	—	—
1623 GF Rare	—	—	—	—	—	—
1625 Rare	—	—	—	—	—	—
1626 Rare	—	—	—	—	—	—

KM# 59 2 SCUDI

76.0000 g., Silver **Obv:** Crown breaks legend, griffins with spread wings **Note:** Dav. #LS547. Illustration reduced.

Date	Mintage	VG	F	VF	XF	Unc
1627	—	1,150	2,200	3,400	5,300	—
1628	—	1,150	2,200	3,400	5,300	—
1629	—	1,150	2,200	3,400	5,300	—
1630	—	1,150	2,200	3,400	5,300	—
1631	—	1,150	2,200	3,400	5,300	—
1633	—	1,150	2,200	3,400	5,300	—
1634 IBS	—	1,150	2,200	3,400	5,300	—
1635 IBS	—	1,150	2,200	3,400	5,300	—
1636 IBS	—	1,150	2,200	3,400	5,300	—
1637 IBS	—	1,150	2,200	3,400	5,300	—

KM# 82 2 SCUDI

76.0000 g., Silver **Obv:** Ornate cross with cherub heads and wings in angles **Rev:** Madonna and child on cloud, two cherubs above **Note:** Dav. #LS553. Illustration reduced.

Date	Mintage	VG	F	VF	XF	Unc
1638 IBS	—	500	800	1,500	2,500	—
1640 CS	—	500	800	1,500	2,500	—
1642 CS	—	500	800	1,500	2,500	—
1645 IBS	—	500	800	1,500	2,500	—
1649 IBN	—	500	800	1,500	2,500	—
1650 IBN	—	500	800	1,500	2,500	—
1652 IAB	—	500	800	1,500	2,500	—
1653 IAB	—	500	800	1,500	2,500	—
1664 AB	—	500	800	1,500	2,500	—
1666 AB	—	500	800	1,500	2,500	—
1670 ISS	—	500	800	1,500	2,500	—
1676 ILM	—	500	800	1,500	2,500	—
1680 SM	—	500	800	1,500	2,500	—
1681 SM	—	500	800	1,500	2,500	—
1682 SM	—	500	800	1,500	2,500	—
1684 PBM	—	2,250	4,000	6,500	—	—
1685 GLM	—	500	800	1,500	2,500	—
1687 GLM	—	500	800	1,500	2,500	—
1687 GLM	—	500	800	1,500	2,500	—
1689 GLM	—	500	800	1,500	2,500	—
1691 ITC	—	500	800	1,500	2,500	—
1692 ITC	—	500	800	1,500	2,500	—
1693 ITC	—	500	800	1,500	2,500	—
1694 ITC	—	500	800	1,500	2,500	—
1695 ITC	—	500	800	1,500	2,500	—
1697 ITC	—	500	800	1,500	2,500	—
1698 ITC	—	500	800	1,500	2,500	—
1698 IBM	—	500	800	1,500	2,500	—
1699 IBM	—	500	800	1,500	2,500	—
1700 IBM	—	500	800	1,500	2,500	—

KM# 83 3 SCUDI

114.0000 g., Silver **Note:** Similar to 2 Scudi, Dav. #1364. Dav. #1363, #LS552.

Date	Mintage	VG	F	VF	XF	Unc
1638 IBS	—	975	1,900	3,000	4,900	—
1652 IAB	—	975	1,900	3,000	4,900	—
1666 AB	—	975	1,900	3,000	4,900	—
1670 ISS	—	975	1,900	3,000	4,900	—
1680 SM	—	975	1,900	3,000	4,900	—
1682 SM	—	975	1,900	3,000	4,900	—
1684 PBM	—	975	1,900	3,000	4,900	—
1692 ITC	—	975	1,900	3,000	4,900	—
1693 ITC	—	975	1,900	3,000	4,900	—

KM# 58 4 SCUDI

Silver **Note:** Similar to 2 Scudi, Dav. #LS545. Dav. #LS544.

Date	Mintage	VG	F	VF	XF	Unc
1625 Rare	—	—	—	—	—	—

KM# 60 4 SCUDI

Silver **Note:** Similar to 2 Scudi, Dav. #LS547. Dav. #LS546.

Date	Mintage	VG	F	VF	XF	Unc
1628 Rare	—	—	—	—	—	—
1632 Rare	—	—	—	—	—	—
1633 Rare	—	—	—	—	—	—
1634 IBS Rare	—	—	—	—	—	—
1635 IBS Rare	—	—	—	—	—	—
1636 IBS Rare	—	—	—	—	—	—
1637 IBS Rare	—	—	—	—	—	—

KM# 84 4 SCUDI

152.0000 g., Silver **Note:** Similar to 2 Scudi, Dav. #1364. Dav. #1362, #LS551. Illustration reduced.

Date	Mintage	VG	F	VF	XF	Unc
1638 IBS	—	1,500	3,000	5,300	9,000	—
1649 IBN	—	1,500	3,000	5,300	9,000	—
1652 IAB	—	1,500	3,000	5,300	9,000	—
1664 AB	—	1,500	3,000	5,300	9,000	—
1670 ISS	—	1,500	3,000	5,300	9,000	—
1680 SM	—	1,500	3,000	5,300	9,000	—
1681 SM	—	1,500	3,000	5,300	9,000	—
1682 SM	—	1,500	3,000	5,300	9,000	—
1684 PBM	—	1,500	3,000	5,300	9,000	—
1685 GLM	—	1,500	3,000	5,300	9,000	—
1689 GLM	—	1,500	3,000	5,300	9,000	—
1692 ITC	—	1,500	3,000	5,300	9,000	—
1694 ITC	—	1,500	3,000	5,300	9,000	—
1697 ITC	—	1,500	3,000	5,300	9,000	—

KM# 157 5 SCUDI

190.0000 g., Silver **Note:** Similar to 2 Scudi, Dav. #1360. Dav. #LS550.

Date	Mintage	VG	F	VF	XF	Unc
1693 ITC Rare	—	—	—	—	—	—

KM# 158 6 SCUDI

230.0000 g., Silver **Note:** Similar to 2 Scudi, Dav. #1364. Dav. #1361, #LS549.

Date	Mintage	VG	F	VF	XF	Unc
1695 ITC Rare	—	—	—	—	—	—
1697 ITC Rare	—	—	—	—	—	—
1700 IBM Rare	—	—	—	—	—	—

KM# 51 1/8 DOPPIA

0.8750 g., 0.9860 Gold 0.0277 oz. AGW **Obv:** Symbolic castle, date below **Rev:** Ornate cross

Date	Mintage	VG	F	VF	XF	Unc
1621 GF	—	400	700	1,400	2,600	—
1623 GF	—	400	700	1,400	2,600	—
1624 GF	—	400	700	1,400	2,600	—

KM# 105 1/8 DOPPIA

0.8750 g., 0.9860 Gold 0.0277 oz. AGW **Obv:** Madonna and child on cloud in stars, date in legend

Date	Mintage	VG	F	VF	XF	Unc
1641	—	400	725	1,100	2,150	—

KM# 53 1/4 DOPPIA

1.7500 g., 0.9860 Gold 0.0555 oz. AGW **Obv:** Symbolic castle, date below in inner circle **Rev:** Ornate cross

Date	Mintage	VG	F	VF	XF	Unc
1621 GF	—	500	1,000	2,200	3,250	—
1623 GF	—	500	1,000	2,200	3,250	—
1629	—	500	1,000	2,200	3,250	—
1636	—	500	1,000	2,200	3,250	—

KM# 106 1/4 DOPPIA

1.7500 g., 0.9860 Gold 0.0555 oz. AGW **Obv:** Madonna and child on cloud in stars, date in legend **Rev:** Ornate cross

Date	Mintage	VG	F	VF	XF	Unc
1641	—	325	650	1,200	2,000	—

KM# 30 1/2 DOPPIA

3.5000 g., 0.9860 Gold 0.1109 oz. AGW **Ruler:** Conrad II **Obv:** Symbolic castle, date below in inner circle **Rev:** Ornate cross in inner circle

Date	Mintage	VG	F	VF	XF	Unc
1604 IV	—	375	700	1,250	2,250	—
1605 IV	—	375	700	1,250	2,250	—
1613 MC	—	375	700	1,250	2,250	—
1617 IZ	—	375	700	1,250	2,250	—
1618 DN	—	375	700	1,250	2,250	—
1619 DN	—	375	700	1,250	2,250	—
1620 GF	—	375	700	1,250	2,250	—
1623 GF	—	375	700	1,250	2,250	—
1624 GF	—	375	700	1,250	2,250	—
1625	—	375	700	1,250	2,250	—
1626	—	375	700	1,250	2,250	—
1627	—	375	700	1,250	2,250	—
1632	—	375	700	1,250	2,250	—
1637	—	375	700	1,250	2,250	—

KM# 90 1/2 DOPPIA

3.5000 g., 0.9860 Gold 0.1109 oz. AGW **Obv:** Madonna and child on cloud in stars, date in legend **Rev:** Ornate cross in inner circle

Date	Mintage	VG	F	VF	XF	Unc
1639 IBS	—	425	600	900	1,350	—
1640 IBS	—	425	600	900	1,350	—
1641 IBS	—	425	600	900	1,350	—
1648 IBS	—	425	600	900	1,350	—
1652 IAB	—	425	600	900	1,350	—
1655 IAB	—	425	600	900	1,350	—
1656 IAB	—	425	600	900	1,350	—
1658 IBN	—	425	600	900	1,350	—
1664 AB	—	425	600	900	1,350	—
1675 ILM	—	425	600	900	1,350	—
1690 GLM	—	425	600	900	1,350	—
1691 ITC	—	425	600	900	1,350	—
1692 ITC	—	425	600	900	1,350	—
1697 ITC	—	425	600	900	1,350	—

KM# 14.1 DOPPIA (2 Scudi)

7.0000 g., 0.9860 Gold 0.2219 oz. AGW **Obv:** Castle **Obv. Legend:** DVX ET GVB REIP GENV **Rev:** Cross **Rev. Legend:** CONRADVS II RO REX

Date	Mintage	VG	F	VF	XF	Unc
1601 IV	—	400	750	1,350	2,500	—
1602 IV	—	400	750	1,350	2,500	—
1602 PP	—	400	750	1,350	2,500	—
1603 IV	—	400	750	1,350	2,500	—
1604 IV	—	400	750	1,350	2,500	—
1607 HP	—	400	750	1,350	2,500	—
1609 HP	—	400	750	1,350	2,500	—
1613 MC	—	400	750	1,350	2,500	—
1616 IZ	—	400	750	1,350	2,500	—
1617 IZ	—	400	750	1,350	2,500	—
1619 DN	—	400	750	1,350	2,500	—
1621 GF	—	400	750	1,350	2,500	—
1624 GF	—	400	750	1,350	2,500	—
1625	—	400	750	1,350	2,500	—
1626	—	400	750	1,350	2,500	—
1627	—	400	750	1,350	2,500	—
1628	—	400	750	1,350	2,500	—
1629	—	400	750	1,350	2,500	—
1633	—	400	750	1,350	2,500	—
1637	—	400	750	1,350	2,500	—

KM# 14.2 DOPPIA (2 Scudi)

7.0000 g., 0.9860 Gold 0.2219 oz. AGW **Rev:** Ornate cross **Rev. Legend:** IN HOC SALVS MVNDI

Date	Mintage	VG	F	VF	XF	Unc
1624	—	425	800	1,500	2,750	—

KM# 99 DOPPIA (2 Scudi)

7.0000 g., 0.9860 Gold 0.2219 oz. AGW **Obv:** Madonna and child on cloud

Date	Mintage	VG	F	VF	XF	Unc
1640 IBS	—	600	1,200	2,250	4,250	—
1641 IBS	—	600	1,200	2,250	4,250	—
1653 IAB	—	600	1,200	2,250	4,250	—
1654 IAB	—	600	1,200	2,250	4,250	—
1656 IAB	—	600	1,200	2,250	4,250	—
1658 IBN	—	600	1,200	2,250	4,250	—
1670 ISS	—	600	1,200	2,250	4,250	—
1676 ILM	—	600	1,200	2,250	4,250	—
1694 ITC	—	600	1,200	2,250	4,250	—

KM# 28 2 DOPPIE

14.0000 g., 0.9860 Gold 0.4438 oz. AGW **Obv:** Symbolic castle, date below in inner circle **Rev:** Ornate cross in inner circle

Date	Mintage	VG	F	VF	XF	Unc
1603 IV	—	900	1,800	3,600	5,250	—
1608 HP	—	900	1,800	3,600	5,250	—
1609 HP	—	900	1,800	3,600	5,250	—
1612 MC	—	900	1,800	3,600	5,250	—
1617 IZ	—	900	1,800	3,600	5,250	—
1618 IZ	—	900	1,800	3,600	5,250	—
1619 DN	—	900	1,800	3,600	5,250	—
1621 GF	—	900	1,800	3,600	5,250	—
1623 GF	—	900	1,800	3,600	5,250	—
1624 GF	—	900	1,800	3,600	5,250	—
1625 GF	—	900	1,800	3,600	5,250	—
1627	—	900	1,800	3,600	5,250	—
1628	—	900	1,800	3,600	5,250	—
1629	—	900	1,800	3,600	5,250	—
1630	—	900	1,800	3,600	5,250	—
1632	—	900	1,800	3,600	5,250	—
1637 IBS	—	900	1,800	3,600	5,250	—

KM# 85 2 DOPPIE

14.0000 g., 0.9860 Gold 0.4438 oz. AGW **Obv:** Madonna and child on cloud

Date	Mintage	VG	F	VF	XF	Unc
1638 IBS	—	1,500	3,000	5,000	8,100	—
1639 IBS	—	1,500	3,000	5,000	8,100	—
1640 IBS	—	1,500	3,000	5,000	8,100	—
1641 IBS	—	1,500	3,000	5,000	8,100	—
1650 IBN	—	1,500	3,000	5,000	8,100	—
1651 IAB	—	1,500	3,000	5,000	8,100	—
1653 IAB	—	1,500	3,000	5,000	8,100	—
1654 IAB	—	1,500	3,000	5,000	8,100	—
1655 IAB	—	1,500	3,000	5,000	8,100	—
1658 IAB	—	1,500	3,000	5,000	8,100	—
1659	—	1,500	3,000	5,000	8,100	—
1661 AB	—	1,500	3,000	5,000	8,100	—
1662 AB	—	1,500	3,000	5,000	8,100	—
1668 ISS	—	1,500	3,000	5,000	8,100	—
1669 ISS	—	1,500	3,000	5,000	8,100	—
1670 ISS	—	1,500	3,000	5,000	8,100	—
1671 ISS	—	1,500	3,000	5,000	8,100	—
1675 ILM	—	1,500	3,000	5,000	8,100	—
1698 ITC	—	1,500	3,000	5,000	8,100	—

KM# 152 2-1/2 DOPPIE

17.5000 g., 0.9860 Gold 0.5547 oz. AGW **Obv:** Ornate cross in inner circle **Rev:** Madonna and child on cloud in stars, date in legend

Date	Mintage	VG	F	VF	XF	Unc
1675 ILM	—	—	—	6,900	11,500	—
1676 ILM	—	—	—	6,900	11,500	—
1697 ITC	—	—	—	6,900	11,500	—

KM# 39 4 DOPPIE (Quadrupia)

28.0000 g., 0.9860 Gold 0.8876 oz. AGW **Ruler:** Conrad II **Obv:** Castle **Obv. Legend:** DVX ET GVB REIP GEN **Rev:** Cross **Rev. Legend:** CONRADVS II RO REX

Date	Mintage	VG	F	VF	XF	Unc
1613 MC	—	—	—	—	—	—
1614 MC	—	—	—	—	—	—
1615 IZ	—	—	—	—	—	—
1616 IZ	—	—	—	—	—	—

KM# 16 5 DOPPIE

35.0000 g., 0.9860 Gold 1.1095 oz. AGW **Ruler:** Conrad II

Date	Mintage	VG	F	VF	XF	Unc
1613 MC Rare	—	—	—	—	—	—
1615 IZ Rare	—	—	—	—	—	—
1616 IZ Rare	—	—	—	—	—	—
1620 GF Rare	—	—	—	—	—	—
1623 GF Rare	—	—	—	—	—	—
1633 Rare	—	—	—	—	—	—

KM# 100 5 DOPPIE

35.0000 g., 0.9860 Gold 1.1095 oz. AGW **Rev:** Madonna and child on cloud

Date	Mintage	VG	F	VF	XF	Unc
1640 IBS	—	2,500	5,000	10,000	20,000	—
1641 IBS	—	2,500	5,000	10,000	20,000	—
1642 CS	—	2,500	5,000	10,000	20,000	—
1643 CS	—	2,500	5,000	10,000	20,000	—
1644 CS	—	2,500	5,000	10,000	20,000	—
1645 CS	—	2,500	5,000	10,000	20,000	—
1646 CS	—	2,500	5,000	10,000	20,000	—
1647 IBN	—	2,500	5,000	10,000	20,000	—
1649 IBN	—	2,500	5,000	10,000	20,000	—
1650 IBN	—	2,500	5,000	10,000	20,000	—
1651 IBN	—	2,500	5,000	10,000	20,000	—
1652 IAB	—	2,500	5,000	10,000	20,000	—
1653 IAB	—	2,500	5,000	10,000	20,000	—
1655 IAB	—	2,500	5,000	10,000	20,000	—
1673 IBT	—	2,500	5,000	10,000	20,000	—
1675 ILM	—	2,500	5,000	10,000	20,000	—
1679 ILM	—	2,500	5,000	10,000	20,000	—
1685 GLM	—	2,500	5,000	10,000	20,000	—
1691 ITC	—	2,500	5,000	10,000	20,000	—
1692 ITC	—	2,500	5,000	10,000	20,000	—
1697 ITC	—	2,500	5,000	10,000	20,000	—

KM# 107 10 DOPPIE

70.0000 g., 0.9860 Gold 2.2190 oz. AGW **Obv:** Ornate cross in inner circle **Rev:** Madonna and child on cloud in stars, date in legend

Date	Mintage	VG	F	VF	XF	Unc
1641 IBS Rare	—	—	—	—	—	—
1649 IBN Rare	—	—	—	—	—	—

Date	Mintage	VG	F	VF	XF	Unc
1650 IBN Rare	—	—	—	—	—	—
1666 AB Rare	—	—	—	—	—	—
1670 ISS Rare	—	—	—	—	—	—
1694 ITC Rare	—	—	—	—	—	—

KM# 72 12-1/2 DOPPIE

0.9860 Gold **Obv:** Symbolic castle, date below in inner circle **Rev:** Ornate cross in inner circle **Note:** Weight varies: 82.0-85.0 grams. Actual gold weight varies: 2.6000-2.6960 ounces.

Date	Mintage	VG	F	VF	XF	Unc
1632 Rare	—	—	—	—	—	—
1634 Rare	—	—	—	—	—	—
1636 IBS Rare	—	—	—	—	—	—
1637 IBS Rare	—	—	—	—	—	—

KM# 86 12-1/2 DOPPIE

0.9860 Gold **Obv:** Cherubs between ends of cross within circle **Rev:** Madonna and child on cloud in stars, date in legend **Note:** 82-85 grams.

Date	Mintage	VG	F	VF	XF	Unc
1638 IBS Rare	—	—	—	—	—	—
1641 IBS Rare	—	—	—	—	—	—
Note: Stack's International sale 3-88 near XF realized $38,500						
1649 IBN Rare	—	—	—	—	—	—
1650 IBN Rare	—	—	—	—	—	—
1653 IAB Rare	—	—	—	—	—	—
1656 IAB Rare	—	—	—	—	—	—
1680 SM Rare	—	—	—	—	—	—
1694 ITC Rare	—	—	—	—	—	—
1698 ITC Rare	—	—	—	—	—	—

KM# 110 20 DOPPIE

132.0000 g., 0.9860 Gold 4.1843 oz. AGW **Obv:** Ornate cross in inner circle **Rev:** Madonna and child on cloud in stars, date in legend

Date	Mintage	VG	F	VF	XF	Unc
1645 CS Rare	—	—	—	—	—	—

KM# 76 25 DOPPIE

175.0000 g., 0.9860 Gold 5.5474 oz. AGW **Ruler:** Conrad II **Obv:** Symbolic castle, date below in inner circle **Rev:** Ornate cross in inner circle

Date	Mintage	VG	F	VF	XF	Unc
1636 IBS Rare	—	—	—	—	—	—

KM# 87 25 DOPPIE

175.0000 g., 0.9860 Gold 5.5474 oz. AGW **Obv:** Madonna and child on cloud

Date	Mintage	VG	F	VF	XF	Unc
1638 IBS Rare	—	—	—	—	—	—
1642 CS Rare	—	—	—	—	—	—
1653 Rare	—	—	—	—	—	—
1670 Rare	—	—	—	—	—	—
1694 Rare	—	—	—	—	—	—
1697 Rare	—	—	—	—	—	—

TRADE COINAGE

(for Levante)

KM# 125 LIGURINO

Billon **Obv:** Crowned shield with griffin supporters, LIBERTAS on shield **Rev:** Bust of female and Arabic legend

Date	Mintage	VG	F	VF	XF	Unc
1668	—	350	750	1,250	—	—
1669	—	350	750	1,250	—	—

KM# 126 GIUSTINO

2.0000 g., Billon **Obv:** Crowned shield with griffin supporters, LIBERTAS on shield **Rev:** Female seated

Date	Mintage	VG	F	VF	XF	Unc
1668	—	350	500	1,000	—	—
1669	—	350	500	1,000	—	—

KM# 127 GIANUINO

2.2000 g., Billon **Obv:** Crowned shield **Rev:** Janiform head of male and female

Date	Mintage	VG	F	VF	XF	Unc
1668	—	200	400	750	1,250	—

KM# 128 GIORGINO

1.7500 g., Silver **Obv:** Griffin supporting crowned arms, LIBERTAS on shield **Obv. Legend:** DVX ET GVB REIP GENV **Rev:** St. George slaying dragon **Rev. Legend:** S. GEOR PROT BONVIN VII

Date	Mintage	VG	F	VF	XF	Unc
1668	—	850	1,650	3,250	5,500	—

KM# 154 SCUDO

27.2500 g., Silver **Obv:** Crowned shield in palm **Obv. Legend:** DVX ET GVBER REIP GENV **Rev:** Griffin holding shield with Arabic text **Note:** Dav. #3903.

Date	Mintage	VG	F	VF	XF	Unc
1677 ILM Rare	—	—	—	—	—	—

PATTERNS

Including off metal strikes

KM#	Date	Mintage	Identification	Mkt Val
Pn1	1681	—	5 Doppie. Gold.	—

GUASTALLA

Located in Emilia on the southern bank of the Po River in the modern province of Reggio. Guastalla was ruled by the Torelli family from 1403, and in 1539, was sold to Ferranti Gonzaga by the last female descendant of the line. It became a duchy in 1621, but, was united with Parma and Piacenza in 1748 and subsequently followed their history.

RULERS

Ferrante II Gonzaga, 1575-1630
Ferrante III Gonzaga, 1632-1678

DUCHY

STANDARD COINAGE

DAV# 3917A SCUDO

19.0000 g., Silver **Obv:** Bust right, 1664 and GGF below **Rev:** Statue of Ferrante I

Date	Mintage	VG	F	VF	XF	Unc
1664	—	950	1,750	—	—	—

DAV# 3917 2 SCUDI

Silver **Obv:** Bust right, 1664 and GGF below **Rev:** Statue of Ferranti I

Date	Mintage	VG	F	VF	XF	Unc
1664 Rare	—	—	—	—	—	—

DAV# 3905 TALLERO

Silver **Obv:** Half figure right **Obv. Legend:** FERDINANDVS... **Rev:** Crowned arms with date divided above

Date	Mintage	VG	F	VF	XF	Unc
1601	—	1,050	2,100	5,000	—	—
1602	—	1,050	2,100	5,000	—	—
1603	—	850	1,750	4,500	—	—
ND	—	850	1,750	4,500	—	—

DAV# 3910 TALLERO

Silver **Obv:** Bust right dividing date **Obv. Legend:** ...GONZAGA... **Rev:** Crowned arms in order chain **Rev. Legend:** MELFICTI...

Date	Mintage	VG	F	VF	XF	Unc
1619	—	650	1,150	2,250	3,750	—

DAV# 3911 TALLERO
Silver **Obv. Legend:** FERDINANDVS: GONZ: - CAESARIS... **Rev. Legend:** MELFI: PRINC*: - GVA: COMES:

Date	Mintage	VG	F	VF	XF	Unc
1619	—	750	1,250	2,500	4,500	—

DAV# 3912 TALLERO
Silver **Obv:** Bust right in wreath, 16-19 below **Obv. Legend:** ...GONZAGA. **Rev. Legend:** MELFICTI. PRINCEP...

Date	Mintage	VG	F	VF	XF	Unc
1619 Rare	—	—	—	—	—	—

DAV# 3913 TALLERO
Silver

Date	Mintage	VG	F	VF	XF	Unc
1620	—	450	750	1,250	3,000	8,000

DAV# 3914 TALLERO
Silver **Rev:** Without order chain

Date	Mintage	VG	F	VF	XF	Unc
1620	—	500	1,000	2,000	3,500	—

DAV# 3918 TALLERO
Silver **Obv:** Bust right without high collar, long hair hanging on shoulder **Rev:** Spiked wheel with indicator

Date	Mintage	VG	F	VF	XF	Unc
1673 Rare	—	—	—	—	—	—

DAV# 3904 2 TALLERO
Silver **Obv:** Half figure right, date below **Rev:** Crowned arms in order chain

Date	Mintage	VG	F	VF	XF	Unc
MDC Rare	—	—	—	—	—	—

Note: Numismatica Ars Classica Auction 32, 1-06, VF realized approximately $27,780

Date	Mintage	VG	F	VF	XF	Unc
1601 Rare	—	—	—	—	—	—
1603 Rare	—	—	—	—	—	—

DAV# 3907 DUCATONE
Silver **Obv:** Large bust right **Obv. Legend:** FERDIN. GON.-MELF... **Rev:** Annunciation scene, 1610 and MICHI below

Date	Mintage	VG	F	VF	XF	Unc
1610 Rare	—	—	—	—	—	—

DAV# 3909 DUCATONE
Silver **Obv:** Bust right, 1614 below **Obv. Legend:** FERDINANDVS... **Rev:** Statue of Ferrante I, MDCXIII below

Date	Mintage	VG	F	VF	XF	Unc
1614	—	2,500	4,500	—	—	—

DAV# 3915 DUCATONE
Silver **Obv:** Bust right, 3*L*X* below **Obv. Legend:** FERD... **Rev:** Statue of Ferrante I, MDCXXII below

Date	Mintage	VG	F	VF	XF	Unc
1622 Rare	—	—	—	—	—	—

Note: Numismatica Ars Classica Auction 30, 6-05, XF realized approximately $15,970

DAV# 3916 DUCATONE
Silver **Obv:** Bust left **Rev:** Spiked wheel with indicator

Date	Mintage	VG	F	VF	XF	Unc
ND Rare	—	—	—	—	—	—

DAV# 3906 2 DUCATONE
Silver **Obv:** Large bust right **Obv. Legend:** FERDIN. GON.-MELF... **Rev:** Annunciation scene, 1610 and MICHI below

Date	Mintage	VG	F	VF	XF	Unc
1610 Rare	—	—	—	—	—	—

DAV# 3908 2 DUCATONE
Silver **Obv:** Bust right, 1614 below **Obv. Legend:** FERDINAN DVX... **Rev:** Statue of Ferrante I, MDCXIII below

Date	Mintage	VG	F	VF	XF	Unc
1614 Rare	—	—	—	—	—	—

FR# 460 SCUDO D'ORO
3.5000 g., 0.9860 Gold 0.1109 oz. AGW **Obv:** Crowned arms **Rev:** Cross in inner circle

Date	Mintage	VG	F	VF	XF	Unc
ND Rare	—	—	—	—	—	—

FR# 459 DUCAT
3.5000 g., 0.9860 Gold 0.1109 oz. AGW **Obv:** Ferrante standing in inner circle **Rev:** Crowned arms in inner circle

Date	Mintage	VG	F	VF	XF	Unc
ND	—	775	1,650	2,750	3,850	—

FR# A459 4 DOPPIE
26.3000 g., 0.9860 Gold 0.8337 oz. AGW **Obv:** Bust of Ferrante to right in inner circle **Rev:** Annunciation scene in inner circle; date in exergue

Date	Mintage	VG	F	VF	XF	Unc
1604 Rare	—	—	—	—	—	—

FR# 458 10 DOPPIE
66.4100 g., 0.9860 Gold 2.1052 oz. AGW

Date	Mintage	VG	F	VF	XF	Unc
1610 Rare	—	—	—	—	—	—

LIVORNO

Livorno (Leghorn), a city on the Tyrrhenian Sea in western Tuscany, had a mint at which the Medici dukes struck coins with the mark LIBVRNI.

RULERS
Ferdinand II Medici, 1621-1670
Cosimo III Medici, 1670-1723

DUCHY

STANDARD COINAGE

KM# 8 LUIGINO
2.2200 g., Silver **Obv:** Head of Ferdinand right **Rev:** Crowned French shield

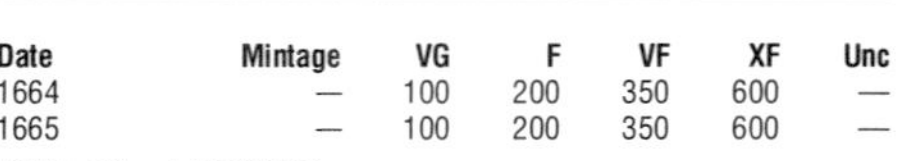

Date	Mintage	VG	F	VF	XF	Unc
1657	—	100	200	350	600	—
1659	—	100	200	350	600	—
1660	—	100	200	350	600	—
1661	—	100	200	350	600	—
1662	—	100	200	350	600	—
1663	—	100	200	350	600	—
1664	—	100	200	350	600	—
1665	—	100	200	350	600	—

KM# 20 LUIGINO
2.2200 g., Silver **Obv:** Bust of Cosimo right **Rev:** Crowned French shield

Date	Mintage	VG	F	VF	XF	Unc
1675	—	150	250	400	725	—
ND	—	150	250	400	725	—

KM# 10 1/4 PEZZA
Silver **Obv:** Crowned oval arms, FERDINANDO **Rev:** Rosebush **Note:** Weight varies: 6.00-6.40 grams.

Date	Mintage	VG	F	VF	XF	Unc
1665	—	165	275	450	725	—

KM# 30 1/4 PEZZA
Silver **Obv:** Crowned arms of Medici, COSMVS **Note:** Weight varies: 6.00-6.40 grams.

Date	Mintage	VG	F	VF	XF	Unc
1697	—	225	400	700	—	—
1699	—	2,250	400	700	—	—

KM# 11 1/2 PEZZA
13.0000 g., Silver **Obv:** Crowned oval arms, FERDINANDO **Rev:** Rosebush

Date	Mintage	VG	F	VF	XF	Unc
1665	—	350	550	900	1,500	—

KM# 31 1/2 PEZZA
13.0000 g., Silver **Obv:** Crowned oval arms of Medici, COSMVS

Date	Mintage	VG	F	VF	XF	Unc
1697	—	275	500	900	1,600	—

KM# 12 PEZZA DELLA ROSA
Silver **Obv:** Crowned arms of Medici, FERDINAND **Rev:** Rosebush **Note:** Dav. #4208.

Date	Mintage	VG	F	VF	XF	Unc
1665	—	1,650	3,250	5,500	9,000	—

KM# 15.1 PEZZA DELLA ROSA
Silver **Obv:** Crowned arms of Medici, unbroken legend **Obv. Legend:** COSMVS III... **Note:** Dav. #4216A.

Date	Mintage	VG	F	VF	XF	Unc
1670	—	300	550	900	1,600	—
1684	—	300	550	900	1,600	—

Note: Varieties exist for the 1684

KM# 15.2 PEZZA DELLA ROSA

Silver **Obv:** Crown breaks legend **Note:** Dav. #4216.

Date	Mintage	VG	F	VF	XF	Unc
1684	—	120	240	425	725	—
1697	—	150	300	475	775	—
1698	—	150	300	475	775	—
1699	—	150	300	475	775	—
1700	—	150	300	475	775	—

KM# 25 1/4 TOLLERO

6.1500 g., Silver **Obv:** Crowned head right **Rev:** Fortress of Livorno

Date	Mintage	VG	F	VF	XF	Unc
1683	—	—	—	—	—	—

KM# 26 1/2 TOLLERO

13.0000 g., Silver **Obv:** Crowned bust right **Rev:** Ship, LIBVRNI below

Date	Mintage	VG	F	VF	XF	Unc
1683	—	175	350	650	—	—

KM# 7.1 TOLLERO

27.0000 g., Silver **Obv:** Head of Ferdinand right, curved crown points **Rev:** Port of Livorno **Note:** Dav. #4204.

Date	Mintage	VG	F	VF	XF	Unc
1656 Rare	—	—	—	—	—	—

KM# 7.2 TOLLERO

27.0000 g., Silver **Obv:** Straight crown points **Note:** Dav. #4206.

Date	Mintage	VG	F	VF	XF	Unc
1659	—	400	750	1,500	—	—
1666	—	500	950	1,850	—	—
1669 Rare	—	—	—	—	—	—

KM# 16.1 TOLLERO

27.0000 g., Silver **Obv:** Crowned bust of Cosmus III right **Note:** Dav. #A4214.

Date	Mintage	VG	F	VF	XF	Unc
1670	—	600	1,200	2,250	4,250	—
1675	—	600	1,200	2,250	4,250	—

KM# 16.2 TOLLERO

27.0000 g., Silver **Obv. Legend:** D. G. MAG. DVX... **Note:** Dav. #4214.

Date	Mintage	VG	F	VF	XF	Unc
1680	—	375	750	1,500	2,500	—

KM# 16.3 TOLLERO

27.0000 g., Silver **Obv:** Without border around wide bust **Obv. Legend:** ...ETRVR. VI. **Note:** Dav. #4215A.

Date	Mintage	VG	F	VF	XF	Unc
1681	—	155	325	550	900	—

KM# 16.4 TOLLERO

27.0000 g., Silver **Obv:** Narrow bust **Note:** Dav. #4215.

Date	Mintage	VG	F	VF	XF	Unc
1683	—	100	210	350	650	—
1685	—	100	210	350	650	—
1687	—	100	210	350	650	—
1688	—	100	210	350	650	—
1692	—	100	210	350	650	—
1694	—	100	210	350	650	—
1695	—	100	210	350	650	—
1697	—	100	210	350	650	—
1698	—	100	210	350	650	—
1699	—	100	210	350	650	—
1700	—	100	210	350	650	—

KM# 5 ONGARO

2.3500 g., Gold **Obv:** Head of Ferdinand right **Rev:** Fortress, DIVERSIS

Date	Mintage	VG	F	VF	XF	Unc
1655 Rare	—	—	—	—	—	—

KM# 6 ONGARO

2.3500 g., Gold **Rev:** Harbor, ET PAVET

Date	Mintage	VG	F	VF	XF	Unc
ND Rare	—	—	—	—	—	—

KM# 17 ONGARO

2.3500 g., Gold **Obv:** Head of Cosimo right

Date	Mintage	VG	F	VF	XF	Unc
ND Rare	—	—	—	—	—	—

Note: Superior Pipito sale 12-87 choice XF realized $42,900

KM# 18 ONGARO

2.3500 g., Gold **Obv:** Grand Duke standing **Rev:** Six-line inscription in cartouche

Date	Mintage	VG	F	VF	XF	Unc
1674	—	300	450	900	1,650	—
1675	—	300	450	900	1,650	—
1676	—	300	450	900	1,650	—
1678	—	300	450	900	1,650	—
1691	—	300	450	900	1,650	—
ND	—	300	450	900	1,650	—

KM# 19 ONGARO

2.3500 g., Gold **Obv:** Grand Duke standing **Rev:** Fame on clouds with stars and rays

Date	Mintage	VG	F	VF	XF	Unc
ND	—	2,000	5,000	7,500	12,500	—

LOANO

Loana, a county in Liguria on the Tyrrhenian Sea, was acquired by Oberti Doria in 1263, but sold by the family in 1505 to Gian Luigi Fieschi. Thru marriage, however, it came back to Giovanni Andrea Doria, who restored the castle and built walls. The mint privilege had been conferred in 1547.

RULERS

Giovanni Andrea Dorea I, 1560-1606
Giovanni Andrea Doria II, 1622-1640
Giovanni Andrea Doria III, 1654-1737

COUNTY

STANDARD COINAGE

KM# 16 LUIGINO

Billon **Rev:** Crowned baroque arms **Rev. Legend:** SPES... **Note:** Weight varies: 1.80-2.45 grams.

Date	Mintage	VG	F	VF	XF	Unc
1665	—	75.00	150	300	550	—
1666	—	75.00	150	300	550	—

KM# 17 LUIGINO

Billon **Rev:** Crowned arms divide date **Rev. Legend:** DEVS... **Note:** Weight varies: 1.80-2.45 grams.

Date	Mintage	VG	F	VF	XF	Unc
1665	—	50.00	120	250	475	850
1666	—	50.00	120	250	475	850

KM# 18 LUIGINO

Billon **Rev:** Crowned arms, date above **Rev. Legend:** DEVS... **Note:** Weight varies: 1.80-2.45 grams.

Date	Mintage	VG	F	VF	XF	Unc
1665	—	65.00	145	285	550	950
1666	—	65.00	145	285	550	950

KM# 15 LUIGINO

Silver **Rev:** Crowned arms divide date **Rev. Legend:** SPES... **Note:** Weight varies: 1.74-2.22 grams.

Date	Mintage	VG	F	VF	XF	Unc
1665	—	85.00	175	350	675	—
1666	—	85.00	175	350	675	—

KM# 23 LUIGINO

Billon **Obv:** Bust right **Obv. Legend:** VIOLANTE... **Rev:** Crowned French arms divide date **Rev. Legend:** DEVS... **Note:** Weight varies: 1.80-2.45 grams.

Date	Mintage	VG	F	VF	XF	Unc
1665	—	—	—	—	—	—
1666	—	35.00	75.00	185	325	—

KM# 15a LUIGINO
Billon **Note:** Weight varies: 1.80-2.45 grams.

Date	Mintage	VG	F	VF	XF	Unc
1666	—	—	—	—	—	—

KM# 22 LUIGINO
Billon **Obv:** Bust of Volante Lomellini, widow of Andrea III right **Obv. Legend:** GRATIOR... **Rev:** Crowned French arms divide date (one lis above two) **Rev. Legend:** SANCTE **Note:** Weight varies: 1.80-2.45 grams.

Date	Mintage	VG	F	VF	XF	Unc
1666	—	35.00	75.00	185	325	—
1667	—	35.00	75.00	185	325	—
1668	—	35.00	75.00	185	325	—

KM# 24 LUIGINO
Billon **Obv:** Bust right **Obv. Legend:** GRATIOR... **Rev:** Crowned French arms divide date (two lis above one) **Note:** Weight varies: 1.80-2.45 grams.

Date	Mintage	VG	F	VF	XF	Unc
1667	—	35.00	75.00	185	325	—
1668	—	35.00	75.00	185	325	—
1669	—	35.00	75.00	185	325	—

KM# 25 LUIGINO
Billon **Obv:** Bust right **Obv. Legend:** PVLCRA... **Rev:** Crowned French arms **Rev. Legend:** BONITAS... **Note:** Weight varies: 1.80-2.45 grams.

Date	Mintage	VG	F	VF	XF	Unc
1668	—	35.00	75.00	185	325	—
1669	—	35.00	75.00	185	325	—

KM# 26 LUIGINO
Billon **Rev:** Crowned arms divide date **Rev. Legend:** SIT NOMEN... **Note:** Weight varies: 1.80-2.45 grams.

Date	Mintage	VG	F	VF	XF	Unc
1669	—	100	200	375	700	—

KM# 27 LUIGINO
Billon **Obv:** Bust right **Obv. Legend:** PVLCRA... **Rev:** Crowned French arms divide date **Rev. Legend:** *TRES **Note:** Weight varies: 1.80-2.45 grams.

Date	Mintage	VG	F	VF	XF	Unc
1669	—	50.00	120	250	475	—

KM# 19 REALE
4.5000 g., Silver **Obv:** Bust of Gio right **Rev:** Crowned arms divide date

Date	Mintage	VG	F	VF	XF	Unc
1665 Rare	—	—	—	—	—	—

KM# 6 SCUDO
Silver **Obv:** Bust left **Rev:** Caduceus and cornucopia **Note:** Weight varies: 31.00-38.00 grams. Dav. #3920.

Date	Mintage	VG	F	VF	XF	Unc
1601 Rare	—	—	—	—	—	—

KM# 30 SCUDO
Silver **Obv:** Bust right, date below **Rev:** Crowned eagle arms **Note:** Weight varies: 31.00-38.00 grams. Dav. #3922.

Date	Mintage	VG	F	VF	XF	Unc
1670 Rare	—	—	—	—	—	—

KM# 7 DUCATONE
42.0400 g., Silver **Obv:** Bust left **Rev:** Crowned eagle arms, date below **Note:** Dav. #3921.

Date	Mintage	VG	F	VF	XF	Unc
1606 Rare	—	—	—	—	—	—

KM# 10 DOPPIA
7.0000 g., 0.9860 Gold 0.2219 oz. AGW **Obv:** Bust of Giovanni andrea Doria II right in inner circle **Rev:** Crowned eagle arms in inner circle

Date	Mintage	VG	F	VF	XF	Unc
1639 Rare	—	—	—	—	—	—

KM# 20 DOPPIA
7.0000 g., 0.9860 Gold 0.2219 oz. AGW **Obv:** Bust of Giovanni Andrea Doria III to right **Rev:** Crowned arms on St. Andrew's cross, date at top

Date	Mintage	VG	F	VF	XF	Unc
1665 Rare	—	—	—	—	—	—

KM# 21 DOPPIA
7.0000 g., 0.9860 Gold 0.2219 oz. AGW **Rev:** Arms divide date

Date	Mintage	VG	F	VF	XF	Unc
1665 Rare	—	—	—	—	—	—

KM# 11 2 DOPPIE
14.0000 g., 0.9860 Gold 0.4438 oz. AGW **Obv:** Bust of Giovanni Andrea Doria II right in inner circle **Rev:** Crowned eagle arms in inner circle

Date	Mintage	VG	F	VF	XF	Unc
1639 Rare	—	—	—	—	—	—

TRADE COINAGE

KM# 8 DUCAT
3.5000 g., 0.9860 Gold 0.1109 oz. AGW **Obv:** Madonna and child **Rev:** Four-line inscription in tablet

Date	Mintage	VG	F	VF	XF	Unc
ND	—	2,500	4,000	7,500	12,500	—

LUCCA

Luca, Lucensis
Lucca and Piombino

A town in Tuscany and the residence of a marquis, was nominally a fief but managed to maintain a *de facto* independence until awarded by Napoleon to his sister Elisa in 1805. In 1814 it was occupied by the Neapolitans, from 1817 to 1847 it was a duchy of the queen of Etruria, after which it became a division of Tuscany. Republic, 1369-1799

MONETARY SYSTEM

2 Quattrini = 1 Duetto
3 Quattrini = 1 Soldo
12 Soldi = 6 Bolognini = 2 Grossi = 1 Barbone
25 Soldi = 1 Santa Croce
2 Scudi D'oro = 1 Doppia

REPUBLIC

STANDARD COINAGE

KM# 5 QUATTRINO
0.7500 g., Copper **Obv:** Large L divides date **Rev:** Head of St. Vultus

Date	Mintage	VG	F	VF	XF	Unc
1601	—	10.00	20.00	40.00	70.00	—
1602	—	10.00	20.00	40.00	70.00	—
1607	—	10.00	20.00	40.00	70.00	—
1610	—	10.00	20.00	40.00	70.00	—
1611	—	10.00	20.00	40.00	70.00	—
1613	—	10.00	20.00	40.00	70.00	—
1614	—	10.00	20.00	40.00	70.00	—
1615	—	10.00	20.00	40.00	70.00	—
1616	—	10.00	20.00	40.00	70.00	—
1620	—	10.00	20.00	40.00	70.00	—
1621	—	10.00	20.00	40.00	70.00	—
1623	—	10.00	20.00	40.00	70.00	—
1625	—	10.00	20.00	40.00	70.00	—
1626	—	10.00	20.00	40.00	70.00	—
1627	—	10.00	20.00	40.00	70.00	—
1628	—	10.00	20.00	40.00	70.00	—
1629	—	10.00	20.00	40.00	70.00	—
1630	—	10.00	20.00	40.00	70.00	—
1631	—	10.00	20.00	40.00	70.00	—
1636	—	10.00	20.00	40.00	70.00	—
1637	—	10.00	20.00	40.00	70.00	—
1638	—	10.00	20.00	40.00	70.00	—
1639	—	10.00	20.00	40.00	70.00	—
1640	—	10.00	20.00	40.00	70.00	—
(16)64	—	10.00	20.00	40.00	70.00	—
1674	—	10.00	20.00	40.00	70.00	—

KM# 42 PANTERINO
Copper **Obv:** Oval republic arms **Rev:** City arms **Note:** Weight varies: 0.60-1.00 grams.

Date	Mintage	VG	F	VF	XF	Unc
1682	—	8.00	16.00	30.00	50.00	—
1683	—	8.00	16.00	30.00	50.00	—
1684	—	8.00	16.00	30.00	50.00	—
1691	—	8.00	16.00	30.00	50.00	—
1692	—	8.00	16.00	30.00	50.00	—

KM# 9 GROSSETTO
Billon **Obv:** L-V-C-A arund center rosette **Rev:** Bust of St. Vultus **Note:** Weight varies: 0.80-1.52 grams.

Date	Mintage	VG	F	VF	XF	Unc
1602	—	55.00	115	225	375	—

KM# 20 GROSSETTO
Billon **Obv:** LIBERTAS in field **Obv. Legend:** CAROLVS **Rev:** St. Peter standing **Note:** Weight varies: 0.80-1.52 grams.

Date	Mintage	VG	F	VF	XF	Unc
1645	—	18.00	37.50	70.00	130	—

KM# 30 GROSSETTO
Billon **Obv:** Arms in cartouche **Obv. Legend:** OTTO **Rev:** St. Peter **Note:** Weight varies: 0.80-1.52 grams.

Date	Mintage	VG	F	VF	XF	Unc
1661	—	11.00	18.00	33.00	60.00	—
1662	—	11.00	18.00	33.00	60.00	—
1675	—	11.00	18.00	33.00	60.00	—

KM# 32 GROSSETTO
Billon **Obv:** L-V-C-A around a rose **Obv. Legend:** OTTO **Note:** Weight varies: 0.80-1.52 grams.

Date	Mintage	VG	F	VF	XF	Unc
1666	—	14.00	25.00	55.00	90.00	—

KM# 40 DUETTO (2 Quattrino)
1.5000 g., Billon **Obv:** LVCA cruciform around center rosette, date at bottom **Obv. Legend:** CARLO L.O.D.I.D.... **Rev:** St. Peter standing

Date	Mintage	VG	F	VF	XF	Unc
1681	—	11.00	18.00	30.00	55.00	—
1682	—	11.00	18.00	30.00	55.00	—
1683	—	11.00	18.00	30.00	55.00	—
1686	—	11.00	18.00	30.00	55.00	—
1691	—	11.00	18.00	30.00	55.00	—
1692	—	11.00	18.00	30.00	55.00	—

KM# 26 SOLDO
Copper **Obv:** Crowned shield **Obv. Legend:** OTTO **Rev:** St. Paul **Note:** Weight varies: 1.81-2.07 grams.

Date	Mintage	VG	F	VF	XF	Unc
1658	—	12.00	22.50	45.00	90.00	—
1681	—	12.00	22.50	45.00	90.00	—

KM# 41 SOLDO
Copper **Obv:** Crowned shield **Obv. Legend:** RESPVBLICA **Note:** Weight varies: 1.81-2.07 grams.

Date	Mintage	VG	F	VF	XF	Unc
1681	—	11.00	18.00	33.00	55.00	—
1682	—	11.00	18.00	33.00	55.00	—
1691	—	11.00	18.00	33.00	55.00	—
1692	—	11.00	18.00	33.00	55.00	—

KM# 33 LUIGINO
Silver **Rev:** Crowned French arms **Note:** Weight varies: 1.50-1.60 grams. Struck for the Levant

Date	Mintage	VG	F	VF	XF	Unc
1668	—	300	600	1,000	—	—

KM# 10 MEZZO (1/2) GROSSO
Billon **Obv:** L-V-C-A around center rosette **Rev:** St. Peter **Note:** Weight varies: 0.96-1.58 grams.

Date	Mintage	VG	F	VF	XF	Unc
1602	—	—	—	—	—	—
1658	—	—	—	—	—	—

KM# 6 GROSSO
Silver **Obv:** L-V-C-A around center rosette **Rev:** St. Vultus **Note:** Weight varies: 3.40-3.50 grams.

Date	Mintage	VG	F	VF	XF	Unc
1601	—	30.00	55.00	150	280	—
1602	—	30.00	55.00	150	280	—
1607	—	30.00	55.00	150	280	—

KM# 11 GROSSO
Silver **Obv:** Crowned arms **Note:** Weight varies: 3.40-3.50 grams.

Date	Mintage	VG	F	VF	XF	Unc
1603	—	30.00	55.00	150	280	—
1605	—	30.00	55.00	150	280	—
1606	—	30.00	55.00	150	280	—

KM# 13 GROSSO
Silver **Obv:** L-V-C-A in Gothic letters **Note:** Weight varies: 3.40-3.50 grams.

Date	Mintage	VG	F	VF	XF	Unc
1609	—	30.00	55.00	150	280	—
1610	—	30.00	55.00	150	280	—
1624	—	30.00	55.00	150	280	—

KM# 25 GROSSO
Silver **Obv:** Oval arms **Rev. Legend:** SANCTVS. VULTVS. DE LVCA. **Note:** Weight varies: 3.40-3.50 grams.

Date	Mintage	VG	F	VF	XF	Unc
1651	—	22.50	37.50	115	225	—

KM# 31 GROSSO
Silver **Obv:** L-V-C-A in garland **Note:** Weight varies: 3.40-3.50 grams.

Date	Mintage	VG	F	VF	XF	Unc
1661	—	22.50	37.50	115	225	—

KM# 34 BARBONE (Grosso - 12 Soldi)
Silver **Obv:** Crowned arms with supporters **Rev:** Justice seated **Note:** Weight varies: 2.94-3.11 grams.

Date	Mintage	VG	F	VF	XF	Unc
1668	—	37.50	75.00	180	300	—
1669	—	37.50	75.00	180	300	—
1682	—	37.50	75.00	180	300	—
1686	—	37.50	75.00	180	300	—
1691	—	37.50	75.00	180	300	—

KM# 16 SANTACROCE (25 Soldi)
8.6400 g., 0.8950 Silver 0.2486 oz. ASW **Obv:** Crowned republic arms, date below **Obv. Legend:** LUCENSIS • RESPUBLICA **Rev:** St. Vultus on cross **Rev. Legend:** ...VULTUS •

Date	Mintage	VG	F	VF	XF	Unc
1615	—	60.00	120	225	375	—
1619	—	60.00	120	225	375	—
1622	—	60.00	120	225	375	—
1625	—	60.00	120	225	375	—

Date	Mintage	VG	F	VF	XF	Unc
1668	—	60.00	120	225	375	—
1682	—	60.00	120	225	375	—

KM# 12 1/4 SCUDO (San Martino - 15 Soldi)

6.1100 g., Silver **Obv:** Oval shield **Rev:** St. Martin on horseback

Date	Mintage	VG	F	VF	XF	Unc
1603	—	48.00	95.00	180	300	—
1604	—	48.00	95.00	180	300	—
1605	—	48.00	95.00	180	300	—
1607	—	48.00	95.00	180	300	—
1610	—	48.00	95.00	180	300	—
1613	—	48.00	95.00	180	300	—
1615	—	48.00	95.00	180	300	—
1623	—	48.00	95.00	180	300	—
1625	—	48.00	95.00	180	300	—

KM# 35 1/4 SCUDO (San Martino - 15 Soldi)

6.1100 g., Silver **Obv:** Crowned arms

Date	Mintage	VG	F	VF	XF	Unc
1668	—	145	265	575	975	—

KM# 15 1/3 SCUDO (San Martino - 25 Soldi)

10.8400 g., Silver **Obv:** Oval arms **Rev:** St. Martin on horseback

Date	Mintage	VG	F	VF	XF	Unc
1613	—	500	800	1,500	—	—

KM# 7 1/2 SCUDO

15.5000 g., Silver **Obv:** Crowned shield **Rev:** St. Martin on horseback

Date	Mintage	VG	F	VF	XF	Unc
1601	—	—	—	—	—	—
1603	—	—	—	—	—	—
1615	—	—	—	—	—	—

KM# 8 SCUDO

Silver **Obv:** Oval arms, LV-CA below **Rev:** St. Martin and beggar **Note:** Dav. #3923.

Date	Mintage	VG	F	VF	XF	Unc
1601	—	1,500	2,650	4,800	—	—
1604	—	1,500	2,650	4,800	—	—
1605	—	1,500	2,650	4,800	—	—
1607	—	1,500	2,650	4,800	—	—

KM# 17 SCUDO

Silver **Obv:** Crowned elongated shield **Note:** Dav. #3924.

Date	Mintage	VG	F	VF	XF	Unc
1615	—	900	1,750	2,800	—	—
1616	—	900	1,750	2,800	—	—
1617	—	900	1,750	2,800	—	—

MACCAGNO

This county in the province of Como south of Lake Lucerne had been in possession of the Mandelli family since 960. The short coinage ceased with the death of Giovanni Francesco in 1668.

RULERS

Giacomo III Mandelli, 1618-1645
Giovanni Francesco Mandelli, 1645-1668

COUNTY

STANDARD COINAGE

KM# 5 SESINO

Billon **Obv:** Bust right **Rev:** Foliate cross **Note:** Weight varies: 0.70-1.30 grams.

Date	Mintage	VG	F	VF	XF	Unc
ND	—	90.00	180	375	—	—

KM# 6 SESINO

Billon **Obv:** Head right in ruffled collar **Rev:** Plain cross **Note:** Weight varies: 0.70-1.30 grams.

Date	Mintage	VG	F	VF	XF	Unc
ND	—	55.00	115	225	—	—

KM# 24 SOLDO

1.1500 g., Silver **Obv:** Crowned double eagle, date below **Rev:** Bust of St. Aloyius

Date	Mintage	VG	F	VF	XF	Unc
1623	—	475	850	1,800	—	—

KM# 7 QUATTRINO

Copper **Obv:** Bust right **Obv. Legend:** IACO **Rev:** Eagle and lion arms **Note:** Weight varies: 1.34-2.29 grams.

Date	Mintage	VG	F	VF	XF	Unc
ND	—	70.00	140	325	—	—

KM# 35 QUATTRINO

Copper **Obv:** Head right, IOA **Rev:** Cross **Note:** Weight varies: 1.34-2.29 grams.

Date	Mintage	VG	F	VF	XF	Unc
ND	—	105	210	375	—	—

KM# 36 QUATTRINO

Copper **Obv:** Head right, IOAN **Note:** Weight varies: 1.34-2.29 grams.

Date	Mintage	VG	F	VF	XF	Unc
ND	—	105	210	375	—	—

KM# 25 DICKEN

6.7100 g., Billon **Obv:** Double eagle, date below **Rev:** St. Aloysius

Date	Mintage	VG	F	VF	XF	Unc
1623	—	—	—	—	—	—

KM# 8 1/2 DUCATONE

15.4300 g., Silver **Obv:** Bust right **Rev:** Crowned multiple arms

Date	Mintage	VG	F	VF	XF	Unc
ND Rare	—	—	—	—	—	—

KM# 9 TALLERO

24.7400 g., Silver **Obv:** Bust right **Rev:** Crowned double eagle **Note:** Dav. #3930.

Date	Mintage	VG	F	VF	XF	Unc
ND Rare	—	—	—	—	—	—

KM# 15 DUCATONE

Silver **Obv:** Warrior behind shield **Obv. Legend:** ...MAN. L. D. MAC*. **Rev:** Rampant lion **Note:** Weight varies: 31.00-32.00 grams. Dav. #3925.

Date	Mintage	VG	F	VF	XF	Unc
1621 Rare	—	—	—	—	—	—
1622 Rare	—	—	—	—	—	—

KM# 16 DUCATONE

Silver **Obv. Legend:** ...M. G. I. V. P*. **Note:** Weight varies: 31.00-32.00 grams. Dav. #3926.

Date	Mintage	VG	F	VF	XF	Unc
1622 Rare	—	—	—	—	—	—

KM# 30 DUCATONE

Silver **Obv:** Armored bust right **Rev:** Crowned arms, date below **Note:** Weight varies: 31.00-32.00 grams. Dav. #3927.

Date	Mintage	VG	F	VF	XF	Unc
1626 Rare	—	—	—	—	—	—

KM# 31 DUCATONE

Silver **Obv:** Bust right **Rev:** Crowned arms, SACRIQ **Note:** Weight varies: 31.00-32.00 grams. Dav. #3928.

Date	Mintage	VG	F	VF	XF	Unc
ND Rare	—	—	—	—	—	—

KM# 32 DUCATONE

Silver **Rev:** Crowned double eagle with Mandelli arms **Note:** Weight varies: 31.00-32.00 grams. Dav. #3929.

Date	Mintage	VG	F	VF	XF	Unc
ND Rare	—	—	—	—	—	—

KM# 10 DOPPIA

7.0000 g., 0.9860 Gold 0.2219 oz. AGW **Obv:** Giacomo standing facing in inner circle **Rev:** Crowned arms in inner circle

Date	Mintage	VG	F	VF	XF	Unc
ND Rare	—	—	—	—	—	—

KM# 29.1 DOPPIA

7.0000 g., 0.9860 Gold 0.2219 oz. AGW **Obv:** Bust of Giacomo right **Obv. Legend:** IACOBVS MANDELLVS... **Rev:** Crowned arms

Date	Mintage	VG	F	VF	XF	Unc
1625 Rare	—	—	—	—	—	—

KM# 29.2 DOPPIA

7.0000 g., 0.9860 Gold 0.2219 oz. AGW **Obv. Legend:** MON. NO. AV...

Date	Mintage	VG	F	VF	XF	Unc
ND Rare	—	—	—	—	—	—

KM# 11 ZECCHINO

3.5000 g., 0.9860 Gold 0.1109 oz. AGW **Obv:** Giacomo

Date	Mintage	VG	F	VF	XF	Unc
ND	—	1,500	3,000	6,000	10,000	—

KM# 22 ZECCHINO

3.5000 g., 0.9860 Gold 0.1109 oz. AGW **Rev:** Crowned arms in inner circle

Date	Mintage	VG	F	VF	XF	Unc
1622	—	750	1,500	3,000	5,300	—
1623	—	750	1,500	3,000	5,300	—

KM# 12 ZECCHINO

3.5000 g., 0.9860 Gold 0.1109 oz. AGW **Rev:** Orb in inner circle

Date	Mintage	VG	F	VF	XF	Unc
ND	—	1,500	3,000	6,000	10,000	—

KM# 17.1 ZECCHINO

3.5000 g., 0.9860 Gold 0.1109 oz. AGW **Obv:** St. Stephen kneeling in inner circle **Rev:** Crowned eagle in inner circle

Date	Mintage	VG	F	VF	XF	Unc
1622	—	600	1,000	2,400	4,500	—

KM# 17.2 ZECCHINO

3.5000 g., 0.9860 Gold 0.1109 oz. AGW **Rev:** Crowned arms in inner circle

Date	Mintage	VG	F	VF	XF	Unc
1622	—	600	1,000	2,400	4,500	—

KM# 18 ZECCHINO

3.5000 g., 0.9860 Gold 0.1109 oz. AGW **Obv:** Helmeted arms in inner circle, date in legend **Rev:** Crowned imperial eagle in inner circle

Date	Mintage	VG	F	VF	XF	Unc
1622	—	600	1,000	2,400	4,500	—
ND	—	600	1,000	2,400	4,500	—

KM# 19 ZECCHINO

3.5000 g., 0.9860 Gold 0.1109 oz. AGW **Rev:** Orb in inner circle

Date	Mintage	VG	F	VF	XF	Unc
1622	—	600	1,000	2,400	4,500	—

KM# 20 ZECCHINO

3.5000 g., 0.9860 Gold 0.1109 oz. AGW **Obv:** Giacomo standing facing in inner circle **Rev:** Crowned arms in inner circle, date above crown

Date	Mintage	VG	F	VF	XF	Unc
1622	—	800	1,800	3,600	6,000	—
ND	—	800	1,800	3,600	6,000	—

KM# 21 ZECCHINO

3.5000 g., 0.9860 Gold 0.1109 oz. AGW **Rev:** Crowned double-headed eagle in inner circle

Date	Mintage	VG	F	VF	XF	Unc
ND	—	800	1,800	3,600	6,000	—

KM# 23 ZECCHINO

3.5000 g., 0.9860 Gold 0.1109 oz. AGW

Date	Mintage	VG	F	VF	XF	Unc
1622	—	1,200	2,400	5,000	9,000	—

KM# 26 ZECCHINO

3.5000 g., 0.9860 Gold 0.1109 oz. AGW **Rev:** Four-line inscription in tablet

Date	Mintage	VG	F	VF	XF	Unc
1623	—	750	1,500	3,000	5,250	—
ND	—	750	1,500	3,000	5,250	—

KM# 27 ZECCHINO

3.5000 g., 0.9860 Gold 0.1109 oz. AGW, 22 mm. **Ruler:** Giacomo III **Obv:** Madonna with child

Date	Mintage	VG	F	VF	XF	Unc
ND	—	825	1,650	3,250	5,600	—

KM# 28 ZECCHINO

3.5000 g., 0.9860 Gold 0.1109 oz. AGW **Obv:** Bishop **Rev:** Crowned imperial eagle in inner circle

Date	Mintage	VG	F	VF	XF	Unc
ND	—	900	1,750	3,400	6,000	—

MANTUA

Mantova
Marquisate and Duchy

Originally of Etruscan foundation, Mantua is situated about 22 miles (37 kilometers) south-southwest of Verona and 36 miles (60 kilometers) east of Cremona. The city was famous in antiquity as the birthplace of Virgil and was made part of the kingdom of the Lombards in 601. Charlemagne made Mantua the seat of a countship, which was combined with the office of the local bishop by the later 9th century. Secular counts ruled Mantua again until the hereditary line died out in 1115 and Mantua became a republic. Elected administrators continually fell under imperial influence and the city was contested by the rival factions of Guelfs and Ghibellines. The family of Bonaccolsi controlled affairs in Mantua for about half a century before they were dispossessed by Luigi Gonzaga in 1328. He founded the dynasty that would rule Mantua and its considerable territory until the early 18th century.

At first, the Gonzagas were content with the title of captain, but the head of the family was named Vicar of the Empire in 1365. Mantua was raised to the status of Marquisate in 1432, but in 1530 the marchese was made duke. The city was sacked by imperial forces in 1630 and during the War of the Spanish Succession. The last duke was forced to allow French troops to occupy Mantua in 1703. The French left Italy in 1707 and the emperor declared the action by the duke to have allowed them entrance earlier as a felony. Invoking his right after the death of the last duke in 1708, the emperor claimed the fief reverted to the crown. It remained an imperial possession until Napoleon besieged and captured the city in 1797. It was returned to Austria in 1814 and became part of united Italy in 1866.

The Gonzagas followed the unusual practice of giving themselves numbers as the first, second, third, etc. marchese, then duke. The numbers are found on most of their coins in the form of Roman numerals and begin over again at 'I' when the marchese became the first duke.

RULERS

Vincenzo I, 1587-1612
Eleonora de'Medici, 1584-1611
Francesco IV, 1612, (Feb.–Dec.)
Ferdinando, 1612-1626
Vincenzo II, 1626-1627
Carlo I, 1627-1637
Carlo II Gonzaga Nevers, 1637-1665
w/his mother Maria as regent, 1637-1647
Ferdinando Carlo, 1665-1707
w/his mother Isabella Clara, as regent, 1665-1707

MONETARY SYSTEM

6 Denari = 1 Sesino
2 Sesini = 1 Soldo
20 Soldi = 1 Lira
12 Lire = 1 Tallero

MINT

Mantua

MINTMASTERS' INITIALS

CT - Carol Torre
GM, GMF - Gaspare Molo

Reference:

V = Alberto Varesi, ***Monete Italiane Regionali: Lombareia, Zecche Minori***. Pavia, 1995.

DUCHY

Gonzaga Family

STANDARD COINAGE

KM# 219 CINQUINTA (1/5 Soldi)

Billon **Ruler:** Carlo I **Obv:** Crowned shield **Obv. Legend:** MANT ANNOSALVTIS **Rev:** CG monogram, IIII below, all in wreath

Date	Mintage	VG	F	VF	XF	Unc
ND(1629)	—	50.00	100	190	350	—

KM# 221 CINQUINTA (1/5 Soldi)

Billon **Obv:** IIII in wreath **Rev:** Reliquary **Rev. Legend:** TABER SANG CHRIS

Date	Mintage	VG	F	VF	XF	Unc
ND(1629)	—	36.00	70.00	130	240	—

KM# 183 QUATTRINO

Copper **Ruler:** Carlo I **Obv:** Ornate cross **Obv. Legend:** CAR I DGD MAN MON ETC. **Rev:** Bust of Virgil right **Rev. Legend:** VIRGILIVS MARO **Note:** Weight varies: 1.30-1.45 grams.

Date	Mintage	VG	F	VF	XF	Unc
ND(1627-37)	—	40.00	80.00	150	300	—

KM# 192 SESINO (1/6 Soldi)

Billon **Ruler:** Carlo I **Obv:** Floriated cross in circle **Obv. Legend:** CAR. I. D. G. D. MAN. MON. ET. C. **Rev:** Laureate bust of Virgil right **Rev. Legend:** VIRGILIVS. MARO. **Note:** Weight varies: 1.00-1.26 g.

Date	Mintage	VG	F	VF	XF	Unc
ND(1627-37)	—	12.00	25.00	45.00	110	—

KM# 305 SESINO (1/6 Soldi)

Billon **Ruler:** Carlo II **Obv:** Head left **Obv. Legend:** CAROLVS II D G DVX **Rev:** MAN/TU/A within crowned wreath **Note:** Weight varies: 0.80-1.10 grams.

Date	Mintage	VG	F	VF	XF	Unc
ND(1647-65)	—	80.00	160	300	500	—

KM# 45 BARBARINA

Billon **Ruler:** Vincenzo I **Obv:** St. Barbara standing **Obv. Legend:** SANCTA BARBRA **Rev:** Plant **Rev. Legend:** IAM NVLLA FVGA **Note:** Weight varies: 1.60-1.70 grams.

Date	Mintage	VG	F	VF	XF	Unc
1605	—	40.00	80.00	150	240	—

KM# 55 BARBARINA

Billon **Ruler:** Francesco IV **Obv:** Crowned shield with FIDES **Obv. Legend:** FRAN IIII DG DVX MAN V ET M F III **Rev:** St. Barbara standing **Rev. Legend:** SANCTA BARBRA **Note:** Weight varies: 1.60-1.70 grams.

Date	Mintage	VG	F	VF	XF	Unc
ND(1612)	—	40.00	80.00	150	240	—

KM# 185 PARPAGLIOLA

Billon **Ruler:** Carlo I **Obv:** Mt. Olympus, FIDES **Obv. Legend:** CAR I D G DVX MAN ETC. **Rev:** St. Charles kneeling before cross **Rev. Legend:** SANCTVS CARLVS **Note:** Weight varies: 2.20-2.60 grams.

Date	Mintage	VG	F	VF	XF	Unc
ND(1627-37)	—	60.00	120	240	400	—

KM# 190 PARPAGLIOLA

Billon **Ruler:** Carlo II **Obv:** 2 angels holding pyx between them, MANTVA in exergue **Obv. Legend:** TABER. SANG. XPI. IESV. **Rev:** Madonna and child in circle **Rev. Legend:** MARIA. MATER. GRATIÆ **Note:** Weight varies: 1.31-2.00 g.

Date	Mintage	VG	F	VF	XF	Unc
ND(1637-47)	—	—	8.00	20.00	30.00	80.00

KM# 307 PARPAGLIOLA

Billon **Ruler:** Carlo II **Obv:** Crowned shield below Mt. Olympus **Obv. Legend:** CAR II D G DVX MANT ET M F **Rev:** St. Barbara standing **Rev. Legend:** SANCTA BARBRA **Note:** Weight varies: 2.20-2.60 grams.

Date	Mintage	VG	F	VF	XF	Unc
ND(1647-65)	—	50.00	100	200	350	—

KM# 353 PARPAGLIOLA

Billon **Obv:** Crowned shield **Obv. Legend:** CARLO II DVX MAN ET MON ETC. **Rev:** St. Patrick standing **Rev. Legend:** SANCTVS PATRITIVS **Note:** Weight varies: 2.20-2.60 grams.

Date	Mintage	VG	F	VF	XF	Unc
1661	—	70.00	130	280	450	—

KM# 14 ANSELMINO (Stretto)

6.5000 g., Billon **Ruler:** Vincenzo I **Obv:** Mt. Olympus above crowned shield **Obv. Legend:** VIN D G DVX MAN III ET MO F II **Rev:** St. Ansel standing **Rev. Legend:** SANCTVS ANSELMVS EPS

Date	Mintage	VG	F	VF	XF	Unc
ND(1587-1612)	—	70.00	140	290	550	—

KM# 16 ANSELMINO (Largo)
Billon **Obv:** Mt. Olympus above crowned shield **Obv. Legend:** VIN D G DVX MAN IIII ET M F II **Rev:** St. Ansel standing **Rev. Legend:** SANCTVS ANSELMVS EP **Note:** Weight varies: 5.70-6.00 grams.

Date	Mintage	VG	F	VF	XF	Unc
ND(1587-1612)	—	50.00	110	220	400	—

KM# 158 SOLDO
Copper **Ruler:** Vincenzo II **Obv:** Two religquaries **Obv. Legend:** NIHIL ISTO TRISTE RECEPTO **Rev:** Elephant, ACCENSVS SANGVINE IN HOSTES

Date	Mintage	VG	F	VF	XF	Unc
ND(1626-27)	—	44.00	90.00	170	350	—

KM# 161 SOLDO
Copper **Obv:** Legend in six lines within wreath **Obv. Legend:** VIN/ II D G/ DVX MAN/ VII ET/ M F/ V **Rev:** Galley **Rev. Legend:** HAC MOSTRANTE VIAM

Date	Mintage	VG	F	VF	XF	Unc
ND(1626-27)	—	250	500	1,000	1,650	—

KM# 163 SOLDO
Copper **Obv:** Four-line legend within crowned shield **Obv. Legend:** IVSTITA/ ET PAX/ OCSVLATAE/ SVNT **Rev:** Sword above olive branch

Date	Mintage	VG	F	VF	XF	Unc
ND(1626-27)	—	150	300	575	1,000	—

KM# 187 SOLDO
Copper **Ruler:** Carlo I **Obv:** Five-line legend within crowned shield **Obv. Legend:** CAR I D/ G MAN/ M F NI/ MAY R/ DVX **Rev:** Crucible in flames **Rev. Legend:** DOMINE PROBASTI

Date	Mintage	VG	F	VF	XF	Unc
ND(1627-37)	—	50.00	115	250	450	—

KM# 186 SOLDO
Copper **Ruler:** Carlo I **Obv:** 5-line inscription **Obv. Inscription:** CAROL / I. D. G. DVX / MAN. TVE / MON. FER / ET. C. **Rev:** Laureate bust of Virgil to left in circle **Rev. Legend:** VIRGILIV(S). MAR. MANT. **Note:** Weight varies: 2.14-4.46 g.

Date	Mintage	VG	F	VF	XF	Unc
ND(1627-37)	—	—	20.00	45.00	80.00	220

KM# 272 SOLDO
Copper **Ruler:** Carlo II **Obv:** Crowned shield, FIDES above **Obv. Legend:** MAR M CAR II D M E T M F E **Rev:** Reliquary **Rev. Legend:** TAB SANG CHRIST IESV

Date	Mintage	VG	F	VF	XF	Unc
ND(1637-47)	—	45.00	90.00	165	325	—

KM# 223 2 SOLDI
Billon **Ruler:** Carlo I **Obv:** Crowned II within wreath **Rev:** Reliquary **Rev. Legend:** TABER SA NG CHRI

Date	Mintage	VG	F	VF	XF	Unc
ND(1629-30)	—	50.00	100	190	375	—

KM# 225 6 SOLDI
2.1000 g., Copper **Ruler:** Carlo I **Obv:** Crowned arms within collar of The Redeemer **Rev:** 6 within oval shield

Date	Mintage	VG	F	VF	XF	Unc
ND(1629)	—	150	300	600	1,050	—

KM# 115 7 SOLDI
2.2000 g., Billon **Ruler:** Ferdinand **Obv:** Crowned shield **Obv. Legend:** FERD D G DVX MAN VI ET M F IV **Rev:** Radiant sun, 7 below **Rev. Legend:** NON MVTVATA LVCE

Date	Mintage	VG	F	VF	XF	Unc
ND(1614)	—	20.00	45.00	100	175	—

KM# A187 7 SOLDI
2.2000 g., Billon **Obv:** Crowned shield **Obv. Legend:** VINS DG DVX MAN VI M F V **Rev:** Radiant sun, 7 below **Rev. Legend:** MONETA LUCE

Date	Mintage	VG	F	VF	XF	Unc
ND(1627)	—	15.00	30.00	60.00	100	—

KM# 227 7 SOLDI
Copper **Obv:** Crowned M, 7 below **Rev:** Seated St. Ansel **Rev. Legend:** SANCTVS ANSELMVS **Note:** Weight varies: 4.90-6.90 g.

Date	Mintage	VG	F	VF	XF	Unc
ND(1629-30)	—	90.00	180	375	675	—

KM# 10 8 SOLDI
Silver **Ruler:** Vincenzo I and Eleonora **Obv:** Crowned oval Medici shield **Obv. Legend:** LEONORA DVCISSAE MANTVA **Rev:** Crowned Gonzaga shield **Rev. Legend:** MONETA DA OTTO SOLDI **Note:** Weight varies: 2.60-2.70 grams.

Date	Mintage	VG	F	VF	XF	Unc
ND(1584-1611)	—	225	425	825	1,800	—

KM# 56 8 SOLDI
3.0000 g., Billon **Ruler:** Ferdinand **Obv:** Legend in six lines **Obv. Inscription:** 8 / FERDIN / DG DVX / MANT VI / ER MONT / F IIII **Rev:** Radiant sun **Rev. Legend:** NON MVTVATA LVCE

Date	Mintage	VG	F	VF	XF	Unc
ND(1612-26)	—	22.50	45.00	90.00	150	—

KM# 117 8 SOLDI
3.0000 g., Billon **Ruler:** Ferdinand **Obv:** Eagle wtihin wreath, 8 below **Obv. Legend:** FER2 CAR D G DVX M VI ET ME F IIII

Date	Mintage	VG	F	VF	XF	Unc
ND(1614)	—	100	190	350	600	—

KM# 309 8 SOLDI
3.0000 g., Billon **Ruler:** Carlo II **Obv:** Legend in six lines **Obv. Inscription:** 8 / CAROLVX / DG DVX / MANT VIIII / ET MONT / F VIIII

Date	Mintage	VG	F	VF	XF	Unc
ND(1647-65)	—	18.00	37.50	75.00	135	—

KM# 12 10 SOLDI
Silver **Ruler:** Vincenzo I and Eleonora **Obv:** Shield, Mt. Olympus on top, FIDES and crown above **Obv. Legend:** VIN DG DVX M IIII ET M F II **Rev:** Shield of Medici **Rev. Legend:** LEONORA DVCISSA MANTVA **Note:** Weight varies: 2.75-3.25 grams.

Date	Mintage	VG	F	VF	XF	Unc
ND(1584-1611)	—	525	1,050	1,900	—	—

KM# 365 15 SOLDI
Billon **Ruler:** Ferdinando **Obv:** Conjoined busts right **Obv. Legend:** ISABELLA CLARA FERD CAR D G D MAN ET M F ET C **Rev:** Radiant sun, clouds and sea **Rev. Legend:** ALTA A LONGE COGNOSCIT **Note:** Weight varies: 3.30-3.50 grams.

Date	Mintage	VG	F	VF	XF	Unc
1666	—	70.00	140	280	500	—

KM# 189 20 SOLDI
Silver **Ruler:** Carlo I **Obv:** Cross with rose in each angle **Obv. Legend:** CAROLVS I D G DVX MANTVAE **Rev:** Mt. Olympus above crowned arms, all in the collar of The Redeemer, 20 below **Rev. Legend:** ET MON FER ETC

Date	Mintage	VG	F	VF	XF	Unc
ND(1627-37) Rare	—	—	—	—	—	—

KM# 191 20 SOLDI
Silver **Ruler:** Carlo II **Obv:** Saint kneeling before reliquary **Obv. Legend:** CAROLVS II D G DVX MANT **Rev:** Tree stump with new growth **Rev. Legend:** GLORIOSA PRODVCTIO

Date	Mintage	VG	F	VF	XF	Unc
ND(1637-65)	—	55.00	100	180	300	—

KM# 57 30 SOLDI (1/4 Scudo)
7.0000 g., Silver **Ruler:** Ferdinand **Obv:** Mt. Olympus above crowned shield, collar of The Redeemer above **Obv. Legend:** FERD D G DVX MAN VI ET M F IV **Rev:** St. Andrew standing with cross and reliquary **Rev. Legend:** NIHIL ISTO TRISTE RECEPTO

Date	Mintage	VG	F	VF	XF	Unc
ND(1612-26)	—	550	1,100	1,900	3,300	—

KM# 311 30 SOLDI (1/4 Scudo)
7.0000 g., Billon **Ruler:** Carlo II **Obv:** Armored bust left, XXX below **Obv. Legend:** CAROLVS II D G DVX MANT **Rev:** Crowned shield in the collar of The Redeemer **Rev. Legend:** ET MONT FERATI ET C

Date	Mintage	VG	F	VF	XF	Unc
ND(1647-65)	—	100	200	400	700	—

KM# 313 30 SOLDI (1/4 Scudo)
7.0000 g., Billon **Ruler:** Carlo II **Obv:** Mt. Olympus, FIDES on banner, XXX below **Obv. Legend:** ET MON FER NIVER RET VMENE ETC

Date	Mintage	VG	F	VF	XF	Unc
ND(1647-65)	—	525	1,050	1,900	—	—

KM# 367 30 SOLDI (1/4 Scudo)
7.0000 g., Billon **Ruler:** Ferdinando **Obv:** Conjoined bust right **Obv. Legend:** ISABELLA CLARA FER CAR D G MAN ET MF ETC. **Rev:** Radiant sun, clouds and sea **Rev. Legend:** ALTA A LONGE COGNOSCIT

Date	Mintage	VG	F	VF	XF	Unc
1666	—	60.00	120	225	400	—

KM# 61 40 SOLDI (2 Lire)
7.7000 g., Silver **Ruler:** Francesco IV **Obv:** Facing busts **Obv. Legend:** FRANCISCVS ET MARGARITA DVCES **Rev:** Crucible in flames **Rev. Legend:** DOMINE PROBASTI

Date	Mintage	VG	F	VF	XF	Unc
1612 Rare	—	—	—	—	—	—

KM# 59 40 SOLDI (2 Lire)
Silver **Ruler:** Ferdinand **Obv:** FIDES above Mt. Olympus, 40 in exergue **Obv. Legend:** FERD D G DVX MANT VI ET M F IV **Rev:** St. Barbara standing **Rev. Legend:** SANCTA BARBRA PROTECTRIX MANTVAE **Note:** Weight varies: 8.10-8.40 grams.

Date	Mintage	VG	F	VF	XF	Unc
ND(1612-26)	—	350	650	1,150	2,000	—

KM# 164 40 SOLDI (2 Lire)
7.7000 g., Silver **Ruler:** Vincenzo II **Obv:** Crowned shield with FIDES and Mt. Olympus **Obv. Legend:** VINC II DG DVX MANT VII ET MFB **Rev:** Aloiis Gonzaga kneeling before angel, 40 below **Rev. Legend:** B ALOIIS GONZ PROT MAN

Date	Mintage	VG	F	VF	XF	Unc
ND(1626-27)	—	300	550	1,050	1,900	—

KM# 165 40 SOLDI (2 Lire)
7.7000 g., Silver **Ruler:** Vincenzo II **Obv:** Bust left **Obv. Legend:** VINC II D G DVX MAN VII ET MFV **Rev:** Dog standing left **Rev. Legend:** FERIS TANTVM INFENSVS

Date	Mintage	VG	F	VF	XF	Unc
1627	—	400	700	1,300	—	—

KM# 167 40 SOLDI (2 Lire)
7.7000 g., Silver **Ruler:** Carlo I **Obv:** Crowned shield with Mt. Olympus, FIDES **Obv. Legend:** CAROL I D G MAN M F NIV MAY RET DVX ETC. **Rev:** Aloiis Gonzaga kneeling before angel **Rev. Legend:** B ALOIIS GONZ PROT MAN

Date	Mintage	VG	F	VF	XF	Unc
ND(1627-37)	—	250	500	1,000	1,800	—

KM# 315 40 SOLDI (2 Lire)
7.7000 g., Silver **Ruler:** Carlo II **Obv:** Crowned arms in collar of The Redeemer **Obv. Legend:** CAROLVX II D G DVX MANT ET M F **Rev:** St. Barbara standing with palm **Rev. Legend:** SANCTA BARBARA PROTECTRIX

Date	Mintage	VG	F	VF	XF	Unc
ND(1647-1665)	—	100	200	400	700	—

KM# 340 40 SOLDI (2 Lire)
7.7000 g., Silver **Ruler:** Carlo II **Obv:** Bust right **Obv. Legend:** CAROL II OG DVX MAN ET M **Rev:** Crowned shield, Mt. Olympus above **Rev. Legend:** SIT NOMEN DOMINI BENEDICTUM

Date	Mintage	VG	F	VF	XF	Unc
1653	—	—	—	—	—	—

KM# 355 40 SOLDI (2 Lire)
7.7000 g., Silver **Ruler:** Carlo II **Rev:** Sun in zodiac, stars, clouds, and earth **Rev. Legend:** NEC RETROGRADIOR NEC DEVIO

Date	Mintage	VG	F	VF	XF	Unc
1663	—	1,200	2,450	4,550	7,700	—

KM# 361 40 SOLDI (2 Lire)
7.7000 g., Silver **Ruler:** Carlo II **Obv:** Crowned oval shield in order collar **Obv. Legend:** CAR II D G DBX MAN ET M FE ETC **Rev:** St. George slaying dragon **Rev. Legend:** PROTECTOR NOSTER ASPICE

Date	Mintage	VG	F	VF	XF	Unc
1664	—	150	300	525	975	—

KM# 426 40 SOLDI (2 Lire)
Billon **Ruler:** Ferdinando **Obv:** Bust right **Obv. Legend:** FERDI CAR D G DVX MANTVAE MON FER CAR VIL GVAS EC. **Rev:** Abundance standing with goods **Rev. Legend:** NON OMNIBVS OMNIA

Date	Mintage	VG	F	VF	XF	Unc
MDCXC (1690)	—	250	500	800	1,500	—

KM# 125 55 SOLDI (1/2 Ducatone)
13.1000 g., Silver **Ruler:** Ferdinand **Obv:** Bust right **Obv. Legend:** FERDINANDVS D G DVX MAN VI MANT **Rev:** Crowned shield with Mt. Olympus, FIDES all in collar of The Redeemer **Rev. Legend:** ET MONTIS FERRAT IV SOLDI 55

Date	Mintage	VG	F	VF	XF	Unc
1616 Rare	—	—	—	—	—	—

KM# 317 60 SOLDI (1/2 Scudo)
Billon **Ruler:** Carlo II **Obv:** Bust left **Obv. Legend:** CAROLUV II D G DVX MANTVE **Rev:** Mt. Olympus, FIDES above, 60 in exergue **Rev. Legend:** ET MON FER NIVER RET VIMEN ETC **Note:** Weight varies: 13.75-14.25 grams.

Date	Mintage	VG	F	VF	XF	Unc
ND(1647-65)	—	975	1,800	3,750	—	—

KM# 369 60 SOLDI (1/2 Scudo)
Billon **Ruler:** Carlo II **Obv:** Conjoined busts right **Obv. Legend:** ISABELLA CLARA FERD CAR DGD MAN ET M ET C **Rev:** Radiant sun, clouds, and sea **Rev. Legend:** ALTO A LONGE COGNOSCIT **Note:** Weight varies: 13.75-14.25 grams.

Date	Mintage	VG	F	VF	XF	Unc
1666	—	85.00	175	300	525	—

KM# 99 80 SOLDI (1/2 Ducatone)
Silver **Ruler:** Ferdinand **Obv:** Eagle within laruel wreath **Rev:** Maltese cross, crown and bishop's hat, 80 below

Date	Mintage	VG	F	VF	XF	Unc
1613 Unique	—	—	—	—	—	—

KM# 193.1 80 SOLDI (1/2 Ducatone)
13.1000 g., Silver **Ruler:** Carlo I **Obv:** Crowned shield with Mt. Olympus in order collar **Obv. Legend:** CAROL I D G DVX MAN ET MON FOR **Rev:** St. Luigi kneeling in prayer to angel **Rev. Legend:** B ALOIIS GONZ PROT MAN

Date	Mintage	VG	F	VF	XF	Unc
ND(1627-37)	—	180	350	650	1,100	—

KM# 193.2 80 SOLDI (1/2 Ducatone)
13.1000 g., Silver **Ruler:** Carlo I **Obv:** Crowned shield. **Obv. Legend:** CAROLVS I D G MAN MONF NIV MAY RET DVX ETC **Rev:** St. Luigi kneeling in prayer to angel **Rev. Legend:** B ALOIIS GONZ PROT MAN

Date	Mintage	VG	F	VF	XF	Unc
ND(1627-37)	—	180	350	650	1,100	—

KM# 229 80 SOLDI (1/2 Ducatone)
Silver **Ruler:** Carlo I **Obv:** Crowned shield **Obv. Legend:** MANTVAE ANNO SALVTIS **Rev:** Sunflower within beaded circle all within wreath, 80 below **Note:** Weight varies: 14.75-15.00 grams.

Date	Mintage	VG	F	VF	XF	Unc
1629	—	1,200	2,250	4,500	7,500	—

KM# 318 80 SOLDI (1/2 Ducatone)
Silver **Ruler:** Carlo II **Obv:** Crowned arms in collar of The Redeemer **Obv. Legend:** CAROLVS II D G DVX MANT ET M F **Rev:** St.

Barbara standing with palm, 80 below **Rev. Legend:** SANCTA BARBARA PROTECTRIX **Note:** Weight varies: 14.75-15.00 grams.

Date	Mintage	VG	F	VF	XF	Unc
ND(1647-65)	—	150	270	500	800	—

KM# 49 110 SOLDI
25.7000 g., Silver **Ruler:** Ferdinand **Obv:** Armored bust right **Obv. Legend:** FERDINANDVS D G DVX MAN VI MANT **Rev:** Crowned shieLd with Mt. Olympus and FIDES above, 110 below **Rev. Legend:** ET MONTIS FERRATI IV **Note:** Dav. #3941.

Date	Mintage	VG	F	VF	XF	Unc
1607(1617)	—	—	—	—	—	—
1617	—	1,650	3,250	6,500	—	—
Note: Error: 100 in reverse exergue						
1618	—	—	—	—	—	—

KM# 127 110 SOLDI
25.7000 g., Silver **Ruler:** Ferdinand **Obv:** Armored bust right **Obv. Legend:** FERDINANDVS DG DVX MAN VI **Rev:** Crowned arms in collar of The Redeemer, value below **Rev. Legend:** ET MONTIS FERRAT IV **Note:** Dav. #3939.

Date	Mintage	VG	F	VF	XF	Unc
1616	—	900	1,800	3,250	—	—
1618	—	900	1,800	3,250	—	—

KM# 63 120 SOLDI (Tallero)
Silver **Ruler:** Francesco IV **Obv:** Crowned arms with Mt. Olympus, FIDES in collar of The Redemmer **Obv. Legend:** FRAN IIII DG DVX MAN V ET MON III **Rev:** Kneeling St. Andrew receives reliquary from St. Andrew **Rev. Legend:** NIHIL ISTO TRISTE RECRPTO **Note:** Dav. #3932.

Date	Mintage	VG	F	VF	XF	Unc
1612 Rare	—	—	—	—	—	—

KM# 65.1 120 SOLDI (Tallero)
Silver **Ruler:** Ferdinand **Obv:** Cardinal's hat tops crowned shield with Mt. Olympus, FIDES within collar **Obv. Legend:** FER S RED CAR D G DVX MAN VI ET MON F IIII **Rev:** St. Andrew and St. Longuino, 120 in exergue below **Rev. Legend:** NIHIL ISTO TRISTE RECRPTO **Note:** Dav. #3933. Obverse legend varieties exist.

Date	Mintage	VG	F	VF	XF	Unc
1612	—	1,150	2,450	4,550	—	—
1613	—	1,150	2,450	4,550	—	—

KM# 65.2 120 SOLDI (Tallero)
Silver **Ruler:** Ferdinand **Rev:** St. Andrew and St. Longuino, decoration in exergue **Note:** Dav. #3934.

Date	Mintage	VG	F	VF	XF	Unc
1613	—	1,150	2,450	4,550	—	—
1615	—	1,150	2,450	4,550	—	—

KM# 101 120 SOLDI (Tallero)
Silver **Ruler:** Ferdinand **Obv:** Crowned shield, no cardinal's hat **Obv. Legend:** FERDINAN DG DVX MANT VI ET MONF IV **Note:** Dav. #3935.

Date	Mintage	VG	F	VF	XF	Unc
1613	—	1,150	2,450	4,550	—	—

KM# 230 160 SOLDI (Scudo)
Silver **Ruler:** Ferdinand **Obv:** Mt. Olympus, FIDES above, 160 below **Rev:** Saint standing before tower, MANTVAE below **Note:** Dav. #3948.

Date	Mintage	VG	F	VF	XF	Unc
ND	—	700	1,500	2,900	5,600	—

KM# 231 160 SOLDI (Scudo)
Silver **Ruler:** Carlo I **Obv:** Crowned shield **Obv. Legend:** MANTVAE ANNO SALVTIS **Rev:** Sunflower within wreath, 160 below **Note:** Dav. #3958.

Date	Mintage	VG	F	VF	XF	Unc
1629	—	1,000	2,000	4,000	6,500	—

Note: Ira & Larry Goldberg Coins & Collectibles Auction 46 - The Millennia Collection, 5-08, AU-55 realized $9,500

KM# 351 LUIGINO
2.4000 g., Silver **Ruler:** Carlo II **Obv:** Bust left **Obv. Legend:** CAR II D G DVX MANT M F ETC **Rev:** Crowned shield, with Mt. Olympus above **Rev. Legend:** AVORVM LILIIS FLORET OLYMPVS

Date	Mintage	VG	F	VF	XF	Unc
1660 Rare	—	—	—	—	—	—

KM# 169 1/2 GROSSETTO
Silver **Ruler:** Vincenzo II **Obv:** Large crowned V **Rev:** Crucible in flames

Date	Mintage	VG	F	VF	XF	Unc
ND(1626-27)	—	60.00	120	240	400	—

KM# 171 1/2 GROSSETTO
Silver **Ruler:** Vincenzo II **Obv:** Four-line legend within crowned shield **Obv. Legend:** VINC/ III DVX/ MANT/ VII **Rev:** Crucible in flames **Rev. Legend:** DOMINO PROBASTI

Date	Mintage	VG	F	VF	XF	Unc
ND(1626-27)	—	40.00	70.00	130	250	—

KM# 195 1/2 GROSSETTO
Silver **Ruler:** Carlo I **Obv:** Five-line legend within crowned shield **Obv. Legend:** CAR I D/ G MAR/ M TVI/ MAV/ DVX **Rev:** Crucible in flames **Rev. Legend:** DOMINE PROBASTI

Date	Mintage	VG	F	VF	XF	Unc
ND(1627-37)	—	40.00	70.00	130	250	—

KM# 18 GROSSETTO
1.5000 g., Silver **Ruler:** Vincenzo I **Obv:** Mt. Olympus, FIDES above **Obv. Legend:** VIN D G DVX M IIII ET M F II **Rev:** Tree **Rev. Legend:** ROBORE SISTIT

Date	Mintage	VG	F	VF	XF	Unc
ND(1587-1612)	—	60.00	110	190	400	—

KM# 173 GROSSETTO
1.5000 g., Silver **Ruler:** Vincenzo II **Obv:** Mt. Olympus above crowned arms **Obv. Legend:** VIN II D G DVX MAN VII ET MFV **Rev:** IIII around sword and palm

Date	Mintage	VG	F	VF	XF	Unc
ND(1626-27)	—	60.00	110	190	400	—

KM# 20 GROSSO
3.2000 g., Silver **Ruler:** Vincenzo I **Obv:** Crowned shield with Mt. Olympus and FIDES **Obv. Legend:** VIN D G DVX MA IIII ET MA F II **Rev:** Reliquary **Rev. Legend:** TABERN SAGVINIS XPI IESV

Date	Mintage	VG	F	VF	XF	Unc
ND(1587-1612)	—	70.00	150	300	500	—

KM# 22 GROSSO
3.2000 g., Silver **Ruler:** Vincenzo II **Obv:** Legend in six lines **Obv. Legend:** VIN/ II D G/ DVX MAN/ VII ET/ MF/ V **Rev:** Galley **Rev. Legend:** HAC MONSTRANTE VIAM

Date	Mintage	VG	F	VF	XF	Unc
ND(1587-1612)	—	225	375	675	1,050	—

KM# 175 GROSSO
3.2000 g., Silver **Ruler:** Vincenzo II **Obv:** Legend in four lines in wreath **Obv. Inscription:** IVSTITIA / ET PAX / OSCVLATAE / SVNT **Rev:** Sword and olive branch

Date	Mintage	VG	F	VF	XF	Unc
ND(1626-27)	—	265	425	725	1,150	—

KM# 177 2 GROSSO
2.7500 g., Silver **Ruler:** Vincenzo II **Obv:** Pair of reliquaries **Obv. Legend:** NIHL ISTO TRISTE RECEPTO **Rev:** Elephant **Rev. Legend:** ACCENSVS SANGVINE IN HOSTES

Date	Mintage	VG	F	VF	XF	Unc
ND(1626-27) Rare	—	—	—	—	—	—

KM# 303 ESCALIN
3.9500 g., Silver **Ruler:** Carlo II **Obv:** Rampant lion **Obv. Legend:** CARLO D G DVX MANTMO AR P **Rev:** Crowned shield divides date **Rev. Legend:** RO ET MO VII ST

Date	Mintage	VG	F	VF	XF	Unc
1646	—	—	—	—	—	—

KM# 264 1/2 GIULIO
Silver **Ruler:** Carlo I **Obv:** Crowned shield, Mt. Olympus above **Obv. Legend:** CAR I D G DVX MAN ET M F **Rev:** St. Lucia standing with palm divides date **Rev. Legend:** SANCTA LVCIA **Note:** Weight varies: 1.35-1.50 grams.

Date	Mintage	VG	F	VF	XF	Unc
1633	—	50.00	100	200	400	—

KM# 24 GIULIO
2.2000 g., Silver **Ruler:** Vincenzo I **Obv:** Reliquary **Obv. Legend:** TABERN SANGVINI CHRIST IESV **Rev:** St. Francis receiving the stigmata **Rev. Legend:** SVB TVVM PRAESIDIVM

Date	Mintage	Good	VG	F	VF	XF
ND	—	80.00	160	300	500	—

KM# 47 GIULIO
2.2000 g., Silver **Ruler:** Vincenzo I **Obv:** Reliquary **Obv. Legend:** CHRISTI IESV TABER SANGVINI **Rev:** St. Francis receiving the stigmata **Rev. Legend:** SVB TVVM PRAESIDIVM

Date	Mintage	Good	VG	F	VF	XF
1601	—	25.00	50.00	90.00	180	350
1605	—	25.00	50.00	90.00	180	350

KM# 266 GIULIO
2.2000 g., Silver **Ruler:** Carlo I **Obv:** Crowned arms with Mt. Olympus, FIDES above **Obv. Legend:** CAR I DG DM ET M F ET C **Rev:** Standing St. Lucia divides date

Date	Mintage	VG	F	VF	XF	Unc
1633	—	50.00	90.00	160	300	—

KM# 67 1/2 LIRE (1/2 Mocenigo)
Silver **Ruler:** Ferdinand **Obv:** Shield **Obv. Legend:** FERDIN D G DVX MAN VI ET MONF IIII **Rev:** St. Longuino with reliquary **Rev. Legend:** AB OMNI MA LO DEFENDE NOS **Note:** Weight varies: 2.80-3.10 grams.

Date	Mintage	VG	F	VF	XF	Unc
ND(1612-26)	—	350	700	1,300	2,000	—

KM# 197 1/2 LIRE (1/2 Mocenigo)
Silver **Ruler:** Carlo I **Obv:** Crowned shield **Obv. Legend:** CA I D G M ET M F ET **Rev:** St. Lucia standing **Rev. Legend:** SANCTA LVCIA **Note:** Weight varies: 2.80-3.10 grams.

Date	Mintage	VG	F	VF	XF	Unc
ND(1627-36) Rare	—	—	—	—	—	—

KM# 69 LIRA
Silver **Ruler:** Francesco IV **Obv:** Crowned shield with Mt. Olympus, FIDES **Obv. Legend:** FRAN IIII D G DVX MAN ET M F IIII **Rev:** St. Ansel standing **Rev. Legend:** SANCTVS ANSELMVS EPS **Note:** Weight varies: 5.90-6.10 grams.

Date	Mintage	VG	F	VF	XF	Unc
ND(1612)	—	90.00	180	325	550	—
1612	—	90.00	180	325	550	—

KM# 419 LIRA
Billon **Ruler:** Ferdinando **Obv:** Bust right **Obv. Legend:** FERDINAN CAR D G DVX **Rev:** Mt. Olympus and FIDES **Rev. Legend:** MANTVAE MON FER CAR VIL GVAST

Date	Mintage	VG	F	VF	XF	Unc
1689	—	75.00	150	255	525	—

KM# 71 TESTONE
8.8000 g., Silver **Ruler:** Francesco IV **Obv:** Crowned shield within collar of The Redeemer **Obv. Legend:** FRANC IIII DVX MANT V ET MO FR III **Rev:** Bust of Madonna **Rev. Legend:** HAC MOSTRANTE VIAM IIII

Date	Mintage	VG	F	VF	XF	Unc
1612 Rare	—	—	—	—	—	—

KM# 301 1/8 SCUDO
Silver **Ruler:** Carlo II **Obv:** Crowned shield in order collar **Obv. Legend:** CAR II DG DVX MAN ET M F ET C **Rev:** St. George slaying dragon **Rev. Legend:** PROTECTOR NOSTER ASPICE

Date	Mintage	VG	F	VF	XF	Unc
1664	—	190	375	600	1,050	—

KM# 233 1/4 SCUDO
Silver **Ruler:** Carlo I **Obv:** Crowned arms **Obv. Legend:** MANTVAE ANNO SALVTIS **Rev:** Sunflower **Note:** Weight varies: 6.50-7.50 grams.

Date	Mintage	VG	F	VF	XF	Unc
1629	—	1,150	2,250	4,400	—	—

KM# 371 1/4 SCUDO
5.2200 g., Silver **Ruler:** Ferdinando **Obv:** Crowned shield of Austria and Gonzaga **Obv. Legend:** ISABELLA CLARA FERD CAROL D G DV **Rev:** Cross with octolobe

Date	Mintage	VG	F	VF	XF	Unc
1666 Rare	—	—	—	—	—	—

KM# 103 1/2 SCUDO (60 Soldi = 1/2 Tallero)
15.4000 g., Silver **Ruler:** Ferdinand **Obv:** Shield with Mt. Olympus, cardinal's cap above **Obv. Legend:** FER SRCD CAR DG DVX MA VI ET MF III **Rev:** St. Longuino and St. Andrew standing **Rev. Legend:** NIHIL ISTO TRISTE RECEPTO

Date	Mintage	VG	F	VF	XF	Unc
1613 Rare	—	—	—	—	—	—

KM# 154 1/2 SCUDO (60 Soldi = 1/2 Tallero)
15.4000 g., Silver **Ruler:** Ferdinand **Obv:** Mt. Olympus **Obv. Legend:** FERD DG DVX MANT VI ET MON F IV **Rev:** St. Barbara holding palm **Rev. Legend:** SANCTA BARBARA PAROTECTRIX

Date	Mintage	VG	F	VF	XF	Unc
1624	—	975	1,900	3,750	6,000	—

KM# 179 1/2 SCUDO (60 Soldi = 1/2 Tallero)
15.4000 g., Silver **Ruler:** Vincenzo II **Obv:** Crowned shield with Mt. Olympus, FIDES **Obv. Legend:** VINCEN II D G DVX MANT VII ET MON FV **Rev:** Kneeling Aloiis gonzaga in prayer to angel with palm **Rev. Legend:** B ALOIIS GONZ PROT MAN

Date	Mintage	VG	F	VF	XF	Unc
ND(1626-27)	—	265	525	975	1,500	—

KM# 237 1/2 SCUDO (60 Soldi = 1/2 Tallero)
9.7700 g., Billon **Ruler:** Carlo I **Obv:** St. Andrew with reliquary **Obv. Legend:** NIHIL ISTO TRISTE RECEPTO **Rev:** Crucible in flames **Rev. Legend:** DOMINE PROBASTI ME ET COGNOVISTI ME

Date	Mintage	VG	F	VF	XF	Unc
ND(1629-30)	—	500	1,000	2,000	4,000	—
1630	—	1,050	2,250	4,050	7,500	—

KM# 235 1/2 SCUDO (60 Soldi = 1/2 Tallero)
Billon **Ruler:** Carlo I **Obv:** St. Andrew with cross and reliquary **Obv. Legend:** IHIL ISTO TRISTE RECEPTO MANTVAE **Rev:** Crucible in flames **Rev. Legend:** DOMINE PROBASTI ME ET COGNOVISTI ME **Note:** Weight varies: 11.90-13.00 grams.

Date	Mintage	VG	F	VF	XF	Unc
ND(1629-30)	—	165	325	575	1,100	—

KM# 237a 1/2 SCUDO (60 Soldi = 1/2 Tallero)
9.9000 g., Billon **Ruler:** Carlo I

Date	Mintage	VG	F	VF	XF	Unc
ND(1629-30)	—	300	525	975	1,750	—

KM# 417 1/2 SCUDO (60 Soldi = 1/2 Tallero)
Silver **Ruler:** Ferdinando **Obv:** Crowned shield **Obv. Legend:** FERDINANDVS CAROLVS D G DVX **Rev:** Cross **Rev. Legend:** MANTVAE MONTISO FERRATI CAROLIVIL ET C **Note:** Weight varies: 10.50-10.70 grams.

Date	Mintage	VG	F	VF	XF	Unc
1675	—	200	400	750	1,250	—
1680	—	200	400	750	1,250	—

KM# 428 1/2 SCUDO (60 Soldi = 1/2 Tallero)
Silver **Ruler:** Ferdinando **Obv:** Bust right **Obv. Legend:** FERDINAN CAR D G DVX **Rev:** Crowned arms in collar of The Redeemer **Rev. Legend:** MANTVAE MON FER CAR VIL G **Note:** Weight varies: 10.50-10.70 grams.

Date	Mintage	VG	F	VF	XF	Unc
1691	—	130	260	525	975	—

KM# 239 SCUDO
Silver **Ruler:** Carlo I **Obv:** St. Andrew with cross and reliquary, MANT(VAE) below, date on base **Rev:** Crucible of gold rods in flames **Note:** Dav. #3956.

Date	Mintage	VG	F	VF	XF	Unc
1629	—	2,000	4,000	6,500	—	—
ND	—	800	1,650	2,750	4,500	—

KM# 260 SCUDO
Silver **Ruler:** Carlo I **Obv:** MAN • OBSES on base, date below saint **Note:** Dav. #3957.

Date	Mintage	VG	F	VF	XF	Unc
1630	—	1,800	3,500	6,000	—	—
ND	—	850	1,750	2,850	4,750	—

KM# 373 SCUDO
26.7000 g., Silver **Ruler:** Ferdinando **Obv:** Crowned shield of Austria and Gonzaga **Obv. Legend:** ISABELLA CLARA FERD CAROL D G DVC **Rev:** Cross within octolobe, legend, date **Rev. Legend:** MANT MON F CARLO VIL RETH ET C **Note:** Dav. #3968.

Date	Mintage	VG	F	VF	XF	Unc
1666	—	500	1,000	1,900	—	—

KM# 406 SCUDO
26.7000 g., Silver **Ruler:** Ferdinando **Obv:** Crowned arms of Austria and Gonzaga **Obv. Legend:** FERDINANDVS CAROLVS D G DVX **Rev:** Cross with items in angles **Rev. Legend:** MANTVAE MONTIS FERRATI CAROLI VIL ET C **Note:** Dav. #3969.

Date	Mintage	VG	F	VF	XF	Unc
1675	—	250	450	1,000	2,500	—
1678/7	—	200	350	750	1,500	—
1678	—	200	350	750	1,500	—
1680	—	200	350	750	1,500	—

KM# 408 SCUDO
26.7000 g., Silver **Ruler:** Ferdinando **Obv:** Armored bust right **Obv. Legend:** FERDINANDVS CAR D G DVX MANTVAE MON FER ET C **Rev:** Radiant sun over landscape, eagle in flight **Rev. Legend:** QVAE MAJOR ORIGO D **Note:** Dav. #3970.

Date	Mintage	VG	F	VF	XF	Unc
1676 Rare	—	—	—	—	—	—

KM# 142 TALLERO
25.7000 g., Silver **Ruler:** Ferdinand **Obv:** Bust right **Obv. Legend:** FERDIN DG DVX MANT VI ET MONT F IV **Rev:** Crowned shield with Mt. Olympus, FIDES **Rev. Legend:** DOMINE PROBASTI **Note:** Dav. #3943.

Date	Mintage	VG	F	VF	XF	Unc
1620 Rare	—	—	—	—	—	—

KM# 144 TALLERO
25.7000 g., Silver **Ruler:** Ferdinand **Rev:** Crowned shield with Mt. Olympus, FIDES, in collar of The Redeemer **Rev. Legend:** ET MONTIS FERRATI IV **Note:** Dav. #3944.

Date	Mintage	VG	F	VF	XF	Unc
1620 Rare	—	—	—	—	—	—

KM# 146 TALLERO
25.7000 g., Silver **Ruler:** Ferdinand **Obv:** Shield wtih four eagles **Rev:** Crowned shield with Mt. Olympus, FIDES, within collar of The Redeemer **Note:** Dav. #3946.

Date	Mintage	VG	F	VF	XF	Unc
1620	—	2,000	4,000	9,000	—	—
1622	—	2,000	4,000	9,000	—	—

KM# 150 TALLERO
25.7000 g., Silver **Ruler:** Ferdinand **Rev:** Crowned shield with four eagles, Mt. Olympus, FIDES within collar of The Redeemer **Note:** Dav. #3945.

Date	Mintage	VG	F	VF	XF	Unc
MDCXXI (1621)	—	900	1,700	3,000	—	—
MDCXXII (1622)	—	900	1,700	3,000	—	—

KM# 268 TALLERO
25.7000 g., Silver **Ruler:** Carlo I **Obv:** Crowned arms, FIDES above **Rev:** Cross in frame, date above **Note:** Dav. #3955.

Date	Mintage	VG	F	VF	XF	Unc
1633 Rare	—	—	—	—	—	—

KM# 357 1/8 DUCATONE
4.0500 g., Silver **Ruler:** Carlo II **Obv:** Crowned arms, FIDES above **Obv. Legend:** CAR II DG DM ET MF ETC **Rev:** St. Lucy standing

Date	Mintage	VG	F	VF	XF	Unc
1663	—	120	250	450	750	—

KM# 198 1/2 DUCATONE
Silver **Ruler:** Ferdinand **Obv:** Bust right wearing cardinal's birretto and cape **Obv. Legend:** FER. CAR. - D. G. - DVX. M. VI. ET. M. F. IIII. **Rev:** Radiant sun face **Rev. Legend:** NON. MVTVATA. LVCE **Note:** Weight varies: 15.34-15.72 g.

Date	Mintage	VG	F	VF	XF	Unc
ND(1612-26)	—	—	850	1,650	3,500	6,600

KM# 199 1/2 DUCATONE
15.5700 g., Silver **Ruler:** Vincenzo II **Obv:** Bust left **Obv. Legend:** VINCII D G DVX MAN VII ET M FV **Rev:** Dog standing left **Rev. Legend:** FERIS TANTVM INFENSVS

Date	Mintage	VG	F	VF	XF	Unc
MDCXXVII (1627)	—	825	1,500	2,650	4,300	—
MDCXXVIII (1628)	—	—	—	—	—	—

KM# 241 1/2 DUCATONE
15.5700 g., Silver **Ruler:** Carlo I **Obv:** Armored bust right **Obv. Legend:** CAROLVS I D G DVX MAN ET M F ETC **Rev:** Sun, zodiac symbols, stars, earth **Rev. Legend:** NEC RETROGRADIOR NEC DEVIO

Date	Mintage	VG	F	VF	XF	Unc
1629	—	—	—	—	—	—
1631	—	750	1,350	2,500	4,150	—

KM# 274 1/2 DUCATONE
15.5700 g., Silver **Ruler:** Carlo II **Obv:** Conjoined busts left, woman veiled **Obv. Legend:** MARIA ET CAR II DGC MAN ET MON FETC **Rev:** Madonna and child **Rev. Legend:** MARIA MATER GRACIAE PROTECTRIX NOSTRA MANTVAE

Date	Mintage	VG	F	VF	XF	Unc
ND(1637-47)	—	1,750	3,150	5,600	—	—

KM# 342 1/2 DUCATONE
15.5700 g., Silver **Ruler:** Carlo II **Obv:** Bust right **Obv. Legend:** CAROL II D G DVX MAN ET M **Rev:** Crowned shield **Rev. Legend:** SIT NOMEN DOMINI BENEDICTVM

Date	Mintage	VG	F	VF	XF	Unc
1653 Rare	—	—	—	—	—	—

KM# 359 1/2 DUCATONE
15.5700 g., Silver **Ruler:** Carlo II **Obv:** Bust left **Obv. Legend:** CAR II D G DVBX MAN ET M F ET C **Rev:** Sun in zodiac, clouds and earth **Rev. Legend:** NEC RETROGRADIOR NEC DEVIO

Date	Mintage	VG	F	VF	XF	Unc
1663	—	1,250	2,500	4,400	7,500	—

KM# 375 1/2 DUCATONE
15.5700 g., Silver **Ruler:** Ferdinando **Obv:** Conjoined busts right **Obv. Legend:** ISABELLA CLARA FERD CAR D G D MAN **Rev:** Radiant sun above clouds and sea

Date	Mintage	VG	F	VF	XF	Unc
1666	—	750	1,350	2,250	3,500	—

KM# 26 DUCATONE
Silver **Ruler:** Vincenzo I **Obv:** Bust left **Obv. Legend:** VIN D G DVX MAN III ET MON FER II **Rev:** St. George slaying dragon **Rev. Legend:** PROTECTOR NOSTER ASPICE MANTVA **Note:** Weight varies: 31.40-31.80 grams.

Date	Mintage	VG	F	VF	XF	Unc
ND(1587-1612)	—	1,900	3,500	5,600	—	—

KM# 28 DUCATONE
Silver **Ruler:** Vincenzo I **Obv:** Bust left **Obv. Legend:** VINCENTIVS D G DVX MANT IIII **Rev:** Crowned shield with Mt. Olympus within fleece collar **Rev. Legend:** ET MONTIS FERRATI II **Note:** Weight varies: 31.40-31.80 grams.

Date	Mintage	VG	F	VF	XF	Unc
ND(1587-1612)	—	800	1,400	2,400	—	—

KM# 30 DUCATONE
Silver **Ruler:** Vincenzo I **Obv:** Bust left **Obv. Legend:** VINCENTIVS D G DVX MANTVAE IIII **Rev:** Crowned shield in fleece collar **Rev. Legend:** ET MONTIS FERRATI **Note:** Weight varies: 31.40-31.80 grams.

Date	Mintage	VG	F	VF	XF	Unc
ND(1587-1612)	—	1,100	1,950	3,250	—	—

KM# 73 DUCATONE

Silver **Ruler:** Francesco IV **Obv:** Armored bust right, date below **Obv. Legend:** FRAN IIII D G DVX MANTV ET M F III **Rev:** St. Francis kneeling with cross, church in distance **Rev. Legend:** PROTECTOR FACTVS EST MIHI **Note:** Weight varies: 31.40-31.80 grams. Dav. #3931.

Date	Mintage	VG	F	VF	XF	Unc
1612	—	600	1,000	2,000	—	—

KM# 75 DUCATONE

Silver **Ruler:** Ferdinand **Obv:** Mt. Olympus with FIDES above **Obv. Legend:** FERD D G DVX MANT VI ET MONT F IV **Rev:** St. Barbara standing with palm **Rev. Legend:** FERIS TANTVM INFENSVS **Note:** Weight varies: 31.40-31.80 grams.

Date	Mintage	VG	F	VF	XF	Unc
ND(1612-26)	—	525	1,150	2,200	4,200	—

KM# 105.1 DUCATONE

Silver **Ruler:** Ferdinand **Obv:** Bust as cardinal left **Obv. Legend:** FERD CARD D G DVX MAN VI ET M F IIII **Rev:** Radiant sun **Rev. Legend:** MON MVTVATA LVCE **Note:** Weight varies: 31.40-31.80 grams. Dav. #3937.

Date	Mintage	VG	F	VF	XF	Unc
1613 Rare	—	—	—	—	—	—
MDCXIIII (1613) Rare	—	—	—	—	—	—
MDCXV (1615) Rare	—	—	—	—	—	—

KM# 105.3 DUCATONE

Silver **Ruler:** Ferdinand **Obv:** Armored bust right **Note:** Weight varies: 31.40-31.80 grams. Dav. #3947.

Date	Mintage	VG	F	VF	XF	Unc
ND(1612-26)	—	800	1,600	3,000	—	—

KM# 105.4 DUCATONE

Silver **Ruler:** Ferdinand **Obv:** Thinner bust **Note:** Weight varies: 31.40-31.80 grams. Dav. #3947A.

Date	Mintage	VG	F	VF	XF	Unc
ND(1612-26)	—	900	1,800	3,200	—	—

KM# 105.2 DUCATONE

Silver **Ruler:** Ferdinand **Obv:** Bust right in inner circle **Note:** Weight varies: 31.40-31.80 grams. Dav. #3940.

Date	Mintage	VG	F	VF	XF	Unc
1617	—	650	1,300	2,350	3,750	—

KM# 201 DUCATONE

Silver **Ruler:** Vincenzo II **Obv:** Armored bust right **Obv. Legend:** PRINC VINCENTIVS GONZA **Rev:** Globe frame in collar **Rev. Legend:** IMMOBILIS IN MOTV **Note:** Weight varies: 31.40-31.80 grams. Dav. #3952.

Date	Mintage	VG	F	VF	XF	Unc
ND Rare	—	—	—	—	—	—

KM# 203.1 DUCATONE

Silver **Ruler:** Vincenzo II **Obv:** Armored bust left in ruff collar, date below **Note:** Weight varies: 31.40-31.80 grams. Dav. #3951.

Date	Mintage	VG	F	VF	XF	Unc
ND	—	1,000	2,000	5,000	—	—
1627	—	1,000	2,000	5,000	—	—

KM# 203.2 DUCATONE

Silver **Ruler:** Vincenzo II **Obv:** Bust left in armor and ruff collar, angel at shoulder **Rev:** Dog standing left, tail pulled in **Note:** Weight varies: 31.40-31.80 grams. Dav. #3951A.

Date	Mintage	VG	F	VF	XF	Unc
ND	—	750	1,450	2,500	3,750	—

KM# 205 DUCATONE

Silver **Ruler:** Vincenzo II **Obv:** Armored bust right **Obv. Legend:** VINCEN II D G DVX MANT VII ET M F V **Rev:** Dog standing left, date below **Rev. Legend:** FERIS TANTVM INFENSVS **Note:** Weight varies: 31.40-31.80 grams. Dav. #3950.

Date	Mintage	VG	F	VF	XF	Unc
MDCXXVII (1627)	—	2,000	3,000	6,000	—	—

KM# 207 DUCATONE

Silver **Ruler:** Vincenzo II **Obv:** Legned in six lines **Obv. Legend:** VINCENTI/ II D G DVX/ MANTVAE VII/ ET MONITS/ FERRATI/ V **Rev:** Galley with oars **Rev. Legend:** HAC MONSTRANTO VIAM **Note:** Weight varies: 31.40-31.80 grams. Dav. #3953.

Date	Mintage	VG	F	VF	XF	Unc
1627 Rare	—	—	—	—	—	—

KM# 213 DUCATONE

Silver **Ruler:** Carlo I **Obv:** Bust right **Obv. Legend:** CAROLVS

I D G DVX MAN ET M F ETC **Rev:** Sun in zodiac, stars, and earth **Note:** Weight varies: 31.40-31.80 grams. Dav. #3954.

Date	Mintage	VG	F	VF	XF	Unc
1628	—	1,000	2,500	6,500	—	—
1631	—	1,000	2,500	6,500	—	—
1632	—	1,000	2,500	6,500	—	—
1633	—	1,000	2,500	6,500	—	—
1636	—	1,000	2,500	6,500	—	—

KM# 276 DUCATONE

Silver **Ruler:** Carlo II **Obv:** Conjoined busts left, woman veiled **Obv. Legend:** MARIA ET CAR II D G D MAN ET MON F ETC **Rev:** Madonna and child **Rev. Legend:** MARIA MATER GRATIAE PROTECTRIX NOSTRA MANTVAE **Note:** Weight varies: 31.40-31.80 grams. Dav. #3961.

Date	Mintage	VG	F	VF	XF	Unc
ND(1637-47)	—	1,450	2,600	4,550	—	—

KM# 319 DUCATONE

Silver **Ruler:** Carlo II **Obv:** Bust left **Obv. Legend:** CAROLVS D G DVX MANT IX **Rev:** Crowned arms in collar of The Redeemer **Rev. Legend:** ET MONTIS FERRATI VII **Note:** Weight varies: 31.40-31.80 grams. Dav. #3963.

Date	Mintage	VG	F	VF	XF	Unc
ND(1647-65)	—	900	1,800	3,250	—	—

KM# 321 DUCATONE

Silver **Ruler:** Carlo II **Obv:** Armored bust left **Obv. Legend:** CAROLVS II D G DVX MAN ET MF ETC **Rev:** Madonna and child **Rev. Legend:** MARIA MATER GRATIAE PROTETRIX NOSTRA MANTVAE **Note:** Weight varies: 31.40-31.80 grams. Dav. #3964.

Date	Mintage	VG	F	VF	XF	Unc
ND(1647-65) Rare	—	—	—	—	—	—

KM# 327 DUCATONE

Silver **Ruler:** Carlo II **Obv:** Armored bust left **Obv. Legend:** CAROLVS II D G DVX MAN ET MF ETC **Rev:** Oval shield in ornate frame **Rev. Legend:** TV AVTEM PERMANES **Note:** Weight varies: 31.40-31.80 grams. Dav. #3962.

Date	Mintage	VG	F	VF	XF	Unc
1649	—	1,700	3,000	6,000	9,500	—

KM# 377 DUCATONE

Silver **Ruler:** Ferdinando **Obv:** Conjoined busts right **Obv. Legend:** ISABELLA CLARA FERD CAR D G MAN ET M F ETC **Rev:** Radiant sun above clouds and sea **Rev. Legend:** ALTA A LONGE COGNOSCIT **Note:** Weight varies: 31.40-31.80 grams. Dav. #3966.

Date	Mintage	VG	F	VF	XF	Unc
1666	—	600	1,200	2,200	3,700	—

KM# 379 DUCATONE

Silver **Ruler:** Ferdinando **Rev:** Madonna and child **Rev. Legend:** MARIA MATER TRATIAE PROTETRIX NOSTRA MANTVAE **Note:** Weight varies: 31.40-31.80 grams. Dav. #3967.

Date	Mintage	VG	F	VF	XF	Unc
1666	—	650	1,300	2,300	3,800	—

KM# 395 DUCATONE (6 Lire)

Silver **Obv:** Crowned arms with FIDES in Order Chain **Obv. Legend:** FERDINAN:... **Rev:** St. Andrea and St. Longino, MANTVAE in exergue **Note:** Weight varies: 31.40-31.80 grams. Dav. #3949.

Date	Mintage	VG	F	VF	XF	Unc
ND Rare	—	—	—	—	—	—

KM# 278 2 DUCATONE

63.5000 g., Silver **Ruler:** Carlo II **Obv:** Conjoined busts left, woman veiled **Obv. Legend:** MARIA ET CAR II DGD MAN ET MON F ETC **Rev:** Madonna and child **Rev. Legend:** MARIA MATER GRATIAE PROTETRIX NOSTRA MANTVAE **Note:** Dav. #3960.

Date	Mintage	VG	F	VF	XF	Unc
ND(1637-47) Rare	—	—	—	—	—	—

KM# A379 2 DUCATONE

63.5000 g., Silver **Ruler:** Ferdinando **Obv:** Conjoined bust right **Obv. Legend:** ISABELLA CLARA FERD CAR D G D MAN ET M F ETC **Rev:** Radiant sun over clouds and sea **Rev. Legend:** ALTA A LONGE DOGNOSCIT **Note:** Dav. #3965.

Date	Mintage	VG	F	VF	XF	Unc
1666 Rare	—	—	—	—	—	—

KM# 280 3 DUCATONE

96.0000 g., Silver **Ruler:** Carlo II **Obv:** Conjoined busts left, woman veiled **Obv. Legend:** MARIA ET CAR II D G MAN ET MON F ETC **Rev:** Madonna and child **Rev. Legend:** MARIA MATER GRATIAE PROTETRIX NOSTRA MANTVAE **Note:** Dav. #3959.

Date	Mintage	VG	F	VF	XF	Unc
ND(1637-47) Rare	—	—	—	—	—	—

KM# 32 OTTAVO SCUDO D'ORO (1/8 Scudo D'oro)

0.3500 g., Gold **Ruler:** Vincenzo I **Obv:** Bust 3/4 right **Obv. Legend:** VERGILIVS MAR **Rev:** Legend, crescent **Rev. Legend:** MANTVAE

Date	Mintage	VG	F	VF	XF	Unc
ND(1587-1612) Rare	—	—	—	—	—	—

KM# 181 SCUDO D'ORO

2.5000 g., Gold **Ruler:** Vincenzo II **Obv:** Legend in six lines **Obv. Legend:** VIN/IL DG/DVX MAN/VII ET/M F/V **Rev:** Galley with oars **Rev. Legend:** HAC MONSTRANTE VIAM

Date	Mintage	VG	F	VF	XF	Unc
ND(1626-27) Rare	—	—	—	—	—	—

KM# 243 SCUDO D'ORO

2.5000 g., Gold **Ruler:** Carlo I **Obv:** St. Andrew with reliquary **Obv. Legend:** NIHL ISTO TRISTE RECEPTO

Date	Mintage	VG	F	VF	XF	Unc
ND(1629)	—	—	—	—	—	—

KM# 245 SCUDO D'ORO

2.5000 g., Gold **Rev:** Crucible in flames **Rev. Legend:** DOMINE PROBASTI ME TAE COGNOVISTI ME

Date	Mintage	VG	F	VF	XF	Unc
ND(1629)	—	—	—	—	—	—

KM# 247 SCUDO D'ORO

2.5000 g., Gold **Obv:** Crowned arms **Obv. Legend:** CAROLVS I D G DVX MAN EMF EC **Rev:** Crowned shield with motto: "in bello" **Rev. Legend:** MANTVAE ANNO SALTIS

Date	Mintage	VG	F	VF	XF	Unc
1629	—	—	—	—	—	—

KM# 77 SCUDO D'SOLE

Gold **Ruler:** Ferdinand **Obv:** Ferdinand standing **Obv. Legend:** FERD D G DVX M VI ET MON F IIII **Rev:** Madonna and shild **Rev. Legend:** TIT SM IN PARTICV SRED CAR **Note:** Weight varies: 3.20-3.37 grams.

Date	Mintage	VG	F	VF	XF	Unc
ND(1612-26) Rare	—	—	—	—	—	—

KM# 33 ONGARO

Gold **Ruler:** Vincenzo I **Obv:** Duke standing right **Obv. Legend:** VINC D G DVX M IIII ET M F II **Rev:** Crowned shield **Rev. Legend:** MONETA NOVA AVREA **Note:** Weight varies: 3.35-3.40 grams.

Date	Mintage	VG	F	VF	XF	Unc
ND(1587-1612)	—	500	1,000	2,000	3,500	—

KM# 79 1/2 ZECCHINO

1.6000 g., 0.9860 Gold 0.0507 oz. AGW **Ruler:** Ferdinand **Obv:** Bust right **Obv. Legend:** FERDINAN D G DVX MANT VI **Rev:** Crowned shield in order collar **Rev. Legend:** ET MONTIS FERRATI IV **Note:** Fr.#562.

Date	Mintage	VG	F	VF	XF	Unc
ND(1612-26) Rare	—	—	—	—	—	—

KM# 34 DOPPIA

6.5000 g., 0.9860 Gold 0.2060 oz. AGW **Ruler:** Vincenzo I **Obv:** Bust right **Obv. Legend:** VIN D G DVX M IIII **Rev:** Crowned shield with supporters **Rev. Legend:** ET MONTIS FERRATI II

Date	Mintage	VG	F	VF	XF	Unc
ND(1587-1612) Rare	—	—	—	—	—	—

KM# 81 DOPPIA

6.5000 g., 0.9860 Gold 0.2060 oz. AGW **Ruler:** Ferdinand **Obv:** Bust left **Obv. Legend:** FERD D G DVX MAN VI ET MF IIII **Rev:** Crowned shield with Mt. Olympus in collar of The Redeemer **Rev. Legend:** ET MONTIS FERRATI IV

Date	Mintage	VG	F	VF	XF	Unc
ND(1612-26)	—	1,600	2,900	5,700	12,500	—

KM# 104 DOPPIA

Gold **Ruler:** Ferdinand **Obv:** High-collared armored bust left **Obv. Legend:** FERDINAN. D. G. DVX. MANT. VI. **Rev:** Crowned 4-fold arms with central shield, chain of order around **Rev. Legend:** ET. MONTIS. FERRATI. IV. **Note:** Weight varies: 6.18-6.45 g.

Date	Mintage	VG	F	VF	XF	Unc
ND(1612-26)	—	—	850	1,650	3,200	5,500

KM# 83 DOPPIA

3.2000 g., 0.9860 Gold 0.1014 oz. AGW **Ruler:** Ferdinand **Obv:** Large rose **Obv. Legend:** FERDIN D G DVX MANT VI ET MON FER IIII **Rev:** Madonna and child **Rev. Legend:** TV GLORIA JERVSALEM **Note:** Fr#566.

Date	Mintage	VG	F	VF	XF	Unc
ND(1612-26)	—	1,000	1,800	3,600	7,000	—

KM# 85 DOPPIA

6.5000 g., 0.9860 Gold 0.2060 oz. AGW **Ruler:** Francesco IV **Obv:** Armored bust right, date below **Obv. Legend:** FRAN IIII D G DVX MANT V **Rev:** Crowned shield with Mt. Olympus, FIDES **Rev. Legend:** ET MONTIS FERRATI III

Date	Mintage	VG	F	VF	XF	Unc
1612 Rare	—	—	—	—	—	—

KM# 107 DOPPIA

6.5000 g., 0.9860 Gold 0.2060 oz. AGW **Ruler:** Ferdinand **Obv:** Bust left **Obv. Legend:** FER CAR DG DVX M VI ET M F IIII **Rev:** St. Andrew and St. Longuino standing **Rev. Legend:** NIHIL ISTO TRISTE RECEPTIO

Date	Mintage	VG	F	VF	XF	Unc
1613 Rare	—	—	—	—	—	—

KM# 119 DOPPIA

6.5000 g., 0.9860 Gold 0.2060 oz. AGW **Ruler:** Ferdinand **Obv:** Bust left as cardinal **Obv. Legend:** FER CAR D G DVX M VI ET MF IIII **Rev:** Pair of angels flank reliquary **Rev. Legend:** NIHIL ISTO TRISTE RECEPTO

Date	Mintage	VG	F	VF	XF	Unc
MDCXIIII (1614)	—	1,500	3,000	7,500	12,000	—

KM# 129 DOPPIA

6.5000 g., 0.9860 Gold 0.2060 oz. AGW **Ruler:** Ferdinand **Obv:** Bust left in armor **Obv. Legend:** FERD: DG: DVX: MAN:

VI • E: M: F: IIII **Rev:** St. Longuino with reliquary **Rev. Legend:** AB OMNI MALO DEFENDE NOS

Date	Mintage	VG	F	VF	XF	Unc
MDCXVI (1616)	—	2,250	4,500	9,000	15,000	—

KM# 209 DOPPIA

6.5000 g., 0.9860 Gold 0.2060 oz. AGW **Ruler:** Vincenzo II **Obv:** Bust of Vincenzo left **Rev:** Crowned arms

Date	Mintage	VG	F	VF	XF	Unc
ND	—	1,900	3,750	7,500	13,500	—
1627	—	1,900	3,750	7,500	13,500	—

KM# 262 DOPPIA

6.5000 g., 0.9860 Gold 0.2060 oz. AGW **Ruler:** Carlo I **Obv:** Armored bust of Carlo I right **Rev:** Crowned arms in Order chain

Date	Mintage	VG	F	VF	XF	Unc
ND	—	1,900	3,750	7,500	13,500	—
1632	—	1,900	3,750	7,500	13,500	—

KM# 282 DOPPIA

6.5000 g., 0.9860 Gold 0.2060 oz. AGW **Ruler:** Carlo II **Obv:** Child bust of Carlo II with mother Maria left **Rev:** Crowned arms in Order chain

Date	Mintage	VG	F	VF	XF	Unc
ND Rare	—	—	—	—	—	—

KM# 323 DOPPIA

6.5000 g., 0.9860 Gold 0.2060 oz. AGW **Obv:** Armored bust left **Obv. Legend:** CAROLVS II D G DVX MAN **Rev:** Crowned shield in collar of The Redeemer **Rev. Legend:** ET MONTIS FERRATI C

Date	Mintage	VG	F	VF	XF	Unc
ND(1647-65) Rare	—	—	—	—	—	—

KM# 36 2 DOPPIE

0.9860 Gold **Ruler:** Vincenzo I **Obv:** Bust right **Obv. Legend:** VINCENTIVS D G DVX MANT IIII **Rev:** Shield with Mt. Olympus above, crowned **Rev. Legend:** ET MONTIS FERRATI II FIDES **Note:** Weight varies: 12.80-12.95 grams. Actual gold weight varies: .4058-.4105 ounces.

Date	Mintage	VG	F	VF	XF	Unc
ND(1587-1612)	—	3,150	6,100	14,500	25,000	—

KM# 87 2 DOPPIE

0.9860 Gold **Ruler:** Francesco IV **Obv:** Armored bust right, date below **Obv. Legend:** FRAN IIII D G DVX MANT V **Rev:** Crowned shield with Mt. Olympus, FIDES in collar of The Redeemer **Rev. Legend:** ET MONTIS FERRAT III **Note:** Weight varies: 12.80-12.95 grams. Actual gold weight varies: .4058-.4105 ounces.

Date	Mintage	VG	F	VF	XF	Unc
1612	—	2,650	5,300	13,500	24,000	—

KM# 89 2 DOPPIE

0.9860 Gold **Ruler:** Ferdinand **Obv:** Armored bust right **Obv. Legend:** FERD D G DVX MAN VI ET MF IIII **Rev:** St. Longuino and St. Pissidenella **Rev. Legend:** AB OMNI MALO DE FENDE NOS **Note:** Weight varies: 12.80-12.95 grams. Actual gold weight varies: .4058-.4105 ounces.

Date	Mintage	VG	F	VF	XF	Unc
ND(1612-26)	—	1,500	2,650	4,900	9,000	—

KM# 91 2 DOPPIE

0.9860 Gold **Ruler:** Ferdinand **Obv:** Armored bust right **Obv. Legend:** FERDIN DG DVX MANT VI **Rev:** Crowned shield with Mt. Olympus in collar of The Redeemer **Rev. Legend:** ET MONTIS FERRATI IV **Note:** Weight varies: 12.80-12.95 grams. Actual gold weight varies: .4058-.4105 ounces.

Date	Mintage	VG	F	VF	XF	Unc
ND(1612-26)	—	1,250	2,200	4,150	7,500	—

KM# 93 2 DOPPIE

0.9860 Gold **Ruler:** Ferdinand **Obv:** Bust of Ferdinand left **Rev:** Crowned arms **Note:** Weight varies: 12.80-12.95 grams. Actual gold weight varies: .4058-.4105 ounces.

Date	Mintage	VG	F	VF	XF	Unc
ND CT	—	2,100	4,400	11,500	21,000	—
ND(1612-26) CT	—	1,550	3,050	7,500	13,000	—

KM# 109 2 DOPPIE

0.9860 Gold **Ruler:** Ferdinand **Obv:** Bust left, as cardinal, GASP M F, in exergue **Obv. Legend:** FER CAR D G DVX m VI ET M F IIII **Rev:** Pair of angels flank reliquary **Rev. Legend:** NIHIL ISTO TRISTE RECEPTIO **Note:** Weight varies: 12.80-12.95 grams. Actual gold weight varies: .4058-.4105 ounces.

Date	Mintage	VG	F	VF	XF	Unc
MDXCIII (1613)	—	2,000	4,800	6,800	14,500	—
MDCXIIII (1614)	—	1,750	4,400	6,400	13,500	—
MDCXV (1615)	—	1,750	4,400	6,400	13,500	—
MDCXIIIII (1615)	—	1,750	4,400	6,400	13,500	—

KM# 111 2 DOPPIE

0.9860 Gold **Ruler:** Ferdinand **Obv:** Crowned shield in collar of The Redeemer **Obv. Legend:** FERD D G DVX MAN VI ET MON FER IIII **Rev:** St. Andrew and St. Longuino standing **Rev. Legend:** NIHIL TRISTE RECEPTO **Note:** Weight varies: 12.80-12.95 grams. Actual gold weight varies: .4058-.4105 ounces.

Date	Mintage	VG	F	VF	XF	Unc
MDCXIII (1613) Rare	—	—	—	—	—	—

KM# 152 2 DOPPIE

0.9860 Gold **Ruler:** Ferdinand **Obv:** Armored bust right **Obv. Legend:** FERD IN D G DVX MAN VI ET M F IIII **Rev:** Crowned shield with Mt. Olympus **Rev. Legend:** ET MONTIS FERRATI VI ET C **Note:** Weight varies: 12.80-12.95 grams. Actual gold weight varies: .4058-.4105 ounces.

Date	Mintage	VG	F	VF	XF	Unc
1621	—	1,500	3,000	5,600	9,800	—

KM# 156 2 DOPPIE

0.9860 Gold **Ruler:** Vincenzo II **Obv:** Armored bust left **Obv. Legend:** VINCEN II D G DVX MANT VII **Rev:** Crowned shield with Mt. Olympus and FIDES within the collar of the Order of the Redeemer **Rev. Legend:** ET MONTIS FERRATI...

Date	Mintage	VG	F	VF	XF	Unc
1625	—	—	—	—	—	—

KM# 211 2 DOPPIE

0.9860 Gold **Ruler:** Vincenzo II **Obv:** Armored bust left **Obv. Legend:** VINCEN II D G DVX MANT VII **Rev:** Crowned shield with Mt. Olympus, FIDES in collar of The Redeemer **Rev. Legend:** ET MONTIS FERRATI V

Date	Mintage	VG	F	VF	XF	Unc
ND	—	—	—	—	—	—
1627	—	4,400	7,900	12,000	30,000	—

KM# 251 2 DOPPIE

0.9860 Gold **Ruler:** Carlo I **Obv:** Armored bust right **Obv. Legend:** CARLOS I D G DVX MAN **Rev:** Crowned shield with Mt. Olympus and FIDES in collar of The Redeemer **Rev. Legend:** ET MONTIS FERRATI ETC **Note:** Weight varies: 12.80-12.95 grams. Actual gold weight varies: .4058-.4105 ounces.

Date	Mintage	VG	F	VF	XF	Unc
1629 Rare	—	—	—	—	—	—
1631 Rare	—	—	—	—	—	—
1636	—	2,650	6,100	9,800	15,000	—

KM# 325 2 DOPPIE

0.9860 Gold **Ruler:** Carlo II **Obv:** Child bust of Carlo II with mother Maria **Rev:** Crowned arms in Order chain **Note:** Weight varies: 12.80-12.95 grams. Actual gold weight varies: .4058-.4105 ounces.

Date	Mintage	VG	F	VF	XF	Unc
ND(1637-47)	—	2,200	5,700	9,000	14,500	—

KM# 284 2 DOPPIE

0.9860 Gold **Ruler:** Carlo II **Obv:** Conjoined busts left, woman veiled **Obv. Legend:** MARIA ET CAR II DGD MAN ET M F ET C **Rev:** Crowned arms with Mt. Olympus, FIDES in collar of The Redeemer **Rev. Legend:** ET MONTIS FERRATI ET C **Note:** Weight varies: 12.80-12.95 grams. Actual gold weight varies: .4058-.4105 ounces.

Date	Mintage	VG	F	VF	XF	Unc
ND(1637-47)	—	2,200	5,700	9,000	14,500	—

KM# 363 2 DOPPIE

0.9860 Gold **Ruler:** Carlo II **Obv:** Bust of Carlo II left **Rev:** Crowned arms in Order chain **Note:** Weight varies: 12.80-12.95 grams. Actual gold weight varies: .4058-.4105 ounces.

Date	Mintage	VG	F	VF	XF	Unc
ND(1647-65) Rare	—	—	—	—	—	—

KM# 381 2 DOPPIE

0.9860 Gold **Ruler:** Ferdinando **Obv:** Conjoined busts right **Obv. Legend:** ISABELLA CLARA FERD CAR D G D MAN ET M ET C **Rev:** Radiant sun above clouds and sea **Note:** Weight varies: 12.80-12.95 grams. Actual gold weight varies: .4058-.4105 ounces.

Date	Mintage	VG	F	VF	XF	Unc
1666 Rare	—	—	—	—	—	—

KM# 393 2 DOPPIE

0.9860 Gold **Ruler:** Ferdinando **Obv:** Bust of Ferdinand Carol right in inner circle **Rev:** Crowned arms in inner circle **Note:** Weight varies: 12.80-12.95 grams. Actual gold weight varies: .4058-.4105 ounces.

Date	Mintage	VG	F	VF	XF	Unc
ND(1668-1707) Rare	—	—	—	—	—	—

KM# 95 4 DOPPIE

26.0000 g., 0.9860 Gold 0.8242 oz. AGW **Ruler:** Ferdinand **Obv:** Bust right of cardinal **Obv. Legend:** FER CAR D G DVX M VI ET M FIIII **Rev:** Sun **Rev. Legend:** NON MATVATA LVCE

Date	Mintage	VG	F	VF	XF	Unc
ND(1612-26)	—	5,300	10,500	19,500	33,000	—

KM# 286 4 DOPPIE

26.0000 g., 0.9860 Gold 0.8242 oz. AGW **Ruler:** Carlo II **Obv:** Conjoined busts, woman veiled **Obv. Legend:** MARIA ET CAR II DGD MAN ET MON F ETC **Rev:** Madonna and child **Rev. Legend:** MARIA MATER GRATIAE PROTETRIX NOSTRA MANTVAE

Date	Mintage	VG	F	VF	XF	Unc
ND(1637) Rare	—	—	—	—	—	—

KM# 383 4 DOPPIE

26.0000 g., 0.9860 Gold 0.8242 oz. AGW **Ruler:** Ferdinando **Obv:** Conjoined busts left **Obv. Legend:** ISABELLA CLARA FERD CAR DGD MAN ET M F ETC **Rev:** Radiant sun above clouds and sea **Rev. Legend:** ALTA A LONGE COGNOSCIT

Date	Mintage	VG	F	VF	XF	Unc
1666 Rare	—	—	—	—	—	—

Note: Bowers and Merena Guia sale 3-88 AU realized $20,900

KM# 97 5 DOPPIE

32.7000 g., 0.9860 Gold 1.0366 oz. AGW **Ruler:** Francesco IV **Obv:** Crowned shield with Mt. Olympus, FIDES **Obv. Legend:** FRAN IIII D G DVX MAN V ET MON III **Rev:** St. Andrew and St. Longuino with reliquary **Rev. Legend:** NIHIL ISTO TRISTE RECEPTO

Date	Mintage	VG	F	VF	XF	Unc
1612 Rare	—	—	—	—	—	—

KM# 270 5 DOPPIE

32.7000 g., 0.9860 Gold 1.0366 oz. AGW **Ruler:** Carlo I **Obv:** Armored bust right **Obv. Legend:** CARLOVS I D G DVX MAN ET MF **Rev:** Sun in zodian, stars, clouds, and moon **Rev. Legend:** NEC RET5ROGRADIOR REC DEVIO

Date	Mintage	VG	F	VF	XF	Unc
1636 Rare	—	—	—	—	—	—

KM# 285 5 DOPPIE

32.7000 g., 0.9860 Gold 1.0366 oz. AGW **Ruler:** Carlo II **Obv:** Conjoined busts left **Obv. Legend:** MARIA ET CAR II DGD MAN ET MON F ETC **Rev:** Madonna and child **Rev. Legend:** MARIA MATER GRATIAE PROTECTIRX NOSTRA MANTVAE

Date	Mintage	VG	F	VF	XF	Unc
ND(1637-47) Rare	—	—	—	—	—	—

KM# 288 5 DOPPIE (10 Zecchini)

32.7000 g., Gold **Obv:** Armored bust left **Obv. Legend:** CAROLUS II DG DVX MAN ET MF ETC **Rev:** Radiant sun/rain clouds in oval shiedl with ornate frame **Rev. Legend:** TV AVTEM PERMANES

Date	Mintage	VG	F	VF	XF	Unc
1649 Rare	—	—	—	—	—	—

KM# 329 5 DOPPIE (10 Zecchini)

5.6000 g., Gold **Ruler:** Carlo II **Obv:** Armored bust left **Obv. Legend:** CARLOVS II D G DVX MAN ET MF ET C **Rev:** Oval shield within ornate frame **Rev. Inscription:** TV AVTEM PERMANES

Date	Mintage	VG	F	VF	XF	Unc
1649 Rare	—	—	—	—	—	—

KM# 385 5 DOPPIE (10 Zecchini)

32.7000 g., Gold **Ruler:** Ferdinando **Obv:** Conjoined busts right **Obv. Legend:** ISABELLA CLARA FERD CAR D G D MAN ET M F ETC **Rev:** Radiant sun above clouds and sea **Rev. Legend:** ALTA A LONGE COGNOSCIT

Date	Mintage	VG	F	VF	XF	Unc
1666 Rare	—	—	—	—	—	—

KM# 113 6 DOPPIE (12 Scudo D'oro)

39.0000 g., 0.9860 Gold 1.2363 oz. AGW **Ruler:** Ferdinand **Obv:** Bust right as cardinal **Obv. Legend:** FERDI CARD D G DVX MAN VI ET M F IIII **Rev:** Radiant sun **Rev. Legend:** NON MVTVATA LVCE

Date	Mintage	VG	F	VF	XF	Unc
1613 Rare	—	—	—	—	—	—
MDCXIV (1614) Rare	—	—	—	—	—	—
MDCXV (1615) Rare	—	—	—	—	—	—

KM# 121 6 DOPPIE (12 Scudo D'oro)

39.0000 g., 0.9860 Gold 1.2363 oz. AGW **Obv:** Bust right as cardinal **Obv. Legend:** FERDINANDVS SRED CRAD D G DVX **Rev:** Madonna and child **Rev. Legend:** TIT SM INPORTICV SRE DIAC

Date	Mintage	VG	F	VF	XF	Unc
MDCXIIII (1614) Rare	—	—	—	—	—	—

KM# 131 6 DOPPIE (12 Scudo D'oro)

39.0000 g., 0.9860 Gold 1.2363 oz. AGW **Obv:** Armored bust right **Obv. Legend:** FERDINANDVS D G DVX MAN VI MAN TVAE **Rev:** Crowned shield in collar of the Order of the Redeemer **Rev. Legend:** ET MONITS FERRATI IV

Date	Mintage	VG	F	VF	XF	Unc
1616 Rare	—	—	—	—	—	—

KM# 148 6 DOPPIE (12 Scudo D'oro)

39.0000 g., 0.9860 Gold 1.2363 oz. AGW **Obv:** Shield of four eagles in octalobe **Obv. Legend:** FERDINANDVS D G DVX MANT VI **Rev:** Crowned shield in collar of The Redeemer **Rev. Legend:** ET MONTI FERRATI IV

Date	Mintage	VG	F	VF	XF	Unc
1620 Rare	—	—	—	—	—	—

KM# 215 6 DOPPIE (12 Scudo D'oro)

39.0000 g., 0.9860 Gold 1.2363 oz. AGW **Ruler:** Carlo I **Obv:** Armored bust right **Obv. Legend:** CAROLVS I DG DVX MAN ET M F ET C **Rev:** Sun in zodiac, stars, cloud, and earth **Rev. Legend:** NEC RETROGRADIOR

Date	Mintage	VG	F	VF	XF	Unc
1628 Rare	—	—	—	—	—	—
1632 Rare	—	—	—	—	—	—

KM# 290 6 DOPPIE (12 Scudo D'oro)

39.0000 g., 0.9860 Gold 1.2363 oz. AGW **Ruler:** Carlo II **Obv:** Conjoined busts left, woman veiled **Obv. Legend:** MARIA ET CAR II D G D MAN ET MON F ETC **Rev:** Madonna and child **Rev. Legend:** MARIA MATER GRATIAE PROTECTRIX NOSTRA MANTVAE

Date	Mintage	VG	F	VF	XF	Unc
ND(1637-47) Rare	—	—	—	—	—	—

KM# 331 6 DOPPIE (12 Scudo D'oro)

39.0000 g., 0.9860 Gold 1.2363 oz. AGW **Ruler:** Carlo II **Obv:** Armored bust left **Obv. Legend:** CAROLVS II D G DVX MAN ET M F ET C **Rev:** Oval shield with ornate frame **Rev. Legend:** TV AVTEM PERMANES

Date	Mintage	VG	F	VF	XF	Unc
1649 Rare	—	—	—	—	—	—
1669 Error; rare	—	—	—	—	—	—

KM# 387 6 DOPPIE (12 Scudo D'oro)

39.0000 g., 0.9860 Gold 1.2363 oz. AGW **Ruler:** Ferdinando **Obv:** Conjoined busts right **Obv. Legend:** ISABELLA CLARA FERD CAR D G D MAN ET M F **Rev:** Madonna and child **Rev. Legend:** MARIA MATER GRATIAE PROTECTRIX MOSTRA MANTVAE

Date	Mintage	VG	F	VF	XF	Unc
1666 Rare	—	—	—	—	—	—

KM# 389 6 DOPPIE (12 Scudo D'oro)

39.0000 g., 0.9860 Gold 1.2363 oz. AGW **Obv:** Conjoined busts right **Obv. Legend:** ISABELLA CLARA FERD CAR D G D MAN ET M F ETC **Rev:** Sun above clouds and sea **Rev. Legend:** ALTA ALONGE COGNOSCIT

Date	Mintage	VG	F	VF	XF	Unc
1666 Rare	—	—	—	—	—	—

KM# 217 8 DOPPIE

52.4000 g., 0.9860 Gold 1.6610 oz. AGW **Ruler:** Carlo I **Obv:** Armored bust right **Obv. Legend:** CAROLVS I D DVX MAN ET M F ETC **Rev:** Sun in zodiac, clouds and earth **Rev. Legend:** NEC RETROGRADIOR NEC DEVIO

Date	Mintage	VG	F	VF	XF	Unc
1628 Rare	—	—	—	—	—	—

KM# 292 8 DOPPIE

52.4000 g., 0.9860 Gold 1.6610 oz. AGW **Ruler:** Carlo II **Obv:** Conjoined busts left, veiled woman **Obv. Legend:** MARIA ET CAR II D G MAN ET MONT ETC **Rev:** Madonna and child **Rev. Legend:** MARIA MATER GRATIAE PROTETRIX NOSTRA MANTVAE

Date	Mintage	VG	F	VF	XF	Unc
ND(1637-47) Rare	—	—	—	—	—	—

KM# 410 8 DOPPIE

52.4000 g., 0.9860 Gold 1.6610 oz. AGW **Ruler:** Ferdinando **Obv:** Armored bust right **Obv. Legend:** FERDINANDVS CAR D G DVX MANTVAE MON FER ETC **Rev. Legend:** QVAE MAIOR ORIGO

Date	Mintage	VG	F	VF	XF	Unc
1679 Rare	—	—	—	—	—	—

KM# 38 10 DOPPIE

60.3000 g., 0.9860 Gold 1.9115 oz. AGW **Ruler:** Vincenzo I **Obv:** Bust right **Obv. Legend:** VINCENTIVS GONZAGA **Rev:** St. George slaying dragon **Rev. Legend:** PROTEC NOSTER ASPICE

Date	Mintage	VG	F	VF	XF	Unc
ND(1587-1612) Rare	—	—	—	—	—	—

KM# 133 10 DOPPIE

60.3000 g., 0.9860 Gold 1.9115 oz. AGW **Ruler:** Ferdinand **Obv:** Bust of Ferdinando right **Rev:** Radiant sun face in inner circle

Date	Mintage	VG	F	VF	XF	Unc
1617 CT Rare	—	—	—	—	—	—

KM# 123 12 DOPPIE

72.0000 g., 0.9860 Gold 2.2824 oz. AGW **Ruler:** Ferdinand **Obv:** Robed bust of Ferdinando with scepter left **Rev:** Madonna and child in branches

Date	Mintage	VG	F	VF	XF	Unc
1614 GM Rare	—	—	—	—	—	—

KM# 391 12 DOPPIE

72.0000 g., 0.9860 Gold 2.2824 oz. AGW **Ruler:** Ferdinando **Obv:** Conjoined busts right **Obv. Legend:** ISABELLA CLARA FERD CAR D G D MAN ET M F ETC **Rev:** Radiant sun above clouds and sea **Rev. Legend:** ALTA A LONGE COGNOSCIT

Date	Mintage	VG	F	VF	XF	Unc
1666 Rare	—	—	—	—	—	—

PATTERNS

Including off metal strikes

KM#	Date	Mintage	Identification	Mkt Val
Pn1	MDCXIIII (1614)	—	Ducatone. Copper. Similar to KM#105.1.	—

MASEGRA

FORTRESS

The castle of Masegra was located in the vicinity of Sondrio, north of Bergamo, in the foothills of the Alps. The place was a fief of the Beccaria, a family of possible Germanic origins. They struck a few small copper coins during the 17th century.

Reference: V = Alberto Varesi, ***Monete Italiane Regionali: Lombardia, Zecche Minori***, Pavia, 1995.

FORTRESS

STANDARD COINAGE

KM# 1 1/2 QUATTRINO (Mezzo Quatrrino)

0.4000 g., Copper, 9.5 mm. **Obv:** 2-line inscription **Obv. Inscription:** (checkmark) / QVATR. **Rev:** 3-line inscription **Rev. Inscription:** DI/BECCA/RIA. **Note:** V#778.

Date	Mintage	F	VF	XF	Unc	BU
ND(16xx)	—	150	275	575	825	—

KM# 2 QUATTRINO

Copper, 11 mm. **Obv:** 3-line inscription **Obv. Inscription:** 1/QVATRI/NO. **Rev:** 3-line inscription **Rev. Inscription:** DI/BECCA/RIA **Note:** V#777. Weight varies: 0.56-0.65g.

Date	Mintage	F	VF	XF	Unc	BU
ND(16xx)	—	150	275	575	825	—

MASSA DI LUNIGIANO

Massa was a city north of Pisa and Lucca. In 1559 Ferdinand I had given the mint right to Prince Alberico I Cybo Malaspina, who subsequently inherited the marquisate of Massa thru his mother. Father, son and grandson coined until 1667.

RULERS

Alberico I Cybo Malaspina, prince of Massa, 1568-1623
Carlo I Cybo Malaspina, 1623-1662
Alberico II Cybo Malaspina, 1662-1690

MARQUISATE

STANDARD COINAGE

KM# 7 QUATTRINO

0.5600 g., Copper **Obv:** Cybo arms **Rev:** Pyramid

Date	Mintage	VG	F	VF	XF	Unc
1616	—	30.00	60.00	120	—	—
1617	—	30.00	60.00	120	—	—
ND	—	30.00	60.00	120	—	—

KM# 8 QUATTRINO

0.5600 g., Copper **Rev:** Thornbush

Date	Mintage	VG	F	VF	XF	Unc
ND	—	30.00	60.00	120	—	—

KM# 9 CRAZIA

0.7300 g., Silver **Obv:** Cybo arms **Rev:** .S./.R.I.ET./MASS./.P.I.

Date	Mintage	VG	F	VF	XF	Unc
ND	—	—	—	—	—	—

KM# 10 DUETTO

Copper **Obv:** Cybo arms **Rev:** Thornbush

Date	Mintage	VG	F	VF	XF	Unc
1616	—	35.00	75.00	150	—	—

KM# 11 DUETTO

Copper **Rev:** St. Peter **Note:** Weight varies: 1.09-1.50 grams.

Date	Mintage	VG	F	VF	XF	Unc
ND	—	35.00	75.00	150	—	—

KM# 12 1/2 BOLOGNINO

0.3500 g., Silver **Obv:** Cybo arms **Rev:** Cross

Date	Mintage	VG	F	VF	XF	Unc
ND	—	—	—	—	—	—

KM# 13 BOLOGNINO (2 Soldi)

Silver **Obv:** Cybo arms **Rev:** Cross in cartouche **Note:** Weight varies: 0.60-0.95 grams.

Date	Mintage	VG	F	VF	XF	Unc
ND	—	175	350	600	—	—

KM# 40 7 BOLOGNINI

2.1300 g., Silver **Obv:** Bust right, VII or 7 below **Rev:** Crowned Cybo arms

Date	Mintage	VG	F	VF	XF	Unc
1666	—	—	—	—	—	—
1667	—	350	900	2,250	4,500	—

KM# 41 7 BOLOGNINI

2.1300 g., Silver **Obv:** Facing head

Date	Mintage	VG	F	VF	XF	Unc
1666 Rare	—	—	—	—	—	—

KM# 35 8 BOLOGNINI

2.2700 g., Silver **Obv:** Bust right **Rev:** Peacock

Date	Mintage	VG	F	VF	XF	Unc
1662	—	—	—	—	—	—

KM# 36 8 BOLOGNINI

2.2700 g., Silver

Date	Mintage	VG	F	VF	XF	Unc
1662	—	45.00	100	275	450	—
1663	—	45.00	100	275	450	—

KM# 38 8 BOLOGNINI

2.2700 g., Silver **Obv:** 8 below bust

Date	Mintage	VG	F	VF	XF	Unc
1664	—	35.00	90.00	225	400	—
1665	—	35.00	90.00	225	400	—

KM# 39 8 BOLOGNINI

2.2700 g., Silver **Obv:** Bust right **Obv. Legend:** ...DVX...

Date	Mintage	VG	F	VF	XF	Unc
1664	—	45.00	100	275	450	—
1665	—	45.00	100	275	450	—
1666	—	45.00	100	275	450	—

KM# 37 16 BOLOGNINI

4.8900 g., Silver **Obv:** Bust right, 16 below **Rev:** Similar to 8 Bolognini, KM#36

Date	Mintage	VG	F	VF	XF	Unc
1663	—	100	200	400	650	—
1664	—	100	200	400	650	—

KM# 25 CERVIA

2.3100 g., Silver **Obv:** Bust right **Rev:** Stag left

Date	Mintage	VG	F	VF	XF	Unc
1617 Rare	—	—	—	—	—	—
1618 Rare	—	—	—	—	—	—

KM# 26 4 CERVIA

5.3400 g., Silver **Obv:** Bust right, date below **Rev:** St. Peter standing

Date	Mintage	VG	F	VF	XF	Unc
1618	—	—	—	—	—	—

KM# 14 PAOLA

2.5400 g., Silver **Obv:** Arms **Rev:** St. Peter

Date	Mintage	VG	F	VF	XF	Unc
ND	—	700	1,200	2,100	—	—

KM# 15 PAOLA

2.5400 g., Silver **Obv:** Cybo arms **Rev:** Crowned double eagle

Date	Mintage	VG	F	VF	XF	Unc
ND	—	500	900	1,750	—	—

KM# 16 1/4 LIRA

Silver **Obv:** Cybo arms **Rev:** Cross in circle **Note:** Weight varies: 2.70-3.21 grams.

Date	Mintage	VG	F	VF	XF	Unc
ND	—	850	1,400	2,450	—	—

KM# 17 TESTONE (2 Lire - 20 Bolognini)

9.4000 g., Silver **Obv:** Bust right **Rev:** Legend, burning barrel **Rev. Legend:** VON. GVETTEN: IN . PESSER.

Date	Mintage	VG	F	VF	XF	Unc
ND Rare	—	—	—	—	—	—

KM# 18 80 SOLDI (Tallero)

Base Silver **Obv:** Knight behind shield **Rev:** Rampant lion **Rev. Legend:** ...SOL * LXXX **Note:** Dav. #A3973.

Date	Mintage	Good	VG	F	VF	XF
ND	—	450	950	2,150	3,600	—

KM# 19 80 SOLDI (Tallero)

Base Silver **Rev:** Rampant lion **Rev. Legend:** ...SOLD. 80 **Note:** Dav. #B3973.

Date	Mintage	Good	VG	F	VF	XF
ND	—	500	1,000	2,250	3,750	—

KM# 5 DUCATONE

32.1600 g., Silver **Obv:** Bust right **Rev:** Crowned double eagle with arms **Note:** Dav. #3971.

Date	Mintage	Good	VG	F	VF	XF
1601 Rare	—	—	—	—	—	—

Note: Numismatica Ars Classica Auction 35, XF, 12-06 realized approximately $37,310

KM# 6 DUCATONE

32.1600 g., Silver **Obv:** Bust of Alberico right **Rev:** Three stags swimming left **Note:** Dav. #3972.

Date	Mintage	Good	VG	F	VF	XF
ND Rare	—	—	—	—	—	—

KM# 30 DUCATONE

32.1600 g., Silver **Obv:** Bust of Carlo right **Rev:** Crowned Cybo arms **Note:** Dav. #3973.

Date	Mintage	Good	VG	F	VF	XF
ND Rare	—	—	—	—	—	—

KM# 20 1/2 SCUDO D'ORO

1.6800 g., Gold **Obv:** Cybo arms **Rev:** Pyramid with sun above

Date	Mintage	VG	F	VF	XF	Unc
ND	—	900	1,800	3,750	6,000	—

KM# 21 SCUDO D'ORO (1/2 Doppia)

3.3100 g., Gold **Obv:** Oval arms **Rev:** Ornate cross

Date	Mintage	VG	F	VF	XF	Unc
ND	—	1,800	3,500	7,000	11,000	—

KM# 22 SCUDO D'ORO (1/2 Doppia)

3.3100 g., Gold **Obv:** Cybo arms **Rev. Legend:** DVRABO

Date	Mintage	VG	F	VF	XF	Unc
ND	—	1,800	3,500	7,000	11,000	—

KM# 23 DOPPIA

6.8300 g., Gold **Obv:** Cybo arms **Obv. Legend:** ALB... **Rev:** Crowned double eagle

Date	Mintage	VG	F	VF	XF	Unc
ND	—	2,000	4,000	8,000	13,000	—

KM# 24 2 DOPPIE

13.9000 g., Gold **Obv:** Bust right **Obv. Legend:** ALBERICVS... **Rev:** Crowned double eagle with Cybo arms

Date	Mintage	VG	F	VF	XF	Unc
ND	—	2,500	4,500	9,000	15,000	—

KM# 31 5 DOPPIE

Gold **Obv:** Bust of Carlo right **Rev:** Crowned Cybo arms

Date	Mintage	VG	F	VF	XF	Unc
ND Rare	—	—	—	—	—	—

MESSERANO

(Masserano)

(Lordship, Countship, Marquisate, Principality)

The small village of Messerano, situated in Piedmont about 9 miles (15 kilometers) east of Biella, came under the control of the bishop of Vercelli in the 9th century. The bishop in turn sold the lordship of Messerano to the town of Vercelli in 1240, but it eventually passed to the Fieschi family in 1381, who also acquired nearby Crevacuore (which see) in 1394. The Fieschi became counts of Messerano in 1508 and the countship passed by inheritance to the Ferrero dynasty in 1532. The feudal domain was raised by Pope Paolo III to a marquisate in 1547 and Crevacuore was sold to Savoy in 1554. Pope Clement VIII made Messerano a principality in 1598. After the production of an extensive coinage spanning much of the 16th and 17th centuries, the mint of Messerano was closed in 1690. Prince Vittorio Filippo sold the sovereignty of Messerano to Savoy in 1767 and the Ferrero dynasty became extinct in 1833.

RULERS

Ferrero Dynasty

Francesco Filiberto, 1584-1629

Paolo Besso, 1629-1667

Francesco Ludovico, 1667-1685

Maria Cristina Simiana, wife of Francesco Ludovico

Carlo Besso, 1685-1720

Reference: Alberto Varesi, ***Monete Italiane Regionali: Piemonte, Sardegna, Liguria, Isola di Corsica.*** Pavia, 1996.

PRINCIPALITY

STANDARD COINAGE

KM# 5 QUATTRINO

0.6300 g., Billon, 15-16 mm. **Ruler:** Francesco Filiberto 1584-1629 **Obv:** Armored bust to right **Obv. Legend:** FRANCISCVS **Rev:** Shield of arms **Rev. Legend:** PRINCIPE **Note:** Varesi 799.

Date	Mintage	VG	F	VF	XF	Unc
ND(1584-1629)	—	85.00	165	375	500	—

KM# 6.1 QUATTRINO

0.4000 g., Billon, 13 mm. **Obv:** Armored bust to right **Obv. Legend:** FRANCISCVS **Rev:** Cross in circle **Rev. Legend:** NON. NO. D......GL **Note:** Previously KM #6. Varesi 800.

Date	Mintage	VG	F	VF	XF	Unc
ND(1584-1629)	—	85.00	165	375	500	—

KM# 6.2 QUATTRINO

0.4100 g., Billon, 14 mm. **Ruler:** Francesco Filiberto 1584-1629 **Obv:** Armored bust to right **Obv. Legend:** FRANCISCVS **Rev:** Floriated cross in circle **Rev. Legend:** SALVS. NOSTRA **Note:** Varesi 801.

Date	Mintage	VG	F	VF	XF	Unc
ND(1584-1629)	—	85.00	165	375	500	—

KM# 4 QUATTRINO

1.0000 g., Copper, 17 mm. **Ruler:** Francesco Filiberto 1584-1629 **Obv:** Rosette in center, FF above, M below, D left and M right. **Rev:** Large cross in circle, small cross in each angle **Note:** Varesi 802.

Date	Mintage	VG	F	VF	XF	Unc
ND(1584-1629	—	60.00	110	225	330	—

KM# 51 QUATTRINO

Copper Weight varies, 1.81-1.82g, 18 mm. **Ruler:** Paolo Besso 1629-1667 **Obv:** High collared bust to right **Obv. Legend:** P. FE. FL. II. P. MEN. M **Rev:** Crowned serpent **Rev. Legend:** MARCHI. CREP. ET. C **Note:** Varesi 827.

Date	Mintage	VG	F	VF	XF	Unc
ND(1629-67)	—	60.00	110	225	330	—

KM# 50 QUATTRINO

Billon Weight varies, 1.37-1.98g, 15 mm. **Ruler:** Paolo Besso 1629-1667 **Obv:** Bust to right **Obv. Legend:** P. FE. FL. II. P. MEN. M **Rev:** Shield of 4-fold arms **Rev. Legend:** MARCHI. CREP. ET. C **Note:** Varesi 828.

Date	Mintage	VG	F	VF	XF	Unc
ND(1629-67)	—	30.00	65.00	135	195	—

KM# 80 QUATTRINO

Billon, 15 mm. **Ruler:** Francesco Ludovico 1667-1685 **Obv:** Head to right **Obv. Legend:** ... RIN. MESSE **Rev:** Cross with trefoil ends in circle **Rev. Legend:** MARCH(IO) ... **Note:** Varesi 836.

Date	Mintage	VG	F	VF	XF	Unc
ND(1667-85)	—	40.00	80.00	170	250	—

KM# 81 QUATTRINO

Billon Weight varies, 1.77-2.45g, 16 mm. **Ruler:** Francesco Ludovico 1667-1685 **Obv:** Head to right **Obv. Legend:** FRAN. LVD. FER... PR. M **Rev:** Crowned serpent **Rev. Legend:** MARC. CR. COM. LAVA **Note:** Varesi 837.

Date	Mintage	VG	F	VF	XF	Unc
ND(1667-85)	—	40.00	80.00	170	250	—

KM# 101 QUATTRINO

0.6600 g., Copper, 14 mm. **Obv:** Standing figure of St. Teonesto facing left **Obv. Legend:** S. THEONESTVS. PRO. NOBIS **Rev:** Lion of St. Mark in circle **Rev. Legend:** NON. NOBIS. D....O **Note:** Varesi 844.

Date	Mintage	VG	F	VF	XF	Unc
ND(17th c.)	—	50.00	100	150	210	—

KM# 102 QUATTRINO

Copper Weight varies, 0.96-1.16g, 18 mm. **Obv:** Winged lion holding sword and scales of justice **Obv. Legend:** FACTVS. MAIOR. VEHITVR **Rev:** Lion of St. Mark walking to left **Rev. Legend:** DILIGITE. IVSTITIAM **Note:** Varesi 845.

Date	Mintage	VG	F	VF	XF	Unc
ND(17th c.)	—	50.00	100	150	210	—

KM# 100 QUATTRINO

Billon, 18 mm. **Ruler:** Carlo Besso 1685-1720 **Obv:** Bust to right **Obv. Legend:** CAR. BESS. PRIN. MESSERA **Rev:** Crowned shield of 4-fold arms with central shield, date at top **Rev. Legend:** MARCHIO. CREP. COM. LAVA. **Note:** Varesi 843.

Date	Mintage	VG	F	VF	XF	Unc
1689	—	90.00	195	375	550	—

KM# 7 QUARTO

0.6200 g., Billon, 13-14 mm. **Ruler:** Francesco Filiberto 1584-1629 **Obv:** Crowned FF with rosette between the two letters **Rev:** Cross with trefoil ends in quatrefoil **Note:** Varesi 798.

Date	Mintage	VG	F	VF	XF	Unc
ND(1584-1629)	—	50.00	110	225	330	—

KM# 59 TRILLINA

Billon **Ruler:** Paolo Besso 1629-1667 **Obv:** Crown over PBF **Obv. Legend:** P. MESS. ... **Rev:** Crowned oval shield of arms **Rev. Legend:** ... CREP. ET. C.... **Note:** Varesi 826.

Date	Mintage	VG	F	VF	XF	Unc
ND(1629-67)	—	115	225	450	650	—

KM# 10 1/2 SOLDO
1.3500 g., Billon, 18 mm. **Ruler:** Paolo Besso 1629-1667 **Obv:** Crowned shield of 4-fold arms with central shield, chain of order around **Obv. Legend:** P. FER. FLIS. PRIN. MESS **Rev:** Ornate floriated cross **Rev. Legend:** SALVS. MONDO **Note:** Varesi 825.

Date	Mintage	VG	F	VF	XF	Unc
ND(1629-67)	—	50.00	110	200	275	—

KM# 82 1/2 SOLDO
Billon, 15-16 mm. **Ruler:** Francesco Ludovico 1667-1685 **Obv:** Head to right **Obv. Legend:** FRAN. LVD. ... **Rev:** Cross with lily ends **Rev. Legend:** MAR. CREP. ET. COM. LAV **Note:** Varesi 835.

Date	Mintage	VG	F	VF	XF	Unc
ND(1667-85)	—	55.00	110	225	330	—

KM# 83 1/2 SOLDO
1.3500 g., Billon **Rev:** St. Maurice cross

Date	Mintage	VG	F	VF	XF	Unc
ND(1667)	—	25.00	50.00	110	225	—

KM# 84 1/2 SOLDO
1.3500 g., Billon **Obv:** Bust of Francesco right **Rev:** Crowned serpent

Date	Mintage	VG	F	VF	XF	Unc
ND(1667)	—	25.00	50.00	110	225	—

KM# 41 SOLDO
Billon **Obv:** Crowned arms **Rev:** Ornate cross **Note:** Weight varies: 1.50-1.80 grams.

Date	Mintage	VG	F	VF	XF	Unc
1614	—	75.00	150	275	450	—

KM# 11 SOLDO
Billon Weight varies, 1.50-1.85g, 20 mm. **Ruler:** Paolo Besso 1629-1667 **Obv:** Crowned 4-fold arms in baroque frame with central shield of rampant lion left **Obv. Legend:** P. B. F. ... PRI. MESSE **Rev:** Cross with trefoil ends in baroque frame **Rev. Legend:** ADM. ... GLORIA **Note:** Varesi 824.

Date	Mintage	VG	F	VF	XF	Unc
ND(1629-67)	—	80.00	165	300	440	—

KM# 90.2 SOLDO
Billon, 20 mm. **Ruler:** Francesco Ludovico 1667-1685 **Obv:** Crowned shield of 4-fold arms **Obv. Legend:** MONETA ... **Rev:** Ornate cross **Rev. Legend:** ... (M)ESSERANO... **Note:** Varesi 834.

Date	Mintage	VG	F	VF	XF	Unc
ND(1667-85)	—	100	195	325	550	—

KM# 90.1 SOLDO
1.7900 g., Billon, 19 mm. **Ruler:** Francesco Ludovico 1667-1685 **Obv:** Bust to right, date below **Obv. Legend:** FRA. LVD. F. F. PRIN. MES **Rev:** Cross in circle **Rev. Legend:** COME. LAVA. MARC. CREP **Note:** Previously KM #90. Varesi 833.

Date	Mintage	VG	F	VF	XF	Unc
1672	—	115	220	550	825	—

KM# 30 3 KREUZER
1.4700 g., Billon, 19 mm. **Ruler:** Francesco Filiberto 1584-1629 **Obv:** Shield of 3-fold arms, date above **Obv. Legend:** MONETA. NOVA. PRINC. MESSE **Rev:** Crowned imperial eagle, 3 in orb on breast **Rev. Legend:** DOMINE. SALVA. NOS. SPES **Note:** Varesi 795.

Date	Mintage	VG	F	VF	XF	Unc
1603	—	100	195	325	550	—

KM# 8 6 DENARI
Billon, 16-17 mm. **Ruler:** Francesco Filiberto 1584-1629 **Obv:** Crowned shield of 2-fold arms **Obv. Legend:** CARV. IMPER. GRATIA **Rev:** Sword vertical withi point downwards **Rev. Legend:** MONETA. F - ACTA. MESS **Note:** Varesi 793.

Date	Mintage	VG	F	VF	XF	Unc
ND(1584-1629)	—	170	330	550	825	—

KM# 31 3 GROSSI
1.5200 g., Billon, 20 mm. **Ruler:** Francesco Filiberto 1584-1629 **Obv:** Crowned shield of 4-fold arms **Obv. Legend:** FRAN. FIL. FER. FLI. PRINC. MESSE **Rev:** Crowned imperial eagle, 3 in orb on breast, G in margin at bottom **Rev. Legend:** CAROLI. QVIN. IMP. GRATIA **Note:** Varesi 785.

Date	Mintage	VG	F	VF	XF	Unc
ND(1584-1629)	—	100	200	250	500	—

KM# 32 3 GROSSI
Billon **Obv:** Double eagle **Rev:** Bust of St. Theodor **Note:** Weight varies: 1.47-1.52 grams.

Date	Mintage	VG	F	VF	XF	Unc
ND	—	35.00	75.00	150	250	—

KM# 33 3 GROSSI
Billon **Obv:** Quadruple arms **Rev:** Seated woman **Note:** Weight varies: 1.47-1.52 grams.

Date	Mintage	VG	F	VF	XF	Unc
ND	—	20.00	35.00	75.00	150	—

KM# 34 3 GROSSI
Billon **Obv:** Head left **Rev:** St. Maurice cross **Note:** Weight varies: 1.47-1.52 grams.

Date	Mintage	VG	F	VF	XF	Unc
ND	—	20.00	35.00	75.00	150	—

KM# 35 3 GROSSI
Billon **Obv:** Cross with globes **Rev:** St. Mark lion **Note:** Weight varies: 1.47-1.52 grams.

Date	Mintage	VG	F	VF	XF	Unc
ND	—	20.00	35.00	65.00	125	—

KM# 9 18 GROSSI
Silver **Obv:** Bust of Francesco right **Rev:** Crowned double eagle with G. XFIII

Date	Mintage	VG	F	VF	XF	Unc
ND	—	45.00	90.00	175	300	—

KM# 91 LUIGINO
Silver, 21 mm. **Ruler:** Maria Cristina Simiana 1672-1685 **Obv:** Bust to right **Obv. Legend:** MARIA. CRISTINA. SIMIANA **Rev:** Crowned shield of arms, date above **Rev. Legend:** PRINCIPESA. MESSERANI **Note:** Varesi 838.

Date	Mintage	VG	F	VF	XF	Unc
1672	—	125	250	450	750	—

KM# 38 1/17 SCUDO
2.0400 g., Silver, 16-17 mm. **Ruler:** Paolo Besso 1629-1667 **Obv:** Cross with star in each angle **Obv. Legend:** PRNI. MES. MAR. CREP. CO. L **Rev:** Madonna and Child in circle, date at end of legend **Rev. Legend:** PROTECT. NOSTRA **Note:** Varesi 823.

Date	Mintage	VG	F	VF	XF	Unc
1662	—	100	195	315	475	—

KM# 12 2 SOLDI
2.0400 g., Silver **Obv:** Cross with stars in angles **Rev:** Madonna and child

Date	Mintage	VG	F	VF	XF	Unc
ND	—	60.00	120	250	400	—

KM# 13 4 SOLDI
Billon Weight varies, 4.27-4.97g, 25-26 mm. **Ruler:** Paolo Besso 1629-1667 **Obv:** Crowned shield of 4-fold arms with central shield **Obv. Legend:** PAVLVS. FERRERIVS. P. MA **Rev:** Cross with trefoil ends, rosette in each angle **Rev. Legend:** + MONETA. NOVA. DA. SOL. 4 **Note:** Varesi 822.

Date	Mintage	VG	F	VF	XF	Unc
ND(1629-67)	—	225	415	775	1,100	—

KM# 14 4-1/2 SOLDI
Billon Weight varies, 2.93-3.66g, 28 mm. **Ruler:** Paolo Besso 1629-1667 **Obv:** Crowned shield of 4-fold arms in baroque frame with central shield **Obv. Legend:** P. FER. FLISC. PRINC. MES **Rev:** Full-length standing figure of St. Paul, G between feet **ev. Legend:** PROTECTOR - NOSTER **Note:** Varesi 821.

Date	Mintage	VG	F	VF	XF	Unc
ND(1629-67)	—	200	360	675	1,000	—

KM# 15 5 SOLDI
Billon Weight varies, 3.87-5.55g, 28-29 mm. **Ruler:** Paolo Besso 1629-1667 **Obv:** Crowned oval shield of manifold arms in baroque frame **Obv. Legend:** P. BES. FER. FLIS. PRIN. MESS. II **Rev:** Full-length standing figure of Blessed Andreas holding shield with B./AN/DRE/AS **Rev. Legend:** NON. NOB. DOM. SE - D. NOM. TVO. DA. GLO **Note:** Varesi 820.

Date	Mintage	VG	F	VF	XF	Unc
ND(1629-67)	—	135	275	550	825	—

KM# 110 LIRA
5.6700 g., Silver, 28 mm. **Ruler:** Carlo Besso 1685-1720 **Obv:** Bust to right **Obv. Legend:** CAR. BESS. PRIN. MESSERANI **Rev:** Crowned shield of 4-fold arms withi central shield, date at top **Rev. Legend:** MARCHIO. CREP. COM. LAVAN **Note:** Varesi 842.

Date	Mintage	VG	F	VF	XF	Unc
1690	—	750	1,100	2,300	3,250	—

KM# 16 FIORINO
Silver **Obv:** Lion with banner **Rev:** Bust of Pope right **Note:** Weight varies: 4.00-5.00 grams.

Date	Mintage	VG	F	VF	XF	Unc
ND	—	200	400	750	1,250	—

KM# 85 FIORINO
Silver **Obv:** Crowned double eagle, FRANC **Rev:** Crowned quadruple arms **Rev. Legend:** AVILIVM **Note:** Weight varies: 4.00-5.00 grams.

Date	Mintage	VG	F	VF	XF	Unc
ND(1667)	—	100	225	450	900	—

KM# 86 FIORINO
Silver **Obv:** Crowned multiple arms, EXEMPLVM **Rev:** Crowned double eagle **Note:** Weight varies: 4.00-5.00 grams.

Date	Mintage	VG	F	VF	XF	Unc
ND	—	100	225	450	900	—

KM# 17 FIORINO
Silver **Obv:** Fleur-de-lis **Rev:** Ornate cross **Note:** Weight varies: 4.00-5.00 grams.

Date	Mintage	VG	F	VF	XF	Unc
ND	—	—	—	—	—	—

KM# 18 FIORINO
Silver **Obv:** Crowned multiple arms, MONETA **Rev:** Crowned double eagle, NON NOB **Note:** Weight varies: 4.00-5.00 grams.

Date	Mintage	VG	F	VF	XF	Unc
ND	—	75.00	150	300	600	—

KM# 87 FIORINO
Silver **Obv:** Crowned quadruple arms, MONETA **Rev:** Crowned double eagle, PRAESIDIO **Note:** Weight varies: 4.00-5.00 grams.

Date	Mintage	VG	F	VF	XF	Unc
ND	—	100	225	450	900	—

KM# 19 FIORINO
Silver **Obv. Legend:** FRAN FIL. **Rev. Legend:** EXPECTANS. **Note:** Weight varies: 4.00-5.00 grams.

Date	Mintage	VG	F	VF	XF	Unc
ND	—	85.00	175	350	750	—

KM# 20 FIORINO
Silver **Obv. Legend:** MONETA **Note:** Weight varies: 4.00-5.00 grams.

Date	Mintage	VG	F	VF	XF	Unc
ND	—	85.00	175	350	750	—

KM# 21 2 FIORINO
Silver **Obv:** Bust of Francesco right **Rev:** Crowned arms, EX VIROQVE **Note:** Weight varies: 7.00-8.00 grams.

Date	Mintage	VG	F	VF	XF	Unc
ND	—	500	1,000	2,000	—	—

KM# 22 2 FIORINO
Silver **Rev. Legend:** VIRTUS **Note:** Weight varies: 7.00-8.00 grams.

Date	Mintage	VG	F	VF	XF	Unc
ND Rare	—	—	—	—	—	—

KM# 23 2 FIORINO
Silver **Rev:** Crowned arms with liions at sides **Rev. Legend:** MONETA **Note:** Weight varies: 7.00-8.00 grams.

Date	Mintage	VG	F	VF	XF	Unc
ND Rare	—	—	—	—	—	—

KM# 24 2 FIORINO
Silver **Obv:** Crowned double eagle with shield **Rev:** St. Stephan standing **Note:** Weight varies: 7.00-8.00 grams.

Date	Mintage	VG	F	VF	XF	Unc
ND	—	500	1,000	2,000	—	—

KM# 103 TESTONE
Silver, 31-32 mm. **Ruler:** Carlo Besso 1685-1720 **Obv:** Bust to right **Obv. Legend:** CAR. BESS. PRIN. MESSERANI **Rev:** Crowned shield of 4-fold arms with central shield, date at top **Rev. Legend:** MARCHIO. CREP. COM. LAVAN **Note:** Varesi 841.

Date	Mintage	VG	F	VF	XF	Unc
1686 Rare	—	—	—	—	—	—

KM# 94 1/2 SCUDO
12.8600 g., Silver, 32 mm. **Ruler:** Francesco Ludovico 1667-1685 **Obv:** Bust to right **Obv. Legend:** FRA. LVD. F.F. PRIN. MESSERANI **Rev:** Crowned shield of 4-fold arms with central shield, date at top in margin **Rev. Legend:** MARCHIO. CREP. COM. LAVANIÆ **Note:** Varesi 832.

Date	Mintage	VG	F	VF	XF	Unc
1672 Rare	—	—	—	—	—	—
1673 Rare	—	—	—	—	—	—

KM# 25 1/4 TALLERO
Silver **Obv:** Armored bust right **Obv. Legend:** NON NOBIS **Rev:** Crowned double-headed imperial eagle with shield on breast **Note:** Weight varies: 5.39-6.50 grams.

Date	Mintage	VG	F	VF	XF	Unc
ND	—	250	500	950	—	—

KM# 26 1/4 TALLERO
Silver **Obv:** Crowned double eagle **Obv. Legend:** VIRTVTVS **Note:** Weight varies: 5.39-6.50 grams.

Date	Mintage	VG	F	VF	XF	Unc
ND	—	400	900	1,750	—	—

KM# 52 1/2 TALLERO
15.8000 g., Silver, 35 mm. **Ruler:** Paolo Besso 1629-1667 **Obv:** Bust wearing high collar to right **Obv. Legend:** P. FER. MES. P. ET. MAR. CREP. III. S. XII **Rev:** St. George on horseback to right, slaying dragon below, in exergue S. G. CASNIL **Rev. Legend:** PROTECTOR. NOSTER. ASPICE **Note:** Varesi 818.

Date	Mintage	VG	F	VF	XF	Unc
ND(1629-67)	—	1,250	2,200	4,250	6,500	—

KM# 53 1/2 TALLERO

15.8500 g., Silver, 37-38 mm. **Ruler:** Paolo Besso 1629-1667 **Obv:** Bust wearing high collar to right **Obv. Legend:** P. FER. MES. P. ET. MAR. CREP. III. S. XII **Rev:** Sun with stars around in Zodiac, clouds and earth below **Rev. Legend:** NVN. QVAM. RETRO. CVRSVM. VERTO **Note:** Varesi 819.

Date	Mintage	VG	F	VF	XF	Unc
ND(1629-67)	—	1,250	2,200	4,250	6,500	—

KM# 92 SCUDO

Silver, 40-41 mm. **Ruler:** Francesco Ludovico 1667-1685 **Obv:** Draped bust to right **Obv. Legend:** FRA. LVD. F. F. PRIN. MESSERANI **Rev:** Four small shields of arms in cruciform around small shield of arms in circle in center, fleur-de-lis in each angle, date divided to outer edge above crowns of arms **Rev. Legend:** MARC - CREP - COME - LAVA **Note:** Dav. #3994; Varesi 831.

Date	Mintage	VG	F	VF	XF	Unc
1672 Rare	—	—	—	—	—	—

KM# 104 SCUDO

Silver, 43 mm. **Ruler:** Carlo Besso 1685-1720 **Obv:** Draped bust to right **Obv. Legend:** CAR. BESS. PRIN. MESSERANI **Rev:** Crowned shield of 4-fold arms with central shield, date in margin at top **Rev. Legend:** MARCHIO. CREP. COM. LAVAN **Note:** Dav. #3995; Varesi 840.

Date	Mintage	VG	F	VF	XF	Unc
1686 Rare	—	—	—	—	—	—

KM# 104a SCUDO

Copper

Date	Mintage	VG	F	VF	XF	Unc
1686 Proof; Rare	—	—	—	—	—	—

KM# 46.2 TALLERO

Silver, 42 mm. **Ruler:** Francesco Filiberto 1584-1629 **Obv:** Half-length armored figure to right **Obv. Legend:** FRANC. FIL. FERR. FLI. PRINCE. MESS. ET. M **Rev:** Crowned imperial eagle, oval shield of 2-fold arms on breast, B. 12 in cartouche at bottom **Rev. Legend:** NON. NOBIS. DNE. SED - NOM. TVO. DA. GLORIAM **Note:** Dav. 3978A.

Date	Mintage	VG	F	VF	XF	Unc
ND(1584-1629)	—	350	700	1,250	—	—

KM# 46.3 TALLERO

Silver, 41-42 mm. **Ruler:** Francesco Filiberto 1584-1629 **Obv:** Half-length armored figure to right **Obv. Legend:** + F. D. G. SAC. ROMAN. IMP. PRIN. M. C. ET. I. M. **Rev:** Crowned displayed eagle, shield of 4-fold arms on breast **Rev. Legend:** SAC. E. MA. A. COM. CAM. ET. A. P. S. P. O. R **Note:** Varesi 764.

Date	Mintage	VG	F	VF	XF	Unc
ND(1584-1629) Rare	—	—	—	—	—	—

KM# 47.1 TALLERO

Silver, 44 mm. **Ruler:** Francesco Filiberto 1584-1629 **Obv:** Half-length armored figure to right **Obv. Legend:** PRINC. PRIMVS. MESSERANI. ET. MAR **Rev:** Crowned imperial eagle, ornate shield of arms on breast **Rev. Legend:** STABILITAS. ALTA. PETIT. F. VII **Note:** Dav. #3979; Varesi 765.

Date	Mintage	VG	F	VF	XF	Unc
ND(1584-1629)	—	900	1,650	3,500	6,000	—

KM# 47.2 TALLERO

23.3300 g., Silver, 43-45 mm. **Ruler:** Francesco Filiberto 1584-1629 **Obv:** Half-length armored figure to right **Obv. Legend:** FRAN. PRINCEPS. PRIMVS. M. ET. M **Rev:** Crowned imperial eagle, oval shield of arms on breast **Rev. Legend:** STABILITAS. ALTA. PETIT. F. VI **Note:** Dav. #3980; Varesi 766.

Date	Mintage	VG	F	VF	XF	Unc
ND(1584-1629)	—	1,800	3,000	5,000	—	—

KM# 48 TALLERO

Silver Weight varies, 27.28-27.88g, 41-43 mm. **Ruler:** Francesco Filiberto 1584-1629 **Obv:** Half-length armored figure to right **Obv. Legend:** FRANCIS. FILIB. S. R. S. PRIN. MESSERANI **Rev:** Crowned shield of 4-fold arms with central shield of displayed eagle, all in wreath **Rev. Legend:** MARCHIO. CREPACORI. COM. LAVANI **Note:** Dav. #3981; Varesi 768.

Date	Mintage	VG	F	VF	XF	Unc
ND(1584-1629)	—	800	1,550	2,750	4,500	—

KM# 49 TALLERO

26.4500 g., Silver, 42 mm. **Ruler:** Francesco Filiberto 1584-1629 **Obv:** Armored bust to left **Obv. Legend:** FRAN. FIL. FERR. FLIS. PRINC. MESSERA **Rev:** Crowned shield of 4-fold arms in baroque frame with central shield of displayed eagle, chain of order around, X - II below in margin **Rev. Legend:** NON. NOBIS. DNE. SED. - NOM. TVO. DA. GLORIA **Note:** Dav. #3982; Varesi 769.

Date	Mintage	VG	F	VF	XF	Unc
ND(1584-1629)	—	1,500	3,250	5,500	9,500	—

KM# 45.2 TALLERO

Silver **Ruler:** Francesco Filiberto 1584-1629 **Obv:** Half-length armored figure to right **Obv. Legend:** FRANC. FLI. PRINCE. MESSERA **Rev:** Crowned imperial eagle, oval shield of 2-fold arms on breast, F. VIII in cartouche at bottom **Rev. Legend:** CAROLI. QVINTI. - IMPERATOR. GRA **Note:** Dav. #3976.

Date	Mintage	VG	F	VF	XF	Unc
ND(1584-1629)	—	475	950	1,800	3,000	—

KM# 45.3 TALLERO

Silver, 41-42 mm. **Ruler:** Francesco Filiberto 1584-1629 **Obv:** Half-length armored figure to right **Obv. Legend:** FRANC. FIL. FERR. FLI. PRINCE. MESSERA **Rev:** Crowned imperial eagle, oval shield of 2-fold arms on breast **Rev. Legend:** CAROLI. QVINTI. IMPERATOR. GRATIA **Note:** Dav. #3977.

Date	Mintage	VG	F	VF	XF	Unc
ND(1584-1629)	—	300	600	1,150	2,000	—

KM# 46.1 TALLERO

Silver Weight varies, 25.34-26.40g, 42 mm. **Obv:** Half-length armored figure to right **Obv. Legend:** FRANC. FIL. FERR. FLI. PRINCE. MESSERA **Rev:** Crowned imperial eagle, oval shield of 2-fold arms on breast, B. 12 in cartouche at bottom **Rev. Legend:** NON. NOBIS. DNE. SED - NOM. TVO. DA. GLORIAM **Note:** Previously KM #46. Dav. #3978; Varesi 763.

Date	Mintage	VG	F	VF	XF	Unc
ND(1584-1629)	—	500	925	2,300	5,500	—

KM# 40 TALLERO

Silver Weight varies, 26.77-27.39g, 42 mm. **Ruler:** Francesco Filiberto 1584-1629 **Obv:** Half-length armored figure to right **Obv. Legend:** FRANC. FIL. FER(R). FLI. PRINCE. MESSERA **Rev:** Crowned imperial eagle, oval shield of 2-fold arms on breast, date divided to lower left and right, F. VIII in cartouche at bottom **Rev. Legend:** CAROLI. QVINTI. - IMPERATOR. GRA(TIA) **Note:** Dav. #3974; Varesi 762.

Date	Mintage	VG	F	VF	XF	Unc
ND(1584-1629)	—	260	500	1,450	2,850	—
1612	—	260	500	1,450	2,850	—
1613	—	260	500	1,450	2,850	—

KM# 45.1 TALLERO

Silver, 40-42 mm. **Ruler:** Francesco Filiberto 1584-1629 **Obv:** Half-length armored figure to right **Obv. Legend:** FRAN. PRINCEPS. PRIMVS. M. ET. M **Rev:** Crowned imperial eagle, shield of arms on breast, crown divides date **Rev. Legend:** STABILITAS. ALTA. PETIT. F. S. 9 **Note:** Dav. #3975; Varesi 767.

Date	Mintage	VG	F	VF	XF	Unc
1621	—	900	1,650	3,500	6,000	—

KM# 45.4 TALLERO

Silver **Obv. Legend:** PRINC. PRIMVS. MESS. FT. MAR **Rev. Legend:** STABILITAS. A. LIA. PETIT. F. VI. **Note:** Weight varies: 23.00-27.00 grams.

Date	Mintage	VG	F	VF	XF	Unc
ND	—	900	1,750	3,300	5,400	—

KM# 66.1 TALLERO

Silver Weight varies, 28.55-32.83g, 42-43 mm. **Ruler:** Paolo Besso 1629-1667 **Obv:** Bust with high collar to right, L.I. below shoulder **Obv. Legend:** P. FER. MES. P. ET. MAR. CREP. III. M.DCXXXIII **Rev:** St. George on horseback to right, slaying dragon below, in exergue S. G. C(A)S(NI)L **Note:** Dav. #3983; Varesi 811/1.

Date	Mintage	VG	F	VF	XF	Unc
MDCXXXIII(1633)	—	900	1,650	3,500	6,000	—

KM# 67.1 TALLERO

Silver Weight varies, 30.58-31.29g, 44 mm. **Ruler:** Paolo Besso 1629-1667 **Obv:** Bust with high collar to right, L.I. below shoulder **Obv. Legend:** P. FER. MES. P. ET. MAR. CREP. III. M.DCXXXIII **Rev:** Sun with stars around in Zodiac, clouds and earth below **Rev. Legend:** MVM/ QVAM. RETRO. CVRSVM. VERTO. L. I. **Note:** Dav. #3984; Varesi 813.

Date	Mintage	VG	F	VF	XF	Unc
MDCXXXIII(1633)	—	1,350	2,750	5,500	9,000	—

KM# 68.1 TALLERO

Silver Weight varies, 28.25-30.78g, 44 mm. **Ruler:** Paolo Besso 1629-1667 **Obv:** Bust with high collar to right, L.I. below shoulder **Obv. Legend:** P. FER. MES. P. ET. MAR. CREP. III. M.DCXXXIII **Rev:** Sunface with rays around in circle, B between 2 scrollwork ornaments at bottom **Rev. Legend:** NON. MVTABO. LVCEM. L. I. **Note:** Dav. #3985; Varesi 816/1.

Date	Mintage	VG	F	VF	XF	Unc
MDCXXXIII(1633)	—	1,350	2,750	5,500	9,000	—

KM# 67.4 TALLERO

Silver, 45 mm. **Ruler:** Paolo Besso 1629-1667 **Obv:** Sun with stars around in Zodiac, clouds and earth below **Obv. Legend:** NVN. QVAM. RETRO. CVRSVM. VERTO. L. I. **Rev:** Sunface with rays around in circle, B between two scrollwork ornaments **Rev. Legend:** NON. MVTABO. LVCEM. L. I. **Note:** Mule of reverse die of KM #67.1 and reverse die of KM #68.1. Varesi 817.

Date	Mintage	VG	F	VF	XF	Unc
ND(1633) Rare	—	—	—	—	—	—

KM# 69 TALLERO

Silver **Obv:** Bust right **Obv. Legend:** CAROLI **Rev:** Zodiac **Note:** Weight varies: 23.00-27.00 grams.

Date	Mintage	VG	F	VF	XF	Unc
1635 Rare	—	—	—	—	—	—

KM# 66.2 TALLERO

Silver **Ruler:** Paolo Besso 1629-1667 **Obv:** Bust with high collar to right **Obv. Legend:** P. FER. MA. P. ET. MAR. CRE. III **Rev:** St. George on horseback to right, slaying dragon below, in exergue S. G. CA. SNI. L **Rev. Legend:** PROTECTOR. NOSTER. ASPICE. MDCXXXV **Note:** Dav. #3986; Varesi 811/3.

Date	Mintage	VG	F	VF	XF	Unc
MDCXXXV(1635)	—	900	1,650	3,500	6,000	—

KM# 66.3 TALLERO

Silver Weight varies, 28.55-32.83g, 43-44 mm. **Ruler:** Paolo Besso 1629-1667 **Obv:** Bust with high collar to right **Obv. Legend:** P. FER. MA. P. ET. MAR. CREP. MDCXXXV **Rev:** St. George on horseback to right, slaying dragon below, in exergue S. G. CA. SNI. L **Rev. Legend:** PROTECTOR. NOSTER. ASPICE. MDCXXXV **Note:** Dav. #3987; Varesi 811/4. Dated both sides.

Date	Mintage	VG	F	VF	XF	Unc
MDCXXXV(1635)	—	900	1,650	3,500	6,000	—

KM# 67.2 TALLERO

Silver **Ruler:** Paolo Besso 1629-1667 **Obv:** Armored and mantled bust to right, LI below shoulder **Obv. Legend:** CAROLVS. I. MDCVX. MA. P. E. MAR. CRE. **Rev:** Sun with stars around in Zodiac, clouds and earth below **Rev. Legend:** NVN. QVAM. RETRO. SVRSVM. VERTO. L. I. **Note:** Dav. #3988; Varesi 814.

Date	Mintage	VG	F	VF	XF	Unc
MDCVX(1635) Rare	—	—	—	—	—	—

KM# 68.2 TALLERO

Silver, 43 mm. **Ruler:** Paolo Besso 1629-1667 **Obv:** Armored and mantled bust to right, LI below shoulder **Obv. Legend:** CAROLVS. I. M.DCVS. MA. P. E. MAR. CRE **Rev:** Sunface with rays around in circle, B in margin below between two scrollwork ornaments **Rev. Legend:** NON. MVTABO. LVCEM. L. I. **Note:** Dav. #3989; Varesi 815.

Date	Mintage	VG	F	VF	XF	Unc
MDCVX(1635) Rare	—	—	—	—	—	—

KM# 70.1 TALLERO

Silver Weight varies, 28.25-30.78g, 43 mm. **Ruler:** Paolo Besso 1629-1667 **Obv:** Bust Bust with high collar to right **Obv. Legend:** P. FER. MA. P. ET. MAR. CREP. MDCXXXV **Rev:** Sunface with rays around in circle, B in margin below between two scrollwork ornaments **Rev. Legend:** nON. MVTABO. LVCEM. L. I. **Note:** Dav. #3990; Varesi 816/2.

Date	Mintage	VG	F	VF	XF	Unc
MDCXXXV(1635) Rare	—	1,350	2,750	5,500	9,000	—

KM# 70.2 TALLERO

Silver, 44 mm. **Ruler:** Paolo Besso 1629-1667 **Obv:** Bust with high collar to right, L.I. below shoulder **Obv. Legend:** P. FER. MES. P. ET. MAR. CREP. M.DCXXXV **Rev:** Sunface with rays around in circle, B between two scrollwork ornaments at bottom **Rev. Legend:** NON. MVTABO. LVCEM. L. I. **Note:** Dav. #3991.

Date	Mintage	VG	F	VF	XF	Unc
MDCXXXV(1635) Rare	—	—	—	—	—	—

KM# 66.5 TALLERO

Silver **Ruler:** Paolo Besso 1629-1667 **Obv:** Bust with high collar to right **Obv. Legend:** P. FER. MA. P. ET. MAR. CREP. MDCXXXV **Rev:** St. George on horseback to right, slaying dragon below, in exergue S. G. CA. SNI. L **Rev. Legend:** ROTECTOR. NOSTER. ASPICE. **Note:** Dav. 3987A.

Date	Mintage	VG	F	VF	XF	Unc
MDCXXXV(1635)	—	900	1,650	3,500	6,000	—

KM# 66.6 TALLERO

Silver **Ruler:** Paolo Besso 1629-1667 **Obv:** Bust with high collar to right **Obv. Legend:** P. FER. MES. P. ET. MAR. CREP. MDCXXXV **Rev:** St. George on horseback to right, slaying dragon below, in exergue S. G. CA. SNI. L **Rev. Legend:** PROTECTOR. NOSTER. ASPICE **Note:** Dav. 3987B; Varesi 811/2.

Date	Mintage	VG	F	VF	XF	Unc
MDCXXXV(1635)	—	900	1,650	3,500	6,000	—

KM# 66.7 TALLERO

Silver **Ruler:** Paolo Besso 1629-1667 **Obv:** Bust wearing high collar to right **Obv. Legend:** FER. MA. P. ET. MAR. CRE. III. P **Rev:** St. George on horseback to right, slaying dragon below, in exergue S. G. CA. SNI. L **Rev. Legend:** PROTECTOR. NOSTER. ASPICE **Note:** Dav. 3987C.

Date	Mintage	VG	F	VF	XF	Unc
MDCXXXV(1635)	—	900	1,650	3,500	6,000	—

KM# 66.4 TALLERO

Silver Weight varies, 28.55-32.83g, 43-44 mm. **Ruler:** Paolo Besso 1629-1667 **Obv:** Bust with high collar to right **Obv. Legend:** FER. MA. P. ET. MAR. CRE. III. P **Rev:** St. George on horseback to right, slaying dragon below, in exergue S. G. CASL. **Rev. Legend:** PROTECTOR. NOSTER. ASPICE. M.DCVXIII **Note:** Dav. #3992; Varesi 811/5.

Date	Mintage	VG	F	VF	XF	Unc
MDCVXIII(1638)	—	900	1,650	3,500	6,000	—

KM# 67.3 TALLERO

Silver, 44 mm. **Ruler:** Paolo Besso 1629-1667 **Obv:** Bust wearing high collar to right **Obv. Legend:** P. FER. MA. CRE. EC. D. S. P. B. F. MDCVXVIII. P. **Rev:** Sun with stars around in Zodiac, clouds and earth below **Rev. Legend:** NVNQVAM RETRORSVM. VERTO **Note:** Dav. #3993; Varesi 812.

Date	Mintage	VG	F	VF	XF	Unc
MDCVXVIII(1638) Rare	—	—	—	—	—	—

KM# 75 SCUDO D'ORO

3.2000 g., Gold, 22 mm. **Ruler:** Paolo Besso 1629-1667 **Obv:** High collared bust to right **Obv. Legend:** P. FER. MA. D. ET. MAR. CREP. MDCXL. **Rev:** Crowned shield of 4-fold arms with central shield, all within chain of order **Rev. Legend:** MON. NOR. D. O. RA. SO. LVI. D. FLOR. **Note:** Fr. 624; Varesi 805.

Date	Mintage	VG	F	VF	XF	Unc
MDCXL(1640)	—	1,500	3,000	5,500	9,500	—

KM# 55.2 DUCAT

Gold, 23 mm. **Ruler:** Paolo Besso 1629-1667 **Obv:** Full-length figure of armored prince turned slightly to right., holding sword with point down **Obv. Legend:** P. FER. MES. PRIN. M. - CREP. MO. AVR. D. IIII. **Rev:** Square tablet with 5-line inscription in ornate frame **Rev. Inscription:** PAV. FER/MES. PRI/MAR. CR/P. MON. AVR/DA. IIII. **Note:** Previously KM #55. Varesi 806.

Date	Mintage	VG	F	VF	XF	Unc
ND(1629-67)	—	550	1,200	2,000	3,000	—

KM# 55.1 DUCAT

Gold, 23 mm. **Ruler:** Paolo Besso 1629-1667 **Obv:** Full-length figure of armored prince, head turned to right, holding sword over right shoulder and bundle of arrows in left hand, divides date **Obv. Legend:** DE. PVGNABO - SIC. PROFII. **Rev:** Square tablet with 5-line inscription in ornate frame. **Rev. Inscription:** P. B. FER./D. MA. A./C. R. EF/MO. DO/DA. SOL. X. **Note:** Varesi 807.

Date	Mintage	VG	F	VF	XF	Unc
1632	—	550	1,200	2,000	3,000	—

KM# 56 DUCAT

Gold Weight varies, 3.30-3.47g, 22.5 mm. **Ruler:** Paolo Besso 1629-1667 **Obv:** Full-length figure of armored prince turned slightly to right., holding sword with point down **Obv. Legend:** F. FER. MES. PRIN. M. CREP. MO. AVR. DA. VII. **Rev:** Square tablet with 5-line inscription in ornamented frame **Rev. Inscription:** MONE/TA/NOVA/AVREA/CO. LAV. **Note:** Varesi 808.

Date	Mintage	VG	F	VF	XF	Unc
ND(1629-67)	—	900	1,650	3,500	5,000	—

KM# 57 DUCAT

3.2400 g., Gold, 21-21.5 mm. **Ruler:** Paolo Besso 1629-1667 **Obv:** Full-length figure of armored prince turned slightly to right., holding sword with point down **Obv. Legend:** P. FER. MES. PRIN. M. CREP. MO. AVR. DA. L. III. **Rev:** Square tablet with 5-line inscription in ornamented frame **Rev. Inscription:** P. FER. MES/PRIN. M/CREP. MO/AVR. DA. L. III/F. **Note:** Varesi 809.

Date	Mintage	VG	F	VF	XF	Unc
ND(1629-67)	—	900	1,650	3,500	5,000	—

KM# 58 DUCAT

Gold, 23.5 mm. **Ruler:** Paolo Besso 1629-1667 **Obv:** Square tablet with 5-line inscription in ornamented frame **Obv. Inscription:** MONE/TA/NOVA/AVREA/CO. LA. **Rev:** Crowned imperial eagle, shield of arms on breast **Rev. Legend:** SVB. VMBRA. ALARVM. TVARVM **Note:** Fr. 626; Varesi 810.

Date	Mintage	VG	F	VF	XF	Unc
ND(1629-67)	—	550	1,200	2,000	3,000	—

KM# 27 DOPPIA

6.4000 g., Gold **Obv:** Bust of Francesco right **Rev:** Annunciation

Date	Mintage	VG	F	VF	XF	Unc
ND Rare	—	—	—	—	—	—

KM# 28 DOPPIA

6.4000 g., Gold **Rev:** Crowned multiple arms

Date	Mintage	VG	F	VF	XF	Unc
ND	—	2,000	3,500	6,500	11,000	—

KM# 88 DOPPIA

Gold, 25 mm. **Ruler:** Francesco Ludovico 1667-1685 **Obv:** Draped bust to right **Obv. Legend:** FRANN. LVD. FER. FL. PRI. MESS **Rev:** Crowned shield of 4-fold arms with central shield, date above crown **Rev. Legend:** MARH. CREP. - COM. LAVA **Note:** Fr. 627; Varesi 830.

Date	Mintage	VG	F	VF	XF	Unc
1667 Rare	—	—	—	—	—	—

KM# 105 DOPPIA

Gold, 26 mm. **Ruler:** Carlo Besso 1685-1720 **Obv:** Bust to right **Obv. Legend:** CAR. BESS. PRIN. MESSERA **Rev:** Crowned shield of 4-fold arms with central shield, date above crown **Rev. Legend:** MARCHIO. CREP. COM. LAVA **Note:** Fr. 629; Varesi 839.

Date	Mintage	VG	F	VF	XF	Unc
1689 Rare	—	—	—	—	—	—

KM# 54 2 DOPPIE

12.6000 g., Gold, 32 mm. **Ruler:** Paolo Besso 1629-1667

Obv: Bust right wearing high collar **Obv. Legend:** P. FER. MA. L. DVX. A. C. S. R. E. F. E. V. **Rev:** Crowned shield of 4-fold arms with central shield within chain of order **Rev. Legend:** AV. MO. D. V. FLOR. **Note:** Fr. 623a; Varesi 804.

Date	Mintage	VG	F	VF	XF	Unc
ND(1629-67)	—	3,500	5,500	9,500	16,000	—

KM# 29 2 DOPPIE

Gold **Obv:** Bust of Francesco right **Rev:** Annunciation

Date	Mintage	VG	F	VF	XF	Unc
ND Rare	—	—	—	—	—	—

KM# 71 5 DOPPIE

Gold, 43 mm. **Ruler:** Paolo Besso 1629-1667 **Obv:** Mantled bust to left, date behind shoulder in margin **Obv. Legend:** PAVLVS. BESSVS. FERRERIVS. FLISCVS. **Rev:** Crowned shield of 4-fold arms with central shield within baroque frame **Rev. Legend:** PRINC. MESSERANI. MARCHIO. CREPAC. LAV. C. **Note:** Fr. 623; Varesi 803.

Date	Mintage	VG	F	VF	XF	Unc
1638 Rare	—	—	—	—	—	—

KM# 93 5 DOPPIE

Gold, 40-41 mm. **Ruler:** Francesco Ludovico 1667-1685 **Obv:** Draped bust to right **Obv. Legend:** FRA. LVD. F. F. PRIN. MESSERANI **Rev:** Four small crowned shields of arms in cruciform around small shield of arms in circle in center, fleur-de-lis in each angle, date divided to outer edge above crownes of arms **Rev. Legend:** MARC - CREP - COME - LAVA **Note:** Fr. 628; Varesi 829.

Date	Mintage	VG	F	VF	XF	Unc
1672 Rare	—	—	—	—	—	—

MILAN

A city in Lombardy, was ruled by the Lombards before falling to the Franks in 774. It was a dependency of the Spanish Crown from 1535 until the War of the Spanish Succession in 1714. Then it was handed over to Austria who ruled over it until the Napoleonic campaign of 1796 and then became part of the Cisalpine Republic in 1797. In 1802 it became part of the Italian Republic and was part of the Kingdom of Napoleon from 1805 to 1814. From 1814 it was incorporated within Lombardy-Venetia, again under Austrian rule. The Lombard campaign of 1859 restored Milan under the Kingdom of Italy.

RULER
Spanish, until 1714

SPANISH ADMINISTRATION

STANDARD COINAGE

DAV# 3998 FILIPPO

Silver **Obv:** Uncrowned bust with ruffled collar right, date below **Rev:** Crowned complex arms, 100 in exergue below

Date	Mintage	VG	F	VF	XF	Unc
1604	—	160	325	600	1,100	—
1605	—	160	325	600	1,100	—
1606	—	160	325	600	1,100	—
1607	—	160	325	600	1,100	—
ND	—	160	325	600	1,100	—

DAV# 4003 FILIPPO

Silver **Obv:** High unruffled collar on bust **Rev:** Crowned complex arms

Date	Mintage	VG	F	VF	XF	Unc
1652	—	170	325	650	1,200	—
1657	—	170	325	650	1,200	—

DAV# 4004 FILIPPO

Silver **Obv:** Accolated busts right, date below

Date	Mintage	VG	F	VF	XF	Unc
1666	—	170	325	650	1,200	—

DAV# 4005 FILIPPO

Silver **Obv:** Bust of Charles II right

Date	Mintage	VG	F	VF	XF	Unc
1676	—	140	270	500	1,000	—

DAV# 4007 FILIPPO

Silver **Obv:** Older bust **Rev:** Simpler frame for arms

Date	Mintage	VG	F	VF	XF	Unc
1694	—	150	290	550	1,050	—

DAV# 4006 2 FILIPPI

Silver **Note:** Similar to 1 Filippo, Dav. #4007.

Date	Mintage	VG	F	VF	XF	Unc
1694 Rare	—	—	—	—	—	—

DAV# 3997 DUCATONE

Silver **Obv:** Crowned bust right, date below **Obv. Legend:** PHILIPPVS. III... **Rev:** Crowned arms of Milan

Date	Mintage	VG	F	VF	XF	Unc
1602	—	160	325	600	1,100	—
1603	—	160	325	600	1,100	—
1605	—	160	325	600	1,100	—
1606	—	160	325	600	1,100	—
1608	—	160	325	600	1,100	—

DAV# 4001 DUCATONE

Silver **Obv:** Crowned bust right, date below **Obv. Legend:** PHILIPPVS IIII...

Date	Mintage	VG	F	VF	XF	Unc
1622	—	140	270	500	1,000	—
1625	—	140	270	500	1,000	—
1630	—	140	270	500	1,000	—
ND	—	140	270	500	1,000	—

DAV# 3996 2 DUCATONE

Silver **Note:** Similar to 1 Ducatone, Dav. #3997.

Date	Mintage	VG	F	VF	XF	Unc
1603 Rare	—	—	—	—	—	—

DAV# 4000 2 DUCATONE

Silver **Note:** Similar to 1 Ducatone, Dav. #4001.

Date	Mintage	VG	F	VF	XF	Unc
1622 Rare	—	—	—	—	—	—
1630 Rare	—	—	—	—	—	—

DAV# 4002 2 DUCATONE
Silver **Obv:** Crowned bust right in border **Rev:** Differently shaped shield

Date	Mintage	VG	F	VF	XF	Unc
1641 Rare	—	—	—	—	—	—
1643 Rare	—	—	—	—	—	—

DAV# 3999 3 DUCATONE
Silver **Note:** Similar to 1 Ducatone, Dav. #4001.

Date	Mintage	VG	F	VF	XF	Unc
1630 Rare	—	—	—	—	—	—

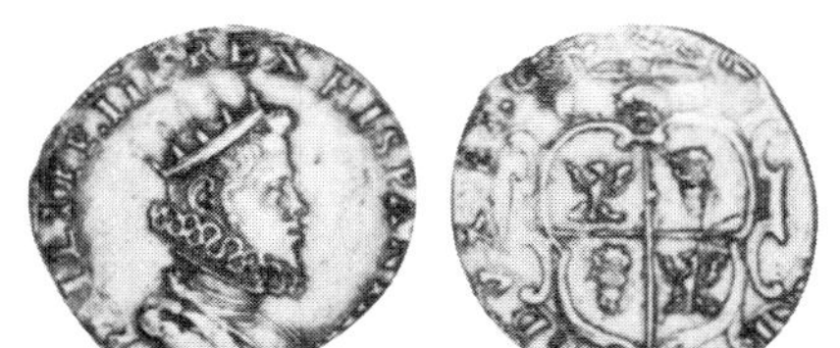

FR# 721 DOPPIA
6.3000 g., 0.9100 Gold 0.1843 oz. AGW **Obv:** Crowned bust of Philip III right, date below **Rev:** Crowned arms

Date	Mintage	VG	F	VF	XF	Unc
1617	—	1,450	2,650	5,400	9,600	—
ND	—	1,450	2,650	5,400	9,600	—

FR# 725 DOPPIA
6.3000 g., 0.9100 Gold 0.1843 oz. AGW **Obv:** Crowned young bust of Philip IV right

Date	Mintage	VG	F	VF	XF	Unc
ND	—	950	2,400	3,900	6,600	—

FR# A725 DOPPIA
6.3000 g., 0.9100 Gold 0.1843 oz. AGW **Obv:** Older bust of Philip IV right

Date	Mintage	VG	F	VF	XF	Unc
1630 Rare	—	—	—	—	—	—

FR# 727 DOPPIA
6.3000 g., 0.9100 Gold 0.1843 oz. AGW **Obv:** Crowned young bust of Charles II right

Date	Mintage	VG	F	VF	XF	Unc
1676	—	2,200	4,950	9,900	17,500	—

FR# 728 DOPPIA
6.3000 g., 0.9100 Gold 0.1843 oz. AGW **Obv:** Older bust of Charles II right

Date	Mintage	VG	F	VF	XF	Unc
1698 Rare	—	—	—	—	—	—

Note: Bowers and Merena Guia sale 3-88 choice VF realized $26,400

FR# 720 2 DOPPIE
12.6000 g., 0.9100 Gold 0.3686 oz. AGW **Subject:** Philip III

Date	Mintage	VG	F	VF	XF	Unc
1610	—	650	1,100	4,950	7,700	—
1617	—	650	1,100	4,950	7,700	—
ND	—	650	1,100	4,700	7,200	—

FR# 724 2 DOPPIE
12.6000 g., 0.9100 Gold 0.3686 oz. AGW **Subject:** Philip IV

Date	Mintage	VG	F	VF	XF	Unc
1630	—	650	1,200	2,250	4,500	—
ND	—	650	1,200	2,250	4,500	—

FR# 726 2 DOPPIE
12.6000 g., 0.9100 Gold 0.3686 oz. AGW **Obv:** Conjoined busts of Charles II and Maria Anna (his mother), date below

Date	Mintage	VG	F	VF	XF	Unc
1666	—	2,200	4,400	8,800	15,500	—

FR# 722 4 DOPPIE
0.9860 Gold **Obv:** Bust of Philip IV right, date below **Rev:** City of Milan in center circle

Date	Mintage	VG	F	VF	XF	Unc
1630 Rare	—	—	—	—	—	—

FR# 723 20 ZECCHINI
65.6000 g., 0.9100 Gold 1.9192 oz. AGW **Obv:** Bust of Philip IV

Date	Mintage	VG	F	VF	XF	Unc
1643	—	—	—	—	—	—

Note: Bowers and Merena Guia sale 3-88 XF realized $82,500

PIEFORTS

KM#	Date	Mintage	Identification	Mkt Val
P1	1622	—	2 Ducatone. Silver. Dav. 4000	—
P2	1630	—	2 Ducatone. Silver. Dav. 4000	—
P3	1630	—	3 Ducatone. Silver. Dav. 3999.	—

MIRANDOLA

Mirandola, a duchy in Modena, was originally associated with an abbey. It belonged to several families before coming into possession of the Pico. Minting rights were granted in 1515. The scudo coinage is confined to the two dukes of the 17th century. It was sold to the Estes in Modena sometime after 1708.

RULERS
Alessandro I Pico, 1602-1637
Alessandro II Pico, 1637-1691

DUCHY

STANDARD COINAGE

DAV# 4008 SCUDO
Silver **Obv:** Bust left, date below **Obv. Legend:** ALEXANDER. DVX. MIRANDVLAE **Rev:** Crowned arms in order chain **Rev. Legend:** CONCORDIAE**MARCHIO*III

Date	Mintage	VG	F	VF	XF	Unc
1613 Rare	—	—	—	—	—	—

DAV# 4010 SCUDO
Silver **Obv:** Bust left, date below **Obv. Legend:** ALEXAN*PICVS*MIRANDVLAE*DVX*I **Rev:** Figure standing on globe, spray in hand **Rev. Legend:** ...NVNC*PEDE...CERTO

Date	Mintage	VG	F	VF	XF	Unc
1617 Rare	—	—	—	—	—	—

Note: Numismatica Ars Classica Auction 44, 11-07, VF realized approximately $34,130

DAV# 4011 SCUDO
Silver **Obv. Legend:** ALEXAN*MIRANDVLA(E)*DUX. I.

Date	Mintage	VG	F	VF	XF	Unc
1618 Rare	—	—	—	—	—	—

DAV# 4012 SCUDO
Silver **Obv:** Bust left dividing date **Obv. Legend:** ALEXANDER. DUX MIRANDVLAE. **Rev:** Crowned arms in order chain **Rev. Legend:** CONCORDIAE*MARCHIO*III

Date	Mintage	VG	F	VF	XF	Unc
1618	—	1,850	3,250	5,500	—	—

DAV# 4013 SCUDO
Silver **Obv:** Bust right, date below legend **Obv. Legend:** ALEX. DUX. MIR... **Rev. Legend:** INSIGNA ANTIQUI-SSIMA ET MATERNO

Date	Mintage	VG	F	VF	XF	Unc
1622	—	1,800	3,000	5,000	—	—

DAV# 4014 SCUDO
Silver **Obv. Legend:** ALEXANDER. PICVS. DVS. MIR **Rev:** Crowned arms **Rev. Legend:** CONCORDIAE. MARCHIO. III.

Date	Mintage	VG	F	VF	XF	Unc
1633 Rare	—	—	—	—	—	—

DAV# 4019 SCUDO
Silver **Obv. Legend:** ALEX. PICVS. DVX. MIRA: I: E. C. **Rev:** Crowned arms **Rev. Legend:** S. ALEX. MON. -DA. BOL. TREN.

Date	Mintage	VG	F	VF	XF	Unc
ND Rare	—	—	—	—	—	—

DAV# 4009 2 SCUDI
Silver **Obv:** Bust left, date below **Rev:** Figure standing on globe, spray in hand

Date	Mintage	VG	F	VF	XF	Unc
1617 Rare	—	—	—	—	—	—

DAV# 4015 TALLERO

Silver **Obv:** Half figure of knight behind shield **Obv. Legend:** MO. NOV. DEL. DVC... **Rev:** Lion, legend, date **Rev. Legend:** VICIT. LEO. DE. TRIBV. IVDA.

Date	Mintage	VG	F	VF	XF	Unc
1636	—	850	1,650	3,000	5,000	—

DAV# 4016 TALLERO

Silver **Obv. Legend:** MO. NO. DA. SESIN.-LXX. DEL. DVX. MI.

Date	Mintage	VG	F	VF	XF	Unc
1637	—	950	1,750	3,250	5,500	—

DAV# 4017 TALLERO

Silver **Obv:** Bust right **Obv. Legend:** ALEX*DEI*GRA*AC* SACRI*ROM*IMP*DVX*M*I* **Rev:** Crowned arms in order chain **Rev. Legend:** CONCOR*MAR*III*-*SAN*MART*BARO

Date	Mintage	VG	F	VF	XF	Unc
ND Rare	—	—	—	—	—	—

Note: Numismatica Ars Classica Auction 32, 1-06, VF realized approximately $25,400

DAV# 4018 TALLERO

Silver **Obv. Legend:** ALEX. DVX. MIR. I. CON. MAR. III. S. MART. IN. SPI. DOM. **Rev. Legend:** ANTIQVISSIMAE FA-MI...

Date	Mintage	VG	F	VF	XF	Unc
ND Rare	—	—	—	—	—	—

Note: Numismatica Ars Classica Auction 35, 12-06, XF realized approximately $27,980

DAV# 4020 DUCATONE

Silver **Obv:** Bust of Alessandro II right **Rev:** Phoenix rising from flames

Date	Mintage	VG	F	VF	XF	Unc
ND Rare	—	—	—	—	—	—

Note: Numismatica Ars Classica Auction 32, 1-06, XF realized approximately $75,400

KM# 25 24 SCUDI D'ORO

78.7800 g., Gold **Obv:** Armored bust of Alexander I left in inner circle, date below **Rev:** Crowned arms in order collar in inner circle

Date	Mintage	VG	F	VF	XF	Unc
1618 Rare	—	—	—	—	—	—

KM# 27 2 DOPPIE

13.0900 g., Gold **Obv:** Bust of Alexander II right **Rev:** St. Savinus kneeling 3/4 facing left

Date	Mintage	VG	F	VF	XF	Unc
ND Unique	—	—	—	—	—	—

MODENA

Mutina

The ancient Mutina is a territorial division of Italy fronting on the Adriatic Sea between Venetia and Marches which became Roman in 215-212 B.C. Ravaged by Attila and Lombard attacks, it was rebuilt in the 9th century. Obizzo d'Este became its lord in 1288 and it was constituted a duchy in favor of Borso d'Este in 1452. Modena was included in the Napoleonic complex from 1796 to 1813, after which it was governed by the House of Austria-Este. Modena began coining in the 13th century and ceased in 1796.

RULERS

Cesare d'Este, 1598-1628
Francesco I d'Este, 1629-1658
Alfonso IV d'Este, 1658-1662
Francesco II d'Este, 1662-1694
Rinaldo D'Este, 1694-1737

DUCHY

STANDARD COINAGE

DAV# 4027 4 LIRE (Levant)

Silver **Obv:** Half-figure left **Obv. Legend:** CAESAR. DVX. MVT. REG. E. C. **Rev:** Crowned arms in order chain, L4 below **Rev. Legend:** NOBILITAS.-ESTENSIS

Date	Mintage	VG	F	VF	XF	Unc
ND Rare	—	—	—	—	—	—

DAV# 4026 SCUDO

Silver **Obv:** Bust left **Obv. Legend:** CASEAR. DUX. MVT. REG. E. C. **Rev:** Crowned arms in order chain **Rev. Legend:** NOBILITAS. ESTENSIS

Date	Mintage	VG	F	VF	XF	Unc
1613	—	1,850	3,500	6,000	9,500	—

DAV# 4039 SCUDO

26.4400 g., 0.9100 Silver 0.7735 oz. ASW, 42.6 mm. **Obv:** Bust right, 103 below **Obv. Legend:** FR(A) (N). (I). MV (T)... **Rev:** Crowned arms in frame **Rev. Legend:** LIBRAT. AFFERT. ET. EFERT. **Note:** Varieties exist.

Date	Mintage	VG	F	VF	XF	Unc
ND	—	1,250	2,500	4,500	7,500	—

DAV# 4038 2 SCUDI

Silver **Obv:** Bust right, 103 below **Obv. Legend:** FR(A) (N). (I). MV (T)... **Rev:** Crowned arms in frame **Rev. Legend:** LIBRAT. AFFERT. ET. EFERT.

Date	Mintage	VG	F	VF	XF	Unc
ND Rare	—	—	—	—	—	—

DAV# 4021 TALLERO (Levant)

25.8100 g., 0.9100 Silver 0.7551 oz. ASW **Obv:** Bust right, date below **Obv. Legend:** CAESAR. DVX.-MVT. REG. E. C. **Rev:** Crowned arms in frame **Rev. Legend:** NOBILITAS.-ESTENSIS

Date	Mintage	VG	F	VF	XF	Unc
1601 Rare	—	—	—	—	—	—
1602 Rare	—	—	—	—	—	—

DAV# 4022 MEZZO (1/2) DUCATONE

Silver **Obv:** Bust right **Obv. Legend:** CAESAR. DVX.-MVTINAE... **Rev:** Abundance with cornucopia **Rev. Legend:** FIRMISSIMAE...

Date	Mintage	VG	F	VF	XF	Unc
1603	—	1,400	2,700	5,100	—	—
1605	—	1,400	2,700	5,100	—	—

DAV# 4025 DUCATONE

Silver **Obv:** Bust right with LS below **Obv. Legend:** CAESAR. DVX. MVT. REG. EC. . **Rev:** Abundance with cornucopia **Rev. Legend:** FIRMISSIMAE. SPEI.

Date	Mintage	VG	F	VF	XF	Unc
1610	—	1,600	3,000	5,700	—	—
1611	—	1,600	3,000	5,700	—	—
1612	—	1,600	3,000	5,700	—	—

DAV# 4036 DUCATONE

Silver **Obv. Legend:** FR(AN) (CISCVS). I. MV(T)*R(EG)-E(T). C. DV(X). VIII.

Date	Mintage	VG	F	VF	XF	Unc
ND	—	1,700	3,200	6,000	—	—

DAV# 4036A DUCATONE

Silver **Obv:** Large draped bust

Date	Mintage	VG	F	VF	XF	Unc
ND	—	1,700	3,200	6,000	—	—

DAV# 4037 DUCATONE
Silver **Obv:** Bust right **Rev:** FRANCISCVS. I. MVT. RE(G) E(VS). C. DVX. VIII.

Date	Mintage	VG	F	VF	XF	Unc
ND Rare	—	—	—	—	—	—

DAV# 4031 DUCATONE
Silver **Obv:** Bust right with date below **Obv. Legend:** FRANCISCVS. I. MVT. REG. ET. C. DVX. VIII **Rev:** Ship with stars above, legend, date below **Rev. Legend:** NON. ALIO. SIDERE

Date	Mintage	VG	F	VF	XF	Unc
1631	—	2,000	4,000	7,500	—	—
1632	—	2,000	4,000	7,500	—	—
1633	—	2,000	4,000	7,500	—	—
1634	—	2,000	4,000	7,500	—	—
1637	—	2,000	4,000	7,500	—	—
ND	—	2,000	4,000	7,500	—	—

DAV# 4031A DUCATONE
Silver **Obv:** Bust right **Rev:** Date below

Date	Mintage	VG	F	VF	XF	Unc
1633	—	2,000	4,000	7,500	—	—
1634	—	2,000	4,000	7,500	—	—
1637	—	2,000	4,000	7,500	—	—

DAV# 4032 DUCATONE
Silver **Obv:** Bust left **Obv. Legend:** FRAN*I*... **Rev:** Date in legend

Date	Mintage	VG	F	VF	XF	Unc
1639	—	1,700	3,200	6,000	—	—

DAV# 4034 DUCATONE
Silver **Obv:** Bust left breaking legend at top **Obv. Legend:** FR*I*MVT*RE-E*C...

Date	Mintage	VG	F	VF	XF	Unc
1640	—	1,700	3,200	6,000	—	—
1646	—	1,700	3,200	6,000	—	—
1649	—	1,700	3,200	6,000	—	—
ND	—	1,700	3,200	6,000	—	—

DAV# 4040 DUCATONE
Silver **Obv:** Bust right with date and ET below **Obv. Legend:** ALPH. IV. MV. RE. E. C. DVX. IX. **Rev:** Sword in spray circle **Rev. Legend:** ALTERVTRVM...

Date	Mintage	VG	F	VF	XF	Unc
1659 Rare	—	—	—	—	—	—

Note: Numismatica Ars Classica Auction 32, 1-06, XF realized approximately $39,685

DAV# 4024 2 DUCATONE
Silver **Obv:** Bust right with LS below **Obv. Legend:** CAESAR... **Rev:** Abundance with cornucopia, date below **Rev. Legend:** FIRMISSIMAE. SPEI.

Date	Mintage	VG	F	VF	XF	Unc
1612 Rare	—	—	—	—	—	—

DAV# 4028 2 DUCATONE
Silver **Obv:** Bust right with date and BS below **Obv. Legend:** FR*I*MV*R*-E*C*DV*VIII

Date	Mintage	VG	F	VF	XF	Unc
1630 Rare	—	—	—	—	—	—

DAV# 4030 2 DUCATONE
Silver **Obv:** Bust right with date bwlow **Obv. Legend:** FRANCISCVS. I... **Rev:** Ship with stars above **Rev. Legend:** NON. ALIO. SIDERE.

Date	Mintage	VG	F	VF	XF	Unc
1631	—	3,000	6,000	10,000	—	—
1632	—	3,000	6,000	10,000	—	—
1633	—	3,000	6,000	10,000	—	—
1634	—	3,000	6,000	10,000	—	—
1637	—	3,000	6,000	10,000	—	—
1640	—	3,000	6,000	10,000	—	—

DAV# 4030A 2 DUCATONE
Silver **Obv:** Bust right **Rev:** Date below

Date	Mintage	VG	F	VF	XF	Unc
1633	—	3,000	6,000	10,000	—	—
1634	—	3,000	6,000	10,000	—	—
1637	—	3,000	6,000	10,000	—	—

DAV# 4033 2 DUCATONE
Silver **Obv:** Bust left **Obv. Legend:** FR(AN) (CISCVS)...

Date	Mintage	VG	F	VF	XF	Unc
1649	—	3,000	6,000	10,000	—	—
ND	—	3,000	6,000	10,000	—	—

DAV# 4035 2 DUCATONE
Silver **Obv:** Without initials below bust **Rev:** Without initials in exergue

Date	Mintage	VG	F	VF	XF	Unc
ND Rare	—	—	—	—	—	—

Note: Numismatica Ars Classica Auction 32, 1-06, VF/XF realized approximately $18,255

DAV# 4035A 2 DUCATONE
Silver **Obv:** Large draped bust **Obv. Legend:** FR*I*MV*R*...

Date	Mintage	VG	F	VF	XF	Unc
ND Rare	—	—	—	—	—	—

DAV# 4029 3 DUCATONE
Silver **Obv:** Bust right, legend, date below **Obv. Legend:** FRANCISCVS... **Rev:** Ship with stars above and initials in exergue

Date	Mintage	VG	F	VF	XF	Unc
1633 Rare	—	—	—	—	—	—

FR# 791 1/3 SCUDO D'ORO (103 Soldi)
0.7800 g., 0.9860 Gold 0.0247 oz. AGW **Obv:** Shield **Rev:** Displayed eagle

Date	Mintage	VG	F	VF	XF	Unc
ND	—	175	325	550	900	—

FR# 785 1/2 SCUDO D'ORO
1.7500 g., 0.9860 Gold 0.0555 oz. AGW **Obv:** Bust of Francesco I right **Rev:** Displayed eagle

Date	Mintage	VG	F	VF	XF	Unc
ND Rare	—	—	—	—	—	—

FR# A784 SCUDO D'ORO
3.5000 g., 0.9860 Gold 0.1109 oz. AGW **Obv:** Bust of Francesco I right in inner circle **Rev:** Crowned arms in inner circle

Date	Mintage	VG	F	VF	XF	Unc
1651	—	775	1,400	2,100	4,200	—

FR# 784 SCUDO D'ORO
3.5000 g., 0.9860 Gold 0.1109 oz. AGW **Obv:** Bust of Francesco I right **Rev:** Displayed eagle

Date	Mintage	VG	F	VF	XF	Unc
ND Rare	—	—	—	—	—	—

FR# 779 2 SCUDI D'ORO
7.0000 g., 0.9860 Gold 0.2219 oz. AGW **Obv:** Bust of Francesco I right in inner circle **Rev:** Madonna facing child in inner circle

Date	Mintage	VG	F	VF	XF	Unc
1631	—	800	2,000	3,750	6,000	—
ND	—	800	2,000	3,750	6,000	—

FR# 783 2 SCUDI D'ORO
7.0000 g., 0.9860 Gold 0.2219 oz. AGW **Rev:** Displayed eagle

Date	Mintage	VG	F	VF	XF	Unc
ND	—	5,300	8,300	13,500	—	—

FR# A783 2 SCUDI D'ORO
7.0000 g., 0.9860 Gold 0.2219 oz. AGW **Obv:** Bust of Alfonso right **Rev:** Crowned arms on eagle

Date	Mintage	VG	F	VF	XF	Unc
1660 Rare	—	—	—	—	—	—
ND Rare	—	—	—	—	—	—

FR# 778.2 4 SCUDI D'ORO
14.0000 g., 0.9860 Gold 0.4438 oz. AGW **Obv:** Bust of Francesco I right with ruffled collar **Rev:** Madonna facing child in inner circle **Note:** Varieties exist.

Date	Mintage	VG	F	VF	XF	Unc
ND(1629-58) IT	—	2,400	4,200	6,000	11,500	—

FR# 778.1 4 SCUDI D'ORO
14.0000 g., 0.9860 Gold 0.4438 oz. AGW **Obv:** Bust of Francesco I right **Rev:** Madonna with child

Date	Mintage	VG	F	VF	XF	Unc
1632	—	775	1,500	2,400	5,300	—
1634	—	775	1,500	2,400	5,300	—
ND GFM	—	775	1,500	2,400	5,300	—

FR# 782 4 SCUDI D'ORO
14.0000 g., 0.9860 Gold 0.4438 oz. AGW **Rev:** Displayed eagle

Date	Mintage	VG	F	VF	XF	Unc
ND Rare	—	—	—	—	—	—

FR# A782 4 SCUDI D'ORO
14.0000 g., 0.9860 Gold 0.4438 oz. AGW **Obv:** Bust of Alfonso right **Rev:** Crowned arms on eagle

Date	Mintage	VG	F	VF	XF	Unc
1660 Rare	—	—	—	—	—	—

FR# 776 6 SCUDI D'ORO
21.0000 g., 0.9860 Gold 0.6657 oz. AGW **Obv:** Bust of Francesco I left **Rev:** Sailing ship

Date	Mintage	VG	F	VF	XF	Unc
ND	—	3,500	7,000	12,500	20,000	—

FR# 775 8 SCUDI D'ORO
28.0000 g., 0.9860 Gold 0.8876 oz. AGW **Obv:** Bust of Francesco I left **Rev:** Sailing ship

Date	Mintage	VG	F	VF	XF	Unc
1631 Rare	—	—	—	—	—	—
1633 Rare	—	—	—	—	—	—
ND Rare	—	—	—	—	—	—

Note: Stack's International sale 3-88 VF realized $14,300

FR# 777 8 SCUDI D'ORO
28.0000 g., 0.9860 Gold 0.8876 oz. AGW **Obv:** Bust of Francesco I left **Rev:** Madonna with child

Date	Mintage	VG	F	VF	XF	Unc
1631 Rare	—	—	—	—	—	—

FR# 773 12 SCUDI D'ORO
42.0000 g., 0.9860 Gold 1.3314 oz. AGW **Obv:** Bust of Francesco I right **Rev:** Madonna with child

Date	Mintage	VG	F	VF	XF	Unc
1633 Rare	—	—	—	—	—	—

Note: Stack's International sale 3-88 XF realized $28,600

FR# 770 24 SCUDI D'ORO
84.0000 g., 0.9860 Gold 2.6627 oz. AGW **Obv:** Bust of Francesco I left **Rev:** Sailing ship

Date	Mintage	VG	F	VF	XF	Unc
1631 Rare	—	—	—	—	—	—
ND Rare	—	—	—	—	—	—

Note: Bowers and Merena Guia sale 3-88 choice VF realized $48,400

FR# 765 DOPPIA
7.0000 g., 0.9860 Gold 0.2219 oz. AGW **Obv:** Cesare **Rev:** Patience

Date	Mintage	VG	F	VF	XF	Unc
1605	—	1,800	3,750	6,800	11,500	—
1606	—	1,800	3,750	6,800	11,500	—
1608	—	1,800	3,750	6,800	11,500	—
1609	—	1,800	3,750	6,800	11,500	—

FR# 787 DOPPIA
7.0000 g., 0.9860 Gold 0.2219 oz. AGW **Obv:** Francesco I standing right divides date **Rev:** Double-headed eagle

Date	Mintage	VG	F	VF	XF	Unc
1639 Rare	—	—	—	—	—	—

FR# 780 DOPPIA
3.5000 g., 0.9860 Gold 0.1109 oz. AGW **Obv:** Bust of Francesco I right in inner circle **Rev:** Crowned arms in inner circle

Date	Mintage	VG	F	VF	XF	Unc
1651 Rare	—	—	—	—	—	—

FR# 766 2 DOPPIE
14.0000 g., 0.9860 Gold 0.4438 oz. AGW **Obv:** Bust of Cesare right in inner circle **Rev:** Woman standing

Date	Mintage	VG	F	VF	XF	Unc
1608 Rare	—	—	—	—	—	—

FR# 767 4 DOPPIE
28.0000 g., 0.9860 Gold 0.8876 oz. AGW **Obv:** Bust of Cesare right in inner circle **Rev:** Soldier seated left in inner circle

Date	Mintage	VG	F	VF	XF	Unc
1612 Rare	—	—	—	—	—	—

FR# 768 4 DOPPIE
28.0000 g., 0.9860 Gold 0.8876 oz. AGW **Obv:** Bust of Cesare left in inner circle **Rev:** Crowned displayed eagle wtih head left

Date	Mintage	VG	F	VF	XF	Unc
ND Rare	—	—	—	—	—	—

TRADE COINAGE

FR# 764 1/4 DUCAT
0.8750 g., 0.9860 Gold 0.0277 oz. AGW **Obv:** Cesare standing right **Rev:** Crowned arms

Date	Mintage	VG	F	VF	XF	Unc
ND Rare	—	—	—	—	—	—

FR# 786 DUCAT
3.5000 g., 0.9860 Gold 0.1109 oz. AGW **Obv:** Francesco I standing right **Rev:** Value and date in tablet

Date	Mintage	VG	F	VF	XF	Unc
1649	—	425	825	1,450	2,550	—

FR# 788 DUCAT
3.5000 g., 0.9860 Gold 0.1109 oz. AGW **Obv:** Francesco I standing divides date **Rev:** Double-headed eagle

Date	Mintage	VG	F	VF	XF	Unc
1649	—	450	875	1,550	3,200	—

FR# 789 DUCAT
3.5000 g., 0.9860 Gold 0.1109 oz. AGW **Rev:** Displayed eagle with shield of arms on breast

Date	Mintage	VG	F	VF	XF	Unc
1649	—	425	825	1,450	3,000	—

KM# A789 DUCAT
3.5000 g., 0.9860 Gold 0.1109 oz. AGW **Ruler:** Francesco I d'Este **Obv:** Francesco I standing, divides date **Obv. Legend:** FRA(retro N)C • I • MV • & • E • C • DV : X • VIII **Rev:** Crowned shield, small eagle at top of shield **Rev. Legend:** NOBILITAS ESTENSIS

Date	Mintage	VG	F	VF	XF	Unc
1649 Rare	—	—	—	—	—	—

Note: Auktionshaus H. D. Rauch GmbH Auction 82, 4-08, VF+ realized approximately $12,700; Baldwin's Auctions Ltd. Auction 48, 9-06, VF+ realized approximately $6,825.

FR# 795 DUCAT
3.5000 g., 0.9860 Gold 0.1109 oz. AGW **Ruler:** Francesco II d'Este

Date	Mintage	VG	F	VF	XF	Unc
ND	—	800	1,200	3,000	6,000	—

NAPLES & SICILY

Two Sicilies

Consisting of Sicily and the south of Italy, Naples & Sicily came into being in 1130. It passed under Spanish control in 1502; Naples was conquered by Austria in 1707. In 1733 Don Carlos of Spain was recognized as king. From then until becoming part of the United Kingdom of Italy, Naples and Sicily, together and separately, were contested for by Spain, Austria, France, and the republican and monarchial factions of Italy.

RULERS

Spanish

Philip IV, 1621-1665
Charles II, 1665-1700

MINT OFFICIALS' INITIALS

Initial	Date	Name
AC	1676, 78-83	Antonio Caputo
AG	1683-1714	Andrea Giovane
B, FB	1622-25	Fabrizio Biblia
DC	1648-?	Domenico Caropreso
GAC	1636-48	Giovanni Andrea Cavo
GM	1647-48	Giuseppe Maffei
MC	1621-26	Michele Cavo
O	1635-36	Orazio Calentano
OC	1677	Ottavio Caropreso
P	1625-31	Pietro Palomera
S	1631-35	Lorenzo Salomone

ASSAYERS' INITIALS

Initial	Date	Name
A	1676, 78-83	F. Antonio Ariani
C	1621-30	Constantino Di Costanzo
C	1631-35	Antonio Di Costanzo
C	1635	G. Antonio Consolo
N	1642-47, 48	Germano De Novellis
P	1647	Geronimo Pontecorvo

ENGRAVERS' INITIALS

Usually found on the obverse below the portrait.

Initial	Date	Name
AH	1674	Arina Amerani
IM	1688	Giovanni Montemein
NG	1621	Nicola Galoti at the Torre Annunziata Mint

KINGDOM OF NAPLES

Spanish Rule

STANDARD COINAGE

KM# 55 3 TORNESI
7.0500 g., Copper, 29 mm. **Subject:** Republican issue **Obv:** Crowned arms **Rev:** Bundled vegetation **Edge:** Plain **Note:** irregular shape

Date	Mintage	VG	F	VF	XF	Unc
1648 GAC-S	—	350	750	1,250	—	—

DAV# 4041 SCUDO
Silver **Obv:** Bust right **Obv. Legend:** PHILIPPVS.-III. DEI... **Rev:** Crowned diamond shaped arms dividing initials, legend, date **Rev. Legend:** SICILIAE. ET. HIS. REX

Date	Mintage	VG	F	VF	XF	Unc
1610	—	150	300	650	1,500	—
1611	—	150	300	650	1,500	—
1612	—	150	300	650	1,500	—

DAV# 4042 SCUDO

Silver **Obv:** Without inner circle, IC/C behind bust, date below **Rev:** Crowned eagle **Rev. Legend:** QVOD + VIS +...

Date	Mintage	VG	F	VF	XF	Unc
1617	—	1,500	3,000	5,250	—	—

DAV# 4043 DUCATO

Silver **Obv:** Bust right, MC/C behind and date below **Obv. Legend:** PHILIPPVS. IIII. D(EI). G(RA). **Rev:** Crowned arms **Rev. Legend:** HISP. VIRIVSQ.-SICILIE. REX.

Date	Mintage	VG	F	VF	XF	Unc
1622 Rare	—	—	—	—	—	—

DAV# 4044 DUCATO

Silver **Obv:** Accolated bust right of King Charles II and regent mother Maria Anna, date below **Rev:** Crowned arms in sprays **Rev. Legend:** ET. MARIAN...

Date	Mintage	VG	F	VF	XF	Unc
1674 Rare	—	—	—	—	—	—

DAV# 4045 DUCATO

Silver **Obv:** Bust of Charles II right **Rev:** Crowned scepter dividing hemispheres, date and AG/A below

Date	Mintage	VG	F	VF	XF	Unc
1684	—	90.00	175	350	800	—

DAV# 4046 DUCATO

Silver **Obv:** Crowned bust right, AG/A behind **Obv. Legend:** CAROLVS.II... **Rev:** Crowned arms, date divided below

Date	Mintage	VG	F	VF	XF	Unc
1689	—	85.00	165	325	750	—

DAV# 4047 DUCATO

Silver **Obv:** Smaller bust **Obv. Legend:** CAR. II. D. G. REX.. **Rev:** Date, value and Ag/ A in fancy frame

Date	Mintage	VG	F	VF	XF	Unc
1693	—	65.00	145	350	600	—

FR# 840 SCUDO D'ORO

3.5000 g., 0.9860 Gold 0.1109 oz. AGW **Ruler:** Philip IV

Date	Mintage	VG	F	VF	XF	Unc
1622 MC C	—	425	650	1,200	2,000	—
1623 BC	—	425	650	1,200	2,000	—
1624 BC	—	425	650	1,200	2,000	—
1625 G	—	425	650	1,200	2,000	—
1626 MC C	—	425	650	1,200	2,000	—
1626 MC C DD	—	425	650	1,200	2,000	—
1626 MC C V	—	425	650	1,200	2,000	—
1626 MC C R	—	425	650	1,200	2,000	—
1627 MC C	—	425	650	1,200	2,000	—
1628 MC C C	—	425	650	1,200	2,000	—
1628 MC C D	—	425	650	1,200	2,000	—
1628 MC C Y	—	425	650	1,200	2,000	—
1629	—	425	650	1,200	2,000	—

FR# 841 SCUDO D'ORO

3.5000 g., 0.9860 Gold 0.1109 oz. AGW

Date	Mintage	VG	F	VF	XF	Unc
1642 GAC N	—	600	1,200	2,200	3,750	—
1642 GAC NX	—	600	1,200	2,200	3,750	—
1642 GAC NY	—	600	1,200	2,200	3,750	—
1647 GAC N	—	600	1,200	2,200	3,750	—
1647 GAC N H	—	600	1,200	2,200	3,750	—
1647 GAC N O	—	600	1,200	2,200	3,750	—
1647 GAC N P	—	600	1,200	2,200	3,750	—
1647 GAC N H	—	600	1,200	2,200	3,750	—
1649 GAC N H	—	600	1,200	2,200	3,750	—
1649 GAC N G	—	600	1,200	2,200	3,750	—

FR# 842 DUCAT

3.5000 g., 0.9860 Gold 0.1109 oz. AGW **Obv:** Cronwed bust of Charles II left in inner circle, date below **Rev:** Crowned arms in order collar in inner circle

Date	Mintage	VG	F	VF	XF	Unc
1665 X Rare	—	—	—	—	—	—

PAPAL STATES

During many centuries prior to the formation of the unified Kingdom of Italy, when Italy was divided into numerous independent papal and ducal states, the Popes held temporal sovereignty over an area in central Italy comprising some 17,000 sq. mi. (44,030 sq. km.) including the city of Rome. At the time of the general unification of Italy under the Kingdom of Sardinia, 1861, the papal dominions beyond Rome were acquired by that kingdom diminishing the Pope's sovereignty to Rome and its environs. In 1870, while France's opposition to papal dispossession was neutralized by its war with Prussia, the Italian army seized weakly defended Rome and made it the capital of Italy, thereby abrogating the last vestige of papal temporal power. In 1871, the Italian Parliament enacted the Law of Guarantees, which guaranteed a special status for the Vatican area, and spiritual freedom and a generous income for the Pope. Pope Pius IX and his successors adamantly refused to acknowledge the validity of these laws and voluntarily "imprisoned" themselves in the Vatican. The impasse between State and Church lasted until the signing of the Lateran Treaty, Feb. 11, 1929, by which Italy recognized the sovereignty and independence of the new Vatican City state.

PONTIFFS

Clement VIII, 1592-1605
Sede Vacante, (March 5 - April 1) 1605
Leo XI, (April 1 - April 28) 1605
Sede Vacante, (April 28 - May 16) 1605
Paul V, 1605-1621
Sede Vacante, 1621
Gregory XV, 1621-1623
Sede Vacante, 1623
Urban VIII, 1623-1644
Sede Vacante, 1644
Innocent X, 1644-1655
Sede Vacante, 1655
Alexander VII, 1655-1667
Sede Vacante, 1667
Clement IX, 1667-1669
Sede Vacante, 1669-1670
Clement X, 1670-1676
Sede Vacante, 1676
Innocent XI, 1676-1689
Sede Vacante, 1689
Alexander VIII, 1689-1691
Sede Vacante, 1691
Innocent XII, 1691-1700
Sede Vacante, 1700
Clement XI, 1700-1721

MINT MARKS

B - Bologna
R – Rome

MONETARY SYSTEM

(Until 1860)

5 Quattrini = 1 Baiocco
5 Baiocchi = 1 Grosso
6 Grossi = 4 Carlini = 3 Giulio = 3 Paoli = 1 Testone.
14 Carlini = 1 Piastre
100 Baiocchi = 1 Scudo
10 Testone = Doppia

PAPACY

STANDARD COINAGE

KM# 19 QUATTRINO

Copper **Ruler:** Clement VIII **Obv:** Arms **Rev:** Veronica's veil

Date	Mintage	Good	VG	F	VF	XF
1602 Unique	—	—	—	—	—	—

KM# 21 QUATTRINO

Copper **Ruler:** Paul V **Rev:** St. Paul standing holding sword downward left, book right

Date	Mintage	Good	VG	F	VF	XF
ND(1605)-I Rare	—	—	—	—	—	—
ND(1606)-II	—	10.00	20.00	35.00	60.00	—
ND	—	10.00	20.00	35.00	60.00	—

KM# 22 QUATTRINO

Copper **Ruler:** Paul V **Rev:** St. Paul standing holding hand downward

Date	Mintage	Good	VG	F	VF	XF
ND(1605)-I	—	10.00	20.00	35.00	60.00	—

KM# 35 QUATTRINO

Copper **Ruler:** Paul V **Rev:** St. Paul standing holding book at left and sword upward at right

Date	Mintage	Good	VG	F	VF	XF
ND(1606)-II	—	10.00	20.00	35.00	60.00	—
ND(1607)-III	—	10.00	20.00	35.00	60.00	—
ND(1608)-IIII	—	10.00	20.00	35.00	60.00	—
ND(1609)-V	—	10.00	20.00	35.00	60.00	—
ND(1610)-VI	—	10.00	20.00	35.00	60.00	—
ND(1611)-VII	—	10.00	20.00	35.00	60.00	—
ND(1612)-VIII	—	10.00	20.00	35.00	60.00	—
ND(1613)-VIIII	—	10.00	20.00	35.00	60.00	—
ND	—	10.00	20.00	35.00	60.00	—

KM# 64 QUATTRINO

Copper **Ruler:** Paul V **Rev:** St. Paul standing both hands holding sword

Date	Mintage	Good	VG	F	VF	XF
ND(1611)-VII	—	10.00	20.00	35.00	60.00	—
ND(1612)-VIII	—	10.00	20.00	35.00	60.00	—

KM# 72 QUATTRINO

Copper **Ruler:** Paul V **Rev:** St. Paul standing, book left, sword downward at right

Date	Mintage	Good	VG	F	VF	XF
ND(1615)-XI	—	10.00	20.00	35.00	60.00	—
ND(1616)XII	—	10.00	20.00	35.00	60.00	—
ND	—	10.00	20.00	35.00	60.00	—

KM# 90 QUATTRINO

Copper **Ruler:** Paul V **Obv:** Arms

Date	Mintage	Good	VG	F	VF	XF
ND(1621)	—	15.00	30.00	55.00	90.00	—

KM# 101 QUATTRINO

Copper **Ruler:** Gregory XV **Obv:** Bust of Gregory XV right **Rev:** Radiant Virgin Mary standing on crescent

Date	Mintage	Good	VG	F	VF	XF
ND(1622)-II	—	30.00	50.00	85.00	145	—

KM# 106 QUATTRINO

Copper **Obv:** Arms of Cardinal Ippolito Aldobrandini **Rev:** Christ standing in rays **Note:** Sede Vacante issue.

Date	Mintage	Good	VG	F	VF	XF
1623	—	50.00	100	175	320	—

KM# 128 QUATTRINO

Copper **Ruler:** Urban VIII **Obv:** Arms **Rev:** Holy Door with Veronica's veil **Rev. Legend:** ...TVVM **Note:** Holy year issue.

Date	Mintage	Good	VG	F	VF	XF
1625-I	—	10.00	22.00	40.00	70.00	—
1625-II	—	10.00	22.00	40.00	70.00	—

KM# 129 QUATTRINO

Copper **Ruler:** Urban VIII **Rev:** Holy Door with Veronica's veil **Rev. Legend:** ...MACVLA **Note:** Holy year issue.

Date	Mintage	Good	VG	F	VF	XF
ND(1625)	—	10.00	22.00	40.00	70.00	—

KM# 130 QUATTRINO

Copper **Ruler:** Urban VIII **Rev:** Holy Door with Veronica's veil, date at sides **Note:** Holy year issue.

Date	Mintage	Good	VG	F	VF	XF
1625-II	—	12.00	25.00	45.00	80.00	—

KM# 131 QUATTRINO

Copper **Ruler:** Urban VIII **Rev:** Holy Door, ROMA at sides within wreath **Note:** Holy year issue.

Date	Mintage	Good	VG	F	VF	XF
ND(1625)-I	—	10.00	22.00	40.00	70.00	—
ND(1625)-II	—	10.00	22.00	40.00	70.00	—

KM# 132 QUATTRINO

Copper **Ruler:** Urban VIII **Rev:** Radiant Virgin Mary standing on crescent

Date	Mintage	Good	VG	F	VF	XF
ND(1625) Rare	—	—	—	—	—	—

KM# 150 QUATTRINO

Copper **Ruler:** Urban VIII **Note:** Busts of SS. Peter and Paul. An error legend exists with PETERVS repeated.

Date	Mintage	Good	VG	F	VF	XF
ND(1626)-II	—	10.00	20.00	35.00	65.00	—
ND(1627)-III	—	10.00	20.00	35.00	65.00	—
ND(1628)-IIII	—	10.00	20.00	35.00	65.00	—

KM# 155 QUATTRINO

Copper **Ruler:** Urban VIII **Rev:** Bust of St. Peter left

Date	Mintage	Good	VG	F	VF	XF
ND(1628)-IIII	—	12.00	25.00	45.00	80.00	—

KM# 186 QUATTRINO

Copper **Ruler:** Urban VIII **Obv:** Bust right **Rev:** St. Michael the Archangel expelling Lucifer

Date	Mintage	Good	VG	F	VF	XF
ND(1636)-XIII	—	10.00	22.00	40.00	70.00	—
ND(1637)-XIIII	—	10.00	22.00	40.00	70.00	—

KM# 187 QUATTRINO

Copper **Ruler:** Urban VIII **Obv:** Arms

Date	Mintage	Good	VG	F	VF	XF
ND(1636)-XIII	—	10.00	20.00	35.00	60.00	—
ND(1637)-XIIII	—	10.00	20.00	35.00	60.00	—

KM# 200 QUATTRINO

Copper **Ruler:** Urban VIII **Obv:** Bust right **Rev:** Papal arms in wreath

Date	Mintage	Good	VG	F	VF	XF
ND(1641)-XVIII	—	10.00	20.00	40.00	70.00	—

KM# 206 QUATTRINO

Copper **Ruler:** Innocent X **Obv:** Arms **Rev:** Bust of St. Paul **Rev. Legend:** ...APOS ALMA

Date	Mintage	Good	VG	F	VF	XF
ND(1644)-I	—	10.00	22.00	40.00	70.00	—

KM# 207 QUATTRINO

Copper **Ruler:** Innocent X **Rev:** Bust of St. Paul **Rev. Legend:** ...ALMA

Date	Mintage	Good	VG	F	VF	XF
ND(1644)-I	—	10.00	22.00	40.00	70.00	—
ND(1645)-II	—	10.00	22.00	40.00	70.00	—

KM# 224 QUATTRINO

Copper **Ruler:** Innocent X **Rev:** Bust of St. Paul in wreath **Rev. Legend:** ...APOS • ALMA

Date	Mintage	Good	VG	F	VF	XF
ND(1645)-II	—	15.00	30.00	45.00	80.00	—

KM# 225 QUATTRINO

Copper **Ruler:** Innocent X **Rev:** St. Paul standing in wreath **Rev. Legend:** ...SANCT PAVLVS

Date	Mintage	Good	VG	F	VF	XF
ND(1645)-II	—	10.00	22.00	35.00	65.00	—

KM# 226 QUATTRINO

Copper **Ruler:** Innocent X **Rev:** St. Paul standing in wreath **Rev. Legend:** S. PAVLVS APOS.

Date	Mintage	Good	VG	F	VF	XF
ND(1645)-II	—	12.00	25.00	40.00	75.00	—

KM# 20 MEZZO (1/2) BAIOCCO

Copper **Obv:** Arms divide RO-MA **Rev:** Facing bust of St. Paul wearing tiara

Date	Mintage	Good	VG	F	VF	XF
1602 Rare	—	—	—	—	—	—

KM# 65 MEZZO (1/2) BAIOCCO

Copper **Ruler:** Paul V **Obv:** Arms **Rev:** Value: MEZO/BAIOCCO

Date	Mintage	Good	VG	F	VF	XF
ND(1611)-VI	—	12.00	22.00	45.00	70.00	—
MDCXI (1611)-VI	—	12.00	22.00	45.00	70.00	—
ND(1617)-XII	—	12.00	22.00	45.00	70.00	—
1617-XII	—	12.00	22.00	45.00	70.00	—
1619-XII	—	12.00	22.00	45.00	70.00	—

KM# 133 MEZZO (1/2) BAIOCCO

Copper **Ruler:** Urban VIII **Rev:** Holy Door with Veronica's veil **Note:** Holy year issue.

Date	Mintage	Good	VG	F	VF	XF
MDCXXV (1625)-II	—	10.00	20.00	40.00	65.00	—

KM# 23 1/2 GROSSO

Silver **Obv:** Arms **Rev:** Bust of St. Peter **Rev. Legend:** ...ALMA ROM

Date	Mintage	Good	VG	F	VF	XF
ND(1605-21)	—	12.00	22.00	45.00	75.00	—

KM# 24 1/2 GROSSO

Silver **Rev:** Bust of St. Peter **Rev. Legend:** ...ROMA

Date	Mintage	Good	VG	F	VF	XF
ND(1605-21)	—	12.00	22.00	45.00	75.00	—

KM# 36 1/2 GROSSO

Silver **Ruler:** Paul V **Rev:** Bust of Christ left

Date	Mintage	Good	VG	F	VF	XF
ND(1606)-II	—	12.00	25.00	50.00	90.00	—
ND	—	12.00	25.00	50.00	90.00	—

KM# 37 1/2 GROSSO

Silver **Ruler:** Paul V **Rev:** Bust of St. Paul right

Date	Mintage	Good	VG	F	VF	XF
ND(1606)-II	—	12.00	22.00	45.00	75.00	—
ND(1607)-III	—	12.00	22.00	45.00	75.00	—
ND(1608)-IIII	—	12.00	22.00	45.00	75.00	—
ND(1609)-V	—	12.00	22.00	45.00	75.00	—
ND(1610)-VI	—	12.00	22.00	45.00	75.00	—
ND(1611)-VII	—	12.00	22.00	45.00	75.00	—
ND(1612)-VIII	—	12.00	22.00	45.00	75.00	—
ND(1613)-VIIII	—	12.00	22.00	45.00	75.00	—
ND(1614)-X	—	12.00	22.00	45.00	75.00	—
ND(1615)-XI	—	12.00	22.00	45.00	75.00	—

KM# 38 1/2 GROSSO

Silver **Ruler:** Paul V **Rev:** Bust of St. Paul left

Date	Mintage	Good	VG	F	VF	XF
ND(1606)-II	—	12.00	22.00	45.00	75.00	—
ND(1607)-III	—	12.00	22.00	45.00	75.00	—
ND(1608)-IIII	—	12.00	22.00	45.00	75.00	—
ND(1609)-V	—	12.00	22.00	45.00	75.00	—
ND(1610)-VI	—	12.00	22.00	45.00	75.00	—
ND(1611)-VII	—	12.00	22.00	45.00	75.00	—
ND(1612)-VIII	—	12.00	22.00	45.00	75.00	—
ND(1613)-VIIII	—	12.00	22.00	45.00	75.00	—
ND(1614)-X	—	12.00	22.00	45.00	75.00	—
ND(1615)-XI	—	12.00	22.00	45.00	75.00	—

KM# 77 1/2 GROSSO

Silver **Ruler:** Paul V **Rev:** St. Paul standing

Date	Mintage	Good	VG	F	VF	XF
ND(1616)-XII	—	12.00	22.00	45.00	75.00	—
ND	—	12.00	22.00	45.00	75.00	—

KM# 78 1/2 GROSSO

Silver **Ruler:** Paul V **Obv:** Bust right

Date	Mintage	Good	VG	F	VF	XF
ND(1616)-XII	—	20.00	40.00	80.00	135	—
ND(1617)-XIII	—	20.00	40.00	80.00	135	—
ND(1618)-XIIII	—	20.00	40.00	80.00	135	—

KM# 91 1/2 GROSSO

Silver **Ruler:** Gregory XV **Obv:** Arms **Rev:** St. Paul standing

Date	Mintage	Good	VG	F	VF	XF
ND(1621-23)	—	20.00	40.00	80.00	135	—

KM# 92 1/2 GROSSO

Silver **Ruler:** Gregory XV **Rev:** Radiant Virgin Mary standing on crescent

Date	Mintage	Good	VG	F	VF	XF
ND(1621-23)	—	20.00	40.00	80.00	135	—

KM# 102 1/2 GROSSO

Silver **Ruler:** Gregory XV **Obv:** Bust right

Date	Mintage	Good	VG	F	VF	XF
ND(1622)-II	—	30.00	60.00	120	185	—
ND(1623)-III	—	30.00	60.00	120	185	—
ND	—	30.00	60.00	120	185	—

KM# 108 1/2 GROSSO

Silver **Obv:** Bust right **Rev:** Busts of SS. Peter and Paul

Date	Mintage	Good	VG	F	VF	XF
ND(1623-44)	—	20.00	40.00	80.00	135	—

KM# 109 1/2 GROSSO

Silver **Obv:** Arms **Rev:** Radiant Virgin Mary standing on crescent

Date	Mintage	Good	VG	F	VF	XF
ND(1623-44)	—	20.00	40.00	80.00	135	—

KM# 107 1/2 GROSSO

Silver **Obv:** Arms of Cardinal Ippolito Aldobrandini **Rev:** Christ standing with banner **Note:** Sede Vacante issue.

Date	Mintage	Good	VG	F	VF	XF
1623	—	65.00	125	225	350	—

KM# 123 1/2 GROSSO

Silver **Ruler:** Urban VIII **Obv:** Arms

Date	Mintage	Good	VG	F	VF	XF
ND(1624)-II	—	18.00	35.00	55.00	95.00	—
ND(1625)-III	—	18.00	35.00	55.00	95.00	—
ND(1626)-IIII	—	18.00	35.00	55.00	95.00	—
ND(1627)-V	—	18.00	35.00	55.00	95.00	—
ND(1628)-VI	—	18.00	35.00	55.00	95.00	—
ND	—	18.00	35.00	55.00	95.00	—

KM# 134 1/2 GROSSO

Silver **Ruler:** Urban VIII **Rev:** Bust of Madonna right

Date	Mintage	Good	VG	F	VF	XF
ND(1625)-III	—	18.00	35.00	55.00	95.00	—
ND(1626)-V	—	18.00	35.00	55.00	95.00	—
ND(1627)-VI	—	18.00	35.00	55.00	95.00	—

KM# 135 1/2 GROSSO

Silver **Ruler:** Urban VIII **Rev:** Holy Door **Note:** Holy year issue.

Date	Mintage	Good	VG	F	VF	XF
1625-III	—	20.00	40.00	65.00	110	—
ND	—	20.00	40.00	65.00	110	—

KM# 136 1/2 GROSSO

Silver **Ruler:** Urban VIII **Rev:** Holy Door, 1625 and ROMA at sides within wreath **Note:** Holy year issue.

Date	Mintage	Good	VG	F	VF	XF
1625	—	18.00	35.00	55.00	95.00	—

KM# 137 1/2 GROSSO

Silver **Ruler:** Urban VIII **Rev:** Holy Door inscribed 1625 in wreath **Note:** Holy year issue.

Date	Mintage	Good	VG	F	VF	XF
1625	—	18.00	35.00	55.00	95.00	—

KM# 138 1/2 GROSSO

Silver **Ruler:** Urban VIII **Rev:** Holy Door, 1625 at sides in wreath **Note:** Holy year issue.

Date	Mintage	Good	VG	F	VF	XF
1625	—	20.00	40.00	65.00	110	—

KM# 179 1/2 GROSSO

Silver **Ruler:** Urban VIII **Obv:** Bust left **Rev:** St. Peter standing

Date	Mintage	Good	VG	F	VF	XF
ND(1634)-X	—	20.00	40.00	80.00	135	—

KM# 180 1/2 GROSSO

Silver **Ruler:** Urban VIII **Obv:** Arms

Date	Mintage	Good	VG	F	VF	XF
ND(1634)-X	—	18.00	35.00	55.00	95.00	—

KM# 204 1/2 GROSSO

Silver **Ruler:** Urban VIII **Rev:** Bust of Madonna right

Date	Mintage	Good	VG	F	VF	XF
1643-XX	—	18.00	35.00	55.00	95.00	—
1644-XXI	—	18.00	35.00	55.00	95.00	—
ND	—	18.00	35.00	55.00	95.00	—

KM# 208 1/2 GROSSO

Silver **Ruler:** Innocent X **Rev:** Radiant Virgin Mary standing on crescent

Date	Mintage	Good	VG	F	VF	XF
ND(1644)-I	—	12.00	22.00	45.00	80.00	—

KM# 209 1/2 GROSSO

Silver **Ruler:** Innocent X **Subject:** Immaculate Conception **Rev:** Half-length figure of Madonna with child

Date	Mintage	Good	VG	F	VF	XF
ND(1644)-I	—	12.00	22.00	45.00	80.00	—
ND(1645)-II	—	12.00	22.00	45.00	80.00	—
ND(1646)-III	—	12.00	22.00	45.00	80.00	—
ND(1647)-IIII	—	12.00	22.00	45.00	80.00	—
ND(1648)-V	—	12.00	22.00	45.00	80.00	—

KM# 210 1/2 GROSSO

Silver **Ruler:** Innocent X **Rev:** Bust of Madonna right

Date	Mintage	Good	VG	F	VF	XF
ND(1644)-I	—	12.00	22.00	45.00	80.00	—
ND(1645)-II	—	12.00	22.00	45.00	80.00	—

KM# 250 1/2 GROSSO

Silver **Ruler:** Innocent X **Rev:** Holy Door, 1650 in exergue **Note:** Holy year issue.

Date	Mintage	Good	VG	F	VF	XF
1650-VI	—	12.00	25.00	50.00	90.00	—
1650-VII	—	12.00	25.00	50.00	90.00	—

KM# 255 1/2 GROSSO

Silver **Ruler:** Innocent X **Rev:** Holy Door with cross, 1651 in exergue **Note:** Holy year issue.

Date	Mintage	Good	VG	F	VF	XF
1651-VII	—	12.00	25.00	50.00	90.00	—
1651-VIII	—	12.00	25.00	50.00	90.00	—

KM# 258 1/2 GROSSO

Silver **Ruler:** Innocent X **Rev:** Bust of St. Paul left

Date	Mintage	Good	VG	F	VF	XF
ND(1652)-IX	—	12.00	22.00	45.00	80.00	—
ND(1653)-X	—	12.00	22.00	45.00	80.00	—

KM# 265 1/2 GROSSO

Silver **Ruler:** Alexander VII **Obv:** Arms **Rev:** Legend on ornate shield **Rev. Legend:** TEMPE/RATO/SPLEN/DEAT/VSV

Date	Mintage	Good	VG	F	VF	XF
ND(1655-67)	—	9.00	18.00	35.00	60.00	—

KM# 266 1/2 GROSSO

Silver **Ruler:** Alexander VII **Rev:** Inscription on simple shield

Date	Mintage	Good	VG	F	VF	XF
ND(1655-67)	—	9.00	18.00	35.00	60.00	—

KM# 267 1/2 GROSSO

Silver **Ruler:** Alexander VII **Subject:** Immaculate Conception **Rev:** Radiant Virgin Mary standing on crescent

Date	Mintage	Good	VG	F	VF	XF
ND(1655-67)	—	10.00	20.00	40.00	65.00	—

KM# 264 1/2 GROSSO

Silver **Obv:** Arms of Cardinal Antonio Barberini **Rev:** Radiant dove **Note:** Sede Vacante issue.

Date	Mintage	Good	VG	F	VF	XF
ND(1655)	—	30.00	60.00	125	220	—

KM# 301 1/2 GROSSO

Silver **Ruler:** Clement IX **Rev:** SACROS / BASILIC / LATERAN / POSSESS in round cartouche **Note:** Lateran issue.

Date	Mintage	Good	VG	F	VF	XF
1667	—	16.00	32.00	65.00	110	—

KM# 300 1/2 GROSSO

Silver **Ruler:** Clement IX **Rev:** Head of St. Peter right

Date	Mintage	Good	VG	F	VF	XF
ND(1667-69)	—	10.00	20.00	40.00	65.00	—

KM# 315 1/2 GROSSO

Silver **Obv:** Arms of Cardinal Antonio Barberini **Rev:** Radiant dove **Note:** Sede Vacante issue.

Date	Mintage	Good	VG	F	VF	XF
MDCLXIX (1669)	—	12.00	25.00	45.00	80.00	—

KM# 330 1/2 GROSSO

Silver **Ruler:** Clement X **Obv:** Arms **Rev:** SACROSAN / BASILIC / LATERAN / POSSESS in round cartouche **Note:** Lateran issue.

Date	Mintage	Good	VG	F	VF	XF
MDCLXX (1670)	—	9.00	18.00	35.00	60.00	—

KM# 331 1/2 GROSSO

Silver **Ruler:** Clement X **Obv:** Capped bust left **Rev:** Papal arms within wreath

Date	Mintage	Good	VG	F	VF	XF
ND(1670)	—	20.00	40.00	80.00	125	—

KM# 332 1/2 GROSSO

Silver **Ruler:** Clement X **Obv:** Capped bust right

Date	Mintage	Good	VG	F	VF	XF
ND(1670)	—	10.00	20.00	40.00	70.00	—

KM# 333 1/2 GROSSO

Silver **Ruler:** Clement X **Obv:** Arms **Rev:** St. Peter standing

Date	Mintage	Good	VG	F	VF	XF
ND(1670)	—	8.00	16.00	32.00	55.00	—

KM# 334 1/2 GROSSO

Silver **Ruler:** Clement X **Rev:** CVMME / LAVDARENT / SIMVL ASTRA / MATVTINA within wreath

Date	Mintage	Good	VG	F	VF	XF
ND(1670)	—	8.00	16.00	32.00	55.00	—

KM# 357 1/2 GROSSO

Silver **Ruler:** Clement X **Rev:** Holy Door open **Note:** Holy year issue.

Date	Mintage	Good	VG	F	VF	XF
1675	—	9.00	18.00	35.00	60.00	—

KM# 358 1/2 GROSSO

Silver **Ruler:** Clement X **Rev:** Holy Door closed **Note:** Holy year issue.

Date	Mintage	Good	VG	F	VF	XF
1675	—	9.00	18.00	35.00	60.00	—

KM# 383 1/2 GROSSO

Silver **Ruler:** Innocent XI **Rev:** Inscription: SACROSAN / BASILIC / LATERAN / POSSESS **Note:** Lateran issue.

Date	Mintage	Good	VG	F	VF	XF
MDCLXXVI (1676)	—	5.00	12.00	22.00	40.00	—

KM# 378 1/2 GROSSO

Silver **Obv:** Arms of Cardinal Paluzzo Paluzzi-Altieri **Rev:** Radiant dove **Note:** Sede Vacante issue.

Date	Mintage	Good	VG	F	VF	XF
MDCLXXVI (1676)	—	18.00	35.00	55.00	95.00	—

KM# 379 1/2 GROSSO

Silver **Ruler:** Innocent XI **Obv:** Arms **Rev:** Bust of St. Paul right **Rev. Legend:** SAN PALVS

Date	Mintage	Good	VG	F	VF	XF
ND(1676-89)	—	5.00	10.00	20.00	35.00	—

KM# 380 1/2 GROSSO

Silver **Ruler:** Innocent XI **Rev:** Bust of St. Paul right **Rev. Legend:** SANC PAVLVS. AP.

Date	Mintage	Good	VG	F	VF	XF
ND(1676-89)	—	5.00	10.00	20.00	35.00	—

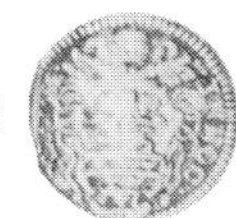

KM# 381 1/2 GROSSO

Silver **Ruler:** Innocent XI **Rev:** Bust of St. Paul right with halo

Date	Mintage	Good	VG	F	VF	XF
ND(1676-89)	—	5.00	10.00	20.00	35.00	—

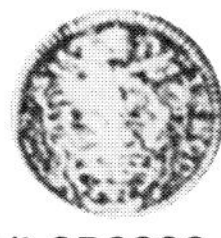

KM# 382 1/2 GROSSO

Silver **Ruler:** Innocent XI **Rev:** Bust of St. Paul left

Date	Mintage	Good	VG	F	VF	XF
ND(1676-89)	—	5.00	10.00	20.00	35.00	—

KM# 459 1/2 GROSSO

Silver **Ruler:** Innocent XI **Rev:** Inscription: QVID / PRODEST / STVLTO in cartouche

Date	Mintage	Good	VG	F	VF	XF
ND(1685-88)	—	4.00	8.00	18.00	30.00	—

KM# 460 1/2 GROSSO

Silver **Ruler:** Innocent XI **Rev:** Inscription on palm wreath

Date	Mintage	Good	VG	F	VF	XF
ND(1685-88)	—	4.00	8.00	18.00	30.00	—

KM# 461 1/2 GROSSO

Silver **Ruler:** Innocent XI **Rev:** Inscription in laurel wreath

Date	Mintage	Good	VG	F	VF	XF
ND(1685-88)	—	4.00	8.00	18.00	30.00	—

KM# 462 1/2 GROSSO

Silver **Ruler:** Innocent XI **Rev:** Inscription in cartouche **Rev. Inscription:** NOCET / MINVS

Date	Mintage	Good	VG	F	VF	XF
1685	—	3.00	7.00	15.00	25.00	—
1686	—	3.00	7.00	15.00	25.00	—
1687	—	3.00	7.00	15.00	25.00	—
1688	—	3.00	7.00	15.00	25.00	—
ND	—	3.00	7.00	15.00	25.00	—

KM# 463 1/2 GROSSO

Silver **Ruler:** Innocent XI **Rev:** Inscription in palm wreath

Date	Mintage	Good	VG	F	VF	XF
1685	—	3.00	7.00	15.00	25.00	—

KM# 464 1/2 GROSSO

Silver **Ruler:** Innocent XI **Rev:** Inscription in laurel wreath

Date	Mintage	Good	VG	F	VF	XF
1685	—	3.00	7.00	15.00	25.00	—
ND	—	3.00	7.00	15.00	25.00	—

KM# 482 1/2 GROSSO

Silver **Ruler:** Alexander VII **Obv:** Arms **Rev:** Bust of St. Peter right

Date	Mintage	Good	VG	F	VF	XF
1689	—	8.00	16.00	32.00	55.00	—

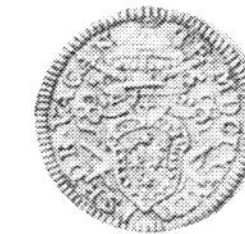

KM# 481 1/2 GROSSO

Silver **Obv:** Arms of Cardinal Paluzzo Paluzzi-Altieri **Rev:** Radiant dove **Note:** Sede Vacante issue.

Date	Mintage	Good	VG	F	VF	XF
MDCLXXXIX (1689)	—	10.00	20.00	40.00	65.00	—

KM# 483 1/2 GROSSO

Silver **Ruler:** Alexander VII **Rev:** Inscription in cartouche **Rev. Inscription:** SACROS / BASILIC / LATERAN / POSSESS **Note:** Lateran issue.

Date	Mintage	Good	VG	F	VF	XF
1689	—	10.00	20.00	40.00	65.00	—

KM# 521 1/2 GROSSO

Silver **Obv:** Arms of Cardinal Paluzzo Paluzzi-Altieri **Rev:** Radiant dove ascending **Note:** Sede Vacante issue.

Date	Mintage	Good	VG	F	VF	XF
MDCLXXXXI (1690)	—	10.00	20.00	45.00	70.00	—

KM# 531 1/2 GROSSO

Silver **Obv:** Arms of Cardinal Paluzzo Paluzzi-Altieri **Rev:** Radiant dove flying left **Note:** Sede Vacante issue.

Date	Mintage	Good	VG	F	VF	XF
MDCLXXXXI (1690)	—	10.00	20.00	45.00	70.00	—
1690	—	—	2,000	4,000	7,000	11,500

KM# 532 1/2 GROSSO

Silver **Ruler:** Innocent XII **Obv:** Arms **Rev:** Head of St. Peter, halo behind

Date	Mintage	Good	VG	F	VF	XF
1691	—	6.00	12.00	25.00	45.00	—

KM# 543 1/2 GROSSO

Silver **Ruler:** Innocent XII **Rev:** Head of St. Peter, halo above

Date	Mintage	Good	VG	F	VF	XF
1692	—	6.00	12.00	25.00	45.00	—

KM# 544 1/2 GROSSO

Silver **Ruler:** Innocent XII **Rev. Inscription:** SACRO ISAN / BASILIC / LATERAN / POSSESS **Note:** Lateran issue.

Date	Mintage	Good	VG	F	VF	XF
MDCXCII (1692)	—	6.00	12.00	25.00	45.00	—

KM# 548 1/2 GROSSO

Silver **Ruler:** Innocent XII **Rev:** Inscription in cartouche **Rev. Inscription:** FAC / VT / IVVET

Date	Mintage	Good	VG	F	VF	XF
1692	—	6.00	12.00	25.00	45.00	—

KM# 560 1/2 GROSSO

Silver **Ruler:** Innocent XII **Rev:** St. Paul's head right

Date	Mintage	Good	VG	F	VF	XF
ND(1693)-III	—	6.00	12.00	25.00	45.00	—

KM# 564 1/2 GROSSO

Silver **Ruler:** Innocent XII **Rev:** Bust of St. Peter left

Date	Mintage	Good	VG	F	VF	XF
ND(1693)-III	—	6.00	12.00	25.00	45.00	—

KM# 570 1/2 GROSSO

Silver **Ruler:** Innocent XII **Rev:** Inscription in palm wreath **Rev. Inscription:** VT/OCTVR

Date	Mintage	Good	VG	F	VF	XF
1694	—	5.00	10.00	22.00	35.00	—

KM# 571 1/2 GROSSO

Silver **Ruler:** Innocent XII **Rev:** Inscription in laurel wreath

Date	Mintage	Good	VG	F	VF	XF
1694	—	5.00	10.00	22.00	35.00	—

KM# 581 1/2 GROSSO

Silver **Ruler:** Innocent XII **Rev:** Inscription in olive or laurel wreath **Rev. Inscription:** DA / PAVPERI

Date	Mintage	Good	VG	F	VF	XF
1695-V	—	5.00	10.00	22.00	35.00	—

KM# 582 1/2 GROSSO

Silver **Ruler:** Innocent XII **Rev:** Inscription in carotuche ornamented by vases

Date	Mintage	Good	VG	F	VF	XF
1695	—	5.00	10.00	22.00	35.00	—

KM# 589 1/2 GROSSO

Silver **Ruler:** Innocent XII **Rev:** Inscription curved in carotuche

Date	Mintage	Good	VG	F	VF	XF
1696	—	5.00	10.00	22.00	35.00	—

KM# 604 1/2 GROSSO

Silver **Ruler:** Innocent XII **Rev:** Inscription between foliage

Date	Mintage	Good	VG	F	VF	XF
1698	—	5.00	10.00	22.00	35.00	—

KM# 50 GROSSO

Silver **Ruler:** Paul V **Obv:** Arms **Obv. Legend:** ...P.M. **Rev:** St. Paul standing holding sword and book at right

Date	Mintage	Good	VG	F	VF	XF
ND(1608)-IIII	—	14.00	28.00	55.00	95.00	—
ND	—	14.00	28.00	55.00	95.00	—

KM# 73 GROSSO

Silver **Ruler:** Paul V **Obv:** Arms **Obv. Legend:** ...PONT•MAXIM

Date	Mintage	Good	VG	F	VF	XF
1615-XI	—	12.00	25.00	50.00	90.00	—
1615-XII	—	12.00	25.00	50.00	90.00	—

KM# 74 GROSSO

Silver **Ruler:** Paul V **Obv:** Bust right

Date	Mintage	Good	VG	F	VF	XF
1615-XI	—	20.00	40.00	75.00	135	—
1615-XII	—	20.00	40.00	75.00	135	—

KM# 75 GROSSO

Silver **Ruler:** Paul V **Rev:** St. Paul standing, sword at right, book at left

Date	Mintage	Good	VG	F	VF	XF
ND(1615)-XI Unique	—	—	—	—	—	—

KM# 93 GROSSO

Silver **Ruler:** Gregory XV **Rev:** St. Paul standing

Date	Mintage	Good	VG	F	VF	XF
ND(1621-23)	—	25.00	50.00	95.00	175	—

KM# 94 GROSSO

Silver **Ruler:** Gregory XV **Rev:** Radiant Virgin Mary standing on crescent

Date	Mintage	Good	VG	F	VF	XF
ND(1621-23)	—	22.00	45.00	90.00	170	—

KM# 111 GROSSO

Silver **Obv:** Arms **Rev:** ROMA below

Date	Mintage	Good	VG	F	VF	XF
ND(1623-44)	—	15.00	30.00	60.00	110	—

KM# 110 GROSSO

Silver **Obv:** Arms of Cardinal Ippolito Aldobrandini **Rev:** Christ standing in rays **Note:** Sede Vacante issue.

Date	Mintage	Good	VG	F	VF	XF
1623	—	85.00	165	325	600	—

KM# 139 GROSSO

Silver **Ruler:** Urban VIII **Rev:** Holy Door with Veronica's veil, 1625 at sides **Note:** Holy year issue.

Date	Mintage	Good	VG	F	VF	XF
1625-II	—	15.00	30.00	60.00	110	—

KM# 140 GROSSO

Silver **Ruler:** Urban VIII **Rev:** Date in exergue **Note:** Holy year issue.

Date	Mintage	Good	VG	F	VF	XF
1625-II	—	15.00	30.00	60.00	110	—

KM# 151 GROSSO

Silver **Ruler:** Urban VIII **Rev:** St. Paul standing
Rev. Legend: ...ALMA ROMA

Date	Mintage	Good	VG	F	VF	XF
ND(1627)-VI	—	15.00	30.00	60.00	110	—
ND	—	15.00	30.00	60.00	110	—

KM# 152 GROSSO

Silver **Ruler:** Urban VIII **Rev:** Radiant Virgin Mary standing on crescent

Date	Mintage	Good	VG	F	VF	XF
ND(1627)-VI	—	15.00	30.00	60.00	110	—
ND(1628)-VII	—	15.00	30.00	60.00	110	—
ND	—	15.00	30.00	60.00	110	—

KM# 156 GROSSO

Silver **Ruler:** Urban VIII **Rev:** Bust of Christ left

Date	Mintage	Good	VG	F	VF	XF
ND(1628)-VII	—	15.00	30.00	60.00	110	—
ND(1630)-XVIII	—	15.00	30.00	60.00	110	—
ND	—	15.00	30.00	60.00	110	—

KM# 192 GROSSO

Silver **Ruler:** Urban VIII **Rev:** St. Paul standing
Rev. Legend: ...ALMA ROMA

Date	Mintage	Good	VG	F	VF	XF
ND(1639)-XVIII	—	15.00	30.00	60.00	110	—
ND(1641)-XX	—	15.00	30.00	60.00	110	—
1642-XX	—	15.00	30.00	60.00	110	—
ND(1644)-XXI	—	15.00	30.00	60.00	110	—

KM# 213 GROSSO

Silver **Ruler:** Innocent X **Rev:** Bust of St. Paul, ROMA in exergue

Date	Mintage	Good	VG	F	VF	XF
ND(1644)-I	—	20.00	40.00	85.00	150	—
ND(1645)-II	—	20.00	40.00	85.00	150	—
ND(1652)-IX	—	20.00	40.00	85.00	150	—
ND(1653)-X	—	20.00	40.00	85.00	150	—

KM# 214 GROSSO

Silver **Ruler:** Innocent X **Subject:** Immaculate Conception
Rev: Radiant Virgin Mary standing on crescent

Date	Mintage	Good	VG	F	VF	XF
ND(1644)-I	—	18.00	35.00	70.00	125	—
ND(1645)-II	—	18.00	35.00	70.00	125	—

KM# 211 GROSSO

Silver **Ruler:** Urban VIII **Rev:** St. Paul standing
Rev. Legend: ...APOSTOL

Date	Mintage	Good	VG	F	VF	XF
ND(1644)-XXI	—	15.00	30.00	60.00	110	—

KM# 212 GROSSO

Silver **Ruler:** Urban VIII **Rev:** Head of St. Peter left

Date	Mintage	Good	VG	F	VF	XF
ND(1644)-XXI	—	18.00	35.00	70.00	125	—

KM# 215 GROSSO

Silver **Ruler:** Innocent X **Rev:** St. Paul standing
Rev. Legend: ...ALMA ROMA

Date	Mintage	Good	VG	F	VF	XF
ND(1644)-I	—	20.00	40.00	85.00	150	—

KM# 227 GROSSO

Silver **Ruler:** Innocent X **Rev. Legend:** ...AP

Date	Mintage	Good	VG	F	VF	XF
ND(1645)-II	—	18.00	35.00	70.00	125	—

KM# 229 GROSSO

Silver **Ruler:** Innocent X **Rev. Legend:** ...ALMA ROMA

Date	Mintage	Good	VG	F	VF	XF
ND(1645)-II	—	18.00	35.00	70.00	125	—
ND(1648)-V	—	18.00	35.00	70.00	125	—

KM# 228 GROSSO

Silver **Ruler:** Innocent X **Rev. Legend:** ...AP ROMA

Date	Mintage	Good	VG	F	VF	XF
ND(1645)-II	—	18.00	35.00	70.00	125	—

KM# 251 GROSSO

Silver **Ruler:** Innocent X **Rev:** Holy Door **Note:** Holy year issue.

Date	Mintage	Good	VG	F	VF	XF
1650-VI	—	20.00	40.00	85.00	150	—
MDCL (1650)-VI	—	20.00	40.00	85.00	150	—
1650-VII	—	20.00	40.00	85.00	150	—

KM# 289 GROSSO

Silver **Ruler:** Innocent X **Rev. Legend:** ...APOSTOLVS

Date	Mintage	Good	VG	F	VF	XF
ND(1653)-X	—	20.00	40.00	85.00	160	—

KM# 268 GROSSO

Silver **Obv:** Arms of Cardinal Antonio Barberini **Rev:** Radiant dove **Note:** Sede Vacante issue.

Date	Mintage	Good	VG	F	VF	XF
ND(1655)	—	80.00	165	300	500	—

KM# 269 GROSSO

Silver **Ruler:** Alexander VII **Obv:** Arms **Rev:** Inscription on shield
Rev. Inscription: HILAREM / DATOREM / DILIGIT / DEVS

Date	Mintage	VG	F	VF	XF	Unc
ND(1655-67)	—	22.00	45.00	85.00	160	—

KM# 270 GROSSO

Silver **Ruler:** Alexander VII **Rev:** Inscription on simple shield

Date	Mintage	VG	F	VF	XF	Unc
ND(1655-67)	—	22.00	45.00	85.00	160	—

KM# 271 GROSSO

Silver **Ruler:** Alexander VII **Rev:** Inscription without shield

Date	Mintage	VG	F	VF	XF	Unc
ND(1655-67)	—	22.00	45.00	85.00	160	—

KM# 272 GROSSO

Silver **Ruler:** Alexander VII **Subject:** Immaculate Conception
Rev: Radiant Virgin Mary standing on crescent

Date	Mintage	VG	F	VF	XF	Unc
ND(1655-67)	—	28.00	55.00	100	175	—

KM# 302 GROSSO

Silver **Ruler:** Clement IX **Rev:** Bust of St. Peter

Date	Mintage	VG	F	VF	XF	Unc
1667 Rare	—	—	—	—	—	—
ND Rare	—	—	—	—	—	—

KM# 304 GROSSO

Silver **Ruler:** Clement IX **Rev:** Inscription in round cartouche

Date	Mintage	VG	F	VF	XF	Unc
1667	—	28.00	55.00	100	175	—

KM# 303 GROSSO

Silver **Ruler:** Clement IX **Rev. Inscription:** SACROS / BASILIC / LATERAN / POSSESS **Note:** Lateran issue.

Date	Mintage	VG	F	VF	XF	Unc
1667	—	28.00	55.00	100	175	—

KM# 316 GROSSO

Silver **Obv:** Arms of Cardinal Antonio Barberini **Rev:** Radiant dove **Note:** Sede Vacante issue.

Date	Mintage	VG	F	VF	XF	Unc
MDCLXIX (1669)	—	35.00	70.00	125	200	—

KM# 335 GROSSO

Silver **Ruler:** Clement X **Obv:** Capped bust right **Rev:** St. Peter crowned by angel

Date	Mintage	VG	F	VF	XF	Unc
MDCLXX (1670)	—	28.00	55.00	100	175	—

KM# 336 GROSSO

Silver **Ruler:** Clement X **Obv:** Arms **Rev. Inscription:** SACROS / BASILIC / LATERAN / POSSESS **Note:** Lateran issue.

Date	Mintage	VG	F	VF	XF	Unc
MDCLXX (1670)	—	20.00	40.00	75.00	125	—

KM# 337 GROSSO

Silver **Ruler:** Clement X **Obv:** Capped bust right **Rev:** Half-figure of Madonna and child

Date	Mintage	VG	F	VF	XF	Unc
ND(1670-76)	—	25.00	50.00	90.00	165	—

KM# 338 GROSSO

Silver **Ruler:** Clement X **Rev:** St. Paul standing

Date	Mintage	VG	F	VF	XF	Unc
ND(1670-76)	—	22.00	45.00	80.00	140	—

KM# 339 GROSSO

Silver **Ruler:** Clement X **Rev:** Papal arms

Date	Mintage	VG	F	VF	XF	Unc
ND(1670-76)	—	22.00	45.00	85.00	150	—

KM# 359 GROSSO

Silver **Ruler:** Clement X **Rev:** Holy Door closed **Note:** Holy year issue.

Date	Mintage	VG	F	VF	XF	Unc
1675	—	22.00	45.00	80.00	140	—

KM# 360 GROSSO

Silver **Ruler:** Clement X **Rev:** Holy Door open **Note:** Holy year issue.

Date	Mintage	VG	F	VF	XF	Unc
1675	—	22.00	45.00	80.00	140	—

KM# 384 GROSSO

Silver **Obv:** Arms of Cardinal Paluzzo Paluzzi-Altieri
Rev: Radiant dove **Note:** Sede Vacante issue.

Date	Mintage	VG	F	VF	XF	Unc
MDCLXXVI (1676)	—	35.00	70.00	125	200	—

KM# 385 GROSSO

Silver **Ruler:** Innocent XI **Obv:** Arms **Rev. Inscription:** SACROSAN / BASILIC / LATERAN / POSSESS **Note:** Lateran issue.

Date	Mintage	VG	F	VF	XF	Unc
MDCLXXVI (1676)	—	12.00	25.00	45.00	80.00	—

KM# 386 GROSSO

Silver **Ruler:** Innocent XI **Rev:** Bust of St. Peter

Date	Mintage	VG	F	VF	XF	Unc
ND(1676-85)	—	12.00	22.00	40.00	70.00	—

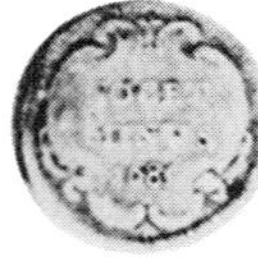

KM# 465 GROSSO

Silver **Ruler:** Innocent XI **Rev:** Inscription in ornate cartouche
Rev. Inscription: NOCET / MINVS

Date	Mintage	VG	F	VF	XF	Unc
1685	—	10.00	20.00	35.00	65.00	—

KM# 468 GROSSO

Silver **Ruler:** Innocent XI **Rev:** Inscription on palm wreath

Date	Mintage	VG	F	VF	XF	Unc
1685	—	10.00	20.00	35.00	65.00	—
ND	—	10.00	20.00	35.00	65.00	—

KM# 466 GROSSO

Silver **Ruler:** Innocent XI **Rev:** Inscription in plain cartouche

Date	Mintage	VG	F	VF	XF	Unc
1685	—	10.00	20.00	35.00	65.00	—

KM# 467 GROSSO

Silver **Ruler:** Innocent XI **Rev:** Inscription in cartouche turned inward at top

Date	Mintage	VG	F	VF	XF	Unc
ND(1685-88)	—	10.00	20.00	35.00	65.00	—

KM# 476 GROSSO

Silver **Ruler:** Innocent XI **Rev:** St. Peter's head left

Date	Mintage	VG	F	VF	XF	Unc
1686	—	22.00	45.00	85.00	150	—

KM# 480 GROSSO

Silver **Ruler:** Innocent XI **Rev:** Inscription in ornate cartouche

Date	Mintage	VG	F	VF	XF	Unc
1688	—	10.00	20.00	35.00	65.00	—

KM# 487 GROSSO

Silver **Ruler:** Alexander VIII **Rev:** St. Peter standing

Date	Mintage	VG	F	VF	XF	Unc
1689	—	22.00	45.00	85.00	150	—

KM# 484 GROSSO

Silver **Obv:** Arms of Cardinal Paluzzo Paluzzi-Altieri **Rev:** Radiant dove **Note:** Sede Vacante issue.

Date	Mintage	VG	F	VF	XF	Unc
MDCLXXXIX (1689)	—	28.00	55.00	100	175	—

KM# 485 GROSSO

Silver **Ruler:** Alexander VIII **Obv:** Arms **Rev:** Inscription in cartouche **Rev. Inscription:** SACROS / BASILIC / LATERAN / POSSESS / 1689 **Note:** Lateran issue.

Date	Mintage	VG	F	VF	XF	Unc
1689	—	25.00	50.00	90.00	165	—

KM# 486 GROSSO

Silver **Ruler:** Alexander VIII **Rev:** Inscription in palm wreath **Note:** Lateran issue.

Date	Mintage	VG	F	VF	XF	Unc
1689	—	28.00	55.00	100	175	—

KM# 533 GROSSO

Silver **Obv:** Arms of Cardinal Paluzzo Paluzzi-Altieri **Rev:** Radiant dove ascending **Note:** Sede Vacante issue.

Date	Mintage	VG	F	VF	XF	Unc
MDCLXXXXI (1691)	—	25.00	50.00	90.00	165	—

KM# 547 GROSSO

Silver **Rev:** St. Peter's head 3/4 left, upwards

Date	Mintage	VG	F	VF	XF	Unc
ND(1691-1700)	—	14.00	28.00	55.00	95.00	—

KM# 534 GROSSO

Silver **Rev:** Dove flying left

Date	Mintage	VG	F	VF	XF	Unc
MDCLXXXXI (1691)	—	25.00	50.00	90.00	165	—

KM# 546 GROSSO

Silver **Rev:** St. Peter's head left

Date	Mintage	VG	F	VF	XF	Unc
1691	—	14.00	28.00	55.00	95.00	—

KM# A548 GROSSO

Silver **Ruler:** Innocent XII **Obv:** Arms **Rev. Inscription:** SACRO / SAN BASILIC / LATERAN / POSSESS **Note:** Lateran issue.

Date	Mintage	VG	F	VF	XF	Unc
MDCXCII (1692)	—	14.00	28.00	55.00	95.00	—

KM# 549 GROSSO

Silver **Ruler:** Innocent XII **Rev. Inscription:** PECCATA / REDIME

Date	Mintage	VG	F	VF	XF	Unc
1692	—	14.00	28.00	50.00	90.00	—

KM# 565 GROSSO

Silver **Ruler:** Innocent XII **Rev:** St. Paul's head right

Date	Mintage	VG	F	VF	XF	Unc
ND(1693)-III	—	14.00	28.00	55.00	95.00	—

KM# 572 GROSSO

Silver **Ruler:** Innocent XII **Rev:** Inscription in laurel wreath **Rev. Inscription:** CVM / EGENIS

Date	Mintage	VG	F	VF	XF	Unc
1694	—	14.00	28.00	55.00	95.00	—

KM# 573 GROSSO

Silver **Ruler:** Innocent XII **Rev:** Inscription in palm wreath

Date	Mintage	VG	F	VF	XF	Unc
1694	—	14.00	28.00	55.00	95.00	—

KM# 583 GROSSO

Silver **Ruler:** Innocent XII **Rev:** Inscription in polygonal cartouche **Rev. Inscription:** EGENIO / SPEIS

Date	Mintage	VG	F	VF	XF	Unc
1695	—	12.00	25.00	48.00	85.00	—

KM# 584 GROSSO

Silver **Ruler:** Innocent XII **Rev:** Inscription in oval cartouche

Date	Mintage	VG	F	VF	XF	Unc
1695	—	12.00	25.00	48.00	85.00	—

KM# 590 GROSSO

Silver **Ruler:** Innocent XII **Rev:** Inscription in floral wreath, seraph above

Date	Mintage	VG	F	VF	XF	Unc
1696	—	12.00	25.00	48.00	85.00	—

KM# 591 GROSSO

Silver **Ruler:** Innocent XII **Rev:** Inscription in floral wreath without seraph

Date	Mintage	VG	F	VF	XF	Unc
1696	—	12.00	25.00	48.00	85.00	—
1697	—	12.00	25.00	48.00	85.00	—

KM# 592 GROSSO

Silver **Ruler:** Innocent XII **Rev:** Inscription in palm wreath

Date	Mintage	VG	F	VF	XF	Unc
1696	—	12.00	25.00	48.00	85.00	—
1697	—	12.00	25.00	48.00	85.00	—

KM# 600 GROSSO

Silver **Ruler:** Innocent XII **Rev:** Inscription in cartouche with dot above

Date	Mintage	VG	F	VF	XF	Unc
1697	—	12.00	25.00	48.00	85.00	—

KM# 605 GROSSO

Silver **Ruler:** Innocent XII **Rev:** Inscription in olive wreath

Date	Mintage	VG	F	VF	XF	Unc
1698	—	12.00	25.00	48.00	85.00	—

KM# 609 GROSSO

Silver **Ruler:** Innocent XII **Rev:** Holy Door **Rev. Legend:** PORTA AVREA **Note:** Holy year issue.

Date	Mintage	VG	F	VF	XF	Unc
1699	—	14.00	28.00	50.00	90.00	—

KM# 610 GROSSO

Silver **Ruler:** Innocent XII **Rev:** Holy Door **Rev. Legend:** PORTA COELI **Note:** Holy year issue.

Date	Mintage	VG	F	VF	XF	Unc
1699	—	15.00	30.00	55.00	95.00	—

KM# 611 GROSSO

Silver **Ruler:** Innocent XII **Rev:** Holy Door **Rev. Legend:** PORTA PARADISI **Note:** Holy year issue.

Date	Mintage	VG	F	VF	XF	Unc
1699	—	15.00	30.00	55.00	95.00	—

KM# 635 GROSSO

Silver **Ruler:** Clement XI **Obv:** Papal arms **Rev:** Inscription in cartouche **Rev. Inscription:** DEDIT / PAVPE / RIBVS

Date	Mintage	VG	F	VF	XF	Unc
ND(1700-21)	—	10.00	22.00	38.00	60.00	100

KM# 636 GROSSO

Silver **Ruler:** Clement XI **Obv:** Papal arms **Rev:** Inscription in cartouche **Rev. Inscription:** ESVRI / ENTEM / NE / DESPRE / XERIS

Date	Mintage	VG	F	VF	XF	Unc
ND(1700-21)	—	10.00	22.00	38.00	60.00	100

KM# 637 GROSSO

Silver **Ruler:** Clement XI **Obv:** Papal arms **Rev:** Inscription without cartouche

Date	Mintage	VG	F	VF	XF	Unc
ND(1700-21)	—	10.00	22.00	38.00	60.00	100

KM# 714 GROSSO

Silver **Ruler:** Clement XI **Obv:** Papal arms **Rev:** Inscription in cartouche **Rev. Inscription:** DEDIT / PAVPE / RIBVS

Date	Mintage	VG	F	VF	XF	Unc
ND(1700-21)	—	10.00	22.00	38.00	60.00	100

KM# 26 GIULIO

Silver **Ruler:** Paul V **Obv:** Arms **Rev:** St. Paul standing with sword and book

Date	Mintage	Good	VG	F	VF	XF
ND(1605)-I	—	20.00	40.00	85.00	160	—
ND(1606)-II	—	20.00	40.00	85.00	160	—
ND(1607)-III	—	20.00	40.00	85.00	160	—
ND(1608)-IIII	—	20.00	40.00	85.00	160	—
ND(1609)-V	—	20.00	40.00	85.00	160	—
ND(1610)-VI	—	20.00	40.00	85.00	160	—
ND(1611)-VII	—	20.00	40.00	85.00	160	—
ND(1612)-VIII	—	20.00	40.00	85.00	160	—
ND(1613)-VIIII	—	20.00	40.00	85.00	160	—
ND(1614)-X	—	20.00	40.00	85.00	160	—
ND(1615)-XI	—	20.00	40.00	85.00	160	—
ND	—	20.00	40.00	85.00	160	—

KM# 27 GIULIO

Silver **Ruler:** Paul V **Rev:** St. Paul seated left

Date	Mintage	Good	VG	F	VF	XF
ND(1605)-I Rare	—	—	—	—	—	—
ND(1606)-II	—	28.00	50.00	85.00	160	—
ND(1607)-III	—	28.00	50.00	85.00	160	—

KM# 25 GIULIO

Silver **Obv:** Arms of Cardinal Pietro Aldobrandini **Rev:** St. Paul standing **Note:** Sede Vacante issue.

Date	Mintage	Good	VG	F	VF	XF
MDCV (1605)	—	100	200	325	500	—

KM# 39 GIULIO

Silver **Ruler:** Paul V **Rev:** St. Paul standing right

Date	Mintage	Good	VG	F	VF	XF
ND(1606)-II	—	28.00	50.00	85.00	160	—
ND(1607)-III	—	28.00	50.00	85.00	160	—

KM# 40 GIULIO

Silver **Ruler:** Paul V **Rev:** St. Paul standing with hand raised

Date	Mintage	Good	VG	F	VF	XF
ND(1606)-II	—	35.00	60.00	100	165	—
ND(1607)-III	—	35.00	60.00	100	165	—
ND(1608)-IIII	—	35.00	60.00	100	165	—
ND(1609)-V	—	35.00	60.00	100	165	—
ND(1610)-VI	—	35.00	60.00	100	165	—
ND(1611)-VII	—	35.00	60.00	100	165	—
ND(1612)-VIII	—	35.00	60.00	100	165	—
ND(1613)-VIIII	—	35.00	60.00	100	165	—
ND(1614)-X	—	35.00	60.00	100	165	—

KM# 60 GIULIO

Silver **Ruler:** Paul V **Obv:** Bust left

Date	Mintage	Good	VG	F	VF	XF
ND(1610)-VI	—	35.00	60.00	100	165	—
ND(1611)-VII	—	35.00	60.00	100	165	—

KM# 96 GIULIO

Silver **Ruler:** Gregory XV **Obv:** Arms **Rev:** Radiant Virgin Mary standing on crescent

Date	Mintage	Good	VG	F	VF	XF
ND(1621-23)	—	40.00	70.00	115	185	—

KM# 95 GIULIO

Silver **Obv:** Arms of Cardinal Pietro Aldobrandini **Rev:** Faith standing **Note:** Sede Vacante issue.

Date	Mintage	Good	VG	F	VF	XF
1621	—	65.00	120	200	300	—

KM# 112 GIULIO

Silver **Ruler:** Alexander VIII **Obv:** Arms of Cardinal Ippolito Aldobrandini **Rev:** Radiant Christ standing **Note:** Sede Vacante issue.

Date	Mintage	Good	VG	F	VF	XF
1623	—	140	250	425	650	—

KM# 113 GIULIO

Silver **Ruler:** Urban VIII **Obv:** Arms **Rev:** SS. Peter and Paul, dove above

Date	Mintage	Good	VG	F	VF	XF
ND(1623) (i)(P)	—	22.00	40.00	70.00	120	—
ND(1624)-II	—	22.00	40.00	70.00	120	—
ND(1625)-III	—	22.00	40.00	70.00	120	—
ND(1626)-IIII	—	22.00	40.00	70.00	120	—
ND(1627)-V	—	22.00	40.00	70.00	120	—
ND(1628)-VI	—	22.00	40.00	70.00	120	—
ND(1629)-VII	—	22.00	40.00	70.00	120	—
ND(1630)-VIII	—	22.00	40.00	70.00	120	—

KM# 141 GIULIO

Silver **Ruler:** Urban VIII **Rev:** Holy Door with Veronica's veil **Rev. Legend:** QVI DILIGVNT NOMEN TVVM **Note:** Holy year issue.

Date	Mintage	Good	VG	F	VF	XF
ND(1625)	—	22.00	40.00	70.00	120	—

KM# 142 GIULIO

Silver **Ruler:** Urban VIII **Rev:** Date in exergue **Rev. Legend:** QVI INGREDITVR SINE MACVLA **Note:** Holy year issue.

Date	Mintage	Good	VG	F	VF	XF
MDCXXV(1625)	—	22.00	40.00	70.00	120	—
MDCXX (1620) Error	—	22.00	40.00	70.00	120	—

KM# 143 GIULIO

Silver **Ruler:** Urban VIII **Rev:** Holy Door with Veronica's veil, date below veil **Note:** Holy year issue.

Date	Mintage	Good	VG	F	VF	XF
MDCXXV (1625)-II	—	22.00	40.00	70.00	120	—
MDCXXV (1625)-III	—	22.00	40.00	70.00	120	—

KM# 144 GIULIO

Silver **Ruler:** Urban VIII **Rev:** Date divided by Holy Door **Note:** Holy year issue.

Date	Mintage	Good	VG	F	VF	XF
MDCXXV (1625)-II	—	22.00	40.00	70.00	120	—
MDCXXV (1625)-III	—	22.00	40.00	70.00	120	—

KM# 161 GIULIO

Silver **Ruler:** Urban VIII **Rev:** Half-figure of Madonna with child

Date	Mintage	Good	VG	F	VF	XF
ND(1629)-VII	—	22.00	40.00	70.00	120	—
ND(1630)-VIII	—	22.00	40.00	70.00	120	—
ND(1631)-VIIII	—	22.00	40.00	70.00	120	—
ND(1632)-X	—	22.00	40.00	70.00	120	—
ND(1633)-XI	—	22.00	40.00	70.00	120	—
ND(1634)-XII	—	22.00	40.00	70.00	120	—
ND(1635)-XIII	—	22.00	40.00	70.00	120	—
ND(1636)-XIIII	—	22.00	40.00	70.00	120	—
ND(1637)-XV	—	22.00	40.00	70.00	120	—
ND(1638)-XVI	—	22.00	40.00	70.00	120	—
ND(1639)-XVII	—	22.00	40.00	70.00	120	—
ND(1640)-XVIII	—	22.00	40.00	70.00	120	—
ND(1641)-XVIIII	—	22.00	40.00	70.00	120	—
ND(1642)-XX	—	22.00	40.00	70.00	120	—

KM# 170 GIULIO

Silver **Ruler:** Urban VIII **Rev:** Pope kneeling left, before St. Michael the Archangel in clouds

Date	Mintage	Good	VG	F	VF	XF
ND(1630)-VIII	—	40.00	80.00	125	200	—
ND(1631)-VIIII	—	40.00	80.00	125	200	—

KM# 177 GIULIO

Silver **Ruler:** Urban VIII **Rev:** Without door

Date	Mintage	Good	VG	F	VF	XF
1633	—	22.00	40.00	70.00	120	—

KM# 201 GIULIO

Silver **Ruler:** Urban VIII **Rev:** Radiant Virgin Mary standing on crescent

Date	Mintage	Good	VG	F	VF	XF
ND(1642)-XX	—	22.00	40.00	70.00	120	—

Date	Mintage	Good	VG	F	VF	XF
ND(1643)-XXI	—	22.00	40.00	70.00	120	—
ND	—	22.00	40.00	70.00	120	—

KM# 216 GIULIO

Silver **Ruler:** Innocent X **Rev:** St. Paul standing with sword right **Rev. Legend:** S • PAVLVS ALMA ROMA

Date	Mintage	Good	VG	F	VF	XF
ND(1644)-I	—	35.00	60.00	100	165	—
ND(1645)-II	—	35.00	60.00	100	165	—
ND(1652)-VIIII	—	35.00	60.00	100	165	—
ND(1653)-X	—	35.00	60.00	100	165	—

KM# 217 GIULIO

Silver **Ruler:** Innocent X **Rev. Legend:** S PAVLVS AP ALMA ROMA

Date	Mintage	Good	VG	F	VF	XF
ND(1644)-I	—	35.00	60.00	100	165	—

KM# 230 GIULIO

Silver **Ruler:** Innocent X **Subject:** Immaculate Conception **Rev:** Radiant Virgin Mary standing on crescent

Date	Mintage	Good	VG	F	VF	XF
ND(1644)-I	—	35.00	60.00	100	165	—
ND(1645)-II	—	35.00	60.00	100	165	—

KM# 231 GIULIO

Silver **Ruler:** Innocent X **Rev:** St. Paul standing with sword left **Rev. Legend:** S PAVLVS ALMA ROMA

Date	Mintage	Good	VG	F	VF	XF
ND(1645)-II	—	35.00	60.00	100	165	—
ND(1646)-III	—	35.00	60.00	100	165	—

KM# 245 GIULIO

Silver **Ruler:** Innocent X **Rev:** Confronted busts of SS. Peter and Paul

Date	Mintage	Good	VG	F	VF	XF
ND(1646)-II	—	40.00	70.00	115	185	—

KM# 252 GIULIO

Silver **Ruler:** Innocent X **Rev:** Holy Door with Veronica's veil **Note:** Holy year issue.

Date	Mintage	Good	VG	F	VF	XF
ND(1650)-VII	—	40.00	70.00	115	185	—

KM# 273 GIULIO

Silver **Obv:** Arms of Cardinal Antonio Barberini **Rev:** Radiant dove **Note:** Sede Vacante issue.

Date	Mintage	Good	VG	F	VF	XF
MDCLV (1655)	—	100	200	325	500	—

KM# 274 GIULIO

Silver **Ruler:** Alexander VII **Obv:** Arms **Rev:** Table with coins

Date	Mintage	VG	F	VF	XF	Unc
ND(1655-67)	—	40.00	85.00	150	250	—

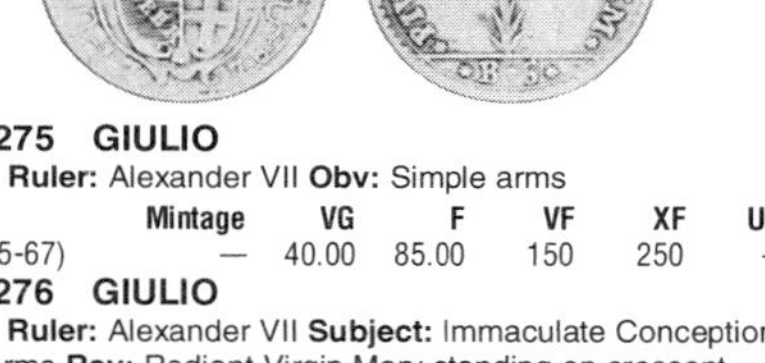

KM# 275 GIULIO

Silver **Ruler:** Alexander VII **Obv:** Simple arms

Date	Mintage	VG	F	VF	XF	Unc
ND(1655-67)	—	40.00	85.00	150	250	—

KM# 276 GIULIO

Silver **Ruler:** Alexander VII **Subject:** Immaculate Conception **Obv:** Arms **Rev:** Radiant Virgin Mary standing on crescent

Date	Mintage	VG	F	VF	XF	Unc
ND(1655-56)	—	35.00	75.00	135	225	—

KM# 305 GIULIO

Silver **Obv:** Arms of Cardinal Antonio Barberini **Rev:** Radiant dove **Note:** Sede Vacante issue.

Date	Mintage	VG	F	VF	XF	Unc
MDCLXVII (1667)	—	55.00	110	200	325	—

KM# 306 GIULIO

Silver **Ruler:** Clement IX **Rev:** St. Peter walking right

Date	Mintage	VG	F	VF	XF	Unc
ND(1667-69)	—	40.00	85.00	150	250	—

KM# 307 GIULIO

Silver **Ruler:** Clement IX **Rev:** Inscription in cartouche, wreath below **Rev. Inscription:** SACROSAN / BASILIC / LATERAN / POSSESS **Note:** Lateran issue.

Date	Mintage	VG	F	VF	XF	Unc
MDCLXVII (1667)	—	50.00	95.00	175	285	—

KM# 317 GIULIO

Silver **Obv:** Arms of Cardinal Antonio Barberini **Rev:** Radiant dove **Note:** Sede Vacante issue.

Date	Mintage	VG	F	VF	XF	Unc
MDCLXIX (1669)	—	50.00	95.00	175	285	—

KM# 340 GIULIO

Silver **Obv:** Bust of Clement X right **Rev:** St. Peter standing crowned by angel

Date	Mintage	VG	F	VF	XF	Unc
MDCLXX (1670)-I	—	70.00	140	250	400	—

KM# 341 GIULIO

Silver **Subject:** Immaculate Conception **Obv:** Arms **Rev:** Radiant Virgin Mary standing on crescent

Date	Mintage	VG	F	VF	XF	Unc
ND(1670-76)	—	55.00	110	200	325	—

KM# 348 GIULIO

Silver **Rev:** Inscription in round cartouche **Rev. Inscription:** SACROSAN / BASILIC / LATERAN / POSSESS **Note:** Lateran issue.

Date	Mintage	VG	F	VF	XF	Unc
MDCLXX (1670)	—	60.00	125	225	375	—

KM# 352 GIULIO

Silver **Obv:** Capped bust right **Rev:** Inscription in wreath **Rev. Inscription:** DA PACEM / DOMINE / IN DIEBVS / NOSTRIS

Date	Mintage	VG	F	VF	XF	Unc
MDCLXXII (1672)-III	—	50.00	100	185	300	—

KM# 354 GIULIO

Silver **Rev:** St. Venantius standing

Date	Mintage	VG	F	VF	XF	Unc
MDCLXXIII (1673)-IIII	—	120	225	400	650	—

KM# 361 GIULIO

Silver **Obv:** Arms **Rev:** Holy Door open **Note:** Holy year issue.

Date	Mintage	VG	F	VF	XF	Unc
1675	—	55.00	110	200	325	—

KM# 362 GIULIO

Silver **Rev:** Holy Door closed **Note:** Holy year issue.

Date	Mintage	VG	F	VF	XF	Unc
1675	—	55.00	110	200	325	—

KM# 387 GIULIO

Silver **Obv:** Arms of Cardinal Paluzzo Paluzzi-Altieri **Rev:** Radiant dove **Note:** Sede Vacante issue.

Date	Mintage	VG	F	VF	XF	Unc
MDCLXXVI (1676)	—	35.00	70.00	125	200	—

KM# 388 GIULIO

Silver **Ruler:** Innocent XI **Obv:** Arms **Rev:** Inscription in cartouche **Rev. Inscription:** DELECTA BOR / IN / MVLTTVDINE / PACIS

Date	Mintage	VG	F	VF	XF	Unc
ND(1676-89)	—	22.00	45.00	85.00	150	—

KM# 409 GIULIO

Silver **Ruler:** Innocent XI **Rev:** Inscription in cartouche **Rev. Inscription:** SACROSAN / BASILIC / LATERAN / POSSESS **Note:** Lateran issue.

Date	Mintage	VG	F	VF	XF	Unc
MDCLXXVI (1676)	—	25.00	50.00	90.00	160	—

KM# 396 GIULIO

Silver **Ruler:** Innocent XI **Rev:** Bust of Innocent XI right

Date	Mintage	VG	F	VF	XF	Unc
1677-II	—	28.00	55.00	100	165	—
ND-III	—	28.00	55.00	100	165	—

KM# 405 GIULIO

Silver **Ruler:** Innocent XI **Rev:** Inscription on drapery **Rev. Inscription:** MODICVM / IVSTO

Date	Mintage	VG	F	VF	XF	Unc
ND(1679)-IIII	—	25.00	50.00	90.00	160	—

KM# 420 GIULIO

Silver **Ruler:** Innocent XI **Rev:** Cartouche replaces drapery

Date	Mintage	VG	F	VF	XF	Unc
ND(1680)-V	—	22.00	45.00	85.00	150	—

KM# 423 GIULIO

Silver **Ruler:** Innocent XI **Rev:** Inscription within laurel wreath **Rev. Inscription:** QVID / PRODEST / HOMINI

Date	Mintage	VG	F	VF	XF	Unc
ND(1681)-VI	—	22.00	45.00	85.00	150	—

KM# 535 GIULIO

Silver **Obv:** Arms of Cardinal Paluzzo Paluzzi-Altieri **Rev:** Radiant dove **Note:** Sede Vacante issue.

Date	Mintage	VG	F	VF	XF	Unc
MDCLXXXI (1681)	—	28.00	55.00	100	175	—

KM# 432 GIULIO

Silver **Ruler:** Innocent XI **Rev:** Inscription in cartouche **Rev. Inscription:** QVI DAT / PAVPERI / NON / TNDIGEBIT

Date	Mintage	VG	F	VF	XF	Unc
1684-VIII	—	22.00	45.00	80.00	140	—
1685-X	—	22.00	45.00	80.00	140	—
1686-XI	—	22.00	45.00	80.00	140	—
1688-XIII	—	22.00	45.00	80.00	140	—
ND	—	22.00	45.00	80.00	140	—

KM# 477 GIULIO

Silver **Ruler:** Innocent XI **Rev:** Inscription in palm wreath

Date	Mintage	VG	F	VF	XF	Unc
1686-XI	—	22.00	45.00	80.00	140	—

KM# 478 GIULIO

Silver **Ruler:** Innocent XI **Rev:** Inscription in ornamental wreath

Date	Mintage	VG	F	VF	XF	Unc
1686-XI	—	22.00	45.00	80.00	140	—

KM# 489 GIULIO

Silver **Ruler:** Alexander VIII **Obv:** Arms **Rev:** St. Paul standing

Date	Mintage	VG	F	VF	XF	Unc
1689-I	—	28.00	55.00	100	175	—
1690-II	—	28.00	55.00	100	175	—

KM# 488 GIULIO

Silver **Obv:** Arms of Cardinal Paluzzo Paluzzi-Altieri **Rev:** Radiant dove **Note:** Sede Vacante issue.

Date	Mintage	VG	F	VF	XF	Unc
MDCLXXXIX (1689)	—	35.00	70.00	125	200	—

KM# 490 GIULIO

Silver **Ruler:** Alexander VIII **Rev. Inscription:** SACROS / BASLIC / LATERAN / POSSESS **Note:** Lateran issue.

Date	Mintage	VG	F	VF	XF	Unc
1689	—	28.00	55.00	100	175	—

KM# 491 GIULIO

Silver **Ruler:** Alexander VIII **Rev:** St. Bruno kneeling right

Date	Mintage	VG	F	VF	XF	Unc
1689	—	35.00	65.00	120	200	—

KM# 553 GIULIO

Silver **Ruler:** Innocent XII **Obv:** Arms **Rev:** Inscription in cartouche **Rev. Inscription:** QVI / VIDET TE / REDDET / TIBI

Date	Mintage	VG	F	VF	XF	Unc
ND(1692)-II	—	25.00	50.00	90.00	160	—

KM# 536 GIULIO

Silver **Ruler:** Innocent XII **Obv:** Arms **Rev:** Legend in cartouche **Rev. Inscription:** SACRO • SAN / BASILIC / LATERAN / POSSESS **Note:** Lateran issue.

Date	Mintage	VG	F	VF	XF	Unc
MDCXCII (1692)	—	20.00	55.00	100	175	—

KM# 566 GIULIO

Silver **Ruler:** Innocent XII **Rev:** Inscription in cartouche **Rev. Inscription:** NE / OBLIVISCARIS / PAAVPERVM

Date	Mintage	VG	F	VF	XF	Unc
1693	—	25.00	50.00	90.00	160	—

KM# 523 GIULIO

Silver **Ruler:** Innocent XII **Rev:** St. Paul standing

Date	Mintage	VG	F	VF	XF	Unc
1694	—	28.00	55.00	100	175	—

KM# 574 GIULIO

Silver **Ruler:** Innocent XII **Rev:** Cannon firing right, artillery man standing left

Date	Mintage	VG	F	VF	XF	Unc
(16)94-IIII	—	40.00	85.00	150	250	—

KM# 585 GIULIO

Silver **Ruler:** Innocent XII **Rev:** Inscription in cartouche **Rev. Inscription:** ELEVAT / PAVPEREM

Date	Mintage	VG	F	VF	XF	Unc
1695-V	—	28.00	55.00	100	175	—

KM# 586 GIULIO

Silver **Ruler:** Innocent XII **Rev:** Three vases above cartouche

Date	Mintage	VG	F	VF	XF	Unc
1695-V	—	25.00	50.00	90.00	160	—

KM# 587 GIULIO

Silver **Ruler:** Innocent XII **Rev:** Inscription on drapery without vases

Date	Mintage	VG	F	VF	XF	Unc
1695-V	—	25.00	50.00	90.00	160	—

KM# 593 GIULIO

Silver **Ruler:** Innocent XII **Rev:** Inscription curved upward or downward in cartouche

Date	Mintage	VG	F	VF	XF	Unc
1696-V	—	25.00	50.00	90.00	150	—
1697-VII	—	25.00	50.00	90.00	150	—

KM# 612 GIULIO

Silver **Ruler:** Innocent XII **Rev:** Inscription in cartouche **Rev. Inscription:** PECCATA / ELEEMOSYNIS / REDIME

Date	Mintage	VG	F	VF	XF	Unc
1699	—	25.00	50.00	90.00	150	—

KM# 639 GIULIO

Silver **Ruler:** Innocent XII **Rev:** Holy Door with four columns **Note:** Holy Year issue.

Date	Mintage	VG	F	VF	XF	Unc
MDCC (1700)-IX	—	35.00	70.00	125	200	—

KM# 640 GIULIO

Silver **Ruler:** Innocent XII **Rev:** Holy Door with two columns **Note:** Holy Year issue.

Date	Mintage	VG	F	VF	XF	Unc
MDCC (1700)-IX	—	35.00	65.00	120	200	—

KM# 643 GIULIO

Silver **Ruler:** Clement XI **Obv:** Arms **Rev:** Holy Door, triangular or curved top **Note:** Holy Year issue.

Date	Mintage	VG	F	VF	XF	Unc
MDCC (1700)-I	—	30.00	60.00	110	185	—

KM# 642 GIULIO

Silver **Ruler:** Innocent XII **Obv:** Arms of Cardinal Giovanni Spinola **Rev:** Radiant dove upwards **Note:** Sede Vacante issue.

Date	Mintage	VG	F	VF	XF	Unc
MDCC (1700)	—	50.00	95.00	175	285	—

KM# 641 GIULIO

Silver **Obv:** Arms of Cardinal Giovanni Spinola **Rev:** Radiant dove upwards **Note:** Sede Vacante issue.

Date	Mintage	VG	F	VF	XF	Unc
MDCC (1700)	—	50.00	95.00	175	285	—

KM# 31 TESTONE (30 Baiocchi)

9.5960 g., 0.9160 Silver 0.2826 oz. ASW **Ruler:** Paul V **Obv:** Arms **Rev:** Miracle of the Snakes

Date	Mintage	Good	VG	F	VF	XF
ND(1605)-I	—	35.00	70.00	135	225	—
ND(1606)-II	—	35.00	70.00	135	225	—
ND(1607)-III	—	35.00	70.00	135	225	—

KM# 32 TESTONE (30 Baiocchi)

9.5960 g., 0.9160 Silver 0.2826 oz. ASW **Ruler:** Paul V **Obv:** Bust left **Rev:** Bust of St. Paul left

Date	Mintage	Good	VG	F	VF	XF
ND(1605-21)	—	35.00	70.00	125	200	—

KM# 33 TESTONE (30 Baiocchi)

9.5960 g., 0.9160 Silver 0.2826 oz. ASW **Ruler:** Paul V **Obv:** Papal arms supported by two angels **Rev:** Madonna and child seated on altar, SS. Peter and Paul at sides

Date	Mintage	Good	VG	F	VF	XF
ND(1605-21)	—	320	525	875	1,400	—

KM# 28 TESTONE (30 Baiocchi)

9.5960 g., 0.9160 Silver 0.2826 oz. ASW **Obv:** Arms of Cardinal Pietro Aldobrandini **Rev:** St. Peter standing **Note:** Sede Vacante issue.

Date	Mintage	Good	VG	F	VF	XF
ND(1605)	—	150	300	475	750	—

KM# 29 TESTONE (30 Baiocchi)

9.5960 g., 0.9160 Silver 0.2826 oz. ASW **Obv:** Arms of Cardinal Pietro Aldobrandini **Rev:** Confronted busts of SS. Peter and Paul **Note:** Sede Vacante issue.

Date	Mintage	Good	VG	F	VF	XF
ND(1605)	—	200	400	650	1,000	—

KM# 30 TESTONE (30 Baiocchi)

9.5960 g., 0.9160 Silver 0.2826 oz. ASW **Obv:** Arms of Cardinal Pietro Aldobrandini **Rev:** SS. Peter and Paul standing **Note:** Sede Vacante issue.

Date	Mintage	Good	VG	F	VF	XF
MDCV (1605)	—	200	400	650	1,000	—

KM# 41 TESTONE (30 Baiocchi)

9.5960 g., 0.9160 Silver 0.2826 oz. ASW **Ruler:** Paul V **Rev:** SS. Peter and Paul standing

Date	Mintage	Good	VG	F	VF	XF
ND(1606)-II	—	25.00	45.00	75.00	125	—
ND(1607)-III	—	25.00	45.00	75.00	125	—
ND(1608)-IIII	—	25.00	45.00	75.00	125	—

KM# 46 TESTONE (30 Baiocchi)

9.5960 g., 0.9160 Silver 0.2826 oz. ASW **Ruler:** Paul V **Obv:** Bust left

Date	Mintage	Good	VG	F	VF	XF
ND(1607)-III	—	60.00	120	200	300	—

KM# 47 TESTONE (30 Baiocchi)

9.5960 g., 0.9160 Silver 0.2826 oz. ASW **Ruler:** Paul V **Obv:** Bust left

Date	Mintage	Good	VG	F	VF	XF
ND(1607)-III	—	45.00	90.00	145	225	—

KM# 51 TESTONE (30 Baiocchi)

9.5960 g., 0.9160 Silver 0.2826 oz. ASW **Ruler:** Paul V **Obv:** Arms **Rev:** St. Paul standing with sword left, book right

Date	Mintage	Good	VG	F	VF	XF
ND(1608)-IIII	—	25.00	45.00	75.00	125	—
ND(1609)-IIIII	—	25.00	45.00	75.00	125	—
ND(1610)-VI	—	25.00	45.00	75.00	125	—
ND(1611)-VII	—	25.00	45.00	75.00	125	—

KM# 52 TESTONE (30 Baiocchi)

9.5960 g., 0.9160 Silver 0.2826 oz. ASW **Ruler:** Paul V **Obv:** Bust left **Rev:** St. Paul standing holding sword and book

Date	Mintage	Good	VG	F	VF	XF
ND(1608)-IIII	—	45.00	90.00	145	225	—
ND(1609)-IIIII	—	45.00	90.00	145	225	—

KM# 61 TESTONE (30 Baiocchi)

9.5960 g., 0.9160 Silver 0.2826 oz. ASW **Ruler:** Paul V **Rev:** St. Paul seated with sword

Date	Mintage	Good	VG	F	VF	XF
ND(1610)-VI	—	25.00	50.00	100	165	—
1610	—	25.00	50.00	100	165	—
ND(1611)-VII	—	25.00	50.00	100	165	—
1611	—	25.00	50.00	100	165	—
MDCII (1602) error for 1612	—	25.00	50.00	100	165	—
ND(1612)-VIII	—	25.00	50.00	100	165	—
ND	—	25.00	50.00	100	165	—

KM# 62 TESTONE (30 Baiocchi)

9.5960 g., 0.9160 Silver 0.2826 oz. ASW **Ruler:** Paul V
Rev: St. Paul seated without sword

Date	Mintage	Good	VG	F	VF	XF
ND(1610)-VI	—	25.00	50.00	100	165	—
ND(1611)-VII	—	25.00	50.00	100	165	—
ND(1612)-VIII	—	25.00	50.00	100	165	—
ND(1613)-VIIII	—	25.00	50.00	100	165	—
ND(1614)-X	—	25.00	50.00	100	165	—
ND(1615)-XI	—	25.00	50.00	100	165	—

KM# 66 TESTONE (30 Baiocchi)

9.5960 g., 0.9160 Silver 0.2826 oz. ASW **Ruler:** Paul V
Rev: St. Paul seated with sword right and book left

Date	Mintage	Good	VG	F	VF	XF
ND(1611)-VII	—	25.00	50.00	100	165	—
1612-VIII	—	25.00	50.00	100	165	—
1613-VIIII	—	25.00	50.00	100	165	—
1614-X	—	25.00	50.00	100	165	—
1615-XI	—	25.00	50.00	100	165	—
1616-XII	—	25.00	50.00	100	165	—
1617-XIII	—	25.00	50.00	100	165	—
ND	—	25.00	50.00	100	165	—

KM# 63 TESTONE (30 Baiocchi)

9.5960 g., 0.9160 Silver 0.2826 oz. ASW **Ruler:** Paul V
Obv: Papal arms supported by two angels, no legend
Rev: St. Paul seated with sword and book

Date	Mintage	Good	VG	F	VF	XF
ND	—	300	500	800	1,250	—

KM# 68 TESTONE (30 Baiocchi)

9.5960 g., 0.9160 Silver 0.2826 oz. ASW **Ruler:** Paul V
Rev: St. Paul seated without sword

Date	Mintage	Good	VG	F	VF	XF
1612	—	300	500	800	1,250	—

KM# 69 TESTONE (30 Baiocchi)

9.5960 g., 0.9160 Silver 0.2826 oz. ASW **Ruler:** Paul V
Obv: Bust of Paul V left **Obv. Legend:** PAVLVS • V • P • M •
Rev: Papal arms supported by two angels

Date	Mintage	Good	VG	F	VF	XF
ND(1612)-VIII	—	50.00	100	165	250	—
ND(1613)-VIIII	—	50.00	100	165	250	—
1613	—	50.00	100	165	250	—

KM# 70 TESTONE (30 Baiocchi)

9.5960 g., 0.9160 Silver 0.2826 oz. ASW **Ruler:** Paul V **Obv:** Arms

Date	Mintage	Good	VG	F	VF	XF
ND(1612)-VIII	—	100	200	325	500	—
ND(1615)-XI	—	100	200	325	500	—

KM# 71 TESTONE (30 Baiocchi)

9.5960 g., 0.9160 Silver 0.2826 oz. ASW **Ruler:** Paul V
Obv. Legend: PAVLVS V PONT OPT MAX

Date	Mintage	Good	VG	F	VF	XF
ND(1614)-IX	—	50.00	100	165	250	—
MDCXIV (1614)	—	50.00	100	165	250	—

KM# 76 TESTONE (30 Baiocchi)

9.5960 g., 0.9160 Silver 0.2826 oz. ASW **Ruler:** Paul V
Obv: Arms **Rev:** Madonna and child seated on altar, SS. Peter and Paul at sides

Date	Mintage	Good	VG	F	VF	XF
ND(1615)-XI	—	300	500	800	1,250	—
ND(1616)-XII	—	300	500	800	1,250	—
ND	—	300	500	800	1,250	—

KM# 79 TESTONE (30 Baiocchi)

9.5960 g., 0.9160 Silver 0.2826 oz. ASW **Ruler:** Paul V
Obv: Bust right **Rev:** Conversion of St. Paul

Date	Mintage	Good	VG	F	VF	XF
ND(1616)-XII	—	200	400	650	1,000	—

KM# 98 TESTONE (30 Baiocchi)

9.5960 g., 0.9160 Silver 0.2826 oz. ASW **Ruler:** Gregory XV
Obv: Arms **Rev:** St. Paul standing

Date	Mintage	Good	VG	F	VF	XF
ND(1621-23)	—	70.00	135	225	350	—

KM# 100 TESTONE (30 Baiocchi)

9.5960 g., 0.9160 Silver 0.2826 oz. ASW **Ruler:** Gregory XV
Rev: Radiant Virgin Mary standing on crescent

Date	Mintage	Good	VG	F	VF	XF
ND(1621-23)	—	40.00	80.00	150	225	—

KM# 97 TESTONE (30 Baiocchi)

9.5960 g., 0.9160 Silver 0.2826 oz. ASW **Obv:** Arms of Cardinal Pietro Aldobrandini **Rev:** Faith standing **Note:** Sede Vacante issue.

Date	Mintage	Good	VG	F	VF	XF
1621	—	115	225	400	600	—

KM# 99 TESTONE (30 Baiocchi)

9.5960 g., 0.9160 Silver 0.2826 oz. ASW **Ruler:** Gregory XV
Rev: Madonna and child seated on altar, Sts. Peter and Paul at sides **Note:** Legend varieties exist.

Date	Mintage	Good	VG	F	VF	XF
ND(1621-33)	—	50.00	100	185	280	—

KM# 114 TESTONE (30 Baiocchi)

9.5960 g., 0.9160 Silver 0.2826 oz. ASW **Obv:** Arms of Cardinal Ippolito Aldobrandini **Rev:** Christ standing with banner
Note: Sede Vacante issue.

Date	Mintage	Good	VG	F	VF	XF
1623	—	175	350	575	900	—

KM# 115 TESTONE (30 Baiocchi)

9.5960 g., 0.9160 Silver 0.2826 oz. ASW **Obv:** Arms of Cardinal Ippolito Aldobrandini **Rev:** Radiant Christ standing with banner
Note: Sede Vacante issue.

Date	Mintage	Good	VG	F	VF	XF
1623	—	250	450	775	1,200	—

KM# 116 TESTONE (30 Baiocchi)

9.5960 g., 0.9160 Silver 0.2826 oz. ASW **Ruler:** Urban VIII
Obv: Arms **Rev:** Sts. Peter and Paul standing, keys to left

Date	Mintage	Good	VG	F	VF	XF
ND(1623)-I	—	25.00	60.00	85.00	165	—
ND(1624)-II	—	25.00	60.00	85.00	165	—
ND(1625)-III	—	25.00	60.00	85.00	165	—
ND(1626)-IIII	—	25.00	60.00	85.00	165	—
ND(1627)-V	—	25.00	60.00	85.00	165	—
ND(1628)-VI	—	25.00	60.00	85.00	165	—
ND(1629)-VII	—	25.00	60.00	85.00	165	—
ND	—	25.00	60.00	85.00	165	—

KM# 124 TESTONE (30 Baiocchi)

9.5960 g., 0.9160 Silver 0.2826 oz. ASW **Ruler:** Urban VIII
Rev: SS. Peter and Paul standing, keys at right

Date	Mintage	Good	VG	F	VF	XF
ND(1624)-II	—	30.00	60.00	110	175	—
ND(1625)-III	—	30.00	60.00	110	175	—
ND(1626)-IIII	—	30.00	60.00	110	175	—
ND(1627)-V	—	30.00	60.00	110	175	—
ND(1628)-VII	—	30.00	60.00	110	175	—
ND(1629)-VIII	—	30.00	60.00	110	175	—
ND	—	30.00	60.00	110	175	—

KM# 145 TESTONE (30 Baiocchi)

9.5960 g., 0.9160 Silver 0.2826 oz. ASW **Ruler:** Urban VIII
Rev: Holy Door with Veronica's veil, dove above **Note:** Holy Year issue.

Date	Mintage	Good	VG	F	VF	XF
1625-II	—	30.00	60.00	110	175	—

KM# 147 TESTONE (30 Baiocchi)

9.5960 g., 0.9160 Silver 0.2826 oz. ASW **Ruler:** Urban VIII
Rev: Holy Door with Veronica's veil **Note:** Holy Year issue.

Date	Mintage	Good	VG	F	VF	XF
1625-II	—	35.00	70.00	115	185	—

KM# 146 TESTONE (30 Baiocchi)

9.5960 g., 0.9160 Silver 0.2826 oz. ASW **Ruler:** Urban VIII
Rev: Holy Door with Veronica's veil, Madonna above **Note:** Holy Year issue.

Date	Mintage	Good	VG	F	VF	XF
1625-II	—	25.00	50.00	100	150	—
1625-III	—	25.00	50.00	100	150	—

KM# 157 TESTONE (30 Baiocchi)

9.5960 g., 0.9160 Silver 0.2826 oz. ASW **Ruler:** Urban VIII **Obv:** Bust right **Rev:** SS. Peter and Paul standing, dove above

Date	Mintage	Good	VG	F	VF	XF
ND(1628)-V	—	40.00	80.00	125	200	—
ND(1628)-VI	—	40.00	80.00	125	200	—
1628	—	40.00	80.00	125	200	—

KM# 172 TESTONE (30 Baiocchi)

9.5960 g., 0.9160 Silver 0.2826 oz. ASW **Ruler:** Urban VIII **Rev:** Roma seated right

Date	Mintage	Good	VG	F	VF	XF
ND(1631)-VIII	—	50.00	100	165	250	—

KM# 173 TESTONE (30 Baiocchi)

9.5960 g., 0.9160 Silver 0.2826 oz. ASW **Ruler:** Urban VIII **Obv:** Arms

Date	Mintage	Good	VG	F	VF	XF
ND(1631)-VIII	—	30.00	60.00	125	200	—
ND(1632)-VIIII	—	30.00	60.00	125	200	—

KM# 175 TESTONE (30 Baiocchi)

9.5960 g., 0.9160 Silver 0.2826 oz. ASW **Ruler:** Urban VIII **Obv:** Bust left

Date	Mintage	Good	VG	F	VF	XF
1632-VIIII	—	45.00	90.00	150	235	—

KM# 176 TESTONE (30 Baiocchi)

9.5960 g., 0.9160 Silver 0.2826 oz. ASW **Ruler:** Urban VIII **Obv:** Arms

Date	Mintage	Good	VG	F	VF	XF
ND(1632)-VIII	—	30.00	60.00	115	180	—
1632	—	30.00	60.00	115	180	—
1633	—	30.00	60.00	115	180	—
ND	—	30.00	60.00	115	180	—

KM# 174 TESTONE (30 Baiocchi)

9.5960 g., 0.9160 Silver 0.2826 oz. ASW **Ruler:** Urban VIII **Obv:** Bust right **Rev:** St. Peter seated

Date	Mintage	Good	VG	F	VF	XF
1632-VIII	—	45.00	90.00	150	235	—
1632-VIIII	—	45.00	90.00	150	235	—

KM# 191 TESTONE (30 Baiocchi)

9.5960 g., 0.9160 Silver 0.2826 oz. ASW **Ruler:** Urban VIII **Obv:** Bust right **Rev:** Radiant Virgin Mary standing on crescent

Date	Mintage	Good	VG	F	VF	XF
ND(1636)-XII	—	50.00	100	165	250	—
ND(1637)-XIII	—	50.00	100	165	250	—
ND(1638)-XIIII	—	50.00	100	165	250	—
ND(1639)-XV	—	50.00	100	165	250	—
ND(1640)-XVI	—	50.00	100	165	250	—
ND(1641)-XVII	—	50.00	100	165	250	—
ND(1642)-XVIII	—	50.00	100	165	250	—
1642	—	50.00	100	165	250	—
ND(1643)-XVIIII	—	50.00	100	165	250	—
ND(1644)-XX	—	50.00	100	165	250	—

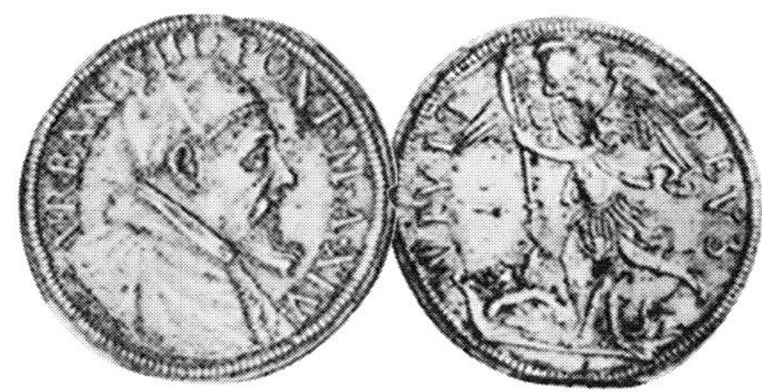

KM# 193 TESTONE (30 Baiocchi)

9.5960 g., 0.9160 Silver 0.2826 oz. ASW **Ruler:** Urban VIII **Rev:** St. Michael defeating Lucifer

Date	Mintage	Good	VG	F	VF	XF
ND(1638)-XIV	—	70.00	135	225	350	—
1643	—	70.00	135	225	350	—
ND(1644)-XX	—	70.00	135	225	350	—

KM# 218 TESTONE (30 Baiocchi)

9.5960 g., 0.9160 Silver 0.2826 oz. ASW **Ruler:** Urban VIII **Obv:** Arms **Note:** Varieties in placement of rays exist.

Date	Mintage	Good	VG	F	VF	XF
1642	—	30.00	60.00	125	185	—
ND(1644)-XX	—	30.00	60.00	125	185	—
ND(1645)-XXI	—	30.00	60.00	125	185	—

KM# 219 TESTONE (30 Baiocchi)

9.5960 g., 0.9160 Silver 0.2826 oz. ASW **Ruler:** Urban VIII **Obv:** Arms

Date	Mintage	Good	VG	F	VF	XF
ND(1644)-XX	—	35.00	70.00	130	200	—

KM# 221 TESTONE (30 Baiocchi)

9.5960 g., 0.9160 Silver 0.2826 oz. ASW **Ruler:** Innocent X **Obv:** Arms **Rev:** Justice seated right in legend

Date	Mintage	Good	VG	F	VF	XF
ND(1644)-I	—	35.00	70.00	115	180	—
ND(1645)-II	—	35.00	70.00	115	180	—
ND(1653)-X	—	35.00	70.00	115	180	—

KM# 222 TESTONE (30 Baiocchi)

9.5960 g., 0.9160 Silver 0.2826 oz. ASW **Ruler:** Innocent X **Rev:** Justice seated right in wreath

Date	Mintage	Good	VG	F	VF	XF
ND(1644)-I	—	35.00	70.00	115	180	—
ND(1645)-II	—	35.00	70.00	115	180	—
ND(1652)-IX	—	35.00	70.00	115	180	—
ND(1653)-X	—	35.00	70.00	115	180	—

KM# 220 TESTONE (30 Baiocchi)

9.5960 g., 0.9160 Silver 0.2826 oz. ASW **Obv:** Arms of Cardinal Antonio Barberini **Rev:** Half figure of Madonna and child **Note:** Sede Vacante issue.

Date	Mintage	Good	VG	F	VF	XF
1644	—	600	1,000	1,650	2,500	—
ND	—	600	1,000	1,650	2,500	—

KM# 237 TESTONE (30 Baiocchi)

9.5960 g., 0.9160 Silver 0.2826 oz. ASW **Ruler:** Innocent X **Obv:** Arms **Note:** Varieties exist with angel in exergue.

Date	Mintage	Good	VG	F	VF	XF
ND(1645)-II	—	40.00	80.00	125	200	—

KM# 232 TESTONE (30 Baiocchi)

9.5960 g., 0.9160 Silver 0.2826 oz. ASW **Ruler:** Innocent X **Obv:** Bust right **Rev:** Justice seated right in legend

Date	Mintage	Good	VG	F	VF	XF
ND(1645)-II	—	185	375	625	950	—

KM# 233 TESTONE (30 Baiocchi)

9.5960 g., 0.9160 Silver 0.2826 oz. ASW **Ruler:** Innocent X **Obv:** Arms **Rev:** St. Paul standing

Date	Mintage	Good	VG	F	VF	XF
ND(1645)-II	—	35.00	70.00	115	185	—

KM# 234 TESTONE (30 Baiocchi)

9.5960 g., 0.9160 Silver 0.2826 oz. ASW **Ruler:** Innocent X **Obv:** Bust right **Rev:** St. Paul seated right

Date	Mintage	Good	VG	F	VF	XF
1645-II	—	70.00	135	225	365	—

KM# 235 TESTONE (30 Baiocchi)

9.5960 g., 0.9160 Silver 0.2826 oz. ASW **Ruler:** Innocent X **Obv:** Arms

Date	Mintage	Good	VG	F	VF	XF
ND(1645)-II	—	35.00	70.00	115	185	—

KM# 236 TESTONE (30 Baiocchi)

9.5960 g., 0.9160 Silver 0.2826 oz. ASW **Ruler:** Innocent X **Obv:** Bust right **Rev:** St. Paul seated left

Date	Mintage	Good	VG	F	VF	XF
ND(1645)-II Rare	—	—	—	—	—	—

KM# 238 TESTONE (30 Baiocchi)

9.5960 g., 0.9160 Silver 0.2826 oz. ASW **Ruler:** Innocent X **Rev:** Virgin Mary standing on crescent, angels at sides

Date	Mintage	Good	VG	F	VF	XF
ND(1645)-II	—	115	225	400	625	—

KM# 239 TESTONE (30 Baiocchi)

9.5960 g., 0.9160 Silver 0.2826 oz. ASW **Ruler:** Innocent X **Rev:** Without angels at sides

Date	Mintage	Good	VG	F	VF	XF
ND(1645)-II Unique	—	—	—	—	—	—

KM# 240 TESTONE (30 Baiocchi)

9.5960 g., 0.9160 Silver 0.2826 oz. ASW **Ruler:** Innocent X **Subject:** Immaculate Conception **Rev:** Radiant Virgin Mary standing on crescent

Date	Mintage	Good	VG	F	VF	XF
ND(1645)-II	—	40.00	80.00	125	200	—

KM# 253 TESTONE (30 Baiocchi)

9.5960 g., 0.9160 Silver 0.2826 oz. ASW **Ruler:** Innocent X **Rev:** Holy Door with Veronica's veil **Note:** Holy Year issue.

Date	Mintage	Good	VG	F	VF	XF
MDCL (1650)-VI	—	100	200	325	500	—

KM# 277 TESTONE (30 Baiocchi)

9.5960 g., 0.9160 Silver 0.2826 oz. ASW **Obv:** Arms of Cardinal Antonio Barberini **Rev:** Radiant dove **Note:** Sede Vacante issue.

Date	Mintage	VG	F	VF	XF	Unc
MDCLV (1655)	—	250	450	775	1,250	—

KM# 278.1 TESTONE (30 Baiocchi)

9.5960 g., 0.9160 Silver 0.2826 oz. ASW **Ruler:** Alexander VII **Obv:** Arms **Rev:** Hand of God holding scale

Date	Mintage	VG	F	VF	XF	Unc
ND(1655-67)	—	65.00	130	235	400	—

KM# 278.2 TESTONE (30 Baiocchi)

9.5960 g., 0.9160 Silver 0.2826 oz. ASW **Ruler:** Alexander VII **Obv:** Baroque shield

Date	Mintage	VG	F	VF	XF	Unc
ND(1655-67)	—	65.00	130	235	400	—

KM# 309 TESTONE (30 Baiocchi)

9.5960 g., 0.9160 Silver 0.2826 oz. ASW **Ruler:** Clement IX **Obv:** Arms **Rev:** St. Peter seated

Date	Mintage	VG	F	VF	XF	Unc
ND(1667-69)	—	60.00	125	225	385	—

KM# 308 TESTONE (30 Baiocchi)

9.5960 g., 0.9160 Silver 0.2826 oz. ASW **Obv:** Arms of Cardinal Antonio Barberini **Rev:** Radiant dove **Note:** Sede Vacante issue.

Date	Mintage	VG	F	VF	XF	Unc
MDCLXVII (1667)	—	70.00	140	250	425	—

KM# 318 TESTONE (30 Baiocchi)

9.5960 g., 0.9160 Silver 0.2826 oz. ASW **Obv:** Arms of Cardinal Antonio Barberini **Rev:** Radiant dove **Note:** Sede Vacante issue.

Date	Mintage	VG	F	VF	XF	Unc
MDCLXIX (1669)	—	70.00	140	250	425	—

KM# 342 TESTONE (30 Baiocchi)

9.5960 g., 0.9160 Silver 0.2826 oz. ASW **Ruler:** Clement X **Obv:** Arms **Rev:** Half-length figure of Christ holding orb

Date	Mintage	VG	F	VF	XF	Unc
ND(1670-76)	—	300	550	900	1,600	—

KM# 343 TESTONE (30 Baiocchi)

9.5960 g., 0.9160 Silver 0.2826 oz. ASW **Rev:** Tiara in front of Pope kneeling left

Date	Mintage	VG	F	VF	XF	Unc
ND(1670-76)	—	85.00	165	300	550	—

KM# 349 TESTONE (30 Baiocchi)

9.5960 g., 0.9160 Silver 0.2826 oz. ASW **Obv:** Capped bust of Clement X right **Rev:** Standing St. Peter being crowned by angel

Date	Mintage	VG	F	VF	XF	Unc
MDCLXX (1670)-I	—	85.00	165	300	550	—
MDCLXXI (1671)-II	—	85.00	165	300	550	—

KM# 350 TESTONE (30 Baiocchi)

9.5960 g., 0.9160 Silver 0.2826 oz. ASW **Obv:** Arms **Rev:** King David seated playing harp

Date	Mintage	VG	F	VF	XF	Unc
ND	—	85.00	165	300	550	—

KM# 363 TESTONE (30 Baiocchi)

9.5960 g., 0.9160 Silver 0.2826 oz. ASW **Obv:** Capped bust right **Rev:** Holy Door open with pilgrims **Note:** Holy Year issue.

Date	Mintage	VG	F	VF	XF	Unc
1675	—	100	200	350	600	—

KM# 364 TESTONE (30 Baiocchi)

9.5960 g., 0.9160 Silver 0.2826 oz. ASW **Obv:** Arms **Rev:** Holy Door open with pilgrims **Note:** Holy Year issue.

Date	Mintage	VG	F	VF	XF	Unc
1675	—	45.00	90.00	175	325	—

KM# 365 TESTONE (30 Baiocchi)

9.5960 g., 0.9160 Silver 0.2826 oz. ASW **Obv:** Capped bust right **Rev:** Closed Holy Door **Note:** Holy Year issue.

Date	Mintage	VG	F	VF	XF	Unc
1675	—	100	200	350	600	—

KM# 366 TESTONE (30 Baiocchi)

9.5960 g., 0.9160 Silver 0.2826 oz. ASW **Obv:** Arms **Note:** Holy Year issue.

Date	Mintage	VG	F	VF	XF	Unc
1675	—	45.00	100	200	350	—

KM# 389 TESTONE (30 Baiocchi)

9.5960 g., 0.9160 Silver 0.2826 oz. ASW **Obv:** Arms of Cardinal Paluzzo Paluzzi-Altieri **Rev:** Radiant dove **Note:** Sede Vacante issue.

Date	Mintage	VG	F	VF	XF	Unc
MDCLXXVI (1676)	—	65.00	125	235	400	—

KM# 390 TESTONE (30 Baiocchi)

9.5960 g., 0.9160 Silver 0.2826 oz. ASW **Ruler:** Innocent XI **Obv:** Arms **Rev:** Madonna and child seated

Date	Mintage	VG	F	VF	XF	Unc
ND(1676)-I	—	50.00	100	200	350	—

KM# 397 TESTONE (30 Baiocchi)

9.5960 g., 0.9160 Silver 0.2826 oz. ASW **Ruler:** Innocent XI **Rev:** St. Peter helping invalid

Date	Mintage	VG	F	VF	XF	Unc
1677-II	—	70.00	135	250	425	—
ND(1680)-V	—	70.00	135	250	425	—

KM# 401 TESTONE (30 Baiocchi)

9.5960 g., 0.9160 Silver 0.2826 oz. ASW **Ruler:** Innocent XI **Rev:** Inscription in palm wreath **Rev. Inscription:** NOLITE / COR / APPONERE

Date	Mintage	VG	F	VF	XF	Unc
ND(1678)-III	—	25.00	50.00	100	175	—

KM# 402 TESTONE (30 Baiocchi)

9.5960 g., 0.9160 Silver 0.2826 oz. ASW **Ruler:** Innocent XI **Rev:** Inscription in cartouche **Rev. Inscription:** NOLT / ANXIVS / ESSE

Date	Mintage	VG	F	VF	XF	Unc
ND(1678)-III	—	25.00	50.00	100	175	—
ND(1679)-IIII	—	25.00	50.00	100	175	—
ND(1680)-V	—	25.00	50.00	100	175	—

KM# 424 TESTONE (30 Baiocchi)

9.5960 g., 0.9160 Silver 0.2826 oz. ASW **Ruler:** Innocent XI **Rev:** Inscription in cartouche

Date	Mintage	VG	F	VF	XF	Unc
ND(1681)-VI	—	25.00	50.00	100	175	—

KM# 434 TESTONE (30 Baiocchi)

9.5960 g., 0.9160 Silver 0.2826 oz. ASW **Ruler:** Innocent XI **Rev:** Cartouche with pellets at top and bottom of frame

Date	Mintage	VG	F	VF	XF	Unc
1684-VIII	—	25.00	50.00	100	175	—

KM# 435 TESTONE (30 Baiocchi)

9.5960 g., 0.9160 Silver 0.2826 oz. ASW **Ruler:** Innocent XI **Rev:** Cartouche without pellet ornamentation

Date	Mintage	VG	F	VF	XF	Unc
1684-VIII	—	20.00	45.00	90.00	165	—

KM# 436 TESTONE (30 Baiocchi)

9.5960 g., 0.9160 Silver 0.2826 oz. ASW **Ruler:** Innocent XI **Rev:** Cartouche ends left, pellets and flora around

Date	Mintage	VG	F	VF	XF	Unc
1684-VIII	—	25.00	50.00	100	175	—

KM# 437 TESTONE (30 Baiocchi)

9.5960 g., 0.9160 Silver 0.2826 oz. ASW **Ruler:** Innocent XI

Date	Mintage	VG	F	VF	XF	Unc
1684	—	30.00	60.00	120	200	—

KM# 438 TESTONE (30 Baiocchi)

9.5960 g., 0.9160 Silver 0.2826 oz. ASW **Ruler:** Innocent XI

Date	Mintage	VG	F	VF	XF	Unc
1684	—	25.00	50.00	100	175	—

KM# 439 TESTONE (30 Baiocchi)
9.5960 g., 0.9160 Silver 0.2826 oz. ASW **Ruler:** Innocent XI
Rev: Laurel and branch ornamentation

Date	Mintage	VG	F	VF	XF	Unc
1684	—	25.00	50.00	100	175	—

KM# 440 TESTONE (30 Baiocchi)
9.5960 g., 0.9160 Silver 0.2826 oz. ASW **Ruler:** Innocent XI
Rev: Floral leaves

Date	Mintage	VG	F	VF	XF	Unc
1684	—	25.00	50.00	100	175	—

KM# 441 TESTONE (30 Baiocchi)
9.5960 g., 0.9160 Silver 0.2826 oz. ASW **Ruler:** Innocent XI

Date	Mintage	VG	F	VF	XF	Unc
ND(1684-86)	—	25.00	85.00	110	185	—

KM# 442 TESTONE (30 Baiocchi)
9.5960 g., 0.9160 Silver 0.2826 oz. ASW **Ruler:** Innocent XI

Date	Mintage	VG	F	VF	XF	Unc
ND(1684-86)	—	25.00	55.00	110	185	—

KM# 443 TESTONE (30 Baiocchi)
9.5960 g., 0.9160 Silver 0.2826 oz. ASW **Ruler:** Innocent XI

Date	Mintage	VG	F	VF	XF	Unc
ND(1684-86)	—	30.00	60.00	120	200	—

KM# 444 TESTONE (30 Baiocchi)
9.5960 g., 0.9160 Silver 0.2826 oz. ASW **Ruler:** Innocent XI

Date	Mintage	VG	F	VF	XF	Unc
ND(1684-86)	—	25.00	55.00	110	185	—

KM# 445 TESTONE (30 Baiocchi)
9.5960 g., 0.9160 Silver 0.2826 oz. ASW **Ruler:** Innocent XI

Date	Mintage	VG	F	VF	XF	Unc
ND(1684-86)	—	25.00	55.00	110	185	—

KM# 446 TESTONE (30 Baiocchi)
9.5960 g., 0.9160 Silver 0.2826 oz. ASW **Ruler:** Innocent XI
Rev: Inscription in flora, shield below

Date	Mintage	VG	F	VF	XF	Unc
ND(1684-86)	—	20.00	45.00	90.00	165	—

KM# 447 TESTONE (30 Baiocchi)
9.5960 g., 0.9160 Silver 0.2826 oz. ASW **Ruler:** Innocent XI
Rev: Legend in frame

Date	Mintage	VG	F	VF	XF	Unc
ND(1684-86)	—	25.00	50.00	100	175	—

KM# 448 TESTONE (30 Baiocchi)
9.5960 g., 0.9160 Silver 0.2826 oz. ASW **Ruler:** Innocent XI
Rev: Legend in cartouche

Date	Mintage	VG	F	VF	XF	Unc
ND(1684-86)-VII	—	20.00	45.00	90.00	165	—

KM# 449 TESTONE (30 Baiocchi)
9.5960 g., 0.9160 Silver 0.2826 oz. ASW **Ruler:** Innocent XI

Date	Mintage	VG	F	VF	XF	Unc
1684	—	20.00	45.00	90.00	165	—

KM# 450 TESTONE (30 Baiocchi)
9.5960 g., 0.9160 Silver 0.2826 oz. ASW **Ruler:** Innocent XI
Rev: Legend in plaque, wreath behind

Date	Mintage	VG	F	VF	XF	Unc
1684	—	25.00	50.00	100	175	—

KM# 433 TESTONE (30 Baiocchi)
9.5960 g., 0.9160 Silver 0.2826 oz. ASW **Ruler:** Innocent XI
Rev: Cartouche with seraphim above, bottom tip curls left
Note: Reform weight.

Date	Mintage	VG	F	VF	XF	Unc
1684	—	30.00	60.00	120	200	—

KM# 469 TESTONE (30 Baiocchi)
9.5960 g., 0.9160 Silver 0.2826 oz. ASW **Ruler:** Innocent XI
Rev: Cartouche with two laurel sprigs, top curves outwards

Date	Mintage	VG	F	VF	XF	Unc
1685-IX	—	25.00	50.00	100	175	—

KM# 470 TESTONE (30 Baiocchi)
9.5960 g., 0.9160 Silver 0.2826 oz. ASW **Ruler:** Innocent XI
Rev: Cartouche with two laurel sprigs, top curves inwards

Date	Mintage	VG	F	VF	XF	Unc
1685-IX	—	30.00	60.00	120	200	—

KM# 471 TESTONE (30 Baiocchi)
9.5960 g., 0.9160 Silver 0.2826 oz. ASW **Ruler:** Innocent XI
Rev: Bands with pellets at top and sides

Date	Mintage	VG	F	VF	XF	Unc
1685-IX	—	25.00	50.00	100	175	—

KM# 472 TESTONE (30 Baiocchi)
9.5960 g., 0.9160 Silver 0.2826 oz. ASW **Ruler:** Innocent XI

Date	Mintage	VG	F	VF	XF	Unc
1685-IX	—	20.00	45.00	90.00	165	—

KM# 473 TESTONE (30 Baiocchi)
9.5960 g., 0.9160 Silver 0.2826 oz. ASW **Ruler:** Innocent XI

Date	Mintage	VG	F	VF	XF	Unc
1685-XI	—	25.00	50.00	100	175	—

KM# 474 TESTONE (30 Baiocchi)
9.5960 g., 0.9160 Silver 0.2826 oz. ASW **Ruler:** Innocent XI
Rev: Rectangular shield in leaves

Date	Mintage	VG	F	VF	XF	Unc
1685-XI	—	25.00	50.00	100	175	—

KM# 492 TESTONE (30 Baiocchi)
9.5960 g., 0.9160 Silver 0.2826 oz. ASW **Ruler:** Innocent XI

Date	Mintage	VG	F	VF	XF	Unc
1686-X	—	25.00	50.00	100	175	—

KM# 493 TESTONE (30 Baiocchi)
9.5960 g., 0.9160 Silver 0.2826 oz. ASW **Ruler:** Innocent XI

Date	Mintage	VG	F	VF	XF	Unc
1686-X	—	30.00	60.00	120	200	—

KM# 494 TESTONE (30 Baiocchi)
9.5960 g., 0.9160 Silver 0.2826 oz. ASW **Ruler:** Innocent XI

Date	Mintage	VG	F	VF	XF	Unc
1686-X	—	30.00	60.00	120	200	—

KM# 507 TESTONE (30 Baiocchi)
9.5960 g., 0.9160 Silver 0.2826 oz. ASW **Ruler:** Innocent XI

Date	Mintage	VG	F	VF	XF	Unc
1686-X	—	30.00	60.00	120	200	—

KM# 495 TESTONE (30 Baiocchi)
9.5960 g., 0.9160 Silver 0.2826 oz. ASW **Ruler:** Innocent XI

Date	Mintage	VG	F	VF	XF	Unc
1687-XI	—	25.00	55.00	110	185	—

KM# 505 TESTONE (30 Baiocchi)
9.5960 g., 0.9160 Silver 0.2826 oz. ASW **Rev:** SS. Peter and Paul standing, dove above

Date	Mintage	VG	F	VF	XF	Unc
1689-I	—	165	300	550	900	—

KM# 506 TESTONE (30 Baiocchi)
9.5960 g., 0.9160 Silver 0.2826 oz. ASW **Obv:** Capped bust right **Rev:** St. Bruno kneeling right

Date	Mintage	VG	F	VF	XF	Unc
1689-I	—	50.00	100	200	350	—

KM# 522 TESTONE (30 Baiocchi)
9.5960 g., 0.9160 Silver 0.2826 oz. ASW **Ruler:** Alexander VIII
Obv: Arms

Date	Mintage	VG	F	VF	XF	Unc
1689	—	50.00	100	185	325	—
1690-I	—	50.00	100	185	325	—
1690	—	50.00	100	185	325	—

KM# A495 TESTONE (30 Baiocchi)
9.5960 g., 0.9160 Silver 0.2826 oz. ASW **Ruler:** Innocent XI
Obv: Papal Arms **Rev:** Legend within palm wreath **Rev. Legend:** MELIVS / EST •DARE / QVAM / ACCIPERE /(date)

Date	Mintage	VG	F	VF	XF	Unc
1689-XIII	—	—	—	—	—	—

KM# 496 TESTONE (30 Baiocchi)
9.5960 g., 0.9160 Silver 0.2826 oz. ASW **Obv:** Arms of Cardinal Paluzzo Paluzzi-Altieri **Rev:** Radiant dove **Note:** Sede Vacante issue.

Date	Mintage	VG	F	VF	XF	Unc
MDCLXXXIX (1689)	—	20.00	45.00	90.00	165	—

KM# A523 TESTONE (30 Baiocchi)
9.5960 g., 0.9160 Silver 0.2826 oz. ASW **Ruler:** Alexander VIII
Rev: SS. Magnus and Bruno standing

Date	Mintage	VG	F	VF	XF	Unc
ND(1690)-II	—	50.00	100	200	350	—
1690-II	—	50.00	100	200	350	—

KM# 524 TESTONE (30 Baiocchi)
9.5960 g., 0.9160 Silver 0.2826 oz. ASW **Ruler:** Alexander VIII
Obv: Capped bust right **Rev:** Two oxen right

Date	Mintage	VG	F	VF	XF	Unc
MDCXC (1690)-I	—	70.00	145	275	450	—

KM# 538 TESTONE (30 Baiocchi)
9.5960 g., 0.9160 Silver 0.2826 oz. ASW **Rev:** Radiant dove flying upwards

Date	Mintage	VG	F	VF	XF	Unc
MDCLXXXXI (1691)	—	50.00	100	200	350	—

KM# 539 TESTONE (30 Baiocchi)
9.5960 g., 0.9160 Silver 0.2826 oz. ASW **Rev:** Radiant dove flying downwards

Date	Mintage	VG	F	VF	XF	Unc
MDCLXXXXI (1691)	—	50.00	100	200	350	—

KM# 540 TESTONE (30 Baiocchi)
9.5960 g., 0.9160 Silver 0.2826 oz. ASW **Ruler:** Innocent XII **Obv:** Arms **Rev:** Inscription in cartouche **Rev. Inscription:** NOLI / AMARE / NE / PERDAS

Date	Mintage	VG	F	VF	XF	Unc
ND(1691)-I	—	25.00	50.00	100	175	—

KM# 541 TESTONE (30 Baiocchi)
9.5960 g., 0.9160 Silver 0.2826 oz. ASW **Ruler:** Innocent XII **Rev:** Inscription in cartouche **Rev. Inscription:** TANQVAM / LVTVM / AESTIMABITVR

Date	Mintage	VG	F	VF	XF	Unc
ND(1691)-I	—	25.00	50.00	100	175	—

KM# 537 TESTONE (30 Baiocchi)
9.5960 g., 0.9160 Silver 0.2826 oz. ASW **Obv:** Arms of Cardinal Paluzzo Paluzzi-Altieri **Rev:** Radiant dove flying right **Note:** Sede vacante issue.

Date	Mintage	VG	F	VF	XF	Unc
MDCLXXXXI (1691)	—	50.00	100	200	350	—

KM# 552 TESTONE (30 Baiocchi)
9.5960 g., 0.9160 Silver 0.2826 oz. ASW **Ruler:** Innocent XII **Rev:** Inscription in cartouche **Rev. Inscription:** NON SIT/TECVM IN/ PERDIT/ONEM

Date	Mintage	VG	F	VF	XF	Unc
(1692)-II	—	25.00	50.00	100	175	—

KM# A553 TESTONE (30 Baiocchi)
9.5960 g., 0.9160 Silver 0.2826 oz. ASW **Ruler:** Innocent XII **Rev:** Inscription in cartouche

Date	Mintage	VG	F	VF	XF	Unc
1692-II	—	25.00	50.00	100	175	—
1693-III	—	25.00	50.00	100	175	—

KM# 567 TESTONE (30 Baiocchi)
9.5960 g., 0.9160 Silver 0.2826 oz. ASW **Ruler:** Innocent XII **Rev:** Eagle with two eaglets

Date	Mintage	VG	F	VF	XF	Unc
1693-III	—	65.00	135	250	450	—

KM# 575 TESTONE (30 Baiocchi)
9.5960 g., 0.9160 Silver 0.2826 oz. ASW **Ruler:** Innocent XII **Rev:** Abundance standing

Date	Mintage	VG	F	VF	XF	Unc
1694-III	—	50.00	100	175	325	—

KM# 588 TESTONE (30 Baiocchi)
9.5960 g., 0.9160 Silver 0.2826 oz. ASW **Ruler:** Innocent XII **Rev:** Pope listening to peace exhortation

Date	Mintage	VG	F	VF	XF	Unc
1695-V	—	60.00	125	225	400	—

KM# 595 TESTONE (30 Baiocchi)
9.5960 g., 0.9160 Silver 0.2826 oz. ASW **Ruler:** Innocent XII **Rev:** Straight inscription in cartouche

Date	Mintage	VG	F	VF	XF	Unc
1696-VI	—	25.00	50.00	100	175	—

KM# 594 TESTONE (30 Baiocchi)
9.5960 g., 0.9160 Silver 0.2826 oz. ASW **Ruler:** Innocent XII **Rev:** Inscription in arched cartouche **Rev. Inscription:** ROGATE EA / QVAE AD PACEM / SVNT

Date	Mintage	VG	F	VF	XF	Unc
1696-V	—	25.00	50.00	100	175	—
1696-VI	—	25.00	50.00	100	175	—

KM# 606 TESTONE (30 Baiocchi)
9.5960 g., 0.9160 Silver 0.2826 oz. ASW **Ruler:** Innocent XII **Rev:** Christ standing with orb

Date	Mintage	VG	F	VF	XF	Unc
1698-VII	—	50.00	100	185	325	—

KM# 648 TESTONE (30 Baiocchi)
9.5960 g., 0.9160 Silver 0.2826 oz. ASW **Obv:** Rounded bottom shield **Note:** Holy Year Issue.

Date	Mintage	VG	F	VF	XF	Unc
ND (1700)	—	165	300	500	850	—

KM# 645 TESTONE (30 Baiocchi)
9.5960 g., 0.9160 Silver 0.2826 oz. ASW **Obv:** Arms of Cardinal Giovanni Spinola **Rev:** Radiant dove flying upwards **Note:** Sede Vacante issue.

Date	Mintage	VG	F	VF	XF	Unc
MDCC (1700)	—	165	300	550	900	—

KM# 646 TESTONE (30 Baiocchi)
9.5960 g., 0.9160 Silver 0.2826 oz. ASW **Rev:** Radiant dove flying left **Note:** Sede Vacante issue.

Date	Mintage	VG	F	VF	XF	Unc
MDCC (1700)	—	165	300	550	900	—

KM# 644 TESTONE (30 Baiocchi)
9.5960 g., 0.9160 Silver 0.2826 oz. ASW **Ruler:** Innocent XII **Rev:** Holy Door **Note:** Holy Year issue.

Date	Mintage	VG	F	VF	XF	Unc
1700-IX	—	45.00	95.00	185	300	—

KM# 647 TESTONE (30 Baiocchi)
9.5960 g., 0.9160 Silver 0.2826 oz. ASW **Ruler:** Clement XI **Obv:** Arms **Rev:** Holy Door **Note:** Holy Year issue.

Date	Mintage	VG	F	VF	XF	Unc
1700-I	—	75.00	150	285	475	—

KM# A18 1/2 PIASTRE
Silver **Ruler:** Clement VIII **Obv:** Bust of Clement VIII left **Rev:** Holy Door **Note:** Holy Year issue.

Date	Mintage	VG	F	VF	XF	Unc
ND(1601)-X Rare	—	—	—	—	—	—

KM# 429 1/2 PIASTRE
Silver **Ruler:** Innocent XI **Obv:** Arms **Rev:** In cartouche **Rev. Inscription:** AVARVS / NON / IMPLEBITVR

Date	Mintage	VG	F	VF	XF	Unc
ND(1683)-VII	—	50.00	100	200	350	—
ND	—	50.00	100	200	350	—

KM# 430 1/2 PIASTRE
Silver **Ruler:** Innocent XI **Rev:** Seraphin above and below, lion's head at sides

Date	Mintage	VG	F	VF	XF	Unc
ND(1683)-VII	—	50.00	100	200	350	—

KM# 431 1/2 PIASTRE
Silver **Ruler:** Innocent XI **Rev:** Inscription in palm wreath

Date	Mintage	VG	F	VF	XF	Unc
ND(1683)-VII	—	50.00	100	200	350	—

KM# 554 1/2 PIASTRE
Silver **Ruler:** Innocent XII **Obv:** Capped bust right **Rev:** The Church seated in clouds

Date	Mintage	VG	F	VF	XF	Unc
ND(1692)-II	—	100	200	325	575	—

KM# 555 1/2 PIASTRE
Silver **Ruler:** Innocent XII **Obv:** Arms **Rev:** Pelican right feeding young

Date	Mintage	VG	F	VF	XF	Unc
1692-II	—	80.00	175	285	500	—

KM# 556 1/2 PIASTRE
Silver **Ruler:** Innocent XII **Obv:** Capped bust right **Rev:** Peace standing

Date	Mintage	VG	F	VF	XF	Unc
1692-II	—	85.00	185	300	525	—

KM# 568 1/2 PIASTRE

Silver **Ruler:** Innocent XII **Obv:** Arms **Rev:** Pelican feeding young

Date	Mintage	VG	F	VF	XF	Unc
1693-III	—	80.00	175	285	500	—

KM# 596 1/2 PIASTRE

Silver **Ruler:** Innocent XII **Rev:** Pope kneeling right in prayer

Date	Mintage	VG	F	VF	XF	Unc
1696-V Rare	—	—	—	—	—	—

KM# 597 1/2 PIASTRE

Silver **Ruler:** Innocent XII **Obv:** Capped bust right **Rev:** Pope kneeling left in prayer

Date	Mintage	VG	F	VF	XF	Unc
1696-V	—	85.00	185	300	525	—

KM# 601 1/2 PIASTRE

Silver **Ruler:** Innocent XII **Obv:** Arms

Date	Mintage	VG	F	VF	XF	Unc
ND(1697)-VI	—	75.00	150	265	450	—
ND(1698)-VII	—	75.00	150	265	450	—

KM# 607 1/2 PIASTRE

Silver **Ruler:** Innocent XII **Subject:** Signing of the Peace of Ryswick **Obv:** Bust right **Rev:** Noah's Ark

Date	Mintage	VG	F	VF	XF	Unc
ND(1698)-VII	—	150	350	600	1,000	—

KM# 613 1/2 PIASTRE

Silver **Ruler:** Innocent XII **Obv:** Capped bust right **Rev:** St. John the Baptist preaching to crowd

Date	Mintage	VG	F	VF	XF	Unc
1699-IX	—	85.00	185	300	525	—

KM# 650 1/2 PIASTRE

Silver **Ruler:** Innocent XII **Rev:** Holy Door **Note:** Holy Year issue.

Date	Mintage	VG	F	VF	XF	Unc
MDCC (1700)-IX	—	100	200	350	600	—

KM# 178 PIASTRA (Scudo of 80 Bolognini)

Silver **Ruler:** Urban VIII **Obv:** Bust right, ANXI in legend **Rev:** St. Michael the Archangel fighting four demons **Note:** Dav. #4055. Pope's collar in floral or St. Peter design.

Date	Mintage	VG	F	VF	XF	Unc
ND(1633)-XI	—	250	450	800	1,400	—

KM# 181 PIASTRA (Scudo of 80 Bolognini)

Silver **Ruler:** Urban VIII **Obv:** Bust right, ANXII below **Note:** Dav. #4056. Pope's collar in floral or St. Peter design.

Date	Mintage	VG	F	VF	XF	Unc
ND(1634)-XII	—	250	450	800	1,400	—

KM# 184 PIASTRA (Scudo of 80 Bolognini)

Silver **Ruler:** Urban VIII **Rev:** Radiant Virgin Mary standing on crescent **Note:** Dav. #4057.

Date	Mintage	VG	F	VF	XF	Unc
ND(1634)-XII	—	275	525	875	1,500	—
ND(1643)-XX	—	275	525	875	1,500	—

KM# 182 PIASTRA (Scudo of 80 Bolognini)

Silver **Ruler:** Urban VIII **Rev:** St. Michael the Archangel fighting one demon, arms in exergue **Note:** Dav. #4058.

Date	Mintage	VG	F	VF	XF	Unc
ND(1634)-XII	—	250	450	800	1,450	—

KM# 183 PIASTRA (Scudo of 80 Bolognini)

Silver **Ruler:** Urban VIII **Rev:** Pope kneeling left before St. Michael the Archangel in clouds left **Note:** Dav. #4060.

Date	Mintage	VG	F	VF	XF	Unc
ND(1634)-XII	—	400	700	1,250	2,000	—
1643-XII GM	—	400	700	1,250	2,000	—

KM# 190 PIASTRA (Scudo of 80 Bolognini)

Silver **Ruler:** Urban VIII **Rev:** St. Michael the Archangel fighting one demon, mint mark (arms) in left field **Note:** Dav. #4059.

Date	Mintage	VG	F	VF	XF	Unc
ND(1637)-XV	—	250	450	800	1,450	—
1643-XX	—	250	450	800	1,450	—

KM# 205 PIASTRA (Scudo of 80 Bolognini)

Silver **Ruler:** Urban VIII **Rev:** Busts of SS. Peter and Paul, radiant dove above **Note:** Dav. #4061.

Date	Mintage	VG	F	VF	XF	Unc
1643-XXI GM	—	275	500	850	1,750	—

KM# 241 PIASTRA (Scudo of 80 Bolognini)

Silver **Ruler:** Urban VIII **Obv:** Bust of Innocent X right **Rev:** Jesus standing, blessing St. Peter kneeling right **Note:** Dav. #4064. Varieties exist in ornamentation of collar.

Date	Mintage	VG	F	VF	XF	Unc
ND(1645)-II	—	450	750	1,350	2,500	—
ND(1646)-III	—	450	750	1,350	2,500	—
ND(1647)-IV	—	450	750	1,350	2,500	—

KM# 254 PIASTRA (Scudo of 80 Bolognini)

Silver **Ruler:** Urban VIII **Obv:** Bust wearing tiara right **Rev:** Holy Door with Veronica's veil **Note:** Dav. #4065. Holy Year issue.

Date	Mintage	VG	F	VF	XF	Unc
MDCL (1650)-VII	—	750	1,350	2,250	4,250	—

KM# 279 PIASTRA (Scudo of 80 Bolognini)

Silver **Ruler:** Urban VIII **Rev:** Jesus standing, blessing St. Peter kneeling right **Note:** Dav. #4066.

Date	Mintage	VG	F	VF	XF	Unc
ND(1653)-IX	—	500	900	1,500	2,700	—
ND(1654)-X	—	500	900	1,500	2,700	—

KM# 280 PIASTRA (Scudo of 80 Bolognini)
Silver **Obv:** Arms of Cardinal Antonio Barberini **Rev:** Radiant dove **Note:** Dav. #4069. Sede Vacante issue.

Date	Mintage	VG	F	VF	XF	Unc
MDCLV (1655)	—	175	350	675	1,150	—

KM# 290 PIASTRA (Scudo of 80 Bolognini)
Silver **Ruler:** Alexander VII **Obv:** Arms, St. Peter reclining above **Rev:** St. Thomas of Villanova giving alms to beggar **Note:** Dav. #4070.

Date	Mintage	VG	F	VF	XF	Unc
ND(1658)	—	225	400	850	1,500	—

KM# 310 PIASTRA (Scudo of 80 Bolognini)
Silver **Obv:** Arms of Cardinal Antonio Barberini **Rev:** Radiant dove **Note:** Dav. #4071. Sede Vacante issue.

Date	Mintage	VG	F	VF	XF	Unc
MDCLXVII (1667)	—	125	250	500	100	1,750

KM# 311 PIASTRA (Scudo of 80 Bolognini)
Silver **Ruler:** Clement IX **Obv:** Arms **Rev:** Chair of St. Peter between four seraphim **Note:** Dav. #4072.

Date	Mintage	VG	F	VF	XF	Unc
ND(1667-69)	—	175	350	600	1,000	—

KM# 319 PIASTRA (Scudo of 80 Bolognini)
Silver **Ruler:** Clement X **Obv:** Arms of Cardinal Antonio Barberini **Rev:** Radiant dove **Note:** Dav. #4073. Sede Vacante issue.

Date	Mintage	VG	F	VF	XF	Unc
MDCLXIX (1669)	—	120	225	425	800	—

KM# 351 PIASTRA (Scudo of 80 Bolognini)
Silver **Obv:** Capped bust of Clement X right **Rev:** Clemency and Abundance standing **Note:** Dav. #4074.

Date	Mintage	VG	F	VF	XF	Unc
MDCLXXI (1671)-II	—	350	550	900	1,500	—
MDCLXXII (1672)-II	—	350	550	900	1,500	—

KM# 353 PIASTRA (Scudo of 80 Bolognini)
Silver **Obv:** Arms **Rev:** Port of Civitavecchia **Note:** Dav. #4075.

Date	Mintage	VG	F	VF	XF	Unc
MDCLXXII (1672)	—	350	600	950	1,600	—

KM# 355 PIASTRA (Scudo of 80 Bolognini)
Silver **Subject:** Beautification of Pius V **Obv:** Capped bust right **Rev:** St. Pius kneeling right by altar, angel holding Battle of Lepanto shround **Note:** Dav. #4076.

Date	Mintage	VG	F	VF	XF	Unc
MDCLXXIII (1673)-IIII	—	200	375	700	1,250	—

KM# 367 PIASTRA (Scudo of 80 Bolognini)
Silver **Rev:** Portico of St. Peter with pilgrims **Note:** Dav. #4077.

Date	Mintage	VG	F	VF	XF	Unc
MDCLXXV (1675-IV)	—	120	225	425	700	—

KM# 368 PIASTRA (Scudo of 80 Bolognini)
Silver **Obv:** Arms **Note:** Dav. #4078.

Date	Mintage	VG	F	VF	XF	Unc
MDCLXXV (1675)	—	120	225	425	700	—

KM# 369 PIASTRA (Scudo of 80 Bolognini)
Silver **Obv:** Capped bust right **Rev:** Holy Door closed **Rev. Legend:** CIAVSIS FORBVS... **Note:** Dav. #4079.

Date	Mintage	VG	F	VF	XF	Unc
MDCLXXV (1675)	—	150	300	600	1,250	—

KM# 371 PIASTRA (Scudo of 80 Bolognini)
Silver **Rev:** Holy Door closed **Rev. Legend:** DABIT FRVCTVM... **Note:** Dav. #4081. Holy Year issue.

Date	Mintage	VG	F	VF	XF	Unc
MDCLXXV (1675)	—	100	225	500	950	—

KM# 370 PIASTRA (Scudo of 80 Bolognini)
Silver **Obv:** Arms **Note:** Holy Year issue. Dav.#4080.

Date	Mintage	VG	F	VF	XF	Unc
MDCLXXV (1675)	—	100	225	500	950	—

KM# 391 PIASTRA (Scudo of 80 Bolognini)
Silver **Obv:** Arms of Cardinal Paluzzo Paluzzi-Altieri **Rev:** Radiant dove **Note:** Sede Vacante issue. Dav.#4084.

Date	Mintage	VG	F	VF	XF	Unc
MDCLXXVI (1676)	—	125	275	550	1,000	—

KM# 392 PIASTRA (Scudo of 80 Bolognini)
Silver **Ruler:** Innocent XI **Obv:** Capped bust right **Rev:** St. Mathew standing on chair, angel left **Note:** Dav. #4085.

Date	Mintage	VG	F	VF	XF	Unc
ND(1676)-I	—	120	225	450	800	—

KM# 393 PIASTRA (Scudo of 80 Bolognini)
Silver **Ruler:** Innocent XI **Rev:** St. Matthew standing on cloud, angel left **Note:** Dav. #4086.

Date	Mintage	VG	F	VF	XF	Unc
ND(1676)-I	—	125	250	475	850	—

KM# 408 PIASTRA (Scudo of 80 Bolognini)
Silver **Ruler:** Innocent XI **Rev:** Inscription within palm wreath **Note:** Dav. #4095.

Date	Mintage	VG	F	VF	XF	Unc
ND(1676-89)	—	85.00	175	325	600	—

KM# 407 PIASTRA (Scudo of 80 Bolognini)
Silver **Ruler:** Innocent XI **Obv:** Arms **Rev:** Inscription in wreath **Rev. Inscription:** NON / TRODERVNT / IN DIE / VLTIONIS **Note:** Dav. #4096.

Date	Mintage	VG	F	VF	XF	Unc
ND(1676-89)	—	120	225	375	775	—

KM# 398 PIASTRA (Scudo of 80 Bolognini)
Silver **Ruler:** Innocent XI **Obv:** Capped bust right **Rev:** Façade of St. Peter's Basilica **Note:** Dav. #4087.

Date	Mintage	VG	F	VF	XF	Unc
ND(1677)-II	—	250	450	800	1,350	—

KM# 399 PIASTRA (Scudo of 80 Bolognini)
Silver **Ruler:** Innocent XI **Obv:** Arms **Rev:** Façade of St. Peter's **Note:** Dav. #4088.

Date	Mintage	VG	F	VF	XF	Unc
ND(1677)-II	—	250	450	825	1,400	—

KM# 403 PIASTRA (Scudo of 80 Bolognini)
Silver **Ruler:** Innocent XI **Obv:** Capped bust right **Rev:** Christ on boat with apostles, calming the storm **Note:** Dav. #4089.

Date	Mintage	VG	F	VF	XF	Unc
ND(1678)-III	—	265	475	850	1,450	—

KM# 421.1 PIASTRA (Scudo of 80 Bolognini)
Silver **Ruler:** Innocent XI **Obv:** Pointed arms **Rev:** St. Peter enthroned **Note:** Dav. #4090.

Date	Mintage	VG	F	VF	XF	Unc
1680	—	125	240	450	800	—
1681	—	125	240	450	800	—

KM# 421.2 PIASTRA (Scudo of 80 Bolognini)
Silver **Ruler:** Innocent XI **Obv:** Curved arms

Date	Mintage	VG	F	VF	XF	Unc
1680	—	125	240	450	800	—
1681	—	125	240	450	800	—

KM# 426 PIASTRA (Scudo of 80 Bolognini)
Silver **Ruler:** Innocent XI **Rev:** Inscription in cartouche with seraph at top **Rev. Inscription:** NON / PRODERVNT / IN DIE / VLTIONIS **Note:** Dav. #4091.

Date	Mintage	VG	F	VF	XF	Unc
ND(1682)-VII	—	120	240	425	700	—

KM# 427 PIASTRA (Scudo of 80 Bolognini)
Silver **Ruler:** Innocent XI **Rev:** Without seraph at top **Note:** Dav. #4092.

Date	Mintage	VG	F	VF	XF	Unc
ND(1682)-VII	—	120	240	425	700	—

KM# 452.1 PIASTRA (Scudo of 80 Bolognini)
Silver **Ruler:** Innocent XI **Rev:** Inscription and date in palm wreath **Note:** Dav. #4094.

Date	Mintage	VG	F	VF	XF	Unc
1684-IX	—	110	220	385	625	1,150

KM# 451.1 PIASTRA (Scudo of 80 Bolognini)
Silver **Ruler:** Innocent XI **Obv:** Capped bust right **Rev:** Inscription in palm sprays, date below **Rev. Inscription:** DEXTERA / TVA DOMINE / PERCVSSIT / INIMICVM **Note:** Dav. #4093.

Date	Mintage	VG	F	VF	XF	Unc
1684-VIII	—	110	220	385	625	1,150

KM# 451.2 PIASTRA (Scudo of 80 Bolognini)
Silver **Ruler:** Innocent XI **Rev:** Date in palm sprays **Note:** Dav. #4093A.

Date	Mintage	VG	F	VF	XF	Unc
1684-VIII	—	110	220	385	625	1,150

KM# 451.3 PIASTRA (Scudo of 80 Bolognini)
Silver **Ruler:** Innocent XI **Rev:** Without date **Note:** Dav. #4093B.

Date	Mintage	VG	F	VF	XF	Unc
ND(1684)-VIII	—	110	220	385	625	1,150

KM# 451.4 PIASTRA (Scudo of 80 Bolognini)
Silver **Ruler:** Innocent XI **Rev:** Inscription in palm wreath **Note:** Dav. #4093C.

Date	Mintage	VG	F	VF	XF	Unc
1684-VIII	—	110	220	385	625	1,150
1684-IX	—	110	220	385	625	1,150

KM# 452.2 PIASTRA (Scudo of 80 Bolognini)
Silver **Ruler:** Innocent XI **Rev:** Date below palm wreath **Note:** Dav. #4094A.

Date	Mintage	VG	F	VF	XF	Unc
1684-IX	—	110	220	385	625	1,150

KM# 497 PIASTRA (Scudo of 80 Bolognini)
Silver **Obv:** Arms of Cardinal Paluzzo Paluzzi-Altieri **Rev:** Radiant dove **Note:** Dav. #4098. Sede Vacante issue.

Date	Mintage	VG	F	VF	XF	Unc
MDCLXXXIX (1689)	—	125	200	450	750	—

KM# 498.1 PIASTRA (Scudo of 80 Bolognini)
Silver **Ruler:** Alexander VIII **Rev:** SS. Peter and Paul standing, radiant dove above **Note:** Dav. #4099.

Date	Mintage	VG	F	VF	XF	Unc
ND(1689)-I	—	750	1,500	3,000	5,000	—

KM# 498.2 PIASTRA (Scudo of 80 Bolognini)
Silver **Ruler:** Alexander VIII **Rev. Legend:** S. PAVLVS. **Note:** Dav. #4099A.

Date	Mintage	VG	F	VF	XF	Unc
ND(1689)-I	—	—	—	—	—	—

KM# 528 PIASTRA (Scudo of 80 Bolognini)
Silver **Ruler:** Alexander VIII **Obv:** Capped bust right **Rev:** Church standing left, holding church and standard **Note:** Dav. #4100.

Date	Mintage	VG	F	VF	XF	Unc
MDCXC (1690)-I	—	300	575	950	1,550	—
MDCXCI (1691)-II	—	300	575	950	1,550	—

KM# 557 PIASTRA (Scudo of 80 Bolognini)
Silver **Ruler:** Innocent XII **Obv:** Capped bust right **Rev:** St. Michael defeating Lucifer **Note:** Dav. #4102.

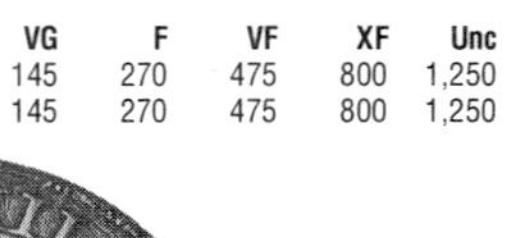

Date	Mintage	VG	F	VF	XF	Unc
1692-II	—	145	270	475	800	1,250
1693-II	—	145	270	475	800	1,250

KM# 558 PIASTRA (Scudo of 80 Bolognini)

Silver **Ruler:** Innocent XII **Rev:** Radiant throne of St. Peter, supported by angels **Note:** Dav. #4101.

Date	Mintage	VG	F	VF	XF	Unc
ND(1692)-II	—	400	700	1,250	2,000	—

KM# 569 PIASTRA (Scudo of 80 Bolognini)

Silver **Ruler:** Innocent XII **Rev:** Charity seated right, nursing infant **Note:** Dav. #4103.

Date	Mintage	VG	F	VF	XF	Unc
1693-III	—	225	425	600	1,250	—

KM# 576 PIASTRA (Scudo of 80 Bolognini)

Silver **Ruler:** Innocent XII **Rev:** Woman seated left, leaning on altar **Note:** Dav. #4104.

Date	Mintage	VG	F	VF	XF	Unc
1694-IIII	—	225	425	600	1,250	—

KM# 598 PIASTRA (Scudo of 80 Bolognini)

Silver **Ruler:** Innocent XII **Rev:** Enthroned Pope facing Consistory **Rev. Legend:** LOQVETVR PAC... **Note:** Dav. #4106.

Date	Mintage	VG	F	VF	XF	Unc
1696-V	—	225	425	600	1,250	2,500
1696-VI	—	225	425	600	1,250	2,500

KM# 599 PIASTRA (Scudo of 80 Bolognini)

Silver **Ruler:** Innocent XII **Rev:** Enthroned Pope right in Consistory **Rev. Legend:** PACEM LOQVETUR... **Note:** Dav. #4105.

Date	Mintage	VG	F	VF	XF	Unc
ND(1696)-V	—	225	425	675	1,350	—
ND(1696)-VI	—	225	425	675	1,350	—

KM# 608 PIASTRA (Scudo of 80 Bolognini)

Silver **Ruler:** Innocent XII **Subject:** First Anniversary - Peace of Ryswick **Rev:** St. Peter blessing reclining crowd **Note:** Dav. #4107.

Date	Mintage	VG	F	VF	XF	Unc
1698-VIII	—	265	475	700	1,400	—

KM# 614 PIASTRA (Scudo of 80 Bolognini)

Silver **Ruler:** Innocent XII **Subject:** Reduction of Tax on Wheat Flour **Rev:** Israelites gathering manna **Note:** Dav. #4108.

Date	Mintage	VG	F	VF	XF	Unc
MDCIC (1699)-VIII	—	225	425	725	1,600	—

KM# 615 PIASTRA (Scudo of 80 Bolognini)

Silver **Ruler:** Innocent XII **Subject:** Restoration of the Port of Anzio **Rev:** Port of Anzio **Note:** Dav. #4109.

Date	Mintage	VG	F	VF	XF	Unc
MDCXCIX (1699)-VIII	—	550	950	1,750	3,400	—

KM# 649 PIASTRA (Scudo of 80 Bolognini)

Silver **Ruler:** Innocent XII **Rev:** Holy Door flanked by standing angels **Note:** Dav. #4110. Holy Year issue.

Date	Mintage	VG	F	VF	XF	Unc
MDCC (1700)-IX	—	265	475	700	1,400	—

KM# 651 PIASTRA (Scudo of 80 Bolognini)

Silver **Obv:** Arms of Cardinal Giovanni Spinola, pointed bottom shield **Rev:** Radiant dove **Note:** Dav. #4112. Sede Vacante issue.

Date	Mintage	VG	F	VF	XF	Unc
MDCC (1700)	—	260	450	750	1,150	—

KM# 652 PIASTRA (Scudo of 80 Bolognini)
Silver **Obv:** Arms of Cardinal Giovanni Spinola, rounded bottom shield **Note:** Dav. #4113. Sede Vacante issue.

Date	Mintage	VG	F	VF	XF	Unc
MDCC (1700)	—	260	450	750	1,150	—

KM# 653 PIASTRA (Scudo of 80 Bolognini)
Silver **Ruler:** Clement XI **Rev:** Holy Door **Note:** Holy Year issue. Dav.#1428.

Date	Mintage	VG	F	VF	XF	Unc
MDCC (1700)-I	—	300	550	900	1,500	—

KM# 577 1/2 SCUDO D'ORO
Silver **Ruler:** Innocent XII **Obv:** Papal arms **Rev:** Bust of St. Peter left

Date	Mintage	VG	F	VF	XF	Unc
ND(1694)-III	—	725	1,400	3,000	4,500	—

KM# 578 1/2 SCUDO D'ORO
Silver **Ruler:** Innocent XII **Rev:** Holy Door

Date	Mintage	VG	F	VF	XF	Unc
ND(1694)-III	—	725	1,400	3,000	4,500	—

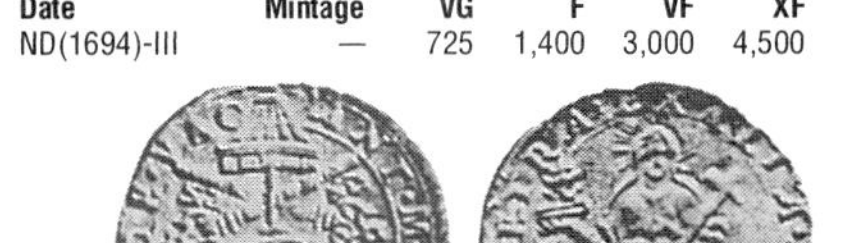

KM# 34 SCUDO D'ORO
3.5000 g., 0.9860 Gold 0.1109 oz. AGW **Obv:** Arms of Cardinal Pietro Aldobrandini **Note:** Sede Vacante issue.

Date	Mintage	VG	F	VF	XF	Unc
MDCV (1605) Rare	—	—	—	—	—	—

KM# 42 SCUDO D'ORO
3.5000 g., 0.9860 Gold 0.1109 oz. AGW, 23 mm. **Ruler:** Paul V **Obv:** Papal arms of Paul V **Rev:** St. Paul seated left

Date	Mintage	VG	F	VF	XF	Unc
ND(1606)-II	—	375	875	1,750	3,000	—

KM# 43 SCUDO D'ORO
3.5000 g., 0.9860 Gold 0.1109 oz. AGW **Ruler:** Paul V **Rev:** Year in exergue

Date	Mintage	VG	F	VF	XF	Unc
ND(1606)-III	—	385	880	1,750	3,000	—

KM# 48 SCUDO D'ORO
3.5000 g., 0.9860 Gold 0.1109 oz. AGW, 19 mm. **Ruler:** Paul V **Rev:** St. Paul bust right

Date	Mintage	VG	F	VF	XF	Unc
ND(1607)-III	—	300	575	1,150	2,100	—
ND(1612)-VIII	—	300	575	1,150	2,100	—
ND(1615)-XI	—	300	575	1,150	2,100	—
ND(1616)-XII	—	300	575	1,150	2,100	—

KM# 53 SCUDO D'ORO
3.5000 g., 0.9860 Gold 0.1109 oz. AGW **Ruler:** Paul V **Rev:** Conjoined busts of SS. Peter and Paul left

Date	Mintage	VG	F	VF	XF	Unc
ND(1608)-IV	—	450	875	2,100	3,300	—

KM# 80 SCUDO D'ORO
3.5000 g., 0.9860 Gold 0.1109 oz. AGW **Ruler:** Paul V **Obv:** Bust right **Rev:** St. Paul standing

Date	Mintage	VG	F	VF	XF	Unc
ND(1617)-XIII	—	600	1,250	2,700	4,200	—

KM# 103 SCUDO D'ORO
3.5000 g., 0.9860 Gold 0.1109 oz. AGW **Ruler:** Gregory XV **Rev:** Santa Maria Maggiore church façade

Date	Mintage	VG	F	VF	XF	Unc
ND(1622)-II	—	550	1,100	2,400	3,900	—

KM# 104 SCUDO D'ORO
3.5000 g., 0.9860 Gold 0.1109 oz. AGW **Ruler:** Paul V **Rev:** Radiant Madonna standing

Date	Mintage	VG	F	VF	XF	Unc
ND(1622)-II	—	550	1,100	2,400	3,900	—

KM# 105 SCUDO D'ORO
3.5000 g., 0.9860 Gold 0.1109 oz. AGW **Ruler:** Paul V **Obv:** Papal arms **Rev:** Facing busts of SS. Peter and Paul

Date	Mintage	VG	F	VF	XF	Unc
ND Rare	—	—	—	—	—	—

KM# 148 SCUDO D'ORO
3.5000 g., 0.9860 Gold 0.1109 oz. AGW **Ruler:** Urban VIII **Obv:** Bust right **Rev:** Holy Door divides date **Note:** Holy Year issue.

Date	Mintage	VG	F	VF	XF	Unc
1625	—	325	725	1,500	2,400	—

KM# 149 SCUDO D'ORO
3.5000 g., 0.9860 Gold 0.1109 oz. AGW **Ruler:** Urban VIII **Rev:** Holy Door, date in exergue **Note:** Holy Year issue.

Date	Mintage	VG	F	VF	XF	Unc
1625-II Rare	—	—	—	—	—	—

KM# A149 SCUDO D'ORO
3.5000 g., 0.9860 Gold 0.1109 oz. AGW **Ruler:** Urban VIII **Obv:** Papal arms **Rev:** Holy Door with Veronica's veil, date flanking, ROMA in exergue **Note:** Holy Year issue.

Date	Mintage	VG	F	VF	XF	Unc
1625 Rare	—	—	—	—	—	—

KM# 154 SCUDO D'ORO
3.5000 g., 0.9860 Gold 0.1109 oz. AGW **Ruler:** Urban VIII **Rev:** Madonna standing

Date	Mintage	VG	F	VF	XF	Unc
ND(1627)-IIII	—	725	1,300	2,700	3,900	—
ND(1636)-XIII	—	725	1,300	2,700	3,900	—
ND(1638)-XV	—	725	1,300	2,700	3,900	—
ND	—	725	1,300	2,700	3,900	—

KM# 153 SCUDO D'ORO
3.5000 g., 0.9860 Gold 0.1109 oz. AGW **Ruler:** Urban VIII **Obv:** Papal arms **Rev:** Bust of St. Paul right

Date	Mintage	VG	F	VF	XF	Unc
ND(1627)-IIII	—	550	1,100	2,400	3,900	—

KM# 159 SCUDO D'ORO
3.5000 g., 0.9860 Gold 0.1109 oz. AGW **Ruler:** Urban VIII **Rev:** St. Michael slaying the devil

Date	Mintage	VG	F	VF	XF	Unc
ND(1629)-VI	—	500	1,000	2,150	3,400	—

KM# 171 SCUDO D'ORO
3.5000 g., 0.9860 Gold 0.1109 oz. AGW **Ruler:** Urban VIII **Rev:** Bust of Christ

Date	Mintage	VG	F	VF	XF	Unc
ND(1630)-VII	—	550	1,100	2,400	3,900	—

KM# 202 SCUDO D'ORO
3.5000 g., 0.9860 Gold 0.1109 oz. AGW **Ruler:** Urban VIII **Obv:** Papal arms **Rev:** Radiant Madonna standing

Date	Mintage	VG	F	VF	XF	Unc
1642-XX	—	725	1,300	2,700	3,900	—
1643-XXI	—	725	1,300	2,700	3,900	—
ND	—	725	1,300	2,700	3,900	—

KM# 203 SCUDO D'ORO
3.5000 g., 0.9860 Gold 0.1109 oz. AGW **Ruler:** Urban VIII **Rev:** St. Michael slaying the devil

Date	Mintage	VG	F	VF	XF	Unc
1642-XX	—	500	1,000	2,150	3,400	—
ND(1643)-XXI	—	500	1,000	2,150	3,400	—

KM# 243 SCUDO D'ORO
3.5000 g., 0.9860 Gold 0.1109 oz. AGW **Ruler:** Innocent X **Subject:** Immaculate Conception **Rev:** Radiant Madonna standing

Date	Mintage	VG	F	VF	XF	Unc
ND(1645)-II Unique	—	—	—	—	—	—

KM# 242 SCUDO D'ORO
3.5000 g., 0.9860 Gold 0.1109 oz. AGW, 20 mm. **Ruler:** Innocent X **Rev:** St. Peter holding keys

Date	Mintage	VG	F	VF	XF	Unc
1644-I	—	1,800	3,300	6,000	9,600	—

KM# 244 SCUDO D'ORO
3.5000 g., 0.9860 Gold 0.1109 oz. AGW **Ruler:** Innocent X **Rev:** Madonna standing in inner circle, date below

Date	Mintage	VG	F	VF	XF	Unc
ND(1645)-II	—	1,800	3,300	6,000	9,600	—
1652-VIII	—	1,800	3,300	6,000	9,600	—
ND(1653)-VIIII	—	1,800	3,300	6,000	9,600	—

KM# 248 SCUDO D'ORO
3.5000 g., 0.9860 Gold 0.1109 oz. AGW **Ruler:** Innocent X **Rev:** Without date

Date	Mintage	VG	F	VF	XF	Unc
ND(1653)-IX	—	1,800	3,300	6,000	9,600	—

KM# 261 SCUDO D'ORO
3.5000 g., 0.9860 Gold 0.1109 oz. AGW **Ruler:** Alexander VII **Rev:** Inscription in cartouche **Rev. Inscription:** DEVS / DAT OMNI / BVS...NON IMPRO / PERAT

Date	Mintage	VG	F	VF	XF	Unc
ND	—	725	2,200	4,200	7,200	—

KM# 262 SCUDO D'ORO
3.5000 g., 0.9860 Gold 0.1109 oz. AGW **Ruler:** Alexander VII **Rev:** Simple Papal arms

Date	Mintage	VG	F	VF	XF	Unc
ND	—	725	2,200	4,200	7,200	—

KM# 263 SCUDO D'ORO
3.5000 g., 0.9860 Gold 0.1109 oz. AGW, 19 mm. **Ruler:** Alexander VII

Date	Mintage	VG	F	VF	XF	Unc
ND	—	875	2,750	4,800	7,800	—

KM# 312 SCUDO D'ORO
3.5000 g., 0.9860 Gold 0.1109 oz. AGW **Obv:** Arms of Cardinal Antonio Barberini **Note:** Sede Vacante issue.

Date	Mintage	VG	F	VF	XF	Unc
MDCLXVII (1667)	—	1,800	3,300	6,000	9,600	—

KM# 313 SCUDO D'ORO
3.5000 g., 0.9860 Gold 0.1109 oz. AGW **Ruler:** Clement IX **Obv:** Papal arms **Rev:** Madonna standing in inner circle

Date	Mintage	VG	F	VF	XF	Unc
ND	—	600	2,000	3,600	6,000	—

KM# 320 SCUDO D'ORO
3.5000 g., 0.9860 Gold 0.1109 oz. AGW **Obv:** Arms of Cardinal Antonio Barberini **Rev:** Radiant and flaming dove **Note:** Sede Vacante issue.

Date	Mintage	VG	F	VF	XF	Unc
MDCLXIX (1669)	—	875	2,750	4,800	7,800	—

KM# 321 SCUDO D'ORO
3.5000 g., 0.9860 Gold 0.1109 oz. AGW **Ruler:** Clement IX **Obv:** Papal arms **Rev:** St. Peter standing facing

Date	Mintage	VG	F	VF	XF	Unc
ND	—	550	1,100	2,400	3,900	—

KM# 322 SCUDO D'ORO
3.5000 g., 0.9860 Gold 0.1109 oz. AGW, 21 mm. **Ruler:** Clement X **Rev:** Madonna and child on clouds

Date	Mintage	VG	F	VF	XF	Unc
ND Rare	—	—	—	—	—	—

KM# 372 SCUDO D'ORO
3.5000 g., 0.9860 Gold 0.1109 oz. AGW **Ruler:** Clement X **Rev:** Closed Holy Door **Note:** Holy Year issue.

Date	Mintage	VG	F	VF	XF	Unc
1675	—	500	1,000	2,150	3,400	—

KM# 373 SCUDO D'ORO
3.5000 g., 0.9860 Gold 0.1109 oz. AGW **Ruler:** Clement X **Rev:** Open Holy Door **Note:** Holy Year issue.

Date	Mintage	VG	F	VF	XF	Unc
1675	—	500	1,000	2,150	3,400	—

KM# 374 SCUDO D'ORO
3.5000 g., 0.9860 Gold 0.1109 oz. AGW **Ruler:** Innocent XI **Rev:** Head of St. Peter right

Date	Mintage	VG	F	VF	XF	Unc
ND	—	550	1,100	2,400	3,900	—

KM# 375 SCUDO D'ORO
3.5000 g., 0.9860 Gold 0.1109 oz. AGW **Ruler:** Innocent XI **Subject:** Immaculate Conception **Rev:** Radiant Madonna standing

Date	Mintage	VG	F	VF	XF	Unc
ND	—	550	1,100	2,400	3,900	—

KM# 376 SCUDO D'ORO
3.5000 g., 0.9860 Gold 0.1109 oz. AGW **Ruler:** Innocent XI **Rev:** Madonna and child in clouds

Date	Mintage	VG	F	VF	XF	Unc
ND	—	550	1,100	2,400	3,900	—

KM# 377 SCUDO D'ORO
3.5000 g., 0.9860 Gold 0.1109 oz. AGW **Ruler:** Innocent XI **Rev:** Inscription in wreath **Rev. Inscription:** NEQVE / DIVITIAS

Date	Mintage	VG	F	VF	XF	Unc
ND	—	250	550	1,100	1,800	—

KM# 453 SCUDO D'ORO
3.5000 g., 0.9860 Gold 0.1109 oz. AGW **Ruler:** Innocent XI **Rev:** Date below inscription in cartouche **Rev. Inscription:** POSSIDE / SAPIENTIAM

Date	Mintage	VG	F	VF	XF	Unc
1684	—	220	550	1,100	1,800	—
1685 Unique	—	—	—	—	—	—

KM# 454 SCUDO D'ORO
3.5000 g., 0.9860 Gold 0.1109 oz. AGW **Ruler:** Innocent XI **Rev:** Inscription in wreath **Rev. Inscription:** POSSIDE / SAPIENTIAM

Date	Mintage	VG	F	VF	XF	Unc
ND	—	250	575	1,150	1,900	—

KM# 455 SCUDO D'ORO
3.5000 g., 0.9860 Gold 0.1109 oz. AGW **Ruler:** Innocent XI **Rev:** Inscription in cartouche, small shield at bottom **Rev. Inscription:** PRO / PRETIO / ANIMAE

Date	Mintage	VG	F	VF	XF	Unc
ND	—	220	550	1,100	1,800	—

KM# 456 SCUDO D'ORO
3.5000 g., 0.9860 Gold 0.1109 oz. AGW **Ruler:** Innocent XI **Rev:** Different small shield at bottom

Date	Mintage	VG	F	VF	XF	Unc
ND	—	220	550	1,100	1,800	—

KM# 499 SCUDO D'ORO
3.5000 g., 0.9860 Gold 0.1109 oz. AGW **Ruler:** Alexander VIII **Rev:** St. Peter standing facing, date in exergue

Date	Mintage	VG	F	VF	XF	Unc
1689-I	—	725	1,450	2,650	4,200	—

KM# 529 SCUDO D'ORO
3.5000 g., 0.9860 Gold 0.1109 oz. AGW **Ruler:** Alexander VIII **Rev:** Conjoined busts of SS. Peter and Paul right, date in exergue

Date	Mintage	VG	F	VF	XF	Unc
MDCXC (1690)-I	—	500	1,000	2,100	3,300	—

KM# A544 SCUDO D'ORO
3.5000 g., 0.9860 Gold 0.1109 oz. AGW **Ruler:** Innocent XII **Rev:** Head of St. Peter right

Date	Mintage	VG	F	VF	XF	Unc
ND(1691)-I	—	725	1,450	2,650	4,200	—

KM# 559 SCUDO D'ORO
3.5000 g., 0.9860 Gold 0.1109 oz. AGW **Ruler:** Innocent XII **Rev:** Head of St. Peter with halo right, date below

Date	Mintage	VG	F	VF	XF	Unc
1692-II	—	550	1,100	2,400	3,900	—

KM# 579 SCUDO D'ORO
3.5000 g., 0.9860 Gold 0.1109 oz. AGW **Ruler:** Innocent XII **Rev:** Sunflower on stalk with sun at upper left, date at lower right

Date	Mintage	VG	F	VF	XF	Unc
1694-III	—	1,250	2,400	4,800	8,100	—

KM# 602 SCUDO D'ORO
3.5000 g., 0.9860 Gold 0.1109 oz. AGW **Ruler:** Innocent XII **Rev:** Sheaf of grain, date in exergue

Date	Mintage	VG	F	VF	XF	Unc
1697-VII	—	550	1,100	2,400	3,900	—

KM# 654 SCUDO D'ORO
3.5000 g., 0.9860 Gold 0.1109 oz. AGW **Ruler:** Innocent XII **Rev:** Holy Door, date in exergue **Note:** Holy Year issue.

Date	Mintage	VG	F	VF	XF	Unc
MDCC (1700)	—	550	1,100	2,400	3,900	—

KM# 655 SCUDO D'ORO
3.5000 g., 0.9860 Gold 0.1109 oz. AGW **Obv:** Arms of Cardinal Giovanni Spinola, date in legend **Rev:** Radiant dove **Note:** Sede Vacante issue.

Date	Mintage	VG	F	VF	XF	Unc
1700	—	1,100	2,200	4,200	7,200	—

KM# 117 DOPPIA (2) SCUDO D'ORO
7.0000 g., 0.9860 Gold 0.2219 oz. AGW **Ruler:** Paul V **Rev:** St. Paul

Date	Mintage	VG	F	VF	XF	Unc
ND	—	875	1,750	3,900	6,600	—

KM# 118 DOPPIA (2) SCUDO D'ORO
7.0000 g., 0.9860 Gold 0.2219 oz. AGW **Ruler:** Paul V **Rev:** Radiant Madonna with wide rays in inner circle

Date	Mintage	VG	F	VF	XF	Unc
ND	—	1,800	3,600	7,200	11,000	—

KM# 119 DOPPIA (2) SCUDO D'ORO
7.0000 g., 0.9860 Gold 0.2219 oz. AGW **Ruler:** Paul V **Rev:** Short rays

Date	Mintage	VG	F	VF	XF	Unc
ND	—	1,800	3,600	7,200	11,000	—

KM# 120 DOPPIA (2) SCUDO D'ORO
7.0000 g., 0.9860 Gold 0.2219 oz. AGW **Ruler:** Paul V **Rev:** St. Paul standing

Date	Mintage	VG	F	VF	XF	Unc
ND Unique	—	—	—	—	—	—

KM# 121 DOPPIA (2) SCUDO D'ORO
7.0000 g., 0.9860 Gold 0.2219 oz. AGW **Obv:** Arms of Cardinal Ippolito Aldobrandini **Rev:** Christ standing with banner **Note:** Sede Vacante issue.

Date	Mintage	VG	F	VF	XF	Unc
1623 Rare	—	—	—	—	—	—

KM# 125 DOPPIA (2) SCUDO D'ORO
7.0000 g., 0.9860 Gold 0.2219 oz. AGW **Ruler:** Urban VIII **Rev:** Madonna standing

Date	Mintage	VG	F	VF	XF	Unc
ND(1624)-I	—	650	1,300	2,400	4,200	—

KM# 126 DOPPIA (2) SCUDO D'ORO
7.0000 g., 0.9860 Gold 0.2219 oz. AGW **Ruler:** Urban VIII **Obv:** Bust **Rev:** Facing busts of SS. Peter and Paul

Date	Mintage	VG	F	VF	XF	Unc
1624-I Rare	—	—	—	—	—	—

KM# 127 DOPPIA (2) SCUDO D'ORO
7.0000 g., 0.9860 Gold 0.2219 oz. AGW **Ruler:** Urban VIII **Obv:** Papal arms

Date	Mintage	VG	F	VF	XF	Unc
1624-I	—	2,200	4,400	8,400	12,000	—

KM# 256 DOPPIA (2) SCUDO D'ORO
7.0000 g., 0.9860 Gold 0.2219 oz. AGW **Ruler:** Innocent X **Rev:** Holy Door divides RO-MA, date in exergue

Date	Mintage	VG	F	VF	XF	Unc
MDCLI (1651)-VII Unique	—	—	—	—	—	—

KM# 257 DOPPIA (2) SCUDO D'ORO
7.0000 g., 0.9860 Gold 0.2219 oz. AGW **Ruler:** Innocent X
Rev: Holy Door divides date, ROMA in exergue

Date	Mintage	VG	F	VF	XF	Unc
1651-VII Rare	—	—	—	—	—	—

KM# 259 DOPPIA (2) SCUDO D'ORO
7.0000 g., 0.9860 Gold 0.2219 oz. AGW **Ruler:** Innocent X
Rev: Bust of St. Peter in inner circle, date below

Date	Mintage	VG	F	VF	XF	Unc
1652-VIII Rare	—	—	—	—	—	—

KM# 281 DOPPIA (2) SCUDO D'ORO
7.0000 g., 0.9860 Gold 0.2219 oz. AGW **Obv:** Arms of Cardinal Antonio Barberini, date in legend **Rev:** Radiant and flaming dove, ROMA in exergue **Note:** Sede Vacante issue.

Date	Mintage	VG	F	VF	XF	Unc
MDCLV (1655)	—	2,750	5,500	11,000	16,000	—

KM# 282 DOPPIA (2) SCUDO D'ORO
7.0000 g., 0.9860 Gold 0.2219 oz. AGW **Ruler:** Alexander VII
Obv: Quartered Papal arms **Rev. Inscription:** NON EX / TRISTITIA / AVT EX / NECESSITA / TE

Date	Mintage	VG	F	VF	XF	Unc
ND Rare	—	—	—	—	—	—

KM# 283 DOPPIA (2) SCUDO D'ORO
7.0000 g., 0.9860 Gold 0.2219 oz. AGW **Ruler:** Alexander VII
Obv: Simple Papal arms

Date	Mintage	VG	F	VF	XF	Unc
ND Rare	—	—	—	—	—	—

KM# 284 DOPPIA (2) SCUDO D'ORO
7.0000 g., 0.9860 Gold 0.2219 oz. AGW **Ruler:** Clement IX
Rev: Madonna standing

Date	Mintage	VG	F	VF	XF	Unc
ND	—	1,500	3,050	6,000	9,600	—

KM# 323 DOPPIA (2) SCUDO D'ORO
7.0000 g., 0.9860 Gold 0.2219 oz. AGW **Obv:** Arms of Cardinal Antonio Barberini **Note:** Sede Vacante issue.

Date	Mintage	VG	F	VF	XF	Unc
MDCLXIX (1669)	—	2,400	4,700	9,000	14,000	—

KM# 344 DOPPIA (2) SCUDO D'ORO
7.0000 g., 0.9860 Gold 0.2219 oz. AGW **Ruler:** Clement X
Obv: Bust right **Rev:** St. Peter standing being crowned by an angel, date in exergue

Date	Mintage	VG	F	VF	XF	Unc
MDCLXX (1670)-I Rare	—	—	—	—	—	—

KM# 345 DOPPIA (2) SCUDO D'ORO
7.0000 g., 0.9860 Gold 0.2219 oz. AGW **Ruler:** Clement X
Rev: St. Venantius standing holding banner

Date	Mintage	VG	F	VF	XF	Unc
ND	—	1,250	2,400	4,800	7,800	—

KM# 346 DOPPIA (2) SCUDO D'ORO
7.0000 g., 0.9860 Gold 0.2219 oz. AGW **Ruler:** Clement X
Rev: SS. Peter and Paul standing, RO-MA in exergue

Date	Mintage	VG	F	VF	XF	Unc
ND	—	1,250	2,400	4,800	7,800	—

KM# 400 DOPPIA (2) SCUDO D'ORO
7.0000 g., 0.9860 Gold 0.2219 oz. AGW **Ruler:** Innocent XI
Rev: Inscription in cartouche **Rev. Inscription:** MVLTOS / PERDIDIT / AVRVM

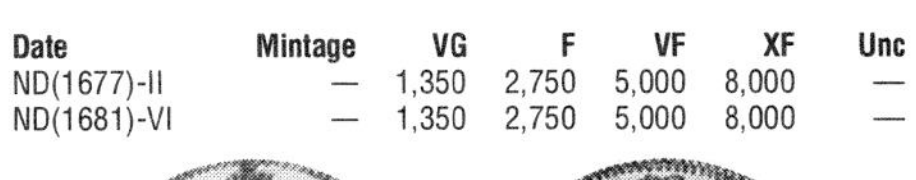

Date	Mintage	VG	F	VF	XF	Unc
ND(1677)-II	—	1,350	2,750	5,000	8,000	—
ND(1681)-VI	—	1,350	2,750	5,000	8,000	—

KM# 406 DOPPIA (2) SCUDO D'ORO
7.0000 g., 0.9860 Gold 0.2219 oz. AGW **Ruler:** Innocent XI
Rev: Inscription in cartouche **Rev. Inscription:** NIHIL AVARO / SCELESTIVS

Date	Mintage	VG	F	VF	XF	Unc
ND(1679)-IIII	—	1,500	3,050	6,000	9,600	—

KM# 422 DOPPIA (2) SCUDO D'ORO
7.0000 g., 0.9860 Gold 0.2219 oz. AGW **Ruler:** Innocent XI
Rev: Different cartouche for motto

Date	Mintage	VG	F	VF	XF	Unc
ND(1680)-V	—	1,500	3,050	6,000	9,600	—

KM# 457 DOPPIA (2) SCUDO D'ORO
7.0000 g., 0.9860 Gold 0.2219 oz. AGW **Ruler:** Innocent XI
Rev: Date in cartouche **Rev. Inscription:** QVI / CONFIDIT / IN.DIVITIIS / CORRVET

Date	Mintage	VG	F	VF	XF	Unc
1684-IX	—	1,500	3,050	6,000	9,600	—

KM# 458 DOPPIA (2) SCUDO D'ORO
7.0000 g., 0.9860 Gold 0.2219 oz. AGW **Ruler:** Innocent XI
Rev: Different cartouche for motto

Date	Mintage	VG	F	VF	XF	Unc
1684-XI	—	1,500	3,050	6,000	9,600	—

KM# 475 DOPPIA (2) SCUDO D'ORO
7.0000 g., 0.9860 Gold 0.2219 oz. AGW **Ruler:** Innocent XI
Rev: Different Papal arms

Date	Mintage	VG	F	VF	XF	Unc
1685-IX	—	1,500	3,050	6,000	9,600	—

KM# 500 DOPPIA (2) SCUDO D'ORO
7.0000 g., 0.9860 Gold 0.2219 oz. AGW **Ruler:** Innocent XI
Obv: Papal arms **Rev:** Date in cartouche **Rev. Inscription:** DIVES / IN / HUMILITATE

Date	Mintage	VG	F	VF	XF	Unc
1687-XII Rare	—	—	—	—	—	—

KM# 501 DOPPIA (2) SCUDO D'ORO
7.0000 g., 0.9860 Gold 0.2219 oz. AGW **Obv:** Arms of Cardinal Paluzzo Paluzzi-Altieri **Rev:** Radiant and flaming dove, RO-MA divided below **Note:** Sede Vacante issue.

Date	Mintage	VG	F	VF	XF	Unc
MDCLXXXIX (1689) Unique	—	—	—	—	—	—

KM# 502 DOPPIA (2) SCUDO D'ORO
7.0000 g., 0.9860 Gold 0.2219 oz. AGW **Ruler:** Alexander VIII
Obv: Papal arms **Rev:** St. Bruno in clouds, date divided at bottom

Date	Mintage	VG	F	VF	XF	Unc
1689-I	—	1,100	2,200	4,300	7,200	—
ND(1689)-I	—	1,100	2,200	4,300	7,200	—

KM# 530 DOPPIA (2) SCUDO D'ORO
7.0000 g., 0.9860 Gold 0.2219 oz. AGW **Ruler:** Alexander VIII
Rev: Altar with garlands, date in exergue

Date	Mintage	VG	F	VF	XF	Unc
MDCXC (1690)	—	1,250	2,400	4,800	7,800	—

KM# 545 DOPPIA (2) SCUDO D'ORO
7.0000 g., 0.9860 Gold 0.2219 oz. AGW **Obv:** Arms of Cardinal Paluzzi-Altieri **Rev:** Radiant dove, RO-MA divided below **Note:** Sede Vacante issue.

Date	Mintage	VG	F	VF	XF	Unc
MDCXCI (1691) Rare	—	—	—	—	—	—

KM# 562 DOPPIA (2) SCUDO D'ORO
7.0000 g., 0.9860 Gold 0.2219 oz. AGW **Ruler:** Innocent XII **Obv:** Papal arms **Rev:** St. Paul standing holding sword, date in exergue

Date	Mintage	VG	F	VF	XF	Unc
1692	—	1,500	3,050	6,000	9,600	—

KM# 603 DOPPIA (2) SCUDO D'ORO
7.0000 g., 0.9860 Gold 0.2219 oz. AGW **Ruler:** Innocent XII
Obv: Bust right **Rev:** Noah's ark with dove in flight with olive branch

Date	Mintage	VG	F	VF	XF	Unc
ND(1697)-VI	—	1,800	3,600	7,200	11,000	—

Note: Superior Pipito sale 12-87 about XF realized $10,120

KM# 616 DOPPIA (2) SCUDO D'ORO
7.0000 g., 0.9860 Gold 0.2219 oz. AGW **Ruler:** Innocent XII
Obv: Papal arms **Rev:** Holy Door, date in exergue

Date	Mintage	VG	F	VF	XF	Unc
1699-IX	—	1,800	3,600	7,200	11,000	—

KM# 656 DOPPIA (2) SCUDO D'ORO
7.0000 g., 0.9860 Gold 0.2219 oz. AGW **Ruler:** Clement XI
Obv: Bust right **Rev:** Closed Holy Door **Note:** Holy Year issue.

Date	Mintage	VG	F	VF	XF	Unc
ND(1700)-I	—	875	1,800	3,600	6,000	—

KM# 44 QUADRUPLA (4) SCUDO D'ORO
14.0000 g., 0.9860 Gold 0.4438 oz. AGW **Ruler:** Paul V
Obv: Bust left **Rev:** St. Paul reclining holding sword vertically

Date	Mintage	VG	F	VF	XF	Unc
ND(1606)-II	—	2,200	4,400	8,400	14,000	—

KM# 45 QUADRUPLA (4) SCUDO D'ORO
14.0000 g., 0.9860 Gold 0.4438 oz. AGW **Ruler:** Paul V
Obv: Bust left **Rev:** St. Paul seated holding sword at an angle

Date	Mintage	VG	F	VF	XF	Unc
ND(1606)-II	—	2,200	4,400	8,400	14,000	—

KM# 49 QUADRUPLA (4) SCUDO D'ORO
14.0000 g., 0.9860 Gold 0.4438 oz. AGW **Ruler:** Paul V
Obv: Bust left **Rev:** St. Paul seated holding sword at an angle

Date	Mintage	VG	F	VF	XF	Unc
ND(1607)-III	—	2,200	4,400	8,400	14,000	—

KM# 55 QUADRUPLA (4) SCUDO D'ORO
14.0000 g., 0.9860 Gold 0.4438 oz. AGW **Ruler:** Paul V **Obv:** Papal arms **Rev:** Bust of St. Paul left in inner circle, date in exergue

Date	Mintage	VG	F	VF	XF	Unc
MDCVIII (1608)-IV	—	1,250	2,500	5,400	9,000	—
MDCIX (1609)-IV	—	1,250	2,500	5,400	9,000	—
MDCIX (1609)-V	—	1,250	2,500	5,400	9,000	—

KM# 54 QUADRUPLA (4) SCUDO D'ORO
14.0000 g., 0.9860 Gold 0.4438 oz. AGW **Ruler:** Paul V
Rev: St. Paul standing in inner circle

Date	Mintage	VG	F	VF	XF	Unc
ND(1608)-III	—	2,200	4,400	8,400	14,000	—

KM# 67 QUADRUPLA (4) SCUDO D'ORO
14.0000 g., 0.9860 Gold 0.4438 oz. AGW **Ruler:** Paul V
Obv: Papal arms **Rev:** St. Paul seated right, date in exergue

Date	Mintage	VG	F	VF	XF	Unc
1611-VI	—	1,100	2,200	4,500	7,500	—

KM# 81 QUADRUPLA (4) SCUDO D'ORO
14.0000 g., 0.9860 Gold 0.4438 oz. AGW **Ruler:** Paul V **Obv:** Bust right **Rev:** St. Paul seated right, without date in exergue

Date	Mintage	VG	F	VF	XF	Unc
ND(1617)-XIII	—	1,100	2,200	4,500	7,500	—

KM# 82 QUADRUPLA (4) SCUDO D'ORO
14.0000 g., 0.9860 Gold 0.4438 oz. AGW **Ruler:** Paul V **Obv:** Bust of Paul V right in inner circle, ROMA below

Date	Mintage	VG	F	VF	XF	Unc
ND	—	1,100	2,200	4,500	7,500	—

KM# 83 QUADRUPLA (4) SCUDO D'ORO
14.0000 g., 0.9860 Gold 0.4438 oz. AGW **Ruler:** Gregory XV **Obv:** Papal arms **Rev:** Radiant Madonna standing **Note:** Varieties exist in shield shape.

Date	Mintage	VG	F	VF	XF	Unc
ND	—	2,500	4,950	9,600	15,000	—

KM# 122 QUADRUPLA (4) SCUDO D'ORO
14.0000 g., 0.9860 Gold 0.4438 oz. AGW **Obv:** Arms of Cardinal Ippolito Aldobrandini **Rev:** Christ standing holding banner **Note:** Sede Vacante issue.

Date	Mintage	VG	F	VF	XF	Unc
1623 Rare	—	—	—	—	—	—

KM# 185 QUADRUPLA (4) SCUDO D'ORO
14.0000 g., 0.9860 Gold 0.4438 oz. AGW **Ruler:** Urban VIII **Obv:** Bust right in inner circle **Rev:** St. Michael slaying the devil, date in exergue

Date	Mintage	VG	F	VF	XF	Unc
1634-XII	—	3,300	6,600	11,500	17,500	—

KM# 189 QUADRUPLA (4) SCUDO D'ORO
14.0000 g., 0.9860 Gold 0.4438 oz. AGW **Ruler:** Urban VIII **Obv:** Bust right **Rev:** Madonna standing, RO-MA in exergue

Date	Mintage	VG	F	VF	XF	Unc
1636-XIV	—	3,300	6,600	11,500	17,500	—

KM# 246 QUADRUPLA (4) SCUDO D'ORO
14.0000 g., 0.9860 Gold 0.4438 oz. AGW **Ruler:** Innocent X **Obv:** Bust right in inner circle, date below **Rev:** Papal arms

Date	Mintage	VG	F	VF	XF	Unc
1647-III Rare	—	—	—	—	—	—

KM# 285 QUADRUPLA (4) SCUDO D'ORO
14.0000 g., 0.9860 Gold 0.4438 oz. AGW **Obv:** Arms of Cardinal Antonio Barberini **Rev:** Radiant and flaming dove in inner circle, ROMA in exergue **Note:** Sede Vacante issue.

Date	Mintage	VG	F	VF	XF	Unc
MDCLV (1655) Rare	—	—	—	—	—	—

KM# 286 QUADRUPLA (4) SCUDO D'ORO
14.0000 g., 0.9860 Gold 0.4438 oz. AGW **Obv:** Arms of Cardinal Antonio Barberini **Rev:** Radiant and flaming dove in inner circle, Without ROMA in exergue **Note:** Roman numeral date. Sede Vacante issue.

Date	Mintage	VG	F	VF	XF	Unc
MDCLV (1655) Rare	—	—	—	—	—	—

Note: Superior Pipito sale 12-87 XF realized $34,100

KM# 287 QUADRUPLA (4) SCUDO D'ORO
14.0000 g., 0.9860 Gold 0.4438 oz. AGW **Ruler:** Alexander VII **Obv:** Papal arms **Rev:** Chest with bags of coins inside

Date	Mintage	VG	F	VF	XF	Unc
ND Rare	—	—	—	—	—	—

KM# 288 QUADRUPLA (4) SCUDO D'ORO
14.0000 g., 0.9860 Gold 0.4438 oz. AGW **Ruler:** Clement IX **Obv:** Papal arms **Rev:** Madonna standing in inner circle

Date	Mintage	VG	F	VF	XF	Unc
ND Rare	—	—	—	—	—	—

KM# 324 QUADRUPLA (4) SCUDO D'ORO
14.0000 g., 0.9860 Gold 0.4438 oz. AGW **Obv:** Arms of Cardinal Antonio Barberini **Rev:** Radiant and flaming dove in inner circle, ROMA in exergue **Note:** Sede Vacante issue.

Date	Mintage	VG	F	VF	XF	Unc
MDCLXIX (1669) Rare	—	—	—	—	—	—

KM# 347 QUADRUPLA (4) SCUDO D'ORO
14.0000 g., 0.9860 Gold 0.4438 oz. AGW **Ruler:** Clement X **Obv:** Papal arms

Date	Mintage	VG	F	VF	XF	Unc
ND(1670-76) Rare	—	—	—	—	—	—

KM# 356 QUADRUPLA (4) SCUDO D'ORO
14.0000 g., 0.9860 Gold 0.4438 oz. AGW **Ruler:** Clement X **Obv:** Bust right **Rev:** King David seated right, playing harp

Date	Mintage	VG	F	VF	XF	Unc
MDCLXXIII (1673)-IIII Rare	—	—	—	—	—	—

KM# 394 QUADRUPLA (4) SCUDO D'ORO
14.0000 g., 0.9860 Gold 0.4438 oz. AGW **Ruler:** Innocent XI **Rev:** Madonna seated with child on throne

Date	Mintage	VG	F	VF	XF	Unc
ND(1676)-I Rare	—	—	—	—	—	—

KM# 395 QUADRUPLA (4) SCUDO D'ORO
14.0000 g., 0.9860 Gold 0.4438 oz. AGW **Ruler:** Innocent XI **Obv:** Bust of Innocent XI right **Rev:** Enthroned Madonna and child with SS. Lawrence and Augustine at left and SS. Stephen and Francis of Asisis at right

Date	Mintage	VG	F	VF	XF	Unc
ND(1676)-I Rare	—	—	—	—	—	—
ND(1677)-II Rare	—	—	—	—	—	—

KM# 404 QUADRUPLA (4) SCUDO D'ORO
14.0000 g., 0.9860 Gold 0.4438 oz. AGW **Ruler:** Innocent XI **Subject:** Immaculate Conception **Rev:** Radiant Madonna on clouds above rainbow

Date	Mintage	VG	F	VF	XF	Unc
ND(1678)-III Rare	—	—	—	—	—	—

KM# 425 QUADRUPLA (4) SCUDO D'ORO
14.0000 g., 0.9860 Gold 0.4438 oz. AGW **Ruler:** Innocent XI **Rev:** Inscription in cartouche **Rev. Inscription:** VBI / THESAVRVS / IBI COR

Date	Mintage	VG	F	VF	XF	Unc
ND(1681)-VI Rare	—	—	—	—	—	—

KM# 428 QUADRUPLA (4) SCUDO D'ORO
14.0000 g., 0.9860 Gold 0.4438 oz. AGW **Ruler:** Innocent XI **Rev:** Inscription and date in wreath

Date	Mintage	VG	F	VF	XF	Unc
ND(1682)-VII Rare	—	—	—	—	—	—
1685-X Rare	—	—	—	—	—	—

Note: Superior Pipito sale 12-87 AU realized $17,050

KM# 479 QUADRUPLA (4) SCUDO D'ORO
14.0000 g., 0.9860 Gold 0.4438 oz. AGW **Ruler:** Innocent XI **Obv:** Papal arms **Rev:** Date in cartouche

Date	Mintage	VG	F	VF	XF	Unc
1687-XII Rare	—	—	—	—	—	—

KM# 504 QUADRUPLA (4) SCUDO D'ORO
14.0000 g., 0.9860 Gold 0.4438 oz. AGW **Ruler:** Alexander VIII **Obv:** Bust right **Rev:** SS. Peter and Paul standing below radiant dove, date in exergue

Date	Mintage	VG	F	VF	XF	Unc
1689-I	—	2,200	4,400	8,400	14,000	—

KM# 503 QUADRUPLA (4) SCUDO D'ORO
14.0000 g., 0.9860 Gold 0.4438 oz. AGW **Obv:** Arms of Cardinal Paluzzo Paluzzi-Altieri **Rev:** Radiant and flaming dove, RO-MA divided below **Note:** Sede Vacante issue.

Date	Mintage	VG	F	VF	XF	Unc
MDCLXXXIX (1689) Rare	—	—	—	—	—	—

KM# A531 QUADRUPLA (4) SCUDO D'ORO
14.0000 g., 0.9860 Gold 0.4438 oz. AGW **Ruler:** Alexander VIII **Rev:** SS. Magnus and Bruno standing facing, date in exergue

Date	Mintage	VG	F	VF	XF	Unc
1690-II	—	2,200	4,400	8,400	14,000	—

KM# A532 QUADRUPLA (4) SCUDO D'ORO
14.0000 g., 0.9860 Gold 0.4438 oz. AGW **Ruler:** Innocent XII **Rev:** Two oxen right

Date	Mintage	VG	F	VF	XF	Unc
MDCXC (1690)-I	—	1,550	3,100	6,000	10,000	—

KM# A533 QUADRUPLA (4) SCUDO D'ORO
14.0000 g., 0.9860 Gold 0.4438 oz. AGW **Ruler:** Alexander VIII **Rev:** St. Bruno in clouds

Date	Mintage	VG	F	VF	XF	Unc
ND(1690)-I Rare	—	—	—	—	—	—

KM# 580 QUADRUPLA (4) SCUDO D'ORO
14.0000 g., 0.9860 Gold 0.4438 oz. AGW **Ruler:** Alexander VIII **Subject:** Papal aid to Venice **Obv:** Bust right **Rev:** Church standing with building and standard

Date	Mintage	VG	F	VF	XF	Unc
(MD)CXC (1690)-I Rare	—	—	—	—	—	—

KM# 617 QUADRUPLA (4) SCUDO D'ORO
14.0000 g., 0.9860 Gold 0.4438 oz. AGW **Ruler:** Innocent XII **Obv:** Bust right **Rev:** Fountain of Sancta Maria in Trastevere, divided date in exergue

Date	Mintage	VG	F	VF	XF	Unc
1694-IIII	—	2,400	4,700	9,000	15,000	—

PATTERNS

Including off metal strikes

KM#	Date	Mintage	Identification	Mkt Val
Pn1	NDYr. III	—	Baiocco. Copper Around Silver. Arms. Veronica's veil.	—

PAPAL CITY STATES

The 21 Papal City States spanned the Papal states from one end to the other. Most of the cities had been the holy see for hundreds of years. Many of them housed religious architecture and relics that were a veritable history of the church. Many had strong local families that helped administrate the city and occasionally opposed the Papal authority. Most of these cities stayed in the Papal states until 1860 when Papal territories began to crumble due to the move for unification of all Italy.

MINTS

17 of the mints functioned only during the Napoleonic period.

1. Ancona
2. Ascoli
3. Bologna
4. Civitavecchia
5. Fano
6. Fermo
7. Ferrara
8. Foligno
9. Gubbio
10. Macerata
11. Matelica
12. Montaito
13. Pergola
14. Perugia
15. Ravenna
16. Ronciglione
17. San Severino
18. Spoleto
19. Terni
20. Tivoli
21. Viterbo

EXTRINSIC MINT
Avignon (Southern France)

PONTIFFS
Refer to Papal States.

MONETARY SYSTEM
6 Quattrini = 1 Bolognino or Baiocco
5 Baiocchi = 1 Grossi
2 Grossi = 1 Giuli = 1 Paoli
3 Giulio = 3 Paoli = 1 Testone
10 Giulio = 10 Paoli = 1 Scudo
3 Scudi = 1 Doppia

PAPAL STATES-AVIGNON

A commercial and manufacturing city located in southeastern France, near the confluence of the Rhone and Durance rivers. Leading industries are chemicals, leather products and soap. It is the sight of an ancient cathedral and papal palace.

Founded as Phocaean colony; later conquered by the Romans, Goths, Burgundians, Ostrogoths, and finally the Franks. Part of kingdom of Arles it became a republic in 1135-46. Later as part of Venaissin it was sold by Joanna I of Naples to Pope Clement VI 1348. It became the seat of the papacy from 1309-77 and of the Avignonese popes during Western Schism from 1378-1417; remaining in the possession of the popes until finally being annexed to France in 1791.

RULER
Papal, until 1791

CITY

STANDARD COINAGE

KM# 1 PATARD
Copper Or Billon **Subject:** Clement VIII **Obv:** Crossed keys **Rev:** Cross in quadrilobe **Rev. Legend:** S • PETRVS • ET • PAVLVS • AVEN:

Date	Mintage	Good	VG	F	VF	XF
1601	—	15.00	25.00	40.00	65.00	—
1602	—	15.00	25.00	40.00	65.00	—
1603	—	15.00	25.00	40.00	65.00	—
ND	—	15.00	25.00	40.00	65.00	—

KM# 21 PATARD
Copper Or Billon **Subject:** Paul V **Obv:** Crossed keys **Rev:** Cross in quadrilobe

Date	Mintage	Good	VG	F	VF	XF
1614	—	15.00	25.00	40.00	65.00	—
ND	—	15.00	25.00	40.00	65.00	—

KM# 30 PATARD
Copper Or Billon **Subject:** Gregory XV **Obv:** Crossed keys **Rev:** Cross in quadrilobe

Date	Mintage	Good	VG	F	VF	XF
1621	—	20.00	32.00	50.00	80.00	—
1622	—	20.00	32.00	50.00	80.00	—

KM# 41 PATARD
Copper Or Billon **Subject:** Urban VIII **Obv:** Crossed keys **Rev:** Cross in quadrilobe

Date	Mintage	Good	VG	F	VF	XF
ND	—	14.00	24.00	38.00	65.00	—

KM# 67 PATARD
Copper Or Billon **Subject:** Innocent X **Obv:** Crossed keys, fleur-de-lis above **Rev:** Cross in quadrilobe

Date	Mintage	Good	VG	F	VF	XF
ND	—	12.00	22.00	35.00	60.00	—

KM# 73 PATARD
Copper Or Billon **Obv:** Crossed keys without fleur-de-lis

Date	Mintage	Good	VG	F	VF	XF
ND Rare	—	—	—	—	—	—

KM# 86 PATARD
Copper Or Billon **Subject:** Alexander VII **Obv:** Crossed keys **Rev:** Cross in quadrilobe

Date	Mintage	Good	VG	F	VF	XF
ND	—	12.00	22.00	35.00	60.00	—

KM# 53 DOUBLE TOURNOIS
Copper **Obv:** Bust of Urban VIII right **Rev:** Three bees

Date	Mintage	Good	VG	F	VF	XF
1635	—	10.00	20.00	30.00	50.00	—
1636	—	10.00	20.00	30.00	50.00	—
1637	—	10.00	20.00	30.00	50.00	—
1638	—	10.00	20.00	30.00	50.00	—
1639	—	10.00	20.00	30.00	50.00	—
1640	—	10.00	20.00	30.00	50.00	—
ND	—	10.00	20.00	30.00	50.00	—

KM# 42 LIARD
Billon **Subject:** Urban VIII **Obv:** Tiara above V among three bees **Rev:** Maltese cross

Date	Mintage	Good	VG	F	VF	XF
ND	—	6.00	12.00	22.00	40.00	—

KM# 43 LIARD
Billon **Obv:** Tiara above M among three bees

Date	Mintage	Good	VG	F	VF	XF
ND	—	6.00	12.00	22.00	40.00	—

KM# 2 DOUZAIN
Billon **Subject:** Clement VIII **Obv:** Cross surmounted by tiara, A at sides **Rev:** Cross with eagles in angles

Date	Mintage	Good	VG	F	VF	XF
1601	—	27.50	45.00	75.00	125	—
1602	—	27.50	45.00	75.00	125	—
1603	—	27.50	45.00	75.00	125	—
ND	—	27.50	45.00	75.00	125	—

KM# 3 DOUZAIN
Billon **Note:** Similar to KM#2 but without A at sides.

Date	Mintage	Good	VG	F	VF	XF
1601 Rare	—	—	—	—	—	—
1602 Rare	—	—	—	—	—	—
1603 Rare	—	—	—	—	—	—
ND Rare	—	—	—	—	—	—

KM# 11 DOUZAIN
Billon **Subject:** Paul V **Obv:** Arms surmounted by tiara, A's flanking **Rev:** Cross, eagles, and dragons in angles **Rev. Legend:** SCIPIO BURGHESIVS CARD LEG AVEN

Date	Mintage	Good	VG	F	VF	XF
1609 Rare	—	—	—	—	—	—
1610 Rare	—	—	—	—	—	—
1611 Rare	—	—	—	—	—	—
1612 Rare	—	—	—	—	—	—
ND Rare	—	—	—	—	—	—

KM# 22 DOUZAIN
Billon **Obv:** Arms surmounted by tiara **Rev:** Cross, eagles, and oaks in angles **Rev. Legend:** PHI • S • R • E • CARD • PHILONARDVS • P • LEG • AVEN

Date	Mintage	Good	VG	F	VF	XF
1614 Rare	—	—	—	—	—	—

KM# 45 DOUZAIN
Billon **Subject:** Urban VIII **Obv:** Shield surmounted by tiara **Rev:** Floral cross, bee in angle **Rev. Legend:** FRANC • CARD...

Date	Mintage	Good	VG	F	VF	XF
1624 Rare	—	—	—	—	—	—
1625 Rare	—	—	—	—	—	—

KM# 51 DOUZAIN
Billon **Obv:** A'a flanking shield

Date	Mintage	Good	VG	F	VF	XF
1632 Rare	—	—	—	—	—	—
1633 Rare	—	—	—	—	—	—

KM# 54 DOUZAIN
Billon **Obv:** Shield surmounted by tiara **Rev:** Floral cross **Rev. Legend:** ANTONIV. S CAR...

Date	Mintage	Good	VG	F	VF	XF
1635 Rare	—	—	—	—	—	—

KM# 44 JULES (Barberino)
Silver **Subject:** Uban VIII **Obv:** Arms **Rev:** Half-length figure of St. Peter

Date	Mintage	Good	VG	F	VF	XF
1623	—	20.00	40.00	65.00	100	—
1624	—	20.00	40.00	65.00	100	—
1625	—	20.00	40.00	65.00	100	—
1626	—	20.00	40.00	65.00	100	—
1627	—	20.00	40.00	65.00	100	—
1628	—	20.00	40.00	65.00	100	—
1629	—	20.00	40.00	65.00	100	—
1630	—	20.00	40.00	65.00	100	—
1631	—	20.00	40.00	65.00	100	—
1632	—	20.00	40.00	65.00	100	—
1633	—	20.00	40.00	65.00	100	—
1634	—	20.00	40.00	65.00	100	—
1635	—	20.00	40.00	65.00	100	—
1636	—	20.00	40.00	65.00	100	—
1637	—	20.00	40.00	65.00	100	—

KM# 4 1/3 FRANC (1/8 Piastre)
Silver **Obv:** Bust of Clement VIII right **Rev:** Shield

Date	Mintage	Good	VG	F	VF	XF
1601 Unique	—	—	—	—	—	—

KM# 88 LUIGINO
Silver **Obv:** Bust of Alexander VII right **Rev:** Shield **Rev. Legend:** FLAVIVS CARD GHISIVS LEGATVS

Date	Mintage	VG	F	VF	XF	Unc
1658	—	105	210	500	800	—

KM# 91 LUIGINO
Silver **Obv:** Bust right with different shield on shoulder

Date	Mintage	VG	F	VF	XF	Unc
1659	—	105	210	500	800	—
1660	—	105	210	500	800	—

KM# 92 LUIGINO
Silver **Rev:** Crowned shield **Rev. Legend:** PAX • ORIETVR • EX • MONTIBVS

Date	Mintage	VG	F	VF	XF	Unc
1660	—	105	210	500	800	—
1661	—	105	210	500	800	—
1662	—	105	210	500	800	—
1663	—	105	210	500	800	—
1664	—	105	210	500	800	—
1665	—	105	210	500	800	—
1666	—	105	210	500	800	—

KM# 94 LUIGINO
Silver **Rev:** Shield as octalobe **Rev. Legend:** EXUMONTIBVS PAX ORIETVR

Date	Mintage	VG	F	VF	XF	Unc
1662	—	75.00	150	350	725	—
1663	—	75.00	150	350	725	—
1664	—	75.00	150	350	725	—
1665	—	75.00	150	350	725	—

KM# 96 LUIGINO
Silver **Obv:** Bust right with different shield on shoulder

Date	Mintage	VG	F	VF	XF	Unc
1666	—	85.00	170	350	550	—

KM# 99 LUIGINO

Silver **Obv:** Bust of Cardinal Chigi **Obv. Legend:** FLAVIVS • CAR • GHISIVS • LE • A • **Rev:** Crowned shield **Rev. Legend:** AB • STELLA • LVX • ORITVR •

Date	Mintage	VG	F	VF	XF	Unc
1666	—	85.00	170	350	550	—
1667	—	85.00	170	350	550	—

KM# 100 LUIGINO

Silver **Rev:** Crowned shield **Rev. Legend:** PAX • MONTIBVS • EX • MONTIBVS

Date	Mintage	VG	F	VF	XF	Unc
1666 Rare	—	—	—	—	—	—

KM# 14 1/4 FRANC

Silver **Obv:** Bust of Paul V right **Rev:** Floral cross **Rev. Legend:** SCIPIO • BVRGHESIVS • CARD • LEG • AVEN

Date	Mintage	Good	VG	F	VF	XF
1611	—	180	300	650	1,000	—
1612	—	180	300	650	1,000	—
1613	—	180	300	650	1,000	—

KM# 56 1/4 FRANC

Silver **Obv:** Bust of Urban VIII right **Rev:** Floral cross

Date	Mintage	Good	VG	F	VF	XF
1636 Rare	—	—	—	—	—	—

KM# 8 1/2 FRANC

Silver **Obv:** Bust of Paul V right **Rev:** Shield of cardinal **Rev. Legend:** SCIPIO • BVRGHESIVS • CARD • LEG • AVEN

Date	Mintage	Good	VG	F	VF	XF
1608	—	100	180	400	750	—
1609	—	100	180	400	750	—
1610	—	100	180	400	750	—
1611	—	100	180	400	750	—
1612	—	100	180	400	750	—
1613	—	100	180	400	750	—

KM# 12 1/2 FRANC

Silver **Obv:** Bust of Paul V right **Rev:** Floral cross

Date	Mintage	Good	VG	F	VF	XF
1609	—	100	180	400	750	—
1617/XIII	—	100	180	400	750	—
1618/XIII	—	100	180	400	750	—
ND(1618)/XIII	—	100	180	400	750	—

KM# 16 1/2 FRANC

Silver **Obv:** Bust of Paul V left **Rev:** Floral cross **Rev. Legend:** PHILIP • PHILONARD • CARD • P.LEG • AVEN

Date	Mintage	Good	VG	F	VF	XF
1612 Rare	—	—	—	—	—	—

KM# 31 1/2 FRANC

Silver **Obv:** Bust of Gregory XV right **Rev:** Floral cross

Date	Mintage	Good	VG	F	VF	XF
1621 Rare	—	—	—	—	—	—

KM# 57 1/2 FRANC

Silver **Obv:** Bust of Urban VIII right **Rev:** Floral cross

Date	Mintage	Good	VG	F	VF	XF
1636	—	125	300	800	2,000	—
1637	—	125	300	800	2,000	—
1638	—	125	300	800	2,000	—
1639	—	125	300	800	2,000	—
1640	—	125	300	800	2,000	—

KM# 61 1/2 FRANC

Silver **Obv:** Bust of Urban VIII right **Rev:** Floral cross, V at center

Date	Mintage	Good	VG	F	VF	XF
1641 Rare	—	—	—	—	—	—
1642 Rare	—	—	—	—	—	—

KM# 87 CARLIN

Silver **Subject:** Alexander VII **Obv:** Arms **Rev:** Half-length figure of St. Peter above arms

Date	Mintage	Good	VG	F	VF	XF
1656	—	25.00	45.00	75.00	125	—
1657	—	25.00	45.00	75.00	125	—
1658	—	25.00	45.00	75.00	125	—
1659	—	25.00	45.00	75.00	125	—
1660	—	25.00	45.00	75.00	125	—
1661	—	25.00	45.00	75.00	125	—
1662	—	25.00	45.00	75.00	125	—

KM# 5 TESTONE

Silver **Obv:** Bust of Clement VIII right **Rev:** Shield

Date	Mintage	Good	VG	F	VF	XF
1601	—	190	325	500	825	—

KM# 9 TESTONE

Silver **Obv:** Bust of Paul V right, arms below **Rev:** Arms

Date	Mintage	Good	VG	F	VF	XF
1608	—	350	650	1,100	1,700	—

KM# 13 TESTONE

Silver **Rev:** Floral cross, different from mintmark below

Date	Mintage	Good	VG	F	VF	XF
1610	—	400	750	1,250	2,000	—

KM# 17 TESTONE

Silver **Rev:** View of Avignon **Rev. Legend:** AVENIO 1612

Date	Mintage	Good	VG	F	VF	XF
1612 Rare	—	—	—	—	—	—

KM# 18 TESTONE

Silver **Rev. Legend:** PHILIP PHILONARD CARD P. LEG AVEN.

Date	Mintage	Good	VG	F	VF	XF
1612 Rare	—	—	—	—	—	—
1613 Rare	—	—	—	—	—	—

KM# 20 TESTONE

Silver **Rev. Legend:** PHI • S • R • E • CARD • PHILONARDVS P. LEG AVEN 1613

Date	Mintage	Good	VG	F	VF	XF
1613 Unique	—	—	—	—	—	—

KM# 24 TESTONE

Silver **Rev. Legend:** SCIPIO • BVRGHESIVS • CARD • LEG • AVEN

Date	Mintage	Good	VG	F	VF	XF
1617 Rare	—	—	—	—	—	—
1618 Rare	—	—	—	—	—	—
ND(1618)/XIII Rare	—	—	—	—	—	—

KM# 48 TESTONE

Silver **Obv:** Bust of Urban VIII right **Rev:** Shield

Date	Mintage	VG	F	VF	XF	Unc
1629	—	105	205	375	625	—
1630	—	105	205	375	625	—
1631	—	105	205	375	625	—
1632	—	105	205	375	625	—
1633	—	105	205	375	625	—
1634	—	105	205	375	625	—

KM# 49 TESTONE

Silver **Obv:** Bust of Urban VIII right **Rev:** Shield

Date	Mintage	VG	F	VF	XF	Unc
1631	—	120	225	400	650	—

KM# 105 1/12 ECU

Silver **Obv:** Bust of Innocent XII capped right with shield on shoulder **Rev:** Shield **Rev. Legend:** PETRVS • CARD • OTTHOBONVS • LEGAT

Date	Mintage	VG	F	VF	XF	Unc
1692/II	—	75.00	150	350	575	—
1693/II	—	75.00	150	350	575	—

KM# 106 1/12 ECU

Silver **Rev:** PCL monogram

Date	Mintage	VG	F	VF	XF	Unc
1692/II	—	70.00	140	250	400	—

KM# 107 1/12 ECU

Silver **Rev:** Papal arms

Date	Mintage	VG	F	VF	XF	Unc
1693/II	—	60.00	120	200	325	—

KM# 68 1/2 ECU

Silver **Obv:** Bust of Innocent X right **Rev:** Floral cross

Date	Mintage	Good	VG	F	VF	XF
1645 Rare	—	—	—	—	—	—

Note: Numismatica Ars Classica Auction 44, 11-07, XF realized approximately $28,195

Date	Mintage	Good	VG	F	VF	XF
1646 Rare	—	—	—	—	—	—
1647 Rare	—	—	—	—	—	—

KM# 77 1/2 ECU

Silver **Obv:** Bust right with different shield at shoulder **Rev. Legend:** CAMILLVS • CARD...

Date	Mintage	Good	VG	F	VF	XF
1651	—	700	1,200	2,050	3,050	—

KM# 81 1/2 ECU

Silver **Rev. Legend:** CAMILLVS • PRES • CARD

Date	Mintage	Good	VG	F	VF	XF
1652	—	975	1,750	3,000	4,500	—

KM# 80 ECU

Silver **Rev. Legend:** CAMILLVS • PRES • CAR • PAMPH. LIVS...

Date	Mintage	VG	F	VF	XF	Unc
1651 Rare	—	—	—	—	—	—

KM# 79 ECU

Silver **Obv:** Large bust with large shield on shoulder **Rev. Legend:** CAMILLVS • CARD • PAMPHILIVS... **Note:** Dav. #4067.

Date	Mintage	VG	F	VF	XF	Unc
1651	—	3,400	6,900	12,500	21,500	—

KM# 78 ECU

Silver **Obv:** Bust of Innocent X right **Rev:** Shield **Rev. Legend:** CAMILLVS • CARD • PAMPHILLIVS... **Note:** Dav. #4068.

Date	Mintage	VG	F	VF	XF	Unc
1651	—	3,000	5,600	10,000	—	—
1652	—	3,000	5,600	10,000	—	—

KM# 26 1/2 PIASTRE

Silver **Obv:** Bust of Paul V right **Rev:** Shield

Date	Mintage	Good	VG	F	VF	XF
MDCXVIII/XIIII (1618) Rare	—	—	—	—	—	—
MDCXVIIII/XIIII (1619) Rare	—	—	—	—	—	—

KM# 32 1/2 PIASTRE

Silver **Obv:** Bust of Gregory XV right **Obv. Legend:** ...MAX

Date	Mintage	Good	VG	F	VF	XF
1621 Rare	—	—	—	—	—	—
1622 Rare	—	—	—	—	—	—

KM# 35 1/2 PIASTRE

Silver **Obv:** Bust of Gregory XV right **Obv. Legend:** Ends: ... OPT • MAX •

Date	Mintage	Good	VG	F	VF	XF
1622 Rare	—	—	—	—	—	—
ND Rare	—	—	—	—	—	—

KM# 62 1/2 PIASTRE

Silver **Obv:** Bust of Urban VIII right **Rev:** Floral cross, V at center

Date	Mintage	Good	VG	F	VF	XF
1641	—	1,500	3,000	4,900	7,500	—
1642	—	1,500	3,000	4,900	7,500	—
1643	—	1,500	3,000	4,900	7,500	—

KM# 27 PIASTRE

Silver **Obv:** Bust of Paul V right **Rev:** Shield **Rev. Legend:** SCIPIO • BVRGHESIVS • CARD • LEG • AVEN

Date	Mintage	Good	VG	F	VF	XF
MDCXVIII/XIIII (1618) Rare	—	—	—	—	—	—
MDCXVIIII/XIIII (1619) Rare	—	—	—	—	—	—

KM# 33 PIASTRE

Silver **Obv:** Bust of Gregory XV left **Rev. Legend:** LVD CARD LVDOVISIVS LEGATVS AVEN **Note:** Dav. #4052.

Date	Mintage	Good	VG	F	VF	XF
1621 Unique	—	—	—	—	—	—

Note: Numismatica Ars Classica Auction 44, 11-07, near XF realized approximately $54,905

KM# 34 PIASTRE

Silver **Obv:** Bust of Gregory XV right **Rev. Legend:** ...CAMER. LEG. AVEN. **Note:** Dav. #4053.

Date	Mintage	Good	VG	F	VF	XF
1621 Rare	—	—	—	—	—	—
1622 Rare	—	—	—	—	—	—

KM# 6 DOPPIA

7.0000 g., 0.9860 Gold 0.2219 oz. AGW **Obv:** Bust of Clement VIII right **Rev:** Shield

Date	Mintage	VG	F	VF	XF	Unc
1602	—	2,200	3,600	6,000	10,000	—

KM# 10 DOPPIA

7.0000 g., 0.9860 Gold 0.2219 oz. AGW **Obv:** Bust of Paul V right in inner circle, date in legend **Rev:** Arms, legend of Papal legate, Scipio Borghese

Date	Mintage	VG	F	VF	XF	Unc
1608	—	1,000	1,900	3,400	5,600	—

KM# 23 DOPPIA

7.0000 g., 0.9860 Gold 0.2219 oz. AGW **Obv:** Bust of Paul V left in inner circle, date in legend **Rev:** Legend of Papal legate, Scipio Borghese

Date	Mintage	VG	F	VF	XF	Unc
1614 Rare	—	—	—	—	—	—

KM# 25 DOPPIA

7.0000 g., 0.9860 Gold 0.2219 oz. AGW **Obv:** Bust of Paul V right, shield in inner circle, date below **Rev:** Floreate cross in inner circle

Date	Mintage	VG	F	VF	XF	Unc
1617/XIII Rare	—	—	—	—	—	—

KM# 59 DOPPIA

7.0000 g., 0.9860 Gold 0.2219 oz. AGW **Obv:** Bust of Urban VIII right in inner circle, date in legend **Rev:** Arms, legend of Papal legate, Antonio Barberini

Date	Mintage	VG	F	VF	XF	Unc
1639	—	1,600	3,100	5,700	9,500	—

KM# 60 DOPPIA

7.0000 g., 0.9860 Gold 0.2219 oz. AGW **Obv:** Bust of Urban VIII right in inner circle, date below

Date	Mintage	VG	F	VF	XF	Unc
1640 Rare	—	—	—	—	—	—

KM# 69 DOPPIA

7.0000 g., 0.9860 Gold 0.2219 oz. AGW **Obv:** Bust of Innocent X right in inner circle **Rev:** Arms, legend of Papal legate, Lorenzo Corsi

Date	Mintage	VG	F	VF	XF	Unc
1644	—	3,500	6,500	11,000	18,500	—

KM# 70 DOPPIA

7.0000 g., 0.9860 Gold 0.2219 oz. AGW **Obv:** Bust of Alexander VII right in inner circle **Rev:** Arms, legend of Papal legate, Fabio Chigi

Date	Mintage	VG	F	VF	XF	Unc
1664	—	1,000	2,000	3,700	6,000	—

KM# 15 QUADRUPLA

14.0000 g., 0.9860 Gold 0.4438 oz. AGW **Obv:** Bust of Paul V right in inner circle, date in legend **Rev:** Arms, legend of Papal legate, Scipio Borghese

Date	Mintage	VG	F	VF	XF	Unc
1611 Unique	—	—	—	—	—	—

KM# 19 QUADRUPLA

14.0000 g., 0.9860 Gold 0.4438 oz. AGW **Obv:** Bust of Paul V right, date below **Rev:** Arms, legend of Papal legate, Philip Filonardi

Date	Mintage	VG	F	VF	XF	Unc
1612 Rare	—	—	—	—	—	—

KM# 28 QUADRUPLA

14.0000 g., 0.9860 Gold 0.4438 oz. AGW **Rev:** Floriate cross in inner circle

Date	Mintage	VG	F	VF	XF	Unc
1618/XIII	—	2,250	4,000	6,500	10,000	—

KM# 46 QUADRUPLA

14.0000 g., 0.9860 Gold 0.4438 oz. AGW **Obv:** Bust of Urban VIII right in inner circle, date in legend **Rev:** Arms, legend of Papal legate, Francis Barberini

Date	Mintage	VG	F	VF	XF	Unc
1624	—	2,250	4,000	6,500	10,000	—
1628	—	2,250	4,000	6,500	10,000	—
1629	—	2,250	4,000	6,500	10,000	—
1631	—	2,250	4,000	6,500	10,000	—
1632	—	2,250	4,000	6,500	10,000	—

KM# 47 QUADRUPLA

14.0000 g., 0.9860 Gold 0.4438 oz. AGW **Rev:** Arms, legend of Papal legate, Cosimo Bardi

Date	Mintage	VG	F	VF	XF	Unc
1626 Rare	—	—	—	—	—	—

KM# 50 QUADRUPLA

14.0000 g., 0.9860 Gold 0.4438 oz. AGW **Obv:** Bust of Urban VIII right **Rev. Legend:** FRANCIVCVS CAR. BARBERINVS...

Date	Mintage	VG	F	VF	XF	Unc
1631 Rare	—	—	—	—	—	—
1632 Rare	—	—	—	—	—	—

KM# 52 QUADRUPLA

14.0000 g., 0.9860 Gold 0.4438 oz. AGW **Obv:** Bust of Urban VIII right in inner circle, date in exergue **Rev:** Arms, legend of Papal legate, Antonio Barberini

Date	Mintage	VG	F	VF	XF	Unc
1634 Unique	—	—	—	—	—	—

KM# 55 QUADRUPLA

14.0000 g., 0.9860 Gold 0.4438 oz. AGW **Obv:** Bust of Urban VIII right in inner circle, date in legend

Date	Mintage	VG	F	VF	XF	Unc
1635 Rare	—	—	—	—	—	—
1636 Rare	—	—	—	—	—	—

KM# 58 QUADRUPLA

14.0000 g., 0.9860 Gold 0.4438 oz. AGW **Obv:** Different shield on bust

Date	Mintage	VG	F	VF	XF	Unc
1637	—	1,750	3,250	5,000	8,000	—
1638	—	1,750	3,250	5,000	8,000	—
1639	—	1,750	3,250	5,000	8,000	—
1640	—	1,750	3,250	5,000	8,000	—
1641	—	1,750	3,250	5,000	8,000	—
1642	—	1,750	3,250	5,000	8,000	—
1643	—	1,750	3,250	5,000	8,000	—
1644	—	1,750	3,250	5,000	8,000	—

KM# 71 QUADRUPLA

14.0000 g., 0.9860 Gold 0.4438 oz. AGW **Obv:** Bust of Innocent X right in inner circle, date in legend **Rev:** Legend of Papal legate, Antonio Barberini

Date	Mintage	VG	F	VF	XF	Unc
1644	—	1,500	2,500	4,400	7,500	—

KM# 72 QUADRUPLA

14.0000 g., 0.9860 Gold 0.4438 oz. AGW **Obv:** Tall bust of Innocent X right in inner circle, date in legend **Rev:** Arms, legend of Papal legate, Camillo Pamphilj

Date	Mintage	VG	F	VF	XF	Unc
1644	—	1,500	2,500	4,400	7,500	—

KM# 74 QUADRUPLA

14.0000 g., 0.9860 Gold 0.4438 oz. AGW **Obv:** Different shield on shoulder

Date	Mintage	VG	F	VF	XF	Unc
1645 Rare	—	—	—	—	—	—
1646 Rare	—	—	—	—	—	—
1647 Rare	—	—	—	—	—	—

KM# 75 QUADRUPLA

14.0000 g., 0.9860 Gold 0.4438 oz. AGW **Rev:** Shield on Maltese cross

Date	Mintage	VG	F	VF	XF	Unc
1645 Rare	—	—	—	—	—	—
1646 Rare	—	—	—	—	—	—

KM# 76 QUADRUPLA

14.0000 g., 0.9860 Gold 0.4438 oz. AGW **Obv:** Large bust of Innocent X right in inner circle, date in legend **Rev:** Arms, legend of Papal legate, Lorenzo Corsi

Date	Mintage	VG	F	VF	XF	Unc
1647 Unique	—	—	—	—	—	—

KM# 89 QUADRUPLA

14.0000 g., 0.9860 Gold 0.4438 oz. AGW **Rev:** Papal arms **Rev. Legend:** PONTIFICATVS-SVI-ANNO. II. 1657.

Date	Mintage	VG	F	VF	XF	Unc
1657 Rare	—	—	—	—	—	—

KM# 90 QUADRUPLA

14.0000 g., 0.9860 Gold 0.4438 oz. AGW **Obv:** Bust of Alexander VII right in inner circle **Rev:** Arms, legend of Papal legate, Fabio Chigi

Date	Mintage	VG	F	VF	XF	Unc
1658	—	2,050	3,750	6,000	10,000	—
1659 Rare	—	—	—	—	—	—
1662	—	2,050	3,750	6,000	10,000	—

KM# 95 QUADRUPLA

14.0000 g., 0.9860 Gold 0.4438 oz. AGW **Obv:** Different shield on shoulder

Date	Mintage	VG	F	VF	XF	Unc
1665 Rare	—	—	—	—	—	—

KM# 36 OCTUPLE

28.0000 g., 0.9860 Gold 0.8876 oz. AGW **Obv:** Bust of Gregory XV **Rev. Legend:** LVD. CARD. LVDOVISIVS...

Date	Mintage	VG	F	VF	XF	Unc
1622 Rare	—	—	—	—	—	—

PAPAL STATES-BOLOGNA

(Bolonia)

A city in Emilia, began as an independent commune, and after serving under various masters became a papal possession in 1506. Except for the Napoleonic period (1797-1815) and the revolutions of 1821 and 1831, it remained a papal state until 1860.

MINT OFFICIALS' INITIALS

MINT MARK

Initial	Date	Name
BP	1644-76	Bartolomeo Provagli
CF	1700-21	Carlo Falconi
GB	1700-21	Girolamo Bevilacqua
GCG	1691-1700	Giovan Carlo Gualchierl
LS	1623-44	Ludovico Salvatici

B – Bologna

MONETARY SYSTEM

(Until 1777)

6 Quattrini = 1 Bolognino
12 Bolognini = 1 Giulio = 1 Bianco
80 to 108 Bolognini = 1 Scudo

CITY

STANDARD COINAGE

KM# 5 QUATTRINO

Copper **Subject:** Clement VIII **Obv:** Crowned lion ramant left with banner **Rev:** BONO/NIA/DOCET

Date	Mintage	Good	VG	F	VF	XF
1604	—	16.00	25.00	40.00	75.00	—

KM# 13 QUATTRINO

Copper **Subject:** Paul V **Obv:** Lion rampant left with banner **Rev:** BONO INIA/DOCET

Date	Mintage	Good	VG	F	VF	XF
1607	—	8.00	12.50	22.00	40.00	—
1608	—	8.00	12.50	22.00	40.00	—
1609	—	8.00	12.50	22.00	40.00	—
1610	—	8.00	12.50	22.00	40.00	—
1611	—	8.00	12.50	22.00	40.00	—
1612	—	8.00	12.50	22.00	40.00	—
1613	—	8.00	12.50	22.00	40.00	—
1614	—	8.00	12.50	22.00	40.00	—
1615	—	8.00	12.50	22.00	40.00	—
1616	—	8.00	12.50	22.00	40.00	—
1617	—	8.00	12.50	22.00	40.00	—
1618	—	8.00	12.50	22.00	40.00	—
1619	—	8.00	12.50	22.00	40.00	—
1620	—	8.00	12.50	22.00	40.00	—

KM# 30 QUATTRINO

Copper **Subject:** Gregory XV **Obv:** Lion rampant left with banner **Rev:** BONO/NIA/DOCET

Date	Mintage	Good	VG	F	VF	XF
1621	—	10.00	16.50	25.00	45.00	—
1622	—	10.00	16.50	25.00	45.00	—

KM# 32 QUATTRINO

Copper **Subject:** Urban VII **Obv:** Lion rampant left with banner **Rev:** BONO/NIA/DOCET

Date	Mintage	Good	VG	F	VF	XF
1624	—	8.00	12.50	22.00	5.00	—
1625	—	8.00	12.50	22.00	5.00	—
1626	—	8.00	12.50	22.00	5.00	—
1627	—	8.00	12.50	22.00	5.00	—
1628	—	8.00	12.50	22.00	5.00	—
1629	—	8.00	12.50	22.00	5.00	—
1630	—	8.00	12.50	22.00	5.00	—
1631	—	8.00	12.50	22.00	5.00	—
1632	—	8.00	12.50	22.00	5.00	—
1633	—	8.00	12.50	22.00	5.00	—
1634	—	8.00	12.50	22.00	5.00	—
1635	—	8.00	12.50	22.00	5.00	—
1636	—	8.00	12.50	22.00	5.00	—
1637	—	8.00	12.50	22.00	5.00	—
1638	—	8.00	12.50	22.00	5.00	—
1639	—	8.00	12.50	22.00	5.00	—
1640	—	8.00	12.50	22.00	5.00	—
1641	—	8.00	12.50	22.00	5.00	—
1642	—	8.00	12.50	22.00	5.00	—

KM# 40 QUATTRINO

Copper **Subject:** Innocent X **Obv:** Lion rampant left with banner **Rev. Inscription:** BONO / NIA / DOCET

Date	Mintage	Good	VG	F	VF	XF
1646	—	6.00	10.00	16.50	30.00	—
1647	—	6.00	10.00	16.50	30.00	—

Date	Mintage	Good	VG	F	VF	XF
1648	—	6.00	10.00	16.50	30.00	—
1649	—	6.00	10.00	16.50	30.00	—

KM# 67 QUATTRINO

Copper **Subject:** Alexander VII **Obv:** Lion rampant left with banner **Rev. Inscription:** BONO / NIA / DOCET

Date	Mintage	VG	F	VF	XF	Unc
1663	—	10.00	18.00	32.00	60.00	—
1664	—	10.00	18.00	32.00	60.00	—
1665	—	10.00	18.00	32.00	60.00	—
1666	—	10.00	18.00	32.00	60.00	—
1667	—	10.00	18.00	32.00	60.00	—

KM# 75 QUATTRINO

Copper **Subject:** Clement IX **Obv:** Lion rampant left with banner **Rev. Inscription:** BONO / NIA / DOCET

Date	Mintage	VG	F	VF	XF	Unc
1668	—	12.00	20.00	35.00	65.00	—
1669	—	12.00	20.00	35.00	65.00	—

KM# 88 QUATTRINO

Copper **Subject:** Clement X **Obv:** Lion rampant left with banner **Rev. Inscription:** BONO / NIA / DOCET

Date	Mintage	VG	F	VF	XF	Unc
1676	—	10.00	18.00	32.00	60.00	—

KM# 90 QUATTRINO

Copper **Subject:** Innocent XI **Obv:** Lion rampant left with banner **Rev. Inscription:** BONO / NIA / DOCET

Date	Mintage	VG	F	VF	XF	Unc
1677	—	10.00	18.00	32.00	65.00	—
1678	—	10.00	18.00	32.00	65.00	—
1679	—	10.00	18.00	32.00	65.00	—
1680	—	10.00	18.00	32.00	65.00	—
1681	—	10.00	18.00	32.00	65.00	—
1682	—	10.00	18.00	32.00	65.00	—
1683	—	10.00	18.00	32.00	65.00	—
1684	—	10.00	18.00	32.00	65.00	—
1685	—	10.00	18.00	32.00	65.00	—
1686	—	10.00	18.00	32.00	65.00	—
1687	—	10.00	18.00	32.00	65.00	—
1688	—	10.00	18.00	32.00	65.00	—
1689	—	10.00	18.00	32.00	65.00	—

KM# 110 QUATTRINO

Copper **Subject:** Alexander VIII **Obv:** Lion rampant left with banner **Rev. Inscription:** BONO / NIA / DOCET

Date	Mintage	VG	F	VF	XF	Unc
1690	—	9.00	16.00	27.50	50.00	—

KM# 114 QUATTRINO

Copper **Subject:** Innocent XII **Obv:** Lion rampant left with banner showing cross **Rev. Inscription:** BONO / NIA / DOCET

Date	Mintage	VG	F	VF	XF	Unc
1691	—	9.00	16.00	26.00	50.00	—
1692	—	9.00	16.00	26.00	50.00	—
1693	—	9.00	16.00	26.00	50.00	—
1694	—	9.00	16.00	26.00	50.00	—
1695	—	9.00	16.00	26.00	50.00	—
1696	—	9.00	16.00	26.00	50.00	—
1697	—	9.00	16.00	26.00	50.00	—
1698	—	9.00	16.00	26.00	50.00	—
1699	—	9.00	16.00	26.00	50.00	—
1700	—	9.00	16.00	26.00	50.00	—

KM# 120 QUATTRINO

Copper **Obv:** Lion rampant left with banner showing LIBER

Date	Mintage	VG	F	VF	XF	Unc
1692	—	9.00	16.00	26.00	50.00	—
1693	—	9.00	16.00	26.00	50.00	—
1694	—	9.00	16.00	26.00	50.00	—
1695	—	9.00	16.00	26.00	50.00	—
1696	—	9.00	16.00	26.00	50.00	—
1697	—	9.00	16.00	26.00	50.00	—
1698	—	9.00	16.00	26.00	50.00	—
1699	—	9.00	16.00	26.00	50.00	—
1700	—	9.00	16.00	26.00	50.00	—

KM# 130 QUATTRINO

Copper **Obv:** Shield below canopy and keys **Rev. Inscription:** LI / BER / TAS **Note:** Sede Vacante issue.

Date	Mintage	VG	F	VF	XF	Unc
ND(1700)	—	40.00	75.00	140	195	—

KM# 20 1/2 BOLOGNINO

Copper **Subject:** Paul V **Obv:** Shield **Obv. Legend:** BONONIA DOCET **Rev:** Half lion rampant left above legend in cartouche **Rev. Legend:** MEZO BOLOGNINO

Date	Mintage	Good	VG	F	VF	XF
MDCXII (1612)	—	12.50	20.00	32.00	60.00	—
MDCXIII (1613)	—	12.50	20.00	32.00	60.00	—
MDCIIII (1614)	—	12.50	20.00	32.00	60.00	—
MDCXV (1615)	—	12.50	20.00	32.00	60.00	—
MDCXVI (1616)	—	12.50	20.00	32.00	60.00	—
MDCXVII (1617)	—	12.50	20.00	32.00	60.00	—
MDCXVIII (1618)	—	12.50	20.00	32.00	60.00	—
MDCXVIIII (1619)	—	12.50	20.00	32.00	60.00	—
MDCXX (1620)	—	12.50	20.00	32.00	60.00	—

KM# 31 1/2 BOLOGNINO

Copper **Subject:** Gregory XV **Obv:** Shield **Obv. Legend:** BONONIA DOCET **Rev:** Half lion rampant left **Rev. Legend:** MEZO BOLOGNINO

Date	Mintage	Good	VG	F	VF	XF
MDCXXI (1621)	—	20.00	32.00	50.00	80.00	—
MDCXXII (1622)	—	20.00	32.00	50.00	80.00	—

KM# 33 1/2 BOLOGNINO

Copper **Subject:** Urban VIII **Obv:** Shield, BONONIA DOCET **Rev:** MEZO BOLOGNINO, half lion rampant left

Date	Mintage	Good	VG	F	VF	XF
1624	—	10.00	18.00	28.00	55.00	—
1625	—	10.00	18.00	28.00	55.00	—
1626	—	10.00	18.00	28.00	55.00	—
1627	—	10.00	18.00	28.00	55.00	—
1628	—	10.00	18.00	28.00	55.00	—
1629	—	10.00	18.00	28.00	55.00	—
1630	—	10.00	18.00	28.00	55.00	—
1631	—	10.00	18.00	28.00	55.00	—

KM# 41 1/2 BOLOGNINO

Copper **Subject:** Innocent X **Obv:** Shield, BONONIA DOCET **Rev:** MEZO BOLOGNINO, half lion rampant left

Date	Mintage	Good	VG	F	VF	XF
1647	—	9.00	16.00	25.00	55.00	—
1648	—	9.00	16.00	25.00	55.00	—
1649	—	9.00	16.00	25.00	55.00	—

KM# 95 1/2 BOLOGNINO

Copper **Subject:** Innocent XI **Obv:** BONONIA DOCET, shield **Rev:** MEZO BOLOGNINO, half lion rampant left

Date	Mintage	VG	F	VF	XF	Unc
1680	—	14.00	25.00	40.00	70.00	—
1681	—	14.00	25.00	40.00	70.00	—
1682	—	14.00	25.00	40.00	70.00	—
1683	—	14.00	25.00	40.00	70.00	—
1684	—	14.00	25.00	40.00	70.00	—
1685	—	14.00	25.00	40.00	70.00	—
1686	—	14.00	25.00	40.00	70.00	—
1687	—	14.00	25.00	40.00	70.00	—
1688	—	14.00	25.00	40.00	70.00	—
1689	—	14.00	25.00	40.00	70.00	—

KM# 111 1/2 BOLOGNINO

Copper **Subject:** Alexander VIII **Obv:** BONONIA DOCET and shield **Rev:** MEZO BOLOGNINO, half lion rampant left

Date	Mintage	VG	F	VF	XF	Unc
1690	—	14.00	25.00	40.00	70.00	—
ND	—	14.00	25.00	40.00	70.00	—

KM# 115 1/2 BOLOGNINO

Copper **Subject:** Innocent XII **Obv:** Shield, BONONIA DOCET **Rev:** MEZO BOLOGNINO, half lion rampant left

Date	Mintage	VG	F	VF	XF	Unc
1691	—	14.00	25.00	40.00	70.00	—
1692	—	14.00	25.00	40.00	70.00	—
1693	—	14.00	25.00	40.00	70.00	—
1694	—	14.00	25.00	40.00	70.00	—
1695	—	14.00	25.00	40.00	70.00	—
1696	—	14.00	25.00	40.00	70.00	—
1697	—	14.00	25.00	40.00	70.00	—
1698	—	14.00	25.00	40.00	70.00	—
1699	—	14.00	25.00	40.00	70.00	—

KM# 121 1/2 BOLOGNINO

Copper **Obv:** Different shield

Date	Mintage	VG	F	VF	XF	Unc
1692	—	16.50	30.00	50.00	80.00	—

KM# 127 1/2 BOLOGNINO

Copper **Obv:** SENAT • POP • QVE • BONONIE, shield below canopy and keys **Rev:** LI/BER/TAS **Note:** Sede Vacante issue.

Date	Mintage	VG	F	VF	XF	Unc
ND	—	50.00	85.00	165	250	—

KM# 132 BOLOGNINO

Billon **Subject:** Clement XI **Obv:** BONONIA MATER, lion rampant left with banner **Rev:** STVDIORVM, crossed keys

Date	Mintage	VG	F	VF	XF	Unc
ND	—	10.00	20.00	40.00	70.00	—

KM# 131 BOLOGNINO

Billon **Obv:** SENAT • POP • QVE • BONONIE, shield below canopy and keys **Rev:** LI/BER/TAS **Note:** Sede Vacante issue.

Date	Mintage	VG	F	VF	XF	Unc
ND(1700)	—	35.00	60.00	120	210	—

KM# 42 2 BOLOGNINI

Billon **Obv:** Bust of Innocent X right **Rev:** St. Petronius standing

Date	Mintage	Good	VG	F	VF	XF
1647	—	14.00	28.00	45.00	75.00	—
1648	—	14.00	28.00	45.00	75.00	—
1649	—	14.00	28.00	45.00	75.00	—

KM# 49 2 BOLOGNINI

Billon **Obv:** Bust of Alexander VII right

Date	Mintage	Good	VG	F	VF	XF
ND	—	7.00	15.00	25.00	45.00	—

KM# 71 2 BOLOGNINI

Billon **Obv:** Capped bust of Clement IX right

Date	Mintage	Good	VG	F	VF	XF
ND(1667-69)	—	30.00	60.00	120	180	—

KM# 80 2 BOLOGNINI

Billon **Obv:** Bust of Clement X right

Date	Mintage	Good	VG	F	VF	XF
ND(1670-76)	—	12.00	25.00	42.00	75.00	—

KM# 89 2 BOLOGNINI

Billon **Obv:** Bust of Innocent XI right

Date	Mintage	VG	F	VF	XF	Unc
ND(1676-89)	—	10.00	20.00	36.00	70.00	—

KM# 104 2 BOLOGNINI

Billon **Obv:** Bust of Alexander VIII right

Date	Mintage	VG	F	VF	XF	Unc
ND(1689-91)	—	10.00	22.00	45.00	80.00	—

KM# 117 2 BOLOGNINI

Billon **Obv:** Bust of Innocent XII right

Date	Mintage	VG	F	VF	XF	Unc
ND(1691-1700)	—	12.00	25.00	60.00	120	—

KM# 116 2 BOLOGNINI

Billon **Obv:** Two shields below canopy and keys **Note:** Sede Vacante issue.

Date	Mintage	VG	F	VF	XF	Unc
ND(1691)	—	15.00	30.00	75.00	150	—

KM# 133 2 BOLOGNINI

Billon **Obv:** Two shields below canopy and keys **Note:** Sede Vacante issue.

Date	Mintage	VG	F	VF	XF	Unc
1700	—	20.00	35.00	65.00	120	—

KM# 6 2-1/2 BOLOGNIA (1/2 Carlino)

Billon **Subject:** Paul V **Obv:** Arms **Rev:** BONO/NIA/DOCET within wreath

Date	Mintage	Good	VG	F	VF	XF
ND	—	28.00	50.00	85.00	140	—

KM# 7 2-1/2 BOLOGNIA (1/2 Carlino)

Billon **Obv:** Bust of St. Petronius **Rev:** BONO/NIA/DOCET

Date	Mintage	Good	VG	F	VF	XF
ND	—	22.00	40.00	70.00	120	—

KM# 8 5 BOLOGNINI (Carlino)

Silver **Subject:** Paul V **Obv:** Arms **Rev:** Madonna with child **Rev. Legend:** PRAE SIDIVM ET DECVS

Date	Mintage	Good	VG	F	VF	XF
ND	—	35.00	70.00	120	185	—

KM# 9 5 BOLOGNINI (Carlino)

Silver **Obv:** Shield **Obv. Legend:** BONONIA DOCET

Date	Mintage	Good	VG	F	VF	XF
ND	—	27.00	50.00	85.00	140	—

KM# 10 5 BOLOGNINI (Carlino)

Silver **Obv:** Shield **Obv. Legend:** BONONIA • DOCET **Rev:** Bust of Madonna with child

Date	Mintage	Good	VG	F	VF	XF
ND	—	18.00	35.00	55.00	110	—

KM# 81 5 BOLOGNINI (Carlino)

Silver **Subject:** Clement X **Rev:** Half-length figure of Madonna with child

Date	Mintage	Good	VG	F	VF	XF
1671	—	16.50	32.50	55.00	110	—
1672	—	16.50	32.50	55.00	110	—
1673	—	16.50	32.50	55.00	110	—
1674	—	16.50	32.50	55.00	110	—
1675	—	16.50	32.50	55.00	110	—
1676	—	16.50	32.50	55.00	110	—

KM# 91 5 BOLOGNINI (Carlino)

Silver **Subject:** Innocent XI

Date	Mintage	Good	VG	F	VF	XF
1677	—	16.50	32.50	55.00	110	—
1678	—	16.50	32.50	55.00	110	—
1679	—	16.50	32.50	55.00	110	—
1680	—	16.50	32.50	55.00	110	—
1681	—	16.50	32.50	55.00	110	—
1682	—	16.50	32.50	55.00	110	—
1683	—	16.50	32.50	55.00	110	—
1684	—	16.50	32.50	55.00	110	—
1685	—	16.50	32.50	55.00	110	—
1686	—	16.50	32.50	55.00	110	—
1687	—	16.50	32.50	55.00	110	—
1688	—	16.50	32.50	55.00	110	—
1689	—	16.50	32.50	55.00	110	—

KM# 112 5 BOLOGNINI (Carlino)

Silver **Subject:** Alexander VII

Date	Mintage	Good	VG	F	VF	XF
1690	—	18.00	35.00	55.00	110	—

KM# 122 5 BOLOGNINI (Carlino)
Silver **Subject:** Innocent XII

Date	Mintage	Good	VG	F	VF	XF
1692	—	18.00	35.00	55.00	110	—

KM# 11 8 BOLOGNINI (Giulio)
Silver **Obv:** Bust of Paul V left **Rev:** Shield **Rev. Legend:** BONONIA DOCET

Date	Mintage	Good	VG	F	VF	XF
ND	—	50.00	85.00	160	295	—

KM# 12 8 BOLOGNINI (Giulio)
Silver **Obv:** BO/NONIA/DO/CET in quadrilobe **Rev:** St. Petronius enthroned

Date	Mintage	Good	VG	F	VF	XF
ND Rare	—	—	—	—	—	—

KM# 22 10 BOLOGNINI (Bianca)
Silver **Obv:** Bust of Paul V left **Rev:** Lion rampant left, holding banner, Paul on shield

Date	Mintage	Good	VG	F	VF	XF
1615	—	65.00	120	220	400	—
1616	—	65.00	120	220	400	—
1617	—	65.00	120	220	400	—
1618	—	65.00	120	220	400	—
1619	—	65.00	120	220	400	—

KM# 23 10 BOLOGNINI (Bianca)
Silver **Obv:** Bust of St. Petronius

Date	Mintage	Good	VG	F	VF	XF
1615	—	40.00	70.00	125	230	—

KM# 24 10 BOLOGNINI (Bianca)
Silver **Obv:** Half-length figure of St. Petronius **Rev:** Lion rampant left, holding banner

Date	Mintage	Good	VG	F	VF	XF
ND	—	40.00	70.00	125	230	—

KM# 35 10 BOLOGNINI (Bianca)
Silver **Obv:** Bust of Urban VIII right **Rev:** Shield **ev. Legend:** BONONIA DOCET

Date	Mintage	Good	VG	F	VF	XF
MDCXXV (1625)	—	45.00	85.00	160	295	—

KM# 50 10 BOLOGNINI (Bianca)
Silver **Subject:** Alexander VII **Obv:** Arms **Rev:** Bust of Madonna with child, shields at side

Date	Mintage	Good	VG	F	VF	XF
ND	—	55.00	100	180	325	—

KM# 51 10 BOLOGNINI (Bianca)
Silver **Rev:** Different shields

Date	Mintage	Good	VG	F	VF	XF
ND	—	55.00	100	180	325	—

KM# 98 10 BOLOGNINI (Bianca)
Silver **Obv:** Bust of Innocent XI right **Rev:** Lion rampant left with banner **Rev. Legend:** BONONIA DOCET MATER STVD

Date	Mintage	Good	VG	F	VF	XF
1686	—	45.00	75.00	140	260	—

KM# 99 10 BOLOGNINI (Bianca)
Silver **Obv:** Capped bust right

Date	Mintage	Good	VG	F	VF	XF
1686	—	45.00	75.00	140	260	—

KM# 21 20 BOLOGNINI (Lira)
Silver **Subject:** Paul V **Obv:** Felsina standing with pennant **Rev:** St. Petronius enthroned

Date	Mintage	Good	VG	F	VF	XF
MDCXIIII (1614)	—	55.00	100	180	325	—
MDCXV (1615)	—	55.00	100	180	325	—

KM# 25 20 BOLOGNINI (Lira)
Silver **Obv:** Arms, BOL/XX

Date	Mintage	Good	VG	F	VF	XF
MDCXV (1615)	—	45.00	85.00	160	295	—
MDCXIX (1619)	—	45.00	85.00	160	295	—

KM# 45 20 BOLOGNINI (Lira)
Silver **Subject:** Innocent X **Obv:** St. Petronius enthroned **Rev:** Lion rampant left

Date	Mintage	Good	VG	F	VF	XF
1650 Rare	—	—	—	—	—	—

KM# 52 20 BOLOGNINI (Lira)
Silver **Subject:** Alexander VII **Obv:** Arms **Rev:** Lion rampant left, two shields **Rev. Legend:** BONONIA DOCET

Date	Mintage	Good	VG	F	VF	XF
1655	—	60.00	115	200	300	—
1656	—	60.00	115	200	300	—
1657	—	60.00	115	200	300	—
1658	—	60.00	115	200	300	—

KM# 56 20 BOLOGNINI (Lira)
Silver **Rev:** Different shields

Date	Mintage	Good	VG	F	VF	XF
1658	—	60.00	115	200	300	—
1659	—	60.00	115	200	300	—
1660	—	60.00	115	200	300	—
1661	—	60.00	115	200	300	—

KM# 65 20 BOLOGNINI (Lira)
Silver **Rev:** Different shields

Date	Mintage	Good	VG	F	VF	XF
1662	—	60.00	115	200	300	—
1663	—	60.00	115	200	300	—
1664	—	60.00	115	200	300	—
1665	—	60.00	115	200	300	—

KM# 68 20 BOLOGNINI (Lira)
Silver **Rev:** Different shields

Date	Mintage	Good	VG	F	VF	XF
1665	—	60.00	115	200	300	—
1666	—	60.00	115	200	300	—

KM# 73 20 BOLOGNINI (Lira)
Silver **Subject:** Clement IX **Obv:** Arms **Rev:** St. Petronius standing

Date	Mintage	Good	VG	F	VF	XF
1667 Rare	—	—	—	—	—	—

KM# 72 20 BOLOGNINI (Lira)
Silver **Obv:** Two shields below canopy and keys **Rev:** St. Petronius kneeling left, XX in exergue **Note:** Sede Vacante issue.

Date	Mintage	Good	VG	F	VF	XF
1667	—	80.00	145	270	500	—

KM# 82 20 BOLOGNINI (Lira)
Silver **Subject:** Clement X **Obv:** Arms, shields at sides **Rev:** Lion rampant left with banner

Date	Mintage	VG	F	VF	XF	Unc
1671	—	60.00	120	220	425	—
1672	—	60.00	120	220	425	—
1673	—	60.00	120	220	425	—

KM# 84 20 BOLOGNINI (Lira)
Silver **Obv:** Different shields

Date	Mintage	VG	F	VF	XF	Unc
1673	—	60.00	120	220	425	—
1674	—	60.00	120	220	425	—

KM# 96 20 BOLOGNINI (Lira)
Silver **Subject:** Innocent XI **Obv:** Arms with shields at sides **Rev:** Rampant lion with banner left **Rev. Legend:** BONONIA DOCET

Date	Mintage	VG	F	VF	XF	Unc
1682	—	60.00	120	220	425	—
1683	—	60.00	120	220	425	—

KM# 100 20 BOLOGNINI (Lira)
Silver **Obv:** Arms with different shields at sides

Date	Mintage	VG	F	VF	XF	Unc
1686	—	60.00	120	220	425	—
1687	—	60.00	120	220	425	—

KM# 105 20 BOLOGNINI (Lira)
Silver **Obv:** Arms with different shields at sides

Date	Mintage	VG	F	VF	XF	Unc
1689	—	85.00	150	275	550	—

KM# 106 20 BOLOGNINI (Lira)
Silver **Subject:** Alexander VIII **Obv:** Arms, shields at sides **Rev:** Rampant lion with banner left

Date	Mintage	VG	F	VF	XF	Unc
1689	—	75.00	135	250	500	—
1690	—	75.00	135	250	500	—

KM# 118 20 BOLOGNINI (Lira)
Silver **Obv:** Two shields below canopy and keys **Rev:** St. Petronius kneeling left

Date	Mintage	VG	F	VF	XF	Unc
1691	—	75.00	135	250	500	—

KM# 123 20 BOLOGNINI (Lira)
Silver **Subject:** Innocent XII **Obv:** Arms, two shields at sides **Rev:** Rampant lion wtih banner left

Date	Mintage	VG	F	VF	XF	Unc
1692	—	60.00	120	220	425	—
ND	—	60.00	120	220	425	—

KM# 124 20 BOLOGNINI (Lira)
Silver **Obv:** Arms, two different shields at sides

Date	Mintage	VG	F	VF	XF	Unc
ND	—	60.00	120	220	425	—

KM# 134 20 BOLOGNINI (Lira)
Silver **Obv:** Two shields below canopy and keys **Rev:** St. Petronius kneeling left **Note:** Sede Vacante issue.

Date	Mintage	VG	F	VF	XF	Unc
1700 Unique	—	—	—	—	—	—

KM# 101 24 BOLOGNINI
Silver **Subject:** Innocent XI **Obv:** Arms, shields at sides **Rev:** St. Petronius enthroned

Date	Mintage	VG	F	VF	XF	Unc
1686	—	50.00	100	195	375	—
1687	—	50.00	100	195	375	—

KM# 107 24 BOLOGNINI
Silver **Obv:** Arms, three different shields at sides

Date	Mintage	VG	F	VF	XF	Unc
1689	—	65.00	125	250	500	—

KM# 34 26 BOLOGNINI (Gabellone)
12.0560 g., Silver **Obv:** Bust of Urban VIII right **Rev:** Shield **Rev. Legend:** BONONIA DOCET

Date	Mintage	Good	VG	F	VF	XF
1624	—	220	350	750	1,500	—
1625	—	220	350	750	1,500	—

KM# 26 30 BOLOGNINI (Testone)
Silver **Obv:** Bust of Paul V left **Rev:** Shield **Rev. Legend:** BONONIA DOCET

Date	Mintage	Good	VG	F	VF	XF
MDCXV (1615)	—	200	325	700	1,350	—

KM# 97 30 BOLOGNINI (Testone)
Silver **Obv:** Bust of Innocent XI right **Rev:** Radiant cross, shields **Rev. Legend:** BONONIA DOCET

Date	Mintage	VG	F	VF	XF	Unc
1683	—	50.00	100	220	425	—

KM# 102 30 BOLOGNINI (Testone)

Silver **Obv:** Capped bust of Paul V right

Date	Mintage	VG	F	VF	XF	Unc
1686	—	60.00	120	250	500	—

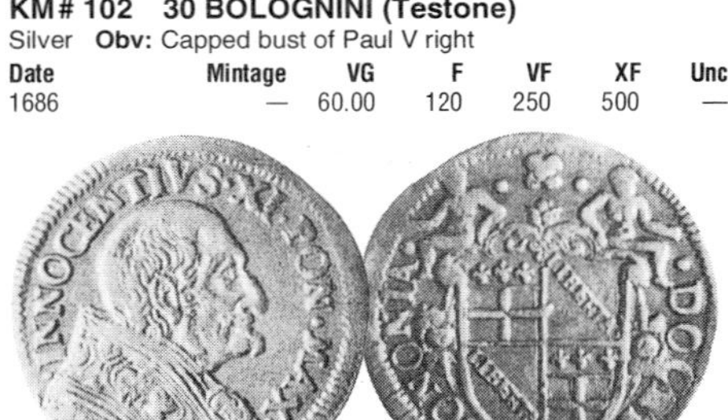

KM# 119 30 BOLOGNINI (Testone)

Silver **Obv:** Capped bust of Innocent XII right **Rev:** Shield **Rev. Legend:** BONONIA DOCET

Date	Mintage	VG	F	VF	XF	Unc
ND	—	60.00	120	250	500	—

KM# 85 40 BOLOGNINI (1/2 Scudo - 2 Lire)

Silver **Subject:** Clement X **Obv:** Arms **Rev:** Floral cross, two shields **Rev. Legend:** BONONIA DOCET

Date	Mintage	VG	F	VF	XF	Unc
1673	—	205	375	625	1,250	—

KM# 86 40 BOLOGNINI (1/2 Scudo - 2 Lire)

Silver **Rev:** Different shields

Date	Mintage	VG	F	VF	XF	Unc
1673	—	205	375	625	1,250	—
1674	—	205	375	625	1,250	—
1675	—	205	375	625	1,250	—

KM# 113 40 BOLOGNINI (1/2 Scudo - 2 Lire)

Silver **Subject:** Alexander VIII **Rev:** Floral cross, two shields **Rev. Legend:** BONONIA DOCET

Date	Mintage	VG	F	VF	XF	Unc
1690 Rare	—	—	—	—	—	—

KM# 125 40 BOLOGNINI (1/2 Scudo - 2 Lire)

Silver **Subject:** Innocent XII

Date	Mintage	VG	F	VF	XF	Unc
1692 Rare	—	—	—	—	—	—

KM# 83 80 BOLOGNIA (4 Lire - Scudo)

Silver **Subject:** Clement X **Obv:** Arms **Rev:** Floral cross, shields **Rev. Legend:** BONONIA DOCET **Note:** Dav. #4082.

Date	Mintage	VG	F	VF	XF	Unc
1671	—	2,000	4,000	7,000	—	—
1672	—	2,000	4,000	7,000	—	—
1673	—	2,000	4,000	7,000	—	—

KM# 87 80 BOLOGNIA (4 Lire - Scudo)

Silver **Rev:** Different shields **Note:** Dav. #4083.

Date	Mintage	VG	F	VF	XF	Unc
1673	—	2,000	4,000	7,000	—	—
1674	—	2,000	4,000	7,000	—	—

KM# 103 80 BOLOGNIA (4 Lire - Scudo)

Silver **Subject:** Innocent XI **Rev:** Radiant cross **ev. Legend:** BONONIA DOCET **Note:** Dav. #4097.

Date	Mintage	VG	F	VF	XF	Unc
1687	—	—	—	—	—	—
ND Rare	—	—	—	—	—	—

KM# 126 80 BOLOGNIA (4 Lire - Scudo)

Silver **Subject:** Innocent XII **Rev:** Floral cross, two shields **Rev. Legend:** BONONIA DOCET **Note:** Dav. #4111.

Date	Mintage	VG	F	VF	XF	Unc
1692 Rare	—	—	—	—	—	—

KM# 46 SCUDO D'ORO

3.5000 g., 0.9860 Gold 0.1109 oz. AGW **Subject:** Innocent X **Obv:** Papal arms divide date **Rev:** Floriate cross with two small shields at bottom

Date	Mintage	VG	F	VF	XF	Unc
1654 Rare	—	—	—	—	—	—

KM# 53 SCUDO D'ORO

3.5000 g., 0.9860 Gold 0.1109 oz. AGW **Obv:** Papal arms **Rev:** Floriate cross divides date, two small shields at bottom

Date	Mintage	VG	F	VF	XF	Unc
1655	—	600	1,000	1,800	3,000	—
1656	—	600	1,000	1,800	3,000	—
1657	—	600	1,000	1,800	3,000	—
1658	—	600	1,000	1,800	3,000	—

KM# 57 SCUDO D'ORO

3.5000 g., 0.9860 Gold 0.1109 oz. AGW **Rev:** Different shields

Date	Mintage	VG	F	VF	XF	Unc
1658	—	600	1,000	1,800	3,000	—
1659	—	600	1,000	1,800	3,000	—
1660	—	600	1,000	1,800	3,000	—
1661	—	600	1,000	1,800	3,000	—
1662	—	600	1,000	1,800	3,000	—

KM# 66 SCUDO D'ORO

3.5000 g., 0.9860 Gold 0.1109 oz. AGW **Rev:** Different shields

Date	Mintage	VG	F	VF	XF	Unc
1662	—	600	1,000	1,800	3,000	—
1663	—	600	1,000	1,800	3,000	—
1664	—	600	1,000	1,800	3,000	—

KM# 70 SCUDO D'ORO

3.5000 g., 0.9860 Gold 0.1109 oz. AGW **Rev:** Different shields **Note:** Varieties exist.

Date	Mintage	VG	F	VF	XF	Unc
1666	—	600	1,000	1,800	3,000	—

KM# 47 DOPPIA D'ORO

7.0000 g., 0.9860 Gold 0.2219 oz. AGW **Subject:** Innocent X **Obv:** Papal arms **Rev:** Floriate cross with two small shields at bottom

Date	Mintage	VG	F	VF	XF	Unc
1654 Rare	—	—	—	—	—	—

KM# 54 DOPPIA D'ORO

7.0000 g., 0.9860 Gold 0.2219 oz. AGW **Subject:** Alexander VII **Obv:** Papal arms **Rev:** Floriate arms divide date, two small shields at bottom

Date	Mintage	VG	F	VF	XF	Unc
1655	—	950	1,750	3,000	5,000	—
1656	—	950	1,750	3,000	5,000	—
1657	—	950	1,750	3,000	5,000	—
1658	—	950	1,750	3,000	5,000	—

KM# 58 DOPPIA D'ORO

7.0000 g., 0.9860 Gold 0.2219 oz. AGW **Rev:** Different shields

Date	Mintage	VG	F	VF	XF	Unc
1658	—	950	1,750	3,000	5,000	—
1659	—	950	1,750	3,000	5,000	—
1660	—	950	1,750	3,000	5,000	—
1661	—	950	1,750	3,000	5,000	—

KM# 69 DOPPIA D'ORO

7.0000 g., 0.9860 Gold 0.2219 oz. AGW

Date	Mintage	VG	F	VF	XF	Unc
1665	—	950	1,750	3,000	5,000	—
1666	—	950	1,750	3,000	5,000	—

KM# 48 4 DOPPIE D'ORO (Quadrupla)

14.0000 g., 0.9860 Gold 0.4438 oz. AGW **Subject:** Innocent X **Obv:** Papal arms divide date **Rev:** Floriate cross, two small shields at bottom

Date	Mintage	VG	F	VF	XF	Unc
1654 Rare	—	—	—	—	—	—

KM# 55 QUADRUPLA (4 Scudi D'oro)

14.0000 g., 0.9860 Gold 0.4438 oz. AGW **Subject:** Alexander VII **Obv:** Papal arms in inner circle **Rev:** Floriate cross divides date, two small shields at bottom **Note:** Varieties exist.

Date	Mintage	VG	F	VF	XF	Unc
1655	—	1,350	2,800	4,000	6,500	—
1656	—	1,350	2,800	4,000	6,500	—
1657	—	1,350	2,800	4,000	6,500	—

KM# 59 QUADRUPLA (4 Scudi D'oro)

14.0000 g., 0.9860 Gold 0.4438 oz. AGW **Rev:** Two different small shields at bottom

Date	Mintage	VG	F	VF	XF	Unc
1659	—	1,350	2,500	4,000	6,500	—
1660	—	1,350	2,500	4,000	6,500	—
1661	—	1,350	2,500	4,000	6,500	—

KM# 74 QUADRUPLA (4 Scudi D'oro)

14.0000 g., 0.9860 Gold 0.4438 oz. AGW **Subject:** Clement IX **Obv:** Papal arms in inner circle **Rev:** Floriate cross divides arms, two small shields at bottom

Date	Mintage	VG	F	VF	XF	Unc
1667 Rare	—	—	—	—	—	—

PAPAL STATES-FERRARA

A city located in northeastern Italy in Emalia. With the Papacy 1598-1859.

MINT OFFICIALS' INITIALS

Initial	Date	Name
FR	1605-21	Nicolo Franchini and Agostino Rivarola
NF	1621-23	Nicolo Franchini
TA, TAB, (TA)B	1621-44	Tommaso and Agostino Bellegrandi

CITY

STANDARD COINAGE

KM# 5 QUATTRINO

Copper **Subject:** Paul V **Obv:** Arms **Rev:** FERRARI

Date	Mintage	Good	VG	F	VF	XF
ND	—	13.50	22.50	40.00	80.00	—

KM# 6 QUATTRINO

Copper **Rev:** FER/RARI

Date	Mintage	Good	VG	F	VF	XF
ND	—	13.50	22.50	40.00	80.00	—

KM# 7 QUATTRINO

Copper **Obv:** Capped bust of Pual V left, PP in legend **Rev:** St. George slaying dragon **Rev. Legend:** FERRARIAE • PROTECTOR

Date	Mintage	Good	VG	F	VF	XF
ND	—	15.00	25.00	38.00	70.00	—

KM# 15 QUATTRINO

Copper **Obv:** Legend without • PP •

Date	Mintage	Good	VG	F	VF	XF
1612	—	15.00	25.00	38.00	70.00	—
1613	—	15.00	25.00	38.00	70.00	—

KM# 16 QUATTRINO

Copper **Rev. Legend:** • PROTECTCTOR • FERRARIAE

Date	Mintage	Good	VG	F	VF	XF
1613	—	15.00	25.00	38.00	70.00	—
ND	—	15.00	25.00	38.00	70.00	—

KM# 17 QUATTRINO

Copper **Rev. Legend:** S • GEOR • PROT • FERRARIAE

Date	Mintage	Good	VG	F	VF	XF
1613	—	15.00	25.00	38.00	70.00	—

KM# 18 QUATTRINO

Copper **Obv:** Legend without • PP •

Date	Mintage	Good	VG	F	VF	XF
1613	—	15.00	26.00	40.00	75.00	—

KM# 40 QUATTRINO

Copper **Subject:** Gregory XV **Obv:** Arms **Rev. Inscription:** FER / RARI / 1622

Date	Mintage	Good	VG	F	VF	XF
1622	—	15.00	26.00	40.00	75.00	—

KM# 42 QUATTRINO

Copper **Obv:** Bust right **Rev:** FER/RARI/date

Date	Mintage	Good	VG	F	VF	XF
1622	—	35.00	55.00	85.00	135	—
1623	—	35.00	55.00	85.00	135	—

KM# 41 QUATTRINO

Copper **Rev:** FER/RARI within wreath

Date	Mintage	Good	VG	F	VF	XF
ND	—	15.00	26.00	40.00	75.00	—

KM# 46 QUATTRINO
Copper **Obv:** Arms of Cardinal **Rev:** CIVITAS • FERRARIAE • 1623 **Note:** Sede Vacante Issue.

Date	Mintage	Good	VG	F	VF	XF
1623	—	70.00	115	175	275	—

KM# 47 QUATTRINO
Copper **Obv:** Capped bust of Urban VIII right **Rev:** St. George slaying dragon

Date	Mintage	Good	VG	F	VF	XF
1623	—	13.50	22.50	35.00	65.00	—

KM# 60 QUATTRINO
Copper **Obv:** Arms **Rev:** Within wreath **Rev. Inscription:** FER / RARI

Date	Mintage	Good	VG	F	VF	XF
1636	—	9.00	15.00	22.00	50.00	100
ND	—	9.00	15.00	22.00	50.00	100

KM# 65 QUATTRINO
Copper **Subject:** Innocent X **Obv:** Arms, A • X **Rev. Inscription:** FER / RARI

Date	Mintage	Good	VG	F	VF	XF
ND	—	10.00	16.50	25.00	55.00	—

KM# 78 QUATTRINO
Copper **Rev:** Fer/RARIAE/date within wreath

Date	Mintage	Good	VG	F	VF	XF
1655	—	6.50	13.50	25.00	50.00	—
1656	—	6.50	13.50	25.00	50.00	—

KM# 79 QUATTRINO
Copper **Rev:** St. George slaying dragon

Date	Mintage	Good	VG	F	VF	XF
1655	—	6.50	13.50	25.00	50.00	—

KM# 76 QUATTRINO
Copper **Obv:** Arms of Cardinal **Rev:** FER/RARI within wreath **Note:** Sede Vacante Issue.

Date	Mintage	Good	VG	F	VF	XF
1655	—	60.00	100	150	250	—

KM# 77 QUATTRINO
Copper **Subject:** Alexander VII **Obv:** Arms

Date	Mintage	VG	F	VF	XF	Unc
ND Unique	—	—	—	—	—	—

KM# 91 QUATTRINO
Copper **Subject:** Clement X **Rev:** FER/RARI

Date	Mintage	Good	VG	F	VF	XF
1675	—	6.50	13.50	25.00	45.00	—
1676	—	6.50	13.50	25.00	45.00	—

KM# 92 QUATTRINO
Copper **Rev:** FER/RARI within wreath

Date	Mintage	Good	VG	F	VF	XF
1675	—	6.50	13.50	25.00	45.00	—

KM# 93 QUATTRINO
Copper **Rev:** Wreath

Date	Mintage	Good	VG	F	VF	XF
1675	—	6.50	13.50	25.00	45.00	—
1676	—	6.50	13.50	25.00	45.00	—

KM# 95 QUATTRINO
Copper **Obv:** Arms of Cardinal **Rev:** FER/RARI/1676 **Note:** Sede Vacante Issue.

Date	Mintage	Good	VG	F	VF	XF
1676	—	13.50	27.50	50.00	90.00	—

KM# 98 QUATTRINO
Copper **Obv:** FER/RARI/1677 **Rev:** St. George slaying dragon

Date	Mintage	Good	VG	F	VF	XF
1677	—	6.50	13.50	25.00	50.00	—

KM# 33 1/2 BAIOCCO
Copper **Subject:** Gregory XV **Obv:** Arms **Rev:** FER/RARI/1621 within wreath

Date	Mintage	Good	VG	F	VF	XF
1621	—	22.50	40.00	60.00	95.00	—

KM# 43 1/2 BAIOCCO
Copper **Rev:** FER/RARI/date without wreath

Date	Mintage	Good	VG	F	VF	XF
1622	—	22.50	40.00	60.00	100	—
1623	—	22.50	40.00	60.00	100	—

KM# 49 1/2 BAIOCCO
Copper **Subject:** Urban VIII **Obv:** Arms **Rev:** FER/RARI/1623

Date	Mintage	Good	VG	F	VF	XF
1623	—	8.00	16.00	30.00	55.00	—

KM# 48 1/2 BAIOCCO
Copper **Obv:** Arms of Cardinal **Rev:** CIVITAS FERRARIAE 1623 **Note:** Sede Vacante issue.

Date	Mintage	VG	F	VF	XF	Unc
1623 Rare	—	—	—	—	—	—

KM# 70 1/2 BAIOCCO
Copper **Subject:** Innocent X **Rev:** FER/RARI

Date	Mintage	Good	VG	F	VF	XF
1654(sic)	—	12.00	25.00	45.00	85.00	—

KM# 90 1/2 BAIOCCO
Copper **Subject:** Clement X **Note:** Varieties exist.

Date	Mintage	Good	VG	F	VF	XF
1674	—	8.00	16.00	32.00	70.00	175
1675	—	8.00	16.00	32.00	70.00	175
1676	—	8.00	16.00	32.00	70.00	175
ND	—	8.00	16.00	32.00	70.00	175

KM# 94 1/2 BAIOCCO
Copper **Rev:** St. George slaying dragon

Date	Mintage	Good	VG	F	VF	XF
1675	—	8.00	16.00	30.00	65.00	175
1676	—	8.00	16.00	30.00	65.00	175

KM# 96 1/2 BAIOCCO
Copper **Obv:** Arms of Cardinal **Rev:** FER/RARI/1676 **Note:** Sede Vacante issue.

Date	Mintage	Good	VG	F	VF	XF
1676	—	20.00	40.00	70.00	135	—

KM# 97 1/2 BAIOCCO
Copper **Obv:** Arms of Cardinal **Rev:** FER/RARI/date **Note:** Sede Vacante issue.

Date	Mintage	Good	VG	F	VF	XF
1676	—	7.00	14.00	25.00	50.00	—
1677	—	7.00	14.00	25.00	50.00	—

KM# 8 1/2 GROSSO
Silver **Obv:** Bust right **Rev:** FER/RARI in wreath

Date	Mintage	Good	VG	F	VF	XF
ND	—	35.00	60.00	100	180	—

KM# 9 1/2 GROSSO
Silver **Rev:** FER/RARI in arabesque border

Date	Mintage	Good	VG	F	VF	XF
ND	—	35.00	60.00	100	180	—

KM# 34 1/2 GROSSO
Silver **Obv:** Bust of Gregory XV right **Rev:** FER/RARI within wreath

Date	Mintage	Good	VG	F	VF	XF
1621	—	40.00	70.00	115	210	—
1622	—	40.00	70.00	115	210	—
1623	—	40.00	70.00	115	210	—

KM# 35 1/2 GROSSO
Silver **Obv:** Bust of Gregory XV right **Rev:** FER/RARI in arabesque border

Date	Mintage	Good	VG	F	VF	XF
1621	—	40.00	70.00	115	210	—
1622	—	40.00	70.00	115	210	—
1623	—	40.00	70.00	115	210	—

KM# 71 1/2 GROSSO
Silver **Subject:** Innocent X **Obv:** Arms **Rev:** Within wreath **Rev. Inscription:** FER / RARI

Date	Mintage	Good	VG	F	VF	XF
1654/X	—	20.00	40.00	65.00	120	—
1655/X	—	20.00	40.00	65.00	120	—
ND	—	20.00	40.00	65.00	120	—

KM# 72 1/2 GROSSO
Silver **Subject:** Alexander VII **Rev. Inscription:** FER / RARI / 1654

Date	Mintage	Good	VG	F	VF	XF
1654	—	18.00	35.00	60.00	100	—

KM# 10 GROSSO
Silver **Subject:** Paul V **Obv:** Arms **Rev:** St. George slaying dragon

Date	Mintage	Good	VG	F	VF	XF
ND	—	25.00	50.00	80.00	150	250

KM# 36 GROSSO
Silver **Subject:** Gregory XV

Date	Mintage	Good	VG	F	VF	XF
1621 NF	—	40.00	80.00	130	240	—
1622 TAB	—	40.00	80.00	130	240	—
1623 TAB	—	40.00	80.00	130	240	—
1624(sic) TAB	—	40.00	80.00	130	240	—

KM# 50 GROSSO
Silver **Obv:** Arms of Cardinal **Rev:** CIVITAS FERRARIAE 1623 **Note:** Sede Vacante issue.

Date	Mintage	Good	VG	F	VF	XF
1623	—	70.00	135	225	425	—

KM# 52 GROSSO
Silver **Subject:** Urban VIII **Obv:** Arms **Obv. Legend:** PONT MAX **Rev:** St. George slaying dragon

Date	Mintage	Good	VG	F	VF	XF
1624 TAB	—	35.00	60.00	100	180	—

KM# 53 GROSSO
Silver **Obv:** Arms **Obv. Legend:** PM

Date	Mintage	Good	VG	F	VF	XF
1624	—	35.00	60.00	100	180	—

KM# 73 GROSSO
Silver **Subject:** Innocent X **Obv:** Arms

Date	Mintage	Good	VG	F	VF	XF
1654	—	35.00	60.00	100	180	—

KM# 81 GROSSO
Silver **Subject:** Alexander VII **Obv:** Arms **Rev:** St. George slaying dragon

Date	Mintage	Good	VG	F	VF	XF
1655	—	35.00	60.00	100	180	—
1656	—	35.00	60.00	100	180	—
ND	—	35.00	60.00	100	180	—

KM# 80 GROSSO
Silver **Obv:** Arms of Cardinal **Rev:** Shield and CIVITAS FERRARIAE 1655 **Note:** Sede Vacante issue.

Date	Mintage	Good	VG	F	VF	XF
1655	—	90.00	175	300	550	—

KM# 20 GIULIO
Silver **Subject:** Paul V **Obv:** Arms **Rev:** St. George slaying dragon

Date	Mintage	Good	VG	F	VF	XF
1619	—	40.00	70.00	125	225	—
1620	—	40.00	70.00	125	225	—
1621	—	40.00	70.00	125	225	—

KM# 37 GIULIO
Silver **Obv:** Arms of Cardinal **Rev:** CIVITAS FERRARIAE 1621 **Note:** Sede Vacante issue.

Date	Mintage	Good	VG	F	VF	XF
1621	—	80.00	160	290	525	—

KM# 44 GIULIO
Silver **Subject:** Gregory XV **Obv:** Arms **Rev:** St. George slaying dragon

Date	Mintage	Good	VG	F	VF	XF
1622 TAB	—	70.00	135	250	450	—

KM# 51 GIULIO
Silver **Obv:** Arms of Cardinal **Rev:** CIVITAS FERRARIAE 1623 **Note:** Sede Vacante issue.

Date	Mintage	Good	VG	F	VF	XF
1623	—	250	500	1,000	1,850	—

KM# 74 GIULIO
Silver **Subject:** Innocent X **Obv:** Arms **Rev:** St. George slaying dragon

Date	Mintage	Good	VG	F	VF	XF
1654	—	40.00	80.00	145	260	—

KM# 83 GIULIO
Silver **Subject:** Alexander VII **Obv:** Arms **Rev:** St. George slaying dragon

Date	Mintage	Good	VG	F	VF	XF
1655	—	30.00	60.00	110	180	—
1656	—	30.00	60.00	110	180	—

KM# 82 GIULIO
Silver **Obv:** Arms of Cardinal **Rev:** Shield and CIVITAS FERRARIE 1655 **Note:** Sede Vacante issue.

Date	Mintage	Good	VG	F	VF	XF
1655	—	100	200	350	650	—

KM# 21 TESTONE
Silver **Obv:** Capped bust of Paul V right **Rev:** St. George slaying dragon

Date	Mintage	Good	VG	F	VF	XF
1619	—	100	200	425	—	—
1620	—	100	200	425	—	—

KM# 38 TESTONE
Silver **Obv:** Arms of Cardinal **Rev:** CIVITAS FERRARIAE 1621 **Note:** Sede Vacante issue.

Date	Mintage	Good	VG	F	VF	XF
1621	—	200	350	600	1,000	—

KM# 45 TESTONE
Silver **Obv:** Capped bust of Gregory XV right **Rev:** St. George slaying dragon

Date	Mintage	Good	VG	F	VF	XF
1622 TAB	—	100	200	400	800	—

KM# 75 TESTONE
Silver **Subject:** Innocent X

Date	Mintage	Good	VG	F	VF	XF
1654	—	75.00	135	270	550	—

KM# 85 TESTONE
Silver **Subject:** Alexander VII **Obv:** Arms **Rev:** St. George slaying dragon

Date	Mintage	Good	VG	F	VF	XF
1655	—	50.00	100	200	400	—

KM# 86 TESTONE
Silver **Obv:** Different arms

Date	Mintage	Good	VG	F	VF	XF
1655	—	50.00	100	200	400	—

KM# 84 TESTONE
Silver **Obv:** Arms of Cardinal **Rev:** CIVITAS FERRARIAE 1655 and shield **Note:** Sede Vacante issue.

Date	Mintage	Good	VG	F	VF	XF
1655	—	200	350	650	1,000	—

KM# 87 TESTONE
Silver **Obv:** Bust of Alexander VII right

Date	Mintage	Good	VG	F	VF	XF
1656	—	50.00	100	200	400	—

KM# 19 PIASTRA
Silver **Obv:** Capped bust of Paul V right **Rev:** Arms of Cardinal Borghese **Note:** Dav. #4048.

Date	Mintage	VG	F	VF	XF	Unc
MDCXVIII/XIIII (1618)	—	750	1,500	2,500	4,500	—
MDCXVIII (1618)	—	750	1,500	2,500	4,500	—

KM# 22 PIASTRA

Silver **Obv:** Capped bust right, legend starts at lower left **Rev:** St. George slaying dragon, exergue line **Note:** Dav. #4049.

Date	Mintage	VG	F	VF	XF	Unc
1619	—	750	1,500	2,500	4,500	—

KM# 23 PIASTRA

Silver **Rev:** St. George slaying dragon without exergue line below **Note:** Dav. #4050.

Date	Mintage	VG	F	VF	XF	Unc
1619	—	750	1,500	2,500	4,500	—

KM# 30 PIASTRA

Silver **Obv:** Capped bust right, legend starts above bust **Rev:** St. George slaying dragon with exergue line below **Note:** Dav. #4051.

Date	Mintage	VG	F	VF	XF	Unc
1620	—	750	1,500	2,500	4,500	—

KM# 39 PIASTRA

Silver **Obv:** Capped bust of Gregory XV right **Note:** Dav. #4054.

Date	Mintage	VG	F	VF	XF	Unc
1621 NF	—	3,000	6,000	10,000	16,500	—
1622 TAB	—	3,000	6,000	10,000	16,500	—
1623 TAB	—	3,000	6,000	10,000	16,500	—

KM# 54 PIASTRA

Silver **Obv:** Capped bust of Urban VIII right **Note:** Dav. #4062.

Date	Mintage	VG	F	VF	XF	Unc
1624	—	4,500	7,500	11,500	—	—

KM# 55 PIASTRA

Silver **Rev:** Without exergue line **Note:** Dav. #4063.

Date	Mintage	VG	F	VF	XF	Unc
1624	—	4,500	7,500	11,500	—	—

KM# 31 DOPPIA

Gold **Obv:** Capped bust of Paul V right **Rev:** St. George slaying dragon **Note:** Withdrawn issue.

Date	Mintage	VG	F	VF	XF	Unc
1620 Rare	—	—	—	—	—	—

KM# 32 QUADRUPLA

14.0000 g., 0.9860 Gold 0.4438 oz. AGW **Obv:** Bust of Paul V right in inner circle, date in legend **Rev:** St. George and St. Maurelius facing standing **Note:** Withdrawn issue.

Date	Mintage	VG	F	VF	XF	Unc
1620 Rare	—	—	—	—	—	—

PAPAL STATES-GUBBIO

A city in Umbria, was part of the donation of Charlemagne to the pope in 774. It became a consul-governed republic in 1151, came under the dukes of Urbino in 1387, and was ceded to the pope in 1624.

NOTE: For later issues see Roman Republic-Gubbio.

CITY

STANDARD COINAGE

KM# 5 QUATTRINO

Copper, 19.8 mm. **Subject:** Innocent X **Obv:** Arms **Rev:** St. Paul standing **Rev. Legend:** SANCTVS PAVIVS. AP.

Date	Mintage	VG	F	VF	XF	Unc
ND(1645)/II	—	15.00	28.00	55.00	85.00	—
ND(1646)/III	—	15.00	28.00	55.00	85.00	—
ND(1647)/IIII	—	15.00	28.00	55.00	85.00	—
ND(1648)/V	—	15.00	28.00	55.00	85.00	—
ND(1649)/VI	—	15.00	28.00	55.00	85.00	—
ND(1650)/VII	—	15.00	28.00	55.00	85.00	—
ND(1651)/VIII	—	15.00	28.00	55.00	85.00	—
ND(1652)/VIIII	—	15.00	28.00	55.00	85.00	—
ND(1653)/X	—	15.00	28.00	55.00	85.00	—

KM# 6 QUATTRINO

Copper **Rev:** Without AP at end of legend

Date	Mintage	VG	F	VF	XF	Unc
ND(1646)/III	—	15.00	28.00	55.00	85.00	—
ND(1647)/IIII	—	15.00	28.00	55.00	85.00	—
ND(1652)/IX	—	15.00	28.00	55.00	85.00	—

KM# 10 QUATTRINO

Copper **Obv:** Arms, FG at sides **Rev:** Holy Door open **Note:** Holy Year Issue.

Date	Mintage	VG	F	VF	XF	Unc
1650/VI	—	16.50	30.00	60.00	90.00	—

KM# 11 QUATTRINO

Copper **Rev:** Holy door closed **Note:** Holy Year Issue.

Date	Mintage	VG	F	VF	XF	Unc
1650/VI	—	16.50	30.00	60.00	90.00	—

KM# 12 QUATTRINO

Copper **Subject:** Alexander VII **Obv:** Arms **Rev:** St. Paul standing

Date	Mintage	VG	F	VF	XF	Unc
ND(1655)/I	—	16.50	30.00	60.00	90.00	—

KM# 13 QUATTRINO

Copper **Rev:** Without AP in legend

Date	Mintage	VG	F	VF	XF	Unc
ND(1655)/I	—	16.50	30.00	60.00	90.00	—

KM# 14 QUATTRINO

Copper **Obv:** Simple arms

Date	Mintage	VG	F	VF	XF	Unc
ND(1655)/I	—	15.00	28.00	55.00	85.00	—

KM# 15 QUATTRINO

Copper **Rev:** Virgin Mary standing on crescent

Date	Mintage	VG	F	VF	XF	Unc
ND(1655)/I	—	16.50	30.00	60.00	90.00	—

KM# 25 QUATTRINO

Copper **Subject:** Clement IX **Obv:** Arms **Rev:** St. Paul standing

Date	Mintage	VG	F	VF	XF	Unc
ND(1667)/I	—	22.00	40.00	70.00	110	—
ND	—	22.00	40.00	70.00	110	—

KM# 32 QUATTRINO

Copper **Rev:** Holy Door open

Date	Mintage	VG	F	VF	XF	Unc
ND	—	20.00	35.00	65.00	100	—

KM# 31 QUATTRINO

Copper **Subject:** Clement X **Rev:** Closed Holy Door **Note:** Holy Year Issue.

Date	Mintage	VG	F	VF	XF	Unc
ND	—	20.00	35.00	65.00	100	—

KM# 33 QUATTRINO

Copper **Rev:** Bust of St. Paul left, ROMA in exergue **Note:** Varieties in quality of engraving.

Date	Mintage	VG	F	VF	XF	Unc
ND	—	16.50	30.00	60.00	90.00	—

KM# 34 QUATTRINO

Copper **Rev:** Bust of SS. Peter and Paul

Date	Mintage	VG	F	VF	XF	Unc
ND	—	16.50	30.00	60.00	90.00	—

KM# 35 QUATTRINO

Copper **Subject:** Innocent XI **Rev:** St. Paul standing, sword right

Date	Mintage	VG	F	VF	XF	Unc
ND(1676/I	—	12.00	22.00	45.00	70.00	—

KM# 36 QUATTRINO

Copper **Rev:** St. Peter standing

Date	Mintage	VG	F	VF	XF	Unc
ND(1677)/II	—	12.00	22.00	45.00	70.00	—
ND(1678)/III	—	12.00	22.00	45.00	70.00	—

KM# 38 QUATTRINO

Copper **Rev:** Half-length figure of Madonna and child **ev. Legend:** MONSTRA • TE • ESSEIMATR

Date	Mintage	VG	F	VF	XF	Unc
ND(1678)/III	—	12.00	22.00	45.00	70.00	—

KM# 40 QUATTRINO

Copper **Rev:** St. Paul standing, sword left

Date	Mintage	VG	F	VF	XF	Unc
ND(1680)/V	—	12.00	22.00	45.00	70.00	—

KM# 41 QUATTRINO

Copper **Rev:** Half-length figure of Madonna and child **Rev. Legend:** SVB • TVVM PRAESIDIVM

Date	Mintage	VG	F	VF	XF	Unc
ND(1680)/V	—	14.00	27.00	50.00	80.00	—

KM# 43 QUATTRINO

Copper **Obv:** INNOCE/NTVS/XIPM/(year) on cartouche **Rev:** Papal arms

Date	Mintage	VG	F	VF	XF	Unc
ND(1682)/VII	—	14.00	27.00	50.00	80.00	—
ND(1683)/VIII	—	14.00	27.00	50.00	80.00	—
ND(1684)/VIIII	—	14.00	27.00	50.00	80.00	—
ND(1685)/X	—	14.00	27.00	50.00	80.00	—
ND(1686)/XI	—	14.00	27.00	50.00	80.00	—
ND(1687)/XII	—	14.00	27.00	50.00	80.00	—

KM# 44 QUATTRINO

Copper **Subject:** Alexander VIII **Obv:** Arms **Rev:** St. Paul standing

Date	Mintage	VG	F	VF	XF	Unc
ND	—	13.50	25.00	45.00	70.00	—

KM# 51 QUATTRINO

Copper **Rev:** AP at end of legend

Date	Mintage	VG	F	VF	XF	Unc
ND	—	13.50	25.00	45.00	70.00	—

KM# 52 QUATTRINO

Copper **Obv:** Arms, without legend

Date	Mintage	VG	F	VF	XF	Unc
ND	—	13.50	25.00	45.00	70.00	—

KM# 50 QUATTRINO

Copper **Rev:** St. Paul standing without AP at end of legend

Date	Mintage	VG	F	VF	XF	Unc
ND(1690)/II	—	13.50	25.00	45.00	70.00	—

KM# 54 QUATTRINO

Copper **Subject:** Innocent XII **Obv:** Within wreath **Rev:** Papal arms **Rev. Inscription:** INNOC / XII / PONT • M / AI

Date	Mintage	VG	F	VF	XF	Unc
ND(1691)/I	—	14.00	27.00	50.00	75.00	—

KM# 55 QUATTRINO

Copper **Obv:** Arms **Rev:** St. Paul standing

Date	Mintage	VG	F	VF	XF	Unc
ND(1692)/II	—	10.00	20.00	40.00	65.00	—

KM# 56 QUATTRINO
Copper **Rev:** St. Paul standing

Date	Mintage	VG	F	VF	XF	Unc
ND(1692)/II	—	10.00	20.00	40.00	65.00	—

KM# 57 QUATTRINO
Copper **Rev:** St. Paul standing, sword right

Date	Mintage	VG	F	VF	XF	Unc
ND(1693)/III	—	4.00	10.00	22.00	40.00	—
ND(1694)/IIII	—	4.00	10.00	22.00	40.00	—
ND(1695)/V	—	4.00	10.00	22.00	40.00	—
ND(1696)/VI	—	4.00	10.00	22.00	40.00	—
ND(1697)/VII	—	4.00	10.00	22.00	40.00	—
ND(1698)/VIII	—	4.00	10.00	22.00	40.00	—
ND(1699)/IX	—	4.00	10.00	22.00	40.00	—
ND(1700)/10	—	4.00	10.00	22.00	40.00	—

KM# 58 QUATTRINO
Copper **Rev:** St. Paul seated right

Date	Mintage	VG	F	VF	XF	Unc
ND(1693)/III	—	4.00	10.00	22.00	40.00	—

KM# 59 QUATTRINO
Copper **Rev:** St. Paul standing facing, holding keys right

Date	Mintage	VG	F	VF	XF	Unc
ND(1693)/III	—	4.00	10.00	22.00	40.00	—

KM# 60 QUATTRINO
Copper **Rev:** St. Paul standing right, keys right

Date	Mintage	VG	F	VF	XF	Unc
ND(1693)/III	—	4.00	10.00	22.00	40.00	—

KM# 61 QUATTRINO
Copper **Rev:** St. Paul standing facing, keys left, book right

Date	Mintage	VG	F	VF	XF	Unc
ND(1693)/III	—	4.00	10.00	22.00	40.00	—

KM# 62 QUATTRINO
Copper **Rev:** St. Paul standing facing without keys or book

Date	Mintage	VG	F	VF	XF	Unc
ND(1693)/III	—	4.00	10.00	22.00	40.00	—

KM# 63 QUATTRINO
Copper **Rev:** St. Paul standing, keys lower left, book right

Date	Mintage	VG	F	VF	XF	Unc
ND(1694)/IIII	—	4.00	10.00	22.00	40.00	—
ND(1695)/V	—	4.00	10.00	22.00	40.00	—
ND(1696)/VI	—	4.00	10.00	22.00	40.00	—
ND(1697)/VII	—	4.00	10.00	22.00	40.00	—
ND(1698)/VIII	—	4.00	10.00	22.00	40.00	—
ND(1699)/VIIII	—	4.00	10.00	22.00	40.00	—
ND(1700)/10	—	4.00	10.00	22.00	40.00	—

KM# 64 QUATTRINO
Copper **Rev:** St. Paul standing, keys upper left, book right

Date	Mintage	VG	F	VF	XF	Unc
ND(1694)/IIII	—	10.00	20.00	40.00	70.00	—
ND(1695)/V	—	10.00	20.00	40.00	70.00	—
ND(1696)/VI	—	10.00	20.00	40.00	70.00	—
ND(1697)/VII	—	10.00	20.00	40.00	70.00	—
ND(1698)/VIII	—	10.00	20.00	40.00	70.00	—
ND(1699)/IX	—	10.00	20.00	40.00	70.00	—
ND(1700)/10	—	10.00	20.00	40.00	70.00	—

KM# 65 QUATTRINO
Copper **Rev:** St. Paul standing, both hands on sword

Date	Mintage	VG	F	VF	XF	Unc
ND(1694)IIII	—	10.00	20.00	40.00	65.00	—

KM# 67 QUATTRINO
Copper **Rev:** St. Paul standing, sword left

Date	Mintage	VG	F	VF	XF	Unc
ND(1697)/VII	—	10.00	20.00	40.00	65.00	—

KM# 68 QUATTRINO
Copper **Rev:** St. Paul seated, sword left

Date	Mintage	VG	F	VF	XF	Unc
ND(1699)/IX	—	10.00	20.00	40.00	65.00	—
ND(1700)/10	—	10.00	20.00	40.00	65.00	—

KM# 75 QUATTRINO
Copper **Rev:** St. Paul seated, EVG in exergue

Date	Mintage	VG	F	VF	XF	Unc
ND(1700)/10	—	10.00	20.00	40.00	65.00	—

KM# 76 QUATTRINO
Copper **Rev:** St. Paul seated, with sword left, EVG in exergue

Date	Mintage	VG	F	VF	XF	Unc
ND(1700)/10	—	10.00	20.00	40.00	65.00	—

KM# 7 1/2 BAIOCCO
Copper **Subject:** Innocent X **Obv:** Arms **Rev:** MEZZO/BAIOC/CO within wreath

Date	Mintage	VG	F	VF	XF	Unc
ND(1648)/V	—	10.00	20.00	40.00	65.00	—
ND(1649)/VI	—	10.00	20.00	40.00	65.00	—
ND(1650)/VII	—	10.00	20.00	40.00	65.00	—
ND(1651)/VIII	—	10.00	20.00	40.00	65.00	—
ND(1652)/VIIII	—	10.00	20.00	40.00	65.00	—
ND(1653)/X	—	10.00	20.00	40.00	65.00	—

KM# 16 1/2 BAIOCCO
Copper **Subject:** Alexander VII **Rev:** In laurel wreath
Rev. Inscription: MEZO / BAIOC / CO

Date	Mintage	VG	F	VF	XF	Unc
ND	—	10.00	20.00	40.00	65.00	—

KM# 17 1/2 BAIOCCO
Copper **Obv:** Simple arms

Date	Mintage	VG	F	VF	XF	Unc
ND	—	12.00	22.00	45.00	70.00	—

KM# 18 1/2 BAIOCCO
Copper **Obv:** Arms **Rev:** Legend in oak wreath

Date	Mintage	VG	F	VF	XF	Unc
ND	—	10.00	20.00	40.00	65.00	—

KM# 19 1/2 BAIOCCO
Copper **Obv:** Simple arms

Date	Mintage	VG	F	VF	XF	Unc
ND	—	12.00	22.00	45.00	70.00	—

KM# 26 1/2 BAIOCCO
Copper **Subject:** Clement IX **Obv:** Arms **Rev:** MEZO/BAIOC/CO within laurel wreath **Note:** Varieties exist.

Date	Mintage	VG	F	VF	XF	Unc
ND	—	15.00	30.00	60.00	90.00	—

KM# 27 1/2 BAIOCCO
Copper **Rev:** MEZO/BAIOC/CO within oak wreath

Date	Mintage	VG	F	VF	XF	Unc
ND	—	15.00	30.00	60.00	90.00	—

KM# 30 1/2 BAIOCCO
Copper **Subject:** Clement X **Rev:** MEZO/BAIOC/CO within laurel wreath

Date	Mintage	VG	F	VF	XF	Unc
ND	—	9.00	18.00	35.00	55.00	—

KM# 37 1/2 BAIOCCO
Copper **Subject:** Innocnet XI **Rev:** MEZZO/BAIOC/CO in cartouche, symbol above and/or below

Date	Mintage	VG	F	VF	XF	Unc
ND(1677)/II	—	8.00	15.00	28.00	50.00	—
ND(1678)/III	—	8.00	15.00	28.00	50.00	—
ND(1679)/IIII	—	8.00	15.00	28.00	50.00	—
ND(1680)/V	—	8.00	15.00	28.00	50.00	—
ND(1681)/VI	—	8.00	15.00	28.00	50.00	—
ND(1682)/VII	—	8.00	15.00	28.00	50.00	—
ND(1683)/VIII	—	8.00	15.00	28.00	50.00	—
ND(1684)/IX	—	8.00	15.00	28.00	50.00	—
ND	—	8.00	15.00	28.00	50.00	—

KM# 42 1/2 BAIOCCO
Copper **Rev:** Legend within laurel wreath

Date	Mintage	VG	F	VF	XF	Unc
ND(1680)V	—	8.00	15.00	28.00	50.00	—
ND(1681)/VI	—	8.00	15.00	28.00	50.00	—
ND(1682)/VII	—	8.00	15.00	28.00	50.00	—
ND(1683)/VIII	—	8.00	15.00	28.00	50.00	—
ND(1684)IX	—	8.00	15.00	28.00	50.00	—
ND(1685)/X	—	8.00	15.00	28.00	50.00	—
ND(1686)/XI	—	8.00	15.00	28.00	50.00	—

KM# 45 1/2 BAIOCCO
Copper **Subject:** Alexander VIII **Rev:** MEZO/BAIOC/CO in laurel wreath

Date	Mintage	VG	F	VF	XF	Unc
ND(1689)/I	—	9.00	18.00	35.00	55.00	—

KM# 53 1/2 BAIOCCO
Copper **Subject:** Innocent XII

Date	Mintage	VG	F	VF	XF	Unc
ND(1690)/II	—	8.00	15.00	28.00	50.00	—
ND(1691)/III	—	8.00	15.00	28.00	50.00	—
ND(1692)/IIII	—	8.00	15.00	28.00	50.00	—
ND(1693)/V	—	8.00	15.00	28.00	50.00	—
ND(1694)/VI	—	8.00	15.00	28.00	50.00	—
ND(1695)/VII	—	8.00	15.00	28.00	50.00	—
1696	—	8.00	15.00	28.00	50.00	—

KM# 66 1/2 BAIOCCO
Copper **Rev:** MEZO/BAIOC/CO in palm wreath

Date	Mintage	VG	F	VF	XF	Unc
ND(1694)/VI	—	8.00	15.00	28.00	50.00	—
1696	—	8.00	15.00	28.00	50.00	—
ND	—	8.00	15.00	28.00	50.00	—

PARMA

A town in Emilia, which was a papal possession from 1512 to 1545, was seized by France in 1796, and was attached to the Napoleonic Empire in 1808. In 1814, Parma was assigned to Marie Louise, empress of Napoleon I. It was annexed to Sardinia in 1860.

RULERS
Ranuccio Farnese I, 1592-1622
Odardo Farnese, 1622-1646
Ranuccio Farnese II, 1646-1694
Francesco Farnese I, 1694-1727

CITY

STANDARD COINAGE

DAV# 4120 SCUDO
Silver **Ruler:** Odardo Farnese **Obv:** Bust right, date below **Obv. Legend:** ODOARDVS. FAR. PAR. ET. PLA. DVX. V **Rev:** Half figure right, SCVDO below **Rev. Legend:** S. VITALIS. PARME. PROTECTOR.

Date	Mintage	VG	F	VF	XF	Unc
1626	—	300	650	1,350	3,500	—
1627	—	300	650	1,350	3,500	—
1628	—	300	650	1,350	3,500	—
1629	—	300	650	1,350	3,500	—
ND	—	300	650	1,350	3,500	—

DAV# 4125 SCUDO
Silver **Ruler:** Ranuccio Farnese II **Obv. Legend:** RAN. FAR. PAR. ET. PLA. DVX. VI. **Rev. Legend:** S. VITALIS. PARMAE. PROT.

Date	Mintage	VG	F	VF	XF	Unc
ND	—	350	700	1,450	3,750	—

DAV# 4117 TALLERO (10 Guillie)
Silver **Ruler:** Odardo Farnese **Obv:** Crowned arms in Order chain **Rev:** Half-length figure of saint right

Date	Mintage	VG	F	VF	XF	Unc
ND	—	1,200	2,000	4,000	—	—

DAV# 4115 DUCATON

25.7040 g., 0.9020 Silver 0.7454 oz. ASW **Ruler:** Ranuccio Farnese I **Obv. Legend:** RAIN. FA(R) (N). PAR. ET. PLAC. DVX. IIII or IV **Rev:** Pallas and Mars holding crown above trees

Date	Mintage	VG	F	VF	XF	Unc
1603	—	1,000	2,000	4,000	—	—
1604	—	1,000	2,000	4,000	—	—
1605	—	1,000	2,000	4,000	—	—
1606	—	1,000	2,000	4,000	10,000	—
1607	—	1,000	2,000	4,000	—	—
1614	—	750	1,500	3,000	5,000	—
1615	—	750	1,500	3,000	5,000	—
1616	—	750	1,500	3,000	5,000	—
1617	—	750	1,500	3,000	5,000	—
1624	—	750	1,500	3,000	5,000	—

DAV# 4116 DUCATON

25.7040 g., 0.9020 Silver 0.7454 oz. ASW **Ruler:** Ranuccio Farnese I **Obv:** Different bust left **Rev:** Ship with date below **Rev. Legend:** ADVERSIS. PROVECTA. NOTIS.

Date	Mintage	VG	F	VF	XF	Unc
1621 Rare	—	—	—	—	—	—

DAV# 4118 DUCATON

25.7040 g., 0.9020 Silver 0.7454 oz. ASW **Ruler:** Odardo Farnese **Obv:** Bust right with or without border **Obv. Legend:** ODOARDVS... **Rev:** Cherubs above Madonna and child **ev. Legend:** MILLE. CLYPEI-PENDENT*

Date	Mintage	VG	F	VF	XF	Unc
1623	—	1,250	2,500	6,500	—	—
1624	—	1,250	2,500	6,500	—	—
1625	—	1,000	2,250	6,000	—	—
1626	—	1,000	2,250	6,000	—	—
1629	—	1,500	3,000	7,000	—	—
ND	—	1,000	2,000	5,000	—	—

DAV# 4121 DUCATON

25.7040 g., 0.9020 Silver 0.7454 oz. ASW **Ruler:** Odardo Farnese **Obv:** A flanking date in exergue **Rev:** PARME below legend **Rev. Legend:** MILE...

Date	Mintage	VG	F	VF	XF	Unc
1629	—	1,250	2,500	6,500	—	—
1638	—	1,250	2,500	6,500	—	—

DAV# 4123 DUCATON

25.7040 g., 0.9020 Silver 0.7454 oz. ASW **Ruler:** Ranuccio Farnese II **Obv:** Bust of Ranuccio II left **Obv. Legend:** RAN(V). II. FAR. PAR. ET. PLA. DVX. W. **Rev:** Roman numerals below Pallas and Mars **Rev. Legend:** QVESITAM. **. MERITAS.

Date	Mintage	VG	F	VF	XF	Unc
1660	—	1,650	2,750	5,500	—	—
1673	—	1,250	2,200	4,550	—	—
1674	—	1,250	2,200	4,550	—	—
1676	—	1,250	2,200	4,550	—	—
1677	—	1,250	2,200	4,550	—	—

DAV# 4124 DUCATON

25.7040 g., 0.9020 Silver 0.7454 oz. ASW **Ruler:** Ranuccio Farnese II **Obv:** Bust of Ranuccio II left **Obv. Inscription:** Roman numeral date below bust **Rev:** Fleur-de-lis below Pallas and Mars

Date	Mintage	VG	F	VF	XF	Unc
1692	—	1,400	2,500	4,800	—	—

DAV# 4114 2 DUCATONE

Silver **Ruler:** Ranuccio Farnese I **Obv:** Bust of Ranuccio II left

Date	Mintage	VG	F	VF	XF	Unc
1604	—	2,000	4,000	7,000	13,000	—
1614	—	2,000	4,000	7,000	13,000	—
1615	—	2,000	4,000	7,000	13,000	—
1616	—	2,000	4,000	7,000	13,000	—
1617	—	2,000	4,000	7,000	13,000	—

DAV# 4119 2 DUCATONE

14.2820 g., Silver **Ruler:** Odardo Farnese **Obv:** Bust of Odoardo left **Rev:** Madonna seated and child under crown held by two cherubs

Date	Mintage	VG	F	VF	XF	Unc
1626	—	3,000	5,600	9,000	16,000	—
ND	—	3,000	5,600	9,000	16,000	—

DAV# 4122 2 DUCATONE

14.2820 g., Silver **Ruler:** Ranuccio Farnese II **Note:** Similar to 1 Ducatone, Dav. #4123.

Date	Mintage	VG	F	VF	XF	Unc
1660	—	7,000	15,000	25,000	—	—

FR# 912 DOPPIA

7.1410 g., 0.8910 Gold 0.2046 oz. AGW **Ruler:** Odardo Farnese **Obv:** Bust of Odoardo right in inner circle **Rev:** Madonna and child under crown held by two cherubs

Date	Mintage	VG	F	VF	XF	Unc
ND	—	900	1,800	3,600	8,400	—

FR# 920 DOPPIA

7.1410 g., 0.8910 Gold 0.2046 oz. AGW **Ruler:** Ranuccio Farnese II **Obv:** Bust of Ranuccio II left **Rev:** Saint Viyae standing, date below

Date	Mintage	VG	F	VF	XF	Unc
1687	—	2,400	4,800	9,600	—	—

FR# 921 DOPPIA

7.1410 g., 0.8910 Gold 0.2046 oz. AGW **Ruler:** Ranuccio Farnese II **Obv:** Bust of Ranuccio II left, date below **Rev:** Head of wind blowing from right to left into clouds

Date	Mintage	VG	F	VF	XF	Unc
1692 GG	—	3,000	5,400	11,000	—	—

FR# 925 DOPPIA

7.1410 g., 0.8910 Gold 0.2046 oz. AGW **Ruler:** Francesco Farnese I **Obv:** Bust of Francesco right **Rev:** Crowned arms

Date	Mintage	VG	F	VF	XF	Unc
1695 GG	—	3,600	6,000	11,500	—	—

FR# 911.1 2 DOPPIE

0.8910 Gold **Ruler:** Odardo Farnese **Obv:** Large bust of Odoardo **Rev:** Madonna and child under crown held by two cherubs

Date	Mintage	VG	F	VF	XF	Unc
1625 AA	—	1,200	2,000	4,500	8,000	—
1639 VC	—	1,200	2,000	4,500	8,000	—

FR# 911.2 2 DOPPIE

0.8910 Gold **Ruler:** Odardo Farnese **Obv:** Small bust of Odoardo right

Date	Mintage	VG	F	VF	XF	Unc
ND	—	1,200	2,000	3,750	6,500	—

FR# 919 2 DOPPIE

0.8910 Gold **Ruler:** Ranuccio Farnese II **Obv:** Bust of Ranuccio II left, date below

Date	Mintage	VG	F	VF	XF	Unc
1658 Rare	—	—	—	—	—	—
ND Rare	—	—	—	—	—	—

FR# 914 3 DOPPIE

21.4230 g., 0.8910 Gold 0.6137 oz. AGW **Ruler:** Odardo Farnese **Obv:** Bust of Odoardo right in inner circle **Rev:** Three nude graces standing, date 1574 above in legend

Date	Mintage	VG	F	VF	XF	Unc
1633 AC Rare	—	—	—	—	—	—

Note: First 3 retrograde

FR# 901 DUCAT

3.5000 g., 0.9860 Gold 0.1109 oz. AGW **Ruler:** Ranuccio Farnese I **Obv:** Ranuccio I standing left **Rev:** Crowned arms in Order collar

Date	Mintage	VG	F	VF	XF	Unc
1602 LS	—	400	650	1,000	1,500	—
1603 LS	—	400	650	1,000	1,500	—

FR# 902 DUCAT

3.5000 g., 0.9860 Gold 0.1109 oz. AGW **Ruler:** Ranuccio Farnese I **Rev:** Madonna and child facing

Date	Mintage	VG	F	VF	XF	Unc
ND	—	800	1,200	2,500	3,750	—

FR# 910 6 DUCAT

0.9860 Gold **Ruler:** Odardo Farnese **Obv:** Youthful, ruffled and armored bust right **Rev:** Crown supported by two cherubs above Madonna and child

Date	Mintage	VG	F	VF	XF	Unc
ND(1622-46) Rare	—	—	—	—	—	—

PIACENZA

Placentia

A town and episcopal see that is located in the northwestern corner of the Italian territorial division of Emilia. It was made a Roman colony in 218 B.C., later becoming an important road center of the Roman Empire. Once a leading member of the Lombard League, it was united with Parma in 1545 to form a hereditary duchy in favor of the son of Pope Paul III. In 1731 it passed to Parma, then to the house of Hapsburg, and finally back to Parma in 1748.

RULERS

Ranuccio I Farnese, 1592-1622
Odoardo Farnese, 1622-1646
Ranuccio II Farnese, 1646-1694

DUCHY

STANDARD COINAGE

DAV# 4126 SCUDO (Stretto)

Silver **Obv:** Bust of Alessandro Farnese right **Note:** Posthumous issue.

Date	Mintage	VG	F	VF	XF	Unc
1601	—	280	525	1,200	2,650	—
1603	—	280	525	1,200	2,650	—
1604 Retrograde 4	—	280	525	1,200	2,650	—
1605	—	280	525	1,200	2,650	—
1609	—	280	525	1,200	2,650	—
1620	—	280	525	1,200	2,650	—
ND	—	280	525	1,200	2,650	—

DAV# 4127 SCUDO (Stretto)

Silver **Obv:** Bust of Odoardo right **Rev:** Saint on horseback

Date	Mintage	VG	F	VF	XF	Unc
1626	—	350	750	1,650	2,750	—

DAV# 4128 SCUDO (Stretto)

Silver **Rev:** Saint standing left with standard

Date	Mintage	VG	F	VF	XF	Unc
1628	—	225	450	850	1,600	—
1629	—	225	450	850	1,600	—
1630	—	225	450	850	1,600	—
1631	—	225	450	850	1,600	—
1632	—	225	450	850	1,600	—
1636	—	225	450	850	1,600	—

DAV# 4129 SCUDO (Stretto)

Silver **Rev:** Saint on horseback **Rev. Legend:** S. ANTO-NINs-...

Date	Mintage	VG	F	VF	XF	Unc
1629	—	350	750	1,650	2,750	—
16XXX3 (1633)	—	350	750	1,650	2,750	—

DAV# 4130 SCUDO (Stretto)

Silver **Obv:** Bust of Ranuccio II left **Rev. Legend:** S. ANTON. -MART. PROT. PLAC.

Date	Mintage	VG	F	VF	XF	Unc
1676	—	2,000	4,000	7,000	12,000	—

FR# 906 DOPPIA

7.0000 g., 0.9860 Gold 0.2219 oz. AGW **Obv:** Bust of Ranuccio I left **Rev:** Head of wind blowing from right to left into clouds, date in exergue

Date	Mintage	VG	F	VF	XF	Unc
1612 Rare	—	—	—	—	—	—
ND Rare	—	—	—	—	—	—

FR# 918 DOPPIA

7.0000 g., 0.9860 Gold 0.2219 oz. AGW **Obv:** Bust of Odoardo right in inner circle **Rev:** Crown over she-wolf in front of lilies, date in exergue

Date	Mintage	VG	F	VF	XF	Unc
1626 Rare	—	—	—	—	—	—

FR# 905 2 DOPPIE

14.0000 g., 0.9860 Gold 0.4438 oz. AGW **Ruler:** Ranuccio I Farnese **Rev:** Head of wind blowing from right to left into clouds, date in exergue

Date	Mintage	VG	F	VF	XF	Unc
1612	—	2,000	3,500	6,000	9,000	—
1613	—	2,000	3,500	6,000	9,000	—

FR# 907 2 DOPPIE

14.0000 g., 0.9860 Gold 0.4438 oz. AGW

Date	Mintage	VG	F	VF	XF	Unc
1601	—	500	1,000	2,000	4,000	—
1602	—	500	1,000	2,000	4,000	—
1604	—	500	1,000	2,000	4,000	—
1607	—	500	1,000	2,000	4,000	—
1608	—	500	1,000	2,000	4,000	—
1609	—	500	1,000	2,000	4,000	—
1610	—	500	1,000	2,000	4,000	—
1611	—	500	1,000	2,000	4,000	—
1613	—	500	1,000	2,000	4,000	—
1614	—	500	1,000	2,000	4,000	—
1615	—	500	1,000	2,000	4,000	—
1616	—	500	1,000	2,000	4,000	—
1617	—	500	1,000	2,000	4,000	—
1618	—	500	1,000	2,000	4,000	—
1619	—	500	1,000	2,000	4,000	—
1622	—	500	1,000	2,000	4,000	—

FR# 915 2 DOPPIE

14.0000 g., 0.9860 Gold 0.4438 oz. AGW **Obv:** Odoardo

Date	Mintage	VG	F	VF	XF	Unc
1623	—	4,000	6,000	10,000	20,000	—
1624	—	4,000	6,000	10,000	20,000	—

FR# 917.1 2 DOPPIE

14.0000 g., 0.9860 Gold 0.4438 oz. AGW **Obv:** * L • X * below bust **Rev:** Crown over she-wolf in front of lilies, date in exergue

Date	Mintage	VG	F	VF	XF	Unc
1626	—	750	1,500	2,500	4,500	—
1631	—	750	1,500	2,500	4,500	—

FR# 917.2 2 DOPPIE

14.0000 g., 0.9860 Gold 0.4438 oz. AGW **Rev:** Crown over she-wolf in front of lilies, date and • L • X • in exergue

Date	Mintage	VG	F	VF	XF	Unc
MDCXXVI (1626)	—	750	1,500	2,500	4,500	—

FR# 904 4 DOPPIE

0.9860 Gold **Obv:** Bust of Ranuucio I left **Rev:** Head of wind blowing from right to left into clouds, date in exergue

Date	Mintage	VG	F	VF	XF	Unc
1601 Rare	—	—	—	—	—	—

TRADE COINAGE

FR# 908 DUCAT

3.5000 g., 0.9860 Gold 0.1109 oz. AGW **Obv:** Ranuccio I standing in inner circle **Rev:** Four-line inscription in tablet

Date	Mintage	VG	F	VF	XF	Unc
1601 Rare	—	—	—	—	—	—

PIOMBINO

Piombino, a seaport near Leghorn in Tuscany opposite Elba, was variously owned and occupied but under general Pisan jurisdiction. A mint was opened in 1509. When Pisa was ceded to the Visconti, the Appiani family kept Piombino and Elba, and it was made an independent princedom in 1594 by Rudolph II. It passed to the Ludovici family, and finally thru marriage to the Boncompagni family. Its last coinage occurred in the Ludovici period by a father and son.

RULERS
Niccolo Ludovici, 1634-1665
Giovanni Baptiste Ludovisi, 1665-1699

PRINCIPALITY

STANDARD COINAGE

KM# 15 CRAZIA

Billon **Obv:** Crowned Ludovici arms, ASTRIS **Rev:** Madonna standing **Note:** Weight varies: 0.77-0.85 grams.

Date	Mintage	VG	F	VF	XF	Unc
1651	—	45.00	90.00	180	375	—
1652	—	45.00	90.00	180	375	—
ND	—	37.50	75.00	155	325	—

KM# 21 CRAZIA

Billon **Obv:** Ludovici arms **Rev:** St. Anastasia **Note:** Weight varies: 0.77-0.85 grams.

Date	Mintage	VG	F	VF	XF	Unc
1668	—	—	—	—	—	—

KM# 28 CRAZIA

Billon **Obv:** Crowned Ludovici arms D. IO. BAT. **Rev:** Madonna and child **Note:** Weight varies: 0.77-0.85 grams.

Date	Mintage	VG	F	VF	XF	Unc
1694	—	30.00	55.00	125	300	—
1695	—	30.00	55.00	125	300	—
1696	—	30.00	55.00	125	300	—

KM# 16 QUATTRINO

Copper **Obv:** Bust left, NICOL **Rev:** Crowned Ludovici arms **Note:** Weight varies: 0.90-1.20 grams.

Date	Mintage	VG	F	VF	XF	Unc
1651	—	60.00	105	215	400	—
1654	—	60.00	105	215	400	—
ND	—	55.00	90.00	180	350	—

KM# 25 QUATTRINO

Copper **Obv:** Crowned Ludovici arms **Rev:** PRINC./PLVMB./ date **Note:** Weight varies: 0.90-1.20 grams.

Date	Mintage	VG	F	VF	XF	Unc
1692	—	37.50	60.00	135	325	—
1693	—	37.50	60.00	135	325	—
1694	—	37.50	60.00	135	325	—

KM# 26 QUATTRINO

Copper **Obv:** Bust of Gio left, IO:BAT **Rev:** Crowned Ludovici arms, ASTRIS **Note:** Weight varies: 0.90-1.20 grams.

Date	Mintage	VG	F	VF	XF	Unc
ND	—	30.00	55.00	125	300	—

KM# 29 DUETTA (2 Quattrino)

Copper **Obv:** Crowned Ludovici arms **Rev:** 1694 in circle **Note:** Weight varies: 0.98-1.16 grams.

Date	Mintage	VG	F	VF	XF	Unc
1694	—	55.00	90.00	180	375	—

KM# 27 SOLDO (3 Quattrino)

1.8700 g., Copper **Obv:** Crowned Ludovici arms **Rev:** PRINC./PLVMB./date

Date	Mintage	VG	F	VF	XF	Unc
1693	—	60.00	105	80.00	400	—
1694	—	60.00	105	80.00	400	—
1695	—	60.00	105	80.00	400	—

KM# 8 1/2 PAOLA

1.4700 g., Silver **Obv:** Bust left **Obv. Legend:** NICOL. **Rev:** Crowned Ludovici arms

Date	Mintage	VG	F	VF	XF	Unc
1642	—	—	—	—	—	—
1643	—	—	—	—	—	—

KM# 9 1/2 PAOLA

1.4700 g., Silver **Obv:** Crowned multiple arms **Rev:** MA monogram

Date	Mintage	VG	F	VF	XF	Unc
ND	—	—	—	—	—	—

KM# 10 1/2 PAOLA

1.4700 g., Silver **Obv:** Crowned Ludovici arms **Rev:** B in cartouche

Date	Mintage	VG	F	VF	XF	Unc
ND	—	—	—	—	—	—

KM# 20 PAOLA

Silver **Obv:** Bust of Gio right **Rev:** Crowned multiple arms **Note:** Weight varies: 2.05-2.75 grams.

Date	Mintage	VG	F	VF	XF	Unc
ND(1665)	—	—	—	—	—	—

KM# 7 TESTONE

8.9000 g., Silver **Obv:** Bust left **Rev:** Crowned multiple arms

Date	Mintage	VG	F	VF	XF	Unc
1641	—	—	—	—	—	—
1651	—	—	—	—	—	—

KM# 30 TESTONE

8.9000 g., Silver **Obv:** Bust right **Obv. Legend:** PRINCEPS. **Rev:** Crowned Ludovici arms

Date	Mintage	VG	F	VF	XF	Unc
1695	—	—	—	—	—	—
ND	—	—	—	—	—	—

KM# 35 1/2 PIASTRE

13.1100 g., Silver **Obv:** Crowned multiple arms **Rev:** Sea with two fortresses

Date	Mintage	VG	F	VF	XF	Unc
1697 Rare	—	—	—	—	—	—

KM# 31 PIASTRE

25.6100 g., Silver **Obv:** Bust right **Rev:** Harbor and city view **Note:** Dav. #4133.

Date	Mintage	VG	F	VF	XF	Unc
1695 Rare	—	—	—	—	—	—

KM# 5 1/2 SCUDO

15.9000 g., Silver **Obv:** Bust right **Rev:** Crowned Ludovici arms

Date	Mintage	VG	F	VF	XF	Unc
1640 Rare	—	—	—	—	—	—

KM# 6 SCUDO

32.0000 g., Silver **Obv:** Bust left, date below **Rev:** Crowned multiple arms **Note:** Dav. #4131.

Date	Mintage	VG	F	VF	XF	Unc
1640 Rare	—	—	—	—	—	—

KM# 18 SCUDO

32.0000 g., Silver **Obv:** Bust right **Rev:** Crowned multiple arms divide date **Note:** Dav. #4132.

Date	Mintage	VG	F	VF	XF	Unc
1654 Rare	—	—	—	—	—	—

KM# 32 ZECCHINO

3.3800 g., 0.9860 Gold 0.1071 oz. AGW **Obv:** Head of Giovanni Baptiste right, date below **Rev:** Crowned arms

Date	Mintage	VG	F	VF	XF	Unc
1695 Rare	—	—	—	—	—	—

KM# 33 ZECCHINO

3.3800 g., 0.9860 Gold 0.1071 oz. AGW **Obv:** Head of Giovanni Baptiste right **Rev:** Crowned and mantled arms, date divided at top

Date	Mintage	VG	F	VF	XF	Unc
1696 Rare	—	—	—	—	—	—

KM# 11 DOPPIA

7.0000 g., 0.9860 Gold 0.2219 oz. AGW **Obv:** Crowned Ludovici arms **Rev:** Madonna standing

Date	Mintage	VG	F	VF	XF	Unc
1644 Rare	—	—	—	—	—	—

KM# 34 DOPPIA

7.0000 g., 0.9860 Gold 0.2219 oz. AGW **Obv:** Bust of Giovanni Baptiste right, date below **Rev:** Crowned arms in Order collar

Date	Mintage	VG	F	VF	XF	Unc
1695 Rare	—	—	—	—	—	—

KM# 17 2 DOPPIE

13.2700 g., Gold **Obv:** Crowned arms **Rev:** Madonna standing

Date	Mintage	VG	F	VF	XF	Unc
1651 Rare	—	—	—	—	—	—

PISA

A city located on the Arno River in western Tuscany on the Tyrrhenian Sea, site of the famous leaning tower and mint. Rebelled against Florentine rule 1494-1509 and was under the Medici lineage of the Tuscan Grand Dukes, except for the French occupation between 1807-14. It joined the Kingdom of Italy in 1860.

GRAND DUKES
Ferdinand I de'Medici, 1595-1608
Cosimo II de'Medici, 1608-1620
Ferdinand II de'Medici, 1620-1670
Cosimo III de'Medici, 1670-1723

MINT NAME
Pisa

CITY

STANDARD COINAGE

KM# 5 CRAZIA

Billon **Obv:** Medici arms **Rev:** Pisan cross **Note:** Weight varies: 0.62-1.06 grams.

Date	Mintage	VG	F	VF	XF	Unc
ND	—	—	—	—	—	—

KM# 6 2 QUATTRINI (1 Duetto)

Billon **Obv:** Pisan cross **Rev:** QVAT/TRI/NI/II **Note:** Weight varies: 0.65-1.18 grams.

Date	Mintage	VG	F	VF	XF	Unc
ND	—	—	—	—	—	—

KM# 35 2 QUATTRINI (1 Duetto)

Copper **Ruler:** Fian Gastone **Obv:** Medici arms **Obv. Legend:** QVATTRIN. II. **Rev:** Pisan cross, date **Note:** Weight varies: 1.06-1.40 grams.

Date	Mintage	VG	F	VF	XF	Unc
1679	—	12.00	22.00	45.00	80.00	—
1680	—	12.00	22.00	45.00	80.00	—
1681	—	12.00	22.00	45.00	80.00	—
1682	—	12.00	22.00	45.00	80.00	—
1687	—	12.00	22.00	45.00	80.00	—
1689	—	12.00	22.00	45.00	80.00	—

KM# 7 3 QUATTRINI (1 Soldo)

Billon **Obv:** Pisan cross **Rev. Inscription:** QVATTRI / NI / III **Note:** Weight varies: 1.14-1.18 grams.

Date	Mintage	VG	F	VF	XF	Unc
ND	—	—	—	—	—	—

KM# 36 3 QUATTRINI (1 Soldo)

Billon **Ruler:** Fian Gastone **Obv:** Medici arms **Obv. Legend:** QVATTRINI. III **Rev:** Pisan cross **Note:** Weight varies: 1.14-1.18 grams.

Date	Mintage	VG	F	VF	XF	Unc
1679	—	15.00	25.00	50.00	90.00	—
1680	—	15.00	25.00	50.00	90.00	—
1681	—	15.00	25.00	50.00	90.00	—
1687	—	15.00	25.00	50.00	90.00	—

KM# 8 4 QUATTRINI

Billon **Obv:** Pisan cross **Rev:** QUATTRI/NI/IIII **Note:** Weight varies: 1.07-1.10 grams.

Date	Mintage	VG	F	VF	XF	Unc
ND	—	—	—	—	—	—

KM# 9 10 SOLDI

2.5100 g., Silver **Obv:** Crowned Medici arms **Rev:** Arms of Florence **Note:** Struck for the Levant.

Date	Mintage	VG	F	VF	XF	Unc
ND	—	—	—	—	—	—

KM# 10 10 SOLDI

2.5100 g., Silver **Rev:** Grand Duke standing, three figures kneeling

Date	Mintage	VG	F	VF	XF	Unc
ND	—	—	—	—	—	—

KM# 15 TALLERO

Silver **Ruler:** Ferdinand I de'Medici **Note:** Weight varies: 25.38-28.72 grams. Dav. #4186.

Date	Mintage	VG	F	VF	XF	Unc
1601	—	150	300	600	1,000	2,500
1603	—	150	300	600	1,000	2,500
1604	—	150	300	600	1,000	2,500
1605	—	150	300	600	1,000	2,500
1606	—	150	300	600	1,000	2,500
1607	—	150	300	600	1,000	2,500
1608	—	150	300	600	1,000	2,500

KM# 16.1 TALLERO

Silver **Obv:** Half figure right, 1609 below **Obv. Legend:** COSMVS. MED. MAGN. ETR. DVX. IIII. **Rev. Legend:** PISA. INVETVSTAE. MAIESTATIS. MEMORIAM. **Note:** Weight varies: 23.98-29.50 grams. Dav. #4193.

Date	Mintage	VG	F	VF	XF	Unc
1609	—	250	500	1,000	1,750	—

KM# 16.2 TALLERO

Silver **Obv:** Larger bust **Note:** Weight varies: 23.98-29.50 grams. Dav. #4194.

Date	Mintage	VG	F	VF	XF	Unc
1611	—	250	500	1,000	1,750	—
1612	—	250	500	1,000	1,750	—

KM# 16.3 TALLERO

Silver **Note:** Weight varies: 23.98-29.50 grams. Dav. #4195.

Date	Mintage	VG	F	VF	XF	Unc
1614	—	85.00	175	350	750	—
1615	—	85.00	175	350	750	—
1616	—	85.00	175	350	750	—
1618	—	85.00	175	350	750	—
1619	—	85.00	175	350	750	—
1620	—	85.00	175	350	750	—

KM# 20 TALLERO

Silver **Obv:** Bust of Ferdinand II right **Rev:** Crowned Medici arms **Note:** Weight varies: 27.95-28.31 grams. Dav. #4197.

Date	Mintage	VG	F	VF	XF	Unc
1621	—	100	200	500	1,000	3,500
1623	—	100	200	500	1,000	3,500
1629	—	100	200	500	1,000	3,500

KM# 16.4 TALLERO

Silver **Note:** Varieties exist. Certain dies were re-engraved, sometimes leaving the earlier ruler's name quite discernable.Weight varies: 23.98-29.50 grams. Dav. #4196.

Date	Mintage	VG	F	VF	XF	Unc
1621	—	85.00	175	350	750	—
ND	—	85.00	175	350	750	—

KM# 29 TALLERO

Silver **Obv:** Mature bust **Note:** Weight varies: 27.95-28.31 grams. Dav. #4203.

Date	Mintage	VG	F	VF	XF	Unc
1648	—	85.00	175	350	750	—
1654	—	85.00	175	350	750	—

KM# 25 1/2 DOPPIA

Gold **Obv:** Pisan cross **Rev:** Ascension of the Virgin Mary **Note:** Weight varies: 3.06-3.25 grams.

Date	Mintage	VG	F	VF	XF	Unc
1643	—	550	850	1,750	3,250	—
ND	—	550	850	1,750	3,250	—

KM# 26 DOPPIA

6.5300 g., Gold **Obv:** Pisan cross **Rev:** Ascension of the Virgin Mary

Date	Mintage	VG	F	VF	XF	Unc
1641	—	550	875	1,750	5,500	—
1644	—	550	875	1,750	5,500	—
1647	—	550	875	1,750	5,500	—
1655	—	550	875	1,750	5,500	—
ND	—	550	875	1,750	5,500	—

KM# 27 DOPPIA

6.5300 g., Gold **Obv:** Plain cross **Obv. Legend:** COSMVS

Date	Mintage	VG	F	VF	XF	Unc
ND	—	3,000	5,400	7,800	12,000	—

KM# 28 2 DOPPIE

13.2000 g., Gold **Obv:** Pisan cross **Rev:** Ascension of the Virgin Mary

Date	Mintage	VG	F	VF	XF	Unc
ND Rare	—	—	—	—	—	—

RETEGNO

(Trivulzio)

A commune in the province of Milan, it was made a barony in 1654 by Ferdinand II. The mint right was given to Cardinal Gian Giacomo Teodoro Trivulzio. The family held the county of Misox in Switzerland.

RULERS

Hercules Teodoro Trivulzio, 1656-1664
Antonio Teodoro Trivulzio, 1676-1678
Antonio Gaetano Trivulzio-Gallio, 1679-1705

BARONY

STANDARD COINAGE

KM# 5 1/4 FILIPPO

6.9500 g., Silver **Obv:** Bust of Hercules Teodoro right **Obv. Legend:** THEO. **Rev:** Crowned arms

Date	Mintage	VG	F	VF	XF	Unc
ND(1656)	—	700	1,350	3,000	—	—

KM# 10 1/4 FILIPPO

Silver **Obv:** Bust of Antonio Teodor right **Obv. Legend:** THEODORVS. **Rev:** Arms in cartouche, VNICA/MENS at sides **Note:** Weight varies: 5.89-6.70 grams.

Date	Mintage	VG	F	VF	XF	Unc
1676	—	350	700	1,850	—	—

KM# 25 1/4 FILIPPO

Silver **Obv:** Bust of Antonio Gaetano right **Obv. Legend:** ANT. **Rev:** Crowned arms above two shields, date in legend **Note:** Weight varies: 6.75-6.90 grams.

Date	Mintage	VG	F	VF	XF	Unc
1686	—	350	750	1,950	—	—

KM# 6 1/2 FILIPPO

13.9000 g., Silver, 43 mm. **Obv:** Bust of Hercules Teodoro right **Obv. Legend:** THEO. **Rev:** Crowned arms

Date	Mintage	VG	F	VF	XF	Unc
ND(1656)	—	650	1,250	3,000	—	—

KM# 11 1/2 FILIPPO

13.5000 g., Silver **Obv:** Bust of Antonio Teodoro right **Obv. Legend:** THEOD(O).

Date	Mintage	VG	F	VF	XF	Unc
1676	—	250	600	1,850	—	—

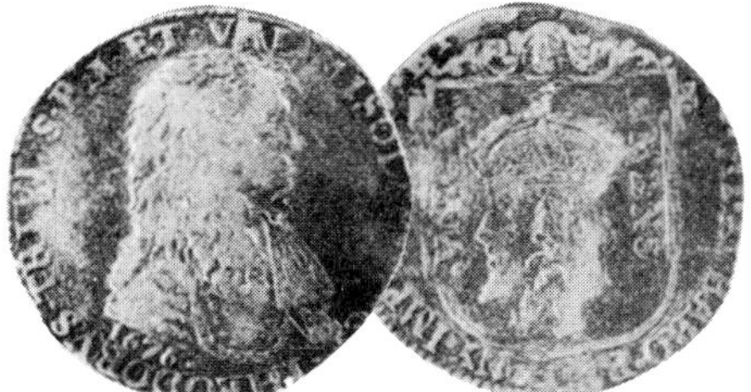

KM# 12 1/2 FILIPPO

Silver, 43 mm. **Ruler:** Antonio Teodoro Trivulzio **Note:** Weight varies: 13.32-13.85 grams.

Date	Mintage	VG	F	VF	XF	Unc
1676	—	200	500	1,500	2,500	—

KM# 26 1/2 FILIPPO

13.5000 g., Silver **Obv:** Bust of Antonio Gaetano right **Obv. Legend:** ANT. **Rev:** Crowned arms above two shields, date in legend

Date	Mintage	VG	F	VF	XF	Unc
1686	—	350	650	1,650	2,750	—

KM# 13 FILIPPO (Largo)
Silver, 51 mm. **Obv. Legend:** THEODORVS... **Note:** Weight varies: 27.28-27.50 grams. Similar to KM#14. Dav. #4136.

Date	Mintage	VG	F	VF	XF	Unc
1676	—	300	600	1,150	2,250	—

KM# 14 FILIPPO (Stretto)
Silver, 40 mm. **Obv. Legend:** THEOD(O). **Note:** Weight varies: 27.28-27.50 grams. Dav. #4137.

Date	Mintage	VG	F	VF	XF	Unc
1676	—	300	550	1,000	1,850	—

KM# 28 FILIPPO (Stretto)
28.5000 g., Silver **Obv:** Bust of Antonio right, .130. below **Note:** Dav. #4141.

Date	Mintage	VG	F	VF	XF	Unc
1686	—	300	600	1,450	2,750	—

KM# 27 FILIPPO (Stretto)
28.5000 g., Silver **Note:** Similar to KM#28. Dav. #4140.

Date	Mintage	VG	F	VF	XF	Unc
1686	—	300	600	1,400	2,700	—

KM# 15.1 2 FILIPPI (Largo)
Silver, 50 mm. **Obv:** Bust of Antonio Teodoro right **Obv. Legend:** THEON(ORVS). **Note:** Weight varies: 55.34-55.50 grams. Dav. #4135.

Date	Mintage	VG	F	VF	XF	Unc
1676	—	350	650	1,350	2,500	—

KM# 15.2 2 FILIPPI (Stretto)
Silver, 50 mm. **Note:** Weight varies: 55.34-55.50 grams. Dav. #4138.

Date	Mintage	VG	F	VF	XF	Unc
1677 Rare	—	—	—	—	—	—

KM# 15.3 2 FILIPPI (Stretto)
Silver, 50 mm. **Note:** Weight varies: 55.34-55.50 grams. Dav. #4138A.

Date	Mintage	VG	F	VF	XF	Unc
1677 Rare; restrike	—	—	—	—	—	—

KM# 16 3 FILIPPI
Silver **Obv:** Bust of Antonio Teodaro right **Obv. Legend:** THEODORVS **Rev:** Supported arms **Note:** Weight varies: 82.20-83.20 grams. Dav. #4134.

Date	Mintage	VG	F	VF	XF	Unc
1676	—	1,200	2,500	4,500	7,500	—

KM# 29 3 FILIPPI
83.2500 g., Silver **Obv:** Bust of Antonio Gaetano right **Obv. Legend:** ANT. **Rev:** Crowned arms above two shields, date in legend **Note:** Dav. #4139.

Date	Mintage	VG	F	VF	XF	Unc
1686	—	1,500	3,000	5,500	8,500	—

KM# 17 4 FILIPPI
Silver **Obv:** Bust of Antonio Teodoro right **Obv. Legend:** THEODORVS. **Rev:** Supported arms

Date	Mintage	VG	F	VF	XF	Unc
1676 Rare	—	—	—	—	—	—

Note: Numismatica Ars Classica Auction 32, 1-06, VF realized approximately $16,270

KM# 30 2 DOPPIE
7.0000 g., 0.9860 Gold 0.2219 oz. AGW **Obv:** Soldier standing right in circle with 12 rays, three Volti with imperial crown **Rev:** Seven-line inscription

Date	Mintage	VG	F	VF	XF	Unc
1686 Rare	—	—	—	—	—	—

KM# 18 ZECCHINO
3.5000 g., 0.9860 Gold 0.1109 oz. AGW **Obv:** Equestrian figure of Antonio Teodoro right **Rev:** Tied bundle of corn ears

Date	Mintage	VG	F	VF	XF	Unc
1676	—	1,650	3,250	5,500	8,500	—

KM# 19 10 ZECCHINI
35.0000 g., 0.9860 Gold 1.1095 oz. AGW **Obv:** Teodoro

Date	Mintage	VG	F	VF	XF	Unc
1677	—	—	—	25,000	35,000	—

Note: Stack's International sale 3-88 VF realized $20,900

KM# 31 10 ZECCHINI
35.0000 g., 0.9860 Gold 1.1095 oz. AGW **Obv:** Bust of Antonio Gaetano **Rev:** Elaborately crested helmet above arms, date in legend

Date	Mintage	VG	F	VF	XF	Unc
1686	—	—	—	20,000	30,000	—

Note: Bowers and Merena Guia sale 3-88 Unc. realized $17,600

TRADE COINAGE

KM# 20 DUCAT
3.5000 g., 0.9860 Gold 0.1109 oz. AGW **Obv:** Soldier standing right in inner circle **Rev:** 6-line inscription in tablet **Note:** Fr. #988.

Date	Mintage	VG	F	VF	XF	Unc
1677	—	2,000	3,500	6,000	10,000	—

KM# 32 DUCAT
3.5000 g., 0.9860 Gold 0.1109 oz. AGW **Ruler:** Antonio GaetanoTrivulzio-Gallio **Obv:** Soldier standing right divides date **Rev:** 6-line inscription in tablet **Note:** Fr. #992.

Date	Mintage	VG	F	VF	XF	Unc
1686	—	800	2,000	3,500	5,500	—
ND(1686)	—	800	2,000	3,500	5,500	—

KM# 21 2 DUCAT
7.0000 g., 0.9860 Gold 0.2219 oz. AGW **Obv:** Soldier standing right in inner circle **Rev:** 6-line inscription in tablet **Note:** Fr. #987.

Date	Mintage	VG	F	VF	XF	Unc
1677	—	2,500	4,000	7,500	12,500	—

KM# 33 2 DUCAT
7.0000 g., 0.9860 Gold 0.2219 oz. AGW **Ruler:** Antonio GaetanoTrivulzio-Gallio **Obv:** Soldier standing right divdies date **Rev:** 6-line inscription in tablet **Note:** Fr. #991.

Date	Mintage	VG	F	VF	XF	Unc
1686	—	1,500	3,000	5,000	8,000	—
ND(1686)	—	1,500	3,000	5,000	8,000	—

RONCO

This county in Liguria north of Genoa belonged to a branch of the Spinola family. Mint privileges were obtained from Ferdinand III. Napoleon and his grandson, who were also marquises of Roccaforte were the only members of the family to strike coins. The mint was closed in 1699.

RULERS
Napoleone Spinola, 1647-1672
Carlo Spinola, 1699-1720

COUNTY

STANDARD COINAGE

KM# 10 LUIGINO
Silver **Obv:** Bust right, 8S below **Rev:** Crowned double eagle, shield divides date **Note:** Weight varies: 1.90-2.22 grams.

Date	Mintage	VG	F	VF	XF	Unc
1668	—	225	450	900	1,650	—
1669	—	225	450	900	1,650	—

KM# 11 LUIGINO
Silver **Obv:** Crowned double eagle **Rev:** Crowned double eagle **Note:** Weight varies: 1.90-2.22 grams.

Date	Mintage	VG	F	VF	XF	Unc
1668	—	125	250	400	750	—

KM# 12 LUIGINO
Silver **Obv:** Bust right, date below **Rev:** Crowned double eagle **Note:** Weight varies: 1.90-2.22 grams.

Date	Mintage	VG	F	VF	XF	Unc
1668	—	235	475	950	1,750	—

KM# 5 1/4 SCUDO
Silver **Obv:** Bust left, date below **Rev:** Crowned double eagle with shield **Note:** Weight varies: 5.45-7.75 grams.

Date	Mintage	VG	F	VF	XF	Unc
1647	—	500	1,000	2,200	4,000	—

KM# 14 1/4 SCUDO
Silver **Obv:** Bust right **Rev:** Crowned double eagle with shield, date in legend **Note:** Weight varies: 5.45-7.75 grams.

Date	Mintage	VG	F	VF	XF	Unc
1669	—	650	1,250	2,750	5,000	—

KM# 20 1/4 SCUDO
Silver **Obv:** Bust of Carlo right **Note:** Weight varies: 5.45-7.75 grams.

Date	Mintage	VG	F	VF	XF	Unc
1699	—	1,000	2,000	4,000	6,500	—

KM# 21 1/2 SCUDO
19.2200 g., Silver **Obv:** Bust right, *B:VII:12 below **Rev:** Crowned double eagle with shield

Date	Mintage	VG	F	VF	XF	Unc
1699 Rare	—	—	—	—	—	—

KM# 15 SCUDO
Silver **Obv:** Napoleone standing **Rev:** Crowned double eagle with shield **Note:** Dav. #4142. Weight varies: 28.90-37.50 grams.

Date	Mintage	VG	F	VF	XF	Unc
1669 Rare	—	—	—	—	—	—

Note: Numismatica Ars Classica Auction 32, planchet flaw, otherwise XF/near Unc realized approximately $24,605

KM# 16 SCUDO
Silver **Obv:** Bust of Napoleone right **Note:** Dav. #4143. Weight varies: 28.90-37.50 grams.

Date	Mintage	VG	F	VF	XF	Unc
1669	—	3,500	6,500	12,500	—	—

KM# 22 SCUDO
Silver **Obv:** Bust of Carlo right **Note:** Dav. #4144. Weight varies: 28.90-37.50 grams.

Date	Mintage	VG	F	VF	XF	Unc
1699 Rare	—	—	—	—	—	—

KM# 23 DOPPIA
7.0000 g., 0.9860 Gold 0.2219 oz. AGW **Obv:** Bust of Carlo right **Rev:** Crowned arms on crowned imperial eagle

Date	Mintage	VG	F	VF	XF	Unc
ND(1699) Rare	—	—	—	—	—	—

KM# 6 2 DOPPIE
12.2800 g., Gold **Obv:** Bust of Napoleone left **Rev:** Crowned double eagle with Spinola arms

Date	Mintage	VG	F	VF	XF	Unc
1647 Rare	—	—	—	—	—	—

TRADE COINAGE

KM# 13 DUCAT
3.5000 g., 0.9860 Gold 0.1109 oz. AGW **Obv:** Bust of Napoleone right **Rev:** Crowned imperial eagle with crowned arms on chest

Date	Mintage	VG	F	VF	XF	Unc
1668 Rare	—	—	—	—	—	—

KM# 7 4 DUCAT
14.0000 g., 0.9860 Gold 0.4438 oz. AGW **Obv:** Bust of Napoleone left, date below **Rev:** Crowned imperial eagle with crowned arms on breast

Date	Mintage	VG	F	VF	XF	Unc
1647 Rare	—	—	—	—	—	—

ROVEGNO

A small territory in the province of Pavia in Lombardy. It was in the possession of the Doria of Genoa. The young prince, who was also Count of Loana, struck a piece in imitation of the Dutch lion dollar.

RULER
Giovanni Andrea III Doria, 1654-1700

PRINCIPALITY

STANDARD COINAGE

KM# 1 TALLERO
Silver **Obv:** Knight behind shield **Rev:** Rampant lion **Note:** Dav. #4145

Date	Mintage	VG	F	VF	XF	Unc
1669 Rare	—	—	—	—	—	—

SABBIONETA

The village of Sabbioneta was founded in ancient times and was ceded by the Venetians to Duke Gianfrancesco II Gonzaga of Mantua in 1426. His grandson, Gianfrancesco the Younger, established a cadet line of the Gonzagas in Sabbioneta and died in 1496. The ruling captain in 1565 was raised to the rank of marchese, then to prince in 1574 and finally to duke in 1577. The line of Gonzagas died out in 1637, but the titles were inherited through marriage to a Spaniard, Ramiro de Guzmán. His son died without heirs and the coinage came to an end. In 1748, Sabbioneta was acquired by the Duke of Parma.

RULERS
Isabella, 1591-1637
Luigi Carafa de Stigliano, 1591-1638
Anna, 1638-1644
Ramiro de Guzmán, Duke of Medinas les Torres, 1644-1668
Nicolò Ramirez de Guzmán, 1644-1684

Reference:
V = Alberto Varesi, ***Monete Italiane Regionali: Lombardia, Zecche Minori***. Pavia, 1995.

DUCHY

STANDARD COINAGE

KM# 8 QUATTRINO
0.7500 g., Billon **Obv:** Large S, *CRVX **Rev:** St. Nicholaus, SAN AVGVST **Note:** Weight varies: 0.54-0.91 grams.

Date	Mintage	VG	F	VF	XF	Unc
ND	—	30.00	60.00	100	—	—

KM# 5 SESINO
Billon **Obv:** Head left **Rev:** St. Nicholaus standing **Note:** Weight varies: 0.54-0.91 grams.

Date	Mintage	VG	F	VF	XF	Unc
ND	—	25.00	40.00	80.00	150	—

KM# 6 SESINO
Billon **Obv:** Large S, *ALOY **Note:** Weight varies: 0.54-0.91 grams.

Date	Mintage	VG	F	VF	XF	Unc
ND	—	50.00	95.00	200	—	—

KM# 7 SESINO
Billon **Obv:** Large S **Note:** Weight varies: 0.54-0.91 grams.

Date	Mintage	VG	F	VF	XF	Unc
ND	—	20.00	35.00	70.00	145	—

KM# 9 SOLDO
Billon **Obv:** Crowned arms **Rev:** St. Nicholaus standing **Note:** Weight varies: 0.95-1.47 grams.

Date	Mintage	VG	F	VF	XF	Unc
ND	—	30.00	50.00	90.00	165	—

KM# 10 SOLDO
Billon **Rev:** Large S **Note:** Weight varies: 0.95-1.47 grams.

Date	Mintage	VG	F	VF	XF	Unc
ND	—	30.00	60.00	125	250	—

KM# 11 CAVALOTTO
Billon **Obv:** Crowned arms **Rev:** Horse right **Note:** Weight varies: 1.82-2.16 grams.

Date	Mintage	VG	F	VF	XF	Unc
ND	—	45.00	85.00	165	275	—

KM# 15 DUCATO
21.4000 g., Billon **Obv:** Double eagle, LIBERTAS on band **Rev:** Madonna and child, date below

Date	Mintage	VG	F	VF	XF	Unc
1605 Rare	—	—	—	—	—	—

KM# 12 TALLERO
25.3500 g., Billon **Obv:** Knight behind shield **Rev:** Rampant lion

Date	Mintage	VG	F	VF	XF	Unc
ND	—	3,000	6,000	9,000	—	—

KM# 13 TALLERO
25.3500 g., Billon **Obv:** Knight behind shield, 50-80

Date	Mintage	VG	F	VF	XF	Unc
ND Rare	—	—	—	—	—	—

KM# 20 TALLERO
25.3500 g., Billon **Obv:** Knight behind shield

Date	Mintage	VG	F	VF	XF	Unc
1637 Rare	—	—	—	—	—	—

KM# 25 DUCATONE
31.3200 g., Billon, 44.3 mm. **Obv:** Crowned arms in chain **Obv. Legend:** • NICOLAVS • D • G • SABLONET – DVX • ET • OBSTIL • PRIN • ET • C • **Rev:** Madonna and child in rays **Rev. Legend:** • - LVNA • SVB • PE • – • DIBVS • EIVS • - • **Note:** Dav. #4146.

Date	Mintage	VG	F	VF	XF	Unc
1666 Rare	—	—	—	—	—	—

Note: Numismatica Ars Classica Auction 32, 1-06, XF realized approximately $24,605; Astarte S.A. Auction XIX, 5-06, VF realized approximately $17,510

SAN MARTINO

A commune in the province of Mantua was a fief given to the Gonzaga family who were also lords of Bozzolo.

RULER
Scipione Gonzaga, prince of Bozzolo

COMMUNE

STANDARD COINAGE

KM# 5 QUATTRINO
Copper **Obv:** Head right **Rev:** SANTO/MARTIN in cartouche **Note:** Weight varies: 0.46-0.70 grams.

Date	Mintage	VG	F	VF	XF	Unc
ND	—	160	300	550	—	—

KM# 6 2 QUATTRINI
1.4700 g., Billon **Obv:** Head right **Rev:** SANTO/MARTIN in cartouche

Date	Mintage	VG	F	VF	XF	Unc
ND	—	240	500	900	—	—

SARDINIA

Sardinia is an island located in the Mediterranean Sea, west of the southern Italian peninsula, 9,301 sq. mi.; population 1,645,192. Along with some minor islands, it constitutes an autonomous region of Italy separated on the north from Corsica, France by the Strait of Bonifacio.

Settled by Phoenician's and Greeks before it came under control of Carthage during 600 BC; taken by the Romans in 238 BC; in the Vandal Kingdom during the5th century; re-conquered by the Byzantine Empire in533 AD. From the 8th century it was frequently raided by Muslims whose threat was eliminated by Pisa in 1016 as an object of a competitor's bet. The Genoese and Pisans were driven out by the Aragonese during the 14th-15th centuries, remaining under Spanish rule until 1708; held by Austria 1708-17, regained by the Spanish in 1717 until it was finally ceded to Savoy in 1720 in exchange for Sicily, after which the ruler of Savoy and Piedmont took the title as King of Sardinia.

RULERS
Carlo Emanuele I, 1580-1630
Vittorio Amedeo I, 1630-1637
Francesco Hyacint, 1637-1638
Under regency of his mother, Maria Cristina
Carlo Emanuele II, 1638-1675
Under regency of his mother, Maria Cristina, 1639-1648
Under supposed regency of Maurice and Thomas, 1639-1641
Alone as Duke, 1649-1675
Vittorio Amedeo II, 1675-1730
Under regency of his mother, Maria Giovanna Battista, 1675-1680
Alone as Duke, 1680-1713
as King of Sicily, 1713-1718
as King of Sardinia, 1718-1730

MINTMASTER'S INITIALS
P – Pietro Perrinet, 1640-42

MINTMASTERS' MARKS
P in oval = Andrea O Luca Podesta
L in diamond = Felippo Lavy
P in shield = Giovanni Parodi
B in shield = Tommaso Battilana

MONETARY SYSTEM
12 Denari = 6 Cagliarese = 1 Soldo
50 Soldi = 10 Reales = 2 1/2 Lire = 1 Scudo Sardo
20 Soldi = 1 Lira
6 Lire = 1 Scudo
2 Scudi Sardi = 1 Doppietta
Commencing 1816
100 Centesimi = 1 Lira

KINGDOM

ISLAND COINAGE

KM# 1 REALE

Silver **Obv:** Carlos II **Rev:** Island arms **Note:** CNI-48.

Date	Mintage	F	VF	XF	Unc	BU
1690CI	—	—	—	—	—	—

DAV# 4147 10 REALES

Silver **Obv:** Crowned bust divided C/X-A, date below **Rev:** Cross with dots or X in angles

Date	Mintage	Good	VG	F	VF	XF
1641	—	55.00	110	210	400	—
1642	—	55.00	110	210	400	—
1643	—	55.00	110	210	400	—
1644	—	120	240	425	775	—
1646	—	120	240	425	775	—
1647	—	120	240	425	775	—
1650	—	60.00	120	265	525	—
1652	—	60.00	120	265	525	—
1653	—	60.00	120	265	525	—
1664	—	60.00	120	265	525	—

DAV# 4148 10 REALES

Silver **Obv:** Bust of Charles II right divides C/X-R, date below **Rev:** Cross with flowerettes in angles

Date	Mintage	Good	VG	F	VF	XF
1671	—	120	240	475	975	—
1672	—	120	240	475	975	—
1674	—	120	240	475	975	—
ND	—	120	240	475	975	—

DAV# 4149 10 REALES

Silver **Obv. Legend:** CAROLVS*II*ARAG. E. SARDIE. REX.

Date	Mintage	Good	VG	F	VF	XF
1674	—	120	240	475	975	—
1675	—	180	350	650	1,150	—
1677	—	120	240	475	975	—
1678	—	120	240	475	975	—
1683	—	120	240	475	975	—
1684	—	120	240	475	975	—
1685	—	180	350	650	1,150	—
1689	—	180	350	650	1,150	—

SAVOY

Historical region of southeastern France and northwestern Italy of varying limits, now chiefly in the French departments of Haute-Savoie and Savoie, its' chief city is Chambery.

From 11th century the counts of Savoy ruled this area located in the western Alps as part of kingdom of Arles. It became predominantly independent and expanded its territory to encircle Lake Geneva and later included Piedmont in Italy. It was elevated to a duchy in 1416 by Emperor Sigismund. The scene of fighting in many wars; at times allied with France, sometimes with Italy; involved in wars between France and Spain with alternating allegiances. Under Charles Emmanuel I, it lost territories beyond the Rhone. Later joined Grand Alliance in 1704.By the Treaty of Utrecht 1713 it received island of Sicily and held it until 1720 when that was exchanged for the island of Sardinia forming the Kingdom of Sardinia (included Piedmont, Savoy, and island of Sardinia), the dukes of Savoy becoming Kings of Sardinia. The Kingdom of Sardinia sided with Royalists during the French Revolution and as a result lost the territory of Savoy in 1792 and later Piedmont in 1796 which was restored to Victor Emmanuel I by the Congress of Vienna in 1815 with Genoa added. In 1860 Sardinia, Genoa, and Piedmont joined other states of Italy to form Kingdom of Italy with the House of Savoy as rulers, while the territory of Savoy along with Nice was ceded to France.

RULERS

Carlo Emanuele I, 1580-1630
Vittorio Amedeo I, 1630-1637
Francesco Hyacint, 1637-1638
 under regency of his mother, Maria Cristina
Carlo Emanuele II, 1638-1675
 under regency of his mother,
 Maria Cristina, 1639-1648
 under supposed regency of Maurice
 and Thomas, 1639-1641
 alone as Duke, 1649-1675
Vittorio Amedeo II, 1675-1720
 under regency of his mother,
 Maria Giovanna Battista, 1675-1680
 alone as Duke, 1680-1713

MINTMASTER'S INITIALS

P - Pietro Perrinet, 1640-1642

MONETARY SYSTEM

9 Fiorini = 1 Scudo

DUCHY

STANDARD COINAGE

DAV# 4155 SCUDO (9 Fiorini)

Silver **Obv:** Bust of Carlo Emanuele I right, date below **Rev:** St. Amedeo standing, **ff*9* below

Date	Mintage	VG	F	VF	XF	Unc
1609	—	600	1,200	2,500	7,500	—
1610	—	600	1,200	2,500	7,500	—
1619	—	450	1,150	2,250	7,500	—
1620	—	450	1,150	2,250	7,500	—
1624	—	500	1,200	2,500	7,500	—
1628	—	500	1,200	2,500	7,500	—
1629	—	500	1,200	2,500	7,500	—

DAV# 4159 SCUDO (9 Fiorini)

Silver **Rev:** St. Amedeo standing with shield with 8-line inscription, ff.9 in exergue

Date	Mintage	VG	F	VF	XF	Unc
1612	—	500	1,250	2,500	8,500	—
1619	—	500	1,250	2,500	8,500	—
1620	—	500	1,250	2,500	8,500	—

DAV# 4157 SCUDO (9 Fiorini)

Silver **Rev:** St. Charles standing with cross, S • CAROLVS in exergue

Date	Mintage	VG	F	VF	XF	Unc
1614	—	650	1,350	3,250	9,750	—
1615	—	650	1,350	3,250	9,750	—
1618	—	650	1,350	3,250	9,750	—

DAV# 4158 SCUDO (9 Fiorini)

Silver **Rev:** St. Maurice standing. S. MAVR. in exergue

Date	Mintage	VG	F	VF	XF	Unc
1616 Rare	—	—	—	—	—	—
1618 Rare	—	—	—	—	—	—
ND Rare	—	—	—	—	—	—

DAV# 4156 SCUDO (9 Fiorini)
Silver **Obv:** Circle within **Rev:** Circle within; B. AMEDEVS in exergue below St. Amedeo

Date	Mintage	VG	F	VF	XF	Unc
1616 Rare	—	—	—	—	—	—
1618 Rare	—	—	—	—	—	—

DAV# 4160 SCUDO (9 Fiorini)
Silver **Obv:** Larger bust breaks legend at top D:G. -DVX. **Rev:** Seven-line inscription in shield, date added in exergue

Date	Mintage	VG	F	VF	XF	Unc
1629 Rare	—	—	—	—	—	—

Note: Numismatica Ars Classica Auction 32, 1-06, XF realized approximately $23,020

DAV# 4169 SCUDO (Bianco)
Silver **Rev:** Crowned arms in Order chain

Date	Mintage	VG	F	VF	XF	Unc
1659 Rare	—	—	—	—	—	—

DAV# 4170 SCUDO (Bianco)
Silver **Rev:** Crowned and supported arms, date below

Date	Mintage	VG	F	VF	XF	Unc
1667 Rare	—	—	—	—	—	—

DAV# 4171 SCUDO (Bianco)
Silver **Obv:** Conjoined busts of Vittorio Amedeo II and his regent mother, Maria Giovanni Battista

Date	Mintage	VG	F	VF	XF	Unc
1675	—	700	1,500	3,500	10,000	—
1680	—	700	1,500	3,500	10,000	—

DAV# 4172 SCUDO (Bianco)
Silver **Obv:** Bust of Vittorio Amedeo II right

Date	Mintage	VG	F	VF	XF	Unc
1680	—	1,650	3,250	9,500	—	—
1681	—	1,650	3,250	9,500	—	—
1682	—	1,650	3,250	9,500	—	—

DAV# 4173 SCUDO (Bianco)
Silver **Obv:** Older bust right

Date	Mintage	VG	F	VF	XF	Unc
1690	—	1,850	3,750	10,000	—	—
1695	—	1,850	3,750	10,000	—	—

DAV# 4164 SCUDO (Soadino)
Silver **Rev:** Arm with sword from cloud, cartouche below

Date	Mintage	VG	F	VF	XF	Unc
ND	—	1,650	3,250	6,500	11,500	—

DAV# 4164A SCUDO (Soadino)
Silver **Rev:** Without cartouche, blank exergue

Date	Mintage	VG	F	VF	XF	Unc
ND	—	1,750	3,500	7,000	12,000	—

DAV# 4164B SCUDO (Soadino)
Silver **Rev:** Cartouche with St. Maurice cross

Date	Mintage	VG	F	VF	XF	Unc
ND	—	2,500	5,000	9,000	—	—

DAV# 4150 DUCATONE
Silver **Obv:** Bust right, T and date below **Rev:** Crowned arms dividing FE-RT

Date	Mintage	VG	F	VF	XF	Unc
1601 Rare	—	—	—	—	—	—
1603 Rare	—	—	—	—	—	—
1604	—	1,150	2,250	4,500	8,500	—

DAV# 4151 DUCATONE
Silver **Obv:** Bust in ruffled collar

Date	Mintage	VG	F	VF	XF	Unc
1607 Rare	—	—	—	—	—	—

DAV# 4152 DUCATONE
Silver **Rev:** Crowned ornate arms, without FERT

Date	Mintage	VG	F	VF	XF	Unc
1608 Rare	—	—	—	—	—	—

DAV# 4153 DUCATONE
Silver **Obv:** Different bust **Rev:** Crowned arms divide FE-RT

Date	Mintage	VG	F	VF	XF	Unc
1609 Rare	—	—	—	—	—	—
1610 Rare	—	—	—	—	—	—
1611 Rare	—	—	—	—	—	—

DAV# 4154 DUCATONE
Silver **Obv:** Different bust **Note:** Varieties exist.

Date	Mintage	VG	F	VF	XF	Unc
1620	—	850	1,750	3,500	7,500	—
1621	—	850	1,750	3,500	7,500	—
1622	—	850	1,750	3,500	7,500	—
1627	—	850	1,750	3,500	7,500	—

DAV# 4161 DUCATONE
Silver **Obv. Legend:** ...SABAVDIAE. **Rev:** Compass

Date	Mintage	VG	F	VF	XF	Unc
1621 Rare	—	—	—	—	—	—
1627 Rare	—	—	—	—	—	—

Note: Numismatica Ars Classica Auction 32, 1-06, XF realized approximately $66,675

DAV# A4155 DUCATONE
Silver **Obv. Legend:** CAR. EM. D. G. DVX. S. A. B. P. PED. E. C.

Date	Mintage	VG	F	VF	XF	Unc
1627	—	500	1,200	2,500	7,500	—

DAV# 4163 DUCATONE
Silver **Obv. Legend:** CAROLVS. EM. D: G: DVX. SABAVDIE P. P. **Rev:** Crowned amrs dividing legend at top and FE-RT at center

Date	Mintage	VG	F	VF	XF	Unc
1628 Rare	—	—	—	—	—	—

Note: Numismatica Ars Classica Auction 32, 1-06, Fine realized approximately $11,115

DAV# 4165 DUCATONE
Silver **Obv:** Bust of Vittorio Amedeo I right **Obv. Legend:** ... D: G DVX SABAVDIÆ **Rev:** Crowned arms in Order Collar of the Annunziata **Rev. Legend:** ET PRINCEPS PEDEMONTIVM

Date	Mintage	VG	F	VF	XF	Unc
1632	—	1,250	2,500	5,000	9,000	—
1633	—	1,250	2,500	5,000	9,000	—

DAV# 4167 DUCATONE
Silver **Obv:** Conjoined busts of Carlo Emanuele II and his regent mother, Cristina, date below **Rev:** Crowned arms

Date	Mintage	VG	F	VF	XF	Unc
1641	—	2,750	5,500	9,000	—	—
1642 Rare	—	—	—	—	—	—

Note: Numismatica Ars Classica Auction 32, 1-06, XF/Unc realized approximately $28,575

Date	Mintage	VG	F	VF	XF	Unc
1643 Rare	—	—	—	—	—	—

DAV# 4168 DUCATONE
Silver **Obv:** Bust of Carlo Emanuele II right **Rev:** Crowned arms in Order Collar of the Annunziata

Date	Mintage	VG	F	VF	XF	Unc
1649 Rare	—	—	—	—	—	—

DAV# 4162 2 DUCATONE
Silver **Obv:** Bust of Carlo Emanuele I right, date below **Rev:** Crowned arms dividing legend at top and FE-RT at center

Date	Mintage	VG	F	VF	XF	Unc
1628 Rare	—	—	—	—	—	—

DAV# 4166 2 DUCATONE
Silver **Obv:** Accolated busts of Carlo Emanuele II and his regent mother, Maria, date below **Rev:** Crowned arms

Date	Mintage	VG	F	VF	XF	Unc
1641 Rare	—	—	—	—	—	—
1642 Rare	—	—	—	—	—	—
1643 Rare	—	—	—	—	—	—

TRADE COINAGE

KM# 8 1/2 SCUDO
Gold **Obv:** Winged lion head above shield of arms **Rev:** Cross in inner circle, date in legend

Date	Mintage	VG	F	VF	XF	Unc
1610 Rare	—	—	—	—	—	—

FR# 1051 1/2 SCUDO
1.7600 g., 0.9860 Gold 0.0558 oz. AGW **Obv:** Bust of Carlo Emanuele I right in inner circle **Rev:** Cross of St. Maurice in inner circle, date in legend

Date	Mintage	VG	F	VF	XF	Unc
1627 T Rare	—	—	—	—	—	—

FR# 1076 1/2 SCUDO
1.6900 g., 0.9860 Gold 0.0536 oz. AGW **Obv:** Conjoined busts of Carlo Emanuele II and Mother Maria Cristina right **Rev:** Four interlinked C's with crowns at top, bottom and sides

Date	Mintage	VG	F	VF	XF	Unc
ND	—	2,500	4,500	7,000	11,500	—

FR# 1085 1/2 SCUDO
1.6900 g., 0.9860 Gold 0.0536 oz. AGW **Obv:** Bust of Carlo Emanuele II right **Rev:** Crowned arms in order collar, date in legend

Date	Mintage	VG	F	VF	XF	Unc
1649 Rare	—	—	—	—	—	—

FR# 1050 SCUDO (Bianco)
Gold **Obv:** Carlo Emanuele I

Date	Mintage	VG	F	VF	XF	Unc
1627 Rare	—	—	—	—	—	—

FR# 1052 SCUDO (Bianco)
Gold **Rev:** Legend in wreath **Rev. Inscription:** CRESCIT / CRESCEN / TIBVS / ANNIS

Date	Mintage	VG	F	VF	XF	Unc
ND Rare	—	—	—	—	—	—

FR# A1052 SCUDO (Bianco)
3.1900 g., 0.9860 Gold 0.1011 oz. AGW **Subject:** Death of the Duke **Rev:** Legend in inner circle, date in outer legend
Rev. Inscription: BENE / DICES / CORONAE / ANNI

Date	Mintage	VG	F	VF	XF	Unc
1630 Rare	—	—	—	—	—	—

FR# 1075 SCUDO (Bianco)
3.1900 g., 0.9860 Gold 0.1011 oz. AGW **Obv:** Crowned arms in inner circle **Rev:** Crowned cruciform C monograms

Date	Mintage	VG	F	VF	XF	Unc
ND	—	3,000	5,000	7,500	12,000	—

FR# 1088 SCUDO (Bianco)
3.1900 g., 0.9860 Gold 0.1011 oz. AGW **Obv:** Young bust of Carlo Emanuele II right **Rev:** Cross of St. Maurice

Date	Mintage	VG	F	VF	XF	Unc
ND Rare	—	—	—	—	—	—

FR# 1086 SCUDO (Bianco)
3.1900 g., 0.9860 Gold 0.1011 oz. AGW **Obv:** Head of Carlo Emanuele II right, date below **Rev:** Cross of eight linked C's with crowns at top, bottom and sides

Date	Mintage	VG	F	VF	XF	Unc
1670 Rare	—	—	—	—	—	—

FR# 1056 DUCATO
3.2200 g., 0.9860 Gold 0.1021 oz. AGW **Obv:** Crowned arms in Order Collar of the Annunziata in inner circle, date divided at bottom

Date	Mintage	VG	F	VF	XF	Unc
1601	—	250	475	900	1,650	—
1602	—	250	475	900	1,650	—
1603	—	250	475	900	1,650	—

KM# 75 4 SCUDI (Quadrupla)
12.9700 g., 0.9860 Gold 0.4111 oz. AGW **Obv:** Small bust of Carlo Emanuele I right **Rev:** Crowned arms in inner circle, date in legend

Date	Mintage	VG	F	VF	XF	Unc
1601 Rare	—	—	—	—	—	—
1605 Rare	—	—	—	—	—	—
1607 Rare	—	—	—	—	—	—
1610 Rare	—	—	—	—	—	—
ND Rare	—	—	—	—	—	—

KM# 77 4 SCUDI (Quadrupla)
12.9700 g., 0.9860 Gold 0.4111 oz. AGW **Obv:** Larger bust **Rev:** Without inner circle

Date	Mintage	VG	F	VF	XF	Unc
ND Rare	—	—	—	—	—	—

FR# 1058 4 SCUDI (Quadrupla)
13.2000 g., 0.9860 Gold 0.4184 oz. AGW **Obv:** Bust of Vittorio Amedeo I right in inner circle, date below **Obv. Legend:** V. AMEDEVS D G DVX SAB P PED. **Rev:** Three banners in crown in inner circle, value SCUDI 4 in exergue

Date	Mintage	VG	F	VF	XF	Unc
1633 Rare	—	—	—	—	—	—

FR# A1058 4 SCUDI (Quadrupla)
13.3500 g., 0.9860 Gold 0.4232 oz. AGW **Obv:** Vittorio Amedeo II

Date	Mintage	VG	F	VF	XF	Unc
1633 Rare	—	—	—	—	—	—
1634 Rare	—	—	—	—	—	—

FR# 1063 4 SCUDI (Quadrupla)
13.3500 g., 0.9860 Gold 0.4232 oz. AGW **Rev:** Crowned arms in Order Collar of the Annunziata

Date	Mintage	VG	F	VF	XF	Unc
1634 Rare	—	—	—	—	—	—
ND Rare	—	—	—	—	—	—

FR# 1067 4 SCUDI (Quadrupla)
13.0300 g., 0.9860 Gold 0.4130 oz. AGW **Obv:** Accolated busts of Francesco Hyacint and Mother Maria Christina right **Rev:** Madonna and child in laurel wreath

Date	Mintage	VG	F	VF	XF	Unc
ND	—	3,500	6,000	10,000	16,500	—

FR# 1071.1 4 SCUDI (Quadrupla)
13.0700 g., 0.9860 Gold 0.4143 oz. AGW **Obv:** Conjoined busts of Carlo Emanuele II and Mother Maria Christina di Francia in inner circle **Rev:** Crowned arms

Date	Mintage	VG	F	VF	XF	Unc
1639	—	700	1,500	3,000	5,000	—
1640	—	700	1,500	3,000	5,000	—
1641	—	700	1,500	3,000	5,000	—
1642	—	700	1,500	3,000	5,000	—
1643	—	700	1,500	3,000	5,000	—
1644	—	700	1,500	3,000	5,000	—
1644 I (sic)	—	700	1,500	3,000	5,000	—
1648	—	700	1,500	3,000	5,000	—

FR# 1078 4 SCUDI (Quadrupla)
13.1400 g., 0.9860 Gold 0.4165 oz. AGW **Obv:** Young bust of Carlo Emanuele II right in inner circle **Rev:** Crowned arms in inner circle, date in legend

Date	Mintage	VG	F	VF	XF	Unc
1639 Rare	—	—	—	—	—	—
1640 Rare	—	—	—	—	—	—

FR# 1071.3 4 SCUDI (Quadrupla)
13.1400 g., 0.9860 Gold 0.4165 oz. AGW **Note:** Date at bottom on both sides.

Date	Mintage	VG	F	VF	XF	Unc
1641//1641	—	800	1,600	3,200	5,000	—
1641//1642	—	800	1,600	3,200	5,000	—
1642//1641	—	800	1,600	3,200	5,000	—
1643//1642	—	800	1,600	3,200	5,000	—

FR# 1071.2 4 SCUDI (Quadrupla)
13.1400 g., 0.9860 Gold 0.4165 oz. AGW
Rev. Legend: PRINCIPES • PEDEM • REGIS • CYPRI

Date	Mintage	VG	F	VF	XF	Unc
1641//1642	—	800	1,600	3,200	5,000	—
1643//1642	—	800	1,600	3,200	5,000	—

FR# 1071.4 4 SCUDI (Quadrupla)
13.1400 g., 0.9860 Gold 0.4165 oz. AGW **Obv:** Without inner circles **Rev:** Without inner circles **Rev. Legend:** DVCE • SAR • PP • PEDE • ...

Date	Mintage	VG	F	VF	XF	Unc
1641 P	—	1,200	2,400	4,800	7,500	—
1642 P	—	1,200	2,400	4,800	7,500	—
1643 P Rare	—	—	—	—	—	—

Note: Bowers and Merena Guia sale 3-88 XF realized $13,860

FR# 1073 4 SCUDI (Quadrupla)
13.1400 g., 0.9860 Gold 0.4165 oz. AGW **Obv:** Date in exergue **Rev:** Value S X in exergue

Date	Mintage	VG	F	VF	XF	Unc
1642 Rare	—	—	—	—	—	—

FR# 1083 4 SCUDI (Quadrupla)
13.2400 g., 0.9860 Gold 0.4197 oz. AGW **Obv:** Bust of Carlo Emanuele II right in inner circle, date below **Rev:** Crowned arms in Order Collar of the Annunziata in inner circle

Date	Mintage	VG	F	VF	XF	Unc
1650 Rare	—	—	—	—	—	—
1652 Rare	—	—	—	—	—	—
1654 Rare	—	—	—	—	—	—

FR# A1083 4 SCUDI (Quadrupla)
13.2400 g., 0.9860 Gold 0.4197 oz. AGW **Obv:** Without inner circle **Rev:** Date in legend

Date	Mintage	VG	F	VF	XF	Unc
1654 Rare	—	—	—	—	—	—

FR# 1092 4 SCUDI (Quadrupla)
13.2600 g., 0.9860 Gold 0.4203 oz. AGW **Obv:** Accolated busts of Vittorio Amedeo II and Mother Maria Giovanna Battista right **Rev:** Seated Madonna facing, child standing at right with orb, date in exergue

Date	Mintage	VG	F	VF	XF	Unc
1675 Rare	—	—	—	—	—	—
1676 Rare	—	—	—	—	—	—
1677	—	3,500	6,000	10,000	22,000	—

FR# 1096 4 SCUDI (Quadrupla)
13.2600 g., 0.9860 Gold 0.4203 oz. AGW **Obv:** Bust of Vittorio Amedeo II right **Rev:** Crowned arms in Order Collar of the Annunziata, arms divide date

Date	Mintage	VG	F	VF	XF	Unc
1680 Rare	—	—	—	—	—	—

FR# 1066 8 SCUDI
26.3100 g., 0.9860 Gold 0.8340 oz. AGW **Obv:** Francesco Hyacint and Mother Maria Cristina

Date	Mintage	VG	F	VF	XF	Unc
ND Rare	—	—	—	—	—	—

FR# 1070 8 SCUDI
26.1100 g., 0.9860 Gold 0.8277 oz. AGW **Obv:** Carlo Emanuele II and Mother Maria Cristina

Date	Mintage	VG	F	VF	XF	Unc
1641 Rare	—	—	—	—	—	—
ND	—	5,000	9,000	15,000	25,000	—

FR# 1046 10 SCUDI
33.1700 g., 0.9860 Gold 1.0515 oz. AGW **Obv:** Bust of Carlo Emanuele I right in inner circle, date below **Rev:** Crowned arms in Order Collar of the Annunziata in inner circle

Date	Mintage	VG	F	VF	XF	Unc
1607 T Rare	—	—	—	—	—	—
1610 Rare	—	—	—	—	—	—
1618 Rare	—	—	—	—	—	—

FR# A1046 10 SCUDI
33.2700 g., 0.9860 Gold 1.0546 oz. AGW **Obv:** Wide date below bust **Rev:** Without order collar, arms divide FE-RT

Date	Mintage	VG	F	VF	XF	Unc
1610 Rare	—	—	—	—	—	—

FR# B1046 10 SCUDI
32.4300 g., 0.9860 Gold 1.0280 oz. AGW **Obv:** Small date below bust

Date	Mintage	VG	F	VF	XF	Unc
1618 Rare	—	—	—	—	—	—
1619 HA Rare	—	—	—	—	—	—
1619 Rare	—	—	—	—	—	—
1621 Rare	—	—	—	—	—	—
1623 Rare	—	—	—	—	—	—
1627 Rare	—	—	—	—	—	—
1627 T Rare	—	—	—	—	—	—

FR# C1046 10 SCUDI
32.4300 g., 0.9860 Gold 1.0280 oz. AGW

Date	Mintage	VG	F	VF	XF	Unc
1628 V Rare	—	—	—	—	—	—

FR# 1053 10 SCUDI
33.3200 g., 0.9860 Gold 1.0562 oz. AGW **Rev:** Compass in inner circle

Date	Mintage	VG	F	VF	XF	Unc
1628 Rare	—	—	—	—	—	—

FR# A1053 10 SCUDI
33.3200 g., 0.9860 Gold 1.0562 oz. AGW **Rev:** Compass in inner circle

Date	Mintage	VG	F	VF	XF	Unc
1630 Rare	—	—	—	—	—	—

FR# D1046 10 SCUDI
32.4300 g., 0.9860 Gold 1.0280 oz. AGW **Note:** Varieties exist.

Date	Mintage	VG	F	VF	XF	Unc
1630 Rare	—	—	—	—	—	—

FR# 1062 10 SCUDI
33.0200 g., 0.9860 Gold 1.0467 oz. AGW **Obv:** Bust of Vittorio Amedeo I right in inner circle, date below **Rev:** Crowned arms in Order Collar of the Annunziata in inner circle

Date	Mintage	VG	F	VF	XF	Unc
1633 Rare	—	—	—	—	—	—
1634 Rare	—	—	—	—	—	—
1635 Rare	—	—	—	—	—	—
1636 Rare	—	—	—	—	—	—

FR# 1057 10 SCUDI
33.2600 g., 0.9860 Gold 1.0543 oz. AGW **Rev:** Three banners through crown in inner circle

Date	Mintage	VG	F	VF	XF	Unc
1633 Rare	—	—	—	—	—	—

FR# 1065 10 SCUDI
32.9600 g., 0.9860 Gold 1.0448 oz. AGW **Rev:** Cruciform knots with letters F-E-R-T, one in each knot, clasped hands in angles, all in double inner circle

Date	Mintage	VG	F	VF	XF	Unc
1635 Rare	—	—	—	—	—	—

FR# 1077 10 SCUDI
33.2500 g., 0.9860 Gold 1.0540 oz. AGW **Obv:** Young bust of Carlo Emanuele II right in inner circle **Rev:** Crowned arms in inner circle

Date	Mintage	VG	F	VF	XF	Unc
1639 Rare	—	—	—	—	—	—

FR# 1069 10 SCUDI
33.5300 g., 0.9860 Gold 1.0629 oz. AGW **Obv:** Accolated busts of Carlo Emanuele II and Mother Maria Cristina right, in inner circle **Rev:** Crowned arms in inner cirlce

Date	Mintage	VG	F	VF	XF	Unc
1641 Rare	—	—	—	—	—	—

Note: Bowers and Merena Guia sale 3-88 AU realized $30,800

Date	Mintage	VG	F	VF	XF	Unc
1648 Rare	—	—	—	—	—	—

FR# A1069 10 SCUDI
33.5300 g., 0.9860 Gold 1.0629 oz. AGW

Date	Mintage	VG	F	VF	XF	Unc
1641 Rare	—	—	—	—	—	—

FR# 1082 10 SCUDI
32.9100 g., 0.9860 Gold 1.0432 oz. AGW **Obv:** Bust of Carlo Emanuele II right in inner circle, date below **Rev:** Crowned arms in collar of the annunziata in inner circle **Note:** Varieties exist.

Date	Mintage	VG	F	VF	XF	Unc
1649 Rare	—	—	—	—	—	—
1650 Rare	—	—	—	—	—	—
1654 Rare	—	—	—	—	—	—
1656 Rare	—	—	—	—	—	—
1658 Rare	—	—	—	—	—	—
1660 Rare	—	—	—	—	—	—

FR# A1082 10 SCUDI
32.9100 g., 0.9860 Gold 1.0432 oz. AGW **Obv:** Without date below bust

Date	Mintage	VG	F	VF	XF	Unc
ND Rare	—	—	—	—	—	—

FR# B1082 10 SCUDI
33.1400 g., 0.9860 Gold 1.0505 oz. AGW **Obv:** Mature bust right, date in legend

Date	Mintage	VG	F	VF	XF	Unc
1663 Rare	—	—	—	—	—	—

Note: Bowers and Merena Guia sale 3-88 VF realized $61,600

FR# C1082 10 SCUDI
33.1400 g., 0.9860 Gold 1.0505 oz. AGW **Obv:** Date below bust

Date	Mintage	VG	F	VF	XF	Unc
1665 Rare	—	—	—	—	—	—

FR# D1082 10 SCUDI
33.0500 g., 0.9860 Gold 1.0477 oz. AGW **Rev:** Small square arms, date in legend

Date	Mintage	VG	F	VF	XF	Unc
1668 Rare	—	—	—	—	—	—

FR# E1082 10 SCUDI
33.1300 g., 0.9860 Gold 1.0502 oz. AGW **Obv:** Older bust right **Rev:** Crowned arms wtih lion supporters, date in exergue

Date	Mintage	VG	F	VF	XF	Unc
1670 Rare	—	—	—	—	—	—
1671 Rare	—	—	—	—	—	—

FR# 1094 10 SCUDI
33.1300 g., 0.9860 Gold 1.0502 oz. AGW **Obv:** Young armored bust of Vittorio Amedeo II right

Date	Mintage	VG	F	VF	XF	Unc
1680 Rare	—	—	—	—	—	—

KM# 140 20 SCUDI
33.1300 g., 0.9860 Gold 1.0502 oz. AGW **Obv:** Bust of Carlo Emanuele I right in inner circle, date below bust **Rev:** Crowned arms divide FE-RT in inner circle

Date	Mintage	VG	F	VF	XF	Unc
1610 Rare	—	—	—	—	—	—

FR# 1061 20 SCUDI
Gold **Obv:** Bust of Vittorio Amedeo I right in inner circle, date below bust **Rev:** Crowned arms in Order Collar of the Annunziata in inner circle

Date	Mintage	VG	F	VF	XF	Unc
1635 Rare	—	—	—	—	—	—

FR# 1068 20 SCUDI
Gold **Obv:** Accolated bust of Carlo Emanuele II right in inner circle, date below **Rev:** Crowned arms in inner circle

Date	Mintage	VG	F	VF	XF	Unc
1641 Rare	—	—	—	—	—	—

FR# 1081 20 SCUDI
66.3700 g., 0.9860 Gold 2.1039 oz. AGW **Obv:** Bust of Carlo Emanuele II in elaborate cape to right in inner circle, date below bust **Rev:** Crowned arms in Order Collar of the Annunziata in inner circle

Date	Mintage	VG	F	VF	XF	Unc
1649 Rare	—	—	—	—	—	—

FR# A1081 20 SCUDI
66.3500 g., 0.9860 Gold 2.1032 oz. AGW **Obv:** Armored bust of Carlo Emanuele II right in inner circle, date below bust

Date	Mintage	VG	F	VF	XF	Unc
1656 Rare	—	—	—	—	—	—
1657 Rare	—	—	—	—	—	—

FR# B1081 20 SCUDI
66.5000 g., 0.9860 Gold 2.1080 oz. AGW **Obv:** Bust of Carlo Emanuele II in elaborate armor right in inner circle, date below bust

Date	Mintage	VG	F	VF	XF	Unc
1660 Rare	—	—	—	—	—	—
1667 Rare	—	—	—	—	—	—

FR# C1081 20 SCUDI

66.4200 g., 0.9860 Gold 2.1055 oz. AGW **Obv:** Older bust of Carlo Emanuele II right **Rev:** Crowned arms iwth lion supporters, date in exergue

Date	Mintage	VG	F	VF	XF	Unc
1671 Rare	—	—	—	—	—	—

FR# 1093 20 SCUDI

67.2000 g., 0.9860 Gold 2.1302 oz. AGW **Obv:** Young armored bust of Vittorio Amedeo II right **Rev:** Crowned arms with lion supporters, date in exergue

Date	Mintage	VG	F	VF	XF	Unc
1684 Rare	—	—	—	—	—	—

FR# 1060 30 SCUDI

Gold **Obv:** Bust of Vittorio Amedeus I right in inner circle, date below bust **Rev:** Crowned arms in Order Collar of the Annunziata in inner circle

Date	Mintage	VG	F	VF	XF	Unc
1635 Rare	—	—	—	—	—	—

FR# 1080 30 SCUDI

Gold **Obv:** Bust of Carlo Emanuele II right in inner circle, date below bust

Date	Mintage	VG	F	VF	XF	Unc
1656 Rare	—	—	—	—	—	—

FR# 1079 40 SCUDI

Gold **Obv:** Bust of Carlo Emanuele II right in inner circle, date below bust **Rev:** Crowned arms in Order Collar of the Annunziata in inner circle

Date	Mintage	VG	F	VF	XF	Unc
1656 Rare	—	—	—	—	—	—

FR# 1091 1/2 DOPPIA

3.3000 g., 0.9860 Gold 0.1046 oz. AGW **Obv:** Conjoined busts of Vittorio Amedeo II and Mother Maria Giovanna Battista right **Rev:** Crowned arms in Order Collar of the Annunziata, date in legend

Date	Mintage	VG	F	VF	XF	Unc
1675	—	625	1,250	2,300	4,250	—
1676	—	625	1,250	2,300	4,250	—
1677	—	625	1,250	2,300	4,250	—
1678	—	625	1,250	2,300	4,250	—
1679	—	625	1,250	2,300	4,250	—

FR# 1098 1/2 DOPPIA

3.3200 g., 0.9860 Gold 0.1052 oz. AGW **Obv:** Young bust of Vittorio Amedeo II right **Rev:** Crowned arms in Order Collar of the Annunziata, date in legend

Date	Mintage	VG	F	VF	XF	Unc
1679	—	550	1,200	2,000	4,000	—

FR# A1098 1/2 DOPPIA

3.2900 g., 0.9860 Gold 0.1043 oz. AGW **Obv:** Young armored bust of Vittorio Amedeo II right

Date	Mintage	VG	F	VF	XF	Unc
1680 Rare	—	—	—	—	—	—
1681 Rare	—	—	—	—	—	—

FR# 1100 1/2 DOPPIA

3.2900 g., 0.9860 Gold 0.1043 oz. AGW **Ruler:** Vittorio Amedeo II **Obv:** Mature bust right **Rev:** Crowned arms in Order Collar of the Annunziata, date in legend

Date	Mintage	Good	VG	F	VF	XF
1692 Rare	—	—	—	—	—	—

FR# 1049.1 DOPPIA

6.6700 g., 0.9860 Gold 0.2114 oz. AGW **Obv:** Carlo Emanuele I

Date	Mintage	VG	F	VF	XF	Unc
1601	—	800	1,600	3,500	6,000	—
1604	—	800	1,600	3,500	6,000	—

FR# 1049.2 DOPPIA

6.5500 g., 0.9860 Gold 0.2076 oz. AGW **Obv:** Carlo Emanuele I

Date	Mintage	VG	F	VF	XF	Unc
1610	—	800	1,600	3,500	6,000	—
1611	—	800	1,600	3,500	6,000	—

FR# 1049.4 DOPPIA

6.6200 g., 0.9860 Gold 0.2098 oz. AGW **Obv:** Date below bust

Date	Mintage	VG	F	VF	XF	Unc
1611	—	800	1,600	3,500	6,000	—
ND	—	800	1,600	3,500	6,000	—

FR# 1064 DOPPIA

6.5200 g., 0.9860 Gold 0.2067 oz. AGW **Obv:** Vittorio Amedeo

Date	Mintage	VG	F	VF	XF	Unc
ND Rare	—	—	—	—	—	—

FR# 1049.3 DOPPIA

6.6200 g., 0.9860 Gold 0.2098 oz. AGW **Rev:** Crowned arms in inner circle

Date	Mintage	VG	F	VF	XF	Unc
ND	—	800	1,600	3,500	6,000	—

KM# 170 DOPPIA

6.6200 g., 0.9860 Gold 0.2098 oz. AGW **Obv:** Young head of Carlo Emanuele II right in inner circle

Date	Mintage	VG	F	VF	XF	Unc
1640	—	1,500	2,750	—	—	—

FR# 1072.1 DOPPIA

6.6200 g., 0.9860 Gold 0.2098 oz. AGW **Obv:** Accolated busts of Carlo Emanuele II and Mother Maria Cristina left, date below **Rev:** Crowned arms in inner circle

Date	Mintage	VG	F	VF	XF	Unc
1640	—	1,500	2,750	—	—	—

FR# 1072.2 DOPPIA

6.6900 g., 0.9860 Gold 0.2121 oz. AGW **Obv:** Accolated busts of Carlo Emanuele II and Mother Maria Cristina right **Rev:** Crowned arms in inner circle, date in legend

Date	Mintage	VG	F	VF	XF	Unc
1641 Rare	—	—	—	—	—	—

FR# 1084.1 DOPPIA

6.5700 g., 0.9860 Gold 0.2083 oz. AGW **Obv:** Bust of Carlo Emanuele II right in inner circle, date below bust **Rev:** Crowned arms in Order Collar of the Annunziata

Date	Mintage	VG	F	VF	XF	Unc
1650 Rare	—	—	—	—	—	—

FR# 1084.2 DOPPIA

6.6000 g., 0.9860 Gold 0.2092 oz. AGW **Obv:** Bust of Carlo Emanuele II right

Date	Mintage	VG	F	VF	XF	Unc
1653 Rare	—	—	—	—	—	—
1654	—	2,250	5,750	6,500	12,000	—
1655 Rare	—	—	—	—	—	—

FR# 1085a DOPPIA

6.6000 g., 0.9860 Gold 0.2092 oz. AGW **Obv:** Head of Carlo Emanuele II right, date below **Rev:** Cross of eight linked C's with crowns at top, bottom and sides

Date	Mintage	VG	F	VF	XF	Unc
1670 Rare	—	—	—	—	—	—

FR# 1087 DOPPIA

6.6500 g., 0.9860 Gold 0.2108 oz. AGW **Rev:** Crowned arms in Order Collar of the Annunziata

Date	Mintage	VG	F	VF	XF	Unc
1675	—	900	1,800	4,000	6,500	—

FR# 1090 DOPPIA

6.6690 g., 0.9860 Gold 0.2114 oz. AGW **Obv:** Accolated busts of Vittorio Amedeo II and Mother Maria Giovanna Battista

Date	Mintage	VG	F	VF	XF	Unc
1675	—	450	850	2,000	4,900	—
1676	—	450	850	2,000	4,900	—
1677	—	450	850	2,000	4,900	—
1678	—	450	850	2,000	4,900	—
1679	—	450	850	2,000	4,900	—
1680	—	450	850	2,000	4,900	—

FR# 1097 DOPPIA

6.5900 g., 0.9860 Gold 0.2089 oz. AGW **Obv:** Vittorio Amedeo II

Date	Mintage	VG	F	VF	XF	Unc
1680 Rare	—	—	—	—	—	—
1681 Rare	—	—	—	—	—	—
1682	—	1,650	2,950	4,900	7,200	—

FR# A1099 DOPPIA

6.6000 g., 0.9860 Gold 0.2092 oz. AGW **Obv:** Tall bust of Vittorio Amedeo II right, date below

Date	Mintage	VG	F	VF	XF	Unc
1690 Rare	—	—	—	—	—	—
1691 Rare	—	—	—	—	—	—

FR# A1092 2 DOPPIE

Gold **Obv:** Vittorio Amadeo II and Mother Giovanna Battista

Date	Mintage	VG	F	VF	XF	Unc
1677 Rare	—	—	—	—	—	—

FR# 1089 5 DOPPIE

33.1300 g., 0.9860 Gold 1.0502 oz. AGW **Obv:** Accolated busts of Bittorio Amedeo II and Mother Giovanna Battista right **Rev:** Crowned arms, date in legend

Date	Mintage	VG	F	VF	XF	Unc
1675 Rare	—	—	—	—	—	—
1678 Rare	—	—	—	—	—	—

FR# 1095 5 DOPPIE

33.1300 g., 0.9860 Gold 1.0502 oz. AGW **Obv:** Equestrian figure of Bittorio Amedeo II left, date in exergue **Rev:** Seated Justice facing on cloud holding sword and scales

Date	Mintage	VG	F	VF	XF	Unc
1694 Rare	—	—	—	—	—	—

SEBORGA

Seborga, a commune in the province of Porto Maurizio, was a fief of the Benedictine Monastery of Lerino. The abbot coined luigini without authorization.

COMMUNE

STANDARD COINAGE

KM# 5 LUIGINI

Silver **Obv:** Bust right **Rev:** Crowned arms, date above **Rev. Legend:** SVBVMBAR **Note:** Weight varies: 2.09-3.05 grams.

Date	Mintage	VG	F	VF	XF	Unc
1667	—	200	375	850	1,750	—
1668	—	200	375	850	1,750	—

KM# 6 LUIGINI

Silver **Rev:** Crowned arms in sprays **Rev. Legend:** MONAST. **Note:** Weight varies: 2.09-3.05 grams.

Date	Mintage	VG	F	VF	XF	Unc
1668	—	200	375	850	1,750	—

KM# 7 LUIGINI

Silver **Obv:** Bust right **Obv. Legend:** DECVS **Rev:** Crowned arms divide date **Note:** Weight varies: 2.09-3.05 grams.

Date	Mintage	VG	F	VF	XF	Unc
1669	—	250	450	950	2,000	—
1671	—	150	325	750	1,600	—

SICILY

Has a history of occupation extending back to the ancient Phoenicians. In more recent times it was part of the Kingdom of Naples and Sicily.

RULER
Charles II (of Spain), 1665-1700

MONETARY SYSTEM
6 Cavalli = 1 Grano
20 Grani = 2 Carlini = 1 Tari
12 Tari = 1 Piastra
15 Tari = 1 Scudo
2 Scudi = 1 Oncia

KINGDOM

STANDARD COINAGE

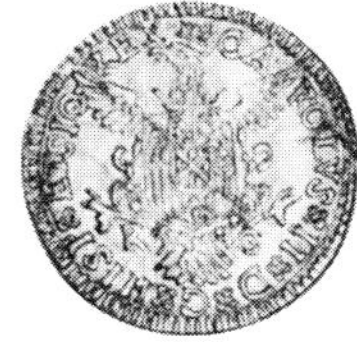

FR# 881 SCUDO RICCIO
Gold **Ruler:** Charles II **Obv:** Head of Charles right in crowned cartouche, date below **Rev:** Crowned eagle with arms on breast

Date	Mintage	VG	F	VF	XF	Unc
1697 RC	—	600	1,200	2,100	4,500	—

SOLFERINO

A commune in the province of Mantua.

RULER
Carlo Gonzaga, 1640-1678

COMMUNE

STANDARD COINAGE

KM# 5 SESINO
0.4500 g., Billon **Obv:** Head right **Rev:** MVNI/ SESIN

Date	Mintage	VG	F	VF	XF	Unc
ND	—	65.00	120	200	400	—

KM# 6 MURAILO
1.3600 g., Billon **Obv:** Bust of Pontiff right **Rev:** St. Nicholas

Date	Mintage	VG	F	VF	XF	Unc
ND	—	70.00	125	220	425	—

KM# 7 QUATTRINO
Copper **Obv:** Armored bust right **Rev:** Ornate cross **Note:** Weight varies: 0.70-1.71 grams.

Date	Mintage	VG	F	VF	XF	Unc
ND	—	50.00	90.00	165	325	—

KM# 8 QUATTRINO
Copper **Obv:** Bust right **Rev:** Eagle **Note:** Weight varies: 0.70-1.71 grams.

Date	Mintage	VG	F	VF	XF	Unc
ND	—	30.00	70.00	140	275	—

KM# 9 QUATTRINO
Copper **Obv:** Crowned arms **Rev:** Head of saint right **Note:** Weight varies: 0.70-1.71 grams.

Date	Mintage	VG	F	VF	XF	Unc
ND	—	50.00	90.00	165	325	—

KM# 21 QUATTRINO
Copper **Obv:** MARCH/ SVL FARINI/ 1643 **Rev:** Rampant lion **Note:** Weight varies: 0.70-1.71 grams.

Date	Mintage	VG	F	VF	XF	Unc
1643	—	35.00	75.00	150	300	—

KM# 10 SOLDO
Billon **Obv:** Bust right **Rev:** Cross with sun in center **Note:** Weight varies: 1.60-1.80 grams.

Date	Mintage	VG	F	VF	XF	Unc
ND	—	40.00	80.00	150	300	—

KM# 11 SOLDO
Billon **Rev:** Radiant sun **Note:** Weight varies: 1.60-1.80 grams.

Date	Mintage	VG	F	VF	XF	Unc
ND	—	45.00	95.00	175	335	—

KM# 12 SOLDO
Billon **Rev:** Sun with long rays **Note:** Weight varies: 1.60-1.80 grams.

Date	Mintage	VG	F	VF	XF	Unc
ND	—	45.00	95.00	175	335	—

KM# 13 SOLDO
Billon **Obv:** Crowned arms **Rev:** Soldier standing **Note:** Weight varies: 1.60-1.80 grams.

Date	Mintage	VG	F	VF	XF	Unc
ND	—	40.00	80.00	150	300	—

KM# 14 SOLDO
Billon **Obv:** Head left **Rev:** Sun with rays **Note:** Weight varies: 1.60-1.80 grams.

Date	Mintage	VG	F	VF	XF	Unc
ND	—	50.00	100	175	335	—

KM# 15 SOLDO
Billon **Obv:** Crowned arms **Rev:** Tabernacle **Note:** Weight varies: 1.60-1.80 grams.

Date	Mintage	VG	F	VF	XF	Unc
ND	—	40.00	90.00	165	325	—

KM# 16 GUIGINO
Billon **Obv:** Bust right **Rev:** Saint kneeling in prayer **Note:** Weight varies: 1.54-2.45 grams.

Date	Mintage	VG	F	VF	XF	Unc
ND	—	40.00	90.00	185	350	—

KM# 20 SCUDO
31.3400 g., Silver **Obv:** Bust left **Rev:** St. Aloisius kneeling **Note:** Dav. #4174.

Date	Mintage	VG	F	VF	XF	Unc
1640 Rare	—	—	—	—	—	—

KM# 17 2 FLORIN D'ORO
7.0000 g., 0.9860 Gold 0.2219 oz. AGW **Obv:** Bust of Carlo left **Rev:** Crowned arms

Date	Mintage	VG	F	VF	XF	Unc
ND Rare	—	—	—	—	—	—

KM# 18 DUCAT
3.5000 g., 0.9860 Gold 0.1109 oz. AGW **Obv:** Carlo standing right in inner circle **Rev:** Crowned arms in order collar in inner circle

Date	Mintage	VG	F	VF	XF	Unc
ND Rare	—	—	—	—	—	—

TASSAROLO

Countship

Tassarolo is a town of ancient origin which was already a possession of the marchese of Gavi by 1192 and, afterwards, of the Republic of Genoa. It was transferred to Alessandria in 1227, but later subjected to Genoa again and became a possession of the Spinola family in 1454. Tassarolo was erected into a countship by Emperor Ferdinand I in 1560 for the Spinolas' benefit, and received the mint right at that time. The production of coinage in Tassarolo ended in 1688.

RULERS
Augostino Spinola, 1604-1616
Filippo Spinola, 1616-1688
Livia Centurioni Oltremarini, wife of Filippo

Reference: Alberto Varesi, ***Monete Italiane Regionali: Piemonte, Sardegna, Liguria, Isola di Corsica.*** Pavia, 1996.

COUNTSHIP

STANDARD COINAGE

KM# 22 PARAGLIOLA
Billon, 22-23 mm. **Ruler:** Agostino **Obv:** Crowned displayed eagle in circle **Obv. Legend:** AVG. SPI. COM. TASS. **Rev:** St. Francis kneeling and receiving the stigmata, date in exergue **Rev. Legend:** SPES. FIRMA. **Note:** Varesi 973.

Date	Mintage	VG	F	VF	XF	Unc
1614	—	150	325	700	1,000	—

KM# 48.1 LUIGINO
Silver Weight varies: 1.41-2.16g, 20-21 mm. **Ruler:** Livia **Obv:** Bust to right **Obv. Legend:** MAR. LIV. COM. PALAT. SOW. DOM. **Rev:** Crowned shield of arms divides date, "7" at bottom **Rev. Legend:** DNS. ILLVMINAT. ET. SALVS. MEA. **Note:** Varesi 994.

Date	Mintage	VG	F	VF	XF	Unc
1658	—	60.00	100	165	250	—

KM# 48.2 LUIGINO
Silver Weight varies: 1.41-2.16g, 20-21 mm. **Ruler:** Livia **Obv:** Bust to right **Obv. Legend:** MAR. LLIV. COM. PALAT. SOW. DOM. **Rev:** Crowned shield of arms divides date, "5" at bottom **Rev. Legend:** DNS. ILLVMINAT. ET. SALVS. MEA. **Note:** Varesi 994/1.

Date	Mintage	VG	F	VF	XF	Unc
1658	—	60.00	100	165	250	—

KM# 50 LUIGINO
Silver Weight varies: 1.97-2.22g, 20 mm. **Ruler:** Filippo **Obv:** Bust to right **Obv. Legend:** PHILIPPVS. D.G. COMES. TASS. **Rev:** Crowned shield of arms, date at end of legend **Rev. Legend:** CIRCVMDEDISTI - ME. LÆTITIA. **Note:** Varesi 992/1-5

Date	Mintage	VG	F	VF	XF	Unc
1660	—	225	385	875	1,400	—
1662	—	225	385	875	1,400	—
1663	—	225	385	875	1,400	—
1665	—	225	385	875	1,400	—
1666	—	225	385	875	1,400	—

KM# 51 LUIGINO
Silver Weight varies: 1.95-2.06g, 19-20 mm. **Ruler:** Filippo **Obv:** Bust to right **Obv. Legend:** PHILIPPVS. D.G. TASS. COMES. **Rev:** Crowned shield of arms, date above **Rev. Legend:** IN. TE. DOMINE. SPERAVI. **Note:** Varesi 993.

Date	Mintage	VG	F	VF	XF	Unc
1665	—	100	200	450	650	—

KM# 52.1 LUIGINO
Silver Weight varies: 2.06-2.13g, 21-22 mm. **Ruler:** Livia **Obv:** Bust to right **Obv. Legend:** LIV. MA. PRI. SP. COM. T. SOW. DOM. **Rev:** Crowned shield of arms divides date, "ToA" at bottom **Rev. Legend:** DNS. ADIVTOR. ET. REDEM. MEVS. **Note:** Varesi 995.

Date	Mintage	VG	F	VF	XF	Unc
1666	—	25.00	55.00	100	165	—

KM# 52.2 LUIGINO
Silver Weight varies: 2.06-2.13g, 21-22 mm. **Ruler:** Livia **Obv:** Bust to right **Obv. Legend:** MAR. LIV. COM. PALAT. SOW. DOM. **Rev:** Crowned shield of arms divides date, "ToA" at bottom **Rev. Legend:** DNS. ADIVTOR. ET. REDEM. MEVS. **Note:** Varesi 995/1.

Date	Mintage	VG	F	VF	XF	Unc
1666	—	45.00	80.00	135	195	—

KM# 52.3 LUIGINO
1.9800 g., Silver, 21 mm. **Ruler:** Livia **Obv:** Bust to right **Obv. Legend:** AN. MAIOV. PRINC. SOW. DE. DOM. **Rev:** Crowned shield of arms divides date, "T" at bottom **Rev. Legend:** DNS. ADIVTOR. ET. REDEM. MEVS. **Note:** Varesi 996.

Date	Mintage	VG	F	VF	XF	Unc
1667	—	45.00	80.00	120	165	—

KM# A13 7 SOLDI
2.2500 g., Billon, 22 mm. **Ruler:** Agostino **Obv:** Bust to right, date below **Obv. Legend:** AVGVST. SPIN. COMES. TASS. **Rev:** Crowned imperial eagle, shield of Austrian arms on breast **Rev. Legend:** MONETA. DA. SOLDI. SETTE. **Note:** Varesi 972.

Date	Mintage	VG	F	VF	XF	Unc
1605 Rare	—	—	—	—	—	—

KM# 25 1/8 SCUDO
3.2000 g., Silver, 24 mm. **Ruler:** Agostino **Obv:** Cross in circle **Obv. Legend:** AVGVSTINVS. SPINOLA. **Rev:** Crowned shield of arms **Rev. Legend:** COMES. TASSAROLI. **Note:** Varesi 971.

Date	Mintage	VG	F	VF	XF	Unc
ND(1604-16) Rare	—	—	—	—	—	—

KM# 24 1/8 SCUDO
Silver Weight varies: 3.06-3.40g, 24 mm. **Ruler:** Agostino **Obv:** Half-length armored figure to right **Obv. Legend:** AVGVSTINVS. SPIN. COMES. TASS. **Rev:** Crowned imperial eagle, shield of Austrian arms on breast **Rev. Legend:** VIRTVTE. CAESAREA. DVCE. **Note:** Varesi 970.

Date	Mintage	VG	F	VF	XF	Unc
ND(1604-16)	—	120	250	600	1,500	—

KM# 53 1/8 SCUDO
2.4000 g., Silver, 21 mm. **Ruler:** Filippo **Obv:** Bust to right **Obv. Legend:** PHILIP. SPINV. TASS. COMES. **Rev:** Crowned imperial eagle, shield of arms on breast, date divided at top **Rev. Legend:** DEVS. MEVS. IN. TE. CONFIDO. **Note:** Varesi 990.

Date	Mintage	VG	F	VF	XF	Unc
1667	—	500	825	1,700	2,750	—

KM# 54 1/8 SCUDO
1.9800 g., Silver, 21 mm. **Ruler:** Filippo **Obv:** Bust to right **Obv. Legend:** PHILIP. D.G. COMES. PALAT. **Rev:** Crowned imperial eagle, shield of arms on breast, date divided at top. **Rev. Legend:** VIRT. DVCE. CES. FORTVN. **Note:** Varesi 991.

Date	Mintage	VG	F	VF	XF	Unc
1667	—	500	825	1,700	2,750	—

KM# 14 1/4 SCUDO
7.9600 g., Silver, 30-31 mm. **Ruler:** Agostino **Obv:** Armored bust to right, date below shoulder **Obv. Legend:** AVGVS. SPIN. COM. PALATIN. **Rev:** Crowned ornate shield of 4-fold arms with central shield **Rev. Legend:** NOSTRÆ. SPES - VNA. SALVTIS. **Note:** Varesi 968.

Date	Mintage	VG	F	VF	XF	Unc
1606 Rare	—	—	—	—	—	—

KM# 17 1/4 SCUDO
Silver Weight varies: 6.28-7.25g, 27-28 mm. **Ruler:** Agostino **Obv:** Half-length armored figure to right, date below, where present **Obv. Legend:** AVGVSTI(NVS). SPIN. COMES. TASS. **Rev:** Crowned imperial eagle, oval shield of Austrian arms on breast **Rev. Legend:** VIRTVTE. CAESAREA. DVCE. **Note:** Varesi 969/1-2.

Date	Mintage	VG	F	VF	XF	Unc
1607	—	125	250	650	1,100	—
ND(1607-10)	—	125	250	650	1,100	—

KM# 31 1/4 SCUDO

7.8100 g., Silver, 29-30 mm. **Ruler:** Filippo **Obv:** Armored bust to right **Obv. Legend:** PHILIPPVS. SPINVLA. **Rev:** Crowned shield of arms in baroque frame, date at end of legend **Rev. Legend:** COMES. TASSAROLI. **Note:** Varesi 988.

Date	Mintage	VG	F	VF	XF	Unc
1629	—	650	1,000	2,150	3,350	—

KM# A51 1/4 SCUDO

Silver, 30 mm. **Ruler:** Filippo **Obv:** Large armored bust to right **Obv. Legend:** PHIL. SPIN. COM. TASS. **Rev:** Imperial eagle withi shield of arms on breast, large crown above, date at end of legend **Rev. Legend:** IN. TE. DOMINE. SPERAVI. **Note:** Varesi 989.

Date	Mintage	VG	F	VF	XF	Unc
1663 Rare	—	—	—	—	—	—

KM# 8 1/2 SCUDO

14.6200 g., Silver, 35-36 mm. **Ruler:** Agostino **Obv:** Armored bust to right, date below shoulder **Obv. Legend:** AVGVSTINVS. SPINVLA. **Rev:** Shield of family arms in baroque frame, large crown above **Rev. Legend:** COMES - TASSAROLI. **Note:** Varesi 967.

Date	Mintage	VG	F	VF	XF	Unc
1604 Rare	—	—	—	—	—	—

KM# 39 1/2 SCUDO

15.7100 g., Silver, 35-36 mm. **Ruler:** Filippo **Obv:** Armored bust to right **Obv. Legend:** PHILIPPVS. SPIN. COM. TASS. **Rev:** St. George on horseback to right slaying dragon below, date in exergue **Rev. Legend:** SPES. NON. CONFVNDIT. **Note:** Varesi 987.

Date	Mintage	VG	F	VF	XF	Unc
1639	—	750	1,100	2,850	4,400	—

KM# 9 SCUDO

Silver Weight varies: 27.30-31.84g, 42 mm. **Ruler:** Agostino **Obv:** Armored bust to right, date below shoulder **Obv. Legend:** AVGVSTINVS. SPINVLA. **Rev:** Crowned shield of family arms in baroque frame **Rev. Legend:** COMES. TAS - SAROLI. **Note:** Dav. #4175;Varesi 963.

Date	Mintage	VG	F	VF	XF	Unc
1604	—	2,200	4,500	8,500	—	—

KM# 10.1 SCUDO

Silver Weight varies: 25.96-27.15g, 39-40 mm. **Ruler:** Agostino **Obv:** Armored bust to right, date below shoulder **Obv. Legend:** AVGVST. SPINVLA. COMES. TASSAR. **Rev:** Crowned shield of manifold arms, Order of Golden Fleece around **Rev. Legend:** NIL. NISI. AVGVST. AVSPICE. AVGVSTO. **Note:** Dav. #4176; Varesi 964.

Date	Mintage	VG	F	VF	XF	Unc
1604	—	1,200	2,250	4,500	7,500	—

KM# 10.2 SCUDO

Silver Weight varies: 25.96-27.15g, 39-40 mm. **Ruler:** Agostino **Obv:** Armored bust to right, date below shoulder **Obv. Legend:** AVGVSTINVS. SPINVLA. COMES. TASSAROL. **Rev:** Crowned shield of manifold arms, Order of Golden Fleece around **Rev. Legend:** NIL. NISI. AVGVST. AVSPICE. AVGVSTO. **Note:** Dav. #4176A.

Date	Mintage	VG	F	VF	XF	Unc
1604	—	1,200	2,250	4,500	7,500	—

KM# 16.1 SCUDO

Silver Weight varies: 21.00-28.42g, 40-41 mm. **Ruler:** Agostino **Obv:** Half-length armored figure to right **Obv. Legend:** AVGVSTINVS. SPINV. COMES. TASS. **Rev:** Crowned imperial eagle, shield of Austrian arms on breast, "C.XV." below in margin **Rev. Legend:** SVB. TVVM. - PRESIDIVM. **Note:** Dav. #4178; Varesi 966.

Date	Mintage	VG	F	VF	XF	Unc
ND(1604-16)	—	425	950	2,250	5,000	—

KM# 16.2 SCUDO

Silver Weight varies: 21.00-28.42g, 40-41 mm. **Ruler:** Agostino **Obv:** Half-length armored figure to right **Obv. Legend:** AVGVSTINVS. SPINV. COMES. TASS. **Rev:** Crowned imperial eagle, shield of Spinola family arms on breast, "C.XV." below margin **Rev. Legend:** SVB. TVVM. - PRESIDIVM. **Note:** Varesi 966/1.

Date	Mintage	VG	F	VF	XF	Unc
ND(1604-16)	—	650	950	2,000	3,250	—

KM# 15 SCUDO

Silver, 39 mm. **Ruler:** Agostino **Obv:** Armored bust to right, date below shoulder **Obv. Legend:** AVGVS. SPIN. COM. PALATINVS. **Rev:** Large crown above shield of 4-fold arms withi central shield in baroque frame **Rev. Legend:** NOSTRÆ. SPES. - VNA. SALVTIS. **Note:** Dav. #4177; Varesi 965.

Date	Mintage	VG	F	VF	XF	Unc
1606 Rare	—	—	—	—	—	—

KM# 30 SCUDO

Silver Weight varies: 31.05-31.57g, 42-43 mm. **Ruler:** Filippo **Obv:** Armored bust to right **Obv. Legend:** PHILIPPVS. SPINVLA. **Rev:** Crowned shield of family arms in baroque frame, date at end of legend **Rev. Legend:** COMES. TASSAROLI. **Note:** Dav. #4179; Varesi 983/1-3. Varieties exist.

Date	Mintage	VG	F	VF	XF	Unc
1620 Rare	—	—	—	—	—	—
1622 Rare	—	—	—	—	—	—
1629 Rare	—	—	—	—	—	—

KM# 40 SCUDO

Silver Weight varies: 28.55-31.80g, 42-43 mm. **Ruler:** Filippo **Obv:** Armored bust to right **Obv. Legend:** PHILIPPVS. SPIN. COMES. TASS. **Rev:** St. George on horseback to right, slaying dragon below, date in exergue **Rev. Legend:** SPES. NON. - CONFVNDIT. **Note:** Dav. #4180; Varesi 984/1-3.

Date	Mintage	VG	F	VF	XF	Unc
1639	—	275	450	1,100	2,500	—
1640	—	275	450	1,100	2,500	—
1642	—	275	450	1,100	2,500	—

KM# 47 SCUDO

Silver Weight varies: 29.97-31.59g, 43-44 mm. **Ruler:** Agostino **Obv:** Armored bust to right **Obv. Legend:** PHILIP. SPINVLA. COM. TASSARO. **Rev:** Large crown above shield with crowned imperial eagle, shield of arms on breast, date at end of legend **Rev. Legend:** IN. TE. DOMINE. SPERAVI. **Note:** Dav. #4181; Varesi 985/1.

Date	Mintage	VG	F	VF	XF	Unc
1643 Rare	—	—	—	—	—	—

KM# 55 SCUDO

Silver Weight varies: 29.97-31.59g, 43-44 mm. **Ruler:** Filippo **Obv:** Armored bust to right **Obv. Legend:** PHILIP. SPINVLA. COM. TASSA. **Rev:** Large crown above shield in baroque frame crowned imperial eagle, shield of arms on breast, date at end of legend **Rev. Legend:** IN. TE. DOMINE. SPERAVI. **Note:** Dav. #4182; Varesi 985/2.

Date	Mintage	VG	F	VF	XF	Unc
1663 Rare	—	—	—	—	—	—

KM# 26 TALLERO OF 96 SOLDI

26.3500 g., Base Silver, 40-42 mm. **Ruler:** Filippo **Obv:** Half-length armored figure behind shield of lion arms below **Obv. Legend:** MON. DA. SOL. 96 - COM. PALAT. **Rev:** Rampant lion to left in circle **Rev. Legend:** CONFI. IN. DOM. NON. PERIB. IN. ETER. **Note:** Dav. #4183; Varesi 986. Previous KM #5. Imitation of United Netherlands Daalder.

Date	Mintage	VG	F	VF	XF	Unc
ND(1616-88)	—	900	1,750	3,000	—	—

KM# 27 TALLERO OF 96 SOLDI

26.3500 g., Base Silver, 40-42 mm. **Ruler:** Filippo **Obv:** Half-length armored figure behind shield of lion arms below **Obv. Legend:** MO. ARG. PRO. CON - FOE. BELG. HOL. **Rev:** Rampant lion to left in circle **Rev. Legend:** CONFI. IN. DOM. NON, PERIB. IN. ETER. **Note:** Dav. #4183A. Previous KM #6. Imitation of United Netherlands Daalder.

Date	Mintage	VG	F	VF	XF	Unc
ND(1616-88)	—	1,000	2,000	3,500	—	—

KM# 5 DUCAT

Gold Weight varies: 3.37-3.42g, 24 mm. **Ruler:** Agostino **Obv:** Full-length armored figure of count looking toright, holding sword pointed downwards in left hand **Obv. Legend:** AVGVSTI. SPI. COMES. TASSA. **Rev:** Crowned imperial eagle, oval shield of Austrian arms on breast **Rev. Legend:** AVGVSTINVS. SPI. COMES. TAS. **Note:** Fr. -; Varesi 960.

Date	Mintage	VG	F	VF	XF	Unc
ND(1604-16)	—	750	1,100	2,250	3,300	—

KM# 6 DUCAT

3.2900 g., Gold, 23-24 mm. **Ruler:** Agostino **Obv:** Full-length armored figure of count looking toright, holding sword pointed downwards in left hand **Obv. Legend:** AGV. SPI. - COM. PALA. **Rev:** Crowned imperial eagle in circle **Rev. Legend:** SVB. VMBRA. ALARVM. TVARVM. **Note:** Fr. -; Varesi 962.

Date	Mintage	VG	F	VF	XF	Unc
ND(1604-16)	—	750	1,100	2,250	3,300	—

KM# 12 DUCAT

3.3000 g., Gold, 22 mm. **Ruler:** Agostino **Obv:** Crowned imperial eagle, oval shield of Austrian arms on breast **Obv. Legend:** AVGVSTINVS. SPI. COMES. TAS. **Rev:** Laureate bust to right, date below shoulder **Rev. Legend:** RVDOLPHVS. II. D.G. ROM. IMP. **Note:** Fr. 1175; Varesi 956.

Date	Mintage	VG	F	VF	XF	Unc
1604 Rare	—	—	—	—	—	—

KM# 13.1 DUCAT

Gold Weight varies: 3.31-3.45g, 22-23 mm. **Ruler:** Agostino **Obv:** Full-length armored figure of count looking to right, holding sword pointed downwards in left hand **Obv. Legend:** AVGVST. SPI. - COMES. TASSA. **Rev:** Crowned imperial eagle, oval shield of family arms on breast **Rev. Legend:** VIRTVTE. CAESAREA. DVCE. **Note:** Fr. 1177; Varesi 959.

Date	Mintage	VG	F	VF	XF	Unc
ND(1604-16)	—	500	825	1,350	2,250	—

KM# 13.2 DUCAT

Gold Weight varies: 3.31-3.45g, 22-23 mm. **Ruler:** Agostino **Obv:** Full-length armored figure of count looking to right, holding sword pointed downwards in left hand **Obv. Legend:** AVGVST. SPI. - COMES. TASSA. **Rev:** Crowned imperial eagle, oval shield of Austrian arms on breast **Rev. Legend:** VIRTVTE. CAESAREA. DVCE. **Note:** Fr. -; Varesi 959/1. Previoius KM #13.

Date	Mintage	VG	F	VF	XF	Unc
ND(1604-16)	—	500	825	1,350	2,250	—

KM# 21 DUCAT

Gold Weight varies: 3.29-3.44g, 22-23 mm. **Ruler:** Agostino **Obv:** Full-length armored figure of count looking toright, holding sword pointed downwards in left hand **Obv. Legend:** AGVS. SPIN. - COM. PAL. **Rev:** Crowned shield of 8-fold arms in circle **Rev. Legend:** VIRTVTE. CAESAREA. DVCE. **Note:** Fr. 1178; Varesi 961.

Date	Mintage	VG	F	VF	XF	Unc
ND(1604-16)	—	750	1,100	2,250	3,300	—

KM# 20 DUCAT

Gold Weight varies: 3.35-3.38g, 23-24 mm. **Ruler:** Agostino **Obv:** 5-line inscription in ornamented square tablet **Obv. Inscription:** MO. NO. AV/ORDINI/AVG. SPI/COM. PAL/PRO. IMP. **Rev:** Full-length armored figure of count turned slightly to right, holding sword over right shoulder, divides date **Rev. Legend:** CONCORDIA. PAR - RES. CRESCV. **Note:** Fr. 1176; Varesi 958/1-3.

Date	Mintage	VG	F	VF	XF	Unc
1611	—	750	1,100	2,250	3,300	—
1612	—	750	1,100	2,250	3,300	—

KM# 23 DUCAT

Gold, 23 mm. **Ruler:** Agostino **Obv:** Madonna and Child, date in exergue **Obv. Legend:** MO. NOVA. AOVS. SPICO. PAL. **Rev:** Crowned shield of 8-fold arms **Rev. Legend:** VIRTVTE. CAESAREA. DVCE. **Note:** Fr. 1179; Varesi 957.

Date	Mintage	VG	F	VF	XF	Unc
1614	—	1,500	2,500	4,500	8,000	—

KM# 37.1 DUCAT

3.3500 g., Gold, 21-22 mm. **Ruler:** Filippo **Obv:** Full-length armored figure of count between two small shields of arms **Obv. Legend:** PHILIPPVS. SP. - D.G. COM. PAL. **Rev:** 5-line inscription in ornamented square tablet **Rev. Inscription:** NON. NOB/DNE. NON/NOB. SED/NOI. TVO/DA. GLAM. **Note:** Fr. -; Varesi 980.

Date	Mintage	VG	F	VF	XF	Unc
ND(1616-88)	—	750	1,100	2,250	3,300	—

KM# 37.2 DUCAT

Gold Weight varies: 3.34-3.50g, 21-22 mm. **Ruler:** Filippo **Obv:** 5-line inscription in ornamented square tablet **Obv. Inscription:** FER. IMP/SEM. AVG/PHI. SPA/COM. TAS/FIL. PER. **Rev:** Full-length armored figure of count holding sword pointed downwards in right hand **Rev. Legend:** PARS. MEA. DEVS. - IN. ÆTERNVM. **Note:** Fr. -; Varesi 981. Previous KM #37.

Date	Mintage	VG	F	VF	XF	Unc
ND(1616-88)	—	650	1,000	1,850	2,750	—

KM# 37.3 DUCAT

Gold Weight varies: 3.34-3.50g, 21-22 mm. **Ruler:** Filippo **Obv:** 5-line inscription in ornamented square tablet **Obv. Inscription:** FER. IMP/ROM. AVG/PHI. SPA/COM. TAS/FIL.PER. **Rev:** Full-length armored figure of count holdling sword in right hand pointed downwards **Rev. Legend:** PARS. MEA. DEVS. - IN. ÆTERNVM. **Note:** Fr. -; Varesi 981/1.

Date	Mintage	VG	F	VF	XF	Unc
ND(1616-88)	—	650	1,000	1,850	2,750	—

KM# 38 DUCAT

3.3800 g., Gold, 21 mm. **Ruler:** Filippo **Obv:** 5-line inscription in ornamented square tablet **Obv. Inscription:** FER. IMP.SEM. AVG/PHI. SPA/COM. TAS/FIL. PER. **Rev:** large rose in circular garland **Rev. Legend:** IN. OR9REM. DVRRVNT. QVI. DILI. **Note:** Fr. 1187; Varesi 982.

Date	Mintage	VG	F	VF	XF	Unc
ND(1616-88)	—	650	1,150	2,250	3,750	—

KM# 36 DUCAT

Gold Weight varies: 3.32-3.35g, 21 mm. **Ruler:** Filippo **Obv:** Full-length armored figure of count between two small shields of arms **Obv. Legend:** PHILIPPVS. SP. - D.G. COM. PAL. **Rev:** Crowned imperial eagle, shield of arms on breast, date at end of legend **Rev. Legend:** SVB. VMBRA. ALAR. TVAR. PROT. **Note:** Fr. 1185; Varesi 979.

Date	Mintage	VG	F	VF	XF	Unc
1637	—	650	1,000	1,850	2,750	—

KM# 7 DOPPIA

6.8000 g., Gold, 27 mm. **Ruler:** Agostino **Obv:** Crowned imperial eagle **Obv. Legend:** AVGS. SPI. COM. PALAT. MO. NO. AV. **Rev:** Facing figure of St. Nicholas standing behind ornate shield of 4-fold arms with central shield, below **Rev. Legend:** SANTVS. NICOLAVS. PROTECTOR. NOV. **Note:** Fr. 1180; Varesi 955.

Date	Mintage	VG	F	VF	XF	Unc
ND(1604-16)	—	3,000	5,000	9,000	16,500	—

KM# 35 DOPPIA

6.5500 g., Gold, 25 mm. **Ruler:** Filippo **Obv:** Bust to right **Obv. Legend:** PHILIPPVS. SPINVLA. **Rev:** Crowned oval shield of family arms in baroque frame, date at end of legend **Rev. Legend:** COMES. TAS - SAROLI. **Note:** Fr. 1182; Varesi 977.

Date	Mintage	VG	F	VF	XF	Unc
1630	—	2,500	4,500	7,500	12,500	—

KM# 45 DOPPIA

6.5500 g., Gold, 25 mm. **Ruler:** Filippo **Obv:** Armored bust to right. **Obv. Legend:** PHILIPPVS. COMES. TASS. **Rev:** Facing figure of San Carlo Spinola in flames, date in exergue **Rev. Legend:** P. CAROLVS. - SPIN. M. SOC. IESV. **Note:** Fr. 1184; Varesi 978.

Date	Mintage	VG	F	VF	XF	Unc
1640	—	2,500	4,500	7,500	12,500	—

KM# 11 2 DOPPIE

14.0000 g., Gold, 30 mm. **Ruler:** Agostino **Obv:** Bust to right, date below shoulder **Obv. Legend:** AVGVSTINVS. SPINVLA. **Rev:** Crowned shield of family arms in baroque frame **Rev. Legend:** COMES. TASSAROLI. **Note:** Fr. 1174; Varesi 954.

Date	Mintage	VG	F	VF	XF	Unc
1604 Rare	—	—	—	—	—	—

KM# 28 2 DOPPIE

13.2300 g., Gold, 28 mm. **Ruler:** Filippo **Obv:** Crowned imperial eagle, shield of family arms on breast **Obv. Legend:** PHIL. SPIN. COM. PALAT. MO. AV. **Rev:** Facing figure of St. Nicholas behind shield of 4-fold arms with central shield below **Rev. Legend:** SANTVS. NICOLAVS. PROTECTOR. NOS. **Note:** Fr. 1188; Varesi 976.

Date	Mintage	VG	F	VF	XF	Unc
ND(1616-88) Rare	—	—	—	—	—	—

KM# 32 2 DOPPIE

Gold Weight varies: 13.0-13.14g, 29 mm. **Ruler:** Filippo **Obv:** Armored bust to right **Obv. Legend:** PHILIPPVS. SPINVLA. **Rev:** Crowned shield of family arms in baroque frame, date at end of legend **Rev. Legend:** COMES. TASSAROLI. **Note:** Fr. 1181; Varesi 974.

Date	Mintage	VG	F	VF	XF	Unc
1629 Rare	—	—	—	—	—	—

KM# 46 2 DOPPIE

Gold Weight varies: 13.06-13.10g, 31 mm. **Ruler:** Filippo **Obv:** Armored bust to right **Obv. Legend:** PHILIPPVS. COMES. TASS. **Rev:** Figure of San Carlo Spinola being burnt at the stake, date in exergue **Rev. Legend:** P. CAROLVS. - SPIN. M. SOC. IESV. **Note:** Fr. 1183; Varesi 975/1-2.

Date	Mintage	VG	F	VF	XF	Unc
1640 Rare	—	—	—	—	—	—
1645 Rare	—	—	—	—	—	—

KM# 3 5 DOPPIE

34.2700 g., Gold, 42 mm. **Ruler:** Agostino **Obv:** Armored bust to right, date below shoulder **Obv. Legend:** AVGVSTINVS. SPINVLA. **Rev:** Crowned shield of family armes in baroque frame **Rev. Legend:** COMES. TAS - SAROLI. **Note:** Fr. 1173; Varesi 953. Struck from Scudo dies, KM #9.

Date	Mintage	VG	F	VF	XF	Unc
1604 Rare	—	—	—	—	—	—

TORRIGLIA

A Doria marquisate in the mountains of Liguria from which the Princess Violante had coins struck in four years.

RULER

Violante, widow of Prince Andrea III

MARQUISATE

STANDARD COINAGE

KM# 5 LUIGINI

Silver **Ruler:** Violante **Obv:** Female head right **Obv. Legend:** VIOLANTE... **Rev:** Crowned French arms divide date **Rev. Legend:** DEVS... **Note:** Struck for the Levant.

Date	Mintage	VG	F	VF	XF	Unc
1665	—	45.00	90.00	200	425	—
1666	—	45.00	90.00	200	425	—

KM# 6 LUIGINI

Silver **Ruler:** Violante **Obv:** Head right **Obv. Legend:** DON VI... **Rev:** Crowned French arms **Rev. Legend:** DOMINVS...

Date	Mintage	VG	F	VF	XF	Unc
1665	—	45.00	90.00	200	400	—

KM# 7 LUIGINI

Silver **Ruler:** Violante **Obv:** Head right **Obv. Legend:** PVLCRA... **Rev:** Crowned French arms **Rev. Legend:** SIMVL...

Date	Mintage	VG	F	VF	XF	Unc
1666	—	40.00	80.00	165	375	—
1667	—	40.00	80.00	165	375	—
1668	—	40.00	80.00	165	375	—

TRESANA

Tresana, a marquisate near Massa and Carrara in Tuscany was in the possession of the Malaspina family, who were also lords of Fosdinovo. A mint was opened in 1571 and closed at Guglielmo's death in 1651.

RULER

Guglielmo II Malaspina, 1613-1651

MARQUISATE

STANDARD COINAGE

DAV# 4184 TALLERO

Silver **Obv:** Bust right dividing date **Rev:** Crowned 4-part shield

Date	Mintage	VG	F	VF	XF	Unc
1621 Rare	—	—	—	—	—	—

FR# 1192 DUCAT

3.5000 g., 0.9860 Gold 0.1109 oz. AGW **Obv:** Soldier standing divides date **Rev:** 5-line inscription in tablet

Date	Mintage	VG	F	VF	XF	Unc
1619 Rare	—	—	—	—	—	—

FR# 1190 DUCAT

3.5000 g., 0.9860 Gold 0.1109 oz. AGW **Obv:** St. Ladislaus standing in inner circle **Rev:** Madonna and child facing in inner circle

Date	Mintage	VG	F	VF	XF	Unc
1620 Rare	—	—	—	—	—	—

FR# 1191 DUCAT

3.5000 g., 0.9860 Gold 0.1109 oz. AGW **Obv:** St. Louis standing in inner circle **Rev:** Crowned eagle in inner circle

Date	Mintage	VG	F	VF	XF	Unc
ND Rare	—	—	—	—	—	—

FR# 1193 DIRHEM

Gold **Obv:** Arabic legend **Rev:** Arabic legend **Note:** Struck for trade in the Middle East.

Date	Mintage	VG	F	VF	XF	Unc
ND Rare	—	—	—	—	—	—

TRICERRO

Village

A small place in Piedmont near Vercelli, Tricerro was a feudal dependency of the Tizzone family of Desana.

RULER

Carlo Giuseppe Francesco Tizzone, 1641-1676

Reference: Alberto Varesi, ***Monete Italiane Regionali: Piemonte, Sardegna, Liguria, Isola di Corsica***. Pavia, 1996.

VILLAGE

REGULAR COINAGE

KM# 1 SOLDINO

Billon, 15-16mm mm. **Ruler:** Carlo Giuseppe Tizzoni 1641-1676 **Obv:** Bust to right in circle, date at end of legend **Obv. Legend:** CAROL. II. T.C.D.S. **Rev:** Ornate cross in circle **Rev. Legend:** MARCHIO. TRISC. ET. C. **Note:** Varesi 1031.

Date	Mintage	VG	F	VF	XF	Unc
1670 Rare	—	—	—	—	—	—

TUSCANY

Etruria

An Italian territorial division on the west-central peninsula, belonged to the Medici from 1530 to 1737, when it was given to Francis, duke of Lorraine. In 1800 the French established it as part of the Spanish dominions; from 1807 to 1809 it was a French department. After the fall of Napoleon it reverted to its pre-Napoleonic owner, Ferdinand III.

RULERS

Ferdinand I, 1587-1609
Cosimo II, 1609-1621
Ferdinand II, 1621-1670
Cosimo III, 1670-1723

MINT MARKS

FIRENZE - Florence
LEGHORN - Livorno
PISIS – Pisa

MONETARY SYSTEM

Until 1826

12 Denari = 3 Quattrini = 1 Soldo
20 Soldi = 1 Lira
10 Lire = 1 Dena
40 Quattrini = 1 Paolo
1-1/2 Paoli = 1 Lira
10 Paoli = 1 Francescone, Scudo, Tallero
3 Zecchini = 1 Ruspone = 40 Lire

GRAND DUCHY

STANDARD COINAGE

DAV# 4185 PIASTRE

Silver **Ruler:** Ferdinand I **Obv:** Bust right **Rev:** St. John baptizing Christ, date in exergue

Date	Mintage	VG	F	VF	XF	Unc
1601	—	300	600	1,250	3,250	—
1604	—	300	600	1,250	3,250	—
1608	—	300	600	1,250	3,250	—
1609	—	300	600	1,250	3,250	—

DAV# 4187 PIASTRE

Silver **Ruler:** Cosimo II **Obv:** Bust right, stars below **Rev:** Baptism scene with Christ standing, date in exergue

Date	Mintage	VG	F	VF	XF	Unc
1608 Rare	—	—	—	—	—	—
1609 Rare	—	—	—	—	—	—

DAV# 4188 PIASTRE

Silver **Ruler:** Cosimo II **Obv:** Bust right **Rev:** Christ kneeling in baptism scene, date below

Date	Mintage	VG	F	VF	XF	Unc
1609 Rare	—	—	—	—	—	—
1610 Rare	—	—	—	—	—	—

DAV# 4189 PIASTRE

Silver **Ruler:** Cosimo II **Obv:** Bust right, date below **Rev:** Christ standing in baptism scene, date below

Date	Mintage	VG	F	VF	XF	Unc
1609/1609 Rare	—	—	—	—	—	—
1610/1609 Rare	—	—	—	—	—	—
1610/1610 Rare	—	—	—	—	—	—

DAV# 4190 PIASTRE

Silver **Ruler:** Cosimo II **Obv:** Bust right **Rev:** Christ standing in baptism scene, date below

Date	Mintage	VG	F	VF	XF	Unc
1610/1610 Rare	—	—	—	—	—	—

DAV# 4191 PIASTRE

Silver **Ruler:** Cosimo II **Obv:** Bust right **Rev:** St. John standing, date below

Date	Mintage	VG	F	VF	XF	Unc
1611	—	1,850	3,750	7,500	—	—
1613	—	1,850	3,750	7,500	—	—
1615	—	1,850	3,750	7,500	—	—
1618	—	1,850	3,750	7,500	—	—

DAV# 4192 PIASTRE

Silver **Ruler:** Cosimo II **Obv:** Bust left **Rev:** St. John standing

Date	Mintage	VG	F	VF	XF	Unc
1611	—	300	1,000	2,750	5,500	—
1612	—	300	1,000	2,750	5,500	—
1613	—	300	1,000	2,750	5,500	—

DAV# 4198 PIASTRE

Silver **Ruler:** Ferdinand II **Obv:** Bust right, date below **Rev:** St. John standing

Date	Mintage	VG	F	VF	XF	Unc
1623/1623	—	1,000	2,000	4,000	6,500	—

DAV# 4199A PIASTRE

Silver **Ruler:** Ferdinand II **Obv:** Bust with ruffled collar, cape and armor, right, date below **Rev:** St. John standing

Date	Mintage	VG	F	VF	XF	Unc
1624/1623	—	1,000	2,000	4,000	6,500	—

DAV# 4199 PIASTRE

Silver **Ruler:** Ferdinand II **Obv:** Bust with ruffled collar, cape and armor, right **Rev:** St. John standing

Date	Mintage	VG	F	VF	XF	Unc
1625/1620	—	175	325	800	3,000	—
1625/1623	—	175	325	800	3,000	—
1625/1626	—	175	325	800	3,000	—
1628	—	175	325	800	3,000	—

DAV# 4200 PIASTRE

Silver **Ruler:** Ferdinand II **Obv:** Bust with ruffled collar and armor, right **Rev:** St. John standing

Date	Mintage	VG	F	VF	XF	Unc
1629	—	175	325	800	3,000	—
1630	—	175	325	800	3,000	—
1630 Retrograde 3	—	175	325	800	3,000	—
1633	—	175	325	800	3,000	—

DAV# 4201 PIASTRE

Silver **Ruler:** Ferdinand II **Obv:** Bust with ruffled collar, mustache and armor, right, date below **Rev:** St. John standing

Date	Mintage	VG	F	VF	XF	Unc
1633/1630	—	1,150	2,250	4,500	7,500	—
1633	—	1,150	2,250	4,500	7,500	—
1634	—	1,150	2,250	4,500	7,500	—
1635	—	1,150	2,250	4,500	7,500	—
1638	—	1,150	2,250	4,500	7,500	—
1641	—	1,150	2,250	4,500	7,500	—

DAV# 4202 PIASTRE

Silver **Ruler:** Ferdinand II **Obv:** Bust with ruffled collar, mustache and armor, right **Rev:** St. John standing, date below

Date	Mintage	VG	F	VF	XF	Unc
1635	—	150	300	750	3,000	—
1638/1635	—	150	300	750	3,000	—
1638/1685	—	150	300	750	3,000	—
1642	—	150	300	750	3,000	—
1642/1642	—	150	300	750	3,000	—
1645/1642	—	150	300	750	3,000	—
1649/1642	—	150	300	750	3,000	—

DAV# 4207 PIASTRE

Silver **Ruler:** Ferdinand II **Obv:** Older bust right, date below

Date	Mintage	VG	F	VF	XF	Unc
1663 Rare	—	—	—	—	—	—

DAV# 4209 PIASTRE

Silver **Ruler:** Cosimo III **Obv:** Bust right, date below **Rev:** Christ standing in baptism scene

Date	Mintage	VG	F	VF	XF	Unc
1675	—	90.00	185	375	650	3,750
1676	—	90.00	185	375	650	3,750
1677	—	90.00	185	375	650	3,750
1678	—	90.00	185	375	650	3,750
1679	—	90.00	185	375	650	3,750

DAV# 4210 PIASTRE

Silver **Ruler:** Cosimo III **Obv:** Wide drapped bust right

Date	Mintage	VG	F	VF	XF	Unc
1680	—	225	450	900	1,650	—
1680/1681	—	225	450	900	1,650	—
ND	—	225	450	900	1,650	—

DAV# 4211 PIASTRE

Silver **Ruler:** Cosimo III **Obv:** Older and larger head, beaded inner circle

Date	Mintage	VG	F	VF	XF	Unc
1680	—	175	350	700	1,250	—
1680/1680	—	175	350	700	1,250	—

DAV# 4212 PIASTRE

Silver **Ruler:** Cosimo III **Obv:** Small bust right within linear circle, large date below

Date	Mintage	VG	F	VF	XF	Unc
1683	—	100	200	400	800	4,000

Date	Mintage	VG	F	VF	XF	Unc
1684	—	100	200	400	800	4,000
1694	—	100	200	400	800	4,000

DAV# 4213 PIASTRE
Silver **Ruler:** Cosimo III **Obv:** Armored bust right **Rev:** St. John seated, lamb at left

Date	Mintage	VG	F	VF	XF	Unc
1684	—	1,200	2,500	5,500	9,000	—

FR# 314 FLORINO
Gold **Ruler:** Cosimo II **Obv:** Elaborate fleur-de-lis **Rev:** St. John the Baptist standing, date in legend

Date	Mintage	VG	F	VF	XF	Unc
1608	—	175	280	525	975	—
1610	—	175	280	525	975	—
1611	—	175	280	525	975	—
1614	—	175	280	525	975	—

FR# 319 FLORINO
Gold **Ruler:** Ferdinand II

Date	Mintage	VG	F	VF	XF	Unc
1655	—	250	400	750	1,400	—
ND	—	250	400	750	1,400	—

FR# 318 1/8 DOPPIA
0.8750 g., 0.9860 Gold 0.0277 oz. AGW **Ruler:** Cosimo II **Obv:** Crowned arms **Rev:** Ornate cross

Date	Mintage	VG	F	VF	XF	Unc
ND	—	400	725	1,550	3,250	—

FR# 321 1/8 DOPPIA
0.8750 g., 0.9860 Gold 0.0277 oz. AGW **Ruler:** Ferdinand II **Obv:** Crowned arms without legend **Rev:** Bust of St. John the Baptist facing without legend

Date	Mintage	VG	F	VF	XF	Unc
ND	—	—	—	—	—	—

FR# 311 1/4 DOPPIA
1.7500 g., 0.9860 Gold 0.0555 oz. AGW **Ruler:** Cosimo II **Obv:** Bust right, date below **Rev:** Ornate cross

Date	Mintage	VG	F	VF	XF	Unc
1609 Rare	—	—	—	—	—	—

FR# 320 1/4 DOPPIA
1.7500 g., 0.9860 Gold 0.0555 oz. AGW **Ruler:** Ferdinand II **Obv:** Crowned arms, date divided near top **Rev:** Bust of St. John the Baptist facing

Date	Mintage	VG	F	VF	XF	Unc
1663	—	750	1,200	2,000	4,000	—
1668	—	750	1,200	2,000	4,000	—

FR# 317 1/2 DOPPIA
3.5000 g., 0.9860 Gold 0.1109 oz. AGW **Ruler:** Ferdinand II **Obv:** Crowned arms **Obv. Legend:** FERD II... **Rev:** Ornate cross

Date	Mintage	VG	F	VF	XF	Unc
ND	—	750	1,250	2,250	4,500	—

FR# 324 1/2 DOPPIA
3.5000 g., 0.9860 Gold 0.1109 oz. AGW **Ruler:** Cosimo III **Obv. Legend:** COSMVS III ...

Date	Mintage	VG	F	VF	XF	Unc
ND	—	1,000	2,000	3,500	6,500	—

FR# 312 DOPPIA
7.0000 g., 0.9860 Gold 0.2219 oz. AGW **Ruler:** Cosimo II **Obv:** Crowned arms **Obv. Legend:** COS II...

Date	Mintage	VG	F	VF	XF	Unc
1608 Rare	—	—	—	—	—	—
ND	—	350	500	1,000	2,000	—

FR# 316 DOPPIA
7.0000 g., 0.9860 Gold 0.2219 oz. AGW **Ruler:** Ferdinand II **Obv. Legend:** FERDIN II...

Date	Mintage	VG	F	VF	XF	Unc
ND	—	300	450	850	1,500	—

FR# 322 2 DOPPIE
14.0000 g., 0.9860 Gold 0.4438 oz. AGW **Obv:** Crowned arms **Rev:** Ornate cross **Note:** Struck at Florence.

Date	Mintage	VG	F	VF	XF	Unc
1676 Rare	—	—	—	—	—	—

URBINO

This duchy in central Italy was under Church rule in the Middle Ages. It was ceded to the Montefeltro family under whom it became a center of Renaissance culture. The Della Rovere family inherited Urbino through the feminine line. They extended its domains but moved the capital of the duchy to Pesaro. In 1626 Francesco Maria, the last of the line, abdicated and the duchy with all of its lands fell to Pope Urban VIII and was included in the Papal States.

RULER
Francesco Maria II, 1574-1624

DUCHY

STANDARD COINAGE

DAV# 4217 SCUDO (20 Grossi)
Silver **Ruler:** Francesco Maria II **Obv:** Bust right, date below **Rev:** Crowned arms in order chain

Date	Mintage	VG	F	VF	XF	Unc
1601 Rare	—	—	—	—	—	—

DAV# 4220 SCUDO (20 Grossi)
Silver **Ruler:** Francesco Maria II **Obv:** Crowned arms **Rev:** 1621 / GROSSI / XX in baroque cartouche, L-X divided below

Date	Mintage	VG	F	VF	XF	Unc
1621 Rare	—	—	—	—	—	—

DAV# 4222 SCUDO (20 Grossi)
Silver **Ruler:** Francesco Maria II **Obv:** Crowned shield **Rev:** GROSSI / XX in frame, LX divided below

Date	Mintage	VG	F	VF	XF	Unc
ND	—	700	1,350	2,250	—	—

DAV# 4218 SCUDO (18 Grossi)
Silver **Ruler:** Francesco Maria II **Obv:** Bust left, Roman numeral date below **Obv. Legend:** M. SEDECINAR... **Rev:** Crowned eagle with arms

Date	Mintage	VG	F	VF	XF	Unc
1603 Rare	—	—	—	—	—	—

DAV# 4219 SCUDO (18 Grossi)
Silver **Ruler:** Francesco Maria II **Obv. Legend:** FRANCISCVS. MARIA. II. **Rev:** Crowned arms in frame **Rev. Legend:** VRBINI-DVX. VI. ET. C.

Date	Mintage	VG	F	VF	XF	Unc
1603 Rare	—	—	—	—	—	—
1604 Rare	—	—	—	—	—	—

Note: Numismatica Ars Classica Auction 32, 1-06, VF realized approximately $31,750

DAV# 4219A SCUDO (18 Grossi)
Silver **Ruler:** Francesco Maria II **Rev:** Roman numeral date at bottom

Date	Mintage	VG	F	VF	XF	Unc
MDCIII (1603) Rare	—	—	—	—	—	—

DAV# 4221 SCUDO (18 Grossi)
Silver **Ruler:** Francesco Maria II **Obv:** Bust right **Rev:** Crowned arms

Date	Mintage	VG	F	VF	XF	Unc
ND Rare	—	—	—	—	—	—

FR# 1207 SCUDO D'ORO
3.5000 g., 0.9860 Gold 0.1109 oz. AGW **Ruler:** Francesco Maria II **Obv:** Bust left **Rev:** Crowned arms

Date	Mintage	VG	F	VF	XF	Unc
ND	—	1,250	2,250	3,000	5,000	—

FR# 1209 SCUDO D'ORO
3.5000 g., 0.9860 Gold 0.1109 oz. AGW **Ruler:** Francesco Maria II **Obv:** Tree in pastoral scene **Rev:** Crowned arms in order collar in inner circle

Date	Mintage	VG	F	VF	XF	Unc
ND	—	1,500	2,500	4,000	6,500	—

FR# 1210 SCUDO D'ORO
3.5000 g., 0.9860 Gold 0.1109 oz. AGW **Ruler:** Francesco Maria II **Obv:** Crowned arms **Rev:** St. Michael standing left, holding scales of justice, spearing dragon below

Date	Mintage	VG	F	VF	XF	Unc
ND	—	800	1,600	2,750	4,750	—

FR# 1211 SCUDO D'ORO
3.5000 g., 0.9860 Gold 0.1109 oz. AGW **Ruler:** Francesco Maria II **Obv:** St. Francis of Assisi standing **Rev:** Fortress

Date	Mintage	VG	F	VF	XF	Unc
ND	—	1,850	3,250	5,000	7,000	—

FR# 1208 4 SCUDI D'ORO
14.0000 g., 0.9860 Gold 0.4438 oz. AGW **Ruler:** Francesco Maria II **Obv:** Tree in pastoral scene **Rev:** Crowned arms in order collar in inner circle

Date	Mintage	VG	F	VF	XF	Unc
ND	—	3,000	5,000	8,000	16,000	—

VENICE

Venezia

A seaport of Venetia was founded by refugees from the Hun invasions. From that time until the arrival of Napoleon in 1797, it maintained an enormous foreign trade involving the possession of many islands in the Mediterranean while keeping a state of quasi-independence despite the antagonism of jealous Italian states and the Ottoman Turks. During the French Occupation Napoleon handed it over to Austria. Later, upon the defeat of the Austrians by Prussia in 1860, Venice then became a part of the United Kingdom of Italy.

RULERS
Marino Grimani, 1595-1605
Leonardo Donato, 1605-1612
Marcantonio Memmo, 1612-1615
Giovanni Bembo, 1615-1618
Nicolo Donato, 1618
Antonio Priuli, 1618-1623
Francesco Contarini, 1623-1624
Giovanni Corner, 1625-1629
Nicolo Contarini, 1630-1631
Francesco Erizzo, 1631-1646
Francesco Molin, 1646-1655
Carlo Contarini, 1655-1656
Francesco Corner, 1656
Bertuccio Valiero, 1656-1658
Giovanni Pesaro, 1658-1659
Domenico II Contarini, 1659-1674
Nicolo Sagredo, 1675-1676
Luigi Contarini, 1676-1684
Marcantonio Giustinian, 1684-1688
Francesco Morosini, 1688-1694
Silvestro Valiero, 1694-1700
Alvise II Mocenigo, 1700-1709

MINT MARKS
A - Vienna
F - Hall
V - Venice
ZV - Zecca Venezia - Venice
None - Venice

MINTMASTERS' INITIALS FOR SILVER

Initials	Date	Name
AB	1697-98	Gian Andrea Baffo
AB	1642-43	Anzolo Balbi
AC	1684-85	Alvise Gabriel (Cabriel)
AC	1698	Anzolo Cicogna
AC	1679	Alessandro Contarini
AC	1612-13	Antonio Contarini
AD	1666-67	Anzolo Dolfin
AD	1683-84	Antonio Dona
AF	1625-27	Andrea Falier
AG	1688	Alvise Gritti
AL	1643	Andrea Lippomano
AL	1643	Andrea Lippomano
AM	1613-14	Alvise Minio
AS	1667	Alessandro Salamon
AS	1667-68	Agustin Soranzo
AZ	1675	Agustin Zolio
AZ	1634-36	Alvise Zusto
BB	1659-60	Benetto Balbi
BB	1636	Bernardo Balbi
BC	1699	Benetto Civran
BC	1633-34	Benetto Contarini
BC	1650	Benetto Corner
BM	1612	Bernardo Morosini
BV	1656-57	Bernardino Vizzamano
CA	1649	Clandio Avogaro
CD	1621	Carlo Dona
CG	1614-15	Carlo Gritti
CP	1607-08	Constantin Pasqualigo
CZ	1609-12	Constantin Zorzi
DB	1629-30	Domenego Basadonna
DB	1637	Donato Bembo
DG	1663	Domenego Gritti
DM	1632	Domenego Michiel
DM	1609	Daniele Morosini
DM	1625	Tomaso da Mosta
DP	1685	Domenego Pizzamano
DT	1683	Domenego Trevisan
FC	1655-56	Francesco Corner
FM	1624-25	Ferigo da Molin
FM M	1624	Francesco Maria Malipiero
FP	1641-42	Francesco Pasqualigo
FR	1652-54	Francesco da Riva
FS	1612	Fantino Soranzo
FT	1693	Francesco Trevisan
FZ	1671	Fantino Zancariol
GAB	1697-98	Gian Andrea Baffo
GAB	1694-95	Gian Antonio Benzon
GB	1699-1701	Gerolamo Barbaro
GB	1632-33	Giacomo Barozzi
GBZ	1654-55	Giovan Battista Zorzi
GC	1628, 39-40, 72	Gerolamo Contarini
GD	1662-63	Gerolamo Dandolo
GD	1640-41	Gerolamo Dolfin
GD	1675	Giulio Dona
GL	1672	Gabriele Lombardo
GM	1693	Gerolamo Malipiero
GM	1681-82	Gerolamo Marcello
GM	1695	Giuseppe Minotto
GM	1691-92	Giacomo Morosini
GP IP	1627-28	Giacomo Pesaro
GR	1665-66	Giacomo da Riva
GR IR	1618-20	Giacomo Renier
GV	1685-86	Gerolamo Venier
GZ	1679-81	Gerolamo Zorzi
HZ	1620-21	Gerolamo Zorzi
IAM MAI	1627	Zan Alvise Minotto
IB	1691	Iseppo Baseggio
IBC BC ZC	1623-24	Zan Battista Contarini
IM	1659	Jacopo Malipiero
IM	1616-17	Jacopo da Molin
LF	1630-32	Luca Falier
LP	1668	Lorenzo Pisani
LP	1687-88	Lunardo Pisani
LV	1615-16	Leonardo Vendramin
MAM	1634	Marcantonio Malipiero
MAS SAM	1658-59	Marco Aurelio Soranzo
MAV MV AV	1613	Marcantonio Venier
MB	1692-93	Mattio Balbi
MB	1645-46	Marino Boldu
MM	1663	Marino da Molin
MM	1664	Marco Morosini
MQ	1678	Marchio Querini
MV	1671	Marino Vizzamano
MZ	1656	Marino Zen
MZ	1650-51	Marco Zorzi
NC	1658	Nicolo Contarini
ND	1682	Nicolo Dona
NF FN	1630	Nicolo Foscarini
OZ	1641	Ottaviano Zorzi
PB	1617	Paolo Balbi
PB	1618	Pietro Barbaro
PC	1612	Paulo Capello
PG	1649-50	Piero Gritti
PL	1675-77	Piero Lion
PM	1681	Piero Malipiero
PM	1698-99	Paolo Minotto
PM	1694	Piero Minotto
PP	1690-91	Paolo Pisani
PZ PZ60	1673	Pietro Zaguri VI
SB	1628-29	Sebastiano Badoer
SB	1677	Sebastiano Badoer
SB	1677	Stefano Barbaro
TB	1661	Tomaso Barbarigo
TB	1617-18	Tomaso Bragadin
VC	1620	Vicenzo Correr
VD	1638	Vicenzo Diedo
VE	1614	Vicenzo Emo
VM	1630	Urbano Malipiero
VV	1637-38	Valerio Valier
ZAB IAB	1646	Zan Alvise Battagia
ZAL	1686-87	Zan Andrea Loredan
ZAP	1608	Zuan Arsenio Priuli
ZAS	1651	Zan Antonio Semitecolo
ZAV	1621-22	Zan Antonio Venier
ZAZ	1647	Zan Antonio zorzi
ZB	1647-49	Zuane Barozzi
ZD	1633	Zuane Diedo
ZD ID	1622-23	Zuane Dolfin
ZL	1638-39	Zuane Loredan
ZM	1609	Zuane Marcello
ZMB	1643-44	Zan Marco Balbi
ZP	1674-75	Zuane Priuli
ZPS	1607	Zan Piero Sagredo
ZQ	1669, 1689	Zuane Querini
ZR	1693-94	Zuane da Riva
ZV	1636-37	Zaccaria Valier

MINTMASTERS' INITIALS FOR GOLD

Initials	Date	Name
FT	1693	Francesco Trevisan
LP	1673-75	Lorenzo Pisani

MONETARY SYSTEM

6 Denari = 1 Bezzo
12 Denari = 1 Soldo
20 Soldi = 1 Lira
30 Soldi = 1 Lirazza
124 Soldi = 1 Ducatone = 1 Ducato
140 Soldi = 1 Scudo = 1 Tallero = 1 Zecchino
160 Soldi = 1 Scudo
2 Scudi = 1 Doppia

WEIGHTS

Zechhino = 3.45 g
Doppia = 6.90 g

NOTE: Venice struck many types of gold coins using billon or silver coinage dies. They also struck many denominations from the same dies, so it is most important to check the weight to determine the proper denomination.

DIE VARIETIES

Throughout this series there is great variety in the abbreviation within the legends while various stars, dots, colons, diamonds, rosettes and other devices were used in separating them.

REPUBLIC

STANDARD COINAGE

DAV# 4267 DUCATO

23.4000 g., 0.8264 Silver 0.6217 oz. ASW **Ruler:** Domenico II Contarini **Obv:** Legend around St. Mark blessing kneeling Doge **Obv. Legend:** S • M • VEN • DOMIN • CON DVX **Rev:** Legend around lion **Rev. Legend:** DVCATVS • VENETVS **Note:** Legend varieties exist.

Date	Mintage	VG	F	VF	XF	Unc
ND(1663) MM	—	50.00	90.00	200	350	—
ND(1665) GR	—	50.00	90.00	200	350	—
ND(1666) AD	—	50.00	90.00	200	350	—
ND(1667) AS	—	50.00	90.00	200	350	—
ND(1668) LP	—	50.00	90.00	200	350	—
ND(1669) ZQ	—	50.00	90.00	200	350	—
ND(1671) FZ	—	50.00	90.00	200	350	—
ND(1671) MV	—	50.00	90.00	200	350	—
ND(1672) GC	—	50.00	90.00	200	350	—
ND(1673) PZ6o	—	50.00	90.00	200	350	—

DAV# 4270 DUCATO

23.4000 g., 0.8264 Silver 0.6217 oz. ASW **Ruler:** Nicolo Sagredo **Obv. Legend:** S • M • V • NICOLA • SAGREDO • D **Note:** Legend varieties exist.

Date	Mintage	VG	F	VF	XF	Unc
ND(1675) GD	—	150	265	450	750	—
ND(1675) AZ	—	150	265	450	750	—
ND(1675) AZ	—	150	265	450	750	—
Note: With obverse legend retrograde N						
ND(1675-76) PL	—	150	265	450	750	—

DAV# 4274 DUCATO

23.4000 g., 0.8264 Silver 0.6217 oz. ASW **Ruler:** Luigi Contarini **Obv. Legend:** S • M • V • ALOYSIVS • CONT • D **Note:** Legend varieties exist.

Date	Mintage	VG	F	VF	XF	Unc
ND(1676) AZ	—	50.00	90.00	200	350	—
ND(1676-77) PL	—	50.00	90.00	200	350	—
ND(1677) SB	—	50.00	90.00	200	350	—
ND(1679) AC	—	50.00	90.00	200	350	—
Note: Obverse legend retrograde N						
ND(1679) AC	—	50.00	90.00	200	350	—
Note: Obverse legend normal N						
ND(1679-81) GZ	—	50.00	90.00	200	350	—
Note: Obverse legend retrograde N						
ND(1679-81) GZ	—	50.00	90.00	200	350	—
Note: Obverse legend normal N						
ND(1681) PM	—	50.00	90.00	200	350	—
ND(1682) ND	—	50.00	90.00	200	350	—

DAV# 4277 DUCATO

23.4000 g., 0.8264 Silver 0.6217 oz. ASW **Ruler:** Marcantonio Giustinian **Obv. Legend:** • S • M • V • M • ANT • IVSTINIANVS • D

Date	Mintage	VG	F	VF	XF	Unc
ND(1684) AD	—	65.00	110	215	350	—
ND(1685-86) GV	—	65.00	110	215	350	—
ND(1686-87) ZAL	—	65.00	110	215	350	—

DAV# 4280 DUCATO

23.4000 g., 0.8264 Silver 0.6217 oz. ASW **Ruler:** Francesco Morosini **Obv. Legend:** • S • M • V • FRAN • MAVROC • D **Note:** Legend varieties exist.

Date	Mintage	VG	F	VF	XF	Unc
ND(1688) AG	—	50.00	90.00	200	350	—
ND(1689) ZQ	—	50.00	90.00	200	350	—
ND(1691-92) GM	—	50.00	90.00	200	350	—
ND(1692-93) MB	—	50.00	90.00	200	350	—

DAV# 4286 DUCATO

23.4000 g., 0.8264 Silver 0.6217 oz. ASW **Ruler:** Silvestro Valiero **Obv. Legend:** • S • M • V • SILV • VALERIO • DVX • V **Note:** Legend varieties exist.

Date	Mintage	VG	F	VF	XF	Unc
ND(1694) FT	—	50.00	90.00	200	350	—
ND(1698-99) PM	—	50.00	90.00	200	350	—

DAV# 1527 DUCATO

23.4000 g., 0.8264 Silver 0.6217 oz. ASW **Ruler:** Alvise II Mocenigo **Obv. Legend:** * S * M * V * ALOY * MOCENICO • DV * **Note:** Legend varieties exist.

Date	Mintage	VG	F	VF	XF	Unc
ND(1700) BC	—	50.00	90.00	200	350	—

DAV# 4226 DUCATO MOZZO (120 Soldi)

27.2500 g., 0.9480 Silver 0.8305 oz. ASW **Ruler:** Marino Grimani **Obv:** Christ blessing kneeling Doge **Obv. Legend:** • PROTEGENOS MARIN: GRIM **Rev:** Winged lion seated with gospels **Note:** Two legend varieties.

Date	Mintage	VG	F	VF	XF	Unc
ND (1595)	—	300	500	825	1,350	—

DAV# A4226 DUCATO MOZZO (120 Soldi)

27.2500 g., 0.9480 Silver 0.8305 oz. ASW **Ruler:** Marino Grimani **Obv:** Legend around Christ blessing kneeling Doge **Obv. Legend:** • PROTEGE. NOS. *. MARIN: GRIM **Rev:** Lion seated with book **Note:** Legend varieties exist.

Date	Mintage	VG	F	VF	XF	Unc
ND(1595-1605) NT	—	300	500	825	1,350	—

DAV# 4228 DUCATONE (124 Soldi)

26.2000 g., 0.9480 Silver 0.7985 oz. ASW **Ruler:** Marino Grimani **Obv:** Legend around St. Mark standing with kneeling Doge **Obv. Legend:** • MARINVS • GRIMANO • S • M... **Rev:** Legend around standing Christ **Rev. Legend:** TIBI * SOLI * - GLORIA *

Date	Mintage	VG	F	VF	XF	Unc
ND(1595-1605)	—	300	500	825	1,350	—

DAV# 4225 DUCATONE (124 Soldi)

28.1030 g., 0.9480 Silver 0.8565 oz. ASW **Ruler:** Marino Grimani **Obv:** Legend around Doge kneeling before lion **Obv. Legend:** *S. M. VENET. MARIN: GRIMA... **Rev:** St. Justina standing between sailing ships **Note:** Legend varieties exist, some with inverted "V" for "A".

Date	Mintage	VG	F	VF	XF	Unc
ND(1595-1605)	—	135	225	350	600	—

DAV# 4232 DUCATONE (124 Soldi)

28.1030 g., 0.9480 Silver 0.8565 oz. ASW **Ruler:** Leonardo Donato **Obv. Legend:** *S: M: VENET: LEON: DONAT. * **Note:** Four legend varieties exist.

Date	Mintage	VG	F	VF	XF	Unc
ND(1605-12) Retrograde 4	—	135	225	350	600	—
ND(1605-12) Normal 4	—	135	225	350	600	—

DAV# 4241 DUCATONE (124 Soldi)

28.1030 g., 0.9480 Silver 0.8565 oz. ASW **Ruler:** Antonio Priuli **Obv. Legend:** * S • M • VENET• ANT • PRIOL • **Note:** Legend varieties exist.

Date	Mintage	VG	F	VF	XF	Unc
ND(1618-23)	—	135	225	350	600	—

DAV# 4243 DUCATONE (124 Soldi)

28.1030 g., 0.9480 Silver 0.8565 oz. ASW **Ruler:** Francesco Contarini **Obv. Legend:** • S • M • VEN • FRANC • CONT... **Note:** Legend varieties exist.

Date	Mintage	VG	F	VF	XF	Unc
ND(1623-24)	—	135	225	350	600	—

DAV# 4245 DUCATONE (124 Soldi)

28.1030 g., 0.9480 Silver 0.8565 oz. ASW **Ruler:** Giovanni Corner **Obv. Legend:** • S • M • V • IOAN • CORNEL... **Note:** Legend varieties exist.

Date	Mintage	VG	F	VF	XF	Unc
ND(1625-29)	—	135	225	350	600	—

DAV# 4250 DUCATONE (124 Soldi)

28.1030 g., 0.9480 Silver 0.8565 oz. ASW **Ruler:** Francesco Erizzo **Obv. Legend:** • S • M • VEN • FRANC • ERIZZO DVX **Note:** Legend varieties exist.

Date	Mintage	VG	F	VF	XF	Unc
ND(1634) MAM	—	50.00	90.00	200	350	—

DAV# 4250A DUCATONE (124 Soldi)

28.1030 g., 0.9480 Silver 0.8565 oz. ASW **Ruler:** Francesco Erizzo **Obv:** DVX of legend in exergue

Date	Mintage	VG	F	VF	XF	Unc
ND(1634)	—	—	—	—	—	—

DAV# 4253 DUCATONE (124 Soldi)

28.1030 g., 0.9480 Silver 0.8565 oz. ASW **Ruler:** Francesco Molin **Obv. Legend:** • S • M • VEN • FRANC • MOLINO • D

Date	Mintage	VG	F	VF	XF	Unc
ND(1646) MB	—	50.00	90.00	200	350	—

DAV# 4255 DUCATONE (124 Soldi)

28.1030 g., 0.9480 Silver 0.8565 oz. ASW **Ruler:** Carlo Contarini **Obv. Legend:** S • M • V • CAROL • CONTAR...

Date	Mintage	VG	F	VF	XF	Unc
ND(1655) GBZ	—	55.00	100	215	350	—

DAV# 4257 DUCATONE (124 Soldi)

28.1030 g., 0.9480 Silver 0.8565 oz. ASW **Ruler:** Francesco Corner **Obv. Legend:** S • M • V • FRANC • CORNEL • D •

Date	Mintage	VG	F	VF	XF	Unc
ND(1656) FC	—	55.00	100	215	350	—

DAV# 4259 DUCATONE (124 Soldi)

28.1030 g., 0.9480 Silver 0.8565 oz. ASW **Ruler:** Bertuccio Valiero **Obv. Legend:** S • M • VEN • BERT • VALER • D •

Date	Mintage	VG	F	VF	XF	Unc
ND(1656) FC	—	100	170	325	525	—
ND(1656) FCM	—	100	170	325	525	—

DAV# 4261 DUCATONE (124 Soldi)

28.1030 g., 0.9480 Silver 0.8565 oz. ASW **Ruler:** Giovanni Pesaro **Obv. Legend:** S • M • VEN • IOAN • PISAVRO • D • **Note:** Two legend varieties exist.

Date	Mintage	VG	F	VF	XF	Unc
ND(1658) BV	—	55.00	100	215	350	—

DAV# 4265 DUCATONE (124 Soldi)

28.1030 g., 0.9480 Silver 0.8565 oz. ASW **Ruler:** Domenico II Contarini **Obv. Legend:** • S • M • VEN • DOMIN • CONT • D • **Note:** Many legend varieties exist.

Date	Mintage	VG	F	VF	XF	Unc
ND(1659) MAS	—	55.00	100	215	350	—
ND(1662-63) GD	—	55.00	100	215	350	—
ND(1663) DG	—	55.00	100	215	350	—

DAV# 4269 DUCATONE (124 Soldi)

28.1030 g., 0.9480 Silver 0.8565 oz. ASW **Ruler:** Nicolo Sagredo **Obv. Legend:** S • M • V • NICO • SAGREDO • X •

Date	Mintage	VG	F	VF	XF	Unc
ND(1675) GD	—	165	270	450	750	—

DAV# 4273 DUCATONE (124 Soldi)

28.1030 g., 0.9480 Silver 0.8565 oz. ASW **Ruler:** Luigi Contarini **Obv. Legend:** S • M • V • ALOYSIVS • CONT • D •

Date	Mintage	VG	F	VF	XF	Unc
ND(1676) AZ	—	135	225	375	650	—

DAV# 4276 DUCATONE (124 Soldi)

28.1030 g., 0.9480 Silver 0.8565 oz. ASW **Ruler:** Marcantonio Giustinian **Obv. Legend:** S • M • V • M • ANT • IVSTINIANVS •

Date	Mintage	VG	F	VF	XF	Unc
ND(1685-86) GV	—	135	225	375	650	—

DAV# 4279 DUCATONE (124 Soldi)

28.1030 g., 0.9480 Silver 0.8565 oz. ASW **Ruler:** Francesco Morosini **Obv. Legend:** S • M • V • FRANC • MAVROCENVS • D •

Date	Mintage	VG	F	VF	XF	Unc
ND(1690-91) PP	—	135	225	375	650	—

DAV# 4284 DUCATONE (124 Soldi)

28.1030 g., 0.9480 Silver 0.8565 oz. ASW **Ruler:** Silvestro Valiero **Obv. Legend:** S • M • V • SILVE • VALERIO • DVX *

Date	Mintage	VG	F	VF	XF	Unc
ND(1694) FT	—	135	225	375	650	—

DAV# 4236 REALE

28.8200 g., Silver **Ruler:** Marcantonio Memmo **Obv:** Arms within order collar, ducal cap above **Obv. Legend:** MARCUS • ANTONINVS • MEMMO... **Rev:** St. Mark with book and lion

Date	Mintage	VG	F	VF	XF	Unc
1614	—	900	1,500	2,250	—	—

DAV# 4224 SCUDO (140 Soldi)

31.8290 g., 0.9480 Silver 0.9701 oz. ASW **Ruler:** Marino Grimani **Obv:** Legend around lion shield **Obv. Legend:** MARINVS • GRIMAN • DVX... **Rev:** Ornate cross with lis in corners **Note:** Legend varieties exist, many with inverted "V" for "A" which also appears in mintmaster initials.

Date	Mintage	VG	F	VF	XF	Unc
ND(1595-1605) GV	—	55.00	100	215	350	—
ND(1595-1605) SM	—	55.00	100	215	350	—
ND(1595-1605) MD	—	55.00	100	215	350	—
ND(1595-1605) MV	—	55.00	100	215	350	—
ND(1595-1605) ZE	—	55.00	100	215	350	—
ND(1595-1605) AM	—	55.00	100	215	350	—
ND(1595-1605) AR	—	55.00	100	215	350	—
ND(1595-1605) PC	—	55.00	100	215	350	—
ND(1595-1605) FG	—	55.00	100	215	350	—
ND(1595-1605) ZFL	—	55.00	100	215	350	—
ND(1595-1605) SC	—	55.00	100	215	350	—
ND(1595-1605) AT	—	55.00	100	215	350	—

DAV# 4227 SCUDO (140 Soldi)

31.8290 g., 0.9480 Silver 0.9701 oz. ASW **Ruler:** Marino Grimani **Obv:** Legend around ornate cross **Obv. Legend:** MARINVS • GRIMANO • DVX... **Rev:** Winged lion with gospel book

Date	Mintage	VG	F	VF	XF	Unc
ND(1595-1605) AT	—	55.00	100	215	350	—

DAV# 4229 SCUDO (140 Soldi)

31.8290 g., 0.9480 Silver 0.9701 oz. ASW **Ruler:** Leonardo Donato **Obv:** Legend around ornate cross **Obv. Legend:** LEON • DONATO • DVX... **Rev:** Lion with shield **Note:** Legend varieties exist.

Date	Mintage	VG	F	VF	XF	Unc
ND(1605-12) AT	—	55.00	100	215	350	—
ND(1605-12) SC	—	55.00	100	215	350	—
ND(1609) ZM	—	55.00	100	215	350	—
ND(1609-12) CZ	—	55.00	100	215	350	—
ND(1609) DM	—	55.00	100	215	305	—

DAV# 4234 SCUDO (140 Soldi)

31.8290 g., 0.9480 Silver 0.9701 oz. ASW **Ruler:** Marcantonio Memmo **Obv. Legend:** M • ANTON • MEMMO • DVX • VEN **Note:** Varieties of flowers at mintmaster initials exist.

Date	Mintage	VG	F	VF	XF	Unc
ND(1612) BM	—	105	195	325	550	—
ND(1612-15) AV	—	105	195	325	550	—
ND(1613-14) AM	—	105	195	325	550	—
ND(1614) VE	—	105	195	325	550	—
ND(1614-15) CG	—	105	195	325	550	—

DAV# 4237 SCUDO (140 Soldi)

31.8290 g., 0.9480 Silver 0.9701 oz. ASW **Ruler:** Giovanni Bembo **Obv. Legend:** IOANNES • BEMBO... **Note:** Legend varieties exist.

Date	Mintage	VG	F	VF	XF	Unc
ND(1614-15) CG	—	165	270	450	750	—
ND(1615) LV	—	165	270	450	750	—
Note: With inverted "A" for "V"						
ND(1615) LV	—	165	270	450	750	—
ND(1616) IM	—	165	270	450	750	—

DAV# 4239 SCUDO (140 Soldi)

31.8290 g., 0.9480 Silver 0.9701 oz. ASW **Ruler:** Antonio Priuli **Obv. Legend:** ANTON • PRIOL... **Note:** Legend varieties exist.

Date	Mintage	VG	F	VF	XF	Unc
ND(1618) TB	—	55.00	100	210	350	—
ND(1618-20) GR	—	55.00	100	210	350	—
ND(1620) VC	—	55.00	100	210	350	—
ND(1620-21) HZ	—	55.00	100	210	350	—
ND(1621) CD	—	55.00	100	210	350	—
ND(1621-22) ZAV	—	55.00	100	210	350	—
ND(1622-23) ZD	—	55.00	100	210	350	—

DAV# 4238 SCUDO (140 Soldi)

31.8290 g., 0.9480 Silver 0.9701 oz. ASW **Ruler:** Nicolo Donato **Obv. Legend:** NICOL • DONATO...

Date	Mintage	VG	F	VF	XF	Unc
ND(1618) TB	—	195	325	650	1,100	—

DAV# 4242 SCUDO (140 Soldi)

31.8290 g., 0.9480 Silver 0.9701 oz. ASW **Ruler:** Francesco Contarini **Obv. Legend:** FRANC • CONT(AR)... **Note:** Legend varieties exist.

Date	Mintage	VG	F	VF	XF	Unc
ND(1623) ZD	—	55.00	100	210	350	—
ND(1623) IBC	—	55.00	100	210	350	—
ND(1624) FMM	—	55.00	100	210	350	—
ND(1624) FM	—	55.00	100	210	350	—

DAV# 4244 SCUDO (140 Soldi)

31.8290 g., 0.9480 Silver 0.9701 oz. ASW **Ruler:** Giovanni Corner **Obv. Legend:** IOAN • CORNEL... **Note:** Legend varieties exist.

Date	Mintage	VG	F	VF	XF	Unc
ND(1625) FM	—	55.00	100	210	350	—
ND(1625) DM	—	55.00	100	210	350	—
ND(1626) AF	—	55.00	100	210	350	—
ND(1627) IAM	—	55.00	100	210	350	—
ND(1627) GP	—	55.00	100	210	350	—
ND(1628) GC	—	55.00	100	210	350	—
ND(1629) NF	—	55.00	100	210	350	—
ND(1629) DB	—	55.00	100	210	350	—

DAV# 4246 SCUDO (140 Soldi)

31.8290 g., 0.9480 Silver 0.9701 oz. ASW **Ruler:** Nicolo Contarini **Obv. Legend:** NICOL • CONTAR... **Note:** Legend varieties exist.

Date	Mintage	VG	F	VF	XF	Unc
ND(1630) DB	—	55.00	100	210	350	—
ND(1630) DB	—	55.00	100	210	350	—
Note: With obverse legend CVX (error)						
ND(1630) VM	—	55.00	100	210	350	—
ND(1630) AM	—	55.00	100	210	350	—

DAV# 4249 SCUDO (140 Soldi)

31.8290 g., 0.9480 Silver 0.9701 oz. ASW **Ruler:** Francesco Erizzo **Obv. Legend:** FRANC • ERIZZO... **Note:** Legend varieties exist.

Date	Mintage	VG	F	VF	XF	Unc
ND(1631) VM	—	55.00	90.00	200	350	—
ND(1632) DM	—	55.00	90.00	200	350	—
ND(1634) MAM	—	55.00	90.00	200	350	—
ND(1635) AZ	—	55.00	90.00	200	350	—
ND(1636) BB	—	55.00	90.00	200	350	—
ND(1637) DB	—	55.00	90.00	200	350	—
ND(1638) VV	—	55.00	90.00	200	350	—
ND(1638-39) ZL	—	55.00	90.00	200	350	—
ND(1639-40) GC	—	55.00	90.00	200	350	—
ND(1641) OZ	—	55.00	90.00	200	350	—
ND(1642-43) AB	—	55.00	90.00	200	350	—

DAV# 4252 SCUDO (140 Soldi)

31.8290 g., 0.9480 Silver 0.9701 oz. ASW **Ruler:** Francesco Molin **Obv. Legend:** FRANC • MOLINO... **Note:** Legend varieties exist.

Date	Mintage	VG	F	VF	XF	Unc
ND(1646) MB	—	55.00	90.00	200	350	—
ND(1646) ZAB	—	55.00	90.00	200	350	—
ND(1647) ZAZ	—	55.00	90.00	200	350	—
ND(1649-50) PG	—	55.00	90.00	200	350	—
ND(1652-54) FR	—	55.00	90.00	200	350	—

DAV# 4254 SCUDO (140 Soldi)

31.8290 g., 0.9480 Silver 0.9701 oz. ASW **Ruler:** Carlo Contarini **Obv. Legend:** CAROL • CONTAR... **Note:** Four varieties of ornaments at value exist.

Date	Mintage	VG	F	VF	XF	Unc
ND(1655) GBZ	—	55.00	100	210	350	—

DAV# 4256 SCUDO (140 Soldi)
31.8290 g., 0.9480 Silver 0.9701 oz. ASW **Ruler:** Francesco Corner **Obv. Legend:** FRANC • CORNEL...

Date	Mintage	VG	F	VF	XF	Unc
ND(1656) FC	—	75.00	125	240	400	—

DAV# 4258 SCUDO (140 Soldi)
31.8290 g., 0.9480 Silver 0.9701 oz. ASW **Ruler:** Bertuccio Valiero **Obv. Legend:** BERTVC • VALERIO...

Date	Mintage	VG	F	VF	XF	Unc
ND(1656) FC	—	135	225	350	600	—
ND(1656-57) BV	—	135	225	350	600	—

DAV# 4260 SCUDO (140 Soldi)
31.8290 g., 0.9480 Silver 0.9701 oz. ASW **Ruler:** Giovanni Pesaro **Obv. Legend:** IOANNES • PISAVRO... **Note:** Two legend varieties exist.

Date	Mintage	VG	F	VF	XF	Unc
ND(1658) BV	—	55.00	100	210	350	—

DAV# 4263 SCUDO (140 Soldi)
31.8290 g., 0.9480 Silver 0.9701 oz. ASW **Ruler:** Domenico II Contarini **Obv. Legend:** DOMINIC • CONTAR... **Note:** Legend varieties exist.

Date	Mintage	VG	F	VF	XF	Unc
ND(1659) IM	—	55.00	100	210	350	—
ND(1659-60) BB	—	55.00	100	210	350	—
ND(1662-63) GD	—	55.00	100	210	350	—
ND(1664) MM	—	55.00	100	210	350	—
ND(1665-66) GR	—	55.00	100	210	350	—
ND(1666-67) AD	—	55.00	100	210	350	—
ND(1668) LP	—	55.00	100	210	350	—
ND(1671) MV	—	55.00	100	210	350	—
ND(1672) GL	—	55.00	100	210	350	—
ND(1673) PZ6o	—	55.00	100	210	350	—

DAV# 4268 SCUDO (140 Soldi)
31.8290 g., 0.9480 Silver 0.9701 oz. ASW **Ruler:** Nicolo Sagredo **Obv. Legend:** NICOLAVS • SAGRE • DVX • VENET * P • Z • 6° *

Date	Mintage	VG	F	VF	XF	Unc
ND(1675) PZ6o	—	210	350	600	975	—
ND(1675) ZP	—	210	350	600	975	—

DAV# 4272 SCUDO (140 Soldi)
31.8290 g., 0.9480 Silver 0.9701 oz. ASW **Ruler:** Luigi Contarini **Obv. Legend:** ALOYSIVS CONTARENDO... **Note:** Legend varieties exist.

Date	Mintage	VG	F	VF	XF	Unc
ND(1676-77) PL	—	55.00	100	200	350	—
ND(1677) SB	—	55.00	100	200	350	—
ND(1678) MQ	—	55.00	100	200	350	—
ND(1679-81) GZ	—	55.00	100	200	350	—

DAV# 4275 SCUDO (140 Soldi)
31.8290 g., 0.9480 Silver 0.9701 oz. ASW **Ruler:** Marcantonio Giustinian **Obv. Legend:** M • ANTON • IVSTINIANVS... **Note:** Legend varieties exist.

Date	Mintage	VG	F	VF	XF	Unc
ND(1684) DT	—	75.00	125	240	400	—
ND(1685) DP	—	75.00	125	240	400	—

DAV# 4278 SCUDO (140 Soldi)
31.8290 g., 0.9480 Silver 0.9701 oz. ASW **Ruler:** Francesco Morosini **Obv. Legend:** FRAN • MAVROCENVS...

Date	Mintage	VG	F	VF	XF	Unc
ND(1688) AG	—	70.00	120	225	350	—
ND(1691-92) GM	—	70.00	120	225	350	—

DAV# 4283 SCUDO (140 Soldi)
31.8290 g., 0.9480 Silver 0.9701 oz. ASW **Ruler:** Silvestro Valiero **Obv. Legend:** SILVESTER * VALERIO... **Note:** Legend varieties exist.

Date	Mintage	VG	F	VF	XF	Unc
ND(1694) FT	—	70.00	120	225	350	—
ND(1698-99) PM	—	70.00	120	225	350	—

DAV# 1524 SCUDO (140 Soldi)
31.8290 g., 0.9480 Silver 0.9701 oz. ASW **Ruler:** Alvise II Mocenigo **Obv:** Floral cross, leaves in angles, B•C below

Obv. Legend: ALOYSIV * MOCENICO * DVX * VENET
Rev: Winged lion holding gospel in shield above value
Rev. Legend: SANCTVS • MARCVS • VENET •

Date	Mintage	VG	F	VF	XF	Unc
ND(1700) BC	—	70.00	120	225	350	—

DAV# 4223 SCUDO (160 Soldi)
36.3800 g., 0.9480 Silver 1.1088 oz. ASW **Ruler:** Marino Grimani **Obv:** St. Mark seated blessing kneeling Doge **Obv. Legend:** * DVX • S • M • VENET • MARIN:' GRIMA * **Rev:** St. Junstina with palm and book, lion behind

Date	Mintage	VG	F	VF	XF	Unc
ND(1595-1605) GV	—	300	500	825	1,400	—

DAV# 4233 SCUDO (160 Soldi)
36.3800 g., 0.9480 Silver 1.1088 oz. ASW **Ruler:** Marcantonio Memmo **Obv. Legend:** * S • M • VENETVS • M • ANT • MEMO • DV *

Date	Mintage	VG	F	VF	XF	Unc
ND(1612-13) AC	—	300	500	825	1,400	—

FR# 1457 SCUDO D'ORO
3.3310 g., 0.9170 Gold 0.0982 oz. AGW **Ruler:** Antonio Priuli **Obv. Legend:** ANT • PRIOL • DVX • VENETIAR

Date	Mintage	VG	F	VF	XF	Unc
ND(1618-23) Rare	—	—	—	—	—	—

FR# 1459 SCUDO D'ORO
3.3310 g., 0.9170 Gold 0.0982 oz. AGW **Ruler:** Francesco Contarini **Obv. Legend:** FRANC • CONTARENO • DVX • VEN

Date	Mintage	VG	F	VF	XF	Unc
ND(1623-24)	—	850	1,800	3,400	5,400	—

FR# 1461 SCUDO D'ORO
3.3310 g., 0.9170 Gold 0.0982 oz. AGW **Ruler:** Giovanni Corner **Obv. Legend:** IOAN • CORNEL • DVX • VENET

Date	Mintage	VG	F	VF	XF	Unc
ND(1625-29) Rare	—	—	—	—	—	—

FR# 1463 SCUDO D'ORO
3.3310 g., 0.9170 Gold 0.0982 oz. AGW **Ruler:** Nicolo Contarini **Obv. Legend:** NICOL CONTAR • DVX • VEN

Date	Mintage	VG	F	VF	XF	Unc
ND(1630-31) Rare	—	—	—	—	—	—

FR# 1465 SCUDO D'ORO
3.4030 g., 0.9170 Gold 0.1003 oz. AGW **Ruler:** Francesco Erizzo **Obv. Legend:** FRANC • ERIZZO • DVX • VENE

Date	Mintage	VG	F	VF	XF	Unc
ND(1631-46) Rare	—	—	—	—	—	—

FR# 1466 SCUDO D'ORO
3.4030 g., 0.9170 Gold 0.1003 oz. AGW **Ruler:** Francesco Corner **Obv. Legend:** FRANC • CORNEL • DVX • VENET

Date	Mintage	VG	F	VF	XF	Unc
ND(1656) Rare	—	—	—	—	—	—

FR# 1470 SCUDO D'ORO
3.3810 g., 0.9170 Gold 0.0997 oz. AGW **Ruler:** Silvestro Valiero **Obv. Legend:** SILVESTER • VALERIO • DVX • VE

Date	Mintage	VG	F	VF	XF	Unc
ND(1694) FT Rare	—	—	—	—	—	—

FR# 1456 2 SCUDI
6.7620 g., 0.9170 Gold 0.1994 oz. AGW **Ruler:** Antonio Priuli **Obv. Legend:** ANTON • PRIOL • DVX • VENETIAR

Date	Mintage	VG	F	VF	XF	Unc
ND(1618-23)	—	1,800	3,000	5,400	7,800	—

FR# 1458 2 SCUDI
6.7620 g., 0.9170 Gold 0.1994 oz. AGW **Ruler:** Francesco Contarini **Obv. Legend:** FRANC • CONTARENO • DVX • VENET

Date	Mintage	VG	F	VF	XF	Unc
ND(1623-24)	—	650	1,350	2,650	3,750	—

FR# 1460 2 SCUDI
6.7620 g., 0.9170 Gold 0.1994 oz. AGW **Ruler:** Giovanni Corner **Obv. Legend:** IOAN • CORNEL • DVX • VENET

Date	Mintage	VG	F	VF	XF	Unc
ND(1625-29)	—	650	1,350	2,650	3,750	—

FR# 1462 2 SCUDI
6.7620 g., 0.9170 Gold 0.1994 oz. AGW **Ruler:** Nicolo Contarini **Obv. Legend:** NICOL • CONTAR • DVX • VENE

Date	Mintage	VG	F	VF	XF	Unc
ND(1630-31)	—	700	1,500	2,750	4,500	—

FR# 1464 2 SCUDI
6.8060 g., 0.9170 Gold 0.2006 oz. AGW **Ruler:** Francesco Erizzo **Obv. Legend:** FRANC • ERIZZO • DVX • VENET

Date	Mintage	VG	F	VF	XF	Unc
ND(1631-46) Rare	—	—	—	—	—	—

FR# 1467 2 SCUDI
6.8060 g., 0.9170 Gold 0.2006 oz. AGW **Ruler:** Bertuccio Valiero **Obv. Legend:** BERTVCCIVS • VALERIO • DVX • VEN •

Date	Mintage	VG	F	VF	XF	Unc
ND(1656-58) Rare	—	—	—	—	—	—

FR# 1468 2 SCUDI
6.8060 g., 0.9170 Gold 0.2006 oz. AGW **Ruler:** Nicolo Sagredo **Obv. Legend:** NICOLAVS • SAGRE • DVX • VENE

Date	Mintage	VG	F	VF	XF	Unc
ND(1675) LP Rare	—	—	—	—	—	—

FR# 1469 2 SCUDI
6.8060 g., 0.9170 Gold 0.2006 oz. AGW **Ruler:** Silvestro Valiero **Obv. Legend:** SILVESTER • VALERIO • DVX • VEN

Date	Mintage	VG	F	VF	XF	Unc
ND(1694) FT Rare	—	—	—	—	—	—

DAV# 4282 LEONE
27.1200 g., 0.7390 Silver 0.6443 oz. ASW **Ruler:** Francesco Morosini **Obv. Legend:** FRAN • MAVROC... **Rev:** Lion holds cross and palm frond in front

Date	Mintage	VG	F	VF	XF	Unc
ND(1688-94)	—	250	425	725	1,150	—
ND(1691) IB	—	250	425	725	1,150	—

DAV# 4281 LEONE
27.1200 g., 0.7390 Silver 0.6443 oz. ASW **Ruler:** Francesco Morosini **Obv:** Legend around St. Mark standing blessing kneeling Doge **Obv. Legend:** FRAN • MAVRO... **Rev:** Legend around rearing lion holding cross behind and palm frond in front **Rev. Legend:** FIDES ET VICTORIA **Note:** Legend varieties exist.

Date	Mintage	VG	F	VF	XF	Unc
ND(1688) AG	—	250	425	725	1,150	—

DAV# 4287 LEONE
27.1200 g., 0.7390 Silver 0.6443 oz. ASW **Ruler:** Silvestro Valiero **Obv. Legend:** SILV • VALERIO... **Note:** Legend varieties exist.

Date	Mintage	VG	F	VF	XF	Unc
ND(1694) FT	—	250	425	725	1,150	—
ND(1697-98) GAB	—	250	425	725	1,150	—
ND(1698-99) PM	—	250	425	725	1,150	—
ND(1698) AC	—	250	425	725	1,150	—
ND(1699) AZ	—	250	425	725	1,150	—

FR# 1276.2 1/4 ZECCHINO
0.8730 g., 0.9990 Gold 0.0280 oz. AGW **Ruler:** Marino Grimani **Obv:** Doge kneeling before St. Mark, legend in outer border **Obv. Legend:** MARIN GRIMANI DVX **Rev:** Christ standing in starred field

Date	Mintage	VG	F	VF	XF	Unc
ND(1595-1605)	—	110	170	325	550	—

FR# A1276 1/4 ZECCHINO
0.8730 g., 0.9990 Gold 0.0280 oz. AGW **Ruler:** Marino Grimani **Obv:** Legend in outer border **Obv. Legend:** MARIN GRIMANI DVX

Date	Mintage	VG	F	VF	XF	Unc
ND(1595-1605)	—	110	170	325	550	—

FR# 1276.1 1/4 ZECCHINO
0.8730 g., 0.9990 Gold 0.0280 oz. AGW **Ruler:** Marino Grimani **Obv:** Doge kneeling before St. Mark **Obv. Legend:** MAR GRIM... **Rev:** Christ standing in starred field

Date	Mintage	VG	F	VF	XF	Unc
ND(1595-1605)	—	110	170	325	550	—

FR# 1280 1/4 ZECCHINO
0.8730 g., 0.9990 Gold 0.0280 oz. AGW **Ruler:** Leonardo Donato **Obv. Legend:** LEONAR DONATO...

Date	Mintage	VG	F	VF	XF	Unc
ND(1605-12)	—	95.00	170	300	475	—

FR# 1283 1/4 ZECCHINO
0.8730 g., 0.9990 Gold 0.0280 oz. AGW **Ruler:** Marcantonio Memmo **Obv. Legend:** M ANTO MEMMO...

Date	Mintage	VG	F	VF	XF	Unc
ND(1612-15)	—	210	425	650	1,150	—

FR# 1286 1/4 ZECCHINO
0.8730 g., 0.9990 Gold 0.0280 oz. AGW **Ruler:** Giovanni Bembo **Obv. Legend:** IOAN BEMBO...

Date	Mintage	VG	F	VF	XF	Unc
ND(1615-18) Rare	—	—	—	—	—	—

FR# 1288 1/4 ZECCHINO
0.8730 g., 0.9990 Gold 0.0280 oz. AGW **Ruler:** Nicolo Donato **Obv. Legend:** NICOL DONATO...

Date	Mintage	VG	F	VF	XF	Unc
ND(1618)	—	600	1,200	2,400	4,500	—

FR# 1293 1/4 ZECCHINO
0.8730 g., 0.9990 Gold 0.0280 oz. AGW **Ruler:** Antonio Priuli **Obv. Legend:** ANTON PRIOLO...

Date	Mintage	VG	F	VF	XF	Unc
ND(1618-23)	—	110	210	350	600	—

FR# 1296 1/4 ZECCHINO
0.8730 g., 0.9990 Gold 0.0280 oz. AGW **Ruler:** Francesco Contarini **Obv. Legend:** FRANC CONTAR...

Date	Mintage	VG	F	VF	XF	Unc
ND(1623-24)	—	350	775	1,500	3,400	—

FR# 1299 1/4 ZECCHINO
0.8730 g., 0.9990 Gold 0.0280 oz. AGW **Ruler:** Giovanni Corner **Obv. Legend:** IOAN CORN...

Date	Mintage	VG	F	VF	XF	Unc
ND(1625-29)	—	350	775	1,500	3,400	—

FR# 1309 1/4 ZECCHINO
0.8730 g., 0.9990 Gold 0.0280 oz. AGW **Ruler:** Nicolo Contarini **Obv. Legend:** NICOL CONT...

Date	Mintage	VG	F	VF	XF	Unc
ND(1630-31)	—	425	850	1,900	3,900	—

FR# 1312 1/4 ZECCHINO
0.8730 g., 0.9990 Gold 0.0280 oz. AGW **Ruler:** Francesco Erizzo **Obv. Legend:** FRANC ERIZZO...

Date	Mintage	VG	F	VF	XF	Unc
ND(1631-46)	—	120	240	425	900	—

FR# 1320 1/4 ZECCHINO
0.8730 g., 0.9990 Gold 0.0280 oz. AGW **Ruler:** Francesco Molin **Obv. Legend:** FRANC MOLINO...

Date	Mintage	VG	F	VF	XF	Unc
ND(1646-55)	—	240	475	1,000	2,400	—

FR# 1323 1/4 ZECCHINO
0.8730 g., 0.9990 Gold 0.0280 oz. AGW **Ruler:** Carlo Contarini **Obv. Legend:** CAROL CONT...

Date	Mintage	VG	F	VF	XF	Unc
ND(1655-56)	—	475	950	1,800	3,600	—

FR# A1323 1/4 ZECCHINO
0.8730 g., 0.9990 Gold 0.0280 oz. AGW **Ruler:** Francesco Corner **Obv. Legend:** FRANC CORNEL...

Date	Mintage	VG	F	VF	XF	Unc
ND(1656)	—	475	950	1,800	3,600	—

FR# 1328 1/4 ZECCHINO
0.8730 g., 0.9990 Gold 0.0280 oz. AGW **Ruler:** Bertuccio Valiero **Obv. Legend:** BERTVC VALER...

Date	Mintage	VG	F	VF	XF	Unc
ND(1656-58)	—	350	650	1,200	2,400	—

FR# 1331 1/4 ZECCHINO
0.8730 g., 0.9990 Gold 0.0280 oz. AGW **Ruler:** Giovanni Pesaro **Obv. Legend:** IOANNES PISAVRO...

Date	Mintage	VG	F	VF	XF	Unc
ND(1658-59)	—	300	600	1,200	2,650	—

FR# 1334 1/4 ZECCHINO
0.8730 g., 0.9990 Gold 0.0280 oz. AGW **Ruler:** Domenico II Contarini **Obv. Legend:** DOMIN CONTAR... **Note:** Varieties exist.

Date	Mintage	VG	F	VF	XF	Unc
ND(1659-74)	—	110	180	325	575	—

FR# 1337 1/4 ZECCHINO
0.8730 g., 0.9990 Gold 0.0280 oz. AGW **Ruler:** Nicolo Sagredo **Obv. Legend:** NICOL SAGREDO...

Date	Mintage	VG	F	VF	XF	Unc
ND(1675-76) Rare	—	—	—	—	—	—

FR# 1340 1/4 ZECCHINO
0.8730 g., 0.9990 Gold 0.0280 oz. AGW **Ruler:** Luigi Contarini **Obv. Legend:** ALOYSI CONTA...

Date	Mintage	VG	F	VF	XF	Unc
ND(1676-84)	—	120	180	325	575	—

FR# 1343 1/4 ZECCHINO
0.8730 g., 0.9990 Gold 0.0280 oz. AGW **Ruler:** Marcantonio Giustinian **Obv. Legend:** M ANTON IVSTIN...

Date	Mintage	VG	F	VF	XF	Unc
ND(1684-88)	—	325	625	1,250	2,600	—

FR# 1349 1/4 ZECCHINO
0.8730 g., 0.9990 Gold 0.0280 oz. AGW **Ruler:** Francesco Morosini **Obv. Legend:** FRAN MAVROC...

Date	Mintage	VG	F	VF	XF	Unc
ND(1688-94)	—	325	650	1,300	2,600	—

FR# 1356 1/4 ZECCHINO
0.8730 g., 0.9990 Gold 0.0280 oz. AGW **Ruler:** Silvestro Valiero **Obv. Legend:** SILVEST VALERIO...

Date	Mintage	VG	F	VF	XF	Unc
ND(1694-1700)	—	325	575	1,150	2,350	—

FR# 1360 1/4 ZECCHINO
0.8730 g., 0.9990 Gold 0.0280 oz. AGW **Ruler:** Alvise II Mocenigo **Obv:** Doge kneeling before St. Mark **Obv. Legend:** ALOY • MOC... **Rev:** Christ standing in starred field **Rev. Legend:** EGO • SVM • LVX • MVN •

Date	Mintage	VG	F	VF	XF	Unc
ND(1700-09)	—	90.00	120	300	525	—

FR# 1275 1/2 ZECCHINO
1.7470 g., 0.9990 Gold 0.0561 oz. AGW **Ruler:** Marino Grimani **Obv:** Doge kneeling before St. Mark **Obv. Legend:** MARIN GRI... **Rev:** Christ standing in starred field

Date	Mintage	VG	F	VF	XF	Unc
ND(1595-1605)	—	110	170	350	600	—

FR# 1279 1/2 ZECCHINO
1.7470 g., 0.9990 Gold 0.0561 oz. AGW **Ruler:** Leonardo Donato **Obv. Legend:** LEON DON...

Date	Mintage	VG	F	VF	XF	Unc
ND(1605-12)	—	95.00	155	325	550	—

FR# 1282 1/2 ZECCHINO
1.7470 g., 0.9990 Gold 0.0561 oz. AGW **Ruler:** Marcantonio Memmo **Obv. Legend:** M A MEMMO...

Date	Mintage	VG	F	VF	XF	Unc
ND(1612-15)	—	210	425	725	1,200	—

FR# 1285 1/2 ZECCHINO
1.7470 g., 0.9990 Gold 0.0561 oz. AGW **Ruler:** Giovanni Bembo **Obv. Legend:** IO BEMBO...

Date	Mintage	VG	F	VF	XF	Unc
ND(1615-18) Rare	—	—	—	—	—	—

FR# 1292 1/2 ZECCHINO
1.7470 g., 0.9990 Gold 0.0561 oz. AGW **Ruler:** Antonio Priuli **Obv. Legend:** ANT PRI...

Date	Mintage	VG	F	VF	XF	Unc
ND(1618-23)	—	110	170	350	600	—

FR# 1295 1/2 ZECCHINO
1.7470 g., 0.9990 Gold 0.0561 oz. AGW **Ruler:** Francesco Contarini **Obv. Legend:** FRA CONT...

Date	Mintage	VG	F	VF	XF	Unc
ND(1623-24)	—	350	775	1,600	3,600	—

FR# 1298 1/2 ZECCHINO
1.7470 g., 0.9990 Gold 0.0561 oz. AGW **Ruler:** Giovanni Corner **Obv. Legend:** IO CORN...

Date	Mintage	VG	F	VF	XF	Unc
ND(1625-29)	—	350	775	1,550	3,500	—

FR# 1308 1/2 ZECCHINO
1.7470 g., 0.9990 Gold 0.0561 oz. AGW **Ruler:** Nicolo Contarini **Obv. Legend:** NIC CONT...

Date	Mintage	VG	F	VF	XF	Unc
ND(1630-31)	—	525	1,050	2,500	5,000	—

FR# 1311 1/2 ZECCHINO
1.7470 g., 0.9990 Gold 0.0561 oz. AGW **Ruler:** Francesco Erizzo **Obv. Legend:** FRA ERI...

Date	Mintage	VG	F	VF	XF	Unc
ND(1631-46)	—	150	270	450	975	—

FR# 1319 1/2 ZECCHINO
1.7470 g., 0.9990 Gold 0.0561 oz. AGW **Ruler:** Francesco Molin **Obv. Legend:** FRANC MOL...

Date	Mintage	VG	F	VF	XF	Unc
ND(1646-55)	—	350	650	1,350	3,050	—

FR# 1322 1/2 ZECCHINO
1.7470 g., 0.9990 Gold 0.0561 oz. AGW **Ruler:** Carlo Contarini **Obv. Legend:** CAROL CON...

Date	Mintage	VG	F	VF	XF	Unc
ND(1655-56)	—	425	850	1,600	3,600	—

FR# 1325 1/2 ZECCHINO
1.7470 g., 0.9990 Gold 0.0561 oz. AGW **Ruler:** Francesco Corner **Obv. Legend:** FRANC CORN...

Date	Mintage	VG	F	VF	XF	Unc
ND(1656) Rare	—	—	—	—	—	—

FR# 1327 1/2 ZECCHINO

1.7470 g., 0.9990 Gold 0.0561 oz. AGW **Ruler:** Bertuccio Valiero **Obv. Legend:** BERT VAL...

Date	Mintage	VG	F	VF	XF	Unc
ND(1656-58)	—	600	1,200	2,550	5,100	—

FR# 1330 1/2 ZECCHINO

1.7470 g., 0.9990 Gold 0.0561 oz. AGW **Ruler:** Giovanni Pesaro **Obv. Legend:** IO PISAVR...

Date	Mintage	VG	F	VF	XF	Unc
ND(1658-59)	—	500	1,000	2,150	4,200	—

FR# 1333 1/2 ZECCHINO

1.7470 g., 0.9990 Gold 0.0561 oz. AGW **Ruler:** Domenico II Contarini **Obv. Legend:** COMIN CON...

Date	Mintage	VG	F	VF	XF	Unc
ND(1659-74)	—	110	190	350	600	—

FR# 1336 1/2 ZECCHINO

1.7470 g., 0.9990 Gold 0.0561 oz. AGW **Ruler:** Nicolo Sagredo **Obv. Legend:** NICOL SAG...

Date	Mintage	VG	F	VF	XF	Unc
ND(1675-76)	—	650	1,300	2,700	5,300	—

FR# 1339 1/2 ZECCHINO

1.7470 g., 0.9990 Gold 0.0561 oz. AGW **Ruler:** Luigi Contarini **Obv. Legend:** ALOYS CO...

Date	Mintage	VG	F	VF	XF	Unc
ND(1676-84) Rare	—	—	—	—	—	—

FR# 1342 1/2 ZECCHINO

1.7470 g., 0.9990 Gold 0.0561 oz. AGW **Ruler:** Marcantonio Giustinian **Obv. Legend:** M A IVSTIN...

Date	Mintage	VG	F	VF	XF	Unc
ND(1684-88)	—	245	500	1,050	2,300	—

FR# 1348 1/2 ZECCHINO

1.7470 g., 0.9990 Gold 0.0561 oz. AGW **Ruler:** Francesco Morosini **Obv. Legend:** FR MAVROC...

Date	Mintage	VG	F	VF	XF	Unc
ND(1688-94)	—	300	575	1,200	2,650	—

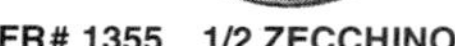

FR# 1355 1/2 ZECCHINO

1.7470 g., 0.9990 Gold 0.0561 oz. AGW **Ruler:** Silvestro Valiero **Obv. Legend:** SIL VALERI...

Date	Mintage	VG	F	VF	XF	Unc
ND(1694-1700)	—	350	650	1,400	3,000	—

FR# 1359 1/2 ZECCHINO

1.7470 g., 0.9990 Gold 0.0561 oz. AGW **Ruler:** Alvise II Mocenigo **Obv:** Doge kneeling before St. Mark **Obv. Legend:** ALOY • MOC... **Rev:** Christ standing in starred field **Rev. Legend:** * LVX * MVN * EGO * SVM *

Date	Mintage	VG	F	VF	XF	Unc
ND(1700-09)	—	110	170	300	550	—

FR# 1274 ZECCHINO

3.4940 g., 0.9990 Gold 0.1122 oz. AGW **Ruler:** Marino Grimani **Obv:** Doge kneeling before St. Mark **Obv. Legend:** MARIN GRIM... **Rev:** Christ standing in starred field

Date	Mintage	VG	F	VF	XF	Unc
ND(1595-1605)	—	70.00	110	240	475	—

FR# 1278 ZECCHINO

3.4940 g., 0.9990 Gold 0.1122 oz. AGW **Ruler:** Leonardo Donato **Obv. Legend:** LEON DON...

Date	Mintage	VG	F	VF	XF	Unc
ND(1605-12)	—	130	265	450	900	—

DAV# 4230 ZECCHINO

45.4700 g., 0.9480 Silver 1.3858 oz. ASW **Ruler:** Leonardo Donato **Obv:** St. Mark seated blessing kneeling Doge **Obv. Legend:** S. M. VENET: LEONARS: DONAT: DVX **Rev:** Legend around Christ standing in oval and stars **Rev. Legend:** SIT • T • XPE • DAT • Q • TV... **Note:** Two legend varieties exist.

Date	Mintage	VG	F	VF	XF	Unc
ND(1607) ZPS	—	300	525	900	1,500	—

DAV# 4231 ZECCHINO

45.4700 g., 0.9480 Silver 1.3858 oz. ASW **Ruler:** Leonardo Donato **Obv:** Legend around St. Mark standing blessing kneeling Doge **Obv. Legend:** LEONAR • DONATO... **Note:** Two legend varieties exist.

Date	Mintage	VG	F	VF	XF	Unc
ND(1607) ZPS	—	300	500	825	1,350	—
ND(1607-08) CP	—	300	500	825	1,350	—
ND(1609-12) CZ	—	300	500	825	1,350	—

DAV# 4235 ZECCHINO

45.4700 g., 0.9480 Silver 1.3858 oz. ASW **Ruler:** Marcantonio Memmo **Obv. Legend:** M • ANT • MEMO...

Date	Mintage	VG	F	VF	XF	Unc
ND(1612-13) AC	—	300	525	900	1,500	—

FR# 1281 ZECCHINO

3.4940 g., 0.9990 Gold 0.1122 oz. AGW **Ruler:** Marcantonio Memmo **Obv. Legend:** M • A • MEMMO...

Date	Mintage	VG	F	VF	XF	Unc
ND(1612-18)	—	300	800	1,200	2,000	—

FR# 1284 ZECCHINO

3.4940 g., 0.9990 Gold 0.1122 oz. AGW **Ruler:** Giovanni Bembo **Obv. Legend:** IO BEMBO...

Date	Mintage	VG	F	VF	XF	Unc
ND(1615-18)	—	500	1,000	2,000	3,000	—

FR# 1287 ZECCHINO

3.4940 g., 0.9990 Gold 0.1122 oz. AGW **Ruler:** Nicolo Donato **Obv. Legend:** NIC DONATO...

Date	Mintage	VG	F	VF	XF	Unc
ND(1618)	—	2,200	3,300	6,100	9,900	—

FR# 1291 ZECCHINO

3.4940 g., 0.9990 Gold 0.1122 oz. AGW **Ruler:** Antonio Priuli **Obv. Legend:** ANT PRIOL...

Date	Mintage	VG	F	VF	XF	Unc
ND(1618-23)	—	110	220	425	850	—

DAV# 4240 ZECCHINO

45.4700 g., 0.9480 Silver 1.3858 oz. ASW **Ruler:** Antonio Priuli **Obv. Legend:** ANT: PRIOL...

Date	Mintage	VG	F	VF	XF	Unc
ND(1618-20) GR	—	300	500	825	1,350	—
ND(1620-21) HZ	—	300	500	825	1,350	—

FR# 1294 ZECCHINO

3.4940 g., 0.9990 Gold 0.1122 oz. AGW **Ruler:** Francesco Contarini **Obv. Legend:** FRANC CONT...

Date	Mintage	VG	F	VF	XF	Unc
ND(1623-24)	—	2,200	3,300	6,100	9,900	—

FR# 1297 ZECCHINO

3.4940 g., 0.9990 Gold 0.1122 oz. AGW **Ruler:** Giovanni Corner **Obv. Legend:** IO CORNEL...

Date	Mintage	VG	F	VF	XF	Unc
ND(1625-29) Rare	—	—	—	—	—	—

FR# 1307 ZECCHINO

3.4940 g., 0.9990 Gold 0.1122 oz. AGW **Ruler:** Nicolo Contarini **Obv. Legend:** NIC CONT...

Date	Mintage	VG	F	VF	XF	Unc
ND(1630-31)	—	3,000	4,800	7,800	12,000	—

DAV# 4247 ZECCHINO
45.4700 g., 0.9480 Silver 1.3858 oz. ASW **Ruler:** Nicolo Contarini **Obv. Legend:** NICOL • CONT...

Date	Mintage	VG	F	VF	XF	Unc
ND(1630) DB	—	300	525	900	1,500	—

FR# 1310 ZECCHINO
3.4940 g., 0.9990 Gold 0.1122 oz. AGW **Ruler:** Francesco Erizzo **Obv. Legend:** FRANC ERIZZ...

Date	Mintage	VG	F	VF	XF	Unc
ND(1631-46)	—	110	180	375	750	—

FR# 1318 ZECCHINO
3.4940 g., 0.9990 Gold 0.1122 oz. AGW **Ruler:** Francesco Molin **Obv. Legend:** FRANC MOLINO...

Date	Mintage	VG	F	VF	XF	Unc
ND(1646-55)	—	110	130	240	475	—

FR# 1321 ZECCHINO
3.4940 g., 0.9990 Gold 0.1122 oz. AGW **Ruler:** Carlo Contarini **Obv. Legend:** CAROL CONT...

Date	Mintage	VG	F	VF	XF	Unc
ND(1655-56)	—	140	280	450	900	—

FR# 1324 ZECCHINO
3.4940 g., 0.9990 Gold 0.1122 oz. AGW **Ruler:** Francesco Corner **Obv. Legend:** FRANC CORN...

Date	Mintage	VG	F	VF	XF	Unc
ND(1656)	—	2,200	3,300	6,100	9,900	—

FR# 1326 ZECCHINO
3.4940 g., 0.9990 Gold 0.1122 oz. AGW **Ruler:** Bertuccio Valiero **Obv. Legend:** BERT VALER...

Date	Mintage	VG	F	VF	XF	Unc
ND(1656-58)	—	110	150	300	600	—

FR# 1329 ZECCHINO
3.4940 g., 0.9990 Gold 0.1122 oz. AGW **Ruler:** Giovanni Pesaro **Obv. Legend:** IOAN PISAVRO...

Date	Mintage	VG	F	VF	XF	Unc
ND(1658-59)	—	150	325	625	1,150	—

FR# 1332 ZECCHINO
3.4940 g., 0.9990 Gold 0.1122 oz. AGW **Ruler:** Domenico II Contarini **Obv. Legend:** DOMIN CONT... **Note:** Varieties exist.

Date	Mintage	VG	F	VF	XF	Unc
ND(1659-74)	—	110	130	225	575	—

FR# 1335 ZECCHINO
3.4940 g., 0.9990 Gold 0.1122 oz. AGW **Ruler:** Nicolo Sagredo **Obv. Legend:** NICOL SAGREDO...

Date	Mintage	VG	F	VF	XF	Unc
ND(1675-76)	—	190	375	750	1,250	—

FR# 1338 ZECCHINO
3.4940 g., 0.9990 Gold 0.1122 oz. AGW **Ruler:** Luigi Contarini **Obv. Legend:** ALOYSIVS CONT...

Date	Mintage	VG	F	VF	XF	Unc
ND(1676-84)	—	110	130	225	575	—

FR# 1341 ZECCHINO
3.4940 g., 0.9990 Gold 0.1122 oz. AGW **Ruler:** Marcantonio Giustinian **Obv. Legend:** M ANT IVSTIN...

Date	Mintage	VG	F	VF	XF	Unc
ND(1684-88)	—	110	135	300	600	—

FR# 1347 ZECCHINO
3.4940 g., 0.9990 Gold 0.1122 oz. AGW **Ruler:** Francesco Morosini **Obv. Legend:** FRAN MABROC...

Date	Mintage	VG	F	VF	XF	Unc
ND(1688-94)	—	110	150	300	650	—

FR# 1354 ZECCHINO
3.4940 g., 0.9990 Gold 0.1122 oz. AGW **Ruler:** Silvestro Valiero **Obv. Legend:** SILV VALERIO...

Date	Mintage	VG	F	VF	XF	Unc
ND(1694-1700)	—	110	150	300	650	—

FR# 1358 ZECCHINO
3.4940 g., 0.9990 Gold 0.1122 oz. AGW **Ruler:** Alvise II Mocenigo **Obv:** Doge kneeling before St. Mark **Obv. Legend:** ALOY * MOCENI * ... **Rev:** Christ standing in starred field **Rev. Legend:** SIT • T • XPE • DAT • Q • TV REGIS • ISTE • ĐVCA

Date	Mintage	VG	F	VF	XF	Unc
ND(1700-09)	—	110	130	180	450	—

FR# 1290 2 ZECCHINI
6.9880 g., 0.9990 Gold 0.2244 oz. AGW **Ruler:** Antonio Priuli **Obv. Legend:** S • M • VENET • ANT • PRIOL • DVX •

Date	Mintage	VG	F	VF	XF	Unc
ND(1618-23) Rare	—	—	—	—	—	—

FR# 1306 2 ZECCHINI
6.9100 g., 0.9990 Gold 0.2219 oz. AGW **Ruler:** Nicolo Contarini **Obv. Legend:** NIC CONT... **Rev:** Christ standing in starred field

Date	Mintage	VG	F	VF	XF	Unc
ND(1630-31) Rare	—	—	—	—	—	—

FR# 1305 3 ZECCHINI
10.4820 g., 0.9990 Gold 0.3367 oz. AGW **Ruler:** Nicolo Contarini **Obv. Legend:** NIC CONT...

Date	Mintage	VG	F	VF	XF	Unc
ND(1630-31) Rare	—	—	—	—	—	—

FR# 1378 4 ZECCHINI
13.9700 g., 0.9990 Gold 0.4487 oz. AGW **Ruler:** Alvise II Mocenigo **Obv:** Doge kneeling before St. Mark **Obv. Legend:** ALOYS * MOCEN * ... **Rev:** Christ standing in starred field **Rev. Legend:** SIT * T * XPE * DAT * Q * T V ...

Date	Mintage	VG	F	VF	XF	Unc
ND(1700-09)	—	1,200	2,900	4,800	9,000	—

FR# 1289 5 ZECCHINI
17.3700 g., 0.9990 Gold 0.5579 oz. AGW **Ruler:** Antonio Priuli **Obv. Legend:** ANT PRIOL...

Date	Mintage	VG	F	VF	XF	Unc
ND(1618-23) Rare	—	—	—	—	—	—

FR# 1346 6 ZECCHINI
20.2800 g., 0.9990 Gold 0.6513 oz. AGW **Ruler:** Francesco Morosini **Obv:** Doge kneeling before St. Mark **Obv. Legend:** FRAN MAVROC... **Rev:** Christ standing in starred field **Note:** Varieties exist.

Date	Mintage	VG	F	VF	XF	Unc
ND (1688)	—	3,600	6,000	10,000	15,000	—

FR# 1317 7 ZECCHINI
24.2900 g., 0.9990 Gold 0.7801 oz. AGW **Ruler:** Francesco Molin **Obv:** Doge kneeling before St. Mark **Obv. Legend:** FRANC MOLINO... **Rev:** Christ standing in starred field

Date	Mintage	VG	F	VF	XF	Unc
ND(1646-55) Rare	—	—	—	—	—	—

FR# 1345 8 ZECCHINI
27.9400 g., 0.9990 Gold 0.8974 oz. AGW **Ruler:** Francesco Morosini **Obv:** Doge kneeling before St. Mark **Obv. Legend:** FRAN MAVROC... **Rev:** Christ standing in starred field

Date	Mintage	VG	F	VF	XF	Unc
ND(1688-94) Rare	—	—	—	—	—	—

FR# A1303 10 ZECCHINI
34.6500 g., 0.9990 Gold 1.1129 oz. AGW, 30 mm. **Ruler:** Francesco Contarini

Date	Mintage	VG	F	VF	XF	Unc
ND(1623-24) Rare	—	—	—	—	—	—

FR# 1303 10 ZECCHINI
34.6500 g., 0.9990 Gold 1.1129 oz. AGW **Ruler:** Francesco Contarini **Obv:** Doge kneeling before St. Mark

Date	Mintage	VG	F	VF	XF	Unc
ND(1623-24) Rare	—	—	—	—	—	—

FR# 1316 10 ZECCHINI
34.6500 g., 0.9990 Gold 1.1129 oz. AGW **Ruler:** Francesco Molin **Obv. Legend:** FRANC MOLINO... **Rev:** Christ standing in starred field **Note:** Varieties exist.

Date	Mintage	VG	F	VF	XF	Unc
ND(1646-55)	—	2,400	4,200	9,000	14,500	—

FR# 1344 10 ZECCHINI
34.6500 g., 0.9990 Gold 1.1129 oz. AGW **Ruler:** Francesco Morosini

Date	Mintage	VG	F	VF	XF	Unc
ND(1688-94) Rare	—	—	—	—	—	—

FR# 1353 10 ZECCHINI
34.6500 g., 0.9990 Gold 1.1129 oz. AGW **Ruler:** Silvestro Valiero **Obv. Legend:** SILV VALERIO...

Date	Mintage	VG	F	VF	XF	Unc
ND(1694-1700) Rare	—	—	—	—	—	—

FR# 1357 10 ZECCHINI
34.7500 g., 0.9990 Gold 1.1161 oz. AGW **Ruler:** Alvise II Mocenigo **Obv. Legend:** ALOY. MOCENI...

Date	Mintage	VG	F	VF	XF	Unc
ND(1700-09)	—	2,400	6,000	10,000	15,000	—

FR# 1315 12 ZECCHINI
41.8000 g., 0.9990 Gold 1.3425 oz. AGW **Ruler:** Francesco Molin **Obv:** Doge kneeling before St. Mark **Obv. Legend:** FRANC MOLINO... **Rev:** Christ standing in starred field

Date	Mintage	VG	F	VF	XF	Unc
ND(1646-55) Rare	—	—	—	—	—	—

FR# 1352 12 ZECCHINI
41.5700 g., 0.9990 Gold 1.3351 oz. AGW **Ruler:** Silvestro Valiero **Obv. Legend:** SILV VALERIO...

Date	Mintage	VG	F	VF	XF	Unc
ND(1694-1700) Rare	—	—	—	—	—	—

FR# 1351 15 ZECCHINI
52.1000 g., 0.9990 Gold 1.6733 oz. AGW **Ruler:** Silvestro Valiero **Obv:** Doge kneeling before St. Mark **Obv. Legend:** SILV VALERIO... **Rev:** Christ standing in starred field

Date	Mintage	VG	F	VF	XF	Unc
ND(1694-1700) Rare	—	—	—	—	—	—

FR# 1313 20 ZECCHINI
69.6000 g., 0.9990 Gold 2.2354 oz. AGW **Ruler:** Francesco Molin **Obv:** Doge kneeling before St. Mark **Obv. Legend:** FRANC MOLINO... **Rev:** Christ standing in starred field

Date	Mintage	VG	F	VF	XF	Unc
ND(1646-55) Rare	—	—	—	—	—	—

FR# 1494 1/2 DUCAT
1.0830 g., 0.9990 Gold 0.0348 oz. AGW **Ruler:** Leonardo Donato **Obv:** Doge kneeling before seated figure of St. Mark **Obv. Legend:** S • M • VEN • LEON • DONAT **Rev:** Lion of St. Mark in inner circle

Date	Mintage	VG	F	VF	XF	Unc
ND(1605-12)	—	300	650	1,300	2,400	—

FR# 1493 DUCAT
2.1660 g., 0.9990 Gold 0.0696 oz. AGW **Ruler:** Leonardo Donato **Obv:** Doge kneeling before seated figure of St. Mark **Obv. Legend:** S • M • VEN • LEON • DONAT • DVX **Rev:** Lion of St. Mark in inner circle

Date	Mintage	VG	F	VF	XF	Unc
ND(1605-12)	—	425	775	1,450	2,400	—

FR# 1499 DUCAT
2.1660 g., 0.9990 Gold 0.0696 oz. AGW **Ruler:** Leonardo Donato **Obv:** Doge kneeling before lion of St. Mark **Obv. Legend:** S • M • VEN • LEON • DONAT • DVX **Rev:** St. Justina standing with palm and cross in inner circle

Date	Mintage	VG	F	VF	XF	Unc
ND(1605-12) Rare	—	—	—	—	—	—

FR# 1500 DUCAT
2.1660 g., 0.9990 Gold 0.0696 oz. AGW **Ruler:** Leonardo Donato **Obv:** Doge kneeling before St. Mark **Obv. Legend:** S • M • VEN • LEONAR • DONAT • DVX **Rev:** Christ standing facing on pedestal in inner circle

Date	Mintage	VG	F	VF	XF	Unc
ND(1605-12) Rare	—	—	—	—	—	—

FR# 1495 DUCAT
2.1660 g., 0.9990 Gold 0.0696 oz. AGW **Ruler:** Nicolo Donato **Obv:** Doge kneeling before seated figure of St. Mark **Obv. Legend:** S • M • VEN • NIC • DONATO • DVX **Rev:** Lion of St. Mark in inner circle

Date	Mintage	VG	F	VF	XF	Unc
ND(1618) Rare	—	—	—	—	—	—

FR# 1496 DUCAT
2.1660 g., 0.9990 Gold 0.0696 oz. AGW **Ruler:** Antonio Priuli **Obv:** Doge kneeling before seated figure of St. Mark **Obv. Legend:** S • M • VEN • ANT • PRIOL • DVX **Rev:** Lion of St. Mark in inner circle

Date	Mintage	VG	F	VF	XF	Unc
ND(1618-23) Rare	—	—	—	—	—	—

FR# 1497 DUCAT
2.1660 g., 0.9990 Gold 0.0696 oz. AGW **Ruler:** Giovanni Corner **Obv:** Doge kneeling before seated figure of St. Mark **Obv. Legend:** S • M • VEN • IO • CORN • DVX **Rev:** Lion of St. Mark in inner circle

Date	Mintage	VG	F	VF	XF	Unc
ND(1625-29)	—	3,000	4,800	7,800	11,500	—

FR# 1492 2 DUCATS
4.3320 g., 0.9990 Gold 0.1391 oz. AGW **Ruler:** Leonardo Donato **Obv:** Doge kneeling before seated figure of St. Mark **Obv. Legend:** S • M • VEN • LEON • DONAT • DVX **Rev:** Lion of St. Mark in inner circle

Date	Mintage	VG	F	VF	XF	Unc
ND(1605-12) Rare	—	—	—	—	—	—

PATTERNS

Including off metal strikes

KM#	Date	Mintage	Identification	Mkt Val
Pn1	ND(1612) FS	—	Zecchino. Gold. 52.1500 g. Leonardo Dona. Dav. #4231.	—
Pn2	ND(1623-24)	—	Piastre. 0.9480 Silver. 26.9100 g. Francesco Contarini.	—
Pn3	ND(1623-24)	—	Reale. 0.9480 Silver. 26.7500 g. Francesco Contarini.	—
Pn4	ND(1631-46)	—	4 Soldi. Billon. 3.9850 g. Francesco Erizzo.	—
Pn5	ND(1631-46)	—	5 Soldi. Billon. 2.1700 g. Francesco Erizzo.	—
Pn6	ND(1645-46) MB	—	72 Soldi. 13.1300 g. Francesco Erizzo.	—

KM#	Date	Mintage	Identification	Mkt Val
Pn7	1644 ZMB	—	Reale. Silver. 13.9300 g. Francesco Erizzo.	—
Pn8	ND(1639-40) GC	—	2 Scudi. Silver. 64.0000 g. Francesco Erizzo. Dav. #4248.	2,000
Pn9	ND(1641) OZ	—	2 Scudi. Silver. 64.0000 g. Francesco Erizzo. Dav. #4248.	2,000
Pn10	ND(1646) MB	—	2 Scudi. Silver. 64.0000 g. Francesco Molin. Dav. #4251.	2,000
Pn11	ND(1659-60) BB	—	2 Scudi. Silver. 64.0000 g. Domenico Contarini. Dav. #4262.	2,000
Pn12	ND(1662-63) GD	—	2 Ducatone. Silver. 56.0000 g. Domenico Contarini. Dav. #4264.	1,000
Pn13	ND(1666-67) AD	—	2 Ducato. Silver. 47.0000 g. Domenico Contarini. Dav. #4266.	1,000
Pn14	ND(1668) LP	—	2 Ducato. Silver. 47.0000 g. Domenico Contarini. Dav. #4266.	1,000
Pn15	ND(1679-81) GZ	—	2 Scudi. Silver. 64.0000 g. Alvise Contarini. Dav. #4271.	2,000
Pn16	ND(1679) AC	—	2 Ducato. Silver. 47.0000 g. Alvise Contarini. Dav. #A4274.	1,000
Pn17	ND(1694-1700) FT	—	2 Ducato. Silver. 47.0000 g. Silvestro Valier. Dav. #4285.	1,000
Pn18	ND(1700-09)	—	2 Ducato. Silver. 47.0000 g. Alvise Mociengo II; Dav.#1526.	—

VERCELLI

MARQUISATE

SIEGE COINAGE

1617

Struck while Vercelli, with the Marquis di Caluso as commander, was besieged in 1617, by the Spanish, commanded by Don Pedro of Toledo.

KM# 1 DOPPIA FIORINO

Billon **Obv:** Bust of Charles Emanuel in ruffled collar **Rev:** Three-line legend and date in ornamental frame

Date	Mintage	VG	F	VF	XF	Unc
1617	—	1,000	2,000	4,000	—	—

KM# 2 4 SCUDI D'ORO

13.2000 g., 0.9860 Gold 0.4184 oz. AGW **Obv:** Bust of Charles Emanuel in ruffled collar right **Rev:** Three-line legend and date in ornamental frame

Date	Mintage	VG	F	VF	XF	Unc
1617 Rare	—	—	—	—	—	—

SIEGE COINAGE

1638

Struck during a second Spanish siege of Vercelli, with the troops of Francesco Giacinto defending the city.

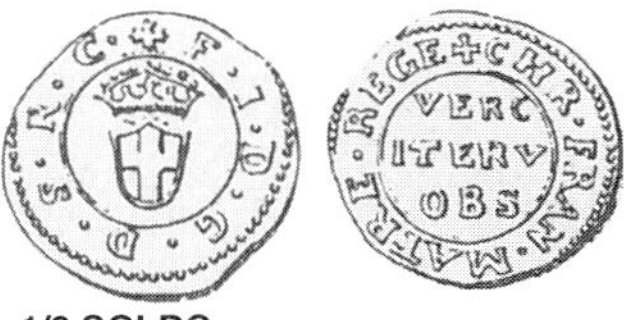

KM# 3 1/2 SOLDO

Billon **Obv:** Crowned shield **Rev:** Three-line legend

Date	Mintage	VG	F	VF	XF	Unc
ND	—	850	1,450	2,500	—	—

KM# 4.1 1/4 LIRA

Billon **Obv:** Crowned shield divide date **Rev:** Four-line legend in frame, • S:V • below

Date	Mintage	VG	F	VF	XF	Unc
1638	—	3,500	7,000	12,750	—	—

KM# 4.2 1/4 LIRA

Billon **Rev:** Four-line legend, • S:S • below

Date	Mintage	VG	F	VF	XF	Unc
1638	—	2,500	6,000	10,000	—	—

KM# 4.3 1/4 LIRA

Billon **Obv:** Crowned shield divides date **Rev:** Four-line inscription in frame •S•V below **Note:** Small flan without legends.

Date	Mintage	VG	F	VF	XF	Unc
1638	—	1,650	2,750	5,000	—	—

FR# 5 DOPPIA

6.7600 g., 0.9860 Gold 0.2143 oz. AGW **Obv:** Crowned arms divide date in inner circle **Rev:** Four-line legend in inner circle

Date	Mintage	VG	F	VF	XF	Unc
1638 Rare	—	—	—	—	—	—

VERGAGNI

Marquisate

Vergagni was a castle in the Valle Borbera, between Roccaforte and Mongiardino and held as a feudal possession of the Spinola family of Genoa from medieval times. In 1676, the feudal barony was raised to a marquisate by Emperor Leopold I. However, when the marchese committed an act of cowardice, Emperor Carlo VI stripped him of his possession of Vergagni and awarded it to Urbano Fieschi.

RULER

Giovanni Battista Spinola, 1676-1712

Reference: Alberto Varesi, ***Monete Italiane Regionali: Piemonte, Sardegna, Liguria, Isola di Corsica***. Pavia, 1996.

MARQUISATE

STANDARD COINAGE

KM# 1 LUIGINO

3.9800 g., Silver, 23 mm. **Ruler:** Giovanni Battista Spinola 1676-1712 **Obv:** Armored bust to left, date below **Obv. Legend:** IO. BAPTIS. SPINVLA. **Rev:** Crowned shield of arms between two palm fronds **Rev. Legend:** MARC. S.R.I. ET. VERGAGNI. PRIM. COM. P. ET. **Note:** Varesi 1038.

Date	Mintage	VG	F	VF	XF	Unc
1680 Rare	—	—	—	—	—	—

KM# 2 2 LUIGINO
6.4000 g., Silver, 25.5 mm. **Ruler:** Giovanni Battista Spinola 1676-1712 **Obv:** Armored bust to left, date below **Obv. Legend:** IO. BAPTIS. SPINVLA. **Rev:** Crowned shield of arms between two palm fronds **Rev. Legend:** MARC. S.R.I. ET. VERGAGNI. PRIM. COM. P. ET. **Note:** Varesi 1037.

Date	Mintage	VG	F	VF	XF	Unc
1680 Rare	—	—	—	—	—	—

KM# 3 SCUDO
26.3500 g., Silver, 41-42 mm. **Ruler:** Giovanni Battista Spinola 1676-1712 **Obv:** Armored bust to left **Obv. Legend:** IOANNES. BAPTISTA. SPINVLA. **Rev:** Crowned imperial eagle, crowned shield of arms on breast **Rev. Legend:** MARC. S.R.I. ET VERGAGNI. PRIM. COM. P. ETc. **Note:** Dav. #4288; Varesi 1036.

Date	Mintage	VG	F	VF	XF	Unc
ND(1680) Rare	—	—	—	—	—	—

PROVAS

KM#	Date	Mintage	Identification	Mkt Val
Pr1	1697	—	Scudo. Silver. Crowned arms.	—

JAPAN

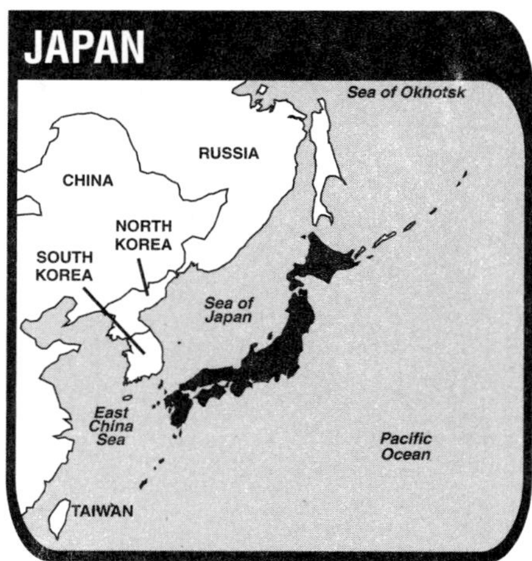

Japan, founded (so legend holds) in 660 B.C. by a direct descendant of the Sun Goddess, was first brought into contact with the west by a storm-blown Portuguese ship in 1542. European traders and missionaries proceeded to enlarge the contact until the Shogunate, sensing a military threat in the foreign presence, expelled all foreigners and restricted relations with the outside world in the 17th century. After Commodore Perry's U.S. flotilla visited in 1854, Japan rapidly industrialized, abolished the Shogunate and established a parliamentary form of government, and by the end of the 19th century achieved the status of a modern economic and military power.

Many of the provinces of Japan issued their own definitive coinage under the Shogunate.

RULERS

Shoguns

Iyeyasu Tokugawa, 1603-1605
Hidetada, 1605-1623
Iyemitsu, 1623-1651
Iyetsuna, 1651-1680
Tsunayoshi, 1680-1709

MONETARY SYSTEM

Until 1870

Prior to the Meiji currency reform, there was no fixed exchange rate between the various silver, gold and copper "cash" coins (which previously included Chinese "cash") in circulation. Each coin exchanged on the basis of its own merits and the prevailing market conditions. The size and weight of the copper coins and the weight and fineness of the silver and gold coins varied widely. From time to time the government would declare an official exchange rate, but this was usually ignored. For gold and silver, nominal equivalents were:

16 Shu = 4 Bu = 1 Ryo

MONETARY UNITS

Momme 匁 Ryo 両

Bu 分 Shu 朱 Mon 文

MINT MARKS ON MON

A - Edo (Tokyo) 文

LEGENDS

Reading top-bottom, right-left

Kan'ei Tsuho

Bunkyu-Eiho

SHOGUNATE

CAST COINAGE

KM# 5 MON
Cast Copper **Obv. Inscription:** Kei-Cho Tsu-Ho **Rev:** Plain

Date	Mintage	VG	F	VF	XF	Unc
ND(1606)	—	50.00	75.00	150	200	—

KM# 10 MON
Cast Copper **Obv. Inscription:** "Gen-Wa (Genna) Tsu-Ho" **Rev:** Character "ichi" ("one") at bottom

Date	Mintage	VG	F	VF	XF	Unc
ND(1617)	—	700	1,200	1,650	2,250	—

KM# 15 MON
Cast Copper **Obv:** First horizontal stroke of bottom character extends far to right of vertical **Obv. Inscription:** "Kwan-Ei (Kanei) Tsu-Ho"

Date	Mintage	VG	F	VF	XF	Unc
ND(1626)	—	300	325	375	500	—

C# 1.1 MON
Cast Copper, Bronze Or Brass **Obv. Inscription:** "Kwan-Ei (Kanei) Tsu-Ho" **Rev:** Plain **Note:** Cast at Edo (Tokyo) and Sakamoto.

Date	Mintage	VG	F	VF	XF	Unc
ND(1636-56)	—	0.25	0.50	1.00	1.50	—

C# 1.2 MON
Cast Copper, Bronze Or Brass **Rev:** "Bun" above

Date	Mintage	VG	F	VF	XF	Unc
ND(1668-1700)	—	0.25	0.50	1.00	1.50	—

BULLION COINAGE

KM# 6.1 MAMEITA GIN
0.8000 Silver **Obv:** One or more thin-line characters; without "God of Plenty" **Rev:** Chop marks **Note:** Keicho era.

Date	Mintage	VG	F	VF	XF	Unc
ND(1601-1695)	—	300	400	600	800	—

KM# 6.2 MAMEITA GIN
0.8000 Silver **Obv:** "God of Plenty" drawn within lines; without era designators **Note:** Keicho era.

Date	Mintage	VG	F	VF	XF	Unc
ND(1601-1695)	—	400	600	900	1,200	—

KM# 7 MAMEITA GIN
0.8000 Silver **Obv:** "God of Plenty" design, without era designators **Rev:** "God of Plenty" design, without era designators **Note:** Keicho era.

Date	Mintage	VG	F	VF	XF	Unc
ND(1601-1695) Rare	—	—	—	—	—	—

KM# 20.1 MAMEITA GIN
0.6400 Silver **Obv:** One or more characters, without "God of Plenty"; era designator "gen" between characters **Rev:** Chop marks **Note:** Genroku era.

Date	Mintage	VG	F	VF	XF	Unc
ND(1695-1706)	—	400	600	800	1,000	—

KM# 20.2 MAMEITA GIN
0.6400 Silver **Obv:** "God of Plenty" with other characters; era designator "gen" between characters and on God's belly **Note:** Genroku era.

Date	Mintage	VG	F	VF	XF	Unc
ND(1695-1706)	—	250	500	750	1,000	—

KM# 21 MAMEITA GIN
0.6400 Silver **Obv:** "God of Plenty" design, era designator on belly **Rev:** "God of Plenty" design, era designator on belly **Note:** Genroku era.

Date	Mintage	VG	F	VF	XF	Unc
ND(1695-1706)	—	300	750	1,100	1,500	—

KM# 22 MAMEITA GIN
0.6400 Silver **Obv:** "God of Plenty" design, with era designator on belly **Rev:** Many small or one large character "gen" **Note:** Genroku era.

Date	Mintage	VG	F	VF	XF	Unc
ND(1695-1706)	—	1,200	1,750	2,100	2,750	—

KM# 48 CHO GIN
0.8000 Silver **Obv:** Miscellaneous characters and designs of thin strokes finely drawn throughout **Rev:** Chop marks **Note:** Keicho era. Illustration reduced by 50%.

Date	Mintage	VG	F	VF	XF	Unc
ND(1601-1695)	—	3,000	4,000	5,000	6,000	—

KM# 49.1 CHO GIN
0.8000 Silver **Obv:** Edges completely covered with 12-14 stamps, mostly of characters, a few of "God of Plenty" **Rev:** Chop marks **Note:** Keicho era.

Date	Mintage	VG	F	VF	XF	Unc
ND(1601-1695) Rare	—	—	—	—	—	—

KM# 49.2 CHO GIN
0.8000 Silver **Obv:** Edges completely covered with 12 stamps of "God of Plenty" **Rev:** Chop marks **Note:** Keicho era.

Date	Mintage	VG	F	VF	XF	Unc
ND(1601-1695) Rare	—	—	—	—	—	—

KM# 50 CHO GIN
0.6400 Silver **Obv:** Era marks at each end; miscellaneous characters and designs elsewhere **Rev:** Chop marks **Note:** Genroku era. Illustration reduced by 50%.

Date	Mintage	VG	F	VF	XF	Unc
ND(1695-1706)	—	5,000	6,000	8,000	10,000	—

KM# 51 CHO GIN
0.6400 Silver **Obv:** Edges completely covered with 12-14 stamps, mostly of characters, a few of "God of Plenty" **Rev:** Chop marks **Note:** Genroku era.

Date	Mintage	VG	F	VF	XF	Unc
ND(1695-1706) Rare	—	—	—	—	—	—

KM# 52 CHO GIN
0.6400 Silver **Obv:** Edges completely covered with 12 stamps of "God of Plenty" **Rev:** Chop marks **Note:** Genroku era.

Date	Mintage	VG	F	VF	XF	Unc
ND(1695-1706) Rare	—	—	—	—	—	—

HAMMERED COINAGE

FR# 33 2 SHU (Nishu Gin)
2.2100 g., Gold And Silver .564 gold and .436 silver **Subject:** xyz **Note:** Genroku era.

Date	Mintage	VG	F	VF	XF	Unc
ND(1695-1710)	—	800	1,200	1,900	2,000	—

FR# 24 BU (Ichibu)

4.4300 g., Gold And Silver **Rev:** Without characters in top corners **Note:** .857 Gold and .143 Silver. Keicho era.

Date	Mintage	VG	F	VF	XF	Unc
ND(1601-95)	—	600	800	1,000	1,200	—

FR# 24a BU (Ichibu)

4.4300 g., Gold And Silver **Rev:** Character in top right corner **Note:** .857 Gold and .143 Silver. Keicho era.

Date	Mintage	VG	F	VF	XF	Unc
ND(1601-95)	—	1,000	1,300	2,200	2,400	—

FR# 24b BU (Ichibu)

4.4300 g., Gold And Silver **Rev:** 2 characters, top right and left corners **Note:** .857 Gold and .143 Silver. Keicho era.

Date	Mintage	VG	F	VF	XF	Unc
ND(1601-95)	—	6,000	8,000	10,000	12,000	—

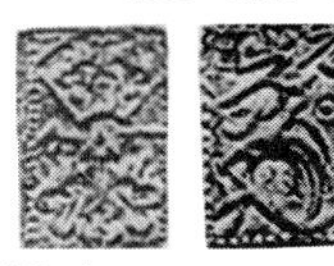

FR# 25 BU (Ichibu)

4.4600 g., Gold And Silver **Subject:** xyz **Note:** .564 Gold and .436 Silver. Genroku era.

Date	Mintage	VG	F	VF	XF	Unc
ND(1695-1710)	—	800	1,000	1,600	1,800	—

FR# 9.1 KOBAN (1 Ryo)

17.7300 g., Gold And Silver **Subject:** xyz **Obv:** Fine crenulations **Note:** .857 Gold and .143 Silver. Keicho era.

Date	Mintage	VG	F	VF	XF	Unc
ND(1601-95)	—	9,000	10,000	12,000	15,000	—

FR# 9.2 KOBAN (1 Ryo)

17.7300 g., Gold And Silver **Obv:** Coarse crenulations **Note:** .857 Gold and .143 Silver. Keicho era.

Date	Mintage	VG	F	VF	XF	Unc
ND(1602-95)	—	9,000	10,000	11,000	12,000	—

FR# 10 KOBAN (1 Ryo)

17.8100 g., Gold And Silver **Note:** .564 Gold and .436 Silver. Genroku era.

Date	Mintage	VG	F	VF	XF	Unc
ND(1695-1710)	13,936,000	10,000	12,000	14,000	18,000	—

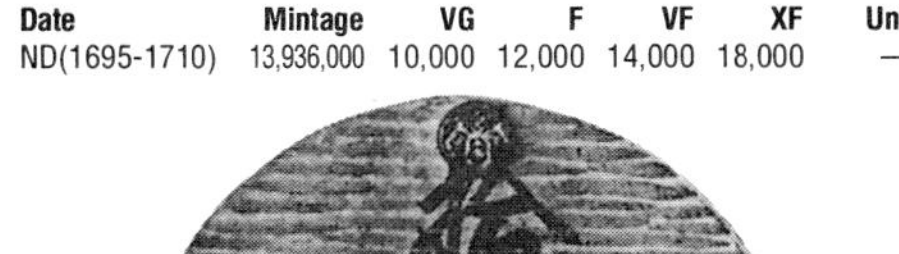

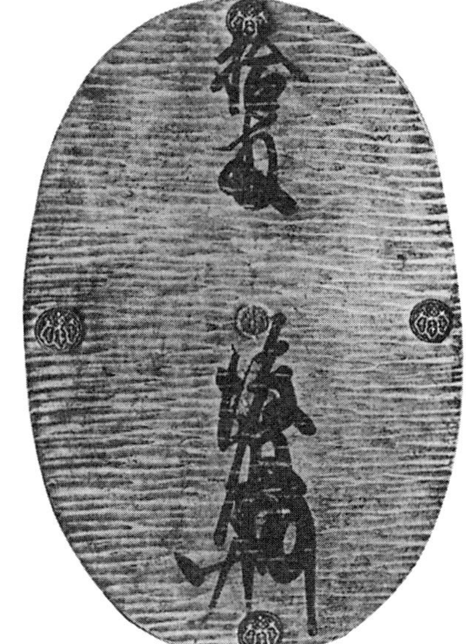

FR# 1 OBAN

165.4000 g., Gold And Silver **Note:** Illustration reduced. Tensho era. .730 Gold and .270 Silver.

Date	Mintage	VG	F	VF	XF	Unc
ND(1573-1609) Rare	—	—	—	—	—	—

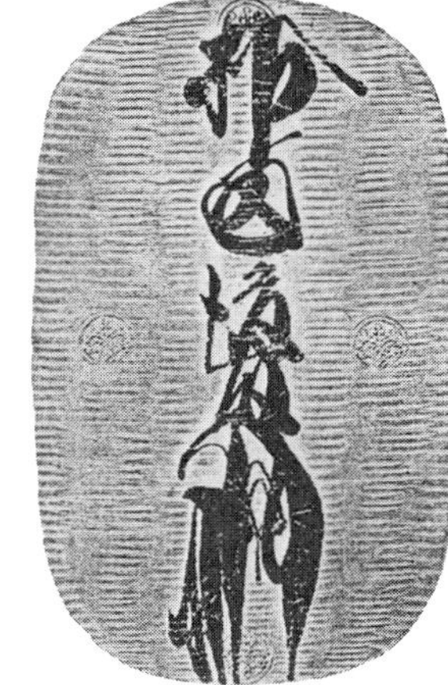

FR# A3 OBAN

165.1800 g., Gold And Silver **Note:** .672 Gold and .294 Silver. Keicho-Sasagaki era. Illustration reduced by 50%.

Date	Mintage	VG	F	VF	XF	Unc
ND(1601)	—	—	—	200,000	300,000	—

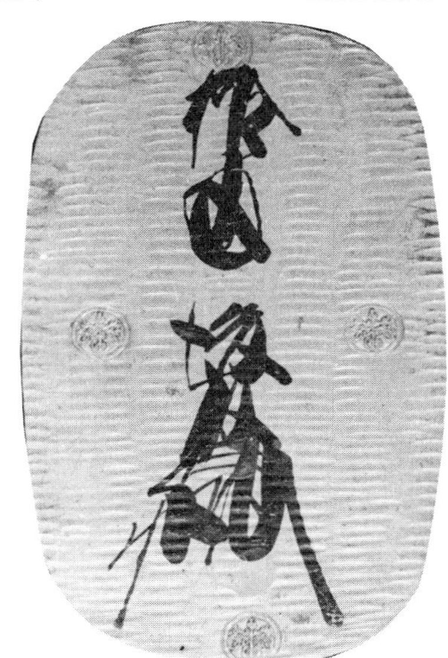

FR# 3 OBAN

165.1800 g., Gold And Silver **Note:** .672 Gold and .294 Silver. Keicho era.

Date	Mintage	VG	F	VF	XF	Unc
ND(1601)	17,000	—	—	125,000	165,000	—

FR# A4 OBAN

165.1800 g., Gold And Silver **Note:** .670 Gold and .276 Silver. Meireki era. Illustration reduced by 50%.

Date	Mintage	VG	F	VF	XF	Unc
ND(1658)	—	—	—	100,000	140,000	—

FR# 4 OBAN

164.5600 g., Gold And Silver **Subject:** xyz **Note:** .521 Gold and .449 Silver. Genroku era. Illustration reduced by 50%.

Date	Mintage	VG	F	VF	XF	Unc
ND(1695-1716)	30,000	—	—	180,000	275,000	—

KOSHU

A province, (formal name Kai, now Yamanashi Prefecture), located in central Honshu west of Tokyo.

The following listings are representative of a very complex series of gold coinage. Other obscure or odd denominations may exist. This series contains many varieties. The characters usually found stamped on the reverse are hallmarks.

PROVINCE

PROVINCIAL COINAGE

KM# 90 KAKU SHU-NAKA KIN (Rectangular Half Shu Gold)

0.4000 g., Gold, 6x8 mm.

Date	Mintage	VG	F	VF	XF	Unc
ND	—	700	900	1,200	1,600	—

KM# 91 SHU-NAKA KIN (Half Shu Gold)

Gold, 8.5-9.5 mm. **Note:** Similar to Ichi-Bu KM#94. Weight varies: 0.40-0.50 grams. Size varies.

Date	Mintage	VG	F	VF	XF	Unc
ND	—	3,000	5,000	5,500	6,500	—

KM# 92 ISSHU KIN (One Shu Gold)

Gold, 11-12 mm. **Note:** Similar to Ichi-Bu KM#94. Weight varies: 0.90-1.00 grams. Size varies.

Date	Mintage	VG	F	VF	XF	Unc
ND	—	425	650	850	1,100	—

KM# 93 NISSHU KIN (Two Shu Gold)

1.9000 g., Gold, 12-13 mm. **Note:** Similar to Ichi-Bu KM#94. Size varies.

Date	Mintage	VG	F	VF	XF	Unc
ND	—	500	600	700	800	—

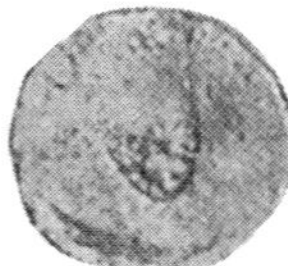

KM# 94 ICHI-BU KIN (One Bu Gold)

Gold, 14-17 mm. **Note:** Similar to Ichi-Bu KM#94. Weight varies: 3.70-4.00 Size varies.

Date	Mintage	VG	F	VF	XF	Unc
ND	—	600	700	900	1,100	—

KM# 95 ICHI-BU ISSHU KIN (One Bu One Shu Gold)

4.8000 g., Gold, 18 mm. **Note:** Similar to Ichi-Bu KM#94.

Date	Mintage	VG	F	VF	XF	Unc
ND Rare	—	—	—	—	—	—

KM# 96 ICHI-BU NISSHU KIN (One Bu Two Shu Gold)

5.0000 g., Gold, 16 mm. **Note:** Similar to Ichi-Bu KM#94.

Date	Mintage	VG	F	VF	XF	Unc
ND Rare	—	—	—	—	—	—

KM# 97 NI-BU KIN (Two Bu Gold)

Gold, 18-19 mm. **Note:** Similar to Ichi-Bu KM#94. Weight varies: 7.00-7.50 grams. Size varies.

Date	Mintage	VG	F	VF	XF	Unc
ND Rare	—	—	—	—	—	—

KM# 98 NI-BU ISSHU KIN (Two Bu One Shu Gold)

8.8000 g., Gold, 24 mm. **Note:** Similar to Ichi-Bu KM#94.

Date	Mintage	VG	F	VF	XF	Unc
ND Rare	—	—	—	—	—	—

KM# 99 RYO KIN (One Ryo Gold)

Gold, 16-19 mm. **Note:** Rounded "nugget" shape with stamps, similar to Ichi-Bu KM#94. Weight varies: 14.70-15.30 grams. Size varies.

Date	Mintage	VG	F	VF	XF	Unc
ND Rare	—	—	—	—	—	—

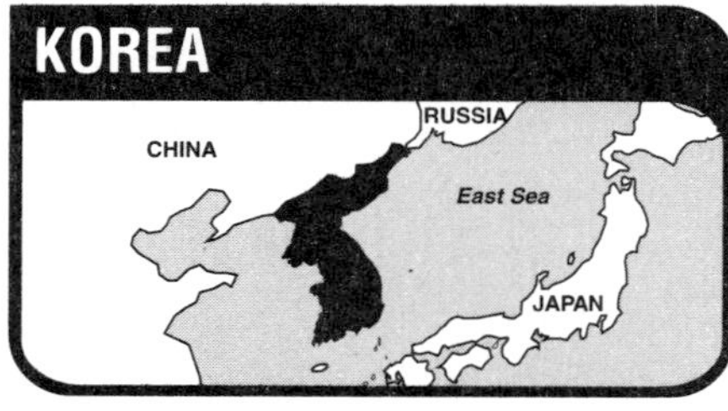

Korea, 'Land of the Morning Calm', occupies a mountainous peninsula in northeast Asia bounded by Manchuria, the Yellow Sea and the Sea of Japan.

According to legend, the first Korean dynasty, that of the House of Tangun, ruled from 2333 B.C. to 1122 B.C. It was followed by the dynasty of Kija, a Chinese scholar, which continued until 193 B.C. and brought a high civilization to Korea. The first recorded period in the history of Korea, the period of the Three Kingdoms, lasted from 57 B.C. to 935 A.D. and achieved the first political unification of the peninsula. The Kingdom of Koryo, from which Korea derived its name, was founded in 935 and continued until 1392, when it was superseded by the Yi Dynasty of King Yi. Sung Kye was to last until the Japanese annexation in 1910.

At the end of the 16th century Korea was invaded and occupied for 7 years by Japan, and from 1627 until the late 19th century it was a semi-independent tributary of China. Japan replaced China as the predominant foreign influence at the end of the Sino-Japanese War (1894-95), only to find her position threatened by Russian influence from 1896 to 1904. The Russian threat was eliminated by the Russo-Japanese War (1904-05) and in 1905 Japan established a direct protectorate over Korea. On Aug. 22,1910, the last Korean ruler signed the treaty that annexed Korea to Japan as a government-generalcy in the Japanese Empire. Japanese suzerainty was maintained until the end of World War II.

From 1633 to 1891 the monetary system of Korea employed cast coins with a square center hole. Fifty-two agencies were authorized to procure these coins from a lesser number of coin foundries. They exist in thousands of varieties. Seed, or mother coins, were used to make the impressions in the molds in which the regular cash coins were cast. Czarist-Russian Korea experimented with Korean coins when Alexiev of Russia, Korea's Financial Advisor, founded the First Asian Branch of the Russo-Korean Bank on March 1, 1898, and authorized the issuing of a set of new Korean coins with a crowned Russian-style quasi-eagle. British-Japanese opposition and the Russo-Japanese War operated to end the Russian coinage experiment in 1904.

RULERS

Yi Kweng (Sonjo Sog Yung), 1568-1609
Yi Hon (Kwang hae gun), 1609-1623
Yi Chong (Injo Honmun), 1623-1650
Yi Ho (Hyojong Sonmun), 1650-1660
Yi Yun (Hyonjong Sohyu), 1660-1675
Yi Sun (Sukjong Hyonui), 1675-1721

MONETARY UNITS

Mun	文	Yang, Niang	兩
Fun	分	Hwan, Warn	圜
Chon	錢	Won Whan, Hwan	圜

SEED COINS

Seed coins are specially prepared examples, perfectly round, with sharp characters, used in the preparation of clay or sand molds. Seed types for value 2 and 5 Mun are not included as they are very scarce and seldom are encountered in today's market.

MINT MARKS

Ho	戶	Treasury Department
Kong	工	Ministry of Industry
Kyong	冏	Bureau of Royal Transportation
Hyang	向	Food Supply Office
Ch'ong	摠	General Military Office
Yong	營 or 営	Special Army Unit
Hun	訓 or 訓	Military Training Command
Ch'o	抄	Commando Military Unit
Kae	開	Kaesong Township Military Office
Won	原	Wonju Township Military Office
P'yong	平	P'yongan Provincial Office
P'yong	平	P'yongan Military Fort
Sang	尙	Kyongsang Provincial Office
Sang Su	尙水	Kyongsang Naval Station
Sang U	尙右	Kyongsang Right Naval Base
Sang Chwa	尙左	Kyongsang Left Naval Base
Chon	全	Cholla Provincial Office
Chon Pyong	全兵	Cholla Military Fort
Chon U	全右	Cholla Right Naval Base
Chon Chwa	全左	Cholla Left Naval Base

NOTE: For earlier issues refer to *Cast Coinage of Korea* by the late Edgar J. Mandel.

KINGDOM

TREASURY DEPARTMENT

(Ho Jo)

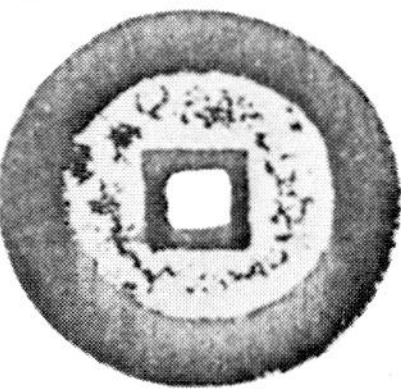

KM# 3 MUN

Cast Copper, 24 mm. **Note:** Uniface. Legend "Clerkly" characters: "Cho Son T'ong Bo".

Date	Mintage	Good	VG	F	VF	XF
ND(1625-33)	—	25.00	35.00	50.00	100	—

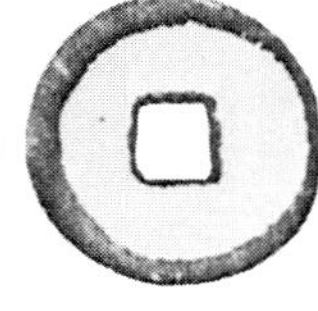

KM# 4 MUN

Cast Copper, 20 mm. **Obv. Legend:** Sang P'yong T'ong Bo

Date	Mintage	Good	VG	F	VF	XF
ND(1633)	—	225	300	450	600	—

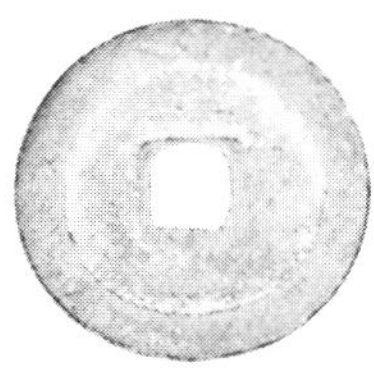

KM# 5 MUN

Cast Copper **Note:** Size varies: 23-24 mm.

Date	Mintage	Good	VG	F	VF	XF
ND(1633)	—	225	300	450	600	—

KM# 6 MUN

Cast Copper Or Bronze **Obv. Legend:** "Sang P'yong T'ong Bo" **Rev:** "Ho" at top

Date	Mintage	Good	VG	F	VF	XF
ND(1678)	—	35.00	65.00	120	180	—

KM# 6s MUN

Cast Copper Or Bronze

Date	Mintage	Good	VG	F	VF	XF
ND(1678)	—	—	—	—	—	325

KM# 7 MUN

Cast Copper Or Bronze **Rev:** "Ho" at top in different style

Date	Mintage	Good	VG	F	VF	XF
ND(1678)	—	35.00	65.00	120	180	—

KM# 7s MUN

Cast Copper Or Bronze

Date	Mintage	Good	VG	F	VF	XF
ND(1678)	—	—	—	—	—	250

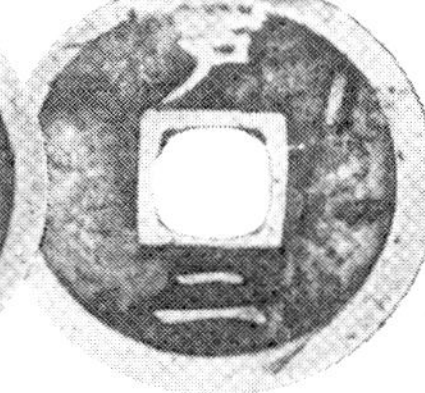

KM# 74 2 MUN

Cast Copper Or Brass **Rev:** "I" (2) at bottom **Note:** Weight varies 8.00-9.00 grams.

Date	Mintage	Good	VG	F	VF	XF
ND(1679-1752)	—	4.00	5.00	8.00	13.00	—

MINISTRY OF INDUSTRY

(Kong Jo)

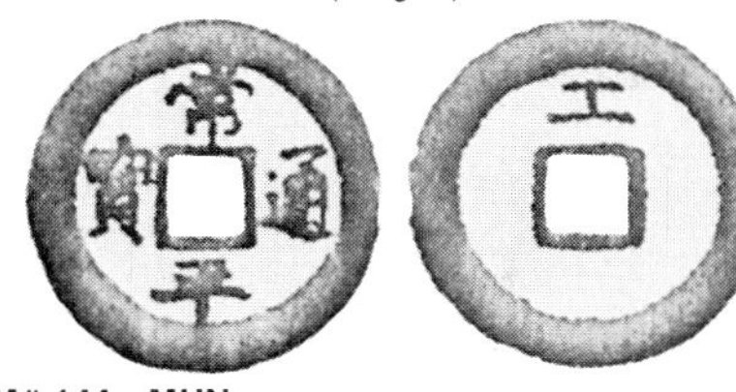

KM# 144 MUN

4.5000 g., Cast Copper **Rev:** "Kong" at top

Date	Mintage	Good	VG	F	VF	XF
ND(1685-1752) Rare	—	—	—	—	—	—

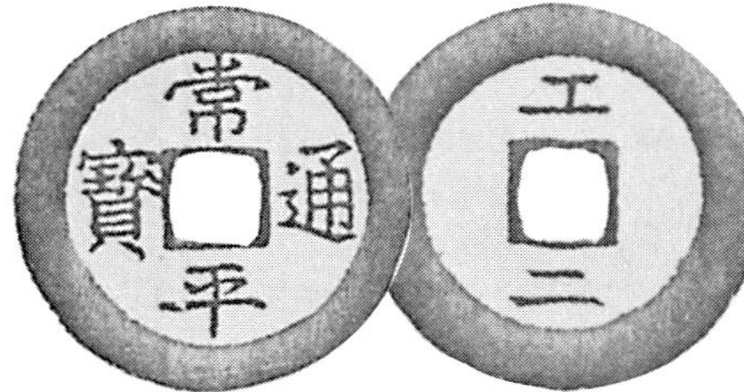

KM# 145 2 MUN

Cast Copper **Rev:** "Kong" at top, "I" (2) at bottom **Note:** Weight varies 8.00-9.00 grams.

Date	Mintage	Good	VG	F	VF	XF
ND(1685-1752)	—	3.00	5.00	8.00	15.00	—

KM# 146 2 MUN

Cast Copper **Rev:** Dot at right **Note:** Weight varies 8.00-9.00 grams.

Date	Mintage	Good	VG	F	VF	XF
ND(1685-1752)	—	10.00	15.00	25.00	48.00	—

BUREAU OF ROYAL TRANSPORTATION

(Kyong Saboksi)

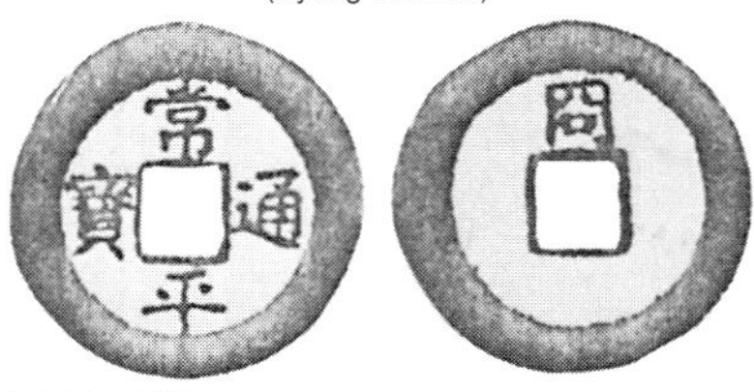

KM# 154 MUN

4.5000 g., Cast Copper **Rev:** "Kyong" at top **Note:** Small characters.

Date	Mintage	Good	VG	F	VF	XF
ND(1678-95) Rare	—	—	—	—	—	—

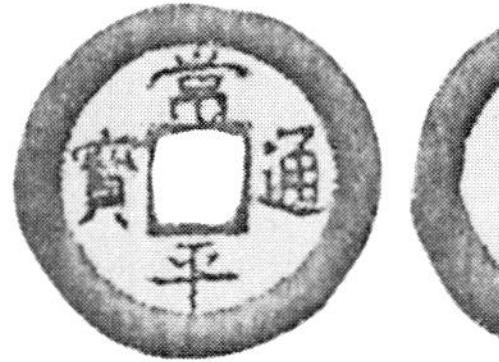

KM# 155 MUN

4.5000 g., Cast Copper **Note:** Large characters.

Date	Mintage	Good	VG	F	VF	XF
ND(1678-95) Rare	—	—	—	—	—	—

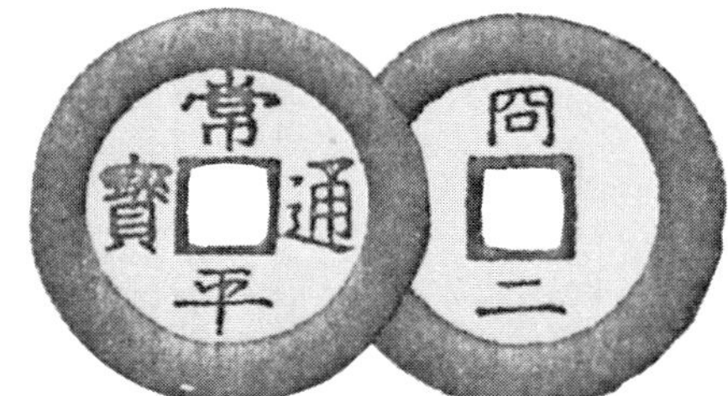

KM# 156 2 MUN

Cast Copper **Rev:** "I" (2) at bottom **Note:** Weight varies 8.00-9.00 grams.

Date	Mintage	Good	VG	F	VF	XF
ND(1679-1752) Rare	—	—	—	—	—	—

SEOUL CHARITY OFFICE

(Chinh Yu Chong)

KM# 160 2 MUN

Cast Copper **Rev:** "I" (2) at bottom **Note:** Weight varies: 8.00-9.00 grams. Inside diameter: 23-24 mm.

Date	Mintage	Good	VG	F	VF	XF
ND(1679-95)	—	4.00	7.00	11.00	14.00	—

KM# 161 2 MUN

Cast Copper **Note:** Weight varies: 8.00-9.00 grams. Inside diameter: 21 mm.

Date	Mintage	Good	VG	F	VF	XF
ND(1679-95)	—	4.00	6.00	9.00	17.00	—

KM# 161s 2 MUN

Cast Copper **Note:** Weight varies: 8.00-9.00 grams. Seed type.

Date	Mintage	Good	VG	F	VF	XF
ND(1679-95)	—	—	—	—	—	125

KM# 162 2 MUN

Cast Copper **Rev:** Dot at left **Note:** Weight varies: 8.00-9.00 grams.

Date	Mintage	Good	VG	F	VF	XF
ND(1695)	—	4.00	7.00	11.00	14.00	—

KM# 163 2 MUN

Cast Copper, 32-33 mm. **Rev:** Circle at right **Note:** Weight varies 8.00-9.00 grams. Size varies.

Date	Mintage	Good	VG	F	VF	XF
ND(1695-1742)	—	4.00	7.00	11.00	14.00	—

KM# 165 2 MUN

Cast Copper **Rev:** Circle at left **Note:** Weight varies 8.00-9.00 grams.

Date	Mintage	Good	VG	F	VF	XF
ND(1695-1742)	—	10.00	25.00	35.00	70.00	—

KM# 166 2 MUN

Cast Copper, 32-33 mm. **Note:** Weight varies 8.00-9.00 grams. Size varies.

Date	Mintage	Good	VG	F	VF	XF
ND(1695-1742)	—	4.00	7.00	11.00	14.00	—

KM# 168 2 MUN

Cast Copper **Rev:** Small crescent at left **Note:** Weight varies 8.00-9.00 grams.

Date	Mintage	Good	VG	F	VF	XF
ND(1695-1742)	—	4.00	7.00	11.00	14.00	—

KM# 169 2 MUN

Cast Copper, 32-33 mm. **Rev:** Dot in crescent at left **Note:** Weight varies 8.00-9.00 grams. Size varies.

Date	Mintage	Good	VG	F	VF	XF
ND(1695-1742)	—	4.00	6.00	8.00	14.00	—

FOOD SUPPLY OFFICE

(Yang Hyang Ch'ong)

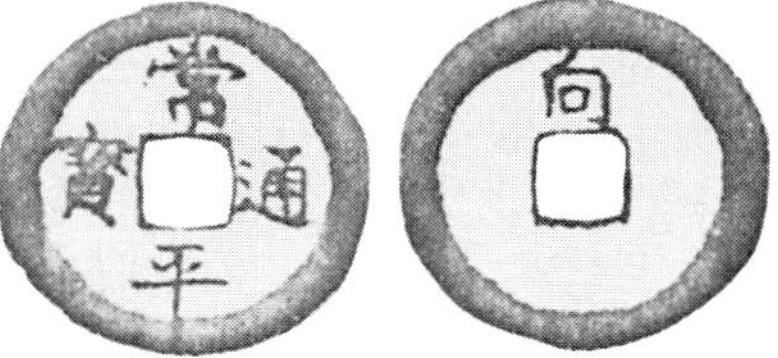

KM# 171 MUN

4.5000 g., Cast Copper **Rev:** "Hyang" at top

Date	Mintage	Good	VG	F	VF	XF
ND(1695-1742) Rare	—	—	—	—	—	—

GENERAL MILITARY OFFICE

(Ch'ong Yung Ch'ong)

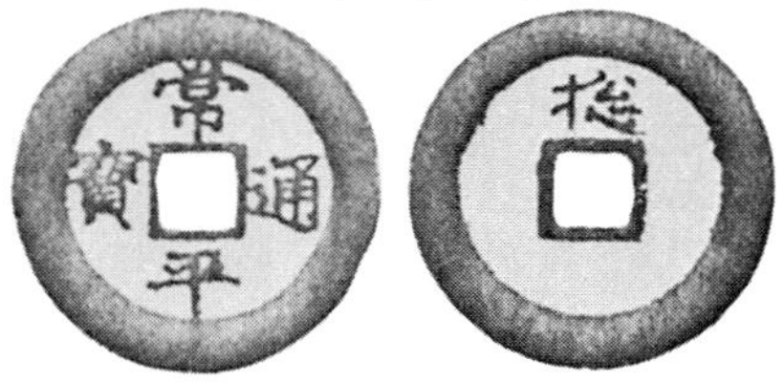

KM# 217 MUN

4.5000 g., Cast Copper **Rev:** "Ch'ong" at top

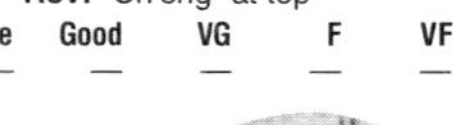

Date	Mintage	Good	VG	F	VF	XF
ND(1692) Rare	—	—	—	—	—	—

KM# 225 2 MUN

Cast Copper **Rev:** "I" (2) at bottom **Note:** Weight varies 8.00-9.00 grams.

Date	Mintage	Good	VG	F	VF	XF
ND(1692-1752)	—	4.00	6.00	8.00	14.00	—

KM# 226 2 MUN

Cast Copper **Rev:** Dot at right **Note:** Weight varies 8.00-9.00 grams.

Date	Mintage	Good	VG	F	VF	XF
ND(1692-1752)	—	13.00	25.00	39.00	65.00	—

KM# 227 2 MUN

Cast Copper **Rev:** Dot at left **Note:** Weight varies 8.00-9.00 grams.

Date	Mintage	Good	VG	F	VF	XF
ND(1692-1752)	—	18.00	30.00	48.00	70.00	—

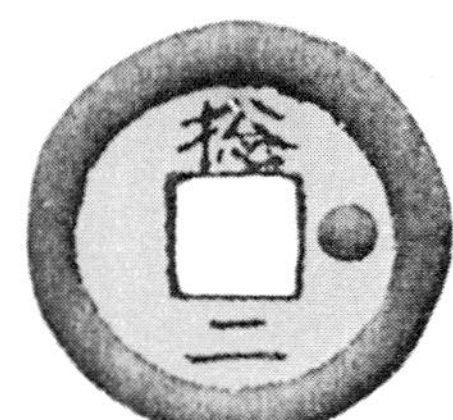

KM# 228 2 MUN

Cast Copper **Rev:** Large filled circle at right **Note:** Weight varies 8.00-9.00 grams.

Date	Mintage	Good	VG	F	VF	XF
ND(1692-1752)	—	37.50	65.00	95.00	155	—

SPECIAL ARMY UNIT

(O Yong Ch'ong)

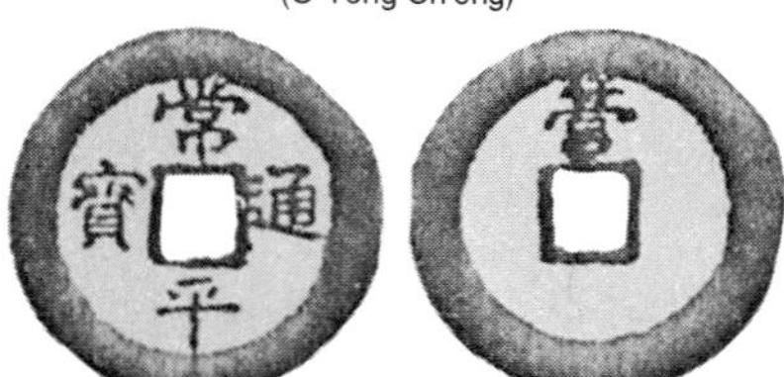

KM# 269 MUN

4.5000 g., Cast Copper **Rev:** "Yong" at top

Date	Mintage	Good	VG	F	VF	XF
ND(1678-1742) Rare	—	—	—	—	—	—

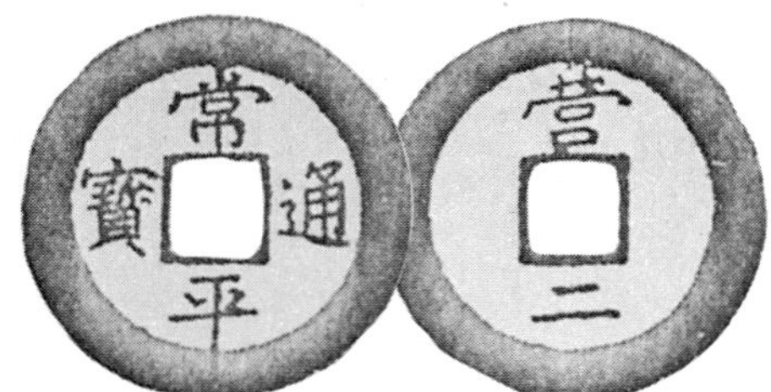

KM# 281 2 MUN

Cast Copper, 32 mm. **Rev:** "I" (2) at bottom **Note:** Weight varies: 8.00-9.00 grams. Large characters.

Date	Mintage	Good	VG	F	VF	XF
ND(1679)	—	13.00	19.00	31.25	50.00	—

MILITARY TRAINING COMMAND

(Hul Lyu On Do Gam)

Obverse Character

P'yong variety I: 平

P'yong variety II: 平

T'ong variety I - top:

T'ong variety II - top:

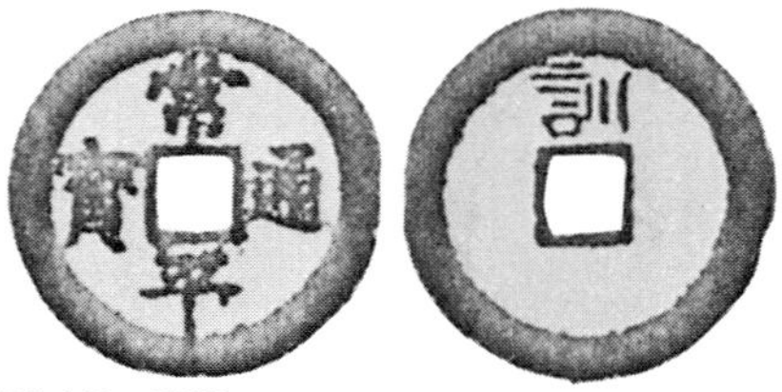

KM# 446 MUN

4.5000 g., Cast Copper **Rev:** "Hun" at top

Date	Mintage	Good	VG	F	VF	XF
ND(1678) Rare	—	—	—	—	—	—

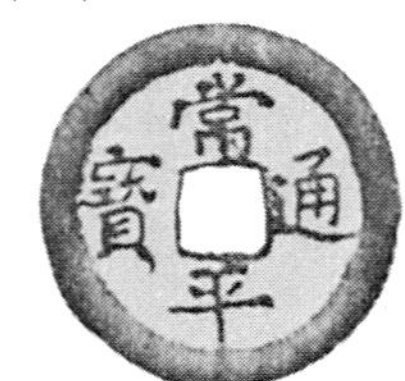

KM# 447 MUN

4.5000 g., Cast Copper **Rev:** "Hun" in different style

Date	Mintage	Good	VG	F	VF	XF
ND(1678) Rare	—	—	—	—	—	—

KM# 477 2 MUN

Cast Copper **Obv:** "T'ong" variety I **Rev:** "Hun" at top, "I" (2) at bottom **Note:** Weight varies: 8.00-9.00 grams. Size varies.

Date	Mintage	Good	VG	F	VF	XF
ND(1679)	—	5.00	10.00	15.00	25.00	—

KM# 477s 2 MUN

Cast Copper **Note:** Weight varies: 8.00-9.00 grams. Size varies: 31-32 mm.

Date	Mintage	Good	VG	F	VF	XF
ND(1679)	—	—	—	—	—	150

KM# 478 2 MUN

Cast Copper **Note:** Size varies: 28-30 mm.

Date	Mintage	Good	VG	F	VF	XF
ND(1679)	—	6.00	12.00	18.00	25.00	—

KM# 478s 2 MUN

Cast Copper **Note:** Size varies: 28-30 mm.

Date	Mintage	Good	VG	F	VF	XF
ND(1679)	—	—	—	—	—	150

COMMANDO MILITARY UNIT

(Chong Ch'o Ch'ong)

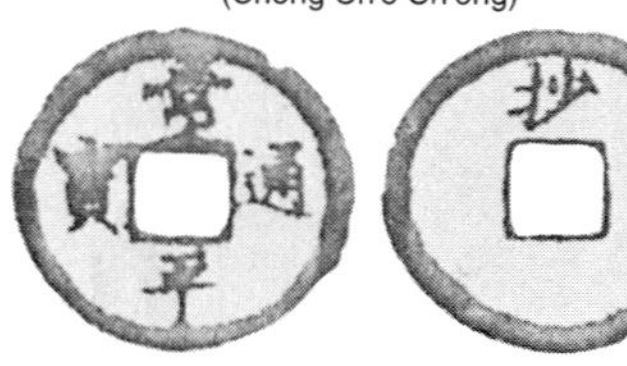

KM# 565 MUN

4.5000 g., Cast Copper **Rev:** "Ch'o" at top

Date	Mintage	Good	VG	F	VF	XF
ND(1678) Rare	—	—	—	—	—	—

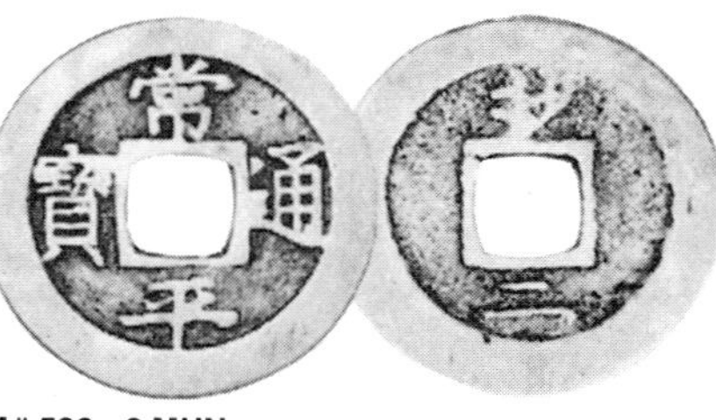

KM# 566 2 MUN

Cast Copper **Rev:** "I" (2) at bottom **Note:** Weight varies: 8.00-9.00 grams.

Date	Mintage	Good	VG	F	VF	XF
ND(1679)	—	6.00	9.00	13.00	19.00	—

KM# 566a 2 MUN

Cast Copper **Obv:** "P'yong" with hooks **Note:** Weight varies: 8.00-9.00 grams.

Date	Mintage	Good	VG	F	VF	XF
ND(1679)	—	6.00	9.00	13.00	19.00	—

KAESONG TOWNSHIP MILITARY OFFICE

(Kae Song Kwal Li Yong)

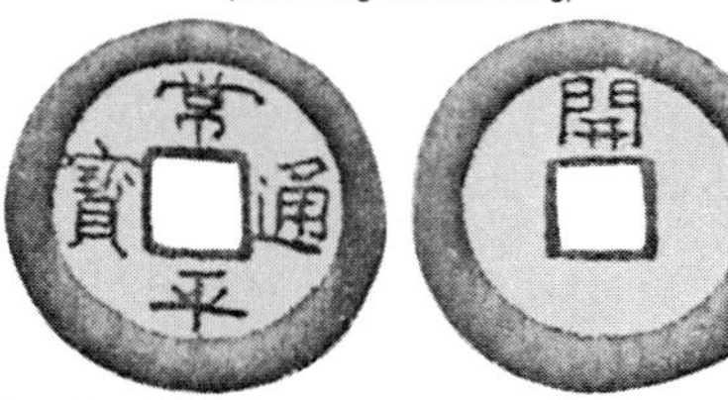

KM# 780 MUN

4.5000 g., Cast Copper Or Bronze, 26 mm. **Obv:** Large characters **Rev:** "Kae" at top

Date	Mintage	Good	VG	F	VF	XF
ND(1678-1742) Rare	—	—	—	—	—	—

KM# A780 MUN

4.5000 g., Cast Copper Or Bronze, 25 mm. **Obv:** Medium characters **Note:** Reduced size.

Date	Mintage	Good	VG	F	VF	XF
ND(1678-1742) Rare	—	—	—	—	—	—

KM# 781 MUN

4.5000 g., Cast Copper Or Bronze, 24 mm. **Obv:** Small characters **Note:** Reduced size.

Date	Mintage	Good	VG	F	VF	XF
ND(1678-1742) Rare	—	—	—	—	—	—

KM# 782 MUN

4.5000 g., Cast Copper Or Bronze **Rev:** Dot at lower right

Date	Mintage	Good	VG	F	VF	XF
ND(1678-1742) Rare	—	—	—	—	—	—

KM# 783 MUN

4.5000 g., Cast Copper Or Bronze **Rev:** Dot at bottom

Date	Mintage	Good	VG	F	VF	XF
ND(1678-1742) Rare	—	—	—	—	—	—

KM# 784 MUN

4.5000 g., Cast Copper Or Bronze **Rev:** 2 dots at bottom

Date	Mintage	Good	VG	F	VF	XF
ND(1678-1742) Rare	—	—	—	—	—	—

KM# 785 MUN

4.5000 g., Cast Copper Or Bronze **Rev:** Circle at lower right

Date	Mintage	Good	VG	F	VF	XF
ND(1678-1742) Rare	—	—	—	—	—	—

KM# 786 MUN

4.5000 g., Cast Copper Or Bronze **Rev:** Circle at left

Date	Mintage	Good	VG	F	VF	XF
ND(1678-1742) Rare	—	—	—	—	—	—

KM# 787 MUN

4.5000 g., Cast Copper Or Bronze **Rev:** 2 circles at bottom

Date	Mintage	Good	VG	F	VF	XF
ND(1678-1742) Rare	—	—	—	—	—	—

KM# 788 MUN

4.5000 g., Cast Copper Or Bronze **Rev:** Crescent at bottom

Date	Mintage	Good	VG	F	VF	XF
ND(1678-1742) Rare	—	—	—	—	—	—

KM# 789 MUN

4.5000 g., Cast Copper Or Bronze **Rev:** Circle at right, crescent at left

Date	Mintage	Good	VG	F	VF	XF
ND(1678-1742) Rare	—	—	—	—	—	—

KM# 790 MUN

4.5000 g., Cast Copper Or Bronze **Rev:** Vertical line at bottom

Date	Mintage	Good	VG	F	VF	XF
ND(1678-1742) Rare	—	—	—	—	—	—

SONG (SONG DO KWAL LI YONG)

(Song Do is another name for Kae Song)

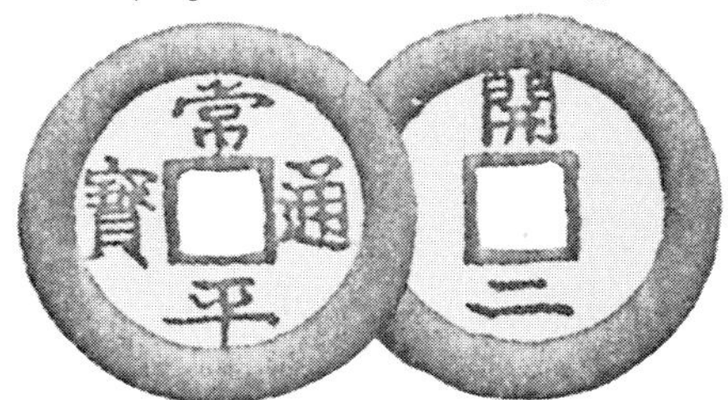

KM# 806 2 MUN

Cast Copper, 32 mm. **Rev:** "Kae" at top, "I" (2) at bottom **Note:** Weight varies 8.00-9.00 grams.

Date	Mintage	Good	VG	F	VF	XF
ND(1679-1752)	—	5.00	10.00	20.00	40.00	—

KM# 806a 2 MUN

Cast Copper, 31 mm. **Rev:** Star at lower left **Note:** Weight varies 8.00-9.00 grams.

Date	Mintage	Good	VG	F	VF	XF
ND(1679-1752)	—	—	—	—	—	—

KM# 806b 2 MUN

Cast Copper, 30 mm. **Rev:** Star at lower left **Note:** Weight varies 8.00-9.00 grams.

Date	Mintage	Good	VG	F	VF	XF
ND(1679-1752)	—	—	—	—	—	—

KM# 807 2 MUN

Cast Copper **Rev:** Dot at right **Note:** Weight varies 8.00-9.00 grams.

Date	Mintage	Good	VG	F	VF	XF
ND(1679-1752)	—	7.00	10.00	13.00	20.00	—

KM# 808 2 MUN

Cast Copper **Rev:** Circle at right **Note:** Weight varies 8.00-9.00 grams.

Date	Mintage	Good	VG	F	VF	XF
ND(1679-1752)	—	7.00	10.00	13.00	20.00	—

KM# 809 2 MUN

Cast Copper **Rev:** Circle at right, crescent at left **Note:** Weight varies 8.00-9.00 grams.

Date	Mintage	Good	VG	F	VF	XF
ND(1679-1752)	—	7.00	10.00	13.00	20.00	—

KM# A809 2 MUN

Cast Copper **Rev:** Circle at right, dot at left **Note:** Weight varies 8.00-9.00 grams.

Date	Mintage	Good	VG	F	VF	XF
ND(1679-1752)	—	—	—	—	—	—

KM# 810 2 MUN

Cast Copper **Rev:** "Il" (1) at right **Note:** Weight varies 8.00-9.00 grams.

Date	Mintage	Good	VG	F	VF	XF
ND(1679-1752)	—	31.25	65.00	100	155	—

KM# 811 2 MUN

Cast Copper **Rev:** Vertical line at right **Note:** Weight varies 8.00-9.00 grams.

Date	Mintage	Good	VG	F	VF	XF
ND(1679-1752)	—	5.00	12.00	22.00	30.00	—

KM# 811a 2 MUN

Cast Copper **Rev:** Star at upper right **Note:** Weight varies 8.00-9.00 grams.

Date	Mintage	Good	VG	F	VF	XF
ND(1679-1752)	—	—	—	—	—	—

KM# 812 2 MUN

Cast Copper **Rev:** Vertical line at left **Note:** Weight varies 8.00-9.00 grams.

Date	Mintage	Good	VG	F	VF	XF
ND(1679-1752)	—	48.00	80.00	120	210	—

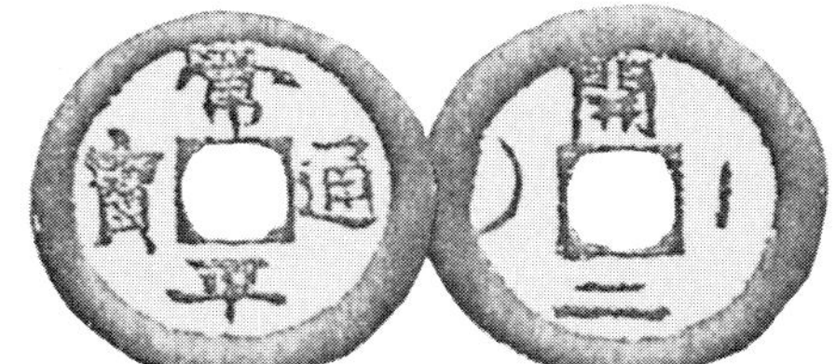

KM# 813 2 MUN

Cast Copper **Rev:** Vertical line at right, crescent at left **Note:** Weight varies 8.00-9.00 grams.

Date	Mintage	Good	VG	F	VF	XF
ND(1679-1752)	—	20.00	39.00	80.00	130	—

WONJU TOWNSHIP MILITARY OFFICE

(Won Ju Kwal Li Yong)

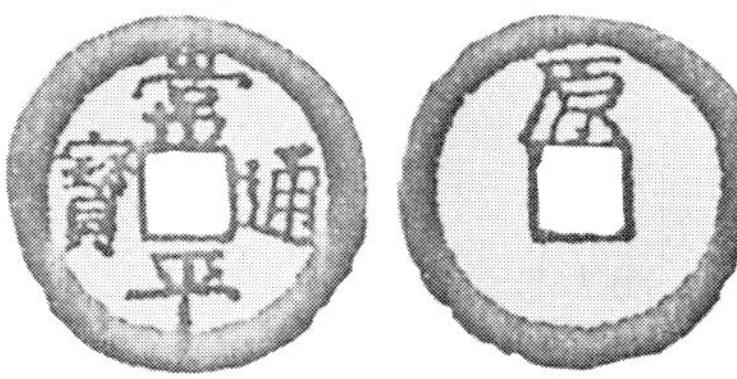

KM# 859 MUN

4.5000 g., Cast Copper **Rev:** "Won" at top **Note:** Large characters.

Date	Mintage	Good	VG	F	VF	XF
ND(1678) Rare	—	—	—	—	—	—

P'YONGAN PROVINCIAL OFFICE

(P'yong An Kam Yong)

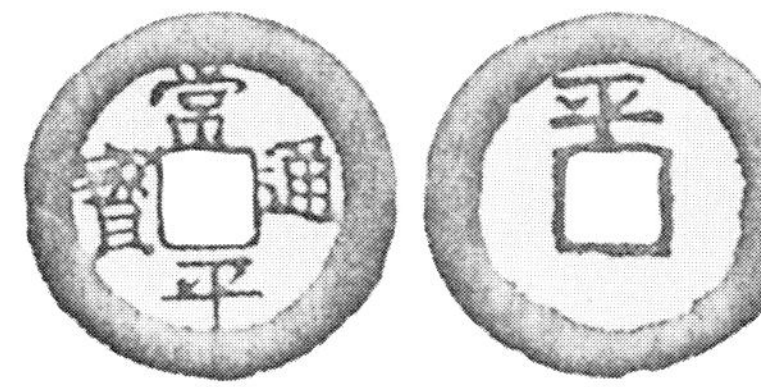

KM# 913 MUN

4.5000 g., Cast Copper **Rev:** "P'yong" at top

Date	Mintage	Good	VG	F	VF	XF
ND(1678-95) Rare	—	—	—	—	—	—

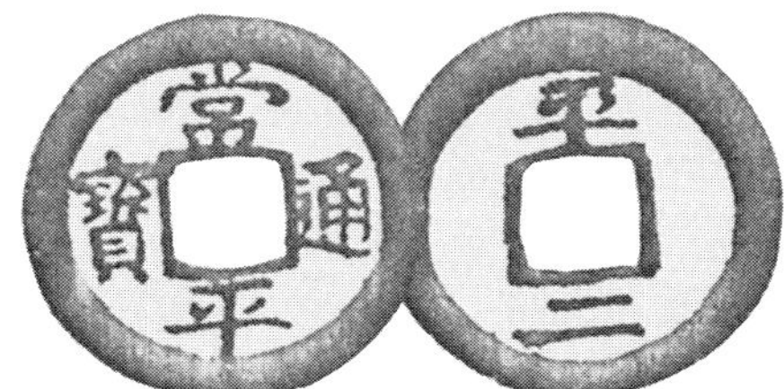

KM# 925 2 MUN

Cast Copper **Rev:** "P'yong" at top, "I" (2) at bottom **Note:** Weight varies 8.00-9.00 grams.

Date	Mintage	Good	VG	F	VF	XF
ND(1679-1742)	—	5.00	8.00	10.00	13.00	—

P'YONGAN MILITARY FORT

(P'yong An Pyong Yong)

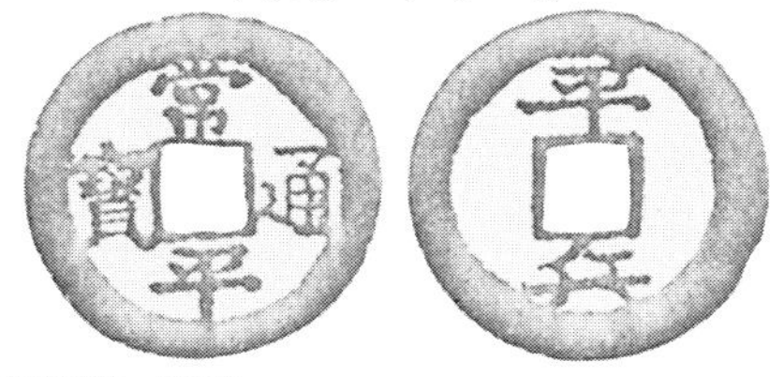

KM# 971 MUN

4.5000 g., Cast Copper **Rev:** "P'yong" at top, "Pyong" at bottom

Date	Mintage	Good	VG	F	VF	XF
ND(1678) Rare	—	—	—	—	—	—

KM# 972 2 MUN

Cast Copper **Rev:** "P'yong" at top, "Pyong" at bottom, "I" (2) at right **Note:** Weight varies: 8.00-9.00 grams.

Date	Mintage	Good	VG	F	VF	XF
ND(1679)	—	85.00	125	175	250	—

KYONGSANG PROVINCIAL OFFICE

(Kyong Sang Kam Yong)

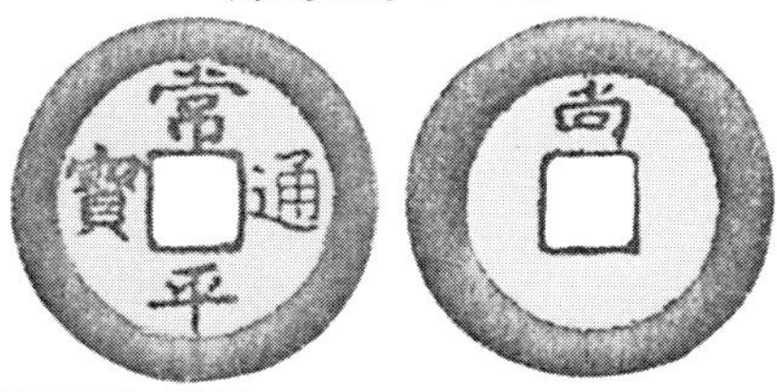

KM# 1010 MUN

4.5000 g., Cast Copper **Rev:** "Sang" at top

Date	Mintage	Good	VG	F	VF	XF
ND(1695-1727) Rare	—	—	—	—	—	—

KM# 1011 2 MUN

Cast Copper **Rev:** "Sang" at top, "I" (2) a t bottom **Note:** Weight varies 8.00-9.00 grams.

Date	Mintage	Good	VG	F	VF	XF
ND(1695-1742)	—	5.00	7.00	10.00	13.00	—

KYONGSANG NAVAL STATION

(Kyong Sang Su Yong)

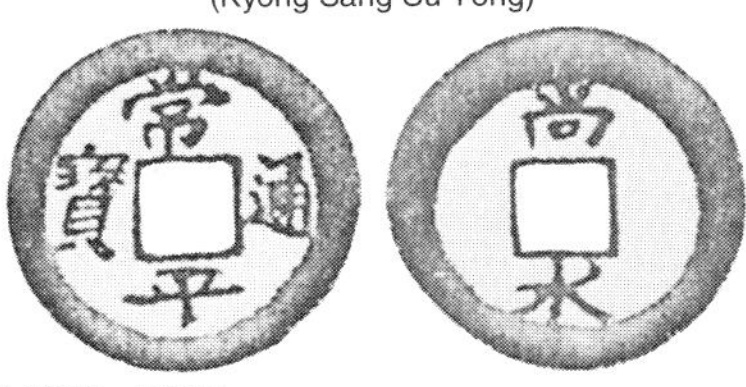

KM# 1037 MUN

4.5000 g., Cast Copper **Rev:** "Sang" at top, "Su" at bottom

Date	Mintage	Good	VG	F	VF	XF
ND(1695-1742) Rare	—	—	—	—	—	—

KM# 1038 2 MUN

Cast Copper **Rev:** "Sang" at top, "Su" at bottom, "I" (2) at right **Note:** Weight varies 8.00-9.00 grams.

Date	Mintage	Good	VG	F	VF	XF
ND(1695-1742) Rare	—	—	—	—	—	—

KYONGSANG RIGHT NAVAL BASE

(Kyong Sang U Yong)

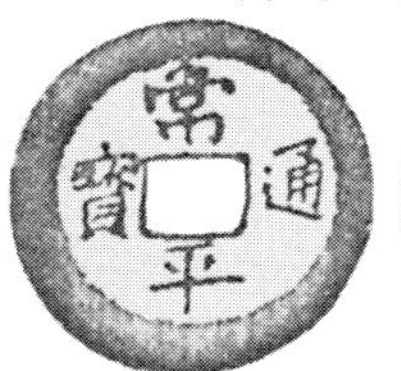

KM# 1039 MUN

4.5000 g., Cast Copper **Rev:** "Sang" at top, "U" at bottom

Date	Mintage	Good	VG	F	VF	XF
ND(1695-1742) Rare	—	—	—	—	—	—

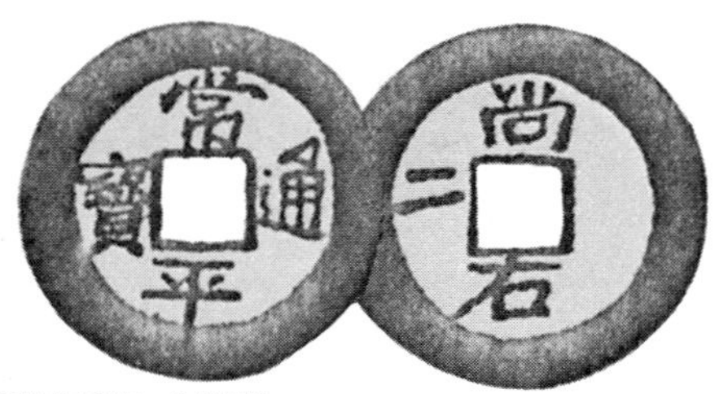

KM# 1040 2 MUN
Cast Copper **Rev:** "Sang" at top, "U" at bottom, "I" (2) at left **Note:** Weight varies 8.00-9.00 grams.

Date	Mintage	Good	VG	F	VF	XF
ND(1695-1742) Rare	—	—	—	—	—	—

KYONGSANG LEFT NAVAL BASE
(Kyong Sang Chwa Yong)

KM# 1041 MUN
4.5000 g., Cast Copper **Rev:** "Sang" at top, "Chwa" at bottom

Date	Mintage	Good	VG	F	VF	XF
ND(1695-1742) Rare	—	—	—	—	—	—

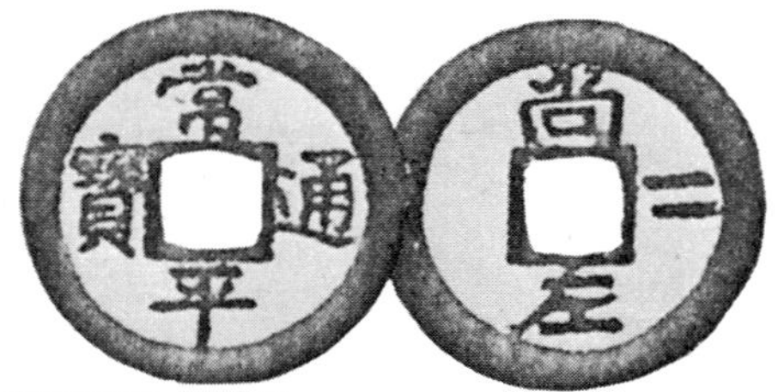

KM# 1042 2 MUN
Cast Copper **Rev:** "Sang" at top, "Chwa" at bottom, "I" (2) at right **Note:** Weight varies 8.00-9.00 grams.

Date	Mintage	Good	VG	F	VF	XF
ND(1695-1742) Rare	—	—	—	—	—	—

KM# 1043 2 MUN
Cast Copper **Rev:** "Sang" at top, "Chwa" at bottom, "I" (2) at left **Note:** Weight varies 8.00-9.00 grams.

Date	Mintage	Good	VG	F	VF	XF
ND(1695-1742) Rare	—	—	—	—	—	—

KM# 1043a 2 MUN
Cast Copper **Rev:** Star at lower left **Note:** Weight varies 8.00-9.00 grams.

Date	Mintage	Good	VG	F	VF	XF
ND(1695-1742)	—	—	—	—	—	—

CHOLLA PROVINCIAL OFFICE
(Chol La Kam Yong)

KM# 1044 MUN
4.5000 g., Cast Copper **Rev:** "Chon" at top

Date	Mintage	Good	VG	F	VF	XF
ND(1682-1727) Rare	—	—	—	—	—	—

KM# 1045 2 MUN
Cast Copper **Rev:** "Chon" at top, "I" (2) at bottom **Note:** Weight varies: 8.00-9.00 grams. Size varies: 29-32 mm.

Date	Mintage	Good	VG	F	VF	XF
ND(1679-95)	—	4.00	7.00	10.00	15.00	—

KM# 1045a 2 MUN
Cast Copper, 30 mm. **Rev:** Star at lower right **Note:** Weight varies: 8.00-9.00 grams.

Date	Mintage	Good	VG	F	VF	XF
ND(1679-95)	—	—	—	—	—	—

KM# 1046 2 MUN
Cast Copper, 27 mm. **Note:** Weight varies: 8.00-9.00 grams. Reduced size.

Date	Mintage	Good	VG	F	VF	XF
ND(1679-95)	—	4.00	10.00	15.00	20.00	—

CHOLLA MILITARY FORT
(Chol La Pyong Yong)

KM# 1072 MUN
4.5000 g., Cast Copper **Rev:** "Chon" at top, "Pyong" at bottom

Date	Mintage	Good	VG	F	VF	XF
ND(1678) Rare	—	—	—	—	—	—

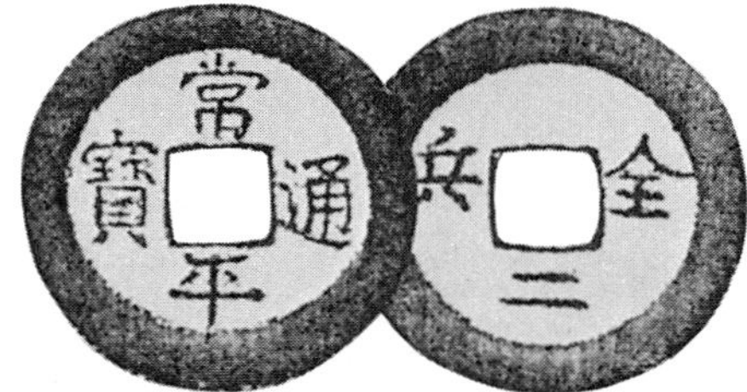

KM# 1073 2 MUN
Cast Copper **Rev:** "Chon" at right, "Pyong" at left, "I" (2) at bottom **Note:** Weight varies 8.00-9.00 grams.

Date	Mintage	Good	VG	F	VF	XF
ND(1679-1742) Rare	—	—	—	—	—	—

CHOLLA RIGHT NAVAL BASE
(Choi La U Yong)

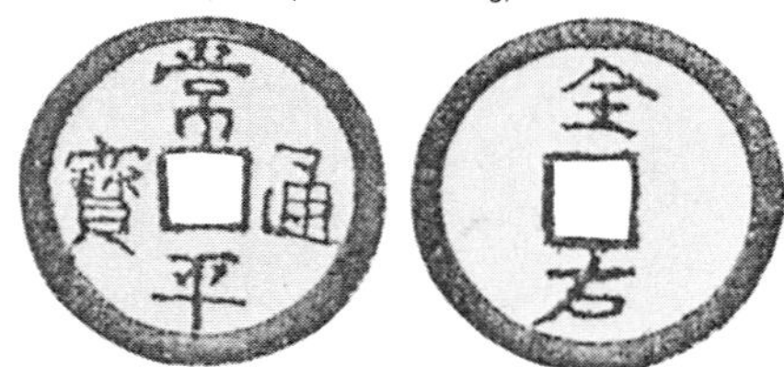

KM# 1074 MUN
4.5000 g., Cast Copper **Rev:** "Chon" at top, "U" at bottom

Date	Mintage	Good	VG	F	VF	XF
ND(1678) Rare	—	—	—	—	—	—

CHOLLA LEFT NAVAL BASE
(Chol La Chwa Yong)

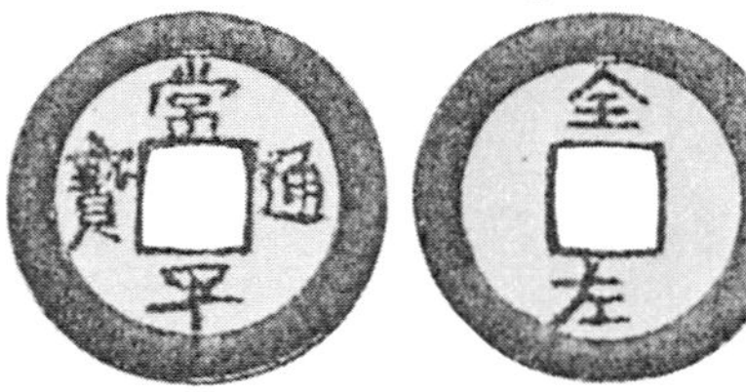

KM# 1075 MUN
4.5000 g., Cast Copper **Rev:** "Chon" at top, "Chwa" at bottom

Date	Mintage	Good	VG	F	VF	XF
ND(1678) Rare	—	—	—	—	—	—

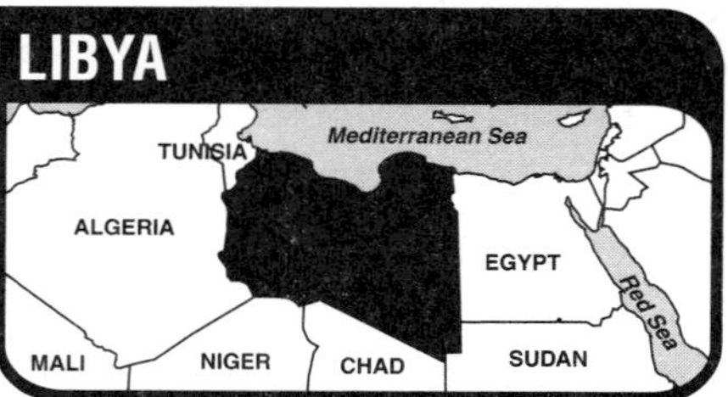

Libya has been subjected to foreign rule throughout most of its history, various parts of it having been ruled by the Phoenicians, Carthaginians, Vandals, Byzantines, Greeks, Romans, Egyptians, and in the following centuries the Arabs' language, culture and religion were adopted by the indigenous population. Libya was conquered by the Ottoman Turks in 1553, and remained under Turkish domination, becoming a Turkish vilayet in 1835, until it was conquered by Italy and made into a colony in 1911. The name 'Libya', the ancient Greek name for North Africa exclusive of Egypt, was given to the colony by Italy in1934

TITLES

المملكة الليبية

al-Mamlaka(t) al-Libiya(t)

الجمهورية الليبية

al-Jomhuriya(t) al-Arabiya(t) al-Libiya(t)

TRIPOLI

Tripoli (formerly Ottoman Empire Area of antique Tripolitania, 700-146 B.C.), the capital city and chief port of the Libyan Arab Jamahiriya, is situated on the North African coast on a promontory stretching out into the Mediterranean Sea. It was probably founded by Phoenicians from Sicily, but was under Roman control from 146 B.C. until 450 A.D. Invasion by Vandals and conquest by the Byzantines preceded the Arab invasions of the 11th century which, by destroying the commercial centers of Sabratha and Leptis, greatly enhanced the importance of Tripoli, an importance maintained through periods of Norman and Spanish control. Tripoli fell to the Turks, who made it the capital of the vilayet of Tripoli in 1551 and remained in their hands until 1911, when it was occupied by the Italians who made it the capital of the Italian province of Tripolitania. British forces entered the city on Jan. 23, 1943, and administered it until establishment of the independent Kingdom of Libya on Dec. 24, 1951.

RULERS
Ottoman, until 1911
refer to Turkey

MINT NAMES

طرابلس

Tarabalus

طرابلس غرب

Tarabalus Gharb = (Tripoli West)

The appellation *west* serving to distinguish it from Tripoli in Lebanon, which had been an Ottoman Mint in the 16th century. On some of the copper coins, *Gharb* is omitted; several types come both with and without *Gharb*. The mint closed between the 28th and 29th year of the reign of Mahmud II.

MONETARY SYSTEM

The monetary system of Tripoli was confused and is poorly understood. Theoretically, 40 Para were equal to one Piastre, but due to the debasement of the silver coinage, later issues are virtually pure copper, though the percentage of alloy varies radically even within a given year. The 10 Para and 20 Para pieces were a little heavier than the copper Paras, with which they could easily be confounded, except that the copper Paras were generally thicker, and bear simpler inscriptions. It is not known how many of the coppers were tariffed to the debased Piastre and its fractions. Some authorities consider the copper pieces to be Beshliks (5 Para coins).

The gold coinage came in two denominations, the Zeri Mahbub (2.4-2.5 g), and the Sultani Altin (3.3-3.4 g). The ratio of the billon Piastres to the gold coins fluctuated from day to day.

BARBARY STATE

Murad IV

OTTOMAN COINAGE

KM# 2 MANGIR
Copper **Note:** Size varies 13-16mm.

Date	Mintage	VG	F	VF	XF	Unc
AH1039	—	31.25	65.00	—	—	—
AH1041	—	31.25	65.00	—	—	—

KM# 1 SULTANI

Gold **Note:** Weight varies 3.40-3.50 grams. Size varies 22-23mm.

Date	Mintage	VG	F	VF	XF	Unc
AH1032	—	450	650	775	—	—
AH1033	—	450	650	775	—	—

Ibrahim

OTTOMAN COINAGE

KM# 3 MANGIR

Copper, 12 mm.

Date	Mintage	VG	F	VF	XF	Unc
AH(10)49	—	31.25	65.00	—	—	—

KM# 4 SULTANI

Gold **Note:** Weight varies 2.90-3.40 grams. Size varies 28-29mm.

Date	Mintage	VG	F	VF	XF	Unc
AH1049	—	450	650	775	—	—
AH1053	—	450	650	775	—	—

Mehmed IV

OTTOMAN COINAGE

KM# 7 MANGIR

Copper **Note:** Size varies 11-1/2-12-1/2mm.

Date	Mintage	VG	F	VF	XF	Unc
ND 6-pointed star	—	25.00	37.50	—	—	—
ND Hexagram ++ 40	—	25.00	37.50	—	—	—
AH(10)94	—	25.00	37.50	—	—	—
AH(10)95	—	31.25	50.00	—	—	—
AH(10)97	—	25.00	37.50	—	—	—
AH(10)98	—	25.00	37.50	—	—	—

KM# 8 PARA

Copper **Note:** Weight varies 2.46-3.60 grams. Size varies 13-15mm.

Date	Mintage	VG	F	VF	XF	Unc
AH(1)076	—	25.00	43.75	65.00	—	—
AH(10)78	—	25.00	43.75	65.00	—	—
AH(10)83	—	25.00	43.75	65.00	—	—
AH(10)84	—	25.00	43.75	65.00	—	—
AH(10)87	—	25.00	43.75	65.00	—	—
AH(10)91	—	25.00	43.75	65.00	—	—
AH(10)94	—	25.00	43.75	65.00	—	—

KM# 9.1 5 PARA (Beshlik)

1.4100 g., Silver, 18 mm.

Date	Mintage	VG	F	VF	XF	Unc
AH1059	—	65.00	80.00	100	145	—

KM# 9.2 5 PARA (Beshlik)

1.5000 g., Silver

Date	Mintage	VG	F	VF	XF	Unc
AH1083	—	65.00	80.00	100	145	—

KM# 10 1/2 SULTANI

1.6000 g., Gold, 17 mm.

Date	Mintage	VG	F	VF	XF	Unc
AH1078	—	100	165	325	525	—
AH1098	—	100	165	325	525	—

KM# 11 SULTANI

3.4000 g., Gold, 23 mm.

Date	Mintage	VG	F	VF	XF	Unc
AH1078	—	—	400	575	850	—

Suleyman II

OTTOMAN COINAGE

KM# 13 MANGIR

Copper, 12-1/2 mm.

Date	Mintage	VG	F	VF	XF	Unc
AH(1)102 8-pointed star	—	37.50	55.00	100	—	—

KM# 18 SULTANI

3.3900 g., Gold **Note:** Size varies 22-24mm.

Date	Mintage	VG	F	VF	XF	Unc
AH1099	—	—	800	1,350	—	—

Mustafa II

OTTOMAN COINAGE

KM# 20 MANGIR

Copper **Note:** Weight varies 1.15-1.35 grams. Size varies 12-13mm.

Date	Mintage	VG	F	VF	XF	Unc
AH118 Error for 1108	—	32.00	44.00	65.00	95.00	—

KM# 21 5 PARA (Beshlik)

1.0000 g., Billon, 19 mm.

Date	Mintage	VG	F	VF	XF	Unc
AH1108	—	100	190	270	—	—

KM# 22 10 PARA

1.5300 g., Copper, 23 mm.

Date	Mintage	VG	F	VF	XF	Unc
AH1107	—	110	210	—	—	—

LIEGE

Situated along the Meuse, Ourthe, and Sambre rivers, Liege was a bishopric which geographically completely divided the Austro-Spanish Netherlands.

Traditionally founded in the 7th Century by St. Lambert, Liege became a bishopric in 721 and by1000, under Bishop Notga, thrived as an intellectual hub of the west and center for Mosan art. Internal struggles between citizens' guilds and prince-bishops did not weaken Liege to self-destruction. She resisted two sacks by Charles the Bold during 15th Century Burgundian domination of the Netherlands and completely rebuilt the city upon his death in 1477.

Liege was bombarded by the French in 1691, and during the War of Spanish Succession was taken by the English in 1702. After the death of Johann Theodor (Bishop, 1744-1763) there were no coin issues of the bishops. The only coin issues were the *Sede Vacante* issues of 1763, 1771, 1784 and 1792.

Ultimately the rule of the nobles ended in 1789 by a bloodless revolution which was followed by her annexation to France in 1795 and assignment with the rest of Belgium to the Netherlands in 1815.

Since Belgium's independence in 1830, Liege is again recognized as a major river port, rail center and cosmopolitan hub for art, education and industry.

RULERS

Ernest of Bavaria, 1581-1612
Ferdinand of Bavaria, 1612-1650
Maximilian Henry of Bavaria, 1650-1688
Sede Vacante, 1688
John Louis Eldern, 1688-1694
Sede Vacante, 1694
Joseph Clement of Bavaria, 1694-1723

MONETARY SYSTEM

6 Sols = 1 Escalin
48 Sols = 1 Patagon

BISHOPRIC

STANDARD COINAGE

KM# 1 6 SOLS

Copper **Ruler:** Ernest **Obv:** Capped ornate four-fold arms on crossed sword and crozier **Obv. Legend:** ER NES BA • DV EP LEO **Rev:** Monument divides two shields **Rev. Legend:** AVDIATVR • ALTERA • PARS **Edge:** Plain **Mint:** Liege

Date	Mintage	VG	F	VF	XF	Unc
ND(1581-1612)	—	25.00	50.00	95.00	225	—

KM# 2 6 SOLS

Copper **Ruler:** Ernest **Obv:** Monument divides two shields **Obv. Legend:** ERNEST • BA • DVX • EPS • LEOD **Rev:** Capped oval ornate four-fold arms on crossed sword and crozier **Rev. Legend:** A VDIAT VR • ALT PAR :/: S **Edge:** Plain **Mint:** Liege

Date	Mintage	VG	F	VF	XF	Unc
ND(1581-1612)	—	25.00	50.00	95.00	225	—

KM# 3 6 SOLS (6 Sous - 1/4 Liara)

Copper **Ruler:** Ernest **Obv:** Capped ornate arms on crossed sword and scepter **Obv. Legend:** ER NES BA • DV EP LE O **Rev:** Monument between two shields **Rev. Legend:** AVDIATVR • ALTERA • PARS **Edge:** Plain **Mint:** Liege

Date	Mintage	VG	F	VF	XF	Unc
ND(1581-1612)	—	25.00	50.00	95.00	225	—

KM# 4 6 SOLS (6 Sous - 1/4 Liara)

Copper **Ruler:** Ernest **Obv:** Ornate capped four-fold arms on crossed sword and crozier **Obv. Legend:** A VDIAT VR • ALT PAR •/: S **Rev:** Monument between two shields **Rev. Legend:** ERNEST • BA • DVX • EPS • LEOD **Edge:** Plain **Mint:** Liege

Date	Mintage	VG	F	VF	XF	Unc
ND(1581-1612)	—	25.00	50.00	95.00	225	—

KM# A6 12 SOLS (Sous - 1/ 2 Liard)

Copper **Ruler:** Ernest **Obv:** Four-fold arms on long cross divides legend **Obv. Legend:** ERNE BA x DV X x EPS LEOD **Rev:** Monument divides value XII - SVS **Rev. Legend:** AVDIATVR x ALTERA x PARS xxx **Edge:** Plain **Mint:** Liege **Note:** Varieties in denomination exist: SVS, SOV, SOS, SO, SOVS.

Date	Mintage	VG	F	VF	XF	Unc
ND(1581-1612)	—	37.50	75.00	150	325	—

KM# 20 VI (6) SOLS (1/4 Liard)

Copper **Ruler:** Ferdinand **Obv:** Capped four-fold arms on crossed sword and scepter **Obv. Legend:** (Rosette) FERDINAN • ELEC • COL • EPIS • LEO **Rev:** Monument divides two shield and denomination V-I **Rev. Legend:** V • DVX • BAVARI • MAR • FRANCHT **Mint:** Liege

Date	Mintage	VG	F	VF	XF	Unc
ND(1612-50)	—	65.00	115	225	450	—

KM# 5 VIII (8) SOLS (1/3 Liard)

Copper **Ruler:** Ernest **Obv:** Capped four-fold arms **Obv. Legend:** ERNEST • BAVA • DVX • EPS • LEOD • **Rev:** Cross with fleur de lis at ends divides legend **Rev. Legend:** DVX • BVLL • M • FR • • C • LO(S) • **Mint:** Liege

Date	Mintage	VG	F	VF	XF	Unc
ND(1581-1612)	—	43.75	80.00	155	350	—

KM# 21 XII (12) SOLS (1/2 Liard)

Copper **Ruler:** Ferdinand **Obv:** Capped Bavarian arms **Obv. Legend:** FERD(I) • D • G • EP • LEO(D) **Rev:** Three shields below crown, denomination X-II divided at bottom **Mint:** Liege

Date	Mintage	VG	F	VF	XF	Unc
ND(1612-50)	—	13.00	25.00	50.00	120	—

KM# 22 XII (12) SOLS (1/2 Liard)

Copper **Ruler:** Ferdinand **Rev:** Without denomination

Date	Mintage	VG	F	VF	XF	Unc
ND(1612-50)	—	37.50	75.00	150	325	—

KM# 23 XII (12) SOLS (1/2 Liard)

Copper **Ruler:** Ferdinand **Obv:** Capped four-fold arms divide denomination X-II **Obv. Legend:** FERDINAN • ELEC • COL • EP • LE(O) • **Rev:** Large crown above three shields, date divided at bottom **Rev. Legend:** •:• MAR • FRANCHI • COMES • HORNE • (Z) **Mint:** Liege

Date	Mintage	VG	F	VF	XF	Unc
1614	—	13.00	25.00	50.00	120	—
1615	—	13.00	25.00	50.00	120	—
ND	—	13.00	25.00	50.00	120	—

KM# 55 1/3 LIARD

Copper **Ruler:** Ferdinand **Obv:** Crowned FB divides date **Obv. Legend:** (Monument) FERD • PR • ELEC(T) • COL • EP • LEOD **Rev:** Crowned arms on fleur de lis cross **Rev. Legend:** SVR • DVX • BVL • COMES • LOSS **Mint:** Liege

Date	Mintage	VG	F	VF	XF	Unc
1615	—	13.00	25.00	50.00	120	—

KM# 6 1/2 LIARD

Copper **Ruler:** Ernest **Obv:** Bust of Ernest left **Obv. Legend:** ERNEST • BAVA • DVX • EPS • LEOD • **Rev:** Capped four-fold arms, legend divided by cap **Rev. Legend:** DVX • • BVLL • • M • FR • • C • LO(S) • **Mint:** Liege

Date	Mintage	VG	F	VF	XF	Unc
ND(1581-1612)	—	37.50	75.00	150	325	—

KM# 7 1/2 LIARD

Copper **Ruler:** Ernest **Obv:** Bust of Ernest left **Obv. Legend:** (Acorn) • ERNESTVS • DVX • BAVARIE **Rev:** Small shield above capped four-fold arms **Rev. Legend:** COMES • LOSSENSIS **Mint:** Maeseyck

Date	Mintage	VG	F	VF	XF	Unc
ND(1581-1612)	—	37.50	75.00	150	325	—

KM# 8 1/2 LIARD

Copper **Ruler:** Ernest **Obv:** Bust of Ernest left **Obv. Legend:** (Acorn) ERNESTVS • DVX • BAVARIE **Rev:** Capped five-fold arms, legend divided by cap **Rev. Legend:** COMES • LOSSENSIS **Mint:** Maeseyck

Date	Mintage	VG	F	VF	XF	Unc
ND(1581-1612)	—	37.50	75.00	150	325	—

KM# A9 1/2 LIARD

Copper **Ruler:** Ernest **Obv:** Capped four-fold arms **Obv. Legend:** (Lion) ERNEST • BAVA (monument) DV X • D • G • EPIC(C) **Rev:** Bust of Ernest left **Rev. Legend:** (Lion) LEODIE • DVX • BVLL • CO • LOS(S) • **Edge:** Plain **Mint:** Liege

Date	Mintage	VG	F	VF	XF	Unc
ND(1581-1612)	—	40.00	80.00	155	350	—

KM# 9 1/2 LIARD

Copper **Ruler:** Ernest **Obv:** Crowned laureate four-fold arms **Rev:** Crowned laureate arms of Bouillon **Rev. Legend:** BVL LONEN SIS **Edge:** Plain

Date	Mintage	VG	F	VF	XF	Unc
ND(1581-1612)	—	43.75	90.00	175	375	—

KM# 27 1/2 LIARD

Copper **Ruler:** Ferdinand **Obv:** Bust of Ferdinand left **Obv. Legend:** (Branch) FERDI • D • G • EP • LEO • D • BVL **Rev:** Crowned five-fold arms **Rev. Legend:** • COMES • LOSSENSIS •

Date	Mintage	VG	F	VF	XF	Unc
ND(1612-50)	—	50.00	95.00	180	375	—

KM# 28 1/2 LIARD

Copper **Ruler:** Ferdinand **Obv:** Bust of Ferdinand left **Obv. Legend:** (Rosette) FERDINAND • D • G • EP • LEO •

Date	Mintage	VG	F	VF	XF	Unc
ND(1612-50)	—	50.00	95.00	180	375	—

KM# 24 1/2 LIARD

Copper **Ruler:** Ferdinand **Obv:** Bust of Ferdinand left **Obv. Legend:** (Acorn) FERDINANDVS • DVX • BAVARIE **Rev:** Capped five-fold arms **Rev. Legend:** COMES LOSSENSIS **Mint:** Maeseyck

Date	Mintage	VG	F	VF	XF	Unc
ND(1612-50)	—	50.00	95.00	180	375	—

KM# 25 1/2 LIARD

Copper **Ruler:** Ferdinand **Obv:** Capped ornate fivd-fold arms on crossed sword and crozier **Obv. Legend:** FERD D • G • EP • LEOD **Rev:** Capped F-B divided by monument **Rev. Legend:** DV . BV . MAR . FRANC . CO . LO . **Mint:** Liege

Date	Mintage	VG	F	VF	XF	Unc
ND(1612-50)	—	43.75	80.00	155	350	—

KM# 26 1/2 LIARD

Copper **Ruler:** Ferdinand **Obv:** Capped five-fold arms on crossed sword and crozier **Obv. Legend:** FERD D • G • EP LEOD • **Rev:** Capped F ★ B, monument below **Rev. Legend:** DV . BV . MAR . FRA . CO . LO . H **Mint:** Liege

Date	Mintage	VG	F	VF	XF	Unc
1641	—	19.00	37.50	70.00	150	—
ND	—	19.00	37.50	70.00	150	—

KM# 70 1/2 LIARD

Copper **Ruler:** Maximilian Henry **Obv:** Crowned shield, titles of Maximilian **Rev:** Crown on sword and scepter above shield

Date	Mintage	VG	F	VF	XF	Unc
ND(1650-88)	—	13.00	25.00	50.00	120	—

KM# 14 LIARD

Copper, 28 mm. **Ruler:** Ernest **Obv:** Capped bust of Ernest left **Obv. Legend:** • ERNESTVS • D • G • ARCHIEPIS • COL(L) **Rev:** Capped four-fold arms **Rev. Legend:** EPIS • LEO DIE (monument) N • (monument) • V • BAVA(RI) • DVX **Mint:** Liege

Date	Mintage	VG	F	VF	XF	Unc
ND(1581-1612)	—	19.00	37.50	70.00	150	—

KM# 10 LIARD

Copper **Ruler:** Ernest **Obv:** Larger capped bust of Ernest left **Obv. Legend:** (Monument) ERNESTV(S) • D • (monument) G • ARCHIEPIS • COL **Rev:** Capped four-fold arms **Rev. Legend:** EPIS • LEO DIE(N) • V • BAV(A) RIE • DVX **Mint:** Liege

Date	Mintage	VG	F	VF	XF	Unc
ND(1581-1612)	—	19.00	37.50	70.00	150	—

KM# 12 LIARD

Copper **Ruler:** Ernest **Obv:** Capped bust of Ernest left **Obv. Legend:** ERNESTVS • BAVA • DVX • D • GRA • EIP **Rev:** Capped four-fold arms betweem two dots, small shield at top **Rev. Legend:** LEODIEN • DVX • BVLL • CO • LOSSE **Mint:** Maeseyck

Date	Mintage	VG	F	VF	XF	Unc
ND(1581-1612) Acorn	—	15.00	31.25	55.00	130	—

KM# 13 LIARD

Copper **Ruler:** Ernest **Obv:** Capped bust of Ernest left **Obv. Legend:** ERNESTVS • DVX • BAVARIE **Rev:** Capped five-fold arms, legend divided by cap **Rev. Legend:** COMES • LOSSENSIS **Mint:** Maeseyck

Date	Mintage	VG	F	VF	XF	Unc
ND(1581-1612) Acorn	—	13.00	25.00	47.50	105	—

KM# 11 LIARD

Copper **Ruler:** Ernest **Obv:** Capped four-fold arms **Obv. Legend:** (Lion) ERNESTVS • BAVA (monument) DVX • D • G • EPISC • CO **Rev:** Capped bust of Ernest left **Rev. Legend:** (Lion) LEODIENSIS • DVX • BVLL • CO • LOS **Edge:** Plain **Mint:** Liege

Date	Mintage	VG	F	VF	XF	Unc
ND(1581-1612)	—	19.00	37.50	70.00	150	—

KM# 15 LIARD

Copper **Ruler:** Ernest **Obv:** Capped bust of Ernest left **Obv. Legend:** (Monument) ERNESTVS • D • (monument) G • ARCHIEPIS • COL **Rev:** Capped four-fold arms divide date **Rev. Legend:** EPIS • LEO DIEN • V • BAVAR • DVX **Mint:** Liege **Note:** Prev. KM#11.

Date	Mintage	VG	F	VF	XF	Unc
1610	—	13.00	25.00	47.50	105	—
1611	—	13.00	25.00	47.50	105	—
1612	—	13.00	25.00	47.50	105	—

KM# A32 LIARD

Copper, 25.5 mm. **Ruler:** Ferdinand **Obv:** Crowned bust to left **Obv. Legend:** FERDINAND. D.G. ARC. COL **Rev:** Crowned four-fold arms of Bavaria-Pfalz **Rev. Legend:** PR. L. ET S. CO. P.R. D. BAV

Date	Mintage	VG	F	VF	XF	Unc
ND	—	10.00	20.00	40.00	90.00	—

KM# 32 LIARD

Copper **Ruler:** Ferdinand **Obv:** Bust of Ferdinand with cap left **Obv. Legend:** • FERDINANDVS • D • G • ARC • COL **Rev:** Capped four-fold arms **Rev. Legend:** • PR • L • ET • S • CO • P • R • D • BAV • **Mint:** Liege

Date	Mintage	VG	F	VF	XF	Unc
ND(1612-50)	—	9.00	19.00	37.50	85.00	—

KM# 33 LIARD

Copper **Ruler:** Ferdinand **Obv:** Bust of Ferdinand left divides legend **Obv. Legend:** • FERDINANDVS • D • G • EPISCO(P) LEO(DI) **Rev:** Capped five-fold arms **Rev. Legend:** • DVX • BVLLONIENSIS •

Date	Mintage	VG	F	VF	XF	Unc
ND(1612-50)	—	9.00	19.00	37.50	85.00	—

KM# 34 LIARD

Copper **Ruler:** Ferdinand **Obv:** Bust of Ferdinand with cap left **Obv. Legend:** ⁜ FERDINAND • D • G • EPISCOPVS • LEODI **Rev. Legend:** • DVX • BVLLONIENSIS • **Mint:** Liege

Date	Mintage	VG	F	VF	XF	Unc
ND(1612-50)	—	9.00	19.00	37.50	85.00	—

KM# 30 LIARD

Copper **Ruler:** Ferdinand **Obv:** Large bust of Ferdinand left **Obv. Legend:** • FERDINANDVS • D • G • EPISCOP • LEODI **Rev:** Capped four-fold arms **Rev. Legend:** FERDINAN ELEC COL EP LEO

Date	Mintage	VG	F	VF	XF	Unc
ND(1612-50) Rare	—	10.00	20.00	40.00	90.00	—

KM# 40 LIARD

Copper **Ruler:** Ferdinand **Obv:** Bust of Ferdinand with cap left **Obv. Legend:** (Branch) FERDINAND • D • G • EP • LEO • D • BVL • **Rev:** Different center shield **Rev. Legend:** • COMES • LOSSENSIS • **Mint:** Hasselt

Date	Mintage	VG	F	VF	XF	Unc
ND(1612-50)	—	10.00	20.00	40.00	90.00	—

KM# 41 LIARD

Copper **Ruler:** Ferdinand **Obv. Legend:** h FERDINAND • D • G • EPISCOPVS • LEOD **Rev. Legend:** • COMES • LOSSENSIS • **Mint:** Hasselt

Date	Mintage	VG	F	VF	XF	Unc
ND(1612-50)	—	10.00	20.00	40.00	90.00	—

KM# 31 LIARD

Copper **Ruler:** Ferdinand **Obv:** Capped four-fold arms **Obv. Legend:** FERDINAN • ELEC • COL • EP(IS) • LEO(D) **Rev:** Crown above three shields, date divided below **Rev. Legend:** •:• MAR • FRANCH(I) • COMES • DE • HORNE **Mint:** Liege

Date	Mintage	VG	F	VF	XF	Unc
1614	—	8.00	15.00	31.25	75.00	—
ND	—	8.00	15.00	31.25	75.00	—

KM# 29 LIARD

Copper, 26 mm. **Ruler:** Ferdinand **Obv:** Bust of Ferdinand left **Obv. Legend:** (Rosette) FERDINAN ELEC COL EP LEO **Rev:** Capped four-fold arms dividing date **Rev. Legend:** EPIS • LEODIEN • V • BAVAR • DVX

Date	Mintage	VG	F	VF	XF	Unc
1617 Rare	—	10.00	20.00	40.00	90.00	—

KM# 38 LIARD

Copper **Ruler:** Ferdinand **Obv:** Bust of Ferdinand with cap left **Obv. Legend:** (Lion) FERDINAND • D • G • EPISCOP • LEO **Rev:** Capped five-fold arms **Rev. Legend:** • DVX • BVLLONIENSIS • **Mint:** Dinant

Date	Mintage	VG	F	VF	XF	Unc
ND(1640)	—	13.00	25.00	47.50	105	—

KM# 39 LIARD

Copper **Ruler:** Ferdinand **Obv:** Bust of Ferdinand with cap left **Obv. Legend:** FERDINAND • D • G • EPIS...LEOD **Rev:** Capped five-fold arms **Rev. Legend:** • DVX • BVLLONIENSIS • **Mint:** Visè

Date	Mintage	VG	F	VF	XF	Unc
ND(1640)	—	25.00	50.00	95.00	225	—

KM# 35 LIARD

Copper **Ruler:** Ferdinand **Obv:** Capped ornate five-fold arms on crossed sword and crozier divides date **Obv. Legend:** FERDINAND • D • G • EP • LEOD(IE) **Rev:** Capped *F*B*, monument below **Rev. Legend:** • DVX • BVL • MAR • FRANCH • CO • LO • HO(R) **Mint:** Liege

Date	Mintage	VG	F	VF	XF	Unc
1641	—	9.00	19.00	35.00	85.00	—
1642	—	9.00	19.00	35.00	85.00	—
1643	—	9.00	19.00	35.00	85.00	—

KM# 36 LIARD

Copper **Ruler:** Ferdinand **Obv:** Crowned five-fold arms on crossed sword and crozier divides date **Obv. Legend:** FERDINAND • D • G • EP • LEO • **Rev. Legend:** DVX • BVL • MAR • FRANCH • CO • LO • (HO) **Mint:** Maeseyck

Date	Mintage	VG	F	VF	XF	Unc
1641	—	9.00	19.00	35.00	85.00	—
1642	—	9.00	19.00	35.00	85.00	—
1643	—	9.00	19.00	35.00	85.00	—

KM# 37 LIARD

Copper **Ruler:** Ferdinand **Obv:** Capped five-fold arms on crossed sword and crozier divides date **Obv. Legend:** FERDINAND • D • G • EP • LEO **Rev:** Capped monument divides F-B **Rev. Legend:** • DVX • BVL • MAR • FRANCHI • CO • LO • **Mint:** Liege

Date	Mintage	VG	F	VF	XF	Unc
1641	—	9.00	19.00	35.00	85.00	—
1642	—	9.00	19.00	35.00	85.00	—
1643	—	9.00	19.00	35.00	85.00	—
ND	—	9.00	19.00	35.00	85.00	—

KM# 42 LIARD

Copper **Ruler:** Ferdinand **Obv:** Capped five-fold arms on crossed sword and crozier divides date **Obv. Legend:** FERDINAND • D • G • EP • LEO • **Rev:** Capped monument divides • F-B • in inner circle **Rev. Legend:** ❉ DVX • BVL • MAR • FRANCH • CO • LO • HO **Mint:** Maeseyck

Date	Mintage	VG	F	VF	XF	Unc
1641	—	9.00	19.00	35.00	85.00	—
1642	—	9.00	19.00	35.00	85.00	—
1643	—	9.00	19.00	35.00	85.00	—
ND	—	9.00	19.00	35.00	85.00	—

KM# 43 LIARD

Copper **Ruler:** Ferdinand **Obv. Legend:** FERDINAND • D • G • EP • LE • **Rev. Legend:** • DVX • BVL • MAR • FRANCH • CO • LO **Mint:** Hasselt

Date	Mintage	VG	F	VF	XF	Unc
1643	—	10.00	20.00	40.00	90.00	—

KM# 71 LIARD

Copper, 26-27 mm. **Ruler:** Maximilian Henry **Obv:** Capped shield on crossed sword **Obv. Legend:** MAXIM • • HENRI : D. G • ARCHI • COL • **Rev:** Crowned four-fold arms **Rev. Legend:** • EPISC • ET • PRINC • LEO : D • BVL • **Mint:** Hasselt

Date	Mintage	VG	F	VF	XF	Unc
ND(1650-88)	—	25.00	50.00	100	240	—

KM# 72 LIARD

Copper, 23 mm. **Ruler:** Maximilian Henry **Obv:** Crowned Bavarian arms **Obv. Legend:** MAXIM • HEN • D • G • ARC • CO(L) **Rev:** Capped shield on crossed sword and scepter **Rev. Legend:** • EPS ET PRINC • LEO(D) • DV(X) • BV • (L) **Mint:** Hasselt

Date	Mintage	VG	F	VF	XF	Unc
ND(1650-88)	—	10.00	20.00	37.50	90.00	—

KM# 73 LIARD

Copper, 23 mm. **Ruler:** Maximilian Henry **Obv:** Crowned Bavarian arms without inner circle, legend with small letters **Obv. Legend:** MAX • HEN • D • G • ARC • COL • **R ev. Legend:** • EP • ET • PRIN • LEO • DVX • BVL

Date	Mintage	VG	F	VF	XF	Unc
ND(1650-88)	—	9.00	19.00	35.00	85.00	—

KM# 66 LIARD

Copper **Ruler:** Maximilian Henry **Obv:** Cap on crossed sword and crozier, date below **Obv. Legend:** MAXIM HENRI • D • G • ARC HI : COL • **Rev:** Capped arms **Rev. Legend:** EPIS • ET • PRIN : LEO • D • BVL **Edge:** Plain **Mint:** Liege

Date	Mintage	VG	F	VF	XF	Unc
1650	—	—	—	—	—	—

KM# 95 LIARD

Copper, 23-24 mm. **Obv:** Bust of St. Lambert left **Obv. Legend:** S • LAMBERT • PATRO • LEOD • **Rev:** Capped arms divides date **Rev. Legend:** (Rosette) DEC • ET • CAP • LEOD • SEDE • VACANTE **Mint:** Liege **Note:** Sede Vacante issue.

Date	Mintage	VG	F	VF	XF	Unc
1688	—	8.00	15.00	31.25	75.00	—

KM# 96 LIARD

Copper **Ruler:** John Louis **Obv:** Capped arms of Jean Louis on crossed sword and crozier, dates above **Obv. Legend:** IO • LVD • D • G • EP • ET • PRIN • LEO(D) • **Rev:** Radial cross of five shields **Rev. Legend:** DVX • BVL • MAR • FRA • COM • LOS • HOR **Mint:** Liege

Date	Mintage	VG	F	VF	XF	Unc
1688	—	8.00	15.00	31.25	75.00	—
1691	—	8.00	15.00	31.25	75.00	—
1692	—	8.00	15.00	31.25	75.00	—

KM# 97 LIARD

Copper **Ruler:** John Louis **Rev:** Shields in cross horizontally aligned **Mint:** Liege

Date	Mintage	VG	F	VF	XF	Unc
1688	—	8.00	15.00	31.25	75.00	—
1691	—	8.00	15.00	31.25	75.00	—
1692	—	8.00	15.00	31.25	75.00	—

KM# 107 LIARD

Copper, 24 mm. **Ruler:** Joseph Clement **Obv:** Crowned four-fold arms **Obv. Legend:** IOSEPH • CLEM • D • G • ARC • COL **Rev:** Without date in angles of shields **Rev. Legend:** * EP • ET • PRI • LEO • DVX • BVL • M • F • C • L • H **Mint:** Liege

Date	Mintage	VG	F	VF	XF	Unc
ND(1694-1723)	—	8.00	15.00	31.25	75.00	—

KM# 106 LIARD

Copper **Obv:** Bust of St. Lambert left **Obv. Legend:** S : LAMBERTTVS • PATRO(NVS) • LEO(D) : **Rev:** Cross of shields, date in angles **Rev. Legend:** ❉ DEC • ET • CAP • LEOD • SEDE • VACANTE **Note:** Sede Vacante issue.

Date	Mintage	VG	F	VF	XF	Unc
1694	—	25.00	50.00	105	250	—

KM# 107a LIARD

Silver, 24 mm. **Ruler:** Joseph Clement **Obv:** Crowned 4-fold arms, titles of Joseph **Rev:** Without date in angles of shields

Date	Mintage	VG	F	VF	XF	Unc
ND(1694-1723)	—	—	—	—	—	—

KM# B36 SOUVERAIN

Silver **Ruler:** Ferdinand **Obv:** Arms on floriate cross with F and B in angles **Obv. Legend:** (Rosette) FERDINANDVS • D • G • ARCHI • COL • PRINC • ELECTOR **Rev. Legend:** EPISC • ET • PRINC • LEO • VTR • BAV • ET • S • BVL • DVX **Edge:** Plain **Mint:** Liege

Date	Mintage	VG	F	VF	XF	Unc
ND(1612-50) Rare	—	—	—	—	—	—

KM# 17 TESTON (15 Sols)

Silver **Ruler:** Ernest **Obv:** Bust of Ernest left **Obv. Legend:** • ERNESTVS • D(E) • G(R) • EPICSOPVS • LEODI(E) **Rev:** Capped shield over crossed sword and crozier divides date, value XV below **Rev. Legend:** (Annulet) DVX † BVLLONIENSIS (annulet) **Edge:** Plain **Mint:** Bouillon

Date	Mintage	VG	F	VF	XF	Unc
1611	—	325	500	875	—	—
161Z	—	325	500	875	—	—

KM# 18.1 2 TESTONS

Silver **Ruler:** Ernest **Obv:** Bust of Ernest left **Obv. Legend:** (Annulet) ERNESTVS • DEI • GR • EPICSOPVS • LEODIE **Rev:** Capped shield on crossed sword and crozier, crozier divides date at upper left **Rev. Legend:** DVX :: BVILLONIENSIS :: **Edge:** Plain **Mint:** Bouillon

Date	Mintage	VG	F	VF	XF	Unc
1611	—	275	475	825	—	—

KM# 18.2 2 TESTONS

Silver **Ruler:** Ernest **Obv:** Bust of Ernest left **Obv. Legend:** (Annulet) ERNESTVS • DEI • GR • EPISC(O)PVS • LEODIE **Rev:** Capped shield over crossed sword and crozier, cap divides date **Rev. Legend:** DVX (annulet) BVILLONIENSIS **Edge:** Plain **Mint:** Bouillon

Date	Mintage	VG	F	VF	XF	Unc
1611	—	250	450	750	—	—
1612	—	250	450	750	—	—

KM# 19 4 TESTONS

Silver **Ruler:** Ernest **Obv:** Bust of Ernest left **Obv. Legend:** (Annulet) ERNESTVS • DEI • GR • EPISCOPVS • LEODIE **Rev:** Capped shield on crossed sword and crozier **Rev. Legend:** DVX (annulet) BVLLONIENSIS **Edge:** Plain **Mint:** Bouillon

Date	Mintage	VG	F	VF	XF	Unc
1611	—	375	625	1,050	—	—

KM# 48 4 TESTONS

Silver **Ruler:** Ferdinand **Obv:** Bust of Ferdinand left **Obv. Legend:** •:• FERDINANDVS • D : G • EPISCOPVS • LEODIE **Rev:** Crowned arms over crossed sword and crozier **Mint:** Bouillon **Note:** Dav. #4290.

Date	Mintage	VG	F	VF	XF	Unc
1613 Rare	—	—	—	—	—	—

KM# 44 TESTON OF 15 PATARDS

Silver **Ruler:** Ferdinand **Obv:** Bust of Ferdinand left **Obv. Legend:** (Annulet) FERDINANDVS • DEI • G • EPISCOPVS • LEODI **Rev:** Capped ornate arms on crossed sword and crozier, value XV below **Rev. Legend:** (Rosette) DVX • BVLLONIENSIS (Rosette) **Edge:** Plain **Mint:** Hasselt

Date	Mintage	VG	F	VF	XF	Unc
1612	—	65.00	115	205	450	—

KM# 45.1 2 TESTON OF 30 PATARDS

Silver **Ruler:** Ferdinand **Obv:** Bust of Ferdinand left, value XXX below **Obv. Legend:** •:• FERDINANDVS • DEI • G • EPISCOPVS • LEODI(E) **Rev:** Capped arms over crossed sword and crozier **Rev. Legend:** •:• DVX • BVLLONIENSIS **Edge:** Plain **Mint:** Bouillon

Date	Mintage	VG	F	VF	XF	Unc
161Z	—	55.00	95.00	155	375	—

KM# 45.2 2 TESTON OF 30 PATARDS

Silver **Ruler:** Ferdinand **Obv:** Bust of Ferdinand left **Obv. Legend:** •:• FERDINANDVS • DEI • G • EPISCOPVS • LEODI(E) **Rev:** Capped ornate arms over crossed sword and crozier **Rev. Legend:** •:• • DVX • BVLLONIENSIS **Edge:** Plain **Mint:** Bouillon

Date	Mintage	VG	F	VF	XF	Unc
1613	—	55.00	95.00	155	375	—

KM# D53.1 1/2 DALER OF 15 PATARDS

Silver **Ruler:** Ferdinand **Obv:** Bust of Ferdinand left **Obv. Legend:** •:• FERNANDVS • D(EI) • G • ARCHI • COL • PRI • ELE C **Rev:** Capped arms divides crowned F-B, without value or date below **Rev. Legend:** •:• EPIS • ET • PRIN(C) • LEOD • SVPR • DVX • BVLIONENSIS **Edge:** Plain **Mint:** Liege **Note:** Legend varieties exist.

Date	Mintage	VG	F	VF	XF	Unc
ND(1612-50)	—	155	325	575	—	—

KM# B53 1/2 DALER OF 15 PATARDS

Silver **Ruler:** Ferdinand **Obv:** Crowned rampant lion with sword and shield left **Obv. Legend:** (Rosette) FERDINANDUS • DEI • G • ARCHI • COL • PRIN • ELEC(T) **Rev:** Capped arms divides crowned F-B, value XV and date below **Rev. Legend:** •:• EPIS • ET • PRINC • LEOD : SVPR • DVX • BVLIONENSIS **Edge:** Plain **Mint:** Hasselt

Date	Mintage	VG	F	VF	XF	Unc
1614	—	220	375	625	—	—

KM# D53.2 1/2 DALER OF 15 PATARDS

Silver **Ruler:** Ferdinand **Obv:** Bust of Ferdinand left **Obv. Legend:** •:• FERNANDVS • D(EI) • G • ARCHI • COL • PRI • ELE C **Rev:** Capped arms divides crowned F-B, value XV and date below **Rev. Legend:** •:• EPIS • ET • PRINC • LEOD • SVPR • DVX • BVLIONENSIS **Edge:** Plain **Mint:** Visè **Note:** Legend varieties exist.

Date	Mintage	VG	F	VF	XF	Unc
1615	—	155	325	575	—	—

KM# D53.3 1/2 DALER OF 15 PATARDS

Silver **Ruler:** Ferdinand **Obv:** Bust of Ferdinand left **Obv. Legend:** •:• FERNANDVS • D(EI) • G • ARCHI • COL • PRI • ELE C **Rev:** Capped arms divides crowned F-B, value XV and date below **Rev. Legend:** •:• EPIS • ET • PRINC • LEOD • SVPR • DVX • BVLIONENSIS **Edge:** Plain **Mint:** Liege **Note:** Legend varieties exist.

Date	Mintage	VG	F	VF	XF	Unc
1619	—	105	220	450	—	—
1625	—	105	220	450	—	—
1635	—	105	220	450	—	—

KM# 69 1/2 DALER OF 15 PATARDS

Silver **Ruler:** Ferdinand **Obv:** Bust of Ferdinand left **Obv. Legend:** (Rosette) FERDINANDVS • D • G • ARCHI • COL • PRINC • ELE C **Rev:** Capped arms divide crowned F-B, date and vlaue XXXVIII below **Rev. Legend:** EPIS • ET • PRIN • LEO • SVPRE... **Edge:** Plain **Mint:** Liege

Date	Mintage	VG	F	VF	XF	Unc
1645	—	115	230	475	—	—

KM# 68 1/2 DALER OF 15 PATARDS

Silver **Ruler:** Ferdinand **Obv:** Bust of Ferdinand left **Obv. Legend:** (Rosette) FERDINANDVS... **Rev:** Capped arms divide crowned F-B, date and vlaue XVIII below **Rev. Legend:** •:• EPIS • ET • PRINC... **Edge:** Plain **Mint:** Liege

Date	Mintage	VG	F	VF	XF	Unc
1645	—	115	230	475	—	—

KM# C53 DALER OF 30 PATARDS

Silver **Ruler:** Ferdinand **Obv:** Crowned rampant lion with sword and shield left **Obv. Legend:** •:• FERDINANDVS • DEI G : ARCHI : COL : PRIN(C)(:)(EP)(S) : ELEC(T) **Rev:** Capped arms divides crowned F-B, value and date below **Rev. Legend:** EPIS(C) • ET • PRINC • LEOD • SVPR(E) • DVX • BVLIONENSIS **Edge:** Plain **Mint:** Hasselt

Date	Mintage	VG	F	VF	XF	Unc
1614	—	90.00	165	300	600	—

KM# 60.1 DALER OF 30 PATARDS

Silver **Ruler:** Ferdinand **Obv:** Bust of Ferdinand left **Obv. Legend:** •:•FERDINANDVS • DEI • G • ARCHI • COL • PRIN(C) • (ELEC)(T) • LEO **Rev:** Capped ornate arms divides crowned F and B, XXX - date below **Rev. Legend:** EPIS • ET • PRIN • LEOD • SUPRE • DVX • BVLIONENSIS **Edge:** Plain **Mint:** Hasselt **Note:** Dav. #4291. Reverse legend varieties exist.

Date	Mintage	VG	F	VF	XF	Unc
1614	—	95.00	175	325	650	—

KM# 60.2 DALER OF 30 PATARDS

Silver **Ruler:** Ferdinand **Obv:** Bust of Ferdinand left **Obv. Legend:** •:•FERDINANDVS • DEI • G • ARCHI • COL • PRIN(C) • (ELEC)(T) • LEO **Rev:** Capped ornate arms divides crowned F and B, XXX - date below **Rev. Legend:** EPIS • ET • PRIN • LEOD • SUPRE • DVX • BVLIONENSIS **Edge:** Plain **Mint:** Visè **Note:** Dav. #4291. Reverse legend varieties exist.

Date	Mintage	VG	F	VF	XF	Unc
1615	—	95.00	175	325	650	—

KM# 60.4 DALER OF 30 PATARDS

Silver **Ruler:** Ferdinand **Obv:** Bust of Ferdinand left **Obv. Legend:** •:•FERDINANDVS • DEI • G • ARCHI • COL • PRIN(C) • (ELEC)(T) • LEO **Rev:** Capped ornate arms divides crowned F and B, XXX - date below **Rev. Legend:** EPIS • ET • PRIN • LEOD • SUPRE • DVX • BVLIONENSIS **Edge:** Plain **Mint:** Liege **Note:** Dav. #4291. Reverse legend varieties exist.

Date	Mintage	VG	F	VF	XF	Unc
1619	—	80.00	155	280	575	—
1621	—	80.00	155	280	575	—
1622	—	80.00	155	280	575	—
1624	—	80.00	155	280	575	—
1625	—	80.00	155	280	575	—
1630	—	80.00	155	280	575	—
1634	—	80.00	155	280	575	—
1636	—	80.00	155	280	575	—
1637	—	80.00	155	280	575	—
1641	—	80.00	155	280	575	—
1645	—	80.00	155	280	575	—
1646	—	80.00	155	280	575	—

KM# 60.3 DALER OF 30 PATARDS

Silver **Ruler:** Ferdinand **Obv:** Bust of Ferdinand left **Obv. Legend:** •:•FERDINANDVS•DEI•G•ARCHI•COL•PRIN(C) • (ELEC)(T) • LEO **Rev:** Capped ornate arms divides crowned F and B, XXX - date below **Rev. Legend:** EPIS • ET • PRIN • LEOD • SUPRE • DVX • BVLIONENSIS **Edge:** Plain **Mint:** Dinant **Note:** Dav. #4291. Reverse legend varieties exist.

Date	Mintage	VG	F	VF	XF	Unc
1631 Rare	—	—	—	—	—	—
1633 Rare	—	—	—	—	—	—

KM# 64.1 1/2 ESCALIN

Silver **Ruler:** Ferdinand **Obv:** Floreate cross **Obv. Legend:** FERDINANDVS • D • G • ARCH • COL... **Rev:** Capped arms divides date **Rev. Legend:** EPIS • ET • PRIN(C) • LEO :... N • BAV • S • BVL • DVX **Edge:** Plain **Mint:** Liege

Date	Mintage	VG	F	VF	XF	Unc
1636 Rare	—	—	—	—	—	—

KM# 64.2 1/2 ESCALIN

Silver **Ruler:** Ferdinand **Obv:** Floreate cross **Obv. Legend:** FERDINANDVS • D • G • ARCH • COL... **Rev:** Capped arms divides date **Rev. Legend:** EPIS • ET • PRIN(C) • LEO • SVBR • DVX • BV... **Edge:** Plain **Mint:** Liege

Date	Mintage	VG	F	VF	XF	Unc
1636 Rare	—	—	—	—	—	—

KM# 75 1/2 ESCALIN

Silver **Ruler:** Maximilian Henry **Obv:** Floreate cross, rosette in center **Obv. Legend:** (Rosette) MAXIM • HENRI • D • G • ARCHIE • COL(LON) (BA DVX) **Rev:** Capped Bavarian arms, shield of Bouillon at center in multiple foils **Rev. Legend:** • EPISC • ET • PRIN • LEOD(I) • DVX • BVL • (LO)(NI) • **Edge:** Plain **Mint:** Bouillon

Date	Mintage	VG	F	VF	XF	Unc
1651	—	19.00	37.50	75.00	180	—
1652	—	19.00	37.50	75.00	180	—

Date	Mintage	VG	F	VF	XF	Unc
1654	—	19.00	37.50	75.00	180	—
1656	—	19.00	37.50	75.00	180	—
1658	—	19.00	37.50	75.00	180	—
1659	—	19.00	37.50	75.00	180	—
1660	—	19.00	37.50	75.00	180	—
1662	—	19.00	37.50	75.00	180	—

KM# 59 ESCALIN

Silver **Ruler:** Ferdinand **Obv:** Rampant lion with shield left **Obv. Legend:** FERDINANDVS • D • G • ARCHI • COL • PRIN • ELEC **Rev:** Capped shield divides date in double outline **Rev. Legend:** • EPIS • ET • PRIN • LEO • VT • BA • ET •... **Edge:** Plain

Date	Mintage	VG	F	VF	XF	Unc
1633	—	—	—	—	—	—

KM# 58 ESCALIN

Silver **Ruler:** Ferdinand **Obv:** Rampant lion with sword and shield left **Obv. Legend:** FERDINANDVS • D • G • ARC(HI) • COL • P(RIN) • EL(EC) **Rev:** Capped shield on floreate cross divides date **Rev. Legend:** • EP(S) • ET • PRI(N) • • LEO • • (ET) • S • DVX • BVL • **Edge:** Plain **Mint:** Liege **Note:** Reverse legend varieties exist.

Date	Mintage	VG	F	VF	XF	Unc
1636	—	31.25	55.00	100	250	—
1637	—	31.25	55.00	100	250	—
1640	—	31.25	55.00	100	250	—
1641	—	31.25	55.00	100	250	—
1646	—	31.25	55.00	100	250	—
1650	—	31.25	55.00	100	250	—

KM# 76 ESCALIN

Silver **Ruler:** Maximilian Henry **Obv:** Rampant lion with sword and shield left **Obv. Legend:** (Rosette) MAX(IM) • HEN(RI) • D • G • ARC(HIE) • COL • (B) **Rev:** Capped arms of Bavarian, shield of Bouillon at center on floreate cross dividing legend, shield divides date **Rev. Legend:** • EPS ET • PRI NC • LEO • ET • S • BV DVX **Edge:** Plain **Mint:** Liege

Date	Mintage	VG	F	VF	XF	Unc
1651	—	25.00	50.00	90.00	225	—
1652	—	25.00	50.00	90.00	225	—
1653	—	25.00	50.00	90.00	225	—
1654	—	25.00	50.00	90.00	225	—
1656	—	25.00	50.00	90.00	225	—
1657	—	25.00	50.00	90.00	225	—
1658	—	25.00	50.00	90.00	225	—

KM# 77 ESCALIN

Silver **Ruler:** Maximilian Henry **Obv:** Rampant lion with sword and shield left **Obv. Legend:** (Rosette) MAXIM • HENRI • D • G • ARCHI • COL • **Rev:** Capped arms of Bavarian, shield of Bouillon at center on floreate cross dividing legend, shield divides date, cap also divides legend **Rev. Legend:** • EP • ET • P RIN • LEO ET • (S) • BV • D(V) • (X) **Edge:** Plain **Mint:** Liege

Date	Mintage	VG	F	VF	XF	Unc
1660	—	31.25	55.00	100	250	—
1661	—	31.25	55.00	100	250	—

KM# 65 DALER OF 40 PATARDS

Silver **Ruler:** Ferdinand **Obv:** Capped four-fold arms on crossed sword and crozier, capped shield at right **Rev:** St. Lambert and the Virgin with child standing **Mint:** Liege **Note:** Dav. #4293.

Date	Mintage	VG	F	VF	XF	Unc
1646 Rare	—	—	—	—	—	—

KM# 79 1/2 PATAGON

Silver **Ruler:** Maximilian Henry **Obv:** Bust of Maximlian Henry right **Obv. Legend:** MAX • HEN • D • G • ARC • COL • PRIN • EL **Rev:** Capped five-fold arms **Rev. Legend:** (Rosette) EP • ET • PRIN • LEOD • DVX • BVL • MAR • FR • LO • **Edge:** Plain **Mint:** Liege

Date	Mintage	VG	F	VF	XF	Unc
1663 Rare	—	—	—	—	—	—

KM# 61 PATAGON

Silver **Ruler:** Ferdinand **Obv:** Floriate cross with shield of Bouillon at center, crowned F's and crowned B's in angles **Obv. Legend:** FERDINANDVS • D • G • ARCHI • COL • PRINC • ELECTOR • **Rev:** Capped ornate oval Bavarian arms with shield of Bouillon at center **Rev. Legend:** • EPISC • ET • PRINC • LEO • VTR • BAV • ET • S • BVL • DVX **Note:** Dav. #4292.

Date	Mintage	VG	F	VF	XF	Unc
1635 Rare	—	—	—	—	—	—

KM# 80 PATAGON

Silver **Ruler:** Maximilian Henry **Obv:** Bust of Maximilian Henry right **Obv. Legend:** MAX • H(EA)N • D • G • ARC • COL • PRIN(C) • E(LR) • **Rev:** Capped eight-fold arms, date above **Rev. Legend:** • EP • ET • PRIN(C) • LEO(D) • DVX... **Mint:** Liege **Note:** Dav. #4294.

Date	Mintage	VG	F	VF	XF	Unc
1662	—	75.00	150	350	575	—
1663	—	75.00	150	350	575	—
1664	—	75.00	150	350	575	—
1665	—	75.00	150	350	575	—
1666	—	75.00	150	350	575	—
1667	—	75.00	150	350	575	—
1668	—	75.00	150	350	575	—
1669	—	75.00	150	350	575	—
1670	—	75.00	150	350	575	—
1671	—	75.00	150	350	575	—
1672	—	75.00	150	350	575	—
1673	—	75.00	150	350	575	—
1674	—	75.00	150	350	575	—
1675	—	75.00	150	350	575	—
1676	—	75.00	150	350	575	—
1677	—	75.00	150	350	575	—
1678	—	75.00	150	350	575	—
1679	—	75.00	150	350	575	—
1680	—	75.00	150	350	575	—
1681	—	75.00	150	350	575	—
1682	—	75.00	150	350	575	—
1683	—	75.00	150	350	575	—
1685	—	75.00	150	350	575	—
1686	—	75.00	150	350	575	—

KM# 99 PATAGON

Silver **Obv:** Capped four-fold arms **Rev:** Bust of St. Lambert left **Mint:** Liege **Note:** Sede Vacante issue. Dav. #4298.

Date	Mintage	VG	F	VF	XF	Unc
1688	—	325	575	1,300	2,200	—

KM# 98 PATAGON

Silver **Obv:** Capped four-fold arms **Rev:** Bust of St. Lambert left in ornate oval frame **Mint:** Liege **Note:** Sede Vacante issue. Struck at Liege. Dav. #4297.

Date	Mintage	VG	F	VF	XF	Unc
1688	—	325	575	1,300	2,200	—

KM# 102 PATAGON

Silver **Ruler:** John Louis **Obv:** Bust of John Louis Eldern right **Obv. Legend:** IOAN • LVD • D • G • EP • ET • PRIN • LEO **Rev:** Capped five-fold arms with date above **Rev. Legend:** • DVX • BVL(L) • MAR • FRA • COM • LO(S) • HO(R) • **Mint:** Liege **Note:** Dav. #4300.

Date	Mintage	VG	F	VF	XF	Unc
1689	—	250	450	1,050	1,600	—
1690	—	250	450	1,050	1,600	—

Date	Mintage	VG	F	VF	XF	Unc
1691	—	250	450	1,050	1,600	—
1692	—	250	450	1,050	1,600	—
1693	—	250	450	1,050	1,600	—

KM# 109 PATAGON

Silver **Ruler:** Joseph Clement **Obv:** Bust of Joseph Clement right breaking upper legend **Obv. Legend:** IOSEPH • CLE • D • G • AR • COL • P • EL • **Rev:** Capped eight-fold arms, date above **Rev. Legend:** ⁜ EP • ET • PRINC • LEOD • DVX •... **Mint:** Liege **Note:** Dav. #4302.

Date	Mintage	VG	F	VF	XF	Unc
1694 Rare	—	—	—	—	—	—
1695 Rare	—	—	—	—	—	—

KM# 108 PATAGON

Silver **Obv:** Capped five-fold arms with date above **Rev:** Bust of St. Lambert left **Mint:** Liege **Note:** Sede Vacante issue. Dav. #4301.

Date	Mintage	VG	F	VF	XF	Unc
1694	—	325	575	1,300	2,200	—

KM# 112.1 PATAGON

Silver **Ruler:** Joseph Clement **Obv:** Smaller bust of Joseph Clement right, legend continuous **Obv. Legend:** IOSEPH • CLEM • D • G • AR • COL • P • EL • **Rev:** Capped nine-fold arms, date above **Mint:** Liege **Note:** Dav. #4303.

Date	Mintage	F	VF	XF	Unc	BU
1694	—	500	1,050	1,750	—	—
1695	—	500	1,050	1,750	—	—

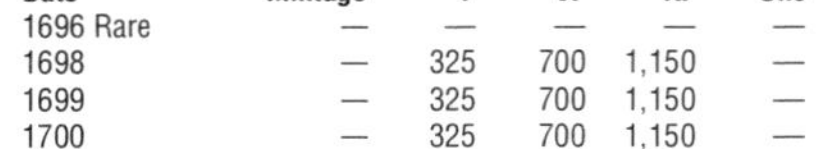

Date	Mintage	F	VF	XF	Unc	BU
1696 Rare	—	—	—	—	—	—
1698	—	325	700	1,150	—	—
1699	—	325	700	1,150	—	—
1700	—	325	700	1,150	—	—

KM# 112.2 PATAGON

Silver **Ruler:** Joseph Clement **Rev:** Quarters of Bavaria-Palatinant in small shield reversed

Date	Mintage	VG	F	VF	XF	Unc
1700	—	250	450	1,050	1,600	—

KM# 84 DUCATONE

Silver **Ruler:** Maximilian Henry **Obv:** Capped bust of Maximilian Henry right **Obv. Legend:** MAX • HEN • D • G • A • C • P... **Rev:** Capped, supported five-fold arms **Rev. Legend:** SVPR(E)MV(S) BVLLONIEN SIS • DVX **Mint:** Liege **Note:** Dav. #4296.

Date	Mintage	VG	F	VF	XF	Unc
1666	—	75.00	150	350	575	—
1667	—	75.00	150	350	575	—
1668	—	75.00	150	350	575	—
1669	—	75.00	150	350	575	—
1670	—	75.00	150	350	575	—
1671	—	75.00	150	350	575	—
1673	—	75.00	150	350	575	—
1674	—	75.00	150	350	575	—
1675	—	75.00	150	350	575	—
1676	—	75.00	150	350	575	—
1677	—	75.00	150	350	575	—
1678	—	75.00	150	350	575	—
1680	—	75.00	150	350	575	—
1681	—	75.00	150	350	575	—
1682	—	75.00	150	350	575	—
1683	—	75.00	150	350	575	—

KM# 101 DUCATONE

Silver **Ruler:** John Louis **Obv:** Bust of John Louis Eldern right, date **Obv. Legend:** • IOAN • LVD • D • G • EP • PRIN • LEOD• **Rev:** Capped and supported arms **Rev. Legend:** SVPREMVS BVLLONIEN SIS • DVX **Edge:** Plain **Mint:** Liege **Note:** Dav. #4299.

Date	Mintage	VG	F	VF	XF	Unc
1689	—	250	450	1,050	1,600	—
1690	—	250	450	1,050	1,600	—
1691	—	250	450	1,050	1,600	—

KM# 103 DUCATONE

Silver **Ruler:** John Louis **Obv:** Similar to KM#101 **Rev:** Similar to KM#101 **Rev. Legend:** SVPREMV... **Edge Lettering:** AD PRINCIPIS GLORIAM ET POPULI SECURITATEM **Mint:** Liege **Note:** Dav. #4299A.

Date	Mintage	VG	F	VF	XF	Unc
1689	—	350	625	1,500	2,200	—

KM# 90 2 DUCATONE

Silver **Ruler:** Maximilian Henry **Obv:** Capped bust of Maximilian Henry right **Obv. Legend:** MAX • HEN • D • G • A • C • P • **Rev:** Capped, supported five-fold arms **Mint:** Liege **Note:** Struck at Liege. Dav. #4295.

Date	Mintage	VG	F	VF	XF	Unc
1671 Rare	—	—	—	—	—	—

KM# G35 2 DALER

Silver **Ruler:** Ferdinand **Obv:** Bust of Ferdinand **Obv. Legend:** (Rosette) FERDINANDVS • DEI • G • ARCHI • COL • PRINC • ELECT **Rev:** Five-fold arms with lion supporters **Rev. Legend:** (Rosette) EPISC • ET • PRIN • LEOD • VTR • BAT • ET • SVPREMVS • BVL • DVX **Edge:** Plain **Mint:** Dinant

Date	Mintage	VG	F	VF	XF	Unc
ND(1612-50) Rare	—	—	—	—	—	—

KM# 16 1/2 REAL

Silver **Ruler:** Ernest **Obv:** Capped four-fold arms **Obv. Legend:** ERNESTVS • D • G • ARCHIEP • C **Rev:** Floriate cross **Rev. Legend:** † EPIS • LEODIEN • V • BAVARIE • DV **Edge:** Plain **Mint:** Liege

Date	Mintage	VG	F	VF	XF	Unc
ND(1581-1612)	—	—	—	—	—	—

KM# E35 1/2 REAL

Silver **Ruler:** Ferdinand **Obv:** Capped five-fold arms **Obv. Legend:** FERDINANDVS • DE • GRATIA **Rev:** Long floreate cross divides legend, crosses in angles **Rev. Legend:** EPIS LEOD DVX BVLI **Edge:** Plain

Date	Mintage	VG	F	VF	XF	Unc
ND(1612-50)	—	170	350	750	—	—

KM# C35 1/2 REAL

Silver **Ruler:** Ferdinand **Obv:** Capped arms **Obv. Legend:** FERDINA • ELEC • COL • EPIS • LEO • Z **Rev:** Long floreate cross, crosses in angles, imperial eagle at center **Rev. Legend:** MATH ROMA IMPE S • AVG **Edge:** Plain **Mint:** Liege

Date	Mintage	VG	F	VF	XF	Unc
ND(1612-19)	—	170	350	750	—	—

KM# B35 1/2 REAL

Silver **Ruler:** Ferdinand **Obv:** Capped arms **Obv. Legend:** FERDINAN • ELEC • COL • EPIS • LEO : Z **Rev:** Long floreate cross, perrons in angles, imperial eagle at center **Rev. Legend:** MATH ROMA IMPE S • AVG **Edge:** Plain **Mint:** Liege

Date	Mintage	VG	F	VF	XF	Unc
ND(1612-19) Rare	—	170	350	750	—	—

KM# F35.1 1/2 REAL

Silver **Ruler:** Ferdinand **Obv:** Ornate four-fold arms **Obv. Legend:** FERD • DE • GRA • DVX • EP • LEOD • DVX • BVL • COM(E)S • LOS **Rev:** Long floreate cross divides legend, floreate ends repeated in angles, imperial eagle at center **Rev. Legend:** FERD II • ROM IMPE SEM • AV **Edge:** Plain **Mint:** Liege

Date	Mintage	VG	F	VF	XF	Unc
ND(1619-37) Rare	—	—	—	—	—	—

KM# F35.2 1/2 REAL

Silver **Ruler:** Ferdinand **Obv:** Ornate four-fold arms **Obv. Legend:** FERD • DE • G • EPS • ET • PRIN • COL **Rev:** Long floreate cross divides legend, floreate ends repeated in quarters, imperial eagle at center **Rev. Legend:** FERD II • ROM IMPE SEM • AV **Edge:** Plain **Mint:** Liege

Date	Mintage	VG	F	VF	XF	Unc
ND(1619-37) Rare	—	—	—	—	—	—

KM# A56 REAL

Silver **Ruler:** Ferdinand **Obv:** Ornate four-fold arms divides date **Obv. Legend:** FERD • D • G • EPS • ET • PRINC • LEOD • VTR • BA • ET • B • DVX **Rev:** Long floreate cross divides legend, floreate ends repeated in angles, imperial eagle at center **Rev. Legend:** FERD II • ROM IMPE SEM • AV **Edge:** Plain **Mint:** Liege

Date	Mintage	VG	F	VF	XF	Unc
1629	—	155	325	675	—	—
1630	—	155	325	675	—	—
1631	—	155	325	675	—	—

KM# A36 REAL

Silver **Ruler:** Ferdinand **Obv:** Ornate four-fold arms divides date **Obv. Legend:** FERDINANDVS • DE • G...LEO **Rev:** Long floreate cross divides legend, lis in angles **Rev. Legend:** EPI...PRI...VT • BA • ET SV • B • DVX **Edge:** Plain **Mint:** Dinant

Date	Mintage	VG	F	VF	XF	Unc
1631 Rare	—	—	—	—	—	—

KM# A3 PATARD (Sol)

Billon **Ruler:** Ernest **Obv:** Capped four-fold arms divides value I-S **Obv. Legend:** (Acorn) ERNESTVS • D • G • ARCHIE • COL **Rev:** Imperial eagle on cross divides legend **Rev. Legend:** EPIS LEODI • COMES LOSSE **Edge:** Plain **Mint:** Maeseyck

Date	Mintage	VG	F	VF	XF	Unc
ND(1581-1612) Rare	—	—	—	—	—	—

KM# B3 2 PATARDS (2 Sols)

Billon **Ruler:** Ernest **Obv:** Capped four-fold arms **Obv. Legend:** ERNESTVS • D • G • ARCHIE • COL **Rev:** Acorn above three shields, lower shield divides value II-S **Rev. Legend:** EPIS • LEODIEN • COMES • LOSSEN • **Edge:** Plain **Mint:** Maeseyck

Date	Mintage	VG	F	VF	XF	Unc
ND(1581-1612) Rare	—	—	—	—	—	—

KM# D35 2 PATARDS (2 Sols)

Silver **Ruler:** Ferdinand **Obv:** Capped arms divides value II-S **Obv. Legend:** FERDINAN • ELEC • COL • EPI(S) • LE(OD) • Z **Rev:** Crowned imperial eagle **Rev. Legend:** MATHIAS • ROMANO • IMPE • SEMP • AV(G) **Edge:** Plain **Mint:** Liege

Date	Mintage	VG	F	VF	XF	Unc
ND(1612-19)	—	80.00	155	425	—	—

KM# A35 4 PATARDS (4 Sols)

Billon **Ruler:** Ferdinand **Obv:** Capped ornate arms, value IIIS below **Obv. Legend:** FERDINAN • ELEC • COL • EPIS • LEO • Z **Rev:** Crowned imperial eagle **Rev. Legend:** MATHIAS • ROMANO • IMPE • SEM • AVG **Edge:** Plain **Mint:** Liege

Date	Mintage	VG	F	VF	XF	Unc
ND(1612-19) Rare	—	—	—	—	—	—

TRADE COINAGE

KM# B20 FLORIN D'OR

3.5000 g., 0.9860 Gold 0.1109 oz. AGW **Ruler:** Ernest **Obv:** Bust of Ernest right in inner circle **Obv. Legend:** (Acorn) ERNEST • BA • DVX • EP • LE • DVX • B • CO • LOS **Rev:** Capped arms divides legend **Rev. Legend:** AV...TR ALTERA PARS... **Mint:** Maeseyck **Note:** Fr. #210a.

Date	Mintage	VG	F	VF	XF	Unc
ND(1581-1612)	—	2,250	3,750	6,800	11,500	—

KM# A20 FLORIN D'OR

3.5000 g., 0.9860 Gold 0.1109 oz. AGW **Ruler:** Ernest **Obv:** Bust of Ernest left **Obv. Legend:** •:• ERNESTVS • D • G • EPISCOPVS • LEODIEN **Rev:** Capped arms on crossed sword and crozier, date above **Mint:** Bouillon **Note:** Fr. #210.

Date	Mintage	VG	F	VF	XF	Unc
1612	—	2,250	3,750	6,800	11,500	—

KM# 46 FLORIN D'OR

3.5000 g., 0.9860 Gold 0.1109 oz. AGW **Ruler:** Ferdinand **Obv:** Bust of Ferdinand left **Obv. Legend:** (Rosette) FERDINAN(DVS) • D • G • EPISCOPVS • LEOD(IE) **Rev:** Capped arms on crossed sword and crozier **Rev. Legend:** DVX • BV(I)LLONIENSIS **Mint:** Bouillon **Note:** Fr. #211.

Date	Mintage	VG	F	VF	XF	Unc
1612	—	300	750	1,500	2,500	—
1613	—	300	750	1,500	2,500	—

KM# 47 FLORIN D'OR

3.5000 g., 0.9860 Gold 0.1109 oz. AGW **Ruler:** Ferdinand **Obv:** Ferdinand enthroned facing in electoral robes, arms below **Obv. Legend:** •:• FERD : D : G : ARCH(I) • COL • PRIN(C) : ELE(C) •:• **Rev:** Trilobe with four-fold arms at center and F-B-D in trilobe **Mint:** Hasselt **Note:** Fr. #216.

Date	Mintage	VG	F	VF	XF	Unc
ND(1614) F-B-D	—	525	1,150	2,200	3,750	—

KM# 52 COURONNE D'OR

11.0600 g., 0.9190 Gold 0.3268 oz. AGW **Ruler:** Ferdinand **Obv:** Floreated cross with Fs in angles and crowns at ends **Obv. Legend:** •:• FERD(INAND) • D • G • ARCH(I) • COL • P(RINCEPS) **Rev:** Capped five-fold arms, date divided below **Rev. Legend:** EPISC : ET • PR : LEO : SV • (D) • BVL **Mint:** Hasselt **Note:** Fr. #215.

Date	Mintage	VG	F	VF	XF	Unc
1614	—	525	1,150	2,200	3,750	—

KM# 49 ECU D'OR

3.3600 g., 0.9520 Gold 0.1028 oz. AGW **Ruler:** Ferdinand **Obv:** Crowned arms over crossed sword and crozier **Obv. Legend:** + FERDINANDVS • D(EI) • G • EPISCOPVS • LEODIE **Rev:** Ornamental cross with B at center **Rev. Legend:** + SVPREMVS • DVX • BVLLONIENSIS **Mint:** Bouillon **Note:** Fr. #214.

Date	Mintage	VG	F	VF	XF	Unc
1613	—	525	1,150	1,900	3,400	—

KM# 53 ECU D'OR

3.3600 g., 0.9520 Gold 0.1028 oz. AGW **Ruler:** Ferdinand **Obv:** Floreated cross with F's in angles and crowns at ends **Obv. Legend:** •:• FERD • D • G • ARCHI • COL • PRINCEP(S) • ELECT **Rev:** Capped ornate spade-shaped five-fold arms on crossed sword and crozier, date divided by cap **Rev. Legend:** EPISC • ET • PRINC • LEO • SV • D • BVL **Mint:** Hasselt **Note:** Fr. #215.

Date	Mintage	VG	F	VF	XF	Unc
1614	—	525	1,150	1,900	3,400	—

KM# 54.1 ECU D'OR

3.3600 g., 0.9520 Gold 0.1028 oz. AGW **Ruler:** Ferdinand **Obv:** Floreated cross with F's in angles and crowns at ends **Obv. Legend:** FERDINANDVS • DEI • G • ARCHI • COL • PRIN • ELE **Rev:** Capped ornate spade-shaped Bavarian arms with shield of Bouillon at center, cap divides date **Rev. Legend:** EPISC • ET • PR • LEO • VTR • BA • ET • S • B • D • **Mint:** Liege

Date	Mintage	VG	F	VF	XF	Unc
1631	—	375	750	1,500	3,000	—

KM# 54.2 ECU D'OR
3.3600 g., 0.9520 Gold 0.1028 oz. AGW **Ruler:** Ferdinand **Obv:** Floreated cross with F's in angles and crowns at ends **Obv. Legend:** FERDINANDVS • D(EI) • G • ARCH(I) • COL • P(RINC) • ELE(C) **Mint:** Liege

Date	Mintage	VG	F	VF	XF	Unc
1631	—	225	500	1,050	1,750	—
1635	—	225	500	1,050	1,750	—
1636	—	225	500	1,050	1,750	—
1637	—	225	500	1,050	1,750	—
1639	—	225	500	1,050	1,750	—
1640	—	225	500	1,050	1,750	—
1641	—	225	500	1,050	1,750	—
1643	—	225	500	1,050	1,750	—
1644	—	225	500	1,050	1,750	—

KM# 62 ECU D'OR
3.3600 g., 0.9520 Gold 0.1028 oz. AGW **Ruler:** Ferdinand **Obv:** Floreated cross with F's in angles and crowns at ends **Obv. Legend:** • FERDINANDVS • D • G • ARCHI • COL • PRINC • ELEC **Rev:** Capped ornate arms divides date below **Rev. Legend:** EPS • ETPR • LEO • VT • BA • ET • S • BV • DVX • **Mint:** Liege

Date	Mintage	VG	F	VF	XF	Unc
1635 Rare	—	—	—	—	—	—

KM# 51 2 ECU D'OR
6.7200 g., 0.9520 Gold 0.2057 oz. AGW **Ruler:** Ferdinand **Obv:** Crowned arms **Obv. Legend:** •:• FERDINANDVS • D : G • EPISCOPVS • LEODI(E) **Rev:** Ornamental cross with B at center **Rev. Legend:** •:• SVPREMVS • DVX • BVILLIONIENSIS **Mint:** Bouillon

Date	Mintage	VG	F	VF	XF	Unc
1613 Rare	—	—	—	—	—	—

KM# 50 2 ECU D'OR
6.7200 g., 0.9520 Gold 0.2057 oz. AGW **Ruler:** Ferdinand **Obv:** Crowned arms over crossed sword and crozier **Obv. Legend:** FERDINANDVS • D : G • EPISCOPVS • • LEOD(IE) **Rev:** Ornamental cross with B at center **Rev. Legend:** SVPREMVS • DVX • BVILLIONIENSIS **Mint:** Bouillon **Note:** Fr. #213.

Date	Mintage	VG	F	VF	XF	Unc
1613	—	1,150	2,200	3,750	6,800	—

KM# 63 DUCAT
3.5000 g., 0.9860 Gold 0.1109 oz. AGW **Ruler:** Ferdinand **Obv:** Capped ornate four-fold arms **Obv. Legend:** FE RDI • ELEC • COL • EPS • LEO(D) • BAV(A)DV X **Rev:** Inscription in tablet, date divided at sides **Rev. Inscription:** DVCATVS / NOWS DVC / BVLLONI / ENSIS **Mint:** Liege

Date	Mintage	VG	F	VF	XF	Unc
1638	—	525	1,300	2,650	3,750	—

KM# 74 DUCAT
3.5000 g., 0.9860 Gold 0.1109 oz. AGW **Ruler:** Maximilian Henry **Obv:** Capped ornate five-fold arms **Obv. Legend:** MAX : HEN : ELEC • COL • EPS • LEO • BA(V)-D **Rev:** Tablet **Rev. Inscription:** DVCATVS / NOWS DV(C) / BVLLONI / ENSIS **Mint:** Liege

Date	Mintage	VG	F	VF	XF	Unc
1651	—	375	975	2,250	3,400	—
1652	—	375	975	2,250	3,400	—
1653	—	375	975	2,250	3,400	—
1654	—	375	975	2,250	3,400	—
1656	—	375	975	2,250	3,400	—
1658	—	375	975	2,250	3,400	—
1661	—	375	975	2,250	3,400	—

KM# 81 DUCAT
3.5000 g., 0.9860 Gold 0.1109 oz. AGW **Ruler:** Maximilian Henry **Obv:** Bust of Maximilian Henry right, date below **Obv. Legend:** MAX • HEN • D • G • ARC • COL • PR(•)E(L) **Rev:** Capped ornate five-fold arms **Mint:** Liege

Date	Mintage	VG	F	VF	XF	Unc
ND	—	450	1,150	2,500	3,750	—
1663	—	450	1,150	2,500	3,750	—
1664 Rare	—	—	—	—	—	—
1666 Rare	—	—	—	—	—	—
1667 Rare	—	—	—	—	—	—
1668	—	450	1,150	2,500	3,750	—
1669 Rare	—	—	—	—	—	—
1670	—	450	1,150	2,500	3,750	—
1671 Rare	—	—	—	—	—	—
1672 Rare	—	—	—	—	—	—
1674 Rare	—	—	—	—	—	—

KM# 82 DUCAT
3.5000 g., 0.9860 Gold 0.1109 oz. AGW **Ruler:** Maximilian Henry **Obv:** Bust of Maximilian Henry right **Obv. Legend:** MAX • HEN • D • G • ARC • COL • PR • EL **Rev:** Capped ornate five-fold arms **Mint:** Liege

Date	Mintage	VG	F	VF	XF	Unc
1664 Rare	—	—	—	—	—	—

KM# 83 2 DUCAT
7.0000 g., 0.9860 Gold 0.2219 oz. AGW **Ruler:** Maximilian Henry **Obv:** Bust of Maximilian Henry right **Obv. Legend:** MAX • HEN • D • G • ARC • COL • PRIN • EL (dog) **Rev:** Capped ornate five-fold arms **Mint:** Liege

Date	Mintage	VG	F	VF	XF	Unc
ND(1650-88)	—	4,500	7,500	11,500	15,000	—

KM# 100 2 DUCAT
7.0000 g., 0.9860 Gold 0.2219 oz. AGW **Obv:** Crowned four-fold arms divide date **Rev:** Bust of St. Lambert left **Mint:** Liege **Note:** Sede Vacante issue.

Date	Mintage	VG	F	VF	XF	Unc
1688	—	4,500	7,500	11,500	15,000	—

KM# 105 2 DUCAT
7.0000 g., 0.9860 Gold 0.2219 oz. AGW **Ruler:** John Louis **Obv:** Bust of John Louis right **Obv. Legend:** IOZN • LVD • D • G • EP • ET • PRIN • LEO **Rev:** Crowned five-fold arms, date above **Mint:** Liege

Date	Mintage	VG	F	VF	XF	Unc
1690	—	5,300	8,300	13,000	18,000	—

KM# 110 2 DUCAT
7.0000 g., 0.9860 Gold 0.2219 oz. AGW **Obv:** Capped five-fold arms **Obv. Legend:** • MO • AVREA • CAP • LEO • SEDE • VACANTE • **Rev:** Bust of St. Lambert left **Mint:** Liege **Note:** Sede Vacante issue.

Date	Mintage	VG	F	VF	XF	Unc
1694	—	4,500	7,500	11,500	15,000	—

KM# 111 3 DUCAT
10.5000 g., 0.9860 Gold 0.3328 oz. AGW **Ruler:** Joseph Clement **Obv:** Bust of Joseph Clement right, date at lower left **Obv. Legend:** (Rosette) IOSEPH • CLEM • D • G • ARC • COL • PRIN • ELEC • **Rev:** Crowned eight-fold arms, value 3 below **Mint:** Liege

Date	Mintage	VG	F	VF	XF	Unc
1695 Rare	—	—	—	—	—	—
1700 Rare	—	—	—	—	—	—

PATTERNS

Including off metal strikes

KM#	Date	Mintage	Identification	Mkt Val
PnA1	ND(1694-1723)	—	Liard. Silver. KM#107.	—

LITHUANIA

Lithuania emerged as a grand duchy in the 14th century. In the 15th century it was a major power of central Europe, stretching from the Baltic to the Black Sea. It was joined with Poland in 1569, but lost Smolensk, Chernigovsk, and the left bank of the river Dnepr Ukraina in 1667. Following the third partition of Poland by Austria, Prussia and Russia, 1795, Lithuania came under Russian domination and did not regain its independence until shortly before the end of World War I when it declared itself a sovereign republic on Feb. 16, 1918. In fall of 1920, Poland captured Vilna (Vilnius). The republic was occupied by Soviet troops and annexed to the U.S.S.R. in 1940. Following the German occupation of 1941-44, it was retaken by Russia and reestablished as a member republic of the Soviet Union. Western countries, including the United States, did not recognize Lithuania's incorporation into the Soviet Union.

Lithuania declared its independence March 11, 1990and it was recognized by the United States on Sept. 2,1991, followed by the Soviet government in Moscow on Sept. 6. They were seated in the UN General Assembly on Sept. 17, 1991.

RULERS

Kings of Poland
Sigismund III, (Zygimantas) 1587-1632
Wladislaus, (Vladislavas) 1632-1648
Johann Casimir, (Jan II Kazimieras) 1648-1668
Michael Korybut, 1669-1673
John III Sobieski, (Jan III Sobieski) 1674-1696
Augustus II, (Augustas II) 1697-1704

MINT MARKS

LMK – Vilna

MINT OFFICIALS' INITIALS

Initial	Date	Name
LMK	1600-03	? – Vina
HT	1618-23	Jonusas Trilneris
II, I I – VE	1623-27	Jokubas Jakobsenas van Emdenas
RL (monogram)	1623-27	Rudolf Lehman
IT	1639	Jonusas Trilneris
TLB	1660-66	Titus Livijus Boratinis, Tenant
	1664-66	Brzesc. Litewski, C. Bandine, Tenant
GFH	1665-66	Georgas Fon Hornis
TZH	1665-66	Teodor Horn, Kovno

PRIVY MARKS

Mark	Date	Name
hook	1599-1604	Zacharias Boll
(a) – swan	1598-1604	Anorius Zrvisa
(b) – HW or 2 arrows	1605-18	Jeronimas Valavicius
Arrow up	1606-18	Jonusas Stypla
(c) – 2 fish	1618-30	Kristupas Narvsevicius
	1630-35	Steponas Pacas
	1636-44	Mykolas Kiska
(d) – lily	1644-52	Mykolms Georonas Tryzna
(e) – bird w/ring	1652-62	Vincentas Gonsievskis
(f) – KHPL or buck's head	1663-76	Jeronimas Kryspinas Kirsensteinas
	1676-1703	Benediktas Povilas Sapiega

GRAND DUCHY

STANDARD COINAGE

KM# 8 2 DENARI

Silver **Obv:** Crowned S monogram divides date, value below **Rev:** Vytis on horseback to left, mint mark below

Date	Mintage	VG	F	VF	XF	Unc
1606	—	100	150	175	200	—
1607	—	100	150	175	200	—
1609	—	20.00	40.00	50.00	75.00	—
1611	—	10.00	20.00	40.00	60.00	—
1612	—	10.00	20.00	40.00	60.00	—
1613	—	10.00	20.00	40.00	60.00	—
1614	—	125	175	200	225	—

KM# 15.1 2 DENARI

Silver **Rev:** H below Vytis

Date	Mintage	VG	F	VF	XF	Unc
1612 H	—	150	200	225	275	—
1614 H	—	125	175	200	245	—

KM# 15.2 2 DENARI

Silver **Note:** Without mint mark.

Date	Mintage	VG	F	VF	XF	Unc
1619	—	35.00	45.00	65.00	100	—

KM# 15.3 2 DENARI

Silver **Rev:** Two fish privy mark

Date	Mintage	VG	F	VF	XF	Unc
1620 (c)	—	15.00	20.00	30.00	65.00	—
1621 (c)	—	15.00	20.00	30.00	65.00	—
1622 (c) Rare	—	—	—	—	—	—
1623 (c) Rare	—	—	—	—	—	—
1626 (c) Rare	—	—	—	—	—	—

KM# 30 2 DENARI

Silver **Obv:** Eagle within circle **Rev:** Vytis on horse left within circle, two-digit date in legend

Date	Mintage	VG	F	VF	XF	Unc
1623	—	15.00	30.00	50.00	75.00	—
(16)23	—	15.00	30.00	50.00	75.00	—
1624	—	15.00	30.00	50.00	75.00	—

KM# 31 2 DENARI

Silver **Obv:** Crowned S monogram in inner circle **Rev:** Crown above two shields of arms in inner circle, date in legend **Note:** Five varieties known for 1624.

Date	Mintage	VG	F	VF	XF	Unc
1624	—	15.00	20.00	40.00	70.00	—
1625	—	15.00	20.00	40.00	70.00	—
1626	—	15.00	20.00	40.00	70.00	—
1627	—	15.00	20.00	40.00	70.00	—

KM# 41 2 DENARI

Billon **Obv:** Crowned ICR monogram in inner circle **Rev:** Vytis on horseback left in inner circle, date in legend **Note:** Legend and crown varieties exist.

Date	Mintage	VG	F	VF	XF	Unc
(16)52	—	15.00	22.50	45.00	75.00	—
(16)52	—	15.00	22.50	45.00	75.00	—
1653	—	15.00	22.50	45.00	75.00	—
16(53)	—	15.00	22.50	45.00	75.00	—
1654 Rare	—	—	—	—	—	—
1661 Rare	—	—	—	—	—	—

KM# 16.1 SCHILLING

Silver **Obv:** Crowned monogram divides date **Rev:** Crown above two shields

Date	Mintage	VG	F	VF	XF	Unc
(16)12 Rare	—	—	—	—	—	—
(16)14	—	12.50	30.00	47.50	75.00	—
(16)15	—	15.00	20.00	35.00	45.00	—
(16)16	—	15.00	20.00	35.00	45.00	—

KM# 16.2 SCHILLING

Silver **Obv:** S divides four-digit date

Date	Mintage	VG	F	VF	XF	Unc
1615	—	15.00	20.00	25.00	35.00	—
1616	—	15.00	20.00	25.00	35.00	—
1617	—	15.00	20.00	25.00	35.00	—

KM# 16.3 SCHILLING

Silver **Obv:** S divides two-digit date **Note:** Crown varieties exist.

Date	Mintage	VG	F	VF	XF	Unc
(16)17	—	15.00	20.00	35.00	45.00	—
(16)18	—	15.00	20.00	25.00	35.00	—
(16)19	—	15.00	20.00	25.00	35.00	—

KM# 25 SCHILLING

Silver **Rev:** Two-digit date in legend

Date	Mintage	VG	F	VF	XF	Unc
(16)20 Rare	—	—	—	—	—	—
(16)21 Rare	—	—	—	—	—	—
(16)22	—	15.00	20.00	25.00	35.00	—
(16)23	—	15.00	20.00	25.00	35.00	—

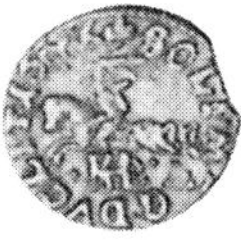

KM# 50 SCHILLING

Copper **Obv:** Laureate head of Johann Casimir right, TLB or GFH below head **Rev:** Vytis on horseback left, date in legend **Note:** Legend varieties exist.

Date	Mintage	VG	F	VF	XF	Unc
1660 TLB	7,000	7.50	12.50	25.00	40.00	—
1661 TLB	Inc. above	7.50	12.50	25.00	40.00	—
1663 GFH	—	7.50	12.50	25.00	40.00	—
1664 GFH	—	10.00	15.00	30.00	50.00	—
1664 TLB/HKPL	Inc. above	7.50	12.50	25.00	40.00	—
1665 GFH	—	7.50	12.50	25.00	40.00	—
1665 TLB/HKPL	Inc. above	7.50	12.50	25.00	40.00	—
1666 TLB/HKPL	Inc. above	7.50	12.50	25.00	40.00	—
1666 GFH	—	7.50	12.50	25.00	40.00	—

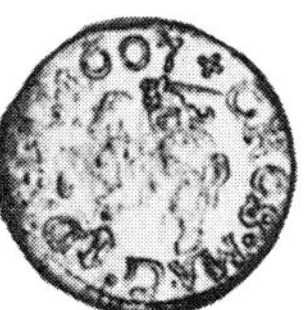

KM# 9 GROSZ

Silver **Obv:** Crowned bust of Sigismund III right in inner circle **Obv. Legend:** SIG III D G REX PO M D L - GROS MAG DV LIT **Rev:** Vytis on horseback left in inner circle, date in legend

Date	Mintage	VG	F	VF	XF	Unc
1607 with shield under Vytis	—	25.00	40.00	75.00	95.00	—
1607 without shield under Vytis	—	85.00	100	175	250	—
1608	—	25.00	40.00	75.00	95.00	—

KM# 10 GROSZ

Silver **Obv:** Displayed eagle in inner circle **Note:** Legend varieties exist.

Date	Mintage	VG	F	VF	XF	Unc
1608	—	30.00	45.00	65.00	95.00	—
1609	—	30.00	45.00	65.00	95.00	—
1610	—	30.00	45.00	65.00	95.00	—
1611	—	30.00	45.00	65.00	95.00	—
1612	—	30.00	45.00	65.00	95.00	—
1613	—	30.00	45.00	65.00	95.00	—
1614	—	30.00	45.00	65.00	95.00	—
1615	—	30.00	45.00	65.00	95.00	—
(16)15	—	30.00	45.00	65.00	95.00	—

KM# 11 GROSZ

Silver **Note:** Klippe.

Date	Mintage	VG	F	VF	XF	Unc
1610 Rare	—	—	—	—	—	—

KM# 32 GROSZ

Silver **Obv:** Crowned bust of Sigismund III right **Rev:** Vytis on horseback left in inner circle, date in legend **Note:** Legend and crown varieties exist.

Date	Mintage	VG	F	VF	XF	Unc
1625	—	17.50	25.00	50.00	75.00	—
1262 Error for 1626	—	50.00	60.00	80.00	125	—
1626	—	15.00	20.00	20.00	50.00	—
1627	—	15.00	20.00	20.00	50.00	—

KM# 42 GROSZ

Silver **Obv:** Crowned bust of Johann Casimir right **Rev:** Vytis on horseback left, date in legend **Note:** Three varieties known.

Date	Mintage	VG	F	VF	XF	Unc
1652	—	60.00	80.00	125	175	—

KM# 20 1-1/2 GROSZY

Silver **Obv:** Crowned arms, titles of Sigismund III **Rev:** Orb with value within and below divides two-digit date in inner circle **Note:** Two varieties known.

Date	Mintage	VG	F	VF	XF	Unc
1619	—	75.00	100	150	200	—
1620	—	85.00	135	200	275	—

KM# 40 1-1/2 GROSZY

Silver **Obv:** Crowned arms in inner circle, titles of Johann Casimir **Rev:** Orb with value in inner circle, date in legend

Date	Mintage	VG	F	VF	XF	Unc
1650	—	75.00	150	175	250	—
1652	—	250	450	550	700	—

KM# 5 3 GROSZY

Silver **Obv:** Crowned bust right **Rev:** Value,divided date, symbols and two-line inscription between

Date	Mintage	VG	F	VF	XF	Unc
1600	—	75.00	125	150	200	—
1601 W	—	75.00	125	150	200	—
1601 V	—	50.00	75.00	175	350	—
1602	—	75.00	125	200	375	—
1602 V	—	75.00	125	200	375	—
1603 V	—	125	200	400	575	—
1608	—	75.00	125	150	225	—

KM# 6 3 GROSZY

Silver **Note:** Klippe.

Date	Mintage	VG	F	VF	XF	Unc
1602 V Rare	—	—	—	—	—	—

KM# 43 3 GROSZY

Silver **Obv:** Laureate bust of Johann Casimir right in inner circle **Rev:** Value at top, divided date at bottom, three-line inscription between

Date	Mintage	VG	F	VF	XF	Unc
1652	—	150	250	350	500	—
1664 TLB/HKLP	—	100	150	225	300	—
1665 TLB/HKLP	—	125	200	275	350	—

KM# 44 6 GROSZY

Silver **Obv:** Crowned bust of Johann Casimir right in inner circle **Rev:** Vytis on horseback left, 1-5 below in inner circle, date in legend

Date	Mintage	VG	F	VF	XF	Unc
1652	—	250	375	425	500	—

KM# 51 6 GROSZY
Silver **Obv:** Crowned head reaches to edge of coin at top **Rev:** Value below Vytis

Date	Mintage	VG	F	VF	XF	Unc
1664 TLB	—	50.00	75.00	125	200	—
1665 TLB	—	50.00	75.00	125	200	—
1666 TLB	—	50.00	75.00	125	200	—
1668 TLB	—	50.00	75.00	125	200	—

KM# 52 6 GROSZY
Silver **Note:** Value as IV.

Date	Mintage	VG	F	VF	XF	Unc
1664 TLB	—	50.00	75.00	125	210	—

KM# 51.2 6 GROSZY
Silver **Obv:** Long, narrow bust

Date	Mintage	VG	F	VF	XF	Unc
1666	—	50.00	75.00	125	200	—

KM# 60 6 GROSZY
Silver **Obv:** Laureate bust right **Rev:** Crowned Vytis on horse left, value below within circle, date in legend

Date	Mintage	VG	F	VF	XF	Unc
1679 TLB Rare	—	—	—	—	—	—

KM# 53 ORT (18 Groszy; 1/2 Thaler)
Silver **Obv:** Laureate bust of Johann Casimir right, with or without inner circle **Rev:** Crowned Vytis on horseback left above value in inner circle, date in legend

Date	Mintage	VG	F	VF	XF	Unc
1664 TLB	—	250	325	400	600	—
1665 TLB	—	250	325	400	600	—

KM# 55 GULDEN (Zloty)
Silver **Obv:** Crowned ICR monogram in inner circle **Rev:** Crowned Vytis on horseback left above value XXX, date in legend

Date	Mintage	VG	F	VF	XF	Unc
1666 TLB Rare	—	—	—	—	—	—

TRADE COINAGE

KM# 54.1 1/2 DUCAT (Czerwony Zloty)
1.7500 g., 0.9860 Gold 0.0555 oz. AGW **Obv:** Laureate head of Johann Casimir right **Obv. Legend:** IOA CAS REX PO S MON AVR MAG DVC LIT

Date	Mintage	VG	F	VF	XF	Unc
1664 TLB/HKPL	—	800	1,500	2,500	4,000	—
1665 TLB/HKPL	—	800	1,500	2,500	4,000	—

KM# 54.2 1/2 DUCAT (Czerwony Zloty)
1.7500 g., 0.9860 Gold 0.0555 oz. AGW **Obv:** Smaller head **Obv. Legend:** ...MON AVREA MAG D L

Date	Mintage	VG	F	VF	XF	Unc
1665 TLB/HKPL	—	775	1,500	2,500	4,000	—

KM# 4 DUCAT (Dukaty)
3.5000 g., 0.9860 Gold 0.1109 oz. AGW **Obv:** Crowned bust right **Rev:** Crowned arms in inner circle

Date	Mintage	VG	F	VF	XF	Unc
1590	—	325	1,000	2,750	4,250	—
1591	—	325	1,000	2,750	4,250	—
ND	—	325	1,000	2,750	4,250	—

KM# 56 DUCAT (Dukaty)
3.5000 g., 0.9860 Gold 0.1109 oz. AGW **Obv:** Small laureate head of Johann Casimir in branches **Rev:** Rider left above HKPL monogram in branches, date in legend

Date	Mintage	VG	F	VF	XF	Unc
1666 TLB/HKPL	—	1,500	2,500	5,000	7,500	—

KM# 17 3 DUCATS
10.5000 g., 0.9860 Gold 0.3328 oz. AGW **Obv:** Crowned bust of Sigismund in inner circle **Rev:** Crowned arms in Order collar in inner circle

Date	Mintage	VG	F	VF	XF	Unc
1615 Rare	—	—	—	—	—	—

KM# 18 5 DUCATS (Dukaton)
17.5000 g., 0.9860 Gold 0.5547 oz. AGW **Obv:** Crowned bust right within circle **Obv. Legend:** SIGI SMVND III D G REX POL M D LI **Rev:** Crowned arms in Order collar in inner circle, crown divides date in legend

Date	Mintage	VG	F	VF	XF	Unc
161Z	—	—	—	—	—	—
1618	—	1,500	1,950	5,000	8,000	—

KM# 26 5 DUCATS (Dukaton)
17.5000 g., 0.9860 Gold 0.5547 oz. AGW **Obv. Legend:** ...MAG DVX LIT **Note:** Smaller planchet.

Date	Mintage	VG	F	VF	XF	Unc
1621 HT	—	2,000	4,000	7,000	10,000	—

KM# 27 5 DUCATS (Dukaton)
17.5000 g., 0.9860 Gold 0.5547 oz. AGW **Rev:** Crown divides date in inner circle

Date	Mintage	VG	F	VF	XF	Unc
1622	—	2,000	4,000	7,000	10,000	—
1623	—	2,000	4,000	7,000	10,000	—

KM# 7.1 10 DUCATS
34.6980 g., 0.9860 Gold 1.0999 oz. AGW **Obv:** Sigismund III bust facing right

Date	Mintage	VG	F	VF	XF	Unc
1604 Struck in 1614, Rare	—	—	—	—	—	—
1616 Rare	—	—	—	—	—	—
1617 Rare	—	—	—	—	—	—

KM# 7.2 10 DUCATS
34.6980 g., 0.9860 Gold 1.0999 oz. AGW **Rev:** Privy marks above crown

Date	Mintage	VG	F	VF	XF	Unc
1616	—	—	—	15,000	25,000	—

KM# 19 10 DUCATS
34.6980 g., 0.9860 Gold 1.0999 oz. AGW **Rev:** Date in legend at upper left

Date	Mintage	VG	F	VF	XF	Unc
1618	—	—	—	15,000	25,000	—

KM# 28 10 DUCATS
34.6980 g., 0.9860 Gold 1.0999 oz. AGW **Rev:** Date above shield divided by crown

Date	Mintage	VG	F	VF	XF	Unc
1621	—	—	—	15,000	25,000	—

KM# 29 10 DUCATS
34.6980 g., 0.9860 Gold 1.0999 oz. AGW **Rev:** Date in legend divided by shield

Date	Mintage	VG	F	VF	XF	Unc
1622	—	—	—	15,000	25,000	—

KM# 35 10 DUCATS
34.6980 g., 0.9860 Gold 1.0999 oz. AGW **Obv:** Crowned bust of Wladislaus half right **Rev:** Crowned arms in Order collar in inner circle

Date	Mintage	VG	F	VF	XF	Unc
1639 IT Rare	—	—	—	—	—	—

A former province of Russia, now partly in Latvia and partly in southern Estonia.

The division of Livonia left the northern part governed by Russia while the southern part fell under the dominion of Poland. In 1621 it was the theatre of a war between Sweden and Poland. Being conquered by Sweden, Livonia enjoyed 25 years of milder rule.

RULERS

Polish, until 1628
Swedish, until 1720

MINT OFFICIALS' MARKS

Mark	Desc.	Date	Name
(d)=	Dog	1647-56	Heinrich Jager
(h)=	Helmet	1644-47	Marsilius Philipson
(o)=	Helmet in heart outline	1644-47	Marsilius Philipson
IM		1661-97	Joachim Meinekes

RIGA

Polish Occupation

Founded in 1158, it became a bishopric in 1198 and joined the Hanseatic League in 1282. It came under Polish rule in 1581, was occupied by Sweden in 1621 and remained a Swedish possession until 1710. Ceded to Russia after the battle of Poltava, it was a part of the Treaty of Nystad in 172l. Riga is an important seaport and capital of modern Latvia.

RULERS

Polish, until 1621
Swedish, until 1721

MINT OFFICIALS' INITIALS

Initial	Date	Name
AH, GAH	1700-01	Georg Albrekt Hille
HW	1625-50	A. Winhelmann, warden
HW	1633-59	Henrik Wulff, Tenant
SD	Ca. 1645	Sebastian Dattler, engraver
IM	1652-73	Joachim Meinecke
	1652-63	As warden
	1663-68	As mintmaster
IH	1660	Jost Haltermann, mintmaster
MW	1621-33	Martin Wulff, mintmaster

STANDARD COINAGE

KM# 5 SCHILLING (Silins)

Silver **Obv:** Large S monogram divides date **Obv. Legend:** SIG III D G REX PO D LI - SOLIDVS CIVI RIGENS **Rev:** Crowned arms **Note:** Legend varieties exist.

Date	Mintage	VG	F	VF	XF	Unc
(1)601	—	5.00	12.00	20.00	35.00	—
(1)602	—	5.00	12.00	20.00	35.00	—
(1)603	—	5.00	12.00	20.00	35.00	—
(1)604	—	5.00	12.00	20.00	35.00	—
(1)605	—	5.00	12.00	20.00	35.00	—
(1)606	—	5.00	12.00	20.00	35.00	—
(1)607	—	5.00	12.00	20.00	35.00	—
1609	—	5.00	12.00	20.00	35.00	—
(1)610	—	5.00	12.00	20.00	35.00	—
1610	—	5.00	12.00	20.00	35.00	—
(1)611	—	5.00	12.00	20.00	35.00	—
(16)12	—	5.00	12.00	20.00	35.00	—
1613	—	5.00	12.00	20.00	35.00	—
1614	—	5.00	12.00	20.00	35.00	—
1615	—	5.00	12.00	20.00	35.00	—
1616	—	5.00	12.00	20.00	35.00	—
1617	—	5.00	12.00	20.00	35.00	—
(16)18	—	5.00	12.00	20.00	35.00	—
1619	—	5.00	12.00	20.00	35.00	—
(16)20	—	5.00	12.00	20.00	35.00	—
(1)620	—	5.00	12.00	20.00	35.00	—
1620	—	5.00	12.00	20.00	35.00	—
(16)21	—	5.00	12.00	20.00	35.00	—
(16)22	—	5.00	12.00	20.00	35.00	—
ND	—	5.00	12.00	20.00	35.00	—

KM# 7 GROSCHEN (Grasis, Grosze)

Silver **Obv:** Shield of arms **Obv. Legend:** SIGIS III DG REX POL M L GROS ARGEN CIVI RIGE **Rev:** Orb, crossed keys below **Rev. Legend:** GROS AEGE (N) CIVI RIG.

Date	Mintage	VG	F	VF	XF	Unc
(16)16	—	10.00	22.00	45.00	75.00	—
(16)17	—	15.00	30.00	75.00	125	—

KM# A6 3 GROSCHEN

Silver **Obv:** Crowned bust of Sigismund III to right **Rev. Legend:** III / GR-OS / ARG. TRIP / CIVI. RI / GE.

Date	Mintage	VG	F	VF	XF	Unc
1601	—	—	—	—	—	—
1603	—	—	—	—	—	—
1619	—	12.00	25.00	50.00	150	650
ND	—	10.00	20.00	40.00	130	—

KM# A9 DUCAT

Gold

Date	Mintage	VG	F	VF	XF	Unc
1619 Rare	—	—	—	—	—	—

RIGA

Swedish Occupation

STANDARD COINAGE

KM# 17 3 POLKER (3 Pelheri)

Silver **Note:** Struck at Bromberg (Bydgoszcz) Mint.

Date	Mintage	VG	F	VF	XF	Unc
1625	—	15.00	30.00	60.00	120	—

KM# 9 SOLIDUS (Schilling, Silins)

Silver **Obv:** Crowned GA monogram in inner circle **Obv. Legend:** GVSTA ADOL D G REX S SOLIDVS CIVI RIGENSIS **Rev:** Arms in cartouche in inner circle, date in legend **Note:** Legend varieties exist.

Date	Mintage	VG	F	VF	XF	Unc
1621	—	8.00	20.00	40.00	80.00	—
16Z1	—	8.00	20.00	40.00	80.00	—
162.1	—	8.00	20.00	40.00	80.00	—
1622 Rare	—	—	—	—	—	—
1623	—	—	—	—	—	—
(16)24	—	5.00	10.00	16.00	30.00	—
1625	—	5.00	10.00	16.00	30.00	—
1626	—	5.00	10.00	16.00	30.00	—
(16)27	—	5.00	10.00	16.00	30.00	—
1627 Rare	—	—	—	—	—	—
1628	—	5.00	10.00	16.00	30.00	—
1629 Rare	—	—	—	—	—	—
1630	—	5.00	10.00	16.00	30.00	—
1631	—	5.00	10.00	16.00	30.00	—
1632	—	5.00	10.00	16.00	30.00	—
(16)33	—	5.00	10.00	16.00	30.00	—
1634	—	5.00	10.00	16.00	30.00	—
ND	—	5.00	10.00	16.00	30.00	—

KM# 21 SOLIDUS (Schilling, Silins)

Silver **Obv:** Crowned C with Vasa arms within inner circle **Obv. Legend:** CHRISTINA D G DR S SOLIDUS CIVI RIGENSIS

Date	Mintage	VG	F	VF	XF	Unc
1634 Rare	—	—	—	—	—	—
1635	—	5.00	10.00	16.00	30.00	—
1636	—	5.00	10.00	16.00	30.00	—
1637	—	5.00	10.00	16.00	30.00	—
(16)83 Error for 1638	—	6.00	12.00	17.00	33.50	—
(16)38	—	5.00	10.00	18.00	30.00	—
1639	—	6.50	12.00	18.00	36.00	—
(16)40	—	6.50	12.00	18.00	36.00	—
1640	—	6.50	12.00	18.00	36.00	—
1641	—	6.50	12.00	18.00	36.00	—
(16)42	—	6.50	12.00	18.00	36.00	—
(16)43	—	6.50	12.00	18.00	36.00	—
1644	—	6.50	12.00	18.00	36.00	—
1645	—	6.50	12.00	18.00	36.00	—
1646	—	6.50	12.00	18.00	36.00	—
(16)47	—	6.50	12.00	18.00	36.00	—
(16)48	—	6.50	12.00	18.00	36.00	—
1649	—	6.50	12.00	18.00	36.00	—
(16)50	—	6.50	12.00	18.00	36.00	—
1651	—	13.00	32.00	60.00	120	—
(16)51	—	6.50	12.00	18.00	36.00	—
1652	—	13.00	32.00	60.00	120	—
(16)52	—	6.50	12.00	18.00	36.00	—
1653	—	6.50	12.00	18.00	36.00	—
1654	—	6.50	12.00	18.00	36.00	—

KM# 25 SOLIDUS (Schilling, Silins)

Silver **Rev:** Last two digits of date in Roman numerals

Date	Mintage	VG	F	VF	XF	Unc
16XL(1640)	—	10.00	25.00	50.00	100	—

KM# 50 SOLIDUS (Schilling, Silins)

Silver **Obv:** Crowned CG monogram in inner circle

Date	Mintage	VG	F	VF	XF	Unc
1654	—	7.00	15.00	30.00	60.00	—
1655	—	7.00	15.00	30.00	60.00	—
1656	—	7.00	15.00	30.00	60.00	—
1657	—	7.00	15.00	30.00	60.00	—
1658	—	7.00	15.00	30.00	60.00	—
1659	—	7.00	15.00	30.00	60.00	—
1660	—	7.00	15.00	30.00	60.00	—

KM# 53 SOLIDUS (Schilling, Silins)

Silver **Obv:** Without inner circle

Date	Mintage	VG	F	VF	XF	Unc
1657	—	16.00	40.00	90.00	180	—

KM# 55 SOLIDUS (Schilling, Silins)

Silver **Obv:** Crowned CR monogram in inner circle **Note:** 1666-68 dates are contemporary counterfeits generaly produced at Suczava.

Date	Mintage	VG	F	VF	XF	Unc
1660	—	5.00	10.00	30.00	90.00	—
1661	—	5.00	10.00	30.00	90.00	—
1662	—	5.00	10.00	30.00	90.00	—
(16)63	—	5.00	10.00	30.00	90.00	—
1664	—	5.00	10.00	30.00	90.00	—
(16)65	—	5.00	10.00	30.00	90.00	—
1666	—	5.00	10.00	30.00	90.00	—
(16)66	—	5.00	10.00	30.00	90.00	—
1668	—	5.00	10.00	30.00	90.00	—
(1)668	—	5.00	10.00	30.00	90.00	—
ND	—	5.00	10.00	30.00	90.00	—

KM# 12 1-1/2 SCHILLING

Silver **Obv:** Riga arms in inner circle **Rev:** Crossed keys divide date in inner circle

Date	Mintage	VG	F	VF	XF	Unc
(16)23	—	35.00	85.00	175	350	—

KM# 10 1/24 THALER (1/24 Dalderi, Trispelher)

Silver **Obv:** Crowned arms in inner circle **Obv. Legend:** GVST ADOLP D G REX S MON NOV CIVI RIGE **Rev:** Orb with value within divides date in inner circle

Date	Mintage	VG	F	VF	XF	Unc
(16)22	—	8.00	20.00	40.00	85.00	—
(16)23	—	7.00	15.00	30.00	65.00	—
(16)24	—	7.00	15.00	30.00	65.00	—
1625	—	7.00	15.00	30.00	65.00	—
(16)26	—	7.00	15.00	30.00	65.00	—
(16)27	—	7.00	15.00	30.00	65.00	—
(16)28	—	7.00	15.00	30.00	65.00	—
1629	—	7.00	15.00	30.00	65.00	—
1633	—	7.00	15.00	30.00	65.00	—

Date	Mintage	VG	F	VF	XF	Unc
1634	—	7.00	15.00	30.00	65.00	—
1635	—	7.00	15.00	30.00	65.00	—

KM# 31 1/24 THALER (1/24 Dalderi, Trispelher)
Silver **Obv. Legend:** CHRISTINA D G REG SV-MON NOVA CIVI RIGE **Note:** Legend varieties exist.

Date	Mintage	VG	F	VF	XF	Unc
(16)44	—	9.00	22.50	45.00	120	—
(16)47	—	12.00	30.00	60.00	160	—
(16)48	—	9.00	22.50	45.00	120	—
(16)49	—	15.00	37.50	75.00	200	—

KM# A69 1/24 THALER (1/24 Dalderi, Trispelher)
Silver **Obv. Legend:** CHRISTINA D G R S MON NOVA LIVONI

Date	Mintage	VG	F	VF	XF	Unc
1662	—	35.00	80.00	160	300	—

KM# 69 1/24 THALER (1/24 Dalderi, Trispelher)
Silver **Obv:** Titles of Charles XI

Date	Mintage	VG	F	VF	XF	Unc
(16)69	—	27.50	70.00	140	265	—

KM# 90 1/24 THALER (1/24 Dalderi, Trispelher)
Silver **Obv:** Center shield of arms with Bavarian lozenges; Titles of Charles XII

Date	Mintage	VG	F	VF	XF	Unc
1700	—	43.75	105	210	425	—

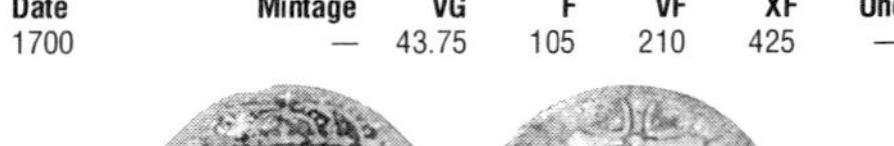

KM# 91 1/24 THALER (1/24 Dalderi, Trispelher)
Silver **Obv:** Center shield of arms with lion

Date	Mintage	VG	F	VF	XF	Unc
1700	—	20.00	55.00	105	210	—

KM# 8 3 POLKER (1 1/2 Groschen)
Silver **Obv:** 3 at bottom **Rev:** Orb, crossed keys below, with keys and/or fox at end of legend **Rev. Legend:** MONE NOVA CIVI RIGE **Note:** Legend varieties exist.

Date	Mintage	VG	F	VF	XF	Unc
(16)Z0 fox	—	7.00	16.00	28.00	50.00	—
(16)Z0 keys	—	7.00	16.00	28.00	50.00	—
(16)Z0 fox & keys	—	8.00	20.00	30.00	60.00	—
(16)24	—	—	—	—	—	—

KM# 64 1/4 THALER
Silver **Obv:** Draped bust of Charles XI to right in inner circle **Rev:** Arms of Riga divide date in inner circle

Date	Mintage	VG	F	VF	XF	Unc
1668 IM Rare	—	—	—	—	—	—

KM# 65 1/3 THALER
Silver **Obv:** Bust of Charles XI right **Rev:** Arms of Riga divide date in inner circle

Date	Mintage	VG	F	VF	XF	Unc
1668 IM Rare	—	—	—	—	—	—

KM# 15 1/2 THALER
Silver **Note:** Similar to 1 Thaler, KM#16. Varieties exist.

Date	Mintage	VG	F	VF	XF	Unc
1629	—	3,000	5,000	9,000	—	—

KM# A15 1/2 THALER
Silver

Date	Mintage	VG	F	VF	XF	Unc
1630	—	3,500	6,500	11,000	—	—
1631 Rare	—	—	—	—	—	—

KM# A40 1/2 THALER
Silver **Note:** Similar to 1 Thaler, KM#33.

Date	Mintage	VG	F	VF	XF	Unc
1645 Rare	—	—	—	—	—	—
1648 Rare	—	—	—	—	—	—

KM# 66 1/2 THALER
Silver **Obv:** Draped bust of Charles XI right in inner circle **Rev:** Arms of Riga divide date in inner circle

Date	Mintage	VG	F	VF	XF	Unc
1668 IM Rare	—	—	—	—	—	—

KM# 14 THALER (Dalderi)
Silver **Obv:** Crowned bust of Gustavus Adolphus right in inner circle **Rev:** Arms of Riga with lion supporters divide date in inner circle **Note:** Dav. #4586.

Date	Mintage	VG	F	VF	XF	Unc
1628 MN Rare	—	—	—	—	—	—

KM# 16 THALER (Dalderi)
Silver **Note:** Dav. #4587.

Date	Mintage	VG	F	VF	XF	Unc
1629 MW	—	2,000	4,000	6,500	—	—

KM# 20 THALER (Dalderi)
Silver **Note:** Dav. #4588.

Date	Mintage	VG	F	VF	XF	Unc
1630 MW	—	1,750	3,500	6,000	9,500	—
1631 MW	—	2,000	4,000	7,000	—	—

KM# 23 THALER (Dalderi)
Silver **Obv:** Without lace collar **Note:** Dav. #4589.

Date	Mintage	VG	F	VF	XF	Unc
1639 HW	—	1,000	2,250	4,950	9,800	—

KM# 22 THALER (Dalderi)
Silver **Note:** Similar to KM#23 but with lace collar.

Date	Mintage	VG	F	VF	XF	Unc
1639 HW	—	1,000	2,250	4,800	9,800	—

KM# 26 THALER (Dalderi)
Silver **Note:** Dav. #4590. Small letters in legends.

Date	Mintage	VG	F	VF	XF	Unc
1643 HW	—	1,200	2,550	5,300	10,500	—

KM# 32.1 THALER (Dalderi)
Silver **Rev. Legend:** MON: NOVA ARGENT: CIVIT: RIGEN: **Note:** Dav. #4592. Large letters in legends.

Date	Mintage	VG	F	VF	XF	Unc
1644 HW	—	2,250	4,500	7,000	—	—

KM# 32.2 THALER (Dalderi)
Silver **Rev. Legend:** ...CIVIT: RIGENSIS: **Note:** Dav. #4592A.

Date	Mintage	VG	F	VF	XF	Unc
1644 HW Rare	—	—	—	—	—	—

Note: Fritz Rudolf Künker Münzenhandlung Auction 134, 1-08, VF-XF realized approximately $19,200

KM# 33 THALER (Dalderi)
Silver **Note:** Dav. #4594.

Date	Mintage	VG	F	VF	XF	Unc
1644 HW	—	900	2,400	4,950	9,800	—
1645 HW	—	1,500	3,600	7,500	15,000	—

KM# 41 THALER (Dalderi)
Silver **Obv:** Half figure of Christina right in inner circle **Note:** Dav. #4595.

Date	Mintage	VG	F	VF	XF	Unc
1646 HW	—	1,500	3,600	7,500	15,000	—
1648 HW	—	1,650	3,750	7,800	15,500	—

KM# 56.1 THALER (Dalderi)
Silver **Rev:** Towers have double pennants **Note:** Dav. #A4596.

Date	Mintage	VG	F	VF	XF	Unc
1660 IM Rare	—	—	—	—	—	—

KM# 56.2 THALER (Dalderi)
Silver **Rev:** Towers have single pennants **Note:** Dav. #4596.

Date	Mintage	VG	F	VF	XF	Unc
1660 IM Rare	—	—	—	—	—	—

Note: Fritz Rudolf Künker Münzenhandlung Auction 134, 1-08, XF-Unc realized approximately $16,245

KM# 67 THALER (Dalderi)
Silver **Obv:** Older draped bust of Charles XI right in inner circle **Rev. Legend:** MONETA NOVA ARGENTEA CIVITATIS RIGENSIS **Note:** Dav. #4597.

Date	Mintage	VG	F	VF	XF	Unc
1668 IM Rare	—	—	—	—	—	—

KM# 75 THALER (Dalderi)
Silver **Obv:** Young armored bust of Charles XI right in inner circle **Note:** Dav. #4598.

Date	Mintage	VG	F	VF	XF	Unc
1672 IM Rare	—	—	—	—	—	—

KM# 34 2 THALER
Silver **Note:** Dav. #A4591. Similar to 1 Thaler, KM#32.

Date	Mintage	VG	F	VF	XF	Unc
1644 HW Rare	—	—	—	—	—	—

KM# 39 2 THALER
Silver **Note:** Dav. #4593. Similar to 1 Thaler, KM#33.

Date	Mintage	VG	F	VF	XF	Unc
1645 HW Rare	—	—	—	—	—	—

KM# 48 3 THALER
Silver **Note:** Dav. #4591. Similar to 1 Thaler, KM#32.

Date	Mintage	VG	F	VF	XF	Unc
1644 Rare	—	—	—	—	—	—

KM# 35 3 THALER
Silver **Note:** Dav. #B4591. Similar to 1 Thaler, KM#32.

Date	Mintage	VG	F	VF	XF	Unc
1644 HW Unique	—	—	—	—	—	—

TRADE COINAGE

KM# 13 DUCAT
3.5000 g., 0.9860 Gold 0.1109 oz. AGW **Obv:** Crowned bust of Gustavus Adolphus left **Rev:** Supported arms in inner circle, date in legend

Date	Mintage	VG	F	VF	XF	Unc
1623 Rare	—	—	—	—	—	—

KM# 27 DUCAT
3.5000 g., 0.9860 Gold 0.1109 oz. AGW **Obv:** Bust of Christina facing half left in inner circle

Date	Mintage	VG	F	VF	XF	Unc
1643 HW Rare	—	—	—	—	—	—

KM# 36 DUCAT
3.5000 g., 0.9860 Gold 0.1109 oz. AGW **Obv:** Bust of Christina left in inner circle **Obv. Legend:** CHRISTINA D G SVE GOVA Q D REG PRIN H **Rev:** Supported arms in inner circle **Rev. Legend:** MONETA AUREA CIVITATIS RIGENSIS **Note:** Legend varieties exist.

Date	Mintage	VG	F	VF	XF	Unc
1644 HW Rare	—	—	—	—	—	—

Note: Fritz Rudolf Künker Münzenhandlung Auction 139, 3-08, XF-Unc realized approximately $24,935

Date	Mintage	VG	F	VF	XF	Unc
1645 HW Rare	—	—	—	—	—	—

KM# 42 DUCAT
3.5000 g., 0.9860 Gold 0.1109 oz. AGW **Obv:** Bust of Christina right

Date	Mintage	VG	F	VF	XF	Unc
1646 HW Rare	—	—	—	—	—	—

KM# 61 DUCAT
3.5000 g., 0.9860 Gold 0.1109 oz. AGW **Obv:** Bust of Charles XI right in inner circle **Rev:** Crowned arms in inner circle divide date

Date	Mintage	VG	F	VF	XF	Unc
1664 IM Rare	—	—	—	—	—	—

KM# 68 DUCAT
3.5000 g., 0.9860 Gold 0.1109 oz. AGW **Obv:** Bust of Charles XI right without inner circle

Date	Mintage	VG	F	VF	XF	Unc
1668 IM Rare	—	—	—	—	—	—

KM# 76 DUCAT
3.5000 g., 0.9860 Gold 0.1109 oz. AGW **Obv:** Large bust of Charles XI right in inner circle

Date	Mintage	VG	F	VF	XF	Unc
1673 Rare	—	—	—	—	—	—

Note: Fritz Rudolf Künker Münzenhandlung Auction 139, 3-08, nearly Unc, realized approximately $21,820

KM# 80 DUCAT
3.5000 g., 0.9860 Gold 0.1109 oz. AGW **Obv:** Large bust of Charles XI right without inner circle

Date	Mintage	VG	F	VF	XF	Unc
1681 Unique	—	—	—	—	—	—

KM# 92 DUCAT
3.5000 g., 0.9860 Gold 0.1109 oz. AGW **Obv:** Draped bust right **Obv. Legend:** CAROLVS • XII • D • G • REX • SVE • **Rev:** Crown above towers divides date within circle **Rev. Legend:** CIVITAT • RIGENSIS & MON • NOVA • AUREA

Date	Mintage	VG	F	VF	XF	Unc
1700 Rare	—	—	—	—	—	—

KM# 28 2 DUCAT
7.0000 g., 0.9860 Gold 0.2219 oz. AGW **Obv:** Bust of Christiana facing half left in inner circle **Rev:** Supported arms in inner circle, date in legend

Date	Mintage	VG	F	VF	XF	Unc
1643 HW Rare	—	—	—	—	—	—

KM# 43 2 DUCAT
7.0000 g., 0.9860 Gold 0.2219 oz. AGW **Obv:** Bust of Christiana right in inner circle **Rev:** Supported arms with date below in inner circle

Date	Mintage	VG	F	VF	XF	Unc
1646 HW Rare	—	—	—	—	—	—

KM# 62 2 DUCAT
7.0000 g., 0.9860 Gold 0.2219 oz. AGW **Obv:** Fine style bust of Charles XI right in inner circle **Rev:** Crowned arms in inner circle divide date

Date	Mintage	VG	F	VF	XF	Unc
1664 IM Rare	—	—	—	—	—	—

KM# 63 2 DUCAT
7.0000 g., 0.9860 Gold 0.2219 oz. AGW **Obv:** Bust of Charles XI

Date	Mintage	VG	F	VF	XF	Unc
1667 IM Rare	—	—	—	—	—	—

Note: Fritz Rudolf Künker Münzenhandlung Auction 135, 1-08, nearly Unc realized approximately $44,300

KM# 29 3 DUCAT
10.5000 g., 0.9860 Gold 0.3328 oz. AGW **Obv:** Bust of Christina

Date	Mintage	VG	F	VF	XF	Unc
1643 HW Rare	—	—	—	—	—	—

KM# 37 3 DUCAT
10.5000 g., 0.9860 Gold 0.3328 oz. AGW **Obv:** Bust of Christina right in inner circle **Rev:** Supported arms with date below in inner circle

Date	Mintage	VG	F	VF	XF	Unc
1644 HW Rare	—	—	—	—	—	—

KM# A38 3 DUCAT
10.5000 g., 0.9860 Gold 0.3328 oz. AGW **Obv. Legend:** CHRISTINA D G SVE GO VAN Q REGINA & PRINCIP HAE M D F **Rev. Legend:** EX AVRO SOLIDO REGIA CIVITAS RIGENSIS FIERI F

Date	Mintage	VG	F	VF	XF	Unc
1646 Rare	—	—	—	—	—	—

Note: Fritz Rudolf Künker Münzenhandlung Auction 135, 1-08, XF realized approximately $38,395

KM# 44 4 DUCAT
14.0000 g., 0.9860 Gold 0.4438 oz. AGW **Obv:** Bust of Christina right in inner circle **Rev:** Supported arms with date below in inner circle

Date	Mintage	VG	F	VF	XF	Unc
1646 HW Rare	—	—	—	—	—	—

KM# 45 ROSE RYAL (4 Ducat)
14.0000 g., 0.9860 Gold 0.4438 oz. AGW **Obv:** Christina enthroned in inner circle **Rev:** Crowned arms in branches in inner circle

Date	Mintage	VG	F	VF	XF	Unc
ND Rare	—	—	—	—	—	—

KM# 40 5 DUCAT
17.5000 g., 0.9860 Gold 0.5547 oz. AGW **Obv:** Bust of Christina

Date	Mintage	VG	F	VF	XF	Unc
1645 Rare	—	—	—	—	—	—

KM# 51 5 DUCAT
17.5000 g., 0.9860 Gold 0.5547 oz. AGW **Obv:** Bust of Charles X

Date	Mintage	VG	F	VF	XF	Unc
1645(1654) Rare	—	—	—	—	—	—

Note: Fritz Rudolf Künker Münzenhandlung Auction 135, 1-08, attractive example realized approximately $103,370

Date	Mintage	VG	F	VF	XF	Unc
1655 Rare	—	—	—	—	—	—

Note: Altered date

KM# 38 6 DUCAT
21.0000 g., 0.9860 Gold 0.6657 oz. AGW **Obv:** Bust of Christina facing half left in inner circle **Rev:** Supported arms, radiant "Jehovah" at top, date in exergue

Date	Mintage	VG	F	VF	XF	Unc
1644 HW Rare	—	—	—	—	—	—

KM# 52 6 DUCAT
21.0000 g., 0.9860 Gold 0.6657 oz. AGW **Obv:** Crowned bust of Charles right **Rev:** City of Riga in inner circle **Note:** Deleted.

Date	Mintage	VG	F	VF	XF	Unc
1645(1654) Rare	—	—	—	—	—	—
1655 Rare	—	—	—	—	—	—

Note: Altered date

KM# 11 7 DUCAT
24.5000 g., 0.9860 Gold 0.7766 oz. AGW **Obv:** Half-length figure of Gustavus Adolphus left with orb and scepter **Rev:** Supported arms in inner circle, Roman numeral date in legend

Date	Mintage	VG	F	VF	XF	Unc
1622 Unique	—	—	—	—	—	—

KM# 30 10 DUCAT
35.0000 g., 0.9860 Gold 1.1095 oz. AGW **Obv:** Christine **Rev:** Radiant "Jehovah" above supported arms

Date	Mintage	VG	F	VF	XF	Unc
1643 HW Unique	—	—	—	—	—	—
1644 HW Rare	—	—	—	—	—	—
1645 HW Rare	—	—	—	—	—	—

KM# 57 10 DUCAT
35.0000 g., 0.9860 Gold 1.1095 oz. AGW **Obv:** Child bust of Charles XI right **Rev:** Crowned arms in inner circle divide date

Date	Mintage	VG	F	VF	XF	Unc
1660 IM Rare	—	—	—	—	—	—

LIVONIA

Swedish Occupation

STANDARD COINAGE

KM# 1 SOLIDUS (Schilling, Silins)
Silver **Obv:** Crowned CR monogram in inner circle **Rev:** Vasa arms in cartouche in inner circle, date in legend **Note:** Varieties exist.

Date	Mintage	VG	F	VF	XF	Unc
1644 Rare	—	—	—	—	—	—
1645 Rare	—	—	—	—	—	—
1645 (o) Rare	—	—	—	—	—	—

KM# 2 SOLIDUS (Schilling, Silins)
Silver **Obv:** Crowned C with Vasa arms within inner circle **Rev:** Arms in cartouche in inner circle, date in legend **Note:** Varieties exist.

Date	Mintage	VG	F	VF	XF	Unc
1645 (h)	—	20.00	50.00	100	200	—
1645 (o)	—	20.00	50.00	100	200	—
1645	—	12.00	30.00	60.00	120	—
1647	—	6.00	12.00	18.00	30.00	—
1648	—	6.00	12.00	18.00	30.00	—
1649	—	6.00	12.00	18.00	30.00	—
1650	—	6.00	12.00	18.00	30.00	—
1651	—	6.00	12.00	18.00	30.00	—
1652	—	6.00	12.00	18.00	30.00	—
1653	—	6.00	12.00	18.00	30.00	—
1654	—	6.00	12.00	18.00	30.00	—

KM# 4 SOLIDUS (Schilling, Silins)
Silver **Obv:** Crowned CG monogram inner circle

Date	Mintage	VG	F	VF	XF	Unc
1654	—	7.00	15.00	30.00	60.00	—
1655	—	7.00	15.00	30.00	60.00	—
1656	—	7.00	15.00	30.00	60.00	—
1657	—	7.00	15.00	30.00	60.00	—
1658	—	7.00	15.00	30.00	60.00	—
1659	—	7.00	15.00	30.00	60.00	—

KM# A5 SOLIDUS (Schilling, Silins)
Silver **Obv:** Crowned CR monogram inner circle **Note:** Obverse legend varieties exist.

Date	Mintage	VG	F	VF	XF	Unc
(16)60	—	7.00	15.00	30.00	60.00	—
(16)61	—	7.00	15.00	30.00	60.00	—
1662	—	7.00	15.00	30.00	60.00	—
1663	—	7.00	15.00	30.00	60.00	—
1664	—	7.00	15.00	30.00	60.00	—
1665	—	7.00	15.00	30.00	60.00	—

KM# 3 1/24 THALER (1/24 Daldieri)
Silver **Obv:** Crowned arms in inner circle, titles of Christina **Rev:** Orb with value within divides date in inner circle **Note:** Varieties exist.

Date	Mintage	VG	F	VF	XF	Unc
(16)47	—	20.00	50.00	100	200	—
(16)48	—	20.00	50.00	100	200	—
(16)48 (d)	—	8.00	20.00	40.00	80.00	—

KM# 6 1/24 THALER (1/24 Daldieri)
Silver **Obv:** Titles of Charles XI

Date	Mintage	VG	F	VF	XF	Unc
(16)69	—	16.00	40.00	80.00	160	—

PATTERNS

Including off metal strikes

KM#	Date	Mintage	Identification	Mkt Val
Pn1	1645(1654)	—	5 Ducat. Silver. KM#51.	500

JOHORE

Johore (Johor) is a state with numerous small islands located between the South China Sea and the Strait of Malacca, with the capital of Johor Baharu. Ala'uddin, son of Sultan Mahmud, who fled Malacca after the Portuguese conquest of 1511, declared himself the first Sultan of Johore. Johore later was captured by Acheh, Sumatra, in 1564 and became its vassel state until the collapse of the Acheh Empire in 1641. In 1717, Raja Kechil of Siak, captured Johore, but was later defeated by Bugis forces in 1722. The Dutch defeated the Bugis forces in 1784 and subjected Johore to their control. Johore was later split by Dutch and English influence with the Anglo-Dutch Treaty of 1824. Johore came under British protection as one of the unfederated Malay States by the Anglo-Johore Treaty of 1885. By the end of January 1942 until 1945, Japanese forces occupied Johore. In April 1946, Johore joined the short-lived Malayan Union. In 1948 Johore became part of the Federation of Malaya, attained independence in 1957, and in 1963 became one of the component States of Malaysia.

REFERENCE: (SS#) – *"The Coins of Malaysia, Singapore and Brunei, 1400-1986"* by Saran Singh.

RULERS

Sultans of Johore (Malacca Royal Line)
Ala'udin Riayat Shah II, 1597-1613
Abdullah Ha'ayat Shah, 1615-1623
Abdul Jalil Shah III, 1623-1677
Ibrahim Shah, 1677-1685
Mahmud Shah II, 1685-1699

Sultans of Johore (Bendahara Line)
Abdul Jalil Riayat Shah IV, 1700-1719

MONETARY SYSTEM
25 Katun = 1 Penjuru
2 Penjuru = 1 Kupang
4 Kupang = 1 Mas

STATE

HAMMERED COINAGE

KM# 4 1/4 PENJURU

0.4500 g., Silver, 12 mm. **Ruler:** Abdul Jalil Shah III 1623 - 1677 **Obv:** Inscription in Arabic **Obv. Inscription:** "Sultan Abdul Jalil Shah" **Rev:** Inscription in Arabic **Rev. Inscription:** "Khalifatul Muminin" **Edge:** Plain **Shape:** Octagonal **Note:** SS#20a.

Date	Mintage	Good	VG	F	VF	XF
ND(1623-77)	—	200	375	650	900	—

KM# 5 KUPANG

0.6400 g., Gold, 13 mm. **Ruler:** Abdul Jalil Shah III 1623 - 1677 **Obv:** Inscription in Arabic **Obv. Inscription:** "Sultan Abdul Jalil Shah" **Rev:** Inscription in Arabic **Rev. Inscription:** "Khalifatul Muminin" **Edge:** Plain **Shape:** Octagonal **Note:** SS#14.

Date	Mintage	Good	VG	F	VF	XF
ND(1623-77)	—	150	275	450	650	—

KM# 8 KUPANG

0.6200 g., Gold **Ruler:** Mahmud Shah II 1685 - 1699 **Obv:** Inscription in Arabic **Obv. Inscription:** "Sultan Mahmud" **Rev:** Inscription in Arabic **Rev. Inscription:** "Khalifatul Muminin" **Edge:** Plain **Shape:** Octagonal **Note:** SS#16; Size varies 11 - 12 mm.

Date	Mintage	Good	VG	F	VF	XF
ND(1685-99)	—	450	850	1,350	2,000	—

KM# 2 MAS

2.6000 g., Gold, 17 mm. **Ruler:** Abdullah Ha'ayat Shah 1615 - 1623 **Obv:** Arabic inscription in octagonal border and circle of dots **Obv. Inscription:** "Sultan Abdullah Riayat Shah" **Rev:** Arabic inscription in octagonal border and circle of dots **Rev. Inscription:** "Khalifatul Muminin" **Edge:** Plain **Note:** SS#11.

Date	Mintage	Good	VG	F	VF	XF
ND(1615-1623)	—	1,350	2,750	4,500	6,500	—

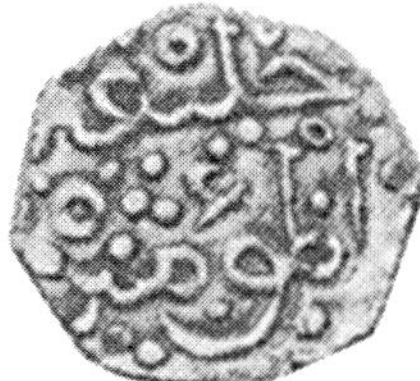

KM# 6 MAS

2.4600 g., Gold, 16.8 mm. **Ruler:** Abdul Jalil Shah III 1623 - 1677 **Obv:** Inscription in Arabic **Obv. Inscription:** "Sultan Abdul Jalil Shah" **Rev:** Inscription in Arabic **Rev. Inscription:** "Khalifatul Muminin" **Edge:** Plain **Shape:** Octagonal **Note:** SS#12.

Date	Mintage	Good	VG	F	VF	XF
ND(1623-77)	—	500	1,000	1,750	2,500	—

KM# 6a MAS

1.8000 g., Gilt Copper, 16.8 mm. **Ruler:** Abdul Jalil Shah III 1623 - 1677 **Subject:** Funeral of Sultan Abdul Jalil Shah III **Obv:** Inscription in Arabic **Obv. Inscription:** "Sultan Abdul Jalil Shah" **Rev:** Inscription in Arabic **Rev. Inscription:** "Khalifatul Muminin" **Edge:** Plain **Shape:** Octagonal **Note:** SS#13.

Date	Mintage	Good	VG	F	VF	XF
ND(1677)	—	500	1,000	1,750	2,500	—

KM# 9 MAS

2.5500 g., Gold, 16 mm. **Ruler:** Mahmud Shah II 1685 - 1699 **Obv:** Inscription in Arabic **Obv. Inscription:** "Sultan Mahmud Shah" **Rev:** Inscription in Arabic **Rev. Inscription:** "Khalifatul Muminin" **Edge:** Plain **Shape:** Octagonal **Note:** SS#15.

Date	Mintage	Good	VG	F	VF	XF
ND(1685-99)	—	1,000	2,000	3,200	4,500	—

KEDAH

A state in northwestern Malaysia. Islam introduced in 15th century. Subject to Thailand from 1821-1909. Coins issued under Governor Tengku Anum.

TITLES

Kedah

SULTANS
Dhiauddin Mukarram Shah, 1661-1687
Abdullah al-Muazzam Shah I, 1698-1706

SULTANATE

HAMMERED COINAGE

KM# 3 TARRA

Copper, 30 mm. **Obv:** Inscription in Arabic **Obv. Inscription:** "Al-Sultan Dhiauddin Mukarram Shah" **Note:** Arabic legend. SS#5a.

Date	Mintage	Good	VG	F	VF	XF
ND Rare	—	—	—	—	—	—

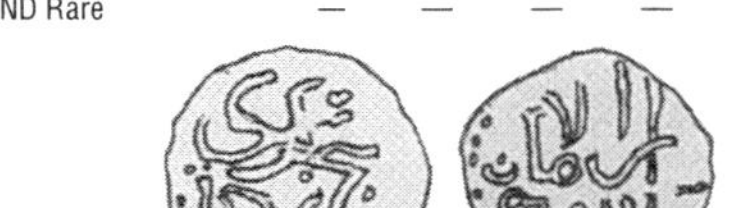

KM# 7 TARRA

Copper, 18 mm. **Obv:** Inscription in Arabic **Obv. Inscription:** "Belanja Negeri Kedah" **Rev:** Inscription in Arabic **Rev. Inscription:** "Darul Aman Sanat" **Note:** Arabic legend. SS#6.

Date	Mintage	Good	VG	F	VF	XF
AH1110 Rare	—	—	—	—	—	—

KM# 6 1/4 REAL

0.7700 g., 0.7000 Silver 0.0173 oz. ASW **Obv:** Inscription in Arabic **Obv. Inscription:** "Dhiauddin" **Rev:** Inscription in Arabic **Rev. Inscription:** "Sultan Sanat" **Note:** Arabic legend. SS#4.

Date	Mintage	Good	VG	F	VF	XF
AH1077 Rare	—	—	—	—	—	—

KM# 1 KUPANG

0.4500 g., Gold, 12 mm. **Ruler:** Dhiauddin Mukarram Shah **Obv:** Arabic inscription **Obv. Inscription:** "Sultan Abdullah Shah" **Rev:** Arabic inscription **Rev. Inscription:** "Khalifatul Muminin" **Shape:** Hexagonal

Date	Mintage	VG	F	VF	XF	Unc
ND Rare	—	—	—	—	—	—

KM# 5 KUPANG

0.5000 g., Gold, 8 mm. **Obv:** Inscription in Arabic **Obv. Inscription:** "Dhiauddin" **Rev:** Inscription in Arabic **Rev. Inscription:** "Shah Mukarram" **Note:** Arabic legend

Date	Mintage	VG	F	VF	XF	Unc
ND Rare	—	—	—	—	—	—

KM# 4 KUPANG

0.5000 g., Gold, 9 mm. **Obv:** Inscription in Arabic **Obv. Inscription:** "Dar'ul-Aman" **Rev:** Inscription in Arabic **Rev. Inscription:** "Fil al-Quds"

Date	Mintage	VG	F	VF	XF	Unc
ND Rare	—	—	—	—	—	—

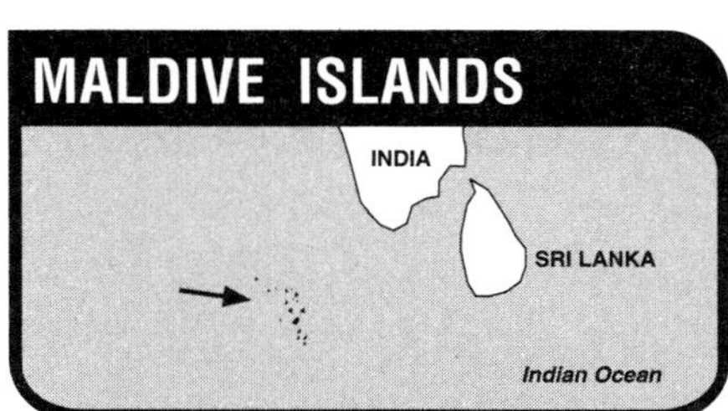

The Republic of Maldives, an archipelago of 2,000 coral islets in the northern Indian Ocean 417 miles (671 km.) west of Ceylon, has an area of 116 sq. mi. (298 sq. km.).

The Maldive Islands were visited by Arab traders and converted to Islam in 1153. After being harassed in the16th and 17th centuries by Mopla pirates of the Malabar coast and Portuguese raiders, the Maldivians voluntarily placed themselves under the suzerainty of Ceylon. In 1887 the islands became an internally self-governing British protectorate and a nominal dependency of Ceylon. Traditionally a sultanate, the Maldives became a republic in 1953 but restored the sultanate in 1954. The Sultanate of the Maldive Islands attained complete internal and external autonomy on July 26, 1965, and on Nov. 11,1968, again became a republic.

RULERS
Muhammad Imad al-Din I, AH1030-1058/1620-1648AD
Ibrahim Iskandar I bin Muhammad, AH1058-1098/1648-1687AD
Muhammad bin Ibrahim, AH1098-1102/1687-1690AD (no coinage known)
Muhammad Muhi al-Din bin Fulan, AH1102-1103/1690-1691AD
Muhammad Shams al-Din al-Hamawi, AH1103-1104/1691-1692AD
Muhammad al-Hajji bin Ali, AH1104-1112/1692-1700AD

MINT NAME

Mahle (Male)

NOTE: The metrology of the early coinage is problematical. There seem to have been three denominations: a double Larin of 8-10 g, a Larin of approximately 4.8 g, and a half Larin that varied from 1.1 to 2.4 g, known as the Bodu Larin, Larin and Kuda Larin, respectively. In some years probably when copper was cheap (AH1276 & 1294),the Kuda (1/2) Larin is found with weights as high as 3.5 g. During the rule of Muhammad Imad Al-Din II Al-Muzaffar Bin Muhammad (1704-1721AD) additional denominations in the form of the 1/4, 1/8 and 1/16 Larin (1.17 g, 0.55 g and 0.29 g) were introduced on an experimental basis. This experiment was not followed by later rulers with the exception of Muhammad Imad Al-Din IV (1835-1882AD) who struck some light weight coins of about 1.1 g which can be considered 1/4 Larins.

SULTANATE

Muhammad Imad al-Din I

AH 1030-58 / 1620-48 AD

STANDARD COINAGE

KM# 1 LARIN

Silver **Mint:** Mahle (Malé) **Note:** Countermarked bent silver wire.

Date	Mintage	Good	VG	F	VF	XF
AHxxxx Rare	—	—	—	—	—	—

Note: O.N.S. Newsletter #89, April, 1984

Ibrahim Iskandar I bin Muhammad

AH 1058-98 / 1648-87 AD

STANDARD COINAGE

KM# 2.1 LARIN

4.8000 g., Silver **Mint:** Mahle (Malé)

Date	Mintage	Good	VG	F	VF	XF
AH1070	—	7.50	12.50	18.00	25.00	—
AH1074	—	7.50	12.50	18.00	25.00	—
ND	—	7.50	12.50	18.00	25.00	—

KM# 2.2 LARIN

4.8000 g., Silver **Mint:** Mahle (Malé)

Date	Mintage	Good	VG	F	VF	XF
AH1096	—	10.00	17.00	25.00	35.00	—

Muhammad Muhi al-Din bin Fulan
AH 1102-03 / 1690-91 AD

STANDARD COINAGE

KM# 6 LARIN
4.8000 g., Silver **Mint:** Mahle (Malé) **Note:** Varieties exist.

Date	Mintage	Good	VG	F	VF	XF
ND	—	13.00	22.00	32.00	45.00	—

Muhammad Shams al-Din al-Hamawi
AH 1103-04 / 1691-92 AD

STANDARD COINAGE

KM# 8 LARIN
4.8000 g., Silver **Mint:** Mahle (Malé)

Date	Mintage	Good	VG	F	VF	XF
ND	—	12.00	20.00	28.00	40.00	—

Muhammad al-Hajji bin Ali
AH 1104-12 / 1692-1700 AD

STANDARD COINAGE

KM# 9 1/2 LARIN (Kuda)
2.4000 g., Silver

Date	Mintage	Good	VG	F	VF	XF
AH1105	—	4.50	7.50	11.50	16.50	—

KM# 10 LARIN
4.8000 g., Silver **Mint:** Mahle (Malé)

Date	Mintage	Good	VG	F	VF	XF
AH1104	—	5.00	8.50	12.50	18.00	—

ORDER OF MALTA

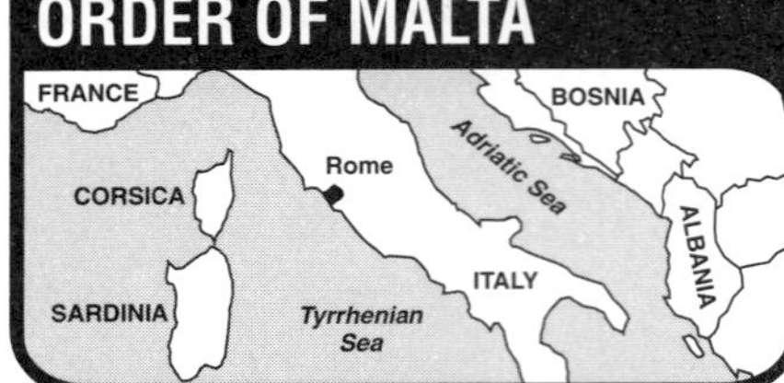

The Order of Malta, modern successor to the Sovereign Military Hospitaller Order of St. John of Jerusalem (the crusading Knights Hospitallers), derives its sovereignty from grants of extraterritoriality by Italy (1928) and the Vatican City (1953), and from its supranational character as a religious military order owing suzerainty to the Holy See. Its territory is confined to Palazzo Malta on Via Condotti, Villa Malta and the crest of the Aventine Hill, all in the city of Rome. The Order maintains diplomatic relations with about 35 governments, including Italy, Spain, Austria, State of Malta, Portugal, Brazil, Guatemala, Panama, Peru, Iran, Lebanon, Philippines, Liberia, Ethiopia, etc.

The Knights Hospitallers were founded in 1099 just before the crusaders' capture of Jerusalem. Father Gerard (died 1120) was the founder and first rector of the Jerusalem hospital. The headquarters of the Order were successively at Jerusalem 1099-1187; Acre 1187-1291;Cyprus 1291-1310; Rhodes 1310-1522; Malta 1530-1798;Trieste 1798-1799; St. Petersburg 1799-1803; Catania1803-1825; Ferrara 1826-1834; Rome 1834-Present.

The symbolic coins issued by the Order since 1961 are intended to continue the last independent coinage of the Order on Malta in 1798. In traditional tari and scudi denominations, they are issued only in proof condition. They have a theoretical fixed exchange value with the Italian lira, but are not used in commerce.

These medallic issues are perhaps the world's last major symbolic coinage, just as their issuer is the world's last sovereign order of knighthood. Proceeds from the sale of this coinage maintain the Order's hospitals, clinics and leprosariums around the world.

RULERS

Martin Garzes, 1595-1601
Alof de Wignacourt, 1601-1622
Luis Mendes de Vasconcellos, 1622-1623
Antoine de Paule, 1623-1636
Jean-Paul Lascaris Castellar, 1636-1657
Martin de Redin, 1657-1660
Annet de Clermont Gessan, 1660
Rafael Cotoner, 1660-1663
Nicolas Cotoner, 1663-1680
Gregorio Carafa, 1680-1690
Adrien de Wignacourt, 1690-1697
Ramon Perellos y Roccaful, 1697-1720

MONETARY SYSTEM

(Until ca. 1800)

20 Grani = 1 Tari
12 Tari = 1 Scudo

SOVEREIGN HOSPITAL ORDER

STANDARD COINAGE

KM# 5 PICCIOLO (Diniere)
Copper **Obv:** Circular arms of Alof de Wignacourt **Rev:** Maltese cross **Rev. Legend:** ORDO HOSPITALI HIERVSA

Date	Mintage	Good	VG	F	VF	XF
ND(1601-22)	—	—	25.00	48.00	90.00	—

KM# 6 PICCIOLO (Diniere)
Copper **Rev:** Maltese cross **Rev. Legend:** ORDO • OSP • S • IOA HIERV **Note:** Varieties exist.

Date	Mintage	Good	VG	F	VF	XF
ND(1602-22) Rare	—	—	—	—	—	—

KM# 7 PICCIOLO (Diniere)
Copper **Obv:** Circular arms **Obv. Legend:** S • JOAN BAP ORD PRO NO **Rev:** Maltese cross **Rev. Legend:** S • IOA HIERVSA **Note:** Varieties exist.

Date	Mintage	Good	VG	F	VF	XF
ND(1602-22) Unique	—	—	—	—	—	—

KM# 40 PICCIOLO (Diniere)
Copper **Obv:** Arms of Antoine de Paule **Rev:** Maltese cross

Date	Mintage	Good	VG	F	VF	XF
ND(1623-36)	—	—	18.00	36.00	80.00	120

KM# 61 PICCIOLO (Diniere)
Copper **Obv:** Arms of Lascaris **Rev:** Maltese cross

Date	Mintage	Good	VG	F	VF	XF
ND(1636-57)	—	—	20.00	40.00	75.00	—

KM# 125 PICCIOLO (Diniere)
Copper **Obv:** Shield of Adrien de Wignacourt in pellet circle **Rev:** Maltese cross

Date	Mintage	Good	VG	F	VF	XF
1693	—	—	25.00	48.00	90.00	—

KM# 8 3 PICCIOLI
Copper **Obv:** Circular arms of Alof de Wignacourt **Rev:** 3 in circle **Rev. Legend:** HOSPITALI HIERVSA **Note:** Varieties exist.

Date	Mintage	Good	VG	F	VF	XF
ND(1602-22)	—	—	38.50	60.00	120	220

KM# 35 3 PICCIOLI
Copper **Obv:** Circular arms of Vasconcellos **Rev:** 3 in circle **Rev. Legend:** HOSPITALI HIERVS

Date	Mintage	Good	VG	F	VF	XF
ND(1622-23)	—	—	55.00	100	210	—

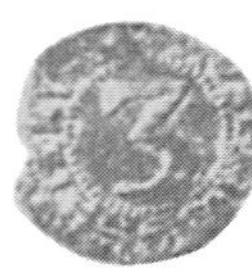

KM# 41 3 PICCIOLI
Copper **Obv:** Arms of de Paule **Rev:** 3 in circle **Rev. Legend:** HOSPITALI HIERVSA **Note:** Legend varieties exist.

Date	Mintage	Good	VG	F	VF	XF
ND(1623-36)	—	—	38.50	60.00	120	215

KM# 42 3 PICCIOLI
Copper **Rev:** Maltese cross **Note:** Varieties exist.

Date	Mintage	Good	VG	F	VF	XF
ND(1623-36)	—	—	38.50	60.00	120	215

KM# 43 3 PICCIOLI
Copper **Obv:** 3 and small Maltese cross **Rev:** Maltese cross and four stars **Note:** Varieties exist.

Date	Mintage	Good	VG	F	VF	XF
ND(1623-36) Unique	—	—	—	—	—	—

KM# 44 3 PICCIOLI
Copper **Obv. Legend:** F DE PAULA D. WIGNACO. **Note:** Varieties exist.

Date	Mintage	Good	VG	F	VF	XF
ND(1623-36) Unique	—	—	—	—	—	—

Note: An engraver error combining names of two grand masters

KM# 62 3 PICCIOLI
Copper **Obv:** Circular arms of Lascaris **Obv. Legend:** 3 in circle, M • M • HOSPITALI • HIERVS

Date	Mintage	Good	VG	F	VF	XF
ND(1636-57)	—	—	38.50	60.00	120	—

KM# 9 GRANO
Copper **Obv:** Circular arms of Wignacourt **Rev:** Inner: VT / COMMO / DIVS; outer: HOSPITALIS HIERVSALEM

Date	Mintage	Good	VG	F	VF	XF
ND(1601-22)	—	—	15.00	30.00	55.00	100

KM# 36 GRANO
Copper **Obv:** Circular arms of Vasconcellos **Note:** Varieties exist.

Date	Mintage	Good	VG	F	VF	XF
ND(1622-23)	—	—	60.00	115	210	300

KM# 49 GRANO

Copper **Obv:** Arms of de Paule **Rev:** HOSPITALI HIERVSALEM around VT/COMMO/DIVS

Date	Mintage	Good	VG	F	VF	XF
ND(1623-26)	—	—	45.00	75.00	130	—

KM# 50 GRANO

Copper **Obv:** Arms of de Paule **Rev:** Plain cross of the Order, date in angles

Date	Mintage	Good	VG	F	VF	XF
1626	—	—	22.50	42.00	75.00	135
1628	—	—	22.50	42.00	75.00	135
1629	—	—	22.50	42.00	75.00	135

KM# 51 GRANO

Copper **Obv:** Legend around PVB / COMMO / DIT **Rev:** Maltese cross, date in angles

Date	Mintage	Good	VG	F	VF	XF
1629	—	—	45.00	75.00	115	180

KM# 70 GRANO

Copper **Obv:** Arms of Lascaris **Rev:** Maltese cross

Date	Mintage	Good	VG	F	VF	XF
1637	—	—	18.00	37.50	60.00	120
1638	—	—	18.00	37.50	60.00	120

KM# 124 GRANO

Copper **Obv:** Circular arms of Adrien Wignacourt **Rev:** Maltese cross, date in angles

Date	Mintage	Good	VG	F	VF	XF
1692	—	—	15.00	30.00	55.00	100
1693	—	—	15.00	30.00	55.00	100
1694	—	—	15.00	30.00	55.00	100
1695	—	—	15.00	30.00	55.00	100

KM# 10 2-1/2 GRANI (1/2 Cinquina)

Silver **Obv:** Circular arms of Alof Wignacourt **Rev:** Cross

Date	Mintage	VG	F	VF	XF	Unc
ND(1602-22)	—	120	200	400	650	—

KM# 11 V (5) GRANI (Cinquina)

Silver **Obv:** Circular arms of Alouf Wignacourt **Rev:** Arms of the Order

Date	Mintage	VG	F	VF	XF	Unc
ND(1602-22)	—	80.00	150	240	375	—

KM# 26 V (5) GRANI (Cinquina)

Copper **Obv:** Fleur-de-lis and two stars above arms of Vasconcellos **Rev:** Two clasped hands, V below

Date	Mintage	Good	VG	F	VF	XF
1619	—	—	55.00	85.00	155	220

KM# 52 V (5) GRANI (Cinquina)

Copper **Obv:** Fleur-de-lis above arms of de Paule **Rev:** Two clasped hands, V below

Date	Mintage	Good	VG	F	VF	XF
1629	—	—	36.00	60.00	110	180

KM# 12 X (10) GRANI (Carlino)

Silver **Obv:** Arms of Alof Wignacourt **Rev:** Arms of the Order

Date	Mintage	VG	F	VF	XF	Unc
ND(1601-22)	—	60.00	110	200	375	—

KM# 27 X (10) GRANI (Carlino)

Copper **Obv:** Crown above arms of Alof Wignacourt **Rev:** Two clasped hands, X below

Date	Mintage	Good	VG	F	VF	XF
1619	—	—	25.00	50.00	100	180

KM# 37 X (10) GRANI (Carlino)

Silver **Obv:** Arms of de Vasconcellos **Obv. Legend:** + F • L • MEN: DE VASCONCELOS • M • M • H **Rev:** Ornamental arms of the Order **Rev. Legend:** + S • IOAN • BAP • ORA • PRONOBIS

Date	Mintage	VG	F	VF	XF	Unc
ND(1622-23)	—	50.00	100	175	275	—

KM# 46 X (10) GRANI (Carlino)

Silver **Obv:** Arms of de Paule **Rev:** Shield of the Order

Date	Mintage	VG	F	VF	XF	Unc
ND(1623-36)	—	40.00	90.00	170	300	—

KM# 53 X (10) GRANI (Carlino)

Copper **Obv:** Crown above arms of de Paule **Rev:** Two clasped hands, X below

Date	Mintage	Good	VG	F	VF	XF
1629	—	—	25.00	50.00	95.00	175

KM# 63 X (10) GRANI (Carlino)

Silver **Obv:** Crown above arms of Lascaris **Rev:** Shield of the Order **Note:** Legend spacing varieties exist.

Date	Mintage	VG	F	VF	XF	Unc
ND(1636-57)	—	60.00	135	225	300	—

KM# 85 X (10) GRANI (Carlino)

Silver **Obv:** Crown above arms of de Redin **Rev:** Arms of the Order

Date	Mintage	VG	F	VF	XF	Unc
ND(1657-1660)	—	85.00	180	240	—	—

KM# 90 X (10) GRANI (Carlino)

Silver **Obv:** Crown above arms of R. Cotoner **Rev:** Shield of the Order

Date	Mintage	VG	F	VF	XF	Unc
ND(1660-1663)	—	48.00	110	180	265	—

KM# 99 X (10) GRANI (Carlino)

Silver **Obv:** Crown above arms of N. Cotoner **Rev:** Shield of the Order **Note:** Legend varieties exist.

Date	Mintage	VG	F	VF	XF	Unc
ND(1663-80)	—	48.00	110	180	265	—

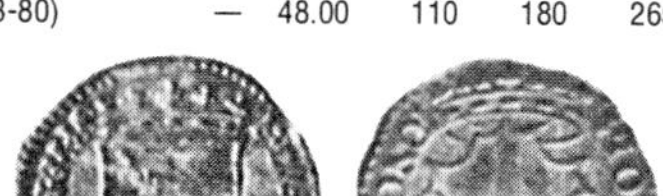

KM# 110 X (10) GRANI (Carlino)

Silver **Obv:** Crown above arms of Carafa **Rev:** Shield of the Order

Date	Mintage	VG	F	VF	XF	Unc
ND(1680-90)	—	48.00	110	180	265	—

KM# 120 X (10) GRANI (Carlino)

Silver **Obv:** Crown above arms of Adrien Wignacourt **Rev:** Arms of the Order **Note:** Legend varieties exist.

Date	Mintage	VG	F	VF	XF	Unc
1690	—	48.00	110	180	240	—
ND(1690-97)	—	48.00	110	180	240	—

KM# 131 X (10) GRANI (Carlino)

Silver **Ruler:** Ramon Perellos y Roccaful **Obv:** Crown above shield of Perellos y Roccafull **Rev:** Arms of the Order

Date	Mintage	VG	F	VF	XF	Unc
ND(1697-1720)	—	120	180	240	300	—

KM# 28 TARI

Copper **Obv:** Crown above arms of Alof Wignacourt **Rev:** Two clasped hands, T I below

Date	Mintage	Good	VG	F	VF	XF
1619	—	—	42.00	80.00	145	240

KM# 38 TARI

Silver **Obv:** Arms of Vasconcellos **Rev:** Arms of the Order

Date	Mintage	VG	F	VF	XF	Unc
ND(1622-23)	—	60.00	120	210	325	—

KM# 71 TARI

Silver **Obv:** Crowned arms of Lascaris **Rev:** Two clasped hands, T I below **Note:** Legend varieties.

Date	Mintage	VG	F	VF	XF	Unc
1639	—	40.00	110	180	240	—

KM# 91 TARI

Silver **Obv:** Crowned arms of R. Cotoner divide TI **Rev:** Paschal Lamb with banner

Date	Mintage	VG	F	VF	XF	Unc
ND(1660-63)	—	45.00	110	210	325	—

KM# 100 TARI

Silver **Obv:** Crowned arms of N. Cotoner divide TI **Rev:** Paschal Lamb with banner

Date	Mintage	VG	F	VF	XF	Unc
ND(1663-80)	—	45.00	110	210	325	—

KM# 111 TARI

Silver **Obv:** Crowned arms of Carafa divide TI **Rev:** Arms of the Order **Note:** Variety in shield (raised or incuse lines).

Date	Mintage	VG	F	VF	XF	Unc
ND(1680-90)	—	—	—	—	—	—

Note: Reported, not confirmed

KM# 25 2 TARI

Silver **Obv:** Crowned arms of Alof Wignacourt divide T2 **Rev:** Head of St. John the Baptist in a stemmed platter

Date	Mintage	VG	F	VF	XF	Unc
1613	—	100	180	350	550	—

KM# 60 2 TARI

Silver **Obv:** Crowned arms of de Paule

Date	Mintage	VG	F	VF	XF	Unc
1634	—	150	240	475	725	—

KM# 64 2 TARI

Silver **Obv:** Crowned arms of Lascaris

Date	Mintage	VG	F	VF	XF	Unc
1636	—	100	180	350	550	—

KM# 65 2 TARI

Copper **Obv:** Crowned arms of Lascaris in legend **Rev:** Two clasped hands, date above, T2 below

Date	Mintage	Good	VG	F	VF	XF
1636	—	—	22.50	44.00	90.00	150
1637	—	—	22.50	44.00	90.00	150
1641	—	—	22.50	44.00	90.00	150
1642	—	—	22.50	44.00	90.00	150
1643	—	—	22.50	44.00	90.00	150

KM# 75 2 TARI

Copper **Obv:** Legend without Castellar

Date	Mintage	Good	VG	F	VF	XF
1643	—	—	22.50	44.00	90.00	150

KM# 13 3 TARI

Silver **Obv:** Crowned arms of Alof Wignacourt **Rev:** Maltese cross, date in angles

Date	Mintage	VG	F	VF	XF	Unc
1609	—	85.00	165	275	450	—
1611	—	85.00	165	275	450	—
1617	—	85.00	165	275	450	—
1620	—	85.00	165	275	450	—
16ZZ	—	70.00	140	220	375	—
ND	—	70.00	140	220	375	—

KM# A46 3 TARI

Silver **Obv:** Arms of Vasconcellos

Date	Mintage	VG	F	VF	XF	Unc
1623	—	220	325	650	1,100	—

KM# 47 3 TARI

Silver **Obv:** Crowned arms of de Paule

Date	Mintage	VG	F	VF	XF	Unc
1623	—	90.00	175	270	475	—
1624	—	90.00	175	270	475	—
1626	—	90.00	175	270	475	—
1627	—	90.00	175	270	475	—
1628	—	90.00	175	270	475	—
1629	—	90.00	175	270	475	—
1632	—	90.00	175	270	475	—
1635	—	90.00	175	270	475	—

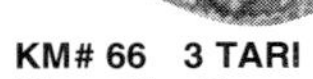

KM# 66 3 TARI

Silver **Obv:** Crowned arms of Lascaris

Date	Mintage	VG	F	VF	XF	Unc
1636	—	80.00	150	240	425	—
1637	—	80.00	150	240	425	—
1638	—	80.00	150	240	425	—
1640	—	80.00	150	240	425	—
1642	—	80.00	150	240	425	—
1648	—	80.00	150	240	425	—
1649	—	80.00	150	240	425	—
1651	—	80.00	150	240	425	—

KM# 86 3 TARI

Silver **Obv:** Crowned arms of the de Redin

Date	Mintage	VG	F	VF	XF	Unc
1658	—	220	325	550	875	—

KM# 92 3 TARI

Silver **Obv:** Coronet above arms of R. Cotoner

Date	Mintage	VG	F	VF	XF	Unc
1660	—	195	300	550	875	—
1662	—	195	300	550	875	—

KM# 101 3 TARI

Silver **Obv:** Crowned arms of N. Cotoner

Date	Mintage	VG	F	VF	XF	Unc
1663/1664	—	65.00	125	220	350	—
1665	—	65.00	125	220	350	—
1666	—	65.00	125	220	350	—

KM# 112 3 TARI

Silver **Obv:** Crowned arms of Carafa

Date	Mintage	VG	F	VF	XF	Unc
1680	—	65.00	125	220	350	—

KM# 14 4 TARI

Silver **Obv:** Crowned arms of Alof Wignacourt dividing T4 **Rev:** Head of St. John the Baptist **Rev. Legend:** S IOAN... **Note:** Varieties exist.

Date	Mintage	VG	F	VF	XF	Unc
1609	—	95.00	180	300	525	—
1611	—	95.00	180	300	525	—
1619	—	95.00	180	300	525	—
16ZZ	—	70.00	140	250	425	—
16Z0	—	70.00	140	250	425	—

KM# 15 4 TARI

Silver **Rev. Legend:** PROPTER...

Date	Mintage	VG	F	VF	XF	Unc
ND	—	—	—	—	—	—

KM# 39 4 TARI

Silver **Obv:** Crowned arms of Vasconcellos

Date	Mintage	VG	F	VF	XF	Unc
16ZZ	—	1,300	2,200	3,850	5,500	—

KM# 48 4 TARI

Silver **Obv:** Crowned arms of de Paule

Date	Mintage	VG	F	VF	XF	Unc
1623	—	65.00	125	220	400	—
1624	—	65.00	125	220	400	—
1625	—	65.00	125	220	400	—
1626	—	65.00	125	220	400	—
1629	—	65.00	125	220	400	—
1634	—	65.00	125	220	400	—

KM# 67 4 TARI

Copper **Obv:** Crowned arms of Lascaris divides sun and moon; legend without CASTELLAR **Obv. Legend:** F • IOANNES • PAVLVS... **Rev:** Two clasped hands, date above, T4 below

Date	Mintage	Good	VG	F	VF	XF
1636	—	—	25.00	65.00	125	205
1637	—	—	25.00	65.00	125	205
1641	—	—	25.00	65.00	125	205

Date	Mintage	Good	VG	F	VF	XF
1642	—	—	25.00	65.00	125	205
1643	—	—	25.00	65.00	125	205
1647	—	—	25.00	65.00	125	205
1651	—	—	25.00	65.00	125	205

KM# 68 4 TARI

Copper **Obv. Legend:** F • IO:PAVLVS • LASCARIS •

Date	Mintage	Good	VG	F	VF	XF
1636	—	—	25.00	65.00	125	205
1637	—	—	25.00	65.00	125	205
1641	—	—	25.00	65.00	125	205
1642	—	—	25.00	65.00	125	205
1643	—	—	25.00	65.00	125	205
1647	—	—	25.00	65.00	125	205

KM# 69 4 TARI

Silver **Obv:** Crowned arms of Lascaris **Note:** Obv. and Rev. legend varieties exist including rotation of each starting at lower left or upper right.

Date	Mintage	VG	F	VF	XF	Unc
1637	—	48.00	95.00	190	325	—
1638	—	48.00	95.00	190	325	—
1639	—	48.00	95.00	190	325	—
1640	—	48.00	95.00	190	325	—
1642	—	48.00	95.00	190	325	—
1643	—	48.00	95.00	190	325	—
1644	—	48.00	95.00	190	325	—
1645	—	48.00	95.00	190	325	—
1646	—	48.00	95.00	190	325	—
1647	—	48.00	95.00	190	325	—
1648	—	48.00	95.00	190	325	—
1649	—	48.00	95.00	190	325	—
1650	—	48.00	95.00	190	325	—
1651	—	48.00	95.00	190	325	—
1656	—	48.00	95.00	190	325	—

KM# 87 4 TARI

Silver **Obv:** Crowned arms of de Redin **Rev:** Head of John the Baptist

Date	Mintage	VG	F	VF	XF	Unc
1658	—	240	475	725	1,200	—

KM# 93 4 TARI

Silver **Obv:** Crowned arms of Gessan

Date	Mintage	VG	F	VF	XF	Unc
1660	—	240	475	725	1,200	—

KM# 94 4 TARI

Silver **Obv:** Crowned arms of R. Cotoner

Date	Mintage	VG	F	VF	XF	Unc
1660	—	210	350	600	1,000	—

KM# 102 4 TARI

Silver **Obv:** Crowned arms of N. Cotoner

Date	Mintage	VG	F	VF	XF	Unc
1663	—	85.00	165	300	500	—
1664	—	85.00	165	300	500	—
1665	—	85.00	165	300	500	—
1666	—	85.00	165	300	500	—
1667	—	85.00	165	300	500	—
1668	—	85.00	165	300	500	—
1673	—	85.00	165	300	500	—

KM# 113 4 TARI

Silver **Obv:** Crowned arms of Carafa

Date	Mintage	VG	F	VF	XF	Unc
1680	—	180	475	725	1,200	—
1681	—	180	475	725	1,200	—
1685	—	180	475	725	1,200	—

KM# 121 4 TARI

Silver **Obv:** Crowned arms of Adrian Wignacourt

Date	Mintage	VG	F	VF	XF	Unc
1691	—	240	425	650	1,150	—

KM# 122 4 TARI

Silver **Obv:** Crowned shield, crown with points, the style of an Eastern crown **Note:** Varieties exist.

Date	Mintage	VG	F	VF	XF	Unc
1691	—	240	475	725	1,200	—

KM# 132 4 TARI

Silver **Obv:** Crowned arms of Perellos y Roccaful **Note:** Varieties with or without HH flanking shield.

Date	Mintage	VG	F	VF	XF	Unc
1697	—	120	300	475	725	—

MB# 80 ZECCHINO

Gold **Ruler:** Martin Garzes **Obv:** St. John presents the banner of the Order of the Kneeling Grand Master, "M.H." in field **Obv. Legend:** F. MARTINVS GARZES **Rev:** Christ standing surrounded by nine stars in dotted oval **Rev. Legend:** DA MICHI. VIRTV(TE) CO(N)TRA HOSTES. T(VO). **Edge:** Plain **Note:** FR#9.

Date	Mintage	Good	VG	F	VF	XF
ND(1595-1601)	—	—	300	550	1,050	1,800

KM# A16 ZECCHINO

3.5000 g., 0.9860 Gold 0.1109 oz. AGW **Obv:** Grand Master kneeling before St. John **Obv. Legend:** F. MARTINVS GARZES **Rev:** Christ in oval with ten stars **Rev. Legend:** DA MICHIVIRTE COTRA...

Date	Mintage	VG	F	VF	XF	Unc
ND(1595-1601)	—	220	325	550	925	—

KM# 16 ZECCHINO

3.5000 g., 0.9860 Gold 0.1109 oz. AGW **Obv:** Grand Master kneeling before St. John **Obv. Legend:** F. ALOPIVS. DE WIGNACOVRT **Rev:** Christ within stars

Date	Mintage	VG	F	VF	XF	Unc
ND(1601-22)	—	275	450	650	1,100	—

KM# 17 ZECCHINO

3.5000 g., 0.9860 Gold 0.1109 oz. AGW **Obv. Legend:** F. L. MENDES DE VASCONCELOS. M. M. H.

Date	Mintage	VG	F	VF	XF	Unc
ND(1622-23)	—	2,200	3,850	6,100	8,800	—

KM# 18 ZECCHINO

3.5000 g., 0.9860 Gold 0.1109 oz. AGW **Obv. Legend:** F. ANTONIUS DE PAULA. M. M. H.

Date	Mintage	VG	F	VF	XF	Unc
ND(1623-36)	—	450	725	2,200	3,300	—

KM# 19 ZECCHINO

3.5000 g., 0.9860 Gold 0.1109 oz. AGW **Obv. Legend:** F. IO. PAULUS LASC CASTELLAR. M. M. H.

Date	Mintage	VG	F	VF	XF	Unc
ND(1636-57)	—	450	725	2,200	3,300	—

KM# 20 ZECCHINO

3.5000 g., 0.9860 Gold 0.1109 oz. AGW **Obv. Legend:** F. D. GREG. CARAFA S. IO. BAPTISTA. **Rev:** Crowned arms of Grand Master

Date	Mintage	VG	F	VF	XF	Unc
ND(1680-90)	—	450	725	1,300	2,750	—

KM# 123 ZECCHINO

3.5000 g., 0.9860 Gold 0.1109 oz. AGW **Obv. Legend:** F. ADR. WIGNAC. S. 10. BAPT.

Date	Mintage	VG	F	VF	XF	Unc
1691	—	325	550	1,100	2,200	—
1694	—	325	550	1,100	2,200	—
1695	—	325	550	1,100	2,200	—
1696	—	325	550	1,100	2,200	—

KM# A133.1 ZECCHINO

3.5000 g., 0.9860 Gold 0.1109 oz. AGW **Ruler:** Ramon Perellos y Roccaful **Obv:** Crowned round shield in sprays **Obv. Legend:** (*) F (•) RAYMUNDV(S) PERELLOS (•) M • M • H • ET • S • S • HIE **Rev:** St. John standing presents Order flag to kneeling Grand Master **Rev. Legend:** PIETATE - VINCES

Date	Mintage	VG	F	VF	XF	Unc
ND(1697-1720)	—	165	240	500	875	—
1699	—	165	240	500	875	—

KM# A133.2 ZECCHINO

3.5000 g., 0.9860 Gold 0.1109 oz. AGW **Ruler:** Ramon Perellos y Roccaful **Obv:** Crowned round shield in sprays **Obv. Legend:** F RAIMUNDVS PERELLOS • M • M • H • ET • S • S • HIE **Rev:** St. John standing presents the flag of the Order to the kneeling Grand Master **Rev. Legend:** PIETATE - VINCES

Date	Mintage	VG	F	VF	XF	Unc
1699	—	165	240	500	875	—

KM# 21 2 ZECCHINO

7.0000 g., 0.9860 Gold 0.2219 oz. AGW **Obv:** Bust of Grand Master Castellar **Obv. Legend:** *F. 10 PAVLVS LASCARIS... **Rev:** Arms of the Grand Master

Date	Mintage	VG	F	VF	XF	Unc
ND(1636-57) Rare	—	—	—	—	—	—

KM# 22 2 ZECCHINO

7.0000 g., 0.9860 Gold 0.2219 oz. AGW **Ruler:** Ramon Perellos y Roccaful **Obv:** Crowned shield within sprigs **Obv. Legend:** F RAIMVNDVS PERELLOS... **Rev:** Knights of the Order holding a flag

Date	Mintage	VG	F	VF	XF	Unc
ND(1697-1720)	—	2,750	3,300	5,500	7,700	—

KM# 126 4 ZECCHINI

14.0000 g., 0.9860 Gold 0.4438 oz. AGW **Obv:** St. John presents flag to kneeling Grand Master **Obv. Legend:** F. ADR. WIGNACOURT **Rev:** Arms of Grand Master

Date	Mintage	VG	F	VF	XF	Unc
1695/4 Rare	—	—	—	—	—	—

KM# 134 4 ZECCHINI

14.0000 g., 0.9860 Gold 0.4438 oz. AGW **Ruler:** Ramon Perellos y Roccaful **Obv:** Crowned arms in palm branches **Rev:** St. John presenting banner to kneeling Grand Master

Date	Mintage	VG	F	VF	XF	Unc
1699	—	1,400	2,050	3,850	6,600	—

COUNTERMARKED COINAGE

For over a century the two and four Tari copper coins struck during the reign of Jean-Paul Lascaris Castellar were countermarked as an expedient against the prevalent forging of these coins both in Malta and Messina.

A total of eight different countermarks were utilized. As many as seven can be found on the 2 Tari and all eight different may be encountered on the 4 Tari.

COUNTERMARKS

I. Imperial eagle in circle.

Initiated May 28, 1646.

II. Head of John the Baptist in oval.

Initiated April 19, 1662.

III. Crowned fleur-de-lis.

Initiated August 27, 1696.

For more information refer to The Coinage of the Knights in Malta by Felice Restelli and Joseph C. Sammut, 1977 by Emmanuel Said Publishers, Valettta, Malta.

NOTE: Coins are properly catalogued by the latest countermark. Obviously certain coins may lack one or more countermarks having been missed during such an extensive countermarking period. Prices for this section are based on common examples, which are likely to show less detail and tend to be cupped. The images shown here are exceptional examples and command premium prices.

KM# 76 2 TARI

Copper **Countermark:** Type I **Obv. Legend:** F • IO : PAVLVS:... **Note:** Countermark on 2 Tari, KM#65.

CM Date	Host Date	Good	VG	F	VF	XF
ND(1646)	1636-43	25.00	41.25	60.00	90.00	—

KM# 77 2 TARI

Copper **Countermark:** Type I **Obv. Legend:** F • IOANNES • PAVLVS •... **Note:** Countermark on 2 Tari, KM#75.

CM Date	Host Date	Good	VG	F	VF	XF
ND(1646)	1643	25.00	41.25	60.00	90.00	—

KM# 96 2 TARI

Copper **Countermark:** Type I and Type II **Obv. Legend:** F • IOANNES • PAVLVS •... **Note:** Countermark on 2 Tari, KM#75.

CM Date	Host Date	Good	VG	F	VF	XF
ND(1662)	1643	22.50	38.50	55.00	75.00	—

KM# 95 2 TARI

Copper **Countermark:** Type I and Type II **Obv. Legend:** F • IO : PAVLVS:... **Note:** Countermark on 2 Tari, KM#65.

CM Date	Host Date	Good	VG	F	VF	XF
ND(1662)	1636-43	22.50	38.50	55.00	75.00	—

KM# 127 2 TARI

Copper **Countermark:** Type I-III **Obv. Legend:** F • IO : PAVLVS :... **Note:** Countermark on 2 Tari, KM#65.

CM Date	Host Date	Good	VG	F	VF	XF
ND(1696)	1636-43	20.00	33.00	46.75	65.00	—

KM# 128 2 TARI

Copper **Countermark:** Type I-III **Obv. Legend:** F • IOANNES • PAVLVS •... **Note:** Countermark on 2 Tari, KM#75.

CM Date	Host Date	Good	VG	F	VF	XF
ND(1696)	1643	20.00	33.00	46.75	65.00	—

KM# 78 4 TARI

Copper **Countermark:** Type I **Obv. Legend:** F • IO : PAVLVS •... **Note:** Countermark on 4 Tari, KM#67.

CM Date	Host Date	Good	VG	F	VF	XF
ND(1646)	1636-51	33.00	55.00	75.00	110	—

KM# 79 4 TARI

Copper **Countermark:** Type I **Obv. Legend:** F • IOANNES • PAVLVS •... **Note:** Countermark on 4 Tari, KM#68.

CM Date	Host Date	Good	VG	F	VF	XF
ND(1646)	1636-47	33.00	55.00	75.00	110	—

KM# 98 4 TARI

Copper **Countermark:** Type I and Type II **Obv. Legend:** F • IOANNES • PAVLVS •... **Note:** Countermark on 4 Tari, KM#68.

CM Date	Host Date	Good	VG	F	VF	XF
ND(1662)	1636-47	25.00	41.25	60.00	90.00	—

KM# 97 4 TARI

Copper **Countermark:** Type I and Type II **Obv. Legend:** F • IO : PAVLVS •... **Note:** Countermark on 4 Tari, KM#67.

CM Date	Host Date	Good	VG	F	VF	XF
ND	1636-51	25.00	41.25	60.00	90.00	—

KM# 129 4 TARI

Copper **Countermark:** Type I-III **Obv. Legend:** F • IO • PAVLVS •... **Note:** Countermark on 4 Tari, KM#67.

CM Date	Host Date	Good	VG	F	VF	XF
ND	1636-51	22.50	38.50	55.00	75.00	—

KM# 130 4 TARI

Copper **Countermark:** Type I-III **Obv. Legend:** F • IOANNES • PAVLVS •... **Note:** Countermark on 4 Tari, KM#68.

CM Date	Host Date	Good	VG	F	VF	XF
ND	1636-47	22.50	38.50	55.00	75.00	—

MEXICO

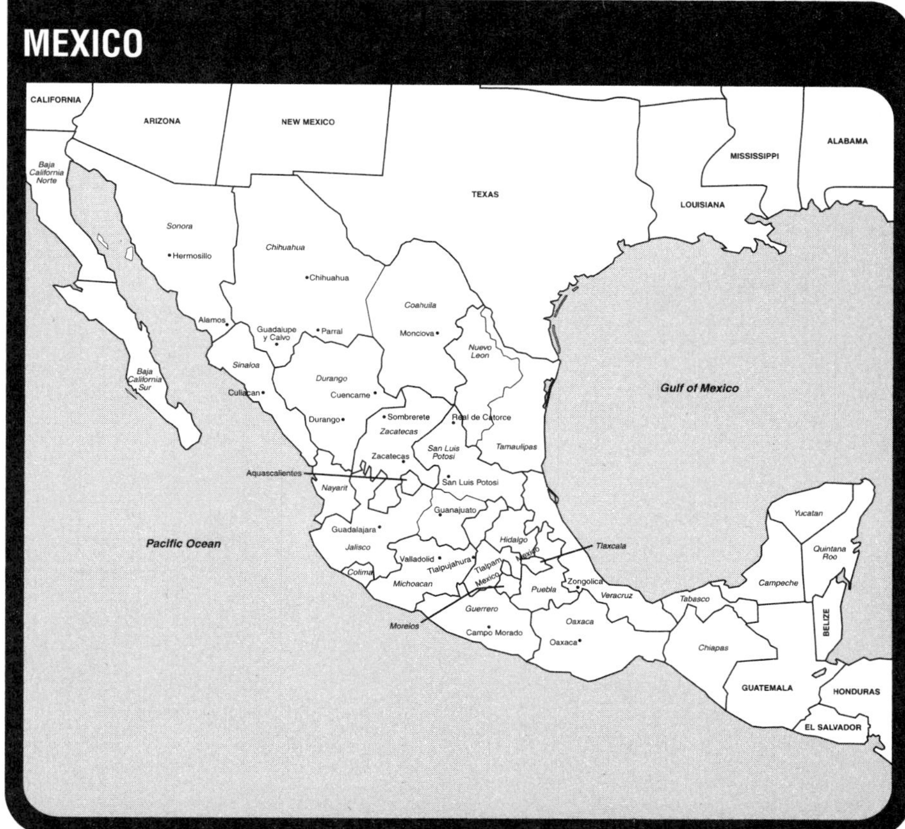

Mexico, located immediately south of the United States has an area of 759,529 sq. mi. (1,967,183 sq. km).

Mexico was the site of highly advanced Indian civilizations 1,500 years before conquistador Hernando Cortes conquered the wealthy Aztec empire of Montezuma,1519-21, and founded a Spanish colony which lasted for nearly 300 years. During the Spanish period, Mexico, then called New Spain, stretched from Guatemala to the present states of Wyoming and California, its present northern boundary having been established by the secession of Texas during 1836 and the war of 1846-48 with the United States.

Independence from Spain was declared by Father Miguel Hidalgo on Sept. 16, 1810, (Mexican Independence Day) and was achieved by General Agustin de Iturbide in 1821. Iturbide became emperor in 1822 but was deposed when a republic was established a year later. For more than fifty years following the birth of the republic, the political scene of Mexico was characterized by turmoil which saw two emperors (including the unfortunate Maximilian), several dictators and an average of one new government every nine months passing swiftly from obscurity to oblivion. The land, social, economic and labor reforms promulgated by the Reform Constitution of Feb. 5, 1917 established the basis for sustained economic development and participative democracy that have made Mexico one of the most politically stable countries of modern Latin America.

Rulers:
Philip III, 1598-1621
Philip IV, 1621-1665
Charles II, 1665-1700

Mint Marks:
M, Mo, oMo, MXo – Mexico City

Assayer's Initials

Initial	Date	Name
A	1608-09	?
F	15??-1608	?
F	1610-15 or 1616	
Ne	1611	?
D	1616 or 1617-34	?
P	1634-65	?
G	1666-77	Geronimo Becerra
L	1677-1705	Martin Lopez

SPANISH COLONY

COB COINAGE

MB# 21 1/2 REAL

1.6900 g., 0.9310 Silver 0.0506 oz. ASW **Ruler:** Philip III
Obv: Legend around crowned arms **Rev:** Legend around cross, lions and castles **Note:** Mint mark M, Mo.

Date	Mintage	Good	VG	F	VF	XF
ND(1598-1606) F	—	—	35.00	65.00	100	225

KM# 21 1/2 REAL

1.6900 g., 0.9310 Silver 0.0506 oz. ASW **Ruler:** Philip III
Obv: Legend around crowned PHILIPVS monogram
Rev: Legend around cross, lions and castles **Note:** Struck at Mexico City Mint, mint mark M, Mo.

Date	Mintage	Good	VG	F	VF	XF
ND(1607-21) Date off flan	—	—	35.00	65.00	100	225
1609 A	—	—	110	185	285	395
1610 F	—	—	110	185	285	395
1614 F	—	—	110	185	285	395
1620 D	—	—	110	185	285	395

KM# 22 1/2 REAL

1.6900 g., 0.9310 Silver 0.0506 oz. ASW **Ruler:** Philip IV
Obv: Legend around crowned PHILIPVS monogram
Rev: Legend around cross, lions and castles **Note:** Struck at Mexico City Mint, mint mark M, Mo.

Date	Mintage	Good	VG	F	VF	XF
ND(1622-67) Date off flan	—	—	25.00	50.00	75.00	175
1622 D	—	—	110	185	285	395
1650 P	—	—	110	185	285	395
1653 P	—	—	110	185	285	395
1654 P	—	—	110	185	285	395
1656 P	—	—	110	185	285	395
1658 P	—	—	110	185	285	395
1659 P	—	—	110	185	285	395
1661 P	—	—	110	185	285	395
1662 P	—	—	110	185	285	395

KM# 23 1/2 REAL

1.6900 g., 0.9310 Silver 0.0506 oz. ASW **Ruler:** Charles II **Obv:** Legend around crowned CAROLVS monogram **Rev:** Legend around cross, lions and castles **Note:** Struck at Mexico City Mint, mark mark M, Mo.

Date	Mintage	Good	VG	F	VF	XF
ND(1668-99) Date off flan	—	—	25.00	50.00	75.00	150
1668 G	—	—	110	185	285	475
1669 G	—	—	110	185	285	475
1671 G	—	—	110	185	285	475
1673 G	—	—	110	185	285	475
1674 G	—	—	110	185	285	475
1677 L	—	—	110	185	285	475
1678 L	—	—	110	185	285	475
1681/0 L	—	—	110	185	285	475
1681 L	—	—	110	185	285	475
1682 L	—	—	110	185	285	475
1683 L	—	—	110	185	285	475
1684 L	—	—	110	185	285	475
1685 L	—	—	110	185	285	475
1687 L	—	—	110	185	285	475
1689 L	—	—	110	185	285	475
1690 L	—	—	110	185	285	475
1692	—	—	110	185	285	475
1694 L	—	—	110	185	285	475
1695 L	—	—	110	185	285	475
1697 L	—	—	110	185	285	475

MB# 27.1 REAL

3.3800 g., 0.9310 Silver 0.1012 oz. ASW **Ruler:** Philip III
Obv: Legend around crowned arms **Obv. Legend:** PHILIPVS III DEI GRATIA **Rev:** Legend around cross, lions and castles
Note: Prev. KM#27.1. Mint mark M, Mo.

Date	Mintage	Good	VG	F	VF	XF
ND(1598-1606) F	—	—	40.00	75.00	150	240

KM# 27.2 REAL

3.3800 g., 0.9310 Silver 0.1012 oz. ASW **Ruler:** Philip III
Obv: Legend and date around crowned arms **Obv. Legend:** PHILIPVS III DEI G **Rev:** Legend around cross, lions and castles
Note: Struck at Mexico City Mint, mint mark M, Mo.

Date	Mintage	Good	VG	F	VF	XF
ND(1607-21) Date off flan	—	—	20.00	40.00	75.00	175
1607 F	—	—	100	175	285	395
1608/7 F	—	—	100	175	285	395
1608 A	—	—	100	175	285	395
1608 F	—	—	100	175	285	395
1609 A	—	—	100	175	285	395
1610/09 F	—	—	100	175	285	395
1610 F	—	—	100	175	285	395
1611/10 F	—	—	100	175	285	395
1611 F	—	—	100	175	285	395
1612/1 F	—	—	100	175	285	395
1612 F	—	—	100	175	285	395
1613 F	—	—	100	175	285	395

KM# 28 REAL

3.3800 g., 0.9310 Silver 0.1012 oz. ASW **Ruler:** Philip IV **Obv:** Legend and date around crowned arms **Obv. Legend:** PHILIPVS IIII DEI G **Note:** Struck at Mexico City Mint, mint mark M, Mo.

Date	Mintage	Good	VG	F	VF	XF
ND(1622-67) Date off flan	—	—	25.00	40.00	85.00	15.00
1622 D	—	—	185	225	375	495
1624/3 D	—	—	185	225	375	495
1627 D	—	—	185	225	375	495
1630 D	—	—	185	225	375	495
1632/29 D	—	—	185	225	375	495
1643 P	—	—	185	225	375	495
1651 P	—	—	185	225	375	495
1652 P	—	—	185	225	375	495
1653 P	—	—	185	225	375	495
1654 P	—	—	185	225	375	495

KM# 29 REAL

3.3800 g., 0.9310 Silver 0.1012 oz. ASW **Ruler:** Charles II **Obv:** Legend and date around crowned arms **Obv. Legend:** CAROLVS II DEI G **Note:** Struck at Mexico City Mint, mint mark M, Mo.

Date	Mintage	Good	VG	F	VF	XF
ND(1668-99) Date off flan	—	—	35.00	60.00	100	125
1668 G	—	—	300	400	500	600
1688 L	—	—	200	300	400	600
1692 L	—	—	200	300	400	600

MB# 32.1 2 REALES

6.7700 g., 0.9310 Silver 0.2026 oz. ASW **Ruler:** Philip III
Obv: Legend around crowned arms **Obv. Legend:** PHILIPVS III DEI GRATIA **Rev:** Legend around cross, lions and castles
Note: Prev. KM#32.1. Mint mark M, Mo.

Date	Mintage	Good	VG	F	VF	XF
ND(1598-1606) F	—	—	75.00	125	200	275

KM# 32.2 2 REALES

6.7700 g., 0.9310 Silver 0.2026 oz. ASW **Ruler:** Philip III **Obv:** Legend around crowned arms **Obv. Legend:** PHILIPVS III DEI G **Rev:** Legend around cross, lions and castles **Note:** Struck at Mexico City Mint, mint mark M, Mo.

Date	Mintage	Good	VG	F	VF	XF
ND(1607-22) Date off flan	—	—	60.00	90.00	120	225
1607 A Rare	—	—	—	—	—	—
1607 F	—	—	150	300	400	500
1608 A	—	—	150	300	400	500
1608/9 A/F Rare	—	—	—	—	—	—
1609 A	—	—	150	300	400	500
1609 F Rare	—	—	—	—	—	—
1611 F	—	—	150	300	400	500
1613 F	—	—	150	300	400	500
1616 F	—	—	150	300	400	500
1620 D	—	—	150	300	400	500
1622 D (retrograde 2's)	—	—	150	300	400	500

KM# 33 2 REALES

6.7700 g., 0.9310 Silver 0.2026 oz. ASW **Ruler:** Philip IV **Obv:** Legend and date around crowned arms **Obv. Legend:** PHILIPVS IIII DEI G **Rev:** Legend around cross, lions and castles **Note:** Struck at Mexico City Mint, mint mark M, Mo.

Date	Mintage	Good	VG	F	VF	XF
ND(1622-67) Date off flan	—	—	50.00	65.00	100	175
1641 P	—	—	150	250	400	500
1653 P	—	—	150	250	400	500
1654 P	—	—	150	250	400	500
1655 P	—	—	150	250	400	500
1657 P	—	—	150	250	400	500

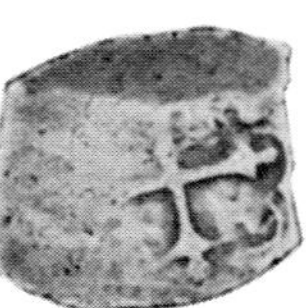

KM# 34 2 REALES

6.7700 g., 0.9310 Silver 0.2026 oz. ASW **Ruler:** Charles II **Obv:** Legend and date around crowned arms **Obv. Legend:** CAROLVS II DEI G **Rev:** Legend around cross, lions and castles **Note:** Struck at Mexico City Mint, mint mark M, Mo.

Date	Mintage	Good	VG	F	VF	XF
ND(1668-99) Date off flan	—	—	60.00	90.00	120	195
1668 G	—	—	300	400	600	750
1669 G	—	—	300	400	600	750
1690 L Unique	—	—	—	—	—	—
1695 L	—	—	300	400	600	750
1699 L	—	—	300	400	600	750

MB# 37.1 4 REALES

13.5400 g., 0.9310 Silver 0.4053 oz. ASW **Ruler:** Philip III **Obv:** Legend around crowned arms **Obv. Legend:** PHILLIPVS III DEI GRATIA **Rev:** Legend around cross, lions and castles **Note:** Prev. KM#37.1. Mint mark M, Mo.

Date	Mintage	Good	VG	F	VF	XF
ND(1598-1607) F	—	—	125	200	300	395

KM# 37.2 4 REALES

13.5400 g., 0.9310 Silver 0.4053 oz. ASW **Ruler:** Philip III **Obv:** Legend and date around crowned arms **Obv. Legend:** PHILIPVS III DEI G **Rev:** Legend around cross, lions and castles **Note:** Struck at Mexico City Mint, mint mark M, Mo.

Date	Mintage	Good	VG	F	VF	XF
ND(1607-21) Date off flan	—	—	90.00	125	250	325
1607 F	—	—	250	450	825	1,250
1608 A	—	—	250	450	825	1,250
1609/8 A Rare	—	—	—	—	—	—
1609 A	—	—	250	400	650	975
1610 F	—	—	250	400	650	975
1611 F	—	—	250	400	650	975
1612 F	—	—	250	450	825	1,250
1613 F	—	—	250	525	1,000	1,500
1614 F	—	—	250	450	825	1,250
1618 D	—	—	250	400	650	975
1620 D	—	—	250	450	825	1,250
1621 D	—	—	250	450	825	1,250

KM# 38 4 REALES

13.5400 g., 0.9310 Silver 0.4053 oz. ASW **Ruler:** Philip IV **Obv:** Legend and date around crowned arms **Obv. Legend:** PHILIPVS III DEI G **Rev:** Legend around cross, lions and castle **Note:** Struck at Mexico City Mint, mint mark M, Mo.

Date	Mintage	Good	VG	F	VF	XF
ND(1622-65) Date off flan	—	—	55.00	75.00	100	225
1622 D	—	—	240	375	600	850
1623/2 D	—	—	240	375	600	850
1623 D	—	—	240	375	600	850
1624 D	—	—	240	375	600	850
1629 D	—	—	240	375	600	850
1631 D	—	—	240	375	600	850
1632 D	—	—	240	375	600	850
1636 P	—	—	240	375	600	850
1639 P	—	—	240	375	600	850
1643 P	—	—	240	375	600	850
1644 P	—	—	240	375	600	850
1645 P	—	—	240	375	600	850
1648 P	—	—	240	375	600	850
1649 P	—	—	240	375	600	850
1650 P	—	—	240	375	600	850
1651 P	—	—	240	375	600	850
1652 P	—	—	200	300	400	500
1653 P	—	—	200	300	400	500
1654 P	—	—	200	300	400	500
1655 P	—	—	240	375	600	850
1656 P	—	—	240	375	600	850
1657 P	—	—	240	375	600	850
1658 P	—	—	240	375	600	850
1659/8 P	—	—	240	375	600	850
1661 P	—	—	240	375	600	850
1665 P	—	—	240	375	600	850

KM# 39 4 REALES

13.5400 g., 0.9310 Silver 0.4053 oz. ASW **Ruler:** Charles II **Obv:** Legend and date around crowned arms **Obv. Legend:** CAROLVS II DEI G **Rev:** Legend around cross, lions and castles **Note:** Struck at Mexico City Mint, mint mark M, Mo.

Date	Mintage	Good	VG	F	VF	XF
ND(1667-99) Date off flan	—	—	100	150	250	325
1678 L	—	—	600	900	1,600	2,000
1679 L	—	—	600	900	1,500	2,000
1682 L	—	—	600	900	1,600	2,000
1683 L	—	—	600	900	1,600	2,000
1685 L	—	—	600	900	1,600	2,000
1689 L	—	—	600	900	1,600	2,000
1690 L	—	—	600	900	1,600	2,000
1691/0 L	—	—	600	900	1,600	2,000
1691 L	—	—	600	900	1,600	2,000
1692 L	—	—	600	900	1,600	2,000
1694 L	—	—	600	900	1,600	2,000
1695 L	—	—	600	900	1,600	2,000
1697 L	—	—	600	900	1,600	2,000
1698 L	—	—	600	900	1,600	2,000

MB# 44.1 8 REALES

27.0700 g., 0.9310 Silver 0.8102 oz. ASW **Ruler:** Philip III **Obv:** Legend around crowned arms **Obv. Legend:** PHILIPVS III DEI GRATIA **Rev:** Legend around cross, lions and castles **Note:** Prev. KM#44.1. Mint mark M, Mo.

Date	Mintage	Good	VG	F	VF	XF
ND(1598-1607) F	—	—	100	150	200	325

MB# 44.2 8 REALES

27.0700 g., 0.9310 Silver 0.8102 oz. ASW **Ruler:** Philip III **Obv:** Legend around crowned arms **Obv. Legend:** PHILIPVS III DEI GRATIA **Rev:** Lions and castles interchanged **Note:** Prev. KM#44.2. Mint mark M, Mo.

Date	Mintage	Good	VG	F	VF	XF
ND(1598-1607) F	—	—	250	400	800	1,250

KM# 44.3 8 REALES

27.0700 g., 0.9310 Silver 0.8102 oz. ASW **Ruler:** Philip III **Obv:** Legend around crowned arms **Obv. Legend:** PHILIPVS III DEI G **Rev:** Legend around cross, lions and castles **Note:** Struck at Mexico City Mint, mint mark M, Mo.

Date	Mintage	Good	VG	F	VF	XF
ND(1607-21) Date off flan	—	—	100	150	200	325
1607 F Date over GRATIA	—	—	400	600	1,000	1,350
1607 F	—	—	300	450	900	1,200
1608/7 F	—	—	500	750	1,300	1,500
1608 A/F	—	—	400	600	1,000	1,350
1608 A	—	—	300	450	900	1,200
1608 F	—	—	500	750	1,300	1,500
1609 A	—	—	300	450	900	1,200
1609 F Rare	—	—	—	—	—	—
1610/9 F	—	—	300	450	900	1,200
1610 F	—	—	300	450	900	1,200
1611/0 F	—	—	600	850	1,650	1,850
1611 F	—	—	600	850	1,650	1,850
1612/1 F	—	—	300	450	900	1,200
1612 F	—	—	300	450	900	1,200
1613 F	—	—	600	850	1,650	1,850
1614 F	—	—	300	450	900	1,200
1615 F	—	—	300	450	900	1,200
1616 F Rare	—	—	—	—	—	—
1617 F Rare	—	—	—	—	—	—
1618 D/F Rare	—	—	—	—	—	—
1618 D	—	—	300	450	900	1,200
1619 D Rare	—	—	—	—	—	—
1620 D	—	—	300	450	900	1,200
1621/0 D	—	—	300	450	900	1,200
1621 D	—	—	300	450	900	1,200

KM# 45 8 REALES

27.0700 g., 0.9310 Silver 0.8102 oz. ASW **Ruler:** Philip IV **Obv:** Legend around crowned arms **Obv. Legend:** PHILIPVS IIII DEI G **Rev:** Legend around cross, lions and castles **Note:** Struck at Mexico City Mint, mint mark M, Mo.

Date	Mintage	Good	VG	F	VF	XF
ND(1621-67) Date off flan	—	—	70.00	90.00	120	200
1621 D	—	—	200	350	500	750
1622/1 D Rare	—	—	—	—	—	—
1622 D	—	—	200	350	500	750
1623/2 D	—	—	200	350	500	750
1623 D	—	—	200	350	500	750
1624/3 D	—	—	200	350	500	750
1624 D	—	—	200	350	500	750
1625/4 D	—	—	200	350	500	750
1625 D	—	—	200	300	500	750
1626/5 D Rare	—	—	—	—	—	—
1626 D	—	—	200	350	500	750
1627/6/5 D	—	—	200	350	500	750
1627/6 D	—	—	200	350	500	750
1627 D	—	—	200	350	500	750
1628/7	—	—	200	350	500	750
1628 D	—	—	200	350	500	750
1629 D	—	—	200	350	500	750
1630 D Rare	—	—	—	—	—	—
1631/0 D Rare	—	—	—	—	—	—
1631 D Rare	—	—	—	—	—	—
1632 D	—	—	200	350	500	750
1634 D	—	—	200	350	500	750
1634 P/D	—	—	200	350	500	750
1634 P	—	—	200	350	500	750
1635 P	—	—	200	350	500	750
1636 P	—	—	200	350	500	750
1637 P	—	—	200	350	500	750
1639/8 P	—	—	200	350	500	750
1639 P	—	—	200	350	500	750
1640/39 P	—	—	200	350	500	750
1640 P	—	—	200	350	500	750
1641/40/39 P	—	—	200	350	500	750
1641 P	—	—	200	350	500	750
1642 P	—	—	200	350	500	750
1643 P	—	—	200	350	500	750
1644 P Rare	—	—	—	—	—	—
1645 P	—	—	200	350	500	750
1646 P	—	—	200	350	500	750
1647/6 P	—	—	200	350	500	750
1647 P	—	—	200	350	500	750
1648/7 P Rare	—	—	—	—	—	—
1648 P	—	—	200	350	500	750
1649/8 P Rare	—	—	—	—	—	—
1649 P	—	—	200	350	500	750
1650 P	—	—	200	350	500	750
1651 P	—	—	175	250	350	500
1652/45 P	—	—	175	250	350	500
1652/48 P	—	—	175	250	350	500
1652/49 P	—	—	165	225	300	475
1652/0 P	—	—	165	225	300	475
1652/1 P	—	—	165	225	300	475
1652 P	—	—	165	225	300	475
1653/2 P	—	—	165	225	300	475
1653 P	—	—	165	225	300	475
1654/3 P	—	—	165	225	300	475
1654 P	—	—	165	225	300	475
1655/4 P	—	—	165	225	300	475
1655 P	—	—	165	225	300	475
1656 P	—	—	165	225	300	475
1657 P	—	—	250	400	600	800
1658/7 P	—	—	250	400	600	800
1658 P	—	—	250	400	600	800
1659 P	—	—	300	500	800	1,000
1660/59 P	—	—	300	500	800	1,000
1660 P	—	—	300	500	800	1,000
1661 /OP Rare	—	—	—	—	—	—
1661 P Rare	—	—	—	—	—	—
1662 P	—	—	300	500	800	1,000
1663 P	—	—	300	500	800	1,000
1664 P	—	—	300	500	800	1,000
1665 P	—	—	300	500	800	1,000
1666 G/P Rare	—	—	—	—	—	—
1666 G Rare	—	—	—	—	—	—

KM# 46 8 REALES

27.0700 g., 0.9310 Silver 0.8102 oz. ASW **Ruler:** Charles II **Obv:** Legend and date around crowned arms **Obv. Legend:** CAROLVS II DEI G **Rev:** Legend around cross, lions and castles **Note:** Struck at Mexico City Mint, mint mark M, Mo.

Date	Mintage	Good	VG	F	VF	XF
ND(1667-1701) Date off flan	—	—	90.00	110	150	200
1667/6 Rare	—	—	—	—	—	—
1667 G	—	—	600	900	1,500	—
1668 G	—	—	600	900	1,500	—
1669 G	—	—	600	900	1,500	—
1670 G	—	—	600	900	1,500	—
1671 G	—	—	700	1,000	1,700	—
1672 G	—	—	700	1,000	1,700	—
1673 G	—	—	700	1,000	1,700	—
1674 G	—	—	600	900	1,500	—
1675 G	—	—	600	900	1,500	—
1676/5 G	—	—	400	600	900	—
1676 G	—	—	400	600	900	—
1677 G	—	—	400	600	900	—
1678 L	—	—	400	600	900	—
1679 L	—	—	400	600	900	—
1680 L	—	—	300	400	600	—
1681 L	—	—	600	400	600	—
1682 L Rare	—	—	—	—	—	—
1683 L Rare	—	—	—	—	—	—
1684 L	—	—	600	900	1,500	—
1685 L	—	—	600	900	1,500	—
1686 L Rare	—	—	—	—	—	—
1687 L	—	—	700	1,000	1,700	—
1688 L	—	—	700	1,000	1,700	—
1689 L	—	—	600	900	1,500	—
1690 L Rare	—	—	—	—	—	—
1691 L Rare	—	—	—	—	—	—
1692 L Rare	—	—	—	—	—	—
1693 L Rare	—	—	—	—	—	—
1694 L Rare	—	—	—	—	—	—
1695 L	—	—	600	900	1,500	—
1697 L Rare	—	—	—	—	—	—
1698 L Rare	—	—	—	—	—	—
1699 L	—	—	600	900	1,500	—
1700 L	—	—	700	1,000	1,700	—

KM# 50 ESCUDO

3.3800 g., 0.9170 Gold 0.0996 oz. AGW **Ruler:** Charles II **Obv:** Legend and date around crowned arms **Obv. Legend:** CAROLVS II DEI G **Rev:** Lions and castles in angles of cross, legend around **Note:** Mint mark MXo.

Date	Mintage	VG	F	VF	XF	Unc
ND(1679-1701) Date off flan	—	—	1,200	1,500	2,000	—
1679MXo L Rare	—	—	—	—	—	—
1690MXo L	—	—	3,000	4,000	5,000	—
1695MXo L	—	—	3,000	4,000	5,000	—
1697MXo L	—	—	3,000	4,000	5,000	—
1698MXo L	—	—	3,000	4,000	5,000	—
1699MXo L	—	—	3,000	4,000	5,000	—
1700MXo L	—	—	3,000	4,000	5,000	—

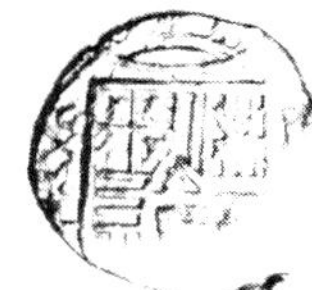

KM# 52 2 ESCUDOS

6.7700 g., 0.9170 Gold 0.1996 oz. AGW **Ruler:** Philip V **Obv:** Legend and date around crowned arms **Obv. Legend:** CAROLVS II DEI G **Rev:** Legend around cross **Note:** Mint mark MXo.

Date	Mintage	VG	F	VF	XF	Unc
ND(1679-1701) Date off flan	—	—	1,300	1,750	2,500	—
1680MXo L	—	—	4,000	5,000	6,000	—
1681MXo L	—	—	4,000	5,000	6,000	—
1695MXo L	—	—	4,000	5,000	6,000	—
1698MXo L	—	—	4,000	5,000	6,000	—

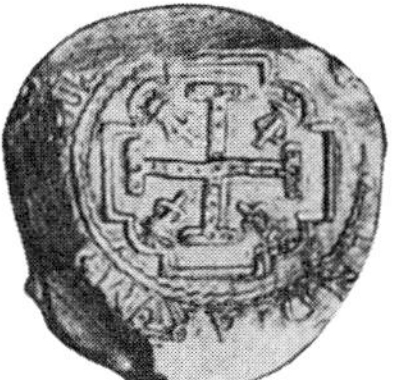

KM# 54 4 ESCUDOS

13.5400 g., 0.9170 Gold 0.3992 oz. AGW **Ruler:** Charles II **Obv:** Legend and date around crowned arms **Obv. Legend:** CAROLVS II DEI G **Rev:** Legend around cross **Note:** Struck at Mexico City Mint, mint mark MXo.

Date	Mintage	VG	F	VF	XF	Unc
ND(1679-1701) Date off flan	—	—	2,500	3,500	4,750	—
1680MXo L Rare	—	—	—	—	—	—
1681MXo L	—	—	4,500	6,000	7,500	—
1683MXo L	—	—	4,500	6,000	7,500	—
1693MXo L	—	—	4,500	6,000	7,500	—
1694MXo L	—	—	4,500	6,000	7,500	—
1695MXo L	—	—	4,500	6,000	7,500	—
1696MXo L	—	—	4,500	6,000	7,500	—
1697MXo L	—	—	4,500	6,000	7,500	—
1698MXo L	—	—	4,500	6,000	7,500	—
1699/8/7MXo L	—	—	4,500	6,000	7,500	—

KM# 56 8 ESCUDOS

27.0700 g., 0.9170 Gold 0.7981 oz. AGW **Ruler:** Philip V **Obv:** Legend and date around crowned arms **Obv. Legend:** CAROLVS II DEI G **Rev:** Legend around cross **Note:** Struck at Mexico City Mint, mark mark MXo.

Date	Mintage	VG	F	VF	XF	Unc
ND(1679-1701) Date off flan	—	—	4,500	6,250	7,000	—
1691MXo L	—	—	6,000	7,500	9,000	—
1694MXo L	—	—	6,000	7,500	9,000	—
1695MXo L	—	—	6,000	7,500	9,000	—
1697/6MXo L	—	—	6,000	7,500	9,000	—
1697MXo L	—	—	6,000	7,500	9,000	—
1698MXo L	—	—	6,000	7,500	9,000	—
1699MXo L	—	—	6,000	7,500	9,000	—
1700MXo L	—	—	6,000	7,500	9,000	—

ROYAL COINAGE

Struck on specially prepared round planchets using well centered dies in excellent condition to prove the quality of the minting to the Viceroy or even to the King.

KM# R28 REAL

3.3834 g., 0.9310 Silver 0.1013 oz. ASW **Ruler:** Philip IV **Obv. Legend:** PHILIPVS IIII DEI G **Note:** Struck at Mexico City Mint, mint mark Mo.

Date	Mintage	Good	VG	F	VF	XF
1643Mo P Rare	—	—	—	—	—	—

KM# R29 REAL

3.3834 g., 0.9310 Silver 0.1013 oz. ASW **Ruler:** Charles II **Obv. Legend:** CAROLVS II DEI G **Note:** Struck at Mexico City Mint, mint mark Mo.

Date	Mintage	Good	VG	F	VF	XF
1699Mo L Rare	—	—	—	—	—	—

KM# R34 2 REALES
6.7668 g., 0.9310 Silver 0.2025 oz. ASW **Ruler:** Charles II
Obv. Legend: CAROLVS II DEI G **Note:** Struck at Mexico City Mint, mint mark Mo.

Date	Mintage	Good	VG	F	VF	XF
1668Mo G Rare	—	—	—	—	—	—

KM# R38 4 REALES
113.5337 g., 0.9310 Silver 3.3982 oz. ASW **Ruler:** Philip III

Date	Mintage	Good	VG	F	VF	XF
ND(1598-1606)Mo Rare	—	—	—	—	—	—

KM# R37.1 4 REALES
13.5337 g., 0.9310 Silver 0.4051 oz. ASW **Ruler:** Philip III
Obv. Legend: PHILLIPVS III DEI GRATIA **Note:** Struck at Mexico City Mint, mint mark Mo.

Date	Mintage	Good	VG	F	VF	XF
NDMo F Rare	—	—	—	—	—	—

KM# R41 4 REALES
13.5337 g., 0.9310 Silver 0.4051 oz. ASW **Ruler:** Philip IV

Date	Mintage	Good	VG	F	VF	XF
1631Mo D Rare	—	—	—	—	—	—
1639Mo P Rare	—	—	—	—	—	—
1643Mo P Rare	—	—	—	—	—	—
1647/6Mo P Rare	—	—	—	—	—	—
1654Mo P Rare	—	—	—	—	—	—

KM# R39 4 REALES
13.5337 g., 0.9310 Silver 0.4051 oz. ASW **Ruler:** Charles II
Obv. Legend: CAROLVS II DEI G

Date	Mintage	Good	VG	F	VF	XF
1678Mo L Rare	—	—	—	—	—	—
1682Mo L Rare	—	—	—	—	—	—
1691/0Mo L Rare	—	—	—	—	—	—
1695Mo L Rare	—	—	—	—	—	—

KM# R44.1 8 REALES
27.0674 g., 0.9310 Silver 0.8102 oz. ASW **Ruler:** Philip III
Obv. Legend: PHILIPVS III DEL GRATIA **Note:** Struck at Mexico City Mint, mint mark Mo.

Date	Mintage	Good	VG	F	VF	XF
ND(1598-1606)Mo F Rare	—	—	—	—	—	—

KM# R44.3 8 REALES
27.0674 g., 0.9310 Silver 0.8102 oz. ASW **Ruler:** Philip III
Obv. Legend: PHILIPVS III DEI G **Note:** Struck at Mexico City Mint, mint mark Mo.

Date	Mintage	Good	VG	F	VF	XF
1607Mo F Rare	—	—	—	—	—	—
1609Mo A Rare	—	—	—	—	—	—
1610Mo F Rare	—	—	—	—	—	—
1613Mo F Rare	—	—	—	—	—	—
1614Mo F Rare	—	—	—	—	—	—
1615Mo F Rare	—	—	—	—	—	—
1617Mo F Rare	—	—	—	—	—	—
1618Mo D/F Rare	—	—	—	—	—	—

KM# R45 8 REALES
27.0674 g., 0.9310 Silver 0.8102 oz. ASW **Ruler:** Philip IV
Obv. Legend: PHILIPVS IIII DEI G **Note:** Struck at Mexico City Mint, mint mark Mo.

Date	Mintage	Good	VG	F	VF	XF
1621Mo D Rare	—	—	—	—	—	—
1629Mo D Rare	—	—	—	—	—	—
1632Mo D Rare	—	—	—	—	—	—
1636Mo D Rare	—	—	—	—	—	—
1639Mo P Rare	—	—	—	—	—	—
1642Mo P Rare	—	—	—	—	—	—
1646Mo P Rare	—	—	—	—	—	—
1650Mo P Rare	—	—	—	—	—	—
1667Mo P Rare	—	—	—	—	—	—

KM# R46 8 REALES
27.0674 g., 0.9310 Silver 0.8102 oz. ASW **Ruler:** Charles II
Obv. Legend: CAROLVS II DEI G **Note:** Mint mark Mo.

Date	Mintage	Good	VG	F	VF	XF
1674Mo G Rare	—	—	—	—	—	—
1678Mo L Rare	—	—	—	—	—	—
1681/0Mo L Rare	—	—	—	—	—	—
1682Mo L Rare	—	—	—	—	—	—
1685Mo L Rare	—	—	—	—	—	—
1689/8Mo L Rare	—	—	—	—	—	—
1690Mo L Rare	—	—	—	—	—	—
1691/0Mo L Rare	—	—	—	—	—	—
1691Mo L Rare	—	—	—	—	—	—
1698Mo L Rare	—	—	—	—	—	—
1699Mo L Rare	—	—	—	—	—	—
1700Mo L Rare	—	—	—	—	—	—

KM# R56 8 ESCUDOS
27.0674 g., 0.9170 Gold 0.7980 oz. AGW **Note:** Fully struck sample specimens referred to as "Royal" strikes are seldom encountered. Struck at Mexico City Mint, mint mark MXo.

Date	Mintage	Good	VG	F	VF	XF
1695MXo L Rare	—	—	—	—	—	—
1698MXo L Rare	—	—	—	—	—	—

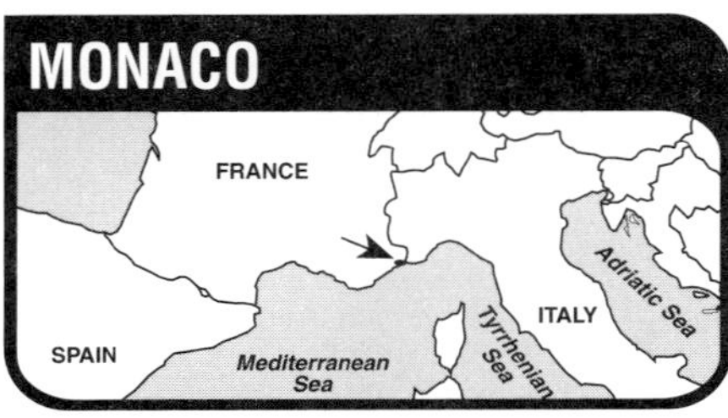

The Principality of Monaco, located on the Mediterranean coast nine miles from Nice, has an area of 0.58 sq. mi. (1.9 sq. km).

Monaco derives its name from Monoikos', the Greek surname for Hercules, the mythological strong man who, according to legend, formed the Monacan headland during one of his twelve labors. Monaco has been ruled by the Grimaldi dynasty since 1297 - Prince Rainier III, the present and 31st monarch of Monaco, is still of that line - except for a period during the French Revolution until Napoleon's downfall when the Principality was annexed to France. Since 1865, Monaco has maintained a customs union with France which guarantees its privileged position as long as the royal line remains intact. Under the new constitution proclaimed on December 17, 1962, the Prince shares his power with an 18-member unicameral National Council.

RULERS
Hercules I, 1589-1604
Honore II, 1604-1662
Louis I, 1662-1701

MINT PRIVY MARKS
(a) - Paris (privy marks only)
(ac) - Acorn, 1660-1664, 1670-1671
(b) - Bird on branch, 1678-1679
(bd) - Bird, diving, 1691
(bf) - Bird in flight, 1691-1693
(bh) - Bird, heraldic, 1683
(bs) - Bird, small, 1670-1674
C and clasped hands - Francois Cabinas, mint director, 1837-1838
(cl) - Cross, Latin, 1681
(cm) - Cross, Maltese, 1654; 1681
(d) - Daisy, stem, 1678-1679
(f) - Flower, 1673
(fb) - Flower buds, 1720
(ff) - Frame, oval with finger, 1683
(h) - Crowned H, 1701
(l) - Lily, stem, 1692-1693
(lr) - Lion, rampant, 1654-1659
(p) - Thunderbolt - Poissy
(q) - Quatrefoil, 1674-1675
(r) - Rosebud, 1648-1653
(s) - Star, 5-pointed, 1654
(sb) - Scale, balance, 1701
(sd) - Star of David, 1665-1669
(sf) - Shield with finger, 1682
(sr) - Sunface, radiant, 1681-1683
(t) - Thistle, 1672-1674

PRINCIPALITY

STANDARD COINAGE

KM# 2 2 PATACCHI (2 Patards)
Copper **Obv:** Bust of Honore II right in inner circle **Rev:** Crowned H in inner cirlce, date in legend

Date	Mintage	VG	F	VF	XF	Unc
1640	—	900	1,800	3,000	4,500	—

KM# 3 4 PATACCHI (4 Patards)
Copper **Obv:** Bust of Honore II right in inner circle **Rev:** Crowned H in inner circle, value in exergue, date in legend

Date	Mintage	VG	F	VF	XF	Unc
1640	—	250	400	750	1,400	—

KM# 52 DENIER TOURNOIS (1 Liard, 2 Deniers)
Copper **Obv:** Bust of Louis I right **Rev:** 5 groups of 3 diamonds

Date	Mintage	VG	F	VF	XF	Unc
1677 Rare	—	—	—	—	—	—

KM# 55 DENIER TOURNOIS (1 Liard, 2 Deniers)
Copper **Obv:** Louis I **Rev:** St. Devote standing, divides date

Date	Mintage	VG	F	VF	XF	Unc
1683	—	125	250	550	1,000	—

KM# 24 2 TOURNOIS
Copper **Obv:** Bust of Honore II right **Rev:** 3 diamonds in inner circle, date in legend

Date	Mintage	VG	F	VF	XF	Unc
1653 Rare	—	—	—	—	—	—

KM# 4 2 GROS
1.9000 g., Billon **Obv:** Bust of Honore II right in inner circle
Rev: St. Devote standing, divides date

Date	Mintage	VG	F	VF	XF	Unc
1640	—	750	1,500	3,000	—	—

KM# 5 6 GROS (1/2 Florin)
3.1300 g., Billon **Obv:** Bust of Honore II right in inner circle, date in exergue **Rev:** Crowned arms in inner circle, value below in legend

Date	Mintage	VG	F	VF	XF	Unc
1640	—	900	1,800	3,750	—	—

KM# 6 12 GROS (Florin)
5.9900 g., Billon **Obv:** Bust of Honore II right in inner circle
Rev: Crowned arms in order collar in inner circle

Date	Mintage	VG	F	VF	XF	Unc
1640	—	2,250	3,750	6,800	—	—

KM# 21 12 GROS (Florin)
5.9900 g., Billon **Obv:** Bust left

Date	Mintage	VG	F	VF	XF	Unc
1640	—	2,400	4,150	7,500	—	—

KM# 9 1-1/2 SOLS (1/2 Pezetta)
1.6500 g., Billon **Obv:** Crowned arms, titles of Honore II
Rev: Maltese cross with diamonds in angles, date in legend

Date	Mintage	VG	F	VF	XF	Unc
1648	—	150	275	550	1,100	—

KM# 10 1-1/2 SOLS (1/2 Pezetta)
1.6500 g., Billon **Rev:** St. Devote standing, divides date

Date	Mintage	VG	F	VF	XF	Unc
1648	—	250	450	900	1,800	—

KM# 50 1-1/2 SOLS (1/2 Pezetta)
1.6500 g., Billon **Obv:** Titles of Louis I **Rev:** Maltese cross with diamonds in angles, date in legend

Date	Mintage	VG	F	VF	XF	Unc
1673 (f)	—	100	220	450	900	—
1683	—	100	220	450	900	—
1693 (bf)	—	125	250	500	1,000	—

KM# 11 3 SOLS (Pezetta)
4.5000 g., Billon **Obv:** Bust of Honore II right **Rev:** Crowned arms, date in legend

Date	Mintage	VG	F	VF	XF	Unc
1648	—	250	450	900	1,800	—

KM# 51 3 SOLS (Pezetta)
4.5000 g., Billon **Obv:** Louis I bust facing right **Rev:** Crowned arms

Date	Mintage	VG	F	VF	XF	Unc
1673 (t)	—	185	375	750	1,500	—
1683 (bh)	—	165	325	625	1,250	—

KM# 60.1 3 SOLS (Pezetta)
4.5000 g., Billon **Rev:** Cross with lozenges in angles

Date	Mintage	VG	F	VF	XF	Unc
1693 (bf//l)	—	250	450	900	1,650	—

KM# 8 5 SOLS (1/12 Ecu)
Obv: Small bust of Honore II right **Rev:** Crowned arms, date in legend at lower right

Date	Mintage	VG	F	VF	XF	Unc
1644	—	—	—	—	—	—

KM# 20 5 SOLS (1/12 Ecu)
2.2000 g., Silver **Obv:** Large bust of Honore II right
Obv. Legend: HONORATVS II **Rev:** Crowned arms, date in legend at upper left

Date	Mintage	VG	F	VF	XF	Unc
1650 (r)	—	165	325	625	1,200	—
1651 (r)	—	165	325	625	1,200	—
1653 (r)	—	165	325	625	1,200	—

KM# 25 5 SOLS (1/12 Ecu)
2.2000 g., Silver **Obv. Legend:** HON. II

Date	Mintage	VG	F	VF	XF	Unc
1654 (s, lr)	—	150	275	550	1,000	—
1655 (lr)	—	150	275	550	1,000	—
1656 (lr)	—	150	275	550	1,000	—
1657 (lr)	—	125	225	500	950	—
1658 (lr)	—	125	225	500	950	—
16558 (lr)	—	750	1,500	3,000	—	—
16658 (lr)	—	750	1,500	3,000	—	—
1659 (lr)	—	125	225	500	950	

KM# 35 5 SOLS (1/12 Ecu)
2.2000 g., Silver **Obv:** Draped bust of Honore II right **Rev. Legend:** DVX. VALENT.PAR $ FRANCIAE & C.

Date	Mintage	VG	F	VF	XF	Unc
1660 (ac)	—	125	225	475	950	—
1661 (ac)	—	125	225	475	950	—
1662 (ac)	—	125	225	475	950	—

KM# 36 5 SOLS (1/12 Ecu)
2.2000 g., Silver **Obv:** Young armored bust of Louis I right

Date	Mintage	VG	F	VF	XF	Unc
1662 (ac)	—	100	175	375	800	—
1663 (ac)	—	100	200	450	900	—
1664 (ac)	—	150	300	650	1,150	—

KM# 39 5 SOLS (1/12 Ecu)
2.2000 g., Silver **Obv:** Draped bust of Louis I left **Rev:** Crowned round arms with 5 vertical rows of diamonds, date in legend at left

Date	Mintage	VG	F	VF	XF	Unc
1665 (sd)	—	125	250	500	975	—

KM# 40 5 SOLS (1/12 Ecu)
2.2000 g., Silver **Rev:** Round arms with 7 vertical rows of diamonds **Note:** Private traders produced debased 5 Sols dated 1667, 1668 and 1669 with obverse bust of Marie Louise of Dombes as well as Louis I and reverse similar to KM#40 for the Levantine trade.

Date	Mintage	VG	F	VF	XF	Unc
1665 (sd)	—	125	250	500	975	—
1666 (sd)	—	125	250	500	975	—

KM# 41.1 5 SOLS (1/12 Ecu)
2.2000 g., Silver **Obv:** Draped bust of Louis I **Rev:** Crowned straight-sided shield of arms with 7 vertical rows of diamonds

Date	Mintage	VG	F	VF	XF	Unc
1665 (sd)	—	90.00	185	375	800	—
1666 (sd)	—	125	275	550	1,100	—

KM# 41.2 5 SOLS (1/12 Ecu)
2.2000 g., Silver **Obv:** Revised bust **Rev:** Crowned straight-sided shield of arms with 5 vertical rows of diamonds

Date	Mintage	VG	F	VF	XF	Unc
1674 (q)	—	200	375	750	1,400	—
1678 (d)	—	175	350	700	1,250	—

KM# 41.3 5 SOLS (1/12 Ecu)
2.2000 g., Silver

Date	Mintage	VG	F	VF	XF	Unc
1681 (cm//sr)	—	175	350	700	1,250	—

KM# 30 10 SOLS (1/6 Ecu)
4.3800 g., Silver **Obv:** Bust of Honore II right **Rev:** Crowned arms, date in legend at upper left

Date	Mintage	VG	F	VF	XF	Unc
1656 (lr)	—	450	350	1,350	2,650	—
1658 (lr)	—	400	600	1,250	2,400	—
1659 (lr)	—	400	600	1,250	2,400	—
1660 (ac)	—	400	600	1,250	2,400	—

KM# 7 1/4 ECU (15 Sols)
7.0000 g., Silver **Obv:** Bust of Honore II right **Rev:** Crowned arms in order chain

Date	Mintage	VG	F	VF	XF	Unc
1643	—	—	—	—	—	—

KM# 12 1/4 ECU (15 Sols)
7.0000 g., Silver **Obv:** Bust of Honore II right within legend **Obv. Legend:** HONORATVS... **Rev:** Crowned arms, date in legend at upper left

Date	Mintage	VG	F	VF	XF	Unc
1648 (r)	—	375	700	1,500	3,400	—
1649 (r)	—	375	700	1,500	3,400	—
1650 (r)	—	350	675	1,350	3,200	—
1651 (r)	—	350	675	1,350	3,200	—

KM# 18.1 1/4 ECU (15 Sols)
7.0000 g., Silver **Obv:** Legend begins at left **Obv. Legend:** HONO: II • D:G:...

Date	Mintage	VG	F	VF	XF	Unc
1652 (r)	—	350	675	1,350	3,200	—
1653 (r)	—	350	675	1,350	3,200	—

KM# 18.2 1/4 ECU (15 Sols)
7.0000 g., Silver **Obv. Legend:** HON • II • D:G...

Date	Mintage	VG	F	VF	XF	Unc
1654 (lr)	—	350	675	1,350	3,200	—
1655 (lr)	—	350	675	1,350	3,200	—
1656 (lr)	—	350	675	1,350	3,200	—
1657 (lr)	—	350	675	1,350	3,200	—
1658 (lr)	—	350	675	1,350	3,200	—
1660 (ac)	—	350	675	1,350	3,200	—
1661 (ac)	—	350	675	1,350	3,200	—

KM# 42.1 1/4 ECU (15 Sols)
7.0000 g., Silver **Obv:** Bust of Louis I right **Rev. Legend:** DVX.VALENT.PAR.FRANCIAE & C.

Date	Mintage	VG	F	VF	XF	Unc
1665 (sd)	—	185	375	750	1,800	—
1666 (sd)	—	200	425	850	2,050	—

KM# 42.2 1/4 ECU (15 Sols)
7.0000 g., Silver **Obv:** Divided by stars

Date	Mintage	VG	F	VF	XF	Unc
1671 (bs//ac)	—	225	450	900	2,200	—

KM# 42.3 1/4 ECU (15 Sols)
7.0000 g., Silver **Obv:** Divided by dots

Date	Mintage	VG	F	VF	XF	Unc
1673 (t)	—	250	500	1,000	2,400	—
1679 (d//b)	—	300	600	1,250	2,800	—
1683 (bh)	—	350	700	1,400	3,250	—

KM# 61 1/4 ECU (15 Sols)
7.0000 g., Silver **Rev:** Date **Rev. Legend:** AVXILIVM MEVM.A.DOMINO

Date	Mintage	VG	F	VF	XF	Unc
1693 (bf//l)	—	500	1,000	2,000	4,200	—

KM# 13 1/2 ECU (30 Sols)
13.5500 g., Silver **Obv:** Honore II within legend **Rev:** HONORATVS • II • D • G...

Date	Mintage	VG	F	VF	XF	Unc
1648 (r)	—	375	750	1,600	3,400	—
1649 (r)	—	375	750	1,600	3,400	—
1650 (r//r)	—	375	750	1,600	3,400	—
1651 (r//r)	—	375	750	1,600	3,400	—
16648 (r)	—	375	750	1,600	3,400	—

KM# 22.1 1/2 ECU (30 Sols)
13.5500 g., Silver **Obv:** HONO:II:D:G...

Date	Mintage	VG	F	VF	XF	Unc
1652 (r)	—	350	675	1,350	3,200	—

KM# 22.2 1/2 ECU (30 Sols)
13.5500 g., Silver **Obv:** Modified portrait

Date	Mintage	VG	F	VF	XF	Unc
1653 (r)	—	350	675	1,350	3,200	—

KM# 26 1/2 ECU (30 Sols)
13.5500 g., Silver **Obv:** HON • II • D:G... **Note:** Varieties exist.

Date	Mintage	VG	F	VF	XF	Unc
1654 (cm)	—	375	750	1,600	3,400	—
1654 (lr)	—	375	750	1,600	3,400	—
1655 (lr)	—	375	750	1,600	3,400	—
1656 (lr)	—	425	800	1,650	3,850	—
1658 (lr)	—	425	800	1,650	3,850	—
1660 (ac)	—	450	850	1,750	4,400	—

KM# 43.1 1/2 ECU (30 Sols)
13.5500 g., Silver **Obv:** Louis I bust facing right

Date	Mintage	VG	F	VF	XF	Unc
1665 (sd)	—	200	400	800	2,100	—
1666 (sd)	—	175	350	700	2,000	—

KM# 43.2 1/2 ECU (30 Sols)
13.5500 g., Silver **Obv:** Legend divided by stars

Date	Mintage	VG	F	VF	XF	Unc
1674 (bs//t)	—	350	650	1,250	2,700	—

KM# 43.3 1/2 ECU (30 Sols)
13.5500 g., Silver **Obv:** Legend divided by dots with mint mark at upper left

Date	Mintage	VG	F	VF	XF	Unc
1681 (cl//sr)	—	400	750	1,350	3,000	—
1683 (ff//sr)	—	500	1,000	2,000	4,200	—

KM# 14.1 SCUDO (Ecu, 60 Sols)
27.0000 g., Silver **Obv:** Honore II within legend **Obv. Legend:** HONORATVS • II... **Note:** Dav. #4305.

Date	Mintage	VG	F	VF	XF	Unc
1648 (r//r)	—	1,300	2,700	4,950	10,000	—
1649 (r//r)	—	1,150	2,250	4,150	9,300	—
1650 (r//r)	—	1,050	2,050	3,700	8,300	—

KM# 14.2 SCUDO (Ecu, 60 Sols)
27.0000 g., Silver **Obv:** Larger modified bust **Note:** Dav. #A4305.

Date	Mintage	VG	F	VF	XF	Unc
1651 (r//r)	—	550	1,100	2,200	4,800	—

KM# 23 SCUDO (Ecu, 60 Sols)
27.0000 g., Silver **Obv:** Legend begins at left **Obv. Legend:** HONO: II... **Note:** Dav. #4306.

Date	Mintage	VG	F	VF	XF	Unc
1652 (r)	—	400	850	1,950	4,200	—
1653 (r)	—	350	750	1,650	3,600	—

KM# 32 SCUDO (Ecu, 60 Sols)
27.0000 g., Silver **Obv. Legend:** HON • II • D:G... **Note:** Dav. #4307. Varieties exist.

Date	Mintage	VG	F	VF	XF	Unc
1654 (lr)	—	400	850	1,950	4,200	—
1655 (lr)	—	450	950	2,100	4,500	—
1656 (lr)	—	600	1,150	2,500	5,400	—
1658 (lr)	—	1,000	2,000	4,150	8,400	—
1659 (lr)	—	800	1,600	3,300	6,600	—
1660 (ac)	—	900	1,750	3,600	7,200	—
1662 (ac)	—	925	1,850	3,850	7,800	—

KM# 31 SCUDO (Ecu, 60 Sols)
27.0000 g., Silver **Obv:** Honore II within legend **Obv. Legend:** HONORATVS • II... **Note:** Dav. #A4307.

Date	Mintage	VG	F	VF	XF	Unc
1654 (cm, lr)	—	750	1,400	2,800	6,000	—

KM# 37.1 SCUDO (Ecu, 60 Sols)
27.0000 g., Silver **Obv:** Louis I bust facing right **Note:** Dav. #A4308.

Date	Mintage	VG	F	VF	XF	Unc
1662 (ac)	—	600	1,150	2,500	5,400	—
1663 (ac)	—	950	1,850	3,850	7,800	—

KM# 37.2 SCUDO (Ecu, 60 Sols)
27.0000 g., Silver **Obv:** Legend divided by dots with mint mark at upper left **Note:** Dav. #4308.

Date	Mintage	VG	F	VF	XF	Unc
1666 (sd)	—	450	950	2,100	4,500	—
1668 (sd)	—	450	950	2,100	4,500	—
1669 (sd)	—	450	950	2,100	4,500	—

KM# 37.3 SCUDO (Ecu, 60 Sols)
27.0000 g., Silver **Note:** Dav. #B4308.

Date	Mintage	VG	F	VF	XF	Unc
1670 (bs//ac)	—	600	1,150	2,500	5,400	—
1672 (bs//ac)	—	550	1,100	2,200	4,800	—
1673 (bs//t)	—	550	1,100	2,200	4,800	—
1674 (bs//t)	—	550	1,100	2,200	4,800	—
1674 (q, t)	—	550	1,100	2,200	4,800	—
1675 (q//t)	—	700	1,350	2,750	6,000	—

KM# 37.4 SCUDO (Ecu, 60 Sols)
27.0000 g., Silver **Obv:** Legend divided by dots with mint mark at upper left **Note:** Dav. #C4308.

Date	Mintage	VG	F	VF	XF	Unc
1678 (d//b)	—	600	1,150	2,500	5,400	—
1679 (d//b)	—	700	1,350	2,750	6,000	—

KM# 37.5 SCUDO (Ecu, 60 Sols)
27.0000 g., Silver **Obv:** Modified armor **Note:** Dav. #D4308.

Date	Mintage	VG	F	VF	XF	Unc
1681 (cl//sr)	—	700	1,350	2,750	6,000	—
1682 (sf//sr)	—	700	1,350	2,750	6,000	—

KM# 48 SCUDO (Ecu, 60 Sols)
27.0000 g., Silver **Rev. Legend:** AVXILIVM.MEVM...
Note: Dav. #4309.

Date	Mintage	VG	F	VF	XF	Unc
1690	—	900	1,750	3,600	7,200	—
1691 (bf//bd)	—	1,000	2,000	4,150	8,400	—
1692 (bf//I)	—	1,000	2,000	4,150	8,400	—

KM# 27 TALLERO (28 Stuivers)
19.6100 g., Silver **Obv:** Crowned arms **Rev:** Crowned eagle with 28 in circle on breast

Date	Mintage	VG	F	VF	XF	Unc
ND	—	5,000	7,000	12,500	17,500	—

KM# 45 TALLERO (28 Stuivers)
26.1000 g., Silver **Obv:** Standing knight behind lion shield **Rev:** Rampant lion left holding shield with Grimaldi arms
Note: Imitation of the Dutch Lion Thaler.

Date	Mintage	VG	F	VF	XF	Unc
1668 4 known	—	—	—	—	—	—

TRADE COINAGE

KM# 19 1/2 DOPPIA (1/2 Louis D'or)
3.5000 g., 0.9860 Gold 0.1109 oz. AGW **Obv:** Bust of Honore right **Rev:** Crowned H monograms in cruciform, lis in angles, date in legend

Date	Mintage	VG	F	VF	XF	Unc
1650 Rare	—	—	—	—	—	—

KM# 15 DOPPIA (Louis D' or)
7.0000 g., 0.9860 Gold 0.2219 oz. AGW **Obv:** Bust of Honore right **Rev:** Crowned H monograms in cruciform, lis in angles, date in legend

Date	Mintage	VG	F	VF	XF	Unc
1648	—	4,000	8,000	14,500	24,500	—
1649	—	4,000	8,000	14,500	24,500	—

KM# 28.1 DOPPIA (Louis D' or)
7.0000 g., 0.9860 Gold 0.2219 oz. AGW **Rev:** Crowned H in branches

Date	Mintage	VG	F	VF	XF	Unc
1654 (lr)	—	4,500	9,000	16,000	27,500	—
1656 (lr)	—	4,500	9,000	16,000	27,500	—
1657 (lr)	—	4,500	9,000	16,000	27,500	—

KM# 28.2 DOPPIA (Louis D' or)
7.0000 g., 0.9860 Gold 0.2219 oz. AGW **Rev:** Crowned H in branches

Date	Mintage	VG	F	VF	XF	Unc
1660 (ac)	—	4,500	9,000	16,000	27,500	—
1661 (ac)	—	4,500	9,000	16,000	27,500	—

KM# 16 2 DOPPIA (2 Louis D' or)
14.0000 g., 0.9860 Gold 0.4438 oz. AGW **Obv:** Honore II bust facing right

Date	Mintage	VG	F	VF	XF	Unc
1648	—	7,000	13,500	25,000	40,000	—
1649	—	7,000	13,500	25,000	40,000	—
1650	—	7,000	13,500	25,000	40,000	—

KM# 29 2 DOPPIA (2 Louis D' or)
14.0000 g., 0.9860 Gold 0.4438 oz. AGW **Obv:** Armored bust of Honore II right **Rev:** Crowned H in branches

Date	Mintage	VG	F	VF	XF	Unc
1656 (lr)	—	7,500	14,500	27,500	50,000	—

KM# 38 2 DOPPIA (2 Louis D' or)
14.0000 g., 0.9860 Gold 0.4438 oz. AGW **Obv:** Louis I bust facing right

Date	Mintage	VG	F	VF	XF	Unc
1663 (ac)	—	7,000	13,500	25,000	40,000	—
1664 (ac)	—	7,000	13,500	25,000	40,000	—

KM# 17 5 DOPPIA (5 Louis D' or)
35.0000 g., 0.9860 Gold 1.1095 oz. AGW **Obv:** Honore II bust facing right

Date	Mintage	VG	F	VF	XF	Unc
1649 (r//r)	—	15,000	25,000	45,000	65,000	—

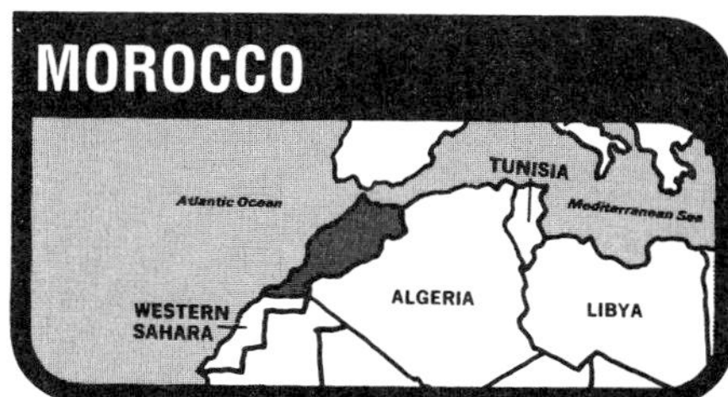

The Kingdom of Morocco, situated on the northwest corner of Africa, has an area of 275,117 sq. mi. (446,550 sq. km.).

Morocco's strategic position at the gateway to western Europe has been the principal determinant of its violent, frequently unfortunate history. Time and again the fertile plain between the rugged Atlas Mountains and the sea has echoed the battle's trumpet as Phoenicians, Romans, Vandals, Visigoths, Byzantine Greeks and Islamic Arabs successively conquered and occupied the land. Modern Morocco is a remnant of an early empire formed by the Arabs at the close of the 7th century which encompassed all of northwest Africa and most of the Iberian Peninsula. During the 17th and 18th centuries, while under the control of native dynasties, it was the headquarters of the famous Sale pirates. Morocco's strategic position involved it in the competition of 19th century European powers for political influence in Africa, and resulted in the division of Morocco into French and Spanish spheres of interest which were established as protectorates in 1912. Morocco became independent on March 2, 1956, after France agreed to end its protectorate. Spain signed similar agreements on April 7 of the same year.

TITLES

المغربية

Al-Maghribiya(t)

المملكة المغربية

Al-Mamlaka(t) al-Maghribiya(t)

المحمدية الشريفة

Al-Mohammediya(t) esh-Sherifiya(t)

RULERS

Sa'dians: Hasani Sharifs
Abu'l-'Abbas Ahmad, AH986-1012/1578-1603AD
Abu Faris 'Abd Allah al-Wathiq, AH1012-1017/1603-1608
The rival sons of Ahmad II
Abu Faris 'Abd Allah al-Wathiq (at Marrakesh), AH1012-1018/1603-1608AD
al-Nasir Zaydan, AH1012-1037/1603-1626AD
Mohammed al-Sheikh al-Ma'mun, AH1012-1022/1603-1612AD
Zaydan al-Nasir, AH1012-1037/1603-1627
Abu'l Mahally al-Mahdi, Userper, AH1021-1022/1612-1613AD
'Abd Allah al-Ghalib, AH1021-1033/1612-1624AD
'Abd al-Malik, al Mu'tasim, AH1033-1036/1623-1626AD
Abu'l-'Abbas Ahmad III, AH1037-1038/1627-1628AD
Abu Marwan 'Abd al-Malik II, AH1037-1040/1627-1629AD
al Walid, AH1040-1045/1629-1634AD
Mohammed al-Shaykh al-Saghir, AH1045-1064/1634-1654AD
Abu'l-'Abbas Ahmad IV, AH1064-1069/1654-1659AD
'Abd al-Karim, AH1069-?/1659-? AD
Filali (or 'Alawi) Sharifs
Mohammed I (at Tafilalt), AH1041-1045/1631-1635AD
Mohammed II, AH1045-1075/1635-1664AD
al-Rashid, AH1075-1082/1664-1672AD
Isma'il, AH1082-1139/1672-1727AD

EARLY COINAGE

Prior to the introduction of modern machine-struck coinage in Morocco in AH1299 (= 1882AD), a variety of primitive cast bronze coins and crudely hammered silver and gold were in circulation, together with considerable quantities of foreign coins.

The cast bronze were produced in several denominations, multiples of the basic unit, the Falus (Felous). The size of the coins is variable, and the distinction of the various denominations is not always clear, particularly on the issues of Sulaiman. The early types are varied, but beginning about AH1218, the reverse bears the seal of Solomon, and the obverse contains the date and/or mint. Several early varieties with the seal of Solomon on both sides exist. The date is inscribed in European numerals, the mint, when present, is written out in Arabic script. Many of the issues are quite barbarous, with illegible dates and mints, and occasionally light in weight. These barbarous issues may have been contemporary counterfeits, and are of little numismatic value. The bronze pieces were cast in "trees", and occasionally, entire or partial trees' are found on the market.

The silver and gold coins usually have the mintname on one side and the date on the other. The silver unit was the dirham of about 2.7 grams (but only about 2.0 grams from circa AH 1266-78), and the gold unit was the benduqi of about 3.25 grams. There were no fixed rates of exchange between coins of different metals.

Prices are for specimens with clearly legible dates and mintnames (if any). Illegible, barbarous, and defectively produced pieces are worth much less.

MINTS

فاس

Fs = Fes (Fas, Fez)

فاس حضره

FH = Fes Hazrat

الكتو ةحضره

KH = al-Kitaoua Hazrat

مراكش

Mr = Marrakesh (Marakesh)

مكناس

Mk = Miknas (Meknes)

سجلماسة

Si = Sijilmasah

سوس

Sus

NOTE: Some of the above forms of the mintnames are shown as they appear on the coins, not in regular Arabic script.

The following coins are divided by reign. However, all of the coins are anonymous, and the distinction by reign is purely artificial. There is much variation within each type, and several of the subtypes overlap more than one reign. The coinage of Sulaiman II and Abd al-Rahman II are listed only by type (dates through AH1276 inclusive); those of Muhammad IV (beginning AH1277 inclusive) and those of Al Hasan I (Moulai Hasan) are broken down by mint and date. The date listings for these two rulers, however, are believed to be very incomplete.

KINGDOM

Sa'Di Sharifs - Hasanid Dynasty

Abu'l-'Abbas Ahmad II

AH986-1012/1578-1603AD

HAMMERED COINAGE

Marrakesh

KM# 3 DINAR

Gold

Date	Mintage	VG	F	VF	XF	Unc
AH1010	—	275	450	750	1,150	—
AH1011	—	275	450	750	1,150	—
AH1012	—	275	450	750	1,150	—

Abu Faris 'Abd Allah al-Wathiq

Rival at Marakesh

HAMMERED COINAGE

Marrakesh

KM# 7 DINAR

Gold **Note:** 3.80-4.40 grams.

Date	Mintage	VG	F	VF	XF	Unc
AH1012	—	275	450	750	1,150	—
AH1013	—	275	450	750	1,150	—
AH1014	—	275	450	750	1,150	—
AH1015	—	275	450	750	1,150	—

Marrakesh

KM# 9 2 DINAR

Gold

Date	Mintage	VG	F	VF	XF	Unc
AH1013	—	300	500	800	1,250	—

Muhammed al-Shaykh al-Ma'mun, rival

AH1012-22/1603-12AD

HAMMERED COINAGE

Fes

KM# 10 DINAR

Gold **Note:** 3.80-4.40 grams.

Date	Mintage	VG	F	VF	XF	Unc
AH1012	—	175	300	500	700	—
AH1013	—	175	300	500	700	—

Marrakesh

KM# 11 DINAR

Gold

Date	Mintage	VG	F	VF	XF	Unc
AH1015	—	200	325	600	800	—

Zaydan al-Nasir

AH1012-37/1603-26AD

HAMMERED COINAGE

Marrakesh

KM# A13 FALUS

Copper **Obv. Legend:** Zaydan al-Nasir

Date	Mintage	VG	F	VF	XF	Unc
AH1034	—	15.00	30.00	50.00	—	—

KM# 12 DIRHAM

1.4500 g., Silver

Date	Mintage	VG	F	VF	XF	Unc
AH1015	—	30.00	75.00	125	—	—

Marrakesh

KM# 14 ECU

26.0000 g., Silver

Date	Mintage	VG	F	VF	XF	Unc
AH1016 Rare	—	—	—	—	—	—

KM# 13 DINAR

Gold **Note:** 3.80-4.40 grams.

Date	Mintage	VG	F	VF	XF	Unc
AH1016	—	125	250	400	600	—
AH1017	—	125	250	400	600	—
AH1018	—	125	250	400	600	—
AH1019	—	125	250	400	600	—
AH1020	—	125	250	400	600	—
AH1021	—	125	250	400	600	—
AH1022	—	125	250	400	600	—
AH1023	—	125	250	400	600	—
AH1024	—	125	250	400	600	—
AH1025	—	125	250	400	600	—
AH1026	—	125	250	400	600	—
AH1027	—	125	250	400	600	—
AH1028	—	125	250	400	600	—
AH1029	—	125	250	400	600	—
AH1030	—	125	250	400	600	—
AH1031	—	125	250	400	600	—

Fes

KM# B13 DINAR

Gold **Note:** 3.80-4.40 grams.

Date	Mintage	VG	F	VF	XF	Unc
AH1015	—	150	275	450	650	—

Marrakesh

KM# A15 DINAR

Gold **Obv:** Central legend in quadralobes **Rev:** Central legend in quadralobes **Note:** 3.80-4.40 grams.

Date	Mintage	VG	F	VF	XF	Unc
AH1015	—	75.00	125	250	400	—
AH1016	—	125	250	400	600	—
AH1017	—	125	250	400	600	—

KM# B15 DINAR

Gold **Obv:** Central legend in inner circles **Rev:** Central legend in inner circles **Note:** 3.80-4.40 grams.

Date	Mintage	VG	F	VF	XF	Unc
AH1018	—	75.00	125	250	400	—

KM# 15 DINAR

Gold **Note:** 3.80-4.40 grams.

Date	Mintage	VG	F	VF	XF	Unc
AH1019	—	125	250	400	600	—
AH1020	—	125	250	400	600	—
AH1021	—	125	250	400	600	—
AH1022	—	125	250	400	600	—
AH1023	—	125	250	400	600	—
AH1024	—	125	250	400	600	—
AH1025	—	125	250	400	600	—
AH1026	—	125	250	400	600	—
AH1027	—	125	250	400	600	—
AH1028	—	125	250	400	600	—
AH1029	—	125	250	400	600	—

Date	Mintage	VG	F	VF	XF	Unc
AH1030	—	125	250	400	600	—
AH1031	—	125	250	400	600	—

Sijilmasah

KM# 16 DINAR

Gold **Note:** 3.80-4.40 grams.

Date	Mintage	VG	F	VF	XF	Unc
AH1023	—	125	250	400	600	—
AH1024	—	125	250	400	600	—
AH1026	—	125	250	400	600	—
AH1027	—	125	250	400	600	—
AH1028	—	125	250	400	600	—
AH1029	—	125	250	400	600	—
AH1030	—	125	250	400	600	—
AH1031	—	125	250	400	600	—
AH1032	—	125	250	400	600	—
AH1033	—	125	250	400	600	—
AH1034	—	125	250	400	600	—

Sus

KM# 17 DINAR

Gold **Note:** 3.80-4.40 grams.

Date	Mintage	VG	F	VF	XF	Unc
AH1012	—	175	300	500	750	—

Abu' Mahally al-Mahdi, Usurper

AH1021-22/1612-13AD

HAMMERED COINAGE

KM# 18 DINAR

Gold **Note:** 3.40-4.40 grams.

Date	Mintage	VG	F	VF	XF	Unc
AH1021	—	175	300	500	700	—

Marrakesh

KM# 19 DINAR

Gold, 16.5 mm. **Note:** 3.40-4.40 grams.

Date	Mintage	VG	F	VF	XF	Unc
AH1021	—	175	300	500	700	—

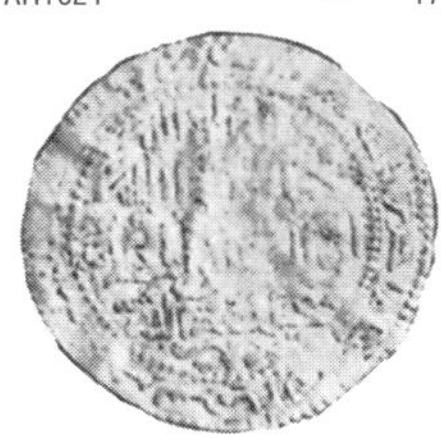

Sijilmasah

KM# A20 DINAR

Gold **Note:** 3.40-4.40 grams.

Date	Mintage	VG	F	VF	XF	Unc
AH1021	—	175	300	500	700	—

Abd Allah al-Ghalib, in Fes

AH1021-33/1612-24AD

HAMMERED COINAGE

KM# B20 DIRHAM

Silver

Date	Mintage	VG	F	VF	XF	Unc
ND	—	25.00	60.00	100	—	—

Fes

KM# 20 DINAR

Gold **Note:** 3.40-4.40 grams.

Date	Mintage	VG	F	VF	XF	Unc
AH1021	—	175	300	500	700	—
AH1022	—	175	300	500	700	—

'Abd al-Malik, al-Mu'tasim, in Fes

AH1033-36/1623-26AD

HAMMERED COINAGE

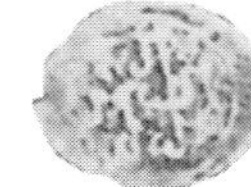

KM# 21 DIRHAM

Silver

Date	Mintage	VG	F	VF	XF	Unc
ND	—	25.00	60.00	100	—	—

Abu Marwan 'Abd al-Malik II

AH1037-40/1626-29AD

HAMMERED COINAGE

KM# A22 DIRHAM

Silver

Date	Mintage	VG	F	VF	XF	Unc
ND	—	25.00	60.00	100	—	—

Marrakesh

KM# 22 DINAR

Gold **Note:** Crescent with 2 palm trees. 3.80-4.40 grams.

Date	Mintage	VG	F	VF	XF	Unc
AH1037	—	260	375	650	900	—
AH1038	—	260	375	650	900	—
AH1039	—	260	375	650	900	—

Abu'l-'Abbas Ahmad III

AH1037-38/1627-28AD

HAMMERED COINAGE

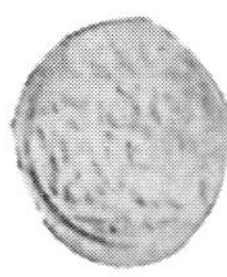

Fes

KM# A21 DIRHAM

Silver **Obv. Legend:** "al-Sultan Ahmad..."

Date	Mintage	VG	F	VF	XF	Unc
ND	—	40.00	75.00	150	—	—

al-Walid

AH1040-45/1630-36AD

HAMMERED COINAGE

KM# 23 DIRHAM

Silver

Date	Mintage	VG	F	VF	XF	Unc
ND	—	20.00	50.00	90.00	—	—

Marrakesh

KM# 24 DINAR

Gold **Note:** 3.80-4.40 grams.

Date	Mintage	VG	F	VF	XF	Unc
AH1040	—	175	300	500	700	—
AH1041	—	175	300	500	700	—
AH1042	—	175	300	500	700	—

Muhammed al-Sheikh al-Saghir

AH1045-64/1636-54AD

HAMMERED COINAGE

Marrakesh

KM# 26 DINAR

Gold **Note:** 3.80-4.40 grams.

Date	Mintage	VG	F	VF	XF	Unc
AH1045	—	175	300	500	700	—
AH1046	—	175	300	500	700	—
AH1047	—	175	300	500	700	—
AH1048	—	175	300	500	700	—
AH1049	—	175	300	500	700	—
AH1050	—	175	300	500	700	—
AH1051	—	175	300	500	700	—
AH1052	—	175	300	500	700	—
AH1053	—	175	300	500	700	—
AH1054	—	175	300	500	700	—
AH1055	—	175	300	500	700	—
AH1056	—	175	300	500	700	—
AH1057	—	175	300	500	700	—
AH1058	—	175	300	500	700	—
AH1059	—	175	300	500	700	—
AH1060	—	175	300	500	700	—
AH1061	—	175	300	500	700	—
AH1062	—	175	300	500	700	—
AH1063	—	175	300	500	700	—
AH1064	—	175	300	500	700	—

KINGDOM

Filali Sharifs - Alawi Dynasty

al-Rashid

AH1075-82/1664-72AD

HAMMERED COINAGE

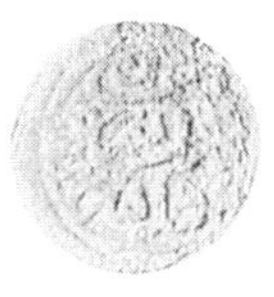

Fes

KM# A27.2 FALUS

3.9700 g., Bronze **Note:** Anonymous issues.

Date	Mintage	Good	VG	F	VF	XF
AH1081	—	20.00	40.00	80.00	—	—
AH1082	—	40.00	80.00	150	—	—

Sijilmasah

KM# A27.1 FALUS

3.9700 g., Bronze **Note:** Anonymous issues.

Date	Mintage	Good	VG	F	VF	XF
AH1081	—	40.00	80.00	150	—	—
AH1082 Rare	—	—	—	—	—	—

Fes Hazrat

KM# 27.1 MUZUNA

1.1700 g., Silver **Note:** Issues with name of ruler.

Date	Mintage	Good	VG	F	VF	XF
AH1079	—	8.00	15.00	30.00	60.00	—
AH1080	—	8.00	15.00	30.00	60.00	—
AH1081	—	25.00	45.00	70.00	120	—
AH1082	—	25.00	45.00	70.00	120	—

Marakesh Hazrat

KM# 27.2 MUZUNA

1.1700 g., Silver **Note:** Issues with name of ruler.

Date	Mintage	Good	VG	F	VF	XF
AH1082	—	8.00	15.00	30.00	60.00	—
AH1083	—	40.00	70.00	120	180	—

Rabat al-Fath

KM# 27.3 MUZUNA

1.1700 g., Silver **Note:** Issues with name of ruler.

Date	Mintage	Good	VG	F	VF	XF
AH1080	—	20.00	40.00	60.00	100	—
AH1081	—	20.00	40.00	60.00	100	—
AH1082	—	20.00	40.00	60.00	100	—

Sijilmasah

KM# 27.4 MUZUNA

1.1700 g., Silver **Note:** Issues with name of ruler.

Date	Mintage	Good	VG	F	VF	XF
AH1079	—	25.00	45.00	70.00	120	—
AH1080	—	8.00	15.00	30.00	60.00	—
AH1081	—	25.00	45.00	70.00	120	—
AH1082	—	40.00	70.00	120	180	—

Isma'il

AH1082-1139/1672-1727AD

HAMMERED COINAGE

Fes

KM# A28.2 FALUS

3.9700 g., Bronze, 18-24 mm. **Note:** Anonymous issue.

Date	Mintage	Good	VG	F	VF	XF
AHxxxx Illegible date	—	20.00	40.00	80.00	—	—
AH1088	—	25.00	50.00	100	—	—
AH1094 Rare	—	—	—	—	—	—
AH1103	—	25.00	50.00	100	—	—

Illegible Mintname

KM# 28 FALUS

3.9700 g., Copper, 18-24 mm. **Note:** Anonymous issue. Most Falus of Isma'il show Obv. and Rev. ornaments composed of interlacing lines in a circle or square with inscriptions around; some issues have octagonal or hexagonal designs besides inscriptions.

Date	Mintage	Good	VG	F	VF	XF
AHxxxx Illegible date	—	20.00	40.00	80.00	—	—

Marrakesh

KM# A28.3 FALUS

3.9700 g., Bronze, 18-24 mm. **Note:** Anonymous issue.

Date	Mintage	Good	VG	F	VF	XF
AHxxxx Illegible date	—	20.00	40.00	80.00	—	—
AH1101	—	30.00	60.00	120	—	—

Meknes Hazrat

KM# A28.4 FALUS

3.9700 g., Bronze, 18-24 mm. **Note:** Anonymous issue.

Date	Mintage	Good	VG	F	VF	XF
AHxxxx Illegible date	—	20.00	40.00	80.00	—	—

Rabat al-Fath

KM# A28.5 FALUS

3.9700 g., Bronze, 18-24 mm. **Note:** Anonymous issues.

Date	Mintage	Good	VG	F	VF	XF
AHxxxx Illegible date	—	20.00	40.00	80.00	—	—
AH1102	—	25.00	50.00	100	—	—
AH1103	—	25.00	50.00	100	—	—

Fes Hazrat

KM# B28.1 MUZUNA

0.9400 g., Silver **Note:** Anonymous issue.

Date	Mintage	Good	VG	F	VF	XF
AH1083	—	10.00	20.00	40.00	80.00	—
AH1084	—	8.00	15.00	30.00	60.00	—
AH1085	—	5.00	10.00	20.00	40.00	—
AH1086 Rare	—	—	—	—	—	—
AH1087	—	12.00	25.00	50.00	100	—
AH1088	—	8.00	15.00	30.00	60.00	—
AH1089	—	5.00	10.00	20.00	40.00	—
AH1090	—	8.00	15.00	30.00	60.00	—
AH1091	—	8.00	15.00	30.00	60.00	—
AH1092	—	8.00	15.00	30.00	60.00	—
AH1093	—	12.00	25.00	50.00	100	—
AH1094	—	5.00	10.00	20.00	40.00	—
AH1095	—	8.00	15.00	30.00	60.00	—
AH1096 Rare	—	—	—	—	—	—
AH1099 Rare	—	—	—	—	—	—
AH1100 Rare	—	—	—	—	—	—
AH1101	—	8.00	15.00	30.00	60.00	—
AH1106 Rare	—	—	—	—	—	—
AH1107 Rare	—	—	—	—	—	—
AH1110 Rare	—	—	—	—	—	—

Marakesh Hazrat

KM# B28.4 MUZUNA

0.9400 g., Silver **Note:** Anonymous issues.

Date	Mintage	Good	VG	F	VF	XF
AH1085	—	5.00	10.00	20.00	40.00	—
AH1086 Rare	—	—	—	—	—	—
AH1100 Rare	—	—	—	—	—	—

Marrakesh

KM# B28.3 MUZUNA

0.9400 g., Silver **Note:** Anonymous issues.

Date	Mintage	Good	VG	F	VF	XF
AH1088	—	5.00	10.00	20.00	40.00	—
AH1089	—	10.00	20.00	40.00	80.00	—
AH1090	—	10.00	20.00	40.00	80.00	—
AH1092	—	12.00	25.00	50.00	100	—

Meknes Hazrat

KM# B28.5 MUZUNA

0.9400 g., Silver **Note:** Anonymous issues.

Date	Mintage	Good	VG	F	VF	XF
AH1111 Rare	—	—	—	—	—	—

Rabat al-Fath

KM# B28.2 MUZUNA

0.9400 g., Silver **Note:** Anonymous issue.

Date	Mintage	Good	VG	F	VF	XF
AH1084	—	8.00	15.00	30.00	60.00	—
AH1085	—	5.00	10.00	20.00	40.00	—
AH1086 Rare	—	—	—	—	—	—
AH1087	—	12.00	25.00	50.00	100	—
AH1088	—	8.00	15.00	30.00	60.00	—
AH1089	—	8.00	15.00	30.00	60.00	—
AH1090	—	5.00	10.00	20.00	40.00	—
AH1091	—	8.00	15.00	30.00	60.00	—
AH1092	—	12.00	25.00	50.00	100	—
AH1094	—	8.00	15.00	30.00	60.00	—

Sijilmasah

KM# B28.6 MUZUNA

0.9400 g., Silver **Note:** Anonymous issue.

Date	Mintage	Good	VG	F	VF	XF
AH1085	—	15.00	30.00	60.00	120	—
AH1088	—	15.00	30.00	60.00	120	—
AH1089	—	15.00	30.00	60.00	120	—
AH1093	—	15.00	30.00	60.00	120	—
AH1094 Rare	—	—	—	—	—	—

KM# 28.3 DINAR

3.5200 g., Gold **Note:** Illegible mintname. Anonymous issues.

Date	Mintage	VG	F	VF	XF	Unc
AH1111	—	120	200	350	500	—
AH1112	—	120	200	350	500	—

Fes Hazrat

KM# 28.1 DINAR

3.5200 g., Gold **Note:** Anonymous issues.

Date	Mintage	VG	F	VF	XF	Unc
AH1089	—	120	200	350	500	—
AH1090	—	120	200	350	500	—
AH1091	—	120	200	350	500	—
AH1092	—	120	200	350	500	—
AH1093	—	120	200	350	500	—
AH1094	—	120	200	350	500	—
AH1095 Rare	—	—	—	—	—	—
AH1096	—	120	200	350	500	—
AH1097 Rare	—	—	—	—	—	—
AH1098 Rare	—	—	—	—	—	—
AH1099	—	120	200	350	500	—
AH1101 Rare	—	—	—	—	—	—
AH1108 Rare	—	—	—	—	—	—
AH1109	—	120	200	350	500	—
AH1111	—	120	200	350	500	—

Meknes Hazrat

KM# 28.2 DINAR

3.5200 g., Gold **Note:** Anonymous issues.

Date	Mintage	VG	F	VF	XF	Unc
AH1095 Rare	—	—	—	—	—	—
AH1096 Rare	—	—	—	—	—	—
AH1104 Rare	—	—	—	—	—	—
AH1106 Rare	—	—	—	—	—	—

NEPAL

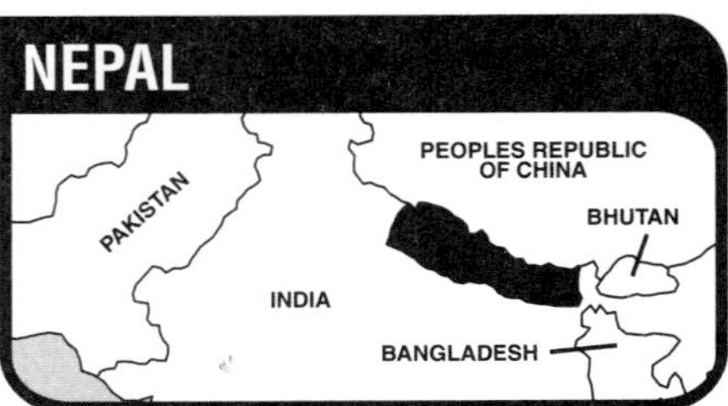

The Kingdom of Nepal, the world's only surviving Hindu kingdom, is a landlocked country occupying the southern slopes of the Himalayas. It has an area of 56,136 sq. mi. (140,800 sq. km.).

Apart from a brief Muslim invasion in the 14th century, Nepal was able to avoid the mainstream of Northern Indian politics, due to its impregnable position in the mountains. It is therefore a unique survivor of the medieval Hindu and Buddhist culture of Northern India which was largely destroyed by the successive waves of Muslim invasions.

Prior to the late 18th century, Nepal, as we know it today, was divided among a number of small states. Unless otherwise stated, the term *Nepal* applies to the small fertile valley, about 4,500 ft. above sea level, in which the three main cities of Kathmandu, Patan and Bhatgaon are situated.

During the reign of King Yaksha Malla (1428-1482AD), the Nepalese kingdom, with capital at Bhatgaon, was extended northwards into Tibet, and also controlled a considerable area to the south of the hills. After Yaksha Malla's death, the Kingdom was divided among his sons, so four kingdoms were established with capitals at Bhatgaon, Patan, Kathmandu and Banepa, all situated within the small valley, less than 20 miles square. Banepa was quickly absorbed within the territory of Bhatgaon, but the other three kingdoms remained until 1769. The internecine strife between the three kings effectively stopped Nepal from becoming a major military force during this period, although with its fertile land and strategic position, it was by far the wealthiest and most powerful of the Himalayan states.

Apart from agriculture, Nepal owed its prosperity to its position on one of the easiest trade routes between the great monasteries of central Tibet, and India. Nepal made full use of this, and a trading community was set up in Lhasa during the 16th century, and Nepalese coins became the accepted currency medium in Tibet.

The seeds of discord between Nepal and Tibet were sown during the first half of the 18th century, when the Nepalese debased the coinage, and the fate of the Malla kings of Nepal was sealed when Prithvi Narayan Shah, King of the small state of Gorkha, to the west of Kathmandu, was able to gain control of the trans-himalayan trade routes during the years after 1750.

Prithvi Narayan spent several years consolidating his position in hill areas before he finally succeeded in conquering the Kathmandu Valley in 1768, where he established the Shah dynasty, and moved his capital to Kathmandu.

After Prithvi Narayan's death a period of political instability ensued which lasted until the 1840's when the Rana family reduced the monarch to a figurehead and established the post of hereditary Prime Minister. A popular revolution in 1950 toppled the Rana family and reconstituted power in the throne. In 1959 King Mahendra declared Nepal a constitutional monarchy, and in 1962 a new constitution set up a system of *panchayat* (village council) democracy. In 1990, following political unrest, the king's powers were reduced. The country then adopted a system of parliamentary democracy.

DATING

Nepal Samvat Era (NS)

All coins of the Malla kings of Nepal are dated in the Nepal Samvat era (NS). Year 1 NS began in 881, so to arrive at the AD date add 880 to the NS date. This era was exclusive to Nepal, except for one gold coin of Prana Narayan of Cooch Behar.

Saka Era (SE)

Up until 1888AD all coins of the Gorkha Dynasty were dated in the Saka era (SE). To convert from Saka to AD take Saka date and add 78 to arrive at the AD date. Coins dated with this era have SE before the date in the following listing.

RULERS

KINGS OF KATHMANDU

Shiva Simha, शिवसिंह

NSc.698-740/c.1578-1620AD

Lakshmi Narasimha, 

NS740-761/1620-1641AD

Pratap Malla, प्रताप मल्ल

NS761-794/1641-1674AD

Chakravartendra Malla, चक्रवर्तेन्द्र मल्ल

NS789/1669AD

Mahipatendra Malla, महीप तेन्द्र मल्ल

Nripendra Malla, नृपेन्द्र मल्ल
NS794-800/1674-1680AD

Parthivendra Malla, पार्थिवेन्द्र मल्ल
NS800-807/1680-1687AD

Bhupalendra Malla, भूपालेन्द्र मल्ल
NS807-820/1687-1700AD

KINGS OF PATAN

Harihara Simha हरि हरसिंह
NSc.720-729/c.1600-1609AD

Shiva Simha, King of Kathmandu शिवसिंह
NSc.729-740/c.1609-1620AD

Siddhi Narasimha सिद्धि नरसिंह
NS740-781/1620-1661AD

Srinivasa Malla श्रीनिवास मल्ल
NS781-805/1661-1685AD

Yoga Narendra Malla, योग नरेन्द्र मल्ल
NS805-825/1685-1705AD

KINGS OF BHATGAON

Trailokya Malla and Tribhuvana Malla, joint rulers, त्रैलोक्य मल्ल
NSc.680-733/c.1560-1613AD

Jagajjotir Malla, जगज्ज्योति मल्ल
NS733-757/1613-1637AD

Naresha Malla, नरेश मल्ल
NS757-764/1637-1644AD

Jagatprakash Malla, जगत्प्रकाश मल्ल
NS764-793/1644-1673AD

Jitamitra Malla, जितामित्र मल्ल
NS783-816/1663-1696AD

Bhupatindra Malla, भूपतीन्द्र मल्ल
NS816-842/1696-1722AD

MONETARY SYSTEM

Tanka Series, c.1560-1639AD

The main Nepalese silver coinage began soon after 1560AD with fine silver coins, struck to a tanka standard of about 10.6 g. Although the first coins were purely Hindu in design, the later issues of tankas were copied from Muslim prototypes, and although Hindu elements were included in the design, the bulk of the field was taken up by debased Arabic legends. This may have been to make the coins acceptable amongst a population used to a currency of Muslim tankas.

While some of the tankas were struck in the names of specific kings, most were anonymous, and it is not known which of the kingdoms of the Nepal Valley was responsible for their issue. However, with Kathmandu dominant at this period, (Shiva Simha being king of both Kathmandu and Patan between at least 1609 and 1620AD) it may be assumed that most of them were struck in Kathmandu.

During the early 17th century many of the tankas struck were in very debased silver. This may have been due to the fact that Ram Shah of Gorkha cut the Valley off from the Tibetan trade during part of this period.

Apart from the coin of Mahendra Malla, the tankas fall into two distinct groups, one may be called the *'Ala-ud-din* type, which has an inscription copied from the tankas of Ala-ud-din Khilji, the Sultan of Delhi, 1295-1315AD, although the inscription reads clock-wise around the coin, quite unlike the prototype. The second main type may be called the *Ghiyas-ud-din* type, as it is copied from coins of the Bengal Sultan Ghiyas-ud-din Mahmud Shah III, 1526-1532AD, although the design is inverted.

The minor denominations of this period present a problem, as surviving specimens do not readily indicate what fraction they represent of the tanka. There are many small pieces with weights ranging from about 0.04 g to 0.14 g but varying very little, if at all, in diameter. If different denominations were intended, they would have been impossible to distinguish in circulation, so they have all been included in this listing under the general term "Dam", which should be a 1/128th part of a tanka, or about 0.08 g.

After 1639AD the tanka coins seem to have been withdrawn from circulation, which probably accounts for their rarity.

Mohar Series

In about 1640 the weight standard of the Nepalese coinage was completely changed, and it is probable that all the old tanka coins were withdrawn from circulation.

The new standard coin was the Mohar, weighing about 5.4 g, or rather more than half the old tanka. The Mohar was subdivided in factors of 2, as follows:

2 Mohar (Rupee) = 10.80 g
1 Mohar = 5.40 g
1/2 Mohar = 2.70 g
1/4 Mohar (Suki) = 1.35 g
1/8 Mohar = 0.67 g
1/16 Mohar = 0.34 g
1/32 Mohar = 0.17 g
1/128 Mohar (Dam) = 0.04-0.08 g
1/512 Mohar (Jawa) = 0.01 g

The weights given above correspond to the average weight of actual specimens, rather than the theoretical weight, which has been said to be 86.4 grains, or 5.60 g.

The coinage was almost entirely of silver, with the tiny Jawa being easily the smallest coin in the world. Gold coins were struck on only one or two occasions during the Madras period, from the same dies as the silver coins, but these were probably only used for ceremonial purposes. Gold after 1777AD was struck in greater quantity.

Initially the coinage was of fine silver, in contrast to the tanka coins, which were frequently debased. During the early 18th century, however, the coins became debased, but the fineness was improved after 1753AD. The coinage was again debased in the first half of the 19th century.

Many of the mohars circulated in Tibet as well as in Nepal, and on a number of occasions coins were struck from bullion supplied by the Tibetan authorities. The smaller denominations never circulated in Tibet, but some of the mohars were cut for use as small change in Tibet.

In these listings only major changes in design have been noted. There are numerous minor varieties of ornamentation or spelling.

4 Dam = 1 Paisa
2 Paisa = 1 Dyak, Adhani

NUMERALS

Nepal has used more variations of numerals on their coins than any other nation. The most common are illustrated in the numeral chart in the introduction. The chart below illustrates some variations encompassing the last four centuries.

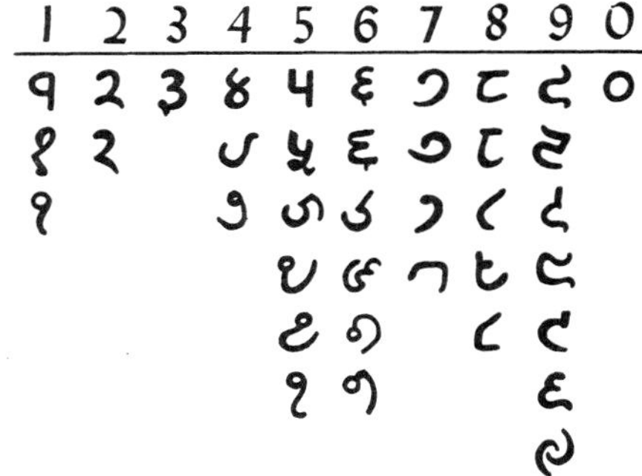

NUMERICS

Half आधा
One एक
Two दुइ
Four चार
Five पाच
Ten दस
Twenty बिस
Twenty-five पचीस
Fifty पचास

OBVERSE

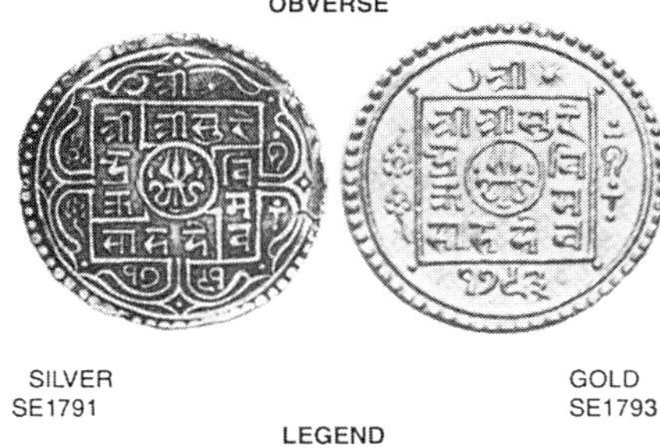

SILVER SE1791 GOLD SE1793

LEGEND

श्री श्रीश्री सुरेन्द्र विक्रम साहदेव

Shri Shri Shri Surendra Vikrama Saha Deva (date)

REVERSE

SILVER GOLD

LEGEND (in center)

श्री ३ भवानी

Shri 3 Bhavani (around outer circle)

श्री श्री श्री गोरषनाथ

Shri Shri Shri Gorakhanatha

KINGDOM OF BHATGAON

Jagajjotir Malla
NS733-757 / 1613-1637AD

TANKA COINAGE

KM# 35 1/128 TANKA
0.0800 g., Silver, 8 mm.

Date	Mintage	Good	VG	F	VF	XF
ND(1613-37)	—	—	—	45.00	75.00	—

Jagatprakash Malla
NS764-793 / 1644-1673AD

MOHAR COINAGE

KM# 40 1/16 MOHAR
0.3300 g., Silver

Date	Mintage	Good	VG	F	VF	XF
ND(1644-73)	—	18.00	45.00	90.00	150	—

KM# 45 1/4 MOHAR
1.3300 g., Silver

Date	Mintage	Good	VG	F	VF	XF
NS775(1655)	—	24.00	60.00	120	200	—

KM# 46 1/4 MOHAR
1.3300 g., Silver **Note:** In the name of Prime Minister, Chandra Sekhar Simha.

Date	Mintage	Good	VG	F	VF	XF
NS782(1662)	—	18.00	45.00	90.00	150	—

KM# 50 MOHAR
5.3400 g., Silver

Date	Mintage	Good	VG	F	VF	XF
NS765(1645)	—	15.00	37.50	75.00	125	—

Jaya Jitamitra Malla
NS783-816 / 1663-1696AD

MOHAR COINAGE

KM# 55 DAM
0.0400 g., Silver **Note:** Uniface.

Date	Mintage	Good	VG	F	VF	XF
ND(1663-96)	—	—	—	15.00	25.00	—

KM# 60 1/16 MOHAR
0.3300 g., Silver

Date	Mintage	Good	VG	F	VF	XF
ND(1663-96)	—	18.00	45.00	90.00	150	—

KM# 61 1/16 MOHAR
0.3300 g., Silver **Note:** In the name of Prime Minister, Jagat Chandra.

Date	Mintage	Good	VG	F	VF	XF
ND(1663-96)	—	30.00	75.00	150	250	—

KM# 63 1/8 MOHAR
0.6600 g., Silver

Date	Mintage	Good	VG	F	VF	XF
ND(1663-96)	—	24.00	60.00	120	200	—

KM# 65 1/4 MOHAR
1.3300 g., Silver

Date	Mintage	Good	VG	F	VF	XF
NS798(1678)	—	30.00	75.00	150	250	—

KM# 70 MOHAR
5.3400 g., Silver **Rev:** Coronation date, "Chaitre Sudi 9,783"

Date	Mintage	Good	VG	F	VF	XF
NS783(1663)	—	100	200	350	500	—

KM# 71 MOHAR
5.3400 g., Silver

Date	Mintage	Good	VG	F	VF	XF
NS783(1663)	—	24.00	60.00	120	200	—

Jaya Bhupatindra Malla
NS816-42 / 1696-1722AD

MOHAR COINAGE

KM# 75 DAM
0.0400 g., Silver **Obv. Inscription:** "Shri Shri Bhupa"

Date	Mintage	Good	VG	F	VF	XF
ND(1696-1722)	—	—	—	20.00	35.00	—

KM# 76 DAM
0.0400 g., Silver **Obv. Inscription:** "Shri Bhupati"

Date	Mintage	Good	VG	F	VF	XF
ND(1696-1722)	—	—	—	15.00	25.00	—

KM# 78 1/16 MOHAR
0.3300 g., Silver

Date	Mintage	Good	VG	F	VF	XF
ND(1696-1722)	—	18.00	45.00	90.00	150	—

KM# 80 1/8 MOHAR
0.6600 g., Silver

Date	Mintage	Good	VG	F	VF	XF
ND(1696-1722)	—	18.00	45.00	90.00	150	—

KM# 82 1/4 MOHAR
1.3300 g., Silver **Note:** Varieties exist.

Date	Mintage	Good	VG	F	VF	XF
NS816(1696)	—	18.00	45.00	90.00	150	—

KM# 84 1/2 MOHAR
2.6700 g., Silver **Obv:** Coronation date, "Bhadra Vadi 11,816"

Date	Mintage	Good	VG	F	VF	XF
NS816(1696)	—	85.00	170	280	400	—

KM# 86 MOHAR
5.3400 g., Silver **Obv:** Three characters in upper two lines

Date	Mintage	Good	VG	F	VF	XF
NS816(1696)	—	20.00	50.00	100	165	—

KM# 87 MOHAR
5.3400 g., Silver **Obv:** Four characters in all three lines **Note:** Varieties exist.

Date	Mintage	Good	VG	F	VF	XF
NS816(1696)	—	10.00	25.00	50.00	80.00	—

KINGDOM OF KATHMANDU

Shiva Simha
NS698-740 / c.1578-1620AD

TANKA COINAGE

KM# 137 DAM
Silver, 9mm, **Obv. Legend:** "Sri Jaya" **Note:** Weight varies: 0.04-0.14grams.

Date	Mintage	Good	VG	F	VF	XF
ND(1578-1620)	—	—	—	45.00	75.00	—

KM# 138 DAM
Silver, 9mm, **Obv. Legend:** "Sri" **Note:** Weight varies: 0.04-0.14grams.

Date	Mintage	Good	VG	F	VF	XF
ND(1578-1620)	—	—	—	45.00	75.00	—

KM# 140 PAISA
Silver, 0.3000 g.

Date	Mintage	Good	VG	F	VF	XF
ND(1578-1620)	—	30.00	75.00	150	250	—

KM# 142 TANKA
Silver, 30mm. **Note:** Weight varies: 0.04-0.14grams.

Date	Mintage	Good	VG	F	VF	XF
ND(1578-1620)	—	100	200	350	500	—

Lakshmi Narasimha
NS740-761 / 1620-1641AD

TANKA COINAGE

KM# 145 1/128 TANKA
0.0800 g., Silver **Rev:** Nara and lion **Note:** Size varies: 8-9 mm.

Date	Mintage	Good	VG	F	VF	XF
ND(1620-41)	—	—	—	24.00	40.00	—

KM# 147 1/4 TANKA
Silver **Note:** Weight varies: 1.90-2.30 grams.

Date	Mintage	Good	VG	F	VF	XF
ND(1620-41)	—	75.00	150	250	350	—

KM# 148 1/4 TANKA
Silver **Note:** Weight varies: 1.90-2.30 grams.

Date	Mintage	Good	VG	F	VF	XF
ND(1620-41)	—	60.00	120	200	300	—

KM# 150 TANKA
Silver **Note:** Weight varies: 8.90-10.00 grams. Ala-ud-din type.

Date	Mintage	Good	VG	F	VF	XF
ND(1620-41)	—	100	200	350	500	—

KM# 151 TANKA
Silver **Note:** Weight varies: 8.90-10.00 grams. Ghiyas-ud-din type.

Date	Mintage	Good	VG	F	VF	XF
ND(1620-41)	—	100	200	350	500	—

MOHAR COINAGE

KM# 158 DAM
0.0400 g., Silver **Note:** Uniface.

Date	Mintage	Good	VG	F	VF	XF
ND(1620-41)	—	—	—	15.00	25.00	—

KM# 160 MOHAR
5.3400 g., Silver **Note:** Size varies: 25-29 milimeters.

Date	Mintage	Good	VG	F	VF	XF
ND(1620-41)	—	12.00	30.00	60.00	100	—

Pratap Malla
NS761-794 / 1641-1674AD

MOHAR COINAGE

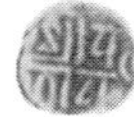

KM# 162 DAM
0.0400 g., Silver **Note:** Uniface.

Date	Mintage	Good	VG	F	VF	XF
ND(1641-74)	—	—	—	15.00	25.00	—

KM# 163 MOHAR
5.3400 g., Silver

Date	Mintage	Good	VG	F	VF	XF
NS761(1641)	—	9.00	18.00	36.00	60.00	—

KM# 164 MOHAR
5.3400 g., Silver **Obv:** Trident at center

Date	Mintage	Good	VG	F	VF	XF
NS775(1655)	—	11.00	27.00	55.00	90.00	—

KM# 166 2 MOHARS
11.1150 g., Silver **Obv:** Trident at center **Shape:** square **Note:** 27x27 mm.

Date	Mintage	Good	VG	F	VF	XF
NS781(1661)	—	165	330	550	800	—

Rupamati Devi
Queen of Pratap Malla, NS769 / 1649AD

MOHAR COINAGE

KM# 168 1/4 MOHAR
1.3300 g., Silver **Obv:** Trident at center **Obv. Inscription:** "Shri Rupamati"

Date	Mintage	Good	VG	F	VF	XF
NS769(1649)	—	18.00	45.00	90.00	150	—

KM# 169 1/4 MOHAR
1.3300 g., Silver **Obv:** Trident at center **Obv. Inscription:** "Shri Rupamati" **Rev. Inscription:** "Bihari Rajkanya"

Date	Mintage	Good	VG	F	VF	XF
NS769(1649)	—	18.00	45.00	90.00	150	—

Chakravartendra Malla
NS789 / 1669AD

MOHAR COINAGE

KM# 171 1/2 MOHAR
2.6700 g., Silver **Obv:** Trident at center

Date	Mintage	Good	VG	F	VF	XF
ND(1669)	—	27.00	67.50	135	225	—

KM# 173 MOHAR
5.3400 g., Silver **Obv:** Five arrows at left of inner circle, bow at right **Obv. Inscription:** "Shri 2 Jaya Cakra Va-" **Rev:** Noose and elephant goad in triangle **Rev. Inscription:** "rtindra Malla"

Date	Mintage	Good	VG	F	VF	XF
NS789(1669)	—	15.00	37.50	75.00	125	—

Mahipatendra Malla
NS790 / 1670AD

MOHAR COINAGE

KM# 175 1/2 MOHAR
2.6700 g., Silver

Date	Mintage	Good	VG	F	VF	XF
ND(1670)	—	45.00	110	220	325	—

KM# 177 MOHAR
5.3400 g., Silver **Obv:** Trident at center **Obv. Inscription:** "Shri Jaya Mahipa-" **Rev:** Sword at center **Rev. Inscription:** "tindra Malla Deva"

Date	Mintage	Good	VG	F	VF	XF
ND(1670)	—	20.00	50.00	100	185	—

Nripendra Malla
NS794-800 / 1674-1680AD

MOHAR COINAGE

KM# 179 DAM
0.0400 g., Silver **Note:** Uniface.

Date	Mintage	Good	VG	F	VF	XF
ND(1674-80)	—	—	—	24.00	40.00	—

KM# 181 1/16 MOHAR
0.3300 g., Silver **Note:** Uniface.

Date	Mintage	Good	VG	F	VF	XF
ND(1674-80)	—	15.00	37.50	75.00	125	—

KM# 183 1/4 MOHAR
1.3300 g., Silver

Date	Mintage	Good	VG	F	VF	XF
NS795(1675)	—	18.00	45.00	90.00	150	—

KM# 185 MOHAR
5.3400 g., Silver **Obv:** Trident at center **Rev:** Sword at center

Date	Mintage	Good	VG	F	VF	XF
NS794(1674)	—	12.00	30.00	60.00	100	—

KM# 186 MOHAR
5.3400 g., Silver **Obv:** Trident at center **Rev:** Sword at center

Date	Mintage	Good	VG	F	VF	XF
NS794(1674)	—	15.00	37.50	75.00	125	—

Parthivendra Malla
NS800-807 / 1680-1687AD

MOHAR COINAGE

KM# 188 DAM
0.0400 g., Silver **Note:** Uniface.

Date	Mintage	Good	VG	F	VF	XF
ND(1680-87)	—	—	—	15.00	25.00	—

KM# 190 1/4 MOHAR
1.3300 g., Silver

Date	Mintage	Good	VG	F	VF	XF
NS800(1680)	—	20.00	50.00	100	175	—

KM# 196 1/4 MOHAR
1.3300 g., Silver **Obv:** Trident at center **Note:** In the names of Parthivendra Malla and Queen Rajya Lakshmi.

Date	Mintage	Good	VG	F	VF	XF
NS802(1682)	—	17.00	42.50	85.00	140	—

KM# 197 1/2 MOHAR
2.6700 g., Silver **Obv:** Pedestal at center **Rev:** Sword at center **Shape:** Square, 17x17 mm **Note:** In the names of Parthivendra Malla and Queen Rajya Lakshmi.

Date	Mintage	Good	VG	F	VF	XF
ND(1680-87)	—	125	250	420	600	—

KM# 194 MOHAR
5.3400 g., Silver **Obv:** Trident at center **Note:** Size varies: 26-27 mm.

Date	Mintage	Good	VG	F	VF	XF
NS800(1680)	—	15.00	37.50	75.00	125	—

KM# 198 MOHAR
5.3400 g., Silver **Rev:** Vase at center **Note:** In the names of Parthivendra Malla and Queen Rajya Lakshmi. Size varies: 26-27 milimeters.

Date	Mintage	Good	VG	F	VF	XF
NS802(1682)	—	11.00	27.50	55.00	90.00	—

Bhupalendra Malla
NS807-820 / 1687-1700AD

MOHAR COINAGE

KM# 202 DAM
0.0400 g., Silver **Note:** Uniface.

Date	Mintage	Good	VG	F	VF	XF
ND(1687-1700)	—	—	—	15.00	25.00	—

KM# 204 1/32 MOHAR
0.1600 g., Silver **Note:** Uniface.

Date	Mintage	Good	VG	F	VF	XF
ND(1687-1700)	—	12.00	30.00	60.00	100	—

KM# 205 1/16 MOHAR
0.3300 g., Silver **Obv. Inscription:** "Shri Bhupalendra" **Note:** Uniface.

Date	Mintage	Good	VG	F	VF	XF
ND(1687-1700)	—	5.00	12.00	24.00	40.00	—

KM# 206 MOHAR
5.3400 g., Silver **Obv:** Trident at center **Rev:** Sword at center

Date	Mintage	Good	VG	F	VF	XF
NS808(1688)	—	20.00	50.00	100	175	—

KM# 207 MOHAR
5.3400 g., Silver **Obv:** Trident at center **Rev:** Sword at center

Date	Mintage	Good	VG	F	VF	XF
NS809(1689)	—	20.00	50.00	100	175	—

KM# 208 MOHAR
5.3400 g., Silver **Obv:** Trident at center **Rev:** Sword at center

Date	Mintage	Good	VG	F	VF	XF
NS812(1692)	—	8.00	20.00	40.00	70.00	—

KM# 209 MOHAR
5.3400 g., Silver **Obv:** Trident at center **Rev:** Sword at center

Date	Mintage	Good	VG	F	VF	XF
NS820(1700)	—	14.00	35.00	70.00	115	—

Riddhi Lakshmi Devi
Regent for Bhupalendra, NS808 / 1688AD

MOHAR COINAGE

KM# 200 1/4 MOHAR
1.3300 g., Silver **Obv:** Trident at center **Obv. Inscription:** "Shri 2 Hrdhi Laksmi Raje" **Rev:** Pedestal at center

Date	Mintage	Good	VG	F	VF	XF
NS808(1688)	—	8.00	20.00	40.00	65.00	—

KINGDOM OF PATAN

KINGDOM

Siddhi Narasimha
NS740-781 / 1620-1661AD

MOHAR COINAGE

KM# 295 DAM
0.0400 g., Silver **Obv:** Four characters **Note:** Uniface.

Date	Mintage	Good	VG	F	VF	XF
ND(1620-61)	—	9.00	22.50	45.00	75.00	—

KM# 296 DAM
0.0400 g., Silver **Obv:** Three characters

Date	Mintage	Good	VG	F	VF	XF
ND(1620-61)	—	5.00	12.00	24.00	40.00	—

KM# 299 1/4 MOHAR
1.3300 g., Silver, 17 mm. **Obv:** Sword at center **Obv. Inscription:** "Shri Shri Siddhi" **Rev:** Lion standing left at center **Rev. Inscription:** "Nara"

Date	Mintage	Good	VG	F	VF	XF
NS774(1654)	—	25.00	60.00	120	200	—

Note: Leather, clay, or gold coins with this design are forgeries

KM# 301 MOHAR
5.3400 g., Silver **Obv:** Sword at center **Obv. Inscription:** "Shri Shri Siddhi" at center **Rev:** Lion left at center **Rev. Inscription:** "Nara" above lion **Note:** Size varies: 26-28 milimeters.

Date	Mintage	Good	VG	F	VF	XF
NS761(1641)	—	7.50	18.00	36.00	60.00	—

TANKA COINAGE

KM# 155 TANKA
10.0000 g., Silver **Note:** Ala-ud-din type.

Date	Mintage	Good	VG	F	VF	XF
ND(1620-61)	—	150	300	500	700	—

KM# 156 TANKA
10.0000 g., Silver **Obv:** Sword at center **Obv. Inscription:** "Shri Shri Siddhi" at center **Rev:** lion left at center **Rev. Inscription:** "Nara" above lion **Note:** Ghiyas-ud-din type.

Date	Mintage	Good	VG	F	VF	XF
NS759(1639)	—	150	300	500	700	—

Srinivasa Malla
NS781-805 / 1661-1685AD

MOHAR COINAGE

KM# 302 DAM
0.0410 g., Silver **Obv. Inscription:** "Shri Nivasa" **Note:** Uniface.

Date	Mintage	Good	VG	F	VF	XF
ND(1661-85)	—	—	—	45.00	75.00	—

KM# 303 1/16 MOHAR
0.3300 g., Silver **Note:** Uniface.

Date	Mintage	Good	VG	F	VF	XF
ND(1661-85)	—	—	—	—	—	—

KM# 304 1/4 MOHAR
1.3300 g., Silver

Date	Mintage	Good	VG	F	VF	XF
ND(1661-85)	—	30.00	75.00	150	250	—

KM# 310 1/4 MOHAR
1.3300 g., Silver **Obv:** Trident at center **Rev:** Sword in center of 6-pointed star **Note:** In the names of Srinivasa Malla and Queen Mrigavati.

Date	Mintage	Good	VG	F	VF	XF
ND(1661-85)	—	30.00	75.00	150	250	—

KM# 306 MOHAR
5.3400 g., Silver **Obv:** Sword in center **Obv. Inscription:** "Shri Shri Jaya" in center **Rev. Inscription:** "Shri Ni-" above, "vasa Malla" in center

Date	Mintage	Good	VG	F	VF	XF
NS781(1661)	—	15.00	36.00	72.00	120	—

KM# 307 MOHAR
5.3400 g., Silver **Obv:** Sword at lower center in 6-pointed star **Obv. Inscription:** "Shri Shri Jaya" in center, "Shri Nivasa Malla" in star points **Rev:** Staff betwen two water jugs with streamers, date below within circle **Rev. Inscription:** "Nepalesvara"

Date	Mintage	Good	VG	F	VF	XF
NS786(1666)	—	9.00	22.50	45.00	75.00	—

KM# 308 MOHAR
5.3400 g., Silver **Obv:** Sword at lower center in 6-pointed star **Obv. Inscription:** "Shri shri Jaya" in center, "Shri Nivasa Malla" in star points **Rev:** Staff between two water jugs with streamers within circle, date below **Rev. Inscription:** "Nepalesvara"

Date	Mintage	Good	VG	F	VF	XF
NS786(1666)	—	9.00	22.50	45.00	75.00	—

Yoga Narendra Malla
NS805-825 / 1685-1705AD

MOHAR COINAGE

KM# 312 DAM
0.0480 g., Silver **Obv. Inscription:** "Shri Yoga" **Note:** Uniface.

Date	Mintage	Good	VG	F	VF	XF
ND(1685-1705)	—	—	—	15.00	25.00	—

KM# 315 1/4 MOHAR
1.3830 g., Silver **Obv:** Shorter inscription

Date	Mintage	Good	VG	F	VF	XF
NS805(1685)	—	15.00	37.50	75.00	125	—

KM# 316 1/4 MOHAR
1.3830 g., Silver **Obv:** Vase, date in square **Obv. Inscription:** "Shri Shri Yoga Narendra Malla" **Rev. Inscription:** "Shri Shri Lokanatha...Shri Talejo"

Date	Mintage	Good	VG	F	VF	XF
ND(1685-1705)	—	25.00	60.00	120	200	—

KM# 317 1/4 MOHAR
1.3830 g., Silver **Obv:** Date in square **Obv. Inscription:** "Shri Yoga Narendra Malla" **Rev. Inscription:** "Shri Shri Lokanatha...Shri Taleju"

Date	Mintage	Good	VG	F	VF	XF
ND(1685-1705)	—	20.00	50.00	100	165	—

KM# 328 1/4 MOHAR
1.3830 g., Silver

Date	Mintage	Good	VG	F	VF	XF
ND(1685-1705)	—	100	200	320	450	—

KM# 314 1/4 MOHAR
1.3830 g., Silver **Obv:** Inscription, date within 4-trefoiled petals around square with staff at center **Obv. Inscription:** "Shri Shri Yoga" within, "Narendra Malla..." around square **Rev:** Curved 5-pointed star **Rev. Inscription:** "Shri Shri Shri Lokanatha...Shri Taleju Sahaya"

Date	Mintage	Good	VG	F	VF	XF
NS807(1687)	—	27.50	67.50	135	225	—

KM# 321 1/2 MOHAR
2.7600 g., Silver **Rev:** Without vase **Note:** In the names of Yoga Lakshmi and Queen Yoga Lakshmi

Date	Mintage	Good	VG	F	VF	XF
NS804(1684)	—	30.00	75.00	150	250	—

KM# 322 1/2 MOHAR
2.7600 g., Silver **Rev:** Vase **Note:** In the names of Yoga Lakshmi and Queen Yoga Lakshmi

Date	Mintage	Good	VG	F	VF	XF
NS805(1685)	—	25.00	60.00	120	200	—

KM# 330 1/2 MOHAR
2.7600 g., Silver

Date	Mintage	Good	VG	F	VF	XF
ND(1685-1705)	—	30.00	75.00	150	275	—

KM# 334 1/2 MOHAR
2.7600 g., Silver

Date	Mintage	Good	VG	F	VF	XF
ND(1685-1705)	—	30.00	75.00	150	275	—

KM# 319 3/4 MOHAR
3.9600 g., Silver **Shape:** Square **Note:** Center hole, 19x19 mm.

Date	Mintage	Good	VG	F	VF	XF
NS804(1684)	—	100	200	350	500	—

KM# 324 MOHAR
5.3400 g., Silver **Note:** In the names of Yoga Lakshmi and Queen Yoga Lakshmi

Date	Mintage	Good	VG	F	VF	XF
NS805(1685)	—	65.00	130	220	325	—

KM# 325 MOHAR
5.3400 g., Silver **Note:** In the names of Yoga Lakshmi and Queen Yoga Lakshmi

Date	Mintage	Good	VG	F	VF	XF
NS805(1685)	—	12.00	30.00	60.00	100	—

KM# 332 MOHAR
5.3400 g., Silver **Note:** In the names of Yoga Narendra Malla and Queen Jaya Lakshmi.

Date	Mintage	Good	VG	F	VF	XF
NS805(1685)	—	10.00	25.00	50.00	85.00	—

KM# 336 MOHAR
5.3400 g., Silver **Note:** In the names of Yoga Narendra Malla and Queen Narendra Lakshmi.

Date	Mintage	Good	VG	F	VF	XF
NS805(1685)	—	10.00	25.00	50.00	85.00	—

KM# 337 MOHAR
5.3400 g., Silver **Note:** In the names of Yoga Narendra Malla and Queen Narendra Lakshmi.

Date	Mintage	Good	VG	F	VF	XF
NS805(1685)	—	8.00	21.00	42.00	70.00	—

KM# 326 MOHAR
5.3400 g., Silver **Note:** In the names of Yoga Lakshmi and Queen Yoga Lakshmi

Date	Mintage	Good	VG	F	VF	XF
NS808(1688)	—	15.00	37.50	75.00	125	—

KM# 320 MOHAR
5.3400 g., Silver

Date	Mintage	Good	VG	F	VF	XF
NS820(1700)	—	12.00	30.00	60.00	100	—

NETHERLANDS

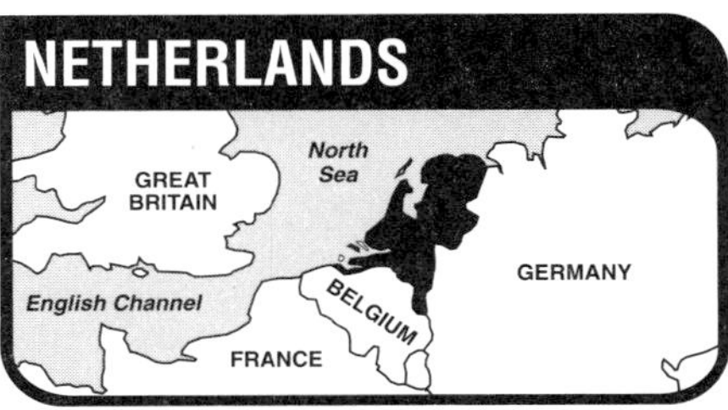

The Kingdom of the Netherlands, a country of western Europe fronting on the North Sea and bordered by Belgium and Germany, has an area of 15,770 sq. mi. (41,500 sq. km

After being a part of Charlemagne's empire in the 8th and 9th centuries, the Netherlands came under control of Burgundy and the Austrian Hapsburgs, and finally was subjected to Spanish dominion in the 16th century. Led by William of Orange, the Dutch revolted against Spain in 1568. The seven northern provinces formed the Union of Utrecht and declared their independence in 1581, becoming the Republic of the United Netherlands. In the following century, the *Golden Age* of Dutch history, the Netherlands became a great sea and colonial power, a patron of the arts and a refuge for the persecuted. The United Dutch Republic ended in 1795 when the French formed the Batavian Republic. Napoleon made his brother Louis, the King of Holland in 1806, however he abdicated in 1810 when Napoleon annexed Holland. The French were expelled in 1813, and all the provinces of Holland and Belgium were merged into the Kingdom of the United Netherlands under William I, in 1814. The Belgians withdrew in 1830 to form their own kingdom, the last substantial change in the configuration of European Netherlands. German forces invaded in 1940 as the royal family fled to England where a government-in-exile was formed. A German High Commissioner, Arthur Seyss-Inquart, was placed in command until 1945 when the arrival of Allied military forces ended the occupation.

RULER
United Netherlands, 1543-1795

MINT PRIVY MARKS

Dordrecht (Holland)

Mark	Date
Rosette	1600-1806

Middelburg (Zeeland)

Mark	Date
Castle	1601-1799

MONETARY SYSTEM
1 Penning = 1/2 Duit
2 Duits = 1 Oord
8 Duits = 1 Stuiver (Stiver)
6 Stuiver = 1 Schelling
20 Stuiver = 1 Gulden (Guilder or Florin)
50 Stuiver = 1 Rijksdaalder (Silver Ducat)
60 Stuiver = 1 Ducaton (Silver Rider)
14 Gulden = 1 Golden Rider

KINGDOM

COUNTERMARKED COINAGE

1693

During the late 17th century many circulating coins were found to be underweight. In 1693 coins meeting the legal requirements were countermarked with a bundle of arrows for general circulation.

KM# 2.1 6 STUIVERS

Silver **Countermark:** Bundle of arrows **Note:** Countermark on Overyssel KM#50.

CM Date	Host Date	Good	VG	F	VF	XF
ND(1693)	1680-96	—	—	—	—	—

KM# 2.2 6 STUIVERS

Silver **Countermark:** Bundle of arrows **Note:** Countermark on Utrecht KM#60.3.

CM Date	Host Date	Good	VG	F	VF	XF
ND(1693)	1679-91	—	—	—	—	—

KM# 2.3 6 STUIVERS

Silver **Countermark:** Bundle of arrows **Note:** Countermark on Zutphen KM#19.

CM Date	Host Date	Good	VG	F	VF	XF
ND(1693)	1688-91	—	—	—	—	—

KM# 3 14 STUIVERS

Silver **Countermark:** Bundle of arrows **Note:** Countermark on Deventer KM#27.

CM Date	Host Date	Good	VG	F	VF	XF
ND(1693)	1618	—	—	—	—	—

KM# 4.9 28 STUIVERS

Silver **Countermark:** Bundle of arrows **Note:** Countermark on Deventer 28 Stuivers, KM#81.1.

CM Date	Host Date	Good	VG	F	VF	XF
ND(1693)	1692	—	—	—	—	—
ND(1693)	1690	—	—	—	—	—
ND(1693)	1686	—	—	—	—	—
ND(1693)	1685	—	—	—	—	—

KM# 4.1 28 STUIVERS

Gold **Countermark:** Bundle of arrows **Note:** Countermark on Deventer KM#79.

CM Date	Host Date	Good	VG	F	VF	XF
ND(1693)	1684	—	—	—	—	—

KM# 4.10 28 STUIVERS

Silver **Countermark:** Bundle of arrows **Note:** Countermark on Friesland, KM#10.

CM Date	Host Date	Good	VG	F	VF	XF
ND(1693)	1683-84	15.00	33.00	66.00	100	—

KM# 4.2 28 STUIVERS

Silver **Countermark:** Bundle of arrows **Note:** Countermark on Groningen KM#38.

CM Date	Host Date	Good	VG	F	VF	XF
ND(1693)	1681	—	—	—	—	—

KM# 4.3 28 STUIVERS

Silver **Countermark:** Bundle of arrows **Note:** Countermark on Groningen KM#50.

CM Date	Host Date	Good	VG	F	VF	XF
ND(1693)	1690	—	—	—	—	—

KM# 4.4 28 STUIVERS

Silver **Countermark:** Bundle of arrows **Note:** Countermark on Groningen KM#52.

CM Date	Host Date	Good	VG	F	VF	XF
ND(1693)	ND	—	—	—	—	—

KM# 4.5 28 STUIVERS

Silver **Countermark:** Bundle of arrows **Note:** Countermark on Kampen KM#76.

CM Date	Host Date	Good	VG	F	VF	XF
ND(1693)	1680-86	—	—	—	—	—

KM# 4.6 28 STUIVERS

Silver **Countermark:** Bundle of arrows **Note:** Countermark on Nijmegen KM#27.

CM Date	Host Date	Good	VG	F	VF	XF
ND(1693)	1685-90	—	—	—	—	—

KM# 4.7 28 STUIVERS

Silver **Countermark:** Bundle of arrows **Note:** Countermark on Zwolle KM#78.

CM Date	Host Date	Good	VG	F	VF	XF
ND(1693)	1679-86	—	—	—	—	—

KM# 4.8 28 STUIVERS

Silver **Countermark:** Bundle of arrows **Note:** Countermark on Overijssel KM#55.

CM Date	Host Date	Good	VG	F	VF	XF
ND(1693)	1685-89	—	—	—	—	—

AMSTERDAM

CITY

STANDARD COINAGE

KM# 2.1 DUCATON

32.7800 g., Silver **Rev:** Amsterdam Arms between date below crowned shield **Note:** Dav. #4933.

Date	Mintage	Good	VG	F	VF	XF
1672	—	40.00	100	200	300	450
1673/72	—	80.00	200	300	500	900
1673	—	40.00	100	200	300	450

KM# 1 DUCATON

32.7800 g., Silver **Obv:** Knight on horseback, Holland arms below **Obv. Legend:** ...HOLLANDIA **Rev:** Amsterdam Arms between date above crowned shield **Note:** Dav. #4933A.

Date	Mintage	Good	VG	F	VF	XF
1672	1,386,230	34.00	85.00	200	350	500

KM# 2.2 DUCATON

Silver **Edge Lettering:** TER GEDACHTENISSE... **Note:** Dav. #4933C.

Date	Mintage	Good	VG	F	VF	XF
1672	—	50.00	125	400	800	1,200
1673	—	50.00	125	400	800	1,200

KM# 3 DUCATON

Silver **Note:** Klippe. Dav. #4933D.

Date	Mintage	Good	VG	F	VF	XF
1673	—	120	300	650	950	1,200

KM# 4 2 DUCATONS

Silver **Obv:** Without inner circle **Rev:** Amsterdam Arms below crowned arms, with inner circle **Note:** Dav. #4932.

Date	Mintage	Good	VG	F	VF	XF
1672	—	160	400	750	1,200	1,850

KM# 5 2 DUCATONS

Silver **Note:** Klippe. Dav. #4932B.

Date	Mintage	Good	VG	F	VF	XF
1672	—	220	550	950	1,500	2,200

KM# 6.1 2 DUCATONS

Silver **Note:** Without inner circle on both sides. Dav. #4932A.

Date	Mintage	Good	VG	F	VF	XF
1673	—	160	400	750	1,200	1,850

KM# 6.2 2 DUCATONS

Silver **Edge Lettering:** TER GEDACHTENISSE **Note:** Dav. #4932D.

Date	Mintage	Good	VG	F	VF	XF
1673	—	160	400	750	1,200	1,850

KM# 7 2 DUCATONS

65.3500 g., Silver **Obv:** Knight on horse holding sword right without inner circle **Rev:** Amsterdam arms below crowned arms **Note:** Klippe. Dav. #4932C. Illustration reduced.

Date	Mintage	Good	VG	F	VF	XF
1673	—	220	550	950	1,500	2,200

KM# 8 3 DUCATONS

Silver **Note:** Klippe. Dav. #4932.

Date	Mintage	Good	VG	F	VF	XF
1673	—	320	800	1,200	1,800	2,500

KM# 10 DUCAT

3.5100 g., Gold **Obv:** 5-line inscripton in tablet, Amsterdam arms below **Rev:** Standing knight divides date

Date	Mintage	VG	F	VF	XF	Unc
1673	57,000	600	1,500	2,200	3,000	—

KM# 11 3 DUCAT

10.5000 g., 0.9860 Gold 0.3328 oz. AGW **Note:** Struck with 1 Ducat dies.

Date	Mintage	VG	F	VF	XF	Unc
1673	—	320	600	1,200	2,000	—

KM# 12 3-1/2 DUCAT

12.2500 g., 0.9860 Gold 0.3883 oz. AGW **Note:** Struck with 1 Ducat dies.

Date	Mintage	VG	F	VF	XF	Unc
1673	—	400	750	1,450	2,500	—

KM# 13 4 DUCAT

14.0000 g., 0.9860 Gold 0.4438 oz. AGW **Note:** Struck with 1 Ducat dies.

Date	Mintage	VG	F	VF	XF	Unc
1673	—	400	750	1,450	2,500	—

KM# 14 4-1/2 DUCAT

15.7500 g., 0.9860 Gold 0.4993 oz. AGW **Note:** Struck with 1 Ducat dies.

Date	Mintage	VG	F	VF	XF	Unc
1673	—	600	1,200	1,750	2,500	—

KM# 15 5 DUCAT

17.5000 g., 0.9860 Gold 0.5547 oz. AGW **Note:** Struck with 1 Ducat dies.

Date	Mintage	VG	F	VF	XF	Unc
1673	—	700	1,400	2,000	2,750	—

BATENBURG

Free Barony

A small free barony in the duchy of Gelders, Batenburg was established as a branch of the lords of Bronckhorst in the early 14th century. Inherited Anhold (see) in the 15th century and then divided into four lines, the last Batenburg line being founded in the mid-16th century. The male line became extinct in 1641 and Batenburg passed by marriage successively to the counts of Horn, then Bentheim in 1694.

RULERS

Hermann Dietrich, 1573-1602
Maximilian, 1602-1641

ARMS

Batenburg – St. Andrew's cross, a pair of scissors with points down in each angle
Bronkhorst – lion rampant to left or right
Stein – 7 lozenges in 2 rows of three each and a single one below

Reference: K = Wilhelm Kraaz, ***Münzen der deutschen Kipperzeit***, Halle, 1924.

COUNTY

STANDARD COINAGE

KM# 1 DUIT

Copper **Ruler:** Maximilian von Bronckhorst **Obv:** Lion in crowned shield **Rev:** Inscription in tulip wreath **Rev. Inscription:** BATEN / BVRV / CVSA

Date	Mintage	Good	VG	F	VF	XF
ND(1616-22)	—	4.00	10.00	20.00	40.00	70.00

KM# 2 DUIT

Copper **Ruler:** Maximilian von Bronckhorst **Obv:** Lion in crowned shield **Rev:** inscription in tulip wreath **Rev. Inscription:** BAT / ENBVRG / GVM

Date	Mintage	VG	F	VF	XF	Unc
ND(1616-22)	—	30.00	75.00	100	150	—

KM# 4 STUIVER

Silver **Ruler:** Hermann Dietrich **Obv:** Cross with HEN/THE/BRO/BA **Rev:** Crowned arms divide IS **Rev. Legend:** MONETA NOVA ARGENT

Date	Mintage	Good	VG	F	VF	XF
ND(1600)	—	16.00	40.00	90.00	150	250

KM# 5 2 STUIVERS

Silver **Ruler:** Maximilian von Bronckhorst **Obv:** Double eagle, 2S **Obv. Legend:** MO NO MAX CO D BR I B. **Rev:** Cross **Rev. Legend:** TANDEM BONA CAVSA TRIVMPHAT

Date	Mintage	VG	F	VF	XF	Unc
1620	—	60.00	150	250	400	—

KM# 6 4 STUIVERS (Arendschelling; Kipper)

Silver **Obv:** Crowned 4-fold arms, value IIII. STV. in legend **Rev:** Imperial eagle, titles of Matthias

Date	Mintage	Good	VG	F	VF	XF
ND	—	20.00	50.00	100	175	300

KM# 7 4 STUIVERS (Arendschelling; Kipper)

Silver **Obv:** Crowned 4-fold arms **Rev:** Imperial eagle, value IV in orb on breast, titles of Matthias

Date	Mintage	Good	VG	F	VF	XF
ND	—	20.00	50.00	100	175	300

KM# 10 3 KREUZER (1 Stuiver)

Silver **Ruler:** Maximilian von Bronckhorst **Obv:** Arms of Bronckhorst, Batenburg and Stein with lion **Obv. Inscription:** MONETA / NOVA / ARG / BAT / I / AST. **Rev:** Imperial eagle, value 3 **Rev. Legend:** MATH I...

Date	Mintage	Good	VG	F	VF	XF
ND	—	20.00	50.00	125	250	400

KM# 20 ROOSSCHELLING (5 Stuiver)

Silver **Ruler:** Maximilian von Bronckhorst **Obv:** Crowned arms, date **Obv. Legend:** MO. NO. AR. MAX. CO. DE. BR. BAT **Rev. Legend:** FIDE / SED / CVI / - VIDE

Date	Mintage	Good	VG	F	VF	XF
1622	—	24.00	60.00	125	200	350

KM# 8 DAALDER

Silver **Ruler:** Maximilian von Bronckhorst **Obv:** Helmeted arms **Obv. Legend:** MAXIM • CO • D: BRONCK • BAT • LI • ... **Rev:** Imperial eagle **Rev. Legend:** MATTHIAS • I • D • G • ELEC • IMP • SEM AVGVS • **Note:** Dav. # 4995.

Date	Mintage	Good	VG	F	VF	XF
1616	—	—	—	—	—	—
	Note: Reported, not confirmed					
1618	—	400	1,000	2,000	3,000	5,000

KM# 9 2 DAALDERS

Silver, 45 x 45 mm. **Ruler:** Maximilian von Bronckhorst **Obv:** Helmeted arms **Obv. Legend:** MAXIM • CO • D: BRONCK • BAT • LI **Rev:** Imperial eagle **Rev. Legend:** MATTHIAS • I • D • G • ELEC • IMP • SEM AVGVS • **Note:** Klippe, illustration reduced. Dav. # A4995.

Date	Mintage	Good	VG	F	VF	XF
1616	—	—	—	—	—	—
1618	—	—	—	—	—	—

PATTERNS

Including off metal strikes

KM#	Date	Mintage	Identification	Mkt Val
Pn1	ND(1616)	—	Duit. Silver. KM#2	—

PIEFORTS

KM#	Date	Mintage	Identification	Mkt Val
P1	ND(1616)	—	Duit. Copper. KM#2	—

BRABANT

A marquisate in medieval time. In 1578 Don John of Austria, the hero of Lepanto, died here. The area and town were much fought over even into modern times.

BREDA

Breda is a town on the Merk River, 14 miles (23 km) west of Tilburg. It received a municipal charter in 1252 when it was a heavily fortified city. The Dutch and Spanish kept taking and retaking the town thru much of the 16th and 17th centuries. Compromise of Breda was signed 1566 by the Dutch and Spanish, retaken by duke of Parma 1581 only to be retaken again by Maurice of Nassau in 1590. The Spanish laid a year-long siege to Breda before the inhabitants surrendered in 1625. The Dutch re-couped their hold in 1637. An amnesty proclamation (Declaration of Breda) was issued in 1660 by exiled Charles II of England. Peace Treaties were concluded in 1667 between Britain, France and the Netherlands.

Breda remained an important city in wars of the French Revolution, 1793-95.

SIEGE COINAGE

KM# 1 STUIVER

1.8600 g., Copper, 14 x 14 mm. **Obv:** B/date/shield divides 1 - S **Note:** Uniface klippe.

Date	Mintage	Good	VG	F	VF	XF
1625	—	26.00	65.00	135	200	350

KM# 2 2 STUIVERS

4.8000 g., Copper **Obv:** Shield divides date, 3-line inscription **Obv. Inscription:** II / BREDA / OBSESSA **Note:** Uniface klippe.

Date	Mintage	Good	VG	F	VF	XF
1625	—	30.00	75.00	150	250	350

KM# 3 20 STUIVERS
5.0000 g., Silver, 20 x 20 mm. **Obv:** Date around shield **Obv. Legend:** BREDA • OBSES • **Note:** Uniface klippe.

Date	Mintage	Good	VG	F	VF	XF
1625	—	64.00	160	320	430	550

KM# 4 40 STUIVERS
Silver **Obv:** Date around rampant lion with sword **Obv. Legend:** BREDA • OBSESSA **Note:** Uniface klippe.

Date	Mintage	Good	VG	F	VF	XF
1625	—	75.00	185	375	450	500

KM# 5 40 STUIVERS
9.8800 g., Silver, 24 x 25 mm. **Obv:** Date at left of crowned shield **Obv. Legend:** BREDA • OBSESSA **Note:** Uniface klippe.

Date	Mintage	Good	VG	F	VF	XF
1625	—	90.00	225	450	600	900

KM# 6.1 60 STUIVERS
Silver, 28 x 29 mm. **Obv:** Rampant lion with sword between 2 shield countermarks, rosette countermark below, value 60 above **Obv. Legend:** BREDA • OBSESSA **Note:** Uniface klippe.

Date	Mintage	Good	VG	F	VF	XF
1625	—	—	—	—	—	—

KM# 6.2 60 STUIVERS
Silver **Obv:** Legend, date **Obv. Legend:** BREDA • BSESSA **Note:** Uniface klippe.

Date	Mintage	Good	VG	F	VF	XF
1625	—	—	—	—	—	—

DEVENTER

PROVINCE

STANDARD COINAGE

KM# 7 DUIT
Copper **Obv:** Crowned arms on cross **Rev:** Inscription in sprays **Rev. Inscription:** DA / VEN / TRIA / date

Date	Mintage	Good	VG	F	VF	XF
1602	—	6.00	15.00	35.00	50.00	80.00
1615	—	12.00	30.00	60.00	100	200
1617	—	6.00	15.00	35.00	50.00	80.00
1618	—	12.00	30.00	60.00	100	200

KM# 47 DUIT
Copper **Obv:** Crowned city arms **Rev:** Inscription **Rev. Inscription:** DA / VEN / TRIA

Date	Mintage	Good	VG	F	VF	XF
ND(1628)	200,000	3.00	10.00	20.00	30.00	50.00

KM# 47a DUIT
Silver **Obv:** Crowned city arms. **Rev:** Inscription **Rev. Inscription:** DA / VEN / TRIA **Note:** Prev. KM #7a.

Date	Mintage	Good	VG	F	VF	XF
ND(1628)	—	6.00	15.00	35.00	70.00	120

KM# 66 DUIT
Copper **Obv:** Crowned arms in sprays **Rev:** Inscription in sprays **Rev. Inscription:** DA / VEN / TRIA / date

Date	Mintage	Good	VG	F	VF	XF
1663	—	4.00	10.00	30.00	40.00	70.00

KM# 66a DUIT
Silver **Obv:** Crowned arms in sprays **Rev:** Inscription in sprays **Rev. Inscription:** DA / VEN / TRIA / date **Note:** Klippe.

Date	Mintage	Good	VG	F	VF	XF
1663	—	—	—	—	—	—

KM# 4 1/8 STUIVER
Silver **Obv:** 4-fold arms **Obv. Inscription:** DAV. **Note:** Uniface.

Date	Mintage	Good	VG	F	VF	XF
ND(1602)	—	35.00	100	200	500	1,200

KM# 60 1/2 STUIVER
1.0000 g., Billon **Obv:** Crowned arms divide value in inner circle, crown divides date **Rev:** Ornate long cross with H-S-D-E in angles in inner circle

Date	Mintage	Good	VG	F	VF	XF
ND(1629)	140,000	8.00	20.00	50.00	100	150

KM# 61 STUIVER
2.0000 g., Billon **Obv:** Crowned arms divide value in inner circle **Rev:** Ornamental long cross with quatrefoil around center

Date	Mintage	Good	VG	F	VF	XF
ND	26,000	10.00	25.00	50.00	150	250
1663	—	10.00	25.00	50.00	150	250

KM# 90 STUIVER
0.8100 g., 0.5830 Silver 0.0152 oz. ASW **Obv:** Crowned arms divide value in sprays **Rev. Inscription:** DAVEN / TRIA / date

Date	Mintage	Good	VG	F	VF	XF
1691	490,000	6.00	15.00	35.00	70.00	110

KM# 8 2 STUIVERS
Billon **Obv:** Arms in inner circle **Rev:** Orb divides date in inner circle

Date	Mintage	Good	VG	F	VF	XF
1602	—	16.00	40.00	80.00	200	500

KM# 77 2 STUIVERS
1.7300 g., 0.5830 Silver 0.0324 oz. ASW **Obv:** Crowned rampant lion left holding sword and arrows, value at sides **Rev:** DAVEN/TRIA/(date) **Note:** Mint mark: Sitting dog.

Date	Mintage	VG	F	VF	XF	Unc
1683	290,000	7.50	25.00	50.00	80.00	—
1685	61,000	7.50	25.00	50.00	80.00	—
1687	—	7.50	25.00	40.00	50.00	—

KM# 31 5 STUIVERS (1/10 Arendsrijksdaalder)
2.9000 g., 0.8850 Silver 0.0825 oz. ASW **Obv:** Crowned double-headed eagle with value on breast in inner circle **Rev:** Sheild of arms with plumed helmet above

Date	Mintage	Good	VG	F	VF	XF
ND(1629)	109,000	20.00	50.00	100	250	400

KM# 6 6 STUIVERS (Roosschelling)
5.2700 g., 0.5830 Silver 0.0988 oz. ASW **Obv:** Crowned arms in wreath in inner circle, date at top in legend, titles of Rudolph II **Rev:** Ornamental cross in inner circle

Date	Mintage	Good	VG	F	VF	XF
1601	—	16.00	40.00	80.00	150	250

KM# 32 6 STUIVERS (Roosschelling)
Billon **Rev:** Titles of Ferdinand II

Date	Mintage	Good	VG	F	VF	XF
ND(1623)	37,000	12.00	30.00	70.00	125	200

KM# 78 6 STUIVERS (Rijderschelling)
0.5830 Silver **Obv:** Crowned arms divide value, date above crown **Rev:** Knight with sword on horseback right **Note:** Mint mark: Sitting dog. Varieties exist. Weight varies 4.71 - 4.95 g.

Date	Mintage	Good	VG	F	VF	XF
1683	16,000	4.00	10.00	30.00	50.00	90.00
1684	—	3.00	7.50	20.00	40.00	60.00
1685	364,000	3.00	7.50	20.00	40.00	60.00
1686	520,000	3.00	7.50	20.00	40.00	60.00
1688	2,000,000	3.00	7.50	20.00	40.00	60.00
1689	350,000	3.00	7.50	20.00	40.00	60.00
1690	764,000	3.00	7.50	20.00	40.00	60.00
1691	540,000	3.00	7.50	20.00	40.00	60.00

KM# 26 8 STUIVERS
8.0000 g., Silver **Obv:** Crowned eagle in inner circle **Rev:** Standing figure of St. Lubvinus divides value in inner circle, date at top in legend **Note:** Mint mark: Shamrock

Date	Mintage	Good	VG	F	VF	XF
1618	105,000	20.00	50.00	150	300	600

KM# 40 8 STUIVERS
Silver **Obv:** Crowned quartered arms **Rev:** Crowned imperial eagle

Date	Mintage	Good	VG	F	VF	XF
ND(1620)	25,000	—	—	—	—	—

KM# 41 8 STUIVERS
Silver **Obv:** Mitred bust of St. Lubvinus left

Date	Mintage	Good	VG	F	VF	XF
ND	Est. 1,500	—	—	—	—	—

KM# 42 8 STUIVERS
Silver **Obv:** Standing knight holding banner behind shield of arms **Rev:** Crowned arms on ornamental cross in inner circle

Date	Mintage	Good	VG	F	VF	XF
ND	—	16.00	40.00	140	225	300

KM# 23 10 STUIVERS (1/5 Arendsrijksdaalder)
5.8000 g., 0.8850 Silver 0.1650 oz. ASW **Obv:** Crowned imperial eagle with value on breast **Rev:** Shield of arms with plumed helmet above

Date	Mintage	Good	VG	F	VF	XF
ND(1617)	—	60.00	150	250	600	1,200
1617	—	60.00	150	250	600	1,200

KM# 27 14 STUIVERS (1/2 Florin)
9.7500 g., 0.6730 Silver 0.2110 oz. ASW **Obv:** Crowned imperial eagle **Rev:** Crowned arms with date below in inner circle **Note:** Mint mark: Shamrock.

Date	Mintage	Good	VG	F	VF	XF
1618	3,700	50.00	125	300	500	1,000

KM# 28 14 STUIVERS (1/2 Florin)
9.7500 g., 0.6730 Silver 0.2110 oz. ASW **Obv:** Date between crown and top of shield

Date	Mintage	Good	VG	F	VF	XF
1618	Inc. above	50.00	125	300	500	1,000

KM# A66 20 STUIVERS (1/2 Ducaton)
16.3000 g., 0.9410 Silver 0.4931 oz. ASW **Obv:** Knight with sword on horseback right, city arms below in inner circle **Rev:** Crowned arms with crowned lion supporters in inner circle, date at top in legend **Note:** Mint mark: Sitting dog.

Date	Mintage	Good	VG	F	VF	XF
1666	—	50.00	125	350	800	1,500

KM# 75 20 STUIVERS (Gulden)
10.6100 g., 0.9200 Silver 0.3138 oz. ASW **Obv:** Crowned eagle arms divide value, date above crown **Rev:** Standing female figure leaning on Bible on column, holding spear with Libertry cap

Date	Mintage	Good	VG	F	VF	XF
1682	—	10.00	25.00	50.00	90.00	150
1686	—	8.00	20.00	40.00	70.00	110
1687	116,000	8.00	20.00	40.00	70.00	110

KM# 91 20 STUIVERS (Gulden)
Silver **Obv:** Crowned lion arms divide value **Rev:** Date at sides

Date	Mintage	Good	VG	F	VF	XF
1698	345,050	12.00	30.00	60.00	120	200

KM# 50 24 STUIVERS (1/2 Lion Daalder)
13.8400 g., 0.7500 Silver 0.3337 oz. ASW **Obv:** Armored knight looking right above eagle shield **Rev:** Rampant lion left in inner circle **Note:** Mint mark: Lily.

Date	Mintage	Good	VG	F	VF	XF
1640Lily	—	20.00	50.00	150	250	350

KM# A51 24 STUIVERS (1/2 Lion Daalder)
Silver **Obv:** Armored knight looking right above eagle shield **Rev:** Rampant lion left in circle **Note:** Klippe. Mint mark: Lily.

Date	Mintage	Good	VG	F	VF	XF
1640Lily	—	—	—	—	1,500	2,500

KM# 67 24 STUIVERS (1/2 Silver Ducat)
14.1200 g., 0.8730 Silver 0.3963 oz. ASW **Obv:** Armored knight standing holding sword behind shield of arms, date at sides in inner circle **Rev:** Crowned arms in inner circle **Note:** Mint mark: Sitting dog.

Date	Mintage	Good	VG	F	VF	XF
1666	—	50.00	125	300	475	600

KM# 14 25 STUIVERS (1/2 Arendsrijksdaalder)
Silver **Note:** Klippe.

Date	Mintage	Good	VG	F	VF	XF
ND(1622)	—	—	—	—	—	—

KM# 13 25 STUIVERS (1/2 Arendsrijksdaalder)
14.5100 g., 0.8850 Silver 0.4128 oz. ASW **Obv:** Shield of arms with plumed helmet above in inner circle **Rev:** Crowned imperial eagle with orb on breast in inner circle

Date	Mintage	Good	VG	F	VF	XF
ND	—	—	—	—	—	—

KM# 25 28 STUIVERS (Florin)
19.5000 g., 0.6730 Silver 0.4219 oz. ASW **Obv:** Date between crown and top of shield **Obv. Legend:** FLOR • ARG • CI - • IMP • DAVENT **Rev:** Crowned imperial eagle with orb on breast in inner circle **Rev. Legend:** MATTH • I • D • G • ROM • IMP • ...

Date	Mintage	Good	VG	F	VF	XF
1617	—	80.00	100	250	500	800
1618/7	—	16.00	40.00	100	150	300
1618	390,000	12.00	30.00	80.00	125	250

KM# 24 28 STUIVERS (Florin)
Silver **Obv:** Crowned arms in inner circle, date above crown, value at bottom **Obv. Legend:** FLOR x ARG x CIV x IMP x DAVENT x **Rev:** Crowned imperial eagle in inner circle, titles of Matthias **Rev. Legend:** MATH. 1 . I. D.G. ROM. IMP. SEM. AVG. **Note:** Mint mark: Shamrock.

Date	Mintage	Good	VG	F	VF	XF
1.6.1.7	—	32.00	80.00	220	400	800
1619	—	20.00	50.00	150	275	400

KM# 29 28 STUIVERS (Florin)
Silver **Rev:** Value "Z8" in orb

Date	Mintage	Good	VG	F	VF	XF
1618	—	10.00	20.00	50.00	80.00	150

KM# 30 28 STUIVERS (Florin)
Silver **Rev:** Value "Z8" in orb **Note:** Klippe

Date	Mintage	Good	VG	F	VF	XF
1618	—	—	—	—	—	—

KM# 43.1 28 STUIVERS (Florin)
Silver **Obv:** Crowned arms **Obv. Legend:** FLOR • ARG • CI - • IMP • DAVEN **Rev:** Crowned imperial eagle with "Z8" in orb on breast **Rev. Legend:** FERDNAND • II • ROM • IMP • ...

Date	Mintage	Good	VG	F	VF	XF
1619	440,000	14.00	35.00	60.00	120	250
1621	170,000	14.00	35.00	60.00	120	250

KM# 43.2 28 STUIVERS (Florin)
Silver **Obv:** Crowned arms **Obv. Legend:** FLOR • ARG • CI - IMP • DAVEN **Rev:** Crowned inperial eagle with error "8Z' in orb on breast **Rev. Legend:** FERDNAND • II • ROM • IMP • ...

Date	Mintage	Good	VG	F	VF	XF
1619	—	40.00	100	170	280	400

KM# 79 28 STUIVERS (Florin)
Silver **Obv:** Crowned arms divide denomination, date at top, titles of Leopold I **Obv. Legend:** FLOR. ARG. CIV. DAVENTRIAE. **Rev:** Crowned imperial eagle with orb on breast **Rev. Legend:** LEOP. IGN. D.G. ELEC. ROM. IMP. SEM. AVG. **Note:** Mint mark: Sitting dog.

Date	Mintage	Good	VG	F	VF	XF
1684	460,000	20.00	50.00	100	220	400

KM# 81.1 28 STUIVERS (Florin)
Silver **Obv:** Crowned arms in inner circle, date above crown, titles of Ferdinand II **Obv. Legend:** FLOR. ARG. CIV. DAVENTRIAE. **Rev:** Crowned imperial eagle in inner circle, value "28" below in cartouche **Rev. Legend:** FERDINAND. II. D.G. ROM. IMP. SEM. AVG. **Note:** Prev. KM#81. This coin appears with countermarks of HOL, FRI, UTR, and G.O.

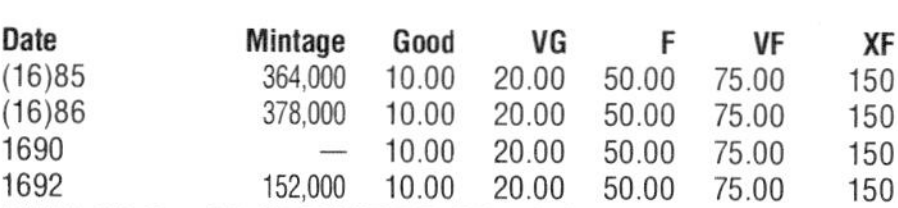

Date	Mintage	Good	VG	F	VF	XF
(16)85	364,000	10.00	20.00	50.00	75.00	150
(16)86	378,000	10.00	20.00	50.00	75.00	150
1690	—	10.00	20.00	50.00	75.00	150
1692	152,000	10.00	20.00	50.00	75.00	150

KM# 81.2 28 STUIVERS (Florin)
Silver **Obv:** Crowned arms in inner circle, date above crown, titles of Ferdinand II **Obv. Legend:** FLOR. ARG. DIV. DAVENTRIAE. **Rev:** Crowned imperial eagle in inner circle, error value "8Z" below in cartouche

Date	Mintage	Good	VG	F	VF	XF
1685	—	16.00	40.00	100	150	300

KM# 83 30 STUIVERS (Daalder)
15.8800 g., 0.9060 Silver 0.4625 oz. ASW **Obv:** Value below arms **Rev:** Standing knight with sword behind crowned arms to left, date in legend

Date	Mintage	Good	VG	F	VF	XF
1685	—	12.00	25.00	65.00	120	200
1686	—	12.00	25.00	65.00	120	200
1687	—	12.00	25.00	65.00	120	200
1688	—	12.00	25.00	65.00	120	200

KM# 82 30 STUIVERS (Daalder)
Silver **Obv:** Crowned arms with lion supporters **Rev:** Standing knight with sword divides value, date in legend **Note:** Mint mark: Sitting dog. Varieties exist.

Date	Mintage	Good	VG	F	VF	XF
1685	387,000	14.00	30.00	70.00	130	240

KM# 62.1 40 STUIVERS (Ducaton)
32.7800 g., 0.9410 Silver 0.9917 oz. ASW **Obv:** Knight with sword on horseback right, city arms below in inner circle **Rev:** Crowned arms with crowned lion supporters in inner circle, date at top in legend **Note:** Mint mark: Moor's head. Dav. #4944.

Date	Mintage	Good	VG	F	VF	XF
1662	—	22.00	40.00	80.00	150	275
1663	—	22.00	40.00	80.00	150	275
1664	13,000	22.00	40.00	80.00	150	275
1666	—	22.00	40.00	80.00	150	275

KM# 62.2 40 STUIVERS (Ducaton)
32.7800 g., 0.9410 Silver 0.9917 oz. ASW **Obv:** Knight on horseback right, city arms below in inner circle **Rev:** Crowned arms with crowned lion supporters in inner circle, date at top in legend. **Note:** Mint mark: Sitting dog. Varieties exist. Dav. #4944.

Date	Mintage	Good	VG	F	VF	XF
1664	Inc. above	22.00	40.00	80.00	150	275
1666	—	22.00	40.00	80.00	150	275
1667	—	22.00	40.00	80.00	150	275
1668	—	22.00	40.00	80.00	150	275

KM# 51 48 STUIVERS (Lion Daalder)
27.6800 g., 0.7500 Silver 0.6674 oz. ASW **Obv:** Rampant lion left in inner circle **Rev:** Armored knight left in inner circle **Note:** Mint mark: Lily. Dav. #4873.

Date	Mintage	Good	VG	F	VF	XF
1640	7,000	20.00	50.00	100	180	300

KM# 52 48 STUIVERS (Lion Daalder)
Silver **Obv:** Rampant lion left in inner circle **Rev:** Armored knight left in inner circle **Note:** Klippe. Mint mark: Lily.Dav. #A4873.

Date	Mintage	Good	VG	F	VF	XF
1640	—	—	—	—	—	—

KM# 63.1 48 STUIVERS (Lion Daalder)
Silver **Obv:** Armored knight looking right above lion shield **Rev:** Rampant lion left **Note:** Mint mark: Moor's head. Dav. #4875.

Date	Mintage	Good	VG	F	VF	XF
1662	7,800	16.00	30.00	80.00	150	250
1663	38,000	16.00	30.00	80.00	150	250
1664	—	16.00	30.00	80.00	150	250

KM# 63.2 48 STUIVERS (Lion Daalder)
Silver **Obv:** Armored knight looking right above lion shield **Rev:** Rampant lion left **Note:** Mint mark: Sitting dog. Dav. #4875.

Date	Mintage	Good	VG	F	VF	XF
1664	20,000	16.00	30.00	80.00	150	250
1666	21,000	16.00	30.00	80.00	150	250
1667	4,400	16.00	30.00	80.00	150	250
1668	20,000	18.00	40.00	100	175	275

KM# 80 48 STUIVERS (Lion Daalder)
Silver **Obv:** Armored knight looking right without plume in knight's helmet **Rev:** Rampant lion left, divided date in legend **Note:** Dav. #4876.

Date	Mintage	Good	VG	F	VF	XF
1684	—	16.00	30.00	80.00	150	250
1685	6,000	16.00	30.00	80.00	150	250
1687	200,000	16.00	30.00	80.00	150	250
1688/7	146,000	18.00	40.00	100	175	300
1688	Inc. above	16.00	30.00	80.00	150	250
1698	17,000	18.00	40.00	100	175	300

KM# 64.1 48 STUIVERS (Silver Ducat)
28.2500 g., 0.8730 Silver 0.7929 oz. ASW **Obv:** Armored knight looking right **Rev:** Crowned lion shield **Note:** Mint mark: Moor's head. Varieties exist. Dav. #4916.

Date	Mintage	Good	VG	F	VF	XF
1662	21,000	20.00	45.00	100	180	300
1663	2,600	22.00	50.00	120	250	400
1666	9,300	20.00	45.00	100	180	300

KM# 64.2 48 STUIVERS (Silver Ducat)
28.2500 g., 0.8730 Silver 0.7929 oz. ASW **Obv:** Armored knight looking right **Rev:** Crowned lion shield **Note:** Mint mark: Sitting dog.

Date	Mintage	Good	VG	F	VF	XF
1662	Inc. above	30.00	75.00	150	275	450
1663	Inc. above	22.00	50.00	120	250	400
1666	Inc. above	22.00	50.00	120	250	400

KM# 92 48 STUIVERS (Silver Ducat)
Silver **Obv:** Armored knight looking right, without inner circle **Rev:** Crowned lion shield divides date, without inner circle **Note:** Dav. #4917.

Date	Mintage	Good	VG	F	VF	XF
1698	126,000	22.00	50.00	120	250	400

KM# 9 50 STUIVERS (Arendsrijksdaalder)
29.0300 g., 0.8850 Silver 0.8260 oz. ASW **Obv:** Arms of Deventer and Oversticht below plumed helmet, date in legend **Rev:** Similar to KM#11 **Note:** Dav. #4974.

Date	Mintage	Good	VG	F	VF	XF
1603	—	250	600	2,000	3,000	4,000

KM# 10 50 STUIVERS (Arendsrijksdaalder)
Silver **Obv:** Shield divided with arms of Deventer and Oversticht below plumed helmet in inner circle **Note:** Dav. #4975.

Date	Mintage	Good	VG	F	VF	XF
ND(1620)	80,000	80.00	200	600	1,000	1,600

KM# 11.1 50 STUIVERS (Arendsrijksdaalder)
Silver **Obv:** Arms of Deventer below plumed helmet in inner circle **Rev:** Crowned imperial eagle **Rev. Legend:** FERDINAND • II • ROM - IMP • SEM • AV • **Note:** Mint mark: Clover leaf. Dav. #4976.

Date	Mintage	Good	VG	F	VF	XF
ND(1622)	—	50.00	125	300	500	750

KM# 11.2 50 STUIVERS (Arendsrijksdaalder)
Silver **Obv:** Arms of Deventer below plumed helmet in inner circle **Rev:** Crowned imperial eagle **Rev. Legend:** FERDINAND • II • ROM - IMP • SEM • AV • **Note:** Mint mark: Lily.

Date	Mintage	Good	VG	F	VF	XF
ND(1627)	15,000	200	500	1,000	2,000	3,000

KM# 84 60 STUIVERS (Double Daalder)
31.7600 g., 0.9060 Silver 0.9251 oz. ASW **Obv:** Crowned arms with lion supporters, value below **Rev:** Standing knight with sword behind crowned arms to left, date in legend **Note:** Mint mark: Sitting dog. Dav. #4978.

Date	Mintage	Good	VG	F	VF	XF
1689	15,500	32.00	80.00	200	350	600

KM# 76 60 STUIVERS (3 Gulden)
31.8200 g., 0.9200 Silver 0.9412 oz. ASW **Obv:** Crowned eagle arms divide value, date above crown **Rev:** Standing female figure leaning on Bible on column, holding spear with Liberty cap **Note:** Dav. #4967. Eagle's head in arms may face left or right.

Date	Mintage	Good	VG	F	VF	XF
1682	Inc. above	40.00	100	300	500	750
1683	—	40.00	100	300	500	750
1686	—	40.00	100	300	500	750
1687	—	40.00	100	300	500	750

KM# 93 60 STUIVERS (3 Gulden)
Silver **Obv:** Crowned lion shield divides value **Rev:** Female figure seated, date below **Note:** Dav. #4968. Varieties exist.

Date	Mintage	Good	VG	F	VF	XF
1698	128,000	28.00	70.00	170	300	450

TRADE COINAGE

KM# 5 FLORIN D'OR
3.5000 g., 0.9860 Gold 0.1109 oz. AGW **Obv:** Crowned imperial eagle in inner circle, date in legend, titles of Rudolf II **Rev:** Helmeted arms in inner circle

Date	Mintage	VG	F	VF	XF	Unc
1600 Rare	—	—	—	—	—	—

KM# 20 FLORIN D'OR
3.5000 g., 0.9860 Gold 0.1109 oz. AGW **Obv:** Helmeted arms in inner circle **Rev:** Crowned imperial eagle in inner circle, date in legend, titles of Matthias as emperor

Date	Mintage	VG	F	VF	XF	Unc
ND(1612-19)	Est. 100,000	150	250	500	800	—

KM# 21 FLORIN D'OR
3.5000 g., 0.9860 Gold 0.1109 oz. AGW **Rev:** Titles of Matthias as king of Hungary and Bohemia

Date	Mintage	VG	F	VF	XF	Unc
ND(1612-19)	—	250	400	650	1,000	—

KM# 22 FLORIN D'OR
3.5000 g., 0.9860 Gold 0.1109 oz. AGW **Note:** Klippe.

Date	Mintage	VG	F	VF	XF	Unc
ND(1618)	—	350	750	1,000	1,400	—

KM# 33 FLORIN D'OR
3.5000 g., 0.9860 Gold 0.1109 oz. AGW **Rev:** Titles of Ferdinand II

Date	Mintage	VG	F	VF	XF	Unc
ND(1619-29)	—	250	400	650	1,000	—

KM# 12 DUCAT
3.5000 g., 0.9860 Gold 0.1109 oz. AGW **Obv:** 5-line inscription in tablet **Rev:** Rudolf II standing right divides date

Date	Mintage	VG	F	VF	XF	Unc
1603	—	150	300	500	700	—
1604	—	150	300	500	700	—
1605	—	150	300	500	700	—

KM# 15 DUCAT
3.5000 g., 0.9860 Gold 0.1109 oz. AGW **Obv:** 5-line inscription in tablet **Rev:** Matthias standing right divides date

Date	Mintage	VG	F	VF	XF	Unc
1615	—	200	400	600	850	—

KM# 45 DUCAT
3.5000 g., 0.9860 Gold 0.1109 oz. AGW **Obv:** 5-line inscription in tablet **Rev:** Ferdinand II standing right divides date

Date	Mintage	VG	F	VF	XF	Unc
1632	—	150	300	400	600	—
1633	12,000	150	300	400	600	—
1634	38,000	150	300	400	600	—
1635	18,000	150	300	400	600	—
1636	6,000	150	300	400	600	—

KM# 65 DUCAT
3.5000 g., 0.9860 Gold 0.1109 oz. AGW **Obv:** 5-line inscription in tablet **Rev:** Leopold I standing right divides date **Note:** Titles of Leopold I.

Date	Mintage	VG	F	VF	XF	Unc
1662	1,000	150	300	500	700	—
1665	1,300	150	300	500	700	—
1666	8,000	150	300	500	700	—

KM# 55 2 DUCAT
7.0000 g., 0.9860 Gold 0.2219 oz. AGW **Obv:** 5-line inscription in tablet **Rev:** Leopold I standing right divides date

Date	Mintage	VG	F	VF	XF	Unc
1656	—	300	600	1,100	1,500	—
1662	500	300	600	1,100	1,500	—
1666	2,000	300	600	1,100	1,500	—

SIEGE COINAGE

KM# 70 1/8 DAALDER
Silver **Obv:** Crowned eagle, date **Note:** Uniface klippe.

Date	Mintage	Good	VG	F	VF	XF
1672	—	50.00	125	185	250	450

KM# 71 1/4 DAALDER
Silver **Obv:** Crowned eagle, date **Note:** Uniface klippe.

Date	Mintage	Good	VG	F	VF	XF
1672	—	100	250	400	700	1,000

KM# 72 1/2 DAALDER
Silver **Obv:** Crowned eagle, date **Note:** Uniface klippe.

Date	Mintage	Good	VG	F	VF	XF
1672	—	70.00	175	300	600	900

KM# 73 DAALDER
Silver **Obv:** Crowned eagle, date **Note:** Uniface klippe.

Date	Mintage	Good	VG	F	VF	XF
1672	—	90.00	225	500	800	1,100

PATTERNS

Including off metal strikes

KM#	Date	Mintage	Identification	Mkt Val
Pn3	1685	—	Schelling. Gold. 7.6000 g. Knight on horse.	—
Pn6	1687	—	Florin. Gold. 13.6000 g.	5,000
Pn7	1688	—	6 Stuivers. Gold. KM#78.	3,000

KM#	Date	Mintage	Identification	Mkt Val
Pn8	(16)88	—	28 Stuivers. Gold. 30.8400 g. KM#81.	—
Pn9	1691	—	Stuiver. Gold. 3.8000 g.	—

PIEFORTS

KM#	Date	Mintage	Identification	Mkt Val
P1	1618	—	28 Stuivers. Silver. Klippe, KM#29.	—
P2	1640	—	40 Stuivers. Silver. Klippe, (triple weight), KM#52.	—
P3	1640	—	48 Stuivers. Silver. Triple weight. Klippe.	—
P4	1660	—	40 Stuivers. Silver. Klippe, KM#62.2.	—
P5	1662	—	48 Stuivers. Silver. KM#63.1.	—
P6	1662	—	48 Stuivers. Silver. KM#64.1.	—
P7	1662	—	48 Stuivers. Silver. KM#64.2.	1,200
P8	1662	—	2 Ducat.	—
P9	1663	—	48 Stuivers. Silver. KM#64.1.	1,200
P10	1664	—	48 Stuivers. Silver. KM#63.1.	1,750
P11	1666	—	48 Stuivers. Silver. KM#64.1.	1,750
P12	1666	—	Ducat. Gold. Klippe, KM#65.	3,500
P13	1682	—	60 Stuivers. Silver. KM#76.	—
P14	1683	—	2 Stuivers. Silver. KM#77.	—
P15	1684	—	28 Stuivers. Silver. KM#79.	—
P16	1685	—	28 Stuivers. Silver. (Triple weight), KM#81.1.	—
P17	1685	—	30 Stuivers. Silver. Triple weight, KM#82.	—
P18	1688	—	30 Stuivers. Silver. Triple weight, KM#83.	—
P19	1689	—	60 Stuivers. Silver. KM#84.	2,000
P20	1689	—	60 Stuivers. Silver. Triple weight. KM#84.	—

ELBURG

TOWNSHIP

STANDARD COINAGE

KM# 1 1/2 DUIT
Copper **Obv:** City gate with 3 towers within wreath
Rev: Inscription **Rev. Inscription:** .1.6. / MONETA / ECCLES / ELBORG / I.S.

Date	Mintage	Good	VG	F	VF	XF
ND(1619-21)	—	7.50	30.00	75.00	150	300

KM# 2 1/2 DUIT
Copper **Obv:** Star above city gate with 3 towers within sprays **Rev:** Inscription **Rev. Inscription:** *** / MONETA / ECCLES / ELBVRG / ***

Date	Mintage	Good	VG	F	VF	XF
ND(1619-21)	—	7.50	30.00	75.00	150	300

KM# 3.1 1/2 DUIT
Copper **Obv:** Crowned city arms **Rev:** Inscription
Rev. Inscription: MONE / ECCLE / ELBV

Date	Mintage	Good	VG	F	VF	XF
ND(1619-21)	—	35.00	100	250	500	1,000

KM# 3.2 1/2 DUIT
Copper **Obv:** Crowned city arms **Rev:** Inscription
Rev. Inscription: ... / MONE / ECCLE / ELBV / ...

Date	Mintage	Good	VG	F	VF	XF
ND(1619-21)	—	7.50	30.00	75.00	150	300

KM# 3.2a 1/2 DUIT
Silver **Obv:** Crowned city arms **Rev:** Inscription
Rev. Inscription: ... / MONE / ECCLE / ELBV / ...

Date	Mintage	Good	VG	F	VF	XF
ND(1619-21)	—	—	—	—	—	—

KM# 5 1/2 DUIT
Copper **Obv:** Arms in beaded circle **Rev:** Inscription in beaded circle **Rev. Inscription:** MONE / ECCLE / ELBV

Date	Mintage	Good	VG	F	VF	XF
ND(1619-21)	—	7.50	30.00	75.00	150	300

KM# 6 1/2 DUIT
Copper **Obv:** Crowned arms in branches **Rev:** Inscription in branches **Rev. Inscription:** MONE / ECCLE / ELBV

Date	Mintage	Good	VG	F	VF	XF
ND(1619-21)	—	7.50	30.00	75.00	150	300

KM# 7 1/2 DUIT
Copper **Obv:** Crowned arms in branches **Rev:** Inscription, date in wreath **Rev. Inscription:** MON / ECCL / ELB

Date	Mintage	Good	VG	F	VF	XF
1621	—	7.50	30.00	75.00	150	300

FRIESLAND

PROVINCE

STANDARD COINAGE

KM# 3 DUIT
Copper **Obv:** Crowned shield **Rev:** Inscription in wreath **Rev. Inscription:** FRI / SIA

Date	Mintage	Good	VG	F	VF	XF
ND(1600-04)	—	5.00	15.00	40.00	100	200

KM# 16 DUIT
Copper **Obv:** Crowned shield **Rev. Inscription:** FRI/SIA/(date) in wreath

Date	Mintage	Good	VG	F	VF	XF
1604	—	4.00	10.00	20.00	40.00	100
1605	—	4.00	10.00	20.00	40.00	100
1606	—	4.00	10.00	20.00	40.00	100
1611	—	4.00	10.00	20.00	40.00	100
1612	—	4.00	10.00	20.00	40.00	100
1613/11	—	6.00	15.00	30.00	60.00	125
1613	—	4.00	10.00	20.00	40.00	100
1616	—	4.00	10.00	20.00	40.00	100
1617	—	4.00	10.00	20.00	40.00	100
1618	—	4.00	10.00	20.00	40.00	100
1619	—	4.00	10.00	20.00	40.00	100
1620	—	4.00	10.00	20.00	40.00	100

KM# 16a DUIT
Silver **Obv:** Crowned shield **Rev. Inscription:** FRI / SIA / (date) in wreath

Date	Mintage	Good	VG	F	VF	XF
1605	—	—	—	—	—	—
1606	—	—	—	—	—	—
1617	—	—	—	—	—	—
1620	—	—	—	—	—	—

KM# 46 DUIT
Copper **Obv:** Wide shield of arms

Date	Mintage	Good	VG	F	VF	XF
1626	—	1.60	4.00	10.00	20.00	40.00
1627	—	2.40	6.00	20.00	50.00	100
1629	—	1.60	4.00	10.00	20.00	40.00
1643	—	1.60	4.00	10.00	20.00	40.00
1644	—	2.40	6.00	20.00	50.00	100
1645	—	2.40	6.00	20.00	40.00	70.00
1646	—	1.60	4.00	10.00	20.00	40.00
1647	—	1.60	4.00	10.00	20.00	40.00
1648	—	1.60	4.00	10.00	20.00	40.00
1653/48	—	1.60	4.00	10.00	20.00	40.00
1653	—	1.60	4.00	10.00	20.00	40.00
1654/48	—	1.60	4.00	10.00	20.00	40.00
1654	—	1.60	4.00	10.00	20.00	40.00
1663	—	2.40	6.00	20.00	40.00	70.00

KM# 46a DUIT
Silver **Obv:** Wide shield of arms **Note:** Weight varies 2.3 - 3.7 g.

Date	Mintage	Good	VG	F	VF	XF
1626	—	—	—	—	—	—
1627	—	—	—	—	—	—
1653	—	—	—	—	—	—

KM# 61 DUIT
Copper **Obv:** Crowned shield **Rev. Inscription:** FRISIA

Date	Mintage	Good	VG	F	VF	XF
1651	—	10.00	25.00	50.00	100	200
1675	—	2.00	5.00	15.00	30.00	40.00
1681	—	2.00	5.00	15.00	30.00	40.00
1682	—	2.00	5.00	15.00	30.00	40.00
1684	—	2.40	6.00	20.00	40.00	50.00
1685	—	2.00	5.00	15.00	30.00	40.00
1686	—	2.00	5.00	15.00	30.00	40.00
1688	—	2.40	6.00	20.00	40.00	50.00

KM# 46b DUIT
3.5000 g., Gold **Obv:** Wide shield of arms

Date	Mintage	Good	VG	F	VF	XF
1653	—	—	—	—	—	—

KM# 60 DUIT
Copper **Obv:** Crowned arms without legend
Rev. Inscription: FRISIA / (date)

Date	Mintage	Good	VG	F	VF	XF
1672	—	4.00	10.00	25.00	50.00	85.00

KM# 61a DUIT
Silver **Obv:** Crowned shield **Rev. Inscription:** FRISIA
Note: Weight varies 2.5 - 2.8 g.

Date	Mintage	Good	VG	F	VF	XF
1675	—	—	—	—	200	300
1681	—	—	—	—	—	—
1685	—	—	—	—	—	—
1690	—	—	—	—	—	—

KM# 8 2 DUIT (Oord)
Copper **Obv:** Crowned arms on ornamental cross in inner circle **Rev:** Frisian farmer with sword on shoulder between F - O (Frisia Ordines) in inner circle

Date	Mintage	Good	VG	F	VF	XF
ND(1606-07)	—	4.00	10.00	30.00	60.00	100

KM# 26 2 DUIT (Oord)

Copper **Obv:** Crowned arms on ornamental cross in inner circle **Rev:** Frisian farmer with sword on shoulder between F - O (Frisia Ordines) in inner circle

Date	Mintage	Good	VG	F	VF	XF
1608	—	3.00	8.00	25.00	40.00	75.00
1609	—	3.00	8.00	25.00	40.00	75.00
1610	—	3.00	8.00	25.00	40.00	75.00

KM# 26a 2 DUIT (Oord)

Silver **Obv:** Crowned arms on ornamental cross in inner circle **Rev:** Frisian farmer with sword on shoulder between F - O (Frisiae Ordines) in inner circle

Date	Mintage	Good	VG	F	VF	XF
1608/7	—	10.00	25.00	50.00	100	250
1608	—	2.00	5.00	20.00	50.00	100
1609	—	2.00	5.00	20.00	50.00	100
1610	—	2.00	5.00	20.00	50.00	100

KM# 18 2 DUIT (Oord)

Copper **Obv:** Crowned arms on ornamental cross in inner circle **Rev:** Frisian farmer with longer sword crossing inner circle between F - O (Frisia Ordines)

Date	Mintage	Good	VG	F	VF	XF
1608	—	2.00	5.00	25.00	60.00	100

KM# 18b 2 DUIT (Oord)

Gold **Obv:** Crowned arms on ornamental cross in inner circle **Rev:** Frisian farmer with longer sword crossing inner circle **Note:** Prev. KM #26b.

Date	Mintage	Good	VG	F	VF	XF
1608	—	—	—	—	—	—

KM# 28 2 DUIT (Oord)

Silver **Obv:** Crowned arms on ornamental cross in inner circle **Rev:** Frisian farmer with sword on shoulder between F - O (Frisiae Ordines) in inner circle **Note:** Klippe. Prev. KM# 26a.2.

Date	Mintage	Good	VG	F	VF	XF
1610	—	—	—	—	—	—

KM# 27 2 DUIT (Oord)

Copper **Rev:** Date in legend at upper left **Note:** Varieties exist.

Date	Mintage	Good	VG	F	VF	XF
1611	—	2.00	5.00	25.00	40.00	90.00
1612	—	2.00	5.00	25.00	40.00	90.00
1616	—	2.00	5.00	25.00	40.00	90.00
ND(1617-19)	—	8.00	10.00	30.00	75.00	125
1618	—	2.00	5.00	30.00	50.00	90.00

KM# 41 2 DUIT (Oord)

Copper **Obv:** Crowned arms on ornamental cross in inner circle, date above **Rev:** Frisian farmer with sword on shoulder between F - O (Frisiae Ordines) in inner circle **Note:** Varieties exist.

Date	Mintage	Good	VG	F	VF	XF
1620	—	3.20	8.00	20.00	40.00	90.00
ND(1626)	—	3.20	8.00	20.00	40.00	90.00
1644	—	8.00	20.00	50.00	100	150
1646	—	4.00	10.00	25.00	60.00	110
1647	—	4.00	10.00	25.00	60.00	110
1648	—	3.20	8.00	20.00	40.00	90.00
1649	—	4.00	10.00	25.00	60.00	90.00

KM# 43 2 DUIT (Oord)

Silver **Obv:** Crowned arms on ornamental cross in inner circle, date above **Rev:** Frisian farmer with sword on shoulder between F - O (Frisiae Ordines) in inner circle **Note:** Klippe.

Date	Mintage	Good	VG	F	VF	XF
1620	—	—	—	—	—	—

KM# 41a 2 DUIT (Oord)

Silver **Obv:** Crowned arms on ornametal cross in inner circle, date above **Rev:** Frisian farmer with sword on shoulder between F - O (Frisiae Ordines) in inner circle

Date	Mintage	Good	VG	F	VF	XF
1620	—	—	—	—	—	—
ND(1626)	—	—	—	—	—	—
1648	—	—	—	—	—	—

KM# 19 1/2 STUIVER

1.0000 g., Billon **Obv:** Crowned arms between F - B in inner circle **Rev:** Ornamental cross in inner circle

Date	Mintage	Good	VG	F	VF	XF
ND	—	14.00	35.00	80.00	100	150

KM# 20 STUIVER

2.0000 g., Billon **Obv:** Crowned arms divide value in inner circle **Rev:** Ornamental cross in quatrefoil in inner circle

Date	Mintage	Good	VG	F	VF	XF
ND	—	20.00	50.00	125	200	300

KM# 42 STUIVER

1.3100 g., 0.3330 Silver 0.0140 oz. ASW **Obv. Inscription:** FRI / SIA **Rev:** Bundle of arrows divides value in wreath **Note:** Varieties exist.

Date	Mintage	Good	VG	F	VF	XF
1619	—	3.00	10.00	20.00	30.00	60.00
1622	—	3.00	10.00	20.00	30.00	60.00
1623	—	3.00	10.00	20.00	30.00	60.00
1627	—	3.00	10.00	20.00	30.00	60.00
1628	—	3.00	10.00	20.00	30.00	60.00
1629	—	3.00	10.00	20.00	30.00	60.00
1630	—	3.00	10.00	20.00	30.00	60.00
1650	—	3.00	10.00	20.00	30.00	60.00
1653	—	3.00	10.00	20.00	30.00	60.00
1660	—	3.00	10.00	20.00	30.00	60.00
1661	—	3.00	10.00	20.00	30.00	60.00
1664	—	3.00	10.00	20.00	30.00	60.00

KM# 5 2 STUIVERS

4.0000 g., Billon **Obv:** Crowned arms divide value in cartouche in inner circle **Rev:** Ornamental cross in inner circle, date in legend

Date	Mintage	Good	VG	F	VF	XF
1601	—	15.00	45.00	120	170	250

KM# 32.1 2 STUIVERS

1.7300 g., 0.5830 Silver 0.0324 oz. ASW **Obv. Inscription:** FRI / SIA / (date) **Rev:** Crowned rampant lion left holding sword and arrows divides value 2 - S **Rev. Inscription:** FRI / SIA /(date) **Note:** Mint mark: Rampant lion.

Date	Mintage	Good	VG	F	VF	XF
1614	—	2.25	7.00	12.00	35.00	50.00

KM# 32.2 2 STUIVERS

1.7300 g., Silver **Obv. Inscription:** FRI / SIA / (date) **Rev:** Crowned rampant lion left holding sword and arrows divides value 2 - S **Note:** Mint mark: Rosette.

Date	Mintage	Good	VG	F	VF	XF
1629	—	1.60	5.00	10.00	30.00	60.00
1652	—	1.60	5.00	10.00	30.00	60.00
1653	—	1.60	5.00	10.00	30.00	60.00
1659	—	1.60	5.00	10.00	30.00	60.00
1662	—	1.60	5.00	10.00	30.00	60.00
1664	—	1.60	5.00	10.00	30.00	60.00
1665	—	1.60	5.00	10.00	30.00	60.00
1666	—	1.60	5.00	10.00	30.00	60.00
1670	—	1.60	5.00	10.00	30.00	60.00
1671	—	1.60	5.00	10.00	30.00	60.00
1673	—	1.60	5.00	10.00	30.00	60.00

KM# 32.3 2 STUIVERS

Silver **Obv. Inscription:** FRI / SIA / (date) **Rev:** Rampant lion left holding sword and arrows divides value 2 - S **Note:** Mint mark: Rampant lion. Varieties exist.

Date	Mintage	VG	F	VF	XF	Unc
1675	—	5.00	10.00	30.00	60.00	—
1676	—	5.00	10.00	30.00	60.00	—
1678	—	5.00	10.00	30.00	60.00	—
1679	—	5.00	10.00	30.00	60.00	—
1680	—	5.00	10.00	30.00	60.00	—
1681	—	5.00	10.00	30.00	60.00	—
1682	—	5.00	10.00	30.00	60.00	—
1683	—	5.00	10.00	30.00	60.00	—

KM# 6 3 STUIVERS (1/2 Snaphaanschelling)

3.3300 g., 0.5000 Silver 0.0535 oz. ASW **Obv:** Arms on ornamental cross **Obv. Legend:** MONE• - NOVA+ - ORDI+ - FRISI+ **Rev:** Helmeted arms **Rev. Legend:** NISI+ DOMINVS+ - NOBISCVM+

Date	Mintage	Good	VG	F	VF	XF
(16)01	—	40.00	125	225	350	500

KM# 30 6 STUIVERS (Snaphaanschelling)

6.6500 g., 0.5000 Silver 0.1069 oz. ASW **Obv:** Arms on ornate cross in inner circle **Obv. Legend:** MONE - NOVA• - ORDI• - FRISI• **Rev:** Knight on horseback left brandishing sword, date in exerque, in inner circle **Rev. Legend:** NISI •DOMENVS• NOBISCVM

Date	Mintage	Good	VG	F	VF	XF
1612	—	20.00	60.00	120	250	400
1621	—	10.00	30.00	60.00	100	150
1622	—	10.00	30.00	60.00	100	150
1623	—	10.00	30.00	60.00	100	150
1625	—	10.00	30.00	60.00	100	150

KM# 34 6 STUIVERS (Arendschelling)

6.0000 g., 0.5000 Silver 0.0964 oz. ASW **Obv:** Crowned arms of 14 states in inner circle **Rev:** Crowned double-headed eagle in inner circle

Date	Mintage	Good	VG	F	VF	XF
ND(1615-17)	—	15.00	45.00	110	170	250

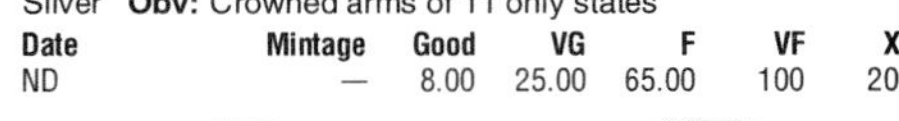

KM# 35 6 STUIVERS (Arendschelling)

Silver **Obv:** Crowned arms of 11 only states

Date	Mintage	Good	VG	F	VF	XF
ND	—	8.00	25.00	65.00	100	200

KM# 65 6 STUIVERS (Ruiterschelling)

4.9500 g., 0.5830 Silver 0.0928 oz. ASW **Obv:** Crowned arms **Rev:** Armored knight horseback right brandishing sword

Date	Mintage	Good	VG	F	VF	XF
1682	—	50.00	150	275	500	850

KM# 7 7 STUIVERS (1/4 Florin)

4.3200 g., 0.7650 Silver 0.1062 oz. ASW **Obv:** Crowned arms on ornate cross in inner circle **Rev:** Frisian farmer right with sword on shoulder divides value 7 - S in inner circle, date in legend in Arabic numerals

Date	Mintage	Good	VG	F	VF	XF
1601	—	15.00	45.00	100	150	200
1604	—	15.00	45.00	100	150	200
1684	—	15.00	45.00	100	150	200
1686	—	15.00	45.00	100	150	200
1688	—	15.00	55.00	150	200	300

KM# 66 7 STUIVERS (1/4 Florin)

4.3200 g., 0.7650 Silver 0.1062 oz. ASW **Obv:** Crowned arms on ornate cross in inner circkle **Rev:** Frisian farmer right with sword on shoulder divides value 7 - S, date in legend in Roman numerals

Date	Mintage	Good	VG	F	VF	XF
1684	—	18.00	55.00	150	200	300

KM# 24 10 STUIVERS

5.9500 g., 0.9170 Silver 0.1754 oz. ASW **Obv:** Armored knight standing holding sword behind shield of arms, date at sides in inner circle **Rev:** Crowned arms divide value in inner circle

Date	Mintage	Good	VG	F	VF	XF
1607	—	30.00	100	300	500	700

KM# 72 10 STUIVERS (1/2 Gulden)

5.3000 g., 0.5000 Silver 0.0852 oz. ASW **Obv:** Crowned arms **Obv. Legend:** MO: ARG: ORD: FÆD: BELG: FRI: **Rev:** Dutch maiden standing with liberty cap on lance leaning on bible on column **Rev. Legend:** HAC: NITIMVR HANC. TVEMVR

Date	Mintage	Good	VG	F	VF	XF
1694	—	18.00	55.00	150	200	300
1696	—	15.00	45.00	100	150	200

KM# 9 14 STUIVERS (1/2 Florin)
Silver **Obv. Legend:** MONETA. NOVA. ORDINVM. FRISIÆ.

Date	Mintage	Good	VG	F	VF	XF
1601	—	16.00	50.00	125	175	300

KM# A8.1 14 STUIVERS (1/2 Florin)
8.6500 g., 0.7650 Silver 0.2127 oz. ASW **Obv:** Crowned arms with ornaments at sides in inner circle **Obv. Legend:** FLORENVS • ARGENT • ORODI • FRIÆ **Rev:** Large bust of Frisian with sword on shoulder divides value in inner circle **Rev. Legend:** NISI • DOMINVS • NOBI SCVM

Date	Mintage	Good	VG	F	VF	XF
1601	—	15.00	45.00	100	150	250
1604	—	15.00	45.00	100	150	250

KM# A8.2 14 STUIVERS (1/2 Florin)
8.6500 g., 0.7650 Silver 0.2127 oz. ASW **Obv:** Crowned arms with ornaments at sides in inner circle **Obv. Legend:** FLORENVS • ARGENT • ORODI • FRIÆ **Rev:** Small bust of Frisian with sword on shoulder right divides value in inner circle **Rev. Legend:** NISI • DOMINVS • NOBI SCVM

Date	Mintage	Good	VG	F	VF	XF
1684	—	15.00	45.00	100	150	250
1686	—	15.00	45.00	100	150	250

KM# 67 14 STUIVERS (1/2 Florin)
Silver **Obv. Legend:** MONETA. ARGEN. ORD. FRIS.

Date	Mintage	Good	VG	F	VF	XF
1688	—	15.00	45.00	100	175	300

KM# 50 20 STUIVERS (1/2 Ducaton)
16.3000 g., 0.9410 Silver 0.4931 oz. ASW **Obv:** Knight horseback right brandishing sword, provincial arms below in inner circle **Rev:** Crowned arms with crowned lion supporters in inner circle, date at top in legend

Date	Mintage	Good	VG	F	VF	XF
1659	—	30.00	100	250	350	600
1660	—	30.00	100	250	350	600
1661	—	30.00	100	250	350	600
1662/0	—	40.00	125	300	550	700
1662	—	30.00	100	250	350	600
1668	—	40.00	125	300	550	700

KM# 51 20 STUIVERS (1/2 Ducaton)
Silver **Obv:** Knight horseback right brandishing sword, provincial arms below in inner circle **Rev:** Crowned arms with crowned lion supporters in inner circle, date at top in legend **Note:** Klippe.

Date	Mintage	Good	VG	F	VF	XF
1659	—	—	—	—	—	—

KM# 73 20 STUIVERS (Gulden)
10.6100 g., 0.9200 Silver 0.3138 oz. ASW **Obv:** Crowned lion shield divides value **Rev:** Standing female figure leaning on Bible on column, holding spear with Liberty cap, date in exerque **Note:** Varieties exist.

Date	Mintage	Good	VG	F	VF	XF
1696	—	20.00	70.00	150	300	500

KM# 12 24 STUIVERS (1/2 Lion Daalder)
13.8400 g., 0.7500 Silver 0.3337 oz. ASW **Obv:** Armored knight looking right above lion shield in inner circle **Rev:** Rampant lion left in inner circle, date at top in legend **Note:** Varieties exist.

Date	Mintage	Good	VG	F	VF	XF
1601/1599	—	16.00	50.00	150	350	600
1601	—	50.00	150	350	800	1,500
1602/1	—	16.00	50.00	150	350	600
1602	—	20.00	65.00	200	400	750
1604	—	16.00	50.00	150	350	600
1607	—	16.00	50.00	150	250	350
1611	—	16.00	50.00	150	250	350
1613	—	12.00	35.00	110	200	250
1614	—	16.00	50.00	150	250	350
1616	—	16.00	50.00	150	250	350
1617	—	12.00	35.00	110	200	250
1619	—	12.00	35.00	110	200	250
1622	—	12.00	35.00	110	200	250
1626	—	12.00	35.00	110	200	250
1628	—	12.00	35.00	110	200	250
1629	—	16.00	50.00	150	250	350
1632	—	12.00	35.00	110	200	250
1659	—	12.00	35.00	110	200	250
1663	—	16.00	50.00	150	250	350
ND	—	12.00	35.00	110	200	250

KM# 21 24 STUIVERS (1/2 Rijksdaalder)
14.5100 g., 0.8850 Silver 0.4128 oz. ASW **Obv:** Laureate 1/2 figure holding sword and arms in inner circle **Rev:** Crowned arms divide date in inner circle

Date	Mintage	Good	VG	F	VF	XF
1606	—	25.00	75.00	200	300	500
1607	—	25.00	75.00	200	300	500
1608	—	25.00	75.00	200	300	500
1609	—	25.00	75.00	200	300	500
1610	—	25.00	75.00	200	300	500
1611	—	25.00	75.00	200	300	500
1619	—	20.00	60.00	100	250	400
1620	—	20.00	60.00	100	250	400
1621	—	20.00	60.00	100	250	400
1622	—	20.00	60.00	100	250	400
1626	—	20.00	60.00	100	250	400
1629	—	20.00	60.00	100	250	400
1630	—	20.00	60.00	100	250	400
1631	—	20.00	60.00	100	250	400
1645	—	20.00	60.00	100	250	400
1649	—	25.00	75.00	200	300	500
1650	—	20.00	60.00	100	250	400
1651	—	20.00	60.00	100	250	400
1661/0	—	25.00	75.00	200	300	500
1661	—	25.00	75.00	200	300	500
1662	—	25.00	75.00	200	300	500
1666	—	25.00	75.00	200	300	500

KM# 55 24 STUIVERS (1/2 Silver Ducat)
14.1200 g., 0.8730 Silver 0.3963 oz. ASW **Obv:** Armored knight standing holding sword behind shield of arms, date at sides in inner circle **Rev:** Crowned arms in inner circle

Date	Mintage	Good	VG	F	VF	XF
1660	—	25.00	75.00	200	300	500

Date	Mintage	Good	VG	F	VF	XF
1672	—	25.00	75.00	200	300	500
1673	—	25.00	75.00	200	300	500

KM# 10 28 STUIVERS (Florin)
17.3000 g., 0.7650 Silver 0.4255 oz. ASW **Obv:** Crowned arms with ornaments **Obv. Legend:** FLORENVS • ARGENT • ORDI • FRISIÆ **Rev:** Farmer with sword **Rev. Legend:** NISI • DOMINVS • NOBISCVM •

Date	Mintage	Good	VG	F	VF	XF
1601	—	25.00	75.00	150	250	400
1602	—	65.00	200	300	450	700
1614/01	—	65.00	200	300	450	700
1614/04	—	65.00	200	300	450	700
1614	—	65.00	200	300	450	700
1664	—	25.00	75.00	150	250	400
1665/4	—	30.00	100	300	450	700
1665	—	25.00	75.00	150	250	400
1666	—	25.00	75.00	150	250	400
1683	—	25.00	75.00	150	250	400
1684	—	25.00	75.00	150	250	400
1688	—	30.00	100	300	450	700
1689	—	30.00	100	300	450	700
1690	—	25.00	75.00	150	250	400
1691	—	25.00	75.00	150	250	400
1694	—	—	—	—	—	—

KM# 71 28 STUIVERS (Florin)
19.5000 g., 0.6730 Silver 0.4219 oz. ASW **Obv:** Crowned arms **Obv. Legend:** MO: ARG: ORD: FÆD: BELG: FRI: **Rev:** Standing Dutch maiden leaning on Bible on column, holding lance with Liberty cap on top **Rev. Inscription:** HAC: NITIMVR HANC. TVEMVR

Date	Mintage	Good	VG	F	VF	XF
1694	—	—	—	—	—	—

KM# 36.1 30 STUIVERS (Arendsdaalder of 60 Groot)
20.6800 g., 0.7500 Silver 0.4986 oz. ASW **Obv:** Ornate arms with upper right shield with diagonal lines left **Rev:** Double-headed eagle with provincial arms on breast in inner circle

Date	Mintage	Good	VG	F	VF	XF
1617	—	25.00	80.00	200	350	650
1618	—	25.00	80.00	200	350	650

KM# 36.2 30 STUIVERS (Arendsdaalder of 60 Groot)
20.6800 g., 0.7500 Silver 0.4986 oz. ASW **Obv:** Ornate arms with upper right shield with diagonal lines right **Rev:** Double-headed eagle with provincial arms on breast in inner circle

Date	Mintage	Good	VG	F	VF	XF
1618	—	25.00	80.00	200	350	650

KM# 4 30 STUIVERS (Koggerdaalder)
Silver **Obv:** Crowned ornate arms **Obv. Legend:** ANTIQVA * VIRTVTE * ET * FIDE * **Rev:** Four crowned shields: Oostergo, Westergo, Sevenwolden and 11-fold with clasped hands holding arrows at center **Rev. Legend:** CONCOR - DIA* FRI - SIÆ*LI - BERTAS+

Date	Mintage	Good	VG	F	VF	XF
1601	—	100	250	600	900	1,800

KM# A66 30 STUIVERS (Koggerdaalder)
19.1900 g., 0.7570 Silver 0.4670 oz. ASW **Obv:** Crowned arms **Obv. Legend:** ANTIGVA•VIRTVTE•ET • FIDE• **Rev:** Four crowned shields: Oostergo, Westergo, Sevenwolden and 11-fold with "OG - WG - SW - ST" in angles, 'OG' under "CONCOR" **Rev. Legend:** CONCOR•FRISIAE•LIBERTAS

Date	Mintage	Good	VG	F	VF	XF
1682	—	40.00	100	240	400	675

KM# A67.1 30 STUIVERS (Koggerdaalder)
Silver **Obv:** Crowned arms **Rev:** 4 crowned shields with bundle of arrows at center **Rev. Legend:** CONGO•FRISI•LIBER-TAS

Date	Mintage	Good	VG	F	VF	XF
1687	—	28.00	110	250	425	700

KM# A67.2 30 STUIVERS (Koggerdaalder)
Silver **Obv:** Crowned arms, legend with retrograde 'N' **Obv. Legend:** ANTIGVA **Rev:** 4 crowned shields with bundle of arrows at center **Rev. Legend:** CONGO • FRISI • LIBER-TAS

Date	Mintage	Good	VG	F	VF	XF
1687	—	28.00	110	250	425	700

KM# 74 30 STUIVERS (1/2 3 Gulden)
15.9100 g., 0.9200 Silver 0.4706 oz. ASW **Obv:** Crowned arms **Obv. Legend:** MO: ARG: ORD: FÆD: BELG: FRI: **Rev:** Dutch maiden standing with liberty cap on lance, leaning on bible on column **Rev. Legend:** HAC: NITIMVR HANC. TVEMVR

Date	Mintage	Good	VG	F	VF	XF
1696	—	14.00	40.00	100	150	250

KM# 52 40 STUIVERS (Ducaton)
32.7800 g., 0.9410 Silver 0.9917 oz. ASW **Obv:** Knight with sword on horseback right, provincial arms below in inner circle **Rev:** Crowned arms with crowned lion supporters in inner circle **Note:** Dav. #4926.

Date	Mintage	Good	VG	F	VF	XF
1659	—	26.00	80.00	200	300	450
1660	—	26.00	80.00	200	300	450
1661	—	26.00	80.00	200	300	450
1662	—	26.00	80.00	200	300	450
1663	—	26.00	80.00	200	300	450
1665	—	26.00	80.00	200	300	450
1668	—	26.00	80.00	200	300	450

KM# 75 40 STUIVERS (2 Guilden)
21.2100 g., 0.9200 Silver 0.6273 oz. ASW **Obv:** Crowned arms divide value **Rev:** Dutch maiden standing with Liberty cap on lance, leaning on bible on column

Date	Mintage	Good	VG	F	VF	XF
1696	26,796	32.00	100	250	350	550

KM# 53 48 STUIVERS (Ducat)
28.2500 g., 0.8730 Silver 0.7929 oz. ASW **Obv:** Amored knight standing holding sword behind shield of arms, date at sides in inner circle **Rev:** Crowned arms in inner circle **Note:** Varieties exist. Dav. #4892.

Date	Mintage	Good	VG	F	VF	XF
1659	—	26.00	80.00	250	375	500
1660	—	26.00	80.00	250	375	500
1661	—	26.00	80.00	250	375	500
1662	—	26.00	80.00	250	375	500
1663	—	26.00	80.00	250	375	500
1672	—	26.00	80.00	250	375	500

KM# 76 48 STUIVERS (Ducat)
Silver **Obv:** Without inner circle **Rev:** Crowned arms divide date, without inner circle **Note:** Dav. #4893.

Date	Mintage	Good	VG	F	VF	XF
1696	—	32.00	100	220	350	500
1698	—	40.00	125	300	500	800

KM# 11 48 STUIVERS (Lion Daalder)
27.6800 g., 0.7500 Silver 0.6674 oz. ASW **Obv:** Armored knight looking right above lion shield in inner circle, date divided at bottom **Obv. Legend:** MO + NO + ORD - FRI + VA + HOL **Rev:** Rampant lion left in inner circle **Note:** Mint mark: Lion arms. Dav. #4851.

Date	Mintage	Good	VG	F	VF	XF
1601	—	13.00	40.00	100	150	300
1602/0	—	15.00	45.00	110	200	350
1602/1	—	15.00	45.00	110	200	350
1602	—	13.00	40.00	100	150	300
1603	—	13.00	40.00	100	150	300
1604	—	13.00	40.00	100	150	300

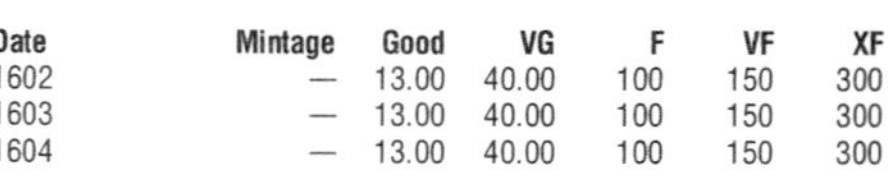

KM# 14 48 STUIVERS (Lion Daalder)
Silver **Obv:** Provincial arms in shield instead of lion **Note:** Mint mark: Arms. Dav. #4852.

Date	Mintage	Good	VG	F	VF	XF
1603	—	13.00	40.00	100	175	225
1604	—	13.00	40.00	100	175	225
1605	—	13.00	40.00	100	175	225
1606	—	13.00	40.00	100	175	225

KM# 23.1 48 STUIVERS (Lion Daalder)
Silver **Obv:** Lion shield instead of provincial arms, mint mark **Rev:** Date at top in legend **Note:** Dav. #4853.

Date	Mintage	Good	VG	F	VF	XF
1606	—	12.00	30.00	75.00	110	150
1607	—	12.00	30.00	75.00	110	150
1608	—	12.00	30.00	75.00	110	150
1609	—	12.00	30.00	75.00	110	150
1610	—	12.00	30.00	75.00	110	150
1601 Error for 1610	—	12.00	35.00	80.00	150	200
1611	—	12.00	30.00	75.00	110	150
1612	—	12.00	30.00	75.00	110	150
1613	—	12.00	30.00	75.00	110	150
1614	—	12.00	30.00	75.00	110	150
1615 date retrograde	—	13.00	40.00	100	200	300
1615	—	12.00	30.00	75.00	110	150
1616	—	12.00	30.00	75.00	110	150
1617	—	12.00	30.00	75.00	110	150
1619/2	—	12.00	30.00	75.00	110	150
1619	—	12.00	30.00	75.00	110	150
1620	—	12.00	35.00	80.00	120	160
1622	—	12.00	35.00	80.00	120	160
1625	—	12.00	35.00	80.00	120	160
1626	—	15.00	45.00	120	200	250
1628	—	12.00	30.00	75.00	110	150
1629/8	—	15.00	45.00	120	230	350
1629	—	12.00	35.00	80.00	120	160
1640	—	26.00	80.00	225	400	700

Date	Mintage	Good	VG	F	VF	XF
1641	—	23.00	70.00	200	300	400
1642	—	23.00	70.00	200	300	400
1643	—	23.00	70.00	200	300	400
1649	—	23.00	70.00	200	300	400
1650	—	23.00	70.00	200	300	400
1653	—	12.00	35.00	80.00	150	200

KM# 33 48 STUIVERS (Lion Daalder)

Silver **Obv:** Date divided at bottom **Note:** Dav. #4854.

Date	Mintage	Good	VG	F	VF	XF
ND	—	12.00	35.00	75.00	110	200
1614	—	12.00	35.00	75.00	110	200
1615	—	12.00	35.00	75.00	110	200
1616	—	12.00	35.00	75.00	110	200
1617	—	12.00	35.00	75.00	110	200
1622	—	12.00	35.00	75.00	110	200

KM# 47 48 STUIVERS (Lion Daalder)

Silver Dav. #4853B. **Obv:** Armored knight looking right behind lion shield, date **Rev:** Rampant lion left, date

Date	Mintage	Good	VG	F	VF	XF
1617	—	13.00	40.00	100	200	250
1628	—	12.00	35.00	75.00	110	150
1629	—	13.00	40.00	100	200	250

KM# 23.2 48 STUIVERS (Lion Daalder)

Silver **Rev:** Mint mark

Date	Mintage	Good	VG	F	VF	XF
1625	—	12.00	35.00	80.00	150	250

KM# 22 48 STUIVERS (Rijksdaalder)

29.0300 g., 0.8850 Silver 0.8260 oz. ASW **Obv:** Laureate 1/2 figure holding sword and arms in inner circle **Rev:** Crowned arms divide date in inner circle **Note:** Dav. #4829. Varieties exist.

Date	Mintage	Good	VG	F	VF	XF
1606	—	20.00	60.00	80.00	130	200
1607	—	20.00	60.00	80.00	130	200
1608	—	16.00	50.00	80.00	160	275
1609	—	16.00	50.00	80.00	160	275
1610	—	16.00	50.00	80.00	160	275
1611	—	16.00	50.00	80.00	160	275
1612	—	16.00	50.00	80.00	160	275
1613	—	16.00	50.00	80.00	160	275
1617	—	16.00	50.00	80.00	160	275
1618	—	16.00	50.00	80.00	160	275

Date	Mintage	Good	VG	F	VF	XF
1619/2	—	16.00	50.00	80.00	160	275
1619	—	20.00	60.00	80.00	130	200
1620	—	16.00	50.00	80.00	160	275
1621/16	—	20.00	60.00	100	200	350
1621/0	—	16.00	50.00	80.00	160	275
1621	—	18.00	55.00	75.00	100	150
1622/0	—	20.00	60.00	80.00	130	200
1622	—	18.00	55.00	75.00	100	150
1626/1	—	20.00	60.00	100	200	350
1626	—	18.00	55.00	75.00	100	150
1629	—	18.00	55.00	75.00	100	150
1630	—	20.00	60.00	80.00	130	200
1650	—	20.00	60.00	80.00	130	200
1651	—	20.00	60.00	80.00	130	200
1661	—	20.00	60.00	80.00	130	200

KM# 15 50 STUIVERS (Arendsrijksdaalder)

29.0300 g., 0.8850 Silver 0.8260 oz. ASW **Obv:** Frisian farmer with sword on shoulder in inner circle, date in legend **Rev:** Crowned double-headed eagle in inner circle **Note:** Lion arms.

Date	Mintage	Good	VG	F	VF	XF
1603	—	65.00	200	600	800	1,100

KM# 77 60 STUIVERS (3 Gulden)

31.8200 g., 0.9200 Silver 0.9412 oz. ASW **Obv:** Crowned arms divide value **Rev:** Standing female figure leaning on Bible on column, holding spear with Liberty cap, date in exergue **Note:** Dav. #4950.

Date	Mintage	Good	VG	F	VF	XF
1696	—	75.00	225	600	800	1,100
1697	—	75.00	225	600	800	1,100
1698	—	75.00	225	600	800	1,100

KM# 39 1/2 ROSE NOBLE

3.9000 g., Gold **Obv:** Ruler in ship holding Friesland shield in inner circle **Rev:** Radiant rose in circle of 4 crowned lis and 4 crowned lions

Date	Mintage	VG	F	VF	XF	Unc
ND(1600-02)	—	400	1,000	2,000	3,000	—

KM# 40 ROSE NOBLE

7.8000 g., Gold **Obv:** Ruler in ship holding Friesland shield in inner circle **Rev:** Radiant rose in circle of 4 crowned lis and 4 crowned lions

Date	Mintage	VG	F	VF	XF	Unc
ND(1600-02)	—	800	2,000	4,000	6,000	—

KM# 45 1/2 CAVALIER D'OR

5.0000 g., 0.9200 Gold 0.1479 oz. AGW **Obv:** Equestrian figure of knight above arms in inner circle **Rev:** Crowned arms in inner circle, date at top

Date	Mintage	VG	F	VF	XF	Unc
1620	—	200	450	800	1,200	—
1622	—	200	450	800	1,200	—
1623	—	200	450	800	1,200	—
1624	—	200	450	800	1,200	—
1626	—	200	450	800	1,200	—
1628	—	200	450	800	1,200	—
1630	—	200	450	800	1,200	—
1644	—	200	450	800	1,200	—

KM# 48 1/2 CAVALIER D'OR

5.0000 g., 0.9200 Gold 0.1479 oz. AGW **Note:** Klippe.

Date	Mintage	VG	F	VF	XF	Unc
1628 Proof	—	Value: 4,500				

KM# 25 CAVALIER D'OR

10.0000 g., 0.9200 Gold 0.2958 oz. AGW **Obv:** Equestrian figure of knight above arms in inner circle **Rev:** Crowned arms in inner circle, date at top

Date	Mintage	VG	F	VF	XF	Unc
1607	—	400	1,000	2,000	3,500	—
1617	—	400	1,000	2,000	3,500	—
1618	—	400	1,000	2,000	3,500	—
1619	—	400	1,000	2,000	3,500	—
1620	—	400	1,000	2,000	3,500	—
1626	—	400	1,000	2,000	3,500	—
1628	—	400	1,000	2,000	3,500	—

TRADE COINAGE

KM# 37 FLORIN D'OR

3.5000 g., 0.9860 Gold 0.1109 oz. AGW **Obv:** Crowned imperial eagle in inner circle **Rev:** 5 shields of arms in quatrefoil, date in legend

Date	Mintage	VG	F	VF	XF	Unc
1617	—	200	500	1,000	1,600	—
1618	—	200	500	1,000	1,600	—
1619	—	200	500	1,000	1,600	—

KM# 38 FLORIN D'OR

3.5000 g., 0.9860 Gold 0.1109 oz. AGW **Rev:** Helmeted arms in inner circle, date in legend

Date	Mintage	VG	F	VF	XF	Unc
1618 Rare	—	—	—	—	—	—
1619 Rare	—	—	—	—	—	—

KM# 13 DUCAT

3.5000 g., 0.9860 Gold 0.1109 oz. AGW **Obv:** Knight holding sword and a bundle of arrows **Rev:** 5-line inscription in tablet

Date	Mintage	VG	F	VF	XF	Unc
1602	—	140	250	500	700	—
1603/596	—	140	250	500	700	—
1603	—	120	150	275	400	—
1605/4	—	150	300	600	1,000	—
1605	—	120	150	275	400	—
1607/3	—	120	150	275	400	—
1607	—	120	150	275	400	—
1608/7	—	120	150	275	400	—
1608	—	120	150	275	400	—
1609	—	120	150	275	400	—
1610	—	120	150	275	400	—
1611	—	120	150	275	400	—
1612/07	—	120	150	275	400	—
1612	—	120	150	275	400	—
1614/1	—	120	150	275	400	—
1614	—	120	150	275	400	—
1615	—	120	150	275	400	—
1616	—	130	200	400	500	—
1619	—	140	250	500	700	—
1620 Rare	—	—	—	—	—	—
1629/8	—	—	—	—	—	—
1629	—	140	250	500	700	—
1630	—	140	250	500	700	—
1631	—	140	250	500	700	—
1633	—	140	250	500	700	—
1634	—	140	250	500	700	—
1635	—	140	250	500	700	—
1636	—	140	250	500	700	—
1638/6	—	140	250	500	700	—
1638	—	140	250	500	700	—
1639	—	140	250	500	700	—
1640/30	—	140	250	500	700	—
1640/33	—	140	250	500	700	—
1640	—	140	250	500	700	—
1643	—	140	250	500	700	—
1645	—	140	250	500	700	—
1648	—	140	250	500	700	—
1650	—	140	250	500	700	—
1652	—	140	250	500	700	—
1653	—	140	250	500	700	—
1654	—	140	250	500	700	—
1657	—	140	250	500	700	—
1666	—	140	250	500	700	—
1668	—	140	250	500	700	—
1676	—	140	250	500	700	—
1693	—	140	250	500	700	—

KM# 17 DUCAT

3.5000 g., 0.9860 Gold 0.1109 oz. AGW **Obv:** Knight standing right holding sword and shield

Date	Mintage	VG	F	VF	XF	Unc
1604	—	225	450	825	1,150	—
1605/4	—	500	1,000	2,000	3,000	—
1605	—	225	450	825	1,150	—

KM# 31 2 DUCAT

7.0000 g., 0.9860 Gold 0.2219 oz. AGW **Obv:** Knight standing right divides date **Rev:** 5-line inscription in tablet

Date	Mintage	VG	F	VF	XF	Unc
1612	—	600	1,500	2,500	3,500	—
1661	—	600	1,500	2,500	3,500	—

KM# A13 6-1/2 DUCAT

Gold **Ruler:** Heinrich Casimer **Obv:** Armored and draped bust right **Obv. Legend:** HENR. CASIM. D.G. PR. NASS. GVB. HÆR. FRIS. **Rev:** Crowned 6-fold arms with central shield, hat above, double chain connecting border of 11 small shields, legend around inside shields **Rev. Legend:** INSIG. PR. NASS. ET. VRB. FRIS.

Date	Mintage	F	VF	XF	Unc	BU
ND(1664-96) Rare	—	—	—	—	—	—

COUNTERMARKED COINAGE

1693

During the late 17th century many circulating coins were found to be underweight. In 1693 coins meeting the legal requirements were countermarked for a specific province or city, such as a crowned shield of Friesland.

KM# 70.1 28 STUIVERS

Silver **Countermark:** Crowned shield **Note:** Countermarked on Deventer KM#81.

CM Date	Host Date	Good	VG	F	VF	XF
ND(1693)	1685-92	—	—	—	—	—

KM# 70.2 28 STUIVERS
Silver **Countermark:** Crowned shield **Note:** Countermarked on Friesland KM#10.

CM Date	Host Date	Good	VG	F	VF	XF
ND(1693)	1601-91	—	—	—	—	—

KM# 70.3 28 STUIVERS
Silver **Countermark:** Crowned shield **Note:** Countermarked on Nijmegen KM#27.

CM Date	Host Date	Good	VG	F	VF	XF
ND(1693)	1685-90	—	—	—	—	—

KM# 70.4 28 STUIVERS
Silver **Countermark:** Crowned shield **Note:** Countermarked on Overyssel KM#55.

CM Date	Host Date	Good	VG	F	VF	XF
ND(1693)	1685-89	—	—	—	—	—

PATTERNS

Including off metal strikes

KM#	Date	Mintage	Identification	Mkt Val
Pn1	1601	—	30 Stuivers. Gold. 94.0000 g.	—
Pn2	1601	—	14 Stuivers. Gold. 12.0000 g. KM#9	—
Pn3	1610	—	2 Ducat. Silver.	—
Pn4	1614/04	—	28 Stuivers. Gold. 21.2000 g. KM#10.	—
Pn5	1614	—	28 Stuivers. Gold. 38.6000 g. KM#10.	—
Pn6	1618	—	30 Stuivers. Gold. 25.6000 g. KM#36.	—
Pn10	1652	—	30 Stuivers. Gold. 36.0000 g.	—
Pn11	1660	—	Stuiver. Gold. 5.2000 g. KM#42.	—
Pn12	1665	—	28 Stuivers. Gold. KM#10	—
Pn13	1675	—	2 Stuivers. Gold. 3.4000 g. KM#32.2.	—
Pn14	1680	—	2 Stuivers. Gold. 3.4000 g. KM#32.2.	—
Pn15	1682	—	6 Stuivers. Gold. 8.7000 g. KM#65.	—
Pn16	1682	—	30 Stuivers. Gold. 17.0000 g.	—
Pn17	1682	—	30 Stuivers. Silver. WG under CONCOR. WG under CONCOR	5,000
Pn18	1688	—	28 Stuivers. Silver. KM#10.	—
PnA19	1688	—	28 Stuivers. Gold. 19.5000 g. KM#10.	—
Pn19	1694	—	2 Gulden. Gold. 23.0000 g. KM#75.	—

PIEFORTS

KM#	Date	Mintage	Identification	Mkt Val
P1	1601	—	30 Stuivers. Silver. 53.6000 g. KM#4.	2,500
P2	1601	—	30 Stuivers. Gold. KM#4.	—
P3	1626	—	Cavalier D'Or. Gold. KM#25.	—
P4	1628	—	Cavalier D'Or. Gold. KM#25.	—
P5	1647	—	Duit. Copper. KM#47.	—
PA6	1647	—	2 Duit. Silver. KM#41a.	—
P6	1652	—	30 Stuivers. Silver.	1,500
P7	1652	—	30 Stuivers. Silver. Triple weight, 42.8-180 g.	—
P8	1659	—	20 Stuivers. Silver. Klippe. KM#51.	—
P9	1659	—	40 Stuivers. Silver. KM#52.	—
P10	1661	—	40 Stuivers. Silver. KM#52.	—
P11	1665	—	28 Stuivers. Silver. KM#10.	—
P12	1675	—	Duit. Silver. 7.6000 g. KM#61a.	—
P13	1684	—	28 Stuivers. Silver. KM#10.	—
P14	1695	—	60 Stuivers. Silver. KM#77.	—

GELDERLAND

Ducatus Gelriae

Gelder, a former duchy, was merged with the Hapsburg dominions in the Netherlands until the revolt of the Low Countries resulted in its partition. In 1579 the greater part of Gelder, comprising the quarters of Nijmegen, Arnhem, and Zutphen, became the province of Gelderland in the Dutch Republic.

PROVINCE

STANDARD COINAGE

KM# 30 DUIT
Copper **Obv:** Provincial arms in cartouche in inner circle **Rev:** Imscription in wreath **Rev. Inscription:** DVC / GEL / (date)

Date	Mintage	Good	VG	F	VF	XF
1626	—	1.60	5.00	10.00	20.00	35.00
1628	—	1.60	6.00	15.00	30.00	55.00
1631	—	1.70	7.00	20.00	40.00	65.00
1633	—	1.60	5.00	10.00	20.00	35.00
1634	—	1.60	5.00	10.00	20.00	35.00
1635	—	1.60	5.00	10.00	20.00	35.00
1636	—	1.60	5.00	10.00	20.00	35.00
1640	—	1.60	5.00	10.00	20.00	35.00

KM# 47 DUIT
Copper **Obv:** Crowned arms of Gelderland **Rev:** Inscription, date in wreath **Rev. Inscription:** .D. / GEL / RIÆ / (date)

Date	Mintage	Good	VG	F	VF	XF
1662	—	1.60	5.00	15.00	30.00	40.00
1663	—	1.30	4.00	10.00	20.00	30.00
1664	—	1.30	4.00	10.00	20.00	30.00
1665	—	1.30	4.00	10.00	20.00	30.00
1666	—	1.60	5.00	15.00	30.00	40.00
1668	—	2.00	6.00	20.00	40.00	60.00
1676	—	1.60	5.00	15.00	30.00	40.00
1678	—	1.30	4.00	10.00	20.00	30.00
1679	—	1.60	5.00	15.00	30.00	40.00
1681	—	1.30	4.00	10.00	20.00	30.00
1684	—	1.30	4.00	10.00	20.00	30.00
1690	—	1.30	4.00	10.00	20.00	30.00
1591 error for 1691	—	—	—	—	—	—
1691	—	1.30	4.00	10.00	20.00	30.00
1692	—	1.60	5.00	15.00	30.00	40.00
1693	—	1.60	5.00	15.00	30.00	40.00

KM# 47a DUIT
Silver **Obv:** Crowned arms of Gelderland **Rev:** Inscription, date in wreath **Rev. Inscription:** .D. / GEL / RIÆ / (date)

Date	Mintage	Good	VG	F	VF	XF
1690	—	—	—	—	—	—
1691	—	8.00	20.00	60.00	125	250
1692	—	—	—	—	—	—
1693	—	—	—	—	—	—
1699	—	—	—	—	—	—

KM# 25 STUIVER
0.8600 g., 0.5830 Silver 0.0161 oz. ASW **Obv:** Crowned rampant lion left holding sword and arrows, value at sides **Rev. Inscription:** GEL / RIA / (date)

Date	Mintage	Good	VG	F	VF	XF
1614	—	1.00	3.00	10.00	20.00	45.00

KM# 35 STUIVER
1.3100 g., 0.5830 Silver 0.0246 oz. ASW **Obv:** Bundle of arrows divides value in wreath **Rev:** Inscription, date in wreath **Rev. Inscription:** GEL / RIA / (date) **Note:** Mint mrk: Lily or cross

Date	Mintage	Good	VG	F	VF	XF
1640	—	1.00	3.00	10.00	30.00	55.00
1642	—	3.00	10.00	25.00	50.00	100

KM# 26.1 2 STUIVERS
1.7300 g., 0.5830 Silver 0.0324 oz. ASW **Obv:** Crowned rampant lion left holding sword and arrows, value at sides **Rev. Inscription:** GEL / RIA / (date) **Note:** Mint mark: Cross

Date	Mintage	Good	VG	F	VF	XF
1614	—	1.60	5.00	12.00	25.00	50.00
1615	—	1.60	5.00	12.00	25.00	50.00
1618	—	1.60	5.00	12.00	25.00	50.00

KM# 26.2 2 STUIVERS
1.7300 g., 0.5830 Silver 0.0324 oz. ASW **Obv:** Crowbed rampant lion left holding sword and arrows, value at sides **Rev. Inscription:** GEL / RIA / (date) **Note:** Mint mark: Lily.

Date	Mintage	Good	VG	F	VF	XF
1646	—	1.60	5.00	12.00	25.00	50.00

KM# 26.3 2 STUIVERS
1.7300 g., 0.5830 Silver 0.0324 oz. ASW **Obv:** Crowned rampant lion left holding sword and arrows, value at sides **Rev. Inscription:** GEL / RIA / (date) **Note:** Mint mark: Dog.

Date	Mintage	Good	VG	F	VF	XF
1678	—	1.60	5.00	12.00	20.00	40.00
1679	—	1.60	5.00	12.00	20.00	40.00
1680	—	1.60	5.00	12.00	20.00	40.00

KM# 6 6 STUIVERS (Roosschelling)
5.2700 g., 0.5830 Silver 0.0988 oz. ASW **Obv:** Crowned arms in wreath in inner circle, date above crown **Rev:** Ornamental cross in inner circle

Date	Mintage	Good	VG	F	VF	XF
1601	—	25.00	75.00	200	400	600
1602/1	—	25.00	75.00	200	400	600
1602	—	25.00	75.00	200	400	600

KM# 55 6 STUIVERS (Rijderschelling)
4.9500 g., 0.5830 Silver 0.0928 oz. ASW **Obv:** Crowned arms divide value in inner circle, date above crown **Rev:** Knight horseback right brandishing sword in inner circle **Note:** Mint mark: Dog.

Date	Mintage	Good	VG	F	VF	XF
1681	—	2.30	7.00	20.00	35.00	50.00
1682	—	2.30	7.00	20.00	35.00	50.00

KM# 60 6 STUIVERS (Rijderschelling)
Silver **Obv:** Crowned arms divides date, without inner cricles **Rev:** Knight horseback right brandishing sword, without inner circles **Note:** Mint mark: Unicorn.

Date	Mintage	Good	VG	F	VF	XF
1691	—	2.00	6.00	17.50	40.00	90.00

KM# 12 10 STUIVERS
5.9500 g., 0.9170 Silver 0.1754 oz. ASW **Obv:** Armored knight standing holding sword behind shield of arms, date at sides in inner circle **Rev:** Crowned arms divide value in inner circle

Date	Mintage	Good	VG	F	VF	XF
1606	—	50.00	150	350	750	1,200

KM# 7 20 STUIVERS (1/2 Prince Daalder)
11.5100 g., 0.8850 Silver 0.3275 oz. ASW **Obv:** Armored bust of William the Silent with sword right in inner circle, date at top in legend **Rev:** Helmeted arms in inner circle

Date	Mintage	Good	VG	F	VF	XF
1601	—	33.00	100	300	600	1,000
1602	—	—	—	—	—	—
1603	—	33.00	100	300	600	1,000
1604	—	33.00	100	300	600	1,000

KM# 45 20 STUIVERS (1/2 Ducaton)
16.3000 g., 0.9410 Silver 0.4931 oz. ASW **Obv:** Knight with sword on horseback to right, provincial arms below in inner circle **Rev:** Crowned arms with crowned lion supporters in inner circle, date divided in legend at top **Note:** Mint mark: Dog. Dav. #4922.

Date	Mintage	Good	VG	F	VF	XF
1661	—	50.00	150	500	750	1,000
1667	—	40.00	125	400	650	850
1668	—	40.00	125	400	650	850
1670/67	—	65.00	200	500	800	1,200
1670	—	40.00	125	400	650	850
1676	—	40.00	125	400	650	850

KM# 65.1 20 STUIVERS (Gulden)
10.6100 g., 0.9200 Silver 0.3138 oz. ASW **Obv:** Crowned lion shield divides value **Rev:** Standing female figure leaning on Bible on column, holding spear with Liberty cap, date in exerque **Note:** Mint mark: Unicorn.

Date	Mintage	Good	VG	F	VF	XF
1694	63,900	6.00	20.00	50.00	100	200

KM# 65.2 20 STUIVERS (Gulden)
10.6100 g., 0.9200 Silver 0.3138 oz. ASW **Obv:** Crowned arms of Gelderland divide value **Rev:** Standing female figure leaning on Bible on column, holding pole with liberty cap, date in exerque **Note:** Mint mark: Knight on horse.

Date	Mintage	Good	VG	F	VF	XF
1697	538,920	—	15.00	30.00	70.00	125
1698	Inc. above	—	15.00	30.00	70.00	125
1699	Inc. above	—	15.00	30.00	70.00	125
1700/99	Inc. above	—	25.00	50.00	100	150
1700	941,775	—	15.00	30.00	70.00	125

KM# 14 24 STUIVERS (1/2 Rijksdaalder)
14.5100 g., 0.8850 Silver 0.4128 oz. ASW **Obv:** Laureate 1/2 figure holding sword and arms in inner circle **Rev:** Crowned arms divide date in inner circle

Date	Mintage	Good	VG	F	VF	XF
1606	—	22.00	70.00	200	300	500
1609	—	30.00	100	250	400	800

Date	Mintage	Good	VG	F	VF	XF
1610	—	12.00	40.00	100	200	250
1611	—	12.00	40.00	100	200	250
1612	—	12.00	40.00	100	200	250
1614/11	—	—	—	—	—	—
1614/12	—	12.00	40.00	100	200	250
1614	—	22.00	70.00	200	300	400
1616/15	—	20.00	60.00	150	250	350
1616	—	20.00	60.00	150	250	350
1618	—	12.00	40.00	100	200	250
1619/8	—	20.00	60.00	150	250	350
1619	—	12.00	40.00	100	200	250
1620	—	22.00	70.00	200	300	500
1621	—	12.00	40.00	100	200	250
1622	—	12.00	40.00	100	200	250
1624	—	20.00	60.00	150	250	350
1625	—	20.00	60.00	150	250	350
1626	—	20.00	60.00	150	250	350

KM# 9 24 STUIVERS (1/2 Lion Daalder)

13.8400 g., 0.7500 Silver 0.3337 oz. ASW **Obv:** Armored knight looking right above lion shield in inner circle, date divide at bottom **Rev:** Rampant lion to left in inner circle

Date	Mintage	Good	VG	F	VF	XF
1602/00	—	22.00	70.00	200	300	400
1602	—	22.00	70.00	200	300	400

KM# 13.1 24 STUIVERS (1/2 Lion Daalder)

Silver **Obv:** Armored knight looking right above lion shield **Rev:** Rampant lion left, date at top in legend

Date	Mintage	Good	VG	F	VF	XF
1606	—	12.00	40.00	125	200	300
1607	—	22.00	70.00	200	300	400
1608	—	32.00	100	250	400	800
1610	—	10.00	30.00	125	150	250
1611	—	12.00	40.00	125	200	300
1615/11	—	12.00	40.00	125	200	300
1615	—	12.00	40.00	125	200	300
1616	—	10.00	30.00	100	150	250
1617	—	10.00	30.00	100	150	250
1620	—	10.00	30.00	100	150	250
1622	—	12.00	40.00	125	200	300
1623	—	12.00	40.00	125	200	300
1626	—	12.00	40.00	125	200	300
1628	—	12.00	40.00	125	150	250
1632	—	12.00	40.00	125	200	300
1633	—	12.00	40.00	125	150	250
1637	—	12.00	40.00	125	150	250

KM# 13.2 24 STUIVERS (1/2 Lion Daalder)

Silver **Obv:** Armored knight looking right above lion shield **Rev:** Rampant lion left with tail left, date at top in legend **Note:** Mint mark: Lily.

Date	Mintage	Good	VG	F	VF	XF
1637	—	12.00	40.00	125	200	300
1638	—	12.00	40.00	125	200	300
1639	—	12.00	40.00	125	200	300
1640	—	10.00	30.00	100	150	250
1641	—	10.00	30.00	60.00	100	175
1643	—	10.00	30.00	100	150	250
1644	—	10.00	30.00	100	150	250
1646	—	10.00	30.00	60.00	100	175
1647	—	26.00	80.00	100	200	400
1648	—	10.00	30.00	60.00	100	125
1649	—	10.00	30.00	60.00	100	125

KM# 13.3 24 STUIVERS (1/2 Lion Daalder)

Silver **Obv:** Armored knight looking right above lion shield **Rev:** Rampant lion left with tail right, date at top in legend **Note:** Mint mark: Lily.

Date	Mintage	Good	VG	F	VF	XF
1646	—	10.00	30.00	60.00	100	175

KM# 13.4 24 STUIVERS (1/2 Lion Daalder)

Silver **Obv:** Armored knight looking right above lion shield **Rev:** Rampant lion left, date at top in legend **Note:** Mint mark: Dog.

Date	Mintage	Good	VG	F	VF	XF
1652	—	10.00	30.00	60.00	100	175

KM# 46 24 STUIVERS (1/2 Silver Ducat)

Silver **Note:** Mint mark: Dog. Similar to 48 Stuivers, KM#42.

Date	Mintage	Good	VG	F	VF	XF
1661	—	40.00	125	350	600	800
1667	—	40.00	125	350	600	800
1664	—	40.00	125	350	600	800

KM# 62 30 STUIVERS (Daalder)

15.8800 g., 0.9060 Silver 0.4625 oz. ASW **Obv:** Standing knight with sword behind crowned arms to left, in inner circle **Rev:** Crowned double-headed eagle in inner circle

Date	Mintage	Good	VG	F	VF	XF
ND(1690-1694) Rare	—	—	—	—	—	—

KM# 61 30 STUIVERS (Daalder)

Silver **Obv:** Crowned provincial arms with lion supporters, value below **Rev:** Standing knight with sword behind crowned arms to left, date in legend

Date	Mintage	Good	VG	F	VF	XF
1693	—	—	—	—	—	—

KM# 8 40 STUIVERS (Prince Daalder)

29.0300 g., 0.8850 Silver 0.8260 oz. ASW **Obv:** Armored bust of William the Silent with sword right in inner circle, date a top in legend **Rev:** Helmeted arms in inner circle

Date	Mintage	Good	VG	F	VF	XF
1601	—	40.00	130	350	550	750
1602	—	25.00	100	250	400	600
1603	—	40.00	130	350	550	750
1604	—	35.00	150	375	600	800

KM# 50 40 STUIVERS (Ducaton)

Silver **Obv:** Armored knight horseback right brandishing sword, shield below **Rev:** Crowned supported arms with empty cartouche below **Note:** Dav. #4924.

Date	Mintage	Good	VG	F	VF	XF
1676	—	25.00	50.00	125	250	400
1677	—	25.00	50.00	125	250	400
1679/7	—	25.00	50.00	125	250	400
1679	—	25.00	50.00	125	250	400
1680	—	25.00	50.00	125	250	400
1681	—	25.00	50.00	125	250	400

KM# 66 40 STUIVERS (2 Gulden)

21.2100 g., 0.9200 Silver 0.6273 oz. ASW **Obv:** Crowned shield divides value 2-GL **Rev:** Date in exergue

Date	Mintage	Good	VG	F	VF	XF
1694	—	20.00	50.00	125	200	400

KM# 67 40 STUIVERS (2 Gulden)

Silver **Obv:** Crowned provincial arms divide value 2-G, date above crown **Rev:** Standing female figure leaning on Bible on column, holding spear with Liberty cap **Note:** Mint mark: Unicorn.

Date	Mintage	Good	VG	F	VF	XF
1694	14,615	32.00	100	175	300	500

KM# 69 40 STUIVERS (2 Gulden)

Silver **Note:** Without value.

Date	Mintage	Good	VG	F	VF	XF
1696	—	32.00	100	175	300	500

KM# 16.1 48 STUIVERS (Rijksdaalder)

29.0300 g., 0.8850 Silver 0.8260 oz. ASW **Obv:** Laureate 1/2 figure right holding sword and arms in inner circle **Rev:** Crowned arms divide date in inner circle **Note:** Mint mark: Ornate cross. Dav. #4828.

Date	Mintage	Good	VG	F	VF	XF
1606	—	20.00	40.00	80.00	175	300
1607	—	20.00	40.00	80.00	175	300
1608	—	20.00	40.00	80.00	175	300
1609	—	20.00	40.00	80.00	175	300
1610/9	—	28.00	60.00	120	200	400
1610	—	20.00	40.00	80.00	175	300
1611/0	—	20.00	40.00	80.00	175	300
1611	—	20.00	40.00	80.00	175	300
1612	—	20.00	40.00	80.00	175	300
1613/1	—	20.00	40.00	80.00	175	300
1613/2	—	20.00	40.00	80.00	175	300
1613	—	20.00	40.00	80.00	175	300
1614/3	—	20.00	40.00	80.00	175	300
1614	—	20.00	40.00	80.00	175	300
1615	—	20.00	40.00	80.00	175	300
1617/4	—	20.00	40.00	80.00	175	300
1617	—	25.00	50.00	100	200	350
1618/7	—	20.00	40.00	80.00	175	300
1618	—	20.00	40.00	80.00	175	300
1619/8	—	25.00	50.00	90.00	200	330
1619	—	20.00	40.00	80.00	175	300
1620	—	20.00	40.00	80.00	175	300
1621/0	—	25.00	50.00	90.00	200	330
1621	—	20.00	40.00	80.00	175	300
16ZZ	—	25.00	50.00	90.00	200	330
1622	—	25.00	50.00	90.00	200	330
1623	—	25.00	50.00	90.00	200	330
1624	—	25.00	50.00	90.00	200	330
1625	—	20.00	40.00	80.00	175	300
1629	—	20.00	40.00	80.00	175	300
1631	—	20.00	40.00	80.00	175	300
1643	—	20.00	40.00	80.00	175	300

KM# 16.5 48 STUIVERS (Rijksdaalder)

29.0300 g., 0.8850 Silver 0.8260 oz. ASW **Obv:** Laureate 1/2 length figure right holding sword and shield in inner circle **Rev:** Crowned arms divide date in inner circle **Note:** Mint mark: Diamond shape. Prev. KM#19. Dav. #4828B.

Date	Mintage	Good	VG	F	VF	XF
1608	—	—	—	—	—	—

KM# 16.2 48 STUIVERS (Rijksdaalder)

29.0300 g., 0.8850 Silver 0.8260 oz. ASW **Obv:** Laureate 1/2 figure right holding sword and arms in inner circle **Rev:** Crowned arms divide date in inner circle **Note:** Mint mark: Lily. Dav. # 4828.

Date	Mintage	Good	VG	F	VF	XF
1648	—	20.00	40.00	80.00	125	200
1649	—	20.00	40.00	80.00	125	200
1650	—	20.00	40.00	80.00	125	200
1651	—	20.00	40.00	80.00	125	200

KM# 16.4 48 STUIVERS (Rijksdaalder)

29.0300 g., Silver **Obv:** Laureate 1/2 length figure right holding sword in inner circle **Rev:** Crowned arms divides date in innner circle **Note:** Mint marks: Obverse Lily, reverse Dog. Dav. # 4828C.

Date	Mintage	Good	VG	F	VF	XF
1652	—	40.00	100	200	400	800
1653	—	25.00	50.00	100	200	350

KM# 16.3 48 STUIVERS (Rijksdaalder)

29.0300 g., 0.8850 Silver 0.8260 oz. ASW **Obv:** Laureate 1/2 figure right holding sword and arms in inner circle **Rev:** Crowned arms divide date in inner circle **Note:** Mint mark: Dog.

Date	Mintage	Good	VG	F	VF	XF
1652	—	20.00	40.00	80.00	125	200
1653	—	20.00	40.00	80.00	125	200
1654	—	25.00	50.00	90.00	150	300
1655	—	20.00	40.00	80.00	125	200
1656	—	20.00	40.00	80.00	125	200
1657	—	25.00	50.00	90.00	150	300
1658	—	20.00	40.00	80.00	125	200
1659	—	25.00	50.00	90.00	150	300
1662	—	35.00	100	200	400	800
1674	—	28.00	60.00	120	200	400
1676	—	28.00	60.00	120	200	400
1680 Rare	—	—	—	—	—	—

KM# 16.6 48 STUIVERS (Rijksdaalder)

Silver **Obv:** Laureate 1/2 length figure right holding sword in inner circle **Rev:** Crowned arms divide date in inner circle **Note:** Mint marks: Obverse dog, reverse Lily. Dav. # 4828.

Date	Mintage	Good	VG	F	VF	XF
1665	—	25.00	50.00	90.00	150	300

KM# 16a 48 STUIVERS (Rijksdaalder)

27.6800 g., 0.7500 Silver 0.6674 oz. ASW **Obv:** Laureate 1/2 figure right holding sword and arms in inner circle **Rev:** Crowned arms divide date in inner circle **Note:** Mint mark: Knight on horse. Prev. KM # 16.4.

Date	Mintage	Good	VG	F	VF	XF
1699	—	25.00	50.00	100	200	400

KM# 10 48 STUIVERS (Lion Daalder)

Silver **Obv:** Armored knight looking right above lion shield in inner circle, date divided at bottom **Rev:** Rampant lion left in inner circle **Note:** Dav. #4847.

Date	Mintage	Good	VG	F	VF	XF
160Z/0	—	22.00	45.00	90.00	150	250
160Z	—	22.00	45.00	90.00	150	250

KM# 15.1 48 STUIVERS (Lion Daalder)

Silver **Obv:** Armored knight looking right above lion shield **Rev:** Rampant lion left, date at top in legend **Note:** With "+" after GEL in legend. Dav. #4849.

Date	Mintage	Good	VG	F	VF	XF
1606	—	18.00	25.00	60.00	80.00	120
1607	—	18.00	25.00	60.00	80.00	120
1608	—	18.00	25.00	60.00	80.00	120
1609/8	—	18.00	25.00	60.00	80.00	120
1610	—	18.00	25.00	60.00	80.00	120
1611	—	18.00	25.00	60.00	80.00	120
1612	—	18.00	25.00	60.00	80.00	120
1613/2	—	35.00	100	200	300	500
1613	—	18.00	25.00	60.00	80.00	120
1614/2	—	22.00	35.00	70.00	120	200
1615/4	—	22.00	45.00	90.00	180	350
1615	—	20.00	35.00	70.00	110	150
1616/5	—	20.00	35.00	70.00	120	200
1616	—	18.00	25.00	60.00	80.00	120
1617/6	—	18.00	25.00	60.00	80.00	120
1617	—	18.00	25.00	60.00	80.00	120
1618	—	20.00	35.00	70.00	110	150
1619	—	20.00	35.00	70.00	110	150
1624	—	18.00	25.00	60.00	80.00	120
1622	—	20.00	35.00	70.00	110	150
1626	—	20.00	35.00	70.00	110	150
1628/18	—	18.00	25.00	60.00	80.00	120
1628/2	—	20.00	35.00	70.00	120	200
1628	—	18.00	25.00	60.00	80.00	120
1629/7	—	20.00	35.00	70.00	110	150
1629	—	18.00	25.00	70.00	80.00	120
1630	—	20.00	35.00	70.00	110	150
1631	—	20.00	35.00	70.00	110	150
1632	—	18.00	25.00	60.00	80.00	120
1633	—	18.00	25.00	60.00	80.00	120
1634	—	18.00	25.00	60.00	80.00	120
1635	—	18.00	25.00	60.00	80.00	120

KM# 15.2 48 STUIVERS (Lion Daalder)

Silver **Obv:** Armored knight looking right above lion shield **Rev:** Rampant lion left **Note:** Without "+" after GEL in legend. Dav. # 4849.

Date	Mintage	Good	VG	F	VF	XF
1635	—	18.00	25.00	60.00	80.00	110
1636	—	18.00	25.00	60.00	80.00	120
1637	—	18.00	25.00	60.00	80.00	110
1638/29	—	18.00	25.00	60.00	80.00	110
1638	—	18.00	25.00	60.00	80.00	110
1639	—	18.00	25.00	60.00	80.00	110
1640	—	18.00	25.00	60.00	80.00	110
1641	—	18.00	25.00	60.00	80.00	110
1642	—	18.00	25.00	60.00	80.00	110
1643	—	18.00	25.00	60.00	80.00	110
1644	—	18.00	25.00	60.00	80.00	110
1645	—	18.00	25.00	60.00	90.00	125
1646	—	18.00	25.00	60.00	80.00	110

KM# 36 48 STUIVERS (Lion Daalder)

Silver **Obv:** Armored knight looking left above lion shield **Rev:** Rampant lion left **Note:** Dav. #4850.

Date	Mintage	Good	VG	F	VF	XF
1646	—	18.00	25.00	60.00	80.00	150
1647	—	18.00	25.00	60.00	80.00	150
1648	—	18.00	25.00	60.00	80.00	150
1649	—	18.00	25.00	60.00	80.00	150
1652	—	18.00	25.00	60.00	80.00	150

KM# 15.3 48 STUIVERS (Lion Daalder)

Silver **Obv:** Armored knight looking right above lion shield **Rev:** Rampant lion left **Note:** Mint mark: Lily. Dav. # 4849.

Date	Mintage	Good	VG	F	VF	XF
1647/6	—	18.00	25.00	60.00	80.00	110
1647	—	18.00	25.00	60.00	80.00	110
1648/88	—	18.00	25.00	60.00	80.00	110
1648	—	18.00	25.00	60.00	80.00	110
1649	—	18.00	25.00	60.00	80.00	110
1651	—	18.00	25.00	60.00	80.00	110

KM# 15.4 48 STUIVERS (Lion Daalder)

Silver **Obv:** Armored knight looking right above lion shield **Rev:** Rampant lion left **Note:** Mint mark: Dog. Dav. # 4849.

Date	Mintage	Good	VG	F	VF	XF
1652	—	20.00	30.00	60.00	80.00	150
1653	—	20.00	30.00	60.00	80.00	150
1654	—	20.00	30.00	60.00	80.00	150
1655	—	20.00	30.00	60.00	80.00	150
1657	—	22.00	35.00	70.00	110	200
1658	—	30.00	65.00	90.00	200	350
1661	—	22.00	35.00	70.00	110	150
1662	—	22.00	25.00	60.00	80.00	150
1663	—	22.00	35.00	70.00	110	150
1666	—	22.00	35.00	70.00	110	200
1667	—	22.00	35.00	70.00	110	200
1668	—	22.00	35.00	70.00	110	150
1674	75,855	22.00	35.00	70.00	110	200
1675	Inc. above	22.00	35.00	70.00	110	150
1676	Inc. above	22.00	35.00	70.00	110	150
1680	Inc. above	30.00	65.00	90.00	200	350

KM# 15.5 48 STUIVERS (Lion Daalder)

Silver **Obv:** Armored knight looking right above lion shield **Rev:** Rampant lion left **Note:** Mint mark: Knight on horse. Dav. # 4849.

Date	Mintage	Good	VG	F	VF	XF
1694	—	20.00	30.00	60.00	100	200
1697	—	20.00	30.00	60.00	100	200
1699	—	30.00	60.00	125	250	400
1700/699	—	25.00	50.00	100	200	300

KM# 42 48 STUIVERS (Silver Ducat)

28.2500 g., 0.8730 Silver 0.7929 oz. ASW **Obv:** Knight standing holding sword and shield divides date **Obv. Legend:** MO.NO.AR.PRO.CON-FOE.BELG:D.GEL.C.Z. **Rev:** Crowned shield **Rev. Legend:** CONCORDIA:RES:PARVAE:CRESCVNT **Note:** Mint mark: Dog. Dav. #4890.

Date	Mintage	Good	VG	F	VF	XF
1659	Inc. above	28.00	60.00	100	200	350
1660	Inc. above	18.00	30.00	60.00	100	200
1661	Inc. above	18.00	30.00	60.00	100	200
1662	Inc. above	25.00	50.00	100	150	250
1663/0	Inc. above	25.00	50.00	100	150	250
1663/62	Inc. above	25.00	50.00	100	150	250
1663	Inc. above	18.00	30.00	60.00	100	200
1664	Inc. above	25.00	50.00	100	150	250
1674	Inc. above	25.00	50.00	100	150	250
1677	Inc. above	30.00	70.00	120	250	450
1680	Inc. above	30.00	70.00	120	250	450

KM# 63.1 48 STUIVERS (Silver Ducat)

Silver **Obv:** Knight standing right, crowned lion shield at feet **Rev:** Crowned arms divide date, without inner circle **Note:** Mint mark: Unicorn. Dav. #4891.

Date	Mintage	Good	VG	F	VF	XF
1693	—	35.00	80.00	175	250	350
1694	—	35.00	80.00	200	300	450

KM# 63.2 48 STUIVERS (Silver Ducat)

Silver **Obv:** Knight standing right, crowned lion shield at feet **Rev:** Crowned arms divide date, without inner circle **Note:** Mint mark: Knight horseback on reverse. Dav. #4891.

Date	Mintage	Good	VG	F	VF	XF
1695	—	35.00	80.00	200	300	450
1696	—	20.00	35.00	75.00	150	300
1698/6	—	35.00	80.00	200	300	450
1698	—	20.00	35.00	75.00	150	300
1699/8	—	35.00	80.00	200	300	450
1699	—	20.00	35.00	75.00	150	300
1700	—	20.00	35.00	75.00	150	300

KM# 70 48 STUIVERS (Silver Ducat)

Silver **Obv:** Knight standing right, crowned lion shield at feet **Rev:** Arms without crown divide date **Note:** Dav. #4891B.

Date	Mintage	Good	VG	F	VF	XF
1696	—	50.00	150	300	500	800

KM# 63.3 48 STUIVERS (Silver Ducat)

Silver **Obv:** Knight standing right, crowned lion shield at feeet. **Rev:** Crowned arms divide date, without inner circle **Note:** Without knight horseback mint mark. Dav. #4891

Date	Mintage	Good	VG	F	VF	XF
1699	—	35.00	80.00	200	300	450

KM# 63.4 48 STUIVERS (Silver Ducat)

Obv: Knight standing right, crowned lion shield at feet **Rev:** Crowned arms divide date, without inner circle **Note:** Mint mark: Knight horseback on obverse. Dav. #4891

Date	Mintage	Good	VG	F	VF	XF
1699	—	35.00	80.00	200	300	450

KM# 63.5 48 STUIVERS (Silver Ducat)

Silver **Obv:** Knight standing right, crowned arms at feet **Rev:** Crowned arms divide date, without inner circle **Note:** Mint mark: Knight horseback on obverse and reverse. Dav. #4891.

Date	Mintage	Good	VG	F	VF	XF
1699	—	35.00	80.00	200	300	450

KM# 56.1 60 STUIVERS (3 Gulden)

31.8200 g., 0.9200 Silver 0.9412 oz. ASW **Obv:** Crowned provincial arms divide value 3-G date above crown **Rev:** Standing female figure leaning on Bible on column, holding spear with Liberty cap **Note:** Mint mark: Dog. Dav. #4948.

Date	Mintage	Good	VG	F	VF	XF
1682	—	40.00	125	350	600	900
1687	—	45.00	135	400	700	1,000

KM# 56.2 60 STUIVERS (3 Gulden)

31.8200 g., 0.9290 Silver 0.9504 oz. ASW **Obv:** Crowned provincial arms divide value 3-G date above crown **Rev:** Standing female figure leaning on Bible on column, holding spear with Liberty cap **Note:** Mint mark. Unicorn. Dav. #4948.

Date	Mintage	Good	VG	F	VF	XF
1694	Inc. above	40.00	125	350	600	900

KM# 68.1 60 STUIVERS (3 Gulden)

Silver **Obv:** Crowned lion arms divide value: 3 - GL **Rev:** Standing female figure leaning on Bible column holding spear with Liberty cap, date in exurgue **Note:** Mint mark: Unicorn. Dav. #4949.

Date	Mintage	Good	VG	F	VF	XF
1694	—	30.00	75.00	200	300	450

KM# 68.2 60 STUIVERS (3 Gulden)

Silver **Obv:** Crowned lion arms divide value: 3 - GL **Rev:** Standing female figure leaning on Bible column holdimg spear with Liberty cap, date in exergue **Note:** Mint mark: Knight horseback. Dav. #4949.

Date	Mintage	Good	VG	F	VF	XF
1696	—	28.00	60.00	150	250	400
1697	—	28.00	60.00	150	250	400

KM# 64 1/2 GULDEN (10 Stuivers)

5.3000 g., 0.9290 Silver 0.1583 oz. ASW **Obv:** Crowned lion shield divides value **Rev:** Standing female figure leaning on Bible on column, holding spear with Liberty cap, date in exergue **Note:** Mint mark: Unicorn.

Date	Mintage	Good	VG	F	VF	XF
1694	44,040	10.00	30.00	80.00	150	250

KM# 33 DOUBLE 3 GULDEN

Silver **Obv:** Crowned double lion arms, date above **Rev:** Standing female figure leaning on Bible column holding spear with Liberty cap. **Note:** Dav. #A4948.

Date	Mintage	Good	VG	F	VF	XF
1682 Rare	—	—	—	—	—	—

KM# 41 DUCATON (Silver Rider)

32.7800 g., 0.9410 Silver 0.9917 oz. ASW **Obv:** Knight with sword on horseback right, provincial arms below in inner circle **Rev:** Crowned arms with crowned lion supporters in inner circle, date divided in legend at top **Note:** Mint mark: Dog. Dav. #4923.

Date	Mintage	Good	VG	F	VF	XF
1659	—	25.00	70.00	200	260	400
1660	—	22.00	40.00	80.00	125	250
1661	—	22.00	40.00	80.00	125	250
1662/1	—	22.00	40.00	80.00	125	250
1662	—	25.00	70.00	200	260	400
1663	—	22.00	40.00	80.00	125	250
1664	—	22.00	40.00	80.00	125	250
1666	—	22.00	40.00	80.00	125	250
1667	—	22.00	40.00	80.00	125	250
1668	—	22.00	40.00	80.00	125	250
1669	—	22.00	40.00	80.00	125	250
1670	—	22.00	40.00	80.00	125	250
1671	—	22.00	40.00	80.00	125	250
1672	—	22.00	40.00	80.00	125	250
1674	—	22.00	40.00	80.00	125	250
1676	—	22.00	40.00	80.00	125	250
1677	—	22.00	40.00	80.00	125	250

KM# 99.1 2 DUCATON

Silver **Obv:** Inner circles **Rev:** Inner circles, date above crowned arms **Note:** Dav. #4922.

Date	Mintage	Good	VG	F	VF	XF
1660 Rare	—	—	—	—	—	—
1662 Rare	—	—	—	—	—	—
1670 Rare	—	—	—	—	—	—
1676 Rare	—	—	—	—	—	—
1680 Rare	—	—	—	—	—	—

KM# 99.2 2 DUCATON

Silver **Obv:** Narrow horse and rider **Rev:** Empty cartouche below crowned arms **Note:** Dav. #A4924.

Date	Mintage	Good	VG	F	VF	XF
1680 Rare	—	—	—	—	—	—

KM# 31 3 DUCATON

Silver **Obv:** Inner circles **Rev:** Inner circles, date above crowned arms **Note:** Dav. #A4922.

Date	Mintage	Good	VG	F	VF	XF
1680 Rare	—	—	—	—	—	—

KM# 28 2 SILVER DUCAT

Silver **Note:** Similar to 1 Silver Ducat, KM#27. Dav. #4889.

Date	Mintage	Good	VG	F	VF	XF
1659 Rare	—	—	—	—	—	—

KM# 29 2 SILVER DUCAT

Silver **Note:** Klippe, similar to 1 Silver Ducat, KM#27. Dav. #4889.

Date	Mintage	Good	VG	F	VF	XF
1660 Rare	—	—	—	—	—	—

KM# 21 RIJKSDAALDER

Silver **Obv:** Armored half bust William the Silent right, with sword, date **Obv. Legend:** VIEILATE. DEO. CON - FIDENTES **Rev:** Helmeted small arms **Rev. Legend:** MO. NO. ARG. GELRIAE. CO ZVT **Note:** Dav. #4821.

Date	Mintage	Good	VG	F	VF	XF
1601	—	80.00	200	400	750	1,200
1604 Rare	—	—	—	—	—	—

KM# 24 2 DUTCH RIJKSDAALDER

Silver **Obv:** Half-figure with sword holding small arms **Obv. Legend:** MO. ARG. PRO. CONFOE. BE1. GEL(R) **Rev:** Crowned arms divide date **Rev. Legend:** CONCORDIA. RES. PARVAE. CRESCVNT **Note:** Klippe. Dav. #4827.

Date	Mintage	Good	VG	F	VF	XF
1608	—	—	—	—	—	—
1612	—	—	—	—	—	—
1615 Rare	—	—	—	—	—	—

KM# 23 2 DUTCH RIJKSDAALDER

Silver **Obv:** Half-figure with sword holding small arms **Obv. Legend:** MO. ARG. PRO. CONFOE. BE1. GEL(R) **Rev:** Crowned arms divide date **Rev. Legend:** CONCORDIA. RES. PARVAE. CRESCVNT **Note:** Dav. #4827.

Date	Mintage	Good	VG	F	VF	XF
1618 Rare	—	—	—	—	—	—

KM# 11 1/2 ROSE NOBLE

3.9000 g., Gold **Obv:** Ruler in ship in inner circle **Rev:** Floriated cross with crowned lions in angles **Note:** Fr. #231.

Date	Mintage	VG	F	VF	XF	Unc
ND(1602)	50,361	300	750	1,000	1,250	—

KM# 17 1/2 CAVALIER D'OR

5.0000 g., 0.9200 Gold 0.1479 oz. AGW **Obv:** Equestrian figure of knight above arms **Rev:** Crowned arms in inner circle, date at top **Note:** Fr. #241.

Date	Mintage	VG	F	VF	XF	Unc
1606	—	250	600	1,300	1,700	—
1607	—	250	600	1,300	1,700	—
1608	—	250	600	1,000	1,400	—
1613	—	250	600	1,000	1,400	—
1614/04	—	250	600	1,000	1,400	—
1614	—	250	600	1,000	1,400	—
1615	—	250	600	1,000	1,400	—
1616	—	250	600	1,000	1,400	—
1617	—	250	600	1,000	1,400	—
1618	—	250	600	1,300	1,700	—
1619	—	250	600	1,000	1,400	—
1620	—	250	600	1,000	1,400	—
1621	—	250	600	1,000	1,400	—
1622	—	250	600	1,000	1,400	—
1623	—	250	600	1,000	1,400	—
1624	—	250	600	1,000	1,400	—
1625	—	250	600	1,000	1,400	—
1641	—	250	600	1,000	1,400	—
1644	—	250	600	1,000	1,400	—

KM# 18 CAVALIER D'OR

10.0000 g., 0.9200 Gold 0.2958 oz. AGW **Obv:** Equestrian figure of knight above arms in inner circle **Rev:** Crowned arms in inner circle, date at top **Note:** Fr. #240.

Date	Mintage	VG	F	VF	XF	Unc
1606	—	320	650	1,150	2,000	—
1607	—	320	650	1,150	2,000	—
1608	—	320	650	1,150	2,000	—
1613	—	320	650	1,150	2,000	—
1614	—	1,500	2,500	3,500	4,000	—
1615	—	320	650	1,150	2,000	—
1616	—	320	650	1,150	2,000	—
1617	—	320	650	1,150	2,000	—
1618	—	320	650	1,150	2,000	—
1619/4	—	320	650	1,150	2,000	—
1619/15	—	320	650	1,150	2,000	—
1619/6	—	320	650	1,150	2,000	—
1619	—	320	650	1,150	2,000	—
1620	—	320	650	1,150	2,000	—
1621	—	320	650	1,150	2,000	—
1623	—	320	650	1,150	2,000	—
1625	—	320	650	1,150	2,000	—
1627	—	320	650	1,150	2,000	—
1628	—	320	650	1,150	2,000	—

TRADE COINAGE

KM# 5 DUCAT

3.4900 g., 0.9860 Gold 0.1106 oz. AGW **Obv:** Armored knight standing right holding sword on shoulder and bundle of arrows **Obv. Legend:** CONCORDIA RES. PAR. CRES. D. G. 8C C. Z. **Rev:** Ornate tablet with inscription **Note:** Fr. #237.

Date	Mintage	VG	F	VF	XF	Unc
1600	—	150	300	600	1,000	—
1602/0	—	120	175	250	350	—
1602	—	120	175	250	350	—
1603/2	—	120	175	250	350	—
1603	—	120	175	250	350	—
1606	—	120	175	250	350	—
1607	—	120	175	250	350	—
1608	—	120	150	200	300	—
1609	—	120	150	200	300	—
1610	—	120	175	250	350	—
1611	—	120	150	200	300	—
1612	—	120	150	200	300	—
1613	—	120	150	200	300	—
1614/3	—	120	200	350	450	—
1617	—	120	150	200	300	—
1618	—	120	150	200	300	—
1619	—	120	150	200	300	—
1622	—	120	200	350	450	—
1628/23	—	120	200	350	450	—
1628	—	120	150	200	300	—
1629	—	120	150	200	300	—
1631/29	—	120	150	200	300	—
1631/23	—	120	150	200	300	—
1631	—	120	150	200	300	—
1632	—	120	150	200	300	—
1633	—	120	150	200	300	—
1634	—	120	150	200	300	—
1635	—	120	150	200	300	—
1636	—	120	150	200	300	—
1637	—	120	150	200	300	—
163-8	—	125	200	300	400	—
1638	—	120	150	200	300	—
1639	—	120	150	200	300	—
1640	—	120	150	200	300	—
1641	—	120	150	200	300	—
1642	—	120	150	200	300	—
1643	—	120	150	200	300	—
1644	—	120	150	200	300	—
1645	—	120	150	200	300	—
1646	—	120	150	200	300	—
1647	—	120	150	200	300	—
1648	—	120	150	200	300	—
1649	—	120	150	200	300	—
1650	—	120	150	200	300	—
1651	—	120	150	200	300	—
1652	—	120	150	200	300	—

Date	Mintage	VG	F	VF	XF	Unc
1653	—	120	150	200	300	—
1654	—	120	150	200	300	—
1655	—	120	150	200	300	—
1656	—	120	150	200	300	—
1657	—	120	150	200	300	—
1658	—	120	150	200	300	—
1659	—	120	150	200	300	—
1660	—	120	150	200	300	—
1661	—	120	150	200	300	—
1662	—	120	150	200	300	—
1663	—	120	150	200	300	—
1664	—	120	200	350	450	—
1665	—	150	275	575	850	—
1666	—	120	200	350	450	—
1667	—	120	200	350	450	—
1686	—	120	200	350	450	—

KM# 40 2 DUCAT
6.9800 g., 0.9860 Gold 0.2213 oz. AGW **Obv:** Knight standing right divides date in inner circle **Rev:** Legend in ornamental tablet **Note:** Fr. #235.

Date	Mintage	VG	F	VF	XF	Unc
1656	—	250	500	800	1,250	—
1658	—	250	500	800	1,250	—
1659	—	250	500	800	1,250	—
1661	—	250	500	800	1,250	—
1662	—	250	500	800	1,250	—
1664	—	250	500	800	1,250	—

PATTERNS

Including off metal strikes

KM#	Date	Mintage	Identification	Mkt Val
Pn5	1646	—	2 Stuivers. Gold. 7.0000 g. Klippe. KM#26.2.	—
Pn6	1681	—	48 Stuivers. Gold. 20.7000 g. KM#15.4.	—
Pn7	1687	—	48 Stuivers. Gold. 20.7000 g. KM#15.4.	—
Pn8	1696	—	40 Stuivers. Gold. 21.5000 g. KM#69.	—

PIEFORTS

KM#	Date	Mintage	Identification	Mkt Val
P1	ND(1601)	—	Rose Noble. Gold.	—
	ND(1601)	—	Rose Noble. Gold.	—
P2	1608	—	48 Stuivers. Silver. 43.0000 g. KM#16.1.	—
P3	1612	—	48 Stuivers. Silver. Klippe, KM16.1	—
P4	1615	—	48 Stuivers. Silver. Klippe, KM16.1.	—
P5	1633	—	48 Stuivers. Silver. KM15.1	1,700
P6	1643	—	Ducat. 0.9860 Gold. 13.9990 g. KM#5, Klippe. Quadruple weight.	—
P7	1659	—	48 Stuivers. Silver. KM#42.	1,700
P8	1660	—	48 Stuivers. Silver. KM#42, Klippe.	—
P9	1660	—	40 Stuivers. Silver. KM41.	—
P10	1662	—	40 Stuivers. Silver. KM41.	—
P11	1662	—	40 Stuivers. Silver. Klippe, KM41.	—
P12	1670	—	40 Stuivers. Silver. KM41.	—
P13	1672	—	40 Stuivers. Silver. Klippe, KM41.	—
P14	1676	—	40 Stuivers. Silver. KM41.	—
P15	1680	—	40 Stuivers. Silver. KM50.	—
P16	1680	—	40 Stuivers. Silver. Triple weight, KM50.	—
P17	1680	—	48 Stuivers. Silver. KM15.4.	—
P18	1682	—	60 Stuivers. Silver. KM56.1.	—

GRONINGEN AND OMMELAND

The province of Groningen is located in northern Netherlands and is drained by numerous rivers and canals.

The early history of Groningen is chiefly one of conflict between the city and the surrounding districts known as the Ommelanden. The city remained loyal to the Spanish king while the surrounding area supported the revolt against Spain. After 1594 Groningen and Ommelanden were united into one republic but it was not until 1795 that they were merged into one province.

The Groningen Mint was closed in 1692. The following coins were struck at the Harderwyk Mint of Gelderland.

CITY

STANDARD COINAGE

KM# 12 DUIT (Plak)
Billon **Obv:** Arms in inner circle, date in legend **Rev:** Double-headed eagle with arms on breast in inner circle

Date	Mintage	Good	VG	F	VF	XF
1609	—	6.00	20.00	50.00	80.00	125
1615	—	6.00	20.00	50.00	80.00	125
1622	—	6.00	20.00	50.00	80.00	125
1623	—	6.00	20.00	50.00	80.00	125

KM# 45 DUIT (Plak)
Copper **Obv:** Crowned arms with lion supporters, date at top **Rev:** CIV/GRONIN/GA in cartouche

Date	Mintage	Good	VG	F	VF	XF
1690	320,000	6.00	20.00	60.00	120	250

KM# 46 DUIT (Plak)
Copper **Obv:** Crowned arms with lion supporters, date at top **Rev:** GRO/NINGA in cartouche

Date	Mintage	Good	VG	F	VF	XF
1690	Inc. above	6.00	20.00	60.00	120	250

KM# 8 2 PLAK
1.1700 g., Billon **Obv:** Arms on long cross in inner circle, date in legend **Rev:** Double-headed eagle with arms on breast in inner circle **Note:** 0.083 silver.

Date	Mintage	Good	VG	F	VF	XF
1602	—	10.00	30.00	75.00	135	250
1609	—	10.00	30.00	75.00	135	250
1612	—	10.00	30.00	75.00	135	250
1614	—	16.00	50.00	100	200	350
1615	—	10.00	30.00	75.00	135	250
1617	—	10.00	30.00	75.00	135	250
1622	—	10.00	30.00	75.00	135	250
1625	—	10.00	30.00	75.00	135	250
1626	—	10.00	30.00	75.00	135	250
1628	—	10.00	30.00	75.00	135	250
1635	—	10.00	30.00	75.00	135	250
1649	—	10.00	30.00	75.00	135	250

KM# 10 1/2 STUIVER (4 Plakken)
1.1700 g., 0.1770 Silver 0.0067 oz. ASW **Obv:** Crowned arms divide value in inner circle **Rev:** Ornamental long cross with S-P-Q-G in angles

Date	Mintage	Good	VG	F	VF	XF
1604	—	10.00	30.00	75.00	150	250
1609	—	10.00	30.00	75.00	150	250
1613	—	10.00	30.00	75.00	150	250
1614	—	10.00	30.00	75.00	150	250
1615	—	10.00	30.00	75.00	150	250
1616	—	10.00	30.00	75.00	150	250
1617	—	10.00	30.00	75.00	150	250
1620	—	10.00	30.00	75.00	150	250
1625	—	10.00	30.00	75.00	150	250
1626	—	10.00	30.00	75.00	150	250
1628	—	10.00	30.00	75.00	150	250
1635	—	10.00	30.00	75.00	150	250
1649	—	10.00	30.00	75.00	150	250

KM# 14 1/2 STUIVER (4 Plakken)
0.1770 Silver **Obv:** Crowned arms divide value in inner circle **Rev:** Ornamental long cross with S-P-Q-G in angles **Note:** Klippe of KM #10.

Date	Mintage	Good	VG	F	VF	XF
1613	—	—	—	—	—	750
1626	—	—	—	—	—	—

KM# 47 STUIVER
0.8100 g., 0.5830 Silver 0.0152 oz. ASW **Obv:** Crowned arms divide value, date above crown **Rev:** Inscription **Rev. Inscription:** CIV / GRONIN / GA

Date	Mintage	Good	VG	F	VF	XF
1690	—	6.00	20.00	40.00	70.00	100
1691	—	10.00	30.00	60.00	150	250

KM# 47a STUIVER
Gold **Obv:** Crowned arms divide value, date above crown **Rev:** Inscription **Rev. Inscription:** CIV / GRONIN / GA

Date	Mintage	Good	VG	F	VF	XF
1690	—	—	—	—	—	700

KM# 5.1 STUIVER (8 Plakken)
1.9200 g., 0.2430 Silver 0.0150 oz. ASW **Obv:** Double-headed eagle with arms on breast in inner circle **Rev:** Ornamental long cross with I-S-B-R in angles, date in legend **Note:** Mint mark: Quatrefoil.

Date	Mintage	Good	VG	F	VF	XF
1601	—	10.00	30.00	75.00	100	150
1602	—	10.00	30.00	75.00	150	250
1604	—	10.00	30.00	75.00	150	250
1605	—	10.00	30.00	75.00	150	250
1609	—	10.00	30.00	75.00	150	250
1613	—	10.00	30.00	75.00	150	250
1615	—	10.00	30.00	75.00	150	250
1622	—	10.00	30.00	75.00	150	250
1625	—	10.00	30.00	75.00	150	250
1627	—	10.00	30.00	75.00	150	250

KM# A16.1 STUIVER (8 Plakken)
Billon **Obv:** Double headed eagle with arms on breast in inner circle **Rev:** Ornamental long cross with I-S-B-R in angles, date in legend **Note:** Mint mark: Quatrefoil. Klippe of KM#5.1.

Date	Mintage	VG	F	VF	XF	Unc
1613	—	—	—	—	—	1,000
1622	—	—	—	—	—	1,000

KM# A16.2 STUIVER (8 Plakken)
0.2430 Silver **Obv:** Double headed eagle with arms on breast in inner circle **Rev:** Ornamental long cross with I-S-B-R in angles, date in legend **Note:** Mint mark: Double eagle. Klippe of KM #5.2.

Date	Mintage	VG	F	VF	XF	Unc
1635	—	—	—	—	—	1,000

KM# 5.2 STUIVER (8 Plakken)
Billon **Obv:** Double-headed eagle with arms on breast in inner circle **Rev:** Ornamental long cross with I-S-B-R in angles, date in legend **Note:** Mint mark: Double eagle.

Date	Mintage	Good	VG	F	VF	XF
1628	—	10.00	30.00	75.00	150	250
1630	—	10.00	30.00	75.00	150	250
1635	—	10.00	30.00	75.00	150	250

KM# 1 JAGER (2 STUIVERS)
1.9200 g., 0.4930 Silver 0.0304 oz. ASW **Obv:** Double headed eagle with arms on breast in inner circle **Obv. Legend:** *MONETA • NOVA • GRONINGENSIS • **Rev:** Ornate cross with arms at center **Rev. Legend:** DOMI - NI • BENE - DICTVM •

Date	Mintage	Good	VG	F	VF	XF
1601	—	—	—	—	—	—

KM# 11.1 JAGER (2 STUIVERS)
1.9200 g., 0.4930 Silver 0.0304 oz. ASW **Obv:** Shield of arms in inner circle, date in legend **Rev:** Ornamental long cross in inner circle **Note:** Mint mark: Quatrefoil.

Date	Mintage	Good	VG	F	VF	XF
1604	—	16.00	50.00	150	225	300
1605	—	16.00	50.00	150	225	300
1606	—	16.00	50.00	150	225	300
1622	—	16.00	50.00	150	225	300

KM# 11.2 JAGER (2 STUIVERS)
1.9200 g., 0.4930 Silver 0.0304 oz. ASW **Obv:** Shield of arms in inner circle, date in legend **Rev:** Ornamental long cross in inner circle **Note:** Mint mark: Double Eagle.

Date	Mintage	Good	VG	F	VF	XF
1627	—	16.00	50.00	150	225	300

KM# 20 JAGER (2 STUIVERS)
Silver **Obv:** Crowned arms divide value **Rev:** Ornamental long cross in inner circle, date in legend

Date	Mintage	Good	VG	F	VF	XF
1635	—	16.00	50.00	150	225	300

KM# 13 4 STUIVERS (Flabbe)
Silver

Date	Mintage	Good	VG	F	VF	XF
1604	—	12.00	35.00	85.00	150	200

KM# 15.1 4 STUIVERS (Flabbe)
Silver **Note:** Mint mark: Quatrefoil. Similar to KM#16 but not Klippe.

Date	Mintage	Good	VG	F	VF	XF
1620	—	10.00	30.00	60.00	120	200
1622	—	10.00	30.00	60.00	120	200

KM# 16 4 STUIVERS (Flabbe)
3.8400 g., 0.4930 Silver 0.0609 oz. ASW **Obv:** Arms with imperial eagle **Rev:** Ornate cross with small shield in center **Note:** Klippe.

Date	Mintage	Good	VG	F	VF	XF
1622	—	100	250	600	1,000	1,500
1623	—	100	250	600	1,000	1,500
1626	—	100	250	600	1,000	1,500
1635	—	100	250	600	1,000	1,500
1653	—	100	250	600	1,000	1,500

KM# 15.2 4 STUIVERS (Flabbe)

Silver **Note:** Mint mark: Double Eagle. Similar to KM#16 but not Klippe.

Date	Mintage	Good	VG	F	VF	XF
1623	—	10.00	30.00	60.00	120	200
1625	—	10.00	30.00	60.00	120	200
1626	—	10.00	30.00	60.00	120	200
1627	—	10.00	30.00	60.00	120	200
1631	—	10.00	30.00	60.00	120	200
1635	—	10.00	30.00	60.00	120	200
1649	—	10.00	30.00	60.00	120	200

KM# 48 6 STUIVER (RYDER SCHELLING)

4.9500 g., 0.5830 Silver 0.0928 oz. ASW **Obv:** Crowned arms divide value, date above crown **Rev:** Knight with sword on horseback to right **Note:** Mint mark: Siren.

Date	Mintage	Good	VG	F	VF	XF
1690	—	3.00	10.00	30.00	50.00	90.00
1691	—	3.00	10.00	30.00	50.00	90.00
1692	—	3.00	10.00	30.00	50.00	90.00
1696	—	3.00	10.00	30.00	50.00	90.00

KM# 17 8 STUIVERS (2 Flabbe)

7.6770 g., 0.4930 Silver 0.1217 oz. ASW **Obv:** Standing figure of St. Martin divides value in inner circle, date in legend **Rev:** Double-headed eagle with arms on breast in inner circle **Note:** Mint mark: Double Eagle.

Date	Mintage	Good	VG	F	VF	XF
1626	—	16.00	50.00	100	200	300
1627	—	8.00	25.00	50.00	100	200

KM# 18 8 STUIVERS (2 Flabbe)

Silver **Obv:** Standing figure of St. Martin divides value in inner circle **Rev:** Double headed eagle with arms on breast in inner circle **Note:** Klippe.

Date	Mintage	Good	VG	F	VF	XF
1627 Rare	—	—	—	—	—	—

KM# 50 28 STUIVERS (Florin)

Silver **Obv. Legend:** MO. NO. ARG. CIV. GRONINGAE

Date	Mintage	Good	VG	F	VF	XF
1690	—	32.00	100	200	400	800

KM# 49 28 STUIVERS (Florin)

19.5000 g., 0.6730 Silver 0.4219 oz. ASW **Obv:** Crowned arms in innr circle, date above crown **Obv. Legend:** FLOR. ARG. CIV. GRONINGAE **Rev:** Crowned double-headed eagle in inner circle **Note:** Mint mark: Siren.

Date	Mintage	Good	VG	F	VF	XF
1690	—	16.00	50.00	125	200	300
1691	—	16.00	50.00	125	200	300
1692	—	16.00	50.00	125	200	300
1962 Error 1692	—	32.00	100	300	450	600

KM# 9 1/2 RYKSDAALDER

14.5100 g., 0.8850 Silver 0.4128 oz. ASW **Note:** Similar to 1 Rijksdaalder KM#7 but not Klippe.

Date	Mintage	Good	VG	F	VF	XF
1602	—	—	—	—	—	—

KM# 7 RYKSDAALDER (48 Stuivers)

35.0000 g., 0.8850 Silver 0.9958 oz. ASW **Obv:** St. John standing facing holding Pascal lamb **Obv. Legend:** MONE: NOVA: ARG GRONINGENSIS **Rev:** Imperial eagle **Rev. Legend:** RVDOL • II • ROMANO: IMPE: SEMPER • AVGV **Note:** Klippe. Dav. #4979A. Illustration reduced.

Date	Mintage	Good	VG	F	VF	XF
1601	—	—	—	—	2,750	4,000
160Z	—	—	—	—	—	3,000

KM# 6 RYKSDAALDER (48 Stuivers)

29.1000 g., Silver **Obv:** St. John standing facing holding Pascal lamb **Obv. Legend:** MONE: NOVA: ARG GRONINGENSIS **Rev:** Imperial eagle **Rev. Legend:** RVDOL • II • ROMANO: IMPE: SEMPER • AVGV **Note:** Similar to KM#7 but not Klippe. Dav. #4979.

Date	Mintage	Good	VG	F	VF	XF
1601	—	160	400	1,000	2,000	3,000
160Z	—	160	400	1,000	2,000	3,000

SIEGE COINAGE

KM# 24 6-1/4 STUIVERS

Silver **Obv:** Crowned arms **Obv. Legend:** IVRE ET TEMPORE **Note:** Uniface, Diamond Klippe.

Date	Mintage	Good	VG	F	VF	XF
1672	—	8.00	25.00	60.00	125	200

KM# 25 12-1/2 STUIVERS

Silver **Obv:** Crowned arms **Obv. Legend:** IVRE ET TEMPORE **Note:** Uniface. Diamond Klippe.

Date	Mintage	Good	VG	F	VF	XF
1672	—	12.00	35.00	70.00	150	300

KM# 26 25 STUIVERS

Silver **Obv:** Crowned arms **Obv. Legend:** IVRE ET TEMPORE **Note:** Uniface, Diamond Klippe.

Date	Mintage	Good	VG	F	VF	XF
1672	—	16.00	50.00	100	200	400

KM# 27.1 50 STUIVERS

Silver **Obv:** Crowned arms **Obv. Legend:** IVRE ET TEMPORE **Note:** Uniface, Klippe, large arms.

Date	Mintage	Good	VG	F	VF	XF
1672	—	25.00	75.00	150	300	500

KM# 27.2 50 STUIVERS

Silver **Obv:** Crowned arms **Obv. Legend:** IVRE ET TEMPORE **Note:** Uniface, Klippe, small arms

Date	Mintage	Good	VG	F	VF	XF
1672	—	20.00	60.00	120	250	400

PROVINCE

STANDARD COINAGE

KM# 28 DUIT

Copper **Obv:** Crowned arms in inner circle **Rev. Inscription:** GRON/ ET OML / (date)

Date	Mintage	Good	VG	F	VF	XF
1673	—	6.00	20.00	60.00	100	150
1674	—	3.00	10.00	30.00	50.00	80.00
1675	—	3.00	10.00	30.00	50.00	80.00
1676	—	3.00	10.00	30.00	50.00	80.00

KM# 28a DUIT

3.8000 g., Gold **Obv:** Crowned arms in inner circle **Rev. Inscription:** GRON / ET OML / (date)

Date	Mintage	Good	VG	F	VF	XF
1674	—	—	—	—	1,200	2,000
1675	—	—	—	—	1,200	2,000
1677	—	—	—	—	1,200	2,000

KM# 35 DUIT

Copper **Obv:** Crowned arms without inner circle **Rev. Inscription:** GRON / ET OML / (date)

Date	Mintage	Good	VG	F	VF	XF
1681	—	3.00	10.00	30.00	60.00	75.00
1682	—	2.00	6.00	20.00	30.00	45.00
1684	—	2.00	6.00	20.00	30.00	45.00
1685/4	—	—	—	—	—	—
1685	—	2.00	6.00	20.00	30.00	45.00
1692	—	2.00	6.00	20.00	30.00	45.00

KM# 36 STUIVER

0.8100 g., 0.5830 Billon 0.0152 oz. **Obv:** Crowned arms divide value **Rev. Inscription:** GRON / ET OML / (date)

Date	Mintage	Good	VG	F	VF	XF
1681	—	3.00	10.00	25.00	50.00	100
1682	—	6.00	20.00	40.00	80.00	150
1683	—	3.00	10.00	25.00	50.00	100
1684	—	3.00	10.00	25.00	50.00	100

KM# 39 1/2 STUIVER

0.4100 g., 0.5830 Billon 0.0077 oz. **Obv:** Crowned arms **Rev. Inscription:** 1/2 / STUVER / 1682

Date	Mintage	Good	VG	F	VF	XF
1682	—	13.00	40.00	80.00	150	400

KM# 29 6 STUIVER (RYDER SCHELLING)

4.9500 g., 0.5830 Silver 0.0928 oz. ASW **Obv:** Crowned arms divide value **Rev:** Knight with sword on horseback right, date in legend

Date	Mintage	Good	VG	F	VF	XF
1673	—	8.00	25.00	40.00	75.00	150
1674	—	5.00	15.00	25.00	50.00	100
1677	—	12.00	32.00	65.00	100	250

KM# 30 6 STUIVER (RYDER SCHELLING)

Silver **Obv:** Crowned arms without value **Rev:** Knight with sword horseback right, date in legend

Date	Mintage	Good	VG	F	VF	XF
1673	—	—	—	—	—	—

KM# 37.1 6 STUIVER (RYDER SCHELLING)

Silver **Obv:** Crowned arms divide value 6 - S, date above crown **Rev:** Knight with sword on horseback right **Note:** Mint mark: Rose.

Date	Mintage	Good	VG	F	VF	XF
1681	—	5.00	15.00	35.00	70.00	100
1682	—	5.00	15.00	35.00	70.00	100
1683	—	5.00	15.00	35.00	70.00	100
1684	—	5.00	15.00	35.00	70.00	100
1685	—	5.00	15.00	35.00	70.00	100
1686	—	5.00	15.00	35.00	70.00	100
1687	—	5.00	15.00	35.00	70.00	100

KM# 37.3 6 STUIVER (RYDER SCHELLING)

Silver **Obv:** Crowned arms divide value S - 6, date above **Rev:** Knight with sword horseback right **Note:** Mint mark: Dog.

Date	Mintage	Good	VG	F	VF	XF
1691	—	6.00	20.00	40.00	80.00	150

KM# A38 6 STUIVER (RYDER SCHELLING)

Silver **Obv:** Crowned arms divide value 6 - S, date above **Rev:** Knight with sword horseback right **Note:** Mint mark: Dog. Klippe.

Date	Mintage	Good	VG	F	VF	XF
1691	—	—	—	—	—	550

KM# 37.2 6 STUIVERS (Schelling)
Silver **Obv:** Crowned arms divide value 6 - S, date above **Rev:** Knight with sword on horseback right **Note:** Mint mark: Dog. Varieties exist.

Date	Mintage	Good	VG	F	VF	XF
1691	—	6.00	20.00	40.00	80.00	150
1692	—	6.00	20.00	40.00	80.00	150

KM# 31.1 28 STUIVERS (Florin)
19.5000 g., 0.6730 Silver 0.4219 oz. ASW **Obv:** Crowned arms in divide value 28 - ST in inner circle **Rev:** Large 1/2-figure of man wearing hat with sword on shoulder right divides date in inner circle

Date	Mintage	Good	VG	F	VF	XF
1673	—	16.00	50.00	125	250	350
1674	—	16.00	50.00	125	250	350
1675	—	16.00	50.00	125	250	350
1676	—	32.00	100	250	350	450
1677	—	32.00	100	200	300	400

KM# 31.2 28 STUIVERS (Florin)
19.5000 g., 0.6730 Silver 0.4219 oz. ASW **Obv:** Crowned arms divide value 28 - ST without inner circle **Rev:** Large 1/2 length figure of man wearing hat with sword on shoulder right divides date in inner circle

Date	Mintage	Good	VG	F	VF	XF
1673	—	16.00	50.00	125	250	350

KM# 32.1 28 STUIVERS (Florin)
19.5000 g., 0.6730 Silver 0.4219 oz. ASW **Obv:** Crowned arms with double headed eagle shields in 1st and 3rd quadrants divides value 28 - ST within legend **Rev:** Large 1/2-figure of man wearing hat with sword on shoulder right divides date **Note:** Prev. KM #38.

Date	Mintage	Good	VG	F	VF	XF
1674	—	26.00	80.00	200	350	500

KM# 32.2 28 STUIVERS (Florin)
19.5000 g., 0.6730 Silver 0.4219 oz. ASW **Obv:** Crowned arms with double headed eagle in 2nd and 4th quadrants divides value 28 - ST within legend **Rev:** Large 1/2-length figure of man wearing hat with sword on shoulder right divides date

Date	Mintage	Good	VG	F	VF	XF
1674	—	26.00	80.00	200	350	500

KM# 38 28 STUIVERS (Florin)
17.3000 g., 0.7650 Silver 0.4255 oz. ASW **Obv:** Crowned arms divide value 28 - ST **Rev:** Clasped hands holding two poles with hat and symbol in rays

Date	Mintage	Good	VG	F	VF	XF
1681	—	20.00	60.00	125	250	500

KM# 42 28 STUIVERS (Florin)
19.5000 g., 0.6730 Silver 0.4219 oz. ASW **Obv:** Crowned arms divide value 28 - ST **Rev:** Small 1/2-figure of man wearing hat with plumes with sword on shoulderright **Note:** Mint mark: Rose.

Date	Mintage	Good	VG	F	VF	XF
1685	—	32.00	100	250	400	600
1686	—	26.00	80.00	200	300	450

KM# 51 28 STUIVERS (Florin)
19.5000 g., 0.6730 Silver 0.4219 oz. ASW **Obv:** Crowned arms divide value 28 - ST **Rev:** Small 1/2 figure of man wearing hat with plumes with sword on shoulder right **Note:** Mint mark: Dog.

Date	Mintage	Good	VG	F	VF	XF
1691	—	100	300	650	1,250	2,500
1692	—	16.00	50.00	125	275	500

KM# 52 28 STUIVERS (Florin)
Silver **Obv:** Crowned arms divide value 28 - ST, date above **Rev:** Double headed eagle with arms on breast

Date	Mintage	Good	VG	F	VF	XF
1692	—	16.00	50.00	75.00	150	250

KM# 40 DUCATON (Silver Rider)
32.7800 g., 0.9410 Silver 0.9917 oz. ASW **Obv:** Crowned arms with crowned lion supporters, date in cartouche below **Rev:** Knight with sword on horseback right

Date	Mintage	Good	VG	F	VF	XF
1682	—	80.00	250	600	1,000	1,500
1683	—	—	—	—	—	—

KM# 40a DUCATON (Silver Rider)
37.1700 g., Gold **Obv:** Crowned arms with crowned lion supporters, date in cartouche below **Rev:** Knight with sword on horseback right

Date	Mintage	Good	VG	F	VF	XF
1682 Rare	—	—	—	—	—	—

Note: Stack's International sale 3-88 AU realized $8,800

KM# 41 SILVER DUCAT
28.2500 g., 0.8730 Silver 0.7929 oz. ASW **Obv:** Armored knight standing holding sword and shield of arms **Rev:** Crowned arms, date above

Date	Mintage	Good	VG	F	VF	XF
1683	—	32.00	100	200	500	900

COUNTERMARKED COINAGE

1693

During the late 17th century many circulating coins were found to be underweight. In 1693 coins meeting the legal requirements were countermarked for a specific province or city, such as G.O. for Groningen and Ommeland.

KM# 53.1 28 STUIVERS
Silver **Countermark:** G.O. **Note:** Countermark on Deventer KM#81.

CM Date	Host Date	Good	VG	F	VF	XF
ND(1693)	1685-92	—	—	—	—	—

KM# 53.2 28 STUIVERS
Silver **Countermark:** G.O. **Note:** Countermark on Friesland KM#10.

CM Date	Host Date	Good	VG	F	VF	XF
ND(1693)	1601-91	—	—	—	—	—

KM# 53.3 28 STUIVERS
Silver **Countermark:** G.O. **Note:** Countermark on Groningen & Ommeland KM#38.

CM Date	Host Date	Good	VG	F	VF	XF
ND(1693)	1681	—	—	—	—	—

KM# 53.4 28 STUIVERS
Silver **Countermark:** G.O. **Note:** Countermark on Groningen & Ommeland KM#50.

CM Date	Host Date	Good	VG	F	VF	XF
ND(1693)	1690	—	—	—	—	—

KM# 53.5 28 STUIVERS
Silver **Countermark:** G.O. **Note:** Countermark on Groningen & Ommeland KM#52.

CM Date	Host Date	Good	VG	F	VF	XF
ND(1693)	1692	—	—	—	—	—

KM# 53.6 28 STUIVERS
Silver **Countermark:** G.O. **Note:** Countermark on Groningen & Ommeland KM#31.

CM Date	Host Date	Good	VG	F	VF	XF
ND(1693)	1673-77	—	—	—	—	—

KM# 53.7 28 STUIVERS
Silver **Countermark:** G.O. **Note:** Countermark on Groningen & Ommeland KM#32.

CM Date	Host Date	Good	VG	F	VF	XF
ND(1693)	1674	—	—	—	—	—

KM# 53.8 28 STUIVERS
Silver **Countermark:** G.O. **Note:** Countermark on Kampen KM#76.

CM Date	Host Date	Good	VG	F	VF	XF
ND(1693)	1680-86	—	—	—	—	—

KM# 53.9 28 STUIVERS
Silver **Countermark:** G.O. **Note:** Countermark on Nijmegen KM#27.

CM Date	Host Date	Good	VG	F	VF	XF
ND(1693)	1685-90	—	—	—	—	—

KM# 53.10 28 STUIVERS
Silver **Countermark:** G.O. **Note:** Countermark on Overyssel KM#55.

CM Date	Host Date	Good	VG	F	VF	XF
ND(1693)	1685-90	—	—	—	—	—

KM# 53.11 28 STUIVERS
Silver **Countermark:** G.O. **Note:** Countermark on West Friesland KM#90.

CM Date	Host Date	Good	VG	F	VF	XF
ND(1693)	1685-87	—	—	—	—	—

KM# 53.12 28 STUIVERS
Silver **Countermark:** G.O. **Note:** Countermark on Zwolle KM#78.

CM Date	Host Date	Good	VG	F	VF	XF
ND(1693)	1679-86	—	—	—	—	—

PATTERNS

Including off metal strikes

KM#	Date	Mintage	Identification	Mkt Val
Pn1	1609	—	2 Plak. Gold. Klippe, KM#8.	800
Pn2	1626	—	2 Plak. Gold. Klippe, KM#8.	800
Pn3	1627	—	8 Stuivers. Gold. 6.6000 g. KM#17.	—
Pn4	1635	—	4 Stuivers. Gold. 6.7000 g. KM#15.2.	—
Pn6	1672	—	6 Stuivers. Gold. 9.0000 g. KM#29.	—
Pn7	1673	—	6 Stuivers. Gold. 9.0000 g. KM#29.	—
Pn8	1673	—	28 Stuivers. Gold. 14.7500 g. KM#31.	—
Pn9	1675	—	28 Stuivers. Gold. 15.5000 g. KM#31.	—
Pn10	1676	—	28 Stuivers. Gold. 15.2500 g. KM#31.	—
Pn11	1677	—	28 Stuivers. Gold. 15.4000 g. KM#31.	—
Pn12	1680	—	Duit. Copper. Klippe.	—
Pn13	1690	—	6 Stuivers. Gold. 9.9000 g. KM#48.	—
Pn14	1691	—	6 Stuivers. Gold. 7.0000 g. KM#37.2.	—

PIEFORTS

KM#	Date	Mintage	Identification	Mkt Val
P1	1601	—	48 Stuivers. Silver. KM6.	3,000
P2	1626	—	8 Stuivers. Silver. Klippe, KM17.	3,000
P3	1681	—	Duit. Copper. Klippe.	—
P4	1682	—	Duit. Copper. Klippe.	—
P5	1683	—	Ducaton. Silver. KM40.	—
P6	1683	—	Silver Ducat. KM41.	2,000
P7	1690	—	Duit. Copper. KM45.	—
P8	1690	—	28 Stuivers. Silver. Triple weight, KM49.	—
P9	1691	—	6 Stuiver (Ryder Schelling). Silver. KM#37.2.	750
P10	1691	—	28 Stuivers. Silver. KM49 with value.	1,000
PA11	1611	—	28 Stuivers. Silver. W/o value.	—
P11	1691	—	28 Stuivers. Silver. Triple weight, KM49.	—
P12	1691	—	28 Stuivers. Silver. KM51.	—
P13	1692	—	28 Stuivers. Silver. 36.8300 g. KM49.	1,500
P15	1692	—	28 Stuivers. Silver. KM52.	2,500
P14	1692	—	28 Stuivers. Silver. Quintuple weight, KM50.	—
P16	1692	—	28 Stuivers. Silver. Quadruple weight, KM52.	—

'S-HEERENBERG

(Stevensweerd)

RULERS
Count Hendrik van den Bergh, 1616-1626
Herman Frederik, 1627-1631

PROVINCE

STANDARD COINAGE

KM# 17 4 HELLER
Copper **Obv:** PROTECTOR/MEVS/IIII in tulip wreath **Rev:** Lion in crowned shield

Date	Mintage	VG	F	VF	XF	Unc
ND(1626-32)	—	30.00	75.00	100	250	—

KM# 36 8 HELLER
Silver **Obv:** VIII **Obv. Legend:** NVMMVS. AD. LEGEM. **Rev:** LXX/VIIII **Rev. Legend:** CVCVC. S. VALORIS 630

Date	Mintage	VG	F	VF	XF	Unc
(1)630	—	75.00	125	200	300	—

KM# 9 GIGOT (Duit)
Copper **Obv:** FRI/DER in tulip wreath with date **Rev:** Crowned arms of Friesland with lion supporters

Date	Mintage	VG	F	VF	XF	Unc
1619	—	30.00	75.00	125	200	—
1620	—	30.00	75.00	125	200	—
1621	—	30.00	75.00	125	200	—
1624	—	30.00	75.00	125	200	—

KM# 16 GIGOT (Duit)
Copper **Obv:** FRI/STA, date in tulip wreath **Rev:** Crowned arms of Friesland with lion supporters

Date	Mintage	VG	F	VF	XF	Unc
1620	—	30.00	75.00	150	250	—
1625	—	30.00	75.00	150	250	—
1626	—	30.00	75.00	150	250	—
1629	—	30.00	75.00	150	250	—
1630	—	30.00	75.00	150	250	—
1631	—	30.00	75.00	150	250	—

KM# 18 GIGOT (Duit)
Copper **Obv:** FRI/STW in tulip wreath **Rev:** Crowned arms of Friesland with lion supporters

Date	Mintage	VG	F	VF	XF	Unc
ND(1626-32)	—	30.00	75.00	150	250	—

KM# 19 GIGOT (Duit)
Copper **Obv:** WER/IND/VSA in tulip wreath **Rev:** Crowned arms of Friesland with lion supporters

Date	Mintage	VG	F	VF	XF	Unc
ND(1626-32)	—	30.00	75.00	150	250	—

KM# 5 24 KREUZER
Silver **Obv:** Armored bust of Count right **Rev:** Displayed eagle with 24 in orb on breast

Date	Mintage	VG	F	VF	XF	Unc
ND	—	20.00	50.00	100	175	—

KM# 23 5 GROOT
Silver **Obv:** Man between 2 shields **Obv. Legend:** S. STEPHA/PROTH. M. **Rev:** Cross **Rev. Legend:** SIT. NOMEN. DNI. BENEDICTVM/S. ST-WER-. V. G. -ROS.

Date	Mintage	VG	F	VF	XF	Unc
ND(1627-31)	—	75.00	125	250	400	—

KM# 6 10 GROOT
Silver **Obv:** Bust of Count wearing coat right **Rev:** Crowned double-headed eagle

Date	Mintage	VG	F	VF	XF	Unc
ND	—	—	—	—	—	—

KM# 10 2 STUIVER
Silver **Obv:** INSV/LA; ST/1619 **Rev:** Lion divides 2S

Date	Mintage	VG	F	VF	XF	Unc
1619	—	75.00	125	250	400	—

KM# 35 8 STUIVER (Langrok)
Silver **Obv:** Mitred Saint divides VIII St **Rev:** Double-headed eagle with shield on breast **Rev. Legend:** MONETA. H. F. C. M. AD LEGEM GRONINGE

Date	Mintage	VG	F	VF	XF	Unc
1630	—	75.00	125	250	400	—

KM# 24 30 STUIVER
Silver

Date	Mintage	VG	F	VF	XF	Unc
1627	—	—	—	—	—	—

KM# 25 50 STUIVER
Silver **Obv:** Crowned and crested helmet above lion shield **Rev:** Crowned double-headed eagle **Note:** Dav. #5000.

Date	Mintage	VG	F	VF	XF	Unc
ND	—	—	—	—	—	—

KM# 8 1/4 SNAPHAAN
Silver **Obv:** Count on horse right **Obv. Legend:** S. P-ER-AMVSM-ELIORA **Rev:** Cross with arms on center **Rev. Legend:** MONET-A NOVA - MONT - ENSIS

Date	Mintage	VG	F	VF	XF	Unc
ND	—	75.00	125	250	400	—

KM# 7 1/2 DAALDER
Silver **Obv:** Armored bust of Count right **Rev:** Crowned and crested helmet above lion sheild

Date	Mintage	VG	F	VF	XF	Unc
ND	—	—	—	—	—	—

KM# 20 DAALDER
Silver **Ruler:** Count Hendrik van den Bergh **Obv:** Armored 1/2-length bust of Count holding baton above arms dividing date **Obv. Legend:** HENRICVS: COMES. D. - MONTE. DNS. IND. ST. W. **Rev:** Crowned and crested helmet above lion sheild **Rev. Legend:** DNS. PROTECTOR. VITAE. MEAE. QVO. TREPIDAB. **Note:** Dav. #4996.

Date	Mintage	VG	F	VF	XF	Unc
1626	—	—	—	—	—	—

KM# 21 DAALDER
Silver **Obv:** Armored bust of Count right **Note:** Dav. #4997.

Date	Mintage	VG	F	VF	XF	Unc
ND	—	40.00	85.00	175	350	—

KM# 22 DAALDER
Silver **Obv:** Larger bust of Count **Note:** Dav. #4999. Varieties in legend exist.

Date	Mintage	VG	F	VF	XF	Unc
ND	—	40.00	85.00	175	350	—
1628	—	40.00	85.00	175	350	—

KM# 26 FLORIN D'OR
3.5000 g., 0.9860 Gold 0.1109 oz. AGW **Obv:** Armored bust of Herman Frederik right holding helmet **Rev:** Quartered arms as 4 shields in inner circle

Date	Mintage	VG	F	VF	XF	Unc
ND Rare	—	—	—	—	—	—

KM# 27 FLORIN D'OR
3.5000 g., 0.9860 Gold 0.1109 oz. AGW **Obv:** Helmeted arms **Rev:** Crowned imperial eagle in inner circle

Date	Mintage	VG	F	VF	XF	Unc
ND Rare	—	—	—	—	—	—

KM# 28 FLORIN D'OR
3.5000 g., 0.9860 Gold 0.1109 oz. AGW **Obv:** St. Stephen **Rev:** Crowned imperial eagle in inner circle **Note:** Imitation of a Metz florin.

Date	Mintage	VG	F	VF	XF	Unc
ND	—	200	350	500	900	—
1634	—	250	450	750	1,250	—

HOLLAND

Hollandia

Holland, a Dutch maritime province fronting on the North Sea, is the most important region of the Netherlands. It is a leader in maritime activities and in efficient agriculture. During the period of Spanish domination, Holland was the bulwark of the Protestant faith in the Netherlands and the focus of the resistance to Spanish tyranny.

MINT MARKS
Rose - Dordrecht
State Arms - Amsterdam

PROVINCE

STANDARD COINAGE

KM# 13 DUIT
2.9300 g., Copper **Obv:** Maiden sitting in enclosed fence with right hand raised, date in legend **Rev:** Inscription in wreath **Rev. Inscription:** HOL / LAN / DIA

Date	Mintage	Good	VG	F	VF	XF
1604	—	3.00	10.00	20.00	50.00	125
1605	—	3.00	10.00	20.00	50.00	125

KM# 13a DUIT
Silver **Obv:** Maiden sitting in enclosed fence with right hand raised **Rev:** Inscription in wreath **Rev. Inscription:** HOL / LAN / DIA

Date	Mintage	Good	VG	F	VF	XF
1605	—	—	—	—	—	—

KM# 30 DUIT
2.9300 g., Copper **Rev:** Inscription in wreath **Rev. Inscription:** HOL / LANDIA / (date)

Date	Mintage	Good	VG	F	VF	XF
1626	—	6.00	20.00	40.00	80.00	175
1627	—	6.00	20.00	40.00	80.00	175

KM# 30b DUIT
2.1000 g., Silver **Rev:** Inscription in wreath **Rev. Inscription:** HOL / LANDIA / (date)

Date	Mintage	VG	F	VF	XF	Unc
1626	—	—	80.00	150	250	—

KM# 30a DUIT
1.4000 g., Silver **Rev:** Inscription in wreath **Rev. Inscription:** HOL / LANDIA / (date)

Date	Mintage	Good	VG	F	VF	XF
1627	—	—	—	—	—	—

KM# 26 STUIVER
0.8600 g., 0.5830 Silver 0.0161 oz. ASW **Obv:** Crowned rampant lion left holding sword and arrows, value at sides **Rev. Inscription:** HOL / LAN / DIA / (date)

Date	Mintage	Good	VG	F	VF	XF
1614	—	2.50	8.00	22.00	40.00	60.00
1616/4	—	8.00	25.00	50.00	90.00	150
1618	—	2.50	8.00	22.00	40.00	60.00

KM# 28 STUIVER
1.3100 g., 0.3330 Silver 0.0140 oz. ASW **Obv:** Bundle of arrows divides value in wreath

Date	Mintage	Good	VG	F	VF	XF
1619	—	3.00	10.00	20.00	45.00	80.00
1628	—	3.00	10.00	20.00	45.00	80.00

KM# 5 2 STUIVERS (1/3 Roosschelling)
1.7600 g., 0.5830 Silver 0.0330 oz. ASW **Obv:** Crowned arms divide value in enclosed fence in inner circle, date at top **Rev:** Ornamental cross with rose at center in inner circle

Date	Mintage	Good	VG	F	VF	XF
1601	—	32.00	100	250	450	750

KM# 27 2 STUIVERS (Double Stuiver)
1.7300 g., 0.5830 Silver 0.0324 oz. ASW **Obv:** Crowned rampant lion left holding sword and arrows, value at sides **Rev. Inscription:** HOL / LAN / DIA / (date)

Date	Mintage	Good	VG	F	VF	XF
1614	—	2.00	6.00	15.00	25.00	50.00
1615	—	2.00	6.00	15.00	25.00	50.00
1616	—	2.00	6.00	15.00	25.00	50.00
1617	—	2.00	6.00	15.00	25.00	50.00
1618	—	2.00	6.00	15.00	25.00	50.00
1619	—	2.00	6.00	15.00	25.00	50.00
1620	—	2.00	6.00	15.00	25.00	50.00
1628	—	2.00	6.00	15.00	25.00	50.00
1670	—	6.00	20.00	40.00	100	250

KM# 48 2 STUIVERS (Double Wapenstuiver)
1.6200 g., 0.5830 Silver 0.0304 oz. ASW **Obv:** Crowned arms of Holland divides value **Rev. Inscription:** HOL/ LAN /DIA / (date)

Date	Mintage	VG	F	VF	XF	Unc
1672	—	3.00	10.00	15.00	40.00	—
1675	—	3.00	10.00	15.00	40.00	—
1676	—	3.00	10.00	15.00	40.00	—
1677	—	3.00	10.00	15.00	40.00	—
1678	—	3.00	10.00	15.00	40.00	—
1680/70	—	—	—	—	—	—
1680	—	3.00	10.00	15.00	40.00	—
1683	—	3.00	10.00	15.00	40.00	—
1697	—	3.00	10.00	15.00	40.00	—
1698	—	3.00	10.00	15.00	40.00	—
1699	—	3.00	10.00	15.00	40.00	—
1700	—	3.00	10.00	15.00	40.00	—

KM# 6 3 STUIVERS (1/2 Roosschelling)
2.6300 g., 0.5830 Silver 0.0493 oz. ASW **Obv:** Crowned arms divide value in enclosed fence in inner circle, date at top **Rev:** Ornamental cross with rose at center in inner circle

Date	Mintage	Good	VG	F	VF	XF
1601	—	16.00	50.00	150	350	650

KM# 70 5 STUIVERS (1/4 Gulden)
2.6500 g., 0.9200 Silver 0.0784 oz. ASW **Obv:** Crowned arms divide value, date above crown **Rev:** Standing female figure leaning on Bible on column, holding spear with Liberty cap

Date	Mintage	Good	VG	F	VF	XF
1692	—	25.00	75.00	200	300	400

KM# 7 6 STUIVERS (Roosschelling)
5.2700 g., 0.5830 Silver 0.0988 oz. ASW **Obv:** Crowned arms **Rev:** Ornate short cross

Date	Mintage	Good	VG	F	VF	XF
1601	—	10.00	30.00	70.00	100	150

KM# 45.1 6 STUIVERS (Scheepjesschelling)
4.9500 g., 0.5830 Silver 0.0928 oz. ASW **Obv:** Without denomination 6 - S

Date	Mintage	Good	VG	F	VF	XF
1670	—	16.00	50.00	150	250	350

KM# 45.2 6 STUIVERS (Scheepjesschelling)
4.9500 g., 0.5830 Silver 0.0928 oz. ASW **Obv:** With denomination 6 - S

Date	Mintage	Good	VG	F	VF	XF
1671	—	2.50	8.00	20.00	50.00	100
1674	—	2.50	8.00	20.00	50.00	100
1675	—	3.00	10.00	25.00	60.00	120
1677	—	2.50	8.00	20.00	50.00	100
1679	—	3.00	10.00	25.00	60.00	120
1680	—	4.00	12.00	32.00	80.00	150
1688	—	4.00	12.00	32.00	80.00	150
1700	—	2.50	8.00	20.00	50.00	100

KM# 45a.2 6 STUIVERS (Scheepjesschelling)
Gold **Obv:** With denomination 6 - S

Date	Mintage	Good	VG	F	VF	XF
1671	—	—	—	—	—	—
1674	—	—	—	—	—	1,000
1684	—	—	—	—	—	1,200

KM# 14 10 STUIVERS
5.9500 g., 0.9170 Silver 0.1754 oz. ASW **Obv:** Knight standing right with sword on shoulder, left hand on lion shield divides date **Rev:** Crowned arms divide value X - S

Date	Mintage	Good	VG	F	VF	XF
1606	—	32.00	100	300	650	950
1607	—	32.00	100	300	650	950

KM# 15 10 STUIVERS
5.9500 g., 0.9170 Silver 0.1754 oz. ASW **Obv:** Knight standing right holding bow in left hand

Date	Mintage	Good	VG	F	VF	XF
1606	—	32.00	100	300	450	750

KM# 59 10 STUIVERS

5.3000 g., 0.9200 Silver 0.1568 oz. ASW **Obv:** Crowned arms divide value, date above **Rev:** Standing female figure leaning on Bible on column holding spear with Liberty cap

Date	Mintage	Good	VG	F	VF	XF
1681	142,900	20.00	60.00	170	350	600
1682	Inc. above	16.00	50.00	125	250	450
1688/1	Inc. above	16.00	50.00	125	250	450
1688	Inc. above	16.00	50.00	125	250	450
1692	Inc. above	26.00	80.00	200	400	700

KM# 59a 10 STUIVERS

Gold **Obv:** Crowned arms divide value, date above **Rev:** Standing female figure leaning on Bible on column holding spear with Liberty cap **Note:** Weight varies 6.90-10.30 g.

Date	Mintage	Good	VG	F	VF	XF
1688	—	—	—	—	1,000	1,800
1689	—	—	—	—	1,000	1,800

KM# 71 28 STUIVERS (Florin)

19.5000 g., 0.6730 Silver 0.4219 oz. ASW **Obv:** Crowned arms of the 7 provinces **Rev:** Standing female figure leaning on Bible on column, holding spear with Liberty cap divides value, date in exergue

Date	Mintage	Good	VG	F	VF	XF
1694	—	—	—	—	2,500	4,000

KM# 71a 28 STUIVERS (Florin)

17.2000 g., Gold **Obv:** Crowned arms of the 7 provinces **Rev:** Standing female figure leaning on Bible on column, holding spear with Liberty cap divides value, date in exergue

Date	Mintage	Good	VG	F	VF	XF
1694	—	—	—	10,000	15,000	20,000

KM# 65 1/2 GULDEN (10 Stuivers)

Silver **Obv:** Without value 10 - S

Date	Mintage	Good	VG	F	VF	XF
1682	—	20.00	65.00	150	300	500

KM# 65a 1/2 GULDEN (10 Stuivers)

10.3000 g., Gold **Obv:** Without value 10 - S , with value 1/2 - GL

Date	Mintage	Good	VG	F	VF	XF
1682	—	—	—	—	2,000	3,000

KM# 72 1/2 GULDEN (10 Stuivers)

5.3000 g., 0.9200 Silver 0.1568 oz. ASW **Obv:** Standing female figure leaning on Bible column, holding spear with Liberty cap **Rev:** Crowned arms divide value

Date	Mintage	Good	VG	F	VF	XF
1694	—	10.00	30.00	75.00	150	250

KM# 55 GULDEN (20 Stuiver)

10.6100 g., 0.9200 Silver 0.3138 oz. ASW **Obv:** Rampant lion left **Rev:** Crowned arms divide value I - G

Date	Mintage	Good	VG	F	VF	XF
1680	—	100	300	700	1,000	1,500

KM# 56 GULDEN (20 Stuiver)

10.6100 g., 0.9200 Silver 0.3138 oz. ASW **Rev:** Standing female figure holding lion shield and spear with Liberty cap, date in exergue

Date	Mintage	Good	VG	F	VF	XF
1680	—	—	—	—	—	3,000

KM# 60 GULDEN (20 Stuiver)

Silver **Obv:** Crowned arms divide value I - G **Rev:** Standing female figure leaning on Bible column, holding spear with Liberty cap

Date	Mintage	Good	VG	F	VF	XF
1681	—	26.00	80.00	250	350	500
1682	—	32.00	100	300	425	600

KM# 61 GULDEN (20 Stuiver)

Silver **Obv:** Crowned arms without value **Rev:** Standing female figure leaning on Bible column, holding spear with Liberty cap

Date	Mintage	Good	VG	F	VF	XF
1681	—	50.00	150	350	550	800

KM# 61a GULDEN (20 Stuiver)

Gold **Obv:** Crowned arms without value **Rev:** Standing female figure leaning on Bible column, holding spear with Liberty cap **Note:** Weight varies 13.80-17.30 g.

Date	Mintage	Good	VG	F	VF	XF
1681	—	—	—	1,500	2,500	4,000

KM# 73 GULDEN (20 Stuiver)

10.6100 g., 0.9200 Silver 0.3138 oz. ASW **Obv:** Crowned arms of Holland divides value I - G **Obv. Legend:** MO: ARG : ORD: FÆD: BELG : HOLL : **Rev:** Standing figure leaning on column, holding pole with cap, date below **Rev. Legend:** HANCTVEMVR HAC NITIMVR

Date	Mintage	VG	F	VF	XF	Unc
1694	—	20.00	60.00	100	200	—

KM# 73a GULDEN (20 Stuiver)

Gold **Obv:** Crowned arms of Holland divides value **Rev:** Standing figure leaning on column, holding pole with cap, date below

Date	Mintage	VG	F	VF	XF	Unc
1694 Rare	—	—	—	—	—	—
1696 Rare	—	—	—	—	—	—

KM# 74 1/2 3 (1-1/2) GULDEN

15.9100 g., 0.9200 Silver 0.4706 oz. ASW **Obv:** Crowned arms divide value (1/2 - 3GL) **Rev:** Standing female figure leaning on Bible on column holding spear with Liberty cap

Date	Mintage	Good	VG	F	VF	XF
1694	—	65.00	200	500	800	1,000

KM# 74a 1/2 3 (1-1/2) GULDEN

Gold **Obv:** Crowned arms divide value 1/2 - 3GL **Rev:** Standing female figure leaning on Bible on column holding spear with Liberty cap **Note:** Weight varies 17.20-20.60 g.

Date	Mintage	VG	F	VF	XF	Unc
1694	—	—	—	—	8,000	10,000

KM# 57 2 GULDEN

21.2100 g., 0.9200 Silver 0.6273 oz. ASW **Obv:** Rampant lion left **Rev:** Crowned arms

Date	Mintage	Good	VG	F	VF	XF
1680	—	100	300	750	1,000	1,250

KM# 62 2 GULDEN

21.2100 g., 0.9200 Silver 0.6273 oz. ASW **Obv:** Crowned arms divides value 2 - G **Rev:** Standing female figure leaning on Bible column, holding spear with Liberty cap

Date	Mintage	Good	VG	F	VF	XF
1681	8,150	40.00	125	250	450	700
1682	—	25.00	75.00	150	250	400
1687	—	28.00	85.00	200	300	500

KM# 75 2 GULDEN

Silver **Obv:** Value 2 - GL **Rev:** Date in exergue

Date	Mintage	Good	VG	F	VF	XF
1694	—	—	—	—	—	—

KM# 58 3 GULDEN (60 Stuiver)

31.8200 g., 0.9200 Silver 0.9412 oz. ASW **Obv:** Rampant lion left **Rev:** Crowned arms divide value 3 - G **Note:** Dav. #4951.

Date	Mintage	Good	VG	F	VF	XF
1680	—	80.00	250	600	900	1,350

KM# 63 3 GULDEN (60 Stuiver)
31.8200 g., 0.9200 Silver 0.9412 oz. ASW **Obv:** Crowned arms divide value 3 - G **Rev:** Standing female figure leaning on Bible column holding spear with Liberty cap **Note:** Dav. #4952.

Date	Mintage	Good	VG	F	VF	XF
1681	—	25.00	75.00	200	400	750
1682	—	25.00	75.00	200	400	750
1694/82	—	50.00	150	375	600	1,000
1694	—	32.00	100	300	500	800

KM# 64 3 GULDEN (60 Stuiver)
31.8200 g., 0.9200 Silver 0.9412 oz. ASW **Obv:** Crowned arms without value **Rev:** Standing female figure leaning on Bible column holding spear with Liberty cap **Note:** Dav. #4952A.

Date	Mintage	Good	VG	F	VF	XF
1681	—	115	350	900	1,250	1,500
1682	—	115	350	900	1,250	1,500

KM# 66 3 GULDEN (60 Stuiver)
31.8200 g., 0.9200 Silver 0.9412 oz. ASW **Obv:** Rampant lion left without value in inner circle **Rev:** Standing female figure leaning on Bible column holding spear with Liberty cap **Note:** Dav. #4953.

Date	Mintage	VG	F	VF	XF	Unc
1684	—	350	900	1,250	1,500	2,000

KM# 152 3 GULDEN (60 Stuiver)
Silver **Obv:** Crowned lion with sword arms divide value 3 - GL **Obv. Legend:** MO: ARG: ORD: FAED: BELG: HOLL **Rev:** Standing female figure leaning on Bible column holding spear with Liberty cap, date below **Note:** Dav. #4954.

Date	Mintage	Good	VG	F	VF	XF
1694	—	25.00	75.00	200	300	450

KM# 40 1/2 DUCATON
Silver **Obv:** Knight with sword on horseback right, provincial arms below in inner circle **Rev:** Crowned arms with crowned lion supporters in inner circle, date at top in legend

Date	Mintage	Good	VG	F	VF	XF
1659	—	30.00	90.00	200	325	450

KM# 41 DUCATON
32.7800 g., 0.9410 Silver 0.9917 oz. ASW **Obv:** Knight horseback right brandishing sword **Rev:** Crowned arms with lion supporters **Note:** Similar to KM#46 but cruder style. Dav. #4928.

Date	Mintage	Good	VG	F	VF	XF
1659	—	20.00	40.00	100	175	265
1660	—	20.00	40.00	100	175	265
1661/0	—	20.00	40.00	100	200	300
1661	—	20.00	40.00	100	175	265
1662	—	20.00	40.00	100	175	265
1666	—	25.00	55.00	125	200	300
1668	—	20.00	40.00	100	175	265

KM# 46 DUCATON
Silver **Obv:** Knight horseback right holding sword upright **Rev:** Crowned arms with lion supporters **Edge:** Lettered **Note:** Dav. #4931.

Date	Mintage	VG	F	VF	XF	Unc
1671	—	300	850	1,300	1,800	—
1672	—	300	800	1,200	1,500	—

KM# 51 DUCATON
32.7800 g., 0.9410 Silver 0.9917 oz. ASW **Obv:** Knight on horseback right holds sword upright, crowned arms below **Obv. Legend:** BELG : PRO : HOLLAND : MO : NO : ARG : CONFOE **Rev:** Crowned arms of Holland, with supporters, date in cartouche below **Rev. Legend:** * CONCORDIA RES PARVAE CRESCUNT : **Note:** Dav. #4930. Similar to KM#90.

Date	Mintage	Good	VG	F	VF	XF
1672	—	22.00	50.00	100	200	300
1673/2	—	22.00	50.00	100	200	300
1673	—	22.00	50.00	100	200	300
1674	—	22.00	50.00	100	200	300
1675	—	22.00	50.00	100	200	300
1676	—	22.00	50.00	100	200	300
1678/6	—	22.00	50.00	100	200	300
1679/69	—	22.00	50.00	100	200	300
1679/6	—	22.00	50.00	100	200	300
1679	—	22.00	50.00	100	200	300
1680	—	22.00	50.00	100	200	300
1687	—	22.00	50.00	100	200	300
1692	—	22.00	50.00	100	200	300
1693	—	22.00	50.00	100	200	300
1694	—	22.00	50.00	100	200	300

KM# 93 2 DUCATON
Silver **Obv:** Knight horseback right brandishing sword **Rev:** Crowned arms with lion supporters **Note:** Dav. #4929.

Date	Mintage	Good	VG	F	VF	XF
1671	—	90.00	275	550	1,000	1,650
1672	—	90.00	275	550	1,000	1,650
1673	—	90.00	275	550	1,000	1,650
1674	—	90.00	275	550	1,000	1,650
1675	—	90.00	275	550	1,000	1,650
1676	—	90.00	275	550	1,000	1,650
1677	—	90.00	275	550	1,000	1,650
1678	—	90.00	275	550	1,000	1,650
1679	—	90.00	275	550	1,000	1,650
1680 Rare	—	—	—	—	—	—
1687	—	90.00	275	550	1,000	1,650
1693	—	90.00	275	550	1,000	1,650

KM# 42 1/2 DUCAT (24 Stuivers)
14.1200 g., 0.8730 Silver 0.3963 oz. ASW **Obv:** Knight standing right with sword on shoulder, left hand on lion shield **Rev:** Crowned arms

Date	Mintage	Good	VG	F	VF	XF
1659	—	32.00	100	250	350	700

KM# 43 DUCAT (48 Stuivers)
28.2500 g., 0.8730 Silver 0.7929 oz. ASW **Obv:** Knight standing right with sword on shoulder, left hand on lion shield **Rev:** Crowned arms **Note:** Dav. #4896.

Date	Mintage	Good	VG	F	VF	XF
1659	594,275	20.00	35.00	70.00	125	200
1660/59	Inc. above	25.00	50.00	100	200	300
1660	Inc. above	20.00	35.00	70.00	125	200
1661	Inc. above	20.00	35.00	70.00	125	200
1662/0	Inc. above	25.00	50.00	100	200	300
1662/1	Inc. above	25.00	50.00	100	200	300
1662	Inc. above	25.00	50.00	100	200	300
1663	Inc. above	25.00	50.00	100	200	300
1664/2	Inc. above	20.00	35.00	70.00	125	200
1664	Inc. above	20.00	35.00	70.00	125	200
1665	Inc. above	25.00	50.00	100	200	300
1666/5	Inc. above	25.00	50.00	100	200	300
1666	Inc. above	25.00	50.00	100	200	300
1668	Inc. above	28.00	70.00	140	250	350
1670	Inc. above	28.00	70.00	140	250	350

KM# 52 DUCAT (48 Stuivers)

Silver **Obv:** Standing armored Knight with crowned shield at feet **Obv. Legend:** BELG : .. : HOL : MONO : ARG : PRO : CONFOE : **Rev:** Crowned arms of Holland divides date **Rev. Legend:** CONCORDIA RES PAR.... **Note:** Dav. #4898 and #1840.

Date	Mintage	VG	F	VF	XF	Unc
1672	—	35.00	70.00	150	250	—
1673	—	35.00	70.00	150	250	—
1674	—	35.00	70.00	150	250	—
1679	—	40.00	80.00	160	275	—
1680/79	—	50.00	125	200	350	—
1680	—	40.00	80.00	160	275	—
1683	—	60.00	125	200	350	—
1684	46,595	40.00	80.00	160	275	—
1693	—	40.00	80.00	160	275	—
1694/3	—	40.00	80.00	160	275	—
1694	—	40.00	80.00	160	275	—
1695/4	—	40.00	80.00	160	275	—
1695	—	50.00	125	200	350	—

KM# 108 2 DUCAT

Silver **Obv:** Armored knight standing right holding bow in left hand **Rev:** Crowned arms divides date **Note:** Dav. #4897.

Date	Mintage	Good	VG	F	VF	XF
1673	—	110	350	650	1,150	1,850
1674	—	110	350	650	1,150	1,850
1683	—	110	350	650	1,150	1,850
1693	—	110	350	650	1,150	1,850
1694	—	110	350	650	1,150	1,850

KM# 8 1/2 DAALDER (Prince 20 Stuiver)

14.5100 g., 0.8850 Silver 0.4128 oz. ASW **Obv:** Armoured bust of William the Silent with sword right in inner circle, date at top in legend **Rev:** Helmeted arms in inner circle

Date	Mintage	Good	VG	F	VF	XF
1601	—	62.00	200	500	750	1,000
1602	—	62.00	200	500	750	1,000

KM# 9 1/2 DAALDER (Lion 24 Stuiver)

13.8400 g., 0.7500 Silver 0.3337 oz. ASW **Obv:** Armored knight looking right above lion shield, date divided at bottom **Rev:** Rampant lion left in inner circle

Date	Mintage	Good	VG	F	VF	XF
1589	—	—	—	—	—	—
1601/0	—	12.00	30.00	70.00	150	250
1601	—	12.00	30.00	70.00	150	250
1602/1	—	12.00	30.00	70.00	150	250
1602	—	12.00	30.00	70.00	150	250
1604	—	12.00	30.00	70.00	150	250
1605/4	—	12.00	30.00	70.00	150	250
1605	—	12.00	30.00	70.00	150	250

KM# 16 1/2 DAALDER (Lion 24 Stuiver)

Silver **Rev:** Date at top in legend

Date	Mintage	Good	VG	F	VF	XF
1606	—	25.00	60.00	120	200	300
1607	—	25.00	60.00	120	200	300
1608	—	25.00	60.00	120	200	300
1609	—	25.00	60.00	120	200	300
1610	—	25.00	60.00	120	200	300
1611	—	25.00	60.00	120	200	300
1615/3	—	25.00	60.00	120	200	300
1616	—	20.00	50.00	100	175	250
1617	—	20.00	50.00	100	175	250
1618	—	20.00	50.00	100	175	250
1622	—	20.00	50.00	100	175	250
1623/2	—	20.00	50.00	100	175	250
1623	—	25.00	60.00	120	200	300
1624/2	—	25.00	60.00	120	200	300
1624	—	25.00	60.00	120	200	300
1626	—	25.00	60.00	120	200	300
1632	—	25.00	60.00	120	200	300
1633	—	25.00	60.00	120	200	300
1634	—	25.00	60.00	120	200	300
1636	—	25.00	60.00	120	200	300
1637	—	25.00	60.00	120	200	300
1640	—	25.00	60.00	120	200	300
1641/0	—	25.00	60.00	120	200	300
1641	—	25.00	60.00	120	200	300
1643	—	25.00	60.00	120	200	300
1645	—	25.00	60.00	120	200	300
1647	—	25.00	60.00	120	200	300
1648/7	—	20.00	50.00	100	175	250
1648	—	20.00	50.00	100	175	250
1650	—	20.00	50.00	100	175	250
1651/0	—	20.00	50.00	100	175	250
1652	—	20.00	50.00	100	175	250
1653/2	—	20.00	50.00	100	175	250
1653	—	20.00	50.00	100	175	250

KM# 25 1/2 DAALDER (Rijks)

14.5100 g., 0.8850 0.4128 oz. **Obv:** Laureate 1/2 figure holding sword and arms in inner circle **Rev:** Crowned arms divide date in inner circle

Date	Mintage	Good	VG	F	VF	XF
1606	—	18.00	50.00	175	250	350
1610	—	18.00	50.00	165	225	300
1611	—	18.00	50.00	165	225	300
1612	—	18.00	50.00	165	225	300
1614	—	18.00	50.00	165	225	300
1620	—	18.00	50.00	165	225	300
1621	—	18.00	50.00	165	225	300
1622	—	18.00	50.00	165	225	300
1623/2	—	18.00	50.00	165	225	300
1623	—	18.00	50.00	165	225	300
1624	—	18.00	50.00	165	225	300
1625/4	—	18.00	50.00	165	225	300
1625	—	18.00	50.00	165	225	300
1628	—	18.00	50.00	165	225	300
1629	—	18.00	50.00	165	225	300
1630	—	18.00	50.00	165	225	300
1632	—	18.00	50.00	165	225	300
1640	—	18.00	50.00	165	225	300
1648	—	18.00	50.00	165	225	300
1649	—	18.00	50.00	165	225	300
1650	—	18.00	50.00	165	225	300
1654	—	18.00	50.00	165	225	300
1657/4	—	18.00	50.00	165	225	300
1657	—	18.00	50.00	165	225	300
1659	—	18.00	50.00	165	225	300

KM# 10 DAALDER (Prince 40 Stuivers)

29.0300 g., 0.8850 Silver 0.8260 oz. ASW **Obv:** Helmeted arms in inner circle **Rev:** Armored half figure of William the Silent with sword right in inner circle, date at top in legend **Note:** Dav. #4822.

Date	Mintage	Good	VG	F	VF	XF
1601	—	40.00	125	350	550	800
1602	—	40.00	125	350	550	800

KM# 11 DAALDER (Lion - 48 Stuivers)

27.6300 g., 0.7500 Silver 0.6662 oz. ASW **Obv:** Armored knight looking right above lion shield, date divided at bottom **Rev:** Rampant lion to left in inner circle **Note:** Dav. #4856.

Date	Mintage	Good	VG	F	VF	XF
1601/1589	—	16.00	30.00	75.00	160	300
1601/1594	—	16.00	30.00	75.00	160	300
1601/0/1599	—	16.00	30.00	75.00	160	300
1601/0	—	16.00	30.00	75.00	160	300
1601	—	16.00	30.00	75.00	160	300
1602/1	—	16.00	30.00	75.00	160	300
1602	—	16.00	30.00	75.00	160	300
1604	—	16.00	30.00	75.00	160	300
1605	—	16.00	30.00	75.00	160	300

KM# 17 DAALDER (Lion - 48 Stuivers)

Silver **Obv:** Armored knight left looking backwards holding bow and resting hand on shield **Rev:** Rampant lion left, date at top in legend **Note:** Dav. #4858.

Date	Mintage	Good	VG	F	VF	XF
1606	—	18.00	35.00	70.00	120	200
1607	—	16.00	30.00	60.00	90.00	150
1608/6	—	16.00	30.00	60.00	90.00	150
1608	—	16.00	30.00	60.00	90.00	150
1609/8	—	16.00	30.00	60.00	90.00	150
1609	—	16.00	30.00	60.00	90.00	150
1610	—	18.00	35.00	70.00	120	200
1611/0	—	16.00	30.00	60.00	90.00	150
1611	—	16.00	30.00	60.00	90.00	150
1612	—	18.00	35.00	70.00	110	190
1614	—	18.00	35.00	70.00	110	190
1616/3	—	16.00	30.00	60.00	90.00	150
1616	—	16.00	30.00	60.00	90.00	150
1617	—	16.00	30.00	60.00	90.00	150
1621	—	18.00	35.00	70.00	120	200
1622	—	18.00	35.00	70.00	120	200
1623/17	—	18.00	35.00	70.00	120	200
1623/19	—	18.00	35.00	70.00	110	190
1623/22	—	18.00	35.00	70.00	110	190
1623	—	18.00	35.00	70.00	110	180
1624	—	18.00	35.00	70.00	110	190
1625	—	18.00	35.00	70.00	110	180
1626	—	18.00	35.00	70.00	110	190
1627/6	—	18.00	35.00	70.00	110	180
1627	—	18.00	35.00	70.00	110	180
1628	—	18.00	35.00	70.00	110	180
1632	—	18.00	35.00	70.00	110	180
1633	—	18.00	35.00	70.00	110	180
1634/3	—	18.00	35.00	70.00	110	180
1634	—	18.00	35.00	70.00	110	180
1635	—	18.00	35.00	70.00	110	180
1636	—	18.00	35.00	70.00	110	180
1637	—	18.00	35.00	70.00	110	180
1638	—	18.00	35.00	70.00	110	190
1639	—	18.00	35.00	70.00	110	190
1641/0	—	25.00	50.00	125	250	500
1640	—	18.00	35.00	70.00	110	190
1641	—	18.00	35.00	70.00	110	190
1643	—	18.00	35.00	70.00	120	200
1644	—	18.00	35.00	70.00	120	200
1645	—	18.00	35.00	70.00	110	190
1647	—	18.00	35.00	70.00	110	190
1648	—	18.00	35.00	70.00	110	180
1649	—	18.00	35.00	70.00	110	180
1650/49	—	18.00	35.00	70.00	110	190
1650	—	18.00	35.00	70.00	110	180
1651	—	18.00	35.00	70.00	110	180
1652	—	18.00	35.00	70.00	110	180
1653	—	18.00	35.00	70.00	120	200
1654	—	18.00	35.00	70.00	120	200
1655	—	18.00	35.00	70.00	120	200
1658	—	18.00	35.00	70.00	120	200
1659	—	18.00	35.00	70.00	120	200
1661	—	18.00	35.00	70.00	120	200
1662/52	—	—	—	—	—	—
1662	—	18.00	35.00	70.00	110	180
1663	—	18.00	35.00	70.00	110	180
1664	—	18.00	35.00	70.00	110	190
1665	—	—	—	—	—	—
1666	—	18.00	35.00	70.00	110	180
1668	—	18.00	35.00	70.00	110	180
1674	—	18.00	35.00	70.00	120	200
1675	—	18.00	35.00	70.00	110	180
1676	—	18.00	35.00	70.00	120	200
1679	—	18.00	35.00	70.00	120	200
1680	—	18.00	35.00	70.00	110	190
1683	—	18.00	35.00	70.00	110	190
1684	—	18.00	35.00	70.00	110	190
1685	—	18.00	35.00	70.00	110	190

Date	Mintage	Good	VG	F	VF	XF
1687	—	18.00	35.00	70.00	110	190
1697	—	22.00	45.00	110	200	350

KM# 18 DAALDER (Rijks)

28.2500 g., 0.8730 Silver 0.7929 oz. ASW **Obv:** Laureate 1/2 figure holding sword and arms in inner circle **Obv. Legend:** * MO: ARG: PRO• - CONFOE: BELG: C: HOL• **Rev:** Crowned arms divide date **Rev. Legend:** CONCORDIA RES PARVAE CRESCUNT **Note:** Dav. #4831.

Date	Mintage	Good	VG	F	VF	XF
1606	—	20.00	40.00	70.00	125	250
1607	—	20.00	40.00	70.00	125	250
1609	—	20.00	40.00	70.00	125	250
1610	—	22.00	45.00	90.00	150	300
1611	—	18.00	35.00	60.00	100	200
1612	—	18.00	35.00	60.00	100	200
1614	—	18.00	35.00	60.00	100	200
1619/8	—	18.00	35.00	60.00	100	200
1619	—	18.00	35.00	60.00	100	200
1620	—	18.00	35.00	60.00	100	200
1621/0	—	20.00	40.00	70.00	125	250
1621	—	18.00	35.00	60.00	100	200
1622	—	18.00	35.00	60.00	100	200
1623/2	—	18.00	35.00	60.00	100	200
1623	—	18.00	35.00	60.00	100	200
1624/2	—	20.00	40.00	70.00	125	250
1624/3	—	20.00	40.00	70.00	125	250
1624	—	18.00	35.00	60.00	100	200
1625	—	18.00	35.00	60.00	100	200
1626	—	18.00	35.00	60.00	100	200
1628	—	18.00	35.00	60.00	100	200
1629	—	18.00	35.00	60.00	100	200
1631/28	—	20.00	40.00	70.00	125	250
1631	—	18.00	35.00	60.00	100	200
1634	—	20.00	40.00	70.00	125	250
1636	—	20.00	40.00	70.00	125	250
1640	—	20.00	40.00	70.00	125	250
1644	—	20.00	40.00	70.00	125	250
1648	—	20.00	40.00	70.00	125	250
1649	—	20.00	40.00	70.00	125	250
1650	—	20.00	40.00	70.00	125	250
1651	—	20.00	40.00	70.00	125	250
1652	—	20.00	40.00	70.00	125	250
1653	—	20.00	40.00	70.00	125	250
1656	—	20.00	40.00	70.00	125	250
1657/6	—	20.00	40.00	70.00	125	250
1657	—	16.00	30.00	50.00	90.00	180
1658	—	16.00	30.00	50.00	90.00	180
1659	—	16.00	30.00	50.00	90.00	180
1662	—	20.00	40.00	70.00	125	250
1674	—	16.00	30.00	50.00	90.00	180
1675	—	16.00	30.00	50.00	90.00	180
1676	—	16.00	30.00	50.00	90.00	180
1683	—	20.00	40.00	70.00	125	250
1684/3	—	16.00	30.00	50.00	90.00	180
1684	—	16.00	30.00	50.00	90.00	180
1687	—	22.00	45.00	90.00	150	300
1693	—	20.00	40.00	70.00	125	250

KM# 88 2 DAALDERS (Lion)

Silver **Obv:** Armored knight left looking backwards holding bow and lion shield **Rev:** Rampant lion left, date above in legend **Note:** Dav. #4857.

Date	Mintage	Good	VG	F	VF	XF
1636	—	200	600	1,000	1,750	2,500
1640	—	200	600	1,000	1,750	2,500
1641	—	200	600	1,000	1,750	2,500
1645	—	200	600	1,000	1,750	2,500
1674	—	200	600	1,000	1,750	2,500
1676/4	—	200	600	1,000	1,750	2,500
1676	—	200	600	1,000	1,750	2,500

KM# 86 2 DAALDERS (Rijks)

Silver **Obv:** Armored knight right with sword on shoulder holding bow **Rev:** Crowned arms divides date **Note:** Dav. #4830.

Date	Mintage	Good	VG	F	VF	XF
1631 Rare	—	—	—	—	—	—
1649 Rare	—	—	—	—	—	—
1674 Rare	—	—	—	—	—	—
1687 Rare	—	—	—	—	—	—

KM# 87 2 DAALDERS (Rijks)

Silver **Obv:** Armored knight with sword on shoulder holding bow **Rev:** Crowned arms divides date **Note:** Klippe. Dav. #4830A.

Date	Mintage	Good	VG	F	VF	XF
1631 Rare	—	—	—	—	—	—

KM# 20 1/2 CAVALIER D'OR

5.0000 g., 0.9200 Gold 0.1479 oz. AGW **Obv:** Knight horseback right brandishing sword **Rev:** Crowned arms, date above **Note:** Fr. # 252.

Date	Mintage	VG	F	VF	XF	Unc
1607	—	200	350	600	1,000	—
1608	—	200	350	600	1,000	—

Date	Mintage	VG	F	VF	XF	Unc
1617	—	200	350	600	1,000	—
1621	—	200	350	600	1,000	—
1622	—	200	350	600	1,000	—
1623	—	250	450	800	1,500	—
1632/22	—	250	450	800	1,500	—
1632/1	—	250	450	800	1,500	—
1634	—	250	450	800	1,500	—
1644	—	200	350	600	1,000	—
1645	—	200	350	600	1,000	—

KM# 19 CAVALIER D'OR

10.0000 g., 0.9200 Gold 0.2958 oz. AGW **Obv:** Knight horseback right brandishing sword **Rev:** Crowned arms, date above **Note:** Fr. # 251.

Date	Mintage	VG	F	VF	XF	Unc
1606	—	450	1,200	2,000	3,000	—
1607	—	450	1,200	2,000	3,000	—
1608	—	450	1,200	2,000	3,000	—
1621	—	450	1,200	2,000	3,000	—
1622	—	450	1,200	2,000	3,000	—
1623	—	450	1,200	2,000	3,000	—
1624	—	450	1,200	2,000	3,000	—
1625	—	450	1,200	2,000	3,000	—
1629	—	450	1,200	2,000	3,000	—
1632	—	450	1,200	2,000	3,000	—

TRADE COINAGE

KM# 12 DUCAT

3.4900 g., 0.9860 Gold 0.1106 oz. AGW **Obv:** Armored, standing Knight holding bundle of arrows, divides date **Obv. Legend:** CONCORDIA • RES PAR • CRES • HOL • **Rev:** Inscription within ornamented square **Rev. Inscription:** MO:ORD:/ PROVIN./ FOEDER BELGAD/ LEGIMP. **Note:** Fr. #249, 250.

Date	Mintage	VG	F	VF	XF	Unc
1603	—	120	160	225	350	—
1604	—	150	170	300	450	—
1605	—	120	160	225	350	—
1606	—	120	160	225	350	—
1608	—	120	160	225	350	—
1609	—	120	160	225	350	—
1610	—	120	160	225	350	—
1611	—	120	160	225	350	—
1621	—	175	275	400	600	—
1622	—	175	275	400	600	—
1631	—	120	150	200	300	—
1632	—	120	150	200	300	—
1633	—	120	150	200	300	—
1634/3	—	120	150	200	300	—
1634	—	120	150	200	300	—
1635	—	120	150	200	300	—
1636	—	120	150	200	300	—
1637	—	120	150	200	300	—
1638	—	120	150	200	300	—
1639	—	120	150	200	300	—
1640	—	175	250	400	600	—
1641	—	120	150	200	300	—
1642	—	120	150	200	300	—
1643	—	120	150	200	300	—
1644	—	120	150	200	300	—
1645	—	120	150	200	300	—
1646/5	—	175	350	600	800	—
1646	—	120	150	200	300	—
1647	—	120	150	200	300	—
1648	—	175	350	600	800	—

Date	Mintage	VG	F	VF	XF	Unc
1649	—	120	150	200	300	—
1650	—	120	150	200	300	—
1651/0	—	120	150	200	300	—
1651	—	120	150	200	300	—
1652	—	120	150	200	300	—
1653	—	120	150	200	300	—
1654	—	120	150	200	300	—
1655	—	120	150	200	300	—
1657	—	175	350	600	800	—
1658	—	175	350	600	800	—
1659/5	—	120	150	200	300	—
1659	—	120	150	200	300	—
1660	—	120	150	200	300	—
1661	—	175	350	600	800	—
1662	—	140	200	400	600	—
1663	—	175	350	600	800	—
1664	—	175	350	600	800	—
1665	—	175	350	400	600	—
1666	—	140	175	275	400	—
1668	—	175	350	600	800	—
1672	—	120	150	200	300	—
1673	—	120	150	200	300	—
1674/3	—	140	250	400	500	—
1674	—	120	150	200	300	—
1683	—	120	150	200	300	—
1685	—	175	350	600	800	—
1686	—	120	150	200	300	—
1688	—	120	150	200	300	—
1691	—	120	150	200	300	—
1692	—	120	150	200	300	—
1693	—	120	150	200	300	—
1694/1	—	120	150	200	300	—
1698	—	175	350	600	800	—
1699	—	120	150	200	300	—

KM# 35 2 DUCAT

6.9800 g., 0.9860 Gold 0.2213 oz. AGW **Obv:** Standing knight wearing helmet **Rev:** Tablet with five line inscription **Note:** Fr. #247.

Date	Mintage	VG	F	VF	XF	Unc
1645	—	250	500	800	1,250	—
1646	—	250	500	800	1,250	—
1647	—	250	500	800	1,250	—
1648	—	250	500	800	1,250	—
1649	—	250	500	800	1,250	—
1650	—	250	500	800	1,250	—
1651	—	250	500	800	1,250	—
1652	—	250	500	800	1,250	—
1653	—	250	500	800	1,250	—
1654	—	275	450	850	1,500	—
1655/4	—	275	450	850	1,500	—
1655	—	250	400	650	1,250	—
1656	—	300	600	1,000	1,750	—
1657/0	—	275	450	800	1,500	—
1657	—	250	500	800	1,250	—
1658	—	300	600	1,000	1,750	—
1659	—	250	500	800	1,250	—
1660	—	250	500	800	1,250	—
1661	—	250	500	800	1,250	—
1662	—	250	500	800	1,250	—
1663	—	300	600	1,000	1,750	—

KM# 47 2 DUCAT

6.9800 g., 0.9860 Gold 0.2213 oz. AGW **Obv:** Standing, armored knight holding bundle of arrows, divides date within broken circle **Obv. Legend:** CONCORDIA • RES PAR • CRES • HOL • **Rev:** Inscription within ornamented square **Rev. Inscription:** MO:ORD:/ PROVIN./ FOEDER/ BELG•AD/ LEG•IMP• **Edge:** Plain

Date	Mintage	VG	F	VF	XF	Unc
1671	—	250	400	600	1,000	—
1672	—	250	400	600	1,000	—
1673	—	250	400	600	1,000	—
1674	—	250	400	600	1,000	—
1687	—	300	900	1,300	2,200	—
1694	—	400	800	1,200	2,000	—

COUNTERMARKED COINAGE

1693

During the late 17th century many circulating coins were found to be underweight. In 1693 coins meeting the legal requirements were countermarked for a specific province or city, such as HOL for Holland.

KM# 68 14 STUIVERS

Silver **Countermark:** HOL **Note:** Countermark on Friesland KM#67.

CM Date	Host Date	Good	VG	F	VF	XF
ND(1693)	1688	—	—	—	—	—

KM# 69.18 28 STUIVERS

Silver **Countermark:** HOL **Note:** Countermarked on Deventer 28 Stuivers KM # 81.2.

CM Date	Host Date	Good	VG	F	VF	XF
ND(1693)	1685	—	—	—	—	—

KM# 69.1 28 STUIVERS

Silver **Countermark:** HOL **Note:** Countermark on Deventer KM#79.

CM Date	Host Date	Good	VG	F	VF	XF
ND(1693)	1684	—	—	—	—	—

KM# 69.2 28 STUIVERS

Silver **Countermark:** HOL **Note:** Countermark on Deventer KM#81.

CM Date	Host Date	Good	VG	F	VF	XF
ND(1963)	1685-92	—	—	—	—	—

KM# 69.3 28 STUIVERS

Silver **Countermark:** HOL **Note:** Countermark on Friesland KM#10.

CM Date	Host Date	Good	VG	F	VF	XF
ND(1693)	1601-91	30.00	60.00	100	160	—

KM# 69.6 28 STUIVERS

Silver **Countermark:** HOL **Note:** Countermark on Groningen & Ommeland KM#31.

CM Date	Host Date	Good	VG	F	VF	XF
ND(1693)	1673-77	—	—	200	—	—

KM# 69.7 28 STUIVERS

Silver **Countermark:** HOL **Note:** Countermark on Groningen & Ommeland KM#33.

CM Date	Host Date	Good	VG	F	VF	XF
ND(1693)	1674	—	—	—	—	—

KM# 69.19 28 STUIVERS

Silver **Countermark:** HOL **Note:** Countermark on Groningen & Ommeland 28 Stuiver, KM#42.

CM Date	Host Date	Good	VG	F	VF	XF
ND(1693)	1685-86	—	—	—	—	—

KM# 69.8 28 STUIVERS

Silver **Countermark:** HOL **Note:** Countermark on Groningen & Ommeland KM#47.

CM Date	Host Date	Good	VG	F	VF	XF
ND(1693)	1685-86	75.00	150	250	—	—

KM# 69.4 28 STUIVERS

Silver **Countermark:** HOL **Note:** Countermark on Groningen & Ommeland KM#49.

CM Date	Host Date	Good	VG	F	VF	XF
ND(1693)	1690-92	—	—	—	—	—

KM# 69.5 28 STUIVERS

Silver **Countermark:** HOL **Note:** Countermark on Groningen & Ommeland KM#50.

CM Date	Host Date	Good	VG	F	VF	XF
ND(1693)	1690	—	—	—	—	—

KM# 69.9 28 STUIVERS

Silver **Countermark:** HOL **Note:** Countermark on Groningen & Ommeland KM#52.

CM Date	Host Date	Good	VG	F	VF	XF
ND(1693)	1692	—	—	—	—	—

KM# 69.10 28 STUIVERS

Silver **Countermark:** HOL **Note:** Countermark on Kampen KM#23.

CM Date	Host Date	Good	VG	F	VF	XF
ND(1693)	1616-19	—	—	—	—	—

KM# 69.11 28 STUIVERS

Silver **Countermark:** HOL **Note:** Countermark on Kampen KM#76.

CM Date	Host Date	Good	VG	F	VF	XF
ND(1693)	1680-86	—	—	—	—	—

KM# 69.12 28 STUIVERS

Silver **Countermark:** HOL **Note:** Countermark on Nijmegen KM#27.

CM Date	Host Date	Good	VG	F	VF	XF
ND(1693)	1685-90	—	—	—	—	—

KM# 69.13 28 STUIVERS

Silver **Countermark:** HOL **Note:** Countermark on Overyssel KM#55.

CM Date	Host Date	Good	VG	F	VF	XF
ND(1693)	1685-89	—	—	—	—	—

KM# 69.14 28 STUIVERS

Silver **Countermark:** HOL **Note:** Countermark on West Friesland KM#90.

CM Date	Host Date	Good	VG	F	VF	XF
ND(1693)	1685-87	—	—	—	—	—

KM# 69.17 28 STUIVERS

Silver, 37 mm. **Countermark:** HOL **Note:** c/m on West Friesland, 28 Stuivers.

CM Date	Host Date	Good	VG	F	VF	XF
ND(1693)	ND	60.00	120	200	300	—

KM# 69.15 28 STUIVERS

Silver **Countermark:** HOL **Note:** Countermark on Zutphen KM#25.

CM Date	Host Date	Good	VG	F	VF	XF
ND(1693)	1690	—	—	—	—	—

KM# 69.16 28 STUIVERS

Silver **Countermark:** HOL **Note:** Countermark on Zwolle KM#78.

CM Date	Host Date	Good	VG	F	VF	XF
ND(1693)	1679-86	—	—	—	—	—

PATTERNS

Including off metal strikes

KM#	Date	Mintage	Identification	Mkt Val
Pn1	1670	—	6 Stuivers. Gold. 7.0000 g. KM#45.2.	—
Pn2	1671	—	6 Stuivers. Gold. 7.0000 g. KM#45.2.	—
Pn3	1672	—	Ducaton. Gold. 34.7000 g. KM#51.	—
Pn4	1672	—	Ducaton. Gold. 38.3000 g. KM#51.	—
Pn5	1672	—	Ducaton. Gold. 62.3000 g. KM#51.	—
Pn6	1672	—	Ducaton. Gold. 40.8000 g. KM#49.1.	—
Pn7	1673	—	Ducaton. Gold. 30.5000 g. KM#49.1.	—
Pn8	1674	—	6 Stuivers. Gold. 7.0000 g. KM#45.2.	—
Pn9	1680	—	Ducaton. Gold. 38.3000 g.	—
Pn10	ND	—	2 Gulden. Gold. 27.6000 g. KM#62.	—
Pn11	1681	—	3 Gulden. Gold. KM#63.	10,000
Pn12	1681	—	Ducaton. Gold. 38.4000 g. KM#63.	—
Pn13	1684	—	6 Stuivers. Gold. 7.0000 g. KM#45.2.	—
Pn14	1684	—	3 Gulden. Gold. KM#66.	—
Pn15	1684	—	Daalder. Gold. 35.0000 g. KM#17.	—
Pn16	1687	—	Ducaton. Gold. 34.5000 g. KM#51.	10,000
Pn17	1692	—	5 Stuivers. Gold. KM#70.	2,000
Pn18	1692	—	Gulden. Gold. 13.8000 g. KM#61.	—
Pn19	1687	—	Daalder. Gold. 34.5000 g. KM#18.	30,000
Pn20	1694	—	1/2 Gulden. Gold. KM#72.	—
Pn21	1696	—	1/2 Gulden. Gold. 10.3000 g. KM#65a.	—
Pn22	1697	—	2 Stuivers. Gold. 1697.0000 g. KM#48a.	—
Pn23	1697	—	2 Gulden. Gold. KM#62.	—
Pn24	1697	—	2 Gulden. Gold. 27.5000 g. KM#75.	—
Pn25	1698	—	1/2 3 (1-1/2) Gulden. Gold. 20.6000 g. KM#74a.	—
Pn26	1698	—	1/2 Gulden. Gold. 10.3000 g. KM#65a.	—

PIEFORTS

KM#	Date	Mintage	Identification	Mkt Val
P1	1631	—	Daalder. Silver. KM18.	—
P2	1631	—	Daalder. Silver. Klippe, KM18.	—
P3	1636	—	Lion Daalder. Silver. KM17.	—
P4	1640	—	Lion Daalder. Silver. KM17.	—
P5	1645	—	Lion Daalder. Silver. KM17.	—
P6	1649	—	Daalder. Silver. KM18.	—
P7	1672	—	Ducaton. Silver. KM49.	700
PA8	1672	—	Ducaton. Silver. Klippe, KM49.2.	—
P8	1672	—	Ducaton. Silver. Klippe, KM50.	—
P9	1672	—	Ducaton. Silver. KM51.	1,500
P10	1673	—	Ducaton. Silver. KM49.	—
P11	1673	—	Ducaton. Silver. Klippe, KM50.	—
P12	1673	—	Ducaton. Silver. Klippe, triple weight, KM50.	—
P13	1673	—	Ducaton. Silver. KM51.	2,000
P14	1673	—	Silver Ducat. KM52.	2,000
P15	1674	—	Ducaton. Silver. KM51.	1,500
P16	1674	—	Silver Ducat. KM52.	—
P17	1674	—	Lion Daalder. Silver. KM17.	—
P18	1674	—	Daalder. Silver. KM18.	1,500
P19	1675	—	Ducaton. Silver. KM51.	—
P20	1676	—	Ducaton. Silver. KM51.	—
P21	1676/4	—	Lion Daalder. Silver. KM17.	—
P22	1676	—	Lion Daalder. Silver. KM17.	—
P23	1678/6	—	Ducaton. Silver. KM51.	2,000
P24	1678	—	Ducaton. Silver. KM51.	—
P25	1679/6	—	Ducaton. Silver. KM51.	2,000
P26	1679	—	Ducaton. Silver. KM51.	—
P27	1680	—	Ducaton. Silver. KM51.	—
PA27	1680	—	6 Stuivers. Silver. KM45.2	500
P28	1682	—	3 Gulden. Silver. KM63, Dav.#A4952.	2,000
P29	1683	—	Silver Ducat. KM52.	2,500

KM#	Date	Mintage	Identification	Mkt Val
P30	1684	—	3 Gulden. Silver. KM66, Dav.#A4953.	2,000
PA31	1687	—	Daalder. Gold. KM#18, Rare.	—
PB31	1687	—	Ducaton. Gold. KM#51.	2,000
P31	1687	—	Ducaton. Silver. KM51.	—
P32	1692	—	5 Stuivers. Gold.	2,000
P33	1693	—	Ducaton. Silver. KM51.	2,500
P34	1693	—	Silver Ducat. KM52.	2,000
P35	1694	—	Silver Ducat. KM52.	2,000
P36	1697	—	2 Stuivers. Silver. KM48	500

HUIZEN

COMMUNE

STANDARD COINAGE

KM# 5 DUIT

Copper **Obv:** Crowned arms **Rev:** Inscription in wreath **Rev. Inscription:** IN / HVES / SEN

Date	Mintage	Good	VG	F	VF	XF
ND(1611-13)	800	3.00	10.00	30.00	50.00	75.00

KM# 6 DUIT

Copper **Obv:** Crowned arms **Rev:** Inscription in wreath **Rev. Inscription:** CVSA / HVNS / SIÆ

Date	Mintage	Good	VG	F	VF	XF
ND(1611-13)	Inc. above	—	10.00	30.00	50.00	75.00

KM# 7 2 DUIT (Oord)

Copper **Obv:** Crowned arms **Obv. Legend:** IVSTITIA . THRONVM . FIR **Rev:** Cross, date **Rev. Legend:** MO: POSS: PRIN IVL. E. MON

Date	Mintage	Good	VG	F	VF	XF
1609	—	5.00	15.00	40.00	60.00	85.00
1611	—	3.00	10.00	30.00	50.00	75.00

KM# 8 STUIVER

Silver

Date	Mintage	Good	VG	F	VF	XF
ND(1620)	—	8.00	25.00	70.00	100	150

KM# 9 ARENDSCHILLING

Silver **Note:** Titles of Rudolph II.

Date	Mintage	Good	VG	F	VF	XF
ND	—	12.00	40.00	100	150	225

KAMPEN

PROVINCE

STANDARD COINAGE

KM# 36 DUIT

Copper **Obv:** Arms in beaded circle **Rev:** CAM/PEN/1639 in wreath

Date	Mintage	VG	F	VF	XF	Unc
1639	—	12.00	30.00	60.00	100	—

KM# 36a DUIT

12.6000 g., Silver **Obv:** Arms in beaded circle **Rev:** CAM/PEN/ 1639 in wreath

Date	Mintage	VG	F	VF	XF	Unc
1639	—	—	—	—	—	—

KM# 40 DUIT

Copper **Obv:** Arms in wreath

Date	Mintage	VG	F	VF	XF	Unc
1644	—	13.00	32.50	65.00	110	—

KM# 40a DUIT

Gold **Obv:** Arms in wreath

Date	Mintage	VG	F	VF	XF	Unc
1644	—	—	—	—	—	—

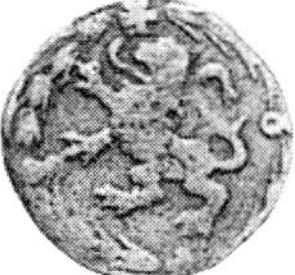

KM# 41 DUIT

Copper **Obv:** CAM/DEN, date below in ornamental circle **Rev:** Rampant lion left in wreath

Date	Mintage	VG	F	VF	XF	Unc
1644	—	18.00	45.00	90.00	180	—

KM# 51 DUIT

Copper **Obv:** City arms in wreath **Rev:** CAM/DEN(date) in ornamental circle **Note:** Varieties exist.

Date	Mintage	VG	F	VF	XF	Unc
1655	—	12.00	20.00	35.00	55.00	—
1658	—	15.00	25.00	45.00	90.00	—
1659	—	12.00	25.00	40.00	85.00	—
1660	—	10.00	17.50	25.00	60.00	—
1661	—	10.00	15.00	22.50	50.00	—
1662	—	10.00	15.00	22.50	50.00	—
1663	—	10.00	15.00	22.50	50.00	—
1664	—	10.00	15.00	22.50	50.00	—
1665	—	10.00	12.50	20.00	50.00	—
1666	—	10.00	12.50	20.00	50.00	—
1668	—	12.00	20.00	35.00	75.00	—
1669	—	10.00	12.50	20.00	50.00	—
1670	—	10.00	12.50	20.00	50.00	—
1671	—	10.00	12.50	20.00	50.00	—

KM# 53 DUIT

Copper **Obv:** Crowned city arms

Date	Mintage	VG	F	VF	XF	Unc
1658	—	15.00	30.00	60.00	85.00	—
1659	—	10.00	12.50	35.00	70.00	—
1660 Error	—	15.00	30.00	60.00	85.00	—
1660	—	10.00	12.50	35.00	70.00	—
1661	—	10.00	12.50	35.00	70.00	—
1662	—	10.00	12.50	35.00	70.00	—

KM# 51a DUIT

Silver **Obv:** City arms in wreath **Rev:** CAM/DEN(date) in ornamental circle

Date	Mintage	VG	F	VF	XF	Unc
1659	—	—	—	—	—	—

KM# 5 STUIVER

2.0000 g., Billon **Obv:** Crowned arms divide value in inner circle **Rev:** Ornamental long cross with quatrefoil around center **Note:** Varieties exist.

Date	Mintage	VG	F	VF	XF	Unc
ND(ca.1621)	—	10.00	25.00	60.00	125	—

KM# 71 2 STUIVERS

1.7300 g., 0.5830 Silver 0.0324 oz. ASW **Obv:** Crowned rampant lion left holding sword and arrows, value at sides **Rev:** CAM/PEN/(date)

Date	Mintage	VG	F	VF	XF	Unc
1677	—	7.50	20.00	40.00	100	—
1678	—	7.50	20.00	40.00	100	—
1679	—	7.50	20.00	40.00	100	—
1680	—	7.50	20.00	40.00	100	—
1681	—	7.50	20.00	40.00	100	—

KM# 6 3 STUIVERS (1/2 Schelling)

3.0000 g., 0.5000 Silver 0.0482 oz. ASW **Obv:** Crowned arms in inner circle **Rev:** Crowned double-headed eagle in inner circle

Date	Mintage	VG	F	VF	XF	Unc
ND	—	35.00	100	200	400	—

KM# 7 6 STUIVERS (Schelling)

6.0000 g., 0.5000 Silver 0.0964 oz. ASW **Obv:** Crowned arms within circle **Rev:** Crowned double-headed imperial eagle within circle, titles of Rudolf II

Date	Mintage	VG	F	VF	XF	Unc
ND	—	10.00	22.00	45.00	75.00	—

KM# 22 6 STUIVERS (Schelling)

Silver **Obv:** Titles of Matthias I

Date	Mintage	VG	F	VF	XF	Unc
ND	—	10.00	22.00	45.00	75.00	—

KM# 45 6 STUIVERS (Schelling)

Silver **Obv:** Titles of Ferdinand III

Date	Mintage	VG	F	VF	XF	Unc
ND	—	10.00	25.00	40.00	95.00	—

KM# 67 6 STUIVERS (Schelling)

Silver **Obv:** Titles of Leopold I

Date	Mintage	VG	F	VF	XF	Unc
1675	—	15.00	40.00	70.00	100	—

KM# 75 6 STUIVERS (Schelling)

Silver **Obv:** Crowned arms with lion supporters in inner circle, date at top **Rev:** Knight with sword on horseback right **Note:** Mint mark: Rider.

Date	Mintage	VG	F	VF	XF	Unc
1680	—	15.00	35.00	60.00	150	—

KM# 77 6 STUIVERS (Schelling)

4.9500 g., 0.5830 Silver 0.0928 oz. ASW **Obv:** Crowned arms divide value, date above crown **Rev:** Knight with sword on horseback right, crowned arms below horse

Date	Mintage	VG	F	VF	XF	Unc
1681	—	7.50	12.50	30.00	60.00	—
1682	—	7.50	12.50	30.00	60.00	—
1683	—	15.00	30.00	60.00	150	—
1684	—	15.00	30.00	60.00	150	—
1686	—	7.50	12.50	30.00	60.00	—
1688	—	15.00	30.00	60.00	150	—
1689	—	7.50	12.50	30.00	60.00	—
1690	—	7.50	12.50	30.00	60.00	—
1691	—	7.50	12.50	30.00	60.00	—

KM# 23 28 STUIVERS (Florin)

19.5000 g., 0.6730 Silver 0.4219 oz. ASW **Obv:** Crowned arms within circle, date above crown, value below **Rev:** Crowned double-headed imperial eagle within circle, titles of Matthias **Note:** Mint mark: Rosette.

Date	Mintage	VG	F	VF	XF	Unc
1616	—	50.00	125	250	350	—
1618	—	40.00	100	200	300	—
1619	—	50.00	125	250	350	—
ND(1665)	—	35.00	75.00	175	250	—

KM# 30 28 STUIVERS (Florin)

Silver **Obv:** Titles of Ferdinand II

Date	Mintage	VG	F	VF	XF	Unc
1628	—	40.00	100	200	300	—

KM# 76 28 STUIVERS (Florin)

Silver **Obv:** Titles of Matthias I **Note:** Mint mark: Rider.

Date	Mintage	VG	F	VF	XF	Unc
1680/60	—	25.00	70.00	120	250	—
1680	—	25.00	70.00	120	250	—
(16)81	—	25.00	60.00	100	200	—
1682	—	20.00	60.00	100	200	—
(16)83	—	20.00	60.00	100	200	—
(16)84	—	20.00	60.00	100	200	—
(16)85	—	15.00	50.00	100	200	—
(16)86	—	15.00	50.00	100	200	—

KM# 64 1/2 DUCATON

16.8900 g., 0.9410 Silver 0.5110 oz. ASW

Date	Mintage	VG	F	VF	XF	Unc
1670	—	75.00	150	250	550	—

KM# 54 DUCATON (40 Stuiver - Silver Rider)

32.7800 g., 0.9410 Silver 0.9917 oz. ASW **Note:** Mint mark: Lily

Date	Mintage	VG	F	VF	XF	Unc
1659	207,715	50.00	125	200	350	—
1660	Inc. above	50.00	125	200	350	—
1661	—	50.00	125	200	350	—
1662	—	50.00	125	200	350	—
1663	—	50.00	125	200	350	—

KM# 61.1 DUCATON (40 Stuiver - Silver Rider)

Silver **Obv:** Smaller knight, city arms below in inner circle **Note:** Dav. #4945. Mint mark: Moor's head.

Date	Mintage	VG	F	VF	XF	Unc
1664	—	50.00	125	200	350	—
1665	—	60.00	125	250	400	—
1666	—	50.00	125	200	350	—
1667	—	60.00	125	250	400	—
1668	—	50.00	125	200	350	—
1669	—	60.00	125	250	400	—
1670	—	50.00	125	200	350	—
1675	—	50.00	125	200	350	—

KM# 61.2 DUCATON (40 Stuiver - Silver Rider)

Silver **Obv:** Smaller knight, city arms below in inner circle **Note:** Dav. #4945. Mint mark: Rider. Varieties exist.

Date	Mintage	VG	F	VF	XF	Unc
1676	155,515	30.00	100	150	300	—
1677	Inc. above	30.00	100	150	300	—
1678	Inc. above	30.00	100	150	300	—
1679/6	Inc. above	30.00	100	150	300	—
1679	Inc. above	30.00	100	150	300	—
1680/79	Inc. above	40.00	125	200	350	—
1680	Inc. above	30.00	100	150	300	—

KM# 78 3 GULDEN (60 Stuiver)

31.8200 g., 0.9200 Silver 0.9412 oz. ASW **Obv:** Crowned arms divide value, date above crown **Rev:** Standing female figure leaning on Bible on column, holding spear with Liberty cap **Note:** Dav. #4969. Mint mark: Rider

Date	Mintage	VG	F	VF	XF	Unc
1682	193,695	80.00	200	350	550	—
1862 error	Inc. above	100	250	450	700	—
1683	Inc. above	80.00	200	350	550	—
1686	Inc. above	80.00	200	350	550	—
1687	Inc. above	80.00	200	350	550	—

KM# 55.1 DUCAT (48 Stuiver)

28.2500 g., 0.8730 Silver 0.7929 oz. ASW **Note:** Dav. #4918. Mint mark: Lily.

Date	Mintage	VG	F	VF	XF	Unc
1659	—	25.00	50.00	100	250	—
1660	—	25.00	50.00	100	250	—
1661	—	25.00	50.00	100	250	—
1662	—	25.00	50.00	150	250	—
1662/1	—	40.00	80.00	200	350	—
1663	—	200	400	800	1,500	—
1664	—	40.00	80.00	200	350	—

KM# 55.2 DUCAT (48 Stuiver)

28.2500 g., 0.8730 Silver 0.7929 oz. ASW **Rev:** Lion without sword and arrows **Note:** Dav. #4918. Mint mark: Lily.

Date	Mintage	VG	F	VF	XF	Unc
1659	—	40.00	80.00	175	300	—

KM# 68 DUCAT (48 Stuiver)

Silver **Obv:** Armored knight standing behind shield looking right with sword on shoulder **Rev:** Crowned lion shield divides date **Note:** Dav. #4919. Mint mark: Rider.

Date	Mintage	VG	F	VF	XF	Unc
1676	15,820	40.00	80.00	175	350	—
1677	Inc. above	40.00	80.00	175	350	—

KM# 79 DUCAT (48 Stuiver)

Silver **Obv:** Armored knight standing behind shield looking right with sword on shoulder **Rev:** Crowned lion shield, date above **Note:** Dav. #4920.

Date	Mintage	VG	F	VF	XF	Unc
1679	7,810	50.00	100	200	400	—
1684	Inc. above	40.00	80.00	125	175	—

KM# 87 DUCAT (48 Stuiver)

Silver **Obv:** Armored knight standing behind shield looking right with sword on shoulder and ribbon bow in other hand **Rev:** Crowned lion shield divides date

Date	Mintage	VG	F	VF	XF	Unc
1693	—	50.00	100	200	400	—

KM# 2 1/5 DAALDER (Philip - 10 Stuiver)

6.8500 g., 0.8330 Silver 0.1834 oz. ASW **Obv:** Crowned arms on ornamental cross in inner circle **Rev:** Bust of Rudolph II left in inner circle

Date	Mintage	VG	F	VF	XF	Unc
ND(1601)	—	250	600	1,500	3,000	—

KM# 3 1/2 DAALDER (Philip - 25 Stuiver)

17.1300 g., 0.8330 Silver 0.4587 oz. ASW **Obv:** Crowned arms on ornamental cross in inner circle **Rev:** Bust of Rudolph II left in inner circle

Date	Mintage	VG	F	VF	XF	Unc
ND(1601)	—	—	—	—	—	—

KM# 43 1/2 DAALDER (Lion - 24 Stuiver)

13.8400 g., 0.7500 Silver 0.3337 oz. ASW **Obv:** Armored knight looking to right above lion shield **Rev:** Rampant lion left in inner circle, date divided at top **Note:** Mint mark: Lily

Date	Mintage	VG	F	VF	XF	Unc
1646	—	60.00	150	220	350	—
1647	—	60.00	150	220	350	—
1648	—	80.00	175	250	400	—
1657	—	60.00	150	220	350	—

KM# 8 DAALDER (Philip - 50 Stuiver)

34.2770 g., 0.8330 Silver 0.9180 oz. ASW **Obv:** Crownd arms on ornamental cross in inner circle **Rev:** Bust of Rudolph II left in inner circle **Note:** Dav. #4984.

Date	Mintage	VG	F	VF	XF	Unc
ND(1601)	—	—	—	—	—	—

KM# 21 DAALDER (Arendsrijks 50 Stuiver)

Silver **Obv:** City arms with digits of date between towers in inner circle **Rev:** Crowned double-headed eagle in inner circle, titles of Matthias **Note:** Dav. #4980.

Date	Mintage	VG	F	VF	XF	Unc
1614	—	—	—	—	—	—
1615	—	—	—	—	—	—

KM# 35.1 DAALDER (Lion - 48 Stuiver)

27.6800 g., 0.7500 Silver 0.6674 oz. ASW **Obv:** Armored knight looking right behind lion shield **Rev:** Rampant lion left **Note:** Dav. #4879. Without mint mark.

Date	Mintage	VG	F	VF	XF	Unc
1637	—	30.00	60.00	120	200	—
1642	—	30.00	60.00	120	200	—
1643	—	30.00	60.00	120	200	—
1656	—	60.00	150	250	450	—
1671	—	30.00	80.00	150	300	—

KM# 42.1 DAALDER (Lion - 48 Stuiver)

27.6800 g., 0.7500 Silver 0.6674 oz. ASW **Obv:** Armored knight looking left behind lion shield **Rev:** Rampant lion left **Note:** Without mint mark. Dav. # 4879.

Date	Mintage	VG	F	VF	XF	Unc
1644	—	60.00	120	200	400	—
1646	—	30.00	60.00	100	200	—
1656	—	75.00	150	300	600	—

KM# 42.2 DAALDER (Lion - 48 Stuiver)

27.6800 g., 0.7500 Silver 0.6674 oz. ASW **Obv:** Armored knight looking left behind lion shield **Rev:** Rampant lion left **Note:** Mint mark: Lily. Dav. # 4879.

Date	Mintage	VG	F	VF	XF	Unc
1646/3	—	65.00	120	225	350	—
1646	—	30.00	70.00	100	175	—
1647/4	—	30.00	70.00	100	175	—
1647	—	30.00	70.00	100	175	—
1648/7	—	30.00	70.00	100	175	—
1648	—	30.00	70.00	100	175	—
1649	—	30.00	70.00	100	175	—
1650	—	30.00	70.00	100	175	—

KM# 35.2 DAALDER (Lion - 48 Stuiver)

27.6800 g., 0.7500 Silver 0.6674 oz. ASW **Obv:** Armored knight looking right behind lion shield **Rev:** Rampant lion left **Note:** Dav. #4879. Mint mark: Lily.

Date	Mintage	VG	F	VF	XF	Unc
1650	—	25.00	60.00	80.00	150	—
1651	—	25.00	60.00	80.00	150	—
1652	—	25.00	60.00	80.00	150	—
1653	—	25.00	60.00	80.00	150	—
1654	—	45.00	80.00	150	300	—
1655	—	45.00	80.00	150	300	—
1657	—	45.00	80.00	150	300	—
1662	—	45.00	80.00	150	300	—
1664	—	45.00	80.00	150	300	—

KM# 35.3 DAALDER (Lion - 48 Stuiver)

27.6800 g., 0.7500 Silver 0.6674 oz. ASW **Note:** Dav. #4879. Mint mark: Moor's head.

Date	Mintage	VG	F	VF	XF	Unc
1664	—	25.00	60.00	80.00	170	—
1666	—	55.00	100	250	400	—
1667	—	25.00	60.00	80.00	170	—
1668	—	25.00	60.00	80.00	170	—

KM# 35.4 DAALDER (Lion - 48 Stuiver)

27.6800 g., 0.7500 Silver 0.6674 oz. ASW **Note:** Dav. #4879. Mint mark: Rider.

Date	Mintage	VG	F	VF	XF	Unc
1675	—	35.00	80.00	140	200	—
1676	—	30.00	70.00	110	175	—
1677	—	25.00	60.00	80.00	175	—
1679	—	30.00	70.00	110	175	—
1681	—	25.00	60.00	80.00	175	—
1682/1	—	35.00	80.00	140	200	—
1682	—	25.00	60.00	80.00	175	—
1683	—	25.00	60.00	80.00	175	—
1684	—	25.00	60.00	80.00	175	—
1685	—	25.00	60.00	80.00	175	—
1686	—	25.00	60.00	80.00	175	—
1687	—	25.00	60.00	80.00	175	—
1688	—	25.00	60.00	80.00	175	—
1689	—	30.00	70.00	110	200	—
1690	—	30.00	70.00	110	200	—
1691	—	30.00	70.00	130	150	—
1692	—	25.00	60.00	80.00	175	—
1693	—	25.00	60.00	80.00	175	—

KM# 34 DAALDER (Rijks - 48 Stuiver)

29.0300 g., 0.8850 Silver 0.8260 oz. ASW **Rev:** Titles of Ferdinand III **Note:** Dav. #4983.

Date	Mintage	VG	F	VF	XF	Unc
1633	—	100	200	350	700	—
1649	—	80.00	150	300	600	—
1651	—	80.00	150	300	600	—
1653	—	80.00	150	300	600	—
1654	—	80.00	150	300	600	—

KM# 52 DAALDER (Rijks - 48 Stuiver)

29.0300 g., 0.8850 Silver 0.8260 oz. ASW **Note:** Dav. #4985.

Date	Mintage	VG	F	VF	XF	Unc
1655	—	50.00	150	300	600	—
1657	—	50.00	150	300	600	—

KM# 65 DAALDER (Lion)

Silver **Obv:** Armored knight right holding shield with city arms **Note:** Dav. #4880.

Date	Mintage	VG	F	VF	XF	Unc
1671	—	40.00	100	200	400	—
1672	—	40.00	100	200	400	—

KM# 70 DAALDER (Rijks)

29.0300 g., 0.8850 Silver 0.8260 oz. ASW **Note:** Dav. #4845. Without inner circle.

Date	Mintage	VG	F	VF	XF	Unc
1676	8,420	200	500	1,000	2,000	—

KM# 69 DAALDER (Rijks)

Silver **Obv:** Laureate half figure holding sword and arms in inner circle **Rev:** Crowned arms divide date in inner circle **Note:** Dav. #4845A. Mint mark: Rider.

Date	Mintage	VG	F	VF	XF	Unc
1676	—	100	300	500	700	—

KM# 85 DAALDER (30 Stuiver)

Silver **Obv:** Crowned arms with lion supporters, value below. **Rev:** Standing knight with sword behind crowned arms to left, date in legend

Date	Mintage	VG	F	VF	XF	Unc
1690	—	80.00	250	400	800	—
1692	—	40.00	125	200	300	—

KM# 9 1/4 NOBLE

Gold **Obv:** Ruler in ship in inner circle **Rev:** Floriated cross with crowned lions in angles **Note:** Fr. #153.

Date	Mintage	VG	F	VF	XF	Unc
ND(ca.1600)	—	1,000	2,000	3,000	4,000	—

KM# 11 1/2 NOBLE

Gold **Rev:** Radiant rose in circle of 4 crowned lis and 4 crowned lions **Note:** Fr. 152.

Date	Mintage	VG	F	VF	XF	Unc
ND(1600-02)	—	500	700	800	1,200	—

KM# 10 1/2 NOBLE

Gold **Obv:** Ruler in ship in inner circle **Rev:** Floriated cross with crowned lions in angles **Note:** Fr. 152a.

Date	Mintage	VG	F	VF	XF	Unc
ND	—	500	700	800	1,200	—

KM# 13 NOBLE

Gold **Rev:** Radiant rose in circle of 4 crowned lis and 4 crowned lions **Note:** Fr. 151.

Date	Mintage	VG	F	VF	XF	Unc
ND(1600-02)	—	600	850	1,000	1,450	—

KM# 12 NOBLE

Gold **Obv:** Ruler in ship in inner circle **Rev:** Floriated cross with crowned lions in angles **Note:** Fr. 151a.

Date	Mintage	VG	F	VF	XF	Unc
ND	—	600	850	1,000	1,450	—

KM# 14 2 ROSE NOBLE

15.6000 g., Gold **Obv:** Enthroned ruler holding orb and scepter in innr circle **Rev:** Full blown rose with arms at center in inner circle

Date	Mintage	VG	F	VF	XF	Unc
ND(1600-02) Rare	—	—	—	—	—	—

SIEGE COINAGE

Struck after the city was under siege by Christoph Bernard von Galen, the Bishop of Munster

KM# 66 DAALDER

Obv: City arms with CAMPEN below **Rev:** NE/CESSITAS/ALTERA/1672 **Note:** Dav. #4987.

Date	Mintage	VG	F	VF	XF	Unc
1672	—	500	700	1,000	1,500	—

TRADE COINAGE

KM# A20 FLORIN D'OR

3.5000 g., 0.9860 Gold 0.1109 oz. AGW **Obv:** Three shields with tops touching in inner circle **Rev:** Orb in trilobe, titles of Matthias **Note:** Fr. #158.

Date	Mintage	VG	F	VF	XF	Unc
ND(1612-19)	—	175	300	500	1,000	—

KM# 4 DUCAT

3.5000 g., 0.9860 Gold 0.1109 oz. AGW **Rev:** Titles of Rudolph II **Note:** Fr. #161.

Date	Mintage	VG	F	VF	XF	Unc
1600	—	130	250	350	550	—
1601/599	—	125	175	225	400	—
1601	—	125	175	225	400	—
1602	—	125	175	225	400	—
1603/597	—	125	175	250	450	—
1603/02	—	125	175	225	400	—
1603	—	125	175	225	400	—

KM# 24 DUCAT

3.5000 g., 0.9860 Gold 0.1109 oz. AGW **Obv:** Matthias standing right divides date **Rev:** 5-line inscription in tablet

Date	Mintage	VG	F	VF	XF	Unc
1616	—	125	250	350	550	—
1619	—	125	250	350	550	—

KM# 44 DUCAT

3.5000 g., 0.9860 Gold 0.1109 oz. AGW **Obv:** Inscription within ornamented square **Rev:** Ferdinand III, armored standing figure divides date

Date	Mintage	VG	F	VF	XF	Unc
1646	—	125	175	225	400	—
1647	—	125	175	225	400	—
1648	—	125	175	225	400	—
1649	—	125	175	225	400	—
1650	—	125	275	350	550	—
1651	—	125	175	225	400	—
1652/1/0	—	125	275	350	550	—
1652	—	125	175	225	400	—
1653	—	125	175	225	400	—
1654	—	125	175	225	400	—
1655	—	125	175	225	400	—
1656	—	100	275	350	550	—
1658	—	125	175	225	400	—
1659	—	125	175	225	400	—
1660	—	125	175	225	400	—

KM# 60 DUCAT

3.5000 g., 0.9860 Gold 0.1109 oz. AGW **Obv:** Leopold standing right divides date

Date	Mintage	VG	F	VF	XF	Unc
1662	—	80.00	150	200	350	—
1664	—	80.00	150	200	350	—
1666	—	125	250	500	800	—
1668	17,000	80.00	150	200	350	—
1675	—	80.00	150	200	350	—
1676	3,640	80.00	150	200	350	—

KM# 50 2 DUCAT

7.0000 g., 0.9860 Gold 0.2219 oz. AGW **Obv:** Inscription within ornamented square **Rev:** Ferdinand III standing right, divides date **Note:** FR. #160.

Date	Mintage	VG	F	VF	XF	Unc
1650	—	300	600	850	1,250	—
1655	—	300	600	850	1,250	—
1656	—	300	600	850	1,250	—
1657	—	300	600	850	1,250	—
1658	—	300	600	850	1,250	—

PATTERNS

Including off metal strikes

KM#	Date	Mintage	Identification	Mkt Val
Pn1	1615	—	Rijksdaalder. Gold. 6.5000 g. Eagle.	—
Pn2	1618	—	28 Stuivers. Silver. Klippe. KM#23.	—
Pn3	ND(1621)	—	Stuiver. Gold. KM#5.	3,000
Pn4	ND(1621)	—	6 Stuivers. Silver. Klippe. KM#22.	500
Pn5	ND(1621)	—	6 Stuivers. Silver. Octagonal klippe. KM#22.	1,250
Pn6	1639	—	Duit. Tin. 2.0000 g. KM#36.	—
Pn7	1644	—	Duit. Gold.	—
Pn8	1667	—	1/2 Daalder. Silver. Klippe. KM#63.	—
Pn9	ND	—	6 Stuivers. Gold. 6.6500 g. KM#7.	5,000
Pn10	1689	—	Lion Daalder. Gold.	—

PIEFORTS

KM#	Date	Mintage	Identification	Mkt Val
P2	1614	—	Daalder. Silver. Towered building facade, towers divide date. Crowned double-headed imperial eagle, orb on breast. Klippe, KM21.	1,750
P3	1615	—	Daalder. Silver. Klippe, KM21.	—
P4	1616	—	Daalder. Silver. Towered building facade, towers divide date. Imperial double-headed eagle, titles of Ferdinand I. Klippe, KM#21.	—
P5	ND	—	28 Stuivers. Silver. Crowned ornate shield. Crowned double-headed imperial eagle, orb on breast. KM23.	—
P6	1618	—	28 Stuivers. Silver. KM23.	—
P7	1618	—	28 Stuivers. Silver. Diamond planchet, KM23.	—
P8	1618	—	28 Stuivers. Silver. Square planchet, KM23.	1,750
P9	1634	—	Daalder. Silver. KM#34.	—
PA9	1634	—	Daalder. Silver. Klippe, titles of Ferdinand I, KM34.	—
PA10	1639	—	Duit. Copper. KM36.	—
PB10	1639	—	Duit. Copper. KM#36. Klippe.	1,000
P10	1647	—	Lion Daalder. Silver. KM#35.2.	3,000
P11	1648	—	Lion Daalder. Silver. Klippe, KM35.2.	4,000
P12	1649	—	Daalder. Silver. KM45.	—
PA13	1649	—	Daalder. Silver. KM#34.	—
P13	1650	—	Lion Daalder. Silver. Klippe, KM42.	—

KM#	Date	Mintage	Identification	Mkt Val
PA14	1652		Ducat (48 Stuiver) Gold. KM#44.	—
P14	1659	—	Ducaton. Silver. KM54.	2,000
P15	1659	—	Silver Ducat. KM55.	2,500
PA15	1661	—	Ducaton. Silver. KM#54.	3,000
P16	1664	—	Ducaton. Silver. KM54.	2,500
P17	1669	—	Ducaton. Silver. KM61.	—
P18	1670	—	Ducaton. Silver. KM61.	—
P19	1670	—	Ducaton. Silver. Klippe, KM61.	—
P20	1672	—	Duit. Copper. Klippe, KM51.	—
P21	1679	—	Lion Daalder. Silver. KM#36.6.	—
P22	1680	—	28 Stuivers. Silver. Triple weight, KM76.	—
P23	1681	—	28 Stuivers. Silver. KM76.	—
P24	1682	—	28 Stuivers. Silver. KM76.	1,500
P25	1682	—	28 Stuivers. Silver. Triple weight, KM76.	—
P26	1682	—	3 Gulden. Silver. KM78.	—
PA27	1682	—	3 Gulden. Silver. KM#78. Klippe.	5,000
P27	1689	—	Lion Daalder. Silver. KM36.6.	—
P28	1689	—	Ryderschelling. Silver. KM#77.	750

LEEUWARDEN

A commercial and industrial city located on the Ee River. It is noted for its manufactures in gold and silver.

CITY

COUNTERMARKED COINAGE

1693

During the late 17th century many circulating coins were found to be underweight. In 1693 coins meeting the legal requirements were countermarked for a specific province or city, such as L for Leeuwarden.

KM# 5.8 28 STUIVERS

Silver **Countermark:** L **Note:** Countermark L/HOL on Deventer, KM#81.

CM Date	Host Date	Good	VG	F	VF	XF
ND(1693)	(16)85	—	—	—	—	—

KM# 5.1 28 STUIVERS

Silver **Countermark:** L **Note:** Countermark on Deventer KM#81.

CM Date	Host Date	Good	VG	F	VF	XF
ND(1693)	1685-92	—	—	—	—	—

KM# 5.2 28 STUIVERS

Silver **Countermark:** L **Note:** Countermark on Friesland KM#10.

CM Date	Host Date	Good	VG	F	VF	XF
ND(1693)	1601-91	—	—	—	—	—

KM# 5.3 28 STUIVERS

Silver **Countermark:** L **Note:** Countermark on Groningen KM#50.

CM Date	Host Date	Good	VG	F	VF	XF
ND(1693)	1690	—	—	—	—	—

KM# 5.4 28 STUIVERS

Silver **Countermark:** L **Note:** Countermark on Groningen KM#52.

CM Date	Host Date	Good	VG	F	VF	XF
ND(1693)	1692	—	—	—	—	—

KM# 5.5 28 STUIVERS
Silver **Countermark:** L **Note:** Countermark on Nijmegen KM#27.

CM Date	Host Date	Good	VG	F	VF	XF
ND(1693)	1685-90	—	—	—	—	—

KM# 5.6 28 STUIVERS
Silver **Countermark:** L **Note:** Countermark on West Friesland KM#90.

CM Date	Host Date	Good	VG	F	VF	XF
ND(1693)	1685-87	—	—	—	—	—

KM# 5.7 28 STUIVERS
Silver **Countermark:** L **Note:** Countermark on Zwolle KM#78.

CM Date	Host Date	Good	VG	F	VF	XF
ND(1693)	1679-86	—	—	—	—	—

NIJMEGEN

PROVINCE

STANDARD COINAGE

KM# 3 DUIT
Copper **Obv:** Inscription within tulip wreath **Obv. Inscription:** NOV / IMA / GVM **Rev:** Woman with one hand raised supports shield with double eagle **Rev. Legend:** BEA. GNS. CV. DNS. SPS. E.

Date	Mintage	VG	F	VF	XF	Unc
ND(1618-20)	—	10.00	25.00	45.00	80.00	—

KM# 5 DUIT
Copper **Obv:** Inscription within tulip wreath **Obv. Inscription:** NOV / IMA / GVM **Rev:** Woman with one hand raised supports shield with double eagle, all in inner circle **Rev. Legend:** BEATA • GNS • CVI • DNS • SPS • EI **Note:** Legend varieties exist.

Date	Mintage	VG	F	VF	XF	Unc
(16)18	—	10.00	25.00	45.00	80.00	—
(16)19	—	10.00	25.00	45.00	80.00	—
(16)20	—	10.00	25.00	45.00	80.00	—

KM# 4 DUIT
Copper **Obv:** NOV/IMA/GVM in tulip wreath **Rev:** Woman sitting in fenced-in area, holding sword, one arm raised, shield with double eagle below **Rev. Legend:** BEA. GNS. CVIVS. DNS. SPS. EIV. **Note:** Legend varieties exist.

Date	Mintage	VG	F	VF	XF	Unc
ND(1618-20)	—	10.00	25.00	45.00	80.00	—

KM# 2 2 DUIT (Oord)
Copper **Obv:** Inscription within tulip wreath **Obv. Inscription:** NO / VIMA / GVM **Rev:** Woman with one hand raised, behind shield with double eagle **Rev. Legend:** BEA.GNS.C. DNS.SPS. E. **Note:** Struck over Spanish Netherlands 2 Duit of Albert and Isabella.

Date	Mintage	VG	F	VF	XF	Unc
ND(1602-1605)	—	15.00	35.00	60.00	100	—

KM# 6.1 1/4 STUIVER
Billon **Obv:** Crowned double-headed eagle in inner circle **Rev:** Ornamental cross with 4 at center, in inner circle **Rev. Legend:** NVLLA. SALYS. BELIO.

Date	Mintage	VG	F	VF	XF	Unc
ND	—	20.00	50.00	100	250	—

KM# 6.2 1/4 STUIVER
1.0000 g., Billon **Rev. Legend:** PACEM. TE. POSCI. OMNE.

Date	Mintage	VG	F	VF	XF	Unc
ND	—	20.00	50.00	100	250	—

KM# A5 1/2 STUIVER
Billon **Obv:** Crowned arms divide value in inner circle, crown divides date **Rev:** Ornate long cross with H-S-V-N in angles in inner circle

Date	Mintage	VG	F	VF	XF	Unc
1601	—	20.00	50.00	100	150	—
1602	—	20.00	50.00	100	150	—
1603	—	20.00	50.00	100	150	—
1620	—	20.00	50.00	100	150	—

KM# 7 STUIVER
4.0000 g., Billon **Obv:** Crowned arms divide value in inner circle, crown divides date **Rev:** Ornamental long cross with quatrefoil around center

Date	Mintage	VG	F	VF	XF	Unc
1602	—	30.00	80.00	150	250	—
1619	—	30.00	80.00	150	250	—
1620	—	30.00	80.00	150	250	—

KM# 15 2 STUIVERS
Silver **Obv:** Crowned arms divide value in inner circle, crown divides date **Rev:** Ornate cross in inner circle

Date	Mintage	VG	F	VF	XF	Unc
1619	—	25.00	60.00	150	275	—
16Z0	—	25.00	60.00	150	275	—

KM# 25 2 STUIVERS
1.7300 g., 0.8530 Silver 0.0474 oz. ASW **Obv:** Crowned rampant lion left holding sword and arrows, value at sides **Rev:** Inscription **Rev. Inscription:** NOVIO / MAGUM / (date) **Note:** Mint mark: Moor's head.

Date	Mintage	VG	F	VF	XF	Unc
1681	—	10.00	25.00	50.00	100	—
1685	—	10.00	25.00	50.00	100	—
1686	—	10.00	25.00	50.00	100	—
1688	—	10.00	25.00	50.00	100	—

KM# 8 3 STUIVERS (1/2 Arend-Schelling)
3.0000 g., 0.5000 Silver 0.0482 oz. ASW **Obv:** Crowned imperial eagle with arms on breast in inner circle **Rev:** Crowned arms in inner circle, crown divides date in legend **Note:** Mint mark: Pomegranate.

Date	Mintage	VG	F	VF	XF	Unc
1602	—	50.00	100	200	400	—
1604	—	50.00	100	200	400	—

KM# 9 3 STUIVERS (1/2 Arend-Schelling)
3.0000 g., Silver **Obv:** Ornate cross within circle **Rev:** Crowned double-headed eagle with arms on breast

Date	Mintage	VG	F	VF	XF	Unc
ND	—	60.00	125	250	500	—

KM# 10.1 6 STUIVERS (Arend-Schelling)
6.0000 g., 0.5000 Silver 0.0964 oz. ASW **Obv:** Crowned arms within circle, crown divides date in legend **Rev:** Crowned imperial eagle with arms on breast within circle, titles of Rudoph II **Note:** Mint mark: Pomegranate.

Date	Mintage	VG	F	VF	XF	Unc
1602	—	50.00	100	200	400	—
1603	—	50.00	100	200	400	—
1604	—	50.00	100	200	400	—
ND	—	50.00	100	200	400	—

KM# 10.2 6 STUIVERS (Arend-Schelling)
6.0000 g., 0.5000 Silver 0.0964 oz. ASW **Obv:** Titles of Matthias I **Note:** Varieties exist.

Date	Mintage	VG	F	VF	XF	Unc
1605	—	50.00	100	200	400	—

KM# 26.2 6 STUIVERS (Arend-Schelling)
Silver **Rev:** Sitting dog below knight

Date	Mintage	VG	F	VF	XF	Unc
1685	—	10.00	20.00	30.00	40.00	—

KM# 26.1 6 STUIVERS (Arend-Schelling)
4.9500 g., 0.5830 Silver 0.0928 oz. ASW **Obv:** Crowned arms divide value, last two digits of date right of crown **Rev:** Knight with sword on horseback right **Note:** Mint mark: Moor's head.

Date	Mintage	VG	F	VF	XF	Unc
(16)85	—	12.50	27.50	40.00	75.00	—
(16)86	—	12.50	27.50	40.00	75.00	—
(16)88/6	—	15.00	30.00	60.00	125	—
(16)88	—	12.50	27.50	40.00	75.00	—
(16)89	—	12.50	27.50	40.00	75.00	—
(16)90	—	12.50	27.50	40.00	75.00	—
(16)91	—	12.50	27.50	40.00	75.00	—

KM# 26.3 6 STUIVERS (Arend-Schelling)
Silver **Rev:** Eagle with one head

Date	Mintage	VG	F	VF	XF	Unc
1691	—	10.00	20.00	30.00	40.00	—

KM# 16 8 STUIVERS (Langrok)
Silver **Obv:** Standing figure of St. Stephen **Rev:** Crowned imperial eagle with arms on breast

Date	Mintage	VG	F	VF	XF	Unc
1619	—	50.00	80.00	125	200	—

KM# 27 28 STUIVERS (Florin)
19.5000 g., 0.6730 Silver 0.4219 oz. ASW **Obv:** Crowned arms **Rev:** Imperial eagle **Note:** Mint mark: Moor's head. This coin appears with countermarks of HOL, UTR, L, G.O., arms, lion, and bundle of arrows.

Date	Mintage	VG	F	VF	XF	Unc
1685	—	50.00	100	200	400	—
1686	—	50.00	100	200	400	—
1688	—	60.00	125	250	500	—
1690	—	50.00	100	250	400	—

KM# 29 GULDEN (20 Stuiver)
10.6100 g., 0.9200 Silver 0.3138 oz. ASW **Obv:** Crowned arms divide value, date above crown **Rev:** Standing female figure leaning on Bible on column, holding spear with Liberty cap **Note:** Mint mark: Moor's head.

Date	Mintage	VG	F	VF	XF	Unc
1687	69,510	25.00	70.00	110	250	—
1691	Inc. above	20.00	60.00	90.00	200	—
ND	Inc. above	25.00	70.00	110	250	—

KM# 28 3 GULDEN (60 Stuiver)
31.8200 g., 0.9200 Silver 0.9412 oz. ASW **Obv:** Crowned arms divide value, date above crown **Rev:** Standing knight with sword behind crowned arms left, date in legend **Note:** Dav. #4971. Mint mark: Moor's head.

Date	Mintage	VG	F	VF	XF	Unc
1686	13,860	150	300	600	1,200	—
1687	Inc. above	150	400	800	1,600	—
1689	Inc. above	150	400	800	1,600	—
1690	Inc. above	150	300	600	1,200	—

KM# 11 DAALDER (Rijks)
29.0300 g., 0.8850 Silver 0.8260 oz. ASW **Obv:** Crowned imperial eagle in inner circle **Rev:** Crowned arms with lion supporters, date below in inner circle

Date	Mintage	VG	F	VF	XF	Unc
1602	—	100	200	450	900	—

KM# 30 DAALDER (30 Stuivers)
15.8800 g., 0.9060 Silver 0.4625 oz. ASW **Obv:** Crowned arms

with lion supporters, value below **Rev:** Standing knight with sword behind crowned arms left, date in legend **Note:** Mint mark: Moor's head.

Date	Mintage	VG	F	VF	XF	Unc
1688	94,895	60.00	125	175	300	—
1689	Inc. above	70.00	150	200	375	—

KM# 32 DAALDER (Lion - 48 Stuivers)

27.6800 g., 0.7500 Silver 0.6674 oz. ASW **Obv:** Knight standing behind shield in inner circle **Rev:** Rampant lion left in inner circle, date above in legend **Note:** Dav. #4887.

Date	Mintage	VG	F	VF	XF	Unc
1692	234,325	35.00	100	175	350	—

KM# 31 60 STUIVERS 2 DAALDERS

31.7600 g., 0.9060 Silver 0.9251 oz. ASW **Obv:** Crowned arms with lion supporters, value below **Rev:** Standing knight with sword behind crowned arms left, date in legend **Note:** Dav. #4988. Mint mark: Moor's head.

Date	Mintage	VG	F	VF	XF	Unc
1688	7,735	250	500	1,000	1,750	—
1689	Inc. above	250	500	1,000	1,750	—

KM# 12 FLORIN

3.5000 g., 0.9860 Gold 0.1109 oz. AGW **Obv:** Crowned imperial eagle in inner circle, titles of Rudolf II **Rev:** Crowned arms with lion supporters, date in exergue in inner circle

Date	Mintage	VG	F	VF	XF	Unc
1602 Rare	—	—	—	—	—	—

KM# 20 FLORIN

3.5000 g., 0.9860 Gold 0.1109 oz. AGW **Obv:** Titles of Ferdinand II

Date	Mintage	VG	F	VF	XF	Unc
1620 Rare	—	—	—	—	—	—

PATTERNS

Including off metal strikes

KM#	Date	Mintage	Identification	Mkt Val
Pn1	1685	—	2 Stuivers. Gold. KM#25.	—
Pn2	1686	—	Schelling. Gold. 7.5000 g. KM#26.1.	—
Pn3	1688	—	Schelling. Gold. 7.5000 g. KM#26.1.	—

PIEFORTS

KM#	Date	Mintage	Identification	Mkt Val
P2	1685	—	28 Stuivers. Silver. Triple weight, KM27.	—
P4	1688	—	28 Stuivers. Silver. Triple weight, KM27.	—
P5	1688/6	—	28 Stuivers. Silver. KM27.	—
P6	1688	—	Daalder. Silver. Triple weight, KM30.	—
P8	1692	—	Lion Daalder. Silver. Triple weight, KM32.	—

OVERYSSEL

Overijsel, Transisulania

Overyssel is a province in northeastern Netherlands whose name means *beyond the Issel*, a tributary of the Rhine. Originally known as the lordship of Overstticht it was a part of the holdings of the bishops of Utrecht. It was sold to Charles V in 1527 and made a part of the Habsburg domain. Three of its cities - Kampen, Deventer and Zwolle were important Hanseatic towns of the medieval period.

PROVINCE

STANDARD COINAGE

KM# A9 1/2 DUIT

1.5000 g., Copper, 20 mm. **Obv:** Crowned arms with rampant lion facing to right **Rev:** Three line inscription TRAN / INSV / LA in wreath **Edge:** Plain

Date	Mintage	VG	F	VF	XF	Unc
ND(1606-12)	—	—	—	—	—	—

KM# 22 DUIT

Copper **Rev:** TRANS/SISVLA/NIA/ (date) in wreath

Date	Mintage	VG	F	VF	XF	Unc
1619	—	5.00	20.00	30.00	40.00	—
1626	—	5.00	20.00	30.00	40.00	—
1628	—	4.00	10.00	20.00	30.00	—
1629	—	5.00	20.00	30.00	40.00	—
1633	—	5.00	20.00	30.00	40.00	—
1635	—	5.00	20.00	30.00	40.00	—

KM# 22a DUIT

5.2500 g., Gold **Rev. Inscription:** TRANS / SISVLA / NIA / date in wreath

Date	Mintage	VG	F	VF	XF	Unc
1628 Rare	—	—	—	—	—	—

KM# 18 2 DUIT (Oord)

Copper **Obv:** Bust of Rudolph II left **Obv. Legend:** MONE • NOVA - ORDI • TRAS **Rev:** Crowned arms

Date	Mintage	VG	F	VF	XF	Unc
1607/6 Rare	—	—	—	—	—	—
1607	—	10.00	20.00	40.00	150	—

KM# 23 STUIVER

1.3100 g., 0.3330 Silver 0.0140 oz. ASW **Obv:** Bundle of arrows divides value in wreath, value outside bow **Rev:** TRA/ISVLA/NIA(date) in wreath

Date	Mintage	VG	F	VF	XF	Unc
1619	—	10.00	20.00	45.00	100	—
1621	—	4.00	10.00	25.00	50.00	—
1625	—	4.00	10.00	25.00	50.00	—
1628	82,800	5.00	15.00	32.50	65.00	—
1629	Inc. above	10.00	20.00	45.00	100	—
1633	Inc. above	4.00	10.00	25.00	50.00	—
1634	Inc. above	30.00	80.00	150	300	—

KM# 24 STUIVER

Billon **Obv:** Value inside bow

Date	Mintage	VG	F	VF	XF	Unc
1619	—	4.00	10.00	25.00	50.00	—
1628	—	4.00	10.00	25.00	50.00	—
1653	—	4.00	10.00	25.00	50.00	—
1665	—	4.00	10.00	25.00	50.00	—
1666	—	4.00	10.00	25.00	50.00	—

KM# 19 2 STUIVERS

1.9300 g., 0.5830 Silver 0.0362 oz. ASW **Obv:** Crowned rampant lion left holding sword and arrows divides value 2 - S **Rev:** Inscription. date **Rev. Inscription:** TRS / ISS / VLA or TRAS / ISVLA / • NIA • **Note:** Mint marks: lion, lily or cross.

Date	Mintage	VG	F	VF	XF	Unc
1612	—	10.00	25.00	50.00	100	—
1615	—	6.00	15.00	50.00	100	—
1616	—	6.00	15.00	50.00	100	—
1617	—	6.00	15.00	50.00	100	—
1618	—	6.00	15.00	50.00	100	—
1619	—	6.00	15.00	50.00	100	—
1620	—	6.00	15.00	50.00	100	—
1622	—	6.00	15.00	50.00	100	—
1627	—	6.00	15.00	50.00	100	—
1628	—	6.00	15.00	50.00	100	—
1630	—	6.00	15.00	50.00	100	—
1631	—	6.00	15.00	50.00	100	—
1632	—	6.00	15.00	50.00	100	—
1633	—	6.00	15.00	50.00	100	—
1634	—	6.00	15.00	50.00	100	—

KM# 25 2 STUIVERS

Billon **Obv:** Rampant lion left holding sword and arrows **Rev:** Inscription, date **Rev. Inscription:** TRAS / ISVLA / • NIA • **Note:** Klippe.

Date	Mintage	VG	F	VF	XF	Unc
1619	—	—	—	175	300	—

KM# 48 2 STUIVERS

1.6200 g., 0.5830 Silver 0.0304 oz. ASW **Obv:** Crowned shield with rampant lion left holding sword and arrows divides value 2 - S **Rev:** Inscription, date **Rev. Inscription:** TRAS / ISVLA / NIA **Note:** Mint marks: lion, lily or cross,

Date	Mintage	VG	F	VF	XF	Unc
1677	—	10.00	25.00	50.00	100	—
1678	—	10.00	25.00	50.00	100	—
1679	—	10.00	25.00	50.00	100	—
1680	—	10.00	25.00	50.00	100	—
1681	—	10.00	25.00	50.00	100	—

KM# 30 6 STUIVERS (Roosschelling)

5.2700 g., 0.5830 Billon 0.0988 oz. **Obv:** Crowned arms in inner circle, date above crown **Rev:** Floreated cross in inner circle

Date	Mintage	VG	F	VF	XF	Unc
1639	—	40.00	100	200	400	—

KM# 47 6 STUIVERS (Rijderschelling)

4.9500 g., 0.5830 Billon 0.0928 oz. **Obv:** Crowned arms divide value in inner circle, date above crown **Rev:** Knight with sword on horseback to right

Date	Mintage	VG	F	VF	XF	Unc
1679	—	15.00	40.00	75.00	100	—
1680	—	15.00	40.00	75.00	100	—
1681	—	15.00	40.00	75.00	100	—

KM# 50 6 STUIVERS (Rijderschelling)

Billon **Note:** Mint mark: Rose. Small planchet

Date	Mintage	VG	F	VF	XF	Unc
1680	—	7.50	17.50	30.00	80.00	—
1682	—	7.50	17.50	30.00	80.00	—
1683	—	7.50	17.50	30.00	80.00	—
1684	—	7.50	17.50	30.00	80.00	—
1685	—	7.50	17.50	30.00	80.00	—
1686	—	7.50	17.50	30.00	80.00	—
1688	—	7.50	17.50	30.00	80.00	—
1689	—	7.50	17.50	30.00	80.00	—
1690	—	7.50	17.50	30.00	80.00	—
1691	—	7.50	17.50	30.00	80.00	—
1696	—	7.50	17.50	30.00	80.00	—

KM# 55a 28 STUIVERS (Florin)

30.5000 g., Gold **Obv:** Crowned arms in inner circle, date at top above crown **Rev:** Crowned double-headed eagle with value in orb on breast in inner circle **Note:** Mint mark: Rose.

Date	Mintage	VG	F	VF	XF	Unc
1685	—	—	—	5,000	7,000	—

KM# 55 28 STUIVERS (Florin)

19.5000 g., 0.6730 Silver 0.4219 oz. ASW **Obv:** Crowned arms in inner circle, date at top above crown **Rev:** Crowned double-headed eagle with value in orb on breast in inner circle **Note:** Mint mark: Rose. This coin appears with countermarks of HOL, FRI, UTR, TRAN and G.O.

Date	Mintage	VG	F	VF	XF	Unc
1685	228,000	40.00	85.00	150	300	—
1686	Inc. above	40.00	85.00	150	300	—
1688	Inc. above	60.00	140	200	400	—
1689	Inc. above	40.00	85.00	150	300	—

KM# 56 30 STUIVERS (1 Daalder)
15.8800 g., 0.9060 Silver 0.4625 oz. ASW **Obv:** Standing knight with sword behind crowned arms to left **Rev:** Crowned arms of Deventer, Zwolle and Kampen in triangle in inner circle, value and date in angles **Note:** Mint mark: Rose.

Date	Mintage	VG	F	VF	XF	Unc
1685	—	40.00	100	175	350	—
1686	—	40.00	100	175	350	—
1689	—	40.00	100	175	350	—
1690	—	40.00	100	175	350	—
1691	—	40.00	100	175	350	—
1692	—	40.00	100	175	350	—

KM# 56a 30 STUIVERS (1 Daalder)
27.7600 g., Gold **Obv:** Standing knight with sword behind crowned arms to left **Rev:** Crowned arms of Deventer, Zwolle and Kampen in triangle in inner circle, value and date in angles

Date	Mintage	VG	F	VF	XF	Unc
1690 1 known	—	—	—	—	12,000	—

KM# 63.1 GULDEN
10.6100 g., 0.9200 Silver 0.3138 oz. ASW **Obv:** Crowned arms of Overyssel divide value **Rev:** Standing female figure leaning on Bible on column, holding spear with Liberty cap, date below figure **Note:** Mint mark: Rose.

Date	Mintage	VG	F	VF	XF	Unc
1698	88,170	15.00	30.00	60.00	120	—

KM# 62 2 GULDEN
21.2100 g., 0.9200 Silver 0.6273 oz. ASW **Obv:** Crowned arms divide value **Rev:** Standing female figure leaning on Bible on column, holding spear with Liberty cap, date below figure

Date	Mintage	VG	F	VF	XF	Unc
1697	—	60.00	150	350	650	—

KM# 52 3 GULDEN (60 Stuiver)
Silver **Rev:** Figure divides date **Note:** Dav. #4956.

Date	Mintage	VG	F	VF	XF	Unc
1681	Inc. above	60.00	120	250	400	—
1682	Inc. above	60.00	120	250	400	—
1683	Inc. above	60.00	120	250	400	—
1684	Inc. above	150	300	700	1,250	—

KM# 51 3 GULDEN (60 Stuiver)
31.8200 g., 0.9200 Silver 0.9412 oz. ASW **Obv:** Crowned arms divide value, date above **Rev:** Standing female figure leaning on Bible column, holding spear with Liberty cap **Note:** Mint mark: Rose. Dav. #4955.

Date	Mintage	VG	F	VF	XF	Unc
1681	215,697	50.00	150	300	450	—
1682	Inc. above	50.00	150	300	450	—
1683	Inc. above	50.00	150	300	450	—

KM# 54 3 GULDEN (60 Stuiver)
31.8200 g., 0.9200 Silver 0.9412 oz. ASW **Note:** Date on obverse and reverse.

Date	Mintage	VG	F	VF	XF	Unc
1682	Inc. above	125	350	700	900	—

KM# 60 3 GULDEN (60 Stuiver)
Silver **Obv:** Crowned arms of Overyssel divide value **Rev:** Standing female figure leaning on Bible on column, holding spear with Liberty cap, date below figure **Note:** Mint mark: Rose. Dav. #4957.

Date	Mintage	VG	F	VF	XF	Unc
1694	892,876	40.00	100	175	250	—
1695	Inc. above	40.00	100	200	300	—
1697	Inc. above	40.00	100	175	250	—

KM# 46 1/2 DUCATON ((20 Stuiver))
16.3000 g., 0.9410 Silver 0.4931 oz. ASW **Obv:** Knight with sword on horseback right, provincial arms below in inner circle **Rev:** Crowned arms with crowned lion supporters in inner circle, date at top in legend

Date	Mintage	VG	F	VF	XF	Unc
1677	—	150	450	750	1,000	—

KM# 35 DUCATON (40 Stuiver)
32.7800 g., 0.9410 Silver 0.9917 oz. ASW **Obv:** Knight with sword on horseback right, provincial arms below in inner circle **Rev:** Crowned arms with crowned lion supporters in inner circle, date at top in legend **Note:** Mint mark: Sun. Dav. #4935.

Date	Mintage	VG	F	VF	XF	Unc
1659	—	50.00	110	170	300	—
1660	—	50.00	110	170	300	—
1661	—	50.00	110	170	300	—
1662	—	40.00	90.00	125	275	—
1663/2	—	80.00	175	250	500	—
1663	—	40.00	90.00	125	275	—
1664	—	40.00	90.00	125	275	—
1665	—	60.00	150	200	400	—
1666	—	40.00	90.00	125	275	—
1668	—	40.00	90.00	125	275	—
1669	—	60.00	150	200	400	—

KM# 41 DUCATON (40 Stuiver)
Silver **Obv:** Smaller knight and horse with crowned arms below **Note:** Mint mark: Rose. Dav. #4936.

Date	Mintage	VG	F	VF	XF	Unc
1675	—	60.00	120	200	350	—
1676	—	60.00	120	200	350	—
1677	—	60.00	120	200	350	—
1678	—	60.00	120	200	350	—
1679	—	60.00	120	200	350	—
1680	—	60.00	120	200	350	—
1682	—	60.00	120	200	350	—

KM# 36.1 DUCAT (48 Stuiver)
28.2500 g., 0.8730 Silver 0.7929 oz. ASW **Obv:** Armoured knight standing holding sword behind shield of arms, date at sides in inner circle **Rev:** Crowned arms in inner circle **Note:** Mint mark: Sun. Dav. #4899.

Date	Mintage	VG	F	VF	XF	Unc
1659	256,710	40.00	125	200	400	—
1660	Inc. above	40.00	125	200	400	—
1661	Inc. above	50.00	175	250	450	—
1662	Inc. above	40.00	125	200	400	—
1663	Inc. above	50.00	175	250	450	—
1664	Inc. above	50.00	175	250	450	—

KM# 36.2 DUCAT (48 Stuiver)
Silver **Obv:** Armoured knight standing holding sword behind shield of arms, date at sides in inner circle **Rev:** Crowned arms in inner circle **Note:** Mint mark: Rose. Varieties exist.

Date	Mintage	VG	F	VF	XF	Unc
1676	—	50.00	175	250	350	—
1677	—	50.00	175	250	350	—

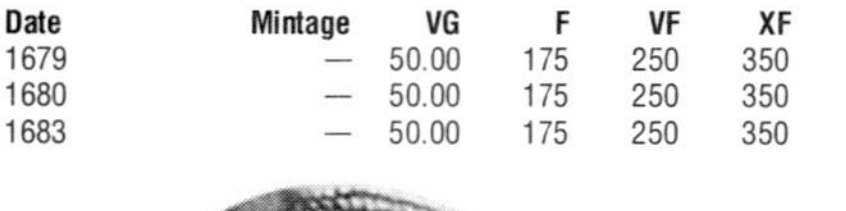

Date	Mintage	VG	F	VF	XF	Unc
1679	—	50.00	175	250	350	—
1680	—	50.00	175	250	350	—
1683	—	50.00	175	250	350	—

KM# 61 DUCAT (48 Stuiver)

Silver **Obv:** Standing, armored knight with crowned shield at feet **Rev:** Crowned arms of Overyssel divides date **Note:** Mint mark: Rose. Dav. #4900.

Date	Mintage	VG	F	VF	XF	Unc
1695	1,650,901	40.00	100	175	250	—
1698	Inc. above	40.00	100	175	250	—
1699/5	Inc. above	60.00	120	200	400	—
1699	Inc. above	40.00	100	175	250	—
1700	Inc. above	40.00	100	175	250	450

KM# 10 1/2 DAALDER (Rijks - 24 Stuiver)

14.5100 g., 0.8850 Silver 0.4128 oz. ASW **Obv:** Laureate 1/2 figure holding sword and arms in inner circle **Rev:** Crowned arms divide date in inner circle

Date	Mintage	VG	F	VF	XF	Unc
1606	—	45.00	100	200	300	—
1610	—	45.00	100	200	300	—
1612	—	45.00	100	200	300	—
1613	—	45.00	100	200	300	—
1614/13	—	45.00	100	200	300	—
1614	—	45.00	100	200	300	—
1616	—	45.00	100	200	300	—
1618	—	45.00	100	200	350	—
1619	—	45.00	100	200	350	—
1620	—	45.00	100	200	300	—
1621	—	45.00	100	200	300	—
1628	—	45.00	100	200	300	—
1629	—	45.00	100	200	300	—

KM# 11 1/2 DAALDER (Lion - 24 Stuiver)

13.8400 g., 0.7500 Silver 0.3337 oz. ASW **Obv:** Armoured knight looking to right above lion shield in inner circle **ev:** Rampant lion to left in inner circle, date at top in legend

Date	Mintage	VG	F	VF	XF	Unc
1606	—	35.00	100	150	300	—
1608	—	30.00	80.00	110	250	—
1610	—	35.00	100	150	300	—
1611	—	35.00	100	150	300	—
1612	—	35.00	100	150	300	—
1613/2	—	45.00	110	200	450	—
1614	—	30.00	80.00	110	250	—
1615/2	—	45.00	110	200	350	—
1615	—	30.00	80.00	110	250	—
1616/Z	—	35.00	100	150	200	—
1616	—	30.00	80.00	110	150	—
1617	—	—	—	—	—	—
1622	—	50.00	150	250	300	—
1629/8	—	45.00	110	200	350	—
1629	—	45.00	110	200	350	—
1633	—	30.00	80.00	110	250	—
1637	—	30.00	80.00	110	250	—
1639	—	30.00	80.00	110	250	—
1640	—	30.00	80.00	110	250	—
1641	—	30.00	80.00	110	250	—
1643	—	50.00	150	250	400	—

KM# 12 DAALDER (Lion - 24 Stuiver)

27.6800 g., 0.7500 Silver 0.6674 oz. ASW **Rev:** Date at top in legend

Date	Mintage	VG	F	VF	XF	Unc
1606	90,125	35.00	90.00	150	250	—
1607	Inc. above	25.00	60.00	100	175	—
1608/7	—	25.00	60.00	100	175	—
1608	—	25.00	60.00	100	175	—
1610	—	25.00	60.00	100	175	—
1611/08	—	35.00	90.00	150	250	—
1611	—	25.00	60.00	100	175	—
1612	—	25.00	60.00	100	175	—
1613/1	—	35.00	90.00	150	250	—
1613/2	—	35.00	90.00	150	250	—
1613	—	25.00	60.00	100	175	—
1614	—	25.00	60.00	100	175	—
1615/2/08	—	35.00	90.00	150	250	—
1615/2	—	25.00	60.00	150	250	—
1615	—	25.00	60.00	150	250	—
1616/2	—	25.00	60.00	150	250	—
1616/3	—	25.00	60.00	100	175	—
1616	100,000	25.00	60.00	150	250	—
1617/6	—	25.00	60.00	150	250	—
1617	—	25.00	60.00	150	250	—
1619	—	25.00	60.00	150	250	—
1621/13	—	35.00	90.00	150	250	—
16ZZ	—	40.00	65.00	100	200	—
1622	—	40.00	65.00	100	200	—
1623/1	—	35.00	90.00	150	250	—
1623/2	—	35.00	90.00	150	250	—
1623	—	35.00	90.00	150	250	—
1628/2	—	35.00	90.00	150	250	—
1628	—	35.00	90.00	150	250	—
1629/16	—	35.00	90.00	150	250	—
1629/2	—	35.00	90.00	150	250	—
1629/7	—	35.00	90.00	150	250	—
1629/8/2	—	60.00	125	150	250	—
1629/8	—	35.00	90.00	150	250	—
1629	—	35.00	90.00	150	250	—
1631	—	35.00	90.00	150	250	—
1632	—	35.00	90.00	150	250	—
1633	—	25.00	60.00	100	175	—
1634	—	35.00	90.00	150	250	—
1636	—	25.00	60.00	100	175	—
1637	—	25.00	60.00	100	175	—
1639	—	25.00	60.00	100	175	—
1640	—	25.00	60.00	100	175	—
1641	—	25.00	60.00	100	175	—
1642	—	35.00	90.00	150	250	—
1643/2	—	25.00	60.00	100	175	—
1643	—	25.00	60.00	100	175	—
1644	—	30.00	85.00	150	250	—
1645	—	30.00	85.00	150	250	—
1647	—	30.00	85.00	150	250	—
1656	—	30.00	85.00	150	250	—
1663	—	30.00	85.00	150	250	—
1666	—	30.00	85.00	150	250	—

KM# 13 DAALDER (Rijks)

29.0300 g., 0.8850 Silver 0.8260 oz. ASW **Obv:** Laureate 1/2 figure holding sword and arms in inner circle **Rev:** Crowned arms divide date **Note:** Mint mark: Rose.

Date	Mintage	VG	F	VF	XF	Unc
1606	345,155	50.00	110	175	250	—
1607	Inc. above	35.00	80.00	125	250	—
1610/07	Inc. above	35.00	80.00	125	250	—
1610	Inc. above	35.00	80.00	125	250	—
1611/0	Inc. above	75.00	150	250	450	—
1612	Inc. above	35.00	80.00	125	250	—
1614/2	Inc. above	50.00	110	175	300	—
1614	Inc. above	50.00	110	175	300	—
1616	Inc. above	50.00	110	175	300	—
1617	Inc. above	75.00	150	250	450	—
1618	Inc. above	35.00	80.00	125	250	—
1619	Inc. above	35.00	80.00	125	250	—
1620	Inc. above	35.00	80.00	125	250	—
1621	Inc. above	35.00	80.00	125	250	—
1622	Inc. above	50.00	110	175	350	—
1623/2	Inc. above	100	200	400	650	—
1623	Inc. above	50.00	110	175	300	—
1628	Inc. above	50.00	110	175	300	—
1629	Inc. above	75.00	150	250	350	—
1651	Inc. above	—	—	—	—	—

KM# 44.1 DAALDER (Rijks)

Silver **Rev:** Date at top in legend **Note:** Varieties exist.

Date	Mintage	VG	F	VF	XF	Unc
1676	42,130	70.00	200	375	650	—
1677	Inc. above	70.00	200	375	650	—

KM# 44.2 DAALDER (Rijks)

Silver **Rev:** Date at top in legend

Date	Mintage	VG	F	VF	XF	Unc
1688	14,750	70.00	200	375	650	—

KM# 64 DAALDER (Rijks)

Silver **Rev:** Crowned arms divide date in inner circle **Note:** Dav. #4861.

Date	Mintage	VG	F	VF	XF	Unc
1699	9,830	80.00	250	400	750	—

KM# 42.1 DAALDER (Lion)

27.6800 g., 0.7500 Silver 0.6674 oz. ASW **Obv:** Knight without plume in helmet **Note:** Mint mark: Rose.

Date	Mintage	VG	F	VF	XF	Unc
1675/1	216,531	40.00	80.00	160	350	—
1675	Inc. above	30.00	70.00	90.00	250	—
1676	Inc. above	30.00	65.00	85.00	225	—
1677	Inc. above	25.00	60.00	80.00	220	—
1678	Inc. above	40.00	80.00	160	350	—
1679	Inc. above	25.00	60.00	80.00	220	—
1680	Inc. above	30.00	75.00	100	250	—
1681	Inc. above	30.00	75.00	100	250	—
1682	—	30.00	70.00	90.00	235	—
1683	—	30.00	75.00	100	250	—
1684	—	40.00	90.00	175	400	—
1685	—	40.00	90.00	175	400	—
1688	—	30.00	65.00	85.00	225	—
1689/8	—	30.00	65.00	85.00	225	—
1689	—	30.00	65.00	85.00	225	—
1690	—	65.00	175	275	425	—
1692	—	40.00	90.00	125	200	—
1697	—	45.00	95.00	135	220	—
1698	—	65.00	175	275	425	—
1699	—	65.00	175	275	425	—
1700	—	50.00	150	225	375	—

KM# 42.2 DAALDER (Lion)

Silver **Obv:** Knight without plume in helmet **Note:** Without mint mark.

Date	Mintage	VG	F	VF	XF	Unc
1676	—	25.00	60.00	120	210	—
1683	—	25.00	60.00	120	210	—
1684	—	35.00	85.00	150	250	—

KM# 5 DAALDER (Lion - 48 Stuivers)

Silver **Obv:** Armored knight looking to right above lion shield in inner circle, date divided at bottom **Rev:** Rampant lion to left in inner circle

Date	Mintage	VG	F	VF	XF	Unc
1602	—	40.00	75.00	200	350	—

KM# 6 DAALDER (Leicester - 48 Stuivers)

29.2400 g., 0.8880 Silver 0.8348 oz. ASW **Obv:** Laureate bust of Leicester holding sword and arrows in inner circle. **Rev:** Shield of arms of the 7 provinces with date above in inner circle

Date	Mintage	VG	F	VF	XF	Unc
1603	—	300	700	1,100	1,750	—

KM# 14 1/2 CAVALIER D'OR

5.0000 g., 0.9200 Gold 0.1479 oz. AGW **Obv:** Equestrian knight right above arms in inner circle **Rev:** Crowned arms in inner circle, date at top **Note:** Fr. #272.

Date	Mintage	VG	F	VF	XF	Unc
1606	—	225	400	625	900	—
1067 (error)	23,480	225	400	625	900	—
1607	Inc. above	225	400	625	900	—
1609	—	225	400	625	900	—
1610	—	225	400	625	900	—
1616	—	225	400	625	900	—

KM# 16 CAVALIER D'OR

10.0000 g., 0.9200 Gold 0.2958 oz. AGW **Obv:** Equestrian knight above arms in inner circle **Rev:** Crowned arms in inner circle, date at top **Note:** FR. #271.

Date	Mintage	VG	F	VF	XF	Unc
1067 (error)	—	450	750	140	2,200	—
1607	—	350	650	1,200	2,000	—
1616/07	—	350	650	1,200	2,000	—
1616	—	350	650	1,200	2,000	—
1617	—	350	650	1,200	2,000	—
1620	—	350	650	1,200	2,000	—

TRADE COINAGE

KM# 7 DUCAT

3.5000 g., 0.9860 Gold 0.1109 oz. AGW **Obv:** Knight standing right divides date in inner circle **Rev:** 5-line inscripton on tablet **Note:** Fr. #268.

Date	Mintage	VG	F	VF	XF	Unc
1603	—	135	250	350	600	—
1604	—	120	150	200	300	—
1606	—	120	150	200	300	—
1607	—	120	150	200	300	—
1608/7	—	125	210	300	480	—
1608	—	120	150	200	300	—
1610	—	125	210	300	480	—
1611	—	135	250	350	600	—
1612	—	120	150	200	300	—
1613/2	—	120	150	200	300	—
1613	—	120	150	200	300	—
1614/3	—	125	210	300	480	—
1614	—	120	150	200	300	—
1616	—	120	150	200	300	—
1630	—	125	250	350	600	—
1631/16	—	125	210	300	480	—
1631/0	—	125	210	300	480	—
1631	—	120	150	200	300	—
1633/11	—	125	210	300	480	—
1633	—	120	150	200	300	—
1634	—	135	250	350	600	—
1635	—	135	250	350	600	—
1636/1	—	135	250	350	600	—
1636/3	—	135	250	350	600	—
1636	—	135	250	350	600	—
1637	—	120	150	200	300	—
1638	—	135	250	350	600	—
1640	—	135	250	350	600	—
1646	—	135	250	350	600	—
1660	—	135	250	350	600	—
1662	—	135	250	350	600	—
1664	—	135	250	350	600	—
1666	—	135	250	350	600	—

KM# 21 DUCAT

3.5000 g., 0.9860 Gold 0.1109 oz. AGW **Note:** Klippe. Fr. # 268a.

Date	Mintage	VG	F	VF	XF	Unc
1615	—	—	—	2,500	4,000	5,000
1616	—	—	—	2,500	4,000	5,000

KM# 40 DUCAT

3.5000 g., 0.9860 Gold 0.1109 oz. AGW **Rev:** Rosette in small shield below tablet

Date	Mintage	VG	F	VF	XF	Unc
1673	—	150	325	600	1,000	—
1675	—	150	325	600	1,000	—
1676	—	150	325	600	1,000	—
1678	—	150	325	600	1,000	—

KM# 53 DUCAT

3.5000 g., 0.9860 Gold 0.1109 oz. AGW **Obv:** Knight standing right divides date, without inner circle **Rev:** 5-line inscription on tablet **Note:** Fr. #268.

Date	Mintage	VG	F	VF	XF	Unc
1681	—	125	250	400	600	—
1688/6	—	125	250	400	600	—
1688	—	125	250	400	600	—

PATTERNS

Including off metal strikes

KM#	Date	Mintage	Identification	Mkt Val
Pn2	1628	—	Duit. Copper. KM#22. Klippe.	250
Pn3	1628	—	Duit. Gold. KM#22.	—
Pn5	1631	—	2 Stuivers. Gold. 6.9000 g.	—
Pn6	1679	—	6 Stuivers. Gold. 10.5000 g. KM#476.	—

PIEFORTS

KM#	Date	Mintage	Identification	Mkt Val
P1	1607	—	2 Ducat. Gold. KM7.	—
PA2	1616	—	Ducat. Gold. KM#7. Klippe.	6,000
P2	1616	—	Cavalier D'Or. Gold. KM16	—
P3	1620	—	24 Stuivers. Silver. Klippe, KM10.	2,000
P4	1628	—	Duit. Copper. Klippe, KM22.	—
P5	1633	—	Daalder. Silver. KM12. Klippe.	—
P6	1660	—	Ducaton. Silver. KM35	—
P7	1660	—	Ducat. Silver. KM36.1.	2,000
P8	1661	—	Ducaton. Silver. KM35	—
P9	1668	—	Ducaton. Silver. KM35.	3,000
P10	1680	—	Ducaton. Silver. KM41	3,000

UTRECHT

Trajectum

Utrecht (Trajectum), the smallest Netherlands province, represents the bulk of a see founded in 722. It was one of the seven provinces that signed the Union of Utrecht against Spain, a treaty regarded as the foundation of the Dutch Republic and later kingdom of the Netherlands.

CITY

STANDARD COINAGE

KM# 22 DUIT

2.0000 g., Copper **Obv:** Shield of arms on floral long cross **Rev:** TRA/IEC/TVM/(date) in wreath

Date	Mintage	VG	F	VF	XF	Unc
1617 (error)	—	10.00	25.00	50.00	100	—
1619	—	5.00	15.00	30.00	80.00	—
1625	—	4.00	12.50	20.00	60.00	—
1626	—	6.00	20.00	40.00	70.00	—
1628	—	6.00	20.00	40.00	70.00	—
1631	—	6.00	20.00	40.00	70.00	—
1634	—	4.00	12.50	20.00	40.00	—
1637	—	4.00	12.50	20.00	40.00	—
1637/4	—	6.00	20.00	40.00	70.00	—
1654 (error)	—	—	—	—	—	—

KM# 43.1 DUIT

Copper **Obv:** Crowned arms with lion supporters, CIV • TRA below **Rev:** U/TRECHT and date in quatrefoil

Date	Mintage	VG	F	VF	XF	Unc
1657	—	10.00	40.00	60.00	90.00	—

KM# 43.2 DUIT

Copper **Obv:** UTRECHT below **Rev:** CIV/TRAIECT/1657

Date	Mintage	VG	F	VF	XF	Unc
1657	—	10.00	40.00	60.00	90.00	—
1659	—	15.00	60.00	90.00	120	—

KM# 43.2a DUIT

3.5000 g., Silver **Obv:** UTRECHT below **Rev:** CIV/TRAIECT/1657

Date	Mintage	VG	F	VF	XF	Unc
1657	—	—	—	200	300	—

KM# 44 DUIT

Copper **Obv:** Crowned arms with horizontal stripes

Date	Mintage	VG	F	VF	XF	Unc
1657	—	5.00	17.50	30.00	45.00	—
1659	—	4.00	12.50	20.00	30.00	—
1661	—	4.00	12.50	20.00	30.00	—
1663	—	4.00	12.50	20.00	30.00	—
1664	—	4.00	12.50	20.00	30.00	—
1665	—	4.00	12.50	20.00	30.00	—
1666	—	4.00	12.50	20.00	30.00	—
1667	—	5.00	15.00	25.00	35.00	—
1668	—	5.00	15.00	25.00	35.00	—
1670	—	3.00	10.00	17.50	30.00	—
1671	—	5.00	15.00	25.00	35.00	—
1676	—	3.00	10.00	17.50	30.00	—
1677	—	3.00	10.00	17.50	30.00	—
1681	—	3.00	10.00	17.50	30.00	—
1683	—	5.00	15.00	25.00	35.00	—
1684	—	3.00	10.00	17.50	30.00	—
1685	—	3.00	10.00	17.50	30.00	—
1687	—	10.00	25.00	50.00	100	—

KM# 44a DUIT

3.3000 g., Silver **Obv:** Crowned arms with horizontal stripes

Date	Mintage	VG	F	VF	XF	Unc
1659/7	—	—	—	—	—	—
1659	—	—	—	200	400	—
1663	—	—	—	—	—	—
1665	—	—	—	—	—	—
1671	—	—	—	—	—	—
1676	—	—	—	—	—	—
1681	—	—	—	—	—	—

KM# 44b DUIT

3.5000 g., Gold **Obv:** Crowned arms with horizontal stripes

Date	Mintage	VG	F	VF	XF	Unc
1659 Rare	—	—	—	—	—	—
1678 Rare	—	—	—	—	—	—
1680	—	—	—	—	—	—

KM# 43.2b DUIT

3.5000 g., Gold **Obv:** UTRECHT below **Rev:** CIV / TRAIECT / 1657

Date	Mintage	VG	F	VF	XF	Unc
1659	—	—	—	650	1,000	2,000

KM# 66 DUIT

Copper **Obv:** Vertical stripes in arms

Date	Mintage	VG	F	VF	XF	Unc
1681	—	8.00	25.00	50.00	75.00	—
1683	—	8.00	25.00	50.00	75.00	—
1684	—	6.00	20.00	40.00	65.00	—
1686	—	6.00	20.00	40.00	65.00	—
1687	—	5.00	15.00	25.00	35.00	—
1689	—	5.00	15.00	25.00	35.00	—
1690	—	—	—	—	—	—

KM# 66b DUIT

3.5000 g., Gold **Obv:** Vertical stripes in arms

Date	Mintage	VG	F	VF	XF	Unc
1687	—	—	—	800	1,200	1,600
1689	—	—	—	—	—	—
1690	—	—	—	800	1,200	1,600
1691	—	—	—	—	—	—

KM# 66a DUIT

2.1500 g., Silver **Obv:** Vertical stripes in arms

Date	Mintage	VG	F	VF	XF	Unc
1687	—	—	—	100	150	300
1690	—	—	—	100	150	300
1691	—	—	—	—	—	—

KM# 25 1/2 STUIVER

1.0000 g., Billon **Obv:** Crowned arms, date at top **Rev:** Ornamental cross

Date	Mintage	VG	F	VF	XF	Unc
1627	—	40.00	150	300	450	—

KM# 26 STUIVER

1.5000 g., Billon **Obv:** Crowned arms divide value, date at top **Rev:** Cross in ornamental cartouche

Date	Mintage	VG	F	VF	XF	Unc
1627	—	30.00	50.00	100	200	—

KM# 50 STUIVER

1.3000 g., Billon **Note:** Reduced size.

Date	Mintage	VG	F	VF	XF	Unc
1665	—	20.00	50.00	100	200	—
1666	—	20.00	50.00	100	200	—

PROVINCE

COPIED COINAGE

KM# A22 DUIT

1.2100 g., Copper, 18.7 mm. **Obv:** Ornamented coat of arms **Rev:** TRA / REC / HEM in wreath **Edge:** Plain

Date	Mintage	VG	F	VF	XF	Unc
ND (1578-1617)	—	—	—	—	—	—

STANDARD COINAGE

KM# 20 STUIVER

0.8600 g., 0.5830 Silver 0.0161 oz. ASW **Obv:** Crowned rampant lion left holding sword and arrows, value at sides **Rev. Inscription:** TRA / IEC / TVM / date

Date	Mintage	VG	F	VF	XF	Unc
1614	—	8.00	15.00	40.00	70.00	—
1618	—	8.00	15.00	40.00	70.00	—

KM# 21 2 STUIVERS

1.7300 g., 0.5830 Silver 0.0324 oz. ASW **Obv:** Crowned rampant lion left holding sword and arrows, value at sides **Rev. Inscription:** TRA / IC / TVM / date

Date	Mintage	VG	F	VF	XF	Unc
1614	—	10.00	20.00	40.00	100	—
1615	—	10.00	20.00	40.00	100	—
1616	—	10.00	20.00	40.00	100	—
1617	—	10.00	20.00	40.00	100	—
1618	—	10.00	20.00	40.00	100	—

KM# 55 2 STUIVERS

Silver **Obv:** Rampant lion without crown and weapons

Date	Mintage	VG	F	VF	XF	Unc
1646	—	20.00	40.00	80.00	200	—
1674	—	10.00	20.00	40.00	100	—
1675	—	10.00	20.00	40.00	100	—

KM# 27 3 STUIVERS (1/2 Roosschelling)

2.6300 g., 0.5830 Silver 0.0493 oz. ASW **Obv:** Crowned arms in inner circle, date above crown **Rev:** Ornamental quatrefoil with rose at center, in inner circle

Date	Mintage	VG	F	VF	XF	Unc
1627	—	40.00	100	200	400	—

KM# 8 6 STUIVERS (Roosschelling)

5.2700 g., 0.5830 Silver 0.0988 oz. ASW **Obv:** Crowned arms in inner circle, date above crown **Rev:** Ornamental quatrefoil with rose at center, in inner circle

Date	Mintage	VG	F	VF	XF	Unc
1601	—	10.00	30.00	60.00	100	—
1627	—	20.00	50.00	100	150	—
1629/7	—	30.00	75.00	150	250	—
1629	—	20.00	50.00	100	150	—
1630	—	20.00	50.00	100	150	—
1631	—	20.00	50.00	100	150	—
1632	—	20.00	50.00	100	150	—

KM# 60.1 6 STUIVERS (Rijderschelling)

4.9500 g., 0.5830 Silver 0.0928 oz. ASW **Obv:** Crowned quartered arms divide value in branches, date above crown **Rev:** Knight with sword on horseback to right **Note:** Mint mark: Agnus Dei on obverse.

Date	Mintage	VG	F	VF	XF	Unc
1675	—	15.00	35.00	75.00	150	—

KM# 60.2 6 STUIVERS (Rijderschelling)

4.9500 g., 0.5830 Silver 0.0928 oz. ASW **Rev:** Mint mark **Note:** Mint mark: Agnus Dei on reverse.

Date	Mintage	VG	F	VF	XF	Unc
1676	—	15.00	40.00	60.00	100	—
1677	—	15.00	40.00	60.00	100	—
1678	—	15.00	40.00	60.00	100	—

KM# 60.3 6 STUIVERS (Rijderschelling)

Silver **Note:** Mint mark: Rosette. Varieties exist.

Date	Mintage	VG	F	VF	XF	Unc
1679	—	5.00	15.00	25.00	45.00	—
1680	—	5.00	15.00	25.00	45.00	—
1681	—	5.00	15.00	25.00	45.00	—
1682	—	15.00	45.00	60.00	100	—
1686/81	—	15.00	45.00	60.00	100	—
1686	—	5.00	15.00	25.00	45.00	—
1691	—	5.00	15.00	25.00	45.00	—

KM# 80 6 STUIVERS (Scheepjesschelling)

4.9500 g., 0.5830 Silver 0.0928 oz. ASW **Obv:** Crowned quartered arms with center shield divide value, branches below arms **Rev:** Ship sailing to right, date in legend

Date	Mintage	VG	F	VF	XF	Unc
1700	—	15.00	30.00	60.00	100	160

KM# 69 10 STUIVERS (1/2 Gulden)

5.3000 g., 0.9200 Silver 0.1568 oz. ASW

Date	Mintage	VG	F	VF	XF	Unc
1682	8,815	40.00	100	200	450	—

KM# 67 GULDEN

10.6100 g., 0.9200 Silver 0.3138 oz. ASW **Obv:** Crowned quartered arms divide value 1 - G **Rev:** Standing female figure leaning on Bible on column, holding spear with Liberty cap, date on column

Date	Mintage	VG	F	VF	XF	Unc
1681	—	75.00	200	350	500	—

KM# 70 GULDEN

Silver **Obv:** Date above crown

Date	Mintage	VG	F	VF	XF	Unc
1682	—	45.00	125	200	250	—
1683	—	45.00	125	200	250	—
1684	—	45.00	125	200	250	—
1687	—	45.00	125	200	250	—

KM# 76 GULDEN

Silver

Date	Mintage	VG	F	VF	XF	Unc
1697/4	63,275	15.00	30.00	60.00	125	—
1697	Inc. above	15.00	30.00	60.00	125	—
1698	Inc. above	15.00	30.00	60.00	125	—

KM# 68 3 GULDEN (60 Stuiver)

31.8200 g., 0.9200 Silver 0.9412 oz. ASW **Obv:** Crowned arms divide value **Rev:** Standing female figure leaning on Bible on column, holding spear with Liberty cap, date on column **Note:** Dav. #4958.

Date	Mintage	VG	F	VF	XF	Unc
1681	—	125	400	650	850	—

KM# 71 3 GULDEN (60 Stuiver)

Silver **Obv:** Date above crown **Note:** Dav. #4959.

Date	Mintage	VG	F	VF	XF	Unc
1682	432,085	60.00	150	225	450	—
1683	Inc. above	60.00	150	225	450	—
1684	Inc. above	60.00	150	225	450	—
1685	Inc. above	60.00	150	225	450	—
1686	Inc. above	60.00	150	225	450	—
1687	Inc. above	60.00	150	225	450	—
1689/7	Inc. above	—	—	—	—	—
1689	Inc. above	60.00	150	225	450	—

KM# 75 3 GULDEN (60 Stuiver)

Silver **Rev:** Date in exergue **Note:** Dav. #4960.

Date	Mintage	VG	F	VF	XF	Unc
1693	—	50.00	100	200	400	—
1694	—	50.00	100	200	400	—
1695	—	50.00	100	200	400	—
1696	—	50.00	100	200	300	—
1697	—	50.00	100	200	400	—

KM# 45 1/2 DUCATON (20 Stuiver)

16.3900 g., 0.9410 Silver 0.4958 oz. ASW **Note:** Similar to 1 Ducaton, KM#46.1

Date	Mintage	VG	F	VF	XF	Unc
1659	—	90.00	200	350	500	—
1660	—	75.00	175	300	400	—
1661	—	90.00	200	300	500	—
1662	—	75.00	175	300	400	—
1663	—	90.00	200	350	500	—
1664	—	90.00	200	350	500	—
1666	—	90.00	200	350	500	—
1667	—	90.00	200	350	500	—
1668	—	75.00	175	300	400	—
1669	—	90.00	200	350	500	—
1670	—	90.00	200	350	500	—
1671	—	75.00	175	300	400	—
1672	—	90.00	200	350	500	—

KM# 56.1 1/2 DUCATON (20 Stuiver)

Silver **Note:** Without inner circles on both sides. Mint mark: Agnus Dei.

Date	Mintage	VG	F	VF	XF	Unc
1674	—	75.00	175	300	500	—
1675	—	75.00	175	300	400	—
1676	—	75.00	175	300	400	—

KM# 56.2 1/2 DUCATON (20 Stuiver)

Silver **Note:** Mint mark: Rosette. Varieties exist.

Date	Mintage	VG	F	VF	XF	Unc
1679	—	75.00	175	300	450	—
1680	—	75.00	175	300	450	—

KM# 46.1 DUCATON (60 Stuiver - Silver Rider)

32.7800 g., 0.9410 Silver 0.9917 oz. ASW **Note:** Dav. #4937.

Date	Mintage	VG	F	VF	XF	Unc
1659	—	40.00	100	200	400	—
1660	—	40.00	100	200	400	—
1661	—	50.00	150	300	600	—
1662	—	50.00	150	300	600	—
1664	—	50.00	150	300	600	—
1665	—	40.00	100	300	400	—
1666	—	30.00	70.00	150	275	—
1667	—	30.00	70.00	150	275	—
1668	—	30.00	70.00	150	275	—
1669	—	50.00	150	300	600	—
1670	—	30.00	70.00	110	275	—
1671	—	40.00	100	200	400	—
1672	—	40.00	100	200	400	—
1673	—	40.00	100	200	400	—

KM# 46.2 DUCATON (60 Stuiver - Silver Rider)

32.7800 g., 0.9410 Silver 0.9917 oz. ASW **Note:** Mint mark: Agnus Dei. Without inner circles.

Date	Mintage	VG	F	VF	XF	Unc
1674	63,450	50.00	130	250	350	—
1675	Inc. above	50.00	130	250	350	—
1676	Inc. above	50.00	150	250	350	—

KM# 63 DUCATON (60 Stuiver - Silver Rider)
Silver **Rev:** Date in cartouche below arms **Note:** Mint mark: Rossette. Dav. #4938.

Date	Mintage	VG	F	VF	XF	Unc
1679	—	50.00	100	175	300	—
1680	—	50.00	100	175	300	—
1681	—	50.00	100	175	300	—
1682	—	50.00	100	175	300	—
1692	—	50.00	100	175	300	—

KM# 47 1/2 SILVER DUCAT (24 Stuiver)
14.1200 g., 0.8730 Silver 0.3963 oz. ASW **Obv:** Armored knight standing, holding sword behind shield of arms, date at sides in inner circle **Rev:** Crowned arms in inner circle

Date	Mintage	VG	F	VF	XF	Unc
1659	—	75.00	200	400	650	—
1660	—	75.00	200	400	650	—
1661	—	75.00	200	400	650	—
1662	—	75.00	200	400	650	—
1663	—	75.00	200	400	650	—
1664	—	75.00	200	400	650	—
1669/4	—	—	—	—	—	—
1669	—	75.00	200	400	650	—
1673	—	75.00	200	400	650	—

KM# 58 1/2 SILVER DUCAT (24 Stuiver)
Silver **Note:** Without inner circles on both sides. Mint mark: Agnus Dei.

Date	Mintage	VG	F	VF	XF	Unc
1674	—	100	300	500	750	—

KM# 48.1 SILVER DUCAT (48 Stuiver)
28.2500 g., 0.8730 Silver 0.7929 oz. ASW **Obv:** Armored knight standing holding sword behind shield of arms, date at sides in inner circle **Rev:** Crowned arms in inner circle **Note:** Dav. #4902.

Date	Mintage	VG	F	VF	XF	Unc
1659	353,865	60.00	150	300	400	—
1660	Inc. above	40.00	100	200	300	—
1661	Inc. above	40.00	100	200	300	—
1662	Inc. above	40.00	100	200	300	—
1663	Inc. above	60.00	150	300	400	—
1664	Inc. above	40.00	100	200	300	—
1668	Inc. above	60.00	150	300	400	—
1669	Inc. above	60.00	150	300	400	—
1671	Inc. above	70.00	175	325	450	—
1672	Inc. above	70.00	175	325	450	—
1673	—	70.00	175	325	450	—
1674	—	80.00	200	350	500	—

KM# 48.2 SILVER DUCAT (48 Stuiver)
28.2500 g., 0.8730 Silver 0.7929 oz. ASW **Note:** Mint mark: Agnus Dei.

Date	Mintage	VG	F	VF	XF	Unc
1674	—	80.00	200	350	500	—

KM# 65 SILVER DUCAT (48 Stuiver)
Silver **Note:** Without inner circles on both sides. Mint mark: Rosette. Dav. #4904.

Date	Mintage	VG	F	VF	XF	Unc
1679	1,702,895	70.00	175	325	450	—
1680	Inc. above	70.00	175	325	450	—
1681	Inc. above	40.00	100	200	300	—
1682	Inc. above	35.00	75.00	125	180	—
1683	Inc. above	35.00	75.00	125	180	—
1684	Inc. above	35.00	75.00	125	180	—
1687	Inc. above	35.00	75.00	150	250	—
1688	Inc. above	70.00	150	300	500	—
1692	Inc. above	35.00	75.00	150	250	—
1693	Inc. above	35.00	75.00	150	250	—
1694	Inc. above	35.00	75.00	150	250	—
1695	Inc. above	35.00	75.00	150	250	—
1696/5	Inc. above	70.00	150	300	500	—
1696	Inc. above	70.00	150	300	500	—
1697	Inc. above	35.00	75.00	150	250	—
1698	Inc. above	35.00	75.00	150	250	—
1699	Inc. above	35.00	75.00	150	250	—

KM# 11 1/2 DAALDER (Rijks - 24 Stuiver)
14.5100 g., 0.8850 Silver 0.4128 oz. ASW **Note:** Similar to 1 Daalder, KM#14. With dotted inner circles on both sides.

Date	Mintage	VG	F	VF	XF	Unc
1606	—	65.00	150	250	350	—
1607	—	80.00	200	300	400	—
1610	—	65.00	150	250	350	—
1611/08	—	65.00	150	250	350	—
1611	—	65.00	150	250	350	—
1612	—	65.00	150	250	350	—
1613	—	65.00	150	250	350	—
1618	—	65.00	150	250	350	—
1619	—	40.00	100	175	275	—
1620	—	40.00	100	175	275	—
1621	—	40.00	100	175	275	—
1622	—	40.00	100	175	275	—
1623	—	65.00	150	250	350	—
1624	—	40.00	100	175	275	—
1625	—	65.00	150	250	350	—
1626	—	40.00	100	175	275	—
1629	—	40.00	100	175	275	—
1645	—	65.00	150	250	350	—
1650	—	—	—	—	—	—

KM# 12 1/2 DAALDER (Lion)
13.8400 g., 0.7500 Silver 0.3337 oz. ASW **Note:** Similar to 1 Daalder, KM#30. With dotted inner circles on both sides.

Date	Mintage	VG	F	VF	XF	Unc
1606	—	40.00	100	175	300	—
1607	—	40.00	100	175	300	—
1608	—	40.00	100	175	300	—
1609	—	40.00	100	175	300	—
1610	—	40.00	100	175	300	—
1611	—	40.00	100	175	300	—
1613	—	65.00	150	250	450	—
1614/13	—	45.00	125	200	400	—
1614	—	40.00	100	175	300	—
1616	—	30.00	75.00	125	250	—
1617	—	30.00	75.00	125	250	—
1618	—	30.00	75.00	125	250	—
1626	—	40.00	100	175	350	—
1628	—	40.00	100	175	350	—
1629/1	—	40.00	100	175	350	—
1629/8	—	40.00	100	175	350	—
1629	—	30.00	75.00	125	250	—
1633	—	40.00	100	175	350	—
1634	—	40.00	100	175	350	—
1636	—	30.00	75.00	125	250	—
1639	—	30.00	75.00	125	250	—
1640	—	30.00	75.00	125	250	—
1641	—	30.00	75.00	125	250	—
1642/1	—	40.00	100	175	350	—
1642	—	30.00	75.00	125	250	—
1643	—	30.00	75.00	125	250	—
1644/3	—	—	—	—	—	—
1644	—	40.00	100	175	350	—
1645	—	40.00	100	175	350	—
1646	—	30.00	75.00	125	250	—
1647	—	30.00	75.00	125	250	—
1648	—	30.00	75.00	125	250	—
1649	—	30.00	75.00	125	250	—
1650	—	30.00	75.00	125	250	—

KM# 31 1/2 DAALDER (Lion)
Silver **Rev:** Crowned lion

Date	Mintage	VG	F	VF	XF	Unc
1636	—	40.00	100	175	350	—
1640	—	30.00	75.00	125	250	—

KM# 35.1 1/2 DAALDER (Lion)
Silver **Rev:** Lion without crown **Note:** With solid inner circles on both sides.

Date	Mintage	VG	F	VF	XF	Unc
1644	—	40.00	100	175	350	—
1645	—	40.00	100	175	350	—
1646	—	30.00	75.00	125	250	—
1647	—	30.00	75.00	125	250	—
1648	26,610	30.00	75.00	125	250	—
1649	—	30.00	75.00	125	250	—
1650	—	30.00	75.00	125	250	—
1654	—	40.00	100	175	350	—
1658/4	—	40.00	100	175	350	—
1660	—	30.00	75.00	125	250	—
1661	—	30.00	75.00	125	250	—
1663	—	30.00	75.00	125	250	—
1664	—	40.00	100	175	350	—
1667	—	30.00	75.00	125	250	—

KM# 35.2 1/2 DAALDER (Lion)
Silver **Note:** Mint mrk: Agnus Dei. With solid inner circles on both sides.

Date	Mintage	VG	F	VF	XF	Unc
1674	—	75.00	175	250	400	—
1676	—	75.00	175	250	400	—

KM# 41 1/2 DAALDER (Rijks)
14.5100 g., 0.8850 Silver 0.4128 oz. ASW **Note:** Without solid inner circles on both sides. Similar to 1 Daalder, KM#14.

Date	Mintage	VG	F	VF	XF	Unc
1650	—	50.00	125	200	300	—
1651	—	50.00	125	200	300	—
1654	—	50.00	125	200	300	—
1656	—	50.00	125	200	300	—
1657	—	50.00	125	200	300	—
1658	—	50.00	125	200	300	—
1659	—	50.00	125	200	300	—
1663	—	50.00	125	200	300	—
1668	21,530	50.00	125	200	300	—

KM# 61 1/2 DAALDER (Rijks)
Silver **Note:** Without inner circles on both sides.

Date	Mintage	VG	F	VF	XF	Unc
1675	26,235	50.00	125	200	300	—

KM# 9 DAALDER (Prince - 40 Stuiver)
29.0300 g., 0.8850 Silver 0.8260 oz. ASW **Obv:** Helmeted arms in inner circle. **Rev:** Armored bust of William the Silent with sword to right in inner circle, date divided at top **Note:** Dav. #4823.

Date	Mintage	VG	F	VF	XF	Unc
1601/0	—	60.00	200	325	500	—
1601	—	50.00	150	250	450	—
1603	—	70.00	225	375	600	—

KM# 10 DAALDER (Lion - 48 Stuiver)
27.6800 g., 0.7500 Silver 0.6674 oz. ASW **Note:** Similar to KM#30 but date divided at bottom on obverse. Dav. #4862.

Date	Mintage	VG	F	VF	XF	Unc
1601/1598	—	30.00	60.00	150	300	—
1601	—	30.00	60.00	120	250	—
1602	—	30.00	60.00	150	300	—
1603	—	30.00	60.00	150	300	—

KM# 13 DAALDER (Lion - 48 Stuiver)
27.6800 g., 0.7500 Silver 0.6674 oz. ASW **Rev:** Lion shield without crown **Note:** Similar to KM#30. Dav. #4863.

Date	Mintage	VG	F	VF	XF	Unc
1606	—	25.00	60.00	80.00	160	—
1607/06	—	25.00	60.00	80.00	160	—
1607	—	25.00	60.00	80.00	160	—
1608/7	—	25.00	60.00	80.00	160	—
1608	—	25.00	60.00	80.00	160	—
1609	—	25.00	60.00	80.00	160	—
1610	—	25.00	60.00	80.00	160	—
1611/0	—	35.00	75.00	125	250	—
1612/08	—	35.00	75.00	125	320	—
1612/09	—	30.00	70.00	90.00	250	—
1612/0	—	35.00	75.00	125	320	—
1612	—	35.00	75.00	125	320	—
1613	—	25.00	60.00	80.00	160	—

Date	Mintage	VG	F	VF	XF	Unc
1614/3	—	25.00	60.00	80.00	160	—
1614	—	25.00	60.00	80.00	160	—
1615	—	25.00	60.00	80.00	160	—
1616/5	—	25.00	60.00	80.00	160	—
1616	—	25.00	60.00	80.00	160	—
1617/4	—	30.00	70.00	90.00	250	—
1617/5	—	30.00	70.00	90.00	250	—
1617/6	—	30.00	70.00	90.00	250	—
1617	—	25.00	60.00	80.00	160	—
1618/6	—	55.00	100	175	350	—
1618/7	—	30.00	70.00	90.00	250	—
1618	—	25.00	60.00	80.00	160	—
1623	—	35.00	75.00	125	250	—
1626/3	—	25.00	60.00	80.00	160	—
1626	—	25.00	60.00	80.00	160	—
1627/5	—	35.00	75.00	125	250	—
1627/6	—	35.00	75.00	125	250	—
1628	—	25.00	60.00	80.00	160	—
1629/6	—	25.00	60.00	80.00	160	—
1629/8	—	25.00	60.00	80.00	160	—
1629	—	25.00	60.00	80.00	160	—
1632/29	—	25.00	60.00	80.00	160	—
1632	—	25.00	60.00	80.00	160	—
1633	—	35.00	75.00	125	250	—
1634/3	—	35.00	75.00	125	250	—
1634	—	35.00	75.00	125	250	—

KM# 14 DAALDER (Rijks)
29.0300 g., 0.8850 0.8260 oz. **Note:** Dav. #4836.

Date	Mintage	VG	F	VF	XF	Unc
1606	—	40.00	150	200	250	—
1607/06	—	40.00	150	200	250	—
1607	—	40.00	150	200	250	—
1608	—	50.00	170	225	300	—
1609	—	40.00	150	200	250	—
1610	—	40.00	150	200	250	—
1611/0	—	40.00	150	200	250	—
1611	—	40.00	150	200	250	—
1612	—	30.00	75.00	100	150	—
1613	—	40.00	150	200	250	—
1614/3	—	40.00	150	200	250	—
1614	—	30.00	75.00	100	150	—
1616/3	—	—	—	—	—	—
1616	—	50.00	170	225	300	—
1617	—	40.00	150	200	250	—
1618	—	30.00	75.00	100	150	—
1619/8	—	30.00	75.00	100	150	—
1619	—	30.00	75.00	100	150	—
1620	—	30.00	75.00	100	150	—
1621	—	30.00	75.00	100	150	—
1622	—	30.00	75.00	100	150	—
1623	—	30.00	75.00	100	150	—
1624	—	30.00	75.00	100	150	—
1625	—	30.00	75.00	100	150	—
1626	—	30.00	75.00	100	150	—
1629/24	—	30.00	75.00	100	150	—
1629/25	—	30.00	75.00	100	150	—
1629/3	—	30.00	75.00	100	150	—
1629	—	30.00	75.00	100	150	—
1631	—	50.00	170	225	300	—
1648	—	40.00	150	200	250	—
1652	—	40.00	150	200	250	—
1688	—	40.00	150	200	250	—

KM# 40 DAALDER (Rijks)
29.0300 g., 0.8850 Silver 0.8260 oz. ASW **Note:** Similar to KM#14 but plain inner circles. Dav. #4838.

Date	Mintage	VG	F	VF	XF	Unc
1650	—	50.00	125	175	250	—
1651	—	50.00	125	175	250	—
1652	—	60.00	150	250	350	—
1653	—	50.00	125	175	250	—
1654	—	50.00	125	175	250	—
1655	—	50.00	125	175	250	—
1656	—	50.00	125	175	250	—
1657/0	—	50.00	125	175	250	—
1657	—	50.00	125	175	250	—
1658	—	50.00	125	175	250	—
1659	—	50.00	125	175	250	—

KM# A41 DAALDER (Rijks)
28.5600 g., Silver **Obv:** 1/2-length figure of knight right holding sword upright **Obv. Legend:** MO • ARG • PRO • CONFOE • BEL • TRA **Rev:** Crowned shield **Rev. Legend:** + CONCORDIA RES PARVAE CRESCVNT **Note:** Klippe.

Date	Mintage	Good	VG	F	VF	XF
1656	—	—	—	—	—	—

KM# 62.1 DAALDER (Rijks)
Silver **Note:** Mint mark: Agnus Dei. Similar to KM#14 but without inner circles. Dav. #4839.

Date	Mintage	VG	F	VF	XF	Unc
1675	—	55.00	125	200	275	—
1676	—	55.00	125	200	275	—

KM# 62.2 DAALDER (Rijks)
Silver **Note:** Mint mark: Rosette.

Date	Mintage	VG	F	VF	XF	Unc
1683/77	—	60.00	130	225	300	—
1683	—	55.00	125	200	275	—
1687/3	—	55.00	125	200	275	—
1687	—	55.00	125	200	275	—
1688	—	55.00	125	200	275	—
1693/82	—	55.00	125	200	275	—
1693/86	—	80.00	175	250	350	—
1693/2	—	80.00	175	250	350	—
1693	—	80.00	175	250	350	—
1694	—	55.00	125	200	275	—
1695	—	55.00	125	200	275	—
1700	—	60.00	130	225	300	—

KM# 30 DAALDER (Lion)
27.6800 g., 0.7500 Silver 0.6674 oz. ASW **Rev:** Crowned lion shield in inner circle **Note:** Dav. #4863.

Date	Mintage	VG	F	VF	XF	Unc
1635	—	10.00	50.00	100	200	—
1636	—	10.00	40.00	80.00	160	—
1637	—	10.00	40.00	80.00	160	—
1638	—	10.00	40.00	80.00	160	—
1639/7	—	25.00	60.00	125	250	—
1639	—	10.00	40.00	80.00	160	—
1640	—	10.00	40.00	80.00	160	—
1641	—	10.00	40.00	80.00	160	—
1642/1	—	25.00	60.00	125	250	—
1642	—	10.00	40.00	80.00	260	—
1643/1	—	25.00	60.00	125	250	—
1643	—	10.00	40.00	80.00	160	—
1644/04	—	10.00	40.00	80.00	160	—
1644/3	—	10.00	40.00	80.00	160	—
1644	—	10.00	40.00	80.00	160	—
1645/4	—	10.00	40.00	80.00	160	—
1645	—	10.00	40.00	80.00	160	—
1646/5	—	10.00	40.00	80.00	160	—
1646	—	10.00	40.00	80.00	160	—
1647	—	10.00	40.00	80.00	160	—
1648	—	10.00	40.00	80.00	160	—
1649	—	10.00	40.00	80.00	160	—
1650	—	10.00	40.00	80.00	125	—
1651	—	10.00	40.00	80.00	125	—
1652	—	10.00	40.00	80.00	125	—

KM# 32 DAALDER (Lion)
Silver **Obv:** Armored knight behind lion shield in inner dotted circle **Rev:** Rampant lion left in inner dotted circle **Note:** Mint mark: Rosette.

Date	Mintage	VG	F	VF	XF	Unc
1636	—	—	—	—	—	—
1641	—	10.00	50.00	80.00	160	—
1645	—	35.00	50.00	200	400	—
1647	—	10.00	50.00	80.00	160	—
1648	—	10.00	40.00	80.00	160	—
1649/8	—	10.00	40.00	80.00	160	—
1649	—	10.00	40.00	80.00	160	—
1650	—	10.00	40.00	80.00	160	—
1651	—	10.00	40.00	80.00	160	—
1652	—	10.00	40.00	80.00	160	—
1653	—	10.00	40.00	80.00	160	—
1654	—	10.00	40.00	80.00	160	—
1655	—	10.00	40.00	80.00	160	—
1656	—	10.00	40.00	80.00	160	—
1658	—	10.00	40.00	80.00	160	—
1659	—	10.00	40.00	80.00	160	—
1660	—	10.00	40.00	80.00	160	—
1661	—	10.00	40.00	80.00	160	—
1662	—	10.00	40.00	80.00	160	—
1663	—	10.00	40.00	80.00	160	—
1664	—	10.00	40.00	80.00	160	—
1666	—	25.00	70.00	150	300	—
1667	—	25.00	70.00	150	300	—
1668/7	—	20.00	50.00	100	200	—
1669/86/67	—	40.00	90.00	180	400	—

KM# 59.1 DAALDER (Lion)

Note: Mint mrk: Agnus Dei. Similar to kM#30 but without inner circles. Dav. #4838.

Date	Mintage	VG	F	VF	XF	Unc
1674	—	30.00	75.00	130	300	—
1675	—	30.00	75.00	130	300	—
1676	—	30.00	75.00	130	300	—

KM# 72 DAALDER (Lion)

Silver **Obv:** Without plume on knight's helmet **Note:** Similar to KM#30. Dav. #4866.

Date	Mintage	VG	F	VF	XF	Unc
1679	—	45.00	100	150	250	—
1680	—	45.00	100	150	250	—
1681	—	45.00	100	150	250	—
1682	—	45.00	100	150	250	—
1683	—	25.00	60.00	80.00	150	—
1685/83	—	45.00	100	150	250	—
1685	—	25.00	60.00	80.00	150	—
1686	—	25.00	60.00	80.00	150	—
1687	—	25.00	60.00	80.00	150	—
1688	—	25.00	60.00	80.00	150	—
1689	—	25.00	60.00	80.00	150	—
1690	—	65.00	125	225	300	—
1690/81	—	65.00	125	225	300	—
1690/86	—	65.00	125	225	300	—
1696	—	25.00	60.00	80.00	150	—
1697	—	25.00	60.00	80.00	150	—
1698	—	25.00	60.00	80.00	150	—
1700	—	25.00	60.00	80.00	150	—

KM# 59.2 DAALDER (Lion)

Silver **Obv:** Armored knight looking right behind lion shield **Rev:** Rampant lion left **Note:** Mint mark: Rosette. Varieties exist.

Date	Mintage	VG	F	VF	XF	Unc
1679	—	30.00	75.00	100	200	—
1680/79	—	30.00	75.00	100	200	—
1680	—	30.00	75.00	100	200	—
1681	—	30.00	75.00	100	200	—
1682/80	—	30.00	75.00	100	200	—
1682	—	30.00	75.00	100	200	—
1683	—	30.00	75.00	100	200	—

KM# 73 DAALDER (30 Stuiver)

15.8800 g., 0.9060 Silver 0.4625 oz. ASW

Date	Mintage	VG	F	VF	XF	Unc
1685	1,187,950	30.00	65.00	100	200	—
1686	Inc. above	30.00	65.00	100	200	—
1687	Inc. above	30.00	65.00	100	200	—
1688/6	Inc. above	30.00	65.00	130	250	—
1688	Inc. above	30.00	65.00	100	200	—
1689	Inc. above	30.00	65.00	100	200	—
1690	Inc. above	60.00	120	200	300	—
1691	Inc. above	30.00	65.00	100	200	—
1692	376,885	30.00	65.00	100	200	—

KM# 5 1/2 ROSE NOBLE

3.9000 g., Gold **Obv:** Ruler in ship in inner circle **Rev:** Radiant sun surrounded by crowned lions and lis **Note:** Fr. #279.

Date	Mintage	VG	F	VF	XF	Unc
ND(ca. 1600-02)	189,000	300	550	850	1,350	—

KM# 6 ROSE NOBLE

7.8000 g., Gold **Obv:** Ruler in ship in inner circle **Rev:** Radiant sun surrounded by crowned lions and lis **Note:** Fr. #277.

Date	Mintage	VG	F	VF	XF	Unc
ND(ca. 1600-02)	250,000	500	800	1,300	1,800	—

KM# 16 1/2 CAVALIER D'OR

5.0000 g., 0.9200 Gold 0.1479 oz. AGW **Obv:** Knight on horseback right above arms **Rev:** Crowned arms, date above **Note:** fr. #287.

Date	Mintage	VG	F	VF	XF	Unc
1606	—	200	350	700	1,100	—
1607/6	—	—	—	—	—	—
1607	—	200	350	700	1,100	—
1608	—	200	350	700	1,100	—
1614/06	—	200	350	700	1,100	—
1614/07	—	200	350	700	1,100	—
1614	—	200	350	700	1,100	—
1615/4	—	200	350	700	1,100	—
1615	—	200	350	700	1,100	—
1616	—	200	350	700	1,100	—
1617/07	—	200	350	700	1,100	—
1617	—	200	350	700	1,100	—
1618	—	200	350	700	1,100	—
1622	—	200	350	700	1,100	—
1629	—	200	350	700	1,100	—
1639	—	200	350	700	1,100	—
1644	—	200	350	700	1,100	—

KM# 15 CAVALIER D'OR

10.0000 g., 0.9200 Gold 0.2958 oz. AGW **Note:** Fr. #286.

Date	Mintage	VG	F	VF	XF	Unc
1606	—	400	600	950	1,550	—
1607/6	—	400	600	950	1,550	—
1607	—	400	600	950	1,550	—
1608	—	400	600	950	1,550	—
1614/06	—	400	600	950	1,550	—
1614	—	400	600	950	1,550	—
1615/4	—	400	600	950	1,550	—
1615	—	400	600	950	1,550	—
1616	—	400	650	1,000	1,750	—
1617/0	—	400	650	1,100	1,850	—
1617/6	—	400	650	1,100	1,850	—
1617	—	400	650	1,000	1,750	—
1618	—	400	600	950	1,550	—
1619	—	400	600	950	1,550	—
1620/19	—	400	600	950	1,550	—
1620	—	400	650	1,000	1,750	—
1621	—	400	600	950	1,550	—
1622	—	400	600	950	1,550	—
1623	—	400	600	950	1,550	—
1624	—	400	600	950	1,550	—
1625	—	400	600	950	1,550	—
1627	—	—	—	—	—	—

TRADE COINAGE

KM# 7 DUCAT

3.5000 g., 0.9860 Gold 0.1109 oz. AGW **Obv:** Standing, armored knight holding bundle of arrows, divides date **Obv. Legend:** CONCORDIARES ... **Rev:** Inscription within ornamented tablet **Rev. Inscription:** MO/ ORD/ PROVIN/ FOEDER/ BELGAD/ LEGIMP **Note:** Fr. #284.

Date	Mintage	VG	F	VF	XF	Unc
1602	—	120	175	250	400	—
1603	—	120	175	250	400	—
1604/3	—	—	—	—	—	—
1604	—	120	150	170	300	—
1605	—	120	150	170	300	—
1606/5	—	120	175	250	400	—
1606	—	120	175	250	400	—
1607/5	—	—	—	—	—	—
1607/6	—	120	150	170	300	—
1607	—	120	150	170	300	—
1608/3	—	120	150	170	300	—
1608/7	—	120	150	170	300	—
1608	—	120	150	170	300	—
1609	—	120	150	170	300	—
1610	—	120	150	170	300	—
1611/09	—	120	150	170	300	—
1611	—	120	150	170	300	—
1612	—	120	150	170	300	—
1613/0	—	120	175	250	400	—
1613	—	120	150	170	300	—
1614/3	—	120	150	170	300	—
1614	—	120	150	170	300	—
1615/3	—	120	175	250	400	—
1615/4	—	120	175	250	400	—
1615	—	120	175	250	400	—
1616	—	120	150	170	300	—
1618/07	—	120	150	170	300	—
1620	—	120	175	250	400	—
1622	—	120	175	250	400	—
1623/14	—	120	150	170	300	—
1623/19	—	120	150	170	300	—

Date	Mintage	VG	F	VF	XF	Unc
1623	—	120	150	170	300	—
1624	—	120	175	250	400	—
1629/7	—	120	175	250	400	—
1629	—	120	175	250	400	—
1630/24	—	—	—	—	—	—
1630/29	—	120	175	250	400	—
1630	—	120	150	170	300	—
1631/20	—	120	175	250	400	—
1631	—	120	175	250	400	—
1632	—	120	175	250	400	—
1633/2	—	120	175	250	400	—
1634	—	120	150	170	300	—
1635	—	120	150	170	300	—
1636	—	120	150	170	300	—
1637	—	120	150	170	300	—
1638/7	—	120	150	200	325	—
1638	—	120	150	170	300	—
1639	—	120	175	250	400	—
1640/36	—	120	150	170	300	—
1640	—	120	150	170	300	—
1641	—	120	150	170	300	—
1642	—	120	175	250	400	—
1643/34	—	—	—	—	—	—
1643/0	—	—	—	—	—	—
1643	—	120	150	170	300	—
1644	—	120	175	250	400	—
1645/3	—	120	175	250	400	—
1645	—	120	150	160	265	—
1646	—	120	150	200	300	—
1647	—	120	150	200	300	—
1648	—	120	150	200	300	—
1649	—	120	150	200	300	—
1650	—	120	175	250	400	—
1651	—	120	175	250	400	—
1652	—	120	150	200	300	—
1653	—	120	175	250	400	—
1654	—	120	175	250	400	—
1656	—	120	175	250	400	—
1657	—	120	175	250	400	—
1658	—	120	150	200	300	—
1659	—	120	175	250	400	—
1660	—	120	175	250	400	—
1661	—	120	150	200	300	—
1662	—	120	150	200	300	—
1663	—	120	150	200	300	—
1664	—	120	150	200	300	—
1666	—	120	150	200	300	—
1667	—	120	150	200	300	—
1668	—	120	150	200	300	—
1669	—	120	150	200	300	—
1670	—	120	150	200	265	—
1671	—	120	150	200	300	—
1672	—	120	175	250	400	—
1673	—	120	150	200	300	—
1674 with inner circle	—	120	150	250	400	—
1674 without inner circle	—	125	175	250	400	—
1675	—	125	175	200	300	—
1676/5	—	—	—	—	—	—
1676	—	120	175	250	400	—
1679	—	120	150	200	300	—
1680	—	120	175	250	400	—
1681/0	—	120	175	250	400	—
1681	—	120	175	250	400	—
1682/0	—	120	175	250	400	—
1682	—	120	175	250	400	—
1683	—	120	150	200	300	—
1684	—	120	150	200	300	—
1685	—	120	150	200	300	—
1686	—	120	150	200	300	—
1687	—	120	150	200	300	—
1688	—	120	150	200	300	—
1689	—	120	150	200	300	—
1690	—	120	150	200	300	—
1691	—	120	175	250	400	—
1692	—	120	150	200	300	—
1693/88	—	120	—	—	—	—
1693	—	120	150	200	300	—
1694	—	120	175	250	400	—
1695	—	120	150	200	300	—
1696/3	—	—	—	—	—	—
1696	—	120	175	250	400	—
1697	—	120	175	250	400	—
1698	—	120	175	250	400	—
1699	—	120	175	250	400	—
1700	—	120	200	350	500	—

KM# 42 2 DUCAT

7.0000 g., 0.9860 Gold 0.2219 oz. AGW **Obv:** Standing, armored knight holding bundle of arrows, divides date within broken circle **Obv. Legend:** CONCORDIA RES PAR• CRESTRA• **Rev:** Inscription within ornamented square **Rev. Inscription:** MO:ORD/PROVIN/FOEDER:/BELGAD/LEG.IMP **Note:** Fr. #282.

Date	Mintage	VG	F	VF	XF	Unc
1650	—	300	550	800	1,100	—
1652	—	300	650	1,000	1,500	—
1653	—	250	300	600	850	—
1654	—	250	300	600	850	—
1655	—	250	300	600	850	—
1656	—	250	300	600	850	—
1657	—	250	300	600	850	—
1658	—	300	650	1,000	1,500	—
1660	—	300	550	800	1,100	—
1666	—	300	550	800	1,100	—
1669	—	300	650	1,000	1,500	—
1683	—	250	300	600	850	—
1684	—	250	650	1,000	1,500	—
1688	—	300	650	1,000	1,500	—
1690	—	250	300	600	850	—
1691	—	250	300	600	850	—
1692	—	250	300	600	850	—
1693	—	300	650	1,000	1,500	—
1694	—	300	650	1,000	1,500	—
1695	—	300	650	1,000	1,500	—
1696	—	300	650	1,000	1,500	—
1697	—	300	650	1,000	1,500	—
1699/66	—	300	650	1,000	1,500	—
1699	—	300	650	1,000	1,500	—

COUNTERMARKED COINAGE

1693

During the late 17th century many circulating coins were found to be underweight. In 1693 coins meeting the legal requirements were countermarked for a specific province or city, such as UTR for Utrecht.

KM# 74.1 28 STUIVERS

Silver **Countermark:** UTR **Note:** Countermark on Deventer KM#79.

CM Date	Host Date	Good	VG	F	VF	XF
ND(1693)	1684	—	—	—	—	—

KM# 74.2 28 STUIVERS

Silver **Countermark:** UTR **Note:** Countermark on Deventer KM#81.

CM Date	Host Date	Good	VG	F	VF	XF
ND(1693)	1685-92	—	—	—	—	—

KM# 74.3 28 STUIVERS

Silver **Countermark:** UTR **Note:** Countermark on Friesland KM#10.

CM Date	Host Date	Good	VG	F	VF	XF
ND(1693)	1601-91	—	—	—	—	—

KM# 74.4 28 STUIVERS

Silver **Countermark:** UTR **Note:** Countermark on Groningen KM#50.

CM Date	Host Date	Good	VG	F	VF	XF
ND(1693)	1690	—	—	—	—	—

KM# 74.5 28 STUIVERS

Silver **Countermark:** UTR **Note:** Countermark on Groningen and Ommeland KM#52.

CM Date	Host Date	Good	VG	F	VF	XF
ND(1693)	1692	—	—	—	—	—

KM# 74.6 28 STUIVERS

Silver **Countermark:** UTR **Note:** Countermark on Groningen and Ommeland KM#31.

CM Date	Host Date	Good	VG	F	VF	XF
ND(1693)	1673-77	—	—	—	—	—

KM# 74.7 28 STUIVERS

Silver **Countermark:** UTR **Note:** Countermark on Nijmegen KM#27.

CM Date	Host Date	Good	VG	F	VF	XF
ND(1693)	1685-90	—	—	—	—	—

KM# 74.8 28 STUIVERS

Silver **Countermark:** UTR **Note:** Countermark on Overyssel KM#55.

CM Date	Host Date	Good	VG	F	VF	XF
ND(1693)	1685-89	—	—	—	—	—

KM# 74.9 28 STUIVERS

Silver **Countermark:** UTR **Note:** Countermark on West Friesland KM#90.

CM Date	Host Date	Good	VG	F	VF	XF
ND(1693)	1685-87	—	—	—	—	—

KM# 74.10 28 STUIVERS

Silver **Countermark:** UTR **Note:** Countermark on Zwolle KM#78.

CM Date	Host Date	Good	VG	F	VF	XF
ND(1693)	1679-86	—	—	—	—	—

KM# 74.11 28 STUIVERS

Silver **Countermark:** UTR **Note:** Countermark on Groningen and Ommeland KM#50

CM Date	Host Date	Good	VG	F	VF	XF
ND(1693)	1690	—	—	—	—	—

PATTERNS

Including off metal strikes

KM#	Date	Mintage	Identification	Mkt Val
Pn1	1673	—	Rijksdaalder. Silver. Prince William III	—
Pn4	1682	—	1/2 Gulden. Gold. 10.4000 g. KM#69.	2,000
Pn5	1682	—	Gulden. Gold. 13.8000 g. KM#70.	4,750
Pn6	1684	—	3 Gulden. Gold. 41.8000 g. KM#71.	—

KM#	Date	Mintage	Identification	Mkt Val
Pn7	1685	—	Daalder. Gold. 21.8000 g. KM#73.	3,000
Pn8	1687	—	Daalder. Gold. 21.8000 g. KM#73.	—

PIEFORTS

KM#	Date	Mintage	Identification	Mkt Val
P1	1606	—	Cavalier D'Or. Gold. 19.9000 g. KM15.	—
PA2	1620	—	Cavalier D'Or. Gold. 19.9000 g. KM15	—
P2	1629	—	Cavalier D'Or. Gold. 19.9000 g. KM15.	—
P3	1653	—	Rijksdaalder. Silver. KM40	2,000
P4	1656	—	Rijksdaalder. Silver. KM40, not klippe	2,000
PA5	1657	—	Duit. Copper. KM43.2	—
PB5	1657	—	Duit. Copper. KM43.2, triple weight	—
P5	1659	—	Ducaton. Silver. KM46.1, round version.	1,200
P6	1659	—	Silver Ducat. KM48.1, Dav. #4901.	—
P7	1660	—	Ducaton. Silver. KM48.1, round version.	—
P8	1660	—	Ducaton. Silver. Klippe, KM46.1	2,000
P9	1660	—	Silver Ducat. KM48.1, Dav. #4901.	—
P10	1661	—	Ducaton. Silver. KM46.1, round version	1,000
P11	1661	—	Ducaton. Silver. Klippe, KM46.1.	1,200
P12	1662	—	Ducaton. Silver. KM46.1, round version	—
P13	1662	—	Ducaton. Silver. Klippe, KM46.1	—
P14	1662	—	Silver Ducat. KM48.1, Dav. #4901.	—
P15	1664	—	Ducaton. Silver. KM46.1, but not Klippe	—
P16	1664	—	Silver Ducat. KM48.1, Dav. #4901.	800
PA17	1668	—	1/2 Ducaton. Silver. KM45	2,500
P17	1668	—	Ducaton. Silver. 65.1100 g. KM46 but not Klippe	2,000
P18	1669	—	2 Ducat. Gold. KM42	—
P19	1670	—	Ducaton. Silver. KM46.2	2,500
P20	1672	—	Ducaton. Silver. KM46.2	—
P21	1679	—	Ducaton. Silver. KM63.	—
P22	1680	—	Ducaton. Silver. KM63.	—
PA22	1682	—	1/2 Gulden. Gold. 10.5000 g. KM69	1,000
P23	1687	—	Silver Ducat. KM65, Dav. #4903.	—
PA24	1689	—	Duit. Copper. KM66	—
P24	1692	—	Ducaton. Silver. KM63.	—
P-A24	1693	—	2 Ducat. Gold. 13.8300 g. KM42.	—

WEST FRIESLAND

West Frisia

West Friesland (West Frisia), also known as North Holland, is part of the province of Holland, and is not associated with the province of Friesland.

PROVINCE

STANDARD COINAGE

KM# 56 1/2 DUIT

1.0000 g., Copper **Obv:** Crowned arms **Rev:** WEST/FRISIAE/ (date) in branches

Date	Mintage	VG	F	VF	XF	Unc
1663	—	6.00	25.00	45.00	100	—

KM# 10 DUIT

2.0000 g., Copper **Obv:** Crowned arms **Rev:** WEST/FRISIAE/ (date) in wreath

Date	Mintage	VG	F	VF	XF	Unc
ND(1603)	—	10.00	25.00	55.00	80.00	—
1604	—	5.00	15.00	35.00	50.00	—
1605	—	8.00	20.00	45.00	75.00	—

KM# 40 DUIT

Copper **Note:** Klippe. Weight varies 4-12 grams.

Date	Mintage	VG	F	VF	XF	Unc
1626	—	—	—	—	300	—
1645	—	—	—	—	400	—
1658	—	—	—	—	300	—
1660	—	—	—	—	400	—
1661	—	—	—	—	—	—
1663	—	—	—	—	300	—
1665	—	—	—	—	400	—

KM# 29 DUIT

Copper **Obv:** Crowned arms **Rev:** Larger wreath **Note:** Varieties exist.

Date	Mintage	VG	F	VF	XF	Unc
1626	—	5.00	15.00	25.00	50.00	—
1627	—	7.00	20.00	30.00	60.00	—
1658	—	4.00	12.50	20.00	45.00	—
1659	—	15.00	50.00	100	250	—
1660	—	4.00	12.50	20.00	45.00	—
1663	—	4.00	12.50	20.00	45.00	—
1664	—	7.00	20.00	30.00	60.00	—

KM# 40a DUIT

Silver

Date	Mintage	VG	F	VF	XF	Unc
1626	—	20.00	50.00	75.00	100	—
1645	—	20.00	50.00	100	200	—
1660	—	20.00	50.00	75.00	100	—
1663	—	20.00	50.00	75.00	100	—
1665	—	20.00	50.00	75.00	100	—

KM# 29a DUIT

Silver

Date	Mintage	VG	F	VF	XF	Unc
1645	—	—	—	—	200	—
1658	—	—	—	—	—	—
1660	—	—	—	—	—	—

KM# 45 DUIT

2.0000 g., Copper **Obv:** Arms of Enkhuizen, Hoorn and Medemblik **Obv. Legend:** DEVS. FORTI. E. SP. NOS.

Date	Mintage	VG	F	VF	XF	Unc
1658	—	15.00	35.00	70.00	110	—

KM# 45a DUIT

Silver

Date	Mintage	VG	F	VF	XF	Unc
1658	—	—	—	—	200	—
1660	—	—	—	—	200	—

KM# 45b DUIT

3.5000 g., Gold **Obv:** Crowned shield **Obv. Legend:** DEVS. FORT. ET. SP. NOS. **Rev:** 3 shields of Enkhuizen, Hoorn and Medemblik

Date	Mintage	VG	F	VF	XF	Unc
1660	—	—	—	—	—	—

KM# 11 2 DUIT

Copper **Obv:** Crowned arms **Rev. Inscription:** WEST / FRISIAE / date in wreath

Date	Mintage	VG	F	VF	XF	Unc
1604	—	6.00	20.00	35.00	70.00	—

KM# 20 STUIVER

0.8600 g., 0.3330 Silver 0.0092 oz. ASW **Obv:** Crowned rampant lion to left holding sword and arrows, value at sides **Rev:** W/FRISIA/(date)

Date	Mintage	VG	F	VF	XF	Unc
1614	—	10.00	20.00	40.00	90.00	—
1615	—	10.00	20.00	40.00	90.00	—
1628	—	10.00	20.00	40.00	90.00	—

KM# 38 STUIVER

1.3190 g., 0.3330 Silver 0.0141 oz. ASW **Obv:** Bundle of arrows divides value in wreath **Rev:** W/FRI/SIA/(date) in wreath

Date	Mintage	VG	F	VF	XF	Unc
1639	—	7.00	15.00	25.00	40.00	—
1641/39	—	10.00	20.00	35.00	60.00	—
1641	—	7.00	15.00	25.00	40.00	—

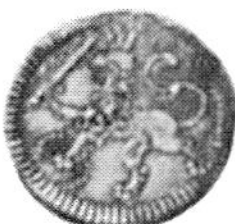

KM# 60 STUIVER

Silver **Obv:** Crowned rampant lion to left holding sword and arrows **Rev:** Small shield with 3 herrings at top **Rev. Inscription:** WEST / FRISIA / 1 STUIVER / (date) **Note:** Struck at private mint of Dirk Bosch in Enkhuizen.

Date	Mintage	VG	F	VF	XF	Unc
1673	—	50.00	125	175	275	—

KM# 69 STUIVER

Silver **Obv:** Crowned rampant lion to left holding sword and arrows **Rev. Inscription:** W / FRISIA / 1 STUIVER / BANKG / (date) **Note:** Struck at private mint of Dirk Bosch in Enkhuizen.

Date	Mintage	VG	F	VF	XF	Unc
1675	—	50.00	125	175	300	—

KM# 71 STUIVER

Silver **Obv:** Crowned arms divide B-P (Bank Payment) **Rev. Inscription:** WEST / FRISIA / 1 STUIVER / BANKG / (date) **Note:** Struck at private mint of Dirk Bosch in Enkhuizen.

Date	Mintage	VG	F	VF	XF	Unc
1676	—	15.00	40.00	75.00	125	—
1677	—	10.00	35.00	60.00	90.00	—

KM# 74 STUIVER

Silver **Obv:** Crowned arms divides value **Rev. Inscription:** WEST / FRISIA / (date) **Note:** Struck at private mint of Dirk Bosch in Enkhuisen.

Date	Mintage	VG	F	VF	XF	Unc
1677	—	8.00	30.00	50.00	80.00	—
1678	—	8.00	30.00	50.00	80.00	—

KM# 21.1 2 STUIVERS

Silver **Obv:** Crowned rampant lion to left holding sword and arrows, value at sides **Rev. Inscription:** W / FRI / SIA / (date) **Note:** Mint mark: Lily.

Date	Mintage	VG	F	VF	XF	Unc
1614	—	5.00	15.00	25.00	50.00	—
1615	—	5.00	15.00	25.00	50.00	—
1616	—	5.00	15.00	25.00	50.00	—
1639	—	5.00	15.00	25.00	50.00	—
1641/39	—	8.00	20.00	40.00	80.00	—
1641	—	5.00	15.00	25.00	50.00	—
1646/1	—	10.00	20.00	40.00	80.00	—
1646	—	5.00	15.00	40.00	50.00	—

KM# 21.2 2 STUIVERS

1.7300 g., 0.5830 Silver 0.0324 oz. ASW **Obv:** Crowned rampant lion to left holding sword and arrows, value at sides **Rev. Inscription:** W / FRI / SIA / (date) **Note:** Mint mark: Rosette.

Date	Mintage	VG	F	VF	XF	Unc
1625	—	5.00	15.00	25.00	50.00	—
1628	—	5.00	15.00	25.00	50.00	—

KM# 21.3 2 STUIVERS

1.7300 g., 0.5830 Silver 0.0324 oz. ASW **Obv:** Crowned rampant lion to left holding sword and arrows, value at sides **Rev. Inscription:** W / FRI / SIA / (date) **Note:** Mint mark: Cinquefoil. Varieties exist.

Date	Mintage	VG	F	VF	XF	Unc
1653	—	5.00	12.50	22.50	45.00	—
1670	—	5.00	12.50	22.50	45.00	—
1671	—	5.00	10.00	20.00	40.00	—
1672	—	5.00	10.00	20.00	40.00	—
1673	—	5.00	10.00	20.00	40.00	—
1674	—	5.00	10.00	20.00	40.00	—
1675	—	6.00	15.00	35.00	70.00	—
1677	—	5.00	10.00	20.00	40.00	—
1678	—	5.00	10.00	20.00	40.00	—
1679	—	5.00	10.00	20.00	40.00	—
1699	—	5.00	10.00	20.00	40.00	—
1700	—	5.00	10.00	20.00	40.00	—

KM# 61 2 STUIVERS

Silver **Note:** Struck at private mint of Dirk Bosch in Enkhuizen.

Date	Mintage	VG	F	VF	XF	Unc
1673	—	40.00	100	250	500	—

KM# 65 2 STUIVERS

Silver **Obv:** Provincial arms of West Friesland **Note:** Struck at private mint of Dirk Bosch in Enkhuizen.

Date	Mintage	VG	F	VF	XF	Unc
1674	—	100	400	600	1,000	—

KM# 70 2 STUIVERS

Silver **Obv:** Crowned rampant lion to left holding sword and arrows **Rev:** WEST/FRISIA/II STUIVERS/BANKGELT/1675 **Note:** Struck at private mint of Dirk Bosch in Enkhuizen.

Date	Mintage	VG	F	VF	XF	Unc
1675	—	60.00	150	300	600	—

KM# 72 2 STUIVERS

Silver **Obv:** Crowned arms divide B - P (Bank Payment) **Rev:** WEST/FRISIA/2 STUIVERS/ (date) **Note:** Struck at private mint of Dirk Bosch in Enkhuizen.

Date	Mintage	VG	F	VF	XF	Unc
1676	—	30.00	75.00	150	300	—
1677	—	30.00	75.00	150	300	—

KM# 75 2 STUIVERS

Silver **Obv:** Crowned arms divide value 2 - S **Rev. Inscription:** WEST / FRISIA / (date) **Note:** Struck at private mint of Dirk Bosch in Enkhuizen.

Date	Mintage	VG	F	VF	XF	Unc
1677	—	10.00	25.00	40.00	70.00	—
1678	—	10.00	25.00	40.00	70.00	—

KM# 79 1/2 ROOSSCHELLING (3 Stuivers)

5.2700 g., Silver **Obv:** Crowned provincial arms, date above within dotted circle **Rev:** Ornate cross with rosette at center

Date	Mintage	VG	F	VF	XF	Unc
1682	—	80.00	150	300	600	—

KM# 66 6 STUIVERS (Lion Schelling)

3.3000 g., 0.8750 Silver 0.0928 oz. ASW **Note:** Struck at private mint of Dirk Bosch in Enkhuizen.

Date	Mintage	VG	F	VF	XF	Unc
1674	—	100	250	500	800	—
1676	—	100	250	500	800	—

KM# 5.1 6 STUIVERS (Roosschelling)

5.2700 g., 0.5830 Silver 0.0988 oz. ASW **Obv:** Crowned arms in branches in inner circle, date above crown **Rev:** Ornamental cross with rose at center in inner circle

Date	Mintage	VG	F	VF	XF	Unc
1601	—	15.00	45.00	75.00	125	—
1629	—	15.00	45.00	75.00	125	—
1653	—	15.00	45.00	75.00	125	—
1680	—	15.00	45.00	75.00	125	—

KM# 5.2 6 STUIVERS (Roosschelling)

5.2700 g., 0.5830 Silver 0.0988 oz. ASW **Obv:** Crowned arms in branches in inner circle, date above crown **Rev:** Ornamental cross with rose at center in inner circle **Note:** Mint mark: Bull. Varieties exist.

Date	Mintage	VG	F	VF	XF	Unc
1682	—	25.00	75.00	125	250	—
1683	—	25.00	75.00	125	250	—

KM# 62 6 STUIVERS (Scheepjesschelling)

3.3000 g., 0.8750 Silver 0.0928 oz. ASW **Obv:** Crowned arms divide date **Rev:** Sailing ship to right **Note:** Struck at private mint of Dirk Bosch in Enkhuizen.

Date	Mintage	VG	F	VF	XF	Unc
1673	—	125	275	500	750	—

KM# 77 6 STUIVERS (Scheepjesschelling)

3.3900 g., Silver **Obv:** Rampant lion left holding sword and bundle of arrows **Obv. Legend:** MONET•NO ORD•FOEDERATÆ•BELG• **Rev. Inscription:** WEST / FRISIA / VI • STUIVERS / BANKGELD / (date) **Note:** Struck at the private mint of Dirk Bosch in Enkhuizen.

Date	Mintage	VG	F	VF	XF	Unc
1674	—	100	200	400	800	—

KM# 77a 6 STUIVERS (Scheepjesschelling)

3.2000 g., Gold **Obv:** Rampant lion left holding sword and bundle of arrows **Obv. Legend:** MONET• NO ORD•FOEDERATÆ•BELG• **Rev. Inscription:** WEST / FRISIA / VI • STUIVERS / BANKGELD / (date) **Note:** Struck at the private mint of Dirk Bosch in Enkhuizen.

Date	Mintage	VG	F	VF	XF	Unc
1674	—	—	—	—	—	2,000

KM# 73 6 STUIVERS (Scheepjesschelling)

3.3000 g., 0.8750 Silver 0.0928 oz. ASW **Obv:** Crowned arms divide value 6 - S and B - P (Bank Payment) **Rev:** Sailing ship to right **Note:** Struck at private mint of Dirk Bosch in Enkhuizen.

Date	Mintage	VG	F	VF	XF	Unc
1676	—	55.00	125	200	350	—
1677	—	55.00	125	200	350	—

KM# 73a 6 STUIVERS (Scheepjesschelling)

3.5000 g., Gold **Obv:** Crowned arms divide value 6 - s and B - P (Bank Payment) **Rev:** Sailing ship **Note:** Struck at private mint of Dirk Bosch in Enkhuizen.

Date	Mintage	VG	F	VF	XF	Unc
1676	—	—	—	—	—	—
1677	—	—	—	—	—	—

KM# 76 6 STUIVERS (Scheepjesschelling)

3.3000 g., 0.8750 Silver 0.0928 oz. ASW **Obv:** Without B-P **Rev:** Sailing ship to right **Note:** Struck at private mint of Dirk Bosch in Enkhuizen.

Date	Mintage	VG	F	VF	XF	Unc
1677	—	10.00	25.00	50.00	100	—
1678/7	—	10.00	25.00	50.00	100	—
1678	—	8.00	20.00	30.00	60.00	—
1679	—	10.00	25.00	50.00	100	—

KM# 3 10 STUIVERS

5.9500 g., Silver **Obv:** Armored knight standing behind shield with sword on shoulder **Obv. Legend:** MO•ARG•PRO•CON - FOE•BELG•WESTF **Rev:** Crowned lion shield divides value X - S **Rev. Legend:** +CON CORDIA • RES • PARVÆ • CRESCVNT•

Date	Mintage	VG	F	VF	XF	Unc
1606	—	—	—	—	—	—

KM# 80 10 STUIVERS (1/2 Gulden)

5.3000 g., 0.9200 Silver 0.1568 oz. ASW **Obv:** Crowned arms divide value 10 - S, date above crown **Rev:** Standing female figure leaning on Bible on column, holding spear with Liberty cap

Date	Mintage	VG	F	VF	XF	Unc
1682	—	50.00	150	300	500	—

KM# 81 GULDEN

10.6100 g., 0.9200 Silver 0.3138 oz. ASW

Date	Mintage	VG	F	VF	XF	Unc
1682	Inc. below	50.00	150	250	500	—
1687	26,240	50.00	150	250	500	—

KM# 97.1 GULDEN

10.6100 g., 0.9200 Silver 0.3138 oz. ASW **Obv:** Crowned arms of Friesland divide value **Obv. Legend:** MO: ARG: ORD: FÆD: ... **Rev:** Standing figure leaning on column with cap on pole, date in exergue below **Rev. Legend:** HAC NITIMVR HANCTVEMVR **Note:** Mint mark: Cinquefoil. Similar to 3 Gulden, KM#141.

Date	Mintage	VG	F	VF	XF	Unc
1699	—	12.50	30.00	50.00	75.00	—

KM# 83 2 GULDEN (40 Stuiver)

Silver **Note:** Klippe.

Date	Mintage	VG	F	VF	XF	Unc
1682	—	—	—	—	—	—

KM# 82 2 GULDEN (40 Stuiver)

21.2100 g., Silver **Note:** Similar to KM#83 but not Klippe.

Date	Mintage	VG	F	VF	XF	Unc
1682	—	150	400	600	1,200	—

KM# 84 3 GULDEN (60 Stuiver)

31.8200 g., 0.9200 Silver 0.9412 oz. ASW **Obv:** Crowned arms of West Friesland divide value, date above crown **Rev:** Standing female figure leaning on Bible on column, holding spear with Liberty cap **Note:** Dav. #4961.

Date	Mintage	VG	F	VF	XF	Unc
1682	77,420	100	300	400	600	—
1687	Inc. above	125	350	500	675	—
1687/2	Inc. above	150	400	600	750	—

KM# 95.1 3 GULDEN (60 Stuiver)

31.8200 g., 0.9200 Silver 0.9412 oz. ASW **Rev:** Date in exergue **Note:** Mint mark: Ship. Dav. #4963.

Date	Mintage	VG	F	VF	XF	Unc
1694	—	50.00	125	200	300	—

KM# 95.2 3 GULDEN (60 Stuiver)

31.8200 g., 0.9200 Silver 0.9412 oz. ASW **Obv:** Crowned arms of United Netherlands **Note:** Mint mark: Cinquefoil. Similar to KM#141.

Date	Mintage	VG	F	VF	XF	Unc
1695/4	—	50.00	125	200	300	—
1695	—	30.00	60.00	100	200	—
1696	—	30.00	60.00	100	200	—
1697	—	30.00	60.00	100	200	—

Date	Mintage	VG	F	VF	XF	Unc
1698	—	30.00	60.00	100	200	—
1700	—	30.00	60.00	100	250	350

KM# 96 3 GULDEN (60 Stuiver)

Silver **Note:** Klippe.

Date	Mintage	VG	F	VF	XF	Unc
1697	—	—	—	—	1,500	—

KM# 51 1/2 DUCATON (20 Stuiver)

16.3900 g., 0.9410 Silver 0.4958 oz. ASW **Note:** Mint mark: Cinquefoil. Similar to 1 Ducaton, KM#46.

Date	Mintage	VG	F	VF	XF	Unc
1660	—	75.00	175	300	400	—
1661	—	75.00	175	300	400	—
1662	—	75.00	175	300	400	—
1663	—	75.00	175	300	400	—
1664	—	75.00	175	300	400	—
1666	—	75.00	175	300	400	—
1667	—	75.00	175	300	400	—
1669	—	—	—	—	—	—
1670	—	75.00	175	300	400	—
1672	—	75.00	175	300	400	—
1673	—	75.00	175	300	400	—
1674	—	75.00	175	300	400	—
1679	—	100	200	350	450	—

KM# 57 1/2 DUCATON (20 Stuiver)

Silver **Note:** Klippe.

Date	Mintage	VG	F	VF	XF	Unc
1664	—	—	—	—	—	—

KM# 67 1/2 DUCATON (20 Stuiver)

Silver **Obv:** Without inner circle **Rev:** Date above crown in inner circle

Date	Mintage	VG	F	VF	XF	Unc
1673	—	75.00	150	250	350	—
1674	—	100	250	450	600	—
1679	—	75.00	150	250	350	—

KM# 46 DUCATON

32.7800 g., 0.9410 Silver 0.9917 oz. ASW **Obv:** Provincial arms below in inner circle **Note:** Mint mark: Cinquefoil. Dav. #4939.

Date	Mintage	VG	F	VF	XF	Unc
1659	—	30.00	90.00	125	250	—
1660/59	—	45.00	125	200	350	—
1660	—	30.00	90.00	125	225	—
1661/0	—	35.00	100	150	250	—
1661	—	35.00	100	150	250	—
1662	—	30.00	90.00	125	225	—
1663/2	—	35.00	100	150	250	—
1663	—	30.00	90.00	125	225	—
1664	—	30.00	90.00	125	225	—
1665	—	30.00	90.00	125	225	—
1666	—	30.00	90.00	125	225	—
1668	—	30.00	90.00	125	225	—
1669	—	30.00	90.00	125	225	—

Date	Mintage	VG	F	VF	XF	Unc
1670	—	20.00	75.00	100	200	—
1671	—	45.00	125	200	350	—
1672	—	30.00	90.00	125	225	—
1673	—	30.00	90.00	125	225	—
1674	—	30.00	90.00	125	225	—

KM# 68 DUCATON

Silver **Note:** Dav. #4940. Mint mark: Cinquefoil. Similar to KM#107.1.

Date	Mintage	VG	F	VF	XF	Unc
1672	499,170	—	—	—	—	—
1674	Inc. above	30.00	90.00	125	225	—
1675	Inc. above	35.00	100	150	300	—
1676	Inc. above	30.00	90.00	125	225	—
1677	Inc. above	30.00	90.00	125	225	—
1678	Inc. above	30.00	90.00	125	225	—
1679	Inc. above	30.00	90.00	125	225	—
1692	Inc. above	85.00	200	300	400	—

KM# 63.1 DUCATON

32.7800 g., 0.9410 Silver 0.9917 oz. ASW **Rev:** Small arms of Enkhuisen (3 herrings) below shield **Note:** Struck at a private mint of Dirk Hosch in Enkhuizen. Dav. #4941.

Date	Mintage	VG	F	VF	XF	Unc
1673	—	250	600	1,000	1,400	—

KM# 63.2 DUCATON

32.7800 g., 0.9410 Silver 0.9917 oz. ASW **Edge:** Lettered **Note:** Struck at private mint of Dirk Bosch in Enkhuizen.

Date	Mintage	VG	F	VF	XF	Unc
1673	—	—	1,250	2,500	3,500	—

KM# 55 1/2 SILVER DUCAT

Silver **Shape:** Klippe

Date	Mintage	VG	F	VF	XF	Unc
1660	—	—	—	—	—	—
1662	—	—	—	—	—	—
1665	—	—	—	—	—	—

KM# 52 1/2 SILVER DUCAT

14.1200 g., 0.8730 Silver 0.3963 oz. ASW **Note:** Mint mark: Cinquefoil. Similar to 1 Silver Ducat, KM#47.

Date	Mintage	VG	F	VF	XF	Unc
1660	—	100	250	400	600	—
1661	—	100	250	400	600	—
1662	—	100	250	400	600	—
1663/2	—	100	250	400	600	—
1664	—	100	250	400	600	—
1665	—	100	250	400	600	—
1672	—	100	250	400	600	—
1673/2	—	100	250	500	700	—
1673	—	100	250	400	600	—

KM# 47 SILVER DUCAT

28.2500 g., 0.8730 Silver 0.7929 oz. ASW **Obv:** Knight standing facing right holding broad sword upwards and shield **Rev:** Crowned shield **Note:** Mint mark: Cinquefoil. Dav. #4906.

Date	Mintage	VG	F	VF	XF	Unc
1659	—	30.00	75.00	125	175	—
1660	—	30.00	75.00	125	175	—
1661	—	30.00	75.00	125	175	—
1662	—	30.00	75.00	125	175	—
1663/2	—	40.00	100	200	300	—
1663	—	30.00	75.00	125	175	—
1664	—	30.00	75.00	125	175	—
1665	—	40.00	100	200	300	—
1666	—	30.00	75.00	125	175	—
1668	—	30.00	75.00	125	175	—
1669/8/2	—	40.00	100	200	300	—
1669	—	40.00	100	200	300	—
1672	—	30.00	75.00	125	175	—
1673	—	30.00	75.00	125	175	—
1674	—	30.00	75.00	125	175	—
1675	—	40.00	100	200	300	—
1687	—	40.00	100	200	300	—

KM# 54 SILVER DUCAT

Silver **Shape:** Klippe **Note:** Weight 42.4 grams, heavier 1662 exists at 56.5 grams.

Date	Mintage	VG	F	VF	XF	Unc
1661	—	—	—	—	—	—
1662	—	—	—	—	—	—

KM# 64.2 SILVER DUCAT

Silver **Obv:** Knight standing facing right holding broad sword downwards and shield **Rev:** Crowned shield **Edge:** Lettered **Note:** Struck at private mint of Dirk Bosch in Enkhuizen. Prev. KM #62.3.

Date	Mintage	VG	F	VF	XF	Unc
1673	—	170	350	800	1,500	—
1678	—	170	350	800	1,500	—

KM# 64.1 SILVER DUCAT

28.2500 g., Silver **Obv:** Knight standing facing right holding broad sword downwards and shield **Obv. Legend:** MO • NO • ARG • PRO - CONFOE • BEL • WES **Rev:** Crowned shield **Note:** Struck at the private mint of Dirk Hosch in Enkhuizen. Dav. #4910.

Date	Mintage	VG	F	VF	XF	Unc
1673	—	150	350	700	1,250	—
1676	—	125	250	500	750	—
1677	—	125	250	500	750	—
1678	—	125	250	500	750	—

KM# 85.1 SILVER DUCAT

Silver **Rev:** Crowned arms divide date **Note:** Mint mark: Bull. Without inner circles. Dav. #4908.

Date	Mintage	VG	F	VF	XF	Unc
1683	42,860	60.00	175	275	350	—
1687/3	Inc. above	60.00	175	275	350	—
1687/6	Inc. above	60.00	175	275	350	—
1687	Inc. above	50.00	125	225	300	—

KM# 85.2 SILVER DUCAT

Silver **Note:** Mint mark: Rosette.

Date	Mintage	VG	F	VF	XF	Unc
1683	—	60.00	175	275	350	—
1687/3	—	60.00	175	275	350	—
1687	—	60.00	175	275	350	—
1688	—	60.00	175	275	350	—
1692	—	60.00	175	275	350	—

KM# 85.3 SILVER DUCAT

Silver **Note:** Mint mark: Ship.

Date	Mintage	VG	F	VF	XF	Unc
1693/2	—	50.00	125	225	300	—
1693	—	30.00	75.00	125	160	—
1694	—	30.00	75.00	125	160	—
1695	—	30.00	75.00	125	160	—

KM# 85.4 SILVER DUCAT

Silver **Obv:** Standing armored knight with crowned shield at feet **Obv. Legend:** MO: NO: ARG: TRO: CONFOE: .... **Rev:** Crowned arms of Friesland divide date **Rev. Legend:** CONCORDIA RESPARVÆ ... **Note:** Mint mark: Cinquefoil. Similar to KM#128. Varieties exist.

Date	Mintage	VG	F	VF	XF	Unc
1695	—	30.00	75.00	125	160	—
1696/5	—	60.00	150	250	325	—
1696	—	60.00	150	250	325	—
1698	—	30.00	75.00	125	160	—
1699	—	30.00	75.00	125	160	—

KM# 90 FLORIN (28 Stuiver)

19.5000 g., 0.6730 Silver 0.4219 oz. ASW **Obv:** Crowned arms in inner circle, date above crown, value at bottom **Rev:** Crowned double-headed eagle in inner circle

Date	Mintage	VG	F	VF	XF	Unc
1685	—	100	250	400	700	—
1686	—	100	250	400	700	—
1687/6	—	125	300	500	800	—

KM# 91 FLORIN (28 Stuiver)

Silver **Shape:** Diamond klippe

Date	Mintage	VG	F	VF	XF	Unc
1685	—	—	—	—	—	—

KM# 92 FLORIN (28 Stuiver)

Silver **Shape:** Octagonal klippe

Date	Mintage	VG	F	VF	XF	Unc
1686	—	—	—	—	—	—

KM# 9 1/2 DAALDER (Lion - 24 Stuiver)

13.8400 g., 0.7500 Silver 0.3337 oz. ASW **Note:** Similar to 1 Daalder, KM#12.

Date	Mintage	VG	F	VF	XF	Unc
1603	—	70.00	200	300	450	—
1604	—	50.00	150	200	250	—
1605/4	—	70.00	200	300	450	—
1605	—	50.00	150	200	250	—

KM# 22.4 1/2 DAALDER (Lion - 24 Stuiver)

13.8400 g., Silver **Note:** Without mint mark.

Date	Mintage	VG	F	VF	XF	Unc
1606	—	50.00	100	200	350	—
1608	—	100	200	400	600	—
1613/2	—	100	200	400	600	—
1613	—	100	200	400	600	—
1616	—	50.00	100	200	350	—
1617	—	50.00	100	200	350	—
1618/6	—	50.00	100	200	350	—
1618	—	50.00	100	200	350	—
1622	—	75.00	150	300	500	—
1623	—	50.00	100	200	350	—
1624	—	100	200	400	600	—
1625	—	50.00	100	200	350	—
1626	—	50.00	100	200	350	—
1627/6	—	50.00	100	200	350	—
1629	—	75.00	150	300	500	—
1643	—	50.00	100	200	350	—
1650	—	50.00	100	200	350	—

KM# 22.1 1/2 DAALDER (Lion - 24 Stuiver)

13.8400 g., 0.7500 Silver 0.3337 oz. ASW **Note:** Mintmark: Lily. Similar to KM#35.1 but not Klippe

Date	Mintage	VG	F	VF	XF	Unc
1616	—	35.00	100	175	250	—
1617	—	35.00	100	175	250	—
1623	—	35.00	100	175	250	—
1629/8	—	70.00	200	300	450	—
1629	—	35.00	100	175	250	—
1631	—	40.00	120	250	350	—
1632	—	35.00	100	175	250	—
1633/1	—	35.00	100	175	250	—
1633	—	35.00	100	175	250	—
1634	—	60.00	150	300	500	—
1635	—	60.00	150	300	500	—
1636	—	60.00	150	300	500	—
1637	—	35.00	100	175	250	—
1638	—	35.00	100	175	250	—
1639	—	35.00	100	175	250	—
1640	—	35.00	100	175	250	—
1641	—	35.00	100	175	250	—
1642	—	35.00	100	175	250	—
1643	—	35.00	100	175	250	—
1644	—	35.00	100	175	250	—
1645/1	—	60.00	150	300	500	—
1645	—	35.00	100	175	250	—
1646/3	—	60.00	150	300	500	—
1646	—	35.00	100	175	250	—
1647/6	—	60.00	150	300	500	—
1647	—	35.00	100	175	250	—
1648	—	35.00	100	175	250	—

KM# 22.3 1/2 DAALDER (Lion - 24 Stuiver)

13.8400 g., 0.7500 Silver 0.3337 oz. ASW **Note:** Mintmark: Cinquefoil. Varieties exist.

Date	Mintage	VG	F	VF	XF	Unc
1629	—	60.00	150	300	500	—
1650	—	35.00	100	175	250	—
1651	—	45.00	125	200	300	—
1652	—	45.00	125	200	300	—
1654	—	45.00	125	200	300	—
1661	—	45.00	125	200	300	—
1662	—	45.00	125	200	300	—
1664	—	45.00	125	200	300	—
1666	—	45.00	125	200	300	—
1668	—	45.00	125	200	300	—

KM# 35.1 1/2 DAALDER (Lion - 24 Stuiver)

20.7600 g., Silver **Note:** Mint mark: Lily. Klippe.

Date	Mintage	VG	F	VF	XF	Unc
1632	—	—	—	1,200	2,000	—
1634	—	—	—	1,200	2,000	—
1635	—	—	—	1,200	2,000	—
1637	—	—	—	1,200	2,000	—
1638	—	—	—	1,200	2,000	—
1639	—	—	—	1,200	2,000	—
1640	—	—	—	1,200	2,000	—
1641	—	—	—	1,200	2,000	—
1642	—	—	—	1,200	2,000	—
1645	—	—	—	1,200	2,000	—
1646	—	—	—	1,200	2,000	—
1649	—	—	—	1,200	2,000	—

KM# 35.2 1/2 DAALDER (Lion - 24 Stuiver)

20.7600 g., Silver **Note:** Mint mark: Cinquefoil. Klippe.

Date	Mintage	VG	F	VF	XF	Unc
1666	—	—	—	—	—	—

KM# 13.1 1/2 DAALDER (Rijks)

14.5100 g., 0.8850 Silver 0.4128 oz. ASW **Note:** Mintmark: Rosette. Similar to 1 Daalder, KM#15.

Date	Mintage	VG	F	VF	XF	Unc
1606	—	20.00	60.00	175	350	—
1607	—	20.00	60.00	175	350	—
1609	—	20.00	60.00	175	350	—
1610	—	20.00	60.00	175	350	—
1611	—	30.00	90.00	250	450	—
1612	—	20.00	60.00	175	350	—
1614	—	20.00	60.00	175	350	—
1615	—	20.00	60.00	175	350	—
1616	—	30.00	90.00	250	450	—
1618	—	20.00	50.00	125	225	—
1619	—	20.00	50.00	125	225	—
1620	—	20.00	50.00	125	225	—
1621	—	20.00	50.00	125	225	—
1622	—	20.00	50.00	125	225	—
1623	—	20.00	50.00	125	225	—
1624	—	20.00	50.00	125	225	—
1625	—	20.00	60.00	175	350	—

KM# 13.2 1/2 DAALDER (Rijks)

14.5100 g., 0.8850 Silver 0.4128 oz. ASW **Note:** Mintmark: Lily. Similar to 1 Daalder, KM#15.

Date	Mintage	VG	F	VF	XF	Unc
1618	—	20.00	50.00	125	250	—
1619	—	20.00	50.00	125	250	—
1644/22	—	30.00	75.00	150	300	—
1644	—	20.00	50.00	125	250	—
1646/5	—	30.00	75.00	150	300	—
1648	—	20.00	50.00	125	250	—
1649	—	20.00	50.00	125	250	—

KM# 28 1/2 DAALDER (Rijks)

Silver **Note:** Klippe.

Date	Mintage	VG	F	VF	XF	Unc
1623	—	—	—	1,200	2,000	—
1636	—	—	—	1,200	2,000	—
1638	—	—	—	1,200	2,000	—
1646	—	—	—	1,200	2,000	—

KM# 13.3 1/2 DAALDER (Rijks)

14.5100 g., 0.8850 Silver 0.4128 oz. ASW **Note:** Mint mark: Cinquefoil. Similar to 1 Daalder, KM#15. Varieties exist.

Date	Mintage	VG	F	VF	XF	Unc
1649	—	20.00	50.00	125	250	—
1650	—	20.00	50.00	125	250	—
1651	—	20.00	50.00	125	250	—
1656	—	20.00	50.00	125	250	—
1657	—	20.00	50.00	125	250	—
1658	—	20.00	50.00	125	250	—
1659	—	20.00	50.00	125	250	—
1662	—	20.00	50.00	125	250	—

KM# 6 DAALDER (Prince - 40 Stuiver)

29.0300 g., 0.8850 Silver 0.8260 oz. ASW **Obv:** Armored bust of William the Silent with sword to right in inner circle, date at top in legend **Rev:** Helmeted arms in inner circle **Note:** Dav. #4824.

Date	Mintage	VG	F	VF	XF	Unc
1601	—	100	300	450	750	—

KM# 7 DAALDER (Lion - 48 Stuiver)

27.6800 g., 0.7500 Silver 0.6674 oz. ASW **Note:** Similar to KM#12 but date divided below shield. Dav. #4867.

Date	Mintage	VG	F	VF	XF	Unc
1601	—	45.00	125	175	400	—
ND	—	45.00	125	175	400	—
1603	268,860	45.00	125	175	400	—
1609/3	—	45.00	125	175	400	—

KM# 12 DAALDER (Lion - 48 Stuiver)
27.6800 g., 0.7500 Silver 0.6674 oz. ASW **Obv:** Date at sides of shield **Note:** Province Liondaalder. Dav. #4868.

Date	Mintage	VG	F	VF	XF	Unc
1604	—	20.00	45.00	100	250	—
1605/4	—	20.00	45.00	100	250	—
1605	—	20.00	45.00	100	250	—

KM# 14.1 DAALDER (Lion - 48 Stuiver)
27.6800 g., 0.7500 Silver 0.6674 oz. ASW **Rev:** Date at top in legend **Note:** Without mint mark. Dav. #4870.

Date	Mintage	VG	F	VF	XF	Unc
1606	—	25.00	60.00	125	250	—
1608	—	25.00	60.00	125	250	—
1609/6	—	25.00	40.00	100	200	—
1609/8	—	25.00	40.00	100	200	—
1609	—	25.00	60.00	125	250	—
1610	—	25.00	60.00	100	200	—
1611	—	25.00	60.00	100	200	—
1612/09	—	25.00	60.00	100	200	—
1612	—	25.00	60.00	100	200	—
1613/2	—	25.00	60.00	100	200	—
1613	—	25.00	—	—	—	—
1614	—	25.00	40.00	60.00	200	—
1615	—	25.00	60.00	100	200	—
1618/7	—	25.00	60.00	100	200	—
1618	—	25.00	60.00	100	200	—
1621	—	25.00	60.00	100	200	—
1622	—	25.00	60.00	100	200	—
1623/2	—	25.00	60.00	125	250	—
1623	—	25.00	60.00	100	200	—
1624/2	—	25.00	60.00	125	250	—
1624/3	—	25.00	60.00	100	200	—
1624	—	25.00	60.00	100	200	—
1625	—	25.00	60.00	100	200	—
1627	—	25.00	60.00	100	200	—
1628/7	—	25.00	60.00	100	200	—
1628	—	25.00	60.00	100	200	—
1630	—	25.00	60.00	100	200	—
1650	—	25.00	60.00	100	200	—

KM# 14.2 DAALDER (Lion - 48 Stuiver)
27.6800 g., 0.7500 Silver 0.6674 oz. ASW **Rev:** Date at top in legend **Note:** Mint mark: Lily.

Date	Mintage	VG	F	VF	XF	Unc
1616	—	15.00	35.00	75.00	150	—
1617	—	15.00	35.00	75.00	150	—
1631	—	15.00	35.00	75.00	150	—
1632	—	15.00	35.00	75.00	150	—
1633	—	15.00	35.00	75.00	150	—
1634	—	15.00	35.00	75.00	150	—
1635/3	—	15.00	35.00	75.00	150	—
1635	—	15.00	35.00	75.00	150	—
1636	—	15.00	35.00	75.00	150	—
1637	—	15.00	35.00	75.00	150	—
1638	—	15.00	35.00	75.00	150	—
1639	—	15.00	35.00	75.00	150	—
1640	—	15.00	35.00	75.00	150	—
1641	—	15.00	35.00	75.00	150	—
1642	—	15.00	35.00	75.00	150	—
1643/1	—	15.00	35.00	75.00	150	—
1643	—	15.00	35.00	75.00	150	—
1644/2	—	15.00	40.00	100	200	—
1644	—	15.00	35.00	75.00	150	—
1645	—	15.00	40.00	100	200	—
1646/3	—	15.00	40.00	100	200	—
1646	—	15.00	35.00	75.00	150	—
1647	—	15.00	35.00	75.00	150	—
1648/7	—	15.00	40.00	100	200	—
1648	—	15.00	35.00	75.00	150	—
1649	—	15.00	40.00	100	200	—

KM# 14.5 DAALDER (Lion - 48 Stuiver)
27.6800 g., 0.7500 Silver 0.6674 oz. ASW **Rev:** Date at top in legend **Note:** Mint mark: Rosette.

Date	Mintage	VG	F	VF	XF	Unc
1616	—	15.00	40.00	100	200	—
1622/13	—	15.00	40.00	100	200	—
1622	—	20.00	50.00	125	250	—
1623/2	—	25.00	60.00	150	300	—
1623	—	15.00	40.00	100	200	—
1624/3	—	25.00	60.00	150	300	—
1624	—	15.00	40.00	100	200	—
1626	—	15.00	40.00	100	200	—
1627	—	25.00	60.00	150	300	—
1628/7	—	15.00	35.00	75.00	150	—
1628	—	15.00	35.00	75.00	150	—
1629	—	15.00	40.00	125	250	—

KM# 37 DAALDER (Lion - 48 Stuiver)
27.6800 g., 0.7500 Silver 0.6674 oz. ASW **Note:** Klippe.

Date	Mintage	VG	F	VF	XF	Unc
1637	—	—	—	—	—	—
1638	—	—	—	—	—	—
1639	—	—	—	—	—	—
1650	—	—	—	—	1,500	2,000
1652	—	—	—	—	—	—
1667	—	—	—	—	—	—

KM# 14.3 DAALDER (Lion - 48 Stuiver)
27.6800 g., 0.7500 Silver 0.6674 oz. ASW **Rev:** Date at top in legend **Note:** Mint mark: Cinquefoil.

Date	Mintage	VG	F	VF	XF	Unc
1649/0	—	25.00	50.00	100	200	—
1649	—	25.00	60.00	125	250	—
1650/49	—	25.00	50.00	100	200	—
1650	—	15.00	35.00	75.00	150	—
1651	—	15.00	35.00	75.00	150	—
1652	—	15.00	35.00	75.00	150	—
1654/3	—	15.00	35.00	75.00	150	—
1654	—	15.00	35.00	75.00	150	—
1655	—	25.00	60.00	125	250	—
1657	—	25.00	60.00	125	250	—
1658	—	25.00	60.00	125	250	—
1661	—	25.00	60.00	125	250	—
1662	—	15.00	35.00	75.00	150	—
1663	—	25.00	60.00	125	250	—
1664	—	25.00	60.00	125	250	—
1665	—	15.00	40.00	100	200	—
1666	—	15.00	40.00	100	200	—
1667	—	40.00	80.00	125	250	—
1668	—	15.00	40.00	100	200	—
1670	—	15.00	40.00	100	200	—
1671	—	15.00	40.00	100	200	—
1672	—	15.00	40.00	100	200	—
1674	—	15.00	40.00	100	200	—
1675	—	15.00	40.00	100	200	—
1676	—	25.00	60.00	125	250	—
1677	—	15.00	40.00	100	200	—
1678	—	15.00	40.00	100	200	—
1679	—	15.00	40.00	100	200	—
1697	—	25.00	60.00	125	250	—
1698	—	25.00	60.00	125	250	—
1699	—	25.00	60.00	125	250	—
1700	—	25.00	60.00	125	250	—

KM# 14.4 DAALDER (Lion - 48 Stuiver)
27.6800 g., 0.7500 Silver 0.6674 oz. ASW **Rev:** Date at top in legend **Note:** Mint mark: Bull. Varieties exist.

Date	Mintage	VG	F	VF	XF	Unc
1682	30,630	25.00	60.00	150	300	—
1687	—	50.00	100	200	400	—

KM# 86 DAALDER (30 Stuivers)
15.8800 g., 0.9060 Silver 0.4625 oz. ASW **Obv:** Three opposed crowned shields **Rev:** Knight standing behind shield brandishing sword, with inner circle

Date	Mintage	VG	F	VF	XF	Unc
1684	878,540	45.00	100	200	400	—

KM# 87 DAALDER (30 Stuivers)
15.8800 g., 0.9060 Silver 0.4625 oz. ASW **Obv:** Three opposed crowned shields **Rev:** Knight standing behind shield looking left brandishing sword **Note:** Klippe.

Date	Mintage	VG	F	VF	XF	Unc
1684	—	—	—	—	—	—

KM# 89 DAALDER (30 Stuivers)
15.8800 g., 0.9060 Silver 0.4625 oz. ASW **Obv:** Three opposed crowned shields **Rev:** Knight standing behind shield looking right brandishing sword **Note:** Klippe.

Date	Mintage	VG	F	VF	XF	Unc
1684	—	—	—	—	—	—

KM# 88.2 DAALDER (30 Stuivers)
15.8800 g., 0.9060 Silver 0.4625 oz. ASW **Obv:** Three opposed crowned shields **Rev:** Knight standing behind left brandishing sword **Note:** Mint mark: Cinquefoil.

Date	Mintage	VG	F	VF	XF	Unc
1684	—	35.00	100	150	250	—
1685	—	35.00	100	150	250	—
1686	—	35.00	100	150	250	—
1687	—	35.00	100	150	250	—

KM# 88.3 DAALDER (30 Stuivers)
15.8800 g., 0.9060 Silver 0.4625 oz. ASW **Obv:** Three opposed crowned shields **Rev:** Knight standing behind shield brandishing sword **Note:** Mint mark: Shield of Medenblik.

Date	Mintage	VG	F	VF	XF	Unc
1684	—	35.00	100	150	250	—
1685	—	35.00	100	150	250	—

KM# 88.1 DAALDER (30 Stuivers)
15.8800 g., 0.9060 Silver 0.4625 oz. ASW **Obv:** Three opposed crowned shields **Rev:** Knight standing behind shield brandishing sword **Note:** Without mint mark.

Date	Mintage	VG	F	VF	XF	Unc
1684	—	35.00	100	150	250	—
1685	—	35.00	100	150	250	—

KM# 15.1 DAALDER (Rijks)
29.0300 g., 0.8850 Silver 0.8260 oz. ASW **Note:** Mint mark: Rosette. Dav. #4842.

Date	Mintage	VG	F	VF	XF	Unc
1607	—	30.00	65.00	125	250	—
1608	—	30.00	65.00	125	250	—
1609	—	30.00	65.00	110	200	—
1610	—	30.00	65.00	110	200	—
1611	—	30.00	65.00	110	200	—
1612/1	—	30.00	65.00	110	200	—
1612	—	30.00	65.00	110	200	—
1613	—	30.00	65.00	110	200	—
1614/1	—	30.00	65.00	110	200	—
1614	—	30.00	65.00	110	200	—
1615/3	—	30.00	65.00	110	200	—
1615	—	30.00	65.00	110	200	—
1616	—	30.00	65.00	110	200	—
1618	—	30.00	65.00	110	200	—
1619	—	30.00	65.00	110	200	—
1620	—	30.00	65.00	110	200	—
1621	—	30.00	65.00	110	200	—
1622	—	30.00	65.00	110	200	—
1623	—	30.00	65.00	110	200	—
1624/2	—	30.00	65.00	110	200	—
1624/3	—	30.00	65.00	110	200	—
1624	—	30.00	65.00	110	200	—
1625	—	30.00	65.00	110	200	—
1626	—	40.00	100	150	225	—
1628	—	40.00	100	150	225	—
1629	—	40.00	100	150	225	—

KM# 15.2 DAALDER (Rijks)

29.0300 g., 0.8850 Silver 0.8260 oz. ASW **Note:** Mint mark: Lily.

Date	Mintage	VG	F	VF	XF	Unc
1616	—	30.00	65.00	110	200	—
1619	—	30.00	65.00	110	200	—
1644	—	30.00	65.00	110	200	—
1646	—	30.00	65.00	110	200	—
1649	—	30.00	65.00	110	200	—

KM# 25 DAALDER (Rijks)

Silver **Note:** Klippe.

Date	Mintage	VG	F	VF	XF	Unc
1620	—	—	—	—	—	—
1626	—	—	—	—	—	—

KM# 15.4 DAALDER (Rijks)

Silver **Note:** Without mint mark.

Date	Mintage	VG	F	VF	XF	Unc
1622	—	30.00	50.00	100	200	—
1623	—	30.00	50.00	100	200	—

KM# 15.3 DAALDER (Rijks)

29.0300 g., 0.8850 Silver 0.8260 oz. ASW **Note:** Mint mark: Cinquefoil. Varieties exist.

Date	Mintage	VG	F	VF	XF	Unc
1649	—	25.00	80.00	100	200	—
1650	—	25.00	80.00	100	200	—
1651	—	25.00	80.00	100	200	—
1652	—	65.00	125	275	350	—
1653	—	25.00	80.00	100	200	—
1654/3	—	30.00	85.00	110	200	—
1654	—	25.00	80.00	100	200	—
1655	—	30.00	85.00	110	200	—
1656	—	25.00	80.00	100	200	—
1657	—	25.00	80.00	100	200	—
1658	—	25.00	80.00	100	200	—
1659	—	25.00	80.00	100	200	—
1668	—	25.00	80.00	100	200	—
1675	—	25.00	80.00	100	200	—
1683	—	65.00	125	275	350	—
1693	—	65.00	125	275	350	—

KM# 26 1/2 CAVALIER D'OR

5.0000 g., 0.9200 Gold 0.1479 oz. AGW **Obv:** Equestrian figure of knight above arms in inner circle **Rev:** Crowned arms in inner circle, date at top **Note:** Fr. #297.

Date	Mintage	VG	F	VF	XF	Unc
1621	—	350	700	1,500	2,500	—
1626	—	350	700	1,500	2,500	—
1632	—	250	500	1,000	2,000	—
1644	—	500	800	1,700	2,700	—

KM# 27 CAVALIER D'OR

10.0000 g., 0.9200 Gold 0.2958 oz. AGW **Obv:** Equestrian figure of knight above arms in inner circle **Rev:** Crowned arms in inner circle, date at top **Note:** Fr. #296.

Date	Mintage	VG	F	VF	XF	Unc
1621	—	320	400	900	2,000	—
1623	—	320	450	1,000	2,250	—
1627	—	320	400	900	2,000	—

TRADE COINAGE

KM# 8 DUCAT

3.5000 g., 0.9860 Gold 0.1109 oz. AGW **Obv:** Ruler standing divides date in inner circle **Rev:** Crowned arms in inner circle, date at top **Note:** Fr. #294.

Date	Mintage	VG	F	VF	XF	Unc
1596	—	125	210	300	500	—
1601	327,600	125	210	300	500	—
1603	Inc. above	150	275	375	600	—
1604	Inc. above	120	175	275	400	—
1605/1	Inc. above	125	210	300	500	—
1605	Inc. above	120	175	275	400	—

KM# 16 DUCAT

3.5000 g., 0.9860 Gold 0.1109 oz. AGW **Obv:** Ruler standing facing in inner circle **Rev:** Crowned arms in inner circle, date at top **Note:** Varieties exist. Fr. #294, 295.

Date	Mintage	VG	F	VF	XF	Unc
1607	180,880	120	150	200	300	—
1608	Inc. above	120	150	200	300	—
1609	Inc. above	120	150	200	300	—
1610/09	—	120	150	200	300	—
1610	Inc. above	120	150	200	300	—
1611	Inc. above	120	150	200	300	—
1612	Inc. above	120	150	200	300	—
1619	30,480	120	150	200	300	—
1622	Inc. above	120	150	200	300	—
1624	—	120	150	200	300	—
1631	—	120	150	200	300	—
1632	—	120	150	200	300	—
1633	—	120	150	200	300	—
1634/3	—	120	150	200	300	—
1634	—	120	150	200	300	—
1635	—	120	150	200	300	—
1636	—	120	150	200	300	—
1637	—	120	150	200	300	—
1638	—	120	150	200	300	—
1639	—	120	150	200	300	—
1640	—	120	150	200	300	—
1641	—	120	150	200	300	—
1642	—	120	150	200	300	—
1643	—	120	150	200	300	—
1644	—	120	150	200	300	—
1645	—	120	150	200	300	—
1646	—	120	150	200	300	—
1647/6	—	120	150	200	300	—
1647	—	120	150	200	300	—
1648	—	120	150	200	300	—
1649 Lily	—	120	150	200	300	—
1649 Rose	—	120	150	200	300	—
1650	—	120	150	200	300	—
1651	—	120	150	200	350	—
1652	—	120	150	200	350	—
1653/2	—	120	150	200	350	—
1653	—	120	150	200	350	—
1654	—	120	150	200	350	—
1655	—	120	150	200	350	—
1656	—	120	150	200	350	—
1657	—	120	150	200	350	—
1658	—	120	150	200	350	—
1659	—	125	275	400	600	—
1661	174,650	120	225	300	500	—
1662	Inc. above	120	225	300	500	—
1664	Inc. above	125	275	400	600	—
1666	Inc. above	125	275	400	600	—
1667	Inc. above	125	275	400	600	—
1668	Inc. above	120	200	300	475	—
1669	Inc. above	125	275	400	600	—
1670	Inc. above	125	275	400	600	—
1671	—	120	150	200	300	—
1672	—	120	150	200	300	—
1673	—	120	150	200	300	—
1674	—	120	150	200	300	—
1675	—	120	150	200	300	—

KM# 93 DUCAT

3.5100 g., 0.9860 Gold 0.1113 oz. AGW **Obv:** Standing armored knight divides date **Obv. Legend:** CONCORDIA RES PAR • CRES .... **Rev:** Inscription within ornamented square **Rev. Inscription:** MO:ORD/PROVIN/FOEDER/BELGAD/LEG IMP **Note:** Fr. #295.

Date	Mintage	VG	F	VF	XF	Unc
1683	—	—	—	—	—	—
1684	—	120	150	200	200	—
1686/5/4	—	120	150	200	350	—
1686	—	120	150	200	350	—
1689	—	150	275	400	600	—
1690	—	150	275	400	600	—
1692	5,355	120	150	200	300	—
1693/2	—	150	275	400	600	—
1693	—	120	150	200	300	—
1694	—	150	275	600	600	—
1696	—	120	150	300	300	—
1697	—	150	275	400	600	—

KM# 36 2 DUCAT

0.9860 Gold **Obv:** Knight standing right with sword and bundle of arrows **Rev:** Tablet with five-line inscription **Note:** Klippe. Struck with 1 Ducat dies, KM#16. Weight varies 6.76 - 7.02 grams.

Date	Mintage	VG	F	VF	XF	Unc
1635	—	—	—	2,300	2,800	—
1637	—	—	—	2,300	2,800	—
1662	—	—	—	—	—	—

KM# 53.1 2 DUCAT

7.0200 g., 0.9860 Gold 0.2225 oz. AGW **Obv:** Standing armored knight holding bundle of arrows divides date within broken circle **Obv. Legend:** CONCORDIA RES PAR CRES • WF • **Rev:** Inscription within ornamented square **Rev. Inscription:** MO:ORD/PROVIN/FOEDER/BELG•AD/LEG•IMP **Note:** Without mint mark. Fr. #292.

Date	Mintage	VG	F	VF	XF	Unc
1660	—	200	400	750	1,000	—
1661	—	300	600	1,000	1,200	—
1662	—	300	650	1,100	1,500	—
1664	—	300	600	1,000	1,200	—
1666	—	200	400	750	1,000	—
1672	—	200	400	750	1,000	—
1673	—	175	325	500	700	—
1684	—	300	600	1,000	1,200	—
1694/84	—	200	400	750	1,000	—
1694	—	200	400	750	1,000	—
1696	—	200	400	750	1,000	—

KM# 53.2 2 DUCAT

7.0200 g., 0.9860 Gold 0.2225 oz. AGW **Obv:** Armored knight standing holding bundle of arrows, divides date within broken circle **Obv. Legend:** CONCORDIA RES PAR CRES • WF • **Rev:** Inscription on ornamented tablet **Rev. Inscription:** MO: ORD / PROVIN / FOEDER / BELG • AD / LEG • IMP **Note:** Mint mark: Cinquefoil. Fr. #292.

Date	Mintage	VG	F	VF	XF	Unc
1662	—	300	650	1,100	1,850	—
1666	—	250	400	750	1,500	—
1672	—	250	400	750	1,500	—

KM# 94 2 DUCAT

7.0200 g., 0.9860 Gold 0.2225 oz. AGW **Obv:** Knight standing holding bundle of arrows divides date **Obv. Legend:** CONCORDIA RES PAR CRES • WF • **Rev:** Inscription on ornamented tablet **Rev. Inscription:** MO: ORD / PROVIN / FOEDER / BELG • AD / LEG • IMP **Note:** Without mint mark. Fr. #293.

Date	Mintage	VG	F	VF	XF	Unc
1684	—	300	600	1,000	1,800	—
1694/84	—	250	400	750	1,500	—
1694	—	250	400	750	1,500	—
1696	—	250	400	750	1,500	—

PATTERNS

Including off metal strikes

KM#	Date	Mintage	Identification	Mkt Val
Pn4	1639	—	Stuiver. Gold. Klippe, KM#39.	2,000
Pn5	1686	—	Ducaton. Gold. 41.7300 g. KM#68.	—

PIEFORTS

KM#	Date	Mintage	Identification	Mkt Val
P1	1609	—	Lion Daalder. Silver. KM14.1.	—
PA2	1609/8	—	Daalder. Silver.	—
PB2	1633	—	Daalder. Silver. 41.5000 g.	—
PC2	1639	—	Daalder. Silver. 41.5000 g.	—
PD2	1639	—	Stuiver. Gold. 4.0400 g. KM 38, Klippe	2,000
PE2	1645	—	Duit. Silver. 6.0000 g. KM#29.	300
P2	1646	—	Rijks Daalder. Silver. KM15.2	—
P3	1649	—	Lion Daalder. Silver. Km14.1	—
P4	1650	—	Rijks Daalder. Silver. Klippe, KM15.3.	—
P5	1651	—	Rijks Daalder. Silver. Quadruple weight, KM15.3.	—
PA6	1652	—	Daalder. Silver. 55.3600 g. KM#14.1.	—
PB6	1658	—	Duit. Copper. Klippe, KM29.	—
P6	1659	—	Ducaton. Silver. KM#46.	—

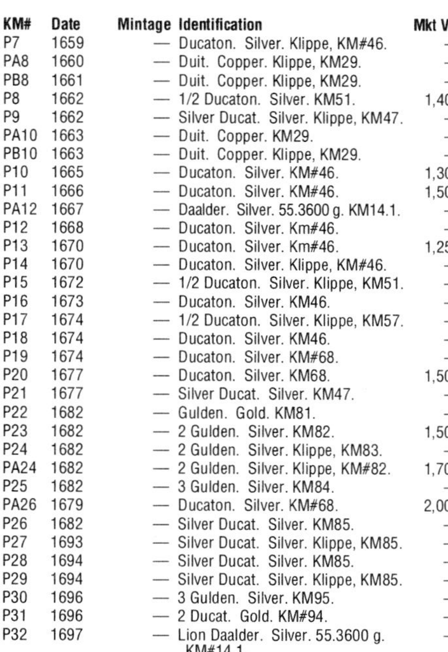

KM#	Date	Mintage	Identification	Mkt Val
P7	1659	—	Ducaton. Silver. Klippe, KM#46.	—
PA8	1660	—	Duit. Copper. Klippe, KM29.	—
PB8	1661	—	Duit. Copper. Klippe, KM29.	—
P8	1662	—	1/2 Ducaton. Silver. KM51.	1,400
P9	1662	—	Silver Ducat. Silver. Klippe, KM47.	—
PA10	1663	—	Duit. Copper. KM29.	—
PB10	1663	—	Duit. Copper. Klippe, KM29.	—
P10	1665	—	Ducaton. Silver. KM#46.	1,300
P11	1666	—	Ducaton. Silver. KM#46.	1,500
PA12	1667	—	Daalder. Silver. 55.3600 g. KM14.1.	—
P12	1668	—	Ducaton. Silver. Km#46.	—
P13	1670	—	Ducaton. Silver. Km#46.	1,250
P14	1670	—	Ducaton. Silver. Klippe, KM#46.	—
P15	1672	—	1/2 Ducaton. Silver. Klippe, KM51.	—
P16	1673	—	Ducaton. Silver. KM46.	—
P17	1674	—	1/2 Ducaton. Silver. Klippe, KM57.	—
P18	1674	—	Ducaton. Silver. KM46.	—
P19	1674	—	Ducaton. Silver. KM#68.	—
P20	1677	—	Ducaton. Silver. KM68.	1,500
P21	1677	—	Silver Ducat. Silver. KM47.	—
P22	1682	—	Gulden. Gold. KM81.	—
P23	1682	—	2 Gulden. Silver. KM82.	1,500
P24	1682	—	2 Gulden. Silver. Klippe, KM83.	—
PA24	1682	—	2 Gulden. Silver. Klippe, KM#82.	1,700
P25	1682	—	3 Gulden. Silver. KM84.	—
PA26	1679	—	Ducaton. Silver. KM#68.	2,000
P26	1682	—	Silver Ducat. Silver. KM85.	—
P27	1693	—	Silver Ducat. Silver. Klippe, KM85.	—
P28	1694	—	Silver Ducat. Silver. KM85.	—
P29	1694	—	Silver Ducat. Silver. Klippe, KM85.	—
P30	1696	—	3 Gulden. Silver. KM95.	—
P31	1696	—	2 Ducat. Gold. KM#94.	—
P32	1697	—	Lion Daalder. Silver. 55.3600 g. KM#14.1.	—

ZEELAND

Zelandia

Zeeland (Zelandia), the southernmost maritime province of the Netherlands, consists of a strip of the Flanders mainland and six islands.

MINT MARK

Castle

PROVINCE

COPIED COINAGE

KM# 15.2 OORD (2 Duit)

3.1000 g., Copper, 25 mm. **Obv:** Bust of Prince Maurice right **Rev:** Crowned shield, crown divides date **Edge:** Plain **Note:** Contemporary copy of similar but altered design.

Date	Mintage	F	VF	XF	Unc	BU
1657	—	—	—	—	—	—

STANDARD COINAGE

KM# 14a 1/2 DUIT

Center Weight: 1.5000 g. **Center Composition:** Silver **Obv:** Inscription within wreath **Obv. Inscription:** ZE / LAN / DIA **Rev:** Maiden standing within sprays, shield below

Date	Mintage	VG	F	VF	XF	Unc
ND	—	—	—	—	—	—
1626	—	—	—	—	—	—
1632	—	—	—	—	—	—
1637	—	—	—	—	—	—

KM# 14 DUIT

Center Weight: 2.0400 g. **Center Composition:** Copper **Obv:** Inscription within wreath **Obv. Inscription:** ZE / LAN / DIA **Rev:** Maiden standing within sprays, shield below

Date	Mintage	VG	F	VF	XF	Unc
ND	—	8.00	20.00	40.00	100	—
1601	—	8.00	20.00	45.00	120	—
1604	—	6.00	17.50	30.00	70.00	—
1609	—	8.00	20.00	40.00	100	—
1626	—	6.00	17.50	30.00	70.00	—
1632	—	6.00	17.50	40.00	120	—
1636	—	5.00	15.00	25.00	60.00	—
1637	—	5.00	15.00	35.00	100	—

KM# 14b DUIT

Center Weight: 3.5000 g. **Center Composition:** Gold **Obv:** Inscription within wreath **Rev:** Maiden standing within sprays, shield below **Rev. Inscription:** ZE / LAN / DIA

Date	Mintage	VG	F	VF	XF	Unc
1637 Rare	—	—	—	—	—	—

KM# 33 DUIT

2.0400 g., Copper **Obv:** Inscripion within wreath **Obv. Inscription:** ZEE / LAN / DIA **Rev:** Maiden seated within fence, crowned shield below

Date	Mintage	VG	F	VF	XF	Unc
1641	—	5.00	15.00	35.00	80.00	—
1642/1	—	8.00	20.00	40.00	100	—
1642	—	5.00	15.00	30.00	70.00	—
1643	—	8.00	20.00	40.00	100	—
1645	—	5.00	15.00	30.00	70.00	—
1647	—	5.00	15.00	30.00	70.00	—
1648	—	5.00	15.00	30.00	70.00	—
1649	—	5.00	15.00	30.00	70.00	—
1653	—	5.00	15.00	30.00	70.00	—
1654	—	8.00	20.00	40.00	100	—
1657	—	5.00	15.00	35.00	95.00	—
1658	—	8.00	20.00	40.00	100	—
1663	—	5.00	15.00	30.00	70.00	—
1664	—	5.00	15.00	30.00	70.00	—
1665	—	8.00	20.00	40.00	100	—
1669	—	5.00	15.00	35.00	70.00	—
1670	—	6.00	17.50	35.00	80.00	—

KM# 33a DUIT

1.5000 g., Silver **Obv:** Inscription within wreath **Obv. Inscription:** ZEE / LAN / DIA **Rev:** Maiden seated within fence, crowned shield below

Date	Mintage	VG	F	VF	XF	Unc
1641	—	—	—	—	—	—
1647	—	—	—	—	—	—

KM# 33b DUIT

3.5000 g., Gold **Obv:** Inscription within wreath **Obv. Inscription:** ZEE / LAN / DIA **Rev:** Maiden seated within fence

Date	Mintage	VG	F	VF	XF	Unc
1647 Rare	—	—	—	—	—	—

KM# 55 DUIT

Center Composition: Copper **Obv:** Inscription in wreath **Obv. Inscription:** ZEE / LAN / DIA / date **Rev:** Figure seated within fence, shield below

Date	Mintage	VG	F	VF	XF	Unc
1680	—	5.00	15.00	25.00	40.00	—
1681	—	5.00	15.00	25.00	40.00	—
1683	—	5.00	15.00	25.00	40.00	—
1684	—	5.00	15.00	25.00	40.00	—
1685	—	5.00	15.00	25.00	40.00	—
1686/5	—	6.00	17.50	30.00	50.00	—
1686	—	5.00	15.00	25.00	40.00	—
1689	—	5.00	15.00	25.00	40.00	—

KM# 55a DUIT

Center Weight: 5.5000 g. **Center Composition:** Silver **Obv:** ZEE/LAN/DIA/(date) in wreath **Rev:** Figure seated

Date	Mintage	VG	F	VF	XF	Unc
1683	—	—	—	—	—	—

KM# 55b DUIT

Center Weight: 3.5000 g. **Center Composition:** Gold **Obv:** ZEE / LAN / DIA / date in wreath

Date	Mintage	VG	F	VF	XF	Unc
1681 Rare	—	—	—	—	—	—
1684 Rare	—	—	—	—	—	—
1686 Rare	—	—	—	—	—	—
1689	—	—	—	—	—	2,000

KM# 5 OORD (2 Duit)

Center Weight: 5.1000 g. **Center Composition:** Copper **Obv:** Bust of Prince William of Orange right **Rev:** Crowned arms of Zeeland, castle divides date above crown

Date	Mintage	VG	F	VF	XF	Unc
1601	—	7.00	22.50	65.00	100	—
1602	—	7.00	22.50	65.00	100	—
1603	—	15.00	45.00	100	200	—

KM# 15.1 OORD (2 Duit)

Center Composition: Copper Weight varies, 4.3 grams to 1663, 3.9 grams 1669. 1671. **Obv:** Bust of Prince Maurice right **Rev:** Crowned shield, crown divides date

Date	Mintage	VG	F	VF	XF	Unc
1604	—	7.00	22.50	65.00	100	—
1608	—	15.00	45.00	100	200	—
1626	—	7.00	22.50	65.00	100	—
1636	—	7.00	22.50	65.00	100	—
1637	—	15.00	45.00	100	200	—
1641	—	7.00	27.50	75.00	150	—
1642	—	7.00	22.50	65.00	120	—
1643	—	7.00	22.50	65.00	120	—
1645	—	7.00	22.50	65.00	120	—
1649	—	7.00	22.50	65.00	120	—
1653/43	—	7.00	27.50	75.00	150	—
1653	—	7.00	22.50	65.00	120	—
1655	—	7.00	22.50	65.00	120	—
1657/3	—	7.00	22.50	65.00	120	—
1657/5	—	7.00	22.50	65.00	120	—
1657	—	7.00	22.50	65.00	120	—
1659	—	7.00	22.50	65.00	120	—
1663	—	7.00	22.50	35.00	100	—
1669	—	9.00	30.00	60.00	100	—
1671	—	10.00	40.00	75.00	150	—

KM# 8 STUIVER

Center Weight: 1.3000 g. **Center Composition:** 0.3000 Silver 0.0125 oz. ASW **Obv:** Crowned arms divide value in inner circle **Rev:** Ornate cross with castle at center in quatrefoil in inner circle

Date	Mintage	VG	F	VF	XF	Unc
1602	—	30.00	80.00	175	350	—

KM# 27 STUIVER

Center Weight: 0.8600 g. **Center Composition:** 0.5830 Silver 0.0161 oz. ASW **Obv:** ZEE/LAN/DIA/(date) **Rev:** Crowned rampant lion left holding sword and arrows, value at sides

Date	Mintage	VG	F	VF	XF	Unc
1614	—	15.00	40.00	75.00	150	—
1615	—	15.00	40.00	75.00	150	—

KM# 58 STUIVER

1.3000 g., 0.2710 Silver 0.0113 oz. ASW **Obv:** Arms of Zeeland **Rev:** Inscription above date **Rev. Inscription:** ZEE/LAN/DIA

Date	Mintage	VG	F	VF	XF	Unc
1681	—	6.00	15.00	40.00	85.00	—
1683	—	6.00	15.00	40.00	85.00	—
1684	—	6.00	15.00	40.00	85.00	—
1685	—	6.00	15.00	40.00	85.00	—

KM# 28 STUIVER (Bezem)

0.8600 g., 0.5830 Silver 0.0161 oz. ASW **Obv:** Bundle of arrows divide value within wreath **Rev:** Inscription above date **Rev. Inscription:** ZEE/LAN/DIA • **Note:** Varieties exist.

Date	Mintage	VG	F	VF	XF	Unc
1614	—	6.00	15.00	35.00	75.00	—
1619	—	6.00	15.00	35.00	75.00	—
1628	—	6.00	15.00	35.00	75.00	—
1629	—	6.00	15.00	35.00	75.00	—

KM# 29 2 STUIVER

Center Weight: 1.7300 g. **Center Composition:** 0.5830 Silver 0.0324 oz. ASW **Obv:** ZEE/LAN/DIA/(date) **Rev:** Crowned rampant lion left holding sword and arrow, value at sides

Date	Mintage	VG	F	VF	XF	Unc
1614	—	6.00	17.50	30.00	60.00	—
1615	—	6.00	17.50	30.00	60.00	—
1616	—	6.00	17.50	30.00	60.00	—
1617	—	6.00	17.50	30.00	60.00	—
1618	—	6.00	17.50	30.00	60.00	—
1619	—	6.00	17.50	30.00	60.00	—
1622	—	6.00	17.50	30.00	60.00	—
1624	—	6.00	17.50	30.00	60.00	—
1625	—	6.00	17.50	30.00	60.00	—
1626	—	6.00	17.50	30.00	60.00	—
1627	—	6.00	17.50	30.00	60.00	—
1628	—	6.00	17.50	30.00	60.00	—
1637	—	6.00	17.50	30.00	60.00	—
1639	—	6.00	17.50	30.00	60.00	—
1640	—	6.00	17.50	30.00	60.00	—
1641	—	6.00	17.50	30.00	60.00	—
1646	—	6.00	17.50	30.00	60.00	—
1653	—	6.00	17.50	30.00	60.00	—
1669	—	6.00	17.50	30.00	60.00	—
1670	—	6.00	17.50	30.00	60.00	—
1672	—	6.00	17.50	30.00	60.00	—
1675	—	6.00	17.50	30.00	60.00	—

KM# 59 2 STUIVER

1.6200 g., 0.5830 Silver 0.0304 oz. ASW **Obv:** Crowned arms of Zeeland divide value **Rev:** Inscription above date **Rev. Inscription:** ZEE/LAN/DIA

Date	Mintage	VG	F	VF	XF	Unc
1681	—	2.00	6.00	15.00	25.00	—
1683	—	2.00	6.00	15.00	25.00	—
1684	—	2.00	6.00	15.00	25.00	—
1686	—	2.00	6.00	15.00	25.00	—
1690	—	2.00	6.00	15.00	25.00	—
1695	—	2.00	6.00	15.00	25.00	—
1696	—	2.00	6.00	15.00	25.00	—
1699	—	2.00	6.00	15.00	25.00	—
1700	—	2.00	6.00	10.00	17.50	—

KM# 9 2-1/2 STUIVER (1/12 Arendsdaalder)
Center Weight: 1.7200 g. **Center Composition:** 0.7500 Silver 0.0415 oz. ASW **Obv:** Garnished arms with date above in inner circle **Rev:** Doulbe-headed eagle with arms on breat in inner circle

Date	Mintage	VG	F	VF	XF	Unc
1602	—	80.00	200	400	750	—

KM# 6 3 STUIVERS (1/2 Roosschelling)
Center Weight: 2.6300 g. **Center Composition:** 0.5830 Silver 0.0493 oz. ASW **Obv:** Crowned Zeeland arms in inner circle, date above crown **Rev:** Ornate cross in inner circle with castle at center

Date	Mintage	VG	F	VF	XF	Unc
1601	—	35.00	75.00	175	350	—
1603	—	35.00	75.00	175	350	—
1614	—	35.00	75.00	175	350	—

KM# 10 5 STUIVERS (1/6 Arendsdaalder)
Center Weight: 3.4500 g. **Center Composition:** 0.7500 Silver 0.0832 oz. ASW **Obv:** Garnished arms with date above in inner circle **Rev:** Double-headed eagle with arms on breast in inner circle

Date	Mintage	VG	F	VF	XF	Unc
1602	—	60.00	175	400	700	—

KM# 7 6 STUIVERS (Roosschelling)
Center Weight: 5.2700 g. **Center Composition:** 0.5830 Silver 0.0988 oz. ASW **Obv:** Crowned Zeeland arms in inner circle, date above crown **Rev:** Ornate cross in inner circle with castle at center

Date	Mintage	VG	F	VF	XF	Unc
1601	—	30.00	80.00	150	250	—
1603	—	30.00	80.00	150	250	—
1613	—	30.00	80.00	150	250	—
1614	—	30.00	80.00	150	250	—
1615	—	30.00	80.00	150	250	—
1646	—	30.00	80.00	150	250	—
1653	—	30.00	80.00	150	250	—

KM# 47 6 STUIVERS (Snaphaanschilling)
Center Weight: 6.5300 g. **Center Composition:** 0.5000 Silver 0.1050 oz. ASW **Obv:** Armored knight standing holding sword behind shield of arms, date divided at top **Rev:** Ornate cross in inner circle with castle at center

Date	Mintage	VG	F	VF	XF	Unc
1669	—	30.00	100	250	400	—
1670	—	30.00	100	250	400	—

KM# 50 6 STUIVERS (Hoedjesschelling)
4.9500 g., 0.5830 Silver 0.0928 oz. ASW **Obv:** Crowned arms of Zeeland divide date **Rev:** Reclining lion holding pole with cap

Date	Mintage	VG	F	VF	XF	Unc
1672	—	10.00	25.00	75.00	125	—
1677	—	10.00	25.00	75.00	125	—
1678	—	10.00	25.00	75.00	125	—
1680	—	10.00	25.00	75.00	125	—
1681	—	10.00	25.00	75.00	125	—
1682	—	10.00	25.00	75.00	125	—
1683	—	10.00	25.00	75.00	125	—
1684	—	10.00	25.00	75.00	125	—
1685	—	10.00	25.00	75.00	125	—
1687	—	10.00	25.00	75.00	125	—
1692	—	10.00	25.00	75.00	125	—
1699	—	10.00	25.00	75.00	125	—
1700	—	10.00	25.00	75.00	125	—

KM# 50a 6 STUIVERS (Hoedjesschelling)
6.8000 g., Gold **Obv:** Crowned arms of Zeeland divide date **Rev:** Reclining lion holding pole with cap

Date	Mintage	VG	F	VF	XF	Unc
1684 Rare	—	—	—	—	—	—
1685 Rare	—	—	—	—	2,500	—

KM# 50b 6 STUIVERS (Hoedjesschelling)
Center Weight: 17.0000 g. **Center Composition:** Gold **Obv:** Crowned arms divide date **Rev:** Reclining lion to left holding spear with Liberty cap **Note:** Prev. KM#50c. Weight varies, 1681 - 14.4 grams, 1687 - 10.5 grams.

Date	Mintage	VG	F	VF	XF	Unc
1681 Rare	—	—	—	—	—	—
1687	—	—	—	—	—	—

KM# 26 10 STUIVERS
Center Weight: 5.9500 g. **Center Composition:** 0.9170 Silver 0.1754 oz. ASW **Obv:** Armored knight standing behind shield with sword on shoulder **Rev:** Crowned arms divide value X - S

Date	Mintage	VG	F	VF	XF	Unc
1613	—	75.00	250	500	1,000	—

KM# 11 10 STUIVERS (1/3 Arendsdaalder)
Center Weight: 6.9000 g. **Center Composition:** 0.7500 Silver 0.1664 oz. ASW **Obv:** Garnished arms with date above in inner circle **Rev:** Double-headed eagle with arms on breast in iner circle

Date	Mintage	VG	F	VF	XF	Unc
1602	—	40.00	100	300	450	—

KM# 12 30 STUIVERS (Arendsdaalder of 60 Groot)
Center Weight: 20.6800 g. **Center Composition:** 0.7500 Silver 0.4986 oz. ASW **Obv:** Garnished arms with date above in inner circle **Rev:** Double-headed eagle with arms on breast in inner circle

Date	Mintage	VG	F	VF	XF	Unc
1602	—	50.00	150	200	350	—
1618/02	—	60.00	175	250	450	—
1618	—	50.00	150	200	350	—
1619	—	50.00	150	200	350	—

KM# 53 30 STUIVERS (Daalder)
Center Weight: 15.8800 g. **Center Composition:** 0.9060 Silver 0.4625 oz. ASW

Date	Mintage	VG	F	VF	XF	Unc
1676	422,670	35.00	90.00	150	250	—
1677	Inc. above	35.00	90.00	150	250	—
1678	Inc. above	35.00	90.00	150	250	—
1679	725,540	35.00	90.00	150	250	—
1680	—	35.00	90.00	150	250	—
1681	—	35.00	90.00	150	250	—
1682/0	147,793	35.00	100	175	300	—
1682	Inc. above	35.00	90.00	150	250	—

KM# 60 30 STUIVERS (Daalder)
Center Weight: 15.8800 g. **Center Composition:** 0.9060 Silver 0.4625 oz. ASW

Date	Mintage	VG	F	VF	XF	Unc
1682	—	35.00	90.00	150	250	—
1683	—	35.00	90.00	150	250	—
1684/3	—	35.00	90.00	150	250	—
1684	—	35.00	90.00	150	250	—
1685/3	—	50.00	100	175	300	—
1685	—	35.00	90.00	150	250	—
1686/2	—	50.00	100	175	300	—
1686/5	—	50.00	100	175	300	—
1686	—	35.00	90.00	150	250	—

KM# 64 30 STUIVERS (5 Schelling = 1 Daalder)
Center Weight: 15.8500 g. **Center Composition:** 0.9060 Silver 0.4617 oz. ASW **Obv:** Value appears as 5 - SC

Date	Mintage	VG	F	VF	XF	Unc
1685	—	60.00	150	250	350	—
1686	60,047	50.00	125	200	300	—
1687	—	60.00	150	250	350	—

KM# 70 3 GULDEN
Center Composition: Silver **Obv:** Crowned arms of Zeeland **Note:** Dav. #4965.

Date	Mintage	VG	F	VF	XF	Unc
1685	—	200	500	800	1,200	—
1694	—	150	400	600	800	—

KM# 71 3 GULDEN
Center Weight: 31.8200 g. **Center Composition:** 0.9200 Silver 0.9412 oz. ASW **Obv:** Different crowned lion shield divides value 3 - GL **Rev:** Date in exergue **Note:** Dav. #4966.

Date	Mintage	VG	F	VF	XF	Unc
1694	—	125	300	400	500	—
1698	—	125	300	400	500	—

KM# 66 15 GULDEN
10.2000 g., Gold **Obv:** Crowned arms divide date **Obv. Legend:** MO. NO. AUR... **Rev:** Reclining lion to left holding spear with Liberty cap **Note:** Previously listed as 6 Stuiver, KM50b, gold strike.

Date	Mintage	VG	F	VF	XF	Unc
1687	—	—	—	—	7,000	10,000

KM# A65 30 GULDEN
20.8000 g., Gold **Obv:** 6 shields around center shield, between 30-G. **Obv. Legend:** MO. NO. AUR. ORDIN. ZEELANDIAE *1684* **Rev:** Armored standing knight, looking to right, holding sword, behind shield of arms

Date	Mintage	VG	F	VF	XF	Unc
1684	—	—	—	—	8,500	—
1687	—	—	—	—	8,500	—

KM# B65 30 GULDEN
Center Weight: 20.8000 g. **Center Composition:** Gold **Obv:** Without denominatjon

Date	Mintage	VG	F	VF	XF	Unc
1687 Rare	—	—	—	—	—	—

KM# 65 60 GULDEN
34.4000 g., Gold **Obv:** Circle of shields flanked by denomination **Rev:** Standing knight holding sword, behind arms

Date	Mintage	VG	F	VF	XF	Unc
1684 Rare	—	—	—	—	—	—

KM# 25 1/2 DAALDER (Rijks - 24 Stuiver)
Center Weight: 14.5100 g. **Center Composition:** 0.8850 Silver 0.4128 oz. ASW **Obv:** Laureate 1/2 figure holding sword and arms in inner circle **Rev:** Crowned arms divide date in inner circle

Date	Mintage	VG	F	VF	XF	Unc
1610	—	100	250	400	500	—
1601 (error)	—	—	—	—	—	—

Date	Mintage	VG	F	VF	XF	Unc
1612	—	65.00	175	300	400	—
1613	—	65.00	175	300	400	—
1619/3	—	65.00	175	300	400	—
1619/6	—	65.00	175	300	400	—
1619	—	65.00	175	300	400	—
1620	—	65.00	175	300	400	—
1621	—	65.00	175	300	400	—
1622	—	65.00	175	300	400	—
1623	—	65.00	175	300	400	—
1625	—	100	250	400	500	—
1626	—	100	250	400	500	—
1628	—	100	250	400	500	—
1629	—	100	250	400	500	—
1631	—	65.00	175	300	400	—
1634	—	65.00	175	300	400	—
1635	—	65.00	175	300	400	—
1646/3	—	65.00	175	300	400	—
1646	—	65.00	175	300	400	—
1647	—	65.00	175	300	400	—
1648	—	65.00	175	300	400	—
1649	—	65.00	175	300	400	—
1650	—	65.00	175	300	400	—
1651	—	65.00	175	300	400	—
1652	—	65.00	175	300	400	—
1653	—	65.00	175	300	400	—
1655/2	—	65.00	175	300	400	—
1655	—	65.00	175	300	400	—
1656	—	65.00	175	300	400	—
1657	—	65.00	175	300	400	—
1658	—	65.00	175	300	400	—
1659	—	65.00	175	300	400	—
1660	—	65.00	175	300	400	—
1661	—	65.00	175	300	400	—
1662/1	—	65.00	175	300	400	—
1662	—	65.00	175	300	400	—

KM# 30 1/2 DAALDER (1/2 Lion)
Center Weight: 13.8400 g. **Center Composition:** 0.7500 Silver 0.3337 oz. ASW **Obv:** Armoured knight looking right above lion shield in inner circle **Rev:** Rampant lion left in inner circle, date at top in legend

Date	Mintage	VG	F	VF	XF	Unc
1609	—	65.00	175	300	600	—
1614	—	50.00	125	200	400	—
1615	—	50.00	125	200	400	—
1616	—	50.00	125	200	400	—
1617	—	50.00	125	200	400	—
1618	—	50.00	125	200	400	—
1619	—	50.00	125	200	400	—
1623	—	50.00	125	200	400	—
1625/4	—	65.00	175	300	600	—
1628	—	50.00	125	200	650	—
1632/0	—	65.00	175	250	500	—
1634	—	75.00	200	400	800	—
1635	—	75.00	200	400	800	—
1638	—	50.00	125	250	500	—
1639	—	75.00	200	600	800	—
1641	—	75.00	200	400	800	—
1645	—	65.00	175	300	600	—
1648	—	65.00	175	300	600	—
1649/8	—	75.00	200	400	800	—
1649	—	65.00	175	300	600	—
1650	—	50.00	125	200	400	—
1651	—	50.00	125	200	400	—
1652	—	50.00	125	200	400	—
1653	—	50.00	125	200	400	—

KM# 13 DAALDER (Prince - 40 Stuiver)
Center Weight: 29.0300 g. **Center Composition:** 0.8850 Silver 0.8260 oz. ASW **Obv:** Armored bust of Prince Maurice with sword right in inner circle, date at top **Rev:** Helmeted provincial arms in inner circle **Note:** Dav. #4825.

Date	Mintage	VG	F	VF	XF	Unc
1603	2,410	100	300	600	1,000	—

KM# 16 DAALDER (Lion)
Center Weight: 27.6800 g. **Center Composition:** 0.7500 Silver 0.6674 oz. ASW **Obv:** Armored knight looking right above lion shield in inner circle **Rev:** Rampant lion left in inner circle, date at top in legend **Note:** Dav. #4872.

Date	Mintage	VG	F	VF	XF	Unc
1606	46,770	25.00	50.00	100	200	—
1607	Inc. above	45.00	85.00	150	300	—
1609/7	—	45.00	85.00	120	240	—
1609	—	45.00	85.00	120	240	—
1611	—	45.00	85.00	120	240	—
1612	—	25.00	50.00	100	200	—
1613	—	25.00	50.00	100	200	—
1614	—	25.00	50.00	100	200	—
1615	—	25.00	50.00	100	200	—
1616	—	25.00	50.00	100	200	—
1617	—	25.00	50.00	100	200	—
1618	—	45.00	85.00	150	300	—
16222 (error)	—	—	—	—	—	—
1623	—	25.00	50.00	100	240	—
1624	—	45.00	85.00	150	300	—
1627/5	—	45.00	85.00	150	300	—
1628	—	25.00	65.00	120	240	—
1629	—	45.00	85.00	150	300	—
1631/0	—	55.00	120	175	275	—
1633	—	25.00	50.00	100	200	—
1634	—	45.00	85.00	120	240	—
1635	—	45.00	85.00	150	300	—
1636	—	45.00	85.00	120	240	—
1637	—	45.00	85.00	120	240	—
1638	—	45.00	85.00	120	240	—
1640/30	—	25.00	50.00	100	240	—
1640	—	25.00	50.00	100	240	—
1644	—	40.00	85.00	150	300	—
1645/3	—	40.00	85.00	150	300	—
1645	—	40.00	85.00	150	300	—
1646	—	40.00	85.00	120	240	—
1647	—	40.00	85.00	150	300	—
1648	—	25.00	50.00	100	240	—
1649	—	25.00	50.00	100	240	—
1650/49	—	25.00	50.00	100	240	—
1650	—	25.00	50.00	100	240	—
1651	—	25.00	50.00	100	240	—
1652	—	25.00	50.00	100	240	—
1653	—	40.00	85.00	150	300	—
1655	—	70.00	175	250	350	—
1658	—	25.00	50.00	80.00	200	—

KM# 17 DAALDER (Rijks)
Center Weight: 29.0300 g. **Center Composition:** 0.8850 Silver 0.8260 oz. ASW **Obv:** Laureate 1/2 figure holding sword and arms in inner circle **Rev:** Crowned arms divide date in inner circle **Note:** 1606-51 mint mark: castle; 1652-71 without mint mark. Dav. #4844.

Date	Mintage	VG	F	VF	XF	Unc
1606	—	40.00	100	150	245	—
1607	—	40.00	100	150	245	—
1610	—	60.00	150	200	325	—
1612/1	—	60.00	150	200	325	—
1612	—	40.00	100	150	245	—
1613	—	40.00	100	150	245	—
1616	—	40.00	100	150	245	—
1617	—	40.00	100	150	245	—
1619	—	40.00	100	150	245	—
1620	—	40.00	100	150	245	—
1621	—	40.00	100	150	245	—
1622	—	40.00	100	150	245	—
1623	—	40.00	100	150	245	—
1624	—	40.00	100	150	245	—
1625	—	40.00	100	150	245	—
1626	—	40.00	100	150	245	—
1628/6	—	40.00	100	150	245	—
1629	—	40.00	100	150	245	—
1630	—	40.00	100	150	245	—
1631/0	—	40.00	100	150	245	—
1631	—	40.00	100	150	245	—
1635	—	75.00	175	250	375	—
1638	—	40.00	100	150	245	—
1642	—	40.00	100	150	245	—

Date	Mintage	VG	F	VF	XF	Unc
1643	—	75.00	175	250	375	—
1644	—	40.00	100	150	245	—
1646	—	40.00	100	150	245	—
1647	—	40.00	100	150	245	—
1648	—	40.00	100	150	245	—
1649	—	40.00	100	150	245	—
1650	—	40.00	100	150	245	—
1651	—	40.00	100	150	245	—
1652	—	40.00	100	150	245	—
1653	—	60.00	150	200	325	—
1654	—	40.00	100	150	245	—
1655	—	40.00	100	150	245	—
1656	—	40.00	100	150	245	—
1657	—	40.00	100	150	245	—
1658	—	40.00	100	150	245	—
1659	—	40.00	100	150	245	—
1660	—	40.00	100	150	245	—
1661	—	40.00	100	150	245	—
1662	—	40.00	100	150	245	—
1664	—	60.00	150	200	325	—
1671	—	60.00	150	200	325	—

KM# 63 2 DAALDERS (60 Stuiver - 10 Schelling, Escalins)

Center Weight: 31.7600 g. **Center Composition:** 0.9060 Silver 0.9251 oz. ASW **Note:** Dav. #4973.

Date	Mintage	VG	F	VF	XF	Unc
1685	350,756	75.00	200	300	450	—
1685 Proof	—	—	—	—	—	—
1687	Inc. above	75.00	200	300	450	—
1688	104,307	100	250	400	550	—
1689/8	Inc. above	75.00	200	300	450	—
1689	Inc. above	50.00	125	200	325	—
1690	Inc. above	50.00	125	200	325	—
1692	Inc. above	50.00	125	200	325	—
1693	Inc. above	75.00	200	300	450	—

KM# 45 1/2 SILVER DUCAT

Center Weight: 14.1200 g. **Center Composition:** 0.8730 Silver 0.3963 oz. ASW **Obv:** Armored knight standing holding sword behind shield o f arms, date at sides in inner circle **Rev:** Crowned arms in inner circle

Date	Mintage	VG	F	VF	XF	Unc
1659	—	170	250	400	550	—
1660	—	100	250	400	550	—
1661/0	—	100	275	450	650	—
1661	—	100	250	400	550	—
1662/1	—	100	275	450	650	—
1662	—	100	250	400	550	—
1663	—	100	250	400	550	—
1668	—	100	275	450	650	—

KM# 51 1/2 SILVER DUCAT

14.1200 g., 0.8730 Silver 0.3963 oz. ASW **Obv:** Standing armored knight with crowned shield at feet **Obv. Legend:** MON • NOV • ARG • PRO • CONFOED • BELG • COM • ZEL • **Rev:** Crowned arms of Zeeland divide date **Rev. Legend:** CONCORDIA RES PARVÆ CRESCUNT

Date	Mintage	VG	F	VF	XF	Unc
1672	—	40.00	80.00	120	250	—
1673	—	40.00	80.00	120	250	—
1675	—	40.00	80.00	120	250	—

KM# 40 SILVER DUCAT

28.2500 g., 0.8730 Silver 0.7929 oz. ASW **Obv:** Armored kniht standing holding sword behind shield of arms, date at sides in inner circle **Rev:** Crowned arms in inner circle **Note:** Dav. #4912.

Date	Mintage	VG	F	VF	XF	Unc
1659	—	55.00	125	175	300	—
1660	—	55.00	125	175	300	—
1661/0	—	55.00	125	175	300	—
1661	—	55.00	125	175	300	—
1662	—	55.00	125	175	300	—
1663	—	55.00	125	175	300	—
1664	—	95.00	200	300	450	—
1667	—	55.00	125	175	300	—
1668	—	95.00	200	300	450	—

KM# 52.1 SILVER DUCAT

28.2500 g., 0.8730 Silver 0.7929 oz. ASW **Obv:** Standing armored Knight with crowned shield at feet **Obv. Legend:** MO • NO • ARG • PRO : CON • FOE • BELG • COM • ZEEL • **Rev:** Crowned arms of Zeeland divide date **Rev. Legend:** CONCORDIA • RES • PARVÆ • CRESCUNT **Note:** Dav. #4914.

Date	Mintage	VG	F	VF	XF	Unc
ND	—	20.00	60.00	125	225	—
1672	—	20.00	60.00	125	225	—
1673	—	20.00	60.00	125	225	—
1674	—	20.00	60.00	125	225	—
1675/3	—	20.00	60.00	125	225	—
1675	—	20.00	60.00	125	225	—
1676	—	20.00	60.00	125	225	—
1677	—	20.00	60.00	125	225	—
1678	—	20.00	60.00	125	225	—
1679/6	—	20.00	60.00	125	225	—
1679	—	20.00	60.00	125	225	—
1680	—	20.00	60.00	125	225	—
1693	—	20.00	60.00	125	225	—
1694	—	20.00	60.00	125	225	—
1695	—	20.00	60.00	125	225	—
1696	—	20.00	60.00	125	225	—
1697/5	—	20.00	60.00	125	225	—
1697/6	—	20.00	60.00	125	225	—
1697	—	20.00	60.00	125	225	—
1698	—	20.00	60.00	125	225	—
1699	—	20.00	60.00	125	225	—
1700	—	20.00	60.00	125	225	300

KM# 46 1/2 DUCATON (20 Stuiver)

16.3900 g., 0.9410 Silver 0.4958 oz. ASW **Obv:** Knight with sword on horseback right, provincial arms below in inner circle **Rev:** Crowned arms with crowned lion supporters in inner circle, date at top in legend

Date	Mintage	VG	F	VF	XF	Unc
1660	—	60.00	175	250	400	—
1661	—	60.00	175	250	400	—
1662	—	60.00	175	250	400	—
1663	—	60.00	175	250	400	—
1664	—	70.00	200	300	450	—
1670	—	70.00	200	300	450	—
1672	—	80.00	200	350	500	—
1673	—	80.00	200	350	500	—

KM# 41.1 DUCATON (40 Stuiver)

32.7800 g., 0.9410 Silver 0.9917 oz. ASW **Obv:** Knight with sword on horseback right, provincial arms below in inner circle **Rev:** Crowned arms with crowned lion supporters in inner circle, date at top in legend **Note:** Dotted inner circle 1659-66; solid inner circle 1668-72. Dav. #4942.

Date	Mintage	VG	F	VF	XF	Unc
1659	—	60.00	150	200	300	—
1660	—	70.00	200	275	400	—
1661	—	60.00	150	200	300	—
1662	—	60.00	150	200	300	—
1663	—	60.00	150	200	300	—
1664	—	60.00	150	200	300	—
1666	—	60.00	150	200	300	—
1668	—	60.00	150	200	300	—
1670	—	60.00	150	200	300	—
1671	—	70.00	200	275	400	—
1672	—	70.00	200	275	400	—

KM# 41.2 DUCATON (40 Stuiver)

32.7800 g., 0.9410 Silver 0.9917 oz. ASW **Obv:** Knight with sword on horseback right, provincial arms below in inner circle **Rev:** Crowned arms with crowned lion supporters in inner circle, date at top in legend **Edge:** Lettered **Edge Lettering:** LVCT(OR) ET.EMERGO.

Date	Mintage	VG	F	VF	XF	Unc
1670	—	—	—	—	—	—
1672	—	—	—	—	—	—

KM# 56 DUCATON (40 Stuiver)

Silver **Obv:** Without ground under the horse's legs **Note:** Dav. #4943.

Date	Mintage	VG	F	VF	XF	Unc
1680	—	40.00	100	225	450	—
1683	—	—	—	—	—	—

KM# 57 DUCATON (Silver Rider)

32.7800 g., 0.9410 Silver 0.9917 oz. ASW **Obv:** Armored Knight on horse above crowned shield **Obv. Legend:** MON: NOV: ARG: PRO: CON FOED: BELG: COM: ZEL • **Rev:** Crowned arms of Zeeland with supporters, date in cartouche below **Rev. Legend:** CONCORDIA RES • PARVÆ • CRESCUNT •

Date	Mintage	VG	F	VF	XF	Unc
1670	—	—	—	—	—	—
1671	—	—	—	—	—	—
1672	—	—	—	—	—	—
1675	—	—	—	—	—	—
1680	—	40.00	115	225	325	—
1683	—	40.00	115	225	325	—

KM# 3 1/2 ROSE NOBLE

3.8200 g., Gold **Obv:** Ruler in ship facing holding sword upright and provincial shield **Obv. Legend:** ... COMITAT • ZELAN **Rev:** Radiant sun surrounded by crowned lions and lis **Note:** FR#303.

Date	Mintage	Good	VG	F	VF	XF
ND(1602)	—	—	300	600	900	1,500

KM# 4 ROSE NOBLE

7.6400 g., Gold **Obv:** Ruler in ship facing holding sword upright and provincial shield **Obv. Legend:** ... COMITAT • ZELAN **Rev:** Radiant sun surrounded by crowned lions and lis **Note:** FR.#302.

Date	Mintage	Good	VG	F	VF	XF
ND(1602)	—	—	400	800	1,500	2,500

KM# 19 1/2 CAVALIER D'OR

5.0000 g., 0.9200 Gold 0.1479 oz. AGW **Note:** Date divided by mint mark 1645-48. Fr. #312.

Date	Mintage	VG	F	VF	XF	Unc
1609	—	275	500	900	1,300	—
1610	—	275	500	900	1,300	—
1611	—	275	500	900	1,300	—
1614	—	275	500	900	1,300	—
1615	—	250	400	650	900	—
1617	—	250	400	650	900	—
1618	—	250	450	700	1,100	—
1621	—	250	400	650	900	—
1622	—	250	400	650	900	—
1623	—	250	400	650	900	—
1625	—	250	400	650	900	—
1626	—	275	500	900	1,300	—
1627	—	250	400	650	900	—
1628	—	275	500	900	1,300	—
1629	—	250	400	650	900	—
1630	—	250	400	650	900	—
1631	—	900	1,100	1,800	2,500	—
1634	—	275	650	900	1,300	—
1635	—	250	400	650	900	—
1638	—	250	400	650	900	—
1639	—	250	400	650	900	—
1640	—	250	400	650	900	—
1641	—	250	400	650	900	—
1644	—	250	400	650	900	—
1645	—	250	400	650	900	—
1647	—	250	400	650	900	—
1648	—	250	400	650	900	—

KM# 18 CAVALIER D'OR

10.0000 g., 0.9200 Gold 0.2958 oz. AGW **Obv:** Equestrian figure of knight above arms in inner circle **Rev:** Crowned arms in inner circle, date at top **Note:** Fr. #311.

Date	Mintage	VG	F	VF	XF	Unc
1606	—	350	750	1,500	2,500	—
1615	—	350	750	1,500	2,500	—
1621	—	350	750	1,500	2,500	—
1624	—	350	750	1,500	2,500	—
1630	—	450	1,000	2,500	3,500	—
1638	—	350	750	1,500	2,500	—
1644/38	—	350	750	1,500	2,500	—
1644	—	350	750	1,500	2,500	—

TRADE COINAGE

KM# 20 DUCAT

3.5000 g., 0.9860 Gold 0.1109 oz. AGW **Obv:** 5-line inscription in tablet **Rev:** Standing figure of knight to right divides date in inner circle **Note:** Fr. #307.

Date	Mintage	VG	F	VF	XF	Unc
1609	—	120	150	200	350	—
1621	—	120	150	200	350	—
1631	—	120	150	200	350	—
1632	—	120	150	200	350	—
1635	—	130	175	265	400	—
1638	—	120	150	200	350	—
1641	—	120	150	200	350	—
1642	—	120	150	200	350	—
1643	—	120	150	200	350	—
1645	—	130	200	300	500	—
1648	—	130	200	300	500	—
1649	—	120	150	200	350	—
1650	—	130	200	300	500	—
1651	—	130	200	300	500	—
1654	—	120	150	200	350	—
1658	—	120	150	200	350	—
1659	—	120	150	200	350	—

KM# 62 DUCAT

3.5000 g., 0.9860 Gold 0.1109 oz. AGW **Obv:** Knight standing to right divides date within inner circle **Rev:** Tablet on full-blown rose **Note:** Fr. #307.

Date	Mintage	VG	F	VF	XF	Unc
1682	—	120	150	225	400	—
1683	—	120	150	225	400	—
1686	—	130	200	300	500	—
1687/3	—	120	150	225	400	—
1687	—	120	150	225	400	—
1690	—	120	150	225	400	—

KM# 35 2 DUCAT

7.0000 g., 0.9860 Gold 0.2219 oz. AGW **Obv:** Knight standing right divides date in inner circle **Rev:** 5-line inscription in tablet **Note:** FR. #306.

Date	Mintage	VG	F	VF	XF	Unc
1645	—	350	600	1,000	1,500	—
1646	—	250	400	700	1,100	—
1647/6	—	350	600	1,000	1,500	—
1647	—	350	400	700	1,100	—
1648	—	350	400	700	1,100	—
1649	—	350	400	700	1,100	—
1649/7	—	300	600	1,000	1,500	—
1650	—	250	400	700	1,100	—
1651	—	250	400	700	1,100	—
1652	—	250	400	700	1,100	—
1653	—	250	400	700	1,100	—
1654	—	250	400	700	1,100	—
1655	—	250	400	700	1,100	—
1656	—	250	400	700	1,000	—
1658	—	250	400	700	1,100	—
1658/6	—	350	600	1,000	1,500	—
1659	—	350	600	1,000	1,500	—
1660	—	250	400	700	1,100	—
1661	—	350	600	1,000	1,500	—
1662	—	250	400	700	1,100	—
1668	—	350	600	1,000	1,500	—
1672	—	350	6,000	1,000	1,500	—
1673	—	350	600	1,000	1,500	—

KM# 61 2 DUCAT

7.0000 g., 0.9860 Gold 0.2219 oz. AGW **Obv:** Without inner circle **Rev:** Tablet on full blown rose **Note:** FR. #306.

Date	Mintage	VG	F	VF	XF	Unc
1673	—	275	500	1,000	1,800	—
1682	—	275	500	1,000	1,800	—
1683	—	275	500	1,000	1,800	—
1684	—	275	500	1,000	1,800	—
1689	—	275	500	1,000	1,800	—
1690	—	275	500	1,000	1,800	—

SIEGE COINAGE

Middelburg - 1573

FR# 164 DUCAT

Gold **Countermark:** Zeeland shield and middelburg shield **Obv. Legend:** DEO / REGI / ... / MIDDELB: **Note:** Klippe, uniface.

Date	Mintage	F	VF	XF	Unc	BU
1573	—	—	2,100	3,000	—	—
1574	—	—	2,100	3,000	—	—

FR# 163 2 DUCAT

Gold **Countermark:** Zeeland shield and Middelburg shield **Obv. Legend:** DEO / REGI / ... / MIDDELB: **Note:** Klippe, uniface.

Date	Mintage	F	VF	XF	Unc	BU
1573	—	—	3,100	4,000	—	—

FR# 162 4 DUCAT

Gold **Countermark:** Zeeland shield and Middelburg shield **Obv. Legend:** DEO / REGI / ... / MIDDELB: **Note:** Klippe, uniface

Date	Mintage	F	VF	XF	Unc	BU
1573 Rare	—	—	—	—	—	—

PATTERNS

Including off metal strikes

KM#	Date	Mintage	Identification	Mkt Val
Pn3	1682	—	Daalder. Gold. 34.6000 g. KM#17.	—
Pn6	1684	—	Daalder. Gold. 34.6000 g. KM#17.	—
Pn7	1685/3	—	30 Gulden. Silver.	—
Pn8	1685/3	—	30 Stuivers. Silver. 30St over 30G, ARG over AUR.	—
Pn10	1686	—	Daalder. Gold. 42.0000 g. KM#17.	—
Pn11	1687	—	Daalder. Silver. 36.6000 g. KM#52.1.	—
Pn12	1687	—	2 Daalders. Gold. 35.0000 g. KM#63.	—
Pn13	1687	—	2 Daalders. Gold. 21.0000 g. KM#63.	—
Pn14	1689	—	Stuiver. Gold. 3.4000 g. KM#58.	—
Pn15	1689	—	2 Stuiver. Gold. 3.4500 g. KM#59a.	—

PIEFORTS

KM#	Date	Mintage	Identification	Mkt Val
P3	1627	—	2 Stuiver.	200
P4	1659	—	Ducaton. Silver. KM41.1. \	1,200
P5	1660	—	Ducaton. KM#41.1.	1,500
P6	1661	—	Ducaton.	—
P7	1662	—	Ducaton.	—
P8	1663	—	Ducaton.	—
P9	1664	—	Ducaton.	—
P10	1666	—	Ducaton. KM#61.1.	1,500
P11	1668	—	Ducaton. KM#61.1.	1,500
P12	1669	—	Duit. Copper. KM14.	—
P13	1676	—	10 Stuivers.	—
P14	1676	—	Daalder. Silver. KM#53.	—
P18	1683	—	Ducaton. KM#57.	—
P15	1683	—	10 Stuivers. Silver.	1,500
P16	1683	—	30 Gulden. Gold. 42.0000 g.	3,000
	1683	—	30 Gulden. Gold. 42.0000 g.	3,000
P19	1683	—	2 Ducaton.	2,250
P17	1683	—	Daalder. Silver. KM#60.	1,500
P20	1685	—	Daalder. Silver. KM#60.	1,500
P22	1687	—	Daalder. Silver. KM#64.	900
P23	1687	—	2 Daalders. KM#63.	1,750
P21	1687	—	30 Stuivers.	—
P24	1688	—	2 Daalders. Silver. KM#63.	1,750
PA26	1690	—	2 Daalders. Silver. KM#63. Triple weight.	—
P25	1690	—	2 Daalders. Silver. KM#63.	1,750
P26	1693	—	2 Daalders. KM#63.	1,750
P27	1694	—	3 Gulden. Silver. KM#70.	3,000
P28	1694	—	3 Gulden. Silver. KM#71.	—

ZUTPHEN

COMMUNE

STANDARD COINAGE

KM# 4 1/4 STUIVER

Silver **Obv:** City arms in dotted circle **Obv. Legend:** + MONE. VET. VRB. ZVTPH **Rev:** Rampant lion **Rev. Legend:** FATA. VIAM. INVENIENT

Date	Mintage	VG	F	VF	XF	Unc
ND(1605)	—	100	200	500	1,000	—

KM# 2 PEERDEKE (1/4 Snaphaan)

Silver **Obv:** City arms on long cross **Obv. Legend:** MO: NE - NOVA - CIVITA - ZVTPHA **Rev:** Equestrian knight right brandishing sword **Rev. Legend:** VIAM.IN - VENIENT - FA - TA+

Date	Mintage	VG	F	VF	XF	Unc
1604	—	25.00	75.00	200	500	—
1605	—	25.00	75.00	200	500	—

KM# 10 SNAPHAAN

Silver **Obv:** Armored knight on horseback right in inner circle, date below in cartouche **Rev:** Arms on long cross in inner circle

Date	Mintage	VG	F	VF	XF	Unc
1604	—	35.00	80.00	140	200	—

KM# 3 SNAPHAAN

Silver **Obv:** City arms on long cross **Obv. Legend:** DEO * ET - VIRTVT - E* DVCI - BVS* **Rev:** Equestrian knight right brandishing sword **Rev. Legend:** + TANDEM • BONA • CAVSA • TRIVMPHAT

Date	Mintage	VG	F	VF	XF	Unc
1604	—	—	—	—	—	—

KM# 5 DUIT

Copper **Obv:** Crowned rampant lion left in inner circle **Rev:** 3-line inscription in wreath

Date	Mintage	VG	F	VF	XF	Unc
ND(1604-05)	—	15.00	35.00	60.00	100	—

KM# 16 DUIT

Copper **Obv:** Crowned arms with lion supporters with last 2 digits of date ave crown **Rev:** Inscription in cartouche **Rev. Inscription:** CIV / ZVTPHA / NIA

Date	Mintage	VG	F	VF	XF	Unc
ND	—	10.00	30.00	60.00	110	—
(16)87	—	10.00	30.00	60.00	110	—
(16)87/88	—	15.00	50.00	90.00	160	—

KM# 16a.1 DUIT

Silver **Obv:** Crowned arms with lion supporters with last 2 digits of date ave crown **Rev:** CIV/ZVTPHA/NIA in cartouche

Date	Mintage	VG	F	VF	XF	Unc
1687	—	—	—	—	—	—

KM# 16b DUIT

Gold **Obv:** Date under shield **Rev:** CIV/ZVTPHA/NIA in cartouche

Date	Mintage	VG	F	VF	XF	Unc
1687	—	—	—	—	—	—

KM# 16a.2 DUIT

Silver **Obv:** Date under shield

Date	Mintage	VG	F	VF	XF	Unc
1687	—	—	—	—	—	—

KM# 6 1/2 STUIVER

Silver **Obv:** 3 towered castle in inner circle **Rev:** Arms on long cross in inner circle

Date	Mintage	VG	F	VF	XF	Unc
ND(1604-05)	—	100	200	300	400	—

KM# 7 STUIVER

2.0000 g., Silver **Obv:** Crowned arms divide value in innr circle, crown divides date **Rev:** Ornamental long cross with arms at center in inner circle

Date	Mintage	VG	F	VF	XF	Unc
1605	—	30.00	75.00	120	170	—

KM# 8 STUIVER (1/4 Snaphaan)

Silver **Obv:** Armored knight on horseback right in inner circle, date below in cartouche **Rev:** Arms on long cross in inner circle

Date	Mintage	VG	F	VF	XF	Unc
1505 (error)	—	—	—	—	—	—
1605	—	35.00	90.00	150	210	—

KM# 9 2 STUIVERS

4.0000 g., Silver **Obv:** Crowned arms divide value in inner circle, date below **Rev:** Ornamental long cross with arms at center in inner circle

Date	Mintage	VG	F	VF	XF	Unc
1605	—	30.00	75.00	150	250	—

KM# 11 3 STUIVERS (1/2 Roosschelling)

2.6300 g., Silver **Obv:** Crowned arms divide value in inner circle, crown divides date **Rev:** Floreated cross with rose at center in inner circle

Date	Mintage	VG	F	VF	XF	Unc
1605	—	75.00	150	250	450	—

KM# 19 6 STUIVERS (Rijderschelling)

4.7100 g., Silver **Obv:** Crowned arms divide value, date above crown **Rev:** Armored knight on horseback right **Note:** Mint mark: Antlers.

Date	Mintage	VG	F	VF	XF	Unc
1668 (error for 1688)	—	20.00	50.00	100	200	—
1688	—	10.00	25.00	50.00	125	—
1689	—	10.00	25.00	50.00	125	—
1690	—	10.00	25.00	50.00	125	—
1691	—	10.00	25.00	50.00	125	—

KM# 25 28 STUIVERS (Florin)

19.5000 g., 0.6730 Silver 0.4219 oz. ASW **Obv:** Crowned arms, date above crown **Rev:** Crowned double-headed eagle with value on breast **Note:** Mint mark: Antlers.

Date	Mintage	VG	F	VF	XF	Unc
1660 (error)	28,920	50.00	150	250	350	—
1690	Inc. above	50.00	150	250	350	—

KM# 20 30 STUIVERS (Daalder)

15.8800 g., 0.9060 Silver 0.4625 oz. ASW **Obv:** Crowned arms with lion supporters, value below **Rev:** Standing knight with sword behind crowned arms to left, date in legend

Date	Mintage	VG	F	VF	XF	Unc
1688	—	70.00	200	450	600	—
1689/8	—	—	—	—	—	—
1689	—	70.00	200	450	600	—
1692	—	70.00	200	450	600	—

KM# 17 1/2 GULDEN (10 Stuiver)

5.3000 g., 0.9200 Silver 0.1568 oz. ASW **Note:** Mint mark: Antlers. Similar to 3 Gulden, KM#15.

Date	Mintage	VG	F	VF	XF	Unc
1687	4,460	40.00	100	175	350	—

KM# 18 GULDEN (20 Stuiver)

Silver **Note:** Mint marks: Antlers. Similar to 3 Gulden, KM#15.

Date	Mintage	VG	F	VF	XF	Unc
ND	57,935	100	200	400	1,000	—
1687	Inc. above	40.00	100	175	350	—

KM# 15 3 GULDEN (60 Stuiver)

31.8200 g., 0.9200 Silver 0.9412 oz. ASW **Note:** Mint marks: Antlers. Dav. #4972.

Date	Mintage	VG	F	VF	XF	Unc
1686	4,625	175	500	800	1,200	—
1687	Inc. above	175	500	800	1,200	—

KM# 26 DAALDER (Liom - 48 Stuiver)

27.6800 g., 0.7500 Silver 0.6674 oz. ASW **Obv:** Armored knight looking right above lion shield in inner circle **Rev:** Rampant lion left in inner circle, date divided at top **Note:** Mint mark: Antlers. Dav. #4888.

Date	Mintage	VG	F	VF	XF	Unc
1690	—	500	1,500	3,000	4,500	—
1691	—	500	1,500	3,000	4,500	—
1692	—	500	1,500	3,000	4,500	—

PATTERNS

Including off metal strikes

KM#	Date	Mintage	Identification	Mkt Val
Pn1	1690	—	Ducat D'Argent. Silver.	—

PIEFORTS

KM#	Date	Mintage	Identification	Mkt Val
P1	1604	—	Peerdeke. Silver. KM#2.	—
P2	1604	—	Snaphaan. Silver. KM#3. Klippe.	—
P3	1687	—	Gulden. Silver. KM#18.	—
P4	1687	—	Duit. Silver. KM#16a.1.	—
P5	1688	—	Daalder. Silver. Triple weight. KM#30.	—
P6	1688	—	Daalder. Silver. Quadruple weight. KM#30.	—
P7	1689	—	Daalder. Silver. Triple weight. KM#30.	—
P8	1690	—	Florin. Silver. Triple weight. KM#28.	—
P9	1690	—	3 Gulden. Silver. KM#15.	—
P10	1692	—	Daalder. Silver. Triple weight. KM#30.	—

ZWOLLE

COMMUNE

STANDARD COINAGE

KM# 21 DUIT

Copper **Obv:** Shield of Zwolle arms (St. Michael holding sword and shield) **Rev:** ZW/OLLAE/1 (shield) 8 in wreath

Date	Mintage	VG	F	VF	XF	Unc
1618	—	7.50	15.00	30.00	60.00	—

KM# 37 DUIT

Copper **Obv:** Shield of Zwolle arms **Obv. Legend:** DEVS. REFVGIVM. NOSTRVM. **Rev:** ZW/OLLAE/3 (shield) 9 in wreath

Date	Mintage	VG	F	VF	XF	Unc
(16)36	—	9.00	20.00	30.00	50.00	—
(16)39	—	7.50	15.00	25.00	35.00	—

KM# 69 DUIT
Copper **Obv:** Shield of Zwolle arms in wreath **Rev:** ZW/OLLAE/6 (shield) 3 in wreath

Date	Mintage	VG	F	VF	XF	Unc
1663	—	9.00	20.00	35.00	55.00	—

KM# 4 1/8 STUIVER
Silver **Obv:** City arms (ZWO / 2 lions) **Note:** Uniface.

Date	Mintage	VG	F	VF	XF	Unc
ND(1590-1606)	—	100	250	600	1,200	—

KM# 7 2 STUIVERS
Billon **Obv:** Orb with value divides date in inner circle **Rev:** Arms with St. Michael above in inner circle

Date	Mintage	VG	F	VF	XF	Unc
1601	—	30.00	100	150	250	—
1602	—	50.00	150	200	350	—

KM# 76 2 STUIVERS
1.7300 g., 0.5830 Silver 0.0324 oz. ASW **Obv:** Crowned rampant lion left divides value **Rev:** ZW/OLLA/ (date divided by arms)

Date	Mintage	VG	F	VF	XF	Unc
1672	—	10.00	15.00	30.00	45.00	—
1674	—	10.00	15.00	30.00	45.00	—
1677	—	10.00	15.00	30.00	45.00	—
1678	—	10.00	15.00	30.00	45.00	—
1679	—	10.00	15.00	30.00	45.00	—

KM# 8 3 STUIVERS (1/2 Arendschelling)
Billon **Obv:** Crowned imperial eagle in inner circle **Rev:** Shield of arms with elaborate helmet above in inner circle

Date	Mintage	VG	F	VF	XF	Unc
ND	—	25.00	150	250	500	—

KM# 70 1/2 SCHELLING
Silver **Obv:** Crowned city arms **Obv. Legend:** MONETA. ARGENTEA. CIVIT. ZW **Rev:** Laureate male right **Rev. Legend:** DA. PAC. Domin. IN. DIEB. NOS

Date	Mintage	VG	F	VF	XF	Unc
1662	—	50.00	100	250	500	—
1664	—	50.00	100	250	500	—

KM# 15 6 STUIVERS (Arendschelling)
Billon **Obv:** Crowned arms in inner circle **Rev:** Crowned imperial eagle in inner circle, titles of Rudolph II

Date	Mintage	VG	F	VF	XF	Unc
ND(1601)	—	15.00	25.00	40.00	75.00	—

KM# 15a 6 STUIVERS (Arendschelling)
5.0400 g., Gold **Obv:** Crowned arms in inner circle **Rev:** Crowned imperial eagle, titles of Rudolph II

Date	Mintage	VG	F	VF	XF	Unc
ND(1601)	—	—	—	2,500	4,000	—

KM# 16 6 STUIVERS (Arendschelling)
Billon **Rev:** Titles of Matthias

Date	Mintage	VG	F	VF	XF	Unc
ND(1613)	—	15.00	25.00	40.00	75.00	—
1618	—	15.00	25.00	40.00	65.00	—
1678 (error for 1618)	—	20.00	40.00	60.00	100	—

KM# 75 6 STUIVERS (Arendschelling)
Billon **Rev. Legend:** Da: DAC: DOM: IN: DIEB: NOST

Date	Mintage	VG	F	VF	XF	Unc
1670	—	15.00	25.00	40.00	55.00	—
1675	—	25.00	45.00	75.00	100	—
1678	—	20.00	35.00	55.00	70.00	—
1679	—	14.00	25.00	40.00	55.00	—

KM# 85 6 STUIVERS (Rijderschelling)
4.9500 g., 0.5830 Billon 0.0928 oz. **Obv:** Crowned arms divide value **Rev:** Knight with sword on horseback to right, crowned arms below horse, date with Arabic numerals in legend

Date	Mintage	VG	F	VF	XF	Unc
1680	—	10.00	15.00	25.00	50.00	—
1681	—	10.00	15.00	25.00	50.00	—
1682	—	10.00	15.00	25.00	50.00	—
1683	—	10.00	15.00	25.00	50.00	—
1691	—	10.00	15.00	25.00	50.00	—

KM# 87 6 STUIVERS (Rijderschelling)
4.7100 g., 0.5830 Billon 0.0883 oz. **Obv:** Crowned arms divide value **Rev:** Date in Roman style numerals

Date	Mintage	VG	F	VF	XF	Unc
1685	—	15.00	30.00	50.00	100	—
1686	—	10.00	15.00	25.00	50.00	—
1687	—	10.00	15.00	25.00	50.00	—
1688	—	10.00	15.00	25.00	50.00	—

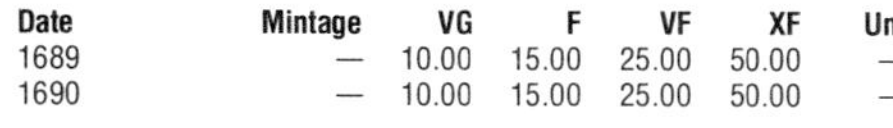

Date	Mintage	VG	F	VF	XF	Unc
1689	—	10.00	15.00	25.00	50.00	—
1690	—	10.00	15.00	25.00	50.00	—

KM# 17 28 STUIVERS (Florin)
19.5000 g., 0.6730 Silver 0.4219 oz. ASW **Obv:** Crowned arms in inner circle, date at top above crown **Rev:** Crowned imperial eagle with value in orb on breast in inner circle

Date	Mintage	VG	F	VF	XF	Unc
1619	—	25.00	70.00	100	200	—
1620 (error, value "82")	—	—	—	—	—	—
1620	—	25.00	70.00	100	200	—
1621	—	25.00	70.00	100	200	—
1626	—	25.00	70.00	100	200	—
1628	—	—	—	—	—	—
ND(1650-65)	—	15.00	50.00	75.00	125	—

KM# 22 28 STUIVERS (Florin)
Silver **Obv:** Crowned arms in inner circle, date above **Rev:** Crowned imperial eagle with value in orb on breast in inner circle **Note:** Klippe.

Date	Mintage	VG	F	VF	XF	Unc
1619	—	—	—	—	—	—

KM# 78.1 28 STUIVERS (Florin)
Silver **Obv:** Crowned arms in inner circle **Obv. Legend:** FLOR • ARG • CIVITA • IMP • ZWOLLÆ **Rev:** Crowned imperial eagle with orb on breast in inner circle, partial date at upper left **Rev. Legend:** DA • PAC • DOM • IN • DIEB • NOSTRIS •

Date	Mintage	VG	F	VF	XF	Unc
(16)79	70,020	15.00	50.00	75.00	150	—
(16)80	Inc. above	15.00	50.00	75.00	150	—

KM# 78.2 28 STUIVERS (Florin)
Silver **Obv:** Crowned arms in inner circle, partial date above **Obv. Legend:** FLOR • ARG • CIVITA • IMP • ZWOLLÆ **Rev:** Crowned imperial eagle with orb on breast with value 28 **Rev. Legend:** DA • PAC • DOM • IN • DIEB • NOSTRIS •

Date	Mintage	VG	F	VF	XF	Unc
1680	Inc. above	—	15.00	50.00	75.00	150
1683/0	Inc. above	—	15.00	50.00	75.00	150
1683	Inc. above	—	15.00	50.00	75.00	150
1685	Inc. above	—	25.00	70.00	125	250

KM# 78.3 28 STUIVERS (Florin)
Silver **Obv:** Crowned arms, date above **Obv. Legend:** FLOR • ARG • CIVITA • IMP • ZWOLLÆ **Rev:** Crowned imperial eagle with orb on breast with value 28 **Rev. Legend:** DA • PAC • DOM • IN • DIEB • NOSTRIS •

Date	Mintage	VG	F	VF	XF	Unc
1684	Inc. above	15.00	50.00	75.00	150	—
1685	Inc. above	15.00	50.00	75.00	150	—
1686	Inc. above	15.00	50.00	75.00	150	—

KM# 88 30 STUIVERS (Daalder)
15.8800 g., 0.9610 Silver 0.4906 oz. ASW **Obv:** Crowned arms divide value, date in legend **Rev:** Standing knight with sword behind crowned arms to left **Note:** Mint mark: Rosette.

Date	Mintage	VG	F	VF	XF	Unc
1685	91,650	60.00	100	175	300	—

KM# 89 30 STUIVERS (Daalder)

Silver **Obv:** Crowned quartered arms divide value, date in legend

Date	Mintage	VG	F	VF	XF	Unc
1686	—	40.00	85.00	125	200	—
1688	—	40.00	85.00	125	200	—
1692/1	—	40.00	85.00	125	200	—
1692	—	40.00	85.00	125	200	—

KM# 90 GULDEN

10.6100 g., 0.9200 Silver 0.3138 oz. ASW **Obv:** Crowned arms divide value, date above crown **Rev:** Standing female figure leaning on Bible on column, holding spear with Liberty cap

Date	Mintage	VG	F	VF	XF	Unc
1687	21,555	125	250	500	800	—

KM# 86 3 GULDEN (60 Stuiver)

31.8200 g., 0.9200 Silver 0.9412 oz. ASW **Obv:** Crowned arms divide value, date above crown **Rev:** Standing female figure leaning on Bible on column, holding spear with Liberty cap **Note:** Mint mark: Rosette. Dav. #4970.

Date	Mintage	VG	F	VF	XF	Unc
1682	40,595	200	400	800	1,000	—
1686	Inc. above	150	300	600	800	—
1687	Inc. above	150	300	600	800	—
1689	Inc. above	150	300	600	800	—
1690	Inc. above	150	300	600	800	—

KM# 18 1/2 DAALDER (Arendsrijks - 25 Stuiver)

14.5100 g., 0.8850 Silver 0.4128 oz. ASW **Obv:** Shield of arms with elaborate helmet above in inner circle **Rev:** Crowned imperial eagle with orb on breast in inner circle, titles of Rudolph II

Date	Mintage	VG	F	VF	XF	Unc
1612	—	175	500	800	1,000	—

KM# 19 1/2 DAALDER (Arendsrijks - 25 Stuiver)

Silver **Rev:** Titles of Matthias

Date	Mintage	VG	F	VF	XF	Unc
ND	—	150	400	600	800	—
1612	—	—	—	—	—	—
1620	—	—	—	—	—	—
1647	—	—	—	—	—	—

KM# 50 1/2 DAALDER (Arendsrijks - 25 Stuiver)

Silver **Rev:** Titles of Ferdinand III

Date	Mintage	VG	F	VF	XF	Unc
1647	—	—	—	—	—	—
1649	—	—	—	—	—	—

KM# 31 1/2 DAALDER (Lion - 24 Stuiver)

27.6800 g., 0.7500 Silver 0.6674 oz. ASW **Obv:** Armored knight looking right above lion sheild in inner circle **Rev:** Rampant lion left divides date in inner circle

Date	Mintage	VG	F	VF	XF	Unc
1633	—	75.00	200	450	850	—

KM# 35 1/2 DAALDER (Lion - 24 Stuiver)

Silver **Obv:** Armored knight looking right above Zwolle arms in inner circle

Date	Mintage	VG	F	VF	XF	Unc
1637	—	35.00	100	150	250	—
1639	—	35.00	100	150	250	—
1641	—	35.00	100	150	250	—
1642	—	35.00	100	150	250	—
1644	—	35.00	100	150	250	—

KM# 45 1/2 DAALDER (Lion - 24 Stuiver)

Silver **Rev:** Date in legend

Date	Mintage	VG	F	VF	XF	Unc
1641	—	30.00	80.00	130	200	—
1642	—	45.00	100	170	300	—
1644	—	30.00	80.00	130	200	—
1646	—	30.00	80.00	130	200	—
1648	—	30.00	80.00	130	200	—
1649	—	30.00	80.00	130	200	—
1650	—	30.00	80.00	130	200	—
1651	—	30.00	80.00	130	200	—
1652	—	45.00	100	170	300	—

KM# 57 1/2 DAALDER (Rijks)

14.5100 g., 0.8850 Silver 0.4128 oz. ASW **Obv:** Laureate 1/2 figure holding sword and arms in inner circle **Rev:** Crowned arms divide date in inner circle

Date	Mintage	VG	F	VF	XF	Unc
1653	—	—	—	—	—	—

KM# 10 DAALDER (Arendsrijks - 50 Stuiver)

29.0300 g., 0.8850 Silver 0.8260 oz. ASW **Obv:** Shield of arms with elaborate helmet above in inner circle, divided at bottom **Rev:** Crowned imperial eagle with orb on breast in inner circle, titles of Rudolph II **Note:** Dav. #4989.

Date	Mintage	VG	F	VF	XF	Unc
ND	—	70.00	200	300	600	—
1601	—	70.00	200	300	500	—
1612	—	125	250	500	1,000	—
1613	—	—	—	—	—	—

KM# 20 DAALDER (Arendsrijks - 50 Stuiver)

Silver **Rev:** Titles of Matthias **Note:** Dav. #4990.

Date	Mintage	VG	F	VF	XF	Unc
ND	—	100	250	325	700	—
1613	—	125	300	450	900	—
1620	—	125	300	450	900	—

KM# 25.1 DAALDER (Arendsrijks - 50 Stuiver)

Silver **Obv:** Shield of arms with elaborate helmet above in inner circle, date near helmet **Rev:** Crowned imperial eagle with orb on breast in inner circle, titles of Ferdinand II **Note:** Dav. #4991.

Date	Mintage	VG	F	VF	XF	Unc
ND	—	—	—	—	—	—
1628	—	125	300	450	750	—
1629	—	125	300	450	750	—
1631	—	175	500	1,250	1,500	—
1636	—	175	500	1,250	1,500	—

KM# 32 DAALDER (Arendsrijks - 50 Stuiver)

Silver **Rev:** Titles of Ferdinand III (or 3) in legend **Note:** Dav. #4992.

Date	Mintage	VG	F	VF	XF	Unc
ND	—	100	300	450	800	—
1646	—	—	—	—	—	—
1647	—	100	300	450	800	—
1649	—	100	300	450	800	—
1652	—	100	300	450	800	—
1653	—	100	300	450	800	—

KM# 25.2 DAALDER (Arendsrijks - 50 Stuiver)

Silver **Obv:** Shield of arms with elaborate helmet above in inner circle **Rev:** Crowned imperial eagle with orb on breast in inner circle, date in legend, titles of Ferdinand II

Date	Mintage	VG	F	VF	XF	Unc
1636	—	125	300	450	800	—

KM# 33 DAALDER (Lion - 48 Stuiver)

27.6800 g., 0.7500 Silver 0.6674 oz. ASW **Obv:** Similar to KM#36 but with lion on sheild **Rev:** Similar to KM#36 but smaller sheild on lion's side **Note:** Dav. #4881.

Date	Mintage	VG	F	VF	XF	Unc
1633	—	30.00	50.00	125	300	—

KM# 36 DAALDER (Lion - 48 Stuiver)
Silver **Obv:** Shield with St. Michael **Rev:** Larger shield on lion's side **Note:** Dav. #4882.

Date	Mintage	VG	F	VF	XF	Unc
1637	—	35.00	75.00	175	350	—
1639	—	30.00	50.00	125	250	—

KM# 38 DAALDER (Lion - 48 Stuiver)
Silver **Obv:** Shield with St. Michael **Rev:** Without shield on lion's side **Note:** Dav. #4883.

Date	Mintage	VG	F	VF	XF	Unc
1639	—	20.00	40.00	100	175	—
1640	—	20.00	40.00	100	175	—
1641	—	20.00	40.00	100	175	—
1642	—	20.00	40.00	100	175	—
1644	—	20.00	40.00	100	175	—
1646	—	20.00	40.00	100	175	—

KM# 46 DAALDER (Lion - 48 Stuiver)
Silver **Rev:** Date in legend **Note:** Varieties exist. Dav. #4885.

Date	Mintage	VG	F	VF	XF	Unc
1641	—	15.00	30.00	75.00	150	—
1642	—	15.00	30.00	75.00	150	—
1644	—	15.00	30.00	75.00	150	—
1646	—	15.00	30.00	75.00	150	—
1647	—	15.00	30.00	75.00	150	—
1648	—	15.00	30.00	75.00	150	—
1649	—	15.00	30.00	75.00	150	—
1650	—	15.00	30.00	75.00	150	—
1651	—	15.00	30.00	75.00	150	—
1652	—	15.00	30.00	75.00	150	—
1653	—	15.00	30.00	75.00	150	—
1654/1	—	20.00	50.00	100	200	—
1654	—	15.00	30.00	75.00	150	—
1655	—	15.00	30.00	75.00	150	—

KM# 48 DAALDER (Lion - 48 Stuiver)
Silver **Rev:** Date behind lion **Note:** Dav. #4884.

Date	Mintage	VG	F	VF	XF	Unc
1642	—	20.00	40.00	100	175	—
1644	—	20.00	40.00	100	175	—

KM# 56 DAALDER (Rijks)
29.0300 g., 0.8850 Silver 0.8260 oz. ASW **Obv:** Crowned lion shield divides date **Obv. Legend:** MONETA • ARG • CIVITATES • ZWOL(L) • **Rev:** 1/2 length armored knight right **Rev. Legend:** FERDINA III - • DG • RO... **Note:** Dav. #4993.

Date	Mintage	VG	F	VF	XF	Unc
1650	—	80.00	135	250	500	—
1652	—	80.00	135	250	500	—
1654	—	80.00	135	250	500	—
1655	—	80.00	135	250	500	—
1656	—	80.00	135	250	500	—

KM# 55 DAALDER (Rijks)
Silver **Obv:** Crowned bust of Ferdinand III **Note:** Mint mark: Flower. Dav. #4994.

Date	Mintage	VG	F	VF	XF	Unc
1650	—	100	250	450	700	—

KM# 77 DAALDER (Rijks)
Silver **Obv:** Laureate 1/2 figure holding sword and arms **Rev:** Crowned arms divide date in inner circle **Note:** Dav. #4846.

Date	Mintage	VG	F	VF	XF	Unc
1676	63,960	125	300	550	750	—

KM# 66 DAALDER (Lion)
Silver **Note:** Dav. #4886.

Date	Mintage	VG	F	VF	XF	Unc
1661	—	25.00	50.00	80.00	150	—
1662	—	25.00	50.00	80.00	150	—
1663	—	25.00	50.00	80.00	150	—
1664	—	25.00	50.00	80.00	150	—
1665	—	25.00	60.00	100	175	—
1666	—	25.00	60.00	100	175	—
1667	—	—	—	—	—	—
1674	—	40.00	80.00	160	225	—
1676	—	40.00	80.00	160	225	—
1677	—	25.00	50.00	80.00	150	—
1679	—	40.00	80.00	160	225	—
1685/7	—	25.00	50.00	80.00	150	—
1685	—	—	—	—	—	—
1688/7	—	25.00	50.00	80.00	150	—
1692	—	75.00	150	275	425	—

KM# 59 SILVER DUCAT
28.2500 g., 0.8730 Silver 0.7929 oz. ASW **Note:** Mint mark: Flower.

Date	Mintage	VG	F	VF	XF	Unc
1656 (error, inverted 9)	443,655	60.00	175	260	400	—
1659	—	60.00	175	250	375	—
1660	—	60.00	175	275	450	—

KM# 60 SILVER DUCAT
Silver **Rev. Legend:** CONCORDIA. RES. PARVAE. CRESCVNT. **Note:** Dave. #4921.

Date	Mintage	VG	F	VF	XF	Unc
1659	—	60.00	175	250	400	—
1660	—	60.00	175	250	400	—
1661	—	60.00	175	250	400	—
1662	—	60.00	175	250	400	—
1664	—	150	350	500	750	—
1667	—	60.00	175	250	400	—
1668	—	60.00	175	250	400	—
1669	—	60.00	175	250	400	—

KM# 67 1/2 DUCATON (20 Stuiver)
16.3900 g., 0.9410 Silver 0.4958 oz. ASW **Obv:** Knight with sword on horseback right, city arms below in inner circle
Rev: Crowned arms with crowned lion supporters in innr circle, date at top in legend

Date	Mintage	VG	F	VF	XF	Unc
1661	—	150	300	600	1,000	—

KM# 61 DUCATON (40 Stuiver)
32.7800 g., 0.9410 Silver 0.9917 oz. ASW **Obv:** Knight with sword on horseback right, city arms below in inner circle
Rev: Crowned arms with crowned lion supporters in innr circle, date at top in legend **Note:** Mint mark: Flower. Dav. #4946.

Date	Mintage	VG	F	VF	XF	Unc
1659	262,695	35.00	100	200	400	—
1660	Inc. above	35.00	100	200	400	—

KM# 65.1 DUCATON (40 Stuiver)
Silver **Rev. Legend:** CONCORDIA. RES. PARVAE. CRESCVNT. **Note:** Dav. #4947. Varieties exist.

Date	Mintage	VG	F	VF	XF	Unc
1660	—	35.00	100	175	350	—
1661	—	25.00	60.00	150	300	—
1662	—	25.00	60.00	150	300	—

Date	Mintage	VG	F	VF	XF	Unc
1663	—	25.00	60.00	150	300	—
1664	—	25.00	60.00	100	200	—
1665	—	25.00	60.00	100	200	—
1666	—	25.00	60.00	100	200	—
1667	—	25.00	60.00	100	200	—
1668	—	25.00	70.00	125	250	—
1669	—	35.00	100	175	350	—
1670	—	35.00	100	175	350	—
1671	—	35.00	100	175	350	—
1674	—	35.00	100	175	350	—
1675	—	30.00	70.00	150	300	—
1676	—	30.00	70.00	150	300	—
1677	—	25.00	60.00	125	250	—
1682	—	25.00	60.00	150	300	—
1686	—	35.00	70.00	175	350	—

KM# 65.2 DUCATON (40 Stuiver)

Silver **Rev. Legend:** CONCORDIA - RES - PARVAE - CRESCVNT **Note:** Struck with special dies by C. Adolphi.

Date	Mintage	VG	F	VF	XF	Unc
1662 Proof	—	Value: 1,500				

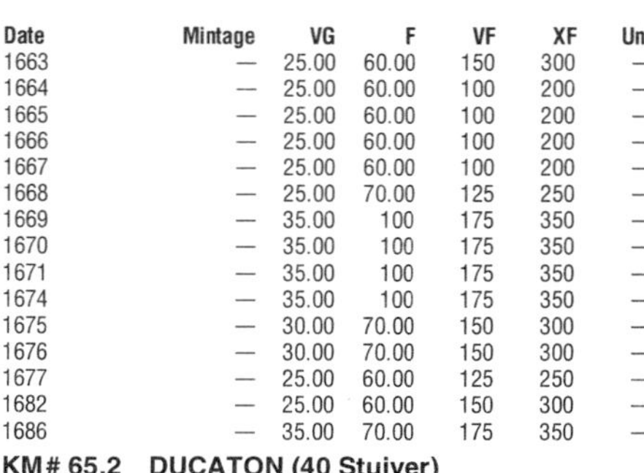

KM# 11 FLORIN D'OR

3.5000 g., 0.9860 Gold 0.1109 oz. AGW **Obv:** Helmeted arms in innr circle **Rev:** Crowned imperial eagle in inner circle, titles of Rudolf II

Date	Mintage	VG	F	VF	XF	Unc
ND(1590-1612)	—	125	200	350	700	—

KM# 49 1/2 CAVALIER D'OR

5.0000 g., 0.9200 Gold 0.1479 oz. AGW **Obv:** Equestrian figure of knight above arms in inner circle **Rev:** Crowned arms in inner circle, date at top **Note:** Fr. #215.

Date	Mintage	VG	F	VF	XF	Unc
1644	—	500	1,500	3,000	7,000	—

KM# 51 CAVALIER D'OR

10.0000 g., 0.9200 Gold 0.2958 oz. AGW **Note:** FR. # 214.

Date	Mintage	VG	F	VF	XF	Unc
1644	—	—	—	6,500	10,000	—

TRADE COINAGE

KM# 12 DUCAT

3.5000 g., 0.9860 Gold 0.1109 oz. AGW **Obv:** Titles of Rudolf II **Rev:** 5-line inscription in tablet. **Note:** FR. #211.

Date	Mintage	VG	F	VF	XF	Unc
ND(1590-1612)	—	120	150	200	300	—

KM# 30 DUCAT

3.5000 g., 0.9860 Gold 0.1109 oz. AGW **Obv:** 5-line inscription in tablet **Rev:** Titles of Ferdinand II **Note:** Fr. #213.

Date	Mintage	VG	F	VF	XF	Unc
1630	—	120	150	225	350	—
1631	—	120	150	225	350	—
1632	—	120	150	225	350	—
1633	—	120	150	225	350	—
1634	—	120	150	225	350	—
1636	—	120	150	225	350	—
1637	—	120	150	225	350	—
1638	—	120	150	225	350	—

KM# 34 DUCAT

3.5000 g., 0.9860 Gold 0.1109 oz. AGW **Obv:** 4-line inscription in tablet

Date	Mintage	VG	F	VF	XF	Unc
1633	—	120	150	225	350	—
1634	—	120	150	225	350	—
1636	—	120	150	225	350	—
1638	—	130	200	300	500	—
1639	—	120	150	225	350	—
1640	—	120	150	225	350	—
1641/1461	—	120	150	225	350	—
1641	—	120	150	225	350	—
1642	—	120	150	225	350	—
1644	—	120	150	225	350	—
1645	—	120	150	225	350	—
1646	—	120	150	200	350	—
1647	—	120	150	200	350	—
1648	—	130	200	300	500	—
1649	—	120	150	200	350	—
1650	—	120	150	200	350	—
1652	—	120	150	200	350	—
1653	—	120	150	200	350	—
1654	—	120	150	200	350	—
1655	—	120	150	200	350	—
1656	—	120	150	200	300	—
1659	—	120	150	200	300	—
1660/50	—	120	150	200	300	—
1660	—	120	150	200	300	—
1661	—	130	200	300	500	—
1662	—	120	150	200	300	—
1676/5	—	150	300	600	1,000	—
1676	—	150	300	600	1,000	—

KM# 68 DUCAT

3.5000 g., 0.9860 Gold 0.1109 oz. AGW **Rev:** Titles of Ferdinand III, date in legend **Note:** Fr. # 213.

Date	Mintage	VG	F	VF	XF	Unc
1662	—	130	200	350	700	—
1664	—	130	200	350	700	—
1666	—	120	200	300	400	—
1668	—	120	150	200	300	—
1674	—	130	250	400	800	—

KM# 58.1 2 DUCAT

7.0000 g., 0.9860 Gold 0.2219 oz. AGW **Obv:** 5-line inscription in tablet **Rev:** Standing figure of knight to right divides date in inner circle **Note:** Fr. # 212.

Date	Mintage	VG	F	VF	XF	Unc
1655	—	200	400	800	1,300	—
1656	—	200	400	800	1,300	—
1662	—	200	400	800	1,300	—

KM# 58.2 2 DUCAT

7.0000 g., 0.9860 Gold 0.2219 oz. AGW **Obv:** 4-line inscription in tablet **Rev:** Standing figure of knight to right divides date in inner circle **Note:** Fr. #212.

Date	Mintage	VG	F	VF	XF	Unc
1662	—	—	—	1,500	2,500	—

KM# 47 10 DUCAT (Portugaleser)

35.0000 g., 0.9860 Gold 1.1095 oz. AGW **Obv:** Crowned arms in inner circle, double circled legend **Rev:** Cross in inner circle

Date	Mintage	VG	F	VF	XF	Unc
1641 Rare	—	—	—	—	—	—

PATTERNS

Including off metal strikes

KM#	Date	Mintage	Identification	Mkt Val
Pn1	ND(1601)	—	Arendschelling. Silver. KM#15. Klippe.	800
Pn2	1677	—	Schelling. Gold. 14.0000 g. KM#75.	—

PIEFORTS

KM#	Date	Mintage	Identification	Mkt Val
P1	1637	—	Lion Daalder. Silver. KM#36.	—
PA2	(16)39	—	Duit. Copper. KM37	—
P2	1648	—	Lion Daalder. Silver. KM#46. Klippe.	3,000
P3	1650	—	Rijksdaalder. Silver. KM#55.	3,000
P4	1653	—	Rijksdaalder. Silver. KM#55.	—
P5	1660	—	Silver Ducat. KM#60.	—
P6	1664	—	Ducaton. Silver. KM#65.1.	—
P7	1682	—	3 Gulden. Silver. KM#86.	3,000
P8	1685	—	Ryderschelling. KM#87. Klippe.	900

NETHERLANDS EAST INDIES

The Republic of Indonesia, the world's largest archipelago, extends for more than 3,000 miles (4,827 km.) along the equator from the mainland of Southeast Asia to Australia. The 17,508 islands comprising the archipelago have a combined area of 788,425 sq. mi. (1,919,440 sq.km.) and a population of 205 million, including East Timor.

Portuguese traders established posts in the 16th century, but they were soon outnumbered by the Dutch who arrived in 1596 and gradually asserted control over the islands comprising present-day Indonesia. Dutch dominance, interrupted by British incursions during the Napoleonic Wars, established the Netherlands East Indies as one of the richest colonial possessions in the world.

The VOC (United East India Company) struck coins and emergency issues for the Indonesian Archipelago and for the islands at various mints in the Netherlands and the islands. In 1798 the VOC was subsumed by the Dutch government, which issued VOC type transitional and regal types during the Batavian Republic and the Kingdom of the Netherlands until independence.

RULERS

United East India Company, 1602-1799

UNITED AMSTERDAM COMPANY

COLONIAL COINAGE

KM# 5 1/4 REAL

0.8100 g., 0.9170 Silver 0.0239 oz. ASW **Obv:** Crowned Holland arms with one dot on each side **Rev:** Crowned Amsterdam arms with lion supporters

Date	Mintage	VG	F	VF	XF	Unc
ND(1601) 16 known	—	150	375	500	700	—

KM# 6 1/2 REAL

1.7100 g., 0.9170 Silver 0.0504 oz. ASW **Obv:** Crowned Holland arms with 2 dots at each side **Obv. Legend:** INSIGNIA • HOLLANDIAE **Rev:** Crowned Amsterdam arms with lion supporters **Rev. Legend:** ET • CIVITATIS • AMSTELREDAMEMSIS

Date	Mintage	VG	F	VF	XF	Unc
ND(1601) 21 known	—	250	600	850	1,000	—

KM# 7 REAL

3.4100 g., 0.9170 Silver 0.1005 oz. ASW **Obv:** Crowned Holland arms with four dots at each side **Obv. Legend:** INSIGNIA • HOLLANDIAE **Rev:** Crowned Amsterdam arms with lion supporters

Date	Mintage	VG	F	VF	XF	Unc
1601 17 known	—	350	1,000	1,700	2,000	—

KM# 8 2 REALS (Quarter Daalder)

6.8300 g., 0.9170 Silver 0.2014 oz. ASW **Obv:** Crowned Holland arms with "I" at each side **Obv. Legend:** INSIGNIA • HOLLANDIAE **Rev:** Crowned Amsterdam arms with lion supporters **Rev. Legend:** ET • CIVITATIS • AMSTELREDAMENSIS

Date	Mintage	VG	F	VF	XF	Unc
1601 18 known	—	500	1,500	2,000	2,500	—

KM# 9 4 REALS (Half Daalder)
13.6500 g., 0.9170 Silver 0.4024 oz. ASW **Ruler:** United East India Company **Obv:** Crowned Holland arms with "II" at each side **Obv. Legend:** INSIGNIA • HOLLANDIAE **Rev:** Crowned Amsterdam arms with lion supporters **Rev. Legend:** ET • CIVITATIS • AMSTELREDAMENSIS

Date	Mintage	VG	F	VF	XF	Unc
1601 22 known	—	850	1,900	2,500	3,400	—

KM# 10 8 REALS (Daalder)
27.3100 g., 0.9170 Silver 0.8051 oz. ASW **Ruler:** United East India Company **Obv:** Crowned Holland arms with "IIII" at each side **Obv. Legend:** INSIGNIA • HOLLANDIAE **Rev:** Crowned Amsterdam arms with lion supporters **Rev. Legend:** ET • CIVITATIS • AMSTELREDAMENSIS **Note:** Dav. #413.

Date	Mintage	VG	F	VF	XF	Unc
1601 22 known	—	2,000	4,000	6,500	10,000	—

Note: Ira and Larry Goldberg Goodman sale 6-02, XF or better realized $12,650.

UNITED ZEELAND COMPANY

COLONIAL COINAGE

KM# 20 8 REALS (Daalder)
Silver **Ruler:** United East India Company **Obv:** Garnished arms of Zeeland and nobility in inner circle **Obv. Legend:** MONE • ARG • ORDI • ZEELANDIAE **Rev:** Crowned arms of Zeeland divide value, date above crown **Rev. Legend:** LVCTOR • ET EMERGO **Note:** Dav. #414. Only five examples known.

Date	Mintage	VG	F	VF	XF	Unc
1602 Rare	10,800	—	—	—	—	—

Note: Spink Zurich Salvesen sale 10-88, VF realized $22,780

UNITED EAST INDIA COMPANY

CAST COINAGE

Emergency Issue

KM# 30 1/4 STUIVER
Cast Copper **Obv:** Upright sword of Batavia **Rev:** Value above VOC monogram

Date	Mintage	VG	F	VF	XF	Unc
1644	—	150	225	320	450	—

KM# 31 1/2 STUIVER
Cast Copper **Obv:** Upright sword of Batavia in inner circle, date at top in legend **Rev:** Value above VOC monogram

Date	Mintage	VG	F	VF	XF	Unc
1644	—	45.00	85.00	150	275	—

KM# 32 12 STUIVERS (1/4 Daalder)
6.0500 g., 0.9990 Cast Silver 0.1943 oz. **Obv:** Arms of Batavia in inner circle, date at top in legend **Rev:** Value above VOC monogram

Date	Mintage	VG	F	VF	XF	Unc
1645 Rare	—	—	—	—	—	—

KM# 33 24 STUIVERS (1/2 Daalder)
12.1100 g., 0.9990 Cast Silver 0.3889 oz. **Obv:** Arms of Batavia in inner circle, date at top in legend **Rev:** Value above VOC monogram

Date	Mintage	VG	F	VF	XF	Unc
1645 Rare	—	—	—	—	—	—

Note: Laurens Schulman Auction #104-93 XF realized $10,425

KM# 34 48 STUIVERS (Daalder)
24.2239 g., 0.9990 Cast Silver 0.7780 oz. **Obv:** Arms of Batavia in inner circle, date at top in legend **Rev:** Value above VOC monogram **Note:** Dav. #415.

Date	Mintage	VG	F	VF	XF	Unc
1645 Rare	—	—	—	—	—	—

Note: D.A.P. Coins private sale 3-89 XF $32,000

COUNTERMARKED COINAGE

1686-1692

KM# 27 1/2 DUCATOON
Silver **Countermark:** Knight on horseback riding left **Note:** Circular or square indent countermark on Brabant 1/2 Ducatoon.

CM Date	Host Date	Good	VG	F	VF	XF
ND(1686-92)	1638 Unique	—	—	—	—	—
ND(1686-92)	1640 Unique	—	—	—	—	—

KM# 35 1/2 DUCATOON
Silver **Countermark:** Knight on horseback riding left **Note:** Circular or square indent countermark on Antwerp 1/2 Ducatoon.

CM Date	Host Date	Good	VG	F	VF	XF
ND(1686-92)	1649 Unique	—	—	—	—	—

KM# 41 1/2 DUCATOON
Silver **Countermark:** Knight on horseback riding left **Note:** Circular or square indent countermark on Zeeland 1/2 Ducatoon.

CM Date	Host Date	Good	VG	F	VF	XF
ND(1686-92)	1662 Unique	—	—	—	—	—

KM# 40 DUCATOON
Silver **Countermark:** Knight on horseback riding left **Note:** Dav. #416. Circular or square indent countermark on Spanish Netherlands, Brabant Ducatoon, Dav. #4444.

CM Date	Host Date	Good	VG	F	VF	XF
ND(1686-92)	1631 Unique	—	—	—	—	—

KM# 45 DAALDER
Silver **Countermark:** Knight on horseback riding left **Note:** Dav. #416. Circular or square indent countermark on Friesland Eagle Daalder, Dav. #8811.

CM Date	Host Date	Good	VG	F	VF	XF
ND(1686-92)	1584 Rare	—	—	—	—	—

COUNTERMARKED COINAGE

1687

KM# 43 STUIVER
Silver **Countermark:** Swimming lion **Note:** Countermark on Zeeland Stuiver, KM#50.

CM Date	Host Date	Good	VG	F	VF	XF
ND(1687)	1681-85 Unique	—	—	—	—	—

COUNTERMARKED COINAGE

1690

KM# 42 10 RIXDALER
17.7300 g., Gold And Silver **Countermark:** Rampant lion facing left in square **Note:** .857 Gold/.143 Silver. Countermark on Japan Keicho Koban, Fr. #9.1.

CM Date	Host Date	Good	VG	F	VF	XF
ND(1690)	1673-95 Rare	—	—	—	—	—

Note: 6 examples are known, four of which reside in the British Museum. The debased Genroku Koban would not have met the gold content standard for this host type. Counterfeit Kobans and debased Genroku Kobans were used as hosts for private imitations of the official Rampant Lion countermark

COUNTERMARKED COINAGE

1693-1694

KM# 44 RUPEE
11.4400 g., 0.9840 Silver 0.3619 oz. ASW **Countermark:** Knight on horseback riding left **Note:** Shield or square indent countermark on India Rupee of Mughul Emperor Aurangzeb Alamgir, Surat Mint, KM#300.86.

CM Date	Host Date	Good	VG	F	VF	XF
1693-94	ND(AH1102)/34	—	200	325	475	750
1693-94	ND(AH1104)/36	—	200	325	475	750
1693-94	ND(AH1104)/37	—	200	325	475	750
1693-94	ND(AH1105)/38	—	200	325	475	750

BENCULEN

Bengkulu

The British established a settlement at Benculen on the southwest coast of Sumatra in 1684. By 1685 they had built Fort York and solidified their hold on the region, setting up a healthy trade in pepper and other spices. This burgeoning outpost was moved three miles to the south with the construction of Fort Marlborough in 1714.

BRITISH EAST INDIA COMPANY

FT. YORK ISSUES

KM# 1 CASH
Copper **Obv:** Bale mark **Rev:** Anglish Kompany

Date	Mintage	VG	F	VF	XF	Unc
ND(1687) Rare	—	—	—	—	—	—
ND(1695) Rare	—	—	—	—	—	—

KM# 2 FANAM

1.0600 g., Silver **Obv:** Bale mark **Rev:** Anglish Kompany

Date	Mintage	VG	F	VF	XF	Unc
ND(1693) Rare	—	—	—	—	—	—

KM# 4 2 FANAMS

2.1600 g., Silver **Obv:** Bale mark **Rev:** Anglish Kompany

Date	Mintage	VG	F	VF	XF	Unc
ND(1695) Rare	—	—	—	—	—	—

KM# 3 3 FANAMS

Silver

Date	Mintage	VG	F	VF	XF	Unc
ND(1693) Rare	—	—	—	—	—	—

JAVA

LOCAL COINAGE

A mountainous island, 661 miles long by 124 miles at widest part, in greater Sunda island group. Early cultural influence from India. Islam introduced in late 1400's. Java was mainly a Dutch possession from 1619 to 1947 with the exception of a few periods of British occupation, principally 1811-1816.

MONETARY SYSTEM

4 Duit = 1 Stiver
30 Stivers = 1 Rupee (Silver)
66 Stivers = 1 Dollar

DATING SYSTEM

The coins listed are found with AD (Christian) dates, AD and AH (Hejira) dates, and with AD, AH and AS (Aji Saka = Javanese) dates which are explained in the introduction in this catalog.

UNITED EAST INDIA COMPANY

COUNTERMARKED COINAGE

1760

By order of the home authorities of the Company the countermarking of Ducats was stopped in 1761. Countermark: Java in Arabic in circular indent.

KM# 168 RUPEE

11.4400 g., 0.9840 Silver 0.3619 oz. ASW **Countermark:** *Java*"
Note: Prev. KM#44. Countermark on Rupee, KM#44.

CM Date	Host Date	Good	VG	F	VF	XF
ND	1693-94//38 Rare	—	—	—	—	—

NORWAY

The Kingdom of Norway (*Norge, Noreg*) is located in northwestern Europe, has an area of 150,000sq. mi. (324,220 sq. km.), including the island territories of Spitzbergen (Svalbard) and Jan Mayen

A united Norwegian kingdom was established in the 9th century, the era of the indomitable Norse Vikings who ranged far and wide, visiting the coasts of northwestern Europe, the Mediterranean, Greenland and North America. In the 13th century the Norse kingdom was united briefly with Sweden, then passed through inheritance in 1380 to the rule of Denmark which was maintained until 1814. In 1814 Norway fell again under the rule of Sweden. The union lasted until 1905 when the Norwegian Parliament arranged a peaceful separation and invited a Danish prince (King Haakon VII) to ascend the throne of an independent Kingdom of Norway.

RULER

Danish, until 1814

MINT MARK

(h) - Crossed hammers – Kongsberg

MINT OFFICIALS' INITIALS

Christiania, 1628-1695

Initial	Date	Name
FG, bottle (b)	1651-59	Frederik Gruner
FG, clover leaf on hill (c)	1659-94	Frederik Gruner
PG, clover leaf on hill	1643-50	Peter Gruner
(C) Clover leaf	1628-42	Anders Pedersen
(R) Rose	1643	Anders Pedersen

Kongsberg, 1686-

Initial	Date	Name
HCM plus Flower (f)	1687-1718	Henning Christofer Meyer
IAR		Angrid Austlid Rise, engraver

Lettered Edges for Kongsberg Mint

Number	Edges
1	HAEC BOREAS CYMBRO FERT ORNAMENTO LABORUM
2	DET KLIPPERNE YDER VOR BERGMAND UDBRYDER HVA HYTTEN DA GYDER AF MYNTEN VI NYDER
3	DANNER KONGIS NORDSKE FIELDE SLIGE FRUGTER HAR I VAELDE
4	I DETTE ANSIGT DANNEMARK OG NORGE SKUER SIN MONARK
5	NICHT AUS SILBER-SUCHT DIESE NORDENS-FRUCHT WIRD ZU GOTTES EHR GESUCHT
6	STORE KONGE NORDENS AERE LAD DE FRUGTER YNDIG VAERE SOM DIG NORSKE KLIPPER BAERE VAERE SOM DIG NORSKE
7	SAADAN NORDENS SKAT GUD GIEMTE TIL KONG CHRISTIAN DEND FEMTE

MONETARY SYSTEM

Until 1794

96 Skilling = 1 Speciedaler

KINGDOM

STANDARD COINAGE

KM# 133 1/2 SKILLING

0.7500 g., 0.1250 Silver 0.0030 oz. ASW **Obv:** Lion **Rev:** 1/2 SKILING/DANSKE/ year

Date	Mintage	VG	F	VF	XF	Unc
1676	262,000	75.00	150	250	550	—

KM# 149 1/2 SKILLING

0.7300 g., 0.1250 Silver 0.0029 oz. ASW **Obv:** Lion **Rev:** 1 HAL SKILING/DANSKE/ year

Date	Mintage	VG	F	VF	XF	Unc
1682	64,000	200	350	600	1,500	—

KM# 23 SKILLING

0.9200 g., 0.1560 Silver 0.0046 oz. ASW **Obv:** Crowned lion
Obv. Legend: CHRISTIAN... **Rev:** 1/SKILI/NGDA/NSK
Note: Legend varieties exist.

Date	Mintage	VG	F	VF	XF	Unc
1643 (c)	207,000	45.00	100	175	350	—
1644 (c)	205,000	45.00	100	175	350	—
1645 (c) Unique	—	—	—	—	—	—
1646 (c)	47,000	40.00	75.00	150	300	—
1647 (c)	123,000	40.00	75.00	150	300	—
1648 (c)	255,000	40.00	75.00	150	300	—

KM# 29 SKILLING

0.9200 g., 0.1560 Silver 0.0046 oz. ASW **Rev. Legend:** NOR GOT REX...

Date	Mintage	VG	F	VF	XF	Unc
1649 (c)	1,074,000	15.00	25.00	70.00	200	—
1650 (c)	Inc. above	15.00	25.00	70.00	200	—
1651 (b)	Inc. above	15.00	25.00	70.00	200	—
1652 (b)	372,000	15.00	25.00	70.00	200	—
1653 (b)	419,000	15.00	25.00	70.00	200	—
1654 (b)	262,000	15.00	25.00	70.00	200	—
1655 (b)	484,000	15.00	25.00	70.00	200	—
1656 (b)	554,000	15.00	25.00	70.00	200	—
1657 (b)	368,000	15.00	25.00	70.00	200	—
1658 (b)	475,000	15.00	25.00	70.00	200	—
1659 (b) Rare	—	—	—	—	—	—
1659	359,000	15.00	25.00	70.00	200	—
1660	376,000	15.00	25.00	70.00	200	—
1661	259,000	15.00	25.00	70.00	200	—
1662	211,000	—	25.00	70.00	200	—
1663	229,000	15.00	25.00	70.00	200	—
1664	305,000	15.00	25.00	70.00	200	—
1665	175,000	15.00	25.00	70.00	200	—
1666	157,000	15.00	25.00	70.00	200	—
1667	175,000	15.00	25.00	70.00	200	—
1668	112,000	15.00	25.00	70.00	200	—
1669	208,000	15.00	25.00	70.00	200	—
1670 Rare; only 3 known	55,000	—	—	—	—	—

KM# 90 SKILLING

0.9200 g., 0.1560 Silver 0.0046 oz. ASW **Obv:** Lion
Rev: NOR/VAN/GOT/REX.

Date	Mintage	VG	F	VF	XF	Unc
1670	31,000	65.00	100	250	500	—

KM# 91 SKILLING

0.8100 g., 0.1560 Silver 0.0041 oz. ASW **Obv:** Lion
Rev: DAN/NOR/VAN/GOT

Date	Mintage	VG	F	VF	XF	Unc
1670	Inc. above	100	225	500	900	—

KM# 130 SKILLING

0.8100 g., 0.2500 Silver 0.0065 oz. ASW **Rev:** 1/SKILLING/ DANSKE/ year

Date	Mintage	VG	F	VF	XF	Unc
1675 (ch)	402,000	30.00	50.00	100	250	—
1682 PG	26,000	200	350	625	—	—

KM# 152 SKILLING

1.1100 g., 0.1880 Silver 0.0067 oz. ASW **Obv:** Crowned C5 monogram

Date	Mintage	VG	F	VF	XF	Unc
1686	14,000	125	250	600	1,200	—
1687	77,000	75.00	150	350	750	—

KM# 159 SKILLING

1.1100 g., 0.1880 Silver 0.0067 oz. ASW **Obv:** Crowned script C5 monogram

Date	Mintage	VG	F	VF	XF	Unc
1687	Inc. above	65.00	150	300	600	—
1688	41,000	60.00	125	275	550	—

KM# 173 SKILLING

1.1100 g., 0.1880 Silver 0.0067 oz. ASW

Date	Mintage	VG	F	VF	XF	Unc
1688	Inc. above	50.00	100	250	500	—
1690	23,000	50.00	100	250	500	—
1691	72,000	35.00	75.00	200	400	—
1692	15,000	100	200	425	725	—
1693	18,000	35.00	75.00	200	400	—
1694	10,000	50.00	100	250	500	—
1695	26,000	50.00	100	250	500	—
1696	36,000	50.00	100	250	500	—
1697	20,000	100	200	425	725	—
1698	12,000	50.00	100	250	500	—
1699	40,000	50.00	100	250	500	—

KM# 205 SKILLING

1.1100 g., 0.1880 Silver 0.0067 oz. ASW **Obv:** Crowned monogram **Rev:** Value, crossed hammers divides date below

Date	Mintage	VG	F	VF	XF	Unc
1700	21,000	75.00	200	425	800	—

KM# 20 2 SKILLING

0.5900 g., 0.8750 Silver 0.0166 oz. ASW **Obv:** Crowned lion
Rev: II/SKILIN/G:DANS/year **Note:** Legend varieties exist.

Date	Mintage	VG	F	VF	XF	Unc
1641 (f)	13,000	35.00	70.00	130	300	—
1642 (f)	91,000	20.00	40.00	80.00	150	—

KM# 24 2 SKILLING

1.3000 g., 0.2810 Silver 0.0117 oz. ASW **Rev:** II/SKILI/ NGDA/NSK in inner circle **Note:** Legend varieties exist.

Date	Mintage	VG	F	VF	XF	Unc
1643 (c)	60,000	20.00	40.00	80.00	175	—
1644 (c)	170,000	17.50	35.00	70.00	150	—
1646 (c)	17,000	20.00	40.00	80.00	175	—
1647 (c)	245,000	15.00	30.00	60.00	120	—
1648 (c)	302,000	15.00	30.00	60.00	120	—

KM# 30 2 SKILLING

1.3000 g., 0.2810 Silver 0.0117 oz. ASW
Obv. Legend: FRIDERIC III... **Note:** Legend varieties exist.

Date	Mintage	VG	F	VF	XF	Unc
1649 (c)	913,000	7.00	20.00	55.00	150	—
1650 (c)	Inc. above	7.00	20.00	55.00	150	—
1651 (b)	Inc. above	7.00	20.00	55.00	150	—
1651 (c)	Inc. above	25.00	75.00	150	425	—
1652 (b)	244,000	7.00	20.00	55.00	150	—
1653 (b)	247,000	7.00	20.00	55.00	150	—
1654 (b)	421,000	7.00	20.00	55.00	150	—
1655 (b)	336,000	7.00	20.00	55.00	150	—
1656 (b)	286,000	7.00	20.00	55.00	150	—
1657 (b)	332,000	7.00	20.00	55.00	150	—
1658 (b)	299,000	7.00	20.00	55.00	150	—
1659 (b)	—	100	225	—	—	—
1659 (b+ch)	—	100	225	—	—	—
1659 (ch)	283,000	7.00	20.00	55.00	150	—
1660	351,000	7.00	20.00	55.00	150	—
1660 (ch)	Inc. above	7.00	20.00	55.00	150	—
1661	479,000	7.00	20.00	55.00	150	—
1662	554,000	7.00	20.00	55.00	150	—
1663	634,000	7.00	20.00	55.00	150	—

Date	Mintage	VG	F	VF	XF	Unc
1664	497,000	7.00	20.00	55.00	150	—
1665	473,000	7.00	20.00	55.00	150	—
1666	440,000	7.00	20.00	55.00	150	—
1667	496,000	7.00	20.00	55.00	150	—

KM# 82 2 SKILLING

1.3000 g., 0.2810 Silver 0.0117 oz. ASW **Obv:** Crowned lion with shield

Date	Mintage	VG	F	VF	XF	Unc
1667	Inc. above	200	350	700	1,400	—
1668	Inc. above	200	350	700	1,400	—

KM# 85 2 SKILLING

1.2200 g., 0.2810 Silver 0.0110 oz. ASW **Obv:** Crowned lion in inner circle **Note:** Legend varieties exist.

Date	Mintage	VG	F	VF	XF	Unc
1668	491,000	7.00	22.50	50.00	125	—
1669	708,000	7.00	22.50	50.00	125	—
1670	116,000	7.00	22.50	50.00	125	—

KM# 92 2 SKILLING

1.2200 g., 0.2810 Silver 0.0110 oz. ASW **Obv. Legend:** CHRISTIAN... **Rev:** II/SKILL/INGDA/NSK in inner circle

Date	Mintage	VG	F	VF	XF	Unc
1670	88,000	12.00	25.00	75.00	225	—
1671	—	25.00	65.00	150	400	—
1672 Rare	—	—	—	—	—	—

KM# 114 2 SKILLING

1.3000 g., 0.2810 Silver 0.0117 oz. ASW **Rev:** II/SKILLING/ DANSKE/year

Date	Mintage	VG	F	VF	XF	Unc
1673 (ch)	43,000	60.00	125	275	550	—
1673 FG	195,000	70.00	140	300	600	—

KM# 115 2 SKILLING

1.0900 g., 0.4060 Silver 0.0142 oz. ASW **Obv:** Crowned C5 monogram **Rev:** II/SKILLING/DANSKE/year divided by lion

Date	Mintage	VG	F	VF	XF	Unc
1673	151,000	15.00	50.00	125	325	—

KM# 116 2 SKILLING

1.0900 g., 0.4060 Silver 0.0142 oz. ASW **Rev:** Lion

Date	Mintage	VG	F	VF	XF	Unc
1673 Rare	—	—	—	—	—	—

KM# 131 2 SKILLING

1.0900 g., 0.4060 Silver 0.0142 oz. ASW

Date	Mintage	VG	F	VF	XF	Unc
1675 (ch)	272,000	7.00	22.50	50.00	140	—
1676 (ch)	95,000	7.00	22.50	50.00	140	—
1677 (ch)	89,000	10.00	27.50	75.00	150	—
1678 (ch)	370,000	7.00	22.50	50.00	140	—
1679 (ch)	499,000	10.00	27.50	75.00	140	—
1680 (ch)	528,000	7.00	22.50	50.00	140	—
1681 (ch)	441,000	7.00	22.50	50.00	140	—
1682 (ch)	331,000	7.00	22.50	50.00	140	—
1682 PG	Inc. above	10.00	27.50	75.00	150	—
1683 PG	246,000	7.00	22.50	50.00	140	—

KM# 135 2 SKILLING

2.7800 g., 0.1250 Silver 0.0112 oz. ASW **Obv:** Crowned C5 monogram

Date	Mintage	VG	F	VF	XF	Unc
1677 (ch)	89,000	75.00	200	325	750	—

KM# 151 2 SKILLING

1.2200 g., 0.3440 Silver 0.0135 oz. ASW **Rev:** II/SKILLING/ DANSKE/year divided by lion

Date	Mintage	VG	F	VF	XF	Unc
1684 PG	214,000	10.00	25.00	90.00	250	—
1685 PG	586,000	10.00	25.00	90.00	250	—
1686 PG	231,000	15.00	30.00	110	275	—

KM# 153 2 SKILLING

1.2200 g., 0.3440 Silver 0.0135 oz. ASW **Obv:** Crowned double C5 monogram **Rev:** Crowned arms in rectangular shield dividing date **Note:** Varieties exist.

Date	Mintage	VG	F	VF	XF	Unc
1686	—	30.00	60.00	200	550	—
1687	503,000	15.00	30.00	60.00	200	—

KM# 160 2 SKILLING

1.2200 g., 0.3440 Silver 0.0135 oz. ASW **Obv:** Crowned double CV monogram **Note:** Varieties exist.

Date	Mintage	VG	F	VF	XF	Unc
1687	Inc. above	20.00	50.00	175	600	—
1688	660,000	17.50	40.00	135	400	—

KM# 161 2 SKILLING

1.2200 g., 0.3440 Silver 0.0135 oz. ASW **Obv:** Crowned double CV monogram, date below

Date	Mintage	VG	F	VF	XF	Unc
1687	Inc. above	80.00	225	525	1,000	—

KM# 174 2 SKILLING

1.2200 g., 0.3440 Silver 0.0135 oz. ASW **Obv:** Crowned ornate double C5 monogram **Rev:** Lion in circle **Note:** Varieties exist.

Date	Mintage	VG	F	VF	XF	Unc
1688	Inc. above	15.00	30.00	75.00	225	—
1689	728,000	10.00	20.00	55.00	175	—
1690	898,000	10.00	20.00	50.00	150	—
1691	959,000	10.00	20.00	40.00	135	—
1692	334,000	10.00	20.00	50.00	150	—
1693	306,000	12.50	20.00	55.00	175	—
1694	370,000	10.00	30.00	75.00	225	—
1695	357,000	12.50	20.00	50.00	150	—
1696	371,000	10.00	30.00	75.00	225	—
1697	455,000	10.00	20.00	55.00	175	—
1698	396,000	10.00	20.00	50.00	150	—
1699	483,000	10.00	20.00	50.00	150	—

KM# 206 2 SKILLING

1.2200 g., 0.3440 Silver 0.0135 oz. ASW **Obv:** Crowned double F4 monogram

Date	Mintage	VG	F	VF	XF	Unc
1700	613,000	10.00	22.50	65.00	300	—

KM# 21.1 4 SKILLING

1.1800 g., 0.8750 Silver 0.0332 oz. ASW **Obv:** Crowned lion **Rev:** IIII/SKILI/NGDA/NS

Date	Mintage	Good	VG	F	VF	XF
1641 (f)	12,000	50.00	85.00	175	350	—
1642 (f)	90,000	25.00	50.00	110	225	—

KM# 21.2 4 SKILLING

1.1800 g., 0.8750 Silver 0.0332 oz. ASW **Rev:** SCKILING DANSK

Date	Mintage	Good	VG	F	VF	XF
1641 (f)	Inc. above	—	—	—	—	—

KM# 21.1a 4 SKILLING

1.1700 g., 0.7500 Silver 0.0282 oz. ASW **Note:** Mint mark: Cloverleaf.

Date	Mintage	Good	VG	F	VF	XF
1643 (c) Rare	—	—	—	—	—	—

KM# 136 4 SKILLING

5.8500 g., 0.1250 Silver 0.0235 oz. ASW **Obv:** Crowned C5 monogram **Rev:** IIII/SKILLING/DANSKE/year

Date	Mintage	VG	F	VF	XF	Unc
1677	128,000	45.00	80.00	175	450	—

KM# 22 8 SKILLING (1/2 Mark)

2.3900 g., 0.8750 Silver 0.0672 oz. ASW **Note:** Similar to KM#26.1. Legend varieties exist.

Date	Mintage	VG	F	VF	XF	Unc
1641 (f)	3,100	90.00	200	425	900	—
1642 (f)	17,000	65.00	125	250	600	—

KM# 22a 8 SKILLING (1/2 Mark)

2.3400 g., 0.7500 Silver 0.0564 oz. ASW

Date	Mintage	VG	F	VF	XF	Unc
1643 (c)	42,000	30.00	75.00	150	400	—

KM# 26.1 8 SKILLING (1/2 Mark)

2.3400 g., 0.7500 Silver 0.0564 oz. ASW **Obv:** Mintmaster's initials

Date	Mintage	VG	F	VF	XF	Unc
1644 (c)	80,000	200	400	700	—	—

KM# 26.2 8 SKILLING (1/2 Mark)

2.3400 g., 0.7500 Silver 0.0564 oz. ASW **Obv:** Mintmaster's initials **Rev:** Mintmaster's initials

Date	Mintage	VG	F	VF	XF	Unc
1644 (c)	Inc. above	110	250	500	—	—

KM# 26.3 8 SKILLING (1/2 Mark)

2.3400 g., 0.7500 Silver 0.0564 oz. ASW **Rev:** Mintmaster's initials **Note:** Legend varieties exist.

Date	Mintage	VG	F	VF	XF	Unc
1644 (c)	Inc. above	25.00	50.00	125	300	—

KM# 31 8 SKILLING (1/2 Mark)

2.7800 g., 0.6720 Silver 0.0601 oz. ASW

Date	Mintage	VG	F	VF	XF	Unc
1649 (c)	—	50.00	100	250	575	—
1650 (c)	—	100	200	400	800	—
1651 (c)	—	50.00	100	250	575	—
1651 (b)	—	50.00	100	250	575	—
1652 (b)	—	50.00	100	250	575	—
1653 (b)	—	65.00	125	250	600	—
1654 (b)	—	65.00	125	250	600	—
1655 (b)	—	65.00	125	250	600	—
1656 (b)	—	65.00	125	250	600	—
1657 (b)	—	110	225	450	800	—
1658 (b)	—	40.00	100	250	575	—
1659 (ch)	—	45.00	80.00	200	500	—
1660 (ch)	—	45.00	90.00	200	500	—
Note: Crown breaks inner circle						
1660 (ch)	—	45.00	90.00	185	400	—
Note: Crown within inner circle						
1661	—	45.00	100	250	450	—
1661	—	45.00	90.00	250	450	—
1663 (ch)	—	90.00	150	300	650	—
1665	—	50.00	100	200	500	—
1668	—	125	250	550	1,200	—

KM# 93 8 SKILLING (1/2 Mark)

2.6600 g., 0.6670 Silver 0.0570 oz. ASW **Obv:** Crowned C5 monogram within inner circle **Rev:** Crowned lion within inner circle, date in legend

Date	Mintage	VG	F	VF	XF	Unc
1670	—	100	225	450	900	—

KM# 93a 8 SKILLING (1/2 Mark)

2.7800 g., 0.6720 Silver 0.0601 oz. ASW

Date	Mintage	VG	F	VF	XF	Unc
1672	—	100	225	500	1,200	—
1675	—	125	250	500	1,200	—

KM# 145 8 SKILLING (1/2 Mark)

2.7800 g., 0.6720 Silver 0.0601 oz. ASW **Obv:** Crowned C5 monogram divides date **Rev:** Lion within branches **Note:** Varieties exist.

Date	Mintage	VG	F	VF	XF	Unc
1681	—	90.00	175	350	800	—
1682 PG	—	85.00	165	350	800	—
1683 PG	—	85.00	165	285	700	—
1685 PG	—	165	325	650	1,400	—
1689 PG	—	200	400	800	1,750	—

KM# 207 8 SKILLING (1/2 Mark)

3.0600 g., 0.5620 Silver 0.0553 oz. ASW **Obv:** Bust of Frederic IV, right **Rev:** Crown

Date	Mintage	VG	F	VF	XF	Unc
1700 (f)	423,000	10.00	25.00	55.00	135	—

KM# 27 16 SKILLING (1 Mark)

5.5700 g., 0.5930 Silver 0.1062 oz. ASW **Obv:** Crowned C4 monogram **Rev:** IUSTUS/"Jehovah"/IUDEX

Date	Mintage	VG	F	VF	XF	Unc
1644 (c)	45,000	35.00	70.00	175	425	—
1645 (c)	48,000	45.00	90.00	200	450	—
1646 (c)	9,475	45.00	90.00	200	450	—
1647 (c)	7,707	50.00	100	225	525	—

KM# 32.1 16 SKILLING (1 Mark)

5.5700 g., 0.6720 Silver 0.1203 oz. ASW **Obv. Legend:** ...DANSK

Date	Mintage	VG	F	VF	XF	Unc
1648 Unique	—	—	—	—	—	—
1649 (c)	—	30.00	60.00	125	300	—
1650 (c)	—	30.00	60.00	125	300	—
1651 (b)	—	30.00	60.00	125	300	—
1651 (c)	—	65.00	130	250	575	—
1652 (b)	—	30.00	60.00	125	300	—
1653 (b)	—	30.00	60.00	125	300	—
1654 (b)	—	30.00	60.00	125	300	—
1655 (b)	—	30.00	60.00	125	300	—
1656 (b)	—	30.00	60.00	125	300	—
1657 (b)	—	30.00	60.00	125	300	—
1658 (b)	—	30.00	60.00	125	300	—
1659 (b)	—	65.00	130	300	650	—
1659 (ch)	—	45.00	90.00	175	425	—
1660 (ch)	—	45.00	90.00	175	425	—
1660	—	45.00	90.00	175	425	—
1661	—	45.00	90.00	175	425	—

KM# 32.2 16 SKILLING (1 Mark)

5.5700 g., 0.6720 Silver 0.1203 oz. ASW **Obv. Legend:** ...DANSKE

Date	Mintage	VG	F	VF	XF	Unc
1648 Unique	—	—	—	—	—	—
1663 (ch)	—	65.00	130	250	575	—
1663 Rare	—	—	—	—	—	—
Note: Inverted N in DOMINVS						
ND(1663)	—	175	350	700	1,500	—
1665 (ch)	—	35.00	70.00	140	350	—

Date	Mintage	VG	F	VF	XF	Unc
1666 (ch) PROUIDEBIT	—	35.00	70.00	140	350	—
1667 (ch)	—	35.00	70.00	140	350	—
1668 (ch)	—	35.00	70.00	140	350	—
1669 (ch)	—	40.00	80.00	160	400	—

KM# 94 16 SKILLING (1 Mark)
5.3100 g., 0.6670 Silver 0.1139 oz. ASW

Date	Mintage	VG	F	VF	XF	Unc
1670	—	100	250	475	1,200	—

KM# 94a 16 SKILLING (1 Mark)
5.5700 g., 0.6720 Silver 0.1203 oz. ASW

Date	Mintage	VG	F	VF	XF	Unc
1671	—	125	250	500	1,100	—
1673	—	125	250	500	1,100	—
1674	—	900	1,300	2,250	—	—
1675	—	75.00	150	300	750	—
1676	—	75.00	150	300	750	—
1679	—	125	250	425	950	—

KM# 146 MARK (16 Skilling)
5.5700 g., 0.6720 Silver 0.1203 oz. ASW **Obv:** Crowned C5 monogram divides date **Rev:** Crowned lion between laurel branches

Date	Mintage	VG	F	VF	XF	Unc
1681	—	100	175	425	950	—
1681 PG Unique	—	—	—	—	—	—
1682 PG	—	100	175	425	950	—
1683 PG	—	165	350	700	1,200	—
1684	—	100	175	425	950	—
1685 PG	—	165	350	700	1,200	—
1686 PG	—	165	350	700	1,200	—

KM# 155 MARK (16 Skilling)
5.5700 g., 0.6720 Silver 0.1203 oz. ASW **Obv:** Crowned, more ornate monogram

Date	Mintage	VG	F	VF	XF	Unc
1686 Rare	—	—	—	—	—	—

KM# 154 MARK (16 Skilling)
5.5700 g., 0.6720 Silver 0.1203 oz. ASW **Obv:** Crowned double C5 monogram **Rev:** Crowned lion in shield with rectangular sides **Note:** Varieties exist.

Date	Mintage	VG	F	VF	XF	Unc
1686	—	125	250	500	1,000	—

KM# 162 MARK (16 Skilling)
5.5700 g., 0.6720 Silver 0.1203 oz. ASW **Rev:** Crowned lion in shield with oval sides divides HC M **Note:** Varieties exist.

Date	Mintage	VG	F	VF	XF	Unc
1687 HCM	—	125	250	500	1,000	—

KM# 175 MARK (16 Skilling)
5.5700 g., 0.6720 Silver 0.1203 oz. ASW **Rev:** Crowned lion, smaller shield

Date	Mintage	VG	F	VF	XF	Unc
1688 HCM	—	175	350	700	1,400	—

KM# 176 MARK (16 Skilling)
5.5700 g., 0.6720 Silver 0.1203 oz. ASW **Obv:** More ornate monogram **Rev:** Crowned lion within laurel branches, HCM inside branches

Date	Mintage	VG	F	VF	XF	Unc
1688 HCM	—	400	800	1,600	3,500	—

KM# 185.1 MARK (16 Skilling)
5.5700 g., 0.6720 Silver 0.1203 oz. ASW **Rev:** HCM outside branches **Edge:** Plain

Date	Mintage	VG	F	VF	XF	Unc
1689 HCM	—	275	550	1,100	2,250	—
1690 HCM Rare	—	—	—	—	—	—

KM# 185.2 MARK (16 Skilling)
5.5700 g., 0.6720 Silver 0.1203 oz. ASW **Edge:** Milled
Note: Edge varieties exist.

Date	Mintage	VG	F	VF	XF	Unc
1691 HCM	—	175	350	700	1,400	—
1692 HCM	—	85.00	175	350	700	—
1693 HCM Rare	—	—	—	—	—	—
1694 HCM	—	100	200	400	850	—
1695 HCM	—	100	200	400	850	—
1697 HCM	—	85.00	175	350	700	—
1698 HCM	—	85.00	175	350	700	—
1699 HCM Rare	—	—	—	—	—	—

KM# 197 MARK (16 Skilling)
4.5000 g., 0.8330 Silver 0.1205 oz. ASW **Obv:** Portrait of Christian V **Rev:** Crown

Date	Mintage	VG	F	VF	XF	Unc
1699 HCM(f)	—	150	300	600	1,200	—

KM# 28 2 MARK
11.1400 g., 0.5930 Silver 0.2124 oz. ASW **Obv:** Crowned C4 monogram **Rev:** IUSTUS/"Jehova"/IUDEX

Date	Mintage	VG	F	VF	XF	Unc
1644 WM	—	45.00	90.00	225	525	—
1644 (c)	—	45.00	70.00	200	450	—
1645 (c)	—	50.00	100	250	550	—
1646 (c)	—	70.00	140	300	700	—
1647 (c)	—	75.00	150	300	775	—

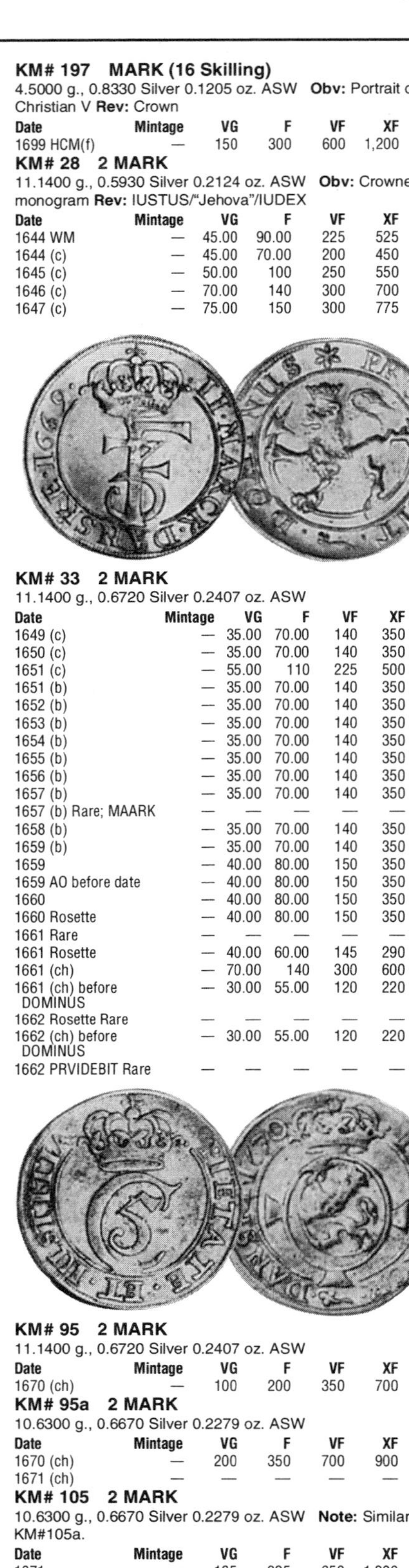

KM# 33 2 MARK
11.1400 g., 0.6720 Silver 0.2407 oz. ASW

Date	Mintage	VG	F	VF	XF	Unc
1649 (c)	—	35.00	70.00	140	350	—
1650 (c)	—	35.00	70.00	140	350	—
1651 (c)	—	55.00	110	225	500	—
1651 (b)	—	35.00	70.00	140	350	—
1652 (b)	—	35.00	70.00	140	350	—
1653 (b)	—	35.00	70.00	140	350	—
1654 (b)	—	35.00	70.00	140	350	—
1655 (b)	—	35.00	70.00	140	350	—
1656 (b)	—	35.00	70.00	140	350	—
1657 (b)	—	35.00	70.00	140	350	—
1657 (b) Rare; MAARK	—	—	—	—	—	—
1658 (b)	—	35.00	70.00	140	350	—
1659 (b)	—	35.00	70.00	140	350	—
1659	—	40.00	80.00	150	350	—
1659 AO before date	—	40.00	80.00	150	350	—
1660	—	40.00	80.00	150	350	—
1660 Rosette	—	40.00	80.00	150	350	—
1661 Rare	—	—	—	—	—	—
1661 Rosette	—	40.00	60.00	145	290	—
1661 (ch)	—	70.00	140	300	600	—
1661 (ch) before DOMINUS	—	30.00	55.00	120	220	—
1662 Rosette Rare	—	—	—	—	—	—
1662 (ch) before DOMINUS	—	30.00	55.00	120	220	—
1662 PRVIDEBIT Rare	—	—	—	—	—	—

KM# 95 2 MARK
11.1400 g., 0.6720 Silver 0.2407 oz. ASW

Date	Mintage	VG	F	VF	XF	Unc
1670 (ch)	—	100	200	350	700	—

KM# 95a 2 MARK
10.6300 g., 0.6670 Silver 0.2279 oz. ASW

Date	Mintage	VG	F	VF	XF	Unc
1670 (ch)	—	200	350	700	900	—
1671 (ch)	—	—	—	—	—	—

KM# 105 2 MARK
10.6300 g., 0.6670 Silver 0.2279 oz. ASW **Note:** Similar to KM#105a.

Date	Mintage	VG	F	VF	XF	Unc
1671	—	165	325	650	1,300	—

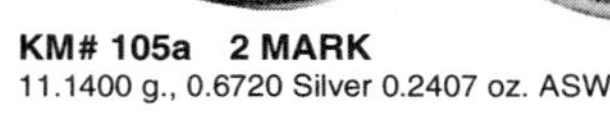

KM# 105a 2 MARK
11.1400 g., 0.6720 Silver 0.2407 oz. ASW

Date	Mintage	VG	F	VF	XF	Unc
1672	—	135	275	500	1,150	—
1673 Rare	—	—	1,500	2,300	—	—
Note: Four known						
1674 Rare	—	—	1,650	2,500	—	—
Note: Two known						

KM# 147 2 MARK
11.1400 g., 0.6720 Silver 0.2407 oz. ASW **Obv:** Crowned C5 monogram divides date **Rev:** Lion between laurel branches

Date	Mintage	VG	F	VF	XF	Unc
1681	—	500	950	2,000	3,500	—

KM# 150 2 MARK
11.1400 g., 0.6720 Silver 0.2407 oz. ASW **Rev:** Lion divides PG

Date	Mintage	VG	F	VF	XF	Unc
1682 PG Rare	—	—	1,750	2,800	—	—
Note: Three known						
1683 PG Rare	—	—	1,750	2,800	—	—
Note: Three known						
1685 PG	—	900	1,500	2,300	4,500	—

KM# 156 2 MARK
11.1400 g., 0.6720 Silver 0.2407 oz. ASW **Obv:** Crowned double monogram **Rev:** Crowned arms in rectangular shield **Note:** Varieties exist.

Date	Mintage	VG	F	VF	XF	Unc
1686	—	300	600	1,250	2,500	—

KM# 165 2 MARK
11.1400 g., 0.6720 Silver 0.2407 oz. ASW **Obv:** Ornate double monogram **Rev:** Crossed hammers mint mark **Note:** Varieties exist.

Date	Mintage	VG	F	VF	XF	Unc
1687 HCM	—	250	650	1,250	2,500	—

KM# 163 2 MARK
11.1400 g., 0.6720 Silver 0.2407 oz. ASW **Rev:** Crowned arms in shield with bowed sides divide HCM

Date	Mintage	VG	F	VF	XF	Unc
1687 HCM Rare	—	—	—	—	—	—

KM# 164 2 MARK
11.1400 g., 0.6720 Silver 0.2407 oz. ASW **Rev:** Crowned arms in smaller shield

Date	Mintage	VG	F	VF	XF	Unc
1687 HCM Rare	—	—	—	—	—	—

KM# 166 2 MARK
11.1400 g., 0.6720 Silver 0.2407 oz. ASW **Rev:** Without mint mark

Date	Mintage	VG	F	VF	XF	Unc
1687 HCM Rare	—	—	—	—	—	—

KM# 177 2 MARK
11.1400 g., 0.6720 Silver 0.2407 oz. ASW **Rev:** Star instead of rosette

Date	Mintage	VG	F	VF	XF	Unc
1688 HCM Rare	—	—	—	—	—	—

KM# 178 2 MARK
11.1400 g., 0.6720 Silver 0.2407 oz. ASW **Obv:** Crowned more ornate double monogram **Rev:** Crowned lion with HCM inside laurel branches

Date	Mintage	VG	F	VF	XF	Unc
1688 HCM	—	—	—	—	—	—

KM# 179.1 2 MARK
11.1400 g., 0.6720 Silver 0.2407 oz. ASW **Rev:** HCM outside laurel branches **Edge:** Milled

Date	Mintage	VG	F	VF	XF	Unc
1688 HCM Rare	—	—	—	—	—	—
1689 HCM	—	600	1,200	2,500	4,000	—
1693 HCM	—	600	1,200	2,500	4,000	—
1695 HCM	—	500	1,000	2,000	3,750	—
1697 HCM	—	500	1,000	2,000	3,750	—
1698 HCM	—	600	1,200	2,500	4,000	—
1699 HCM	—	600	1,200	2,500	4,000	—

KM# 179.2 2 MARK
11.1400 g., 0.6720 Silver 0.2407 oz. ASW **Edge:** Plain

Date	Mintage	VG	F	VF	XF	Unc
1690 HCM Rare	—	—	—	—	—	—
1691 HCM Rare	—	—	—	—	—	—
1692 HCM	—	500	1,000	2,000	3,750	—
1693 HCM	—	350	700	1,500	3,000	—
1694 HCM	—	500	1,000	2,000	3,750	—
1696 HCM	—	600	1,200	2,500	4,000	—

KM# 198 2 MARK
8.9900 g., 0.8330 Silver 0.2408 oz. ASW **Obv:** Portrait of Christian V **Rev:** Crown

Date	Mintage	VG	F	VF	XF	Unc
1699 HCM(f)	—	150	300	600	1,200	—

KM# 208 2 MARK
8.9900 g., 0.8330 Silver 0.2408 oz. ASW

Date	Mintage	VG	F	VF	XF	Unc
1700 (f)	—	200	425	950	1,800	—

KM# 96 4 MARK (1 Krone)
22.2700 g., 0.6720 Silver 0.4811 oz. ASW **Note:** Dav. #3662. Edge varieties exist.

Date	Mintage	VG	F	VF	XF	Unc
1669 FG	—	900	1,750	3,350	6,500	—
1670 FG	—	50.00	100	200	400	—
1670 EG 3 known	—	650	1,000	1,500	—	—
1671 FG	—	50.00	100	200	400	—
1671 Rare	—	750	1,150	1,850	—	—
1672 FG	—	50.00	100	200	400	—
1673 FG	—	50.00	100	200	400	—
1674 FG	—	90.00	180	350	700	—
1676 PG	—	100	200	400	850	—
1677 PG	—	80.00	160	325	700	—
1678 PG	—	50.00	100	200	400	—
1679 PG	—	50.00	100	200	400	—
1680 PG	—	50.00	100	200	400	—

KM# 96a 4 MARK (1 Krone)
21.2600 g., 0.6720 Silver 0.4593 oz. ASW

Date	Mintage	VG	F	VF	XF	Unc
1670 FG Rare	—	—	—	—	—	—
1671 FG Rare	—	—	—	—	—	—

KM# 148.1 4 MARK (1 Krone)
22.2700 g., 0.6720 Silver 0.4811 oz. ASW **Note:** Dav. #3663.

Date	Mintage	VG	F	VF	XF	Unc
1681 PG	—	50.00	100	200	400	—
1682 PG	—	50.00	100	200	400	—
1683 PG	—	50.00	100	200	400	—
1684 PG	—	50.00	100	200	400	—
1685 PG	—	90.00	180	350	700	—
1686 PG	—	165	325	650	1,425	—
1687 PG	—	65.00	130	250	575	—
1688 PG	—	65.00	130	250	575	—
1689 PG	—	55.00	115	225	425	—
1690 PG	—	55.00	115	225	425	—
1691 PG	—	55.00	115	225	425	—
1692 PG	—	65.00	130	250	575	—
1693 PG	—	50.00	100	200	450	—
1694 PG	—	50.00	100	200	450	—
1695 PG	—	—	1,800	2,800	—	—

KM# 148.2 4 MARK (1 Krone)
11.1400 g., 0.6720 Silver 0.2407 oz. ASW **Obv:** Crowned C5 in cartouche, lions **Rev:** Cross

Date	Mintage	VG	F	VF	XF	Unc
1683 PG	—	175	500	900	2,000	—

KM# A148.2 4 MARK (1 Krone)
22.2700 g., 0.6720 Silver 0.4811 oz. ASW **Obv:** Crowned C5 monogram in inner circle

Date	Mintage	VG	F	VF	XF	Unc
1683 PG	—	45.00	90.00	165	420	—

KM# 158 4 MARK (1 Krone)
22.2700 g., 0.6720 Silver 0.4811 oz. ASW **Obv:** More ornate double monogram

Date	Mintage	VG	F	VF	XF	Unc
1686	—	285	575	1,100	2,200	—

KM# 157 4 MARK (1 Krone)
22.2700 g., 0.6720 Silver 0.4811 oz. ASW **Obv:** Crowned double C5 monogram **Rev:** Crowned lion in shield with rectangular sides **Note:** Varieties exist.

Date	Mintage	VG	F	VF	XF	Unc
1686	56,000	150	300	550	1,100	—

KM# 167 4 MARK (1 Krone)
22.2700 g., 0.6720 Silver 0.4811 oz. ASW **Note:** Varieties exist.

Date	Mintage	VG	F	VF	XF	Unc
1687	44,000	150	300	550	1,150	—

KM# 168 4 MARK (1 Krone)
22.2700 g., 0.6720 Silver 0.4811 oz. ASW **Obv:** Star before "PIETATE" **Note:** Dav. #3665. Edge varieties exist.

Date	Mintage	VG	F	VF	XF	Unc
1687 Rare	—	—	—	—	—	—

KM# 169 4 MARK (1 Krone)
22.2700 g., 0.6720 Silver 0.4811 oz. ASW **Obv:** Smaller shield dividing HC M **Note:** Dav. #3665A. Varieties exist.

Date	Mintage	VG	F	VF	XF	Unc
1687 HCM	—	175	350	500	900	—
1688 HCM Rare	—	—	—	—	—	—

KM# 170 4 MARK (1 Krone)
22.2700 g., 0.6720 Silver 0.4811 oz. ASW **Obv:** Star before "PIETATE"

Date	Mintage	VG	F	VF	XF	Unc
1687 HCM Rare	—	—	—	—	—	—

KM# 171 4 MARK (1 Krone)
22.2700 g., 0.6720 Silver 0.4811 oz. ASW **Rev:** Crowned Danish coat of arms

Date	Mintage	VG	F	VF	XF	Unc
1687 Rare	—	—	—	—	—	—

KM# 182 4 MARK (1 Krone)
22.2700 g., 0.6720 Silver 0.4811 oz. ASW **Obv:** Point instead of mint mark

Date	Mintage	VG	F	VF	XF	Unc
1688 HCM Rare	—	—	—	—	—	—

KM# 180 4 MARK (1 Krone)
22.2700 g., 0.6720 Silver 0.4811 oz. ASW **Obv:** More ornate double monogram, flower after "JUSTITIA"

Date	Mintage	VG	F	VF	XF	Unc
1688 HCM Rare	26,000	—	—	—	—	—

KM# 183 4 MARK (1 Krone)
22.2700 g., 0.6720 Silver 0.4811 oz. ASW **Rev:** Divided HCM outside laurel branches **Note:** Dav. #3666.

Date	Mintage	VG	F	VF	XF	Unc
1688 HCM(f) Rare	—	—	—	—	—	—
1689 HCM(f)	19,000	70.00	140	275	550	—
1690 HCM(f)	14,000	70.00	140	275	550	—
Note: Edge varieties exist						
1691 HCM(f)	16,000	175	350	700	1,400	—
1692 HCM(f)	19,000	90.00	175	350	800	—
Note: Edge varieties exist						
1693 HCM(f)	25,000	65.00	125	250	600	—
1694 HCM(f)	27,000	65.00	125	250	600	—
1695 HCM(f)	29,000	70.00	140	275	600	—
Note: Edge varieties exist						
1696 HCM(f)	45,000	65.00	125	250	525	—
1697 HCM(f)	76,000	65.00	125	250	525	—
1698 HCM(f)	65,000	65.00	125	250	525	—
1699 HCM(f)	56,000	70.00	140	275	550	—

KM# 181 4 MARK (1 Krone)
22.2700 g., 0.6720 Silver 0.4811 oz. ASW **Rev:** Crowned lion and HCM within laurel branches **Note:** Vareieties exist.

Date	Mintage	VG	F	VF	XF	Unc
1688 HCM	—	90.00	170	320	620	—

KM# 199 4 MARK (1 Krone)
17.9900 g., 0.8330 Silver 0.4818 oz. ASW **Obv:** Portrait of Christian V **Rev:** Crown **Note:** Dav. #3648.

Date	Mintage	VG	F	VF	XF	Unc
1699 HCM(f)	—	125	250	450	750	—

KM# 200.1 4 MARK (1 Krone)
17.9900 g., 0.8330 Silver 0.4818 oz. ASW **Rev:** Swedish, Danish, and Norwegian arms in ovals **Edge Lettering:** ET NORDENS LYYS GIK UD. ET ANDET TAENDTE GUD

Date	Mintage	VG	F	VF	XF	Unc
1699 (f)	—	300	650	1,300	2,500	—
1700 (f)	—	—	—	—	—	—

KM# 200.2 4 MARK (1 Krone)

17.9900 g., 0.8330 Silver 0.4818 oz. ASW
Edge Lettering: SERVANT ET DECORANT

Date	Mintage	VG	F	VF	XF	Unc
1700 (F)	17,000	125	275	550	1,100	—

KM# 5 1/8 SPECIE DALER

3.2500 g., 0.9690 Silver 0.1012 oz. ASW **Obv:** Crowned portrait **Rev:** Lion **Note:** See 1 Specie daler, KM#8 for mintage information

Date	Mintage	VG	F	VF	XF	Unc
1628 (f)	—	325	600	1,100	2,000	—
1629 (f)	—	225	450	800	1,500	—

KM# 9 1/8 SPECIE DALER

3.6500 g., 0.8820 Silver 0.1035 oz. ASW **Note:** Varieties exist.

Date	Mintage	VG	F	VF	XF	Unc
1629 (f)	—	200	375	725	1,500	—
1630 (f)	—	150	300	700	1,500	—
1631 (f)	—	150	300	700	1,500	—
1632 (f)	—	150	300	700	1,500	—
1633 (f) Unique	—	—	—	—	—	—
1634 (f)	—	—	1,100	2,200	—	—
1635 (f) Unique	—	—	—	—	—	—
1636 (f)	—	—	1,100	2,200	—	—
1637 (f)	—	—	1,100	2,200	—	—
1638 (f)	—	—	1,100	2,200	—	—
1639 (f)	—	150	400	950	1,250	—
1640 (f)	—	300	325	650	1,600	—
1641 (f)	—	165	600	950	1,450	—
1642 (f)	—	300	400	700	1,900	—
1643 (c) before FAC	—	175	400	700	1,500	—
1643 (c) after FAC Rare	—	—	—	—	—	—
1643 (c) Rare	—	—	—	—	—	—
1646 PG(c)	—	—	1,100	2,200	—	—
1647 (PG(c)	—	—	1,100	2,200	—	—

KM# 34 1/8 SPECIE DALER

3.5900 g., 0.8750 Silver 0.1010 oz. ASW, 27 mm. **Rev:** Lion with two tails **Note:** Larger planchet.

Date	Mintage	VG	F	VF	XF	Unc
1649 PG(c) Rare	—	—	—	—	—	—
1650 PG(c) Rare	—	—	—	—	—	—

KM# 49 1/8 SPECIE DALER

3.6000 g., 0.8750 Silver 0.1013 oz. ASW, 25 mm. **Rev:** Lion in smaller circle **Note:** Smaller planchet.

Date	Mintage	VG	F	VF	XF	Unc
1654 FG(b) Rare	—	—	—	—	—	—

KM# 60 1/8 SPECIE DALER

3.6000 g., 0.8750 Silver 0.1013 oz. ASW **Obv:** Crowned facing portrait without inner circle **Rev:** Lion with one tail within laurel branches

Date	Mintage	VG	F	VF	XF	Unc
1660 FG Rare	—	—	—	—	—	—

KM# 62 1/8 SPECIE DALER

3.6000 g., 0.8750 Silver 0.1013 oz. ASW **Obv:** Different crowned facing portrait in inner circle **Rev:** Lion in inner circle

Date	Mintage	VG	F	VF	XF	Unc
1661 FG	—	500	850	2,000	3,000	—

KM# 63 1/8 SPECIE DALER

3.6000 g., 0.8750 Silver 0.1013 oz. ASW **Rev:** Lion within laurel branches

Date	Mintage	VG	F	VF	XF	Unc
1661 FG Rare	—	—	—	—	—	—

KM# 68 1/8 SPECIE DALER

3.6000 g., 0.8750 Silver 0.1013 oz. ASW

Date	Mintage	VG	F	VF	XF	Unc
1663 FG	—	400	950	1,750	3,000	—

KM# 71 1/8 SPECIE DALER

3.6000 g., 0.8750 Silver 0.1013 oz. ASW **Rev:** Lion within crowned oval shield

Date	Mintage	VG	F	VF	XF	Unc
1665	—	350	700	1,400	2,500	—

KM# 104 1/8 SPECIE DALER

3.6100 g., 0.8750 Silver 0.1016 oz. ASW **Obv:** Laureate bust of Christian V **Rev:** Lion in crowned shield

Date	Mintage	VG	F	VF	XF	Unc
1671	—	250	500	1,000	2,000	—

KM# 6 1/4 SPECIE DALER

6.5000 g., 0.9690 Silver 0.2025 oz. ASW **Note:** See 1 Specie daler, KM#8 for mintage information.

Date	Mintage	VG	F	VF	XF	Unc
1628 (f)	—	250	625	1,275	2,600	—
1629 (f)	—	350	700	1,500	3,000	—

KM# 10 1/4 SPECIE DALER

7.3100 g., 0.8820 Silver 0.2073 oz. ASW **Note:** Varieties exist.

Date	Mintage	VG	F	VF	XF	Unc
1629 (f)	—	175	350	700	1,400	—
1630 (f)	—	175	350	700	1,400	—
1631 (f)	—	175	350	750	1,600	—
1632 (f)	—	175	350	750	1,600	—
1633 (f)	—	175	350	750	1,600	—
1634 (f)	—	175	350	700	1,400	—
1635 (f)	—	175	350	700	1,400	—
1636 (f)	—	175	350	700	1,600	—
1637 (f)	—	175	350	700	1,600	—
1638 (f)	—	175	350	700	1,400	—
1639 (f)	—	175	350	700	1,400	—
1640 (f)	—	175	350	700	1,400	—
1641 (f)	—	175	350	700	1,400	—
1642 (f)	—	175	350	700	1,400	—
1643 (f)	—	350	500	900	2,000	—
1643 (c)	—	225	450	900	2,000	—
1646 PG(c)	—	225	450	900	2,000	—
1647 PG(c)	—	225	450	900	2,000	—

KM# 10a 1/4 SPECIE DALER

7.1800 g., 0.8750 Silver 0.2020 oz. ASW

Date	Mintage	VG	F	VF	XF	Unc
1648 PG(c)	—	175	325	550	1,200	—
1648 PG	—	175	325	550	1,200	—

KM# 35 1/4 SPECIE DALER

7.1800 g., 0.8750 Silver 0.2020 oz. ASW **Obv:** Crowned bust of Frederick III **Rev:** Crowned lion with two tails whithin inner circle

Date	Mintage	VG	F	VF	XF	Unc
1649 PG(c)	—	600	950	1,750	3,500	—
1650 PG(c)	—	600	950	1,800	3,500	—
1651 FG(b)	—	600	950	1,800	3,500	—

KM# 45.1 1/4 SPECIE DALER

7.1800 g., 0.8750 Silver 0.2020 oz. ASW **Obv:** Small bust wtih drapery **Obv. Legend:** ...DG DA NO VA

Date	Mintage	VG	F	VF	XF	Unc
1652 FG(b)	—	600	900	1,800	3,500	—
1653 FG(b)	—	600	900	1,800	3,500	—
1654 FG(b) 2 known	—	—	—	—	—	—

KM# 45.2 1/4 SPECIE DALER

7.1800 g., 0.8750 Silver 0.2020 oz. ASW **Obv. Legend:** ...DG DA NO V G REX

Date	Mintage	VG	F	VF	XF	Unc
1655 FG(b) 3 known	—	—	—	—	—	—
1656 FG(b) 2 known	—	—	—	—	—	—

KM# 69 1/4 SPECIE DALER

7.1800 g., 0.8750 Silver 0.2020 oz. ASW **Obv:** Large bust **Rev:** Lion with one tail within laurel branches

Date	Mintage	VG	F	VF	XF	Unc
1663 FG Unique	—	—	—	—	—	—

KM# 106 1/4 SPECIE DALER

7.2200 g., 0.8750 Silver 0.2031 oz. ASW **Obv:** Laureate bust **Rev:** Lion in crowned oval shield divides date

Date	Mintage	VG	F	VF	XF	Unc
1671 FG	—	1,800	3,000	4,500	7,500	—
1675 FG Only 4 known	—	—	—	—	—	—

KM# 7 1/2 SPECIE DALER

12.9900 g., 0.9690 Silver 0.4047 oz. ASW **Note:** Similar to KM#11 but without legend in inner circle around bust. See 1 Specie daler, KM#8 for mintage information.

Date	Mintage	VG	F	VF	XF	Unc
1628 (f)	—	1,100	1,800	3,250	4,500	—
1629 (f) Rare	—	—	—	—	—	—

KM# 11 1/2 SPECIE DALER

14.6200 g., 0.8820 Silver 0.4146 oz. ASW

Date	Mintage	VG	F	VF	XF	Unc
1629 (f)	—	650	1,000	2,000	3,300	—
1630 (f)	—	650	1,000	2,000	3,300	—
1631 (f)	—	650	1,000	2,000	3,300	—
1632 (f) Rare	—	—	—	—	—	—
1633 (f)	—	650	1,000	2,000	3,300	—
1634 (f)	—	650	1,000	2,000	3,300	—
1635 (f)	—	650	1,000	2,000	3,300	—
1636 (f) Rare	—	—	—	—	—	—
1637 (f)	—	650	1,000	2,000	3,300	—
1638 (f)	—	650	1,000	2,000	3,300	—
1639 (f)	—	650	1,000	2,000	3,300	—
1640 (f)	—	650	1,000	2,000	3,300	—
1641 (f) DANI NOR Rare	—	—	—	—	—	—
1641 (f) DAN NOR Rare	—	—	—	—	—	—
1642 (f)	—	700	1,200	2,200	3,700	—
1643 (f) Rare	—	—	—	—	—	—
1644 (f) Rare	—	—	—	—	—	—
1644 PG(c) Rare	—	—	—	—	—	—
1645 PG(c) Rare	—	—	—	—	—	—
1646 PG(c)	—	—	—	2,000	—	—
1646 PG Rare	—	600	1,000	2,000	3,500	—
1647 PG	—	600	1,000	2,000	3,500	—
1647 PG(c) Rare	—	600	1,000	2,000	3,500	—

KM# 11a 1/2 SPECIE DALER

14.3600 g., 0.8750 Silver 0.4040 oz. ASW

Date	Mintage	VG	F	VF	XF	Unc
1648 PG(c)	—	600	1,000	2,000	3,500	—
1648 PG	—	600	1,000	2,000	3,500	—

KM# 36 1/2 SPECIE DALER

14.3600 g., 0.8750 Silver 0.4040 oz. ASW **Obv:** Bust of Frederic III **Rev:** Lion with two tails **Note:** Varieties exist.

Date	Mintage	VG	F	VF	XF	Unc
1649 PG(c)	—	1,750	3,250	5,500	8,000	—
1650 PG(c)	—	1,750	3,250	5,500	8,000	—
1651 FG(b)	—	1,750	3,250	5,500	8,000	—
1651 FG(b)	—	1,750	3,250	5,500	8,000	—
1652 FG(b)	—	1,750	3,250	5,500	8,000	—
1653 FG(b)	—	1,750	3,250	5,500	8,000	—

KM# 47 1/2 SPECIE DALER

14.3600 g., 0.8750 Silver 0.4040 oz. ASW **Obv:** Larger bust **Note:** Varieties exist.

Date	Mintage	VG	F	VF	XF	Unc
1653 FG(b)	—	1,750	3,250	5,500	8,000	—
1654 FG(b)	—	1,750	3,250	5,500	8,000	—
1655 FG(b)	—	1,750	3,250	5,500	8,000	—
1656 FG(b)	—	1,750	3,250	5,500	8,000	—

Date	Mintage	VG	F	VF	XF	Unc
1657 FG(b)	—	1,750	3,250	5,500	8,000	—
1658 FG(b)	—	1,750	3,250	5,500	8,000	—

KM# 53 1/2 SPECIE DALER

14.3900 g., 0.8750 Silver 0.4048 oz. ASW **Rev:** Lion with one tail

Date	Mintage	VG	F	VF	XF	Unc
1659 FG	—	2,200	3,700	7,000	10,000	—
1660 FG	—	2,200	3,700	7,000	10,000	—

KM# 72 1/2 SPECIE DALER

14.3900 g., 0.8750 Silver 0.4048 oz. ASW **Obv:** Laureate and cuirassed bust **Rev:** Lion within crowned oval shield
Note: Varieties exist.

Date	Mintage	VG	F	VF	XF	Unc
1665 FG	—	2,000	3,500	6,000	9,500	—
1667 FG	—	2,000	3,500	6,000	9,500	—

KM# 87 1/2 SPECIE DALER

14.3900 g., 0.8750 Silver 0.4048 oz. ASW **Obv:** Draped bust

Date	Mintage	VG	F	VF	XF	Unc
1669 FG	—	2,000	3,500	6,000	9,500	—

KM# 107 1/2 SPECIE DALER

14.4500 g., 0.8750 Silver 0.4065 oz. ASW **Obv:** Laureate bust of Christian V

Date	Mintage	VG	F	VF	XF	Unc
1671 FG Rosettes	—	2,000	3,500	6,000	9,500	—
1673 FG Stars	—	2,000	3,500	6,000	9,500	—
1674 FG Stars, Rare	—	—	—	—	—	—

KM# 191 1/2 SPECIE DALER

14.4500 g., 0.8750 Silver 0.4065 oz. ASW **Rev:** National arms amid eight provincial arms

Date	Mintage	VG	F	VF	XF	Unc
1693 HCM	—	700	1,200	1,800	3,250	—

KM# 4 LION DALAR

Silver **Obv:** Knight behind arms **Rev:** Lion on battle axe **Note:** Dav. #3515. This has come to be considered a Danish coin

Date	Mintage	VG	F	VF	XF	Unc
1608 Rare	—	—	—	—	—	—

KM# 8 SPECIE DALER

25.9800 g., 0.9690 Silver 0.8093 oz. ASW **Note:** Dav. #3529. Mintage figures reflect combined totals of KM#5-8, 1/8 Speciedaler through 1 Speciedaler respectively.

Date	Mintage	VG	F	VF	XF	Unc
1628	Est. 43,000	500	850	1,500	3,000	—
1629	Est. 78,000	700	1,250	2,500	5,500	—

KM# 12 SPECIE DALER

29.2300 g., 0.8820 Silver 0.8288 oz. ASW **Ruler:** Christian IV **Obv:** Bust right **Rev:** Lion left on battle axe divides date
Note: Dav. #3534. Varieties exist in the king's bust and the lion.

Date	Mintage	VG	F	VF	XF	Unc
1629	—	450	750	950	1,800	—
1630	—	450	750	950	1,800	—
1631	53,000	450	750	950	1,800	—
1632	32,000	450	750	950	1,800	—
1633	33,000	450	750	950	1,800	—
1634	39,000	450	750	950	1,800	—
1635	50,000	450	750	950	1,800	—
1636	50,000	450	750	950	1,800	—
1637	57,000	450	750	950	1,800	—
1638	50,000	450	750	950	1,800	—
1639	52,000	450	750	950	1,800	—
1640	50,000	450	750	950	1,800	—
1641	45,000	450	750	950	1,800	—
1642	38,000	450	750	950	1,800	—
1643	7,834	450	800	1,000	1,900	—
1643 (c)	6,206	450	800	1,000	1,900	—
1644 P(c)G	14,000	475	850	1,400	2,600	—
1644 PG	—	475	850	1,400	2,600	—
1645 PG	21,000	450	750	950	1,900	—
1646 PG	55,000	450	750	950	1,900	—
1647 PG	62,000	450	750	950	1,900	—
1648 PG	62,000	450	650	950	1,500	—

KM# 12a SPECIE DALER

28.7200 g., 0.8750 Silver 0.8079 oz. ASW **Obv:** Frederick III

Date	Mintage	VG	F	VF	XF	Unc
1648 PG Rare	55,000	—	—	—	—	—

KM# 37 SPECIE DALER

28.7200 g., 0.8750 Silver 0.8079 oz. ASW **Obv:** Crowned bust of Frederick III **Note:** Dav. #3583.

Date	Mintage	VG	F	VF	XF	Unc
1649 PG(c)	—	400	900	1,400	2,300	—
1650 PG(c)	45,000	400	900	1,400	2,300	—
1651 PG(c) Rare	—	—	—	—	—	—

KM# 40 SPECIE DALER

28.7200 g., 0.8750 Silver 0.8079 oz. ASW **Obv:** Crowned bust of Frederick III with longer hair **Note:** Dav. #3590. Varieties exist.

Date	Mintage	VG	F	VF	XF	Unc
1651 FG(b)	—	400	900	1,400	2,300	—
1652 FG(b)	15,000	400	900	1,400	2,300	—

KM# A46 SPECIE DALER

28.7800 g., 0.8750 Silver 0.8096 oz. ASW **Note:** Dav. #3592. Varieties exist.

Date	Mintage	VG	F	VF	XF	Unc
1652 FG(b) Rare	15,000	—	—	—	—	—
1653 FG(b)	Inc. above	400	900	1,400	2,200	—

KM# 48 SPECIE DALER

28.7800 g., 0.8750 Silver 0.8096 oz. ASW **Obv:** Higher crown **Note:** Dav. #3595.

Date	Mintage	VG	F	VF	XF	Unc
1653 FG(b)	—	350	750	1,200	1,900	—
1654 FG(b)	23,000	350	750	1,200	1,900	—
1655 FG(b)	20,000	350	750	1,200	1,900	—
1656 FG(b)	18,000	500	950	1,400	2,500	—

KM# A41 SPECIE DALER

28.7800 g., 0.8750 Silver 0.8096 oz. ASW **Obv:** Smaller bust in circle, continuous legend **Note:** Dav. #3597.

Date	Mintage	VG	F	VF	XF	Unc
1655 Unique	—	—	—	—	—	—
1656	—	350	750	1,200	1,900	—
1657	—	450	900	1,300	2,200	—

KM# A42 SPECIE DALER

28.7800 g., 0.8750 Silver 0.8096 oz. ASW **Rev:** Smaller lettering, flowers at top **Note:** Dav. #3601. Varieties exist.

Date	Mintage	VG	F	VF	XF	Unc
1657 FG(b)	17,000	500	750	1,150	1,800	—
1658 FG(b)	18,000	550	800	1,250	2,000	—

KM# A43 SPECIE DALER

28.7800 g., 0.8750 Silver 0.8096 oz. ASW **Obv:** Small bust in inner circle **Rev:** Frame border around lion with tail **Note:** Dav. #3603.

Date	Mintage	VG	F	VF	XF	Unc
1658	—	750	1,100	1,800	3,250	—

KM# 51 SPECIE DALER

28.7800 g., 0.8750 Silver 0.8096 oz. ASW **Rev:** Lion with one tail **Note:** Dav. #3604. Varieties exist.

Date	Mintage	VG	F	VF	XF	Unc
1658 (b)	15,000	750	1,100	2,000	3,500	—
1659 FG(b) Rare	—	—	—	—	—	—
1659 FG(f)	—	750	1,100	2,000	3,500	—
1659 FG	—	750	1,100	2,000	3,500	—

KM# 54 SPECIE DALER

28.7800 g., 0.8750 Silver 0.8096 oz. ASW **Note:** Dav. #3607. Varieties exist.

Date	Mintage	VG	F	VF	XF	Unc
1659 FG	—	550	900	1,800	2,500	—
1660 FG	18,000	550	900	1,800	2,500	—
1661 FG	22,000	550	900	1,800	2,500	—
1662 FG	24,000	550	900	1,800	2,500	—

KM# 64 SPECIE DALER

28.7800 g., 0.8750 Silver 0.8096 oz. ASW **Subject:** Akershus Castle in Oslo **Note:** Dav. #3609.

Date	Mintage	VG	F	VF	XF	Unc
ND(1661) Rare	—	—	—	—	—	—

KM# 56 SPECIE DALER

28.7800 g., 0.8750 Silver 0.8096 oz. ASW **Obv:** Large crowned bust **Rev:** Lion in wreath **Note:** Dav. #3611.

Date	Mintage	VG	F	VF	XF	Unc
1661 Unique	—	—	—	—	—	—
1662	—	500	850	1,600	2,850	—

KM# A57 SPECIE DALER

28.7800 g., 0.8750 Silver 0.8096 oz. ASW **Obv:** Bust with bow knot on back and armored sleeve **Note:** Dav. #3614.

Date	Mintage	VG	F	VF	XF	Unc
1662	—	—	—	—	—	—
1663	—	—	—	—	—	—
1664	—	—	—	—	—	—

KM# 58 SPECIE DALER

28.7800 g., 0.8750 Silver 0.8096 oz. ASW **Obv:** Crowned armored bust right in laurel border **Note:** Dav. #3615.

Date	Mintage	VG	F	VF	XF	Unc
1662 Unique	—	—	—	—	—	—

KM# 67 SPECIE DALER

28.7800 g., 0.8750 Silver 0.8096 oz. ASW **Note:** Dav. #3617. Varieties exist.

Date	Mintage	VG	F	VF	XF	Unc
1662 FG	—	565	1,125	2,300	4,150	—
1663 FG	24,000	565	1,125	2,300	4,150	—
1664 FG	—	565	1,125	2,300	4,150	—

KM# 70 SPECIE DALER

28.7800 g., 0.8750 Silver 0.8096 oz. ASW **Obv:** Laureate bust with angels holding crown above **Note:** Dav. #3618.

Date	Mintage	VG	F	VF	XF	Unc
1664 FG	23,000	1,200	2,750	4,250	6,500	—

KM# 59 SPECIE DALER

28.7800 g., 0.8750 Silver 0.8096 oz. ASW **Obv:** Laureate bust without angels, leafy inner circle **Rev:** Crowned Norwegian lion on cross **Note:** Dav. #3619.

Date	Mintage	VG	F	VF	XF	Unc
1665	—	—	—	—	—	—

KM# 73 SPECIE DALER

28.7800 g., 0.8750 Silver 0.8096 oz. ASW **Obv:** Laureate bust within laurel branches **Rev:** Lion in crowned rectangular shield within laurel branches **Note:** Dav. #3621. Varieties exist.

Date	Mintage	VG	F	VF	XF	Unc
1665 FG	19,000	1,200	2,750	4,250	6,500	—

KM# 74 SPECIE DALER

28.7800 g., 0.8750 Silver 0.8096 oz. ASW **Obv:** Laureate and cuirassed bust **Rev:** Lion in crowned oval shield **Note:** Dav. #3623. Varieties exist.

Date	Mintage	VG	F	VF	XF	Unc
1665 FG	—	500	950	1,800	3,000	—
1666 FG	—	—	—	—	—	—
1667 FG	18,000	500	950	1,800	3,000	—

KM# 83 SPECIE DALER

28.7800 g., 0.8750 Silver 0.8096 oz. ASW **Obv:** Laureate, draped bust **Note:** Dav. #3625.

Date	Mintage	VG	F	VF	XF	Unc
1667 FG	32,000	500	950	1,800	3,000	—
1668 FG	12,000	500	950	1,800	3,000	—
1669 FG	13,000	500	950	1,800	3,000	—

KM# 97 SPECIE DALER

28.7800 g., 0.8750 Silver 0.8096 oz. ASW **Obv:** Crowned bust in armor **Rev:** Lion in crowned oval shield, date in legend **Note:** Dav. #3650. Varieties exist.

Date	Mintage	VG	F	VF	XF	Unc
1670 FG	3,149	1,400	2,800	5,300	9,500	—

KM# 98 SPECIE DALER

28.7800 g., 0.8750 Silver 0.8096 oz. ASW **Rev:** Date divided by shield **Note:** Dav. #3650A.

Date	Mintage	VG	F	VF	XF	Unc
1670 FG Rare	—	—	—	—	—	—

KM# 99 SPECIE DALER

28.7800 g., 0.8750 Silver 0.8096 oz. ASW **Obv:** Laureate bust **Rev:** Date in legend **Note:** Dav. #3651.

Date	Mintage	VG	F	VF	XF	Unc
1670 FG 3 known	—	—	—	—	—	—

KM# 108 SPECIE DALER

28.8900 g., 0.8750 Silver 0.8127 oz. ASW **Rev:** Motto within legend **Note:** Dav. #3653.

Date	Mintage	VG	F	VF	XF	Unc
1671 FG	7,728	1,000	1,300	2,700	5,000	—
1672 FG	7,728	700	1,200	2,200	3,500	—

KM# 109 SPECIE DALER

28.7800 g., 0.8750 Silver 0.8096 oz. ASW **Obv:** Laureate bust, Roman style **Rev:** Crown divides rosettes **Note:** Dav. #3656.

Date	Mintage	VG	F	VF	XF	Unc
1671 FG Rare	7,728	800	1,500	3,000	4,500	—
1672 FG	10,000	500	950	2,200	3,700	—
1674 FG	35,000	500	750	1,800	3,200	—

KM# 132 SPECIE DALER

28.7800 g., 0.8750 Silver 0.8096 oz. ASW **Obv:** Draped bust

Date	Mintage	VG	F	VF	XF	Unc
1675 PG	29,000	650	1,100	1,900	3,700	—
1676 PG	31,000	650	1,100	1,900	3,700	—
1677 PG	18,000	900	1,500	3,000	5,500	—
1678 PG	12,000	750	1,300	2,700	5,000	—
1679 PG	16,000	900	1,500	3,000	5,500	—
1680 PG Rare	13,000	—	—	—	—	—

KM# 172 SPECIE DALER

28.8900 g., 0.8750 Silver 0.8127 oz. ASW **Obv:** Cuirassed bust **Rev:** Crowned national arms amid eight provincial arms **Note:** Dav. #3657.

Date	Mintage	VG	F	VF	XF	Unc
1687 HCM 2 known, (1)	—	—	—	—	—	—

KM# 184 SPECIE DALER

28.8900 g., 0.8750 Silver 0.8127 oz. ASW **Obv:** Roman style portrait with long hair **Note:** Dav. #3658.

Date	Mintage	VG	F	VF	XF	Unc
1688 HCM 3 known, (1)	126	—	—	—	—	—
1690 HCM 3 known, (1)	44	—	—	—	—	—

KM# 190 SPECIE DALER

28.8900 g., 0.8750 Silver 0.8127 oz. ASW **Obv:** Laureate Roman style portrait **Note:** Dav. #3659.

Date	Mintage	VG	F	VF	XF	Unc
1692 HCM (1)	—	350	600	950	1,800	—
1692 HCM (2)	—	350	600	950	1,800	—
1692 HCM (3)	13,000	350	600	950	1,800	—
1692 HCM (4), Rare	—	—	—	—	—	—
1692 HCM (5), 2 known	—	—	—	—	—	—
1692 HCM (6)	—	350	600	950	1,800	—
1693 HCM (1)	22,000	350	600	950	1,800	—
1693 HCM (2)	—	350	600	950	1,800	—
1693 HCM (3)	—	350	600	950	1,800	—
1693 HCM (4), 2 known	—	—	—	—	—	—
1693 HCM (6), 2 known	—	—	—	—	—	—

KM# 192 SPECIE DALER

28.8900 g., 0.8750 Silver 0.8127 oz. ASW **Rev:** Crowned arms within Order of the Elephant **Note:** Dav. #3660.

Date	Mintage	VG	F	VF	XF	Unc
1693 HCM (1)	—	1,500	2,500	5,000	7,500	—
1693 HCM (2)	—	1,500	2,500	5,000	7,500	—
1693 HCM (3)	—	1,500	2,500	5,000	7,500	—

KM# 193 SPECIE DALER

28.8900 g., 0.8750 Silver 0.8127 oz. ASW **Obv:** Draped portrait without Order of the Elephant **Note:** Dav. #3661.

Date	Mintage	VG	F	VF	XF	Unc
1693 HCM Unique, (1)	—	—	—	—	—	—
1693 HCM Unique, (2)	—	—	—	—	—	—
1693 HCM Unique, (3)	—	—	—	—	—	—
1694 HCM (1)	—	350	750	1,300	2,500	—
1694 HCM (2)	—	350	750	1,300	2,500	—
1694 HCM (3)	—	350	750	1,300	2,500	—
1694 HCM 4 known, (6)	—	—	—	—	—	—

KM# 194 SPECIE DALER

28.8900 g., 0.8750 Silver 0.8127 oz. ASW **Obv:** Draped portrait with Order of the Elephant

Date	Mintage	VG	F	VF	XF	Unc
1694 HCM (1)	—	250	500	850	1,300	—
1694 HCM (2)	—	250	500	850	1,300	—
1694 HCM (3)	—	250	500	850	1,300	—
1694 HCM (7)	—	250	500	850	1,300	—
1694 HCM 3 known, (4)	—	—	—	—	—	—
1694 HCM 4 known, (6)	—	—	—	—	—	—
1694 HCM Unique, (5)	—	—	—	—	—	—
1695 HCM (1)	—	250	500	850	1,300	—
1695 HCM (2)	—	250	500	850	1,300	—
1695 HCM (3)	—	250	500	850	1,300	—
1695 HCM (7)	—	250	500	850	1,300	—
1695 HCM 2 known, (5)	—	—	—	—	—	—
1695 HCM 3 known, (4)	—	—	—	—	—	—
1695 HCM Unique, (6)	—	—	—	—	—	—
1696 HCM (1)	16,000	250	500	850	1,300	—
1696 HCM (2)	Inc. above	250	500	850	1,300	—
1696 HCM (3)	Inc. above	250	500	850	1,300	—
1696 HCM 3 known, (4)	Inc. above	—	—	—	—	—
1696 HCM 3 known, (6)	Inc. above	—	—	—	—	—

Date	Mintage	VG	F	VF	XF	Unc
1696 HCM 4 known, (5)	Inc. above	—	—	—	—	—
1696 HCM Rare, (7)	Inc. above	250	500	850	1,300	—

KM# 16 1 1/2 SPECIE DALER
Silver **Note:** Similar to 1 Specie Daler, KM#12.

Date	Mintage	VG	F	VF	XF	Unc
1630	—	—	—	—	—	—

KM# 13 2 SPECIE DALER
58.4600 g., 0.8820 Silver 1.6577 oz. ASW **Obv:** Crowned portrait of Christian IV **Rev:** Lion with two tails **Note:** Dav. #3532.

Date	Mintage	VG	F	VF	XF	Unc
1629 (f) Unique	—	—	—	—	—	—
1630 (f) Unique	—	—	—	—	—	—
1631 (f) Rare	—	—	—	—	—	—
1632 (f) Rare	—	—	—	—	—	—
1633 (f) Unique	—	—	—	—	—	—
1634 (f) Unique	—	—	—	—	—	—
1635 (f) Unique	—	—	—	—	—	—
1636 (f) Rare	—	—	—	—	—	—
1637 (f) Rare	—	—	—	—	—	—
1638 (f) Rare	—	—	—	—	—	—
1639 (f) Unique	—	—	—	—	—	—
1640 (f) Unique	—	—	—	—	—	—
1641 (f) Rare	—	—	—	—	—	—
1642 (f) Rare	—	—	—	—	—	—
1644 PG(c) Rare	—	—	—	—	—	—
1645 PG(c) Rare	—	—	—	—	—	—
1646 PG(c)	—	1,750	3,500	7,500	15,000	—
1647 PG(c)	—	1,750	3,500	7,500	15,000	—

KM# 13a 2 SPECIE DALER
57.4300 g., 0.8750 Silver 1.6155 oz. ASW

Date	Mintage	VG	F	VF	XF	Unc
1648 PG(c)	—	2,000	4,000	7,500	15,000	—

KM# 38 2 SPECIE DALER
57.4300 g., 0.8750 Silver 1.6155 oz. ASW **Obv:** Bust of Frederick III **Note:** Dav. #3587. Similar to 1 Specie Daler, KM#37.

Date	Mintage	VG	F	VF	XF	Unc
1649 PG(c)	—	3,000	6,500	11,000	16,500	—
1650 PG(c)	—	3,000	6,500	11,000	16,500	—

KM# 44 2 SPECIE DALER
57.4300 g., 0.8750 Silver 1.6155 oz. ASW **Note:** Dav. #3589. Similar to 1 Specie Daler, KM#37. Varieties exist.

Date	Mintage	VG	F	VF	XF	Unc
1651 FG(b) 3 known	—	—	—	—	—	—
1652 FG(b)	—	3,000	6,500	11,000	16,500	—

KM# 46 2 SPECIE DALER
57.4300 g., 0.8750 Silver 1.6155 oz. ASW **Note:** Dav. #3591. Similar to 1 Specie Daler, KM#A46.

Date	Mintage	VG	F	VF	XF	Unc
1653 Rare	—	—	—	—	—	—

KM# 38a 2 SPECIE DALER
57.5500 g., 0.8750 Silver 1.6189 oz. ASW **Obv:** Large bust breaking legend at top **Note:** Dav. #3594. Similar to 1 Specie Daler, KM#48.

Date	Mintage	VG	F	VF	XF	Unc
1653 FG(b) Unique	—	—	—	—	—	—
1654 FG(b) 2 known	—	—	9,000	14,000	20,000	—
1655 FG(b) Unique	—	—	—	—	—	—
1656 FG(b) 2 known	—	—	9,000	14,000	20,000	—

KM# 41 2 SPECIE DALER
57.5500 g., 0.8750 Silver 1.6189 oz. ASW **Note:** Dav. #3596. Similar to 1 Specie Daler, KM#A41.

Date	Mintage	VG	F	VF	XF	Unc
1656 FG(b) Unique	—	—	—	—	—	—
1657 FG(b) Unique	—	—	—	—	—	—

KM# 42 2 SPECIE DALER
57.5500 g., 0.8750 Silver 1.6189 oz. ASW **Note:** Dav. #3600. Similar to 1 Specie Daler, KM#A42. Varieties exist.

Date	Mintage	VG	F	VF	XF	Unc
1657 FG(b) 2 known	—	—	—	—	—	—
1658 FG(b) 7 known	—	—	—	—	—	—

KM# B52 2 SPECIE DALER
57.5500 g., 0.8750 Silver 1.6189 oz. ASW **Obv:** Small bust in inner circle **Rev:** Frame border around lion with one tail **Note:** Dav. #3602.

Date	Mintage	VG	F	VF	XF	Unc
1658 (b) 4 known	—	—	—	—	—	—

KM# A52 2 SPECIE DALER
57.5500 g., 0.8750 Silver 1.6189 oz. ASW **Note:** Dav. #3606. Similar to 1 Specie Daler, KM#54.

Date	Mintage	VG	F	VF	XF	Unc
1659 FG 5 known	—	—	—	—	—	—
1660 FG 3 known	—	—	—	—	—	—
1661 FG 2 known	—	—	—	—	—	—
1662 FG Unique	—	—	—	—	—	—

KM# 65 2 SPECIE DALER
57.5500 g., 0.8750 Silver 1.6189 oz. ASW **Subject:** Akershus Castle in Oslo **Note:** Dav. #3608. Similar to 1 Specie Daler, KM#64.

Date	Mintage	VG	F	VF	XF	Unc
ND(1661) 3 known	—	—	—	—	—	—

KM# 89 2 SPECIE DALER
57.5500 g., 0.8750 Silver 1.6189 oz. ASW **Obv:** Large crowned bust **Rev:** Lion in wreath **Note:** Dav. #3610.

Date	Mintage	VG	F	VF	XF	Unc
1662 Rare	—	—	—	—	—	—

KM# 57 2 SPECIE DALER
57.5500 g., 0.8750 Silver 1.6189 oz. ASW **Note:** Dav. #3613. Similar to 1 Specie Daler, KM#A57.

Date	Mintage	VG	F	VF	XF	Unc
1662 Rare	—	—	—	—	—	—
1663 Rare	—	—	—	—	—	—
1664 Rare	—	—	—	—	—	—

KM# 52 2 SPECIE DALER
57.5500 g., 0.8750 Silver 1.6189 oz. ASW **Note:** Dav. #3613. Similar to 1 Specie Daler, KM#67.

Date	Mintage	VG	F	VF	XF	Unc
1663 FG Rare	—	—	—	—	—	—
1664 FG Rare	—	—	—	—	—	—

KM# 76 2 SPECIE DALER
57.5500 g., 0.8750 Silver 1.6189 oz. ASW **Obv:** Cuirrassed bust **Rev:** Lion within oval shield **Note:** Dav. #3622. Similar to 1 Specie Daler, KM#74.

Date	Mintage	VG	F	VF	XF	Unc
1665 FG Rare	—	—	—	—	—	—
1666 FG Rare	—	—	—	—	—	—
1667 FG Rare	—	—	—	—	—	—

KM# 75 2 SPECIE DALER
57.5500 g., 0.8750 Silver 1.6189 oz. ASW **Rev:** Lion within crowned shield

Date	Mintage	VG	F	VF	XF	Unc
1665 FG Rare	—	—	—	—	—	—

KM# 84 2 SPECIE DALER
57.5500 g., 0.8750 Silver 1.6189 oz. ASW **Obv:** Draped bust **Note:** Dav. #3624. Similar to 1 Specie Daler, KM#83.

Date	Mintage	VG	F	VF	XF	Unc
1667 FG	—	4,250	7,000	12,500	18,000	—
1668 FG	—	4,250	7,000	12,500	18,000	—
1669 FG Unique	—	—	—	—	—	—

KM# 100 2 SPECIE DALER
57.5500 g., 0.8750 Silver 1.6189 oz. ASW **Obv:** Crowned bust of Christian V in armor **Rev:** Lion in crowned oval shield, date in legend **Note:** Dav. #3649.

Date	Mintage	VG	F	VF	XF	Unc
1670 FG 2 known	—	—	—	—	—	—

KM# 101 2 SPECIE DALER
57.5500 g., 0.8750 Silver 1.6189 oz. ASW **Rev:** Lion in oval shield divides date **Note:** Dav. #3649A.

Date	Mintage	VG	F	VF	XF	Unc
1670 FG 2 known	—	—	—	—	—	—

KM# 102 2 SPECIE DALER
57.5500 g., 0.8750 Silver 1.6189 oz. ASW **Obv:** Cuirassed and laureate bust **Rev:** Date in legend

Date	Mintage	VG	F	VF	XF	Unc
1670 FG Unique	—	—	—	—	—	—

KM# A110 2 SPECIE DALER
57.5500 g., 0.8750 Silver 1.6189 oz. ASW **Rev:** Motto around crowned shield within legend **Note:** Dav. #3652. Similar to 1 Specie Daler, KM#108.

Date	Mintage	VG	F	VF	XF	Unc
1671 FG Unique	—	—	—	—	—	—
1672 FG Unique	—	—	—	—	—	—

KM# 110 2 SPECIE DALER
57.5500 g., 0.8750 Silver 1.6189 oz. ASW **Note:** Dav. #3655. Similar to 1 Specie Daler, KM#109. Varieties exist.

Date	Mintage	VG	F	VF	XF	Unc
1672 FG 2 known	—	4,200	7,250	12,500	17,500	—
1674 FG 4 known	—	4,200	7,250	12,500	17,500	—
1675 PG Unique	—	—	—	—	—	—
1676 PG Unique	—	—	—	—	—	—
1677 PG Rare	—	3,500	7,000	12,500	17,500	—
1678 PG 2 known	—	4,200	7,250	12,500	17,500	—
1679 PG 2 known	—	4,200	7,250	12,500	17,500	—
1680 PG Unique	—	—	—	—	—	—

KM# 25 3 SPECIE DALER
87.7000 g., 0.8820 Silver 2.4868 oz. ASW **Obv:** Crowned portrait of Christian IV **Rev:** Lion **Note:** Dav. #3531. Similar to 1 Specie Daler, KM#12.

Date	Mintage	VG	F	VF	XF	Unc
1643 (f) Unique	—	—	—	—	—	—
1644 PG(c) Unique	—	—	—	—	—	—

KM# A39 3 SPECIE DALER
86.1500 g., 0.8750 Silver 2.4235 oz. ASW **Obv:** Crowned portrait of Frederick III **Rev:** Lion with two tails within circle **Note:** Dav. #3586.

Date	Mintage	VG	F	VF	XF	Unc
1649 PG(c) 3 known	—	—	—	—	—	—
1650 PG(c) 3 known	—	—	—	—	—	—

KM# 39 3 SPECIE DALER
86.1500 g., 0.8750 Silver 2.4235 oz. ASW **Note:** Dav. #A3589. Similar to 1 Specie Daler, KM#40. Varieties exist.

Date	Mintage	VG	F	VF	XF	Unc
1651 FG(b) Unique	—	—	—	—	—	—
1652 FG(b) Unique	—	—	—	—	—	—

KM# A39a 3 SPECIE DALER
86.3200 g., 0.8750 Silver 2.4282 oz. ASW **Note:** Dav. #A3591. Similar to 1 Specie Daler, KM#A46.

Date	Mintage	VG	F	VF	XF	Unc
1652 FG(b) Unique	—	—	—	—	—	—

KM# B39a 3 SPECIE DALER
86.3200 g., 0.8750 Silver 2.4282 oz. ASW **Note:** Dav. #3593. Similar to 1 Specie Daler, KM#48.

Date	Mintage	VG	F	VF	XF	Unc
1654 FG(b) 4 known	—	—	—	—	—	—
1655 FG(b) Unique	—	—	—	—	—	—
1656 FG(b) Unique	—	—	—	—	—	—

KM# 39a 3 SPECIE DALER
86.3200 g., 0.8750 Silver 2.4282 oz. ASW **Note:** Dav. #3599. Similar to 1 Specie Daler, KM#A42. Varieties exist.

Date	Mintage	VG	F	VF	XF	Unc
1657 FG(b) Unique	—	—	—	—	—	—
1658 FG(b) 2 known	—	—	—	—	—	—

KM# A55 3 SPECIE DALER
86.3200 g., 0.8750 Silver 2.4282 oz. ASW **Rev:** Lion with one tail **Note:** Dav. #3605. Similar to 1 Specie Daler, KM#54.

Date	Mintage	VG	F	VF	XF	Unc
1659 FG(b) 2 known	—	—	—	—	—	—
1660 FG 2 known	—	—	—	—	—	—

KM# 55 3 SPECIE DALER
86.3200 g., 0.8750 Silver 2.4282 oz. ASW **Note:** Dav. #3612. Similar to 1 Specie Daler, KM#A57.

Date	Mintage	VG	F	VF	XF	Unc
1663 FG Unique	—	—	—	—	—	—
1664 FG 2 known	—	—	—	—	—	—

KM# A67 3 SPECIE DALER
86.3200 g., 0.8750 Silver 2.4282 oz. ASW **Note:** Dav. #A3616. Similar to 1 Specie Daler, KM#67.

Date	Mintage	VG	F	VF	XF	Unc
1663 2 known	—	—	—	—	—	—

KM# 79 3 SPECIE DALER
86.3200 g., 0.8750 Silver 2.4282 oz. ASW **Obv:** Laureate bust **Rev:** Crowned lion in shield

Date	Mintage	VG	F	VF	XF	Unc
1666 FG Unique	—	—	—	—	—	—
1667 FG Unique	—	—	—	—	—	—
1668 FG Unique	—	—	—	—	—	—

KM# 128 3 SPECIE DALER
86.6800 g., 0.8750 Silver 2.4384 oz. ASW **Obv:** Christian V **Note:** Dav. #3654. Similar to 1 Specie Daler, KM#109.

Date	Mintage	VG	F	VF	XF	Unc
1674 FG Unique	—	—	—	—	—	—
1678 PG Unique	—	—	—	—	—	—
1679 PG 2 known	—	—	—	—	—	—
1680 PG 3 known	—	—	—	—	—	—

KM# 15 4 SPECIE DALER
116.9300 g., 0.8820 Silver 3.3156 oz. ASW **Obv:** Christian IV **Rev:** Lion **Note:** Dav. #3530. Similar to 1 Specie Daler, KM#12.

Date	Mintage	VG	F	VF	XF	Unc
1634 (f) Unique	—	—	—	—	—	—
1644 PG(c) 3 known	—	—	—	—	—	—
1645 PG(c) Unique	—	—	—	—	—	—

KM# 15a 4 SPECIE DALER
114.8800 g., 0.8750 Silver 3.2317 oz. ASW

Date	Mintage	VG	F	VF	XF	Unc
1648 PG Unique	—	—	—	—	—	—

KM# A50 4 SPECIE DALER
115.1000 g., 0.8750 Silver 3.2378 oz. ASW **Obv:** Portrait of Frederick III **Rev:** Lion with two tails within circle **Note:** Dav. #A3596. Similar to 1 Specie Daler, KM#A41.

Date	Mintage	VG	F	VF	XF	Unc
1656 FG(b) 2 known	—	—	—	—	—	—

KM# 50 4 SPECIE DALER
115.1000 g., 0.8750 Silver 3.2378 oz. ASW **Note:** Dav. #A3596. Similar to 1 Specie Daler, KM#A42.

Date	Mintage	VG	F	VF	XF	Unc
1657 FG(b) 2 known	—	—	—	—	—	—
1658 FG(b) Unique	—	—	—	—	—	—

KM# 66 4 SPECIE DALER
115.1000 g., 0.8750 Silver 3.2378 oz. ASW **Rev:** Lion with one tail within laurel wreath

Date	Mintage	VG	F	VF	XF	Unc
1661 FG Unique	—	—	—	—	—	—

KM# 129 4 SPECIE DALER
115.5700 g., 0.8750 Silver 3.2511 oz. ASW **Obv:** Portrait of Christian V **Rev:** Crowned lion in shield **Note:** Dav. #A3654.

Date	Mintage	VG	F	VF	XF	Unc
1674 FG Unique	—	—	—	—	—	—
1678 PG Unique	—	—	—	—	—	—
1679 PG Unique	—	—	—	—	—	—
1680 PG 3 known	—	—	—	—	—	—

TOKEN COINAGE

KM# Tn1 12 SKILLING
4.1800 g., 0.6720 Silver 0.0903 oz. ASW **Subject:** Summer Transport Token

Date	Mintage	VG	F	VF	XF	Unc
1689	—	125	250	500	1,100	—

KM# Tn2 16 SKILLING
5.5700 g., 0.6720 Silver 0.1203 oz. ASW **Subject:** Winter Transport Token

Date	Mintage	VG	F	VF	XF	Unc
1689	—	400	700	1,000	2,000	—

TRADE COINAGE

KM# 80 1/2 DUCAT
1.4900 g., 0.9790 Gold 0.0469 oz. AGW **Obv:** Draped, laureate bust of Frederick right **Rev:** Crowned arms mounted on cross **Note:** Struck at Christiania Mint.

Date	Mintage	VG	F	VF	XF	Unc
1666 3 known	—	—	—	—	—	—

KM# 103 1/2 DUCAT
1.4900 g., 0.9790 Gold 0.0469 oz. AGW **Obv:** Laureate bust of Christian right

Date	Mintage	VG	F	VF	XF	Unc
ND Rare	—	—	—	—	—	—

KM# 81 1/2 DUCAT
1.4900 g., 0.9790 Gold 0.0469 oz. AGW **Obv:** Roman style bust of Frederick III right

Date	Mintage	VG	F	VF	XF	Unc
ND(f)	—	2,000	3,000	6,000	9,000	—

KM# 61 DUCAT
3.4900 g., 0.9790 Gold 0.1098 oz. AGW **Obv:** Crowned bust right of Frederick **Note:** Struck at Christiania Mint.

Date	Mintage	VG	F	VF	XF	Unc
1660 FG Unique	—	—	—	—	—	—

KM# 77 DUCAT
3.4900 g., 0.9790 Gold 0.1098 oz. AGW **Obv:** Frederick

Date	Mintage	VG	F	VF	XF	Unc
1665 3 known	—	—	—	40,000	60,000	—

KM# 86 DUCAT
3.4900 g., 0.9790 Gold 0.1098 oz. AGW **Obv:** Draped bust of Frederick right

Date	Mintage	VG	F	VF	XF	Unc
1668 Unique	—	—	—	—	—	—

KM# 88 DUCAT
3.4900 g., 0.9790 Gold 0.1098 oz. AGW **Obv:** Large Roman bust of Frederick right **Rev:** Crowned arms mounted on cross, date below

Date	Mintage	VG	F	VF	XF	Unc
1669 FG(ch) Unique	—	—	—	—	—	—

KM# 117 DUCAT
3.4900 g., 0.9790 Gold 0.1098 oz. AGW **Obv:** Laureate bust of Christian V right **Rev:** Crowned arms mounted on cross, date divided below

Date	Mintage	VG	F	VF	XF	Unc
1673 Unique	—	—	—	—	—	—
ND 2 known	—	—	—	—	—	—

KM# 118 DUCAT
3.4900 g., 0.9790 Gold 0.1098 oz. AGW **Rev:** Crowned arms mounted on cross **Note:** Small planchet.

Date	Mintage	VG	F	VF	XF	Unc
ND Unique	—	—	—	—	—	—

KM# 195 DUCAT
3.4900 g., 0.9790 Gold 0.1098 oz. AGW **Obv:** Bust of Christian V right **Rev:** Six-line inscription **Note:** Struck at Kongsberg Mint.

Date	Mintage	VG	F	VF	XF	Unc
1697 HCM 2 known	—	—	—	—	—	—

KM# 78 2 DUCAT
6.9800 g., 0.9790 Gold 0.2197 oz. AGW **Obv:** Armored bust of Frederick right **Obv. Legend:** FREDERIC: III: D: G: DAN: NOR: **Rev:** Crowned arms mounted on cross, date in legend **Rev. Legend:** VANDAL: GOTO: REX:

Date	Mintage	VG	F	VF	XF	Unc
1665 2 known, Rare	—	—	—	—	—	—

KM# 119 2 DUCAT
6.9800 g., 0.9790 Gold 0.2197 oz. AGW **Obv:** Laureate bust of Christian V right **Rev:** Crowned arms mounted on cross, date divided below

Date	Mintage	VG	F	VF	XF	Unc
1673 Unique	—	—	—	—	—	—
ND 2 known	—	—	—	—	—	—

KM# 121 2 DUCAT
6.9800 g., 0.9790 Gold 0.2197 oz. AGW **Obv:** Equestrian figure of Christian V

Date	Mintage	VG	F	VF	XF	Unc
1673 Rare	—	—	—	—	—	—

KM# 122 2 DUCAT
6.9800 g., 0.9790 Gold 0.2197 oz. AGW **Obv:** Laureate head of Christian V right, date below

Date	Mintage	VG	F	VF	XF	Unc
1673 Rare	—	—	—	—	—	—

KM# 123 2 DUCAT
6.9800 g., 0.9790 Gold 0.2197 oz. AGW **Rev:** Three C5 monograms among six crowns at border

Date	Mintage	VG	F	VF	XF	Unc
1673 Rare	—	—	—	—	—	—

KM# 120 2 DUCAT
6.9800 g., 0.9790 Gold 0.2197 oz. AGW **Rev:** Crowned arms mounted on cross **Note:** Small thick planchet.

Date	Mintage	VG	F	VF	XF	Unc
ND 3 known	—	—	—	—	—	—

KM# 137 2 DUCAT
6.9800 g., 0.9790 Gold 0.2197 oz. AGW **Obv:** Larger head of Christian

Date	Mintage	VG	F	VF	XF	Unc
1678 Unique	—	—	—	—	—	—

KM# 138 2 DUCAT
6.9800 g., 0.9790 Gold 0.2197 oz. AGW **Obv:** Draped bust of Christian right

Date	Mintage	VG	F	VF	XF	Unc
ND Unique	—	—	—	—	—	—

KM# 196 2 DUCAT
6.9800 g., 0.9790 Gold 0.2197 oz. AGW **Obv:** Bust of Christian V right **Rev:** Six-line inscription **Note:** Struck at Kongsberg Mint.

Date	Mintage	VG	F	VF	XF	Unc
1697 HCM 2 known	—	—	—	—	—	—

KM# 111 3 DUCAT
10.4700 g., 0.9790 Gold 0.3295 oz. AGW **Obv:** Laureate bust of Christian V right **Rev:** Crowned arms mounted on cross divide date **Note:** Struck at Christiania Mint.

Date	Mintage	VG	F	VF	XF	Unc
1671 FB Unique	—	—	—	—	—	—

KM# 124 3 DUCAT
10.4700 g., 0.9790 Gold 0.3295 oz. AGW **Rev:** Crowned arms mounted on cross, date divided below

Date	Mintage	VG	F	VF	XF	Unc
1673 Unique	—	—	—	—	—	—

KM# 125 3 DUCAT
10.4700 g., 0.9790 Gold 0.3295 oz. AGW **Obv:** Equestrian figure of Christian V left **Rev:** Crowned arms, date in legend

Date	Mintage	VG	F	VF	XF	Unc
1673 4 known	—	—	—	—	—	—

KM# 126 3 DUCAT
10.4700 g., 0.9790 Gold 0.3295 oz. AGW **Obv:** Equestrian figure of Christian V right **Rev:** Elephant with arms on side cloth, date in exergue

Date	Mintage	VG	F	VF	XF	Unc
1673 Unique	—	—	—	—	—	—

KM# 127 3 DUCAT
10.4700 g., 0.9790 Gold 0.3295 oz. AGW **Obv:** Three C5 monograms among six crowns at border

Date	Mintage	VG	F	VF	XF	Unc
1673 Rare	—	—	—	—	—	—

KM# 139 3 DUCAT
10.4700 g., 0.9790 Gold 0.3295 oz. AGW **Obv:** Three C5 monograms among six crowns at border

Date	Mintage	VG	F	VF	XF	Unc
1678 3 known	—	—	—	—	—	—

KM# A140 3-3/8 DUCAT
11.8500 g., 0.9790 Gold 0.3730 oz. AGW

Date	Mintage	VG	F	VF	XF	Unc
1684 Rare	—	—	—	—	—	—

KM# 112 4 DUCAT
13.9600 g., 0.9790 Gold 0.4394 oz. AGW **Obv:** Christian V

Date	Mintage	VG	F	VF	XF	Unc
1671 FG Unique	—	—	—	—	—	—

LARGESSE COINAGE

KM# A107.1 1/4 SPECIE DALER
7.2200 g., 0.8750 Silver 0.2031 oz. ASW **Subject:** Royal Visit to Norway **Obv. Legend:** CVRDNVG IN MEMORIAM

Date	Mintage	VG	F	VF	XF	Unc
1685 Rare	—	—	—	—	—	—

KM# A107.2 1/4 SPECIE DALER
7.2200 g., 0.8750 Silver 0.2031 oz. ASW
Obv. Legend: CVRDNVG TERPAMARI

Date	Mintage	VG	F	VF	XF	Unc
1685 Rare	—	—	—	—	—	—

PATTERNS
Including off metal strikes

KM#	Date	Mintage	Identification	Mkt Val
Pn1	ND	—	12 Skilling. 0.6720 Silver. King on horseback, crowned C5 monogram	550
Pn2	ND	—	1/2 Ducat. 0.9790 Gold. Head of king, crowned arms.	—
Pn3	ND	—	Ducat. Gold. King on horseback, knight and lion.	—
Pn4	ND	—	Ducat. Silver. King on horseback, knight and lion.	300
Pn5	ND	—	Ducat. Gold. King on horseback, crowned monograms.	—
Pn6	ND	—	Ducat. Silver. King on horseback, lion.	300
Pn7	ND	—	Ducat. Gold. Head of king, crowned arms.	—
Pn8	ND	—	Ducat. Silver. Head of king, crowned arms.	—
Pn9	ND	—	2 Ducat. Silver. King on horseback, arms.	500
Pn10	ND	—	2 Ducat. Gold. King on horseback, crowned monograms.	—
Pn11	ND	—	2 Ducat. Silver. King on horseback, crowned monograms.	200
Pn12	ND	—	2 Ducat. Gold. King on horseback, crowned monograms.	—
Pn13	ND	—	2 Ducat. Silver. King on horseback, crowned monograms.	—
Pn14	ND	—	2 Ducat. Silver. Head of king, crowned monograms.	—
Pn15	ND	—	2 Ducat. Silver. Head of king, crowned monograms.	—
Pn16	ND	—	2 Ducat. Gold. Head of king, crowned monograms.	—
Pn17	ND	—	4 Ducat. Gold. King on horseback, crowned monograms.	—
Pn18	ND	—	4 Ducat. Silver. King on horseback, crowned monograms.	750
PnA19	ND	—	10 Ducat. 35.5000 Gold.	—
PnB19	1644	—	4 Skilling. Copper. IIII/SKL/D	—
PnC19	1660	—	1/8 Specie Daler. Gold. KM#60.	—
Pn19	1660	—	Ducat. Gold. KM#61.	—
PnA20	1664	—	10 Ducat. 35.0000 Gold. Struck with Specidaler dies, KM#10.	—
PnB20	1665	—	7-7/8 Ducat. 28.0000 Gold. Struck with Speciedaler dies, KM#73.	—
PnC20	1665	—	10 Ducat. 33.8000 Gold. Struck with Speciedaler dies, KM#74.	—
PnD20	1668	—	10 Ducat. 35.5000 Gold. Struck with Speciedaler dies, KM#83.	—
PnE20	1669	—	12 Ducat. 40.7000 Gold. Struck with Speciedaler dies, KM#83.	—
Pn22	1673	—	3 Ducat. 40.7000 Silver. Equestrian figure.	—
Pn20	1673	—	2 Ducat. 40.7000 Silver. Laureate head.	1,200
Pn21	1673	—	2 Ducat. 40.7000 Silver. C5 monograms.	1,000
PnA23	1674	—	5 Ducat. 17.5000 Gold. Struck with Speciedaler dies, KM#109.	—
PnB23	1675	—	4-3/16 Ducat. 14.6500 Gold. Struck with Speciedaler dies, KM#132.	—
Pn23	1678	—	2 Ducat. Gold. Head of king, monograms and crowns.	—
Pn24	1678	—	2 Ducat. Gold. Head of king, elephant.	—
Pn25	1678	—	3 Ducat. Silver. C5 monograms.	—
Pn26	1678	—	3 Ducat. Gold. Head of king, elephant.	—
Pn27	1681	—	12 Skilling. Head of king, lion in branches.	—
Pn28	1683	—	4 Mark. Monogram and lion, Dannenbrog cross.	2,500
Pn29	1684	—	Mark. Monogram and lion, Dannebrog cross.	1,300
Pn30	1685	—	1/2 Mark. Monogram and lion; Dannebrog cross.	550
PnA31	1685	—	16-5/8 Ducat. 58.0000 Gold. Struck with Speciedaler dies.	—
PnB31	1690	—	12 Ducat. 58.0000 Gold. Struck with Speciedaler dies, KM#184.	—
Pn31	1697 HCM	—	Ducat. Silver.	—

PERU

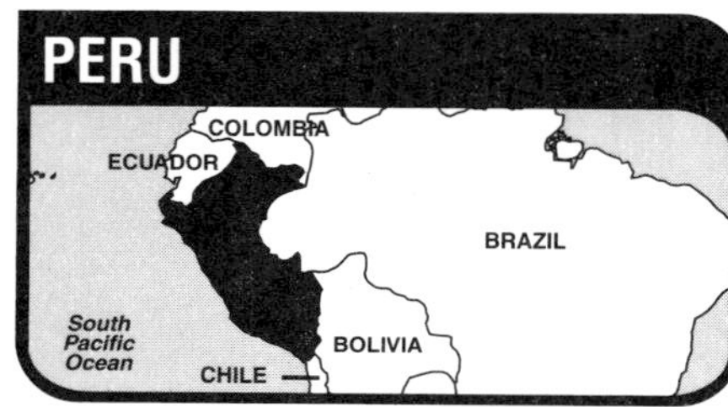

The Republic of Peru, located on the Pacific coast of South America, has an area of 496,225 sq. mi. (1,285,220sq. km).

Once part of the great Inca Empire that reached from northern Ecuador to central Chile, the conquest of Peru by Francisco Pizarro began in 1531. Desirable as the richest of the Spanish viceroyalties, it was torn by warfare between avaricious Spaniards until the arrival in 1569 of Francisco de Toledo, who initiated 2-1/2 centuries of efficient colonial rule, which made Lima the most aristocratic colonial capital and the stronghold of Spain's American possessions. Jose de San Martin of Argentina proclaimed Peru's independence on July 28, 1821;Simon Bolivar of Venezuela secured it in December, 1824 when he defeated the last Spanish army in South America. After several futile attempts to re-establish its South American empire, Spain recognized Peru's independence in 1879.

Andres de Santa Cruz, whose mother was a high-ranking Inca, was the best of Bolivia's early presidents, and temporarily united Peru and Bolivia 1836-39, thus realizing his dream of a Peruvian/Bolivian confederation. This prompted the separate coinages of North and South Peru. Peruvian resistance and Chilean intervention finally broke up the confederation, sending Santa Cruz into exile. A succession of military strongman presidents ruled Peru until Marshall Castilla revitalized Peruvian politics in themid-19th century and repulsed Spain's attempt to reclaim its one-time colony. Subsequent loss of southern territory to Chile in the War of the Pacific, 1879-81, and gradually increasing rejection of foreign economic domination, combined with recent serious inflation, affected the country numismatically.

As a result of the discovery of silver at Potosi in 1545, a mint was eventually authorized in 1565 with the first coinage taking place in 1568. The mint had an uneven life span during the Spanish Colonial period from 1568-72. It was closed from 1573-76, reopened from 1577-88. It remained closed until 1659-1660 when an unauthorized coinage in both silver and gold were struck. After being closed in 1660, it remained closed until 1684 when it struck cob style coins until 1752.

RULER
Spanish until 1822

MINT MARKS
(L) = London

NOTE: The LIMAE monogram appears in three forms. The early LM monogram form looks like a dotted L with M. The later LIMAE monogram has all the letters of LIMAE more readily distinguishable. The third form appears as an M monogram during early Republican issues.

MINT ASSAYERS' INITIALS

Initial	Date	Name
H, Ho	1696-1705,	?
M	1694	?
N	1699-1706	Joaquin Negrow
R	1698-1701	
V	1659-60	Francesco Villegas
V	1684, 1689-90	
V	1692-93	

The letter(s) following the dates of Peruvian coins are the assayer's initials appearing on the coins. They generally appear at the 11 o'clock position on the Colonial coinage and at the 5 o'clock position along the rim on the obverse or reverse on the Republican coinage.

MONETARY SYSTEM
16 Reales = 2 Pesos = 1 Escudo

SPANISH COLONY

COLONIAL COB COINAGE

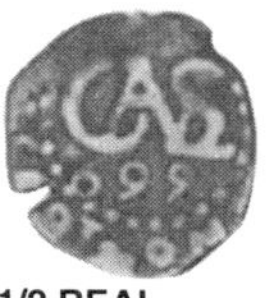

KM# 22 1/2 REAL
1.6917 g., 0.9310 Silver 0.0506 oz. ASW **Ruler:** Charles II **Obv:** CAROLVS monogram, date below **Rev:** Cross of Jerusalem, lions and castles in quarters

Date	Mintage	Good	VG	F	VF	XF
ND(1684-1700) Date off flan	—	10.00	15.00	30.00	50.00	—
1684L	—	30.00	50.00	70.00	110	—
1685L	—	30.00	50.00	70.00	110	—
1686L	—	30.00	50.00	70.00	110	—
1687L	—	30.00	50.00	70.00	110	—
1688L	—	30.00	50.00	70.00	110	—
1689L	—	30.00	50.00	70.00	110	—
1690L	—	30.00	50.00	70.00	110	—
1691L	—	30.00	50.00	70.00	110	—
1692L	—	30.00	50.00	70.00	110	—
1693L	—	30.00	50.00	70.00	110	—
1694L	—	30.00	55.00	70.00	110	—
1695L	—	30.00	55.00	70.00	110	—
1696L	—	30.00	50.00	70.00	110	—
1697L	—	30.00	50.00	70.00	110	—
1698L	—	32.00	50.00	70.00	110	—
1699L	—	30.00	50.00	75.00	135	—
1700L	—	38.00	55.00	95.00	155	—

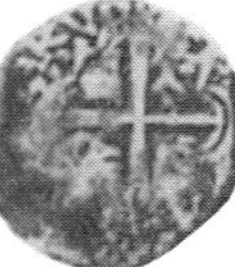

KM# 15 REAL
3.3834 g., 0.9310 Silver 0.1013 oz. ASW **Obv:** Pillars and waves, star above mint mark and date **Obv. Legend:** PHILIPPVS IIII DEI

Date	Mintage	Good	VG	F	VF	XF
1659L*M V	—	200	300	475	725	—
1660L*M V	—	275	550	1,100	1,850	—

KM# 20 REAL
3.3834 g., 0.9310 Silver 0.1013 oz. ASW **Ruler:** Charles II **Obv:** Cross of Jerusalem, lions and castles in quarters **Rev:** Pillars and waves

Date	Mintage	Good	VG	F	VF	XF
ND(1684-1700)L Date off flan	—	15.00	20.00	35.00	60.00	—
1684L V	—	30.00	70.00	90.00	125	—

Date	Mintage	Good	VG	F	VF	XF
1685L R	—	30.00	70.00	90.00	125	—
1686L R	—	30.00	70.00	90.00	125	—
1687L R	—	30.00	70.00	90.00	125	—
1688L R	—	30.00	70.00	90.00	125	—
1689L V	—	30.00	70.00	90.00	125	—
1690L V	—	30.00	70.00	90.00	125	—
1690L R	—	30.00	70.00	90.00	125	—
1691L R	—	30.00	70.00	90.00	125	—
1692L V	—	30.00	70.00	90.00	125	—
1693L V	—	30.00	70.00	90.00	125	—
1694L M	—	30.00	70.00	90.00	125	—
1695L R	—	30.00	70.00	90.00	125	—
1696L H	—	30.00	70.00	90.00	125	—
1697L H	—	30.00	70.00	90.00	125	—
1698L H	—	30.00	70.00	90.00	125	—
1699L R	—	30.00	70.00	90.00	125	—
1700L H	—	30.00	70.00	90.00	125	—

KM# 16 2 REALES

6.7668 g., 0.9310 Silver 0.2025 oz. ASW
Obv. Legend: PHILIPPVS IIII DEI. G

Date	Mintage	Good	VG	F	VF	XF
1659L*M V Rare	—	—	—	—	—	—
1659LI*M V Rare	—	—	—	—	—	—
1660L*M V Rare	—	—	—	—	—	—

KM# 21 2 REALES

6.7668 g., 0.9310 Silver 0.2025 oz. ASW **Obv:** Cross of Jerusalem, lions and castles in quarters, mint mark **Obv. Legend:** CAROLVS II D • G • HISPANIARVM REX **Rev:** Pillars, assayer's initial, date, PLVS VLTRA within

Date	Mintage	Good	VG	F	VF	XF
ND(1684-1700)L Date off flan	—	20.00	30.00	45.00	75.00	—
1684L V	—	60.00	90.00	150	250	—
1685L R	—	60.00	90.00	150	250	—
1686L R	—	60.00	90.00	150	250	—
1687L R	—	60.00	90.00	150	250	—
1688L R	—	60.00	90.00	150	250	—
1689L V	—	60.00	90.00	150	250	—
1690L R	—	60.00	90.00	150	250	—
1691L R	—	60.00	90.00	150	250	—
1692L V	—	60.00	90.00	150	250	—
1693L V	—	60.00	90.00	150	250	—
1694L M	—	60.00	90.00	150	250	—
1695L R	—	60.00	90.00	150	250	—
1696L H	—	60.00	90.00	150	250	—
1696L Ho Rare	—	—	—	—	—	—
1697L H	—	60.00	90.00	150	250	—
1698L H	—	60.00	90.00	150	250	—
1699L R	—	60.00	90.00	150	250	—
1700L H	—	60.00	90.00	150	250	—

KM# 17 4 REALES

13.5337 g., 0.9310 Silver 0.4051 oz. ASW **Obv:** Pillars and waves, star above mint mark and date **Obv. Legend:** PHILIPPVS IIII DEI. G **Rev. Inscription:** ...PLVS/• * •/VLTRA/660.

Date	Mintage	Good	VG	F	VF	XF
1659LIMA V Star above mint mark, rare	—	—	—	—	—	—
1659L*M V Rare	—	—	—	—	—	—
1660L*M V Rare	—	—	—	—	—	—
(1)660L V Rare	—	—	—	—	—	—

KM# 23 4 REALES

13.5337 g., 0.9310 Silver 0.4051 oz. ASW **Obv:** Cross of Jerusalem, lions and castles in quarters **Obv. Legend:** CAROLVS II D • G • HISPANIARVM REX **Rev:** Pillars with mint mark, value and assayer's initial between

Date	Mintage	Good	VG	F	VF	XF
ND(1684-1700)L Date off flan	—	50.00	75.00	90.00	125	—
1684L V	—	125	200	350	550	—
1685L R	—	110	180	285	480	—
1686L R	—	110	180	285	480	—
1687L R	—	110	180	285	480	—
1688L R	—	110	180	285	480	—
1689L V Rare	—	—	—	—	—	—
1689L R	—	—	—	—	—	—
Note: Reported, not confirmed						
1690L R Rare	—	—	—	—	—	—
1691L R	—	125	200	350	550	—
1692L V	—	125	200	350	550	—
1693L V	—	125	200	350	550	—
1695L R Rare	—	—	—	—	—	—
1696L H	—	125	220	400	580	—
1697L H	—	110	170	270	435	—
1698L H	—	110	170	270	435	—
1699L H	—	—	—	—	—	—
Note: Reported, not confirmed						
1699L R Rare	—	—	—	—	—	—
1700L H	—	110	170	270	435	—

KM# 18.1 8 REALES

27.0674 g., 0.9310 Silver 0.8102 oz. ASW **Obv:** Pillars and waves, star above mint mark and date **Obv. Legend:** PHILIPPVS IIII DEI. G **Note:** Struck at Lima.

Date	Mintage	Good	VG	F	VF	XF
1659LIMA V LIMA 8 V left and right; Rare	—	—	—	—	—	—
Note: Swiss Bank Coins of Peru Auction #20 9-88 VF realized $13,400.						
1659LIMA V Lima V left, 8 right	—	900	1,500	2,500	3,500	—
1659L*M V 8-pointed star	—	900	1,500	2,500	3,500	—

KM# 18.2 8 REALES

27.0674 g., 0.9310 Silver 0.8102 oz. ASW **Obv:** PLVS/ • * • /VLTRA/660 between pillars **Obv. Legend:** PHILIPPVS IIII DEI. G

Date	Mintage	Good	VG	F	VF	XF
660 (1) 660 • * • 6-pointed star	—	2,000	3,000	4,000	5,000	—

Note: Clear, sharply struck examples of KM#18.1 and KM#18.2, along with other denominations of the Star of Lima coinage, have been known to bring much higher prices for examples which may exceed a VF grade

KM# 24 8 REALES

27.0674 g., 0.9310 Silver 0.8102 oz. ASW **Ruler:** Charles II **Obv:** Cross of Jerusalem, lions and castles in quarters **Rev:** PLV/ SVL/ TRA between pillars

Date	Mintage	Good	VG	F	VF	XF
ND(1684-1701)L Date off flan	—	75.00	90.00	110	150	—
1684L V	—	150	250	350	500	—
1685L R	—	150	250	350	500	—
1685L V Rare	—	—	—	—	—	—
1686/5L R Rare	—	—	—	—	—	—
1686L R	—	150	250	350	500	—
1687L R	—	150	250	350	500	—
1688L R	—	150	250	350	500	—
1689L V	—	150	250	350	500	—
1690L V	—	150	250	350	500	—
1690L R	—	150	250	350	500	—
1691L R	—	150	250	350	500	—
1692L V	—	150	250	350	500	—
1693L V	—	150	250	350	500	—
1694L M	—	175	275	375	575	—
1695L R	—	150	250	350	500	—
1696L H	—	150	250	350	500	—
1696L Ho Rare	—	—	—	—	—	—
1697L H	—	150	250	350	500	—
1698L H	—	150	250	350	500	—
1699L R	—	150	250	350	500	—
1700L H	—	150	250	350	500	—

KM# 27 ESCUDO

3.3834 g., 0.9170 Gold 0.0997 oz. AGW **Ruler:** Charles II **Obv:** Castle divides L H, date as 698 below **Rev:** Cross of Jerusalem, dots in quarters **Note:** See pattern section of 1696 date.

Date	Mintage	VG	F	VF	XF	Unc
ND(1696-1700)L Date off flan	—	—	2,000	2,500	4,000	—
1697/6L H	—	—	3,000	4,000	6,000	—
1698L H	575	—	3,000	4,000	6,000	—
1698L R	Inc. above	—	3,000	4,000	6,000	—
1699L R	748	—	3,000	4,000	6,000	—
1700L R	427	—	3,000	4,000	6,000	—

KM# A27 ESCUDO

3.3834 g., 0.9170 Gold 0.0997 oz. AGW **Obv:** Castle **Rev:** Cross of Jerusalem, X's in quarters

Date	Mintage	VG	F	VF	XF	Unc
ND(1698)C M Date off flan	—	—	3,000	3,500	5,000	—
1698C M	—	—	4,000	5,000	7,500	—

KM# 29 2 ESCUDOS

6.7668 g., 0.9170 Gold 0.1995 oz. AGW **Ruler:** Charles II **Obv:** Cross of Jerusalem with lions and castles in quarters **Obv. Legend:** C • II D • G • HISPANIARVM **Rev:** Pillars and waves

Date	Mintage	VG	F	VF	XF	Unc
ND(1696-1701)L Date off flan	—	—	1,500	2,500	3,500	—
1696L H	32,979	—	4,000	5,000	7,000	—
1697L H	39,472	—	4,000	5,000	7,000	—
1698L H	912	—	4,000	5,000	7,000	—
1699L H	1,788	—	4,000	5,000	7,000	—
1699L R	Inc. above	—	4,000	5,000	7,000	—
1700L H	6,315	—	4,000	5,000	7,000	—

KM# 28 2 ESCUDOS

6.7668 g., 0.9170 Gold 0.1995 oz. AGW **Ruler:** Charles II **Obv:** Cross of Jerusalem with lions and castles in quarters **Obv. Legend:** C • II D • G • HISPANIARVM **Rev:** Pillars, PVA and date, mintmark

Date	Mintage	VG	F	VF	XF	Unc
ND(1698)	—	—	1,500	2,500	3,500	—
1698C M	—	—	4,000	5,000	7,000	—

KM# 25 4 ESCUDOS

13.5337 g., 0.9170 Gold 0.3990 oz. AGW **Ruler:** Charles II **Obv:** Cross of Jerusalem with castles and lions in quarters **Obv. Legend:** C • II D • G • HISPANIARVM **Rev:** Pillars and waves

Date	Mintage	VG	F	VF	XF	Unc
ND(1696-1701)L Date off flan	—	—	5,000	6,250	7,500	—
1696L H	—	—	9,000	12,000	15,000	—
1697L H	—	—	9,000	12,000	15,000	—
1698L H	1,260	—	9,000	12,000	15,000	—
1699L R	1,636	—	9,000	12,000	15,000	—
1700L H	2,006	—	9,000	12,000	15,000	—

KM# 19 8 ESCUDOS

27.0674 g., 0.9170 Gold 0.7980 oz. AGW **Obv:** Arms, pillars **Obv. Legend:** PHILIPPVS IIII D • G • HISPANIARVM **Rev:** Cross of Jerusalem, legend and date around

Date	Mintage	VG	F	VF	XF	Unc
1659L V Rare	1,617	—	—	—	—	—
1660L V Rare	846	—	—	—	—	—

KM# 26.1 8 ESCUDOS

27.0674 g., 0.9170 Gold 0.7980 oz. AGW **Ruler:** Charles II **Obv:** Cross of Jerusalem with castles and lions in quarters **Obv. Legend:** C • II D • G • HISPANIARVM **Rev:** Pillars, P. V. A., date and mint mark

Date	Mintage	VG	F	VF	XF	Unc
1697L H	—	—	8,000	10,000	12,000	—
1698L H	5,898	—	8,000	10,000	12,000	—
1699L R	15,656	—	8,000	10,000	12,000	—

KM# 26.2 8 ESCUDOS

27.0674 g., 0.9170 Gold 0.7980 oz. AGW **Ruler:** Charles II **Obv:** Cross of Jerusalem, lions and castles in quarters **Obv. Legend:** C • II D • G • HISPANIARVM **Rev:** Pillars, PVA, date and mint mark

Date	Mintage	VG	F	VF	XF	Unc
ND(1696-1701)L Date off flan	—	—	5,000	6,250	7,500	—
1696L H	—	—	8,000	10,000	12,500	—
1697L H	—	—	8,000	10,000	12,500	—
1698L H	—	—	8,000	10,000	12,500	—
1699L R	Inc. above	—	8,000	10,000	12,500	—
1700L H	10,350	—	8,000	10,000	12,500	—

ROYAL COINAGE

KM# R21 2 REALES

6.7668 g., 0.9310 Silver 0.2025 oz. ASW **Ruler:** Charles II **Note:** Struck at Lima.

Date	Mintage	Good	VG	F	VF	XF
1685L R Rare	—	—	—	—	—	—

KM# R18 8 REALES

27.0674 g., 0.9310 Silver 0.8102 oz. ASW

Date	Mintage	Good	VG	F	VF	XF
1659 Rare	—	—	—	—	—	—

KM# R24 8 REALES

Ruler: Charles II **Note:** Struck at Lima.

Date	Mintage	Good	VG	F	VF	XF
1684L V Rare	—	—	—	—	—	—
1686L R Rare	—	—	—	—	—	—
1687L R Rare	—	—	—	—	—	—
1688L R Rare	—	—	—	—	—	—
1689L V Rare	—	—	—	—	—	—
1691L R Rare	—	—	—	—	—	—
1692L V Rare	—	—	—	—	—	—
1693L V Rare	—	—	—	—	—	—
1694L M Rare	—	—	—	—	—	—
1695L R Rare	—	—	—	—	—	—
1697L H Rare	—	—	—	—	—	—

PATTERNS

Including off metal strikes

KM#	Date	Mintage	Identification	Mkt Val
PnA1	ND(1696)	—	Escudo. Gold.	—

POLAND

The Republic of Poland, located in central Europe, has an area of 120,725 sq. mi. (312,680 sq. km).

Poland began as a Slavic duchy in the 10th century and reached its peak of power between the 14th and 16th centuries. In the 17th century it has had a turbulent history of invasion, occupation or partition by Mongols (13th century), Turkey (14th century), Transylvania, Sweden (17th century), Austria, Prussia and Russia (18th century)

RULERS

Zygmunt III Waza, 1587-1632
Wladyslaw IV Waza, 1633-1648
Jan II Kazimierz Waza, 1649-1668
Michal Korybut Wisniowiecki, 1669-1673
Jan III Sobieski, 1674-1696
August II Mocny Wettin, 1697-1733

MINT MARKS

MW - Moneta Wschovensis, 1650-1655

Other letters appearing with date denote the Mintmaster at the time the coin was struck.

Mintmasters' Initials, Marks and Symbols

Mintmasters initials usually appear flanking the shield or by the date.

BYDGOSZCZ MINT
(Bromberg)

Initial	Date	Name
B		Bydgoszcz mint
(u) or SC	1594-1601	Stanislaw Cikowski, mint contractor
VI	1595-?	Walenteg (Valentin Jahns, mint contractor
(v)	Ca.1614	Stanislaw Koniecpolski, mintmaster
AS or SA	1614-17	Samuel Amman, die-cutter
CG	1650-52	Christoph Guttman
DS	1622	Daniel Seiler
GG	1640-44	Gabriel Gorloff
II or II-VE	1616-24	Jacob Jacobson van Emden
MH	1671-85	Michael Haderman
MRVM	1639	Mathias Rippers von Meiningen
MS	1640-42	Melchior Schirmer, mint official
BS	Ca. 1640-44	Benedykt Stefani, die-cutter
TT	1660	Thomas Timpf
EPH	1693-1714	Ernst Peter Hecht

ELBLAG MINT
(Elbing)

Initial	Date	Name
MP	1628-35	Marek (Marsilius) Philippson, mint contractor
BS	Ca. 1631-36	Benedykt Stefani, die-cutter
WVE or VE	1650-52	Wilhelm von Eck, mintmaster
NH	1652-65	Mikolaj Hennig, mintmaster
IP	1665-67	Jan Paulson, mintmaster
CS	1671-73	Chrystian Schultz, mintmaster

GDANSK MINT
(Danzig)

Initial	Date	Name
(x) = arm holding dagger	1582-1610	Philipp Klüwer, mintmaster
PK (in ligature)		
(w) = bear paw	1608-18	Daniel Klüwer, mintmaster
DC		
FB	Ca. 1610	Unknown die-cutter
SA	1613-21	Samuel Amman, medailleur and die-cutter
SB or BS	1618-35	Stanislaw Berman, mintmaster
DG	Ca. 1623	Unknown mint official
KHW	Ca. 1623	Unknown mint official
II or II-VE	1630-39	Jakub Jakobson van Emden, mint contractor
CS	1636-60	Chrystian Schirmer, Sr., warden
GR	1639-56	Gerard Rogge, mintmaster
IH/h	Ca. 1644-58	Jan Hoehn, die-cutter
DL	1656-85	Daniel Lesse, mintmaster
CS	1664-91	Chrystian Schirmer, Jr., warden

KRAKOW MINT
(Cracow)

Initial	Date	Name
(p) = lion rampant left or IF	1590-1609	Jan Firlej, royal mint director
(s) or HR	1595-1601	Hermann Rüdiger, royal mint contractor
(m)	1609-15	Baltazar Stanislawski, royal mint director
TKA/TA	1614-24	Tomasz Altenberger, royal mint contractor
W	1614-16	Stanislaw Warszycki, royal mint director
(o)	1616-24	Nikolaus Danillowicz, royal mint director
SA	1621	Samuel Amman, die-cutter
(n) = donkey head	1624-32	Hermolaus Ligeza, royal mint director
II or II-VE	1624-30	Jakub Jacobson van Emden, mint contractor
(y)	1632-50	Jan Danillowicz, royal mint director
CDC	1644-46	Claudius de Canotti
GP	1647-50	Gerhard Pyrami
(aa) = ox head facing	1650-59	Boguslaw Leszczynski, royal mint director
AT or ACPT	1650-67	Andrzej Tymf, royal mint contractor
SCH	1655-58	Stanislaw Chrzastowski, mint administrator
IT	1655-61	Jan Thamm, mintmaster & warden
IC	1656	Jakub Chamer, mintmaster
TLB	1658-87	Tytus Liwiusz Boratini, mintmaster
(z) = bird on horseshoe	1659-68	Jan Kazimierz Krasinski, royal mint director
(bb)	1668-83	Jan Andrzej Morsztyn, royal mint director
(cc)	1683-89	Marcin Zamojski, royal mint director
B	Ca. 1685	Gotfryd Bartsch, mint contractor
(dd)	1689-92	Markus Matczynski, royal mint director

LOBZENICA MINT
(Lobsenz)

Initial	Date	Name
L		Lobzenica mint
AK	1612	Andrzej Krotoski, mintmaster
	1612-15	Jan Beker, mintmaster

LWÓW MINT
(Lvov in Ukraine, Ger. Lemberg)

Initial	Date	Name
GBA or BGA	1661-63	Giovanni Battista Amuretti, mint contractor

OLKUSZ MINT

Initial	Date	Name
(i) = clover	Ca. 1680	Unknown

POZNAN
(Posen)

Initial	Date	Name
RL (usually ligature)	1599-1601	Rudolph Lehmann, medailleur and warden
GC	Ca. 1610	Unknown moneyer
AT	1650-60	Andrzej Tymp (Tümfe, Tümpfe), mint contractor
NG	1660-62	Mikolaj (Nicolaus) Gille, mint administrator

TORUN MINT
(Thorn)

Initial	Date	Name
HH	1629-31	Henryk Hema, warden
HL	1630	Jan (Hans) Lippe, mintmaster
II or II-VE	1630-39	Jakub Jakobson van Emden, mint contractor
MS	1640-42	Melchior Schirmer, mintmaster
GR	1643-49	Gerard Rogge, mintmaster
HDL	1649-69	Jan (Hans) Dawid Lauer, mint contractor
HIL	1653-55	Jan (Hans) Jakub Lauer, mintmaster
HS	1668-72	Henryk Sievert, mintmaster

UJAZDOW MINT

Initial	Date	Name
TLB	1659-65	Tytus Liwiusz Boratini, mintmaster

WSCHOWA MINT
(Fraustadt)

Initial	Date	Name
HR	1595-1601	Herman Rüdiger
RL (usually ligature)	1599-1603	Rudolph Lehmann, medailleur and warden

ARMS as Found on Coins of Poland
Batory dynasty – wolf's jawbone with 3 teeth
Elblag – shield divided horizontally with cross in each half, lower half shaded
Gdansk – crown over 2 crosses, 1 above the other
Jagiellon dynasty – double-barred cross
Lithuania – knight on horseback to left
Prussia – eagle usually holding sword over head with claw
Torun – triple-towered city gate
Waza dynasty – sheaf of grain
Wschowa – double-barred cross, annulet to either side between bars

MONETARY SYSTEM

Until 1815

1 Solidus = 1 Schilling
3 Solidi = 2 Poltura = 1 Grosz
3 Poltura = 1-1/2 Grosze = 1 Polturak
6 Groszy = 1 Szostak
18 Groszy = 1 Tympf = 1 Ort
30 Groszy = 4 Silbergroschen = 1 Zloty
1 Talar = 1 Zloty
6 Zlotych = 1 Reichsthaler
8 Zlotych = 1 Speciesthaler
5 Speciesthaler = 1 August D'or
3 Ducats = 1 Stanislaus D'or

KINGDOM

STANDARD COINAGE

KM# 34 DENAR (Solidus, Obol, Halerz)

Silver **Ruler:** Sigismund III **Obv:** Crowned large S **Rev:** Three shields

Date	Mintage	Good	VG	F	VF	XF
(16)12	—	—	—	—	—	—
(16)18	—	30.00	60.00	115	—	—
(16)19	—	34.50	70.00	140	—	—
(16)20	—	34.50	70.00	140	—	—
(16)21	—	30.00	60.00	115	—	—
(16)ZZ	—	30.00	60.00	115	—	—
(16)22	—	30.00	60.00	115	—	—
(16)Z3	—	17.00	34.50	70.00	—	—
(16)23	—	—	—	—	—	—
(16)Z4	—	17.00	34.50	70.00	—	—
(16)24	—	—	—	—	—	—

KM# 1 DENAR (Solidus, Obol, Halerz)

Silver **Ruler:** Sigismund III **Obv:** Three shields

Date	Mintage	Good	VG	F	VF	XF
ND	—	14.00	25.00	50.00	—	—

KM# 3 3 DENAR (Trzeciak, Ternar)

Silver **Ruler:** Sigismund III **Obv:** Large S, shield at center **Rev:** Three shields, crown above

Date	Mintage	Good	VG	F	VF	XF
1601 Rare	—	—	—	—	—	—

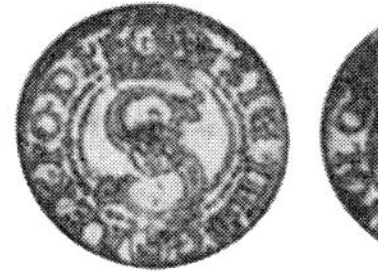

KM# 4 SOLIDUS (Szelag, Schilling)

Silver **Ruler:** Sigismund III **Obv:** Crowned large S, dividing date and initials **Rev:** Crown above two or three shields **Note:** Struck at Bromberg, Fraustadt, Marborg, Krakow and Poznan mints.

Date	Mintage	Good	VG	F	VF	XF
1601 Inverted F	—	6.00	17.00	34.50	70.00	—
1601 F	—	6.00	17.00	34.50	70.00	—
1601	—	6.00	17.00	34.50	70.00	—
1601 BB	—	9.00	17.00	34.50	70.00	—
1601 B	—	6.00	12.00	22.50	50.00	—
1601 B-B	—	9.00	17.00	34.50	70.00	—
1601 FF	—	3.00	7.00	14.00	22.50	—
1601 C	—	3.00	7.00	14.00	22.50	—
1601 D	—	3.00	7.00	14.00	22.50	—
1601 G	—	3.00	7.00	14.00	22.50	—
1601 K	—	3.00	7.00	14.00	30.00	—
1601 M	—	3.00	7.00	14.00	22.50	—
1601 N	—	3.00	7.00	14.00	22.50	—
1613	—	3.00	6.00	12.00	20.00	—
1616 F	—	3.00	6.00	12.00	20.00	—
1616 P	—	3.00	6.00	12.00	20.00	—
1619 F	—	3.00	6.00	12.00	20.00	—

KM# 25 SOLIDUS (Szelag, Schilling)

Silver **Ruler:** Sigismund III **Obv:** Crowned large SR **Rev:** Legend and date **Note:** Varieties exist.

Date	Mintage	Good	VG	F	VF	XF
1601K	—	—	—	—	—	—
1616K	—	3.00	9.00	17.00	30.00	—
1622K	—	3.00	9.00	17.00	30.00	—
16ZZK	—	3.00	9.00	17.00	30.00	—
1623K	—	3.00	9.00	17.00	30.00	—
1624K	—	3.00	9.00	17.00	30.00	—
1625K	—	3.00	9.00	17.00	30.00	—
1626K	—	2.25	6.00	12.00	20.00	—
1627K	—	6.00	17.00	34.50	70.00	—
1631K Unique	—	—	—	—	—	—
NDK	—	3.00	9.00	17.00	30.00	—

KM# 16 SOLIDUS (Szelag, Schilling)

Silver **Ruler:** Sigismund III **Obv:** Eagle with shield on breast **Rev:** Crowned large S, shield at center dividing date **Note:** Legend varieties exist.

Date	Mintage	Good	VG	F	VF	XF
(16)13	—	3.00	7.00	14.00	22.50	—
(16)14 Rare	—	—	—	—	—	—
(1)614	—	3.00	7.00	14.00	22.50	—
1616 SR	—	7.00	14.00	27.50	60.00	—
(16)16	—	3.00	7.00	14.00	22.50	—
(16)17	—	—	—	—	—	—
(16)19	—	12.00	34.50	85.00	175	—
(16)21 Rare	—	—	—	—	—	—
(16)25	—	3.00	7.00	14.00	22.50	—

KM# 24 SOLIDUS (Szelag, Schilling)

Silver **Ruler:** Sigismund III **Obv:** Three shields **Rev:** Crowned large S, shield at center dividing date

Date	Mintage	Good	VG	F	VF	XF
1616	—	—	—	—	—	—

KM# 28 SOLIDUS (Szelag, Schilling)

Silver **Ruler:** Sigismund III **Rev:** Three-line inscription

Date	Mintage	Good	VG	F	VF	XF
1617	—	3.00	7.00	14.00	22.50	—

KM# 36 SOLIDUS (Szelag, Schilling)

Silver **Ruler:** Sigismund III **Obv:** Eagle with shield on breast **Rev:** Large crown

Date	Mintage	Good	VG	F	VF	XF
1620	—	4.00	8.00	16.00	30.00	—
1621	—	4.00	8.00	16.00	30.00	—

KM# A37 SOLIDUS (Szelag, Schilling)

Silver **Ruler:** Sigismund III **Obv:** Five-fold arms in inner circle **Obv. Legend:** SIGIS•III•D•G•REX•POLONIA• **Rev:** Crowned S with shield in center divides date **Rev. Legend:** SOLIDVS REGNI POLO

Date	Mintage	Good	VG	F	VF	XF
(16)25	—	5.00	9.00	18.00	36.75	—
(16)26	—	5.00	9.00	18.00	36.75	—

KM# 83 SOLIDUS (Szelag, Schilling)

Copper **Ruler:** Johann Casimir **Obv:** Crowned JCR monogram **Rev:** Inscription, date below

Date	Mintage	Good	VG	F	VF	XF
1650	—	60.00	80.00	140	290	—

KM# 84 SOLIDUS (Szelag, Schilling)

Copper **Ruler:** Johann Casimir **Obv:** Crowned JCR monogram in circle **Rev:** Crowned eagle with shield on breast

Date	Mintage	Good	VG	F	VF	XF
1650	—	60.00	80.00	140	290	—

KM# 100 SOLIDUS (Szelag, Schilling)

Copper **Ruler:** Johann Casimir **Obv:** Crowned eagle with shield on breast **Rev:** Crowned large S, shield in center

Date	Mintage	Good	VG	F	VF	XF
1652 Rare	—	—	—	—	—	—
1653 Rare	—	—	—	—	—	—

KM# 110 SOLIDUS (Szelag, Schilling)

Copper **Ruler:** Johann Casimir **Obv:** Bust right **Rev:** Crowned eagle with shield on breast

Date	Mintage	Good	VG	F	VF	XF
1659	—	2.25	5.00	10.00	22.50	—
1660	—	2.25	5.00	10.00	20.00	—
1661	—	2.25	5.00	10.00	20.00	—

KM# 20 3 POLKER (3 Poltorak - 1 Kruzierz)

Silver **Ruler:** Sigismund III **Obv:** Eagle with shield on breast **Rev:** 24 within orb dividing date **Note:** Varieties exist.

Date	Mintage	Good	VG	F	VF	XF
(16)14 W	—	12.00	22.50	40.25	60.00	—

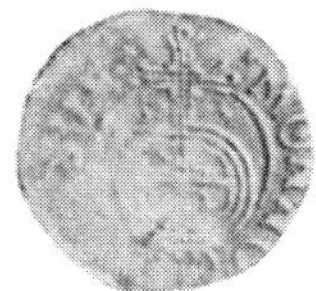

KM# 41 3 POLKER (3 Poltorak - 1 Kruzierz)

Silver **Ruler:** Sigismund III **Obv:** Crowned shield **Rev:** 24 within orb dividing date **Note:** Varieties exist.

Date	Mintage	Good	VG	F	VF	XF
(16)14	—	7.00	22.50	46.00	70.00	—
1614	—	3.00	14.00	30.00	46.00	—
1615	—	3.00	14.00	30.00	46.00	—
(16)15	—	3.00	14.00	30.00	46.00	—
(16)16	—	3.00	14.00	30.00	46.00	—
(16)17	—	3.00	14.00	30.00	46.00	—
(16)18	—	3.00	14.00	30.00	46.00	—
(16)19	—	3.00	14.00	30.00	46.00	—
16Z0	—	2.25	7.00	14.00	22.50	—
(16)20	—	2.25	7.00	14.00	22.50	—
(16)21	—	2.25	6.00	12.00	17.00	—
(16)22	—	1.25	3.00	7.00	12.00	—
(16)23	—	1.25	3.00	7.00	12.00	—
(16)24	—	1.25	3.00	7.00	12.00	—
(16)25	—	1.25	3.00	7.00	12.00	—
(16)26	—	1.25	3.00	7.00	12.00	—
16Z7	—	1.75	3.00	7.00	12.00	—
(16)27	—	1.25	3.00	7.00	12.00	—
16Z8	—	12.00	22.50	60.00	85.00	—
(16)28	—	12.00	22.50	60.00	85.00	—
ND	—	6.00	12.00	22.50	40.25	—

KM# 105 3 POLKER (3 Poltorak - 1 Kruzierz)

Silver **Ruler:** Johann Casimir **Obv:** Crowned shield **Rev:** 60 within orb **Note:** Varieties exist with 60 or 61 in orb.

Date	Mintage	Good	VG	F	VF	XF
(16)54 Rare	—	—	—	—	—	—
(16)58 Rare	—	—	—	—	—	—
(16)59	—	40.25	100	200	325	—
(16)61	—	30.00	60.00	115	200	—
(16)62	—	22.50	34.50	60.00	115	—
(16)66 Rare	—	—	—	—	—	—

KM# 23 3 KREUZER

Silver **Ruler:** Sigismund III **Obv:** Crowned bust right **Rev:** Crowned shield **Note:** Varieties exist.

Date	Mintage	Good	VG	F	VF	XF
1615	—	7.00	14.00	31.00	46.00	—
1616	—	7.00	14.00	31.00	46.00	—
1617	—	7.00	14.00	31.00	46.00	—
1618	—	12.00	17.00	40.25	80.00	—

KM# 5 GROSCHEN (1/24 Thaler, 7-1/2 Groszy, Srebrnik)

Silver **Ruler:** Sigismund III **Obv:** Crowned half-length bust right, lion in shield below **Rev:** Crown above three shields, eagle **Note:** Varieties exist.

Date	Mintage	Good	VG	F	VF	XF
1601	—	9.00	17.00	39.25	65.00	—
1603	—	9.00	17.00	39.25	65.00	—
1604	—	6.00	12.00	17.00	39.25	—
1605	—	6.00	12.00	17.00	39.25	—
1605	—	6.00	12.00	17.00	39.25	—
Note: Legend error: G POSSVS...						
1606	—	6.00	12.00	17.00	39.25	—
1607	—	6.00	12.00	17.00	39.25	—
1607	—	6.00	12.00	17.00	39.25	—
Note: Legend error: ...POLONI/ND...						

KM# 11 GROSCHEN (1/24 Thaler, 7-1/2 Groszy, Srebrnik)

Silver **Ruler:** Sigismund III **Obv:** Large crown above legend **Rev:** Eagle with shield on breast, lion in shield below **Note:** Varieties exist.

Date	Mintage	Good	VG	F	VF	XF
1601 Error 10	—	30.00	46.00	90.00	175	—
1603	—	30.00	46.00	90.00	175	—
1604	—	6.00	12.00	22.50	34.50	—
1605	—	6.00	12.00	22.50	34.50	—
1606	—	6.00	12.00	22.50	34.50	—
1607	—	6.00	12.00	22.50	34.50	—
1608	—	30.00	46.00	90.00	175	—
1609	—	6.00	12.00	22.50	34.50	—
1610	—	6.00	12.00	22.50	34.50	—
1611	—	6.00	12.00	22.50	34.50	—
1612	—	6.00	12.00	22.50	34.50	—
1613	—	6.00	12.00	22.50	34.50	—
1614	—	6.00	12.00	22.50	34.50	—
1615	—	6.00	12.00	22.50	34.50	—
1616	—	—	—	—	—	—
1617	—	—	—	—	—	—
1621 Error 12	—	—	—	—	—	—
1623	—	2.25	6.00	12.00	30.00	—

Date	Mintage	Good	VG	F	VF	XF
1624	—	2.25	6.00	12.00	30.00	—
1625	—	2.25	6.00	12.00	30.00	—
1626	—	2.25	6.00	12.00	30.00	—
1627	—	2.25	6.00	12.00	30.00	—
ND	—	12.00	22.50	40.25	75.00	—

KM# 8 GROSCHEN (1/24 Thaler, 7-1/2 Groszy, Srebrnik)

Silver **Ruler:** Sigismund III **Obv:** Crowned bust left **Rev:** Eagle with shield on breast, lion in shield below **Note:** Varieties exist.

Date	Mintage	Good	VG	F	VF	XF
1604	—	7.00	14.00	31.00	46.00	—
1607	—	5.00	9.00	22.50	41.50	—
1608	—	5.00	9.00	22.50	41.50	—

KM# 85 GROSCHEN (1/24 Thaler, 7-1/2 Groszy, Srebrnik)

Silver **Ruler:** Johann Casimir **Obv:** Crowned eagle with shield on breast **Rev:** Crown above date and legend **Note:** Struck at Krakow and Bydgoszcz; Varieties exist.

Date	Mintage	Good	VG	F	VF	XF
1650 Rare	—	—	—	—	—	—
1666 Rare	—	—	—	—	—	—

KM# 86 2 GROSCHEN (1/12 Thaler, 15 Groszy, Polzlotek)

Silver **Ruler:** Johann Casimir **Obv:** Crowned eagle with shield on breast **Rev:** Crown above legend and date

Date	Mintage	Good	VG	F	VF	XF
1650 CG	—	17.00	34.50	70.00	140	—

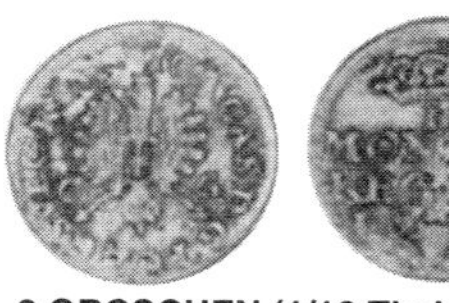

KM# 97 2 GROSCHEN (1/12 Thaler, 15 Groszy, Polzlotek)

Silver **Ruler:** Johann Casimir **Rev:** Crown above value, legend and date **Note:** Varieties exist.

Date	Mintage	Good	VG	F	VF	XF
1651 CG	—	—	17.00	34.50	85.00	175
1652	—	—	22.50	60.00	115	230
1654 Rare	—	—	—	—	—	—

KM# 88.1 18 GROSZY (Tympf)

Silver **Ruler:** Johann Casimir **Obv:** Laureate bust right **Rev:** Crowned shield dividing 18 **Note:** Numerious varieties exist.

Date	Mintage	Good	VG	F	VF	XF
1650 CGDAL Rare	—	—	—	—	—	—
1650 CG/BA Rare	—	—	—	—	—	—
1650 GP Rare	—	—	—	—	—	—
1650 CG Rare	—	—	—	—	—	—
1650	—	17.00	30.00	80.00	140	—
1651 MW	—	17.00	30.00	80.00	140	—
1651 MW (monogram)	—	14.00	25.00	75.00	115	—
1651 CG	—	17.00	40.25	115	230	—
1651 AT	—	34.50	75.00	175	350	—
1652	—	17.00	30.00	80.00	140	—
1652 MW	—	17.00	30.00	80.00	140	—
1652 CG Rare	—	—	—	—	—	—
1652 AT	—	17.00	40.25	85.00	230	—
1653 MW	—	17.00	30.00	80.00	140	—
1653 MW (monogram)	—	14.00	25.00	75.00	115	—
1653 AT	—	14.00	30.00	80.00	140	—
1654 MW	—	17.00	30.00	80.00	115	—
1654 MW (monogram)	—	17.00	30.00	80.00	140	—
1654 AT	—	17.00	40.25	105	140	—
1655 MW (monogram)	—	14.00	20.00	70.00	140	—
1655 IT	—	14.00	20.00	70.00	175	—
1655 AT	—	17.00	30.00	80.00	125	—
1655 SCH	—	14.00	20.00	70.00	125	—

KM# 88.2 18 GROSZY (Tympf)

Silver **Ruler:** Johann Casimir **Rev:** 22 flanking shield

Date	Mintage	Good	VG	F	VF	XF
1650 CG	—	70.00	115	215	350	—

KM# 88.3 18 GROSZY (Tympf)

Silver **Ruler:** Johann Casimir **Rev:** 21 flanking shield

Date	Mintage	Good	VG	F	VF	XF
1650 CG	—	70.00	115	215	350	—

KM# A94 18 GROSZY (Tympf)

Silver **Ruler:** Johann Casimir **Obv:** Crowned portrait bust right **Rev:** Crowned shield **Note:** Numerious varieties exist. Prev. KM#88.4.

Date	Mintage	Good	VG	F	VF	XF
1651 AT	—	34.50	75.00	145	290	—
1652 AT	—	17.00	40.25	85.00	175	—
1653 AT	—	17.00	40.25	85.00	175	—
1654 AT	—	17.00	40.25	75.00	145	—
1655 IT	—	14.00	20.00	40.25	85.00	—
1655 AT	—	17.00	30.00	50.00	100	—
1656 AT	—	34.50	85.00	175	350	—
1656 IT/IC	—	17.00	30.00	50.00	100	—
1656 IDV/IC Rare	—	—	—	—	—	—
1656 Lion	—	60.00	115	175	350	—
1657 AT	—	14.00	20.00	30.00	85.00	—
1657 IT/SCH	—	14.00	20.00	40.25	85.00	—
1657 Lion	—	—	—	—	—	—
1658 AT, "18"	—	14.00	20.00	100	200	—
1658	—	17.00	34.50	70.00	175	—
1658 AT	—	14.00	20.00	70.00	115	—
1658 "18"	—	14.00	20.00	70.00	115	—
1658 IT/SCH	—	14.00	20.00	80.00	140	—
1658 TLB/IT	—	17.00	30.00	70.00	115	—
1658 TLB	—	14.00	20.00	70.00	115	—
1659 AT	—	14.00	20.00	70.00	115	—
1659 TLB	—	14.00	20.00	70.00	115	—
1660 GBA Rare	—	—	—	—	—	—
1660 Lion Rare	—	—	—	—	—	—
1663 AT	—	14.00	20.00	70.00	115	—
1664 AT	—	14.00	20.00	70.00	115	—
1667 TLB	—	14.00	20.00	70.00	115	—
1668 TLB	—	14.00	20.00	70.00	115	—

KM# 126 18 GROSZY (Tympf)

Silver **Ruler:** Johann III Sobieski **Obv:** Laureate armored bust right **Rev:** Crowned shield, 18 flanking shield **Note:** For previously listed 18 Groszy, KM#134, see 1/4 Thaler, KM#677, Saxony-German States.

Date	Mintage	Good	VG	F	VF	XF
1677	—	22.50	46.00	105	175	—
1677 SB	—	12.00	20.00	70.00	125	—
1677 MH	—	17.00	30.00	80.00	140	—
1678	—	12.00	20.00	70.00	125	—
1678 SB	—	17.00	30.00	80.00	140	—
1678 MN Rare	—	—	—	—	—	—
1679	—	17.00	30.00	80.00	140	—
1679 TLB	—	17.00	30.00	80.00	150	—
1680	—	30.00	60.00	115	175	—
1684 TLB	—	12.00	20.00	70.00	115	—
1685	—	46.00	70.00	145	175	—
1686	—	60.00	85.00	175	290	—

KM# 32 ORT (18 Groszy - 1/4 Thaler)

Silver **Ruler:** Sigismund III **Obv:** Crowned half-length figure right **Rev:** Crowned shield within fleece collar

Date	Mintage	Good	VG	F	VF	XF
1618 Rare	—	—	—	—	—	—

KM# 37 ORT (18 Groszy - 1/4 Thaler)

Silver **Ruler:** Sigismund III **Rev:** Crowned shield **Note:** Varieties exist.

Date	Mintage	Good	VG	F	VF	XF
1620 IIVE Rare	—	—	—	—	—	—
1620/21	—	—	—	—	—	—
1621 IIVE	—	—	—	—	—	—
1622	—	14.00	25.00	46.00	80.00	—
1623	—	12.00	17.00	30.00	60.00	—
1624	—	12.00	17.00	30.00	60.00	—
1625 Rare	—	—	—	—	—	—
1628 11 Rare	—	—	—	—	—	—
ND	—	—	—	—	—	—

KM# A6 3 GROSCHEN

Silver **Ruler:** Sigismund III **Obv:** Large crowned bust left **Rev:** Value and armorials above inscription, date

Date	Mintage	Good	VG	F	VF	XF
1601 K	—	6.00	12.00	22.00	45.00	—

KM# 6 3 GROSCHEN

Silver **Ruler:** Sigismund III **Obv:** Crowned bust right **Rev:** Value and armorial above legend, date and mintmaster below **Note:** Varieties exist.

Date	Mintage	Good	VG	F	VF	XF
1601 K	—	7.00	14.00	25.00	50.00	—
1601 FI	—	12.00	17.00	33.75	70.00	—
1601 P	—	6.00	12.00	22.50	50.00	—
1601 F	—	6.00	12.00	22.50	50.00	—
1601 B	—	6.00	12.00	22.50	50.00	—
1601 L/IF	—	12.00	17.00	33.75	70.00	—
1601 L Rare	—	—	—	—	—	—
1601 IF Rare	—	—	—	—	—	—
1602 K	—	17.00	39.25	85.00	170	—
1603 K	—	17.00	39.25	85.00	170	—
1604 K	—	7.00	14.00	25.00	50.00	—
1605 K	—	7.00	14.00	25.00	50.00	—
1606 K	—	22.50	46.75	90.00	195	—
1607 K	—	7.00	14.00	25.00	42.50	—
1608 Rare	—	—	—	—	—	—
1614 TKA Rare	—	—	—	—	—	—
ND	—	12.00	17.00	33.75	70.00	—

KM# 31 3 GROSCHEN

Silver **Ruler:** Sigismund III **Rev:** Value, armorials and date above legend **Note:** Varieties exist.

Date	Mintage	Good	VG	F	VF	XF
1618	—	6.00	12.00	22.50	41.50	—
1619	—	6.00	12.00	22.50	41.50	—
1620	—	6.00	12.00	22.50	41.50	—
1621	—	6.00	12.00	22.50	41.50	—
1622	—	6.00	12.00	22.50	41.50	—
1623	—	6.00	12.00	22.50	41.50	—
1624	—	6.00	12.00	22.50	41.50	—
ND	—	12.00	17.00	34.50	75.00	—

KM# 87 3 GROSCHEN

Silver **Ruler:** Johann Casimir **Obv:** Bust of Johann Casimir right **Rev:** Crown dividing date above value and legend

Date	Mintage	Good	VG	F	VF	XF
1650 CG Rare	—	—	—	—	—	—
1657 Rare	—	—	—	—	—	—
1658 Rare	—	—	—	—	—	—

KM# 114 3 GROSCHEN

Silver **Ruler:** Johann Casimir **Obv:** Crowned bust right **Rev:** Value above armorials, date and legend **Note:** Varieties exist.

Date	Mintage	Good	VG	F	VF	XF
1660 Rare	—	—	—	—	—	—
1661 AT Rare	—	—	—	—	—	—
1662 AT	—	40.25	75.00	145	290	—
1665 AT Rare	—	—	—	—	—	—

KM# 130 3 GROSCHEN

Silver **Ruler:** Johann Casimir **Obv:** Laureate bust of Johann III Sobieski right **Rev:** Value and armorials above legend and date

Date	Mintage	Good	VG	F	VF	XF
1684 C	—	34.50	70.00	145	290	—
1684 B	—	—	—	—	—	—
1685 B	—	34.50	70.00	145	290	—

KM# 7.1 6 GROSCHEN

Silver **Ruler:** Sigismund III **Obv:** Crowned bust right **Rev:** Value and armorials above legend and date

Date	Mintage	Good	VG	F	VF	XF
1601 (P)	—	17.00	40.25	75.00	140	—

KM# 7.2 6 GROSCHEN

Silver **Ruler:** Sigismund III

Date	Mintage	Good	VG	F	VF	XF
1601 (P)-M	—	17.00	40.25	75.00	140	—

KM# 42 6 GROSCHEN

Silver **Ruler:** Sigismund III **Rev:** Crown above three shields
Note: Varieties exist.

Date	Mintage	Good	VG	F	VF	XF
1623	—	8.00	16.00	30.00	65.00	—
1624	—	8.00	16.00	30.00	65.00	—
1625	—	8.00	16.00	30.00	65.00	—
1626	—	8.00	16.00	30.00	65.00	—
1627	—	8.00	16.00	30.00	65.00	—
ND	—	10.00	17.00	34.50	75.00	—

KM# 91 6 GROSCHEN

Silver **Ruler:** Johann Casimir **Obv:** Large crowned bust right in linear circle **Rev:** Crown above three shields **Note:** Varieties exist.

Date	Mintage	Good	VG	F	VF	XF
1650	—	40.25	75.00	145	290	—
1656 IT	—	7.00	14.00	32.25	60.00	—
1657 IT	—	7.00	14.00	32.25	60.00	—
1658 IT Rare	—	—	—	—	—	—
1658 TLB	—	30.00	60.00	115	230	—
1659	—	7.00	14.00	32.25	60.00	—
1660	—	7.00	14.00	32.25	60.00	—
1660 GBA	—	7.00	14.00	32.25	60.00	—
1660 TT	—	7.00	14.00	32.25	60.00	—
1660 TLB	—	7.00	14.00	32.25	60.00	—
1660 LT	—	7.00	14.00	32.25	60.00	—
1661 TLB	—	7.00	14.00	32.25	60.00	—
1661 GBA	—	7.00	14.00	32.25	60.00	—
1661 NG	—	7.00	14.00	32.25	60.00	—
1661 AT	—	7.00	14.00	32.25	60.00	—
1661 TT	—	7.00	14.00	32.25	60.00	—
1662 AT	—	7.00	14.00	32.25	60.00	—
1662 ACPT	—	12.00	22.50	46.00	100	—
1662 NG	—	7.00	14.00	32.25	60.00	—
1662 TT	—	7.00	14.00	32.25	60.00	—
1662	—	7.00	14.00	32.25	60.00	—
1662 BGA	—	12.00	22.50	46.00	100	—
1662 GBA	—	7.00	14.00	32.25	60.00	—
1663 AT	—	7.00	14.00	32.25	60.00	—
1663 ACPT	—	12.00	22.50	46.00	100	—
1664 AT	—	7.00	14.00	32.25	60.00	—
1664 ACPT Rare	—	—	—	—	—	—
1664 TLB Rare	—	—	—	—	—	—
1665 AT	—	6.00	14.00	32.25	60.00	—
1666 AT	—	6.00	14.00	32.25	60.00	—
1666 TLB Rare	—	—	—	—	—	—
1667 TLB	—	12.00	22.50	46.00	90.00	—

KM# 89 6 GROSCHEN

Silver **Ruler:** Johann Casimir **Obv:** Small bust of Johann Casimir right **Rev:** Crown above three shields

Date	Mintage	Good	VG	F	VF	XF
1650	—	—	—	—	—	—

KM# 90 6 GROSCHEN

Silver **Ruler:** Johann Casimir **Obv:** Large bust right **Rev:** Crowned eagle with shield on breast

Date	Mintage	Good	VG	F	VF	XF
1650 CG	—	50.00	105	205	325	—

KM# 121 6 GROSCHEN

Silver **Ruler:** Johann Casimir **Obv:** Crowned bust within pellet circle

Date	Mintage	Good	VG	F	VF	XF
1667 TLB	—	7.00	14.00	32.25	60.00	—
1667 AT	—	7.00	14.00	32.25	60.00	—
1668 TLB	—	7.00	14.00	32.25	60.00	—
ND TLB	—	17.00	30.00	50.00	100	—
ND AT	—	17.00	30.00	50.00	100	—

KM# 122 6 GROSCHEN

Silver **Ruler:** Johann III Sobieski **Obv:** Crowned bust right **Rev:** Crown above three shields **Note:** Varieties exist.

Date	Mintage	Good	VG	F	VF	XF
1677	—	7.00	17.00	36.75	70.00	—
1677 SB Rare	—	—	—	—	—	—
1677 TLB Rare	—	—	—	—	—	—
1678	—	7.00	17.00	36.75	70.00	—
1679 TLB	—	7.00	17.00	36.75	70.00	—
1680 TLB/C	—	12.00	22.50	46.00	100	—
1680 K Rare	—	—	—	—	—	—
1680 IT Rare	—	—	—	—	—	—
1681 TLB	—	7.00	17.00	36.75	70.00	—
1681 TLB/C	—	7.00	17.00	36.75	70.00	—
1682 TLB without C	—	7.00	17.00	36.75	70.00	—
1682 C with TLB only	—	17.00	34.50	70.00	140	—

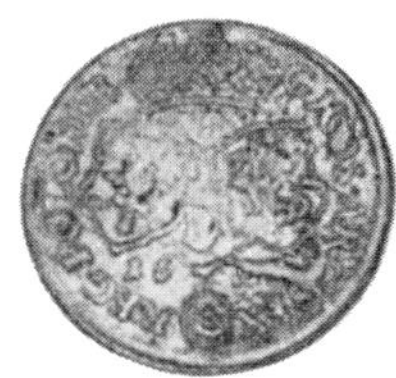

KM# 128 6 GROSCHEN

Silver **Ruler:** Johann III Sobieski **Obv:** Laureate armored bust right

Date	Mintage	Good	VG	F	VF	XF
1682 TLB	—	7.00	17.00	40.25	75.00	—
1683 TLB/C	—	7.00	17.00	40.25	75.00	—
1683 C	—	7.00	17.00	40.25	75.00	—
1684 TLB	—	7.00	17.00	40.25	75.00	—
1684 SVP	—	17.00	30.00	50.00	100	—
1684 SP	—	7.00	17.00	40.25	80.00	—
1684 C	—	17.00	30.00	50.00	100	—
1685 B	—	7.00	17.00	40.25	80.00	—
1686 TLB	—	30.00	60.00	115	290	—
1687 TLB	—	30.00	60.00	115	290	—

KM# 135 6 GROSCHEN

Silver **Ruler:** August II **Obv:** Small crowned bust of August II right **Rev:** Crown above three shields

Date	Mintage	VG	F	VF	XF	Unc
1698EPH Rare	—	—	—	—	—	—

KM# 120 GULDEN (30 Groschen - 1/3 Thaler - Tympf)

Silver **Ruler:** Johann Casimir **Obv:** Crowned monogram **Rev:** Crowned shield, XXX GRO on shield

Date	Mintage	VG	F	VF	XF	Unc
1633 AT Rare, error 63	—	—	—	—	—	—
1661 Rare	—	—	—	—	—	—
1663	—	12.00	25.00	40.00	80.00	—
1663 AT	—	12.00	25.00	40.00	80.00	—
1664 AT	—	12.00	25.00	40.00	80.00	—
1665 AT	—	12.00	25.00	40.00	80.00	—
1665/1665	—	12.00	25.00	40.00	80.00	—
1666 AT	—	12.00	25.00	40.00	80.00	—

KM# 123 GULDEN (30 Groschen - 1/3 Thaler - Tympf)

Silver **Ruler:** Johann Casimir **Obv:** Laureate bust of Michael Korybut right **Rev:** Crowned shield, date divided by crown, 1/3 in shield below

Date	Mintage	VG	F	VF	XF	Unc
1671 MH Rare	—	—	—	—	—	—

KM# 38 1/2 THALER (4 Zlotych - 1/2 Talar)

Silver **Ruler:** Sigismund III **Obv:** Crowned half-length figure right **Rev:** Crowned shield within fleece collar **Rev. Legend:** SAM LIV NE NO SVE GOT VAD Q HRI REX **Note:** Varieties exist.

Date	Mintage	VG	F	VF	XF	Unc
1620 IIVE Rare	—	—	—	—	—	—
1622 IIVE Rare	—	—	—	—	—	—
1628	—	115	175	450	975	—
1628 11	—	115	230	525	1,050	—
1629 II	—	115	230	525	1,050	—
1630	—	115	175	450	975	—
1631 II	—	115	175	450	975	—
1632 II Rare	—	—	—	—	—	—

KM# 55 1/2 THALER (4 Zlotych - 1/2 Talar)

Silver **Ruler:** Wladislaus IV **Obv:** Crowned bust right **Obv. Legend:** VLADISLS IIII D G REX POL M D L LIT RVS PRVS MAS **Rev:** Crowned arms within fleece collar **Note:** Varieties exist.

Date	Mintage	VG	F	VF	XF	Unc
1633 Rare	—	—	—	—	—	—
1634 Rare	—	—	—	—	—	—
1640 GG Rare	—	—	—	—	—	—
1640 BS Rare	—	—	—	—	—	—
1641 GG Rare	—	—	—	—	—	—
1642 GG Rare	—	—	—	—	—	—
164Z BS Rare	—	—	—	—	—	—
1644 CDC Rare	—	—	—	—	—	—
1645 CDC Rare	—	—	—	—	—	—
1646 CDC Rare	—	—	—	—	—	—
1646 GGT Rare	—	—	—	—	—	—
1647 GP Rare	—	—	—	—	—	—

KM# 70 1/2 THALER (4 Zlotych - 1/2 Talar)

Silver **Ruler:** Wladislaus IV **Obv:** Large laureate bust of Johann Casimir right **Rev:** Crowned oval shield

Date	Mintage	VG	F	VF	XF	Unc
1649 GP Rare	—	—	—	—	—	—
1649 GR Rare	—	—	—	—	—	—
1651 Rare	—	—	—	—	—	—
1652 MW Rare	—	—	—	—	—	—

KM# 71 1/2 THALER (4 Zlotych - 1/2 Talar)

Silver **Ruler:** Wladislaus IV **Obv:** Smaller crowned bust right **Rev:** Crowned shield **Note:** For previously listed 1/2 Thaler, KM#158, see KM#928, Saxony-German States.

Date	Mintage	VG	F	VF	XF	Unc
ND1652 GP Rare	—	—	—	—	—	—

KM# 17 THALER

Silver **Ruler:** Sigismund III **Rev:** Crowned arms in fleece collar **Note:** Dav. #4311.

Date	Mintage	VG	F	VF	XF	Unc
ND Rare	—	—	—	—	—	—
1613 Rare	—	—	—	—	—	—
1614	—	350	700	1,250	2,300	—
1616 Rare	—	—	—	—	—	—

KM# A17 THALER

Silver **Ruler:** Sigismund III **Obv:** Bust of Sigismund III right **Rev:** Crowned arms in ornate frame **Note:** Dav. #A4310.

Date	Mintage	VG	F	VF	XF	Unc
1612	—	—	—	—	—	—

KM# 18 THALER

Silver **Ruler:** Sigismund III **Note:** Klippe. Dav.#4311A.

Date	Mintage	VG	F	VF	XF	Unc
1613 Rare	—	—	—	—	—	—
1614 Rare	—	—	—	—	—	—
1616 Rare	—	—	—	—	—	—
1617 SA Rare	—	—	—	—	—	—
1617 IIVE Rare	—	—	—	—	—	—
1617 MS Rare	—	—	—	—	—	—
1617 AS Rare	—	—	—	—	—	—

KM# 33.1 THALER

Silver **Ruler:** Sigismund III **Obv:** Crowned half-length figure right **Rev:** Crowned shield above 6-0 dividing date **Note:** Dav. #4313.

Date	Mintage	VG	F	VF	XF	Unc
1618 MS Unique	—	—	—	—	—	—
1620	—	260	525	975	1,600	—
1620 IIVE	—	260	525	975	1,600	—
1621 IIVE	—	260	525	975	1,600	—

KM# 33.2 THALER

Silver **Ruler:** Sigismund III **Rev:** Crowned shield above 3-0 dividing date **Note:** Legend varieties exist.

Date	Mintage	VG	F	VF	XF	Unc
1621 IIVE Rare	—	—	—	—	—	—
1622 IIVE	—	625	1,250	2,500	3,500	—
1623 IIVE	—	625	1,250	2,500	3,500	—

KM# 43 THALER

Silver **Ruler:** Sigismund III **Rev:** Crowned shield with ornamented sides above divided date **Note:** Dav. #4314.

Date	Mintage	VG	F	VF	XF	Unc
1623 IIVE	—	575	1,150	2,300	3,200	—
1624 IIVE	—	575	1,150	2,300	3,200	—

KM# 44 THALER

Silver **Ruler:** Sigismund III **Note:** Dav. #4315.

Date	Mintage	VG	F	VF	XF	Unc
1625 IIVE	—	575	1,150	2,300	3,200	—
1625 Crowned STR Rare	—	—	—	—	—	—
1626 IIVE	—	575	1,150	2,300	3,200	—
1626 STR Rare	—	—	—	—	—	—
1627 Crowned STR Rare	—	—	—	—	—	—
1627 IIVE	—	80.00	185	290	450	—
1627	—	80.00	185	290	450	—
1628	—	—	—	—	—	—
1629	—	—	—	—	—	—

KM# 48.1 THALER

Silver **Ruler:** Sigismund III **Obv:** Similar but with small bull's head shield (of treasurer, Hormolaus Lipezy) in legend at six o'clock **Note:** Dav. #4316.

Date	Mintage	VG	F	VF	XF	Unc
1627 IIVE	—	90.00	200	325	500	—
1627 II	—	90.00	200	325	500	—
1627	—	90.00	200	325	500	—
1628 II	—	90.00	200	325	500	—
1629 II	—	90.00	200	325	500	—
1629 Crowned STR Rare	—	—	—	—	—	—
1630 II	—	90.00	200	350	625	—
1631 II	—	90.00	200	325	500	—

KM# 48.2 THALER

Silver **Ruler:** Sigismund III **Rev:** Small bull's head shield below arms

Date	Mintage	VG	F	VF	XF	Unc
1630 II	—	90.00	200	325	500	—

KM# 48.3 THALER

Silver **Ruler:** Sigismund III **Obv:** Small bull's head shield **Rev:** Small bull's head shield

Date	Mintage	VG	F	VF	XF	Unc
1630 II	—	90.00	200	325	500	—

KM# 48.4 THALER

Silver **Ruler:** Sigismund III **Obv:** Without small bull's head shield **Rev:** Without small bull's head shield

Date	Mintage	VG	F	VF	XF	Unc
1630 II	—	90.00	200	325	500	—

KM# 48.5 THALER

Silver **Ruler:** Sigismund III **Obv:** Bust with ornamentation on armor and bull's head shield at six o'clock **Rev:** Without small bull's head shield **Note:** Crown, portrait and legend varieties exist.

Date	Mintage	VG	F	VF	XF	Unc
1630 II	—	90.00	200	325	500	—
1630	—	90.00	200	325	500	—
1631 II	—	90.00	200	325	500	—
1632 II	—	90.00	200	325	500	—
16xx II	—	90.00	200	325	500	—
1633 II	—	90.00	200	325	500	—
ND	—	250	575	1,150	2,200	—

KM# 52 THALER

Silver **Ruler:** Sigismund III **Obv:** Bare-headed bust **Note:** Dav. #4322.

Date	Mintage	VG	F	VF	XF	Unc
ND Rare	—	—	—	—	—	—

KM# 54 THALER

Silver **Ruler:** Wladislaus IV **Obv:** Crowned half-figure of Ladislaus IV **Note:** Dav. #4326. Legend and crown varieties exist.

Date	Mintage	VG	F	VF	XF	Unc
1633 II	—	125	250	450	700	—
1634 II	—	125	250	450	700	—
1635 II	—	125	250	450	700	—
1636 II	—	125	250	450	700	—
1637 II	—	125	250	450	700	—
1638 II Rare	—	—	—	—	—	—
1639 II Rare	—	—	—	—	—	—
1640 BS	—	190	325	575	1,150	—

KM# 58 THALER

Silver **Ruler:** Wladislaus IV **Obv:** Bust right **Rev:** Crowned oval shield within fleece collar, cupid supporters **Note:** Dav. #4327.

Date	Mintage	VG	F	VF	XF	Unc
1635	—	825	1,550	2,800	4,400	—

KM# 59 THALER

Silver **Ruler:** Wladislaus IV **Rev:** Crowned oval shield without cupid supporters **Note:** Dav. #4328.

Date	Mintage	VG	F	VF	XF	Unc
1636 II	—	950	1,700	3,050	4,700	—
1636 IH	—	950	1,700	3,050	4,700	—

KM# 62 THALER

Silver **Ruler:** Wladislaus IV **Obv:** Crowned bust right **Note:** Dav. #4329.

Date	Mintage	VG	F	VF	XF	Unc
ND GGBS	—	—	—	—	—	—
1640 GGBS	—	190	325	500	875	—
1641 GGBS	—	125	250	450	700	—
164Z GGBS	—	125	250	450	700	—
1642 GGBS	—	125	250	450	700	—
1643 GGBS	—	125	250	450	700	—
1644 CDC-FS	—	190	350	575	1,050	—
1644 DC-BS	—	190	350	575	1,050	—
1644 DC-BL	—	190	350	575	1,050	—
1644 CDC-BL	—	190	350	575	1,050	—
1645 CDC-BS	—	190	350	575	1,050	—
1645 CDC-BS	—	190	350	575	1,050	—
1646 GP-BS	—	190	350	575	1,050	—
1647 GG	—	190	350	575	1,050	—

KM# 64 THALER
Silver **Ruler:** Wladislaus IV **Obv:** Smaller crowned bust right in inner circle **Note:** Dav. #4330.

Date	Mintage	VG	F	VF	XF	Unc
1640 GG	—	125	325	500	875	—
1641 GG	—	125	325	500	875	—
1642 GG	—	125	325	500	875	—

KM# 68 THALER
Silver **Ruler:** Wladislaus IV **Rev:** Shield between vertical date **Note:** Dav. #4332.

Date	Mintage	VG	F	VF	XF	Unc
1644 CDC	—	1,050	1,800	3,300	5,000	—

KM# 67 THALER
Silver **Ruler:** Wladislaus IV **Obv:** Crowned half-length figure, 3/4 facing **Rev:** Crowned shield in fleece collar **Note:** Dav. #4331. Varieties exist.

Date	Mintage	VG	F	VF	XF	Unc
1644 BS	—	—	—	—	—	—
1644 BL	—	—	—	—	—	—
1644 CDC	—	950	1,700	3,050	4,700	—
1645 CDC	—	950	1,700	3,050	4,700	—
1645 BS	—	950	1,700	3,050	4,700	—
1645 BL	—	950	1,700	3,050	4,700	—

KM# 74 THALER
Silver **Ruler:** Johann Casimir **Obv:** Tall crowned half-length bust right **Rev. Legend:** SA • LI • SM • SEV • CZE ... **Note:** Dav. #4335. Varieties exist.

Date	Mintage	VG	F	VF	XF	Unc
1649 GP	—	375	625	1,450	3,150	—
1650 GP	—	375	625	1,450	3,150	—

KM# 76 THALER
Silver **Ruler:** Johann Casimir **Obv:** Large crowned bust right **Rev. Legend:** PM S(A) S (E) CZN ... **Note:** Dav. #4336. Varieties exist.

Date	Mintage	VG	F	VF	XF	Unc
1649 GP	—	250	500	1,050	2,200	—
1650 GP	—	250	500	1,050	2,200	—

KM# 77 THALER
Silver **Ruler:** Johann Casimir **Rev. Legend:** P • M • S • CZ • NE • N... **Note:** Dav. #4337.

Date	Mintage	VG	F	VF	XF	Unc
1649 GP	—	325	575	1,150	2,250	—
1650 CP	—	325	575	1,150	2,250	—

KM# 78 THALER
Silver **Ruler:** Johann Casimir **Rev. Legend:** P • M • L • SA(SE) • CZ(E)N ... **Note:** Dav. #4338.

Date	Mintage	VG	F	VF	XF	Unc
1649 GP	—	375	625	1,450	3,150	—
1650 CP	—	375	625	1,450	3,150	—

KM# 72 THALER
Silver **Ruler:** Johann Casimir **Obv:** Tall crowned half-length bust of Johann Casimir right with scepter and orb **Rev. Legend:** SA: SE • CZ ... **Note:** Dav. #4333.

Date	Mintage	VG	F	VF	XF	Unc
1649 GP	—	250	500	1,050	2,200	—

KM# 73 THALER
Silver **Ruler:** Johann Casimir **Rev. Legend:** SM(O) • SE(V) • CZ(E) (R)... **Note:** Dav. #4334

Date	Mintage	VG	F	VF	XF	Unc
1649	—	250	500	875	1,900	—

KM# 75 THALER
Silver **Ruler:** Johann Casimir **Rev. Legend:** SM • SE • CZ • NEC ... **Note:** Dav. #A4336.

Date	Mintage	VG	F	VF	XF	Unc
1649 GP	—	250	500	875	1,900	—

KM# 93 THALER
Silver **Ruler:** Johann Casimir **Rev:** Small arms below shield **Note:** Dav. #4339.

Date	Mintage	VG	F	VF	XF	Unc
1650 GP Rare	—	—	—	—	—	—
1650 CP Rare	—	—	—	—	—	—

KM# 98 THALER
Silver **Ruler:** Johann Casimir **Obv:** Laureate, armored bust of Johann Casimir right **Rev:** Crowned shield **Note:** Dav. #4340.

Date	Mintage	VG	F	VF	XF	Unc
1651 Rare	—	—	—	—	—	—

KM# 99 THALER
Silver **Ruler:** Johann Casimir **Rev:** Crowned oval shield **Note:** Dav. #4341. Varieties exist.

Date	Mintage	VG	F	VF	XF	Unc
1651 Rare	—	—	—	—	—	—
1652 Rare	—	—	—	—	—	—

KM# 101 THALER
Silver **Ruler:** Johann Casimir **Obv:** Small crowned bust right

Date	Mintage	VG	F	VF	XF	Unc
1652 AT Rare	—	—	—	—	—	—

KM# A115 THALER
Silver **Ruler:** Johann Casimir **Rev:** Crowned ornate oval arms **Note:** Dav. #4342.

Date	Mintage	VG	F	VF	XF	Unc
1661	—	—	—	—	—	—

KM# B115 THALER
Silver **Ruler:** Johann Casimir **Obv:** Crowned ornate arms **Note:** Dav. #4343.

Date	Mintage	VG	F	VF	XF	Unc
1661	—	—	—	—	—	—

KM# 115 THALER
Silver **Ruler:** Johann Casimir **Obv:** Large crowned bust right **Rev:** Crowned oval shield, ornate border **Note:** Dav. #4344.

Date	Mintage	VG	F	VF	XF	Unc
1661 GBA	—	750	1,450	2,500	4,050	—

KM# 131 THALER
Silver **Ruler:** Johann III Sobieski **Obv:** Laureate bust of Johann III Sobieski right **Rev:** Crowned shield **Note:** Dav. #4345.

Date	Mintage	VG	F	VF	XF	Unc
ND(1684) Rare	—	—	—	—	—	—

KM# 21 1-1/2 THALER
Silver **Ruler:** Sigismund III **Note:** Similar to 1 Thaler, KM#50. Dav. #A4311. Klippe.

Date	Mintage	VG	F	VF	XF	Unc
1614 Rare	—	—	—	—	—	—

KM# 22 2 THALER
Silver **Ruler:** Sigismund III **Obv:** Bust of Sigismund III right **Rev:** Crowned arms in collar of the Golden Fleece **Note:** Dav. #4310.

Date	Mintage	VG	F	VF	XF	Unc
1614 Rare	—	—	—	—	—	—

KM# 29 2 THALER
Silver **Ruler:** Sigismund III **Obv:** Bust with tall collar right **Rev:** Crowned ornate arms dividing date at top **Note:** Dav. #4312.

Date	Mintage	VG	F	VF	XF	Unc
1617 Rare	—	—	—	—	—	—

KM# A30 2 THALER
Silver **Ruler:** Sigismund III **Obv:** Armored bust right **Rev:** Crowned arms **Rev. Legend:** MAGNVS • DUX • LITVA... **Note:** Dav. #A4313.

Date	Mintage	VG	F	VF	XF	Unc
ND	—	—	—	—	—	—

KM# 30 2 THALER
Silver **Ruler:** Sigismund III **Obv:** Large bust right **Rev:** Crowned arms divide II-VI at center **Note:** Dav. #4323.

Date	Mintage	VG	F	VF	XF	Unc
ND Rare	—	—	—	—	—	—

KM# 56 2 THALER
Silver **Ruler:** Wladislaus IV **Note:** Dav. #4325. Similar to 1 Thaler, KM#58.

Date	Mintage	VG	F	VF	XF	Unc
1633 Rare	—	—	—	—	—	—
1634 Rare	—	—	—	—	—	—
1635 Rare	—	—	—	—	—	—
1636 Rare	—	—	—	—	—	—

KM# 65 2 THALER
Silver **Ruler:** Wladislaus IV **Note:** Dav. #A4329. Similar to 1 Thaler, KM#61.

Date	Mintage	VG	F	VF	XF	Unc
1641 Rare	—	—	—	—	—	—
1643 Rare	—	—	—	—	—	—
1647 Rare	—	—	—	—	—	—

TRADE COINAGE

KM# 104 1/2 DUCAT (1/2 Czerwenego Zlotego)
1.7500 g., 0.9860 Gold 0.0555 oz. AGW **Ruler:** Johann Casimir **Obv:** Crowned bust of Johann Casimir right **Rev:** Crowned displayed eagle, date in legend

Date	Mintage	VG	F	VF	XF	Unc
1653 MW	—	500	900	1,750	3,500	—
1654 MW	—	500	900	1,750	3,500	—
ND IC	—	500	900	1,750	3,500	—

KM# 109 1/2 DUCAT (1/2 Czerwenego Zlotego)
1.7500 g., 0.9860 Gold 0.0555 oz. AGW **Ruler:** Johann Casimir **Rev:** Crowned arms, date in legend

Date	Mintage	VG	F	VF	XF	Unc
1657 IT	—	500	900	1,750	3,500	—

KM# 112 1/2 DUCAT (1/2 Czerwenego Zlotego)
1.7500 g., 0.9860 Gold 0.0555 oz. AGW **Ruler:** Johann Casimir **Obv:** Head laureate right **Rev:** Eagle **Note:** Reverse legend varieties exist.

Date	Mintage	VG	F	VF	XF	Unc
1660 TLB	—	500	900	1,750	3,500	—
1661 TLB	—	500	900	1,750	3,500	—
1662 AT	—	500	900	1,750	3,500	—
ND MW	—	500	900	1,750	3,500	—

KM# 9 DUCAT
3.5000 g., 0.9860 Gold 0.1109 oz. AGW **Ruler:** Sigismund III **Obv:** Large crowned bust right **Rev:** Crowned arms within fleece collar

Date	Mintage	VG	F	VF	XF	Unc
1609	—	850	1,700	3,500	5,600	—
1610	—	850	1,700	3,500	5,600	—
1611	—	850	1,700	3,500	5,600	—
1612	—	850	1,700	3,500	5,600	—

KM# 19 DUCAT
3.5000 g., 0.9860 Gold 0.1109 oz. AGW **Ruler:** Sigismund III **Obv:** Smaller bust right

Date	Mintage	VG	F	VF	XF	Unc
1613 IIVE	—	850	1,700	3,500	5,600	—
1623 II/VE	—	850	1,700	3,500	5,600	—

KM# 47 DUCAT
3.5000 g., 0.9860 Gold 0.1109 oz. AGW **Ruler:** Sigismund III **Obv:** Crowned longer bust right

Date	Mintage	VG	F	VF	XF	Unc
1628 II	—	900	1,750	3,850	6,300	—

KM# 49 DUCAT
3.5000 g., 0.9860 Gold 0.1109 oz. AGW **Ruler:** Sigismund III **Rev:** Five shields above date in inner circle

Date	Mintage	VG	F	VF	XF	Unc
1630	—	900	1,750	3,850	6,300	—

KM# 50 DUCAT
3.5000 g., 0.9860 Gold 0.1109 oz. AGW **Ruler:** Sigismund III **Rev:** Four-line inscription in tablet

Date	Mintage	VG	F	VF	XF	Unc
ND	—	900	1,750	3,850	6,300	—

KM# 61 DUCAT
3.5000 g., 0.9860 Gold 0.1109 oz. AGW **Ruler:** Wladislaus IV **Obv:** Crowned bust right in inner circle **Rev:** Crowned arms in inner circle, crown divides date at top

Date	Mintage	VG	F	VF	XF	Unc
1639 MR-VM	—	775	1,600	3,150	5,300	—
1640 GG-BS	—	775	1,600	3,150	5,300	—
1641 GG-BS	—	775	1,600	3,150	5,300	—
1642 GG-BS	—	775	1,600	3,150	5,300	—
1644 C-DC	—	775	1,600	3,150	5,300	—

KM# 69 DUCAT

3.5000 g., 0.9860 Gold 0.1109 oz. AGW **Ruler:** Wladislaus IV **Obv:** Heavier crowned bust right **Rev:** Crowned arms in Order collar in inner circle

Date	Mintage	VG	F	VF	XF	Unc
1647 GP	—	775	1,600	3,150	5,300	—
ND	—	775	1,600	3,150	5,300	—

KM# 79 DUCAT

3.5000 g., 0.9860 Gold 0.1109 oz. AGW **Ruler:** Johann Casimir **Obv:** Laureate bust right

Date	Mintage	VG	F	VF	XF	Unc
1649 GP	—	700	1,400	2,800	4,550	—

KM# 80 DUCAT

3.5000 g., 0.9860 Gold 0.1109 oz. AGW **Ruler:** Johann Casimir **Obv:** Johann standing in inner circle **Note:** Varieties exist, including an obverse legend error.

Date	Mintage	VG	F	VF	XF	Unc
1649 GP	—	1,900	3,850	7,700	12,500	—

KM# 81 DUCAT

3.5000 g., 0.9860 Gold 0.1109 oz. AGW **Ruler:** Johann Casimir **Obv:** Crowned bust right in inner circle

Date	Mintage	VG	F	VF	XF	Unc
1649 GP	—	700	1,400	2,800	4,550	—

KM# 95 DUCAT

3.5000 g., 0.9860 Gold 0.1109 oz. AGW **Ruler:** Johann Casimir **Obv:** Laureate bust right **Rev:** Crowned displayed eagle, date divided at top **Note:** Legend varieties exist.

Date	Mintage	VG	F	VF	XF	Unc
1650	—	700	1,400	2,800	4,550	—
1651 AT	—	700	1,400	2,800	4,550	—
1651 CG	—	700	1,400	2,800	4,550	—
1651 MW	—	700	1,400	2,800	4,550	—

KM# 102 DUCAT

3.5000 g., 0.9860 Gold 0.1109 oz. AGW **Ruler:** Johann Casimir **Obv:** Crowned bust right in inner circle, finer style **Rev:** Crowned arms in inner circle, date in legend **Note:** Legend varieties exist.

Date	Mintage	VG	F	VF	XF	Unc
1652 AT	—	700	1,400	2,800	4,550	—
1652 MW	—	700	1,400	2,800	4,550	—
1653 AT	—	700	1,400	2,800	4,550	—
1653 MW	—	700	1,400	2,800	4,550	—
1654 AT	—	700	1,400	2,800	4,550	—
1654 MW	—	700	1,400	2,800	4,550	—
1655 MW	—	700	1,400	2,800	4,550	—
1655 IT/SCH	—	700	1,400	2,800	4,550	—

KM# 108 DUCAT

3.5000 g., 0.9860 Gold 0.1109 oz. AGW **Ruler:** Johann Casimir **Obv:** Coarse crowned bust right

Date	Mintage	VG	F	VF	XF	Unc
1655 SCH	—	700	1,400	2,800	4,550	—
1657 IT	—	700	1,400	2,800	4,550	—
1658 IT/SCH	—	700	1,400	2,800	4,550	—
1658 TLB	—	700	1,400	2,800	4,550	—
1659 TLB	—	700	1,400	2,800	4,550	—

KM# 107 DUCAT

3.5000 g., 0.9860 Gold 0.1109 oz. AGW **Ruler:** Johann Casimir **Obv:** Crowned bust right, without inner circle **Rev:** Crowned shield, without inner circle

Date	Mintage	VG	F	VF	XF	Unc
1656 IT/IC	—	700	1,400	2,800	4,550	—

KM# 113 DUCAT

3.5000 g., 0.9860 Gold 0.1109 oz. AGW **Ruler:** Johann Casimir **Obv:** Older crowned bust right **Note:** Legend varieties exist.

Date	Mintage	VG	F	VF	XF	Unc
1660 TLB	—	700	1,400	2,800	4,550	—
1660 NG	—	700	1,400	2,800	4,550	—
1661 TT	—	700	1,400	2,800	4,550	—
1661 GBA	—	700	1,400	2,800	4,550	—
1662 AT	—	700	1,400	2,800	4,550	—
1668	—	700	1,400	2,800	4,550	—

KM# 124 DUCAT

3.5000 g., 0.9860 Gold 0.1109 oz. AGW **Ruler:** Michael Korybut **Obv:** Laureate bust right in inner circle **Rev:** Crowned arms within scroll

Date	Mintage	VG	F	VF	XF	Unc
1671 MH	—	1,050	2,100	3,850	7,000	—

KM# 127 DUCAT

3.5000 g., 0.9860 Gold 0.1109 oz. AGW **Ruler:** Johann III Sobieski **Obv:** Laureate bust right **Rev:** Crowned arms in inner circle, date in legend **Note:** Legend varieties exist.

Date	Mintage	VG	F	VF	XF	Unc
1681	—	850	1,750	3,200	6,000	—
1682	—	700	1,400	3,000	5,600	—
1685 BIC	—	700	1,400	3,000	5,600	—

KM# 129 DUCAT

3.5000 g., 0.9860 Gold 0.1109 oz. AGW **Ruler:** Johann III Sobieski **Rev:** Crowned shield, without inner circle

Date	Mintage	VG	F	VF	XF	Unc
1683 TLB	—	700	1,400	3,000	5,600	—

KM# A129 DUCAT

3.5000 g., 0.9860 Gold 0.1109 oz. AGW **Ruler:** August II **Subject:** Coronation of August II **Obv. Inscription:** PRO REGNO, ID-DG / AUGUSTUS II / CORON IN REG / POLON & MDL / I SEPT / 1697

Date	Mintage	VG	F	VF	XF	Unc
1697 Rare	—	—	—	—	—	—

KM# 10 2 DUCAT

7.0000 g., 0.9860 Gold 0.2219 oz. AGW **Ruler:** Sigismund III **Obv:** Crowned bust right in inner circle **Rev:** Crowned arms in Order collar in inner circle, date in legend

Date	Mintage	VG	F	VF	XF	Unc
1609 Rare	—	—	—	—	—	—
1610	—	1,750	3,500	5,600	9,100	—

KM# 96 2 DUCAT

7.0000 g., 0.9860 Gold 0.2219 oz. AGW **Ruler:** Johann Casimir **Obv:** Large laureate bust of Johann Casimir right **Note:** Legend varieties exist.

Date	Mintage	VG	F	VF	XF	Unc
1650	—	850	1,700	3,500	6,000	—
1651 MW	—	850	1,700	3,500	6,000	—
1652 AT	—	850	1,700	3,500	6,000	—
1652 MW	—	850	1,700	3,500	6,000	—
1653 MW	—	850	1,700	3,500	6,000	—
1654	—	850	1,700	3,500	6,000	—
1655 IT	—	850	1,700	3,500	6,000	—

KM# 106 2 DUCAT

7.0000 g., 0.9860 Gold 0.2219 oz. AGW **Ruler:** Johann Casimir **Obv:** Crowned bust of Johann Casimir right in inner circle **Rev:** Crowned arms in Order collar in inner circle, date in legend **Note:** Legend varieties exist.

Date	Mintage	VG	F	VF	XF	Unc
1654	—	500	975	2,100	4,200	—
1654 AT	—	500	975	2,100	4,200	—
1654 MW	—	550	1,050	2,250	4,500	—
1655 AT	—	500	975	2,100	4,200	—
1655 IT/SCH	—	500	975	2,100	4,200	—
1656 IT/IC	—	500	975	2,100	4,200	—
1657 IT/SCH Rare	—	—	—	—	—	—
1657 IT/IC Rare	—	—	—	—	—	—
1658 AT	—	500	850	1,700	3,500	—
1658 TLB	—	500	850	1,700	3,500	—
1658 IT/SCH	—	500	850	1,700	3,500	—

KM# 111.1 2 DUCAT

7.0000 g., 0.9860 Gold 0.2219 oz. AGW **Ruler:** Johann Casimir **Rev:** Without Order collar

Date	Mintage	VG	F	VF	XF	Unc
1659 TLB	—	500	975	2,100	4,200	—
1659 AT	—	500	975	2,100	4,200	—
1660 TLB	—	500	850	1,400	2,800	—
1660 TT	—	500	850	1,400	2,800	—
1660 GBA	—	550	1,050	2,100	4,200	—
1661 TLB	—	500	850	2,100	4,200	—
1661 GBA	—	500	850	2,100	4,200	—
1661 NG	—	500	850	2,100	4,200	—
1661 AT	—	550	1,050	2,100	4,200	—

KM# 111.2 2 DUCAT

7.0000 g., 0.9860 Gold 0.2219 oz. AGW **Ruler:** Johann Casimir **Rev:** Different arms **Note:** Legend varieties and inner circle varieties (dotted, plain) exist.

Date	Mintage	VG	F	VF	XF	Unc
1659 TLB	—	625	1,200	2,450	4,900	—

KM# 116 2 DUCAT

7.0000 g., 0.9860 Gold 0.2219 oz. AGW **Ruler:** Johann Casimir **Obv:** Laureate bust of Johann Casimir right **Rev:** Crowned eagle displayed with four-fold arms on breast in inner circle, date in legend **Rev. Legend:** ARCUS FORTIUM...

Date	Mintage	VG	F	VF	XF	Unc
1661 NG	—	625	1,200	2,450	4,900	—
1662 NG	—	625	1,200	2,450	4,900	—

KM# 117 2 DUCAT

7.0000 g., 0.9860 Gold 0.2219 oz. AGW **Ruler:** Johann Casimir **Rev:** Without inner circle, date at sides of eagle **Rev. Legend:** NON EST FORTIS...

Date	Mintage	VG	F	VF	XF	Unc
1661 NG	—	625	1,200	2,450	4,900	—

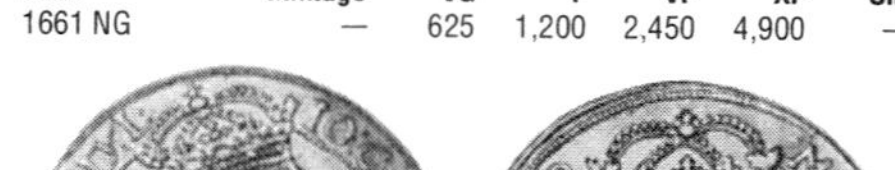

KM# 119 2 DUCAT

7.0000 g., 0.9860 Gold 0.2219 oz. AGW **Ruler:** Johann Casimir **Obv:** Crowned bust of Johann Casimir right **Rev:** Crowned arms in order collar **Note:** Legend varieties exist.

Date	Mintage	VG	F	VF	XF	Unc
1662 NG	—	625	1,050	2,100	4,200	—
1662 AT	—	625	1,050	2,100	4,200	—
1663 AT	—	625	1,050	2,100	4,200	—
1664 AT	—	625	1,050	2,100	4,200	—
1666 AT	—	625	1,100	2,450	4,900	—
1667 TLB Rare	—	—	—	—	—	—

KM# 125 2 DUCAT

7.0000 g., 0.9860 Gold 0.2219 oz. AGW **Ruler:** Michael Korybut **Obv:** Bust of Michael Korybut right **Rev:** Crowned arms

Date	Mintage	VG	F	VF	XF	Unc
1671 MH	—	3,500	5,600	9,100	14,000	—

KM# 132 2 DUCAT

7.0000 g., 0.9860 Gold 0.2219 oz. AGW **Ruler:** Michael Korybut **Obv:** Crowned bust of Johann Sobieski right **Rev:** Crowned arms divides date

Date	Mintage	VG	F	VF	XF	Unc
1681 TB	—	2,100	3,500	5,900	9,800	—
1683	—	2,100	3,500	5,900	9,800	—
1685 B	—	2,100	3,500	5,900	9,800	—

KM# 133 2 DUCAT

7.0000 g., 0.9860 Gold 0.2219 oz. AGW **Ruler:** Johann III Sobieski **Obv:** Laureate head of Johann Sobieski right in inner circle

Date	Mintage	VG	F	VF	XF	Unc
ND	—	2,100	3,500	5,900	9,800	—

KM# 14 3 DUCAT

10.5000 g., 0.9860 Gold 0.3328 oz. AGW **Ruler:** Sigismund III **Obv:** Crowned bust right in inner circle **Rev:** Crowned arms in Order collar in inner circle, date in legend

Date	Mintage	VG	F	VF	XF	Unc
1612	—	1,750	3,150	5,600	9,800	—

KM# 15 4 DUCAT

14.0000 g., 0.9860 Gold 0.4438 oz. AGW **Ruler:** Sigismund III **Obv:** Crowned bust right in inner circle **Rev:** Crowned arms in Order collar in inner circle, date in legend

Date	Mintage	VG	F	VF	XF	Unc
1611	—	2,800	4,900	8,400	13,500	—
1612	—	2,800	4,900	8,400	13,500	—

KM# A97 4 DUCAT

14.0000 g., 0.9860 Gold 0.4438 oz. AGW **Ruler:** Johann Casimir

Date	Mintage	VG	F	VF	XF	Unc
1650 Rare	—	—	—	—	—	—

KM# A126 4 DUCAT

14.0000 g., 0.9860 Gold 0.4438 oz. AGW **Ruler:** Johann III Sobieski **Subject:** January 3 Commemorative

Date	Mintage	VG	F	VF	XF	Unc
1677 Rare	—	—	—	—	—	—

KM# 12 5 DUCAT

17.5000 g., 0.9860 Gold 0.5547 oz. AGW **Ruler:** Sigismund III **Subject:** January 3 Commemorative

Date	Mintage	VG	F	VF	XF	Unc
1611 Rare	—	—	—	—	—	—
1612 Rare	—	—	—	—	—	—
1613 Rare	—	—	—	—	—	—
1614 Rare	—	—	—	—	—	—

KM# 26 5 DUCAT

17.5000 g., 0.9860 Gold 0.5547 oz. AGW **Ruler:** Sigismund III

Date	Mintage	VG	F	VF	XF	Unc
1616 Rare	—	—	—	—	—	—

KM# 45 5 DUCAT

17.5000 g., 0.9860 Gold 0.5547 oz. AGW **Ruler:** Sigismund III **Obv:** Crowned bust right with sword and orb in inner circle **Rev:** Crowned arms divides date in Order collar and inner circle

Date	Mintage	VG	F	VF	XF	Unc
1623 Rare	—	—	—	—	—	—
ND Rare	—	—	—	—	—	—

KM# 57 5 DUCAT

17.5000 g., 0.9860 Gold 0.5547 oz. AGW **Ruler:** Wladislaus IV **Obv:** Bust right **Rev:** Crowned arms in order chain **Note:** Fr. #85.

Date	Mintage	VG	F	VF	XF	Unc
1633	—	—	—	10,500	17,000	—
1642 GG	—	—	2,800	4,900	9,800	—
1644 CDC	—	—	2,800	4,900	9,800	—
1645 CDC	—	—	2,800	4,900	9,800	—
1646 CDC	—	—	2,800	4,900	9,800	—
1647 GP	—	—	2,800	4,900	9,800	—

KM# 13 10 DUCAT

35.0000 g., 0.9860 Gold 1.1095 oz. AGW **Ruler:** Sigismund III **Obv:** Crowned bust right in inner circle **Rev:** Crowned arms in inner circle, date in legend

Date	Mintage	VG	F	VF	XF	Unc
1611 Rare	—	—	—	—	—	—
1612 Rare	—	—	—	—	—	—

KM# 27 10 DUCAT

35.0000 g., 0.9860 Gold 1.1095 oz. AGW **Ruler:** Sigismund III

Date	Mintage	VG	F	VF	XF	Unc
1616 Rare	—	—	—	—	—	—
1617 Rare	—	—	—	—	—	—
1617 SA Rare	—	—	—	—	—	—
1618 SA Rare	—	—	—	—	—	—
1620 SA Rare	—	—	—	—	—	—
1622 Rare	—	—	—	—	—	—

KM# 35 10 DUCAT

35.0000 g., 0.9860 Gold 1.1095 oz. AGW **Ruler:** Sigismund III **Obv:** Bust of sigismund right without inner circle **Note:** Varieties exist.

Date	Mintage	VG	F	VF	XF	Unc
ND Rare	—	—	—	—	—	—

KM# 60 10 DUCAT

35.0000 g., 0.9860 Gold 1.1095 oz. AGW **Ruler:** Wladislaus IV

Date	Mintage	VG	F	VF	XF	Unc
1636 II Rare	—	—	—	—	—	—

KM# 103 10 DUCAT

35.0000 g., 0.9860 Gold 1.1095 oz. AGW **Ruler:** Johann Casimir **Obv:** Laureate bust of Casimir inside outer laurel border **Rev:** Crowned oval arms in ornamental frame, half Order collar below outside laurel border

Date	Mintage	VG	F	VF	XF	Unc
1652 Rare	—	—	—	—	—	—

KM# 118 10 DUCAT

35.0000 g., 0.9860 Gold 1.1095 oz. AGW **Ruler:** Johann Casimir **Obv:** Crowned bust of Johann Casimir in Order collar **Rev:** Crowned oval arms in ornamental frame, crown divides date

Date	Mintage	VG	F	VF	XF	Unc
1661 TT Rare	—	—	—	—	—	—

KM# A42 20 DUCAT

70.0000 g., 0.9860 Gold 2.2190 oz. AGW **Ruler:** Sigismund III

Date	Mintage	VG	F	VF	XF	Unc
1614 Rare	—	—	—	—	—	—
1617 AS Rare	—	—	—	—	—	—
1621 II VE Rare	—	—	—	—	—	—
1621 SA Rare	—	—	—	—	—	—
1622 DS Rare	—	—	—	—	—	—

KM# A43 30 DUCAT

105.0000 g., 0.9860 Gold 3.3284 oz. AGW **Ruler:** Sigismund III

Date	Mintage	VG	F	VF	XF	Unc
1621 II VE Rare	—	—	—	—	—	—
1621 SA Rare	—	—	—	—	—	—

KM# B43 40 DUCAT

140.0000 g., 0.9860 Gold 4.4379 oz. AGW, 68.5 mm. **Ruler:** Sigismund III **Note:** Illustration reduced.

Date	Mintage	VG	F	VF	XF	Unc
1621 II VE Rare	—	—	—	—	—	—
1621 SA Rare	—	—	—	—	—	—

KM# C43 50 DUCAT

175.0000 g., 0.9860 Gold 5.5474 oz. AGW **Ruler:** Sigismund III

Date	Mintage	VG	F	VF	XF	Unc
1621 II AE Rare	—	—	—	—	—	—

Date	Mintage	VG	F	VF	XF	Unc
1621 SA Rare	—	—	—	—	—	—
1621 Rare	—	—	—	—	—	—

KM# D43 60 DUCAT

210.0000 g., 0.9860 Gold 6.6569 oz. AGW **Ruler:** Sigismund III

Date	Mintage	VG	F	VF	XF	Unc
1621 II AE Rare	—	—	—	—	—	—
1621 SA Rare	—	—	—	—	—	—

KM# E43 70 DUCAT

245.0000 g., 0.9860 Gold 7.7663 oz. AGW **Ruler:** Sigismund III

Date	Mintage	VG	F	VF	XF	Unc
1621 II AE Rare	—	—	—	—	—	—
1621 SA Rare	—	—	—	—	—	—

KM# F43 80 DUCAT

280.0000 g., 0.9860 Gold 8.8758 oz. AGW **Ruler:** Sigismund III

Date	Mintage	VG	F	VF	XF	Unc
1621 II AE Rare	—	—	—	—	—	—
1621 SA Rare	—	—	—	—	—	—

KM# G43 90 DUCAT

315.0000 g., 0.9860 Gold 9.9853 oz. AGW **Ruler:** Sigismund III

Date	Mintage	VG	F	VF	XF	Unc
1621 II VE Rare	—	—	—	—	—	—
1621 SA Rare	—	—	—	—	—	—

KM# H43 100 DUCAT

350.0000 g., 0.9860 Gold 11.094 oz. AGW **Ruler:** Sigismund III

Date	Mintage	VG	F	VF	XF	Unc
1621 II VE Rare	—	—	—	—	—	—
1621 SA Rare	—	—	—	—	—	—

PATTERNS

Including off metal strikes

KM#	Date	Mintage	Identification	Mkt Val
Pn1	1601	—	3 Groschen. Klippe.	—
Pn2	1609	—	2 Ducaton.	—
Pn3	1610	—	2 Ducaton.	—
Pn4	1613	—	Thaler. Klippe.	—
Pn5	1614	—	Thaler. Weight of 2 Thaler.	—
Pn6	1614	—	Thaler. Klippe.	—

KM#	Date	Mintage	Identification	Mkt Val
Pn7	1614	—	Thaler. Gold.	—
Pn8	1616	—	Thaler. Klippe.	—
Pn9	1617	—	2 Thaler. Gold.	—
Pn10	1620	—	Thaler. Gold.	—
Pn11	1621	—	Orte. Klippe.	—
Pn12	1621	—	Thaler. Gold.	—
Pn13	1622	—	Schilling. Gold.	—
Pn14	1622	—	Schilling. Klippe.	—
Pn15	1622	—	Thaler. Gold.	—
Pn16	1624	—	Thaler. Gold.	—
Pn17	1628	—	Thaler. Gold. Gedenk.	—
Pn18	1629	—	Thaler. Gold. Gedenk.	—
Pn19	1633	—	Thaler. Weight of 2 Thaler.	—
Pn20	1635	—	3 Groschen.	—
Pn21	1635	—	6 Groschen.	—
Pn22	1635	—	Ort.	—
Pn23	1642	—	1/2 Thaler. Gold.	—
Pn24	1643	—	Thaler. Weight of 2 Thaler.	—
Pn25	1645	—	1/2 Thaler. Gold.	—
Pn26	1647	—	1/2 Thaler. Gold.	—
Pn27	1647	—	Thaler. Weight of 2 Thaler.	—
Pn28	1649	—	1/2 Thaler. Gold.	—
Pn29	1651	—	Thaler. Gold.	—
Pn30	ND	—	1/2 Thaler. Gold.	—
Pn31	1652	—	1/2 Thaler. Gold.	—
Pn32	1652 AT	—	Thaler. Gold.	—
Pn33	1661 TT	—	Thaler. Gold. Weight of 5 Dukat.	—
Pn34	1661 TT	—	Thaler. Gold. Weight of 10 Dukat.	—
Pn35	1668	—	Dukat. Silver. Fr. 20, Casimer	—

BROMBERG

North of Poznan by about 67 mi., Bromberg originated as a commercial center for the Teutonic Knights. It was under Prussian rule from 1772-1919 and thrived during the reign of Frederik the Great.

ORDER

STANDARD COINAGE

KM# 1 THALER

Silver **Obv:** DEVS PROVIDEBIT above crown, crossed sword and scepter, orb below **Rev:** Crowned arms divide date **Rev. Legend:** SAM • LIV • NE • SVE-GOT • VAD • Q • HR • REX **Note:** Dav. #4346.

Date	Mintage	VG	F	VF	XF	Unc
1632	—	500	950	1,750	2,900	—

KM# 2 THALER

Silver **Obv:** Laureate bust right **Obv. Legend:** IOAN CASIM D G POL & SUEC REX M D L RUS PR. **Rev:** Crowned arms **Rev. Legend:** MON ARGENT CIVIT BIDGOSTIENS **Note:** Dav. #4347.

Date	Mintage	VG	F	VF	XF	Unc
1650 Rare	—	—	—	—	—	—

DANZIG

Danzig is an important seaport on the northern coast of Poland with access to the Baltic Sea. It has at different times belonged to the Teutonic Knights, Pomerania, Russia, and Prussia. It was part of the Polish Kingdom from 1587-1772.

Danzig (Gdansk) was a free city from 1919 to 1939 during which most of its modern coinage was made.

RULERS

Sigismund III, 1587-1632
Wladislaus IV, 1632-1648
Johann Casimir, 1648-1669
Michael Korybut, 1669-1673
Johann III Sobieski, 1674-1696
August II (of Saxony), 1697-1733

MINT OFFICIALS' INITIALS

Initial	Date	Name
CS	1636-60	Christian Schirmer, Sr.
CS	1664-91	Christian Schirmer, Jr.
DC	1623	Daniel Cluwer
DL	1657-85	Daniel Lesse
DS	1661	Daniel Sailer
FB	1610	?
GR	1639-56	Gerhard Rogge
IH	?	Jan Hoem
II, JJ	1630	Jakob Jacobson
PK		Philipp Kluwer
SA	1613-22	Samuel Amman
SB	1618-35	Stanislaw Berman

MONETARY SYSTEM

3 Schilling (Szelag) = 1 Groschen (Grosz)

KINGDOM

STANDARD COINAGE

KM# 10 TERNAR (3 Denarii - 1 Pfennig)

Silver **Obv:** Oval arms divide date, value above **Rev:** Prussian eagle

Date	Mintage	VG	F	VF	XF	Unc
1613	—	10.00	20.00	40.00	—	—
1616 SA	—	15.00	35.00	80.00	—	—

KM# 57 SZELAG (12 Danarii)

Silver **Obv:** ICR monogram divides date in inner circle **Rev:** Oval arms in cartouche in inner circle, date in legend

Date	Mintage	VG	F	VF	XF	Unc
1657	—	20.00	40.00	70.00	—	—

KM# 58 SZELAG (12 Danarii)

Silver **Obv:** Crowned ICR monogram

Date	Mintage	VG	F	VF	XF	Unc
1657	—	15.00	30.00	60.00	—	—
1658	—	15.00	30.00	60.00	—	—

KM# 70 SZELAG (12 Danarii)

Silver **Obv:** Crowned MR monogram

Date	Mintage	VG	F	VF	XF	Unc
1670	—	20.00	60.00	120	—	—

KM# 77 SZELAG (12 Danarii)

Silver **Obv:** Crowned I3R monogram

Date	Mintage	VG	F	VF	XF	Unc
1688	128,000	15.00	30.00	60.00	—	—

KM# 11 GROSZ

Silver **Obv:** Crowned bust of Sigismund III right **Rev:** Oval arms in inner circle, date in legend **Note:** Varieties exist.

Date	Mintage	VG	F	VF	XF	Unc
1623 SB	—	12.50	25.00	45.00	—	—
1623	—	25.00	50.00	100	—	—
1624	—	12.50	25.00	45.00	—	—
1625	—	12.50	25.00	45.00	—	—
1626	—	12.50	25.00	45.00	—	—
1627	—	12.50	25.00	45.00	—	—

KM# 45 2 GROSZE

Silver **Subject:** Johann Casimir **Note:** Varieties exist.

Date	Mintage	VG	F	VF	XF	Unc
1651 GR	—	17.50	35.00	65.00	120	—
1652 GR	—	25.00	75.00	150	350	—
1653 GR Rare	—	—	—	—	—	—

KM# 6 ORT (1/4 Thaler - 10 Groszy)

Silver **Ruler:** Sigismund III **Obv:** Sigismund III in ruff collar

Date	Mintage	VG	F	VF	XF	Unc
1608 Rare	—	—	—	—	—	—
1609	—	15.00	30.00	60.00	100	—
1610	—	15.00	35.00	100	150	—
1611	—	35.00	70.00	140	250	—
1612	—	35.00	70.00	140	250	—
1613	—	15.00	30.00	60.00	100	—
1614	—	15.00	30.00	60.00	100	—
1615 SA	—	10.00	25.00	60.00	100	—
1616 SA	—	10.00	25.00	60.00	100	—

KM# 14 ORT (1/4 Thaler - 10 Groszy)

Silver **Obv:** Sigismund III without ruff collar

Date	Mintage	VG	F	VF	XF	Unc
1617 SA	—	12.50	30.00	55.00	90.00	—
1618 SA/SB	—	12.50	30.00	55.00	90.00	—
1618 SB	—	12.50	30.00	55.00	90.00	—
1619 SA/SB	—	12.50	30.00	55.00	90.00	—
1619 SB/SA	—	12.50	30.00	55.00	90.00	—
1620 SA	—	12.50	30.00	55.00	90.00	—
1621 SB/SA	—	15.00	32.50	60.00	100	—

KM# 15.1 ORT (1/4 Thaler - 10 Groszy)

Silver **Obv:** Sigismund III in ruff collar divides 1-6 **Rev:** Date repeated in legend

Date	Mintage	VG	F	VF	XF	Unc
1623	—	22.00	45.00	90.00	150	—

KM# 15.2 ORT (1/4 Thaler - 10 Groszy)

Silver **Obv:** Sigismund III in ruff collar divides 1-6

Date	Mintage	VG	F	VF	XF	Unc
1623	—	12.50	28.00	55.00	85.00	—
1623 (SB) Rare	—	—	—	—	—	—
1623 SA Rare	—	—	—	—	—	—
1624/35	—	12.50	28.00	55.00	85.00	—
1624 SA	—	10.00	28.00	55.00	85.00	—
1625 SA	—	10.00	28.00	55.00	85.00	—
1626/55A	—	15.00	30.00	60.00	100	—
1626 SA	—	10.00	28.00	55.00	85.00	—

KM# 46 ORT (1/4 Thaler - 10 Groszy)

Silver **Subject:** Johann Casimir

Date	Mintage	VG	F	VF	XF	Unc
1650 GR Rare	—	—	—	—	—	—
1651 GR	—	25.00	50.00	90.00	150	—

KM# 54 ORT (1/4 Thaler - 10 Groszy)

Silver **Obv:** Inner circles added **Rev:** Inner circles added

Date	Mintage	VG	F	VF	XF	Unc
1652 GR	—	75.00	125	250	450	—
1654 GR Rare	—	—	—	—	—	—
1655 GR	—	50.00	100	150	225	—
1656 GR	—	50.00	100	150	225	—
1657 DL	—	25.00	45.00	75.00	125	—
1658 DL	—	25.00	45.00	75.00	125	—
1659 DL	—	25.00	45.00	75.00	150	—
1660 DL	—	25.00	45.00	75.00	150	—
1661 DL	—	25.00	45.00	75.00	125	—
1662 DL	—	25.00	45.00	75.00	125	—
1663 DL	—	25.00	45.00	75.00	125	—
1664 DL	—	25.00	45.00	75.00	125	—
1666 DL	—	50.00	100	200	400	—
1667 DL Rare	—	—	—	—	—	—

KM# 26.1 1/2 THALER

Silver **Subject:** Wladislaus IV

Date	Mintage	VG	F	VF	XF	Unc
1639 GR	—	350	600	—	—	—
1640 GR	—	350	600	—	—	—
1641 GR	—	350	600	—	—	—
1646 GR	—	350	600	—	—	—

KM# 39 1/2 THALER

Silver **Obv:** Crowned bust of Johann Casimir right in inner circle

Date	Mintage	VG	F	VF	XF	Unc
1649 GR Rare	—	—	—	—	—	—
1650 GR Rare	—	—	—	—	—	—

KM# 48 1/2 THALER

Silver **Note:** Octagonal klippe.

Date	Mintage	VG	F	VF	XF	Unc
1650 GR Rare	—	—	—	—	—	—

KM# 22 THALER

Silver **Rev:** Date divided in legend at top **Note:** Dav. #4350.

Date	Mintage	VG	F	VF	XF	Unc
1636 II	—	1,000	2,000	3,500	6,000	—
1637 II/CS	—	1,000	2,000	3,500	6,000	—

KM# 21 THALER

Silver **Subject:** Wladislaus IV **Note:** Dav. #4351.

Date	Mintage	VG	F	VF	XF	Unc
1636 II	—	1,000	2,000	3,500	6,000	—

KM# 23 THALER

Silver **Rev:** Date divided below shield **Note:** Dav. #4352.

Date	Mintage	VG	F	VF	XF	Unc
1638 II	—	1,000	2,000	3,500	6,000	—

KM# 24 THALER

Silver **Obv:** Crowned bust of Wladislaus IV right in inner circle **Rev:** Date in cartouche below arms **Note:** Dav. #4353.

Date	Mintage	VG	F	VF	XF	Unc
1638 II	—	475	950	1,700	2,850	—
1639 II	—	350	600	1,250	2,000	—
1639 GR	—	350	500	1,000	1,850	—
1640 GR	—	450	900	1,650	2,750	—

KM# 27 THALER

Silver **Note:** Dav. #4356. Varieties exist.

Date	Mintage	VG	F	VF	XF	Unc
1640 GR	—	125	250	450	800	—
1641 GG	—	100	200	400	700	—
1642 GG	—	100	200	400	700	—
1643 GR	—	350	500	950	1,850	—
1644 GR	—	350	500	950	1,850	—
1645 GR	—	450	900	1,650	2,750	—
1646 GR	—	400	650	1,100	2,200	—
1647 GR Rare	—	—	—	—	—	—
1648 GR	—	150	250	450	850	—

KM# 38 THALER

Silver **Rev:** Cherubs above city view of Danzig, date **Note:** Dav. #4357.

Date	Mintage	VG	F	VF	XF	Unc
1643 GR Rare	—	—	—	—	—	—

KM# 40 THALER

Silver **Subject:** Johann Casimir **Note:** Dav. #4358. Varieties exist.

Date	Mintage	VG	F	VF	XF	Unc
1649 GR	—	100	200	375	650	—

KM# 49 THALER

Silver **Rev. Legend:** MON... **Note:** Dav. #4360.

Date	Mintage	VG	F	VF	XF	Unc
1650 GR	—	80.00	180	325	600	—
1651 GR Rare	—	—	—	—	—	—
1652 GR Rare	—	—	—	—	—	—
1655 GR Rare	—	—	—	—	—	—

KM# 76 THALER

Silver **Subject:** Johann III Sobieski **Note:** Dav. #4361.

Date	Mintage	VG	F	VF	XF	Unc
1685 DL	200	750	1,250	2,250	3,750	—

KM# 28 2 THALER

Silver **Obv:** Crowned bust of Wladislaus IV right in inner circle **Rev:** Similar to KM#50 **Note:** Dav. #4355.

Date	Mintage	VG	F	VF	XF	Unc
1639 GR Rare	—	—	—	—	—	—

KM# 50 2 THALER

Silver **Subject:** Johann Casimir **Note:** Dav. #4359.

Date	Mintage	VG	F	VF	XF	Unc
1650 GR	—	1,000	2,000	3,500	6,000	—

KM# 5.1 DUCAT

3.5000 g., 0.9860 Gold 0.1109 oz. AGW

Date	Mintage	VG	F	VF	XF	Unc
1601	—	300	750	1,500	2,000	—

KM# 5.2 DUCAT

3.5000 g., 0.9860 Gold 0.1109 oz. AGW **Obv:** Bust divides legend between DG and REX

Date	Mintage	VG	F	VF	XF	Unc
1609	—	350	750	1,750	2,500	—

KM# 5.3 DUCAT

3.5000 g., 0.9860 Gold 0.1109 oz. AGW **Obv:** Bust divides legend between D and G

Date	Mintage	VG	F	VF	XF	Unc
1610	—	150	200	400	750	—

KM# 5.4 DUCAT

3.5000 g., 0.9860 Gold 0.1109 oz. AGW

Date	Mintage	VG	F	VF	XF	Unc
1610 FB	—	150	200	400	750	—
1610 PK	—	150	200	400	750	—
1611	—	150	200	400	750	—
1612	—	150	200	400	750	—
1614 PK with angel head Rare	—	—	—	—	—	—

KM# 5.5 DUCAT

3.5000 g., 0.9860 Gold 0.1109 oz. AGW **Obv:** Tall, smaller bust, closed crown

Date	Mintage	VG	F	VF	XF	Unc
1614 S-A	—	150	300	750	1,500	—
1619 S-B Rare	—	—	—	—	—	—
1621 S-B	—	150	350	900	1,750	—
1622 S-B	—	150	300	600	1,200	—
1623 S-B	—	150	300	750	1,500	—
1623 DG/S-B	—	150	300	750	1,500	—
1623 DG Rare	—	—	—	—	—	—
1625 S-B	—	150	300	600	1,200	—
1626 S-B	—	300	750	1,650	2,500	—
1627 S-B Rare	—	—	—	—	—	—
1628 S-B	—	300	750	1,650	2,500	—
1629 S-B	—	150	270	450	800	—
1630 S-B	—	150	200	375	700	—
1631 S-B	—	150	200	375	700	—

KM# 5.6 DUCAT

3.5000 g., 0.9860 Gold 0.1109 oz. AGW **Obv:** Open crown

Date	Mintage	VG	F	VF	XF	Unc
ND	—	150	200	375	700	—
1632 S-B	—	150	200	375	700	—

KM# 20.1 DUCAT
3.5000 g., 0.9860 Gold 0.1109 oz. AGW **Subject:** Wladislaus IV **Obv:** Larger tall, thin bust

Date	Mintage	VG	F	VF	XF	Unc
1633 SB	—	150	200	500	950	—
1634 SB	—	150	200	500	950	—
1635 SB	—	150	200	500	950	—

KM# 20.2 DUCAT
3.5000 g., 0.9860 Gold 0.1109 oz. AGW

Date	Mintage	VG	F	VF	XF	Unc
1636 CS	—	150	200	425	850	—
1638 II	—	150	225	600	1,200	—
1639 II	—	150	200	475	900	—

KM# 20.3 DUCAT
3.5000 g., 0.9860 Gold 0.1109 oz. AGW **Obv:** Small, short, fat bust

Date	Mintage	VG	F	VF	XF	Unc
1639 GR	—	150	200	475	900	—
1640 GR Rare	—	—	—	—	—	—
1641 GR	—	150	300	800	1,600	—
1642 GR	—	150	200	425	800	—
1643 GR	—	150	200	475	900	—
1644 GR	—	150	300	800	1,600	—
1645 GR	—	150	200	475	900	—
1646 GR	—	150	300	800	1,600	—
1647 GR	—	150	200	425	800	—

KM# 20.4 DUCAT
3.5000 g., 0.9860 Gold 0.1109 oz. AGW **Obv:** Small head

Date	Mintage	VG	F	VF	XF	Unc
1642 GR Rare	—	—	—	—	—	—

KM# 53 DUCAT
3.5000 g., 0.9860 Gold 0.1109 oz. AGW **Rev:** Date below arms

Date	Mintage	VG	F	VF	XF	Unc
1651 GR	—	150	250	500	950	—

KM# 41.1 DUCAT
3.5000 g., 0.9860 Gold 0.1109 oz. AGW **Subject:** Johann Casimir

Date	Mintage	VG	F	VF	XF	Unc
1649 GR	—	150	200	400	750	—
1650 GR	—	150	200	400	750	—
1651 GR	—	150	200	400	750	—
1652 GR	—	150	200	600	1,200	—
1653 GR	—	150	200	550	1,000	—
1655 GR	—	150	200	400	750	—
1656 GR	—	150	200	400	750	—
1657 DL	—	150	200	400	750	—

KM# 41.2 DUCAT
3.5000 g., 0.9860 Gold 0.1109 oz. AGW **Obv:** No knot at shoulder

Date	Mintage	VG	F	VF	XF	Unc
1658 DL	—	150	200	450	800	—
1659 DL	—	200	400	1,000	2,200	—
1660 DL	—	150	250	500	975	—
1661 DL	—	150	200	375	700	—
1662 DL	—	150	200	375	700	—
1663 DL	—	150	200	375	700	—

KM# 41.3 DUCAT
3.5000 g., 0.9860 Gold 0.1109 oz. AGW **Obv:** Knot at shoulder

Date	Mintage	VG	F	VF	XF	Unc
1666 DL	—	150	200	375	700	—
1667 DL	—	150	200	375	700	—
1668 DL	—	150	200	400	750	—

KM# 71.1 DUCAT
3.5000 g., 0.9860 Gold 0.1109 oz. AGW **Subject:** Michael Korybut

Date	Mintage	VG	F	VF	XF	Unc
1670 DL	—	250	400	1,000	1,750	—

KM# 71.2 DUCAT
3.5000 g., 0.9860 Gold 0.1109 oz. AGW

Date	Mintage	VG	F	VF	XF	Unc
1672 DL	—	250	350	700	1,150	—
1673 DL	—	250	350	700	1,150	—
ND	—	250	350	700	1,150	—

KM# 72.1 DUCAT
3.5000 g., 0.9860 Gold 0.1109 oz. AGW **Subject:** Johann III Sobieski

Date	Mintage	VG	F	VF	XF	Unc
1676 DL	—	250	350	950	1,500	—

KM# 72.2 DUCAT
3.5000 g., 0.9860 Gold 0.1109 oz. AGW

Date	Mintage	VG	F	VF	XF	Unc
1677 DL	—	225	300	600	1,000	—
1682 DL	—	225	300	750	1,200	—

KM# 75.1 DUCAT
3.5000 g., 0.9860 Gold 0.1109 oz. AGW

Date	Mintage	VG	F	VF	XF	Unc
1683 DL	—	225	300	600	1,000	—
1688/6	—	225	300	600	1,000	—
1688	—	225	300	600	1,000	—

KM# 75.2 DUCAT
3.5000 g., 0.9860 Gold 0.1109 oz. AGW

Date	Mintage	VG	F	VF	XF	Unc
1692	—	225	300	650	1,250	—

KM# 83 DUCAT
3.5000 g., 0.9860 Gold 0.1109 oz. AGW **Subject:** August II

Date	Mintage	VG	F	VF	XF	Unc
1698	—	425	850	1,650	2,750	—

KM# 84 DUCAT
3.5000 g., 0.9860 Gold 0.1109 oz. AGW **Obv:** Small bust of Augustus II with continuous legend

Date	Mintage	VG	F	VF	XF	Unc
1698	—	425	850	1,650	2,750	—

KM# A21 1-1/2 DUCAT
Gold **Subject:** Wladislaus IV

Date	Mintage	VG	F	VF	XF	Unc
1634	—	285	450	850	1,600	—
1644	—	285	450	850	1,600	—
1645	—	285	450	850	1,600	—
1646	—	285	450	850	1,600	—
1647	—	285	450	850	1,600	—

KM# 59 1-1/2 DUCAT
Gold **Subject:** Johann Casimir

Date	Mintage	VG	F	VF	XF	Unc
1658 DL	—	750	1,500	2,750	4,500	—
1661 DL	—	750	1,500	2,750	4,500	—

KM# 35 2 DUCAT
7.0000 g., 0.9860 Gold 0.2219 oz. AGW **Obv:** Crowned bust of Wladislaus IV in inner circle **Rev:** City of Danzig in inner circle, date and arms in exergue

Date	Mintage	VG	F	VF	XF	Unc
1634	—	250	500	950	1,800	—
1635	—	250	500	950	1,800	—
1636	—	250	500	950	1,800	—
1637	—	250	500	950	1,800	—
1638	—	250	500	950	1,800	—
1639	—	250	500	950	1,800	—
1640	—	250	500	950	1,800	—

Date	Mintage	VG	F	VF	XF	Unc
1641	—	250	500	950	1,800	—
1642	—	250	500	950	1,800	—
1643	—	250	500	950	1,800	—
1644	—	250	500	950	1,800	—
1645	—	250	500	950	1,800	—
1646	—	250	500	950	1,800	—
1647	—	250	500	950	1,800	—

KM# 56.1 2 DUCAT

7.0000 g., 0.9860 Gold 0.2219 oz. AGW **Subject:** Johann Casimir

Date	Mintage	VG	F	VF	XF	Unc
1651 Rare	—	—	—	—	—	—
1655 DL	—	500	1,000	2,000	3,500	—
1658 DL	—	500	1,000	2,000	3,500	—
1661 DS	—	500	1,000	2,000	3,500	—

KM# 56.2 2 DUCAT

7.0000 g., 0.9860 Gold 0.2219 oz. AGW

Date	Mintage	VG	F	VF	XF	Unc
ND GR	—	—	—	—	—	—

KM# 65 2 DUCAT

7.0000 g., 0.9860 Gold 0.2219 oz. AGW **Subject:** Michael Korybut

Date	Mintage	VG	F	VF	XF	Unc
ND Rare	—	—	—	—	—	—

KM# 80.1 2 DUCAT

7.0000 g., 0.9860 Gold 0.2219 oz. AGW **Subject:** Johann III Sobieski

Date	Mintage	VG	F	VF	XF	Unc
1692	—	750	1,500	3,000	6,000	—
ND DL	—	750	1,500	3,000	6,000	—

KM# 80.2 2 DUCAT

7.0000 g., 0.9860 Gold 0.2219 oz. AGW

Date	Mintage	VG	F	VF	XF	Unc
ND	—	750	1,500	3,000	6,000	—

KM# 81 2 DUCAT

7.0000 g., 0.9860 Gold 0.2219 oz. AGW **Obv:** Laureate bust of Johann III Sobieski right

Date	Mintage	VG	F	VF	XF	Unc
ND DL	—	750	1,500	3,000	6,000	—

KM# 85 2 DUCAT

7.0000 g., 0.9860 Gold 0.2219 oz. AGW **Subject:** August II

Date	Mintage	VG	F	VF	XF	Unc
1698	—	600	1,200	2,500	5,000	—
1699	—	—	—	—	—	—

KM# 34 2-1/2 DUCAT

8.7500 g., 0.9860 Gold 0.2774 oz. AGW

Date	Mintage	VG	F	VF	XF	Unc
1645 GR Rare	—	—	—	—	—	—

KM# 16 3 DUCAT

10.5000 g., 0.9860 Gold 0.3328 oz. AGW

Date	Mintage	VG	F	VF	XF	Unc
1617 Rare	—	—	—	—	—	—

KM# 36 3 DUCAT

10.5000 g., 0.9860 Gold 0.3328 oz. AGW **Subject:** Wladislaus IV

Date	Mintage	VG	F	VF	XF	Unc
1634	—	850	1,750	3,250	5,500	—
1640	—	850	1,750	3,250	5,500	—
1641	—	850	1,750	3,250	5,500	—
1642	—	850	1,750	3,250	5,500	—
1647 GR	—	850	1,750	3,250	5,500	—

KM# 51.1 3 DUCAT

10.5000 g., 0.9860 Gold 0.3328 oz. AGW **Ruler:** Johann Casimir **Obv:** Laureate bust right in inner circle **Rev:** City view, arms below

Date	Mintage	VG	F	VF	XF	Unc
ND(1649-68)	—	900	1,850	3,500	6,000	—
1650	—	900	1,850	3,500	6,000	—
1658	—	900	1,850	3,500	6,000	—

KM# A66 3 DUCAT

10.5000 g., 0.9860 Gold 0.3328 oz. AGW **Ruler:** Michael Korybut **Obv:** Laureate bust right without inner circle **Rev:** City view, arms below, without value 3 at top

Date	Mintage	VG	F	VF	XF	Unc
ND(1669-73)	—	1,350	2,750	5,000	9,000	—

KM# 37 4 DUCAT

14.0000 g., 0.9860 Gold 0.4438 oz. AGW **Obv:** Crowned bust of Wladislaus IV in inner circle **Rev:** City of Danzig in inner circle, arms below **Note:** Legend varieties exist.

Date	Mintage	VG	F	VF	XF	Unc
1641	—	750	1,350	2,850	5,500	—
1642	—	750	1,350	2,850	5,500	—
1643	—	750	1,350	2,850	5,500	—
1644	—	750	1,350	2,850	5,500	—
1645	—	750	1,350	2,850	5,500	—

KM# 44 4 DUCAT

14.0000 g., 0.9860 Gold 0.4438 oz. AGW **Subject:** Johann Casimir

Date	Mintage	VG	F	VF	XF	Unc
1650 GR	—	650	1,200	2,650	5,000	—
ND GR	—	650	1,200	2,650	5,000	—

KM# 82 4 DUCAT

14.0000 g., 0.9860 Gold 0.4438 oz. AGW **Subject:** Johann Sobieski

Date	Mintage	VG	F	VF	XF	Unc
1692	—	1,200	2,500	4,500	7,500	—

KM# 7 5 DUCAT (1/2 Portugaloser)

16.8620 g., 0.9860 Gold 0.5345 oz. AGW **Subject:** Sigismund III

Date	Mintage	VG	F	VF	XF	Unc
ND(1614)	—	2,500	4,000	7,000	11,500	—

KM# 55.1 5 DUCAT (1/2 Portugaloser)
16.8620 g., 0.9860 Gold 0.5345 oz. AGW **Subject:** Johann Casimir

Date	Mintage	VG	F	VF	XF	Unc
1649 GR	—	—	—	—	—	—
1654 GR	—	2,000	3,500	6,000	9,500	—

KM# 55.2 5 DUCAT (1/2 Portugaloser)
16.8620 g., 0.9860 Gold 0.5345 oz. AGW **Rev:** 5 added above all seeing eye above modified city view

Date	Mintage	VG	F	VF	XF	Unc
1656 GR	—	2,000	3,500	6,000	9,500	—

KM# A33 6 DUCAT
Gold **Subject:** Wladislaus IV

Date	Mintage	VG	F	VF	XF	Unc
1644	—	1,200	2,500	4,000	6,500	—
1645	—	1,200	2,500	4,000	6,500	—

KM# B33 7 DUCAT
Gold **Subject:** Wladislaus IV

Date	Mintage	VG	F	VF	XF	Unc
1644	—	1,500	2,750	4,500	7,000	—
1645	—	1,500	2,750	4,500	7,000	—

KM# 12 8 DUCAT
28.0000 g., 0.9860 Gold 0.8876 oz. AGW **Subject:** Sigismund III **Note:** Struck from 5 Ducat dies.

Date	Mintage	VG	F	VF	XF	Unc
1614	—	3,000	5,000	8,000	13,500	—

KM# C33 8 DUCAT
28.0000 g., 0.9860 Gold 0.8876 oz. AGW **Subject:** Wladislaus IV

Date	Mintage	VG	F	VF	XF	Unc
1644	—	2,000	3,250	5,500	8,500	—
1645	—	2,000	3,250	5,500	8,500	—

KM# 4 10 DUCAT
35.0000 g., 0.9860 Gold 1.1095 oz. AGW **Subject:** Sigismund III

Date	Mintage	VG	F	VF	XF	Unc
1613//1614 Rare	—	—	—	—	—	—

KM# 33 10 DUCAT
35.0000 g., 0.9860 Gold 1.1095 oz. AGW **Subject:** Wladislaus IV

Date	Mintage	VG	F	VF	XF	Unc
1644 GR	—	—	—	8,000	12,500	—

KM# 52 10 DUCAT
35.0000 g., 0.9860 Gold 1.1095 oz. AGW **Subject:** Johann Casimir

Date	Mintage	VG	F	VF	XF	Unc
1650 GR Rare	—	—	—	—	—	—
1651 GR Rare	—	—	—	—	—	—
ND	—	—	—	—	—	—

KM# A53 12 DUCAT
Gold **Subject:** Johann Casimir

Date	Mintage	VG	F	VF	XF	Unc
1650 Rare	—	—	—	—	—	—

KM# 13 15 DUCAT
52.5000 g., 0.9860 Gold 1.6642 oz. AGW **Subject:** Sigismund III

Date	Mintage	VG	F	VF	XF	Unc
ND(1614) Rare	—	—	—	—	—	—

KM# 17 20 DUCAT
69.7400 g., 0.9860 Gold 2.2107 oz. AGW **Subject:** Sigismund III

Date	Mintage	VG	F	VF	XF	Unc
1613//1614 Rare	—	—	—	—	—	—

Note: Bowers and Merena Guia sale 3-88 VF realized $14,300

TRADE COINAGE

KM# 51.2 3 DUCAT
10.5000 g., 0.9860 Gold 0.3328 oz. AGW **Ruler:** Johann Casimir **Obv:** Laureate bust right without inner circle **Rev:** City view, arms below, without value 3 at top

Date	Mintage	VG	F	VF	XF	Unc
ND(1649-68)	—	650	1,150	2,500	4,750	—

KM# A59 4 DUCAT
14.0000 g., 0.9860 Gold 0.4438 oz. AGW, 37 mm. **Ruler:** Johann Casimir **Obv:** Crowned bust right **Rev:** Hebrew and script in sunburst over city view, supported arms below **Note:** Fr. #29.

Date	Mintage	Good	VG	F	VF	XF
ND(ca. 1657)	—	—	—	—	5,000	8,000

PIEFORTS

KM#	Date	Mintage	Identification	Mkt Val
P1	1616	—	Orte. Silver.	—

PATTERNS

Including off metal strikes

KM#	Date	Mintage	Identification	Mkt Val
Pn1	1613	—	Ternar. Gold. KM#10.	—
Pn2	1640	—	1/2 Thaler. Gold. KM#26.	—
Pn3	1641	—	1/2 Thaler. Gold. KM#26. Weight of 2 Ducat.	—
Pn4	1641	—	1/2 Thaler. Gold. KM#26. Weight of 3 Ducat.	—
Pn5	1641	—	1/2 Thaler. Gold. KM#26. Weight of 4 Ducat.	—
Pn6	1657	—	Schilling. Gold. KM#57.	—
Pn7	1659 DL	—	Ducat. Silver. KM#41.	100
Pn8	1661 DL	—	Ducat. Lead. KM#41.	100

ELBING

Elbing is an important industrial city and seaport in northern Poland and was founded in 1237 (Elblag). They later joined the Hanseatic League. The city was under Polish control from 1454-1772 when it was annexed to Prussia. They produced their own coinage from 1454-1763.

RULERS
Polish, 1454-1626, 1636-1655, 1660-
Swedish, 1626-1636, 1655-1660

MINT OFFICIALS' INITIALS

Initials or Mark	Desc.	Date	Name
CS		1671-73	Christian Schultz
IP		1665-67	Jan Paulson
WVE		1650-52	Wilhelm von Eck
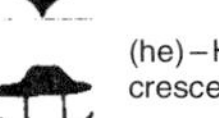	MP, (ha) – Heart with crossed arrows		
	(he) – Helmet above crescent		
	(hf) – Heart with flag	1628-35	Marsilius Philipsen
NH		1656-60	Nicholaus Henning
Without mint mark		1631	Benedikt Steffen

MONETARY SYSTEM
1-1/2 Groschen (Grosze) = Poltorak (1630-1633)

POLISH AUTHORITY

STANDARD COINAGE

KM# 5 SOLIDUS (Schilling)
Silver **Obv:** Crowned large S monogram

Date	Mintage	VG	F	VF	XF	Unc
(16)14	—	—	—	—	—	—

KM# 86 SOLIDUS (Schilling)
Silver **Obv:** Crowned ICR monogram divides date
Rev. Legend: SOLID / CIVITAT / ELBIN

Date	Mintage	VG	F	VF	XF	Unc
1666	—	34.50	60.00	105	175	—

KM# 90 SOLIDUS (Schilling)
Silver **Obv:** Crowned MR monogram with date
Rev. Legend: SOLID / CIVITAT / ELBINGE, arms below

Date	Mintage	VG	F	VF	XF	Unc
1671	—	70.00	140	290	450	—
1672	—	30.00	60.00	115	230	—
1673	—	17.00	40.25	70.00	145	—
ND	—	17.00	40.25	70.00	145	—

KM# 54 2 GROSCHEN (2 Groschen = 1 Poltorak)
Silver **Subject:** John Casimir

Date	Mintage	VG	F	VF	XF	Unc
1651 WE	—	60.00	85.00	175	260	—
1651 WVE	—	60.00	85.00	175	260	—

KM# 50 ORTE
Silver **Subject:** John Casimir

Date	Mintage	VG	F	VF	XF	Unc
1650 WVE Rare	—	—	—	—	—	—
1651 WVE Rare	—	—	—	—	—	—

KM# 51 ORTE
Silver **Note:** Klippe.

Date	Mintage	VG	F	VF	XF	Unc
1650 WVE Rare	—	—	—	—	—	—

KM# 53 ORTE
Silver **Note:** Klippe.

Date	Mintage	VG	F	VF	XF	Unc
1651 WVE	—	—	—	—	—	—

KM# 52 ORTE
Silver **Rev:** 1-8 at top of arms

Date	Mintage	VG	F	VF	XF	Unc
1651 WVE	—	70.00	140	290	450	—
1660 WVE	—	30.00	60.00	115	230	—
1661 NH	—	30.00	60.00	115	230	—

KM# 85 ORTE
Silver **Subject:** John Casimir

Date	Mintage	VG	F	VF	XF	Unc
1662 NH	—	30.00	60.00	115	230	—
1665 IP	—	40.25	85.00	175	350	—
1666 IP	—	40.25	85.00	175	350	—
1667 IP Rare	—	—	—	—	—	—

KM# A52 1/2 THALER
Silver **Subject:** John Casimir

Date	Mintage	VG	F	VF	XF	Unc
1650 WVE Rare	—	—	—	—	—	—
1651 WVE Rare	—	—	—	—	—	—

KM# 48 THALER
Silver **Obv:** Facing bust of Wladislaus IV in inner circle
Rev: Oval arms in wreath, date at top **Note:** Dav. #4362.

Date	Mintage	VG	F	VF	XF	Unc
1635 II	—	600	1,150	2,250	4,050	—
1636/5 II	—	600	1,150	2,250	4,050	—
1636 II	—	600	1,150	2,250	4,050	—

KM# 55 THALER

Silver **Subject:** John Casimir **Note:** Dav. #4364.

Date	Mintage	VG	F	VF	XF	Unc
1651 WVE	—	800	1,500	2,700	4,750	—

KM# 91 THALER

Silver **Subject:** Michael Korybut **Note:** Dav. #4365.

Date	Mintage	VG	F	VF	XF	Unc
1671 CS Rare	—	—	—	—	—	—

KM# 92 THALER

Silver **Note:** Weight of 1/2 Thaler. Dav. #4365A.

Date	Mintage	VG	F	VF	XF	Unc
1671 CS Rare	—	—	—	—	—	—

KM# 56 1-1/2 THALER

43.2600 g., Silver **Note:** Dav. #4364A.

Date	Mintage	VG	F	VF	XF	Unc
1651 WVE Rare	—	—	—	—	—	—

KM# B57 2 THALER

57.6800 g., Silver **Note:** Dav. #4364B.

Date	Mintage	VG	F	VF	XF	Unc
1651 WVE Rare	—	—	—	—	—	—

KM# A57 2 THALER

Silver **Note:** Similar to 1 Tharler, KM#55. Dav. #4563.

Date	Mintage	VG	F	VF	XF	Unc
1651 WVE Rare	—	—	—	—	—	—

TRADE COINAGE

KM# 76 DUCAT

3.5000 g., 0.9860 Gold 0.1109 oz. AGW **Subject:** John Casimir

Date	Mintage	VG	F	VF	XF	Unc
1658 NH	—	2,500	4,900	8,300	13,500	—
1660	—	2,500	4,900	8,300	13,500	—
1661	—	2,500	4,900	8,300	13,500	—
1663	—	2,500	4,900	8,300	13,500	—

KM# 93 DUCAT

3.5000 g., 0.9860 Gold 0.1109 oz. AGW **Subject:** Michael Korybut

Date	Mintage	VG	F	VF	XF	Unc
1671 CS	—	2,500	4,900	8,300	13,500	—
1672 CS	—	2,500	4,900	8,300	13,500	—

KM# 94 2 DUCAT

7.0000 g., 0.9860 Gold 0.2219 oz. AGW **Subject:** Michael Korybut

Date	Mintage	VG	F	VF	XF	Unc
1672 CS	—	3,000	5,300	9,000	14,500	—

SWEDISH AUTHORITY

STANDARD COINAGE

KM# 23 SOLIDUS (Schilling)

Silver **Obv:** Crowned GA monogram, titles of Gustavus Adolphus

Date	Mintage	VG	F	VF	XF	Unc
1629 Rare	—	—	—	—	—	—
1630	—	9.00	17.00	30.00	70.00	—
1631	—	9.00	17.00	30.00	70.00	—
1632	—	9.00	17.00	30.00	70.00	—

KM# 38 SOLIDUS (Schilling)

Silver **Obv:** Crowned GA monogram in inner circle

Date	Mintage	VG	F	VF	XF	Unc
1632 MP	—	14.00	30.00	50.00	115	—
1633 MP	—	20.00	40.25	75.00	175	—

KM# 46 SOLIDUS (Schilling)

Silver **Obv:** Crowned CR monogram in inner circle, titles of Christina

Date	Mintage	VG	F	VF	XF	Unc
1633 Rare	—	—	—	—	—	—
1634	—	12.00	22.50	40.25	100	—
1635	—	12.00	22.50	40.25	100	—

KM# 45 SOLIDUS (Schilling)

Silver **Note:** Posthumous issue.

Date	Mintage	VG	F	VF	XF	Unc
1633	—	9.00	17.00	30.00	70.00	—
1634	—	17.00	34.50	70.00	140	—

KM# 57 SOLIDUS (Schilling)

Silver **Obv:** Crowned CG monogram in inner circle **Rev:** Three crowns, two above one, in inner circle; date in legend

Date	Mintage	VG	F	VF	XF	Unc
1656 Rare	—	—	—	—	—	—
1657 Rare	—	—	—	—	—	—

KM# 65 SOLIDUS (Schilling)

Silver **Obv:** Crowned CG monogram in inner circle, titles of Charles X **Rev:** Arms in carotuche in inner circle, date in legend **Rev. Legend:** SOLIDVS PRUSSIAE

Date	Mintage	VG	F	VF	XF	Unc
1657 Rare	—	—	—	—	—	—

KM# 66 SOLIDUS (Schilling)

Silver **Rev. Legend:** SOLIDVS ELBING

Date	Mintage	VG	F	VF	XF	Unc
1657 Rare	—	—	—	—	—	—

KM# 10 GROSCHEN (Grosz)

Silver **Obv:** Crown above three-line inscription **Rev:** Oval arms in inner circle, date in legend

Date	Mintage	VG	F	VF	XF	Unc
1628 Rare	—	—	—	—	—	—

KM# 24 GROSCHEN (Grosz)

Silver **Obv:** Crowned bust of Gustavus Adolphus right

Date	Mintage	VG	F	VF	XF	Unc
1629	—	17.00	40.25	80.00	145	—
(16)29	—	17.00	34.50	60.00	115	—
1630	—	17.00	34.50	60.00	115	—

KM# 39 GROSCHEN (Grosz)

Silver **Obv:** Crowned bust of Gustavus Adolphus right in inner circle

Date	Mintage	VG	F	VF	XF	Unc
1632	—	46.00	90.00	190	400	—

KM# 30 3 GROSCHEN

Silver **Obv:** Crowned bust of Gustavus Adolphus right **Rev:** Value and date above three-line inscription **Note:** Varieties exist.

Date	Mintage	VG	F	VF	XF	Unc
1631 (ha)	—	40.25	75.00	145	300	—
1631 (hc)	—	17.00	40.25	75.00	155	—
1632 Rare	—	—	—	—	—	—

KM# 40 3 GROSCHEN

Silver **Obv:** Crowned bust of Gustav Adolf II right **Rev:** Supported arms divide date, three-line inscription below

Date	Mintage	VG	F	VF	XF	Unc
1632	—	17.00	40.25	75.00	155	—
1633	—	60.00	115	175	290	—

KM# 73 6 GROSCHEN

Silver **Obv:** Crowned bust of Charles X right in inner circle **Rev:** Value above Elbing arms in inner circle, date in legend

Date	Mintage	VG	F	VF	XF	Unc
1658	—	85.00	175	350	700	—
1659	—	70.00	140	275	550	—

KM# 58 18 GROSCHEN

Silver **Obv:** Laureate bust of Charles X left **Rev:** Rampant lion surrounded by three crowns, without value

Date	Mintage	VG	F	VF	XF	Unc
ND(1656)	—	85.00	175	350	700	—

KM# 62 18 GROSCHEN

Silver **Obv:** Laureate bust of Charles X right **Rev:** Oval arms in cartouche divides value, date in legend

Date	Mintage	VG	F	VF	XF	Unc
1656 NH	—	85.00	175	350	700	—

KM# 63 18 GROSCHEN

Silver **Obv:** Laureate bust of Charles X right **Rev:** Angel above oval arms divides value in inner circle, date in legend

Date	Mintage	VG	F	VF	XF	Unc
1656 Rare	—	—	—	—	—	—

KM# 64 18 GROSCHEN

Silver **Obv:** Bust in inner circle **Rev:** Without inner circle

Date	Mintage	VG	F	VF	XF	Unc
1656 Rare	—	—	—	—	—	—
1657	—	70.00	140	275	550	—
1658/7 Rare	—	—	—	—	—	—

KM# 59 18 GROSCHEN

Silver **Rev:** Value added

Date	Mintage	VG	F	VF	XF	Unc
ND(1656)	—	85.00	175	350	700	—
ND(1656) NH	—	70.00	140	275	550	—

KM# 60 18 GROSCHEN

Silver **Obv:** Laureate bust of Charles X left in inner circle

Date	Mintage	VG	F	VF	XF	Unc
ND(1656) NH	—	70.00	140	275	550	—

KM# 61 18 GROSCHEN

Silver **Obv:** Laureate bust of Charles X right in inner circle

Date	Mintage	VG	F	VF	XF	Unc
ND(1656)	—	85.00	175	350	700	—

KM# 69 18 GROSCHEN

Silver **Obv:** S • G • V at end of legend

Date	Mintage	VG	F	VF	XF	Unc
1657	—	70.00	140	275	550	—

KM# 67 18 GROSCHEN

Silver **Note:** Inner circles on both sides.

Date	Mintage	VG	F	VF	XF	Unc
1657	—	60.00	115	230	450	—

KM# 68 18 GROSCHEN

Silver **Note:** Klippe.

Date	Mintage	VG	F	VF	XF	Unc
1657 Rare	—	—	—	—	—	—

KM# 11 1/24 THALER

Silver **Obv:** Crowned arms in inner circle, titles of Gustavus Adolphus **Rev:** Orb with value within divides date in inner circle **Note:** City issue.

Date	Mintage	VG	F	VF	XF	Unc
(16)28	—	30.00	60.00	115	230	—
(16)29	—	14.00	30.00	60.00	115	—
(16)30	—	14.00	30.00	60.00	115	—
(16)31	—	14.00	30.00	60.00	115	—
(16)32	—	14.00	30.00	60.00	115	—

KM# 42 1/24 THALER

Silver **Note:** Error: 60 instead of 24 as value.

Date	Mintage	VG	F	VF	XF	Unc
1632	—	60.00	115	230	450	—

KM# 43 1/24 THALER

Silver **Obv:** Titles of Christina

Date	Mintage	VG	F	VF	XF	Unc
1632 Rare	—	—	—	—	—	—
1634	—	22.50	46.00	90.00	185	—
1635	—	22.50	46.00	90.00	185	—

KM# 41 1/24 THALER

Silver **Obv:** Crowned arms, titles of Gustav Adolf II **Rev:** Orb with value within divides two-digit date **Note:** Royal issue.

Date	Mintage	VG	F	VF	XF	Unc
(16)32	—	17.00	34.50	70.00	140	—
(16)33	—	22.50	46.00	90.00	185	—
(16)34 Unique	—	—	—	—	—	—
(16)35 Rare	—	—	—	—	—	—

KM# 47 1/24 THALER

Silver **Note:** Posthumous issue.

Date	Mintage	VG	F	VF	XF	Unc
(16)33 Rare	—	—	—	—	—	—

KM# 70 1/24 THALER

Silver **Obv:** Titles of Charles X

Date	Mintage	VG	F	VF	XF	Unc
1657 Rare	—	—	—	—	—	—
1658 Rare	—	—	—	—	—	—

KM# 12 1/4 THALER

Silver **Obv:** Crowned Swedish arms in inner circle **Rev:** Oval arms in cartouche divides date in inner circle

Date	Mintage	VG	F	VF	XF	Unc
1628 Rare	—	—	—	—	—	—

KM# 31 1/4 THALER

Silver **Obv:** Crowned bust of Gustavus Adolphus right in inner circle **Rev:** Oval arms with lion supporters in inner circle, date in legend

Date	Mintage	VG	F	VF	XF	Unc
1631 MP Rare	—	—	—	—	—	—

KM# 32 1/4 THALER

Silver **Obv:** Bust divides 1-6 within linear circle **Rev:** 24 above lion supported arms

Date	Mintage	VG	F	VF	XF	Unc
1631 Unique	—	—	—	—	—	—

KM# 13 1/2 THALER

Silver **Obv:** Crowned Swedish arms with lion supporters **Rev:** Angel above oval arms in cartouche, date above legend

Date	Mintage	VG	F	VF	XF	Unc
1628 Rare	—	—	—	—	—	—

KM# 15 THALER

Silver **Note:** Date on both sides. Dav. #4565.

Date	Mintage	VG	F	VF	XF	Unc
1628	—	400	800	1,600	3,250	—

KM# 14 THALER

Silver **Obv:** Crowned Swedish arms with lion supporters **Rev:** Angel above oval arms in cartouche, date above angel **Note:** Dav. #4567.

Date	Mintage	VG	F	VF	XF	Unc
1628	—	550	1,000	2,050	3,700	—

KM# 16 THALER

Silver **Note:** Klippe. Dav. #4565A. Struck wtih 1/2 Thaler dies, KM#13.

Date	Mintage	VG	F	VF	XF	Unc
1628 Rare	—	—	—	—	—	—

KM# 74 THALER

Silver **Obv:** Crowned bust of Charles X right in inner circle **Rev:** Angel above arms in inner circle, date in legend **Note:** Dav. #4369.

Date	Mintage	VG	F	VF	XF	Unc
1658 Rare	—	—	—	—	—	—

KM# 75 1-1/4 THALER

Silver **Obv:** Crowned bust of Charles X right in inner circle **Rev:** Angel above arms in inner circle, date in legend **Note:** Klippe. Dav. #4568.

Date	Mintage	VG	F	VF	XF	Unc
1658 Rare	—	—	—	—	—	—

KM# 17 1-1/2 THALER

Silver **Obv:** Crowned Swedish arms in inner circle **Rev:** Angel above oval arms in cartouche, date divided above angel **Note:** Dav. #4562.

Date	Mintage	VG	F	VF	XF	Unc
1628 Rare	—	—	—	—	—	—

KM# 18 1-1/2 THALER

Silver **Obv:** Crowned Swedish arms with lion supporters **Note:** Dav. #4564.

Date	Mintage	VG	F	VF	XF	Unc
1628 Rare	—	—	—	—	—	—

KM# 19 2 THALER

Silver **Obv:** Crowned Swedish arms with lion supporters **Rev:** Angel above oval arms in cartouche, date divided above angel **Note:** Dav. #4563.

Date	Mintage	VG	F	VF	XF	Unc
1628 Rare	—	—	—	—	—	—

KM# 20 3 THALER

Silver **Obv:** Crowned Swedish arms in inner circle **Rev:** Angel above oval arms in cartouche, date divided above angel **Note:** Dav. #A4562.

Date	Mintage	VG	F	VF	XF	Unc
1628 Unique	—	—	—	—	—	—

KM# 21 3 THALER

Silver **Obv:** Crowned Swedish arms with lion supporters **Note:** Dav. #A4563.

Date	Mintage	VG	F	VF	XF	Unc
1628 Unique	—	—	—	—	—	—

TRADE COINAGE

KM# 71 DUCAT

3.5000 g., 0.9860 Gold 0.1109 oz. AGW **Obv:** Crowned bust of Charles right in inner circle **Rev:** Garnished arms in inner circle

Date	Mintage	VG	F	VF	XF	Unc
1657 NH	—	3,500	6,300	9,800	17,000	—
1658 NH	—	3,500	6,300	9,800	17,000	—

KM# 72 DUCAT

3.5000 g., 0.9860 Gold 0.1109 oz. AGW **Rev:** Garnished arms without inner circle

Date	Mintage	VG	F	VF	XF	Unc
ND	—	3,500	6,300	9,800	17,000	—

KM# 77 1-1/2 DUCAT

0.9860 Gold **Obv:** Crowned bust of Charles right in inner circle **Rev:** Arms held by angel above, date in legend

Date	Mintage	VG	F	VF	XF	Unc
1658 NH Rare	—	—	—	—	—	—

KM# 78 2 DUCAT

7.0000 g., 0.9860 Gold 0.2219 oz. AGW **Obv:** Crowned bust of Charles right in inner circle **Rev:** Arms held by angel above, date in legend

Date	Mintage	VG	F	VF	XF	Unc
1658 Rare	—	—	—	—	—	—
ND Rare	—	—	—	—	—	—

KM# 33 3 DUCAT

10.5000 g., 0.9860 Gold 0.3328 oz. AGW **Obv:** Crowned bust of Gustavus Adolphus right **Rev:** Supported arms in inner circle, date in legend

Date	Mintage	VG	F	VF	XF	Unc
1631 MP Rare	—	—	—	—	—	—

KM# 34 3 DUCAT

10.5000 g., 0.9860 Gold 0.3328 oz. AGW **Obv:** Crowned draped bust of Gustavus Adolphus right

Date	Mintage	VG	F	VF	XF	Unc
1631 MP Unique	—	—	—	—	—	—

KM# 22 4 DUCAT

14.0000 g., 0.9860 Gold 0.4438 oz. AGW **Obv:** Crowned Swedish arms in inner circle **Rev:** Garnished Elbing arms, date divided at top

Date	Mintage	VG	F	VF	XF	Unc
1628 Rare	—	—	—	—	—	—

KM# 35 4 DUCAT

13.8000 g., 0.9860 Gold 0.4375 oz. AGW **Obv:** Crowned bust of Gustavus Adolphus right **Rev:** Supported arms in inner circle, date in legend

Date	Mintage	VG	F	VF	XF	Unc
1631 MP Unique	—	—	—	—	—	—

KM# 36 5 DUCAT

17.5000 g., 0.9860 Gold 0.5547 oz. AGW **Obv:** Crowned bust of Gustavus Adolphus right **Rev:** Supported arms in inner circle, date in legend

Date	Mintage	VG	F	VF	XF	Unc
1631 Rare	—	—	—	—	—	—

KM# 37 5 DUCAT
17.5000 g., 0.9860 Gold 0.5547 oz. AGW **Obv:** Crowned draped bust of Gustavus Adolphus right

Date	Mintage	VG	F	VF	XF	Unc
1631 Rare	—	—	—	—	—	—

KM# 79 5 DUCAT
17.5000 g., 0.9860 Gold 0.5547 oz. AGW **Obv:** Crowned bust of Charles right **Rev:** Arms held by angel above in inner circle, date in legend

Date	Mintage	VG	F	VF	XF	Unc
1658 Rare	—	—	—	—	—	—

KM# 44 10 DUCAT
35.0000 g., 0.9860 Gold 1.1095 oz. AGW **Obv:** Bust of Gustavus Adolphus facing half-right in inner circle **Rev:** Ornamental Swedish arms divide date

Date	Mintage	VG	F	VF	XF	Unc
1632 Rare	—	—	—	—	—	—

KM# 80 10 DUCAT
35.0000 g., 0.9860 Gold 1.1095 oz. AGW **Obv:** Crowned bust of Charles right **Rev:** Arms held by angel above in inner circle, date in legend

Date	Mintage	VG	F	VF	XF	Unc
1658 Rare	—	—	—	—	—	—

PATTERNS

Including off metal strikes

KM#	Date	Mintage	Identification	Mkt Val
PnA1	1630	—	Ducat. Silver. Klippe.	—
Pn1	1631	—	3 Groschen. Gold. KM#30.	—
Pn2	1632	—	Solidus. Gold. KM#38. Weight of 1/2 Ducat.	—
Pn3	1635	—	1/24 Thaler. Gold. KM#43. Weight of 3/4 Ducat.	—
Pn4	1658	—	18 Groschen. Gold. KM#67. Weight of 3 Ducat.	—
PnA5	1658	—	Ducat. Silver. Klippe.	—

FRAUSTADT

(Wschowa)

MINT MARK
W - Wschowa (Fraustadt)

MINT OFFICIALS' INITIALS

Initial or Mark	Date	Name
(a) rose	1595-1601	Herman Rudiger
(b)	1599-1603	Rudolf Lehman

CITY

STANDARD COINAGE

KM# 5 DENARE
Silver **Obv:** Crowned displayed eagle **Rev:** Crowned arms divide date, CW above

Date	Mintage	VG	F	VF	XF	Unc
1600 Rare	—	—	—	—	—	—
(1)60Z Rare	—	—	—	—	—	—
160Z	—	30.00	50.00	85.00	—	—
(16)03	—	30.00	50.00	85.00	—	—
(16)04	—	115	200	290	—	—

KM# 6 DENARE
Silver **Note:** Uniface. Two shields of arms, date above, W below.

Date	Mintage	VG	F	VF	XF	Unc
1608	—	40.25	70.00	140	—	—
1609	—	22.50	40.25	70.00	—	—

KM# 7 DENARE
Silver **Obv:** Crowned displayed eagle **Rev:** Crowned arms divide two-digit date, W above

Date	Mintage	VG	F	VF	XF	Unc
(16)10	—	30.00	50.00	85.00	—	—
(16)11	—	40.25	70.00	140	—	—
(16)1Z	—	30.00	50.00	85.00	—	—

KM# 8 DENARE
Silver **Note:** Uniface. Two shields of arms, W below.

Date	Mintage	VG	F	VF	XF	Unc
ND(1608-10) Rare	—	—	—	—	—	—

LOBSENZ

(Lobzenica)

MINT MARK
L - Lobsenz (Lobzenica)

MINT OFFICIALS' INITIALS

Initial	Date	Name
AK crowned	1612-30	Andrzej Krotoski
(b)	1612-16	Jan Beker

CITY

STANDARD COINAGE

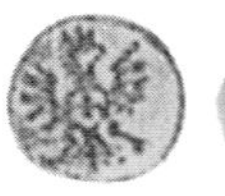

KM# 5 DENAR
Silver

Date	Mintage	VG	F	VF	XF	Unc
(16)12 Rare	—	—	—	—	—	—
(16)13 Rare	—	—	—	—	—	—
(16)14 Rare	—	—	—	—	—	—

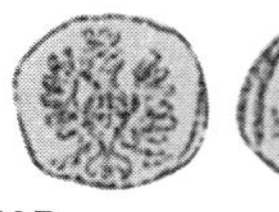

KM# 6 DENAR
Silver

Date	Mintage	VG	F	VF	XF	Unc
(16)13 Rare	—	—	—	—	—	—
(16)15L Rare	—	—	—	—	—	—

KM# 7 DENAR
Silver

Date	Mintage	VG	F	VF	XF	Unc
(16)22	—	75.00	150	250	—	—
(16)23	—	43.75	95.00	150	—	—
(16)24	—	65.00	125	220	—	—
ND	—	—	—	—	—	—

KM# 8 DENAR
Silver **Note:** Klippe.

Date	Mintage	VG	F	VF	XF	Unc
(16)23 Rare	—	—	—	—	—	—
ND Rare	—	—	—	—	—	—

KM# 9 TERNAR (3 Denarii, Pfennig = 1/6 Grosy)
Silver

Date	Mintage	VG	F	VF	XF	Unc
1623	—	17.00	80.00	175	—	—

KM# 10 TERNAR (3 Denarii, Pfennig = 1/6 Grosy)
Silver **Note:** Varieties exist.

Date	Mintage	VG	F	VF	XF	Unc
1624	—	14.00	60.00	115	—	—
16Z4	—	14.00	25.00	60.00	—	—
1625	—	14.00	25.00	60.00	—	—
16Z5	—	14.00	25.00	60.00	—	—
1626	—	14.00	25.00	60.00	—	—
16Z6	—	14.00	25.00	60.00	—	—

KM# 11 TERNAR (3 Denarii, Pfennig = 1/6 Grosy)
Silver **Note:** Legend varieties exist.

Date	Mintage	VG	F	VF	XF	Unc
1626L	—	14.00	25.00	46.00	—	—
16Z6	—	14.00	25.00	46.00	—	—
1627L	—	14.00	25.00	46.00	—	—
16Z7	—	14.00	25.00	46.00	—	—
1630	—	14.00	25.00	46.00	—	—

KM# 12 TERNAR (3 Denarii, Pfennig = 1/6 Grosy)
Silver

Date	Mintage	VG	F	VF	XF	Unc
1627	—	14.00	25.00	46.00	—	—
16Z7	—	14.00	25.00	46.00	—	—
1628	—	14.00	25.00	46.00	—	—
16Z8	—	14.00	25.00	46.00	—	—
16Z9	—	14.00	25.00	46.00	—	—
1630	—	14.00	25.00	46.00	—	—

POSEN

Posen was part of Poland until 1793, then a province of Prussia from 1793-1918. It became part of the Grand Duchy of Warsaw (Warszawa). Returned to Prussia after the Congress of Vienna (1815). A special coin issue was made as a provincial issue for the Grand Duchy (Frederich August, Grand Duke) of Posen by Prussia immediately after repossession.

RULER
Friedrich Wilhelm III (of Prussia), 1797-1840

MINT MARKS
A - Berlin
B - Breslau

KINGDOM

STANDARD COINAGE

KM# 5 DENAR
Silver

Date	Mintage	VG	F	VF	XF	Unc
(16)01 Unique	—	—	—	—	—	—
(16)02 Rare	—	—	—	—	—	—
(16)03	—	35.00	90.00	220	—	—
1603	—	50.00	125	325	—	—
(16)04 Rare	—	—	—	—	—	—
(16)05	—	35.00	90.00	220	—	—
(16)06	—	40.00	100	250	—	—
(16)07	—	27.50	75.00	190	—	—
(16)08	—	35.00	90.00	220	—	—
(16)09	—	27.50	75.00	190	—	—
(16)10	—	27.50	75.00	190	—	—
(16)11	—	35.00	90.00	220	—	—
(16)12	—	27.50	75.00	190	—	—
(16)1Z	—	—	—	—	—	—
(16)13	—	35.00	90.00	220	—	—
(16)14 Rare	—	—	—	—	—	—
ND Rare	—	—	—	—	—	—

KM# 6 TERNAR (3 Denarii - Pfennig)
Silver **Obv:** Large S monogram

Date	Mintage	VG	F	VF	XF	Unc
(16)03 Rare	—	—	—	—	—	—

KM# 7 TERNAR (3 Denarii - Pfennig)
Silver **Obv:** Displayed eagle

Date	Mintage	VG	F	VF	XF	Unc
1603	—	—	—	—	—	—
(16)03 Rare	—	—	—	—	—	—
(16)04 Rare	—	—	—	—	—	—

KM# 8 TERNAR (3 Denarii - Pfennig)
Silver **Obv:** Large S monogram divides date **Rev:** Three shields of arms

Date	Mintage	VG	F	VF	XF	Unc
(16)03 P Rare	—	—	—	—	—	—

KM# 9 TERNAR (3 Denarii - Pfennig)
Silver **Note:** Varieties exist.

Date	Mintage	VG	F	VF	XF	Unc
(16)05 P	—	60.00	140	290	—	—
(16)05	—	60.00	140	290	—	—
(16)06 P	—	60.00	140	290	—	—
(16)06	—	60.00	140	290	—	—
(16)08 P	—	60.00	140	290	—	—
(16)08	—	60.00	140	290	—	—
(16)09 P Rare	—	—	—	—	—	—
(16)10	—	60.00	140	290	—	—
(16)10 GC	—	80.00	175	400	—	—
(16)11	—	60.00	140	290	—	—
(16)13 Rare	—	—	—	—	—	—
(16)15	—	60.00	140	290	—	—
(16)16	—	60.00	140	290	—	—

KM# 15 TERNAR (3 Denarii - Pfennig)
Silver

Date	Mintage	VG	F	VF	XF	Unc
(16)16	—	60.00	140	290	—	—
(16)17	—	—	—	—	—	—
(16)18	—	—	—	—	—	—
(16)19	—	—	—	—	—	—

KM# 20 TERNAR (3 Denarii - Pfennig)
Silver

Date	Mintage	VG	F	VF	XF	Unc
(16)20	—	—	—	—	—	—

KM# 21 TERNAR (3 Denarii - Pfennig)
Silver **Obv:** Displayed eagle **Rev:** Crossed keys divide two-digit date

Date	Mintage	VG	F	VF	XF	Unc
(16)Z4	—	46.00	115	230	—	—

KM# 22 TERNAR (3 Denarii - Pfennig)
Silver **Note:** Varieties exist.

Date	Mintage	VG	F	VF	XF	Unc
1624	—	46.00	115	230	—	—
1626	—	46.00	115	230	—	—

KM# 23 TERNAR (3 Denarii - Pfennig)
Silver

Date	Mintage	VG	F	VF	XF	Unc
1626	—	46.00	115	230	—	—
1627	—	30.00	70.00	140	—	—

KM# 25 THALER
Silver **Subject:** Johann Casimir **Note:** Dav. #4366.

Date	Mintage	VG	F	VF	XF	Unc
1652 (aa)-AT Rare	—	—	—	—	—	—

THORN

Thorn is an industrial city in north-central Poland which was founded in 1231. They became a member of the Hanseatic League. The city came under Polish suzerainty (Torun) in 1454 and remained until they were absorbed by Prussia in 1793, except for brief periods of Swedish Occupation from1655-58 and during the Great Northern War (1703) when they were ruled by Sweden.

The city of Thorn was the birthplace of the astronomer, Copernicus. The last city coinage was struck in 1765.

RULERS
Sigismund III, 1587-1632
Wladislaus IV, 1632-1648
Johann Casimir, 1648-1655, 1658-1668
Swedish, 1655-1658
Michael Korybut, 1669-1673
August II of Saxony, 1697-1733

MINT OFFICIALS' INITIALS

Initial	Date	Name
GR	1643-49	Gerhard Rogge, tenant
HDL	1649-68	Hans Daniel Lauer, tenant during Swedish Occupation
HH	1629-31	Jenryk Hema, warden
HIL	1653-55	Hans Jacob Lauer
HL	1630	Hans Lippe, tenant
HS	1668-72	Heinrich Sievert
II	1630	Jacob Jacobson van Emden
MS	1640-42	Melchior Schirmer, tenant

CITY

STANDARD COINAGE

KM# 46 SOLIDUS
Silver **Obv:** Bust of Carl X Gustavus left, crowned ICR monogram divides date **Rev:** 3 crowns of Sweden **Rev. Legend:** SOLIDVS / CIVITATIS / THORVN

Date	Mintage	VG	F	VF	XF	Unc
1665 Rare	—	—	—	—	—	—
1666	—	14.00	30.00	55.00	95.00	—
1668	—	14.00	30.00	55.00	95.00	—

KM# 50 SOLIDUS
Silver **Obv:** Crowned MR monogram

Date	Mintage	VG	F	VF	XF	Unc
1671	—	18.00	42.00	70.00	120	—
ND(ca.1673)	—	18.00	42.00	70.00	120	—

KM# 36 2 GROSCHEN (2 Grosze)
Silver **Subject:** John Casimir

Date	Mintage	VG	F	VF	XF	Unc
1651 HDL	—	25.00	48.00	80.00	150	—

KM# 35 18 GROSZY (Ort)
Silver **Subject:** John Casimir

Date	Mintage	VG	F	VF	XF	Unc
1650 HDL	—	65.00	130	260	575	—
1651 HDL	—	45.50	100	195	400	—
1653 HDL	—	32.50	65.00	130	260	—
1654 HDL	—	32.50	65.00	130	260	—
1655 HDL	—	18.00	36.50	65.00	115	—
1655 HIL	—	32.50	65.00	130	260	—
1659 HDL	—	20.00	39.00	70.00	130	—
1660 HDL	—	18.00	36.50	65.00	115	—
1661 HDL	—	18.00	36.50	65.00	115	—
1662 HDL	—	18.00	36.50	65.00	115	—
1663 HDL	—	18.00	36.50	65.00	115	—
1664 HDL	—	18.00	36.50	65.00	115	—
1665 HDL	—	25.00	60.00	115	230	—
1666 HDL	—	25.00	60.00	115	230	—
1667 HDL	—	65.00	130	260	525	—
1668 HDL Unique	—	—	—	—	—	—
1668 HS Rare	—	—	—	—	—	—

KM# 38 18 GROSZY (Ort)
Silver **Ruler:** Carl X Gustavus **Note:** Swedish Occupation.

Date	Mintage	VG	F	VF	XF	Unc
ND(1656) Rare	—	—	—	—	—	—

KM# 15 1/4 THALER (Ort)
Silver **Subject:** Sigismund III

Date	Mintage	VG	F	VF	XF	Unc
1630 HL Rare	—	—	—	—	—	—

KM# 16 1/2 THALER (1/2 Talar)
Silver **Note:** Similar to 1/4 Thaler, KM#15.

Date	Mintage	VG	F	VF	XF	Unc
1629 HH	—	195	400	975	1,950	—
1630 HL	—	195	400	975	1,950	—
1630 II	—	130	260	575	1,250	—
1631 II	—	130	260	575	1,250	—
1632 II	—	195	400	775	1,550	—

KM# 30 1/2 THALER (1/2 Talar)
Silver **Note:** Similar to 1 Thaler, KM#24.

Date	Mintage	VG	F	VF	XF	Unc
1640 MS	—	450	975	1,950	3,900	—
1642 MS Rare	—	—	—	—	—	—

KM# 8 THALER
Silver **Rev:** Without angel behind arms

Date	Mintage	VG	F	VF	XF	Unc
1629	—	650	1,150	2,150	3,600	—

KM# 5 THALER
Silver **Note:** Seige Thaler. Dav. #4367.

Date	Mintage	VG	F	VF	XF	Unc
1629 HL Rare	—	—	—	—	—	—

KM# 6 THALER

Silver **Obv:** City of Torn in flames in inner circle **Rev:** Angel holding arms above six-line inscription **Note:** Seige Thaler. Dav. #4368.

Date	Mintage	VG	F	VF	XF	Unc
1629 HH//HL	—	950	1,650	2,750	4,350	—

KM# 7 THALER

Silver **Obv:** Small angel holding city arms above 7-line inscription **Rev:** City of Thorn in flames, ten ships in river in inner circle **Note:** Seige Thaler. Dav. #4369.

Date	Mintage	VG	F	VF	XF	Unc
1629	—	725	1,300	2,400	4,000	—

KM# 9 THALER

Silver **Obv:** Small angel holding oval city arms above 7-line inscription **Rev:** Two small angels above city of Thorn in flames in inner circle **Note:** Seige Thaler. Dav. #4370.

Date	Mintage	VG	F	VF	XF	Unc
1629	—	725	1,300	2,400	4,000	—

KM# 17 THALER

Silver **Subject:** Sigismund III **Note:** Dav. #4371.

Date	Mintage	VG	F	VF	XF	Unc
1630 HL/HH	—	110	215	400	650	—
1631 HH	—	110	215	400	650	—

KM# 18 THALER

Silver **Rev:** Amgel holding city arms divides date in inner circle **Note:** Dav. #4372.

Date	Mintage	VG	F	VF	XF	Unc
1630 II	—	110	215	450	850	—
1631 II	—	110	215	450	850	—
1632 II	—	110	215	425	775	—

KM# 20 THALER

Silver **Note:** Interregnum Issue. Dav. #4373.

Date	Mintage	VG	F	VF	XF	Unc
1632 II Rare	—	—	—	—	—	—

KM# 21 THALER

Silver **Subject:** Wladislaus IV **Note:** Dav. #4374.

Date	Mintage	VG	F	VF	XF	Unc
1633 II	—	195	325	625	1,250	—
1634 II	—	230	400	725	1,500	—
1635 II	—	195	325	575	1,150	—
1636 II	—	260	450	875	1,650	—
1637 II	—	130	260	450	775	—
1638 II	—	130	260	450	775	—

KM# 24 THALER

Silver **Subject:** Wladislaus IV **Note:** Dav. #4375.

Date	Mintage	VG	F	VF	XF	Unc
1638 II	—	130	295	500	650	—
1639 II	—	130	295	500	650	—
1640 MS	—	130	295	500	700	—
1641 MS	—	130	295	500	700	—
1642 MS	—	130	295	500	650	—

KM# 31 THALER

Silver **Obv:** Crowned bust of Wladislaus IV right in inner circle **Note:** Dav. #4376.

Date	Mintage	VG	F	VF	XF	Unc
1643 GR	—	260	450	875	1,650	—
1644 GR Rare	—	—	—	—	—	—
1645 GR Rare	—	—	—	—	—	—
1646 GR Rare	—	—	—	—	—	—
1647 GR Rare	—	—	—	—	—	—
1648 GR	—	260	450	875	1,650	—

KM# 32 THALER

Silver **Subject:** John Casimir **Note:** Dav. #4377.

Date	Mintage	VG	F	VF	XF	Unc
1649 GR	—	260	450	875	1,650	—
1649 HDL	—	195	325	625	1,150	—
1650 HDL	—	195	400	825	1,300	—
1659 HDL	—	195	325	625	1,250	—
1663 HDL Rare	—	—	—	—	—	—

KM# 23 2 THALER

Silver **Obv:** Crowned half-figure of Wladislaus IV right holding orb and sword in inner circle **Rev:** Angel holding oval city arms divides date in inner circle **Note:** Dav. #A4374.

Date	Mintage	VG	F	VF	XF	Unc
1637 II	—	1,550	2,600	4,550	7,800	—
1639 II	—	1,550	2,600	4,550	7,800	—

KM# 25 2 THALER

Silver **Note:** Dav. #B4374. Klippe.

Date	Mintage	VG	F	VF	XF	Unc
1639 II Rare	—	—	—	—	—	—

TRADE COINAGE

KM# 19 DUCAT (Dukat)

3.5000 g., 0.9860 Gold 0.1109 oz. AGW **Subject:** Sigismund

Date	Mintage	VG	F	VF	XF	Unc
1630 HL	—	1,050	2,200	4,150	6,800	—
1630 II	—	1,050	2,200	4,150	6,800	—

KM# 22.1 DUCAT (Dukat)

3.5000 g., 0.9860 Gold 0.1109 oz. AGW **Subject:** Wladislaus IV **Note:** Small bust.

Date	Mintage	VG	F	VF	XF	Unc
1633 II	—	900	1,800	3,400	5,600	—
1634 II	—	750	1,500	3,000	4,900	—
1635 II	—	750	1,500	3,000	4,900	—
1637 II	—	750	1,500	3,000	4,900	—
1638 II	—	750	1,500	3,000	4,900	—
1639 II	—	750	1,650	3,300	5,300	—

KM# 22.2 DUCAT (Dukat)

3.5000 g., 0.9860 Gold 0.1109 oz. AGW **Note:** Medium bust.

Date	Mintage	VG	F	VF	XF	Unc
1640 MS	—	650	1,300	2,600	4,250	—

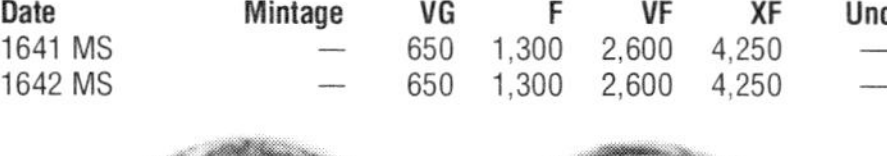

Date	Mintage	VG	F	VF	XF	Unc
1641 MS	—	650	1,300	2,600	4,250	—
1642 MS	—	650	1,300	2,600	4,250	—

KM# 22.3 DUCAT (Dukat)

3.5000 g., 0.9860 Gold 0.1109 oz. AGW **Note:** Large bust.

Date	Mintage	VG	F	VF	XF	Unc
1643 GR Rare	—	—	—	—	—	—
1645 GR	—	650	1,300	2,600	4,250	—
1646 GR Rare	—	—	—	—	—	—
1647 GR	—	775	1,550	2,950	4,900	—
1648 GR	—	650	1,300	2,600	4,250	—

KM# 33 DUCAT (Dukat)

3.5000 g., 0.9860 Gold 0.1109 oz. AGW **Subject:** Johann Casimir

Date	Mintage	VG	F	VF	XF	Unc
1649 GR	—	850	1,650	3,100	5,200	—
1649 HDL	—	775	1,550	2,950	4,900	—
1650 HDL	—	650	1,300	2,600	4,250	—
1651 HDL	—	650	1,300	2,600	4,250	—
1653 HIL, HDL	—	650	1,300	2,600	4,250	—
1654 HIL	—	650	1,450	2,800	4,550	—
1655 HIL	—	650	1,300	2,600	4,250	—
1655 HDL	—	650	1,300	2,600	4,250	—
1659 HDL	—	650	1,300	2,600	4,250	—
1660 HDL	—	650	1,300	2,600	4,250	—
1661 HDL	—	650	1,300	2,600	4,250	—
1666 HDL	—	775	1,550	2,950	4,900	—
1667 HDL	—	1,050	1,950	3,600	5,900	—
1668 HS Rare	—	—	—	—	—	—

KM# 45 2 DUCAT

7.0000 g., 0.9860 Gold 0.2219 oz. AGW **Subject:** Johann Casimir **Note:** Legend varieties exist.

Date	Mintage	VG	F	VF	XF	Unc
1660 HDL	—	1,300	2,600	5,200	9,100	—
1662 HDL	—	1,300	2,600	5,200	9,100	—
1663 HDL	—	1,300	2,600	5,200	9,100	—
1664 HDL	—	1,300	2,600	5,200	9,100	—
1665 HDL	—	1,300	2,600	5,200	9,100	—
1667 HDL	—	1,300	2,600	5,200	9,100	—
1668 HS	—	1,550	2,950	5,900	10,500	—

KM# 51 2 DUCAT

7.0000 g., 0.9860 Gold 0.2219 oz. AGW **Subject:** Michael Korybut

Date	Mintage	VG	F	VF	XF	Unc
1670 HS	—	2,250	4,150	7,900	12,500	—
1671 HS	—	2,250	4,150	7,900	12,500	—

KM# 52 2 DUCAT

7.0000 g., 0.9860 Gold 0.2219 oz. AGW **Obv:** Laureate bust of Michael Korybut right in inner circle **Rev:** City of Thorn

Date	Mintage	VG	F	VF	XF	Unc
ND(ca.1670) HDL	—	1,200	2,250	4,250	6,750	—

KM# 10 3 DUCAT

10.5000 g., 0.9860 Gold 0.3328 oz. AGW **Subject:** Siege of Thorn in 1629 **Obv:** Burning city of Thorn in inner circle **Rev:** Five-line inscription and Roman numeral date, arms above

Date	Mintage	VG	F	VF	XF	Unc
1629 HH	—	3,000	6,000	10,500	17,500	—
1630 HH	—	3,000	6,000	10,500	17,500	—
1631 HH	—	3,000	6,000	10,500	17,500	—

KM# 37 3 DUCAT

10.5000 g., 0.9860 Gold 0.3328 oz. AGW **Subject:** Johann Casimir

Date	Mintage	VG	F	VF	XF	Unc
1655	—	2,400	4,500	8,300	13,500	—

KM# 39 3 DUCAT

10.5000 g., 0.9860 Gold 0.3328 oz. AGW

Date	Mintage	VG	F	VF	XF	Unc
1659 H	—	1,900	3,750	7,500	12,000	—

KM# 53 3 DUCAT

10.5000 g., 0.9860 Gold 0.3328 oz. AGW **Obv:** Laureate bust of Michael Korybut right **Rev:** Arms of Thorn with angel above in inner circle, date in legend

Date	Mintage	VG	F	VF	XF	Unc
1671 HS Rare	—	—	—	—	—	—

KM# 40 4 DUCAT

14.0000 g., 0.9860 Gold 0.4438 oz. AGW

Date	Mintage	VG	F	VF	XF	Unc
1655 HL	—	4,150	6,800	12,000	21,000	—
1659 HL	—	4,150	6,800	12,000	21,000	—

KM# 41 5 DUCAT

17.5000 g., 0.9860 Gold 0.5547 oz. AGW

Date	Mintage	VG	F	VF	XF	Unc
1655 HL	—	6,000	9,000	15,000	24,000	—
1659 HL	—	6,000	9,000	15,000	24,000	—

KM# 44 6 DUCAT

21.0000 g., 0.9860 Gold 0.6657 oz. AGW, 38 mm.

Ruler: Johann Casimir **Obv:** Crowned bust right **Rev:** City, harbor view **Note:** Fr. #61.

Date	Mintage	Good	VG	F	VF	XF
1659	—	—	—	—	9,000	12,000

PATTERNS

Including off metal strikes

KM#	Date	Mintage	Identification	Mkt Val
Pn1	1629 HH/HL	—	Thaler. Gold. KM#6.	—
Pn2	1629	—	Thaler. Gold. KM#7.	—

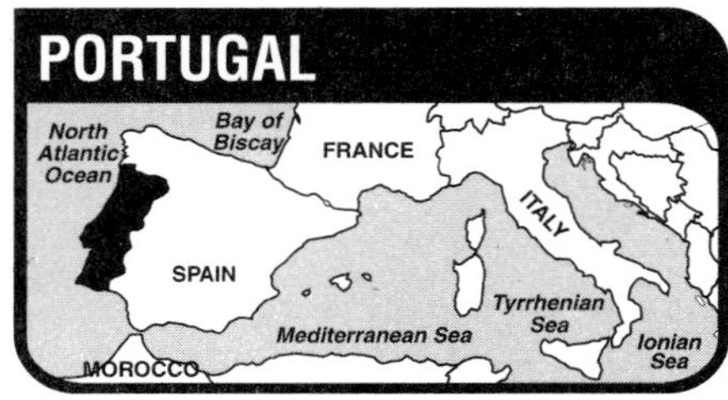

Portugal, located in the western part of the Iberian Peninsula in southwestern Europe, has an area of 35,553 sq. mi. (92,080 sq. km

After centuries of domination by Romans, Visigoths and Moors, Portugal emerged in the 12th century as an independent kingdom financially and philosophically prepared for the great period of exploration that would soon follow. Attuned to the inspiration of Prince Henry the Navigator (1394-1460), Portugal's daring explorers of the 15th and 16th centuries roamed the world's oceans from Brazil to Japan in an unprecedented burst of energy and endeavor that culminated in 1494 with Portugal laying claim to half the transoceanic world. Unfortunately for the fortunes of the tiny kingdom, the Portuguese population was too small to colonize this vast territory. Less than a century after Portugal laid claim to half the world, English, French and Dutch trading companies had seized the lion's share of the world's colonies and commerce, and Portugal's place as an imperial power was lost forever. The monarchy was overthrown in 1910 and a republic was established.

RULERS

Philip II (Philip III of Spain), 1598-1621
Philip III (Philip IV of Spain), 1621-1640
John IV, 1640-1656
Alfonso VI, 1656-1683
Peter, as Prince Regent, (for Alfonso VI), 1667-1683
Peter II, 1683-1706

NOTE: The coins of Philip II and Philip III are so similar that it is not possible to give an absolute attribution. Portuguese authorities rely on legend variants and many times these are lacking in certainty. The "Philippvs" name is attributed to both rulers but it is likely that "Philipvs" is only Philip III.

MINT MARKS

E - Evora
L - Lisbon
P - Porto
No Mint mark – Lisbon

MONETARY SYSTEM

Until 1825

20 Reis = 1 Vintem
100 Reis = 1 Tostao
480 Reis = 24 Vintens = 1 Cruzado
1600 Reis = 1 Escudo
6400 Reis = 4 Escudos = 1 Peca

NOTE: The primary denomination was the Peca, weighing14.34 g, tariffed at 6400 Reis until 1825, and at 7500 Reis after 1826. The weight was not changed.

KINGDOM

DUMP COINAGE

KM# 25 1-1/2 REIS
Copper **Obv:** Crowned arms **Obv. Legend:** IOANNES IIII... **Rev:** 1-1/2 within circle **Note:** Varieties exist.

Date	Mintage	VG	F	VF	XF	Unc
ND(1640-56)	—	25.00	42.00	70.00	145	—

KM# 95 1-1/2 REIS
Center Composition: Copper **Obv. Legend:** PETRVS... **Note:** Varieties exist.

Date	Mintage	VG	F	VF	XF	Unc
1670	—	—	—	—	—	—
1673	—	42.00	90.00	220	450	—
1674	—	42.00	90.00	220	450	—
1675	—	42.00	90.00	220	450	—
1676	—	18.00	38.50	65.00	130	—

Date	Mintage	VG	F	VF	XF	Unc
1677	—	18.00	38.50	65.00	130	—
1678	—	42.00	90.00	220	450	—

KM# 26 3 REIS
Copper **Obv:** Crowned arms **Obv. Legend:** IOANNES IIII... **Rev:** 3 within circle **Note:** Varieties exist.

Date	Mintage	VG	F	VF	XF	Unc
ND(1640-56)	—	27.50	55.00	90.00	190	—

KM# 96 3 REIS
Copper **Obv:** Crowned arms **Obv. Legend:** PETRVS... **Rev:** 3 within circle

Date	Mintage	VG	F	VF	XF	Unc
1675	—	36.00	70.00	180	350	—
1676	—	18.00	38.50	65.00	130	—
1677	—	18.00	36.00	60.00	120	—

KM# 27 5 REIS
Copper **Obv:** Crowned arms **Obv. Legend:** IOANNES IIII... **Rev:** V within circle **Note:** Varieties exist.

Date	Mintage	VG	F	VF	XF	Unc
ND(1640-56)	—	22.50	42.00	70.00	150	—

KM# 97 5 REIS
Copper **Obv:** Crowned arms **Obv. Legend:** PETRVS... **Rev:** V within circle

Date	Mintage	VG	F	VF	XF	Unc
1675	—	30.00	60.00	180	350	—
1676	—	20.00	55.00	90.00	170	—
1677	—	18.00	38.50	65.00	130	—

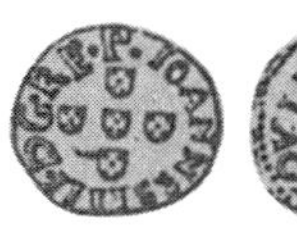

KM# 28 10 REIS (1/2 Vinten)
Silver **Obv:** 4 shields in cruciform **Obv. Legend:** IOANNES... **Rev:** Cross of Jerusalem with dots in angles **Note:** Varieties exist.

Date	Mintage	VG	F	VF	XF	Unc
ND(1640-56)	—	450	750	1,250	2,000	—

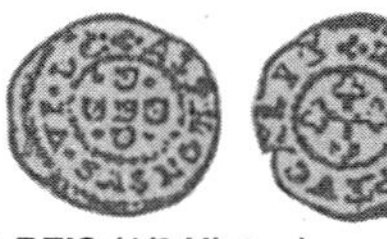

KM# 65 10 REIS (1/2 Vinten)
Silver **Obv:** 4 shields in cruciform **Obv. Legend:** ALPHONSVS... **Rev:** Without dots **Note:** Varieties exist.

Date	Mintage	VG	F	VF	XF	Unc
ND(1656-83)	—	275	450	700	1,200	—

KM# 66 10 REIS (1/2 Vinten)
Silver **Obv:** X and dots within inner circle **Obv. Legend:** ALPHONSVS... **Rev:** Without dots **Note:** Varieties exist.

Date	Mintage	VG	F	VF	XF	Unc
ND(1656-83)	—	225	400	650	1,000	—

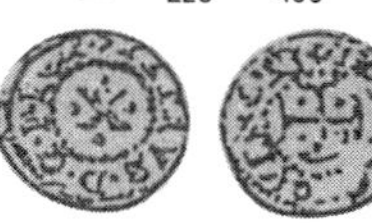

KM# 98 10 REIS (1/2 Vinten)
Silver **Obv:** X and dots within inner circle **Obv. Legend:** PETRVS... **Rev:** Cross of Jerusalem with dots in angles **Note:** Varieties exist.

Date	Mintage	VG	F	VF	XF	Unc
ND(1663)	—	300	500	800	1,500	—

KM# 99 10 REIS (1/2 Vinten)
Copper **Obv:** Crowned arms **Obv. Legend:** PETRVS... **Rev:** X and annulets within inner circle

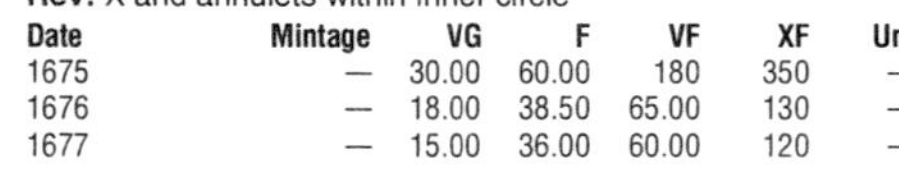

Date	Mintage	VG	F	VF	XF	Unc
1675	—	30.00	60.00	180	350	—
1676	—	18.00	38.50	65.00	130	—
1677	—	15.00	36.00	60.00	120	—

KM# 15 20 REIS (Vinten)
Silver **Obv:** Crowned arms **Obv. Legend:** PHILIPVS... **Rev:** F above XX **Note:** Struck at Lisbon.

Date	Mintage	VG	F	VF	XF	Unc
ND	—	40.00	85.00	165	275	—

KM# 29 20 REIS (Vinten)
Silver **Obv:** Crowned arms **Obv. Legend:** IOANNES... **Rev:** I above XX **Note:** Varieties exist.

Date	Mintage	VG	F	VF	XF	Unc
ND	—	25.00	50.00	90.00	165	—

KM# 30 20 REIS (Vinten)
Silver **Obv:** Crowned arms **Obv. Legend:** IOANNES... **Rev:** I above XPX **Note:** Varieties exist.

Date	Mintage	VG	F	VF	XF	Unc
ND	—	35.00	75.00	150	250	—

KM# 31 20 REIS (Vinten)
Silver **Obv:** Crowned arms **Obv. Legend:** IOANNES... **Rev:** I/XX/E **Note:** Varieties exist.

Date	Mintage	VG	F	VF	XF	Unc
ND	—	50.00	100	195	300	—

KM# 67 20 REIS (Vinten)
Silver **Obv:** A above XX **Obv. Legend:** ALPHONSVS... **Rev:** Crowned arms **Note:** Varieties exist.

Date	Mintage	VG	F	VF	XF	Unc
ND	—	40.00	90.00	180	300	—

KM# 32 20 REIS (Vinten)
Silver **Obv:** I above XX **Obv. Legend:** IOANNES... **Rev:** Crowned arms **Rev. Legend:** ALPHONSVS...

Date	Mintage	VG	F	VF	XF	Unc
ND	—	120	240	425	—	—

KM# 68 20 REIS (Vinten)
Silver **Obv:** XX within circle **Rev:** Cross of Jerusalem in inner circle **Note:** Varieties exist.

Date	Mintage	VG	F	VF	XF	Unc
ND	—	20.00	40.00	70.00	130	—

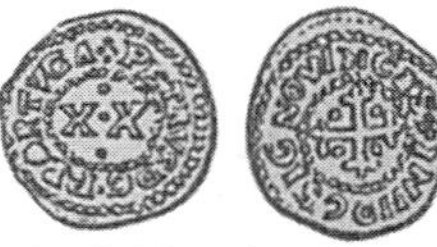

KM# 100 20 REIS (Vinten)
Silver **Obv:** XX within circle **Obv. Legend:** PETRVS... **Rev:** Dots in angles of cross **Note:** Varieties exist.

Date	Mintage	VG	F	VF	XF	Unc
ND	—	20.00	30.00	55.00	100	—

KM# 33 40 REIS (2 Vintens)
Silver **Obv:** Crown above JO IIII / XXXX **Rev:** Annulets, fleur de lis or dots in angles of St. George cross **Note:** Varieties exist.

Date	Mintage	VG	F	VF	XF	Unc
ND	—	20.00	40.00	70.00	165	—

KM# 34 40 REIS (2 Vintens)
Silver **Obv:** Crown above JO IIII / XXXX **Rev:** P in angles of cross **Note:** Varieties exist.

Date	Mintage	VG	F	VF	XF	Unc
NDP	—	30.00	60.00	110	275	—

KM# 35 40 REIS (2 Vintens)
Silver **Obv:** Crown above JO IIII / XXXX **Rev:** E in angles of cross **Note:** Varieties exist.

Date	Mintage	VG	F	VF	XF	Unc
ND	—	60.00	120	225	550	—

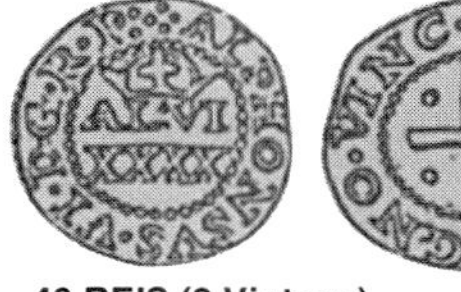

KM# 69 40 REIS (2 Vintens)
Silver **Obv:** Crown above AL. VI / XXXX **Rev:** Cross of St. George with dots in angles

Date	Mintage	VG	F	VF	XF	Unc
ND	—	1,000	1,650	2,500	—	—

KM# 70 40 REIS (2 Vintens)
Silver **Obv:** Crown above XXXX **Obv. Legend:** ALPHONSVS... **Rev:** Cross of Jerusalem with dots in angles **Note:** Varieties exist.

Date	Mintage	VG	F	VF	XF	Unc
ND	—	30.00	50.00	95.00	195	—

KM# 101 40 REIS (2 Vintens)
Silver **Obv:** Crown above XXXX **Obv. Legend:** PETRVS... **Rev:** Cross of Jerusalem with dots in angles **Note:** Varieties exist.

Date	Mintage	VG	F	VF	XF	Unc
ND	—	20.00	35.00	70.00	165	—

KM# 5 50 REIS (1/2 Tostao)
Silver **Obv:** 4 shields in cruciform within beaded circle **Obv. Legend:** PHILIPPVS... **Rev:** Cross of St. George within beaded circle

Date	Mintage	VG	F	VF	XF	Unc
ND	—	20.00	40.00	70.00	165	—

KM# 16 50 REIS (1/2 Tostao)
Silver **Obv:** 4 shields in cruciform within beaded circle **Obv. Legend:** PHILIPVS... **Rev:** Cross with or without dots in angles **Note:** Varieties exist.

Date	Mintage	VG	F	VF	XF	Unc
ND	—	20.00	40.00	70.00	165	—

KM# 36 50 REIS (1/2 Tostao)
Silver **Obv:** Design in angles of cruciform **Obv. Legend:** JOANNES IIII... **Rev:** Cross with date in bottom angles, annulets in top angles **Note:** Varieties exist.

Date	Mintage	VG	F	VF	XF	Unc
1641	—	35.00	75.00	140	325	—

KM# 37 50 REIS (1/2 Tostao)
Silver **Obv:** Design in angles of cruciform **Obv. Legend:** JOANNES IIII... **Rev:** Cross with date in angles

Date	Mintage	VG	F	VF	XF	Unc
1641	—	20.00	35.00	70.00	175	—
1642	—	20.00	35.00	70.00	175	—

KM# 38 50 REIS (1/2 Tostao)
Silver **Obv:** Design in angles of cruciform **Obv. Legend:** JOANNES IIII... **Rev:** Cross with P in angles **Note:** Varieties exist. Struck at Porto.

Date	Mintage	VG	F	VF	XF	Unc
ND	—	25.00	45.00	85.00	205	—

KM# 39 50 REIS (1/2 Tostao)
Silver **Obv:** Design in angles of cruciform **Obv. Legend:** JOANNES IIII... **Rev:** Cross with E in angles **Note:** Varieties exist.

Date	Mintage	VG	F	VF	XF	Unc
ND	—	25.00	40.00	75.00	250	—

KM# 71 50 REIS (1/2 Tostao)
Silver **Obv:** Design in angles of cruciform **Obv. Legend:** ALPHONSVS... **Rev:** Dots in angles of cross

Date	Mintage	VG	F	VF	XF	Unc
ND	—	180	325	550	—	—

KM# 72 50 REIS (1/2 Tostao)
Silver **Obv:** Crowned arms in baroque frame **Obv. Legend:** ALPHONSVS... **Rev:** Cross of Jerusalem **Note:** Varieties exist.

Date	Mintage	VG	F	VF	XF	Unc
ND	—	15.00	32.00	60.00	140	—

KM# 102 50 REIS (1/2 Tostao)
Silver **Obv:** Crowned arms in baroque frame **Obv. Legend:** PETRVS... **Rev:** Cross of Jerusalem with dots in angles

Date	Mintage	VG	F	VF	XF	Unc
ND	—	20.00	40.00	70.00	165	—

KM# 40 80 REIS (4 Vintens)
Silver **Obv:** Crown above JO IIII / LXXX **Rev:** Annulets, fleur de lis or dots in angles of St. George cross **Note:** Varieties exist.

Date	Mintage	VG	F	VF	XF	Unc
ND	—	25.00	45.00	90.00	165	—

KM# 41 80 REIS (4 Vintens)
Silver **Obv:** Crown above JO IIII / LXXX **Rev:** P in angles of cross **Note:** Varieties exist.

Date	Mintage	VG	F	VF	XF	Unc
ND	—	75.00	160	285	550	—

KM# 42 80 REIS (4 Vintens)
Silver **Obv:** Crown above JO IIII / LXXX **Rev:** E in angles of cross **Note:** Varieties exist.

Date	Mintage	VG	F	VF	XF	Unc
ND	—	100	200	350	650	—

KM# 73 80 REIS (4 Vintens)
Silver **Obv:** Crown above AL. VI / LXXX **Rev:** Annulets in angles of cross **Note:** Varieties exist.

Date	Mintage	VG	F	VF	XF	Unc
ND	—	1,000	2,000	3,000	—	—

KM# 74 80 REIS (4 Vintens)
Silver **Obv:** Crown above LXXX **Rev:** Cross of Jerusalem with or without dots in angles **Note:** Varieties exist.

Date	Mintage	VG	F	VF	XF	Unc
ND	—	35.00	60.00	110	205	—

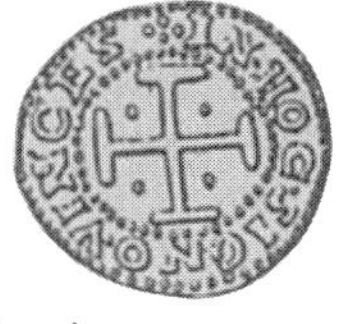

KM# 103 80 REIS (4 Vintens)
Silver **Obv:** Crown above LXXX **Obv. Legend:** PETRVS... **Rev:** Cross of Jerusalem with or without dots in angles

Date	Mintage	VG	F	VF	XF	Unc
ND	—	30.00	50.00	95.00	180	—

KM# 6 100 REIS (Tostao)
Silver **Obv:** Crowned arms with mintmark at left and right **Obv. Legend:** PHILIPPVS... **Rev:** Cross of Jerusalem in inner circle with or without dots **Note:** Varieties exist.

Date	Mintage	VG	F	VF	XF	Unc
ND L	—	300	650	1,200	2,000	—
ND LB	—	200	400	750	1,250	—

KM# 17 100 REIS (Tostao)
Silver **Obv:** Crowned arms with mintmark at left and right **Obv. Legend:** PHILIPPVS... **Rev:** Cross of Jerusalem in inner circle with five dots in each angle **Note:** Varieties exist.

Date	Mintage	VG	F	VF	XF	Unc
ND LB	—	125	275	500	850	—

KM# 43 100 REIS (Tostao)
Silver **Obv:** Crowned arms with or without fleur de lis or dots **Obv. Legend:** JOANNES IIII... **Rev:** Cross of St. George with or without dots in angles

Date	Mintage	VG	F	VF	XF	Unc
ND(1640)INCM LC	—	250	500	850	1,500	—
ND(1640)INCM LS	—	650	1,200	2,000	3,500	—

KM# 44 100 REIS (Tostao)
Silver **Obv:** Crowned arms with or without annulets **Obv. Legend:** JOANNES IIII... **Rev:** P in angles of cross **Note:** Varieties exist.

Date	Mintage	VG	F	VF	XF	Unc
ND(1640)	—	45.00	90.00	160	300	—

KM# 45 100 REIS (Tostao)
Silver **Obv:** Crowned arms with or without annulets **Obv. Legend:** JOANNES IIII... **Rev:** E in angles of cross **Note:** Varieties exist.

Date	Mintage	VG	F	VF	XF	Unc
ND(1640)	—	100	200	350	650	—

KM# 46 100 REIS (Tostao)
Silver **Obv:** Crowned arms with or without annulets **Obv. Legend:** JOANNES IIII... **Rev:** Cross of Jerusalem with or without dots in angles **Note:** Varieties exist.

Date	Mintage	VG	F	VF	XF	Unc
1641	—	350	750	1,200	2,000	—

KM# 47 100 REIS (Tostao)
Silver **Obv:** Crowned arms with mint mark at left and right **Obv. Legend:** JOANNES IIII... **Rev:** Cross of Jerusalem with date in bottom of angles **Note:** Varieties exist.

Date	Mintage	VG	F	VF	XF	Unc
1641 LC	—	450	900	1,500	2,500	—
1641	—	30.00	50.00	100	200	—
1642	—	35.00	60.00	120	275	—

KM# 48 100 REIS (Tostao)
Silver **Obv:** Crowned arms with or without fleur de lis or dots **Obv. Legend:** JOANNES IIII... **Rev:** Cross of St. George with or without dots **Note:** Varieties exist.

Date	Mintage	VG	F	VF	XF	Unc
ND	—	30.00	60.00	120	275	—

KM# 75 100 REIS (Tostao)
Silver **Obv:** Crowned arms **Obv. Legend:** ALPHONSVS... **Rev:** Cross with dots in angles **Note:** Varieties exist.

Date	Mintage	VG	F	VF	XF	Unc
ND	—	300	550	950	—	—

KM# 76 100 REIS (Tostao)
Silver **Obv:** Crowned arms in baroque frame **Obv. Legend:** ALPHONSVS... **Rev:** Cross of Jerusalem in inner circle **Note:** Varieties exist.

Date	Mintage	VG	F	VF	XF	Unc
ND	—	20.00	40.00	75.00	150	—

KM# 104 100 REIS (Tostao)
Silver **Obv:** Crowned arms in baroque frame **Obv. Legend:** PETRVS... **Rev:** Cross of Jerusalem in inner circle

Date	Mintage	VG	F	VF	XF	Unc
ND	—	750	1,250	2,000	—	—

KM# 49 200 REIS (1/2 Cruzado)
Silver **Obv:** Crowned arms, value at right **Obv. Legend:** IOANNES... **Rev:** Cross of Jerusalem with dots in angles **Note:** Varieties exist.

Date	Mintage	VG	F	VF	XF	Unc
ND	—	40.00	85.00	150	285	—

KM# 50 200 REIS (1/2 Cruzado)
Silver **Obv:** Crowned arms, value at right **Obv. Legend:** IOANNES... **Rev:** Cross with P in angles **Note:** Varieties exist.

Date	Mintage	VG	F	VF	XF	Unc
ND	—	75.00	165	325	550	—

KM# 51 200 REIS (1/2 Cruzado)
Silver **Obv:** Crowned arms, value at right **Obv. Legend:** IOANNES... **Rev:** Cross with E in angles **Note:** Varieties exist.

Date	Mintage	VG	F	VF	XF	Unc
ND	—	125	250	450	750	—

KM# 77 200 REIS (1/2 Cruzado)
Silver **Obv:** Crowned arms, value at right **Obv. Legend:** ALPHONSVS... **Rev:** Dots in angles of cross **Note:** Varieties exist.

Date	Mintage	VG	F	VF	XF	Unc
ND	—	150	275	500	—	—

KM# 82 200 REIS (1/2 Cruzado)
Silver **Obv:** Crowned arms, value at right **Obv. Legend:** ALPHONSVS... **Rev:** Date in angles of cross

Date	Mintage	VG	F	VF	XF	Unc
1663	—	20.00	40.00	90.00	200	—
1664	—	22.00	45.00	100	225	—
1665	—	25.00	55.00	125	250	—
1666	—	30.00	65.00	150	325	—

KM# 105 200 REIS (1/2 Cruzado)
Silver **Obv:** Crowned arms, value at right **Obv. Legend:** PETRVS... **Rev:** Date in angles of cross

Date	Mintage	VG	F	VF	XF	Unc
1676	—	—	—	—	—	—

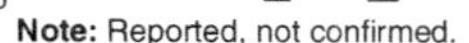

Note: Reported, not confirmed.

KM# 52 400 REIS (Cruzado)
Silver **Obv:** Crowned arms, value at right **Obv. Legend:** JOANNES... **Rev:** Cross of Jerusalem with dots in angles **Note:** Dav. #4380. Varieties exist.

Date	Mintage	VG	F	VF	XF	Unc
ND	—	75.00	150	285	530	—

KM# 53 400 REIS (Cruzado)
Silver **Obv:** Crowned arms, value at right **Obv. Legend:** JOANNES... **Rev:** Cross with P in angles **Note:** Dav. #4381. Varieties exist.

Date	Mintage	VG	F	VF	XF	Unc
ND	—	125	250	450	850	—

KM# 54 400 REIS (Cruzado)
Silver **Obv:** Crowned arms, value at right **Obv. Legend:** JOANNES... **Rev:** Cross with E in angles **Note:** Dav. #4382. Varieties exist.

Date	Mintage	VG	F	VF	XF	Unc
ND	—	400	900	2,250	4,500	—

KM# 78 400 REIS (Cruzado)
Silver **Obv:** Crowned arms, value at right **Obv. Legend:** ALPHONSVS... **Rev:** Dots in angles of cross **Note:** Dav. #4383

Date	Mintage	VG	F	VF	XF	Unc
ND	—	2,500	4,500	7,000	—	—

KM# 83 400 REIS (Cruzado)
Silver **Obv:** Crowned arms, value at right **Obv. Legend:** ALPHONSVS... **Rev:** Date in angles of cross **Note:** Dav. #4384

Date	Mintage	VG	F	VF	XF	Unc
1663	—	80.00	200	550	1,000	—
1664	—	100	250	650	1,200	—
1665	—	100	250	650	1,200	—
1666	—	80.00	200	550	1,000	—

KM# 84 1000 REIS

3.0600 g., 0.9170 Gold 0.0902 oz. AGW **Obv:** Crowned arms with date and value at sides, titles of Alphonso VI **Rev:** Jerusalem cross with annulets in angles in inner circle

Date	Mintage	VG	F	VF	XF	Unc
1663 Rare	—	—	—	—	—	—
1666 Rare	—	—	—	—	—	—

KM# 87 1100 REIS (1/4 Moeda)

3.0600 g., 0.9170 Gold 0.0902 oz. AGW **Obv:** Crowned arms with date and value at sides, titles of Peter as Prince Regent **Rev:** Jerusalem cross in quatrefoil in inner circle

Date	Mintage	VG	F	VF	XF	Unc
1668 Rare	—	—	—	—	—	—
Note: Sotheby's Geneva Sale 11-86 Fine realized $23,750						
1671 Rare	—	—	—	—	—	—

KM# 85 2000 REIS (1/2 Moeda)

6.1200 g., 0.9170 Gold 0.1804 oz. AGW **Obv:** Crowned arms with date and value at sides, titles of Alphonso VI **Rev:** Jerusalem cross with annulets in angles

Date	Mintage	VG	F	VF	XF	Unc
1663 Rare	—	—	—	—	—	—
1666 Rare	—	—	—	—	—	—

KM# 88 2200 REIS

6.1200 g., 0.9170 Gold 0.1804 oz. AGW **Obv:** Crowned arms with date and value at sides, titles of Peter as Prince Regent **Rev:** Jerusalem cross in quatrefoil in inner circle

Date	Mintage	VG	F	VF	XF	Unc
1668 Rare	—	—	—	—	—	—
1669 Rare	—	—	—	—	—	—
Note: Sotheby's Geneva Sale 11-86 Fine realized $22,450						
1671 Rare	—	—	—	—	—	—
1674 Rare	—	—	—	—	—	—

KM# 86 4000 REIS

12.2400 g., 0.9170 Gold 0.3608 oz. AGW **Obv:** Crowned arms with date and value at sides, titles of Alphonso VI **Rev:** Jerusalem cross with annulets in angles in inner circle

Date	Mintage	VG	F	VF	XF	Unc
1663 Rare	—	—	—	—	—	—
1664 Rare	—	—	—	—	—	—
1665 Rare	—	—	—	—	—	—
1666 Rare	—	—	—	—	—	—

KM# 89 4400 REIS (Moeda)

12.2400 g., 0.9170 Gold 0.3608 oz. AGW **Obv:** Crowned arms with date and value at sides, titles of Peter as Prince Regent **Rev:** Jerusalem cross in quatrefoil in inner circle

Date	Mintage	VG	F	VF	XF	Unc
1668 Rare	—	—	—	—	—	—
1669 Rare	—	—	—	—	—	—
Note: Sotheby's Geneva Sale 11-86 Fine realized $22,450						
1670 Rare	—	—	—	—	—	—
1671 Rare	—	—	—	—	—	—
1672 Rare	—	—	—	—	—	—
1673 Rare	—	—	—	—	—	—
1674 Rare	—	—	—	—	—	—

KM# 7 CRUZADO

3.0600 g., 0.9220 Gold 0.0907 oz. AGW **Obv:** Crowned arms with mint mark at left and value at right **Rev:** Cross of St. George in inner circle, single dots in angles

Date	Mintage	VG	F	VF	XF	Unc
ND LB Rare	—	—	—	—	—	—

KM# 55 CRUZADO

3.0600 g., 0.9170 Gold 0.0902 oz. AGW **Obv:** Crowned arms with large crown, titles of John IV **Rev:** Cross of St. George with date in angles, center turned 90 degrees

Date	Mintage	VG	F	VF	XF	Unc
1642 Rare	—	—	—	—	—	—

KM# 58 CRUZADO

3.0600 g., 0.9170 Gold 0.0902 oz. AGW **Obv:** Small crown on arms **Rev:** Cross of St. George with date in angles, center turned 90 degrees

Date	Mintage	VG	F	VF	XF	Unc
1642 Rare	—	—	—	—	—	—
1647 Rare	—	—	—	—	—	—

KM# 8 2 CRUZADOS

6.1200 g., 0.9220 Gold 0.1814 oz. AGW **Obv:** Crowned arms with mint mark at left and value at right **Rev:** Cross of St. George in inner circle, 5 dots in each angle

Date	Mintage	VG	F	VF	XF	Unc
ND L Rare	—	—	—	—	—	—
ND LB Rare	—	—	—	—	—	—

KM# 56 2 CRUZADOS

6.1200 g., 0.9170 Gold 0.1804 oz. AGW **Obv:** Crowned arms, titles of John VI **Rev:** Cross of St. George with date in angles, center turned 90 degrees **Note:** Varieties exist with large and small crowns.

Date	Mintage	VG	F	VF	XF	Unc
1642 Rare	—	—	—	—	—	—

KM# 59 2 CRUZADOS

Obv: Small crown on arms

Date	Mintage	VG	F	VF	XF	Unc
1642 Rare	—	—	—	—	—	—
1646 Rare	—	—	—	—	—	—
1647 Rare	—	—	—	—	—	—

KM# 80 2 CRUZADOS

6.1200 g., 0.9170 Gold 0.1804 oz. AGW **Obv:** Titles of Alphonso VI **Rev:** Cross of St. George with date in angles, center turned 90 degrees

Date	Mintage	VG	F	VF	XF	Unc
1660 Rare	—	—	—	—	—	—

KM# 9.2 4 CRUZADOS

12.2400 g., 0.9220 Gold 0.3628 oz. AGW **Ruler:** Philip II **Obv:** Crowned arms with mint mark at left and value at right. **Obv. Legend:** ...PORTVGALIA ET **Rev:** Cross of St. George in inner circle, 5 dots in each angle

Date	Mintage	VG	F	VF	XF	Unc
ND(1598-1620) LB Rare	—	—	—	—	—	—

KM# 18 4 CRUZADOS

12.2400 g., 0.9220 Gold 0.3628 oz. AGW **Ruler:** Philip III **Obv:** Crowned arms. **Obv. Legend:** PHILIPVS.. **Rev:** Cross of St. George in inner circle, 5 dots in each angle **Note:** Varieties exist.

Date	Mintage	VG	F	VF	XF	Unc
ND L Rare	—	—	—	—	—	—
ND LB Rare	—	—	—	—	—	—

KM# 60 4 CRUZADOS

12.2400 g., 0.9170 Gold 0.3608 oz. AGW **Ruler:** John IV **Obv:** Crowned arms, titles of John IV **Rev:** Cross of St. George with date in angles in inner circle **Note:** Varieties exist.

Date	Mintage	VG	F	VF	XF	Unc
1642 Rare	—	—	—	—	—	—
1645 Rare	—	—	—	—	—	—
1646 Rare	—	—	—	—	—	—
1647 Rare	—	—	—	—	—	—
1648 Rare	—	—	—	—	—	—
1652 Rare	—	—	—	—	—	—

KM# 57 4 CRUZADOS

12.2400 g., 0.9170 Gold 0.3608 oz. AGW **Ruler:** John IV **Obv:** Crowned arms flanked by quatrefoils, titles of John IV **Rev:** Cross of St. George with date in angles, center turned 90 degrees

Date	Mintage	VG	F	VF	XF	Unc
1642 Rare	—	—	—	—	—	—

KM# 9.1 4 CRUZADOS

12.2400 g., 0.9220 Gold 0.3628 oz. AGW **Ruler:** Philip II **Obv:** Crowned arms with mint mark at left and value at right **Obv. Legend:** PHILIPPVS... **Rev:** Cross of St. George in inner circle, 5 dots in each angle

Date	Mintage	VG	F	VF	XF	Unc
ND LB Rare	—	—	—	—	—	—
ND L Rare	—	—	—	—	—	—

KM# 81 4 CRUZADOS

12.2400 g., 0.9170 Gold 0.3608 oz. AGW **Ruler:** Alfonso VI **Obv:** Crowned arms with date and value at sides, titles of Alfonso VI **Rev:** Jerusalem cross with date in angles in inner circle **Note:** Varieties exist.

Date	Mintage	VG	F	VF	XF	Unc
1660 Rare	—	—	—	—	—	—
1663 Rare	—	—	—	—	—	—

KM# A82 4 CRUZADOS
12.2400 g., 0.9170 Gold 0.3608 oz. AGW **Ruler:** Alfonso VI **Obv:** 4000 Reis KM#86 **Rev:** 4 Cruzados KM#81 **Note:** Mule.

Date	Mintage	VG	F	VF	XF	Unc
1663 Rare	—	—	—	—	—	—

MILLED COINAGE

KM# 128 1-1/2 REIS
Copper **Obv:** Crowned shield in baroque frame **Obv. Legend:** PETRVS... **Rev:** 1-1/2 in cartouche, date above

Date	Mintage	VG	F	VF	XF	Unc
1683	—	200	400	750	1,250	—

KM# 165 1-1/2 REIS
Copper **Ruler:** Peter II **Obv:** Crown above P:II within wreath **Obv. Legend:** D • G • PORT • ET • ALG • REX **Rev:** Value within wreath, date above **Rev. Legend:** VTILITATI • PVBLICÆ **Note:** Varieties exist with center turned 180 degrees.

Date	Mintage	VG	F	VF	XF	Unc
1699	—	10.00	20.00	45.00	90.00	—

KM# 132 20 REIS (Vinten)
Silver **Obv:** Globe **Rev:** Cross of Jerusalem with quatrefoils in angles

Date	Mintage	VG	F	VF	XF	Unc
ND(1686)INCM	—	40.00	80.00	150	250	—

KM# 129 3 REIS (III)
Copper **Obv:** Crowned arms on baroque frame

Date	Mintage	VG	F	VF	XF	Unc
1683	—	60.00	120	250	450	—

KM# 166 3 REIS (III)
Copper **Ruler:** Peter II **Obv:** Crown above PII within wreath **Rev:** Value within wreath **Note:** Varieties exist.

Date	Mintage	VG	F	VF	XF	Unc
1699	—	10.00	25.00	50.00	100	—

KM# 130 5 REIS (V)
Copper **Obv:** Crowned shield in baroque frame

Date	Mintage	VG	F	VF	XF	Unc
1683	—	70.00	150	300	550	—

KM# 167 5 REIS (V)
Copper **Ruler:** Peter II **Obv:** Crown above P II within wreath **Obv. Legend:** D • G • PORT • ET • ALG • REX **Rev:** Value within wreath, date above **Rev. Legend:** PVBLICÆ ....

Date	Mintage	VG	F	VF	XF	Unc
1699	—	10.00	25.00	50.00	100	—

KM# 131 10 REIS (X; 1/2 Vinten)
Copper **Obv:** Crowned shield in baroque frame

Date	Mintage	VG	F	VF	XF	Unc
1683	—	100	200	400	700	—

KM# 168 10 REIS (X; 1/2 Vinten)
Copper **Ruler:** Peter II **Obv:** Crowned PII within broken rope wreath **Obv. Legend:** D • G • PORT ET • ALG • REX **Rev:** Value (X) within wreath, date above **Rev. Legend:** VTILITATI .... **Note:** Varieties exist.

Date	Mintage	VG	F	VF	XF	Unc
1699	—	10.00	25.00	55.00	110	—

KM# 133 20 REIS (Vinten)
Silver **Obv:** Globe **Rev:** Cross with P in angles **Note:** Varieties exist.

Date	Mintage	VG	F	VF	XF	Unc
ND(1688)P	—	12.00	20.00	35.00	75.00	—

KM# 118 40 REIS (Pataco)
Silver **Obv:** Crown above XXXX **Obv. Legend:** PETRVS... **Rev:** Cross with rosettes in angles **Note:** Varieties exist.

Date	Mintage	VG	F	VF	XF	Unc
ND	—	12.50	25.00	65.00	135	—
(1)679	—	250	450	900	1,600	—

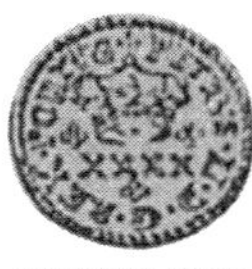

KM# 134 40 REIS (Pataco)
Silver **Obv:** Crown above XXXX **Obv. Legend:** PETRVS II... **Rev:** Cross with rosettes in angles **Note:** Varieties exist.

Date	Mintage	VG	F	VF	XF	Unc
ND	—	7.50	15.00	30.00	65.00	—

KM# 110 50 REIS (1/2 Tostao)
Silver **Obv:** Crowned arms **Obv. Legend:** PETRVS... **Rev:** Cross of Jerusalem with dots in angles **Note:** Varieties exist.

Date	Mintage	VG	F	VF	XF	Unc
ND(1667-83)	—	25.00	50.00	110	225	—

KM# 135 50 REIS (1/2 Tostao)
Silver **Obv:** Crowned arms **Obv. Legend:** PETRVS II... **Rev:** Cross of Jerusalem with dots in angles **Note:** Varieties exist.

Date	Mintage	VG	F	VF	XF	Unc
ND(1683-1706)	—	20.00	40.00	85.00	175	—

KM# 136 50 REIS (1/2 Tostao)
Silver **Obv:** Value: XXXX, crown above **Obv. Legend:** PETRVS II... **Rev:** Cross of St. George with quatrefoils in angles **Note:** Varieties exist.

Date	Mintage	VG	F	VF	XF	Unc
ND(1683-1706)	—	10.00	20.00	45.00	90.00	—

KM# 137 50 REIS (1/2 Tostao)
Silver **Obv:** Value: XXXX, crown above **Obv. Legend:** PETRVS II... **Rev:** Cross with P in angles **Note:** Varieties exist.

Date	Mintage	VG	F	VF	XF	Unc
ND(1683-1706)P	—	10.00	20.00	45.00	90.00	—

KM# 138 60 REIS (3 Vintens)
Silver **Obv:** Crowned arms **Obv. Legend:** PETRVS II... **Rev:** Cross of Jerusalem with quatrefoils or rosettes in angles **Note:** Varieties exist.

Date	Mintage	VG	F	VF	XF	Unc
ND	—	10.00	25.00	50.00	100	—

KM# 139 60 REIS (3 Vintens)
Silver **Obv:** Crowned arms **Obv. Legend:** PETRVS II... **Rev:** Cross with P in angles **Note:** Varieties exist.

Date	Mintage	VG	F	VF	XF	Unc
ND	—	10.00	25.00	50.00	100	—

KM# 111 80 REIS
Silver **Obv:** Crown with LXXX below **Obv. Legend:** PETRVS... **Rev:** Cross of St. George with rosettes in angles **Note:** Varieties exist.

Date	Mintage	VG	F	VF	XF	Unc
ND(1667-83)	—	20.00	40.00	85.00	175	—

KM# 140 80 REIS
Silver **Obv:** Crown with LXXX below **Obv. Legend:** PETRVS II... **Rev:** Cross of St. George with rosettes in angles **Note:** Varieties exist.

Date	Mintage	VG	F	VF	XF	Unc
ND(1676-1706)	—	20.00	40.00	85.00	175	—

KM# 112 80 REIS (LXXX; Tostao)

Silver **Obv:** Crowned arms **Obv. Legend:** PETRVS... **Rev:** Cross of Jerusalem with quatrefoils in angles **Note:** Worth 100 Reis, though marked LXXX = 80 Reis. Varieties exist.

Date	Mintage	VG	F	VF	XF	Unc
ND(1663-83)	—	25.00	50.00	100	200	—
1681	—	300	550	1,000	1,850	—

KM# 141 80 REIS (LXXX; Tostao)

Silver **Obv:** Crowned arms **Obv. Legend:** PETRVS II. D G. REX. PORTVOA **Rev:** Rosettes in angles of cross

Date	Mintage	VG	F	VF	XF	Unc
ND(1683-1706)	—	20.00	40.00	85.00	175	—

KM# 142 80 REIS (LXXX; Tostao)

Silver **Obv:** Crowned above LXXX **Obv. Legend:** PETRVS II. D G. PORT. ET. AL. REX **Rev:** Cross of St. George with rosettes in angles of cross **Note:** Varieties exist.

Date	Mintage	VG	F	VF	XF	Unc
ND(1683-1706)	—	12.00	25.00	55.00	110	—

KM# 157 80 REIS (LXXX; Tostao)

Silver **Ruler:** Peter II **Obv:** Crown above LXXX, date below **Obv. Legend:** • PETRVS • II • D • G • REX • PORTVG • **Rev:** Cross with P in angles **Rev. Legend:** IN HOC SIGNO VINCES **Note:** Varieties exist.

Date	Mintage	VG	F	VF	XF	Unc
1689	—	7.00	15.00	32.00	75.00	—
1690	—	7.00	15.00	32.00	75.00	—
1691	—	7.00	15.00	32.00	75.00	—
1692	—	12.00	25.00	50.00	100	—
1693	—	15.00	30.00	60.00	120	—
1696	—	20.00	40.00	85.00	200	—
1697	—	20.00	40.00	85.00	200	—
1699	—	60.00	120	250	450	—
1700	—	7.00	15.00	32.00	75.00	—

KM# 143 120 REIS (6 Vintens)

Silver **Obv:** Crowned arms **Obv. Legend:** PETRVS II... **Rev:** Jerusalem cross with rosettes in angles

Date	Mintage	VG	F	VF	XF	Unc
ND(1673-1706)	—	20.00	40.00	85.00	175	—

KM# 158 120 REIS (6 Vintens)

Silver **Obv:** Crowned arms **Obv. Legend:** PETRVS II... **Rev:** P in angles of cross

Date	Mintage	VG	F	VF	XF	Unc
1689	—	17.50	30.00	50.00	95.00	—
1690	—	17.50	30.00	50.00	95.00	—
1691	—	20.00	35.00	55.00	110	—
1693	—	25.00	40.00	65.00	125	—
1698	—	30.00	50.00	100	225	—

KM# 113 200 REIS (1/2 Cruzado)

Silver **Obv:** Crowned arms, value at left, date at right **Obv. Legend:** PETRVS... **Rev:** Cross of Jerusalem with rosettes in angles **Note:** Varieties exist.

Date	Mintage	VG	F	VF	XF	Unc
1677	—	550	1,150	2,250	4,250	—
1679	—	450	1,000	2,000	4,000	—
1681	—	125	250	500	950	—
1682	—	300	650	1,250	2,500	—

KM# 144 200 REIS (1/2 Cruzado)

Silver **Obv:** Crowned arms, value at left, date at right **Obv. Legend:** PETRVS II... **Rev:** Cross of Jerusalem with rosettes in angles **Note:** Varieties exist.

Date	Mintage	VG	F	VF	XF	Unc
1683	—	300	625	1,250	2,250	—
1684	—	275	575	1,150	2,150	—

KM# 148 200 REIS (12 Vintens, 200 = 240 Reis)

Silver **Obv:** Crowned arms, value at left, date at right **Obv. Legend:** PETRVS II... **Rev:** Cross of Jerusalem with rosettes in angles **Note:** Varieties exist.

Date	Mintage	VG	F	VF	XF	Unc
1686	—	25.00	60.00	125	285	—
1687	—	15.00	35.00	75.00	200	—
1688	—	15.00	35.00	75.00	200	—
1689	—	15.00	35.00	75.00	200	—
1690	—	40.00	85.00	175	350	—
1691	—	40.00	85.00	175	350	—
1692	—	150	300	550	1,150	—
1693	—	300	650	1,350	2,500	—
1696	—	70.00	150	300	550	—
1697	—	85.00	175	350	600	—

KM# 153 200 REIS (12 Vintens, 200 = 240 Reis)

Silver **Obv:** Crowned arms, value at left, date at right **Obv. Legend:** PETRVS II... **Rev:** Cross of Jerusalem, P in angles **Note:** Varieties exist.

Date	Mintage	VG	F	VF	XF	Unc
1688	—	50.00	100	225	450	—
1689	—	18.00	35.00	75.00	150	—
1690	—	20.00	45.00	90.00	185	—
1699 Rare	—	—	—	—	—	—

KM# 114.1 400 REIS (Cruzado)

Silver **Obv:** Crowned arms, value at left, date at right **Obv. Legend:** PETRVS... **Rev:** Cross of St. George with rosettes in angles **Note:** Dav. #4386

Date	Mintage	VG	F	VF	XF	Unc
1677 Rare	—	—	—	—	—	—
1679 Rare	—	—	—	—	—	—
1681	—	1,650	3,000	5,000	9,000	—

KM# 114.2 400 REIS (Cruzado)

Silver **Obv:** Dots or rosettes before and after date and value **Obv. Legend:** PETRVS... **Rev:** Cross of St. George with rosettes in angles **Note:** Varieties exist.

Date	Mintage	VG	F	VF	XF	Unc
1681	—	450	950	1,850	3,250	—
1682	—	450	950	1,850	3,250	—
1683	—	450	950	1,850	3,250	—

KM# 145.1 400 REIS (Cruzado)

Silver **Obv:** Prince's crown above arms **Obv. Legend:** PETRVS II... **Rev:** Cross of St. George with rosettes in angles **Note:** Dav. #4388

Date	Mintage	VG	F	VF	XF	Unc
1683	—	400	800	1,750	3,500	—
1684	—	300	650	1,600	3,350	—
1686	—	1,000	2,000	3,500	5,500	—

KM# 145.2 400 REIS (Cruzado)

Silver **Obv:** Arms with King's crown above **Obv. Legend:** PETRVS II... **Rev:** Cross of St. George with rosettes in angles **Note:** Dav. #4389. Varieties exist.

Date	Mintage	VG	F	VF	XF	Unc
1686	—	150	300	650	1,250	—
1687	—	35.00	75.00	150	350	—

KM# 154.2 400 REIS (Cruzado Novo, 400 = 480 Reis)

Silver **Obv:** Crowned arms, value at left, date at right **Obv. Legend:** PETRVS II... **Rev:** Cross of St. George with rosettes in angles **Note:** Dav. #4390

Date	Mintage	VG	F	VF	XF	Unc
1688INCM	—	35.00	75.00	150	350	—
1689	—	35.00	75.00	150	350	—
1690	—	55.00	125	250	500	—
1691	—	500	1,000	2,000	4,000	—
1692	—	400	900	1,750	3,500	—
1693 Rare	—	—	—	—	—	—

KM# 154.1 400 REIS (Cruzado Novo, 400 = 480 Reis)

Silver **Obv:** Crowned arms, value at left, date at right **Obv. Legend:** PETRVS II... **Rev:** Cross of St. George with P in angles **Note:** Dav. #4392; 1702 is Dav. #1625.

Date	Mintage	VG	F	VF	XF	Unc
1688	—	150	300	650	1,250	—
1689	—	30.00	70.00	125	250	—
1690	—	30.00	70.00	125	250	—
1691	—	35.00	75.00	135	275	—
1692	—	75.00	150	300	600	—
1693	—	90.00	175	350	700	—
1694	—	100	200	400	850	—
1695	—	350	750	1,500	2,500	—
1696	—	100	200	400	850	—
1697	—	125	250	500	950	—
1698	—	125	250	500	950	—
1700 Rare	—	—	—	—	—	—

KM# 154.3 400 REIS (Cruzado Novo, 400 = 480 Reis)
Silver **Ruler:** Peter II **Obv:** Crowned arms, flanked by vertical date and value **Obv. Legend:** PETRVS • II • ... **Rev:** Maltese cross, quatrefoil in angles **Rev. Legend:** • IN HOC SIGNO VINCES • **Note:** Dav. #4391; 1700s are Dav. #1627. Varieties exist.

Date	Mintage	VG	F	VF	XF	Unc
1696	—	225	450	950	1,850	—
1697	—	650	1,250	2,750	4,500	—

KM# 115 1000 REIS (Quartinho, 1200 Reis)
2.6900 g., 0.9170 Gold 0.0793 oz. AGW **Obv:** Crowned arms with value at side, titles of Peter as Prince Regent **Rev:** Jerusalem cross with quatrefoils in angles, date at top

Date	Mintage	VG	F	VF	XF	Unc
1677	—	650	1,350	2,500	4,000	—
1678	—	275	550	1,000	2,000	—
1679	—	400	800	1,500	2,500	—
1681	—	400	800	1,500	2,500	—

KM# 146 1000 REIS (Quartinho, 1200 Reis)
2.6900 g., 0.9170 Gold 0.0793 oz. AGW **Obv:** Crowned narrow shield with value at side, titles of Peter II **Rev:** Jerusalem cross with quatrefoils in angles, date at top

Date	Mintage	VG	F	VF	XF	Unc
1683	—	1,000	2,000	3,500	6,500	—

KM# 155 1000 REIS (Quartinho, 1200 Reis)
2.6900 g., 0.9170 Gold 0.0793 oz. AGW **Ruler:** Peter II **Obv:** Crowned arms with vertical value at left side, titles of Peter II at right **Obv. Legend:** PETRVS • II • .... **Rev:** Maltese cross, quatrefoil in angles, date above **Rev. Legend:** IN HOC SIGNO VINCES

Date	Mintage	VG	F	VF	XF	Unc
1688	—	225	450	850	1,500	—
1689	—	150	300	550	1,000	—
1690	—	175	375	700	1,250	—
1691	—	125	250	400	750	—
1698	—	175	375	700	1,250	—
1699	—	150	300	550	1,000	—

KM# 116 2000 REIS
5.3800 g., 0.9170 Gold 0.1586 oz. AGW **Obv:** Crowned arms with value at side, titles of Peter as Prince Regent **Rev:** Jerusalem crown with quatrefoils in angles **Note:** Varieties exist.

Date	Mintage	VG	F	VF	XF	Unc
1677	—	925	1,750	3,050	4,950	—
1678	—	500	1,050	1,950	3,300	—
1680	—	500	1,050	1,950	3,300	—
1681	—	500	1,050	1,950	3,300	—
1682	—	600	1,200	2,200	3,850	—

KM# 147 2000 REIS
5.3800 g., 0.9170 Gold 0.1586 oz. AGW **Ruler:** Peter II **Obv:** Crowned arms with vertical value at left, titles of Peter II at right **Rev:** Maltese cross with quatrefoils in angles **Note:** Similar to 4000 Reis, KM#156. Varieties exist.

Date	Mintage	VG	F	VF	XF	Unc
1683	—	1,350	2,500	4,000	6,500	—
1684	—	1,100	2,000	3,500	6,000	—
1688	—	375	725	1,300	2,200	—
1689	—	195	375	725	1,250	—
1690	—	195	375	725	1,250	—
1691	—	250	500	875	1,500	—
1692	—	165	325	600	1,100	—
1699	—	250	500	875	1,500	—

KM# 117 4000 REIS
10.7600 g., 0.9170 Gold 0.3172 oz. AGW **Obv:** Crowned arms, value at sides, titles of Peter as Prince Regent **Rev:** Jerusalem cross with quatrefoils in angles **Note:** Varieties exist.

Date	Mintage	VG	F	VF	XF	Unc
1677	—	1,000	2,000	3,500	6,500	—
1678	—	1,150	2,250	3,750	7,000	—
1680/78	—	1,000	2,000	3,500	6,500	—
1680	—	1,000	2,000	3,500	6,500	—
1681	—	1,000	2,000	3,500	6,500	—
1682	—	1,000	2,000	3,500	6,500	—

KM# 156 4000 REIS
10.7600 g., 0.9170 Gold 0.3172 oz. AGW **Ruler:** Peter II **Obv:** Crowned arms, vertical value at left, titles of Peter II at right **Obv. Legend:** PETRVS • II • D • G • PORT • E • TALG • REX **Rev:** Maltese cross with quatrefoils in angles, date above **Rev. Legend:** IN HOC SIGNO VINCES

Date	Mintage	VG	F	VF	XF	Unc
1683 Rare	—	—	—	—	—	—
1688	—	550	1,050	2,000	3,300	—
1689	—	450	875	1,300	2,050	—
1690	—	250	500	875	1,500	—
1691	—	550	1,050	2,000	3,300	—
1692/90	—	—	—	—	—	—
1692	—	250	500	875	1,500	—
1693	—	450	875	1,300	2,050	—
1694	—	450	875	1,300	2,050	—
1695	—	250	500	875	1,500	—
1696	—	250	500	875	1,500	—
1697	—	250	500	875	1,500	—

COUNTERMARKED COINAGE - TYPE I

Authorized by Decree of March 3, 1642 on Portuguese coins of Philip II, Philip III and John IV.

KM# 416 50 REIS
Silver **Countermark:** 50 in rectangle **Note:** Countermark Type I on Portugal 40 Reis, KM#34.

CM Date	Host Date	Good	VG	F	VF	XF
ND(1642)	ND	38.50	70.00	140	250	—

KM# 420.1 60 REIS
Silver **Countermark:** 60 in rectangle **Note:** Countermark on Portugal 1/2 Tostao, KM#16.

CM Date	Host Date	Good	VG	F	VF	XF
ND(1642)	ND	33.00	65.00	120	185	—

KM# 420.2 60 REIS
Silver **Countermark:** 60 in rectangle **Note:** Countermark Type I on Portugal 1/2 Tostao, KM#36.

CM Date	Host Date	Good	VG	F	VF	XF
ND(1642)	ND	38.50	70.00	140	250	—

KM# 429.1 120 REIS
Silver **Countermark:** 120 in rectangle **Note:** Countermark Type I on Portugal 100 Reis, 1 Tostao, KM#17.

CM Date	Host Date	Good	VG	F	VF	XF
ND(1642)	ND	38.50	70.00	140	250	—

KM# 429.2 120 REIS
Silver **Countermark:** 120 in rectangle **Note:** Countermark Type I on Portugal 100 Reis, 1 Tostao, KM#43.

CM Date	Host Date	Good	VG	F	VF	XF
ND(1642)	ND	150	300	600	1,100	—

COUNTERMARKED COINAGE - TYPE III

KM# 417.1 50 REIS
Silver **Countermark:** 50 in crowned square **Note:** Countermark Type III on Portugal 40 Reis, KM#33.

CM Date	Host Date	Good	VG	F	VF	XF
ND(1663)	ND	49.50	100	165	250	—

KM# 417.2 50 REIS
Silver **Countermark:** 50 in crowned square **Note:** Countermark Type III on Portugal 40 Reis, KM#35.

CM Date	Host Date	Good	VG	F	VF	XF
ND(1663)	ND	55.00	110	195	300	—

KM# 417.3 50 REIS
Silver **Countermark:** 50 in crowned square **Note:** Countermark Type III on Portugal 40 Reis, KM#34.

CM Date	Host Date	Good	VG	F	VF	XF
ND(1663)	ND	38.50	70.00	120	185	—

KM# 417.4 50 REIS
Silver **Countermark:** 50 in crowned square **Note:** Countermark Type III on Portugal 40 Reis, KM#69.

CM Date	Host Date	Good	VG	F	VF	XF
ND(1663)	ND	220	500	1,000	1,650	—

KM# 426.1 100 REIS
Silver **Countermark:** 100 in crowned rectangle **Note:** Countermark Type III on Portugal 80 Reis, KM#40.

CM Date	Host Date	Good	VG	F	VF	XF
ND(1663)	ND	49.50	100	165	250	—

KM# 426.2 100 REIS
Silver **Countermark:** 100 in crowned rectangle **Note:** Countermark Type III on Portugal 80 Reis, KM#42.

CM Date	Host Date	Good	VG	F	VF	XF
ND(1663)	ND	55.00	110	195	300	—

KM# 426.3 100 REIS
Silver **Countermark:** 100 in crowned rectangle
Note: Countermark Type III on Portugal 80 Reis, KM#41.

CM Date	Host Date	Good	VG	F	VF	XF
ND(1663)	ND	49.50	100	165	250	—

KM# 426.4 100 REIS
Silver **Countermark:** 100 in crowned rectangle
Note: Countermark Type III on Portugal 80 Reis, KM#73.

CM Date	Host Date	Good	VG	F	VF	XF
ND(1663)	ND	195	425	825	1,400	—

KM# 434.1 250 REIS
Silver **Countermark:** 250 in crowned rectangle **Note:** Countermark Type III on Portugal 200 Reis, KM#49.

CM Date	Host Date	Good	VG	F	VF	XF
ND(1663)	ND	55.00	110	180	270	—

KM# 434.2 250 REIS
Silver **Countermark:** 250 in crowned rectangle
Note: Countermark Type III on Portugal 200 Reis, KM#51.

CM Date	Host Date	Good	VG	F	VF	XF
ND(1642)	ND	90.00	180	300	475	—

KM# 434.3 250 REIS
Silver **Countermark:** 250 in crowned rectangle
Note: Countermark Type III on Portugal 200 Reis, KM#50.

CM Date	Host Date	Good	VG	F	VF	XF
ND(1663)	ND	60.00	120	210	325	—

KM# 434.4 250 REIS
Silver **Countermark:** 250 in crowned rectangle
Note: Countermark Type III on Portugal 200 Reis, KM#77.

CM Date	Host Date	Good	VG	F	VF	XF
ND(1642)	ND	70.00	145	240	425	—

KM# 437.1 500 REIS

Silver **Countermark:** 500 in crowned rectangle
Note: Countermark Type III on Portugal 400 Reis, KM#52.

CM Date	Host Date	Good	VG	F	VF	XF
ND(1663)	ND	85.00	160	270	425	—

KM# 437.2 500 REIS

Silver **Countermark:** 500 in crowned rectangle
Note: Countermark Type III on Portugal 400 Reis, KM#54.

CM Date	Host Date	Good	VG	F	VF	XF
ND(1663)	ND	300	650	1,200	2,000	—

KM# 437.3 500 REIS

Silver **Countermark:** 500 in crowned rectangle
Note: Countermark Type III on Portugal 400 Reis, KM#53.

CM Date	Host Date	Good	VG	F	VF	XF
ND(1663)	ND	120	240	400	650	—

KM# 437.4 500 REIS

Silver **Countermark:** 500 in crowned rectangle
Note: Countermark Type III on Portugal 400 Reis, KM#78.

CM Date	Host Date	Good	VG	F	VF	XF
ND(1663)	ND Rare	—	—	—	—	—

COUNTERMARKED COINAGE - TYPE IV

KM# 418.1 50 REIS

Silver **Countermark:** 50 in crowned square **Note:** Countermark Type IV on Portugal 40 Reis, KM#33.

CM Date	Host Date	Good	VG	F	VF	XF
ND(1663)	ND	44.00	75.00	130	220	—

KM# 418.2 50 REIS

Silver **Countermark:** 50 in crowned square **Note:** Countermark Type IV on Portugal 40 Reis, KM#35.

CM Date	Host Date	Good	VG	F	VF	XF
ND(1663)	ND	55.00	110	195	300	—

KM# 418.3 50 REIS

Silver **Countermark:** 50 in crowned square **Note:** Countermark Type IV on Portugal 40 Reis, KM#34.

CM Date	Host Date	Good	VG	F	VF	XF
ND(1663)	ND	49.50	100	165	250	—

KM# 418.4 50 REIS

Silver **Countermark:** 50 in crowned square **Note:** Countermark Type IV on Portugal 40 Reis, KM#69.

CM Date	Host Date	Good	VG	F	VF	XF
ND(1663)	ND	220	500	1,000	1,650	—

KM# 427.1 100 REIS

Silver **Countermark:** 100 in crowned rectangle
Note: Countermark Type IV on Portugal 80 Reis, KM#40.

CM Date	Host Date	Good	VG	F	VF	XF
ND(1663)	ND	49.50	100	165	250	—

KM# 427.2 100 REIS

Silver **Countermark:** 100 in crowned rectangle
Note: Countermark Type IV on Portugal 80 Reis, KM#42.

CM Date	Host Date	Good	VG	F	VF	XF
ND(1663)	ND	65.00	130	220	350	—

KM# 427.3 100 REIS

Silver **Countermark:** 100 in crowned rectangle
Note: Countermark Type IV on Portugal 80 Reis, KM#41.

CM Date	Host Date	Good	VG	F	VF	XF
ND(1663)	ND	49.50	100	165	250	—

KM# 427.4 100 REIS

Silver **Countermark:** 100 in rectangle **Note:** Countermark Type IV on Portugal 80 Reis, KM#73.

CM Date	Host Date	Good	VG	F	VF	XF
ND(1663)	ND	195	425	825	1,400	—

KM# 435.1 250 REIS

Silver **Countermark:** 250 in crowned rectangle
Note: Countermark Type IV on Portugal 200 Reis, KM#49.

CM Date	Host Date	Good	VG	F	VF	XF
ND(1663)	ND	49.50	100	165	250	—

KM# 435.2 250 REIS

Silver **Countermark:** 250 in crowned rectangle
Note: Countermark Type IV on Portugal 200 Reis, KM#51.

CM Date	Host Date	Good	VG	F	VF	XF
ND(1663)	ND	85.00	165	275	450	—

KM# 435.3 250 REIS

Silver **Countermark:** 250 in crowned rectangle
Note: Countermark Type IV on Portugal 200 Reis, KM#50.

CM Date	Host Date	Good	VG	F	VF	XF
ND(1663)	ND	55.00	110	195	300	—

KM# 435.4 250 REIS

Silver **Countermark:** 250 in crowned rectangle
Note: Countermark Type IV on Portugal 200 Reis, KM#82.

CM Date	Host Date	Good	VG	F	VF	XF
ND(1663)	ND	100	200	350	600	—

KM# 438.1 500 REIS

Silver **Countermark:** 500 in crowned rectangle
Note: Countermark Type IV on Portugal 400 Reis, KM#52.

CM Date	Host Date	Good	VG	F	VF	XF
ND(1663)	ND	90.00	175	300	500	—

KM# 438.2 500 REIS

Silver **Countermark:** 500 in crowned rectangle
Note: Countermark Type IV on Portugal 400 Reis, KM#54.

CM Date	Host Date	Good	VG	F	VF	XF
ND(1663)	ND	375	775	1,400	2,500	—

KM# 438.3 500 REIS

Silver **Countermark:** 500 in crowned rectangle
Note: Countermark Type IV on Portugal 400 Reis, KM#53.

CM Date	Host Date	Good	VG	F	VF	XF
ND(1663)	ND	120	225	400	650	—

KM# 438.4 500 REIS

Silver **Countermark:** 500 in crowned rectangle
Note: Countermark Type IV on Portugal 400 Reis, KM#83.

CM Date	Host Date	Good	VG	F	VF	XF
ND(1663)	ND	775	1,300	2,200	3,850	—

COUNTERMARKED COINAGE - TYPE II

Authorized by Decree of November 20, 1662 on Portuguese coins of John IV and Alfonso VI.

KM# 450.1 1000 REIS

3.0600 g., 0.9170 Gold 0.0902 oz. AGW **Countermark:** Crowned 1 in square frame **Note:** Countermark Type II on 1 Cruzado, KM#55.

CM Date	Host Date	Good	VG	F	VF	XF
ND(1662)	1642 Rare	—	—	—	—	—

KM# 450.2 1000 REIS

3.0600 g., 0.9170 Gold 0.0902 oz. AGW **Countermark:** Crowned 1 in square frame **Note:** Countermark Type II on 1 Cruzado, KM#58.

CM Date	Host Date	Good	VG	F	VF	XF
ND(1662)	1642, 1647 Rare	—	—	—	—	—

KM# 451.1 2000 REIS

6.1200 g., 0.9170 Gold 0.1804 oz. AGW **Countermark:** Crowned 1, 2, or 4 in square frame **Note:** Countermark Type II on 2 Cruzados, KM#59.

CM Date	Host Date	Good	VG	F	VF	XF
ND(1662)	1642, 1646, 1647 Rare	—	—	—	—	—

KM# 451.2 2000 REIS

6.1200 g., 0.9170 Gold 0.1804 oz. AGW **Countermark:** Crowned 1, 2, or 4 in square frame **Note:** Countermark Type II on 2 Cruzados, KM#80.

CM Date	Host Date	Good	VG	F	VF	XF
ND(1662)	1660 Rare	—	—	—	—	—

KM# 452.1 4000 REIS

12.2400 g., 0.9170 Gold 0.3608 oz. AGW **Countermark:** Crowned 4 in square frame **Note:** Countermark Type II on 4 Cruzados of Philip I.

CM Date	Host Date	Good	VG	F	VF	XF
ND(1662)	ND Rare	—	—	—	—	—

KM# 452.2 4000 REIS

12.2400 g., 0.9170 Gold 0.3608 oz. AGW **Countermark:** Crowned 4 in square frame **Note:** Countermark Type II on 4 Cruzados, KM#9.

CM Date	Host Date	Good	VG	F	VF	XF
ND(1662)	ND Rare	—	—	—	—	—

KM# 452.3 4000 REIS

12.2400 g., 0.9170 Gold 0.3608 oz. AGW **Countermark:** Crowned 4 in square frame **Note:** Countermark Type II on 4 Cruzados, KM#18.

CM Date	Host Date	Good	VG	F	VF	XF
ND(1662)	ND Rare	—	—	—	—	—

KM# 452.4 4000 REIS

12.2400 g., 0.9170 Gold 0.3608 oz. AGW **Countermark:** Crowned 4 in square frame **Note:** Countermark Type II on 4 Cruzados, KM#60.

CM Date	Host Date	Good	VG	F	VF	XF
ND(1662)	1642-1652 Rare	—	—	—	—	—

KM# 452.5 4000 REIS

12.2400 g., 0.9170 Gold 0.3608 oz. AGW **Countermark:** Crowned 4 in square frame **Note:** Countermark Type II on 4 Cruzados, KM#81.

CM Date	Host Date	Good	VG	F	VF	XF
ND(1662)	1660, 1663 Rare	—	—	—	—	—

COUNTERMARKED COINAGE - TYPE V

Authorized by Decree of April 12, 1668 on Portuguese coins of John IV and Alfonso VI.

Countermark: Crowned 1100, 2200, or 4400 in rectangle.

KM# 453.1 1100 REIS

3.0600 g., 0.9220 Gold 0.0907 oz. AGW **Countermark:** Crowned 1100 in rectangle **Note:** Countermark Type V on 1 Cruzado, KM58.

CM Date	Host Date	Good	VG	F	VF	XF
ND(1668)	1642 Rare	—	—	—	—	—
ND(1668)	1647 Rare	—	—	—	—	—

KM# 453.2 1100 REIS

3.0600 g., 0.9220 Gold 0.0907 oz. AGW **Countermark:** Crowned 1100 in rectangle **Note:** Countermark Type V on 1000 Reis, KM450.2.

CM Date	Host Date	Good	VG	F	VF	XF
ND(1668)	1642, 1647 Rare	—	—	—	—	—

KM# 453.3 1100 REIS

3.0600 g., 0.9170 Gold 0.0902 oz. AGW **Countermark:** Crowned 1100 in rectangle **Note:** Countermark Type V on 1000 Reis, KM#84.

CM Date	Host Date	Good	VG	F	VF	XF
ND(1668)	1663, 1666 Rare	—	—	—	—	—

KM# 454.1 2200 REIS

6.1200 g., 0.9170 Gold 0.1804 oz. AGW **Countermark:** Crowned 2200 in rectangle **Note:** Countermark Type V on 2 Cruzados, KM#59.

CM Date	Host Date	Good	VG	F	VF	XF
ND(1668)	1642, 1646, 1647 Rare	—	—	—	—	—

KM# 454.2 2200 REIS

6.1200 g., 0.9170 Gold 0.1804 oz. AGW **Countermark:** Crowned 2200 in rectangle **Note:** Countermark Type V on 2000 Reis, KM#451.1

CM Date	Host Date	Good	VG	F	VF	XF
ND(1668)	1642, 1646, 1647 Rare	—	—	—	—	—

KM# 454.3 2200 REIS

6.1200 g., 0.9170 Gold 0.1804 oz. AGW **Countermark:** Crowned 2200 in rectangle **Note:** Countermark Type V on 2000 Reis, KM#451.2.

CM Date	Host Date	Good	VG	F	VF	XF
ND(1668)	1660 Rare	—	—	—	—	—

KM# 454.4 2200 REIS

6.1200 g., 0.9170 Gold 0.1804 oz. AGW **Countermark:** Crowned 2200 in rectangle **Note:** Countermark Type V on 2 Cruzados, KM#80.

CM Date	Host Date	Good	VG	F	VF	XF
ND(1668)	1660 Rare	—	—	—	—	—

KM# 454.5 2200 REIS

6.1200 g., 0.9170 Gold 0.1804 oz. AGW **Countermark:** Crowned 2200 in rectangle **Note:** Countermark Type V on 2000 Reis, KM#85.

CM Date	Host Date	Good	VG	F	VF	XF
ND(1668)	1663, 1666 Rare	—	—	—	—	—

KM# 455.1 4400 REIS

12.2400 g., 0.9220 Gold 0.3628 oz. AGW **Countermark:** Crowned 4400 in rectangle **Note:** Countermark Type V on 4 Cruzados, KM#60.

CM Date	Host Date	Good	VG	F	VF	XF
ND(1668)	1642-1652 Rare	—	—	—	—	—

KM# 455.2 4400 REIS

12.2400 g., 0.9220 Gold 0.3628 oz. AGW **Countermark:** Crowned 4400 in rectangle **Note:** Countermark Type V on 4000 Reis, KM#452.1.

CM Date	Host Date	Good	VG	F	VF	XF
ND(1668)	ND Rare	—	—	—	—	—

KM# 455.3 4400 REIS

12.2400 g., 0.9220 Gold 0.3628 oz. AGW **Countermark:** Crowned 4400 in rectangle **Note:** Countermark Type V on 4000 Reis, KM#452.2.

CM Date	Host Date	Good	VG	F	VF	XF
ND(1668)	ND Rare	—	—	—	—	—

KM# 455.4 4400 REIS

12.2400 g., 0.9220 Gold 0.3628 oz. AGW **Countermark:** Crowned 4400 in rectangle **Note:** Countermark Type V on 4000 Reis, KM#452.3.

CM Date	Host Date	Good	VG	F	VF	XF
ND(1668)	ND Rare	—	—	—	—	—

KM# 455.5 4400 REIS

12.2400 g., 0.9220 Gold 0.3628 oz. AGW **Countermark:** Crowned 4400 in rectangle **Note:** Countermark Type V on 4000 Reis, KM#452.4.

CM Date	Host Date	Good	VG	F	VF	XF
ND(1668)	1642-1652 Rare	—	—	—	—	—

KM# 455.6 4400 REIS

12.2400 g., 0.9220 Gold 0.3628 oz. AGW **Countermark:** Crowned 4400 in rectangle **Note:** Countermark Type V on 4000 Reis, KM#452.5.

CM Date	Host Date	Good	VG	F	VF	XF
ND(1668)	ND Rare	—	—	—	—	—

KM# 455.7 4400 REIS

12.2400 g., 0.9220 Gold 0.3628 oz. AGW **Countermark:** Crowned 4400 in rectangle **Note:** Countermark Type V on 4 Cruzados, KM#81.

CM Date	Host Date	Good	VG	F	VF	XF
ND(1668)	1660, 1663 Rare	—	—	—	—	—

KM# 455.8 4400 REIS

12.2400 g., 0.9170 Gold 0.3608 oz. AGW **Countermark:** Crowned 4400 in rectangle **Note:** Countermark Type V on 4000 Reis, KM#86.

CM Date	Host Date	Good	VG	F	VF	XF
ND(1668)	1663-1666 Rare	—	—	—	—	—

COUNTERMARKED COINAGE - TYPE VII

Authorized by Decree of August 9, 1686 on Portuguese coins of Alfonso IV and Peter as Prince Regent.

Countermark: Crowned globe.

KM# 456 CRUZADO

3.0600 g., 0.9170 Gold 0.0902 oz. AGW **Countermark:** Crowned globe **Note:** Countermark Type VII on 1000 Reis, KM#84.

CM Date	Host Date	Good	VG	F	VF	XF
ND(1686)	1663, 1666 Rare	—	—	—	—	—

KM# 456.2 CRUZADO

3.0600 g., 0.9170 Gold 0.0902 oz. AGW **Countermark:** Crowned globe **Note:** Countermark Type VII on 1100 Reis, KM#453.2.

CM Date	Host Date	Good	VG	F	VF	XF
ND(1686)	1642 Rare	—	—	—	—	—

KM# 456.3 CRUZADO

3.0600 g., 0.9220 Gold 0.0907 oz. AGW **Countermark:** Crowned globe **Note:** Countermark Type VII on 1100 Reis, KM#453.3.

CM Date	Host Date	Good	VG	F	VF	XF
ND(1686)	1663, 1666 Rare	—	—	—	—	—

KM# 456.4 CRUZADO

3.0600 g., 0.9170 Gold 0.0902 oz. AGW **Countermark:** Crowned globe **Note:** Countermark Type VII on 1100 Reis, KM#87..

CM Date	Host Date	Good	VG	F	VF	XF
ND(1686)	1668, 1671 Rare	—	—	—	—	—

KM# 457.1 2 CRUZADOS

6.1200 g., 0.9170 Gold 0.1804 oz. AGW **Countermark:** Crowned globe **Note:** Countermark Type VII on 2000 Reis, KM#85.

CM Date	Host Date	Good	VG	F	VF	XF
ND(1686)	1663, 1666 Rare	—	—	—	—	—

KM# 457.2 2 CRUZADOS

6.1200 g., 0.9170 Gold 0.1804 oz. AGW **Countermark:** Crowned globe **Note:** Countermark Type VII on 2200 Reis, KM#454.3.

CM Date	Host Date	Good	VG	F	VF	XF
ND(1686)	1642 Rare	—	—	—	—	—

KM# 457.3 2 CRUZADOS

6.1200 g., 0.9170 Gold 0.1804 oz. AGW **Countermark:** Crowned globe **Note:** Countermark Type VII on 2200 Reis, KM#454.5.

CM Date	Host Date	Good	VG	F	VF	XF
ND(1686)	1663, 1666 Rare	—	—	—	—	—

KM# 457.4 2 CRUZADOS

6.1200 g., 0.9170 Gold 0.1804 oz. AGW **Countermark:** Crowned globe **Note:** Countermark Type VII on 2200 Reis, KM#88.

CM Date	Host Date	Good	VG	F	VF	XF
ND(1686)	1668-1674 Rare	—	—	—	—	—

KM# 458.1 4 CRUZADOS

12.2400 g., 0.9170 Gold 0.3608 oz. AGW **Countermark:** Crowned globe **Note:** Countermark Type VII on 4000 Reis, KM #86.

CM Date	Host Date	Good	VG	F	VF	XF
ND(1686)	1663, 1666 Rare	—	—	—	—	—

KM# 458.2 4 CRUZADOS

12.2400 g., 0.9170 Gold 0.3608 oz. AGW **Countermark:** Crowned globe **Note:** Countermark Type VII on 4400 Reis, KM#455.1

CM Date	Host Date	Good	VG	F	VF	XF
ND(1686)	1642-1652 Rare	—	—	—	—	—

KM# 458.3 4 CRUZADOS

12.2400 g., 0.9170 Gold 0.3608 oz. AGW **Countermark:** Crowned globe **Note:** Countermark Type VII on 4400 Reis, KM#455.2.

CM Date	Host Date	Good	VG	F	VF	XF
ND(1686)	ND Rare	—	—	—	—	—

KM# 458.4 4 CRUZADOS

12.2400 g., 0.9170 Gold 0.3608 oz. AGW **Countermark:** Crowned globe **Note:** Countermark Type VII on 4400 Reis, KM#455.3.

CM Date	Host Date	Good	VG	F	VF	XF
ND(1686)	ND Rare	—	—	—	—	—

KM# 458.5 4 CRUZADOS

12.2400 g., 0.9170 Gold 0.3608 oz. AGW **Countermark:** Crowned globe **Note:** Countermark Type VII on 4400 Reis, KM#455.4.

CM Date	Host Date	Good	VG	F	VF	XF
ND(1686)	ND Rare	—	—	—	—	—

KM# 458.6 4 CRUZADOS

12.2400 g., 0.9170 Gold 0.3608 oz. AGW **Countermark:** Crowned globe **Note:** Countermark Type VII on 4400 Reis, KM#455.5.

CM Date	Host Date	Good	VG	F	VF	XF
ND(1686)	1642-1652 Rare	—	—	—	—	—

KM# 458.7 4 CRUZADOS

12.2400 g., 0.9170 Gold 0.3608 oz. AGW **Countermark:** Crowned globe **Note:** Countermark Type VII on 4400 Reis, KM#455.7.

CM Date	Host Date	Good	VG	F	VF	XF
ND(1686)	1663-1666 Rare	—	—	—	—	—

KM# 458.8 4 CRUZADOS

12.2400 g., 0.9170 Gold 0.3608 oz. AGW **Countermark:** Crowned globe **Note:** Countermark Type VII on 4400 Reis, KM#455.8.

CM Date	Host Date	Good	VG	F	VF	XF
ND(1686)	ND Rare	—	—	—	—	—

KM# 458.9 4 CRUZADOS

12.2400 g., 0.9170 Gold 0.3608 oz. AGW **Countermark:** Crowned globe **Note:** Countermark Type VII on 4400 Reis, KM#89.

CM Date	Host Date	Good	VG	F	VF	XF
ND(1686)	1668-1674 Rare	—	—	—	—	—

PATTERNS

Including off metal strikes

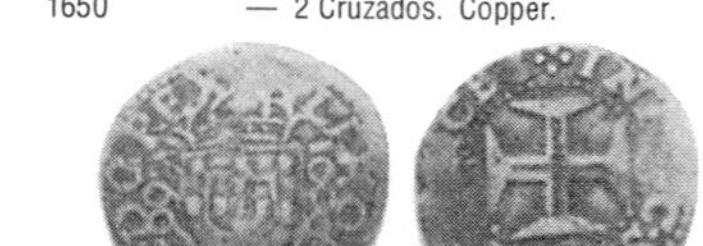

KM#	Date	Mintage	Identification	Mkt Val
Pn1	1650	—	2 Cruzados. Copper.	—
Pn2	1660	—	1000 Reis. Silver. Similar to KM#84.	1,150
Pn4	1682	—	5 Reis. Copper.	2,250
Pn5	1682	—	10 Reis. Copper.	2,250

KM#	Date	Mintage Identification	Mkt Val
Pn3	1682	— 3 Reis. Copper.	2,750
Pn6	1688	— 1-1/2 Real. Copper.	3,000
Pn7	1688	— 3 Reis. Copper.	900
Pn8	1688	— 5 Reis. Copper.	700

KM#	Date	Mintage Identification	Mkt Val
Pn9	1688	— 10 Reis. Copper.	1,250
Pn10	1688	— Cruzado. Copper.	—
Pn11	1696	— 4000 Reis. Copper. As KM156.	—

RAGUSA

A port city in Croatia on the Dalmatian coast of the Adriatic Sea. Ragusa was once a great mercantile power, the merchant fleets of which sailed as far abroad as India and America.

Refugees from the destroyed Latin communities of Salona and Epidaurus, and a colony of Slavs colonized the island rock of Ragusa during the 7th century. For four centuries Ragusa successfully defended itself against attacks by foreign powers, but from 1205 to 1358 recognized Venetian suzerainty. From 1358 to 1526, Ragusa was a vassal state of Hungary. The fall of Hungary in 1526 freed Ragusa, permitting it to become one of the foremost commercial powers of the Mediterranean and a leader in the development of literature and art. After this period its importance declined, due in part to the discovery of America, which reduced the importance of Mediterranean ports. A measure of its former economic importance was regained during the Napoleonic Wars when the republic, by adopting a policy of neutrality (1800-1805), became the leading carrier of the Mediterranean. This favored position was terminated by French seizure in 1805. In 1814 Ragusa was annexed by Austria, remaining a part of the Austrian Empire until its incorporation in the newly formed state of Yugoslavia in 1918. Croatia proclaimed its independence in 1991.

MONETARY SYSTEM

6 Soldi = 1 Grosetto
12 Grosetti = 1 Perpero
3 Perpero = 1 Scudo
36 Grosetti = 1 Scudo
40 Grosetti = 1 Ducato
60 Grosetti = 1 Tallero
5 Perpero = 1 Tallero

REPUBLIC

STANDARD COINAGE

KM# 6 SOLDO

Copper **Obv:** Bust of Saint, facing above brick-like design **Rev:** Christ flanked by designs within circle of stars **Note:** Varieties exist.

Date	Mintage	VG	F	VF	XF	Unc
1678	—	10.00	20.00	45.00	100	—
1682	—	10.00	20.00	45.00	100	—
1689	—	10.00	20.00	45.00	100	—

KM# 5 GROSETTO

Billon **Obv:** St. Blaze **Rev:** Christ within stars **Note:** Varieties exist.

Date	Mintage	VG	F	VF	XF	Unc
1626	—	10.00	20.00	32.00	65.00	—
1627	—	10.00	20.00	32.00	65.00	—
1628	—	10.00	20.00	32.00	65.00	—
1629	—	10.00	20.00	32.00	65.00	—
1630	—	10.00	20.00	32.00	65.00	—
1631	—	10.00	20.00	32.00	65.00	—
1635	—	10.00	20.00	32.00	65.00	—
1642	—	10.00	20.00	32.00	65.00	—
1643	—	10.00	20.00	32.00	65.00	—
1644	—	10.00	20.00	32.00	65.00	—
1645	—	10.00	20.00	32.00	65.00	—
1646	—	10.00	20.00	32.00	65.00	—
1647	—	10.00	20.00	32.00	65.00	—
1648	—	10.00	20.00	32.00	65.00	—
1649	—	10.00	20.00	32.00	65.00	—
1650	—	10.00	20.00	32.00	65.00	—
1651	—	10.00	20.00	32.00	65.00	—
1652	—	10.00	20.00	32.00	65.00	—
1653	—	10.00	20.00	32.00	65.00	—
1654	—	10.00	20.00	32.00	65.00	—
1655	—	10.00	20.00	32.00	65.00	—
1656	—	10.00	20.00	32.00	65.00	—
1657	—	10.00	20.00	32.00	65.00	—
1658	—	10.00	20.00	32.00	65.00	—
1659	—	10.00	20.00	32.00	65.00	—
1660	—	10.00	20.00	32.00	65.00	—
1661	—	10.00	20.00	32.00	65.00	—
1662	—	10.00	20.00	32.00	65.00	—
1663	—	10.00	20.00	32.00	65.00	—
1664	—	10.00	20.00	32.00	65.00	—
1665	—	10.00	20.00	32.00	65.00	—
1666	—	10.00	20.00	32.00	65.00	—
1667	—	10.00	20.00	32.00	65.00	—
1676	—	10.00	20.00	32.00	65.00	—
1677	—	10.00	20.00	32.00	65.00	—
1678	—	10.00	20.00	32.00	65.00	—
1679	—	10.00	20.00	32.00	65.00	—
1680	—	10.00	20.00	32.00	65.00	—
1681	—	10.00	20.00	32.00	65.00	—
1682	—	10.00	20.00	32.00	65.00	—
1683	—	10.00	20.00	32.00	65.00	—
1684	—	10.00	20.00	32.00	65.00	—
1685	—	10.00	20.00	32.00	65.00	—
1686	—	10.00	20.00	32.00	65.00	—
1687	—	10.00	20.00	32.00	65.00	—
1688	—	10.00	20.00	32.00	65.00	—
1689	—	10.00	20.00	32.00	65.00	—
1690	—	10.00	20.00	32.00	65.00	—
1691	—	10.00	20.00	32.00	65.00	—
1692	—	10.00	20.00	32.00	65.00	—
1694	—	10.00	20.00	32.00	65.00	—
1695	—	10.00	20.00	32.00	65.00	—
1696	—	10.00	20.00	32.00	65.00	—
1697	—	10.00	20.00	32.00	65.00	—
1698	—	10.00	20.00	32.00	65.00	—
1699	—	10.00	20.00	32.00	65.00	—
1700	—	10.00	20.00	32.00	65.00	—

KM# 4 3 GROSETTI (Alltilucho)

1.1200 g., Billon **Obv:** Head of Saint, right **Obv. Legend:** S • BLASIVS • RAGVSII **Rev:** Legend **Rev. Legend:** GROS • ARGE / TRIP / CIVI / RAGV **Note:** Varieties exist.

Date	Mintage	VG	F	VF	XF	Unc
1627	—	30.00	60.00	125	275	—
1628	—	30.00	60.00	125	275	—
1629	—	30.00	60.00	125	275	—
1630	—	30.00	60.00	125	275	—
1631	—	30.00	60.00	125	275	—
1632	—	30.00	60.00	125	275	—
1633	—	30.00	60.00	125	275	—
1635	—	30.00	60.00	125	275	—
1642	—	30.00	60.00	125	275	—
1643	—	30.00	60.00	125	275	—
1644	—	30.00	60.00	125	275	—
1645	—	30.00	60.00	125	275	—
1646	—	30.00	60.00	125	275	—
1647	—	30.00	60.00	125	275	—
1648	—	30.00	60.00	125	275	—
1649	—	30.00	60.00	125	275	—
1654	—	30.00	60.00	125	275	—
1675	—	30.00	60.00	125	275	—
1683	—	30.00	60.00	125	275	—
1684	—	30.00	60.00	125	275	—
1685	—	30.00	60.00	125	275	—
1686	—	30.00	60.00	125	275	—
1692	—	30.00	60.00	125	275	—

KM# 7 PERPERO

Billon **Obv:** St. Blaze divides date and S B **Obv. Legend:** PROT • RAEIP • RHAGVSINAE **Rev:** Christ within stars

Date	Mintage	VG	F	VF	XF	Unc
1683	—	25.00	45.00	95.00	175	—
1692	—	25.00	45.00	95.00	175	—

Russia, formerly the central power of the Union of Soviet Socialist Republics and now of the Commonwealth of Independent States occupies the northern part of Asia and the eastern part of Europe, has an area of 17,075,400 sq. km. Capital: Moscow.

The first Russian dynasty was founded in Novgorod by the Viking Rurik in 862 A.D. under Yaroslav the Wise (1019-54). The subsequent Kievan state became one of the great commercial and cultural centers of Europe before falling to the Mongols of the Batu Khan, 13th century, who were suzerains of Russia until late in the 15th century when Ivan III threw off the Mongol yoke. The Russian Empire was enlarged, solidified and Westernized during the reigns of Ivan the Terrible, Peter the Great and Catherine the Great, and by 1881 extended to the Pacific and into Central Asia. Contemporary Russian history began in March of 1917 when Tsar Nicholas II abdicated under pressure and was replaced by a provisional government composed of both radical and conservative elements. This government rapidly lost ground to the Bolshevik wing of the Socialist Democratic Labor Party which attained power following the Bolshevik Revolution which began on Nov. 7, 1917. After the Russian Civil War, the regional governments, national states and armies became federal republics of the Russian Socialist Federal Soviet Republic. These autonomous republics united to form the Union of Soviet Socialist Republics that was established as a federation under the premiership of Lenin on Dec. 30, 1922.

EMPIRE

RULERS

Boris Godunov, 1598-1605
Fedor II, 1605
Dmitri, 1605-1606
Michael I, 1613-1645
Aleksei, 1645-1676
Fedor III, 1676-1682
Ivan V, 1682-1689
Peter I (The Great), 1689-1725

MINT MARKS

ДМ - Moscow, Dvor Zamoskvoretsky, Naval Mint, 1700

MONETARY SYSTEM

1/4 Kopek = Polushka ПОЛУШКА
1/2 Kopek = Denga, Denezhka ДЕНГА, ДЕНЕЖКА
Kopek = КОП_ИКА
(2, 3 & 4) Kopeks КОП_ИКИ
(5 and up) Kopeks КОП_ЕКЪ
(1924 – 5 and up) Kopeks КОПЕЕК
50 Kopeks = Poltina, Poltinnik ПОЛТИНА,...ПОЛРУБЛЪ
100 Kopeks = Rouble, Ruble РУБЛЪ
10 Roubles = Imperial ИМПЕРІАЛЪ
10 Roubles = Chervonetz ЧЕРВОНЕЦ

NOTE: For silver or gold coins with Zlotych, Kopek or Ruble denominations, see Poland.

NOTE: Gold coins of 1 Ducat or Chervonetz denomination with both multiples and fractions are known before Peter I. Most Russian authorities agree that these pieces were not meant to be coins but were only made as awards for the military. The higher the rank of the individual the larger the gold piece. Thus the range was from a gold denga for a common soldier to a "Portugal" or 10 Ducat size for a high ranking officer.

LEGENDS

Peter I

Obverse with full title:
ЦРЬ И ВЕЛИКИИ КНЗЬ ПЕТРЬ АЛЕЗІЕВИЧЪ
"Tsar and Grand Duke Peter Alexievich"
Obverse with short title:
ЦРЬ ПЕТРЬ АЛЕЗІЕВИЧЪ
"Tsar Peter Alexievich"
Reverse with full title:
ВСЕА ВЕЛІКІА И МЛЫА И ВЕЛЫА РОСИИ САМОДЕРЖЕЦЪ
"of All Great, Little & White Russias Autocrat"
Reverse with short title:
ВСЕА РОСИИ САМОДЕРЖЕЦЪ
"of All Russias Autocrat"
ВСЕА РОСИИ ПОВЕЛИТЕЛЬ
"of All Russias Ruler"

EDGE INSCRIPTIONS

Peter 1

МАНЭТЪНАГО ДЕНЕЖЪНАГО ДВОРА 1701
МОСКОВЪСКАА КАПЕИКА X МАНЕТНОГО ДЕНЕЖНОГО ДВОРА
КОПЕИКА МАНЕТНОГО ДЕНЕЖЪНАГО ДВОРА 1710
КОПЕИКА МАНЕТНОГО . . . ДЕНЕЖЪНАГО ДВОРА
КОПЕИКА МАНЕТНОГО ДЕНЕЖНОГО ДВРОА

STANDARD COINAGE

KM# 102 DENGA (1/2 Kopek)

6.4000 g., Copper **Ruler:** Peter I **Obv:** Crowned double-headed eagle, legend around **Obv. Legend:** CZAR PETER ALEXIEVITCH **Rev:** Value, date withinn circle, legend around **Rev. Legend:** AUTOCRAT OF ALL THE RUSSIAS

Date	Mintage	VG	F	VF	XF	Unc
ND(1700)	—	45.00	75.00	150	300	—

KM# 22 KOPEK

0.5650 g., Gold **Ruler:** Fedor II

Date	Mintage	VG	F	VF	XF	Unc
ND(1606-10)	—	675	1,500	3,000	4,900	—

KM# 40 KOPEK

0.4290 g., Gold **Ruler:** Aleksei

Date	Mintage	VG	F	VF	XF	Unc
ND(1645-76)	—	525	1,150	2,200	3,600	—

TRADE COINAGE

FR# 43 DUCAT

3.5000 g., 0.9860 Gold 0.1109 oz. AGW **Ruler:** Fedor III

Date	Mintage	VG	F	VF	XF	Unc
ND(1676-82)	—	675	1,450	2,650	4,300	—

COUNTERMARKED COINAGE

In 1654 the Ukraine was united to Russia under Czar Alexis; this was the pretext for a Russo-Polish war that lasted several years. It was decided to countermark European thalers with the figure of the czar on horseback and the date, for use primarliy in the Ukraine. The value was set at 64 Kopeks. About 800,000 of these thalers were issued in 1655, the majority of which were from German mints, although many were from the Netherlands. Others were countermarked on thalers of Austria, the Scandinavian states, and Switzerland. A few are known from other European regions, such as Poland and the Italian states. Their legal tender status was abrogated by Czar Alexis in 1659; most existing specimens derive from hoards found in the Ukraine in the nineteenth century.

KM# 440 TALER

Silver **Ruler:** Aleksei **Series:** Swiss Thaler **Countermark:** Czar horseback right in dotted circle, date in rectangle **Note:** Countermark on Saint Gall Thaler, KM#61; Dav. #4677.

CM Date	Host Date	Good	VG	F	VF	XF
1655	1645-76	1,350	2,250	3,250	4,500	—

KM# 407 YEFIMOK

Silver **Ruler:** Aleksei **Series:** French State Thaler **Countermark:** Czar horseback right in dotted circle, date in rectangle **Note:** Countermark on Alsace Thaler; Dav. #3346.

CM Date	Host Date	Good	VG	F	VF	XF
1655	1621-25	1,000	1,600	2,250	3,250	—

KM# 434 YEFIMOK

Ruler: Aleksei **Series:** French Local Issue Thaler **Countermark:** Czar horseback right in dotted circle, date in rectangle **Note:** Countermark on Alsace-Metz Thaler, Dav. #5583A.

CM Date	Host Date	Good	VG	F	VF	XF
1655	1638-41, 43, 45-47, 50	2,250	3,750	5,500	7,500	—

KM# 424 YEFIMOK

Silver **Ruler:** Aleksei **Series:** Spanish Netherlands Patagon **Countermark:** Czar horseback right in dotted circle, date in rectangle **Note:** Countermark on Brabant Patagon, Dav. #4432.

CM Date	Host Date	Good	VG	F	VF	XF
1655	1612-21	850	1,500	2,000	3,000	—

KM# 425 YEFIMOK

Silver **Ruler:** Aleksei **Series:** Spanish Netherlands Patagon **Countermark:** Czar horseback right in dotted circle, date in rectangle **Note:** Countermark on Brabant Patagon, Dav. #4462.

CM Date	Host Date	Good	VG	F	VF	XF
1655	1621-53	650	1,000	1,500	2,250	—

KM# 423 YEFIMOK

Silver **Ruler:** Aleksei **Series:** Germanic Thaler **Countermark:** Czar horseback right in dotted circle, date in rectangle **Note:** Countermark on Brunswick-Luneberg-Celle Thaler, Dav. #6521.

CM Date	Host Date	Good	VG	F	VF	XF
1655	1649-53	1,000	1,600	2,250	3,250	—

KM# 400 YEFIMOK

Silver **Ruler:** Aleksei **Series:** Germanic Thaler **Countermark:** Czar horseback right in dotted circle, date in rectangle **Note:** Countermark on Brunswick-Wolfenbuttel Thaler, Dav. #6303.

CM Date	Host Date	Good	VG	F	VF	XF
1655	1613-28	1,250	1,950	2,750	3,750	—

KM# 410 YEFIMOK

Silver **Ruler:** Aleksei **Series:** Spanish Netherlands Patagon **Countermark:** Czar horseback right in dotted circle, date in rectangle **Note:** Countermark on Flanders Patagon, Dav. #4464.

CM Date	Host Date	Good	VG	F	VF	XF
1655	1622-53	650	1,000	1,500	2,250	—

KM# 431 YEFIMOK

Silver **Ruler:** Aleksei **Series:** Germanic Thaler **Countermark:** Czar horseback right in dotted circle, date in rectangle **Note:** Countermark on Frankfurt Thaler, Dav. #5296.

CM Date	Host Date	Good	VG	F	VF	XF
1655	1647	1,350	2,250	3,250	4,750	—

KM# 421 YEFIMOK

Silver **Ruler:** Aleksei **Series:** United Netherlands Lion and Rijksdaalder **Countermark:** Czar horseback right in dotted circle, date in rectangle **Note:** Countermark on Gelderland Lion Daalder, Dav. #4829.

CM Date	Host Date	Good	VG	F	VF	XF
1655	1606-53	750	1,250	1,750	2,500	—

KM# 420 YEFIMOK

Silver **Ruler:** Aleksei **Series:** United Netherlands Lion and Rijksdaalder **Countermark:** Czar horseback right in dotted circle, date in rectangle **Note:** Countermark on Gelderland Rijksdaalder, Dav. #4828.

CM Date	Host Date	Good	VG	F	VF	XF
1655	1606-53	650	1,000	1,500	2,250	—

KM# 429 YEFIMOK

Silver **Ruler:** Aleksei **Series:** Netherlands Free City Rijksdaalder **Countermark:** Czar horseback right in dotted circle, date in rectangle **Note:** Countermark on Kampen Rijksdaalder, Dav. #4983.

CM Date	Host Date	Good	VG	F	VF	XF
1655	1633-58	1,350	2,250	3,250	4,750	—

KM# 432 YEFIMOK

Silver **Ruler:** Aleksei **Series:** Germanic Thaler **Countermark:** Czar horseback right in dotted circle, date in rectangle **Note:** Countermark on Lubeck Thaler, Dav. #5438.

CM Date	Host Date	Good	VG	F	VF	XF
1655	1606-07	1,500	2,500	3,500	5,000	—

KM# 403 YEFIMOK

Silver **Ruler:** Aleksei **Series:** Germanic Thaler **Countermark:** Czar horseback right in dotted circle, date in rectangle **Note:** Countermark on Lubeck Thaler, Dav.#9405.

CM Date	Host Date	Good	VG	F	VF	XF
1655	1549	1,850	2,250	3,250	4,750	—

KM# 405 YEFIMOK

Silver **Ruler:** Aleksei **Series:** Germanic Thaler **Countermark:** Czar horseback right in dotted circle, date in rectangle **Note:** Countermark on Nurnberg Thaler, KM#52; Dav. #5636.

CM Date	Host Date	Good	VG	F	VF	XF
ND(1655)	1621-28	1,500	2,500	3,500	5,000	—

KM# 426 YEFIMOK

Silver **Ruler:** Aleksei **Series:** United Netherlands Lion and Rijksdaalder **Countermark:** Czar horseback right in dotted circle, date in rectangle **Note:** Countermark on Overijssel Rijksdaalder, Dav. #4832.

CM Date	Host Date	Good	VG	F	VF	XF
1655	1606-29	650	1,000	1,500	2,250	—

KM# 401 YEFIMOK

Silver **Ruler:** Aleksei **Series:** Germanic Thaler **Countermark:** Czar horseback right in dotted circle, date in rectangle **Note:** Countermark on Saxony Thaler, Dav. #7601.

CM Date	Host Date	Good	VG	F	VF	XF
1655	1620-38	1,100	1,750	2,500	3,500	—

KM# 436 YEFIMOK

Silver **Ruler:** Aleksei **Series:** Germanic Thaler **Countermark:** Czar horseback right in dotted circle, date in rectangle **Note:** Countermark on Saxony Thaler, Dav. #7612.

CM Date	Host Date	Good	VG	F	VF	XF
1655	1638-56	1,100	1,750	2,500	3,500	—

KM# 430 YEFIMOK

Silver **Ruler:** Aleksei **Series:** Polish Thaler **Countermark:** Czar horseback right in dotted circle, date in rectangle **Note:** Countermark on Thorn Thaler, Dav. #4374.

CM Date	Host Date	Good	VG	F	VF	XF
1655	1633-38	3,000	5,000	6,500	9,500	—

KM# 435 YEFIMOK

Silver **Ruler:** Aleksei **Series:** Spanish Netherlands Patagon **Countermark:** Czar horseback right in dotted circle, date in rectangle **Note:** Countermark on Tournai Patagon, Dav. #4470.

CM Date	Host Date	Good	VG	F	VF	XF
1655	1621-26, 28-37, 41, 43-65	150	250	400	650	—

KM# 439 YEFIMOK

Silver **Series:** United Netherlands Lion and Rijksdaalder **Countermark:** Czar on horseback in circle, date in rectangle **Note:** Countermark on Utrecht Rijksdaalder, KM#40; Dav. #4838.

CM Date	Host Date	Good	VG	F	VF	XF
1655	1650-51	650	1,000	1,500	2,250	—

KM# 422 YEFIMOK

Silver **Ruler:** Aleksei **Series:** United Netherlands Lion and Rijksdaalder **Countermark:** Czar horseback right in dotted circle, date in rectangle **Note:** Countermark on West Friesland Rijksdaalder, Dav. #4829.

CM Date	Host Date	Good	VG	F	VF	XF
1655	1606-53	650	1,000	1,500	2,250	—

KM# 427 YEFIMOK
Silver **Ruler:** Aleksei **Series:** United Netherlands Lion and Rijksdaalder **Countermark:** Czar horseback right in dotted circle, date in rectangle **Note:** Countermark on Zeeland Rijksdaalder, Dav. #4844.

CM Date	Host Date	Good	VG	F	VF	XF
1655	1606-53	750	1,250	1,750	2,500	—

KM# 428 YEFIMOK
Silver **Ruler:** Michael I **Series:** Netherlands Free City Rijksdaalder **Countermark:** Czar horseback right in dotted circle, date in rectangle **Note:** Countermark on Zwolle Rijksdaalder, Dav. #4992.

CM Date	Host Date	Good	VG	F	VF	XF
1655	1636-53	1,350	2,250	3,250	4,750	—

KM# 406 JEFIMOK
Silver **Ruler:** Aleksei **Series:** Germanic Thaler **Countermark:** Czar horseback right in dotted circle, date in rectangle **Note:** Countermark on Nürnberg Thaler; Dav. #5654.

CM Date	Host Date	Good	VG	F	VF	XF
1655	1635-37	3,000	5,000	6,500	9,000	—

KM# 408 JEFIMOK
Silver **Ruler:** Aleksei **Series:** Germanic Thaler **Countermark:** Czar horseback right in dotted circle, date in rectangle **Note:** Countermark on Strasburg Thaler; Dav. #5842.

CM Date	Host Date	Good	VG	F	VF	XF
1655	ND(1617)	2,000	3,250	4,500	6,500	—

NOVODELS

KM#	Date	Mintage	Identification	Mkt Val

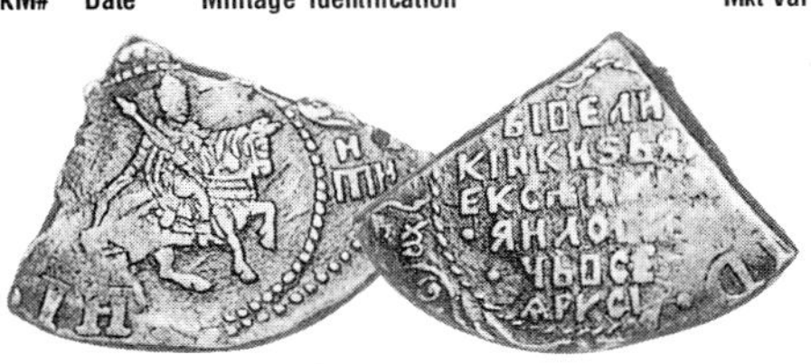

KM#	Date	Mintage	Identification	Mkt Val
N-AA1	1654	—	Poltina.	—
N-AA2	ND(1654)	—	Rouble.	—
N-A1	ND(1685)	—	3 Kopeks. Silver.	—
N-A2	ND(1697)	—	3 Kopeks. Silver.	—
N-A3	ND(1698)	—	3 Kopeks. Silver.	—
N-A4	ND(1699)	—	3 Kopeks. Silver.	—
N-A5	ND(1700)	—	Denga. Copper. Portrait.	—
N-A6	ND(1700)	—	Denga. Copper. Eagle.	—

PATTERNS

Including off metal strikes

KM#	Date	Mintage	Identification	Mkt Val
PnA1	1699	—	1/2 Rouble. Silver.	—

SCOTLAND

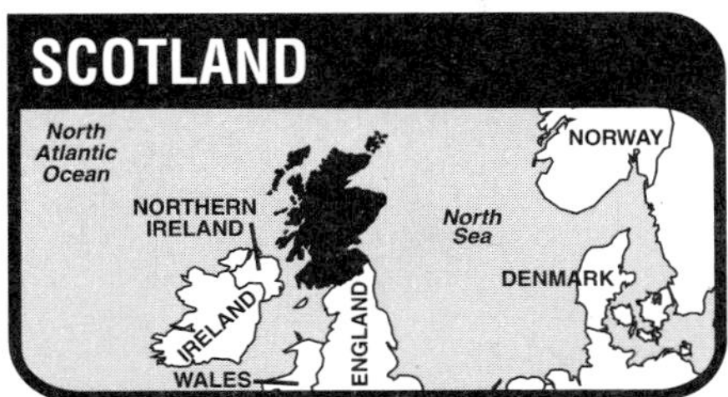

Scotland is located on the northern part of the island of Great Britain. It has an area of 30,414 square miles (78,772 sq. km.

Scotland was the traditional home of the Picts in ancient times. The Romans invaded the area after 80 A.D. and Hadrian's Wall was built from 122-126 A.D. to keep the Picts from the Roman settlements to the south. In the 5th century Scotland had 4 kingdoms: Northumbria (Anglo-Saxon), Picts, Scots (of Irish extraction) and Strathclyde. St. Columba converted the Picts to Christianity in the late 6th century. Norse invasions started in the late 8th century. The Picts conquered the Scots in the 9th century and under Malcolm II (1005-1034) the Scottish kingdoms were united. The Scottish King became a vassal of the English king in 1174 (a circumstance that was to lead to many disputes). The Scots gained independence in 1314 at Bannockburn under Robert Bruce. From 1371-1714 it was ruled by the Stuarts, and in 1603 when James VI of Scotland succeeded Elizabeth I as James I, King of England, a personal union of the two kingdoms was formed. Parliamentary Act in 1707 made final union of the two kingdoms.

RULERS
James IV, 1488-1513
James V, 1513-1542
Mary, 1542-1567
Mary and Henry Darnley, 1565-1567
James VI (I), 1567-1625
Charles I, 1625-1649
Charles II, 1649-1685
James VII (II), 1685-1689
William and Mary, 1689-1694
William II (III), 1694-1702

MINTS
Edinburgh
Holyrood
Stirling

MINT OFFICIALS' INITIALS

Initial	Date	Name
A		Acheson, mintmaster
IG	1553	Jacobus Gubernator, Earl of Arran, Regent

KINGDOM

HAMMERED COINAGE

KM# 22 1/2 CROWN
1.1250 g., 0.9170 Gold 0.0332 oz. AGW **Ruler:** James VI (I) **Obv:** Crowned bust right **Rev:** Crowned arms, Scottish arms in 1st and 4th quarters **Note:** S#5470.

Date	Mintage	Good	VG	F	VF	XF
ND(1609-29)	—	185	350	750	1,650	2,750

KM# 21 1/2 CROWN
1.1250 g., 0.9170 Gold 0.0332 oz. AGW **Ruler:** James VI (I) **Obv:** Crowned bust of King James VI right **Rev:** Crowned arms, English arms in 1st and 4th quarters **Note:** S#5469.

Date	Mintage	Good	VG	F	VF	XF
ND(1604-09)	—	325	600	1,150	2,250	3,500

KM# 48 BRITAIN 1/2 CROWN
1.1250 g., 0.9170 Gold 0.0332 oz. AGW **Ruler:** Charles I **Obv:** Crowned head of Charles left **Rev:** Crowned arms, B above crown **Note:** S#5538.

Date	Mintage	Good	VG	F	VF	XF
ND(1637-42)	—	185	350	775	1,850	3,000

KM# 49 BRITAIN 1/2 CROWN
1.1250 g., 0.9170 Gold 0.0332 oz. AGW **Ruler:** Charles I **Obv:** B below crowned head **Rev:** Crowned arms **Note:** S#5539.

Date	Mintage	Good	VG	F	VF	XF
ND(1637-42)	—	200	375	800	2,000	3,200

KM# 23 BRITAIN CROWN
2.2500 g., 0.9170 Gold 0.0663 oz. AGW **Ruler:** James VI (I) **Obv:** Crowned bust of James VI right **Rev:** Crowned arms, English arms in 1st and 4th quarters **Note:** S#5467.

Date	Mintage	Good	VG	F	VF	XF
ND(1604-09)	—	425	850	1,750	3,500	6,500

KM# 24 BRITAIN CROWN
2.2500 g., 0.9170 Gold 0.0663 oz. AGW **Ruler:** James VI (I) **Obv:** Crowned bust of King James VI **Rev:** Crowned arms, Scottish arms in 1st and 4th quarters **Note:** S#5470.

Date	Mintage	Good	VG	F	VF	XF
ND(1609-25)	—	175	325	650	1,250	2,250

KM# 50 BRITAIN CROWN
2.2500 g., 0.9170 Gold 0.0663 oz. AGW **Ruler:** Charles I **Obv:** Crowned bust of Charles right **Rev:** Crowned arms **Note:** S#5529.

Date	Mintage	Good	VG	F	VF	XF
ND(1625-36)	—	1,250	2,250	4,500	8,500	—

KM# 51 BRITAIN CROWN
2.2500 g., 0.9170 Gold 0.0663 oz. AGW **Ruler:** Charles I **Obv:** Crowned bust of King Charles left, B at end of legend **Rev:** Crowned arms **Note:** S#5536.

Date	Mintage	Good	VG	F	VF	XF
ND(1637-40)	—	650	1,250	2,500	4,750	9,000

KM# 52 BRITAIN CROWN
2.2500 g., 0.9170 Gold 0.0663 oz. AGW **Ruler:** Charles I **Obv:** Crowned bust left, B at beginning of legend **Rev:** Crowned arms **Note:** S#5537.

Date	Mintage	Good	VG	F	VF	XF
ND(1637-42)	—	700	1,350	2,650	5,000	9,500

KM# 26 DOUBLE CROWN
4.5000 g., 0.9170 Gold 0.1327 oz. AGW **Ruler:** James VI (I) **Obv:** Crowned bust of James VI right **Rev:** Crowned arms, English arms in 1st and 4th quarters **Note:** S#5465.

Date	Mintage	Good	VG	F	VF	XF
ND(1604-09)	—	750	1,250	2,500	4,500	7,500

KM# 27.1 DOUBLE CROWN
4.5000 g., 0.9170 Gold 0.1327 oz. AGW **Ruler:** James VI (I) **Obv:** Crowned bust of King James VI right **Obv. Legend:** IA. D. G... **Rev:** Crowned arms, Scottish arms in 1st and 4th quarters **Note:** S#5466.

Date	Mintage	Good	VG	F	VF	XF
ND(1609-25)	—	450	850	1,750	3,500	6,000

KM# 27.2 DOUBLE CROWN
4.5000 g., 0.9170 Gold 0.1327 oz. AGW **Ruler:** James VI (I) **Obv:** Crowned bust right **Obv. Legend:** IACOBVS. D. G... **Rev:** Crowned arms, Scottish arms in 1st and 4th quarters **Note:** S#5466v.

Date	Mintage	Good	VG	F	VF	XF
ND(1609-25)	—	500	950	1,850	3,750	6,500

KM# 53 DOUBLE CROWN
Gold, 20 mm. **Ruler:** Charles I **Obv:** Crowned bust of Charles I right **Rev:** Crowned arms **Note:** Britain Crown. S#5529.

Date	Mintage	Good	VG	F	VF	XF
ND(1625-36)	—	3,500	6,500	10,000	—	—

KM# 25 THISTLE CROWN
2.2500 g., 0.9170 Gold 0.0663 oz. AGW **Ruler:** James VI (I) **Obv:** Crowned rose **Rev:** Crowned thistle **Note:** S#5471.

Date	Mintage	Good	VG	F	VF	XF
ND(1604-25)	—	150	320	650	1,350	2,500

KM# 17 1/2 RIDER (50 Shillings)
2.0450 g., 0.9170 Gold 0.0603 oz. AGW **Ruler:** James VI (I) **Obv:** King in armor with raised sword, right on horseback **Obv. Legend:** IACOBVS • 6 • D • G • R... **Rev:** Crowned shield **Rev. Legend:** SPERO • MELIORA **Note:** Seventh Coinage. S#5459.

Date	Mintage	Good	VG	F	VF	XF
1601	—	250	500	1,000	2,000	—

KM# 19 1/2 SWORD & SCEPTRE
2.0450 g., 0.9170 Gold 0.0603 oz. AGW **Ruler:** James VI (I) **Obv:** Crowned arms **Rev:** Crown over crossed sword and sceptre **Note:** S#5462.

Date	Mintage	Good	VG	F	VF	XF
1601	—	100	200	400	800	1,800
1602	—	125	225	450	900	2,000
1603	—	350	700	1,500	3,000	4,500
1604	—	150	300	600	1,200	2,250

KM# 18 RIDER (100 Shillings)
5.0900 g., 0.9170 Gold 0.1501 oz. AGW **Ruler:** James VI (I) **Obv:** King in armor with raised sword, right on horseback **Obv. Legend:** IACOBVS•6•D•G•R... **Rev:** Crowned shield **Rev. Legend:** SPERO•MELIORA **Note:** Seventh Coinage; Similar to 1/2 Rider, KM#17; S#5458.

Date	Mintage	Good	VG	F	VF	XF
1601	—	350	675	1,350	3,500	—

KM# 20 SWORD AND SCEPTRE
5.0900 g., 0.9170 Gold 0.1501 oz. AGW **Ruler:** James VI (I) **Obv:** Crossed arms **Note:** S#5460.

Date	Mintage	Good	VG	F	VF	XF
1601	—	145	285	575	1,200	2,200
1602	—	145	285	575	1,150	2,100
1603	—	250	400	800	1,600	3,500
1604	—	250	400	850	1,650	3,600

KM# 54 1/2 UNIT
Gold **Ruler:** Charles I **Obv:** Crowned bust of Charles I left, B below bust **Rev:** Crowned arms **Note:** Briot Coinage. S#5534.

Date	Mintage	Good	VG	F	VF	XF
ND(1637-42)	—	450	900	1,800	3,650	5,750

KM# 55 1/2 UNIT
Gold **Ruler:** Charles I **Obv:** Crowned bust of Charles I left, F at end of legend **Rev:** Crowned arms **Note:** Falconer Coinage. S#5535.

Date	Mintage	Good	VG	F	VF	XF
ND(1637-42)	—	2,000	3,500	6,500	10,000	—

KM# 28 UNIT
9.0000 g., 0.9170 Gold 0.2653 oz. AGW **Ruler:** James VI (I) **Obv:** Crowned 1/2 length figure of James VI right with scepter and orb in inner circle **Rev:** Crowned arms, English arms in 1st and 4th quarters **Note:** S#5463.

Date	Mintage	Good	VG	F	VF	XF
ND(1604-09)	—	275	500	925	1,800	3,600

KM# 29 UNIT
9.0000 g., 0.9170 Gold 0.2653 oz. AGW **Ruler:** James VI (I) **Obv:** Crowned 1/2-length figure of James VI right with sceptre and orb in inner circle **Rev:** Cowned arms, Scottish arms in 1st and 4th quarters **Note:** S#5464.

Date	Mintage	Good	VG	F	VF	XF
ND(1609-25)	—	220	350	775	1,550	3,150

KM# 56 UNIT
9.0000 g., 0.9170 Gold 0.2653 oz. AGW **Ruler:** Charles I **Obv:** Crowned 1/2-length figure of Charles I right with sceptre and orb in inner circle **Rev:** Crowned arms **Note:** S#5527.

Date	Mintage	Good	VG	F	VF	XF
ND(1625-49)	—	500	900	1,750	3,150	6,300

KM# 57 UNIT
9.0000 g., 0.9170 Gold 0.2653 oz. AGW **Ruler:** Charles I **Obv:** Fine style crowned 1/2-length figure of Charles right with sceptre and orb, thistle and B after legend **Note:** Briot Coinage. S#5531.

Date	Mintage	Good	VG	F	VF	XF
ND(1637-42)	—	425	775	1,600	2,800	5,600

KM# 58 UNIT
9.0000 g., 0.9170 Gold 0.2653 oz. AGW **Ruler:** Charles I **Obv:** Crowned 1/2-length figure of Charles I right with sceptre and orb, B at beginning of legend and thistle at end **Rev:** Crowned arms **Note:** S#5532.

Date	Mintage	Good	VG	F	VF	XF
ND(1637-42)	—	1,450	2,400	4,000	6,800	—

KM# 59 UNIT
9.0000 g., 0.9170 Gold 0.2653 oz. AGW **Ruler:** Charles I **Obv:** Crowned 1/2-length figure of Charles I right with sceptre and orb, thistle and F after legend **Rev:** Crowned arms **Note:** S#5533.

Date	Mintage	Good	VG	F	VF	XF
ND(1637-42)	—	2,200	4,150	7,700	12,500	—

STERLING COINAGE

KM# 36 PENNY
Copper **Obv:** Three thistles in inner circle **Obv. Legend:** IACOBV5. DEI... **Rev:** Crowned rampant lion left, pellet behind, in inner circle **Rev. Legend:** FRANCIE ET HIBERNIE REX

Date	Mintage	VG	F	VF	XF	Unc
ND(1614)	—	35.00	65.00	250	—	—

KM# 40 PENNY
Copper **Rev. Legend:** FRAN & HIB REX

Date	Mintage	VG	F	VF	XF	Unc
ND(1623)	—	40.00	75.00	275	—	—

KM# 60 PENNY
Copper, 13.5 mm. **Obv:** Three thistles in inner circle **Obv. Legend:** CAROLVS... **Rev:** Crowned rampant lion left, pellet behind, in inner circle

Date	Mintage	VG	F	VF	XF	Unc
ND(1629)	—	60.00	150	375	—	—

KM# 37 2 PENCE

Copper, 18 mm. **Obv:** Three thistles in inner circle **Obv. Legend:** JACOBVS... **Rev:** Crowned rampant lion left, two pellets behind, in inner circle **Rev. Legend:** FRANCIE ET HIBERNIE REX

Date	Mintage	VG	F	VF	XF	Unc
ND(1614)	—	20.00	40.00	100	—	—

KM# 41 2 PENCE

Copper **Rev. Legend:** FRAN & HIB REX

Date	Mintage	VG	F	VF	XF	Unc
ND(1623)	—	20.00	35.00	85.00	—	—

KM# 61 2 PENCE

Copper **Obv:** Three thistles in inner circle **Obv. Legend:** CAROLVS... **Rev:** Crowned rampant lion left, two pellets behind, in inner circle

Date	Mintage	VG	F	VF	XF	Unc
ND(1629)	—	20.00	40.00	90.00	—	—

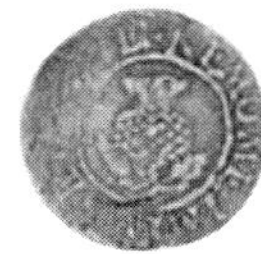

KM# 65 2 PENCE

Copper **Obv:** "English" crown above C. II. R in inner circle **Rev:** Thistle in inner circle

Date	Mintage	VG	F	VF	XF	Unc
ND(1632-39)	—	20.00	35.00	65.00	—	—

KM# 66 2 PENCE

Copper **Obv:** Scottish crown (jeweled band and arches)

Date	Mintage	VG	F	VF	XF	Unc
ND(1632-39)	—	20.00	40.00	90.00	—	—

KM# 67 2 PENCE

Copper **Obv:** Scottish crown (plain band and arches)

Date	Mintage	VG	F	VF	XF	Unc
ND(1632-39)	—	20.00	40.00	90.00	—	—

KM# 68 2 PENCE

Copper **Obv:** Crown with five crosses

Date	Mintage	VG	F	VF	XF	Unc
ND(1632-39)	—	20.00	40.00	90.00	—	—

KM# 69 2 PENCE

Copper **Obv:** Crowned C.R in inner circle **Note:** Varieties exist.

Date	Mintage	VG	F	VF	XF	Unc
ND(1642-50)	—	20.00	40.00	90.00	—	—

KM# 100 2 PENCE

Copper **Obv:** Crowned C.R with II at right in inner circle

Date	Mintage	VG	F	VF	XF	Unc
ND(1663)	—	25.00	45.00	100	200	—

KM# 114 2 PENCE

Copper **Obv:** Crown above crossed sword and scepter **Rev:** Thistle in inner circle, date at top in legend **Note:** Various misspellings occur.

Date	Mintage	VG	F	VF	XF	Unc
1677	—	75.00	135	325	—	—
1678	—	75.00	135	325	—	—
1679	—	75.00	135	325	—	—

KM# 130 2 PENCE

Copper **Obv:** Crowned script W M monogram **Rev:** Crowned thistle, date in legend at upper left

Date	Mintage	VG	F	VF	XF	Unc
1691	—	25.00	45.00	110	350	—
1692	—	25.00	45.00	110	350	—
1693	—	25.00	45.00	110	350	—
1694	—	25.00	45.00	110	350	—

KM# 137 2 PENCE

Copper **Obv:** Crown above sword and secpter, crossed at flat angle **Rev:** Crowned large thistle

Date	Mintage	VG	F	VF	XF	Unc
1695	—	30.00	50.00	185	450	—
1696	—	30.00	50.00	185	450	—

KM# 138 2 PENCE

Copper **Obv:** Sword and scepter crossed at right angles **Rev:** Crowned small thistle

Date	Mintage	VG	F	VF	XF	Unc
1695	—	30.00	50.00	185	450	—
1696	—	30.00	50.00	185	450	—
1697	—	30.00	50.00	185	450	—

KM# 115 6 PENCE

Copper, 25 mm. **Obv:** Laureate bust of Charles II left **Rev:** Crowned thistle, date in legend at upper left **Note:** Varieties exist.

Date	Mintage	VG	F	VF	XF	Unc
1677	—	40.00	60.00	275	650	—
1678	—	40.00	60.00	220	550	—
1679	—	40.00	60.00	185	450	—

KM# 131 6 PENCE

Copper **Obv:** Conjoined laureate busts of William and Mary left **Note:** Varieties exist.

Date	Mintage	VG	F	VF	XF	Unc
1691	—	45.00	65.00	220	550	—
1692	—	45.00	65.00	275	650	—
1693	—	45.00	65.00	220	550	—
1694	—	45.00	65.00	220	550	—

KM# 139 6 PENCE

Copper **Obv:** Laureate bust of William III left **Note:** Varieties exist.

Date	Mintage	VG	F	VF	XF	Unc
1695	—	60.00	120	500	1,250	—
1696	—	60.00	120	500	1,250	—
1697	—	70.00	150	650	1,500	—

KM# 5 SHILLING

Silver **Obv:** Displayed rose in inner circle **Obv. Legend:** I. D. G... **Rev:** Thistle in inner circle **Note:** Mint mark: Thistle.

Date	Mintage	VG	F	VF	XF	Unc
ND(1605)	—	50.00	90.00	250	—	—

KM# 42 SHILLING

Silver **Obv:** C above I in legend **Note:** First Coinage (1625-1634).

Date	Mintage	VG	F	VF	XF	Unc
ND(1625)	—	150	250	450	—	—

KM# 70 20 PENCE

Silver **Obv:** Crowned bust of Charles I left with value behind head, in inner circle **Rev:** Crowned thistle in inner circle **Note:** Second Coinage (Briot's hammered 1636).

Date	Mintage	VG	F	VF	XF	Unc
ND(1636)	—	35.00	100	275	—	—

KM# 73 20 PENCE

Silver **Obv:** Bust to edge of coin **Note:** Third Coinage, 1637-1642. Briot's issue.

Date	Mintage	VG	F	VF	XF	Unc
ND(1637)	—	25.00	40.00	90.00	—	—

KM# 74 20 PENCE

Silver **Obv:** Bust breaks inner circle **Note:** Third Coinage, 1637-1642. Falconer's Second issue.

Date	Mintage	VG	F	VF	XF	Unc
ND(1637)	—	25.00	50.00	100	—	—

KM# 75 20 PENCE

Silver **Obv:** Bust within inner circle

Date	Mintage	VG	F	VF	XF	Unc
ND(1637)	—	30.00	60.00	120	—	—

KM# 3 30 PENCE

1.5000 g., 0.9160 Silver 0.0442 oz. ASW, 17 mm. **Obv:** Armored bust right **Obv. Legend:** IACOBVS • 6 • D • G • R... **Rev:** Crown over triple-headed thistle **Rev. Legend:** NEMO ME IMPUNE LACESSET **Note:** Seventh Coinage, 1593-1601

Date	Mintage	VG	F	VF	XF	Unc
1601	—	250	650	1,150	—	—

KM# 6 2 SHILLINGS

Silver, 17 mm. **Obv:** Crowned displayed rose **Obv. Legend:** I.D.G. ROSA SINE SPINA **Rev:** Crowned thistle **Rev. Legend:** TVEATVR **Note:** Mint mark: Thistle.

Date	Mintage	VG	F	VF	XF	Unc
ND(1605)	—	35.00	65.00	150	—	—

KM# 43 2 SHILLINGS

Silver **Obv. Legend:** C.D.G...

Date	Mintage	VG	F	VF	XF	Unc
ND(1625)	—	55.00	100	250	—	—

KM# 95 2 SHILLINGS

Silver **Obv:** Crowned bust of Charles I left with value behind head in inner circle **Rev:** Crowned arms in inner circle

Date	Mintage	VG	F	VF	XF	Unc
ND(1642)	—	30.00	65.00	165	—	—

KM# 96 3 SHILLING

Silver **Obv:** Crowned bust of Charles I left iwth thistle behind head in inner circle **Rev:** Crowned arms in inner circle **Note:** Fourth Coinage.

Date	Mintage	VG	F	VF	XF	Unc
ND(1642)	—	35.00	85.00	325	—	—

KM# 71 40 PENCE

Silver, 20 mm. **Obv:** Crowned bust of Charles I left iwth thistle behind head in inner circle **Rev:** Crowned thistle in inner circle **Note:** Second Coinage (Briot's hammered issue 1636).

Date	Mintage	VG	F	VF	XF	Unc
ND(1636)	—	35.00	70.00	175	—	—

KM# 76 40 PENCE

Silver **Rev:** B above crown **Note:** Third Coinage 1637-1642. Briot's issue.

Date	Mintage	VG	F	VF	XF	Unc
ND(1637)	—	40.00	90.00	225	—	—

KM# 77 40 PENCE

Silver **Rev:** F above crown **Note:** Falconer's First Issue. Varieties exist.

Date	Mintage	VG	F	VF	XF	Unc
ND(1637)	—	25.00	60.00	150	—	—

KM# 4 5 SHILLINGS

2.9900 g., 0.9160 Silver 0.0881 oz. ASW, 25 mm. **Obv:** Armored bust right **Obv. Legend:** IA COBVS • 6 • D • G • R... **Rev:** Crown over triple-headed thistle **Rev. Legend:** NEMO ME IM PUNE LACESSET **Note:** Seventh Coinage, 1596-1601.

Date	Mintage	VG	F	VF	XF	Unc
1601	—	700	1,500	2,500	—	—

KM# 132 5 SHILLINGS

2.9900 g., 0.9160 Silver 0.0881 oz. ASW, 19 mm. **Obv:** Conjoined laureate busts of William and Mary left **Rev:** Crowned script W M monogram with value below

Date	Mintage	VG	F	VF	XF	Unc
1691	—	60.00	200	650	1,350	—

KM# 136 5 SHILLINGS

2.9900 g., 0.9160 Silver 0.0881 oz. ASW **Obv:** Value below busts

Date	Mintage	VG	F	VF	XF	Unc
1694	—	40.00	120	375	900	—

KM# 140 5 SHILLINGS

Silver, 19 mm. **Ruler:** William II (III) **Obv:** Laureate bust left, value below **Rev:** Crown above 3 thistles, date in legend at upper left **Note:** Varieties exist.

Date	Mintage	VG	F	VF	XF	Unc
1695	—	40.00	100	325	—	—
1696	—	36.00	70.00	160	—	—
1697	—	40.00	100	325	—	—
1699	—	60.00	160	500	—	—
1700	—	50.00	120	400	—	—

KM# 30 6 SHILLING

Silver **Obv:** Crowned bust of James I right, with value behind head, in inner circle **Rev:** Shield with arms of England in 1st and 4th quarters, date above in inner circle

Date	Mintage	VG	F	VF	XF	Unc
1605	—	400	800	1,800	—	—
1606	—	350	700	1,600	—	—
1609/7	—	350	700	1,600	—	—

KM# 35 6 SHILLING

Silver **Rev:** Arms of Scotland in 1st and 4th quarters

Date	Mintage	VG	F	VF	XF	Unc
1610	—	300	600	1,250	—	—
1611	—	300	600	1,250	—	—
1612	—	300	600	1,250	—	—
1613	—	300	600	1,250	—	—
1614	—	300	600	1,250	—	—
1615	—	300	600	1,250	—	—
1616	—	325	650	1,500	—	—
1617	—	325	650	1,500	—	—
1618	—	325	650	1,500	—	—
1619	—	250	500	1,200	—	—
1622	—	250	500	1,200	—	—

KM# 44 6 SHILLING

Silver **Obv:** Crowned bust of Charles I right, value behind head, in inner circle **Rev:** Shield of arms with date above in inner circle **Note:** First Coinage (1625-1634).

Date	Mintage	VG	F	VF	XF	Unc
1625	—	200	525	1,500	—	—
1626	—	200	525	1,500	—	—
1627	—	200	525	1,500	—	—
1628	—	200	525	1,500	—	—
1630	—	200	525	1,500	—	—
1631	—	200	525	1,500	—	—
1632	—	200	525	1,500	—	—
1633	—	200	525	1,500	—	—
1634	—	200	525	1,500	—	—

KM# 78 6 SHILLING

Silver **Obv:** Crowned bust of Charles I left, value behind head, in inner circle, bust to edge of coin **Rev:** Crowned arms divide C-R in inner circle **Note:** Third Coinage (1637-1642) Briot's issue.

Date	Mintage	VG	F	VF	XF	Unc
ND(1637-42)	—	40.00	95.00	325	—	—

KM# 81 6 SHILLING

Silver **Obv:** New narrow bust of Charles I **Note:** Falconer's Anonymous Issue (without F).

Date	Mintage	VG	F	VF	XF	Unc
ND(1637-42)	—	40.00	95.00	325	—	—

KM# 79 6 SHILLING
Silver **Rev:** F above crown **Note:** Falconer's First Issue.

Date	Mintage	VG	F	VF	XF	Unc
ND(1637-42)	—	40.00	95.00	325	—	—

KM# 80 6 SHILLING
Silver **Obv:** Bust within inner circle **Note:** Falconer's Second Issue.

Date	Mintage	VG	F	VF	XF	Unc
ND(1637-42)	—	40.00	95.00	325	—	—

KM# A5 10 SHILLINGS
5.9800 g., 0.9160 Silver 0.1761 oz. ASW, 25 mm. **Obv:** Armored bust right **Obv. Legend:** IACOBVS • 6 • D • G • R... **Rev:** Crown over triple-headed thistle **Rev. Legend:** NEMO ME IMPUNE LACESSET **Note:** Seventh Coinage, 1593-1601.

Date	Mintage	VG	F	VF	XF	Unc
1601	—	400	1,000	2,250	—	—

KM# 121 10 SHILLINGS
5.9800 g., 0.9160 Silver 0.1761 oz. ASW **Obv:** Laureate bust of James VII right, value below bust **Rev:** Cruciform arms divided by St. Andrew's cross, date divided at top

Date	Mintage	VG	F	VF	XF	Unc
1687	—	48.00	120	550	—	—
1688	—	65.00	220	875	—	—

KM# 124 10 SHILLINGS
5.9800 g., 0.9160 Silver 0.1761 oz. ASW **Obv:** Conjoined laureate busts of William and Mary left, value below busts **Rev:** English crown on small shield, date in legend at upper left

Date	Mintage	VG	F	VF	XF	Unc
1689	—	160	475	—	—	—
1690	—	95.00	215	550	—	—

KM# 133 10 SHILLINGS
5.9800 g., 0.9160 Silver 0.1761 oz. ASW **Rev:** Scottish crown on large shield **Note:** Varieties exist.

Date	Mintage	VG	F	VF	XF	Unc
1691	—	85.00	200	450	—	—
1692	—	100	295	650	—	—
1694	—	90.00	265	875	—	—

KM# 141 10 SHILLINGS
5.9800 g., 0.9160 Silver 0.1761 oz. ASW **Obv:** William III, value below bust

Date	Mintage	VG	F	VF	XF	Unc
1695	—	43.75	115	375	—	—
1696	—	43.75	115	375	—	—
1697	—	43.75	115	375	—	—
1698	—	43.75	115	375	—	—
1699	—	65.00	190	625	—	—

KM# 7 12 SHILLING
Silver, 31 mm. **Obv:** Bust of James VI right, value behind head, in inner circle **Rev:** Shield of arms with English arms in 1st and 4th quarters, in inner circle

Date	Mintage	VG	F	VF	XF	Unc
ND(1603)	—	105	270	600	—	—

KM# 8 12 SHILLING
Silver **Rev:** Scottish arms in 1st and 4th quarters

Date	Mintage	VG	F	VF	XF	Unc
ND(1603)	—	105	270	600	—	—

KM# 45 12 SHILLING
Silver, 31 mm. **Obv:** Crowned bust of Charles I right, value behind head, in inner circle **Rev:** Shield of arms in inner circle **Note:** First Coinage 1625-1634

Date	Mintage	VG	F	VF	XF	Unc
ND(1625-34)	—	75.00	180	525	—	—

KM# 86 12 SHILLING
Silver **Obv:** Bust completely within inner circle

Date	Mintage	VG	F	VF	XF	Unc
ND(1637-42)	—	35.00	125	375	—	—

KM# 84 12 SHILLING
Silver **Rev:** F above crown **Note:** Falconer's First Issue.

Date	Mintage	VG	F	VF	XF	Unc
ND(1637-42)	—	35.00	125	375	—	—

KM# 85 12 SHILLING
Silver **Obv:** Bust breaks bottom of inner circle, F after legend **Note:** Falconer's Second Issue.

Date	Mintage	VG	F	VF	XF	Unc
ND(1637-42)	—	35.00	125	375	—	—

KM# 83 12 SHILLING
Silver **Rev:** Thistle above crown **Note:** Intermediate issue.

Date	Mintage	VG	F	VF	XF	Unc
ND(1637-42)	—	35.00	125	375	—	—

KM# 82 12 SHILLING
Silver **Obv:** Charles I, B before and after **Note:** Third Coinage 1637-1642, Briot's issue.

Date	Mintage	VG	F	VF	XF	Unc
ND(1637-42)	—	35.00	125	375	—	—

KM# 13 1/8 MERK
0.0850 g., 0.9160 Silver 0.0025 oz. ASW, 15 mm. **Obv:** Crowned shield **Rev:** Crowned thistle

Date	Mintage	VG	F	VF	XF	Unc
1601	—	30.00	85.00	250	—	—
1602	—	28.00	65.00	200	—	—
1603	—	75.00	185	—	—	—

KM# 14 1/4 MERK
1.7000 g., 0.9160 Silver 0.0501 oz. ASW, 20 mm. **Obv:** Crowned shield **Rev:** Crowned thistle

Date	Mintage	VG	F	VF	XF	Unc
1601	—	25.00	70.00	250	—	—
1602	—	25.00	60.00	200	—	—
1603	—	35.00	175	450	—	—
1604	—	45.00	350	500	—	—

KM# 116 1/4 MERK
1.7000 g., 0.9160 Silver 0.0501 oz. ASW **Obv:** Laureate bust of Charles II left **Rev:** Crown on St. Andrew's cross with national emblems in angles, date in legend at upper left

Date	Mintage	VG	F	VF	XF	Unc
1677	—	50.00	180	350	—	—
1678/7	—	60.00	140	375	—	—
1679/7 Rare	—	—	—	—	—	—
1680	—	150	350	900	—	—
1680	—	175	400	1,000	—	—
1681	—	70.00	175	450	—	—

KM# 15 1/2 MERK
3.4000 g., 0.9160 Silver 0.1001 oz. ASW, 28 mm. **Obv:** Crowned shield **Rev:** Crowned thistle

Date	Mintage	VG	F	VF	XF	Unc
1601	—	30.00	75.00	250	—	—
1602	—	30.00	75.00	250	—	—
1603	—	40.00	110	275	—	—
1604	—	50.00	225	550	—	—

KM# 72 1/2 MERK
3.4000 g., 0.9160 Silver 0.1001 oz. ASW **Obv:** Crowned bust of Charles I left, value VI behind head, in inner circle **Rev:** Crowned arms in inner circle **Note:** Second Coinage (1636) Briot's Hammered Issue.

Date	Mintage	VG	F	VF	XF	Unc
ND(1636)	—	35.00	90.00	325	—	—

KM# 93 1/2 MERK
3.4000 g., 0.9160 Silver 0.1001 oz. ASW **Rev:** Crowned arms divide C-R in inner circle, B after legend **Note:** Third Coinage (1637-42) Briot's Issue.

Date	Mintage	VG	F	VF	XF	Unc
ND(1637-42)	—	40.00	105	245	—	—

KM# 101 1/2 MERK
3.4000 g., 0.9160 Silver 0.1001 oz. ASW **Obv:** Laureate bust of Charles II right **Rev:** Cruciform arms with value at center, crowned linked C's in angles, date in legend at upper right **Note:** Varieties exist.

Date	Mintage	VG	F	VF	XF	Unc
1664	—	130	275	—	—	—
1664 Rare	—	—	—	—	—	—
Note: Stamped 1665						
1665	—	130	275	—	—	—
1666	—	155	325	—	—	—
1667	—	130	275	—	—	—
1668	—	110	220	450	—	—
1669	—	90.00	175	400	—	—
1670	—	90.00	175	400	—	—
1671	—	90.00	175	400	—	—
1672	—	100	200	425	—	—
1673	—	100	200	425	—	—
1675	—	110	220	450	—	—

KM# 105 1/2 MERK
3.4000 g., 0.9160 Silver 0.1001 oz. ASW **Rev:** Arms of England and Ireland transposed **Note:** Error.

Date	Mintage	VG	F	VF	XF	Unc
1665	—	150	375	1,100	—	—
1666 Rare	—	275	650	—	—	—

KM# 112 1/2 MERK
3.4000 g., 0.9160 Silver 0.1001 oz. ASW **Obv:** Charles II **Note:** Second Coinage.

Date	Mintage	VG	F	VF	XF	Unc
1676	—	40.50	135	375	—	—
1677	—	48.00	160	400	—	—
1678/7 Rare	—	—	—	—	—	—
1679	—	175	450	1,200	—	—
1680	—	48.00	160	400	—	—
1682	—	175	450	1,200	—	—

KM# 120 1/2 MERK
3.4000 g., 0.9160 Silver 0.1001 oz. ASW **Rev:** Arms of Scotland and France transposed **Note:** Error.

Date	Mintage	VG	F	VF	XF	Unc
1680	—	275	675	1,750	—	—

KM# 16 MERK

6.7900 g., 0.9160 Silver 0.2000 oz. ASW, 32 mm. **Obv:** Crowned shield **Rev:** Crowned thistle

Date	Mintage	VG	F	VF	XF	Unc
1601	—	35.00	130	375	—	—
1602	—	35.00	130	375	—	—
1603	—	35.00	130	375	—	—
1604	—	50.00	200	500	—	—

KM# 102.1 MERK
6.7900 g., 0.9160 Silver 0.2000 oz. ASW, 25 mm. **Obv:** Charles II, thistle below bust **Note:** First Coinage. Varieties exist.

Date	Mintage	VG	F	VF	XF	Unc
1664	—	80.00	180	375	—	—
1665	—	80.00	225	450	—	—
1666	—	90.00	250	575	—	—
1668	—	80.00	170	375	—	—
1669	—	80.00	170	350	—	—
1670	—	80.00	170	350	—	—
1671	—	80.00	170	350	—	—
1672	—	80.00	170	350	—	—
1673	—	80.00	170	350	—	—
1674	—	90.00	225	575	—	—

KM# 102.2 MERK
6.7900 g., 0.9160 Silver 0.2000 oz. ASW **Obv:** F below bust

Date	Mintage	VG	F	VF	XF	Unc
1674	—	100	275	750	—	—
1675	—	90.00	235	650	—	—

KM# 102.3 MERK
6.7900 g., 0.9160 Silver 0.2000 oz. ASW **Obv:** Plain below bust

Date	Mintage	VG	F	VF	XF	Unc
1675	—	150	375	1,150	—	—

KM# 110.1 MERK
6.7900 g., 0.9160 Silver 0.2000 oz. ASW **Obv:** Laureate bust of Charles II left **Rev:** Cruciform arms with linked C's at center, thistles in angles, date divided at top **Note:** Second Coinage.

Date	Mintage	VG	F	VF	XF	Unc
1675	—	110	300	700	—	—
1676	—	95.00	205	425	—	—
1677/6	—	95.00	235	—	—	—
1677	—	95.00	250	425	—	—
1678	—	95.00	250	550	—	—
1679	—	95.00	205	425	—	—
1680	—	95.00	205	425	—	—
1681	—	95.00	205	425	—	—
1682	—	95.00	220	475	—	—

KM# 110.2 MERK
6.7900 g., 0.9160 Silver 0.2000 oz. ASW **Rev:** Arms of Ireland in 1st shield

Date	Mintage	VG	F	VF	XF	Unc
1682	—	175	450	1,250	—	—

KM# 103.2 2 MERKS
Silver **Obv:** Thistle below bust

Date	Mintage	VG	F	VF	XF	Unc
1664	—	225	550	1,650	—	—
1670	—	150	375	1,150	—	—
1673	—	140	350	1,100	—	—
1674	—	175	450	1,400	—	—

KM# 103.1 2 MERKS
Silver, 33 mm. **Obv:** Laureate bust of Chalres II right, thistle above head **Rev:** Cruciform arms with value at center, crowned linked C's in angles, date in legend at upper left **Note:** First Coinage.

Date	Mintage	VG	F	VF	XF	Unc
1664	—	185	450	1,350	—	—

KM# 103.4 2 MERKS
Silver **Obv:** F below bust

Date	Mintage	VG	F	VF	XF	Unc
1673 Rare	—	—	—	—	—	—
1674	—	200	400	1,200	—	—
1675	—	160	325	1,150	—	—

KM# 111 2 MERKS
Silver **Obv:** Laureate bust of Charles II left **Rev:** Cruciform arms with linked C's at center, thistles in angles, date divided at top **Note:** Second Coinage.

Date	Mintage	VG	F	VF	XF	Unc
1675	—	200	400	1,000	—	—
1676	—	375	750	1,650	—	—
1681	—	205	425	900	—	—

KM# 104.2 4 MERKS
Silver **Obv:** Thistle below bust

Date	Mintage	VG	F	VF	XF	Unc
1664	—	375	1,350	—	—	—
1665 Rare	—	—	—	—	—	—
1670	—	325	800	1,750	—	—
1673	—	325	800	1,750	—	—

KM# 104.1 4 MERKS
Silver, 38 mm. **Obv:** Laureate bust of Charles II right, thistle above head **Rev:** Cruciform arms with value at center, crowned linked C's in angles, date in legend at upper left **Note:** First Coinage.

Date	Mintage	VG	F	VF	XF	Unc
1664	—	650	1,250	2,250	—	—

KM# 104.3 4 MERKS
Silver **Obv:** F below bust

Date	Mintage	VG	F	VF	XF	Unc
1674	—	300	750	1,650	—	—
1675	—	650	1,250	—	—	—

KM# 113 4 MERKS
Silver **Obv:** Charles II **Note:** Second Coinage.

Date	Mintage	VG	F	VF	XF	Unc
1676	—	250	650	1,850	—	—
1679	—	225	550	1,650	—	—
1680	—	350	850	2,750	—	—
1681	—	250	650	1,850	—	—
1682	—	185	450	1,500	—	—

KM# 135 20 SHILLINGS
Silver, 28.5 mm. **Obv:** William and Mary, value below busts

Date	Mintage	VG	F	VF	XF	Unc
1693	—	175	400	1,250	—	—
1694	—	400	800	2,500	—	—

KM# 142 20 SHILLINGS
Silver **Obv:** Laureate bust of William III left, value below bust

Date	Mintage	VG	F	VF	XF	Unc
1695	—	100	350	675	—	—
1696	—	100	350	675	—	—
1697	—	150	550	—	—	—
1698	—	110	325	750	—	—
1699	—	130	325	—	—	—

KM# 9 30 SHILLINGS
Silver, 35 mm. **Obv:** James VI on horseback with sword on shoulder, right in inner circle **Rev:** Shield of arms with English arms in 1st and 4th quarters, in inner circle

Date	Mintage	VG	F	VF	XF	Unc
ND(1603)	—	42.00	160	425	—	—

KM# 10 30 SHILLINGS
Silver **Rev:** Scottish arms in 1st and 4th quarters

Date	Mintage	VG	F	VF	XF	Unc
ND(1603)	—	42.00	160	425	—	—

KM# 46 30 SHILLINGS
Silver **Obv:** Charles I **Rev:** Scottish arms in 1st and 4th quarters **Note:** First Coinage 1625-1634.

Date	Mintage	VG	F	VF	XF	Unc
ND(1625-34)	—	60.00	230	500	—	—

KM# 88 30 SHILLINGS
Silver **Obv:** Without B **Rev:** Without B **Note:** Intermediate issue.

Date	Mintage	VG	F	VF	XF	Unc
ND(1637-42)	—	30.00	100	225	650	—

KM# 87 30 SHILLINGS
Silver **Obv:** Charles I on horseback with sword erect, left in inner circle, B and rosette at top **Rev:** Crowned arms in inner circle, B and thistle before legend **Note:** Third Coinage 1637-1642, Briot's Issue.

Date	Mintage	VG	F	VF	XF	Unc
ND(1637-42)	—	30.00	100	225	650	—

KM# 90.1 30 SHILLINGS

Silver **Obv:** Horse on rough ground, F under horse's rear raised hoof

Date	Mintage	VG	F	VF	XF	Unc
ND(1637-42)	—	30.00	100	225	650	—

KM# 90.2 30 SHILLINGS

Silver **Obv:** Charles I on horseback on rough ground **Rev:** F over the crown

Date	Mintage	VG	F	VF	XF	Unc
ND(1637-42)	—	40.00	130	275	750	—

KM# 91 30 SHILLINGS

Silver **Obv:** Without F **Obv. Legend:** CAROLVS • D:G • MAG • BRIT • FRAN • & • HIB • REX **Note:** Falconer's Anonymous Issue.

Date	Mintage	VG	F	VF	XF	Unc
ND(1637-42)	—	30.00	100	225	650	—

KM# 89 30 SHILLINGS

Silver **Obv:** Horse on smooth ground, F under raised rear hoof **Note:** Falconer's Second Issue.

Date	Mintage	VG	F	VF	XF	Unc
ND(1637-42)	—	25.00	100	175	650	—

KM# 122 40 SHILLING

Silver, 35 mm. **Obv:** Laureate bust of James VII right, value below bust **Rev:** Crowned arms, crown divides date **Note:** Varieties exist.

Date	Mintage	VG	F	VF	XF	Unc
1687	—	100	300	750	1,300	—
1688	—	150	450	900	—	—

KM# 125 40 SHILLING

Silver **Obv:** Conjoined laureate busts of William and Mary left, value below busts **Rev:** Crowned arms, date in legend at upper left **Note:** Varieties exist.

Date	Mintage	VG	F	VF	XF	Unc
1689	—	175	350	875	—	—
1690	—	105	265	800	—	—
1691	—	90.00	245	625	—	—
1692	—	105	265	800	—	—
1693	—	140	300	475	—	—
1694	—	195	400	550	—	—

KM# 143 40 SHILLING

Silver **Obv:** William III **Note:** Varieties exist.

Date	Mintage	VG	F	VF	XF	Unc
1695	—	120	280	750	—	—
1696	—	110	270	700	—	—
1697	—	130	300	825	—	—
1698	—	95.00	270	650	—	—
1699	—	150	325	475	—	—
1700 Rare	—	—	—	—	—	—

KM# 11 60 SHILLING

Silver, 42 mm. **Obv:** James VI **Rev:** English arms in 1st and 4th quarters

Date	Mintage	VG	F	VF	XF	Unc
ND(1603)	—	145	550	1,350	2,950	—

KM# 12 60 SHILLING

Silver **Rev:** Scottish arms in 1st and 4th quarters

Date	Mintage	VG	F	VF	XF	Unc
ND(1603)	—	160	700	1,500	3,300	—

KM# 47 60 SHILLING

Silver **Obv:** Charles I **Rev:** Scottish arms in 1st and 4th quarters **Note:** First Coinage 1625-1634.

Date	Mintage	VG	F	VF	XF	Unc
ND(1625-34)	—	325	875	2,250	5,000	—

KM# 92 60 SHILLING

Silver **Obv:** Charles I **Note:** Third Coinage 1637-1642. Briot's Issue.

Date	Mintage	VG	F	VF	XF	Unc
ND(1637-42)	—	145	475	1,450	3,250	—

KM# 134 60 SHILLING

Silver **Obv:** William and Mary

Date	Mintage	VG	F	VF	XF	Unc
1691	—	375	675	2,100	4,500	—
1692	—	225	450	1,500	3,600	—

KM# 134a 60 SHILLING

Copper

Date	Mintage	VG	F	VF	XF	Unc
1691 Rare	—	—	—	—	—	—

PATTERNS

Including off metal strikes

KM#	Date	Mintage	Identification	Mkt Val
Pn1	ND	—	2 Pence. Copper. Crowned C-R. Thistle.	—
Pn2	ND	—	3 Pence. Silver. Crowned C-R. Thistle.	—
Pn3	ND	—	3 Pence. Silver. Bust of Charles I. Thistle.	—
Pn4	ND	—	20 Pence. Silver. Bust of Charles I. Crowned thistle, C-R.	—
Pn5	ND	—	40 Pence. Silver. Bust of Charles I. Crowned thistle, C-R.	—
Pn6	1636	—	1/2 Merk. Silver. Bust of Charles I. Crowned thistle, C-R.	—

The Spanish State, forming the greater part of the Iberian Peninsula of southwest Europe, has an area of 195,988 sq. mi. (504,714 sq. km.) and a population of 39.4 million including the Balearic and the Canary Islands. Capital: Madrid. The economy is based on agriculture, industry and tourism. Machinery, fruit, vegetables and chemicals are exported.

It isn't known when man first came to the Iberian Peninsula - the Altamira caves off the Cantabrian coast approximately 50 miles west of Santander were fashioned in Paleolithic times. Spain was a battleground for centuries before it became a united nation, fought for by Phoenicians, Carthaginians, Greeks, Celts, Romans, Vandals, Visigoths and Moors. Ferdinand and Isabella destroyed the last Moorish stronghold in 1492, freeing the national energy and resources for the era of discovery and colonization that would make Spain the most powerful country in Europe during the 16th century. After the destruction of the Spanish Armada, 1588, Spain never again played a major role in European politics.

RULERS

Philip III, 1598-1621
Philip IV, 1621-1665
Charles II, 1665-1700

HOMELAND MINT MARKS

Until 1851

B - Burgos

B, BA – Barcelona

(c) - Scalloped shell – Coruna

C, CA (monogram) – Cuenca

G – Granada

M, crowned M, ligate MD – Madrid

S, SL – Seville

T, To (monogram) – Toledo

VD, VDL, VL, VLL – Valladolid

Crowned C – Cadiz

Aqueduct – Segovia

(f) Flags - Valladolid

MINTMASTERS' INITIALS

BURGOS MINT

A	1650-51	Pedro Arce
BR	1651	Bernardo de Pedrera y Negrete
R	1661-64	?

CUENCA MINT

CA	1651	?
E	1628-33	?
I	1600-02	?
JJ	1725	Juan Jose Garcia Caballero

MADRID MINT

A	1650-51, 1660-61	Agustin Mayens
AI	1651	Agustin Mayens and Ipolito de Santo Domingo
G	1620	?
IB	1644-45	Ipolito de Santo Domingo
M	1632, 1638	?
OP	1639	Oracio Levanto
P	1630-37	?
S	1660-64	?
TR	1661, 1680, 1686	?
C	1621-27	?
V+	1642	?
Y	1660-64	?

SEGOVIA MINT

A	1617	?
A+	1616-21	Andres de Pedrera
AR	1614	?
B	1613, 31	?
BR	1659-91	Bernardo de Pedrera y Negrete
Castle Tower (t)	1599-1619	Melchor Rodriquez del Castillo
C	1599-1611	Melchor Rodriquez del Castillo
CA	1610	Melchor Rodriquez del Castillo
F	1699	Francisco de Pedrera y Negrete
I	1651	Ipolito de Santo Domingo
P	1625-30	Esteban de Pedrera
R	1632-39	Rafael Salvan
S	1660-64	?
X	1655	?

SEVILLE MINT

B	1592-1611	Juan Vicente Bravo
D	1612	?
G	1615-21	Gaspar de Talavera
M	1668-70, 1673-74	Manuel Duarte
M	1686-1703, 1707-19	?
R	1621-65	?
V	1613-16	?

TOLEDO MINT

C	1593-1601	Melchor Rodriquez del Castillo
C	1663-64	?
M	1663-64	?
P	1619-35	?
V	1611-18	?
Y	1651-55	?

MONETARY SYSTEM

34 Maravedi = 1 Real (of Silver)
16 Reales = 1 Escudo

NOTE: The early coinage of Spain is listed by denomination based on a system of 16 Reales de Plata (silver) = 1 Escudo (gold).

KINGDOM

REAL COINAGE

KM# 21 DINERO

Copper **Obv:** Castle **Rev:** Rampant lion **Mint:** Seville

Date	Mintage	VG	F	VF	XF	Unc
1602	—	14.00	30.00	50.00	120	—
1603	—	16.00	33.75	65.00	135	—

KM# 63 DINERO

Copper **Obv:** Castle **Rev:** Long cross, pellets and circle in angles **Mint:** Seville

Date	Mintage	VG	F	VF	XF	Unc
1615	—	9.00	22.50	43.50	80.00	—
1616	—	16.00	33.75	65.00	145	—
1617	—	9.00	22.50	43.50	80.00	—
1618	—	9.00	20.00	43.50	80.00	—
1619	—	9.00	22.50	43.50	80.00	—
1621	—	9.00	22.50	43.50	80.00	—

KM# 77 DINERO

Copper **Obv:** Bust of Philip IV left **Rev:** Long cross with circle and pellets in angles **Mint:** Barcelona

Date	Mintage	VG	F	VF	XF	Unc
1622	—	14.00	27.50	55.00	110	—
1625	—	8.00	16.00	36.25	70.00	—
1628	—	8.00	16.00	36.25	70.00	—
1629	—	8.00	16.00	36.25	70.00	—
1632	—	8.00	16.00	36.25	70.00	—
1633	—	8.00	16.00	36.25	70.00	—
1634	—	8.00	16.00	36.25	70.00	—
1635	—	8.00	16.00	36.25	70.00	—

Note: Coins dated 1640 and 1652 were struck for Catalonia

KM# 55 ARDITE

Copper **Obv:** Bust of Philip III dividing AR **Rev:** Diamond-shaped arms, date at upper left **Mint:** Barcelona

Date	Mintage	VG	F	VF	XF	Unc
1612	—	16.00	33.75	65.00	160	—
1613	—	8.00	16.00	36.25	70.00	—
1614	—	8.00	16.00	36.25	70.00	—
1615	—	8.00	16.00	36.25	70.00	—
1616	—	8.00	16.00	36.25	70.00	—
1617	—	9.00	20.00	43.50	90.00	—
1618	—	12.00	25.00	50.00	120	—
1619	—	16.00	33.75	75.00	160	—
1620	—	16.00	33.75	75.00	160	—
1621	—	27.50	55.00	130	325	—

KM# 78 ARDITE

Copper **Obv:** Bust of Philip IV left dividing AR **Rev:** Diamond-shaped arms, date at upper left **Mint:** Barcelona

Date	Mintage	VG	F	VF	XF	Unc
1622	—	14.00	27.50	60.00	120	—
1623	—	14.00	27.50	60.00	120	—
1624	—	9.00	22.50	43.50	80.00	—
1625	—	8.00	16.00	36.25	70.00	—
1626	—	8.00	16.00	36.25	70.00	—
1627	—	9.00	20.00	43.50	80.00	—
1628	—	8.00	16.00	36.25	70.00	—
1629	—	8.00	16.00	36.25	70.00	—
1632	—	8.00	16.00	36.25	70.00	—
1633	—	8.00	16.00	36.25	70.00	—
1634	—	8.00	16.00	36.25	70.00	—
1635	—	8.00	16.00	36.25	70.00	—
1653	—	9.00	20.00	43.50	80.00	—
1654	—	8.00	16.00	36.25	70.00	—
1655	—	8.00	16.00	36.25	70.00	—

Note: Coins dated 1640 and 1652 were struck for Catalonia

KM# 103 1/2 MARAVEDI

Copper **Obv:** Crowned PHILIPPVS monogram, date below **Rev:** Castle and lions **Mint:** Segovia

Date	Mintage	VG	F	VF	XF	Unc
1631	—	205	375	825	1,500	—

KM# 104 1/2 MARAVEDI

Copper **Obv:** Crowned PHILIPPVS monogram, date below **Rev:** BI-ON/CA, facing lion **Mint:** Segovia

Date	Mintage	VG	F	VF	XF	Unc
1631	—	115	235	475	875	—

KM# 6 MARAVEDI

Copper **Obv:** Crowned monogram **Rev:** Castle **Mint:** Cuenca **Note:** Mint mark: Aqueduct.

Date	Mintage	VG	F	VF	XF	Unc
1602	—	33.75	70.00	145	280	—
1606	—	70.00	135	290	525	—
1610	—	100	215	425	800	—

KM# 5.1 MARAVEDI

Copper **Obv:** Castle **Rev:** Rampant lion left **Mint:** Cuenca

Date	Mintage	VG	F	VF	XF	Unc
1601	—	14.00	27.50	50.00	105	—
1602	—	14.00	27.50	50.00	105	—

KM# 105 MARAVEDI

Copper **Obv:** Castle in quatrolobe **Rev:** Lion rampant left in quatrolobe **Mint:** Segovia

Date	Mintage	VG	F	VF	XF	Unc
1631	—	110	225	425	800	—

KM# 9 2 MARAVEDIS

Copper **Obv:** Castle **Rev:** Lion **Mint:** Valladolid **Note:** Machine struck, large flan. Mint mark: Aqueduct.

Date	Mintage	VG	F	VF	XF	Unc
1601 C	—	8.00	16.00	36.25	70.00	—
1602 C	—	8.00	16.00	36.25	70.00	—

KM# 7.5 2 MARAVEDIS

Copper **Obv:** Castle, mint mark L, value II, R **Rev:** Lion rampant left **Mint:** Madrid **Note:** Mint mark: Aqueduct.

Date	Mintage	VG	F	VF	XF	Unc
1602	—	14.00	27.50	50.00	95.00	—
1603	—	16.00	33.75	60.00	120	—

KM# 7.1 2 MARAVEDIS

Copper **Obv:** Castle, mint mark L, value II, R **Rev:** Lion rampant right

Date	Mintage	VG	F	VF	XF	Unc
1602B	—	8.00	16.00	36.25	70.00	—
1603B	—	8.00	16.00	36.25	70.00	—
1604B	—	8.00	16.00	36.25	70.00	—
1605B	—	9.00	22.50	43.50	80.00	—
1606B	—	9.00	22.50	43.50	80.00	—
1607B	—	9.00	22.50	43.50	80.00	—
1608B	—	9.00	22.50	43.50	80.00	—
1618B	—	9.00	22.50	43.50	80.00	—
1619B	—	9.00	22.50	43.50	80.00	—

KM# 7.3 2 MARAVEDIS

Copper **Obv:** Castle, mint mark L, value II, R **Rev:** Lion rampant right **Mint:** Granada

Date	Mintage	VG	F	VF	XF	Unc
1602	—	20.00	40.50	80.00	160	—
1603	—	20.00	40.50	80.00	160	—
1604	—	27.50	55.00	95.00	200	—

KM# 7.4 2 MARAVEDIS

Copper **Obv:** Castle, mint mark L, value II, R **Rev:** Lion rampant right **Mint:** Madrid

Date	Mintage	VG	F	VF	XF	Unc
1618	—	12.00	27.50	50.00	90.00	—
1619	—	12.00	27.50	50.00	90.00	—
1620	—	12.00	27.50	50.00	90.00	—

KM# 7.6 2 MARAVEDIS

Copper **Obv:** Castle, mint mark L, value II, R **Rev:** Lion rampant right **Mint:** Madrid

Date	Mintage	VG	F	VF	XF	Unc
1602	—	20.00	40.50	80.00	160	—
1603	—	20.00	40.50	80.00	160	—
1604	—	20.00	40.50	80.00	160	—

KM# 7.7 2 MARAVEDIS

Copper **Obv:** Castle, mint mark L, value II, R **Rev:** Lion rampant right **Mint:** Madrid

Date	Mintage	VG	F	VF	XF	Unc
1601 I	—	9.00	22.50	43.50	80.00	—
1602 C	—	8.00	16.00	36.25	70.00	—
1602 I	—	9.00	22.50	43.50	80.00	—
1603 C	—	9.00	22.50	43.50	80.00	—
1604 C	—	9.00	22.50	43.50	80.00	—
1605 C	—	9.00	22.50	43.50	80.00	—
1606 C	—	9.00	22.50	43.50	80.00	—
1607 C	—	9.00	22.50	43.50	80.00	—
1608 C	—	9.00	22.50	43.50	80.00	—
1618 C	—	9.00	22.50	43.50	80.00	—
1619 C	—	9.00	22.50	43.50	80.00	—
1620 C	—	9.00	22.50	43.50	80.00	—

KM# 7.2 2 MARAVEDIS

Copper **Obv:** Castle, mint mark L, value II, R **Rev:** Lion rampant right **Mint:** Coruna **Note:** Struck at Coruna.

Date	Mintage	VG	F	VF	XF	Unc
ND	—	70.00	135	290	—	—

KM# 10 2 MARAVEDIS

Copper **Obv:** Castle **Rev:** Lion **Mint:** Valladolid **Note:** Machine struck, small flan. Mint mark: Aqueduct.

Date	Mintage	VG	F	VF	XF	Unc
1602	—	8.00	16.00	36.25	70.00	—
1603	—	8.00	16.00	36.25	70.00	—
1604	—	8.00	16.00	36.25	70.00	—
1605	—	8.00	16.00	36.25	70.00	—
1606	—	8.00	16.00	36.25	70.00	—
1607	—	8.00	16.00	36.25	70.00	—
1608	—	8.00	16.00	36.25	70.00	—
1609	—	8.00	16.00	36.25	70.00	—
1610	—	8.00	16.00	36.25	70.00	—
1611	—	9.00	22.50	43.50	80.00	—
1612	—	8.00	16.00	36.25	70.00	—
1613	—	9.00	22.50	43.50	80.00	—
1614	—	9.00	22.50	43.50	80.00	—
1615	—	8.00	16.00	36.25	70.00	—
1616	—	8.00	16.00	36.25	70.00	—
1617	—	9.00	22.50	43.50	80.00	—
1618	—	9.00	22.50	43.50	80.00	—
1619	—	8.00	16.00	36.25	70.00	—
1620	—	9.00	22.50	43.50	80.00	—

KM# 71.1 2 MARAVEDIS

Copper **Obv:** Castle, value at left **Rev:** Lion rampant left **Mint:** Burgos

Date	Mintage	VG	F	VF	XF	Unc
1621	—	14.00	33.75	60.00	105	—
1622	—	14.00	33.75	60.00	105	—
1623	—	14.00	33.75	60.00	105	—
1624	—	14.00	33.75	60.00	105	—
1625	—	14.00	33.75	60.00	105	—

KM# 71.2 2 MARAVEDIS

Copper **Obv:** Castle, value at left **Rev:** Lion rampant left **Mint:** La Coruna

Date	Mintage	VG	F	VF	XF	Unc
1624	—	27.50	55.00	110	230	—
1625	—	27.50	55.00	110	230	—
1626	—	27.50	55.00	110	230	—

KM# 71.3 2 MARAVEDIS

Copper **Obv:** Castle, value at left **Rev:** Lion rampant left **Mint:** Cuenca

Date	Mintage	VG	F	VF	XF	Unc
1621	—	14.00	33.75	65.00	120	—
1622	—	14.00	33.75	65.00	120	—
1623	—	14.00	33.75	65.00	120	—
1624	—	14.00	33.75	65.00	120	—
1625	—	14.00	30.00	60.00	110	—
1626	—	14.00	33.75	65.00	120	—

KM# 71.4 2 MARAVEDIS

Copper **Obv:** Castle, value at left **Rev:** Lion rampant left **Mint:** Granada

Date	Mintage	VG	F	VF	XF	Unc
1621	—	14.00	33.75	65.00	120	—
1622	—	14.00	33.75	65.00	120	—
1623	—	14.00	33.75	65.00	120	—
1624	—	14.00	33.75	65.00	120	—
1625	—	14.00	33.75	65.00	120	—
1626	—	14.00	33.75	65.00	120	—

KM# 71.5 2 MARAVEDIS

Copper **Obv:** Castle, value at left **Rev:** Lion rampant left **Mint:** Madrid

Date	Mintage	VG	F	VF	XF	Unc
1621	—	16.00	37.75	75.00	130	—
1622	—	16.00	37.75	75.00	130	—
1623	—	16.00	37.75	75.00	130	—
1624	—	16.00	37.75	75.00	130	—
1625	—	16.00	37.75	75.00	130	—
1626	—	16.00	37.75	75.00	130	—

KM# 71.7 2 MARAVEDIS

Copper **Obv:** Castle, value at left **Rev:** Lion rampant left **Mint:** Seville

Date	Mintage	VG	F	VF	XF	Unc
1621	—	12.00	30.00	50.00	90.00	—
1622	—	12.00	30.00	50.00	90.00	—
1623	—	12.00	30.00	50.00	90.00	—
1624	—	12.00	30.00	50.00	90.00	—
1625	—	12.00	30.00	50.00	90.00	—
1626	—	12.00	30.00	50.00	90.00	—

KM# 71.8 2 MARAVEDIS

Copper **Obv:** Castle, value at left **Rev:** Lion rampant left **Mint:** Toledo

Date	Mintage	VG	F	VF	XF	Unc
1621	—	14.00	33.75	60.00	105	—
1622	—	14.00	33.75	60.00	105	—
1623	—	14.00	33.75	60.00	105	—
1624	—	14.00	33.75	60.00	105	—
1625	—	14.00	33.75	60.00	105	—
1626	—	14.00	33.75	60.00	105	—

KM# 71.9 2 MARAVEDIS

Copper **Obv:** Castle, value at left **Rev:** Lion rampant left **Mint:** Valladolid

Date	Mintage	VG	F	VF	XF	Unc
1621	—	14.00	33.75	60.00	105	—
1622	—	14.00	33.75	60.00	105	—
1623	—	14.00	33.75	60.00	105	—
1624	—	14.00	33.75	60.00	105	—
1625	—	14.00	33.75	60.00	105	—
1626	—	14.00	33.75	60.00	105	—

KM# 71.6 2 MARAVEDIS

Copper **Obv:** Castle, value at left **Rev:** Lion rampant left **Mint:** Madrid **Note:** Mint mark: Aqueduct.

Date	Mintage	VG	F	VF	XF	Unc
1621	—	47.25	95.00	180	350	—

KM# 79 2 MARAVEDIS

Copper **Obv:** Small head right **Rev:** Castles and lions in circles **Mint:** Madrid **Note:** Milled coinage, small flan. Mint mark: Aqueduct.

Date	Mintage	VG	F	VF	XF	Unc
1622	—	90.00	170	325	600	—

KM# 106 2 MARAVEDIS

Copper **Obv:** Small head of Philip IV right **Rev:** Castles and lions in quatrefoil **Mint:** Madrid **Note:** Milled, large flan. Mint mark: Aqueduct.

Date	Mintage	VG	F	VF	XF	Unc
1631	—	100	195	400	725	—

KM# 141 2 MARAVEDIS

Copper **Obv:** PHILIPPVS monogram **Rev:** Crowned REX **Mint:** Madrid **Note:** Mint mark: Aqueduct.

Date	Mintage	VG	F	VF	XF	Unc
1656	—	90.00	170	325	600	—

KM# 142 2 MARAVEDIS

Copper **Obv:** Crowned Philip monogram in octolobe **Rev:** Crowned REX, date below, all in octolobe **Mint:** Madrid **Note:** Mint mark: Aqueduct.

Date	Mintage	VG	F	VF	XF	Unc
1658	—	75.00	150	290	525	—

KM# 154.1 2 MARAVEDIS

Copper **Obv:** Bust right of Philip IV **Rev:** Crowned shield of Leon **Mint:** Madrid **Note:** Mint mark: Aqueduct.

Date	Mintage	VG	F	VF	XF	Unc
1661 S	—	95.00	190	375	675	—
1662 S	—	95.00	190	375	675	—
1663 BR	—	70.00	135	270	475	—
1664 BR	—	95.00	190	375	675	—

KM# 154.2 2 MARAVEDIS

Copper **Obv:** Bust of Philip IV right **Rev:** Crowned shield of Leon **Mint:** Seville

Date	Mintage	VG	F	VF	XF	Unc
1661 R	—	60.00	115	240	450	—
1662 R	—	60.00	115	240	450	—
1663 R	—	60.00	115	240	450	—
1664 R	—	60.00	115	240	450	—

KM# 154.3 2 MARAVEDIS

Copper **Obv:** Bust of Philip IV right **Rev:** Crowned shield of Leon **Mint:** Trujillo

Date	Mintage	VG	F	VF	XF	Unc
1661 M	—	55.00	100	195	350	—
1662 M	—	55.00	100	195	350	—
1663 M	—	47.25	90.00	175	325	—
1664 M	—	55.00	100	195	350	—

KM# 155.1 2 MARAVEDIS

Copper **Obv:** Bust of Philip IV right in inner circle **Rev:** Crowned shield of Leon **Mint:** Toledo

Date	Mintage	VG	F	VF	XF	Unc
1661 M	—	60.00	100	195	350	—
1662 M	—	60.00	100	195	350	—
1663 M	—	60.00	100	195	350	—
1664 M	—	60.00	100	195	350	—

KM# 155.2 2 MARAVEDIS

Copper **Obv:** Bust of Philip IV right in inner circle **Rev:** Crowned shield of Leon **Mint:** Valladolid

Date	Mintage	VG	F	VF	XF	Unc
1662 M	—	47.25	90.00	175	325	—
1663 M	—	55.00	110	220	400	—
1664 M	—	47.25	90.00	175	325	—

KM# 169.1 2 MARAVEDIS

Copper **Obv:** Bust of Philip IV right in circle **Rev:** Crowned shield of Leon **Mint:** Burgos

Date	Mintage	VG	F	VF	XF	Unc
1662 R	—	47.25	90.00	175	325	—
1663 R	—	47.25	90.00	175	325	—
1664 R	—	55.00	100	195	350	—

KM# 169.2 2 MARAVEDIS

Copper **Obv:** Bust of Philip IV right in circle **Rev:** Crowned shield of Leon **Mint:** La Coruna

Date	Mintage	VG	F	VF	XF	Unc
1662 R	—	47.25	90.00	175	325	—
1661 R	—	47.25	90.00	175	325	—
1663 R	—	47.25	90.00	175	325	—
1664 R	—	47.25	90.00	175	325	—

KM# 169.3 2 MARAVEDIS

Copper **Obv:** Bust of Philip IV right in circle **Rev:** Crowned shield of Leon **Mint:** Cuenca

Date	Mintage	VG	F	VF	XF	Unc
1662	—	47.25	90.00	175	325	—
1663	—	47.25	90.00	175	325	—
1664	—	47.25	90.00	175	325	—

KM# 169.4 2 MARAVEDIS

Copper **Obv:** Bust of Philip IV right in circle **Rev:** Crowned shield of Leon **Mint:** Granada

Date	Mintage	VG	F	VF	XF	Unc
1662 M	—	70.00	135	255	450	—
1661 M	—	70.00	135	255	450	—
1663 M	—	47.25	90.00	175	325	—

KM# 174 2 MARAVEDIS

Copper **Obv:** Bust of Philip IV right **Rev:** Crowned shield of Leon **Mint:** Granada

Date	Mintage	VG	F	VF	XF	Unc
1663 M	—	47.25	90.00	175	325	—

KM# 175 2 MARAVEDIS

Copper **Obv:** Small head of Philip IV right **Rev:** Crowned shield of Castile **Mint:** Madrid

Date	Mintage	VG	F	VF	XF	Unc
1663 S	—	40.50	80.00	160	290	—
1663 Y	—	40.50	80.00	160	290	—
1664 S	—	40.50	80.00	160	290	—
1664 Y	—	40.50	80.00	160	290	—

KM# 190.2 2 MARAVEDIS

Copper **Obv:** Crowned shield of Castile **Rev:** Crowned shield of Leon **Mint:** Coruna

Date	Mintage	VG	F	VF	XF	Unc
1680	—	8.00	16.00	30.00	55.00	—
1681	—	9.00	20.00	36.25	70.00	—
1682	—	11.00	27.50	43.50	80.00	—
1683	—	11.00	27.50	43.50	80.00	—
1684	—	8.00	16.00	30.00	55.00	—
1685	—	8.00	16.00	30.00	55.00	—
1694	—	9.00	20.00	36.25	70.00	—
1695	—	9.00	20.00	36.25	70.00	—
1696	—	8.00	16.00	30.00	55.00	—

KM# 190.3 2 MARAVEDIS

Copper **Obv:** Crowned shield of Castile **Rev:** Crowned shield of Leon **Mint:** Cuenca

Date	Mintage	VG	F	VF	XF	Unc
1680	—	11.00	27.50	46.50	80.00	—
1681	—	14.00	33.75	60.00	105	—
1682	—	14.00	33.75	60.00	105	—
1683	—	14.00	33.75	60.00	105	—
1684	—	14.00	33.75	60.00	105	—
1685	—	14.00	33.75	60.00	105	—

KM# 190.4 2 MARAVEDIS

Copper **Obv:** Crowned shield of Castile **Rev:** Crowned shield of Leon **Mint:** Granada

Date	Mintage	VG	F	VF	XF	Unc
1680	—	11.00	27.50	50.00	90.00	—
1681	—	14.00	33.75	60.00	105	—
1682	—	14.00	33.75	60.00	105	—
1683	—	14.00	33.75	60.00	105	—
1684	—	14.00	33.75	60.00	105	—
1685	—	11.00	27.50	46.50	80.00	—
1686	—	11.00	27.50	50.00	90.00	—

KM# 190.5 2 MARAVEDIS
Copper **Ruler:** Philip V **Obv:** Crowned shield of Castile **Rev:** Crowned shield of Leon **Mint:** Linares

Date	Mintage	VG	F	VF	XF	Unc
1692	—	8.00	20.00	32.00	50.00	—
1693	—	7.00	15.00	25.00	45.00	—
1694	—	6.00	12.00	20.00	35.00	—
1695	—	6.00	12.00	20.00	35.00	—
1696	—	7.00	15.00	25.00	45.00	—
1697	—	7.00	15.00	25.00	45.00	—
1698	—	8.00	20.00	32.00	50.00	—
1699	—	6.00	12.00	20.00	35.00	—
1700	—	7.00	15.00	25.00	45.00	—

KM# 190.6 2 MARAVEDIS
Copper **Obv:** Crowned shield of Castile **Rev:** Crowned shield of Leon **Mint:** Madrid

Date	Mintage	VG	F	VF	XF	Unc
1680	—	9.00	20.00	40.50	80.00	—
1681	—	14.00	33.75	60.00	105	—
1682	—	14.00	33.75	60.00	105	—
1683	—	14.00	33.75	60.00	105	—
1684	—	14.00	33.75	60.00	105	—
1686	—	14.00	33.75	60.00	105	—

KM# 190.7 2 MARAVEDIS
Copper **Obv:** Crowned shield of Castile **Rev:** Crowned shield of Leon **Mint:** Segovia

Date	Mintage	VG	F	VF	XF	Unc
1680	—	11.00	27.50	50.00	90.00	—
1681	—	14.00	33.75	60.00	105	—
1682	—	14.00	33.75	60.00	105	—
1683	—	14.00	33.75	60.00	105	—
1684	—	14.00	33.75	60.00	105	—
1685	—	14.00	33.75	60.00	105	—
1691	—	20.00	33.75	75.00	135	—

KM# 190.8 2 MARAVEDIS
Copper **Obv:** Crowned shield of Castile **Rev:** Crowned shield of Leon **Mint:** Seville

Date	Mintage	VG	F	VF	XF	Unc
1680	—	11.00	27.50	43.50	80.00	—
1681	—	11.00	27.50	43.50	80.00	—
1682	—	11.00	27.50	43.50	80.00	—
1683	—	11.00	27.50	43.50	80.00	—
1684	—	11.00	27.50	43.50	80.00	—
1685	—	11.00	27.50	43.50	80.00	—

KM# 190.9 2 MARAVEDIS
Copper **Obv:** Crowned shield of Castile **Rev:** Crowned shield of Leon **Mint:** Toledo

Date	Mintage	VG	F	VF	XF	Unc
1680	—	11.00	27.50	46.50	80.00	—
1681	—	11.00	27.50	50.00	90.00	—
1682	—	11.00	27.50	50.00	90.00	—
1683	—	11.00	27.50	50.00	90.00	—
1684	—	14.00	33.75	60.00	105	—
1685	—	11.00	27.50	50.00	90.00	—

KM# 190.10 2 MARAVEDIS
Copper **Obv:** Crowned shield of Castile **Rev:** Crowned shield of Leon **Mint:** Seville

Date	Mintage	VG	F	VF	XF	Unc
1680	—	11.00	27.50	46.50	80.00	—
1681	—	11.00	27.50	46.50	80.00	—
1682	—	14.00	33.75	60.00	105	—
1683	—	14.00	33.75	60.00	105	—
1684	—	14.00	33.75	60.00	105	—
1685	—	14.00	33.75	60.00	105	—
1686	—	11.00	27.50	50.00	95.00	—

KM# 190.11 2 MARAVEDIS
Copper **Obv:** Crowned shield of Castile **Rev:** Crowned shield of Leon **Mint:** Seville

Date	Mintage	VG	F	VF	XF	Unc
1680VD//L	—	14.00	33.75	60.00	105	—
1680VLL//L	—	11.00	27.50	50.00	90.00	—
1681VD//L	—	14.00	33.75	60.00	105	—
1682VLL//L	—	14.00	33.75	60.00	105	—
1683VLL//L	—	14.00	33.75	60.00	105	—
1864VLL//L	—	14.00	33.75	60.00	105	—
1685VLL//L	—	14.00	33.75	60.00	105	—
1686VLL//L	—	14.00	33.75	60.00	105	—

KM# 190.1 2 MARAVEDIS
Copper **Obv:** Crowned shield of Castile **Rev:** Crowned shield of Leon **Mint:** Burgos

Date	Mintage	VG	F	VF	XF	Unc
1680	—	8.00	16.00	30.00	55.00	—
1681	—	11.00	27.50	43.50	80.00	—
1682	—	11.00	27.50	43.50	80.00	—
1683	—	11.00	27.50	43.50	80.00	—
1684	—	11.00	27.50	43.50	80.00	—
1685	—	11.00	27.50	43.50	80.00	—

KM# 22 3 MARAVEDIS
Copper **Obv:** Castle **Rev:** Rampant lion left **Mint:** Toledo

Date	Mintage	VG	F	VF	XF	Unc
1602	—	55.00	110	200	350	—

MB# 13 4 MARAVEDIS
Copper **Obv:** Castle in octolobe **Rev:** Rampant lion in octolobe **Mint:** Valladolid **Note:** Milled, large flan. Mint mark: Aqueduct.

Date	Mintage	VG	F	VF	XF	Unc
1601 C	—	8.00	16.00	36.25	65.00	—
1602 C	—	8.00	16.00	36.25	65.00	—

KM# 12.3 4 MARAVEDIS
Copper **Obv:** Castle **Rev:** Rampant lion left **Mint:** Valladolid

Date	Mintage	VG	F	VF	XF	Unc
1602 C	—	8.00	16.00	32.00	65.00	—
1603 C	—	8.00	16.00	32.00	65.00	—
1604 C	—	9.00	19.00	36.25	70.00	—
1605 C	—	8.00	16.00	32.00	65.00	—
1606 C	—	11.00	22.50	40.50	75.00	—
1607 C	—	8.00	16.00	32.00	65.00	—
1608 C	—	14.00	27.50	43.50	80.00	—
1618 C	—	14.00	27.50	43.50	80.00	—
1619 C	—	8.00	16.00	32.00	65.00	—
1620 C	—	14.00	27.50	46.50	90.00	—

KM# 11.3 4 MARAVEDIS
Copper **Obv:** Castle **Rev:** Rampant lion left **Mint:** Segovia **Note:** Hammered.

Date	Mintage	VG	F	VF	XF	Unc
1601	—	11.00	22.50	43.50	80.00	—
1604	—	11.00	22.50	43.50	90.00	—
1605	—	14.00	27.50	50.00	95.00	—
1606	—	14.00	27.50	50.00	95.00	—
1607	—	14.00	27.50	50.00	95.00	—
1608	—	14.00	27.50	50.00	95.00	—
1609	—	19.00	37.75	65.00	120	—
1610	—	25.00	47.25	80.00	145	—
1618	—	25.00	47.25	80.00	145	—
1619	—	14.00	27.50	50.00	95.00	—
1620	—	14.00	27.50	50.00	95.00	—

KM# 11.4 4 MARAVEDIS
Copper **Obv:** Castle **Rev:** Rampant lion left **Mint:** Toledo **Note:** Hammered.

Date	Mintage	VG	F	VF	XF	Unc
1602	—	8.00	16.00	30.00	55.00	—
1603	—	9.00	19.00	36.25	65.00	—
1604	—	14.00	27.50	43.50	80.00	—
1605	—	14.00	27.50	43.50	80.00	—
1606	—	14.00	27.50	43.50	80.00	—
1607	—	14.00	27.50	43.50	80.00	—
1608	—	14.00	27.50	43.50	80.00	—
1618	—	9.00	19.00	36.25	65.00	—
1619	—	14.00	27.50	43.50	80.00	—
1620	—	19.00	37.75	65.00	105	—

KM# 11.1 4 MARAVEDIS
Copper **Obv:** Castle **Rev:** Rampant lion left

Date	Mintage	VG	F	VF	XF	Unc
1602	—	12.00	16.00	40.50	70.00	—
1603	—	8.00	14.00	30.00	55.00	—
1604	—	8.00	14.00	30.00	55.00	—
1605	—	14.00	27.50	43.50	80.00	—
1606	—	14.00	27.50	43.50	80.00	—
1607	—	14.00	27.50	43.50	80.00	—
1608	—	14.00	27.50	43.50	80.00	—
1618	—	8.00	14.00	30.00	55.00	—
1619	—	8.00	14.00	30.00	55.00	—

KM# 11.2 4 MARAVEDIS
Copper **Obv:** Castle **Rev:** Lion rampant left

Date	Mintage	VG	F	VF	XF	Unc
1618MD	—	14.00	27.50	43.50	80.00	—
1619MD	—	14.00	27.50	43.50	80.00	—
1620MD	—	14.00	27.50	43.50	80.00	—

KM# 12.1 4 MARAVEDIS
Copper **Obv:** Castle **Rev:** Rampant lion left **Mint:** Valladolid

Date	Mintage	VG	F	VF	XF	Unc
1602	—	14.00	27.50	43.50	80.00	—
1603	—	14.00	27.50	43.50	80.00	—
1604	—	14.00	27.50	43.50	80.00	—
1605	—	14.00	27.50	43.50	80.00	—
1606	—	14.00	27.50	43.50	80.00	—
1607	—	14.00	27.50	43.50	80.00	—
1608	—	14.00	27.50	43.50	80.00	—
1618	—	9.00	19.00	36.25	70.00	—
1619	—	9.00	19.00	36.25	70.00	—
1620	—	14.00	27.50	43.50	80.00	—

KM# 12.2 4 MARAVEDIS
Copper **Obv:** Castle in octolobe **Rev:** Rampant lion left **Mint:** Valladolid

Date	Mintage	VG	F	VF	XF	Unc
1601 I	—	9.00	19.00	36.25	65.00	—
1602 I	—	8.00	16.00	32.00	55.00	—

KM# 14 4 MARAVEDIS
Copper **Obv:** Castle **Rev:** Rampant lion left **Mint:** Valladolid **Note:** Smaller flan. Mint mark: Aqueduct.

Date	Mintage	VG	F	VF	XF	Unc
1602	—	10.00	20.00	40.50	70.00	—
1603	—	8.00	16.00	36.25	65.00	—
1604	—	12.00	25.00	43.50	80.00	—
1605	—	12.00	25.00	43.50	80.00	—
1605/4	—	12.00	25.00	43.50	80.00	—
1606	—	10.00	20.00	40.50	70.00	—
1607	—	10.00	20.00	40.50	70.00	—
1608	—	10.00	20.00	40.50	70.00	—
1609	—	16.00	33.75	60.00	105	—
1610	—	16.00	33.75	60.00	105	—
1611	—	16.00	33.75	60.00	105	—
1612	—	10.00	20.00	40.50	70.00	—
1613	—	10.00	20.00	40.50	70.00	—
1614	—	12.00	25.00	43.50	80.00	—
1615	—	12.00	25.00	43.50	80.00	—
1616	—	10.00	20.00	40.50	70.00	—
1617	—	10.00	20.00	40.50	70.00	—
1618	—	8.00	16.00	32.00	65.00	—
1619	—	10.00	20.00	40.50	70.00	—
1620	—	10.00	20.00	40.50	70.00	—

KM# 72.2 4 MARAVEDIS
Copper **Obv:** Castle with IIII at right, mint mark at left **Rev:** Rampant lion left **Mint:** Valladolid **Note:** Mint mark: Crown.

Date	Mintage	VG	F	VF	XF	Unc
1624	—	19.00	37.75	65.00	120	—
1625	—	19.00	37.75	65.00	120	—
1626	—	19.00	37.75	65.00	120	—

KM# 72.7 4 MARAVEDIS
Copper **Obv:** Castle with IIII at right, mint mark at left **Rev:** Rampant lion left **Mint:** Segovia **Note:** Milled coinage.

Date	Mintage	VG	F	VF	XF	Unc
1622	—	12.00	25.00	40.50	70.00	—
1625	—	33.75	60.00	115	265	—
1626	—	16.00	33.75	60.00	105	—

KM# 72.1 4 MARAVEDIS
Copper **Obv:** Castle with IIII at right, mint mark at left **Rev:** Rampant lion left **Mint:** Valladolid

Date	Mintage	VG	F	VF	XF	Unc
1621B	—	27.50	50.00	85.00	160	—
1622B	—	11.00	22.50	43.50	80.00	—
1623B	—	11.00	22.50	43.50	80.00	—
1624B	—	11.00	22.50	43.50	80.00	—
1625B	—	11.00	22.50	43.50	80.00	—
1626B	—	16.00	33.75	60.00	105	—

KM# 72.3 4 MARAVEDIS
Copper **Obv:** Castle with IIII at right, mint mark at left **Rev:** Rampant lion left **Mint:** Valladolid

Date	Mintage	VG	F	VF	XF	Unc
1621C	—	14.00	27.50	50.00	90.00	—
1622C	—	14.00	27.50	50.00	90.00	—
1623C	—	14.00	27.50	50.00	90.00	—
1624C	—	14.00	27.50	50.00	90.00	—
1625C	—	14.00	27.50	50.00	90.00	—
1626C	—	14.00	27.50	50.00	90.00	—

KM# 72.4 4 MARAVEDIS
Copper **Obv:** Castle with IIII at right, mint mark at left **Rev:** Rampant lion left **Mint:** Granada

Date	Mintage	VG	F	VF	XF	Unc
1621	—	20.00	40.50	75.00	135	—
1622	—	20.00	40.50	75.00	135	—
1623	—	20.00	40.50	75.00	135	—
1624	—	20.00	40.50	75.00	135	—
1625	—	16.00	33.75	60.00	110	—
1626	—	20.00	40.50	75.00	135	—

KM# 72.5 4 MARAVEDIS
Copper **Obv:** Castle with IIII at right, mint mark at left **Rev:** Rampant lion left **Mint:** Madrid

Date	Mintage	VG	F	VF	XF	Unc
1621	—	11.00	22.50	43.50	70.00	—
1622	—	11.00	22.50	43.50	70.00	—
1623	—	11.00	22.50	43.50	70.00	—
1624	—	11.00	22.50	50.00	90.00	—
1625	—	16.00	33.75	60.00	105	—
1626	—	16.00	33.75	60.00	105	—

KM# 72.6 4 MARAVEDIS
Copper **Obv:** Castle with IIII at right, mint mark at left **Rev:** Rampant lion left **Mint:** Segovia

Date	Mintage	VG	F	VF	XF	Unc
1621	—	14.00	27.50	43.50	80.00	—
1622	—	12.00	25.00	36.25	70.00	—
1623	—	14.00	27.50	43.50	80.00	—
1624	—	14.00	27.50	43.50	80.00	—
1625	—	14.00	27.50	43.50	80.00	—
1626	—	9.00	19.00	32.00	65.00	—

KM# 72.8 4 MARAVEDIS
Copper **Obv:** Castle with IIII at right, mint mark at left **Rev:** Rampant lion left **Mint:** Seville

Date	Mintage	VG	F	VF	XF	Unc
1621	—	16.00	33.75	60.00	105	—
1622	—	16.00	33.75	60.00	105	—
1623	—	16.00	33.75	60.00	105	—
1624	—	16.00	33.75	60.00	105	—
1625	—	16.00	33.75	60.00	105	—
1626	—	16.00	33.75	60.00	105	—

KM# 72.9 4 MARAVEDIS
Copper **Obv:** Castle with IIII at right, mint mark at left **Rev:** Rampant lion left **Mint:** Toledo

Date	Mintage	VG	F	VF	XF	Unc
1621	—	19.00	37.75	65.00	120	—
1622	—	11.00	22.50	40.50	80.00	—
1623	—	19.00	37.75	65.00	120	—
1624	—	19.00	37.75	65.00	120	—
1625	—	11.00	22.50	40.50	80.00	—
1626	—	19.00	37.75	65.00	120	—

KM# 72.10 4 MARAVEDIS
Copper **Obv:** Castle with IIII at right, mint mark at left **Rev:** Rampant lion left **Mint:** Valladolid

Date	Mintage	VG	F	VF	XF	Unc
1621	—	19.00	37.75	65.00	120	—
1622	—	19.00	37.75	65.00	120	—
1623	—	16.00	33.75	60.00	105	—
1624	—	19.00	37.75	65.00	120	—

Date	Mintage	VG	F	VF	XF	Unc
1625	—	19.00	37.75	65.00	120	—
1626	—	19.00	37.75	65.00	120	—

KM# 143 4 MARAVEDIS

Copper **Obv:** Crowned PHILIPPVS monogram in octolobe within flora **Rev:** Crowned REX in octolobe within flora **Mint:** Segovia

Date	Mintage	VG	F	VF	XF	Unc
1658	—	265	450	750	1,350	—

KM# 150 4 MARAVEDIS

Copper **Obv:** Bust of Philip IV right **Rev:** Castle, value below **Mint:** Madrid

Date	Mintage	VG	F	VF	XF	Unc
1660 A	—	27.50	55.00	95.00	175	—
1661	—	70.00	135	255	450	—
1661 A	—	20.00	40.50	75.00	130	—
1661 Y	—	20.00	40.50	75.00	130	—

KM# 151 4 MARAVEDIS

Copper **Obv:** Bust of Philip IV right **Rev:** Crowned shield of Castile **Mint:** Segovia

Date	Mintage	VG	F	VF	XF	Unc
1660 S	—	16.00	33.75	60.00	105	—
1661 S	—	14.00	27.50	50.00	95.00	—
1662 S	—	25.00	47.25	80.00	145	—
1663 S	—	25.00	47.25	80.00	145	—
1663 BR	—	16.00	33.75	60.00	105	—
1664 BR	—	20.00	40.50	65.00	110	—

KM# 159 4 MARAVEDIS

Copper **Obv:** Head of Philip IV right **Rev:** Castle **Mint:** Toledo

Date	Mintage	VG	F	VF	XF	Unc
1661 M	—	33.75	60.00	115	265	—
1662 M	—	33.75	60.00	115	265	—
1663 M	—	33.75	60.00	115	265	—
1664 M	—	33.75	60.00	115	265	—

KM# 160 4 MARAVEDIS

Copper **Obv:** Tall bust of Philip IV right **Rev:** Castle, value below **Mint:** Toledo

Date	Mintage	VG	F	VF	XF	Unc
1661 M	—	19.00	37.75	65.00	120	—
1662 M	—	19.00	37.75	65.00	120	—
1663 M	—	19.00	37.75	65.00	120	—
1664 M	—	19.00	37.75	65.00	120	—

KM# 156.2 4 MARAVEDIS

Copper **Obv:** Bust of Philip IV right in inner circle, legend around **Rev:** Crowned shield of Castile **Mint:** Segovia **Note:** Mint mark: Crown.

Date	Mintage	VG	F	VF	XF	Unc
1661 R	—	19.00	37.75	65.00	110	—
1662 R	—	16.00	33.75	60.00	105	—
1663 R	—	16.00	33.75	60.00	105	—
1664 R	—	19.00	37.75	65.00	110	—

KM# 156.1 4 MARAVEDIS

Copper **Obv:** Bust of Philip IV right in inner circle, legend around **Rev:** Crowned shield of Castile **Mint:** Segovia **Note:** Mint mark: B.

Date	Mintage	VG	F	VF	XF	Unc
1661B R	—	14.00	27.50	60.00	95.00	—
1662B R	—	14.00	27.50	60.00	95.00	—
1663B R	—	16.00	33.75	65.00	105	—
1963B R (error)	—	20.00	40.50	75.00	130	—
1664B R	—	16.00	33.75	65.00	105	—

KM# 158 4 MARAVEDIS

Copper **Obv:** Bust of Philip IV right in inner circle **Rev:** IIII below castle in inner circle **Mint:** Granada

Date	Mintage	VG	F	VF	XF	Unc
1661 N	—	16.00	33.75	65.00	110	—
1662 N	—	16.00	33.75	60.00	105	—
1663 N	—	20.00	40.50	75.00	120	—
1664 N	—	25.00	47.25	80.00	145	—

KM# 156.3 4 MARAVEDIS

Copper **Obv:** Bust of Philip IV right in inner circle, legend around **Rev:** Crowned shield of Castile **Mint:** Cuenca

Date	Mintage	VG	F	VF	XF	Unc
1662	—	20.00	40.50	75.00	135	—
1663	—	16.00	33.75	60.00	105	—
1664	—	16.00	33.75	60.00	105	—

KM# 156.4 4 MARAVEDIS

Copper **Obv:** Bust of Philip IV right in inner circle, legend around **Rev:** Crowned shield of Castile **Mint:** Madrid

Date	Mintage	VG	F	VF	XF	Unc
1663 S	—	19.00	37.75	65.00	120	—
1663 Y	—	19.00	37.75	65.00	120	—
1664 S	—	16.00	33.75	60.00	105	—
1664 Y	—	16.00	33.75	60.00	105	—

KM# 156.5 4 MARAVEDIS

Copper **Obv:** Bust of Philip IV right in inner circle, legend around **Rev:** Crowned shield of Castile **Mint:** Seville

Date	Mintage	VG	F	VF	XF	Unc
1661 R	—	20.00	40.50	75.00	130	—
1662 R	—	27.50	50.00	85.00	160	—
1663 R	—	20.00	40.50	75.00	130	—
1664 R	—	27.50	50.00	85.00	160	—

KM# 156.6 4 MARAVEDIS

Copper **Obv:** Bust of Philip IV right in inner circle, legend around **Rev:** Crowned shield of Castile **Mint:** Valladolid

Date	Mintage	VG	F	VF	XF	Unc
1661 M	—	30.00	55.00	95.00	175	—
1662 M	—	30.00	55.00	95.00	175	—
1663 M	—	30.00	55.00	95.00	175	—
1664 M	—	30.00	55.00	95.00	175	—

KM# 157 4 MARAVEDIS

Copper **Obv:** Bust of PHilip IV right **Rev:** IIII below castle **Mint:** Cuenca

Date	Mintage	VG	F	VF	XF	Unc
1661	—	55.00	105	175	325	—

KM# 170 4 MARAVEDIS

Copper **Obv:** Tall bust of Philip IV right in circle **Rev:** Crowned shield of Castile **Mint:** Trujillo

Date	Mintage	VG	F	VF	XF	Unc
1662 M	—	14.00	27.50	50.00	90.00	—
1664 M	—	40.50	80.00	145	295	—

KM# 176 4 MARAVEDIS

Copper **Obv:** Tall bust of Philip IV right **Rev:** Crowned shield of Castile **Mint:** Trujillo

Date	Mintage	VG	F	VF	XF	Unc
1663 M	—	14.00	27.50	50.00	90.00	—

KM# 220 4 MARAVEDIS

Copper **Obv:** Crowned shield of Castile and Leon **Rev:** Crown above IHS **Mint:** Valladolid

Date	Mintage	VG	F	VF	XF	Unc
1691	—	120	200	400	—	—

KM# 15.4 8 MARAVEDIS

Copper **Obv:** Crowned shield of Castile **Rev:** Crowned shield of Leon

Date	Mintage	VG	F	VF	XF	Unc
1620MD	—	19.00	36.25	65.00	135	—
1618MD	—	19.00	36.25	65.00	135	—
Note: 1618 issues had a horizontal (rather than vertical) date variety						
1619MD	—	17.00	32.75	65.00	120	—
1621	—	32.75	65.00	95.00	200	—

KM# 15.6 8 MARAVEDIS

Copper **Obv:** Crowned shield of Castile **Rev:** Crowned shield of Leon

Date	Mintage	VG	F	VF	XF	Unc
1602	—	25.00	50.00	80.00	145	—
1603	—	25.00	50.00	80.00	145	—
1604	—	15.00	30.00	50.00	90.00	—
1605	—	15.00	30.00	50.00	90.00	—
1606	—	15.00	30.00	50.00	90.00	—
1607	—	20.00	40.50	65.00	110	—
1608	—	20.00	40.50	65.00	110	—
1618	—	15.00	30.00	50.00	90.00	—
1619	—	15.00	30.00	50.00	90.00	—

KM# 15.7 8 MARAVEDIS

Copper **Obv:** Crowned shield of Castile **Rev:** Crowned shield of Leon **Mint:** Valladolid

Date	Mintage	VG	F	VF	XF	Unc
1602	—	17.00	36.25	60.00	95.00	—
1603	—	17.00	36.25	60.00	95.00	—
1604	—	15.00	30.00	50.00	90.00	—
1605	—	13.00	25.00	46.50	80.00	—
1606	—	17.00	36.25	60.00	95.00	—
1607	—	17.00	36.25	60.00	95.00	—
1608	—	17.00	36.25	60.00	95.00	—
1618	—	12.00	22.50	43.50	70.00	—
1619	—	12.00	22.50	43.50	70.00	—
1620	—	13.00	25.00	46.50	80.00	—

KM# 15.5 8 MARAVEDIS

Copper **Obv:** Crowned shield of Castile **Rev:** Crowned shield of Leon **Note:** Hammered; varieties exist in placement of value and date. Mint mark: Aqueduct.

Date	Mintage	VG	F	VF	XF	Unc
1604	—	13.00	25.00	46.50	80.00	—
1605	—	13.00	25.00	46.50	80.00	—
1606	—	13.00	25.00	46.50	80.00	—
1607	—	15.00	30.00	50.00	90.00	—
1608	—	15.00	30.00	50.00	90.00	—
1609	—	17.00	36.25	60.00	95.00	—
1618	—	15.00	30.00	50.00	90.00	—
1618/168	—	22.50	43.50	75.00	130	—
1619	—	13.00	25.00	46.50	80.00	—
1619 A	—	17.00	36.25	60.00	95.00	—

KM# 15.1 8 MARAVEDIS

Copper **Obv:** Crowned shield of Castile **Rev:** Crowned shield of Leon

Date	Mintage	VG	F	VF	XF	Unc
1602B	—	10.00	20.00	40.50	75.00	—
1603B	—	10.00	20.00	40.50	75.00	—
Note: 1603 issues have a date position variety						
1604B	—	10.00	20.00	40.50	75.00	—
1605B	—	10.00	20.00	40.50	75.00	—
1606B	—	12.00	22.50	46.50	85.00	—
1607B	—	10.00	20.00	40.50	75.00	—
1608B	—	10.00	20.00	40.50	75.00	—
1609	—	30.00	60.00	85.00	150	—
1618B	—	10.00	20.00	40.50	75.00	—
1619B	—	10.00	20.00	40.50	75.00	—

KM# 15.2 8 MARAVEDIS

Copper **Obv:** Crowned shield of Castile **Rev:** Crowned shield of Leon

Date	Mintage	VG	F	VF	XF	Unc
1602C	—	15.00	30.00	50.00	90.00	—
1603C	—	17.00	36.25	60.00	105	—
1604C	—	10.00	20.00	40.50	75.00	—
1605C	—	12.00	22.50	46.50	85.00	—
1606C	—	12.00	22.50	46.50	85.00	—
1607C	—	12.00	22.50	46.50	85.00	—
1609C	—	15.00	30.00	55.00	100	—
1619C	—	12.00	22.50	46.50	85.00	—
1620C	—	15.00	30.00	55.00	100	—

KM# 16 8 MARAVEDIS

Copper **Obv:** Crowned shield of Castile **Rev:** Crowned shield of Leon **Mint:** Valladolid **Note:** Milled coinage; Mint mark varieties of 3 or 4 arches in aqueduct exist. Mint mark: Aqueduct.

Date	Mintage	VG	F	VF	XF	Unc
1601	—	15.00	30.00	50.00	90.00	—
1602	—	15.00	30.00	50.00	90.00	—
1603	—	17.00	36.25	60.00	95.00	—
1604	—	13.00	25.00	46.50	80.00	—
1605	—	13.00	25.00	46.50	80.00	—
1606	—	13.00	25.00	46.50	80.00	—
1607	—	13.00	25.00	46.50	80.00	—
1608	—	13.00	25.00	46.50	80.00	—
1609	—	17.00	36.25	60.00	95.00	—
1610	—	22.50	43.50	75.00	130	—
1611	—	25.00	50.00	80.00	145	—
1612	—	13.00	25.00	46.50	80.00	—
1613	—	15.00	32.00	50.00	90.00	—
1614	—	15.00	32.00	50.00	90.00	—
1615	—	13.00	25.00	46.50	80.00	—
1616	—	13.00	25.00	46.50	80.00	—
1617	—	13.00	25.00	46.50	80.00	—
1618/7	—	15.00	32.00	50.00	90.00	—
1618	—	13.00	25.00	46.50	80.00	—
1619	—	13.00	25.00	46.50	80.00	—
1620	—	17.00	36.25	60.00	95.00	—

KM# 15.3 8 MARAVEDIS

Copper **Obv:** Crowned shield of Castile **Rev:** Crowned shield of Leon

Date	Mintage	VG	F	VF	XF	Unc
1616G	—	60.00	100	180	325	—

KM# A98 8 MARAVEDIS

Silver **Obv:** Crowned shield of Castile **Rev:** Crowned shield of Leon **Note:** Milled coinage, large flan. Prev. KM#98.

Date	Mintage	VG	F	VF	XF	Unc
1621MD	—	15.00	32.00	50.00	90.00	—
1622MD	—	15.00	32.00	50.00	90.00	—
1623MD	—	15.00	32.00	50.00	90.00	—
1624MD	—	15.00	32.00	50.00	90.00	—
1625MD	—	15.00	32.00	50.00	90.00	—
1626MD	—	15.00	32.00	50.00	90.00	—

KM# 73.2 8 MARAVEDIS

Copper **Obv:** Crowned shield of Castile **Rev:** Crowned shield of Leon **Mint:** Burgos **Note:** Mint mark: Crown.

Date	Mintage	VG	F	VF	XF	Unc
1624	—	22.50	43.50	75.00	130	—
1625	—	22.50	43.50	75.00	130	—
1626	—	17.00	36.25	60.00	105	—

KM# 73.1 8 MARAVEDIS

Copper **Obv:** Crowned shield of Castile **Rev:** Crowned shield of Leon **Mint:** Burgos

Date	Mintage	VG	F	VF	XF	Unc
1621	—	12.00	22.50	40.50	70.00	—
1622	—	12.00	22.50	40.50	70.00	—
1623	—	12.00	22.50	40.50	70.00	—
1624	—	12.00	22.50	40.50	70.00	—
1625	—	15.00	30.00	46.50	80.00	—
1626	—	12.00	22.50	40.50	70.00	—

KM# 73.3 8 MARAVEDIS

Copper **Obv:** Crowned shield of Castile **Rev:** Crowned shield of Leon **Mint:** Cuenca

Date	Mintage	VG	F	VF	XF	Unc
1621	—	17.00	36.25	60.00	105	—
1622	—	17.00	36.25	60.00	105	—
1623	—	17.00	36.25	60.00	105	—
1624	—	17.00	36.25	60.00	105	—
1625	—	17.00	36.25	60.00	105	—
1626	—	25.00	50.00	80.00	145	—

KM# 73.4 8 MARAVEDIS

Copper **Obv:** Crowned shield of Castile **Rev:** Crowned shield of Leon **Mint:** Cuenca

Date	Mintage	VG	F	VF	XF	Unc
1621G	—	17.00	36.25	60.00	105	—
1622G	—	15.00	30.00	50.00	80.00	—
1623G	—	15.00	30.00	50.00	80.00	—
1624G	—	15.00	30.00	50.00	80.00	—
1625G	—	15.00	30.00	50.00	80.00	—
1626G	—	15.00	30.00	50.00	80.00	—

KM# 73.5 8 MARAVEDIS

Copper **Obv:** Crowned shield of Castile **Rev:** Crowned shield of Leon **Mint:** Madrid

Date	Mintage	VG	F	VF	XF	Unc
1621	—	17.00	36.25	60.00	95.00	—
1622	—	17.00	36.25	60.00	95.00	—
1623	—	17.00	36.25	60.00	95.00	—
1624	—	17.00	36.25	60.00	95.00	—
1625	—	17.00	36.25	60.00	95.00	—
1626	—	17.00	36.25	60.00	95.00	—

KM# 73.6 8 MARAVEDIS

Copper **Obv:** Crowned shield of Castile **Rev:** Crowned shield of Leon **Mint:** Segovia

Date	Mintage	VG	F	VF	XF	Unc
1621	—	15.00	30.00	50.00	90.00	—
1261 Error	—	36.25	75.00	115	255	—
1622	—	15.00	30.00	50.00	90.00	—

Note: The 1622 issue comes with date on obverse and reverse, without value on reverse. Additional varieties exist

Date	Mintage	VG	F	VF	XF	Unc
1623	—	17.00	36.25	60.00	95.00	—
1624	—	15.00	30.00	50.00	90.00	—
1625	—	15.00	30.00	50.00	90.00	—
1626	—	17.00	36.25	60.00	95.00	—

KM# 73.7 8 MARAVEDIS

Copper **Obv:** Crowned shield of Castile **Rev:** Crowned shield of Leon **Mint:** Segovia

Date	Mintage	VG	F	VF	XF	Unc
1621S	—	15.00	30.00	50.00	80.00	—
1622S	—	15.00	30.00	50.00	80.00	—
1623S	—	15.00	30.00	50.00	80.00	—
1624S	—	15.00	30.00	50.00	80.00	—
1625S	—	15.00	30.00	50.00	80.00	—
1626S	—	15.00	30.00	50.00	80.00	—

KM# 73.8 8 MARAVEDIS

Copper **Obv:** Crowned shield of Castile **Rev:** Crowned shield of Leon **Mint:** Segovia

Date	Mintage	VG	F	VF	XF	Unc
1621	—	15.00	30.00	50.00	90.00	—
1622	—	15.00	30.00	50.00	90.00	—
1623	—	15.00	30.00	50.00	90.00	—
1624	—	15.00	30.00	50.00	90.00	—
1625	—	15.00	30.00	50.00	90.00	—
1626	—	15.00	30.00	50.00	90.00	—

KM# 73.9 8 MARAVEDIS

Copper **Obv:** Crowned shield of Castile **Rev:** Crowned shield of Leon **Mint:** Valladolid

Date	Mintage	VG	F	VF	XF	Unc
1621	—	17.00	36.25	60.00	95.00	—
1622	—	17.00	36.25	60.00	95.00	—
1623	—	17.00	36.25	60.00	95.00	—
1624	—	17.00	36.25	60.00	95.00	—
1625	—	22.50	43.50	75.00	130	—
1626	—	17.00	36.25	60.00	95.00	—

KM# 124 8 MARAVEDIS

Silver **Obv:** Large VIII, mint mark below **Rev:** Cross with castles and lions in angles

Date	Mintage	VG	F	VF	XF	Unc
1643MD B	—	350	650	1,050	—	—

KM# 152 8 MARAVEDIS

Copper **Obv:** Bust right within circle **Rev:** VIII within crowned pillars **Mint:** Burgos

Date	Mintage	VG	F	VF	XF	Unc
1660	—	280	450	750	—	—

KM# 161.1 8 MARAVEDIS

Copper **Obv:** Bust of Philip IV right within circle **Rev:** Crowned shield of Spain, VIII to right **Mint:** Burgos

Date	Mintage	VG	F	VF	XF	Unc
1661 R	—	105	200	350	600	—

KM# 171.1 8 MARAVEDIS

Copper **Obv:** Bust of Philip IV right within circle **Rev:** Crowned shield of Spain, 8 at right **Mint:** Madrid

Date	Mintage	VG	F	VF	XF	Unc
1662B R	—	14.00	27.50	46.50	80.00	—
1663B R	—	14.00	27.50	46.50	90.00	—
1664B R	—	14.00	27.50	46.50	90.00	—

KM# 171.2 8 MARAVEDIS

Copper **Obv:** Bust of Philip IV right within circle **Rev:** Crowned shield of Spain, 8 at right **Mint:** Cuenca

Date	Mintage	VG	F	VF	XF	Unc
1661	—	16.00	30.00	55.00	95.00	—
1662	—	14.00	27.50	50.00	90.00	—
1663	—	14.00	27.50	50.00	90.00	—
1664	—	14.00	27.50	50.00	90.00	—

KM# 171.3 8 MARAVEDIS

Copper **Obv:** Bust of Philip IV right within circle **Rev:** Crowned shield of Spain, 8 at right

Date	Mintage	VG	F	VF	XF	Unc
1661 N	—	11.00	22.50	40.50	65.00	—
1662 N	—	11.00	22.50	40.50	65.00	—
1663 N	—	11.00	22.50	40.50	65.00	—
1664 N	—	14.00	27.50	46.50	80.00	—

KM# 162 8 MARAVEDIS

Copper **Obv:** Bust of Philip IV right within legend **Rev:** Crowned shield of Castile and Leon **Mint:** Segovia **Note:** Value as 8.

Date	Mintage	VG	F	VF	XF	Unc
1661M S	—	11.00	22.50	40.50	65.00	—

Note: A variety of 1661 exists with lions and castles switched in the reverse.

Date	Mintage	VG	F	VF	XF	Unc
1662M S	—	14.00	30.00	50.00	90.00	—
1663M S	—	12.00	25.00	43.50	70.00	—
1663M BR	—	12.00	25.00	43.50	70.00	—
1664M S	—	14.00	30.00	50.00	90.00	—
1664M BR	—	14.00	30.00	50.00	90.00	—

KM# 171.5 8 MARAVEDIS

Copper **Obv:** Bust of Philip IV right within circle **Rev:** Crowned shield of Spain, 8 at right **Mint:** Granada **Note:** Value as VIII.

Date	Mintage	VG	F	VF	XF	Unc
1660MD A	—	14.00	27.50	46.50	80.00	—
1661MD A	—	14.00	27.50	50.00	90.00	—
1661MD	—	14.00	27.50	50.00	90.00	—
1661MD Y	—	14.00	27.50	46.50	80.00	—
1662MD A	—	16.00	33.75	60.00	95.00	—
1662MD Y	—	14.00	27.50	46.50	80.00	—
1663MD Y	—	14.00	27.50	50.00	90.00	—
1664MD Y	—	14.00	27.50	46.50	80.00	—

KM# 171.4 8 MARAVEDIS

Copper **Obv:** Bust of Philip IV right within circle **Rev:** Crowned shield of Spain, 8 at right **Mint:** Granada **Note:** Varieties exist with B vertical or horizontal.

Date	Mintage	VG	F	VF	XF	Unc
1662M S	—	16.00	33.75	60.00	95.00	—
1662M Y	—	14.00	27.50	50.00	90.00	—
1663M S	—	14.00	27.50	50.00	90.00	—
1663M Y	—	14.00	27.50	50.00	90.00	—
1664M S	—	14.00	27.50	46.50	80.00	—
1664M Y	—	14.00	27.50	46.50	80.00	—

KM# 163 8 MARAVEDIS

Copper **Obv:** Bust of Philip IV right within legend **Rev:** Crowned shield of Castile and Leon **Mint:** Seville **Note:** Milled.

Date	Mintage	VG	F	VF	XF	Unc
1661 R	—	14.00	27.50	46.50	80.00	—
1662 R	—	14.00	27.50	46.50	80.00	—
1663 R	—	14.00	27.50	46.50	90.00	—
1664 R	—	14.00	27.50	46.50	90.00	—

KM# 164.1 8 MARAVEDIS

Copper **Obv:** Bust of Philip IV right within legend **Rev:** Crowned shield of Castile and Leon **Mint:** Toledo **Note:** Milled.

Date	Mintage	VG	F	VF	XF	Unc
1661 M	—	14.00	27.50	46.50	80.00	—
1662 M	—	14.00	27.50	46.50	80.00	—
1663 M	—	14.00	27.50	46.50	80.00	—
1664 M	—	14.00	27.50	46.50	80.00	—

KM# 164.2 8 MARAVEDIS

Copper **Obv:** Bust of Philip IV right within legend **Rev:** Crowned shield of Castile and Leon **Mint:** Trujillo **Note:** Milled.

Date	Mintage	VG	F	VF	XF	Unc
1661 M	—	14.00	30.00	50.00	90.00	—
1662 M	—	14.00	30.00	50.00	90.00	—
1663 M	—	14.00	30.00	50.00	90.00	—
1664 M	—	14.00	30.00	50.00	90.00	—

KM# 164.3 8 MARAVEDIS

Copper **Obv:** Bust of Philip IV right within legend **Rev:** Crowned shield of Castile and Leon **Mint:** Valladolid **Note:** Milled.

Date	Mintage	VG	F	VF	XF	Unc
1662 M	—	20.00	40.50	75.00	130	—
1663 M	—	16.00	33.75	60.00	95.00	—
1664 M	—	16.00	33.75	60.00	95.00	—

KM# 165 8 MARAVEDIS

Copper **Obv:** Small bust of Philip IV right within circle **Rev:** Crowned shield of Castile and Leon **Mint:** Cuenca **Note:** Milled coinage.

Date	Mintage	VG	F	VF	XF	Unc
1661 R	—	12.00	25.00	43.50	70.00	—
1662 R	—	11.00	22.50	40.50	65.00	—
1663 R	—	11.00	22.50	40.50	65.00	—
1664 R	—	11.00	22.50	40.50	65.00	—

KM# 167.1 8 MARAVEDIS

Silver **Obv:** Bust of Philip IV right **Rev:** Crowned shield of Castile and Leon **Mint:** Seville **Note:** Irregular flan.

Date	Mintage	VG	F	VF	XF	Unc
1661 R	—	70.00	135	215	350	—
1661	—	70.00	135	215	350	—

KM# 161.2 8 MARAVEDIS

Copper **Obv:** Bust of Philip IV right within circle **Rev:** Crowned shield of Spain, VIII to right **Mint:** Madrid **Note:** Milled, large flan.

Date	Mintage	VG	F	VF	XF	Unc
1664 Y	—	80.00	160	290	475	—

KM# 166.1 8 MARAVEDIS

Copper **Obv:** Bust of Philip IV right **Rev:** Crowned arms of Castile and Leon **Mint:** Burgos **Note:** Milled coinage.

Date	Mintage	VG	F	VF	XF	Unc
1661	—	55.00	110	200	325	—

KM# 166.2 8 MARAVEDIS

Copper **Obv:** Bust of Philip IV right **Rev:** Crowned arms of Castile and Leon **Mint:** Granada

Date	Mintage	VG	F	VF	XF	Unc
1661 N	—	70.00	145	265	450	—

KM# 167.2 8 MARAVEDIS

Silver **Obv:** Bust of Philip IV right **Rev:** Crowned shield of Castile and Leon **Mint:** Toledo **Note:** Irregular flan.

Date	Mintage	VG	F	VF	XF	Unc
1661	—	80.00	160	265	450	—

KM# 167.3 8 MARAVEDIS

Silver **Obv:** Bust of Philip IV right **Rev:** Crowned shield of Castile and Leon **Mint:** Trujillo **Note:** Irregular flan.

Date	Mintage	VG	F	VF	XF	Unc
1661 F	—	70.00	135	200	325	—

KM# 167.4 8 MARAVEDIS

Silver **Obv:** Bust of Philip IV right **Rev:** Crowned shield of Castile and Leon **Mint:** Valladolid **Note:** Irregular flan.

Date	Mintage	VG	F	VF	XF	Unc
1661 M	—	105	200	350	600	—

KM# 221 8 MARAVEDIS

Copper **Obv:** Crowned shield of Castile and Leon **Rev:** Crown above IHS **Mint:** Valladolid

Date	Mintage	VG	F	VF	XF	Unc
1691	—	240	400	675	—	—

KM# 153.1 16 MARAVEDIS

Copper **Obv:** Large bust of Philip IV right **Rev:** Crowned shield, 16 at right **Mint:** Valladolid

Date	Mintage	VG	F	VF	XF	Unc
1960MD A (error)	—	12.00	25.00	50.00	110	—
1660MD A	—	9.00	20.00	36.25	70.00	—
1661MD A	—	9.00	20.00	36.25	70.00	—
1661MD Y	—	9.00	20.00	36.25	70.00	—

KM# 153.2 16 MARAVEDIS

Copper **Obv:** Large bust of Philip IV right **Rev:** Crowned shield, 16 at right **Mint:** Trujillo

Date	Mintage	VG	F	VF	XF	Unc
1661 F	—	80.00	160	290	475	—

KM# 172.1 16 MARAVEDIS

Copper **Obv:** Smaller bust of Philip IV right **Rev:** Crowned arms, 16 at right **Mint:** Trujillo

Date	Mintage	VG	F	VF	XF	Unc
1662B R	—	5.00	11.00	22.50	55.00	—
1663B R	—	5.00	11.00	22.50	55.00	—
1664B R	—	5.00	11.00	22.50	55.00	—

KM# 172.4 16 MARAVEDIS

Copper **Obv:** Smaller bust of Philip IV right **Rev:** Crowned arms, 16 at right **Mint:** Granada

Date	Mintage	VG	F	VF	XF	Unc
1661 N	—	12.00	25.00	50.00	105	—
1662 N	—	5.00	11.00	22.50	55.00	—
1663 N	—	5.00	11.00	22.50	55.00	—

Note: Coin dated 1663 also exists with N inverted

Date	Mintage	VG	F	VF	XF	Unc
1664 N	—	5.00	11.00	22.50	55.00	—

KM# 172.6 16 MARAVEDIS

Copper **Obv:** Smaller bust of Philip IV right **Rev:** Crowned arms, 16 at right **Mint:** Segovia

Date	Mintage	VG	F	VF	XF	Unc
1661 S	—	5.00	11.00	22.50	55.00	—
1661 BR	—	7.00	14.00	30.00	65.00	—
1662 S	—	5.00	11.00	22.50	55.00	—
1662 BR	—	7.00	14.00	30.00	65.00	—
1663 S	—	7.00	14.00	30.00	65.00	—
1663 BR	—	5.00	11.00	22.50	55.00	—
1664 S	—	7.00	14.00	30.00	65.00	—
1664 BR	—	5.00	11.00	22.50	55.00	—

KM# 172.7 16 MARAVEDIS

Copper **Obv:** Smaller bust of Philip IV right **Rev:** Crowned arms, 16 at right **Mint:** Segovia

Date	Mintage	VG	F	VF	XF	Unc
1661S R	—	5.00	11.00	22.50	55.00	—
1662S R	—	5.00	11.00	22.50	55.00	—
1663S R	—	5.00	11.00	22.50	55.00	—
1664S R	—	7.00	11.00	22.50	55.00	—
1664S R Reversed 4	—	9.00	16.00	36.25	70.00	—

KM# 172.8 16 MARAVEDIS

Copper **Obv:** Smaller bust of Philip IV right **Rev:** Crowned arms, 16 at right **Mint:** Toledo

Date	Mintage	VG	F	VF	XF	Unc
1661 M	—	9.00	19.00	40.50	90.00	—
1662 M	—	9.00	19.00	40.50	90.00	—
1663	—	7.00	14.00	30.00	65.00	—
1663 M	—	7.00	14.00	30.00	65.00	—
1664 M	—	7.00	14.00	30.00	65.00	—

KM# 172.10 16 MARAVEDIS

Copper **Obv:** Smaller bust of Philip IV right **Rev:** Crowned arms, 16 at right **Mint:** Valladolid

Date	Mintage	VG	F	VF	XF	Unc
1661 M	—	16.00	33.75	65.00	135	—
1662 M	—	14.00	27.50	60.00	120	—
1663 M	—	20.00	40.50	80.00	160	—
1963 M Error	—	16.00	33.75	65.00	135	—
1664 M	—	14.00	27.50	60.00	120	—

KM# 172.2 16 MARAVEDIS

Copper **Obv:** Smaller bust of Philip IV right **Rev:** Crowned arms, 16 at right **Mint:** Trujillo **Note:** Mint mark: Scalloped shell.

Date	Mintage	VG	F	VF	XF	Unc
1661 R	—	7.00	14.00	30.00	70.00	—
1662 R	—	5.00	11.00	22.50	55.00	—
1663 R	—	5.00	11.00	22.50	55.00	—
1664 R	—	5.00	11.00	22.50	55.00	—

KM# 172.3 16 MARAVEDIS

Copper **Obv:** Smaller bust of Philip IV right **Rev:** Crowned arms, 16 at right **Mint:** Trujillo **Note:** Mint mark: Star above chalice.

Date	Mintage	VG	F	VF	XF	Unc
1661	—	8.00	16.00	36.25	80.00	—
1662	—	5.00	11.00	22.50	55.00	—
1663	—	5.00	11.00	22.50	55.00	—
1664	—	5.00	11.00	22.50	55.00	—

KM# 172.5 16 MARAVEDIS

Copper **Obv:** Smaller bust of Philip IV right **Rev:** Crowned arms, 16 at right **Mint:** Granada **Note:** Varieties exist.

Date	Mintage	VG	F	VF	XF	Unc
1662M S	—	5.00	11.00	22.50	55.00	—
1662M Y	—	7.00	14.00	30.00	65.00	—
1663M S	—	7.00	14.00	30.00	70.00	—
1663M Y	—	7.00	14.00	30.00	65.00	—
1664M S	—	5.00	11.00	22.50	55.00	—
1664M Y	—	5.00	11.00	22.50	55.00	—

KM# 172.9 16 MARAVEDIS

Copper **Obv:** Smaller bust of Philip IV right **Rev:** Crowned arms, 16 at right **Mint:** Trujillo **Note:** Varieties exist.

Date	Mintage	VG	F	VF	XF	Unc
1661 M	—	7.00	14.00	30.00	65.00	—
1662 M	—	8.00	16.00	36.25	80.00	—
1663 M	—	8.00	16.00	36.25	80.00	—
1664 M	—	8.00	16.00	36.25	80.00	—

KM# 34 1/4 REAL (1/4 Croat)

0.8583 g., 0.9306 Silver 0.0257 oz. ASW **Obv:** Bust of Philip III left **Rev:** Long cross, pellets and circle in quarters **Rev. Legend:** BA / RC / INO / 1609 **Mint:** Barcelona

Date	Mintage	VG	F	VF	XF	Unc
1609	—	525	975	1,500	—	—

KM# 23 1/2 REAL (1/2 Croat)

1.7167 g., 0.9306 Silver 0.0514 oz. ASW **Obv:** Crowned PHILIPPVS monogram **Rev:** Cross with castles and lions in quarters **Mint:** Segovia

Date	Mintage	VG	F	VF	XF	Unc
1602	—	40.50	70.00	145	325	—
1609 C	—	40.50	70.00	145	325	—
1611 C	—	40.50	70.00	220	475	—
1611 A/C	—	70.00	135	175	400	—
1613 AR	—	55.00	110	240	550	—
1614 AR	—	19.00	37.75	75.00	160	—
1620	—	19.00	37.75	75.00	160	—
1621/0	—	14.00	27.50	60.00	130	—
1621	—	19.00	37.75	75.00	160	—

KM# 35 1/2 REAL (1/2 Croat)

1.7167 g., 0.9306 Silver 0.0514 oz. ASW **Obv:** Bust of Philip III left **Rev:** Long cross with circles and pellets in angles **Mint:** Barcelona **Note:** Hammered.

Date	Mintage	VG	F	VF	XF	Unc
1609	—	115	235	400	725	—
1620	—	100	225	400	750	—
1621	—	180	350	650	1,200	—

KM# 46 1/2 REAL (1/2 Croat)

1.7167 g., 0.9306 Silver 0.0514 oz. ASW **Obv:** Crowned PHILIPPVS monogram, mintmaster's mark below **Rev:** Cross with castles and lions in quarters **Mint:** Seville **Note:** Hammered.

Date	Mintage	VG	F	VF	XF	Unc
1609 B	—	47.25	90.00	175	325	—
1610 B	—	20.00	40.50	75.00	145	—
1611 B	—	27.50	47.25	85.00	160	—

KM# 45 1/2 REAL (1/2 Croat)

1.7167 g., 0.9306 Silver 0.0514 oz. ASW **Obv:** Crowned PHILIPPVS monogram **Rev:** Cross with castles and lions in quarters **Mint:** Segovia **Note:** Hammered.

Date	Mintage	VG	F	VF	XF	Unc
1610 A	—	60.00	110	240	525	—
1614 AR	—	55.00	100	220	475	—

KM# 51 1/2 REAL (1/2 Croat)

1.7167 g., 0.9306 Silver 0.0514 oz. ASW **Obv:** Bust of Philip III left **Rev:** Short cross with circles and pellets in angles **Mint:** Barcelona **Note:** Date varieties exist.

Date	Mintage	VG	F	VF	XF	Unc
1611	—	27.50	47.25	95.00	200	—
1612	—	16.00	25.00	65.00	120	—
1613	—	27.50	47.25	95.00	200	—
1614	—	115	235	425	800	—
1617	—	33.75	55.00	115	265	—
1618	—	27.50	47.25	95.00	200	—
1619	—	27.50	47.25	95.00	200	—

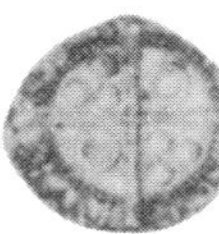

KM# 50 1/2 REAL (1/2 Croat)

1.7167 g., 0.9306 Silver 0.0514 oz. ASW **Obv:** Bust of Philip III left **Rev:** Long cross, circles and pellets in angles **Mint:** Barcelona **Note:** Hammered.

Date	Mintage	VG	F	VF	XF	Unc
1611	—	17.00	33.75	60.00	120	—

KM# 56.1 1/2 REAL (1/2 Croat)

1.7167 g., 0.9306 Silver 0.0514 oz. ASW **Obv:** Crowned PHILIPPVS monogram, mintmaster's mark left **Rev:** Short cross, with castles and lions in angles **Mint:** Barcelona **Note:** Hammered.

Date	Mintage	VG	F	VF	XF	Unc
1612 V	—	19.00	37.75	75.00	145	—
1615 V	—	19.00	37.75	75.00	145	—
1615 G	—	27.50	55.00	110	240	—
1620 R	—	19.00	37.75	75.00	145	—
1621 R	—	19.00	37.75	75.00	145	—

KM# 56.2 1/2 REAL (1/2 Croat)

1.7167 g., 0.9306 Silver 0.0514 oz. ASW **Obv:** Crowned PHILIPPVS monogram, mintmaster's mark left **Rev:** Short cross, with castles and lions in angles **Mint:** Barcelona

Date	Mintage	VG	F	VF	XF	Unc
1612T C	—	55.00	110	255	550	—

KM# 85 1/2 REAL (1/2 Croat)

1.7167 g., 0.9306 Silver 0.0514 oz. ASW **Obv:** Bust of Philip IV left **Rev:** Long cross, with circles and pellets in angles **Mint:** Barcelona

Date	Mintage	VG	F	VF	XF	Unc
1626	—	17.00	33.75	60.00	120	—

KM# 86.1 1/2 REAL (1/2 Croat)

1.7167 g., 0.9306 Silver 0.0514 oz. ASW **Obv:** Crowned PHILIPPVS monogram **Rev:** Cross with castles and lions in angles **Mint:** Barcelona

Date	Mintage	VG	F	VF	XF	Unc
ND(1621-64)G N	—	220	375	575	1,050	—

KM# 86.2 1/2 REAL (1/2 Croat)

1.7167 g., 0.9306 Silver 0.0514 oz. ASW **Obv:** Crowned PHILIPPVS monogram **Rev:** Cross with castles and lions in angles **Mint:** Barcelona **Note:** Large nodule.

Date	Mintage	VG	F	VF	XF	Unc
1627MD	—	255	375	575	1,100	—

KM# 86.3 1/2 REAL (1/2 Croat)

1.7167 g., 0.9306 Silver 0.0514 oz. ASW **Obv:** Crowned PHILIPPVS monogram **Rev:** Cross with castles and lions in angles **Mint:** Madrid **Note:** Small nodule.

Date	Mintage	VG	F	VF	XF	Unc
1651	—	195	290	425	800	—

KM# 88 1/2 REAL (1/2 Croat)

1.7167 g., 0.9306 Silver 0.0514 oz. ASW **Obv:** Crowned PHILIPPVS monogram **Rev:** Cross with castle and lions in angles **Mint:** Madrid **Note:** Milled, mint mark: Aqueduct.

Date	Mintage	VG	F	VF	XF	Unc
1622 A	—	40.50	70.00	130	240	—
1623 A	—	55.00	95.00	180	325	—
1627 A	—	16.00	33.75	65.00	120	—
1627 P	—	14.00	27.50	50.00	90.00	—
1631 R	—	33.75	55.00	110	200	—
1632 R	—	60.00	110	195	350	—
1633 R	—	55.00	95.00	180	325	—
1651 BR	—	16.00	33.75	65.00	120	—
1651 I	—	33.75	55.00	100	190	—
1691 I (Error)	—	55.00	95.00	180	325	—
1652 BR	—	16.00	33.75	65.00	120	—
1652 BB	—	70.00	115	220	400	—
1653 BB	—	27.50	47.25	85.00	160	—
1654 BR	—	90.00	170	325	600	—
1659 BR	—	14.00	27.50	50.00	90.00	—
1663 BR	—	16.00	33.75	65.00	120	—
1664 BR	—	27.50	47.25	85.00	160	—

KM# 87 1/2 REAL (1/2 Croat)

1.7167 g., 0.9306 Silver 0.0514 oz. ASW **Obv:** Crowned PHILIPPVS monogram **Rev:** Cross with castles and lions in angles **Mint:** Seville **Note:** Hammered.

Date	Mintage	VG	F	VF	XF	Unc
1627 D	—	60.00	115	220	475	—
1627 R	—	60.00	115	220	475	—

KM# 89 1/2 REAL (1/2 Croat)

1.7167 g., 0.9306 Silver 0.0514 oz. ASW **Obv:** Crowned PHILIPPVS monogram **Rev:** Cross with castles and lions in angles **Mint:** Segovia **Note:** Milled.

Date	Mintage	VG	F	VF	XF	Unc
1627 P	—	255	475	800	1,550	—

KM# 100 1/2 REAL (1/2 Croat)

1.7167 g., 0.9306 Silver 0.0514 oz. ASW **Obv:** Bust of Philip IV left **Rev:** Short cross, with circles and pellets in angles **Mint:** Barcelona

Date	Mintage	VG	F	VF	XF	Unc
1630	—	27.50	55.00	115	240	—
1632	—	14.00	27.50	65.00	120	—
1633	—	17.00	33.75	80.00	160	—

KM# 109 1/2 REAL (1/2 Croat)

1.7167 g., 0.9306 Silver 0.0514 oz. ASW **Obv:** Bust right **Rev:** Short cross, with circles and pellets in angles **Mint:** Segovia

Date	Mintage	VG	F	VF	XF	Unc
1631	—	400	750	1,300	2,500	—
1632	—	475	800	1,400	2,650	—

KM# 110 1/2 REAL (1/2 Croat)

1.7167 g., 0.9306 Silver 0.0514 oz. ASW **Obv:** Large bust of Philip IV left **Rev:** Short cross, with circles and pellets in angles **Mint:** Segovia

Date	Mintage	VG	F	VF	XF	Unc
1632	—	70.00	135	255	475	—
1635	—	70.00	135	255	475	—

KM# 121 1/2 REAL (1/2 Croat)

1.7167 g., 0.9306 Silver 0.0514 oz. ASW **Obv:** Bust of Philip IV right **Rev:** Cross with castles and lions in angles **Mint:** Madrid **Note:** Hammered.

Date	Mintage	VG	F	VF	XF	Unc
1643	—	115	225	400	750	—

KM# 203 1/2 REAL (1/2 Croat)

1.7167 g., 0.9306 Silver 0.0514 oz. ASW **Obv:** Crowned arms **Obv. Legend:** CAROLVS • II • D • G **Rev:** Cross with castles and lions in angles **Mint:** Segovia **Note:** Varieties exist in shape of crown.

Date	Mintage	VG	F	VF	XF	Unc
1685 BR	—	47.25	90.00	180	350	—
1686 BR	—	47.25	90.00	180	350	—

KM# 222 1/2 REAL (1/2 Croat)

1.7167 g., 0.9306 Silver 0.0514 oz. ASW **Obv:** Crowned arms **Rev:** Cross above AM monogram **Mint:** Madrid

Date	Mintage	VG	F	VF	XF	Unc
1691 BR	—	170	270	500	950	—
1699 BR	—	205	375	725	1,350	—

KM# 27 REAL (Croat)

3.4335 g., 0.9306 Silver 0.1027 oz. ASW **Obv:** Crowned Spanish shield **Obv. Legend:** PHILIPPVS • III • D • G •

Rev: Arms of Castile and Leon in octolobe **Mint:** Barcelona **Note:** Milled. Mint mark: Aqueduct.

Date	Mintage	VG	F	VF	XF	Unc
1607 C	—	22.50	47.25	85.00	200	—
1608 C	—	27.50	55.00	100	240	—
1612 AR	—	37.75	75.00	145	325	—
1613 AR	—	47.25	90.00	175	400	—
1614 AR	—	37.75	75.00	145	325	—
1617	—	30.00	55.00	115	265	—
1621	—	33.75	60.00	125	280	—

KM# 52.1 REAL (Croat)

3.4335 g., 0.9306 Silver 0.1027 oz. ASW **Obv:** Crowned arms **Rev:** Cross with castles and lions in angles in octolobe **Mint:** Granada **Note:** Milled.

Date	Mintage	VG	F	VF	XF	Unc
1611 M	—	27.50	55.00	110	265	—
1612 M	—	27.50	55.00	110	265	—
1614 M	—	120	235	475	950	—

KM# 52.2 REAL (Croat)

3.4335 g., 0.9306 Silver 0.1027 oz. ASW **Obv:** Crowned arms **Rev:** Cross with castles and lions in angles in octolobe **Mint:** Grenada **Note:** Hammered. Mint mark: Aqueduct.

Date	Mintage	VG	F	VF	XF	Unc
1612 A	—	47.25	90.00	180	400	—
ND S	—	80.00	160	290	650	—

KM# 52.3 REAL (Croat)

3.4335 g., 0.9306 Silver 0.1027 oz. ASW **Obv:** Crowned arms **Rev:** Cross with castles and lion in angles in octolobe **Mint:** Grenada

Date	Mintage	VG	F	VF	XF	Unc
1601S B	—	27.50	47.25	85.00	190	—
1602S B	—	27.50	47.25	85.00	190	—
1603S B	—	27.50	47.25	85.00	190	—
1604S B	—	27.50	47.25	85.00	190	—
1605S B	—	27.50	47.25	85.00	190	—
1607S B	—	33.75	55.00	110	240	—
1609S B	—	27.50	47.25	85.00	190	—
1610S B	—	20.00	33.75	65.00	145	—
1611S B	—	20.00	33.75	65.00	145	—
1612S B	—	27.50	47.25	85.00	190	—
1612S D	—	27.50	47.25	85.00	190	—
1613S V	—	47.25	75.00	145	325	—
1614S B	—	27.50	47.25	85.00	190	—
1615S B	—	27.50	47.25	85.00	190	—
1615S V	—	27.50	47.25	85.00	190	—
1618S G	—	33.75	55.00	110	240	—
1620S B	—	27.50	47.25	95.00	200	—

KM# 52.4 REAL (Croat)

3.4335 g., 0.9306 Silver 0.1027 oz. ASW **Obv:** Crowned arms **Rev:** Cross with castles and lions in angles in octolobe **Mint:** Grenada

Date	Mintage	VG	F	VF	XF	Unc
1601T C	—	60.00	110	220	475	—
1605T C	—	27.50	47.25	95.00	200	—
1606T C	—	40.50	70.00	130	290	—
1609T C	—	33.75	55.00	100	215	—
1609T D	—	60.00	110	220	475	—
1612T C	—	33.75	55.00	115	240	—
1615T C	—	33.75	55.00	110	215	—
1616T C	—	33.75	55.00	110	215	—
1620T P	—	47.25	80.00	160	350	—
1621T P	—	33.75	55.00	100	215	—

KM# 52.5 REAL (Croat)

3.4335 g., 0.9306 Silver 0.1027 oz. ASW **Obv:** Crowned arms **Rev:** Cross with castles and lions in angles in octolobe **Mint:** Granada

Date	Mintage	VG	F	VF	XF	Unc
1609 B	—	70.00	120	245	550	—

KM# 130.1 REAL (Croat)

3.4335 g., 0.9306 Silver 0.1027 oz. ASW **Obv:** Crowned arms **Rev:** Cross with castles and lions in angles in octolobe **Mint:** Madrid **Note:** Hammered.

Date	Mintage	VG	F	VF	XF	Unc
1651 A	—	225	350	600	1,050	—

KM# 130.2 REAL (Croat)

3.4335 g., 0.9306 Silver 0.1027 oz. ASW **Obv:** Crowned arms **Rev:** Cross with castles and lions in angles in octolobe **Mint:** Madrid **Note:** Mint mark: Aqueduct.

Date	Mintage	VG	F	VF	XF	Unc
ND R	—	70.00	135	290	550	—

KM# 130.3 REAL (Croat)

3.4335 g., 0.9306 Silver 0.1027 oz. ASW **Obv:** Crowned Spanish shield **Rev:** Arms of Castile and Leon in octolobe **Mint:** Madrid **Note:** Mint mark: S

Date	Mintage	VG	F	VF	XF	Unc
1625S R	—	55.00	115	230	450	—
1627S D	—	40.50	90.00	180	350	—
1628S R	—	40.50	90.00	195	375	—
1635S R	—	60.00	120	260	500	—

KM# 92 REAL (Croat)

3.4335 g., 0.9306 Silver 0.1027 oz. ASW **Obv:** Crowned arms **Obv. Legend:** PHILIPPVS • IIII • D • G • **Rev:** Cross with castles and lions in angles in octolobe **Mint:** Madrid **Note:** Milled, Mint mark: Aqueduct.

Date	Mintage	VG	F	VF	XF	Unc
1627 A	—	20.00	37.75	65.00	145	—
1627 P	—	16.00	27.50	50.00	110	—
1628 A	—	19.00	37.75	75.00	160	—
1628 A/BR	—	33.75	70.00	130	290	—
1628 P	—	14.00	25.00	46.50	105	—
1629 P	—	14.00	27.50	50.00	110	—
1651 I	—	90.00	170	290	550	—
1652 BR	—	20.00	37.75	65.00	145	—
1653 BR	—	20.00	37.75	75.00	160	—
1659 BR	—	20.00	37.75	65.00	145	—
1660 BR	—	22.50	43.25	85.00	190	—
1660	—	135	270	500	950	—

KM# 91 REAL (Croat)

3.4335 g., 0.9306 Silver 0.1027 oz. ASW **Obv:** PHILIPPVS monogram crowned **Rev:** Cross with castles and lions in angles in octolobe **Mint:** Madrid

Date	Mintage	VG	F	VF	XF	Unc
1627 V	—	205	425	650	—	—
1628 V	—	205	425	650	—	—
1651 A	—	205	425	650	—	—

KM# 130.4 REAL (Croat)

3.4335 g., 0.9306 Silver 0.1027 oz. ASW **Obv:** Crowned arms **Rev:** Cross with castles and lions in octolobe **Mint:** Toledo

Date	Mintage	VG	F	VF	XF	Unc
1621 P	—	75.00	145	270	525	—
1627	—	50.00	100	195	450	—

KM# 122 REAL (Croat)

3.4335 g., 0.9306 Silver 0.1027 oz. ASW **Obv:** Bust of Philip IV right **Rev:** Cross with castles and lions in angles in octolobe **Mint:** Madrid **Note:** Milled.

Date	Mintage	VG	F	VF	XF	Unc
1643 B	—	110	220	400	825	—

Note: Varieties with inverted "B" and retrograde "4" also exist

KM# 181.1 REAL (Croat)

3.4335 g., 0.9306 Silver 0.1027 oz. ASW **Obv:** Bust of Charles II left within pellet border **Rev:** Long cross, circle and pellets in angles **Mint:** Barcelona **Note:** Legend varieties exist.

Date	Mintage	VG	F	VF	XF	Unc
1674	—	16.00	30.00	50.00	110	—
1675	—	25.00	40.50	75.00	145	—
1677	—	27.50	47.25	85.00	175	—
1682	—	25.00	40.50	75.00	145	—
1687	—	70.00	120	255	475	—
1688	—	25.00	40.50	80.00	160	—

KM# 181.2 REAL (Croat)

3.4335 g., 0.9306 Silver 0.1027 oz. ASW **Obv:** Bust of Charles II left within pellet border **Rev:** Long cross, circle and pellets in angles **Rev. Legend:** BARCINONE **Mint:** Barcelona

Date	Mintage	VG	F	VF	XF	Unc
1674	—	110	205	375	675	—

KM# 183 REAL (Croat)

3.4335 g., 0.9306 Silver 0.1027 oz. ASW **Obv:** Crowned arms **Rev:** Cross with castles and arms in octolobe **Rev. Legend:** CARLOS SECVNDO... **Mint:** Segovia

Date	Mintage	VG	F	VF	XF	Unc
1675 BR	—	60.00	110	220	475	—

KM# 192 REAL (Croat)

3.4335 g., 0.9306 Silver 0.1027 oz. ASW **Obv:** Crowned arms **Obv. Legend:** CAROLVS•II•D•G• **Rev:** Cross with castles and lions in angles in octolobe **Mint:** Madrid

Date	Mintage	VG	F	VF	XF	Unc
1682 M	—	270	500	825	—	—

KM# 193 REAL (Croat)

3.4335 g., 0.9306 Silver 0.1027 oz. ASW **Obv:** Crowned shield of Castile and Leon **Obv. Legend:** CAROLVS • II • D • G • **Rev:** Crowned CAROLVS monogram **Mint:** Segovia

Date	Mintage	VG	F	VF	XF	Unc
1681 R	—	95.00	180	325	725	—

KM# 198 REAL (Croat)

3.4335 g., 0.9306 Silver 0.1027 oz. ASW **Obv:** Crowned Spanish shield **Obv. Legend:** CAROLVS • II • D • G • **Rev:** Cross with castles and lions in angles in octolobe **Mint:** Segovia

Date	Mintage	VG	F	VF	XF	Unc
1683 BR	—	55.00	100	220	475	—

KM# 202 REAL (Croat)

3.4335 g., 0.9306 Silver 0.1027 oz. ASW **Obv:** Shield with arms of Portugal **Obv. Legend:** CAROLVS • II • D • G • **Rev:** Cross with castles and lionsin angles in octolobe **Mint:** Segovia

Date	Mintage	VG	F	VF	XF	Unc
1684 BR	—	55.00	100	220	475	—
1685 BR	—	70.00	135	290	650	—

KM# 204.1 REAL (Croat)

3.4335 g., 0.9306 Silver 0.1027 oz. ASW **Obv:** Crowned shield of Castile and Leon **Obv. Legend:** CAROLVS • II • D • G • **Rev:** Cross above AM monogram **Mint:** Segovia

Date	Mintage	VG	F	VF	XF	Unc
1686 BR	—	75.00	150	300	600	—
1687 BR	—	180	290	475	1,100	—

KM# 204.2 REAL (Croat)

3.4335 g., 0.9306 Silver 0.1027 oz. ASW **Obv:** Crowned arms **Obv. Legend:** CAROLVS • II • D • G • **Rev:** Cross above AM monogram **Mint:** Seville

Date	Mintage	VG	F	VF	XF	Unc
1690 M	—	110	220	400	750	—
1691 M	—	110	220	400	750	—
1692 M	—	110	220	400	750	—
1694 M	—	110	220	400	750	—
1699 M	—	110	220	400	750	—

KM# 228 REAL (Croat)

3.4335 g., 0.9306 Silver 0.1027 oz. ASW **Obv:** Crowned arms **Rev:** Cross above AM monogram **Mint:** Madrid

Date	Mintage	VG	F	VF	XF	Unc
1691 BR	—	425	750	1,300	—	—
1699 BR	—	220	375	625	—	—

KM# 225 REAL (Croat)

Silver **Obv:** Large bust breaks legend at bottom

Date	Mintage	VG	F	VF	XF	Unc
1693	—	20.00	33.75	65.00	135	—
1698	—	27.50	47.25	85.00	190	—

KM# 240 REAL (Croat)

3.4335 g., 0.9306 Silver 0.1027 oz. ASW **Obv:** Crowned shield of Castile and Leon **Obv. Legend:** CAROLVS II **Rev:** Cross above AM monogram **Mint:** Seville **Note:** Milled, Two varieties exist, dot or rossetes in legends in inner circle.

Date	Mintage	VG	F	VF	XF	Unc
1700 M	—	115	225	425	750	—

KM# 241 REAL (Croat)

3.4335 g., 0.9306 Silver 0.1027 oz. ASW **Obv:** Crowned shield of Castile and Leon **Rev:** Circle around cross and monogram **Mint:** Seville **Note:** Milled, Cross above AM monogram in inner circle in legends.

Date	Mintage	VG	F	VF	XF	Unc
1700 M	—	115	225	375	675	—

KM# 17.6 2 REALES

6.8670 g., 0.9306 Silver 0.2054 oz. ASW **Obv:** Crowned arms, II at right **Obv. Legend:** PHILIPPVS **Rev:** Cross with castles and lions in angles in octolobe **Mint:** Granada

Date	Mintage	VG	F	VF	XF	Unc
1601S B	—	27.50	60.00	115	225	—
1602S B	—	27.50	60.00	115	225	—
1603S B	—	27.50	60.00	115	225	—
1604S B	—	27.50	60.00	115	225	—
1605S B	—	27.50	60.00	115	225	—
1607S B	—	27.50	47.25	95.00	185	—
1611S B	—	27.50	47.25	95.00	185	—
1612S B	—	27.50	55.00	110	200	—
1612S V	—	27.50	55.00	115	215	—
1612S D	—	27.50	55.00	110	200	—
1613S V/D	—	40.50	80.00	160	325	—
1613S V	—	27.50	55.00	115	215	—

Date	Mintage	VG	F	VF	XF	Unc
1614S V	—	27.50	55.00	115	215	—
1615S D	—	27.50	55.00	115	215	—
1615S V	—	27.50	55.00	115	215	—
1616S D	—	80.00	120	255	450	—
1617S D	—	27.50	55.00	115	215	—
1618S D	—	55.00	110	230	400	—
1619S R	—	47.25	90.00	180	350	—
1619S G	—	60.00	120	255	450	—
1620S D	—	27.50	55.00	115	215	—

KM# 17.8 2 REALES

6.8670 g., 0.9306 Silver 0.2054 oz. ASW **Obv:** Crowned Spanish shield, II at right **Obv. Legend:** PHILIPPVS **Rev:** Cross with castles and lions in angles in octolobe **Mint:** Valladolid **Note:** Mint mark: 3 banners.

Date	Mintage	VG	F	VF	XF	Unc
1602 Do	—	120	240	450	750	—
1605 Do	—	100	205	375	675	—
1606 Do	—	135	280	525	950	—
1611 H	—	120	240	450	750	—
1613 H	—	150	300	575	975	—
1621 V	—	150	300	575	975	—

KM# 17.5 2 REALES

6.8670 g., 0.9306 Silver 0.2054 oz. ASW **Obv:** Crowned arms, II at right **Obv. Legend:** PHILIPPVS **Rev:** Cross with castles and lions in angles in octolobe **Mint:** Granada **Note:** Mint mark: Castle.

Date	Mintage	VG	F	VF	XF	Unc
ND(1599-1613)	—	300	525	975	—	—
1608	—	225	375	675	1,200	—
1611 A	—	190	300	525	975	—
1613 B	—	130	265	425	725	—

KM# 17.1 2 REALES

6.8670 g., 0.9306 Silver 0.2054 oz. ASW **Obv:** Crowned Spanish shield, II at right **Obv. Legend:** PHILIPPVS **Rev:** Cross with castles and lions in angles in octolobe **Note:** Mint mark: Castle.

Date	Mintage	VG	F	VF	XF	Unc
1601	—	190	300	575	975	—
1602	—	250	425	750	1,350	—

KM# 17.7 2 REALES

6.8670 g., 0.9306 Silver 0.2054 oz. ASW **Obv:** Crowned Spanish shield, II at right **Obv. Legend:** PHILIPPVS **Rev:** Cross with castles and lions in angles in octolobe **Mint:** Toledo

Date	Mintage	VG	F	VF	XF	Unc
1602 C	—	47.25	90.00	175	325	—
1603 C	—	47.25	90.00	175	325	—
1604 C	—	47.25	90.00	175	325	—
1607 C	—	55.00	100	195	400	—
1609 C	—	47.25	90.00	175	325	—
1610 C	—	55.00	100	195	400	—
1612 C	—	40.50	70.00	145	280	—
1613 C	—	47.25	90.00	180	350	—
1614 C	—	40.50	70.00	145	280	—
1617 V	—	47.25	90.00	175	325	—
1618 V	—	47.25	90.00	175	325	—
1620 P	—	47.25	90.00	175	325	—

KM# 17.4 2 REALES

6.8670 g., 0.9306 Silver 0.2054 oz. ASW **Obv:** Crowned arms, II at right **Rev:** Cross with castles and lions in angles in octolobe **Mint:** Granada

Date	Mintage	VG	F	VF	XF	Unc
1620MD Go	—	190	300	525	975	—
1620MD CG	—	250	425	750	1,350	—
1621MD V	—	115	225	425	725	—

KM# 17.3 2 REALES

6.8670 g., 0.9306 Silver 0.2054 oz. ASW **Obv:** Crowned Spanish shield, II at left or right **Obv. Legend:** PHILIPPVS **Rev:** Cross with castles and lions in angles in octolobe **Mint:** Granada **Note:** G/M appears at left or right of crowned shield.

Date	Mintage	VG	F	VF	XF	Unc
1601G M	—	33.75	70.00	145	325	—
1602G M	—	47.25	90.00	180	350	—
1603G M	—	33.75	70.00	145	325	—
1604G M	—	47.25	90.00	180	350	—
1605G M	—	60.00	115	230	450	—
1607G M	—	27.50	47.25	110	240	—
1608G M	—	27.50	47.25	110	240	—
1613G M	—	27.50	55.00	125	280	—
1615G D	—	90.00	170	375	600	—

KM# 17.2 2 REALES

6.8670 g., 0.9306 Silver 0.2054 oz. ASW **Obv:** Crowned Spanish shield, II at right **Obv. Legend:** PHILIPPVS **Rev:** Cross with castles and lion in angles in octolobe **Mint:** Cuenca

Date	Mintage	VG	F	VF	XF	Unc
1603 I	—	225	375	725	1,200	—

KM# 32 2 REALES

6.8670 g., 0.9306 Silver 0.2054 oz. ASW **Obv:** Crowned arms, II at right **Obv. Legend:** PHILIPPVS • III • D • G **Rev:** Cross with castles and lions in angles in octolobe **Note:** Milled. Large regular flan. Mint mark: Aqueduct.

Date	Mintage	VG	F	VF	XF	Unc
1608 C	—	70.00	135	255	450	—
1611 A	—	55.00	100	220	400	—
1614 AR	—	60.00	120	240	450	—
1620 AR	—	70.00	135	255	450	—
1621/08	—	55.00	110	220	400	—
1621/08 A/C	—	55.00	110	220	400	—
1621/09 A/C	—	55.00	110	220	400	—
1621/11	—	55.00	110	220	400	—
1621/14	—	47.25	90.00	180	350	—

KM# 60 2 REALES

6.8670 g., 0.9306 Silver 0.2054 oz. ASW **Obv:** Crowned arms, II at right **Rev:** Cross with castles and lions in angles in octolobe **Note:** Small irregular flan. Mint mark: Castle.

Date	Mintage	VG	F	VF	XF	Unc
1614/10 AR	—	265	425	750	1,300	—
1614 S	—	225	400	725	1,250	—

KM# 61 2 REALES

6.8670 g., 0.9306 Silver 0.2054 oz. ASW **Obv:** Crowned arms, II at right **Rev:** Cross with castles and lion in angles in octolobe **Note:** Large regular flan.

Date	Mintage	VG	F	VF	XF	Unc
NDT C	—	115	225	350	575	—

KM# 83 2 REALES

6.8670 g., 0.9306 Silver 0.2054 oz. ASW **Obv:** Crowned arms **Rev:** Cross with castles and lions in angles inverted in octolobe **Mint:** Segovia **Note:** Cob type.

Date	Mintage	VG	F	VF	XF	Unc
1623 R	—	170	350	650	1,200	—
1625 R	—	135	270	500	950	—

KM# 93.1 2 REALES

6.8670 g., 0.9306 Silver 0.2054 oz. ASW **Obv:** Crowned arms **Rev:** Cross with castles and lions in angles in octolobe **Mint:** Segovia **Note:** Milled.

Date	Mintage	VG	F	VF	XF	Unc
1627	—	55.00	110	195	400	—
1627 P	—	33.75	60.00	125	265	—
1628 P	—	27.50	55.00	110	230	—
1652/20 BR	—	25.00	47.25	85.00	190	—
1652/22 BR	—	25.00	47.25	85.00	190	—
1652/29 BR	—	27.50	47.25	95.00	215	—
1652 BR	—	25.00	43.25	80.00	175	—
1659/28 BR	—	25.00	43.25	80.00	175	—
1659/29 BR	—	27.50	47.25	95.00	215	—
1659 BR	—	27.50	55.00	100	240	—

KM# 93.2 2 REALES

6.8670 g., 0.9306 Silver 0.2054 oz. ASW **Obv:** Crowned arms **Rev:** Cross with castles and lions in angles in octolobe **Mint:** Toledo **Note:** Milled.

Date	Mintage	VG	F	VF	XF	Unc
1621 P	—	27.50	47.25	95.00	200	—
1622 P	—	27.50	40.50	80.00	175	—
1623 P	—	27.50	40.50	80.00	175	—
1627 P	—	33.75	55.00	110	265	—
1628 P	—	27.50	47.25	95.00	200	—
1635 P	—	27.50	47.25	95.00	200	—

Date	Mintage	VG	F	VF	XF	Unc
1641 C	—	27.50	55.00	100	240	—
1651 Y	—	27.50	55.00	100	240	—
1652 Y	—	60.00	115	220	450	—
1657 Y	—	55.00	100	195	400	—

KM# 97 2 REALES

6.8670 g., 0.9306 Silver 0.2054 oz. ASW **Obv:** Crowned arms **Rev:** Cross with castles and lions in angles in octolobe **Mint:** Seville **Note:** Cob Type.

Date	Mintage	VG	F	VF	XF	Unc
1627 D	—	19.00	37.75	75.00	160	—
1628 R	—	25.00	47.25	85.00	190	—
1629 R	—	25.00	47.25	85.00	190	—
1633 R	—	19.00	37.75	75.00	160	—
1634 R	—	25.00	47.25	85.00	190	—
1636 R	—	25.00	47.25	85.00	190	—

KM# 131.2 2 REALES

6.8670 g., 0.9306 Silver 0.2054 oz. ASW **Obv:** Crowned arms **Rev:** Cross with castles and lions in angles in octolobe **Mint:** Madrid **Note:** Cob Type.

Date	Mintage	VG	F	VF	XF	Unc
1628 V	—	100	205	400	725	—
1629 M	—	170	350	650	1,200	—
1629 BI	—	170	270	500	950	—
1630 BI	—	170	270	500	950	—
1634 BI	—	205	375	725	1,350	—
1639 BI	—	115	225	425	800	—
1641 BI	—	170	270	500	950	—
1650 A	—	70.00	120	255	525	—
1651 A	—	70.00	120	255	525	—
1654 A	—	70.00	120	255	525	—

KM# 123 2 REALES

6.8670 g., 0.9306 Silver 0.2054 oz. ASW **Obv:** Bust of Philip IV right **Rev:** Cross with castles and lions in angles in octolobe **Mint:** Madrid **Note:** Cob type.

Date	Mintage	VG	F	VF	XF	Unc
1643 B	—	115	205	375	650	—
1643 IB	—	235	450	800	1,500	—

KM# 131.1 2 REALES

6.8670 g., 0.9306 Silver 0.2054 oz. ASW **Obv:** Crowned arms **Rev:** Cross with castles and lions in angles in octolobe **Mint:** Burgos **Note:** Cob Type.

Date	Mintage	VG	F	VF	XF	Unc
1651 BR	—	170	270	550	1,000	—

KM# 184 2 REALES

6.8670 g., 0.9306 Silver 0.2054 oz. ASW **Obv:** Crowned arms **Obv. Legend:** CARLOS SECVNDO... **Rev:** Cross with castles and lions in angles in octolobe **Mint:** Segovia **Note:** Cob Type.

Date	Mintage	VG	F	VF	XF	Unc
1675 BR	—	115	225	400	750	—

KM# 194 2 REALES

6.8670 g., 0.9306 Silver 0.2054 oz. ASW **Obv:** Crowned arms **Rev:** Cross with castles and lions in angles in octolobe **Mint:** Madrid **Note:** Hammered.

Date	Mintage	VG	F	VF	XF	Unc
1681 M	—	205	350	700	1,350	—
1681 BR	—	235	400	750	1,450	—
1682/1 BR	—	235	400	750	1,500	—

KM# 195 2 REALES

6.8670 g., 0.9306 Silver 0.2054 oz. ASW **Obv:** Cross with castles and lions in angles in octolobe **Rev:** Crowned CAROLVS monogram **Mint:** Segovia

Date	Mintage	VG	F	VF	XF	Unc
1682 M	—	16.00	27.50	50.00	120	—

KM# 199 2 REALES

6.8670 g., 0.9306 Silver 0.2054 oz. ASW **Obv:** Crowned arms **Obv. Legend:** CAROLVS II... **Rev:** Cross with castles and lions in angles in octolobe **Mint:** Segovia **Note:** Varieties exist.

Date	Mintage	VG	F	VF	XF	Unc
1683 BR	—	16.00	27.50	50.00	120	—
1684 BR	—	16.00	27.50	50.00	120	—
1685 BR	—	16.00	27.50	50.00	120	—
1686 BR	—	16.00	27.50	50.00	120	—

KM# 205 2 REALES

6.8670 g., 0.9306 Silver 0.2054 oz. ASW **Obv:** Crowned arms of Castile and Leon **Obv. Legend:** CAROLVS • III • D • G • HISPANIAR • REX **Rev:** Cross above AM monogram **Mint:** Seville **Note:** Hammered; varieties exist.

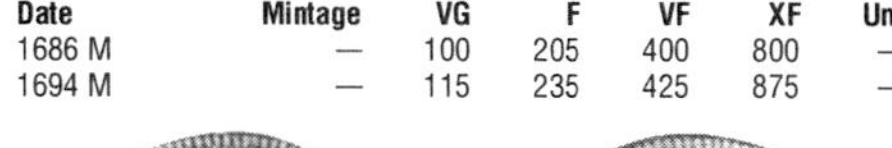

Date	Mintage	VG	F	VF	XF	Unc
1686 M	—	100	205	400	800	—
1694 M	—	115	235	425	875	—

KM# 208 2 REALES

6.8670 g., 0.9306 Silver 0.2054 oz. ASW **Obv:** Crowned arms of Castile and Leon **Rev:** Cross above AM monogram **Mint:** Segovia

Date	Mintage	VG	F	VF	XF	Unc
1687 BR	—	135	270	475	925	—

KM# 223 2 REALES

6.8670 g., 0.9306 Silver 0.2054 oz. ASW **Obv:** Crowned arms of Castile and Leon **Rev:** Cross above AM monogram **Mint:** Madrid

Date	Mintage	VG	F	VF	XF	Unc
1691 BR	—	235	400	750	1,500	—
1694 M	—	205	350	650	1,200	—
1699 BR	—	205	350	625	1,100	—

KM# 229 2 REALES

6.8670 g., 0.9306 Silver 0.2054 oz. ASW **Obv:** Crowned arms of Castile and Leon **Rev:** Cross above AM monogram **Mint:** Madrid **Note:** Milled, Large flan.

Date	Mintage	VG	F	VF	XF	Unc
1699S BR	—	600	1,150	1,900	3,000	—

KM# 242 2 REALES

6.8670 g., 0.9306 Silver 0.2054 oz. ASW **Obv:** Crowned arms of Castile and Leon **Rev:** Cross above AM monogram **Mint:** Madrid **Note:** Small flan. Varieties exist with and without pellets in circle on reverse.

Date	Mintage	VG	F	VF	XF	Unc
1700S M	—	180	300	625	1,100	—

KM# 36.3 4 REALES

13.7341 g., 0.9306 Silver 0.4109 oz. ASW **Obv:** Crowned arms, IIII vertical at right **Rev:** Cross with castles and lions in quarters **Mint:** Toledo **Note:** Cob type.

Date	Mintage	VG	F	VF	XF	Unc
1602 C	—	220	325	525	1,100	—
1609 C	—	220	325	500	1,050	—
1610 C	—	220	325	525	1,100	—
1611 C	—	220	325	500	1,050	—
1611 V	—	220	325	550	1,150	—
1613 C	—	220	325	500	1,050	—
1613 V	—	220	325	525	1,100	—
1615 V	—	220	325	500	1,050	—
1617 V	—	220	325	550	1,150	—
1618 V	—	220	325	525	1,100	—
1619 P	—	180	290	475	1,050	—
1620 P	—	180	290	475	1,050	—
1620 IP	—	180	325	575	1,300	—
1621 P	—	180	290	475	1,050	—

KM# 36.4 4 REALES

13.7341 g., 0.9306 Silver 0.4109 oz. ASW **Obv:** Crowned arms, IIII vertical at right **Rev:** Cross wiht castles and lions in quarters **Mint:** Valladolid **Note:** Cob Type.

Date	Mintage	VG	F	VF	XF	Unc
1609 V	—	425	825	1,450	3,050	—
1611 H	—	325	550	1,050	2,250	—
1612 F	—	325	550	1,050	2,250	—
1613/2 F	—	350	575	1,100	2,300	—
1613 F	—	—	—	—	—	—

KM# 36.2 4 REALES

13.7341 g., 0.9306 Silver 0.4109 oz. ASW **Obv:** Crowned arms, IIII vertical at right **Rev:** Cross with castles and lions in quarters **Note:** Cob Type. Mint mark: S.

Date	Mintage	VG	F	VF	XF	Unc
1601S B	—	255	425	725	1,650	—
1610S V	—	220	425	700	1,550	—
1611S B	—	220	425	700	1,550	—
1612S B	—	220	425	700	1,550	—
1612S D	—	145	290	425	900	—
1612S V	—	145	290	425	900	—
1613S D	—	145	290	425	900	—
1613S V/D	—	145	290	500	1,050	—
1613S V	—	145	290	425	875	—
1614S V	—	145	290	425	875	—
1615S D	—	145	290	425	900	—
1615S V	—	145	290	425	900	—
1616S D	—	145	290	425	900	—
1617S D	—	145	290	425	875	—
1617S G	—	145	290	425	900	—
1618S G	—	145	290	425	875	—
1619S G	—	145	290	425	875	—
1620S G	—	145	290	425	900	—
1621S G	—	145	290	425	900	—

KM# 36.1 4 REALES

13.7341 g., 0.9306 Silver 0.4109 oz. ASW **Obv:** Crowned Spanish shield, IIII vertical at left **Rev:** Cross with castles and lions in quarters **Note:** Cob Type. Mint mark: G.

Date	Mintage	VG	F	VF	XF	Unc
1609 M	—	375	625	1,100	2,400	—
1610 M	—	375	625	1,100	2,400	—

KM# 53.4 4 REALES

13.7341 g., 0.9306 Silver 0.4109 oz. ASW **Obv:** Crowned arms, IIII vertical at right **Rev:** Cross with castles and lions in quarters **Mint:** Granada **Note:** Mint mark: M. Prev. KM#53.2.

Date	Mintage	VG	F	VF	XF	Unc
1615 Go	—	325	550	950	2,000	—
1620 Go	—	325	550	950	2,000	—
1621 V	—	290	500	875	1,850	—

KM# 53.3 4 REALES

13.7341 g., 0.9306 Silver 0.4109 oz. ASW **Obv:** Crowned arms, IIII vertical at right **Obv. Legend:** PHILIPPVS • III • D • G **Rev:** Cross with castles and lions in fields **Mint:** Granada **Note:** A 1599 date exists for this type. Mint mark: Aqueduct.

Date	Mintage	VG	F	VF	XF	Unc
1611 A	—	500	950	1,650	3,300	—
1612 A	—	425	750	1,600	3,300	—
1613 TB	—	425	725	1,450	3,050	—

KM# 53.2 4 REALES

13.7341 g., 0.9306 Silver 0.4109 oz. ASW **Obv:** Crowned arms, IIII vertical at right **Rev:** Cross with castles and lions in fields **Mint:** Granada

Date	Mintage	VG	F	VF	XF	Unc
1611 M	—	255	425	800	1,900	—
1612 M	—	240	400	750	1,800	—
1613 M	—	240	400	750	1,800	—
1615 M	—	240	400	750	1,800	—
1621 M	—	255	425	800	2,000	—

KM# 62 4 REALES

13.7341 g., 0.9306 Silver 0.4109 oz. ASW **Obv:** Crowned arms, IIII vertical at right **Obv. Legend:** PHILIPPVS • III • D • G **Rev:** Cross with castles **Mint:** Granada **Note:** Milled. Mint mark: Aqueduct.

Date	Mintage	VG	F	VF	XF	Unc
1614 AR	—	425	750	1,600	3,300	—
1616	—	240	400	725	1,650	—
1617	—	290	475	875	1,900	—
1620	—	240	400	750	1,800	—
1621	—	290	475	875	1,900	—

KM# 98 4 REALES

13.7341 g., 0.9306 Silver 0.4109 oz. ASW **Obv:** Crowned arms **Obv. Legend:** PHILIPPVS • IIII • D • G **Rev:** Cross with castles and lions in fields **Mint:** Granada **Note:** Milled. Mint mark: Aqueduct.

Date	Mintage	VG	F	VF	XF	Unc
1621 A	—	220	375	650	1,300	—
1625 P	—	145	290	500	950	—
1628 P	—	110	195	375	650	—
1630 P	—	110	195	375	700	—
1632 R	—	145	290	500	950	—
1633 R	—	145	290	500	950	—
1635 R	—	145	255	475	900	—
1635 R/1625 P	—	180	375	650	1,250	—
1636 R	—	145	255	475	900	—
1651 I	—	145	325	625	1,100	—
1659 BR	—	145	290	500	950	—
1660 BR	—	145	290	500	1,000	—

KM# 132.4 4 REALES

13.7341 g., 0.9306 Silver 0.4109 oz. ASW **Obv:** Crowned arms **Rev:** Cross with castles and lions in fields **Mint:** Granada **Note:** Mint mark: Aqueduct. Cob type.

Date	Mintage	VG	F	VF	XF	Unc
1624 R	—	270	475	900	1,750	—
1643 BR	—	475	800	1,450	2,900	—
1644 BR	—	350	575	1,000	2,000	—
1654 BR	—	350	650	1,250	2,300	—
1659 M	—	350	575	1,000	2,000	—
1662 BR	—	270	475	900	1,750	—

KM# 132.3 4 REALES

13.7341 g., 0.9306 Silver 0.4109 oz. ASW **Obv:** Crowned arms **Rev:** Cross with castles and lions in fields **Mint:** Granada **Note:** Cob type. Mint mark: MD (ligate).

Date	Mintage	VG	F	VF	XF	Unc
1626 V	—	235	400	825	1,550	—
1627 V	—	270	475	975	1,800	—
1628 V	—	235	400	825	1,500	—
1639 B	—	235	450	875	1,600	—
1642 B	—	235	400	800	1,450	—
1643 B	—	235	400	800	1,450	—
1644 B	—	270	500	1,000	1,850	—
1644 IB	—	235	450	825	1,600	—
1649 BI	—	205	375	725	1,350	—
1650/49 BI	—	270	500	1,000	1,850	—
1650 A	—	235	400	750	1,400	—
1651 A	—	205	375	725	1,350	—
1651 A/BI	—	270	500	1,000	1,850	—
1659 G	—	270	500	1,000	1,850	—
1662 G	—	270	500	1,000	1,850	—
ND M	—	270	500	1,000	1,850	—

KM# 132.6 4 REALES

13.7341 g., 0.9306 Silver 0.4109 oz. ASW **Ruler:** Philip IV **Obv:** Crowned arms, IIII vertical at right **Rev:** Cross with castles and lions in quarters **Mint:** Granada

Date	Mintage	VG	F	VF	XF	Unc
1621 P	—	80.00	160	280	475	—
1622 P	—	70.00	145	240	450	—
1623 P	—	80.00	160	450	850	—
1624 P	—	70.00	145	240	450	—
1626 P	—	70.00	145	240	450	—
1627 P	—	70.00	145	240	450	—
1628 P	—	80.00	160	450	850	—
1632 P	—	70.00	145	240	450	—
1635 P	—	160	280	475	800	—
1651 Y	—	200	400	650	1,050	—
1655 Y	—	200	400	650	1,050	—
ND	—	55.00	120	200	325	—

KM# 133 4 REALES

13.7341 g., 0.9306 Silver 0.4109 oz. ASW **Obv:** Crowned shield of Castile and Leon **Rev:** Cross above AM monogram **Mint:** Madrid

Date	Mintage	VG	F	VF	XF	Unc
ND BR	—	1,000	1,750	2,900	—	—
168x	—	1,150	1,950	3,250	—	—
1693	—	1,150	1,950	3,250	—	—

KM# 132.2 4 REALES

13.7341 g., 0.9306 Silver 0.4109 oz. ASW **Obv:** Crowned arms, IIII vertical at right **Rev:** Cross with castles and lions in quarters **Mint:** Granada **Note:** Cob type; mint mark: G.

Date	Mintage	VG	F	VF	XF	Unc
1621 N	—	450	850	1,500	2,800	—
1652 N	—	450	850	1,500	2,800	—
1652/1 N	—	600	1,100	2,000	3,600	—

KM# 132.5 4 REALES

13.7341 g., 0.9306 Silver 0.4109 oz. ASW **Obv:** Crowned arms **Rev:** Cross with castles and lions in fields **Mint:** Granada **Note:** Mint mark: S. Cob type.

Date	Mintage	VG	F	VF	XF	Unc
1621 N	—	375	700	1,600	3,200	—
1622 D	—	75.00	150	290	650	—
1622 N	—	375	700	1,600	3,200	—
1622/51 N	—	375	700	1,600	3,200	—
1624 R	—	75.00	150	290	650	—
1626 G	—	120	225	425	950	—
1627 R	—	70.00	120	240	450	—
1628 R	—	70.00	135	255	475	—
1629 R	—	70.00	135	255	475	—
1631 R	—	70.00	135	255	475	—
1632 R	—	70.00	120	240	450	—
1633 R	—	70.00	120	240	450	—
1634 R	—	70.00	120	240	450	—
1636 R	—	70.00	120	240	450	—
1637 R	—	70.00	120	240	450	—
1641 R	—	70.00	120	240	450	—
1642 R	—	70.00	120	240	450	—
1643 R	—	70.00	120	240	450	—
1644 R	—	70.00	120	240	450	—
1648 R	—	70.00	135	270	550	—

KM# 132.1 4 REALES

13.7341 g., 0.9306 Silver 0.4109 oz. ASW **Obv:** Crowned arms **Rev:** Cross wtih castles and lions in fields **Mint:** Burgos **Note:** Cob type.

Date	Mintage	VG	F	VF	XF	Unc
1651 BR	—	550	950	1,950	3,750	—

KM# 200 4 REALES

13.7341 g., 0.9306 Silver 0.4109 oz. ASW **Obv:** Crowned Spanish shield **Rev:** Arms of Castile and Leon in octolobe **Mint:** Madrid **Note:** Mint mark varieties of 3 or 4 arches exist. Mint mark: Aqueduct.

Date	Mintage	VG	F	VF	XF	Unc
1683 BR	—	205	350	650	1,200	—
1684 BR	—	135	235	550	1,050	—
1684/3 BR	—	135	270	575	1,100	—
1684/63 BR	—	270	475	950	1,850	—
1685 BR	—	160	270	625	1,100	—
1685/4 BR	—	180	375	725	1,300	—

KM# 209 4 REALES

13.7341 g., 0.9306 Silver 0.4109 oz. ASW **Obv:** Crowned shield of Castile and Leon **Rev:** Cross above AM monogram **Mint:** Madrid **Note:** Mint mark: Aqueduct.

Date	Mintage	VG	F	VF	XF	Unc
1687 BR	—	270	500	975	2,000	—
1691 BR	—	550	1,000	1,950	3,600	—
1699 BR	—	350	600	1,200	2,650	—

KM# 213 4 REALES

13.7341 g., 0.9306 Silver 0.4109 oz. ASW **Obv:** Crowned shield of Castile and Leon **Rev:** Cross above AM monogram **Mint:** Seville **Note:** Hammered.

Date	Mintage	VG	F	VF	XF	Unc
1689 M	—	875	1,350	2,550	—	—
1692 M	—	950	1,500	2,700	—	—

KM# 230 4 REALES

13.7341 g., 0.9306 Silver 0.4109 oz. ASW **Obv:** Crowned shield of Castile and Leon **Rev:** Cross above AM monogram **Mint:** Seville **Note:** Milled.

Date	Mintage	VG	F	VF	XF	Unc
1699 M	—	700	1,250	2,400	4,400	—

KM# 243 4 REALES

13.7341 g., 0.9306 Silver 0.4109 oz. ASW **Obv:** Crowned shield of Castile and Leon **Rev:** Cross above AM monogram in pellet border **Mint:** Seville **Note:** Milled.

Date	Mintage	VG	F	VF	XF	Unc
1700 M	—	675	1,200	2,250	4,250	—

KM# 18 8 REALES

27.4682 g., 0.9306 Silver 0.8218 oz. ASW **Obv:** Crowned Spanish shield **Obv. Legend:** PHILIPPUS • D • G • OMNIUM **Rev:** Arms of Castile and Leon **Rev. Legend:** HISPAN • REGNORUM • REX **Mint:** Seville **Note:** Dav. #4395.

Date	Mintage	Good	VG	F	VF	XF
1601S B	—	180	375	700	1,100	—
1602S B	—	180	375	700	1,100	—
1603S B	—	375	650	1,100	1,800	—
1604S B	—	475	875	1,450	2,550	—
1607S B	—	180	375	700	1,100	—
1608S B	—	180	375	700	1,100	—
1609S B	—	180	375	700	1,100	—

KM# 28.4 8 REALES

27.4682 g., 0.9306 Silver 0.8218 oz. ASW **Obv:** Crowned Spanish shield; 2-tier aqueduct, mintmaster's symbol - castle tower **Rev:** Arms of Castile and Leon, Roman numeral ones in date **Rev. Legend:** PHILIPVS • III • D • G **Mint:** Toledo **Note:** Mint mark: Aqueduct.

Date	Mintage	Good	VG	F	VF	XF
1619 (t)	—	1,450	2,900	5,400	8,000	—

KM# 19 8 REALES

27.4682 g., 0.9306 Silver 0.8218 oz. ASW **Obv:** Crowned Spanish shield **Obv. Legend:** PHILIPPUS • D • G • OMNIUM **Rev:** Arms of Castile and Leon **Rev. Legend:** HISPAN • REGNORUM • REX **Mint:** Segovia **Note:** Dav. #4398.

Date	Mintage	Good	VG	F	VF	XF
1601To C	—	450	775	1,350	2,100	—
1608To C	—	625	1,250	2,150	3,100	—
1609To C	—	425	725	1,250	2,050	—
1615To P	—	350	625	1,150	1,900	—
1620To P	—	375	675	1,250	2,050	—
1621To P	—	280	550	1,000	1,800	—

KM# 25 8 REALES

27.4682 g., 0.9306 Silver 0.8218 oz. ASW **Obv:** Crowned Spanish shield **Obv. Legend:** PHILIPPUS • D • G • OMNIUM **Rev:** Arms of Castile and Leon **Rev. Legend:** HISPAN • REGNORUM • REX **Mint:** Toledo **Note:** Dav. #4397.

Date	Mintage	Good	VG	F	VF	XF
1605 C	—	550	1,000	1,750	3,250	—

KM# 28.5 8 REALES

27.4682 g., 0.9306 Silver 0.8218 oz. ASW **Obv:** Crowned Spanish shield, 2-tier aqueduct, mintmaster's symbol - castle tower **Rev:** Arms of Castile and Leon, Roman numeral ones in date **Rev. Legend:** PHILIPPVS • III • D • G **Mint:** Toledo **Note:** Dav. #4393. Mint mark: Ligate MD.

Date	Mintage	Good	VG	F	VF	XF
1620 G	—	700	1,250	2,500	3,600	—
1621 VI	—	280	550	1,100	2,000	—
1621 V	—	775	1,350	2,800	3,900	—

KM# 28.1 8 REALES

27.4682 g., 0.9306 Silver 0.8218 oz. ASW **Obv:** Crowned Spanish shield, narrow crown **Obv. Legend:** PHILIPPVS • III • D • G **Rev:** Arms of Castile and Leon, letter J used for 1 in date **Mint:** Toledo **Note:** Dav. #4394. Mint mark: Aqueduct.

Date	Mintage	VG	F	VF	XF	Unc
1607 C	—	575	1,100	1,600	2,700	—
1608 C	—	575	1,200	1,700	2,900	—
1610 C	—	725	1,450	2,000	3,400	—

KM# 28.3 8 REALES

27.4682 g., 0.9306 Silver 0.8218 oz. ASW **Obv:** Crowned Spanish shield, wide crown **Obv. Legend:** PHILIPPVS • III • D • G **Rev:** Arms of Castile and Leon, Roman numeral ones in date **Mint:** Toledo **Note:** Mint mark: Aqueduct.

Date	Mintage	VG	F	VF	XF	Unc
1610 C	—	650	1,300	1,800	3,000	—
1611/09 C	—	575	1,150	1,700	2,700	—
1611 C	—	500	1,100	1,500	2,400	—
1613 AR	—	575	1,250	1,700	2,800	—
1614/07 AR/C	—	475	1,000	1,450	2,400	—
1614 AR	—	375	750	1,000	1,750	—
1617 A+ Punctuated date	—	400	800	1,100	1,800	—
1617 A+	—	325	575	900	1,500	—
1618 A+	—	290	500	725	1,200	—
1620 A+ V in HISPANIARVM inverted A	—	290	500	725	1,200	—
1620 A+ V in PHILIPAVS inverted A	—	290	500	725	1,200	—
1620 A+ Inverted A on obverse and reverse	—	325	575	900	1,500	—
1620 A+	—	290	500	725	1,200	—
1621 A+	—	2,200	3,650	4,800	7,800	—

KM# 28.2 8 REALES

27.4682 g., 0.9306 Silver 0.8218 oz. ASW **Obv:** Crowned Spanish shield, wide crown **Obv. Legend:** PHILIPPVS • III • D • G **Rev:** Arms of Castile and Leon, letter J used for 1 in date **Mint:** Toledo **Note:** Mint mark: Aqueduct.

Date	Mintage	VG	F	VF	XF	Unc
1608 C	—	425	925	1,600	2,750	—

KM# 54 8 REALES

27.4682 g., 0.9306 Silver 0.8218 oz. ASW **Obv:** Crowned Spanish shield, 2-tier aqueduct, mintmaster's symbol - castle tower **Obv. Legend:** PHILIPPVS • III • D • G • **Rev:** Arms of Castile and Leon, Roman numeral ones in date **Rev. Legend:** HISPANIARVM • REX • **Mint:** Seville **Note:** Dav. #4396.

Date	Mintage	Good	VG	F	VF	XF
1611 B	—	145	220	400	600	—
1612 B	—	145	220	400	600	—
1612 D	—	145	220	400	600	—
1614 D	—	180	290	650	950	—
1615 D	—	145	255	425	625	—
1617/5 V/D	—	180	290	575	825	—
1618 D	—	145	220	475	650	—
1619 V/D	—	255	500	1,100	1,450	—
1620 D	—	175	255	500	750	—
1620 G	—	220	375	800	1,050	—
1621 D	—	145	220	475	650	—
1621 G	—	220	425	950	1,250	—

KM# 57 8 REALES

27.4682 g., 0.9306 Silver 0.8218 oz. ASW **Obv:** KM#18 **Rev:** KM#54 **Mint:** Toledo **Note:** Mule. Dav. #4395.

Date	Mintage	Good	VG	F	VF	XF
1613S D	—	180	325	625	850	—

KM# 76 8 REALES

27.4682 g., 0.9306 Silver 0.8218 oz. ASW **Obv:** Crowned Spanish shield, mint mark vertical **Obv. Legend:** PHILIPPVS • IIII • D • G • **Rev:** Arms of Castile and Leon **Rev. Legend:** HISPANIARVM • REX • **Mint:** Toledo **Note:** Dav. #4408. Mint mark: Aqueduct.

Date	Mintage	VG	F	VF	XF	Unc
1621 A	—	1,100	2,250	3,350	5,100	—
1630 P	—	280	500	850	1,600	—
1651 I	—	280	550	950	1,850	—
1659 BR	—	280	525	900	1,750	—
1660 BR	—	350	700	1,100	2,100	—

KM# 74 8 REALES

27.4682 g., 0.9306 Silver 0.8218 oz. ASW **Obv:** Crowned Spanish shield, denomination as VIII **Obv. Legend:** PHILIPPVS • IIII • D • G • **Rev:** Arms of Castile and Leon **Rev. Legend:** HISPANIARVM • REX • **Mint:** Toledo **Note:** Dav. #4404. Mint mark: Ligate MD.

Date	Mintage	Good	VG	F	VF	XF
1621 V	—	550	950	1,700	2,600	—
1627 V	—	600	975	1,750	2,700	—
1627 M	—	425	850	1,600	2,400	—
1631 M	—	425	850	1,600	2,400	—
1633 M	—	350	600	1,350	1,900	—
1635 M	—	350	600	1,350	1,900	—

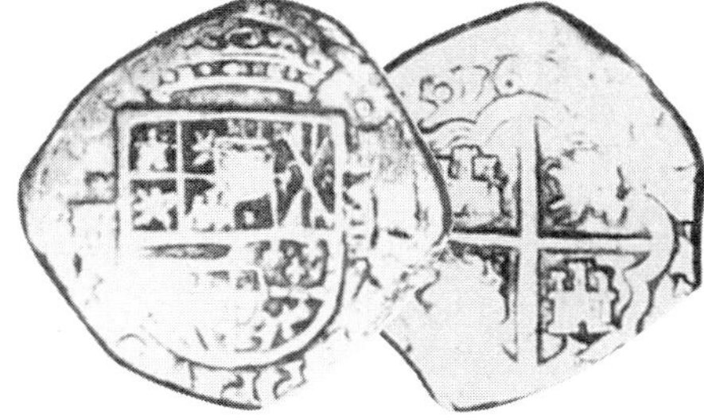

KM# 75 8 REALES

27.4682 g., 0.9306 Silver 0.8218 oz. ASW **Obv:** Large crowned Spanish shield, 2-tier, 4-arch aqueduct, denomination as VIII **Obv. Legend:** PHILIPPVS • IIII • D • G • **Rev:** Arms of Castile and Leon **Rev. Legend:** HISPANIARVM • REX • **Mint:** Toledo **Note:** Dav. #4407. Mint mark: Aqueduct.

Date	Mintage	Good	VG	F	VF	XF
1621 R	—	325	625	1,250	1,800	—
1623 R	—	325	625	1,250	1,800	—
1624/3 R	—	245	425	850	1,200	—
1624 R Lions and castles inverted	—	245	425	850	1,200	—
1624 R	—	245	425	850	1,200	—
1625 R	—	245	425	850	1,200	—
1627 R	—	210	350	700	1,100	—
1628 R	—	280	450	900	1,400	—
1642 BR	—	425	850	1,700	2,400	—

KM# 80 8 REALES

27.4682 g., 0.9306 Silver 0.8218 oz. ASW **Obv:** Crowned Spanish shield, denomination as VIII **Obv. Legend:** PHILIPPVS • IIII • D • G • **Rev:** Arms of Castile and Leon **Rev. Legend:** HISPANIARVM • REX • **Mint:** Toledo **Note:** Dav. #4410.

Date	Mintage	VG	F	VF	XF	Unc
1622S D	—	180	375	625	1,050	—
1623S D	—	180	325	525	875	—
1624S D	—	180	325	525	875	—
1625S D	—	220	375	575	950	—
1625S R	—	180	325	500	825	—
1627/6S R	—	220	375	575	950	—
1628S R	—	220	375	575	950	—
1629S R	—	180	325	500	825	—
1630S R	—	180	325	525	875	—
1631S R	—	180	325	500	825	—
1632S R	—	180	325	500	825	—
1633S R	—	220	375	575	950	—
1634S R	—	180	375	625	1,050	—
1635S R	—	180	325	500	825	—
1637S R	—	180	375	625	1,050	—
1638/7S R	—	180	325	500	850	—
1642S R	—	180	325	500	825	—
1643S R	—	180	325	500	850	—
1644S R	—	180	325	500	825	—
1651S R	—	220	375	575	950	—
1653S R	—	180	375	625	1,050	—
1655S R	—	180	325	500	850	—
1656S R	—	180	375	625	1,050	—
1657S R	—	180	325	500	850	—
1659S R	—	220	375	575	950	—
1662S R	—	180	375	625	1,050	—
1665S M	—	220	425	750	1,250	—

KM# 101 8 REALES

27.4682 g., 0.9306 Silver 0.8218 oz. ASW **Obv:** Crowned Spanish shield, denomination as VIII **Obv. Legend:** PHILIPPVS • IIII • D • G • **Rev:** Arms of Castile and Leon **Rev. Legend:** HISPANIARVM • REX • **Mint:** Toledo **Note:** Dav. #4411.1.

Date	Mintage	Good	VG	F	VF	XF
1630To P	—	210	350	725	1,100	—
1631To P	—	210	350	775	1,150	—
1632To P	—	210	350	775	1,150	—
1634To P	—	210	350	775	1,150	—
1635To P	—	210	350	775	1,150	—
1639To P	—	210	350	775	1,150	—
1651To Y	—	210	350	775	1,200	—
1652To Y	—	245	425	875	1,300	—
1655To Y	—	210	350	775	1,150	—
1659To CA	—	500	975	2,050	3,000	—
1660/59To Y	—	280	500	975	1,500	—
1662To CA	—	775	1,550	3,100	4,500	—
1662To Y	—	210	350	775	1,150	—

KM# 111 8 REALES

27.4682 g., 0.9306 Silver 0.8218 oz. ASW **Obv:** Crowned Spanish shield, 2-tier, 4-arch aqueduct, denomination as 8 **Obv. Legend:** PHILIPPVS • IIII • D • G • **Rev:** Arms of Castile and Leon **Rev. Legend:** HISPANIARVM • REX • **Mint:** Toledo **Note:** Dav. #4409. Mint mark: Aqueduct.

Date	Mintage	VG	F	VF	XF	Unc
1632 R	—	280	525	900	1,500	—
1633 R	—	325	600	1,000	1,450	—
1635 R PHILIPXXS	—	625	1,250	1,800	3,000	—
1635 R HISPANIARAM	—	350	625	1,100	1,800	—
1635 R HISPANIARVM	—	280	500	800	1,400	—
1636/5 R	—	280	550	925	1,600	—
1651 I	—	280	525	900	1,500	—
1652 BR	—	350	700	1,200	2,100	—
1659/32 BR	—	280	525	900	1,500	—
1659/35 BR	—	280	550	950	1,700	—
1659/56 BR	—	350	625	1,100	1,800	—
1659 BR Crosses separate legend	—	425	850	1,450	2,400	—
1659 BR	—	350	625	1,100	1,800	—
1659 I	—	625	1,250	1,800	3,000	—
1660 BR Crosses separate legend	—	280	500	850	1,450	—
1660 BR Crosses flank 8	—	280	525	900	1,500	—

KM# 114 8 REALES

27.4682 g., 0.9306 Silver 0.8218 oz. ASW **Obv:** Large crowned Spanish shield **Obv. Legend:** PHILIPPVS • IIII • D • G •

Rev: Arms of Castile and Leon **Rev. Legend:** HISPANIARVM • REX • **Mint:** Toledo **Note:** Mint mark: Ligate MD.

Date	Mintage	Good	VG	F	VF	XF
1639 BI	—	325	625	1,250	1,750	—
1640 B	—	425	875	1,750	2,400	—
1642 B	—	325	625	1,200	1,700	—

KM# 120 8 REALES

27.4682 g., 0.9306 Silver 0.8218 oz. ASW **Obv:** Crowned Spanish shield, denomination as 8 **Obv. Legend:** PHILIPPVS • IIII • D • G • **Rev:** Arms of Castile and Leon **Rev. Legend:** HISPANIARVM • REX • **Mint:** Toledo **Note:** Mint mark: Ligate MD.

Date	Mintage	Good	VG	F	VF	XF
1641 B	—	245	500	975	1,400	—
1642 B	—	245	500	950	1,350	—
1642 B Inverted B and 4	—	325	625	1,250	1,800	—
1642 B Inverted B	—	325	625	1,250	1,800	—
1643 B Inverted B and 4	—	325	625	1,250	1,800	—
1643 B	—	245	500	975	1,400	—
1644/3 B	—	245	500	950	1,350	—
1644 B	—	245	500	950	1,350	—
1644 IB	—	280	550	1,100	1,600	—
1650 A	—	245	500	1,000	1,500	—
1651 A	—	245	450	950	1,400	—
1659 A	—	280	525	1,100	1,550	—

KM# 132.7 8 REALES

Silver **Mint:** Valladolid

Date	Mintage	VG	F	VF	XF	Unc
16xx	—	575	1,000	1,800	2,900	—

KM# 134.4 8 REALES

27.4682 g., 0.9306 Silver 0.8218 oz. ASW **Obv:** Crowned Spanish shield, denomination as 8 **Obv. Legend:** PHILIPPVS • IIII • D • G • **Rev:** Arms of Castile and Leon **Rev. Legend:** HISPANIARVM • REX • **Mint:** Toledo **Note:** Mint mark: Aqueduct.

Date	Mintage	Good	VG	F	VF	XF
1659 M	—	350	675	1,350	1,900	—
1661 B	—	245	500	950	1,450	—
1662 B	—	325	600	1,150	1,750	—

KM# 134.1 8 REALES

27.4682 g., 0.9306 Silver 0.8218 oz. ASW **Obv:** Crowned Spanish shield, denomination as 8 **Obv. Legend:** PHILIPPVS • IIII • D • G • **Rev:** Arms of Castile and Leon **Rev. Legend:** HISPANIARVM • REX • **Mint:** Toledo **Note:** Dav. #4400.

Date	Mintage	Good	VG	F	VF	XF
1651B BR	—	950	1,950	3,250	5,100	—

KM# 134.2 8 REALES

27.4682 g., 0.9306 Silver 0.8218 oz. ASW **Obv:** Crowned Spanish shield, denomination as 8 **Obv. Legend:** PHILIPPVS • IIII • D • G • **Rev:** Arms of Castile and Leon **Rev. Legend:** HISPANIARVM • REX • **Mint:** Toledo **Note:** Dav. #4402.

Date	Mintage	Good	VG	F	VF	XF
1651C CA	—	725	1,450	2,900	5,100	—

KM# 134.3 8 REALES

27.4682 g., 0.9306 Silver 0.8218 oz. ASW **Obv:** Crowned Spanish shield, denomination as 8 **Obv. Legend:** PHILIPPVS • IIII • D • G • **Rev:** Arms of Castile and Leon **Rev. Legend:** HISPANIARVM • REX • **Mint:** Toledo **Note:** Dav. #4403.

Date	Mintage	Good	VG	F	VF	XF
1651G Retrograde N	—	700	1,400	2,700	4,150	—
1651G N	—	625	1,250	2,300	3,750	—

KM# 134.5 8 REALES

27.4682 g., 0.9306 Silver 0.8218 oz. ASW **Obv:** Crowned Spanish shield, denomination as 8 **Obv. Legend:** PHILIPPVS • IIII • D • G • **Rev:** Arms of Castile and Leon **Rev. Legend:** HISPANIARVM • REX • **Mint:** Toledo **Note:** Dav. #4411.2

Date	Mintage	Good	VG	F	VF	XF
1651 Y	—	255	500	975	1,650	—

KM# 134.6 8 REALES

27.4682 g., 0.9306 Silver 0.8218 oz. ASW **Obv:** Crowned Spanish shield, denominationm as 8 **Obv. Legend:** PHILIPPVS • IIII • D • G • **Rev:** Arms of Castile and Leon **Rev. Legend:** HISPANIARVM • REX • **Mint:** Toledo **Note:** Dav. #4412. Mint mark: Flags.

Date	Mintage	Good	VG	F	VF	XF
1651 F	—	1,550	2,800	4,700	7,500	—

KM# 176.1 8 REALES

27.4682 g., 0.9306 Silver 0.8218 oz. ASW **Obv:** Crowned Spanish shield, denomination as VIII **Obv. Legend:** PHILIPPVS • IIII • D • G • **Rev:** Arms of Castile and Leon **Rev. Legend:** HISPANIARVM • REX • **Mint:** Toledo **Note:** Mint mark: Ligate MD.

Date	Mintage	Good	VG	F	VF	XF
1666 R	—	1,050	2,100	3,550	5,400	—

KM# 176.2 8 REALES

27.4682 g., 0.9306 Silver 0.8218 oz. ASW **Obv:** Crowned Spanish shield, denomination as VIII **Obv. Legend:** PHILIPPVS • IIII • D • G • **Rev:** Arms of Castile and Leon **Rev. Legend:** HISPANIARVM • REX • **Mint:** Toledo **Note:** Dav. #4417.

Date	Mintage	Good	VG	F	VF	XF
1668S M	—	175	350	675	1,000	—
1670S M	—	210	425	800	1,150	—
1671S M	—	210	425	800	1,150	—
1673S M	—	210	375	775	1,150	—
1680S S	—	175	350	700	1,000	—
16xxS G	—	245	500	975	1,450	—

KM# 191.1 8 REALES

27.4682 g., 0.9306 Silver 0.8218 oz. ASW **Obv:** Crowned Spanish shield, denomination as 8 **Obv. Legend:** PHILIPPVS • IIII • D • G • **Rev:** Arms of Castile and Leon **Rev. Legend:** HISPANIARVM • REX • **Mint:** Toledo **Note:** Dav. #4414.

Date	Mintage	Good	VG	F	VF	XF
1680B	—	1,700	3,450	5,600	8,400	—

KM# 191.2 8 REALES

27.4682 g., 0.9306 Silver 0.8218 oz. ASW **Obv:** Crowned Spanish shield, denomination as 8 **Obv. Legend:** PHILIPPVS • IIII • D • G • **Rev:** Arms of Castile and Leon **Rev. Legend:** HISPANIARVM • REX • **Mint:** Toledo **Note:** Dav. #4415. Mint mark: Flower.

Date	Mintage	Good	VG	F	VF	XF
1679	—	1,050	2,050	3,400	5,000	—

KM# 191.3 8 REALES

27.4682 g., 0.9306 Silver 0.8218 oz. ASW **Obv:** Crowned Spanish shield, denomination as 8 **Obv. Legend:** PHILIPPVS • IIII • D • G • **Rev:** Arms of Castile and Leon **Rev. Legend:** HISPANIARVM • REX • **Mint:** Toledo **Note:** Dav. #4416. Mint mark: Aqueduct.

Date	Mintage	Good	VG	F	VF	XF
1682 M Rosettes in legend	—	280	500	800	1,150	—
1682 M Dots in legend	—	375	600	950	1,350	—

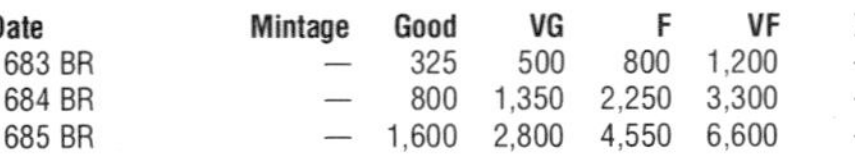

Date	Mintage	Good	VG	F	VF	XF
1683 BR	—	325	500	800	1,200	—
1684 BR	—	800	1,350	2,250	3,300	—
1685 BR	—	1,600	2,800	4,550	6,600	—

KM# 206 8 REALES

27.4682 g., 0.9306 Silver 0.8218 oz. ASW **Obv:** Crowned shield of Castile and Leon in collar of The Golden Fleece **Obv. Legend:** PHILIPPVS • IIII • D • G • **Rev:** Cross above MA monogram **Rev. Legend:** HISPANIARVM • REX • **Mint:** Toledo **Note:** Dav. #4420.

Date	Mintage	Good	VG	F	VF	XF
1686S M	—	245	425	675	925	—
1689S M	—	245	425	675	925	—
1690S M	—	245	425	675	950	—
1691S M	—	280	450	700	1,050	—
1692S M	—	280	450	725	1,100	—
1692S M Inverted 2	—	425	625	1,050	1,500	—
1693S M	—	280	450	725	1,100	—
1694S M	—	280	450	725	1,100	—
1695S M	—	245	425	675	925	—
1697S M	—	325	500	775	1,150	—
1698S M	—	325	500	775	1,100	—
1699S M	—	280	425	700	1,050	—
16xxS J	—	500	775	1,250	1,800	—

KM# 210.2 8 REALES

27.4682 g., 0.9306 Silver 0.8218 oz. ASW **Obv:** Crowned shield of Castile and Leon in collar of The Golden Fleece **Obv. Legend:** PHILIPPVS • IIII • D • G • **Rev:** Cross above MA monogram **Rev. Legend:** HISPANIARVM • REX • **Mint:** Toledo **Note:** Dav. #4419. Mint mark: Aqueduct.

Date	Mintage	VG	F	VF	XF	Unc
1687 BR	—	350	675	1,000	1,800	—
Note: Several varieties of 1687 exist						
1691 BR	—	775	1,600	2,400	4,200	—

KM# 210.1 8 REALES

27.4682 g., 0.9306 Silver 0.8218 oz. ASW **Obv:** Crowned shield of Castile and Leon in collar of The Golden Fleece **Obv. Legend:** PHILIPPVS • IIII • D • G • **Rev:** Cross above MA monogram **Rev. Legend:** HISPANIARVM • REX • **Mint:** Toledo **Note:** Dav. #4418. Mint mark: Ligate MD.

Date	Mintage	Good	VG	F	VF	XF
1689 BR Value R8	—	1,000	1,750	2,900	4,700	—
1699 BR Value 8R	—	1,000	1,750	2,900	4,700	—

KM# 227 8 REALES

27.4682 g., 0.9306 Silver 0.8218 oz. ASW **Obv:** Crowned Spanish shield, Portugal shield removed

Obv. Legend: PHILIPPVS • IIII • D • G • **Rev:** Arms of Castile and Leon **Rev. Legend:** HISPANIARVM • REX • **Mint:** Toledo **Note:** Dav. #4416. Mint mark: Aqueduct.

Date	Mintage	VG	F	VF	XF	Unc
1697/82 F/M	—	450	875	1,200	2,400	—
1697 F 4 lines in first quarter of arms of Sicily	—	850	1,400	2,100	3,600	—
1697 F	—	450	875	1,200	2,400	—

KM# 244 8 REALES

27.4682 g., 0.9306 Silver 0.8218 oz. ASW **Obv:** Crowned Spanish shield in collar of The Golden Fleece, mint mark right, assayer initial left **Obv. Legend:** PHILIPPVS • IIII • D • G • **Rev:** Cross above MA monogram with floral separations **Rev. Legend:** HISPANIARVM • REX • **Mint:** Toledo **Note:** Dav. #4421.

Date	Mintage	VG	F	VF	XF	Unc
1700S M HISPANIAR	—	950	1,650	2,900	4,700	—

Note: Three varieties in the spelling of HISPANIAR exist

KM# 37 50 REALES

170.0000 g., 0.9306 Silver 5.0861 oz. ASW **Obv:** Crowned Spanish shield in inner circle **Rev:** Arms of Castile and Leon **Note:** Dav. #LS566. Mint mark: Aqueduct.

Date	Mintage	VG	F	VF	XF	Unc
1609 C Rare. 2 known	—	—	—	—	—	—
1610 C Rare. 3 known	—	—	—	—	—	—
1613 AR Rare. 2 known	—	—	—	—	—	—
1614 AR Rare. 3 known	—	—	—	—	—	—

KM# 65 50 REALES

170.0000 g., 0.9306 Silver 5.0861 oz. ASW **Obv:** Crowned Spanish shield overlaps inner circle **Rev:** Arms of Castile and Leon **Note:** Dav. #LS566. Mint mark: Aqueduct. Illustration reduced.

Date	Mintage	VG	F	VF	XF	Unc
1617 A+ Rare	—	—	—	—	—	—
1618/7 A+ Rare	—	—	—	—	—	—
1620 A+ Rare	—	—	—	—	—	—

KM# 81.1 50 REALES

170.0000 g., 0.9306 Silver 5.0861 oz. ASW **Obv:** Crowned Spanish shield overlaps inner circle **Obv. Legend:** PHILIPPVS • IIII • D • G • **Rev:** Arms of Castile and Leon **Note:** Dav. #LS567. Mint mark: Aqueduct.

Date	Mintage	VG	F	VF	XF	Unc
1622 A+ Unique	—	—	—	—	—	—
1623 A+ Rare	—	—	—	—	—	—

KM# 81.2 50 REALES

170.0000 g., 0.9306 Silver 5.0861 oz. ASW **Obv:** Crowned Spanish shield, floral crown, floral stops **Obv. Legend:** PHILIPPVS • IIII • D • G • **Rev:** Arms of Castile and Leon, floral stops in legend **Note:** Dav. #LS567. Mint mark: Aqueduct.

Date	Mintage	VG	F	VF	XF	Unc
1626 A+ Rare	—	—	—	—	—	—
1628 A+ Rare	—	—	—	—	—	—

Note: UBS Gold & Numismatics Auction 55, 9-02, VF realized approximately $7,945

Date	Mintage	VG	F	VF	XF	Unc
1631 A+ Rare	—	—	—	—	—	—

KM# 81.3 50 REALES

170.0000 g., 0.9306 Silver 5.0861 oz. ASW **Obv:** Crowned Spanish shield, 2-tier, 6-arch aqueduct mint mark **Obv. Legend:** PHILIPPVS • IIII • D • G • **Rev:** Arms of Castile and Leon, floral stops in legend **Note:** Dav. #LS567. Mint mark: Aqueduct.

Date	Mintage	VG	F	VF	XF	Unc
1632 R Rare	—	—	—	—	—	—
1633/32 R Rare	—	—	—	—	—	—

KM# 81.4 50 REALES

170.0000 g., 0.9306 Silver 5.0861 oz. ASW **Obv:** 2-tier, 4-arch aqueduct mint mark **Obv. Legend:** PHILIPPVS • IIII • D • G • **Rev:** Floral stops **Note:** Dav. #LS567. Mint mark: Aqueduct.

Date	Mintage	VG	F	VF	XF	Unc
1633 R Rare	—	—	—	—	—	—

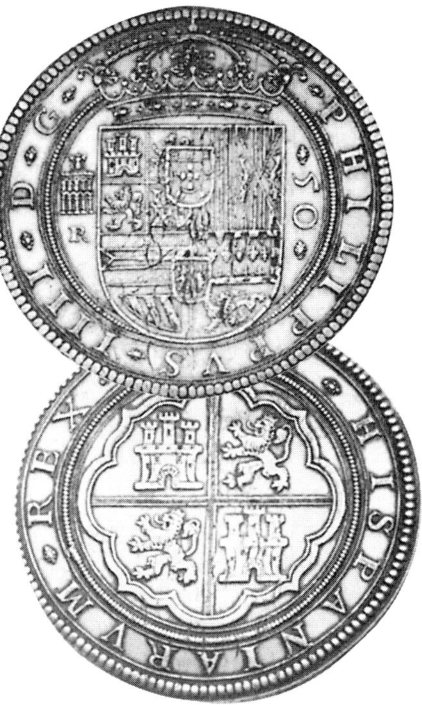

KM# 81.5 50 REALES

170.0000 g., 0.9306 Silver 5.0861 oz. ASW **Obv:** Crowned Spanish shield, 2-tier, 8-arch aqueduct mint mark **Obv. Legend:** PHILIPPVS • IIII • D • G • **Rev:** Arms of Castile and Leon, floral stops in legend **Note:** Dav. #LS567. Mint mark: Aqueduct. Illustration reduced.

Date	Mintage	VG	F	VF	XF	Unc
1635 R Rare, 12 known	—	—	—	—	—	—

Note: Ira & Larry Goldberg Coins & Collectibles Auction 46 - The Millennia Collection, 5-08, MS-60 realized $57,500

Date	Mintage	VG	F	VF	XF	Unc
1636 R Rare, 6-8 known	—	—	—	—	—	—

Note: Akers J. J. Pittman sale 8-99 VF realized $143,750

Date	Mintage	VG	F	VF	XF	Unc
1651 I Rare	—	—	—	—	—	—
1652 BR Rare, 3 known	—	—	—	—	—	—
1659/32 BR	—	—	—	—	—	—

Note: The 1659 BR has been reported as 1659/31, 1659/51 and 1659/36 by various authorities

KM# 196 50 REALES

170.0000 g., 0.9306 Silver 5.0861 oz. ASW **Subject:** Titles of Charles II **Obv:** 2-tier, 8-arch aqueduct mint mark **Obv. Legend:** PHILIPPVS • IIII • D • G • **Rev:** Floral stops **Mint:** Segovia

Date	Mintage	VG	F	VF	XF	Unc
1682 M Rare	—	—	—	—	—	—

KM# 99.1 100 REALES

340.0000 g., 0.9306 Silver 10.172 oz. ASW **Obv:** Crowned arms in inner circle **Rev:** Cross in quatrefoil **Mint:** Segovia **Note:** Mint mark: Aqueduct.

Date	Mintage	VG	F	VF	XF	Unc
1623 AR Unique	—	—	—	—	—	—

KM# 99.2 100 REALES

340.0000 g., 0.9306 Silver 10.172 oz. ASW **Obv:** Revised crown **Rev:** Cross in quatrefoil **Mint:** Segovia **Note:** Mint mark: Aqueduct.

Date	Mintage	VG	F	VF	XF	Unc
1633 R 4 known	—	—	—	—	—	—

KM# 29 ESCUDO

3.4335 g., 0.9167 Gold 0.1012 oz. AGW **Obv:** Crowned arms **Rev:** Cross in quatrefoil **Mint:** Segovia **Note:** Mint mark: Aqueduct.

Date	Mintage	VG	F	VF	XF	Unc
1607 C	—	500	900	1,400	2,000	—
1608 C	—	500	900	1,400	2,000	—

KM# 48.1 ESCUDO

3.4335 g., 0.9167 Gold 0.1012 oz. AGW **Obv:** Crowned arms **Rev:** Cross in quatrefoil **Mint:** Segovia **Note:** Mint mark: S, S/L.

Date	Mintage	VG	F	VF	XF	Unc
1610 B	—	500	900	1,400	2,000	—
1611 V	—	450	800	1,300	1,900	—

Date	Mintage	VG	F	VF	XF	Unc
1617 G	—	600	1,000	—	—	—
1618	—	600	1,000	—	—	—

KM# 48.2 ESCUDO

3.4335 g., 0.9167 Gold 0.1012 oz. AGW **Obv:** Crowned arms **Rev:** Cross in quatrefoil **Mint:** Segovia **Note:** Mint mark: Aqueduct.

Date	Mintage	VG	F	VF	XF	Unc
1615 R	—	400	900	1,400	2,000	—

KM# 68 ESCUDO

3.4335 g., 0.9167 Gold 0.1012 oz. AGW **Obv:** Crowned arms **Rev:** Cross in quatrefoil **Mint:** Segovia **Note:** Mint mark: S, S/L.

Date	Mintage	VG	F	VF	XF	Unc
1623 C	—	450	800	1,250	1,900	—
1623 D	—	450	800	1,200	1,800	—
1628 D	—	500	900	1,400	2,000	—
1659 R	—	500	900	1,400	2,000	—

KM# 94.1 ESCUDO

3.4335 g., 0.9167 Gold 0.1012 oz. AGW **Obv:** Crowned arms **Rev:** Cross in quatrefoil **Mint:** Segovia **Note:** Mint mark: Crowned M.

Date	Mintage	VG	F	VF	XF	Unc
1627 V	—	450	1,100	1,800	2,700	—
1639 R	—	725	1,600	2,500	3,800	—

KM# 94.2 ESCUDO

3.4335 g., 0.9167 Gold 0.1012 oz. AGW **Obv:** Crowned arms **Rev:** Cross in quatrefoil **Mint:** Segovia **Note:** Mint mark: Aqueduct.

Date	Mintage	VG	F	VF	XF	Unc
1628 P Rare	—	—	—	—	—	—

KM# 94.3 ESCUDO

3.4335 g., 0.9167 Gold 0.1012 oz. AGW **Obv:** Crowned arms **Rev:** Cross in quatrefoil

Date	Mintage	VG	F	VF	XF	Unc
1646 D	—	250	500	750	1,100	—

KM# 173 ESCUDO

3.4335 g., 0.9167 Gold 0.1012 oz. AGW **Obv:** Crowned arms **Rev:** Cross in quatrefoil

Date	Mintage	VG	F	VF	XF	Unc
1662B A	—	3,500	5,500	—	—	—

KM# 180 ESCUDO

3.4335 g., 0.9167 Gold 0.1012 oz. AGW **Obv:** Crowned arms **Rev:** Cross in quatrefoil, date at top **Note:** Mint mark: S, S/L.

Date	Mintage	VG	F	VF	XF	Unc
1672 M	—	170	230	350	1,100	—
1675 M	—	180	240	450	1,300	—
1686 G	—	180	240	450	1,300	—

KM# 182 ESCUDO

3.4335 g., 0.9167 Gold 0.1012 oz. AGW **Obv:** Crowned arms **Rev:** Cross in quatrefoil **Note:** Mint mark: Aqueduct.

Date	Mintage	VG	F	VF	XF	Unc
1674 BR	—	700	1,650	2,650	3,950	—
1679 BR	—	700	1,650	2,650	3,950	—
1683 BR	—	700	1,650	2,650	3,950	—

KM# 214 ESCUDO

3.4335 g., 0.9167 Gold 0.1012 oz. AGW **Obv:** Crowned arms **Rev:** Cross in quatrefoil, date at top **Note:** Mint mark: Crowned M.

Date	Mintage	VG	F	VF	XF	Unc
1689 M	—	250	500	750	1,100	—
1690 M	—	250	500	750	1,100	—

KM# 224 ESCUDO

3.4335 g., 0.9167 Gold 0.1012 oz. AGW **Obv:** Crowned Spanish shield, 5 divisions **Rev:** Cross in quatrefoil, date above **Note:** Mint mark: S, S/L.

Date	Mintage	VG	F	VF	XF	Unc
1691 M	—	800	1,900	3,000	4,500	—

KM# 231.1 ESCUDO

3.4335 g., 0.9167 Gold 0.1012 oz. AGW **Obv:** Crowned arms **Obv. Legend:** ...GRAC **Rev:** Cross in quatrefoil, date at top **Note:** Mint mark: S, S/L.

Date	Mintage	VG	F	VF	XF	Unc
1699 M	—	650	1,400	2,200	3,700	—

KM# 231.2 ESCUDO

3.4335 g., 0.9167 Gold 0.1012 oz. AGW **Obv:** Crowned arms **Obv. Legend:** ...GRAT **Rev:** Cross in quatrefoil, date at top **Note:** Mint mark: S, S/L.

Date	Mintage	VG	F	VF	XF	Unc
1699 M	—	600	1,300	2,200	3,700	—

KM# 245 ESCUDO

3.4335 g., 0.9167 Gold 0.1012 oz. AGW **Ruler:** Philip V **Obv:** Crowned arms, pointed bottom **Rev:** Cross is quatrefoil, date at top **Note:** Mint mark: S, S/L.

Date	Mintage	VG	F	VF	XF	Unc
1700 M	—	550	1,150	2,000	3,300	—

KM# 20 2 ESCUDOS

6.8670 g., 0.9167 Gold 0.2024 oz. AGW **Obv:** Crowned arms **Rev:** Cross in quatrefoil in inner circle **Note:** Mint mark: S, S/L.

Date	Mintage	VG	F	VF	XF	Unc
1601 B	—	450	900	1,400	2,000	—
1610 B	—	300	500	800	1,300	—
1611 B	—	300	500	800	1,300	—
1611 V	—	300	500	800	1,300	—
1612 D	—	300	500	800	1,300	—
1612 V	—	300	500	800	1,300	—
1613 B	—	350	700	1,000	1,600	—
1613 V	—	300	500	800	1,300	—
1617 D	—	300	500	800	1,300	—
1620 G	—	300	500	800	1,300	—
1620 R	—	300	500	800	1,300	—

KM# 24.2 2 ESCUDOS

6.8670 g., 0.9167 Gold 0.2024 oz. AGW **Obv:** Crowned arms **Rev:** Cross in quatrefoil **Note:** Mint mark: T, To.

Date	Mintage	VG	F	VF	XF	Unc
1603 C	—	400	800	1,500	2,500	—
1614 P	—	400	800	1,500	2,500	—

KM# 24.1 2 ESCUDOS

6.8670 g., 0.9167 Gold 0.2024 oz. AGW **Obv:** Crowned arms **Rev:** Cross in quatrefoil

Date	Mintage	VG	F	VF	XF	Unc
1605G	—	1,400	2,900	4,800	7,000	—
1606G	—	1,250	2,650	4,400	6,700	—

KM# 30 2 ESCUDOS

6.8670 g., 0.9167 Gold 0.2024 oz. AGW **Obv:** Crowned arms in inner circle **Rev:** Cross in quatrefoil in inner circle, date at top **Note:** Mint mark: Aqueduct.

Date	Mintage	VG	F	VF	XF	Unc
1607 C	—	1,750	3,500	6,100	8,800	—
1610 A	—	1,750	3,500	6,100	8,800	—
1610 C	—	1,750	3,500	6,100	8,800	—
1610 CA	—	1,750	3,500	6,100	8,800	—

KM# 64.1 2 ESCUDOS

6.8670 g., 0.9167 Gold 0.2024 oz. AGW **Obv:** Crowned arms **Rev:** Cross in quatrefoil in inner circle **Note:** Mint mark: Crowned M.

Date	Mintage	VG	F	VF	XF	Unc
1615 G	—	650	1,200	2,000	3,000	—
1616 G	—	650	1,200	1,700	2,700	—
1620 G	—	550	950	1,500	2,500	—

KM# 64.2 2 ESCUDOS

6.8670 g., 0.9167 Gold 0.2024 oz. AGW **Obv:** Crowned arms **Rev:** Cross in quatrefoil in inner circle **Note:** Mint mark: Aqueduct.

Date	Mintage	VG	F	VF	XF	Unc
1615 R	—	500	1,000	1,500	2,500	—

KM# 82.1 2 ESCUDOS

6.8670 g., 0.9167 Gold 0.2024 oz. AGW **Obv:** Crowned arms **Rev:** Cross in quatrefoil **Note:** Mint mark: S, S/L.

Date	Mintage	VG	F	VF	XF	Unc
1622 E	—	300	500	800	1,300	—
1623 R	—	250	400	600	1,000	—
1624 R	—	300	500	800	1,300	—
1627 R	—	300	500	800	1,300	—
1629 R	—	250	400	600	1,000	—
1634 R	—	250	400	600	1,000	—
1640 D	—	250	400	600	1,000	—
1644 R	—	250	400	600	1,000	—
1645 R	—	300	500	800	1,300	—
1651 R	—	300	500	800	1,300	—
1652 C	—	250	400	600	1,000	—
1661 D	—	250	400	600	1,000	—

KM# 82.2 2 ESCUDOS

6.8670 g., 0.9167 Gold 0.2024 oz. AGW **Obv:** Crowned arms **Rev:** Cross in quatrefoil **Note:** Mint mark: Crowned M.

Date	Mintage	VG	F	VF	XF	Unc
1625 V	—	400	800	1,200	1,800	—
1626 V	—	400	800	1,200	1,800	—
1627 V	—	400	800	1,200	1,800	—
1628 V	—	400	800	1,200	1,800	—
1644 A	—	600	1,200	1,800	2,700	—
1646 A	—	700	1,350	2,000	3,000	—
1651 A	—	400	800	1,200	1,800	—
1661 A	—	400	800	1,200	1,800	—

KM# 82.3 2 ESCUDOS

6.8670 g., 0.9167 Gold 0.2024 oz. AGW **Obv:** Crowned arms **Rev:** Cross in quatrefoil

Date	Mintage	VG	F	VF	XF	Unc
1628CA E	—	350	700	1,100	1,700	—
1629CA E	—	350	700	1,100	1,700	—
1630CA E	—	350	700	1,100	1,700	—
1631CA E	—	350	700	1,100	1,700	—
1632CA E	—	350	700	1,100	1,700	—
1633CA E	—	350	700	1,100	1,700	—

KM# 135 2 ESCUDOS

6.8670 g., 0.9167 Gold 0.2024 oz. AGW **Obv:** Crowned arms in inner circle **Rev:** Cross in quatrefoil in inner circle, date at top **Note:** Mint mark: Aqueduct.

Date	Mintage	VG	F	VF	XF	Unc
1651 I	—	1,100	2,700	4,500	6,800	—

KM# 137 2 ESCUDOS

6.8670 g., 0.9167 Gold 0.2024 oz. AGW **Obv:** Crowned arms without inner circle **Rev:** Cross in quatrefoil in inner circle, date at top **Note:** Mint mark: Aqueduct.

Date	Mintage	VG	F	VF	XF	Unc
1652 BR	—	1,100	2,700	4,500	6,800	—

KM# 140.2 2 ESCUDOS

6.8670 g., 0.9167 Gold 0.2024 oz. AGW **Obv:** Crowned arms without inner circle **Rev:** Cross in quatrefoil **Note:** Mint mark: Flower over G.

Date	Mintage	VG	F	VF	XF	Unc
ND	—	1,800	3,600	6,300	9,900	—

KM# 140.1 2 ESCUDOS

6.8670 g., 0.9167 Gold 0.2024 oz. AGW **Obv:** Crowned arms without inner circle **Rev:** Cross in quatrefoil **Note:** Mint mark: B, BA.

Date	Mintage	VG	F	VF	XF	Unc
1656 A	—	1,100	2,700	4,500	6,800	—

KM# 201 2 ESCUDOS

6.8670 g., 0.9167 Gold 0.2024 oz. AGW **Obv:** Crowned arms without inner circle **Rev:** Cross in quatrefoil, date at top **Note:** Mint mark: Aqueduct.

Date	Mintage	VG	F	VF	XF	Unc
1683 BR	—	1,250	2,900	4,950	7,700	—

KM# 207 2 ESCUDOS
6.8670 g., 0.9167 Gold 0.2024 oz. AGW **Obv:** Crowned arms without inner circle **Rev:** Cross in quatrefoil, date at top **Note:** Mint mark: Aqueduct.

Date	Mintage	VG	F	VF	XF	Unc
1686 M	—	700	1,400	2,400	3,700	—
1693 B	—	700	1,400	2,400	3,700	—

KM# 211 2 ESCUDOS
6.8670 g., 0.9167 Gold 0.2024 oz. AGW **Obv:** Crowned arms without inner circle **Rev:** Cross in quatrefoil **Note:** Mint mark: S, S/L.

Date	Mintage	VG	F	VF	XF	Unc
1688 G	—	300	600	1,000	1,500	—
1689 M	—	300	500	700	1,000	—
1690 G	—	300	500	700	1,000	—
1699 M Large crown	—	300	600	1,000	1,500	—
1699 M Small crown	—	300	600	1,000	1,500	—

KM# 31 4 ESCUDOS
13.7341 g., 0.9167 Gold 0.4048 oz. AGW **Obv:** Crowned arms in inner circle **Rev:** Cross in quatrefoil in inner circle, date at top **Note:** Mint mark: Aqueduct.

Date	Mintage	VG	F	VF	XF	Unc
1607 C Rare	—	—	—	—	—	—
1608 C Rare	—	—	—	—	—	—
1610 C Rare	—	—	—	—	—	—
1611 C Rare	—	—	—	—	—	—

KM# 58.1 4 ESCUDOS
13.7341 g., 0.9167 Gold 0.4048 oz. AGW **Obv:** Crowned arms **Rev:** Cross in quatrefoil **Note:** Mint mark: S, S/L.

Date	Mintage	VG	F	VF	XF	Unc
1613 B	—	1,200	2,050	2,950	4,400	—
1615 V	—	625	1,100	1,450	2,150	—

KM# 58.2 4 ESCUDOS
13.7341 g., 0.9167 Gold 0.4048 oz. AGW **Obv:** Crowned arms **Rev:** Cross in quatrefoil **Note:** Mint mark: Aqueduct.

Date	Mintage	VG	F	VF	XF	Unc
1615 R	—	1,100	2,150	3,250	4,850	—

KM# 58.3 4 ESCUDOS
13.7341 g., 0.9167 Gold 0.4048 oz. AGW **Obv:** Crowned arms **Rev:** Cross in quatrefoil **Note:** Mint mark: T, To.

Date	Mintage	VG	F	VF	XF	Unc
1615 CA	—	1,250	2,500	3,600	5,800	—

KM# 107.2 4 ESCUDOS
13.7341 g., 0.9167 Gold 0.4048 oz. AGW **Obv:** Crowned arms **Rev:** Cross in quatrefoil **Note:** Mint mark: S, S/L.

Date	Mintage	VG	F	VF	XF	Unc
1630 R	—	700	1,400	2,450	3,500	—
1631 R	—	700	1,400	2,450	3,500	—
1634 R	—	700	1,400	2,450	3,500	—
1643 R	—	700	1,400	2,450	3,500	—
1647 R	—	700	1,400	2,450	3,500	—

KM# 107.1 4 ESCUDOS
13.7341 g., 0.9167 Gold 0.4048 oz. AGW **Obv:** Crowned arms **Rev:** Cross in quatrefoil **Note:** Mint mark: Crowned M.

Date	Mintage	VG	F	VF	XF	Unc
ND(1631-51) M	—	450	700	1,050	1,600	—
1631 V	—	1,400	3,050	4,800	7,000	—
1638 M	—	1,400	3,050	4,800	7,000	—
1641 IB	—	1,750	3,950	6,100	8,800	—
1642 V	—	1,600	3,500	5,400	7,900	—
1642 IB	—	1,750	3,950	6,100	8,800	—
1644 IB	—	1,400	3,050	4,800	7,000	—
1646 A	—	1,250	2,650	4,400	6,100	—
1648 A	—	1,400	3,050	4,800	7,000	—
1651 A	—	1,400	3,050	4,800	7,000	—

KM# 108 4 ESCUDOS
13.7341 g., 0.9167 Gold 0.4048 oz. AGW **Obv:** Bust of Philip VI right in inner circle **Rev:** Crowned arms **Note:** Mint mark: PA, PL.

Date	Mintage	VG	F	VF	XF	Unc
ND	—	2,650	6,100	9,600	14,000	—

KM# 136 4 ESCUDOS
13.7341 g., 0.9167 Gold 0.4048 oz. AGW **Obv:** Crowned arms **Rev:** Cross in quatrefoil in inner circle, date at top **Note:** Mint mark: Aqueduct.

Date	Mintage	VG	F	VF	XF	Unc
1651 I Rare	—	—	—	—	—	—
1655 BR Rare	—	—	—	—	—	—

KM# 144.1 4 ESCUDOS
13.7341 g., 0.9167 Gold 0.4048 oz. AGW **Obv:** Crowned arms **Rev:** Cross in quatrefoil **Note:** Mint mark: Aqueduct.

Date	Mintage	VG	F	VF	XF	Unc
1659 R Rare	—	—	—	—	—	—

KM# 144.2 4 ESCUDOS
13.7341 g., 0.9167 Gold 0.4048 oz. AGW **Obv:** Crowned arms **Rev:** Cross in quatrefoil **Note:** Mint mark: Crowned M.

Date	Mintage	VG	F	VF	XF	Unc
1665 A	—	875	1,750	3,500	6,100	—
1665 M	—	875	1,750	3,500	6,100	—

KM# 144.3 4 ESCUDOS
13.7341 g., 0.9167 Gold 0.4048 oz. AGW **Obv:** Crowned arms **Rev:** Cross in quatrefoil **Note:** Mint mark: S, S/L.

Date	Mintage	VG	F	VF	XF	Unc
1667 M	—	—	—	—	—	—
1688 G	—	—	—	—	—	—

KM# 185.1 4 ESCUDOS
13.7341 g., 0.9167 Gold 0.4048 oz. AGW **Obv:** Crowned arms in order collar **Rev:** Cross in quatrefoil in inner collar, date at top

Date	Mintage	VG	F	VF	XF	Unc
1676B A	—	1,300	2,650	5,300	8,800	—
1679B A	—	1,300	2,550	5,200	8,500	—
1684B A	—	1,300	2,650	5,300	8,800	—
1697B A	—	1,150	2,200	4,400	7,400	—
1699B A	—	1,150	2,200	4,400	7,400	—

KM# 185.2 4 ESCUDOS
13.7341 g., 0.9167 Gold 0.4048 oz. AGW **Obv:** Crowned arms in order collar **Rev:** Cross in quatrefoil in inner collar, date at top **Note:** Mint mark: Aqueduct.

Date	Mintage	VG	F	VF	XF	Unc
1683 BR Rare	—	—	—	—	—	—
1686 BR Rare	—	—	—	—	—	—
1687/6 BR	—	2,800	6,000	9,100	13,000	—
1687 BR	—	2,100	4,550	6,700	9,600	—
1699 M	—	700	1,400	2,450	3,500	—
1700 M Rare	—	—	—	—	—	—

KM# 232.1 4 ESCUDOS
13.7341 g., 0.9167 Gold 0.4048 oz. AGW **Obv:** Crowned arms **Obv. Legend:** ...GRAT **Rev:** Cross in quatrefoil in inner collar, date at top **Note:** Mint mark: S, S/L.

Date	Mintage	VG	F	VF	XF	Unc
1699 M	—	600	1,000	1,800	2,900	—
1700 M	—	600	1,000	1,800	2,900	—

KM# 232.2 4 ESCUDOS
13.7341 g., 0.9167 Gold 0.4048 oz. AGW **Obv:** Crowned arms **Obv. Legend:** ...GRAC **Rev:** Cross in quatrefoil in inner collar, date at top **Note:** Mint mark: S, S/L.

Date	Mintage	VG	F	VF	XF	Unc
1699 M	—	1,100	1,700	3,000	4,300	—

KM# 49 8 ESCUDOS
27.4682 g., 0.9167 Gold 0.8095 oz. AGW **Obv:** Crowned arms in inner circle **Rev:** Cross in quatrefoil in inner circle, date at top **Note:** Mint mark: Aqueduct.

Date	Mintage	VG	F	VF	XF	Unc
1610 CA Monogram; Rare	—	—	—	—	—	—
1611 C Rare	—	—	—	—	—	—
1614 AR Ligate, Rare	—	—	—	—	—	—
1615 A	—	3,500	7,000	9,600	15,000	—

KM# 59.1 8 ESCUDOS
27.4682 g., 0.9167 Gold 0.8095 oz. AGW **Obv:** Crowned arms **Rev:** Cross in quatrefoil **Note:** Mint mark: S, S/L.

Date	Mintage	VG	F	VF	XF	Unc
1613 V	—	1,050	1,800	2,800	4,000	—

KM# 59.2 8 ESCUDOS
27.4682 g., 0.9167 Gold 0.8095 oz. AGW **Obv:** Crowned arms **Rev:** Cross in quatrefoil **Note:** Mint mark: Aqueduct.

Date	Mintage	VG	F	VF	XF	Unc
1615 R	—	3,950	7,000	11,000	16,000	—

KM# 59.3 8 ESCUDOS
27.4682 g., 0.9167 Gold 0.8095 oz. AGW **Obv:** Crowned arms **Rev:** Cross in quatrefoil **Note:** Mint mark: T, To.

Date	Mintage	VG	F	VF	XF	Unc
1615 CA	—	4,100	7,900	11,500	16,000	—

KM# 59.4 8 ESCUDOS
27.4682 g., 0.9167 Gold 0.8095 oz. AGW **Obv:** Crowned arms **Rev:** Cross in quatrefoil **Note:** Mint mark: Crowned M.

Date	Mintage	VG	F	VF	XF	Unc
ND S	—	900	1,400	2,000	3,000	—

KM# 95 8 ESCUDOS
27.4682 g., 0.9167 Gold 0.8095 oz. AGW **Obv:** Crowned arms in inner circle, 2 arches in mint mark **Rev:** Cross in quatrefoil in inner circle, date at top **Note:** Mint mark: Aqueduct.

Date	Mintage	VG	F	VF	XF	Unc
1627 A Rare	—	—	—	—	—	—
1632 R Rare	—	—	—	—	—	—
1633 R Rare	—	—	—	—	—	—
1635 R Rare	—	—	—	—	—	—
1636 R Rare	—	—	—	—	—	—
1637 R Rare	—	—	—	—	—	—
1638 R Rare	—	—	—	—	—	—
1639 R Rare	—	—	—	—	—	—
1651 I Rare	—	—	—	—	—	—
1652 BR Rare	—	—	—	—	—	—

KM# 96 8 ESCUDOS
27.4682 g., 0.9167 Gold 0.8095 oz. AGW **Obv:** Crowned arms in inner circle **Rev:** Cross in quatrefoil **Note:** Mint mark: S, S/L.

Date	Mintage	VG	F	VF	XF	Unc
1627 R Unique	—	—	—	—	—	—
1631 R	—	1,500	3,050	4,400	6,100	—

KM# 102 8 ESCUDOS
27.4682 g., 0.9167 Gold 0.8095 oz. AGW **Obv:** Crowned arms **Rev:** Cross in quatrefoil, date at top **Note:** Mint mark: Crowned M.

Date	Mintage	VG	F	VF	XF	Unc
1632 M Unique	—	—	—	—	—	—
1632 PM Unique	—	—	—	—	—	—
1633 M	—	3,500	6,100	8,800	13,000	—
1634 M	—	2,200	4,400	6,100	9,600	—
1635 M	—	3,500	6,100	8,800	13,000	—
1637 M	—	1,750	3,500	5,300	7,900	—
1639 OP	—	3,500	6,100	8,800	13,000	—
1640 B	—	1,750	3,500	5,300	7,900	—
1641 B	—	1,750	3,500	5,300	7,900	—
1642 B	—	2,100	3,850	6,100	8,800	—
1643 B	—	2,650	4,750	7,000	10,500	—
1644 B	—	2,650	4,750	7,000	10,500	—
1645 B	—	1,750	3,500	5,300	7,900	—
1645 IB	—	2,200	4,400	6,700	9,600	—
1646 A	—	2,200	4,400	6,700	9,600	—
1648 A	—	2,100	3,850	6,100	8,800	—
1649 A	—	1,750	3,500	5,300	7,900	—
1650 A	—	1,750	3,500	5,300	7,900	—
1651 A	—	1,750	3,500	5,300	7,900	—
1654 A	—	2,450	4,800	7,400	11,500	—
1655 A	—	3,500	6,600	9,600	15,000	—
1656 A	—	3,500	6,600	9,600	15,000	—
1657 A	—	3,500	7,000	10,500	15,500	—
1661 A	—	1,750	3,500	5,300	7,900	—
1662 A	—	2,100	3,850	6,100	8,800	—
1663/1 A Unique	—	—	—	—	—	—

KM# 112 8 ESCUDOS
27.4682 g., 0.9167 Gold 0.8095 oz. AGW **Obv:** Crowned arms in inner circle **Rev:** Cross in quatrefoil with squares in corners **Note:** Mint mark: S, S/L.

Date	Mintage	VG	F	VF	XF	Unc
1634 R	—	2,650	4,400	6,100	8,800	—
1637 R Unique	—	—	—	—	—	—
1638 R	—	1,300	2,650	3,700	5,300	—
1639 R	—	1,300	2,650	3,700	5,300	—
1640 R Unique	—	—	—	—	—	—
1642 R	—	1,150	2,100	3,050	4,400	—

Date	Mintage	VG	F	VF	XF	Unc
1643 R	—	1,750	3,500	5,300	7,900	—
1644 R	—	1,150	2,100	3,050	4,400	—
1645 R	—	975	1,750	2,650	3,850	—
1646 R	—	1,300	2,650	3,700	5,300	—
1647 R	—	1,300	2,650	3,700	5,300	—
1649 R	—	1,150	2,100	3,050	4,400	—
1653 R Unique	—	—	—	—	—	—
1654 R	—	1,150	2,100	3,050	4,400	—
1657 R Unique	—	—	—	—	—	—
1659 R	—	1,150	2,100	3,050	4,400	—
1661 BPR Unique	—	—	—	—	—	—

KM# 138 8 ESCUDOS

27.4682 g., 0.9167 Gold 0.8095 oz. AGW **Obv:** Crowned arms of Navarre in inner circle **Rev:** Cross in ornamental cartouche in inner circle, date in legend **Note:** Mint mark: PA, PP.

Date	Mintage	VG	F	VF	XF	Unc
1652 AP Rare	—	—	—	—	—	—

KM# 139 8 ESCUDOS

27.4682 g., 0.9167 Gold 0.8095 oz. AGW **Obv:** Crowned arms in inner circle, 3 arches in mint mark **Rev:** Cross in quatrefoil in inner circle, date at top **Note:** Mint mark: Aqueduct. Varieties exist.

Date	Mintage	VG	F	VF	XF	Unc
1655 BRx	—	—	—	62,500	—	—

KM# 145 8 ESCUDOS

27.4682 g., 0.9167 Gold 0.8095 oz. AGW **Obv:** Crowned arms **Rev:** Cross in quatrefoil with fleur-de-lis in corners **Note:** Mint mark: S, S/L.

Date	Mintage	VG	F	VF	XF	Unc
1659 R	—	1,150	2,100	3,050	4,400	—
1663 A	—	1,500	3,050	4,400	6,100	—
1663 R	—	1,150	2,100	3,050	4,400	—
1664 R	—	975	1,750	2,650	3,850	—
1665 R	—	1,150	2,100	3,050	4,400	—

KM# 168.1 8 ESCUDOS

27.4682 g., 0.9167 Gold 0.8095 oz. AGW **Obv:** Crowned arms **Rev:** Cross in quatrefoil **Note:** Mint mark: Crowned M.

Date	Mintage	VG	F	VF	XF	Unc
1661 A Rare	—	—	—	—	—	—
1668 AS	—	2,250	4,500	7,500	12,000	—
1686 M	—	2,250	4,500	7,500	12,000	—
1693 B	—	3,000	5,600	8,300	13,000	—

KM# 168.2 8 ESCUDOS

27.4682 g., 0.9167 Gold 0.8095 oz. AGW **Obv:** Crowned arms **Rev:** Cross in quatrefoil **Note:** Mint mark: S, S/L. Varieties exist.

Date	Mintage	VG	F	VF	XF	Unc
1666 R Unique	—	—	—	—	—	—
1666 M Unique	—	—	—	—	—	—
1667 M	—	975	2,200	3,500	5,300	—
1668 M	—	975	2,200	3,500	5,300	—
1669 M	—	975	2,200	3,500	5,300	—
1670 M	—	975	2,200	3,500	5,300	—
1673 M	—	975	2,200	3,500	5,300	—
1674 M	—	975	2,200	3,500	5,300	—
1675/4 M	—	975	2,200	3,500	5,300	—
1676 M Unique	—	—	—	—	—	—
1676 S Unique	—	—	—	—	—	—
1678 M Unique	—	—	—	—	—	—
1680 S Unique	—	—	—	—	—	—
1683 S Unique	—	—	—	—	—	—
1684 S Unique	—	—	—	—	—	—
1685 S Unique	—	—	—	—	—	—
1686 S Unique	—	—	—	—	—	—
1686 G	—	975	2,200	3,500	5,300	—
1687 G Unique	—	—	—	—	—	—
1688 M	—	975	2,200	3,500	5,300	—
1689/8 M	—	975	2,200	3,500	5,300	—
1689 M/S	—	975	2,200	3,500	5,300	—
1690 M	—	975	2,200	3,500	5,300	—
1691 M	—	975	2,200	3,500	5,300	—
1692 M	—	975	2,200	3,500	5,300	—
1694 M Unique, 8 reales style obverse shield	—	—	—	—	—	—
1698 M	—	975	2,200	3,500	5,300	—
1699 M	—	975	2,200	3,500	5,300	—

KM# 197 8 ESCUDOS

27.4682 g., 0.9167 Gold 0.8095 oz. AGW **Obv:** Crowned arms **Rev:** Cross in quatrefoil **Note:** Mint mark: Aqueduct.

Date	Mintage	VG	F	VF	XF	Unc
1682 M Rare	—	—	—	—	—	—
1683 BR Rare	—	—	—	—	—	—
1687/3 BR	—	2,250	5,300	8,300	13,500	—
1687 BR	—	2,250	5,300	8,300	13,500	—
1688 BR Rare	—	—	—	—	—	—

KM# 212 8 ESCUDOS

27.4682 g., 0.9167 Gold 0.8095 oz. AGW **Obv:** Crowned arms **Rev:** Cross in quatrefoil **Note:** Mint mark: T, To.

Date	Mintage	VG	F	VF	XF	Unc
1688 P Rare	—	—	—	—	—	—

KM# 226 8 ESCUDOS

27.4682 g., 0.9167 Gold 0.8095 oz. AGW **Obv:** Crowned arms **Rev:** Cross in quatrefoil in inner circle

Date	Mintage	VG	F	VF	XF	Unc
1693B A Unique	—	—	—	—	—	—
1694B A Unique	—	—	—	—	—	—
1697B A Unique	—	—	—	—	—	—
1699B A	—	1,800	3,800	5,600	8,000	—

KM# 233.1 8 ESCUDOS

27.4682 g., 0.9167 Gold 0.8095 oz. AGW **Obv:** Crowned arms in order collar **Obv. Legend:** CAROLVS II.DEI.GRAT **Rev:** Cross in quatrefoil, date at top **Rev. Legend:** HISPANIARVM.REX **Note:** Mint mark: S, S/L.

Date	Mintage	VG	F	VF	XF	Unc
1699 M	—	2,250	4,900	7,500	12,000	—
1699 M DEI.GRAC (error)	—	2,250	4,900	7,500	12,000	—

KM# 233.2 8 ESCUDOS

27.4682 g., 0.9167 Gold 0.8095 oz. AGW **Ruler:** Charles II **Obv:** Crowned arms in order collar **Obv. Legend:** ...GRAC **Rev:** Cross in quatrefoil **Note:** Mint mark: S, S/L.

Date	Mintage	VG	F	VF	XF	Unc
1699 M	—	2,300	4,900	7,000	12,500	—

KM# 258 8 ESCUDOS

27.4682 g., 0.9167 Gold 0.8095 oz. AGW **Obv:** Crowned arms in order collar **Rev:** Cross in quatrefoil

Date	Mintage	VG	F	VF	XF	Unc
x70xB Unique	—	—	—	—	—	—

KM# 233.3 8 ESCUDOS

27.4682 g., 0.9167 Gold 0.8095 oz. AGW **Ruler:** Charles II **Obv:** Crowned arms in order collar **Obv. Legend:** CAROLVS II • DEI • GRAT **Rev:** Cross in quatrefoil within inner circle **Mint:** Seville

Date	Mintage	VG	F	VF	XF	Unc
1700S M	—	—	—	—	—	—

KM# 38 100 ESCUDOS

0.9167 Gold **Obv:** Crowned arms in inner circle **Rev:** Cross in quatrefoil in inner circle, date at top **Note:** Mint mark: Aqueduct.

Date	Mintage	VG	F	VF	XF	Unc
1609 C Rare	—	—	—	—	—	—
1618 AR Rare	—	—	—	—	—	—

KM# 84 100 ESCUDOS

0.9167 Gold **Obv:** Crowned arms in inner circle, 5 arches in mint mark **Rev:** Cross in quatrefoil in inner circle, date at top **Note:** Mint mark: Aqueduct.

Date	Mintage	VG	F	VF	XF	Unc
1623 AR Unique	—	—	—	—	—	—

KM# 113 100 ESCUDOS

0.9167 Gold **Obv:** Crowned arms in inner circle, 10 arches in mint mark **Rev:** Cross in quatrefoil in inner circle, date at top **Note:** Mint mark: Aqueduct.

Date	Mintage	VG	F	VF	XF	Unc
1633 R Rare	—	—	—	—	—	—

PATTERNS

Including off metal strikes

KM#	Date	Mintage	Identification	Mkt Val
Pn1	1631	—	Maravedi. Copper. Monogram: PH-IL-P-P-V-S. Castle and lion. Struck at Segovia.	—
Pn2	1631	—	Maravedi. Copper. Castle in quatrefoil. Lion in quatrefoil. Struck at Segovia.	1,150
Pn3	1631	—	2 Maravedis. Copper. Castle in circle. Lion in circle. Struck at Segovia.	—
Pn4	1660	—	8 Maravedis. Copper. Struck at Madrid. MD between crowned pillars	—
Pn5	1660	—	8 Maravedis. Copper. VIII between crowned pillars	—
Pn6	1660	—	8 Maravedis. Copper. VIII between crowned pillars	—
Pn7	1663S	—	8 Reales. Silver.	—
Pn8	1663S	—	8 Reales. Silver.	—
Pn9	1663S	—	8 Reales. Silver.	—

ARAGON

Aragon, bordered by Navarre on the west and Catalonia on the east, was an influential Christian Kingdom in Northern Spain. Even after unification the main city of Zaragoza, name of the mint, retained its prominence in the region.

RULERS
Philip III, 1598-1621
Philip IV, 1621-1665
Charles II, 1665-1700
Philip V, 1700-1746

MINT MARKS
C, CA, Z – Zaragoza

PROVINCE

STANDARD COINAGE

KM# 5 DINERO

Copper **Obv:** Small head right **Rev:** Crowned arms of Aragon **Mint:** Granollers

Date	Mintage	VG	F	VF	XF	Unc
ND	—	14.00	20.00	42.00	70.00	—

KM# 6 DINERO

Copper **Obv:** Large head left **Rev:** Crowned arms of Aragon **Mint:** Granollers

Date	Mintage	VG	F	VF	XF	Unc
1601	—	17.00	27.50	49.00	100	—
1602	—	17.00	27.50	49.00	100	—
1616	—	17.00	27.50	49.00	100	—

KM# 7 DINERO

Copper **Obv:** PP monogram **Rev:** St. John the Baptist standing with lamb **Mint:** Perpinan

Date	Mintage	VG	F	VF	XF	Unc
ND	—	100	190	350	—	—

KM# 25 DINERO

Copper **Obv:** Bust of Philip IV right **Rev:** Diamond-shaped shield **Mint:** Perpinan

Date	Mintage	VG	F	VF	XF	Unc
1632	—	—	—	—	—	—

KM# 50 DINERO

Copper **Obv:** Crowned bust of Charles II left **Rev:** Cross in inner circle, date in legend

Date	Mintage	VG	F	VF	XF	Unc
1670CA	—	11.00	19.00	42.00	70.00	—
1671CA	—	11.00	19.00	42.00	70.00	—
1672CA	—	11.00	19.00	42.00	70.00	—
1673CA	—	11.00	19.00	42.00	70.00	—
1674CA	—	11.00	19.00	42.00	70.00	—
1675CA	—	11.00	19.00	42.00	70.00	—
1676CA	—	11.00	19.00	42.00	70.00	—
1677CA	—	11.00	19.00	42.00	70.00	—
1678CA	—	11.00	19.00	42.00	70.00	—
1679CA	—	11.00	19.00	42.00	70.00	—
1680CA	—	11.00	19.00	42.00	70.00	—

KM# 15 3 DINEROS (Ternet)

Copper **Obv:** PP monogram **Rev:** St. John the Baptist with lamb **Mint:** Perpinan

Date	Mintage	VG	F	VF	XF	Unc
1611	—	70.00	135	265	—	—

KM# 55 5 DINEROS (Cinquen)

Copper **Obv:** Crowned bust right **Rev:** Crowned diamond-shaped shield **Mint:** Ibiza

Date	Mintage	VG	F	VF	XF	Unc
1686	—	55.00	90.00	190	—	—

KM# 8 6 DINEROS

Copper **Obv:** Bust right **Rev:** Castle **Mint:** Ibiza **Note:** Legend varieties exist.

Date	Mintage	VG	F	VF	XF	Unc
ND	—	37.50	75.00	150	—	—

KM# 19 1/2 REAL

Silver **Obv:** Crowned shield **Rev:** Tree, cross above, date in legend **Mint:** Zaragoza

Date	Mintage	VG	F	VF	XF	Unc
1612	—	95.00	155	250	375	—

KM# 35 1/2 REAL

Silver **Obv:** Crowned shield **Rev:** Four heads in angles of cross

Date	Mintage	VG	F	VF	XF	Unc
1651	—	155	250	475	825	—

KM# 16 REAL

Silver **Obv:** Crowned shield of Aragon **Rev:** Head in each quarter round arms, date in legend **Mint:** Zaragoza

Date	Mintage	VG	F	VF	XF	Unc
1611CA	—	125	190	325	525	—
1612CA	—	125	190	325	525	—

KM# 36 REAL

Silver **Obv:** Crowned shield

Date	Mintage	VG	F	VF	XF	Unc
1651	—	375	675	1,200	—	—

KM# 37 REAL

Silver

Date	Mintage	VG	F	VF	XF	Unc
1651	—	150	300	575	—	—

KM# 38 2 REALES

Silver **Obv:** Crowned shield of Aragon **Rev:** Zaragoza arms, date in legend **Mint:** Zaragoza

Date	Mintage	VG	F	VF	XF	Unc
1651	—	265	525	1,050	—	—

KM# 39 2 REALES

Silver **Obv:** Dotted inner circle around shield

Date	Mintage	VG	F	VF	XF	Unc
1651	—	265	525	1,050	—	—

KM# 40 2 REALES

Silver

Date	Mintage	VG	F	VF	XF	Unc
1651	—	225	425	825	—	—
1652	—	265	450	900	—	—

KM# 45 2 REALES

Silver

Date	Mintage	VG	F	VF	XF	Unc
1669	—	450	825	1,450	2,500	—

KM# 17 4 REALES

Silver **Mint:** Zaragoza **Note:** Similar to 8 Reales, KM#18

Date	Mintage	VG	F	VF	XF	Unc
1611 Rare	—	—	—	—	—	—

KM# 41 4 REALES

Silver **Note:** Similar to 8 Reales, KM#42. Exists as a cob or a round coin.

Date	Mintage	VG	F	VF	XF	Unc
1651	—	975	1,900	3,000	—	—

KM# 18.1 8 REALES

Silver **Obv:** Crowned ornamental arms of Aragon, denomination as VIII **Obv. Legend:** PHILIPPVS • II • DEI • G **Rev:** Ornamental quartered arms with crowned heads **Rev. Legend:** ARAGONVM • REX • **Mint:** Zaragoza

Date	Mintage	Good	VG	F	VF	XF
1611CA Rare	—	—	—	—	—	—

KM# 18.2 8 REALES

Silver **Obv:** Crowned ornamental arms of Aragon, denomination as VII, dot in center of arms **Obv. Legend:** PHILIPPVS • II • DEI • G **Rev:** Ornamental quartered arms with crowned heads **Rev. Legend:** ARAGONVM • REX • **Mint:** Zaragoza **Note:** Dav. #4399.

Date	Mintage	Good	VG	F	VF	XF
1611CA Rare	—	—	—	—	—	—

KM# 42 8 REALES

Silver **Obv:** Crowned plain arms, denomination 8 **Obv. Legend:** PHILIPPVS • IV • DEI • G **Rev:** Plain quartered arms **Mint:** Zaragoza

Date	Mintage	Good	VG	F	VF	XF
1651	—	1,250	2,500	5,000	7,500	—
1652	—	1,550	3,150	5,600	8,100	—

BARCELONA

Barcelona was a maritime province located in northeast Spain. The city was the provincial capital of Barcelona. Barcelona is a major port and commercial center.

RULERS
Philip III, 1598-1621
Philip IV, 1621-1665
French Occupation
Louis XIII, 1641-1643
Louis XIV, 1643-1659
Charles II, 1665-1700

MINT MARK
Ba – Barcelona

MONETARY SYSTEM
4 Quartos = 1 Sueldo
6 Sueldos = 1 Peseta

FRENCH OCCUPATION

SIEGE

KM# 39 10 REALES
Silver **Ruler:** Louis XIV French Occupation **Obv:** Laureate bust right divides value X-R **Obv. Legend:** LVD•XIIII•D•G•R•F•C•B• **Rev:** Short cross with circles and dots in angles **Rev. Legend:** BARCINO CIVIT OBSESSA

Date	Mintage	Good	VG	F	VF	XF
1652	—	225	450	900	1,500	2,500

STANDARD COINAGE

KM# 34 MENUT
Copper **Ruler:** Louis XIV French Occupation **Obv:** Laureate bust right **Obv. Legend:** L9 - D • G **Rev:** Cross, circles and dots in angles **Rev. Legend:** BAR - CINO - CIVI

Date	Mintage	Good	VG	F	VF	XF
1644	—	—	—	—	—	—

KM# 36 MENUT
Copper **Ruler:** Louis XIV French Occupation **Obv:** Laureate bust right **Obv. Legend:** LVD • XIIII • D • G • **Rev:** Cross, circles and dots in angles **Rev. Legend:** BAR - CIN - CIVI

Date	Mintage	Good	VG	F	VF	XF
1645	—	—	—	—	—	—

KM# 35 1/2 SEIZAIN
Copper **Ruler:** Louis XIV French Occupation **Obv:** Bust right divides A-R **Rev:** Diamond Catalonian shield **Rev. Legend:** BARCINO - CIVI

Date	Mintage	Good	VG	F	VF	XF
1644	—	12.00	25.00	50.00	100	150

KM# 37 SEIZAIN
Copper **Ruler:** Louis XIV French Occupation **Obv:** Laureate bust right **Obv. Legend:** LVD•XIII•D•G•R•F•ET•CO•B **Rev:** Dianmond Catalnoian shield on cross, head of St. Eulalie above, lis below **Rev. Legend:** BARCINO - CIVI

Date	Mintage	Good	VG	F	VF	XF
1648	—	10.00	20.00	40.00	75.00	125

KM# 38 SEIZAIN
Copper **Ruler:** Louis XIV French Occupation **Obv:** Laureate bust right with pearl necklace **Obv. Legend:** LVD•XIII•D•G•R•F• ET•CO•B **Rev:** Diamond Catalonian shield on cross, head of St. Eulalie above, lis below **Rev. Legend:** BARCINO - CIVI

Date	Mintage	Good	VG	F	VF	XF
1648	—	—	—	—	—	—

FRENCH OCCUPATION - VICH

STANDARD COINAGE

KM# 6 1/2 SEIZAIN
Copper **Ruler:** Louis XIV French Occupation **Obv:** Laureate bust right **Obv. Legend:** + LVDOVIC • D • G • R • FRANC **Rev:** Diamond shield **Rev. Legend:** CIVITAS • VICEN •

Date	Mintage	Good	VG	F	VF	XF
1644	—	—	—	—	—	—

PROVINCE

COUNTERMARKED COINAGE

KM# 18 TRENTIN
Gold, 29 mm. **Countermark:** "B" mint mark between facing busts **Note:** Countermark on Trentin, KM#17.1.

CM Date	Host Date	Good	VG	F	VF	XF
ND(1622-40)	1622B	—	675	1,350	2,250	3,750
ND(1635-40)	1626B	—	525	1,050	1,900	3,300

KM# 19 TRENTIN
Gold **Ruler:** Philip IV **Countermark:** Barcelona diamond shield between facing busts **Note:** Countermarked on Spanish 2 Excellentes.

CM Date	Host Date	Good	VG	F	VF	XF
ND(1622-40)	ND	—	—	—	—	—

HAMMERED COINAGE

KM# 5 1/3 TRENTIN
Gold **Ruler:** Philip III **Obv:** Bust of Philip III right **Obv. Legend:** PHILIPP.D GRAT **Rev:** Crowned shield of Barcelona within inner circle **Rev. Legend:** CIVIT **Mint:** Barcelona **Note:** Size varies 16-17mm.

Date	Mintage	VG	F	VF	XF	Unc
1618B	—	300	600	1,150	2,250	—

KM# A14 1/3 TRENTIN
Gold **Ruler:** Philip IV **Obv:** Bust of Philip IV left **Obv. Legend:** PHILIPP.D GRATIA **Rev:** Crowned shield of Barcelona within inner circle **Rev. Legend:** AR...CIV... **Mint:** Barcelona **Note:** Weight varies 15-16 grams.

Date	Mintage	VG	F	VF	XF	Unc
16Z3B	—	600	1,200	2,050	3,400	—
16Z5B	—	525	975	1,900	3,000	—
16Z5	—	750	1,500	2,800	4,900	—

KM# 6.1 1/2 TRENTIN
Gold, 22 mm. **Ruler:** Philip III **Obv:** Facing busts of Ferdinand and Isabella, star above and between **Obv. Legend:** FERNANDVS ELISABET D.G.RES **Rev:** Crowned arms **Rev. Legend:** SVDVMBRA **Note:** Imitation of Spanish 1 Excelente of 1476-1516.

Date	Mintage	VG	F	VF	XF	Unc
ND(1598-1621)	—	575	1,150	1,900	3,250	—

KM# 6.2 1/2 TRENTIN
Gold, 22 mm. **Ruler:** Philip III **Obv:** Facing busts of Ferdinand and Isabella, star above and between **Obv. Legend:** FERNANDVS ELISABET REGS **Rev:** Crowned arms **Rev. Legend:** SVBVMBRA **Note:** Imitation of Spanish 1 Excelente of 1476-1516.

Date	Mintage	VG	F	VF	XF	Unc
ND(1598-1621)	—	575	1,150	1,900	3,250	—

KM# 15.1 1/2 TRENTIN
Gold, 24 mm. **Ruler:** Philip IV **Obv:** Facing busts of Ferdinand and Isabella, star between **Obv. Legend:** FERNANDVS ET ISABET DG RGS **Rev:** Crowned arms **Rev. Legend:** SVBVM BRA **Note:** Imitation of Spanish 1 Excelente of 1476-1516.

Date	Mintage	VG	F	VF	XF	Unc
16Z3	—	600	1,200	2,050	3,400	—
16Z5	—	600	1,200	2,050	3,400	—
16Z6	—	600	1,200	2,050	3,400	—

KM# 16.2 1/2 TRENTIN
Gold, 24 mm. **Ruler:** Philip IV **Obv:** Facing busts of Ferdinand and Isabella, mint mark between **Obv. Legend:** FERNAN DVS ELISABET **Rev:** Crowned arms **Rev. Legend:** SVBVMBRA **Note:** Imitation of Spanish 1 Excelente of 1476-1516.

Date	Mintage	VG	F	VF	XF	Unc
1626B	—	600	1,200	2,050	3,400	—
1627B	—	675	1,350	2,250	3,750	—
1630B	—	600	1,200	2,050	3,400	—
1631B	—	600	1,200	2,050	3,400	—
1632B	—	600	1,200	2,050	3,400	—

KM# A7 TRENTIN
Gold, 30 mm. **Ruler:** Philip III **Obv:** Facing busts of Ferdinand and Isabella, star above and between **Obv. Legend:** FERDANDVS.ET.ELISABET.REX.ET.REG(INA) **Rev:** Winged crowned arms **Rev. Legend:** SVBVMBRA•A... **Mint:** Barcelona **Note:** Imitation of Spanish 2 Excelentes of 1476-1516.

Date	Mintage	VG	F	VF	XF	Unc
ND(1598-1621)	—	525	1,050	1,800	3,000	—

KM# 8 TRENTIN
Gold, 30 mm. **Ruler:** Philip III **Obv:** Facing busts of Ferdinand and Isabella, star above **Obv. Legend:** FERNANDVS ET ELISABET REX • ET • REGI + **Rev:** Eagle with wings spread behind crowned arms **Rev. Legend:** SVBVMBRA•A **Note:** Imitation of Spanish 2 Excellentes of 1476-1516.

Date	Mintage	VG	F	VF	XF	Unc
ND(1598-1621)	—	600	1,200	2,050	3,400	—

KM# 17.1 TRENTIN
Gold, 29 mm. **Ruler:** Philip IV **Obv:** Facing busts of Ferdinand and Isabella, star above and between **Obv. Legend:** FERNANDVS ET ELISABET REGES **Rev:** Eagle with wings spread behind crowned arms **Rev. Legend:** SVBVMBRA **Note:** Imitation of Spanish 2 Excellentes of 1476-1516.

Date	Mintage	VG	F	VF	XF	Unc
1622	—	525	1,050	1,800	3,250	—
1625	—	525	1,050	1,800	3,250	—
1626	—	525	1,050	1,800	3,250	—
1627	—	750	1,450	2,400	4,150	—
1628	—	525	1,050	1,800	3,250	—

KM# 17.2 TRENTIN
Gold, 29 mm. **Ruler:** Philip IV **Obv:** Facing busts of Ferdinand and Isabella, star above, mint mark between **Obv. Legend:** FERNANDVS ET ELISABET REGES **Rev:** Eagle with wings spread behind crowned arms **Rev. Legend:** SVBVMBRA **Note:** Imitation of Spanish 2 Excellentes of 1476-1516.

Date	Mintage	VG	F	VF	XF	Unc
16ZZ	—	600	1,200	2,050	3,400	—
1628	—	600	1,200	2,050	3,400	—
1629	—	600	1,200	2,050	3,400	—
1630	—	675	1,350	2,250	3,750	—
1631	—	600	1,200	2,050	3,400	—
1632	—	600	1,200	2,050	3,400	—
1633	—	600	1,200	2,050	3,400	—

KM# 9 5 TRENTIN
Gold **Ruler:** Philip III **Obv:** Facing busts of Ferdinand and Isabella **Obv. Legend:** FERNANDVS ET ELISABET REX ET REGINA **Rev:** Eagle with wings spread behind crowned arms **Rev. Legend:** SVBVM BRA **Note:** Imitation of Spanish 10 Excellentes of 1476-1516. Size varies 40-42mm.

Date	Mintage	VG	F	VF	XF	Unc
ND(1598-1621) Rare	—	—	—	—	—	—

STANDARD COINAGE

KM# 14 DINERO (Menut)
Silver **Obv:** Bust of Philip III left **Rev:** Cross with dots and annulets in angles **Mint:** Barcelona **Note:** Varieties exist.

Date	Mintage	VG	F	VF	XF	Unc
1615	—	10.00	20.00	39.25	75.00	—
1616	—	18.00	35.00	55.00	105	—
1617	—	10.00	20.00	39.25	75.00	—
1618	—	10.00	20.00	39.25	75.00	—
1619	—	10.00	20.00	39.25	75.00	—
162 Error	—	10.00	20.00	39.25	75.00	—
1621	—	10.00	20.00	39.25	75.00	—

KM# 20 DINERO (Menut)
Silver **Obv:** Bust of Philip IV left **Mint:** Barcelona **Note:** Titles of Philip IV

Date	Mintage	VG	F	VF	XF	Unc
1622	—	18.00	35.00	55.00	105	—
1623	—	20.00	42.00	70.00	140	—
1625	—	8.00	17.00	35.00	70.00	—
1628	—	8.00	17.00	35.00	70.00	—
1629	—	8.00	17.00	35.00	70.00	—
1632	—	8.00	17.00	35.00	70.00	—
1633	—	8.00	17.00	35.00	70.00	—
1634	—	8.00	17.00	35.00	70.00	—
1635	—	8.00	17.00	35.00	70.00	—

KM# 13 ARDITE
Copper **Obv:** Bust of Philip III left between A - R **Rev:** Quartered diamond arms in inner circle **Mint:** Barcelona **Note:** Prev. KM#16.

Date	Mintage	VG	F	VF	XF	Unc
1612 AR	—	18.00	35.00	55.00	105	—
1613 AR	—	8.00	17.00	35.00	70.00	—
1614 AR	—	8.00	17.00	35.00	70.00	—
1615 AR	—	8.00	17.00	35.00	70.00	—
1616 AR	—	8.00	17.00	35.00	70.00	—
1617 AR	—	11.00	20.00	42.00	75.00	—
1618 AR	—	8.00	22.50	44.75	85.00	—
1619 AR	—	14.00	27.50	49.00	100	—
1620 AR	—	14.00	27.50	49.00	100	—
1621 AR	—	27.50	55.00	85.00	170	—

KM# 21 ARDITE
Copper **Obv:** Bust of Philip IV left between A - R

Date	Mintage	VG	F	VF	XF	Unc
1622	—	20.00	42.00	70.00	140	—
1623	—	20.00	42.00	70.00	140	—
1624	—	8.00	17.00	35.00	70.00	—
1625	—	8.00	17.00	35.00	70.00	—
1626	—	8.00	17.00	35.00	70.00	—
1627	—	8.00	17.00	35.00	70.00	—
1628	—	8.00	17.00	35.00	70.00	—
1629	—	8.00	17.00	35.00	70.00	—
1630	—	8.00	17.00	35.00	70.00	—
1631	—	8.00	17.00	35.00	70.00	—
1632	—	8.00	17.00	35.00	70.00	—
1633	—	8.00	17.00	35.00	70.00	—
1634	—	8.00	17.00	35.00	70.00	—
1635	—	8.00	17.00	35.00	70.00	—
1653	—	8.00	17.00	35.00	70.00	—
1654	—	8.00	17.00	35.00	70.00	—
1655	—	8.00	17.00	35.00	70.00	—

KM# 33 SEISENO
Copper **Obv:** Bust of Philip IV left in inner circle **Rev:** Diamond arms in inner circle, date in legend **Mint:** Barcelona

Date	Mintage	VG	F	VF	XF	Unc
1640 SI	—	17.00	35.00	65.00	120	—
1640	—	17.00	35.00	65.00	120	—
1641 SI	—	17.00	35.00	65.00	120	—
1641	—	20.00	42.00	70.00	140	—
1642	—	20.00	42.00	70.00	140	—

KM# 12 1/4 REAL (1/4 Croat)
Silver **Obv:** Bust of Philip III left in inner circle

Date	Mintage	VG	F	VF	XF	Unc
1611	—	—	—	—	—	—

KM# 3 1/2 REAL (1/2 Croat)
Silver **Obv:** Head of Philip III left in inner circle **Rev:** Long cross with dots and annulets in angles, date in legend **Mint:** Barcelona **Note:** Prev. KM#5.

Date	Mintage	VG	F	VF	XF	Unc
1609	—	125	190	350	575	—
1611	—	125	190	350	575	—
1620	—	125	220	375	625	—

KM# 11 1/2 REAL (1/2 Croat)
Silver **Obv:** Bust of Philip III left in inner circle **Note:** Varieties exist.

Date	Mintage	VG	F	VF	XF	Unc
1611	—	17.00	35.00	65.00	105	—
1612	—	17.00	35.00	65.00	105	—
1613	—	27.50	55.00	105	175	—
1614	—	100	195	350	525	—
1615	—	35.00	70.00	140	230	—
1617	—	27.50	55.00	105	175	—
1618	—	20.00	42.00	75.00	140	—
1619	—	20.00	42.00	75.00	140	—

KM# 22 1/2 REAL (1/2 Croat)
Silver **Obv:** Titles of Philip IV

Date	Mintage	VG	F	VF	XF	Unc
1626	—	20.00	42.00	70.00	140	—
ND	—	20.00	42.00	70.00	140	—

KM# 25 1/2 REAL (1/2 Croat)
Silver **Obv:** Bust of Philip III

Date	Mintage	VG	F	VF	XF	Unc
1632	—	20.00	42.00	70.00	140	—

KM# 26 1/2 REAL (1/2 Croat)
Silver **Obv:** Bust of Philip IV left in inner circle **Rev:** Cross with dots and annulets in angles in inner circle, date in legend

Date	Mintage	VG	F	VF	XF	Unc
1632	—	49.00	105	170	280	—
1633	—	49.00	105	170	280	—
1635	—	49.00	105	170	280	—

KM# 4 REAL (Croat)
0.9310 g., Silver **Obv:** Bust of Philip III left in inner circle **Rev:** Long cross with dots and annulets in angles in inner circle, date in legend **Mint:** Barcelona **Note:** Prev. KM#6.

Date	Mintage	VG	F	VF	XF	Unc
1607	—	49.00	105	210	425	—
1609	—	35.00	70.00	120	280	—
1610	—	49.00	105	210	425	—
1611	—	49.00	105	210	425	—
1612	—	49.00	105	210	425	—
1613	—	49.00	105	210	425	—
1620	—	35.00	70.00	120	280	—
16NO	—	42.00	85.00	140	325	—
1621	—	49.00	105	210	425	—

KM# 23.2 REAL (Croat)
0.9310 Silver **Obv:** Bust of Philip IV left in inner circle **Obv. Legend:** PHILIPP **Rev. Legend:** BARCINO CIVI, date **Note:** Titles of Philip IV.

Date	Mintage	VG	F	VF	XF	Unc
1626	—	25.00	44.75	75.00	155	—
1630	—	25.00	49.00	85.00	170	—
1631	—	25.00	44.75	75.00	155	—
1632	—	25.00	44.75	75.00	155	—
1633	—	25.00	44.75	75.00	155	—
1636	—	25.00	44.75	75.00	155	—
1637	—	25.00	44.75	75.00	155	—
1637 Date on both sides	—	35.00	70.00	140	280	—
1638	—	25.00	44.75	75.00	155	—
1639	—	25.00	44.75	75.00	155	—
1640	—	25.00	44.75	75.00	155	—
1653	—	27.50	55.00	100	175	—
1654	—	25.00	44.75	75.00	155	—
1655	—	25.00	49.00	85.00	170	—
1658	—	25.00	49.00	85.00	170	—

KM# 23.1 REAL (Croat)
Silver **Obv:** Bust of Philip IV left in inner circle **Obv. Legend:** PHILIPUS

Date	Mintage	VG	F	VF	XF	Unc
1626	—	25.00	49.00	85.00	170	—

KM# 28 REAL (Croat)
0.9310 Silver **Obv:** Bust of Philip IV left **Rev:** Long cross, circle and 3 pellets in angles **Rev. Legend:** BARCINO CIVITAS, date **Note:** Bust of Philip II.

Date	Mintage	VG	F	VF	XF	Unc
1630	—	—	—	—	—	—
1632	—	65.00	120	245	400	—
1633	—	65.00	120	245	400	—
1635	—	35.00	55.00	105	175	—
1636	—	49.00	90.00	175	325	—

KM# 40 REAL (Croat)
Silver **Obv:** Small crude bust of Charles II left in inner circle **Rev:** Long cross with dots and annulets in angles, date in legend **Note:** Varieties exist

Date	Mintage	VG	F	VF	XF	Unc
1667	—	49.00	90.00	175	280	—
1674	—	49.00	90.00	175	280	—
1675	—	25.00	49.00	85.00	155	—
1677	—	25.00	49.00	85.00	155	—
1682	—	25.00	49.00	85.00	155	—
1687	—	55.00	100	190	375	—
1688	—	25.00	49.00	85.00	155	—

KM# 45 REAL (Croat)
0.9310 Silver **Obv:** Large crude bust of Charles II left in inner circle **Rev:** Long cross with pellets and circle in angles, date **Rev. Legend:** BARCINO CIVI

Date	Mintage	VG	F	VF	XF	Unc
1687	—	30.75	55.00	90.00	160	—

KM# 50 REAL (Croat)
0.9310 Silver **Obv:** Finer style bust of Chalres II left **Obv. Legend:** CARLOS II **Rev:** Cross above AM monogram

Date	Mintage	VG	F	VF	XF	Unc
1693	—	20.00	35.00	65.00	125	—
1698	—	27.50	49.00	85.00	155	—

CATALONIA

Catalonia, a triangular territory forming the northeast corner of the Iberian Peninsula, was formerly a province of Spain and also formerly a principality of Aragon. In 1833 the region was divided into four provinces, Barcelona, Gerona, Lerida and Tarragona.

RULERS
Philip III of Spain, 1598-1621
Philip IV of Spain, 1621-1665
Louis XIII of France,
As Count of Barcelona, 1641-1643

MINT MARK
C – Catalonia

MONETARY SYSTEM
12 Ardites (Dineros) = 8 Ochavos =
4 Quartos = 1 Sueldo
6 Sueldos = 1 Peseta
5 Pesetas = 1 Duro

FRENCH OCCUPATION

STANDARD COINAGE

KM# 5 DINERO
Copper **Obv:** Head right **Rev:** Long cross with pellets and circles in angles **Mint:** Agramont

Date	Mintage	VG	F	VF	XF	Unc
164x	—	110	215	375	—	—
1641	—	110	215	375	—	—
1642	—	100	185	350	—	—
1643	—	100	185	350	—	—
1646	—	120	230	425	—	—

KM# 6 DINERO
Copper **Obv:** Head left **Mint:** Agramont

Date	Mintage	VG	F	VF	XF	Unc
164x	—	110	215	375	—	—
1642	—	110	215	375	—	—

KM# 8 DINERO
Copper **Obv:** Bust right **Rev:** Long cross with pellets and circles in angles **Mint:** Cervera

Date	Mintage	VG	F	VF	XF	Unc
164x	—	60.00	120	220	—	—
1641	—	80.00	160	300	—	—
1642	—	70.00	140	250	—	—
ND	—	36.00	70.00	120	—	—

KM# 9 DINERO
Copper **Obv:** Bust left **Mint:** Cervera

Date	Mintage	VG	F	VF	XF	Unc
164x	—	75.00	155	300	—	—
ND	—	75.00	155	300	—	—

KM# 7 DINERO
Copper **Obv:** Bust right **Mint:** Barcelona **Note:** The 1640 date uses bust of Philip IV, 1642-43 uses bust of Luis XIII, a second 1643 uses name of Luis XIV and the 1646 and 1648 use bust of Luis XIV.

Date	Mintage	VG	F	VF	XF	Unc
1640	—	75.00	155	300	—	—
1642	—	37.50	75.00	140	250	—
1643	—	45.00	90.00	150	275	—
1646	—	25.00	50.00	90.00	190	—
1648	—	25.00	50.00	90.00	190	—

KM# 10 DINERO
Copper **Obv:** Bust right **Rev:** Shield **Mint:** Olot

Date	Mintage	VG	F	VF	XF	Unc
ND	—	60.00	120	215	—	—

KM# 22 DINERO
Copper **Obv:** Crowned arms divide date **Rev:** Long cross with pellets and pebbles in angles **Mint:** Cervera

Date	Mintage	VG	F	VF	XF	Unc
1641	—	80.00	160	300	—	—
1642	—	70.00	140	250	—	—

KM# 23 DINERO
Copper **Obv:** Head left **Rev:** Shield **Mint:** Puigcerda

Date	Mintage	VG	F	VF	XF	Unc
1641	—	30.00	65.00	115	215	—

KM# 24 DINERO
Copper **Obv:** Head left, date at top **Rev:** Long cross with pellets and circles in angles **Mint:** Solsona

Date	Mintage	VG	F	VF	XF	Unc
1641	—	30.00	65.00	115	215	—
1643	—	35.00	70.00	140	250	—

KM# 25 DINERO
Copper **Rev:** Long cross with two bars **Mint:** Solsona

Date	Mintage	VG	F	VF	XF	Unc
1641	—	30.00	65.00	115	215	—
1651	—	35.00	70.00	140	250	—

KM# 26 DINERO
Copper **Obv:** Bust left **Rev:** Castle above waves **Mint:** Tarrega

Date	Mintage	VG	F	VF	XF	Unc
1641	—	90.00	165	300	500	—
1642	—	65.00	100	190	375	—

KM# 76 DINERO
Copper **Obv:** Crowned shield **Rev:** Saint bust facing **Mint:** Camprodon

Date	Mintage	VG	F	VF	XF	Unc
1642	—	120	230	375	—	—

KM# 77 DINERO
Copper **Obv:** Bust right **Rev:** Long cross, pellets and circles in angles **Mint:** Oliana

Date	Mintage	VG	F	VF	XF	Unc
1642	—	120	230	375	—	—

KM# 78 DINERO
Copper **Obv:** Shield **Rev:** Fleur de Lis **Mint:** Puigcerda

Date	Mintage	VG	F	VF	XF	Unc
1642	—	70.00	150	250	—	—
1644	—	70.00	150	250	—	—

KM# 79 DINERO
Copper **Obv:** Bust right **Rev:** Long cross **Mint:** Tarrega

Date	Mintage	VG	F	VF	XF	Unc
1642	—	65.00	100	190	375	—

KM# 80 DINERO
Copper **Obv:** Bust right **Rev:** Diamond shield **Mint:** Vic

Date	Mintage	VG	F	VF	XF	Unc
1642	—	35.00	70.00	125	250	—
1643	—	35.00	70.00	125	250	—
1644	—	35.00	70.00	125	250	—
1645	—	35.00	70.00	125	250	—
1646	—	35.00	70.00	125	250	—

KM# 97 DINERO
Copper **Ruler:** Louis XIV of France As count of Barcelona **Obv:** Fleur de lis **Obv. Legend:** ACRIMONI **Rev:** Short cross with circles and dots in angles **Mint:** Agramont

Date	Mintage	VG	F	VF	XF	Unc
1643	—	110	215	375	—	—
1645	—	—	—	—	—	—

KM# 98 DINERO
Copper **Obv:** Bust right **Rev:** 3-leaf plant **Mint:** Lerida

Date	Mintage	VG	F	VF	XF	Unc
1643	—	255	475	775	—	—

KM# A97 DINERO
Copper **Ruler:** Louis XIV of France As count of Barcelona **Obv:** Bust of Louis XIV right **Obv. Legend:** LVDOVIC. D. G. FRA. **Rev:** Crowned oval arms of Catalonia **Rev. Legend:** VILL. AGRANV **Mint:** Agramont

Date	Mintage	Good	VG	F	VF	XF
ND(1643-59)	—	—	—	—	—	—

KM# 99 DINERO
Copper **Obv:** Bust facing **Rev:** Arms **Mint:** Perpinya

Date	Mintage	VG	F	VF	XF	Unc
1644	—	30.00	65.00	115	215	—
1645	—	30.00	65.00	115	215	—
1646	—	30.00	65.00	115	215	—
1647	—	30.00	65.00	115	215	—
1648	—	30.00	65.00	115	215	—
1654	—	30.00	65.00	115	215	—

KM# A100 DINERO
Copper **Ruler:** Louis XIV of France As count of Barcelona **Obv:** Lis **Rev:** Long cross wtih two annulets in first and fourth quarters, three circles in second and third quarters **Mint:** Agramont

Date	Mintage	Good	VG	F	VF	XF
1645	—	—	—	—	—	—

KM# 11 ARDITE
Copper **Obv:** Bust left dividing A - R **Rev:** Diamond shield **Mint:** Barcelona

Date	Mintage	VG	F	VF	XF	Unc
1640	—	9.00	18.00	35.00	70.00	—

KM# 100 ARDITE
Copper **Obv:** Bust right dividing A - R **Mint:** Barcelona

Date	Mintage	VG	F	VF	XF	Unc
1644	—	25.00	50.00	100	150	—
1647	—	25.00	50.00	100	150	—
1648	—	25.00	50.00	100	150	—

KM# 101 SUELDO
Copper **Obv:** Facing figure **Rev:** Crowned shield **Mint:** Perpinya

Date	Mintage	VG	F	VF	XF	Unc
1644	—	30.00	65.00	115	215	—
1645	—	25.00	55.00	100	200	—
1647	—	65.00	100	190	350	—

KM# 102 2 SUELDOS
Copper **Obv:** Saint standing **Rev:** Crowned diamond shield **Mint:** Perpinya

Date	Mintage	VG	F	VF	XF	Unc
1644	—	25.00	55.00	100	200	—
Note: 1644 date has value as 2 or II						
1645	—	25.00	55.00	100	200	—
1646	—	25.00	55.00	100	200	—
1647	—	25.00	55.00	100	200	—
1648	—	25.00	55.00	100	200	—
1654	—	30.00	65.00	115	215	—

KM# 13 SEISENO
Copper **Obv:** Small bust left **Rev:** Crowned diamond shield

Date	Mintage	VG	F	VF	XF	Unc
1640	—	35.00	70.00	125	225	—
1641	—	30.00	55.00	100	200	—

Note: 1641 with and without SI on reverse

KM# 14 SEISENO
Copper **Obv:** Crowned Catalonian arms in inner circle **Rev:** Diamond arms, date in legend **Mint:** Girona **Note:** Varieties exist.

Date	Mintage	VG	F	VF	XF	Unc
1640	—	25.00	50.00	90.00	175	—
1641	—	25.00	50.00	90.00	175	—
1642	—	25.00	50.00	90.00	175	—

KM# 34 SEISENO
Copper **Obv:** Crowned Catalonian arms in inner circle **Rev:** Diamond arms in inner circle, date in legend **Mint:** Tarrasa **Note:** Legend varieties exist.

Date	Mintage	VG	F	VF	XF	Unc
ND	—	30.00	65.00	115	215	—
1641	—	30.00	65.00	115	215	—
1642	—	30.00	65.00	115	215	—

KM# 27 SEISENO
Copper **Obv:** Large bust right in circle of dots **Rev:** Diamond arms in inner circle, date in legend **Mint:** Barcelona

Date	Mintage	VG	F	VF	XF	Unc
1641	—	42.00	85.00	150	255	—
1642	—	42.00	85.00	150	255	—
1643	—	30.00	60.00	105	210	—
1644	—	20.00	40.00	75.00	125	—
1645	—	20.00	40.00	75.00	125	—
1646	—	20.00	40.00	75.00	125	—
1647	—	20.00	40.00	75.00	125	—
1648	—	20.00	40.00	75.00	125	—
1649	—	20.00	40.00	75.00	125	—
1650	—	20.00	40.00	75.00	125	—
1651	—	20.00	40.00	75.00	125	—
1652	—	45.00	90.00	165	270	—

KM# 28 SEISENO
Copper **Rev:** Large bust right

Date	Mintage	VG	F	VF	XF	Unc
1641	—	30.00	65.00	115	215	—
1642	—	25.00	50.00	90.00	175	—

KM# 29 SEISENO
Copper **Obv:** Crowned Catalonian arms **Rev:** Cross of Lorraine in inner circle, date in legend **Mint:** Besalu

Date	Mintage	VG	F	VF	XF	Unc
1641	—	65.00	100	190	350	—

KM# 30 SEISENO
Copper **Rev:** Cross of Lorraine on left half of shield

Date	Mintage	VG	F	VF	XF	Unc
1641	—	65.00	100	190	350	—
1642	—	65.00	125	225	400	—

KM# 31 SEISENO
Copper **Obv:** Crowned Catalonian arms in inner circle **Rev:** Diamond arms in inner circle, date in legend **Mint:** Caldas

Date	Mintage	VG	F	VF	XF	Unc
1641	—	100	175	300	525	—

KM# 32 SEISENO
Copper **Obv:** Crowned Catalonian arms in inner circle **Rev:** Diamond shield **Mint:** Solsona

Date	Mintage	VG	F	VF	XF	Unc
1641	—	37.50	75.00	140	225	—
1642	—	65.00	125	200	350	—

KM# 33 SEISENO
Copper **Obv:** Bust right **Rev:** Diamond shield

Date	Mintage	VG	F	VF	XF	Unc
1641	—	37.50	75.00	140	225	—

KM# 35 SEISENO
Copper **Mint:** Tarrega

Date	Mintage	VG	F	VF	XF	Unc
1641	—	45.00	90.00	150	250	—

KM# 36 SEISENO
Copper **Obv:** Laureate head right

Date	Mintage	VG	F	VF	XF	Unc
1641	—	50.00	100	190	325	—

KM# 81 SEISENO
Copper **Obv:** Laureate head right **Rev:** Diamond shield **Mint:** Bellpuig

Date	Mintage	VG	F	VF	XF	Unc
1642	—	70.00	125	225	425	—

KM# 82 SEISENO
Copper **Obv:** Head right **Mint:** Girona

Date	Mintage	VG	F	VF	XF	Unc
1642	—	30.00	55.00	100	200	—
1643	—	30.00	55.00	100	200	—
1646	—	125	250	450	700	—

KM# 83 SEISENO
Copper **Obv:** Bust left

Date	Mintage	VG	F	VF	XF	Unc
1642	—	375	725	1,200	—	—

KM# 84 SEISENO
Copper **Obv:** Narrow crowned Catalonian arms **Rev:** Narrow diamond arms, date in legend **Mint:** Manresa

Date	Mintage	VG	F	VF	XF	Unc
1642	—	50.00	100	190	—	—

KM# 85 SEISENO
Copper **Obv:** Wider arms **Rev:** Wider arms

Date	Mintage	VG	F	VF	XF	Unc
1642	—	35.00	70.00	140	—	—

KM# 86 SEISENO
Copper **Obv:** Laureate head right **Rev:** Diamond shield **Mint:** Sanahuja

Date	Mintage	VG	F	VF	XF	Unc
1642	—	115	200	350	—	—

KM# 87 SEISENO
Copper **Obv:** Bust right **Rev:** Diamond shield on long cross **Mint:** Vallis

Date	Mintage	VG	F	VF	XF	Unc
1642	—	155	300	500	—	—

KM# 88 SEISENO
Copper **Obv:** Laureate bust of Louis XIII right divides 5 - E in inner circle **Rev:** Crowned Catalonian arms in inner circle, date in legend **Mint:** Vila Franca del Penedes

Date	Mintage	VG	F	VF	XF	Unc
1642	—	115	215	350	575	—

KM# 89 SEISENO
Copper **Obv:** Bust right **Rev:** Diamond shield

Date	Mintage	VG	F	VF	XF	Unc
1642	—	140	250	450	725	—

KM# 37 1/2 CROAT
Silver **Obv:** Bust right **Rev:** Short cross with pellets and circles in angles **Mint:** Vich **Note:** Legend varieties exist.

Date	Mintage	VG	F	VF	XF	Unc
1641	—	500	900	1,600	2,800	—
1642	—	350	625	1,200	2,100	—

KM# 15 CROAT
Silver **Obv:** Bust of Felipe IV right **Rev:** Long cross with pellets and circles in angles **Mint:** Barcelona

Date	Mintage	VG	F	VF	XF	Unc
1640	—	125	250	450	750	—

KM# 16 CROAT
Silver **Obv:** Bust left **Mint:** Ileida

Date	Mintage	VG	F	VF	XF	Unc
1640	—	1,050	1,900	3,150	—	—

KM# 18 5 SOUS
Silver **Obv:** Crowned shield **Rev:** Long cross with pellets and circle in angle **Mint:** Girona

Date	Mintage	VG	F	VF	XF	Unc
1640	—	1,100	2,100	3,850	—	—
1641	—	700	1,250	2,450	—	—

KM# 17 5 SOUS
Silver **Obv:** Crowned arms dividing V - S **Rev:** Long cross with pellets and circles in angles, date in legend **Mint:** Barcelona **Note:** Legend varieties exist.

Date	Mintage	VG	F	VF	XF	Unc
1640	—	500	900	1,700	—	—
1641	—	625	1,200	2,100	—	—

KM# 39 5 SOUS
Silver **Rev:** Long cross with diamond shield of city at juncture **Mint:** Banyoles **Note:** Legend varieties exist.

Date	Mintage	VG	F	VF	XF	Unc
1641	—	875	1,600	3,150	—	—

KM# 52 5 SOUS
Silver **Rev:** Long cross with diamond shield of city at juncture **Note:** Legend varieties exist.

Date	Mintage	VG	F	VF	XF	Unc
1641	—	900	1,750	3,150	—	—

KM# 41 5 SOUS
Silver **Obv:** Bust of Louis XIII right dividing V - S **Rev:** Long cross with diamond shield of city at juncture **Mint:** Barcelona **Note:** Legend and design varieties exist for 1642 and 1643 date coins.

Date	Mintage	VG	F	VF	XF	Unc
1641	—	900	1,700	3,500	—	—
1642	—	525	950	1,750	—	—
1643	—	675	1,250	2,450	—	—

KM# 38 5 SOUS
Silver **Obv:** Crowned Catalonian arms dividing V - S **Rev:** Long cross with pellets and circles in angle **Mint:** Balaguer

Date	Mintage	VG	F	VF	XF	Unc
1641	—	875	1,650	3,300	—	—

KM# 40 5 SOUS
Silver **Rev:** Long cross with diamond shield of city at Juncture

Date	Mintage	VG	F	VF	XF	Unc
1641	—	1,250	2,300	4,200	—	—

KM# 42 5 SOUS
Silver **Obv:** Crowned arms dividing V - S **Rev:** Long cross with pellets and circles in angles **Mint:** Berga

Date	Mintage	VG	F	VF	XF	Unc
1641	—	875	1,650	3,300	—	—

KM# 43 5 SOUS
Silver **Rev:** Long cross with diamond shield of city at juncture **Mint:** Bisbal

Date	Mintage	VG	F	VF	XF	Unc
1641	—	875	1,600	3,150	—	—

KM# 44 5 SOUS
Silver **Rev:** Long cross with pellets and circles in angles **Mint:** Cervera

Date	Mintage	VG	F	VF	XF	Unc
1641	—	1,100	2,100	4,000	—	—

KM# 45 5 SOUS
Silver **Obv:** Bust right

Date	Mintage	VG	F	VF	XF	Unc
1641	—	1,350	2,450	4,550	—	—

KM# 46 5 SOUS
Silver **Obv:** Crowned arms **Rev:** Long cross with diamond shield of city at juncture **Mint:** Girona

Date	Mintage	VG	F	VF	XF	Unc
1641	—	500	900	1,750	—	—

KM# 47 5 SOUS
Silver **Rev:** Long cross with pellets and circle in angles **Mint:** Manresa

Date	Mintage	VG	F	VF	XF	Unc
1641	—	1,250	2,300	4,200	—	—

KM# 48 5 SOUS
Silver **Mint:** Olot

Date	Mintage	VG	F	VF	XF	Unc
1641	—	1,350	2,450	4,550	—	—

KM# 49 5 SOUS
Silver **Rev:** Pellets around circles in angles

Date	Mintage	VG	F	VF	XF	Unc
1641	—	1,250	2,300	4,200	—	—

KM# 50 5 SOUS
Silver **Rev:** Long cross with pellets and circle in angles **Mint:** Puigcerda

Date	Mintage	VG	F	VF	XF	Unc
1641	—	875	1,600	3,150	—	—

KM# 51 5 SOUS
Silver **Mint:** Vich

Date	Mintage	VG	F	VF	XF	Unc
1641	—	900	1,700	3,500	—	—

KM# 90 5 SOUS
Silver **Rev:** Long cross with pellets and circles in angles **Mint:** Besalu

Date	Mintage	VG	F	VF	XF	Unc
1642	—	900	1,750	3,150	—	—

KM# 91 5 SOUS
Silver **Mint:** Camprodon

Date	Mintage	VG	F	VF	XF	Unc
1642	—	1,550	3,000	6,000	—	—

KM# 92 5 SOUS
Silver **Mint:** Vich **Note:** Louis XIII.

Date	Mintage	VG	F	VF	XF	Unc
1642	—	1,100	2,300	4,200	—	—

KM# 20 5 REAL (1/2 Libra)
Silver **Rev:** Long cross with di amond city shield at juncture **Mint:** Bisbal

Date	Mintage	VG	F	VF	XF	Unc
164x	—	1,250	2,300	3,850	—	—
1641	—	900	1,700	3,150	—	—

KM# 19 5 REAL (1/2 Libra)
Silver **Obv:** Crowned shield dividing V - R **Obv. Legend:** PHILIPP, D.G. R HISP **Rev:** Long cross with pellets and circle in angles **Rev. Legend:** BARC INO.C IVITAS **Mint:** Barcelona **Note:** Legend and design varieties exist.

Date	Mintage	VG	F	VF	XF	Unc
1640	—	375	675	1,250	—	—
1641	—	325	525	950	—	—
1642	—	325	550	975	—	—

KM# 21 5 REAL (1/2 Libra)
Silver **Mint:** Girona **Note:** Philip II. Legend and design varieties exist.

Date	Mintage	VG	F	VF	XF	Unc
1640	—	350	625	1,200	—	—
1641	—	280	500	900	—	—

KM# 53 5 REAL (1/2 Libra)
Silver **Obv:** Crowned shield of Catalongia-Aragon **Obv. Legend:** PRINCIPAT VS CATALONIE **Rev:** Long cross with pellets and circle in angles **Rev. Legend:** SITNO MIRCA ALLIV **Mint:** Agramont **Note:** Legend varieties exist for 1641 dates.

Date	Mintage	VG	F	VF	XF	Unc
1461 Error for 1641	—	675	1,250	2,300	—	—
1642	—	625	1,200	2,100	—	—

KM# 75 5 REAL (1/2 Libra)
Silver **Rev:** Long cross with pellets and circle in angles **Mint:** Vila Franca del Penedes **Note:** Legend varieties exist with 1642.

Date	Mintage	VG	F	VF	XF	Unc
1641	—	1,700	2,800	4,550	—	—
1642	—	1,350	2,450	4,200	—	—

KM# 61 5 REAL (1/2 Libra)
Silver **Mint:** Cervera **Note:** Legend varieties exist.

Date	Mintage	VG	F	VF	XF	Unc
1641	—	280	525	1,000	—	—

KM# 63 5 REAL (1/2 Libra)

Silver **Obv:** Crowned shield dividing V - R **Mint:** Figueres **Note:** Legend varieties exist.

Date	Mintage	VG	F	VF	XF	Unc
1641	—	850	1,550	3,150	—	—

KM# 66 5 REAL (1/2 Libra)

Silver **Mint:** Igualada **Note:** Legend varieties exist.

Date	Mintage	VG	F	VF	XF	Unc
1641	—	325	600	1,100	—	—
1642	—	325	625	1,100	—	—

KM# 54 5 REAL (1/2 Libra)

Silver **Rev:** Long cross with pellets and circles in angles **Mint:** Balaguer **Note:** Legend and design varieties exist.

Date	Mintage	VG	F	VF	XF	Unc
1641	—	450	850	1,550	—	—

KM# 68 5 REAL (1/2 Libra)

Silver **Mint:** Mataro **Note:** Legend and design varieties exist.

Date	Mintage	VG	F	VF	XF	Unc
1641	—	280	525	1,050	—	—
1642	—	450	875	1,600	—	—

KM# 72 5 REAL (1/2 Libra)

Silver **Mint:** Tarrasa **Note:** Legend and design varieties exist.

Date	Mintage	VG	F	VF	XF	Unc
1641	—	775	1,400	2,600	—	—
1642	—	280	550	1,200	—	—

KM# 73 5 REAL (1/2 Libra)

Silver **Mint:** Vich **Note:** Legend and design varieties exist.

Date	Mintage	VG	F	VF	XF	Unc
1641	—	425	850	1,600	—	—

KM# A53 5 REAL (1/2 Libra)

Silver **Obv:** Crowned shield of Catalonia-Arzgon **Obv. Legend:** PHILIPP. D • G R HISPANIA **Rev:** Long cross with pellets and circles in angles **Rev. Legend:** VILLA-AGRIM-ONST

Date	Mintage	VG	F	VF	XF	Unc
1641	—	625	1,200	2,100	—	—

KM# B53 5 REAL (1/2 Libra)

Silver **Obv:** Crowned shield of Catalonia-Aragon **Obv. Legend:** PRINCIPAT VS CATALONI (A)E **Rev:** Long cross with pellets and circles in angles **Rev. Legend:** VILLA ACRIM ONSTS

Date	Mintage	VG	F	VF	XF	Unc
1641	—	550	1,100	2,050	—	—

KM# 70 5 REAL (1/2 Libra)

Silver **Mint:** Puigcerda **Note:** Design varieties exist.

Date	Mintage	VG	F	VF	XF	Unc
1641	—	1,050	1,750	3,000	—	—

KM# 58 5 REAL (1/2 Libra)

Silver **Obv:** Bust of Luis XIII right dividing V- R **Mint:** Barcelona **Note:** Legend and bust varieties exist.

Date	Mintage	VG	F	VF	XF	Unc
1641	—	375	750	1,400	—	—
1642	—	325	625	1,150	—	—
1643	—	325	625	1,150	—	—

KM# 55 5 REAL (1/2 Libra)

Silver **Mint:** Banyoles

Date	Mintage	VG	F	VF	XF	Unc
1641	—	525	950	1,700	—	—

KM# 56 5 REAL (1/2 Libra)

Silver **Rev:** Long cross with diamond city shield at juncture

Date	Mintage	VG	F	VF	XF	Unc
1641	—	625	1,200	2,100	—	—

KM# 57 5 REAL (1/2 Libra)

Silver **Obv. Legend:** PRINCIPATV S CATALONIE **Rev. Legend:** BARC INOC IVITAS **Mint:** Barcelona

Date	Mintage	VG	F	VF	XF	Unc
1641	—	300	600	1,250	2,500	—

KM# 59 5 REAL (1/2 Libra)

Silver **Obv:** Crowned shield dividing V - R **Rev:** Long cross with pellets and circles in angles **Mint:** Berga

Date	Mintage	VG	F	VF	XF	Unc
1641	—	1,050	1,900	3,700	—	—

KM# 60 5 REAL (1/2 Libra)

Silver **Mint:** Besalu

Date	Mintage	VG	F	VF	XF	Unc
1641	—	1,250	2,300	3,850	—	—
1642	—	425	850	1,550	—	—

KM# 62 5 REAL (1/2 Libra)

Silver **Obv:** Bust of Louis XIII right

Date	Mintage	VG	F	VF	XF	Unc
1641	—	525	1,000	1,750	—	—
1642	—	450	850	1,550	—	—

KM# 64 5 REAL (1/2 Libra)

Silver **Rev:** Long cross with diamond city shield at juncture **Mint:** Girona

Date	Mintage	VG	F	VF	XF	Unc
1641	—	280	550	1,050	—	—

KM# 65 5 REAL (1/2 Libra)

Silver **Rev:** Long cross with pellets and circle in angles **Mint:** Granollers

Date	Mintage	VG	F	VF	XF	Unc
1641	—	550	975	1,750	—	—
1642	—	850	1,550	2,600	—	—

KM# 67 5 REAL (1/2 Libra)

Silver **Mint:** Manresa

Date	Mintage	VG	F	VF	XF	Unc
1641	—	350	700	1,350	—	—

KM# 69 5 REAL (1/2 Libra)

Silver **Mint:** Olot

Date	Mintage	VG	F	VF	XF	Unc
1641	—	850	1,700	2,800	—	—

KM# 71 5 REAL (1/2 Libra)
Silver **Mint:** Tarrega

Date	Mintage	VG	F	VF	XF	Unc
1641	—	850	1,700	2,800	—	—
1642	—	550	975	1,900	—	—

KM# 74 5 REAL (1/2 Libra)
Silver **Rev:** Long cross with diamond city arms at center

Date	Mintage	VG	F	VF	XF	Unc
1641	—	1,250	2,300	3,850	—	—

KM# 94 5 REAL (1/2 Libra)
Silver **Rev:** Long cross with pellets and circles in angles **Mint:** Argentona **Note:** Legend and design varieties exist.

Date	Mintage	VG	F	VF	XF	Unc
1642	—	500	900	1,600	—	—

KM# 95 5 REAL (1/2 Libra)
Silver **Rev:** Pellets around circles in angles **Mint:** Besalu **Note:** Legend varieties exist.

Date	Mintage	VG	F	VF	XF	Unc
1642	—	425	775	1,350	—	—

KM# 96 5 REAL (1/2 Libra)
Silver **Mint:** Vich **Note:** Titles of Luis XIII.

Date	Mintage	VG	F	VF	XF	Unc
1642	—	1,250	2,250	3,700	—	—

KM# 103 5 REAL (1/2 Libra)
Silver **Obv:** Bust of Louis XIV right dividing V - R **Rev:** Long cross with diamond city shield **Mint:** Barcelona

Date	Mintage	VG	F	VF	XF	Unc
1644	—	1,250	2,300	3,850	—	—

KM# 104 5 REAL (1/2 Libra)
Silver **Rev:** Pellets around circles in angles **Mint:** Olot

Date	Mintage	VG	F	VF	XF	Unc
1646	—	850	1,700	2,800	—	—

KM# 110 5 REAL (1/2 Libra)
Silver **Obv:** Crowned shield of Spain **Rev:** Bust left **Mint:** Girona

Date	Mintage	VG	F	VF	XF	Unc
1653 Rare	—	—	—	—	—	—

KM# 106 10 REALES
Silver **Obv:** Bust of Louis XIIII right **Obv. Legend:** LVD • XIIII • D • G • R • F • C • B **Rev:** Cross with pellets and circles in angles **Rev. Legend:** BARCINO CIVIT OBBESSA

Date	Mintage	VG	F	VF	XF	Unc
1652/1	—	350	700	1,250	—	—
1652	—	325	625	1,150	—	—

KM# 121 LOUIS D'OR
Gold **Ruler:** Louis XIII of France As Count of Barcelona **Obv:** Laureate head **Obv. Legend:** LVD•XIII•D•G - FR•ET•NAV•REX **Rev:** Crowned cruciform double L monograms with lys in angles, date in legend **Rev. Legend:** CATA-LONIS-

Date	Mintage	VG	F	VF	XF	Unc
1642 Rare	—	—	—	—	—	—

KM# 109 1/12 ECU
Silver, 20.5 mm. **Ruler:** Louis XIII of France As Count of Barcelona **Obv:** Laureate bust right **Obv. Legend:** LVDOVICVS• XIII•D•G•FR•ET NAV•REX **Rev:** Crowned arms **Rev. Legend:** CATALONIAE • COMES

Date	Mintage	VG	F	VF	XF	Unc
1642 Rare	—	—	—	—	—	—

KM# 111 1/4 ECU
Silver, 26 mm. **Ruler:** Louis XIII of France As Count of Barcelona **Obv:** Laureate bust right **Obv. Legend:** LVDOVICVS•XIII•D•G•FR•ET NAV•REX **Rev:** Crowned arms **Rev. Legend:** CATALONIAE • COMES

Date	Mintage	VG	F	VF	XF	Unc
1642 Rare	—	—	—	—	—	—

KM# 112 1/2 ECU
Silver, 31.2 mm. **Ruler:** Louis XIII of France As Count of Barcelona **Obv:** Laureate bust right **Obv. Legend:** LVDOVICVS•XIII•D•G•FR•ET NAV•REX **Rev:** Crowned arms **Rev. Legend:** CATALONIAE • COMES

Date	Mintage	VG	F	VF	XF	Unc
1642 Rare	—	—	—	—	—	—

KM# 113 ECU
Silver, 37.5 mm. **Ruler:** Louis XIII of France As Count of Barcelona **Obv:** Laureate bust right **Obv. Legend:** LVDOVICVS•XIII•D•G•FR•ET NAV•REX **Rev:** Crowned arms **Rev. Legend:** CATALONIAE • COMES

Date	Mintage	VG	F	VF	XF	Unc
1642 Rare	—	—	—	—	—	—

KM# 114 ECU
Silver, 39 mm. **Ruler:** Louis XIII of France As Count of Barcelona **Obv:** Laureate bust right **Obv. Legend:** LVDOVICVS• XIII•D•G•FR•ET NAV•REX **Rev:** Crowned arms of France, Navarre and Catalonia **Rev. Legend:** CATALONIAE PRINCEPS **Note:** Possibly a pattern.

Date	Mintage	VG	F	VF	XF	Unc
1642 Rare	—	—	—	—	—	—

PROVINCE

COUNTERMARKED COINAGE

KM# 1.2 1/3 TRENTIN
Gold **Countermark:** Diamond-shaped shield **Note:** Countermark on Barcelona, KM#14.

CM Date	Host Date	Good	VG	F	VF	XF
ND(1640-59)	16Z5	—	975	1,900	3,400	6,000

KM# 1.1 1/3 TRENTIN
Gold **Countermark:** Diamond-shaped shield **Note:** Countermark on Barcelona, KM#5.

CM Date	Host Date	Good	VG	F	VF	XF
ND(1640-59)	1618B	—	900	1,800	3,000	5,300

KM# 2.4 1/2 TRENTIN
Gold **Countermark:** Diamond-shaped shield **Note:** Countermark on Barcelona, KM#.

CM Date	Host Date	Good	VG	F	VF	XF
ND(1640-59)	1631B	—	750	1,500	3,000	5,300

KM# 2.3 1/2 TRENTIN
Gold **Countermark:** Diamond-shaped shield **Note:** Countermark on Barcelona, KM#15.

CM Date	Host Date	Good	VG	F	VF	XF
ND(1640-59)	1623	—	750	1,500	3,000	5,300

KM# 2.1 1/2 TRENTIN
Gold **Countermark:** Diamond-shaped shield **Note:** Countermark on Barcelona, KM#6.1.

CM Date	Host Date	Good	VG	F	VF	XF
ND(1640-59)	ND(1598-1621)	—	975	1,900	3,750	6,400

KM# 2.2 1/2 TRENTIN
Gold **Countermark:** Diamond-shaped shield **Note:** Countermark on Barcelona, KM#6.2.

CM Date	Host Date	Good	VG	F	VF	XF
ND(1640-59)	ND(1598-1621)	—	975	1,900	3,750	6,400

KM# 3.3 TRENTIN
Gold **Countermark:** Diamond-shaped shield **Note:** Countermark on Barcelona, KM#17.1.

CM Date	Host Date	Good	VG	F	VF	XF
ND(1640-59)	1625	—	900	1,800	3,400	5,600
ND(1640-59)	1626	—	900	1,800	3,400	5,600
ND(1640-59)	1628	—	900	1,800	3,400	5,600

KM# 3.4 TRENTIN
Gold **Countermark:** Diamond-shaped shield **Note:** Countermark on Barcelona, KM#17.2.

CM Date	Host Date	Good	VG	F	VF	XF
ND(1640-59)	1628	—	900	1,800	3,400	5,600
ND(1640-59)	1629	—	900	1,800	3,400	5,600
ND(1640-59)	1632	—	900	1,800	3,400	5,600
ND(1640-59)	1633	—	900	1,800	3,400	5,600

KM# 3.1 TRENTIN
Gold **Countermark:** Diamond-shaped shield **Note:** Countermark on Barcelona, KM#7.

CM Date	Host Date	Good	VG	F	VF	XF
ND(1640-59)	ND(1598-1621)	—	1,050	2,050	4,150	6,800

KM# 3.2 TRENTIN
Gold **Countermark:** Diamond-shaped shield **Note:** Countermark on Barcelona, KM#8.

CM Date	Host Date	Good	VG	F	VF	XF
ND(1640-59)	ND(1598-1621)	—	1,050	2,050	4,150	6,800

KM# 3.5 TRENTIN
Gold **Countermark:** Diamond-shaped shield **Note:** Countermark on Segovia 2 Excellente of Ferdinand and Isabel.

CM Date	Host Date	Good	VG	F	VF	XF
ND(1640-59)	ND(1474-1504)	—	2,250	3,750	6,000	10,500

PATTERNS

Including off metal strikes

KM#	Date	Mintage	Identification	Mkt Val
Pn1	ND(ca 1643)	—	2 Louis D'Or. Gold. Struck at Barcelona Mint.	—

GERONA

PROVINCE

PROVISIONAL COINAGE

KM# 5 DINERO

Copper **Obv:** Bust of Philip III right **Rev:** Diamond shield **Mint:** Gerona

Date	Mintage	VG	F	VF	XF	Unc
ND	—	19.00	35.25	65.00	130	—

STANDARD COINAGE

KM# 6 DINERO

Copper **Obv:** Bust of Philip III right **Rev:** Shield of Olot **Mint:** Olot

Date	Mintage	VG	F	VF	XF	Unc
ND	—	30.00	55.00	95.00	175	—

KM# 7 MENUT

Copper **Obv:** Bust of Philip III right **Rev:** Crowned shield of Aragon **Mint:** Olot

Date	Mintage	VG	F	VF	XF	Unc
ND	—	70.00	145	280	450	—

MAJORCA

(Yslas Baleares)
Majorca

The Balearic Islands, an archipelago located in the Mediterranean Sea off the east coast of Spain including Majorca, Minorca, Cabrera, Ibiza, Formentera and a number of islets. Majorca, largest of the Balearic Islands is famous for its 1,000-year-old olive trees.

RULERS

Philip III of Spain, 1598-1621
Philip IV of Spain, 1621-1665
Charles II, 1665-1700
Philip V, 1700-1746
Louis I, 1723-1726
Pretender, Charles III, 1700-1720

MONETARY SYSTEM

12 Dineros = 6 Doblers = 1 Sueldo (Sou)
30 Sueldos = 1 Duro

PROVINCE

STANDARD COINAGE

KM# 33 DINAR

Copper, 12 mm. **Ruler:** Philip V **Obv:** Small bust of Philip V left, "I" behind **Rev:** Cross with castles and lions in angles **Mint:** Palma de Mallorca

Date	Mintage	VG	F	VF	XF	Unc
ND(1700-1746)	—	50.00	95.00	175	—	—

KM# 32 DINAR

Copper **Ruler:** Philip V **Obv:** Large bust of Philip V left **Rev:** Cross, "II" at lower right **Mint:** Palma de Mallorca **Note:** Size varies 14-15 mm.

Date	Mintage	VG	F	VF	XF	Unc
ND(1700-1746)	—	43.75	80.00	160	280	—

KM# 1.1 DOBLER

Copper, 16 mm. **Ruler:** Philip III of Spain **Obv:** Crowned bust of Philip III **Obv. Legend:** PHILIPVS... **Rev:** Cross within inner circle **Mint:** Palma de Mallorca

Date	Mintage	VG	F	VF	XF	Unc
ND(1598-1621)	—	10.00	20.00	42.00	—	—

KM# 1.2 DOBLER

Copper **Ruler:** Philip III of Spain **Obv:** Crowned bust of Philip III left **Obv. Inscription:** PHILIPUS... **Rev:** Cross within inner circle **Mint:** Palma de Mallorca

Date	Mintage	VG	F	VF	XF	Unc
ND(1598-1621)	—	13.00	25.00	49.00	—	—

KM# 11 DOBLER

Copper **Ruler:** Philip IV of Spain **Obv:** Crowned bust of Philip IV left **Rev:** Cross **Mint:** Palma de Mallorca **Note:** Size varies 15-16 mm.

Date	Mintage	VG	F	VF	XF	Unc
ND(1621-1665)	—	31.25	55.00	120	—	—

KM# 18 DOBLER

Copper **Ruler:** Charles II **Obv:** Crowned bust of Charles II right **Rev:** Cross **Mint:** Palma de Mallorca **Note:** Size varies 15-16 MM.

Date	Mintage	VG	F	VF	XF	Unc
ND(1665-1700)	—	18.00	35.00	65.00	—	—

KM# 19 DOBLER

Copper **Ruler:** Charles II **Obv:** Crowned bust of Charles II right **Rev:** Cross **Mint:** Palma de Mallorca **Note:** Size varies 15-16 mm.

Date	Mintage	VG	F	VF	XF	Unc
ND(1665-1700)	—	19.00	37.50	70.00	—	—

KM# 34 DOBLER

Copper **Ruler:** Philip V **Obv:** Bust of Philip V left **Rev:** Cross with figure at lower left, "II" at lower right **Mint:** Palma de Mallorca **Note:** Size varies 14-15 mm.

Date	Mintage	VG	F	VF	XF	Unc
ND(1700-1746)	—	55.00	100	190	325	—

KM# 35.1 DOBLER

Copper, 14 mm. **Ruler:** Philip V **Obv:** Bust of Philip V left, "2" behind **Rev:** Crowned shield of Castile and Leon, fleur-de-lis at center **Mint:** Palma de Mallorca

Date	Mintage	VG	F	VF	XF	Unc
ND(1700-1746)	—	37.50	75.00	140	250	—

KM# 2 1/2 REAL

Silver, 17 mm. **Ruler:** Philip III of Spain **Obv:** Crowned bust of Philip III left **Obv. Legend:** PHILIPPVS REX ARAGONVM **Rev:** Diamond - shaped shield within inner circle **Rev. Legend:** MAIORICARVM CATOLIC **Mint:** Palma de Mallorca

Date	Mintage	VG	F	VF	XF	Unc
ND(1598-1621)	—	220	400	775	—	—

KM# 20 1/2 REAL

Silver, 16 mm. **Ruler:** Charles II **Obv:** Crowned bust of Charles II IV left **Rev:** Diamond-shaped shield **Mint:** Palma de Mallorca

Date	Mintage	VG	F	VF	XF	Unc
ND(1665-1700)	—	205	375	700	—	—

KM# 21 1/2 REAL

Silver, 16 mm. **Ruler:** Charles II **Obv:** Crowned bust of Charles II right **Rev:** Diamond-shaped shield **Mint:** Palma de Mallorca

Date	Mintage	VG	F	VF	XF	Unc
ND(1665-1700)	—	190	350	675	—	—

KM# 12 REAL (Croat)

Silver **Ruler:** Philip IV of Spain **Obv:** Crowned bust of Philip IV left **Obv. Legend:** PHILIPPVS REX... **Rev:** Diamond-shaped shield within inner circle **Rev. Legend:** MALORICARVM CATOLICVS **Mint:** Palma de Mallorca **Note:** Size varies 21-22 mm.

Date	Mintage	VG	F	VF	XF	Unc
ND(1621-1665)	—	250	500	1,050	1,750	—

KM# 3 REAL

Silver **Ruler:** Philip III of Spain **Obv:** Crowned bust of Philip III left **Obv. Legend:** PHILIPPVS REX ARAGONVM **Rev:** Diamond-shape shield within inner circle **Mint:** Palma de Mallorca **Note:** Size varies 18-20 mm.

Date	Mintage	VG	F	VF	XF	Unc
ND(1598-1621)	—	280	575	1,100	—	—

KM# 4 REAL

Silver **Ruler:** Philip III of Spain **Obv:** Crowned bust of Philip III right **Obv. Legend:** PHILIPPVS REX ARAGONVM **Rev:** Diamond - shaped shield within inner circle **Rev. Legend:** MAIORICARVM CATOLIC **Mint:** Palma de Mallorca **Note:** Size varies 20-21 mm.

Date	Mintage	VG	F	VF	XF	Unc
ND(1598-1621)	—	170	350	700	—	—

KM# 9 REAL

Silver **Ruler:** Philip IV of Spain **Obv:** Crowned bust of Philip III right **Obv. Legend:** PHILIPPVS REX ARAGONVM **Rev:** Diamond - shaped shield within inner circle **Rev. Legend:** MAIORICARVM... VS **Mint:** Palma de Mallorca **Note:** Size varies 18-19 mm.

Date	Mintage	VG	F	VF	XF	Unc
1617	—	375	700	1,350	—	—

KM# 4.1 2 REAL

Silver **Ruler:** Philip III of Spain **Obv:** Crowned bust of Philip III right **Obv. Legend:** PHILIPPVS REX ARAGONVM **Rev:** Diamond-shaped shield within inner circle **Rev. Legend:** MALORICARUM CATOLIC **Mint:** Palma de Mallorca **Note:** Size varies 23-24 mm.

Date	Mintage	VG	F	VF	XF	Unc
ND(1598-1621)	—	375	700	1,250	—	—

KM# 4.2 2 REAL

Silver **Ruler:** Philip III of Spain **Obv:** Crowned bust of Philip III right, shield **Obv. Legend:** PHILIPPVS REX ARAGONVM **Rev:** Diamond-shaped shield within inner circle **Rev. Legend:** MALORICARVM CATOLIC **Mint:** Palma de Mallorca **Note:** Size varies 23-24 mm.

Date	Mintage	VG	F	VF	XF	Unc
ND(1598-1621)	—	375	700	1,250	—	—

KM# 5 2 REAL

Silver **Ruler:** Philip III of Spain **Obv:** Crowned bust of Philip III left, shield **Obv. Legend:** PHILIPPVS REX ARAGONVM **Rev:** Diamond-shaped shield within inner circle **Rev. Legend:** MALORICARVM CATOLIC **Mint:** Palma de Mallorca **Note:** Size varies 23-24 mm.

Date	Mintage	VG	F	VF	XF	Unc
ND(1598-1621)	—	400	750	1,400	—	—

KM# 13 2 REAL

Silver **Ruler:** Philip IV of Spain **Obv:** Crowned bust of Philip IV left **Obv. Legend:** PHILIPPVS... **Rev:** Diamond-shaped shield within inner circle **Rev. Legend:** MALORICARVM CATOLIC **Mint:** Palma de Mallorca **Note:** Size varies 23-25 mm.

Date	Mintage	VG	F	VF	XF	Unc
ND(1621-1665)	—	170	350	700	—	—

KM# 22 2 REAL

Ruler: Charles II **Obv:** Short crowned bust of Charles II IV left **Obv. Legend:** CAROLVS•II•ARAGONVM **Rev:** Diamond-shaped shield **Rev. Legend:** MALORICARVM CATOLICVS **Mint:** Palma de Mallorca **Note:** Size varies 24-25 mm.

Date	Mintage	VG	F	VF	XF	Unc
ND(1665-1700)	—	350	625	1,250	2,100	—

KM# 23 2 REAL

Silver **Ruler:** Charles II **Obv:** Tall crowned bust of Charles II left **Rev:** Diamond-shaped shield **Mint:** Palma de Mallorca **Note:** Size varies 28-29 mm.

Date	Mintage	VG	F	VF	XF	Unc
ND(1665-1700)	—	500	950	1,900	3,150	—

KM# 6.1 4 REAL

Silver **Ruler:** Philip III of Spain **Obv:** Crowned bust of Philip III right **Obv. Legend:** PHILIPPVS REX ARAGONVM **Rev:** Diamond-shaped shield within inner circle **Rev. Legend:** MALORICARVM CATOLIC **Mint:** Palma de Mallorca **Note:** Size varies 30-31 mm.

Date	Mintage	VG	F	VF	XF	Unc
ND(1598-1621)	—	600	1,200	2,200	—	—
1600	—	975	1,800	3,000	—	—
1607	—	975	1,800	3,000	—	—

KM# 6.2 4 REAL

Silver **Ruler:** Philip III of Spain **Obv:** Crowned bust of Philip III right **Obv. Legend:** PHILIPPVS REX ARAGONMD **Rev:** Diamond-shaped shield within inner circle **Rev. Legend:** MALORICARVM CATOLIC **Mint:** Palma de Mallorca **Note:** Size varies 30-31 mm.

Date	Mintage	VG	F	VF	XF	Unc
1617	—	975	1,800	3,000	—	—

KM# 14 4 REAL

Silver, 32 mm. **Ruler:** Philip IV of Spain **Obv:** Crowned bust of Philip IV left **Obv. Legend:** PHILIPPVS...REX ARAGONVM... **Rev:** Diamond-shaped shield within inner circle **Rev. Legend:** MALORICARVM...CVTO **Mint:** Palma de Mallorca

Date	Mintage	VG	F	VF	XF	Unc
ND(1621-1665)	—	1,150	2,250	4,150	6,800	—
1633	—	1,150	2,250	4,150	6,800	—
1648	—	1,150	2,250	4,150	6,800	—

KM# 24 4 REAL

Silver **Ruler:** Charles II **Obv:** Crowned bust of Charles II right **Obv. Legend:** CAROLVS... **Rev:** Diamond-shaped shield **Rev. Legend:** MAIORICARVM CATOLICVS **Mint:** Palma de Mallorca **Note:** Size varies 30-31 mm.

Date	Mintage	VG	F	VF	XF	Unc
ND(1665-1700)	—	1,500	3,000	5,300	9,000	—

KM# 25 4 REAL

Silver **Ruler:** Charles II **Obv:** Crowned bust of Charles II IV left **Rev:** Diamond-shaped shield **Mint:** Palma de Mallorca **Note:** Size varies 33-34 mm.

Date	Mintage	VG	F	VF	XF	Unc
ND(1665-1700)	—	2,250	4,500	7,500	11,500	—

KM# 26 1/2 ESCUDO

1.6917 g., 0.9170 Gold 0.0499 oz. AGW **Ruler:** Charles II **Obv:** Crowned arms divide date **Rev:** Diamond-shaped shield **Note:** Previous Fr.#67.

Date	Mintage	VG	F	VF	XF	Unc
1695	—	600	1,200	2,250	3,750	—

KM# 40 1/2 ESCUDO

1.6917 g., 0.9170 Gold 0.0499 oz. AGW **Ruler:** Philip V **Obv:** Bust of Philip V right, legend at right **Obv. Legend:** PHILIPVS... **Rev:** Diamond shield topped by cross **R ev. Legend:** MAIORIC - ARVM CA **Note:** Previous Fr.#71.

Date	Mintage	VG	F	VF	XF	Unc
ND(1700-1746)	—	1,300	2,650	3,750	5,300	—

KM# 27 ESCUDO

3.3834 g., 0.9170 Gold 0.0997 oz. AGW **Ruler:** Charles II **Obv:** Crowned arms in inner circle, date in legend **Rev:** Diamond-shaped shield **Note:** Previous Fr.#66.

Date	Mintage	VG	F	VF	XF	Unc
1698	—	700	1,300	2,000	3,500	—

KM# 41 ESCUDO

3.3834 g., 0.9170 Gold 0.0997 oz. AGW **Ruler:** Philip V **Obv:** Large bust of Philip V right **Obv. Legend:** PHILIPVS... **Rev:** Crowned arms, tree at left **Mint:** Palma de Mallorca **Note:** Fr.#70.

Date	Mintage	VG	F	VF	XF	Unc
ND(1700-1746)	—	500	950	1,700	2,750	—

KM# 42 ESCUDO

3.3834 g., 0.9170 Gold 0.0997 oz. AGW **Ruler:** Philip V **Obv:** Small bust of Philip V right **Rev:** Crowned arms, tree at left **Mint:** Palma de Mallorca **Note:** Fr.#70a.

Date	Mintage	VG	F	VF	XF	Unc
ND(1700-1746)	—	500	1,000	1,650	2,750	—

KM# 7 2 ESCUDOS

6.7667 g., 0.9170 Gold 0.1995 oz. AGW **Ruler:** Philip III of Spain **Obv:** Crowned arms in inner circle, titles of Philip III **Rev:** Diamond shaped shield **Note:** Previous Fr.#59.

Date	Mintage	VG	F	VF	XF	Unc
ND	—	2,050	4,150	7,500	13,000	—

KM# 15 2 ESCUDOS

6.7667 g., 0.9170 Gold 0.1995 oz. AGW **Ruler:** Philip IV of Spain **Obv:** Crowned arms in inner circle, titles of Philip IV **Rev:** Diamond-shaped shield **Mint:** Palma de Mallorca

Date	Mintage	VG	F	VF	XF	Unc
1660	—	2,050	4,150	7,500	13,000	—

KM# 28 2 ESCUDOS

6.7667 g., 0.9170 Gold 0.1995 oz. AGW **Ruler:** Charles II **Obv:** Crowned arms in ornamental cartouche in inner circle, date in legend **Note:** Previous Fr.#65.

Date	Mintage	VG	F	VF	XF	Unc
1678	—	1,700	3,300	5,500	8,400	—
1689	—	1,600	3,000	4,500	7,000	—
1695	—	1,900	3,600	6,000	10,000	—
1698	—	1,900	3,600	6,000	10,000	—

KM# 8 4 ESCUDOS

13.5334 g., 0.9170 Gold 0.3990 oz. AGW **Ruler:** Philip III of Spain **Obv:** Crowned arms in inner circle, titles of Philip III **Rev:** Diamond shield in inner circle **Note:** Previous Fr.#58.

Date	Mintage	VG	F	VF	XF	Unc
1607 Rare	—	—	—	—	—	—

KM# 16 4 ESCUDOS

13.5334 g., 0.9170 Gold 0.3990 oz. AGW **Ruler:** Philip IV of Spain **Obv:** Titles of Philip IV **Note:** Previous Fr.#61.

Date	Mintage	VG	F	VF	XF	Unc
1648 Rare	—	—	—	—	—	—

KM# 29 4 ESCUDOS

13.5334 g., 0.9170 Gold 0.3990 oz. AGW **Ruler:** Charles II **Obv:** Titles of Charles II **Note:** Previous Fr.#64.

Date	Mintage	VG	F	VF	XF	Unc
1698	—	2,250	3,750	6,800	10,500	—

KM# 30 8 ESCUDOS

27.0674 g., 0.9170 Gold 0.7980 oz. AGW **Ruler:** Charles II **Obv:** Crowned arms in ornamental cartouche in inner circle, date in legend **Obv. Legend:** CAROLVS III **Rev:** Diamond shield in inner circle, cross on top **Note:** Previous Fr.#63.

Date	Mintage	VG	F	VF	XF	Unc
1689 Rare	—	—	—	—	—	—

NAVARRE

Navarre, a frontier province of northern Spain and a former kingdom lies on the western end of the border between France and Spain. From the 10th through the12th centuries Navarre was a solid power in the region. After 1234 the kingdom fell under French dominance. In 1516 Ferdinand annexed Navarre to Spain and it was under this vice royalty that coinage was struck at the mint in Pamplona.

The Kingdom of Navarre was ultimately divided and absorbed by France and Spain.

PROVINCE

STANDARD COINAGE

KM# 5 DINERO

Copper **Obv:** Crowned bust right **Rev:** Diamond shield of Banolas **Mint:** Banyoles **Note:** Legend varieties exist.

Date	Mintage	VG	F	VF	XF	Unc
1600	—	25.00	42.00	80.00	150	—
ND	—	14.00	30.00	55.00	120	—

KM# 6 4 CORNADOS

Copper **Obv:** Crowned FI monogram, value below in inner circle, titles of Philip III **Rev:** Crowned arms in inner circle **Mint:** Pamplona **Note:** Varieties exist.

Date	Mintage	VG	F	VF	XF	Unc
1608	—	14.00	27.50	48.00	95.00	—
168 Error	—	17.00	33.50	60.00	110	—
169 Error	—	17.00	33.50	60.00	110	—
16x Error	—	14.00	30.00	55.00	100	—
1610	—	14.00	27.50	48.00	95.00	—
1611	—	14.00	27.50	48.00	95.00	—
1611 PA	—	14.00	27.50	48.00	95.00	—
1612	—	14.00	27.50	48.00	95.00	—
1613	—	14.00	27.50	48.00	95.00	—
1614	—	14.00	27.50	48.00	95.00	—
1615 P	—	14.00	27.50	48.00	95.00	—
1615 PA	—	14.00	27.50	48.00	95.00	—
1616 PA	—	14.00	27.50	48.00	95.00	—
1617 PA	—	14.00	27.50	48.00	95.00	—
1618 PA	—	14.00	27.50	48.00	95.00	—
1619 PA	—	14.00	27.50	48.00	95.00	—
1620 PA	—	14.00	27.50	48.00	95.00	—
1621 PA	—	17.00	33.50	60.00	110	—

KM# 10 4 CORNADOS

Copper **Note:** Without inner circle.

Date	Mintage	VG	F	VF	XF	Unc
1611	—	14.00	30.00	55.00	100	—

KM# 11 4 CORNADOS

Copper **Obv:** Crowned FI monogram in inner circle, titles of Philip IV **Rev:** Crowned pointed arms in inner circle **Mint:** Pamplona

Date	Mintage	VG	F	VF	XF	Unc
NDPP PP	—	90.00	150	265	—	—

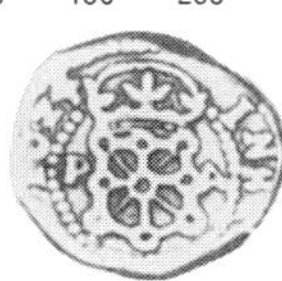

KM# 20 4 CORNADOS

Copper **Obv:** Crowned FI monogram, value 4 between, in pellet circle **Rev:** Crowned arms of Navarre in pellet circle

Date	Mintage	VG	F	VF	XF	Unc
1622	—	27.50	55.00	100	180	—
1624	—	25.00	48.00	90.00	150	—
1625	—	27.50	55.00	100	180	—
1626	—	27.50	55.00	100	180	—
1627	—	25.00	48.00	90.00	150	—
1641	—	25.00	48.00	90.00	150	—

KM# 30 4 CORNADOS

Copper **Rev:** Without pellet circles

Date	Mintage	VG	F	VF	XF	Unc
1641	—	30.00	60.00	110	200	—
1644	—	27.50	55.00	100	180	—
1645	—	27.50	55.00	100	180	—
1650	—	25.00	48.00	90.00	150	—
1651	—	30.00	60.00	110	200	—
1652	—	30.00	60.00	110	200	—
1653	—	30.00	60.00	110	200	—

KM# 31 4 CORNADOS

Copper **Obv:** Crowned Philip monogram **Rev:** Crowned arms of Navarre

Date	Mintage	VG	F	VF	XF	Unc
1644	—	38.50	80.00	140	220	—
1645	—	38.50	80.00	140	220	—
1646	—	38.50	80.00	140	220	—
1649	—	38.50	80.00	140	220	—
1650	—	38.50	80.00	140	220	—
1653	—	38.50	80.00	140	220	—
1654	—	38.50	80.00	140	220	—
1655	—	38.50	80.00	140	220	—
1659	—	38.50	80.00	140	220	—
1663	—	38.50	80.00	140	220	—
1664	—	38.50	80.00	140	220	—
1665	—	55.00	110	210	325	—

KM# 12 8 CORNADOS

Copper **Obv:** Crowned FI monogram in inner circle, titles of Philip IV **Rev:** Crowned pointed arms in inner circle **Mint:** Pamplona

Date	Mintage	VG	F	VF	XF	Unc
ND PP	—	100	190	300	—	—

KM# 13 REAL

Silver **Obv:** Crowned arms of Navarre, 1 at right **Rev:** Cross in cartouche

Date	Mintage	VG	F	VF	XF	Unc
1611 P	—	220	350	600	1,200	—
1612 P	—	250	400	700	1,450	—

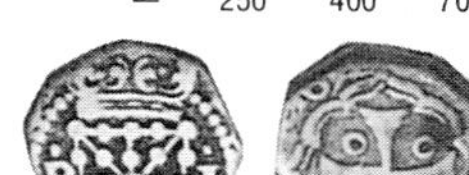

KM# 35 REAL

Silver **Obv:** Crowned arms of Navarre in inner circle dividing P - I **Rev:** Cross in cartouche, circles in angles, date in legend **Mint:** Pamplona

Date	Mintage	VG	F	VF	XF	Unc
1651P A	—	150	280	450	825	—
1652P A	—	150	280	450	825	—

KM# 14 2 REALES

Silver **Obv:** Crowned arms in inner circle, titles of Philip III **Rev:** Cross in cartouche, date in legend **Mint:** Pamplona

Date	Mintage	VG	F	VF	XF	Unc
1611 P	—	400	650	1,150	2,200	—
1612 PA	—	450	700	1,250	2,400	—

KM# 36 2 REALES

Silver **Obv:** Titles of Philip IV **Mint:** Pamplona

Date	Mintage	VG	F	VF	XF	Unc
1651 PA	—	190	325	500	875	—
1652 PA	—	190	325	525	900	—

KM# 15 4 REALES

Silver **Obv:** Crowned arms of Navarre, IIII vertical at left **Rev:** Short cross in cartouche, pellets and ovals in quarters, date in legend **Mint:** Pamplona

Date	Mintage	VG	F	VF	XF	Unc
1612 Rare	—	—	—	—	—	—

KM# 41 4 REALES

Silver **Obv:** Crowned eight equal part shield **Rev:** Cross divides date in lower quadrants **Mint:** Pamplona

Date	Mintage	Good	VG	F	VF	XF
1659	—	600	1,200	2,000	3,000	—

KM# 37 8 REALES

Silver **Obv:** Crowned eight equal part shield **Obv. Legend:** PHILIPPVS • D • GRACIA • REX • **Rev:** Cross, ovals at corners **Rev. Legend:** CASTELLE • ET • NAVARRE

Date	Mintage	VG	F	VF	XF	Unc
1651 A	—	—	—	—	—	—

KM# 38 8 REALES

Silver **Obv. Legend:** PHILIPPVS • VI • D • GRACIA **Rev:** Cross, ovals at corners **Rev. Legend:** NAVARRE • REX

Date	Mintage	Good	VG	F	VF	XF
1652 A	—	1,500	3,000	5,300	7,500	—

KM# 40 8 REALES

Silver **Obv:** Similar to KM#37 **Rev:** Similar to KM#38

Date	Mintage	Good	VG	F	VF	XF
1658	—	1,500	3,000	5,300	7,500	—

KM# 39 50 REALES

Silver **Obv:** Crowned arms of Navarre dividing PA - 50 **Rev:** Cross with ovals in angles, date in legend

Date	Mintage	Good	VG	F	VF	XF
1652 Rare	—	—	—	—	—	—

Note: This is a cast coin and forgeries are known to exist

ROUSSILLON

FRENCH OCCUPATION - PERPIGNAU

STANDARD COINAGE

KM# 14 MENUT
Copper **Ruler:** Louis XIV **Obv:** Double "P" monogram **Obv. Legend:** LVDOVICVS •-• XIIII **Rev:** St. John the Baptist standing facing **Rev. Legend:** + ECCE * AGNVS • DELx

Date	Mintage	Good	VG	F	VF	XF
1648	—	25.00	40.00	70.00	120	—

KM# 11 SOL
Billon **Ruler:** Louis XIV **Obv:** Crowned diamond arms divides date **Obv. Legend:** PERPINIANI VILE **Rev:** St. John the Baptist standing facing, lis below, retrograde value "2" at left **Rev. Legend:** + INTER NATOS - MVLIERVM

Date	Mintage	Good	VG	F	VF	XF
1644	—	—	—	—	—	—

KM# 13 SOL
Billon **Ruler:** Louis XIV **Obv:** Crowned arms with lis at center divides date **Obv. Legend:** PERPINIANI * VILLE **Rev:** St. John the Baptist standing facing, value "1" at left **Rev. Legend:** + INTER NATOS. MVLIERVM

Date	Mintage	Good	VG	F	VF	XF
1645	—	15.00	25.00	45.00	85.00	—

KM# 12.1 2 SOLS
Billon **Ruler:** Louis XIV **Obv:** Crowned diamond arms divides date **Obv. Legend:** PERPINIANI VILE **Rev:** St. John the Baptist standing facing, lis below, value "2" at left **Rev. Legend:** + INTER NATOS - MVLIERVM

Date	Mintage	Good	VG	F	VF	XF
1644	—	20.00	30.00	50.00	90.00	—

KM# 12.2 2 SOLS
Billon **Ruler:** Louis XIV **Obv:** Crowned diamond arms divides date **Obv. Legend:** PERPINIANI VILE **Rev:** St. John the Baptist standing facing, lis below, retrograde value "2" at left **Rev. Legend:** + INTER NATOS - MVLIERVM

Date	Mintage	Good	VG	F	VF	XF
1644	—	20.00	30.00	50.00	90.00	—

SPANISH OCCUPATION - PERPIGNAU

STANDARD COINAGE

KM# 5 MENUT (Denero)
Copper **Ruler:** Philip III **Obv:** Double "P" monogram **Rev:** St. John the Baptist standing facing

Date	Mintage	Good	VG	F	VF	XF
1611	—	75.00	150	300	—	—

KM# 15 TRENET (3 Deneros)
Copper **Ruler:** Philip III **Obv:** Double P monogram, A above **Rev:** St. John the Baptist standing facing, divides date

Date	Mintage	Good	VG	F	VF	XF
1611	—	50.00	100	200	—	—

VALENCIA

Valencia is a maritime province of eastern Spain with a capital city of Valencia. Once a former kingdom, Valencia included the present provinces of Castellon de la Plana and Alicante.

RULERS
Philip III of Spain, 1598-1621
Philip IV of Spain, 1621-1665
Charles II of Spain, 1665-1700
Philip V of Spain, 1700-1746

PROVINCE

STANDARD COINAGE

KM# 5 DINERO (Menudo, Menut)
Copper **Obv:** Bust of Philip right in inner circle **Rev:** Lily plant in center circle, date in legend **Mint:** Valencia

Date	Mintage	VG	F	VF	XF	Unc
1610	—	16.00	32.00	60.00	120	—

KM# 16 DINERO (Menudo, Menut)
Copper **Obv:** Crowned bust right in inner circle **Mint:** Valencia

Date	Mintage	VG	F	VF	XF	Unc
1624	—	36.00	65.00	120	200	—
1634	—	25.00	50.00	90.00	160	—
1646	—	25.00	50.00	90.00	160	—
1651	—	20.00	40.00	70.00	140	—
1652	—	16.00	32.00	60.00	130	—
1653	—	16.00	32.00	60.00	130	—
1654	—	16.00	32.00	60.00	130	—
1655	—	16.00	32.00	60.00	130	—
1660	—	16.00	32.00	100	200	—
1661	—	20.00	40.00	70.00	140	—
1662	—	20.00	40.00	70.00	140	—
1663	—	16.00	32.00	60.00	130	—
1664	—	16.00	32.00	60.00	130	—
1665	—	16.00	32.00	60.00	130	—

KM# 35 DINERO (Menudo, Menut)
Copper **Obv:** Crowned bust of Charles II left in inner circle **Mint:** Valencia

Date	Mintage	VG	F	VF	XF	Unc
1667	—	16.00	30.00	50.00	100	—
1668	—	12.00	25.00	40.00	80.00	—
1669	—	12.00	25.00	40.00	80.00	—
1670	—	12.00	25.00	40.00	80.00	—
1671	—	12.00	25.00	40.00	80.00	—
1672	—	12.00	25.00	40.00	80.00	—
1673	—	12.00	25.00	40.00	80.00	—
1680	—	18.00	36.00	60.00	120	—
1681	—	12.00	25.00	40.00	80.00	—
1682	—	12.00	25.00	40.00	80.00	—
1683	—	14.00	25.00	44.00	90.00	—
1684	—	12.00	25.00	40.00	80.00	—
1685	—	14.00	25.00	44.00	90.00	—
1686	—	14.00	25.00	44.00	90.00	—
1687	—	14.00	25.00	44.00	90.00	—
1688	—	12.00	25.00	40.00	80.00	—
1689	—	14.00	25.00	44.00	90.00	—
1690	—	12.00	25.00	40.00	80.00	—
1691	—	12.00	25.00	40.00	80.00	—
1692	—	12.00	25.00	40.00	80.00	—
1693	—	12.00	25.00	40.00	80.00	—
1694	—	12.00	25.00	40.00	80.00	—
1695	—	12.00	25.00	40.00	80.00	—
1696	—	12.00	25.00	40.00	80.00	—
1697	—	12.00	25.00	40.00	80.00	—
1698	—	12.00	25.00	40.00	80.00	—
1699	—	12.00	25.00	40.00	80.00	—

KM# 6 1/2 REAL
Silver **Obv:** Crowned facing bust of Philip III in inner circle **Rev:** Arms divide date in inner circle **Mint:** Valencia

Date	Mintage	VG	F	VF	XF	Unc
1610	—	70.00	140	250	450	—

KM# 17 1/2 REAL
Silver **Obv:** Crowned facing bust of Philip IV

Date	Mintage	VG	F	VF	XF	Unc
1624	—	265	450	800	—	—
1650	—	265	450	800	—	—

KM# 45 1/2 REAL
Silver **Obv:** Crowned facing bust of Charles II **Rev:** Crowned arms with value, divide date

Date	Mintage	VG	F	VF	XF	Unc
1681	—	120	200	350	550	—
1682	—	60.00	120	180	350	—

KM# 48 1/2 REAL
Silver **Rev:** Without value

Date	Mintage	VG	F	VF	XF	Unc
1682	—	44.00	90.00	150	300	—
1684	—	120	200	350	550	—

KM# 7 REAL
Silver **Obv:** Crowned facing bust of Philip III **Rev:** Crowned arms, date divided near top **Mint:** Valencia **Note:** Varieties exist.

Date	Mintage	VG	F	VF	XF	Unc
1610	—	40.00	80.00	140	280	—
1616	—	40.00	80.00	150	300	—
1618	—	40.00	80.00	130	260	—
1619	—	40.00	80.00	130	260	—
1620	—	40.00	80.00	140	280	—

KM# 15 REAL
Silver **Obv:** Crowned facing bust of Philip IV **Note:** Varieties exist.

Date	Mintage	VG	F	VF	XF	Unc
1621	—	25.00	60.00	100	200	—
1622	—	25.00	60.00	100	200	—
1623	—	25.00	60.00	100	200	—
1624/2	—	25.00	70.00	120	240	—
1624	—	25.00	60.00	100	200	—
1625	—	80.00	160	290	500	—
1638	—	100	200	350	550	—
1639	—	100	200	350	550	—
1640	—	70.00	140	260	400	—
1641	—	30.00	60.00	100	200	—
1642	—	30.00	60.00	100	200	—
1643	—	36.00	70.00	120	240	—
1644	—	30.00	60.00	100	200	—
1645	—	36.00	70.00	120	240	—
1646	—	36.00	70.00	120	240	—
1647	—	70.00	140	260	400	—
1648	—	30.00	60.00	100	200	—
1649	—	30.00	60.00	100	200	—
1650	—	30.00	60.00	100	200	—
1651	—	30.00	60.00	100	200	—
1652	—	30.00	60.00	100	200	—
1653	—	30.00	60.00	100	200	—
1654	—	70.00	140	280	450	—
1655	—	90.00	180	325	525	—
1656	—	120	240	400	700	—
1657	—	120	240	400	700	—
1658	—	120	240	400	700	—
1659	—	70.00	140	260	400	—

KM# 46 REAL
Silver **Obv:** Crowned bust of Charles II right **Note:** Varieties exist.

Date	Mintage	VG	F	VF	XF	Unc
1681	—	225	450	825	1,450	—
1682	—	300	600	1,150	1,900	—
1683	—	265	525	975	1,650	—
1686	—	265	525	975	1,650	—
1687	—	265	525	1,000	1,750	—

KM# 47 REAL
Silver **Obv:** Crowned facing bust of Charles II **Note:** Varieties exist.

Date	Mintage	VG	F	VF	XF	Unc
1681	—	30.00	60.00	100	200	—
1682	—	30.00	60.00	100	200	—
1683	—	36.00	70.00	120	240	—
1684	—	30.00	60.00	100	200	—
1685	—	36.00	70.00	120	240	—
1686	—	36.00	70.00	120	240	—
1687	—	30.00	60.00	100	200	—
1688	—	30.00	60.00	100	200	—
1689	—	30.00	60.00	100	200	—
1690	—	55.00	100	180	350	—
1691	—	55.00	100	180	350	—
1692	—	30.00	60.00	100	200	—
1695	—	60.00	120	200	400	—
1697	—	60.00	120	200	400	—
1698	—	120	240	400	750	—
1699	—	80.00	160	300	600	—

KM# 49 2 REALES
Silver **Obv:** Crowned bust of Charles II right, shield below **Rev:** Crowned arms **Mint:** Valencia

Date	Mintage	VG	F	VF	XF	Unc
1683	—	950	1,600	2,800	4,550	—

KM# 51 ESCUDO
3.3834 g., 0.9170 Gold 0.0997 oz. AGW **Obv:** Crowned diamond shield with vertical stripes, L at each side in inner circle **Rev:** Cross in quadrolobe in inner circle, titles of Philip IV

Date	Mintage	VG	F	VF	XF	Unc
ND	—	325	575	1,150	2,050	—

KM# 52 ESCUDO
3.3834 g., 0.9170 Gold 0.0997 oz. AGW **Rev:** Titles of Charles II

Date	Mintage	VG	F	VF	XF	Unc
1688	—	325	625	1,250	2,250	—
1693	—	325	600	1,150	2,050	—
1694	—	325	625	1,250	2,250	—
1695	—	325	575	1,050	1,950	—
1700	—	400	825	1,550	2,700	—

KM# 53 ESCUDO
3.3834 g., 0.9170 Gold 0.0997 oz. AGW **Rev:** Dragon on helmet

Date	Mintage	VG	F	VF	XF	Unc
1688	—	625	1,250	2,500	4,400	—

SPANISH NETHERLANDS

The Netherlands as an entity perhaps came into being when Philip the Good, duke of Burgundy (1419-1467) called all the Burgundian states together for a common session at Bruges in 1464. Charles the Bold continued to add to the territory and consolidated his power, which, however reverted to the States General at his death in 1477. His daughter Mary married the Austrian archduke Maximilian, and was succeeded by her only son, Philip the Handsome (1494-1506). He married Joanna of Spain, daughter of Ferdinand and Isabella, and their oldest son, Charles V, became king of Aragon and Castile in 1520, head of the Austrian house of Habsburg, and Holy Roman Emperor. The Netherlands passed under the regency of his aunts Margaret of Austria (1519-30) and Mary of Hungary (1531-55). Philip II (1556-98) was a Spaniard and resented by many of the Netherlanders, especially the Protestants and the higher nobility and clergy. The ruthless savagery of his governor the duke of Alba led to continued revolts, and finally to the Pacification of Ghent 1576, a union which was short lived. By the Union of Utrecht (1579) the northern provinces to all intents and purposes were separated from the southern ones.

The Spanish under Farnese, the duke of Parma, gradually regained supremacy in the southern provinces. Philip gave the provinces as dowry when his daughter, Isabella, married the archduke Albert of Austria in 1598. The Spanish Netherlands was to be an independent state based on Catholicism as the only recognized religion, and strong central government. Albert died in 1621 and Isabella in 1633, childless, and the provinces reverted to Philip IV of Spain. War with the United Netherlands and France followed until by the Peace Westphalia, concluding the Thirty Years War in1648, Philip recognized the independence of the northern states. By the Peace of the Pyrenes in 1659 and the Peace of Aix-la-Chapelle in 1668 Louis XIV of France acquired Artois and other border districts. On the death of Charles II in 1700 the southern Netherlands passed to the new Bourbon king of Spain, the French duke Philip of Anjou. In 1701, Louis XIV compelled his grandson to turn the territory over to France, but by the Treaty of Utrecht concluding the War of the Spanish Succession, the provinces were given to Austria.

ARTOIS

(Aire-sur-la-Lys)

A town in north France on the Lys, lies in a low and marshy area at the junction of 3 canals.

In the middle ages, Artois belonged to the counts of Flanders and a charter of 1188 is still extant. It was given to France by the peace of Utrecht in 1713. In World War I, it was one of the headquarters of the British Army Expeditionary Forces.

RULER
Spanish

MINT MARK
Rat - Arras

NOTE: See also France-Aire.

COUNTY

HAMMERED COINAGE

KM# 6 GIGOT

Copper **Obv:** St. Andrew's cross, crown above, fleece below **Rev:** Crowned shield of Philip IV **Rev. Legend:** ...DVX BVRG CO ART Z

Date	Mintage	Good	VG	F	VF	XF
1627	—	12.00	30.00	60.00	150	275
1628	—	12.00	30.00	60.00	150	275
1638	—	12.00	30.00	60.00	150	275
1639	—	12.00	30.00	60.00	150	275
1640	—	12.00	30.00	60.00	150	275

KM# 7 LIARD

Copper **Obv:** Crowne and shields of Burgundy, Brabant, and Breda **Rev:** Crowned shield divides date **Rev. Legend:** ...DVX BVRG CO ART Z

Date	Mintage	Good	VG	F	VF	XF
1627	—	6.00	15.00	25.00	40.00	70.00
1628	—	6.00	15.00	25.00	40.00	70.00
1629	—	8.00	20.00	35.00	55.00	95.00

KM# 1 LIARD

Copper **Obv:** Philip IV

Date	Mintage	VG	F	VF	XF	Unc
ND	—	20.00	40.00	75.00	—	—

KM# 19 LIARD

Copper **Obv:** Bust of Philip IV right **Rev:** Crowned shield of Artois

Date	Mintage	Good	VG	F	VF	XF
1636	—	12.00	30.00	55.00	110	205
1637	—	10.00	25.00	45.00	90.00	160
1638	—	10.00	25.00	45.00	90.00	160
1639	—	10.00	25.00	45.00	90.00	160
1640	—	10.00	25.00	45.00	90.00	160

KM# 2 ESCALIN

5.2600 g., 0.5820 Silver 0.0984 oz. ASW **Obv:** Lion **Rev:** St. Andrew's cross of Bourgogne

Date	Mintage	Good	VG	F	VF	XF
ND	—	12.00	30.00	60.00	120	—

KM# 3 ESCALIN

5.2600 g., 0.5820 Silver 0.0984 oz. ASW **Obv:** Lion rampant left with sword and shield **Rev:** Crowned shield of Philip IV on St. Andrew's cross **Rev. Legend:** ...DVX BVR C ART Zc

Date	Mintage	Good	VG	F	VF	XF
1623	—	8.00	20.00	40.00	85.00	150
1624	—	10.00	25.00	50.00	100	195
1625	—	8.00	20.00	40.00	85.00	150
1626	—	10.00	25.00	50.00	100	195
1627	—	7.50	18.00	35.00	70.00	130
1628	—	8.00	20.00	40.00	85.00	150
1631	—	10.00	25.00	50.00	100	195
1634	—	10.00	25.00	50.00	100	195
1635	—	9.00	22.00	45.00	90.00	180

KM# 5 1/4 PATAGON

7.0300 g., 0.8750 Silver 0.1978 oz. ASW **Obv:** St. Andrew's cross, shield at center, crown above, fleece below, divides date **Rev:** Crowned shield of Philip IV in collar of the Golden Fleece **Rev. Legend:** ...DVX BVRG CO ART Zc

Date	Mintage	Good	VG	F	VF	XF
1624	—	50.00	125	250	500	925
1625	—	60.00	150	300	600	1,100
1626	—	60.00	150	300	600	1,100
1634	—	50.00	125	250	500	925
1635	—	60.00	150	300	600	1,100

KM# 8 1/2 PATAGON

14.0500 g., 0.8750 Silver 0.3952 oz. ASW **Obv:** St. Andrew's cross, shield at center, crown above, fleece below, divides date **Rev:** Crowned shield of Philip IV in collar of the Golden Fleece **Rev. Legend:** ...DVX BVRG CO ART Zc

Date	Mintage	Good	VG	F	VF	XF
1627	—	50.00	125	250	500	925
1628	—	60.00	150	300	600	1,100
1629	—	60.00	150	300	600	1,100
1634	—	70.00	175	350	700	1,250
1635	—	70.00	175	350	700	1,250

KM# 4 PATAGON

28.1000 g., 0.8750 Silver 0.7905 oz. ASW **Obv:** St. Andrew's cross, crown above, fleece below, divides pair of crowned double C monograms **Rev:** Crowned shield in collar of the Golden Fleece **Rev. Legend:** ...DVX BVRG CO ART Zc **Note:** Dav. #4466.

Date	Mintage	Good	VG	F	VF	XF
1623	—	50.00	115	225	450	850
1624	—	60.00	135	270	550	1,000
1625	—	60.00	135	270	550	1,000
1627	—	35.00	75.00	160	325	600
1628/7	—	45.00	105	205	400	700
1629	—	50.00	115	225	450	850
1634	—	60.00	135	270	550	1,000
1635	—	60.00	135	270	550	1,000

KM# 9 2 PATAGON

56.2000 g., 0.8750 Silver 1.5809 oz. ASW **Obv:** St. Andrew's cross, crown above, fleece below, divides pair of crowned double C monograms **Rev:** Crowned shield in collar of the Golden Fleece **Rev. Legend:** ... DVX BVRG CO ART Zc **Note:** Dav. #4465.

Date	Mintage	Good	VG	F	VF	XF
1623	1,623	—	—	—	—	—
1624	—	—	—	—	—	—
1634	—	—	—	—	—	—

KM# 16 1/2 DUCATONE

16.2400 g., 0.9440 Silver 0.4929 oz. ASW **Obv:** Bust of Philip IV right in ruffled collar **Rev:** Crowned shield with lion supporters **Rev. Legend:** ...DVX BVRG CO ART Zc

Date	Mintage	Good	VG	F	VF	XF
1635	—	250	450	850	1,750	2,850

KM# 17 DUCATONE

32.4800 g., 0.9440 Silver 0.9857 oz. ASW **Obv:** Bust of Philip IV right in ruffled collar; mint mark divides date in top legend **Rev:** Lions support crowned shield **Rev. Legend:** ...DVX BVRG CO ART Z **Note:** Dav. #4448.

Date	Mintage	Good	VG	F	VF	XF
1635	—	110	280	550	1,200	2,250

KM# 18 2 DUCATONE

Silver **Note:** Similar to KM#17. Dav. #4447.

Date	Mintage	Good	VG	F	VF	XF
1635 Rare	—	—	—	—	—	—

KM# 15 2 SOUVERAIN D'OR

22.1200 g., 0.9190 Gold 0.6535 oz. AGW **Obv:** Crowned bust of Philip IV in ruffled collar in inner circle; date at top **Rev:** Crowned arms in collar of the Golden Fleece

Date	Mintage	Good	VG	F	VF	XF
1632 Rare	—	—	—	—	—	—
1634 Rare	—	—	—	—	—	—

SIEGE COINAGE

1641

NOTE: OBS = Obsessa, Obsidione (Obsidional)

KM# 25 REAL

3.5000 g., Silver **Obv:** Inscription in six lines **Obv. Inscription:** PHIL. IIII / REX / PATER / PATRIAE / ARIA OBS / 1641 **Note:** Uniface.

Date	Mintage	Good	VG	F	VF	XF
1641	—	100	250	450	650	1,000

KM# 26 2 REALES

6.2000 g., Silver **Obv:** Inscription in six lines **Obv. Inscription:** PHIL. IIII / REX / PATER / PATRIAE / ARIA OBS / 1641.II. **Note:** Uniface.

Date	Mintage	Good	VG	F	VF	XF
1641	—	100	250	450	650	1,000

KM# 27 4 REALES

Silver **Obv:** Inscription in six lines **Obv. Inscription:** PHIL. IIII. / REX / PATER • / PATRIAE. / ARIA OBSESSA./1641.VIII.

Date	Mintage	Good	VG	F	VF	XF
ND(1641)	—	1,200	2,000	3,500	5,500	8,000

BRABANT

A marquisate in medieval time. In 1578 Don John of Austria, the hero of Lepanto, died here. The area and town were much fought over even into modern times.

RULERS

Spanish

Albert and Elizabeth, 1598-1621
Philip IV, 1621-65
Charles II, 1665-1700
Philip V, 1700-1712

Austrian

Archduke Charles
as Charles III, Pretender to
the Spanish Throne, 1703-1711
as Charles VI, Emperor, 1711-1740

MINT MARKS

Hand - Antwerp
Angel face - Brussels
Star - Maastricht
Tree - 's Hertogenbosch

SPANISH RULE

STANDARD COINAGE

KM# 28 DENIER (4 Mites)

Copper **Obv:** Crowned AE monogram **Rev:** Crowned shield of Austria and Bourgonne on St. Andrews's cross **Mint:** Antwerp

Date	Mintage	VG	F	VF	XF	Unc
1606	—	10.00	20.00	60.00	200	—
1607	—	10.00	20.00	60.00	200	—

Note: Legend varieties exist for 1607

KM# 29 2 DENIER (8 Mites)

Copper **Obv:** Crowned AE monogram **Obv. Legend:** Ends: BVRG ET. BRA. **Rev:** Crowned shield of Austria and Bourgonne on St. Andrew's cross **Mint:** Antwerp

Date	Mintage	VG	F	VF	XF	Unc
1606	—	10.00	15.00	20.00	65.00	—
1607	—	10.00	15.00	20.00	65.00	—

KM# 22 1/2 LIARD (6 Mites, Gigot)

Copper **Obv:** Crowned shield of Albert and Elizabeth flanked by stars **Rev:** Cross floree, shield of Maastricht on top **Mint:** Maastricht

Date	Mintage	VG	F	VF	XF	Unc
ND(1598-1612)	—	10.00	15.00	40.00	85.00	—

KM# 23 1/2 LIARD (6 Mites, Gigot)

Copper **Obv:** Crowned shield of Albert and Elizabeth **Rev:** Shield of 's Hertogenbosch **Mint:** s Hertogenbosch

Date	Mintage	VG	F	VF	XF	Unc
1602	—	15.00	30.00	100	300	—
1603	—	20.00	40.00	125	350	—
1604	—	20.00	40.00	125	350	—
1605	—	20.00	40.00	125	350	—
1607	—	25.00	50.00	175	525	—

KM# 32.1 1/2 LIARD (6 Mites, Gigot)

Copper **Obv:** Crowned shield of Austria and Burgundy, lion at center **Obv. Legend:** ...BVRG ET B **Rev:** St. Andrew's cross, crown on top, fleece below **Mint:** Antwerp

Date	Mintage	VG	F	VF	XF	Unc
1608	—	10.00	15.00	25.00	75.00	—
1609	—	10.00	15.00	25.00	75.00	—
1615	—	10.00	15.00	20.00	75.00	—
1616	—	10.00	15.00	20.00	55.00	—
1618	—	10.00	15.00	35.00	130	—
1619	—	10.00	15.00	35.00	130	—

KM# 32.2 1/2 LIARD (6 Mites, Gigot)

Copper **Obv. Legend:** Ends: BVRG Z **Mint:** Brabant

Date	Mintage	VG	F	VF	XF	Unc
1615	—	10.00	15.00	25.00	65.00	—
1616	—	10.00	15.00	25.00	65.00	—

KM# 32.3 1/2 LIARD (6 Mites, Gigot)

Copper **Obv. Legend:** ...BVRG ET B. Z. **Mint:** s Hertogenbosch

Date	Mintage	VG	F	VF	XF	Unc
1615	—	10.00	20.00	50.00	150	—
1616	—	20.00	35.00	95.00	300	—

KM# 32.4 1/2 LIARD (6 Mites, Gigot)

Copper **Obv. Legend:** ...BVRG BRA Z **Mint:** Maastricht

Date	Mintage	VG	F	VF	XF	Unc
1616	—	10.00	15.00	45.00	135	—
1617	—	10.00	15.00	35.00	100	—
1618	—	10.00	15.00	35.00	110	—
1619	—	10.00	15.00	40.00	120	—

KM# 55.2 1/2 LIARD (6 Mites, Gigot)

Copper **Mint:** Maastricht

Date	Mintage	VG	F	VF	XF	Unc
1624	—	35.00	65.00	200	600	—
1625	—	45.00	90.00	275	825	—
1626	—	45.00	90.00	275	825	—

KM# 55.3 1/2 LIARD (6 Mites, Gigot)

Copper **Mint:** Brabant

Date	Mintage	VG	F	VF	XF	Unc
1626	—	25.00	50.00	150	450	—
1650	—	20.00	35.00	100	300	—
1655	—	15.00	30.00	90.00	275	—

KM# 55.1 1/2 LIARD (6 Mites, Gigot)

Copper **Obv:** St. Andrew's cross, crown above, fleece below **Rev:** Crowned shield of Philippe IV **Rev. Legend:** ...DVX BVRG BRAB Z **Mint:** Antwerp

Date	Mintage	VG	F	VF	XF	Unc
1626	—	15.00	30.00	75.00	225	—
1628	—	30.00	60.00	175	525	—
1644	—	—	—	—	—	—
1646	—	—	—	—	—	—
1650	—	25.00	45.00	125	350	—
1654	—	30.00	55.00	175	475	—
1656	—	20.00	40.00	90.00	275	—

KM# 100.1 1/2 LIARD (6 Mites, Gigot)

Copper **Obv:** Fleece separates date **Rev:** Crowned shield of Austria and Burgundy, small lion at center **Rev. Legend:** ...DVX BVRG BRAB Z **Mint:** Antwerp

Date	Mintage	VG	F	VF	XF	Unc
1681	—	25.00	45.00	100	200	—
1685	—	20.00	30.00	60.00	125	—
1686	—	25.00	45.00	100	200	—

KM# 100.2 1/2 LIARD (6 Mites, Gigot)

Copper **Mint:** Brabant

Date	Mintage	VG	F	VF	XF	Unc
1685	—	35.00	70.00	175	450	—
1688	—	75.00	150	375	875	—

KM# 118 1/2 LIARD (6 Mites, Gigot)

Copper **Rev:** Crowned shield separates date **Rev. Legend:** ...DVX BVRG BRAB Z **Mint:** Antwerp

Date	Mintage	VG	F	VF	XF	Unc
1696	—	10.00	12.50	15.00	25.00	—
1700	—	10.00	12.50	15.00	25.00	—

KM# 33.2 LIARD (12 Mites)

Copper **Mint:** Maastricht

Date	Mintage	VG	F	VF	XF	Unc
ND(1598-1612)	—	10.00	15.00	35.00	65.00	—

KM# 24.1 LIARD (12 Mites)

Copper **Obv:** Crowned shield of Albert and Elizabeth **Rev:** Shield of 's Hertogenbosch, date above **Mint:** s Hertogenbosch

Date	Mintage	VG	F	VF	XF	Unc
1602	—	15.00	25.00	60.00	175	—
1603	—	15.00	25.00	60.00	175	—
1604	—	15.00	30.00	90.00	250	—
1605	—	—	—	—	—	—

KM# 24.2 LIARD (12 Mites)

Copper **Mint:** Maastricht

Date	Mintage	VG	F	VF	XF	Unc
1603	—	10.00	15.00	40.00	85.00	—
1604	—	10.00	15.00	35.00	65.00	—
1605	—	10.00	15.00	40.00	80.00	—
1606	—	10.00	15.00	40.00	85.00	—
1607	—	10.00	15.00	30.00	75.00	—
1608	—	10.00	15.00	35.00	65.00	—
1609	—	10.00	15.00	45.00	80.00	—
1611	—	10.00	15.00	40.00	80.00	—
1612	—	10.00	15.00	30.00	60.00	—
1613	—	10.00	20.00	50.00	95.00	—
1614	—	10.00	15.00	35.00	65.00	—
1615	—	10.00	15.00	35.00	65.00	—

KM# 30 LIARD (12 Mites)

Copper **Rev:** Shield of 's Hertogenbosch on St. Andrew's cross divides date **Mint:** s Hertogenbosch

Date	Mintage	VG	F	VF	XF	Unc
1607	—	10.00	20.00	55.00	150	—
1609	—	10.00	20.00	55.00	150	—

KM# 33.1 LIARD (12 Mites)

Copper **Obv:** Crowned shield of Albert and Elizabeth **Obv. Legend:** ...BVRG ET B **Rev:** Crown and shields of Austria, Burgundy and Brabant **Mint:** Antwerp

Date	Mintage	VG	F	VF	XF	Unc
1608	—	10.00	15.00	20.00	65.00	—
1610	—	10.00	12.50	15.00	55.00	—
1617	—	15.00	30.00	90.00	250	—

KM# 40 LIARD (12 Mites)

Billon **Obv:** Crowned shield of Austria and Burgundy **Rev:** Cross floree **Mint:** Antwerp **Note:** Legend varieties exist.

Date	Mintage	VG	F	VF	XF	Unc
1614	—	275	450	875	1,750	—

KM# 63 LIARD (12 Mites)

Copper **Obv:** Crown and shields of Austria, Brabant and Breda **Mint:** Antwerp

Date	Mintage	VG	F	VF	XF	Unc
1626	—	—	—	—	—	—

KM# 62.1 LIARD (12 Mites)

Copper **Obv:** Crown and shields of Austria, Burgundy and Brabant **Rev:** Crowned shield divides date **Mint:** Antwerp

Date	Mintage	VG	F	VF	XF	Unc
1626	—	—	—	—	—	—
1643	—	10.00	12.50	15.00	45.00	—
1650	—	10.00	15.00	30.00	80.00	—
1652	—	10.00	15.00	20.00	50.00	—
1653	—	10.00	15.00	25.00	65.00	—
1654	—	10.00	15.00	20.00	50.00	—
1656	—	10.00	15.00	20.00	50.00	—

KM# 62.2 LIARD (12 Mites)

Copper **Mint:** Maastricht

Date	Mintage	VG	F	VF	XF	Unc
1629	—	10.00	15.00	30.00	95.00	—
1630	—	10.00	15.00	20.00	65.00	—
1632	—	10.00	15.00	20.00	65.00	—

KM# 62.3 LIARD (12 Mites)

Copper **Mint:** Brabant

Date	Mintage	VG	F	VF	XF	Unc
1643	—	10.00	12.50	15.00	50.00	—
1644	—	10.00	12.50	15.00	50.00	—
1647	—	10.00	15.00	25.00	80.00	—
1648	—	10.00	15.00	25.00	80.00	—
1650	—	10.00	15.00	30.00	95.00	—
1652	—	10.00	15.00	20.00	55.00	—
1653	—	10.00	15.00	25.00	80.00	—
1654	—	10.00	15.00	25.00	80.00	—
1655	—	10.00	15.00	30.00	95.00	—
1656	—	10.00	15.00	25.00	80.00	—

KM# 91.1 LIARD (12 Mites)

Copper **Obv:** Crown and shields of Austria, Burgundy and Brabant **Rev:** Crowned shield of Charles II divides date **Rev. Legend:** ...DVX BVRG BRAB Z **Mint:** Antwerp

Date	Mintage	VG	F	VF	XF	Unc
1679	—	10.00	15.00	30.00	65.00	—
1680	—	10.00	15.00	20.00	45.00	—
1683	—	15.00	30.00	75.00	160	—
1685	—	10.00	12.50	15.00	35.00	—

KM# 91.2 LIARD (12 Mites)

Copper **Mint:** Brabant

Date	Mintage	VG	F	VF	XF	Unc
1685	—	10.00	12.50	15.00	35.00	—
1690	—	10.00	12.50	15.00	35.00	—
1691	—	10.00	15.00	25.00	55.00	—

KM# 93.2 LIARD (12 Mites)

Copper **Mint:** Brabant

Date	Mintage	VG	F	VF	XF	Unc
1690	—	10.00	12.50	15.00	35.00	—
1691	—	10.00	12.50	15.00	35.00	—
1692	—	10.00	12.50	15.00	35.00	—
1693	—	10.00	12.50	15.00	35.00	—

KM# 93.3 LIARD (12 Mites)

Copper **Rev. Legend:** ARC D...

Date	Mintage	VG	F	VF	XF	Unc
1691	—	—	—	—	—	—

KM# 93.1 LIARD (12 Mites)

Copper **Obv:** Crown divides date in legend **Obv. Legend:** Ends: ...DVX BVRG BRAB Z **Mint:** Antwerp

Date	Mintage	VG	F	VF	XF	Unc
1692	—	10.00	12.50	15.00	35.00	—
1693	—	10.00	12.50	15.00	35.00	—
1695	—	—	—	—	—	—
1698	—	—	—	—	—	—

KM# 41.1 1/2 PATARD

Billon **Obv:** Cross floree, AE monogram **Rev:** Crowned shield of Albert and Elizabeth **Rev. Legend:** ...BVRG BR(AB) Z **Mint:** Antwerp

Date	Mintage	VG	F	VF	XF	Unc
ND(1614-19)	—	30.00	50.00	100	300	—
1614	—	45.00	75.00	150	300	—
1616	—	45.00	75.00	150	300	—

KM# 41.3 1/2 PATARD

Billon **Mint:** s Hertogenbosch

Date	Mintage	VG	F	VF	XF	Unc
1614	—	35.00	65.00	150	275	—
1616	—	35.00	65.00	150	275	—
1617	—	35.00	65.00	150	275	—
1618	—	35.00	65.00	150	275	—
1619	—	35.00	65.00	150	275	—

KM# 41.2 1/2 PATARD

Billon **Mint:** Brabant **Note:** Legend varieties exist.

Date	Mintage	VG	F	VF	XF	Unc
1614	—	35.00	50.00	75.00	200	—
1618	—	25.00	45.00	90.00	175	—
1619	—	25.00	45.00	90.00	175	—

KM# 42.1 PATARD

Billon **Obv:** Cross floree, AE monogram **Rev:** Crowned shield of Albert and Elizabeth divides date **Rev. Legend:** ...BVRG BR Z **Mint:** Antwerp

Date	Mintage	VG	F	VF	XF	Unc
ND(1613-16)	—	25.00	45.00	90.00	175	—
1614	—	25.00	45.00	90.00	175	—
1615	—	30.00	60.00	125	250	—
1616	—	25.00	45.00	90.00	175	—

KM# 42.2 PATARD

Billon **Mint:** Brabant

Date	Mintage	VG	F	VF	XF	Unc
1614	—	—	—	—	—	—
1615	—	25.00	35.00	65.00	150	—
1616	—	25.00	35.00	65.00	150	—

KM# 42.3 PATARD
Billon **Mint:** s Hertogenbosch

Date	Mintage	VG	F	VF	XF	Unc
1614	—	25.00	35.00	65.00	150	—
1615	—	30.00	50.00	100	200	—
1616	—	—	—	—	—	—
1617	—	30.00	50.00	100	200	—
1618	—	30.00	50.00	100	200	—
1619	—	30.00	50.00	100	200	—
1620	—	30.00	50.00	100	200	—
1621	—	30.00	50.00	100	200	—

KM# 70.2 PATARD
Billon **Mint:** Brabant

Date	Mintage	VG	F	VF	XF	Unc
1631	—	40.00	75.00	150	300	—
1633	—	90.00	150	275	550	—

KM# 70.1 PATARD
Billon **Obv:** Linear cross **Rev:** Crowned shield of Philip IV divides date **Rev. Legend:** ...DVX BVRG BRAB Z **Mint:** Antwerp

Date	Mintage	VG	F	VF	XF	Unc
1632	—	40.00	75.00	150	300	—
1646	—	75.00	125	225	450	—

KM# 92.2 PATARD
Billon **Obv:** Long, linear cross, mint mark at center **Rev:** Crowned shield divides date **Rev. Legend:** ...DVX BRAB Zc **Mint:** Antwerp

Date	Mintage	VG	F	VF	XF	Unc
1679	—	40.00	75.00	200	400	—

KM# 92.3 PATARD
Billon **Mint:** Brabant

Date	Mintage	VG	F	VF	XF	Unc
1679	—	20.00	40.00	100	200	—

KM# 120 2 PATARDS
2.4500 g., 0.3850 Silver 0.0303 oz. ASW **Obv:** Linear cross with lion in center, lion and crown in angles **Rev:** Crowned shield divides date **Mint:** Antwerp

Date	Mintage	VG	F	VF	XF	Unc
1698	—	350	575	1,150	2,300	—

KM# 45.1 3 PATARDS
2.6300 g., 0.5820 Silver 0.0492 oz. ASW **Obv:** Cross floree, lion at center **Rev:** Crowned shield in octolobe **Rev. Legend:** ...BVR BRAB Z **Mint:** Antwerp

Date	Mintage	VG	F	VF	XF	Unc
1616	—	18.00	30.00	60.00	125	—
1617	—	15.00	25.00	50.00	100	—
1620	—	10.00	18.00	40.00	75.00	—
1621	—	10.00	18.00	40.00	75.00	—

KM# 45.3 3 PATARDS
2.6300 g., 0.5820 Silver 0.0492 oz. ASW **Mint:** Brabant

Date	Mintage	VG	F	VF	XF	Unc
1616	—	15.00	25.00	45.00	90.00	—
1617	—	10.00	18.00	40.00	75.00	—
1618	—	10.00	18.00	40.00	75.00	—
1619	—	10.00	18.00	40.00	75.00	—
1620	—	—	—	—	—	—

KM# 45.4 3 PATARDS
2.6300 g., 0.5820 Silver 0.0492 oz. ASW **Mint:** s Hertogenbosch

Date	Mintage	VG	F	VF	XF	Unc
1616	—	30.00	55.00	125	225	—
1617	—	30.00	55.00	125	225	—
1618	—	35.00	65.00	150	275	—
1619	—	35.00	65.00	150	275	—
1620	—	25.00	45.00	90.00	175	—
1621	—	25.00	45.00	90.00	175	—

KM# 45.2 3 PATARDS
2.6300 g., 0.5820 Silver 0.0492 oz. ASW **Mint:** Maastricht

Date	Mintage	VG	F	VF	XF	Unc
1617	—	525	875	1,750	3,450	—

KM# 45.5 3 PATARDS
2.6300 g., 0.5820 Silver 0.0492 oz. ASW **Rev. Legend:** ...DVX BVRG BRAB Z **Mint:** Brabant

Date	Mintage	VG	F	VF	XF	Unc
1623	—	—	—	—	—	—

KM# 121 4 PATARDS
4.9000 g., 0.3850 Silver 0.0606 oz. ASW **Obv:** St. Andrew's cross divides date, crown above, fleece below **Rev:** Crowned shield **Rev. Legend:** ...DVX BVRG BRAB Z **Mint:** Antwerp

Date	Mintage	VG	F	VF	XF	Unc
1698	—	50.00	95.00	220	375	—
1700	—	125	175	350	650	—

KM# 26.1 1/4 REAL
1.7400 g., 0.3960 Silver 0.0222 oz. ASW **Obv:** Crowned shield of Albert and Elizabeth **Rev:** Crowned shield divides date **Rev. Legend:** ...BVRG ET BRAB Z **Mint:** Antwerp

Date	Mintage	VG	F	VF	XF	Unc
1604	—	35.00	65.00	150	275	—
1605	—	25.00	45.00	90.00	175	—

KM# 26.2 1/4 REAL
1.7400 g., 0.3960 Silver 0.0222 oz. ASW **Mint:** s Hertogenbosch

Date	Mintage	VG	F	VF	XF	Unc
1609	—	150	250	475	925	—

KM# 31 1/2 REAL
3.4800 g., 0.3960 Silver 0.0443 oz. ASW **Obv:** Crowned shield of St. Andrew's cross divides date **Obv. Legend:** ...BVRG ET BRA **Rev:** Crowned shield **Mint:** Antwerp **Note:** Legend varieties exist.

Date	Mintage	VG	F	VF	XF	Unc
1607	—	40.00	80.00	175	325	—
1609	—	40.00	80.00	175	325	—

KM# 25.1 REAL
3.0600 g., 0.8960 Silver 0.0881 oz. ASW **Obv:** Crowned shield in collar of the Golden Fleece **Rev:** St. Andrew's cross, crown above, fleece below **Rev. Legend:** ...DVCES BVRG ET BRAB Z **Mint:** Antwerp

Date	Mintage	VG	F	VF	XF	Unc
ND(1603-07)	—	18.00	30.00	60.00	125	—

KM# 25.2 REAL
3.0600 g., 0.8960 Silver 0.0881 oz. ASW
Obv. Legend: ...DVCES BVRG ET B **Mint:** Maastricht

Date	Mintage	VG	F	VF	XF	Unc
ND(1603-10)	—	90.00	150	300	600	—

KM# 25.3 REAL
3.0600 g., 0.8960 Silver 0.0881 oz. ASW **Obv. Legend:** ...DVCES BVRG ET BRAB **Mint:** s Hertogenbosch

Date	Mintage	VG	F	VF	XF	Unc
ND(1606-09)	—	275	450	875	1,750	—

KM# 20 1/4 FLORIN
4.2700 g., 0.6670 Silver 0.0916 oz. ASW **Obv:** Confronted busts of Albert and Elizabeth, crown above, V below **Rev:** Crowned shield in collar of the Golden Fleece **Mint:** Brabant

Date	Mintage	VG	F	VF	XF	Unc
1601	—	525	875	1,750	3,450	—

KM# 47.2 ESCALIN
5.2600 g., 0.5820 Silver 0.0984 oz. ASW **Mint:** Brabant

Date	Mintage	VG	F	VF	XF	Unc
ND(1612-21)	—	15.00	30.00	90.00	400	—
1618	—	35.00	65.00	200	700	—
1620	—	15.00	25.00	75.00	350	—
1621	—	15.00	25.00	75.00	350	—

KM# 47.3 ESCALIN
5.2600 g., 0.5820 Silver 0.0984 oz. ASW **Mint:** s Hertogenbosch

Date	Mintage	VG	F	VF	XF	Unc
1617	—	300	500	1,000	2,000	—

KM# 47.1 ESCALIN
5.2600 g., 0.5820 Silver 0.0984 oz. ASW **Obv:** Eagle with shield of Austria, Burgundy on breast **Rev:** Crowned shield of Albert and Elizabeth on St. Andrew's cross **Rev. Legend:** ...BVRG ET BR Z **Mint:** Antwerp

Date	Mintage	VG	F	VF	XF	Unc
ND(1619-21)	—	15.00	30.00	90.00	400	—
1620	—	35.00	65.00	200	700	—
1621	—	25.00	45.00	150	475	—

KM# 52.1 ESCALIN
5.2600 g., 0.5820 Silver 0.0984 oz. ASW **Obv:** Lion rampant left with sword and shield **Rev:** Crowned shield of Philip IV on St. Andrew's cross **Rev. Legend:** ...DVX BVRG BR Zc **Mint:** s Hertogenbosch

Date	Mintage	VG	F	VF	XF	Unc
1621	—	40.00	65.00	125	375	—
1622	—	15.00	25.00	45.00	125	—
1623	—	15.00	25.00	45.00	125	—
1624	—	15.00	25.00	45.00	125	—
1625	—	15.00	25.00	45.00	125	—
1626	—	25.00	45.00	90.00	275	—
1627	—	40.00	80.00	175	475	—
1628	—	15.00	25.00	45.00	125	—
1629	—	18.00	30.00	60.00	175	—
1630	—	18.00	30.00	60.00	175	—
1631	—	30.00	60.00	125	350	—
1637	—	30.00	45.00	90.00	275	—
1638	—	—	—	—	—	—
1639	—	18.00	30.00	60.00	175	—
1641	—	30.00	45.00	90.00	275	—
1644	—	18.00	30.00	60.00	175	—
1645	—	15.00	25.00	45.00	125	—
1650	—	18.00	30.00	60.00	175	—
1651	—	18.00	30.00	60.00	175	—
1652	—	30.00	60.00	125	350	—
1654	—	40.00	80.00	175	475	—
1657	—	30.00	60.00	125	350	—

KM# 52.3 ESCALIN
5.2600 g., 0.5820 Silver 0.0984 oz. ASW **Mint:** Brabant

Date	Mintage	VG	F	VF	XF	Unc
1621	—	18.00	30.00	55.00	150	—
1622	—	18.00	30.00	55.00	150	—
1623	—	15.00	25.00	45.00	125	—
1624	—	15.00	25.00	45.00	125	—
1625	—	15.00	25.00	45.00	125	—
1626	—	30.00	50.00	100	300	—
1628	—	15.00	25.00	45.00	125	—
1629	—	15.00	25.00	45.00	125	—
1630	—	25.00	40.00	75.00	225	—
1637	—	25.00	40.00	75.00	225	—
1641	—	75.00	125	225	650	—
1643	—	30.00	60.00	125	350	—
1645	—	25.00	35.00	65.00	200	—
1646	—	30.00	50.00	100	300	—
1650	—	30.00	60.00	125	350	—
1651	—	30.00	45.00	90.00	275	—
1652	—	40.00	65.00	125	375	—

KM# 52.4 ESCALIN
5.2600 g., 0.5820 Silver 0.0984 oz. ASW **Mint:** s Hertogenbosch

Date	Mintage	VG	F	VF	XF	Unc
1622	—	55.00	90.00	175	525	—
1623	—	30.00	50.00	100	300	—
1624	—	30.00	60.00	125	350	—

KM# 52.2 ESCALIN
5.2600 g., 0.5820 Silver 0.0984 oz. ASW **Mint:** Maastricht

Date	Mintage	VG	F	VF	XF	Unc
1623	—	—	—	—	—	—
1624	—	125	175	325	950	—
1625	—	90.00	150	300	875	—
1628	—	60.00	100	200	600	—
1629	—	75.00	125	250	775	—
1632	—	125	200	275	1,100	—

KM# 119.1 ESCALIN
5.2600 g., 0.5820 Silver 0.0984 oz. ASW **Obv:** Lion rampant left wtih sword, shield of Austria-Burgundy **Rev:** Crowned shield of Charles II divides date over St. Andrew's cross **Rev. Legend:** ...DVX BVRG BRAB Z **Mint:** Antwerp

Date	Mintage	VG	F	VF	XF	Unc
1698	—	45.00	75.00	150	300	—
1699	—	75.00	125	250	475	—

KM# 119.2 ESCALIN
5.2600 g., 0.5820 Silver 0.0984 oz. ASW **Rev:** Cross above crown **Rev. Legend:** ...DVX BVRG BRAB Z **Mint:** Antwerp

Date	Mintage	VG	F	VF	XF	Unc
1700	—	60.00	100	200	550	—

KM# 21.1 1/2 FLORIN
8.5300 g., 0.6670 Silver 0.1829 oz. ASW **Obv:** Confronted busts of Albert and Elizabeth, crown above, date below **Rev:** St. Andrew's cross, crown above, X below **Mint:** Antwerp

Date	Mintage	VG	F	VF	XF	Unc
1601	—	90.00	150	275	550	—
1602	—	125	200	400	775	—

KM# 21.3 1/2 FLORIN
8.5300 g., 0.6670 Silver 0.1829 oz. ASW **Mint:** Brabant

Date	Mintage	VG	F	VF	XF	Unc
ND(1601)	—	125	200	400	775	—
1601	—	125	175	325	650	—

KM# 21.2 1/2 FLORIN
8.5300 g., 0.6670 Silver 0.1829 oz. ASW **Mint:** Maastricht

Date	Mintage	VG	F	VF	XF	Unc
1603	—	750	1,250	2,450	5,000	—

KM# 34.2 1/4 PATAGON
7.0300 g., 0.8750 Silver 0.1978 oz. ASW **Mint:** Brabant

Date	Mintage	VG	F	VF	XF	Unc
ND(1612-16)	—	25.00	40.00	75.00	150	—

KM# 34.1 1/4 PATAGON
7.0300 g., 0.8750 Silver 0.1978 oz. ASW **Obv:** St. Andrew's cross, crown above, fleece below **Rev:** Crowned shield in collar of the Golden Fleece **Rev. Legend:** ...BVRG ET BRAB Z **Mint:** Antwerp **Note:** Legend varieties exist.

Date	Mintage	VG	F	VF	XF	Unc
ND(1613-20)	—	25.00	35.00	65.00	150	—
1616	—	30.00	60.00	125	250	—
1617	—	25.00	40.00	80.00	175	—

KM# 34.3 1/4 PATAGON
7.0300 g., 0.8750 Silver 0.1978 oz. ASW **Mint:** s Hertogenbosch

Date	Mintage	VG	F	VF	XF	Unc
ND(1614-19)	—	300	500	1,000	2,000	—
1617	—	275	450	900	1,800	—
1620	—	300	575	1,150	2,300	—

KM# 54.1 1/4 PATAGON
7.0300 g., 0.8750 Silver 0.1978 oz. ASW **Rev. Legend:** ...DVX BVRG BRAB Zc **Mint:** Antwerp

Date	Mintage	VG	F	VF	XF	Unc
1623	—	50.00	95.00	200	375	—
1631	—	—	—	—	—	—
1632	—	125	175	350	650	—
1633	—	—	—	—	—	—
1645	—	40.00	75.00	150	300	—
1656	—	75.00	125	225	450	—

KM# 54.3 1/4 PATAGON

7.0300 g., 0.8750 Silver 0.1978 oz. ASW **Mint:** Brabant

Date	Mintage	VG	F	VF	XF	Unc
1623	—	40.00	80.00	175	325	—
1624	—	90.00	150	300	575	—
1626	—	40.00	80.00	175	325	—
1627	—	75.00	125	225	450	—
1628	—	75.00	125	225	450	—
1629	—	125	200	375	725	—
1631	—	40.00	80.00	175	325	—
1632	—	225	375	725	1,450	—
1634	—	—	—	—	—	—
1635	—	—	—	—	—	—
1645	—	40.00	80.00	175	325	—
1654	—	200	325	650	1,300	—
1655	—	150	250	475	950	—
1656	—	—	—	—	—	—
1660	—	225	375	725	1,450	—

KM# 54.2 1/4 PATAGON

7.0300 g., 0.8750 Silver 0.1978 oz. ASW **Mint:** Maastricht

Date	Mintage	VG	F	VF	XF	Unc
1625	—	800	1,300	2,600	5,200	—

KM# 27 3 REAL

9.1900 g., 0.8960 Silver 0.2647 oz. ASW **Obv:** Busts of Albert and Elizabeth conjoined left **Obv. Legend:** ...DVCES BVRG ET BRABAN **Rev:** Crowned shield on St. Andrew's cross **Mint:** Antwerp

Date	Mintage	VG	F	VF	XF	Unc
1605	—	125	200	400	800	—
1606	—	90.00	150	300	575	—
1607	—	125	175	325	650	—
1608	—	90.00	150	300	575	—
1610	—	125	200	400	800	—

KM# 7.1 FLORIN

13.5400 g., 0.8330 Silver 0.3626 oz. ASW **Obv:** Confronted busts of Albert and Elizabeth **Rev:** Crowned shield in collar of the Golden Fleece **Mint:** Antwerp

Date	Mintage	VG	F	VF	XF	Unc
1601	—	225	375	725	1,450	—

KM# 14 FLORIN DE 20 SOLS

13.5400 g., 0.8750 Silver 0.3809 oz. ASW **Obv:** Bust of Philip IV right **Rev:** Lin seated facing with sword and sceptre behind crowned shield **Mint:** Brabant

Date	Mintage	VG	F	VF	XF	Unc
1631	—	2,200	3,600	7,200	14,250	—

KM# 46.1 1/2 PATAGON

14.0500 g., 0.8750 Silver 0.3952 oz. ASW **Obv:** St. Andrew's cross, crown above, fleece below **Rev:** Crowned shield in collar of the Golden Fleece **Rev. Legend:** ...BVRG (ET) BRAB Z **Mint:** Antwerp

Date	Mintage	VG	F	VF	XF	Unc
ND(1612-21)	—	25.00	40.00	75.00	150	—
1616	—	30.00	60.00	125	250	—
1617	—	30.00	50.00	95.00	200	—
1618	—	30.00	60.00	125	250	—
1619	—	25.00	40.00	80.00	175	—

KM# 46.2 1/2 PATAGON

14.0500 g., 0.8750 Silver 0.3952 oz. ASW **Mint:** Brabant

Date	Mintage	VG	F	VF	XF	Unc
ND(1612-21)	—	30.00	50.00	100	200	—
1616	—	35.00	65.00	150	275	—
1617	—	40.00	75.00	150	300	—
1620	—	30.00	50.00	100	200	—
1621	—	30.00	50.00	95.00	200	—

KM# 46.3 1/2 PATAGON

14.0500 g., 0.8750 Silver 0.3952 oz. ASW **Mint:** s Hertogenbosch

Date	Mintage	VG	F	VF	XF	Unc
ND(1614-21)	—	675	1,100	2,150	4,300	—
1617	—	875	1,450	2,900	5,750	—
1619	—	875	1,450	2,900	5,750	—

KM# 46.6 1/2 PATAGON

14.0500 g., 0.8750 Silver 0.3952 oz. ASW **Mint:** Brabant

Date	Mintage	VG	F	VF	XF	Unc
1622	—	70.00	115	205	450	—
1623	—	270	425	850	1,900	—
1628	—	180	270	525	1,150	—
1631	—	115	160	325	700	—
1632	—	70.00	115	205	450	—
1633	—	80.00	135	250	500	—
1634	—	70.00	115	205	450	—
1635	—	70.00	115	205	450	—
1636	—	115	160	325	700	—
1645	—	270	425	850	1,900	—
1651	—	180	270	525	1,150	—
1652	—	180	270	525	1,150	—
1653	—	160	250	450	1,000	—
1654	—	135	205	400	875	—
1655	—	—	—	—	—	—
1656	—	—	—	—	—	—

KM# 46.4 1/2 PATAGON

14.0500 g., 0.8750 Silver 0.3952 oz. ASW **Rev. Legend:** ...DVX BVRG BRAB Zc **Mint:** Antwerp

Date	Mintage	VG	F	VF	XF	Unc
1623	—	45.00	85.00	180	375	—
1625	—	—	—	—	—	—
1627	—	115	160	325	650	—
1628	—	205	325	325	1,300	—
1629	—	—	—	—	—	—
1631	—	45.00	85.00	180	375	—
1632	—	45.00	85.00	180	375	—
1633	—	70.00	115	205	450	—
1635	—	70.00	115	205	450	—
1636	—	80.00	135	250	500	—
1637	—	80.00	135	250	500	—
1639	—	115	160	325	650	—
1645	—	80.00	135	250	500	—
1649	—	—	—	—	—	—
1651	—	80.00	135	250	500	—
1652	—	—	—	—	—	—
1653	—	80.00	135	250	500	—
1655	—	160	250	500	1,100	—
1656	—	—	—	—	—	—

KM# 46.5 1/2 PATAGON

14.0500 g., 0.8750 Silver 0.3952 oz. ASW **Mint:** Maastricht

Date	Mintage	VG	F	VF	XF	Unc
1625	—	—	—	—	—	—
1627	—	—	—	—	—	—
1628	—	—	—	—	—	—
1629	—	—	—	—	—	—
1630	—	—	—	—	—	—
1631	—	—	—	—	—	—
1632	—	—	—	—	—	—

KM# 78.1 1/2 PATAGON

14.0500 g., 0.8750 Silver 0.3952 oz. ASW **Obv:** St. Andrew's cross divides date, crown above, fleece below **Rev:** Crowned shield of Charles II in collar of the Golden Fleece **Rev. Legend:** ...DVX BVRG BRAB Zc **Mint:** Antwerp

Date	Mintage	VG	F	VF	XF	Unc
1672	—	200	325	625	1,250	—
1673	—	300	500	1,000	2,000	—
1677	—	400	650	1,300	2,600	—

KM# 78.2 1/2 PATAGON

14.0500 g., 0.8750 Silver 0.3952 oz. ASW **Mint:** Brabant

Date	Mintage	VG	F	VF	XF	Unc
1666	—	—	—	—	—	—
1671	—	350	550	1,100	2,150	—
1672	—	350	550	1,100	2,150	—
1673	—	225	375	725	1,450	—
1679	—	200	300	575	1,150	—
1685	—	300	500	1,000	2,000	—

KM# A117.1 1/2 PATAGON

14.0500 g., 0.8750 Silver 0.3952 oz. ASW **Ruler:** Charles II **Obv:** St. Andrew's cross, crown above, fleece below divides pair of crowned C monograms **Rev. Legend:** ...BVRG BRABAN Z **Mint:** Antwerp

Date	Mintage	VG	F	VF	XF	Unc
1694	—	300	500	1,000	2,000	—
1698	—	1,050	1,750	3,300	6,600	—

KM# 48.1 1/2 DUCATON

16.2400 g., 0.9440 Silver 0.4929 oz. ASW **Obv:** Busts of Albert and Elizabeth conjoined right **Rev:** Lions supporting crowned shield **Mint:** Antwerp

Date	Mintage	VG	F	VF	XF	Unc
1618	—	500	800	1,600	3,150	—
1619	—	350	575	1,150	2,300	—

KM# 48.2 1/2 DUCATON

16.2400 g., 0.9440 Silver 0.4929 oz. ASW **Mint:** Brabant

Date	Mintage	VG	F	VF	XF	Unc
1618	—	500	800	1,600	3,150	—
1619	—	450	750	1,450	2,900	—
1621	—	450	750	1,450	2,900	—

KM# 60.2 1/2 DUCATON

16.2400 g., 0.9440 Silver 0.4929 oz. ASW **Mint:** Brabant

Date	Mintage	VG	F	VF	XF	Unc
1624	—	875	1,450	2,750	5,450	—
1631	—	600	1,000	2,000	4,000	—
1632	—	400	650	1,300	2,600	—
1633	—	225	350	650	1,300	—
1634	—	525	875	1,750	3,450	—
1635	—	275	525	1,100	2,150	—
1636	—	225	375	725	1,450	—
1637	—	—	—	—	—	—

KM# 60.1 1/2 DUCATON

16.2400 g., 0.9440 Silver 0.4929 oz. ASW **Obv:** Bust of Philip IV right in ruffled collar **Rev:** Lions supporting crowned shield **Rev. Legend:** ...DVX BVRG BRAB Zc **Mint:** Antwerp

Date	Mintage	VG	F	VF	XF	Unc
1628	—	525	950	1,900	3,750	—
1631	—	350	650	1,300	2,600	—
1632	—	225	400	800	1,600	—
1633	—	205	375	725	1,450	—
1634	—	180	300	575	1,150	—
1635	—	115	175	350	1,250	—
1636	—	135	250	500	975	—
1637	—	180	300	600	1,200	—

KM# 73.1 1/2 DUCATON

16.2400 g., 0.9440 Silver 0.4929 oz. ASW **Obv:** Date below bust of Philip IV **Rev:** One lion with swords behind crowned shield **Rev. Legend:** ...DVX BVRG BRAB Zc **Mint:** Antwerp

Date	Mintage	VG	F	VF	XF	Unc
1637	—	135	225	475	925	—
1638	—	135	225	475	925	—
1639	—	115	160	325	650	—
1640	—	135	205	450	875	—
1643	—	250	400	875	1,750	—
1646	—	135	225	475	925	—
1647	—	135	225	475	925	—
1648	—	270	425	950	1,900	—
1649	—	115	180	375	725	—
1650	—	135	225	475	925	—
1651	—	180	295	625	1,250	—
1652	—	180	270	575	1,150	—
1654	—	135	225	475	925	—
1656	—	160	250	550	1,100	—
1658	—	205	350	725	1,400	—
1659	—	135	225	475	925	—
1660	—	135	205	450	875	—
1661	—	205	350	725	1,450	—
1662	—	135	205	450	875	—
1663	—	160	250	550	1,100	—
1665	—	135	205	450	875	—

KM# 73.2 1/2 DUCATON

16.2400 g., 0.9440 Silver 0.4929 oz. ASW **Mint:** Brabant

Date	Mintage	VG	F	VF	XF	Unc
1637	—	275	450	875	1,750	—
1639	—	225	350	650	1,300	—
1640	—	400	650	1,300	2,600	—
1642	—	—	—	—	—	—
1649	—	225	375	725	1,450	—
1650	—	350	550	1,100	2,150	—
1652	—	300	475	950	1,900	—
1654	—	275	450	875	1,750	—
1658	—	275	450	875	1,750	—
1661	—	275	450	875	1,750	—
1662	—	275	450	875	1,750	—
1664	—	275	450	875	1,750	—
1665	—	300	475	950	1,900	—
1666	—	300	475	950	1,900	—

KM# 102 1/2 DUCATON

16.2400 g., 0.9440 Silver 0.4929 oz. ASW **Obv:** Youthful bust of Charles II right with long hair and cravat **Mint:** Brabant

Date	Mintage	VG	F	VF	XF	Unc
1682	—	3,000	5,000	10,000	20,000	—

KM# 104.1 1/2 DUCATON

16.2400 g., 0.9440 Silver 0.4929 oz. ASW **Obv:** Youthful bust of Charles II with long hair and court robe **Rev. Legend:** ...DVX BRAB Z **Mint:** Antwerp

Date	Mintage	VG	F	VF	XF	Unc
1684	—	1,900	3,150	6,150	12,150	—

KM# 104.2 1/2 DUCATON

16.2400 g., 0.9440 Silver 0.4929 oz. ASW **Mint:** Brabant

Date	Mintage	VG	F	VF	XF	Unc
1684	—	1,900	3,150	6,150	12,150	—

KM# 9.1 2 FLORIN

27.0800 g., 0.8330 Silver 0.7252 oz. ASW **Obv:** Confronted busts of Albert and Elizabeth **Obv. Legend:** ...DEI GRA **Rev:** Crowned shield in collar of the Golden Fleece **Mint:** Antwerp **Note:** Dav. #4422.

Date	Mintage	VG	F	VF	XF	Unc
1601	—	—	—	—	—	—

KM# 9.3 2 FLORIN

27.0800 g., 0.8330 Silver 0.7252 oz. ASW **Mint:** Maastricht **Note:** Dav. #4425.

Date	Mintage	VG	F	VF	XF	Unc
1603	—	2,800	4,650	9,300	18,600	—

Date	Mintage	VG	F	VF	XF	Unc
1604	—	3,250	5,400	10,750	21,450	—
1605	—	3,250	5,400	10,750	21,450	—

KM# 9.2 2 FLORIN

27.0800 g., 0.8330 Silver 0.7252 oz. ASW **Obv. Legend:** ...DEI • GRATIA **Mint:** Antwerp

Date	Mintage	VG	F	VF	XF	Unc
1602	—	—	—	—	—	—

KM# 35.1 PATAGON

28.1000 g., 0.8750 Silver 0.7905 oz. ASW **Obv:** St. Andrew's cross, crown above, fleece below divide pairs of crowned C monograms **Rev:** Crowned shield in collar of the Golden Fleece **Rev. Legend:** ...BVRG ET BRAB (Zc) **Mint:** Antwerp

Date	Mintage	VG	F	VF	XF	Unc
ND(1612-21)	—	50.00	90.00	175	350	—
1612	—	85.00	150	300	575	—
1616	—	55.00	100	200	400	—
1617	—	45.00	95.00	200	375	—
1618	—	70.00	125	225	450	—
1619	—	70.00	125	225	450	—
1620	—	85.00	95.00	200	375	—
1621	—	—	—	—	—	—

KM# 35.2 PATAGON

28.1000 g., 0.8750 Silver 0.7905 oz. ASW **Mint:** Maastricht

Date	Mintage	VG	F	VF	XF	Unc
ND(1612-21)	—	2,800	4,650	9,300	18,600	—

KM# 35.3 PATAGON

28.1000 g., 0.8750 Silver 0.7905 oz. ASW **Mint:** Brabant

Date	Mintage	VG	F	VF	XF	Unc
ND(1612-21)	—	35.00	65.00	150	300	—
1616	—	45.00	80.00	175	350	—
1617	—	45.00	80.00	175	350	—
1618	—	45.00	80.00	175	350	—
1619	—	45.00	80.00	175	350	—
1620	—	45.00	80.00	175	350	—
1621	—	30.00	70.00	175	325	—

KM# 35.4 PATAGON

28.1000 g., 0.8750 Silver 0.7905 oz. ASW **Mint:** s Hertogenbosch

Date	Mintage	VG	F	VF	XF	Unc
ND(1614-21)	—	3,000	5,000	10,000	20,000	—
1617	—	3,900	6,450	12,900	25,750	—

KM# 53.3 PATAGON

28.1000 g., 0.8750 Silver 0.7905 oz. ASW **Mint:** Brabant

Date	Mintage	VG	F	VF	XF	Unc
1621	—	115	200	375	725	—
1622	—	80.00	150	275	500	—
1623	—	115	175	350	650	—
1624	—	80.00	150	275	500	—
1625	—	115	175	350	650	—
1628	—	215	350	650	1,300	—
1629	—	240	400	800	1,600	—
1630	—	80.00	150	300	575	—
1631	—	80.00	150	300	575	—
1632	—	115	200	400	800	—
1633	—	80.00	150	300	575	—
1634	—	80.00	150	275	500	—
1635	—	80.00	150	275	500	—
1636	—	140	225	450	875	—
1637	—	115	200	375	725	—
1638	—	265	450	875	1,750	—
1639	—	115	175	350	650	—
1645	—	115	200	400	800	—
1647	—	215	350	650	1,300	—
1649	—	140	225	450	875	—
1651	—	80.00	150	300	575	—
1652	—	215	350	650	1,300	—
1653	—	115	175	350	650	—
1654	—	80.00	150	300	575	—
1655	—	115	200	400	800	—
1657	—	115	175	350	650	—
1660	—	240	400	800	1,600	—

KM# 53.1 PATAGON

28.1000 g., 0.8750 Silver 0.7905 oz. ASW **Obv:** Crowned shield of Philip IV in fleece collar **Rev. Legend:** ...DVX BVRG BRAB Zc **Mint:** Antwerp

Date	Mintage	VG	F	VF	XF	Unc
1622	—	80.00	150	275	500	—
1623	—	80.00	150	275	500	—
1624	—	115	175	350	650	—
1625	—	115	175	350	650	—
1626	—	115	200	400	800	—
1627	—	115	175	350	650	—
1628	—	140	250	475	950	—
1629	—	—	—	—	—	—
1630	—	—	—	—	—	—
1631	—	80.00	150	275	500	—
1632	—	80.00	150	275	500	—
1633	—	80.00	150	300	575	—
1634	—	80.00	150	275	500	—
1635	—	80.00	150	275	500	—
1636	—	80.00	150	275	500	—
1637	—	140	225	450	875	—
1638	—	80.00	150	275	500	—
1639	—	115	200	375	725	—
1645	—	240	400	800	1,600	—
1646	—	80.00	150	300	575	—
1647	—	115	200	375	725	—
1648	—	290	475	950	1,900	—
1649	—	115	200	375	725	—
1650	—	165	275	550	1,100	—
1651	—	80.00	150	300	575	—
1652	—	115	200	375	725	—
1653	—	115	175	350	650	—
1654	—	80.00	150	275	500	—
1655	—	140	225	450	875	—
1656	—	115	175	350	650	—
1657	—	140	250	475	950	—
1658	—	115	200	375	725	—
1661	—	165	275	550	1,100	—
1663	—	140	250	475	950	—
1664	—	240	400	800	1,600	—
1665	—	115	200	400	800	—

KM# 53.2 PATAGON

28.1000 g., 0.8750 Silver 0.7905 oz. ASW **Mint:** Maastricht

Date	Mintage	VG	F	VF	XF	Unc
1625	—	350	550	1,100	2,150	—
1626	—	275	450	875	1,750	—
1627	—	275	450	875	1,750	—
1628	—	300	500	1,000	2,000	—
1629	—	275	450	875	1,750	—
1630	—	300	500	1,000	2,000	—
1631	—	350	575	1,150	2,300	—
1632	—	—	—	—	—	—

KM# 81.2 PATAGON

28.1000 g., 0.8750 Silver 0.7905 oz. ASW **Mint:** Brabant

Date	Mintage	VG	F	VF	XF	Unc
1669	—	270	475	950	1,900	—
1670	—	160	275	550	1,100	—
1671	—	160	275	550	1,100	—
1672	—	325	550	1,100	2,150	—
1673	—	115	200	375	725	—
1675	—	325	550	1,100	2,150	—
1676	—	205	375	725	1,450	—
1677	—	400	725	1,450	2,900	—
1678	—	160	275	550	1,100	—
1679	—	400	725	1,450	2,900	—
1680	—	350	650	1,300	2,600	—
1681	—	400	725	1,450	2,900	—
1682	—	205	375	725	1,450	—
1685	—	205	375	725	1,450	—

KM# 81.1 PATAGON

28.1000 g., 0.8750 Silver 0.7905 oz. ASW **Obv:** St. Andrew's cross, crown above, fleece below, divides date **Rev:** Crowned shield of Charles II **Rev. Legend:** ...DVX BVRG BRAB Zc **Mint:** Antwerp

Date	Mintage	VG	F	VF	XF	Unc
1670	—	—	—	—	—	—
1671	—	—	—	—	—	—
1672	—	115	200	375	725	—
1673	—	115	200	375	725	—
1676	—	325	550	1,100	2,150	—
1677	—	160	275	550	1,100	—
1680	—	—	—	—	—	—
1684	—	205	375	725	1,450	—
1686	—	400	725	1,450	2,900	—

KM# 107.2 PATAGON

28.1000 g., 0.8750 Silver 0.7905 oz. ASW **Mint:** Brabant

Date	Mintage	VG	F	VF	XF	Unc
1686	—	725	1,150	2,600	5,150	—
1687	—	350	5,900	1,300	2,600	—
1688	—	550	900	2,000	4,000	—
1692	—	525	850	1,900	3,750	—
1694	—	350	575	1,300	2,600	—
1695	—	—	—	—	—	—

KM# 115 PATAGON

28.1000 g., 0.8750 Silver 0.7905 oz. ASW **Rev. Legend:** ...DVX BVRGVN BRABAN Zc **Mint:** Brabant

Date	Mintage	VG	F	VF	XF	Unc
1691	—	—	—	—	—	—

KM# 81.3 PATAGON

28.1000 g., 0.8750 Silver 0.7905 oz. ASW **Rev. Legend:** ...DVX BVRGVN BRABAN Zc **Mint:** Brabant

Date	Mintage	VG	F	VF	XF	Unc
1691	—	2,000	3,600	7,150	14,300	—

KM# 107.1 PATAGON

28.1000 g., 0.8750 Silver 0.7905 oz. ASW **Obv:** St. Andrew's cross, crown above, fleece below, divides pair of double crowned C monograms **Rev:** Crowned shield in collar of the Golden Fleece divides date **Rev. Legend:** ...DVX BVRG BRABAN Zc **Mint:** Antwerp

Date	Mintage	VG	F	VF	XF	Unc
1694	—	—	—	—	—	—
1695	—	270	450	1,000	2,000	—
1698	—	—	—	—	—	—
1699	—	600	1,000	2,150	4,300	—
1700	—	400	650	1,450	2,900	—

KM# 49.2 DUCATON

32.4800 g., 0.9440 Silver 0.9857 oz. ASW **Mint:** Brabant

Date	Mintage	VG	F	VF	XF	Unc
1618	—	350	600	1,250	2,600	—
1619	—	350	600	1,250	2,600	—
1620	—	300	525	1,100	2,300	—
1621	—	300	500	1,050	2,150	—

KM# 49.1 DUCATON

32.4800 g., 0.9440 Silver 0.9857 oz. ASW **Obv:** Busts of Albert and Elizabeth conjoined right, mint mark divides date above **Rev:** Lions support crowned shield **Rev. Legend:** ...BVRG BRAB Zc **Mint:** Antwerp **Note:** Dav. #4428.

Date	Mintage	VG	F	VF	XF	Unc
1618	—	350	600	1,250	2,600	—
1619	—	300	525	1,100	2,300	—

KM# 49.3 DUCATON

32.4800 g., 0.9440 Silver 0.9857 oz. ASW **Mint:** s Hertogenbosch

Date	Mintage	VG	F	VF	XF	Unc
1619	—	—	—	—	—	—

KM# 56.1 DUCATON

32.4800 g., 0.9440 Silver 0.9857 oz. ASW **Obv:** Bust of Phillip IV in ruffled collar, mint mark divides date above **Rev:** Lions supporting crowned shield **Rev. Legend:** ...DVX BVRG BRAB Zc **Mint:** Antwerp

Date	Mintage	VG	F	VF	XF	Unc
1622	—	—	—	—	—	—
1623	—	—	—	—	—	—
1631	—	200	350	700	1,450	—
1632	—	150	250	500	1,050	—
1633	—	150	250	500	1,050	—
1634	—	150	250	500	1,050	—
1635	—	125	200	425	575	—
1636	—	100	175	350	725	—

KM# 56.2 DUCATON

32.4800 g., 0.9440 Silver 0.9857 oz. ASW **Mint:** Brabant

Date	Mintage	VG	F	VF	XF	Unc
1624	—	425	700	1,400	2,900	—
1629	—	—	—	—	—	—
1631	—	275	450	875	1,800	—
1633	—	150	250	500	1,100	—
1634	—	125	200	400	875	—
1636	—	125	200	400	875	—

KM# 72.2 DUCATON

32.4800 g., 0.9440 Silver 0.9857 oz. ASW **Mint:** Brabant

Date	Mintage	VG	F	VF	XF	Unc
1636	—	100	175	325	675	—
1637	—	100	175	350	750	—
1638	—	100	175	350	750	—
1640	—	100	175	350	750	—
1642	—	150	250	450	1,050	—
1644	—	150	250	450	1,050	—
1645	—	200	325	600	1,250	—
1648	—	100	175	350	750	—
1649	—	100	175	325	675	—
1650	—	125	200	400	825	—
1651	—	100	175	325	675	—
1652	—	100	175	325	825	—
1653	—	100	175	350	675	—
1654	—	125	225	425	675	—
1655	—	150	250	450	750	—
1656	—	125	200	400	900	—
1657	—	125	200	400	950	—
1658	—	150	250	450	825	—
1659	—	100	175	350	825	—
1660	—	125	200	400	950	—
1661	—	100	175	350	750	—
1662	—	100	175	325	675	—
1663	—	125	225	425	900	—
1664	—	100	175	325	675	—
1665	—	125	225	425	900	—

KM# 72.1 DUCATON

32.4800 g., 0.9440 Silver 0.9857 oz. ASW **Obv:** Bust of Philip IV in thin collar right **Mint:** Antwerp **Note:** Dav. #4454.

Date	Mintage	VG	F	VF	XF	Unc
1636	—	100	150	275	600	—
1637	—	65.00	125	225	500	—
1638	—	65.00	125	225	500	—
1639	—	100	175	325	700	—
1640	—	100	175	325	700	—
1641	—	100	175	325	700	—
1642	—	150	250	500	1,050	—
1644	—	125	225	425	900	—
1647	—	100	175	325	700	—
1648	—	65.00	125	225	500	—
1649	—	100	150	300	650	—
1650	—	100	150	300	650	—
1651	—	100	175	325	700	—
1652	—	100	175	325	700	—
1653	—	65.00	125	225	500	—
1654	—	100	175	325	700	—
1655	—	100	175	325	700	—
1656	—	125	200	400	825	—
1657	—	100	175	350	750	—
1658	—	125	200	400	825	—
1659	—	100	150	275	600	—
1660	—	125	200	400	825	—
1661	—	100	175	325	675	—
1662	—	125	200	400	825	—
1663	—	100	175	350	750	—
1664	—	100	175	325	700	—
1665	—	100	175	325	700	—

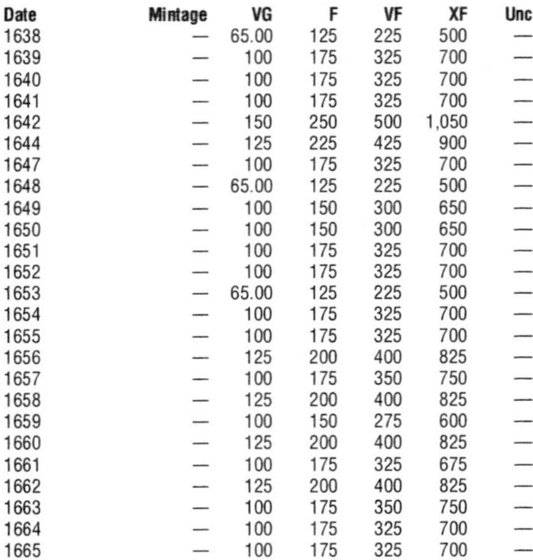

KM# 79.1 DUCATON

32.4800 g., 0.9440 Silver 0.9857 oz. ASW **Obv:** Child's bust of Charles II right **Rev:** Crowned shield of Charles II with lion supporters **Rev. Legend:** ...DVX BVRG BRAB Z **Mint:** Antwerp

Date	Mintage	VG	F	VF	XF	Unc
1665	—	—	—	—	—	—
1666	—	160	250	550	1,100	—
1667	—	160	250	550	1,100	—
1668	—	135	225	500	1,000	—
1670	—	180	295	625	1,250	—
1671	—	160	250	550	1,100	—
1672	—	180	295	625	1,250	—
1673	—	135	225	500	1,000	—
1676	—	225	350	800	1,600	—

KM# 79.2 DUCATON

32.4800 g., 0.9440 Silver 0.9857 oz. ASW **Mint:** Brabant

Date	Mintage	VG	F	VF	XF	Unc
1666	—	205	325	650	1,300	—
1667	—	250	400	875	1,750	—

Date	Mintage	VG	F	VF	XF	Unc
1668	—	160	250	500	1,000	—
1670	—	90.00	180	550	1,100	—
1673	—	160	250	500	1,000	—
1676	—	270	425	950	1,900	—
1677	—	325	500	1,100	2,150	—
1678	—	—	—	—	—	—
1679	—	160	250	500	1,000	—
1680	—	600	1,000	2,150	4,300	—

KM# 103.2 DUCATON

32.4800 g., 0.9440 Silver 0.9857 oz. ASW **Mint:** Brabant

Date	Mintage	VG	F	VF	XF	Unc
1682	—	1,300	2,150	4,300	8,600	—
1683	—	700	1,150	2,300	4,600	—
1684	—	875	1,450	2,900	5,750	—

KM# 103.1 DUCATON

32.4800 g., 0.9440 Silver 0.9857 oz. ASW **Obv:** Youthful bust of Charles II right with long hair and large cravat **Rev. Legend:** ...DVX BVRG BRAB Zc **Mint:** Antwerp

Date	Mintage	VG	F	VF	XF	Unc
1683	—	800	1,300	2,600	5,000	—
1684	—	675	1,100	2,150	4,300	—

KM# 105.1 DUCATON

32.4800 g., 0.9440 Silver 0.9857 oz. ASW **Obv:** Youthful bust of Charles II in court robes **Mint:** Antwerp

Date	Mintage	VG	F	VF	XF	Unc
1684	—	675	1,100	2,150	4,300	—
1700	—	—	—	—	—	—

KM# 105.2 DUCATON

32.4800 g., 0.9440 Silver 0.9857 oz. ASW **Mint:** Brabant

Date	Mintage	VG	F	VF	XF	Unc
1684	—	1,050	1,750	3,450	6,900	—

KM# 106.1 DUCATON

32.4800 g., 0.9440 Silver 0.9857 oz. ASW **Obv:** Mature bust right **Rev. Legend:** ...DVX BVRG BRABAN Zc **Mint:** Antwerp

Date	Mintage	VG	F	VF	XF	Unc
1684	—	—	—	—	—	—
1700	—	—	—	—	—	—

KM# 106.2 DUCATON

32.4800 g., 0.9440 Silver 0.9857 oz. ASW **Mint:** Brabant

Date	Mintage	VG	F	VF	XF	Unc
1686	—	1,750	2,900	5,750	11,450	—
1687	—	2,200	3,600	7,150	14,300	—
1689	—	1,750	2,900	5,750	11,450	—
1692	—	—	—	—	—	—
1693	—	2,200	3,600	7,150	14,300	—
1694	—	1,950	3,250	6,450	12,900	—
1698	—	—	—	—	—	—

KM# 50.1 2 DUCATON

Silver **Mint:** Antwerp **Note:** Similar to 1 Ducaton, KM#49.1.

Date	Mintage	VG	F	VF	XF	Unc
1618	—	—	—	—	—	—

KM# 50.2 2 DUCATON

Silver **Mint:** Brabant **Note:** Similar to 1 Ducaton, KM#49.2.

Date	Mintage	VG	F	VF	XF	Unc
1618	—	—	—	—	—	—
1619	—	—	—	—	—	—
1620	—	—	—	—	—	—

KM# 57.1 2 DUCATON

Silver **Mint:** Antwerp **Note:** Similar to 1 Ducaton, KM#56.1. Dav. #4453.

Date	Mintage	VG	F	VF	XF	Unc
1623	—	500	900	1,750	3,000	—
1628	—	500	900	1,750	3,000	—
1631	—	500	900	1,750	3,000	—
1632	—	500	900	1,750	3,000	—
1633	—	500	900	1,750	3,000	—
1634	—	500	900	1,750	3,000	—
1635	—	500	900	1,750	3,000	—
1636	—	500	900	1,750	3,000	—

KM# 57.2 2 DUCATON

Silver **Mint:** Brabant **Note:** Similar to 1 Ducaton, KM#56.2.

Date	Mintage	VG	F	VF	XF	Unc
1623	—	550	1,000	1,850	3,250	—
1624	—	550	1,000	1,850	3,250	—
1631	—	550	1,000	1,850	3,250	—
1632	—	550	1,000	1,850	3,250	—
1633	—	550	1,000	1,850	3,250	—
1634	—	550	1,000	1,850	3,250	—
1635	—	550	1,000	1,850	3,250	—
1636	—	550	1,000	1,850	3,250	—

KM# 75.1 2 DUCATON

Silver **Ruler:** Philip IV **Mint:** Antwerp **Note:** Similar to 1 Ducaton, KM#72.1, Dav. #4454.

Date	Mintage	VG	F	VF	XF	Unc
1636	—	450	850	1,650	2,850	—
1640	—	450	850	1,650	2,850	—
1642	—	450	850	1,650	2,850	—
1644	—	450	850	1,650	2,850	—
1645	—	450	850	1,650	2,850	—
1646	—	450	850	1,650	2,850	—
1647	—	450	850	1,650	2,850	—
1648	—	450	850	1,650	2,850	—
1650	—	450	850	1,650	2,850	—
1651	—	450	850	1,650	2,850	—
1652	—	450	850	1,650	2,850	—
1654	—	450	850	1,650	2,850	—
1656	—	450	850	1,650	2,850	—
1658	—	450	850	1,650	2,850	—
1662	—	450	850	1,650	2,850	—

KM# 75.2 2 DUCATON

Silver **Ruler:** Philip IV **Mint:** Brabant **Note:** Similar to 1 Ducaton, KM#72.2, Dav. #4454.

Date	Mintage	VG	F	VF	XF	Unc
1636	—	500	900	1,750	3,000	—
1638	—	500	900	1,750	3,000	—
1639	—	500	900	1,750	3,000	—
1640	—	500	900	1,750	3,000	—
1644	—	500	900	1,750	3,000	—
1645	—	500	900	1,750	3,000	—
1646	—	500	900	1,750	3,000	—
1647	—	500	900	1,750	3,000	—
1648	—	500	900	1,750	3,000	—
1649	—	500	900	1,750	3,000	—
1650	—	500	900	1,750	3,000	—
1653	—	500	900	1,750	3,000	—
1654	—	500	900	1,750	3,000	—
1655	—	500	900	1,750	3,000	—
1658	—	500	900	1,750	3,000	—
1659	—	500	900	1,750	3,000	—
1662	—	500	900	1,750	3,000	—
1664	—	500	900	1,750	3,000	—
1673	—	500	900	1,750	3,000	—

KM# A75.2 2 DUCATON

Silver **Ruler:** Philip IV **Mint:** Brabant **Note:** Similar to 1 Ducaton, KM#72.2, Dav. #4454.

Date	Mintage	VG	F	VF	XF	Unc
1636	—	—	—	—	—	—
1638	—	—	—	—	—	—
1646	—	—	—	—	—	—
1648	—	—	—	—	—	—
1658	—	—	—	—	—	—

KM# B75.2 2 DUCATON

Silver **Ruler:** Philip IV **Mint:** Brabant **Note:** Similar to 1 Ducaton, KM#72.2, Dav. #4454.

Date	Mintage	VG	F	VF	XF	Unc
1636	—	—	—	—	—	—
1662	—	—	—	—	—	—

KM# A75.1 2 DUCATON

Silver **Ruler:** Philip IV **Mint:** Antwerp **Note:** Similar to 1 Ducaton, KM#72.1, Dav. #4454.

Date	Mintage	VG	F	VF	XF	Unc
1637	—	—	—	—	—	—
1638	—	—	—	—	—	—
1639	—	—	—	—	—	—
1640	—	—	—	—	—	—
1642	—	—	—	—	—	—
1648	—	—	—	—	—	—
1650	—	—	—	—	—	—
1653	—	—	—	—	—	—
1657	—	—	—	—	—	—

KM# B75.1 2 DUCATON

Silver **Ruler:** Philip IV **Mint:** Antwerp **Note:** Similar to 1 Ducaton, KM#72.1, Dav. #4454.

Date	Mintage	VG	F	VF	XF	Unc
1637 Rare	—	—	—	—	—	—
1639 Rare	—	—	—	—	—	—
1640 Rare	—	—	—	—	—	—
1648 Rare	—	—	—	—	—	—
1649 Rare	—	—	—	—	—	—
1650 Rare	—	—	—	—	—	—
1653 Rare	—	—	—	—	—	—

KM# C75.1 2 DUCATON

Silver **Ruler:** Philip IV **Mint:** Antwerp **Note:** Similar to 1 Ducaton, KM#72.1, Dav. #4454.

Date	Mintage	VG	F	VF	XF	Unc
1638 Rare	—	—	—	—	—	—

KM# 51.1 3 DUCATON

Silver **Mint:** Antwerp **Note:** Similar to 1 Ducaton, KM#49.1.

Date	Mintage	VG	F	VF	XF	Unc
1619	—	—	—	—	—	—

KM# 51.2 3 DUCATON

Silver **Mint:** Brabant **Note:** Similar to 1 Ducaton, KM#49.2.

Date	Mintage	VG	F	VF	XF	Unc
1619	—	—	—	—	—	—
1620	—	—	—	—	—	—

KM# 58.1 3 DUCATON
Silver **Mint:** Antwerp **Note:** Similar to 1 Ducaton, KM#56.1.

Date	Mintage	VG	F	VF	XF	Unc
1623	—	—	—	—	—	—
1631	—	—	—	—	—	—
1632	—	—	—	—	—	—
1633	—	—	—	—	—	—
1634	—	—	—	—	—	—

KM# 58.2 3 DUCATON
Silver **Mint:** Brabant **Note:** Similar to 1 Ducaton, KM#56.2.

Date	Mintage	VG	F	VF	XF	Unc
1633	—	—	—	—	—	—
1634	—	—	—	—	—	—
1635	—	—	—	—	—	—
1636	—	—	—	—	—	—

KM# 59.1 4 DUCATON
Silver **Mint:** Antwerp **Note:** Similar to 1 Ducaton, KM#56.1.

Date	Mintage	VG	F	VF	XF	Unc
1623 Rare	—	—	—	—	—	—
1631 Rare	—	—	—	—	—	—
1634 Rare	—	—	—	—	—	—

KM# 59.2 4 DUCATON
Silver **Mint:** Brabant **Note:** Similar to 1 Ducaton, KM#56.2.

Date	Mintage	VG	F	VF	XF	Unc
1633	—	—	—	—	—	—
1634	—	—	—	—	—	—

KM# 71 5 DUCATON
Silver **Mint:** Antwerp **Note:** Similar to 1 Ducaton, KM#56.1.

Date	Mintage	VG	F	VF	XF	Unc
1632 Rare	—	—	—	—	—	—
1633 Rare	—	—	—	—	—	—

KM# 8.1 ALBERTIN (2/3 Ducat, Corona)
2.9200 g., 0.7920 Gold 0.0743 oz. AGW **Obv:** Crowned arms in collar of the Golden Fleece **Rev:** Crowned floral St. Andrew's cross; date at sides, Golden Fleece at bottom **Note:** Mint mark: Hand.

Date	Mintage	VG	F	VF	XF	Unc
1600	231,000	140	195	350	550	—

KM# 8.2 ALBERTIN (2/3 Ducat, Corona)
2.9200 g., 0.7920 Gold 0.0743 oz. AGW **Obv:** Crowned arms in collar of the Golden Fleece **Rev:** Crowned floral St. Andrew's cross; date at sides, Golden Fleece at bottom **Mint:** Maastricht **Note:** Mint mark: Star.

Date	Mintage	VG	F	VF	XF	Unc
1601	—	220	375	650	1,100	—
1603	—	220	375	650	1,100	—
1604	—	220	375	650	1,100	—
1605	—	220	375	650	1,100	—

KM# 10.1 2 ALBERTIN (4/3 Ducat)
5.1500 g., 0.8950 Gold 0.1482 oz. AGW **Obv:** Crowned shield in collar of the Golden Fleece **Rev:** St. Andrew's cross, crown above, fleece below **Mint:** Antwerp **Note:** Mint mark: Hand.

Date	Mintage	VG	F	VF	XF	Unc
1601	Inc. above	195	300	450	650	—
1602	356,000	195	300	450	650	—
1603	173,000	195	300	450	650	—
1604	235,000	195	300	450	650	—
1605	195,000	195	300	450	650	—
1606	Inc. above	195	300	450	650	—
1607	66,000	195	300	450	650	—
1608	32,000	195	325	550	875	—
1609	16,000	250	450	650	1,000	—

KM# 10.2 2 ALBERTIN (4/3 Ducat)
5.1500 g., 0.8950 Gold 0.1482 oz. AGW **Mint:** Maastricht **Note:** Mint mark: Star.

Date	Mintage	VG	F	VF	XF	Unc
1601	Inc. above	275	550	825	1,200	—
1602	69,000	220	450	725	1,100	—
1603	Inc. above	220	450	725	1,100	—
1607 Rare	924	—	—	—	—	—
1608 Rare	Inc. above	—	—	—	—	—

KM# 10.3 2 ALBERTIN (4/3 Ducat)
5.1500 g., 0.8950 Gold 0.1482 oz. AGW **Mint:** Brussels **Note:** Mint mark: Angel face.

Date	Mintage	VG	F	VF	XF	Unc
1601	15,000	325	550	875	1,500	—

KM# 36.1 1/2 SOUVERAIN OU LION D'OR
2.8000 g., 0.9190 Gold 0.0827 oz. AGW **Obv:** Crowned arms of Austria-Burgundy in inner circle **Rev:** Crowned imperial arms between crowned AE monograms in inner circle **Mint:** Antwerp **Note:** Mint mark: Hand.

Date	Mintage	VG	F	VF	XF	Unc
ND(1613)	840	2,400	4,200	6,600	9,600	—

KM# 36.2 1/2 SOUVERAIN OU LION D'OR
2.8000 g., 0.9190 Gold 0.0827 oz. AGW **Mint:** Brussels **Note:** Mint mark: Angel face.

Date	Mintage	VG	F	VF	XF	Unc
ND	1,433	1,900	3,600	6,000	9,000	—

KM# 65 1/2 SOUVERAIN OU LION D'OR
2.8000 g., 0.9190 Gold 0.0827 oz. AGW **Rev:** Crowned monograms replaced by crowned clasps

Date	Mintage	VG	F	VF	XF	Unc
ND	Inc. above	1,900	3,600	6,000	9,000	—

KM# 38 SOUVERAIN OU LION D'OR
5.1600 g., 0.9880 Gold 0.1639 oz. AGW **Obv:** Conjoined half figures of Albert and Elizabeth right **Rev:** Crowned arms in collar of the Golden Fleece **Mint:** Brussels **Note:** Mint mark: Angel face.

Date	Mintage	VG	F	VF	XF	Unc
ND	2,630	3,000	4,800	7,200	12,000	—

KM# 77.1 SOUVERAIN OU LION D'OR
5.1600 g., 0.9880 Gold 0.1639 oz. AGW **Obv. Legend:** PHIL IIII... **Mint:** Antwerp

Date	Mintage	VG	F	VF	XF	Unc
1648	40,000	150	250	525	1,150	—
1649/8	—	200	350	750	1,200	—
1649	35,000	200	350	750	1,200	—
1650	31,000	200	350	750	1,200	—
1651	10,000	200	350	750	1,200	—
1652	9,000	200	350	750	1,200	—
1653	31,000	200	350	750	1,200	—
1655	20,000	200	350	750	1,200	—
1656	44,000	200	350	750	1,200	—
1657	55,000	200	350	750	1,200	—
1658	64,000	200	350	750	1,200	—
1659	31,000	200	350	750	1,200	—
1660	Inc. above	200	350	750	1,200	—
1662	10,000	200	350	750	1,200	—
1663	—	500	1,000	2,000	3,000	—
1664	9,000	200	350	750	1,200	—
1665	Inc. above	350	525	875	1,450	—

KM# 77.2 SOUVERAIN OU LION D'OR
5.1600 g., 0.9880 Gold 0.1639 oz. AGW **Mint:** Brussels

Date	Mintage	VG	F	VF	XF	Unc
1648	5,631	200	350	750	1,200	—
1649	23,000	200	350	750	1,200	—
1650	49,000	200	350	750	1,200	—
1651	37,000	200	350	750	1,200	—
1652	110,000	200	350	750	1,200	—
1653	Inc. above	200	350	750	1,200	—
1654	Inc. above	200	350	750	1,200	—
1655	37,000	200	350	750	1,200	—
1656	33,000	200	350	750	1,200	—
1657	22,000	200	350	750	1,200	—
1658	42,000	200	350	750	1,200	—
1659	21,000	200	350	750	1,200	—
1661	23,000	200	350	750	1,200	—
1662	11,000	200	350	750	1,200	—
1663	Inc. above	200	350	750	1,200	—
1664	10,000	200	350	750	1,200	—
1665	Inc. above	200	350	750	1,200	—

KM# 80.1 SOUVERAIN OU LION D'OR
5.1600 g., 0.9880 Gold 0.1639 oz. AGW **Mint:** Antwerp

Date	Mintage	VG	F	VF	XF	Unc
1666	9,145	650	1,200	2,250	4,050	—
1684	1,005	800	1,500	3,000	5,600	—
1694	3,976	750	1,300	2,500	4,700	—

KM# 80.2 SOUVERAIN OU LION D'OR
5.1600 g., 0.9880 Gold 0.1639 oz. AGW **Note:** Mint mark: Angel face.

Date	Mintage	VG	F	VF	XF	Unc
1666	4,125	650	1,200	2,250	4,050	—
1667	Inc. above	650	1,200	2,250	4,050	—
1676	4,663	650	1,200	2,250	4,050	—
1681	4,631	650	1,200	2,250	4,050	—
1684	Inc. above	650	1,200	2,250	4,050	—
1686	1,793	800	1,500	2,500	4,700	—
1691	2,222	1,000	1,750	2,750	5,300	—

Note: Machine struck

KM# 43.2 COURONNE D'OR
3.3100 g., 0.9190 Gold 0.0978 oz. AGW **Mint:** Brussels **Note:** Mint mark: Angel face.

Date	Mintage	VG	F	VF	XF	Unc
1614	—	625	1,250	1,850	3,550	—
1616	2,261	625	1,250	1,850	3,550	—
ND	5,442	625	1,250	1,850	3,550	—

KM# 43.1 COURONNE D'OR
3.3100 g., 0.9190 Gold 0.0978 oz. AGW **Obv:** Cruciform crowned AE monograms in inner circle **Rev:** Crowned arms in inner circle, date at top **Mint:** Antwerp **Note:** Mint mark: Hand.

Date	Mintage	VG	F	VF	XF	Unc
1614	38,000	525	1,300	1,800	3,500	—
1616	Inc. above	525	1,300	1,800	3,500	—

KM# 43.3 COURONNE D'OR
3.3100 g., 0.9190 Gold 0.0978 oz. AGW **Mint:** s Hertogenbosch **Note:** Mint mark: Tree.

Date	Mintage	VG	F	VF	XF	Unc
1617 Rare	284	—	—	—	—	—

KM# A57.1 COURONNE D'OR
3.3100 g., 0.9190 Gold 0.0978 oz. AGW **Obv:** Floreated cross in inner circle; date in legend **Rev:** Crowned arms in inner circle **Mint:** Brussels **Note:** Mint mark: Angel face.

Date	Mintage	VG	F	VF	XF	Unc
1622	4,784	350	675	950	1,650	—
1623	11,000	350	675	950	1,650	—
1624	10,000	350	675	950	1,650	—
1625 Rare	3,308	—	—	—	—	—
1629	7,881	350	675	950	1,650	—
1630 Rare	25,000	—	—	—	—	—
1631	Inc. above	350	675	950	1,650	—
1632	14,000	350	675	950	1,650	—
1633	25,000	350	675	950	1,650	—
1635	1,155	350	675	950	1,650	—
1637	4,963	350	675	950	1,650	—
1639	13,000	350	675	950	1,650	—

KM# A57.2 COURONNE D'OR
3.3100 g., 0.9190 Gold 0.0978 oz. AGW **Mint:** Antwerp **Note:** Mint mark: Hand.

Date	Mintage	VG	F	VF	XF	Unc
1623	2,195	350	675	950	1,650	—
1624	3,375	350	675	950	1,650	—
1625	1,121	350	675	950	1,650	—
1627	2,370	350	675	950	1,650	—
1631	12,000	350	675	950	1,650	—
1634	1,979	350	675	950	1,650	—
1637	35,000	350	675	950	1,650	—
1638	11,000	350	675	950	1,650	—
1639	19,000	350	675	950	1,650	—

KM# 57.3 COURONNE D'OR
3.3100 g., 0.9190 Gold 0.0978 oz. AGW **Mint:** s Hertogenbosch **Note:** Mint mark: Tree.

Date	Mintage	VG	F	VF	XF	Unc
1623 Rare	1,056	—	—	—	—	—

KM# 90.1 DUCATON D'OR

0.9480 Gold **Obv:** Child's bust of Charles II right **Rev:** Lions supporting crowned shield of Charles II **Rev. Legend:** ...DVX BVRG BRAB Zc **Mint:** Antwerp

Date	Mintage	VG	F	VF	XF	Unc
1676 Rare	—	—	—	—	—	—

KM# 90.2 DUCATON D'OR

0.9480 Gold **Mint:** Brussels

Date	Mintage	VG	F	VF	XF	Unc
1676 Rare	—	—	—	—	—	—

KM# 109.2 DUCATON D'OR

0.9480 Gold **Mint:** Brabant

Date	Mintage	VG	F	VF	XF	Unc
1687 Rare	—	—	—	—	—	—
1689 Rare	—	—	—	—	—	—
1692 Rare	—	—	—	—	—	—
1694 Rare	—	—	—	—	—	—

KM# 109.1 DUCATON D'OR

0.9480 Gold **Obv:** Mature bust right **Rev. Legend:** ...DVX BVRG BRABAN Zc **Mint:** Antwerp

Date	Mintage	VG	F	VF	XF	Unc
1693 Rare	—	—	—	—	—	—
1698 Rare	—	—	—	—	—	—

KM# 76 DUCAT

3.5000 g., 0.9860 Gold 0.1109 oz. AGW **Mint:** Antwerp **Note:** Similar to 2 Ducat, KM#11. Mint mark: Hand.

Date	Mintage	VG	F	VF	XF	Unc
ND(1600-11)	500	2,500	3,750	6,000	9,000	—

KM# 11 2 DUCAT

7.0000 g., 0.9900 Gold 0.2228 oz. AGW **Obv:** Confronted busts of Albert and Isabella **Rev:** Crowned shield in collar of the Golden Fleece **Rev. Legend:** ...BRAB. Zc. **Mint:** Antwerp

Date	Mintage	VG	F	VF	XF	Unc
ND(1600-11)	250,000	250	500	900	1,650	—

KM# 16 4 DUCATS

20.9600 g., 0.9860 Gold 0.6644 oz. AGW **Note:** Similar to 2 Ducat, KM#13.

Date	Mintage	VG	F	VF	XF	Unc
ND(1600-11) Rare	—	—	—	—	—	—

KM# 12 6 DUCAT

21.0000 g., 0.9900 Gold 0.6684 oz. AGW **Mint:** Antwerp **Note:** Similar to 2 Ducat, KM#11.

Date	Mintage	VG	F	VF	XF	Unc
ND(1600-11) Rare	—	—	—	—	—	—

KM# 37 2/3 SOUVERAIN D'OR

7.7334 g., 0.9190 Gold 0.2285 oz. AGW **Obv:** Albert and Elizabeth walking right **Rev:** Crowned arms in collar of the Golden Fleece **Mint:** Brussels **Note:** Mint mark: Angel face.

Date	Mintage	VG	F	VF	XF	Unc
ND Rare	168	—	—	—	—	—

KM# 39.1 2 SOUVERAIN D'OR

11.0600 g., 0.9190 Gold 0.3268 oz. AGW **Mint:** Brussels **Note:** Mint mark: Angel face.

Date	Mintage	VG	F	VF	XF	Unc
ND	7,919	550	1,225	2,400	4,250	—
1612	993	575	1,250	2,500	4,500	—
1613	572	600	1,275	2,650	4,750	—
1614	—	575	1,250	2,500	4,500	—
1615	1,809	550	1,225	2,400	4,250	—
1616 Rare	342	—	—	—	—	—
1617 Rare	—	—	—	—	—	—
1618	2,393	550	1,225	2,400	4,250	—
1619	3,226	600	1,275	2,650	4,750	—
1620	Inc. above	550	1,225	2,400	4,250	—

KM# 39.3 2 SOUVERAIN D'OR

11.0600 g., 0.9190 Gold 0.3268 oz. AGW **Mint:** Maastricht **Note:** Mint mark: Star.

Date	Mintage	VG	F	VF	XF	Unc
1612 Rare	59	—	—	—	—	—
1613 Rare	Inc. above	—	—	—	—	—

KM# 39.2 2 SOUVERAIN D'OR

11.0600 g., 0.9190 Gold 0.3268 oz. AGW **Note:** Mint mark: Hand.

Date	Mintage	VG	F	VF	XF	Unc
ND	8,843	—	—	—	—	—
1614	1,640	575	1,250	2,500	5,000	—

KM# 64.1 2 SOUVERAIN D'OR

11.0600 g., 0.9190 Gold 0.3268 oz. AGW **Obv:** Philip IV in ruffled collar **Mint:** Brussels **Note:** Mint mark: Angel face.

Date	Mintage	VG	F	VF	XF	Unc
1626	930	600	1,500	2,750	5,000	—
1627	4,360	500	1,200	2,250	4,750	—
1629	4,987	500	1,200	2,250	4,750	—
1634	3,464	500	1,200	2,250	4,750	—
1635	4,003	500	1,200	2,250	4,750	—
1636	5,389	500	1,200	2,250	4,750	—

KM# 64.2 2 SOUVERAIN D'OR

11.0600 g., 0.9190 Gold 0.3268 oz. AGW **Mint:** Antwerp **Note:** Mint mark: Hand.

Date	Mintage	VG	F	VF	XF	Unc
1628	1,352	500	1,200	2,250	4,750	—
1636	25,000	500	1,200	2,250	4,750	—
1637	Inc. above	500	1,200	2,250	4,750	—

KM# 74.1 2 SOUVERAIN D'OR

11.0600 g., 0.9190 Gold 0.3268 oz. AGW **Obv:** Philip IV in flat collar **Mint:** Antwerp **Note:** Mint mark: Hand.

Date	Mintage	VG	F	VF	XF	Unc
1637	40,000	325	675	1,300	2,400	—
1638	33,000	325	675	1,300	2,400	—
1639	29,000	325	675	1,300	2,400	—
1640	42,000	325	675	1,300	2,400	—
1641	35,000	325	675	1,300	2,400	—
1642	82,000	325	675	1,300	2,400	—
1643	Inc. above	325	675	1,300	2,400	—
1644	Inc. above	325	675	1,300	2,400	—
1645	138,000	325	675	1,300	2,400	—
1646	Inc. above	325	675	1,300	2,400	—
1647	Inc. above	325	675	1,300	2,400	—

KM# 74.2 2 SOUVERAIN D'OR

11.0600 g., 0.9190 Gold 0.3268 oz. AGW **Mint:** Brussels **Note:** Mint mark: Angel face.

Date	Mintage	VG	F	VF	XF	Unc
1637	23,000	325	675	1,300	2,400	—
1638	20,000	325	675	1,300	2,400	—
1640	8,000	325	675	1,300	2,400	—
1641	39,000	325	675	1,300	2,400	—
1642	17,000	325	675	1,300	2,400	—
1643	47,000	325	675	1,300	2,400	—
1644	Inc. above	325	675	1,300	2,400	—
1645	14,000	325	675	1,300	2,400	—
1646	Inc. above	325	675	1,300	2,400	—
1647	Inc. above	325	675	1,300	2,400	—

KM# 82.2 2 SOUVERAIN D'OR

11.0600 g., 0.9190 Gold 0.3268 oz. AGW **Mint:** Brussels **Note:** Mint mark: Angel face.

Date	Mintage	VG	F	VF	XF	Unc
1667	2,076	1,000	2,000	3,500	6,000	—
1668	Inc. above	1,000	2,000	3,500	6,000	—
1671	3,374	1,000	2,000	3,500	6,000	—
1673	2,002	1,000	2,000	3,500	6,000	—
1686	3,098	1,000	2,000	3,500	6,000	—
1687	Inc. above	1,000	2,000	3,500	6,000	—

KM# 82.1 2 SOUVERAIN D'OR

11.0600 g., 0.9190 Gold 0.3268 oz. AGW **Obv:** Crowned child bust of Charles II right in inner circle, date below **Mint:** Antwerp **Note:** Mint mark: Hand.

Date	Mintage	VG	F	VF	XF	Unc
1667	1,836	1,000	2,000	3,500	6,000	—
1669	1,252	1,000	2,000	3,500	6,000	—
1671	1,623	1,000	2,000	3,500	6,000	—
1675	3,248	1,000	2,000	3,500	6,000	—
1681 Rare	394	—	—	—	—	—
1684 Rare	538	—	—	—	—	—
1694	11,000	1,000	2,000	3,500	6,000	—

KM# 101.1 2 SOUVERAIN D'OR

11.0600 g., 0.9190 Gold 0.3268 oz. AGW **Obv:** Large crowned bust of Charles II right, mint mark below **Rev:** Crowned arms in collar of the Golden Fleece, divided date at top **Mint:** Brussels **Note:** Mint mark: Angel face.

Date	Mintage	VG	F	VF	XF	Unc
1689	15,000	800	1,600	2,800	5,000	—
1690	Inc. above	800	1,600	2,800	5,000	—
1691	Inc. above	800	1,600	2,800	5,000	—
1692	7,096	800	1,600	2,800	5,000	—
1693	Inc. above	800	1,600	2,800	5,000	—
1694	Inc. above	800	1,600	2,800	5,000	—

KM# 101.2 2 SOUVERAIN D'OR

11.0600 g., 0.9190 Gold 0.3268 oz. AGW **Obv:** Crowned bust of Charles II right, mint mark below **Mint:** Antwerp **Note:** Mint mark: Hand.

Date	Mintage	VG	F	VF	XF	Unc
1697	—	800	1,600	2,800	5,000	—
1699	14,000	800	1,600	2,800	5,000	—
1700	5,711	800	1,600	2,800	5,000	—

KM# 70 4 SOUVERAIN D'OR

Gold **Note:** Similar to 2 Souverain d'Or, KM#64.1.

Date	Mintage	VG	F	VF	XF	Unc
1628 Rare	—	—	—	—	—	—
1636 Rare	—	—	—	—	—	—

KM# A76 4 SOUVERAIN D'OR

Gold **Note:** Similar to 2 Souverain d'Or, KM#64.2.

Date	Mintage	VG	F	VF	XF	Unc
1644 Rare	—	—	—	—	—	—

KM# 90 4 SOUVERAIN D'OR

Gold **Note:** Similar to 2 Souverain d'Or, KM#101.2.

Date	Mintage	VG	F	VF	XF	Unc
1697	—	—	—	—	—	—

Note: Reported, not confirmed

KM# 45 6 SOUVERAIN D'OR

Gold

Date	Mintage	VG	F	VF	XF	Unc
1616 Rare	—	—	—	—	—	—

KM# 117.1 8 SOUVERAIN D'OR

14.0500 g., 0.8750 Silver 0.3952 oz. ASW **Obv:** Bust right **Obv. Legend:** CAROL•II•D•G•HISP•ET•INDIAR•REX **Rev:** Crowned supported arms **Rev. Legend:** ...ARCHID • AVST. - DVX • BURG - BRABANT **Mint:** Brussels **Note:** Mint mark: Angel face. Fr.#114.

Date	Mintage	VG	F	VF	XF	Unc
1687 Rare	—	—	—	—	—	—
1689 Rare	—	—	—	—	—	—
1692 Rare	—	—	—	—	—	—
1694 Rare	—	—	—	—	—	—

KM# 117.2 8 SOUVERAIN D'OR

44.3600 g., Gold **Ruler:** Charles II **Obv:** Bust right **Obv. Legend:** CAROL • II • D • G • HISP • ET • INDIAR • REX **Rev:** Crowned supported arms **Rev. Legend:** ARCHID • AVST • DVX • BURG BRABANT **Mint:** Antwerp **Note:** Fr. #115.

Date	Mintage	VG	F	VF	XF	Unc
1693 Rare	—	—	—	—	—	—
Note: Bowers and Marena Guia sale 3-88 AU realized $17,600.						
1698 Rare	—	—	—	—	—	—

PIEFORTS

KM#	Date	Mintage	Identification	Mkt Val
P1	1624	—	1/2 Ducaton. KM#60.2.	—
P2	1631	—	1/2 Ducaton. KM#60.2.	—
P3	1637	—	1/2 Ducaton. KM#60.2.	—
P4	1643	—	1/2 Ducaton. KM#73.1.	—
P5	1648	—	1/2 Ducaton. KM#73.1.	—
P6	1657	—	1/2 Ducaton. KM#73.1. 48.72g.	—

FLANDERS

A coastal county of modern Belgium first mentioned in 862 which by the Renaissance had become the industrial and commercial center of northern Europe. It was the target of dynastic maneuvering between Burgundy, Spain and France.

RULERS

Albert and Elizabeth, 1598-1621
Philip IV, 1621-1665
Charles II, 1665-1700

MINT MARK

Lis - Bruges (Flanders)

COUNTY

STANDARD COINAGE

KM# 7 DENIER (4 Mites)

Copper **Obv:** Crowned AE monogram **Rev:** Crowned shield of Austria and Burgundy on St. Andrew's cross

Date	Mintage	VG	F	VF	XF	Unc
1607	—	16.00	32.00	60.00	100	—
1608	—	16.00	32.00	60.00	100	—
1609	—	16.00	32.00	60.00	100	—
1610	—	16.00	32.00	60.00	100	—
1615	—	14.00	28.00	50.00	85.00	—
1616	—	14.00	28.00	50.00	85.00	—

KM# 38 GIGOT (6 Mites)

Copper **Obv:** St. Andrew's cross, crown above, fleece below **Rev:** Crowned shield of Philip IV **Rev. Legend:** ...DVX BVR(G) ET CO FL(AN) Z

Date	Mintage	VG	F	VF	XF	Unc
1625	—	28.00	55.00	100	175	—
1626	—	32.00	65.00	120	200	—
1627	—	32.00	65.00	120	200	—
1645	—	40.00	80.00	150	250	—
1655	—	32.00	65.00	120	200	—

KM# 101 GIGOT (6 Mites)

Copper **Rev:** Crowned shield of Austria and Burgundy, small lion in center **Rev. Legend:** ...DVX BVRG C(O) FLAN Z

Date	Mintage	VG	F	VF	XF	Unc
1700	—	10.00	16.00	30.00	55.00	—

KM# 6 2 DENIER (8 Mites)

Copper **Obv:** Crowned AE monogram **Rev:** Crowned shield of Austria and Burgundy on St. Andrew's cross **Rev. Legend:** ...BVRG Z CO(M) F(LA)

Date	Mintage	VG	F	VF	XF	Unc
1606	—	10.00	15.00	25.00	45.00	—
1607	—	10.00	15.00	20.00	35.00	—
1608	—	10.00	20.00	40.00	65.00	—
1609	—	10.00	20.00	40.00	65.00	—
1610	—	10.00	15.00	30.00	50.00	—
1615	—	10.00	15.00	20.00	35.00	—
1616	—	10.00	15.00	20.00	30.00	—

KM# 36 LIARD (12 Mites)

Copper **Obv:** Crown and shields of Austria, Burgundy, and Flanders **Rev. Legend:** ...BVRG ET CO FL(AN) Z (variations exist)

Date	Mintage	VG	F	VF	XF	Unc
1623	—	10.00	15.00	28.00	45.00	—
1633	—	10.00	20.00	40.00	65.00	—
1643	—	10.00	15.00	20.00	35.00	—
1644	—	10.00	15.00	20.00	35.00	—
1645	—	10.00	15.00	20.00	35.00	—
1650	—	10.00	15.00	30.00	50.00	—
1653	—	10.00	15.00	20.00	35.00	—
1654	—	10.00	15.00	20.00	35.00	—
1655	—	10.00	15.00	20.00	35.00	—
1656	—	10.00	15.00	20.00	35.00	—
1657	—	10.00	15.00	20.00	35.00	—
1658	—	10.00	15.00	20.00	35.00	—
1659	—	10.00	15.00	20.00	35.00	—

KM# 81.1 LIARD (12 Mites)

Copper **Rev. Legend:** ...DVX BVRG C(O) FLAN Z

Date	Mintage	VG	F	VF	XF	Unc
1680	—	10.00	15.00	25.00	35.00	—
1681	—	10.00	20.00	40.00	65.00	—
1685	—	10.00	15.00	25.00	35.00	—
1686	—	10.00	15.00	25.00	35.00	—

KM# 81.2 LIARD (12 Mites)

Copper **Rev. Legend:** ...DVX BVRG C(O) FL(AN Z)

Date	Mintage	VG	F	VF	XF	Unc
1691	—	10.00	15.00	20.00	30.00	—
1692	—	10.00	15.00	20.00	30.00	—
1693	—	10.00	15.00	20.00	30.00	—
1694	—	10.00	15.00	20.00	30.00	—
1695	—	10.00	15.00	20.00	30.00	—
1696	—	10.00	15.00	28.00	45.00	—
1698	—	10.00	15.00	20.00	30.00	—
1699	—	10.00	15.00	20.00	30.00	—
1700	—	10.00	15.00	20.00	30.00	—

KM# 19 1/2 PATARD (1/2 Sol)

Billon **Obv:** Cross floree, AE monogram at center **Rev:** Crowned shield of Albert and Elizabeth **Rev. Legend:** ...BVRG CO FL(A) Z

Date	Mintage	VG	F	VF	XF	Unc
1615	—	30.00	60.00	110	200	—

KM# 17 PATARD

Billon **Obv:** Cross floree, AE monogram at center **Rev:** Crowned shield of Albert and Elizabeth divides dates **Rev. Legend:** ...BVRG CO F(L) Z

Date	Mintage	VG	F	VF	XF	Unc
1614	—	12.50	25.00	50.00	85.00	—
1615	—	12.50	25.00	50.00	85.00	—
1616	—	15.00	30.00	60.00	100	—
ND	—	15.00	30.00	60.00	100	—

KM# 47.1 PATARD

Billon **Obv:** Linear cross **Rev:** Crowned shield of Philip IV divides date **Rev. Legend:** ...HISP. INDIAR Z

Date	Mintage	VG	F	VF	XF	Unc
1633	—	70.00	135	250	400	—

KM# 47.2 PATARD

Billon **Rev. Legend:** ...HIS. INDIA Z

Date	Mintage	VG	F	VF	XF	Unc
1644	—	80.00	150	270	450	—

KM# 75 PATARD

Billon **Obv:** Long cross, mint mark in center **Rev:** Crowned shield divides date **Rev. Legend:** ...DVX BVRG CO FL(AN) Zc

Date	Mintage	VG	F	VF	XF	Unc
1679	—	18.00	35.00	70.00	125	—
1680	—	28.00	55.00	100	175	—

KM# 5 1/4 REAL

1.7400 g., 0.3960 Silver 0.0222 oz. ASW **Obv:** Crowned shield of Albert and Elizabeth in fleece collar **Rev:** Crowned shield divides date **Rev. Legend:** ...BVRG COM FL(A)

Date	Mintage	VG	F	VF	XF	Unc
1603	—	225	400	650	1,000	—
1604	—	120	225	425	700	—
1605	—	165	300	500	800	—
1606	—	275	500	1,000	1,650	—
1611 Rare	—	—	—	—	—	—

KM# 9 1/2 REAL

3.4800 g., 0.3960 Silver 0.0443 oz. ASW **Obv:** Crowned shield on St. Anthony's cross divides date **Rev:** Crowned shield with fleece below **Rev. Legend:** ...BVRG Z COM FLA

Date	Mintage	VG	F	VF	XF	Unc
1609	—	325	675	1,250	2,000	—
1610	—	450	900	1,600	2,500	—
ND	—	265	525	950	1,500	—

KM# 1 STOTER (1/8 Florin)

3.4200 g., 0.4170 Silver 0.0458 oz. ASW **Obv:** Crowned shield in fleece collar **Rev:** Cross floree, lion and crown in angles

Date	Mintage	VG	F	VF	XF	Unc
1601	—	225	400	650	1,000	—

KM# 21 3 PATARDS

2.6300 g., 0.5820 Silver 0.0492 oz. ASW **Obv:** Cross floree, lion at center **Rev:** Crowned shield in octolobe **Rev. Legend:** ...BVRG Z CO FL

Date	Mintage	VG	F	VF	XF	Unc
1616	—	15.00	25.00	40.00	60.00	—
1617	—	15.00	25.00	45.00	75.00	—
1620	—	15.00	25.00	40.00	60.00	—

KM# 94 4 PATARDS

4.9000 g., 0.3850 Silver 0.0606 oz. ASW **Obv:** St. Andrew's cross, crown above, fleece below, divides date **Rev:** Crowned shield **Rev. Legend:** ...DVX BVRG C FLAND Z

Date	Mintage	VG	F	VF	XF	Unc
1698	—	25.00	45.00	80.00	135	—
1700	—	35.00	65.00	120	200	—

KM# 23 ESCALIN

5.2600 g., 0.5820 Silver 0.0984 oz. ASW **Obv:** Eagle with shield of Austria, Burgundy on breast **Rev:** Crowned shield of Albert and Elizabeth on St. Andrew's cross **Rev. Legend:** ...BVRG Z CO FL(A) (Z)

Date	Mintage	VG	F	VF	XF	Unc
1619	—	50.00	100	185	300	—
1620	—	15.00	25.00	40.00	65.00	—
1621	—	15.00	25.00	40.00	65.00	—
ND	—	15.00	25.00	40.00	65.00	—

KM# 31 ESCALIN

5.2600 g., 0.5820 Silver 0.0984 oz. ASW **Obv:** Lion rampant left with sword and shield **Rev:** Crowned shield of Philip IV on St. Andrew's cross **Rev. Legend:** ...DVX BVR CO FL(A) Zc

Date	Mintage	VG	F	VF	XF	Unc
1621	—	50.00	100	185	300	—
1622	—	15.00	25.00	40.00	65.00	—
1623	—	15.00	25.00	40.00	65.00	—
1624	—	35.00	75.00	150	250	—
1625	—	15.00	30.00	60.00	100	—
1628	—	50.00	100	185	300	—
1633	—	70.00	140	275	450	—
1646	—	40.00	85.00	165	275	—
1658	—	135	250	425	650	—

KM# 95 ESCALIN

5.2600 g., 0.5820 Silver 0.0984 oz. ASW **Obv:** Lion rampant left with sword, paw on globe **Rev:** Crowned shield on St. Andrew's cross of Charles II **Rev. Legend:** ...DVX BVRG C FLAN (D) Z

Date	Mintage	VG	F	VF	XF	Unc
1698	—	28.00	55.00	100	175	—

KM# 102 ESCALIN

5.2600 g., 0.5820 Silver 0.0984 oz. ASW **Rev. Legend:** ...DVX BVRG C FLAN Z

Date	Mintage	VG	F	VF	XF	Unc
1700	—	135	250	425	650	—

KM# 15 1/4 PATAGON

7.0300 g., 0.8750 Silver 0.1978 oz. ASW **Obv:** St. Andrew's cross, crown above, fleece below divides pair of crowned triple C monograms **Rev:** Crowned shield in fleece collar **Rev. Legend:** ...BVRG ET CO(M) FL(A) Z

Date	Mintage	VG	F	VF	XF	Unc
ND(1598-1621)	—	20.00	35.00	60.00	100	—
1612	—	150	300	550	950	—
1620	—	125	250	500	850	—

KM# 37 1/4 PATAGON

7.0300 g., 0.8750 Silver 0.1978 oz. ASW **Obv:** St. Andrew's cross, crown above, fleece below divides date **Rev:** Crowned shield of Philip IV in fleece collar **Rev. Legend:** ...DVX BVRG ET CO FL(AN) Z

Date	Mintage	VG	F	VF	XF	Unc
1624	—	32.00	65.00	120	200	—
1625	—	80.00	165	300	500	—
1628	—	100	200	350	600	—
1629	—	135	265	475	800	—
1631	—	32.00	65.00	120	200	—
1632	—	40.00	80.00	150	250	—
1638	—	110	220	400	650	—
1640	—	65.00	135	250	400	—
1644	—	80.00	165	300	500	—
1654	—	50.00	100	180	300	—
1655	—	50.00	100	180	300	—
1657	—	80.00	165	300	500	—
1660	—	55.00	110	200	350	—
1663	—	100	200	350	600	—

KM# 8 3 REAL (15 Sols)

9.1900 g., 0.8960 Silver 0.2647 oz. ASW **Obv:** Busts of Albert and Elizabeth conjoined left **Rev:** Crowned arms with fleece below covers St. Andrew's cross and divides date **Rev. Legend:** ...DVCES BVRG ET COM FLAN

Date	Mintage	VG	F	VF	XF	Unc
1607	—	1,000	2,000	3,500	6,000	—
1608	—	1,000	2,000	3,500	6,000	—

KM# 3 FLORIN

13.8700 g., 0.8330 Silver 0.3714 oz. ASW **Obv:** Busts of Albert and Elizabeth confronted **Rev:** Crowned shield within fleece collar

Date	Mintage	VG	F	VF	XF	Unc
1602 Rare	—	—	—	—	—	—

KM# 30 1/2 PATAGON (24 Sols)

14.0500 g., 0.8750 Silver 0.3952 oz. ASW **Obv:** St. Andrew's cross, crown above, fleece below, divides pair of crowned triple C monograms **Rev:** Crowned shield in fleece collar **Rev. Legend:** ...BVRG ET CO FL Z

Date	Mintage	VG	F	VF	XF	Unc
1620 Rare	—	—	—	—	—	—
ND Rare	—	—	—	—	—	—

KM# 33 1/2 PATAGON (24 Sols)

14.0500 g., 0.8750 Silver 0.3952 oz. ASW **Obv:** St. Andrew's cross, crown above, fleece below, divides date **Rev:** Crowned shield of Philip IV in fleece collar **Rev. Legend:** ...DVX BVRG ET CO FL(AN) Zc

Date	Mintage	VG	F	VF	XF	Unc
1622	—	100	200	350	600	—
1623	—	100	200	350	600	—
1631	—	55.00	110	200	350	—
1633	—	40.00	80.00	150	250	—
1635	—	65.00	135	250	400	—
1641	—	100	200	350	600	—
1646	—	75.00	150	275	450	—
1647	—	65.00	135	250	400	—
1648	—	45.00	90.00	165	275	—
1649	—	100	200	350	600	—
1652	—	50.00	100	180	300	—
1653	—	65.00	135	250	400	—
1655	—	65.00	135	250	400	—
1657	—	110	220	400	650	—
1658	—	150	300	575	950	—
1660	—	135	265	475	800	—
1662	—	100	200	350	600	—
1663	—	100	200	350	600	—
1664	—	110	220	400	650	—
1665	—	50.00	100	180	300	—

KM# 66 1/2 PATAGON (24 Sols)

14.0500 g., 0.8750 Silver 0.3952 oz. ASW **Obv:** St. Andrew's cross, crown above, fleece below, divides date **Rev:** Crowned shield of Charles II in fleece collar **Rev. Legend:** ...DVX BVRG C FLAN(D) Z

Date	Mintage	VG	F	VF	XF	Unc
1667	—	85.00	165	300	500	—
1669	—	110	220	400	650	—
1672	—	85.00	165	300	500	—
1673	—	65.00	135	250	400	—
1674	—	110	220	400	650	—
1675	—	85.00	165	300	500	—
1680	—	85.00	165	300	500	—
1686	—	85.00	165	300	500	—
1687	—	100	200	350	600	—
1689	—	85.00	165	300	500	—

KM# 90 1/2 PATAGON (24 Sols)

14.0500 g., 0.8750 Silver 0.3952 oz. ASW **Ruler:** Charles II **Obv:** St. Andrew's cross, crown above, fleece below, divides pair of crowned double C monograms **Rev. Legend:** ...DVX BVRG C FLAN(D) Zc

Date	Mintage	VG	F	VF	XF	Unc
1694 Rare	—	—	—	—	—	—
1695 Rare	—	—	—	—	—	—
1696 Rare	—	—	—	—	—	—
1699 Rare	—	—	—	—	—	—
1700	—	80.00	175	275	400	—

KM# 45 1/2 DUCATON

16.2400 g., 0.9440 Silver 0.4929 oz. ASW **Obv:** Bust of Philip IV right in ruffled collar **Rev:** Crowned shield supported by lions **Rev. Legend:** ...DVX BVRG CO FLAN Zc

Date	Mintage	VG	F	VF	XF	Unc
1632	—	150	285	475	750	—
1633	—	200	375	600	950	—
1636	—	185	325	550	850	—

KM# 49 1/2 DUCATON

16.2400 g., 0.9440 Silver 0.4929 oz. ASW **Obv:** Bust of Philip IV right in thin collar, date divided by mint mark in exergue **Rev:** Lion with swords behind crowned shield **Rev. Legend:** ...DVX BVRG CO FLAN Zc

Date	Mintage	VG	F	VF	XF	Unc
1637	—	200	375	600	950	—
1639	—	220	400	650	1,000	—
1644	—	220	400	650	1,000	—
1652	—	90.00	160	265	400	—
1654	—	110	200	325	500	—
1660	—	185	325	550	850	—
1662	—	125	225	400	600	—

KM# 67 1/2 DUCATON

16.2400 g., 0.9440 Silver 0.4929 oz. ASW **Obv:** Child's bust of Charles II right **Rev:** Crowned shield supported by lions **Rev. Legend:** ...DVX BVRG CO FLAN Zc

Date	Mintage	VG	F	VF	XF	Unc
1668	—	85.00	165	300	500	—
1670	—	70.00	140	250	425	—
1673	—	60.00	120	220	375	—

KM# 83 1/2 DUCATON

16.2400 g., 0.9440 Silver 0.4929 oz. ASW **Obv:** Youthful bust of Charles II with long hair and court robe **Rev. Legend:** ...DVX BVRG CO FLAN Zc

Date	Mintage	VG	F	VF	XF	Unc
1687 Rare	—	—	—	—	—	—

KM# 22 PATAGON

28.1000 g., 0.8750 Silver 0.7905 oz. ASW **Obv:** St. Andrew's cross, crown above, fleece below, divides pair of crowned CCAV monograms **Rev:** Crowned shield in fleece collar **Rev. Legend:** ...BVRG ET CO FLA (Z) **Note:** Legend varieties exist. Dav. #4435.

Date	Mintage	VG	F	VF	XF	Unc
1616	—	45.00	90.00	165	300	—
1617	—	35.00	65.00	125	275	—
1618	—	35.00	65.00	125	275	—
1619	—	40.00	75.00	135	275	—
1620	—	35.00	65.00	125	275	—
1621	—	45.00	85.00	150	275	—
ND	—	30.00	60.00	125	275	—

KM# 34 PATAGON

28.1000 g., 0.8750 Silver 0.7905 oz. ASW **Obv:** St. Andrew's cross, crown above, fleece below, divides date **Rev:** Crowned shield of Philip IV in fleece collar **Rev. Legend:** ...DVX BVRG ET CO FL(AN) Zc **Note:** Dav. #4464.

Date	Mintage	VG	F	VF	XF	Unc
1622	—	45.00	90.00	165	300	—
1623	—	65.00	125	225	400	—
1626	—	150	300	575	975	—
1628	—	175	325	600	1,000	—
1631	—	50.00	100	180	325	—
1632	—	65.00	125	225	400	—
1633	—	40.00	75.00	135	275	—
1636	—	50.00	100	180	325	—
1638	—	75.00	150	275	475	—
1639	—	90.00	175	325	575	—
1640	—	110	220	400	675	—
1641	—	125	250	450	775	—
1642	—	75.00	150	275	475	—
1644	—	100	200	350	625	—
1645	—	50.00	100	180	325	—

Date	Mintage	VG	F	VF	XF	Unc
1646	—	50.00	100	180	325	—
1647	—	65.00	135	250	425	—
1648	—	65.00	135	250	425	—
1649	—	40.00	75.00	135	275	—
1650	—	65.00	135	350	425	—
1651	—	45.00	85.00	150	275	—
1652	—	40.00	75.00	135	275	—
1653	—	65.00	125	225	400	—
1654	—	50.00	100	180	325	—
1655	—	65.00	135	250	425	—
1656	—	80.00	155	285	500	—
1657	—	55.00	110	200	350	—
1658	—	65.00	135	250	425	—
1659	—	110	220	400	675	—
1660	—	80.00	155	285	500	—
1661	—	85.00	165	300	525	—
1663	—	85.00	165	300	525	—
1664	—	110	220	400	675	—
1665	—	80.00	155	285	500	—

KM# 63 PATAGON

28.1000 g., 0.8750 Silver 0.7905 oz. ASW **Obv:** St. Andrew's cross, crown above, fleece below, divides date **Rev:** Crowned shield of Charles II in fleece collar **Rev. Legend:** ...DVX BVRG CO FLAN Zc **Note:** Dav. #4494.

Date	Mintage	VG	F	VF	XF	Unc
1666	—	45.00	85.00	150	275	—
1667	—	55.00	110	200	350	—
1668	—	45.00	85.00	150	275	—
1669	—	45.00	85.00	150	275	—
1670	—	55.00	110	200	350	—
1671	—	55.00	110	200	350	—
1672	—	32.00	65.00	125	250	—
1673	—	50.00	100	180	325	—
1674	—	50.00	100	180	325	—
1675	—	55.00	110	200	350	—
1676	—	55.00	110	200	350	—
1677	—	55.00	110	200	350	—
1678	—	32.00	65.00	125	250	—
1679	—	45.00	85.00	150	275	—
1680	—	45.00	85.00	150	275	—
1683	—	85.00	165	300	525	—
1684	—	70.00	135	250	425	—
1685	—	45.00	85.00	150	275	—
1686	—	50.00	100	180	325	—
1687	—	45.00	85.00	150	275	—
1688	—	70.00	135	250	425	—
1689	—	55.00	110	200	350	—
1690	—	55.00	110	200	350	—
1691	—	100	200	350	625	—
1692	—	70.00	135	250	425	—

KM# 91 PATAGON

28.1000 g., 0.8750 Silver 0.7905 oz. ASW **Obv:** St. Andrew's cross, crown above, fleece below, divides pair of crowned double C monograms **Rev:** Crowned shield of Charles II in fleece collar **Rev. Legend:** ...DVX BVRG C FLAND Z **Note:** Dav. #4500.

Date	Mintage	VG	F	VF	XF	Unc
1694	—	200	400	650	1,000	—
1699	—	275	550	950	1,450	—
1700	—	250	475	800	1,250	—

KM# 35 DUCATON

32.4800 g., 0.9440 Silver 0.9857 oz. ASW **Obv:** Bust of Philip IV in ruffled collar, mint mark divides date in legend **Rev:** Lions supporting crowned shield **Rev. Legend:** ...DVX BVRG ET CO FL(AN) Zc **Note:** Dav. #4446.

Date	Mintage	VG	F	VF	XF	Unc
1622 Rare	—	—	—	—	—	—
1631	—	175	350	600	1,100	—
1632	—	175	350	600	1,100	—
1633	—	120	225	400	750	—
1634	—	120	225	400	750	—
1635	—	150	265	475	900	—
1636	—	175	350	600	1,100	—

KM# 50 DUCATON

32.4800 g., 0.9440 Silver 0.9857 oz. ASW **Obv:** Bust of Philip IV in thin collar **Rev:** Lions supporting crowned shield **Rev. Legend:** ...DVX BVRG ET CO FL(AN) Zc **Note:** Dav. #4457.

Date	Mintage	VG	F	VF	XF	Unc
1636	—	80.00	165	325	550	—
1637	—	100	210	400	650	—
1638	—	90.00	190	350	600	—
1639	—	115	240	450	750	—
1641	—	75.00	155	300	500	—
1642	—	80.00	165	325	550	—
1644	—	80.00	165	325	550	—
1648	—	80.00	165	325	550	—
1649	—	90.00	190	350	600	—
1650	—	55.00	125	250	400	—
1651	—	65.00	140	275	450	—
1652	—	55.00	125	250	400	—
1653	—	75.00	155	300	500	—
1654	—	55.00	125	250	400	—
1655	—	55.00	125	250	400	—
1656	—	75.00	155	300	500	—
1657	—	55.00	125	250	400	—
1658	—	75.00	155	300	500	—
1659	—	75.00	155	300	500	—
1660	—	75.00	155	300	500	—
1662	—	75.00	155	300	500	—
1664	—	55.00	125	250	400	—
1665	—	55.00	125	250	400	—

KM# 64 DUCATON

32.4800 g., 0.9440 Silver 0.9857 oz. ASW **Obv:** Child's bust of Charles II right **Rev:** Crowned shield supported by lions **Rev. Legend:** ...DVX BVRG CO FLAN Zc **Note:** Dav. #4479.

Date	Mintage	VG	F	VF	XF	Unc
1666	—	85.00	175	325	500	—
1667	—	85.00	175	325	500	—
1668	—	85.00	175	325	500	—
1669	—	95.00	190	350	550	—
1670	—	60.00	125	250	425	—
1672	—	60.00	125	250	425	—
1673	—	60.00	125	250	425	—
1676	—	120	245	450	700	—

KM# 82 DUCATON

32.4800 g., 0.9440 Silver 0.9857 oz. ASW **Obv:** Youthfull bust of Charles II with long hair and large cravat **Rev. Legend:** ...DVX BVRG CO FLAN Z **Note:** Dav. #4482.

Date	Mintage	VG	F	VF	XF	Unc
1684 Rare	—	—	—	—	—	—
1687 Rare	—	—	—	—	—	—
1689 Rare	—	—	—	—	—	—

KM# 84 DUCATON

32.4800 g., 0.9440 Silver 0.9857 oz. ASW **Obv:** Mature bust of Charles II right **Rev. Legend:** ...DVX BVRG C FLAND Zc **Note:** Dav. #4488.

Date	Mintage	VG	F	VF	XF	Unc
1694 Rare	—	—	—	—	—	—

KM# 46 2 DUCATON

Silver **Note:** Similar to 1 Ducaton, KM#50.

Date	Mintage	VG	F	VF	XF	Unc
1632	—	550	1,000	1,750	2,750	—
1634	—	550	1,000	1,750	2,750	—
1639	—	450	800	1,750	2,750	—
1645	—	450	800	1,750	2,750	—
1650	—	450	800	1,750	2,750	—
1652	—	450	800	1,750	2,750	—
1654	—	450	800	1,750	2,750	—
1664	—	450	800	1,750	2,750	—

KM# A84 2 DUCATON

64.9800 g., 0.9440 Silver 1.9721 oz. ASW **Ruler:** Charles II **Obv:** Mature bust of Charles II right **Rev. Legend:** ...DVX BVRG C FLAND Zc **Note:** Dav. #4487.

Date	Mintage	VG	F	VF	XF	Unc
1694	—	—	—	2,250	3,750	5,500

KM# 62 3 DUCATON

Silver **Note:** Similar to 1 Ducaton, KM#50.

Date	Mintage	VG	F	VF	XF	Unc
1665 Rare	—	—	—	—	—	—

KM# 61 4 DUCATON

Silver **Note:** Similar to 1 Ducaton, KM#50.

Date	Mintage	VG	F	VF	XF	Unc
1662 Rare	—	—	—	—	—	—

KM# 4 ALBERTIN (Corona)

2.9200 g., 0.7920 Gold 0.0743 oz. AGW **Obv:** Crowned arms in collar of the Golden Fleece **Rev:** Crowned floral St. Andrew's cross, date at sides, Golden Fleece at bottom

Date	Mintage	VG	F	VF	XF	Unc
1602	19,000	225	450	750	1,300	—

KM# 39 COURONNE D'OR

3.4100 g., 0.8820 Gold 0.0967 oz. AGW **Obv:** Cross of four crowned monograms, lions and crowns in angles **Rev:** Crowned shield of Albert and Isabella divides pair of crowned monograms **Rev. Legend:** ...BVRG CO FL Z

Date	Mintage	VG	F	VF	XF	Unc
1615	9,203	450	900	1,750	3,000	—
1620	3,519	450	900	1,750	3,000	—

KM# 40 COURONNE D'OR

3.4100 g., 0.8820 Gold 0.0967 oz. AGW **Obv:** Cross floree **Rev:** Crowned shield of Philip IV divides pair of crowned monograms **Rev. Legend:** ...DVX BVRG CO FL Zc

Date	Mintage	VG	F	VF	XF	Unc
1627	834	500	1,000	2,000	3,000	—
1628	Inc. above	500	1,000	2,000	3,000	—
1631	13,000	300	625	1,250	2,000	—
1632	Inc. above	300	625	1,250	2,000	—
1640	15,000	300	625	1,250	2,000	—
1642	Inc. above	300	625	1,250	2,000	—

KM# 2.1 2 ALBERTINS

5.1500 g., 0.8950 Gold 0.1482 oz. AGW **Obv:** Crowned arms in collar of the Golden Fleece **Rev:** Crowned floral St. Andrew's cross, date at sides, Golden Fleece at bottom

Date	Mintage	VG	F	VF	XF	Unc
1601	21,000	250	500	1,000	1,600	—
1602	Inc. above	250	500	1,000	1,600	—
1603	Inc. above	250	500	1,000	1,600	—
1607	3,496	250	500	1,000	1,600	—

KM# 2.2 2 ALBERTINS

5.1500 g., 0.8950 Gold 0.1482 oz. AGW **Rev. Legend:** ...COM FLAN

Date	Mintage	VG	F	VF	XF	Unc
1601	—	250	500	1,000	1,600	—

KM# 32 SOUVERAIN D'OR (Lion d'Or)

5.5400 g., 0.9470 Gold 0.1687 oz. AGW **Obv:** Crowned lion with sword and shield left **Rev:** Crowned shield of Philip IV in fleece collar **Rev. Legend:** ...BVRG. CO. FLAN. Z.

Date	Mintage	VG	F	VF	XF	Unc
1621 Rare	—	—	—	—	—	—
1625	—	185	300	600	1,200	—
1644	12,000	185	300	600	1,200	—
1648	48,000	185	300	600	1,200	—
1649	Inc. above	185	300	600	1,200	—
1650	Inc. above	185	300	600	1,200	—
1651	—	185	300	600	1,200	—
1652	—	185	300	600	1,200	—
1653	17,000	185	300	600	1,200	—
1654	Inc. above	185	300	600	1,200	—
1655	14,000	185	300	600	1,200	—
1656	27,000	185	300	600	1,200	—
1657	Inc. above	185	300	600	1,200	—
1658	Inc. above	185	300	600	1,200	—
1660	22,000	185	300	600	1,200	—
1662	7,000	185	300	600	1,200	—
1663	Inc. above	185	300	600	1,200	—
1664	5,000	185	300	600	1,200	—

KM# 65 SOUVERAIN D'OR (Lion d'Or)

5.5400 g., 0.9470 Gold 0.1687 oz. AGW **Obv:** Crowned lion with sword, paw on globe set on pedestal, date in exergue **Rev:** Crowned shield of Charles II in fleece collar **Rev. Legend:** ...DVX BVRG CO FL(AN) Z

Date	Mintage	VG	F	VF	XF	Unc
1666	3,014	600	1,200	2,000	3,000	—
1668	2,940	600	1,200	2,000	3,000	—
1669	2,676	600	1,200	2,000	3,000	—
1672	2,513	600	1,200	2,000	3,000	—
1673	Inc. above	600	1,200	2,000	3,000	—
1674	1,067	600	1,200	2,000	3,000	—
1675	3,148	600	1,200	2,000	3,000	—
1685	2,663	600	1,200	2,000	3,000	—

KM# 103 SOUVERAIN D'OR (Lion d'Or)

5.5400 g., 0.9470 Gold 0.1687 oz. AGW, 25 mm. **Rev. Legend:** ...DVX BVRG C FLAN (D) Zc **Note:** Machine struck.

Date	Mintage	VG	F	VF	XF	Unc
1700	1,938	600	1,500	2,500	4,000	—

KM# 16 2 SOUVERAIN D'OR

11.0800 g., 0.9470 Gold 0.3373 oz. AGW **Obv:** Albert and Elizabeth, seated facing on thrones, date in exergue **Rev:** Crowned shield in fleece collar **Rev. Legend:** ...ET COM(IT) FLA(Z)

Date	Mintage	VG	F	VF	XF	Unc
ND	—	500	1,125	2,150	4,000	—
1612	3,059	575	1,200	2,400	4,400	—
1613	Inc. above	500	1,125	2,150	4,000	—
1614	6,090	550	1,175	2,300	4,150	—
1615	Inc. above	500	1,125	2,150	4,000	—
1616	5,730	500	1,125	2,150	4,000	—
1617	Inc. above	575	1,200	2,400	4,400	—
1618	Inc. above	550	1,175	2,300	4,150	—
1620 Rare	176	—	—	—	—	—

KM# 48 2 SOUVERAIN D'OR

11.0800 g., 0.9470 Gold 0.3373 oz. AGW **Obv:** Crowned bust of Philip IV in ruffled collar right **Rev:** Crowned shield in fleece collar **Rev. Legend:** ...DVX BVRG ET CO FL(AN) Zc

Date	Mintage	VG	F	VF	XF	Unc
1634 Rare	9,035	—	—	—	—	—
1635 Rare	Inc. above	—	—	—	—	—
1636	Inc. above	1,000	2,000	4,500	6,500	—

KM# 51 2 SOUVERAIN D'OR

11.0800 g., 0.9470 Gold 0.3373 oz. AGW **Obv:** Older bust of Philip IV in flat collar

Date	Mintage	VG	F	VF	XF	Unc
1638	19,000	350	750	1,800	3,000	—
1639	Inc. above	350	750	1,800	3,000	—
1640	Inc. above	350	750	1,800	3,000	—
1642	36,000	350	750	1,800	3,000	—
1643	Inc. above	350	750	1,800	3,000	—
1644	Inc. above	350	750	1,800	3,000	—
1645	Inc. above	350	750	1,800	3,000	—
1646	41,000	350	750	1,800	3,000	—
1647	Inc. above	350	750	1,800	3,000	—

KM# 68 2 SOUVERAIN D'OR

11.0800 g., 0.9470 Gold 0.3373 oz. AGW **Obv:** Child's bust of Charles II crowned, right **Rev:** Crowned shield in fleece collar **Rev. Legend:** ...DBX BVRG CO FLAN Zc

Date	Mintage	VG	F	VF	XF	Unc
1668 Rare	508	—	—	—	—	—

KM# 104 2 SOUVERAIN D'OR

11.0800 g., 0.9470 Gold 0.3373 oz. AGW **Obv:** Mature bust of Charles II crowned, right

Date	Mintage	VG	F	VF	XF	Unc
1700 Rare	260	—	—	—	—	—

KM# 93 1/2 DUCATON D'OR (4 Souverain)

0.9480 Gold **Obv:** Mature bust of Charles II right **Rev:** Crowned shield of Charles II, supported by lions

Date	Mintage	VG	F	VF	XF	Unc
1696 Rare	—	—	—	—	—	—
1700 Rare	—	—	—	—	—	—

KM# 92 DUCATON D'OR (8 Souverain)

0.9480 Gold **Obv:** Mature bust of Charles II right **Rev:** Crowned shield of Charles II **Rev. Legend:** ...DVX BVRG C FLAND Zc

Date	Mintage	VG	F	VF	XF	Unc
1694 Rare	—	—	—	—	—	—

Note: Stack's International sale 3-88 AU realized $13,750

PIEFORTS

KM#	Date	Mintage	Identification	Mkt Val
P1	1614	—	2 Souverain D'Or. Gold. Double	—
P2	1615	—	2 Souverain D'Or. Gold. Triple	—
P3	1644	—	2 Souverain. Gold.	—
P4	1646	—	2 Souverain. Gold.	—

LUXEMBOURG

Founded about 963, Luxembourg was a prominent country of the Holy Roman Empire; one of its sovereigns became Holy Roman Emperor as Henry VII, 1308. After being made a duchy by Emperor Charles IV, 1354, Luxembourg passed under the domination of burgundy, Spain, Austria and France, 1443-1815.

DUCHY

Spanish Rule

STANDARD COINAGE

KM# 13 ESCALIN

Silver **Ruler:** Philip IV **Obv:** Rampant lion with sword and shield left **Obv. Legend:** PHIL. IIII. D. G. HISP. ET. INDIAR. REX **Rev:** Crowned arms **Rev. Legend:** ARCHID • AVST •DVX • BVRG • LVXEM • Zc

Date	Mintage	Good	VG	F	VF	XF
1637	—	35.00	85.00	175	250	—

KM# 15 1/4 PATAGON
Silver **Ruler:** Philip IV **Obv:** St. Andrew's cross, crown above divides date **Obv. Legend:** PHIL. IIII. D. G. HISP. ET. INDIAR. REX **Rev:** Crowned arms in Order collar **Rev. Legend:** ARCHID • AVST • DVX • BVRG • LVXEM. Zc

Date	Mintage	Good	VG	F	VF	XF
1632	—	200	550	900	1,300	—

KM# 16 1/2 PATAGON
Silver **Ruler:** Philip IV **Obv:** St. Andrew's cross with crown above divides date **Obv. Legend:** PHIL. IIII. D. G. HISP. ET. INDIAR. REX **Rev:** Crowned arms in order collar **Rev. Legend:** ARCHID • AVST • DVX • BVRG • LUVXEM. Zc

Date	Mintage	Good	VG	F	VF	XF
1632	—	200	550	900	1,300	—
1633	—	200	550	900	1,300	—
1634	—	200	550	900	1,300	—
1635	—	200	550	900	1,300	—
1636	—	200	550	900	1,300	—
1639	—	200	550	900	1,300	—

KM# 10 PATAGON
Silver **Ruler:** Albert and Elizabeth **Obv:** St. Andrew's cross with crown above, crowned monograms at left and right, Order of Golden Fleece below **Obv. Legend:** • ALBERTVS • ET • ELISABET • DEI • GRATIA **Rev:** Crowned arms in Order collar **Rev. Legend:** • ARCHID • AVST • DVCES • BURG • ET • LUXENB • **Note:** Mint mark: Lion.

Date	Mintage	Good	VG	F	VF	XF
ND(1616-19)	—	—	—	—	—	—

KM# 17 PATAGON
Silver **Ruler:** Philip IV **Obv:** St. Andrew's cross with crown above divides date **Obv. Legend:** PHIL. IIII. D. G. HISP. ET. INDIAR. REX **Rev:** Crowned arms in Order collar **Rev. Legend:** ARCHID • AVXT • DVX • BVRG • LVXEM. Zc **Note:** Dav. #4468.

Date	Mintage	Good	VG	F	VF	XF
1632	—	200	550	900	1,300	—
1633	—	200	550	900	1,300	—
1634	—	200	550	900	1,300	—
1635	—	200	550	900	1,300	—
1636	—	200	550	900	1,300	—
1637	—	200	550	900	1,300	—
1639	—	200	550	900	1,300	—
1643	—	200	550	900	1,300	—

KM# 18 2 PATAGON
Silver **Ruler:** Philip IV **Obv:** St. Andrew's cross with crown above divides date **Obv. Legend:** PHIL. IIII. D. G. HISP. ET. INDIAR. REX **Rev:** Crowned arms **Rev. Legend:** ARCHID • AVST • DVX • BVRG. LVXEM. Zc **Note:** Dav. #4467.

Date	Mintage	Good	VG	F	VF	XF
1632	—	—	—	—	—	—
1633	—	—	—	—	—	—
1634	—	—	—	—	—	—
1636	—	—	—	—	—	—
1643	—	—	—	—	—	—

KM# 19 COURONNE D'OR
Gold **Ruler:** Philip IV **Obv:** Rampant lion with sword and shield left **Obv. Legend:** PHIL. IIII. D. G. HISP. ET. INDIAR. REX **Rev:** Crowned arms **Rev. Legend:** ARCHID • AVST • DVX • BVRG. LVXEM. Zc **Note:** Fr. #11.

Date	Mintage	Good	VG	F	VF	XF
1632 Rare	—	—	—	—	—	—

NAMUR

Became an independent duchy in the late 12th century. Divided in 1609- the north becoming part of the United Netherlands, the south staying as Spanish (and later Austrian) Netherlands. Became part of Belgium after 1830.

RULER
Philip V of Spain, 1700-1711

MINT MARK
Lion rampant - Namur

DUCHY

MILLED COINAGE

KM# 1 LIARD
Copper **Obv:** Crowned briquet with arms of Austria, Burgundy and Brabant at sides and below, titles of Charles II **Rev:** Crowned arms **Note:** Imitation of Liards of Brabant.

Date	Mintage	VG	F	VF	XF	Unc
1692	—	45.00	90.00	150	250	—

TOURNAI

Tournai, a city in Hainaut made an episcopal see in 6th century, came under French rule and received its charter in 1187. In the early 16th century it was an English possession for a few years and Henry VIII sold it to Francis I. In 1521 the Count of Nassau took it for Spain. It was frequently besieged in wars in the sixteenth through eighteenth centuries. It was severely damaged during World War 1, being captured by the Germans in 1914 and held until 1918.

RULERS
Albert and Elisabeth, 1599-1621
Philip IV, 1621-1665

MINT MARK
Tower - Tournai

COUNTY

STANDARD COINAGE

KM# 29 DENIER (4 Mites)
Copper **Obv:** Crowned AE monogram **Rev:** Crowned shield of Austria-Burgundy on St. Andrew's cross

Date	Mintage	VG	F	VF	XF	Unc
1616	—	11.50	22.50	40.00	65.00	—
1617	—	11.50	22.50	40.00	65.00	—

KM# 12 2 DENIER
Copper **Obv:** Crowned AE monogram **Rev:** Crowned shield of Austria-Burgundy on St. Andrew's cross **Rev. Legend:** ...BVR(G) DOM TOR(NA Z)

Date	Mintage	VG	F	VF	XF	Unc
1607	—	10.00	20.00	40.00	65.00	—
1608	—	10.00	15.00	28.00	45.00	—
1609	—	10.00	15.00	22.50	35.00	—
1615	—	10.00	20.00	40.00	65.00	—
1616	—	10.00	15.00	22.50	35.00	—
1617	—	20.00	40.00	75.00	125	—

KM# 20 1/2 LIARD (Gigot, 6 Mites)
Copper **Obv:** Crowned shield of Austria and Burgundy, lion at center **Rev:** St. Andrew's cross, crown above, fleece below **Rev. Legend:** ...BVR. DOM TOR (N Z)

Date	Mintage	VG	F	VF	XF	Unc
1610	—	14.00	28.00	50.00	85.00	—
1611	—	10.00	15.00	22.50	35.00	—

KM# 54 1/2 LIARD (Gigot, 6 Mites)
Copper **Obv:** St. Andrew's cross, crown above, fleece below, divides date **Rev:** Crowned shield of Philip IV **Rev. Legend:** ...DVX BVR D TOR Zc

Date	Mintage	VG	F	VF	XF	Unc
1638	—	65.00	135	250	400	—
1640	—	65.00	135	250	400	—
1646	—	32.00	65.00	120	200	—
1647	—	40.00	80.00	150	250	—
1648	—	40.00	80.00	150	250	—
1649	—	32.00	65.00	120	200	—
1650	—	40.00	80.00	150	250	—
1651	—	40.00	80.00	150	250	—
1652	—	32.00	65.00	120	200	—
1653	—	28.00	55.00	100	175	—
1654	—	50.00	100	185	300	—
1655	—	40.00	80.00	150	250	—
1656	—	50.00	100	185	300	—
1657	—	50.00	100	185	300	—
1658	—	50.00	100	185	300	—
1659	—	50.00	100	185	300	—

KM# 21 LIARD (12 Mites)
Copper **Obv:** Crowned shield of Albert and Elizabeth **Rev:** Crown and shields of Austria, Burgundy, and Brabant **Rev. Legend:** ...BVRG DOM TOR

Date	Mintage	VG	F	VF	XF	Unc
1610	—	10.00	20.00	40.00	65.00	—
1611	—	10.00	15.00	28.00	45.00	—

KM# 53 LIARD (12 Mites)
Copper **Obv:** Philip IV bust right **Rev:** Crowned shield of Philip IV

Date	Mintage	VG	F	VF	XF	Unc
1637	—	25.00	50.00	90.00	150	—
1638	—	25.00	50.00	90.00	150	—
1639	—	25.00	50.00	90.00	150	—
1640	—	25.00	50.00	90.00	150	—
1641	—	25.00	50.00	90.00	150	—

KM# 61 LIARD (12 Mites)
Copper **Obv:** Crown and shields of Austria, Burgundy, and Brabant **Rev:** Crowned shield divides date **Rev. Legend:** ...DVX BVR D TOR Z

Date	Mintage	VG	F	VF	XF	Unc
1644	—	10.00	15.00	20.00	35.00	—
1645	—	10.00	15.00	20.00	35.00	—
1649	—	10.00	15.00	20.00	35.00	—
1650	—	10.00	15.00	20.00	35.00	—
1651	—	10.00	15.00	22.00	45.00	—
1652	—	10.00	15.00	22.00	45.00	—
1653	—	10.00	15.00	20.00	35.00	—
1654	—	10.00	15.00	20.00	35.00	—
1655	—	10.00	15.00	20.00	35.00	—
1656	—	10.00	15.00	20.00	35.00	—
1657	—	10.00	15.00	20.00	35.00	—
1658	—	10.00	15.00	20.00	35.00	—
1659	—	10.00	15.00	20.00	35.00	—
1660	—	10.00	15.00	20.00	35.00	—
1664	—	10.00	15.00	20.00	35.00	—
1665	—	10.00	15.00	22.00	45.00	—
1666	—	10.00	16.00	30.00	55.00	—

KM# 27 1/2 PATARD (1/2 Sol)
Billon **Obv:** Cross flores, AE monogram at center **Rev:** Crowned shield of Albert and Elizabeth **Rev. Legend:** ...BVRG DOM TOR

Date	Mintage	VG	F	VF	XF	Unc
ND(1612-18)	—	18.00	35.00	60.00	100	—
1615	—	20.00	40.00	75.00	125	—
1616	—	25.00	50.00	90.00	145	—
1618	—	30.00	60.00	110	175	—

KM# 25 PATARD
Billon **Obv:** AE monogram in center of octolobe design **Rev:** Crowned shield of Albert and Elizabeth divides date **Rev. Legend:** ...BVRG DOM TOR(N) Z

Date	Mintage	VG	F	VF	XF	Unc
ND(1612-18)	—	15.00	25.00	40.00	65.00	—
1614	—	15.00	28.00	50.00	85.00	—
1615	—	15.00	25.00	40.00	65.00	—
1616	—	15.00	25.00	40.00	65.00	—
1617	—	15.00	25.00	40.00	65.00	—
1618	—	15.00	35.00	60.00	100	—

KM# 60 PATARD
Billon **Obv:** Linear cross **Rev:** Crowned shield of Philip IV divides date **Rev. Legend:** ...DVX BVRG D TOR Z

Date	Mintage	VG	F	VF	XF	Unc
1641	—	45.00	90.00	165	275	—
1643	—	32.00	65.00	120	200	—
1644	—	50.00	100	180	300	—

KM# 9 1/4 REAL (1-1/4 Sol)
1.7400 g., 0.3960 Silver 0.0222 oz. ASW **Obv:** Crowned shield of Albert and Elizabeth **Rev:** Crowned shield **Rev. Legend:** ...BVRG DOM TOR

Date	Mintage	VG	F	VF	XF	Unc
1603	—	32.00	65.00	120	200	—
1604	—	30.00	60.00	110	185	—
1605	—	25.00	50.00	90.00	150	—
1606	—	30.00	60.00	110	185	—
1611	—	—	—	—	—	—

KM# 13 1/2 REAL (2-1/2 Sol)
3.4800 g., 0.3960 Silver 0.0443 oz. ASW **Obv:** Crowned shield on St. Andrew's cross divides date **Rev:** Crowned shield **Rev. Legend:** ...DVCE. BVRG. DOM.

Date	Mintage	VG	F	VF	XF	Unc
1607	—	65.00	135	250	400	—
1608	—	60.00	115	200	350	—
1609	—	50.00	100	180	300	—
1610	—	60.00	115	200	350	—
1611	—	65.00	135	250	400	—

KM# 1 STOTER (2-1/2 Sols)
3.4200 g., 0.4170 Silver 0.0458 oz. ASW **Obv:** Crowned shield in fleece collar **Rev:** Cross floree, lion and crown in angles

Date	Mintage	VG	F	VF	XF	Unc
1601	—	30.00	60.00	110	185	—
1602	—	28.00	55.00	100	165	—

KM# 30 3 PATARDS
2.6300 g., 0.5820 Silver 0.0492 oz. ASW **Obv:** Cross floree, lion at center **Rev:** Crowned shield in octolobe **Rev. Legend:** ...BVRG DOM TOR(N) Z

Date	Mintage	VG	F	VF	XF	Unc
1616	—	15.00	25.00	45.00	75.00	—
1617	—	15.00	25.00	45.00	75.00	—
1618	—	18.00	35.00	60.00	100	—
1619	—	15.00	25.00	35.00	60.00	—
1620	—	15.00	25.00	35.00	60.00	—

KM# 11 REAL

3.0600 g., 0.8960 Silver 0.0881 oz. ASW **Obv:** Crowned shield in fleece collar **Rev:** St. Andrew's cross, crown above, fleece below **Rev. Legend:** ...DVCES BVRG ET DOM TOR

Date	Mintage	VG	F	VF	XF	Unc
ND(1604-08)	—	35.00	70.00	125	285	—
1606	—	—	—	—	—	—

KM# 2 1/4 FLORIN (5 Sols)

4.2700 g., 0.6670 Silver 0.0916 oz. ASW **Obv:** Bust of Albert and Elizabeth confronted, crown above, V below **Rev:** Crowned shield in fleece collar

Date	Mintage	VG	F	VF	XF	Unc
1601	—	750	1,350	2,250	3,500	—

KM# 40 ESCALIN (6 Sols)

5.2600 g., 0.5820 Silver 0.0984 oz. ASW **Obv:** Eagle with shield of Austria-Burgundy on breast **Rev:** Crowned shield of Albert and Elizabeth on St. Andrew's cross **Rev. Legend:** ...BVRG DOM TOR(N) Z

Date	Mintage	VG	F	VF	XF	Unc
ND(1612-21)	—	15.00	30.00	60.00	125	—
1621	—	28.00	55.00	100	175	—

KM# 41 ESCALIN (6 Sols)

5.2600 g., 0.5820 Silver 0.0984 oz. ASW **Obv:** Lion rampant left with shield and sword **Rev:** Crowned shield of Philip IV on St. Andrew's cross **Rev. Legend:** ...DVX BVRG D TOR(N) Z

Date	Mintage	VG	F	VF	XF	Unc
1621	—	15.00	25.00	50.00	90.00	—
1622	—	15.00	25.00	50.00	90.00	—
1623	—	15.00	27.50	50.00	90.00	—
1624	—	18.00	35.00	65.00	115	—
1625	—	28.00	55.00	100	165	—
1626	—	18.00	35.00	65.00	115	—
1627	—	22.00	45.00	80.00	135	—
1628	—	15.00	25.00	50.00	90.00	—
1629	—	15.00	25.00	50.00	90.00	—
1630	—	15.00	30.00	60.00	100	—
1636	—	35.00	65.00	120	200	—
1637	—	15.00	25.00	50.00	90.00	—
1638	—	22.00	45.00	80.00	135	—
1640	—	15.00	30.00	60.00	100	—
1642	—	28.00	55.00	100	165	—
1643	—	22.00	45.00	80.00	135	—
1644	—	28.00	55.00	100	165	—
1645	—	20.00	40.00	70.00	120	—
1646	—	35.00	65.00	120	200	—
1649	—	40.00	80.00	150	250	—
1651	—	35.00	65.00	120	200	—
1652	—	28.00	55.00	100	165	—
1659	—	60.00	120	200	350	—
1662	—	75.00	150	250	400	—
1663	—	75.00	150	250	400	—

KM# 3 1/2 FLORIN

8.5300 g., 0.6670 Silver 0.1829 oz. ASW **Obv:** Busts of Albert and Isabella confronted, crown above, date below **Rev:** St. Andrew's cross, crown above, X below **Note:** Legend varieties exist.

Date	Mintage	VG	F	VF	XF	Unc
1601	—	135	275	500	850	—
1602	—	135	275	500	850	—
1603 Rare	—	—	—	—	—	—

KM# 10 3 REALS (15 Sols)

9.1900 g., 0.8960 Silver 0.2647 oz. ASW **Obv:** Conjoined busts of Albert and Elizabeth left **Rev:** Crowned shield, St. Andrew's cross in back **Note:** Legend varieties exist.

Date	Mintage	VG	F	VF	XF	Unc
1605	—	75.00	150	275	450	—
1606	—	75.00	150	275	450	—
1607	—	75.00	150	275	450	—
1608	—	75.00	150	275	450	—
1609	—	100	200	350	600	—
1610 Rare	—	—	—	—	—	—

KM# 44 1/2 DUCATON

16.2400 g., 0.9440 Silver 0.4929 oz. ASW **Obv:** Bust of Philip IV right in ruffled collar **Rev:** Crowned shield supported by lions **Rev. Legend:** ...DUX BVRG DOM TOR Z

Date	Mintage	VG	F	VF	XF	Unc
1623	—	550	1,000	1,650	2,500	—

KM# 42 1/2 DUCATON

16.2400 g., 0.9440 Silver 0.4929 oz. ASW **Obv:** Bust of Philip IV right in thin collar right **Rev:** Lion with two swords supports crowned shield **Rev. Legend:** ...DVX BVRG DOM TOR Zc

Date	Mintage	VG	F	VF	XF	Unc
1647	—	200	400	750	1,250	—
1648	—	200	400	750	1,250	—
1649	—	225	450	800	1,350	—
1651	—	185	375	700	1,150	—
1664 Rare	—	—	—	—	—	—
1665 Rare	—	—	—	—	—	—

KM# 47 1/4 PATAGON

Silver, 33 mm. **Ruler:** Albert and Elisabeth **Obv:** St. Andrew's cross, crown above divides date **Obv. Legend:** • PHIL • IIII • D • G • HISP • ET • **Rev:** Crowned arms in order collar **Rev. Legend:** • ARCHID • AVST • DVX • BVRG • DOM • TORN • Zc **Note:** Mint mark: Tower.

Date	Mintage	VG	F	VF	XF	Unc
1626	—	—	—	—	—	—
1630	—	—	—	—	—	—
1631	—	—	—	—	—	—
1632	—	—	—	—	—	—
1633	—	—	—	—	—	—
1634	—	—	—	—	—	—
1635	—	—	—	—	—	—
1654	—	—	—	—	—	—

KM# 48 1/2 PATAGON

Silver, 36 mm. **Ruler:** Philip IV **Obv:** St. Andrew's cross, crown above divides date **Obv. Legend:** • PHIL • IIII • D • G • HISP • ET • INDIAR • REX **Rev:** Crowned arms in order collar **Rev. Legend:** • ARCHID • AVST • BVRG • DOM • TORN • Zc **Note:** Mint mark: Tower

Date	Mintage	VG	F	VF	XF	Unc
1626	—	—	—	—	—	—
1631	—	—	—	—	—	—
1633	—	—	—	—	—	—
1634	—	—	—	—	—	—
1635	—	—	—	—	—	—
1645	—	—	—	—	—	—
1646	—	—	—	—	—	—
1647	—	—	—	—	—	—
1648	—	—	—	—	—	—
1652	—	—	—	—	—	—
1653	—	—	—	—	—	—
1655	—	—	—	—	—	—
1657	—	—	—	—	—	—
1658	—	—	—	—	—	—
1660	—	—	—	—	—	—
1663	—	—	—	—	—	—
1665	—	—	—	—	—	—

KM# 31 PATAGON (48 Sols)

28.1000 g., 0.8750 Silver 0.7905 oz. ASW **Obv:** St. Andrew's cross, crown above, fleece below, divides pair of crowned monograms **Rev:** Crowned shield in fleece collar **Rev. Legend:** ...DVCES DOM TOR(NA Z) **Note:** Dav. #4438.

Date	Mintage	VG	F	VF	XF	Unc
ND(1612-21)	—	50.00	75.00	145	275	—
1616	—	50.00	75.00	145	275	—
1618	—	50.00	75.00	145	275	—
1620	—	50.00	75.00	145	275	—
1621	—	50.00	75.00	145	275	—

KM# A42 PATAGON (48 Sols)

28.1000 g., 0.8750 Silver 0.7905 oz. ASW **Obv:** Date divided by St. Andrew's cross, crown above **Rev:** Crowned shield of Philip IV in fleece collar **Rev. Legend:** ...DVX BVRG DOM TOR(N) Zc **Note:** Dav. #4470.

Date	Mintage	VG	F	VF	XF	Unc
1621	—	—	—	—	—	—
1622	—	50.00	75.00	145	275	—
1623	—	50.00	75.00	145	275	—
1624	—	55.00	110	220	375	—
1625	—	50.00	75.00	145	275	—
1626	—	50.00	75.00	150	290	—
1628	—	50.00	75.00	145	275	—
1630	—	50.00	75.00	150	290	—
1631	—	50.00	75.00	145	275	—
1632	—	50.00	75.00	145	275	—
1633	—	50.00	75.00	145	275	—
1634	—	50.00	75.00	145	275	—
1635	—	50.00	75.00	145	275	—
1636	—	50.00	75.00	145	275	—
1637	—	—	—	—	—	—
1641	—	—	—	—	—	—
1643	—	50.00	75.00	170	310	—
1644	—	50.00	75.00	170	310	—
1645	—	50.00	75.00	145	275	—
1646	—	50.00	75.00	145	275	—
1647	—	50.00	75.00	145	275	—
1648	—	50.00	75.00	145	275	—
1649	—	50.00	75.00	150	290	—
1650	—	50.00	75.00	145	275	—
1651	—	50.00	80.00	170	310	—
1652	—	50.00	75.00	145	275	—
1653	—	50.00	75.00	145	275	—
1654	—	50.00	75.00	145	275	—
1655	—	50.00	75.00	145	275	—
1656	—	50.00	75.00	145	275	—
1657	—	50.00	100	200	345	—
1658	—	50.00	75.00	145	275	—
1659	—	50.00	75.00	145	275	—
1661	—	50.00	80.00	170	310	—
1662	—	50.00	80.00	170	310	—
1663	—	80.00	145	270	475	—
1664	—	80.00	145	270	475	—
1665	—	80.00	145	270	475	—

KM# 70 PATAGON (48 Sols)

28.1000 g., 0.8750 Silver 0.7905 oz. ASW **Obv:** St. Andrew's cross, crown above, fleece divides date **Rev:** Crowned shield of Charles II in fleece collar **Rev. Legend:** ...DVX BRVG DOM TOR Z **Note:** Dav. #4495.

Date	Mintage	VG	F	VF	XF	Unc
1666	—	125	250	425	700	—
1667	—	125	250	425	700	—

KM# 32 DUCATON

32.4800 g., 0.9440 Silver 0.9857 oz. ASW **Obv:** Conjoined busts of Albert and Elisabeth right **Rev:** Lions supporting crowned shield **Rev. Legend:** ...BVRG DOM TORN Z **Note:** Dav. #4430.

Date	Mintage	VG	F	VF	XF	Unc
1618	—	1,800	3,000	5,100	7,800	—
1620	—	2,000	3,300	5,500	8,400	—

KM# 50 DUCATON

32.4800 g., 0.9440 Silver 0.9857 oz. ASW **Obv:** Bust of Philip IV in ruffled collar right **Rev:** Lions supporting crowned shield **Rev. Legend:** ...DVX BVRG DOM TOR Zc **Note:** Dav. #4450.

Date	Mintage	VG	F	VF	XF	Unc
1631	—	125	275	600	1,100	—
1632	—	100	200	450	850	—
1633	—	150	300	700	1,250	—
1634	—	100	200	450	850	—
1635	—	150	300	700	1,250	—
1636	—	125	275	600	1,100	—

KM# 52 DUCATON

32.4800 g., 0.9440 Silver 0.9857 oz. ASW **Obv:** Bust of Philip IV in thin collar right **Rev. Legend:** ...DVX BVRG DOM TOR Zc **Note:** Dav. #4458.

Date	Mintage	VG	F	VF	XF	Unc
1636	—	100	200	425	800	—
1638	—	100	200	425	800	—
1647	—	80.00	175	350	700	—
1648	—	100	200	425	800	—
1649	—	100	200	425	800	—
1650	—	100	200	425	800	—
1651	—	100	200	425	800	—
1652	—	125	275	600	1,100	—
1664	—	150	300	700	1,250	—
1665	—	150	300	700	1,250	—

KM# A5 ALBERTIN

2.9200 g., 0.7920 Gold 0.0743 oz. AGW **Obv:** Crowned arms in collar of the Golden Fleece **Rev:** Crowned floral St. Andrew's cross, date at side, Golden Fleece at bottom

Date	Mintage	VG	F	VF	XF	Unc
1601	—	150	250	450	750	—
1603	—	150	250	450	750	—

KM# 22 1/2 SOUVERAIN D'OR

2.7700 g., 0.9200 Gold 0.0819 oz. AGW **Obv:** Crowned shield of Austria-Burgundy on cross floree **Rev:** Crowned shield of Albert and Isabella divides pair of crowned monograms **Rev. Legend:** ...BVRG DOM TORN (Z)

Date	Mintage	VG	F	VF	XF	Unc
ND(1612-13) Rare	5,188	—	—	—	—	—

KM# 26 COURONNE D'OR

3.4100 g., 0.8820 Gold 0.0967 oz. AGW **Obv:** Cross of four crowned monograms, lions and crowns in angles **Rev:** Crowned shield of Albert and Elizabeth divides pair of crowned monograms **Rev. Legend:** ...BVRG DOM TORN Z

Date	Mintage	VG	F	VF	XF	Unc
1614	9,082	275	550	1,150	2,000	—
1615	Inc. above	275	550	1,150	2,000	—
1616	—	275	550	1,150	2,000	—
1620	—	275	550	1,150	2,000	—
1621	5,914	275	550	1,150	2,000	—

KM# 43 COURONNE D'OR

3.4100 g., 0.8820 Gold 0.0967 oz. AGW **Obv:** Cross floree **Rev:** Crowned shield of Philip IV **Rev. Legend:** ...DVX BVRG D TOR Zc

Date	Mintage	VG	F	VF	XF	Unc
1622 Rare	214	—	—	—	—	—
1629	5,905	250	500	1,000	1,850	—
1630	94,000	250	500	1,000	1,850	—
1631	11,000	250	500	1,000	1,850	—
1632	5,000	250	500	1,000	1,850	—
1633	Inc. above	250	500	1,000	1,850	—
1636	7,000	250	500	1,000	1,850	—
1640	20,000	250	500	1,000	1,850	—
1641	—	250	500	1,000	1,850	—
1642	—	250	500	1,000	1,850	—
1643	22,000	250	500	1,000	1,850	—
1644	Inc. above	250	500	1,000	1,850	—
1645	—	250	500	1,000	1,850	—
1646	9,000	250	500	1,000	1,850	—
1647	48,000	250	500	1,000	1,850	—
1648	Inc. above	250	500	1,000	1,850	—
1649	Inc. above	250	500	1,000	1,850	—

KM# 6 2 ALBERTIN (Corona)

5.1500 g., 0.8950 Gold 0.1482 oz. AGW **Obv:** St. Andrew's cross, crown above, fleece below, divides date **Obv. Legend:** ...COM TOR **Rev:** Crowned shield in fleece collar

Date	Mintage	VG	F	VF	XF	Unc
1601	—	185	275	500	850	—
1602	—	185	275	500	850	—
1603	—	185	275	500	850	—
1604	84,000	185	275	500	850	—
1605	Inc. above	185	275	500	850	—
1606	13,000	185	275	500	850	—
1607	—	185	275	500	850	—
1610	3,003	185	275	500	850	—

KM# 28 2/3 SOUVERAIN D'OR

3.4900 g., 0.9800 Gold 0.1100 oz. AGW **Obv:** Figures of Albert and Isabella standing right **Rev:** Crowned shield in fleece collar **Rev. Legend:** ...BVRG DOM TOR Z **Note:** Legend varieties exist.

Date	Mintage	VG	F	VF	XF	Unc
ND(1615-18) Rare	2,582	—	—	—	—	—
1616 Rare	Inc. above	—	—	—	—	—

KM# 51 SOUVERAIN OU LION D'OR

5.5400 g., 0.9470 Gold 0.1687 oz. AGW **Obv:** Crowned lion left with sword and shield **Rev:** Crowned shield of Philip IV in fleece collar **Rev. Legend:** ...DVX BVRG DOM TOR Zc

Date	Mintage	VG	F	VF	XF	Unc
1633	—	220	425	850	1,500	—
1634	—	220	425	850	1,500	—
1641	—	220	425	850	1,500	—
1644	—	220	425	850	1,500	—
1645	—	220	425	850	1,500	—
1648	74,000	220	425	850	1,500	—
1649	—	220	425	850	1,500	—
1650	Inc. above	220	425	850	1,500	—
1651	22,000	220	425	850	1,500	—
1652	Inc. above	220	425	850	1,500	—
1653	Inc. above	220	425	850	1,500	—
1654	17,000	220	425	850	1,500	—
1655	14,000	220	425	850	1,500	—
1656	Inc. above	220	425	850	1,500	—
1657	—	220	425	850	1,500	—
1658	Inc. above	220	425	850	1,500	—
1659	16,000	220	425	850	1,500	—
1660	Inc. above	220	425	850	1,500	—
1661	—	220	425	850	1,500	—
1662	—	220	425	850	1,500	—
1663	Inc. above	220	425	850	1,500	—
1665	2,020	220	425	850	1,500	—

KM# 23.1 2 SOUVERAIN D'OR

11.0800 g., 0.9470 Gold 0.3373 oz. AGW **Obv:** Albert and Elisabeth seated on thrones facing, date in exergue **Rev:** Crowned shield in fleece collar **Rev. Legend:** ...ET DOM TORN(A) Z

Date	Mintage	VG	F	VF	XF	Unc
ND(1599-1621)	33,000	600	1,200	2,250	3,750	—

KM# 23.2 2 SOUVERAIN D'OR

11.0800 g., 0.9470 Gold 0.3373 oz. AGW **Obv:** Date added below throne **Note:** Legend varieties exist.

Date	Mintage	VG	F	VF	XF	Unc
1612 Rare	5,618	—	—	—	—	—
1613	Inc. above	450	1,000	2,000	3,500	—

Date	Mintage	VG	F	VF	XF	Unc
1616	23,000	450	1,000	2,000	3,500	—
1617	Inc. above	400	850	1,750	3,000	—
1618	12,000	450	1,000	2,000	3,500	—
1619	Inc. above	400	850	1,750	3,000	—
1620	2,219	500	1,100	2,250	3,850	—

KM# 45 2 SOUVERAIN D'OR

11.0800 g., 0.9470 Gold 0.3373 oz. AGW **Obv:** Young crowned bust of Philip IV in ruffled collar right, date above **Rev:** Crowned arms in collar of the Golden Fleece in inner circle **Rev. Legend:** ...DVX BVRG DOM TOR Zc

Date	Mintage	VG	F	VF	XF	Unc
1623	1,950	650	1,250	2,450	4,000	—
1626 Rare	533	—	—	—	—	—
1630	—	—	—	—	—	—
1632	—	—	—	—	—	—
1637	1,811	650	1,250	2,450	4,000	—

KM# 55 2 SOUVERAIN D'OR

11.0800 g., 0.9470 Gold 0.3373 oz. AGW **Obv:** Older bust of Philip IV in flat collar

Date	Mintage	VG	F	VF	XF	Unc
1638	5,145	400	800	1,875	3,250	—
1643	40,000	400	800	1,875	3,250	—
1644	Inc. above	400	800	1,875	3,250	—
1645	Inc. above	400	800	1,875	3,250	—
1646	16,000	400	800	1,875	3,250	—
1647	Inc. above	400	800	1,875	3,250	—
1650	25,000	400	800	1,875	3,250	—
1651	Inc. above	400	800	1,875	3,250	—
1657	—	400	800	1,875	3,250	—

KM# 24.1 4 SOUVERAIN D'OR

22.1000 g., 0.9190 Gold 0.6530 oz. AGW **Note:** Similar to 2 Souverain D'or, KM#23.1.

Date	Mintage	VG	F	VF	XF	Unc
ND Rare	—	—	—	—	—	—

KM# 24.2 4 SOUVERAIN D'OR

22.1000 g., 0.9190 Gold 0.6530 oz. AGW **Note:** Similar to 2 Souverain D'or, KM#23.2.

Date	Mintage	VG	F	VF	XF	Unc
1613 Rare	—	—	—	—	—	—
1617 Rare	—	—	—	—	—	—
1619 Rare	—	—	—	—	—	—
1620 Rare	—	—	—	—	—	—

KM# 46 4 SOUVERAIN D'OR

Gold **Ruler:** Philip IV **Obv:** Young crowned bust in ruffled collar right, date above **Rev:** Crowned arms in collar of the Golden Fleece in inner circle **Rev. Legend:** ... DVX BURG DOM TOR Zc **Note:** Prev. KM#P6.

Date	Mintage	VG	F	VF	XF	Unc
1623 Rare	—	—	—	—	—	—

TRADE COINAGE

KM# 7.1 2 DUCATS

7.0000 g., 0.9000 Gold 0.2025 oz. AGW **Obv:** Busts of Albert and Elizabeth confronted **Rev:** Crowned shield in fleece collar **Rev. Legend:** ...TOR

Date	Mintage	VG	F	VF	XF	Unc
ND(1599-1611)	—	350	650	1,250	2,000	—

KM# 7.2 2 DUCATS

7.0000 g., 0.9000 Gold 0.2025 oz. AGW **Rev. Legend:** ...TOVR

Date	Mintage	VG	F	VF	XF	Unc
ND(1599-1611)	25,000	350	650	1,250	2,000	—

PIEFORTS

KM#	Date	Mintage	Identification	Mkt Val
P1	ND	—	2 Souverain D'Or. Gold.	—
P2	1613	—	2 Souverain D'Or. Gold.	—
P3	1617	—	2 Souverain D'Or. Gold.	—
P4	1619	—	2 Souverain D'Or. Gold.	—
P5	1620	—	2 Souverain D'Or. Gold.	—
P6	1623	—	2 Souverain D'Or. Gold.	—

The Kingdom of Sweden, a limited constitutional monarchy located in northern Europe between Norway and Finland, has an area of 173,732 sq. mi. (449,960 sq. km).

Sweden was founded as a Christian stronghold by Olaf Skottkonung late in the 10th century. After conquering Finland late in the 13th century, Sweden, together with Norway, came under the rule of Denmark, 1397-1523, in an association known as the Union of Kalmar. Modern Sweden had its beginning in 1523 when Gustaf Vasa drove the Danes out of Sweden and was himself chosen king. Under Gustaf Adolphus II and Charles XII, Sweden was one of the great powers of 17th century Europe – until Charles invaded Russia in 1708, and was defeated at the Battle of Pultowa in June, 1709

RULERS

Carl IX, regent, 1598-1604
Carl IX, 1604-1611
John, Duke of Ostergotland, 1606-1618
Gustaf II Adolphus, 1611-1632
Christina, 1632-1654
Carl X Gustavus, 1654-1660
Carl XI, 1660-1697
Carl XII, 1697-1718

MINT OFFICIALS' INITIALS

Initial	Date	Name
AG	1641-45	Anthony Grooth d.y.
AG	1645-46	Anna Grooth f. Skytte
AS	1684-99	Anders Strommer
DF, D	1672-83	Daniel Faxell
DK	1646-50	Daniel Markusson Kock
GW	1658-64	Goran Wagner
	1663-64	Johan Fredrik Herman
IK	1664-65	Isak Kock
MK	1633-39	Markus Kock
(ca) Crossed axes	1652-58	Michael Hack
(as) Arrow between 2 stars	1665-68	Abraham Kock
(monogram FIRST)	1669-72	Christopher Conradi

KINGDOM

STANDARD COINAGE

KM# 5 FYRK

Silver **Obv:** Three large crowns in inner circle **Rev:** "Jehovah" in radiant circle **Mint:** Stockholm

Date	Mintage	VG	F	VF	XF	Unc
1601	—	45.00	95.00	160	—	—

KM# 6 FYRK

Silver **Obv:** Three smaller crowns in inner circle **Mint:** Stockholm

Date	Mintage	VG	F	VF	XF	Unc
1601	—	70.00	150	285	—	—

KM# 103.1 FYRK

7.1000 g., Copper **Obv:** Sheaf with letters G.A.R. **Rev:** Three crowns, date, value **Mint:** Sater **Note:** Klippe.

Date	Mintage	VG	F	VF	XF	Unc
1624	—	100	225	—	—	—

KM# 103.2 FYRK

7.1000 g., Copper **Mint:** Nykoping and Sater

Date	Mintage	VG	F	VF	XF	Unc
1625 Rare	—	—	—	—	—	—

KM# 110 FYRK

7.1000 g., Copper **Mint:** Arboga

Date	Mintage	VG	F	VF	XF	Unc
1627	—	31.50	65.00	155	—	—

KM# 120 FYRK

7.1000 g., Copper **Obv:** Sheaf with value **Rev:** Crossed arrows, date **Mint:** Sater

Date	Mintage	VG	F	VF	XF	Unc
1628	—	750	—	—	—	—

KM# 121 FYRK

7.1000 g., Copper **Obv:** Sheaf with value **Rev:** Griffin, date above left **Mint:** Nykoping

Date	Mintage	VG	F	VF	XF	Unc
1628	—	125	245	700	—	—
1629	—	85.00	210	525	—	—

KM# 126 FYRK

Copper **Rev:** Date between feet of griffin

Date	Mintage	VG	F	VF	XF	Unc
1629	—	50.00	150	300	—	—

KM# 254 1/6 ORE (S.M.)

Copper **Obv:** Three crowns with letters C.R.S. and date **Rev:** Griffin below crown, value and mint mark **Mint:** Avesta

Date	Mintage	VG	F	VF	XF	Unc
1666 S.M.	35,040,000	55.00	100	350	625	—
1666 S.m.	Inc. above	6.00	20.00	30.00	70.00	—
1667	4,512,000	6.00	22.50	35.75	75.00	—
1668/67	—	11.00	32.50	70.00	175	—
1668	2,846,000	7.00	25.00	39.00	85.00	—
1669/68	—	11.00	32.50	70.00	175	—
1669	7,137,000	8.00	25.00	45.50	90.00	—
1670	14,478,000	6.00	22.50	35.75	75.00	—
1671	12,881,000	6.00	22.50	35.75	75.00	—
1672	2,858,000	7.00	25.00	39.00	85.00	—
1673	6,355,000	8.00	25.00	50.00	100	—
Note: Without star in date						
1673	Inc. above	6.00	22.50	35.75	75.00	—
Note: With star in date						
1674	1,862,000	6.00	22.50	35.75	75.00	—
1675	1,229,000	8.00	25.00	39.00	85.00	—
1676	6,123,000	6.00	22.50	35.75	75.00	—
1677	9,811,000	6.00	20.00	30.00	70.00	—
1680/77	—	13.00	39.00	85.00	190	—
1680	2,090,000	8.00	32.50	45.50	110	—
1681	Inc. above	6.00	22.50	35.75	75.00	—
1682/81	—	11.00	35.75	65.00	140	—
1682	597,000	8.00	25.00	39.00	85.00	—
1683/82	—	11.00	35.75	65.00	140	—
1683	2,057,000	6.00	22.50	35.75	75.00	—
1686/83	—	10.00	35.75	60.00	125	—
1686	1,708,000	6.00	20.00	30.00	70.00	—

KM# 297 1/6 ORE (S.M.)

Copper **Note:** Klippe.

Date	Mintage	VG	F	VF	XF	Unc
1686	—	—	—	—	—	—

KM# 152.1 1/4 ORE

10.6000 g., Copper **Obv:** Three crowns, letters C.R.S. **Rev:** Sheaf on shield below crown divide value and date **Mint:** Nykoping **Note:** Varieties exist.

Date	Mintage	VG	F	VF	XF	Unc
1633	1,971,000	18.00	45.50	130	325	—
1634	37,734,000	11.00	32.50	80.00	175	—

KM# 152.2 1/4 ORE
10.6000 g., Copper **Mint:** Nykoping and Sater

Date	Mintage	VG	F	VF	XF	Unc
1635 Mint mark	59,827,200	8.00	22.50	39.00	105	—
1635 Rose	Inc. above	18.00	39.00	125	425	—
1636	40,488,960	9.00	30.00	50.00	120	—

KM# 160 1/4 ORE
12.9000 g., Copper **Mint:** Sater

Date	Mintage	VG	F	VF	XF	Unc
1637	54,502,400	8.00	32.50	65.00	140	—
1638	5,068,800	8.00	32.50	65.00	140	—
1640	—	13.00	60.00	130	280	—
1641	13,981,449	10.00	80.00	80.00	170	—
1642	7,138,560	11.00	50.00	110	245	—

KM# 188 1/4 ORE
12.9000 g., Copper **Mint:** Avesta **Note:** Varieties exist.

Date	Mintage	VG	F	VF	XF	Unc
1644	4,224,000	8.00	25.00	39.00	90.00	—
1644/45	—	33.50	100	195	425	—
1645	940,000	8.00	25.00	39.00	90.00	—
1653	445,400	8.00	25.00	39.00	90.00	—
1654	1,750,400	8.00	25.00	45.50	120	—

KM# 211 1/4 ORE
12.9000 g., Copper **Obv:** Three crowns with letters C.R.S. **Rev:** Griffin with date, crown and value

Date	Mintage	VG	F	VF	XF	Unc
1654 Rare	—	—	—	—	—	—
1655	1,729,600	18.00	37.50	130	375	—
1656	1,024,000	14.00	30.00	100	325	—
1657	819,200	18.00	37.50	130	375	—
1658	6,144,000	18.00	37.50	130	375	—
1658 Rose	Inc. above	65.00	150	425	—	—
1659	—	14.00	30.00	100	325	—
1660	Inc. above	45.50	115	295	700	—

KM# 7 1/2 ORE
1.6201 g., 0.2030 Silver 0.0106 oz. ASW **Obv:** Three crowns in crowned rectangular shield **Rev:** "Jehovah" in inner circle **Mint:** Stockholm

Date	Mintage	VG	F	VF	XF	Unc
1601	—	37.50	75.00	150	—	—
1602	—	37.50	75.00	150	—	—

KM# 65 1/2 ORE
1.6200 g., 0.2030 Silver 0.0106 oz. ASW **Obv:** Three crowns and value **Rev:** Sheaf with letters G.A.R. **Mint:** Stockholm

Date	Mintage	VG	F	VF	XF	Unc
1615	—	49.00	90.00	195	425	—

KM# 104.1 1/2 ORE
16.2000 g., Copper **Obv:** Sheaf with letters G.A.R. **Rev:** Crossed arrows below crown, value, date **Mint:** Sater **Note:** Klippe.

Date	Mintage	VG	F	VF	XF	Unc
1624	—	105	600	950	2,050	—

KM# 123 1/2 ORE
14.1000 g., Copper **Note:** Klippe.

Date	Mintage	VG	F	VF	XF	Unc
1625	—	105	225	300	775	—

KM# 104.2 1/2 ORE
14.1000 g., Copper **Mint:** Nykoping and Sater

Date	Mintage	VG	F	VF	XF	Unc
1625	—	65.00	135	300	725	—
1626 Value as 1/2	—	42.00	130	285	675	—
1626 Value as 2/1	—	—	—	—	—	—
1627 Value as 1/2	—	75.00	145	375	975	—
1627 Value as 2/1	—	—	—	—	—	—

KM# 111 1/2 ORE
14.1000 g., Copper **Rev:** Crossed arrows below crown, value

Date	Mintage	VG	F	VF	XF	Unc
1627	—	85.00	300	550	—	—
1628	—	1,700	—	—	—	—
1629	—	105	375	625	—	—

KM# 122 1/2 ORE
14.1000 g., Copper **Obv:** Asterisks in field beside shield

Date	Mintage	VG	F	VF	XF	Unc
1627	—	210	—	—	—	—
1628	—	65.00	150	300	625	—
1629	—	49.00	115	260	600	—
1630	—	49.00	115	260	600	—
1631	—	90.00	190	350	700	—

KM# 112 1/2 ORE
14.1000 g., Copper **Obv:** Similar to KM#111 **Rev:** Griffin, value, date **Mint:** Nykoping

Date	Mintage	VG	F	VF	XF	Unc
1627	—	85.00	225	550	1,200	—
1628	—	170	—	—	—	—
1629	—	100	265	625	1,250	—

KM# 113 1/2 ORE
14.1000 g., Copper **Obv:** Three crowns in oval below large crown or crowned arms **Rev:** Eagle **Mint:** Arboga

Date	Mintage	VG	F	VF	XF	Unc
1627	—	120	300	775	1,700	—

KM# 124 1/2 ORE
14.1000 g., Copper **Obv:** Crowned rectangular shield **Mint:** Arboga

Date	Mintage	VG	F	VF	XF	Unc
1628 Rare	—	—	—	—	—	—

KM# 127 1/2 ORE
14.1000 g., Copper **Obv:** Crowned ornate arms **Rev:** Griffin **Mint:** Nykoping

Date	Mintage	VG	F	VF	XF	Unc
1629 Rare	—	—	—	—	—	—

KM# 247 1/2 ORE
Silver **Obv:** C.R. below crown **Rev:** Value, date **Mint:** Stockholm

Date	Mintage	VG	F	VF	XF	Unc
1665 Rare	—	—	—	—	—	—

KM# 231 1/2 ORE (K.M.)
8.9000 g., Copper **Obv:** Three crowns, letters CRS, date **Rev:** Crown above lion rampant, value **Mint:** Avesta

Date	Mintage	VG	F	VF	XF	Unc
1661	—	65.00	135	230	500	—
1662	—	49.00	105	200	425	—
1663/2	—	49.00	105	200	425	—
1663	—	65.00	135	230	500	—
1664	—	65.00	135	230	500	—

KM# 8 ORE
2.7353 g., 0.2500 Silver 0.0220 oz. ASW **Obv:** Three crowns on crowned rectangular shield **Rev:** "Jehovah" in radiant circle **Mint:** Stockholm

Date	Mintage	VG	F	VF	XF	Unc
1601	—	90.00	195	295	—	—
1602	—	170	350	650	—	—
1603	—	85.00	180	260	—	—

KM# 31 ORE
1.6201 g., 0.2500 Silver 0.0130 oz. ASW **Obv:** Sheaf separating letters C R **Rev:** Lion rampant **Mint:** Stockholm

Date	Mintage	VG	F	VF	XF	Unc
1609	—	27.50	45.00	70.00	160	—
1610	—	27.50	45.00	70.00	160	—
1611	—	31.50	55.00	80.00	180	—
ND(1611) Rare	—	—	—	—	—	—
1612 Rare	—	—	—	—	—	—

KM# 32 ORE
1.6201 g., 0.2500 Silver 0.0130 oz. ASW **Obv:** Value in legend **Mint:** Gothenburg

Date	Mintage	VG	F	VF	XF	Unc
1609	—	175	375	725	1,450	—
1610	—	105	190	295	650	—

KM# 33 ORE
1.6201 g., 0.2500 Silver 0.0130 oz. ASW **Obv:** Value in field **Mint:** Gothenburg

Date	Mintage	VG	F	VF	XF	Unc
1609	—	120	225	350	750	—
1610	—	105	190	260	575	—
1611	—	120	210	295	650	—

KM# 50 ORE
1.6201 g., 0.2500 Silver 0.0130 oz. ASW **Note:** "1010" error date variety.

Date	Mintage	VG	F	VF	XF	Unc
1610 Rare	—	105	190	325	625	—
1010 error date	—	105	190	325	625	—

KM# 58 ORE
1.6201 g., 0.2500 Silver 0.0130 oz. ASW **Obv:** Lion rampant, value below **Rev:** GAR around three crown shield **Mint:** Vadstena and Soderkoping

Date	Mintage	VG	F	VF	XF	Unc
ND(1611-17)	—	42.00	90.00	155	325	—

KM# 59 ORE

1.6201 g., 0.2500 Silver 0.0130 oz. ASW **Obv:** Value at lion's side **Mint:** Vadstena and Soderkoping

Date	Mintage	VG	F	VF	XF	Unc
ND(1611-17)	—	55.00	115	180	375	—

KM# 60 ORE

1.6201 g., 0.2500 Silver 0.0130 oz. ASW **Obv:** Without value **Mint:** Vadstena and Soderkoping

Date	Mintage	VG	F	VF	XF	Unc
ND(1611-17)	—	65.00	120	190	375	—

KM# 70 ORE

1.6201 g., 0.2500 Silver 0.0130 oz. ASW **Obv:** Three crowns with value **Rev:** Sheath with date and letters G.A.R. **Mint:** Stockholm

Date	Mintage	VG	F	VF	XF	Unc
1613	—	35.00	90.00	170	350	—

KM# 71.1 ORE

1.6201 g., 0.2500 Silver 0.0130 oz. ASW **Obv:** Lion rampant **Rev:** Sheath with date and letters G.A.R. **Mint:** Stockholm

Date	Mintage	VG	F	VF	XF	Unc
1615	—	35.00	100	170	350	—
1616	—	27.50	75.00	130	280	—
1617	—	27.50	75.00	130	280	—
1618	—	27.50	75.00	130	280	—
1619	—	27.50	75.00	130	280	—
1620	—	27.50	75.00	130	280	—
1621	—	27.50	75.00	130	280	—
1622	—	27.50	75.00	130	280	—
x622	—	35.00	115	155	350	—
xx22	—	35.00	115	155	350	—
1623	—	27.50	75.00	130	280	—
1624	—	25.00	60.00	110	245	—
1625 Rare	—	—	—	—	—	—
ND(1625) Rare	—	—	—	—	—	—

KM# 73 ORE

1.6201 g., 0.2500 Silver 0.0130 oz. ASW **Obv:** Without value **Mint:** Soderkoping

Date	Mintage	VG	F	VF	XF	Unc
(16)17	—	70.00	150	230	450	—

KM# 72 ORE

1.6201 g., 0.2500 Silver 0.0130 oz. ASW **Obv:** Lion rampant, value below **Mint:** Soderkoping

Date	Mintage	VG	F	VF	XF	Unc
1617	—	55.00	115	195	425	—
(16)17	—	65.00	130	230	500	—
1671 Error, rare	—	—	—	—	—	—

KM# 71.2 ORE

1.6201 g., 0.2500 Silver 0.0130 oz. ASW **Mint:** Kalmar **Note:** Varieties of placement of mint marks exist.

Date	Mintage	VG	F	VF	XF	Unc
1623 Rare	—	—	—	—	—	—
1624	—	85.00	180	260	550	—
1625	—	85.00	180	260	550	—
1626	—	—	—	—	—	—
1627	—	—	—	—	—	—

KM# 71.3 ORE

1.6201 g., 0.2500 Silver 0.0130 oz. ASW **Mint:** Gothenburg **Note:** Both dates also known on square planchets.

Date	Mintage	VG	F	VF	XF	Unc
1625	—	90.00	180	295	625	—
1626 Rare	180,000	—	—	—	—	—

KM# 106.1 ORE

28.3000 g., Copper **Mint:** Sater

Date	Mintage	VG	F	VF	XF	Unc
1625	—	90.00	190	325	700	—
1626	—	85.00	150	260	625	—
1627	—	120	265	475	975	—

KM# 106.2 ORE

28.3000 g., Copper **Mint:** Nykoping and Sater

Date	Mintage	VG	F	VF	XF	Unc
1625	—	35.00	85.00	155	550	—
1625 Rare	—	—	—	—	—	—
Note: "S" on reverse						
1626	—	30.75	75.00	150	375	—
1627	—	55.00	120	235	725	—

KM# 114 ORE

28.3000 g., Copper **Obv:** Three crowns, date **Rev:** Griffin, value **Mint:** Arboga

Date	Mintage	VG	F	VF	XF	Unc
1626 Rare	—	—	—	—	—	—
1627	—	850	1,700	3,350	—	—

KM# 71.4 ORE

1.6201 g., 0.2500 Silver 0.0130 oz. ASW **Mint:** Norrkoping **Note:** Varieties exist, including a square planchet.

Date	Mintage	VG	F	VF	XF	Unc
1626	—	325	525	1,050	1,950	—

KM# 115 ORE

28.3000 g., Copper **Obv:** Crown above crossed arrows, value, date in legend **Rev:** Crowned arms **Mint:** Sater **Note:** Varieties of crown types exist.

Date	Mintage	VG	F	VF	XF	Unc
1627	—	20.00	45.00	110	350	—
1628 MDCXXVIII	—	14.00	37.50	80.00	280	—
1628 DCXXVIII	—	105	265	475	975	—
1629	—	14.00	37.50	65.00	210	—
1630	—	—	—	—	—	—
1631	—	—	—	—	—	—

KM# 118 ORE

28.3000 g., Copper, 44 mm. **Obv:** Crown above arms **Rev:** Eagle, value, date **Mint:** Arboga

Date	Mintage	VG	F	VF	XF	Unc
1627	—	195	375	975	1,950	—

KM# 119 ORE

28.3000 g., Copper, 41 mm. **Mint:** Arboga

Date	Mintage	VG	F	VF	XF	Unc
1627	—	75.00	190	30.00	775	—
1628	—	70.00	150	30.00	700	—

KM# 116 ORE

28.3000 g., Copper **Obv:** Arms below crown, sheaf in center **Rev:** Griffin with wings down, value, date **Mint:** Nykoping

Date	Mintage	VG	F	VF	XF	Unc
1627 MDCXXV2 Rare	—	—	—	—	—	—
1627 MDCXXVII	—	210	375	725	1,400	—
1627 Rare, date in field	—	—	—	—	—	—
1627 MDCXX7	—	27.50	60.00	150	500	—

KM# 125 ORE

28.3000 g., Copper **Rev:** Value at griffin's sides **Mint:** Sater

Date	Mintage	VG	F	VF	XF	Unc
1628	—	170	350	1,000	1,750	—

KM# 117 ORE

28.3000 g., Copper **Rev:** Griffin with wings up **Mint:** Nykoping **Note:** Varieties exist.

Date	Mintage	VG	F	VF	XF	Unc
1628 MDCXXVIII	—	55.00	120	210	975	—
1628 DCXXVIII Rare	—	—	—	—	—	—
1629 MDCXXVIIII Rare	—	—	—	—	—	—
1629 MDCXXIX	—	55.00	120	210	975	—

KM# 153 ORE

1.2317 g., 0.3750 Copper 0.0148 oz. **Obv:** Sheaf on shield below crown, date **Rev:** Three crowns on shield, value **Mint:** Stockholm

Date	Mintage	VG	F	VF	XF	Unc
1633 CHRISTINA	683,000	27.50	55.00	100	175	—
1633 CHRITINA	—	105	190	325	625	—
1634	3,216,000	27.50	55.00	100	175	—
1635	1,238,000	25.00	48.75	80.00	170	—
1636	1,395,000	27.50	55.00	100	175	—
1637	—	25.00	48.75	85.00	170	—
1650	—	49.00	75.00	155	325	—
1653	404,000	25.00	48.75	80.00	170	—

KM# 154 ORE

1.2317 g., 0.3750 Copper 0.0148 oz. **Obv:** Shield with ornaments at sides **Mint:** Stockholm

Date	Mintage	VG	F	VF	XF	Unc
1633 Rare	—	—	—	—	—	—

KM# 159 ORE

1.2317 g., 0.3750 Copper 0.0148 oz. **Obv:** Date above shield **Rev:** Griffin **Mint:** Gothenburg

Date	Mintage	VG	F	VF	XF	Unc
1635	—	49.00	115	300	550	—
1636 RE.SVE.	—	45.50	105	215	500	—
1636 REC.SV.	—	70.00	180	475	775	—

KM# 161 ORE

51.5000 g., Copper **Mint:** Sater

Date	Mintage	VG	F	VF	XF	Unc
1638	12,471,000	42.00	105	195	375	—
1639	12,612,000	42.00	105	210	425	—
1640	8,835,000	49.00	120	230	450	—
1641	Inc. above	350	1,250	2,500	4,200	—

KM# 162.1 ORE

51.5000 g., Copper **Obv:** Without ornamentation at sides of arms **Mint:** Sater

Date	Mintage	VG	F	VF	XF	Unc
1638	Inc. above	100	225	400	900	—

KM# 162.2 ORE

51.5000 g., Copper **Mint:** Avesta

Date	Mintage	VG	F	VF	XF	Unc
1644 MDCXLIV	2,798,400	210	375	900	2,100	—
1644 MDCXL4	Inc. above	49.00	115	230	500	—
1645	9,929,600	38.50	90.00	195	425	—
1646	6,893,200	42.00	100	215	450	—
1647	2,622,400	49.00	115	230	500	—
1648	1,780,400	70.00	150	260	550	—
1649	1,914,800	49.00	115	230	500	—
1650	356,400	42.00	100	215	450	—
1651	733,600	49.00	115	260	550	—
1652	542,880	49.00	115	230	500	—
1653	256,000	70.00	150	260	550	—
1653 Small crown	Inc. above	155	375	650	1,250	—

KM# 212 ORE

1.2317 g., 0.3750 Silver 0.0148 oz. ASW **Obv:** Griffin in shield below crown, date **Rev:** Three crowns in shield, value **Mint:** Stockholm **Note:** Three mint mark varieties exist.

Date	Mintage	VG	F	VF	XF	Unc
1654	315,000	75.00	150	295	550	—
1655	145,000	55.00	120	195	375	—
1656	167,000	55.00	120	195	375	—
1657	361,000	55.00	120	195	375	—
1659*	83,000	55.00	120	195	375	—
1660	75,000	65.00	135	230	450	—

KM# 230 ORE

1.2317 g., 0.3750 Silver 0.0148 oz. ASW **Obv. Legend:** CAROLVS ... **Mint:** Stockholm **Note:** Similar to KM#212.

Date	Mintage	VG	F	VF	XF	Unc
1660 Rare	—	—	—	—	—	—
1661	37,000	49.00	130	240	525	—
1662 GW	59,000	49.00	130	230	525	—
1662 Rare	Inc. above	—	115	—	425	—
1663 GW	35,000	75.00	150	295	625	—
1663	—	70.00	150	260	550	—
1664 GW	431,000	70.00	150	260	550	—
1664 IK	—	42.00	115	195	425	—
1664	—	35.00	75.00	130	280	—

KM# 248 ORE

1.2317 g., 0.3130 Silver 0.0124 oz. ASW **Obv:** Crowned CRS monogram **Rev:** Three crowns, date, value **Mint:** Stockholm

Date	Mintage	VG	F	VF	XF	Unc
1665 IK	857,000	35.00	85.00	145	325	—
1665 Arrow	Inc. above	55.00	150	260	550	—

KM# 249 ORE

1.2317 g., 0.3130 Silver 0.0124 oz. ASW **Obv:** Crowned double C monogram **Mint:** Stockholm

Date	Mintage	VG	F	VF	XF	Unc
1665 Rare	Inc. above	—	—	—	—	—
1697	Inc. below	27.50	70.00	110	245	—

KM# 250 ORE

1.2317 g., 0.3130 Silver 0.0124 oz. ASW **Mint:** Stockholm

Date	Mintage	VG	F	VF	XF	Unc
1665	—	25.00	55.00	100	210	—
1666/65	—	20.00	45.00	85.00	175	—
1666	1,864,000	18.00	37.50	65.00	140	—
1667/66	—	25.00	55.00	100	210	—
1667	1,556,000	18.00	37.50	65.00	140	—
1668	3,058,000	18.00	37.50	65.00	140	—
1669	Inc. above	18.00	37.50	65.00	140	—
1669 FIRST	283,000	25.00	55.00	90.00	210	—
1670	606,000	18.00	37.50	65.00	140	—
1671	598,000	20.00	45.00	70.00	170	—
1672 FIRST	1,341,000	18.00	37.50	65.00	140	—
1672 DF	Inc. above	20.00	45.00	70.00	170	—
1673	438,000	18.00	37.50	65.00	140	—
1674	379,000	18.00	37.50	65.00	140	—
1675	Inc. above	20.00	45.00	80.00	175	—
1677	378,000	18.00	37.50	65.00	140	—
1681	204,000	18.00	37.50	65.00	140	—
1682/81	—	25.00	55.00	105	245	—
1682	377,000	14.00	30.00	60.00	125	—
1683	599,000	14.00	30.00	60.00	125	—
1684	726,000	14.00	30.00	60.00	125	—
1685	583,000	14.00	30.00	60.00	125	—

KM# 250a ORE

1.2317 g., 0.2500 Silver 0.0099 oz. ASW **Ruler:** Carl XII **Obv:** XII within C and sprigs, crown above **Rev:** 3 Crowns, divided date, initials and value **Mint:** Stockholm

Date	Mintage	VG	F	VF	XF	Unc
1686/85	—	27.50	40.00	105	—	—
1686	408,000	13.00	33.00	65.00	120	—
1687	335,000	13.00	33.00	60.00	120	—
1688	324,000	14.00	33.00	60.00	120	—
1689	337,000	14.00	33.00	60.00	120	—
1690	329,000	13.00	33.00	50.00	120	—
1691	323,000	18.00	33.00	60.00	120	—
1692	333,000	14.00	33.00	60.00	120	—
1693	319,000	13.00	33.00	60.00	120	—
1694	333,000	13.00	33.00	60.00	120	—
1695	328,000	13.00	33.00	60.00	120	—
1696	422,000	13.00	33.00	60.00	120	—
1697	329,000	25.00	33.00	60.00	120	—
1698	328,000	20.00	33.00	60.00	120	—
1698/7	—	20.00	33.00	60.00	120	—
1699	322,000	20.00	33.00	60.00	120	—
1700	418,000	20.00	33.00	60.00	120	—

KM# 264 ORE (S.M.)

49.4000 g., Copper **Mint:** Avesta

Date	Mintage	VG	F	VF	XF	Unc
1669 Rose	1,983,000	75.00	165	295	625	—
1673 Rose	3,219,000	90.00	190	325	700	—
1673 Large star	Inc. above	49.00	115	175	375	—
1673 Small star	Inc. above	55.00	120	195	425	—
1673 Fleur-de-lis	—	—	—	—	—	—

KM# 264a ORE (S.M.)

42.5000 g., Copper **Mint:** Avesta

Date	Mintage	VG	F	VF	XF	Unc
1675	1,728,000	42.00	90.00	175	375	—
1676	1,595,000	35.00	75.00	155	350	—
1677/76	—	49.00	105	195	425	—
1677	3,286,000	35.00	75.00	155	350	—
1678	1,469,000	38.50	85.00	165	350	—
1679	269,000	85.00	180	350	775	—
1680	630,000	38.50	85.00	155	350	—

KM# 264b ORE (S.M.)

40.5000 g., Copper **Mint:** Avesta

Date	Mintage	VG	F	VF	XF	Unc
1683	336,000	42.00	90.00	170	350	—
1684/83	—	75.00	165	285	600	—
1684	277,000	49.00	105	215	375	—
1685	551,000	42.00	90.00	170	350	—
1686	578,000	38.50	85.00	145	325	—

KM# 232.1 ORE (K.M.)
17.7000 g., Copper **Obv:** C.R.S. above crowned ornamented shield **Mint:** Avesta **Note:** Prev. KM#232.

Date	Mintage	VG	F	VF	XF	Unc
1661 Without square by crown	—	42.00	90.00	175	350	—
1661 Square over arrow	—	45.50	115	215	450	—
1661 Two squares by crown	—	75.00	165	300	675	—
1662	—	42.00	90.00	175	350	—
1663	—	42.00	90.00	175	350	—
1664/63	—	70.00	150	285	625	—
1664	—	49.00	105	215	500	—

KM# 232.2 ORE (K.M.)
17.7000 g., Copper **Obv:** Crowned plain shield **Mint:** Avesta **Note:** Prev. KM#233.

Date	Mintage	VG	F	VF	XF	Unc
1661 Rare	—	—	—	—	—	—

KM# 9 2 ORE
2.9254 g., 0.5000 Silver 0.0470 oz. ASW **Mint:** Stockholm

Date	Mintage	VG	F	VF	XF	Unc
1602	—	295	525	1,050	—	—

KM# 16 2 ORE
1.8805 g., 0.5000 Silver 0.0302 oz. ASW **Obv:** Crown above sheaf, C D R below **Rev:** Three crowns, value, date **Mint:** Stockholm

Date	Mintage	VG	F	VF	XF	Unc
1605 Rare	—	—	—	—	—	—

KM# 28 2 ORE
1.8805 g., 0.5000 Silver 0.0302 oz. ASW **Obv:** Sheaf in shield below crown, date **Rev:** Three crowns in shield, value **Mint:** Stockholm **Note:** Struck at Stockholm Mint.

Date	Mintage	VG	F	VF	XF	Unc
1608	—	45.50	100	195	425	—
1609	—	42.00	90.00	170	350	—
1610	—	42.00	90.00	170	350	—
1611	—	49.00	105	215	450	—

KM# 34 2 ORE
1.8805 g., 0.5000 Silver 0.0302 oz. ASW **Obv:** Shield with ornaments **Mint:** Stockholm

Date	Mintage	VG	F	VF	XF	Unc
1609	—	100	225	350	900	—

KM# 35 2 ORE
1.8805 g., 0.5000 Silver 0.0302 oz. ASW **Obv:** Sheaf in shield below crown, date **Rev:** Lion rampant in shield, value **Mint:** Gothenburg

Date	Mintage	VG	F	VF	XF	Unc
1609	—	350	700	1,400	2,450	—
1610 Rare	—	—	—	—	—	—

KM# 51 2 ORE
1.8805 g., 0.5000 Silver 0.0302 oz. ASW **Mint:** Gothenburg **Note:** Square planchet.

Date	Mintage	VG	F	VF	XF	Unc
1610 Rare	—	—	—	—	—	—

KM# A67 2 ORE
4.8418 g., 0.6250 Silver 0.0973 oz. ASW **Obv:** Hebrew "Jehovah" above crowned bust of Gustaf II Adolf left **Rev:** Crown above three shields **Mint:** Stockholm

Date	Mintage	VG	F	VF	XF	Unc
1618 Rare	—	—	—	—	—	—

KM# 102 2 ORE
1.8805 g., 0.5000 Silver 0.0302 oz. ASW **Mint:** Kalmar **Note:** Square planchet.

Date	Mintage	VG	F	VF	XF	Unc
1623 Rare	—	—	—	—	—	—

KM# 101 2 ORE
1.8805 g., 0.5000 Silver 0.0302 oz. ASW **Obv:** Sheaf in shield below crown, date **Rev:** Three crowns in shield, value **Mint:** Kalmar

Date	Mintage	VG	F	VF	XF	Unc
1623	—	195	325	775	1,400	—
1624	—	280	525	1,000	1,750	—
1625 Rare	—	—	—	—	—	—

KM# 107 2 ORE
58.6000 g., Copper **Obv:** Crown above G A R, S below **Rev:** Sheaf, value, date **Mint:** Säter and Nyköping

Date	Mintage	VG	F	VF	XF	Unc
1625	—	425	1,150	—	—	—
1626	1,020,000	280	875	—	—	—
1627	—	500	1,550	—	—	—

KM# 108 2 ORE
58.6000 g., Copper **Mint:** Nykoping and Sater

Date	Mintage	VG	F	VF	XF	Unc
1626	—	245	375	725	1,400	—
1627	—	375	675	1,250	2,450	—

KM# 241.1 2 ORE
1.7551 g., 0.4440 Silver 0.0251 oz. ASW **Obv:** Crown above C R S, wreath around **Rev:** Three crowns, date, value **Mint:** Stockholm

Date	Mintage	VG	F	VF	XF	Unc
1664 IK, 2	2,639,000	20.00	45.00	85.00	175	—
1664 IAK	576,000	38.50	70.00	175	295	—
1664 IK, II	Inc. above	20.00	45.00	85.00	175	—
1664 IK, II	Inc. above	18.00	30.00	60.00	140	—
1665/65	—	18.00	37.50	70.00	155	—
1665 IK, 2	Inc. above	18.00	37.50	70.00	155	—
1665 With arrow	Inc. above	18.00	37.50	70.00	155	—
1666	2,087,000	14.00	30.00	65.00	140	—
1667	1,313,000	18.00	37.50	70.00	155	—
1669	39,000	31.50	75.00	130	280	—

KM# 241.3 2 ORE
1.7551 g., 0.4440 Silver 0.0251 oz. ASW **Obv:** CXI **Mint:** Stockholm

Date	Mintage	VG	F	VF	XF	Unc
1666 Rare	Inc. above	—	—	—	—	—

KM# 241.2 2 ORE
1.7551 g., 0.4440 Silver 0.0251 oz. ASW **Mint:** Landskrone

Date	Mintage	VG	F	VF	XF	Unc
1675	—	85.00	190	350	775	—
1675	—	180	400	725	1,400	—
1676	—	140	300	525	1,100	—

KM# 234.2 2 ORE (K.M.)
35.4000 g., Copper **Obv:** Crowned plain shield **Mint:** Avesta

Date	Mintage	VG	F	VF	XF	Unc
1661	—	—	—	—	—	—

KM# 234.1 2 ORE (K.M.)
35.4000 g., Copper **Obv:** C R S above crowned ornamented shield, date **Rev:** Crown above shield with three crowns, value **Mint:** Avesta **Note:** Prev. KM#234.

Date	Mintage	VG	F	VF	XF	Unc
1661	—	65.00	135	260	550	—
Note: Shield with ornaments						
1662	—	105	225	475	1,000	—
1663/62	—	85.00	190	350	775	—
1663	—	49.00	105	215	450	—
1664/63	—	85.00	180	350	775	—
1664	—	49.00	105	195	425	—
1665	—	85.00	190	230	500	—

KM# 235 2-1/2 ORE (K.M.)
44.3000 g., Copper **Obv:** C. R. S. above crowned shield **Rev:** Value above threee crowns **Mint:** Avesta

Date	Mintage	VG	F	VF	XF	Unc
1661	—	775	1,400	2,800	4,900	—

KM# 10 4 ORE (1/2 Mark)
4.8418 g., 0.6250 Silver 0.0973 oz. ASW **Mint:** Stockholm

Date	Mintage	VG	F	VF	XF	Unc
1602	—	270	600	950	—	—
1603	—	215	475	700	—	—

KM# 17 4 ORE (1/2 Mark)
4.8418 g., 0.6250 Silver 0.0973 oz. ASW **Obv:** Crown above shield with three crowns, sheaf and lion, value **Rev:** Hebrew "Jehovah", date in outer circle **Mint:** Stockholm

Date	Mintage	VG	F	VF	XF	Unc
1605 Rare	—	—	—	—	—	—
1606	—	135	235	400	775	—

KM# 21 4 ORE (1/2 Mark)
4.8418 g., 0.6250 Silver 0.0973 oz. ASW **Obv:** Hebrew "Jehovah" above crowned bust of Carl IX left **Rev:** Crowned arms, value, date **Mint:** Stockholm

Date	Mintage	VG	F	VF	XF	Unc
1607	—	115	205	325	700	—
1608	—	135	270	400	850	—
1609	—	135	270	400	850	—

KM# 66 4 ORE (1/2 Mark)
4.8418 g., 0.6250 Silver 0.0973 oz. ASW **Obv:** Hebrew "Jehovah" above bust of Gustaf II Adolf left **Rev:** Crown above three shields, lion, value, date **Mint:** Stockholm

Date	Mintage	VG	F	VF	XF	Unc
1615	—	1,100	1,600	2,250	3,850	—
1617	—	975	1,300	1,600	2,800	—

KM# 251 4 ORE (1/2 Mark)
3.5103 g., 0.4440 Silver 0.0501 oz. ASW **Obv:** Doubled C monogram below crown **Rev:** Three crowns, date, value **Mint:** Stockholm

Date	Mintage	VG	F	VF	XF	Unc
1665 Rare	—	—	—	—	—	—
1666 Rare	—	—	—	—	—	—

KM# 257 4 ORE (1/2 Mark)
2.9252 g., 0.3750 Silver 0.0353 oz. ASW **Ruler:** Carl XII **Obv:** Crowned C **Rev:** Three crowns **Note:** Varieties exist.

Date	Mintage	VG	F	VF	XF	Unc
1667	473,000	33.75	70.00	135	245	—
1668	1,102,000	20.00	40.50	90.00	175	—
1669	1,023,000	20.00	40.50	90.00	175	—
1669 AO before date	Inc. above	27.50	55.00	100	210	—
1669 Without mm	Inc. above	27.50	55.00	100	210	—
x669	Inc. above	47.25	100	270	500	—
x670	Inc. above	47.25	100	270	500	—
1670	4,197,000	17.00	33.75	80.00	175	—
1671	3,627,000	20.00	40.50	90.00	190	—
1672	1,055,000	20.00	40.50	90.00	190	—
1672 DF	Inc. above	30.50	60.00	110	245	—
1673	1,052,000	27.50	55.00	100	210	—
1674	356,000	20.00	40.50	90.00	170	—
1675	560,000	20.00	40.50	90.00	170	—
1676	1,196,000	20.00	40.50	90.00	170	—
1677	1,047,000	17.00	33.75	70.00	140	—
1678	1,258,000	17.00	33.75	70.00	140	—
1679/76	—	27.50	55.00	100	210	—
1679	978,000	20.00	40.50	90.00	190	—
1680	103,554	17.00	33.75	70.00	140	—
1681	458,000	20.00	40.50	95.00	210	—
1682	197,000	33.75	70.00	135	280	—
1683	202,000	27.50	55.00	110	225	—
1684	137,000	40.50	80.00	160	325	—

KM# 310 5 ORE (S.M.)
3.5103 g., 0.4440 Silver 0.0501 oz. ASW **Obv:** Crown above doubled large C monogram, date **Rev:** Three crowns, value **Mint:** Stockholm

Date	Mintage	VG	F	VF	XF	Unc
1690	1,678,000	16.00	33.75	75.00	155	—
1691	2,563,000	16.00	33.75	75.00	155	—
1692	1,857,000	22.50	40.50	90.00	190	—
1693/92	—	30.50	55.00	120	245	—
1693	2,368,000	16.00	33.75	75.00	155	—
1694	2,257,000	16.00	33.75	75.00	155	—
1699	1,271,000	16.00	33.75	75.00	155	—
1700	2,195,000	16.00	33.75	75.00	155	—

KM# 158 8 ORE (1 Mark)
5.2004 g., 0.7500 Silver 0.1254 oz. ASW **Obv:** Christina seated holding book and orb **Rev:** Crowned arms divide value **Mint:** Stockholm

Date	Mintage	VG	F	VF	XF	Unc
1634	105,000	235	400	800	1,400	—

KM# 13 MARK (8 Ore)
4.9363 g., 0.0210 Silver 0.0033 oz. ASW **Obv:** Crowned arms divide date **Rev:** Hebrew "Jehovah" in rays at center, value **Mint:** Stockholm

Date	Mintage	VG	F	VF	XF	Unc
1604	—	170	350	750	1,400	—
1605	—	115	235	375	850	—
1606	—	110	205	300	625	—

KM# 22 MARK (8 Ore)
4.9363 g., 0.0210 Silver 0.0033 oz. ASW **Obv:** Hebrew "Jehovah" above half-length crowned figure of Carl IX left **Rev:** Crowned arms divide date **Mint:** Stockholm

Date	Mintage	VG	F	VF	XF	Unc
1607	—	100	170	270	350	—
1608	—	80.00	160	245	300	—
1609	—	100	170	270	375	—
1610	—	110	205	375	700	—
1610 CARLOS	—	170	400	800	1,550	—
1611	—	135	90.00	500	375	—

KM# 61 MARK (8 Ore)
4.9363 g., 0.0210 Silver 0.0033 oz. ASW **Obv:** Hebrew "Jehovah" above laureate bust of Gustaf II Adolf left **Rev:** Triple shield, three crowns, lion, sheaf, date, value **Mint:** Stockholm

Date	Mintage	VG	F	VF	XF	Unc
1613 Rare	—	—	—	—	—	—
1614	—	950	1,350	1,950	4,550	—
1615	—	650	975	1,350	2,450	—
1616 Rare	—	—	—	—	—	—
1617	—	575	950	1,250	2,400	—
1617/19	—	650	975	1,350	2,450	—

KM# 74 MARK (8 Ore)
4.9363 g., 0.0210 Silver 0.0033 oz. ASW **Obv:** Crowned bust of Gustaf II Adolf left **Rev:** Crowned amrs divide value **Mint:** Stockholm

Date	Mintage	VG	F	VF	XF	Unc
1617 Rare	—	—	—	—	—	—
1618	—	1,100	1,350	1,750	3,500	—

KM# 181 MARK (8 Ore)
5.5063 g., 0.7500 Silver 0.1328 oz. ASW **Obv:** Bust of Queen Christina right **Rev:** Crowned arms divide value **Mint:** Stockholm

Date	Mintage	VG	F	VF	XF	Unc
1641	—	—	475	1,200	—	—
1642 Rare	—	—	—	—	—	—
1646 Rare	—	—	—	—	—	—
1647	—	70.00	205	550	1,100	—
1648	—	150	270	800	1,750	—

KM# 191 MARK (8 Ore)
5.2004 g., 0.7500 Silver 0.1254 oz. ASW **Rev:** Curved shield **Mint:** Stockholm

Date	Mintage	VG	F	VF	XF	Unc
1648	—	135	450	1,100	1,950	—

KM# 181a MARK (8 Ore)
5.2004 g., 0.7500 Silver 0.1254 oz. ASW **Obv:** Bust of Christina right **Rev:** Crowned arms **Mint:** Stockholm

Date	Mintage	VG	F	VF	XF	Unc
1649	—	80.00	205	475	850	—
1650	—	80.00	205	475	850	—
1651	—	90.00	225	475	925	—

KM# 182 MARK (8 Ore)
5.2004 g., 0.7500 Silver 0.1254 oz. ASW **Rev:** Three crowns **Mint:** Stockholm

Date	Mintage	VG	F	VF	XF	Unc
ND No mintmark	—	100	225	475	1,050	—
ND (ca) No value	—	70.00	190	450	975	—

KM# 219 MARK (8 Ore)
5.2004 g., 0.7500 Silver 0.1254 oz. ASW **Obv:** Bust of King Carl X Gustaf left **Rev:** Three crowns, value, date **Mint:** Stockholm

Date	Mintage	VG	F	VF	XF	Unc
1655	—	850	1,200	1,700	3,850	—
1656	—	850	1,200	1,700	3,850	—
1658	—	1,100	1,500	2,050	4,550	—
ND	—	1,000	1,350	1,900	4,200	—

KM# 240 MARK (8 Ore)
5.2004 g., 0.6940 Silver 0.1160 oz. ASW **Obv:** Bust of Carl XI left **Rev:** Three crowns **Mint:** Stockholm **Note:** Varieties exist.

Date	Mintage	VG	F	VF	XF	Unc
1663	73,000	150	295	750	1,700	—
1664 GW	—	100	195	600	1,250	—
1664	—	120	245	675	1,550	—
1664 IK	—	90.00	205	475	1,050	—
1664 IAK	—	120	230	675	1,250	—
1665	—	100	235	375	975	—
1669	—	120	285	675	1,550	—
1671	—	110	235	450	1,200	—
1671	—	120	270	450	1,550	—
Note: Error, Carolvs IX						
1672 Rare	—	—	—	—	—	—
1673	—	170	375	800	1,550	—
1674	—	120	285	675	1,550	—

KM# 295 MARK (8 Ore)
5.2004 g., 0.6940 Silver 0.1160 oz. ASW **Obv:** Bust of Carl XI right **Rev:** Three crowns **Mint:** Stockholm

Date	Mintage	VG	F	VF	XF	Unc
1683	—	80.00	160	400	850	—
1684	—	70.00	135	375	775	—
1685	—	47.25	100	235	500	—
1686/5	—	55.00	110	245	525	—
1686	—	47.25	100	235	500	—
1687	—	47.25	100	235	500	—
1688	—	40.50	90.00	205	425	—
1689	—	40.50	90.00	205	425	—
1690	—	40.50	90.00	205	425	—
1691	—	40.50	90.00	205	425	—
1692	—	40.50	90.00	205	425	—
1693	—	40.50	90.00	205	425	—
1694	—	40.50	90.00	205	425	—
1695	—	40.50	90.00	205	425	—
1696	—	40.50	90.00	205	425	—
1697	—	95.00	175	450	900	—

KM# 313 MARK (8 Ore)
0.6940 Silver **Ruler:** Carl XII **Obv:** Bust right **Obv. Inscription:** CAROLVS • XII • D • G • REX • S • V • E • **Rev:** Three crowns, divided date, value **Mint:** Stockholm

Date	Mintage	VG	F	VF	XF	Unc
1697	—	135	270	700	1,250	—
1698	24,000	70.00	135	350	625	—

Date	Mintage	VG	F	VF	XF	Unc
1699	52,000	47.25	100	300	550	—
1700	46,000	47.25	100	300	550	—

KM# 11 2 MARK

Silver **Obv:** Crowned "CDS" **Rev:** Crowned sheaf, dates in corners **Mint:** Kalmar

Date	Mintage	VG	F	VF	XF	Unc
1603	—	270	550	875	1,700	—
1604	—	350	950	1,600	2,500	—

KM# 14 2 MARK

9.8726 g., 0.8210 Silver 0.2606 oz. ASW **Obv:** Crowned arms divides date **Rev:** Hebrew "Jehovah" in rays **Mint:** Stockholm

Date	Mintage	VG	F	VF	XF	Unc
1604	—	205	400	800	1,400	—
Note: An incorrect coat-of-arms is reported dated 1604 and is rare						
1605	—	205	400	800	1,400	—
1606	—	180	350	650	1,100	—

KM# 23 2 MARK

9.8726 g., 0.8210 Silver 0.2606 oz. ASW **Obv:** Hebrew "Jehovah" above half-length crowned figure of Carl IX left **Rev:** Crowned arms divides date **Mint:** Stockholm

Date	Mintage	VG	F	VF	XF	Unc
1607	—	375	675	1,100	1,700	—
1608	—	375	675	1,100	1,700	—
1609	—	450	950	1,500	2,100	—
1610	—	375	800	1,300	1,950	—
1611 Rare	—	—	—	—	—	—

KM# 67 2 MARK

9.8726 g., 0.8210 Silver 0.2606 oz. ASW **Obv:** Hebrew "Jehovah" above laureate bust of King Gustaf II Adolf **Rev:** Triple shield, three crowns, lion, sheaf, value, date **Mint:** Stockholm

Date	Mintage	VG	F	VF	XF	Unc
1615	—	1,100	1,500	2,050	3,500	—
1617	—	900	1,200	1,700	3,150	—
1618 Rare	—	—	—	—	—	—
1619 Rare	—	—	—	—	—	—

KM# 163 2 MARK

11.0126 g., 0.7500 Silver 0.2655 oz. ASW **Obv:** 3/4-figure Queen Christina **Rev:** Crowned arms, value, date **Mint:** Stockholm

Date	Mintage	VG	F	VF	XF	Unc
1638	—	135	325	1,050	1,750	—

KM# 183 2 MARK

11.0126 g., 0.7500 Silver 0.2655 oz. ASW **Obv:** Facing bust of Christina **Mint:** Stockholm

Date	Mintage	VG	F	VF	XF	Unc
1641	—	130	270	900	2,100	—
1642	—	400	950	2,100	3,150	—
1646 Rare	—	—	—	—	—	—

KM# 192 2 MARK

11.0126 g., 0.7500 Silver 0.2655 oz. ASW **Obv:** Laureate bust of Christina with long hair right **Mint:** Stockholm

Date	Mintage	VG	F	VF	XF	Unc
1647 Rare	—	—	—	—	—	—
1648	—	350	750	1,750	—	—

KM# 195 2 MARK

10.4009 g., 0.7500 Silver 0.2508 oz. ASW **Obv:** Laureate bust of Christina with short hair right **Mint:** Stockholm

Date	Mintage	VG	F	VF	XF	Unc
1649	—	100	205	375	775	—
1650 REG	—	60.00	115	215	325	—
1650 REGI	—	60.00	120	215	375	—
1650 REGIN	—	70.00	135	270	500	—
1650 REGINA	—	70.00	130	215	425	—
1651	—	70.00	135	270	375	—

KM# 210 2 MARK

10.4008 g., 0.7500 Silver 0.2508 oz. ASW **Obv:** Head of Christina right **Rev:** Three crowns **Mint:** Stockholm

Date	Mintage	VG	F	VF	XF	Unc
ND(1651) (ca)	—	60.00	120	350	700	—
ND(1651) II M	—	70.00	135	400	850	—
ND(1651) 2 M Rare	—	—	—	—	—	—

KM# 213 2 MARK

10.4008 g., 0.7500 Silver 0.2508 oz. ASW **Obv:** Bust of Carl X Gustaf left **Rev:** Three crowns **Mint:** Stockholm

Date	Mintage	VG	F	VF	XF	Unc
ND(1655)	—	110	190	300	625	—
ND(1655)	—	120	205	350	700	—
Note: Bust with epaulet						
1656	—	135	235	400	850	—
1657	—	170	270	500	1,050	—
1658	—	135	235	400	850	—
1659	—	135	235	400	850	—
1660	62,000	205	300	550	1,100	—

KM# 236 2 MARK

10.4008 g., 0.7500 Silver 0.2508 oz. ASW **Obv:** Bust of Carl XI left **Rev:** Three crowns **Mint:** Stockholm

Date	Mintage	VG	F	VF	XF	Unc
1661	154,000	135	300	675	1,400	—

KM# 237 2 MARK

10.4008 g., 0.7500 Silver 0.2508 oz. ASW **Obv:** Longer laureate bust of Carl XI left **Rev:** Three crowns, value: II M: **Mint:** Stockholm

Date	Mintage	VG	F	VF	XF	Unc
1661	Inc. above	235	475	1,050	2,100	—
1662	171,000	100	205	500	1,100	—
1663 GW	14,000	135	270	650	1,200	—
1663 IFH	Inc. above	205	400	1,050	2,100	—
1663	Inc. above	205	400	950	1,950	—

KM# 237a 2 MARK

10.4008 g., 0.6940 Silver 0.2321 oz. ASW **Obv:** Half-length figure of Carl XI left **Rev:** Three crowns **Mint:** Stockholm

Date	Mintage	VG	F	VF	XF	Unc
1664 IK	—	40.50	90.00	180	350	—
1664 IAK	—	40.50	90.00	180	350	—
1665 IK	—	40.50	90.00	180	400	—
1665 IAK	—	40.50	90.00	180	400	—
1665 (as)	—	40.50	90.00	180	400	—
1666	494,000	33.75	80.00	170	280	—
1667	438,000	33.75	80.00	170	280	—
1668	—	33.75	80.00	170	280	—
1669	—	33.75	80.00	170	280	—

KM# 243 2 MARK

10.4008 g., 0.6940 Silver 0.2321 oz. ASW **Obv:** Youthful draped laureate bust of Carl XI right **Rev:** Three crowns **Mint:** Stockholm

Date	Mintage	VG	F	VF	XF	Unc
1664 IK	—	215	450	950	—	—

KM# 242 2 MARK

10.4008 g., 0.6940 Silver 0.2321 oz. ASW **Obv:** Youthful laureate bust of Carl XI left **Rev:** Three crowns, value: 2. - M: **Mint:** Stockholm **Note:** Varieties exist.

Date	Mintage	VG	F	VF	XF	Unc
1664 IK	—	—	—	—	—	—
1665 (as)	—	—	—	—	—	—
1665 IK	—	—	—	—	—	—
1669 FIRST	—	—	—	—	—	—
1670	802,000	33.75	80.00	170	300	—
1671	—	33.75	80.00	170	280	—
1671 Reversed 2	—	70.00	150	295	625	—
1672	—	40.50	90.00	170	325	—
1674	—	40.50	90.00	170	280	—
1675	240,000	40.50	90.00	170	325	—
1676	115,000	40.50	90.00	170	325	—
1677	76,000	55.00	135	245	500	—

KM# 260 2 MARK

10.4008 g., 0.6940 Silver 0.2321 oz. ASW **Obv:** Young laureate bust of Carl XI right **Mint:** Stockholm

Date	Mintage	VG	F	VF	XF	Unc
1668	—	33.75	75.00	160	325	—

Date	Mintage	VG	F	VF	XF	Unc
1673	—	33.75	75.00	160	325	—
1674	—	33.75	75.00	180	375	—

KM# 282.2 2 MARK

10.4008 g., 0.6940 Silver 0.2321 oz. ASW **Mint:** Landskrone
Note: Prev. KM#282a.2.

Date	Mintage	VG	F	VF	XF	Unc
1675	—	—	—	—	—	—

KM# 282.1 2 MARK

10.4008 g., 0.6940 Silver 0.2321 oz. ASW **Obv:** Mature bust of Carl XI right **Rev:** Three crowns **Mint:** Stockholm

Date	Mintage	VG	F	VF	XF	Unc
1677	Inc. above	80.00	160	350	725	—
1678	35,000	115	255	550	1,100	—
1679	36,000	115	255	550	1,100	—
1680	73,000	60.00	130	270	550	—
1680 with epaulet	—	115	255	550	1,100	—
1681	—	60.00	130	325	700	—
1682	153,000	40.50	75.00	210	450	—
1683	—	40.50	75.00	235	500	—
1684	—	47.25	90.00	250	525	—
1685	—	47.25	90.00	270	550	—
1686	—	40.50	75.00	170	350	—
1687	—	33.75	70.00	160	325	—
1688	—	27.50	60.00	150	300	—
1689	—	27.50	60.00	150	300	—
1690	—	27.50	60.00	150	300	—
1691	—	27.50	60.00	150	300	—
1692	—	27.50	55.00	135	280	—
1693	—	27.50	55.00	135	280	—
1694	—	27.50	55.00	135	280	—
1695	—	27.50	55.00	135	280	—
1696	—	27.50	55.00	135	280	—
1697	—	80.00	160	775	1,700	—

KM# 314 2 MARK

10.4000 g., 0.6940 Silver 0.2320 oz. ASW **Ruler:** Carl XII
Obv: Bust right **Obv. Legend:** CAROLVS • XII • D • G • REX • SVE • **Rev:** Three crowns, value **Mint:** Stockholm

Date	Mintage	VG	F	VF	XF	Unc
1697	—	47.25	205	400	850	—
1698	41,000	60.00	135	300	700	—
1699	365,000	33.75	115	235	525	—
1700	518,000	27.50	100	205	425	—

KM# 12 4 MARK

Silver **Obv:** Crowned "CDS" **Rev:** Crowned sheaf, date in corners **Mint:** Kalmar

Date	Mintage	VG	F	VF	XF	Unc
1603	—	280	550	900	1,800	—
1604	—	375	850	1,700	2,800	—

KM# 15.1 4 MARK

19.7453 g., 0.8210 Silver 0.5212 oz. ASW **Obv:** Half-figure of Charles IX above arms divides date **Rev:** Hebrew "Jehovah" in rays at center **Mint:** Stockholm

Date	Mintage	VG	F	VF	XF	Unc
1604	—	205	400	650	1,200	—
1605	—	180	375	575	1,100	—
1606	—	190	400	600	1,150	—

KM# 15.2 4 MARK

19.7453 g., 0.8210 Silver 0.5212 oz. ASW **Obv:** Shield with lions and crowns incorrectly placed **Mint:** Stockholm

Date	Mintage	VG	F	VF	XF	Unc
1604 Rare	—	—	—	—	—	—

KM# 24 4 MARK

19.7453 g., 0.8210 Silver 0.5212 oz. ASW **Obv:** Hebrew "Jehovah" above half-length crowned figure of Carl IX left **Rev:** Crowned arms divide date **Mint:** Stockholm

Date	Mintage	VG	F	VF	XF	Unc
1607 3 varieties	—	180	300	575	1,100	—
1608 GOLATIM	—	250	450	1,050	2,100	—
1608 GOLATIVN	—	170	270	550	1,050	—
1609	—	180	300	575	1,100	—
1610 MEVM	—	170	270	550	1,050	—
1610 MVEM	—	205	375	600	1,350	—
1611	—	180	300	600	1,350	—

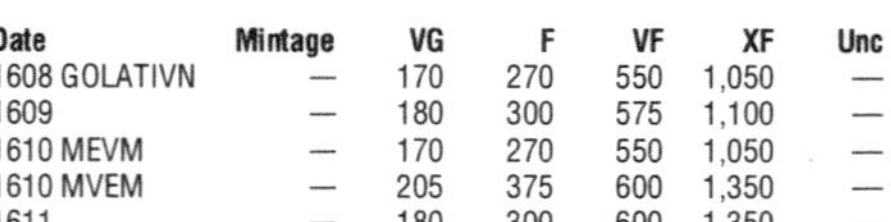

KM# 62 4 MARK

19.7453 g., 0.8210 Silver 0.5212 oz. ASW **Obv:** Half-figure of John, Duke of Ostergotland right, date **Rev:** Triform arms below Hebrew "Jehovah", value **Mint:** Vadstena

Date	Mintage	VG	F	VF	XF	Unc
1613	—	—	—	—	—	—

KM# 63.1 4 MARK

19.7453 g., 0.8210 Silver 0.5212 oz. ASW **Obv:** Bust of John, Duke of Ostergotland left **Rev:** Triform arms below Hebrew "Jehovah" **Mint:** Vadstena

Date	Mintage	VG	F	VF	XF	Unc
1613 Rare	—	—	—	—	—	—
1614	—	1,250	2,100	4,350	8,400	—

KM# 64 4 MARK

19.7453 g., 0.8210 Silver 0.5212 oz. ASW **Obv:** Hebrew "Jehovah" above laureate bust of Gustaf II Adolfus left **Rev:** Three crowned shields **Mint:** Stockholm

Date	Mintage	VG	F	VF	XF	Unc
1613	—	450	750	1,100	2,150	—
1614 GLORIA	—	270	475	575	1,200	—
1614 GLORIA	—	270	475	575	1,200	—
1614 GLORA	—	350	600	850	1,750	—
1614 Reversed 4	—	350	500	750	1,550	—
1615	—	270	475	575	1,200	—
1616	—	295	475	700	1,550	—
1617	—	270	475	650	1,350	—
1618	—	375	600	775	1,600	—
1619 Rare	—	—	—	—	—	—
1620 Rare	—	—	—	—	—	—
1626	—	1,200	2,350	4,050	7,000	—

KM# 63.2 4 MARK

19.7453 g., 0.8210 Silver 0.5212 oz. ASW **Mint:** Soderkoping

Date	Mintage	VG	F	VF	XF	Unc
1617 Rare	—	—	—	—	—	—

KM# 164 4 MARK

22.0252 g., 0.7500 Silver 0.5311 oz. ASW **Obv:** Christina seated left **Rev:** Crowned arms **Mint:** Stockholm

Date	Mintage	VG	F	VF	XF	Unc
1638 Large Collar	—	160	325	875	1,950	—
1638 Over date: III/II Small Collar legend ends ER:HE	—	350	675	1,350	3,500	—

Date	Mintage	VG	F	VF	XF	Unc
1638 Small Collar Legend ends PR: HE	—	170	350	1,600	2,800	—
1638 Small Collar Legend ends ER:HE	—	300	650	1,900	3,500	—

KM# 184 4 MARK

22.0252 g., 0.7500 Silver 0.5311 oz. ASW **Obv:** Facing bust of Queen Christina **Rev:** Crowned arms, date, value **Mint:** Stockholm

Date	Mintage	VG	F	VF	XF	Unc
1641	—	325	450	875	—	—
1642	—	800	1,350	2,700	—	—
1646 Rare	—	—	—	—	—	—

KM# 193 4 MARK

22.0252 g., 0.7500 Silver 0.5311 oz. ASW **Obv:** Bust of Christina right **Rev:** Crowned arms divide date **Mint:** Stockholm **Note:** Varieties exist.

Date	Mintage	VG	F	VF	XF	Unc
1647	—	150	295	725	1,550	—
1647 Small bust	—	205	400	1,050	2,100	—
1648 WAN	—	295	295	725	1,550	—
1648 WAND	—	170	325	875	1,800	—
1649 MDCXLIX	—	205	400	1,100	2,650	—
1649 MDCXLVIIII	—	100	205	750	1,550	—

KM# 244 4 MARK

20.8016 g., 0.6940 Silver 0.4641 oz. ASW **Obv:** Laureate bust of Carl XI left **Rev:** Crowned shield, sprays below **Mint:** Stockholm

Date	Mintage	VG	F	VF	XF	Unc
1664 IK	—	235	675	1,350	3,150	—
1664 IAK	—	205	500	1,100	2,800	—
1664 Carolvs Rex	—	270	450	950	2,650	—
1664 Seven dots below collar	—	350	475	1,000	2,750	—

KM# 261 4 MARK

20.8016 g., 0.6940 Silver 0.4641 oz. ASW **Obv:** Bust of Carl XI left **Rev:** Cruciform of crowned arms **Mint:** Stockholm

Date	Mintage	VG	F	VF	XF	Unc
1668 Rare	—	—	—	—	—	—

KM# 262 4 MARK

20.8016 g., 0.6940 Silver 0.4641 oz. ASW **Obv:** Laureate bust of Carl XI left **Rev:** Crowned arms **Mint:** Stockholm

Date	Mintage	VG	F	VF	XF	Unc
1668	—	205	400	850	2,100	—
1669	—	225	450	900	2,250	—

KM# 279 4 MARK

20.8016 g., 0.6940 Silver 0.4641 oz. ASW **Obv:** Laureate bust of Carl XI right **Rev:** Crowned interlocked "C's" with three crowns **Mint:** Stockholm

Date	Mintage	VG	F	VF	XF	Unc
1673	—	205	450	875	1,800	—
1674 Reversed 4	—	205	450	875	1,800	—

KM# 296 4 MARK

20.8016 g., 0.6940 Silver 0.4641 oz. ASW **Obv:** Mature bust of Carl XI right **Rev:** Crowned shield divides value **Mint:** Stockholm

Date	Mintage	VG	F	VF	XF	Unc
1683	—	110	215	475	975	—
1683 DF	—	100	205	400	850	—
1684/83	—	70.00	135	270	550	—
1684	—	70.00	135	270	550	—
1685	—	70.00	135	270	550	—
1686/85	—	70.00	135	270	550	—
1686	—	70.00	135	270	550	—
1687	—	60.00	120	270	550	—
1688	—	60.00	120	270	550	—
1689	—	60.00	120	270	550	—
1690	—	60.00	115	245	500	—
1691	—	60.00	115	245	500	—
1692/1	—	60.00	115	235	500	—
1692	—	55.00	110	235	500	—
1693	—	55.00	110	235	500	—
1694/93	—	55.00	110	235	500	—
1695	—	55.00	110	235	500	—
1696	—	60.00	115	250	525	—

KM# 315 4 MARK

Silver **Ruler:** Carl XII **Obv:** Bust right **Obv. Legend:** CAROLVS • XII • D • G • REX • SVE • **Rev:** Crowned shield divides value **Rev. Legend:** DOMINVS • PROTECTOR • MEVS • **Mint:** Stockholm

Date	Mintage	VG	F	VF	XF	Unc
1697	—	135	270	550	1,100	—
1698/7	—	110	205	375	850	—
1698	28,000	110	205	400	900	—
1699	91,000	100	170	350	725	—
1700	208,000	80.00	150	350	700	—

KM# 52 5 MARK

1.6365 g., 0.8700 Gold 0.0458 oz. AGW **Obv:** Crowned wheat sheaf divides C-R and U-M **Rev:** Radiant "Jehovah", date in corners **Mint:** Stockholm **Note:** Klippe. Fr. #23.

Date	Mintage	VG	F	VF	XF	Unc
1610 Rare	—	—	—	—	—	—
1611 Rare	—	—	—	—	—	—
1612 Rare	—	—	—	—	—	—

KM# 36 6 MARK

1.8600 g., Gold **Obv:** Hebrew "Jehovah" above crowned bust of Carl IX right

Date	Mintage	VG	F	VF	XF	Unc
1609	—	1,200	2,050	4,050	8,400	—

KM# 37 6 MARK

29.6179 g., 0.8210 Silver 0.7818 oz. ASW **Obv:** Half-figure of Carl IX, with arms and sword **Rev:** Lion rampant in shield in two circles of legends **Mint:** Stockholm **Note:** Dav. #4513.

Date	Mintage	VG	F	VF	XF	Unc
1609	—	800	1,350	2,700	5,300	—

KM# 53 6 MARK

1.8584 g., 0.9790 Gold 0.0585 oz. AGW **Obv:** Hebrew "Jehovah" above crowned bust of Carl IX left **Rev:** Arms of Goteborg in cartouche and inner circle **Mint:** Gothenburg **Note:** Fr. #24.

Date	Mintage	VG	F	VF	XF	Unc
1610 Rare	—	—	—	—	—	—

KM# A11 8 MARK

Gold **Ruler:** Carl IX, Regent **Obv:** Crowned wheat sheaf divides date **Rev:** Three crowns, value **Mint:** Stockholm **Note:** Fr.#14. Klippe.

Date	Mintage	VG	F	VF	XF	Unc
1603 Rare	—	—	—	—	—	—

KM# 29 8 MARK

39.4905 g., 0.8210 Silver 1.0423 oz. ASW **Obv:** Half-figure of Carl IX, with arms and sword left **Rev:** Lion rampant with three crowns **Mint:** Stockholm **Note:** Dav. #4512.

Date	Mintage	VG	F	VF	XF	Unc
1608	—	800	1,600	2,850	6,000	—

KM# 75 8 MARK

39.4905 g., 0.8210 Silver 1.0423 oz. ASW **Rev:** Crowned three shields **Mint:** Stockholm **Note:** Dav. #4518.

Date	Mintage	VG	F	VF	XF	Unc
1617	—	400	875	1,950	4,200	—

KM# 76 8 MARK

39.4905 g., 0.8210 Silver 1.0423 oz. ASW **Obv:** Hebrew "Jehovah" above standing figure of Gustaf II Adolphus **Rev:** Rectangular shield in two circle of shields **Mint:** Stockholm

Date	Mintage	VG	F	VF	XF	Unc
ND(1617)	—	950	1,350	2,150	40.00	—

KM# 77 8 MARK

39.4905 g., 0.8210 Silver 1.0423 oz. ASW **Rev:** Crowned heart-shaped four-fold arms **Mint:** Stockholm

Date	Mintage	VG	F	VF	XF	Unc
ND(1617) Rare	—	—	—	—	—	—

KM# 245 8 MARK

31.3475 g., 0.9220 Silver 0.9292 oz. ASW **Obv:** Laureate bust of Carl XI left **Rev:** Crowned arms divide date **Mint:** Stockholm **Note:** Dav. #4529.

Date	Mintage	VG	F	VF	XF	Unc
1664 IK	1,362	375	850	1,700	3,150	—

KM# 252 8 MARK

31.3475 g., 0.9220 Silver 0.9292 oz. ASW **Mint:** Stockholm **Note:** Dav. #4530.

Date	Mintage	VG	F	VF	XF	Unc
1665	1,801	400	950	1,900	3,550	—

KM# 253 8 MARK

31.3475 g., 0.9220 Silver 0.9292 oz. ASW **Mint:** Stockholm **Note:** Dav. #4531.

Date	Mintage	VG	F	VF	XF	Unc
1666	6,237	270	675	1,500	2,800	—

KM# 255 8 MARK

31.3475 g., 0.9220 Silver 0.9292 oz. ASW **Obv:** Thinner bust, divided legend **Mint:** Stockholm **Note:** Dav. #4532.

Date	Mintage	VG	F	VF	XF	Unc
1666	Inc. above	270	675	1,500	2,800	—

KM# 258 8 MARK

31.3475 g., 0.9220 Silver 0.9292 oz. ASW **Mint:** Stockholm **Note:** Dav. #4533.

Date	Mintage	VG	F	VF	XF	Unc
1667	2,046	400	900	1,900	3,900	—

KM# 259 8 MARK

31.3475 g., 0.9220 Silver 0.9292 oz. ASW **Obv:** Revised bust **Obv. Legend:** DEI GRATIA **Rev:** Interlocking C's between crowned shields in cruciform **Mint:** Stockholm **Note:** Dav. #4534.

Date	Mintage	VG	F	VF	XF	Unc
1667 Rare	Inc. above	—	—	—	—	—

KM# 275 8 MARK

31.3475 g., 0.9220 Silver 0.9292 oz. ASW **Obv:** Laureate bust of Carl XI right **Rev:** Crowned shields in cruciform **Mint:** Stockholm **Note:** Dav. #4535.

Date	Mintage	VG	F	VF	XF	Unc
1670	4,223	270	675	1,350	2,450	—

KM# 276 8 MARK
31.3475 g., 0.9220 Silver 0.9292 oz. ASW **Obv:** Laureate bust of Carl XI right **Rev:** Crowned double C monogram, three crowns in field **Mint:** Stockholm **Note:** Dav. #4536. Both lettered edge and plain edge with small bust and broken legend are known.

Date	Mintage	VG	F	VF	XF	Unc
1670	Inc. above	300	800	1,800	3,150	—

KM# 278 8 MARK
31.3475 g., 0.9220 Silver 0.9292 oz. ASW **Obv:** Wide bust **Rev. Legend:** IMPERIO SVSCEPTO **Mint:** Stockholm **Note:** Dav. #4537.

Date	Mintage	VG	F	VF	XF	Unc
1672	2,024	235	600	1,200	2,450	—

KM# 311 8 MARK
31.3475 g., 0.9220 Silver 0.9292 oz. ASW **Obv:** Draped armored bust of Carl XI right **Mint:** Stockholm **Note:** Dav. #4539. Minor variations in the harness and crown exist.

Date	Mintage	VG	F	VF	XF	Unc
1692 AS	51,000	135	285	625	1,300	—
1693 AS	52,000	135	285	625	1,300	—
1694/3 AS	51,000	150	300	675	1,400	—
1694 AS	Inc. above	135	270	600	1,250	—
1695 AS	24,000	170	375	750	1,550	—
1696 AS	8,000	205	400	875	1,750	—

KM# 316 8 MARK
31.3475 g., 0.9220 Silver 0.9292 oz. ASW **Obv:** Draped armored bust of Carl XII right, curved shoulder armor **Rev:** Crowned shield **Mint:** Stockholm **Note:** Dav. #4540.

Date	Mintage	VG	F	VF	XF	Unc
1697 AS	4,714	400	1,050	2,100	4,200	—
1698 AS	6,448	350	875	1,700	3,150	—

KM# 317 8 MARK
31.3475 g., 0.9220 Silver 0.9292 oz. ASW **Ruler:** Carl XII **Obv:** Armored bust right **Obv. Legend:** CAROLVS • XII • D • G • REX • SVE • **Rev:** Crowned shield divides value **Rev. Legend:** DOMINVS ... **Note:** Dav. #4541, 1712.

Date	Mintage	VG	F	VF	XF	Unc
1697 AS	Inc. above	350	750	1,550	3,150	—

KM# 320 8 MARK
31.3475 g., 0.9220 Silver 0.9292 oz. ASW **Obv:** Ornate harness **Mint:** Stockholm **Note:** Dav. #4541A.

Date	Mintage	VG	F	VF	XF	Unc
1698 AS	Inc. above	350	800	1,550	2,800	—
1700 HZ	6,284	350	825	1,700	3,150	—

KM# 319 8 MARK
31.3475 g., 0.9220 Silver 0.9292 oz. ASW **Obv:** Draped armored bust of Carl XII right, straight shoulder armour **Mint:** Stockholm **Note:** Dav. #4540A.

Date	Mintage	VG	F	VF	XF	Unc
1698 AS	—	—	—	—	—	—
Note: Reported, not confirmed						
1699 AS	6,100	300	775	1,600	3,100	—

KM# 54 10 MARK
3.2728 g., 0.8700 Gold 0.0915 oz. AGW **Obv:** Crowned wheat sheaf divides C-R and X-M **Rev:** Radiant "Jehovah", date in corners **Mint:** Stockholm **Note:** Klippe. Fr.#22.

Date	Mintage	VG	F	VF	XF	Unc
1610	—	1,450	3,000	7,250	—	—

KM# 109 10 MARK
3.2728 g., 0.8700 Gold 0.0915 oz. AGW **Obv:** Crowned wheat sheaf divides G-A and X-M, R below **Rev:** Radiant "Jehovah", date in corners **Mint:** Stockholm **Note:** Fr.#29.

Date	Mintage	VG	F	VF	XF	Unc
16Z6	—	3,350	5,500	8,700	13,000	—

KM# 18 16 MARK
4.9557 g., 0.9790 Gold 0.1560 oz. AGW **Obv:** Laureate bust of Carl IX left with radiant "Jehovah" above **Rev:** Crowned arms divide date **Mint:** Stockholm **Note:** Fr.#18.

Date	Mintage	VG	F	VF	XF	Unc
1606 Rare	—	—	—	—	—	—

KM# 25 16 MARK
4.9557 g., 0.9790 Gold 0.1560 oz. AGW **Obv:** Crowned bust of Carl IX left in inner circle, radiant "Jehovah" at top **Rev:** Crowned arms divide date in inner circle **Mint:** Stockholm **Note:** Fr.#19.

Date	Mintage	VG	F	VF	XF	Unc
1607	—	1,950	3,650	8,400	13,000	—
1608	—	1,950	3,650	8,400	13,000	—
1610	—	1,950	3,650	8,400	13,000	—
1611 Rare	—	—	—	—	—	—

KM# 68 16 MARK
4.9557 g., 0.9790 Gold 0.1560 oz. AGW **Obv:** Laureate bust of Gustaf II Adolf left in inner circle **Rev:** Crown above three shields in inner circle, date in legend **Mint:** Stockholm **Note:** Fr.#28.

Date	Mintage	VG	F	VF	XF	Unc
1615 Rare	—	—	—	—	—	—

Note: Swiss Bank/Spink & Son Zurich Coins of Sweden sale Part I 12-89 two examples, XF and GVF each realized $27,750

KM# 105 16 MARK
4.9557 g., 0.9790 Gold 0.1560 oz. AGW **Obv:** Crowned bust of Gustaf II Adolf left **Rev:** Crown above three shields **Mint:** Stockholm **Note:** Fr.#28.

Date	Mintage	VG	F	VF	XF	Unc
16Z4 Rare	—	—	—	—	—	—
xxZ4 Rare	—	—	—	—	—	—

Note: Swiss Bank/Spink & Sons Zurich Coins of Sweden sale Part I 12-89 VF realized $26,500

KM# A19 20 MARK
98.7260 g., 0.8210 Silver 2.6058 oz. ASW **Obv:** Carl IX standing facing left holding sword and orb, crown at right on table **Obv. Legend:** VERM left of Hebrew "Jehovah" above **Rev:** Crowned five-fold arms surrounded by fifteen shields **Mint:** Stockholm

Date	Mintage	VG	F	VF	XF	Unc
1606	—	1,600	2,700	4,750	8,400	—

KM# 19 20 MARK
98.7264 g., 0.8210 Silver 2.6058 oz. ASW **Obv:** Crowned Carl IX standing facing left holding sword and orb **Obv. Legend:** REX left of Hebrew "Jehovah" above **Mint:** Stockholm **Note:** Dav. #LS574.

Date	Mintage	VG	F	VF	XF	Unc
1606 Unique	—	—	—	—	—	—
1607 Rare	—	—	—	—	—	—
1608	—	35.00	35.00	35.00	7,700	—
1611 Rare	—	—	—	—	—	—

KM# 79 20 MARK
98.7264 g., 0.8210 Silver 2.6058 oz. ASW **Rev:** Crowned heart-shaped shield in two circle legend **Mint:** Stockholm

Date	Mintage	VG	F	VF	XF	Unc
ND(1617) Rare	—	—	—	—	—	—

KM# 78 20 MARK
98.7264 g., 0.8210 Silver 2.6058 oz. ASW **Obv:** Hebrew "Jehovah" above Gustaf II Adolf standing with sword and crown **Mint:** Stockholm

Date	Mintage	VG	F	VF	XF	Unc
1617 Rare	—	—	—	—	—	—
ND(1617) Rare	—	—	—	—	—	—

KM# 80 40 MARK
Silver **Obv:** Hebrew "Jehovah" above Gustaf II Adolf standing with sword and crown, value **Rev:** Similar to 20 Mark, KM#19

Date	Mintage	VG	F	VF	XF	Unc
1617 Unique	—	—	—	—	—	—

KM# 1 1/4 DALER (Ort)
Silver, 32-33 mm. **Ruler:** Carl IX, Regent **Obv:** Half-length bust of Carl IX left holding crowned shield **Obv. Legend:** CAROLVS • D : G • HAER - E •... **Rev:** "Jehovah" in radiant circle **Mint:** Stockholm

Date	Mintage	VG	F	VF	XF	Unc
1603 Rare	—	—	—	—	—	—

KM# 180 1/4 RIKSDALER
7.1926 g., 0.8780 Silver 0.2030 oz. ASW **Obv:** Bust of Queen Christina with hair drawn back facing **Rev:** The Savior with globe, crowned shields at lower left, date **Mint:** Stockholm

Date	Mintage	VG	F	VF	XF	Unc
1640	—	140	300	675	1,100	—
1641	—	210	450	1,150	2,100	—

KM# 185 1/4 RIKSDALER
7.1926 g., 0.8780 Silver 0.2030 oz. ASW **Obv:** Hair hanging long **Mint:** Stockholm

Date	Mintage	VG	F	VF	XF	Unc
1641	—	175	350	775	170	—
1641 Divided date	—	175	350	775	170	—
1642	—	140	300	675	1,400	—
1642 Divided date, Rare	—	—	—	—	—	—
1643	—	175	350	775	1,700	—
1644	—	120	265	650	1,400	—
1645	—	210	450	1,150	2,450	—
1646 AG	—	175	350	775	1,700	—
1646	—	120	265	650	1,400	—
1646 MDCXLVI	—	105	250	575	1,250	—

KM# 2 1/2 DALER
Silver, 35-36 mm. **Ruler:** Carl IX, Regent **Obv:** Half-length bust of Carl IX left holding crowned shield **Obv. Legend:** CAROLVS • D : G • HAER - E •... **Rev:** "Jehovah" in radiant circle **Mint:** Stockholm

Date	Mintage	VG	F	VF	XF	Unc
1601 Rare	—	—	—	—	—	—
1603 Rare	—	—	—	—	—	—

KM# 20 1/2 RIKSDALER
Silver **Obv:** Bust of Carl IX below Hebrew "Jehovah", date **Rev:** Arms below crown **Mint:** Stockholm **Note:** Struck with dies used for 16 Marks in gold, but with not value given.

Date	Mintage	VG	F	VF	XF	Unc
1606 Rare	—	—	—	—	—	—

KM# 140 1/2 RIKSDALER
14.6261 g., 0.8750 Silver 0.4114 oz. ASW **Obv:** Half-figure of Gustaf II Adolf with mace and globe, ornamentation at shoulder **Rev:** The Savior with globe, triform arms left, date **Mint:** Stockholm

Date	Mintage	VG	F	VF	XF	Unc
MDCXXXI (1631) Rare	—	—	—	—	—	—

KM# 141 1/2 RIKSDALER
14.6261 g., 0.8750 Silver 0.4114 oz. ASW **Obv:** Without ornamentation at shoulder **Obv. Legend:** GOTT • MIT • UNS **Rev:** Crowned ornate arms in sprays **Mint:** Stockholm

Date	Mintage	VG	F	VF	XF	Unc
1631	—	550	1,200	2,300	4,700	—
1632	—	625	1,250	2,500	4,900	—

KM# 165 1/2 RIKSDALER
14.3852 g., 0.8780 Silver 0.4061 oz. ASW **Obv:** 3/4-length figure of Christina **Rev:** The Savior standing facing holding orb, crowned shields at left **Mint:** Stockholm

Date	Mintage	VG	F	VF	XF	Unc
1639 MDCXXXVIIII	—	210	450	900	1,950	—
1639 MDCXXXIX	—	280	600	1,250	2,450	—
1640 Small crown	—	245	500	1,000	2,100	—
1640 Large crown	—	245	500	1,000	2,100	—
1641 Small crown Rare	—	210	450	950	2,050	—

KM# 186 1/2 RIKSDALER
14.3852 g., 0.8780 Silver 0.4061 oz. ASW **Obv:** Bust of Christina facing **Mint:** Stockholm

Date	Mintage	VG	F	VF	XF	Unc
1641	—	350	800	1,850	3,500	—
1642	—	190	425	875	1,750	—
1643	—	140	350	775	1,700	—

KM# 186a 1/2 RIKSDALER

14.6261 g., 0.8780 Silver 0.4129 oz. ASW **Mint:** Stockholm

Date	Mintage	VG	F	VF	XF	Unc
1644	—	175	350	775	1,700	—
1645	—	175	350	775	1,700	—
1646	—	175	350	775	1,700	—
1647	—	210	450	900	1,950	—
1652	—	210	450	900	1,950	—

KM# 3 RIKSDALER

Silver **Ruler:** Carl IX, Regent **Obv:** 1/2-length figure holding crowned shield **Rev:** "Jehovah" in rays at center **Mint:** Stockholm **Note:** Dav. #4510.

Date	Mintage	VG	F	VF	XF	Unc
1601 Rare	—	—	—	—	—	—
1603 M IHEHOVA	—	270	550	1,100	1,950	—
1603 VM IHEHOVA	—	270	475	950	1,800	—
1603 M IEHOVA	—	350	675	1,300	2,550	—

KM# 26 RIKSDALER

29.2523 g., 0.8750 Silver 0.8229 oz. ASW **Obv:** Hebrew "Jehovah" above crowned Carl IX standing facing left holding sword and orb, three shields at his fett **Rev:** The Savior, date **Mint:** Stockholm **Note:** Dav. #4511.

Date	Mintage	VG	F	VF	XF	Unc
ND(1607) Rare	—	—	—	—	—	—
1608	—	230	350	1,750	3,650	—
1610 MEV M	—	150	270	1,050	2,100	—
1610 ME VM	—	135	295	1,350	2,800	—
1610 MEVM	—	170	350	1,400	2,950	—
1610 N OS	—	135	295	1,350	2,800	—
1610 NO S	—	135	290	1,300	2,650	—
1611	—	235	350	1,600	3,350	—

KM# 69 RIKSDALER

29.2523 g., 0.8750 Silver 0.8229 oz. ASW **Obv:** Hebrew "Jehovah" above half-length figure of Gustaf II Adolf holding scepter **Rev:** The Savior standing facing holding orb, crowned shields at left **Mint:** Stockholm **Note:** Dav. #4515.

Date	Mintage	VG	F	VF	XF	Unc
1615 HAE	—	205	450	1,300	2,750	—
1615 HAER	—	270	575	1,500	3,200	—
1615 HAERE	—	205	450	1,350	2,900	—
1616	—	235	475	1,350	2,900	—

KM# 82 RIKSDALER

29.2523 g., 0.8750 Silver 0.8229 oz. ASW **Mint:** Stockholm **Note:** Dav. #4516.

Date	Mintage	VG	F	VF	XF	Unc
1617 VANDALOR	—	205	400	1,050	2,200	—
1617 VANDAL	—	235	450	1,150	2,550	—

KM# 83 RIKSDALER

29.2523 g., 0.8750 Silver 0.8229 oz. ASW **Mint:** Sala and Stockholm **Note:** Dav. #4517.

Date	Mintage	VG	F	VF	XF	Unc
1617	—	400	975	1,950	—	—
1618	—	235	475	1,600	—	—
1619	—	235	475	1,600	—	—

KM# 81.2 RIKSDALER

29.2523 g., 0.8750 Silver 0.8229 oz. ASW **Obv:** Small head **Mint:** Soderkoping

Date	Mintage	VG	F	VF	XF	Unc
1617 Rare	—	—	—	—	—	—

KM# 81.1 RIKSDALER

29.2523 g., 0.8750 Silver 0.8229 oz. ASW **Obv:** Half-figure of John, Duke of Ostergotland, large head, date **Rev:** Hebrew "Jehovah" above crowned shields **Mint:** Soderkoping **Note:** Dav. #4514. Prev. KM#81.

Date	Mintage	VG	F	VF	XF	Unc
1617 Large head	—	1,950	3,800	7,200	—	—
1617 Small head	—	1,950	3,800	7,200	—	—

KM# 144 RIKSDALER

29.2523 g., 0.8750 Silver 0.8229 oz. ASW **Obv:** Scepter far away **Mint:** Sala and Stockholm **Note:** Dav. #A4520.

Date	Mintage	VG	F	VF	XF	Unc
1631	—	350	675	1,350	2,550	—

KM# 142 RIKSDALER

29.2523 g., 0.8750 Silver 0.8229 oz. ASW **Mint:** Sala and Stockholm **Note:** Dav. #4519.

Date	Mintage	VG	F	VF	XF	Unc
1631	—	350	675	1,350	2,900	—

KM# 143 RIKSDALER

29.2523 g., 0.8750 Silver 0.8229 oz. ASW **Obv:** Scepter near **Rev:** Roman numeral date **Mint:** Sala and Stockholm **Note:** Dav. #4520.

Date	Mintage	VG	F	VF	XF	Unc
MDCXXXI (1631)	—	205	400	1,050	2,200	—
MDCXXXII (1632)	—	350	675	1,350	2,900	—

KM# 146 RIKSDALER

29.2523 g., 0.8750 Silver 0.8229 oz. ASW **Obv:** Without shoulder bow **Rev:** Christ without robes **Mint:** Sala and Stockholm **Note:** Dav. #4521.1.

Date	Mintage	VG	F	VF	XF	Unc
1631 Rare	—	—	—	—	—	—

KM# 147 RIKSDALER

29.2523 g., 0.8750 Silver 0.8229 oz. ASW **Obv:** Without shoulder bow **Rev:** Christ with robe **Mint:** Sala and Stockholm **Note:** Dav. #4521.2.

Date	Mintage	VG	F	VF	XF	Unc
MDCXXXII (1632)	—	300	600	1,150	2,200	—

KM# 148 RIKSDALER

29.2523 g., 0.8750 Silver 0.8229 oz. ASW **Obv:** Narrow bust **Mint:** Sala and Stockholm **Note:** Dav. #A4521.

Date	Mintage	VG	F	VF	XF	Unc
MDCXXXII (1632)	—	350	675	1,350	2,550	—

KM# 145 RIKSDALER

29.2523 g., 0.8750 Silver 0.8229 oz. ASW **Rev:** Christ with textured robe **Mint:** Sala and Stockholm **Note:** Dav. #B4520.

Date	Mintage	VG	F	VF	XF	Unc
MDCXXXII (1632)	—	1,000	1,700	2,700	—	—

KM# 155 RIKSDALER

29.2523 g., 0.8750 Silver 0.8229 oz. ASW **Mint:** Sala and Stockholm **Note:** Dav. #4522.

Date	Mintage	VG	F	VF	XF	Unc
MDCXXXIII (1633) Rare	—	—	—	—	—	—

Note: Swiss Bank/Spink & Sons Zurich Coins of Sweden sale Part I 12-89 GVF realized $11,300

KM# 168 RIKSDALER

28.7703 g., 0.8780 Silver 0.8121 oz. ASW **Obv:** Large bust, ornate gown, broken inner circle **Mint:** Sala and Stockholm **Note:** Dav. #4523.1.

Date	Mintage	VG	F	VF	XF	Unc
M:DC:XXXIX (1639)	—	400	800	1,500	3,200	—

KM# 169 RIKSDALER

28.7703 g., 0.8780 Silver 0.8121 oz. ASW **Obv:** Small bust, ornate gown, unbroken inner circle **Mint:** Sala and Stockholm **Note:** Dav. #4523.2. Numerous varieties in legend punctuation, gown and jewelry exist for Dav. #4523.

Date	Mintage	VG	F	VF	XF	Unc
M:DC:XXXIX (1639)	—	400	800	1,500	3,200	—
1640 REGI	—	350	675	850	1,800	—
1640 REG	—	300	500	775	1,600	—
1640 RE	—	270	500	775	1,600	—
1641	—	270	475	675	1,450	—

KM# 167 RIKSDALER

28.7703 g., 0.8780 Silver 0.8121 oz. ASW **Obv:** Simple gown, single-edged lace on skirt **Mint:** Sala and Stockholm **Note:** Dav. #B4523.

Date	Mintage	VG	F	VF	XF	Unc
MDCXXXVIIII (1639)	—	325	675	1,000	2,100	—

KM# 166 RIKSDALER

28.7703 g., 0.8780 Silver 0.8121 oz. ASW **Obv:** Simple gown, double-edged lace on skirt **Mint:** Sala and Stockholm **Note:** Dav. #A4523.

Date	Mintage	VG	F	VF	XF	Unc
MDCXXXVIIII (1639)	—	675	1,100	1,600	3,500	—

KM# 187 RIKSDALER

28.7703 g., 0.8780 Silver 0.8121 oz. ASW **Obv:** Bust of Christina left **Mint:** Sala and Stockholm **Note:** Dav. #4525. Variations in Christina's gown occur beginning with the 1646 issue.

Date	Mintage	VG	F	VF	XF	Unc
M.DC.XLI (1641)	—	270	550	850	1,750	—
MDCXLII (1642) AG	—	475	750	1,150	2,300	—
1642 M	—	650	1,100	1,600	3,500	—
1642	—	235	400	600	1,300	—
MDCXLIII (1643) AG	—	235	400	600	1,300	—
MDCXLIV (1644) AG	—	235	400	675	1,450	—
Note: Large or small date varieties						
MDCXLIII (1644) AG	—	700	1,350	2,300	4,350	—
M+DC+XLV (1645) AG	—	270	475	675	1,450	—
1646 SALUATOR SALUA	—	325	550	1,000	2,050	—
1646 AG	—	270	475	750	1,600	—
1646	—	270	475	750	1,600	—
1647	—	270	475	750	1,600	—
1652	—	325	550	975	2,050	—
1653	11,000	1,900	2,700	4,050	8,700	—

KM# 194 RIKSDALER

28.7703 g., 0.8780 Silver 0.8121 oz. ASW **Obv:** Bust of Christina right **Mint:** Sala and Stockholm **Note:** Dav. #4526.

Date	Mintage	VG	F	VF	XF	Unc
1647 Rare	—	—	—	—	—	—

KM# 214 RIKSDALER

28.7703 g., 0.8780 Silver 0.8121 oz. ASW **Obv:** Charles X Gustavus **Mint:** Sala and Stockholm **Note:** Dav. #4528.

Date	Mintage	VG	F	VF	XF	Unc
1654	4,000	675	1,300	1,800	3,650	—

KM# 215 RIKSDALER

28.7703 g., 0.8780 Silver 0.8121 oz. ASW **Mint:** Sala and Stockholm **Note:** Klippe.

Date	Mintage	VG	F	VF	XF	Unc
1654 Rare	—	—	—	—	—	—

KM# 280 RIKSDALER
29.2523 g., 0.8780 Silver 0.8257 oz. ASW **Obv:** Carl XI **Mint:** Sala and Stockholm **Note:** Dav. #4538. Klippe.

Date	Mintage	VG	F	VF	XF	Unc
1676	791	1,350	3,050	5,700	—	—
1676	—	—	325	800	—	—
Note: 19th Century restrike						
1676	—	—	270	675	—	—
Note: Restrike of 1909						

KM# 196 1-1/2 RIKSDALER
Silver **Obv:** Bust of Christina, right **Rev:** Arms below crown, date **Mint:** Stockholm **Note:** Dav. #4527.

Date	Mintage	VG	F	VF	XF	Unc
1649 Rare	—	—	—	—	—	—
Note: Swiss Bank/Spink & Son Zurich Coins of Sweden sale part I 12-89 GXF realized $25,850						

KM# 27 2 RIKSDALER
Silver **Obv:** Full figure of Carl IX with sword and globe below Hebrew legend **Rev:** Arms below crown, double circle of shields, date **Mint:** Stockholm **Note:** Struck with 20 Mark dies.

Date	Mintage	VG	F	VF	XF	Unc
1607 Unique	—	—	—	—	—	—
1611 Unique	—	—	—	—	—	—

KM# 38 2 RIKSDALER
Silver **Obv:** Half-figure of Carl IX with sword and arms below Hebrew legend, date **Rev:** Arms with three cronws in field **Mint:** Stockholm

Date	Mintage	VG	F	VF	XF	Unc
1609 Unique	—	—	—	—	—	—

KM# 55 2 RIKSDALER
Silver **Subject:** Founding of Gothenburg **Obv:** Carl IX with sword below Hebrew legend **Rev:** Panorama with ships and buildings in foreground, tree in background **Mint:** Gothenburg

Date	Mintage	VG	F	VF	XF	Unc
1610	—	1,400	3,500	7,000	15,000	—

KM# 84 2 RIKSDALER
Silver **Obv:** Full figure of Gustaf II Adolf, laurel head **Rev:** Arms below crown, double circle of shields **Mint:** Stockholm

Date	Mintage	VG	F	VF	XF	Unc
1617	—	1,250	2,400	4,900	10,500	—

KM# 85 2 RIKSDALER
Silver **Obv:** Full figure of Gustaf II Adolf, crowned head **Mint:** Stockholm

Date	Mintage	VG	F	VF	XF	Unc
ND	—	1,250	2,400	4,900	10,500	—

KM# 156 2 RIKSDALER
Silver **Obv:** Gustaf II Adolf, mounted **Rev:** Arms below crown, single circle of shields **Mint:** Stockholm **Note:** Illustration reduced.

Date	Mintage	VG	F	VF	XF	Unc
1633	—	850	1,700	3,500	6,000	—

KM# 189 2 RIKSDALER
Silver **Obv:** Bust of Christina **Rev:** The Savior with globe, arms at left, date **Mint:** Stockholm **Note:** Dav. #4524.

Date	Mintage	VG	F	VF	XF	Unc
1644 Rare	—	—	—	—	—	—
1645 Rare	—	—	—	—	—	—
Note: Swiss Bank/Spink & Sons Zurich Coins of Sweden sale Part I 12-89 GVF realized $13,250						
1646 Rare	—	—	—	—	—	—
1647 Rare	—	—	—	—	—	—

KM# 197 2 RIKSDALER
Silver **Obv:** Christina bust right **Rev:** Arms below crown, date **Mint:** Stockholm

Date	Mintage	VG	F	VF	XF	Unc
1649 Rare	—	—	—	—	—	—

KM# 216 2 RIKSDALER
Silver **Obv:** Carl X Gustaf **Rev:** Arms below crown, lions rampant at sides, date **Mint:** Stockholm **Note:** Dav. #A4528.

Date	Mintage	VG	F	VF	XF	Unc
1654 Rare	—	—	—	—	—	—

KM# 56 2-1/2 RIKSDALER
Silver **Subject:** Founding of Gothenburg **Obv:** Charles IX with sword below Hebrew legend **Rev:** Panorama with ships and buildings in foreground, tree in background **Mint:** Gothenburg

Date	Mintage	VG	F	VF	XF	Unc
1610 Rare	—	—	—	—	—	—

KM# 30 3 RIKSDALER
Silver **Obv:** Carl IX with sword and orb below Hebrew legend **Rev:** The Savior with cross and orb, date **Mint:** Stockholm **Note:** Dav. #A4511.

Date	Mintage	VG	F	VF	XF	Unc
1608 Unique	—	—	—	—	—	—

KM# 39 3 RIKSDALER
Silver **Obv:** Carl IX with sword below Hebrew legend **Rev:** The Savior, date **Mint:** Stockholm **Note:** Dav. #B4511.

Date	Mintage	VG	F	VF	XF	Unc
1609 Unique	—	—	—	—	—	—

KM# 57 3 RIKSDALER
Silver **Subject:** Founding of Gothenburg **Obv:** Carl IX with sword below Hebrew legend **Rev:** Panorama with ships and buildings in foreground, tree in background **Mint:** Gothenburg

Date	Mintage	VG	F	VF	XF	Unc
1610	—	1,400	3,500	7,000	—	—

KM# 86 3 RIKSDALER
Silver **Obv:** Gustaf II Adolf with sword and orb below Hebrew legend **Rev:** Arms below crown, rings of multiple shields **Mint:** Sala and Stockholm

Date	Mintage	VG	F	VF	XF	Unc
1617 Rare	—	—	—	—	—	—

KM# 87 3 RIKSDALER
Silver **Rev:** Arms below crown, circle by legends **Mint:** Sala and Stockholm

Date	Mintage	VG	F	VF	XF	Unc
ND(1617) Rare	—	—	—	—	—	—

KM# 88 3 RIKSDALER
Silver **Obv:** Gustaf II Adolf with sword and orb below Hebrew legend **Rev:** Arms below crown, rings of multiple shields **Mint:** Stockholm

Date	Mintage	VG	F	VF	XF	Unc
ND(1617)	—	—	—	—	—	—

KM# 150 3 RIKSDALER
Silver **Obv:** Gustaf II Adolf mounted **Rev:** Arms below crown, ring of shields, date beside crown **Mint:** Stockholm

Date	Mintage	VG	F	VF	XF	Unc
1632 Rare	—	—	—	—	—	—

KM# 151 3 RIKSDALER
Silver **Obv:** City view behind rearing horse **Mint:** Stockholm

Date	Mintage	VG	F	VF	XF	Unc
1632 Rare	—	—	—	—	—	—

KM# 149 3 RIKSDALER
Silver **Obv:** Gustaf II Adolf mounted **Rev:** Arms below crown, ring of multiple shields **Mint:** Sala and Stockholm

Date	Mintage	VG	F	VF	XF	Unc
1632 Rare	—	—	—	—	—	—

KM# 157 3 RIKSDALER
Silver **Rev:** Crowned rectangular shield **Mint:** Stockholm

Date	Mintage	VG	F	VF	XF	Unc
1633	—	2,000	3,500	6,000	—	—

KM# 190 3 RIKSDALER
Silver **Obv:** Queen Christina **Rev:** The Savior, arms at lower left, date **Mint:** Sala and Stockholm **Note:** Dav. #A4524.

Date	Mintage	VG	F	VF	XF	Unc
1646 Rare	—	—	—	—	—	—

PLATE MONEY

The Kingdom of Sweden issued copper plate money, heavy and cumbersome square or rectangular coins ranging in size up to about 13 by 25 inches down to less than 3 by 3 inches, from 1644 to 1776. The kingdom was poor in silver and gold but had rich copper resources. The coins were designed to contain copper bullion in the value of the silver coins they replaced, and were denominated as one, two, four, etc. dalers in silver mint or silver coin.

Although sometimes classed with odd and curious money these were legal tender coins of the realm and although used and exported as bullion, they circulated domestically and were essential in the commerce of Sweden and Finland for more than a century.

They are widely collected, not only in Scandinavia but around the world.

Each denomination is catalogued under the name of the issuing monarch and by the mint mark and or source of the copper. The latter are important in the rarity and thus prices of the coins. The pieces are identified by the center stamp, with the denomination, mint mark, etc., and four identical corner stamps, with the insignia of the king and date.

Many are extremely rare, with only a single specimen or two known, often only a unique survivor in a major museum.

KM# PM15 1/2 DALER S.M.
Copper **Subject:** Charles XI **Mint:** Avesta **Note:** Corner stamps: Crowned C R S, date. Center stamp: 1/2 Daler Solff:Myt, three stars.

Date	Mintage	VG	F	VF	XF	Unc
1681	—	500	1,000	1,750	—	—
1682 Rare	—	500	1,000	1,750	—	—
1683 Rare	—	—	—	—	—	—
1685 Rare	—	—	—	—	—	—
1686 Rare	—	—	—	—	—	—
1687 Rare	—	—	—	—	—	—
1689 Rare	—	—	—	—	—	—
1691 Rare	—	—	—	—	—	—

KM# PM1 DALER S.M.
Copper **Subject:** Queen Christina **Mint:** Avesta **Note:** Corner stamps: Crown above date, legend: CHRISTINA... Center stamp: 1 Daler Solff:Mnt, M K.

Date	Mintage	VG	F	VF	XF	Unc
1649	—	550	2,000	2,200	—	—
1650	—	450	900	1,800	—	—
1651	—	—	—	—	—	—
1652	—	550	1,100	2,200	—	—
1653	—	500	1,000	2,000	—	—
1654	—	550	1,100	2,200	—	—

KM# PM10 DALER S.M.
Copper **Subject:** Carl X Gustaf **Mint:** Avesta **Note:** Corner stamps: Legend: CAROLUS GUSTAVUS...

Date	Mintage	VG	F	VF	XF	Unc
1655	—	700	1,450	2,100	—	—
1656	—	600	1,250	1,800	—	—
1657	—	550	1,150	1,700	—	—
1658	—	550	1,100	1,600	—	—
1659	—	550	1,450	2,100	—	—
1660 Rare	—	800	1,900	2,500	—	—

KM# PM16 DALER S.M.
Copper **Subject:** Carl XI **Mint:** Avesta **Note:** Corner stamps: Legend: CAROLUS... Cemter stamp: 1 DALER Solff:Myt.

Date	Mintage	VG	F	VF	XF	Unc
1660	—	600	1,250	2,500	—	—
1661	—	500	1,050	2,100	—	—
1662	—	550	1,125	2,250	—	—
1663	—	500	1,050	2,100	—	—
1664	—	550	1,125	2,250	—	—
1667	—	600	1,225	2,500	—	—
1668	—	600	1,200	2,400	—	—
1669	—	900	1,850	3,500	—	—
1672	—	650	1,350	2,600	—	—
1673 R/L	—	550	1,175	2,250	—	—
1674	—	550	1,175	2,250	—	—
1674 G	—	550	1,175	2,250	—	—
1675	—	550	1,175	2,250	—	—
1675 K	—	550	1,175	2,250	—	—
1676	—	425	950	2,000	—	—
1677	—	500	1,050	2,100	—	—
1678	—	500	1,050	2,100	—	—
1679	—	500	1,050	2,100	—	—
1680	—	500	1,050	2,100	—	—
1681	—	650	1,350	2,600	—	—
1682	—	800	1,650	3,200	—	—
1683	—	850	1,775	3,500	—	—
1684	—	750	1,550	3,000	—	—
1685	—	750	1,550	3,000	—	—
1686	—	650	1,350	3,000	—	—
1689	—	550	1,175	2,200	—	—
1690	—	550	1,175	2,200	—	—
1691	—	600	1,250	2,500	—	—

KM# PM17 DALER S.M.
Copper **Note:** Copper from Garpenberg.

Date	Mintage	VG	F	VF	XF	Unc
1674 Rare	—	—	—	—	—	—

KM# PMA18 DALER S.M.
Copper **Mint:** Kengis **Note:** Center stamp: AIR monogram below denomination.

Date	Mintage	VG	F	VF	XF	Unc
1675	—	600	1,200	2,400	—	—

KM# PM2 2 DALER S.M.
Copper **Obv:** Queen Christina **Mint:** Avesta **Note:** Center stamp: 2 DALER Solff:Mnt, M.K.

Date	Mintage	VG	F	VF	XF	Unc
1649	—	1,200	3,000	6,000	—	—
1650 Rare	—	—	—	—	—	—
1651 Rare	—	—	—	—	—	—
1652 Rare	—	—	—	—	—	—
1653 Rare	—	—	—	—	—	—
1654 Rare	—	—	—	—	—	—

KM# PM11 2 DALER S.M.
Copper **Obv:** Carl X Gustaf **Mint:** Avesta **Note:** Corner stamps: Crown above date; legend: CAROLUS GUSTAVUS. Center stamp: 2 DALER Solff:Mnt.

Date	Mintage	VG	F	VF	XF	Unc
1658 Rare	—	—	—	—	—	—
1659 Rare	—	—	—	—	—	—

KM# PM18 2 DALER S.M.
Copper **Obv:** Carl XI **Mint:** Avesta **Note:** Corner stamps: Crown above date; legend: CAROLUS... Center stamp: 2 DALER Solff:Myt, shield or rose between stars or lilies, or three stars.

Date	Mintage	VG	F	VF	XF	Unc
1660	—	600	1,250	2,400	—	—
1661	—	800	1,600	3,200	—	—
1662	—	800	1,600	3,200	—	—
1663	—	500	1,000	2,000	—	—
1664	—	800	1,600	3,200	—	—
1667	—	650	1,300	2,600	—	—
1668	—	750	1,550	3,000	—	—
1669	—	600	1,250	2,400	—	—
1672	—	600	1,250	2,400	—	—
1673	—	400	800	1,600	—	—
1674	—	450	950	1,800	—	—
1675	—	375	725	1,400	—	—
1676	—	325	650	1,300	—	—
1677	—	750	775	1,500	—	—
1678	—	750	775	1,500	—	—
1679	—	550	1,100	2,200	—	—
1680	—	400	800	1,600	—	—
1681	—	400	800	1,600	—	—
1682	—	350	700	1,400	—	—
1683	—	350	700	1,400	—	—
1684	—	350	700	1,400	—	—
1685	—	350	700	1,400	—	—
1686	—	350	700	1,400	—	—
1687	—	750	1,450	2,800	—	—
1689	—	350	700	1,400	—	—
1690	—	550	1,050	2,000	—	—
1691	—	450	900	1,800	—	—

KM# PM19 2 DALER S.M.
Copper **Mint:** Avesta **Note:** Center stamp: Star between lilies below denomination. Copper from Garpenberg.

Date	Mintage	VG	F	VF	XF	Unc
1673 Rare	—	—	—	—	—	—
1674 Rare	—	450	950	1,900	—	—

KM# PM20 2 DALER S.M.
Copper **Mint:** Kengis **Note:** Center stamp: Monogram AIR below denomination.

Date	Mintage	VG	F	VF	XF	Unc
1693 Rare	—	—	—	—	—	—

KM# PM41 2 DALER S.M.
Copper **Ruler:** Carl XII **Obv:** Corner stamps: Crown above date, legend CAROLUS... Center stamp: Daler Sölff: Myt, AIR monogram. **Mint:** Kengis

Date	Mintage	VG	F	VF	XF	Unc
1700 Rare	—	—	—	—	—	—

KM# PM21 3 DALER S.M.
Copper **Obv:** Carl XI **Mint:** Avesta **Note:** Corner stamps: Date below crown; legend: CAROLUS XI... Center stamp: 3 DALER Solff:Myt, three stars.

Date	Mintage	VG	F	VF	XF	Unc
1674 Rare	—	—	—	—	—	—

KM# PM3 4 DALER S.M.
Copper **Obv:** Queen Christina **Mint:** Avesta **Note:** Corner stamps: Crown above date; legend: CHRISTINA...Center stamp: 4 DALER Solff:Mnt, MK.

Date	Mintage	VG	F	VF	XF	Unc
1649 Rare	—	—	—	—	—	—
1652 Rare	—	—	—	—	—	—
1653 Rare	—	—	—	—	—	—

KM# PM12 4 DALER S.M.
Copper **Obv:** Carl X Gustaf **Mint:** Avesta **Note:** Corner stamps: Crown above date; legend: CAROLUS... Center stamp: 4 DALER Solff:Mnt, M.K.

Date	Mintage	VG	F	VF	XF	Unc
1656 Rare	—	—	—	—	—	—
1657 Rare	—	—	—	—	—	—
1658 Rare	—	—	—	—	—	—
1659 Rare	—	—	—	—	—	—

KM# PM22 4 DALER S.M.
Copper **Obv:** Carl XI **Mint:** Avesta **Note:** Corner stamps: Crown above date; legend: CAROLUS... Center stamp: 4 DALER Solff:Mnt, M K.

Date	Mintage	VG	F	VF	XF	Unc
1663	—	—	—	—	—	—

KM# PM23 5 DALER S.M.
Copper **Obv:** Carl XI **Mint:** Avesta **Note:** Corner stamps: Crown above date; legend: CAROLUS XI... Center stamp: 5 DALER Solff:Myt, three stars.

Date	Mintage	VG	F	VF	XF	Unc
1674 Rare	—	—	—	—	—	—

KM# PM4 8 DALER S.M.
Copper **Obv:** Queen Christina **Mint:** Avesta **Note:** Corner stamps: Crown above date; legend: CHRISTINA... Center stamp: 8 DALER Solff:Mnt, M K.

Date	Mintage	VG	F	VF	XF	Unc
1652 Rare	—	—	—	—	—	—
1653 Rare	—	—	—	—	—	—

KM# PM13 8 DALER S.M.
Copper **Obv:** Carl X Gustaf **Mint:** Avesta **Note:** Corner stamps: Crown above date; legend: CAROLUS GUSTAVUS. Center stamp: 8 DALER Solff:Mnt, shield between roses.

Date	Mintage	VG	F	VF	XF	Unc
1656 Rare	—	—	—	—	—	—
1657 Rare	—	—	—	—	—	—
1658 Rare	—	—	—	—	—	—
1659	—	25,000	53,000	—	—	—

KM# PM24.1 8 DALER S.M.
Copper **Obv:** Carl XI Gustaf **Mint:** Avesta **Note:** Corner stamps: Crown above date; legend: CAROLUS... Center stamp: 8 DALER Solff:mnt, roses.

Date	Mintage	VG	F	VF	XF	Unc
1660	—	12,500	19,000	37,500	—	—
1661	—	12,500	19,000	37,500	—	—
1662	—	12,500	19,000	37,500	—	—
1663	—	12,500	19,000	37,500	—	—
1674	—	12,500	19,000	37,500	—	—

KM# PM24.2 8 DALER S.M.
Copper **Mint:** Avesta **Note:** Center stamp: 8 DALER Solff:myt, three stars.

Date	Mintage	VG	F	VF	XF	Unc
1681 Rare	—	—	—	—	—	—
1682 Rare	—	—	—	—	—	—

KM# PM5 10 DALER S.M.
Copper **Obv:** Queen Christina **Mint:** Avesta **Note:** Corner stamps: C R S around crown above date. Center stamp: X DALER Solff:Mnt, shield.

Date	Mintage	VG	F	VF	XF	Unc
1644 Rare	—	—	—	—	—	—
1645 Rare	—	—	—	—	—	—

TRADE COINAGE

KM# 312 1/4 DUCAT
0.8703 g., 0.9760 Gold 0.0273 oz. AGW **Obv:** Bust of Carl XI right **Rev:** Crowned double C monogram divides date, value below **Note:** Fr. #46.

Date	Mintage	VG	F	VF	XF	Unc
1692	—	280	400	625	—	—

KM# 330 1/4 DUCAT
0.8703 g., 0.9760 Gold 0.0273 oz. AGW **Obv:** Crowned bust of Carl XII right **Rev:** Crowned arms **Note:** Fr. #52.

Date	Mintage	VG	F	VF	XF	Unc
1700	—	350	450	725	—	—

KM# 217 DUCAT
3.4386 g., 0.9720 Gold 0.1075 oz. AGW **Obv:** Bust of Carl X right, legend begins at bottom **Rev:** Crowned arms divides date near top **Note:** Fr. #36.

Date	Mintage	VG	F	VF	XF	Unc
1654 Rare	—	3,500	5,500	8,500	—	—
ND Rare	—	—	—	—	—	—

KM# 218 DUCAT
3.4386 g., 0.9720 Gold 0.1075 oz. AGW **Obv:** Bust of Carl X Gustavus right **Rev:** Legend begins at top **Note:** Fr. #36.

Date	Mintage	VG	F	VF	XF	Unc
1654 Rare	—	—	—	—	—	—
Note: Swiss Bank/Spink & Son Zurich Coins of Sweden sale Part I 12-89 VF realized $15,750						
ND(1654)	3,649	2,800	5,500	13,000	—	—
1656	2,184	2,800	5,500	13,000	—	—
1657 Rare	1,466	—	—	—	—	—

KM# 220 DUCAT
3.4386 g., 0.9720 Gold 0.1075 oz. AGW **Obv:** Modified bust and legend **Note:** Fr. #36.

Date	Mintage	VG	F	VF	XF	Unc
1658	2,664	3,500	5,500	13,000	—	—
Note: Swiss Bank/Spink & Son Zurich Coins of Sweden sale Part I 12-89 nearly XF realized $20,800						
1660 Rare	423	—	—	—	—	—

KM# 238 DUCAT
3.4386 g., 0.9720 Gold 0.1075 oz. AGW **Obv:** Laureate bust of Carl XI right **Note:** Fr. #40.

Date	Mintage	VG	F	VF	XF	Unc
1662/0 GW Rare	4,255	—	—	—	—	—
1662 GW Rare	Inc. above	—	—	—	—	—
Note: Swiss Bank/Spink & Son Zurich Coins of Sweden sale Part I 12-89 GVF realized $12,600						

KM# 246 DUCAT
3.4813 g., 0.9720 Gold 0.1088 oz. AGW **Obv:** Laureate bust of Carl XI left **Note:** Fr. #41.

Date	Mintage	VG	F	VF	XF	Unc
1664	380	1,250	2,350	5,100	—	—
1665 Rare	4,293	—	—	—	—	—

KM# 256 DUCAT
3.4813 g., 0.9720 Gold 0.1088 oz. AGW **Obv:** Finer style bust of Carl XI left **Rev:** Crowned cruciform arms with entwined C's at bottom **Note:** Varieties exist. Fr. #42.

Date	Mintage	VG	F	VF	XF	Unc
1666	4,222	1,400	2,600	4,650	—	—
1667	—	1,050	2,000	4,650	—	—
1668	4,484	975	1,800	3,750	—	—

KM# 263 DUCAT
3.4813 g., 0.9720 Gold 0.1088 oz. AGW **Obv:** Laureate head of Carl XI left **Note:** Varieties exist. Fr. #42.

Date	Mintage	VG	F	VF	XF	Unc
1668 Rare	—	—	—	—	—	—
1669	6,395	775	1,550	2,900	—	—
1670	4,649	975	1,850	3,750	—	—

KM# 277 DUCAT
3.4813 g., 0.9720 Gold 0.1088 oz. AGW **Note:** Varieties exist. Fr. #43.

Date	Mintage	VG	F	VF	XF	Unc
1671 Rare	3,861	—	—	—	—	—
1672	5,058	1,050	1,950	3,750	7,500	—
1673	Inc. above	850	1,550	2,900	5,800	—
1674 Rare	16,000	—	—	—	—	—
1675	Inc. above	850	1,550	2,900	5,800	—
ND(1675)	Inc. above	850	1,550	2,900	5,800	—
1676	Inc. above	850	1,550	2,900	5,800	—

KM# 281 DUCAT
3.4813 g., 0.9720 Gold 0.1088 oz. AGW **Obv:** Armored bust of Carl XI left **Rev:** Crowned double C monogram, three crowns in field **Note:** Varieties exist. Fr. #44.

Date	Mintage	VG	F	VF	XF	Unc
1676	—	975	1,850	3,750	7,500	—
1677	14,000	975	1,850	3,750	7,500	—

KM# 283 DUCAT
3.4813 g., 0.9720 Gold 0.1088 oz. AGW **Obv:** Draped bust of Carl XI right **Note:** Varieties exist. Fr. #45.

Date	Mintage	VG	F	VF	XF	Unc
1677	Inc. above	700	1,550	2,900	5,800	—
1678	9,001	625	1,450	2,550	5,100	—
1679	16,000	625	1,450	2,550	5,100	—
1680	13,000	625	1,450	2,550	5,100	—
1681	12,000	625	1,450	2,550	5,100	—
1682 Rare	2,617	—	—	—	—	—
1683	11,000	625	1,450	2,550	5,100	—
1684 Rare	3,943	—	—	—	—	—
1685	12,000	625	1,450	2,550	5,100	—
1686	6,312	1,050	1,900	3,400	3,500	—
1687	9,473	1,050	1,900	3,400	3,500	—
1688 Rare	5,513	—	—	—	—	—
1689	3,809	625	1,550	2,550	5,100	—
1690	—	625	1,550	2,900	5,800	—
1691	5,897	625	1,550	2,900	5,800	—
1692	2,385	625	1,550	2,900	5,800	—
1694	3,755	625	1,550	2,900	5,800	—
1695	1,683	625	1,550	2,900	5,800	—

KM# 318 DUCAT
3.5000 g., 0.9760 Gold 0.1098 oz. AGW **Ruler:** Carl XII **Obv:** Draped bust right **Obv. Legend:** CAROLVS • XII • D • G • REX • ... **Rev:** Crowned double C monogram, date below **Note:** Fr. #49.

Date	Mintage	VG	F	VF	XF	Unc
1697	4,781	975	1,900	5,500	11,000	—
1699	6,152	775	1,450	3,050	6,500	—
1700	5,840	975	1,900	5,500	11,000	—

KM# 239 3 DUCAT
10.3158 g., 0.9760 Gold 0.3237 oz. AGW **Obv:** Laureate bust of Carl XI left **Rev:** Three crowns divide date **Note:** Fr. #39.

Date	Mintage	VG	F	VF	XF	Unc
1662 GW Unique	—	—	—	—	—	—

KM# 100 5 DUCAT
17.5000 g., 0.9760 Gold 0.5491 oz. AGW **Obv:** Half-figure of Gustaf II Adolf right in inner circle, radiant "Jehovah" at top **Rev:** Crowned arms with lion supporters, date below in inner circle **Note:** Fr. #30.

Date	Mintage	VG	F	VF	XF	Unc
1620 Rare	—	—	—	—	—	—

KM# A195 5 DUCAT
17.5000 g., 0.9760 Gold 0.5491 oz. AGW, 39 mm.
Ruler: Christina **Obv:** Bust of Christina right **Obv. Legend:** CHRISTINA • D : G • SVE • GOT •... **Rev:** Crowned supported five-fold arms **Mint:** Stockholm **Note:** Fr. #34.

Date	Mintage	VG	F	VF	XF	Unc
1649 Unique	—	—	—	—	—	—

KM# A21 6 DUCAT
20.6316 g., 0.9760 Gold 0.6474 oz. AGW, 50 mm. **Ruler:** Carl IX, Regent **Obv:** Laureate Carl IX standing facing left holding sword and orb, crown on table at right **Rev:** Crowned five-fold arms surrounded by two rows of shields **Mint:** Stockholm **Note:** Fr. #16.

Date	Mintage	VG	F	VF	XF	Unc
1606 Unique	—	—	—	—	—	—

KM# A28 6 DUCAT
20.6316 g., 0.9760 Gold 0.6474 oz. AGW, 51 mm.
Ruler: Carl IX, Regent **Obv:** Crowned Carl IX standing facing left holding sword and orb **Rev:** Crowned five-fold arms surrounded by two rows of shields **Mint:** Stockholm **Note:** Fr. #16.

Date	Mintage	VG	F	VF	XF	Unc
1607 Unique	—	—	—	—	—	—

KM# 40 6 DUCAT
20.6316 g., 0.9760 Gold 0.6474 oz. AGW, 46 mm.
Ruler: Carl IX, Regent **Obv:** Half-length figure of Carl IX holding sword and shield in inner circle **Rev:** Lion shield surrounded by three crowns **Mint:** Stockholm **Note:** Fr. #17.

Date	Mintage	VG	F	VF	XF	Unc
1608 Rare	—	—	—	—	—	—

KM# 41 6 DUCAT
20.6316 g., 0.9760 Gold 0.6474 oz. AGW, 43 mm. **Ruler:** Carl IX **Obv:** Hebrew "Jehovah" above crowned half-length figure of Carl IX holding sword and shield (no inner circle) **Rev:** Lion shield surrounded by three crowns **Mint:** Stockholm **Note:** Fr. #17.

Date	Mintage	VG	F	VF	XF	Unc
1609 Rare	—	—	—	—	—	—

KM# 93 6 DUCAT
20.6316 g., 0.9760 Gold 0.6474 oz. AGW, 50 mm.
Ruler: Carl IX **Obv:** Hebrew "Jehovah" above uncrowned Gustaf II Adolf standing facing left holding sword, crown, and orb **Rev:** Crowned five-fold arms surrounded by two rows of shields **Mint:** Stockholm **Note:** Fr. #27.

Date	Mintage	VG	F	VF	XF	Unc
1617 Rare	—	—	—	—	—	—

KM# 94 10 DUCAT
35.0000 g., 0.9760 Gold 1.0982 oz. AGW, 52 mm.
Ruler: Carl IX **Obv:** Hebrew "Jehovah" above uncrowned Gustaf II Adolf standing facing left holding sword and orb, crown on table at right **Rev:** Crowned five-fold arms surrounded by two rows of shields **Mint:** Stockholm **Note:** Fr. #26.

Date	Mintage	VG	F	VF	XF	Unc
1617 Unique	—	—	—	—	—	—

KM# 95 10 DUCAT
35.0000 g., 0.9760 Gold 1.0982 oz. AGW, 53 mm. **Ruler:** Carl IX **Obv:** Hebrew "Jehovah" above crowned Gustaf II Adolf standing facing left holding sword and orb **Rev:** Crowned five-fold arms surrounded by two rows of shields **Mint:** Stockholm **Note:** Fr. #26.

Date	Mintage	VG	F	VF	XF	Unc
ND(ca.1618) Unique	—	—	—	—	—	—

KM# A219 10 DUCAT
35.0000 g., 0.9760 Gold 1.0982 oz. AGW, 43 mm. **Ruler:** Carl X Gustavus **Obv:** Bust of Carl X Gustaf left **Obv. Legend:** CAROLUS • GUSTAVUS • DECIMUS • D : G : REX • SVECORUM **Rev:** Crowned supported arms **Mint:** Stockholm **Note:** Fr. #35.

Date	Mintage	VG	F	VF	XF	Unc
MDCLIV (1654) Unique	—	—	—	—	—	—

KM# 96 12 DUCAT
42.0000 g., 0.9760 Gold 1.3179 oz. AGW, 52 mm. **Obv:** Hebrew "Jehovah" above uncrowned Gustaf II Adolf standing facing left holding sword and orb, crown on table at right **Rev:** Crowned five-fold arms surrounded by two rows of shields **Mint:** Stockholm **Note:** Fr. #25.

Date	Mintage	VG	F	VF	XF	Unc
ND(ca.1618) Unique	—	—	—	—	—	—

PATTERNS

Including off metal strikes

KM#	Date	Mintage	Identification	Mkt Val
Pn1	1606	—	3 Penningar. Silver.	—
Pn2	16Z5	—	Fyrk. Copper. Klippe.	—
Pn3	(16)Z5	—	1/2 Ore. Copper. Klippe.	—
Pn4	16Z5	—	Ore. Copper. Klippe.	2,000
Pn5	16Z5	—	Ore. Copper. Round planchet.	—
Pn6	16Z9	—	1/2 Ore. Copper. Struck at Nyköping Mint.	750
Pn7	16Z9	—	Ore. Copper. Struck at Sater Mint. Large crowns.	500
Pn8	16Z9	—	Ore. Copper. Small crowns.	750
Pn9	1648	—	Ore. Copper. Date in Roman numerals.	750
Pn10	ND(1660)	—	4 Ore. Silver. Large bust. Struck at Stockholm Mint.	500
Pn11	ND(1660)	—	4 Ore. Silver. Small bust. Struck at Stockholm Mint.	—
Pn12	1665	—	1/2 Ore. Silver. Struck at Stockholm Mint.	—
Pn13	1681	—	4 Mark. Copper. Struck at Stockholm Mint.	—

KRISTIANSTAD

(Christianstad)

Situated in the southwest of Sweden, Kristianstad is a seaport and trade center. Founded in 1614 by Denmark's Christian IV, it was ceded to Sweden in 1658. The Danes occupied the region briefly from 1676 to 1678.

DANISH OCCUPATION

SIEGE COINAGE

KM# 5 2 SKILLING
Copper **Obv:** Crowned C5 monogram in circle **Rev:** Crown above value, date below

Date	Mintage	VG	F	VF	XF	Unc
1677 Rare	—	—	—	—	—	—

KM# 6 2 SKILLING
Copper **Obv:** Value flanking crowned monogram

Date	Mintage	VG	F	VF	XF	Unc
ND(1677-78)	—	375	650	1,000	—	—

KM# 7 4 SKILLING
Copper **Obv:** Value flanking crowned C5 monogram
Note: Uniface.

Date	Mintage	VG	F	VF	XF	Unc
ND(1677-78)	—	450	750	1,150	—	—

KM# 8 8 SKILLING
Copper **Note:** Uniface.

Date	Mintage	VG	F	VF	XF	Unc
ND(1677-78)	—	350	600	900	—	—

KM# 9 MARK
Copper **Obv:** Value flanking crowned C5 monogram
Note: Uniface.

Date	Mintage	VG	F	VF	XF	Unc
ND(1677-78) Rare	—	—	—	—	—	—

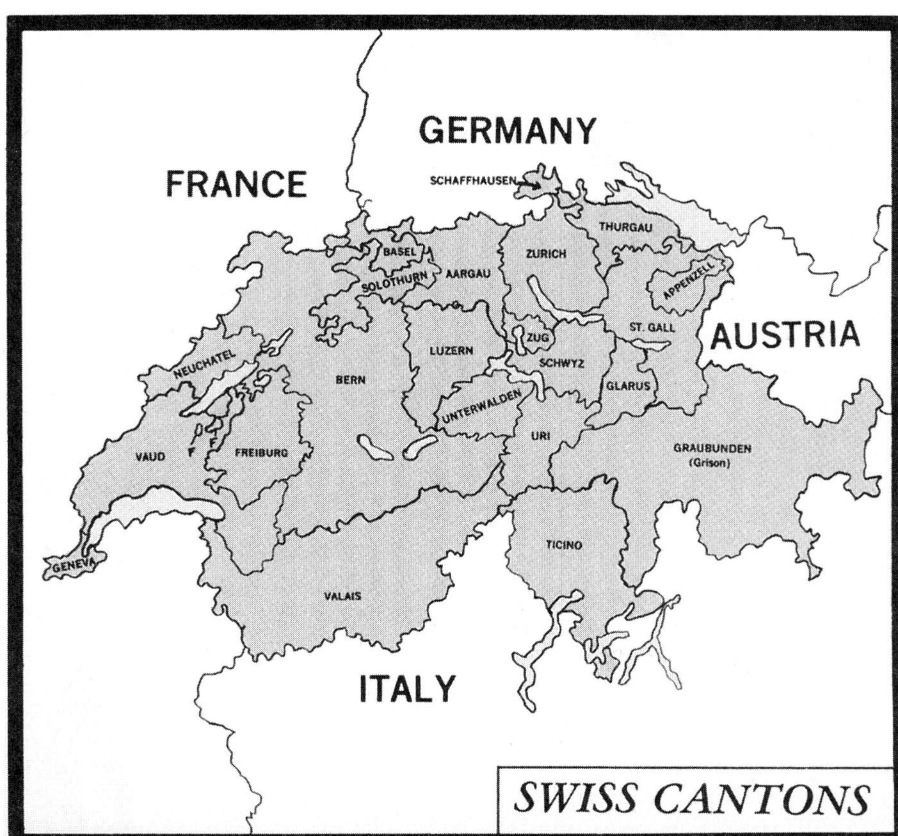

In Switzerland, canton is the name given to each of the 23 states comprising the Swiss Federation. The origin of the cantons is rooted in the liberty-loving instincts of the peasants of Helvetia.

After the Romans departed Switzerland to defend Rome against the barbarians, Switzerland became, in the Middle Ages, a federation of fiefs of the Holy Roman Empire. In 888 it was again united by Rudolf of Burgundy, a minor despot, and for 150 years Switzerland had a king. Upon the death of the last Burgundian king, the kingdom crumbled into a loose collection of feudal fiefs ruled by bishops and ducal families who made their own laws and levied their own taxes. Eventually this division of rule by arbitrary despots became more than the freedom-loving and resourceful peasants could bear. The citizens living in the remote valleys of Uri, Schwyz (from which Switzerland received its name) and Unterwalden decided to liberate themselves from all feudal obligations and become free.

On Aug. 1, 1291, the elders of these three small states met on a tiny heath known as the Rutli on the shores of the Lake of Lucerne and negotiated an eternal pact' which recognized their right to local self-government, and pledged one another assistance against any encroachment upon these rights. The pact was the beginning of the Everlasting League' and the foundation of the Swiss Confederation.

BASEL

BISHOPRIC

A bishopric in northwest Switzerland, founded in the 5th century. The first coinage was c.1000AD. During the Reformation Basel became Protestant and the bishop resided henceforth in the town of Porrentruy. The Congress of Vienna gave the territories of the Bishopric to Bern. Today they form the Canton Jura and the French speaking part of Bern.

RULERS

Johann Franz von Schonau, 1651-1656
Johann Conrad von Roggenbach, 1656-1693

MONETARY SYSTEM

4 Kreuzer = 1 Batzen

STANDARD COINAGE

KM# 8 RAPPEN (Vierer)

Billon **Obv:** Round arms **Obv. Legend:** WILHEL. EPISCO. BASILIENSIS. **Rev:** Cruciform in inner circle, date **Rev. Legend:** FIRMA. NOMEN. DOMINI. **Note:** Uniface.

Date	Mintage	VG	F	VF	XF	Unc
1622 Rare	—	—	—	—	—	—

KM# 11 RAPPEN (Vierer)

Billon **Obv:** Arms on shield, date **Obv. Legend:** WILHEL: EPS: BASI: **Rev:** Cruciform of flowers **Rev. Legend:** FIRMA: MEV: NOM: DNI.

Date	Mintage	VG	F	VF	XF	Unc
1623	—	75.00	150	600	—	—
1624	—	125	225	800	2,000	—

KM# 13 BATZEN

Billon **Obv:** Four-fold arms in cartouche, 1 in circle above **Rev:** Standing Madonna and child

Date	Mintage	VG	F	VF	XF	Unc
1624	—	400	800	2,000	—	—

KM# 17 BATZEN

Billon **Obv:** Four-fold arms on shield, 1 in oval above

Date	Mintage	VG	F	VF	XF	Unc
1654	—	100	200	800	—	—
1655	—	100	200	800	—	—

KM# 21 BATZEN

Billon **Rev:** Half-length standing Madonna and child

Date	Mintage	VG	F	VF	XF	Unc
1655	—	50.00	100	400	—	—
1657	—	65.00	150	600	—	—
1658	—	65.00	150	600	—	—
1659	—	45.00	85.00	325	—	—
1660	—	45.00	85.00	325	—	—
1661	—	45.00	85.00	325	—	—
1662	—	45.00	85.00	325	—	—
1663	—	45.00	85.00	325	—	—

KM# 7 2 BATZEN

Billon **Obv:** Four-fold arms in cartouche, Z in circle above **Rev:** Madonna standing, facing with child

Date	Mintage	VG	F	VF	XF	Unc
1621 Rare	—	—	—	—	—	—
1624	—	200	400	900	—	—
1625	—	200	400	900	—	—

KM# 18 2 BATZEN

Billon **Obv:** Four-fold arms in ornate cartouche, 2 in oval above

Date	Mintage	VG	F	VF	XF	Unc
1654 Rare	—	—	—	—	—	—

KM# 9 1/2 SCHILLING

Billon **Obv:** Two-fold arms in cartouche **Rev:** Saint standing holding a book and flower

Date	Mintage	VG	F	VF	XF	Unc
1622	—	65.00	150	600	—	—

KM# 10 SCHILLING

Billon **Obv:** Four-fold arms **Rev:** Saint standing holding a book and flower

Date	Mintage	VG	F	VF	XF	Unc
1622	—	50.00	150	500	—	—
1623	—	25.00	45.00	150	—	—
1624	—	25.00	45.00	150	—	—

KM# 12 1/4 THALER

Silver **Obv:** Four-fold arms in cartouche **Rev:** Crowned imperial eagle

Date	Mintage	VG	F	VF	XF	Unc
1623	—	2,500	6,000	16,000	—	—

KM# 15 1/2 THALER

Silver **Obv:** Four-fold arms in front of Kaiser Heinrich II **Rev:** Crowned imperial eagle

Date	Mintage	VG	F	VF	XF	Unc
1625 Rare	—	—	—	—	—	—

KM# 14 THALER

Silver **Obv:** Four-fold arms in front of Kaiser Heinrich II **Rev:** Crowned imperial eagle **Note:** Dav. #4657.

Date	Mintage	VG	F	VF	XF	Unc
1624 Rare	—	—	—	—	—	—
1625	—	2,400	6,000	12,000	—	—

KM# 19 THALER

Silver **Obv:** Different four-fold arms **Rev:** Larger eagle **Note:** Dav. #4658.

Date	Mintage	VG	F	VF	XF	Unc
1654	—	1,500	3,200	8,000	16,000	—

KM# 16 2 THALER

Silver **Note:** Dav. #4656. Similar to 1 Thaler, KM#14.

Date	Mintage	VG	F	VF	XF	Unc
1624	—	—	—	—	—	—
1625	—	—	—	—	—	—

KM# A17 2 THALER

Silver **Note:** Klippe.

Date	Mintage	VG	F	VF	XF	Unc
1625	—	—	—	—	—	—

TRADE COINAGE

KM# 20 DUCAT

3.5000 g., 0.9860 Gold 0.1109 oz. AGW **Obv:** Inscription in shield, date divided below **Obv. Inscription:** IOHA/FRAN. D: G/EPIS. BASI/LIEN/SIS **Rev:** St. Heinrich standing with church and scepter in inner circle **Note:** Fr. #88.

Date	Mintage	VG	F	VF	XF	Unc
1654 Rare	—	—	—	—	—	—

KM# 22 DUCAT

3.5000 g., 0.9860 Gold 0.1109 oz. AGW **Obv:** Inscription in shield **Note:** Fr. #89.

Date	Mintage	VG	F	VF	XF	Unc
1659	—	5,000	12,000	30,000	—	—
1662	—	5,000	12,000	30,000	—	—

KM# B17 3 DUCAT

10.5000 g., 0.9860 Gold 0.3328 oz. AGW **Obv:** Four-fold arms in front of Kaiser Heinrich II **Rev:** Crowned imperial eagle **Note:** Struck with 1/2 Thaler dies, KM#15.

Date	Mintage	VG	F	VF	XF	Unc
1625 Rare	—	—	—	—	—	—

CITY

A city in northwest Switzerland, it was founded in 374 by the Roman Emperor Valentinian. It became a Burgundian Mint in the 10th century and obtained the mint right in 1373. It was admitted to the Swiss Confederation in 1501. Developed into a canton.

MONETARY SYSTEM

Until 1798
8 Rappen = 1 Batzen
30 Batzen = 2 Gulden = 1 Thaler
Dicken = 24 Kreuzer

STANDARD COINAGE

KM# 5 STEBLER

Billon, 12.8 mm. **Obv:** Arms on shield, low relief in circle of dots **Note:** Uniface.

Date	Mintage	VG	F	VF	XF	Unc
ND Rare	—	—	—	—	—	—

KM# 6 STEBLER

Billon, 17 mm. **Obv:** Arms on shield, high relief in circle of dots **Note:** Uniface.

Date	Mintage	VG	F	VF	XF	Unc
ND	—	20.00	40.00	160	400	—

KM# 110 ASSIS

Billon **Obv:** Shield **Obv. Legend:** MONETA • NOVA • BASILEENSIS **Rev:** Value, date in center **Rev. Legend:** DOMINE • CONSERVA • NOS • IN • PACE

Date	Mintage	VG	F	VF	XF	Unc
1663	—	5.00	9.00	60.00	120	200
1695	—	5.00	9.00	60.00	120	200
1697	—	5.00	9.00	60.00	120	200
1698	—	5.00	9.00	60.00	120	200

KM# 74 2 ASSIS

Billon **Note:** Similar to 1 Assis KM#135.

Date	Mintage	VG	F	VF	XF	Unc
ND	—	9.00	20.00	45.00	—	—
1623	—	9.00	20.00	45.00	—	—
1624	—	9.00	20.00	45.00	—	—

Date	Mintage	VG	F	VF	XF	Unc
1634	—	50.00	125	500	—	—
1638	—	50.00	125	500	—	—

KM# A75 2 ASSIS
Billon **Note:** Klippe.

Date	Mintage	VG	F	VF	XF	Unc
1624	—	—	—	—	—	—

KM# 74a 2 ASSIS
Billon **Obv:** Shield **Obv. Legend:** MONETA • NOVA • BASILEENSIS **Rev:** Value, date in center **Rev. Legend:** DOMINE • CONSERVA • NOS • IN • PACE **Note:** Klippe.

Date	Mintage	VG	F	VF	XF	Unc
1624	—	—	—	—	—	—

KM# 58 10 KREUZER (1/6 Thaler)
Silver **Obv:** Arms on shield, ornamentation in field within inner circle, legend around **Rev:** Crowned imperial eagle with 10 on breast

Date	Mintage	VG	F	VF	XF	Unc
1606 Rare	—	—	—	—	—	—

KM# 61 12 KREUZER (Zwolfer)
Silver **Obv:** Arms on shield, flourishes in field within circle, legend around **Rev:** Crowned imperial eagle within inner circle, 12 in circle on breast

Date	Mintage	VG	F	VF	XF	Unc
ND	—	150	300	800	1,600	—
1621	—	100	200	475	950	—

KM# 63 12 KREUZER (Zwolfer)
Silver **Obv:** Arms on ornate shield within inner circle

Date	Mintage	VG	F	VF	XF	Unc
ND Rare	—	—	—	—	—	—

KM# 75 12 KREUZER (Zwolfer)
Silver

Date	Mintage	VG	F	VF	XF	Unc
1622	—	175	400	800	1,200	—

KM# 77 12 KREUZER (Zwolfer)
Silver **Obv:** Date in legend at top

Date	Mintage	VG	F	VF	XF	Unc
1622	—	200	400	1,200	2,400	—

KM# 76 12 KREUZER (Zwolfer)
Silver **Note:** Additional ornamentation in fields within circles.

Date	Mintage	VG	F	VF	XF	Unc
1622	—	225	475	1,200	2,400	—

KM# 62 12 KREUZER (Zwolfer)
Silver **Note:** Klippe.

Date	Mintage	VG	F	VF	XF	Unc
ND Rare	—	—	—	—	—	—

KM# 81 12 KREUZER (Zwolfer)
Silver

Date	Mintage	VG	F	VF	XF	Unc
1623	—	60.00	125	275	475	—

KM# 59 60 KREUZER (Guldenthaler)
Silver **Obv:** Arms on shield divide ornamentations, date divided on sides **Obv. Legend:** ✠ MONETA • NOVA • VRBIS • BASILIENSIS **Rev:** Crowned imperial eagle with 60 in orb on breast **Rev. Legend:** ✠ DOMINE • CONSERVA • NOS • IN • PACE **Note:** Dav. #159.

Date	Mintage	VG	F	VF	XF	Unc
1616 Rare	—	1,600	3,500	8,000	15,000	—

KM# 64 DICKEN
Silver **Note:** Klippe. Similar to KM#82.

Date	Mintage	VG	F	VF	XF	Unc
1621 Rare	—	—	—	—	—	—

KM# 82 DICKEN
Silver

Date	Mintage	VG	F	VF	XF	Unc
1623	—	60.00	150	400	800	—
1632	—	60.00	150	400	800	—
1633	—	25.00	50.00	125	250	—
1634	—	25.00	50.00	125	250	—
1635	—	25.00	50.00	125	250	—
1636	—	25.00	50.00	125	250	—

KM# 88 DICKEN
Silver **Obv:** Arms dividing date in cartouche **Rev:** Eagle facing left with 1/4 on breast in circle

Date	Mintage	VG	F	VF	XF	Unc
1640	—	100	225	600	1,200	—

KM# 65 1/2 THALER
Silver **Obv:** Arms divide date in inner circle **Rev:** Eagle facing left in inner circle

Date	Mintage	VG	F	VF	XF	Unc
1621 Rare	—	—	—	—	—	—

KM# 83 1/2 THALER
Silver

Date	Mintage	VG	F	VF	XF	Unc
1623	—	100	225	600	1,200	—
1624	—	125	250	650	1,400	—
1638	—	125	250	650	1,400	—
1639	—	125	250	650	1,400	—

KM# 89 1/2 THALER
Silver

Date	Mintage	VG	F	VF	XF	Unc
1640	—	75.00	150	400	800	—

KM# A66 THALER
Silver **Obv:** Arms divide date **Rev:** Eagle left **Note:** Dav. #4599

Date	Mintage	VG	F	VF	XF	Unc
16Z1	—	60.00	120	325	600	—

KM# 66 THALER
Silver **Obv:** Arms divide date, border of arcs within inner circle **Rev:** Eagle left within inner circle **Note:** Dav. #4601.

Date	Mintage	VG	F	VF	XF	Unc
1621	—	100	200	350	650	—

KM# 68 THALER
Silver **Note:** Klippe.

Date	Mintage	VG	F	VF	XF	Unc
16Z1 Rare	—	—	—	—	—	—

KM# 80 THALER
Silver **Note:** Klippe.

Date	Mintage	VG	F	VF	XF	Unc
Rare	—	—	—	—	—	—
16ZZ	—	35.00	60.00	100	200	—

KM# 67 THALER
Silver **Obv:** Arms supported by two basilisks, date in legend **Note:** Dav. #4603.

Date	Mintage	VG	F	VF	XF	Unc
16ZZ	—	65.00	125	325	600	—

KM# 79.1 THALER
Silver **Obv:** Arms in quatrefoil, four inward lis at angles **Obv. Legend:** + MONETA + NOVA + VRBIS + BASILIEN(SIS)

Rev: Eagle left **Rev. Legend:** (Flower bud) DOMINE + CONSERVA + NOS + IN + PACE **Edge:** Plain **Note:** Dav. #4604.

Date	Mintage	VG	F	VF	XF	Unc
16ZZ	—	50.00	100	240	475	—
1623	—	50.00	100	240	475	—

KM# 79.2 THALER

Silver **Obv:** Arms in quatrefoil, four inward lis at angles **Obv. Legend:** + MONETA + NOVA + VRBIS + BASILIENSIS **Rev:** Eagle left **Rev. Legend:** (Flower bud) DOMINE + CONSERVA + NOS + IN + PACE **Edge:** Plain **Note:** Dav. #4604.

Date	Mintage	VG	F	VF	XF	Unc
1623	—	50.00	80.00	200	400	—
1624	—	55.00	100	250	475	—
1638	—	200	400	1,000	2,000	—
1639	—	100	200	500	1,200	—

KM# 84 THALER

Silver **Obv:** Eagle head right **Note:** Dav. #4605.

Date	Mintage	VG	F	VF	XF	Unc
1624	—	60.00	125	300	500	—

KM# A94 THALER

28.4200 g., Silver **Obv:** Arms in thick ornamental frame, cherub's head at top with full wings **Obv. Legend:** MONETA * NOVA * VRBIS * BASILIENSIS **Rev:** Eagle left **Rev. Legend:** DOMINE * CONSERVA * NOS * IN * PACE **Edge:** Plain **Note:** Dav. #4606.

Date	Mintage	VG	F	VF	XF	Unc
1640	—	60.00	125	300	500	—

KM# B94.1 THALER

Silver **Obv:** Arms in thin ornamental frame, cherub's head at top, wings fold downward **Obv. Legend:** MONETA * NOVA * VRBIS * BASILIENSIS **Rev:** Eagle left **Rev. Legend:** DOMINE * CONSERVA * NOS * IN * PACE **Edge:** Plain **Note:** Dav. #4607.

Date	Mintage	VG	F	VF	XF	Unc
1640	—	60.00	125	300	500	—

KM# 94 THALER

Silver **Obv:** Arms in thick ornamental frame, cherub's head at top, wings drawn upwards **Obv. Legend:** MONETA * NOVA * VRBIS * BASILEESIS **Rev:** Eagle left **Rev. Legend:** DOMINE * CONSERVA * NOS * IN * PACE **Edge:** Plain **Note:** Dav. #4608.

Date	Mintage	VG	F	VF	XF	Unc
1640	—	100	225	500	1,000	—

KM# B94.2 THALER

Silver **Obv:** Similar to KM#B94.1 **Obv. Legend:** MONETA * NOVA * VRBIS * BASILIENSIS **Rev:** Similar to KM#B94.1 **Rev. Legend:** DOMINE * CONSERVA * NOS * IN * PACE **Edge:** Plain **Note:** Dav. #4609.

Date	Mintage	VG	F	VF	XF	Unc
1640	—	60.00	125	300	500	—

KM# B94.3 THALER

Silver **Obv:** Similar to KM#B94.1 **Obv. Legend:** MONETA * NOVA * VRBIS * BASILIEESIS **Rev:** Similar to KM#B94.1 **Rev. Legend:** DOMINE * CONSERVA * NOS * IN * PACE **Edge:** Plain **Note:** Dav. #4610.

Date	Mintage	VG	F	VF	XF	Unc
1640	—	100	225	500	1,000	—

KM# A95 THALER

Silver **Obv:** Arms at center surrounded by eight shields **Obv. Legend:** MONETA + NOVA + VRBIS + BASILENSIS **Rev:** Imperial eagle **Rev. Legend:** DOMINE + CONSERVA + NOS + IN + PACE **Edge:** Plain

Date	Mintage	VG	F	VF	XF	Unc
ND(1640)	—	175	350	600	850	—

KM# 111 THALER

Silver **Obv:** Ornate cartouche around legend, date divided at bottom **Obv. Legend:** MONETA. NOVA/REIPVBLICAE/BASILIENSIS **Rev:** Basilisk left holding pointed shield with arms **Note:** Dav. #4612.

Date	Mintage	VG	F	VF	XF	Unc
1668 Rare	—	—	—	—	—	—

KM# 112 THALER

Silver **Obv:** Date not divided at bottom **Rev:** Arms in ornate circle **Note:** Dav. #4613.

Date	Mintage	VG	F	VF	XF	Unc
1669	—	150	275	650	1,250	—
1676	—	200	400	1,000	—	—

KM# 118 THALER

Silver **Obv:** Date divided at bottom **Rev:** Arms in ornate cartouche, basilisks at both sides **Note:** Dav. #4614.

Date	Mintage	VG	F	VF	XF	Unc
1694	—	125	300	750	1,500	—

KM# A69 1-1/2 THALER

Silver **Obv:** Arms supported by two basillisks **Obv. Legend:** + MONETA + NOVA + VRBIS + BASILIEN : **Rev:** Eagle left **Rev. Legend:** + DOMINE + CONSERVA + NOS + IN + PACE **Edge:** Plain **Note:** Dav. #A4603. Klippe.

Date	Mintage	VG	F	VF	XF	Unc
1621 Rare	—	—	—	—	—	—

KM# A71 1-1/2 THALER

Silver **Note:** Dav. #A4603. Similar to 1 Thaler, KM#67.

Date	Mintage	VG	F	VF	XF	Unc
16Z1 Rare	—	—	—	—	—	—
16Z1 Rare	—	—	—	—	—	—
16ZZ Rare	—	—	—	—	—	—

KM# 70 2 THALER

Silver **Obv:** Arms divide date, border of arcs within inner circle **Note:** Dav. #4600.

Date	Mintage	VG	F	VF	XF	Unc
1621 Rare	—	3,000	6,000	15,000	30,000	—

KM# 69 2 THALER

Silver **Obv:** Two basilisks leaning on shield with arms in inner circle **Rev:** Eagle left in inner circle **Note:** Dav. #4602.

Date	Mintage	VG	F	VF	XF	Unc
1621 Rare	—	2,500	5,000	13,500	26,000	—

KM# 78 2 THALER

Silver **Obv:** 2 basilisks leaning over small shield with arms **Rev:** Large, full eagle **Note:** Dav. #4602.

Date	Mintage	VG	F	VF	XF	Unc
1621	—	225	400	1,000	2,000	—

TRADE COINAGE

KM# 95 1/2 GOLDGULDEN

3.8200 g., 0.9000 Gold 0.1105 oz. AGW **Obv:** Basilisk right holding shield **Rev:** Similar to 1 Goldgulden, KM#132

Date	Mintage	VG	F	VF	XF	Unc
ND(1640)	—	225	400	800	1,600	—

KM# 73 GOLDGULDEN

7.6400 g., 0.9000 Gold 0.2211 oz. AGW **Note:** Varieties exist. Fr. #21.

Date	Mintage	VG	F	VF	XF	Unc
1621	—	750	1,400	2,800	4,500	—
1622	—	750	1,400	2,800	4,500	—
1623	—	1,800	3,500	7,000	12,000	—

KM# 96 GOLDGULDEN

7.6400 g., 0.9000 Gold 0.2211 oz. AGW **Obv:** Similar to KM#100 **Rev:** Eagle right

Date	Mintage	VG	F	VF	XF	Unc
ND(1640) Rare	—	—	—	—	—	—

KM# 100 GOLDGULDEN

7.6400 g., 0.9000 Gold 0.2211 oz. AGW **Note:** Fr. 25a.

Date	Mintage	VG	F	VF	XF	Unc
ND(1644)	—	350	600	1,200	2,000	3,200

KM# 99 GOLDGULDEN

7.6400 g., 0.9000 Gold 0.2211 oz. AGW

Date	Mintage	VG	F	VF	XF	Unc
ND(1648)	—	400	800	1,600	2,800	4,000

KM# 132 GOLDGULDEN

7.6400 g., 0.9000 Gold 0.2211 oz. AGW

Date	Mintage	VG	F	VF	XF	Unc
ND(1700)	—	225	400	800	1,300	2,400

KM# 98 2 GOLDGULDEN

15.2800 g., 0.9000 Gold 0.4421 oz. AGW

Date	Mintage	VG	F	VF	XF	Unc
ND(ca.1645)	—	1,200	2,400	4,500	8,000	—

KM# 109 2 GOLDGULDEN

15.2800 g., 0.9000 Gold 0.4421 oz. AGW

Date	Mintage	VG	F	VF	XF	Unc
ND(ca.1660)	—	800	1,600	3,600	6,000	—

KM# 116 1/2 DUCAT

1.7500 g., 0.9860 Gold 0.0555 oz. AGW **Obv:** Basilisk right holding shield with arms **Rev:** Legend in cartouche **Rev. Legend:** MONETA / NOVA / REIPVB / BASILE / ENSIS

Date	Mintage	VG	F	VF	XF	Unc
ND(1680)	—	2,000	4,000	8,000	—	—

KM# 86 DUCAT

3.5000 g., 0.9860 Gold 0.1109 oz. AGW **Note:** Fr. #46.

Date	Mintage	VG	F	VF	XF	Unc
ND(ca.1635)	—	500	950	2,000	3,200	—

KM# 97 DUCAT

3.5000 g., 0.9860 Gold 0.1109 oz. AGW **Obv:** Oval arms in cartouche, date divided in arms **Rev:** Crowned imperial eagle

Date	Mintage	VG	F	VF	XF	Unc
1640	—	700	1,300	2,400	4,000	—

KM# 102 DUCAT

3.5000 g., 0.9860 Gold 0.1109 oz. AGW **Obv:** Legend in tablet **Rev:** Oval arms in cartouche

Date	Mintage	VG	F	VF	XF	Unc
ND(1650) Rare	—	—	—	—	—	—

KM# 103 DUCAT

3.5000 g., 0.9860 Gold 0.1109 oz. AGW **Obv:** Basilisk right holding shield with arms **Rev:** Legend in curved line in cartouche

Date	Mintage	VG	F	VF	XF	Unc
ND(1650)	—	350	600	1,200	2,000	—

KM# 104 DUCAT

3.5000 g., 0.9860 Gold 0.1109 oz. AGW **Rev:** Legend in straight lines in cartouche

Date	Mintage	VG	F	VF	XF	Unc
ND(1650)	—	350	600	1,200	2,000	—

KM# 105 DUCAT

3.5000 g., 0.9860 Gold 0.1109 oz. AGW **Obv:** Basilisk holding different shield with arms **Rev:** Legend in curved lines in smaller cartouche **Note:** Fr. #52.

Date	Mintage	VG	F	VF	XF	Unc
ND(1650)	—	350	600	1,200	2,400	—

KM# 106 DUCAT

3.5000 g., 0.9860 Gold 0.1109 oz. AGW **Obv:** Date added to legend **Note:** Fr. #51.

Date	Mintage	VG	F	VF	XF	Unc
1653	—	750	1,400	2,800	4,000	—

KM# 107 DUCAT

3.5000 g., 0.9860 Gold 0.1109 oz. AGW **Rev:** Legend in laurel wreath

Date	Mintage	VG	F	VF	XF	Unc
1653 Rare	—	—	—	—	—	—

KM# 133 DUCAT

3.5000 g., 0.9860 Gold 0.1109 oz. AGW

Date	Mintage	VG	F	VF	XF	Unc
ND(ca.1700)	—	250	475	900	2,400	—

KM# 114 2 DUCAT

7.0000 g., 0.9860 Gold 0.2219 oz. AGW **Obv:** Basilisk right holding shield with arms **Rev:** Inscription: MONETA/NOVA... in cartouche, small oval at bottom

Date	Mintage	VG	F	VF	XF	Unc
ND(1675)	—	2,250	4,000	—	—	—

BERN

A city and canton in west central Switzerland. It was founded as a military post in 1191 and became an imperial city with the mint right in 1218. It was admitted to the Swiss Confederation as a canton in 1353.

MINTMASTERS' INITIALS

Initial	Date	Name
BF	1680	
D	1681-84	

MONETARY SYSTEM

Until 1798

8 Vierer = 4 Kreuzer = 1 Batzen

40 Batzen = 1 Thaler

CITY

STANDARD COINAGE

KM# 5 PFENNIG

Billon **Obv:** Bear left, eagle above **Note:** Uniface.

Date	Mintage	VG	F	VF	XF	Unc
ND	—	300	600	1,500	—	—

KM# 10 1/2 KREUZER

Billon **Note:** Similar to 1 Kreuzer, KM#8.

Date	Mintage	VG	F	VF	XF	Unc
ND	—	5.00	10.00	30.00	50.00	—
1617 Rare	—	—	—	—	—	—
1618 Rare	—	—	—	—	—	—
1619 Rare	—	—	—	—	—	—
1620	—	60.00	120	250	750	—
1621 Rare	—	—	—	—	—	—
1622	—	60.00	120	250	750	—
1623	—	60.00	120	250	750	—
1624 Rare	—	—	—	—	—	—

KM# 11 1/2 KREUZER

Billon **Note:** Without inner circle.

Date	Mintage	VG	F	VF	XF	Unc
ND	—	5.00	10.00	30.00	75.00	—

KM# 41 1/2 KREUZER

Billon

Date	Mintage	VG	F	VF	XF	Unc
ND	—	5.00	10.00	30.00	80.00	—
1680	—	20.00	40.00	150	400	—
1684	—	5.00	8.00	25.00	75.00	—
1699	—	20.00	40.00	150	400	—

KM# 40 1/2 KREUZER

Billon **Rev:** Double B's in cruciform, lilies in angles

Date	Mintage	VG	F	VF	XF	Unc
1679	—	9.00	16.00	60.00	150	—

KM# 39 1/2 KREUZER

Billon **Obv:** Bern arms **Rev:** Thicker cross

Date	Mintage	VG	F	VF	XF	Unc
1679	—	5.00	10.00	20.00	30.00	—

KM# 58 1/2 KREUZER

Billon **Rev:** Anchor crosses in angles of cross

Date	Mintage	VG	F	VF	XF	Unc
1684	—	9.00	16.00	60.00	150	—

KM# 8 KREUZER

Billon

Date	Mintage	VG	F	VF	XF	Unc
1612	—	8.00	15.00	40.00	175	—
1613	—	50.00	100	400	—	—
1614	—	50.00	100	400	—	—
1617	—	200	450	1,000	—	—
1618	—	4.00	8.00	30.00	80.00	—
1619	—	4.00	8.00	30.00	80.00	—
1620	—	4.00	8.00	30.00	80.00	—
1621	—	4.00	8.00	30.00	80.00	—
1622	—	25.00	60.00	200	500	—
1623	—	—	—	—	—	—

KM# 25 10 KREUZER

Silver **Obv:** Arms in oval cartouche, date in legend **Rev:** Legend in laurel wreath, 10 below **Rev. Legend:** DEVX / PROVIDE / BIT

Date	Mintage	VG	F	VF	XF	Unc
1656	—	30.00	60.00	125	240	475

KM# 26 10 KREUZER

Silver **Rev:** Crowned imperial eagle with 10 in circle on breast

Date	Mintage	VG	F	VF	XF	Unc
1656	—	20.00	40.00	80.00	125	325
1658	—	20.00	40.00	80.00	125	325
1669	—	400	800	2,000	—	—

KM# 35 10 KREUZER

Silver **Rev:** 10 at top above heads

Date	Mintage	VG	F	VF	XF	Unc
1669	—	20.00	40.00	80.00	175	325

KM# 42 10 KREUZER

Silver **Obv:** Value below arms **Rev:** Legend, date and mintmaster's initials in laurel wreath, 10 below ribbon **Rev. Inscription:** DEVS / PROVIDE / BIT

Date	Mintage	VG	F	VF	XF	Unc
1679 Rare	—	—	—	—	—	—

KM# 17 12 KREUZER

Silver

Date	Mintage	VG	F	VF	XF	Unc
1620	—	75.00	150	400	800	—
1621	—	50.00	100	275	500	—

KM# 27 20 KREUZER

Silver

Date	Mintage	VG	F	VF	XF	Unc
1656	—	20.00	70.00	75.00	150	325
1658	—	30.00	50.00	125	250	500
1659	—	20.00	40.00	75.00	150	325

KM# 43 20 KREUZER

Silver **Obv:** Value below arms **Obv. Legend:** MONETA. REIPVBLICAE. BERNENSIS. **Rev:** Cruciform of intertwined B's, 20 in square in center

Date	Mintage	VG	F	VF	XF	Unc
1679	—	25.00	50.00	100	250	500

KM# 28 30 KREUZER (1/2 Gulden)

Silver

Date	Mintage	VG	F	VF	XF	Unc
ND	—	20.00	40.00	100	200	400
1657	—	25.00	50.00	150	250	500
1680	—	25.00	50.00	150	250	500

KM# 9 1/2 BATZEN

Billon **Obv:** Arms on shield, eagle above, date in legend **Rev:** Cross in inner circle

Date	Mintage	VG	F	VF	XF	Unc
1614	—	50.00	100	400	—	—

KM# 15 BATZEN

Billon **Obv:** Date above cartouche

Date	Mintage	VG	F	VF	XF	Unc
ND	—	8.00	16.00	45.00	150	—
1617	—	8.00	16.00	45.00	150	—
1618	—	8.00	16.00	45.00	150	—
1619	—	50.00	100	175	350	—
1620	—	8.00	16.00	45.00	150	—
1621	—	8.00	16.00	45.00	150	—

Date	Mintage	VG	F	VF	XF	Unc
1622	—	6.00	12.00	40.00	125	—
1623	—	6.00	12.00	40.00	125	—

KM# 13 BATZEN

Billon **Obv:** Arms on shield with decorative flourishes divide date **Rev:** Crowned imperial eagle, breast orb above

Date	Mintage	VG	F	VF	XF	Unc
1617	—	8.00	16.00	45.00	200	—

KM# 14 BATZEN

Billon **Obv:** Arms on shield in cartouche **Rev:** Crowned imperial eagle, date in legend

Date	Mintage	VG	F	VF	XF	Unc
1617	—	100	250	1,000	—	—

KM# 23 BATZEN

Billon **Note:** Klippe.

Date	Mintage	VG	F	VF	XF	Unc
1622	—	—	—	—	—	—

KM# 18 3 BATZEN

Silver **Obv:** Bear walking left, eagle above, 3 in oval below **Rev:** Cross in inner circle, date divided at bottom

Date	Mintage	VG	F	VF	XF	Unc
1620	—	80.00	150	350	800	—
1621	—	50.00	100	250	550	—

KM# 19 1/2 DICKEN

Silver **Obv:** Bear walking left, eagle above **Rev:** Cross in inner circle

Date	Mintage	VG	F	VF	XF	Unc
1620	—	100	200	500	1,000	—

KM# A20 1/2 DICKEN

Silver **Obv:** Ornate arms **Rev:** Imperial eagle

Date	Mintage	VG	F	VF	XF	Unc
1621	—	50.00	100	250	500	—

KM# 12 DICKEN

Silver **Obv:** Arms in cartouche, date in upper legend **Rev:** Crowned imperial eagle in inner circle

Date	Mintage	VG	F	VF	XF	Unc
1617	—	400	800	2,000	—	—
1618	—	500	1,000	2,500	—	—
1620	—	165	325	800	1,600	—
1621	—	400	750	2,000	—	—

KM# 21 DICKEN

Silver **Obv:** Bear walking left, eagle above **Rev:** Cross with ornamentation in angles

Date	Mintage	VG	F	VF	XF	Unc
1620	—	900	2,000	4,000	—	—
1621 Rare	—	—	—	—	—	—
ND(1623)	—	—	—	—	—	—

KM# 20 DICKEN

Silver **Note:** Klippe.

Date	Mintage	VG	F	VF	XF	Unc
1620	—	—	—	—	—	—

KM# 22 DICKEN

Silver **Note:** Klippe.

Date	Mintage	VG	F	VF	XF	Unc
1620	—	—	—	—	—	—

KM# 51 1/4 THALER

Silver **Obv:** Arms in cartouche within inner circle **Rev:** Cross with flowery ornaments in angles, date in legend above and value 1/4 in legend below

Date	Mintage	VG	F	VF	XF	Unc
ND	—	25.00	45.00	100	200	400
1657	—	30.00	60.00	150	300	500
1680	—	30.00	60.00	150	300	500

KM# 44 1/2 THALER

Silver **Note:** Similar to 1 Thaler, KM#46.

Date	Mintage	VG	F	VF	XF	Unc
1679	—	40.00	80.00	200	450	—
1680	—	225	400	1,000	—	—

KM# 37 THALER

Silver **Obv:** Shield with ornamental flourishes **Rev:** Cross with ornamentation in angles **Note:** Dav. #4615.

Date	Mintage	VG	F	VF	XF	Unc
ND(1670)	—	1,200	2,400	4,000	6,000	—

KM# 38 THALER

Silver **Rev:** Bust of the duke of Zahringen right divides date **Rev. Legend:** -:- BERCHT. DVS • ZERING (:) COND. VRB. BERN **Note:** Dav. #4616.

Date	Mintage	VG	F	VF	XF	Unc
ND Rare	—	3,000	6,000	15,000	—	—
1671 Rare	—	—	—	—	—	—

KM# 46.1 THALER

Silver **Obv:** Oval shield in ornate frame **Rev:** Date x1679x **Note:** Dav. #4618.

Date	Mintage	VG	F	VF	XF	Unc
1679 V Small date	—	100	225	600	1,200	2,000

KM# 46.2 THALER

Obv: Similar to KM#46.6 **Note:** Dav. #4618A.

Date	Mintage	VG	F	VF	XF	Unc
1679 V	—	250	500	1,200	—	—

KM# 46.3 THALER

Silver **Obv:** Oval shield with vertical lines in upper and lower fields **Note:** Dav. #4619.

Date	Mintage	VG	F	VF	XF	Unc
1679 V	—	250	500	1,200	—	—

KM# 46.4 THALER

Silver **Obv:** Similar shield to KM#46.3 with P and rosette above **Note:** Dav. #4619A.

Date	Mintage	VG	F	VF	XF	Unc
1679 V	—	250	500	1,200	—	—

KM# 46.5 THALER

Silver **Obv:** Similar shield to KM#46.3 with rosette and P above **Note:** Dav. #4619B.

Date	Mintage	VG	F	VF	XF	Unc
1679	—	250	500	1,200	—	—

KM# 46.6 THALER

Silver **Obv:** Shield with ornamentation in upper and lower fields **Rev:** Rosettes in angles of monogram **Note:** Dav. #4620.

Date	Mintage	VG	F	VF	XF	Unc
1679 C	—	250	500	1,200	—	—

KM# 46.7 THALER

Silver **Obv:** Similar shield to KM#46.3 **Note:** Dav. #4620A.

Date	Mintage	VG	F	VF	XF	Unc
1679 V	—	250	500	1,200	—	—

KM# 45 THALER

Silver **Rev. Legend:** DOMINVS. PROVIDEBIT. **Note:** Similar to KM#46. Dav. #4617.

Date	Mintage	VG	F	VF	XF	Unc
1679 V	—	250	500	1,200	—	—

TRADE COINAGE

KM# 6 1/2 DUCAT

1.7500 g., 0.9860 Gold 0.0555 oz. AGW **Rev:** St. Vincent

Date	Mintage	VG	F	VF	XF	Unc
1601	—	700	1,200	2,400	4,000	6,000
1623 Rare	—	—	—	—	—	—

KM# 29 DUCAT

3.5000 g., 0.9860 Gold 0.1109 oz. AGW **Note:** Fr. #123.

Date	Mintage	VG	F	VF	XF	Unc
1658	—	800	1,500	2,750	4,500	7,000
ND(1658) Rare	—	—	—	—	—	—

KM# 47 DUCAT

3.5000 g., 0.9860 Gold 0.1109 oz. AGW **Rev:** Value and date in branches **Note:** Fr. #126.

Date	Mintage	VG	F	VF	XF	Unc
1679	—	600	1,200	2,500	4,000	6,000

KM# 48 DUCAT

3.5000 g., 0.9860 Gold 0.1109 oz. AGW **Rev:** Value and date in cartouche **Note:** Fr. #127.

Date	Mintage	VG	F	VF	XF	Unc
1679	—	2,000	4,000	8,000	—	—

KM# 59 DUCAT

3.5000 g., 0.9860 Gold 0.1109 oz. AGW **Obv:** Bear and lion supporting oval arms **Rev:** Similar to KM#61

Date	Mintage	VG	F	VF	XF	Unc
1684 Rare	—	—	—	—	—	—

KM# 61 DUCAT

3.5000 g., 0.9860 Gold 0.1109 oz. AGW

Date	Mintage	VG	F	VF	XF	Unc
1696	—	600	1,200	2,500	4,500	7,000

KM# 62 DUCAT

3.5000 g., 0.9860 Gold 0.1109 oz. AGW **Obv:** Crowned, ornate oval arms of Bern **Obv. Legend:** BENEDICTUS • SIT • IEHOVA • DEUS • **Rev:** Inscription, value and date within partial frame flanked by 1/2 figures above **Rev. Inscription:** REIPUBLICA/BERNENSIS/DUCAT **Note:** Fr. #139.

Date	Mintage	VG	F	VF	XF	Unc
1697	—	—	800	1,600	2,750	4,000

KM# A32 2 DUCAT

Note: Fr. #122.

Date	Mintage	VG	F	VF	XF	Unc
ND(1645-65)	—	1,200	2,400	4,500	8,000	12,000

KM# A30 2 DUCAT

7.0000 g., 0.9860 Gold 0.2219 oz. AGW **Obv:** Ornate arms **Rev:** Imperial eagle **Note:** Struck with 1 Ducat dies, KM#29.

Date	Mintage	VG	F	VF	XF	Unc
1658	—	1,200	2,400	4,500	8,000	12,000

KM# 30 2 DUCAT

7.0000 g., 0.9860 Gold 0.2219 oz. AGW **Note:** Fr. #121.

Date	Mintage	VG	F	VF	XF	Unc
ND(1658-59)	—	1,200	2,400	4,500	8,000	12,000

KM# 31 2 DUCAT

7.0000 g., 0.9860 Gold 0.2219 oz. AGW **Note:** Varieties exist. Fr. #121.

Date	Mintage	VG	F	VF	XF	Unc
1659 Rare	—	—	—	—	—	—

KM# 49 2 DUCAT

7.0000 g., 0.9860 Gold 0.2219 oz. AGW **Note:** Fr. #125.

Date	Mintage	VG	F	VF	XF	Unc
1679	—	1,000	2,000	4,000	6,500	9,500

KM# 64 2 DUCAT

7.0000 g., 0.9860 Gold 0.2219 oz. AGW **Obv:** Crowned oval arms **Rev:** Man and woman holding drapery, value and date on drapery **Note:** Fr. #138.

Date	Mintage	VG	F	VF	XF	Unc
1698	—	1,000	2,000	4,000	6,000	9,500

KM# 32 3 DUCAT

10.5000 g., 0.9860 Gold 0.3328 oz. AGW **Obv:** Arms in cartouche, date in legend **Rev:** Crowned imperial eagle **Note:** Fr. #120.

Date	Mintage	VG	F	VF	XF	Unc
ND(1659)	—	1,800	3,500	6,500	12,000	16,500

KM# 52 3 DUCAT

10.5000 g., 0.9860 Gold 0.3328 oz. AGW **Rev. Inscription:** BENEDICTUS/ • SIT • / • IEHOVA • / • DEUS • **Note:** Fr. #132.

Date	Mintage	VG	F	VF	XF	Unc
1680	—	1,200	2,500	4,500	8,000	12,000
1684	—	1,200	2,500	4,500	8,000	12,000
1697	—	1,200	2,500	4,500	8,000	12,000

KM# 63 3 DUCAT

10.5000 g., 0.9860 Gold 0.3328 oz. AGW **Rev. Inscription:** MONEDA / NOVA **Note:** Fr. #133.

Date	Mintage	VG	F	VF	XF	Unc
1697	—	1,200	2,500	4,500	8,000	12,000

KM# 65 3 DUCAT

10.5000 g., 0.9860 Gold 0.3328 oz. AGW **Obv:** Single crowned shield of arms **Note:** Fr. #134.

Date	Mintage	VG	F	VF	XF	Unc
1699	—	1,300	2,400	4,500	8,000	12,000

FR# 116 4 DUCAT

14.0000 g., 0.9860 Gold 0.4438 oz. AGW, 30 mm. **Obv:** Double-headed eagle above bear walking left **Obv. Legend:** MONETA•NO•BERNENSIS **Rev:** Short cross, ornaments in angles **Rev. Legend:** + BERCH:D:ZERING:CONDITO **Note:** Struck with 1 Dicken dies.

Date	Mintage	VG	F	VF	XF	Unc
ND(1600) Rare	—	—	—	—	—	—

KM# 33 4 DUCAT

14.0000 g., 0.9860 Gold 0.4438 oz. AGW **Obv:** Arms in cartouche, date in legend **Rev:** Crowned imperial eagle

Date	Mintage	VG	F	VF	XF	Unc
1659 Rare	—	—	—	—	—	—

KM# 53 4 DUCAT

14.0000 g., 0.9860 Gold 0.4438 oz. AGW **Obv:** Crowned supported arms **Note:** Fr. #131.

Date	Mintage	VG	F	VF	XF	Unc
1680 BF	—	1,500	2,800	5,500	9,000	14,000
1684 D	—	1,500	2,800	5,500	10,000	15,000

KM# 50 5 DUCAT

17.5000 g., 0.9860 Gold 0.5547 oz. AGW **Note:** Similar to 10 Ducat, KM#54.

Date	Mintage	VG	F	VF	XF	Unc
ND(1680) Rare	—	—	—	—	—	—

KM# 55 8 DUCAT

28.0000 g., 0.9860 Gold 0.8876 oz. AGW **Obv:** Crowned arms, palm branches above, being held by lion and bear, garland of flowers below **Rev:** Chain ring on outside, wreath of crosses and flowers around cartouche which contains legend, value and date **Note:** Fr. #130.

Date	Mintage	VG	F	VF	XF	Unc
1681 D	—	—	—	11,000	17,500	—

KM# 54 10 DUCAT

35.0000 g., 0.9860 Gold 1.1095 oz. AGW **Obv:** Crowned arms with bear and lion supporters **Rev:** Ctiy of Bern with arms above

Date	Mintage	VG	F	VF	XF	Unc
ND(1680) Rare	—	—	—	—	—	—

KM# 56 10 DUCAT

35.0000 g., 0.9860 Gold 1.1095 oz. AGW **Obv:** Crowned arms, palm branches above, being held by lion and bear, garland of flowers below **Rev:** Chain ring on outside, wreath of crosses and flowers around cartouche which contains legend, value and date **Note:** Fr. #129; Similar to 20 Ducat, KM#60.

Date	Mintage	VG	F	VF	XF	Unc
1681 D	—	—	12,000	24,000	40,000	60,000

KM# 57 12 DUCAT

42.0000 g., 0.9860 Gold 1.3314 oz. AGW **Obv:** Crowned arms, palm branches above, being held by lion and bear, garland of flowers below **Rev:** Chain ring on outside, wreath of crosses and flowers around cartouche containing legend, value and date **Note:** Fr. #128.

Date	Mintage	VG	F	VF	XF	Unc
1681 D	—	—	14,000	28,000	45,000	60,000

KM# 60 20 DUCAT

70.0000 g., 0.9860 Gold 2.2190 oz. AGW **Note:** Fr. #127a.

Date	Mintage	VG	F	VF	XF	Unc
1681 D Rare	—	—	28,000	55,000	95,000	140,000

CHUR

A former bishopric now part of the canton Graubunden. The mint right was given from 959 until about 1798.

BISHOPRIC

RULERS
Johann V Flugi von Aspermont, 1601-1627
Joseph Mohr von Zernetz, 1627-1635
Johann VI Flugi von Aspermont, 1636-1661
Ulrich VI von Mont, 1661-1692
Ulrich VII von Federspiel, 1692-1728

STANDARD COINAGE

KM# 6 PFENNIG
Billon **Obv:** Bishop's arms with three swan heads right on shield, IEC around within barley corn circle **Note:** Uniface.

Date	Mintage	VG	F	VF	XF	Unc
ND(1601)	—	32.50	65.00	100	200	—

KM# 7 PFENNIG
Billon **Obv:** Three roses around shield **Note:** Uniface.

Date	Mintage	VG	F	VF	XF	Unc
ND(1601)	—	32.50	65.00	100	200	—

KM# 8 PFENNIG
Billon **Obv:** Bishop's family arms on shield with four fields, letters IEC around within pearl circle **Note:** Uniface.

Date	Mintage	VG	F	VF	XF	Unc
ND(1601)	—	32.50	65.00	100	200	—

KM# 9 PFENNIG
Billon **Obv:** Without letters around shield **Note:** Uniface.

Date	Mintage	VG	F	VF	XF	Unc
ND(1601)	—	35.00	70.00	125	250	—

KM# 10 PFENNIG
Billon **Obv:** Bishop's family arms on four-fold shield with swan necks in two fields, IEC around, within crude pearl circle **Note:** Uniface.

Date	Mintage	VG	F	VF	XF	Unc
ND(1601)	—	32.50	65.00	100	200	—

KM# 5 PFENNIG
Billon **Obv:** Bishop's arms with three swan heads left on shield, IEC around within pearl circle **Note:** Uniface. Schussel type.

Date	Mintage	VG	F	VF	XF	Unc
ND(1601)	—	6.00	12.00	32.00	65.00	—

KM# 105 PFENNIG
Billon **Obv:** Bishop's arms with unicorn on shield, letters VEC around within barley corn circle **Note:** Uniface.

Date	Mintage	VG	F	VF	XF	Unc
ND(1661)	—	6.00	12.00	32.00	65.00	—

KM# 106 PFENNIG
Billon **Obv:** Bishop's arms with unicorn on shield, circle around broken by letters VEC within barley corn circle **Note:** Uniface.

Date	Mintage	VG	F	VF	XF	Unc
ND(1661)	—	6.50	12.50	32.00	65.00	—

KM# 107 PFENNIG
Billon **Obv:** Bishop's arms with unicorn on shield, VEC above, flowers at sides within barley corn circle **Note:** Uniface.

Date	Mintage	VG	F	VF	XF	Unc
ND(1661) Rare	—	—	—	—	—	—

KM# 108 PFENNIG
Billon **Obv:** Bishop's arms with unicorn on curved shield, VEC around within barley corn circle **Note:** Uniface.

Date	Mintage	VG	F	VF	XF	Unc
ND(1661)	—	6.50	12.50	32.00	65.00	—

KM# 128 PFENNIG
Billon **Obv:** Arms of Bishopric with Ibex right on curved shield, VEC around **Note:** Uniface.

Date	Mintage	VG	F	VF	XF	Unc
ND(1692)	—	6.00	12.00	32.00	65.00	—

KM# 129 PFENNIG
Billon **Obv:** Ibex left **Note:** Uniface.

Date	Mintage	VG	F	VF	XF	Unc
ND(1692)	—	6.00	12.00	32.00	65.00	—

KM# 11 2 PFENNIG
Billon **Obv:** Three shields, one with swan necks, one with Ibex, one with eagle, 2 in center **Note:** Uniface.

Date	Mintage	VG	F	VF	XF	Unc
ND(1601)	—	6.00	12.00	32.00	65.00	—

KM# 12 2 PFENNIG
Billon **Obv:** Three shields with dot in center **Note:** Uniface.

Date	Mintage	VG	F	VF	XF	Unc
ND(1601)	—	6.00	12.00	32.00	65.00	—

KM# 13 2 PFENNIG
Billon **Obv:** Three shields with two dots in center, 2 below **Note:** Uniface.

Date	Mintage	VG	F	VF	XF	Unc
ND(1601)	—	6.00	12.00	32.00	65.00	—

KM# 14 2 PFENNIG
Billon **Obv:** Three shields, two roses and one eagle in fields between, 2 in center **Note:** Uniface.

Date	Mintage	VG	F	VF	XF	Unc
ND(1601)	—	6.50	12.50	32.00	65.00	—

KM# 15 2 PFENNIG
Billon **Obv:** Three shields joined at center, eagle, rose and 2 in fields **Note:** Uniface.

Date	Mintage	VG	F	VF	XF	Unc
ND(1601)	—	15.00	30.00	80.00	—	—

KM# 16 2 PFENNIG
Billon **Obv:** Three shields joined at center, eagle at top, bishop's arms at left, Bishopric arms at right, 2 below **Note:** Uniface.

Date	Mintage	VG	F	VF	XF	Unc
ND(1601)	—	15.00	30.00	80.00	—	—

KM# 17 2 PFENNIG
Billon **Obv:** Bishopric arms at left, Bishop's arms at right **Note:** Uniface.

Date	Mintage	VG	F	VF	XF	Unc
ND(1601)	—	6.50	12.50	32.00	65.00	—

KM# 109 2 PFENNIG
Billon **Obv:** Three shields, eagle at top, unicorn at left, Ibex at right, 2 below **Note:** Uniface.

Date	Mintage	VG	F	VF	XF	Unc
ND(1661)	—	6.00	12.00	32.00	65.00	—

KM# 110 2 PFENNIG
Billon **Obv:** Ibex at left, unicorn at right **Note:** Uniface.

Date	Mintage	VG	F	VF	XF	Unc
ND(1661)	—	6.00	12.00	32.00	65.00	—

KM# 130 2 PFENNIG
Billon **Obv:** 1/2 stamped on blank reverse **Note:** Uniface.

Date	Mintage	VG	F	VF	XF	Unc
ND(1692)	—	8.00	16.00	40.00	80.00	—

KM# 18 BLUZGER
Billon **Obv:** Wide anchor cross in pearl circle, legend around **Rev:** Bishopric arms with Ibex right on ornamental shield in pearl circle, legend around

Date	Mintage	VG	F	VF	XF	Unc
ND(1602) Rare	—	450	900	2,400	—	—

KM# 19 BLUZGER
Billon **Obv:** Dots at sides and in angles of cross **Rev:** Bust of Madonna holding child, both with halos

Date	Mintage	VG	F	VF	XF	Unc
ND(1601)	—	20.00	40.00	150	—	—

KM# 20 BLUZGER
Billon **Obv:** Maltese cross

Date	Mintage	VG	F	VF	XF	Unc
ND(1601)	—	16.00	32.00	150	—	—

KM# 21 BLUZGER
Billon **Obv:** Cross with prongs at end

Date	Mintage	VG	F	VF	XF	Unc
ND(1601)	—	20.00	40.00	150	—	—

KM# 52 BLUZGER
Billon **Obv:** Cross with ornamentation at ends **Rev:** Madonna and child, date in legend

Date	Mintage	VG	F	VF	XF	Unc
1610 Rare	—	400	800	2,000	—	—
1616	—	150	300	800	—	—
1623	—	60.00	120	300	—	—
1624	—	40.00	80.00	140	—	—

KM# 118 BLUZGER
Billon **Obv:** Four-fold arms in oval cartouche in inner circle **Rev:** Anchor cross in inner circle

Date	Mintage	VG	F	VF	XF	Unc
1680	—	135	275	700	—	—

KM# 120 BLUZGER
Billon **Obv:** Without inner circles **Rev:** Without inner circles

Date	Mintage	VG	F	VF	XF	Unc
1684	—	75.00	150	350	—	—
1691	—	125	250	600	—	—

KM# 131 BLUZGER
Billon **Ruler:** Ulrich VII von Federspiel **Obv:** 4-fold arms in oval cartouche in circle of pearls **Rev:** Anchor cross with ornamentation on arms

Date	Mintage	VG	F	VF	XF	Unc
1693	—	6.50	12.50	32.00	60.00	—
1694	—	6.50	12.50	32.00	60.00	—

KM# 65 KREUZER
Billon

Date	Mintage	VG	F	VF	XF	Unc
1623	—	200	400	1,200	—	—

KM# 73 KREUZER
Billon

Date	Mintage	VG	F	VF	XF	Unc
1627	—	300	500	1,500	—	—

KM# 77 KREUZER
Billon **Obv:** Crowned imperial eagle, one in circle on breast, date below **Rev:** Ibex shield in inner circle **Rev. Legend:** IOSEP...

Date	Mintage	VG	F	VF	XF	Unc
1628	—	100	225	600	—	—

KM# 97 KREUZER
Billon **Obv:** Bust right dividing S-L **Obv. Legend:** IOAN.... **Rev:** Legend, date. **Rev. Legend:** FER.III...

Date	Mintage	VG	F	VF	XF	Unc
1643	—	8.00	16.00	45.00	90.00	—
1644	—	6.00	12.00	45.00	80.00	—
1645	—	8.00	16.00	45.00	90.00	—
1646	—	8.00	16.00	45.00	90.00	—
1649 Rare	—	—	—	—	—	—
1650	—	12.00	25.00	80.00	—	—
1652	—	25.00	50.00	150	—	—

KM# 69 2 KREUZER (1/2 Batzen)
Billon **Obv:** Four-fold arms on shield in inner circle, legend, date **Obv. Legend:** MO.NO... **Rev:** Imperial orb w/2 in inner circle

Date	Mintage	VG	F	VF	XF	Unc
1624 Rare	—	—	—	—	—	—

KM# 71 2 KREUZER (1/2 Batzen)
Billon **Obv:** Legend, date **Obv. Legend:** IOAN. D. G. E. P. CVR

Date	Mintage	VG	F	VF	XF	Unc
1625	—	45.00	90.00	250	—	—
1626	—	45.00	90.00	250	—	—

KM# 99 2 KREUZER (1/2 Batzen)
Billon **Obv:** Four-fold arms on round, with indented sides, shield in inner circle **Obv. Legend:** IOAN. D. G. EPIS. **Rev:** Imperial orb w/2 in center in inner circle, date **Rev. Legend:** FER. III. D.G. R. IM. S.

Date	Mintage	VG	F	VF	XF	Unc
1646	—	8.00	16.00	45.00	90.00	—

KM# 100 2 KREUZER (1/2 Batzen)
Billon **Obv:** Four-fold arms on oval shield in inner circle **Obv. Legend:** IOANNES. D. G. EPIS **Rev:** Legend, date **Rev. Legend:** ...ROM. IM. SEM. A.

Date	Mintage	VG	F	VF	XF	Unc
1648	—	12.00	24.00	80.00	—	—
1649	—	25.00	60.00	120	—	—

KM# 101 2 KREUZER (1/2 Batzen)
Billon **Rev:** Legend, date **Rev. Legend:** MONE. NO. CVRIAE. RETIC.

Date	Mintage	VG	F	VF	XF	Unc
1649	—	75.00	150	400	—	—

KM# 103 2 KREUZER (1/2 Batzen)
Billon **Obv:** Four-fold arms on round with indented sides, shield in inner circle **Rev:** Legend, date **Rev. Legend:** LEOPOLD. I. D. G...

Date	Mintage	VG	F	VF	XF	Unc
1659	—	40.00	80.00	200	—	—

KM# 111 2 KREUZER (1/2 Batzen)
Billon **Obv. Legend:** VDAL. D. G. EPIS. CVR. S. R. I. P.

Date	Mintage	VG	F	VF	XF	Unc
1663	—	16.00	32.00	85.00	175	—

KM# 119 2 KREUZER (1/2 Batzen)
Billon **Obv:** Arms in oval cartouche **Obv. Legend:** ...EP. CVR. D. IN. FV... **Rev. Legend:** LEOPOLDVS...

Date	Mintage	VG	F	VF	XF	Unc
1680	—	200	450	1,200	—	—

KM# 121 2 KREUZER (1/2 Batzen)
Billon **Obv:** Legend, date **Obv. Legend:** D. I. FV. E. G. E. **Rev:** Four-fold arms on ornate shield **Rev. Legend:** LEOPOLD. D. G. R. IM. S. A.

Date	Mintage	VG	F	VF	XF	Unc
1686	—	200	450	1,200	—	—

KM# 22 3 KREUZER (1 Groschen)
Silver **Rev. Legend:** SI DEVS PRO NOB Q CON NOS

Date	Mintage	VG	F	VF	XF	Unc
ND(1601)	—	120	240	600	—	—

KM# 23 3 KREUZER (1 Groschen)
Silver **Rev. Legend:** DO. CONSER. NOS. IN. PAC.

Date	Mintage	VG	F	VF	XF	Unc
ND(1601)	—	200	450	1,200	—	—

KM# 24 3 KREUZER (1 Groschen)
Silver **Obv:** Without bishopric arms in legend

Date	Mintage	VG	F	VF	XF	Unc
ND(1601) Rare	—	—	—	—	—	—

KM# 25 3 KREUZER (1 Groschen)
Silver **Obv:** Without inner circle

Date	Mintage	VG	F	VF	XF	Unc
ND(1601)	—	120	240	600	—	—

KM# 26 3 KREUZER (1 Groschen)
Silver **Obv:** Four-fold arms on ornate shield **Obv. Legend:** IOANNES. DEI... **Rev. Legend:** MATHIAS II D: G. RO. IM. SE. AV. H. B. RE.

Date	Mintage	VG	F	VF	XF	Unc
ND(1601) Rare	—	—	—	—	—	—

KM# 28 3 KREUZER (1 Groschen)
Silver **Obv:** Quartered arms **Obv. Legend:** IOANNES. D. G. EPISC. CVRI **Rev. Legend:** DO. CONSER. NOS. IN. PAC.

Date	Mintage	VG	F	VF	XF	Unc
ND(1601)	—	250	600	1,500	—	—

KM# 29 3 KREUZER (1 Groschen)
Silver **Rev. Legend:** SI DEVS PRO NOB Q CON NOS

Date	Mintage	VG	F	VF	XF	Unc
ND(1601) Rare	—	—	—	—	—	—

KM# 27 3 KREUZER (1 Groschen)
Silver **Note:** Klippe.

Date	Mintage	VG	F	VF	XF	Unc
ND(1601) Rare	—	—	—	—	—	—

KM# 74 3 KREUZER (1 Groschen)
Silver **Obv:** Bust right dividing date in inner circle, 3 in oval shield in legend **Rev:** Three shields, rosette in center within inner circle **Rev. Legend:** DOMI. CONS...

Date	Mintage	VG	F	VF	XF	Unc
1627	—	50.00	100	250	—	—

KM# 75 3 KREUZER (1 Groschen)
Silver **Rev:** Dot at center of shields **Rev. Legend:** DOMINE: CONSER:...

Date	Mintage	VG	F	VF	XF	Unc
1627	—	80.00	160	400	—	—

KM# 78 3 KREUZER (1 Groschen)
Silver **Obv:** 4-fold arms in inner circle **Obv. Legend:** IOSEPHVS. DEI. G... **Rev:** Crowned imperial eagle, 3 on breast, date below

Date	Mintage	VG	F	VF	XF	Unc
1628 Rare	—	500	900	2,400	—	—

KM# 79 3 KREUZER (1 Groschen)
Silver **Obv:** Three shields with lily decorations between in inner circle **Rev:** Imperial orb w/3 on breast of imperial eagle

Date	Mintage	VG	F	VF	XF	Unc
1628	—	40.00	80.00	200	400	—
1631 Rare	—	—	—	—	—	—

KM# 87 3 KREUZER (1 Groschen)
Silver **Rev:** Different shields

Date	Mintage	VG	F	VF	XF	Unc
1633	—	50.00	120	325	—	—

KM# 80 10 KREUZER
Silver **Obv:** Four-fold arms on shield with ornamentation **Rev:** Similar to KM#84

Date	Mintage	VG	F	VF	XF	Unc
1628	—	50.00	80.00	200	400	650
1629	—	30.00	60.00	160	325	475
1630	—	30.00	60.00	160	325	475

KM# 84 10 KREUZER
Silver **Obv:** Capped arms **Rev:** Crowned imperial eagle

Date	Mintage	VG	F	VF	XF	Unc
1630	—	20.00	40.00	90.00	200	325
1632	—	25.00	50.00	125	250	400
1633	—	50.00	60.00	250	450	—
1634	—	30.00	60.00	150	300	450
1635	—	40.00	80.00	200	400	650
1636 Rare	—	—	—	—	—	—

KM# 93 10 KREUZER
Silver **Obv:** Quartered arms, bishop's cap above

Date	Mintage	VG	F	VF	XF	Unc
1637 Rare	—	—	—	—	—	—

KM# 94 10 KREUZER
Silver **Obv:** Half-length figure right, bishop's arms in oval shield at bottom **Rev:** Date in legend divided by crown

Date	Mintage	VG	F	VF	XF	Unc
1637 Rare	—	—	—	—	—	—

KM# 92 10 KREUZER
Silver **Obv:** Bishop's cap above **Note:** Similar to KM#84.

Date	Mintage	VG	F	VF	XF	Unc
1637 Rare	—	—	—	—	—	—

KM# 30 12 KREUZER (1/2 Dicken)
Silver **Obv:** Four-fold mantled arms in inner circle **Rev:** Crowned imperial eagle, 12 on breast

Date	Mintage	VG	F	VF	XF	Unc
ND(1601)	—	400	800	2,000	—	—

KM# 31 12 KREUZER (1/2 Dicken)
Silver **Obv:** Half-length figure right holding scepter and imperial orb **Rev:** 1Z on breast of eagle

Date	Mintage	VG	F	VF	XF	Unc
ND(1601)	—	150	300	800	—	—

KM# 32 12 KREUZER (1/2 Dicken)
Silver **Obv:** Figure divides S-L

Date	Mintage	VG	F	VF	XF	Unc
ND(1601)	—	60.00	125	300	600	—

KM# 122 15 KREUZER
Silver **Obv:** Bust right with bare head in inner circle **Rev:** Similar to KM#135

Date	Mintage	VG	F	VF	XF	Unc
1688	—	35.00	60.00	150	325	—
1689	—	60.00	125	300	—	—
1690	—	70.00	150	400	—	—

KM# 85 20 KREUZER
Silver **Obv:** Bust right dividing S-L **Rev:** Crowned imperial eagle, 20 in orb on breast, date below

Date	Mintage	VG	F	VF	XF	Unc
1631 Rare	—	—	—	—	—	—

KM# 66 24 KREUZER (1 Dicken)
Silver **Obv:** Mantled four-fold arms, bishop's mitre above **Obv. Legend:** MO. NO... **Rev:** Crowned imperial eagle, 24 on breast, date below

Date	Mintage	VG	F	VF	XF	Unc
1623 Rare	—	—	—	—	—	—
1624 Rare	—	—	—	—	—	—

KM# 70 24 KREUZER (1 Dicken)
Silver **Obv:** 24 in shield below arms **Obv. Legend:** IOANNE...

Date	Mintage	VG	F	VF	XF	Unc
1624 Rare	—	—	—	—	—	—

KM# 86 24 KREUZER (1 Dicken)
Silver **Obv:** Half-length saint right with crozier **Rev:** Half-length saint right with crozier

Date	Mintage	VG	F	VF	XF	Unc
1632 Rare	—	1,000	2,000	4,500	—	—

KM# 88 24 KREUZER (1 Dicken)
Silver **Obv:** 24 below crozier **Rev:** 24 below crozier

Date	Mintage	VG	F	VF	XF	Unc
1633 Rare	—	—	—	—	—	—

KM# 33 BATZEN
Billon **Obv:** Shield with Ibex left, eagle above **Obv. Legend:** IOANNES... **Rev:** Anchor corss **Rev. Legend:** MONETA: NOVA: CVRIE

Date	Mintage	VG	F	VF	XF	Unc
ND(1601)	—	60.00	125	325	—	—

KM# 34 BATZEN
Billon **Obv. Inscription:** IOANNES D G EPIS CVR **Rev. Legend:** MONETA NOVA CVR

Date	Mintage	VG	F	VF	XF	Unc
ND(1601) Rare	—	—	—	—	—	—

KM# 35 DICKEN
Silver **Obv:** Half-length figure right divides SI-PEC, shield below **Rev:** Crowned imperial eagle, crown above in legend

Date	Mintage	VG	F	VF	XF	Unc
ND(1601)	—	250	500	1,200	—	—

KM# 36 DICKEN
Silver **Obv:** Smaller figure right, without letters in field

Date	Mintage	VG	F	VF	XF	Unc
ND(1601)	—	200	400	900	—	—

KM# 37 DICKEN
Silver **Rev:** Two shields below figure

Date	Mintage	VG	F	VF	XF	Unc
ND(1601)	—	200	400	900	—	—

KM# 38 DICKEN
Silver **Obv:** Shield below eagle

Date	Mintage	VG	F	VF	XF	Unc
ND(1601)	—	200	450	1,200	—	—

KM# 39 DICKEN
Silver

Date	Mintage	VG	F	VF	XF	Unc
ND(1601)	—	60.00	125	275	550	—

KM# 40 DICKEN
Silver **Obv:** Without shield below figure **Rev:** Shield below eagle

Date	Mintage	VG	F	VF	XF	Unc
ND(1601)	—	60.00	125	275	500	—

KM# 41 DICKEN
Silver **Obv:** Half-length figure divides S-L, shield below

Date	Mintage	VG	F	VF	XF	Unc
ND(1601)	—	60.00	125	275	550	—

KM# 42 DICKEN
Silver **Rev:** Without shield below eagle

Date	Mintage	VG	F	VF	XF	Unc
ND(1601)	—	60.00	125	275	550	—

KM# 59 DICKEN
Silver **Obv:** W/o S-L **Note:** Similar to KM#58.

Date	Mintage	VG	F	VF	XF	Unc
ND	—	60.00	120	200	400	—
1620	—	100	300	700	—	—
1621	—	200	400	900	—	—

KM# 58 DICKEN
Silver **Obv:** 1/2-length figure of Johann V Flugi von Aspermont right **Rev:** Crowned imperial eagle

Date	Mintage	VG	F	VF	XF	Unc
1621	—	125	250	600	—	—
1623 Rare	—	—	—	—	—	—

KM# 63 DICKEN
Silver **Note:** Klippe.

Date	Mintage	VG	F	VF	XF	Unc
1622	—	200	450	1,200	—	—

KM# 43 SCHILLING
Billon **Obv:** Standing figure of saint in inner circle **Rev:** Standing Ibex left in inner circle

Date	Mintage	VG	F	VF	XF	Unc
ND(1601) Rare	—	—	—	—	—	—

KM# 125 1/3 THALER (1/2 Gulden)
Silver **Obv:** Armored bust right **Rev:** Crowned imperial eagle, value in oval shield below

Date	Mintage	VG	F	VF	XF	Unc
1689 Rare	—	1,000	2,400	6,000	—	—

KM# 124 2/3 THALER (1 Gulden)
Silver **Obv:** Bust of Ulrich VI von Mont right **Rev:** Crowned imperial eagle

Date	Mintage	VG	F	VF	XF	Unc
1688	—	125	225	400	700	—
1689 Rare	—	—	—	—	—	—
1690	—	65.00	125	300	550	—

KM# 123 2/3 THALER (1 Gulden)
Silver **Note:** Similar to KM#124 but without inner circles.

Date	Mintage	VG	F	VF	XF	Unc
1688	—	120	240	400	800	—

KM# 126 2/3 THALER (1 Gulden)
Silver **Obv:** 1/2-length figure right **Rev:** Crowned imperial eagle

Date	Mintage	VG	F	VF	XF	Unc
1689	—	50.00	100	250	400	—
1690	—	50.00	100	250	400	—

KM# 60 THALER
Silver **Obv:** Capped arms **Rev:** Bishop seated facing **Note:** Dav. #4661.

Date	Mintage	VG	F	VF	XF	Unc
ND	—	175	325	1,200	2,500	—

KM# 61 THALER
Silver **Rev:** Crowned imperial eagle **Note:** Dav. #4660, 4662.

Date	Mintage	VG	F	VF	XF	Unc
ND(1621) Rare	—	1,200	2,400	6,000	—	—
1622 Rare	—	—	—	—	—	—

KM# 67 THALER
Silver **Obv:** Larger, more ornate shield, large mitre divides date **Rev:** Fully displayed eagle, larger crown above **Note:** Dav. #4663.

Date	Mintage	VG	F	VF	XF	Unc
1623	—	450	950	2,400	—	—

KM# 72 THALER
Silver **Obv:** Small four-fold arms divide date, shorter mantle **Note:** Dav. #4664.

Date	Mintage	VG	F	VF	XF	Unc
1625	—	600	1,200	3,200	—	—
1626	—	450	800	2,000	4,000	—

KM# 82 THALER
Silver **Obv:** Oval arms with bust left in two folds of arms, in ornate cartouche **Rev. Legend:** FERDINANDVS II D G ROM IMP SEM AV **Note:** Dav. #4665.

Date	Mintage	VG	F	VF	XF	Unc
MDCXXVIII (1628)	—	1,500	3,000	7,000	15,000	—

KM# 81 THALER
Silver **Obv:** Date in Roman numerals in legend, oval arms with half-length figure in two folds of arms, in cartouche **Note:** Dav. #4666.

Date	Mintage	VG	F	VF	XF	Unc
1628	—	750	1,400	3,600	7,000	—

KM# 89 THALER
Silver **Obv:** Simpler cartouche **Rev:** Legend, date **Rev. Inscription:** DOMINE... **Note:** Dav. #4667.

Date	Mintage	VG	F	VF	XF	Unc
1633	—	800	1,600	4,000	—	—

KM# 90 THALER
Silver **Obv. Legend:** Legend, date **Rev. Legend:** FERDINANDVS: II: D: G... **Note:** Dav. #4668.

Date	Mintage	VG	F	VF	XF	Unc
1634	—	600	1,250	3,200	6,250	—

KM# 96 THALER
Silver **Obv:** Helmeted arms in inner circle **Note:** Dav. #4669.

Date	Mintage	VG	F	VF	XF	Unc
1642	—	1,500	3,000	8,000	16,000	—

KM# A62 1-1/2 THALER
Silver **Obv:** Similar to 1 Thaler KM#60 **Rev:** Crowned imperial eagle **Note:** Dav. #A4660.

Date	Mintage	VG	F	VF	XF	Unc
ND(1621) Rare	—	—	—	—	—	—

KM# 62 2 THALER
Silver **Obv:** Similar to 1 Thaler, KM#60 **Rev:** Crowned imperial eagle **Note:** Dav. #4659.

Date	Mintage	VG	F	VF	XF	Unc
ND(1621) Rare	—	2,500	4,750	12,000	—	—

TRADE COINAGE

KM# 45 GOLDGULDEN
3.5000 g., 0.9860 Gold 0.1109 oz. AGW **Obv:** St. Luke divides S-L **Obv. Legend:** CVRIEN

Date	Mintage	VG	F	VF	XF	Unc
ND(1601)	—	700	1,400	2,800	4,750	—

KM# 47 GOLDGULDEN
3.5000 g., 0.9860 Gold 0.1109 oz. AGW **Obv:** Bishop standing behind family arms

Date	Mintage	VG	F	VF	XF	Unc
ND Rare	—	—	—	—	—	—

KM# 44 GOLDGULDEN
3.5000 g., 0.9860 Gold 0.1109 oz. AGW **Obv:** St. Luke **Obv. Legend:** ...CVR: **Rev. Legend:** MATH. D. G. R. **Note:** Fr. #196.

Date	Mintage	VG	F	VF	XF	Unc
ND(1601)	—	450	800	1,600	2,800	—

KM# 46 GOLDGULDEN
3.5000 g., 0.9860 Gold 0.1109 oz. AGW **Rev. Legend:** FERDI: D: G: RO:... **Note:** Fr. #197.

Date	Mintage	VG	F	VF	XF	Unc
ND(1601)	—	500	1,000	2,000	3,250	—

KM# 76 DUCAT
3.5000 g., 0.9860 Gold 0.1109 oz. AGW **Obv:** Shield w/bishop's mitre, crozier and stole above **Rev:** Crowned imperial eagle, arms on breast, Order of the Golden Fleece around **Note:** Fr. #202.

Date	Mintage	VG	F	VF	XF	Unc
ND(1627) Rare	—	—	—	—	—	—

KM# 91 DUCAT
3.5000 g., 0.9860 Gold 0.1109 oz. AGW **Obv:** Arms in oval cartouche, titles of Johann VI **Rev:** Crowned imperial eagle in inner circle **Note:** Fr. #204.

Date	Mintage	VG	F	VF	XF	Unc
1636	—	4,000	8,000	18,000	—	—
1649	—	2,200	4,000	9,000	14,000	—
1652	—	2,200	4,000	9,000	14,000	—

KM# 112.1 DUCAT
3.5000 g., 0.9860 Gold 0.1109 oz. AGW **Obv:** Arms on shield, ornamentation on corners **Rev:** W/o inner circle **Note:** Fr. #208.

Date	Mintage	VG	F	VF	XF	Unc
1664	—	2,500	6,000	12,000	20,000	—

KM# 112.2 DUCAT
Gold **Obv:** Arms on shield, ornamentation on corners **Rev:** W/o inner circle **Note:** Fr. #209.

Date	Mintage	VG	F	VF	XF	Unc
1691 Rare	—	—	—	—	—	—

KM# 132 DUCAT
3.5000 g., 0.9860 Gold 0.1109 oz. AGW **Obv:** Shield of arms **Rev:** Crowned imperial eagle, date divided at top **Note:** Fr. #212.

Date	Mintage	VG	F	VF	XF	Unc
1693 Rare	—	—	—	—	—	—

KM# 133 DUCAT
3.5000 g., 0.9860 Gold 0.1109 oz. AGW **Obv:** Ornate oval arms **Rev:** St. Luke

Date	Mintage	VG	F	VF	XF	Unc
1697	—	2,500	6,000	12,000	20,000	—

KM# 48 2 DUCAT
7.0000 g., 0.9860 Gold 0.2219 oz. AGW **Obv:** 4-fold arms in inner circle **Obv. Legend:** IOANNES... **Rev:** Crowned imperial eagle in inner circle **Rev. Legend:** RODL. II...

Date	Mintage	VG	F	VF	XF	Unc
ND(1601)	—	2,500	6,000	12,000	20,000	—

KM# 49 2 DUCAT
7.0000 g., 0.9860 Gold 0.2219 oz. AGW **Obv:** Arms in inner circle **Rev:** Crowned imperial eagle in inner circle, titles of Rudolph II

Date	Mintage	VG	F	VF	XF	Unc
ND	—	2,500	6,000	12,000	20,000	—

KM# 50 2 DUCAT
7.0000 g., 0.9860 Gold 0.2219 oz. AGW **Rev:** Titles of Matthias **Note:** Fr. #201.

Date	Mintage	VG	F	VF	XF	Unc
ND	—	2,500	6,000	12,000	20,000	—

KM# 68 2 DUCAT
7.0000 g., 0.9860 Gold 0.2219 oz. AGW **Obv:** Legend, date **Obv. Legend:** MO NO AVR EPIS CVR **Rev. Legend:** FER II RO IMP SEM AVG **Note:** Fr. #199.

Date	Mintage	VG	F	VF	XF	Unc
1623 Rare	—	—	—	—	—	—

KM# 64 4 DUCAT
14.0000 g., 0.9860 Gold 0.4438 oz. AGW **Obv:** Arms in inner circle **Rev:** Crowned imperial eagle in inner circle **Note:** Fr. #198.

Date	Mintage	VG	F	VF	XF	Unc
ND Rare	—	—	—	—	—	—
1623 Rare	—	—	—	—	—	—

KM# A132 4 DUCAT
14.0000 g., 0.9860 Gold 0.4438 oz. AGW **Obv:** Bust of Ulrich VI von Mont right **Rev:** Crowned imperial eagle **Note:** Struck with 2/3 Thaler dies, KM#124. Fr. #210.

Date	Mintage	VG	F	VF	XF	Unc
1689 Rare	—	—	—	—	—	—

KM# 53 5 DUCAT
17.5000 g., 0.9860 Gold 0.5547 oz. AGW **Note:** Similar to 7 Ducat, KM#55. Fr. #193.

Date	Mintage	VG	F	VF	XF	Unc
1613 Rare	—	—	—	—	—	—

KM# 98 5 DUCAT
17.5000 g., 0.9860 Gold 0.5547 oz. AGW **Obv:** Facing bust of bishop, date **Obv. Legend:** IO EPS CVR DNS... **Rev:** Crowned, helmeted small shield w/arms **Rev. Legend:** DOMINVS... **Note:** Fr. #203.

Date	Mintage	VG	F	VF	XF	Unc
1644 Rare	—	—	—	—	—	—

KM# 113 5 DUCAT
17.5000 g., 0.9860 Gold 0.5547 oz. AGW **Obv:** Larger facing bust of bishop **Obv. Legend:** VDAL: D: G: EP:... **Rev:** Crowned imperial eagle **Rev. Legend:** LEOPOLDUS:... **Note:** Fr. #207.

Date	Mintage	VG	F	VF	XF	Unc
1664 Rare	—	—	—	—	—	—

KM# 114 6 DUCAT
21.0000 g., 0.9860 Gold 0.6657 oz. AGW **Obv:** Facing bust of bishop **Obv. Legend:** VDAL: D: G: EP:... **Rev:** Crowned imperial eagle **Rev. Legend:** LEOPOLDVS:... **Note:** Fr. #205.

Date	Mintage	VG	F	VF	XF	Unc
1664 Rare	—	—	—	—	—	—

FR# 190 7 DUCAT
24.5000 g., 0.9860 Gold 0.7766 oz. AGW, 39 mm. **Obv:** 1/2-length figure of St. Luke right **Obv. Legend:** PETRVS : DEI : GRA : EPISCOPVS **Rev:** Crowned imperial eagle **Rev. Legend:** RODO-L•II•DG. ROM•IMP...

Date	Mintage	VG	F	VF	XF	Unc
(1581-1601)	—	4,500	7,500	16,000	24,000	—

KM# 54 7 DUCAT
24.5000 g., 0.9860 Gold 0.7766 oz. AGW **Obv:** 1/2-length figure of St. Luke **Rev:** Crowned imperial eagle **Note:** Fr. #190.

Date	Mintage	VG	F	VF	XF	Unc
ND(1613)	—	1,500	3,000	5,500	9,500	—

KM# 55 7 DUCAT
24.5000 g., 0.9860 Gold 0.7766 oz. AGW **Rev:** Date divided by crowned imperial eagle **Note:** Fr. #191.

Date	Mintage	VG	F	VF	XF	Unc
1613	—	1,750	3,500	7,000	12,000	—

KM# 56 7 DUCAT
24.5000 g., 0.9860 Gold 0.7766 oz. AGW **Obv:** 1/2-length figure of St. Luke divides date **Rev:** Crowned imperial eagle **Note:** Fr. #194.

Date	Mintage	VG	F	VF	XF	Unc
1615	—	3,250	6,500	13,000	22,000	—

KM# 57 10 DUCAT
35.0000 g., 0.9860 Gold 1.1095 oz. AGW **Note:** Similar to 7 Ducat, KM#56. Fr. #193.

Date	Mintage	VG	F	VF	XF	Unc
1615 Rare	—	—	—	—	—	—

KM# 115 10 DUCAT
35.0000 g., 0.9860 Gold 1.1095 oz. AGW **Obv:** Facing bust of bishop **Obv. Legend:** VDAL: D:G: EP:... **Rev:** Crowned imperial eagle **Rev. Legend:** LEOPOLDVS:... **Note:** Fr. #205.

Date	Mintage	VG	F	VF	XF	Unc
1664 Rare	—	—	—	—	—	—

CITY

STANDARD COINAGE

KM# 200 PFENNIG
Billon **Obv:** Arms with Ibex left, CVR at top and sides **Note:** Uniface. Schussel type.

Date	Mintage	VG	F	VF	XF	Unc
ND(1601)	—	8.00	16.00	40.00	80.00	—

KM# 201 PFENNIG
Billon **Obv:** Arms without CVR **Note:** Uniface.

Date	Mintage	VG	F	VF	XF	Unc
ND(1601) Rare	—	—	—	—	—	—

KM# 202 PFENNIG
Billon **Obv:** Larger arms, CVR at top and sides, large pearl circles around **Note:** Uniface.

Date	Mintage	VG	F	VF	XF	Unc
ND(1601)	—	8.00	16.00	40.00	80.00	—

KM# 203 PFENNIG
Billon **Obv:** Arms without CVR **Note:** Uniface.

Date	Mintage	VG	F	VF	XF	Unc
ND(1601)	—	8.00	16.00	40.00	80.00	—

KM# 204 PFENNIG
Billon **Obv:** Arms with CVR at top and sides, barley corn circle around **Note:** Uniface.

Date	Mintage	VG	F	VF	XF	Unc
ND(1601)	—	8.00	16.00	40.00	80.00	—

KM# 205 PFENNIG
Billon **Obv:** Small arms, Ibex right, CVR at top and sides, barley corn circle around **Note:** Uniface.

Date	Mintage	VG	F	VF	XF	Unc
ND(1601)	—	8.00	16.00	40.00	80.00	—

KM# 206 PFENNIG
Billon **Obv:** Larger arms, Ibex left, CVR at top and sides, inner circle, barley corn circle around **Note:** Uniface.

Date	Mintage	VG	F	VF	XF	Unc
ND(1601)	—	8.50	16.50	45.00	85.00	—

KM# 261 PFENNIG
Billon **Obv:** CUR at top and sides of shield, without inner circle **Note:** Uniface.

Date	Mintage	VG	F	VF	XF	Unc
ND(1700)	—	8.00	16.00	40.00	80.00	—

KM# 262 PFENNIG
Billon **Obv:** CVR at top and sides of shield with Ibex right, without inner circle **Note:** Uniface.

Date	Mintage	VG	F	VF	XF	Unc
ND(1700)	—	8.00	16.00	40.00	80.00	—

KM# 217 BLUZGER
Billon **Obv:** Tall, narrow arms, Ibex left in inner circle **Rev:** Cross in inner circle, date **Rev. Legend:** ...REGNV

Date	Mintage	VG	F	VF	XF	Unc
1624	—	12.00	24.00	80.00	—	—

KM# 224 BLUZGER
Billon **Obv:** City arms with Ibex facing either right or left in inner circle **Rev:** Cross in inner circle, date in legend **Rev. Legend:** DOMINI.EST.REGN

Date	Mintage	VG	F	VF	XF	Unc
1628 Rare	—	—	—	—	—	—
1632	—	6.00	12.00	35.00	60.00	—
1633	—	15.00	30.00	75.00	150	—
1634 Rare	—	—	—	—	—	—
1636	—	15.00	30.00	75.00	150	—
1637	—	20.00	40.00	80.00	150	—
1638	—	6.00	12.00	35.00	60.00	—
1639	—	15.00	35.00	80.00	150	—
1642	—	3.00	4.00	12.00	24.00	—
1643	—	15.00	30.00	80.00	150	—
1644	—	3.00	4.00	12.00	24.00	—
1645	—	25.00	50.00	125	—	—
1652	—	3.00	4.00	12.00	24.00	—
1660	—	3.00	4.00	12.00	24.00	—
1674	—	5.00	10.00	30.00	50.00	—
1677	—	9.00	18.00	40.00	75.00	—
1678	—	9.00	18.00	40.00	75.00	—
1679	—	9.00	18.00	40.00	75.00	—
1680	—	12.00	24.00	50.00	100	—
1684	—	15.00	30.00	75.00	150	—
1691	—	20.00	40.00	125	—	—
1693	—	4.00	8.00	16.00	40.00	—
1694	—	7.00	16.00	35.00	75.00	—

KM# 240 KREUZER
Billon **Obv:** Arms in round border on cross, legend underneath **Rev:** Crowned imperial eagle with halos in inner circle

Date	Mintage	VG	F	VF	XF	Unc
ND(1641) Rare	—	—	—	—	—	—

KM# 242 KREUZER
Billon **Obv:** Double cross, arms on shield at center in inner circle **Rev:** Crowned imperial eagle, 1 in orb on breast in inner circle

Date	Mintage	VG	F	VF	XF	Unc
1642 Rare	—	200	400	1,000	—	—
1643	—	45.00	90.00	225	475	—
1650	—	45.00	90.00	225	475	—

KM# 243 KREUZER
Billon **Obv:** Armored bust of St. Luke right in inner circle **Rev:** Crowned imperial eagle, 1 in orb on breast in inner circle

Date	Mintage	VG	F	VF	XF	Unc
1643	—	15.00	30.00	100	200	—

KM# 218 2 KREUZER (1/2 Batzen)
Silver **Obv:** Large imperial orb w/2 in inner circle **Rev:** Crowned imperial eagle in inner circle

Date	Mintage	VG	F	VF	XF	Unc
1624	—	32.50	65.00	150	300	—
1625	—	20.00	45.00	125	225	—
1626	—	25.00	50.00	150	300	—

KM# 245 2 KREUZER (1/2 Batzen)
Billon **Obv:** Smaller imperial orb, date **Obv. Legend:** MONE. NO. CVRIAE. **Rev. Legend:** FER. III. D. G. ROM. IM. SEM. AVG.

Date	Mintage	VG	F	VF	XF	Unc
1648	—	15.00	30.00	80.00	160	—

KM# 246 2 KREUZER (1/2 Batzen)
Billon **Rev:** Legend, date **Rev. Legend:** FER. III. D. G. ROM. IM. SEM. A.

Date	Mintage	VG	F	VF	XF	Unc
1649	—	100	225	500	—	—

KM# 249 2 KREUZER (1/2 Batzen)
Billon **Obv:** Arms with Ibex left in oval ornate cartouche **Rev:** Large imperial orb with 2, date above

Date	Mintage	VG	F	VF	XF	Unc
1659	—	40.00	80.00	200	400	—
1663	—	22.00	40.00	100	200	—
1686 Rare	—	—	—	—	—	—

KM# 207 3 KREUZER (1 Groschen)
Billon **Obv:** 1/2-length St. Luke right in inner circle **Obv. Legend:** MONETA. C-VRI. **Rev:** Crowned imperial eagle, 3 in orb on breast in inner circle **Rev. Inscription:** DOMIN...

Date	Mintage	VG	F	VF	XF	Unc
ND(1601) Rare	—	—	—	—	—	—

KM# 208 3 KREUZER (1 Groschen)
Billon **Obv. Legend:** DOMINE: E-ST: REGNVM **Rev. Legend:** FER II DEI G ROM IM SEM A

Date	Mintage	VG	F	VF	XF	Unc
ND(1601) Rare	—	—	—	—	—	—

KM# 225 3 KREUZER (1 Groschen)
Silver **Obv. Legend:** MONETA. C-VRIAE: RET. **Rev:** Crowned imperial eagle, orb with 3 on breast, date below **Rev. Legend:** DOMINI-EST. REGN.

Date	Mintage	VG	F	VF	XF	Unc
1628	—	125	250	500	—	—

KM# 226 3 KREUZER (1 Groschen)
Silver **Obv:** Ornamentation on top and sides of shield. **Rev. Legend:** DOMI: CON.-NOS. IN. PA. **Note:** Similar to KM#232.

Date	Mintage	VG	F	VF	XF	Unc
1629	—	30.00	60.00	150	300	—

KM# 231 3 KREUZER (1 Groschen)
Silver **Note:** Similar to KM#232 but ornamentation on top and sides of shield.

Date	Mintage	VG	F	VF	XF	Unc
1631	—	75.00	150	400	—	—

KM# 232 3 KREUZER (1 Groschen)
Silver

Date	Mintage	VG	F	VF	XF	Unc
1631	—	16.00	32.00	75.00	150	325
1633	—	20.00	40.00	90.00	175	—
1634 Rare	—	—	—	—	—	—
1635 Rare	—	—	—	—	—	—

KM# 237 3 KREUZER (1 Groschen)
Silver **Obv:** Half-length of St. Luke right in inner circle **Obv. Legend:** MONE. NOVA... **Rev. Legend:** FERD. III...

Date	Mintage	VG	F	VF	XF	Unc
1637 Rare	—	—	—	—	—	—
1638 Rare	—	—	—	—	—	—

KM# 228 10 KREUZER
Silver **Obv:** 1/2-length figure of St. Luke right **Rev:** Crowned imperial eagle

Date	Mintage	VG	F	VF	XF	Unc
1629	—	16.00	35.00	80.00	150	275
1630	—	16.00	35.00	80.00	150	275
1631	—	16.00	35.00	80.00	150	275
1632	—	16.00	35.00	80.00	150	275
1633	—	16.00	35.00	80.00	150	275
1634	—	16.00	35.00	80.00	150	275
1635	—	16.00	35.00	80.00	150	275
1636	—	16.00	35.00	80.00	150	275
1637	—	225	450	1,000	2,000	—

KM# 227 10 KREUZER
Silver **Obv:** Ornate shield **Rev:** Crowned imperial eagle

Date	Mintage	VG	F	VF	XF	Unc
1629	—	400	800	2,000	4,000	—

KM# 209 12 KREUZER (1/2 Dicken)
Billon **Obv:** 1/2-length St. Luke right in inner circle **Rev:** Crowned imperial eagle with 1Z on round shield on breast

Date	Mintage	VG	F	VF	XF	Unc
ND(1601)	—	300	600	1,500	—	—

KM# 219 24 KREUZER (1 Dicken)
Silver **Obv:** St. Martin riding right, w/o halo **Rev:** Crowned imperial eagle, imperial orb with 24 on breast, date below

Date	Mintage	VG	F	VF	XF	Unc
1624 Rare	—	650	1,200	2,500	4,500	—

KM# 220 24 KREUZER (1 Dicken)
Silver **Obv:** Large halo behind St. Martin's head **Rev:** Crowned imperial eagle without orb on breast, shield divides date below

Date	Mintage	VG	F	VF	XF	Unc
1624 Rare	—	650	1,200	3,600	—	—

KM# 230 24 KREUZER (1 Dicken)
Silver **Obv:** 1/2-length figure of St. Luke right, shield below **Rev:** Crowned imperial eagle, imperial orb with 24 on breast

Date	Mintage	VG	F	VF	XF	Unc
1630 Rare	—	800	1,600	4,000	—	—
1632	—	450	900	2,400	4,500	—
1633	—	350	650	1,400	2,800	—
1638 Rare	—	—	—	—	—	—

KM# 213 DICKEN
Silver **Obv:** 1/2-length figure of St. Luke right in inner circle, date **Obv. Legend:** DOMINI. EST-RENGNVM **Rev:** Crowned imperial eagle in inner circle **Rev. Legend:** MONETA: CVRIAE: RETICAE.

Date	Mintage	VG	F	VF	XF	Unc
ND(1619)	—	90.00	200	475	—	—
1620	—	350	750	2,000	—	—
1621	—	200	400	1,000	—	—

KM# 214 DICKEN
Silver **Obv:** Without halo behind St. Luke's head, arms without shield below figure

Date	Mintage	VG	F	VF	XF	Unc
ND(1619)	—	100	200	450	—	—

KM# 221 SCHILLING
Billon **Obv:** Standing saint in inner circle **Rev:** Crowned imperial eagle, arms on shield divide date below

Date	Mintage	VG	F	VF	XF	Unc
1624	—	100	200	450	900	—

KM# 216 1/2 THALER
Silver **Obv:** Standing angel in inner circle **Rev:** Crowned imperial eagle, arms on shield divide date below

Date	Mintage	VG	F	VF	XF	Unc
1623 Rare	—	4,500	9,000	24,000	—	—

KM# 223 THALER
Silver **Rev:** Ornaments or date at left of crown **Note:** Dav. #4672.

Date	Mintage	VG	F	VF	XF	Unc
1620	—	—	—	—	—	—
ND(1625)	—	125	250	600	1,200	—
1626	—	—	—	—	—	—

KM# A217 THALER
Silver **Obv:** 3/4-length figure of St. Lucius with sceptre and orb right **Obv. Legend:** MONETA NOVA CVRIAE RETICE **Rev:** Crowned imperial eagle **Note:** Dav. #4673.

Date	Mintage	VG	F	VF	XF	Unc
1623	—	—	—	—	—	—

KM# 222 THALER
Silver **Obv:** 1/2-length St. Luke in inner circle, crown divides date above **Rev:** Crowned imperial eagle in inner circle **Note:** Dav. #4674.

Date	Mintage	VG	F	VF	XF	Unc
1624	—	1,650	2,400	6,000	—	—

KM# 233 THALER
Silver **Obv:** Ornate oval shield **Rev:** Crowned imperial eagle **Rev. Legend:** FERDINANDVS • II • D: G: ROM: **Note:** Dav. #4675.

Date	Mintage	VG	F	VF	XF	Unc
1633	—	150	300	700	1,400	2,750
1638/3	—	—	—	—	—	—
1638	—	700	1,375	4,000	8,000	—

TRADE COINAGE

KM# 211 GOLDGULDEN
3.5000 g., 0.9860 Gold 0.1109 oz. AGW **Obv:** St. Luke seated facing **Rev:** Crowned imperial eagle **Rev. Legend:** MATTIAS: I...

Date	Mintage	VG	F	VF	XF	Unc
1618	—	1,500	3,250	6,500	—	—

KM# 212 GOLDGULDEN
3.5000 g., 0.9860 Gold 0.1109 oz. AGW **Obv:** St. Luke **Rev:** Crowned imperial eagle **Rev. Legend:** FERDINANDVS: II... **Note:** Fr. #226.

Date	Mintage	VG	F	VF	XF	Unc
ND(1618-37) Rare	—	—	—	—	—	—

KM# 236 DUCAT
3.5000 g., 0.9860 Gold 0.1109 oz. AGW **Rev:** Crowned imperial eagle **Rev. Legend:** FERDINAND II... **Note:** Fr. #230.

Date	Mintage	VG	F	VF	XF	Unc
1634	—	750	1,400	2,800	4,800	—
1636	—	750	1,400	2,800	4,800	—
1637	—	750	1,400	2,800	4,800	—
1638 Rare	—	—	—	—	—	—

KM# 238 DUCAT
3.5000 g., 0.9860 Gold 0.1109 oz. AGW
Rev. Legend: FERDINAND III...

Date	Mintage	VG	F	VF	XF	Unc
1639	—	1,250	2,000	4,000	—	—

KM# 241 DUCAT
3.5000 g., 0.9860 Gold 0.1109 oz. AGW **Obv:** Modified state shield **Note:** Fr. #231.

Date	Mintage	VG	F	VF	XF	Unc
1641	—	1,200	2,000	4,000	—	—
1642 Rare	—	—	—	—	—	—

KM# 244 DUCAT
3.5000 g., 0.9860 Gold 0.1109 oz. AGW **Obv:** Modified state shield **Note:** Fr. #231.

Date	Mintage	VG	F	VF	XF	Unc
1644	—	1,200	2,000	4,000	—	—
1645 Rare	—	—	—	—	—	—

KM# 248 DUCAT
3.5000 g., 0.9860 Gold 0.1109 oz. AGW **Obv:** Modified state shield **Note:** Fr. #231.

Date	Mintage	VG	F	VF	XF	Unc
1652 Rare	—	—	—	—	—	—

KM# 251 DUCAT
3.5000 g., 0.9860 Gold 0.1109 oz. AGW
Rev. Legend: LEOPOLDBS. I... **Note:** Fr. #231a.

Date	Mintage	VG	F	VF	XF	Unc
1664 Rare	—	—	—	—	—	—

KM# 234 2 DUCAT
7.0000 g., 0.9860 Gold 0.2219 oz. AGW **Obv:** Standing knight in armor with shield in inner circle **Rev:** Crowned imperial eagle in inner circle **Note:** Fr. #228.

Date	Mintage	VG	F	VF	XF	Unc
ND Rare	—	—	—	—	—	—

KM# 235 2 DUCAT
7.0000 g., 0.9860 Gold 0.2219 oz. AGW **Obv:** Arms in cartouche in inner circle **Rev:** Crowned imperial eagle in inner circle **Rev. Legend:** FERDINAND: II... **Note:** Fr. #229.

Date	Mintage	VG	F	VF	XF	Unc
1633	—	3,500	6,000	12,500	—	—

FREIBURG

Friburg, Fribourg, Freyburg

A canton and city located in western Switzerland. The city was founded in 1178 and obtained the mint right in 1422. It joined the Swiss Confederation in 1481. During the Helvetian Republic period it was known as Sarine Et Broye but changed the name back to Freiburg in 1803.

MONETARY SYSTEM

Until 1798

16 Denier = 8 Vierer = 4 Kreuzer = 1 Batzen
56 Kreuzer = 8 Piecette = 1 Gulden
24 Piecette = 1 Thaler

CITY

STANDARD COINAGE

KM# 16 KREUZER
Billon **Obv:** Crowned imperial eagle with shield arms on breast **Rev:** Blossoms in angles of cross

Date	Mintage	VG	F	VF	XF	Unc
ND	—	50.00	125	500	—	—
1622	—	12.00	25.00	100	—	—
1623	—	12.00	25.00	100	—	—
1624	—	12.00	25.00	100	—	—
1625	—	30.00	80.00	250	—	—
1630	—	25.00	60.00	150	—	—
1636	—	25.00	60.00	150	—	—
1650	—	25.00	60.00	150	—	—
1656	—	8.00	16.00	60.00	—	—

CANTON

STANDARD COINAGE

KM# 20 1/2 KREUZER (Vierer)
Billon **Obv:** Tower arms **Obv. Legend:** MO:FRIBVRG **Rev:** Cross, S. NICOLA, date

Date	Mintage	VG	F	VF	XF	Unc
ND	—	350	750	2,000	—	—
1623 Rare	—	750	1,600	4,000	—	—

KM# 8 KREUZER
Billon **Obv:** Tower arms **Rev:** Cross with prongs

Date	Mintage	VG	F	VF	XF	Unc
ND	—	60.00	150	500	—	—
1610	—	30.00	65.00	200	—	—
1612	—	75.00	150	700	—	—

Date	Mintage	VG	F	VF	XF	Unc
1613	—	30.00	60.00	200	—	—
1614	—	30.00	60.00	200	—	—
1615	—	30.00	60.00	200	—	—
1616	—	85.00	175	600	—	—

KM# 9 KREUZER

Billon **Note:** Klippe.

Date	Mintage	VG	F	VF	XF	Unc
ND	—	—	—	—	—	—

KM# 13 12 KREUZER (1/2 Dicken)

Silver **Obv:** Crowned imperial eagle with halos, 12 on breast, tower arms below **Rev:** St. Nicholas bust facing slightly right, holding crozier

Date	Mintage	VG	F	VF	XF	Unc
1620	—	300	550	1,150	—	—
1621 Rare	—	—	—	—	—	—

KM# 22 12 KREUZER (1/2 Dicken)

Silver **Obv:** Crown above eagle **Rev:** Date below saint

Date	Mintage	VG	F	VF	XF	Unc
1635	—	550	1,150	2,150	—	—

KM# 25 20 KREUZER (1/2 Dicken)

Silver **Obv:** Tower arms divide value: 2-0, ealge above, ring below **Rev:** Bust of saint wearing mitre facing forward

Date	Mintage	VG	F	VF	XF	Unc
1658	—	650	1,250	2,500	—	—

KM# 10 BATZEN

Billon **Obv:** Tower arms **Rev:** Cross with flowers in angles

Date	Mintage	VG	F	VF	XF	Unc
ND	—	30.00	65.00	240	—	—
1618 Rare	—	—	—	—	—	—
1619 Rare	—	—	—	—	—	—

KM# 14 BATZEN

Billon **Obv:** 20 in legend **Rev:** Nothing in angles of cross

Date	Mintage	VG	F	VF	XF	Unc
1620	—	50.00	125	400	—	—

KM# 15 BATZEN

Billon **Rev:** Date in legend

Date	Mintage	VG	F	VF	XF	Unc
ND	—	30.00	60.00	225	—	—
1621	—	40.00	80.00	300	—	—
1622	—	40.00	80.00	300	—	—

KM# 17 BATZEN

Billon **Obv:** Tower of arms on shield on top of cross **Rev:** Saint facing forward, date in legend

Date	Mintage	VG	F	VF	XF	Unc
1622	—	35.00	75.00	300	—	—
1623	—	8.00	16.00	60.00	150	—
1630	—	8.00	16.00	60.00	150	—
1631	—	8.00	16.00	60.00	150	—
1639 Rare	—	—	—	—	—	—
1641	—	8.00	16.00	60.00	150	—
1648	—	8.00	16.00	60.00	150	—

KM# 5 1/2 DICKEN

Billon **Obv:** Tower arms **Rev:** Half-length saint right divides date 60-8

Date	Mintage	VG	F	VF	XF	Unc
1608	—	500	1,200	3,000	—	—

KM# 6 DICKEN

Silver

Date	Mintage	VG	F	VF	XF	Unc
1608	—	300	650	1,600	—	—

TRADE COINAGE

KM# 11 GOLDGULDEN

3.5000 g., 0.9860 Gold 0.1109 oz. AGW **Note:** Similar to 1 Duplone, KM#18. Fr. #238.

Date	Mintage	VG	F	VF	XF	Unc
1619 Rare	—	—	—	—	—	—
1620 Rare	—	—	—	—	—	—

KM# 18.1 DUPLONE (Pistole)

7.6400 g., 0.9000 Gold 0.2211 oz. AGW **Note:** Fr. #245.

Date	Mintage	VG	F	VF	XF	Unc
1622 Rare	—	—	—	—	—	—
1623 Rare	—	—	—	—	—	—
1635 Rare	—	—	—	—	—	—

KM# 18.2 DUPLONE (Pistole)

7.6400 g., 0.9000 Gold 0.2211 oz. AGW **Note:** Fr. #246

Date	Mintage	VG	F	VF	XF	Unc
1635	—	2,000	4,000	8,000	13,500	—

KM# 19 2 DUPLONE (Quadrupla)

15.2800 g., 0.9000 Gold 0.4421 oz. AGW **Note:** Similar to 1 Duplone, KM#18. Fr. #244.

Date	Mintage	VG	F	VF	XF	Unc
1622 Rare	—	—	—	—	—	—

PATTERNS

Including off metal strikes

KM#	Date	Mintage	Identification	Mkt Val
PnA1	1610	—	Kreuzer. Gold. KM#8.	—

GENEVA

A canton and city in southwestern Switzerland. The city became a bishopric c.400 AD and was part of the Burgundian Kingdom for 500 years. They became completely independent in 1530. In 1798 they were occupied by France but became independent again in 1813. They joined the Swiss Confederation in 1815.

MINT OFFICIALS' INITIALS

Initial	Date	Name
A-B	1652-55	Augustin Hurtebinet
A-B		Auguste Bovet
AC	1656-64	Andre Capitel
AE	1665-67, 71-76	Andre Emery
AD, D and AD,	1641-43	Ami Deneria and Daniel
DS, SE		Sardes
AE, IE	1677-87	Paul Marcet
B	1644-46	Augustin Baccuet
B		Binet
BG	1638-40	David Guainier and Augustin Baccuet
C	1612-17	Pierre Caille
CL	1692	David Camp and J.A. Lullin
D	1610-12	Jacques Dansse
G, X	1621	Jean Gringalet
G	1621-22, 46-49	Joseph Gringalet
G		Girod
G		Gresset
GR, RG	1622-25	Jean, Richard and Francois Grenus
H		Hoyer
HC	1625-33	Jerome Capitel
IE, Sgr, Srie	1687-89	Jean Emery
IG		Jacques Gresset
JG		Jean Gresset
M	1601-02	Gedeon Morlot
M	1649-51	Jean Mussard
M	1651-52	Augustin Baccuet
NP, NPG	1617-21	Nicolas and Pierre Girard
PB		Paul Binet
PM	1633-37	Pierre du Meurier
TB		Theodore Benneton
W		Charles Wielandy

MONETARY SYSTEM

Until 1794

12 Deniers = 4 Quarts = 1 Sol
12 Sols = 1 Florin
12 Florins, 9 Sols = 1 Thaler
35 Florins = 1 Pistole

CANTON

STANDARD COINAGE

KM# 5 DENIER

Copper **Obv:** Arms **Rev:** I in center **Rev. Legend:** POUR. VN. DENIER.

Date	Mintage	VG	F	VF	XF	Unc
ND	—	25.00	60.00	200	400	—

KM# 16 DENIER

Copper **Obv:** Arms, legend, date **Obv. Legend:** GENEVA. CIVITAS **Rev:** I at center, flowers at sides, dots above and below **Rev. Legend:** POUR. VN. DENIER.

Date	Mintage	VG	F	VF	XF	Unc
1609 Rare	—	—	—	—	—	—

KM# 6 2 DENIERS

Copper **Obv:** Arms **Rev:** II at center, dot above, flower below **Rev. Legend:** POUR. DEUX. DENIERS.

Date	Mintage	VG	F	VF	XF	Unc
ND	—	25.00	60.00	200	400	—

KM# 17 2 DENIERS

Copper **Obv:** Arms, legend, date **Obv. Legend:** GENEVA CIVITAS **Rev:** .I.I. at center, flowers above and below, legend around

Date	Mintage	VG	F	VF	XF	Unc
1609 Rare	—	—	—	—	—	—

KM# 7 3 DENIERS (1 Quart)

Billon **Obv:** Arms, legend, date **Obv. Legend:** GENEVA CIVITAS **Rev:** Ornate cross **Rev. Legend:** POST. TENEBRAS. LVX.

Date	Mintage	VG	F	VF	XF	Unc
1601	—	8.00	16.00	50.00	125	—
1606	—	8.00	16.00	50.00	125	—
1608 Rare	—	—	—	—	—	—
1609	—	8.00	16.00	50.00	125	—
1610 D	—	30.00	70.00	250	500	—
1615	—	8.00	16.00	50.00	125	—
1616	—	8.00	16.00	50.00	125	—
1617 NPG	—	8.00	16.00	50.00	125	—
1619 NPG	—	8.00	16.00	50.00	125	—
1621	—	8.00	16.00	50.00	125	—

KM# 7a 3 DENIERS (1 Quart)

Gold **Obv:** Arms, legend, date **Obv. Legend:** GENEVA CIVITAS **Rev:** Ornate cross **Rev. Legend:** POST. TENEBRAS. LUX.

Date	Mintage	VG	F	VF	XF	Unc
1621 M Rare	—	—	—	—	—	—

KM# 21 4 DENIERS

Billon **Obv:** Arms on shield, legend and date around **Rev:** Inscription at center, legend around **Rev. Inscription:** POVR / IIII / DEN

Date	Mintage	VG	F	VF	XF	Unc
1617	—	35.00	80.00	300	800	—

KM# 12 6 DENIERS (2 Quarts)

Billon **Obv:** IHS in center of radiant sun in inner circle, date in legend **Rev:** Arms on shield, date above, legend around

Date	Mintage	VG	F	VF	XF	Unc
1603	—	8.00	16.00	45.00	125	—
1604	—	8.00	16.00	45.00	125	—
1610 C	—	8.00	16.00	45.00	125	—
1612 C	—	8.00	16.00	45.00	125	—
1613 C	—	8.00	16.00	45.00	125	—
1614 C	—	8.00	16.00	45.00	125	—
1615 C	—	8.00	16.00	45.00	125	—
1616 C	—	8.00	16.00	45.00	125	—
1617 NPG	—	8.00	16.00	45.00	125	—
1618 NPG	—	8.00	16.00	45.00	125	—
1619 NPG	—	8.00	16.00	45.00	125	—
1619 NP	—	8.00	16.00	45.00	125	—
1620 NPG	—	8.00	16.00	45.00	125	—
1620 PG	—	8.00	16.00	45.00	125	—
1645 B	—	8.00	16.00	45.00	125	—
1646 B	—	8.00	16.00	45.00	125	—
1648 G	—	8.00	16.00	45.00	125	—
1649 G	—	25.00	60.00	200	500	—
1650 M	—	6.00	12.00	40.00	95.00	—
1651 M	—	6.00	12.00	40.00	95.00	—
1652 M	—	6.00	12.00	40.00	95.00	—
1653 AB	—	6.00	12.00	40.00	95.00	—
1654 C	—	6.00	12.00	40.00	95.00	—
1654 AB Rare	—	—	—	—	—	—
1677 AE	—	6.00	12.00	40.00	95.00	—
1678 AE	—	6.00	12.00	40.00	95.00	—
1687 IE	—	6.00	12.00	40.00	95.00	—
1688 IE	—	6.00	12.00	40.00	95.00	—

KM# 12a 6 DENIERS (2 Quarts)

Silver

Date	Mintage	VG	F	VF	XF	Unc
1655 AB Rare	—	—	—	—	—	—
1687 IE	—	—	12.00	40.00	90.00	—
1688 IE	—	—	12.00	40.00	90.00	—

KM# 49 6 DENIERS (2 Quarts)

Billon **Rev:** Inscription in center, legend around **Rev. Inscription:** SIX / DENI / ERS

Date	Mintage	VG	F	VF	XF	Unc
1674 AE	—	15.00	30.00	120	250	—

KM# 22 8 DENIERS

Billon **Obv:** Arms on shield, legend and date around **Rev:** Inscription in center, legend around **Rev. Inscription:** POVR / VI. II / DEN:

Date	Mintage	VG	F	VF	XF	Unc
1617	—	15.00	32.00	100	250	—
1618	—	15.00	32.00	100	250	—
1620	—	15.00	32.00	100	250	—

KM# 8 9 DENIERS (3 Quarts)

Billon **Obv:** Anchor cross within quatrefoil **Rev:** Arms, crowned imperial eagle above, date in legend

Date	Mintage	VG	F	VF	XF	Unc
1601 G Rare	—	—	—	—	—	—
1612 C Rare	—	—	—	—	—	—
1613 C	—	15.00	30.00	120	275	—
1614 Rare	—	—	—	—	—	—
1616	—	15.00	30.00	120	275	—
1617	—	15.00	30.00	120	275	—
1619 NP Rare	—	35.00	80.00	300	—	—
1634	—	15.00	30.00	120	200	—
1636	—	18.00	40.00	165	400	—
1637	—	18.00	40.00	165	400	—

KM# 50 9 DENIERS (3 Quarts)

Billon **Obv:** Arms in inner circle, date in legend

Date	Mintage	VG	F	VF	XF	Unc
1678 IE	—	15.00	32.00	125	275	—

KM# 34 18 DENIERS (6 Quarts)

Billon **Obv:** Arms in inner circle, legend and date around **Rev:** Cross of flowers in inner circle, mintmaster's initials above

Date	Mintage	VG	F	VF	XF	Unc
1633 PM	—	18.00	40.00	150	300	—
1634 PM	—	15.00	32.00	125	250	—

KM# 51 18 DENIERS (6 Quarts)

Billon **Rev:** Crowned imperial eagle above arms

Date	Mintage	VG	F	VF	XF	Unc
1678 IE	—	15.00	35.00	125	250	—

KM# 13 UN (1) SOL

Billon **Obv:** Arms on shield, imperial eagle above **Rev:** Anchor cross, flower or mintmaster's initials above

Date	Mintage	VG	F	VF	XF	Unc
1603 Rare	—	—	—	—	—	—
1604	—	25.00	50.00	90.00	185	—
1605	—	25.00	50.00	90.00	185	—
1606	—	25.00	50.00	90.00	185	—
1609	—	25.00	50.00	90.00	185	—
1611 D	—	15.00	32.00	100	250	—
1612 C	—	15.00	32.00	100	250	—
1619 NP	—	20.00	45.00	150	300	—
1619 NP. G	—	20.00	45.00	150	300	—
1621 G	—	20.00	45.00	150	300	—
1622 G	—	15.00	32.00	100	250	—
1622 RG	—	15.00	32.00	100	250	—

KM# 13a UN (1) SOL

Gold **Obv:** Arms on shield, crowned imperial eagle above **Rev:** Anchor cross, flower or mintmaster's initials above

Date	Mintage	VG	F	VF	XF	Unc
1622 RG Rare	—	—	—	—	—	—

KM# 14 3 SOLS

Silver **Obv:** Arms on shield, date above, flower at top **Rev:** POVR / III / SOLS in inner circle, legend around

Date	Mintage	VG	F	VF	XF	Unc
1604	—	90.00	200	450	—	—

KM# 15 3 SOLS

Silver **Obv:** Crowned imperial eagle above arms on shield, date in legend

Date	Mintage	VG	F	VF	XF	Unc
1607	—	50.00	125	300	—	—

KM# 23 3 SOLS

Billon **Obv:** Date above arms on shield **Rev:** Cross on quatrefoil in inner circle

Date	Mintage	VG	F	VF	XF	Unc
1619 NP. G	—	12.00	24.00	80.00	225	—
1620 NP. G	—	12.00	24.00	80.00	225	—
1621 G	—	12.00	24.00	80.00	225	—
1622 G Rare	—	—	—	—	—	—
1624 RG Rare	—	—	—	—	—	—
1633 PM	—	8.00	16.00	60.00	200	—
1634 PM	—	8.00	16.00	60.00	200	—
1636 PM	—	8.00	16.00	60.00	200	—
1637 PM	—	8.00	16.00	60.00	200	—
1638 GB	—	8.00	16.00	60.00	200	—
1638 BG	—	8.00	16.00	60.00	200	—
1639 GB	—	8.00	16.00	60.00	200	—
1639 BG	—	8.00	16.00	60.00	200	—
1640 GB	—	8.00	16.00	60.00	200	—
1640 BG	—	8.00	16.00	60.00	200	—
1641 DS	—	8.00	16.00	60.00	200	—
1641 SD	—	8.00	16.00	60.00	200	—
1641 AD.D.	—	8.00	16.00	60.00	200	—
1642 DS	—	8.00	16.00	60.00	200	—
1642 SD	—	8.00	16.00	60.00	200	—
1643 DS	—	8.00	16.00	60.00	200	—
1643 SD	—	8.00	16.00	60.00	200	—
1644 B	—	8.00	16.00	60.00	200	—
1645 B	—	8.00	16.00	60.00	200	—
1646 B	—	8.00	16.00	60.00	200	—
1661 Rare	—	—	—	—	—	—

KM# 35 3 SOLS

Billon **Obv:** Arms on shield, flower divides date above **Rev:** Radiant sun in inner circle, IHS in circle at center

Date	Mintage	VG	F	VF	XF	Unc
1633 Rare	—	—	—	—	—	—

KM# 52 3 SOLS

Billon

Date	Mintage	VG	F	VF	XF	Unc
1689 SRG	—	20.00	40.00	130	325	—
1689 RGS	—	30.00	60.00	160	400	—
1689 SRIE	—	35.00	80.00	230	500	—

KM# 19 4 SOLS

Silver **Obv:** Arms in shield, radiant sun above, date in legend **Rev:** Inscription, D above in legend **Rev. Inscription:** POVR / II.II / SOLS

Date	Mintage	VG	F	VF	XF	Unc
1610 D	—	85.00	200	475	—	—

KM# 9 6 SOLS

Silver **Obv:** Arms on shield, crowned imperial eagle above, date in legend **Rev:** Inscription in center, legend around **Rev. Inscription:** POVR / SIX / SOLS

Date	Mintage	VG	F	VF	XF	Unc
1602	—	15.00	32.00	80.00	250	—

KM# 10 6 SOLS

Silver **Rev:** Inscription in center **Rev. Inscription:** POVR / VI / SOLS

Date	Mintage	VG	F	VF	XF	Unc
1602 Rare	—	—	—	—	—	—
1603	—	20.00	50.00	125	300	—
1611 D Rare	—	—	—	—	—	—

KM# 29 6 SOLS

Silver **Obv:** Arms in inner circle, 6-S above **Rev:** Crowned imperial eagle, mintmaster's initials above

Date	Mintage	VG	F	VF	XF	Unc
1624 GR Rare	—	—	—	—	—	—

KM# 33 6 SOLS

Billon **Obv:** Arms on shield, VI. S, date above **Rev:** Decorated cross in center, mintmaster's initials above

Date	Mintage	VG	F	VF	XF	Unc
1632 PM Rare	—	—	—	—	—	—
1633 PM	—	15.00	32.00	80.00	—	—
1634 PM	—	15.00	32.00	80.00	—	—
1635 PM	—	30.00	75.00	200	—	—
1638 GB	—	30.00	75.00	200	—	—
1639 GB	—	30.00	75.00	200	—	—
1639 BG	—	30.00	75.00	200	—	—
1640 BG	—	30.00	75.00	200	—	—
1641 DS	—	30.00	75.00	200	—	—
1678 AE	—	15.00	32.00	80.00	—	—
1678 IE	—	15.00	32.00	80.00	—	—

KM# 33a 6 SOLS

Silver

Date	Mintage	VG	F	VF	XF	Unc
1678 IE	—	—	—	—	—	—

KM# 20 8 SOLS

Silver **Obv:** Arms on shield, radiant sun above, date in legend **Rev:** Inscription in inner circle, legend around **Rev. Inscription:** POVR / VIII / SOLS

Date	Mintage	VG	F	VF	XF	Unc
1610 D	—	350	800	2,000	—	—

KM# 30 10 SOLS (Achtelthaler)

Silver **Obv:** Arms in inner circle, date in legend **Rev:** Crowned imperial eagle, mintmaster's initials above

Date	Mintage	VG	F	VF	XF	Unc
1624 GR	—	50.00	100	250	—	—
1624 RG	—	75.00	150	400	—	—
1625 GR	—	75.00	150	400	—	—
1625 HC	—	50.00	100	250	—	—
1626 HC	—	75.00	150	400	—	—
1628 HC Rare	—	—	—	—	—	—

KM# 11 12 SOLS (1 Gulden)

Silver

Date	Mintage	VG	F	VF	XF	Unc
1602	—	65.00	140	300	750	—
1603	—	45.00	100	250	600	—

KM# 38 12 SOLS (1 Gulden)

Silver **Obv:** Arms on shield, imperial eagle above, 12 S below **Rev:** IHS in center of radiant sun in inner circle, date in legend

Date	Mintage	VG	F	VF	XF	Unc
1635 PM	—	175	400	900	2,400	—

KM# 45 12 SOLS (1 Gulden)

Silver **Obv:** Inscription in center, mintmaster's initials above **Obv. Inscription:** POVR / XII / SOLS **Rev:** W/o value, date in legend

Date	Mintage	VG	F	VF	XF	Unc
1654 AB	—	15.00	32.00	80.00	200	—

KM# 36 24 SOLS (2 Guldens)

Silver

Date	Mintage	VG	F	VF	XF	Unc
1634 PM	—	100	250	600	—	—
1635 PM	—	50.00	125	325	—	—
1636 PM	—	80.00	200	475	—	—

KM# 41 24 SOLS (2 Guldens)

Silver

Date	Mintage	VG	F	VF	XF	Unc
1644 B	—	90.00	200	475	—	—
1645 B	—	90.00	200	475	—	—
1647 G Rare	—	—	—	—	—	—

KM# 48 24 SOLS (2 Guldens)

Silver **Obv:** Arms **Obv. Legend:** * GENEVA * CIVITAS * **Rev:** Crowned imperial eagle

Date	Mintage	VG	F	VF	XF	Unc
1657	—	95.00	200	475	—	—

KM# A30 1/16 THALER

Silver

Date	Mintage	VG	F	VF	XF	Unc
1624	—	150	325	800	—	—

KM# 24 1/4 THALER

Silver **Obv:** Arms in inner circle, flower above, date in legend **Rev:** Crowned imperial eagle in inner circle, mintmaster's initials above

Date	Mintage	VG	F	VF	XF	Unc
1619 NPG Rare	—	—	—	—	—	—
1620 NPG Rare	—	—	—	—	—	—
1624 RG	—	350	800	2,000	—	—

KM# 28 1/4 THALER

Silver

Date	Mintage	VG	F	VF	XF	Unc
1623 RG	—	225	475	1,200	—	—
1625 HC	—	350	800	2,000	—	—
1627 HC	—	350	800	2,000	—	—
1633 PM Rare	—	—	—	—	—	—

KM# 27 1/2 THALER

Silver **Obv:** Arms in inner circle, IHS in radiant sun above, divides date **Rev:** Crowned imperial eagle in inner circle, mintmaster's initials divided by crown

Date	Mintage	VG	F	VF	XF	Unc
1621 GI	—	500	1,200	2,750	—	—
1622 GI Rare	—	—	—	—	—	—
1622 RG	—	175	400	900	—	—
1622 GR	—	300	800	2,000	—	—
1623 RG	—	275	600	1,300	—	—
1625 HC	—	600	1,200	3,000	—	—
1626 HC Rare	—	—	—	—	—	—
1627 HC Rare	—	—	—	—	—	—
1629 HC Rare	—	—	—	—	—	—
1630 HC Rare	—	—	—	—	—	—
1633 PM Rare	—	—	—	—	—	—
1638 GB Rare	—	—	—	—	—	—
1640 GB Rare	—	—	—	—	—	—
1641 SD Rare	—	—	—	—	—	—
1641 D-AD	—	275	600	1,300	—	—
1657 AC	—	350	800	2,000	—	—
1659 AC	—	350	800	2,000	—	—

KM# 26 THALER

Silver **Obv:** Arms in inner circle, IHS in radiant sun divide date **Rev:** Crowned imperial eagle in inner circle, mintmaster's initials divided by crown **Note:** Dav. #4621.

Date	Mintage	VG	F	VF	XF	Unc
1620 NPG	—	750	1,600	4,000	—	—
1621 G	—	300	650	1,600	—	—
1622 GI	—	500	1,200	2,800	—	—
1622 GR	—	75.00	165	400	1,200	—
1622 RG	—	110	250	600	—	—
1623 RG	—	75.00	175	475	1,400	—
1625 HC	—	250	600	1,400	—	—
1626 HC	—	250	600	1,400	—	—
1627 HC	—	250	600	1,400	—	—
1628 HC Rare	—	—	—	—	—	—
1629 HC Rare	—	—	—	—	—	—
1630 HC	—	600	1,300	3,000	—	—
1633 PM	—	600	1,300	3,000	—	—
1635 PM	—	600	1,300	3,000	—	—
1638 BG Rare	—	—	—	—	—	—
1638 GB	—	250	600	1,300	3,000	—
1639 GB Rare	—	—	—	—	—	—
1640 GB	—	850	2,000	6,000	—	—
1641 SD	—	850	2,000	6,000	—	—
1641 D-AD	—	850	2,000	6,000	—	—
1642 DS	—	850	2,000	6,000	—	—
1642 SD	—	850	2,000	6,000	—	—
1657 AC	—	750	1,600	4,000	8,000	—
1659 AC	—	750	1,600	4,000	8,000	—

KM# 32 ECU-PISTOLET

0.9170 Gold **Obv:** Radiant sun in inner circle **Rev:** Crowned imperial eagle with shield of arms on breast **Note:** Fr. #250, 251.

Date	Mintage	VG	F	VF	XF	Unc
1630 RG Rare	—	—	—	—	—	—
1634 PM Rare	—	—	—	—	—	—
1638 BG Rare	—	—	—	—	—	—
1639 BG Rare	—	—	—	—	—	—
1642 BD Rare	—	—	—	—	—	—

KM# 39 QUADRUPLA ECU PISTOLET

15.2800 g., 0.9000 Gold 0.4421 oz. AGW **Obv:** Radiant sun in inner circle **Rev:** Crowned imperial eagle with shield of arms on breast **Note:** Fr. #247, 248.

Date	Mintage	VG	F	VF	XF	Unc
1635 PM	—	3,000	6,500	15,000	25,000	—
1637 PM	—	3,000	6,500	15,000	25,000	—
1638 BG	—	3,000	6,500	15,000	25,000	—
1638 GB Rare	—	—	—	—	—	—
1640 GB Rare	—	—	—	—	—	—
1641 SD	—	2,500	6,000	12,000	20,000	—
1642 SD	—	2,500	6,000	12,000	20,000	—
1644 B Rare	—	—	—	—	—	—
1645 B Rare	—	—	—	—	—	—
1646 B Rare	—	—	—	—	—	—
1647 G Rare	—	—	—	—	—	—

KM# 37 PISTOLE

7.6400 g., 0.9000 Gold 0.2211 oz. AGW **Obv:** Radiant sun in inner circle **Rev:** Crowned imperial eagle with shield of arms on breast **Note:** Fr. #252.

Date	Mintage	VG	F	VF	XF	Unc
1634 PM Rare	—	—	—	—	—	—
1636 PM Rare	—	—	—	—	—	—
1637 PM Rare	—	—	—	—	—	—
1638 BG Rare	—	—	—	—	—	—
1639 BG Rare	—	—	—	—	—	—
1640 GB Rare	—	—	—	—	—	—
1641 SD Rare	—	—	—	—	—	—
1642 SD Rare	—	—	—	—	—	—

TRADE COINAGE

KM# 42 DUCAT

3.5000 g., 0.9860 Gold 0.1109 oz. AGW **Note:** Varieties exist. Fr. #256, 257.

Date	Mintage	VG	F	VF	XF	Unc
1644 B	—	800	1,600	3,200	—	—
1645 B Rare	—	—	—	—	—	—
1646 B	—	600	1,600	3,200	—	—
1647 G Rare	—	—	—	—	—	—
1648 G	—	800	2,000	4,000	—	—
1649 G	—	1,000	2,400	4,750	—	—
1650 M	—	1,000	2,400	4,750	—	—
1651 M	—	1,000	2,400	4,750	—	—
1652 M Rare	—	—	—	—	—	—
1654 AB Rare	—	—	—	—	—	—
1657 DS Rare	—	—	—	—	—	—

KM# 46 2 DUCAT

7.0000 g., 0.9860 Gold 0.2219 oz. AGW **Note:** Varieties exist. Fr. #254, 255.

Date	Mintage	VG	F	VF	XF	Unc
1654 AB Rare	—	—	—	—	—	—
1655 AC Rare	—	—	—	—	—	—
1656 AC	—	1,200	2,800	5,000	10,000	—
1657 AC	—	1,200	2,800	5,000	10,000	—
1658 AC Rare	—	—	—	—	—	—
1659 AC Rare	—	—	—	—	—	—
1660 AC Rare	—	—	—	—	—	—
1662 AC Rare	—	—	—	—	—	—
1663 AC Rare	—	—	—	—	—	—
1664 AC Rare	—	—	—	—	—	—
1665 AE Rare	—	—	—	—	—	—
1666 AE Rare	—	—	—	—	—	—
1674 AE Rare	—	—	—	—	—	—
1690 CL Rare	—	—	—	—	—	—
ND AE Rare	—	—	—	—	—	—

GLARUS

A canton in eastern Switzerland. Independence was gained in c.1390 but from 1798-1803 it was occupied by the French. They rejoined the Swiss Confederation in 1803.

MONETARY SYSTEM

3 Rappen = 1 Schilling
100 Rappen = 1 Frank

CANTON

STANDARD COINAGE

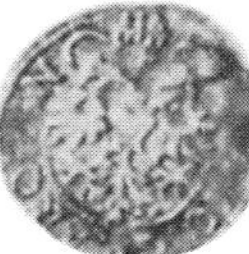

KM# 5 SCHILLING

Billon **Obv:** Standing saint wearing mantle, holding Bible and cane **Rev:** Crowned imperial eagle, cross between heads

Date	Mintage	VG	F	VF	XF	Unc
ND	—	900	2,000	7,000	—	—
1617	—	1,100	2,400	8,000	—	—

KM# 6 SCHILLING

Billon **Note:** Klippe.

Date	Mintage	VG	F	VF	XF	Unc
ND	—	—	—	—	—	—

HALDENSTEIN

Haldenstein was an area in the canton of Graubunden. The rulers were barons who held various estates. They received the mint right in 1612. The property of the barons was mediatized during the French invasion of Graubunden in 1798 and 1799.

RULERS

Thomas I, 1609-1628
Julius Otto, 1628-1666
Georg Philip, 1666-1695

CANTON

STANDARD COINAGE

KM# 6 BLUZGER

Billon **Obv:** Large five-fold arms on Spanish shield in inner circle **Rev:** Plain cross in pearl circle, legend around

Date	Mintage	VG	F	VF	XF	Unc
ND	—	50.00	100	200	—	—

KM# 7 BLUZGER

Billon **Obv. Legend:** THOMAS. L. B. AB. EREN. **Rev. Legend:** DOMINVS. IN. HALDEN

Date	Mintage	VG	F	VF	XF	Unc
ND(1609-20)	—	100	250	600	—	—

KM# 8 BLUZGER

Billon **Obv. Legend:** IVLIVS. OTTO. L. B. AB. EHRE. D. I. H. **Rev. Legend:** MON. NOVA. HALDENSTA.

Date	Mintage	VG	F	VF	XF	Unc
ND(1628-66)	—	125	275	700	—	—

KM# 9 BLUZGER

Billon **Obv:** Arms larger **Rev:** Cross with all four sides broken from center

Date	Mintage	VG	F	VF	XF	Unc
ND	—	110	240	600	—	—

KM# 59 BLUZGER

Billon **Obv:** Five-fold arms in oval decorative cartouche **Obv. Legend:** GEORG. PHLIP. L. B. AB. EHRF. D. I H **Rev:** Cross without inner circle, date in legend

Date	Mintage	VG	F	VF	XF	Unc
1684	—	100	240	600	—	—
1687	—	15.00	35.00	85.00	185	—

KM# 73 BLUZGER

Billon **Obv:** Five-fold arms on Spanish shield in inner circle **Rev:** Cross in inner circle

Date	Mintage	VG	F	VF	XF	Unc
ND	—	35.00	80.00	200	—	—
1693	—	15.00	35.00	80.00	165	—

KM# 45 2 KREUZER (1/2 Batzen)

Billon **Obv:** 2 on imperial orb in inner circle **Rev:** Crowned imperial eagle with halos in inner circle

Date	Mintage	VG	F	VF	XF	Unc
1624 Rare	—	—	—	—	—	—

KM# 51 2 KREUZER (1/2 Batzen)

Billon **Obv:** Five-fold arms on round shield with indented sides **Rev:** 2 on imperial orb

Date	Mintage	VG	F	VF	XF	Unc
1648	—	700	1,600	4,000	—	—

KM# 48 3 KREUZER (1 Groschen)

Silver **Obv:** Bust right **Obv. Legend:** IVLIVS. OTTO. L. B. AB. EHREN **Rev:** Crowned imperial eagle, 3 on imperial orb on breast, date below **Note:** Klippe.

Date	Mintage	VG	F	VF	XF	Unc
1638 Rare	—	—	—	—	—	—

KM# 60 6 KREUZER

Billon **Obv:** Bust right, VI in oval shield below **Rev:** Crowned imperial eagle with crown dividing legend, date in legend

Date	Mintage	VG	F	VF	XF	Unc
1687	—	90.00	200	600	—	—

KM# 61 6 KREUZER

Billon **Obv:** Date in legend at top **Rev:** Crowned imperial eagle withn circle

Date	Mintage	VG	F	VF	XF	Unc
1687 Rare	—	—	—	—	—	—

KM# 63 6 KREUZER

Billon **Obv:** Bust right **Rev:** Crowned five-fold arms on shield between palm branches, date above

Date	Mintage	VG	F	VF	XF	Unc
1688	—	225	475	1,200	—	—

KM# 12 12 KREUZER (1/2 Dicken)

Silver **Obv:** Five-fold arms of Lichtenstein, Grottenstein, Haldenstien, and Herzschild Schauenstein **Rev:** Crowned imperial eagle, 1Z in imperial orb on breast

Date	Mintage	VG	F	VF	XF	Unc
ND	—	110	250	600	—	—

KM# 13 12 KREUZER (1/2 Dicken)

Silver **Rev:** Without orb on breast

Date	Mintage	VG	F	VF	XF	Unc
ND Rare	—	—	—	—	—	—

KM# 44 12 KREUZER (1/2 Dicken)

Silver **Obv:** 1/2-length figure right in innere circle **Rev:** Crowned imperial eagle, 1Z in circle on breast

Date	Mintage	VG	F	VF	XF	Unc
ND	—	75.00	165	400	—	—
1623 Rare	—	—	—	—	—	—

KM# 62 15 KREUZER (1/4 Gulden)

Silver **Obv:** Bust of Georg Philip right **Rev:** Crowned imperial eagle

Date	Mintage	VG	F	VF	XF	Unc
1687	—	65.00	145	325	625	—

KM# 64 15 KREUZER (1/4 Gulden)

Silver **Obv:** Taller figure right **Rev:** Larger shield on eagle's breast, XV in shield below

Date	Mintage	VG	F	VF	XF	Unc
1689	—	65.00	145	325	625	—

KM# 65 15 KREUZER (1/4 Gulden)

Silver **Obv:** Larger bust right **Rev:** Larger eagle

Date	Mintage	VG	F	VF	XF	Unc
1689	—	65.00	140	325	600	—
1690	—	35.00	80.00	200	400	—
1691	—	200	450	1,200	—	—

KM# 66 30 KREUZER (1/2 Gulden)

Silver **Obv:** Bust right in inner circle **Rev:** Crowned five-fold arms between branches, 30 in shield at bottom

Date	Mintage	VG	F	VF	XF	Unc
1689	—	550	1,200	2,800	5,500	—

KM# 14 BATZEN

Billon **Obv:** 1/2-length figure of Thomas I right

Date	Mintage	VG	F	VF	XF	Unc
ND	—	150	325	800	—	—

KM# 15 BATZEN

Billon **Obv:** Similar to KM#14 reverse **Rev:** Cross in inner circle

Date	Mintage	VG	F	VF	XF	Unc
ND	—	250	600	1,600	—	—

KM# 16 BATZEN

Billon **Obv:** Smaller cross in inner circle **Rev:** Smaller five-fold shield, crowned imperial eagle above

Date	Mintage	VG	F	VF	XF	Unc
ND	—	175	400	950	—	—

KM# 17 BATZEN

Billon **Obv:** 5-fold Spanish shield in inner circle **Rev:** Crowned imperial eagle on spanish shield, crosses on both sides, top, and bottom of shield

Date	Mintage	VG	F	VF	XF	Unc
ND	—	160	315	525	—	—

KM# 18 BATZEN

Billon **Obv:** Five-fold arms in inner circle **Rev:** Cross in inner circle

Date	Mintage	VG	F	VF	XF	Unc
ND	—	120	240	400	—	—

KM# A19 1/2 DICKEN

Silver

Date	Mintage	VG	F	VF	XF	Unc
1623 Rare	—	—	—	—	—	—
ND	—	80.00	160	400	—	—

KM# 19 DICKEN

Silver **Obv:** 1/2-length figure right in inner circle **Rev:** Crowned imperial eagle with shield on breast

Date	Mintage	VG	F	VF	XF	Unc
ND	—	400	950	2,400	—	—

KM# 20 DICKEN

Silver **Rev:** Large shield on eagle

Date	Mintage	VG	F	VF	XF	Unc
ND	—	100	200	475	950	—

KM# 21 DICKEN

Silver **Obv:** 1/2-length figure right behind large five-fold shield **Rev:** W/o shield on eagle

Date	Mintage	VG	F	VF	XF	Unc
ND	—	225	475	1,200	—	—

KM# 22 DICKEN

Silver **Obv:** Taller figure with head breaking into legend **Rev:** Narrow legend around larger eagle

Date	Mintage	VG	F	VF	XF	Unc
ND	—	450	950	2,400	—	—

KM# 23 DICKEN

Silver **Obv:** Arms slanting in front of figure

Date	Mintage	VG	F	VF	XF	Unc
ND	—	120	240	550	1,200	—

KM# 24 DICKEN

Silver **Obv:** Shield with two trout in legend below figure

Date	Mintage	VG	F	VF	XF	Unc
ND	—	200	400	750	1,300	—

KM# 25 DICKEN

Silver **Obv:** 1/2-length figure left wearing cardinal's hat

Date	Mintage	VG	F	VF	XF	Unc
ND	—	125	275	600	1,200	—

KM# 26 DICKEN

Silver **Obv:** 1/2-length figure right wearing cardinal's hat

Date	Mintage	VG	F	VF	XF	Unc
ND Rare	—	—	—	—	—	—

KM# 27 DICKEN

Silver **Obv:** 1/2-length figure left wearing cardinal's hat **Rev:** Imperial eagle w/o crown

Date	Mintage	VG	F	VF	XF	Unc
ND	—	200	400	750	1,350	—

KM# 35 DICKEN

Silver **Obv:** Bare-headed 1/2-length figure left, date in legend **Rev:** Crowned imperial eagle

Date	Mintage	VG	F	VF	XF	Unc
ND	—	80.00	160	265	600	—
1617	—	550	1,200	—	—	—

KM# 41 DICKEN

Silver **Obv:** Bare-headed 1/2-length figure right, date in legend

Date	Mintage	VG	F	VF	XF	Unc
1620	—	200	400	950	—	—
1621	—	150	300	600	—	—
1623	—	400	900	2,400	—	—

KM# 42 1/2 THALER

Silver **Obv:** 1/2-length figure of Thomas I right **Rev:** Crowned imperial eagle

Date	Mintage	VG	F	VF	XF	Unc
1620	—	950	2,250	6,000	—	—

KM# 67 60 KREUZER (1 Gulden; 2/3 Thaler)

Silver **Obv:** Bust right in inner circle **Rev:** Crowned imperial eagle, five-fold shield on breast, 60 in oval shield below

Date	Mintage	VG	F	VF	XF	Unc
1689	—	150	325	800	—	—

KM# 68 60 KREUZER (1 Gulden; 2/3 Thaler)

Silver **Obv:** Larger, closer bust right **Rev:** Five-fold shield on cartouche, 60 in oval shield below

Date	Mintage	VG	F	VF	XF	Unc
1689	—	150	325	800	—	—
1690	—	150	325	800	—	—

KM# 70 2/3 THALER

Silver **Obv:** Bust of Georg Philip right **Rev:** 5-fold arms, 2/3 in oval shield below

Date	Mintage	VG	F	VF	XF	Unc
1690	—	60.00	120	275	475	—
1691	—	120	240	600	—	—
1692	—	100	200	475	—	—

KM# 71 2/3 THALER

Silver **Obv:** Bust of Georg Philip right **Rev:** Crowned imperial eagle, 2/3 in oval shield below

Date	Mintage	VG	F	VF	XF	Unc
1690	—	60.00	120	275	475	—
1691	—	50.00	100	250	400	—
1692	—	75.00	140	325	550	—

KM# 43.1 THALER

Silver **Obv:** Bare-headed 1/2-length figure right, date in legend above head **Rev:** Crowned imperial eagle **Note:** Dav. #46789.

Date	Mintage	VG	F	VF	XF	Unc
1621	—	450	800	2,000	—	—

KM# 43.2 THALER

Silver **Obv:** Bare-headed 1/2-length figure right looking up, date in legend to left of head **Note:** Dav. #4679.

Date	Mintage	VG	F	VF	XF	Unc
1623	—	250	500	1,200	—	—

KM# 47 2 THALER

Silver **Obv:** 1/2-length figure right, helmet and Spanish shield in lower margin **Rev:** Crowned imperial eagle, date in legend

Date	Mintage	VG	F	VF	XF	Unc
1637 Rare	—	8,000	16,000	32,000	60,000	—

TRADE COINAGE

KM# 28 GOLDGULDEN

3.5000 g., 0.9860 Gold 0.1109 oz. AGW **Obv:** Orb on eagle's chest **Note:** Legend varieties exist.

Date	Mintage	VG	F	VF	XF	Unc
ND	—	400	1,000	2,000	3,000	—

KM# 29 GOLDGULDEN

3.5000 g., 0.9860 Gold 0.1109 oz. AGW **Obv:** Shield on eagle's chest **Note:** Several varieties exist, all ar rare.

Date	Mintage	VG	F	VF	XF	Unc
ND	—	3,000	5,000	6,500	7,500	—

KM# 49 DUCAT

3.5000 g., 0.9860 Gold 0.1109 oz. AGW **Obv:** Julius Otto standing **Rev:** Crowned imperial eagle **Note:** Fr. #279.

Date	Mintage	VG	F	VF	XF	Unc
1638	—	3,000	6,000	12,000	—	—
1642 Rare	—	—	—	—	—	—
1648 Rare	—	—	—	—	—	—
1649	—	3,000	6,000	12,000	—	—

KM# 55 DUCAT

3.5000 g., 0.9860 Gold 0.1109 oz. AGW **Obv:** 1/2-length figure facing 3/4 front with long hair **Rev:** Crowned imperial eagle w/shield on breast **Note:** Fr. #275.

Date	Mintage	VG	F	VF	XF	Unc
1667 Rare	—	—	—	—	—	—

KM# 36 2 DUCAT

7.0000 g., 0.9860 Gold 0.2219 oz. AGW **Obv:** 1/2-length figure of Thomas I left **Rev:** Crowned imperial eagle **Note:** Fr. #268.

Date	Mintage	VG	F	VF	XF	Unc
1617	—	3,000	6,000	12,000	20,000	—

KM# 37 2 DUCAT

7.0000 g., 0.9860 Gold 0.2219 oz. AGW **Obv:** Shield **Rev:** Crowned imperial eagle **Note:** Fr. #269.

Date	Mintage	VG	F	VF	XF	Unc
ND	—	4,000	8,000	16,000	28,000	—

KM# 72 2 DUCAT

7.0000 g., 0.9860 Gold 0.2219 oz. AGW **Obv:** Bust right w/long hair **Obv. Legend:** GEORG. PHIL. L. B... **Rev:** Crowned imperial eagle, shield on bust **Note:** Fr. #276.

Date	Mintage	VG	F	VF	XF	Unc
1690 Rare	—	—	—	—	—	—

KM# 38 4 DUCAT

14.0000 g., 0.9860 Gold 0.4438 oz. AGW **Obv:** Bust of Thomas left **Rev:** Crowned imperial eagle **Note:** Fr. #267.

Date	Mintage	VG	F	VF	XF	Unc
1617 Rare	—	—	—	—	—	—

KM# 39 7 DUCAT

24.5000 g., 0.9860 Gold 0.7766 oz. AGW **Obv:** 1/2-length figure of Thomas I right **Rev:** Crowned imperial eagle **Note:** Fr. #266.

Date	Mintage	VG	F	VF	XF	Unc
1617	—	3,500	7,000	14,000	24,000	—

LAUFENBURG

A city in northern Switzerland in the canton of Aargau. They received their coinage rights in the early 16th century.

CITY

STANDARD COINAGE

KM# 5 VIERER

Billon **Obv:** Round arms with standing lion in inner circle **Rev:** Floreate cross in inner circle

Date	Mintage	VG	F	VF	XF	Unc
ND Rare	—	—	—	—	—	—

KM# 6 SCHILLING

Billon **Obv:** Arms on shield in inner circle **Rev:** Bust of saint right, lamb in front

Date	Mintage	VG	F	VF	XF	Unc
ND Rare	—	—	—	—	—	—

KM# 7 PLAPPART

Billon **Obv:** Oval arms in cartouche in inner circle **Rev:** Standing saint holding lamb in arms

Date	Mintage	VG	F	VF	XF	Unc
ND Rare	—	—	—	—	—	—

KM# 10 PLAPPART

Billon **Rev:** Half-length figure of saint holding lamb in arms, 1 in circle divides date below

Date	Mintage	VG	F	VF	XF	Unc
1623	—	400	800	—	—	—

KM# 11 PLAPPART

Billon **Rev:** Standing saint in long robe holding lamb in arms, 1 in shield divides date below

Date	Mintage	VG	F	VF	XF	Unc
1623	—	400	800	—	—	—

KM# 9 2 PLAPPART

Billon **Obv:** Standing lion arms on shield, leaf decorations around in inner circle **Rev:** Standing saint in long robe holding lamb and cross divides date in field, Z below

Date	Mintage	VG	F	VF	XF	Unc
1622 Rare	—	—	—	—	—	—

KM# 12 2 PLAPPART

Billon **Obv:** Oval arms in cartouche

Date	Mintage	VG	F	VF	XF	Unc
1623	—	1,000	1,800	2,500	—	—

KM# 13 4 PLAPPART

Billon **Obv:** Oval standing lion arms in cartouche **Rev:** Lamb with halo and cross on round shield, script SVRR - EXIT - IOAN - BAPT in center legend

Date	Mintage	VG	F	VF	XF	Unc
1623 Rare	—	—	—	—	—	—

LUZERN

Lucerne

A canton and city in central Switzerland. The city grew around the Benedictine Monastery which was founded in 750. They joined the Swiss Confederation as the 4th member in 1332. Few coins were issued before the1500s.

MINT OFFICIAL'S INITIALS

Initial	Date	Name
LV	1622	?

MONETARY SYSTEM

Until 1798

240 Angster = 120 Rappen = 40 Schillinge = 1 Gulden
10 Rappen = 1 Batzen
4 Kreuzer = 1 Batzen
10 Batzen = 1 Frank
40 Batzen = 3 Gulden = 1 Thaler
4 Franken = 1 Thaler
12 Gulden = 1 Duplone

CITY

STANDARD COINAGE

KM# 8 SCHILLING

Billon **Obv:** Crowned imperial eagle above arms on shield **Rev:** Bust of saint wearing a mitre

Date	Mintage	VG	F	VF	XF	Unc
1601	—	15.00	32.00	95.00	—	—
1603	—	15.00	32.00	95.00	—	—
1604 Rare	—	—	—	—	—	—
1605	—	8.00	20.00	65.00	165	—

KM# 13 SCHILLING

Billon **Obv:** Larger eagle, date below, small shield of arms in legend at bottom

Date	Mintage	VG	F	VF	XF	Unc
ND	—	15.00	40.00	120	—	—
1609	—	8.00	20.00	65.00	165	—
1610	—	8.00	20.00	65.00	165	—
1611	—	8.00	20.00	65.00	165	—

KM# 17 SCHILLING

Billon **Obv:** Date in legend

Date	Mintage	VG	F	VF	XF	Unc
1611	—	8.00	20.00	65.00	150	—
1612	—	8.00	20.00	65.00	150	—
1613	—	8.00	20.00	65.00	150	—
1614	—	8.00	20.00	65.00	150	—
1615	—	15.00	30.00	80.00	200	—
1616	—	25.00	60.00	120	300	—
1617	—	25.00	60.00	120	300	—
1618	—	25.00	60.00	120	300	—
1619	—	25.00	60.00	120	300	—
1620	—	25.00	60.00	120	300	—
1621	—	8.00	20.00	60.00	150	—
1622	—	8.00	20.00	60.00	150	—

KM# 25 SCHILLING

Billon

Date	Mintage	VG	F	VF	XF	Unc
1623	—	9.00	20.00	60.00	150	—
1634	—	9.00	20.00	60.00	150	—
1638	—	9.00	20.00	60.00	150	—
1639 Rare	—	—	—	—	—	—
1647	—	9.00	20.00	60.00	150	—

KM# 9 3 KREUZER (1 Groschen)

Silver **Obv:** Large shield in inner circle, date in legend **Rev:** Crowned imperial eagle, imperial orb with 3 on breast

Date	Mintage	VG	F	VF	XF	Unc
1601	—	7.00	16.00	32.00	80.00	—
1602	—	7.00	16.00	32.00	80.00	—
1603	—	7.00	16.00	32.00	80.00	—
1604	—	7.00	16.00	32.00	80.00	—
1605	—	7.00	16.00	32.00	80.00	—
1606	—	7.00	16.00	32.00	80.00	—
1613 Rare	—	—	—	—	—	—

KM# 22 BATZEN-10 RAPPEN

Billon **Obv:** Arms, eagle above, with or without L-V at sides of arms, date in legend **Rev:** Cross, fleur-de-lis in angles

Date	Mintage	VG	F	VF	XF	Unc
1622 LV	—	6.00	12.00	40.00	100	—
1622	—	8.00	16.00	50.00	120	—

KM# 29 BATZEN-10 RAPPEN

Billon **Obv:** Large shield in inner circle, date below **Rev:** Large cross in inner circle

Date	Mintage	VG	F	VF	XF	Unc
1638	—	6.00	12.00	40.00	100	—

KM# 21 1/2 DICKEN

Silver **Obv:** Crowned imperial eagle above shield dividing date **Rev:** 1/2-length St. Mauritius in armor right holding swords

Date	Mintage	VG	F	VF	XF	Unc
1620 Rare	—	—	—	—	—	—
1621 Rare	—	—	—	—	—	—
1622 Rare	—	—	—	—	—	—

KM# 23 1/2 DICKEN

Silver **Obv:** Large eagle above small shield **Rev:** Bust of Saint wearing mitre, right

Date	Mintage	VG	F	VF	XF	Unc
1622 Rare	—	—	—	—	—	—

KM# 26 1/2 DICKEN

Silver **Obv:** Large shield in inner circle, date below **Rev:** Half-length saint in armor right holding sword

Date	Mintage	VG	F	VF	XF	Unc
1623	—	35.00	80.00	200	475	—

KM# 15 DICKEN

Silver

Date	Mintage	VG	F	VF	XF	Unc
1610	—	250	600	1,600	—	—

KM# 16 DICKEN

Silver **Obv:** Smaller shield, date divided by eagle's tail **Rev:** Similar to KM#19

Date	Mintage	VG	F	VF	XF	Unc
1610	—	350	800	2,000	—	—
1611	—	35.00	80.00	200	475	—
1612	—	35.00	80.00	200	475	—

KM# 18 DICKEN

Silver **Obv:** Without date **Rev:** Similar to KM#19

Date	Mintage	VG	F	VF	XF	Unc
1612	—	35.00	80.00	200	475	—
1613	—	35.00	80.00	200	475	—
1614	—	35.00	80.00	200	475	—
1615	—	35.00	80.00	200	475	—
1616	—	35.00	80.00	200	475	—

KM# 19 DICKEN

Silver

Date	Mintage	VG	F	VF	XF	Unc
1617	—	75.00	150	400	—	—
1618	—	150	400	950	—	—
1619	—	225	475	125	—	—
1620	—	50.00	125	275	600	—
1621	—	50.00	125	275	600	—
1622	—	50.00	125	275	600	—
1622	—	90.00	165	400	—	—

KM# 27 DICKEN

Silver

Date	Mintage	VG	F	VF	XF	Unc
1623	—	40.00	80.00	200	475	—
1647	—	150	300	800	1,600	—
1656	—	225	475	1,200	—	—

KM# 10 THALER

Silver **Obv:** Eighteen shields of district arms encircle crown above three shields, lion on each side of shields **Rev:** Scene depicting legend of the blinding St. Leodegar **Note:** Dav. #4623.

Date	Mintage	VG	F	VF	XF	Unc
1603 Rare	—	—	—	—	—	—

KM# 24 THALER

Silver **Obv:** Crowned imperial eagle **Rev:** St. Leodegar standing facing **Note:** Dav. #4624.

KM# 40 THALER

Silver **Obv:** Ornate oval shield **Rev:** St. Leodegar standing facing **Note:** Dav. #4625.

Date	Mintage	VG	F	VF	XF	Unc
1698	—	225	475	1,200	2,400	4,000

KM# 11 2 THALER

Silver **Obv:** Eighteen shields of district arms encircle crown above three shields, lion on each side of shields **Rev:** Scene depicting the blinding of the saint **Note:** Dav. #4622.

Date	Mintage	VG	F	VF	XF	Unc
1603 Rare	—	3,000	6,500	16,000	32,000	—

KM# 41 2 THALER

Silver **Note:** Similar to 1 Thaler, KM#40. Dav. #A4625.

Date	Mintage	VG	F	VF	XF	Unc
1698 Rare	—	2,400	4,800	12,000	20,000	—

TRADE COINAGE

KM# 36 DUCAT

3.5000 g., 0.9860 Gold 0.1109 oz. AGW **Obv:** Inscription in cartouche **Rev:** Sts. Leodegar and Maurice standing **Note:** Fr. #302.

Date	Mintage	VG	F	VF	XF	Unc
ND(1695-1700) Rare	—	—	—	—	—	—

KM# 12 2 DUCAT

7.0000 g., 0.9860 Gold 0.2219 oz. AGW **Obv:** Shield of arms with eagle above **Rev:** Facing bust of St. Leodegar **Note:** Fr. #288.

Date	Mintage	VG	F	VF	XF	Unc
1603 Rare	—	—	—	—	—	—

KM# 34 2 DUCAT

7.0000 g., 0.9860 Gold 0.2219 oz. AGW **Obv:** Crowned arms **Rev:** St. Leodegar with church at side **Note:** Fr. #304.

Date	Mintage	VG	F	VF	XF	Unc
1675 Rare	—	—	—	—	—	—

KM# 37 2 DUCAT

7.0000 g., 0.9860 Gold 0.2219 oz. AGW **Obv:** Soldier **Rev:** St. Leodegar **Note:** Fr. #307.

Date	Mintage	VG	F	VF	XF	Unc
1695	—	3,000	6,000	12,000	20,000	—

KM# A37 2 DUCAT

7.0000 g., 0.9860 Gold 0.2219 oz. AGW **Obv:** Inscription in cartouche **Rev:** Sts. Leodegar and Maurice standing **Note:** Fr. #301.

Date	Mintage	VG	F	VF	XF	Unc
ND(1695-1700) Rare	—	—	—	—	—	—

KM# 14 4 DUCAT

14.0000 g., 0.9860 Gold 0.4438 oz. AGW **Obv:** Crowned imperial eagle over shield **Rev:** Bust of St. Leodegar facing **Note:** Struck with 1 Dicken dies, KM#15. Fr. #287.

Date	Mintage	VG	F	VF	XF	Unc
1610 Rare	—	—	—	—	—	—

KM# 20 4 DUCAT

14.0000 g., 0.9860 Gold 0.4438 oz. AGW **Obv:** Crowned imperial eagle over shield **Rev:** Bust of St. Leodegar right **Note:** Struck with 1 Dicken dies, KM#19. Fr. #292.

Date	Mintage	VG	F	VF	XF	Unc
1619 Rare	—	—	—	—	—	—

KM# 38 4 DUCAT

14.0000 g., 0.9860 Gold 0.4438 oz. AGW **Obv:** Soldier seated beside shield **Rev:** St. Leodegar seated **Note:** Fr. #306.

Date	Mintage	VG	F	VF	XF	Unc
1695 Rare	—	—	—	—	—	—

KM# A42 4 DUCAT

14.0000 g., 0.9860 Gold 0.4438 oz. AGW **Obv:** Ornate oval arms **Rev:** St. Leodegar standing facing **Note:** Struck with 1 Thaler dies, KM#40. Fr. #300.

Date	Mintage	VG	F	VF	XF	Unc
1698 Rare	—	—	—	—	—	—

KM# 39 5 DUCAT

17.5000 g., 0.9860 Gold 0.5547 oz. AGW **Obv:** Soldier seated beside shield **Rev:** St. Leodegar seated **Note:** Fr. #305.

Date	Mintage	VG	F	VF	XF	Unc
1695	—	4,000	9,500	20,000	32,000	—

KM# B42 5 DUCAT

17.5000 g., 0.9860 Gold 0.5547 oz. AGW **Obv:** Ornate oval arms **Rev:** St. Leodegar standing facing **Note:** Struck with 1 Thaler dies. KM#40. Fr. #299.

Date	Mintage	VG	F	VF	XF	Unc
1698 Rare	—	—	—	—	—	—

KM# A15 6 DUCAT

21.0000 g., 0.9860 Gold 0.6657 oz. AGW **Obv:** Eighteen shields of district arms encircle crown above three shields with lion on each **Rev:** Scene depicting legend of the blinding of St. Leodegar **Note:** Struck with 1 Thaler dies. KM#10. Fr. 290.

Date	Mintage	VG	F	VF	XF	Unc
1603 Rare	—	—	—	—	—	—

KM# C42 6 DUCAT

21.0000 g., 0.9860 Gold 0.6657 oz. AGW **Obv:** Ornate oval arms **Rev:** St. Leodegar standing facing **Note:** Struck with 1 Thaler dies. KM#40. Fr. #298.

Date	Mintage	VG	F	VF	XF	Unc
1698 Rare	—	—	—	—	—	—

KM# B15 10 DUCAT

35.0000 g., 0.9860 Gold 1.1095 oz. AGW **Obv:** Eighteen shields of district arms encircle crown above three shields with lion on each side **Rev:** Scene depicting legend of the blinding of St. Leodegar **Note:** Struck with 1 Thaler dies. KM#10. Fr. #289.

Date	Mintage	VG	F	VF	XF	Unc
1603 Rare	—	—	—	—	—	—

KM# A25 10 DUCAT

35.0000 g., 0.9860 Gold 1.1095 oz. AGW **Obv:** Crowned imperial eagle **Obv. Legend:** MONETA + NOVA + LVCERNENSIS * **Rev:** St. Leodegar standing facing with crook and borer **Rev. Legend:** SANCTVS * LEODIGARIVS * P * **Note:** Struck with 1 Thaler dies. KM#24. Fr. #291.

Date	Mintage	VG	F	VF	XF	Unc
1622 Rare	—	—	—	—	—	—

KM# 42 10 DUCAT

35.0000 g., 0.9860 Gold 1.1095 oz. AGW **Obv:** Ornate oval arms **Rev:** St. Leodegar standing facing **Note:** Struck with 1 Thaler dies. KM#40. Fr. #297.

Date	Mintage	VG	F	VF	XF	Unc
1698 Rare	—	—	—	—	—	—

PATTERNS

Including off metal strikes

KM#	Date	Mintage	Identification	Mkt Val
Pn1	1621	—	Schilling. Gold. KM#17.	2,000
Pn2	1621	—	1/2 Dicken. Gold. Weight of 2 Goldgulden, KM#21.	—
Pn3	1622	—	1/2 Dicken. Gold. Weight of 1 Goldgulden, KM#21.	—
Pn4	1638	—	Batzen. Gold. 6.6000 g. KM#29.	2,500
Pn5	1639	—	Batzen. Gold. KM#25.	2,000

NEUCHATEL

Nuenberg

A canton on the west central border of Switzerland. The first coins (bracteates) were struck in the 11th century. They were under Prussian rule from 1707 to 1806. France occupied the canton from 1806-1815. They reverted to Prussia until 1857, when they became a full member of the Swiss Confederation.

NOTE: For coins previously listed here dated 1707-1806, see German States, Prussia.

RULERS

Henri II, 1595-1663
Jean Louis, 1663-1671
Charles Paris, 1671-1673
Marie de Orleans-Nemours, 1672-1707

MONETARY SYSTEM

4 Kreuzer = 1 Batzen
7 Kreuzer = 1 Piecette
21 Batzen = 1 Gulden
2 Gulden = 1 Thaler

CANTON

STANDARD COINAGE

KM# 24 1/2 KREUZER

Billon

Date	Mintage	VG	F	VF	XF	Unc
1617 Rare	—	—	—	—	—	—
ND(1666)	—	50.00	125	475	—	—

KM# 6 KREUZER

Billon **Obv:** Crowned four-fold arms divide date **Rev:** Cross wtih forked ends in inner circle

Date	Mintage	VG	F	VF	XF	Unc
1606	—	20.00	48.00	200	—	—
1610	—	20.00	48.00	200	—	—
1611	—	35.00	80.00	275	—	—
1613	—	35.00	80.00	275	—	—
1614	—	35.00	80.00	275	—	—
1615 Rare	—	—	—	—	—	—
1616	—	20.00	48.00	200	—	—
1617	—	20.00	48.00	200	—	—
1618	—	20.00	48.00	200	—	—
1619 Rare	—	—	—	—	—	—

KM# 11 KREUZER

Billon **Obv:** Four fields of arms connected

Date	Mintage	VG	F	VF	XF	Unc
ND	—	22.00	48.00	200	—	—
1621	—	22.00	48.00	200	—	—
1622	—	22.00	48.00	200	—	—
1629	—	22.00	48.00	200	—	—

KM# 15 KREUZER

Billon **Obv:** Crowned two-fold arms divide date **Rev:** Cross with fleur-de-lis in angles

Date	Mintage	VG	F	VF	XF	Unc
1630	—	15.00	32.00	125	—	—
1631	—	15.00	32.00	125	—	—
1640	—	15.00	32.00	125	—	—

KM# 21 10 KREUZER

Silver **Obv:** Armored and draped bust right **Rev:** Crowned two-fold arms

Date	Mintage	VG	F	VF	XF	Unc
ND(1648)	—	40.00	80.00	275	—	—

KM# 25 10 KREUZER

Silver **Obv:** Draped bust with long hair right **Rev:** Crowned two-fold arms divide date

Date	Mintage	VG	F	VF	XF	Unc
1668	—	1,500	3,200	6,500	—	—

KM# 27 16 KREUZER

Silver

Date	Mintage	VG	F	VF	XF	Unc
1694	—	20.00	40.00	125	200	325

KM# 28 20 KREUZER

Silver **Obv:** Bust of Marie right **Rev:** Crowned arms

Date	Mintage	VG	F	VF	XF	Unc
1694 Rare	—	—	—	—	—	—
1695	—	35.00	80.00	200	400	—

KM# 8 1/2 BATZEN

Billon **Obv:** Crowned four-fold arms divide date **Rev:** Cross with prongs at end in inner circle

Date	Mintage	VG	F	VF	XF	Unc
ND Rare	—	—	—	—	—	—
1615 Rare	—	—	—	—	—	—
1619 Rare	—	—	—	—	—	—

KM# 22 1/2 BATZEN

Billon **Obv:** Crowned two-fold arms divide date **Rev:** Cross with prongs at end, fleur-de-lis in angles

Date	Mintage	VG	F	VF	XF	Unc
1648	—	20.00	40.00	165	—	—
1649	—	20.00	40.00	165	—	—

KM# 12 BATZEN

Billon **Obv:** Crowned four-fold arms in inner circle **Rev:** Cross with prongs in inner circle

Date	Mintage	VG	F	VF	XF	Unc
1621 Rare	—	—	—	—	—	—

KM# 13 BATZEN

Billon **Rev:** Date divided by bottom of cross

Date	Mintage	VG	F	VF	XF	Unc
1622	—	20.00	40.00	160	—	—

KM# 9 TESTON (1 Dicken)

Silver **Obv:** Bust left **Obv. Legend:** HEN. DVX. LONGAVIL. CO. S. NEOC. **Rev:** Crowned four-fold arms dividing date **Rev. Legend:** OCVLI. DOMINI. SVPER. IVSTOS.

Date	Mintage	VG	F	VF	XF	Unc
1618 Rare	—	—	—	—	—	—

KM# 16 TESTON (1 Dicken)

Silver **Obv:** Draped bust right **Rev:** Crowned two-fold arms, date below

Date	Mintage	VG	F	VF	XF	Unc
1631	—	3,500	8,000	20,000	—	—

KM# 17 TESTON (1 Dicken)

Silver **Shape:** 8-sided **Note:** Klippe.

Date	Mintage	VG	F	VF	XF	Unc
1631 Rare	—	—	—	—	—	—

KM# 29 1/4 THALER (1/4 Ecu)

Silver **Obv:** Draped bust right **Rev:** Crowned four-fold arms

Date	Mintage	VG	F	VF	XF	Unc
1694	—	300	650	1,600	3,200	—

KM# 19 THALER (1 Ecu)

Silver **Obv:** Draped bust right **Rev:** Crowned two-fold arms divide date **Note:** Dav. #4626.

Date	Mintage	VG	F	VF	XF	Unc
163Z Rare	—	—	—	—	—	—

KM# 5.1 2 PISTOLES

15.2800 g., 0.9000 Gold 0.4421 oz. AGW **Obv:** Bust of Henri II left **Rev:** Crowned arms **Note:** Fr. #335.

Date	Mintage	VG	F	VF	XF	Unc
1603	—	—	20,000	40,000	—	—

KM# 5.2 2 PISTOLES

15.2800 g., 0.9000 Gold 0.4421 oz. AGW **Obv:** Bust of Henri II left **Rev:** Crowned arms **Note:** Fr. #336.

Date	Mintage	VG	F	VF	XF	Unc
1618 Rare	—	—	—	—	—	—

KM# 18 2 PISTOLES

15.2800 g., 0.9000 Gold 0.4421 oz. AGW **Obv:** Bust of Henri II right **Note:** Fr. #337.

Date	Mintage	VG	F	VF	XF	Unc
1631 Rare	—	—	—	—	—	—

KM# 30 2 PISTOLES

15.2800 g., 0.9000 Gold 0.4421 oz. AGW **Obv:** Bust of Marie right **Rev:** Crowned 4-fold arms **Note:** Fr. #339.

Date	Mintage	VG	F	VF	XF	Unc
1694	—	—	12,000	24,000	40,000	—

Note: Bowers and Merena Guia sale 3-88 XF realized $28,600

KM# 31 4 PISTOLES

30.5600 g., 0.9000 Gold 0.8842 oz. AGW **Obv:** Bust of Marie right **Rev:** Crowned 4-fold arms **Note:** Fr. #338.

Date	Mintage	VG	F	VF	XF	Unc
1694 Unique	—	—	—	—	—	—

PATTERNS

Including off metal strikes

KM#	Date	Mintage	Identification	Mkt Val
Pn1	1618	—	Teston. Gold. 12.7500 g. KM#9.	—
Pn2	1618	—	Teston. Gold. 13.8700 g. KM#9.	—
Pn3	1631	—	Teston. Gold. 8.4500 g. KM#16.	—
Pn4	1631	—	Teston. Gold. 13.3500 g. KM#16.	—

SAINT GALL

ABBEY

An abbey in northeast Switzerland, established in c.720. They obtained the mint right in 947 but the first coins were not made until about 100 years later. The power of the abbey dwindled until the last Abbot resigned in 1805.

STANDARD COINAGE

KM# 8 THALER

Silver **Obv:** Crowned imperial eagle, four-fold arms on shield below **Rev:** Half-length saint with bread and staff

Date	Mintage	VG	F	VF	XF	Unc
1622	—	300	650	1,600	3,200	—

KM# 9 THALER

Silver **Note:** Klippe.

Date	Mintage	VG	F	VF	XF	Unc
1622 Rare	—	—	—	—	—	—

KM# 10 2 THALER

Silver **Obv:** Crowned imperial eagle, four-fold arms on shield below **Rev:** Half-length saint with bread and staff

Date	Mintage	VG	F	VF	XF	Unc
1622 Rare	—	3,500	8,000	20,000	—	—

KM# 11 2 THALER

Silver **Note:** Klippe.

Date	Mintage	VG	F	VF	XF	Unc
1622 Rare	—	—	—	—	—	—

CITY

A city located in northeast Switzerland which was built to protect the abbey. It became a free city in 1311 and gained independence from the Abbots in 1457. The first coins were struck in the 1400s and the last ones in 1790.

MINT OFFICIALS' INITIALS

Initials	Date	Name
A		
A-H		
G		
H.G.Z., Z		Hans Georg Zolli Kofer
Z		

STANDARD COINAGE

KM# A51 PFENNIG

Billon **Note:** Uniface.

Date	Mintage	VG	F	VF	XF	Unc
ND	—	15.00	40.00	120	250	—

KM# 51 3 KREUZER

Billon **Obv:** Standing bear left in inner circle **Rev:** Crowned imperial eagle with 3 in circle on breast

Date	Mintage	VG	F	VF	XF	Unc
1618	—	70.00	165	400	800	—
1619	—	70.00	165	400	800	—

KM# 52 3 KREUZER

Billon **Note:** Klippe.

Date	Mintage	VG	F	VF	XF	Unc
1618 Rare	—	—	—	—	—	—

KM# 66 4 KREUZER (1 Batzen)

Billon, 26 mm. **Obv:** Bear standing left divides date, value in oval shield below **Rev:** Eagle on shield on long cross

Date	Mintage	VG	F	VF	XF	Unc
1621	—	70.00	160	475	1,200	—

KM# 67 4 KREUZER (1 Batzen)

Billon, 22 mm. **Obv:** Bear standing left divides value, date below

Date	Mintage	VG	F	VF	XF	Unc
1621	—	30.00	60.00	200	—	—
1622	—	35.00	80.00	225	—	—

KM# 68 4 KREUZER (1 Batzen)

Billon **Note:** Klippe.

Date	Mintage	VG	F	VF	XF	Unc
1621	—	70.00	150	325	700	—
1622	—	70.00	150	325	700	—

KM# 56 3 BATZEN (1/2 Dicken)

Silver **Obv:** Bear standing left, date below **Rev:** Crowned imperial eagle in inner circle, 3 below

Date	Mintage	VG	F	VF	XF	Unc
1619	—	90.00	200	450	—	—
1620	—	450	100	250	—	—
1621	—	22.00	50.00	125	—	—
1622	—	22.00	50.00	125	—	—
1624	—	22.00	50.00	125	—	—

KM# 58 3 BATZEN (1/2 Dicken)

Silver **Note:** Klippe.

Date	Mintage	VG	F	VF	XF	Unc
1620	—	100	250	500	1,000	—
1621	—	100	250	500	1,000	—
1622	—	100	250	500	1,000	—

KM# 53 1/2 DICKEN

Silver **Obv:** Bear standing left, date in legend **Rev:** Crowned imperial eagle in inner circle

Date	Mintage	VG	F	VF	XF	Unc
1618	—	1,000	2,400	6,000	—	—
1619 Rare	—	700	1,600	4,000	—	—

KM# 70 24 KREUZER (6 Batzen - 1 Dicken)

Silver **Obv:** Bear standing left **Rev:** Imperial eagle

Date	Mintage	VG	F	VF	XF	Unc
1631	—	150	325	800	—	—
1633	—	175	400	950	—	—

KM# 54 DICKEN (6 Batzen)

Silver **Note:** Similar to 1/2 Thaler, KM#59.

Date	Mintage	VG	F	VF	XF	Unc
1618	—	70.00	150	325	—	—
1619	—	55.00	120	275	—	—
1620	—	35.00	80.00	200	—	—
1621	—	30.00	65.00	165	—	—

KM# 57 DICKEN (6 Batzen)

Silver **Note:** Klippe.

Date	Mintage	VG	F	VF	XF	Unc
1619	—	200	400	800	1,500	—
1620	—	150	300	600	1,350	—
1621 Rare	—	—	—	—	—	—
1622 Rare	—	—	—	—	—	—

KM# 59 1/2 THALER

Silver **Obv:** Bear standing left **Obv. Legend:** Crowned imperial eagle

Date	Mintage	VG	F	VF	XF	Unc
1620	—	110	240	600	1,200	—

KM# 60 1/2 THALER
Silver **Note:** Klippe. Illustration reduced.

Date	Mintage	VG	F	VF	XF	Unc
1620	—	150	325	800	1,500	—

KM# 62 THALER
Silver **Note:** Klippe. Dav. #4677A.

Date	Mintage	VG	F	VF	XF	Unc
1620	—	100	200	400	800	—
1621	—	70.00	175	350	600	—
1622	—	100	200	400	750	—
1623	—	70.00	175	350	600	—

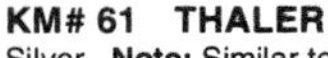

KM# 61 THALER
Silver **Note:** Similar to 1/2 Thaler, KM#59. Dav. #4677.

Date	Mintage	VG	F	VF	XF	Unc
1620	—	35.00	90.00	200	—	—
1621	—	30.00	75.00	165	—	—
1622	—	30.00	75.00	165	—	—
1623	—	35.00	90.00	200	—	—
1624	—	50.00	120	250	—	—

KM# 64 2 THALER
Silver **Obv:** Bear standing left **Rev:** Crowned imperial eagle **Note:** Klippe. Dav. #4676A.

Date	Mintage	VG	F	VF	XF	Unc
1620 Rare	—	—	—	—	—	—
1621 Rare	—	—	—	—	—	—
1622 Rare	—	—	—	—	—	—

KM# 63 2 THALER
Silver **Obv:** Bear standing left **Rev:** Crowned imperial eagle **Note:** Similar to 1/2 Thaler, KM#59. Dav. #4676.

Date	Mintage	VG	F	VF	XF	Unc
1620 Rare	—	—	—	—	—	—
1621	—	950	2,000	4,800	—	—

TRADE COINAGE

KM# A55 2 DUCAT
7.0000 g., 0.9860 Gold 0.2219 oz. AGW **Obv:** Bear standing walking left **Rev:** Imperial eagle **Note:** Fr. #361.

Date	Mintage	VG	F	VF	XF	Unc
1618 Rare	—	—	—	—	—	—
1619 Rare	—	—	—	—	—	—

KM# 69 2 DUCAT
7.0000 g., 0.9860 Gold 0.2219 oz. AGW **Obv:** Bear walking left in inner circle, date in legend **Rev:** Imperial eagle **Note:** Fr. #362.

Date	Mintage	VG	F	VF	XF	Unc
1621	—	1,200	2,400	5,000	8,500	—

KM# 55 3 DUCAT
10.5000 g., 0.9860 Gold 0.3328 oz. AGW **Obv:** Bear walking left in inner circle, date in legend **Rev:** Imperial eagle **Note:** Fr. #360.

Date	Mintage	VG	F	VF	XF	Unc
1618 Unique	—	—	—	—	—	—
1619 Unique	—	—	—	—	—	—

KM# 65 4 DUCAT
14.0000 g., 0.9860 Gold 0.4438 oz. AGW **Obv:** Bear walking left in inner circle, date in legend **Rev:** Crowned imperial eagle **Note:** Klippe. Fr. #359.

Date	Mintage	VG	F	VF	XF	Unc
1620 Unique	—	—	—	—	—	—

PATTERNS

Including off metal strikes

KM#	Date	Mintage	Identification	Mkt Val
PnA1	1621	—	1/2 Dicken. Klippe.	—
Pn1	ND	—	Pfennig. Gold. KM#5	—

KM#	Date	Mintage	Identification	Mkt Val
Pn2	1621	—	2 Ducat. Silver. 6.9500 g. KM#69	400

SCHAFFHAUSEN

A canton located on the north central border of Switzerland. The first coins, which were issued in the 13th century were known as "Ram Bracteates". It joined the Swiss Confederation in 1501.

MONETARY SYSTEM
4 Kreuzer = 1 Batzen

CANTON

STANDARD COINAGE

KM# 5 HELLER
Billon **Note:** Uniface. Schussel type. Ram leaping over town gate.

Date	Mintage	VG	F	VF	XF	Unc
ND	—	150	400	1,600	—	—

KM# 6 4 HELLER (Vierer)
Billon **Obv:** Ram leaping over town gate, three hills above **Rev:** Eagle facing right

Date	Mintage	VG	F	VF	XF	Unc
ND	—	70.00	150	450	1,200	—

KM# 7 4 HELLER (Vierer)
Billon **Rev:** Eagle facing left

Date	Mintage	VG	F	VF	XF	Unc
ND	—	70.00	150	450	1,200	—
1610 Rare	—	—	—	—	—	—
(16)16 Rare	—	—	—	—	—	—

KM# 8 4 HELLER (Vierer)
Billon **Note:** Klippe.

Date	Mintage	VG	F	VF	XF	Unc
ND Rare	—	—	—	—	—	—
(16)16 Rare	—	—	—	—	—	—

KM# 9 4 HELLER (Vierer)
Billon **Rev:** 4 on round shield on eagle's breast

Date	Mintage	VG	F	VF	XF	Unc
ND	—	15.00	30.00	60.00	—	—
1626	—	30.00	75.00	300	—	—
1627	—	30.00	75.00	300	—	—
1628	—	30.00	75.00	300	—	—
1630 Rare	—	—	—	—	—	—

KM# 10 PFENNIG
Billon Or Copper **Note:** Ram jumping out of town gate over grassy bush.

Date	Mintage	VG	F	VF	XF	Unc
ND	—	20.00	40.00	150	400	—

KM# 11 PFENNIG

Billon Or Copper **Note:** Ram jumping out of town gate over three hills.

Date	Mintage	VG	F	VF	XF	Unc
ND	—	50.00	100	450	—	—

KM# 12 PFENNIG

Billon Or Copper **Note:** Upright ram standing left.

Date	Mintage	VG	F	VF	XF	Unc
ND	—	40.00	80.00	300	800	—

KM# 13 KREUZER

Billon **Obv:** Ram standing left **Rev:** Crowned imperial eagle, 1 in round shield on breast

Date	Mintage	VG	F	VF	XF	Unc
ND Rare	—	—	—	—	—	—

KM# 41 2 KREUZER (1/2 Batzen)

Billon **Obv:** Ram jumping from town gate over grassy bush **Rev:** Crowned imperial eagle with 2 on breast

Date	Mintage	VG	F	VF	XF	Unc
1626	—	75.00	150	600	—	—
1698	—	80.00	200	800	1,600	3,000

KM# 59 2 KREUZER (1/2 Batzen)

Billon **Note:** Klippe.

Date	Mintage	VG	F	VF	XF	Unc
1698 Rare	—	—	—	—	—	—

KM# 15 3 KREUZER (1 Groschen)

Silver **Obv:** Ram jumping left from town gate over three hills **Rev:** Crowned imperial eagle with 3 on round shield on breast

Date	Mintage	VG	F	VF	XF	Unc
1605 Rare	—	—	—	—	—	—
1609 Rare	—	—	—	—	—	—
1611	—	10.00	20.00	60.00	125	—
(16)16	—	25.00	45.00	125	275	—
1619	—	35.00	75.00	150	350	—
161x	—	30.00	70.00	150	350	—

KM# 17 3 KREUZER (1 Groschen)

Silver **Note:** Klippe.

Date	Mintage	VG	F	VF	XF	Unc
1607 Rare	—	—	—	—	—	—
1611 Rare	—	—	—	—	—	—
1619 Rare	—	—	—	—	—	—

KM# 27 3 KREUZER (1 Groschen)

Billon **Rev:** Crowned imperial eagle on anchor cross, arms extend into legend

Date	Mintage	VG	F	VF	XF	Unc
ND	—	20.00	45.00	125	200	—
1622	—	25.00	50.00	150	300	—

KM# 28 3 KREUZER (1 Groschen)

Billon **Note:** Klippe.

Date	Mintage	VG	F	VF	XF	Unc
1622	—	—	—	—	—	—

KM# 35 3 KREUZER (1 Groschen)

Silver **Rev:** 3 in round shield divides date at bottom

Date	Mintage	VG	F	VF	XF	Unc
1623	—	20.00	45.00	100	225	—

KM# 36 3 KREUZER (1 Groschen)

Silver **Obv:** Date in legend **Rev:** 3 between ornaments below eagle

Date	Mintage	VG	F	VF	XF	Unc
1624	—	7.00	40.00	100	225	—
1625	—	30.00	75.00	200	400	—
1626	—	15.00	30.00	75.00	150	—
1627	—	15.00	30.00	75.00	150	—
1628	—	15.00	30.00	75.00	150	—
1629	—	15.00	30.00	75.00	150	—
1633	—	15.00	30.00	75.00	150	—
1634	—	15.00	30.00	75.00	150	—

KM# 37 3 KREUZER (1 Groschen)

Silver **Note:** Klippe.

Date	Mintage	VG	F	VF	XF	Unc
1624	—	—	—	—	—	—

KM# 48 4 KREUZER (1 Batzen)

Billon, 23 mm. **Obv:** Crowned ram walking left **Rev:** Crowned imperial eagle with 4 on breast

Date	Mintage	VG	F	VF	XF	Unc
1657	—	20.00	40.00	160	—	—

KM# 50 4 KREUZER (1 Batzen)

Billon, 26 mm.

Date	Mintage	VG	F	VF	XF	Unc
1657	—	30.00	60.00	200	—	—
1658	—	40.00	80.00	300	—	—

KM# 49 4 KREUZER (1 Batzen)

Billon **Note:** Klippe.

Date	Mintage	VG	F	VF	XF	Unc
1657	—	—	—	—	—	—

KM# 51 4 KREUZER (1 Batzen)

Billon **Note:** Klippe.

Date	Mintage	VG	F	VF	XF	Unc
1657	—	—	—	—	—	—

KM# 21 12 KREUZER (1/2 Dicken - Zwolfer)

Silver **Obv:** Ram standing right, date in legend **Rev:** Crowned imperial eagle with 1Z on breast

Date	Mintage	VG	F	VF	XF	Unc
(16)16	—	100	250	500	—	—
1619	—	100	250	500	—	—
1620	—	70.00	150	300	—	—
1621	—	90.00	200	400	—	—

KM# 22 12 KREUZER (1/2 Dicken - Zwolfer)

Silver **Note:** Klippe.

Date	Mintage	VG	F	VF	XF	Unc
(16)16	—	—	—	—	—	—
1619	—	—	—	—	—	—
1621	—	—	—	—	—	—

KM# 31 12 KREUZER (1/2 Dicken - Zwolfer)

Billon **Note:** Klippe.

Date	Mintage	VG	F	VF	XF	Unc
1622	—	—	—	—	—	—

KM# 29 12 KREUZER (1/2 Dicken - Zwolfer)

Billon **Obv:** Ram jumping from town gate over three hills, date above **Rev:** Crowned imperial eagle with 12 on breast

Date	Mintage	VG	F	VF	XF	Unc
1622	—	15.00	30.00	125	—	—

KM# 30 12 KREUZER (1/2 Dicken - Zwolfer)

Billon **Rev:** Date above eagle

Date	Mintage	VG	F	VF	XF	Unc
1622	—	15.00	30.00	125	150	—

KM# 43 12 KREUZER (1/2 Dicken - Zwolfer)

Billon **Obv:** Ram jumping right over three hills **Rev:** Crowned imperial eagle with 12 on breast, date below

Date	Mintage	VG	F	VF	XF	Unc
1627	—	650	1,400	3,000	—	—

KM# 52 15 KREUZER (Ortli)

Silver **Rev:** Value "XV"

Date	Mintage	VG	F	VF	XF	Unc
ND	—	150	300	725	—	—

KM# 53 15 KREUZER (Ortli)

Silver **Obv:** Without ornamentation in legend **Rev:** Without ornamentation in legend, 15 on breast of eagle

Date	Mintage	VG	F	VF	XF	Unc
1657	—	25.00	50.00	125	—	—
1658	—	120	250	500	—	—

KM# 54 15 KREUZER (Ortli)

Silver **Obv. Legend:** DEVS SPES NOSTRA EST **Rev. Legend:** DEVS SPES NOSTRA EST

Date	Mintage	VG	F	VF	XF	Unc
ND	—	100	225	600	—	—

KM# 38 24 KREUZER (1 Dicken)

Silver **Obv:** Ram jumping from town gate over three hills, date in legend **Rev:** Crowned imperial eagle, 24 on round shield on breast

Date	Mintage	VG	F	VF	XF	Unc
1624	—	200	450	1,200	—	—

KM# 39 24 KREUZER (1 Dicken)

Silver **Note:** Klippe.

Date	Mintage	VG	F	VF	XF	Unc
1624	—	—	—	—	—	—

KM# 18 DICKEN

Silver **Rev:** Imperial eagle

Date	Mintage	VG	F	VF	XF	Unc
1611	—	25.00	60.00	125	—	—
1614	—	20.00	80.00	100	—	—
(16)16	—	275	600	1,500	—	—
1617	—	25.00	60.00	150	—	—
1620	—	100	250	600	—	—
1621	—	100	250	600	—	—

KM# 23 DICKEN

Silver **Note:** Klippe.

Date	Mintage	VG	F	VF	XF	Unc
1617	—	—	—	—	—	—
1620	—	—	—	—	—	—
1621	—	—	—	—	—	—

KM# 40 DICKEN

Silver **Obv:** Similar to KM#18 **Rev:** Similar to KM#42

Date	Mintage	VG	F	VF	XF	Unc
1624//1631 Rare	—	—	—	—	—	—

KM# 42 DICKEN

Silver

Date	Mintage	VG	F	VF	XF	Unc
1626	—	500	1,200	2,750	—	—
1627	—	500	1,200	2,750	—	—
1631	—	35.00	80.00	200	400	—
1632	—	35.00	80.00	200	400	—
1633	—	35.00	80.00	200	400	—
1634	—	35.00	80.00	200	400	—
1635 Rare	—	—	—	—	—	—

KM# 45 DICKEN

Silver **Note:** Klippe.

Date	Mintage	VG	F	VF	XF	Unc
1633	—	—	—	—	—	—

KM# 26 1/2 THALER
Silver **Rev:** Imperial eagle

Date	Mintage	VG	F	VF	XF	Unc
1621	—	125	275	625	—	—

KM# 25 THALER
Silver **Obv:** Similar to 1/2 Thaler, KM#26 **Rev:** Imperial eagle **Note:** Dav. #4627.

Date	Mintage	VG	F	VF	XF	Unc
1620	—	35.00	80.00	200	—	—
1621	—	35.00	80.00	200	—	—
1622	—	35.00	80.00	200	—	—
1623	—	35.00	80.00	200	—	—
1624 Rare	—	—	—	—	—	—

KM# 47 THALER
Silver **Obv:** Similar to 1/2 Thaler, KM#26 but date divided at top **Rev:** Crowned imperial eagle **Note:** Dav. #4628.

Date	Mintage	VG	F	VF	XF	Unc
1656 HMA	—	900	2,000	4,750	—	—

COUNTERSTAMPED COINAGE

KM# 55 15 KREUZER
Silver **Countermark:** Crowned ram head in circle **Note:** Counterstamp on KM#52.

CS Date	Host Date	Good	VG	F	VF	XF
ND(1657)	1657	—	22.00	50.00	125	—
ND	1658	—	300	625	1,200	—

KM# 56 15 KREUZER
Silver **Countermark:** Crowned ram head in circle **Note:** Counterstamp on KM#54.

CS Date	Host Date	Good	VG	F	VF	XF
	ND	—	120	240	600	—

TRADE COINAGE

KM# 32 GOLDGULDEN
3.5000 g., 0.9860 Gold 0.1109 oz. AGW **Obv:** Ram leaping to left from doorway in inner circle **Obv. Legend:** MO NO AVREA... **Rev:** Crowned imperial eagle in inner circle **Note:** Fr. #368.

Date	Mintage	VG	F	VF	XF	Unc
1622	—	2,000	4,000	8,000	—	—

KM# 33 GOLDGULDEN
3.5000 g., 0.9860 Gold 0.1109 oz. AGW **Obv. Legend:** MONETA NOVA... **Note:** Fr. #368.

Date	Mintage	VG	F	VF	XF	Unc
1622 Rare	—	—	—	—	—	—
1633 Rare	—	—	—	—	—	—

KM# 34 1/2 DUCAT
1.7500 g., 0.9860 Gold 0.0555 oz. AGW **Obv:** Shield of arms in inner circle **Rev:** Crowned imperial eagle in inner circle **Note:** Fr. #370.

Date	Mintage	VG	F	VF	XF	Unc
ND Rare	—	—	—	—	—	—

KM# 19 DUCAT
3.5000 g., 0.9860 Gold 0.1109 oz. AGW **Rev:** Crowned imperial eagle with two heads **Note:** Fr. #369.

Date	Mintage	VG	F	VF	XF	Unc
1614 Rare	—	—	—	—	—	—

KM# 20 DUCAT
3.5000 g., 0.9860 Gold 0.1109 oz. AGW **Rev:** Crowned imperial eagle with one head **Note:** Fr. #369.

Date	Mintage	VG	F	VF	XF	Unc
1614 Rare	—	—	—	—	—	—

KM# 46 DUCAT
3.5000 g., 0.9860 Gold 0.1109 oz. AGW **Obv:** Modified shield **Note:** Fr. #370.

Date	Mintage	VG	F	VF	XF	Unc
1633	—	450	950	200	3,200	—
1657/33	—	800	1,750	3,600	6,000	—

KM# 57 DUCAT
3.5000 g., 0.9860 Gold 0.1109 oz. AGW **Note:** Fr. #370.

Date	Mintage	VG	F	VF	XF	Unc
ND(1658)	—	550	1,150	2,150	3,600	—

KM# A41 3 DUCAT
10.5000 g., 0.9860 Gold 0.3328 oz. AGW **Obv:** Ram jumping from town gate **Rev:** Imperial eagle with 24 on breast **Note:** Struck with 24 Kreuzer dies, KM#38.

Date	Mintage	VG	F	VF	XF	Unc
1624 Rare	—	—	—	—	—	—

KM# 44 3 DUCAT
10.5000 g., 0.9860 Gold 0.3328 oz. AGW **Obv:** Ram jumping from town gate **Rev:** Imperial eagle, date in exergue **Note:** Struck with 1 Dicken dies, KM#42.

Date	Mintage	VG	F	VF	XF	Unc
1632	—	—	—	20,000	25,000	—

KM# 24 5 DUCAT
17.5000 g., 0.9860 Gold 0.5547 oz. AGW **Obv:** Ram jumping from town gate **Rev:** Imperial eagle **Note:** Struck with 1/2 Thaler dies, KM#26.

Date	Mintage	VG	F	VF	XF	Unc
1621 Rare	—	—	—	—	—	—

KM# A48 20 DUCAT
70.0000 g., 0.9860 Gold 2.2190 oz. AGW **Obv:** Ram jumping from town gate **Rev:** Crowned imperial eagle **Note:** Struck with 1 Thaler dies, KM#47.

Date	Mintage	VG	F	VF	XF	Unc
1656 Rare	—	—	—	—	—	—

PATTERNS

Including off metal strikes

KM#	Date	Mintage	Identification	Mkt Val
Pn1	ND(1630)	—	4 Heller. Gold. Eagle facing right, KM#6.	—
Pn2	ND(1630)	—	4 Heller. Gold. Eagle facing left, klippe, KM#8.	—
Pn3	ND(1630)	—	4 Heller. Gold. 4 on eagle's breast, KM#9.	—
Pn4	ND	—	Pfennig. Gold. KM#10.	—
Pn5	1611	—	Dicken. Gold. Klippe, KM#18.	25,000
Pn6	(16)16	—	12 Kreuzer. Gold. KM#21.	10,000

SCHWYZ

Schwytz, Suitensis

A canton in central Switzerland. In 1291 it became one of the three cantons that would ultimately become the Swiss Confederation and were known as the "Everlasting League". The first coinage was issued in1624.

MONETARY SYSTEM
Until 1798

240 Angster = 120 Rappen
= 40 Schillinge = 1 Gulden
4 Kreuzer = 1 Batzen
40 Batzen = 3 Gulden = 1 Thaler
12 Gulden = 1 Duplone

CANTON

STANDARD COINAGE

KM# 5 RAPPEN
Billon **Note:** Uniface. Square-cornered arms.

Date	Mintage	VG	F	VF	XF	Unc
ND(1650)	—	18.00	40.00	150	400	—

KM# 6 RAPPEN
Billon **Note:** Curved and arched double arms.

Date	Mintage	VG	F	VF	XF	Unc
ND(1675)	—	15.00	30.00	125	250	—

KM# 7 RAPPEN
Billon **Note:** Small arched and curved arms.

Date	Mintage	VG	F	VF	XF	Unc
ND(1695)	—	15.00	30.00	125	250	—

KM# 8 SCHILLING
Billon **Obv:** Crowned imperial eagle, shield divides I-T at bottom **Rev:** Bust of Saint facing forward

Date	Mintage	VG	F	VF	XF	Unc
ND	—	4.00	8.00	40.00	125	—

KM# 15 SCHILLING
Billon **Obv:** Shield divides date at bottom

Date	Mintage	VG	F	VF	XF	Unc
1623	—	4.00	8.00	40.00	125	—
1624	—	4.00	8.00	40.00	125	—
1629	—	4.00	8.00	40.00	125	—
1630	—	4.00	8.00	40.00	125	—
1633	—	4.00	8.00	40.00	125	—
1653	—	4.00	8.00	40.00	125	—
1654	—	4.00	8.00	40.00	125	—
1655	—	4.00	8.00	40.00	125	—
1656	—	12.00	25.00	50.00	200	—
1673	—	18.00	40.00	150	400	—

KM# 12 BATZEN
Billon **Obv:** Spanish shield on anchor cross **Rev:** Crowned imperial eagle

Date	Mintage	VG	F	VF	XF	Unc
1622	—	40.00	95.00	240	—	—

KM# 13 BATZEN
Billon **Obv:** Curved and arched shield on anchor cross

Date	Mintage	VG	F	VF	XF	Unc
1622	—	35.00	80.00	200	—	—

KM# 14 BATZEN
Billon **Obv:** Square-cornered shield on anchor cross

Date	Mintage	VG	F	VF	XF	Unc
1622	—	30.00	65.00	165	—	—

KM# 16 BATZEN
Billon **Obv:** Plain square-cornered shield on anchor corss, date below

Date	Mintage	VG	F	VF	XF	Unc
1623	—	15.00	32.00	80.00	—	—

KM# 17 BATZEN
Billon **Obv:** Ornamentation on shield

Date	Mintage	VG	F	VF	XF	Unc
1623	—	15.00	32.00	80.00	—	—

KM# 18 BATZEN
Billon **Obv:** Plain curved and arched shield on anchor cross, date below

Date	Mintage	VG	F	VF	XF	Unc
1623	—	15.00	32.00	80.00	—	—
1624	—	12.00	24.00	65.00	—	—

KM# 20 BATZEN
Billon **Obv:** Ornamentation on shield

Date	Mintage	VG	F	VF	XF	Unc
1624	—	12.00	25.00	65.00	—	—

KM# 27 4 BATZEN (Ortli)
Silver **Obv:** Square-cornered shield on anchor corss, date in legend **Rev:** Crowned, small imperial eagle

Date	Mintage	VG	F	VF	XF	Unc
1672 Rare	—	700	1,600	3,750	—	—

KM# 28 4 BATZEN (Ortli)
Silver **Obv:** Ornamental arms, rosette on each side

Date	Mintage	VG	F	VF	XF	Unc
1672	—	55.00	120	325	—	—

KM# 29 4 BATZEN (Ortli)
Silver

Date	Mintage	VG	F	VF	XF	Unc
1672	—	55.00	125	325	—	—
1674	—	110	250	600	—	—

KM# 19 DICKEN
Silver

Date	Mintage	VG	F	VF	XF	Unc
1623	—	425	950	2,400	—	—
1629	—	700	1,600	3,600	—	—
1656	—	600	1,400	3,000	—	—

KM# 22 DICKEN

Silver **Rev:** Bust of St. Martin left wearing long robe

Date	Mintage	VG	F	VF	XF	Unc
1630	—	700	1,500	3,500	—	—

KM# 25 1/2 THALER

Silver **Obv:** Crowned imperial eagle, shield divides date below **Rev:** Similar to 1 Dicken, KM#19

Date	Mintage	VG	F	VF	XF	Unc
1656	—	1,000	2,400	5,000	—	—

KM# 24 THALER

Silver **Obv:** Crowned imperial eagle, shield below, date in legend **Rev:** Similar to 1 Dicken, KM#19 **Note:** Dav. #4629.

Date	Mintage	VG	F	VF	XF	Unc
1653	—	225	475	1,200	—	—

TRADE COINAGE

KM# 11.1 DUCAT

3.5000 g., 0.9860 Gold 0.1109 oz. AGW **Obv:** St. Martin on horseback **Obv. Legend:** Madonna standing with child **Note:** Fr. #377.

Date	Mintage	VG	F	VF	XF	Unc
ND(1621)	—	1,100	2,400	4,750	8,000	—
1653	—	1,100	2,400	4,750	8,000	—

KM# 11.2 DUCAT

3.5000 g., 0.9860 Gold 0.1109 oz. AGW **Obv:** St. Martin on horseback **Rev:** Madonna standing with child **Note:** Fr. #378

Date	Mintage	VG	F	VF	XF	Unc
1674 Rare	—	—	—	—	—	—

SITTEN

A canton which was founded in 580 that comprises most of the canton of Valais. Sitten was a Burgundian mint in the 9th century with the first Episcopal coinage being struck c. 1496. They joined the Swiss Confederation as Valais in 1815.

RULER

Hildebrand, 1565-1604

MINT OFFICIAL'S INITIALS

Initial	Date	Name
D-S		David Stedelin

CANTON

STANDARD COINAGE

KM# 5 QUART (Vierer)

Billon **Obv:** X with stars in angles **Rev:** Cross, date in legend

Date	Mintage	VG	F	VF	XF	Unc
1623 Rare	—	—	—	—	—	—
1627 Rare	—	—	—	—	—	—

KM# 23 QUART (Vierer)

Billon **Obv:** Clover in center, ADR and stars around **Rev:** Arms at center, W above, 8-5 at sides

Date	Mintage	VG	F	VF	XF	Unc
1685	—	25.00	60.00	250	600	—

KM# 6 KREUZER

Billon **Obv:** Mitre above crossed sword and crozier **Rev:** Cross in inner circle, date in legend

Date	Mintage	VG	F	VF	XF	Unc
1623	—	35.00	80.00	300	—	—
1624	—	35.00	80.00	300	—	—
1625	—	80.00	200	800	—	—

KM# 7 KREUZER

Billon **Obv:** Mitre above shield with clover leaves on crossed sword and crozier **Rev:** Eagle left above shield with seven stars

Date	Mintage	VG	F	VF	XF	Unc
ND	—	15.00	30.00	150	—	—

KM# 8 KREUZER

Billon **Obv:** Without sword and crozier

Date	Mintage	VG	F	VF	XF	Unc
ND Rare	—	—	—	—	—	—

KM# 9 1/2 BATZEN

Billon **Obv:** Shield with X in center, stars in field on crossed sword and crozier **Rev:** Anchor cross with beams in angles, date in legend

Date	Mintage	VG	F	VF	XF	Unc
1623	—	35.00	80.00	300	—	—
1624	—	35.00	80.00	300	—	—
1625	—	80.00	200	800	—	—
1627	—	35.00	80.00	300	—	—

KM# 15 1/2 BATZEN

Billon **Obv:** Mitre above shield with clover leaves and stars on crossed sword and crozier **Rev:** Eagle above shield with seven stars dividing date

Date	Mintage	VG	F	VF	XF	Unc
1644	—	15.00	30.00	150	—	—
1645	—	15.00	30.00	150	—	—
1646	—	15.00	30.00	150	—	—

KM# 18 1/2 BATZEN

Billon **Note:** Klippe.

Date	Mintage	VG	F	VF	XF	Unc
1646	—	—	—	—	—	—

KM# 20 1/2 BATZEN

Billon **Rev:** Crowned imperial eagle above shield

Date	Mintage	VG	F	VF	XF	Unc
1683	—	9.00	20.00	80.00	—	—
1684	—	9.00	20.00	80.00	—	—
1685	—	9.00	20.00	80.00	—	—

KM# 10 BATZEN

Billon **Obv:** Mitre above shield with X and stars on crossed sword and crozier **Rev:** Bust of saint left wearing mitre and holding sword and crozier

Date	Mintage	VG	F	VF	XF	Unc
1623	—	40.00	90.00	350	—	—
1624	—	40.00	90.00	350	—	—
1625 Rare	—	200	600	1,500	—	—
1627	—	40.00	90.00	350	—	—

KM# 16 BATZEN

Billon **Obv:** Mitre above shield with clover leaves on crossed sword and crozier **Rev:** Eagle above shield with seven stars dividing date

Date	Mintage	VG	F	VF	XF	Unc
1644	—	20.00	40.00	200	—	—

KM# 17 BATZEN

Billon **Note:** Klippe.

Date	Mintage	VG	F	VF	XF	Unc
1644	—	—	—	—	—	—

KM# 21 BATZEN

Billon

Date	Mintage	VG	F	VF	XF	Unc
1683	—	35.00	80.00	300	—	—

KM# 22 BATZEN

Billon **Rev:** Arms divide date in field

Date	Mintage	VG	F	VF	XF	Unc
1683	—	30.00	80.00	300	—	—
1684	—	12.50	25.00	125	—	—
1685	—	12.50	25.00	125	—	—

KM# 11 1/4 THALER (1 Teston)

Silver **Obv:** Mitre above shield with X in center, stars in field on sword and crozier **Rev:** Standing saint holding sword and crozier with foot on devil holding bell

Date	Mintage	VG	F	VF	XF	Unc
1624	—	1,500	3,000	8,000	—	—

KM# 12 1/2 THALER

Silver **Obv:** Mitre above shield with X in center, stars in field on sword and crozier **Rev:** Standing saint holding sword and crozier with foot on devil holding bell

Date	Mintage	VG	F	VF	XF	Unc
1624	—	2,000	4,000	9,000	—	—

TRADE COINAGE

KM# 13 DUCAT

3.5000 g., 0.9860 Gold 0.1109 oz. AGW **Obv:** Ornate cross in inner circle **Rev:** St. Theodolus above arms in inner circle **Note:** Fr. #381.

Date	Mintage	VG	F	VF	XF	Unc
ND(1565-1604) Rare	—	600	12,000	24,000	—	—

REPUBLIK WALLIS

1627-1630

STANDARD COINAGE

KM# 40 KREUZER

Billon **Obv:** Eagle above shield with seven stars **Rev:** Cross in inner circle, date in legend

Date	Mintage	VG	F	VF	XF	Unc
1628	—	35.00	75.00	165	—	—

KM# 41 KREUZER

Silver **Note:** Klippe.

Date	Mintage	VG	F	VF	XF	Unc
1628	—	—	—	—	—	—

KM# 42 1/2 BATZEN

Billon **Obv:** Eagle above shield with seven stars **Rev:** Anchor cross with fleur-de-lis in angles

Date	Mintage	VG	F	VF	XF	Unc
1628	—	15.00	32.00	80.00	—	—

KM# 43 DICKEN

Silver **Obv:** Shield with seven stars in cartouche in inner circle **Rev:** Crowned imperial eagle in inner circle, date below

Date	Mintage	VG	F	VF	XF	Unc
1628 Rare	—	4,000	9,000	20,000	—	—

PATTERNS

Including off metal strikes

KM#	Date	Mintage	Identification	Mkt Val
Pn1	ND	—	Kreuzer. Gold. Sword and crozier, KM#7.	—
Pn2	ND	—	Kreuzer. Silver. Without sword and crozier, KM#8.	—
Pn3	ND	—	Kreuzer. Gold. Without sword and crozier, KM#8.	—
Pn4	1644	—	Batzen. Silver. KM#16.	—
Pn5	1646	—	1/2 Batzen. Silver. KM#15.	—
Pn6	1684	—	Batzen. Gold. KM#22.	5,000

SOLOTHURN

Solodornensis, Soleure

A canton in northwest Switzerland. Bracteates were struck in the 1300s even though the mint right was not officially granted until 1381. They joined the Swiss Confederation in 1481.

MINT OFFICIAL'S INITIALS

Initials	Date	Name
T		Thiebaud

MONETARY SYSTEM

Until 1798

2 Vierer = 1 Kreuzer
4 Kreuzer = 1 Batzen
40 Batzen = 2 Gulden = 1 Thaler

CANTON

STANDARD COINAGE

KM# 5 1/2 KREUZER (Vierer)

Billon **Obv:** Eagle looking left above state arms **Rev:** Cross with prongs at end in inner circle

Date	Mintage	VG	F	VF	XF	Unc
ND	—	75.00	200	600	—	—
1622	—	300	700	2,000	—	—
1623	—	300	700	2,000	—	—
1624	—	150	400	1,000	—	—

KM# 4 KREUZER

Billon **Obv:** Arms divide S-O, Eagle above **Obv. Legend:** MONETA: SOLODORENSIS **Rev:** Short cross with prongs on ends, plain fields **Rev. Legend:** * SANCTVS * SVRBUS * **Note:** Klippe. Previous KM#7.

Date	Mintage	VG	F	VF	XF	Unc
1622 Rare	—	—	—	—	—	—

KM# 3 KREUZER

Billon **Obv:** Arms divide S-O, Eagle above **Obv. Legend:** MON: NO: SLODO **Rev:** Short cross with prongs on ends, plain fields in quarters **Rev. Legend:** SANCT: VRBVS **Note:** Previous KM#6.

Date	Mintage	VG	F	VF	XF	Unc
1622	—	15.00	30.00	125	—	—

KM# 6 KREUZER

Billon **Obv:** Curved, arched arms divide S-O, eagle above **Rev:** Cross with prongs on ends, fleur-de-lis in angles **Note:** Varieites exist.

Date	Mintage	VG	F	VF	XF	Unc
1623	—	10.00	20.00	80.00	200	—
1624	—	10.00	20.00	80.00	200	—
1627	—	15.00	32.00	100	250	—
1628	—	10.00	20.00	80.00	200	—
1629	—	10.00	20.00	80.00	200	—
1637	—	15.00	35.00	150	350	—
1640	—	10.00	20.00	80.00	200	—

KM# 10 1/2 BATZEN (2 Kreuzer)

Billon **Obv:** Curved and arched arms, eagle looking left above **Rev:** Bust of saint right, date in legend

Date	Mintage	VG	F	VF	XF	Unc
1623	—	15.00	32.00	125	275	—
1624	—	15.00	32.00	125	275	—

KM# 11 1/2 BATZEN (2 Kreuzer)

Billon **Note:** Klippe.

Date	Mintage	VG	F	VF	XF	Unc
1623	—	—	—	4,250	7,000	—

KM# 8 BATZEN

Billon **Obv:** Arms on cross in inner circle **Rev:** Bust of saint right dividing date

Date	Mintage	VG	F	VF	XF	Unc
16ZZ	—	350	750	3,000	—	—

KM# 9 BATZEN

Billon **Obv:** Eagle looking left above curved and arched arms **Rev:** Large cross with ornamentation in angles, date in legend

Date	Mintage	VG	F	VF	XF	Unc
16ZZ	—	150	350	1,500	—	—
16Z3	—	28.00	60.00	200	475	—
16Z4	—	35.00	80.00	250	600	—
1630	—	18.00	40.00	150	400	—
1631	—	12.00	25.00	95.00	250	—
1632	—	18.00	40.00	150	400	—
1637	—	35.00	80.00	250	600	—
1638	—	35.00	80.00	250	600	—
1642	—	12.00	25.00	95.00	250	—

KM# 12 BATZEN

Billon **Note:** Klippe.

Date	Mintage	VG	F	VF	XF	Unc
1623	—	—	—	—	—	—
1624	—	—	—	1,500	2,500	—

KM# 15 1/2 DICKEN

Silver **Obv:** Eagle looking left above arms dividing S-O **Rev:** Armored bust of saint right, date below

Date	Mintage	VG	F	VF	XF	Unc
1624 Rare	—	—	—	—	—	—

KM# 25 1/2 DICKEN

Silver **Obv:** Arms dividing S-O **Rev:** Crowned imperial eagle, date below

Date	Mintage	VG	F	VF	XF	Unc
1642 Rare	—	—	—	—	—	—

KM# 16 DICKEN

Silver **Obv:** Eagle looking left above arms dividing date **Rev:** Bust of saint in armor right

Date	Mintage	VG	F	VF	XF	Unc
1624 Rare	—	—	—	—	—	—

KM# 20 DICKEN

Silver **Obv:** Eagle looking left above arms dividing S-O, date below **Rev:** Half-length saint armored right

Date	Mintage	VG	F	VF	XF	Unc
1632 Rare	—	1,750	4,000	9,500	17,500	—

Note: Leu Numismatik Auction 66 5-96 XF realized $15,010

KM# 21 DICKEN

Silver **Obv:** Crowned imperial eagle, date below **Rev:** Half-length saint armored right, arms below

Date	Mintage	VG	F	VF	XF	Unc
1632	—	1,500	3,200	8,000	16,000	—

KM# 22 DICKEN

Silver **Obv:** Imperial eagle with arms on breast, date below **Rev:** Armored bust of saint right

Date	Mintage	VG	F	VF	XF	Unc
1633	—	600	1,200	3,200	6,000	—

KM# 26 DICKEN

Silver **Obv:** Arms on floreate cross **Rev:** Crowned imperial eagle, date below

Date	Mintage	VG	F	VF	XF	Unc
1642	—	850	1,750	3,600	7,200	—

KM# 27 DICKEN

Silver **Obv:** Arms with ornamentation around **Rev:** Imperial eagle

Date	Mintage	VG	F	VF	XF	Unc
1642	—	1,000	2,000	4,000	8,000	—

KM# 13 1/2 THALER

Silver **Obv:** Arms with crowned imperial eagle above divide date and S-O **Rev:** Standing saint in armor

Date	Mintage	VG	F	VF	XF	Unc
1623	—	1,500	3,200	6,500	—	—

KM# 14 THALER

Silver **Obv:** Standing saint in armor **Rev:** Crowned imperial eagle, date in legend **Note:** Dav. #4630.

Date	Mintage	VG	F	VF	XF	Unc
1623 Rare	—	—	—	—	—	—

TRADE COINAGE

KM# 18 1/2 DUCAT

1.7500 g., 0.9860 Gold 0.0555 oz. AGW **Obv:** Arms of Solothurn divides S-O, topped by date in inner circle **Rev:** St. Ursus standing in elongated inner circle **Note:** Fr. #387.

Date	Mintage	VG	F	VF	XF	Unc
1630	—	2,500	4,500	7,500	—	—

Note: Leu Numismatik Auction 66 5-96 VF-XF realized $12,640

KM# 19 DUCAT

3.5000 g., 0.9860 Gold 0.1109 oz. AGW **Obv:** Arms of Solothurn divides S-O below date in inner circle **Rev:** St. Ursus standing in elongated inner circle **Note:** Fr. #386.

Date	Mintage	VG	F	VF	XF	Unc
1630 Rare	—	—	—	—	—	—

KM# 23 DUCAT

3.5000 g., 0.9860 Gold 0.1109 oz. AGW **Obv:** Imperial eagle and arms **Rev:** St. Ursus standing facing **Note:** Fr. #388.

Date	Mintage	VG	F	VF	XF	Unc
ND(ca.1635)	—	4,000	9,000	18,000	32,000	—

Note: Leu Numismatik Auction 66 5-96 VF-XF realized $23,700

PATTERNS

Including off metal strikes

KM#	Date	Mintage	Identification	Mkt Val
Pn1	1623	—	Kreuzer. Gold. Klippe. KM#6.	9,500
Pn2	1624	—	Kreuzer. Gold. KM#6.	3,000
Pn3	1628	—	Kreuzer. Gold. KM#6.	3,000
Pn4	1642	—	Batzen. Gold. KM#9.	3,500

URI

Uranie

A canton in central Switzerland. It is one of the three original cantons which became the Swiss Confederation in 1291. They had their own coinage from the early 1600s until 1811.

MONETARY SYSTEM

10 Rappen = 1 Batzen
10 Batzen = 1 Frank

CANTON

STANDARD COINAGE

KM# 23 KREUZER

Copper **Obv:** Arms in inner circle, date in legend **Rev:** Anchor cross in inner circle

Date	Mintage	VG	F	VF	XF	Unc
1622	—	35.00	80.00	200	475	—
1624	—	35.00	80.00	200	475	—
1627	—	35.00	80.00	200	475	—

KM# 5 SCHILLING

Billon **Obv:** Crowned imperial eagle, arms below, date in legend **Rev:** St. Martin standing facing forward

Date	Mintage	VG	F	VF	XF	Unc
1605	—	12.00	25.00	95.00	225	—
1608	—	12.00	25.00	95.00	225	—
1609	—	12.00	25.00	95.00	225	—
1610	—	12.00	25.00	95.00	225	—
1611	—	12.00	25.00	95.00	225	—
1612	—	9.00	20.00	80.00	200	—
1613	—	9.00	20.00	80.00	200	—
1614	—	9.00	20.00	80.00	200	—
1615	—	9.00	20.00	80.00	200	—
1616 Rare	—	—	—	—	—	—
1618 Rare	—	—	—	—	—	—
1619	—	9.00	20.00	80.00	200	—
1620 Rare	—	—	—	—	—	—
1621	—	30.00	70.00	150	450	—

KM# 24 SCHILLING

Billon **Obv:** Large arms in inner circle

Date	Mintage	VG	F	VF	XF	Unc
1622 Rare	—	—	—	—	—	—

KM# 25 SCHILLING

Billon **Obv:** Crowned double-headed eagle, date below **Rev:** St. Martin standing facing forward in long robe

Date	Mintage	VG	F	VF	XF	Unc
1623	—	8.00	16.00	60.00	150	—
1624	—	8.00	16.00	60.00	150	—
1627	—	8.00	16.00	60.00	150	—
1629	—	8.00	16.00	60.00	150	—
1630	—	8.00	16.00	60.00	150	—
1633	—	8.00	16.00	60.00	150	—
1641	—	30.00	85.00	300	750	—

KM# 20 1/2 BATZEN

Billon **Obv:** Crowned imperial eagle, arms below, date in legend **Rev:** Cross in inner circle

Date	Mintage	VG	F	VF	XF	Unc
1618 Rare	—	—	—	—	—	—

KM# 6 BATZEN-10 RAPPEN

Billon **Obv:** Large arms on Spanish shield, eagle above **Rev:** Anchor cross in inner circle, date in legend

Date	Mintage	VG	F	VF	XF	Unc
1607	—	400	900	2,800	—	—

KM# 15 BATZEN-10 RAPPEN

Billon **Obv:** Crowned imperial eagle above arms **Rev:** Large cross with fleur-de-lis in angles, date in legend

Date	Mintage	VG	F	VF	XF	Unc
1615 Rare	—	—	—	—	—	—

KM# 16 BATZEN-10 RAPPEN

Billon **Obv:** Ornamentation around arms **Rev:** Large cross on plain field

Date	Mintage	VG	F	VF	XF	Unc
1615 Rare	—	—	—	—	—	—
1616 Rare	—	550	1,200	3,200	—	—

KM# 22 BATZEN-10 RAPPEN

Billon **Obv:** Small shield with arms at center of anchor cross, date in legend **Rev:** Crowned imperial eagle

Date	Mintage	VG	F	VF	XF	Unc
1621	—	40.00	125	475	—	—
1622	—	15.00	32.00	125	—	—

KM# 26 BATZEN-10 RAPPEN

Billon **Obv:** Date below cross

Date	Mintage	VG	F	VF	XF	Unc
1624	—	18.00	40.00	125	—	—

KM# 27 BATZEN-10 RAPPEN

Billon **Obv:** Large arms, small eagle above **Rev:** Wide anchor cross in inner circle, date below

Date	Mintage	VG	F	VF	XF	Unc
1624	—	85.00	175	400	—	—

KM# 9 1/2 DICKEN

Silver **Obv:** Crowned imperial eagle above shield of arms divides date **Rev:** Bust of St. Martin in long robe right

Date	Mintage	VG	F	VF	XF	Unc
1610	—	500	1,200	3,000	—	—
1611 Rare	—	—	—	—	—	—

KM# 17 1/2 DICKEN

Silver **Obv:** Large crowned imperial eagle above small arms, date in legend

Date	Mintage	VG	F	VF	XF	Unc
1615 Rare	—	—	—	—	—	—

KM# 28 1/2 DICKEN

Silver **Obv:** Crowned imperial eagle, date below divided by arms

Date	Mintage	VG	F	VF	XF	Unc
1624 Rare	—	—	—	—	—	—

KM# 7 DICKEN

Silver **Obv:** Crowned imperial eagle, arms below divide date **Rev:** Bust of St. Martin in robe right

Date	Mintage	VG	F	VF	XF	Unc
1608 Rare	—	—	—	—	—	—
1610	—	400	800	2,000	—	—
1611 Rare	—	—	—	—	—	—

KM# 10 DICKEN

Silver **Obv:** Similar to KM#18 but without shield below eagle **Rev:** Similar to KM#18 but with shield below saint

Date	Mintage	VG	F	VF	XF	Unc
1612 Rare	—	—	—	—	—	—
1614	—	100	200	450	900	—

KM# 18 DICKEN

Silver

Date	Mintage	VG	F	VF	XF	Unc
1615	—	95.00	200	485	900	—
1616	—	95.00	200	485	900	—
1617	—	95.00	200	485	900	—

KM# 19 DICKEN

Silver **Obv:** Imperial eagle

Date	Mintage	VG	F	VF	XF	Unc
1617	—	95.00	200	485	900	—
1618	—	95.00	200	485	900	—
1619	—	500	1,200	3,000	—	—
1620	—	150	275	600	—	—
1621	—	110	240	550	—	—
1622	—	700	1,600	4,000	—	—

KM# 11 PISTOLE

7.6400 g., 0.9000 Gold 0.2211 oz. AGW **Obv:** Floriated cross with sceptres in angles **Obv. Legend:** MON: AV:... **Rev:** St. Martin on horseback and the beggar **Note:** Fr. #397.

Date	Mintage	VG	F	VF	XF	Unc
ND(1613-16) Rare	—	—	—	—	—	—

KM# 14 PISTOLE

7.6400 g., 0.9000 Gold 0.2211 oz. AGW **Obv:** Floriated cross with sceptres in angles **Obv. Legend:** MO AVREA... **Rev:** St. Martin on horseback and the beggar **Note:** Fr. #397.

Date	Mintage	VG	F	VF	XF	Unc
1613 Rare	—	—	—	—	—	—
1616 Rare	—	—	—	—	—	—

KM# 29 PISTOLE

7.6400 g., 0.9000 Gold 0.2211 oz. AGW **Obv:** Arms on cross **Obv. Legend:** DVO: AV:... **Rev:** St. Martin standing **Note:** Fr. #399.

Date	Mintage	VG	F	VF	XF	Unc
1624 Rare	—	—	—	—	—	—

KM# 31 PISTOLE

7.6400 g., 0.9000 Gold 0.2211 oz. AGW **Obv:** Cross above date **Obv. Legend:** MON: NOVA:... **Rev:** St. Martin on horseback **Note:** Fr. #400.

Date	Mintage	VG	F	VF	XF	Unc
1633 Rare	—	—	—	—	—	—

KM# 32 PISTOLE

7.6400 g., 0.9000 Gold 0.2211 oz. AGW **Obv:** Floriated cross **Obv. Legend:** MO: N(o): AV: REIPV-PLICAE: VRANIE **Rev. Legend:** PATRONS: **Note:** Fr. #398.

Date	Mintage	VG	F	VF	XF	Unc
ND(1635)	—	700	1,450	2,800	4,800	7,200

TRADE COINAGE

KM# 12 1/2 DUCAT

1.7500 g., 0.9860 Gold 0.0555 oz. AGW **Obv:** Imperial eagle **Rev:** St. Martin standing **Note:** Fr. #402.

Date	Mintage	VG	F	VF	XF	Unc
ND Rare	—	—	—	—	—	—

KM# 13 DUCAT

3.5000 g., 0.9860 Gold 0.1109 oz. AGW **Obv:** Imperial eagle **Rev:** St. Martin standing **Note:** Fr. #401.

Date	Mintage	VG	F	VF	XF	Unc
1612 Rare	—	—	—	—	—	—

ZUG

Tugium, Tugiensis

A canton in central Switzerland. They joined the Swiss Confederation in 1352 and had their own coinage from1564 to 1805.

MONETARY SYSTEM

6 Angster = 3 Rappen
= 1 Schilling = 1 Assis

CANTON

STANDARD COINAGE

KM# 36 RAPPEN

Billon **Note:** Uniface

Date	Mintage	VG	F	VF	XF	Unc
ND	—	20.00	45.00	200	475	—

KM# 37 SCHILLING

Billon **Obv:** Crowned imperial eagle, date divided by arms below **Rev:** Bust of saint wearing mitre facing forward

Date	Mintage	VG	F	VF	XF	Unc
1691	—	20.00	40.00	120	400	—

Date	Mintage	VG	F	VF	XF	Unc
1692	—	12.00	25.00	95.00	250	—
1693	—	12.00	25.00	95.00	250	—

KM# 18 10 SCHILLING

Silver **Obv:** Crowned imperial eagle above arms divide date **Rev:** Standing saint, 10 in legend above

Date	Mintage	VG	F	VF	XF	Unc
1602	—	400	800	2,000	4,000	—

KM# 17 3 KREUZER (1 Groschen)

Billon

Date	Mintage	VG	F	VF	XF	Unc
1601	—	8.00	16.00	40.00	140	—
160Z	—	8.00	16.00	40.00	140	—
1603	—	8.00	16.00	40.00	140	—
1604	—	8.00	16.00	40.00	140	—
1605	—	50.00	120	400	—	—
1606	—	8.00	16.00	40.00	140	—
1608	—	12.00	24.00	60.00	160	—

KM# 19 3 KREUZER (1 Groschen)

Billon **Note:** Klippe.

Date	Mintage	VG	F	VF	XF	Unc
1604	—	—	—	—	—	—
1606	—	—	—	—	—	—

KM# 38 3 KREUZER (1 Groschen)

Billon **Obv:** Crowned imperial eagle with arms on breast **Rev:** Armored bust of saint right, 3 in oval below

Date	Mintage	VG	F	VF	XF	Unc
1691	—	400	950	2,400	4,750	—

KM# 47 10 KREUZER

Silver **Obv:** Oval arms in ornate cartouche **Rev:** Crowned imperial eagle, 10 in oval on breast

Date	Mintage	VG	F	VF	XF	Unc
1693	—	150	400	800	—	—
1694	—	200	475	1,200	—	—

KM# 27 12 KREUZER (1/2 Dicken)

Silver

Date	Mintage	VG	F	VF	XF	Unc
1620	—	75.00	160	400	800	—
1621	—	75.00	160	400	800	—

KM# 30 BATZEN

Billon

Date	Mintage	VG	F	VF	XF	Unc
1621	—	20.00	40.00	165	400	—
1622	—	20.00	40.00	165	400	—

KM# 33 BATZEN

Billon **Obv:** Arms with ornamentation, date below **Rev:** Cross with prongs on end, lilies in angles

Date	Mintage	VG	F	VF	XF	Unc
1623	—	15.00	32.00	125	400	—
1624	—	15.00	32.00	125	400	—
1692	—	250	600	2,000	—	—

KM# 20 DICKEN

Silver

Date	Mintage	VG	F	VF	XF	Unc
ND	—	75.00	150	500	1,000	—
1609	—	40.00	80.00	200	400	—
1610	—	40.00	80.00	200	400	—
1611	—	40.00	80.00	200	400	—
1612	—	40.00	80.00	200	400	—
1613	—	150	350	500	1,750	—
1615	—	20.00	40.00	125	250	—
1616	—	20.00	40.00	125	250	—
1617	—	20.00	40.00	125	250	—
1618	—	20.00	40.00	125	250	—
1619	—	50.00	100	300	700	—
1620	—	50.00	100	350	700	—
1621	—	60.00	150	325	650	—
1622	—	120	300	700	1,500	—

KM# 22 DICKEN

Silver **Note:** Klippe.

Date	Mintage	VG	F	VF	XF	Unc
1612	—	—	—	—	—	—

KM# 34 DICKEN

Silver **Rev:** Date below eagle

Date	Mintage	VG	F	VF	XF	Unc
1623	—	300	600	1,500	3,000	—
1624	—	200	400	1,000	2,000	—

KM# 40 20 KREUZER

Silver **Obv:** Oval arms in ornate cartouche, date in legend **Rev:** Crowned imperial eagle, 10 in oval on breast

Date	Mintage	VG	F	VF	XF	Unc
1692	—	225	475	1,200	—	—
1694	—	200	400	900	—	—

KM# 41 1/6 THALER (20 Kreuzers)

Silver **Obv:** Oval arms in cartouche, date in legend **Rev:** Crowned imperial eagle, 1/6 in oval on breast

Date	Mintage	VG	F	VF	XF	Unc
1692	—	300	650	1,200	—	—

KM# 25 1/2 THALER

Silver **Obv:** Half-length armored St. Oswald right with scepter and raven, date in legend **Rev:** Crowned imperial eagle in circle

Date	Mintage	VG	F	VF	XF	Unc
1617 Rare	—	—	—	—	—	—

KM# 28 1/2 THALER

Silver **Obv:** Angel holds shield **Rev:** Imperial eagle

Date	Mintage	VG	F	VF	XF	Unc
1620	—	40.00	80.00	200	450	—
1621	—	30.00	60.00	125	400	—
1622	—	90.00	200	450	800	—

KM# 31 1/2 THALER

Silver **Note:** Klippe.

Date	Mintage	VG	F	VF	XF	Unc
1621	—	—	—	—	—	—

KM# 43 1/2 THALER

Silver **Note:** Klippe.

Date	Mintage	VG	F	VF	XF	Unc
1692	—	—	—	—	—	—

KM# 42 1/2 THALER

Silver **Obv:** Archangel Michael standing holding oval arms **Rev:** Crowned imperial eagle, date in legend

Date	Mintage	VG	F	VF	XF	Unc
1692	—	1,500	3,000	8,000	—	—

KM# 29 THALER

Silver **Note:** Similar to KM#32 but date in legend on obverse. Dav. #4631.

Date	Mintage	VG	F	VF	XF	Unc
1620	—	75.00	125	400	800	—
1621 Rare	—	—	—	—	—	—

KM# 32 THALER

Silver **Obv:** Angel holds shield **Rev:** Crowned impereial eagle **Note:** Dav. #4633.

Date	Mintage	VG	F	VF	XF	Unc
1621	—	60.00	125	300	650	—
1622	—	60.00	125	300	650	—

KM# 35 THALER

Silver **Obv:** Legend, date **Obv. Legend:** MONETA.NOVA. TVGIENSI **Note:** Dav. #4635, 4636.

Date	Mintage	VG	F	VF	XF	Unc
1623	—	95.00	200	525	1,000	—
1624	—	300	600	1,200	3,000	—

TRADE COINAGE

KM# 23 GOLDGULDEN

3.5000 g., 0.9860 Gold 0.1109 oz. AGW **Obv:** Bust of St. Oswald right **Rev:** Crowned imperial eagle and arms **Note:** Fr. #416.

Date	Mintage	VG	F	VF	XF	Unc
1615 Unique	—	—	—	—	—	—

KM# 44 1/4 DUCAT

0.8750 g., 0.9860 Gold 0.0277 oz. AGW **Note:** Similar to 1/2 Ducat, KM#45. Fr. #421.

Date	Mintage	VG	F	VF	XF	Unc
1692	—	2,000	4,500	9,500	16,000	—

KM# 45 1/2 DUCAT

1.7500 g., 0.9860 Gold 0.0555 oz. AGW **Note:** Fr. #420.

Date	Mintage	VG	F	VF	XF	Unc
1692	—	1,500	3,000	7,000	12,000	—

KM# 24 DUCAT

3.5000 g., 0.9860 Gold 0.1109 oz. AGW **Obv:** Crowned imperial eagle **Rev:** 1/2 bust of St. Oswald right

Date	Mintage	VG	F	VF	XF	Unc
1615 Rare	—	—	—	—	—	—

KM# 39 DUCAT

3.5000 g., 0.9860 Gold 0.1109 oz. AGW **Obv:** Bust of St. Oswald right **Rev:** Crowned imperial eagle and arms **Note:** Fr. #415.

Date	Mintage	VG	F	VF	XF	Unc
1691 Rare	—	—	—	—	—	—

KM# 46 1-1/2 DUCAT (Pistole)

5.2500 g., 0.9860 Gold 0.1664 oz. AGW **Obv:** Arms of Zug **Rev:** Seven-line inscription **Note:** Fr. #419.

Date	Mintage	VG	F	VF	XF	Unc
1692 Rare	—	—	—	—	—	—

KM# A48 3 DUCAT

10.5000 g., 0.9860 Gold 0.3328 oz. AGW **Obv:** Archangel Michael standing facing holding oval arms **Rev:** Crowned imperial eagle **Note:** Struck with 1/2 Thaler dies, KM#42. Fr. #418.

Date	Mintage	VG	F	VF	XF	Unc
1692 Rare	—	—	—	—	—	—

KM# 48 6 DUCAT

21.0000 g., 0.9860 Gold 0.6657 oz. AGW **Obv:** Archangel Michael standing facing holding oval arms **Rev:** Crowned imperial eagle **Note:** Struck with 1/2 Thaler dies, KM#42. Fr. #417.

Date	Mintage	VG	F	VF	XF	Unc
1692 Rare	—	—	—	—	—	—

PATTERNS

Including off metal strikes

KM#	Date	Mintage	Identification	Mkt Val
Pn1	1609	—	Dicken. Gold. KM#20.	25,000
Pn2	1609	—	Dicken. Copper. KM#20.	500
Pn3	ND	—	Rappen. Gold. KM#7.	2,000

KM#	Date	Mintage	Identification	Mkt Val
Pn4	ND	—	Rappen. Gold. 45.0000 g. KM#8	2,000

ZURICH

Thicurinae, Thuricensis, Ticurinae, Turicensis

A canton in north central Switzerland. It was the mint for the dukes of Swabia in the 10th and 11th centuries. The mint right was obtained in 1238. The first coinage struck were bracteates and the last coins were struck in 1848. It joined the Swiss Confederation in 1351.

MINT OFFICIALS' INITIALS

B - Bruckmann
AV - A. Vorster

MONETARY SYSTEM

Until 1798

12 Haller = 4 Rappen = 1 Schilling
72 Schillinge = 2 Gulden = 1 Thaler

CANTON

STANDARD COINAGE

KM# 5 HELLER

Billon **Obv:** Arms in Spanish shield, Z above, rosettes at sides **Note:** Uniface.

Date	Mintage	VG	F	VF	XF	Unc
ND	—	6.00	12.00	24.00	60.00	130

KM# 7 ANGSTER

Billon **Obv:** Large arms on Spanish shield, Z above, half moons on both sides

Date	Mintage	VG	F	VF	XF	Unc
ND	—	4.00	8.00	16.00	40.00	80.00

KM# 8 ANGSTER

Billon **Obv:** Mirror image of arms on Spanish shield on clover leaf **Rev:** Eagle in inner circle

Date	Mintage	VG	F	VF	XF	Unc
ND	—	20.00	40.00	85.00	150	—

KM# 9 ANGSTER

Billon **Rev:** Crowned imperial eagle in inner circle

Date	Mintage	VG	F	VF	XF	Unc
ND	—	4.00	8.00	16.00	40.00	—

KM# A12 RAPPEN
Billon **Rev:** Single-headed eagle and double-headed eagle

Date	Mintage	VG	F	VF	XF	Unc
ND	—	30.00	100	300	600	—
Note: single-head eagle						
ND	—	8.00	30.00	80.00	165	—
Note: double-headed eagle						

KM# B12 SECHSER
Billon **Obv:** Arms **Rev:** Double-headed eagle

Date	Mintage	VG	F	VF	XF	Unc
ND	—	40.00	150	400	—	—

KM# 12 SCHILLING
Billon **Obv:** Arms on Spanish shield, four tulip blossoms at top and bottom and sides **Rev:** Crowned imperial eagle in inner circle

Date	Mintage	VG	F	VF	XF	Unc
ND	—	2.00	4.00	20.00	60.00	125

KM# 13 SCHILLING
Billon **Note:** Klippe.

Date	Mintage	VG	F	VF	XF	Unc
ND	—	—	—	—	—	—

KM# 14 SCHILLING
Billon **Obv:** Arms on Spanish shield on long armed cross, ornaments on cross arms in inner circle **Rev:** Eagle in inner circle

Date	Mintage	VG	F	VF	XF	Unc
ND	—	2.00	4.00	24.00	60.00	125

KM# 49 SCHILLING
Billon **Obv:** Arms on spanish shield, tulip blossoms at top, bottom, and sides **Rev:** Crowned imperial eagle

Date	Mintage	VG	F	VF	XF	Unc
1639	—	4.00	8.00	32.00	80.00	200
1640	—	4.00	8.00	32.00	80.00	200
1641	—	4.00	8.00	32.00	80.00	200

KM# 55 SCHILLING
Billon **Note:** Klippe.

Date	Mintage	VG	F	VF	XF	Unc
1640	—	—	—	—	—	—

KM# 85 5 SCHILLINGS
Billon **Obv:** Standing lion holding arms in Spanish shield **Rev:** Inscription, date in circle with six indentations with ornaments **Rev. Inscription:** PRO / DEO Et PA / TRIA

Date	Mintage	VG	F	VF	XF	Unc
1656	—	40.00	80.00	200	400	—

KM# 110 5 SCHILLINGS
Silver **Obv:** Oval arms in cartouche within palm branches **Rev:** S.P.Q.T., date above shield with 5 within laurel branches

Date	Mintage	VG	F	VF	XF	Unc
1693	—	12.00	25.00	60.00	125	300
1694	—	12.00	25.00	60.00	125	300
1697	—	12.00	25.00	60.00	125	300

KM# 115 5 SCHILLINGS
Silver **Obv:** Standing lion holding arms and sword **Rev:** Inscription in ornamented ring **Rev. Inscription:** PRO DEO / ET / PATRIA / (date)

Date	Mintage	VG	F	VF	XF	Unc
1697	—	25.00	60.00	125	225	600
1699	—	12.00	25.00	60.00	125	325
1700	—	12.00	25.00	60.00	125	325

KM# 86 10 SCHILLINGS (1/4 Gulden - Oertli)
Silver **Obv:** Curved, arched arms, roses at sides in inner circle **Rev:** Inscription in ornamented ring **Rev. Inscription:** PRO / DEO / ET PA / TRIA / (date)

Date	Mintage	VG	F	VF	XF	Unc
ND	—	12.00	25.00	60.00	150	300
1656	—	12.00	25.00	60.00	150	300
1677	—	12.00	25.00	60.00	150	300
1700	—	12.00	25.00	60.00	150	300

KM# 15 20 SCHILLINGS (1/2 Gulden)
Silver

Date	Mintage	VG	F	VF	XF	Unc
ND	—	20.00	40.00	80.00	165	400

KM# 28 BATZEN
Billon **Obv:** Large arms on Spanish shield, eagle above **Rev:** Anchor cross in inner circle, date in legend

Date	Mintage	VG	F	VF	XF	Unc
1606	—	12.00	25.00	80.00	240	—
1607	—	10.00	16.00	60.00	200	—
1608	—	10.00	16.00	60.00	200	—

KM# 29 BATZEN
Billon **Note:** Klippe.

Date	Mintage	VG	F	VF	XF	Unc
1607	—	—	—	—	—	—

KM# 36 BATZEN
Billon **Obv:** Smaller arms on Spanish shield, eagle above, roses on sides **Rev:** Anchor cross with small flowers in angles

Date	Mintage	VG	F	VF	XF	Unc
1621	—	4.00	8.00	25.00	150	—
1622	—	4.00	8.00	25.00	150	—

KM# 40 BATZEN
Billon

Date	Mintage	VG	F	VF	XF	Unc
1623	—	4.00	8.00	24.00	150	—
1624	—	4.00	8.00	24.00	150	—
1633	—	12.00	25.00	80.00	200	—

KM# 41 BATZEN
Billon **Note:** Klippe.

Date	Mintage	VG	F	VF	XF	Unc
1623	—	—	—	—	—	—
1624	—	—	—	—	—	—
1633	—	—	—	—	—	—

KM# 51 BATZEN
Billon **Note:** Klippe.

Date	Mintage	VG	F	VF	XF	Unc
1639	—	—	—	—	—	—

KM# 50 BATZEN
Billon **Obv. Legend:** MO-NET-ANO-VA **Rev:** Legend, date **Rev. Legend:** THVRICENSIS

Date	Mintage	VG	F	VF	XF	Unc
1639	—	4.00	8.00	25.00	80.00	—
1640	—	4.00	8.00	25.00	80.00	—
1641	—	4.00	8.00	25.00	80.00	—

KM# A30 1/2 DICKEN
Silver **Obv:** Lion facing left **Rev:** Double-headed eagle, 12 on breast

Date	Mintage	VG	F	VF	XF	Unc
1608 Rare	—	—	—	—	—	—
1620	—	75.00	250	550	—	—
1621	—	75.00	250	550	—	—
1622	—	40.00	125	250	—	—

KM# 30 DICKEN (1/4 Thaler)
Silver

Date	Mintage	VG	F	VF	XF	Unc
1608 Rare	—	—	—	—	—	—
1620	—	60.00	100	200	475	—
1621	—	60.00	100	200	475	—
1622	—	65.00	125	300	600	—

KM# 32 DICKEN (1/4 Thaler)
Silver

Date	Mintage	VG	F	VF	XF	Unc
1620	—	60.00	100	200	475	—
1621	—	60.00	100	200	475	—
1622	—	65.00	125	300	600	—

KM# 33 DICKEN (1/4 Thaler)
Silver **Note:** Klippe.

Date	Mintage	VG	F	VF	XF	Unc
1620	—	—	—	—	—	—
1621	—	—	—	—	—	—

KM# 45 DICKEN (1/4 Thaler)
Silver **Note:** Klippe.

Date	Mintage	VG	F	VF	XF	Unc
1629	—	—	—	—	—	—

KM# 44 DICKEN (1/4 Thaler)
Silver **Obv:** Similar to KM#30 **Rev:** Crowned imperial eagle in inner circle, date below

Date	Mintage	VG	F	VF	XF	Unc
1629	—	50.00	85.00	200	400	—

KM# 80 1/4 THALER (1/2 Gulden)
Silver, 35 mm.

Date	Mintage	VG	F	VF	XF	Unc
1652	—	65.00	125	300	600	—

KM# 81 1/4 THALER (1/2 Gulden)
Silver, 31 mm.

Date	Mintage	VG	F	VF	XF	Unc
1652	—	65.00	120	300	600	—

KM# 100 1/4 THALER (1/2 Gulden)
Silver **Obv:** Standing lion holding arms and sword **Rev:** Inscription in two laurel branches **Rev. Inscription:** DOMINE / CONSERVA / NOS IN / PACE

Date	Mintage	VG	F	VF	XF	Unc
ND	—	65.00	120	300	600	—

KM# 101 1/4 THALER (1/2 Gulden)
Silver

Date	Mintage	VG	F	VF	XF	Unc
1673	—	65.00	120	300	600	—
1674	—	65.00	120	300	600	—

KM# 34 1/2 THALER (1 Gulden - 36 Schillings)
Silver

Date	Mintage	VG	F	VF	XF	Unc
1620	—	65.00	130	300	600	—

KM# 35 1/2 THALER (1 Gulden - 36 Schillings)
Silver

Date	Mintage	VG	F	VF	XF	Unc
ND Rare	—	350	800	2,000	4,000	—
1622	—	65.00	130	300	600	—

KM# 70 1/2 THALER (1 Gulden - 36 Schillings)
Silver **Obv:** Arms on Spanish shield between two standing lions holding a laurel wreath above **Rev:** Cherub's head above DOMINE / CONSERVA / NOS IN / PACE, date in ornamental cartouche

Date	Mintage	VG	F	VF	XF	Unc
1647	—	45.00	80.00	200	400	—
1649	—	45.00	80.00	200	400	—

KM# 82 1/2 THALER (1 Gulden - 36 Schillings)
Silver

Date	Mintage	VG	F	VF	XF	Unc
1652	—	45.00	80.00	200	400	—

KM# 102 1/2 THALER (1 Gulden - 36 Schillings)
Silver **Obv:** Similar to KM#35 but shield curved, 1/2 below lion **Rev:** Cherub's head above inscription in sweeping ornamentation **Rev. Inscription:** DOMINE / CONSERVA / NOS IN PACE / (date)

Date	Mintage	VG	F	VF	XF	Unc
1673	—	85.00	160	350	700	—
1674 Rare	—	—	—	—	—	—
1690	—	60.00	100	250	475	—

KM# 37 THALER
Silver **Obv:** Lion standing left with arms on Spanish shield and sword, date above **Rev:** Crowned imperial eagle **Note:** Dav. #4638.

Date	Mintage	VG	F	VF	XF	Unc
1622	—	75.00	135	300	600	—
1624	—	80.00	150	325	650	—
1645	—	100	200	400	850	—

KM# 56 THALER
Silver **Obv:** Two lions standing holding arms and laurel wreath above, date divided below **Note:** Dav. #4639.

Date	Mintage	VG	F	VF	XF	Unc
1640	—	100	200	475	850	—
1645	—	1,200	2,400	5,500	—	—

KM# 66 THALER
Silver **Obv:** Two pentagonal-shaped arms between two standing lions holding a sword and palm branch **Rev:** Inscription in laurel wreath **Rev. Inscription:** DOMINE / CONSERVA / NOS IN / PACE / (date) **Note:** Dav. #4640.

Date	Mintage	VG	F	VF	XF	Unc
1646	—	80.00	160	400	800	—

KM# 71 THALER
Silver **Rev:** Legend in cartouche, cherub's head at top **Note:** Dav. #4641.

Date	Mintage	VG	F	VF	XF	Unc
1647	—	85.00	165	400	800	—

KM# 72 THALER
Silver **Obv:** Lions holding laurel wreath above arms **Note:** Dav. #4643.

Date	Mintage	VG	F	VF	XF	Unc
1649	—	120	250	550	1,200	—

KM# 76 THALER
Silver **Rev:** View of port city **Note:** Dav. #4645.

Date	Mintage	VG	F	VF	XF	Unc
MDCLI (1651)	—	225	450	1,200	2,450	—

KM# 75 THALER
Silver **Obv:** Lion with sword, orb, and shield on flowered background **Obv. Legend:** MONETA * NOVA * REIPVBLICAE * TIGVRINAE * **Rev:** Inscription within cartouche, cherub head at top **Rev. Inscription:** DOMINE / CONSER- / VA. NOS. / IN. PACE. / (date) **Note:** Dav. #4647.

Date	Mintage	VG	F	VF	XF	Unc
1651	—	110	250	600	1,200	—
1652	—	110	250	600	1,200	—

KM# 88 THALER

Silver **Obv:** Large crowned arms in laurel branches **Obv. Legend:** + MONETA NOVA REIPVBLICAE TIGVRINAE **Rev:** Legend on banner, inscription in center with lily **Rev. Legend:** DOMINE CONSERVA NOS IN PACE **Rev. Inscription:** MDC / LX **Note:** Dav. #4648.

Date	Mintage	VG	F	VF	XF	Unc
MDCLX (1660)	—	150	325	800	1,600	2,800

KM# 89.1 THALER

Silver **Note:** Dav. #4649.

Date	Mintage	VG	F	VF	XF	Unc
1661	—	100	200	475	900	—
1662	—	100	200	475	900	—
1663	—	100	200	475	900	—
1665	—	80.00	165	400	800	—

KM# 103 THALER

Silver **Note:** Dav. #4651.

Date	Mintage	VG	F	VF	XF	Unc
1673	—	80.00	165	400	800	—
1676	—	80.00	165	400	800	—
1677	—	80.00	165	400	800	—
1694	—	50.00	80.00	200	475	—

KM# 113 THALER

Silver **Obv:** Lion holding oval shield and sword **Rev:** City view **Note:** Dav. #4655.

Date	Mintage	VG	F	VF	XF	Unc
ND(ca.1680)	—	250	500	850	1,500	—

KM# 89.2 THALER

Silver **Obv:** Without inner circle **Note:** Dav. #4652.

Date	Mintage	VG	F	VF	XF	Unc
1691	—	65.00	125	325	650	—
1693	—	100	200	400	800	—
1694	—	50.00	80.00	200	425	—

KM# 112 THALER

Silver **Rev:** Similar to KM#89.1 but lion head at top, palm branches at bottom **Note:** Dav. #4653.

Date	Mintage	VG	F	VF	XF	Unc
1695	—	110	200	450	900	—

KM# 38 2 THALER

Silver **Obv:** Lion standing left with arms on Spanish shield and sword, date above **Rev:** Crowned imperial eagle **Note:** Dav. #4637.

Date	Mintage	VG	F	VF	XF	Unc
1622	—	400	800	2,000	4,000	7,200
1624	—	400	800	2,000	4,000	7,200

KM# 57 2 THALER

Silver **Obv:** Two lions standing holding arms and laurel wreath above, date divided below **Note:** Dav. #A4639.

Date	Mintage	VG	F	VF	XF	Unc
1640	—	900	1,900	4,800	10,000	—

KM# 67 2 THALER

Silver **Obv:** Two pentagonal-shaped arms between two standing lions holding a sword and palm branch **Obv. Inscription:** DOMINE / CONSERVA / NOS IN / PACE / (date) **Rev:** Inscription in laurel wreath **Note:** Dav. #A4640.

Date	Mintage	VG	F	VF	XF	Unc
1646	—	700	1,500	4,000	—	—

KM# 73 2 THALER

Silver **Rev:** Legend in cartouche, cherub's head at top **Note:** Dav. #4642.

Date	Mintage	VG	F	VF	XF	Unc
1649	—	2,000	4,000	9,500	—	—

KM# 78 2 THALER

Silver **Rev:** View of port city **Note:** Dav. #4644.

Date	Mintage	VG	F	VF	XF	Unc
MDCLI (1651) Rare	—	—	—	—	—	—

KM# 77 2 THALER

Silver **Note:** Dav. #4646. Similar to 1 Thaler, KM#75.

Date	Mintage	VG	F	VF	XF	Unc
1651	—	1,500	3,200	8,000	—	—
1652 Rare	—	—	—	—	—	—

KM# 111 2 THALER

Silver **Note:** Dav. #4650. Similar to 1 Thaler, KM#103.

Date	Mintage	VG	F	VF	XF	Unc
1694	—	700	1,600	3,600	7,200	—

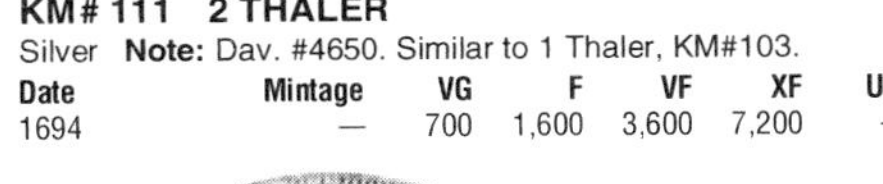

KM# 114 2 THALER

Silver **Obv:** Similar to 1 Thaler, KM#103. **Rev:** Similar to 1 Thaler, KM#89. **Note:** Dav. #4653.

Date	Mintage	VG	F	VF	XF	Unc
1695	—	700	1,600	3,600	7,200	—

KM# 16 1/2 KRONE
Gold **Obv:** Arms on Spanish shield on breast of crowned imperial eagle **Rev:** Floreate cross in inner circle

Date	Mintage	VG	F	VF	XF	Unc
ND	—	450	950	1,900	3,600	4,500

KM# 48 KRONE
Gold **Obv:** Large curved shield of arms in front of crowned imperial eagle in inner circle **Rev:** Floreate cross in inner circle **Note:** Fr. #429.

Date	Mintage	VG	F	VF	XF	Unc
1631	—	2,000	4,000	8,000	—	—

TRADE COINAGE

KM# 39 GOLDGULDEN
3.5000 g., 0.9860 Gold 0.1109 oz. AGW **Obv:** Shield of arms in quatrefoil in inner circle **Rev:** Crowned imperial eagle in inner circle **Note:** Fr. #434.

Date	Mintage	VG	F	VF	XF	Unc
1622	—	900	1,850	3,700	6,000	—

KM# 52 1/4 DUCAT
0.8750 g., 0.9860 Gold 0.0277 oz. AGW **Obv:** Standing knight facing **Rev:** Three-line legend and date in branches **Note:** Fr. # 449.

Date	Mintage	VG	F	VF	XF	Unc
1639	—	900	1,900	4,000	6,500	—

KM# 58 1/4 DUCAT
0.8750 g., 0.9860 Gold 0.0277 oz. AGW **Obv:** Lion holding shield of arms **Rev:** Four-line legend and date in branches **Note:** Varieties exist. Fr. #466.

Date	Mintage	VG	F	VF	XF	Unc
1641	—	100	200	400	600	950
1645	—	80.00	160	325	500	725
1649	—	80.00	160	325	500	725
1651	—	80.00	160	325	500	725
1670	—	65.00	125	250	400	650
1671	—	65.00	125	250	400	650

KM# 83 1/4 DUCAT
0.8750 g., 0.9860 Gold 0.0277 oz. AGW **Note:** Similar to 1/2 Ducat, KM#84. Fr. #475.

Date	Mintage	VG	F	VF	XF	Unc
1654	—	80.00	165	325	475	725
1662	—	80.00	165	325	475	725

KM# 91 1/4 DUCAT
0.8750 g., 0.9860 Gold 0.0277 oz. AGW **Obv:** Lion holding shield of arms and sword **Rev:** MONE / TA NOVA / REIPVB / TIGVRIN / date in ornamental border

Date	Mintage	VG	F	VF	XF	Unc
1666	—	65.00	125	250	400	650

KM# 98 1/4 DUCAT
0.8750 g., 0.9860 Gold 0.0277 oz. AGW **Obv:** Lion holding arms and palm branch **Rev:** ANNO / DOMINI / date in laurel wreath **Note:** Fr. #468.

Date	Mintage	VG	F	VF	XF	Unc
1671	—	65.00	125	250	400	650
1677	—	65.00	125	250	400	650
1692	—	65.00	125	250	400	650

KM# 19 1/2 DUCAT
1.7500 g., 0.9860 Gold 0.0555 oz. AGW **Obv:** Crowned imperial eagle in inner circle **Rev:** Charlemagne standing with sword in inner circle **Note:** Fr. #438.

Date	Mintage	VG	F	VF	XF	Unc
ND(1570) Rare	—	—	—	—	—	—

KM# 20 1/2 DUCAT
1.7500 g., 0.9860 Gold 0.0555 oz. AGW **Obv:** Single-headed eagle **Note:** Fr. #436.

Date	Mintage	VG	F	VF	XF	Unc
ND(ca. 1600)	—	1,500	3,200	5,200	6,500	—

KM# 53 1/2 DUCAT
1.7500 g., 0.9860 Gold 0.0555 oz. AGW **Note:** Fr. #448.

Date	Mintage	VG	F	VF	XF	Unc
1639	—	450	950	2,000	3,200	—

KM# 59 1/2 DUCAT
1.7500 g., 0.9860 Gold 0.0555 oz. AGW **Obv:** Lion holding shield and palm branch **Rev:** Date in laurel branches **Rev. Inscription:** MON. / NO. THV / RICEN / SIS **Note:** Fr. #465.

Date	Mintage	VG	F	VF	XF	Unc
1641	—	100	200	400	650	1,000
1645	—	100	200	400	650	1,000
1649	—	100	200	400	650	1,000
1651	—	100	200	400	650	1,000
1670	—	100	200	400	650	1,000
1671	—	100	200	400	650	1,000

KM# 84 1/2 DUCAT
1.7500 g., 0.9860 Gold 0.0555 oz. AGW **Note:** Fr. #474.

Date	Mintage	VG	F	VF	XF	Unc
1654	—	100	200	400	650	1,000
1662	—	100	200	400	650	1,000

KM# 92 1/2 DUCAT
1.7500 g., 0.9860 Gold 0.0555 oz. AGW **Obv:** Lion holding shield and sword **Rev:** Inscription, date in wide ornate edge **Rev. Inscription:** MONE / TA NOVA / REIPVB / TIGVRIN **Note:** Fr. #465.

Date	Mintage	VG	F	VF	XF	Unc
1666	—	85.00	165	325	550	800

KM# 97 1/2 DUCAT
1.7500 g., 0.9860 Gold 0.0555 oz. AGW **Rev:** Inscription, date in laurel branches **Rev. Inscription:** MON. / NO. THV / RICEN / SIS **Note:** Fr. #465.

Date	Mintage	VG	F	VF	XF	Unc
1670	—	85.00	165	325	550	800

KM# 99 1/2 DUCAT
1.7500 g., 0.9860 Gold 0.0555 oz. AGW **Note:** Fr. #467.

Date	Mintage	VG	F	VF	XF	Unc
1671	—	85.00	165	325	550	800
1677	—	85.00	165	325	550	800
1692	—	85.00	165	325	550	800

KM# 21 DUCAT
3.5000 g., 0.9860 Gold 0.1109 oz. AGW **Obv. Inscription:** S.P.Q. /THVRICEN/SIS **Rev:** Charlemagne enthroned **Note:** Fr. #442.

Date	Mintage	VG	F	VF	XF	Unc
ND(ca. 1620)	—	1,000	1,600	2,500	4,000	—

KM# 22 DUCAT
3.5000 g., 0.9860 Gold 0.1109 oz. AGW **Obv:** Charlemagne enthroned in inner circle **Rev:** Sts. Regula and Felix standing facing holding their heads **Note:** Fr. #440.

Date	Mintage	VG	F	VF	XF	Unc
ND(ca. 1580)	—	1,600	2,800	4,500	6,000	—

KM# 23 DUCAT
3.5000 g., 0.9860 Gold 0.1109 oz. AGW **Obv:** Shield of arms on crowned imperial eagle in inner circle **Rev:** Charlemagne standing left with raised sword in inner circle **Note:** Fr. #437.

Date	Mintage	VG	F	VF	XF	Unc
ND(ca. 1570) Rare	—	—	—	—	—	—

KM# 24 DUCAT
3.5000 g., 0.9860 Gold 0.1109 oz. AGW **Obv:** Shield of arms on crowned imperial eagle in inner circle **Rev:** Charlemagne standing right with sword and orb in inner circle **Note:** Fr. #435.

Date	Mintage	VG	F	VF	XF	Unc
ND(ca. 1600)	—	1,500	2,400	4,000	6,000	—

KM# 60 DUCAT
3.5000 g., 0.9860 Gold 0.1109 oz. AGW **Obv:** Oval arms with lion supporters **Rev:** Four-line legend and date in branches **Note:** Fr. #458.

Date	Mintage	VG	F	VF	XF	Unc
1641	—	400	800	1,400	2,400	3,750
1643	—	400	800	1,400	2,400	3,750

KM# 65 DUCAT
3.5000 g., 0.9860 Gold 0.1109 oz. AGW **Obv:** Standing lion holding shield and palm branch **Rev:** Inscription, date in laurel wreath **Rev. Inscription:** DVCATVS / NOVVS / REIPVBLI / THURICENS / IS **Note:** Fr. #464.

Date	Mintage	VG	F	VF	XF	Unc
1645	—	400	850	2,000	3,200	4,750

KM# 69 DUCAT
3.5000 g., 0.9860 Gold 0.1109 oz. AGW **Note:** Fr. #459.

Date	Mintage	VG	F	VF	XF	Unc
1646	—	400	750	1,400	2,400	3,350
1648	—	400	750	1,400	2,400	3,350
1649	—	400	750	1,400	2,400	3,350
1650	—	400	750	1,400	2,400	3,350

KM# 68 DUCAT
3.5000 g., 0.9860 Gold 0.1109 oz. AGW **Obv:** Two pentagonal-shaped arms between two standing lions holding a sword and palm branch **Rev:** Inscription, date in laurel wreath **Rev. Inscription:** DUCATUS / NOVUS / REIPUBL / TIGURI /

Date	Mintage	VG	F	VF	XF	Unc
1646	—	400	750	1,400	2,400	3,350

KM# 79 DUCAT
3.5000 g., 0.9860 Gold 0.1109 oz. AGW **Note:** Fr. #473.

Date	Mintage	VG	F	VF	XF	Unc
1651	—	400	800	2,000	3,200	4,800
1660 Rare	—	—	—	—	—	—

KM# A90 DUCAT

3.5000 g., 0.9860 Gold 0.1109 oz. AGW **Obv:** Arms **Obv. Legend:** DOMINE ? CONSERVA ? NOS ? IN ? PACE **Rev:** Ornate frame with fruit at bottom **Rev. Inscription:** DVCATUS / NOVV / REIPVBL / TIGVRI **Note:** Prev. KM#90. Fr.#464.

Date	Mintage	VG	F	VF	XF	Unc
ND(c.1660)	—	500	800	1,200	1,800	—

KM# 90 DUCAT

3.5000 g., 0.9860 Gold 0.1109 oz. AGW **Obv:** Arms **Obv. Legend:** * DOMINE • CONSERVA • NOS • IN • PACE * **Rev:** Ornate frame **Rev. Inscription:** DVCATUS / NOVVS / REIPVBL / TIGVRI **Note:** Fr.#464.

Date	Mintage	VG	F	VF	XF	Unc
1661	—	400	800	1,650	2,800	4,000
1662	—	400	800	1,650	2,800	4,000

KM# 105.1 DUCAT

3.5000 g., 0.9860 Gold 0.1109 oz. AGW **Note:** Varieties exist. Fr. #464.

Date	Mintage	VG	F	VF	XF	Unc
1673	—	1,000	2,200	3,500	8,000	—
1676	—	1,000	2,200	3,500	8,000	—
1679	—	1,000	2,200	3,500	8,000	—
1680	—	400	800	1,650	2,800	4,000
1684	—	400	800	1,650	2,800	4,000
1693	—	400	800	1,650	2,800	4,000

KM# 104 DUCAT

3.5000 g., 0.9860 Gold 0.1109 oz. AGW **Rev:** Similar to KM#90 but different legend **Rev. Inscription:** JUSTICIA / ET / CONCORDIA

Date	Mintage	VG	F	VF	XF	Unc
1673 Rare	—	—	—	—	—	—

KM# 105.2 DUCAT

Gold **Obv:** Redesigned lion with sword and shield left **Note:** Fr. #464a.

Date	Mintage	VG	F	VF	XF	Unc
1697	—	400	800	1,650	2,800	4,000

KM# 42 2 DUCAT

7.0000 g., 0.9860 Gold 0.2219 oz. AGW **Obv:** Standing lion with orb holding shield in inner circle, date in legend **Rev:** Crowned imperial eagle in inner circle **Note:** Fr. #446.

Date	Mintage	VG	F	VF	XF	Unc
1624	—	1,200	2,500	4,800	8,000	—

KM# 46 2 DUCAT

7.0000 g., 0.9860 Gold 0.2219 oz. AGW **Rev:** Date in exergue **Note:** Fr. #447.

Date	Mintage	VG	F	VF	XF	Unc
1629	—	1,600	3,000	4,000	6,000	—

KM# 25 2 DUCAT

7.0000 g., 0.9860 Gold 0.2219 oz. AGW **Obv:** Inscription in wreath **Obv. Inscription:** S.P.Q / THURICEN / SIS **Rev:** Charlemagne enthroned in ornamented inner circle **Note:** Fr. #441.

Date	Mintage	VG	F	VF	XF	Unc
ND(ca. 1620) Rare	—	—	—	—	—	—

KM# 26 2 DUCAT

7.0000 g., 0.9860 Gold 0.2219 oz. AGW **Obv:** Charlemagne enthroned in inner circle **Rev:** Sts. Regula and Felix standing facing holding their heads **Note:** Fr. #439.

Date	Mintage	VG	F	VF	XF	Unc
ND(ca. 1580) Rare	—	—	—	—	—	—

KM# 61 2 DUCAT

7.0000 g., 0.9860 Gold 0.2219 oz. AGW **Obv:** Laurel wreath above oval arms supported by two standing lions **Note:** Fr. #457.

Date	Mintage	VG	F	VF	XF	Unc
1641	—	1,200	2,500	4,800	8,000	—

KM# 106 2 DUCAT

7.0000 g., 0.9860 Gold 0.2219 oz. AGW **Obv:** Standing lion with sword holding shield in inner circle, date in legend **Rev:** Value in cartouche **Note:** Fr. #463.

Date	Mintage	VG	F	VF	XF	Unc
1673	—	1,200	2,500	4,800	8,000	—

KM# 108 2 DUCAT

7.0000 g., 0.9860 Gold 0.2219 oz. AGW **Note:** Similar to 1 Ducat, KM#90. Fr. #463.

Date	Mintage	VG	F	VF	XF	Unc
1683	—	2,000	4,000	8,000	13,500	—

KM# 62 3 DUCAT

10.5000 g., 0.9860 Gold 0.3328 oz. AGW **Note:** Similar to 2 Ducat, KM#61. Fr. #456.

Date	Mintage	VG	F	VF	XF	Unc
1641	—	2,000	4,000	8,500	14,000	—

KM# 93 3 DUCAT

10.5000 g., 0.9860 Gold 0.3328 oz. AGW **Obv:** Standing lion with sword in inner circle, legend within laurel wreath **Obv. Legend:** DOMINE CONSERVA NOS IN PACE **Rev:** Inscription, date in baroque frame in laurel wreath **Rev. Inscription:** MONE / TA NOVA / REIPVB / TIGVRIN / **Note:** Fr. #462.

Date	Mintage	VG	F	VF	XF	Unc
1666	—	4,000	8,000	16,000	28,000	—

KM# 31 4 DUCAT

14.0000 g., 0.9860 Gold 0.4438 oz. AGW **Obv:** Standing lion holding sword and shield **Rev:** Imperial eagle **Note:** Struck with 1/2 Thaler dies, KM#35. Fr. #444.

Date	Mintage	VG	F	VF	XF	Unc
1622 Rare	—	—	—	—	—	—

KM# 43 4 DUCAT

14.0000 g., 0.9860 Gold 0.4438 oz. AGW **Obv:** Standing lion with orb holding shield in inner circle, date in legend **Rev:** Crowned imperial eagle in inner circle **Note:** Struck with 1 Thaler dies, KM#37. Fr. #443.

Date	Mintage	VG	F	VF	XF	Unc
1624	—	4,500	9,500	20,000	32,000	—

KM# 47 4 DUCAT

14.0000 g., 0.9860 Gold 0.4438 oz. AGW **Obv:** Lion standing holding sword and shield **Rev:** Crowned imperial eagle, date in exergue **Note:** Struck with 2 Ducat dies, KM#46. Fr. #445.

Date	Mintage	VG	F	VF	XF	Unc
1629	—	4,500	7,500	12,500	18,000	—

KM# A63 4 DUCAT

14.0000 g., 0.9860 Gold 0.4438 oz. AGW **Note:** Similar to 4 Ducat, KM#63. Struck with 1 Thaler dies, KM#56.

Date	Mintage	VG	F	VF	XF	Unc
1640	—	—	—	15,000	30,000	—

KM# 63 4 DUCAT

14.0000 g., 0.9860 Gold 0.4438 oz. AGW **Obv:** Laurel wreath above oval arms at center supported by two standing lions

Date	Mintage	VG	F	VF	XF	Unc
1641	—	2,000	4,000	8,500	13,500	—

KM# 94 4 DUCAT

14.0000 g., 0.9860 Gold 0.4438 oz. AGW **Obv:** Standing lion with sword in inner circle, legend within laurel wreath **Obv. Legend:** DOMINE CONSERVA NOS IN PACE **Rev:** Inscription, date in baroque frame in laurel wreath **Rev. Inscription:** MONE / TA NOVA / REIPVB / TIGVRIN / **Note:** Fr. #461.

Date	Mintage	VG	F	VF	XF	Unc
1666 Rare	—	—	—	—	—	—

KM# 64 5 DUCAT

17.5000 g., 0.9860 Gold 0.5547 oz. AGW **Obv:** Two standing lions holding oval arms at bottom dividing date and laurel wreath at top **Rev:** Crowned imperial eagle in inner circle **Note:** Klippe. Fr. #454.

Date	Mintage	VG	F	VF	XF	Unc
1641 Rare	—	—	—	—	—	—

KM# 95 5 DUCAT

17.5000 g., 0.9860 Gold 0.5547 oz. AGW **Obv:** Standing lion with sword in inner circle **Obv. Legend:** DOMINE CONSERVA NOS IN PACE all within laurel wreath **Rev:** Inscription, date in baroque frame in laurel wreath **Rev. Inscription:** MONE / TA NOVA / REIPVB / TIGVRIN / **Note:** Fr. #460.

Date	Mintage	VG	F	VF	XF	Unc
1666 Rare	—	—	—	—	—	—

KM# A44 6 DUCAT

Gold **Obv:** Lion with sword and shield left **Rev:** Crowned imperial eagle **Note:** Struck with 1 Thaler dies, KM#37. Fr. #442a.

Date	Mintage	VG	F	VF	XF	Unc
1624 Rare	—	—	—	—	—	—

KM# A70 6 DUCAT

21.0000 g., 0.9860 Gold 0.6657 oz. AGW **Obv:** Two pentagonal-shaped arms between two standing lions holding a sword and palm branch **Rev:** Inscription, date in laurel wreath **Rev. Inscription:** DOMINE / CONSERVA / NOS IN / PACE / **Note:** Struck wtih 1 Thaler dies, KM#66. Fr. #472.

Date	Mintage	VG	F	VF	XF	Unc
1646 Rare	—	—	—	—	—	—

KM# 74 6 DUCAT

21.0000 g., 0.9860 Gold 0.6657 oz. AGW **Obv:** Two lions standing holding laurel wreath above arms **Note:** Struck wtih 1 Thaler dies, KM#72. Fr. #472.

Date	Mintage	VG	F	VF	XF	Unc
1649 Rare	—	—	—	—	—	—

KM# A75 7 DUCAT

24.5000 g., 0.9860 Gold 0.7766 oz. AGW **Note:** Similar to 6 Ducat, KM#74. Struck with 1 Thaler dies, KM#72. Fr. #471.

Date	Mintage	VG	F	VF	XF	Unc
1649 Rare	—	—	—	—	—	—

KM# B70 8 DUCAT

28.0000 g., 0.9860 Gold 0.8876 oz. AGW **Note:** Similar to 6 Ducat, KM#A70. Struck with 1 Thaler dies, KM#66. Fr. #470.

Date	Mintage	VG	F	VF	XF	Unc
1646 Rare	—	—	—	—	—	—

KM# B75 8 DUCAT

28.0000 g., 0.9860 Gold 0.8876 oz. AGW **Note:** Similar to 6 Ducat, KM#74. Struck with 1 Thaler dies, KM#72. Fr. #470.

Date	Mintage	VG	F	VF	XF	Unc
1649 Rare	—	—	—	—	—	—

KM# 107 10 DUCAT

35.0000 g., 0.9860 Gold 1.1095 oz. AGW **Obv:** Lion standing holding sword and shield **Rev:** City view **Note:** Struck with 1 Thaler dies, KM#113. Fr. #476.

Date	Mintage	VG	F	VF	XF	Unc
ND(ca.1680) Rare	—	—	—	—	—	—

KM# C75 15 DUCAT

52.5000 g., 0.9860 Gold 1.6642 oz. AGW **Note:** Similar to 8 Ducat, KM#B75. Struck with 1 Thaler dies, KM#72. Fr. #469.

Date	Mintage	VG	F	VF	XF	Unc
1649 Rare	—	—	—	—	—	—

CITY

STANDARD COINAGE

KM# 6 3 HALLER (1 Rappen)

Billon **Obv:** Oval arms between palm and laurel branches **Rev:** Value: 3/Haller in baroque frame

Date	Mintage	VG	F	VF	XF	Unc
ND	—	3.00	5.00	8.00	16.00	40.00

KM# 10 RAPPEN

Billon **Obv:** Arms on Spanish shield on clover leaf, three leaves in field **Rev:** Inscription in palm and laurel branches **Rev. Inscription:** MONETA / NOVA / TIGURI / NA

Date	Mintage	VG	F	VF	XF	Unc
ND	—	3.00	5.00	16.00	40.00	120

KM# 11 RAPPEN

Billon **Obv:** Arms of Zurich within sprigs **Rev:** Inscription within palm and laurel branches **Rev. Inscription:** MONETA / TIGURI / NA

Date	Mintage	VG	F	VF	XF	Unc
ND	—	3.00	5.00	8.00	12.00	20.00

PATTERNS

Including off metal strikes

KM#	Date	Mintage	Identification	Mkt Val

Pn1	1620	—	Dicken. Silver. 14.9900 g. KM#32.	—

Pn2	ND	—	Angster. Gold. 0.8400 g. KM#7.	1,100
Pn3	ND	—	Schilling. Gold. KM#13. Klippe.	1,500
Pn4	1624	—	Batzen. Gold. KM#41.	3,000
Pn5	1694	—	Thaler. Silver.	—

SYRIA

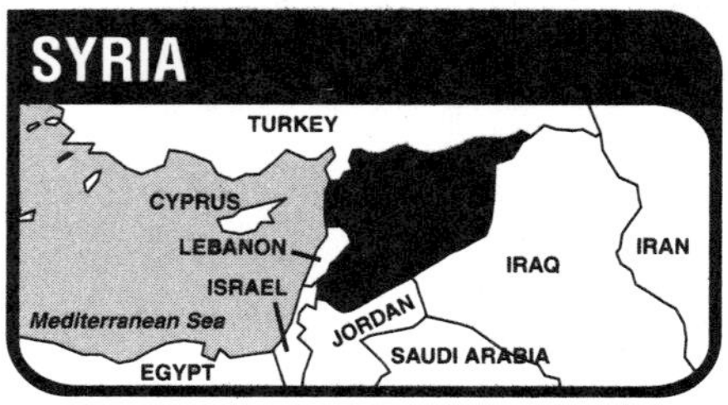

TURKEY CYPRUS LEBANON ISRAEL Mediterranean Sea EGYPT JORDAN SAUDI ARABIA IRAQ IRAN

The Syrian Arab Republic, located in the Near East at the eastern end of the Mediterranean Sea, has an area of 71,498 sq. mi. (185,180 sq. km.).

Ancient Syria, a land bridge connecting Europe, Africa and Asia, has spent much of its history in thrall to the conqueror's whim. Its subjection by Egypt about 1500 B.C. was followed by successive conquests by the Hebrews, Phoenicians, Babylonians, Assyrians, Persians, Macedonians, Romans, Byzantines and finally, in 636 A.D., by the Moslems. The Arabs made Damascus, one of the oldest continuously inhabited cities of the world, the trade center and capital of an empire stretching from India to Spain. In 1516, following the total destruction of Damascus by the Mongols of Tamerlane, Syria fell to the Ottoman Turks and remained a part of Turkey until the end of World War I.

TITLES

الجمهورية السورية

Al-Jumhuriya(t) al-Suriya(t)

RULER

Ottoman, until 1918

MINT NAME

دمشق

Damascus (Dimask)

بلب

Haleb (Aleppo)

MONETARY SYSTEM

100 Piastres (Qirsh) = 1 Pound (Lira)

OTTOMAN EMPIRE

Memed III

AH1003-12/1595-1603AD

HAMMERED COINAGE

Damascus

KM# A1 MANGIR

Copper **Note:** Weight varies: 1.50-3.00 grams.

Date	Mintage	Good	VG	F	VF	XF
AH1003	—	40.00	50.00	60.00	100	—

Haleb

KM# 1 MANGIR

Copper **Note:** Weight varies: 1.50-3.00 grams.

Date	Mintage	Good	VG	F	VF	XF
AH1003	—	22.50	27.50	33.00	55.00	—

Damascus

KM# 2 Akce

0.2000 g., Silver

Date	Mintage	Good	VG	F	VF	XF
AH1003	—	31.25	37.50	50.00	75.00	—

Haleb

KM# 3 Akce

0.2000 g., Silver

Date	Mintage	Good	VG	F	VF	XF
AH1003	—	8.00	12.00	20.00	40.00	—

KM# 5 Medin

Silver **Note:** Weight varies: 1.25-1.30 grams.

Date	Mintage	Good	VG	F	VF	XF
AH1003	—	13.00	25.00	50.00	75.00	—

KM#9 Dirhem

2.4500 g., Silver **Note:** Weight varies: 1.25-1.30 grams.

Date	Mintage	Good	VG	F	VF	XF
AH1003	—	13.00	19.00	25.00	45.00	—

Damascus

KM# 6 Sultani

3.4500 g., Gold

Date	Mintage	Good	VG	F	VF	XF
AH1003	—	100	150	220	350	—

Haleb

KM# 8 Sultani

3.4500 g., Gold

Date	Mintage	Good	VG	F	VF	XF
AH1003	—	100	150	220	350	—

Ahmed I

AH1012-26/1603-17AD

HAMMERED COINAGE

Haleb

KM# 11 MANGIR

1.9000 g., Copper

Date	Mintage	Good	VG	F	VF	XF
AH1012	—	37.50	43.75	65.00	95.00	—

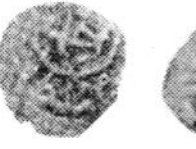

Damascus

KM# 14 AKCE

0.2200 g., Silver

Date	Mintage	Good	VG	F	VF	XF
AH1012	—	22.50	31.25	37.50	65.00	—

Haleb

KM# 15 AKCE

0.2200 g., Silver

Date	Mintage	Good	VG	F	VF	XF
AH1012	—	10.00	13.00	18.00	31.25	—

Haleb

KM# 12 MEDIN

Silver **Note:** Weight varies: 1.25-1.30 grams.

Date	Mintage	Good	VG	F	VF	XF
AH1012	—	13.00	25.00	50.00	75.00	—

Damascus

KM# 17 DIRHEM

Silver **Rev:** Legend in three lines **Note:** Reduced weight varies: 2.10-2.30 grams.

Date	Mintage	Good	VG	F	VF	XF
AH1012	—	30.00	34.50	46.00	80.00	—

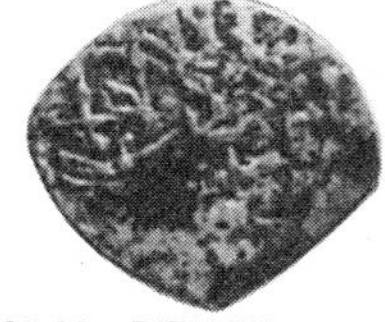

KM# 13 DIRHEM

2.9100 g., Silver **Note:** Size varies: 14-16 millimeters.

Date	Mintage	Good	VG	F	VF	XF
AH1012	—	30.00	40.00	55.00	100	—

Haleb

KM# 16 DIRHEM

Silver **Rev:** Circular legend around mint name **Note:** Weight varies: 2.10-2.18 grams.

Date	Mintage	Good	VG	F	VF	XF
AH1012	—	19.00	25.00	31.25	50.00	—

KM# 18 DIRHEM

Silver **Rev:** Legend around six-pointed star **Note:** Weight varies: 2.10-2.30 grams.

Date	Mintage	Good	VG	F	VF	XF
AH1012	—	20.00	25.00	32.50	50.00	—

Damascus

KM# 21 SULTANI

3.4500 g., Gold **Rev. Inscription:** Darib al-Nasr...

Date	Mintage	VG	F	VF	XF	Unc
AH1012	—	75.00	120	200	300	—

KM# 22 SULTANI

3.4500 g., Gold **Rev. Inscription:** Sultan al-Barrain....

Date	Mintage	VG	F	VF	XF	Unc
AH1012	—	125	150	220	350	—

Haleb

KM# 24 SULTANI

3.4500 g., Gold

Date	Mintage	VG	F	VF	XF	Unc
AH1012	—	100	125	200	325	—
AH10012 Error	—	135	175	275	450	—

Mustafa I

AH1026-27/1617-18AD First Reign

HAMMERED COINAGE

Damascus

KM# A25 AKCE

0.3600 g., Silver, 13 mm.

Date	Mintage	Good	VG	F	VF	XF
AH1026 Rare	—	—	—	—	—	—

Haleb

KM# 25 MEDIN

1.2500 g., Silver

Date	Mintage	Good	VG	F	VF	XF
AH1026 Rare	—	—	—	—	—	—

Haleb

KM# 28 SULTANI

3.4500 g., Gold

Date	Mintage	Good	VG	F	VF	XF
AH1026 Rare	—	—	—	—	—	—

Osman II

AH1027-31/1618-22AD

HAMMERED COINAGE

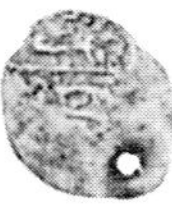

Damascus

KM# 30 AKCE

0.3500 g., Silver

Date	Mintage	Good	VG	F	VF	XF
AH1027	—	40.00	45.00	60.00	100	—

Haleb

KM# 31 AKCE

0.3500 g., Silver

Date	Mintage	Good	VG	F	VF	XF
AH1027	—	15.00	20.00	25.00	50.00	—

Haleb

KM# 34 MEDIN

1.2500 g., Silver

Date	Mintage	Good	VG	F	VF	XF
AH1027	—	20.00	25.00	30.00	60.00	—

Haleb

KM# 32 DIRHEM

Silver **Note:** Weight varies: 2.10-2.18 grams.

Date	Mintage	Good	VG	F	VF	XF
AH1027	—	50.00	60.00	75.00	125	—

Haleb

KM# 33 ONLUK

2.9000 g., Silver **Note:** The Dirham and the Onluk may refer to the same type.

Date	Mintage	Good	VG	F	VF	XF
AH1027	—	50.00	60.00	75.00	125	—

Damascus

KM# 36 SULTANI

3.4500 g., Gold **Note:** Size varies 21-22 mm.

Date	Mintage	Good	VG	F	VF	XF
AH1027	—	—	220	275	350	500

Haleb

KM# 38 SULTANI

3.4500 g., Gold **Note:** Size varies 21-22 mm.

Date	Mintage	Good	VG	F	VF	XF
AH1027	—	—	200	250	325	450

KM# 39 SULTANI

3.4500 g., Gold, 19.5 mm.

Date	Mintage	Good	VG	F	VF	XF
AH1029	—	—	70.00	120	200	300

Mustafa I

AH1031-32/1622-23AD Second Reign

HAMMERED COINAGE

Haleb

KM# 26 DIRHEM

2.7900 g., Silver, 22 mm.

Date	Mintage	Good	VG	F	VF	XF
AH1031	—	70.00	80.00	100	175	—

Damascus

KM# 27 SULTANI

3.4500 g., Gold

Date	Mintage	Good	VG	F	VF	XF
AH1031 Rare	—	—	—	—	—	—

Murad IV

AH1032-49/1623-40AD

HAMMERED COINAGE

Damascus

KM# 40 MANGIR

Copper **Note:** Weight varies: 1.50-3.00 grams.

Date	Mintage	Good	VG	F	VF	XF
AH1032	—	40.00	45.00	55.00	100	—

Haleb

KM# 41 MANGIR

Copper **Note:** Weight varies: 1.50-3.00 grams.

Date	Mintage	Good	VG	F	VF	XF
AH1032	—	7.00	18.00	36.00	60.00	—

Damascus

KM# 43 AKCE

Silver **Note:** Weight varies: 0.35-0.40 grams.

Date	Mintage	Good	VG	F	VF	XF
AH1032	—	25.00	30.00	35.00	60.00	—

Haleb

KM# 42 AKCE

Silver **Note:** Weight varies: 0.35-0.40 grams.

Date	Mintage	Good	VG	F	VF	XF
AH1032	—	10.00	15.00	20.00	40.00	—

Damascus

KM# 45 MEDIN

1.7000 g., Silver

Date	Mintage	Good	VG	F	VF	XF
AH1032	—	30.00	50.00	90.00	150	—

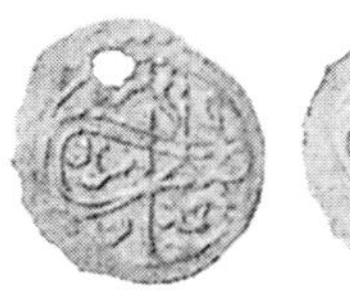

Haleb

KM# 44 MEDIN

1.2000 g., Silver

Date	Mintage	Good	VG	F	VF	XF
AH1032	—	30.00	50.00	90.00	150	—

Damascus

KM# 48 DIRHEM

Silver **Note:** Weight varies: 1.79-1.98 grams.

Date	Mintage	Good	VG	F	VF	XF
AH1032	—	40.00	60.00	100	150	—

Haleb

KM# 46 DIRHEM

2.0600 g., Silver **Note:** Several legend varieties exist.

Date	Mintage	Good	VG	F	VF	XF
AH1032	—	40.00	50.00	60.00	85.00	—

Ibraham

AH1040-58/1640-48AD

HAMMERED COINAGE

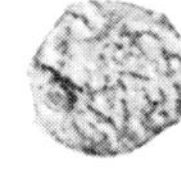

Damascus

KM# 50 AKCE

Silver **Note:** Weight varies: 0.28-0.32 grams.

Date	Mintage	Good	VG	F	VF	XF
AH1049	—	25.00	30.00	40.00	75.00	—

Damascus

KM# 51 BESLIK

Silver **Note:** Weight varies: 1.50-1.55 grams.

Date	Mintage	Good	VG	F	VF	XF
AH1049	—	40.00	60.00	100	150	—

Haleb

KM# A51 BESLIK

Silver **Note:** Weight varies: 1.50-1.55 grams.

Date	Mintage	Good	VG	F	VF	XF
AH1049	—	30.00	35.00	45.00	75.00	—

Mehmed IV

AH1058-99/1648-87AD

HAMMERED COINAGE

Damascus

KM# 54 MANGIR

2.8100 g., Copper, 14 mm.

Date	Mintage	Good	VG	F	VF	XF
AH1058	—	25.00	30.00	40.00	80.00	—

Damascus

KM# 52 AKCE

Silver **Note:** Weight varies: 0.25-0.28 grams. Varieties exist.

Date	Mintage	Good	VG	F	VF	XF
AH1058	—	30.00	35.00	40.00	75.00	—

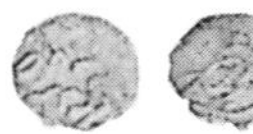

Haleb

KM# 53 AKCE

Silver **Note:** Weight varies: 0.25-0.28 grams.

Date	Mintage	Good	VG	F	VF	XF
AH1058	—	35.00	40.00	50.00	75.00	—

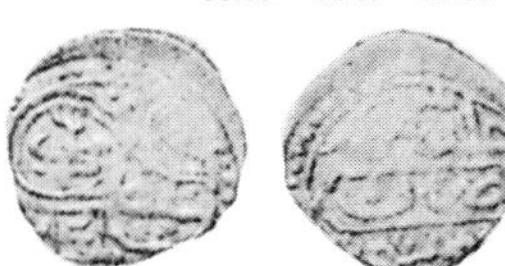

Haleb

KM# 56 MEDIN

0.7800 g., Silver

Date	Mintage	Good	VG	F	VF	XF
AH1058	—	45.00	60.00	70.00	110	—

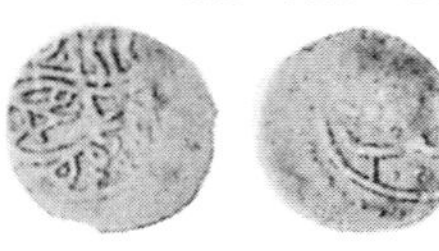

Damascus

KM# 59 BESLIK

Silver **Note:** Weight varies: 1.27-1.35 grams.

Date	Mintage	Good	VG	F	VF	XF
AH1058	—	20.00	25.00	35.00	75.00	—

Haleb

KM# 60 BESLIK

Silver **Note:** Weight varies: 1.27-1.35 grams.

Date	Mintage	Good	VG	F	VF	XF
AH1058	—	22.50	27.50	40.00	80.00	—

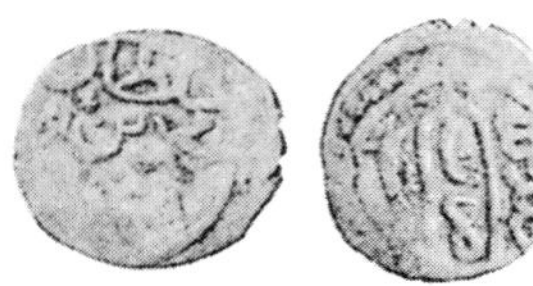

Haleb

KM# 62 DIRHEM

2.2800 g., Silver

Date	Mintage	Good	VG	F	VF	XF
AH1058	—	30.00	35.00	40.00	85.00	—

KM# 63 DIRHEM

2.2800 g., Silver

Date	Mintage	Good	VG	F	VF	XF
AH1058	—	30.00	35.00	40.00	85.00	—

TRANSYLVANIA

Transylvania (Cibin, Siebenburgen) is the plateau region of northwestern Romania, formerly part of Ancient Dacia, a region occupied by the Romans u'nder Emperor Trajan in 100 AD and abandoned to the Goths in 271 AD under Aurelianus. The Romanized population maintained its Latin speech and Christian identity.

In 896 the Hungarians settled into the Carpathian basin, this included Transylvania. While the region remained an autonomous principality, mercenary Saxons enforced the suzerainty of the King of Hungary in exchange for land. When the Hungarian army was defeated by the advancing Turks at Monacs in 1526, the country was divided into three parts under protection of the Sultan. The center was occupied by the Turks, the West by the Hungary Kingdom under the Hapsburgs and Transylvania in the East which became a principality in 1540. Holy Roman Emperor Rudolf II seized control of the territory in 1604 after the murder of Michael the Brave of Wallachia, who had briefly united the Romanian principalities. In 1605 the Diet elected Stephen Bocskaias prince. After George Rakoczi II was defeated in war with Poland, the Turks were able to intervene, deposing the prince and appointing their own vassals. After the defeat of the Ottoman Turks in 1683, the Transylvanian princes then looked to Austria for guidance and protection.

The last Turkish vassal abdicated in 1697, and with the Orthodox Romanians recognizing the authority of the Pope, the Greek-Catholic, or Uniate Church is created. Under these circumstances, and the treaty of Szatmar in 1711, Transylvania was absorbed into the vast Holy Roman Empire. Transylvania continued to be a part of Hungary until the end of World War I. In 1918, Romania occupied Transylvania.

RULERS

Austrian
Michael the Brave of Wallachia, 1601
no monetary issues
Austrian Commissaries, 1602-1603, 1604
no monetary issues
Sigismund Bathori, 1601-1602
coinage of Kronstad
Francis Rakoczi, 1652-1676
no monetary issues
Francis Rhedei, 1657-1658
no monetary issues
George Bannfy I, 1691-1708
Governor and Count of Losoncz
Leopold I, 1690-1705

Local Princes

Moses Szekely, 1603
Stephan Bocskai, 1604-1606
(postmortem issues 1607-1609)
Sigismund Rakoczi, 1606-1608
Gabriel Bathori, 1608-1613
Gabriel Bethlen, 1613-1629
Catherine of Brandenburg, 1629-1630
widow of Gabriel Bethlen
Stephan Bethlen, 1630
George Rakoczi I, 1630-1648
George Rakoczi II, 1648-1660
John Kemeny, 1661-1662

Turkish Vassals

Achatius Barcsai, 1658-1660
Michael Apafi, 1661-1690
Emeric Tokely, 1682-1690
Michael Apafi II, 1690
no monetary issues

MINT MARKS

A-B - Abrud, 1661
A-C - (Arx Claudiopolis), Klausenburg, Cluj, Kolosvar, 1671-1673
AF - (Arx Fogarasch), 1668-89
AI - (Alba Iulia), Karlsburg, 1610-83 (Wissenburg) until 1716
AL-IV - (Alba Iulia), Karlsburg, 1611-13
AZ - (Arx Zalathna), Zlatna
BE \ V - (Besztercze Varos), Bistritz, Bistrita, 1673
BEZ - (Besztercze), Bistritz, Bistrita, 1673
BF – Opole, Polen, 1622-23
BN - Nagybanya
BT - (Besztercze), Bistritz, Bistrita, 1672-73

C - Civitas (Brassoviensis), 1614
CB - (Cibinium), Hermannstadt, 1672
CB - (Claudiolopolis), Klausenburg, Kolosvar, Cluj, 1604-1605
CB - (Civitas Brassoviensis), Kronstadt, Brasov, 1612-60
CB \ crowned roots, 1662-1675
crowned roots, 1601-1674
C-B - (Cibiniu-Sibiu), 1673-1674
CC - (Camera Cassoviensis), Cassovia, Koshice, 1625-1629 (Kaschau), 1574-83, 1693-98, 1705-07
CF - (Civitas Fogarasch), (w/3 fish) Fagaras, 1677
CI, CI-BI, CIBIN, C-B - (Cibinium), Hermannstadt, Sibiu, 1611-13, 1660, 1672
Cor. - (Corona), Kronstadt
CM - (Cibiniensis moneta), Hermannstadt
CM - (Cassoviensis moneta), Cassovia, Koshice, (Kaschau), 1619, 1623-27
CV - (Colosvar), Klausenburg, Cluj, 1636-94
Cor. - (Cibinium), Hermannstadt
D-K – Sibin, 1671
FB - (Felso Banya), Baia Sprie
Fog. - (Fogarasch)
FT - (?), Klausenberg, 1696-1697
HS - Hermannstadt, Sibiu, 1606
KB - (Kormoczbanya), Kremnitz, Kremnica, 1620-22
KO - (Kolosvar), Klausenburg, Cluj, 1613
KS - (Kis-Selyk), Seica-Mica, 1610
KV - (Kolosvar), Klausenburg, Cluj, 1693-1707
M - (Mediasch)
MC - (Moneta Cibiniensis), Hermannstadt, Sibiu, 1672
MC - (Moneta Cassoviensis), Cassovia, Kaschau, Kosice, Slovakia, 1619, 1626-1627
M-M - (Moneta-Munkacsiensis), Mukachiv, Ukraine, 1623
MO \ COM \ N-E - (Moneta Comitatus), Nagy-Enyed, Aiud, 1673-75
MR - Hermannstadt, Sibiu, 1671-72
NB - Nagybanya, Baia-Mare, 1589-1659
NE - Nagy-Enyed, Aiud, 1672
O - (Oravita), Orawitza Banat, 1783, 1812, 1816
P-S – Sibin, 1673
SB - Schassburg, Sighisoara, 1433-1435, 1661, 1664, 1666-1673
SV - Szeben-Varos, Hermannstadt, Sibiu, 1673
SV - Szasz Varos, Orastie, 1672-1675
ZB - Zalathna Banya, Zlatna
Root of the tree under crown – Brasov, 1601-74

HERMANNSTADT MINT OFFICIALS' INITIALS

Initial	Date	Name
A-HR	1605	Anton Huet
GS		Georg Schuler
IR	1660	Johann Ruckinsattel
MR	1671-72	Unknown
PS	1673	Unknown

MONETARY SYSTEM

1 Denar = 2 Obols
1 Kreuzer = 2 Denars
1 Poltura = 3 Denars
1 Groschen = 3 Kreuzer
1 Sechser = 6 Denars
1 Zwolfer = 12 Denars
1 Gulden = 60 Kreuzer
1 Thaler = 2 Gulden

NOTE: Refer also to Austrian listings for common circulation types struck at mints listed above.

PRINCIPALITY

STANDARD COINAGE

KM# 152 MINING PFENNIG (Bergwerkspfennig)

Copper

Date	Mintage	VG	F	VF	XF	Unc
1623	—	90.00	115	150	255	—

KM# 166 MINING PFENNIG (Bergwerkspfennig)

Copper

Date	Mintage	VG	F	VF	XF	Unc
1626 F-B - A-Z	—	70.00	90.00	140	230	—

KM# 197 MINING PFENNIG (Bergwerkspfennig)

Copper

Date	Mintage	VG	F	VF	XF	Unc
1628 I-L - F-K	—	70.00	90.00	140	230	—
1628 Z-B - F-K	—	70.00	90.00	140	230	—

KM# 220 MINING PFENNIG (Bergwerkspfennig)

Copper

Date	Mintage	VG	F	VF	XF	Unc
1630	—	90.00	115	150	255	—

KM# 230 MINING PFENNIG (Bergwerkspfennig)
Copper

Date	Mintage	VG	F	VF	XF	Unc
1634 Z-B	—	90.00	115	150	255	—

KM# 246 MINING PFENNIG (Bergwerkspfennig)
Copper, 25 mm. **Obv:** W.

Date	Mintage	VG	F	VF	XF	Unc
1643	—	90.00	115	150	255	—

KM# 248 MINING PFENNIG (Bergwerkspfennig)
Copper **Obv:** V

Date	Mintage	VG	F	VF	XF	Unc
1643	—	90.00	115	150	255	—

KM# 247 MINING PFENNIG (Bergwerkspfennig)
Copper, 14 mm. **Note:** Reduced size.

Date	Mintage	VG	F	VF	XF	Unc
1643	—	90.00	115	150	255	—

KM# 249 MINING PFENNIG (Bergwerkspfennig)
Copper

Date	Mintage	VG	F	VF	XF	Unc
1644	—	90.00	115	150	255	—

KM# 250 MINING PFENNIG (Bergwerkspfennig)
Copper **Note:** Varieties exist.

Date	Mintage	VG	F	VF	XF	Unc
1663NB Rare	—	115	230	450	925	—

KM# 130 OBOL
0.3000 g., Silver, 11 mm. **Obv:** Date above arms

Date	Mintage	VG	F	VF	XF	Unc
1621KB	—	60.00	90.00	140	230	—

KM# 131 OBOL
0.3000 g., Silver

Date	Mintage	VG	F	VF	XF	Unc
1621NB	—	60.00	90.00	140	230	—
1622KB	—	60.00	90.00	140	230	—

KM# 167 OBOL
0.3000 g., Silver **Obv:** Crowned arms **Rev:** Madonna divides date

Date	Mintage	VG	F	VF	XF	Unc
1626KB	—	60.00	90.00	140	230	—

KM# 76 DENAR
0.5000 g., Silver **Obv:** Hermannstadt arms **Note:** Varieties exist.

Date	Mintage	VG	F	VF	XF	Unc
1611CI	—	34.50	70.00	115	230	—

KM# 87 DENAR
0.5000 g., Silver **Obv:** Different shaped shield with Hermannstadt arms **Note:** Varieties exist.

Date	Mintage	VG	F	VF	XF	Unc
1612CI	—	34.50	70.00	115	230	—

KM# 93 DENAR
0.5000 g., Silver **Obv:** Hermannstadt arms

Date	Mintage	VG	F	VF	XF	Unc
1613CI	—	34.50	70.00	115	230	—

KM# 106 DENAR
0.5000 g., Silver **Obv:** Hermannstadt arms on shield

Date	Mintage	VG	F	VF	XF	Unc
1614	—	34.50	70.00	115	230	—

KM# 107 DENAR
0.5000 g., Silver **Obv:** Hermannstadt arms in center

Date	Mintage	VG	F	VF	XF	Unc
1614	—	34.50	70.00	115	230	—

KM# 120 DENAR
0.5000 g., Silver **Obv:** Hungarian arms **Note:** Varieties exist.

Date	Mintage	VG	F	VF	XF	Unc
1620KB	—	12.00	22.50	40.25	65.00	—
1621 KA	—	12.00	22.50	40.25	65.00	—
1621AI	—	12.00	22.50	40.25	65.00	—
1621KB	—	12.00	22.50	40.25	65.00	—
1621NB	—	12.00	22.50	40.25	65.00	—
1622KB	—	12.00	22.50	40.25	65.00	—
1623BZ	—	12.00	22.50	40.25	65.00	—
1623CM	—	12.00	22.50	40.25	65.00	—
1623NB	—	12.00	22.50	40.25	65.00	—
1623ZB	—	12.00	22.50	40.25	65.00	—
1624NB	—	12.00	22.50	40.25	65.00	—

KM# 162 DENAR
0.5000 g., Silver **Obv:** Crowned Hungarian arms **Note:** Varieties exist.

Date	Mintage	VG	F	VF	XF	Unc
1625NB	—	12.00	22.50	40.25	65.00	—
1626NB	—	12.00	22.50	40.25	65.00	—
1626CC	—	12.00	22.50	40.25	65.00	—

KM# 168 DENAR
Billon

Date	Mintage	VG	F	VF	XF	Unc
1626NB	—	9.00	18.00	34.50	60.00	—
1627NB	—	9.00	18.00	34.50	60.00	—

KM# 210 DENAR
Billon

Date	Mintage	VG	F	VF	XF	Unc
1629NB	—	12.00	22.50	40.25	65.00	—

KM# 288 DENAR
Silver **Obv:** Crowned Hungarian arms **Rev:** Madonna in flame circle

Date	Mintage	VG	F	VF	XF	Unc
1653NB	—	12.00	22.50	40.25	65.00	—

KM# 231 DREI (3) POLKER (= 3 Grosze)
1.2000 g., Silver **Note:** Varieties exist.

Date	Mintage	VG	F	VF	XF	Unc
1636CV	—	40.25	75.00	140	255	—
1637	—	40.25	75.00	140	255	—
1638	—	40.25	75.00	140	255	—

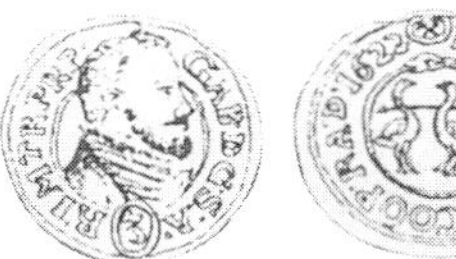

KM# 143 3 KREUZER (Groschen)
Silver, 17 mm. **Note:** Varieties exist. Weight varies: 0.80-1.10 grams.

Date	Mintage	VG	F	VF	XF	Unc
1622	—	30.00	65.00	115	230	—
1622BZ	—	30.00	65.00	115	230	—
1623BZ	—	30.00	65.00	115	230	—

KM# 518 3 KREUZER (Groschen)
Silver **Obv:** Laureate bust of Leopold I right in inner circle, value below **Rev:** Crowned imperial eagle in inner circle, crown divides date **Note:** Varieties exist. Weight varies: 0.80-1.10 grams.

Date	Mintage	VG	F	VF	XF	Unc
1696 FT	—	22.50	50.00	85.00	155	—
1697 FT	—	22.50	50.00	85.00	155	—

KM# 519 3 KREUZER (Groschen)
Silver **Note:** Varieties exist. Weight varies: 0.80-1.10 grams.

Date	Mintage	VG	F	VF	XF	Unc
1696 FT	—	30.00	60.00	100	175	—

KM# 153 24 KREUZER
2.7000 g., Silver **Note:** Varieties exist.

Date	Mintage	VG	F	VF	XF	Unc
1623BZ	—	40.25	85.00	175	290	—
1623ZB	—	40.25	85.00	175	290	—
1623BN	—	40.25	85.00	175	290	—
1.263 BZ Error	—	40.25	85.00	175	290	—
1623 BZ	—	40.25	85.00	175	290	—

KM# 434 SECHSER

Silver **Rev:** Small Hermannstadt arms

Date	Mintage	VG	F	VF	XF	Unc
1673 PS	—	115	200	350	575	—

KM# 435 SECHSER

Silver **Obv:** Larger bust

Date	Mintage	VG	F	VF	XF	Unc
1673CB	—	115	200	350	575	—

KM# 436 SECHSER

Silver **Rev:** Date quartered by arms

Date	Mintage	VG	F	VF	XF	Unc
1673CB	—	115	200	350	575	—

KM# 438 SECHSER

Silver **Rev:** Circle with MO • CO • M at bottom replacing small city arms

Date	Mintage	VG	F	VF	XF	Unc
1673NE	—	115	200	350	575	—

KM# 437 SECHSER

Silver **Rev:** Small arms of Kronstadt **Note:** Varieties exist.

Date	Mintage	VG	F	VF	XF	Unc
1673	—	115	200	350	575	—
1673NE	—	115	200	350	575	—

KM# 455 SECHSER

Silver **Rev:** Circle with MO-C at bottom

Date	Mintage	VG	F	VF	XF	Unc
1674NE	—	115	200	350	575	—

KM# 456 SECHSER

Silver **Rev:** Small Hermannstadt arms **Note:** Varieties exist.

Date	Mintage	VG	F	VF	XF	Unc
1674	—	115	200	350	575	—
1674CI	—	115	200	350	575	—
1674CB	—	115	200	350	575	—

KM# 461 SECHSER

Silver

Date	Mintage	VG	F	VF	XF	Unc
1675 NF	—	115	200	350	575	—

KM# 421 ZWOLFER

Silver **Rev:** Small Kronstadt arms at bottom center **Note:** Varieties exist. Weight varies: 2.60-2.90 grams.

Date	Mintage	VG	F	VF	XF	Unc
1672	—	85.00	145	230	400	—

KM# 417 ZWOLFER

Silver **Note:** Weight varies: 2.60-2.90 grams.

Date	Mintage	VG	F	VF	XF	Unc
1672CI-BI	—	75.00	140	230	425	—

KM# 418 ZWOLFER

Silver **Rev:** Small Hermannstadt arms at bottom **Note:** Weight varies: 2.60-2.90 grams.

Date	Mintage	VG	F	VF	XF	Unc
1672	—	60.00	115	200	350	—

KM# 420 ZWOLFER

Silver **Note:** Weight varies: 2.60-2.90 grams.

Date	Mintage	VG	F	VF	XF	Unc
1672NE Retrograde 2	—	60.00	115	200	350	—

KM# 419 ZWOLFER

Silver **Note:** Varieties exist. Weight varies: 2.60-2.90 grams.

Date	Mintage	VG	F	VF	XF	Unc
1672MC	—	60.00	115	200	350	—
1672NE	—	60.00	115	200	350	—

KM# 441 ZWOLFER

Silver **Note:** Varieties exist. Weight varies: 2.60-2.90 grams.

Date	Mintage	VG	F	VF	XF	Unc
1673SV	—	60.00	115	200	350	—

KM# 443 ZWOLFER

Silver Plated Copper **Rev:** Quartered date

Date	Mintage	VG	F	VF	XF	Unc
1673	—	70.00	115	215	350	—

KM# 444 ZWOLFER

Silver Plated Copper **Rev:** PE-V replacing small Kronstadt arms, date quartered

Date	Mintage	VG	F	VF	XF	Unc
1673 PEV	—	75.00	140	230	400	—

KM# 442 ZWOLFER

Silver **Rev:** Small Hermannstadt arms **Note:** Varieties exist. Weight varies: 2.60-2.90 grams.

Date	Mintage	VG	F	VF	XF	Unc
1673	—	75.00	140	230	400	—
1637 Error	—	75.00	140	230	400	—

KM# 439 ZWOLFER

Silver **Rev:** Small Hermannstadt arms **Note:** Varieties exist. Weight varies: 2.60-2.90 grams.

Date	Mintage	VG	F	VF	XF	Unc
1673	—	60.00	115	200	350	—
1673CI	—	60.00	115	200	350	—
1673SV	—	60.00	115	200	350	—

KM# 440 ZWOLFER

Silver **Rev:** Different Hermannstadt arms **Note:** Varieties exist. Weight varies: 2.60-2.90 grams.

Date	Mintage	VG	F	VF	XF	Unc
1673SV	—	60.00	115	200	350	—
1673SV Inverted date	—	60.00	115	200	350	—
1673 XX	—	60.00	115	200	350	—

KM# 457 ZWOLFER

Silver Plated Copper **Rev:** Small Hermannstadt arms

Date	Mintage	VG	F	VF	XF	Unc
1674	—	60.00	115	215	375	—

KM# 458 ZWOLFER

Silver Plated Copper **Rev:** Small Kronstadt arms, quartered date

Date	Mintage	VG	F	VF	XF	Unc
1674	—	70.00	130	230	400	—

KM# 48 GROSCHEN

Silver **Obv:** Heraldic Transylvanian eagle **Rev:** Fur hat above seven castle towers **Note:** Varieties exist. Weight varies: 1.40-2.20 grams.

Date	Mintage	VG	F	VF	XF	Unc
1608NB	—	25.00	46.00	70.00	100	—
1609NB	—	25.00	46.00	70.00	100	—

KM# 54 GROSCHEN

Silver **Note:** Weight varies: 1.40-2.20 grams.

Date	Mintage	VG	F	VF	XF	Unc
1609NB	—	25.00	46.00	70.00	100	—

KM# 70 GROSCHEN

Silver **Rev:** Five-part arms **Note:** Weight varies: 1.40-2.20 grams.

Date	Mintage	VG	F	VF	XF	Unc
1610NB	—	25.00	50.00	75.00	105	—

KM# 71 GROSCHEN

Silver **Rev:** Four-part arms **Note:** Varieties exist. Weight varies: 1.40-2.20 grams.

Date	Mintage	VG	F	VF	XF	Unc
1610NB	—	25.00	50.00	75.00	105	—

KM# 72 GROSCHEN

Silver **Obv:** Crown above three-line inscription and date **Rev:** Heraldic eagle right **Note:** Varieties exist. Weight varies: 1.40-2.20 grams.

Date	Mintage	VG	F	VF	XF	Unc
1610NB	—	25.00	40.25	70.00	100	—
1611NB	—	25.00	40.25	70.00	100	—
1611	—	25.00	40.25	70.00	100	—
1612NB	—	25.00	40.25	70.00	100	—
1613NB	—	25.00	40.25	70.00	100	—

KM# 109 GROSCHEN

1.9000 g., Silver **Note:** Klippe. Varieties exist.

Date	Mintage	VG	F	VF	XF	Unc
1617 Rare	—	—	—	—	—	—

KM# 110 GROSCHEN

Silver **Note:** Round version of KM#109. Varieties exist.

Date	Mintage	VG	F	VF	XF	Unc
1617	—	40.25	75.00	115	200	—

KM# 112 GROSCHEN

Silver **Note:** Varieties exist.

Date	Mintage	VG	F	VF	XF	Unc
1619	—	25.00	50.00	75.00	105	—

KM# 121 GROSCHEN

Silver **Rev:** Madonna holding child on right side

Date	Mintage	VG	F	VF	XF	Unc
16Z0NB	—	25.00	50.00	75.00	105	—

KM# 122 GROSCHEN

Silver **Rev:** Madonna holding child on left side

Date	Mintage	VG	F	VF	XF	Unc
1620	—	25.00	50.00	75.00	105	—

KM# 123 GROSCHEN

1.4000 g., Silver

Date	Mintage	VG	F	VF	XF	Unc
1620	—	25.00	50.00	75.00	105	—

KM# 132 GROSCHEN

Silver **Obv:** Arms **Rev:** Madonna and child **Note:** Varieties exist.

Date	Mintage	VG	F	VF	XF	Unc
1621NB	—	25.00	50.00	75.00	105	—
16ZZNB	—	25.00	50.00	75.00	105	—
1623CM	—	25.00	50.00	75.00	105	—
1623NB	—	25.00	50.00	75.00	105	—

KM# 144 GROSCHEN

Silver

Date	Mintage	VG	F	VF	XF	Unc
1622 BZ	—	25.00	50.00	75.00	105	—

KM# 154 GROSCHEN

Silver **Rev:** Silesian eagle **Note:** Klippe.

Date	Mintage	VG	F	VF	XF	Unc
1623 BZ Rare	—	—	—	—	—	—

KM# 161 GROSCHEN

Silver **Obv:** Hungarian arms **Rev:** Madonna and child **Note:** Varieties exist.

Date	Mintage	VG	F	VF	XF	Unc
1624CM	—	25.00	50.00	75.00	105	—
1624 MM	—	25.00	50.00	75.00	105	—
1624NB	—	25.00	50.00	75.00	105	—
1624	—	25.00	50.00	75.00	105	—
1625CM	—	25.00	50.00	75.00	105	—
1625NB	—	25.00	50.00	75.00	105	—

KM# 163 GROSCHEN

Silver **Obv:** Madonna and child **Rev:** Crowned Hungarian arms **Note:** Varieties exist.

Date	Mintage	VG	F	VF	XF	Unc
1625NB	—	25.00	50.00	75.00	105	—
1625CC	—	25.00	50.00	75.00	105	—

KM# 164 GROSCHEN

Silver **Note:** Varieties exist.

Date	Mintage	VG	F	VF	XF	Unc
1625	—	25.00	46.00	70.00	100	—
1625NB	—	25.00	46.00	70.00	100	—
1625CC	—	25.00	46.00	70.00	100	—

KM# 169 GROSCHEN

Silver **Obv:** Crowned Hungarian arms **Rev:** Madonna and child **Note:** Varieties exist.

Date	Mintage	VG	F	VF	XF	Unc
1626CC	—	25.00	50.00	75.00	105	—
1626NB	—	25.00	50.00	75.00	105	—
1627MC	—	25.00	50.00	75.00	105	—
1627NB	—	25.00	50.00	75.00	105	—
1628NB	—	25.00	50.00	75.00	105	—
1629NB	—	25.00	50.00	75.00	105	—

KM# 174 GROSCHEN

Silver **Obv:** Transylvania arms **Rev:** Crown above three-line inscription

Date	Mintage	VG	F	VF	XF	Unc
1627 MC	—	25.00	50.00	75.00	105	—

KM# 211 2 GROSCHEN

Silver **Note:** Similar to 1 Groschen, KM#169.

Date	Mintage	VG	F	VF	XF	Unc
1629MC	—	34.50	60.00	100	165	—

KM# 8 3 GROSCHEN

Silver **Note:** Varieties exist. Weight varies: 2.00-2.60 grams.

Date	Mintage	VG	F	VF	XF	Unc
1605	—	34.50	60.00	100	175	—
1606	—	34.50	60.00	100	175	—

KM# 39 3 GROSCHEN
Silver **Note:** Varieties exist. Weight varies: 2.00-2.60 grams.

Date	Mintage	VG	F	VF	XF	Unc
1607	—	40.25	75.00	115	200	—

KM# 38 3 GROSCHEN
Silver **Note:** Klippe. Weight varies: 2.00-2.60 grams.

Date	Mintage	VG	F	VF	XF	Unc
1607 Rare	—	—	—	—	—	—

KM# 49 3 GROSCHEN
Silver **Note:** Varieties exist. Weight varies: 2.00-2.60 grams.

Date	Mintage	VG	F	VF	XF	Unc
1608	—	22.50	40.25	75.00	115	—
1609	—	22.50	40.25	75.00	115	—

KM# 50 3 GROSCHEN
Silver **Note:** Weight varies: 2.00-2.60 grams.

Date	Mintage	VG	F	VF	XF	Unc
1608	—	22.50	40.25	75.00	115	—

KM# 56 3 GROSCHEN
Silver **Note:** Weight varies: 2.00-2.60 grams.

Date	Mintage	VG	F	VF	XF	Unc
1609	—	22.50	40.25	75.00	115	—

KM# 57 3 GROSCHEN
Silver **Note:** Varieties exist. Weight varies: 2.00-2.60 grams.

Date	Mintage	VG	F	VF	XF	Unc
1609	—	22.50	40.25	75.00	115	—
1610	—	22.50	40.25	75.00	115	—

KM# 55 3 GROSCHEN
Silver **Note:** Klippe. Weight varies: 2.00-2.60 grams.

Date	Mintage	VG	F	VF	XF	Unc
1609 Rare	—	—	—	—	—	—

KM# 77 3 GROSCHEN
Silver **Obv:** Bust of Gabriel Bathori right. **Rev:** Value III above shield divides CI-BI and date. **Note:** Klippe. Weight varies: 2.00-2.60 grams.

Date	Mintage	VG	F	VF	XF	Unc
1611 Rare	—	—	—	—	—	—

KM# 80 3 GROSCHEN
Silver **Obv:** Bust of Gabriel Bathori right. **Rev:** Value III above shield divides AL-IV and date.

Date	Mintage	VG	F	VF	XF	Unc
1611	—	22.50	40.25	75.00	115	—
1612	—	22.50	40.25	75.00	115	—
1613	—	22.50	40.25	75.00	115	—

KM# A77 3 GROSCHEN
Silver **Obv:** Bust of Gabriel Bathori right **Rev:** Value III above shield divides CI-BI and date. **Note:** Weight varies, 2.00-2.60 g.

Date	Mintage	VG	F	VF	XF	Unc
1611	—	22.00	35.00	65.00	100	—

KM# 78 3 GROSCHEN
Silver **Note:** Thick Groschen. Weight varies: 8.40-10.00 grams.

Date	Mintage	VG	F	VF	XF	Unc
1611 Rare	—	—	—	—	—	—

KM# 79 3 GROSCHEN
2.5000 g., Silver **Note:** Varieties exist.

Date	Mintage	VG	F	VF	XF	Unc
1611	—	22.50	40.25	75.00	115	—

KM# 94 3 GROSCHEN
Silver

Date	Mintage	VG	F	VF	XF	Unc
1613	—	22.50	40.25	75.00	115	—

KM# 155 3 GROSCHEN
Silver **Note:** Klippe.

Date	Mintage	VG	F	VF	XF	Unc
1623 BZ Rare	—	—	—	—	—	—

KM# 156 3 GROSCHEN
1.7000 g., Silver **Note:** Round version of KM#155.

Date	Mintage	VG	F	VF	XF	Unc
1623 BZ	—	40.25	75.00	115	200	—

KM# 157 3 GROSCHEN
1.5000 g., Silver **Obv:** Crowned portrait **Note:** Varieties exist.

Date	Mintage	VG	F	VF	XF	Unc
1623 BZ	—	40.25	65.00	115	200	—

KM# 233 3 GROSCHEN
1.7000 g., Silver **Obv:** Bust of George Rakoczi I in fur hat

Date	Mintage	VG	F	VF	XF	Unc
1637	—	40.25	65.00	110	190	—

KM# 20 6 GROSCHEN
7.0000 g., Silver

Date	Mintage	VG	F	VF	XF	Unc
1606	—	60.00	90.00	175	350	—

KM# 21 6 GROSCHEN
4.5000 g., Silver **Note:** Varieties exist.

Date	Mintage	VG	F	VF	XF	Unc
1606	—	46.00	80.00	155	325	—

KM# 234 6 GROSCHEN
2.9000 g., Silver **Rev:** Three coats of arms

Date	Mintage	VG	F	VF	XF	Unc
1637	—	40.25	75.00	140	290	—

KM# 235 6 GROSCHEN
2.9000 g., Silver **Rev:** Four coats of arms

Date	Mintage	VG	F	VF	XF	Unc
1637	—	40.25	75.00	140	290	—

KM# 236 1/2 GULDEN
6.8500 g., Silver

Date	Mintage	VG	F	VF	XF	Unc
1637	—	100	190	400	700	—

KM# 237 1/2 GULDEN
6.8500 g., Silver

Date	Mintage	VG	F	VF	XF	Unc
1637	—	100	190	400	700	—

KM# 251 1/2 GULDEN
6.8500 g., Silver

Date	Mintage	VG	F	VF	XF	Unc
1645NB	—	115	230	450	925	—

KM# 252 1/2 GULDEN
6.8500 g., Silver

Date	Mintage	VG	F	VF	XF	Unc
1645NB	—	115	230	450	925	—

KM# 285 1/2 GULDEN
7.2000 g., Silver **Obv:** Armored portrait with fur hat and scepter **Rev:** Crowned Transylvania arms

Date	Mintage	VG	F	VF	XF	Unc
1651NB	—	—	—	—	—	—

KM# 292 1/2 GULDEN
7.4000 g., Silver

Date	Mintage	VG	F	VF	XF	Unc
1656NB	—	290	525	925	1,550	—

KM# 5 GULDEN
Silver **Obv:** Two lions holding sword through crown **Rev:** Three-line inscription within legend

Date	Mintage	VG	F	VF	XF	Unc
1603	—	290	525	975	1,750	—

KM# 9 GULDEN
Silver **Obv:** Armored portrait right wearing fur hat **Rev:** Arm from clouds holding sword through coiled ribbon

Date	Mintage	VG	F	VF	XF	Unc
1605	—	290	525	975	1,750	—

KM# 22 GULDEN
9.8000 g., Silver

Date	Mintage	VG	F	VF	XF	Unc
1606	—	230	400	925	1,650	—

KM# 40 GULDEN
9.8000 g., Silver **Obv:** Armored portrait right with scepter **Rev:** Six-line inscription within legend

Date	Mintage	VG	F	VF	XF	Unc
ND(1607)	—	290	525	975	1,750	—

KM# 51 GULDEN
15.1000 g., Silver

Date	Mintage	VG	F	VF	XF	Unc
1608	—	290	525	975	1,750	—

KM# 58 GULDEN
14.8000 g., Silver **Obv:** Without helmet right of portrait

Date	Mintage	VG	F	VF	XF	Unc
1609	—	230	400	875	1,450	—

KM# 81 GULDEN
14.2000 g., Silver, 40 mm. **Obv:** Crowned arms within circled dragon and legend **Rev:** Five-line inscription

Date	Mintage	VG	F	VF	XF	Unc
1611	—	400	750	1,150	2,150	—

KM# 82 GULDEN
14.3000 g., Silver, 33 mm. **Obv:** Bear claw arms within dragon and legend **Note:** Uniface.

Date	Mintage	VG	F	VF	XF	Unc
1611	—	400	750	1,150	2,150	—

KM# 113 GULDEN
16.1000 g., Silver **Obv:** Bust right wearing cape and fur hat **Rev:** Crown wtih two supporting lions above three coats of arms

Date	Mintage	VG	F	VF	XF	Unc
1619CM	—	—	—	—	—	—

KM# 145 GULDEN
16.1000 g., Silver **Obv:** Bust right **Rev:** Coat of arms

Date	Mintage	VG	F	VF	XF	Unc
1622NB	—	—	—	—	—	—

KM# 158 GULDEN
Silver **Note:** Klippe.

Date	Mintage	VG	F	VF	XF	Unc
1623 BZ Rare	—	—	—	—	—	—

KM# 175 GULDEN
14.1000 g., Silver **Obv:** Armored bust right **Rev:** Crowned arms

Date	Mintage	VG	F	VF	XF	Unc
1627MC	—	—	—	—	—	—

KM# 176 GULDEN
13.9000 g., Silver

Date	Mintage	VG	F	VF	XF	Unc
1627NB	—	575	925	1,500	2,750	—

KM# 177 GULDEN
13.9000 g., Silver **Obv:** Different portrait **Rev:** Different arms

Date	Mintage	VG	F	VF	XF	Unc
1627NB	—	575	925	1,500	2,750	—

KM# 198 GULDEN
Silver **Obv:** Armored bust right **Note:** Weight varies: 12.40-14.60 grams.

Date	Mintage	VG	F	VF	XF	Unc
1628CC	—	625	1,100	1,750	2,900	—
1629CC	—	625	1,100	1,750	2,900	—

KM# 264 GULDEN
Silver **Obv:** Armored bust right in fur hat **Note:** Weight varies: 12.40-14.60 grams.

Date	Mintage	VG	F	VF	XF	Unc
1647NB	—	350	575	975	1,750	—

KM# 289 GULDEN
14.4000 g., Silver **Rev:** Crude crown above arms

Date	Mintage	VG	F	VF	XF	Unc
1654NB	—	—	—	—	—	—

KM# 293 GULDEN
14.0000 g., Silver

Date	Mintage	VG	F	VF	XF	Unc
1656NB	—	—	—	—	—	—

KM# 314 GULDEN
14.0000 g., Silver **Obv:** Barcsais bust right with scepter **Rev:** Crowned arms

Date	Mintage	VG	F	VF	XF	Unc
1659CV	—	525	975	1,750	2,900	—

KM# 313 GULDEN

14.0000 g., Silver **Obv:** Bust right **Rev:** Crowned arms
Note: Varieties exist.

Date	Mintage	VG	F	VF	XF	Unc
1659NB	—	525	975	1,750	2,900	—

KM# 325 GULDEN

14.0000 g., Silver **Obv:** Crowned arms in legend **Rev:** Three-line inscription within double legend **Note:** Octagonal klippe.

Date	Mintage	VG	F	VF	XF	Unc
1660 Rare	—	—	—	—	—	—

KM# 326 GULDEN

14.0000 g., Silver **Note:** Round version of KM#325.

Date	Mintage	VG	F	VF	XF	Unc
1660 Rare	—	—	—	—	—	—
1661	—	—	—	—	—	—

KM# 344 GULDEN

13.8000 g., Silver **Obv:** Crowned arms and legend **Rev:** Angel head above inscription, tree trunk below

Date	Mintage	VG	F	VF	XF	Unc
1661CB	—	550	900	1,100	2,600	—

KM# 361 GULDEN

Silver **Rev:** Crowned arms with Kronstadt arms at bottom

Date	Mintage	VG	F	VF	XF	Unc
1662CB Rare	—	—	—	—	—	—

KM# 360 GULDEN

Silver **Note:** Round version of KM#359.

Date	Mintage	VG	F	VF	XF	Unc
1662	—	550	900	1,400	2,600	—

KM# 359 GULDEN

Silver **Obv:** Armored bust right with fur hat and scepter
Rev: Crowned arms, small Hermannstadt arms at bottom
Shape: Hexagonal. **Note:** Klippe.

Date	Mintage	VG	F	VF	XF	Unc
1662 Rare	—	—	—	—	—	—

KM# 362 GULDEN

Silver **Note:** Varieties exist.

Date	Mintage	VG	F	VF	XF	Unc
1662CB	—	—	—	—	—	—
1663CB	—	—	—	—	—	—

KM# 374 GULDEN

Silver **Note:** Varieties exist.

Date	Mintage	VG	F	VF	XF	Unc
1663CB	—	550	900	1,400	2,800	—
1664CB	—	550	900	1,400	2,800	—
1665CB	—	550	900	1,400	2,800	—
1666	—	550	900	1,400	2,800	—

KM# 386 GULDEN

Silver **Rev:** Small Hermannstadt arms at bottom
Shape: Hexagon **Note:** Klippe.

Date	Mintage	VG	F	VF	XF	Unc
1667 Rare	—	—	—	—	—	—

KM# 387 GULDEN

Silver **Rev:** Crowned arms, small Kronstadt arms at bottom

Date	Mintage	VG	F	VF	XF	Unc
1667 Rare	—	—	—	—	—	—

KM# 410 GULDEN

14.0000 g., Silver **Obv:** Bust right **Rev:** Crowned arms

Date	Mintage	VG	F	VF	XF	Unc
1670KV	—	—	—	—	—	—

KM# 412 GULDEN

14.0000 g., Silver **Obv:** Bust right **Rev:** Crowned arms

Date	Mintage	VG	F	VF	XF	Unc
1671KV	—	—	—	—	—	—

KM# 413 GULDEN

14.0000 g., Silver **Rev:** Crowned arms, small Hermannstadt arms at bottom

Date	Mintage	VG	F	VF	XF	Unc
1671 CT	—	—	—	—	—	—

KM# 422 GULDEN

14.0000 g., Silver **Rev:** Crowned arms above small castle

Date	Mintage	VG	F	VF	XF	Unc
1672	—	—	—	—	—	—

KM# 445 GULDEN

14.0000 g., Silver **Rev:** Crowned arms, small Kronstadt arms at bottom

Date	Mintage	VG	F	VF	XF	Unc
1673	—	—	—	—	—	—

KM# 446 GULDEN

Silver **Note:** Irregular klippe.

Date	Mintage	VG	F	VF	XF	Unc
1673 CW Rare	—	—	—	—	—	—

KM# 496 GULDEN

Silver

Date	Mintage	VG	F	VF	XF	Unc
1689AF	—	—	—	—	—	—

KM# 159 1-1/2 GULDEN

21.4000 g., Silver

Date	Mintage	VG	F	VF	XF	Unc
1623	—	—	—	—	—	—

KM# 23 2 GULDEN

27.5000 g., Silver, 33 mm. **Obv:** Armored bust right
Rev: Crowned arms **Note:** Varieties exist.

Date	Mintage	VG	F	VF	XF	Unc
1606	—	—	—	—	—	—

KM# 179 2 GULDEN

Silver **Note:** Klippe with rounded corners.

Date	Mintage	VG	F	VF	XF	Unc
1627MC	—	700	1,150	1,750	2,600	—

KM# 178 2 GULDEN

28.5000 g., Silver **Note:** Klippe.

Date	Mintage	VG	F	VF	XF	Unc
1627MC	—	700	1,150	1,750	2,600	—

KM# 199 2 GULDEN

28.3000 g., Silver **Note:** Klippe.

Date	Mintage	VG	F	VF	XF	Unc
1628 Rare	—	—	—	—	—	—

KM# 201 2 GULDEN

Silver **Note:** Reduced size.

Date	Mintage	VG	F	VF	XF	Unc
1628	—	—	—	—	—	—

KM# 200 2 GULDEN

28.9000 g., Silver **Note:** Round version on KM#199.

Date	Mintage	VG	F	VF	XF	Unc
1628	—	—	—	—	—	—

KM# 24 3 GULDEN

42.5000 g., Silver **Obv:** Armored bust right **Rev:** Crowned arms

Date	Mintage	VG	F	VF	XF	Unc
1606 Rare	—	—	—	—	—	—

KM# 180 3 GULDEN

42.5000 g., Silver **Note:** Klippe.

Date	Mintage	VG	F	VF	XF	Unc
1627MC Rare	—	—	—	—	—	—

KM# 202 3 GULDEN

43.0000 g., Silver **Note:** Klippe. Varieties exist.

Date	Mintage	VG	F	VF	XF	Unc
1628CC Rare	—	—	—	—	—	—

KM# 203 4 GULDEN

57.2000 g., Silver **Note:** Klippe.

Date	Mintage	VG	F	VF	XF	Unc
1628CC Rare	—	—	—	—	—	—

KM# 212 4 GULDEN

56.0000 g., Silver **Note:** Klippe.

Date	Mintage	VG	F	VF	XF	Unc
1629 Rare	—	—	—	—	—	—

KM# 294 1/4 THALER

Silver **Obv:** Armored bust right with scepter and fur hat **Rev:** Crowned arms

Date	Mintage	VG	F	VF	XF	Unc
1656NB Rare	—	—	—	—	—	—

KM# A83 1/2 THALER

Silver **Note:** Struck with 1 Thaler dies, KM#83.

Date	Mintage	VG	F	VF	XF	Unc
1611CIBIN	—	190	325	525	750	—

KM# A390 1/2 THALER

14.4500 g., Silver **Note:** Struck with 1 Thaler dies, KM#390.

Date	Mintage	VG	F	VF	XF	Unc
1671AC	—	575	975	2,050	3,450	—

KM# 6 THALER

Silver **Obv:** Two lions holding sword through crown within legend **Rev. Legend:** Center: DOMINVS / PROTECToR / MEVS **Note:** Dav. #4685.

Date	Mintage	VG	F	VF	XF	Unc
1603 Rare	—	—	—	—	—	—

KM# 10 THALER

29.7000 g., Silver **Obv. Legend:** STEPHANVS: DEI: GRATIA:... **Rev:** Crowned lion on helmet above three coats of arms **Note:** Varieties exist. Dav. #4689.

Date	Mintage	VG	F	VF	XF	Unc
1605	—	450	825	1,500	2,500	—

KM# 12 THALER

29.7000 g., Silver **Obv:** Coat of arms and date within dragon and legend **Rev:** Madonna and child within legend **Note:** Varieties exist. Dav. #4691.

Date	Mintage	VG	F	VF	XF	Unc
1605NB	—	190	350	625	1,050	—

KM# 11 THALER

29.7000 g., Silver **Obv:** Bust right with fur hat **Obv. Legend:** STEPHANVS. BOCHKAY. D: G... **Rev:** Arm from clouds holding sword throught coiled ribbon **Note:** Varieties exist. Dav. #4692.

Date	Mintage	VG	F	VF	XF	Unc
1605 Rare	—	—	—	—	—	—

KM# 12A THALER

29.7000 g., Silver **Obv. Legend:** *STE. BOCHKAY. D: G:... **Note:** Varieties exist. Dav. #4694.

Date	Mintage	VG	F	VF	XF	Unc
1605	—	325	575	1,050	1,750	—

KM# A25 THALER

27.2000 g., Silver **Obv. Legend:** *STEPHANVS. BOCH:. D. G... **Rev:** Crowned ornamented arms **Note:** Dav. #4696.

Date	Mintage	VG	F	VF	XF	Unc
1606HS Rare	—	—	—	—	—	—

KM# B25 THALER

27.2000 g., Silver **Rev:** Crowned arms without ornaments **Rev. Legend:** ...EICZ **Note:** Dav. #4696A.

Date	Mintage	VG	F	VF	XF	Unc
1606HS Rare	—	—	—	—	—	—

KM# C25 THALER

27.2000 g., Silver **Rev:** Legend divided with small city arms below **Rev. Legend:** C - OMES. ET... **Note:** Dav. #4696B.

Date	Mintage	VG	F	VF	XF	Unc
1606HS Rare	—	—	—	—	—	—

KM# D25 THALER

27.2000 g., Silver **Rev:** Large mint mark **Note:** Dav. #4696C.

Date	Mintage	VG	F	VF	XF	Unc
1606HS Rare	—	—	—	—	—	—

KM# 25 THALER

27.2000 g., Silver **Rev:** Crowned arms without ornaments **Rev. Legend:** ...ETCZ **Note:** Dav. #4696D.

Date	Mintage	VG	F	VF	XF	Unc
1606HS Rare	—	—	—	—	—	—

KM# 26 THALER

27.2000 g., Silver **Obv. Legend:** STEPHANVS: D: G: HVNGARIAE... **Note:** Dav. #4698.

Date	Mintage	VG	F	VF	XF	Unc
1606 Rare	—	—	—	—	—	—

KM# 41 THALER
27.2000 g., Silver **Obv. Legend:** SIGISMVNDVS RAKOCII: D: G: PR:... **Rev:** Six-line inscription within legend **Note:** Dav. #4699.

Date	Mintage	VG	F	VF	XF	Unc
MDCVII Rare	—	—	—	—	—	—

KM# 52 THALER
27.2000 g., Silver **Obv. Legend:** *:GABRIEL: BATHORY: D: G:... **Note:** Dav. #4700.

Date	Mintage	VG	F	VF	XF	Unc
1608	—	190	350	650	1,100	—
1609	—	190	350	650	1,100	—

KM# A52 THALER
27.2000 g., Silver **Note:** Dav. #4700A. Rosettes replace colons in legends.

Date	Mintage	VG	F	VF	XF	Unc
1608	—	190	350	650	1,100	—
1609	—	190	350	650	1,100	—

KM# A53.1 THALER
27.2000 g., Silver **Rev:** Crowned shield of arms **Note:** Dav. #4702.

Date	Mintage	VG	F	VF	XF	Unc
1609NB	—	190	350	650	1,100	—

KM# A53.2 THALER
27.2000 g., Silver **Note:** Dav. #4702A. Retrograde "N's" in legends.

Date	Mintage	VG	F	VF	XF	Unc
1609NB	—	190	350	650	1,100	—

KM# 83.1 THALER
28.6000 g., Silver **Obv. Legend:** ...ET: SI(C). COMES **Note:** Dav. #4703.

Date	Mintage	VG	F	VF	XF	Unc
1611CIBIN	—	125	250	450	—	—

KM# 85 THALER
Silver **Note:** Dav. #4703A. Uniface. Varieties exist in diameter and thickness.

Date	Mintage	VG	F	VF	XF	Unc
1611CIBIN	—	125	250	450	—	—

KM# 83.2 THALER
28.6000 g., Silver **Obv. Legend:** ...ET: SI. COM: **Note:** Dav. #4703B.

Date	Mintage	VG	F	VF	XF	Unc
1611CIBIN	—	125	250	450	—	—

KM# 83.3 THALER
28.6000 g., Silver **Obv. Legend:** ...ET • SI: COMES **Note:** Dav. #4704.

Date	Mintage	VG	F	VF	XF	Unc
1611	—	125	250	450	—	—

KM# 84 THALER
Silver **Note:** Dav. #4705. Uniface.

Date	Mintage	VG	F	VF	XF	Unc
1611CIBIN	—	125	250	450	—	—

KM# 88.1 THALER
Silver **Obv. Legend:** GABRIEL. D. G. PRIN: TRAN:... **Rev:** Date in Latin in legend **Rev. Legend:** Central: PRO / PATRIA / ARIS • ET / FOCIS **Note:** Dav. #4706.

Date	Mintage	VG	F	VF	XF	Unc
ND(1612)CIBIN	—	170	325	575	—	—

KM# 88.2 THALER

Silver **Note:** Dav. #4707. Similar to KM#88.1.

Date	Mintage	VG	F	VF	XF	Unc
ND(1613)CIBIN	—	190	350	625	—	—

KM# 95.1 THALER

Silver **Rev:** Rosette below 1613 **Note:** Dav. #4708.

Date	Mintage	VG	F	VF	XF	Unc
1613	—	190	350	625	—	—

KM# 95.2 THALER

Silver **Rev:** Without rosette below 16.13 **Note:** Dav. #4708A.

Date	Mintage	VG	F	VF	XF	Unc
16.13	—	190	350	625	—	—

KM# 114 THALER

29.6000 g., Silver **Obv. Legend:** *GABRIEL BETH... **Rev:** Crowned arms **Note:** Dav. #4709. Possibly a medallic issue.

Date	Mintage	VG	F	VF	XF	Unc
1619 CM	—	190	350	625	1,050	—

KM# 115 THALER

22.2000 g., Silver **Note:** Dav. #4709A. Possibly a medallic issue. Reduced weight.

Date	Mintage	VG	F	VF	XF	Unc
1619 CM	—	190	350	625	1,050	—

KM# 124 THALER

Silver **Obv. Legend:** *GABRIEL-Madonna-D. G. EL... **Rev. Legend:** TRANS. PRINCEPS. ET... **Note:** Dav. #4710.

Date	Mintage	VG	F	VF	XF	Unc
1620KB	—	125	200	350	500	—

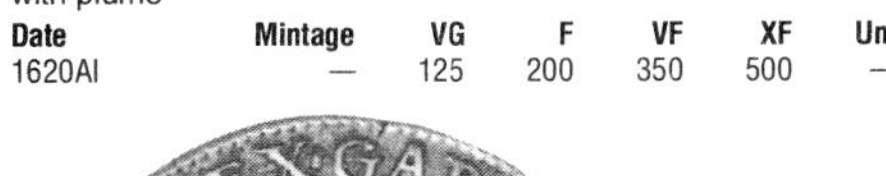

KM# 125 THALER

20.6000 g., Silver **Obv:** Large armored bust right with fur hat with plume

Date	Mintage	VG	F	VF	XF	Unc
1620AI	—	125	200	350	500	—

KM# 134 THALER

28.6000 g., Silver **Note:** Dav. #4710. Varieties exist. Similar to KM#124.

Date	Mintage	VG	F	VF	XF	Unc
1621KB	—	125	200	350	500	—
1622KB	—	125	200	350	500	—

KM# 135 THALER

28.6000 g., Silver **Obv. Legend:** * GABRIEL - Madonna - D:G. EL. HVN... **Note:** Dav. #4711. Varieties exist.

Date	Mintage	VG	F	VF	XF	Unc
1621NB	—	125	200	350	500	—

KM# 136 THALER

28.6000 g., Silver **Obv:** Similar to KM#135 **Obv. Legend:** Ends: DROA-arms-SCL A. REX **Rev:** Modified crowned arms **Note:** Dav. #4712.

Date	Mintage	VG	F	VF	XF	Unc
1621NB	—	125	200	350	500	—

KM# 137 THALER

28.6000 g., Silver **Obv:** Large bust **Note:** Dav. #4713. Varieties exist.

Date	Mintage	VG	F	VF	XF	Unc
16Z1NB	—	125	200	350	500	—
16ZZNB	—	125	200	350	500	—

KM# 146 THALER

28.6000 g., Silver **Obv:** Similar to KM#137, date behind shoulder **Note:** Dav. #4714.

Date	Mintage	VG	F	VF	XF	Unc
16ZZNB	—	125	200	350	500	—

KM# 147 THALER

Silver **Obv:** Harnassed bust with scepter **Note:** Dav. #4715. Varieties exist.

Date	Mintage	VG	F	VF	XF	Unc
16ZZNB	—	125	200	350	500	—

KM# 170 THALER

Silver **Obv. Legend:** :GABR.D: G. SA. R. IMP... **Note:** Varieties exist. Dav. #4717.

Date	Mintage	VG	F	VF	XF	Unc
1626 CC	—	125	200	350	500	—

KM# 182 THALER
Silver **Obv. Legend:** GAB. D. G. SA. RO. IM(P):-.ET... **Note:** Varieties exist. Dav. #4720.

Date	Mintage	VG	F	VF	XF	Unc
1627NB	—	125	200	350	500	—
1628NB	—	125	200	350	500	—

KM# 181 THALER
Silver **Obv. Legend:** *GABR. D. G. SA. R. IMP. ET... **Note:** Varieties exist. Dav. #4721.

Date	Mintage	VG	F	VF	XF	Unc
1627NB	—	125	200	350	500	—

KM# 183 THALER
Silver **Obv:** Divided legend **Obv. Legend:** *GABR. D. G. S(A)R... **Note:** Dav. #4719.

Date	Mintage	VG	F	VF	XF	Unc
1627 MC	—	125	200	350	500	—

KM# A183 THALER
Silver **Obv:** Continuous legend **Note:** Dav. #4719A.

Date	Mintage	VG	F	VF	XF	Unc
1627 MC	—	125	200	350	500	—

KM# A204 THALER
Silver **Obv:** Bare-headed armored bust with scepter **Note:** Dav. #4723.

Date	Mintage	VG	F	VF	XF	Unc
1628 CC	—	125	200	350	500	—

KM# B204 THALER
Silver **Obv:** Similar to KM#204 **Obv. Legend:** GABRIEL. D: G. SA. RO. IMP... **Note:** Dav. #4725.

Date	Mintage	VG	F	VF	XF	Unc
1628NB	—	125	200	350	500	—

KM# 204 THALER
Silver **Obv:** Armored bust right with fur hat with plume and scepter **Obv. Legend:** GAB. D: G. SA. RO. IM... **Rev:** Crowned arms **Note:** Varieties exist. Dav. #4724.

Date	Mintage	VG	F	VF	XF	Unc
1628NB	—	125	200	350	500	—
16Z9NB	—	125	200	350	500	—

KM# C204 THALER
Silver **Obv. Legend:** *GABR*D: G: S*R*IMP*... **Note:** Dav. #4727.

Date	Mintage	VG	F	VF	XF	Unc
1629	—	125	200	350	500	—

KM# 240.1 THALER
Silver **Obv:** Knight left looking back, shield with lion below **Obv. Legend:** MONE • ARGEN • PRO • REG • TRAN **Rev:** Rampant lion left **Rev. Legend:** * CONFIDENS: DOM • NON • MOVETVR • **Note:** Imitation of Netherlands-Overyssel Daalder.

Date	Mintage	VG	F	VF	XF	Unc
1638	—	—	—	—	—	—

KM# 240.2 THALER
Silver **Obv. Legend:** MONE • ARGEN • PRO • REG • TRA **Rev. Legend:** * CONFIDENS • DNO • NON • MOVETVR **Note:** Imitation of Netherlands-Overyssel Daalder.

Date	Mintage	VG	F	VF	XF	Unc
1638	—	—	—	—	—	—
1.6.3.8.	—	—	—	—	—	—
1.638	—	—	—	—	—	—

KM# 254 THALER
Silver **Note:** Dav. #4729. Round version of KM#253. Varieties exist.

Date	Mintage	VG	F	VF	XF	Unc
1645NB	—	250	450	750	1,250	—
1646NB	—	250	450	750	1,250	—

KM# 253 THALER
Silver **Note:** Dav. #4729C. Klippe.

Date	Mintage	VG	F	VF	XF	Unc
1645NB Rare	—	—	—	—	—	—
1646NB Rare	—	—	—	—	—	—

KM# 255 THALER
Silver **Note:** Dav. #4730.

Date	Mintage	VG	F	VF	XF	Unc
1645NB	—	190	350	625	1,050	—

KM# 259 THALER
Silver **Obv:** Similar to 1 Thaler, KM#255. **Rev. Legend:** .PAR. REG. HVNG. DOM. ET. SI. COMES. **Note:** Dav. #4731.

Date	Mintage	VG	F	VF	XF	Unc
1645 NB	—	250	450	750	1,250	—

KM# 260 THALER
Silver **Obv. Legend:** GEORG. RAKO-.D: G. PRI. TRA
Note: Dav. #4732. Varieties exist.

Date	Mintage	VG	F	VF	XF	Unc
1646NB	—	250	450	750	1,050	—
1647NB	—	250	450	750	1,050	—
1648NB	—	250	450	750	1,050	—

KM# A265 THALER
Silver **Obv:** Bust right divides legend at top and bottom with left hand on sword hilt **Note:** Dav. #4734. Varieties exist.

Date	Mintage	VG	F	VF	XF	Unc
1646NB	—	325	500	825	1,150	—
1647NB	—	325	500	825	1,150	—
1648NB	—	325	500	825	1,150	—

KM# A270 THALER
Silver **Obv:** Small bust right divides legend at top with left hand on sword hilt **Note:** Dav. #4736. Varieties exist.

Date	Mintage	VG	F	VF	XF	Unc
1646NB	—	325	500	825	1,150	—
1647NB	—	325	500	825	1,150	—
1648NB	—	325	500	825	1,150	—

KM# A271 THALER
Silver **Obv:** Similar to KM#A265 **Rev:** Crowned ornate shield with mint mark below **Note:** Dav. #A4735.

Date	Mintage	VG	F	VF	XF	Unc
1647NB	—	325	525	875	1,250	—

KM# A269 THALER
Silver **Obv. Legend:** .GEORG: RAKO-: D: G: PRIN: TRA
Note: Dav. #4742.

Date	Mintage	VG	F	VF	XF	Unc
1648NB	—	125	200	350	500	—
1649NB	—	125	200	350	500	—

KM# B269 THALER
Silver **Obv:** Similar to 1 Thaler, KM#269 **Rev:** Similar to 1 Thaler, KM#269C **Note:** Dav. #4742A.

Date	Mintage	VG	F	VF	XF	Unc
1648NB	—	125	200	350	500	—
1649NB	—	125	200	350	500	—

KM# C269 THALER
Silver **Obv. Legend:** .GEOR: RAKO-. D. G: P: TRA
Rev. Legend: ...SIC. COM(ES) **Note:** Dav. #4743.

Date	Mintage	VG	F	VF	XF	Unc
1649NB	—	125	200	350	500	—
1650NB	—	125	200	350	500	—

KM# D269 THALER
Silver **Obv. Legend:** .GEORGIVS.-RAKO: D: G: P: T
Rev: Wheel in center of crowned arms **Note:** Dav. #4744.

Date	Mintage	VG	F	VF	XF	Unc
1649NB	—	125	200	350	500	—

KM# E269 THALER
Silver **Obv:** Similar to 1 Thaler, KM#269C **Rev:** Bird in center of crowned arms **Note:** Dav. #4744A.

Date	Mintage	VG	F	VF	XF	Unc
1649NB	—	125	200	350	500	—

KM# 269 THALER
Silver **Obv. Legend:** GEORGIVS: RA.- D: G: PRI: TRA
Rev: Wheel in center of crowned arms **Note:** Dav. #4745.

Date	Mintage	VG	F	VF	XF	Unc
1649NB	—	125	200	350	500	—

KM# A282 THALER
Silver **Obv. Legend:** .GEOR(G) : RAKO-D. G. P. TRA(N)
Note: Dav. #4746. Varieties exist.

Date	Mintage	VG	F	VF	XF	Unc
1650NB	—	125	200	350	500	—
1651NB	—	125	200	350	500	—

KM# A281 THALER

Silver **Obv. Legend:** .GEORGIVS. -RA: D: G: P: T: **Note:** Dav. #4747. Varieties exist.

Date	Mintage	VG	F	VF	XF	Unc
1650NB	—	125	200	350	500	—

KM# B281 THALER

Silver **Obv. Legend:** GEORGIVS. - RAKO: D:G: P: T: **Note:** Dav. #4747A.

Date	Mintage	VG	F	VF	XF	Unc
1650NB	—	125	200	350	500	—

KM# C281 THALER

Silver **Obv. Legend:** .GEOR: RAKO-: D:G: PRIN: TRA **Rev:** Wheel in center of crowned arms **Note:** Dav. #4748.

Date	Mintage	VG	F	VF	XF	Unc
1650NB	—	125	200	350	500	—

KM# 281 THALER

Silver **Obv:** Similar to 1 Thaler, KM#281B **Rev:** Bird on wheel in center of crowned arms **Note:** Dav. #4748A.

Date	Mintage	VG	F	VF	XF	Unc
1650NB	—	125	200	350	500	—

KM# 280 THALER

Silver **Obv. Legend:** .GEOR: RAKO-. D: G: P: TRA **Note:** Dav. #4749. Square klippe. Illustration reduced.

Date	Mintage	VG	F	VF	XF	Unc
1650NB	—	250	475	875	1,500	—

KM# 282 THALER

Silver **Obv. Legend:** .GEORGIVS.-RA: D: G: P: T: **Rev:** Bird on wheel in center of crowned arms **Note:** Dav. #4750.

Date	Mintage	VG	F	VF	XF	Unc
1650NB	—	125	200	350	500	—
1651NB	—	125	200	350	500	—

KM# 286 THALER

Silver **Obv. Legend:** .GEOR: RAKO... **Note:** Dav. #4751. Varieties exist.

Date	Mintage	VG	F	VF	XF	Unc
1651NB	—	125	200	350	500	—
1652NB	—	125	200	350	500	—
1653NB	—	125	200	350	500	—
1654NB	—	125	200	350	500	—
1655NB	—	125	200	350	500	—
1656NB	—	125	200	350	500	—

KM# B287 THALER

Silver **Note:** Dav. #4752. Round version of KM#A287.

Date	Mintage	VG	F	VF	XF	Unc
1656NB	—	125	200	350	500	—
1657NB	—	125	200	350	500	—
1658NB	—	125	200	350	500	—

KM# C287 THALER

Silver **Obv. Legend:** .GEOR:RAKO-: D: G. P. T. **Rev:** Similar to 1 Thaler, KM#286 **Note:** Dav. #4753.

Date	Mintage	VG	F	VF	XF	Unc
1656NB	—	125	200	350	500	—

KM# 297 THALER

27.3000 g., Silver **Note:** Dav. #4754. Round version of KM#296A. Varieties exist.

Date	Mintage	VG	F	VF	XF	Unc
1657NB Rare	—	—	—	—	—	—

KM# 296 THALER

Silver **Obv. Legend:** GEORGIVS RAKOCI... **Note:** Dav. #4754B. Octagonal klippe.

Date	Mintage	VG	F	VF	XF	Unc
1657NB Rare	—	—	—	—	—	—

KM# 296A THALER

Silver **Note:** Dav. #4754C. Square klippe.

Date	Mintage	VG	F	VF	XF	Unc
1657NB Rare	—	—	—	—	—	—

KM# A287 THALER

Silver **Obv. Legend:** .GEORGIVS... **Shape:** Square **Note:** Dav. #4752A. Klippe.

Date	Mintage	VG	F	VF	XF	Unc
1657ND Rare	—	—	—	—	—	—

KM# 311 THALER

Silver **Note:** Dav. #4755. Round version of KM#309. Varieties exist.

Date	Mintage	VG	F	VF	XF	Unc
1658NB	—	125	200	350	500	—
1659NB	—	125	200	350	500	—

KM# 309 THALER

27.3000 g., Silver **Obv. Legend:** GEORGI.-RA • D:G • P.T. **Note:** Dav. #4755A. Klippe with Denar strikings in three corners.

Date	Mintage	VG	F	VF	XF	Unc
1658NB Rare	—	—	—	—	—	—

KM# 310 THALER

26.5800 g., Silver **Note:** Dav. #4755B. Klippe without Denar strikings.

Date	Mintage	VG	F	VF	XF	Unc
1658NB	—	825	1,400	2,250	3,750	—

KM# 311A THALER

Silver **Obv:** Armored bust right with scepter **Obv. Legend:** GEOR: RA-D: G: P. TR. **Rev:** Ornate crowned arms **Rev. Legend:** • PAR • REG • HVN • DOM • ET • SIC • COM • **Note:** Dav. #4756.

Date	Mintage	VG	F	VF	XF	Unc
1659NB	—	250	450	750	1,250	—
1660NB	—	250	450	750	1,250	—

KM# 320 THALER

Silver **Note:** Dav. #4758. Round version of KM#319. Legend varieties exist.

Date	Mintage	VG	F	VF	XF	Unc
1659CV	—	155	280	525	875	—
1660CV	—	155	280	525	875	—

KM# 319 THALER

Silver **Obv. Legend:** ACHA:BAR-D.G.PR.TR. **Note:** Dav. #4758A. Hexagonal klippe.

Date	Mintage	VG	F	VF	XF	Unc
1659CV Rare	—	—	—	—	—	—

KM# 329.1 THALER

Silver **Obv:** Crowned arms **Obv. Legend:** ACHATIVS BARCSAI. D.G... **Rev. Legend:** Center: *SERVA/NOSQ VIA / PERIMVS* / SCHESBVRGI **Note:** Dav. #4759. Size varies: 39-43mm.

Date	Mintage	VG	F	VF	XF	Unc
1660	—	220	450	750	—	—

KM# 329.2 THALER

Silver **Obv. Legend:** .A CHAT. BAR. D. G. PRI... **Rev. Legend:** ...SCHESSBVRGI **Note:** Dav. #4760.

Date	Mintage	VG	F	VF	XF	Unc
1660	—	250	450	750	—	—

KM# A330 THALER

Silver **Rev. Legend:** DEVS / PROVI / DEBIT **Note:** Dav. #4761.

Date	Mintage	VG	F	VF	XF	Unc
1660 IR	—	220.00	450.00	750.00	—	—

KM# 330.1 THALER

Silver **Obv:** Moon face to left in shield **Rev:** Central legend in small cartouche **Note:** Dav. #4762.

Date	Mintage	VG	F	VF	XF	Unc
1660CB	—	450	750	1,250	—	—

KM# 330.2 THALER

Silver **Obv:** Moon face to right in shield **Rev:** Central legend in large cartouche **Note:** Dav. #4763.

Date	Mintage	VG	F	VF	XF	Unc
1660CB	—	450	750	1,250	—	—

KM# 330.3 THALER

Silver **Obv:** Moon face to left in shield **Rev:** Without cartouche; blossoms before and after SERVA **Note:** Dav. #4764.

Date	Mintage	VG	F	VF	XF	Unc
1660CB	—	375	750	1,250	—	—

KM# 330.4 THALER

Silver **Obv:** Moon face to right **Rev:** Without cartouche; without blossoms before and after SERVA **Note:** Dav. #4765.

Date	Mintage	VG	F	VF	XF	Unc
1660CB	—	450	750	1,250	—	—

KM# 328 THALER

Silver **Note:** Dav. #4757. Round version of KM#327. Varieties exist.

Date	Mintage	VG	F	VF	XF	Unc
1660CV	—	125	200	350	500	—

KM# 327 THALER

Silver **Note:** Dav. #4757A. Hexagonal klippe.

Date	Mintage	VG	F	VF	XF	Unc
1660CV Rare	—	—	—	—	—	—

KM# A345 THALER

Silver **Obv. Legend:** IOAN: KEMENY... **Note:** Dav. #4766.

Date	Mintage	VG	F	VF	XF	Unc
1661	—	900	1,500	2,500	4,400	—

KM# 345 THALER

Silver **Obv. Legend:** IOANNES: KE... **Note:** Dav. #4767. Varieties exist.

Date	Mintage	VG	F	VF	XF	Unc
1661CV	—	400	700	1,150	1,900	—

KM# 346 THALER

Silver **Obv. Legend:** IOANNES. KEM... **Note:** Dav. #4768.

Date	Mintage	VG	F	VF	XF	Unc
1661SB	—	900	1,500	2,500	4,400	—

KM# 347 THALER
Silver **Obv. Legend:** *IOHAN: KEMENY*... **Note:** Dav. #4769. Varieties exist.

Date	Mintage	VG	F	VF	XF	Unc
1661SB Rare	—	—	—	—	—	—

KM# 346A THALER
Silver **Obv:** Similar to 1 Thaler, KM#346 with date below bust **Note:** Dav. #4770.

Date	Mintage	VG	F	VF	XF	Unc
1661SB Rare	—	—	—	—	—	—

KM# 366 THALER
Silver **Note:** Dav. #4771. Round version of KM#365. Varieties exist.

Date	Mintage	VG	F	VF	XF	Unc
1662	—	125	200	350	500	—
1663	—	125	200	350	500	—

KM# 364 THALER
Silver **Shape:** Hexagonal **Note:** Dav. #4771A. Klippe with rounded corners.

Date	Mintage	VG	F	VF	XF	Unc
1662	—	450	750	1,250	2,200	—

KM# 363 THALER
Silver **Obv. Legend:** MICHA • APAFI.-D. G. PR. TR. **Shape:** Hexagonal **Note:** Dav. #4771A. Klippe.

Date	Mintage	VG	F	VF	XF	Unc
1662	—	450	750	1,250	2,200	—
1663	—	450	750	1,250	2,200	—

KM# 365 THALER
Silver **Shape:** Square **Note:** Dav. #4771B. Klippe. Varieties in size exist - 43x42mm and 45x45mm. Illustration reduced.

Date	Mintage	VG	F	VF	XF	Unc
1662	—	450	750	1,250	2,200	—

KM# A375 THALER
Silver **Obv. Legend:** MI. APA. D. G.-PRIN. TRA(N)* **Note:** Dav. #4772.

Date	Mintage	VG	F	VF	XF	Unc
1663CB	—	125	200	350	500	—

KM# 375 THALER
Silver **Rev:** Small Kronstadt arms at bottom **Note:** Dav. #4773. Varieties exist.

Date	Mintage	VG	F	VF	XF	Unc
1663CB Rare	—	—	—	—	—	—

KM# A377 THALER
Silver **Obv. Legend:** * MI * APA * D.G * **Note:** Dav. #4775.

Date	Mintage	VG	F	VF	XF	Unc
1664CB	—	125	200	350	500	—

KM# 377 THALER
Silver **Obv. Legend:** MICHA. APAFI... **Rev:** Kronstadt arms at bottom **Note:** Dav. #4777. Varieties exist.

Date	Mintage	VG	F	VF	XF	Unc
1664	—	125	200	350	500	—
1665	—	125	200	350	500	—
1667	—	125	200	350	500	—

KM# B377 THALER
Silver **Obv. Legend:** *MICHA + APAFI + D +... **Rev. Legend:** PAR + REG + HVN + DOM + ET... **Note:** Dav. #4778.

Date	Mintage	VG	F	VF	XF	Unc
1664SB	—	125	200	350	500	—

KM# A383 THALER
Silver **Obv. Legend:** *MI. APA. D: G*... **Rev. Legend:** .PAR. REG. HV(N). DO(M)... **Note:** Dav. #4780.

Date	Mintage	VG	F	VF	XF	Unc
1665CB	—	125	200	350	500	—
1666CB	—	125	200	350	500	—

KM# B383 THALER
Silver **Obv. Legend:** MIC. APA. D. G... **Rev. Legend:** + PAR. REG. HV(N). DO +... **Note:** Dav. #4782.

Date	Mintage	VG	F	VF	XF	Unc
1665	—	125	200	350	500	—
1666	—	125	200	350	500	—
1667	—	125	200	350	500	—

KM# 383 THALER
Silver **Obv. Legend:** *MICH: APAFII... **Note:** Dav. #4783.

Date	Mintage	VG	F	VF	XF	Unc
1666SB	—	125	200	350	500	—

KM# 388 THALER
Silver **Obv. Legend:** *MIC. APA. D. G... **Rev:** Crowned arms, small Hermannstadt arms at bottom **Note:** Dav. #4785. Varieties exist.

Date	Mintage	VG	F	VF	XF	Unc
1667	—	125	200	350	500	—

KM# 389 THALER
Silver **Obv. Legend:** MICHA. APAFI... **Rev:** Small Kronstadt arms at bottom **Note:** Dav. #4788. Varieties exist.

Date	Mintage	VG	F	VF	XF	Unc
1667	—	125	200	350	500	—

KM# B390 THALER
Silver **Obv. Legend:** *MI(C). APA. D. G. flower... **Rev. Legend:** PAR. REG. HV. DO flower... **Note:** Dav. #4789. Prev. KM#A390.

Date	Mintage	VG	F	VF	XF	Unc
1667	—	125	200	350	500	—

KM# C390 THALER
Silver **Obv. Legend:** Flower MICHA • APAFI... **Rev:** Legend continuous **Note:** Dav. #4790. Prev. KM#B390.

Date	Mintage	VG	F	VF	XF	Unc
1667	—	125	200	350	500	—

KM# 391 THALER
Silver **Obv. Legend:** *MICH: APAFI... **Note:** Dav. #4791.

Date	Mintage	VG	F	VF	XF	Unc
1667SB	—	125	200	350	500	—

KM# 390 THALER
Silver **Obv. Legend:** *MICHAEL. APAFI. D. G... **Note:** Dav. #4793.

Date	Mintage	VG	F	VF	XF	Unc
1667KV	—	125	200	350	500	—
1668KV	—	125	200	350	500	—
1669KV	—	125	200	350	500	—
1670KV	—	125	200	350	500	—
1671AC	—	125	200	350	500	—

KM# 414 THALER
Silver **Obv. Legend:** MICHA. APAFI... **Note:** Dav. #4794. Varieties exist.

Date	Mintage	VG	F	VF	XF	Unc
1671 CT	—	125	200	350	500	—
1671 MR	—	125	200	350	500	—
1671 DK	—	125	200	350	500	—
1672	—	125	200	350	500	—

KM# 415 THALER
Silver **Obv. Legend:** *MICHA: APAFI: D: G:... **Note:** Dav. #4795. Varieties exist.

Date	Mintage	VG	F	VF	XF	Unc
1671 CT	—	125	200	350	500	—

KM# 423 THALER
Silver **Obv. Legend:** *MIC. APA. D. G. PRINCEPS... **Note:** Dav. #4796. Varieties exist.

Date	Mintage	VG	F	VF	XF	Unc
167Z/6ZCB	—	125	200	350	500	—

KM# 426 THALER

Silver **Obv. Legend:** MICA. APAFI. DE. GRA... **Note:** Dav. #4797. Varieties exist.

Date	Mintage	VG	F	VF	XF	Unc
1672	—	125	200	350	500	—

KM# 425 THALER

Silver **Obv. Legend:** + MICH. APAFI. D. G. PRIN... **Rev. Legend:** + PAR. REG. HV. DO... **Note:** Dav. #4798.

Date	Mintage	VG	F	VF	XF	Unc
1672AC	—	125	200	350	500	—

KM# 427 THALER

Silver **Obv. Legend:** MICH: APAFI.-D: G: PR: TR: **Note:** Dav. #4799.

Date	Mintage	VG	F	VF	XF	Unc
1672	—	125	200	350	500	—

KM# 428 THALER

Silver **Obv. Legend:** x MICH x APAFI x - D:G: PR + TR **Note:** Dav. #4800. Varieties exist.

Date	Mintage	VG	F	VF	XF	Unc
167ZSB	—	125	200	350	500	—

KM# 430 THALER

Silver **Obv. Legend:** :MIC: APA: D:G: - .PRIN. TRA. **Note:** Dav. #4804.

Date	Mintage	VG	F	VF	XF	Unc
167ZBT	—	190	350	625	1,050	—

KM# 430A THALER

Silver **Obv. Legend:** *MIC APA: D: G: -:PRIN: TRAN: **Note:** Dav. #4805.

Date	Mintage	VG	F	VF	XF	Unc
1672	—	190	350	625	1,050	—

KM# 429 THALER

Silver **Obv. Legend:** *MICHA: APAFI: *D: G: *PRIN: TRANSIL **Note:** Dav. #4806.

Date	Mintage	VG	F	VF	XF	Unc
167ZBT	—	125	200	350	500	—

KM# 430B THALER

Silver **Obv. Legend:** :MICH: APAFI: D: G:-:PRIN: TRAN* **Note:** Dav. #4807.

Date	Mintage	VG	F	VF	XF	Unc
1672	—	190	350	625	850	—

KM# 424 THALER

Silver **Obv:** Similar to KM#415 **Rev. Legend:** *PAR: REG: HV: DO... **Note:** Dav. #A4796.

Date	Mintage	VG	F	VF	XF	Unc
1672CIBI	—	250	450	750	1,250	—

KM# 428A THALER

Silver **Obv. Legend:** *MIC. APA. D. G.-PRIN. TRAN. **Note:** Similar to 2 Thaler klippe, KM#431. Dav. #4802.

Date	Mintage	VG	F	VF	XF	Unc
1672	—	125	200	350	500	—

KM# 448 THALER

Silver **Note:** Dav. #4809. Round version of KM#447.

Date	Mintage	VG	F	VF	XF	Unc
1673	—	125	200	350	500	—

KM# 447 THALER

Silver **Obv. Legend:** MICHA. APAFI.-D: G. PR. TR. **Note:** Dav. #4809A.

Date	Mintage	VG	F	VF	XF	Unc
1673 Rare	—	—	—	—	—	—

KM# 449 THALER

Silver **Obv. Legend:** MICH: APAFI.-D: G: PR: TR: **Note:** Dav. #4810.

Date	Mintage	VG	F	VF	XF	Unc
1673SB	—	125	200	350	500	—

KM# 450 THALER

Silver **Obv. Legend:** *MICH: APAFI.-*:D: G. PRI: TRA **Note:** Dav. #4811.

Date	Mintage	VG	F	VF	XF	Unc
1673BT Rare	—	—	—	—	—	—

KM# 459 THALER

Silver **Obv. Legend:** MICHAEL * APAFI. D. G. PRIN * TRAN **Rev. Legend:** PAR. REG. HVN. DOM... **Note:** Dav. #4812.

Date	Mintage	VG	F	VF	XF	Unc
1674 Rare	—	—	—	—	—	—

KM# 459A THALER

Silver **Obv. Legend:** MICH. APAFI-D. G. P. T. **Note:** Dav. #4813. Varieties exist.

Date	Mintage	VG	F	VF	XF	Unc
1675 Rare	—	—	—	—	—	—

KM# 465 THALER

Silver **Obv. Legend:** MIC: APAFI-D: G: P: TR: **Note:** Dav. #4814.

Date	Mintage	VG	F	VF	XF	Unc
1677CF	—	125	200	350	500	—

KM# 465A THALER

Silver **Obv. Legend:** MIC: APAFI-D: G: P: T: **Note:** Dav. #4815.

Date	Mintage	VG	F	VF	XF	Unc
1677AI	—	125	200	350	500	—

KM# 465B THALER

Silver **Obv. Legend:** MICH: APAFI*-D*-G: PRIN: TR: **Note:** Dav. #4816.

Date	Mintage	VG	F	VF	XF	Unc
1678AI	—	125	200	350	500	—

KM# 474 THALER

Silver **Obv. Legend:** MIC: APAFI-*D: G: P: T: **Rev. Legend:** ...DO:& SI: COM **Note:** Dav. #4817.

Date	Mintage	VG	F	VF	XF	Unc
1678AI	—	125	200	350	500	—

KM# 474A THALER

Silver **Rev. Legend:** ...:DO-ET. SIC. COM(ES) **Note:** Dav. #4818. Similar to KM#474. Varieties exist.

Date	Mintage	VG	F	VF	XF	Unc
1678AI	—	125	200	350	500	—
1679AI	—	125	200	350	500	—
1680AI	—	125	200	350	500	—

KM# 492 THALER

Silver **Note:** Dav. #4820. Round version of KM#490.

Date	Mintage	VG	F	VF	XF	Unc
1681AI	—	250	450	750	1,250	—
1683AI	—	250	450	750	1,250	—
1684AI	—	250	450	750	1,250	—
1686AI	—	250	450	750	1,250	—
1687AF	—	250	450	750	1,250	—

KM# 490 THALER

Silver **Shape:** Hexagon **Note:** Dav. #4820A. Klippe.

Date	Mintage	VG	F	VF	XF	Unc
1681AI	—	190	375	700	1,150	—
1683AI	—	190	375	700	1,150	—
1684AI	—	190	375	700	1,150	—
1686AI	—	190	375	700	1,150	—

KM# A490 THALER
Silver **Obv. Legend:** MICHAEL • APAFI. DEI. GRATIA... **Shape:** Square **Note:** Dav. #4820B. Klippe.

Date	Mintage	VG	F	VF	XF	Unc
1681AI	—	250	450	750	1,250	—

KM# 491 THALER
Silver **Shape:** Hexagon **Note:** Klippe - clipped nearly round.

Date	Mintage	VG	F	VF	XF	Unc
1686AI	—	150	275	500	875	—

KM# 510 THALER
Silver **Subject:** Leopold I **Note:** Dav. #3277.

Date	Mintage	VG	F	VF	XF	Unc
1694KV Rare	—	—	—	—	—	—
1696KV Rare	—	—	—	—	—	—

KM# 13 1-1/2 THALER
36.2000 g., Silver **Obv:** Shield with lion **Obv. Legend:** STEPHANVS... **Rev:** Madonna and child **Note:** Dav. #4690. Varieties exist.

Date	Mintage	VG	F	VF	XF	Unc
1605NB Rare	—	—	—	—	—	—

KM# 59 1-1/2 THALER
36.2000 g., Silver **Note:** Dav. #4701. Klippe. Similar to 1 Thaler, KM#A53.1.

Date	Mintage	VG	F	VF	XF	Unc
1609NB Rare	—	—	—	—	—	—

KM# 184 1-1/2 THALER
42.5000 g., Silver **Obv. Legend:** GABR. D. G... **Note:** Dav. #4718C. Klippe. Illustration reduced.

Date	Mintage	VG	F	VF	XF	Unc
1627MC	—	375	700	1,250	2,200	—

KM# 185 1-1/2 THALER
36.2000 g., Silver **Obv:** Crowned arms **Rev:** Madonna and child **Note:** Klippe. Struck using 1 Denar (ducat) dies, KM#192.

Date	Mintage	VG	F	VF	XF	Unc
1627NB	—	—	—	—	—	—

KM# 205 1-1/2 THALER
43.0000 g., Silver **Note:** Dav. #4722D. Varieties exist. 46 x 44mm.

Date	Mintage	VG	F	VF	XF	Unc
1628CC	—	350	625	1,150	1,900	—

KM# 270 1-1/2 THALER
42.7000 g., Silver **Note:** Dav. #4735. Similar to 1 Thaler, KM#A270. Illustration reduced.

Date	Mintage	VG	F	VF	XF	Unc
1648 Rare	—	—	—	—	—	—

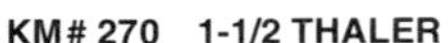

KM# 14 2 THALER
56.5000 g., Silver **Note:** Dav. #4693. Similar to 1 Thaler, KM#12A.

Date	Mintage	VG	F	VF	XF	Unc
1605 Rare	—	—	—	—	—	—

KM# 27 2 THALER
Silver **Note:** Dav. #4695. Similar to 1 Thaler, KM#25.

Date	Mintage	VG	F	VF	XF	Unc
1606 Rare	—	—	—	—	—	—

KM# 138 2 THALER
57.0000 g., Silver **Obv:** Bare headed half-length armored bust right with scepter **Rev:** Crowned arms **Note:** Dav. #A4710. Varieties exist.

Date	Mintage	VG	F	VF	XF	Unc
1621KB Rare	—	—	—	—	—	—

KM# 171.1 2 THALER
58.0000 g., Silver **Obv:** Legend separated at top **Note:** Dav. #4716A. Klippe.

Date	Mintage	VG	F	VF	XF	Unc
1626CC	—	450	825	1,500	2,500	—

KM# 172.1 2 THALER
57.3000 g., Silver **Note:** Dav. #4716B. Round version of KM#171.1.

Date	Mintage	VG	F	VF	XF	Unc
1626CC Rare	—	—	—	—	—	—

KM# 171.2 2 THALER
Silver **Obv:** Legend separated at top and bottom **Note:** Dav. #4718B. Klippe.

Date	Mintage	VG	F	VF	XF	Unc
1627	—	350	625	1,150	1,900	—

KM# 172.2 2 THALER
Silver **Note:** Dav. #4718E. Round version of KM#171.2.

Date	Mintage	VG	F	VF	XF	Unc
1627 Rare	—	—	—	—	—	—

KM# 205B 2 THALER
Silver **Note:** Dav. #4722D. Round version of KM#205A.

Date	Mintage	VG	F	VF	XF	Unc
1628CC Rare	—	—	—	—	—	—

KM# 205A 2 THALER
Silver **Note:** Dav. #4722E. Klippe. Illustration reduced.

Date	Mintage	VG	F	VF	XF	Unc
1628CC	—	350	625	1,150	1,900	—

KM# A207 2 THALER
Silver **Note:** Dav. #4726A. Klippe. Varieties exist. Illustration reduced.

Date	Mintage	VG	F	VF	XF	Unc
1629CC	—	350	625	1,150	1,900	—

KM# 213 2 THALER
Silver **Note:** Dav. #4728.

Date	Mintage	VG	F	VF	XF	Unc
1629 HL	—	575	1,050	1,900	3,150	—

KM# 265 2 THALER
Silver **Obv:** Half-length armored bust right with fur hat and scepter **Rev:** Crowned arms **Note:** Dav. #4733.

Date	Mintage	VG	F	VF	XF	Unc
1647 Rare	—	—	—	—	—	—

KM# 291 2 THALER
Silver **Obv. Legend:** GEOR: RAKO... **Note:** Dav. #A4751.

Date	Mintage	VG	F	VF	XF	Unc
1655NB Rare	—	—	—	—	—	—

KM# D287 2 THALER
Silver **Obv:** Legend with two 1 Denar stampings **Obv. Legend:** GEORGIVS-RAKO. D: G: P. T. **Rev:** Legend with two 1 Denar stampings **Rev. Legend:** PAR • REG • HVN... **Shape:** Rectangular **Note:** Dav. #A4752. Klippe, 95 x 42mm. Prev. KM#C287.

Date	Mintage	VG	F	VF	XF	Unc
1658NB	—	—	—	—	25,000	—

KM# 348 2 THALER
Silver **Obv. Legend:** IOAN: KEMENY... **Note:** Dav. #A4766.

Date	Mintage	VG	F	VF	XF	Unc
1661CV Rare	—	—	—	—	—	—

KM# 379 2 THALER
55.5000 g., Silver **Shape:** Hexagon **Note:** Klippe. 43mm. Varieties exist.

Date	Mintage	VG	F	VF	XF	Unc
1664CB Rare	—	—	—	—	—	—
1665CB Rare	—	—	—	—	—	—
1667CB Rare	—	—	—	—	—	—

KM# 378 2 THALER
56.5000 g., Silver **Obv:** Half-length armored bust right with fur hat and scepter **Rev:** Crowned arms with small Kronstadt arms at bottom **Shape:** Square **Note:** Dav. #4774. Klippe. 44 x 45mm. Varieties exist.

Date	Mintage	VG	F	VF	XF	Unc
1664CB Rare	—	—	—	—	—	—
1665CB Rare	—	—	—	—	—	—
1667CB Rare	—	—	—	—	—	—

KM# 392 2 THALER
Silver **Note:** Dav. #4784. Round version of KM#379.

Date	Mintage	VG	F	VF	XF	Unc
1667CB Rare	—	—	—	—	—	—

KM# 395 2 THALER
Silver **Note:** Dav. #4792.

Date	Mintage	VG	F	VF	XF	Unc
1668AF Rare	—	—	—	—	—	—

KM# 411 2 THALER
56.5000 g., Silver **Obv:** Half-length armored bust right **Rev:** Crowned arms **Shape:** Hexagon **Note:** Klippe.

Date	Mintage	VG	F	VF	XF	Unc
1670KV Rare	—	—	—	—	—	—

KM# 431 2 THALER
56.2000 g., Silver **Obv:** Half-length bust right **Rev:** Crowned arms with small Kronstadt arms at bottom **Shape:** Square **Note:** Dav. #4801. Klippe. 45 x 46mm. Illustration reduced.

Date	Mintage	VG	F	VF	XF	Unc
1672 Rare	—	—	—	—	—	—

KM# 432 2 THALER
56.7000 g., Silver, 43 mm. **Note:** Dav. #4803. Similar to KM#431.

Date	Mintage	VG	F	VF	XF	Unc
1672 Rare	—	—	—	—	—	—

KM# 451 2 THALER
57.5000 g., Silver **Shape:** Hexagon **Note:** Dav. #4808. Klippe.

Date	Mintage	VG	F	VF	XF	Unc
1673AC Rare	—	—	—	—	—	—

KM# 483 2 THALER
Silver **Obv:** Half-length bust right **Rev:** Crowned arms **Shape:** Hexagon **Note:** Dav. #4819. Klippe.

Date	Mintage	VG	F	VF	XF	Unc
1683AI Rare	—	—	—	—	—	—

KM# 186 2-1/2 THALER
71.3000 g., Silver **Obv:** Armored bust right **Rev:** Crowned arms **Note:** Dav. #4718A. Klippe.

Date	Mintage	VG	F	VF	XF	Unc
1627MC Rare	—	—	—	—	—	—

KM# A205B 2-1/2 THALER
71.3000 g., Silver **Note:** Klippe. Dav. #4722B. Prev. KM#205B.

Date	Mintage	VG	F	VF	XF	Unc
1628CC Rare	—	—	—	—	—	—

KM# 187 3 THALER
Silver **Obv:** Armored bust right **Rev:** Crowned arms **Note:** Dav. #4718. Klippe. Weight varies: 86.5-87.5 grams.

Date	Mintage	VG	F	VF	XF	Unc
1627MC Rare	—	—	—	—	—	—

KM# 188 3 THALER
Silver **Note:** Dav. #4718. Round version of KM#187. Weight varies: 86.5-87.5 grams.

Date	Mintage	VG	F	VF	XF	Unc
1627MC Rare	—	—	—	—	—	—

KM# 205C 3 THALER
Silver **Note:** Dav. #4722A. Klippe. Weight varies: 86.5-87.5 grams.

Date	Mintage	VG	F	VF	XF	Unc
1628CC Rare	—	—	—	—	—	—

KM# 205D 3 THALER
Silver **Note:** Dav. #4722E. Round version of KM#205C. Weight varies: 86.5-87.5 grams.

Date	Mintage	VG	F	VF	XF	Unc
1628CC Rare	—	—	—	—	—	—

KM# B207 3 THALER
Silver **Note:** Dav. #4726. Klippe. Weight varies: 86.5-87.5 grams.

Date	Mintage	VG	F	VF	XF	Unc
1629CC Rare	—	—	—	—	—	—

KM# C207 3 THALER
Silver **Note:** Dav. #4726B. Round version of KM#B207. Weight varies: 86.5-87.5 grams.

Date	Mintage	VG	F	VF	XF	Unc
1629CC Rare	—	—	—	—	—	—

KM# A492 3 THALER
83.4700 g., Silver **Obv:** 3/4-length figure of Michael Apafi holding sceptre right **Obv. Legend:** MICHAEL * APAFI. DEI. GRATIA... **Rev:** Crowned ornate arms **Rev. Legend:** . PAR: REG: HVNGARIAE... **Note:** Struck with 1 Thaler dies, KM#492.

Date	Mintage	VG	F	VF	XF	Unc
1681 AI	—	—	—	—	—	—

KM# 173 4 THALER
117.0000 g., Silver **Note:** Dav. #4716. Klippe. Illustration reduced.

Date	Mintage	VG	F	VF	XF	Unc
1626CC Rare	—	—	—	—	—	—

KM# 206 4 THALER

114.1000 g., Silver **Note:** Dav. #4722.

Date	Mintage	VG	F	VF	XF	Unc
1628CC Rare	—	—	—	—	—	—

TRADE COINAGE

KM# 28 1/4 DUCAT

0.8750 g., 0.9860 Gold 0.0277 oz. AGW **Obv:** Arms of Hungary **Obv. Legend:** STEPH. DG HVN TRAN... **Rev:** Madonna and child facing, date below

Date	Mintage	VG	F	VF	XF	Unc
1606	—	70.00	155	350	700	—

KM# 53 1/4 DUCAT

0.8750 g., 0.9860 Gold 0.0277 oz. AGW **Obv:** Ams of Hungary and Dalmetia **Obv. Legend:** SIG: RAKOCY. D. G. P. TRAN.

Date	Mintage	VG	F	VF	XF	Unc
1608	—	70.00	155	350	700	—

KM# 60 1/4 DUCAT

0.8750 g., 0.9860 Gold 0.0277 oz. AGW **Obv:** Coat of arms **Rev:** Madonna and child

Date	Mintage	VG	F	VF	XF	Unc
1609	—	70.00	155	350	700	—
1610	—	70.00	155	350	700	—

KM# 73 1/4 DUCAT

0.8750 g., 0.9860 Gold 0.0277 oz. AGW **Obv. Legend:** GABRI. D. G. PRIN. TRAN. ET. **Rev:** Madonna and child facing on half moon without inner circle

Date	Mintage	VG	F	VF	XF	Unc
1610	—	70.00	140	280	600	—

KM# 89 1/4 DUCAT

0.8750 g., 0.9860 Gold 0.0277 oz. AGW **Obv:** Date in legend

Date	Mintage	VG	F	VF	XF	Unc
1612	—	70.00	140	280	600	—

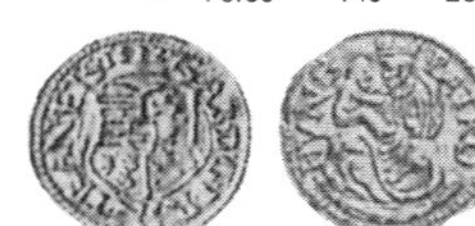

KM# 96 1/4 DUCAT

0.8750 g., 0.9860 Gold 0.0277 oz. AGW **Obv:** Last two digits of date at sides of arms

Date	Mintage	VG	F	VF	XF	Unc
1613	—	70.00	140	280	600	—

KM# 116 1/4 DUCAT

0.8750 g., 0.9860 Gold 0.0277 oz. AGW **Obv:** Oval arms of Transylvania in cartouche in inner circle **Rev:** Madonna and child facing on half moon divide A-I in inner circle, date in legend

Date	Mintage	VG	F	VF	XF	Unc
1619	—	70.00	140	280	600	—
1620	—	70.00	140	280	600	—

KM# 148 1/4 DUCAT

0.8750 g., 0.9860 Gold 0.0277 oz. AGW **Obv:** Arms of Hungary divide N-B in inner circle

Date	Mintage	VG	F	VF	XF	Unc
1622	—	70.00	140	280	600	—
1623	—	70.00	140	280	600	—
1624	—	70.00	140	280	600	—
1626	—	70.00	140	280	600	—

KM# 190 1/4 DUCAT

0.8750 g., 0.9860 Gold 0.0277 oz. AGW **Obv:** Crowned oval arms **Rev:** Madonna and child in circle of flames

Date	Mintage	VG	F	VF	XF	Unc
1627	—	70.00	140	280	600	—

KM# 189 1/4 DUCAT

0.8750 g., 0.9860 Gold 0.0277 oz. AGW **Obv:** Crowned shield-shaped arms **Note:** Varieties exist.

Date	Mintage	VG	F	VF	XF	Unc
1627NB	—	70.00	140	280	600	—
1628NB	—	70.00	140	280	600	—

KM# 245 1/4 DUCAT

0.8750 g., 0.9860 Gold 0.0277 oz. AGW **Obv:** Crowned arms of Hungary divide N-B in inner circle **Obv. Legend:** GEOR. RAKO. D. G. PRI. TRAN **Rev:** Madonna and child facing on half moon with flames below in inner circle

Date	Mintage	VG	F	VF	XF	Unc
1642NB	—	70.00	140	280	600	—
1647NB	—	70.00	140	280	600	—

KM# 283 1/4 DUCAT

0.8750 g., 0.9860 Gold 0.0277 oz. AGW **Obv:** Titles of Georg Rakoczi II

Date	Mintage	VG	F	VF	XF	Unc
1650NB	—	70.00	140	280	600	—
1653NB	—	70.00	140	280	600	—

KM# 29 1/2 DUCAT

1.7500 g., 0.9860 Gold 0.0555 oz. AGW **Obv:** Arms of Hungary **Obv. Legend:** DG HVN TRAN... **Rev:** Madonna and child facing, date below

Date	Mintage	VG	F	VF	XF	Unc
1606	—	175	350	550	1,050	—

KM# 90 1/2 DUCAT

1.7500 g., 0.9860 Gold 0.0555 oz. AGW **Obv:** Arms of Hungary and Dalmatia **Rev:** Madonna and child facing on half moon, date in legend

Date	Mintage	VG	F	VF	XF	Unc
1612	—	140	280	500	875	—

KM# 97 1/2 DUCAT

1.7500 g., 0.9860 Gold 0.0555 oz. AGW **Obv:** Last two digits of date at sides of arms

Date	Mintage	VG	F	VF	XF	Unc
1613	—	140	280	500	875	—

KM# 16 DUCAT

3.5000 g., 0.9860 Gold 0.1109 oz. AGW **Obv:** St. Ladislaus

Date	Mintage	VG	F	VF	XF	Unc
1605 SL	—	230	450	850	1,750	—
1606 SL	—	230	450	850	1,750	—
1607 SL	—	230	450	850	1,750	—

KM# 15 DUCAT

3.5000 g., 0.9860 Gold 0.1109 oz. AGW **Rev:** St. Ladislaus

Date	Mintage	VG	F	VF	XF	Unc
1605	—	230	450	850	1,750	—

KM# 30 DUCAT

3.5000 g., 0.9860 Gold 0.1109 oz. AGW **Rev:** Bocskai arms

Date	Mintage	VG	F	VF	XF	Unc
1606	—	245	500	975	2,100	—

KM# 31 DUCAT

3.5000 g., 0.9860 Gold 0.1109 oz. AGW

Date	Mintage	VG	F	VF	XF	Unc
1606	—	325	625	1,250	2,450	—

KM# 42 DUCAT

3.5000 g., 0.9860 Gold 0.1109 oz. AGW **Obv:** Sigismund Rakoczi **Rev:** AQV ILA and seven towers below in inner circle

Date	Mintage	VG	F	VF	XF	Unc
1607	—	350	700	1,550	3,150	—
1608	—	350	700	1,550	3,150	—

KM# 61 DUCAT

3.5000 g., 0.9860 Gold 0.1109 oz. AGW **Obv:** St. Ladislaus standing divides N-B in inner circle **Rev:** Madonna and child facing on half moon in inner circle, date in legend **Note:** Varieties exist.

Date	Mintage	VG	F	VF	XF	Unc
1609	—	230	450	850	1,750	—
1610	—	230	450	850	1,750	—

KM# 62 DUCAT

3.5000 g., 0.9860 Gold 0.1109 oz. AGW **Obv:** Gabriel Bathori **Rev:** Crowned Bathori arms **Note:** Varieties exist.

Date	Mintage	VG	F	VF	XF	Unc
1609	—	325	625	1,250	2,450	—
1610	—	325	625	1,250	2,450	—
1611/0	—	325	625	1,250	2,450	—
1611	—	325	625	1,250	2,450	—
161Z	—	325	625	1,250	2,450	—
ND	—	325	625	1,250	2,450	—

KM# 74 DUCAT
3.5000 g., 0.9860 Gold 0.1109 oz. AGW **Obv:** Armored bust of Gabriel Bathori right **Rev:** Eagle with Barhori arms on breast **Note:** Varieties exist.

Date	Mintage	VG	F	VF	XF	Unc
1610	—	325	625	1,250	2,450	—
1611	—	325	625	1,250	2,450	—
1612	—	325	625	1,250	2,450	—
1613	—	325	625	1,250	2,450	—

KM# 102 DUCAT
3.5000 g., 0.9860 Gold 0.1109 oz. AGW **Obv:** Gabriel Bethlen **Rev:** Bethlen arms

Date	Mintage	VG	F	VF	XF	Unc
1613	—	245	500	975	2,100	—
1614	—	245	500	975	2,100	—
1615	—	245	500	975	2,100	—
1616	—	245	500	975	2,100	—
1618	—	245	500	975	2,100	—

KM# 98 DUCAT
3.5000 g., 0.9860 Gold 0.1109 oz. AGW **Obv:** Gabriel Bathori **Rev:** Crowned Bathori arms **Note:** Struck at Klausenburg.

Date	Mintage	VG	F	VF	XF	Unc
1613 KO	—	350	700	1,400	3,100	—

KM# 99 DUCAT
3.5000 g., 0.9860 Gold 0.1109 oz. AGW **Obv:** Armored bust of Gabriel Bathori right in inner circle **Rev:** Bathori arms with CIBINI in dragon circle in inner circle, date in legend

Date	Mintage	VG	F	VF	XF	Unc
1613	—	350	700	1,400	3,100	—

KM# 100 DUCAT
3.5000 g., 0.9860 Gold 0.1109 oz. AGW **Rev:** Bathori arms divide C-I in dragon circle in inner circle

Date	Mintage	VG	F	VF	XF	Unc
1613CI	—	350	700	1,400	3,100	—

KM# 101 DUCAT
3.5000 g., 0.9860 Gold 0.1109 oz. AGW

Date	Mintage	VG	F	VF	XF	Unc
ND(1613)CV	—	325	625	1,350	2,800	—

KM# 111 DUCAT
3.5000 g., 0.9860 Gold 0.1109 oz. AGW **Obv:** Gabriel Bethlen **Rev:** Crowned Bethlen arms

Date	Mintage	VG	F	VF	XF	Unc
1618	—	245	500	975	2,100	—
1619	—	245	500	975	2,100	—
1620	—	245	500	975	2,100	—

KM# 128 DUCAT
3.5000 g., 0.9860 Gold 0.1109 oz. AGW **Obv:** Gabriel Bethlen

Date	Mintage	VG	F	VF	XF	Unc
1620	—	245	500	975	2,100	—
1621	—	245	500	975	2,100	—
1622	—	245	500	975	2,100	—

KM# 126 DUCAT
3.5000 g., 0.9860 Gold 0.1109 oz. AGW

Date	Mintage	VG	F	VF	XF	Unc
1620AI	—	325	625	1,250	2,450	—

KM# 127 DUCAT
3.5000 g., 0.9860 Gold 0.1109 oz. AGW **Note:** Similar to KM#101.

Date	Mintage	VG	F	VF	XF	Unc
1620AI	—	260	525	1,050	2,300	—

KM# 139 DUCAT
3.5000 g., 0.9860 Gold 0.1109 oz. AGW **Obv:** Gabriel Bethlen **Note:** Struck at Nagybanya.

Date	Mintage	VG	F	VF	XF	Unc
1621	—	245	500	975	2,100	—
1622	—	245	500	975	2,100	—

KM# 140 DUCAT
3.5000 g., 0.9860 Gold 0.1109 oz. AGW

Date	Mintage	VG	F	VF	XF	Unc
1621NB	—	245	500	975	2,100	—
1622NB	—	245	500	975	2,100	—

KM# 149 DUCAT
3.5000 g., 0.9860 Gold 0.1109 oz. AGW **Obv:** Gabriel Bethlen **Rev:** Crowned arms of Oppeln, Ratibor, and Transylvania

Date	Mintage	VG	F	VF	XF	Unc
1622	—	245	500	975	2,100	—

KM# 160 DUCAT
3.5000 g., 0.9860 Gold 0.1109 oz. AGW **Note:** Varieties exist.

Date	Mintage	VG	F	VF	XF	Unc
1623	—	245	500	975	2,100	—
1624	—	245	500	975	2,100	—
1625	—	245	500	975	2,100	—
1626	—	245	500	975	2,100	—
1627	—	245	500	975	2,100	—

KM# 165 DUCAT
3.5000 g., 0.9860 Gold 0.1109 oz. AGW

Date	Mintage	VG	F	VF	XF	Unc
1625CC	—	230	450	850	1,750	—

KM# 191 DUCAT
3.5000 g., 0.9860 Gold 0.1109 oz. AGW

Date	Mintage	VG	F	VF	XF	Unc
1627	—	245	500	975	2,100	—
1629	—	245	500	975	2,100	—

KM# 192 DUCAT
3.5000 g., 0.9860 Gold 0.1109 oz. AGW **Note:** Struck with 1 Denar dies.

Date	Mintage	VG	F	VF	XF	Unc
1627NB	—	190	375	775	1,600	—

KM# 193 DUCAT
3.5000 g., 0.9860 Gold 0.1109 oz. AGW **Note:** Struck with 1 Denar dies.

Date	Mintage	VG	F	VF	XF	Unc
1627	—	190	375	775	1,600	—

KM# 207 DUCAT
3.5000 g., 0.9860 Gold 0.1109 oz. AGW **Obv:** Bareheaded armored bust right **Obv. Legend:** GAB • D : G • SA • RO • IM • - • ET • TRAN • PRIN **Rev:** Crowned arms **Rev. Legend:** PAR • R • HVN • DOM • SIG - COM • OP • R • DVX • 16Z9 **Note:** Varieties exist.

Date	Mintage	VG	F	VF	XF	Unc
16Z8	—	245	500	975	2,100	—
16Z9/8	—	245	500	975	2,100	—
16Z9	—	245	500	975	2,100	—

KM# 214 DUCAT
3.5000 g., 0.9860 Gold 0.1109 oz. AGW **Obv:** Bust of Gabriel Bethlen in fur hat with plume right divides A-I in inner circle **Rev:** Crowned arms of Hungary and Transylvania in inner circle

Date	Mintage	VG	F	VF	XF	Unc
ND(1629)	—	260	525	1,050	2,300	—

KM# 221 DUCAT

3.5000 g., 0.9860 Gold 0.1109 oz. AGW **Subject:** Catherine Bethlen

Date	Mintage	VG	F	VF	XF	Unc
1630	—	2,450	4,900	7,000	9,100	—

KM# 222 DUCAT

3.5000 g., 0.9860 Gold 0.1109 oz. AGW

Date	Mintage	VG	F	VF	XF	Unc
1630	—	2,800	5,300	8,400	10,500	—

KM# 223 DUCAT

3.5000 g., 0.9860 Gold 0.1109 oz. AGW **Subject:** Stephen Bethlen **Obv:** Crowned Bethlen arms

Date	Mintage	VG	F	VF	XF	Unc
1630CV	—	550	1,150	2,450	3,500	—

KM# 224 DUCAT

3.5000 g., 0.9860 Gold 0.1109 oz. AGW **Obv:** Bust of George Rakoczi I with mace right in inner circle **Rev:** Crowned eagle with sword left, AQV ILA and seven towers below in inner circle

Date	Mintage	VG	F	VF	XF	Unc
MDCXXXI (1631)	—	425	700	1,350	2,600	—

KM# 225 DUCAT

3.5000 g., 0.9860 Gold 0.1109 oz. AGW **Rev:** Arabic date in legend **Note:** Varieties exist.

Date	Mintage	VG	F	VF	XF	Unc
1631	—	425	700	1,350	2,600	—
1632	—	425	700	1,350	2,600	—
1633	—	425	700	1,350	2,600	—
1635	—	425	700	1,350	2,600	—
1636	—	425	700	1,350	2,600	—
1637	—	425	700	1,350	2,600	—

KM# 238 DUCAT

3.5000 g., 0.9860 Gold 0.1109 oz. AGW

Date	Mintage	VG	F	VF	XF	Unc
1639	—	425	700	1,350	2,600	—

KM# 256 DUCAT

3.5000 g., 0.9860 Gold 0.1109 oz. AGW **Subject:** George Rakoczi I **Note:** Varieties exist.

Date	Mintage	VG	F	VF	XF	Unc
1645	—	425	700	1,350	2,600	—

KM# 261 DUCAT

3.5000 g., 0.9860 Gold 0.1109 oz. AGW **Note:** Varieties exist.

Date	Mintage	VG	F	VF	XF	Unc
1646	—	425	700	1,350	2,600	—

KM# 262 DUCAT

3.5000 g., 0.9860 Gold 0.1109 oz. AGW **Obv:** Fur hat with plume added **Note:** Varieties exist.

Date	Mintage	VG	F	VF	XF	Unc
1646	—	425	700	1,350	2,600	—
1648	—	425	700	1,350	2,600	—

KM# 266 DUCAT

3.5000 g., 0.9860 Gold 0.1109 oz. AGW **Obv:** Similar but bust divides lower legend

Date	Mintage	VG	F	VF	XF	Unc
1647NB	—	425	700	1,350	2,600	—

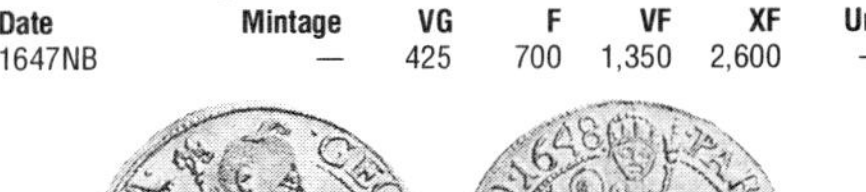

KM# 271 DUCAT

3.5000 g., 0.9860 Gold 0.1109 oz. AGW **Note:** Varieties exist.

Date	Mintage	VG	F	VF	XF	Unc
1648NB	—	425	700	1,350	2,600	—

KM# 272 DUCAT

3.5000 g., 0.9860 Gold 0.1109 oz. AGW

Date	Mintage	VG	F	VF	XF	Unc
1648NB	—	425	700	1,350	2,600	—

KM# 274 DUCAT

3.5000 g., 0.9860 Gold 0.1109 oz. AGW **Subject:** George Rakoczi II **Note:** Varieties exist.

Date	Mintage	VG	F	VF	XF	Unc
1649NB	—	425	700	1,350	2,600	—
1650NB	—	425	700	1,350	2,600	—
1651NB	—	425	700	1,350	2,600	—
1653NB	—	425	700	1,350	2,600	—
1654NB	—	425	700	1,350	2,600	—
1655NB	—	425	700	1,350	2,600	—
1656NB	—	425	700	1,350	2,600	—

KM# 298 DUCAT

3.5000 g., 0.9860 Gold 0.1109 oz. AGW

Date	Mintage	VG	F	VF	XF	Unc
1657NB	—	425	700	1,350	2,600	—

KM# 299 DUCAT

3.5000 g., 0.9860 Gold 0.1109 oz. AGW **Subject:** George Rakoczi II **Rev:** AZV-ILA and seven towers below

Date	Mintage	VG	F	VF	XF	Unc
1657	—	450	775	1,400	2,800	—

KM# A300 DUCAT

3.5000 g., 0.9860 Gold 0.1109 oz. AGW

Date	Mintage	VG	F	VF	XF	Unc
1657AI	—	325	625	1,350	2,450	—

KM# 300 DUCAT

3.5000 g., 0.9860 Gold 0.1109 oz. AGW **Note:** Hexagonal klippe.

Date	Mintage	VG	F	VF	XF	Unc
1657AI	—	625	1,150	2,300	3,500	—

KM# 315 DUCAT

3.5000 g., 0.9860 Gold 0.1109 oz. AGW **Obv:** Bust of Achatius Barcsai with fur hat holding scepter right in inner circle **Rev:** Crowned Triune arms in inner circle

Date	Mintage	VG	F	VF	XF	Unc
1659CV	—	700	1,400	2,950	6,700	—

KM# 316 DUCAT

3.5000 g., 0.9860 Gold 0.1109 oz. AGW **Obv:** Without fur hat

Date	Mintage	VG	F	VF	XF	Unc
1659 G	—	775	1,550	3,000	6,800	—

KM# 331 DUCAT

3.5000 g., 0.9860 Gold 0.1109 oz. AGW

Date	Mintage	VG	F	VF	XF	Unc
1660CIBI	—	550	1,100	2,300	3,500	—

KM# 349 DUCAT

3.5000 g., 0.9860 Gold 0.1109 oz. AGW **Obv. Legend:** IO KEMEN... **Rev:** Crowned arms **Shape:** Hexagon **Note:** Klippe.

Date	Mintage	VG	F	VF	XF	Unc
1661 Rare	—	—	—	—	—	—

KM# 350 DUCAT

3.5000 g., 0.9860 Gold 0.1109 oz. AGW **Note:** Round version of KM#349.

Date	Mintage	VG	F	VF	XF	Unc
1661	—	325	625	1,550	3,150	—

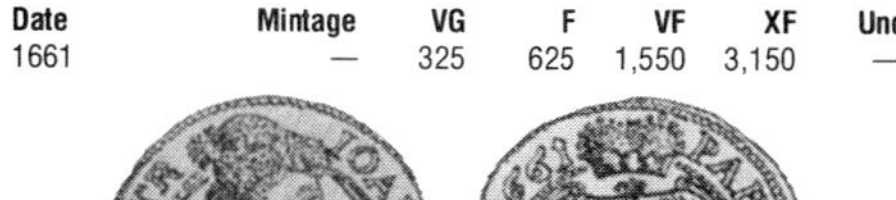

KM# 351 DUCAT

3.5000 g., 0.9860 Gold 0.1109 oz. AGW **Obv. Legend:** IOAN • KEM...

Date	Mintage	VG	F	VF	XF	Unc
1661	—	325	625	1,550	3,150	—

KM# 352 DUCAT

3.5000 g., 0.9860 Gold 0.1109 oz. AGW **Note:** Similar but reverse with oval center arms.

Date	Mintage	VG	F	VF	XF	Unc
1661	—	325	625	1,550	3,150	—

KM# 353 DUCAT

3.5000 g., 0.9860 Gold 0.1109 oz. AGW **Obv:** John Kemeny **Rev:** Crowned Triune arms

Date	Mintage	VG	F	VF	XF	Unc
1661	—	325	625	1,550	3,150	—

KM# 367 DUCAT

3.5000 g., 0.9860 Gold 0.1109 oz. AGW **Obv:** Armored bust of Michael Apafi with fur hat holding scepter right in inner circle **Rev:** Crowned Triune arms in cartouche in inner circle, date in legend

Date	Mintage	VG	F	VF	XF	Unc
1662	—	325	625	1,550	3,150	—
1663	—	325	625	1,550	3,150	—

KM# 368 DUCAT

3.5000 g., 0.9860 Gold 0.1109 oz. AGW **Shape:** Hexagon **Note:** Klippe.

Date	Mintage	VG	F	VF	XF	Unc
1662	—	260	525	1,100	2,450	—
1663	—	260	525	1,100	2,450	—

KM# 384 DUCAT

3.5000 g., 0.9860 Gold 0.1109 oz. AGW **Rev:** Triune arms

Date	Mintage	VG	F	VF	XF	Unc
1666AF	—	260	525	1,100	2,450	—

KM# 393 DUCAT

3.5000 g., 0.9860 Gold 0.1109 oz. AGW **Rev:** Triune arms with large Apafi shield

Date	Mintage	VG	F	VF	XF	Unc
1667	—	260	525	1,100	2,450	—

KM# 396 DUCAT

3.5000 g., 0.9860 Gold 0.1109 oz. AGW **Rev:** Triune arms with large Apafi shield, divided A-F in exergue of inner circle

Date	Mintage	VG	F	VF	XF	Unc
1668AF	—	260	525	1,100	2,450	—

KM# 397 DUCAT

3.5000 g., 0.9860 Gold 0.1109 oz. AGW **Shape:** Hexagon **Note:** Klippe, similar to KM#396.

Date	Mintage	VG	F	VF	XF	Unc
1668AF	—	260	525	1,100	2,450	—

KM# 452 DUCAT

3.5000 g., 0.9860 Gold 0.1109 oz. AGW **Rev:** Crowned Triune arms, A-F in exergue in inner circle, date in legend

Date	Mintage	VG	F	VF	XF	Unc
1673AF	—	350	675	1,400	2,800	—
1675AF	—	350	675	1,400	2,800	—
1676AF	—	350	675	1,400	2,800	—
1676AI	—	350	675	1,400	2,800	—
1677	—	350	675	1,400	2,800	—

KM# 476 DUCAT

3.5000 g., 0.9860 Gold 0.1109 oz. AGW **Note:** Varieties exist.

Date	Mintage	VG	F	VF	XF	Unc
1678AF	—	350	675	1,400	2,800	—
1680AF	—	350	675	1,400	2,800	—
1681AF	—	350	675	1,400	2,800	—
1682	—	350	675	1,400	2,800	—
1683	—	350	675	1,400	2,800	—

KM# 505 DUCAT

3.5000 g., 0.9860 Gold 0.1109 oz. AGW **Note:** Varieties exist.

Date	Mintage	VG	F	VF	XF	Unc
1684AF	—	350	675	1,400	2,800	—
1685	—	350	675	1,400	2,800	—
1686	—	350	675	1,400	2,800	—
1687AF	—	350	675	1,400	2,800	—
1687	—	350	675	1,400	2,800	—
1688	—	350	675	1,400	2,800	—
1689AF	—	350	675	1,400	2,800	—
1690	—	350	675	1,400	2,800	—

KM# 485 DUCAT

3.5000 g., 0.9860 Gold 0.1109 oz. AGW **Shape:** Hexagon **Note:** Klippe. Varieties exist.

Date	Mintage	VG	F	VF	XF	Unc
1684AF	—	500	1,050	2,300	4,550	—
1685	—	500	1,050	2,300	4,550	—
1687AF	—	500	1,050	2,300	4,550	—
1688	—	500	1,050	2,300	4,550	—
1689AF	—	500	1,050	2,300	4,550	—

KM# 506 DUCAT

3.5000 g., 0.9860 Gold 0.1109 oz. AGW **Obv:** Emeric Tokely **Rev:** Triune arms, with helmet and lion crests in inner circle

Date	Mintage	VG	F	VF	XF	Unc
1690	—	525	1,100	2,450	4,900	—

KM# 508 DUCAT

3.5000 g., 0.9860 Gold 0.1109 oz. AGW **Obv:** Titles of Leopold I **Rev:** Crowned arms of Transylvania

Date	Mintage	VG	F	VF	XF	Unc
1692	—	375	775	1,700	3,500	—

KM# 509 DUCAT

3.5000 g., 0.9860 Gold 0.1109 oz. AGW **Subject:** Leopold I **Rev:** Crowned imperial eagle with Transylvania arms on breast **Note:** Varieties exist.

Date	Mintage	VG	F	VF	XF	Unc
1693CV	—	350	625	1,250	2,450	—
1694CV	—	350	625	1,250	2,450	—
1695KV	—	350	625	1,250	2,450	—
1696KV	—	350	625	1,250	2,450	—
1697KV	—	350	625	1,250	2,450	—
1698KV	—	350	625	1,250	2,450	—
1699KV	—	350	625	1,250	2,450	—
1700KV	—	350	625	1,250	2,450	—

KM# 515 DUCAT

3.5000 g., 0.9860 Gold 0.1109 oz. AGW **Shape:** Hexagon **Note:** Klippe.

Date	Mintage	VG	F	VF	XF	Unc
1695	—	525	1,100	2,450	4,900	—

KM# 522 DUCAT

3.5000 g., 0.9860 Gold 0.1109 oz. AGW **Shape:** Octagon **Note:** Klippe.

Date	Mintage	VG	F	VF	XF	Unc
1699	—	525	1,100	2,450	4,900	—

KM# 32 2 DUCAT

7.0000 g., 0.9860 Gold 0.2219 oz. AGW **Obv:** Stephan Bocskai **Rev:** Bocskai arms **Note:** Struck from 1 Ducat dies.

Date	Mintage	VG	F	VF	XF	Unc
1606	—	1,700	3,150	5,900	8,800	—

KM# 33 2 DUCAT
7.0000 g., 0.9860 Gold 0.2219 oz. AGW **Rev:** Crown above crossed swords

Date	Mintage	VG	F	VF	XF	Unc
1606H	—	1,700	3,150	5,900	8,800	—

KM# 43 2 DUCAT
7.0000 g., 0.9860 Gold 0.2219 oz. AGW **Subject:** Sigismund Rakoczi

Date	Mintage	VG	F	VF	XF	Unc
1607CV	—	1,700	3,150	5,900	8,800	—

KM# 75 2 DUCAT
7.0000 g., 0.9860 Gold 0.2219 oz. AGW **Obv:** Bust of Gabriel Bathori right with mace divides C-V in inner circle **Rev:** Crowned Bathori arms in dragon circle in inner circle, date in legend **Note:** Varieties exist.

Date	Mintage	VG	F	VF	XF	Unc
1610 Rare	—	—	—	—	—	—

KM# 91 2 DUCAT
7.0000 g., 0.9860 Gold 0.2219 oz. AGW **Obv:** Half-length armored bust **Note:** Varieties exist.

Date	Mintage	VG	F	VF	XF	Unc
1612 Rare	—	—	—	—	—	—

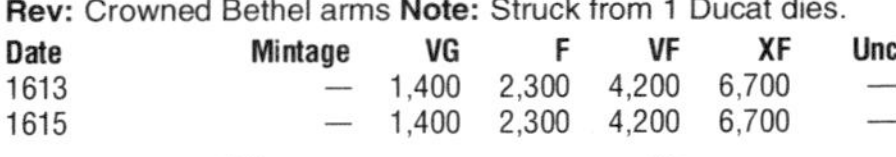

KM# 103 2 DUCAT
7.0000 g., 0.9860 Gold 0.2219 oz. AGW **Obv:** Gabriel Bethlen **Rev:** Crowned Bethel arms **Note:** Struck from 1 Ducat dies.

Date	Mintage	VG	F	VF	XF	Unc
1613	—	1,400	2,300	4,200	6,700	—
1615	—	1,400	2,300	4,200	6,700	—

KM# 194 2 DUCAT
7.0000 g., 0.9860 Gold 0.2219 oz. AGW **Obv:** Armored bust of Gabriel Bethlen **Rev:** Madonna and child in radiance

Date	Mintage	VG	F	VF	XF	Unc
1627	—	1,700	3,150	5,900	8,800	—
1628	—	1,700	3,150	5,900	8,800	—

KM# 229 2 DUCAT
7.0000 g., 0.9860 Gold 0.2219 oz. AGW **Obv:** Bust of George Rakoczi I in fur hat with plume right in inner circle **Rev:** Crowned eagle with sword left, AZV ILA and seven towers below in inner circle, Arabic date in legend

Date	Mintage	VG	F	VF	XF	Unc
1632 Rare	—	—	—	—	—	—

KM# 301 2 DUCAT
7.0000 g., 0.9860 Gold 0.2219 oz. AGW **Obv:** Half-length armored bust right **Rev:** Crowned arms

Date	Mintage	VG	F	VF	XF	Unc
1657AI Rare	—	—	—	—	—	—

KM# 317 2 DUCAT
7.0000 g., 0.9860 Gold 0.2219 oz. AGW **Obv:** Achativs Barcsai **Rev:** Crowned Triune arms **Note:** Struck from 1 Ducat dies.

Date	Mintage	VG	F	VF	XF	Unc
1659 Rare	—	—	—	—	—	—

KM# 318 2 DUCAT
7.0000 g., 0.9860 Gold 0.2219 oz. AGW **Obv:** Without fur hat

Date	Mintage	VG	F	VF	XF	Unc
1659 Rare	—	—	—	—	—	—

KM# 354 2 DUCAT
7.0000 g., 0.9860 Gold 0.2219 oz. AGW **Obv:** Bust of John Kemeny in fur hat with scepter right in inner circle **Note:** Struck from 1 Ducat dies.

Date	Mintage	VG	F	VF	XF	Unc
1661 Rare	—	—	—	—	—	—

KM# 355 2 DUCAT
7.0000 g., 0.9860 Gold 0.2219 oz. AGW **Shape:** Hexagonal **Note:** Klippe.

Date	Mintage	VG	F	VF	XF	Unc
1661 Rare	—	—	—	—	—	—

KM# 369 2 DUCAT
7.0000 g., 0.9860 Gold 0.2219 oz. AGW **Subject:** Michael Apafi **Shape:** Hexagon **Note:** Klippe. Struck from 1 Ducat dies. Varieties exist.

Date	Mintage	VG	F	VF	XF	Unc
1662	—	1,400	2,300	4,200	6,700	—
1668	—	1,400	2,300	4,200	6,700	—
1689	—	—	—	—	—	—

KM# 399 2 DUCAT
7.0000 g., 0.9860 Gold 0.2219 oz. AGW **Note:** 8-pointed star.

Date	Mintage	VG	F	VF	XF	Unc
1668 AF Rare	—	—	—	—	—	—

KM# 400 2 DUCAT
7.0000 g., 0.9860 Gold 0.2219 oz. AGW

Date	Mintage	VG	F	VF	XF	Unc
1668 AF	—	1,400	2,300	4,200	6,700	—

KM# 481 2 DUCAT
7.0000 g., 0.9860 Gold 0.2219 oz. AGW **Obv:** Half-length armored bust right with hat and scepter **Rev:** Crowned arms

Date	Mintage	VG	F	VF	XF	Unc
1682 AF	—	1,400	2,300	4,200	6,700	—

KM# 486 2 DUCAT
7.0000 g., 0.9860 Gold 0.2219 oz. AGW **Note:** Klippe.

Date	Mintage	VG	F	VF	XF	Unc
1684 AF	—	1,400	2,300	4,200	6,700	—

KM# 497 2 DUCAT
7.0000 g., 0.9860 Gold 0.2219 oz. AGW **Shape:** Hexagon **Note:** Klippe.

Date	Mintage	VG	F	VF	XF	Unc
1689 AF	—	1,400	2,300	4,200	6,700	—

KM# 516 2 DUCAT
7.0000 g., 0.9860 Gold 0.2219 oz. AGW **Obv:** Armored bust of Leopold I right in inner circle **Rev:** Crowned imperial eagle with Transylvania arms on breast, date divided at top **Shape:** Hexagon **Note:** Klippe. Struck from 1 Ducat dies.

Date	Mintage	VG	F	VF	XF	Unc
1695	—	625	1,400	3,000	5,300	—
1696	—	625	1,400	3,000	5,300	—

KM# 195 3 DUCAT
10.5000 g., 0.9860 Gold 0.3328 oz. AGW

Date	Mintage	VG	F	VF	XF	Unc
1627NB	—	1,700	3,150	5,900	8,800	—

KM# 302 3 DUCAT
10.5000 g., 0.9860 Gold 0.3328 oz. AGW **Obv:** Bust right with hat and scepter **Rev:** Crowned eagle holding sword

Date	Mintage	VG	F	VF	XF	Unc
1657AI Rare	—	—	—	—	—	—

KM# 356 3 DUCAT
10.5000 g., 0.9860 Gold 0.3328 oz. AGW **Obv:** John Kemeny **Rev:** Crowned Triune arms **Note:** Struck from 1 Ducat dies.

Date	Mintage	VG	F	VF	XF	Unc
1661	—	2,250	3,850	7,700	11,000	—

KM# 376 3 DUCAT
10.5000 g., 0.9860 Gold 0.3328 oz. AGW **Obv:** Armored bust of Michael Apafi in fur hat iwth scepter right in inner circle **Rev:** Crowned Triune arms in cartouche in inner circle, date in legend **Note:** Struck from 1 Ducat dies. Klippe. Varieties exist.

Date	Mintage	VG	F	VF	XF	Unc
1663	—	2,250	3,850	7,700	11,000	—
1684	—	2,250	3,850	7,700	11,000	—

KM# 466 3 DUCAT
10.5000 g., 0.9860 Gold 0.3328 oz. AGW **Shape:** Star **Note:** Klippe.

Date	Mintage	VG	F	VF	XF	Unc
1677AF Rare	—	—	—	—	—	—

KM# 507 3 DUCAT
10.5000 g., 0.9860 Gold 0.3328 oz. AGW **Obv:** Half-length bust right **Rev:** Two lions above crowned arms

Date	Mintage	VG	F	VF	XF	Unc
1690	—	2,300	4,550	8,400	12,500	—

KM# 521 3 DUCAT
10.5000 g., 0.9860 Gold 0.3328 oz. AGW **Obv:** Laureate bust of Leopold I right in inner circle **Rev:** Crowned imperial eagle with Transylvanian arms on breast, date in legend **Note:** Varieties exist.

Date	Mintage	VG	F	VF	XF	Unc
1697	—	1,100	2,300	4,200	8,100	—
1698	—	1,100	2,300	4,200	8,100	—

KM# 196 4 DUCAT
14.0000 g., 0.9860 Gold 0.4438 oz. AGW **Obv:** Portrait right **Rev:** Crowned arms

Date	Mintage	VG	F	VF	XF	Unc
1627 NB Rare	—	—	—	—	—	—

KM# 382 4 DUCAT
14.0000 g., 0.9860 Gold 0.4438 oz. AGW **Obv:** Half-length bust right with hat and scepter **Rev:** Crowned arms, small Kronstadt arms at bottom

Date	Mintage	VG	F	VF	XF	Unc
1665	—	1,100	2,300	4,200	8,100	—

KM# B403 4 DUCAT
14.0000 g., 0.9860 Gold 0.4438 oz. AGW **Note:** Similar to 10 Ducat, KM#403.

Date	Mintage	VG	F	VF	XF	Unc
1668 AF	—	—	—	—	17,500	—

KM# 467 4 DUCAT
14.0000 g., 0.9860 Gold 0.4438 oz. AGW **Obv:** Bust right **Rev:** Crowned arms

Date	Mintage	VG	F	VF	XF	Unc
1677 CF	—	2,250	3,850	7,700	11,000	—

KM# 477 4 DUCAT
14.0000 g., 0.9860 Gold 0.4438 oz. AGW **Subject:** Michael Apafi **Rev:** Crowned Triune arms **Shape:** 8-pointed star **Note:** Struck from 1 Ducat dies.

Date	Mintage	VG	F	VF	XF	Unc
1678	—	2,800	5,400	10,000	16,000	—

KM# 484 4 DUCAT
14.0000 g., 0.9860 Gold 0.4438 oz. AGW **Subject:** Emeric Tokely

Date	Mintage	VG	F	VF	XF	Unc
1683	—	1,550	3,100	6,700	10,500	—

KM# 484A 4 DUCAT
14.0000 g., 0.9860 Gold 0.4438 oz. AGW **Note:** Klippe.

Date	Mintage	VG	F	VF	XF	Unc
1683	—	900	1,550	2,950	4,400	—

KM# 498 4 DUCAT
14.0000 g., 0.9860 Gold 0.4438 oz. AGW **Obv:** Half-length bust of Apafi right **Rev:** Crowned arms

Date	Mintage	VG	F	VF	XF	Unc
1689 AF	—	2,250	3,850	7,700	11,000	—

KM# 520 4 DUCAT
14.0000 g., 0.9860 Gold 0.4438 oz. AGW **Subject:** Leopold I **Shape:** Hexagon **Note:** Klippe. Varieties exist.

Date	Mintage	VG	F	VF	XF	Unc
1696	—	1,400	2,750	5,900	8,800	—
1697	—	1,400	2,750	5,900	8,800	—
1698	—	1,400	2,750	5,900	8,800	—

KM# 34 5 DUCAT
17.0000 g., Gold **Obv:** Armored bust right with secpter **Rev:** Crowned arms

Date	Mintage	VG	F	VF	XF	Unc
1606	—	3,500	6,300	9,800	16,000	—

KM# 150 5 DUCAT
17.0000 g., Gold **Subject:** Gabriel Bethlen **Note:** Struck from 1 Gulden dies.

Date	Mintage	VG	F	VF	XF	Unc
16ZZNB	—	3,500	6,300	9,800	16,000	—

KM# 226 5 DUCAT
17.0000 g., 0.9860 Gold 0.5389 oz. AGW **Subject:** George Rakoczi **Note:** Varieties exist.

Date	Mintage	VG	F	VF	XF	Unc
1631	—	3,500	6,300	9,800	16,000	—
1637	—	3,500	6,300	9,800	16,000	—
1639	—	3,500	6,300	9,800	16,000	—

KM# 332 5 DUCAT
17.0000 g., 0.9860 Gold 0.5389 oz. AGW

Date	Mintage	VG	F	VF	XF	Unc
1660	—	4,550	7,700	13,500	19,000	—

KM# 333 5 DUCAT
17.0000 g., 0.9860 Gold 0.5389 oz. AGW **Note:** Round version of KM#332.

Date	Mintage	VG	F	VF	XF	Unc
1660	—	3,500	6,300	9,800	16,000	—

KM# 357 5 DUCAT
17.0000 g., 0.9860 Gold 0.5389 oz. AGW **Obv:** Half-length armored portrait right **Rev:** Crowned arms

Date	Mintage	VG	F	VF	XF	Unc
1661CV	—	4,900	8,400	14,000	21,000	—

KM# 370 5 DUCAT
17.0000 g., 0.9860 Gold 0.5389 oz. AGW
Obv. Legend: MICHA. APAFI-D • G • PR • TR

Date	Mintage	VG	F	VF	XF	Unc
1662	—	3,150	5,600	9,100	14,000	—

KM# 370A 5 DUCAT
17.0000 g., 0.9860 Gold 0.5389 oz. AGW **Obv. Legend:** + MI + APA + D. G* - PRIN + TRA(N)

Date	Mintage	VG	F	VF	XF	Unc
1663CV	—	3,150	5,600	9,100	14,000	—

KM# 370B 5 DUCAT
17.0000 g., 0.9860 Gold 0.5389 oz. AGW **Obv. Legend:** *MI. APA. D: G*-PRIN. TRAN(S)*

Date	Mintage	VG	F	VF	XF	Unc
1664CV	—	3,150	5,600	9,100	14,000	—

KM# 370C 5 DUCAT
17.0000 g., 0.9860 Gold 0.5389 oz. AGW **Obv. Legend:** *MI. APA. D: G*-PRIN. TRAN(S)*

Date	Mintage	VG	F	VF	XF	Unc
1665CV	—	3,150	5,600	9,100	14,000	—

KM# 370D 5 DUCAT
17.0000 g., 0.9860 Gold 0.5389 oz. AGW **Obv. Legend:** MIC. APA. D. G. -PRIN. TRAN* **Note:** Varieties exist.

Date	Mintage	VG	F	VF	XF	Unc
1666	—	3,150	5,600	9,100	14,000	—

KM# 453 5 DUCAT
17.0000 g., 0.9860 Gold 0.5389 oz. AGW **Obv:** Half-length bust right **Rev:** Crowned arms, small Kronstadt arms at bottom

Date	Mintage	VG	F	VF	XF	Unc
1673	—	3,500	6,300	9,800	16,000	—

KM# 468 5 DUCAT
17.0000 g., 0.9860 Gold 0.5389 oz. AGW **Rev:** Crowned arms, small Fogarasch arms at bottom

Date	Mintage	VG	F	VF	XF	Unc
1677CF	—	4,900	8,400	13,500	20,500	—

KM# 494 5 DUCAT
17.0000 g., 0.9860 Gold 0.5389 oz. AGW **Rev:** Crowned arms

Date	Mintage	VG	F	VF	XF	Unc
1687AI	—	4,900	8,400	13,500	20,500	—

KM# 499 5 DUCAT
17.0000 g., 0.9860 Gold 0.5389 oz. AGW **Shape:** Hexagon **Note:** Klippe.

Date	Mintage	VG	F	VF	XF	Unc
1689AI Rare	—	—	—	—	—	—

KM# 511 5 DUCAT
17.0000 g., 0.9860 Gold 0.5389 oz. AGW **Subject:** Leopold I **Obv:** Crowned imperial eagle with Transylvanian arms on breast

Date	Mintage	VG	F	VF	XF	Unc
1694	—	3,150	5,600	9,100	14,000	—

KM# 512 5 DUCAT
17.0000 g., 0.9860 Gold 0.5389 oz. AGW **Shape:** Octagon **Note:** Klippe.

Date	Mintage	VG	F	VF	XF	Unc
1694KV	—	3,150	5,600	9,100	14,000	—

KM# 104 6 DUCAT
21.0000 g., 0.9860 Gold 0.6657 oz. AGW **Obv:** Armored bust of Gabriel Bathori right in inner circle **Rev:** Displayed eagle with Bathori arms on breast in inner circle, date in legend **Note:** Struck from 1 Ducat dies.

Date	Mintage	VG	F	VF	XF	Unc
1613NB Rare	—	—	—	—	—	—

KM# 267 6 DUCAT
21.0000 g., 0.9860 Gold 0.6657 oz. AGW

Date	Mintage	VG	F	VF	XF	Unc
1647NB	—	4,200	7,000	11,000	15,500	—

KM# 402 6 DUCAT
21.0000 g., 0.9860 Gold 0.6657 oz. AGW **Subject:** Michael Apafi **Shape:** Hexagon **Note:** Klippe. Struck from 1 Ducat dies.

Date	Mintage	VG	F	VF	XF	Unc
1668AF	—	5,600	9,100	14,000	21,500	—

KM# 469 6 DUCAT
21.0000 g., 0.9860 Gold 0.6657 oz. AGW **Obv:** Half-length bust right with hat and scepter **Rev:** Crowned arms **Shape:** Star **Note:** Klippe.

Date	Mintage	VG	F	VF	XF	Unc
1677AF Rare	—	—	—	—	—	—

KM# 493 6 DUCAT
21.0000 g., 0.9860 Gold 0.6657 oz. AGW **Obv:** Half-length armored bust right **Rev:** Crowned arms **Shape:** Hexagon **Note:** Klippe.

Date	Mintage	VG	F	VF	XF	Unc
1686AI Rare	—	—	—	—	—	—

KM# 290 7 DUCAT
24.5000 g., 0.9860 Gold 0.7766 oz. AGW **Subject:** George Rakoczi II

Date	Mintage	VG	F	VF	XF	Unc
1654	—	4,900	7,700	12,500	21,000	—

KM# 334 7 DUCAT
24.5000 g., 0.9860 Gold 0.7766 oz. AGW **Obv:** Crowned arms within legend **Rev:** Three-line inscription within double legend

Date	Mintage	VG	F	VF	XF	Unc
1660	—	5,600	9,100	14,000	21,500	—

KM# 92 8 DUCAT
0.9860 Gold **Obv:** Crown above three coats of arms **Rev:** Four-line inscription within legend

Date	Mintage	VG	F	VF	XF	Unc
1612 CIBIN Rare	—	—	—	—	—	—

KM# 335 9 DUCAT
0.9860 Gold **Obv:** Crowned arms within legend **Rev:** Legend within double legends **Rev. Legend:** DEVS PROVI • DEBIT •

Date	Mintage	VG	F	VF	XF	Unc
1660 Rare	—	—	—	—	—	—

KM# A371 9 DUCAT
0.9860 Gold **Subject:** Michael Apafi

Date	Mintage	VG	F	VF	XF	Unc
1662	—	4,900	8,400	14,000	25,000	—

KM# 7 10 DUCAT
35.0000 g., 0.9860 Gold 1.1095 oz. AGW

Date	Mintage	VG	F	VF	XF	Unc
1603	—	12,500	23,000	35,000	49,000	—

KM# 17 10 DUCAT
35.0000 g., 0.9860 Gold 1.1095 oz. AGW **Subject:** Stephan Bocskai

Date	Mintage	VG	F	VF	XF	Unc
1605 Rare	—	—	—	—	—	—

KM# 18 10 DUCAT
35.0000 g., 0.9860 Gold 1.1095 oz. AGW **Obv. Legend:** STE: BOCHKAY. D: G. HVNGA. TRAN...

Date	Mintage	VG	F	VF	XF	Unc
1605	—	3,500	5,400	9,100	14,000	—

KM# 19 10 DUCAT
35.0000 g., 0.9860 Gold 1.1095 oz. AGW **Obv. Legend:** STEPHANVS BOCHKAY. D: G...

Date	Mintage	VG	F	VF	XF	Unc
1605	—	3,500	5,400	9,100	14,000	—

KM# 35 10 DUCAT
35.0000 g., 0.9860 Gold 1.1095 oz. AGW

Date	Mintage	VG	F	VF	XF	Unc
1606HS Rare	—	—	—	—	—	—

KM# 36 10 DUCAT
35.0000 g., 0.9860 Gold 1.1095 oz. AGW

Date	Mintage	VG	F	VF	XF	Unc
1606	—	7,000	12,500	21,000	35,000	—

KM# 37 10 DUCAT
35.0000 g., 0.9860 Gold 1.1095 oz. AGW

Date	Mintage	VG	F	VF	XF	Unc
1606	—	7,500	12,500	20,000	30,000	—

KM# 44 10 DUCAT
35.0000 g., 0.9860 Gold 1.1095 oz. AGW **Subject:** Sigimund Rakoczi

Date	Mintage	VG	F	VF	XF	Unc
1607	—	6,300	10,500	19,000	31,500	—

KM# 63 10 DUCAT
35.0000 g., 0.9860 Gold 1.1095 oz. AGW **Obv:** Half-length armored bust right **Rev:** Crowned arms circled by dragon

Date	Mintage	VG	F	VF	XF	Unc
1609	—	6,300	10,500	19,000	31,500	—

KM# 86 10 DUCAT
35.0000 g., 0.9860 Gold 1.1095 oz. AGW

Date	Mintage	VG	F	VF	XF	Unc
1611CIBIN	—	7,000	12,500	21,000	35,000	—
1612CIBIN	—	7,000	12,500	21,000	35,000	—
1613CIBIN	—	7,000	12,500	21,000	35,000	—

KM# 105 10 DUCAT
35.0000 g., 0.9860 Gold 1.1095 oz. AGW

Date	Mintage	VG	F	VF	XF	Unc
1613CIBIN	—	7,000	12,500	21,000	35,000	—

KM# 108 10 DUCAT
35.0000 g., 0.9860 Gold 1.1095 oz. AGW **Subject:** Gabriel Bethlen

Date	Mintage	VG	F	VF	XF	Unc
1616	—	5,600	7,400	12,000	20,500	—

KM# 117 10 DUCAT
35.0000 g., 0.9860 Gold 1.1095 oz. AGW **Subject:** Gabriel Bethlen **Rev:** Crowned Triune arms

Date	Mintage	VG	F	VF	XF	Unc
1619	—	4,900	10,500	16,000	26,000	—

KM# 129 10 DUCAT
35.0000 g., 0.9860 Gold 1.1095 oz. AGW

Date	Mintage	VG	F	VF	XF	Unc
1620AI	—	4,900	10,500	17,000	27,500	—

KM# 141 10 DUCAT

35.0000 g., 0.9860 Gold 1.1095 oz. AGW **Subject:** Gabriel Bethlen **Obv. Legend:** ...• DAL • CR shield...

Date	Mintage	VG	F	VF	XF	Unc
1621	—	4,200	9,100	14,000	24,500	—

KM# 208 10 DUCAT

35.1000 g., 0.9860 Gold 1.1126 oz. AGW **Subject:** Gabriel Bethlen

Date	Mintage	VG	F	VF	XF	Unc
16Z8	—	4,200	7,000	11,000	17,500	—

KM# 227 10 DUCAT

35.1000 g., 0.9860 Gold 1.1126 oz. AGW **Subject:** George Rakoczi

Date	Mintage	VG	F	VF	XF	Unc
1631	—	5,600	7,700	13,500	23,000	—

KM# 228 10 DUCAT

35.1000 g., 0.9860 Gold 1.1126 oz. AGW

Date	Mintage	VG	F	VF	XF	Unc
1631CV	—	5,600	7,700	12,500	21,000	—

KM# 232.1 10 DUCAT

35.1000 g., 0.9860 Gold 1.1126 oz. AGW **Subject:** George Rakoczi I **Rev. Legend:** ...ANNO*DOM 1636

Date	Mintage	VG	F	VF	XF	Unc
1636	—	6,300	10,500	17,500	28,000	—

KM# 142 10 DUCAT

35.1000 g., 0.9860 Gold 1.1126 oz. AGW **Obv. Legend:** ...• DAL • CR shield...

Date	Mintage	VG	F	VF	XF	Unc
1621KB	—	4,200	9,100	14,000	24,500	—

KM# 209 10 DUCAT

35.1000 g., 0.9860 Gold 1.1126 oz. AGW **Obv:** Gabriel Bethlen

Date	Mintage	VG	F	VF	XF	Unc
16Z8NB	—	4,900	7,700	13,500	21,000	—

KM# 232.2 10 DUCAT

35.1000 g., 0.9860 Gold 1.1126 oz. AGW

Rev. Legend: ...ANNO * DO 1637

Date	Mintage	VG	F	VF	XF	Unc
1637CV	—	6,300	10,500	17,500	28,000	—

KM# 151 10 DUCAT

35.1000 g., 0.9860 Gold 1.1126 oz. AGW

Date	Mintage	VG	F	VF	XF	Unc
16ZZNB	—	4,900	7,700	13,500	21,000	—

KM# 232.3 10 DUCAT

35.1000 g., 0.9860 Gold 1.1126 oz. AGW

Rev. Legend: ...ANNO * DOMINI 1639

Date	Mintage	VG	F	VF	XF	Unc
1639CV	—	6,300	10,500	17,500	28,000	—

KM# 257 10 DUCAT
35.1000 g., 0.9860 Gold 1.1126 oz. AGW **Obv:** Half-length armored bust right **Rev:** Crowned arms

Date	Mintage	VG	F	VF	XF	Unc
1645NB	—	6,300	10,500	19,000	31,500	—

KM# 263 10 DUCAT
35.1000 g., 0.9860 Gold 1.1126 oz. AGW

Date	Mintage	VG	F	VF	XF	Unc
1646NB	—	6,300	10,500	19,000	31,500	—

KM# 268 10 DUCAT
35.1000 g., 0.9860 Gold 1.1126 oz. AGW **Obv:** Armored bust right **Rev:** Crowned arms

Date	Mintage	VG	F	VF	XF	Unc
1647NB	—	6,300	10,500	19,000	31,500	—

KM# 273 10 DUCAT
35.1000 g., 0.9860 Gold 1.1126 oz. AGW **Obv:** Armored bust right **Rev:** Crowned arms

Date	Mintage	VG	F	VF	XF	Unc
1648NB	—	6,300	10,500	19,000	31,500	—

KM# 275 10 DUCAT
35.1000 g., 0.9860 Gold 1.1126 oz. AGW **Obv:** Half-length armored bust right **Rev:** Crowned arms **Note:** Varieties exist.

Date	Mintage	VG	F	VF	XF	Unc
1649NB	—	4,200	6,300	10,500	17,500	—

KM# 284 10 DUCAT
35.1000 g., 0.9860 Gold 1.1126 oz. AGW

Date	Mintage	VG	F	VF	XF	Unc
1650NB	—	4,200	6,300	10,500	17,500	—
1651NB	—	4,200	6,300	10,500	17,500	—

KM# 287 10 DUCAT
35.1000 g., 0.9860 Gold 1.1126 oz. AGW **Obv. Legend:** • GEOR • RAKO... **Note:** Varieties exist.

Date	Mintage	VG	F	VF	XF	Unc
165Z	—	4,200	6,300	10,500	17,500	—
1653	—	4,200	6,300	10,500	17,500	—
1654	—	4,200	6,300	10,500	17,500	—
1655	—	4,200	6,300	10,500	17,500	—

KM# 295 10 DUCAT
35.1000 g., 0.9860 Gold 1.1126 oz. AGW

Date	Mintage	VG	F	VF	XF	Unc
1656NB	—	4,200	6,300	10,500	17,500	—

KM# 304 10 DUCAT
35.1000 g., 0.9860 Gold 1.1126 oz. AGW **Note:** 4-sided klippe.

Date	Mintage	VG	F	VF	XF	Unc
1657AI Rare	—	—	—	—	—	—

KM# 303 10 DUCAT
35.1000 g., 0.9860 Gold 1.1126 oz. AGW **Note:** Hexagonal klippe.

Date	Mintage	VG	F	VF	XF	Unc
1657AI Rare	—	—	—	—	—	—

KM# 305 10 DUCAT
35.1000 g., 0.9860 Gold 1.1126 oz. AGW **Note:** Round version of KM#303.

Date	Mintage	VG	F	VF	XF	Unc
1657AI	—	4,900	7,400	12,000	19,000	—

KM# 312 10 DUCAT
35.1000 g., 0.9860 Gold 1.1126 oz. AGW **Obv:** Bust right **Rev:** Crowned arms

Date	Mintage	VG	F	VF	XF	Unc
1658NB	—	4,900	7,400	12,000	19,000	—
1659NB	—	4,900	7,400	12,000	19,000	—

KM# 322 10 DUCAT

35.1000 g., 0.9860 Gold 1.1126 oz. AGW

Date	Mintage	VG	F	VF	XF	Unc
1659CV	—	4,900	8,400	14,000	23,000	—
1660CV	—	4,900	8,400	14,000	23,000	—

KM# 323 10 DUCAT

35.1000 g., 0.9860 Gold 1.1126 oz. AGW **Note:** Hexagonal klippe of KM#322.

Date	Mintage	VG	F	VF	XF	Unc
1659CV	—	6,300	9,800	16,000	26,000	—
1659CV Restrike	—	—	—	4,200	6,300	—

KM# 338 10 DUCAT

35.1000 g., 0.9860 Gold 1.1126 oz. AGW **Note:** Round version of KM#336.

Date	Mintage	VG	F	VF	XF	Unc
1660CV	—	4,900	8,400	14,000	21,000	—

KM# 343 10 DUCAT

35.1000 g., 0.9860 Gold 1.1126 oz. AGW **Note:** Round version of KM#342.

Date	Mintage	VG	F	VF	XF	Unc
1660	—	5,600	9,100	15,500	24,500	—

KM# 337 10 DUCAT

35.1000 g., 0.9860 Gold 1.1126 oz. AGW **Note:** Klippe with rounded corners.

Date	Mintage	VG	F	VF	XF	Unc
1660CV Rare	—	—	—	—	—	—

KM# 339 10 DUCAT

35.1000 g., 0.9860 Gold 1.1126 oz. AGW

Date	Mintage	VG	F	VF	XF	Unc
1660	—	4,900	8,400	14,000	22,500	—

KM# 341 10 DUCAT

35.1000 g., 0.9860 Gold 1.1126 oz. AGW

Date	Mintage	VG	F	VF	XF	Unc
1660CB	—	5,600	9,100	17,000	28,000	—

KM# 342 10 DUCAT

35.1000 g., 0.9860 Gold 1.1126 oz. AGW

Date	Mintage	VG	F	VF	XF	Unc
1660	—	6,300	10,500	19,000	31,500	—

KM# 336 10 DUCAT

35.1000 g., 0.9860 Gold 1.1126 oz. AGW

Date	Mintage	VG	F	VF	XF	Unc
1660CV Rare	—	—	—	—	—	—

KM# 340 10 DUCAT
35.1000 g., 0.9860 Gold 1.1126 oz. AGW **Note:** Varieties exist.

Date	Mintage	VG	F	VF	XF	Unc
1660CB	—	9,100	14,000	26,000	39,000	—

KM# 358 10 DUCAT
35.1000 g., 0.9860 Gold 1.1126 oz. AGW **Note:** Varieties exist.

Date	Mintage	VG	F	VF	XF	Unc
1661CV	—	7,000	11,000	19,000	31,500	—

KM# 371 10 DUCAT
35.1000 g., 0.9860 Gold 1.1126 oz. AGW

Date	Mintage	VG	F	VF	XF	Unc
1662	—	5,600	7,700	12,500	21,000	—
1663	—	5,600	7,700	12,500	21,000	—

KM# 373 10 DUCAT
35.1000 g., 0.9860 Gold 1.1126 oz. AGW **Obv:** Half-length armored bust right **Rev:** Crowned arms above small Kronstadt arms

Date	Mintage	VG	F	VF	XF	Unc
1662CB	—	5,600	7,000	12,000	17,000	—
1663CV	—	5,600	7,000	12,000	17,000	—

KM# 372 10 DUCAT
35.1000 g., 0.9860 Gold 1.1126 oz. AGW **Note:** 4-sided klippe. 44 x 44mm.

Date	Mintage	VG	F	VF	XF	Unc
1662	—	5,600	7,700	12,500	21,000	—

KM# 380 10 DUCAT
35.1000 g., 0.9860 Gold 1.1126 oz. AGW **Obv:** Half-length bust right **Rev:** Crowned arms

Date	Mintage	VG	F	VF	XF	Unc
1664CB	—	5,600	7,000	12,000	17,000	—
1665CB	—	5,600	7,000	12,000	17,000	—

KM# 381 10 DUCAT
35.1000 g., 0.9860 Gold 1.1126 oz. AGW

Date	Mintage	VG	F	VF	XF	Unc
1664SB	—	5,600	7,700	12,500	21,000	—

KM# 385 10 DUCAT
35.1000 g., 0.9860 Gold 1.1126 oz. AGW **Subject:** Michael Apafi **Note:** Struck at Kronstadt.

Date	Mintage	VG	F	VF	XF	Unc
1666	—	6,300	8,400	14,000	23,000	—

KM# 394 10 DUCAT
35.1000 g., 0.9860 Gold 1.1126 oz. AGW

Date	Mintage	VG	F	VF	XF	Unc
1667KV	—	4,900	7,000	12,500	21,000	—

KM# A403 10 DUCAT
35.1000 g., 0.9860 Gold 1.1126 oz. AGW **Obv. Legend:** MICHAEL. APAFI. D. G... **Shape:** Hexagon **Note:** Klippe.

Date	Mintage	VG	F	VF	XF	Unc
1668AF	—	—	—	4,200	5,600	—

Note: Believed to be a later strike

KM# 403 10 DUCAT
35.1000 g., 0.9860 Gold 1.1126 oz. AGW **Note:** Round version of KM#A403.

Date	Mintage	VG	F	VF	XF	Unc
1668AF	—	6,000	9,800	14,000	22,500	—
1669AF	—	6,000	9,800	14,000	22,500	—
1670AF	—	6,000	9,800	14,000	22,500	—
1671AF	—	6,000	9,800	14,000	22,500	—

KM# A416 10 DUCAT
35.1000 g., 0.9860 Gold 1.1126 oz. AGW **Obv. Legend:** MICH • APAFI - D. G. P. T.

Date	Mintage	VG	F	VF	XF	Unc
1671	—	4,900	7,400	12,000	21,000	—

KM# 416 10 DUCAT
35.1000 g., 0.9860 Gold 1.1126 oz. AGW

Date	Mintage	VG	F	VF	XF	Unc
1671 CT	—	4,900	7,400	12,000	21,000	—

KM# 433 10 DUCAT
35.1000 g., 0.9860 Gold 1.1126 oz. AGW **Note:** Varieties exist.

Date	Mintage	VG	F	VF	XF	Unc
1672CIBI	—	6,000	9,800	14,000	22,500	—

KM# 454 10 DUCAT
35.1000 g., 0.9860 Gold 1.1126 oz. AGW **Obv. Legend:** MICHA. APAFI-DG • PR • TR

Date	Mintage	VG	F	VF	XF	Unc
1673AC	—	4,900	7,400	12,000	21,000	—
1673	—	4,900	7,400	12,000	21,000	—
1674	—	4,900	7,400	12,000	21,000	—

KM# 462 10 DUCAT

35.1000 g., 0.9860 Gold 1.1126 oz. AGW **Obv. Legend:** *MICHA: APAFI-D. G: PR • TR*

Date	Mintage	VG	F	VF	XF	Unc
1675 AF Rare	—	—	—	—	—	—

KM# 463 10 DUCAT

35.1000 g., 0.9860 Gold 1.1126 oz. AGW **Obv. Legend:** MICH • APAFI - D.G. P. T. **Note:** Varieties exist.

Date	Mintage	VG	F	VF	XF	Unc
1675 AF	—	4,900	7,400	12,000	21,000	—

KM# 471 10 DUCAT

35.1000 g., 0.9860 Gold 1.1126 oz. AGW **Note:** Round version of KM#470.

Date	Mintage	VG	F	VF	XF	Unc
1677AI	—	4,900	7,400	12,000	21,000	—
1678AI	—	4,900	7,400	12,000	21,000	—
1679AI	—	4,900	7,400	12,000	21,000	—
1680AI	—	4,900	7,400	12,000	21,000	—

KM# 470 10 DUCAT

35.1000 g., 0.9860 Gold 1.1126 oz. AGW **Shape:** Hexagon **Note:** Klippe.

Date	Mintage	VG	F	VF	XF	Unc
1677AI Rare	—	—	—	—	—	—

KM# 480 10 DUCAT

35.1000 g., 0.9860 Gold 1.1126 oz. AGW

Date	Mintage	VG	F	VF	XF	Unc
1681AI	—	4,900	7,400	12,000	21,000	—
1683AI	—	4,900	7,400	12,000	21,000	—

KM# 487 10 DUCAT

35.1000 g., 0.9860 Gold 1.1126 oz. AGW **Subject:** Emeric Tokely

Date	Mintage	VG	F	VF	XF	Unc
1683	—	14,000	23,000	35,000	—	—

KM# 488 10 DUCAT

35.1000 g., 0.9860 Gold 1.1126 oz. AGW **Shape:** Hexagon **Note:** Klippe.

Date	Mintage	VG	F	VF	XF	Unc
1684AI	—	8,400	13,500	21,000	26,000	—
1689AF	—	8,400	13,500	21,000	26,000	—

KM# 489 10 DUCAT

35.1000 g., 0.9860 Gold 1.1126 oz. AGW **Note:** Round version of KM#488.

Date	Mintage	VG	F	VF	XF	Unc
1684AI	—	4,900	6,700	9,800	17,500	—
1686AI	—	4,900	6,700	9,800	17,500	—
1687AI	—	4,900	6,700	9,800	17,500	—
1689AF	—	4,900	6,700	9,800	17,500	—

KM# 523 10 DUCAT

35.1000 g., 0.9860 Gold 1.1126 oz. AGW **Obv:** Bust of Leopold I **Rev:** Crowned imperial eagle

Date	Mintage	VG	F	VF	XF	Unc
1694 Rare	—	—	—	—	—	—

KM# 517 10 DUCAT
34.3400 g., 0.9860 Gold 1.0886 oz. AGW **Subject:** Leopold I **Note:** Struck from 1 Thaler dies, KM#510.

Date	Mintage	VG	F	VF	XF	Unc
1695	—	9,100	14,000	21,000	25,000	—
1696	—	9,100	14,000	21,000	25,000	—

KM# 306 12 DUCAT
42.0000 g., 0.9860 Gold 1.3314 oz. AGW **Obv:** Armored bust right with hat and scepter **Rev:** Crowned arms **Note:** Klippe.

Date	Mintage	VG	F	VF	XF	Unc
1657AI Rare	—	—	—	—	—	—

KM# 307 13 DUCAT
45.5000 g., 0.9860 Gold 1.4423 oz. AGW **Obv:** Armored bust right with hat and scepter **Rev:** Crowned arms **Note:** Klippe.

Date	Mintage	VG	F	VF	XF	Unc
1657AI Rare	—	—	—	—	—	—

KM# A227 20 DUCAT
70.0000 g., 0.9860 Gold 2.2190 oz. AGW **Subject:** George Rakoczi I **Note:** Klippe.

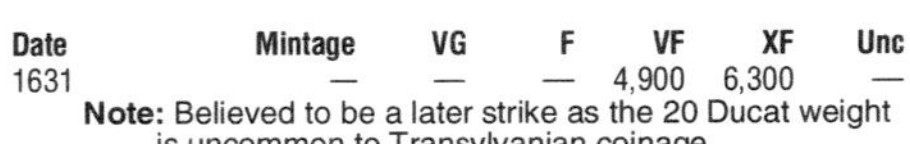

Date	Mintage	VG	F	VF	XF	Unc
1631	—	—	—	4,900	6,300	—

Note: Believed to be a later strike as the 20 Ducat weight is uncommon to Transylvanian coinage

KM# 287A 20 DUCAT
70.0000 g., 0.9860 Gold 2.2190 oz. AGW **Subject:** George Rakoczi II

Date	Mintage	VG	F	VF	XF	Unc
1652NB	—	—	—	4,900	6,300	—

Note: Believed to be a later strike as the 20 Ducat weight is uncommon to Transylvanian coinage

KM# 308 25 DUCAT
87.5000 g., 0.9860 Gold 2.7737 oz. AGW **Note:** Round version of 12 Ducat, KM#306.

Date	Mintage	VG	F	VF	XF	Unc
1657AI Rare	—	—	—	—	—	—

KM# 472 50 DUCAT
175.0000 g., 0.9860 Gold 5.5474 oz. AGW **Note:** Similar to 100 Ducat, KM#473.

Date	Mintage	VG	F	VF	XF	Unc
1677AF Rare	—	—	—	—	—	—

KM# 473 100 DUCAT
350.0000 g., 0.9860 Gold 11.094 oz. AGW, 83 mm. **Subject:** Michael Apafi **Note:** Illustration reduced.

Date	Mintage	VG	F	VF	XF	Unc
1677AF Rare	—	—	—	—	—	—

PATTERNS

Inlcuding off metal strikes

KM#	Date	Mintage	Identification	Mkt Val
Pn1	1606	—	6 Groschen. Gold. 14.0000 g. 4 Ducat.	—
Pn2	1610	—	Groschen. Gold. Broad. 4 Ducat.	—
Pn3	1610	—	Groschen. Gold. Broad. 5 Ducat.	—
Pn4	1620	—	Groschen. Copper. KM#122.	225
Pn5	1630	—	Ducat. Silver. 9.0000 g.	265
Pn6	1657AI	—	10 Ducat. Gold Plated Silver. 34.5000 g. KM#305.	—

KM#	Date	Mintage	Identification	Mkt Val
Pn7	1668	—	Zwolfer. Silver. 1.4000 g. 1 Ducat.	—
Pn8	1677	—	100 Ducat. Silver. 90.8000 g. KM#473.	—
Pn9	1692	—	Ducat. Silver. Leopold I	200

HERMANNSTADT

Hermanstadt (Sibiu), a city located 220 miles northwest of Bucharest, north of the Transylvanian Alps. Originally a Roman colony, refounded by Saxon settlers in the 12th century, became Imperial in 1699.

Occupied by imperial troops - Occupation issues in the name of Rudolph II.

MINT
FT - Hermannstadt

MINTMASTER'S INITIALS

Initial	Date	Name
H, Crowned AHR monogram	1605	Albertus Hutter

CITY

SIEGE COINAGE

1612-1614

KM# 1 GULDEN
15.0000 g., Silver **Note:** Similar to 1 Thaler, KM#2.2.

Date	Mintage	VG	F	VF	XF	Unc
1605 H	—	1,000	1,800	2,500	3,600	—

KM# 2.1 THALER
28.5000 g., Silver **Obv:** Crowned imperial eagle, titles of Rudolf II **Rev:** Crowned swords, legend with rosettes **Rev. Legend:** ...ANNO 1605 **Note:** Dav. #4688.

Date	Mintage	VG	F	VF	XF	Unc
1605 H	—	1,500	2,500	3,750	5,600	—

KM# 2.2 THALER

28.5000 g., Silver **Rev:** Legend with rosette
Rev. Legend: ...ANO 1605

Date	Mintage	VG	F	VF	XF	Unc
1605 H	—	1,500	2,500	3,750	5,600	—

KM# 2.3 THALER

28.5000 g., Silver **Rev:** Legend with Maltese cross
Rev. Legend: ...ANO 1605

Date	Mintage	VG	F	VF	XF	Unc
1605 H	—	1,500	2,500	3,750	5,600	—

KM# 2.4 THALER

28.5000 g., Silver **Rev:** Legend with Maltese cross
Rev. Legend: ...ANNO 1605

Date	Mintage	VG	F	VF	XF	Unc
1605 H	—	1,700	2,800	4,200	6,300	—

KM# 2.5 THALER

28.5000 g., Silver **Rev:** Legend with pointed cross
Rev. Legend: ...ANNO 1605

Date	Mintage	VG	F	VF	XF	Unc
1605 H	—	1,500	2,500	3,750	5,600	—

KM# 3 1-1/2 THALER

Silver **Note:** Similar to 1 Thaler, KM#2.2. Dav. #4687.

Date	Mintage	VG	F	VF	XF	Unc
1605 H Rare	—	—	—	—	—	—

KM# 4 2 THALER

57.0000 g., Silver **Note:** Similar to 1 Thaler, KM#2.2. Dav. #4686.

Date	Mintage	VG	F	VF	XF	Unc
1605 H Rare	—	—	—	—	—	—

KM# 5 DUCAT

3.5000 g., 0.9860 Gold 0.1109 oz. AGW **Obv:** Crowned swords **Rev:** Crowned imperial eagle, titles of Rudolf II **Note:** Fr. #304.

Date	Mintage	VG	F	VF	XF	Unc
1605 H	—	—	5,300	9,100	14,000	—

KM# 6.1 5 DUCAT

17.5000 g., 0.9860 Gold 0.5547 oz. AGW **Rev:** Legend wtih Maltese cross **Rev. Legend:** ...ANNO 1605 **Note:** Similar to 10 Ducats, KM#8.1. Fr. #303.

Date	Mintage	VG	F	VF	XF	Unc
1605 H Rare	—	—	—	—	—	—

KM# 7.2 5 DUCAT

17.5000 g., 0.9860 Gold 0.5547 oz. AGW **Rev:** Legend wtih rosette **Rev. Legend:** ...ANO 1605 **Note:** Similar to 10 Ducats, KM#8.2.

Date	Mintage	VG	F	VF	XF	Unc
1605 H Rare	—	—	—	—	—	—

KM# 8.1 10 DUCAT

35.0000 g., 0.9860 Gold 1.1095 oz. AGW **Obv:** Legend with Maltese cross **Obv. Legend:** ...ANNO 1605 **Rev:** Crowned imperial eagle, titles of Rudolf II **Note:** Fr. #302.

Date	Mintage	VG	F	VF	XF	Unc
1605 H Rare	—	—	—	—	—	—

KM# 8.2 10 DUCAT

35.0000 g., 0.9860 Gold 1.1095 oz. AGW **Obv:** Legend wtih rosette **Obv. Legend:** ...ANO 1605 **Rev:** Crowned imperial eagle **Note:** Fr. #302.

Date	Mintage	VG	F	VF	XF	Unc
1605 H Rare	—	—	—	—	—	—
1605 H Restrike	—	—	—	—	3,000	—

KRONSTADT

Brasov, Brasso

A city located in the foothills of the Transylvanian Alps founded by the Teutonic Order in 1211AD. A leader in Reformation in Transylvania in the 16th century.

Issues of 1601

Struck in support of Sigismund Bathori.

CITY

STANDARD COINAGE

KM# 5 GULDEN

14.1000 g., Silver **Note:** Similar to 1 Thaler, KM#6. Klippe. 36 x 35 millimeters.

Date	Mintage	VG	F	VF	XF	Unc
1601 Rare	—	—	—	—	—	—

KM# 6 THALER

Silver **Obv. Legend:** SIGIS. TRA. NS. ET... **Note:** Dav. #4682. Square klippe. Size varies: 33-38 millimeters. Weight varies: 27.60-28.40 grams.

Date	Mintage	VG	F	VF	XF	Unc
1601	—	1,000	1,700	3,150	—	—

KM# 7 THALER

Silver **Note:** Dav. #4682A. Thick flan, smaller dies. Weight varies: 27.60-28.40 grams.

Date	Mintage	VG	F	VF	XF	Unc
1601	—	1,000	1,700	3,150	—	—

KM# 11 2 THALER

57.2000 g., Silver **Note:** Dav. #4681. Similar to 1 Thaler, KM#6. 39x38 millimeters.

Date	Mintage	VG	F	VF	XF	Unc
1601 Rare	—	—	—	—	—	—

SIEGE COINAGE

1612-1614

KM# 17 GULDEN

15.8000 g., Silver **Note:** Similar to 1 Thaler, KM#18.

Date	Mintage	VG	F	VF	XF	Unc
161ZCB	—	—	—	—	—	—

KM# 18 THALER

28.7000 g., Silver **Obv:** City arms **Obv. Legend:** NOS IN NOM: DOM... **Rev. Legend:** • ILLE • INEQVIS ET **Note:** Dav. #4684.

Date	Mintage	VG	F	VF	XF	Unc
1612CB	—	1,200	2,050	3,850	—	—

KM# 21 2 THALER

56.0000 g., Silver, 45 mm.

Date	Mintage	VG	F	VF	XF	Unc
161ZCB	—	1,400	2,450	4,200	—	—

KM# 20 2 THALER

56.5000 g., Silver, 40 mm. **Note:** Dav. #4683. Round version of KM#19.

Date	Mintage	VG	F	VF	XF	Unc
161ZCB	—	1,400	2,450	4,200	—	—

KM# 19 2 THALER

57.5000 g., Silver **Note:** Dav. #4683A. Similar to 1 Thaler, KM#18. 45x45mm Hexagonal klippe.

Date	Mintage	VG	F	VF	XF	Unc
161ZCB Rare	—	—	—	—	—	—

KM# 15 GROSCHEN

1.5000 g., Silver **Obv:** Crowned city arms **Rev:** Crowned heraldic eagle

Date	Mintage	VG	F	VF	XF	Unc
161Z	—	55.00	100	170	280	—
161ZCB	—	55.00	100	170	280	—

KM# 16 GROSCHEN

1.5000 g., Silver **Rev:** Heraldic eagle without crown

Date	Mintage	VG	F	VF	XF	Unc
161Z	—	55.00	100	170	280	—

KM# 25 GROSCHEN

1.5000 g., Silver **Rev:** Non-heraldic eagle

Date	Mintage	VG	F	VF	XF	Unc
1613	—	55.00	100	170	280	—
1613CB	—	55.00	100	170	280	—
1614CB	—	55.00	100	170	280	—

KM# 29 GROSCHEN

1.5000 g., Silver **Rev:** P on shield

Date	Mintage	VG	F	VF	XF	Unc
1613	—	55.00	100	170	280	—

KM# 30 GROSCHEN

1.5000 g., Silver **Rev:** Uncrowned heraldic eagle with S on shield

Date	Mintage	VG	F	VF	XF	Unc
1613	—	55.00	100	170	280	—

KM# 31 GROSCHEN

1.5000 g., Silver **Rev:** Crowned heraldic eagle with dot on shield

Date	Mintage	VG	F	VF	XF	Unc
1613	—	55.00	100	170	280	—
1613CB	—	55.00	100	170	280	—
1614C	—	55.00	100	170	280	—

KM# 27 GROSCHEN

1.5000 g., Silver **Rev:** Crowned heraldic eagle with empty heart-shaped shield

Date	Mintage	VG	F	VF	XF	Unc
1613	—	55.00	100	170	280	—

KM# 28 GROSCHEN

1.5000 g., Silver **Rev:** H on shield

Date	Mintage	VG	F	VF	XF	Unc
1613	—	55.00	100	170	280	—
1613CB	—	55.00	100	170	280	—

KM# 26 GROSCHEN

1.5000 g., Silver **Rev:** Crowned heraldic eagle with S on shield

Date	Mintage	VG	F	VF	XF	Unc
1613	—	55.00	100	170	280	—
1613B	—	55.00	100	170	280	—
1613CB	—	55.00	100	170	280	—
1613C	—	55.00	100	170	280	—

KM# 31a GROSCHEN

Copper

Date	Mintage	VG	F	VF	XF	Unc
1614C	—	—	—	—	—	—

KM# 33 GROSCHEN

Silver **Note:** Klippe of KM#31.

Date	Mintage	VG	F	VF	XF	Unc
1614CB Rare	—	—	—	—	—	—

KM# 34 GROSCHEN

Silver Plated Copper **Rev:** Heraldic eagle with S on shield

Date	Mintage	VG	F	VF	XF	Unc
1615CB 5 an inverted 2	—	—	—	—	—	—

TRADE COINAGE

KM# 22 DUCAT

3.5000 g., 0.9860 Gold 0.1109 oz. AGW

Date	Mintage	VG	F	VF	XF	Unc
161ZCB	—	—	8,400	14,000	21,000	—

KM# 32 DUCAT

3.5000 g., 0.9860 Gold 0.1109 oz. AGW

Date	Mintage	VG	F	VF	XF	Unc
1613CB	—	—	8,400	14,000	21,000	—

KM# 23 10 DUCATS

34.8000 g., Gold **Note:** Struck with 1 Thaler dies, KM#18.

Date	Mintage	VG	F	VF	XF	Unc
161ZCB Rare	—	—	—	—	—	—

PROVAS

KM#	Date	Mintage	Identification	Mkt Val
Pr1	1612CB	—	10 Ducats. Gold. 59.7000 g. Klippe. KM#23. 45x45 millimeters.	—

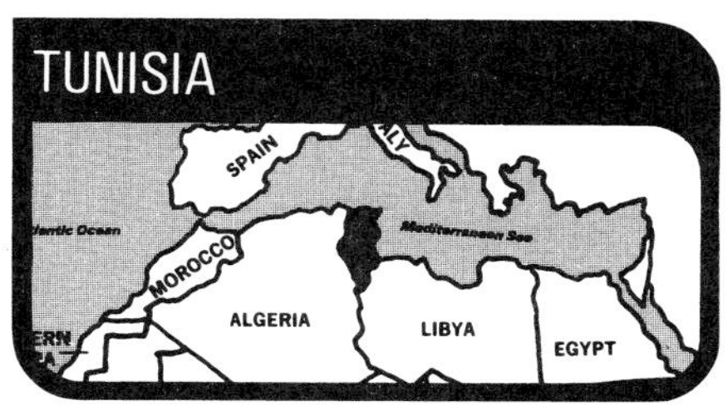

The Republic of Tunisia, located on the northern coast of Africa between Algeria and Libya, has an area of 63,170 sq. mi. (163,610 sq. km.) and a population of *7.9 million. Capital: Tunis. Agriculture is the backbone of the economy. Crude oil, phosphates, olive oil, and wine are exported.

Tunisia, settled by the Phoenicians in the 12th century B.C., was the center of the seafaring Carthaginian Empire. After the total destruction of Carthage, Tunisia became part of Rome's African province. It remained a part of the Roman Empire (except for the 439-533 interval of Vandal conquest) until taken by the Arabs, 648, who administered it until the Turkish invasion of 1570. Under Turkish control, the public revenue was heavily dependent upon the piracy of Mediterranean shipping, an endeavor that wasn't abandoned until 1819 when a coalition of powers threatened appropriate reprisal. Deprived of its major source of income, Tunisia underwent a financial regression that ended in bankruptcy, enabling France to establish a protectorate over the country in 1881.

TUNIS

Tunis, the capital and major seaport of Tunisia, existed in the Carthaginian era, but its importance dates only from the Moslem conquest, following which it became a major center of Arab power and prosperity. Spain seized it in 1535, lost it in 1564, retook it in 1573 and ceded it to the Turks in 1574. Thereafter the history of Tunis merged with that of Tunisia.

RULER

Ottoman, until 1881

MINT

تونس

Tunis

With exceptions noted in their proper place, all coins were struck at Tunis prior to AH1308/1891AD. Thereafter, all coins were struck at Paris with mint mark A until 1928, symbols of the mint from 1929-1957.

MONETARY SYSTEM

Until 1891

6 Burben (Bourbine) = 1 Burbe (Bourbe)
2 Burbe (Bourbe) = 1 Nasri
13 Burbe = 1 Kharub (Caroub)
16 Kharub (Caroub) = 1 Piastre (Rial Sebili)

Arabic name	French name	Value
Qafsi of Falls Raqiq	Bourbine	1/12 Nasri
Fals	Bourbe	6 Qafsi or 1/2 Nasri
Nasri	Asper	1/52 Riyal
Kharub	Caroub	1/16 Riyal
1/8 Riyal	1/8 Piastre	1 Kharub
1/4 Riyal	1/4 Piastre	4 Kharub
1/2 Riyal	1/2 Piastre	8 Kharub
Riyal	Piastre	16 Kharub

OTTOMAN EMPIRE

Mehmed III

AH1003-1012/1595-1603AD

HAMMERED COINAGE

KM# 2 AKCE

0.2500 g., Silver **Mint:** Tunis **Note:** Struck at Tunis.

Date	Mintage	VG	F	VF	XF	Unc
AH1003	—	60.00	100	150	200	—

KM# 3 SULTANI

3.4500 g., Gold **Mint:** Tunis

Date	Mintage	VG	F	VF	XF	Unc
AH1003	—	500	1,500	2,500	4,000	—
AH13(1003)	—	125	200	400	650	—
AH1008 Rare	—	—	—	—	—	—

Ahmed I

AH1012-1026/1603-1617AD

HAMMERED COINAGE

KM# 5 DIRHAM

0.5200 g., Silver **Mint:** Tunis **Note:** Square; 12.5 x 12.5 mm.

Date	Mintage	VG	F	VF	XF	Unc
ND(1603-17)	—	18.00	45.00	80.00	120	—

KM# 7 SULTANI

3.5000 g., Gold, 19 mm. **Mint:** Tunis

Date	Mintage	VG	F	VF	XF	Unc
AH1013	—	700	1,200	2,000	3,000	—
AH1015 Rare	—	—	—	—	—	—

Mustafa I

AH1031-1032/1622-1623AD

HAMMERED COINAGE

KM# 10 BURBE

1.9000 g., Copper **Mint:** Tunis

Date	Mintage	Good	VG	F	VF	XF
AH1031	—	35.00	50.00	75.00	100	—

Murad IV

AH1032-1049/1623-1640AD

HAMMERED COINAGE

KM# 15 BURBE

2.0100 g., Copper **Mint:** Tunis

Date	Mintage	Good	VG	F	VF	XF
AH1033	—	20.00	30.00	50.00	70.00	—
AH1049	—	—	—	—	—	—

KM# 16 NASRI

0.8000 g., Silver **Shape:** Square **Mint:** Tunis

Date	Mintage	Good	VG	F	VF	XF
AH1033	—	30.00	40.00	80.00	150	—

Ibrahim

AH1049-1058/1640-1648AD

HAMMERED COINAGE

KM# 17 BURBE

2.0000 g., Copper **Mint:** Tunis

Date	Mintage	Good	VG	F	VF	XF
AH(10)49	—	15.00	25.00	40.00	60.00	—

KM# A17 NASRI

0.7500 g., Silver **Shape:** Square **Mint:** Tunis

Date	Mintage	VG	F	VF	XF	Unc
AH1049	—	—	—	—	—	—

KM# 18 SULTANI

3.6700 g., Gold **Mint:** Tunis

Date	Mintage	VG	F	VF	XF	Unc
AH1049	—	200	350	500	750	—

Mehmed IV

AH1058-1099/1648-1687AD

HAMMERED COINAOGE

KM# 22 3 BURBEN

Copper **Mint:** Tunis

Date	Mintage	Good	VG	F	VF	XF
AH1058	—	10.00	20.00	30.00	50.00	—
AH1060	—	2.50	7.50	20.00	40.00	—
AH1066	—	10.00	20.00	30.00	50.00	—
AH1067	—	10.00	20.00	30.00	50.00	—
AH1068	—	2.50	7.50	20.00	40.00	—
AH1080	—	10.00	20.00	30.00	50.00	—
AH1085	—	10.00	20.00	30.00	50.00	—
AH1086	—	10.00	20.00	30.00	50.00	—
AH1088	—	10.00	20.00	30.00	50.00	—
AH1089	—	10.00	20.00	30.00	50.00	—
AH1090	—	10.00	20.00	30.00	50.00	—
AH1092	—	10.00	20.00	30.00	50.00	—
AH1095	—	10.00	20.00	30.00	50.00	—

KM# 23 NASRI

0.6300 g., Silver **Mint:** Tunis

Date	Mintage	Good	VG	F	VF	XF
AH1059	—	40.00	80.00	150	180	—

KM# 24 ONLUK

2.9800 g., Silver **Mint:** Tunis

Date	Mintage	Good	VG	F	VF	XF
AH1066	—	—	—	—	800	—

KM# 25 SULTANI

Gold **Mint:** Tunis **Note:** Weight varies: 3.20-3.35 grams.

Date	Mintage	VG	F	VF	XF	Unc
AH1058	—	500	1,000	1,500	2,000	—
AH1061	—	500	1,000	1,500	2,000	—
AH1068	—	500	1,250	1,650	3,000	—
AH1076	—	125	225	350	500	—
AH1087	—	125	225	350	500	—
AH1091	—	1,000	1,500	2,500	3,500	—

Suleyman II

AH1099-1102/1687-1691AD

HAMMERED COINAGE

KM# 28 SULTANI

3.4000 g., Gold **Mint:** Tunis

Date	Mintage	VG	F	VF	XF	Unc
AH1099	—	200	400	600	900	—
AH1100	—	200	400	600	900	—
AH1101	—	200	400	600	900	—
AH1102	—	200	400	600	900	—

Mustafa II

AH1106-15/1695-1703AD

HAMMERED COINAGE

KM# 30 3 BURBEN

Copper **Mint:** Tunis **Note:** Weight varies: 2.44-2.79 grams.

Date	Mintage	Good	VG	F	VF	XF
ND	—	5.00	8.00	25.00	45.00	—
AH1112	—	12.00	18.00	35.00	60.00	—

KM# 31 SULTANI

3.2200 g., Gold, 23 mm. **Mint:** Tunis

Date	Mintage	VG	F	VF	XF	Unc
AH1108	—	150	200	400	600	—
AH1109	—	—	280	400	800	—
AH1111	—	—	280	400	800	—

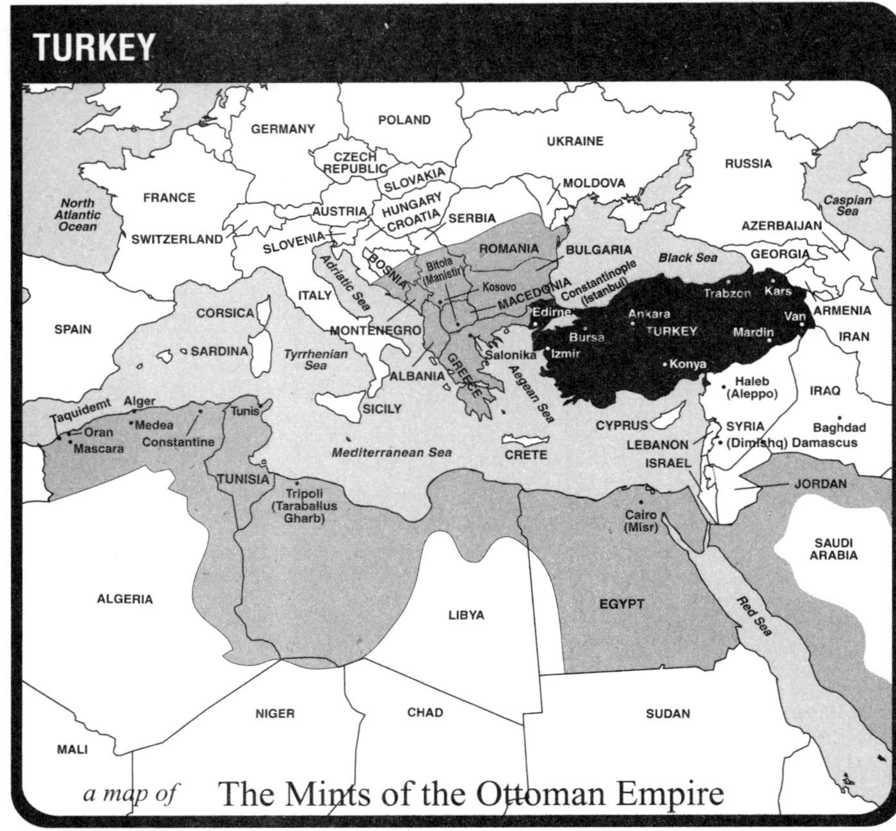

a map of The Mints of the Ottoman Empire

Turkey, located partially in Europe and partially in Asia between the Black and the Mediterranean Seas, has an area of 301,382 sq. mi. (780,580 sq. km).

The Ottoman Turks, a tribe from Central Asia, first appeared in the early 13th century, and by the 17th century had established the Ottoman Empire which stretched from the Persian Gulf to the southern frontier of Poland, and from the Caspian Sea to the Algerian plateau. The defeat of the Turkish navy by the Holy League in 1571, and of the Turkish forces besieging Vienna in 1683, began the steady decline of the Ottoman Empire which, accelerated by the rise of nationalism, contracted its European border, and by the end of World War I deprived it of its Arab lands. The present Turkish boundaries were largely fixed by the Treaty of Lausanne in 1923. The sultanate and caliphate, the political and spiritual ruling institutions of the old empire, were separated and the sultanate abolished in 1922. On Oct. 29, 1923, Turkey formally became a republic.

RULERS

Mehmed III, AH1003-1012/1595-1603AD
Ahmed I, AH1012-1026/1603-1617AD
Mustafa I,
First reign, AH1026-1027/1617-1618AD
Second reign, AH1031-1032/1622-1623AD
Osman II, AH1027-1031/1618-1622AD
Murad IV, AH1032-1049/1623-1640AD
Ibrahim, AH1040-1058/1640-1648AD
Mehmed IV, AH1058-1099/1648-1687AD
Suleyman II, AH1099-1102/1687-1691AD
Ahmed II, AH1102-1106/1691-1695AD
Mustafa II, AH1106-1115/1695-1703AD

MINT NAMES

اماسية
Amasiah

آمد
Amid
Diarbakar
Kara Amid

انگورية انقرية انقرة
Ankara (Anguriyah)

انگوريه
Ayasulik

آزاق آزق
Azak

بغداد
Baghdad - See Iraq-Mesopotamia

بنگالور
Belgrad

بسولے بسولي
Bitlis (Bidlis)

بوسنة سراي
Bosnasaray Saray

كنسا
Canca or Chaniche Gumushhane

قسطنطنية
Constantinople (Qustantiniyah)

Diarbakar - See Amid

ادرنه
Edirne (Adrianople)

روان
Erevan (Erewan, Revan, Yerevan) - See Armenia

ارزروم
Erzerum

فيليپ فلبه
Filibe (Philipopolis - Plovdiv)

گليبولى
Gelibolu (Gallipoli)

كنجه
Genje (Azerbaijan)

گمشخانه
Gumushhane or (Canca)

بلب
Halab (Aleppo) - See Syria

اسلامبول
Islambul or Istanbul

ازمير ازمر
Izmir (Smyrna)

قسطمونى
Kastamonu

(قبريس) قبرس
Kibris (Cyprus)

قونية
Konya (Khanja)

ماردين
Mardin

نخجوان
Nackhchawan - See Azerbaijan

نگبولو
Nigbolu

نوابرده
Novabirda Novar

اوخرى
Ohri

اردو همايون
Ordu-yu Humayun

قراطوه
Qaratova

سكيز ساقز
Sakiz (Scio)

سلانيك
Salonika (Selanik, Saloniki)

بوسنة سراي
Saray Bosnasarzy

سرز سريز
Serez (Siroz)

شماخي شماخه
Shamakhi - See Azerbaijan

شيراز
Shirvan - See Azerbaijan

بسدره قپسى
Sidrekapsi

سيواس
Sivas

صوفية
Sofia

تيره
Tire

توقاط توقات
Tokat

طرابزون طرابزن
Trebizond Trabzon

تونس
Tunis - See Tunisia-Tunis

اسكوپ
Uskub

وان
Van (Wan) - Until AH1032. AH1133-34

ينكى شهر
Yenishehir

زبيد
Zabid - See Yemen

MONETARY EQUIVALENTS
3 Akche = 1 Para
5 Para = Beshlik (Beshparalik)
10 Para = Onluk
20 Para = Yirmilik
30 Para = Zolota
40 Para = Kurush (Piastre)
1-1/2 Kurush (Piastres) = Altmishlik

MONETARY SYSTEM
Silver Coinage
40 Para = 1 Kurush (Piastre)
2 Kurush (Piastres) = 1 Ikilik
2-1/2 Kurush (Piastres) = Yuzluk
3 Kurush (Piastres) = Uechlik
5 Kurush (Piastres) = Beshlik
6 Kurush (Piastres) = Altilik
Gold Coinage
100 Kurush (Piastres) = 1 Turkish Pound (Lira)

This system has remained essentially unchanged since its introduction by Ahmad III in 1688, except that the Asper and Para have long since ceased to be coined. The Piastre, established as a crown-sized silver coin approximately equal to the French Ecu of Louis XIV, has shrunk to a tiny copper coin, worth about 1/15 of a U.S. cent. Since the establishment of the Republic in 1923, the Turkish terms, Kurus and Lira, have replaced the European names Piastres and Turkish Pounds.

OTTOMAN EMPIRE

Mehmed III

AH1003-12/1595-1603AD

HAMMERED COINAGE

Constantinople
KM# 3 MANGIR
3.7800 g., Copper

Date	Mintage	Good	VG	F	VF	XF
AH1003	—	2.00	4.00	10.00	20.00	—

Ankara
KM# 6.1 AKCE
0.3200 g., Silver

Date	Mintage	VG	F	VF	XF	Unc
AH1003	—	3.00	8.00	15.00	25.00	—

Belgrad
KM# 6.2 AKCE
0.3200 g., Silver

Date	Mintage	VG	F	VF	XF	Unc
AH1003	—	3.00	8.00	15.00	25.00	—

Bursa
KM# 6.3 AKCE
0.3200 g., Silver

Date	Mintage	VG	F	VF	XF	Unc
AH1003	—	2.00	5.00	10.00	20.00	—

Canca
KM# 6.4 AKCE
0.3200 g., Silver

Date	Mintage	VG	F	VF	XF	Unc
AH1003	—	2.00	5.00	10.00	20.00	—

Constantinople
KM# 6.5 AKCE
0.3200 g., Silver

Date	Mintage	VG	F	VF	XF	Unc
AH1003	—	2.00	5.00	10.00	20.00	—

Edirne
KM# 6.6 AKCE
0.3200 g., Silver

Date	Mintage	VG	F	VF	XF	Unc
AH1003	—	2.00	5.00	10.00	20.00	—

Filibe
KM# 6.7 AKCE
0.3200 g., Silver

Date	Mintage	VG	F	VF	XF	Unc
AH1003	—	4.00	10.00	20.00	30.00	—

Karatova
KM# 6.10 AKCE
0.3200 g., Silver

Date	Mintage	VG	F	VF	XF	Unc
AH1003	—	3.50	9.00	18.00	28.00	—

Kastamonu
KM# 6.8 AKCE
0.3200 g., Silver

Date	Mintage	VG	F	VF	XF	Unc
AH1003	—	6.00	15.00	20.00	35.00	—

Konya
KM# 6.9 AKCE
0.3200 g., Silver

Date	Mintage	VG	F	VF	XF	Unc
AH1003	—	6.00	15.00	25.00	35.00	—

Novabirda
KM# 6.11 AKCE
0.3200 g., Silver

Date	Mintage	VG	F	VF	XF	Unc
AH1003	—	3.50	9.00	18.00	28.00	—

Ohri
KM# 6.12 AKCE
0.3200 g., Silver

Date	Mintage	VG	F	VF	XF	Unc
AH1003	—	10.00	20.00	30.00	50.00	—

Sakiz
KM# 6.13 AKCE
0.3200 g., Silver

Date	Mintage	VG	F	VF	XF	Unc
AH1003	—	20.00	30.00	60.00	100	—

Salonika
KM# 6.14 AKCE
0.3200 g., Silver

Date	Mintage	VG	F	VF	XF	Unc
AH1003	—	10.00	20.00	30.00	50.00	—

Serez
KM# 6.15 AKCE
0.3200 g., Silver

Date	Mintage	VG	F	VF	XF	Unc
AH1003	—	2.00	5.00	10.00	20.00	—

Sidrekapsi
KM# 6.16 AKCE
0.3200 g., Silver

Date	Mintage	VG	F	VF	XF	Unc
AH1003	—	2.00	5.00	10.00	20.00	—

Tire
KM# 6.17 AKCE
0.3200 g., Silver

Date	Mintage	VG	F	VF	XF	Unc
AH1003	—	22.00	35.00	65.00	125	—

Tukat
KM# 6.18 AKCE
0.3200 g., Silver

Date	Mintage	VG	F	VF	XF	Unc
AH1003	—	12.00	25.00	35.00	60.00	—

Uskub
KM# 6.19 AKCE
0.3200 g., Silver

Date	Mintage	VG	F	VF	XF	Unc
AH1003	—	6.00	15.00	25.00	35.00	—

Yenishehir
KM# 6.20 AKCE
3.2000 g., Silver

Date	Mintage	Good	VG	F	VF	XF
AH1003	—	—	—	—	—	—

Canca
KM# 7.1 DIRHAM
Silver **Note:** Weight varies 2.1 - 3 grams; Prev. KM#7.2.

Date	Mintage	VG	F	VF	XF	Unc
AH1003	—	15.00	35.00	50.00	80.00	—

Haleb
KM# 7.4 DIRHAM
Silver **Note:** Weight varies 2.1 - 3 grams.

Date	Mintage	VG	F	VF	XF	Unc
AH1003	—	10.00	20.00	30.00	50.00	—

Kara Amid
KM# 7.5 DIRHAM
Silver **Note:** Weight varies 2.1 - 3 grams.

Date	Mintage	VG	F	VF	XF	Unc
AH1003	—	12.00	25.00	35.00	60.00	—
AH1009	—	12.00	25.00	35.00	60.00	—

Mardin
KM# 7.6 DIRHAM
Silver **Note:** Weight varies 2.1 - 3 grams.

Date	Mintage	VG	F	VF	XF	Unc
AH1003	—	20.00	45.00	75.00	100	—

Van
KM# 7.7 DIRHAM
Silver **Note:** Weight varies 2.1 - 3 grams.

Date	Mintage	VG	F	VF	XF	Unc
AH1003	—	20.00	45.00	75.00	100	—

Amasiah
KM# 10.1 ALTIN
Gold **Note:** Weight varies: 3.20-3.50 grams.

Date	Mintage	VG	F	VF	XF	Unc
AH1003	—	120	200	300	400	—

Amid
KM# 10.2 ALTIN
Gold **Note:** Weight varies: 3.20-3.50 grams.

Date	Mintage	VG	F	VF	XF	Unc
AH1003	—	100	150	250	350	—

KM# 8 ALTIN
Gold **Rev. Legend:** "Sultan Mehmed bin Sultan Murad..." **Note:** Weight varies: 3.20-3.50 grams.

Date	Mintage	VG	F	VF	XF	Unc
AH1003	—	100	150	250	350	—

Bosnasarzy
KM# 9.1 ALTIN
Gold **Note:** Weight varies: 3.20-3.50 grams.

Date	Mintage	VG	F	VF	XF	Unc
AH1003	—	150	275	450	750	—

Canca
KM# 10.3 ALTIN
Gold **Note:** Weight varies: 3.20-3.50 grams.

Date	Mintage	VG	F	VF	XF	Unc
AH1003	—	50.00	90.00	150	250	—

Constantinople
KM# 10.4 ALTIN
Gold **Note:** Weight varies: 3.20-3.50 grams.

Date	Mintage	VG	F	VF	XF	Unc
AH1003	—	60.00	90.00	150	200	—

KM# 9.2 ALTIN
Gold **Note:** Weight varies: 3.20-3.50 grams.

Date	Mintage	VG	F	VF	XF	Unc
AH1003	—	50.00	90.00	150	200	—

Nackhchawan
KM# 11 ALTIN
Gold **Note:** Weight varies: 3.20-3.50 grams.

Date	Mintage	VG	F	VF	XF	Unc
AHxxxx Rare	—	—	—	—	—	—

Sakiz
KM# 10.5 ALTIN
Gold **Note:** Weight varies: 3.20-3.50 grams.

Date	Mintage	VG	F	VF	XF	Unc
AH1003	—	200	350	550	850	—

Sivas
KM# 10.6 ALTIN
Gold **Note:** Weight varies: 3.20-3.50 grams.

Date	Mintage	VG	F	VF	XF	Unc
AH1003	—	250	400	600	1,000	—

Ahmed I

AH1012-26/1603-17AD

HAMMERED COINAGE

Amid
KM# 13.11 AKCE
0.2700 g., Silver

Date	Mintage	VG	F	VF	XF	Unc
AH1012	—	8.00	12.00	20.00	30.00	—

Belgrad
KM# 13.1 AKCE
0.2700 g., Silver

Date	Mintage	VG	F	VF	XF	Unc
AH1012	—	7.00	15.00	25.00	35.00	—

Bursa
KM# 13.2 AKCE
0.2700 g., Silver

Date	Mintage	VG	F	VF	XF	Unc
AH1012	—	3.00	6.00	10.00	20.00	—

Canca
KM# 13.17 AKCE
0.2700 g., Silver

Date	Mintage	VG	F	VF	XF	Unc
AH1013	—	—	—	—	—	—

Constantinople
KM# 13.3 AKCE
0.2700 g., Silver

Date	Mintage	VG	F	VF	XF	Unc
AH1012	—	3.00	6.00	10.00	20.00	—

Edirne
KM# 13.4 AKCE
0.2700 g., Silver

Date	Mintage	VG	F	VF	XF	Unc
AH1012	—	3.00	6.00	10.00	20.00	—

Erzerum
KM# 13.12 AKCE
0.2700 g., Silver

Date	Mintage	VG	F	VF	XF	Unc
AH1012	—	15.00	20.00	30.00	50.00	—

Filibe
KM# 13.5 AKCE
0.2700 g., Silver

Date	Mintage	VG	F	VF	XF	Unc
AH1012	—	12.00	25.00	35.00	50.00	—

Gelibolu
KM# 13.6 AKCE
0.2700 g., Silver

Date	Mintage	VG	F	VF	XF	Unc
AH1012	—	18.00	35.00	60.00	100	—

Genje
KM# 13.13 AKCE
0.2700 g., Silver

Date	Mintage	VG	F	VF	XF	Unc
AH1012	—	80.00	120	200	300	—

Guzelhisar
KM# 13.14 AKCE
0.2700 g., Silver

Date	Mintage	VG	F	VF	XF	Unc
AH1012	—	150	200	300	500	—

Kibris
KM# 13.15 AKCE
0.2700 g., Silver

Date	Mintage	VG	F	VF	XF	Unc
AH1012	—	30.00	50.00	80.00	150	—

Konya
KM# 13.7 AKCE
0.2700 g., Silver

Date	Mintage	VG	F	VF	XF	Unc
AH1012	—	14.00	28.00	40.00	60.00	—

Novabirda
KM# 13.8 AKCE
0.2700 g., Silver

Date	Mintage	VG	F	VF	XF	Unc
AH1012	—	3.00	6.00	10.00	20.00	—

Serez
KM# 13.9 AKCE
0.2700 g., Silver

Date	Mintage	VG	F	VF	XF	Unc
AH1012	—	3.00	6.00	10.00	20.00	—

Tukat
KM# 13.10 AKCE
0.2700 g., Silver

Date	Mintage	VG	F	VF	XF	Unc
AH1012	—	20.00	35.00	50.00	75.00	—

Van
KM# 13.16 AKCE
0.2700 g., Silver

Date	Mintage	VG	F	VF	XF	Unc
AH1012	—	80.00	120	200	300	—

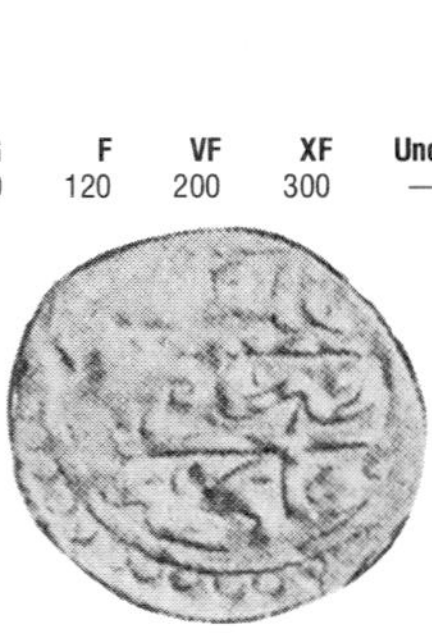

Genje
KM# 15.2 DIRHAM
Silver **Note:** Prev. KM#15; Weight varies 2.1 - 3 grams.

Date	Mintage	VG	F	VF	XF	Unc
AH1012	—	12.00	25.00	35.00	50.00	—

KM# 14 DIRHAM
Silver **Note:** Weight varies 2.1 - 3 grams.

Date	Mintage	VG	F	VF	XF	Unc
AH1012	—	12.00	20.00	30.00	50.00	—

Canca
KM# A14.1 BESHLIK
0.9400 g., Silver

Date	Mintage	VG	F	VF	XF	Unc
AH1012	—	—	—	—	—	—

Erzerum
KM# A14.2 BESHLIK
1.3300 g., Silver

Date	Mintage	VG	F	VF	XF	Unc
AH1014	—	—	—	—	—	—

Kara Amid
KM# A14.3 BESHLIK
1.0200 g., Silver

Date	Mintage	VG	F	VF	XF	Unc
AH1012	—	—	—	—	—	—

Amid
KM# 16.1 ALTIN
3.2000 g., Gold

Date	Mintage	VG	F	VF	XF	Unc
AH1012	—	150	250	450	800	—

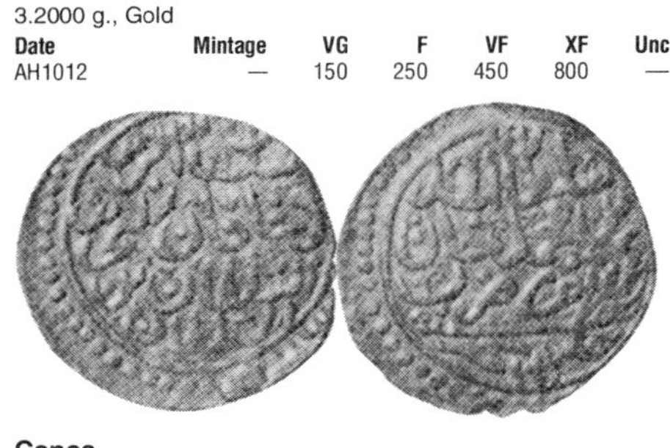

Canca
KM# 16.2 ALTIN
3.2000 g., Gold

Date	Mintage	VG	F	VF	XF	Unc
AH1013	—	150	250	450	800	—

Constantinople
KM# 16.3 ALTIN
3.2000 g., Gold

Date	Mintage	VG	F	VF	XF	Unc
AH1012	—	60.00	150	200	250	—

KM# 19 ALTIN
3.2000 g., Gold

Date	Mintage	VG	F	VF	XF	Unc
AH1012	—	75.00	150	200	300	—

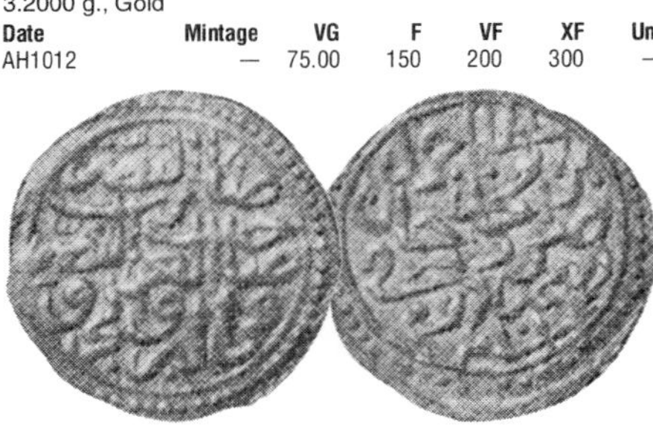

Erzerum
KM# 16.4 ALTIN
3.2000 g., Gold

Date	Mintage	VG	F	VF	XF	Unc
AH1012	—	250	400	600	1,000	—

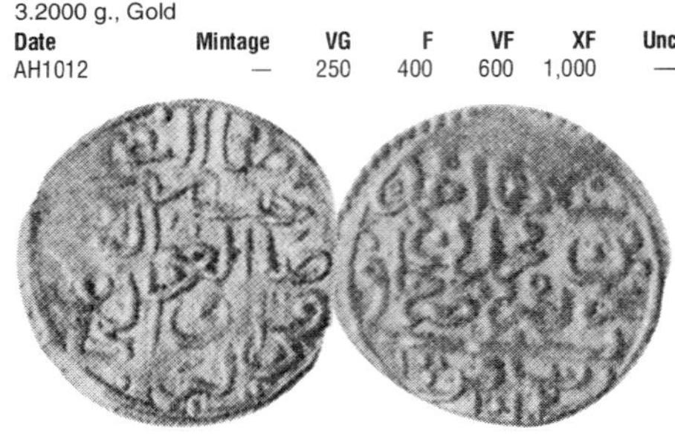

Sakiz
KM# 17 ALTIN
3.2000 g., Gold

Date	Mintage	VG	F	VF	XF	Unc
AH1012	—	175	350	450	800	—

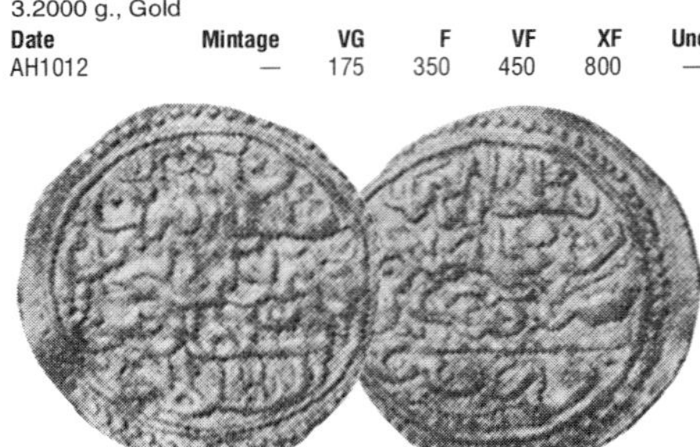

Trebizum
KM# 16.5 ALTIN
3.2000 g., Gold

Date	Mintage	VG	F	VF	XF	Unc
AH1012	—	325	550	900	1,500	—

Tukat
KM# 16.6 ALTIN
3.2000 g., Gold

Date	Mintage	VG	F	VF	XF	Unc
AH1012	—	200	350	500	1,000	—

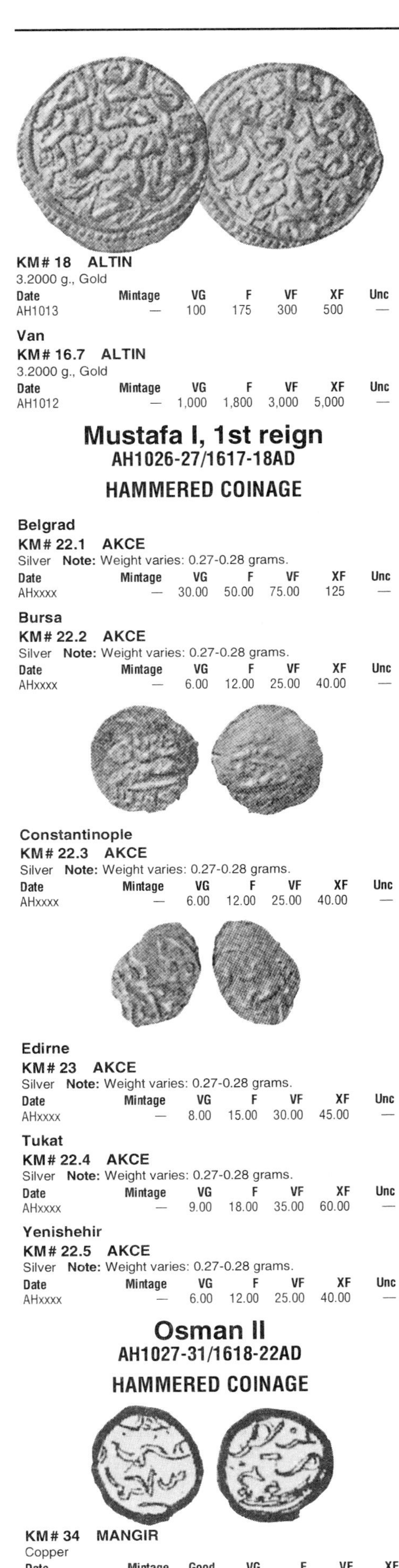

KM# 18 ALTIN
3.2000 g., Gold

Date	Mintage	VG	F	VF	XF	Unc
AH1013	—	100	175	300	500	—

Van
KM# 16.7 ALTIN
3.2000 g., Gold

Date	Mintage	VG	F	VF	XF	Unc
AH1012	—	1,000	1,800	3,000	5,000	—

Mustafa I, 1st reign
AH1026-27/1617-18AD

HAMMERED COINAGE

Belgrad
KM# 22.1 AKCE
Silver **Note:** Weight varies: 0.27-0.28 grams.

Date	Mintage	VG	F	VF	XF	Unc
AHxxxx	—	30.00	50.00	75.00	125	—

Bursa
KM# 22.2 AKCE
Silver **Note:** Weight varies: 0.27-0.28 grams.

Date	Mintage	VG	F	VF	XF	Unc
AHxxxx	—	6.00	12.00	25.00	40.00	—

Constantinople
KM# 22.3 AKCE
Silver **Note:** Weight varies: 0.27-0.28 grams.

Date	Mintage	VG	F	VF	XF	Unc
AHxxxx	—	6.00	12.00	25.00	40.00	—

Edirne
KM# 23 AKCE
Silver **Note:** Weight varies: 0.27-0.28 grams.

Date	Mintage	VG	F	VF	XF	Unc
AHxxxx	—	8.00	15.00	30.00	45.00	—

Tukat
KM# 22.4 AKCE
Silver **Note:** Weight varies: 0.27-0.28 grams.

Date	Mintage	VG	F	VF	XF	Unc
AHxxxx	—	9.00	18.00	35.00	60.00	—

Yenishehir
KM# 22.5 AKCE
Silver **Note:** Weight varies: 0.27-0.28 grams.

Date	Mintage	VG	F	VF	XF	Unc
AHxxxx	—	6.00	12.00	25.00	40.00	—

Osman II
AH1027-31/1618-22AD

HAMMERED COINAGE

KM# 34 MANGIR
Copper

Date	Mintage	Good	VG	F	VF	XF
AHxxxx	—	4.00	8.00	15.00	25.00	—

KM# 35 MANGIR
Copper

Date	Mintage	Good	VG	F	VF	XF
AH1027	—	6.00	12.00	20.00	35.00	—

Constantinople
KM# 33 MANGIR
Copper

Date	Mintage	Good	VG	F	VF	XF
AH102x	—	6.00	12.00	20.00	35.00	—

Amasiah
KM# 38.12 AKCE
0.3000 g., Silver

Date	Mintage	VG	F	VF	XF	Unc
AH1027	—	7.00	15.00	30.00	50.00	—

Belgrad
KM# 38.1 AKCE
0.3000 g., Silver

Date	Mintage	VG	F	VF	XF	Unc
AH1027	—	8.00	15.00	25.00	30.00	—

Bursa
KM# 38.2 AKCE
0.3000 g., Silver

Date	Mintage	VG	F	VF	XF	Unc
AH1027	—	8.00	15.00	30.00	50.00	—

Canca
KM# 38.3 AKCE
0.3000 g., Silver

Date	Mintage	VG	F	VF	XF	Unc
AH1027	—	5.00	10.00	15.00	20.00	—

Constantinople
KM# 38.4 AKCE
0.3000 g., Silver

Date	Mintage	VG	F	VF	XF	Unc
AH1027	—	4.00	7.00	12.00	20.00	—

Konya
KM# 38.5 AKCE
0.3000 g., Silver

Date	Mintage	VG	F	VF	XF	Unc
AH1027	—	9.00	18.00	35.00	60.00	—

Ohri
KM# 38.6 AKCE
0.3000 g., Silver

Date	Mintage	VG	F	VF	XF	Unc
AH1027	—	9.00	18.00	35.00	60.00	—

Serez
KM# 38.7 AKCE
0.3000 g., Silver

Date	Mintage	VG	F	VF	XF	Unc
AH1027	—	4.00	7.00	12.00	20.00	—

Sofia
KM# 38.8 AKCE
0.3000 g., Silver

Date	Mintage	VG	F	VF	XF	Unc
AH1027	—	7.00	15.00	30.00	50.00	—

Tire
KM# 38.15 AKCE
0.3000 g., Silver

Date	Mintage	VG	F	VF	XF	Unc
AH1027	—	—	—	—	—	—

Tokat
KM# 38.13 AKCE
0.3000 g., Silver

Date	Mintage	VG	F	VF	XF	Unc
AH1027	—	18.00	35.00	60.00	85.00	—

Ushkub
KM# 38.10 AKCE
0.3000 g., Silver

Date	Mintage	VG	F	VF	XF	Unc
AH1027	—	5.00	8.00	15.00	25.00	—

Van
KM# 38.14 AKCE
0.3000 g., Silver

Date	Mintage	VG	F	VF	XF	Unc
AH1027	—	60.00	100	150	200	—

Yenishehir
KM# 38.11 AKCE
0.3000 g., Silver

Date	Mintage	VG	F	VF	XF	Unc
AH1027	—	5.00	8.00	15.00	25.00	—

Canca
KM# 42.1 ONLUK
Silver **Note:** Weight varies: 2.60-2.75 grams.

Date	Mintage	VG	F	VF	XF	Unc
AH1027	—	20.00	35.00	60.00	85.00	—

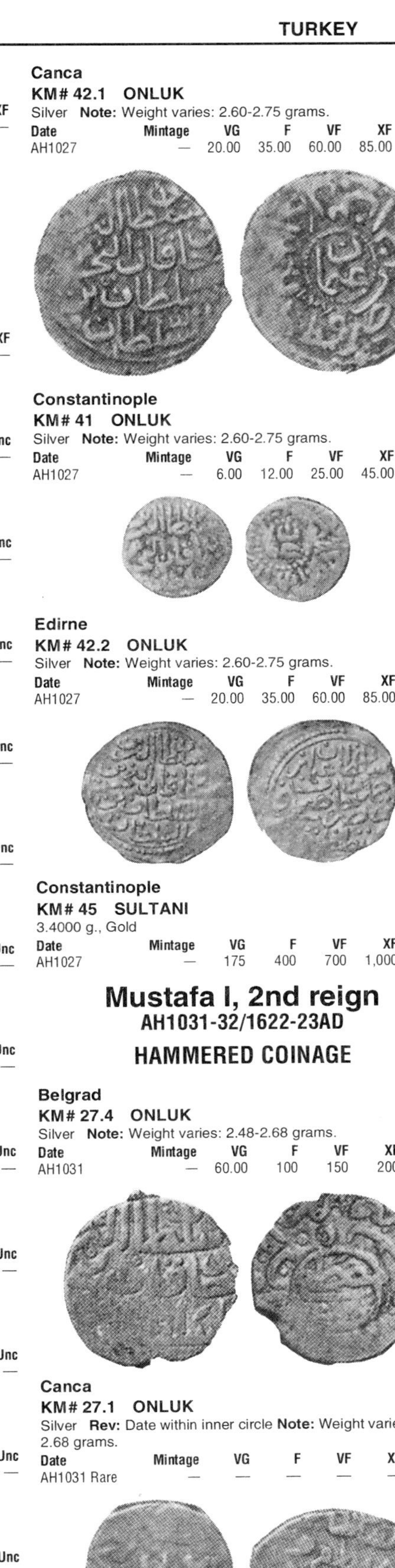

Constantinople
KM# 41 ONLUK
Silver **Note:** Weight varies: 2.60-2.75 grams.

Date	Mintage	VG	F	VF	XF	Unc
AH1027	—	6.00	12.00	25.00	45.00	—

Edirne
KM# 42.2 ONLUK
Silver **Note:** Weight varies: 2.60-2.75 grams.

Date	Mintage	VG	F	VF	XF	Unc
AH1027	—	20.00	35.00	60.00	85.00	—

Constantinople
KM# 45 SULTANI
3.4000 g., Gold

Date	Mintage	VG	F	VF	XF	Unc
AH1027	—	175	400	700	1,000	—

Mustafa I, 2nd reign
AH1031-32/1622-23AD

HAMMERED COINAGE

Belgrad
KM# 27.4 ONLUK
Silver **Note:** Weight varies: 2.48-2.68 grams.

Date	Mintage	VG	F	VF	XF	Unc
AH1031	—	60.00	100	150	200	—

Canca
KM# 27.1 ONLUK
Silver **Rev:** Date within inner circle **Note:** Weight varies: 2.48-2.68 grams.

Date	Mintage	VG	F	VF	XF	Unc
AH1031 Rare	—	—	—	—	—	—

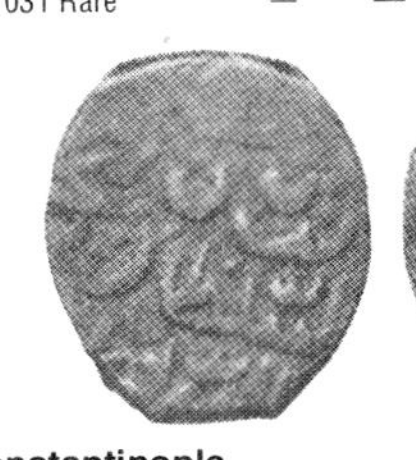

Constantinople
KM# 26 ONLUK
Silver **Note:** Weight varies: 2.48-2.68 grams.

Date	Mintage	VG	F	VF	XF	Unc
AHxxxx	—	10.00	20.00	50.00	75.00	—

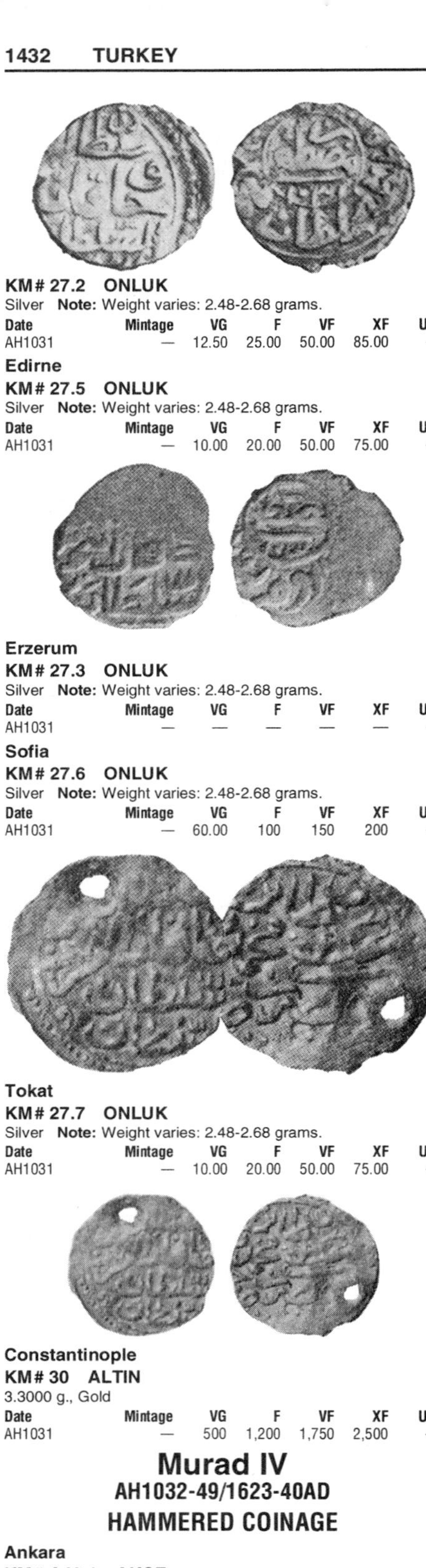

KM# 27.2 ONLUK
Silver **Note:** Weight varies: 2.48-2.68 grams.

Date	Mintage	VG	F	VF	XF	Unc
AH1031	—	12.50	25.00	50.00	85.00	—

Edirne
KM# 27.5 ONLUK
Silver **Note:** Weight varies: 2.48-2.68 grams.

Date	Mintage	VG	F	VF	XF	Unc
AH1031	—	10.00	20.00	50.00	75.00	—

Erzerum
KM# 27.3 ONLUK
Silver **Note:** Weight varies: 2.48-2.68 grams.

Date	Mintage	VG	F	VF	XF	Unc
AH1031	—	—	—	—	—	—

Sofia
KM# 27.6 ONLUK
Silver **Note:** Weight varies: 2.48-2.68 grams.

Date	Mintage	VG	F	VF	XF	Unc
AH1031	—	60.00	100	150	200	—

Tokat
KM# 27.7 ONLUK
Silver **Note:** Weight varies: 2.48-2.68 grams.

Date	Mintage	VG	F	VF	XF	Unc
AH1031	—	10.00	20.00	50.00	75.00	—

Constantinople
KM# 30 ALTIN
3.3000 g., Gold

Date	Mintage	VG	F	VF	XF	Unc
AH1031	—	500	1,200	1,750	2,500	—

Murad IV
AH1032-49/1623-40AD
HAMMERED COINAGE

Ankara
KM# A48.1 AKCE
0.3300 g., Silver

Date	Mintage	VG	F	VF	XF	Unc
AH1032	—	40.00	70.00	120	200	—

Belgrad
KM# 48.1 AKCE
0.3300 g., Silver

Date	Mintage	VG	F	VF	XF	Unc
AH1032	—	7.00	15.00	25.00	40.00	—

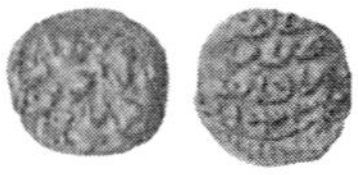

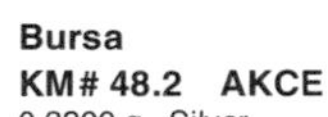

Bursa
KM# 48.2 AKCE
0.3300 g., Silver

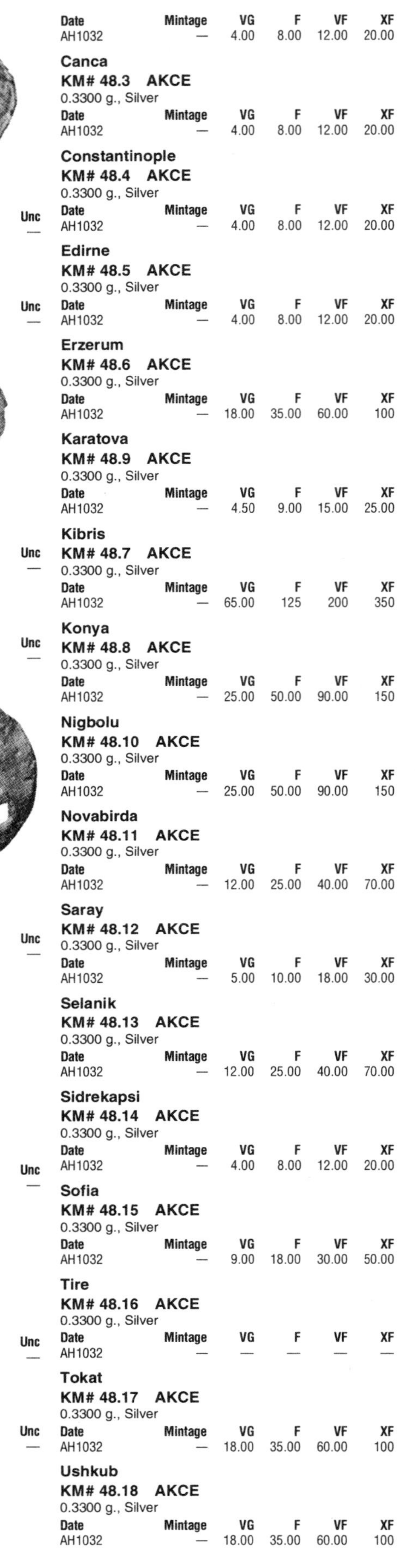

Date	Mintage	VG	F	VF	XF	Unc
AH1032	—	4.00	8.00	12.00	20.00	—

Canca
KM# 48.3 AKCE
0.3300 g., Silver

Date	Mintage	VG	F	VF	XF	Unc
AH1032	—	4.00	8.00	12.00	20.00	—

Constantinople
KM# 48.4 AKCE
0.3300 g., Silver

Date	Mintage	VG	F	VF	XF	Unc
AH1032	—	4.00	8.00	12.00	20.00	—

Edirne
KM# 48.5 AKCE
0.3300 g., Silver

Date	Mintage	VG	F	VF	XF	Unc
AH1032	—	4.00	8.00	12.00	20.00	—

Erzerum
KM# 48.6 AKCE
0.3300 g., Silver

Date	Mintage	VG	F	VF	XF	Unc
AH1032	—	18.00	35.00	60.00	100	—

Karatova
KM# 48.9 AKCE
0.3300 g., Silver

Date	Mintage	VG	F	VF	XF	Unc
AH1032	—	4.50	9.00	15.00	25.00	—

Kibris
KM# 48.7 AKCE
0.3300 g., Silver

Date	Mintage	VG	F	VF	XF	Unc
AH1032	—	65.00	125	200	350	—

Konya
KM# 48.8 AKCE
0.3300 g., Silver

Date	Mintage	VG	F	VF	XF	Unc
AH1032	—	25.00	50.00	90.00	150	—

Nigbolu
KM# 48.10 AKCE
0.3300 g., Silver

Date	Mintage	VG	F	VF	XF	Unc
AH1032	—	25.00	50.00	90.00	150	—

Novabirda
KM# 48.11 AKCE
0.3300 g., Silver

Date	Mintage	VG	F	VF	XF	Unc
AH1032	—	12.00	25.00	40.00	70.00	—

Saray
KM# 48.12 AKCE
0.3300 g., Silver

Date	Mintage	VG	F	VF	XF	Unc
AH1032	—	5.00	10.00	18.00	30.00	—

Selanik
KM# 48.13 AKCE
0.3300 g., Silver

Date	Mintage	VG	F	VF	XF	Unc
AH1032	—	12.00	25.00	40.00	70.00	—

Sidrekapsi
KM# 48.14 AKCE
0.3300 g., Silver

Date	Mintage	VG	F	VF	XF	Unc
AH1032	—	4.00	8.00	12.00	20.00	—

Sofia
KM# 48.15 AKCE
0.3300 g., Silver

Date	Mintage	VG	F	VF	XF	Unc
AH1032	—	9.00	18.00	30.00	50.00	—

Tire
KM# 48.16 AKCE
0.3300 g., Silver

Date	Mintage	VG	F	VF	XF	Unc
AH1032	—	—	—	—	—	—

Tokat
KM# 48.17 AKCE
0.3300 g., Silver

Date	Mintage	VG	F	VF	XF	Unc
AH1032	—	18.00	35.00	60.00	100	—

Ushkub
KM# 48.18 AKCE
0.3300 g., Silver

Date	Mintage	VG	F	VF	XF	Unc
AH1032	—	18.00	35.00	60.00	100	—

Van
KM# 48.20 AKCE
0.3300 g., Silver

Date	Mintage	VG	F	VF	XF	Unc
AH1032 Rare	—	—	—	—	—	—

Yenishehir
KM# 48.19 AKCE
0.3300 g., Silver

Date	Mintage	VG	F	VF	XF	Unc
AH1032	—	5.00	10.00	18.00	30.00	—

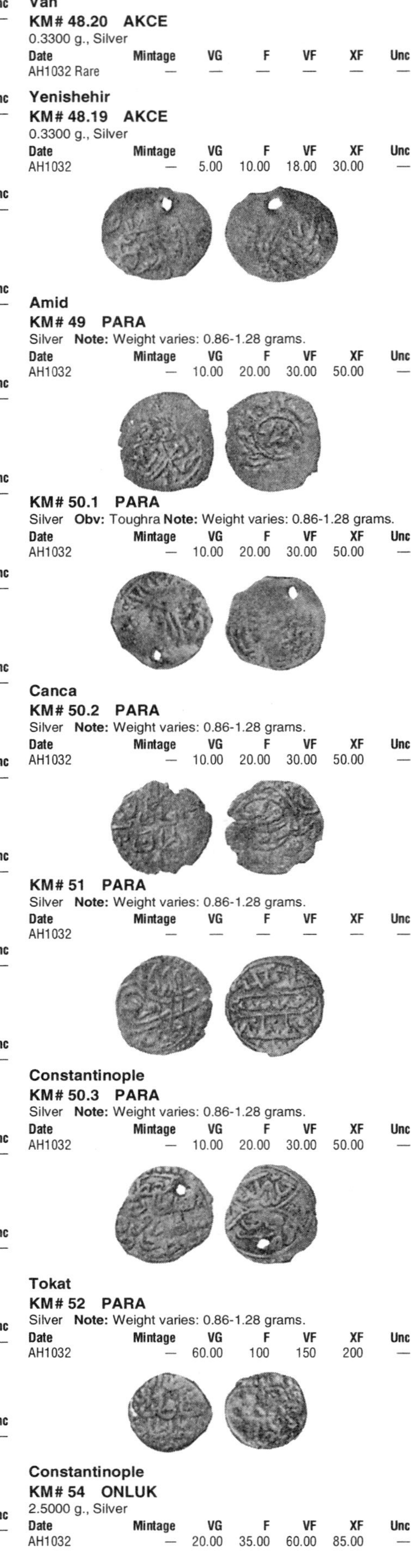

Amid
KM# 49 PARA
Silver **Note:** Weight varies: 0.86-1.28 grams.

Date	Mintage	VG	F	VF	XF	Unc
AH1032	—	10.00	20.00	30.00	50.00	—

KM# 50.1 PARA
Silver **Obv:** Toughra **Note:** Weight varies: 0.86-1.28 grams.

Date	Mintage	VG	F	VF	XF	Unc
AH1032	—	10.00	20.00	30.00	50.00	—

Canca
KM# 50.2 PARA
Silver **Note:** Weight varies: 0.86-1.28 grams.

Date	Mintage	VG	F	VF	XF	Unc
AH1032	—	10.00	20.00	30.00	50.00	—

KM# 51 PARA
Silver **Note:** Weight varies: 0.86-1.28 grams.

Date	Mintage	VG	F	VF	XF	Unc
AH1032	—	—	—	—	—	—

Constantinople
KM# 50.3 PARA
Silver **Note:** Weight varies: 0.86-1.28 grams.

Date	Mintage	VG	F	VF	XF	Unc
AH1032	—	10.00	20.00	30.00	50.00	—

Tokat
KM# 52 PARA
Silver **Note:** Weight varies: 0.86-1.28 grams.

Date	Mintage	VG	F	VF	XF	Unc
AH1032	—	60.00	100	150	200	—

Constantinople
KM# 54 ONLUK
2.5000 g., Silver

Date	Mintage	VG	F	VF	XF	Unc
AH1032	—	20.00	35.00	60.00	85.00	—

Constantinople
KM# 57 ALTIN
3.4000 g., Gold

Date	Mintage	VG	F	VF	XF	Unc
AH1032	—	125	200	300	450	—

Ibrahim
AH1040-58/1640-48AD
HAMMERED COINAGE

Constantinople
KM# 60 MANGIR
1.4500 g., Copper **Obv:** Toughra

Date	Mintage	Good	VG	F	VF	XF
AHxxxx	—	6.00	10.00	20.00	35.00	—

KM# 61 MANGIR
1.4500 g., Copper **Obv:** Toughra

Date	Mintage	Good	VG	F	VF	XF
AH1049	—	6.00	10.00	20.00	35.00	—

KM# 62 MANGIR
1.4500 g., Copper **Obv:** Toughra

Date	Mintage	Good	VG	F	VF	XF
AH1054	—	6.00	10.00	20.00	35.00	—

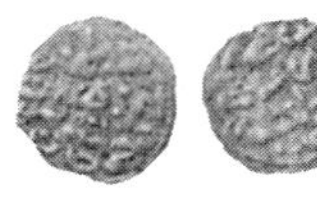

Constantinople
KM# 65 AKCE
0.3200 g., Silver

Date	Mintage	VG	F	VF	XF	Unc
AH1049	—	6.00	12.00	25.00	50.00	—

Kara Amid
KM# 65.2 AKCE
0.3000 g., Silver

Date	Mintage	VG	F	VF	XF	Unc
AHxxxx	—	—	—	—	—	—

Constantinople
KM# 68 PARA
0.6000 g., Silver

Date	Mintage	VG	F	VF	XF	Unc
AHxxxx	—	25.00	50.00	100	150	—

Amid
KM# 71.1 BESHLIK
Silver **Note:** Weight varies: 1.48-1.52 grams.

Date	Mintage	VG	F	VF	XF	Unc
AH1049 Rare	—	—	—	—	—	—

Constantinople
KM# 71.2 BESHLIK
Silver **Note:** Weight varies: 1.48-1.52 grams.

Date	Mintage	VG	F	VF	XF	Unc
AH1049	—	BV	20.00	50.00	100	—

Constantinople
KM# 74 ONLUK
3.0500 g., Silver

Date	Mintage	VG	F	VF	XF	Unc
AHxxxx	—	20.00	35.00	60.00	100	—

Mehmed IV
AH1058-99/1648-87AD
HAMMERED COINAGE

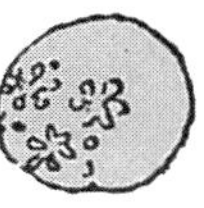

Constantinople
KM# 77 MANGIR
Copper

Date	Mintage	Good	VG	F	VF	XF
AH(1)061	—	6.00	12.00	20.00	40.00	—

Van
KM# 78 MANGIR
Copper

Date	Mintage	VG	F	VF	XF	Unc
AHxxxx	—	—	—	—	—	—

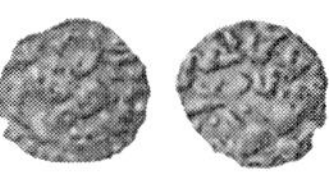

Constantinople
KM# 80 AKCE
0.3200 g., Silver

Date	Mintage	VG	F	VF	XF	Unc
AH1058	—	4.00	8.00	12.00	25.00	—

Constantinople
KM# 82.1 DIRHAM
Silver **Note:** Prev. KM#82

Date	Mintage	VG	F	VF	XF	Unc
AH1058	—	—	—	—	—	—

Halab
KM# 82.2 DIRHAM
Silver

Date	Mintage	VG	F	VF	XF	Unc
AH1058	—	12.00	25.00	35.00	50.00	—

Constantinople
KM# 83 ALTIN
Gold **Note:** Weight varies: 3.45-3.55 grams.

Date	Mintage	VG	F	VF	XF	Unc
AH1058	—	200	400	750	1,000	—

KM# 84 ALTIN
Gold **Note:** Weight varies: 3.45-3.55 grams.

Date	Mintage	VG	F	VF	XF	Unc
AH1058	—	200	400	750	1,000	—

Suleyman II
AH1099-1102/1687-91AD
HAMMERED COINAGE

Bosnasaray
KM# 87.1 MANGIR
Copper

Date	Mintage	Good	VG	F	VF	XF
AH1099	—	—	—	—	—	—

Constantinople
KM# 87.2 MANGIR
Copper

Date	Mintage	Good	VG	F	VF	XF
AH1099	—	2.00	4.00	6.00	12.00	—

Saray
KM# 89 MANGIR
Copper

Date	Mintage	VG	F	VF	XF	Unc
AH1100	—	—	—	—	—	—

Van
KM# 91 MANGIR
Copper

Date	Mintage	VG	F	VF	XF	Unc
AHxxxx	—	—	—	—	—	—

Constantinople
KM# 88 AKCE
Silver

Date	Mintage	VG	F	VF	XF	Unc
AH1099	—	200	300	500	800	—

Constantinople
KM# 90 CEYREK KURUS
6.2500 g., Silver **Note:** Struck at Constantinople.

Date	Mintage	VG	F	VF	XF	Unc
AH1099	—	750	1,000	1,500	2,000	—

Constantinople
KM# 93 YARIM KURUS
9.4000 g., Silver

Date	Mintage	VG	F	VF	XF	Unc
AH1099	—	250	450	750	1,500	—

Constantinople

KM# 96 KURUS

19.3800 g., Silver **Note:** Dav. #314.

Date	Mintage	VG	F	VF	XF	Unc
AH1099	—	50.00	150	200	275	—

Constantinople

KM# 100 SHERIFI ALTIN

3.4500 g., Gold

Date	Mintage	VG	F	VF	XF	Unc
AH1099	—	125	250	500	750	—

KM# 99 SHERIFI ALTIN

3.2500 g., Gold, 27 mm.

Date	Mintage	VG	F	VF	XF	Unc
AHxxxx	—	125	250	500	750	—

Ahmed II
AH1102-1106/1691-95AD
HAMMERED COINAGE

Constantinople

KM# 103 MANGIR

1.3000 g., Copper

Date	Mintage	Good	VG	F	VF	XF
AH1102	—	15.00	30.00	50.00	100	—

Constantinople

KM# 105 AKCE

0.3200 g., Silver

Date	Mintage	VG	F	VF	XF	Unc
AH1102	—	150	250	350	—	—

Constantinople

KM# 107 YARIM KURUS

9.3500 g., Silver

Date	Mintage	VG	F	VF	XF	Unc
AH1102	—	180	250	450	600	—

Constantinople

KM# 110 KURUS

18.7000 g., Silver **Note:** Dav. #316.

Date	Mintage	VG	F	VF	XF	Unc
AH1102	—	100	200	300	500	—

Constantinople

KM# 113 SHERIFI ALTIN

3.4000 g., Gold

Date	Mintage	VG	F	VF	XF	Unc
AH1102	—	200	600	1,000	1,500	—

Mustafa II
AH1106-15/1695-1703AD
HAMMERED COINAGE

Constantinople

KM# 115 PARA

Silver

Date	Mintage	VG	F	VF	XF	Unc
AH1106	—	150	200	300	500	—

Constantinople

KM# 116 YARIM KURUS

9.4300 g., Silver

Date	Mintage	VG	F	VF	XF	Unc
AH1106	—	8.00	12.00	25.00	50.00	—

KM# 116A YARIM KURUS

9.4300 g., Silver **Note:** Without "KAF" in the Mulkehu.

Date	Mintage	VG	F	VF	XF	Unc
AH1106	—	15.00	25.00	50.00	100	—

Edirne

KM# 117.1 YARIM KURUS

9.6200 g., Silver

Date	Mintage	VG	F	VF	XF	Unc
AH1106	—	20.00	40.00	75.00	125	—

Erzerum

KM# 117.2 YARIM KURUS

9.6200 g., Silver

Date	Mintage	VG	F	VF	XF	Unc
AH1106 Rare	—	200	350	500	800	—

Izmir

KM# 117.3 YARIM KURUS

9.6200 g., Silver

Date	Mintage	VG	F	VF	XF	Unc
AH1106	—	75.00	125	200	350	—

KM# 117.3A YARIM KURUS

9.6200 g., Silver **Note:** Without "KAF" in the Mulkehu.

Date	Mintage	VG	F	VF	XF	Unc
AH1106 Rare	—	—	—	—	—	—

Constantinople

KM# 120 KURUS

18.6200 g., Silver **Note:** Dav. #317.

Date	Mintage	VG	F	VF	XF	Unc
AH1106	—	10.00	20.00	50.00	80.00	—

Edirne

KM# 121.1 KURUS

20.0500 g., Silver **Note:** Dav. #318.

Date	Mintage	VG	F	VF	XF	Unc
AH1106	—	20.00	40.00	80.00	120	—

Erzerum

KM# 121.2 KURUS

20.0500 g., Silver **Note:** Dav. #319A.

Date	Mintage	VG	F	VF	XF	Unc
AH1106	—	200	400	600	850	—

Izmir

KM# 121.3 KURUS

20.0500 g., Silver **Note:** Dav. #319.

Date	Mintage	VG	F	VF	XF	Unc
AH1106	—	75.00	100	175	350	—

Constantinople

KM# 124 SHERIFI ALTIN

3.3500 g., Gold

Date	Mintage	VG	F	VF	XF	Unc
AH1106	—	60.00	80.00	125	225	—

Constantinople

KM# 128 ASHRAFI

3.4500 g., Gold

Date	Mintage	VG	F	VF	XF	Unc
AH1106	—	60.00	100	180	250	—

KM# 130 TEK

3.3500 g., Gold, 29 mm.

Date	Mintage	VG	F	VF	XF	Unc
AH1106	—	—	—	—	—	—

Constantinople

KM# 127 TEK

3.3500 g., Gold, 20.5 mm.

Date	Mintage	VG	F	VF	XF	Unc
AH1106	—	60.00	150	250	400	—

Edirne

KM# 129 TEK

3.4500 g., Gold

Date	Mintage	VG	F	VF	XF	Unc
AH1106	—	75.00	150	250	400	—

Izmir

KM# 131 TEK

3.4500 g., Gold

Date	Mintage	VG	F	VF	XF	Unc
AH1106 Rare	—	—	—	—	—	—

Ordu-yu Humayun

KM# A131 TEK

3.4500 g., Gold

Date	Mintage	VG	F	VF	XF	Unc
AH1106 Rare	—	—	—	—	—	—

Constantinople

KM# 132 CIFTE

6.5000 g., Go

Date	Mintage	VG	F	VF	XF	Unc
AH1106 Rare	—	—	—	—	—	—

UNITED STATES OF AMERICA

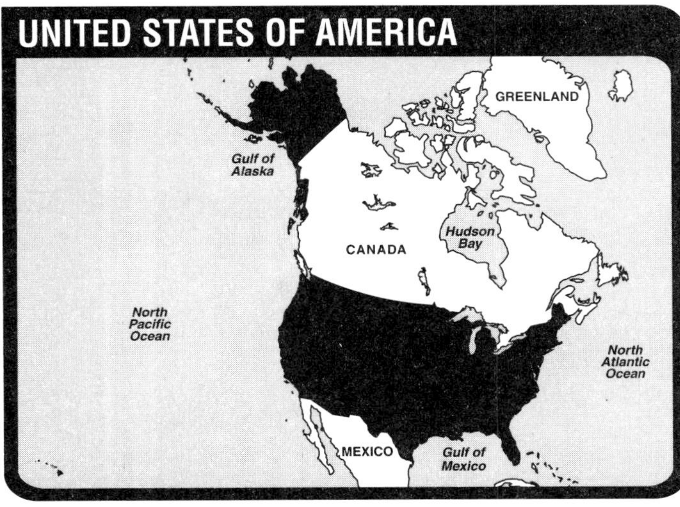

The United States of America as politically organized under the Articles of Confederation consisted of 13 former British-American colonies: New Hampshire, Massachusetts, Rhode Island, Connecticut, New York, New Jersey, Pennsylvania, Delaware, Maryland, Virginia, North Carolina, South Carolina, and Georgia. They were clustered along the eastern seaboard of North America between the forests of Maine (then part of Massachusetts) and the marshes of Georgia.

North America was explored by the Vikings, but it was not until the age of Discovery, that vast colonization began – by the French, Spanish, Dutch, English and Portuguese.

The Spanish would be strongest in Central and South America, taking that whole continent except for Brazil which went to Portugal. The Spanish also would be in Florida, Texas, and California.

The French would settle in the Mississippi River Delta, from New Orleans northward to St. Louis, then east to the Ohio River basin, and west to the Rockies; they would also be to the north, in the St. Lawrence River area in Canada; Quebec and Montreal being their principal cities.

The English would be on the east coast of the United States, from Georgia north to Maine, and east of the Allegheny and Appalachian Mountains. To the north in Canada, they would be in Nova Scotia, Newfoundland, and north of the French in Quebec, Ontario, and with the explorers of the Hudson Bay Company, westward on the plains and to the Pacific.

The Dutch had a presence from the 1620s through 1664, mainly in the New York region, but lost that territory to the English, and never again gained a stronghold on the mainland during this period.

MONETARY SYSTEM

12 Pence = 1 Shilling
5 Shillings = 1 Crown
21 Shillings = 1 Guinea

MARYLAND

Lord Baltimore

PENNY (DENARIUM)

KM# 1 • Copper • Obv. Legend: CAECILIVS Dns TERRAE MARIAE

Date	AG	Good	VG	Fine	VF	XF	Unc
(1659) 5 known	—	—	—	—	—	100,000	—

Note: Stack's Auction 5-04, proof realized $241,500

4 PENCE (GROAT)

KM# 2 • Silver • Obv: Large bust **Obv. Legend:** CAECILIVS Dns TERRAE MARIAE **Rev:** Large shield

Date	AG	Good	VG	Fine	VF	XF	Unc
(1659)	1,250	1,850	3,500	6,250	13,500	20,000	—

KM# 3 • Silver, • Obv: Small bust **Obv. Legend:** CAECILIVS Dns TERRAE MARIAE **Rev:** Small shield

Date	AG	Good	VG	Fine	VF	XF	Unc
(1659) unique	—	—	—	—	—	—	—

Note: Norweb $26,400

6 PENCE

KM# 4 • Silver • Obv: Small bust **Obv. Legend:** CAECILIVS Dns TERRAE MARIAE **Note:** Known in two other rare small-bust varieties and two rare large-bust varieties.

Date	AG	Good	VG	Fine	VF	XF	Unc
(1659)	850	1,400	2,400	4,900	9,000	15,000	—

SHILLING

KM# 6 • Silver • Obv. Legend: CAECILIVS Dns TERRAE MARIAE **Note:** Varieties exist; one is very rare.

Date	AG	Good	VG	Fine	VF	XF	Unc
(1659)	1,100	1,800	3,000	5,750	13,500	20,000	—

MASSACHUSETTS

New England

3 PENCE

KM# 1 • Silver • Obv: NE **Rev:** III

Date	AG	Good	VG	Fine	VF	XF	Unc
(1652) Unique	—	—	—	—	—	—	—

Note: Massachusetts Historical Society specimen

6 PENCE

KM# 2 • Silver • Obv: NE **Rev:** VI

Date	AG	Good	VG	Fine	VF	XF	Unc
(1652) 8 known	—	25,000	50,000	90,000	175,000	—	—

Note: Garrett $75,000

SHILLING

KM# 3 • Silver • Obv: NE **Rev:** XII

Date	AG	Good	VG	Fine	VF	XF	Unc
(1652)	—	35,000	65,000	100,000	200,000	—	—

Oak Tree

2 PENCE

KM# 7 • Silver • Note: Small 2 and large 2 varieites exist.

Date	AG	Good	VG	Fine	VF	XF	Unc
1662	—	500	900	2,000	3,850	6,500	15,000

3 PENCE

KM# 8 • Silver • Note: Two types of legends.

Date	AG	Good	VG	Fine	VF	XF	Unc
1652	350	600	1,000	2,500	5,500	9,000	—

6 PENCE

KM# 9 • Silver • Note: Three types of legends.

Date	AG	Good	VG	Fine	VF	XF	Unc
1652	400	900	1,100	2,700	6,400	9,500	25,000

SHILLING

KM# 10 • Silver • Note: Two types of legends.

Date	AG	Good	VG	Fine	VF	XF	Unc
1652	350	650	1,100	2,600	5,400	8,800	25,000

Pine Tree

3 PENCE

KM# 11 • Silver • Obv: Tree without berries

Date	AG	Good	VG	Fine	VF	XF	Unc
1652	250	500	700	1,650	3,000	5,600	17,500

KM# 12 • Silver • Obv: Tree with berries

Date	AG	Good	VG	Fine	VF	XF	Unc
1652	250	500	700	1,650	3,200	5,750	18,500

6 PENCE

KM# 13 • Silver • Obv: Tree without berries; "spiney tree"

Date	AG	Good	VG	Fine	VF	XF	Unc
1652	400	700	1,400	2,000	3,750	6,500	20,000

KM# 14 • Silver • Obv: Tree with berries

Date	AG	Good	VG	Fine	VF	XF	Unc
1652	300	500	800	1,750	3,500	6,250	18,000

SHILLING

KM# 15 • Silver • Note: Large planchet. Many varieties exist; some are very rare.

Date	AG	Good	VG	Fine	VF	XF	Unc
1652	350	600	950	2,000	4,350	7,500	20,000

KM# 16 • Silver • Note: Small planchet; large dies. All examples are thought to be contemporary fabrications.

Date	AG	Good	VG	Fine	VF	XF	Unc
1652	—	—	—	—	—	—	—

KM# 17 • Silver • Note: Small planchet; small dies. Many varieties exist; some are very rare.

Date	AG	Good	VG	Fine	VF	XF	Unc
1652	285	525	800	1,700	3,750	6,950	22,500

Willow Tree

3 PENCE

KM# 4 • Silver

Date	AG	Good	VG	Fine	VF	XF	Unc
1652 3 known	—	—	—	—	—	—	—

6 PENCE

KM# 5 • Silver

Date	AG	Good	VG	Fine	VF	XF	Unc
1652 14 known	9,000	17,500	30,000	57,500	125,000	200,000	—

SHILLING

KM# 6 • Silver

Date	AG	Good	VG	Fine	VF	XF	Unc
1652	9,800	18,000	34,000	80,000	150,000	225,000	—

NEW JERSEY

St. Patrick or Mark Newby

FARTHING

KM# 1 • Copper • Obv. Legend: FLOREAT REX **Rev. Legend:** QUIESCAT PLEBS

Date	AG	Good	VG	Fine	VF	XF	Unc
(1682)	70.00	125	285	700	2,250	4,500	—

Note: One very rare variety is known with reverse legend: QUIESAT PLEBS

KM# 1a • Silver • Obv. Legend: FLOREAT REX **Rev. Legend:** QUIESCAT PLEBS

Date	AG	Good	VG	Fine	VF	XF	Unc
(1682)	800	1,500	2,200	4,500	8,000	12,500	—

HALFPENNY

KM# 2 • Copper • Obv. Legend: FLOREAT REX **Rev. Legend:** ECCE GREX

Date	AG	Good	VG	Fine	VF	XF	Unc
(1682)	180	365	850	1,650	4,000	10,500	—

EARLY AMERICAN TOKENS

American Plantations

1/24 REAL

KM# Tn5.1 • Tin • Obv. Legend: ET HIB REX

Date	AG	Good	VG	Fine	VF	XF	Unc
(1688)	125	200	300	450	750	2,000	—

KM# Tn5.3 • Tin • Rev: Horizontal 4

Date	AG	Good	VG	Fine	VF	XF	Unc
(1688)	275	400	900	1,500	2,700	5,000	—

KM# Tn5.4 • Tin • Obv. Legend: ET HIB REX

Date	AG	Good	VG	Fine	VF	XF	Unc
(1688)	—	250	450	750	1,400	2,650	9,000

KM# Tn6 • Tin • Rev: Arms of Scotland left, Ireland right

Date	AG	Good	VG	Fine	VF	XF	Unc
(1688)	450	750	1,250	2,000	3,000	6,500	—

KM# Tn5.2 • Tin • Obv: Rider's head left of "B" in legend **Note:** Restrikes made in 1828 from two obverse dies.

Date	AG	Good	VG	Fine	VF	XF	Unc
(1828)	75.00	110	175	275	500	1,000	—

Elephant

UNKNOWN DENOMINATION

KM# Tn1.1 • 15.5500 g., **Copper • Note:** Thick planchet.

Date	AG	Good	VG	Fine	VF	XF	Unc
(1664)	125	200	300	500	1,000	1,750	3,850

KM# Tn1.2 • Copper • Note: Thin planchet.

Date	AG	Good	VG	Fine	VF	XF	Unc
(1664)	175	300	500	850	3,000	5,500	11,750

KM# Tn2 • Copper • Rev: Diagonals tie shield

Date	AG	Good	VG	Fine	VF	XF	Unc
(1664)	250	450	650	2,250	6,500	10,000	17,500

KM# Tn3 • Copper • Rev: Sword right side of shield

Date	AG	Good	VG	Fine	VF	XF	Unc
(1664) 3 known	—	—	—	—	12,500	—	—

Note: Norweb $1,320

KM# Tn4 • Copper • Rev. Legend: LON DON

Date	AG	Good	VG	Fine	VF	XF	Unc
(1684)	340	650	1,000	2,250	4,000	7,000	17,500

KM# Tn7 • Copper • Rev. Legend: NEW ENGLAND

Date	AG	Good	VG	Fine	VF	XF	Unc
(1694) 2 known	—	—	50,000	75,000	95,000	140,000	—

Note: Norweb $25,300

KM# Tn8.1 • Copper • Rev. Legend: CAROLINA (PROPRIETORS)

Date	AG	Good	VG	Fine	VF	XF	Unc
(1694) 5 known	—	—	4,750	6,500	14,000	22,500	—

Note: Norweb $35,200

KM# Tn8.2 • Copper • Rev. Legend: CAROLINA (PROPRIETORS, O over E)

Date	AG	Good	VG	Fine	VF	XF	Unc
1694	1,300	2,500	4,000	6,000	12,000	17,500	—

Note: Norweb $17,600

New Yorke

UNKNOWN DENOMINATION

KM# Tn9 • Brass • Obv. Legend: NEW.YORK.IN. AMERICA

Date	AG	Good	VG	Fine	VF	XF	Unc
1700	1,800	3,500	5,500	13,000	22,500	35,000	—

KM# Tn9a • White Metal • Obv. Legend: NEW. YORK.IN.AMERICA

Date	AG	Good	VG	Fine	VF	XF	Unc
1700 4 known	—	—	6,000	15,000	28,000	50,000	—

VIETNAM (DAI VIET)

In 207 B.C. a Chinese general set up the Kingdom of Nam-Viet on the Red River. This passed to direct Chinese control under the Han and Tang lasting until 968. From that time native clans and dynasties ruled.

In 1407 China again invaded. Forces coalescing around resistance leader Le Loi ousted the Chinese in 1428, founding the Le dynasty. Its capital was Hanoi. Within a century three generals, each at the head of a clan, had splintered off their own rival territories. The Mac were in the north, the Nguyen in the south. The lords Trinh came to dominate the Le kings as puppets, deposing many, but never completely usurping the line.

The weak Le kings, controlled by a virtually parallel Trinh military dynasty, were engaged in constant wars during the 16th century. The Macs occupied nearly the entire country in 1527, claimed the throne and began issuing coins with their own reign titles. Yet by 1593 they had been fought back to two provinces on the Chinese border. Their last kings were permitted by China to make necessity money only. These used the common inscriptions *An-phap nguyen-bao* and *Tai-binh thong-bao*. The scarce Mac An-phap cash can only be differentiated from others by small details. Their Tai-binh cash cannot be attributed at all. The Macs were extinguished in 1667.

In 1599 the Le general Trinh was given the princely title Binh-An-Vuong by the Chinese, and his own sovereignty over 3 former Mac provinces. Coins inscribed Binh-An thong-bao have been attributed to him, but are Japanese trade cash.

In the 1600's the Nguyen clan expanded north and west, establishing their capital at Hue, and annexing Cambodia. While cash were almost certainly cast by them, they were not in their own names. Issues of the Nguyen are not attributable until the 1700's. During this period private casting of cash imitating Chinese and older Vietnamese coins accelerated. Mining and coining licenses were sold by local rulers to Chinese merchants, who then exported the cash in exchange for goods. (Such trade cash were made also in Java, South China and Japan.) Coins formerly attributed to two 17th century Le dynasty kings are now recognized as issues of the Nguyen duke's large mint establishment in the mid 1700's. The Le and Trinh were overturned in the 1780's by the Tayson rebellion. In 1801 a member of the Nguyen triumphed as founder of a new dynasty.

EMPERORS

Thinh Duc, 1653-1658

Vinh Tho, 1658-1662

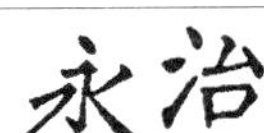

Vinh Tri, 1676-1680

Chinh Hoa, 1680-1705

Khai 啓

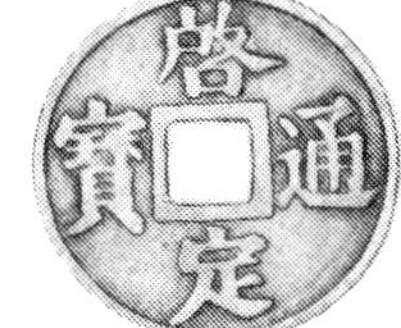

寶 **Bao**

通 **Thong**

Dinh 定

CHARACTER IDENTIFICATION

The Vietnamese used Chinese-style characters for official documents and coins and bars. Some were modified to their liking and will sometimes not match the Chinese character for the same word. The above identification and this table will translate most of the Vietnamese characters (Chinese-style) on their coins and bars described herein.
Chinese/French
Vietnamese/English

An Nam = name of the French protectorate

Dai Nam = name of the country under Gia Long's Nguyen dynasty

Viet Nam = name used briefly During Minh Mang's reign and became the modern name of the country

DAI VIET

CAST COINAGE

KM# 10 PHAN

Cast Copper **Ruler:** Vinh Tho **Obv:** Conventional script inscription **Obv. Inscription:** Vinh-tho Thong-bao **Rev:** Plain

Date	Mintage	Good	VG	F	VF	XF
ND(1658-62)	—	3.50	5.50	12.50	20.00	—

KM# 11 PHAN

Cast Copper **Ruler:** Vinh Tho **Obv:** Conventional script inscription **Obv. Inscription:** Vinh-tho Thong-bao **Rev:** Double rim

Date	Mintage	Good	VG	F	VF	XF
ND(1658-62)	—	5.00	7.50	15.00	25.00	—

KM# 12 PHAN

Cast Copper **Ruler:** Vinh Tho **Obv:** Grassy, cursive and conventional inscription **Obv. Inscription:** Vinh-tho Thong-bao"

Date	Mintage	Good	VG	F	VF	XF
ND(1658-62)	—	6.00	12.50	20.00	35.00	—

KM# 14 PHAN

Cast Copper **Ruler:** Vinh Tho **Obv:** Semi-seal script inscription **Obv. Inscription:** Vinh-tho Thong-bao

Date	Mintage	Good	VG	F	VF	XF
ND(1658-62) Rare	—	—	—	—	—	—

KM# 13 PHAN

Cast Copper **Ruler:** Vinh Tho **Obv:** Cursive inscription **Obv. Inscription:** Vinh-tho Thong-bao **Note:** Numerous script variations may be encountered among "Ving-tho Thong-bao" coins, particularly in the character "VINH".

Date	Mintage	Good	VG	F	VF	XF
ND(1658-62) Rare	—	—	—	—	—	—

KM# 15 PHAN

Cast Zinc **Ruler:** Vinh Tri **Obv:** Conventional script **Rev:** Blank

Date	Mintage	Good	VG	F	VF	XF
ND(1663-71)	—	35.00	50.00	60.00	85.00	—

KM# 25 PHAN

Cast Zinc **Ruler:** Vinh Tri **Obv:** Conventional script with Chi Bao

Date	Mintage	Good	VG	F	VF	XF
ND(1676-80)	—	17.50	30.00	45.00	60.00	—

KM# 19 PHAN

Cast Zinc **Ruler:** Vinh Tri **Obv. Inscription:** Vin-tri Nguyen-bao **Note:** Similar to KM#20.

Date	Mintage	Good	VG	F	VF	XF
ND(1676-80)	—	—	—	—	—	—

KM# 20 PHAN

Cast Copper **Ruler:** Vinh Tri **Obv:** Semi-seal inscription **Obv. Inscription:** Vinh-tri Nguyen-bao

Date	Mintage	Good	VG	F	VF	XF
ND(1676-80)	—	5.00	7.50	15.00	25.00	—

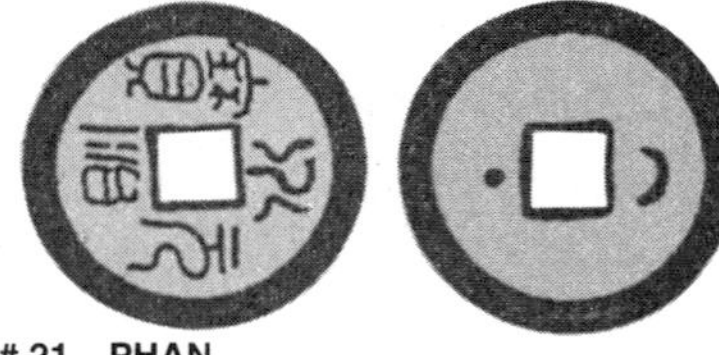

KM# 21 PHAN

Cast Copper **Ruler:** Vinh Tri **Obv:** Seal script with Nguyen Bao **Obv. Inscription:** "Vinh-tri Nguyen-bao" **Rev:** Crescent right, dot left

Date	Mintage	Good	VG	F	VF	XF
ND(1676-80)	—	4.00	6.50	12.50	22.50	—

KM# 22 PHAN

Cast Copper Or Brass **Ruler:** Vinh Tri **Obv:** Conventional script inscription **Obv. Inscription:** Vinh-tri Nguyen-bao

Date	Mintage	Good	VG	F	VF	XF
ND(1676-80)	—	5.00	8.00	17.50	27.50	—

DAI VIET

Capital: Tay Do (Hanoi)

CAST COINAGE

KM# 31 PHAN

Cast Zinc **Ruler:** Chinh Hoa **Obv:** Conventional script with 5-stroke Chanh with Thong Bao **Obv. Inscription:** "Chinh-hoa Thong-bao"

Date	Mintage	Good	VG	F	VF	XF
ND(1676-1705)	—	5.00	8.00	17.50	27.50	—

KM# A33 PHAN

Zinc **Ruler:** Chinh Hoa **Note:** Similar to KM#32.

Date	Mintage	Good	VG	F	VF	XF
ND(1676-1705)	—	—	—	—	—	—

KM# 32 PHAN

Cast Zinc **Ruler:** Chinh Hoa **Obv:** Convention script with 5-stroke Chanh with Thong Bao **Obv. Inscription:** Chinh-hoa Thong-bao **Rev:** Crescent right. **Note:** Only the 5-stroke Chanh of the above Chanh Hoa Thong Bao coins is attributed to the Vietnamese. Those with the 9-stroke Chanh are only copies, of indeterminate date, of chinese Northern Sung coins. Some Vietnamese Chanh Hoa coins may also exist in copper or brass.

Date	Mintage	Good	VG	F	VF	XF
ND(1680-1705)	—	5.00	8.00	17.50	27.50	—

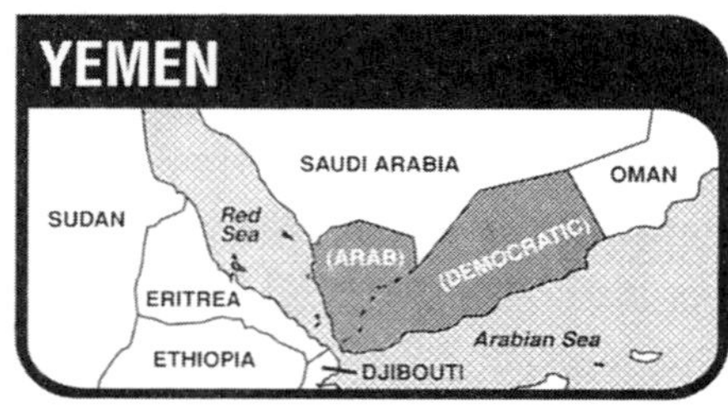

One of the oldest centers of civilization in the Middle East, Yemen was once part of the Minaean Kingdom and of the ancient Kingdom of Sheba, after which it was captured successively by Egyptians, Ethiopians and Romans. It was converted to Islam in 628 A.D. and administered as a caliphate until 1538, when it came under Ottoman occupation in 1849. The second Ottoman occupation which began in 1872 was maintained until 1918 when autonomy was achieved through revolution.

RULERS

Ottoman, until 1625

MINT NAMES

al-Damigh	الدامغ
Adan	عدن
Dhamar	ذمار ذمر
Ibb	ايب
Kawkaban	كوكبان
Rada'	راداء
San'a	صنعاء
Zabid	زبيد

OTTOMAN OCCUPATION

Mehmet III

AH1003-1012 / 1593-1603AD

HAMMERED COINAGE

KM# 105 'UTHMANI

0.6000 g., Silver

Date	Mintage	Good	VG	F	VF	XF
ND(1593-1603) Rare	—	—	—	—	—	—

Ahmed I

AH1012-1026 / 1603-1617AD

HAMMERED COINAGE

KM# 110 'UTHMANI

0.6000 g., Silver

Date	Mintage	Good	VG	F	VF	XF
ND Rare	—	—	—	—	—	—

Osman II

AH1027-1031 / 1618-1622AD

HAMMERED COINAGE

KM# 115 'UTHMANI

0.6000 g., Silver

Date	Mintage	Good	VG	F	VF	XF
ND Rare	—	—	—	—	—	—

Mustafa I

2nd reign, AH1031-1032 / 1622-1623AD

HAMMERED COINAGE

KM# 120 'UTHMANI

0.6000 g., Silver

Date	Mintage	Good	VG	F	VF	XF
ND Rare	—	—	—	—	—	—

Murad IV

in the Yemen, AH1032-1045 / 1623-1635AD

HAMMERED COINAGE

Sana'a

KM# 125 MANGIR

Copper

Date	Mintage	Good	VG	F	VF	XF
AH1032	—	75.00	125	225	500	—

KM# 130 'UTHMANI

0.6000 g., Silver

Date	Mintage	Good	VG	F	VF	XF
ND Date off flan; Rare	—	50.00	100	200	400	—

KINGDOM

al-Mu'ayyad Muhammad I

AH1009-1054 / 1602-1644AD

HAMMERED COINAGE

Dhamar

KM# 140.1 FALS

Copper **Note:** Weight varies: 0.30-0.50 grams.

Date	Mintage	Good	VG	F	VF	XF
ND Date off flan	—	20.00	35.00	60.00	100	—

Ibb

KM# 140.2 FALS

Copper **Note:** Weight varies: 0.30-0.50 grams.

Date	Mintage	Good	VG	F	VF	XF
AH1039	—	45.00	75.00	125	—	—

Al-Damigh

KM# 141.1 BUQSHA

Silver **Obv:** "Muhammad" in circle, titles around **Rev:** Mint and date **Note:** Weight varies: 0.30-0.50 grams.

Date	Mintage	Good	VG	F	VF	XF
ND Date off flan	—	15.00	28.00	45.00	70.00	—
AH1046	—	25.00	50.00	80.00	135	—
AH1047	—	25.00	50.00	80.00	135	—
AH1048	—	25.00	50.00	80.00	135	—
AH1049	—	25.00	50.00	80.00	135	—

Dhamar

KM# 141.2 BUQSHA

Silver **Note:** Weight varies: 0.30-0.50 grams.

Date	Mintage	Good	VG	F	VF	XF
ND Date off flan	—	10.00	18.00	30.00	50.00	—
AH1049	—	16.00	32.00	55.00	90.00	—
AH1050	—	16.00	32.00	55.00	90.00	—
AH1051	—	16.00	32.00	55.00	90.00	—

Ibb

KM# 141.3 BUQSHA

Silver **Note:** Weight varies: 0.30-0.50 grams.

Date	Mintage	Good	VG	F	VF	XF
ND Date off flan	—	8.00	15.00	25.00	40.00	—
AH1039	—	15.00	28.00	45.00	70.00	—
AH1041	—	15.00	28.00	45.00	70.00	—
AH1047	—	15.00	28.00	45.00	70.00	—
AH1048	—	15.00	28.00	45.00	70.00	—
AH1050	—	15.00	28.00	45.00	70.00	—

Kawkaban

KM# 141.4 BUQSHA

Silver **Note:** Weight varies: 0.30-0.50 grams.

Date	Mintage	Good	VG	F	VF	XF
ND Date off flan	—	12.00	25.00	40.00	65.00	—
AH1036	—	25.00	45.00	70.00	120	—

Sana'a

KM# 141.5 BUQSHA

Silver **Note:** Weight varies: 0.30-0.50 grams.

Date	Mintage	Good	VG	F	VF	XF
ND Date off flan	—	15.00	30.00	50.00	85.00	—
AH1047	—	25.00	50.00	80.00	135	—
AH1048	—	25.00	50.00	80.00	135	—

al-Mutawakkil Isma'il

AH1054-1087 / 1644-1676AD

HAMMERED COINAGE

Dhamarmar

KM# 145.1 FALS

Copper

Date	Mintage	Good	VG	F	VF	XF
ND Date off flan	—	16.00	30.00	50.00	80.00	—
AH1083	—	20.00	35.00	60.00	100	—

Sa'da

KM# 145.2 FALS

Copper

Date	Mintage	Good	VG	F	VF	XF
ND Date off flan	—	16.00	30.00	50.00	80.00	—
AH1070	—	20.00	35.00	60.00	100	—

Shihara

KM# 145.3 FALS

Copper

Date	Mintage	Good	VG	F	VF	XF
ND Date off flan	—	16.00	30.00	50.00	80.00	—
AH1064	—	20.00	35.00	60.00	100	—

Al-Damigh
KM# 155.1 BUQSHA
Silver **Obv:** "Isma'il" usually in oval, titles around **Rev:** Mint and date **Note:** Weight varies: 0.20-0.40 grams.

Date	Mintage	Good	VG	F	VF	XF
ND Date off flan	—	8.00	15.00	25.00	40.00	—
AH1069	—	16.00	30.00	50.00	80.00	—

Al-Rawda
KM# 155.2 BUQSHA
Silver **Note:** Weight varies: 0.20-0.40 grams.

Date	Mintage	Good	VG	F	VF	XF
ND Date off flan	—	12.00	25.00	40.00	65.00	—
AH1064	—	35.00	45.00	75.00	125	—
AH1079	—	35.00	45.00	75.00	125	—

Dhamar
KM# 155.3 BUQSHA
Silver **Note:** Weight varies: 0.20-0.40 grams.

Date	Mintage	Good	VG	F	VF	XF
ND Date off flan	—	8.00	15.00	25.00	40.00	—
AH1060	—	12.00	25.00	40.00	65.00	—
AH1062	—	12.00	25.00	40.00	65.00	—
AH1063	—	12.00	25.00	40.00	65.00	—
AH1065	—	12.00	25.00	40.00	65.00	—
AH1066	—	12.00	25.00	40.00	65.00	—
AH1022 Error for 66	—	12.00	25.00	40.00	65.00	—

Dhamarmar
KM# 155.4 BUQSHA
Silver **Note:** Weight varies: 0.20-0.40 grams.

Date	Mintage	Good	VG	F	VF	XF
ND Date off flan	—	20.00	35.00	60.00	100	—
AH1077	—	30.00	60.00	100	175	—

Kawkaban
KM# 155.5 BUQSHA
Silver **Note:** Weight varies: 0.20-0.40 grams.

Date	Mintage	Good	VG	F	VF	XF
ND Date off flan	—	7.00	12.00	20.00	30.00	—
AH1055	—	10.00	20.00	35.00	60.00	—
AH1056	—	10.00	20.00	35.00	60.00	—
AH1057	—	10.00	20.00	35.00	60.00	—
AH1058	—	10.00	20.00	35.00	60.00	—
AH1064	—	10.00	20.00	35.00	60.00	—
AH1065	—	10.00	20.00	35.00	60.00	—
AH1066	—	10.00	20.00	35.00	60.00	—

Rada'
KM# 155.6 BUQSHA
Silver **Note:** Weight varies: 0.20-0.40 grams.

Date	Mintage	Good	VG	F	VF	XF
ND Date off flan	—	7.00	12.00	20.00	45.00	—
AH1070	—	20.00	35.00	60.00	100	—

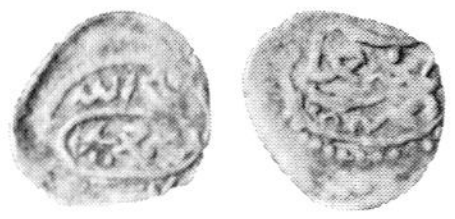

Sana'a
KM# 155.7 BUQSHA
Silver **Note:** Weight varies: 0.20-0.40 grams.

Date	Mintage	Good	VG	F	VF	XF
ND Date off flan	—	6.00	10.00	18.00	30.00	—
AH1054	—	10.00	20.00	35.00	60.00	—
AH1055	—	10.00	20.00	35.00	60.00	—
AH1056	—	10.00	20.00	35.00	60.00	—
AH1057	—	10.00	20.00	35.00	60.00	—
AH1058	—	10.00	20.00	35.00	60.00	—
AH1059	—	10.00	20.00	35.00	60.00	—
AH1064	—	10.00	20.00	35.00	60.00	—
AH1065	—	10.00	20.00	35.00	60.00	—
AH1066	—	10.00	20.00	35.00	60.00	—
AH1067	—	10.00	20.00	35.00	60.00	—
AH1069	—	10.00	20.00	35.00	60.00	—
AH1074	—	10.00	20.00	35.00	60.00	—
AH1075	—	10.00	20.00	35.00	60.00	—
AH1078	—	10.00	20.00	35.00	60.00	—
AH1079	—	10.00	20.00	35.00	60.00	—

Shihara
KM# 155.8 BUQSHA
Silver **Note:** Weight varies: 0.20-0.40 grams.

Date	Mintage	Good	VG	F	VF	XF
ND Date off flan	—	15.00	20.00	45.00	70.00	—
AH1056	—	25.00	45.00	75.00	125	—
AH1057	—	25.00	45.00	75.00	125	—

Dhamar
KM# 150.1 KHUMS KABIR
Silver **Note:** Weight varies: 0.80-1.20 grams.

Date	Mintage	Good	VG	F	VF	XF
ND Date off flan	—	12.00	22.00	35.00	60.00	—
AH1071	—	20.00	35.00	60.00	100	—

Kawkaban
KM# 150.2 KHUMS KABIR
Silver **Note:** Weight varies: 0.80-1.20 grams.

Date	Mintage	Good	VG	F	VF	XF
ND Date off flan	—	10.00	20.00	30.00	50.00	—
AH1074	—	16.00	30.00	50.00	80.00	—

Rada'
KM# 150.3 KHUMS KABIR
Silver **Note:** Weight varies: 0.80-1.20 grams.

Date	Mintage	Good	VG	F	VF	XF
ND Date off flan	—	15.00	25.00	45.00	75.00	—
AH1070	—	25.00	45.00	75.00	125	—

Sana'a
KM# 150.4 KHUMS KABIR
Silver **Note:** Weight varies: 0.80-1.20 grams.

Date	Mintage	Good	VG	F	VF	XF
ND Date off flan	—	8.00	16.00	28.00	45.00	—
AH1066	—	—	—	—	—	—
Note: Reported, not confirmed						
AH1070	—	15.00	28.00	45.00	70.00	—
AH1074	—	15.00	28.00	45.00	70.00	—
AH1075	—	15.00	28.00	45.00	70.00	—

al-Mahdi Ahmad
AH1087-1092 / 1676-1681AD
HAMMERED COINAGE

'Ayyan
KM# 162.1 BUQSHA
0.2000 g., Silver

Date	Mintage	Good	VG	F	VF	XF
ND Date off flan	—	35.00	70.00	120	200	—

Sa'da
KM# 162.2 BUQSHA
0.2000 g., Silver

Date	Mintage	Good	VG	F	VF	XF
AH109x	—	25.00	45.00	75.00	125	—

San'a
KM# 162.3 BUQSHA
Silver **Note:** Weight varies: 1.00-2.00 grams.

Date	Mintage	Good	VG	F	VF	XF
ND	—	—	—	—	80.00	—

KM# 165 BUQSHA (Undetermined denomination)
Gold

Date	Mintage	Good	VG	F	VF	XF
ND Date off flan; Rare	—	—	—	—	—	—

Dhamarmar
KM# 160.1 KHUMS KABIR
Silver **Note:** Weight varies: 0.80-1.00 grams.

Date	Mintage	Good	VG	F	VF	XF
ND Date off flan	—	15.00	28.00	45.00	75.00	—
AH1087	—	28.00	55.00	90.00	150	—

Kawkaban
KM# 160.2 KHUMS KABIR
Silver **Note:** Weight varies: 0.80-1.00 grams.

Date	Mintage	Good	VG	F	VF	XF
ND Date off flan	—	12.00	25.00	45.00	80.00	—
AH1088	—	20.00	35.00	60.00	100	—

al-Mu'ayyad Muhammad II
AH1092-1097 / 1681-1686AD
HAMMERED COINAGE

Rada'
KM# 170 KHUMS KABIR
Silver **Note:** Weight varies: 0.80-1.00 grams.

Date	Mintage	Good	VG	F	VF	XF
ND Date off flan	—	30.00	60.00	100	175	—
AH1093	—	35.00	70.00	120	200	—

al-Nasir Muhammad
First reign AH1098-1105 / 1687-1693AD
HAMMERED COINAGE

Al-Ghiras
KM# 175.1 1/2 FALS
Copper

Date	Mintage	Good	VG	F	VF	XF
ND Date off flan	—	60.00	120	200	350	—

Rada'
KM# 175.2 1/2 FALS
Copper

Date	Mintage	Good	VG	F	VF	XF
ND Date off flan	—	12.00	25.00	40.00	65.00	—
AH1102	—	18.00	35.00	60.00	100	—
AH1103	—	18.00	35.00	60.00	100	—

Rahban
KM# 175.3 1/2 FALS
Copper

Date	Mintage	Good	VG	F	VF	XF
AH1097	—	60.00	120	200	350	—

Al-Hadra'
KM# 180.1 FALS
Copper

Date	Mintage	Good	VG	F	VF	XF
ND Date off flan	—	30.00	60.00	100	175	—

Rada'
KM# 180.2 FALS
Copper

Date	Mintage	Good	VG	F	VF	XF
ND Date off flan	—	9.00	15.00	30.00	40.00	—
AH1101	—	18.00	35.00	60.00	—	—
AH1102	—	18.00	35.00	60.00	—	—
AH1103	—	18.00	35.00	60.00	—	—
AH1104	—	18.00	35.00	60.00	—	—
AH1105	—	18.00	35.00	60.00	—	—

Al-Hadra'
KM# 185.1 KHUMS KABIR
Silver **Note:** Weight varies: 0.80-1.00 grams.

Date	Mintage	Good	VG	F	VF	XF
ND Date off flan	—	20.00	35.00	60.00	100	—
AH1105	—	30.00	60.00	100	175	—

Unknown Mint
KM# 185.2 KHUMS KABIR
Silver **Note:** Probably struck at San'a. Weight varies: 0.80-1.00 gram.

Date	Mintage	Good	VG	F	VF	XF
ND Date off flan	—	12.00	25.00	40.00	65.00	—
AH1102	—	28.00	55.00	90.00	150	—

al-Nasir Muhammad
Second reign as al-Hadi Muhammad
AH1105-1109 / 1693-1697AD
HAMMERED COINAGE

Unknown Mint
KM# 190 1/2 FALS
Copper **Note:** Probably struck at San'a.

Date	Mintage	Good	VG	F	VF	XF
ND Date off flan	—	25.00	45.00	75.00	125	—
AH1108	—	25.00	45.00	75.00	125	—

Al-Hadra'
KM# 195 FALS
Copper

Date	Mintage	Good	VG	F	VF	XF
ND Date off flan	—	25.00	45.00	75.00	125	—

Al-Hadra'
KM# 200.1 KHUMS KABIR
Silver **Note:** Weight varies: 0.80-1.00 grams.

Date	Mintage	Good	VG	F	VF	XF
ND Date off flan	—	16.00	32.00	55.00	90.00	—
AH110x	—	30.00	60.00	100	175	—

Unknown Mint
KM# 200.2 KHUMS KABIR
Silver **Note:** Probably struck at San'a. Weight varies: 0.80-1.00 gram.

Date	Mintage	Good	VG	F	VF	XF
ND Date off flan	—	16.00	32.00	55.00	90.00	—

al-Nasir Muhammad
Third reign as al-Madhi Muhammad
AH1109-1130 / 1697-1718AD
HAMMERED COINAGE

San'a
KM# 215 BUQSHA
Silver **Note:** Weight varies: 0.15-0.20 grams.

Date	Mintage	Good	VG	F	VF	XF
ND Date off flan	—	10.00	20.00	35.00	55.00	—
AH1110	—	15.00	28.00	45.00	75.00	—

San'a
KM# 210 KHUMS KABIR
Silver **Note:** Weight varies: 2.00-3.00 grams.

Date	Mintage	Good	VG	F	VF	XF
ND Date off flan	—	10.00	18.00	30.00	50.00	—
AH1111	—	15.00	28.00	45.00	100	—